Labels
used in the dictionary

The following labels indicate words that express a particular attitude or are appropriate in a particular context.

(approv) Approving expressions show that the user feels approval or admiration, eg *cosy, masterly, petite.*

(derog) Derogatory expressions show that the user feels disapproval or scorn, eg *brat, fuddy-duddy, pedantic.*

(euph) Euphemistic expressions are chosen to refer to something unpleasant or painful in a more pleasant or less direct way, eg *cloakroom* (= a toilet), *pass away* (= to die), *senior citizen* (= an old or retired person).

(fig) Figurative usage is when language is used in a non-literal or metaphorical way. The label is used before examples illustrating such usage, eg *It makes my heart ache* (ie makes me sad) *to see her suffer.*

(fml) Formal expressions are usually only used in serious or official, especially written, language and would be inappropriate in normal everyday conversation. Examples are *disrobe, redoubtable, paucity.*

(infml) Informal expressions are used between friends or people who know each other well, in a relaxed or unofficial context. They are not appropriate for formal situations. Examples are *brainy, dad, umpteen, wallop.*

(ironic) Such usage is when words are used to mean the opposite of or something very different from their apparent meaning, as in *This is a nice mess you've got us into!*

(joc) Jocular expressions are intended to be funny, eg *clodhopper, hanky-panky, long in the tooth, muggins.*

(offensive) Such expressions are used to address or refer to people in a way that is very insulting, especially in connection with their race or religion, eg *nigger, wop, yid.*

(rhet) Rhetorical speech or writing is used in order to sound important, impressive or literary, sometimes in a self-conscious or pompous way. Examples are *attire, doughty, emolument.*

(sexist) Such words express an unfair or patronizing attitude towards a person of the opposite sex. They are usually used by men about women. Examples are *career girl, dolly-bird, looker.*

(sl) Slang is very informal language, mainly used in speaking and sometimes restricted to a particular group of people, eg those who have similar interests or do the same job. Examples are *dope* (= illegal drugs), *the fuzz* (= the police), *lolly* (= money), *naff.*

(⚠) Taboo words are likely to be thought obscene or shocking by many people and should be avoided by learners. Examples are *arse, bloody, shit.*

The following labels indicate other restrictions on the use of words.

(arch) Archaic expressions are no longer in current use, eg *ere, fealty, handmaiden.*

(Brit) This indicates expressions used in British English and not in American English, eg *jumble sale, mackintosh, tombola.*

(catchphrase) Catchphrases are well-known expressions that were often originally used by a public figure, an entertainer, etc and have now passed into more general use, eg *the buck stops here; the plot thickens.*

(dated) Dated expressions are passing out of current use and already seem rather old-fashioned, eg *aerodrome, beatnik, gramophone.*

(dialect) This indicates expressions that are mainly used in particular regions of the British Isles, not including Scotland or Ireland, eg *beck, nowt, sup.*

(propr) Proprietary names are registered trademarks belonging to manufacturing companies, even though they may be commonly used in speech and writing, eg *Babygro, Filofax, Sellotape.*

(saying) Sayings are well-known fixed or traditional phrases, such as proverbs, that are used to make a comment, give advice, issue a warning, etc, eg *look before you leap; you're only young once.*

(Scot) This indicates Scottish expressions, eg *bairn, kirk, loch.*

(techn) Technical expressions are used by people who specialize in a particular field or fields.

(US) This indicates expressions, spellings and pronunciations used in American English and not in British English, eg *drugstore, sidewalk, turnpike.*

There are also many labels for expressions that are normally restricted to specialized use in specific fields, eg **(anatomy)**, **(computing)**, **(grammar)**, **(law)**.

Oxford Advanced
Learner's Dictionary
of Current English

Oxford Advanced Learner's Dictionary
of Current English

A S Hornby

Fifth edition

Editor **Jonathan Crowther**

Assistant Editor Kathryn Kavanagh
Phonetics Editor Michael Ashby

OXFORD UNIVERSITY PRESS

Oxford University Press
Walton Street, Oxford OX2 6DP

Oxford New York
Athens Auckland Bangkok Bombay
Calcutta Cape Town Dar es Salaam Delhi
Florence Hong Kong Istanbul Karachi
Kuala Lumpur Madras Madrid Melbourne
Mexico City Nairobi Paris Singapore
Taipei Tokyo Toronto

and associated companies in
Berlin Ibadan

OXFORD and OXFORD ENGLISH
are trade marks of Oxford University Press

© Oxford University Press 1995
First published 1948 (12 impressions)
Second edition 1963 (19 impressions)
Third edition 1974 (28 impressions)
Fourth edition 1989 (50 impressions)
Fifth edition 1995 (3rd impression)

The British National Corpus is a collaborative project involving Oxford
University Press, Longman, Chambers, the Universities of Oxford and Lancaster
and the British Library.

ISBN 0 19 431421 9 (hardback)
ISBN 0 19 431432 4 (laminated boards)
ISBN 0 19 431180 5 (flexicover)
ISBN 0 19 431422 7 (paperback)
ISBN 0 19 431423 5 (international students' edition)

Illustrations by: David Haldane; Richard Lewington; Martin Lonsdale, Richard
Morris/Hardlines; Vanessa Luff; David More/Linden Artists; Margaret Morgan;
Coral Mula; Oxford Illustrators; Chris Price; John Storey; Technical Graphics
Dept, Oxford University Press; David Williams; Michael Woods.

Maps © Oxford University Press.

Location photography by: Philip Dunn.
We should like to thank Oxford Magistrates Court for their time and assistance.

We should also like to thank the following for permission to reproduce
photographs: Allsport (UK) Ltd/Bob Martin; Associated Press; BBC Photograph
Library; British Library Reproductions; Comstock Photofile Ltd; National
Geographic Ltd; Peter Newark's American Pictures; Photographic Collection of
the Supreme Court of the United States/Franz Jantzen; Press Association/
Topham; Rex Features Ltd/Heimdath; Michelle Smith; Frank Spooner
Pictures Ltd; Universal Pictorial Press & Agency Ltd; Zefa/Messerschmidt.

Designed by Holdsworth Associates, Isle of Wight
Text capture and processing by Oxford University Press
Typesetting by Tradespools Typesetting Ltd, Frome
Printed in Great Britain by
Richard Clay Ltd, Bungay, Suffolk

Contents

Advisory Board

Preface

It is a tribute to the vision and genius of the late A S Hornby that the dictionary which was perhaps his greatest gift to English language learning and teaching still strives to satisfy the same basic needs of foreign students as he perceived them, namely to develop their receptive *and* productive skills, the ability (as Tony Cowie wrote in his preface to the fourth edition) 'to compose as well as to understand'.

In preparing this new edition we have remained true to Hornby's original aims while introducing a number of significant innovations, all designed to give more help to the dictionary user. For the first time we have had at our disposal the British National Corpus, a massive and carefully balanced computer databank of modern written and spoken English developed by a consortium of British publishers led by Oxford University Press. This magnificent new resource has enabled us as never before to determine the relative frequency of words and their meanings, to identify new words and co-occurrences of words, and to present a wholly accurate picture of the syntactic patterns of today's English. In addition the corpus has provided abundant raw material on which to base the illustrative examples which have always been a key feature of the dictionary. Many existing examples were rewritten in the light of the new evidence, and nearly 9 000 new ones were added for this edition.

Another new feature is the introduction of a 3 500-word vocabulary within which definitions are written. The words in the list (given in full as Appendix 10) were chosen principally according to their frequency in the language, as revealed by the corpus, but also as a 'core' vocabulary of real value to students of English. The size of the list was determined by the minimum requirement for producing definitions in natural English that are both accurate and easy to understand. The new language study pages, culture pages and maps also make attractive and, we hope, useful additions to the dictionary.

I am very grateful to Michael Ashby of University College, London, for undertaking a thorough update of the phonetics in the dictionary, and in particular for his overhaul of the treatment of stress in phrasal verbs and idioms, always a difficult area for foreign students. I must also thank Keith Brown for devising the new simplified verb coding scheme introduced in this edition.

The work of revising a major dictionary inevitably involves many helping hands. I am extremely grateful to all those within and outside Oxford University Press who worked on the project, including the following lexicographers: Evadne Adrian-Vallance, Angela Crawley, Gary Dexter, Sarah Hall, Mark Harrison, Fiona McIntosh, Christine Rickards, Allene Tuck, John Williams, and, for her work on the coverage of American English, Coleen Degnan-Veness. Thanks are also due to Margaret Deuter, Penny Stock, Deborah Tempest and Sally Wehmeier for the language notes and study pages; to Jane Taylor, Eunice Gill and Phil Longford for their work on the illustrations and the maps; and to Anna Cotgreave and Kay Pepler for keyboarding most of the text. I am especially indebted to my colleague Kathryn Kavanagh for her hard work, enthusiasm and meticulous attention to detail at every stage of the project.

Jonathan Crowther
January 1995

Key to dictionary entries

headword and pronunciation (see inside back cover)

fender /'fendə(r)/ n **1** a low metal frame placed around a fireplace to prevent burning coal from falling out. **2** a soft solid object such as a mass of rope or a rubber tyre, hung over the side of a boat to prevent damage when it comes next to another boat or to land. **3** (*US*) **(a)** a MUDGUARD over the wheel of a bicycle. **(b)** = WING 4.

meanings separated by numbers or, when closely related, by letters

headwords with same spelling separated by different numbers

ferment¹ /fə'ment/ v to change or make sth change by means of a chemical reaction involving esp YEAST or bacteria: [V] *Fruit juices ferment if they are kept a long time.* ○ (*fig*) *His anger fermented inside him.* [Vn] *Yeast is used in fermenting sugar to produce alcohol.*
▶ **fermentation** /,fɜːmen'teɪʃn/ n [U]: *Sugar is converted into alcohol through (the process of) fermentation.*

ferment² /'fɜːment/ n [U] political or social excitement or uncertainty: *The country was in (a state of) ferment.*

American pronunciation (see inside back cover)

Ferris wheel /'feris wiːl/ (also **big wheel**) n (at a FAIR³(1), etc) a large upright revolving wheel with seats hanging from its edge for people to ride in.

synonym of headword

ferrule /'feruːl; *US* 'ferəl/ n a metal ring or cap placed on the end of a stick, an UMBRELLA, etc to stop it becoming damaged.

word not in defining vocabulary (see Appendix 10)

part of speech (see inside front cover for abbreviations)

ferry /'feri/ n **(a)** a boat that carries people and goods across a stretch of water: *catch/take the ferry* ○ *the cross-channel ferry service.* **(b)** the place where such a service operates: *We waited at the ferry for two hours.*
▶ **ferry** v (*pt, pp* **ferried**) to transport people or goods by boat, aircraft, etc for a short distance, sometimes regularly over a period of time: [Vnp] *Can you ferry us across?* [Vnpr] *ferry goods to the mainland* ○ *ferry the children to and from school* [Vn, Vnpr] *planes ferrying food (to the refugees).*

verb codes before examples that illustrate them (see Study pages B4–8)

fertilize, -ise /'fɜːtəlaɪz/ v [Vn] **1** to introduce POLLEN into a plant so that it develops seed, or SPERM into an egg or a female animal so that a young animal, etc develops inside: *a fertilized egg/cell* ○ *Flowers are often fertilized by bees as they gather nectar.* **2** to make soil, etc more FERTILE(1) by adding a substance such as MANURE to it: *fertilize the garden.*
▶ **fertilization, -isation** /,fɜːtəlaɪ'zeɪʃn; *US* -lə'z-/ n [U]: *successful fertilization by the male.*
fertilizer, -iser n [C, U] a natural or artificial substance added to soil to make it more FERTILE(1): *chemical fertilizers* ○ *a bag of fertilizer* ○ *Get some more fertilizer for the garden.* Compare MANURE.

derivatives section with special symbol ▶

American English spelling of headword

cross-reference to contrasted word

fervour (*US* **fervor**) /'fɜːvə(r)/ n [U] strength or intensity of feeling; enthusiasm: *speak with great fervour* ○ *religious/nationalistic/revolutionary fervour.*

festival /'festɪvl/ n **1** a day or period of religious or other celebration: *Christmas and Easter are Christian festivals.* ○ *a festival atmosphere.* See also HARVEST FESTIVAL. **2** a series of performances of music, drama, films, etc given regularly, esp once a year: *the Edinburgh Festival* ○ *a jazz festival.*

cross-reference to related word

fixed form of noun

festivity /fe'stɪvəti/ n **1** [U] celebration; happiness and enjoyment: *The wedding was an occasion of great festivity.* **2** **festivities** [pl] celebrations; happy and enjoyable events held in honour of sb/sth: *wedding festivities.*

fetch /fetʃ/ v **1** ~ sb/sth (for sb) (*esp Brit*) to go and find and bring back sb/sth: [Vn] *Fetch a doctor at once.* [Vnpr] *I have to fetch the children from school.* [Vnp] *The chair is in the garden — please fetch it in.* [Vnn, Vnpr] *Should I fetch you your coat/fetch your coat for you from upstairs?* **2** (of goods) to be sold for a price: [Vn] *The picture should fetch at least £2 000* *at auction.* [Vn, Vnn] *Those old books won't fetch (you) much.* **3** (*infml*) to hit sb, esp with the hand: [Vnn] *She fetched him a terrific slap in the face.* **IDM** **fetch and ˈcarry (for sb)** to act like a servant for sb; to be busy with small duties: *He expects his daughter to fetch and carry for him all day.* **PHR V** **ˌfetch ˈup** (*Brit infml*) to arrive at a certain place or in a certain position, often by chance: *At lunch-time they all fetched up in the bar of the local pub.*

fetid (also **foetid**) /ˈfetɪd; *Brit also* ˈfiːtɪd/ *adj* smelling very unpleasant; stinking (STINK 1): *fetid air.*

fetish /ˈfetɪʃ/ *n* **1(a)** (*usu derog*) a thing to which more respect or attention is given than is normal or sensible: *He **makes a fetish of** his work.* ○ *She has a fetish about cleanliness.* **(b)** (*techn*) an object or activity that is necessary for or adds to an individual's sexual pleasure. **2** an object that certain people worship, esp because a spirit is believed to live in it.

fetlock /ˈfetlɒk/ *n* the part of a horse's leg above and behind the HOOF, where long hair grows out. ⇨ picture at HORSE.

fetus = FOETUS.

feud /fjuːd/ *n* ~ **(between A and B)**; ~ **(with sb)** a long and bitter quarrel between two people, families or groups: *a long-running feud between the two artists* ○ *Because of a family feud, he never spoke to his wife's parents for years.* See also BLOOD FEUD.

fever /ˈfiːvə(r)/ *n* **1** [C, U] an abnormally high body temperature, esp as a sign of illness: *He has a high fever.* ○ *Aspirin can reduce fever.* **2** [U] (esp in compounds) a specified disease in which a fever occurs: *yellow/typhoid/rheumatic/scarlet fever.* See also HAY FEVER.

▶ **fevered** *adj* [attrib] **1** affected by or suffering from a fever: *She cooled his **fevered brow**.* **2** highly excited: *a fevered imagination* ○ *fevered negotiations.*

■ **ˈfever pitch** *n* [U] a very high level of excitement: *His anxiety reached fever pitch.* ○ *The crowd had been roused to fever pitch by the drama of the game.*

few[1] /fjuː/ *indef det, adj* [usu attrib] **(-er, -est)** (used with *pl* countable *ns* and a *pl v*) not many: *Few people live to be 100.* ○ *a man/woman **of few words*** (ie one who speaks very little) ○ *There are fewer cars parked outside than yesterday.* ○ *The police have very few clues to the murderer's identity.* ○ *The few houses we have seen are in terrible condition.* ○ *There were too few people at the meeting.* ○ *The last few years have been very difficult.* ○ *I visit my parents **every few days/weeks/months*** (ie once in a few days, etc). ○ *Accidents at work are few.* (Compare: *There are few accidents at work.*) ⇨ note at LESS, MUCH[1].

fez /fez/ *n* (*pl* **fezzes**) a red hat with a flat top and a TASSEL but no BRIM(2). ⇨ picture at HAT.

fiancé (*fem* **fiancée**) /fiˈɒnseɪ; *US* ˌfiːɑːnˈseɪ/ *n* a man or woman to whom one is engaged to be married: *her fiancé* ○ *his fiancée.*

fieldsman /ˈfiːldzmən/ *n* (*pl* **-men** /-mən/) (in cricket, etc) a member of the team that is not batting (BAT[1] *v* 1b).

file[1] /faɪl/ *n* **1(a)** any of various types of drawer, shelf, holder, cover, box, etc, usu with a wire or metal rod for keeping loose papers together and in order, so that they can be found easily: *a stack of files* ○ *I bought a file for my letters.* **(b)** a file and its contents: *top secret police files* ○ *a file of cuttings* ○ *Where's the customer order file?* ○ *have/open/keep a confidential file on each member of staff.* **2** an organized collection of related data or material in a computer: *I can't access/update the file on your company because I've forgotten the code.* **IDM** **on ˈfile / on the ˈfiles** kept in a file: *We have all your particulars on file.*

■ **ˈfiling cabinet** (*Brit*) (*US* **ˈfile cabinet**) *n* a piece of office furniture with deep drawers for storing files.

idioms section with special symbol **IDM**

phrasal verbs section with special symbol **PHR V**

alternative written form

alternative British pronunciation

labels giving information about usage (*see inside front cover*)

cross-reference to illustration at different entry

'dummy' entry with reference to main entry elsewhere

information on which prepositions to use with a word

information on different types of noun (*see Study pages* **B1–3**)

examples of use in *italic* type, separated by special symbol ○

information on usage of adjectives (*see Study pages* **B1–3**)

examples of words often used with the headword, separated by special symbol /

compounds section with special symbol ■, and stress shown on compounds

information on comparative and superlative forms of adjectives

common phrase in ***thick type*** in example, with extra explanation in brackets

irregular plural form of noun

alternative American pronunciation (*see inside back cover*)

cross-reference to special sense of word used in definition

word used only in British English, with American English equivalent

NOTE In British English the floor of a building at street level is the **ground floor** and the floor above that is the **first floor**. In American English the street level is often called the **first floor** and the one above is the **second floor**.

[annotation: special note on usage (see Appendix 9)]

floor² /flɔː(r)/ *v* **1** (*infml*) to defeat or confuse sb so that they are unable to respond: [Vn] *Tom was completely floored by two of the questions in the exam.* **2** to knock sb down by hitting them: [Vnpr] *He floored his opponent with a fine punch in the first round.* [also Vn]. **3** to provide a building or room with a floor of a particular type: [Vnpr] *The room is floored with pine.* [also Vn].

[annotation: additional verb pattern for which no example is given]

flop /flɒp/ *v* **(-pp-) 1** to fall, move or hang heavily, loosely or in an awkward way: [Vpr] *The pile of books flopped noisily onto the floor.* ∘ *Her hair flopped over her eyes.* [Vp] *The fish we'd caught were flopping around in the bottom of the boat.* [V] *His head began to flop and seconds later he was asleep.* **2** to sit or lie down heavily and awkwardly because of being tired: [V] *I'm ready to flop.* [Vpr] *Exhausted, he flopped into the nearest chair.* [Vp] *She staggered into the room and flopped down.* **3** (*infml*) to fail totally; to be completely UNSUCCESSFUL: [V] *His first record flopped but his second was a big hit.*

[annotation: doubling of final consonant in -ing and -ed forms]

▶ **flop** *n* **1** (usu *sing*) a flopping movement or sound. See also BELLYFLOP. **2** (*infml*) a total failure; a completely UNSUCCESSFUL thing: *Despite all the publicity, her latest novel was a complete flop.*
flop *adv* with a flop: *fall flop into the water.*
floppy *adj* falling or hanging loosely; soft and flexible; not stiff: *a floppy hat.* — *n* (*infml*) = FLOPPY DISK.

[annotation: sense in which noun is countable but usually singular]

[annotation: derivative with same spelling but different part of speech]

Using your dictionary

Entries

The dictionary contains a great many **entries**, arranged in alphabetical order. Every entry begins with a **headword** and in all main entries this is followed by information on pronunciation and grammar and by one or more **definitions**. These explain the meaning or meanings of the headword and are accompanied in most cases by **examples** showing how the headword is used in context. Different senses are separated by numbers (or, for closely-related meanings, by letters) and are arranged according to their frequency of use in the language, with the main or most common meaning given first.

The definitions are followed, where appropriate, by the **idioms** and/or **phrasal verbs** containing the headword. These sections of the entry are introduced by the symbols **IDM** and **PHR V** respectively. Help with understanding and using idioms and phrasal verbs is given in the Study pages **A2–3** and **A6–7**.

Words which are formed from a simple ('root') word by the addition of a suffix are called **derivatives** and the derivatives of a headword are listed alphabetically in the headword entry after the symbol ▶. In some derivatives the spelling of the root form is changed so that the link between root and derivative is less clear. These derivatives are made headwords in the dictionary. The same is also true for derivatives which have developed distinct meanings from those of their roots. So *satisfy* and its derivative *satisfaction*, and *scarce* and its derivative *scarcely*, are all separate headwords.

Words or expressions which are formed from two or more words functioning as a single unit are called **compounds**. Compounds may be written as unbroken single words (eg *birthplace*) or with a hyphen (eg *bitter-sweet*) or as two or more separate words (eg *boarding card, bird of prey*). In this dictionary compounds spelt with hyphens or as separate words are listed alphabetically in the headword entry, after the symbol ■. Compounds spelt as unbroken single words appear as headwords. More information about compounds is given on Study page **A1**.

Cross-references

The dictionary gives extra help by regularly referring you elsewhere for more information about words. These references may be to other entries, or to pictures, or to notes on usage, or to one of the appendices at the back of the book. They are of various types, as follows. When a word in another entry is referred to, it is given in SMALL CAPITAL LETTERS.

⇨ refers you to another entry where the meaning of a word, an idiom, etc is given, or to a picture or note

= indicates a word with exactly the same meaning

Compare refers you to another word with an opposite or contrasted meaning

See also refers you to another word with a similar or related meaning.

Alternative forms and synonyms

When a word can be spelt in more than one way, or can be replaced by another word with the same meaning, this is shown in the following ways:

blowzy (also **blowsy**) /'blaʊzi/
– different spelling, same pronunciation

barefoot /'beəfʊt/ (also **barefooted** /ˌbeə'fʊtɪd/)
– different form, different pronunciation

basset /'bæsɪt/ (also **basset-hound**)
– longer form

bank-book (also **passbook**)
– synonym

bedsitting room ... (also *infml* **bedsitter, bedsit**)
– informal equivalents

Differences between British and American English are shown in similar ways:

bedhead ... (*Brit*) (*US* **headboard**)
– British and American English words are completely different.

belabour (*US* **belabor**)
– British and American English words have different spellings.

blinkers ... (*US* also **blinders**)
– The word is used in both British and American English but there is a synonym that only occurs in American English.

Irregular forms

The dictionary gives help with certain forms of nouns, verbs and adjectives, especially when these are not what you might expect. These irregular forms are shown near the beginning of the entries.

Nouns
– nouns ending in -*o*
  banjo ... (*pl* **-os**)
  potato ... (*pl* **-oes**)
– nouns ending in -*i*
  semi ... (*pl* **semis**)
– nouns with Latin or Greek endings
  antenna ... (*pl* **antennae**)
  analysis ... (*pl* **analyses**)
– nouns with more than one plural form
  fungus ... (*pl* **fungi** ... or **funguses**)
– nouns with plurals involving a change in the stem
  foot ... (*pl* **feet**)
– nouns whose plural form is the same as the singular form
  sheep ... (*pl* **unchanged**)
– nouns ending in -*ful*
  basketful ... (*pl* **-fuls**)

Verbs
– verbs ending in a consonant which is doubled before -*ing* or -*ed*
  regret ... (**-tt-**)
– verbs whose stem changes in the past tense and/or in the past participle
  drink ... (*pt* **drank** ... *pp* **drunk** ...)
– verbs ending in -*y* after a consonant
  defy ... (*pt, pp* **defied**)

Adjectives
Whenever an adjective can have one-word comparative and superlative forms this is shown. Irregular comparative and superlative forms are shown in full.

plain ... (**-er, -est**)	= **plainer, plainest**
brave ... (**-r, -st**)	= **braver, bravest**
pretty ... (**-ier, -iest**)	= **prettier, prettiest**
big ... (**-gger, -ggest**)	= **bigger, biggest**
good ... (**better** ... **best** ...)	

When no comparative and superlative forms are shown, this means that they are rarely or never found. *More* and *most* are used with the adjective in these cases:

  more difficult, most difficult
not ~~**difficulter, difficultest**~~

Aa

A¹ (also **a**) /eɪ/ n (pl **A's**, **a's** /eɪz/) **1** [C,U] the first letter of the English alphabet: *'Ann' begins with (an) A/'A'*. **2 A** [C,U] (*music*) the 6th note in the scale¹(6) of C major. **3 A** [C,U] an academic mark indicating the highest standard of work: *get (an) A/'A' in biology*. **4 A** [U] (used to represent the first of two or more alternatives): *Let's decide on plan A then.* **5 A** [U] (used to represent a person, eg in an imaginary situation or to conceal her or his identity): *Let's assume A knows B is guilty.* **IDM** **from A to B** from one place to another: *I don't care what a car looks like as long as it gets me from A to B.* **from A to Z** from beginning to end; completely or thoroughly: *know a subject from A to Z.*

A² /eɪ/ symb **1** (used in Britain before a number to refer to a particular major road): *the A34 to Stratford-upon-Avon.* Compare B² 2. **2** (*Brit*) (used before one of a specified set of numbers to indicate standard sizes of paper): *an A4 folder/pad* (ie 297 × 210 mm).

■ **A1** /ˌeɪ ˈwʌn/ adj (*dated infml*) excellent: *I'm feeling A1* (ie very well).

A-OK /ˌeɪ əʊˈkeɪ/ adj [usu pred] (*US infml*) completely satisfactory.

A-road /ˈeɪ rəʊd/ n (*Brit*) a major road, less important than a MOTORWAY but usu wider and straighter than a B-road (B²): *The A-road is much quicker.* See also A² 1.

A³ abbr **1** ampere(s): *13 A* (eg on a FUSE¹(1)). **2** answer. Compare Q².

a¹ /ə; strong form eɪ/ (also **an** /ən; strong form æn/) indef art (The form *a* is used before consonant sounds and the form *an* before vowel sounds. Both are used before [C], [CGp] or [sing] ns that have not already been mentioned.) **1** any one: *a man/horse/girl/committee/unit/U-turn* (Compare: *some men/horses/girls, etc*) ○ *an egg/aunt/uncle/hour/X-ray/MD/L-plate* (Compare: *some eggs/aunts/uncles/hours, etc*) ○ *I can only carry two at a time.* ○ *There's a book on the table — is that the one you want?* **2** (used with an abstract [U] n restricted by an *adj* or by the phrase which follows it): *a strange unease* ○ *We're looking for someone with a good knowledge of German.* ○ *An excess of fat in one's diet can lead to heart disease.* **3** any; every: *A horse is a quadruped.* (Compare: *Horses are quadrupeds.*) ○ *An owl can see* (Compare: *Owls can see*) *in the dark.* **4** (used after a negative) one single; any: *He didn't tell us a thing about his trip.* **5** (used before sb and is not followed by *of* + possess det + n + 's): *He is a friend of my father's* (ie one of my father's friends). ○ *It's a habit of Sally's* (ie one of Sally's habits). **6** (used in front of two ns seen as a single unit): *a cup and saucer* ○ *a knife and fork.* **7** (*infml*) (used instead of *one* before particular numbers and fractions): *a fifth* (ie one fifth) *of the population* ○ *A thousand people attended the concert.* ⇨ App 2. **8** to or for each; per: *pay £2.20 a gallon* ○ *write 800 words a day* ○ *cost 50p a pound.* **9** (*often derog*) a person like sb: *My boss is a little Napoleon.* **10** (used before sb's name to show that the speaker does not know the person): *Do we know a Tim Smith?* ○ *A Mrs Green is waiting to see you.* **11** (used to show membership of a class of people or things): *My mother is a solicitor.* ○ *My father is a Dallas Cowboys supporter.* ○ *The car was a Volvo, not a Saab.* **12** a work of art by the specified artist: *The painting my grandfather gave me turned out to be a Constable.* **13** (used before the names of days of the week to refer to a particular instance of that day): *They were married on a Monday.*

NOTE When saying abbreviations like FM or UN, the way the name of the first letter is said, and not whether it is a vowel or a consonant, determines whether to put **a** or **an** before it. The letter **F** is a consonant but begins with the sound /e/ and so you say: *an FM radio.* The letter **U** is a vowel but begins with the sound /j/ and so you say: *a UN declaration.*

a² /eɪ/ symb (used to label the first section or part of sth. It is usually written *a*) or (*a*).): *A 'jar' means a) a glass container and b) its contents.*

a- pref (forming ns, adjs and advs) not; without: *atheist* ○ *atypical* ○ *asexually.*

AA /ˌeɪ ˈeɪ/ abbr (in Britain) Automobile Association: *members of the AA.*

aback /əˈbæk/ adv **PHRV** **take sb aback** ⇨ TAKE¹.

abacus /ˈæbəkəs/ n (pl **abacuses** /-kəsɪz/) a frame holding a set of parallel rods along which small balls are pushed. It is used for teaching numbers to children, and (in some countries) for counting.

abandon /əˈbændən/ v **1** ~ **sb/sth to sb/sth** (**a**) (often passive) to go away from a person, thing or place not intending to return; to desert sb/sth: [Vn] *a baby abandoned by its parents* ○ *an abandoned car/village* ○ *The fort had long since been abandoned.* ○ *The order came: 'Abandon ship!'* [Vnpr] *They abandoned their lands and property to the invading forces.* (**b**) to withdraw support or help from sb: [Vn] *The country abandoned its political leaders after the war.* [Vnpr] *The poor have been abandoned to their fate.* **2** to stop doing or being involved in sth, or to stop sth happening, esp before it is finished: [Vn] *Have they just postponed the scheme, or abandoned it altogether?* ○ *He urged people who smoke to abandon the habit.* ○ *The match was abandoned because of bad weather.* ○ *The regime has abandoned all/any pretence of democracy.* ○ *He will never abandon hope.* **3** ~ **oneself to sth** (*rhet*) to allow oneself to be completely dominated by an emotion or impulse: [Vnpr] *He abandoned himself to despair.*

▶ **abandon** (also **abandonment**) n [U] freedom from worry or inhibition (INHIBIT): *dance with gay abandon.*

abandoned adj [usu attrib] (of people or behaviour) wild or not following accepted standards.

abandonment n [U] **1** the action of abandoning sb/sth or of being abandoned: *her abandonment of the idea* ○ *the fear of abandonment in old age.* **2** = ABANDON n.

abase /əˈbeɪs/ v [Vn] ~ **oneself/sb** (*fml*) to lower oneself/sb in dignity. ▶ **abasement** n [U].

abashed /əˈbæʃt/ adj [pred] embarrassed and ashamed: *His boss's criticism left him feeling rather abashed.* Compare UNABASHED.

abate /əˈbeɪt/ v (of wind, noise, pain, etc) to become less intense: [V] *The storm showed no signs of abating.* ○ *Public interest in this issue seems to have abated.* ▶ **abatement** n [U].

abattoir /ˈæbətwɑː(r)/ n (*Brit*) = SLAUGHTERHOUSE.

abbess /ˈæbes/ n a woman who is the head of a CONVENT.

abbey /ˈæbi/ n [C] a church associated with other

buildings in which monks or nuns live or formerly lived as a religious community: *Westminster Abbey* ○ *a ruined abbey.*

abbot /'æbət/ *n* a man who is the head of a MONASTERY or an ABBEY.

abbr *abbr* (esp in this dictionary) abbreviation.

abbreviate /ə'briːvieɪt/ *v* **1** ~ **sth** (**to sth**) to make a word, phrase, etc shorter by omitting letters or using only the first letter of each word: [Vnpr] *In writing, the title 'Doctor' is abbreviated to 'Dr'.* *The abbreviated form of 'United States of America' is 'USA'.* **2** to make sth, eg a story, shorter, by omitting details: [Vn] *I gave him an abbreviated account, as there wasn't time to tell him everything.*
▶ **abbreviation** /ə,briːvi'eɪʃn/ *n* **1** [C] (abbreviated as *abbr* in this dictionary) a form of a word, phrase, etc that is shorter than the full form: *a dictionary of abbreviations* ○ *'GB' is the abbreviation of/for 'Great Britain'.* **2** [U] the process of abbreviating sth: *Some abbreviation may be necessary to save space.*

ABC /,eɪ biː 'siː/ *n* [sing] **1** the alphabet, ie all the letters from A to Z, esp as learnt by children: *Do you know your ABC?* **2** the basic facts about a subject: *the ABC of gardening.* **IDM** **as easy as ABC** ⇨ EASY¹.

abdicate /'æbdɪkeɪt/ *v* **1** to resign from being, or choose not to become, king, queen, EMPEROR, etc: [V] *King Edward VIII abdicated in 1936.* **2** (*fml*) to choose not to fulfil a role or duty: [Vn] *This government will not abdicate its responsibility to beat inflation.* [Vpr] *The party decided to abdicate from its role in the coalition government.* ▶ **abdication** /,æbdɪ'keɪʃn/ *n* [C, U].

abdomen /'æbdəmən/ *n* **1** the part of the body below the chest, containing the stomach, bowels, etc. See also INTESTINE. **2** the back part of an insect, SPIDER or CRUSTACEAN: *head, thorax and abdomen.* ⇨ picture at INSECT. ▶ **abdominal** /æb'dɒmɪnl/ *adj*: *abdominal pains* ○ *an abdominal operation.*

abduct /æb'dʌkt/ *v* to take sb away illegally, using force or deception; to KIDNAP sb: [Vn] *He was abducted by four gunmen.* ▶ **abduction** /æb'dʌkʃn/ *n* [U, C]: *child abduction.*

aberrant /æ'berənt/ *adj* not normal or acceptable: *aberrant behaviour/ideas.*

aberration /,æbə'reɪʃn/ *n* [C, U] a temporary change from what is normal or acceptable, esp one that is surprising: *steal sth in a moment of aberration* ○ *The defeat was a temporary aberration — he quickly started winning matches again.*

abet /ə'bet/ *v* (**-tt-**) ~ **sb** (**in sth**) to help or encourage sb to commit an offence or do sth wrong: [Vn, Vnpr] *He was abetted (in the deception) by his wife.* [Vn] *Aiding and abetting suicide is a serious crime.*

abeyance /ə'beɪəns/ *n* [U] a state of not being used or being suspended temporarily: *The scheme is/has been put in abeyance until sufficient funds can be found.* ○ *Legal proceedings are being held/left in abeyance.* ○ *This law falls into abeyance when the country's security is threatened.*

abhor /əb'hɔː(r)/ *v* (**-rr-**) to feel hatred and disgust for sb/sth, esp for moral reasons: [Vn] *abhor terrorism/terrorists.*
▶ **abhorrence** /əb'hɒrəns/ *US* -'hɔːr-/ *n* [U, sing]: *have an abhorrence of war.*
abhorrent /əb'hɒrənt/ *US* -'hɔːr-/ *adj* ~ (**to sb**) causing hatred and disgust: *Violence is abhorrent to him.*

abide /ə'baɪd/ *v* (*pt, pp* abided; in sense 2 also **abode** /ə'bəʊd/) **1** (esp with *can/could*, in negative sentences or questions) to tolerate or bear sb/sth: [Vn] *I can't abide that man.* ○ *How could you abide such awful conditions?* **2** (*arch or fml*) to remain or stay in a place: [Vpr] *abide with sb* ○ *the right to enter and abide in a country.* **PHRV** **a'bide by sth** to accept and act according to a law, agreement, etc; to

be faithful to sth: *abide by a decision/verdict* ○ *If you join a club, you have to abide by its rules.*
▶ **abiding** *adj* enduring; lasting: *an abiding friendship/hatred/mistrust/interest/memory.*

ability /ə'bɪləti/ *n* ~ (**to do sth**) [U, C] the mental or physical capacity, power or skill required to do sth: *a machine with the ability to cope with large loads* ○ *He has the ability to solve complex technical problems.* ○ *I try to do my job to the best of my ability* (ie as well as I can). ○ *A woman of her ability shouldn't have any difficulty getting a good job.* ○ *have musical ability* ○ *pupils of different/mixed abilities* ○ *He was given work more suited to his abilities.*

-ability, -ibility *suff* (forming uncountable *ns* from *adjs* ending in *-able* and *-ible*): *profitability* ○ *capability.*

abject /'æbdʒekt/ *adj* **1** (of conditions or states of mind) terrible; extreme: *living in abject poverty/misery.* **2** (of people) completely without pride or dignity: *an abject coward* ○ *an abject apology* (ie a very HUMBLE(1) one). **3** very poor; completely without success: *The scheme was an abject failure.* ▶ **abjectly** *adv.*

abjure /əb'dʒʊə(r)/ *v* (*fml*) to promise or swear to give up a claim, an opinion, a belief, etc; to RENOUNCE(2) sth formally: [Vn] *abjure one's religion.*

ablaze /ə'bleɪz/ *adj* [pred] **1** burning strongly; completely on fire: *set sth ablaze* ○ *The whole building was soon well ablaze.* **2** ~ (**with sth**) (**a**) very bright and cheerful: *The palace was ablaze with lights.* ○ *The garden was ablaze with flowers.* (**b**) very excited: *His face was ablaze with anger.*

able¹ /'eɪbl/ *adj* **be** ~ **to do sth** (used as a *modal v*) to have the power, skill, intelligence, means or opportunity to do sth: *I wasn't able to lift the suitcase.* ○ *The child is not yet able to walk.* ○ *I've never been able to understand such complicated things.* ○ *Will you be able to come?* ○ *You are better able to do it than I (am).* ⇨ note at CAN².

able² /'eɪbl/ *adj* (**-r** /'eɪblə(r)/; **-st** /'eɪblɪst/) clever and skilful; competent: *an able worker* ○ *the ablest/most able student in the class.*
▶ **ably** /'eɪbli/ *adv* in an able manner: *The organizers of the exhibition were ably assisted by a team of volunteers.*

■ **,able-'bodied** /-'bɒdid/ *adj* healthy, fit and strong.
,able 'seaman *n* a rank in the British Navy. ⇨ App 6.

-able, -ible /-əbl/ *suff* **1** (with *ns* forming *adjs*) having or showing the quality of: *fashionable* ○ *comfortable.* **2** (with *vs* forming *adjs*) (**a**) that may or must be: *eatable* ○ *payable* ○ *reversible.* (**b**) tending to: *changeable* ○ *perishable.* ▶ **-ably, -ibly** (forming *advs*): *noticeably* ○ *incredibly.*

ablutions /ə'bluːʃnz/ *n* [pl] (*fml or joc*) **1** the act of washing the body, face, hands, etc: *perform one's ablutions* (ie wash oneself). **2** (*Brit*) a building or other structure that contains a toilet and facilities for washing.

abnegation /,æbnɪ'geɪʃn/ *n* [U] (*fml*) the action of refusing or not allowing oneself sth that one likes or normally has.

abnormal /æb'nɔːml/ *adj* different, esp in a way that is not desirable, from what is normal, ordinary or expected: *abnormal behaviour/weather conditions* ○ *an abnormal relationship* ○ *be physically/mentally abnormal.* ▶ **abnormality** /,æbnɔː'mæləti/ *n* [U, C]: *tests to detect abnormality at birth* ○ *abnormalities of the heart.* **abnormally** /æb'nɔːməli/ *adv*: *abnormally large feet.*

aboard /ə'bɔːd/ *adv part, prep* on or into a train, a bus, a ship or an aircraft: *We went/climbed aboard.* ○ *Welcome aboard!* ○ *All aboard!* (ie the train, etc is about to depart). ○ *An American airliner has crashed killing all 157 people aboard.* ○ *He was already aboard (the) ship.*

abode¹ /ə'bəʊd/ *n* (usu *sing*) (*fml or rhet or joc*) a house; a home: *one's place of abode* (ie where one lives) ○ *Welcome to our humble abode!* ○ *people of/ with no fixed abode.*

abode² *pt, pp* of ABIDE 2.

abolish /əˈbɒlɪʃ/ *v* to end the existence of a law, a practice, an institution, etc: [Vn] *vote to abolish a tax* ○ *Should the death penalty be abolished?* See also ABROGATE.
▶ **abolition** /ˌæbəˈlɪʃn/ *n* [U]: *campaigns for the abolition of slavery/hanging/vivisection.* **abolitionist** /ˌæbəˈlɪʃənɪst/ *n* a person who favours the abolition of sth.

abominable /əˈbɒmɪnəbl; *US* -mən-/ *adj* **1** (*fml*) causing disgust and horror: *an abominable crime* ○ *abominable behaviour.* **2** (*infml*) very bad or unpleasant: *abominable weather/food/music/people.* ▶ **abominably** /əˈbɒmɪnəbli; *US* -mən-/ *adv*: *I treated my father abominably.* ○ *Her head ached abominably.*
■ **A͵bominable ˈSnowman** *n* = YETI.

abominate /əˈbɒmɪneɪt; *US* -mən-/ *v* [Vn] (*fml*) to feel hatred or disgust for sth/sb.
▶ **abomination** /əˌbɒmɪˈneɪʃn; *US* -məˈn-/ *n* **1** [C] a thing that causes disgust or hatred: *That new concrete building is an abomination.* ○ *For many the death penalty is a moral abomination.* **2** [U] a strong feeling of disgust or hatred.

aboriginal /ˌæbəˈrɪdʒənl/ *adj* (esp of people) existing in a place from a very early period, esp before the arrival of colonists (COLONIST): *aboriginal tribes/ inhabitants* ○ *aboriginal art/culture.*
▶ **aboriginal** *n* (usu **Aboriginal**) an aboriginal inhabitant, esp of Australia.

aborigine /ˌæbəˈrɪdʒəni/ (usu **Aborigine**) *n* an inhabitant of a place, esp Australia, from a very early period: *a Queensland aborigine* ○ *Aborigine art.*

abort /əˈbɔːt/ *v* **1** (*medical*) (**a**) to cause a pregnancy (PREGNANT) to end early in order to prevent the baby from developing and being born alive: [Vn] *abort an expectant mother/a deformed foetus* ○ *In this age-group more than half of all pregnancies are aborted.* (**b**) to give birth to a child or young animal too early for it to survive: [V] *She aborted after four months.* See also MISCARRY. **2** (often passive) to end or cause sth to end before it has been completed, esp because it is likely to fail: [Vn] *abort a space mission* (ie cancel it in space, usu because of mechanical trouble) ○ *Peace talks had to be aborted.* [V] (*computing*) *If no password is given the program aborts.*

abortion /əˈbɔːʃn/ *n* (**a**) [U] the act of causing a pregnancy (PREGNANT) to end early, in order to prevent the baby from developing or being born alive: *Her parents don't approve of abortion.* ○ *abortion laws* ○ *Many people are anti-abortion.* (**b**) [C] an operation to cause a pregnancy to end in this way: *She had an abortion.* Compare MISCARRIAGE 1.
▶ **abortionist** /əˈbɔːʃənɪst/ *n* a person who performs abortions, esp illegally.

abortive /əˈbɔːtɪv/ *adj* failing to produce the intended result; not successful: *an abortive attempt/coup/ mission* ○ *plans that proved abortive.*

abound /əˈbaʊnd/ *v* (**a**) to exist in great numbers or quantities: [V] *Oranges abound here all the year round.* ○ *Rumour/Speculation/Confusion abounds.* (**b**) ~ *in/with* sth to have sth in great numbers or quantities: [Vpr] *a river abounding in/with fish.* See also ABUNDANCE, ABUNDANT.

about¹ /əˈbaʊt/ *adv* **1** (also **around**) a little more or less than; a little before or after; approximately: *It costs about $10.* ○ *He's about the same height as you.* ○ *She drove (for) about ten miles.* ○ *They waited (for) about an hour.* ○ *He arrived (at) about ten o'clock.* **2** (*infml*) nearly; very close to: *I'm (just) about ready.* ○ *This is about the best we can hope for in the circumstances.* ○ *She has (just) about finished her homework.* See also JUST ABOUT. **3** (*infml*) (in emphatic statements) definitely: *I've had (just) about enough* (ie too much) *of your complaining.* ○ *He's been promoted,*

and **about time too** (ie it ought to have happened earlier). See also JUST ABOUT. **IDM** **that's (just) about ¹all; that's (just) about ¹it** that is the end of the subject, conversation, matter, etc: *'Do you have any other comments?' 'No, I think that's about it for now.'* **that's about ¹it / the ¹size of it** (*infml*) that is how I see it or assess the situation.

about² /əˈbaʊt/ *adv part* (in senses 1, 2 and 3 *esp Brit*; in these senses also *esp US* **around**) For the special uses of **about** in phrasal verbs, look at the verb entries. For example, the meaning of **bring sth about** is given in the phrasal verb section of the entry for **bring**. **1**(**a**) (indicating movement) here and there; in many directions: *The children were rushing aˈbout.* ○ *The boys were climbing about on the rocks.* (**b**) (indicating position) here and there in no particular order or arrangement; in various places: *books lying about on the ¹floor* ○ *people sitting about on the ¹grass.* (**c**) doing nothing in particular; doing nothing useful: *I waited about but nobody came.* ○ *People were just standing about on street corners.* (**d**) in many directions from a fixed point: *He looked about, trying to work out where he was.* **2** in circulation; moving from one place to another: *There was nobody aˈbout* (ie Nobody was to be seen). ○ *There's a lot of ¹flu about* (ie Many people are suffering from it). ○ *He'll soon be aˈbout again* (eg after an illness). **3** somewhere near; not far off: *She's ¹somewhere about, I saw her a few minutes ago.* **4** facing the opposite or a different direction: *put the ship aˈbout* ○ *It's the wrong way aˈbout.*
■ **a͵bout-ˈturn** (also **a͵bout-ˈface**) *n* a complete change of opinion, plan, etc: *These new measures indicate an about-turn in government policy.* See also U-TURN.

about³ /əˈbaʊt/ *prep* (in senses 3 and 4 *US* **around**; *Brit* also **around** in these senses) **1**(**a**) on the subject of sb/sth; in connection with sb/sth; concerning sb/sth: *a book about flowers* ○ *Tell me all about it.* ○ *What is he so angry about?* ○ *He is very careful about his personal appearance.* ⇨ note. (**b**) in order to affect or solve sth: *It's happened now and there's nothing you can do about it.* (**c**) relating to sb/sth; in the nature of sb/sth: *There's something strange about the whole affair.* **2** (*esp Brit*) concerned or occupied with sth: *And while you're aˈbout it…* (ie while you're doing that…) ○ *people going about their daily business* ○ *Commerce is all about making money.* **3**(**a**) (indicating movement) here and there in a place; in many directions in a place: *walking about the town* ○ *travelling about the world.* (**b**) (indicating position) here and there in a place; at points throughout sth: *papers strewn about the room.* (**c**) in many directions from a fixed point: *He came out of the door and looked about him.* (**d**) surrounding sb/sth: *He put his arms about her.* ○ *She wore a shawl about her shoulders.* **4** near to a place or point; in the specific area: *She's somewhere about the office.* ○ *I dropped the key somewhere about here.* ○ *He takes no interest in what's going on about him.* **IDM** **be about to do sth** to be intending to do sth; to be on the point of doing sth: *As I was about to say when you interrupted me…* ○ *We're about to start.* ○ *I'm not about to admit defeat* (ie I have no intention of doing so). **how/what about…?** **1** (used when asking for information or to get sb's opinion): *What about his qualifications* (ie Is he qualified) *for the job?* **2** (used when making a suggestion): *How about going to France for our next anniversary?* ○ *What about a cup of tea?*

NOTE Both **about** and **on** can mean 'on the subject of'. A book, film, etc **on** Chinese art, education or early history suggests a serious or formal presentation. A book, discussion or TV programme **about** China, schools or dinosaurs is probably of more general interest and more informal.

---

above¹ /əˈbʌv/ *adv* **1** at or to a higher point: *My bedroom is immediately above.* ○ *Put the books on the shelf above.* ○ *Seen from above, the fields looked like a geometrical pattern.* ○ *A voice called down to us from above.* **2** more; greater in number, level or age: *wage increases of 5% and above* ○ *The competition is open to anyone aged 18 and above.* ○ *Grades C and above are considered satisfactory.* See also OVER¹ 4. **3** earlier or further back in sth written or printed: *As was stated above…* ○ *the points mentioned above* ○ *See above, page 97.* **4** (*rhet or joc*) at a higher rank or level of authority: *act on instructions from above.* Compare BELOW, UNDER, UNDERNEATH.

■ a‚bove-ˈmentioned *adj* [attrib] (*fml*) mentioned or named earlier in the same letter, book, article, etc.

above² /əˈbʌv/ *prep* **1** higher than sth: *The sun rose above the horizon.* ○ *The water came above our knees.* ○ *We were flying above the clouds.* ○ *the people who live in the apartment above mine.* **2** more than sth; greater in number, level or age than sth: *Temperatures have been above average recently.* ○ *inflation above 10%* ○ *Applicants must be above the age of 18.* ⇨ note. **3(a)** higher in rank, position or authority than sb/sth: *A captain in the Navy ranks above a captain in the Army.* ○ *The Head of Section is above the Head of Department.* ○ *They finished the season five places above their local rivals.* (**b**) of greater importance or of higher quality than sb/sth: *Should a soldier value honour above life?* ○ *I rate him above every other player in the sport.* **4** too good, too honest, etc to do sth: *She wouldn't lie — she's above that.* ○ *He thinks he's above* (ie too important for) *such a post.* ○ *Although she's the manager, she's not above asking* (ie she isn't too proud to ask) *for advice.* **5** beyond the reach of sth, because of being too good, too honest, etc: *He is above suspicion* (ie is not suspected because he is completely trusted). ○ *Her behaviour was above criticism.* **6** (*infml*) too difficult for one to understand: *All this maths is above me.* **7** (of a sound) louder or clearer than another sound: *I could hardly hear his voice above the noise in the background.* **8** nearer the source of a river than the specified place: *the waterfall above the bridge.* **IDM** **above ˈall** most important of all; especially: *He longs above all (else) to see his family again.* **aˈbove oneself** having too high an opinion of oneself. Compare BELOW, UNDER, UNDERNEATH.

NOTE When they describe a position higher than something, **above** and **over** can often be used in the same way: *They built a new room above/over the garage.* You can only use **over** when there is movement from one side of something to the other: *She threw the ball over the fence.* ○ *They jumped over the stream.* **Over** can also mean 'covering': *He put a blanket over the sleeping child.*
  Above and **over** can also mean 'more than'. **Above** is used in relation to a minimum level or a fixed point: *2000 feet above sea-level* ○ *He is above average height for his age.* ○ *Temperatures will not rise above zero tonight.* **Over** is used with numbers, ages, money and time: *He's over 50.* ○ *It costs over £100.* ○ *We waited over two hours.* ○ *Over a million people have visited the exhibition.*

---

above³ /əˈbʌv/ *adj* [attrib] mentioned, specified or printed previously in a letter, book, article, etc: *See the above paragraph.* ○ *at the above address.* ▶ **the above** *n*: *If the above is not correct, please inform us immediately.*

abracadabra /ˌæbrəkəˈdæbrə/ *n, interj* a word said by a magician (MAGIC) at the moment of performing a magic trick because it is supposed to make the trick happen.

abrade /əˈbreɪd/ *v* [Vn] to rub or scrape the surface of sth, eg rock or skin, and make it rough.

abrasion /əˈbreɪʒn/ *n* **1** [U] the effect on a surface caused by rubbing or scraping: *wood that is resistant to abrasion.* **2** [C] a damaged area, esp of the skin, caused by rubbing or scraping: *suffer cuts and abrasions.*

abrasive /əˈbreɪsɪv/ *adj* **1** that can scrape or rub sth; rough: *abrasive substances/materials.* **2** tending to hurt other people's feelings; harsh and offensive: *an abrasive person/personality/tone of voice.*
▶ **abrasive** *n* [U,C] a substance used for grinding or polishing surfaces.
abrasively *adv.*
abrasiveness *n* [U].

abreast /əˈbrest/ *adv* ~ (**of sb/sth**) side by side and facing the same way: *cycling two abreast* ○ *The boat came abreast of us and signalled us to stop.* **IDM** **be/keep abreast of sth** to be or remain always aware of the latest news, ideas, developments, etc: *Reading the papers keeps us abreast of current affairs.*

abridge /əˈbrɪdʒ/ *v* to make a book, play, etc shorter by omitting parts: [Vn] *an abridged edition/version of 'War and Peace'.* ▶ **abridgement** (also **abridgment**) *n* [U,C].

abroad /əˈbrɔːd/ *adv* **1** in or to a foreign country or countries; away from one's own country: *be/go/live/travel abroad* ○ *visitors (who have come) from abroad* (ie from another country) ○ *He was much respected, both at home and abroad* (ie in his own country and in other countries). **2** being talked about or felt by many people: *There's a rumour abroad that…* (ie People are saying that…). **3** (*arch or rhet*) out of doors: *Have you ventured abroad yet today?*

abrogate /ˈæbrəɡeɪt/ *v* (*fml*) to cancel or ABOLISH sth: [Vn] *abrogate a law/custom/treaty.* ▶ **abrogation** /ˌæbrəˈɡeɪʃn/ *n* [U].

abrupt /əˈbrʌpt/ *adj* **1** sudden and unexpected: *a road with many abrupt turns* ○ *an abrupt ending/change/departure.* **2** talking very little and often rude or seeming rude; CURT: *He has an abrupt manner* (ie does not spend time being polite). ○ *When I asked her about her new job she was quite abrupt with me.* **3** (of speech, etc) not smooth or flowing evenly; DISJOINTED: *short abrupt sentences* ○ *an abrupt style of writing.* ▶ **abruptly** *adv*: *The interview ended abruptly.* **abruptness** *n* [U].

abscess /ˈæbses/ *n* a swollen part of the body in which a thick yellowish liquid (called *pus*) has collected: *abscesses on the gums.*

abscond /əbˈskɒnd/ *v* to run away suddenly and secretly, esp in order to avoid being taken or held prisoner: [V,Vpr] *He absconded (from police custody) on the way to court.*

abseil /ˈæbseɪl/ *v* to descend a steep slope or rock face attached to a double rope that is fixed at a higher point: [Vpr] *abseil down the mountain* [also V,Vp]. ▶ **abseil** *n.*

absence /ˈæbsəns/ *n* **1** ~ (**from…**) (**a**) [U] the state of being away: *His repeated absence (from school) is worrying.* ○ *It happened in my/her/his/our/your/their absence.* ○ *In the absence of the manager* (ie While she is away) *I shall be in charge.* Compare PRESENCE. (**b**) [C] an occasion or period of being away: *numerous absences from school* ○ *throughout his long absence* ○ *after an absence of three months.* **2** [U] a lack; the fact of not existing or not being available: *in the absence of definite proof* ○ *a complete/total absence of any emotion.* **IDM** **conspicuous by one's absence** ⇨ CONSPICUOUS.

absent¹ /ˈæbsənt/ *adj* **1** ~ (**from sth**) (**a**) not present; at another place: *be absent from school/a meeting/work* ○ *absent friends.* (**b**) not existing; lacking; missing: *Love was totally absent from his childhood.* **2** showing that one is not really thinking about what is being said or done around one: *an absent expression/look.*

▶ **absently** adv without concentrating on what is happening or what one is doing: *stare absently.*

■ ₁**absent-**'**minded** adj not concentrating; tending to forget things: *become absent-minded with age.* ₁**absent-**'**mindedly** adv. ₁**absent-**'**mindedness** n [U].

absent² /æb'sent/ v ~ **oneself (from sth)** (*fml*) to decide not to be present; to stay away: [Vn, Vnpr] *He deliberately absented himself (from the meeting).*

absentee /ˌæbsən'tiː/ n a person who is absent from a place, event, etc where he or she was expected.

▶ **absenteeism** /ˌæbsən'tiːɪzəm/ n [U] frequent absence from school or work, esp without good reason.

■ ₁**absentee** '**landlord** n a person who does not live at and rarely visits the property that he or she lets (LET¹ 4).

absolute /'æbsəluːt/ adj **1** (often used for emphasis) complete; total: *have absolute trust in a person* ○ *tell the absolute truth* ○ *absolute ignorance/ silence* ○ *The darkness was absolute.* ○ *He's an absolute fool!* **2** certain; definite; leaving no doubt: *have absolute proof* ○ *It's an absolute fact.* See also DECREE ABSOLUTE. **3(a)** without limit or restriction: *absolute authority/power.* **(b)** having power without limit or restriction: *an absolute ruler.* **4** existing independently and not in relation to sth else: *There is no absolute standard for beauty.*

▶ **absolute** n an idea or principle that is valid at all times and in all circumstances: *a desire for absolutes in an uncertain world.*

■ ₁**absolute ma**'**jority** n (in an election) a majority over all rivals combined; more than half of the total votes: *The Socialists won/gained an absolute majority.* ○ *33 seats short of an absolute majority.* ₁**absolute** '**zero** n [U] the lowest temperature that is possible in theory.

absolutely /'æbsəluːtli/ adv **1** completely and totally: *Let me make the position **absolutely clear**.* ○ *I'm absolutely convinced that there will be no conflict of interests.* ○ *You're absolutely right.* ○ *I'm not absolutely certain, but…* ○ *I absolutely refuse.* ○ *The money is mine absolutely.* **2** (used with *adjs* or *vs* that express strong emotion or feeling) extremely; very much: *I was absolutely furious.* ○ *She absolutely adores him.* ○ *Her father was absolutely appalled.* **3** (used to give emphasis) positively: *It's absolutely pouring down.* ○ *He did absolutely no work* (ie no work at all). ○ *We had absolutely no intention of following* (ie certainly did not intend to follow) *her advice.* ○ *There is absolutely nothing that anyone can do about it.* **4** /ˌæbsə'luːtli/ (*infml*) (used in answer to a question or as a comment to indicate agreement) yes; certainly: *'Don't you agree?' 'Oh, absolutely!'*

absolution /ˌæbsə'luːʃn/ n [U] (esp in the Christian Church) a formal declaration by a priest that a person's sins have been forgiven: *grant sb absolution.*

absolutism /'æbsəluːtɪzəm/ n [U] (*politics*) the principle that those responsible for government should have power without limit or restriction. ▶ **absolutist** n, adj.

absolve /əb'zɒlv/ v [Vn, Vnpr] ~ **sb (from/of sth) 1** (*fml*) to declare that sb is free of guilt, blame, etc: *The inquiry absolved the driver (of all responsibility for the accident).* **2** to give ABSOLUTION to sb: *absolve repentant sinners (from/of their sins).*

absorb /əb'sɔːb, -'zɔːb/ v [Vn] **1(a)** to take, draw or suck sth in: *absorb heat* ○ *Plants absorb oxygen.* ○ *Dry sand absorbs water.* ○ *Aspirin is quickly absorbed by/into the body.* ○ (*fig*) *absorb the atmosphere of a place* ○ (*fig*) *a society that has absorbed other cultures.* **(b)** (often passive) to include sth/sb as part of itself or oneself; to INCORPORATE sth/sb: *The larger firm gradually absorbed its smaller competitors.* ○ *The surrounding villages have been absorbed by/into*

the growing city. **(c)** to take sth into the mind and learn or understand it: *absorb information* ○ *going to Italy to absorb the language.* **2** to reduce the effect of a blow, etc: *Buffers absorbed most of the impact.* See also SHOCK ABSORBER. **3** to hold sb's attention or interest completely: *His business absorbs him.* **4** to use up a large supply of sth, esp money: *absorb over half of all public expenditure.*

▶ **absorbed** adj [usu pred] with one's attention fully held: *She seemed totally absorbed in her book.* **absorbent** /-ənt/ adj that can absorb sth, esp liquids: *absorbent paper.* **absorbency** n [U]. **absorbing** adj holding the attention fully; extremely interesting: *an absorbing film* ○ *Watching the animals come to drink was utterly absorbing.*

absorption /əb'sɔːpʃn, -'zɔːp-/ n [U] ~ **(in sth)**: *rapid absorption of water* ○ *better shock absorption* ○ *His work suffered because of his total absorption in sport.*

abstain /əb'steɪn/ v [V, Vpr] ~ **(from sth) 1** to choose not to use one's vote: *At the last election he abstained (from voting).* **2** (*fml or joc*) to keep oneself from doing or having sth that one likes or enjoys: *He has been advised to abstain from alcohol.*

▶ **abstainer** n a person who abstains: *a total abstainer* (ie one who never takes alcoholic drinks). See also ABSTENTION, ABSTINENCE.

abstemious /əb'stiːmiəs/ adj not taking much food or drink; not doing or having too much of sth one likes or enjoys: *an abstemious person/lifestyle* ○ *abstemious habits.*

abstention /əb'stenʃn/ n **(a)** [U] ~ **(from sth)** the action or practice of abstaining (ABSTAIN 1), esp of choosing not to use one's vote at an election. **(b)** [C] an instance of this: *five votes in favour of the proposal, three against and two abstentions.*

abstinence /'æbstɪnəns/ n [U] ~ **(from sth)** the practice of abstaining (ABSTAIN 2), esp from food, alcoholic drinks or sex: *total abstinence.*

abstract¹ /'æbstrækt/ adj **1(a)** existing in thought or as an idea but not having a physical or practical existence: *We may talk of abstract things, but beauty itself is abstract.* **(b)** general; not based on any particular person, situation, etc: *talk about sth in abstract terms/in an abstract way* ○ *He has some abstract notion of wanting to change the world.* Compare CONCRETE¹ 1. **2** (of art) not representing people or objects in a realistic way but expressing the artist's ideas and feelings about certain aspects of them: *an abstract painting/painter/design/ballet.*

▶ **abstractly** adv.

■ ₁**abstract** '**noun** n a noun that refers to an abstract¹(1) quality or state, eg *goodness* or *freedom*, not a physical object.

abstract² /'æbstrækt/ n **1** an abstract idea or quality. **2** an example of abstract art: *a painter of abstracts.* **3** a short summary of a book, etc: *an abstract of a lecture.* **IDM** **in the** '**abstract** in a general way, without reference to a particular person, thing, event, situation, etc: *Consider the problem in the abstract.*

abstract³ /æb'strækt/ v **1** ~ **sth (from sth)** to remove sth; to separate sth from sth else: [Vnpr] *Two other points must be abstracted from the argument.* [also Vn]. **2** [Vn] to make a written summary of a book, etc.

abstracted /æb'stræktɪd/ adj thinking of other things; not paying attention: *an abstracted gaze/ smile.* ▶ **abstractedly** adv.

abstraction /æb'strækʃn/ n **1(a)** [C] an abstract idea: *ideological abstractions.* **(b)** [U] the quality of being abstract. **2** [U] the state of thinking of other things and not paying attention; absent-mindedness (ABSENT¹): *a general air of abstraction.* **3** [U] (*fml*) the action of removing sth from sth else; the state of being removed from sth else: *ideas conceived in abstraction from physical observations.*

abstruse /əbˈstruːs, æb-/ *adj* (*fml*) difficult to understand: *abstruse arguments/topics.*

absurd /əbˈsɜːd/ *adj* **1** not reasonable or sensible: *What an absurd idea!* ○ *It was absurd of you to suggest such a thing.* **2** foolish and ridiculous: *That uniform makes them look absurd.*
▶ **the absurd** *n* [sing] things that are or appear absurd: *her sense of the absurd* ○ *Some of his criticisms verge on the absurd.*
absurdity *n* [U, C]: *see the absurdity of a situation.*
absurdly *adv*: *absurdly high prices.*

abundance /əˈbʌndəns/ *n* [U, sing] a quantity that is more than enough; a very large amount: *There was good food* **in abundance**/*an abundance of good food at the party.*

abundant /əˈbʌndənt/ *adj* (**a**) more than enough; great in number or amount: *an abundant supply of fruit* ○ *Fish are abundant in the lake.* ○ *We have abundant proof of his guilt.* (**b**) [pred] ~ **in sth** having plenty of sth; rich in sth: *a land abundant in minerals.* ▶ **abundantly** *adv*: *be abundantly supplied with fruit* ○ *He's made his views abundantly* (ie very) *clear.*

abuse¹ /əˈbjuːz/ *v* **1**(**a**) to make bad or excessive use of sth: [Vn] *abusing drugs/alcohol.* (**b**) to take advantage of one's power, position, etc unfairly or excessively: [Vn] *abuse sb's hospitality.* ○ *abuse one's authority/the confidence placed in one.* **2**(**a**) to treat a person or an animal badly or violently: [Vn] *a hostel for abused and battered women.* Compare MISUSE. (**b**) to have sex with sb illegally or against their will: [Vn] *viciously beaten and sexually abused* ○ *a man who abused his own daughter.* **3** to speak in an insulting or offensive way to or about sb: [Vn] *Journalists had been threatened and abused.* ▶ **abuser** *n*: *a drug abuser* ○ *a child abuser.*

abuse² /əˈbjuːs/ *n* **1**(**a**) [U, C] wrong or excessive use of sth: *drug/solvent abuse* ○ *widespread abuse of computer facilities.* (**b**) [U, sing] wrong or excessive use of one's power, position, etc: *The new system of paying cash bonuses is open to abuse.* ○ *an abuse of trust/privilege/authority.* (**c**) [C] an unfair or illegal practice: *put a stop to political abuses* ○ *abuses of human rights.* **2** [U, C] cruel treatment of a person or animal, esp sexually: *child sex abuse* ○ *physical abuse of horses.* **3** [U] rude and offensive remarks about a person; insults: *verbal abuse* ○ *hurl (a stream/torrent of) abuse at sb* ○ *The word 'bastard' is often used as a term of abuse.*

abusive /əˈbjuːsɪv/ *adj* (of speech or a person) offensive and insulting; criticizing harshly and rudely: *abusive language/remarks* ○ *He became abusive.* ▶ **abusively** *adv*.

abut /əˈbʌt/ *v* (**-tt-**) ~ (**on/onto sth**) (*fml*) (of land or a building) to have a common boundary with sth or a side touching the side of sth: [Vpr] *His land abuts on(to) the motorway.* [also V, Vn].

abysmal /əˈbɪzməl/ *adj* **1** (*infml*) extremely bad: *live in abysmal conditions* ○ *His manners are abysmal.* **2** extreme; very great: *abysmal ignorance.* ▶ **abysmally** *adv*.

abyss /əˈbɪs/ *n* a hole so deep that it seems to have no bottom: (*fig*) *an abyss of ignorance/despair/loneliness.*

AC (also **ac**) /ˌeɪ ˈsiː/ *abbr* **1** (*esp US*) air-conditioning. **2** alternating current. Compare DC 1.

a/c *abbr* (*commerce*) account (current): *charge to a/c 319054* ○ *a/c payee only* (ie written on cheques).

acacia /əˈkeɪʃə/ *n* any of several trees with yellow or white flowers, esp one with a sticky SAP¹ used in making glue.

academe /ˈækədiːm/ *n* [U] (*esp joc*) = ACADEMIA.

academia /ˌækəˈdiːmiə/ *n* [U] the field of learning,

teaching, research, etc, esp at a university: *a career in academia.*

academic /ˌækəˈdemɪk/ *adj* **1** [attrib] of education in schools, universities, etc: *the ˌacademic ˈyear* (ie the total time within a year when teaching is done, usu starting in September or October) ○ *academic dress* ○ *academic life/achievement.* **2**(**a**) [attrib] involving a greater amount of reading and study than technical or practical work: *academic subjects such as history.* (**b**) good at subjects involving reading and study: *She wasn't very academic and hated school.* **3** not relevant to practical affairs; of THEORETICAL interest only: *a matter of academic concern* ○ *The question is purely academic.*
▶ **academic** *n* a teacher at a university, college, etc.
academically /-klɪ/ *adv*.

academician /əˌkædəˈmɪʃn; *US* ˌækədəˈmɪʃn/ *n* a member of an ACADEMY(2).

academy /əˈkædəmi/ *n* **1** a school or college for special training: *an aˌcademy of ˈmusic* ○ *a ˈnaval/ˈmilitary academy.* **2** (usu **Academy**) a society of famous or important artists, scientists, etc; a society for cultivating art, literature, etc, of which membership is an honour: *The Royal Academy (of Arts).*
■ **Aˌcademy Aˈward** *n* one of the awards given every year for achievement in the cinema. They are presented by the US Academy of Motion Picture Arts and Sciences. Compare OSCAR.

ACAS /ˈeɪkæs/ *abbr* (in Britain) Advisory, Conciliation and Arbitration Service (an organization that helps with negotiation during industrial disputes).

accede /əkˈsiːd/ *v* ~ (**to sth**) (*fml*) **1** to take a high position, esp to become king or queen: [Vpr] *accede to the chancellorship* [V, Vpr] *Queen Victoria acceded (to the throne) in 1837.* **2** to agree to a request, proposal, etc: [Vpr] *They will not lightly accede to his request/demand.*

accelerate /əkˈseləreɪt/ *v* **1** to happen or make sth happen faster or earlier: [Vn] *accelerating the rate of growth* [V] *Tests show global warming has accelerated.* **2** (of a vehicle or person) to increase speed rapidly: [Vp] *He accelerated away from the traffic-lights.* [V] *The car accelerated to overtake me.* Compare DECELERATE.
▶ **acceleration** /əkˌseləˈreɪʃn/ *n* **1** [U, sing] ~ (**in sth**) an increase in the rate or speed of sth: *an acceleration in the rate of economic growth.* **2** [U] the ability of a vehicle to gain speed: *a car with good acceleration.*

accelerator /əkˈseləreɪtə(r)/ *n* **1** a device for increasing speed, esp the PEDAL in a vehicle that controls the speed of the engine. ⇨ picture at CAR. **2** (*physics*) an apparatus for making particles (PARTICLE 2) of matter move at high speeds.

accent /ˈæksent, -sənt/ *n* **1** [C] an emphasis given to a syllable or word by means of stress or pitch¹(2): *In the word 'today' the accent is on the second syllable.* **2** [C] a mark or symbol, usu above a letter, used in writing and printing to indicate emphasis or the quality of a vowel sound: *'Café' has an accent on the 'e'.* **3** [C, U] a national, local or individual way of pronouncing words: *speak English with a foreign accent* ○ *have an American accent* ○ *a voice without (a trace of) accent.* Compare DIALECT. **4** [C usu *sing*, U] a special emphasis given to sth: *In all our products the accent is on quality.*
▶ **accent** /ækˈsent/ *v* **1** to pronounce a word or syllable with emphasis or with a foreign accent(3): [Vnadv] *Her English was slow and heavily accented.* [also Vn]. **2** [Vn] to write accents on words, etc. **3** to emphasize a particular feature: [Vn] *eyes accented by make-up.*

accentuate /əkˈsentʃueɪt/ *v* to make sth very noticeable or prominent; to emphasize sth: [Vn] *The* *tight sweater only accentuated his fat stomach.* ▶ **accentuation** /əkˌsentʃuˈeɪʃn/ n [U].

accept /əkˈsept/ v **1(a)** to take willingly sth that is offered: [Vn] *accept a gift/a piece of advice/an apology.* **(b)** to say 'yes' to an offer, invitation, etc: [V, Vn] *She offered me a lift so I accepted (it).* ○ *He proposed marriage and she accepted (him).* **(c)** to receive sth/sb as adequate or suitable: [Vn] *Will you accept a cheque?* ○ *The machine only accepts 10p coins.* ○ *an article accepted for publication* ○ *The college I applied to has accepted me* (ie given me a place on a course). **2** to agree or approve of sth: [Vn] *accept the judge's decision* ○ *They accepted the changes we proposed.* **3(a)** to acknowledge or agree to bear responsibility, etc: [Vn] *He accepts blame for the accident* (ie agrees that it was his fault). ○ *You must accept the consequences of your action.* **(b)** to tolerate sth unpleasant and not try to change or avoid it: [Vn] *accept risks/suffering* ○ *They continue to accept low pay and appalling conditions.* **4** ~ sth **(as sth)** to consider sth as true; to believe sth: [V.that] *I cannot accept that he is to blame.* [Vn] *We do not accept your explanation/what you have said.* ○ *It is an accepted fact* (ie sth that everyone thinks is true). [Vn-n] *Can we accept his account as the true version?* **5** to treat sb/sth as welcome: [Vn] *He was never really accepted by his classmates.*

acceptable /əkˈseptəbl/ adj ~ **(to sb)** **1(a)** adequate or suitable: *socially acceptable behaviour* ○ *Is the proposal acceptable to you?* **(b)** welcome: *A cup of tea would be most acceptable.* **2** that can be tolerated or allowed: *an acceptable risk/sacrifice* ○ *acceptable casualties* ○ *The delay would mean extra costs and this is not acceptable.* Compare UNACCEPTABLE. ▶ **acceptability** /əkˌseptəˈbɪləti/ n [U]. **acceptably** /-bli/ adv.

acceptance /əkˈseptəns/ n **1** [U, C] the action or an instance of accepting a gift, invitation, offer, etc: *a short speech of acceptance* ○ *Since we sent out the invitations we've received five acceptances and one refusal.* **2** [U] the action or process of being accepted or admitted into a group, etc: *acceptance onto a course* ○ *Your acceptance into the pension scheme is guaranteed.* **3** [U] agreement with, approval of, or belief in sth: *her grudging acceptance of his explanation* ○ *The new laws gained widespread acceptance.* **4** [U] willingness to tolerate sth unpleasant: *their calm acceptance of pain/poverty.*

access /ˈækses/ n [U] **1** ~ **(to sth)** a means of approaching or entering a place; a way in: *The only access to the farmhouse is across the fields.* ○ *Some theatres still don't have wheelchair access.* **2** ~ **(to sth/sb)** the opportunity or right to use sth or approach sb: *gain/get access to classified information* ○ *Students must have access to a good library.* ○ *Journalists were denied access to the president.* ▶ **access** v **1** (computing) to open a computer file in order to get information from or put information into it: [Vn] *She accessed three different files to find the correct information.* ○ *Databases were accessed and updated daily.* **2** to approach, enter or use sth: [Vn] *The loft can be accessed by ladder.* ■ **'access road** n (esp US) = SLIP-ROAD. **'access time** n [U] (computing) the time taken to obtain information stored in a computer.

accessible /əkˈsesəbl/ adj ~ **(to sb)** **1** that can be reached, used, etc: *a beach accessible only from the sea* ○ *documents not accessible to the public.* **2** easy to use or understand: *Her poetry is always very accessible.* Compare INACCESSIBLE. ▶ **accessibility** /əkˌsesəˈbɪləti/ n [U].

accession /ækˈseʃn/ n ~ **(to sth)** **1** [U] the reaching or acquiring of a rank or position: *celebrating the queen's accession (to the throne).* Compare SUCCESSION 3. **2** [C] a thing added, esp a new item in a

library, museum, etc: *recent accessions to the art gallery.* See also ACQUISITION 2.

accessory /əkˈsesəri/ n **1** (usu pl) **(a)** a thing that is useful or added as a decoration but is not essential; a small extra part that can be attached to sth: *bicycle accessories* (eg a lamp, pump, etc). **(b)** a small article of (esp women's) dress, eg a belt, bag, etc. **2** ~ **(to sth)** (law) a person who helps another in a crime or knows the details of it: *He was charged with being an accessory to the murder.* **IDM** **accessory before/after the fact** (law) (formerly in Britain) a person who, although not present when a crime is committed, helps the person committing it either before or after it.

accident /ˈæksɪdənt/ n **1** [C] an unpleasant event that happens unexpectedly and causes damage, injury, etc: *be killed in a car/road accident* ○ *I had a slight accident at home and broke some glasses.* ○ *He's very late — I do hope he hasn't met with an accident.* ○ *We reached home without accident* (ie safely). ○ *accident insurance.* **2(a)** [C] an event that happens unexpectedly and is not planned in advance: *Their early arrival was just an accident.* ○ *It is no accident that* (ie not by chance that) *she became a doctor: both her father and grandfather were doctors.* **(b)** [U] chance; FORTUNE(1): *By accident of birth* (ie Because of where he happened to be born) *he is entitled to American citizenship.* **IDM** **accidents will happen** (saying) some unfortunate events must be accepted as inevitable. **by accident** as a result of chance; not planned or organized: *I only found out about it purely by accident.* **a chapter of accidents** ⇨ CHAPTER. ■ **'accident-prone** adj [usu pred] more than usually likely to have accidents: *She was the most accident-prone of the four children.*

accidental /ˌæksɪˈdentl/ adj happening unexpectedly or by chance: *a verdict of accidental death* ○ *an accidental meeting with a friend.* ▶ **accidentally** /-təli/ adv: *The carpet accidentally caught fire.* ○ *The remark slipped out quite accidentally.*

acclaim /əˈkleɪm/ v ~ **sb/sth (as sth)** (esp passive) to welcome or approve of sb/sth enthusiastically; to praise sb/sth publicly: [Vnadv] *a much/widely acclaimed performance* [Vn-n] *It was acclaimed as a great discovery.* [also Vn]. ▶ **acclaim** n [U] enthusiastic welcome or approval; praise: *popular/universal acclaim* ○ *The book received great critical acclaim.*

acclamation /ˌækləˈmeɪʃn/ n [U] loud and enthusiastic approval, esp to honour or welcome sb: *She collected her prize amid great acclamation.*

acclimatize, -ise /əˈklaɪmətaɪz/ v ~ **(oneself/sb/sth) (to sth)** to become able to live in and get used to a new climate or environment, new conditions, etc: [V] *arrive two days early in order to acclimatize* [Vpr, Vnpr] *It takes many months to acclimatize (yourself) to life in the tropics.* [also Vn]. ▶ **acclimatization, -isation** /əˌklaɪmətaɪˈzeɪʃn; US -tɪˈz-/ n [U].

accolade /ˈækəleɪd, ˌækəˈleɪd/ n an award of praise, approval or honour: *To be chosen to represent their country is the highest accolade for most athletes.*

accommodate /əˈkɒmədeɪt/ v **1(a)** to provide a room or place to sleep for sb: [Vn] *The hotel can accommodate up to 500 guests.* **(b)** to provide space for sb/sth: [Vn] *The garden isn't big enough to accommodate livestock.* ○ *Over 70 minutes of music can be accommodated on a CD.* **2** (fml) to take sth into consideration; to take account of sth when planning or calculating, etc: [Vn] *accommodate the special needs of minority groups* ○ *This theory fails to accommodate all the facts.* **3** ~ **(sth/oneself) to sth** (fml) to adjust or adapt oneself/sth to a new situation or to sth else: [Vpr, Vnpr] *accommodate (oneself) to new surroundings.* **4** ~ **sb (with sth)** (fml) to be helpful to sb; to assist sb: [Vn] *I have accommodated the*

press a great deal, giving numerous interviews.
[Vnpr] *The bank will accommodate you with a loan.*
▶ **accommodating** *adj* (of a person) easy to deal
with; willing to help or support: *I found the officials
extremely accommodating to foreign visitors.*

accommodation /əˌkɒməˈdeɪʃn/ *n* **1(a)** [U] (*Brit*)
one or more rooms, esp for living in: *find suitable/
cheap/temporary accommodation* ○ *Hotel accommodation is scarce.* ○ *Wanted — furnished accommodation
for a young married couple.* (**b**) **accommodations**
[pl] (*US*) lodgings, sometimes also including food.
(**c**) [U] the providing of a room, lodgings, etc: *an
organization concerned with the accommodation of
the homeless.* **2** [U] (*fml*) the process of adapting;
adjustment: *It's a matter of mutual accommodation.*
3 [C] (*fml*) a convenient arrangement; a compromise: *The two sides failed to agree on every point but
came to an accommodation.*

accompaniment /əˈkʌmpənimənt/ *n* [C, U] ~ (**to
sth**) **1** a thing that supports or improves another
thing or happens at the same time: *White wine provided the perfect accompaniment to the meal.* ○ *She
made her speech **to the accompaniment of** loud
laughter.* **2** (*music*) a part played by one or more
instruments to support another instrument, voice or
CHOIR(1): *singing with (a) piano accompaniment.*

accompanist /əˈkʌmpənist/ *n* a person who plays
a musical instrument, esp a piano, while sb else
sings or plays the main part of the music.

accompany /əˈkʌmpəni/ *v* (*pt, pp* **-ied**) **1** (*fml*) to
travel or go with sb: [Vn] *I must ask you to accompany me to the police station.* ○ *He was accompanied
on the expedition by his wife.* ○ *Warships will accompany the convoy.* **2(a)** to be present or occur with
sth: [Vn] *strong winds accompanied by heavy rain* ○
Shouts of protest accompanied this announcement.
(**b**) (usu passive) to provide sth in addition to sth
else: [Vn] *Each application should be accompanied
by a stamped addressed envelope.* **3** ~ **sb** (**at/on sth**)
(*music*) to play a musical instrument, esp a piano,
while sb else sings or plays the main part of the
music: [Vn, Vnpr] *The singer was accompanied (at/
on the piano) by her sister.*

accomplice /əˈkʌmplɪs; *US* əˈkɒm-/ *n* a person who
helps another to do sth wrong or against the law:
The police arrested him and his two accomplices.

accomplish /əˈkʌmplɪʃ; *US* əˈkɒm-/ *v* to succeed in
doing sth; to complete sth successfully; to achieve
sth: [Vn] *I don't feel I've accomplished very much
today.* ○ *Such a result can only be accomplished by
hard work.*
▶ **accomplished** *adj* **1** skilled: *an accomplished
dancer/cook/linguist.* **2** (*dated*) well trained or educated in social skills such as conversation, art,
music, etc: *an accomplished young lady.*

accomplishment /əˈkʌmplɪʃmənt; *US* əˈkɒm-/ *n*
1 [U] the successful completing of sth: *the accomplishment of one's objectives.* **2** [C] a thing achieved:
*Winning the competition was a marvellous accom-
plishment.* **3(a)** [U] skill in an activity: *a poet of rare
accomplishment.* (**b**) [C] a social skill that can be
learnt, eg conversation, art, music, etc: *Dancing and
singing were among her many accomplishments.*

accord¹ /əˈkɔːd/ *n* a formal agreement between
groups of people: *a peace accord* ○ *the wages accord
between government, employers and unions* ○ *the
Anglo-Irish accord of November 1985.* **IDM** **in accord
(with sth/sb)** in agreement with sth/sb; in harmony: *Such an act would not be in accord with our
policy.* ○ *We are in complete/perfect accord.* **of one's
own acˈcord** without being asked or forced: *He
came back of his own accord.* **with ˌone acˈcord**
with everybody in agreement or united: *With one
accord they all stood up and cheered.*

accord² /əˈkɔːd/ *v* **1** ~ (**with sth**) (*fml*) (of a thing)

to be in agreement with sth; to correspond to sth:
[Vpr] *This information does not accord with the evidence of earlier witnesses.* [V] *His principles and
actions do not accord.* **2** ~ **sth to sb** (*fml*) to give
authority, rights, status, etc to sb: [Vnn] *Management accorded him permission to attend the seminar.*
[Vnpr] *The powers accorded to the government.*

accordance /əˈkɔːdns/ *n* **IDM** **in accordance
with sth** in agreement or harmony with sth: *in
accordance with sb's wishes* ○ *act in accordance with
custom/the regulations/the law.*

according /əˈkɔːdɪŋ/ **according to** *prep* **1** as stated
or reported by sb/sth: *According to John you were in
Edinburgh last week.* ○ *You've been in prison six
times according to our records.* **2** following or agreeing with sth that has already been decided: *act
according to one's principles* ○ *Everything went according to plan.* ○ *The work was done according to
her instructions.* **3** in relation to sth; in proportion
to sth: *salary according to qualifications and experience* ○ *clothes arranged according to colour.*
▶ **accordingly** *adv* **1** in a manner that is appropriate to the particular circumstances: *I've told you
what the situation is; you must act accordingly.* **2**
(used esp at the beginning of a sentence) for that
reason; therefore: *The cost of materials rose sharply
last year. Accordingly, this increase was passed on to
the consumer in higher prices.*

accordion /əˈkɔːdiən/ (also **piano accordion**) *n* a
musical instrument that is held in the hands. It is
played by pressing keys at one end and buttons at
the other end while the two ends are pressed together and pulled apart to produce sounds. ⇨
picture at CONCERTINA.

accost /əˈkɒst; *US* əˈkɔːst/ *v* [Vn] (**a**) to approach
and speak to sb, esp sb who does not wish to be
approached: *She was accosted in the street by a complete stranger.* (**b**) (of a prostitute) to approach sb in
the street and offer to have sex with them.

account¹ /əˈkaʊnt/ *n* **1** (*abbr* **a/c**) a written statement of money paid or owed for goods or services:
send in an account ○ *settle one's account* (ie pay what
one owes) ○ *keep the accounts* (ie keep a detailed
record of money spent and received) ○ *The accounts
show a profit of $9000.* See also EXPENSE ACCOUNT. **2**
(*abbr* **a/c**) an arrangement made with a bank, etc
which allows sb to leave their money there until
they need it or to borrow money from the bank:
have an account at/with a bank (ie keep money
there and use its facilities) ○ *open/close an account* ○
pay money into/draw money out of an account ○ *I
have £200 in my account.* See also CURRENT ACCOUNT,
DEPOSIT ACCOUNT. **3** = CREDIT ACCOUNT. **4** a report or
description of an event: *She gave the police a full
account of the incident.* ○ *Don't believe the newspaper
account (of what happened).* **IDM** **by/from all accounts** according to what has been said or
reported: *I've never been there but it is, by all accounts, a lovely place.* **by one's own account**
according to what one says oneself: *By his own
account he had a rather unhappy childhood.* **call sb
to account** ⇨ CALL¹. **give a good, poor, etc
acˈcount of oneself** to do or perform well, badly,
etc, esp in a contest: *Our team gave a splendid
account of themselves to win the match.* **of great,
small, no, some, etc acˈcount** of great, small, etc
importance: *a matter of no account.* **on account 1**
as a payment in advance of a larger one: *I'll give you
£20 on account.* **2** to be paid for later: *buy sth on
account.* **on sb's account** for sb's sake: *Don't
change your plans on ¹my account.* **on account of
sth; on this/that account** because of sth; for this/
that reason: *We delayed our departure on account of
the bad weather.* **on no account; not on any account** (used for emphasis) not for any reason: *Don't
on any account leave the house unlocked.* **on one's**

[Vnn] = verb + noun + noun   [V-adj] = verb + adjective   For more help with verbs, see Study pages **B4–8.**

own ac'count 1 for one's own benefit and at one's own risk: *work on one's own account.* **2** on one's own behalf: *I was worried on my own account, not yours.* **put/turn sth to good ac'count** to use money, talent, etc well and in a way that brings benefit or profit: *He turned his artistic gifts to good account by becoming a sculptor.* **settle/square an account/one's account(s) (with sb)** to punish sb or cause them harm because they have caused one harm or suffering. **take account of sth; take sth into account** to consider the importance of a particular factor, consequence, etc when making a decision: *You must take his age into account when you judge his performance.*

account² /ə'kaʊnt/ *v* (*fml*) to think of sb/sth as sth; to consider: [Vn-adj] *In English law a man is accounted innocent until he is proved guilty.* **IDM** **there's no accounting for taste** (*saying*) it is impossible to explain why different people like different things: *She thinks he's wonderful — oh well, there's no accounting for taste* (ie I don't like him and cannot understand why she does). **PHRV** **account for sth 1** to be the explanation of sth; to explain the cause of sth: *His illness accounts for his absence.* ○ *Please account for your disgraceful conduct.* **2** to expect sth; to consider sth likely to happen and make appropriate allowances or arrangements: *She hadn't accounted for becoming ill during the trip.* **3** to be the specified amount or proportion of sth: *The Japanese market accounted for 35% of total sales.* **account for sb/sth 1** to know where sb/sth is or what has happened to them, esp after an accident: *All passengers and crew on the stricken ship have now been accounted for.* ○ *Three files cannot be accounted for.* **2** (*infml*) to kill sb or destroy sth: *Our anti-aircraft guns accounted for five enemy bombers.* **account for sth (to sb)** to give a satisfactory record of money, etc in one's care: *We are required to account (to the company) for every penny we spend on business trips.*

accountable /ə'kaʊntəbl/ *adj* [pred] ~ (**to sb**) (**for sth**) required or expected to give an explanation of one's actions, expenditure, etc; responsible: *Who are you accountable to in the organization?* ○ *He is mentally ill and cannot be held accountable for his actions.* ▶ **accountability** *n* [U]: *the accountability of local government to Parliament* ○ *proposals for greater accountability on the part of the police.*

accountant /ə'kaʊntənt/ *n* a person whose profession is to keep or check financial accounts. ▶ **accountancy** /ə'kaʊntənsi/ *n* [U] the profession of an accountant.

accoutrements /ə'ku:trəmənts/ (*US* **accouterments** /ə'ku:tərmənts/) *n* [pl] (*fml*) extra items of dress, equipment, etc: *an evening dress and all its accoutrements — matching shoes, handbag, etc* ○ (*fig*) *a young man with all the accoutrements* (ie all the necessary personal qualities) *of leadership.*

accredit /ə'kredɪt/ *v* (*fml*) **1** ~ **sb to ...** (usu passive) to appoint sb to an official position, esp as an AMBASSADOR: [Vnpr] *He was accredited to Madrid.* **2** ~ **sth to sb/~ sb with sth** (usu passive) to believe sb to be responsible for doing or saying sth: [Vnpr] *She is accredited with having first introduced this word into the language.* ▶ **accreditation** /ə,kredɪ'teɪʃn/ [U]: *grounds for withholding accreditation* ○ *reporters with false accreditation.*

accredited *adj* [usu attrib] **1** officially appointed or recognized: *our accredited representative* ○ *an accredited journalist/photographer.* **2** officially declared to be of the desired quality or standard: *an accredited school/course.* **3** generally accepted or believed: *the accredited theories.*

accretion /ə'kri:ʃn/ *n* **1** [C] matter which grows on or is added to sth, and accumulates in a layer or mass: *a chimney blocked by an accretion of soot* ○ (*fig*) *Recent research has stripped away many false accretions to historical fact.* **2** [U] the process of growth or increase by means of gradual additions: (*fig*) *the accretion of power.*

accrue /ə'kru:/ *v* (**a**) ~ (**to sb**) (**from sth**) to increase over a period of time: [Vpr] *economic benefits accruing to the country from tourism* [V] *Interest will accrue if you keep your money in a savings account.* (**b**) to allow sth to collect over a period of time; to accumulate sth: [Vn] *The firm had accrued debts of over £6m.*

accumulate /ə'kju:mjəleɪt/ *v* (**a**) to obtain gradually or gather together an increasing number or quantity of sth: [Vn] *I seem to have accumulated a lot of books.* ○ *We need to accumulate enough evidence to ensure his conviction.* ○ *By investing wisely she accumulated a fortune.* ○ *My savings are accumulating interest.* (**b**) to increase in number or quantity: [V] *Dust and dirt soon accumulate if a house is not cleaned regularly.* ○ *Debts soon began to accumulate.* ▶ **accumulation** /ə,kju:mjə'leɪʃn/ *n* [U,C]: *the accumulation of wealth/debt* ○ *an accumulation of toxic chemicals.*

accumulative /ə'kju:mjələtɪv; *US* -leɪtɪv/ *adj* growing or developing by a series of additions: *an accumulative process.*

accuracy /'ækjərəsi/ *n* [U] the state of being correct or exact and without error, esp as a result of careful effort: *She hits the ball with great accuracy* ○ *doubt/question the accuracy of government statistics* ○ *It is impossible to say with any (degree of) accuracy how many people are affected.*

accurate /'ækjərət/ *adj* correct and exact; free from error: *an accurate clock/map* ○ *accurate statistics/measurements/calculations* ○ *accurate information* ○ *an accurate description/account of the event* ○ *Journalists are not always accurate (in what they write).* Compare INACCURATE. ▶ **accurately** *adv*: *The article accurately reflects popular opinion.*

accursed /ə'kɜ:sɪd/ *adj* **1** [usu attrib] (*infml*) (used to indicate one's dislike of or annoyance with the specified person or thing): *those accursed neighbours of ours.* **2** (*dated*) under a curse¹(2).

accusation /,ækju'zeɪʃn/ *n* **1** [C] a statement accusing a person of a fault, wrongdoing or crime: *reject/dismiss an accusation* ○ *Accusations of corruption have been made/brought/laid against him.* **2** [U] the act or process of accusing or being accused: *There was a hint of accusation in her voice.*

accusative /ə'kju:zətɪv/ *n* (*grammar*) (in certain languages) the special form of a noun, a pronoun or an adjective used when it is (part of) the direct object (DIRECT¹) of a verb. ▶ **accusative** *adj*: *The accusative forms of the pronouns 'I', 'we' and 'she' are 'me', 'us' and 'her'.*

accuse /ə'kju:z/ *v* ~ **sb** (**of sth**) to say that sb has done sth wrong, is guilty of sth or has broken the law: [Vnpr] *accuse sb of theft/murder* ○ *She accused him of lying.* ○ *The government was accused of incompetence.* ○ *They stand accused of crimes of the utmost gravity.* [also Vn].

▶ **accusatory** /ə'kju:zətəri, ,ækju'zeɪtəri; *US* -tɔ:ri/ *adj* indicating or suggesting that one believes sb has done sth wrong, etc: *an accusatory glare* ○ *His tone was accusatory.*

the accused *n* (*pl* unchanged) a person on trial for committing a crime: *The accused was/were acquitted of the charge.*

accuser *n*.

accusing *adj*: *a slightly accusing look/stare/face* ○ *His mother's tone was accusing.* ○ (*fig*) *The report points an accusing finger at the insurance industry.* **accusingly** /ə'kju:zɪŋli/ *adv*: *look/point accusingly at sb* ○ *'Edward!' she said accusingly.*

accustom /ə'kʌstəm/ *v* **PHRV** **accustom oneself/sb to sth** to make oneself/sb familiar with sth or

---

[V] = verb used alone   [Vn] = verb + noun   [Vp] = verb + particle   [Vpr] = verb + prepositional phrase

accept sth as normal or usual: *He quickly accustomed himself to this new way of life.*
▶ **accustomed** *adj* **1** [attrib] usual: *He took his accustomed seat by the fire.* **2** [pred] ~ **to sth** familiar with sth; accepting sth as normal or usual: *I soon became/got accustomed to his strange ways.* ○ *My eyes slowly grew accustomed to the darkness.* ○ *This is not the kind of treatment I am accustomed to* (ie not the kind I usually receive).

ace /eɪs/ *n* **1** a PLAYING-CARD with a large single symbol on it, which has either the highest or lowest value, depending on the game: *the ace of spades/hearts/clubs/diamonds.* **2** (*infml*) a person who is very good at a particular activity: *an ace pilot/football player/marksman.* **3** (in tennis) a service (12a) that is too good for the opponent to return. **IDM** **(have) an ace up one's sleeve;** (*US*) **(have) an ace in the hole** (*infml*) to keep a useful plan, piece of information, etc secret and ready to be used when necessary. **hold all the aces** to have all the advantages. **within an ace of sth/doing sth** (*Brit*) very near to (doing) sth: *He came/was within an ace of death/being killed.*
▶ **ace** *adj* [usu pred] (*sl*) very good: *The film was ace!*

acerbic /ə'sɜːbɪk/ *adj* (*fml*) (esp of speech or manner) harsh and sharp; not kind: *an acerbic remark/tone* ○ *She was uncharacteristically acerbic in her response.* ▶ **acerbity** /ə'sɜːbəti/ *n* [U,C].

acetate /'æsɪteɪt/ *n* [U] **1** a chemical compound used in making plastics, etc. **2** a type of smooth artificial cloth.

acetic /ə'siːtɪk/ *adj* of or like VINEGAR.
■ **a,cetic 'acid** *n* [U] the acid in VINEGAR that gives it its taste and smell.

acetylene /ə'setɪliːn/ *n* [U] a gas that burns with a bright flame, used in cutting and welding (WELD) metal.

ache /eɪk/ *n* (often in compounds) a continuous dull pain: ¹*backache* ○ ¹*toothache* ○ *a* ¹*headache* ○ *a* ¹*tummy-ache* ○ *My body was all aches and pains.* ○ *He has an ache in his/the chest.* ○ (*fig*) *an ache of despair/longing.*
▶ **ache** *v* **1** to suffer from a continuous dull pain: [V] *My head aches/is aching.* ○ *I'm aching all over.* ○ (*fig*) *It makes my heart ache* (ie makes me sad) *to see her suffer.* **2** ~ **for sb/sth** to have a strong desire for sb/sth or to do sth: [Vpr, V.to inf] *I was aching for home/aching to go home.*

achieve /ə'tʃiːv/ *v* **1(a)** to succeed in reaching a particular goal, status or standard, esp by effort, skill, courage, etc: [Vn] *achieve success/notoriety/peace of mind* ○ *They could not achieve their target of less than 3% inflation.* **(b)** to succeed in doing sth or causing sth to happen: [Vn] *I've achieved only half of what I'd hoped to do.* ○ *All he managed to achieve was to cause discontent.* **2** to be successful; to perform well: [V] *children whose background gives them little chance of achieving at school.*
▶ **achievable** *adj* (of an aim, purpose, etc) that can be achieved: *Profits of £20m look achievable.*
achievement *n* **1** [C] a thing done successfully, esp with effort and skill: *the greatest scientific achievement of the decade.* ⇨ note at ACT¹. **2** [U] the action or process of achieving sth: *celebrate the achievement of one's aims.*

Achilles /ə'kɪliːz/ *n* **IDM** **an/one's Achilles' 'heel** a weak point or small fault, esp in sb's character, which can be used or attacked by other people to their advantage: *Vanity is his Achilles' heel.*
■ **A,chilles' 'tendon** *n* the TENDON attaching the calf² muscles to the heel.

acid¹ /'æsɪd/ *n* **1** [U,C] (*chemistry*) any of a class of substances containing HYDROGEN that can be replaced by a metal to form a salt. Acids are usu sour and can often destroy things they touch: *Vinegar contains acetic acid.* ○ *Some acids burn holes in wood.* Compare ALKALI. See also AMINO ACID. **2** [C] any sour substance. **3** [U] (*sl*) = LSD. ▶ **acidic** /ə'sɪdɪk/ *adj*: *Some fruit juices are very acidic.* ○ *acidic conditions.*
■ ¹**acid house** *n* [U] a type of electronic music with a strong constant beat, often associated with the taking of harmful drugs: ,*acid house* ¹*parties.*
,**acid 'rain** *n* [U] rain that is made acid by gases released from factories, etc becoming dissolved in it, and that damages trees, crops, buildings, etc.
,**acid 'test** *n* [sing] a test that gives final proof of the value or worth of sth/sb: *The acid test of a good driver is whether he remains calm in an emergency.*

acid² /'æsɪd/ *adj* **1** having a bitter sharp taste; sour: *A lemon is an acid fruit.* ○ *Vinegar has an acid taste.* **2** critical and unkind; sarcastic (SARCASM): *an acid wit* ○ *His remarks were rather acid.* **3(a)** (*chemistry*) having the essential properties (PROPERTY 3) of an acid. **(b)** having a PH value of less than 7: *Rye is tolerant of poor, acid soils.* Compare ALKALINE.
▶ **acidify** /ə'sɪdɪfaɪ/ *v* (*pt, pp* **-ied**) [V, Vn] to become or make sth acid. **acidification** *n* [U].
▶ **acidity** /ə'sɪdəti/ *n* [U] the state or quality of being acid: *suffer from acidity of the stomach.*
acidly *adv* in an unpleasant or critical way: *'Thanks for nothing,' she said acidly.*

acidulous /ə'sɪdjʊləs; *US* -dʒəl-/ *adj* (*fml*) rather sharp or bitter in taste or manner.

acknowledge /ək'nɒlɪdʒ/ *v* **1** to accept the truth of sth; to admit sth: [Vn] *acknowledge the need for reform* ○ *a generally acknowledged fact* ○ *She refused to acknowledge what had happened.* [V.n to inf] *It is generally acknowledged to be true.* [V.that] *She acknowledged that the equipment had been incorrectly installed.* **2** to report that one has received sth: [Vn] *acknowledge (receipt of) a letter.* **3** to express thanks for sth: [Vn] *His services to the country were never officially acknowledged.* ○ *He is always ready to acknowledge his debt to his teachers* (ie to say how much they helped him). **4** to show that one has noticed or recognized sb by a smile, movement of the head, greeting, etc: [Vn] *I was standing right next to her, but she didn't even acknowledge me/my presence.* **5** ~ **sb/sth (as sth)** to accept or recognize sb/sth (as sth): [Vn] *The country acknowledged his claim to the throne.* [Vn-n] *Stephen acknowledged Henry as* (ie recognized his claim to be) *his heir.* [Vn-adj] *beaches acknowledged as the finest on this coast* [V.n to inf] *He is generally acknowledged to be a world-class player.*
▶ **acknowledgement** (also **acknowledgment**) *n* **1** [U, sing] the act of acknowledging sth: *an acknowledgement of the importance of the event* ○ *We are sending you a free copy* **in acknowledgement of** *your valuable help.* **2** [C] (**a**) a thing given or done in return for a service: *These flowers are a small acknowledgement of your great kindness.* (**b**) a letter stating that sth has been received: *I didn't receive an acknowledgement of my application.* **3** [C, U] a statement, esp at the beginning of a book, of an author's thanks to other people or writings that have helped her or him: *a page of acknowledgements* ○ *Her theory was quoted without (an) acknowledgement.*

acme /'ækmi/ *n* (usu *sing*) the highest stage of development; the PEAK² of excellence: *reach the acme of success.*

acne /'ækni/ *n* [U] a skin condition, common among young people, that produces a lot of red spots on the face and neck: *suffer from/have acne.*

acolyte /'ækəlaɪt/ *n* **1** a person who helps a priest in certain church services. **2** (*fml or joc*) an assistant; a faithful follower.

aconite /'ækənaɪt/ *n* [C,U] a plant with yellow or blue flowers and a poisonous root.

acorn /'eɪkɔːn/ *n* the fruit of the OAK tree. It is a

small nut that grows in a base shaped like a cup. ⇨ picture at OAK.

acoustic /əˈkuːstɪk/ adj **1** of or relating to sound or the sense of hearing: *acoustic sensitivity* ○ *the acoustic properties of the music room.* **2** [usu attrib] (of a musical instrument) not electric: *an acoustic guitar.* ⇨ picture at GUITAR.
▶ **acoustic** n [sing] = ACOUSTICS: *The hall has a fine acoustic.*
acoustically adv.
acoustics n **1** [pl] (also **acoustic** [sing]) the qualities of a room, hall, etc that make it good or bad for carrying sound: *The acoustics of the new concert hall are excellent.* **2** [sing v] the scientific study of sound.

acquaint /əˈkweɪnt/ v ~ **sb/oneself with sth** (fml) to make sb/oneself familiar with or aware of sth: [Vnpr] *Please acquaint me with the facts of the case.*
▶ **acquainted** adj [pred] **(a)** ~ **with sth** (fml) familiar with sth: *Are you acquainted with the works of Thoreau?* ○ *You will soon become fully acquainted with the procedures.* **(b)** ~ **(with sb)** knowing sb personally: *I am not acquainted with the lady.* ○ *We are/became acquainted.* ○ *I hope you two will get better acquainted.*

acquaintance /əˈkweɪntəns/ n **1** [U] **(a)** ~ **with sth** slight knowledge of sth: *I have little acquaintance with the Japanese language.* **(b)** ~ **(with sb)** slight knowledge of or friendship with sb: *Their acquaintance began to blossom.* ○ *I was glad to renew my acquaintance with him.* ○ *Nobody of my acquaintance* (ie that I know) *was there.* **2** [C] a person whom one knows but who is not a close friend: *He has a wide circle of acquaintances.* ○ *She's an old acquaintance* (ie I have known her for a long time). **IDM** **have a nodding acquaintance with sb/sth** ⇨ NOD. **make sb's acquaintance/make the acquaintance of sb** to get to know sb; to meet sb personally: *I made his acquaintance at a party.* **on (further) acˈquaintance** when known for a (longer) period of time: *His manner seemed unpleasant at first, but he improved on further acquaintance.*

acquiesce /ˌækwiˈes/ v ~ **(in sth)** (fml) to accept sth without protest; to offer no opposition to a plan, conclusion, etc: [V, Vpr] *His parents will never acquiesce (in such an unsuitable marriage).*
▶ **acquiescence** /ˌækwiˈesns/ n [U].
acquiescent /-ˈesnt/ adj ready to acquiesce: *an acquiescent nature* ○ *She is too acquiescent* (ie too ready to accept sth or sb).

acquire /əˈkwaɪə(r)/ v (fml) **(a)** to gain a skill, habit, etc by one's own ability, efforts or behaviour: [Vn] *acquire a good knowledge of English/a taste for brandy/a reputation for dishonesty.* **(b)** (fml) to obtain sth; to buy or be given sth: [Vn] *Let me tell you how I came to acquire this desk.* ○ *The company has just acquired a further 5% of the shares.* **IDM** **an acquired ˈtaste** a thing that one learns to like gradually: *Abstract art is an acquired taste.*

acquisition /ˌækwɪˈzɪʃn/ n **1** [C] a thing acquired, esp sth useful: *the library's most recent acquisitions* (ie the books it has obtained recently) ○ *His latest acquisition is a racehorse.* See also ACCESSION 2. **2** [U, C] the action or process of acquiring sth: *the acquisition of antiques/knowledge/shares* ○ *theories of language acquisition* ○ *The company has made acquisitions* (ie has bought other companies) *in several EC countries.*

acquisitive /əˈkwɪzətɪv/ adj (often derog) keen to acquire new possessions: *an acquisitive collector* ○ *an acquisitive company* (ie one keen to buy other companies and expand). ▶ **acquisitiveness** n [U].

acquit /əˈkwɪt/ v (-tt-) **1** ~ **sb (of sth)** (law) (often passive) to declare sb to be not guilty of a crime, etc; to free or clear sb of blame, responsibility, etc: [Vnpr] *The jury acquitted him of (the charge of) murder.* [Vn] *Both defendants were acquitted.* Com-

pare CONVICT. **2** ~ **oneself well, badly, etc** to behave or perform in the specified way: [Vnadv] *He acquitted himself splendidly in the exams.*
▶ **acquittal** /əˈkwɪtl/ n (law) **(a)** [C] a judgement that a person is not guilty of the crime with which he or she has been charged: *The case can only result in an acquittal.* **(b)** [U] the action of acquitting sb or of their being acquitted: *Lack of evidence resulted in their acquittal.*

acre /ˈeɪkə(r)/ n **1** a measure of land; 4840 square yards or about 4050 square metres: *a three-acre wood.* ⇨ App 2. **2** (usu pl) a piece of land: *rolling acres of farm land.*
▶ **acreage** /ˈeɪkərɪdʒ/ n [U, C] an area of land measured in acres: *What is the acreage of the farm?*

acrid /ˈækrɪd/ adj **1** having a strongly bitter smell or taste: *acrid fumes from burning rubber tyres.* **2** bitter in temper or manner: *an acrid dispute/remark.*

acrimony /ˈækrɪməni; US -məʊni/ n [U] (fml) angry and bitter feelings or words: *The dispute was settled without acrimony.*
▶ **acrimonious** /ˌækrɪˈməʊniəs/ adj (fml) (esp of arguments) angry and bitter: *an acrimonious meeting/debate/atmosphere.* **acrimoniously** adv.

acrobat /ˈækrəbæt/ n a person, esp at a CIRCUS(1), who performs difficult or unusual physical acts, eg walking on the hands or balancing on a rope fixed high above the ground.
▶ **acrobatic** /ˌækrəˈbætɪk/ adj involving or performing difficult or unusual movements: *acrobatic feats/skills* ○ *an acrobatic dancer.*
acrobatics n **(a)** [pl] acrobatic acts: *perform/do acrobatics* ○ *Her acrobatics were greeted with loud applause.* ○ (fig) *vocal/intellectual acrobatics.* **(b)** [sing v] the art of performing these.

acronym /ˈækrənɪm/ n a word formed from the first letters of a group of words, eg *UNESCO* /juːˈneskəʊ/, ie United Nations Educational, Scientific and Cultural Organization.

across¹ /əˈkrɒs; US əˈkrɔːs/ adv part For the special uses of **across** in phrasal verbs, look at the verb entries. For example, the meaning of **come across** is given in the phrasal verb section of the entry for **come.** **1** from one side to the other side: *Can you swim across?* ○ *I helped the blind man across.* ○ *She called across to the child to wait for her.* ○ *Come across to my office this afternoon.* **2** on the other side: *We leave Dover at ten and we should be across in France by midnight.* **3** in extent; from side to side: *The river is half a mile across* (ie wide). **4** in a particular direction, esp sideways or in front of sb/ sth: *He leaned/reached across and picked up the bottle.* **5** (of a CLUE(2) or an answer in a CROSSWORD) to be read from side to side, not from top to bottom: *Can you do 5 across?* Compare DOWN¹ 3.
■ **across from** prep (esp US) opposite sth: *Just across from our house there's a school.*

across² /əˈkrɒs; US əˈkrɔːs/ prep **1** from one side to the other side of sth: *walk across the street* ○ *row sb across a lake* ○ *A shadow passed across his face.* **2** on the other side of sth: *He shouted to me from across the room.* ○ *My house is just across the street.* **3** extending from one side to the other side of sth: *a bridge across the river* ○ *curtains across a window* ○ *Draw a line across the page.* **4** on or in front of sth so as to cross it or form a cross: *He sat with his arms across his chest.* **5** throughout; everywhere in a place: *an interview broadcast across Europe* ○ *Her family is scattered across the country.* **6** among or involving people from more than one country, culture, political party, etc: *a view held across all sections of the community.*

acrostic /əˈkrɒstɪk; US -ˈkrɔːs-/ n a poem or other

piece of writing in which certain letters in each line form a word or words.

acrylic /ə'krɪlɪk/ *adj* (**a**) made of a substance produced by chemical processes from an ORGANIC(2) acid: *an acrylic sweater* ○ *a moulded acrylic bath.* (**b**) of or created with a type of acrylic paint used by artists: *an acrylic painting.*
▶ **acrylic** *n* [U, C usu *pl*] an acrylic material, plastic or paint: *painted in oils and acrylics.*

act¹ /ækt/ *n* **1** a thing done; a deed: *It is an act of kindness/a kind act to help a blind man across the street.* ○ *an act of terrorism/violence* ○ *This horrific murder is surely the act of a madman.* ⇨ note. **2** a short piece of entertainment, usu one of a series in a programme: *a circus act* ○ *a song and dance act.* **3** any of the main divisions of a play or an opera: *a play in five acts* ○ *The hero dies in Act 4, Scene 3.* **4** a law made by a parliament or similar body(4): *an Act of Congress* ○ *the Health and Safety at Work Act (1974)* ○ *Parliament has passed an act which makes such sports illegal.* **5** (usu *sing*) (*infml*) a way of behaving which is not genuine, but used for the effect it will have on others; a PRETENCE: *Don't take her seriously — it's all an act.* ○ *She's just putting on an act* (ie only pretending). **IDM** **be/get in on the act** (*infml*) to be/become involved in a particular activity, esp for one's own benefit or profit: *She has made a lot of money from the business and now her family want to get in on the act too.* **do a disappearing act** ⇨ DISAPPEAR. **get one's** ¹**act together** (*infml*) to become properly organized in order to be able to deal with or achieve sth: *If you want to do better at school you'll have to get your act together.* **in the (very) act (of doing sth)** while one is doing sth, esp sth wrong: *I caught her in the act (of reading my letters).* ○ *In the act of bending down, he slipped and hurt his back.* **read the Riot Act** ⇨ READ.
■ ¹**act of** ¹**God** *n* (*law*) an event caused by natural forces beyond human control, eg a storm, a flood or an EARTHQUAKE: *insure against all loss or damage including that caused by an act of God.*

NOTE Compare **act**, **deed**, **exploit**, **feat** and **achievement**. An **act** or **action** can be good or bad. The words are close in meaning when **action** is used as a countable noun: *a generous act/action.* **Actions** relate to general behaviour: *Individuals must take responsibility for their actions.* An **act of** something is a specific example of a quality or type of behaviour: *an act of mercy/vandalism.*

Deed is a formal or literary word that refers to a very good or very bad act: *He was guilty of many evil deeds.* **Exploit**, **feat** and **achievement** all describe impressive acts. Both **feat** and **achievement** emphasize that an act is mentally or physically difficult: *Coming top in the exam was quite an achievement.* ○ *The new bridge is a major feat of engineering.* **Exploits** are brave and exciting acts that people talk about: *His exploits as an explorer brought him fame and wealth.*

act² /ækt/ *v* **1**(**a**) to do sth; to perform actions: [V] *The time for talking is past: we must act at once.* [Vadv] *The girl's life was saved because the doctors acted so promptly.* ○ *You acted* (ie behaved) *wisely by/in ignoring such bad advice.* (**b**) to do what is expected of one as a professional or official person; to take action: [V] *The police refused to act until they had more evidence.* **2**(**a**) to perform a part in a play or film; to be an actor: [V] *Have you ever acted?* ○ *She acts well.* (**b**) to take the part of a particular character in a play or film: [V-n, Vn] *Who is acting (the part of) Hamlet?* (**c**) to pretend by one's behaviour to be a certain person or type of person: [V, V-n] *He's not really angry — he's just acting (the stern father).* [V-adj] (*infml*) *Try to act normal!* **IDM** **act/play the**

fool ⇨ FOOL¹. **PHRV** ¹**act as sb/sth** to perform the role or function of sb/sth: *I don't understand their language: you'll have to act as interpreter.*
¹**act for / on behalf of sb** to perform sb's duties, etc on their behalf; to represent sb: *During her illness her attorney has been acting for her in her business affairs.*
¹**act on/upon sth 1** to take action as a result of sth: *Acting on information received, the police raided the club.* **2** to have an effect on sth: *Alcohol acts quickly on the brain.*
,**act sth** ¹**out 1** to act a part, usu in a real situation and for some purpose: *She acted out the role of wronged lover to make him feel guilty.* **2** to perform a drama, ceremony, etc; to ENACT(1) sth: *The ritual of the party conference is acted out in the same way every year.*
,**act** ¹**up** (*infml*) to cause pain or annoyance by functioning or behaving badly: *My sprained ankle has been acting up all week.* ○ *The car's acting up again.* ○ *The kids started acting up.*

acting /'æktɪŋ/ *n* [U] the art or occupation of performing in plays, films, television, etc: *She did a lot of acting while she was at college.*
▶ **acting** *adj* [attrib] having the duties of another person for a time: *the acting manager/headmistress.*

action /'ækʃn/ *n* **1**(**a**) [U] the process of doing sth; using energy or influence; activity: *a man of action* (ie one who achieves things by being bold and active) ○ *I only like films that have got plenty of action.* ○ *The time has come for action.* Compare INACTION. (**b**) [C] a thing done; a deed; an act: *Her quick action saved his life.* ○ *You must judge people by their actions, not by what they say.* ○ *Immediate action must be taken to stop the fire spreading.* ○ *Not wanting to be seen by the others, he quickly took evasive action and hid in the crowd.* ⇨ note at ACT¹. See also COURSE OF ACTION, DIRECT ACTION, INDUSTRIAL ACTION. **2** [U] the events in a story or play: *The action is set in France.* **3** [sing] ~ **on sth** the effect that one substance has on another: *The action of salt on ice causes it to melt.* **4** [U] fighting in battle between troops, ships, etc: *military action* ○ *killed in action* ○ *the destruction caused by enemy action* ○ *He saw* (ie was involved in) *action in North Africa.* **5** [C] a legal process; a LAWSUIT: *a court action* ○ *He brought an action against her* (ie tried to win a case against her in a lawcourt). **6** [C] (**a**) a way of functioning, esp of a part of the body: *study the action of the liver.* (**b**) a way of moving, eg of a sports player, or of a horse when jumping: *a fast bowler with a fine action.* (**c**) the mechanism of an instrument, esp of a gun, piano or clock. **IDM** **actions speak louder than** ¹**words** (*saying*) what sb actually does means more than what they say they will do. **in** ¹**action** in operation or engaging in a typical activity: *I've heard she's a marvellous player but I've never seen her in action.* **into** ¹**action** into operation or a typical activity: *put a plan into action* ○ *At daybreak the troops went into action* (ie started fighting). **out of** ¹**action** no longer able to operate or function; not working: *This machine is out of action.* ○ *The enemy guns put many of our tanks out of action.* ○ *I've been out of action for several weeks with a broken leg.* **a piece/slice of the** ¹**action** (*infml*) being involved in some enterprise, esp in order to get a share of the profits: *I'm only putting money into this outfit if I get a slice of the action.* **swing into action** ⇨ SWING¹. **where the** ¹**action is** (*infml*) any place where life is thought to be busy, enjoyable, profitable, etc: *Life in the country can be very dull — London's where all the action is.*
▶ **actionable** *adj* giving sufficient cause for an action(5) in a lawcourt: *Be careful what you say — your remarks may be actionable.*
■ ¹**action group** *n* (often as part of a name) a group

formed to take active measures, esp in politics: *the Child Poverty Action Group.*

ˈ**action-packed** *adj* full of activity and excitement: *an action-packed holiday.*

ˌ**action** ˈ**replay** *n* the running again of part of a film, often in slow motion, showing a specific incident. Action replays are shown esp during sports matches.

ˈ**action stations** *n* [pl] the positions to which soldiers, etc go when fighting is expected to begin: (*fig*) *Action stations, I can hear the boss coming!*

activate /ˈæktɪveɪt/ *v* to make sth active: [Vn] *The burglar alarm was activated by mistake.* ○ *The gene is activated by a specific protein.* ▶ **activation** /ˌæktɪˈveɪʃn/ *n* [U].

active /ˈæktɪv/ *adj* **1(a)** (in the habit of) doing things; lively: *lead an active life* (ie one full of activity) ○ *Although he's quite old he's still very active.* ○ *She takes an active part* (ie is closely involved) *in local politics.* Compare INACTIVE. **(b)** quick; lively: *have an active brain* ○ *an active debate.* **2** engaged in a particular activity: *politically active* ○ *sexually active teenagers* (ie regularly having sex) ○ *They were active in opposing the closures.* **3** functioning; in operation: *an active volcano* (ie one that is likely to ERUPT(1)) ○ *a virus active within the body.* **4** having an effect; not simply PASSIVE(1): *the active ingredients* ○ *active resistance.* **5** = RADIOACTIVE. **6** (*grammar*) of the form of a verb whose subject is the person or thing that performs the action, as in *He was driving the car* and *The children have eaten the cake.* Compare PASSIVE.

▶ **active** (also **active voice**) *n* [sing] (*grammar*) the active(6) forms of a verb: *In the sentence 'She cleaned the car' the verb is in the active.* Compare PASSIVE *n*.

actively *adv*: *become actively involved in the project* ○ *Your proposal is being actively considered.*

■ **active** ˈ**service** (*US* also **active** ˈ**duty**) *n* [U] full-time service in the armed forces, esp during a war: *be on active service.*

activism /ˈæktɪvɪzəm/ *n* [U] the policy of vigorous action to bring about political change. ▶ **activist** /ˈæktɪvɪst/ *n*: *anti-nuclear/gay/black activists.*

activity /ækˈtɪvəti/ *n* **1** [U] **(a)** the state of being active or lively; functioning: *electrical/sexual/volcanic activity.* **(b)** busy or vigorous action: *The house has been full of activity all day.* Compare INACTIVITY. **2** [C esp *pl*] a specific thing or things done; an action or occupation: *outdoor/recreational/sporting/classroom activities* ○ *Her activities include tennis and painting.* ○ *He was involved in paramilitary activities.*

actor /ˈæktə(r)/ *n* a person who acts on the stage, on television or in films.

actress /ˈæktrəs/ *n* a woman actor.

actual /ˈæktʃuəl/ *adj* existing in fact; real: *What were his actual words?* ○ *The actual cost was much higher than we had expected.* ○ *The preparations for a wedding take weeks though the actual ceremony lasts less than an hour.* ○ *He looks younger than his wife, but in actual fact he's several years older.* ⇨ note at PRESENT¹. **IDM** **your** ˈ**actual ...** (*infml*) the real, genuine or important thing specified: *This ring wasn't cheap, you know. It's your actual silver.*

▶ **actually** /ˈæktʃuəli/ *adv* **1** really; in fact: *The people who actually did the work were not mentioned.* ○ *What did he actually say?* ○ *Actually, I'm busy at the moment — can I phone you back?* **2** though it may seem strange; even: *He actually expected me to pay for his ticket.* ○ *She not only entered the competition — she actually won it!*

actuality /ˌæktʃuˈæləti/ *n* **1** [U] actual existence; reality: *In actuality, I knew about the plan already.* **2** **actualities** [pl] existing conditions; facts: *the grim actualities of prison life.*

actuary /ˈæktʃuəri; *US* -tʃueri/ *n* an expert who

calculates insurance risks and payments by studying how frequently accidents, fires, deaths, etc occur. ▶ **actuarial** /ˌæktʃuˈeəriəl/ *adj.*

actuate /ˈæktʃueɪt/ *v* [Vn] (*fml*) **1** to make a machine, an electrical device, etc move or work; to make a process begin. **2** (usu passive) to make sb act; to MOTIVATE(2) sb: *He was actuated solely by greed.*

acuity /əˈkjuːəti/ *n* [U] (*fml*) the ability to think or perceive clearly; acuteness (ACUTE 2) of thought or the senses.

acumen /ˈækjəmən, əˈkjuːmən/ *n* [U] the ability to understand and judge things quickly and clearly: *business acumen* ○ *have/show/display great political acumen.*

acupuncture /ˈækjupʌŋktʃə(r)/ *n* [U] (*medical*) the method of inserting very thin needles into the skin as a treatment for various diseases or to relieve pain. ▶ **acupuncturist** *n* an expert in acupuncture.

acute /əˈkjuːt/ *adj* (**-r, -st**) **1** very great; severe: *suffer acute hardship* ○ *There's an acute shortage of water.* **2(a)** (of feelings or the senses) keen; sharp: *suffer acute pain/embarrassment/remorse* ○ *Dogs have an acute sense of smell.* **(b)** having or showing a quick and clear understanding; intelligent: *He is an acute observer of the social scene.* ○ *Her judgement is acute.* **3** (of an illness) coming quickly to the most severe or critical stage: *acute appendicitis* ○ *an acute patient* (ie one whose illness has reached this stage). Compare CHRONIC 1. ▶ **acutely** *adv*: *I am acutely aware of the difficulties we face.* **acuteness** *n* [U].

■ **acute** ˈ**accent** *n* a mark (ˊ) over a vowel, as over the *e* in *café.*

acute ˈ**angle** *n* an angle of less than 90°. ⇨ picture at ANGLE.

-acy ⇨ -CY.

AD /ˌeɪ ˈdiː/ *abbr* in the year of Our Lord; of the Christian era (Latin *anno domini*): *in (the year)* ˌ55 *A*ˈ*D*/ˌ*AD* 5ˈ5. Compare BC.

ad /æd/ *n* (*infml*) = ADVERTISEMENT 1: *put an ad in the local paper.*

adage /ˈædɪdʒ/ *n* a traditional phrase expressing a general truth: *According to the old adage, a bad workman always blames his tools.*

adagio /əˈdɑːdʒiəʊ/ *adj, adv* (*music*) in slow time; in a slow and graceful manner.

▶ **adagio** *n* (*pl* **-os**) a piece of music played in a slow and graceful manner.

Adam /ˈædəm/ *n* **IDM** **not know sb from Adam** ⇨ KNOW.

■ ˌ**Adam's** ˈ**apple** *n* the part at the front of the neck, especially prominent in men, that moves up and down when one swallows. ⇨ picture at THROAT.

adamant /ˈædəmənt/ *adj* showing that one refuses to be persuaded or to change one's mind; STUBBORN (1): *an adamant refusal* ○ *She was quite adamant that she would not come.* ○ *On this point I am adamant* (ie my decision will not change). ▶ **adamantly** *adv*: *adamantly opposed to any shift in policy.*

adapt /əˈdæpt/ *v* **1(a)** ~ sth (**for sth**) to make sth suitable for a new use, situation, etc; to MODIFY(1) sth: [Vnpr] *This machine has been specially adapted for use under water.* [Vn.to inf] *These styles can be adapted to suit individual tastes.* [also Vn]. **(b)** ~ sth (**for sth**) (**from sth**) to alter a book or play to make it more suitable for television, the stage, etc: [Vnpr] *This novel has been adapted for radio* (ie translated and changed so that it can be presented on the radio) *from the Russian original.* [also Vn]. **2** ~ (**oneself**) (**to sth**) to become adjusted to new conditions, etc: [Vpr] *Our eyes slowly adapted to the dark.* [Vnpr] *She adapted herself quickly to the new climate.* [also V].

▶ **adaptable** *adj* **(a)** (*approv*) able to adapt oneself/itself to sth: *He is not very adaptable* (ie does not

A

adjust easily to new circumstances, etc). (**b**) that can be adapted. **adaptability** /əˌdæptəˈbɪləti/ n [U].

adaptation /ˌædæpˈteɪʃn/ n **1** [C] a thing made by adapting sth else, esp a text for production on the stage, radio, etc: *an adaptation for children of a play by Shakespeare*. **2** [U] (*esp biology*) the action or process of adapting or being adapted.

adaptive /əˈdæptɪv/ adj (**a**) (*esp biology*) concerned with adapting: *adaptive changes*. (**b**) that can adapt: *an adaptive economic strategy*.

adaptor n **1** a device for connecting pieces of equipment that were not originally designed to be connected. **2** a type of electrical plug that makes it possible to connect several electrical appliances to one SOCKET(2).

ADC /ˌeɪ diː ˈsiː/ abbr aide-de-camp.

add /æd/ v **1** ~ sth (**to sth**) to put sth together with sth else so as to increase the size, number, amount, etc: [Vn] *Whisk the egg and then add the flour.* ○ *If the tea is too strong, add some more water.* ○ *This was an added* (ie an extra, a further) *disappointment.* [Vnpr] *He added his signature to the petition.* ○ *Many words have been added to this edition of the dictionary.* **2** ~ A to B; ~ A and B (**together**) to put numbers or amounts together to get a total: [Vn, Vnp] *If you add 5 and 5 (together), you get 10.* [Vnpr] *Add 9 to the total.* Compare SUBTRACT. **3** ~ sth (**to sth**) to continue to say sth; to make a further remark: [Vn, Vnpr] *I have nothing to add (to my earlier statement).* [V.speech] '*And don't be late,*' she added. [V.that] *As a postscript to his letter he added that he loved her.* **IDM** **add ˌfuel to the ˈflames** to do or say sth that makes people react more strongly or fiercely. **add ˌinsult to ˈinjury** to make one's relationship with sb even worse by offending them as well as actually harming them. **PHRV** **ˌadd sth ˈin** to include sth; to put or pour sth in. **ˌadd sth ˈon (to sth)** to include or attach sth: *add on a 10% service charge.* **ˈadd to sth** to increase sth: *The bad weather only added to our difficulties.* ○ *The house has been added to* (ie New rooms, etc have been built on to it) *from time to time.* **ˌadd ˈup** (*infml*) to seem reasonable or consistent; to make sense: *His story just doesn't add up — he must be lying.* **ˌadd (sth) ˈup** to calculate the total of two or more numbers or amounts: *The waiter can't add up.* ○ *Add up all the money I owe you.* **ˌadd ˈup to sth 1** to amount to sth: *The numbers add up to exactly 100.* **2** (*infml*) to be equivalent to sth; to indicate sth: *These clues don't really add up to very much* (ie give us very little information).
■ **ˈadd-on** n a thing added or included: *add-ons to one's basic pay* ○ *an add-on figure.*

addendum /əˈdendəm/ n (pl **addenda** /-də/) a thing that is added, esp as extra material at the end of a book.

adder /ˈædə(r)/ n a small poisonous snake.

addict /ˈædɪkt/ n **1** a person who is unable to stop taking drugs, alcohol, etc: *a heroin addict.* **2** a person who is extremely interested in sth and spends a lot of time on it: *a chess/TV/football addict.*
▶ **addicted** /əˈdɪktɪd/ adj [pred] ~ (**to sth**) **1** unable to stop taking or using sth as a habit : *become addicted to drugs/alcohol/tobacco.* **2** spending a lot of time on sth as a HOBBY or an interest: *be hopelessly addicted to computer games.*
addiction /əˈdɪkʃn/ n [U, C] ~ (**to sth**) the condition of being an addict: *cocaine addiction* ○ *overcome one's lifelong addiction to alcohol.*
addictive /əˈdɪktɪv/ adj causing one to become an addict: *Heroin is highly addictive.*

addition /əˈdɪʃn/ n **1** [U] the action or skill of adding two or more numbers to find their total: *children learning addition and subtraction.* **2**(**a**) [C] ~ (**to sth**) a person or thing added or joined: *the latest addition to our range of kitchen furniture* ○ *It*

makes a tasty addition to salads. ○ *They've just had an addition to the family* (ie another child). (**b**) [U] the action or process of adding sth to sth else: *the addition of an East European dimension to the EC* ○ *The sauce will be richer **with the addition of** a little brandy.* **IDM** **in addition (to sb/sth)** as an extra person, thing or circumstance: *In addition (to these arrangements), thirty ambulances will be on duty until midnight.*
▶ **additional** /-ʃənl/ adj added; extra: *additional resources/funds/security* ○ *There will be a small additional charge.* ○ *The government is providing an additional £25 million to expand the service.* **additionally** /-ʃənəli/ adv: *Additionally, a shuttle service will run on Sundays from 9 am to 6 pm.*

additive /ˈædətɪv/ n a substance added in small amounts to sth during manufacture, eg to food in order to colour or preserve it: *Vitamin pills often contain additives which can cause allergies.* ○ *additive-free orange juice.*

addled /ˈædld/ adj confused: *His brain was addled from years of drug abuse.*

address[1] /əˈdres; US ˈædres/ n **1** details of where a person lives, works or can be reached, and where letters, etc may be delivered: *a list of useful names and addresses* ○ *Where's my **address book**?* ○ *What's your **name and address**?* ○ *I'll give you my home address.* ○ *My address is 3 West St, Seattle.* **2** a formal speech made to an audience: *tonight's televised presidential address.* See also PUBLIC-ADDRESS SYSTEM.

address[2] /əˈdres/ v **1** ~ sth (**to sb/sth**) to write on a letter, parcel, etc the name and address of the person, firm, etc that it is to be delivered to: [Vnpr] *The card was wrongly addressed to (us at) our old home.* [Vn] *Please enclose a stamped addressed envelope.* **2** to make a speech to a person or an audience, esp formally: [Vn] *The chairman will now address the meeting.* ○ *She was invited to address the rally.* **3** ~ sth **to sb/sth** (*fml*) to direct a remark or written statement to sb/sth: [Vnpr] *Please address all complaints to the manager.* **4** ~ **sb as sth** to use a particular name or title in speaking or writing to sb: [Vn-n] '*How should I address the judge?*' '*Address him as "Your Honour".*' **5** ~ (**oneself to) sth** (*fml*) to direct one's attention to a problem; to deal with sth: [Vnpr] *It is time we addressed ourselves to the main item on the agenda.* [Vn] *Her statement did not address the real issues.*
▶ **addressee** /ˌædreˈsiː/ n a person to whom a letter, etc is addressed.

adduce /əˈdjuːs; US əˈduːs/ v (*fml*) to put sth forward as an example or as proof: [Vn] *adduce evidence/grounds for sth.*

-ade *suff* (with countable ns forming uncountable ns) drink made from or tasting of the specified fruit: *orangeade.*

adenoids /ˈædənɔɪdz/ n [pl] (*anatomy*) pieces of soft tissue between the back of the nose and the throat, often making breathing and speaking difficult. ▶ **adenoidal** /ˌædəˈnɔɪdl/ adj: *an adenoidal voice.*

adept /əˈdept/ adj ~ (**at/in sth/doing sth**) expert or skilful in doing sth: *be very adept at mending clocks* ○ *an adept ball player.*

adequate /ˈædɪkwət/ adj ~ (**to/for sth**) satisfactory in quantity or quality; sufficient: *the lack of adequate provision for disabled students* ○ *take adequate precautions* ○ *adequate car parking facilities* ○ *an adequate supply of trained staff* ○ *She is not adequate to the task.* ○ *Fuel resources are barely adequate for our needs.* ○ *Your work is adequate but I'm sure you could do better.* Compare INADEQUATE. ▶ **adequacy** /ˈædɪkwəsi/ n [U]: *He questioned the adequacy of the security arrangements.* **adequately** adv: *adequately funded projects* ○ *Are you adequately insured?*

adhere /ədˈhɪə(r)/ v **1** ~ **to sth** to obey sth; to hold or follow a set of principles, course of action, etc: [Vpr] *adhere strictly to the terms of a treaty/to a schedule/to the rules*. **2** ~ **(to sth)** to remain attached to sth; to stick by means of glue, etc: [Vpr] *The gold leaf will adhere to any clean metal surface.* [also V]. See also ADHESION, ADHESIVE.

adherent /əd'hɪərənt/ *n* a supporter of a party or set of ideas: *The movement is gaining more and more adherents.* ▶ **adherence** /-rəns/ *n* [U] ~ **(to sth)**: *their strict adherence to traditional values.*

adhesion /əd'hiːʒn/ *n* [U] **1** ~ **(to sth)** the state of being or the ability to become attached to sth: *When you go round a corner too fast the tyres lose their adhesion.* **2** *(fml)* support for a plan, a set of ideas, etc: *adhesion to Labour principles.*

adhesive /əd'hiːsɪv, -'hiːz-/ *adj* that can be made to stick to sth; sticky: *the adhesive side of a stamp* ◦ *adhesive tape/plaster.* ▶ **adhesive** *n* [C, U] a substance that makes things stick: *quick-drying adhesives.* Compare GLUE.

ad hoc /ˌæd 'hɒk/ *adj, adv* **1** made or arranged for a particular purpose only; special: *appoint an ad hoc committee/group to deal with the affair.* **2** happening as necessary and not planned in advance; informal: *ad hoc improvements* ◦ *Problems were solved* **on an ad hoc basis.** ◦ *Contributions for the sick were collected ad hoc.*

adieu /ə'djuː; *US* ə'duː/ *interj* *(arch or rhet)* goodbye: *bid sb adieu.*

ad infinitum /ˌæd ˌɪnfɪ'naɪtəm/ *adv* *(Latin)* without limit; for ever: *I don't want to go on working here ad infinitum.*

adjacent /ə'dʒeɪsnt/ *adj* ~ **(to sth)** situated near or next to sth; close to or touching sth: *We work in adjacent rooms.* ◦ *They began building on the land immediately adjacent to the river.*

■ aˌdjacent 'angles *n* [pl] *(geometry)* angles that share a common line. ⇨ picture at ANGLE.

adjective /'ædʒɪktɪv/ *n* *(grammar)* (abbreviated as *adj* in this dictionary) a word that indicates a quality of the person or thing referred to by a noun, eg *big*, *rotten*, *foreign* in *a big house*, *rotten apples*, *foreign names*: *'Predictable' is an adjective that could never be applied to any of my family.* ◦ *Which adjective best describes the president?* ▶ **adjectival** /ˌædʒek'taɪvl/ *adj* *(grammar)* of or like an adjective: *an adjectival phrase.* **adjectivally** /ˌædʒek'taɪvəli/ *adv*: *a noun used adjectivally.*

adjoin /ə'dʒɔɪn/ *v* to be next to or nearest to sth or joined to it: [V] *We could hear laughter in the adjoining room.* [Vn] *The playing-field adjoins the school.*

adjourn /ə'dʒɜːn/ *v* **1(a)** (usu passive) to stop a meeting, etc for a period of time; to POSTPONE sth: [Vn] *The trial was adjourned for a week/until the following week.* **(b)** (of people at a meeting, in court, etc) to stop the proceedings for a while: [V] *The court will adjourn for lunch.* ◦ *Let's adjourn until tomorrow.* **2** ~ **to ...** *(fml or joc)* (of people who are gathered together socially) to go to another room or place: *After dinner we all adjourned to the bar.* ▶ **adjournment** *n* [C, U]: *The judge granted us a short adjournment.*

adjudge /ə'dʒʌdʒ/ *v* *(fml)* (usu passive) to consider or declare sth to be true or to have happened: [V.n *to* inf] *He adjudged his companion to be a little over 30.* [Vn-adj] *The finance committee was adjudged incompetent.* [Vn-n] *The band's European tour was adjudged a huge success.*

adjudicate /ə'dʒuːdɪkeɪt/ *v* **1** ~ **(between/on sth)** *(fml)* to examine a dispute in detail and give a decision on it: [Vn] *adjudicate sb's claim for damages* [Vpr] *adjudicate on arguments put forward* ◦ *the power to adjudicate between conflicting views* [also V]. **2** to act as judge in a contest: [V] *We would like you to adjudicate at the local flower show.*

▶ **adjudication** /əˌdʒuːdɪ'keɪʃn/ *n* [U] *(fml)*: *The case was referred to a higher court for adjudication.* **adjudicator** *n* a judge, esp in a contest: *refer the case to an adjudicator* ◦ *The adjudicators praised the high standard of all the entries.*

adjunct /'ædʒʌŋkt/ *n* **1** *(grammar)* an adverb or a phrase added to a CLAUSE(1) or sentence to MODIFY(2) the meaning of the verb. In 'He came willingly/at 6 o'clock/by himself/full tilt', *willingly*, *at 6 o'clock*, etc are all adjuncts. **2** ~ **(to/of sth)** a thing that is added or attached to sth else but is less important and not essential: *The scheme was designed as an adjunct to existing health care facilities.*

adjure /ə'dʒʊə(r)/ *v* *(fml)* to request or command sb solemnly to do sth: [Vn.*to* inf] *I adjure you to tell the truth before this court.*

adjust /ə'dʒʌst/ *v* **1** ~ **(sth/oneself) (to sth)** to become or to make sb/sth suited to new conditions; to adapt oneself/sth: [Vpr] *Many former soldiers have difficulty in adjusting to civilian life.* ◦ *It took several seconds for his eyes to adjust to the gloom.* [Vnpr] *The body quickly adjusts itself to changes in temperature.* [V] *She'll be fine, she just needs time to adjust.* [Vn] *adjust one's plans* ◦ *Inform your tax office that you are now married, and they will adjust your tax code.* **2 (a)** to alter sth by a small amount so that it will fit properly or be right for use: [Vn] *adjust the rear mirror/the focus of a camera/the sights of a gun* ◦ *The brakes need adjusting.* **(b)** to move sth slightly so that it looks neat and tidy: [Vn] *He smoothed his hair down and adjusted his tie.* ▶ **adjustable** *adj* that can be adjusted: *adjustable seat-belts* ◦ *The height of the chair is adjustable.* **adjustment** *n* [C, U]: *I've made a few minor adjustments to the seating plan.* ◦ *a period of emotional adjustment* ◦ *Some adjustment of the lens may be necessary.*

adjutant /'ædʒʊtənt/ *n* an army officer responsible for administrative work.

ad lib /ˌæd 'lɪb/ *adj, adv* *(infml)* (esp of speaking and performing in public) without preparation; SPONTANEOUS or in a spontaneous way: *give an ad lib performance* ◦ *He spoke entirely ad lib.* ▶ **ad lib** *v* (**-bb-**) *(infml)* to speak or act without preparation, esp when performing in public; to IMPROVISE: [V] *She often forgot her lines on stage but she was very good at ad libbing.*

adman /'ædmæn/ *n* (*pl* **admen** /'ædmen/) *(infml sometimes derog)* a person who produces commercial advertisements.

admin /'ædmɪn/ *n* [U] *(infml)* administration: *a few admin problems* ◦ *working in admin.*

administer /əd'mɪnɪstə(r)/ *v* **1** to control the affairs of a business, an organization, etc; to manage sth: [Vn] *administer a charity/a trust fund/a school/a project* ◦ *administer a scheme locally/nationally.* **2** *(fml)* to put sth into operation; to apply sth: [Vn] *administer justice/the law.* **3** ~ **sth (to sb)** *(fml)* **(a)** to provide or give sth formally: [Vn] *administer punishment* [Vnpr] *administer relief to famine victims* ◦ *administer the last rites to a dying man.* **(b)** to give sb a drug: [Vnpr, Vnpr] *The dosage administered (to the patient) was 5 milligrams a day for 3 weeks.*

administration /ədˌmɪnɪ'streɪʃn/ *n* **1** [U] the management of public or business affairs: *the day-to-day administration of a company* ◦ *soaring administration costs* ◦ *He works in hospital administration.* ◦ *Deans are more involved in administration than in teaching.* **2** (often **Administration** [C]) **(a)** the part of the government that manages public affairs during the period of office of a President of the USA: *Successive administrations have failed to solve the country's economic problems.* **(b)** the period of office of the leader of a country, esp of the President of the USA: *during the Bush Administration.* **3** [U] the

---

[V.speech] = verb + direct speech   [V.*that*] = verb + *that* clause   [V.*wh*] = verb + *who*, *how*, etc clause

providing, giving or application of sth: *They are responsible for the administration of justice.* ○ *the administration of a drug.*

administrative /əd'mɪnɪstrətɪv; *US* -streɪtɪv/ *adj* of or involving the management of public or business affairs: *an administrative post/problem/error* ○ *Many caterers are finding the Food Safety Act an administrative nightmare.* ▶ **administratively** *adv*: *administratively inconvenient.*

administrator /əd'mɪnɪstreɪtə(r)/ *n* **1** a person responsible for managing public or business affairs: *the administrator of a theatre* ○ *We spoke to the nursing administrator.* ○ *She's an administrator in the housing department.* **2** a person who is good at organizing things: *She's a brilliant organizer and administrator.*

admirable /'ædmərəbl/ *adj* (*fml*) deserving or causing admiration; excellent: *These aims are admirable, but are they realistic?* ○ *His handling of the situation was admirable.* ▶ **admirably** /-əbli/ *adv*: *She coped admirably with a tricky situation.*

admiral /'ædmərəl/ *n* (the title of) a naval officer of very senior rank: *a vice admiral* ○ *The admiral visits the ships under his command by helicopter.* ○ *Admiral of the Fleet Sir John Fieldhouse* ○ *Good morning, Admiral.* ⇨ App 6.
▶ **admiralty** /-əlti/ *n* the **Admiralty** [Gp] (formerly in Britain) the government department controlling the Navy.

admiration /ˌædmə'reɪʃn/ *n* [U] ~ (for sb/sth) a feeling of respect, warm approval or pleasure: *Her handling of the crisis fills me with admiration.* ○ *I have great/the greatest admiration for his courage.* ○ *They stood gazing at the statue, lost in admiration.* ○ *Her achievement won/earned her the admiration of her friends.*

admire /əd'maɪə(r)/ *v* **1** ~ sb/sth (for sth) to regard sb/sth with respect, pleasure or approval: [Vn] *We've been admiring your garden.* [Vnpr] *I admire him for his success in business.* [also V.n ing]. **2** to express one's approval of sb/sth: [Vn] *Aren't you going to admire my new hat?*
▶ **admirer** *n* **(a)** a person who admires sb/sth: *I am not a great admirer of her work.* **(b)** (*dated*) a man who admires and is attracted to a woman: *She has many admirers.*
admiring *adj* showing or feeling admiration: *give sb/receive admiring glances* ○ *be welcomed by admiring fans.* **admiringly** *adv*.

admissible /əd'mɪsəbl/ *adj* that can be allowed or accepted: *admissible evidence* ○ *Such behaviour is not admissible among our staff.* Compare INADMISSIBLE.
▶ **admissibility** /əd,mɪsə'bɪləti/ *n* [U].

admission /əd'mɪʃn/ *n* **1** [C] ~ (of sth); ~ (that...) a statement admitting the truth of sth; a CONFESSION (1): *an admission that one has lied* ○ *Her resignation amounts to an **admission of failure**.* ○ *He is a coward **by his own admission** (ie as he himself has admitted).* **2** [U] ~ (to sth) entering or being allowed to enter a building, society, school, etc: *apply for/seek admission to the European Union* ○ *Admission (to the club) is restricted to members only.* ○ *Admission to university depends on examination results.* ○ *Do they charge for admission?* ○ *How does one gain admission to the archives?* Compare ADMITTANCE. **3** [U] money charged for admitting sb to a public place: *You have to pay £5 admission.* **4** [C] a person needing or wanting to enter a public place, esp a hospital or school: *hospital/university/cinema admissions* ○ *a schools' admissions policy.*

admit /əd'mɪt/ *v* (-tt-) **1** ~ to sth/doing sth to recognize or agree, often unwillingly, that sth is true; to confess sth: [Vpr] *George would never admit to being wrong.* [Vn] *The prisoner has admitted his guilt.* ○ *I wrestled with the problem for weeks but finally had to **admit defeat**.* [Vn, V.*that*] *I admit my*

mistake/(that) I was wrong.* [V.*that*] *I must admit I felt a little nervous.* [V.ing] *He admitted having stolen the car.* [V.n to inf] *It is now generally admitted to have been* (ie Most people agree and accept that it was) *a mistake.* [V.speech] *'You may be right,' she admitted.* **2** ~ sb/sth (to sth) (a) to allow sb/sth to enter: [Vn] *Children are not to be admitted.* ○ *The small window admitted very little light.* [Vnpr] *Each ticket admits two people to the party.* ○ *I was finally **admitted to the great man's presence**.* **(b)** to accept sb into a hospital as a patient, or into a school, etc as a pupil: [Vn] *The music department admits sixty new students every year.* ○ *He was admitted to hospital with minor burns.* **3** (*fml*) (of an enclosed space) to have room for sb/sth: [Vn] *The theatre admits only 250 people.* **4** ~ of sth (*fml*) to allow the possibility of sth; to leave room for sth: [Vpr] *The question admits of only one answer.*
▶ **admittedly** *adv* (esp at the beginning of a clause) as is or must be recognized or agreed: *Admittedly, he didn't know that at the time.* ○ *The plan, admittedly, is not without its difficulties.*

admittance /əd'mɪtns/ *n* [U] ~ (to sth) the right to enter or the act of entering a place: *No admittance — keep out!* ○ *I was refused admittance/unable to **gain admittance** to the house.* Compare ADMISSION 2.

admonish /əd'mɒnɪʃ/ *v* (*fml*) **1** ~ sb (for sth/doing sth) to give a mild but firm warning to sb: [Vnpr] *He was frequently admonished by his teachers for being late.* [also V.speech, Vn]. **2** [Vn.to inf] to advise or urge sb seriously.
▶ **admonishment, admonition** /ˌædmə'nɪʃn/ *ns* [U, C] (*fml*) a warning to sb, esp about their future behaviour: *a letter full of the gravest admonitions.*
admonitory /əd'mɒnɪtri; *US* -tɔːri/ *adj* (*fml*) giving a warning: *an admonitory letter/tone of voice.*

ad nauseam /ˌæd 'nɔːzɪæm/ *adv* (*Latin*) to an excessive or unacceptable extent: *play the same four records ad nauseam* (ie again and again so that it becomes irritating).

ado /ə'duː/ *n* [IDM] **without further/more ado** immediately; without fuss or delay: *And so, without further/more ado, he got into the car and drove off.*

adobe /ə'dəʊbi/ *n* [U] clay that is dried in the sun for use as a building material: *adobe walls.*

adolescence /ˌædə'lesns/ *n* [U] the time in a person's life when he or she develops from a child into an adult: *a happy childhood and adolescence.*
▶ **adolescent** /ˌædə'lesnt/ *adj* of or typical of adolescence: *adolescent boys/crises/attitudes.* — *n* a young person in the process of developing from a child into an adult, ie roughly between the ages of 13 and 17.

adopt /ə'dɒpt/ *v* **1** to take sb else's child into one's family and become its legal parent(s): [V, Vn] *Having no children of their own they were hoping to adopt (an orphan).* [Vn] *Paul's mother had him adopted as a baby because she couldn't look after him herself.* ○ *He is their adopted son.* Compare FOSTER 2. **2** to take over sth and have or use it as one's own: [Vn] *adopt a name/a custom/an idea/a style of dress* ○ *adopt a hard line towards terrorists* ○ *This is her adopted country* (ie not her native country but the one in which she has chosen to live). **3** ~ sb as sth to choose sb as a candidate or representative: [Vn-n] *She has been adopted as Labour candidate for York.* **4** to accept a report, suggestion, etc, esp formally; to approve of sth: [Vn] *Congress voted to adopt the new measures.*
▶ **adoption** /ə'dɒpʃn/ *n* [C, U]: *offer a child for adoption* ○ *her adoption as Labour candidate for York* ○ *the country of her adoption* ○ *the committee's adoption of the proposal.*
adoptive *adj* [usu attrib] related by adoption: *his adoptive parents.*

adorable /ə'dɔːrəbl/ *adj* very attractive; delightful;

charming: *What an adorable child!* ○ *Your dress is absolutely adorable.*

adore /ə'dɔː(r)/ v **1** to love and respect sb very much: [Vn] *He adores his wife and children.* **2** (*infml*) (not used in the continuous tenses) to like sth very much: [Vn] *adore ice-cream/Paris/skiing* ○ *I simply adore that dress!* [V.ing] *I adore going to the theatre.* **3** [Vn] to give worship to God.
▶ **adoration** /ˌædə'reɪʃn/ n [U] great love or worship: *a look of silent adoration* ○ *a picture of the Adoration of the Magi* (ie the Wise Men giving worship to the young child Jesus).
adoring /ə'dɔːrɪŋ/ adj [usu attrib] showing great love: *his adoring grandmother* ○ *give sb an adoring look.*

adorn /ə'dɔːn/ v ~ **sth/sb/oneself (with sth)** to make sth/sb/oneself more attractive or beautiful, esp by adding some type of ornament: [Vn] *admire the paintings that adorn the walls* ○ (*ironic*) *Graffiti adorned the empty train.* [Vnpr] *Her hair was adorned with flowers.* ▶ **adornment** n [U, C]: *a simple dress without adornment* ○ *delicate gold adornments.*

adrenal /ə'driːnl/ adj (*anatomy*) close to the kidneys (KIDNEY 1): *the adrenal glands.*

adrenalin /ə'drenəlɪn/ n [U] (*medical*) (a) a substance produced by the ADRENAL glands (GLAND) when one is excited, afraid or angry. It increases the body's heart rate, level of energy and speed of reactions: *Competitive sports can really get the adrenalin flowing/going.* (b) this substance prepared artificially for medical use.

adrift /ə'drɪft/ adj [pred] **1(a)** (esp of a boat) not tied to anything and floating about without being controlled: *cut a boat adrift from its moorings* ○ *The survivors were adrift on a raft for six days.* (b) having no purpose; lacking direction: *young people adrift in our big cities.* **2** (*Brit infml*) (a) not fixed in position; loose: *Part of the car's bumper had come adrift.* (b) not working or happening as expected; wrong: *Our plans went badly adrift.* **3** ~ **(of sth)** (*Brit*) (esp in sport) behind a score, position or other target aimed at; short¹(5): *They're second in the league, three points adrift of the leaders.* **IDM cast sb adrift** ⇨ CAST¹.

adroit /ə'drɔɪt/ adj skilful; clever: *She succeeded by a combination of adroit diplomacy and sheer good luck.* Compare MALADROIT. ▶ **adroitly** adv: *He adroitly avoided answering my questions.* **adroitness** n [U].

adulation /ˌædju'leɪʃn; US ˌædʒə'l-/ n [U] excessive admiration or praise: *She is treated with wild adulation wherever she goes.* ▶ **adulatory** adj.

adult /'ædʌlt, ə'dʌlt/ adj **1(a)** grown to full size or strength: *adult monkeys* ○ *throughout one's adult life.* (b) mentally and emotionally mature: *His behaviour is not particularly adult.* **2** (*law*) old enough to vote, marry, etc. **3** of or for adults: *the adult population* ○ *adult education* (ie classes available to adults outside the standard educational system).
▶ **adult** n an adult person or animal: *These films are suitable for adults only.* ○ *The bear was a fully grown adult.*
adulthood n [U] the state of being adult: *reach adulthood.*

adulterate /ə'dʌltəreɪt/ v to make sth poorer in quality by adding another substance: [Vn] *adulterated milk* (eg with water added). ▶ **adulteration** /əˌdʌltə'reɪʃn/ n [U].

adultery /ə'dʌltəri/ n [U] sex between a married person and sb who is not that person's husband or wife: *commit adultery.*
▶ **adulterer** /ə'dʌltərə(r)/ n (*fem* **adulteress** /ə'dʌltərəs/) a person who commits adultery.
adulterous /ə'dʌltərəs/ adj of or involving adultery: *have an adulterous liaison/relationship with sb.*

adumbrate /'ædʌmbreɪt/ v [Vn] (*fml*) **1** to give a

faint or general idea of sth. **2** to suggest in advance sth that will happen in the future. ▶ **adumbration** /ˌædʌm'breɪʃn/ n [U, C].

advance¹ /əd'vɑːns; US -'væns/ n **1** [C usu *sing*] a forward movement: *Attempts to halt the rebel army's advance have failed.* ○ (*fig*) *halt the advance of a disease.* **2(a)** [U] progress through time: *the continued advance of civilization.* (b) [C] ~ (**in sth**) an improvement or development: *recent advances in medical science.* **3** [C] money paid before it is due, or for work only partly completed; a loan: *The publishers gave her an advance of $5000.* ○ *She asked for an advance on her salary.* **4** [C] ~ (**on sth**) an increase in price or amount: *'Any advance on* (ie Who will offer more than) *£200?' called the auctioneer.* ○ *Share prices showed significant advances today.* **5 advances** [pl] attempts to start a friendly or sexual relationship with sb: *He made amorous advances to her but she rejected them.* **IDM in advance (of sth) 1** ahead in time: *The rent must be paid in advance.* ○ *Send your luggage on in advance.* ○ *It's impossible to know in advance what will happen.* **2** more highly developed: *Galileo's ideas were well in advance of the age in which he lived.* ○ *That child is far in advance of the rest of the class.*
▶ **advance** adj [attrib] **1** done or provided before sth happens: *give sb advance warning/notice of sth* ○ *make an advance booking* (ie reserve a hotel room, a seat in a theatre, etc before the time when it is needed). **2** going before others: *the advance party* (ie a group of people, eg soldiers, sent ahead of the main group).

advance² /əd'vɑːns; US -'væns/ v **1(a)** ~ (**on/towards sb/sth**) to move forward, often in an aggressive or threatening way: [Vpr] *The mob advanced on/towards us shouting angrily.* [V] *The order came to advance.* [Vn] *The climbers have advanced two miles from base camp.* (b) to move or put sb/sth forward: [Vn] *The general advanced his troops at night.* ○ *He advanced his queen* (ie in a game of CHESS) *to threaten his opponent's king.* Compare RETREAT 1a. **2(a)** to make progress: [V] *advance in one's career* ○ *Has civilization advanced during this century?* (b) to help the progress of sth; to help a person, plan, etc to succeed: [Vn] *advance one's career* ○ *Such conduct is unlikely to advance your interests.* **3** ~ **sth (to sb)** to pay money before it is due to be paid; to lend money: [Vnn] *He asked his employer to advance him a month's salary.* [Vnpr] *The building societies have been advancing too much money to their customers.* **4** (*fml*) to make or present a claim, suggestion, etc for discussion: [Vn] *Scientists have advanced a new theory to explain this phenomenon.* **5** to move an event forward to an earlier date: [Vnpr] *The date of the meeting has been advanced from 10 to 3 June.* [also Vn]. Compare POSTPONE. **6** (of prices, costs, etc) to rise: [V] *Property values continue to advance rapidly.* [Vn, Vnpr] *The share price advanced 6p (to 394p).*
▶ **advanced** adj **1** having reached or developed to a very high level: *advanced weapons* ○ *an advanced state of decay* ○ *Her daughter is very advanced for her age.* ○ *Negotiations have reached a very advanced stage.* **2** involving or capable of a more difficult level of work: *advanced studies* ○ *an advanced student of English.* See also ELEMENTARY 1, INTERMEDIATE 2b. **3** new and not yet generally accepted: *have advanced ideas.* **4** old: *She died at an advanced age.*
■ **ad'vanced level** n = A LEVEL.

advancement /əd'vɑːnsmənt; US -'væns-/ n [U] **1** the process of helping sth to make progress or succeed: *the advancement of learning.* **2** promotion in rank or status: *The job offers good opportunities for advancement.*

advantage /əd'vɑːntɪdʒ; US -'væn-/ n **1(a)** [C]

~ **(over sb)** a condition or circumstance that puts one in a favourable position compared to other people: *gain an advantage over an opponent* ○ *He has the advantage of a steady job.* ○ *Her French upbringing gives her certain advantages over other students.* (**b**) [U] benefit; profit: *Is there any advantage in learning Latin nowadays?* ○ *turn a situation to one's advantage* ○ *The agreement is/works to our advantage.* **2** [sing] (in tennis) the first point scored after DEUCE[1]: *Agassi reached advantage point several times before clinching the set.* **IDM** **have the ad'vantage of sb** (*dated or fml*) to be in a better position than sb, esp in knowing sth that they do not know: *You have the advantage of me, I'm afraid* (eg said when a stranger addresses you by name). **take ad'vantage of sth/sb 1** to make use of sth well, properly, etc: *They took full advantage of the hotel's facilities.* **2** to make use of sb/sth in an unfair or dishonest way to get what one wants; to exploit sb/sth: *She took advantage of my generosity* (eg by taking more than I had intended to give). **to ad'vantage** in a way that shows the best aspects of sth: *The picture may be seen to (its best) advantage against a plain wall.*
▶ **advantage** *v* [Vn] (*fml*) to be of some use or benefit to sb. **advantaged** *adj* having a good social and financial position: *improve opportunities for the least/less advantaged groups.*
▶ **advantageous** /ˌædvən'teɪdʒəs/ *adj* ~ (**to sb**) profitable; BENEFICIAL: *The slump in the housing market is advantageous to home buyers.* **advantageously** *adv.*

advent /'ædvent/ *n* [sing] **1 the ~ of sth/sb** the approach or arrival of an important person, event, etc: *the advent of modern technology.* **2 Advent** the period including four Sundays immediately before Christmas: *Advent hymns.*

adventitious /ˌædven'tɪʃəs/ *adj* (*fml*) not planned; happening accidentally.

adventure /əd'ventʃə(r)/ *n* **1** [C] an unusual, exciting or dangerous experience: *have an adventure* ○ *her adventures in Africa.* **2** [U] excitement associated with danger, taking risks, etc: *a love/spirit/sense of adventure* ○ *a life full of adventure* ○ *adventure stories.*
▶ **adventurer** /əd'ventʃərə(r)/ *n* (*fem* **adventuress** /əd'ventʃərəs/) **1** a person who seeks adventure. **2** (*often derog*) a person who is ready to take risks or act in a dishonest or IMMORAL way for personal gain.
adventurous *adj* **1** (**a**) willing to take risks, test new ideas, experience new situations, etc: *More adventurous investors should look overseas.* ○ *We decided to be more adventurous this year and have a holiday in South America.* (**b**) including new ideas, methods, etc: *an adventurous design/concert programme/advertising campaign.* **2**(**a**) eager for or fond of adventure: *adventurous children.* (**b**) full of danger and excitement: *an adventurous trip/life.* **adventurously** *adv.*
■ **ad'venture playground** *n* (*Brit*) a PLAYGROUND containing ropes and small structures, eg arches, bridges and tunnels, for children to play in or on.

adverb /'ædvɜːb/ *n* (*grammar*) (abbreviated as *adv* in this dictionary) a word that adds more information about place, time, circumstance, manner, cause, degree, etc to a verb, an adjective, a phrase or another adverb: *In 'speak kindly', 'incredibly deep', 'just in time' and 'too quickly', 'kindly', 'incredibly', 'just' and 'too' are all adverbs.*
▶ **adverbial** /æd'vɜːbɪəl/ *adj* of, like or containing an adverb: *'Very quickly indeed' is an adverbial phrase.* **ad,verbial 'particle** *n* (*grammar*) (abbreviated as *adv part* in this dictionary) an adverb used esp after a verb to show position, direction of movement, etc: *In 'come back', 'break down' and 'fall off', 'back', 'down' and 'off' are all adverbial particles.*

adversary /'ædvəsəri; *US* -seri/ *n* an opponent in a contest, an argument or a battle: *He defeated his old adversary.*
▶ **adversarial** /ˌædvə'seəriəl/ *adj* involving conflict or opposition: *an adversarial system of justice* ○ *an adversarial relationship.*

adverse /'ædvɜːs, əd'vɜːs/ *adj* [usu attrib] (**a**) not favourable; contrary; opposing: *adverse winds/weather conditions/circumstances* ○ *The cuts will have an adverse effect on our research programme.* ○ *adverse criticism/comment/publicity* ○ *an adverse reaction to the proposals.* (**b**) harmful: *the adverse effects of drugs* . ▶ **adversely** *adv*: *His health was adversely affected by the climate.*

adversity /əd'vɜːsəti/ *n* [U, C] difficulties; trouble; MISFORTUNE: *remain cheerful in adversity* ○ *face adversity with courage* ○ *She overcame many adversities.*

advert /'ædvɜːt/ *n* (*Brit infml*) = ADVERTISEMENT 1.

advertise /'ædvətaɪz/ *v* **1** to describe a product or service publicly in order to persuade people to buy or use it: [V] *advertise on TV/in a newspaper* [Vn] *advertise soap powder/one's house/one's services* [Vn-adj, Vn-n] *The book was advertised as 'gripping'/'a marvellous read'.* **2**(**a**) to make sth generally or publicly known, eg by placing a notice in a newspaper: [Vn] *advertise a meeting/a concert* ○ *The post has been advertised.* ○ (*fml*) *It may be safer not to advertise your presence* (ie tell people that you are present). [also V]. (**b**) ~ **for sb/sth** to ask for sth or invite sb to apply for a job by placing a notice in a newspaper: [Vpr] *I must advertise for a new secretary.*
▶ **advertisement** /əd'vɜːtɪsmənt; *US* ˌædvər'taɪzmənt/ *n* **1** [C] (also *infml* **advert, ad**) ~ (**for sb/sth**) a public notice offering or asking for goods, services, etc: *a TV advert* ○ *a job ad* ○ *If you want to sell your old sofa, why not put/place an advertisement in the local paper?* ○ (*fig*) *Torn menus and dirty tablecloths are a poor advertisement for* (ie do not attract people to) *a restaurant.* See also CLASSIFIED ADVERTISEMENTS. **2** [U] the action of advertising.
advertiser *n* a person who advertises.
advertising *n* [U] **1** the activity of advertising: *a national advertising campaign* ○ *Cigarette advertising has been banned.* **2** the industry that produces advertisements to be shown on television, printed in magazines, etc: *He works in advertising.* ○ *an advertising agency.*

advice /əd'vaɪs/ *n* [U] **1** the giving of one's opinion about what sb else should do or how they should behave: *act on/follow/take sb's advice* (ie do what sb suggests) ○ *advice on mortgages/financial advice* ○ *You should take legal advice* (ie discuss the problem with a lawyer). ○ *a Citizens' Advice Bureau* ○ *My advice to you would be to wait.* ○ *If you take my advice you'll see a doctor.* ○ *Let me give you a piece/a bit/a few words/a word of advice.* **2** (*esp commerce*) a formal note giving information about a sale, delivery, etc: *We received advice that the goods had been dispatched.* ○ *an advice note.*

advisable /əd'vaɪzəbl/ *adj* [usu pred] ~ (**to do sth**) worth recommending as a course of action; sensible: *Early booking is advisable.* ○ *Do you think it advisable to wait?* Compare INADVISABLE. ▶ **advisability** /əd,vaɪzə'bɪləti/ *n* [U].

advise /əd'vaɪz/ *v* **1** ~ (**sb**) **against sth/doing sth**; ~ **sb (on sth)** to give advice to sb; to recommend sth to sb: [Vn, Vn.*to* inf] *The doctor advised (me to take) a complete rest.* [Vnpr] *They advised her against marrying quickly.* [V, Vpr] *She advises the government (on economic affairs).* [Vn.*to* inf] *We were advised not to drink the water.* [V.*that*, Vn.*to* inf] *We advised that they should start early/advised them to start early.* [V.*to* inf] *I'd advise taking a different approach.* [Vnadv] *You would be well advised* (ie sensible) *to stay indoors.* [V.*wh*, Vn.*wh*] *Can you*

advise (me) what to do next? **2** ~ **sb (of sth)** (*esp commerce*) to inform sb officially: [Vnpr, Vn.*wh*] *Please advise us of the dispatch date/when the goods will be dispatched.* [Vn.*that*] *We were not advised that the date of the meeting had been changed.* [also Vn]. **advisedly** /əd'vaɪzədli/ *adv* (*fml*) after careful thought; deliberately: *I use these words advisedly.*
▶ **adviser** (also *esp US* **advisor**) *n* ~ **(to sb) (on sth)** a person who gives advice, esp sb who is an expert in a particular field: *serve as special adviser to the President on foreign affairs* ○ *a financial adviser.*

advisory /əd'vaɪzəri/ *adj* having the power to advise: *an advisory committee/body/service* ○ *be/act in an advisory capacity/role.*

advocacy /'ædvəkəsi/ *n* [U] **1** ~ **(of sth)** the giving of support to a cause(3): *She is well known for her advocacy of women's rights.* **2** (*law*) the profession or work of an ADVOCATE *n*(2).

advocate /'ædvəkeɪt/ *v* (*fml*) to speak publicly in favour of sth; to recommend or support sth: [Vn] *I advocate a policy of gradual reform.* [V.*ing*] *Do you advocate banning cars in the city centre?* [V.*that*] *He had long advocated that the country should become a republic.* [also V.*n* *ing*].
▶ **advocate** /'ædvəkət/ *n* **1** ~ **(of sth)** a person who supports or speaks in favour of a cause(3), policy, etc: *a lifelong advocate of disarmament.* **2** a lawyer who presents a client's case in a lawcourt. Compare BARRISTER, SOLICITOR. See also DEVIL'S ADVOCATE.

adze (*US* **adz**) /ædz/ *n* a tool similar to an AXE with a curved blade at right angles (RIGHT[1]) to the handle. It is used for cutting or shaping large pieces of wood.

aegis /'iːdʒɪs/ *n* **IDM** **under the aegis of sb/sth** with the protection or support of sb/sth, esp a public institution: *Medical supplies are being flown in under the aegis of the Red Cross.*

aeon (also **eon**) /'iːən/ *n* a very long period of time; many thousands or millions of years: *The earth was formed aeons ago.*

aerate /'eəreɪt/ *v* **1** to add carbon dioxide (CARBON 1) to a liquid under pressure: [Vn] *aerated water.* **2** to expose sth to the chemical action of air: [Vn] *aerate the soil by digging it.* ▶ **aeration** /eə'reɪʃn/ *n* [U].

aerial[1] /'eəriəl/ (*Brit*) (*US* **antenna**) *n* one or more wires or rods for sending or receiving radio or television signals. ⇨ picture at HOUSE[1].

aerial[2] /'eəriəl/ *adj* **1** from aircraft or the air: *aerial bombardment/photography/reconnaissance.* **2** existing or suspended in the air: *an aerial railway.*

aero- *comb form* (forming *adjs* and *ns*) of air or aircraft: *aerodynamic* ○ *aerospace.*

aerobatics /ˌeərə'bætɪks/ *n* **(a)** [pl] difficult and exciting movements performed with aircraft, esp as part of a display, eg flying upside down or in loops: *The aerobatics were the best part of the show.* **(b)** [sing *v*] the art of performing these: *Aerobatics is a dangerous sport.* ▶ **aerobatic** *adj*: *an aerobatic display.*

aerobics /eə'rəubɪks/ *n* [pl] vigorous physical exercises done in order to increase the amount of oxygen taken into the body: *I go to my aerobics class on Wednesdays.* ▶ **aerobic** *adj*: *aerobic fitness.*

aerodrome /'eərədrəum/ *n* (*dated esp Brit*) a small airport used mainly by private aircraft.

aerodynamics /ˌeərəudaɪ'næmɪks/ *n* [pl] **1** [usu sing *v*] the science dealing with the forces acting on solid bodies, eg aircraft or bullets, moving through air. **2** [usu pl *v*] the qualities or properties of a solid body affecting the way it moves through air: *The car's aerodynamics have been improved by 10%.* ▶ **aerodynamic** *adj*: *a smooth, aerodynamic shape.*

aerogramme /'eərəgræm/ *n* = AIR LETTER.

aeronautics /ˌeərə'nɔːtɪks/ *n* [pl, usu sing *v*] the scientific study or practice of constructing and flying aircraft. ▶ **aeronautic, aeronautical** /-'nɔːtɪkl/ *adjs*: *aeronautical engineering/skills.*

aeroplane /'eərəpleɪn/ (also **plane**) (*US* **airplane** /'eərpleɪn/) *n* an aircraft with wings and one or more engines.

aerosol /'eərəsɒl/ *n* a container with a substance inside, eg paint or DEODORANT, that is kept under pressure and released as a fine spray: *ozone-friendly aerosols* ○ *an aerosol can.*

aerospace /'eərəuspeɪs/ *n* [U] the technology involved in making aircraft, spacecraft, missiles, etc: [attrib]: *the aerospace industry.*

aesthete /'iːsθiːt/ (*US* also **esthete** /'esθiːt/) *n* (*sometimes derog*) a person who has or claims to have a love and understanding of art and beauty.

aesthetic /iːs'θetɪk/ (*US* also **esthetic** /es'θetɪk/) *adj* [usu attrib] **1(a)** concerned with beauty and the appreciation of beauty: *aesthetic standards* ○ *an aesthetic sense.* **(b)** appreciating beauty and beautiful things: *an aesthetic person.* **2** pleasing to look at; artistic; showing good taste[1](6): *aesthetic design* ○ *Their furniture was more aesthetic than practical.*
▶ **aesthetic** (*US* also **es-**) *n* **1** a set of principles influencing artistic style or taste: *His aesthetic has remained unchanged since his early films.* **2** **aesthetics** [sing *v*] the branch of philosophy dealing with the principles of beauty and artistic taste.
aesthetically (*US* also **es-**) /-kli/ *adv*: *aesthetically pleasing.*
aestheticism /iːs'θetɪsɪzəm/ (*US* also **es-**) *n* [U].

afar /ə'fɑː(r)/ *adv* **IDM** **from a'far** from a long distance away: *news from afar* ○ (*fig*) *He loved her from afar* (ie did not tell her he loved her).

affable /'æfəbl/ *adj* pleasant and friendly; easy to talk to: *an affable reply* ○ *He found her parents very affable.* ▶ **affability** /ˌæfə'bɪləti/ *n* [U]. **affably** /-əbli/ *adv*.

affair /ə'feə(r)/ *n* **1** [sing] a thing to be done or for which one is responsible; a concern; a matter: *It's not my affair* (ie I am not interested in or responsible for it). **2** **affairs** [pl] **(a)** personal business matters: *put one's affairs in order.* **(b)** matters of public interest and importance: *current/foreign/world affairs* ○ *affairs of state.* **3** [C esp *sing*] **(a)** an event or series of events, esp one connected with a particular person, thing or place: *the Suez affair* ○ *We must try to forget this sad affair.* ○ *The press exaggerated the whole affair wildly.* **(b)** an organized social event: *The wedding was a very grand affair.* **(c)** [C] (*infml*) (following an *adj*) a thing described in a specified way: *Her hat was an amazing affair of ribbons and feathers.* **4** = LOVE AFFAIR: *She's having an affair with her boss.* **IDM** **a state of affairs** ⇨ STATE[1].

affect[1] /ə'fekt/ *v* **1** to have an influence on sb/sth; to produce an effect on sb/sth: [Vn] *The tax increases have affected us all.* ○ *The change in climate may affect your health* (ie be bad for you). ○ *Their opinion will not affect my decision.* ○ *The worst affected areas are the Midlands and North-West.* **2** (of disease) to attack sb/sth; to infect sb/sth: [Vn] *Cancer had affected his lungs.* **3** to cause sb to have feelings of sadness or sympathy: [Vn] *We were deeply affected by the news of her death.*
▶ **affecting** *adj* causing feelings of sadness or sympathy: *The play contains one or two affecting moments but overall it failed to move me.*

NOTE Affect is a verb that means 'to have an influence on': *Alcohol affects drivers' concentration.* Effect, especially in the phrase **have an effect on**, is a noun that means 'a result or influence': *Alcohol has a very bad effect on drivers.* Effect is also a formal verb meaning 'to achieve': *People lack confidence in their ability to effect change in society.* Sometimes people confuse the verbs **affect** and **effect**.

affect² /əˈfekt/ *v* **1** (*derog*) to make an obvious show of using, wearing or liking sth: [Vn] *affect bright colours/bow-ties* ○ *He affects a pretentious use of language* (ie tries to impress people by using unusual or difficult words, etc). **2** to pretend to have or feel sth: [V.to inf] *affect not to know sth* [Vn] *She affected an air of innocence.*

▶ **affected** /əˈfektɪd/ *adj* (*often derog*) not natural or genuine; pretended; artificial: *an affected politeness/cheerfulness* ○ *a highly affected style of writing* ○ *She is so affected.* **affectedly** *adv.*

affectation /ˌæfekˈteɪʃn/ *n* **1** [C, U] (*often derog*) an action or a type of behaviour, manner of speaking, etc, that is not natural but is intended to impress others: *His little affectations irritated her.* ○ *I detest all affectation.* **2** [C usu *sing*] ~ (**of sth**) a deliberate display of sth that is not truly felt; a PRETENCE: *an affectation of interest/indifference.*

affection /əˈfekʃn/ *n* [U, C] ~ (**for sb/sth**) a warm gentle feeling of caring for or loving sb/sth; fondness (FOND): *He felt great affection for his sister.* ○ *The old king was held in great affection.* ○ *She had a deep affection for the countryside.* ○ *I tried to win her affection(s).*

affectionate /əˈfekʃənət/ *adj* showing love or tender feelings for sb; FOND(1): *an affectionate child* ○ *affectionate kisses/words/smiles* ○ *He is very affectionate towards his children.* ▶ **affectionately** *adv*: *Michael ruffled her hair affectionately.* ○ *their son William, known affectionately as Bingo.*

affidavit /ˌæfɪˈdeɪvɪt/ *n* (*law*) a written statement, made by sb who swears that it is true, that can be used as evidence in court: *swear/make/take/sign an affidavit.*

affiliate /əˈfɪlieɪt/ *v* (**a**) ~ **sb/sth** (**with sb/sth**); *Brit* also ~ **sb/sth** (**to sb/sth**) (often passive) to link a person, a society or an institution to a larger organization: [Vnpr] *We are affiliated with the national group.* ○ *The college is affiliated to the university.* [Vn] *affiliated teams/societies/unions.* (**b**) ~ (**with sb/sth**) to become linked to a larger organization: [V, Vpr] *A number of local groups want to affiliate (with the union).*

▶ **affiliate** /əˈfɪliət/ *n* an affiliated person, institution, etc: *affiliate members.*

affiliation /əˌfɪliˈeɪʃn/ *n* [U, C]: *affiliation to the Labour Party* ○ *religious/political affiliations.*

affinity /əˈfɪnəti/ *n* **1** [C] ~ (**for/with sb/sth**); ~ (**between A and B**) a strong feeling of attraction to or interest in sb/sth: *They share a special affinity.* ○ *She has/feels a strong affinity for the music of Delius.* **2** [U, C] ~ (**with sb/sth**); ~ (**between A and B**) a close relationship between two or more people or things that share a common origin, structure, purpose, etc: *There is (a) close affinity between Italian and Spanish.* ○ *Early man shows certain affinities with the ape.*

affirm /əˈfɜːm/ *v* (*fml*) to state formally or confidently that sth is true or correct: [Vn] *She continued to affirm her innocence.* ○ *affirm one's right to speak freely* [V.that] *He affirmed that he was responsible.* [also V.speech]. Compare DENY 1.

▶ **affirmation** /ˌæfəˈmeɪʃn/ *n* **1**(**a**) [U, sing] the action of affirming sth: *The poem is a joyous affirmation of the power of love.* (**b**) [C] a thing that is affirmed; a belief: *the Christian affirmation that God created the world.* **2** [C] (*law*) a solemn declaration made in court instead of an OATH(1).

affirmative /əˈfɜːmətɪv/ *adj* (of words, etc) expressing agreement; indicating 'yes': *an affirmative reply/reaction.* Compare NEGATIVE 1.

▶ **affirmative** *n* [sing] (*fml*) a word or statement that expresses agreement or means 'yes': *The vote was a clear affirmative.* ○ *He replied in the affirmative.*

affirmatively *adv.*

■ **af,firmative 'action** *n* [U] (*esp US*) measures designed to favour people who are at a disadvantage or treated unfairly, esp because of their race or colour, eg to help them obtain employment or accommodation: *an affirmative action programme.* See also POSITIVE DISCRIMINATION.

affix¹ /əˈfɪks/ *v* ~ **sth** (**to/on sth**) (*fml*) to stick, fasten or attach sth: [Vn, Vnpr] *affix a stamp (to an envelope).*

affix² /ˈæfɪks/ *n* (*grammar*) a letter or group of letters added to the beginning or the end of a word to change its meaning or the way it is used. The PREFIX (1) *un-* in *unkind* and the SUFFIX *-less* in *careless* are both affixes.

afflict /əˈflɪkt/ *v* ~ **sb/sth** (**with sth**) (often passive) to cause trouble, pain or distress to sb/sth: [Vnpr] *She is afflicted with* (ie suffers from) *arthritis.* [Vn] *countries afflicted by mounting debts* ○ *Severe drought has afflicted the countryside.*

▶ **affliction** /əˈflɪkʃn/ *n* (*fml*) (**a**) [U] pain; suffering; distress: *help people in affliction.* (**b**) [C] a thing that causes suffering: *Blindness can be a terrible affliction.*

affluence /ˈæfluəns/ *n* [U] the state of having a lot of money and possessions; wealth: *live a life of affluence.*

affluent /ˈæfluənt/ *adj* rich; wealthy: *an affluent lifestyle* ○ *His parents were very affluent.* ○ *an affluent society* (ie one in which most people have a high standard of living).

afford /əˈfɔːd/ *v* **1** (no passive; usu with *can, could* or *be able to*) to have enough money, time, space, etc for a particular purpose: [Vn, V.to inf] *They walked because they couldn't afford (to take) a taxi.* [Vn] *You can't afford* (ie are not in a position to spend) *£90.* ○ *I'd love to go on vacation but I can't afford the time.* ○ *We would give more examples if we could afford the space.* **2** (no passive; usu with *can* or *could*, esp in negative sentences or questions) to be in a position to do sth which may have unpleasant consequences: [V.to inf] *I mustn't annoy my boss because I can't afford to lose my job* (ie must not take the risk of losing my job). ○ *You can ill afford to criticize others when you behave so badly yourself.* [Vn] *The firm cannot afford any more bad publicity.* **3** (*fml*) to give or provide sth: [Vn, Vnn] *The tree afforded (us) welcome shade.* [Vnn] *The scholarship afforded him the opportunity to study in Paris.* [also Vnpr]. ▶ **affordable** /əˈfɔːdəbl/ *adj*: *affordable prices* ○ *an affordable risk.*

afforest /əˈfɒrɪst; *US* əˈfɔːr-/ *v* [Vn] (esp passive) to plant areas of land with trees to form a forest. ▶ **afforestation** /əˌfɒrɪˈsteɪʃn; *US* əˌfɔːr-/ *n* [U].

affray /əˈfreɪ/ *n* (usu *sing*) (*fml or law*) a disturbance caused by fighting, etc in a public place: *The men were charged with causing an affray.*

affront /əˈfrʌnt/ *n* (usu *sing*) ~ (**to sb/sth**) a remark, action, etc, that openly insults or offends sb/sth, esp in public: *His speech was an affront to all decent members of the community.*

▶ **affront** /əˈfrʌnt/ *v* [Vn] (usu passive) to insult sb deliberately and openly; to offend sb. **affronted** *adj*: *He felt deeply affronted at/by her rudeness.*

Afghan /ˈæfɡæn/ *n* **1**(**a**) [C] a native or inhabitant of Afghanistan. (**b**) [U] the official language of Afghanistan. **2 afghan** [C] (**a**) a loose SHEEPSKIN coat. (**b**) (*US*) a type of woollen BLANKET(1). ■ **,Afghan 'hound** *n* a tall breed of dog with long soft hair.

aficionado /əˌfɪsiəˈnɑːdəʊ/ *n* (*pl* **-os**) a person who is very enthusiastic about a particular sport, activity or subject: *an aficionado of modern ballet.*

afield /ə'fiːld/ *adv* **IDM** **far/farther/further a'field** far, etc away, esp from home; to or at a distance: *You can hire a car if you want to explore further afield.* ○ *journalists* **from as far afield as** *China and Brazil* ○ *(fig) To find the culprit we need look no further afield than our own department.*

aflame /ə'fleɪm/ *adj* [pred] **1** in flames; burning: *The whole building was soon aflame.* ○ *(fig) The woods were aflame with autumn colours (eg bright red and orange).* **2** (of people) showing great excitement or embarrassment.

afloat /ə'fləʊt/ *adj* [pred] **1** floating in water: *The boat stuck on a sandbank but we soon got it afloat again.* ○ *The life-jacket kept him afloat* (ie prevented him from sinking). **2** at sea; on a ship: *a holiday afloat.* **3** out of debt or difficulties: *keep the economy afloat* ○ *The firm managed to stay afloat during the recession.*

afoot /ə'fʊt/ *adj* [pred] being planned or prepared: *Great changes are afoot.* ○ *He sensed that something was afoot* (ie something unexpected or suspicious was happening). ○ *There are moves/plans afoot to increase taxation.*

aforementioned /ə,fɔː'menʃənd/ (also **aforesaid** /ə'fɔːsed/, **said**) *adj* [attrib] (*fml*) (esp in legal documents) mentioned or referred to earlier: *The aforementioned 'person/'persons was/were acting suspiciously.*

▶ **the aforementioned** *n* (*pl* unchanged) (*fml*) the person or thing mentioned earlier.

aforethought /ə'fɔːθɔːt/ *adj* **IDM** **with malice aforethought** ⇨ MALICE.

a fortiori /,eɪ ,fɔːti'ɔːraɪ/ *adv* (*fml*) for this stronger reason: *If he can afford a luxury yacht, then a fortiori he can afford to pay his debts.*

afraid /ə'freɪd/ *adj* [pred] **(a)** ~ **(of sb/sth)**; ~ **(of doing sth/to do sth)** feeling fear; frightened of being hurt or of suffering in some way: *Don't be afraid.* ○ *There's nothing to be afraid of.* ○ *Are you afraid of snakes?* ○ *He's afraid of going out/to go out alone at night.* ○ *Don't be afraid* (ie Don't hesitate) *to ask for help if you need it.* **(b)** ~ **of doing sth**; ~ **(that)** ... feeling worry or anxiety about a possible outcome, effect, result, etc: *I didn't mention it because I was afraid of upsetting him/afraid (that) I might upset him.* ○ *I was afraid he would fall asleep.* **(c)** ~ **for sth/sb** feeling fear or worry about things that may put sb in danger or difficulties: *parents afraid for (the safety of) their children* ○ *He's afraid for his job* (ie that he might lose it). **IDM** **I'm afraid (that)** ... (usu without *that*, used to express a polite refusal or when giving a piece of information that may not be welcome) I am sorry to say: *I'm afraid we can't come.* ○ *I can't help you, I'm afraid.* ○ *'Do you have any milk?' 'I'm afraid not.'* ○ *'Have we missed the train?' 'I'm afraid so.'*

NOTE Compare **afraid, frightened** and **scared**. When somebody is **afraid of, frightened of**, or **scared of** something, they dislike that thing and feel fear when they see or experience it: *I've always been afraid of dogs.* ○ *I must admit I'm scared of flying.* ○ *All the kids in the class were frightened of Mr Radley.* When somebody is **scared** or **frightened** they are worried, and fear that something bad will happen: *The earthquake was awful! I have never been so scared in my life.* ○ *She woke up suddenly in the middle of the night feeling very frightened.* **Scared** is often used to describe small fears, especially by children: *I wasn't scared of the wicked witch but Thomas was.* If you are **scared stiff** you are full of fear: *I didn't know anyone at my new school and I was scared stiff.* You can use **scared** and **frightened**, but not **afraid**, before a noun: *The*

worst thing for a frightened child is a frightened adult.

afresh /ə'freʃ/ *adv* again, esp from the very beginning: *Let's start afresh.* ○ *It gives us an opportunity to look afresh at our whole export policy.*

African /'æfrɪkən/ *adj* of Africa or its people or languages.
▶ **African** *n* a native of Africa, esp a black person.
■ **African-American** /,æfrɪkən ə'merɪkən/ *adj* of American Blacks (BLACK² 3) or their culture. — *n* an American Black.

Afrikaans /,æfrɪ'kɑːns/ *n* [U] a language developed from Dutch, spoken in S Africa.

Afrikaner /,æfrɪ'kɑːnə(r)/ *n* a white S African, usu with Dutch ancestors, whose native language is Afrikaans.

Afro /'æfrəʊ/ *adj* (of hair or a HAIRSTYLE) thick and long with very tight curls, like the hair of some black¹(3a) people. ⇨ picture at HAIR.

Afro- *comb form* African; of Africa: *Afro-Asian* (ie of Africa and Asia).

aft /ɑːft; *US* æft/ *adv* in, near or towards the back part of a ship or an aircraft. Compare FORE *adv*.

after¹ /'ɑːftə(r); *US* 'æf-/ *adv* **1** later (in time); afterwards: *The day after, he left the country.* ○ *It reappeared long/soon after.* ○ *They lived happily ever after.* **2** behind (in place): *She followed on after.* Compare BEFORE¹. ⇨ note at BEFORE².

after² /'ɑːftə(r); *US* 'æf-/ *prep* **1(a)** later than sth; following sth in time: *leave after lunch/shortly after six/the day after tomorrow/ the week after next* ○ (*US*) *ten after seven in the morning* (ie 7.10 am). Compare BEFORE² 1. ⇨ note at BEFORE². **(b)** sth (indicating sth happening repeatedly or continuously): *day after day/week after week/year after year/time after time* (ie very often) ○ *He fired shot after shot* (ie many shots). See also ONE AFTER ANOTHER / THE OTHER. **2(a)** behind sb/sth when they have left: *Shut the door after you when you go out.* ○ *I'm always having to clear up after the children* (ie deal with the mess they have left). **(b)** in the direction of sb/sth that has left: *The boys stared after us.* **3** next to and following sb/sth in order, arrangement or importance: *C comes after B in the alphabet.* ○ *Your name comes after mine on the list.* ○ *He's the tallest in the class after Richard.* ○ *After you* (ie Please go in before me, serve yourself first, etc). ○ *After you with the salt.* ⇨ note at BEFORE². **4** in contrast to sth that one has already experienced: *The cottage was beautifully quiet after all the noise and bustle in the town.* **5** as a result of or because of sth that has already happened: *After what he did to my family, I'll never forgive him.* ○ *After your conduct last time, did you really expect to be invited again?* **6** (often indicating surprise or annoyance) in spite of sth; taking sth into account: *After everything I've done for him, he still ignores me.* **7** following behind and trying to reach, find or catch sb/sth: *He ran after her to give her the book.* ○ *The police are after him.* **8** (*infml*) eagerly trying to obtain sth/sb for oneself: *She's after a job in publishing.* **9** about sb/sth; concerning sb/sth: *They inquired after you* (ie asked how you were). **10** in the style of sb/sth; following the example of sb/sth: *a painting after Rubens* ○ *draw up a constitution after the American model* ○ *We've named the baby after you* (ie given it your first name in honour of you). **IDM** **,after 'all 1** in spite of what has been said, done or expected: *So you've come after all!* ○ *After all, what does it matter?* **2** it should be remembered: *He should have offered to pay — he has plenty of money, after all.*

after³ /'ɑːftə(r); *US* 'æf-/ *conj* at or during a time later than sth: *I arrived after he (had) started.* ○ *We'll arrive after you've left.* Compare BEFORE³ 1.

[V] = verb used alone   [Vn] = verb + noun   [Vp] = verb + particle   [Vpr] = verb + prepositional phrase

after⁴ /ˈɑːftə(r); US ˈæf-/ adj [attrib] (fml) later; following: in after years.

■ ˈafter-care n [U] attention or treatment given to a person who has just left hospital, prison, etc: after-care services.

ˈafter-effect n (usu pl) an effect that occurs at a later time than the thing that caused it, and that is usu unexpected or unpleasant: the after-effects of a drug ∘ suffer from/feel no unpleasant after-effects.

ˈafter-taste n [sing] a taste that stays after eating or drinking sth: wine which leaves an unpleasant after-taste (in the mouth).

afterbirth /ˈɑːftəbɜːθ; US ˈæf-/ n (usu the afterbirth [sing]) the material that comes out of a mother's WOMB after giving birth.

afterglow /ˈɑːftəgləʊ; US ˈæf-/ n (usu sing) a light that remains in the sky after the sun has set: (fig) basking in the warm afterglow of their success.

afterlife /ˈɑːftəlaɪf; US ˈæf-/ n [sing] an existence that is thought by some people to follow death: Do you believe in an afterlife?

aftermath /ˈɑːftəmæθ; US ˈæf-; Brit also -mɑːθ/ n (usu sing) the circumstances that follow and are a consequence of an event, esp of an unpleasant one: the rebuilding which took place in the aftermath of the war.

afternoon /ˌɑːftəˈnuːn; US ˌæf-/ n [U,C] the period from MIDDAY to about 6 pm: in/during the afternoon ∘ this/yesterday/tomorrow afternoon ∘ on Sunday afternoon ∘ on the afternoon of 12 May ∘ one afternoon last week ∘ an afternoon sleep/performance/train ∘ afternoon tea ∘ an afternoon's work ∘ have a relaxing afternoon ∘ She goes there two afternoons a week. ∘ Good afternoon, everyone! ⇨ note at MORNING.

▶ **afternoons** adv (esp US) regularly in the afternoon; every afternoon: Afternoons he works at home.

afters /ˈɑːftəz/ n [pl] (Brit infml) a usu sweet course following the main course of a meal: What's for afters? ∘ We had fruit salad for afters. See also DESSERT, PUDDING 1, SWEET² 2.

aftershave /ˈɑːftəʃeɪv; US ˈæf-/ n [U,C] a liquid with a pleasant smell used on a man's face after shaving: Do you use aftershave?

afterthought /ˈɑːftəθɔːt; US ˈæf-/ n a thing that is thought of or added later: The song was originally written as a guitar solo; the words were added as an afterthought. ∘ Mary was a bit of an afterthought — her brothers and sisters are all much older.

afterwards /ˈɑːftəwədz; US ˈæf-/ (US also afterward) adv at a later time: Let's go to the theatre first and eat afterwards. Compare BEFORE¹, BEFOREHAND. ⇨ note at BEFORE².

again /əˈgen, əˈgeɪn/ adv 1 once more; another time; on another occasion: Try again. ∘ Say that again, please. ∘ Here comes Joe, drunk again. ∘ Do call again. ∘ Don't do that again. ∘ This must never happen again. ∘ I've told you again and again (ie repeatedly) not to do that. 2 as before; to or in the original place or condition: He was glad to be ˈhome again. ∘ Back again already? ∘ You'll never get the money ˈback again. ∘ You'll soon be ˈwell again. ∘ I'm glad he's himˈself/his old ˈself again (ie that he has returned to his normal state again after an illness, a shock, etc). 3 (used to emphasize what follows and link it to a previous point, event, etc) (a) similarly; further; also: Again, we have to consider the legal implications. (b) (used to introduce a contrasting point, opinion, etc) on the other hand: I might, and (there/then) again I might not. 4 in addition: I'd like as many/much aˈgain (ie twice as many/much). ∘ ˌhalf as much aˈgain (ie one and a half times as much).

against /əˈgenst, əˈgeɪnst/ prep For the special uses of against in phrasal verbs, look at the verb entries. For example, the meaning of count against sb is given in the phrasal verb section of the entry for

count¹. 1(a) in opposition to sb/sth; contrary to sb/sth; HOSTILE(1) towards sb/sth: fight against enemy forces ∘ We're playing against the league champions next Saturday. ∘ We were rowing against the current. ∘ That's against the law. ∘ She was married against her will. ∘ Some people were for the proposal, but many more were against it. ∘ She is against seeing (ie does not want to see) him. ∘ I'd advise you against doing (ie not to do) that. (b) not to the advantage or favour of sb/sth: The evidence is against him. ∘ The odds are strongly against it. ∘ His age is against him. Compare FOR¹ 7. 2 close to, touching or striking sb/sth: Put the piano there, with its back against the wall. ∘ He was leaning against a tree. ∘ The rain beat against the windows. 3 in order to prevent sth occurring or to reduce the harm or loss caused by sth: take precautions against fire ∘ protect plants against frost ∘ an injection against rabies ∘ be insured against theft. 4 in contrast to sth: silhouetted against the sky ∘ The skier's red clothes stood out clearly against the snow. ∘ House prices here are low against those elsewhere. See also AS AGAINST STH (AS). 5 in relation to sth; in comparison with sth: balance/weigh the advantages against the cost ∘ Check your receipts against the statement. 6 in return for sth: What's the rate of exchange against the dollar? ∘ Tickets are issued only against payment of the full fee. 7 in relation to sth so as to reduce or cancel it: allowances to be set against income.

agape /əˈgeɪp/ adj [pred] (of the mouth) wide open, esp with surprise or wonder: He watched (with mouth) agape.

agate /ˈægət/ n [U,C] a type of very hard stone with bands or patches of colour, used in jewellery: an agate necklace.

age¹ /eɪdʒ/ n 1 [C,U] the length of time that a person has lived or a thing has existed: What age is he? ∘ He's six years of age. ∘ Their ages are six and ten. ∘ At what age did she retire? ∘ I left school at the age of 18. ∘ old/middle age ∘ reach voting age ∘ When I was your age… ∘ We have a son your age. ∘ He lived to a great/an advanced/a ripe old age. ∘ She died at an early age. ∘ Geologists have calculated the age of the earth. ∘ Anyone can enter the contest — there's no age limit (ie no one will be regarded as too old or too young). ⇨ note. 2 [U] the latter part of life; old age: the wisdom that comes with age ∘ His face was wrinkled with age. ∘ Fine wine improves with age. Compare YOUTH 1,2. 3 [C] a period of history with special characteristics or events: the Elizabethan Age (ie the time of Queen Elizabeth I of England) ∘ the modern age/the nuclear age/the age of the microchip. See also THE BRONZE AGE, THE DARK AGES, GOLDEN AGE, ICE AGE, THE IRON AGE, THE MIDDLE AGES, THE STONE AGE. 4 [C usu pl] (infml) a very long time: I waited (for) ages/an age. ∘ He left ages ago. ∘ It took (us) ages to find a place to park. **IDM** ˌbe/ˌact your ˈage (infml) (esp imperative) to behave in a manner appropriate to sb of your age and not as though you were much younger. ˌbe/ˌcome of ˈage 1 to reach the age at which one has an adult's legal rights and obligations. 2 to reach full development and gain acceptance: a literary talent that has come of age. **be of an ˈage** 1 to be at the age when one is expected to do sth: He's of an age when he ought to settle down. 2 to be roughly the same age: The two girls are (very much) of an age. ˌfeel one's age ⇨ FEEL¹. **in this day and age** ⇨ DAY. ˌlook one's ˈage to seem as old as one really is: She doesn't look her age at all (ie appears much younger than she really is). ˌover ˈage too old. ˌunder ˈage not old enough; not yet an adult: You shouldn't sell cigarettes to teenagers who are under age/to under-age teenagers.

■ ˈage group (also ˈage bracket) n people of similar age or within a particular, often specified, range of ages: mix with (people in) one's own age group ∘

Only people in the 20-30 age bracket need apply. ⇨ note.

¹age-long adj [usu attrib] existing for a very long time: *man's age-long struggle for freedom.*

₁age of con'sent n [sing] the age at which sb is considered in law to be old enough to agree to have sex.

₁age-'old adj [usu attrib] having existed for a very long time: *₁age-old 'customs/'ceremonies.*

NOTE There are several ways of saying or writing a person's age in English. In speaking, people usually only use numbers: *'How old are your children?' 'Louise is five and Emma is three.'* ○ *She got married at 16.* You can also refer to **a man/woman/boy/girl of** ...: *They've got a boy of 10 and a girl of 12.* ○ *a young man of 20.*
The expression ...**years old** is used more in writing and descriptions of people. Note that 'old' must always be part of the phrase: *Her parents divorced when she was nine years old.* (NOT *nine years.*) *Police described the driver as white, five feet ten inches tall and about 25 years old.* It is also often used to emphasize somebody's age: *I'm forty years old — I don't need you to tell me what to do!*
...**years old** is also used for things: *My car is ten years old.* ○ *These trees are hundreds of years old.* You can also say **a ...-year-old** or ...**-year-olds** (or similar expressions with **month** and **week**): *a 20-year-old vintage wine* ○ *The volunteers were a group of very bright 18-year-olds on their way to college.* ○ *a two-week-old baby.*
The expression ...**years of age** is used mainly in formal or written contexts: *Children do not start school in some countries until they are seven years of age.* **Under** and **over** are used when describing groups of people who are less than or more than a certain age: *education for the under-fives* ○ *The Third Age refers to people over the age of 60.* ○ *You have to be 21 years old or over before you can do the course.*
The expression **the ...age group** is used to talk about people between certain ages: *Our station's music is aimed at the 18-30 age group* . When describing the approximate age of a person, (ie between 21 and 29, 31 and 39, etc) you say he or she is **in** his or her **teens/twenties**, etc: *She's in her early/mid/late thirties* (ie 31–33/34–36/37–39).
When referring to a specific event, people often say **at/by/before, etc the age of**: *My grandmother died at the age of 86.* ○ *She could read by the age of three.*

age² /eɪdʒ/ v (*pres p* **ageing** or **aging**; *pp* **aged** /eɪdʒd/) **1(a)** to grow old; to show signs of growing old: [V] *an ageing film star* ○ *an ageing population* (ie one with an increasing number of old people) ○ *He's aged a lot recently.* [Vadv] *She's aging gracefully.* **(b)** to make sb become old: [Vn] *The illness has aged him terribly.* ○ *I found her greatly aged.* **2** to become or allow sth to become mature: [V] *allow wine to age* [Vn] *age brandy in casks.*
▶ **aged** adj **1** /eɪdʒd/ [pred] of the age of: *The boy was aged ten.* **2** /'eɪdʒɪd/ [attrib] (*fml*) very old: *an aged man.* **the aged** /'eɪdʒɪd/ n [pl] very old people: *caring for the sick and the aged.* ⇨ note at OLD.
ageing (also **aging**) n [U] the process of growing old: *signs/effects of ageing.*

-age suff (with *ns* and *vs* forming *ns*) **1** a state or condition of : *bondage.* **2** a set or group of: *baggage* ○ *the peerage.* **3** the action or result of: *breakage* ○ *wastage.* **4** the cost of: *postage* ○ *corkage.* **5** a place where: *anchorage* ○ *orphanage.* **6** a quantity or measure of: *mileage* ○ *dosage.*

ageism /'eɪdʒɪzəm/ n [U] (*derog*) the practice of treating people unfairly because of their age, esp because they are considered too old. ▶ **ageist** n, adj.

ageless /'eɪdʒləs/ adj **1** never growing old or never

appearing to grow old: *Her beauty seems ageless.* **2** lasting for ever; ETERNAL(1): *the ageless mystery of the universe.*

agency /'eɪdʒənsi/ n **(a)** a business or organization providing a usu specified service: *an employment/a travel/an advertising/a secretarial agency* ○ *aid/refugee agencies* ○ *Our company has agencies all over the world.* **(b)** (*esp US*) a government office providing a specified service: *the Central Intelligence Agency.* **IDM by/through the agency of sth/sb** (*fml*) as a result of the action of sth/sb: *He obtained his position by/through the agency of friends.*

agenda /ə'dʒendə/ (*pl* **agendas**) n the matters of business to be discussed, esp at a meeting, or a list of these: *What is the next item on the agenda?* ○ (*fig*) *The environment is high on the political agenda at the moment* (ie being widely discussed in politics). ○ (*fig*) *Is there a hidden agenda?* (ie Are there secret motives for sth?)

agent /'eɪdʒənt/ n **1** a person who acts for, or manages the affairs of, other people in business, politics, etc: *an insurance agent* ○ *a travel agent* ○ *a literary agent* ○ *our agents in the Middle East.* **2(a)** a person who does sth or causes sth to happen: *the agent of his own ruin.* **(b)** a force or substance that produces an effect or change: *cleaning/oxidizing agents* ○ *Yeast is the raising agent in bread.* **3** = SECRET AGENT: *an enemy agent.* See also DOUBLE AGENT, ESTATE AGENT, FREE AGENT.

agent provocateur /ˌæʒɒ̃ prəˌvɒkə'tɜː(r)/ n (*pl* **agents provocateurs** /ˌæʒɒ̃ prəˌvɒkə'tɜː(r)/) (*French*) a person employed to help in catching suspected criminals by tempting them to act illegally.

agglomeration /əˌɡlɒmə'reɪʃn/ n a mass of things in a group together in no particular order or arrangement: *an ugly agglomeration of new buildings.*

aggrandizement, -isement /ə'ɡrændɪzmənt/ n [U] (*fml*) increase in a person's power, rank, importance, etc: *His sole aim is personal aggrandizement.*

aggravate /'æɡrəveɪt/ v **1** to make a disease, a situation, an offence, etc worse or more serious: [Vn] *He aggravated his condition by leaving hospital too soon.* ○ *The problem is aggravated by a lack of understanding.* **2** (*infml*) to irritate sb; to annoy sb: *Some of his remarks really aggravate me.*
▶ **aggravating** adj (*infml*) irritating; annoying: *Constant interruptions are very aggravating when you're trying to work.*
aggravation /ˌæɡrə'veɪʃn/ n **1** [U] the action or process of making sth worse or more serious. **2** [U, C] annoyance or a thing that annoys: *minor aggravations.*

aggregate¹ /'æɡrɪɡeɪt/ v (*fml*) to combine separate items, sets of data, etc into a single group or total: [Vn, Vnpr] *The figures are then aggregated (with existing data) to give the final picture.* ▶ **aggregation** /ˌæɡrɪ'ɡeɪʃn/ n [U, C]: *the aggregation of funds.*

aggregate² /'æɡrɪɡət/ n **1** [C] a total number or amount; a mass or an amount of items, data, etc collected together: *the complete aggregate of unemployment figures.* **2** [U, C] (*techn*) material, eg sand or crushed stone, that is mixed with cement and water to make concrete. **IDM in (the) 'aggregate** added together; as a whole: *Businesses are, in the aggregate, deeper in debt than ever before.* **on 'aggregate** taken as a whole; in total: *Our team scored the most goals on aggregate.*
▶ **aggregate** adj [attrib] total; combined: *aggregate data* ○ *the aggregate value/profit.*

aggression /ə'ɡreʃn/ n [U] violent or HOSTILE(1a) feelings or behaviour: *an act of open aggression* ○ *She was always full of aggression as a child.* ○ *Military aggression against our allies cannot be tolerated.*

aggressive /ə'ɡresɪv/ adj **1** (of people or animals) ready or likely to attack or quarrel: *dogs trained to be aggressive* ○ *His aggressive behaviour frightens me* *sometimes.* **2** (*approv*) forceful; promoting an idea, product, etc strongly: *an aggressive advertising campaign* ○ *A good salesman must be aggressive if he wants to succeed.* ► **aggressively** *adv*: *behave/react aggressively* ○ *a new range of pesticides being aggressively marketed in Africa.* **aggressiveness** *n* [U].

aggressor /ə'gresə(r)/ *n* a person or country that attacks first, without being provoked: *armed aggressors* ○ *aggressor nations.*

aggrieved /ə'griːvd/ *adj* ~ (**at/by sth**) feeling that one has been unfairly treated; resentful (RESENT): *feel aggrieved* at losing one's job ○ *be aggrieved by a decision* ○ *the aggrieved party* (eg in a legal case) ○ *I felt rather aggrieved not to be invited.*

aggro /'ægrəʊ/ *n* [U] (*Brit sl*) (**a**) violent aggressive behaviour: *Don't give me any aggro or I'll call the police!* (**b**) trouble; problems and difficulties: *There's a lot of aggro involved in buying a house.*

aghast /ə'gɑːst; *US* ə'gæst/ *adj* [pred] ~ (**at sth**) filled with horror or shock: *Erica looked at him aghast.* ○ *He stood aghast at the terrible sight.*

agile /'ædʒaɪl; *US* 'ædʒl/ *adj* able to move quickly and easily; active: *as agile as a monkey* ○ (*fig*) *an agile mind/brain.* ► **agility** /ə'dʒɪləti/ *n* [U].

aging ⇨ AGE².

agitate /'ædʒɪteɪt/ *v* **1** to make a person feel disturbed, anxious or excited: [Vn] *His appearance at the party had clearly agitated her.* **2** ~ **for/against sth** to demand sth publicly or take part in a campaign for/against sth: [Vpr] *agitate for tax reform/ against nuclear weapons.* **3** to stir or shake a liquid: [Vn] *Agitate the mixture to dissolve the powder.* ► **agitated** *adj* troubled, anxious or excited: *in an agitated condition/state* ○ *He became very agitated and started shouting.* ○ *Don't get all agitated!* **agitation** /ˌædʒɪ'teɪʃn/ *n* **1** [U] a state or feelings of anxiety or excitement: *She was in a state of great agitation.* ○ *He tried to hide his agitation.* **2** [U, C] (a) public protest about or discussion for or against sth: *nationalist agitations* ○ *stir up agitation for equal pay and conditions.*

agitator *n* a person who urges others to protest or take part in a campaign: *a former left-wing agitator.*

aglow /ə'gləʊ/ *adv, adj* [pred] glowing; shining with warmth and colour: *Christmas trees aglow with coloured lights* ○ (*fig*) *happy children's faces all aglow.*

AGM /ˌeɪ dʒiː 'em/ *abbr* (*esp Brit*) annual general meeting. At the AGM of an organization its members elect officers, discuss past and future activities and examine the organization's accounts: *report to the AGM.*

agnostic /æg'nɒstɪk/ *n* a person who is not sure whether or not God exists. Compare ATHEIST. ► **agnostic** *adj*: *an agnostic frame of mind.* **agnosticism** /æg'nɒstɪsɪzəm/ *n* [U].

ago /ə'gəʊ/ *adv* (used in expressions of time after the word or phrase it modifies (MODIFY 2) and with the simple past tense) gone by; in the past: *ten years ago* ○ *not long ago* ○ *It happened a few minutes ago.* ○ *How long ago was it that you last saw her?* ○ *It was seven years ago that my brother died.* ⇨ note at RECENT.

agog /ə'gɒg/ *adj* [pred] eager; excited: *agog with curiosity* ○ *be agog for news/to hear the news* ○ *He was all agog at the surprise announcement.*

agonize, -ise /'ægənaɪz/ *v* ~ (**about/over sth**) to suffer great anxiety or to worry intensely about sth: [Vpr] *agonizing over a decision* ○ *We agonized for days about whether to accept their offer.* [also V]. ► **agonized, -ised** *adj* suffering or expressing severe pain or anxiety: *an agonized look/cry.* **agonizing, -ising** *adj* causing great suffering or anxiety: *an agonizing pain/delay/decision.* **agonizingly, -isingly** *adv* (often used for emphasis) very; extremely: *agonizingly slow progress.*

agony /'ægəni/ *n* [U, C] extreme mental or physical suffering: *The wounded man was in agony.* ○ *They suffered the agony of watching him burn to death.* ○ *be in an agony of indecision/guilt/suspense/embarrassment* ○ *She suffered agonies of remorse.* **IDM** **pile on the agony** ⇨ PILE².

■ **'agony aunt** *n* (*Brit*) (*US* **ad'vice columnist**) (*infml*) a person who replies to letters about people's personal problems sent to and printed in a magazine.

'agony column *n* (*Brit*) (*US* **ad'vice column**) (*infml*) a part of a newspaper or magazine for letters from readers seeking advice about their personal problems.

agoraphobia /ˌægərə'fəʊbiə/ *n* [U] an abnormal fear of being in public places or open spaces. ► **agoraphobic** /-'fəʊbɪk/ *n, adj* (a person) suffering from this fear.

agrarian /ə'greəriən/ *adj* [usu attrib] relating to agricultural land: *agrarian laws/problems/reforms.*

agree /ə'griː/ *v* **1** ~ (**to sth**) to say 'yes'; to say that one is willing to do sth or for sth to happen: [V] *I asked for a pay rise and she agreed.* [V.to inf] *Is he going to agree to our suggestion?* [V.that] *He agreed to let me go/agreed that I could go home early.* Compare REFUSE². **2(a)** ~ (**with sb**) (**about/on sth**); ~ (**with sth**) to have or form a similar opinion to sb; to say that you share sb's opinion of sth: [V] *When he said that, I had to agree.* ○ *'I'm sorry, I don't agree,' he said.* [Vpr] *I agree with his analysis of the situation.* ○ *Do you agree with me about the need for more schools?* [Vpr, V.wh] *We couldn't agree on a date/ agree when to meet.* [V.to inf] *We agreed to start early.* [V.that] *Do we all agree that the proposal is a good one?* [V.speech] *'That's certainly true,' she agreed.* ⇨ note. (**b**) to reach the same opinion on sth; to decide sth: [Vn] *Can we agree a price?* ○ *They met at the agreed time.* Compare DISAGREE 1a. **3** (*esp Brit*) to accept sth as correct; to approve sth: [Vn] *Next year's budget has been agreed.* **4** ~ (**with sth**) to be consistent with sth; to match: [V] *The two accounts do not agree.* [Vpr] *Your account of the affair does not agree with hers.* Compare DISAGREE 1b. **5** ~ (**with sth**) (*grammar*) to correspond with a word or phrase in number(8), GENDER(1) or person(3): [Vpr] *a verb that agrees with its subject* [also V]. **IDM** **a,gree to 'differ** to accept differences of opinion, esp in order to avoid further argument: *We must just agree to differ on this.* **be agreed (on/about sth); be agreed (that...)** (with *it* or a plural subject) to have reached the same opinion: *Are we all agreed on the best course of action?* ○ *It was agreed that another meeting was necessary.* **couldn't agree (with sb) 'more** (used to express complete agreement): *'The plan's bound to fail.' 'I couldn't agree more!'* **PHRV** **a'gree with sb** (esp in negative sentences or questions) to suit sb's health: *The humid climate didn't agree with him.* ○ *I like mushrooms but unfortunately they don't agree with me* (ie they make me ill if I eat them).

NOTE When you have the same opinion as somebody else, you say: *I agree (with you)* (NOT *I am agree*). If you have a different opinion, you say: *I don't agree (with you)/I disagree (with you)* (NOT *I am not agree*). Two or more people can **be agreed on something** if they have the same opinion: *Kate and David are agreed on one thing — they both hate football.*

agreeable /ə'griːəbl/ *adj* **1** pleasant; giving pleasure: *agreeable weather* ○ *agreeable company* ○ *I found him most agreeable.* Compare DISAGREEABLE. **2** [pred] ~ (**to sth**) ready to agree: *If you're agreeable to our proposal, we'll go ahead.* ○ *I'll invite her, if you're agreeable (to her coming).* ► **agreeably** /-əbli/ *adv* pleasantly: *agreeably surprised* ○ *The day passed agreeably.*

agreement /əˈgriːmənt/ n **1** [C] an arrangement, a promise or a contract made with sb: *an international agreement* ○ *Please sign the agreement.* ○ *An agreement with the employers was finally worked out.* ○ *They have broken the agreement between us.* See also GENTLEMAN'S AGREEMENT. **2** [U, C] harmony in opinion or feeling: *The two sides failed to reach (an) agreement.* ○ *There is little agreement as to what our policy should be.* ○ *Are we in agreement about the price?* **3** [U] (*grammar*) having the same number(8), GENDER(1) or person(3): *agreement between subject and verb.*

agri- (also **agro-**) *comb form* (forming *ns* and *adjs*) of farming: *agriculture* ○ *agronomy.*

agribusiness /ˈægrɪbɪznəs/ n [U] the industry concerned with the production, processing and distribution of agricultural products or with farm machinery and services.

agriculture /ˈægrɪkʌltʃə(r)/ n [U] the science or practice of cultivating the land and keeping or breeding animals for food; farming: *the Ministry of Agriculture.* ▶ **agricultural** /ˌægrɪˈkʌltʃərəl/ adj: *agricultural land/workers/machinery.* **agriculturalist** /ˌægrɪˈkʌltʃərəlɪst/ n.

agronomy /əˈgrɒnəmi/ n [U] the science concerned with the relationship between crops and their environment. ▶ **agronomist** /əˈgrɒnəmɪst/ n.

aground /əˈgraʊnd/ adv, adj [pred] (of ships) touching the bottom in shallow water: *The tanker was/went/ran aground.*

ah /ɑː/ interj (used to express surprise, delight, admiration, sympathy, understanding, etc or to introduce a point of disagreement): *Ah, ¹there you are.* ○ *Ah, good, here's the bus.* ○ *Ah, what a lovely baby!* ○ *Ah well, never mind.* ○ *Ah yes, I remember now.* ○ *Ah, but that may not be true.* Compare OH.

aha /ɑːˈhɑː/ interj (used esp to express satisfaction or triumph): *Aha, so that's where she hides her money!*

ahead /əˈhed/ adv part For the special uses of **ahead** in phrasal verbs, look at the verb entries. For example, the meaning of **press ahead (with sth)** is given in the phrasal verb section of the entry for *press²*. **1** further forward in space or time: *look straight ahead* (ie in front) ○ *run ahead* ○ *200 yards ahead* ○ *the way ahead* ○ *We've got a lot of hard work ahead.* ○ *This will create problems for years ahead.* **2** earlier; in advance: *She likes to plan her dinner parties several days ahead.* **3** in the lead; further advanced: *Our team was ahead by six points.* ○ *You need to work hard to keep ahead.*

■ **ahead of** prep **1** further forward in space or time than sb/sth; in front of sb/sth: *Three boys were ahead of us.* ○ *London is about three hours ahead of New York.* ○ *Ahead of us lay ten days of intensive training.* **2** earlier than sb/sth; in advance of sb/ sth: *I finished the work several days ahead of the deadline.* ○ *When we arrived we found they'd got there ahead of us.* **3** further advanced than sb/sth; in front of sb, eg in a race: *She was always well ahead of the rest of the class.* ○ *His ideas were (way) ahead of his time.*

ahem /əˈhem/ interj (used in writing to indicate the noise made when clearing the throat, esp to get sb's attention or express disapproval): *Ahem, might I make a suggestion?*

ahoy /əˈhɔɪ/ interj (a cry used by sailors to attract attention): *Ahoy there!* ○ *Land/Ship ahoy!* (ie There is land/a ship in sight.)

AI /ˌeɪ ˈaɪ/ abbr **1** artificial insemination. **2** artificial intelligence.

aid /eɪd/ n **1** [U] help of any kind: *legal aid* ○ *breathe with the aid of a respirator* ○ *This level of analysis would be impossible without the aid of a computer.* ○ *She came quickly to his aid* (ie to help him). See also FIRST AID. **2** [C] a thing that helps: *a ¹hearing-aid* ○ *¹teaching aids* ○ *a useful aid to giving up*

smoking. **3** [U] food, money, etc sent to a region or country to help it: *How much overseas/foreign aid does Britain give?* ○ *emergency/food/humanitarian aid* ○ *medical ¹aid programmes.* **IDM** **in aid of sth/sb** in support of sth/sb: *collect money in aid of charity.* **what's (all) this, etc in aid of?** (*infml*) what is the purpose of this, etc?: *Now then, what's all this crying in aid of?*

▶ **aid** v ~ **sb/sth (in sth)** (*esp fml*) to help sb/sth: [Vn, Vnpr] *They were accused of aiding his escape/ aiding him in his escape.* [Vn] *The pound, aided by support from the Bank of England, recovered a little today.* ○ *be accused of aiding and abetting a crime* [Vn.to inf] *His absence aided the rebels to gain control of the city.*

aide /eɪd/ n (*esp US*) an assistant to a person: *one of the President's closest aides.*

aide-de-camp /ˌeɪd də ˈkɒ̃; US ˈkæmp/ n (pl **aides-de-camp** /ˌeɪd də ˈkɒ̃/) a naval or military officer who acts as assistant to a senior officer.

Aids (also **AIDS**) /eɪdz/ abbr (*medical*) Acquired Immune Deficiency Syndrome (an often fatal disease marked by severe loss of resistance to infection): *Aids symptoms/patients/research* ○ *Aids is spread mainly by sexual contact.*

ail /eɪl/ v (*arch*) to trouble sb in body or mind: [Vn] *I asked what was ailing her.*

▶ **ailing** adj ill and not improving: *My wife is ailing.* ○ (*fig*) *the ailing economy.*

aileron /ˈeɪlərɒn/ n a part of the wing of an aircraft that moves up and down to control the aircraft's balance while it is flying. ⇨ picture at AIRCRAFT.

ailment /ˈeɪlmənt/ n an illness, esp a slight one: *the treatment of minor ailments.* ⇨ note at ILLNESS.

aim¹ /eɪm/ v **1** ~ (**at/for sth**); ~ (**at doing sth**) to try to achieve sth: [Vadv] *He has always aimed high* (ie been ambitious). [Vpr] *She's aiming at* (ie trying to win) *a scholarship.* [Vpr, V.to inf] *We must aim at increasing/aim to increase exports.* [Vpr] *The company is aiming for a greater share of the home market.* **2** ~ (**sth**) (**at sth/sb**) to point or direct a weapon, blow, missile, etc towards an object: [Vadv] *You're not aiming straight.* [Vpr, Vnpr] *He aimed (his gun) at the target, fired and missed it.* [Vnpr] *The punch was aimed at his opponent's head.* [also Vn]. **3** ~ **sth at sb** to direct a comment, criticism, message, etc at sb: *My remarks were not aimed at you.* ○ *an advertising campaign aimed at young people.*

aim² /eɪm/ n **1** [C] a purpose; an intention: *The aim is to increase sales in Europe.* ○ *He has only one aim in life — to become rich.* ○ *She went to London with the aim of finding a job.* ○ *She failed to achieve her aim.* ○ *What are the aims and objectives of the society?* **2** [U] the action of pointing or directing a weapon, missile, etc at a target: *My aim was accurate.* ○ *Take careful aim* (at the target) *before firing.*

aimless /ˈeɪmləs/ adj having no direction or purpose: *aimless wanderings* ○ *lead an aimless life.* ▶ **aimlessly** adv: *drift aimlessly from job to job.* **aimlessness** n [U].

ain't /eɪnt/ short form (*non-standard or joc*) **1** am/is/ are not: *Things ain't what they used to be.* **2** has/ have not: *You ain't seen nothing yet.*

air¹ /eə(r)/ n **1** [U] the mixture of gases surrounding the earth and breathed by all land animals and plants: *currents of warm air* ○ *air pollution* ○ *Let's go out for some fresh air.* ○ *I need to put some air in my tyres.* **2** [U] (**a**) (usu the **air**) the open space above the earth's surface: *kick a ball high in the air.* (**b**) the atmosphere, esp as the place where aircraft fly: *air travel/transport/traffic/freight* ○ *send goods/travel by air* (ie in an aircraft) ○ *an air-launched missile* (ie launched from an aircraft) ○ *The site of the old fort is clearly visible from the air.* **3** [C] the appearance or manner of sb/sth; the impression

given by sb/sth: *She had a triumphant air.* ○ *The place has an air of mystery (about it)* (ie looks mysterious). **4** [C] (*dated*) (a tune; a MELODY(1): *Bach's Air on the G String.* **5 airs** [pl] (*derog*) an affected manner intended to make one appear more important, educated, elegant, etc: *Stop putting on airs.* ○ *She's always giving herself airs.* ○ *I'm not impressed by his fancy airs and graces.* **IDM** **a breath of fresh air** ⇨ BREATH. **castles in the air/ in Spain** ⇨ CASTLE. **a change of air/climate** ⇨ CHANGE². **clear the air** ⇨ CLEAR³. **float/walk on 'air** to feel very happy. **in the 'air 1** generally present among people; current: *There's (a feeling of) unrest in the air.* **2** uncertain; not yet decided: *Our plans are still (up) in the air.* **in the open air** ⇨ OPEN¹. **light as air/as a feather** ⇨ LIGHT³. **,on/,off the 'air** in/not in the process of broadcasting on radio or television: *This channel comes on the air every morning at 7 am.* ○ *We'll be off the air for the summer and returning for a new series in the autumn.* **over the air** on the radio or television: *They shouldn't use such language over the air.* **,take the 'air** (*dated or fml*) to go outside in order to enjoy the fresh air. **vanish, etc into thin air** ⇨ THIN. **with one's nose in the air** ⇨ NOSE¹.
■ **'air-bed** *n* a MATTRESS that can be filled with air.
'air brake *n* a BRAKE, eg for a bus or train, worked by air pressure.
,Air Chief 'Marshal *n* (the title of) a very senior officer in the Royal Air Force. ⇨ App 6.
,Air 'Commodore *n* (the title of) a senior officer in the Royal Air Force. ⇨ App 6.
'air-conditioning *n* [U] a system that cools and dries the air in a room or building: *turn on the air-conditioning.* **'air-conditioned** *adj*: *an air-conditioned office* ○ *Is the house air-conditioned?* **air-conditioner** *n* an air-conditioning machine.
,air-'cooled *adj* cooled by a current of air: *an ,air-cooled 'engine.*
'air force *n* [CGp] a branch of the armed forces that uses aircraft for attack and defence: *the US Air Force* ○ *air-force officers.*
'air-hostess *n* a woman who serves passengers in an aircraft.
'air letter (also **airmail letter, aerogramme**) *n* a single sheet of light paper folded to form a letter that may be sent by air.
,Air 'Marshal *n* (*Brit*) (the title of) a senior officer in the Royal Air Force. ⇨ App 6.
'air pocket *n* a partial vacuum in the air causing aircraft in flight to drop suddenly.
'air pump *n* a device for pumping air into or out of sth.
'air raid *n* an attack by aircraft dropping bombs: *Many civilians were killed in the air raids on London.* ○ *an air-raid warning/shelter.*
'air rifle *n* = AIRGUN.
,air-sea 'rescue *n* [U, CGp] the process of rescuing people from the sea using aircraft: *an air-sea rescue service with helicopters.*
'air speed *n* the speed of an aircraft relative to the air through which it is moving.
'air terminal *n* a building, usu at an airport, that provides services to passengers arriving and departing by plane.
,air-to-'air *adj* [usu attrib] from one aircraft to another in flight: *an air-to-air missile.*
,air traffic con'troller *n* a person at an airport who gives instructions by radio to pilots of aircraft departing or landing. **,air traffic con'trol** *n* [U] (**a**) the organization that such a person works for: *The pilot contacted French air traffic control.* (**b**) the service provided by this organization: *The new equipment will simplify air traffic control over southern England.*
,Air Vice-'Marshal *n* (*Brit*) (the title of) a senior officer in the Royal Air Force. ⇨ App 6.

'air waves *n* [pl] (*infml*) radio waves used in broadcasting: *A well-known voice came over the air waves.*

air² /eə(r)/ *v* **1(a)** to put clothing, etc in a warm place or the open air in order to dry it thoroughly: [V] *leave the clothes to air* [Vn] *air the sheets.* (**b**) [Vn] to let air into a room, etc to make it cooler and fresher. **2** to express an idea, a complaint, etc publicly: [Vn] *air one's views/opinions/grievances.* ▶ **airing** /'eərɪŋ/ *n* [sing]: *give the bed a good airing* (ie expose it to fresh air or warmth) ○ (*fig*) *give one's views an airing* (ie express them to others).
■ **'airing cupboard** *n* (*Brit*) a warm cupboard in which sheets, towels, etc are kept.

airbase /'eəbeɪs/ *n* a place from which military aircraft operate.

airborne /'eəbɔːn/ *adj* (**a**) [attrib] transported through the air by the wind: *airborne seeds.* (**b**) [pred] (of aircraft) flying in the air after leaving the ground: *Smoking is forbidden until the plane is airborne.* (**c**) [attrib] (of soldiers) specially trained for operations using aircraft: *an airborne division.*

airbrush /'eəbrʌʃ/ *n* a device for spraying paint that works by air pressure.

Airbus /'eəbʌs/ *n* (*propr*) an aircraft operating regularly over short or medium distances.

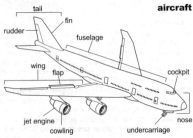

aircraft

aircraft /'eəkrɑːft/ *n* (*pl* unchanged) any machine or structure that can fly in the air and carry goods or passengers: *combat aircraft* ○ *commercial/civil aircraft.* ⇨ picture.
■ **'aircraft-carrier** *n* a ship that carries aircraft and is used as a base for them to land on and take off from.

aircraftman /'eəkrɑːftmən/ *n* (*pl* **-men** /-mən/) the lowest rank in the Royal Air Force. ⇨ App 6.

aircraftwoman /'eəkrɑːftwʊmən/ *n* (*pl* **-women** /-wɪmɪn/) the lowest rank in the Women's Royal Air Force.

aircrew /'eəkruː/ *n* [CGp] the crew of an aircraft.

airfield /'eəfiːld/ *n* an area of open level ground where aircraft can land.

airgun /'eəgʌn/ (also **'air rifle**) *n* a gun that uses air pressure to fire small metal pellets (PELLET 2).

airless /'eələs/ *adj* **1** not having enough fresh air; STUFFY(1): *an airless room.* **2** without any wind; calm and still: *It was a hot, airless evening.*

airlift /'eəlɪft/ *n* the transport of supplies, soldiers, etc by aircraft, esp in an emergency or when other routes are blocked: *an emergency airlift of food to the famine-stricken areas.*
▶ **airlift** *v* ~ **(to sth) (from sth)** to transport people, supplies, etc in this way: [Vnpr] *Civilians trapped in the city have been airlifted to safety.* [also Vn].

airline /'eəlaɪn/ *n* [CGp] a company or service providing regular flights for public use: *an airline pilot.*
▶ **airliner** *n* a large aircraft for carrying passengers.

airlock /'eəlɒk/ *n* **1** a block in the flow of liquid in a pump or pipe, caused by a bubble of air. **2** a small

---

[V.*to* inf] = verb + *to* infinitive   [Vn.inf (no *to*)] = verb + noun + infinitive without *to*   [V.*ing*] = verb + *-ing* form

room with a tightly closed door at each end, providing access to another area at a different pressure, eg on a SUBMARINE.

airmail /ˈeəmeɪl/ n [U] mail carried by air: *send a letter (by) airmail* ○ *an airmail envelope.* ▶ **airmail** v [Vn] to send sth by airmail. ■ ˈ**airmail letter** n = AIR LETTER.

airman /ˈeəmən/ n (*pl* ˈ**airmen** /-mən/) **1** (*Brit*) a member of the Royal Air Force, esp below the rank of an officer. **2** (*US*) a member of one of the four lowest ranks of the US Air Force. ⇨ App 6.

airplane /ˈeəpleɪn/ n (*US*) = AEROPLANE.

airport /ˈeəpɔːt/ n a large area where civil(2) aircraft land and take off, usu with facilities for passengers and goods, and CUSTOMS.

airship /ˈeəʃɪp/ n an aircraft like a large BALLOON(2) filled with a gas lighter than air and driven by engines.

airsick /ˈeəsɪk/ adj feeling sick as a result of travelling in an aircraft. ▶ ˈ**airsickness** n [U].

airspace /ˈeəspeɪs/ n [U] the part of the earth's atmosphere above a country that is legally controlled by that country: *a violation of British airspace by foreign aircraft* (ie by aircraft flying over Britain without permission).

airstrip /ˈeəstrɪp/ (also **landing-field, landing-strip**) n a strip of ground cleared of bushes, etc for aircraft to land on.

airtight /ˈeətaɪt/ adj not allowing air to enter or escape: *Store biscuits in an airtight container.*

airway /ˈeəweɪ/ n **1** a passage for supplying air, eg into a mine or a person's body: *prevent the tongue falling back and obstructing the airway.* **2** a route regularly used by aircraft.

airwoman /ˈeəwʊmən/ n (*pl* **-women** /-wɪmɪn/) (*Brit*) a member of the Women's Royal Air Force, esp below the rank of an officer.

airworthy /ˈeəwɜːði/ adj (of aircraft) fit to fly; in good working order. ▶ **airworthiness** n [U].

airy /ˈeəri/ adj (-ier, -iest) **1** with plenty of fresh air and space: *The office was **light and airy**.* **2** [usu attrib] (**a**) delicate and graceful: *airy church spires.* (**b**) (*usu derog*) not practical or realistic: *airy speculation* ○ *an airy promise* (ie one that is unlikely to be kept). (**c**) showing little concern; not worried: *an airy manner* ○ *an airy disregard for the law.* ▶ **airily** /ˈeərəli/ adv in a casual manner; suggesting lack of concern: *'I don't care,' he said airily.* ■ ˌ**airy-ˈfairy** adj (*Brit infml derog*) not practical or realistic; VAGUE(1): *airy-fairy notions* ○ *The scheme seems a bit airy-fairy to me.*

aisle /aɪl/ n **1** a passage between rows of seats in a church, theatre, railway carriage, etc or between rows of shelves in a shop: *The bride and groom walked slowly down the aisle* (ie after their wedding ceremony). ○ *an aisle seat* (ie one next to the passage in an aircraft, etc). ⇨ picture at CHURCH. **2** a side passage in a church that is divided by a row of pillars from the NAVE in the centre. ⇨ picture at CHURCH. **IDM rolling in the aisles** ⇨ ROLL².

aitch /eɪtʃ/ n the letter H (or h). **IDM drop one's aitches** ⇨ DROP².

ajar /əˈdʒɑː(r)/ adj [pred] (of a door) slightly open: *leave the door ajar* ○ *The door was/stood ajar.*

aka abbr also known as: *Antonio Fratelli, aka 'Big Tony'.*

akimbo /əˈkɪmbəʊ/ adv **IDM with arms akimbo** ⇨ ARM¹. ⇨ picture at ARM¹.

akin /əˈkɪn/ adj [pred] ~ (**to sth**) similar; related: *He felt **something akin** to pity.* ○ *Pity and love are closely akin.*

-al suff **1** (with *ns* forming *adjs*) of or concerning: *magical* ○ *verbal.* **2** (with *vs* forming *ns*) a process or

state of: *recital* ○ *survival.* ▶ **-ally** suff (with sense 1 forming *advs*): *magically* ○ *sensationally.*

à la /ˈɑː lɑː/ prep in the style of sb/sth: *a prime minister à la Margaret Thatcher.*

alabaster /ˈæləbɑːstə(r); *US* -bæs-/ n [U] a type of soft, usu white, stone that looks like marble. Alabaster is often carved to make ornaments. ▶ **alabaster** adj [usu attrib] (**a**) made of alabaster: *an alabaster vase.* (**b**) white or smooth like alabaster: *her alabaster complexion.*

à la carte /ˌɑː lɑː ˈkɑːt/ adv, adj (of a restaurant meal) ordered as separate items from a MENU, not as a complete meal charged at a fixed price: *We only have an à la carte menu.* Compare TABLE D'HÔTE.

alacrity /əˈlækrəti/ n [U] (*fml or rhet*) eagerness or enthusiasm; great willingness: *He accepted her offer with alacrity.*

à la mode /ˌɑː lɑː ˈməʊd/ adj, adv **1** [pred] (of clothes, ideas, etc) fashionable. **2** (following *ns*) (*US*) (of food) served with ice-cream: *apple pie à la mode.*

alarm /əˈlɑːm/ n **1** [U] fear or anxiety that is felt when danger or bad news is expected: *The news filled me with alarm.* ○ *a look of alarm* ○ *He jumped up **in alarm**.* ○ *There's no **cause for alarm**.* **2** [C usu *sing*] a sound or signal that indicates danger, a problem, etc: *give/sound the alarm* ○ ***The alarm was raised*** (eg People told the police) *when the couple failed to return to their hotel.* **3** [C] an apparatus that gives a warning of danger: *set off a burglar/smoke alarm* ○ *When he said he wanted to pay me by cheque, **alarm bells rang/started ringing*** (ie I felt suspicious). See also FALSE ALARM, FIRE-ALARM. **4** [C] = ALARM CLOCK. ▶ **alarm** v to give a warning or feeling of danger to a person or an animal; to frighten or disturb sb: [Vn] *I don't want to alarm you, but there's a strange man in your garden.* ○ *Alarmed by the noise, the birds flew away.* **alarmed** adj [pred] ~ (**at/by sth**) anxious or afraid: *By now she was thoroughly alarmed at the idea/prospect of travelling alone.* ○ *I'm somewhat alarmed (to hear) that you're planning to leave the company.* **alarming** adj causing fear; disturbing: *an alarming increase in the number of car thefts* ○ *The report is most alarming.* **alarmingly** adv: *Prices have risen alarmingly.*

alarmist n (*derog*) a person who alarms others excessively or for no good reason. — adj: *alarmist warnings/forecasts* ○ *We mustn't be alarmist.*

■ aˈ**larm clock** (also **alarm**) n a clock with a device that can be set to ring at a particular time, esp to wake sb from sleep: *set the alarm (clock) for 6 o'clock.*

alas /əˈlæs/ interj (*dated or rhet*) (expressing sorrow or regret): *Alas, we never seem to learn from our mistakes.* ○ *The same, alas, cannot be said of his son.*

albatross /ˈælbətrɒs; *US* also -trɔːs/ n **1** a large white sea bird with long wings, common in the Pacific and Southern Oceans. **2** (usu *sing*) (*infml*) a thing that continually causes difficulties or prevents one doing sth: *No one wanted to buy the house and it became a real albatross (around our necks).*

albeit /ˌɔːlˈbiːɪt/ conj (*dated or fml*) although: *I tried repeatedly, albeit unsuccessfully, to contact him.* ⇨ note at ALTHOUGH.

albino /ælˈbiːnəʊ; *US* -ˈbaɪ-/ n (*pl* **-os**) a person or animal born with no colouring in the skin and hair, which are white, or in the eyes, which are pink: *an albino rabbit.*

album /ˈælbəm/ n **1** a book in which a collection of photographs, stamps, etc can be kept. **2** a record, tape, etc with several items by the same performer: *This is one of the songs from/on her latest album.* Compare SINGLE n 2.

albumen /ˈælbjumɪn; *US* ælˈbjuːmən/ n [U] (*biology*)

the colourless inside part of an egg. ⇨ picture at
EGG. See also WHITE² 3. Compare YOLK.

alchemy /'ælkəmi/ n [U] **(a)** a medieval form of
chemistry. The chief aim of alchemy was to discover
how to change ordinary metals into gold. **(b)** any
mysterious process or change: *the alchemy of love.*
▶ **alchemist** /'ælkəmɪst/ n a person who studied or
practised alchemy.

alcohol /'ælkəhɒl; US -hɔːl/ n [U] **1(a)** a colourless
liquid, contained in drinks such as beer, wine,
spirits, etc, that can make people drunk: *low-alcohol
beer ∘ alcohol-free lager.* **(b)** this liquid used as a fuel
or to dissolve other substances. **2** drinks containing
alcohol: *prohibit the sale of alcohol ∘ alcohol abuse ∘ I
never touch* (ie drink drinks that contain) *alcohol.*
▶ **alcoholic** /ˌælkə'hɒlɪk; US -'hɔːl-/ adj **1** of or
containing alcohol: ˌalcoholic 'drinks ∘ Home-made
wine can be very alcoholic. **2** [attrib] caused by
drinking alcohol: *be in an ˌalcoholic 'stupor.* — n a
person who regularly drinks too much alcohol or
suffers from a physical disorder caused by this.
alcoholism /-ɪzəm/ n [U] a physical disorder
caused by regularly drinking too much alcohol.

alcove /'ælkəʊv/ n a small space in a room formed
by part of the wall being further back from the
centre than the rest; a RECESS(2): *The bed fits neatly
into the alcove.*

alder /'ɔːldə(r)/ n a type of tree that grows in northern regions, usu in wet ground, and that loses its
leaves in winter.

alderman /'ɔːldəmən/ n (pl **-men** /-mən/) **1** (in
Britain formerly) a member of a county or BOROUGH
(1) council, next in rank below the MAYOR. **2** (in
some US cities) a member of the city council, representing a particular part of the city.

ale /eɪl/ n **1(a)** [U,C] (used esp in trade names) a
type of beer, usu sold in bottles or cans: *brown/pale
ale.* See also REAL ALE. **(b)** [C] a glass or bottle of
this: *Two light ales, please.* **2** [U] (*dated or dialect*)
beer generally.

alec ⇨ SMART ALEC.

alehouse /'eɪlhaʊs/ n (pl **-houses** /-haʊzɪz/) (*arch
Brit*) a pub or INN.

alert /ə'lɜːt/ adj ~ (**to sth**) quick to notice things and
to think or act: *be alert to possible dangers ∘ The
alert listener will have noticed the error. ∘ Although
he's over eighty his mind is still remarkably alert.*
▶ **alert** n **1** [sing, U] a situation in which people are
watching for danger and ready to act as required: *a
state of alert ∘ The police/troops were placed/put on
(full) alert. ∘ Police warned the public to* **be on the
alert for** *suspicious packages.* **2** [C] a warning of
danger, of a problem, etc: *a bomb/fire alert.* See also
RED ALERT.
alert v **1** to warn sb that there may be danger,
trouble, etc and that they should be ready to act:
[Vn] *Why weren't the police alerted? ∘ Hospitals were
alerted and staff put on stand-by.* **2** ~ **sb to sth** to
make sb aware of sth: [Vnpr] *alert staff to the crisis
facing the company.*
alertness n [U].

A level /'eɪ levl/ (also **advanced level**) n (in Britain)
an examination or level of academic achievement
that is higher than GCSE and is often used as the
basis for admission to a university: *physics, chemistry and maths A levels ∘ When are you taking A
level/your A levels?*

alfalfa /æl'fælfə/ (also **lucerne**) n [U] a plant used
for feeding farm animals. The young plants are
sometimes also eaten by people as a vegetable. .

alfresco /æl'freskəʊ/ adj, adv in the open air: *an
alfresco lunch ∘ lunching alfresco.*

algae /'ældʒiː, 'ælgiː/ n [pl] (*sing* **alga** /'ælgə/) very
simple plants with no true stems or leaves, found
chiefly in water, including both very small floating

plants and large types of SEAWEED: *a coating of slimy
green algae ∘ blue-green algae.* ▶ **algal** /'ælgəl/ adj:
algal blooms/growth.

algebra /'ældʒɪbrə/ n [U] a branch of MATHEMATICS
in which letters and symbols are used to represent
quantities. ▶ **algebraic** /ˌældʒɪ'breɪɪk/ adj.

algorithm /'ælgərɪðəm/ n (*esp computing*) a set of
rules or procedures that must be followed in solving
a particular problem.

alias /'eɪliəs/ n a name by which a person is called at
other times or in other places; a false name: *The
swindler used a series of aliases.*
▶ **alias** adv also called, usu falsely: *Mick Clark,
alias Sid Brown, is wanted for questioning by the
police.*

alibi /'æləbaɪ/ n (pl **alibis** /'æləbaɪz/) **1** (*law*) a
formal statement or evidence that a person was in
another place at the time of a crime: *a perfect alibi ∘
The suspects all had alibis for the day of the robbery.*
2 (*infml*) an excuse of any kind: *Late again,
Richard? What's your alibi this time?*

alien /'eɪliən/ n **1** (*fml or law*) a person who is not a
citizen of the country in which he or she is living. **2**
a being from another world: *aliens from outer space.*
▶ **alien** adj **1(a)** foreign: *an alien land.* **(b)** not
familiar; strange: *an alien environment ∘ alien
concepts/customs.* **2** [pred] ~ **to sth/sb** contrary to
sth; not at all usual or acceptable to sb: *Such principles are totally alien to our religion. ∘ Cruelty was
quite alien to his nature/to him.*

alienate /'eɪliəneɪt/ v ~ **sb** (**from sb/sth**) **1** to lose
or destroy the friendship, support, sympathy, etc of
sb: [Vn] *The prime minister's policy has alienated
many of his supporters.* [also Vnpr]. **2** to cause sb to
feel different from others and not part of a group:
[Vnpr] *Many artists feel alienated from society.* [also
Vn]. ▶ **alienation** /ˌeɪliə'neɪʃn/ n [U] ~ (**from sb/
sth**): *His criminal activities led to complete alienation
from his family. ∘ Mental illness can create a sense of
alienation from the real world.*

alight¹ /ə'laɪt/ v (*fml*) **1** ~ (**from sth**) to get down
from a horse or vehicle: [Vpr] *Passengers should
never alight from a moving bus.* [also V]. **2** ~ (**on
sth**) (of a bird) to come down from the air and settle
on sth: [Vpr] *The sparrow alighted on a nearby
branch.* [also V]. PHRV **alight on sth** to find sth by
chance; to notice sth: *My eye alighted on a dusty old
book at the back of the shelf.*

alight² /ə'laɪt/ adj [pred] on fire: *A cigarette set the
dry grass alight. ∘ Her dress* **caught alight** *in the
fire. ∘* (*fig*) *Their faces were alight with joy.*

align /ə'laɪn/ v **(a)** ~ **sth** (**with sth**) to place or
arrange a thing or things in a straight line: [Vnpr]
*The columns of printed text are aligned with the edge
of each page.* [also Vn]. **(b)** to put the parts of a
machine into the correct position in relation to each
other, esp in parallel: [Vn] *align the wheels of a car.*
PHRV **align oneself with sb** to become associated
with or join sb as a partner; to come into agreement
with sb: *The Communist Party has aligned itself with
the Socialists.* Compare NON-ALIGNED.
▶ **alignment** n [U,C] **1** arrangement in a straight
line: *The sights of the gun must be in alignment with
the target. ∘ The bathroom tiles are clearly* **out of
alignment.** **2** (esp in politics) an association with
or an agreement to support sb: *the alignment of
Japan with the West.*

alike /ə'laɪk/ adj [pred] like one another; similar:
*These two photographs are almost alike. ∘ They're
twins but they don't look at all alike.*
▶ **alike** adv in the same or a similar way: *treat
everybody exactly alike ∘ Her books are enjoyed by
adults and children alike* (ie by both adults and
children).

alimentary canal /ˌælɪmentəri kə'næl/ n the passage between the mouth and the ANUS through which food passes.

alimony /ˈælɪmənɪ; *US* -məʊnɪ/ *n* [U] the money that a court may order sb to pay regularly to their former wife or husband after a legal separation or DIVORCE¹(1). See also MAINTENANCE 2.

alive /əˈlaɪv/ *adj* [pred] **1** living; not dead: *She was still alive when I reached the hospital.* ○ *Many people are still buried alive after the earthquake.* ○ *He is believed to be the oldest man alive in the country.* **2** lively; alert; excited: *He's looking more alive today.* ○ *She suddenly* **came alive** *when I asked about her children.* ○ *Her eyes were alive and full of fun.* **3 ~ to** sth aware of sth; alert to sth: *He is fully alive to the possible dangers.* **4** in existence; continuing: *Newspaper reports kept interest in the story alive.* ○ *Class prejudice in Britain is still* **alive and well.** **5 ~ with** sth full of living or moving things: *The lake was alive with fish.* **IDM a,live and ˈkicking** (*infml*) still living, in good health and active: *You'll be glad to hear that Bill is alive and kicking.* **eat sb alive** ⇨ EAT. **skin sb alive** ⇨ SKIN *v*.

alkali /ˈælkəlaɪ/ *n* (*pl* **alkalis** /-laɪz/) [C,U] (*chemistry*) any of a class of substances that react with acids to form chemical salts and have a PH of more than 7. When dissolved in water they form solutions that can burn or destroy things they touch: *Caustic soda and ammonia are alkalis.* Compare ACID¹ 1. See also BASE¹ 6.
▶ **alkaline** *adj* (**a**) having the nature of an alkali. (**b**) rich in alkali: *alkaline soil.* Compare ACID³ 3.

alkaloid /ˈælkəlɔɪd/ *n* (*botany or medical*) any of a class of poisonous substances that occur naturally in various plants. Some alkaloids are used as the basis for drugs.

all¹ /ɔːl/ *indef det* **1** (used with plural *ns*. The *n* may be preceded by *the*, *this/that*, *my*, *her*, *his*, etc or a number) the whole number of: *All horses are animals, but not all animals are horses.* ○ *Bullets seemed to be coming from all directions* (ie every direction). ○ *All the people you invited are coming.* ○ *All my plants have died.* ○ *All five men are hard workers.* **2** (used with uncountable *ns*. The *n* may be preceded by *the*, *this/that*, *my*, *her*, *his*, etc) the whole amount of: *All wood tends to shrink.* ○ *You've had all the fun and I've had all the hard work.* ○ *All this mail must be answered.* ○ *He has lost all his money.* **3** (used with singular *ns* indicating a period of time) for the whole period of: *He's worked hard all year/month/week/day* (ie throughout the year, etc). ○ *She was abroad all last summer.* ○ *We were unemployed (for) all that time.* ○ *He has lived all his life in this house.* ⇨ note. **4** the greatest possible: *with all speed/haste* ○ *in all honesty/frankness/sincerity* (ie speaking with the greatest honesty, etc). **5** consisting or appearing to consist of one thing only: *The magazine was all adverts.* ○ *She was all kindness and patience* (ie very kind and patient). **6** any whatever: *He denied all knowledge of the crime.* ○ *She's innocent beyond all doubt* (ie There can be no doubt about it). **IDM and all that** (*jazz, rubbish, etc*) (*infml*) and other similar things: *I'm bored by history — dates and battles and all that stuff.* **for all** ⇨ FOR¹. **not all that good, well, etc** not particularly good, well, etc: *He doesn't sing all that well.* ○ *Her writing isn't all that accurate.* **not as bad(ly), etc as all ˈthat** not to the extent implied: *They're not as rich as all that.* **of ˈall people, things, etc** (*infml*) (used to express surprise because sb/sth seems the least likely person, example, etc): *I didn't think you, of all people, would become a vegetarian.* **of ¡all the ˈcheek, ˈnerve, etc** (*infml*) (used to express anger or annoyance at sth): *I've locked myself out! Of all the stupid things to do!*
■ **ˈall-night** *adj* [attrib] lasting, functioning, etc throughout the night: *an ¡all-night ˈparty/ˈcafé/ˈvigil.*

ˈall-time *adj* [attrib] of all recorded time: *one of the all-time great tennis players* ○ *an all-time record* (ie one that has never been beaten) ○ *Profits are at an all-time low* (ie lower than they have ever been).

NOTE **All** and **half** can be used with countable and uncountable nouns: *The children ate all/half the biscuits and drank all/half the milk.* **Both** can only be used with nouns in the plural, when there are two of something: *Both his parents are teachers.*
All and **both** can be followed by a determiner, eg *the, this, my*: *We've been here all (the) week.* **Half** must be followed by a determiner: *Half this money is yours.*
All and **both** can come after a noun or pronoun: *The audience all applauded.* ○ *We all/both arrived late.*
All, both and **half** can be used with *of* followed by a noun. When they are followed by a pronoun, *of* must be used: *Both (of) her sisters are lawyers.* ○ *All/Both/Half of us wanted to leave early.*

all² /ɔːl/ *indef pron* **1** the whole number or amount (**a**) **~ (of it/them/us/you)** (referring back to sth mentioned previously): *We had several bottles of beer left — all (of them) have disappeared.* ○ *I invited my five sisters but not all (of them) can come.* ○ *Some of the food has been eaten, but not all (of it).* ○ *The last film he made was the best of all (of them).* (**b**) **~ of** sb/sth (referring forward to sth): *All of the mourners were dressed in black/They were all dressed in black.* ○ *All of the toys were broken/They were all broken.* ○ *Take all of the wine/Take it all.* ○ *All of this is yours/This is all yours.* **2** (followed by a relative clause, often without *that*) the only thing; everything: *All I want is peace and quiet.* ○ *He took all there was/all that I had.* **IDM all in ˈall** when everything is considered: *All in all it had been a great success.* **all in ˈone** having two or more uses, functions, etc: *It's a corkscrew and bottle-opener all in one.* **all or ˈnothing** (of a course of action) requiring all one's efforts: *It's all or nothing — if we don't score now we've lost the match.* **and ˈall 1** also; included; in addition: *She jumped into the river, clothes and all* (ie with her clothes on). **2** (*infml*) (used in spoken English) as well; too: *'I'm freezing.' 'Yeah, me and all.'* **(not) at all** in any way; to any extent: *I didn't enjoy it at all.* ○ *There was nothing at all to eat.* ○ *Are you at all worried about the forecast?* **in all** as a total; ALTOGETHER(2): *There were twelve of us in all for dinner.* ○ *That's £25.40 in all.* **¡not at ˈall** (used as a polite reply to an expression of thanks): *'Thanks very much for your help.' 'Not at all, it was a pleasure.'* **one's ˈall** everything one has; one's life: *They gave their all* (ie fought and died) *in the war.*

all³ /ɔːl/ *indef adv* **1** completely: *She was dressed all in white* (ie All the clothes she was wearing were white). ○ *She lives all alone/all by herself.* ○ *The coffee went all over my skirt.* ○ *The party continued all through the night.* **2** (*infml*) very: *She was all excited.* ○ *Now don't get all upset about it.* **3** (used with *too* and *adjs* or *advs*) more than is desirable: *The end of the trip came all too soon.* **4** (in sports and games) to each side: *The score was four all.* **IDM all aˈlong** all the time; from the beginning: *I realized I'd had it in my pocket all along.* **all around** ⇨ ALL ROUND. **all the better, harder, etc** so much better, harder, etc: *We'll have to work all the harder with two members of staff away ill.* **all but 1** almost: *The party was all but over when we arrived.* ○ *It was all but impossible to climb back into the boat.* **2** everything or everybody except sth/sb: *All but one of the plates were damaged.* **all ˈin 1** physically tired; exhausted (EXHAUST²): *At the end of the race he felt all in.* **2** including everything: *The holiday cost £250 all in — that covers travel, accommodation and food.* See also ALL-IN. **all of sth** (*sometimes ironic*) (of size, height, distance, etc) probably more than; fully: *It was all of*

A

two miles to the beach. ○ *That pencil you broke cost me all of 20p.* **all 'one** forming a complete unit: *We don't have a separate dining-room — the living area is all one.* **all 'over 1** everywhere: *We looked all over for the ring.* ○ *I was aching all over after the match.* **2** what one would expect of the person mentioned: *That sounds like my sister all over.* **all 'right** (*infml* or *non-standard* **al'right**) **1** as desired; satisfactory; in a satisfactory manner: *Is the coffee all right?* ○ *Are you getting along all right in your new job?* ○ *Don't worry, it'll be **all right on the night** (ie the performance, event, etc will be satisfactory when the time comes).* **2** safe and well: *I hope the children are all right.* ○ *Do you feel all right?* **3** only just good enough: *Your work is all right but I'm sure you could do better.* **4** (expressing agreement to do what sb has asked): *'Will you post this for me?' 'Yes, all right.'* **5** (*infml*) (emphasizing that one is sure of sth): *That's the man I saw in the car all right.* **all 'round** (*Brit*) (*US* **all a'round**) **1** in every way; in all respects: *a good performance all round.* **2** for each person: *buy drinks all round.* **,all 'there** (*infml*) having a healthy mind; mentally alert: *He behaves very oddly at times — I don't think he's quite all there.* **be all about sb/ sth** to have sb/sth as its subject or main point of interest: *This book is all about ancient Greece.* ○ (*infml*) *Now then, what's this all about?* (ie What is the problem?) **be all for sth / doing sth** to believe strongly that sth is desirable: *She's all for more nursery schools being built.* **be all over ...** to become known by everyone in a place: *News of the holiday was all over the school within minutes.* **be all 'over sb** (*infml*) to show excessive affection for or enthusiasm about sb when in their company: *You can see he's infatuated by her — he was all over her at the party.* **be all up (with sb)** (*infml*) to be the end for sb: *It looks as though it's all up with us now* (ie we are ruined, have no further chances, etc).

■ **all-around** *adj* = ALL-ROUND.

,all-'clear *n* the all-clear (usu *sing*) **1** the signal that danger is over. **2** (*infml*) the permission to do sth: *Have you got the all-clear from Mum to be off school?*

,all-em'bracing *adj* including everything: *an all-embracing theory.*

,all-'in *adj* [attrib] (*Brit*) (of a price) including everything: *an ,all-in 'price.* **,all-in 'wrestling** *n* [U] a type of wrestling (WRESTLE) in which there are few or no restrictions on how one may fight.

,all 'out *adv, adj* [attrib] using all possible strength and resources: *The team is going all out to win the championship.* ○ *make an all-out attempt to meet a deadline.*

,all-'purpose *adj* having many different uses: *an ,all-purpose 'workroom/'vehicle.*

,all-'round *adj* (*Brit*) (*US* **,all-a'round**) [attrib] **1** not specialized; general: *a good ,all-round edu'cation.* **2** (of a person) with a wide range of abilities: *an ,all-round 'sportsman.* **all-'rounder** *n* a person with a wide range of abilities.

'all-star *adj* [attrib] including many famous actors, performers, etc: *an all-star cast.*

all- *pref* (forming compound *adjs* and *advs*) **1** entirely: *an all-electric kitchen* ○ *an all-American show* ○ *an all-inclusive price.* **2** in the highest degree: *all-important* ○ *all-powerful* ○ *all-merciful.*

Allah /'ælə/ *n* the name of God among Muslims and among Arabs of all faiths.

allay /ə'leɪ/ *v* (*fml*) to make sth less; to relieve sth: [Vn] *allay trouble/fears/suffering/doubt/suspicion.*

allegation /,ælə'geɪʃn/ *n* **1** [U] the action of stating sth as a fact without offering proof. **2** [C] a statement made without proof: *These are serious allegations.*

allege /ə'ledʒ/ *v* (*fml*) (often passive) to state sth as a fact but without proof; to give as an argument or excuse: [V.*that*] *The prisoner alleges (that) he was at*

home on the night of the crime. ○ *It is alleged that a number of unauthorized payments were made.* [V.n *to* inf] *We were alleged to have brought goods into the country illegally.* [also Vn]. See also ALLEGATION.

▶ **alleged** *adj* [attrib] stated without being proved: *an alleged criminal* (ie a person said to be a criminal) ○ *alleged tax evasion.* **allegedly** /ə'ledʒɪdli/ *adv*: *The novel was allegedly written by a computer.*

allegiance /ə'liːdʒəns/ *n* [U, C] (*fml*) ~ (**to sb/sth**) support of or loyalty to a government, ruler, cause (3), etc: *swear (an oath of) allegiance to the flag* ○ *political/national/tribal allegiances.*

allegory /'æləgəri; *US* -gɔːr-/ *n* [C, U] a story, play, picture, etc in which the characters and events are meant as symbols, representing eg patience, truth or envy; the use of such symbols: *a political allegory* ○ *His writings are full of allegory.* ▶ **allegorical** /,ælə'gɒrɪkl; *US* ,ælə'gɔːrəkl/ *adj*: *an allegorical figure* ○ *allegorical poetry.* **allegorically** *adv*.

allegro /ə'legrəʊ, -'leɪ-/ *adj, adv* (*music*) in quick time; fast and lively.

▶ **allegro** *n* (*pl* **-os**) a piece of music to be played allegro.

alleluia /,ælɪ'luːjə/ (also **hallelujah**) *n, interj* a song or shout expressing praise to God.

allergy /'ælədʒi/ *n* ~ (**to sth**) a medical condition that causes certain people to react badly or feel ill when they eat or come into contact with particular substances: *Hay fever is caused by an allergy to pollen.* ○ *I have an allergy to certain milk products.*

▶ **allergic** /ə'lɜːdʒɪk/ *adj* **1** [pred] ~ (**to sth**) having an allergy: *I like cats but unfortunately I'm allergic to them.* **2** caused by an allergy: *an allergic rash/reaction.* **3** [pred] ~ **to sth** (*infml joc*) having a strong dislike of sth: *He's allergic to hard work!*

alleviate /ə'liːvieɪt/ *v* to make sth less severe; to ease sth: [Vn] *The doctor gave her an injection to alleviate the pain.* ○ *They tried to alleviate the boredom of waiting by singing songs.* ▶ **alleviation** /ə,liːvi'eɪʃn/ *n* [U].

alley /'æli/ *n* **1** (also **'alley-way**) a narrow passage for people to walk between or behind buildings: *a back alley.* **2** a path with a border of trees or hedges in a garden or park. ⇨ note at ROAD. **3** a long narrow area in which games like BOWLING(1) and skittles (SKITTLE 2) are played, or the building they are played in. **4** (*US*) = TRAMLINES 2. See also BLIND ALLEY.

all-fired /'ɔːl faɪəd/ *adj* (*US infml*) extreme: *He had the all-fired nerve to complain!*

alliance /ə'laɪəns/ *n* **1** [U] the action or state of being joined or associated: *States seek to become stronger through alliance.* ○ *We are working in alliance with our European partners.* **2** [C] a union or an association formed for mutual benefit, esp between countries or organizations: *enter into/break off an alliance with a neighbouring state* ○ *the Nato alliance.*

allied ⇨ ALLY.

alligator /'ælɪgeɪtə(r)/ *n* (**a**) [C] a reptile of the CROCODILE family found esp in the rivers and lakes of tropical America and China. (**b**) [U] its skin made into leather: *an alligator handbag.*

alliteration /ə,lɪtə'reɪʃn/ *n* [U] the same letter or sound occurring at the beginning of two or more words in succession, as in *sing a song of sixpence* or *as thick as thieves.* ▶ **alliterative** /ə'lɪtərətɪv; *US* ə'lɪtəreɪtɪv/ *adj*.

allocate /'æləkeɪt/ *v* ~ **sth** (**to sb/sth**) to distribute sth officially to sb/sth for a special purpose: [V] *allocate funds for repair work* [Vnn, Vnpr] *We allocated each of us our tasks/allocated tasks to each of us.*

▶ **allocation** /,ælə'keɪʃn/ *n* **1** [U] the action of allocating sth: *housing allocation.* **2** [C] an amount of money, space, etc allocated: *We've spent our entire allocation for the year.*

allot /ə'lɒt/ v (-tt-) ~ sth (to sb/sth) to give time, money, duties, etc as a share of what is available: [Vn] *How much cash has been allotted?* [Vn, Vnn] *We did the work within the allotted time/within the time they'd allotted us.* [Vnpr] *Who will she allot the easy jobs to?*
▶ **allotment** n **1** [C] (*esp Brit*) a small area of public land rented for growing vegetables or flowers: *tend one's allotment.* **2** [C] an amount or portion allotted. **3** [U] the action of allotting sth.

allow /ə'laʊ/ v **1(a)** to permit sb/sth to do sth: [V.n to inf] *My boss doesn't allow me to use the telephone for private calls.* ○ *Passengers are not allowed to smoke.* ○ *Allow the water to come to boil.* ○ *I didn't really want to go but I allowed myself to be persuaded.* ⇨ note at MAY¹. (*fig*) *She allowed her mind to wander.* (**b**) to let sth be done or happen: [Vn] *Photography is not allowed in the theatre.* ○ *We don't allow smoking in our house.* ○ *The invention of printing allowed a huge increase in literacy.* (**c**) (usu negative and passive) to permit sb/sth to go in: [Vn] *Dogs not allowed/No dogs allowed* (ie It is not permitted to bring dogs into this park, building, etc). ⇨ note. **2** to let sb have sth: [Vnn] *How much holiday are you allowed?* ○ *I'm not allowed visitors.* ○ *I allow myself one glass of wine a day.* ○ (*fig*) *He allowed his imagination free rein* (ie did not try to control it). **3** ~ sth (for sb/sth) to provide sth or set sth aside for a purpose or in estimating sth: [Vn] *allow four sandwiches each/per head* ○ *I would allow half an hour to get to the station.* [Vnpr] *You must allow three metres for a long-sleeved dress.* **4(a)** to agree that sth is true or correct: [Vn] *The judge allowed my claim.* [V.that] *He allowed that I had the right to appeal.* [also V.speech]. Compare DISALLOW. (**b**) (*fml*) to accept sth; to admit or CONCEDE(1) sth: [V.that] *Even if we allow that the poet was mad ...* [Vnn] *He was very helpful when his mother was ill — I'll allow you that.* **IDM** **allow ¹me** (used in spoken English to offer help politely): *Those bags look heavy — allow me!* **PHRV** **al¹low for sb/sth** to include sb/sth when calculating sth: *It will take you half an hour to get to the station, allowing for traffic delays.* **al₁low sb ¹in, ¹out, ¹up, etc** to permit sb to enter, leave, get up, etc: *She won't allow the children in(to the house) until they've wiped their feet.* ○ *The patient was allowed up* (ie permitted to get out of bed) *after 10 days.* **al¹low of sth** (*fml*) to permit sth; to leave room for sth: *The facts allow of only one explanation.*
▶ **allowable** adj that is or can be allowed by law, the rules, etc: *allowable expenses.*

NOTE Compare **allow**, **permit** and **let**. **Let** is the most common of these verbs, and is often used in the imperative: *Let Grandma sit there.* ○ *Don't let me forget there's a cake in the oven, will you?* ○ *Let me make a note of the phone number.* It is also used to say that a person or thing allows you to do something: *Dad doesn't let me watch that programme.* ○ *The cash machine wouldn't let me get any money out.* **Allow** is frequently used in the passive form **be allowed**: *I'm not allowed to eat any milk products.* ○ *She was allowed home from hospital after being treated for shock.* It can have a thing as a subject as well as a person: *Smoke detectors allow a fire to be dealt with quickly.* **Permit** is used in formal, technical or official written language: *Smoking is not permitted in the coach.* ○ *The mercury content of the fish was above the maximum permitted level.* ○ *You shall not permit the use of the vehicle by any other person.*

allowance /ə'laʊəns/ n [C, U] **1** an amount of sth, esp money, allowed or given regularly: *an allowance of $15 per day* ○ *be paid a clothing/subsistence/travel allowance* (ie money to be spent on clothes, etc) ○ *I didn't receive any allowance from my father.* ○ *bag-*

gage allowance (ie the amount of LUGGAGE a passenger can take free, esp on an aircraft). See also ATTENDANCE ALLOWANCE, MOBILITY ALLOWANCE. **2** an amount of money that can be earned or received free of tax. **IDM** **make allowance(s) for sth** to consider sth when making a decision, etc. **make allowances for sb** to regard sb as deserving to be treated more favourably than others for some reason: *You must make allowances for him because he has been ill.*

NOTE An **allowance** is an amount of money somebody is given regularly for a specific purpose: *a childcare allowance.* **Permission** to do something is given to somebody by a person or an authority: *Did your parents give you permission to use the car?* A **permit** is a document which states that you are allowed to do something, often for a specific period of time: *a three-month work permit* ○ *a permit for fishing.* A **licence** (**license** in American English) is an official document that allows you to use or own something: *Can I see your driving-licence, please?* ○ *He did not have a license for the gun.* A **visa** is an official document that allows you to visit another country: *Do you need a visa to go to Japan?*

alloy¹ /'ælɔɪ/ n [C, U] a metal formed of a mixture of metals or of metal and another substance: *Brass is an alloy of copper and zinc.* ○ *alloy steel.*

alloy² /ə'lɔɪ/ v [Vn, Vnpr] ~ sth (with sth) to mix sth with metal(s) of lower value.

allspice /'ɔ:lspaɪs/ (also **pimento**) n [U] a spice made from the dried berries of a West Indian tree.

allude /ə'lu:d/ v ~ to sb/sth (*fml*) to mention sb/sth briefly or indirectly: [Vpr] *You alluded in your speech to certain developments — what exactly did you mean?* See also ALLUSION.

allure /ə'lʊə(r)/ n [C, U] the quality of being attractive or charming: *sexual allure* ○ *the false allure of big-city life.*
▶ **alluring** adj attractive; charming: *an alluring smile/prospect/person.*

allusion /ə'lu:ʒn/ n ~ (to sb/sth) a brief or indirect reference: *Her writing is full of obscure literary allusions.* ○ *He resents any allusion to his baldness.*
▶ **allusive** adj /ə'lu:sɪv/ containing allusions: *Her allusive style is difficult to follow.*

alluvial /ə'lu:viəl/ adj (usu attrib) made of sand, earth, etc left by rivers or floods: *alluvial deposits/soil/plains.*

ally /ə'laɪ/ v (pt, pp allied) ~ (sb/oneself) with/to sb/sth to join or become joined with sb/sth for mutual benefit: [Vnpr] *Poland has allied itself with western European countries for trade and defence.* [also Vpr].
▶ **allied** /ə'laɪd, 'ælaɪd/ adj ~ (to sth) connected; similar: *a union of 'allied trades* ○ *The increase in violent crimes is al'lied to the rise in unemployment.*
ally /'ælaɪ/ n **1** [C] a person, country, etc joined with another in order to give help and support: *a close ally and friend of the prime minister* ○ *our European/NATO allies.* **2** (usu **the Allies** [pl]) a group of countries fighting on the same side in a war, esp those which fought with Britain in World Wars I and II. **Allied** adj: *Allied troops/prisoners.*

Alma Mater /₁ælmə 'mɑ:tə(r), 'meɪtə(r)/ n (*fml or joc*) the university, school or college that sb attended: *my/her/their Alma Mater.*

almanac (also **almanack**) /'ɔ:lmənæk, 'æl-/ n **1** a book published every year giving information on various subjects, eg sport, the theatre, etc. **2** a book that gives information about the sun, moon, tides, anniversaries, etc for the coming year.

almighty /ɔ:l'maɪti/ adj **1** having complete power: *God Almighty/Almighty God.* **2** [attrib] (*infml*) very

A

great: *an almighty crash/nuisance/row*. **3** (△) (used in the following expressions to show surprise, anger, etc): *Christ/God almighty! What was that noise?*
▶ **the Almighty** *n* [sing] God.

almond /ˈɑːmənd/ *n* (**a**) a type of tree related to the PLUM(1a) and PEACH: *almond blossom*. (**b**) the edible nut inside the fruit of this tree: *almond essence/oil/paste*. ⇨ picture at NUT.

almoner /ˈɑːmənə(r), ˈælm-/ *n* (*dated Brit*) a social worker attached to a hospital, now usu called a *medical social worker*.

almost /ˈɔːlməʊst/ *adv* nearly; not quite (**a**) (used before *advs, ns, adjs, vs, preps, dets* and *prons*): *It's a mistake they almost always make*. ○ *The story is almost certainly false*. ○ *It's almost time to go*. ○ *Dinner's almost ready*. ○ *He slipped and almost fell*. ○ *Their house is almost opposite ours*. ○ *He's almost six feet tall*. ○ *Almost anything will do*. (**b**) (used before *no, nobody, none, nothing, never*): *Almost no one* (ie Hardly anyone) *believed him*. ○ *The speaker said almost nothing* (ie hardly anything) *worth listening to*.

NOTE **Almost**, **nearly**, **scarcely** and **hardly** are adverbs and can be used with verbs, adverbs, adjectives and nouns.
Almost and **nearly** are usually used in positive sentences: *She fell and almost/nearly broke her neck*. ○ *He nearly/almost always arrives late*. **Almost** can be used with negative words. In these cases it can be replaced with **hardly** or **scarcely**: *She ate almost nothing/She ate hardly anything*. ○ *There's almost no space to sit down/There's hardly any space to sit down*.
Hardly is generally preferred to **almost** plus a negative verb: *She sang so quietly that I could hardly hear her* (NOT *I almost couldn't hear her*). In sentences in which one thing happens immediately after another, **hardly** and **scarcely** can be placed at the beginning of the sentence and then the subject and verb are turned around: *Hardly/Scarcely had we arrived, when it began to rain*.

alms /ɑːmz/ *n* [pl] (*dated*) money, clothes, food, etc given to poor people.

almshouse /ˈɑːmzhaʊs/ *n* (*pl* -hɑʊzɪz/) (esp formerly in Britain) a house founded and run by a charity, where poor, usu old, people may live without paying rent.

aloft /əˈlɒft; *US* əˈlɔːft/ *adv* up in the air; upwards: *flags flying aloft* ○ *He held his arms aloft*. ○ *She was borne aloft on the shoulders of her supporters*.

alone /əˈləʊn/ *adj* [pred], *adv* **1**(**a**) without any companions: *I don't like going out alone after dark*. ○ *She lives all alone in that large house*. ○ *Finally the two of us were alone together*. ○ *He is not alone in believing* (ie Others agree with him) *that such a policy is misguided*. ○ (*fig*) *She stands alone* (ie is UNIQUE(1a)) *among modern sculptors*. (**b**) without the help of other people or things: *It will be difficult for one person alone*. ○ *She raised her family quite alone*. ○ *I prefer to work on it alone*. (**c**) lonely and unhappy: *It was my first experience of living away from home and I felt terribly alone*. Compare LONE, LONELY 1. ⇨ note. **2** (following a *n* or *pron*) only: *The shoes alone cost £100*. ○ (*saying*) *Time alone will tell*. ○ *He will be remembered for that one book alone*. ○ *You alone can help me*. **IDM** **go it aˈlone** (to try) to carry out a task or start a difficult project without help from anyone: *He decided to go it alone and start his own business*. **let aˈlone** without considering: *There isn't enough room for* ¹*us*, *let alone a dog and two cats*. ○ *I haven't decided on the* ¹*menu yet, let alone bought the food*. **leave/let sb/sth aˈlone** not to take, touch or interfere with sb/sth; not to try to influence or change sb/sth: *She's asked to be left alone but the press keep pestering her*. ○ *I've told you*

before — leave my things alone! **leave/let well alone** ⇨ WELL¹.

NOTE Compare **alone**, **solitary** and **lonely**. **Alone** and **solitary** describe a person or thing that is separate from others. These words do not necessarily suggest that somebody is unhappy: *I like being alone in the house*. **Alone** cannot be used before a noun, but **solitary** can: *She goes for long, solitary walks*. **On my/our**, etc **own** or **by myself/ourselves**, etc are often used instead of **alone**, especially in speaking: *I'm going on holiday on my own this year*.
Lonely and, in American English, **lonesome** mean that somebody is alone when they do not want to be, and is unhappy: *Sam was very lonely when he first moved to New York*. ○ *She led a solitary life but was seldom lonely*. **Lonely** and **solitary** can also describe places that are isolated or rarely visited: *a lonely/solitary house on the hill*.

along /əˈlɒŋ; *US* əˈlɔːŋ/ *prep* **1** from one end to or towards the other end of sth: *walk along the street* ○ *go along the corridor* ○ *I looked along the shelves for the book I wanted*. **2** close to or parallel with the length of sth: *Flowers grow along the side of the wall*. ○ *You can picnic along the river-bank*.
▶ **along** *adv part* For the special uses of **along** in phrasal verbs, look at the verb entries. For example, the meaning of **get along with sb** is given in the phrasal verb section of the entry for **get**. **1** forward; ONWARD: *The policeman told the crowds to move along*. ○ *Come along or we'll be late*. **2** (*infml*) at sb's company; with sb: *Come to the party and bring some friends along*. ○ *He forgot to take his tools along (with him) to work*. ○ *I'll be along* (ie I will come and join you) *in a few minutes*. **3** towards a better or more advanced position: *The new equipment helped us along enormously*. ○ *The book's coming along nicely*. **IDM** **along with sb/sth** in addition to sb/sth; in the same way as sb/sth: *Tobacco is taxed in most countries, along with alcohol*.

alongside /əˌlɒŋˈsaɪd; *US* -ˌlɔːŋ-/ *adv* close to the side of a ship, PIER, etc: *a boat moored alongside*.
▶ **alongside** *prep* **1** beside sb/sth: *The car drew up alongside the kerb*. **2** together with sb/sth: *Traditional religious beliefs still flourish alongside a modern urban lifestyle*. ○ *The movie starred Nick Nolte alongside Barbra Streisand*.

aloof /əˈluːf/ *adj* [usu pred] ~ (**from sb/sth**) not friendly or interested in other people; distant(3a): *Throughout the conversation he remained silent and aloof*. **IDM** **keep (oneself)/hold (oneself)/stand aloof from sb/sth** to take no part in sth; to show no friendship towards sb: *She kept herself aloof from her fellow students*. ○ *The first generation of immigrants held themselves aloof from British politics*. ▶ **aloofness** *n* [U].

aloud /əˈlaʊd/ *adv* **1** in a voice loud enough to be heard by other people, not in silence or in a WHISPER (1): *children reading aloud* (ie not silently in their heads) ○ *He read his sister's letter aloud*. Compare OUT LOUD (LOUD). **2** loudly enough to be heard at a distance: *laughing aloud* ○ *She called for help*. **IDM** **think aloud** ⇨ THINK¹.

alpaca /ælˈpækə/ *n* (**a**) [C] a South American animal related to the LLAMA. (**b**) [U] the wool of the alpaca, used for making clothes: *an alpaca coat*.

alpha /ˈælfə/ *n* the first letter of the Greek alphabet (A, α), sometimes used as an academic mark indicating the highest standard of work. Compare BETA.
■ ¹**alpha particle** *n* any of the particles (PARTICLE 2) with a positive charge¹(7) produced in a nuclear reaction.

alphabet /ˈælfəbet/ *n* a set of letters or symbols in a fixed order, used when writing a language: *There* are 26 letters in the English alphabet, which begins A, B, C, D, etc.

▶ **alphabetical** /ˌælfəˈbetɪkl/ adj in the order in which letters have their position in the alphabet: *a dictionary listing words in alphabetical order.* **alphabetically** /-kli/ adv: *books arranged alphabetically by author.*

alpine /ˈælpaɪn/ adj of or found in high mountains, esp those in central Europe: *an alpine village* ○ *alpine flowers/sports.*

▶ **alpine** n a plant that grows best in mountain regions.

already /ɔːlˈredi/ adv **1** (used esp with perfect tenses of a v) before now or before a particular time in the past: *I've already seen that film, so I'd rather go and see another one.* ○ *The teacher was already in the room when I arrived.* ○ *She had already left when I phoned.* ○ *There are far too many people here already.* **2** (used in negative sentences or questions, to show surprise) as soon or as early as this: *Have your children started school already?* ○ *Is it 10 o'clock already?* ○ *You're not leaving already, are you?*

NOTE Already and yet are both used to say whether an action has finished or not, or by or before a particular time. They are mostly used with the perfect tenses in British English: *I've already had lunch.* In American English they are also often used with the simple past: *Did you have lunch yet?*

Yet is only used in negative statements and in questions: *I'm not ready yet.* ○ *Are you out of bed yet?*

Already emphasizes that an action is finished. It is usually used in positive statements: *By midday they had already travelled 200 miles.*

Already can be used in questions to express surprise: *Have you finished lunch already? It's only 12 o'clock!*

alright /ɔːlˈraɪt/ adv (*non-standard or infml*) = ALL RIGHT.

Alsatian /ælˈseɪʃn/ n (*US* **German shepherd**) a large dog with smooth hair, often trained to help the police or as a guard dog. ⇨ picture at DOG[1].

also /ˈɔːlsəʊ/ adv **1** (not used with negative vs) in addition; too: *She speaks French and German and also a little Russian.* ○ *He is young and good-looking, and also very rich.* ○ *I teach five days a week and I also teach evening classes.* ○ *She not only plays well, but also writes music.* ○ *It's my favourite restaurant and hers also/also hers.* **2** (*infml*) (used at the beginning of a clause to add a further point or comment): *Sorry I'm late. My alarm didn't go off. Also, I had trouble starting the car.*

■ **'also-ran** n **1** a horse or dog that does not finish first, second or third in a race. **2** a person who is not successful: *I'm afraid John is one of life's also-rans.*

NOTE Compare also, too and as well. Also is the most formal word and usually comes before the main verb (but after 'be' if this is the main verb): *I've met Jane and I've also met her parents.* ○ *She was very rich but she was also very mean.* Too and as well are used more in speaking, and usually come at the end of a clause: *I've read the book and I've seen the film as well/too.* In negative sentences, not...either is used to make the extra point: *They haven't phoned and they haven't written either.*

altar /ˈɔːltə(r)/ n **1** (in Christian churches) a table on which bread and wine are blessed for COMMUNION(1): *an altar cloth.* ⇨ picture at CHURCH. **2** (in some religions) a table on which gifts or sacrifices are offered to a god. **IDM** **at/on the altar of sth** in the cause of sth; for sth considered to be of greater importance: *Moral considerations were sacrificed on the altar of profit.* **lead sb to the altar** ⇨ LEAD[1].

alter /ˈɔːltə(r)/ v to become or make sb/sth different;

to change in character, position, size, etc: [V] *I didn't recognize him because he had altered so much.* [Vn] *She had to alter her clothes after losing weight.* ○ *The plane altered course.* ○ *That alters things* (ie makes the situation different). ⇨ note at CHANGE[1].

▶ **alteration** /ˌɔːltəˈreɪʃn/ n **1** [U] the action or process of changing sth or of making a change: *How much alteration will be necessary?* **2** [C] an act or result of changing sth: *a drastic/radical/substantial alteration of the law* ○ *an alteration in the way local government is financed* ○ *We are making a few alterations to the house.*

altercation /ˌɔːltəˈkeɪʃn/ n [C, U] (*fml*) a noisy argument or disagreement: *Just before half-time there was a brief altercation with the referee.* ⇨ note at ARGUMENT.

alter ego /ˌæltər ˈiːgəʊ, ˌɔːl-/ n (*pl* **alter egos**) (*Latin*) a close friend who is very like oneself: *He's my alter ego — we go everywhere together.*

alternate[1] /ɔːlˈtɜːnət; *US* ˈɔːltərnət/ adj [usu attrib] **1** (of two things) happening or following one after the other: *a dessert made of alternate layers of cream and fruit* ○ *alternate triumph and despair.* **2** one of every two; every second one: *on alternate days* (eg on Monday, Wednesday, Friday, etc and not on the days in between) ○ *I visit them on alternate Sundays* (ie every second Sunday). **3** (*esp US*) that can be used instead of sth else; other; different: *an alternate ending/lifestyle.* ▶ **alternately** adv.

alternate[2] /ˈɔːltəneɪt/ v **~ A and B/~ A with B** to cause things or people to follow one after the other in a regular pattern: [Vn] *Most farmers alternate their crops.* [Vnpr] *He alternated blue beads with white.* **2 ~ (with sth); ~ between A and B** to occur in turn; to consist of two different things in turn: [V] *alternating dry and rainy days* [Vpr] *Rainy days alternated with dry ones.* ○ *The weather alternated between rain and sunshine.* ○ *Their work alternates between London and New York* (ie is first in London, then in New York, then back in London, etc).

▶ **alternation** /ˌɔːltəˈneɪʃn/ n [U, C]: *the alternation of day and night.*

alternator /ˈɔːltəneɪtə(r)/ n a device, used esp in a car, that produces an alternating current.

■ **alternating 'current** n [U, C] (*abbr* **AC**) an electric current that changes direction at regular intervals many times a second. Compare DIRECT CURRENT.

alternate[3] /*US* ˈɔːltərnət/ n (*US*) a person who is given work, authority, etc during sb's absence: *Your alternate will have to go to that meeting.*

alternative /ɔːlˈtɜːnətɪv/ adj [attrib] **1** that can be used instead of sth else; other; different: *find alternative means of transport* ○ *Have you got an alternative suggestion?* **2** not traditional; not following or accepting the usual opinions, methods, styles, etc: *alternative comedy.*

▶ **alternative** n one of two or more possibilities: *One of the alternatives open to you is to resign.* ○ *Caught in the act, he had no alternative but to confess.*

alternatively adv as an alternative: *We could take the train or alternatively go by car.*

■ **al,ternative 'energy** n [U] energy obtained from the power of the sun, wind, water, etc, that does not involve destroying the earth's natural resources. **al,ternative 'medicine** (also **complementary medicine**) n [U] any type of treatment that promotes health without using artificial drugs.

although (also *US infml* **altho**) /ɔːlˈðəʊ/ conj **1** in spite of the fact that; even if: *Although he had only entered the contest for fun, he won first prize.* **2** however; nevertheless; but: *He said they were married, although I'm sure they aren't.* Compare THOUGH.

A

NOTE Compare **although**, **though** and **however**. You use these words to show contrast between two clauses or two sentences. You can use **although** and **(even) though** at the beginning of a sentence or a clause that has a verb: *Although/Though/Even though everyone played well, we lost the game.* ○ *We lost the game although/though/even though everyone played well.*
However can mean the same as although, but is more formal. It is separated by a comma and usually begins or ends a sentence: *Everyone played well. However, we still lost the game./We still lost the game, however.*
Though is used more in speaking and often comes at the end of a sentence, but **although** cannot come at the end of a sentence: *We still lost the game, though.*
Although, **though** (or, in formal contexts, **albeit**) can come before an adjective, adverb or adverbial phrase: *His first acting role, (al)though/albeit small, was a great success.*

altimeter /'æltmiːtə(r); *US* æl'tɪmətər/ *n* an instrument used esp in an aircraft for showing height above sea level.

altitude /'æltɪtjuːd; *US* -tuːd/ *n* **1** [C usu *sing*] the height above sea level: *What is the altitude of this town?* ○ *We are flying at an altitude of 20 000 feet.* **2** [U, C often *pl*] a high place or area: *flying/training at altitude* ○ *There is snow at high altitudes.*

alto /'æltəʊ/ *n* (*pl* **-os**) (*music*) **1(a)** a man's singing voice with a very high range, above TENOR²(b). **(b)** a man with such a voice. **(c)** a musical part written for a singer with an alto voice. Compare COUNTER-TENOR. **2** = CONTRALTO.
▶ **alto** *adj* [attrib] (of a musical instrument) with the second highest pitch¹(2) in its group: *an alto saxophone.*

altogether /ˌɔːltə'geðə(r)/ *adv* **1** entirely; completely; in every way: *The train went slower and slower until it stopped altogether.* ○ *I don't altogether agree with you.* ○ *I am not altogether happy about the decision.* ○ *Their circumstances are altogether different from ours.* **2** including everything: *You owe me £68 altogether.* **3** (used to introduce a summary) considering everything: *The weather was bad and the food dreadful. Altogether the holiday was very disappointing.*
▶ **altogether** *n* **IDM** **in the alto'gether** (*infml*) without any clothes on.

altruism /'æltruːɪzəm/ *n* [U] concern for the needs and feelings of other people above one's own: *an extraordinary example of altruism.* Compare EGOT-ISM 1. ▶ **altruistic** /ˌæltruˈɪstɪk/ *adj*: *altruistic behaviour.*

aluminium /ˌæljə'mɪniəm, ˌælə-/ (*US* **aluminum** /ə'luːmɪnəm/) *n* [U] (*symb* **Al**) a chemical element. Aluminium is a grey metal, light in weight, often used for making pans for cooking: *aluminium window frames* ○ *aluminium foil* (eg for wrapping food). ⇨ App 7.

alumna /ə'lʌmnə/ *n* (*pl* **alumnae** /-niː/) (*US*) a female former student of a school, college or university.

alumnus /ə'lʌmnəs/ *n* (*pl* **alumni** /-naɪ/) (*US*) **1** [C] a male former student of a school, college or university. **2 alumni** [pl] male and female former students of an institution.

alveolar /ˌælvi'əʊlə(r), æl'viːələ(r)/ *adj, n* (*phonetics*) (of) a consonant made with the tongue touching the part of the mouth behind the upper front teeth, eg /t/ or /d/.

always /'ɔːlweɪz/ *adv* **1** at all times; on every occasion: *He nearly always wears a bow-tie.* **2** regularly: *The milkman always comes at 7.30.* ○ *We nearly always go to church on Sundays.* **3(a)** throughout a

period of time; throughout one's life: *She has always loved gardening.* ○ *She was always generous and kind.* ○ *He always did like travelling.* **(b)** for all future time: *Promise me you'll always keep in touch.* ○ *I'll always love you.* **4** (usu with the continuous tenses) again and again in an annoying way; often and repeatedly: *He was always asking for money.* ○ *Why are you always biting your nails?* **5** (with *can/could*) if everything else fails: *You can always leave if you really don't like it.* ○ *They can always go to a bank if they need more money.* **IDM** **as 'always** in a way that is expected because it usu happens like that; as usual: *As always he was late and had to run to catch the bus.* ○ *She sat quietly, as always, in her chair.*

Alzheimer's disease /'æltshaɪməz dɪziːz/ *n* [U] a serious disease of the brain that prevents it functioning normally and causes loss of memory, loss of ability to speak clearly, etc.

AM /ˌeɪ 'em/ *abbr* **1** (*radio*) amplitude modulation (one of the chief methods of sound broadcasting, in which radio waves are modulated (MODULATE 3) by varying the AMPLITUDE(1)). Compare FM 2. **2** (*US*) Master of Arts. Compare MA.

am¹ /əm, m; *strong form* æm/ ⇨ BE¹.

am² (*US* **AM**) /ˌeɪ 'em/ *abbr* in the morning before MIDDAY (Latin *ante meridiem*): *It starts at 10 am.* Compare PM.

amalgam /ə'mælgəm/ *n* **1** [C usu *sing*] a mixture or combination of people or things: *a subtle amalgam of spices* ○ *an amalgam of several political groups.* **2** [U] a mixture of MERCURY with another metal, used esp by dentists (DENTIST) for filling holes in teeth.

amalgamate /ə'mælgəmeɪt/ *v* ~ (**sb/sth**) (**with sb/sth**) to combine or unite, or to make people or things do this: [Vpr] *Our local brewery has amalgamated with another firm.* [V, Vn] *The boys' and girls' schools have (been) amalgamated to form a new coed school.* [Vnpr] *Several colleges were amalgamated into the new university.* ▶ **amalgamation** /əˌmælgə'meɪʃn/ *n* [U, C]: *a process of political amalgamation* ○ *an amalgamation of ethnic groups.*

amass /ə'mæs/ *v* to gather together or collect sth, esp in large quantities: [Vn] *amass a fortune* ○ *They amassed enough evidence to convict him.*

amateur /'æmətə(r), -tʃə(r)/ *n* **1** a person who takes part in a sport or creates sth with artistic skill, etc without receiving money for it: *The tournament is open to leading amateurs as well as professionals.* ○ *an enthusiastic amateur photographer/jockey/musician* ○ *amateur dramatics/athletics* ○ *the Amateur Boxing Association.* Compare PROFESSIONAL *n*. **2** (*usu derog*) a person who is not skilled or experienced in an activity: *The whole house needs rewiring — it's not a job for amateurs.*
▶ **amateurish** /'æmətərɪʃ, -tʃər-/ *adj* (*often derog*) not at all expert; not skilled: *Detectives described the burglary as 'crude and amateurish'.* **amateurishly** /'æmətərɪʃli, -tʃər-/ *adv.*
amateurism /'æmətərɪzəm, -tʃər-/ *n* [U]: *his bumbling amateurism.*

amaze /ə'meɪz/ *v* (often passive) to fill sb with great surprise or wonder: [Vn] *He amazed everyone by passing his driving test.* ○ *It amazed her that he was still alive.* ○ *What amazes me is how keen she still is about the job.* ○ *We were amazed by the change in his appearance.* ▶ **amazed** *adj* ~ (**at sb/sth**): *an amazed silence* ○ *She looked back at him, amazed at how happy she felt.* ○ *He was amazed to find himself sitting on a plane bound for Singapore.* **amazement** *n* [U]: *He looked at me in amazement.* ○ *There, to her amazement, was a gigantic statue of a gorilla.* **amazing** *adj* (*usu approv*): *an amazing speed/player/feat* ○ *I find it amazing that you can't swim.* ○

It is quite amazing how short people's memories are.
amazingly *adv: These tapes are amazingly cheap.* ∘
Amazingly, no one was hurt.

amazon /ˈæməzən; *US* -zɒn/ *n* a tall strong woman.

ambassador /æmˈbæsədə(r)/ *n* a person sent to
live in a foreign country as the senior representative there of her or his own country: *the newly-
appointed British Ambassador to Greece/in Athens* ∘
*(fig) The British Council acts as a cultural ambas-
sador for Britain and for the English language.*
Compare CONSUL 1, HIGH COMMISSIONER. ▶ **ambas-
sadorial** /æmˌbæsəˈdɔːriəl/ *adj.*

amber /ˈæmbə(r)/ *n* [U] (**a**) a hard clear yellowish-
brown substance used for making ornaments or
jewellery: *amber beads.* (**b**) its colour: *The traffic
lights turned to amber.*

ambi- *comb form* referring to both of two: *ambidextrous* ∘ *ambivalent.*

ambidextrous /ˌæmbiˈdekstrəs/ *adj* able to use the
left hand or the right hand equally well.

ambience (also **ambiance**) /ˈæmbiəns/ *n* (usu sing)
the character and atmosphere of a place: *We've tried
to create the ambience of a French bistro.* ∘ *The
Airport Hotel has an ambience all of its own.*

ambient /ˈæmbiənt/ *adj* [attrib] (*fml*) (esp of air) on
all sides; surrounding (SURROUND): *the ambient
temperature/conditions.*

ambiguity /ˌæmbɪˈɡjuːəti/ *n* **1**(**a**) [U] the state of
having more than one possible meaning: *the inherent ambiguity of all language* ∘ *A lot of humour
depends on ambiguity.* (**b**) [C] a word or statement
that can be interpreted in more than one way:
analyse/remove/resolve the ambiguities in the report.
2 [C,U] the state of being confused and difficult to
explain because of involving many different factors:
the ambiguities of class ∘ *the ambiguity of his
mother's attitude.*

ambiguous /æmˈbɪɡjuəs/ *adj* **1** that can be interpreted in more than one way: *an ambiguous message*
∘ *His closing words were deliberately ambiguous.* **2**
not clearly stated or defined: *Their position as consultants is ambiguous.* ▶ **ambiguously** *adv: an
ambiguously worded title.*

ambit /ˈæmbɪt/ *n* [sing] (*fml*) the scope or extent of
the authority, influence, etc of sb/sth: *We aim to
bring these buildings within the ambit of local
government control.*

ambition /æmˈbɪʃn/ *n* ~ (**to be/do sth**) (**a**) [C] a
strong desire to achieve sth: *He finally achieved/
fulfilled his boyhood ambition to become a pilot.* ∘ *She
has a great/burning ambition to succeed in business.*
∘ *sb's political/literary/sporting ambitions.* (**b**) [U]
the desire to be successful, famous, rich, etc: *her
driving ambition* ∘ *He felt his son lacked ambition.*

ambitious /æmˈbɪʃəs/ *adj* **1** ~ (**to be/do sth**); ~
(**for sth**) actively seeking success, wealth, status,
etc: *a ruthlessly/highly ambitious young manager* ∘
be ambitious for one's children. **2** demanding a lot of
effort, money, etc to succeed: *embark on an ambitious programme of expansion* ∘ *Their plans to
complete the project ahead of schedule seem very ambitious to me.* ▶ **ambitiously** *adv.*

ambivalent /æmˈbɪvələnt/ *adj* ~ (**about sb/sth**)
having or showing mixed good and bad feelings
about a particular object, person or situation: *He
has an ambivalent attitude towards his friend's wife.*
∘ *She is ambivalent about her future career.* ▶ **ambivalence** *n* [U,sing] ~ (**about/towards sb/sth**): *an
ambivalence towards foreign tourists* ∘ *There is much
ambivalence about our involvement in the war.*

amble /ˈæmbl/ *v* to move, ride or walk at a slow
relaxed pace: [Vpr] *an old donkey came ambling
down the road.* [Vp] *We ambled along for miles.* ∘
Mark ambled over to the girls. Compare SAUNTER.

ambulance /ˈæmbjələns/ *n* a vehicle equipped to
carry sick or injured people to hospital: *an ambulance crew* ∘ *I'll go and call an ambulance.*
■ **ˈambulance chaser** *n* (*US derog infml*) a lawyer
who encourages people who have been in accidents
to make claims in court for compensation.

ambulanceman /ˈæmbjələnsmən/ (*pl* -**men**
/-mən/) (also **ambulance worker**) *n* a person who
attends emergencies in an AMBULANCE in order to
give immediate medical help before taking the sick
or injured person to hospital.

ambush /ˈæmbʊʃ/ *n* (**a**) [U] the act of waiting in a
hidden position for sb in order to catch them doing
sth illegal, to kill them, etc: *the ambush and shooting
of two senior officers* ∘ *The thieves were lying in
ambush for their victims.* (**b**) [C] a surprise attack
from a hidden position: *killed by/in a terrorist ambush* ∘ *They set up an ambush to trap the aid convoy.*
▶ **ambush** *v* to make a surprise attack on sb/sth
from a hidden position : [Vn] *His car was ambushed
by guerrillas.* ∘ *(fig) She was ambushed by reporters
and cameramen.*

ameliorate /əˈmiːliəreɪt/ *v* (*fml*) to make sth better:
[Vn] *Steps have been taken to ameliorate the situation.* ▶ **amelioration** /əˌmiːliəˈreɪʃn/ *n* [U].

amen /ɑːˈmen, eɪˈmen/ *interj, n* (used esp at the end
of a prayer or hymn) may it be so: *I ask this through
Christ our Lord. Amen.* ∘ *Amen to that* (ie I certainly
agree with that).

amenable /əˈmiːnəbl/ *adj* **1** ~ (**to sth**) (of people)
willing to be influenced or controlled by sb/sth: *I
find him very amenable to reason.* **2** ~ **to sth** that
can be treated in a particular way: *'Hamlet' is the
least amenable of all Shakespeare's plays to being
summarized.*

amend /əˈmend/ *v* to change sth slightly in order to
correct an error; to make an improvement in sth:
[Vn] *amend a document/proposal/law* ∘ *The Official
Secrets Act has been amended to prevent further
leaks.*
▶ **amendment** *n* **1** [C] ~ (**to sth**) a minor change
or addition to a document, etc: *introduce/propose/
move* (ie suggest) *an amendment* ∘ *the fourth Amendment to the US Constitution* ∘ *Parliament debated
several amendments to the bill.* **2** [U] the action or
process of amending sth: *The motion was passed
without further amendment.*

amends /əˈmendz/ *n* [pl] **IDM** **make amends (to
sb) (for sth/doing sth)** to do sth to compensate for
a past mistake, insult or injury: *How can I ever make
amends for the things I said to you last night?*

amenity /əˈmiːnəti ; *US* əˈmenəti/ *n* **1** [C often *pl*] a
feature or facility of a place that makes life there
easy or pleasant: *People who retire to the country
often miss the amenities of a town* (eg libraries, cinemas and shops). **2** [U] (*fml*) the state of being
pleasant or useful: *the amenity value of the river
valley.*

American /əˈmerɪkən/ *adj* of N or S America, esp
the USA: *an American car* ∘ *I'm American.* See also
ANGLO-AMERICAN, LATIN AMERICAN.
▶ **American** *n* **1** [C] a native or citizen of America.
See also AFRICAN-AMERICAN, NATIVE AMERICAN. **2**
(also **American English**) [U] the English language
as spoken in the USA: *'Fag' has different meanings
in British and American English.*

Americana /əˌmerɪˈkɑːnə/ *n* [pl] things connected
with the USA: *She collects fifties Americana.*

Americanism *n* a word or phrase used in American English but not in standard English in Britain.

Americanize, -ise *v* [Vn] to make sb/sth American
in character.
■ **Aˌmerican ˈfootball** *n* [U] (*Brit*) an American
game of football played by two teams of 11 players

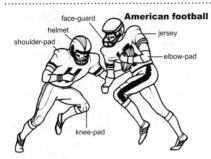

American football

face-guard
helmet
shoulder-pad
jersey
elbow-pad
knee-pad

who advance by running with and passing an OVAL ball. ⇨ picture.

A‚merican 'Indian *n* (*dated*) = NATIVE AMERICAN.

NOTE The continent of **America** is divided into **North America** and **South America**. The narrow region joining North and South America is **Central America**.

North America, which is a geographical term, consists of the **United States of America**, **Canada** and **Mexico**. **Latin America**, a cultural term, refers to the non-English speaking countries of Central and South America, where mainly Portuguese and Spanish is spoken. Mexico is part of Latin America.

The **United States of America** is usually shortened to the **USA**, the **US**, **the States** or simply **America**: *the US President* ○ *Have you ever been to the States?* ○ *She emigrated to America in 1985.* Many people from other parts of the continent dislike this use of **America** to mean just the USA, but it is very common.

American is usually used to talk about somebody or something from the United States of America: *Do you have an American passport?* ○ *American football* ○ *I'm not American, I'm Canadian!* **Latin American** and **South American** are used to refer to other parts of the continent: *Latin American dance music* ○ *Quite a lot of South Americans study here.*

Yank is an informal word for somebody from the United States: *She married a Yank.*

Amerindian /ˌæməˈrɪndiən/ *n* (*dated*) = NATIVE AMERICAN.

amethyst /ˈæməθɪst/ *n* [C,U] a purple precious stone used in making jewellery: *an amethyst ring.*

amiable /ˈeɪmiəbl/ *adj* showing and inspiring a friendly attitude; pleasant: *an amiable character/mood/conversation* ○ *Her parents seemed very amiable.* ► **amiability** /ˌeɪmiəˈbɪləti/ *n* [U]. **amiably** *adv*: *'That's fine', he replied amiably.*

amicable /ˈæmɪkəbl/ *adj* based on or achieved through polite discussion and without quarrelling: *restore amicable relations between the two sides* ○ *An amicable settlement was reached.* ► **amicably** *adv*: *They lived together amicably for several years.*

amid /əˈmɪd/ (also **amidst** /əˈmɪdst/) *prep* in the middle of sth; during sth, esp sth that causes excitement, alarm, etc: *The firm collapsed amid allegations of fraud.* ○ *The dollar fell sharply today amid growing/mounting speculation that the President is about to declare war.*

amidships /əˈmɪdʃɪps/ *adv* in or near the middle of a ship's side: *A torpedo struck them amidships.*

amino acid /əˌmiːnəʊ ˈæsɪd/ *n* (*biology or chemistry*) any of several compounds from which proteins (PROTEIN) found in the bodies of people and animals are formed.

amiss /əˈmɪs/ *adj* [pred], *adv* wrong: *Something seems to be amiss — can I help?* **IDM** **not come/go a'miss** to be useful and appreciated: *A little luck wouldn't come amiss at this stage!* **take sth a'miss**

to be offended by sth: *Would she take it amiss if I offered to help?*

amity /ˈæməti/ *n* [U] (*fml*) a friendly relationship between people or countries.

ammo /ˈæməʊ/ *n* [U] (*infml*) = AMMUNITION.

ammonia /əˈməʊniə/ *n* [U] a colourless gas with a strong smell, used esp in household cleaning substances and for making explosives.

ammunition /ˌæmjuˈnɪʃn/ *n* [U] **1** a supply of bullets, shells, bombs, etc: *an explosion at an ammunition dump* ○ *a haul of hidden weapons, including 500 rounds of live ammunition.* **2** information that can be used in trying to win an argument: *The letter gave her all the ammunition she needed.*

amnesia /æmˈniːziə; US -ˈniːʒə/ *n* [U] partial or total loss of memory: *suffer an attack of amnesia.*

amnesty /ˈæmnəsti/ *n* **1** ~ (**for sb**) an official act of forgiving people who have committed offences against the state and allowing them to go free: *Despite international pressure, the premier refuses to declare/grant an amnesty for political prisoners.* ○ *The rebels returned home under a general amnesty.* **2** a period of time during which people can admit to doing sth wrong without fear of punishment: *Thousands of guns were handed in during last week's amnesty on illegal weapons.*

amniocentesis /ˌæmniəʊsenˈtiːsɪs/ *n* [U, C usu *sing*] (*medical*) a test that involves a sample of fluid being taken from the WOMB of a pregnant woman in order to learn about the condition of her baby.

amoeba /əˈmiːbə/ *n* (*pl* **amoebas** or **amoebae** /-biː/) a tiny living creature consisting of a single cell, which changes shape constantly. Amoebas are found in water or soil.

amok /əˈmɒk/ (also **amuck** /əˈmʌk/) *adv* **IDM** **run amok** to rush about in a state of wild and angry excitement: *The soldiers ran amok and set fire to government buildings.*

among /əˈmʌŋ/ (also **amongst** /əˈmʌŋst/) *prep* (followed by a plural *n* or *pron* or a *n* referring to a group) **1** surrounded by sb/sth: *a house among the trees* ○ *She works among the poor/the sick.* ○ *He found the letters amongst a pile of old books.* **2** included in the group of things or people: *an attitude that is common/widespread among the under-25s* ○ *I was among the last to leave.* ○ *Among the causes of the civil war was a severe famine.* ○ *'What did you object to?' 'Well, among other things, the long working hours.'* ○ *He was only one amongst many who needed help.* **3** to each member of a group: *He handed out the slips of paper among the class.* **4** between people: *Politicians are always arguing amongst themselves.*

NOTE **Among** refers to people or things when you are talking about them as a group: *The books were given out among the class.* ○ *We stood among the crowd watching the tennis match.* ○ *They talked among themselves while they waited.* **Between** refers to two people or things: *They had one book between two pupils.* It can also refer to more than two if each one is considered individually: *She divided her possessions equally between her four children.* ○ *People hung flags across the street between the houses.*

amoral /ˌeɪˈmɒrəl; US -ˈmɔːr-/ *adj* not based on moral standards; not following any moral rules: *a totally amoral person.* Compare IMMORAL, MORAL.

amorous /ˈæmərəs/ *adj* (*fml or euph*) openly showing or feeling love; relating to sexual love: *amorous looks/letters/poetry/experiences* ○ *He became quite amorous at the office party.* ► **amorously** *adv*.

amorphous /əˈmɔːfəs/ *adj* [usu *attrib*] having no definite shape or form; not organized: *an amorphous mass of cells* ○ *an amorphous organization.*

amortize, -ise /ə'mɔːtaɪz; *US* 'æmərtaɪz/ *v* [Vn] (*law*) to make small regular payments over a period in order to pay back a debt. ▶ **amortization, -isation** /ə,mɔːtaɪ'zeɪʃn; *US* ,æmərtə-/ *n* [U, C].

amount /ə'maʊnt/ *v* **PHRV a'mount to sth 1** to add up to sth; to make sth as a total: *The cost amounted to £250.* ○ *Our information doesn't amount to much* (ie We have very little information). **2** to be equal to or the same as sth: *It all amounts to a lot of hard work.* ○ *What you say amounts to a direct accusation.* **IDM amount to / come to / be the same thing** ⇨ SAME¹.
▶ **amount** *n* ~ (**of sth**) (used esp with uncountable ns) **1** a sum of money: *a bill for the full amount* ○ *Can you really afford this amount?* **2** a quantity: *a fair / large amount of work/money/furniture* ○ *Food was provided in varying amounts.* ○ *You have to expect a certain amount of confusion.* ○ *No amount of encouragement would make him jump* (ie Despite much encouragement he refused to jump). **IDM any amount of sth** a large quantity of sth and as much as is necessary or desired: *There's been any amount of research on the subject.*

amour /ə'mʊə(r)/ *n* (*dated or rhet*) a love affair, esp a secret one: *a short story about the amours of a Dublin poet.*

amour propre /,æmʊə 'prɒprə/ (*French*) one's own sense of dignity and worth; SELF-RESPECT: *Try not to offend his amour propre.*

amp /æmp/ *n* **1** (also **ampere** /'æmpeə(r); *US* 'æmpɪər/) the unit for measuring electric current: *a 13 amp fuse/plug.* ⇨ App 8. **2** (*infml*) an amplifier (AMPLIFY).

ampersand /'æmpəsænd/ *n* the sign (&) meaning 'and': *Ampersands are often used in names of companies, eg Brown, Brown & Watkins.*

amphetamine /æm'fetəmiːn/ *n* [C, U] (*medical*) a drug that stimulates the body and makes one feel alert and excited. Amphetamines are sometimes taken illegally.

amphibian /æm'fɪbɪən/ *n* an animal that can live both on land and in water: *Frogs and newts are amphibians.*

amphibious /æm'fɪbɪəs/ *adj* **1** (of military operations, etc) involving troops that land on shore from the sea: *an amphibious raid/landing.* **2** suitable for use on land or water: *amphibious vehicles.* **3** living both on land and in water.

amphitheatre (*US* **-ter**) /'æmfɪθɪətə(r); *US* -θiːətər/ *n* (**a**) a building without a roof containing rows of seats rising in steps round an open space. Amphitheatres were used esp in ancient Greece and Rome for public entertainments. (**b**) a similar arrangement of seats inside a building used eg for lectures.

ample /'æmpl/ *adj* **1** enough or more than enough: *ample time to get to the station* ○ *ample opportunity for discussion* ○ *There is ample evidence to support this view.* ○ *$15 will be ample for my needs.* ○ *an ample salary* ○ *The election was given ample coverage on TV.* **2** (*euph*) large in size: *an ample bosom* ○ *his ample girth.* ▶ **amply** /'æmpli/ *adv*: *amply confirmed/demonstrated/rewarded.*

amplify /'æmplɪfaɪ/ *v* (*pt, pp* **-fied**) **1** to increase sth in strength or intensity, esp sound: [Vn] *amplify a guitar/an electric current/a signal.* **2** to add details to a story, etc: [Vn] *We must ask you to amplify your earlier statement.*
▶ **amplification** /,æmplɪfɪ'keɪʃn/ *n* [U].
amplifier (also *infml* **amp**) *n* a device for amplifying sth, esp sounds or radio signals.

amplitude /'æmplɪtjuːd; *US* -tuːd/ *n* [U] **1** (*techn*) the maximum extent that a sound or radio wave vibrates (VIBRATE 2). **2** (*fml*) the large size, range or scope of sth: *the amplitude of her gestures/movements.*

ampoule (*US* also **ampule**) /'æmpuːl/ *n* (*medical*) a small sealed container holding a liquid, esp one used for an injection (INJECT).

amputate /'æmpjuteɪt/ *v* to cut off a limb in a SURGICAL operation: [Vn] *have a leg amputated* [V, Vn] *Her arm is so badly injured they will have to amputate (it).* ▶ **amputation** /,æmpju'teɪʃn/ *n* [U, C].

amuck = AMOK.

amulet /'æmjʊlət/ *n* a piece of jewellery, etc worn as a charm¹(2) against evil.

amuse /ə'mjuːz/ *v* **1** (often passive) to make sb laugh or smile: [Vn] *Everyone was amused by the story about the dog.* ○ *My funny drawings amused the children.* [Vn.to inf] *We were amused to learn that...* [Vn] *Janet was not amused* (ie rather annoyed). [also V]. **2** to make time pass pleasantly for oneself/sb: [Vn] *These toys will help to keep the baby amused.* ○ *They amused themselves by looking at old photographs.*
▶ **amused** *adj* ~ (**at sth**) perceiving, or showing that one perceives, a situation, etc to be funny: *exchange amused glances* ○ *Helen watched amused.* ○ *Privately, they were amused at his clumsiness.*
amusement *n* **1** [C] a thing that makes time pass pleasantly: *I would never choose to watch golf as an amusement.* ○ *The hotel offers its guests a wide variety of amusements.* **2** [U] the feeling or state of being amused: *She could not disguise her amusement at his mistake.* ○ *To my great amusement his false beard fell off.* ○ *Her eyes twinkled with amusement.* ○ *I only do it for amusement* (ie not for any serious purpose). **a'musement arcade** *n* (*Brit*) a room or hall containing machines operated by coins for playing games. **a'musement park** *n* (*esp US*) an open area with swings, rides, etc; a FAIR³(1).
amusing *adj* causing laughter or smiles; enjoyable: *an amusing story/storyteller* ○ *Our visits to the theatre made the holiday more amusing.* **amusingly** *adv*: *an amusingly written book.*

an ⇨ A¹.

-an ⇨ -IAN.

-ana ⇨ -IANA.

anabolic steroid /,ænəbɒlɪk 'steroɪd, 'stɪə-/ *n* a drug that increases the size of the muscles, sometimes used illegally by athletes (ATHLETE).

anachronism /ə'nækrənɪzəm/ *n* **1** a person, a custom or an idea regarded as old-fashioned or no longer appropriate: *The monarchy is seen by some as an anachronism in present-day society.* **2(a)** the placing of sth in the wrong historical period: *It would be an anachronism to talk of Queen Victoria watching television.* (**b**) a thing placed wrongly in this way: *Modern dress is an anachronism in productions of Shakespeare's plays.* ▶ **anachronistic** /ə,nækrə'nɪstɪk/ *adj.*

anaconda /,ænə'kɒndə/ *n* a large snake of tropical S America that crushes other animals to death before eating them.

anaemia (*US* **anemia**) /ə'niːmiə/ *n* [U] (*medical*) a condition of the blood caused by a lack of red cells. People with anaemia look pale and feel weak.
▶ **anaemic** (*US* **anemic**) /ə'niːmɪk/ *adj* **1** suffering from anaemia: *She looks anaemic.* **2** lacking force or vigour; weak: *an anaemic performance.*

anaerobic /,æneə'rəʊbɪk/ *adj* (*techn*) not having or requiring oxygen: *anaerobic bacteria.*

anaesthesia /,ænəs'θiːzɪə/ (*US* **anesthesia** /-'θiːʒə/) *n* [U] the state of being unable to feel pain, heat, cold, etc, esp as a result of drugs given before a medical operation.
▶ **anaesthetic** (*US* **anesthetic**) /,ænəs'θetɪk/ *n* [C, U] a substance that makes a person or an animal unable to feel pain, heat, cold, etc in the whole body or part of the body: *be under (an) anaesthetic* ○ *give sb a general anaesthetic* (ie cause sb to lose consciousness) ○ *a local anaesthetic* (ie one affecting

only part of the body) *for the removal of a tooth.* — *adj* producing anaesthesia.

anaesthetist (*US* **anesthetist**) /əˈniːsθətɪst/ *n* a person whose job is to give anaesthetics, esp in preparation for a medical operation.

anaesthetize, -ise (*US* **anesthetize**) /əˈniːsθətaɪz/ *v* [Vn] to produce anaesthesia in sb; to make a person unable to feel pain, etc.

anagram /ˈænəgræm/ *n* a word or phrase made by arranging in a different order the letters of another word or phrase: *'Cart-horse' is an anagram of 'orchestra'.*

anal /ˈeɪnl/ *adj* of the ANUS: *the anal region.*

analgesia /ˌænəlˈdʒiːziə; *US* -ʒə/ *n* [U] (*medical*) the loss of ability to feel pain while still conscious.

▶ **analgesic** /ˌænəlˈdʒiːzɪk/ *n* a substance that relieves pain: *Aspirin is a mild analgesic.* — *adj*: *analgesic drugs.*

analogous /əˈnæləgəs/ *adj* ~ (**to/with sth**) partially similar or parallel: *The two processes are not analogous.* ○ *Sleep was sometimes held to be analogous to death.* ○ *The present crisis is analogous with the situation immediately before the war.*

analogue (*US* **analog**) /ˈænəlɒg; *US* -lɔːg/ *n* **1** a thing that is similar to another thing: *Many familiar European mammals have analogues among the Australian marsupials.* **2** (of a computer or an electronic process) using a continuous range of physical quantities, eg weight, length, volume, etc, to represent numbers: *analogue circuits/instruments/systems.* Compare DIGITAL.

analogy /əˈnælədʒi/ *n* **1** [C] ~ (**between sth and sth**); ~ (**with sth**) a similar feature, condition, state, etc shared by two things that are compared: *point to analogies between the two events* ○ *The teacher drew an analogy between the human heart and a pump.* ○ *use the analogy of a human family to explain sth* ○ *There is no analogy with any previous case.* **2** [U] a process of reasoning based on the similar features of two things: *My theory applies to you and by analogy to others like you.* See also ANALOGOUS.

analyse (*US* **analyze**) /ˈænəlaɪz/ *v* **1** to examine the nature or structure of sth, esp by separating it into its parts, in order to understand or explain it: [Vn] *analyse the sample and identify it* ○ *By analysing the parts of the sentence we learn more about English grammar.* ○ *We must try to analyse the causes of the strike.* **2** [Vn] = PSYCHOANALYSE.

analysis /əˈnæləsɪs/ *n* (*pl* **analyses** /-siːz/) **1(a)** [U, C] the study of sth by examining its parts and their relationship: *Textual analysis identified the author as Shakespeare.* ○ *Close/Careful analysis of the sales figures shows clear regional variations.* **(b)** [C] a statement of the result of this: *present a detailed analysis of the situation.* **2** [U] = PSYCHOANALYSIS. **IDM** **in the ˌlast/ˌfinal aˈnalysis** after everything has been considered; in the end: *In the final analysis I think our sympathy lies with the heroine of the play.*

▶ **analytic** /ˌænəˈlɪtɪk/, **analytical** /-kl/ *adjs* using or involving analysis: *an analytic appraisal* ○ *an analytical approach/technique* ○ *He was astute and analytical.* **analytically** /-kli/ *adv.*

analyst /ˈænəlɪst/ *n* **1** a person who is skilled in making analyses: *a political/military/market analyst* ○ *City analysts are forecasting pre-tax profits of £38 million this year.* **2** = PSYCHOANALYST.

anarchy /ˈænəki/ *n* [U] **1** the absence of government or control in society: *The overthrow of the regime was followed by a period of anarchy.* **2** disorder; confusion: *In the absence of their teacher the class was in a state of anarchy.*

▶ **anarchic** /əˈnɑːkɪk/, **anarchical** /-kl/ *adjs.* **anarchism** /ˈænəkɪzəm/ *n* [U] the political belief that there should be no laws or government. **anarchist** /ˈænəkɪst/ *n* a person who believes there

should be no laws or government, or who favours political disorder. **anarchistic** /ˌænəˈkɪstɪk/ *adj.*

anathema /əˈnæθəmə/ *n* **1** [U, C] ~ **to sb/sth** a person or thing that is hated: *Racial prejudice is (an) anathema to me.* **2** [C] (esp formerly) a declaration of the Christian Church condemning sb/sth as evil.

anatomy /əˈnætəmi/ *n* **1(a)** [U] the scientific study of the structure of human or animal bodies: *a professor of anatomy.* **(b)** [C] the structure of an animal or a plant: *the anatomy of the frog.* **2** [C] (*joc*) a person's body: *Various parts of his anatomy were clearly visible.* **3** [C] an analysis or examination of sth: *The book attempts an anatomy of the situation in South Africa.*

▶ **anatomical** /ˌænəˈtɒmɪkl/ *adj*: *anatomical abnormalities.* **anatomically** /-kli/ *adv.*

anatomist /əˈnætəmɪst/ *n* a person who studies anatomy.

-ance, -ence *suff* (with *vs* forming *ns*) an action or a state of: *assistance* ○ *resemblance* ○ *confidence.*

ancestor /ˈænsestə(r)/ *n* **1(a)** any of the people from whom sb is descended, esp those more remote than their grandfather or grandmother: *His ancestors had come to England as refugees.* **(b)** any animal from which modern species have developed: *The mammoth was the ancestor of modern-day elephants.* Compare DESCENDANT. **2** an early form of a machine or structure which later became more developed: *The ancestor of the modern bicycle was called a penny farthing.* Compare FORERUNNER.

▶ **ancestral** /ænˈsestrəl/ *adj* belonging to or inherited from one's ancestors: *her ancestral home* ○ *ancestral species.*

ancestry /ˈænsestri/ *n* (usu *sing*) one's ancestors; the group of people or race from which one is descended: *have a distinguished ancestry* ○ *She was proud of her Scottish ancestry.*

anchor /ˈæŋkə(r)/ *n* **1** a heavy metal device attached to a rope or chain. Anchors are dropped over the side of ships or boats to keep them in the same position on the water: *They brought the boat into the harbour and dropped/cast (the) anchor.* ○ *lie/ride at anchor* (ie be held in a position by the anchor) ○ *We weighed anchor* (ie lifted it out of the water to start sailing) *shortly before midday.* **2** a person or thing that gives security or confidence: *Without the anchor of family support I would never have survived the ordeal.*

▶ **anchor** *v* **1** to lower an anchor; to make sth secure with an anchor: [V, Vn] *We anchored (our boat) close to the shore.* **2** to secure sth firmly in position: [Vn] *anchor a trailer at each end when it is not in use* [Vnpr] *Get your foot anchored around something to prevent you overbalancing.* **3** ~ **sth/sb** (**in/to sth**) to give sth/sb a firm basis or foundation: [Vnpr] *Her poetry is anchored in everyday experience.* ○ *an exchange rate mechanism anchored to the German Bundesbank* [Vn] *His score of 85 helped to anchor the Australian innings.*

▶ **anchorage** /ˈæŋkərɪdʒ/ *n* a place where ships or boats may anchor safely.

anchorite /ˈæŋkəraɪt/ *n* a hermit or religious recluse.

anchorman /ˈæŋkəmæn/ *n* (*pl* **-men** /-men/; *fem* **anchorwoman** /-wʊmən/, *pl* **-women** /-wɪmɪn/) a person who presents a radio or television broadcast, introducing reports and interviews by other people.

anchovy /ˈæntʃəvi; *US* ˈæntʃəʊvi/ *n* a small fish with a strong salty flavour: *a pizza topped with olives, green peppers and anchovies.*

ancient /ˈeɪnʃənt/ *adj* **1** belonging to times that are long past: *ancient civilizations* ○ *ancient history* ○ *an ancient monument* ○ (*joc*) *The incident happened before I was married and that's all ancient history now.* **2** (*often joc*) very old or looking very old: *an ancient woodland* ○ *my ancient green coat* ○ *I feel pretty* *ancient when I see how the younger generation behaves.* ➪ note at OLD.

▶ **the ancients** *n* [pl] the people who lived in ancient times, esp the Egyptians, Greeks and Romans.

ancillary /æn'sɪləri; *US* ˈænsəleri/ *adj* ~ (**to sth**) providing necessary support to the main work or activities of an organization, system, etc: *ancillary staff/duties/services/equipment* ○ *poorly paid ancillary workers in the health service.*

-ancy, -ency *suff* (with *ns, adjs* and *vs* forming *ns*) the state or quality of: *complacency* ○ *constancy* ○ *presidency.*

and /ənd, ən; *also* n, *esp after* t, d; *strong form* ænd/ *conj* (used to connect words of the same part of speech, phrases or clauses) **1(a)** also; in addition to: *bread and butter* ○ *Sue and I have had lunch.* ○ *slowly and carefully* ○ *The children ran in and out.* ○ *able to read and write* ○ *one woman, two men and three children* ○ *shutting doors and opening windows.* (When *and* connects two *ns* standing for things or people that are closely linked, a determiner is not normally repeated before the second *n*, eg *a knife and fork, my father and mother,* but *a knife and a spoon, my father and my uncle.*) **(b)** (*infml*) (used at the beginning of a sentence to introduce or emphasize an additional point): *I walked home after work. And I walked back into town in the evening.* **2** added to; PLUS: *5 and 5 makes 10.* ○ *'What's 47 and 16?' '63.'* (When numbers, except for most dates, are said, *and* is used between the hundreds and any figures that follow, eg *two thousand, two hundred and sixty-four,* ie 2264.) **3** then; following this: *She came in and sat down.* ○ *I pulled the trigger and the gun went off.* **4** as a result of this: *Work hard and* (ie If you work hard) *you will pass your examinations.* ○ *Arrive late once more and* (ie If you arrive late once more) *you're fired.* **5** then again; repeatedly; increasingly: *They talked for hours and hours.* ○ *He tried and tried but without success.* **6** (used to show that not all examples of a thing have the same characteristics): *Don't worry — there are rules and rules* (ie Some rules are less important or easier to ignore than others). **7** but; in contrast: *He wants to go to Scotland and I want to go to Italy.* ○ *I said I would meet him at the post office and then I got delayed at work.* ■ **and/or** *conj* (*infml*) together with or as an alternative to: *He says he will ring the hospital and/or tell his family doctor about it.*

NOTE A few verbs such as **go** and **come** are usually followed by **and** plus a verb instead of the infinitive (**to** plus verb) to show purpose: *Will you go and get me a hammer please?* ○ *Can I come and see you tonight?* ○ *We stayed and had a drink.* ○ *He stopped and bought some flowers.* ○ *I'll try and get you a new one tomorrow.* **Try** can be used in this construction only in the infinitive or imperative form: *I'll try and phone tomorrow morning.* ○ *Try and get a seat at the back of the bus.*

androgynous /æn'drɒdʒənəs/ *adj* having both male and female characteristics: *androgynous faces/models.*

android /ˈændrɔɪd/ *n* a ROBOT that looks like a real person.

anecdote /ˈænɪkdəʊt/ *n* ~ (**about sb/sth**) a short, interesting or amusing story about a real person or event: *He's always telling us anecdotes about his childhood in India.*

▶ **anecdotal** /ˌænɪkˈdəʊtl/ *adj* based on anecdotes and not necessarily true or accurate: *anecdotal evidence.*

anemia ➪ ANAEMIA. ▶ **anemic** ➪ ANAEMIC.

anemone /əˈnemənɪ/ *n* a small plant, often grown in gardens, that has white, red or purple flowers with dark centres.

anesthesia ➪ ANAESTHESIA. ▶ **anesthetic** ➪ ANAESTHETIC.

anew /əˈnjuː;; *US* əˈnuː/ *adv* (*usu rhet*) in a new or different way; again: *ponder anew on life's mysteries.*

angel /ˈeɪndʒl/ *n* **1** (esp in Christian belief) a messenger or servant of God: *An angel appeared to the shepherds.* **2** a beautiful, innocent or kind person: *Mary's three children are all little angels — not like mine!* ○ *Be an angel and make me a sandwich.* ○ *He sings like an angel* (ie very sweetly). See also GUARDIAN ANGEL.

▶ **angelic** /ænˈdʒelɪk/ *adj* of or like an angel: *an angelic smile/voice/face.*

angelica /ænˈdʒelɪkə/ *n* [U] pieces of the stalk of a sweet-smelling plant that have been boiled in sugar and are used to decorate cakes.

anger /ˈæŋgə(r)/ *n* [U] ~ (**at sb/sth**) a strong feeling of annoyance and hostility: *express/voice/vent one's anger* ○ *He was filled with anger and resentment at the way he had been tricked.* ○ *His voice shook/trembled with anger.* ○ *She sensed my growing anger.* ○ *It was said in a moment of anger.* See also ANGRY.

▶ **anger** *v* to fill sb with anger; to make sb angry: [Vn] *He was angered and dismayed by the selfishness of the others.* ○ *The question clearly angered her.*

angina /ænˈdʒaɪnə/ *n* [U] (*medical*) a disease of the heart which causes sharp pains in the chest after physical activity or exercise: *repeated attacks of angina.*

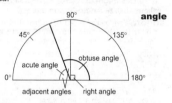

angle

angle¹ /ˈæŋgl/ *n* **1(a)** the amount of distance between the directions of two lines or surfaces where they meet: *an angle of 45°* ○ *form a sharp angle.* ➪ picture. **(b)** a line, direction of movement, etc considered in relation to the ground: *The tower of Pisa leans at an angle.* ○ *the rocket's angle of descent* ○ *The plane was coming in at a steep angle.* ○ *He wore his hat at a jaunty/rakish angle.* See also ACUTE ANGLE, ADJACENT ANGLES, OBTUSE ANGLE, RIGHT ANGLE, WIDE-ANGLE LENS. **(c)** a position from which sth is looked at: *Seen from this angle the woman in the picture is smiling.* See also ANGULAR. **2** the place where two sides of a building, an object, etc meet: *She hit her knee against the angle of the desk.* **3** a particular way of considering an issue, a problem, etc: *We're looking for a new angle for our next advertising campaign.* ○ *Concentrate on the human angle* (eg the emotional aspects) *of the story.*

▶ **angle** *v* **1** to move or place sth so that it is not straight or not directly facing sb/sth: [Vn] *a cleverly angled pass to the left* ○ *Try angling the camera for a more interesting picture.* **2** ~ **sth** (**to/towards sb**) to present information, etc from a particular point of view or for a particular audience: [Vnpr] *This programme is angled towards young viewers.* [also Vn].

angle² /ˈæŋgl/ *v* **1** (usu **go angling**) to catch fish with a line and a hook: [Vpr] *angling for trout* [also V]. **2** ~ **for sth** (*infml*) [Vpr] to try and obtain sth without asking directly but by using hints (HINT 1): *angle for compliments/an invitation/a free ticket.*

▶ **angler** /ˈæŋglə(r)/ *n* a person who goes angling. See also FISHERMAN.

angling *n* [U] the art or sport of fishing with a line and a hook, usu in rivers, lakes, etc rather than in the sea: *an angling club* ○ *Angling is his main hobby.*

A

Anglican /'æŋglɪkən/ n a member of the Church of England or of another Church with the same beliefs and forms of worship. ▶ **Anglican** adj: the Anglican prayer-book.

Anglicize, -ise /'æŋglɪsaɪz/ v to make sb/sth English in character: [Vn] 'Rome' is the Anglicized form of 'Roma'.

Anglo- comb form English or British: Anglo-American ○ Anglophile.

Anglo-American /ˌæŋgləʊ əˈmerɪkən/ n an American person descended from an English family. ▶ **Anglo-American** adj of or concerning England or Britain and America: Anglo-American relations.

Anglo-Catholic /ˌæŋgləʊ ˈkæθlɪk/ n a member of the section of the Church of England that stresses its connection with the early Christian Church and objects to being called Protestant.

Anglophile /'æŋgləʊfaɪl/ n a person who loves England or English things.

Anglophobe /'æŋgləʊfəʊb/ n a person who hates or fears England or English things.

anglophone /'æŋgləʊfəʊn/ n, adj (a person) who speaks English, esp where English is not the only language spoken: anglophone writers from Africa.

Anglo-Saxon /ˌæŋgləʊ ˈsæksn/ n **1** [C] a person whose ancestors were English. **2** [C] an English person of the period before the Norman Conquest. **3** (also **Old English**) [U] the English language before about 1150. ▶ **Anglo-Saxon** adj.

angora /æŋˈgɔːrə/ n **(a)** [C] a breed of cat, goat or rabbit that has long hair. **(b)** [U] cloth made from the hair of angora goats or rabbits: an angora beret.

angry /'æŋgri/ adj (-ier, -iest) ~ **(with sb)** **(at/about sth)** filled with anger: angry protesters/letters/exchanges ○ an angry mob ○ I felt angry that they had left me out. ○ Everything he did made her angry. ○ They got/grew very angry at being delayed/about the delay. ○ I was angry with myself for making such a stupid mistake. ○ (fig) an angry sea/sky. **IDM** an **angry young man** a young man who disagrees openly and strongly with the existing moral, social and political attitudes and tries to change them. ▶ **angrily** /-əli/ adv: hiss/swear/frown angrily ○ Some senators reacted angrily to the President's remarks.

angst /æŋst/ n [U] (German) a feeling of anxiety, guilt or regret, esp about the condition of the world: letters full of teenage angst.

anguish /'æŋgwɪʃ/ n [U] severe distress or mental suffering: tears of anguish ○ He groaned in anguish. ○ Behind all the clowning there is a terrible sense of anguish. ▶ **anguished** adj feeling or expressing anguish: an anguished letter/plea ○ anguished cries.

angular /'æŋgjələ(r)/ adj **1** (of people) thin and having prominent bones: a gaunt, angular face. **2** (of a person's character or manner) stiff and awkward: an angular posture/gait ○ angular movements. **3** having angles or sharp corners: angular blocks of lava.

animal /'ænɪml/ n **1** any living thing, other than a human being, that can feel and move, eg a lion, bird, snake, fish or fly: the plants and animals of the region ○ farm animals ○ hunt/tame a wild animal ○ Animal rights campaigners object to experiments on live animals. **2** a creature with four legs, as distinct from a bird, a reptile, a fish or an insect: Animals were grazing near the river. **3** any living creature, including a human being: Man is unique among animals for having developed the power of speech. **4** a person who behaves in a rough or cruel manner or is very dirty: People who beat up old ladies are animals. **5** a particular type of person, organ-

ization, etc: She's not a political animal. ○ The government which followed the election was a very different kind of animal. See also DUMB ANIMALS, HIGHER ANIMALS.
▶ **animal** adj [attrib] characteristic of animals: studying animal and human brain diseases ○ the instinctive animal desire to be with one's mate.
■ ˌanimal 'husbandry n [U] the care and management of cattle, sheep, horses, etc.
ˌanimal 'magnetism n [U] a strongly attractive quality in sb that draws people towards them.

animate¹ /'ænɪmeɪt/ v **1** to give life to sth/sb; to make sth/sb more lively: [Vn] A smile suddenly animated her face. **2** [Vn] to make people and animals in pictures appear to move, by making pictures of them in different positions and using the sequence of pictures in a cinema film.
▶ **animated** adj **1** lively: an animated conversation/discussion ○ I had rarely seen him so animated. **2** given the appearance of movement: animated cartoons/drawings/waxworks. **animatedly** adv: people talking animatedly.
animation /ˌænɪˈmeɪʃn/ n [U] **1** liveliness: I could see Eleanor talking, with great animation, to Donald. **2** the technique of making people and animals in pictures appear to move: computer animation. See also SUSPENDED ANIMATION.
animator n a person who makes animated films.

animate² /'ænɪmət/ adj living; having life: They see the whole world, animate and inanimate, as God's creation. Compare INANIMATE.

animosity /ˌænɪˈmɒsəti/ n [U,C] ~ **(against/towards sb/sth)**; ~ **(between A and B)** strong dislike or hostility: He felt/harboured no animosity towards his critics. ○ I could sense the animosity between them. ○ the re-emergence of old animosities.

animus /'ænɪməs/ n [U] ~ **(against sb/sth)** (fml) dislike or hostility shown in speech or action: renewed animus against European integration.

anise /'ænɪs/ n [U] a plant with sweet-smelling seeds.

aniseed /'ænəsiːd/ n [U] the seeds of ANISE, used for giving flavour to alcoholic drinks and sweets.

ankle /'æŋkl/ n **1** the joint connecting the foot with the leg: break/sprain/twist an/one's ankle. **2** the thin part of the leg between this joint and the calf²: be ankle-deep in mud ○ ¹ankle socks (ie short socks covering the ankles but no higher). ➪ picture at FOOT¹.
▶ **anklet** /'æŋklət/ n an ornamental chain, ring or band worn round the ankle.

annals /'ænlz/ n [pl] a record of events year by year; historical records: the Annals of the Society ○ a name that will go down in the annals (ie the history) of crime.

annex /əˈneks/ v ~ **sth (to sth)** to take possession and control of a territory, etc, esp by force: [Vn] annex a neighbouring state [Vnpr] Crete was formally annexed to Greece in 1913. ▶ **annexation** /ˌænekˈseɪʃn/ n [U,C]: the annexation of a territory.

annexe (also **annex**) /'æneks/ n **1** a building that is added to or near to a larger one and provides additional accommodation, work space, etc: the annexe to the clinic ○ The hotel was full so we had to sleep in the annexe. **2** an additional section of a document.

annihilate /əˈnaɪəleɪt/ v [Vn] **1** to destroy sb/sth completely: a cure that will annihilate the disease ○ The enemy was completely annihilated. **2** to defeat sb/sth completely: be annihilated in an election ○ She annihilated her opponent, who failed to win a single game. ▶ **annihilation** /əˌnaɪəˈleɪʃn/ n [U]: A full-scale nuclear war could lead to the annihilation of the human race.

anniversary /ˌænɪˈvɜːsəri/ n a date that is exactly a year or a number of years after an event; a celebration of this: the hundredth anniversary of the composer's death ○ our wedding anniversary ○ an anniversary dinner.

annotate /ˈænəteɪt/ v to add notes to a book, text, etc giving explanation or comment: [Vn] *an annotated edition/copy.* ▶ **annotation** /ˌænəˈteɪʃn/ n [C, U]: *make annotations in the margin* ○ *The text required extensive annotation.*

announce /əˈnaʊns/ v **1(a)** to make sth known publicly: [Vn] *They announced their engagement in the local paper.* ○ *(fig) The heavy footsteps announced his arrival.* [Vnpr] *announce the year's sales figures to the staff* [V.that] *The director announced that she would resign.* [Vpr.that] *A spokesman announced to the press that no agreement had yet been reached.* [also V.wh, Vpr.wh]. **(b)** to give information about sth in a public place, esp through a LOUDSPEAKER: [Vn] *Has our flight been announced yet?* ○ *announce the winners of the awards* [V.that] *They announced that the train had been delayed.* **(c)** (at a formal party) to call out the name of sb to indicate that they have arrived: [Vn] *Would you announce the guests as they come in?* **(d)** to say sth in a firm or serious way: [V.speech] *'I've decided to change my lifestyle', he announced one day.* [also V.that]. **2** to introduce or give information about a programme on radio or television: [Vn] *announce the latest news headlines.* ▶ **announcement** n **1** [C] a statement in spoken or written form that makes sth known publicly: *The announcement of further job losses was greeted with dismay.* ○ *Announcements of births, marriages and deaths appear in some newspapers.* ○ *a special announcement on the radio.* **2** [U] the action of announcing sth: *The announcement of the result has been delayed.*

announcer n **1** a person who introduces or gives information about programmes on radio or television. **2** a person who gives information about sth in a public place, esp through a LOUDSPEAKER.

annoy /əˈnɔɪ/ v **1** to make sb fairly angry; to irritate sb: [Vn] *His constant sniffing annoys me.* ○ *It annoys me when people forget to say thank you.* ○ *I was annoyed by his insensitive remarks.* **2** to cause trouble or discomfort to sb; to BOTHER sb: [Vn] *Stop annoying your mother.* ○ *The mosquitoes annoyed me so much I couldn't sleep.*
▶ **annoyance** /-əns/ n **1** [U] the feeling of being annoyed: *a look of annoyance* ○ *much to our annoyance.* **2** [C] a thing that annoys: *One of the annoyances of working here is the difficulty of parking near the office.*
annoyed adj ~ **(with sb)** **(at/about sth)**; ~ **(that... / to do sth)** fairly angry: *He got very annoyed with me about my carelessness.* ○ *I'm extremely annoyed at the way he always stares at me in the office.* ○ *I was annoyed with myself for getting upset over something so trivial.* ○ *Will she be annoyed that you forgot to phone?* ○ *I was annoyed to find they had left without me.*
annoying adj making sb fairly angry: *This interruption is very annoying.* ○ *How annoying, I've left my wallet at home!* **annoyingly** adv.

annual /ˈænjuəl/ adj [usu attrib] **1** happening every year, usu once a year: *an annual event/meeting/report/conference/visit.* **2** calculated over a period of a year: *an annual income/subscription* ○ *annual production/rainfall.* **3** lasting for one year: *the annual course of the sun.*
▶ **annual** n **1** a plant that lives for one year or season. **2** a book or magazine that is published once a year, having the same title each time but different contents.
annually adv once a year: *The exhibition is held annually.*

annualized, -ised /ˈænjuəlaɪzd/ adj (techn) calculated for a period of a year but based on figures for a shorter period: *an annualized deficit.*

annuity /əˈnjuːəti; US -ˈnuː-/ n **(a)** a fixed sum of money paid to sb each year, usu for the rest of their life: *receive a modest annuity.* **(b)** a form of insurance or investment that provides such a regular annual income: *a mortgage annuity scheme.*

annul /əˈnʌl/ v (-ll-) to declare officially that sth is not valid: [Vn] *annul a contract/a marriage/an election.* ▶ **annulment** n [C, U].

annunciation /əˌnʌnsiˈeɪʃn/ n **the Annunciation** [sing] (religion) (in Christianity) the announcement to Mary that she was to be the mother of Christ, celebrated on 25 March.

anode /ˈænəʊd/ n (techn) **1** the TERMINAL n(3) or ELECTRODE by which electric current enters a device. **2** the positive TERMINAL n(3) of a device. Compare CATHODE.

anodyne /ˈænədaɪn/ adj **1** dull; unlikely to cause argument or offence: *He writes rather anodyne articles.* **2** (of drugs, etc) that can relieve pain or mental distress.

anoint /əˈnɔɪnt/ v ~ **sb (with sth)** to put oil on sb or on a part of sb's body as part of a religious or other ceremony: [Vn, Vnpr] *The priest anointed the baby's forehead (with oil).* [Vn-n] *The high priest anointed him king.*

anomalous /əˈnɒmələs/ adj different from what is normal or usual: *He is in an anomalous position as the only part-time worker in the firm.*
▶ **anomaly** /əˈnɒməli/ n ~ **(in sth)** an anomalous thing, event, situation, etc: *the many anomalies in the tax system* ○ *detect any anomalies that have occurred.*

anon¹ /əˈnɒn/ adv (dated or joc) soon: *See you anon.*

anon² /əˈnɒn/ abbr (usu at the end of a piece of writing, etc) anonymous; by an unknown writer.

anonymity /ˌænəˈnɪməti/ n [U] the state of being or remaining unknown to most other people: *the anonymity of city life* ○ *Anyone providing information to the police will be guaranteed anonymity.*

anonymous /əˈnɒnɪməs/ adj **1(a)** with a name that is not known or not made public: *an anonymous donor/buyer/benefactor* ○ *The author wishes to remain anonymous.* **(b)** written or given by sb whose name is not known or revealed: *an anonymous letter/message/gift/phone call.* **2** having no outstanding or unusual features; not particularly noticeable: *anonymous background music* ○ *a somewhat anonymous figure.* ▶ **anonymously** adv.

anorak /ˈænəræk/ n a short coat with a HOOD¹(1) that is worn as a protection against rain, wind and cold. Compare PARKA.

anorexia /ˌænəˈreksiə/ n [U] (medical) **1** a loss of the wish to eat. **2** (also **anorexia nervosa** /nɜːˈvəʊsə/) an illness, esp affecting young women, in which there is an abnormal fear of being fat. This results in a loss of desire to eat, which in turn causes dangerous weight loss.
▶ **anorexic** /ˌænəˈreksɪk/ n, adj (a person who is) suffering from anorexia nervosa.

another /əˈnʌðə(r)/ indef det **1** an additional one or additional ones of the same kind: *Would you like another cup of tea?* ○ *She's going to have another baby.* ○ *In another two weeks it'll be finished.* ○ *We've got another 50 kilometres to go.* **2** a different one or different ones: *We can do it another time.* ○ *She's got another boyfriend.* ○ *That's quite another matter.* ○ *This pen doesn't work — can you lend me another one?* **3** a person or thing of a very similar type or with very similar qualities: *Can he be another Einstein?*
▶ **another** indef pron **1** an additional person or thing: *Can I have another?* ○ *'It's a bill.' 'Oh no, not another!'* ○ *We've had many letters like this — another of them came today.* **2** a different person or thing: *I don't like this room — let's ask for another.* **3** a person or thing of a very similar type or with very

similar qualities: *Shakespeare is the greatest English writer — will there ever be such another?*

answer¹ /ˈɑːnsə(r); *US* ˈæn-/ *n* ~ **(to sb/sth) 1(a)** a thing that is said, written or done as a response, to deal with a question or a situation; a reply: *The answer he gave was quite surprising.* ○ *Have you had an answer to your letter?* ○ *The doctor came in answer to my phone call.* ○ *I rang the bell but there was no answer.* ○ *She had no answer to the accusations.* **(b)** a thing written or said in response to a question in a test, a QUIZ; etc; the correct response to such a question: *Write your answers on the sheet provided.* ○ *What's the right answer to question 12?* ○ *The answers are at the back of the book.* **2** a solution to a problem: *This could be the answer to all our difficulties.* ○ *The only answer was to look for a job elsewhere.* **3** a person or thing from one place that may be considered to have the same role or status as a person or thing from another place: *The Monkees were supposed to be America's answer to the Beatles.* **IDM** **have/know all the ˈanswers** (*infml often derog*) to seem to be cleverer and know a lot more about sth than other people: *He thinks he knows all the answers.*

answer² /ˈɑːnsə(r); *US* ˈæn-/ *v* **1** to say, write or do sth in response to sb/sth: [V] *Think carefully before you answer.* [Vn] *answer a question/a letter/an advertisement* ○ *She didn't answer me.* ○ *answer the door* (ie open the door after sb has knocked or rung the bell) ○ *answer the telephone* (ie pick up the RECEIVER (1) and speak to the person who is calling) ○ *My prayers have been answered* (ie I have got what I wanted). ○ *Nobody answered my call for help.* ○ *How do you answer the charge?* [V.that] *She answered that she preferred to eat alone.* [Vnn] *Can you answer me this?* [V.speech] *'Yes,' she answered softly.* Compare REPLY, RESPOND. **2** to be suitable for sth; to satisfy sth: [Vn] *answer sb's purpose/needs/requirements.* **IDM** **answer (to) the description (of sb/sth)** to match the way sb/sth has been described: *A man answering (to) this description has been seen in the Brighton area.* **answer to the name of sth** (*infml or joc*) (esp of a pet animal) to have as a name; to be called sth: *My dog answers to the name of Spot.* **PHRV** **ˌanswer ˈback** to defend oneself against sth written or said about one: *Following criticisms of his latest film, the director answered back in a scathing article about critics.* **ˌanswer (sb) ˈback** to speak rudely or without respect to sb with authority, esp when being criticized or told to do sth: *Don't answer back!* ○ *He's a rude little boy, always answering his mother back.* **ˈanswer for sb/sth 1** to accept responsibility or blame for sth: *You will have to answer for your crimes one day.* ○ *He has a lot to answer for* (ie He is responsible for many bad things). ○ *I'll answer for the consequences of this decision.* **2** to speak on behalf of sb: *I agree, but I can't answer for my colleagues.* **3** to guarantee that sb has a particular quality: *Knowing her well I can certainly answer for her honesty.* **ˈanswer to sb (for sth)** to be responsible to sb; to be required to explain or justify one's actions to sb: *Who do you answer to in your new job?* ○ *You will answer to me for any damage to the car.*

▶ **answerable** /ˈɑːnsərəbl; *US* ˈæn-/ *adj* **1** [pred] ~ **to sb (for sth)** responsible to sb; required to explain or justify one's actions to sb: *I am answerable to the company for the use of this equipment.* **2** that can be answered.

answerphone /ˈɑːnsəfəʊn; *US* ˈæns-/ *n* a device that automatically answers telephone calls and records any message left by the person calling: *She left her name and number on the answerphone.* ○ *I rang him several times but only got the answerphone.*

ant /ænt/ *n* a very small insect that lives in highly organized groups. There are many different types of ant: *an ant's nest.* ⇨ picture at INSECT.

-ant, -ent *suff* **1** (with *vs* forming *adjs*) that is or does sth: *significant* ○ *different.* **2** (with *vs* forming *ns*) a person or thing that: *inhabitant* ○ *deterrent.*

antagonism /ænˈtægənɪzəm/ *n* [C, U] ~ **(to/towards sb/sth)**; ~ **(between A and B)** a feeling of hostility or opposition: *The antagonism he felt towards his old enemy was still very strong.* ○ *You could sense the antagonism between them.*

antagonist /ænˈtægənɪst/ *n* a person who actively opposes sb/sth; an ADVERSARY: *one of the most formidable antagonists I ever encountered.*

antagonistic /æn,tægəˈnɪstɪk/ *adj* ~ **(to/towards sb/sth)** showing or feeling opposition; HOSTILE(1); aggressive: *be antagonistic towards new ideas.*

antagonize, -ise /ænˈtægənaɪz/ *v* to make sb aggressive or HOSTILE(1); to annoy or irritate sb greatly: [Vn] *It would be dangerous to antagonize him — he has a very nasty temper.*

Antarctic /ænˈtɑːktɪk/ *adj* of the regions around the South Pole: *Antarctic explorers.*
▶ **the Antarctic** *n* [sing] the regions around the South Pole.
■ **the An,tarctic ˈCircle** *n* [sing] the line of LATITUDE 66° 30′ South. ⇨ picture at GLOBE. Compare ARCTIC.

ante /ˈænti/ *n* an amount that is bet before a person receives cards in a gambling game, esp POKER²; a stake(3): *raise/up the ante* ○ *(fig) The announcement merely upped the ante in the take-over battle.*

ante- *pref* (with *ns*, *adjs* and *vs*) (of time or position) before; in front of: *ante-room* ○ *antenatal* ○ *antedate.* Compare POST-, PRE-.

anteater /ˈæntiːtə(r)/ *n* an animal with a long nose and tongue that feeds on ants (ANT).

antecedent /,æntɪˈsiːdnt/ *n* **1** [C] (*fml*) a thing or an event that existed or comes before another: *the antecedent of the current exam system* ○ *The style has strong antecedents in station architecture.* **2** [C] (*grammar*) a word or phrase to which a following word, esp a relative pronoun, refers: *'Which proves I'm right' is not clear unless we know the antecedent of 'which'.* **3** antecedents [pl] a person's ancestors or family and social background.
▶ **antecedent** *adj* (*fml*) previous: *antecedent events.*

antechamber /ˈæntɪtʃeɪmbə(r)/ *n* (*fml*) = ANTEROOM.

antedate /,æntiˈdeɪt/ (also **predate**) *v* [Vn] **1** to put an earlier date on a document, letter, etc than the one at the time of writing. **2** to be before sth/sb in time: *This event antedates the discovery of America by several centuries.* Compare POSTDATE.

antediluvian /,æntidɪˈluːviən/ *adj* (*joc*) very old-fashioned: *His ideas are positively antediluvian!*

antelope /ˈæntɪləʊp/ *n* (*pl* unchanged or **antelopes**) an animal similar to a deer that can run very fast and is found esp in Africa. There are many different types of antelope.

antenatal /,æntiˈneɪtl/ *adj* [usu attrib] (*esp Brit*) (also *esp US* **prenatal**) **(a)** existing or occurring before birth: *Antenatal complications can affect a baby's health.* **(b)** for pregnant women: *antenatal clinics.* Compare POSTNATAL.

antenna /ænˈtenə/ *n* **1** (*pl* antennae /-niː/) either of the two long thin organs on the heads of some insects and sea animals, used for feeling and touching things: *(fig) He has great intelligence and fine political antennae* (ie is very sensitive to trends (TREND), etc in politics). ⇨ picture at BUTTERFLY. **2** (*pl* antennas or **antennae**) (*esp US*) = AERIAL¹: *radar antennas.*

anterior /ænˈtɪəriə(r)/ *adj* [usu attrib] (*fml*) coming before in position or time; nearer the front. Compare POSTERIOR.

ante-room /ˈæntiruːm, -rʊm/ (also **antechamber**) n a room where people can wait before entering a larger or more important room.

anthem /ˈænθəm/ n a short song composed for a group of singers accompanied by an organ²(1), often with words taken from the Bible. See also NATIONAL ANTHEM.

anthill /ˈænthɪl/ n a pile of earth, etc formed by ants (ANT) over their nest.

anthology /ænˈθɒlədʒi/ n a collection of poems or pieces of writing on the same subject or by the same writer: *an anthology of love poetry*.

anthracite /ˈænθrəsaɪt/ n [U] a very hard type of coal that burns without producing a lot of smoke or flames.

anthrax /ˈænθræks/ n [U] a serious disease affecting sheep, cattle and sometimes people. It can cause death.

anthrop(o)- *comb form* of human beings: *anthropology*.

anthropoid /ˈænθrəpɔɪd/ adj resembling a human in form: *anthropoid ancestors of modern humans*.
▶ **anthropoid** n any of a group of large apes (APE) that resemble humans.

anthropology /ˌænθrəˈpɒlədʒi/ n [U] the study of the human race, esp of its origins, development, customs and beliefs.
▶ **anthropological** /ˌænθrəpəˈlɒdʒɪkl/ adj.
anthropologist /ˌænθrəˈpɒlədʒɪst/ n a person who studies anthropology.

anthropomorphic /ˌænθrəpəˈmɔːfɪk/ adj treating gods or animals as human in form and personality.
▶ **anthropomorphism** /ˌænθrəpəˈmɔːfɪzəm/ n [U].

anti /ˈænti/ prep in opposition to sb/sth; against sb/sth: *They're completely anti the new proposals*. Compare PRO¹.

anti- *pref* (used widely with ns and adjs) **1** opposed to; against: *anti-aircraft* ○ *antisocial*. Compare PRO-. **2** the opposite of: *anti-hero* ○ *anticlockwise*. **3** preventing: *antiseptic* ○ *antifreeze*.

anti-aircraft /ˌænti ˈeəkrɑːft; US -kræft/ adj designed to destroy enemy aircraft: *anti-aircraft guns/ missiles*.

antibiotic /ˌæntibaɪˈɒtɪk/ n, adj (a substance, eg PENICILLIN) that can destroy or prevent the growth of bacteria and cure infections: *The doctor has put me on (a course of) antibiotics* (ie told me to take them).

antibody /ˈæntibɒdi/ n a substance formed in the blood to fight against disease.

anticipate /ænˈtɪsɪpeɪt/ v **1(a)** to expect sth: [Vn, V.*ing*] *Do you anticipate (meeting) any trouble?* [V.*that*] *We anticipate that demand is likely to increase*. [also V.n *ing*]. **(b)** to see what is going to happen or what will need to be done and take action to prepare for it in advance: [Vn] *their ability to anticipate and respond to changes in fashion* [V.*that*] *We had anticipated that the weather would turn cold and had taken our coats*. [V.*wh*] *A good general can anticipate what the enemy will do*. **2** (*fml*) to do sth before it can be done by sb else: [Vn] *When Scott reached the South Pole he found Amundsen had anticipated him*. [Vn, V.n *ing*] *We anticipated their (making a) complaint by writing a full report ourselves*. **3** to think with pleasure and excitement about sth that is going to happen: [Vn] *We eagerly anticipated the day we would leave school*. [also V.*ing*]. ▶ **anticipatory** /ænˌtɪsɪˈpeɪtəri/ adj (*fml*): *a fast anticipatory movement by the goalkeeper*.

anticipation /ænˌtɪsɪˈpeɪʃn/ n [U] **1** the action or state of anticipating sth: *In anticipation of bad weather we took plenty of warm clothes*. **2** the excited feeling one has when expecting sth pleasant to happen: *Her eyes were sparkling with excitement and anticipation*.

anticlimax /ˌæntiˈklaɪmæks/ n a disappointing end to an exciting or interesting series of events: *The trip itself was a bit of an anticlimax after all the excitement of planning it*. ▶ **anticlimactic** /ˌæntiklaɪˈmæktɪk/ adj (*fml*).

anticlockwise /ˌæntiˈklɒkwaɪz/ (also *esp US* **counter-clockwise**) adv, adj in the opposite direction to the way in which the hands of a clock move round: *Turn the key anti'clockwise/in an ˌanticlockwise diˈrection*. Compare CLOCKWISE.

antics /ˈæntɪks/ n [pl] strange or silly behaviour which is intended to cause amusement but which sometimes causes disapproval: *laughing at the clown's silly antics* ○ (*fig*) *boardroom antics*.

anticyclone /ˌæntiˈsaɪkləʊn/ n an area of high air pressure which produces settled weather and clear skies. Compare DEPRESSION 4.

antidote /ˈæntidəʊt/ n ~ (**to sth**) **1** a substance that stops or reduces the effects of a poison or disease: *an antidote to snake-bites*. **2** anything that takes away the effects of sth unpleasant: *The holiday was a marvellous antidote to the pressures of work*.

antifreeze /ˈæntifriːz/ n [U] a liquid added to water to prevent it freezing, used esp in the RADIATOR(2) of a motor vehicle.

antigen /ˈæntɪdʒən/ n (*medical*) a substance that, when introduced into the body, can cause disease. The body usu produces antibodies (ANTIBODY) to fight against antigens.

anti-hero /ˈænti hɪərəʊ/ n (pl **-oes**) the main character in a story or play but one who does not have the qualities typically expected, eg courage and strength.

antihistamine /ˌæntiˈhɪstəmiːn/ n [C, U] (*medical*) any of a variety of drugs used to treat allergies (ALLERGY), esp hay fever (HAY).

antimony /ˈæntɪməni; US ˈæntɪməʊni/ n [U] (*symb* **Sb**) a chemical element. Antimony is an easily broken whitish metal used esp in making alloys (ALLOY¹). ⇨ App 7.

antipathy /ænˈtɪpəθi/ n ~ (**to/towards sb/sth**); ~ (**between A and B**) **(a)** [U] a feeling of strong dislike: *She made no attempt to hide her feelings of antipathy*. **(b)** [C usu *sing*] an instance of this: *There exists a profound antipathy between the two men*. ○ *He showed a marked antipathy to foreigners*. ▶ **antipathetic** /ˌæntɪpəˈθetɪk/ adj ~ (**to/towards sb/sth**) (*fml*) showing or feeling antipathy: *deeply antipathetic to Communism*.

anti-personnel /ˌænti ˌpɜːsəˈnel/ adj (of weapons) designed to kill or injure people, not to destroy property, vehicles, etc: *anti-personnel mines*.

antiperspirant /ˌæntiˈpɜːspərənt/ n [C, U] a substance that people use, esp under the arms, to prevent or reduce perspiration (PERSPIRE). See also DEODORANT.

Antipodes /ænˈtɪpədiːz/ n the Antipodes [pl] (*often joc*) (used esp by people in the northern HEMISPHERE) Australia and New Zealand. ▶ **Antipodean** /ˌæntɪpəˈdiːən/ adj: *an Antipodean holiday*.

antiquarian /ˌæntɪˈkweəriən/ adj [usu attrib] of or concerning the study, collection or sale of valuable old objects, esp books: *an antiquarian bookshop*.

antiquary /ˈæntɪkwəri; US ˈæntɪkweri/ (also **antiquarian**) n a person who studies, collects or sells old and valuable objects.

antiquated /ˈæntɪkweɪtɪd/ adj (*usu derog*) (of things or ideas) old-fashioned and no longer appropriate: *an antiquated bus* ○ *antiquated working conditions*.

antique /ænˈtiːk/ adj **1** old and valuable: *an antique vase/fan* ○ *antique jewellery/lace/furniture*. **2(a)** (*sometimes derog*) belonging to the past; old-fashioned: *photographs mounted in an antique style*.

[V.speech] = verb + direct speech   [V.*that*] = verb + *that* clause   [V.*wh*] = verb + *who, how,* etc clause

(b) that has existed for a long time; very old: *an antique farmhouse.* ⇨ note at OLD.

▶ **antique** *n* an object, eg a piece of furniture, that is old and valuable: *an an'tique shop* (ie one that sells antiques) ○ *It appears that the chest is a valuable antique.*

antiquity /æn'tɪkwəti/ *n* **1** [U] the ancient past, esp the times of the Greeks and Romans: *The origins of the practice are lost in antiquity.* ○ *The trade flourished until late classical antiquity.* **2** [U] great age: *Athens is a city of great antiquity* (ie an ancient city). **3** [C usu *pl*] an object from ancient times: *a museum full of Greek and Roman antiquities* (eg coins, statues and ornaments).

anti-Semite /ˌænti 'siːmaɪt; *US* 'sem-/ *n* a person who hates Jews. ▶ **anti-Semitic** /ˌænti sə'mɪtɪk/ *adj*: *anti-Semitic feelings/remarks.* **anti-Semitism** /ˌænti 'semətɪzəm/ *n* [U].

antiseptic /ˌænti'septɪk/ *n* [C,U] a substance that helps to prevent infection in a wound, esp by destroying bacteria: *a bottle of antiseptic.*

▶ **antiseptic** *adj* **1** preventing infection by destroying bacteria: *an ˌantiseptic 'ointment/'cream/'lozenge.* **2** thoroughly clean and free from bacteria: *an ˌantiseptic 'bandage.* **3** clean and tidy but lacking character or excitement: *The room is not helped by its rather antiseptic furnishings.*

antisocial /ˌænti'səʊʃl/ *adj* (*derog*) **1** opposed to the laws and customs of an organized community; causing annoyance and disapproval in other people: *ˌantisocial be'haviour* ○ *antisocial elements* (ie people who show little respect for others). **2** avoiding the company of others; not friendly: *work antisocial hours* (ie at different times from most people, so that it is difficult to meet others socially) ○ *I think it's very antisocial of you not to come to the party.*

anti-tank /ˌænti'tæŋk/ *adj* [attrib] designed to destroy enemy tanks: *ˌanti-tank 'missiles.*

antithesis /æn'tɪθəsɪs/ *n* (*pl* **antitheses** /æn'tɪθəsiːz/) (*fml*) **1(a)** [C usu *sing*] ~ (**of sth/sb**) the exact opposite: *Slavery is the antithesis of freedom.* **(b)** [U] contrast; opposition: *The style of his speech was in complete antithesis to the previous one.* **2** [C,U] the placing together of opposing words or ideas in order to show a contrast: *'Give me liberty, or give me death' is an example of antithesis.* ▶ **antithetical** /ˌænti'θetɪkl/ *adj* ~ (**to sth**): *His approach is antithetical to all modern methods.*

antler /'æntlə(r)/ *n* each of the two horns with short branches that grow on the head of a male deer. ⇨ picture at DEER.

antonym /'æntənɪm/ *n* a word that is opposite in meaning to another word: *'Old' has two possible antonyms: 'young' and 'new'.* Compare SYNONYM.

anus /'eɪnəs/ *n* (*pl* **anuses**) (*anatomy*) the opening through which solid waste matter leaves the body. ⇨ picture at DIGESTIVE SYSTEM. ▶ **anal** /'eɪnl/ *adj*.

anvil /'ænvɪl/ *n* an iron block on which a BLACKSMITH puts hot pieces of metal before hammering them into shape.

anxiety /æŋ'zaɪəti/ *n* **1** ~ (**about/over sth**) **(a)** [U] a nervous feeling caused by fear that sth bad is going to happen; worry: *sleepless nights due to anxiety and depression* ○ *We waited for news with a growing sense of anxiety.* **(b)** [C] a worry or fear about sth: *anxieties about money* ○ *The doctor's report relieved all their anxieties.* **2** [U] ~ **for sth/to do sth** a strong wish for sth or to do sth: *his anxiety to please.*

anxious /'æŋkʃəs/ *adj* **1** ~ (**about sb/sth**) feeling worried or nervous: *an anxious mother* ○ *feel anxious about the future.* **2** [attrib] causing or showing anxiety: *We had a few anxious moments before the plane landed safely.* **3** [pred] ~ **for sth/(for sb) to do sth/that...** wanting sth very much: *anxious for promotion* ○ *I'm very anxious to meet him.* ○ *They are anxious not to give* (ie very much want to

avoid giving) *a bad impression.* ○ *We are very anxious for him to telephone home.* ○ *They are anxious that the report should be published as soon as possible.* ▶ **anxiously** *adv*: *'Don't you like it?' he asked anxiously.*

any¹ /'eni/ *indef det* **1** (used instead of *some* in negative sentences and in questions; after *if/whether*; after *hardly, never, without*, etc; and after such *vs* as *prevent, ban, avoid, forbid*) **(a)** (used with uncountable *ns*) an amount of sth, however large or small: *I didn't eat any meat.* ○ *Do you know any French?* ○ *I've got hardly any money.* ○ *We got home without any difficulty.* ○ *To avoid any delay please phone your order direct.* ○ *It didn't seem to be any distance* (ie It seemed a very short distance) *to the road.* **(b)** (used with plural countable *ns*) one or more: *I've never read any books by Tolstoy.* ○ *Are there any stamps in that drawer?* ○ *I wonder whether you have any suggestions?* ○ *You can't go out without any shoes.* Compare SOME¹. **2(a)** (used with singular countable *ns*) one of a number of things, esp when it does not matter which: *Take any book you like.* ○ *Give me a pen — any colour will do.* ○ *Phone me any day next week.* **(b)** (used with singular countable *ns* in negative sentences or sentences implying doubt; also used after *if, whether*) a; one: *I can't see any door in this room.* ○ *I doubt whether any company could have succeeded.* **3** every; no matter which: *Any fool could tell you that.* ○ *You'll find me here at any hour of the day.* ○ *Any train from this platform stops at Gatwick.* See also IN ANY CASE (CASE¹). See also in ANY EVENT (EVENT). See also AT ANY RATE (RATE¹). **4** (used in negative sentences and after *if* or *whether*) a normal; an ordinary: *It isn't just any day — it's my birthday!*

■ **'any time** *adv* at whatever time you like: *Come round any time.*

any² /'eni/ *indef pron* **1** (used in negative sentences and in questions instead of *some*; after *if/whether*; and after *hardly, never, without*, etc) an amount or number, however large or small: *I can't give you any.* ○ *I need some stamps. Have you got any?* ○ *I wonder whether there are any left.* ○ *Please let me know how many are coming, if any.* ○ *She spent hardly any of the money.* ○ *He returned home without any of the others.* **2** one of a number of people or things, esp when it does not matter which: *If you recognize 'any of the people in the photograph, please tell us.* Compare SOME³. **IDM** **sb isn't 'having any** (*infml*) sb is not interested or does not agree: *I suggested sharing the cost, but he wasn't having any.*

any³ /'eni/ *indef adv* **1** (used esp to emphasize *faster, slower, better*, etc in negative sentences and in questions, and after *if* or *whether*) at all: *I can't run any faster.* ○ *Is your father feeling any better?* ○ *If it were any further we wouldn't be able to get there.* ○ *I can't afford to spend any more on food.* **2** (*US infml*) (used to emphasize negative *vs* or questions) at all: *The dog won't disturb us any.*

■ **any 'more** (*US* **anymore**) *adv* (used in negative sentences and in questions) **(a)** now; still: *She doesn't live here any more.* **(b)** again or any longer starting from now: *I don't want to see you any more.* ○ *Why should I pretend any more?*

anybody /'enibɒdi/ (also **anyone**) *indef pron* **1** (used in negative sentences and in questions instead of *someone*; after *if/whether*; after *hardly, never, without*, etc, and after such *vs* as *prevent, ban, avoid, forbid*) any person; any people: *Did anybody see you?* ○ *Hardly anybody came.* ○ *He left without speaking to anyone else.* **2** any person at all, regardless of who they are: *Anybody can see that it's wrong.* ○ *The exercises are so simple that almost anyone can do them.* **3** (in negative sentences) a person of importance: *She wasn't anybody before she got that job.* Compare NOBODY *n*.

anyhow /'enihaʊ/ *indef adv* (*infml*) **1** (also **anyway**) (used when saying sth to confirm or support an idea or argument just mentioned) in addition; BESIDES: *It's too expensive and anyhow the colour doesn't suit you.* ○ *It's too late now, anyhow.* **2** (also **anyway**) in spite of sth; even so: *The water was cold but I had a bath anyway.* **3** (also **anyway**) (used when changing the subject of a conversation, ending the conversation, or returning to a subject after an interruption): *Anyhow, let's forget about that for the moment.* ○ *Anyway, I'd better go now — I'll see you tomorrow.* ○ *Anyhow, as I was saying...* **4** in a careless and untidy way: *She threw her clothes down all anyhow.*

anyone /'eniwʌn/ *indef pron* = ANYBODY.

anyplace /'enipleɪs/ *indef adv* (*US*) = ANYWHERE.

anything /'eniθɪŋ/ *indef pron* **1** (used in negative sentences and in questions instead of *something*; after *if/whether*; after *hardly, never, without*, etc; and after such *vs* as *prevent, ban, avoid, forbid*) any thing: *Did she tell you anything interesting?* ○ *There's never anything worth watching on TV.* ○ *If you remember anything at all, please let us know.* ○ *Do you want anything else?* **2** any thing of importance: *Is there anything* (ie any truth) *in these rumours?* **3** any thing at all: *I'm very hungry — I'll eat anything.* **IDM** **anything but** definitely not: *The hotel was anything but cheap.* **as happy, quick, etc as anything** (*infml*) very happy, quick, etc: *I felt as pleased as anything.* **not anything like** (*infml*) **1** not at all like; completely different from: *He isn't anything like my first boss.* **2** absolutely not: *The film wasn't anything like as good as ET.* **not for anything** (*infml*) definitely not: *I wouldn't give it up for anything.* **or anything** (*infml*) or another thing of a similar type: *If you want to call a meeting or anything, just let me know.*

anyway /'eniweɪ/ *indef adv* = ANYHOW 1,2,3.

anywhere /'eniweə(r)/ (*US* also **anyplace**) *indef adv* **1** (used in negative sentences and in questions instead of *somewhere*) in, at or to any place: *I can't see it anywhere.* ○ *Did you go anywhere interesting?* ○ *Many of these animals are not found anywhere else.* ○ *He's never been anywhere outside Britain.* **2** in, at or to any place, esp when it does not matter where: *Put the box down anywhere.* ○ *An accident can happen anywhere.*
▶ **anywhere** *indef pron* any place: *I haven't anywhere to stay.* ○ *Do you know anywhere (where) I can buy a second-hand computer?*

aorta /eɪ'ɔːtə/ *n* the main ARTERY that carries blood from the left side of the heart.

apace /ə'peɪs/ *adv* (*dated or rhet*) quickly: *Work is continuing/proceeding apace.*

apart /ə'pɑːt/ *adv part* **1** (of people or things) separated by a distance: *The two houses stood 500 metres apart.* ○ *Her eyes are quite wide/far apart.* ○ *Their birthdays are only three days apart.* ○ (*fig*) *The two sides in the negotiation are still a long way apart* (ie are far from reaching an agreement). **2** to or on one side; aside: *She keeps herself apart from* (ie does not mix with) *other people.* ○ *His tomb stands remote and apart.* ○ *His use of language puts/sets him apart from* (ie makes him better than) *other modern writers.* **3** separate(ly); in different directions: *She and her husband are living apart.* ○ *It's often best to keep friendship and business strictly apart.* ○ *Over the years, Rosie and I had drifted apart.* ○ *I can't tell the twins apart* (ie recognize the difference between them). **4** into pieces: *I'm sorry, the cup just came/fell apart in my hands.* ○ *The bomb ripped the plane apart.* ○ *He enjoys taking old cars apart.* ○ (*fig*) *When his wife died his world fell apart.* **5** (used after a *n* to indicate that sth has been dealt with sufficiently or is being excluded from what follows) except for; excluding: *These considerations apart, the plan seems likely to succeed.* ○ *Edwards apart, there*

were no suitable candidates. ○ *Joking apart, what did you really think of the show?* **IDM** **be worlds apart** ⇨ WORLD.
■ **apart from** (also *esp US* **aside from**) *prep* **1** except for sth: *Apart from being a bit overweight he's quite healthy.* **2** in addition to sb/sth; as well as sb/sth: *Who else was there apart from your parents?* ○ *Apart from going to Italy and Spain, he will also visit Britain.*

apartheid /ə'pɑːthaɪt, -heɪt/ *n* [U] (formerly in S Africa) a political system in which members of different races had different political and social rights and lived, travelled, spent their free time, etc apart from each other.

apartment /ə'pɑːtmənt/ *n* **1** (*US*) = FLAT² 1. **2** a set of rooms rented for a holiday: *self-catering holiday apartments.* **3** (often *pl*) a single room in a house, esp a large or famous one: *You can visit the whole palace except for the private apartments.*
■ **a'partment block** *n* (*Brit*) (*US* **a'partment house**) a tall building with flats on each floor. See also BLOCK¹ 3.

apathy /'æpəθi/ *n* [U] a lack of interest, enthusiasm or concern: *There is a certain apathy about local elections among the public.*
▶ **apathetic** /ˌæpə'θetɪk/ *adj* showing or feeling apathy: *be totally apathetic about world affairs.* **apathetically** /-kli/ *adv.*

apes

gibbon

orang-utan

gorilla

chimpanzee

ape /eɪp/ *n* any of a group of animals similar to large monkeys but without a tail. ⇨ picture.
▶ **ape** *v* to copy sb/sth: [Vn] *A number of actors have tried to ape his style.*

aperitif /əˌperə'tiːf/ *n* a drink, often containing alcohol, that one has before a meal.

aperture /'æpətʃə(r)/ *n* **1** a narrow opening. **2** an opening through which light enters a camera and which can be adjusted in size: *What aperture are you using?*

Apex (also **APEX**) /'eɪpeks/ *abbr* Advance Purchase Excursion (a system that offers cheaper air fares when tickets are reserved a certain time in advance).

apex /'eɪpeks/ *n* [C usu *sing*] the top or highest point: *the apex of a triangle* ○ (*fig*) *At 41 he'd reached the apex of his career.*

aphid /'eɪfɪd/ *n* any of a group of very small insects, eg GREENFLY, that are harmful to plants.

aphorism /'æfərɪzəm/ *n* a short remark which contains a general truth. ▶ **aphoristic** /ˌæfə'rɪstɪk/ *adj.*

aphrodisiac /ˌæfrə'dɪziæk/ *n, adj* (a substance or drug) causing sexual desire.

apiary /'eɪpiəri; *US* -ieri/ *n* a place where bees are kept.

apiece /ə'piːs/ *adv* to, for or by each one of a group: *cakes costing 50p apiece* ○ *The teams scored one goal apiece.*

aplenty /ə'plenti/ adj (fml or rhet) (used after ns) in large amounts: the promise of jobs aplenty.

aplomb /ə'plɒm/ n [U] confidence, esp in difficult situations: The singer performed **with (great) aplomb**.

apocalypse /ə'pɒkəlɪps/ n **1** [C] a REVELATION, esp about the future of the world. **2 the Apocalypse** [sing] the end of the world, esp as described in the Bible. **3** [sing] an event of extraordinary importance or violence: a stock-market apocalypse.
► **apocalyptic** /ə,pɒkə'lɪptɪk/ adj **1** describing or prophesying (PROPHESY) a great disaster or the total destruction of sth, esp the end of the world: apocalyptic visions of the effects of global warming. **2** resembling the end of the world: an apocalyptic event.

apocryphal /ə'pɒkrɪfl/ adj not true; invented: Most of the stories about his life are probably apocryphal.

apogee /'æpədʒiː/ n **1** (astronomy) the position in the ORBIT(1) of the moon, a planet or another object in space when it is furthest from the earth. **2** the highest point of sth; the CLIMAX(1) of sth: at the apogee of his career.

apolitical /,eɪpə'lɪtɪkl/ adj not interested or involved in politics.

apologetic /ə,pɒlə'dʒetɪk/ adj ~ **(about sth)** feeling or showing regret because one has done sth wrong or caused difficulty for sb: an apologetic letter/smile ○ He was very apologetic about arriving late. ► **apologetically** /-kli/ adv: 'I'm afraid the car broke down,' he said apologetically.

apologist /ə'pɒlədʒɪst/ n ~ **(for sth)** a person who defends ideas or beliefs by logical argument: government apologists ○ the apologists for nuclear power.

apologize, -ise /ə'pɒlədʒaɪz/ v ~ **(to sb) (for sth)** to say one is sorry, esp for having done sth wrong: [V] There's no need to apologize. [Vpr] I must apologize for not being able to meet you. ○ Please apologize to your sister and say I'll see her on Tuesday.

apology /ə'pɒlədʒi/ n **1(a)** [C, U] ~ **(to sb) (for sth)** a word or statement to say one is sorry for having done sth wrong or for upsetting sb: offer/make/demand/accept an apology ○ a letter of apology ○ I owe you an apology. ○ Please accept our apologies for the delay. **(b)** [C often pl] an expression of regret that one cannot attend a meeting, etc or must leave early: apologies for absence ○ Apologies were received from Mr Hart and Miss Rowe. ○ I **made my apologies** (to my host) and left early. **2** [C] (fml) an explanation or a defence of one's beliefs or behaviour: I make no apology for this decision. **3** [sing] ~ **for sth** (derog) an inferior example of sth: Please excuse this apology for a letter — I shall write at greater length next week.

apoplexy /'æpəpleksi/ n [U] a sudden loss of the ability to feel or move, caused by an injury to the brain: (fig) His late arrival almost gave the organizers apoplexy (ie made them extremely worried and annoyed). Compare STROKE 8.
► **apoplectic** /,æpə'plektɪk/ adj **1** of or suffering from apoplexy: an apoplectic fit. **2** (infml) red in the face; easily made angry; very angry: apoplectic with fury.

apostasy /ə'pɒstəsi/ n [U] the abandoning of one's religious or political beliefs or principles: be accused of apostasy and blasphemy.
► **apostate** /ə'pɒsteɪt/ n a person who abandons her or his former beliefs or principles.

a posteriori /,eɪ ˌpɒsteri'ɔːraɪ/ adj, adv (fml) (using reasoning that proceeds) from known facts to probable causes, eg saying 'The boys are very tired so they must have walked a long way'. Compare A PRIORI.

apostle /ə'pɒsl/ n **1 Apostle** any of the twelve men sent by Christ to spread news of him and his teaching. **2** a person who strongly supports and promotes

a specified new idea, belief or attitude: an apostle of design/free enterprise.
► **apostolic** /,æpə'stɒlɪk/ adj **1** of the Apostles or their teaching. **2** of the Pope: a report by the church's apostolic visitor.

apostrophe /ə'pɒstrəfi/ n the sign (') used to show that one or more letters or numbers have been omitted (as in can't for cannot, I'm for I am, '76 for 1976, etc), the POSSESSIVE(2) form of nouns (as in the boy's/boys' meaning of the boy/boys), and the PLURAL of letters (as in There are two l's in 'bell'). ⇨ App 3.

apothecary /ə'pɒθəkəri; US -keri/ n (arch) a person who prepared and sold medicines.

apotheosis /ə,pɒθi'əʊsɪs/ n (pl apotheoses /-siːz/) (fml) (usu sing) **1** the highest or most perfect development of sth: The legends of King Arthur represent the apotheosis of chivalry. **2** a declaration that a person has become a god: the apotheosis of a Roman Emperor.

appal (US also **appall**) /ə'pɔːl/ v (-ll-) to make sb feel horror or disgust; to shock sb deeply: [Vn] The newspaper reports of starving children appalled me. [Vn.that] I was appalled that the fire was spreading so rapidly. [Vn.to inf] It appals me to see how many fine old buildings are being knocked down.
► **appalled** adj ~ **(at sth)** feeling or showing horror or disgust: an appalled silence ○ Fanny watched appalled. ○ We were appalled at the prospect of having to miss our son's wedding.
appalling adj (infml) shocking; extremely bad: I've never seen such appalling behaviour. ○ I find much modern architecture quite appalling. **appallingly** adv: appallingly difficult circumstances.

apparatchik /,æpə'rɑːtʃɪk/ n (Russian esp derog or joc) an official in a large, esp political, organization: party/Tory apparatchiks.

apparatus /,æpə'reɪtəs; US -'rætəs/ n (rare pl **apparatuses**) **1** [U] the equipment needed for a particular activity or task: laboratory apparatus ○ Firemen needed breathing apparatus to enter the burning house. ○ The vaulting-horse is a difficult piece of apparatus to master. ⇨ note at MACHINE. **2** [C usu sing] the complex structure of an organization: the party apparatus. **3** [C usu sing] (anatomy) a system of organs in the body: the respiratory/vocal apparatus.

apparel /ə'pærəl/ n [U] (dated or fml) clothing; dress: lords and ladies in rich apparel.

apparent /ə'pærənt/ adj **1** [usu pred] ~ **(in/from sth)**; ~ **(to sb) (that...)** clearly seen or understood; obvious: Certain problems were apparent from the outset. ○ **It became apparent that** she was going to die. ○ Then, **for no apparent reason**, she began to dislike school. ○ Their motives, as will soon become apparent (ie as you will soon see), are completely selfish. **2** [usu attrib] seeming real or true, but not necessarily so: Her apparent indifference made him even more nervous. ○ Their affluence is more apparent than real (ie They are not as rich as they seem to be).
► **apparently** adv according to what one has read or heard; as it seems: He had apparently escaped by bribing a guard. ○ Apparently they're getting divorced.

apparition /,æpə'rɪʃn/ n **1** a ghost or an image of a person who is dead: the apparition of his lost Beatrice ○ You look as though you've seen an apparition. ○ Apparitions of a lady in white robes have been reported. **2** a person or thing that appears strange or not real: a weird apparition in fancy dress.

appeal /ə'piːl/ v **1** ~ **to sb (for sth)**; ~ **for sth** to make a deeply felt, usu urgent request: [Vpr] Nationalist leaders appealed for calm. ○ The organization appealed to the government for financial support. ○ I am appealing on behalf of the famine victims. [Vpr.to inf] The police appealed to the crowd not to panic. [also V.speech]. **2** ~ **(to sb)** to be attractive or interesting to sb: [V, Vpr] *The idea of camping has never appealed (to me).* [Vpr] *Do these paintings appeal to you?* **3** ~ **to sth** to persuade sb to do sth by suggesting that if they want to be good, just, reasonable, etc they must act in a particular way: [Vpr] *appeal to sb's sense of justice* ○ *If you want people to return to the negotiating table, you have to appeal to their better natures, not annoy them further.* **4(a)** ~ **(to sb);** ~ **(against sth)** to ask sb in authority to make a decision, or to change one made by sb less senior than them: [Vpr] *appeal against disqualification* [Vpr, Vpr.*to* inf] *The captain appealed to the umpire (to stop play).* **(b)** ~ **(to sth) (against sth)** (*law*) to take a legal case to a higher court where it can be judged again: [V] *I've decided not to appeal.* [Vpr] *She appealed to the high court against her sentence.*

▶ **appeal** *n* **1(a)** [C] ~ **(for sth)** a deeply felt, usu urgent, request: *make/answer an appeal for help/food/extra staff* ○ *a charity appeal.* **(b)** [U] a request for help or sympathy: *Her eyes held a look of silent appeal.* **2** [U] attraction; interest: *Does jazz hold any appeal for you?* ○ *The new fashion soon lost its appeal.* See also SEX APPEAL. **3** [C] ~ **to sth** an indirect suggestion that any good, just, reasonable, etc person would act in a particular way: *relying on an appeal to his finer feelings.* **4** [C] **(a)** ~ **(against sth)** a request that a decision be changed: *an appeal against the 3-match ban.* **(b)** (*law*) an act of asking for a legal case to be judged again: *lodge an appeal* ○ *have the right of appeal* ○ *an appeal court.* See also COURT OF APPEAL.

appealing *adj* **1** attractive; charming: *I don't find young babies very appealing.* ○ *The idea of a trip abroad is certainly appealing.* **2** making sb feel pity or sympathy: *an appealing glance.* **appealingly** *adv: He looked at her appealingly.*

appear /əˈpɪə(r)/ *v* **1(a)** to come into view; to become visible: [Vpr] *A ship appeared on the horizon.* ○ *A light appeared at the end of the tunnel.* ○ *A new type of glue has appeared in the shops.* [V] *Three days later a rash appeared.* (**b**) to arrive: [V] *He promised to be here at four o'clock but didn't appear until six.* (**c**) to be mentioned: [V, Vpr] *Their names do not appear (on the register).* **2** to begin to exist or be known; to become clear or EVIDENT: [V] *New findings have appeared that cast doubt on her conviction.* [Vpr] *This problem first appeared in the inner cities.* **3** (of a book, piece of writing, programme, etc) to be published or broadcast: [V] *His new book will be appearing in the spring.* ○ *The news appeared next day on the front page.* ○ *These allegations appear in a forthcoming documentary.* **4** to present oneself or be seen publicly: [Vpr] *appear on TV* [V-n] *appear as Falstaff* [V] *The tenor soloist is unable to appear tonight because of illness.* **5(a)** to attend a lawcourt in order to give evidence or answer a charge: [V-n] *appear as a witness* [Vpr] *appear before magistrates* ○ *I have to appear in court (on a charge of drunken driving).* (**b**) ~ **for/on behalf of sb** to act as sb's lawyer in court: [Vpr] *appear for the defendant/prosecution.* **6** to give the impression of being or doing sth; to seem: [V-adj] *The streets appeared deserted.* [V-n] *He appears a perfectly normal person.* [V.*to* inf] *She appears to have many friends.* [V.*to* inf, V.*that*] *There appears to have been/It appears that there has been a mistake.* ○ *You appear to have made/It appears that you have made a mistake.* [V.*that*] *It would appear that they were wrong.* [Vadv] *'Has he been found guilty?' 'It appears so/not.'* ○ *It appears as if/as though she's lost interest in her job.*

appearance /əˈpɪərəns/ *n* **1** [C usu *sing*] the act of becoming visible or noticeable; the arrival of sb/sth: *I don't want to go to the party but I suppose I'd better **put in an appearance** (ie go there and stay a short time).* ○ *The sudden appearance of a policeman*

caused the thief to run away. ○ *the appearance of organic vegetables in supermarkets* ○ *They finally made their appearance* (ie appeared, arrived) *at 11.30.* **2** [C usu *sing*] an act of being published or broadcast: *The appearance of these claims in the media is totally unjustified.* **3** [C] an act of appearing in public as a performer, etc or in a lawcourt: *His first appearance on stage was at the age of three.* **4** [C, U] the outward form sb/sth has; what sb/sth appears to be though in fact they may not be: *Fine clothes added to his strikingly handsome appearance.* ○ *The building was like a prison in appearance.* ○ *She **gave every appearance** of being extremely rich. Don't **judge by appearances** — appearances can be misleading.* ○ *To all appearances he was dead.* ○ *There's no point in **keeping up appearances** (ie hiding the true situation and making a show) when everyone knows we're nearly bankrupt.*

appease /əˈpiːz/ *v* to reduce the intensity of sb's feelings, esp by satisfying their needs or demands partly or in full: [Vn] *measures intended to appease Scottish landowners* ○ *appease sb's anger/hunger/curiosity.* ▶ **appeasement** *n* [U]: *a policy of appeasement.*

appellant /əˈpelənt/ *n* (*law*) a person who appeals to a higher court.

appellation /ˌæpəˈleɪʃn/ *n* (*fml*) a name or title.

append /əˈpend/ *v* ~ **sth (to sth)** (*fml*) to attach or add sth, esp in writing: [Vn, Vnpr] *append one's signature (to a document)* [Vnpr] *append an extra clause to the contract.*

appendage /əˈpendɪdʒ/ *n* a thing that is added to sth larger or that forms a natural part of sth larger: *The elephant's trunk is a highly versatile appendage.* ○ *He treats his wife like a mere appendage.*

appendectomy /ˌæpenˈdektəmi/ *n* [C, U] (*medical*) the removal of the APPENDIX(2) by SURGERY.

appendicitis /əˌpendəˈsaɪtɪs/ *n* [U] a medical condition causing the APPENDIX(2) to swell and become painful.

appendix /əˈpendɪks/ *n* **1** (*pl* **appendices** /-dɪsiːz/) (abbreviated as *app* in this dictionary) a section giving extra information at the end of a book or document: *This dictionary has several appendices, including one on irregular verbs.* **2** (*pl* **appendixes**) a small bag of tissue(1) shaped like a tube that is attached to the INTESTINE. ▷ picture at DIGESTIVE SYSTEM.

appertain /ˌæpəˈteɪn/ *v* **PHRV** **appertain to sb/sth** (*fml*) to belong or relate to sb/sth; to be appropriate to sb/sth: *the duties and privileges appertaining to one's high office* ○ *Paragraph 14 appertains to the recent change in the law.*

appetite /ˈæpɪtaɪt/ *n* **(a)** [U, C usu *sing*] physical desire, esp for food or pleasure: *When I was sick I completely **lost my appetite**.* ○ *Don't spoil your appetite by eating snacks before meals.* ○ *The long walk has given me a good appetite.* ○ *a person of gross sexual appetites.* (**b**) [C] ~ **(for sth)** a strong desire for sth: *He had no appetite for the fight.* ○ *The preview was intended to **whet your appetite**.* ○ *He has an amazing appetite for hard work.*

appetizer, -iser /ˈæpɪtaɪzə(r)/ *n* a thing that is eaten or drunk before a meal to stimulate the appetite: *Olives make a simple appetizer.*

appetizing, -ising /ˈæpɪtaɪzɪŋ/ *adj* (of food, etc) stimulating the appetite: *an appetizing smell from the kitchen* ○ *The list of ingredients sounds very appetizing.* Compare UNAPPETIZING.

applaud /əˈplɔːd/ *v* **1** to show approval of sb/sth by clapping (CLAP[1]) one's hands: [V, Vn] *The crowd applauded (him/the performance) for five minutes.* **2** to praise sb/sth; to approve of sth: [Vn] *I applaud your decision.*

---

applause /ə'plɔːz/ n [U] approval expressed esp by clapping (CLAP¹ 1) the hands: *He sat down amid deafening applause.* ○ *The audience gave her a big* **round of applause.** ○ *The performance received tumultuous applause from the huge crowd.*

apple /'æpl/ n **(a)** a round fruit with firm juicy flesh. Apples have green, red or yellow skin when ripe: *peel an apple* ○ *an apple* '*pie* ○ *apple* '*sauce.* ⇨ picture at FRUIT. See also COOKER 2, EATING APPLE, TOFFEE-APPLE. **(b)** (also '**apple tree**) a tree bearing this fruit. **IDM the ‚apple of sb's 'eye** a person or thing that is loved more than any other: *She is the apple of her father's eye.* **in ‚apple-pie 'order** (*infml*) very neatly arranged.
■ '**apple-cart** n **IDM** upset the/sb's apple-cart ⇨ UPSET.

appliance /ə'plaɪəns/ n an instrument or device for a specific purpose or task: *electrical/kitchen/surgical appliances* ○ *They sell all sorts of domestic appliances — washing-machines, dishwashers, liquidizers and so on.* ⇨ note at MACHINE.

applicable /ə'plɪkəbl, 'æplɪkəbl/ adj [pred] ~ (**to sb/sth**) relevant, appropriate or suitable: *This part of the form is not applicable* (ie does not apply) *to foreign students.* ○ *Give details of children where applicable* (ie if you have any). ▶ **applicability** /ə‚plɪkə'bɪləti, ‚æplɪk-/ n [U]: *the applicability of such judgements to the situation in question.*

applicant /'æplɪkənt/ n ~ (**for sth**) a person who applies for sth, eg for a job, a place on a course, or a loan: *credit card applicants* ○ *There were over 100 applicants for the marketing manager's post.*

application /‚æplɪ'keɪʃn/ n **1(a)** [U] ~ (**to sb**) the action or process of making a formal request: *Keys are available* **on application** *to the principal.* **(b)** [C] ~ (**for sth/to do sth**) a formal request for sth: *a planning/passport/mortgage application* ○ *an application to join the tennis club* ○ *We received 400 applications for the job.* ○ *an application form* (ie a form on which to apply for sth). **2(a)** [U, C] ~ (**of sth**) the action or an instance of putting or spreading sth onto sth else: *lotion for external application only* (ie to be put on the skin, not swallowed) ○ *three applications per day.* **(b)** [C] a substance put onto sth: *an application to relieve muscle pain.* **3** [U] the action or process of making a rule, etc take effect: *the strict application of the law.* **4** [U, C] ~ (**to sth**) the action or an instance of putting a theory, discovery, etc to practical use: *the application of information technology to school management* ○ *a new invention that will have application/a variety of applications in industry.* **5** [C] (*computing*) a PROGRAM designed to perform a particular task for the user: *a database application* ○ *application software.* **6** [U] intense effort; hard work: *Success as a writer demands great application.*

applied ⇨ APPLY.

appliqué /ə'pliːkeɪ; *US* ‚æplə'keɪ/ n [U] a type of NEEDLEWORK in which pieces of one colour or type of material are sewn or stuck to another larger piece in a design or pattern: *an appliqué bedspread.* ▶ **appliquéd** adj decorated with appliqué: *appliquéd cushions/designs.*

apply /ə'plaɪ/ v (*pt, pp* **applied**) **1** ~ (**to sb**) (**for sth**) to make a formal request: [Vpr] *apply to the publishers for permission to reprint an extract* ○ *apply for a job/grant/passport/visa* [V] *You should apply immediately, in person or by letter.* **2** ~ **sth** (**to sth**) to put or spread sth onto sth: [Vn] *apply the ointment sparingly* [Vnpr] *apply the glue to both surfaces.* **3** to make a law, etc operate or become effective in a particular situation: [Vn] *apply a rule/precept/principle* ○ *apply economic sanctions.* **4(a)** ~ (**to sb/sth**) to be relevant to sb/sth; to operate: [V] *Special*

conditions apply. [Vpr] *What I have said applies only to some of you.* **(b)** ~ **sth** (**to sth**) to make use of sth as relevant or appropriate: [Vn] *apply political pressure* [Vnpr] *apply common sense/ingenuity to the problem* ○ *The word 'readable' could never be applied to any of her books.* **5** ~ **sth** (**to sth**) to use pressure in order to operate or have an effect on sth: [Vnpr] *apply force to the lever* [Vn] *I had to apply the brakes hard.* **6** ~ **sth** (**to sth**) to make practical use of sth: [Vnpr] *The results of this research can be applied to car manufacturing.* [also Vn]. **7** ~ **oneself/sth** (**to sth/doing sth**) to concentrate one's thoughts and energy on a task: [Vn, Vnpr] *You will only pass your exams if you really apply yourself (to your work).* [Vnpr] *We applied our minds to finding a solution.* ▶ **applied** /ə'plaɪd/ adj [usu attrib] used in a practical way; not THEORETICAL(1): *applied mathematics* (eg as used by engineers) ○ *applied linguistics.* Compare PURE 6.

appoint /ə'pɔɪnt/ v **1** ~ **sb** (**as/to sth**); ~ **sb** (**to do sth**) to choose sb for a job or position of responsibility: [Vn] *They have appointed Angela Smith/a new manager.* [Vnpr] *He was appointed to the vacant post.* [Vn.to inf] *Who should we appoint (as) chairperson?* [Vn.to inf] *We must appoint somebody to act as secretary.* **2** ~ **sth** (**for sth**) (*fml*) to fix or decide on sth, esp a time or place: [Vnpr] *appoint a date for a meeting* [Vn] *at the time appointed/the appointed time.*
▶ **appointee** /ə‚pɔɪn'tiː/ n a person appointed to a job or position: *a political appointee.*

appointment /ə'pɔɪntmənt/ n **1(a)** [C] ~ (**with sb**) an arrangement to meet or visit sb at a particular time: *make an appointment with sb* ○ *keep/break an appointment* ○ *I have a dental appointment at 3 pm.* **(b)** [U] the action of arranging in advance to meet or visit sb at a particular time: *Viewing is by appointment only.* **2(a)** [C, U] ~ (**as/to sth**) the act of appointing a person to a job or selecting sb for a position of responsibility: *His promotion to manager was a popular appointment.* ○ *his appointment as Foreign Secretary* ○ *the appointment of a new England captain* ○ *Her appointment to the Board is expected soon.* **(b)** [C] a job or position of responsibility: *I'm looking for a permanent appointment.*

apportion /ə'pɔːʃn/ v ~ **sth** (**among/between/to sb**) to divide sth among people; to give a share of sth to sb: [Vn] *apportion costs/damages* [Vnpr] *He apportioned the various tasks among the members of the team.* ○ *I don't wish to* **apportion blame** *to any of you.* [also Vnn]. See also PORTION v. ▶ **apportionment** n [U, sing]: *an apportionment of land.*

apposite /'æpəzɪt/ adj ~ (**to sth**) (*fml*) very appropriate in the circumstances or in relation to sth: *an apposite comment/illustration/example* ○ *I found his speech wholly apposite to the current debate.*

apposition /‚æpə'zɪʃn/ n [U] (*grammar*) the use of a word or phrase immediately following another word or phrase and referring to the same person or thing: *In 'Paris, the capital of France' 'the capital of France' is in apposition to 'Paris'.*

appraise /ə'preɪz/ v to assess the value, quality or nature of sth/sb: [Vn] *appraise a student's work* ○ *an appraising eye/glance* ○ *They carefully appraised the situation before deciding.*
▶ **appraisal** /ə'preɪzl/ n [C, U] a judgement of, or the action of judging, the value, quality or nature of sth/sb: *She gave a detailed appraisal of the situation.* ○ *a staff appraisal scheme.*

appreciable /ə'priːʃəbl/ adj large enough to be noticed or considered important; considerable: *an appreciable drop in temperature* ○ *The change of policy has had no appreciable effect.* ○ *The increase in salary will be appreciable.* ▶ **appreciably** /-əbli/ adv: *He's looking appreciably thinner.*

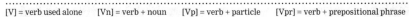

appreciate /əˈpriːʃieɪt/ v **1(a)** to recognize and enjoy the good qualities of sth: [Vn] *You can't fully appreciate foreign literature in translation.* ○ *I really appreciate a good cup of tea.* **(b)** to recognize or show awareness of sb's good qualities: [Vn] *My boss doesn't appreciate me.* **2** to understand sth and show consideration or sympathy: [Vn] *I appreciate your problem, but I don't think I can help you.* [V] *As you will appreciate, we still have a lot of improvements to make.* [V.that] *I appreciate that you may have prior commitments.* [V.wh] *You don't seem to appreciate how busy I am.* **3** to be grateful for sth; to welcome sth: [Vn] *I would appreciate any advice you could give me.* ○ *Your help was greatly appreciated.* ○ *I'd appreciate it if you paid in cash.* [V.n ing] *We'd appreciate her knowing about this as soon as possible.* [V.ing] *They appreciated being invited.* **4** to increase in value over a period of time: [V] *Local property has appreciated (in value) since they built the shopping mall nearby.*
▶ **appreciative** /əˈpriːʃətɪv/ adj **1** ~ **(of sth)** feeling or showing gratitude: *an appreciative letter* ○ *I'm most appreciative of your generosity.* **2** showing one's pleasure or enjoyment: *an appreciative audience/smile* ○ *appreciative laughter.* **appreciatively** adv.

appreciation /əˌpriːʃiˈeɪʃn/ n **1** [U] awareness and enjoyment of the good qualities of sth: *She shows little appreciation of good music.* **2** [U, sing] a full or sympathetic understanding of sth: *Without a proper appreciation of the problems, we can't really comment.* **3** [U] gratitude for sth: *Let me express our appreciation for all your hard work.* ○ *Please accept this gift in appreciation of all you've done for us.* **4** [C] *(fml)* a piece of writing or a discussion in which the qualities or worth of sb/sth are assessed or judged: *write an appreciation of a poet's work.* **5** [U] an increase in value over a period of time: *The pound's rapid appreciation is creating problems for exporters.*

apprehend /ˌæprɪˈhend/ v **1** *(fml)* (esp of the police) to seize or arrest sb: [Vn] *The thief was apprehended in the act of stealing a car.* **2** [Vn, V.that] *(dated or rhet)* to understand sb/sth. See also COMPREHEND.

apprehension /ˌæprɪˈhenʃn/ n **1** [U, C] anxiety about sth in the future; fear that sth will be unpleasant or that sth unpleasant will happen: *filled with apprehension* ○ *I feel a certain apprehension about my interview tomorrow.* ○ *apprehensions of war.* **2** [U] the action of seizing or arresting sb, esp by the police: *the apprehension of the robbers/terrorists.*

apprehensive /ˌæprɪˈhensɪv/ adj ~ **(about/of sth)**; ~ **(that...)** anxious about sth in the future; afraid that sth will be unpleasant or that sth unpleasant will happen: *feel apprehensive about the results of the exams* ○ *apprehensive of failure/that he would fail.* ▶ **apprehensively** adv: *At the door she paused apprehensively.*

apprentice /əˈprentɪs/ n a young person who has agreed to work for a skilled employer for a fixed period, usu for low wages, in return for being taught that person's skill: *an apprentice plumber.*
▶ **apprentice** v ~ **sb (to sb)** (esp passive) to arrange for sb to work as an apprentice: [Vn, Vnpr] *He was apprenticed (to a carpenter) at the age of 16.*
apprenticeship /-tɪʃɪp/ n [C, U] the position or period of being an apprentice: *serve an/one's apprenticeship with a local firm.*

apprise /əˈpraɪz/ v ~ **sb of sth** *(fml)* (esp passive) to inform sb of sth: [Vnpr] *I was apprised of the committee's decision.*

approach /əˈprəʊtʃ/ v **1** to come near or nearer to sb/sth in distance or time: [Vn] *As you approach the town the first building you see is the church.* [V] *The*

time is rapidly/fast approaching when we must think about buying a new car. **2** to come close to sb/sth in quality, level or quantity: [Vn] *No other player approaches her for consistency.* ○ *Few writers even begin to approach Shakespeare's greatness.* ○ *profits approaching $30 million* ○ *Inflation is now approaching 15%.* **3** ~ **sb (about/for sth)** to speak to or make contact with sb, esp in a polite way, in order to ask for or offer sth: [Vnpr] *They approached their bank manager for a loan.* ○ *She approached me about working with her on the project.* [Vn] *approach a number of possible volunteers* ○ *I find him difficult to approach* (ie not easy to talk to in a friendly way). **4** to start dealing with a task, problem, etc in a particular way: [Vn] *Before trying to solve the puzzle, let us consider the best way to approach it.*
▶ **approach** n **1** [C] ~ **(to sth)** a way of dealing with sb/sth; a way of doing sth: *a new approach to language teaching* ○ *adopt a more positive approach* ○ *She took quite the wrong approach in her dealings with them.* **2** [C] an act of speaking to or making contact with sb, esp in a polite way to ask for or offer sth: *The club has made an approach to a local business firm for sponsorship.* ○ *She resented his persistent approaches.* **3** [sing] the action of coming near or nearer in distance or time: *Heavy footsteps signalled the teacher's approach.* ○ *At her approach the children ran off.* ○ *The approach of the exams filled her with anxiety.* **4** [C] a way leading to a place; a path, a road, an entrance, etc: *All the approaches to the palace were guarded by troops.* ○ *Police are patrolling the major approach roads to the stadium.* **5** [C] the part of an aircraft's flight immediately before landing: *begin the final approach to the runway.* **6** [C] ~ **to sth** a thing resembling sth in quality or character: *That's the nearest approach to an apology you'll get from him.*
approachable adj **1** friendly and easy to talk to: *Despite being a big star, she's very approachable.* Compare UNAPPROACHABLE. **2** that can be reached by a particular route or from a particular direction: *The house is only approachable from the south.*

approbation /ˌæprəˈbeɪʃn/ n [U] *(fml)* approval, permission or agreement: *a shout of approbation* ○ *receive official approbation.* Compare DISAPPROBATION.

appropriate¹ /əˈprəʊpriət/ adj ~ **(for/to sth)** suitable, acceptable or correct in the circumstances: *Jeans are not appropriate for a formal party.* ○ *His formal style of speaking was appropriate to the occasion.* ○ *You will be informed of the details at the appropriate time.* ○ *Please debit my Access/Visa/ American Express Card (delete as appropriate).* ○ *It is/seems appropriate that the donation will be used to buy books for the library.* ▶ **appropriately** adv: *dress appropriately* ○ *Appropriately enough, the butcher's name was Mr Lamb.* **appropriateness** n [U].

appropriate² /əˈprəʊprieɪt/ v **1(a)** to take sth for one's own use, esp without permission or illegally: [Vn] *He was accused of appropriating club funds.* **(b)** to use another person's ideas, etc as if they were one's own: [Vn] *appropriate the styles of other musicians* ○ *Some of the opposition's policies have been appropriated by the government.* **2** ~ **sth for sth** to put sth, esp money, on one side for a particular purpose; to ALLOCATE sth to sth: [Vnpr] *$50 000 has been appropriated for a new training programme.*
▶ **appropriation** /əˌprəʊpriˈeɪʃn/ n **1** [U, sing] the action of appropriating sth: *a meeting to discuss the appropriation of funds* ○ *the appropriation of a political cause.* **2** [C] a thing, esp a sum of money, that is appropriated: *make an appropriation of £20 000 for payment of debts* ○ *the US Senate Appropriations Committee* (ie dealing with funds for defence, welfare, etc).

[V] = verb used alone   [Vn] = verb + noun   [Vp] = verb + particle   [Vpr] = verb + prepositional phrase

approval /əˈpruːvl/ n [U] **1** the feeling or opinion that sth is good, acceptable or satisfactory: *have/ retain sb's approval* ○ *a nod of approval* ○ *The crowd showed their approval by cheering loudly.* ○ *Do the plans* **meet with your approval?** **2** [U,C] ~ **(for sth) (from sb)** (esp official) acceptance of or agreement with a proposal, plan, request, etc: *The scheme will go before a committee for approval.* ○ *get/obtain approval for the proposal from the shareholders* ○ *have the formal approval of the President* ○ *give one's approval* ○ *I can't agree to anything without my partner's approval.* ○ *new drug/pesticide approvals* ○ *His report was given the* **seal of approval** (ie formal approval) *by senior management.* **IDM** **on apˈproval** (of goods) supplied to a customer on condition that they may be returned if they are not satisfactory.

approve /əˈpruːv/ v **1** ~ **(of sb/sth)** to feel or believe that sb/sth is good, acceptable or satisfactory: [V, Vpr] *She doesn't want to take her new boyfriend home in case her parents don't approve (of him).* [Vpr] *I approve of your trying to earn some money, but please don't neglect your studies.* **2** to agree to or accept a proposal, plan, request, etc: [Vn] *a proposal approved by a majority of shareholders* ○ *The project will need to be approved by the Board of Directors.* **3** to accept sth as satisfactory or correct: [Vn] *a course approved by the Department of Education* ○ *The auditors approved the company's accounts.*
▶ **approving** adj (abbreviated as *approv* in this dictionary) showing that one believes sb/sth is good, etc: *She received many approving glances.* **approvingly** adv: *smile/nod approvingly.*
■ **apˈproved school** n (esp Brit) (formerly) a place where young people who had committed crimes were sent to be trained and educated. See also BORSTAL, REFORMATORY.

approx abbr approximate; approximately: *a deposit of approx £50* ○ *airport–hotel transfer time approx 30 minutes.*

approximate¹ /əˈprɒksɪmət/ adj fairly correct or accurate but not completely so: *an approximate price/figure/amount* ○ *What is the approximate size of this room?* ▶ **approximately** adv: *It cost approximately £300 — I can't remember the exact figure.* ○ *'How much does he earn?' '£20 000 a year, approximately.'*

approximate² /əˈprɒksɪmeɪt/ v **1** ~ **(to) sth** to be similar to sth in nature, quality, amount, etc but not exactly the same: [Vpr] *Your story approximates to the facts we already know.* [Vn] *They had nothing even approximating the items I was looking for.* **2** to estimate or calculate sth accurately: [Vn] *an attempt to approximate population growth.*
▶ **approximation** /əˌprɒksɪˈmeɪʃn/ n [C] **1** a fairly close estimate of a number or an amount: *3000 students each year would be an approximation of the expected number.* **2** a thing that is similar to sth but is not exactly the same: *a reasonably good approximation of the original style* ○ *an approximation of a smile.*

appurtenance /əˈpɜːtɪnəns/ n (usu pl) (fml or joc) a minor possession or piece of property; an ACCESSORY(1): *It had all the appurtenances of a leading international bank: bright carpets, shiny new counters, smiling staff and state-of-the-art telephones.*

APR /ˌeɪ piː ˈɑː(r)/ abbr annual percentage rate (the amount of interest charged on a loan calculated at a yearly rate): *a rate of 29.8 per cent APR.*

Apr abbr April: *14 Apr 1994.*

après-ski /ˌæpreɪ ˈskiː/ n [U] (French) social activities and entertainment after a day's skiing (SKI v) in a resort: *I enjoyed the après-ski more than the skiing itself.*

apricot /ˈeɪprɪkɒt/ n **1** [C] **(a)** a round yellow or orange fruit with fur on its skin, soft flesh and a large stone inside: *dried apricots* ○ *ˌapricot ˈjam.* **(b)** a tree bearing this fruit. **2** [U] the colour of a ripe apricot.

April /ˈeɪprəl/ n [U,C] (abbr **Apr**) the fourth month of the year, next after March: *She was born in April.* ○ *When were you born? The first of April/April the first/(US) April first.* ○ *We went to Japan last April.*
■ **ˌApril ˈFool** n a person who is the target of a practical joke (PRACTICAL) traditionally played on 1 April (**April Fool's Day**).

a priori /ˌeɪ praɪˈɔːraɪ/ adj, adv (using reasoning that proceeds) from known causes to imagined effects, eg saying 'They've been walking all day so they must be hungry'. Compare A POSTERIORI.

apron

apron   overall
               (US smock)

pinafore

apron /ˈeɪprən/ n **1** a piece of cloth or fabric worn over the front part of the body and tied round the waist to keep one's clothes clean, eg while cooking. ⇨ picture. **2** an area with a hard surface on an airfield, where aircraft are turned round, loaded, etc. **3** (also ˌapron ˈstage) (in a theatre) the part of the stage that extends in front of the curtain. **IDM** **(tied to) one's mother's, wife's, etc apron-strings** (too much under) the influence and control of one's mother, etc: *The British prime minister is too apt to cling to Washington's apron-strings.*

apropos /ˌæprəˈpəʊ/ (also **apropos of**) prep with reference to sb/sth; concerning sth: *my enquiries apropos Mrs Hyde* ○ *Apropos (of) what you were just saying...*
▶ **apropos** adj [pred] appropriate or relevant: *You'll find the last paragraph extremely apropos.*

apse /æps/ n (architecture) a RECESS(3) in the shape of a SEMICIRCLE or with many sides, esp at the east end of a church.

apt /æpt/ adj **1** suitable or appropriate in the circumstances: *an apt quotation* ○ *His choice of music was most apt.* **2** [pred] ~ **to do sth** likely or having a tendency to do sth: *apt to be forgetful/careless/ quick-tempered* ○ *My pen is apt to leak.* **3** ~ **(at doing sth)** quick at learning: *very apt at computer programming* ○ *She showed herself an apt pupil.* ▶ **aptly** adv: *the aptly named Grand Hotel* ○ *As Oscar Wilde so aptly remarked...* **aptness** n [U].

aptitude /ˈæptɪtjuːd; US -tuːd/ n [U,C] ~ **(for sth/ doing sth)** natural ability or skill at doing sth: *Does she show any aptitude for languages?* ○ *He has great aptitude for getting the best out of the people who work for him.*
■ **ˈaptitude test** n a test that is designed to reveal whether sb is suitable for a particular type of work or course of training. Compare INTELLIGENCE TEST.

aqualung /ˈækwəlʌŋ/ n an apparatus used by divers (DIVE¹ 2) to enable them to breathe under water. It consists of a container of air linked to the mouth or nose by tubes.

aquamarine /ˌækwəməˈriːn/ n **1** [C] a pale greenish-blue precious stone. **2** [U] the colour of this.

aquarium /əˈkweəriəm/ n (pl **aquariums** or **aquaria** /-riə/) **(a)** a glass tank in which live fish and other water creatures and plants are kept. **(b)** a building containing such tanks, esp one that is open to the public.

Aquarius /ə'kweəriəs/ n (**a**) [U] the 11th sign of the ZODIAC, the Water-carrier. (**b**) [C] a person born under the influence of this sign. ▶ **Aquarian** n, adj. ⇨ picture at ZODIAC. ⇨ note at ZODIAC.

aquatic /ə'kwætɪk/ adj [usu attrib] **1** (of plants, animals, etc) growing or living in or near water: *aquatic ecosystems* ○ *Many forms of aquatic life inhabit ponds.* **2** (of sports) taking place in or on water: *The resort offers a range of aquatic sports, including swimming and water-skiing.*

aqueduct /'ækwɪdʌkt/ n a structure, esp one built like a bridge, that carries water over a valley or low ground.

aqueous /'eɪkwiəs/ adj (techn) of or like water; containing or produced by water: *chemicals dissolved in an aqueous solution.*

aquifer /'ækwɪfə(r)/ n (geology) a layer of rock or soil that can hold or transmit water.

aquiline /'ækwɪlaɪn/ adj of or like an EAGLE: *an aquiline nose* (ie one curved like an eagle's beak).

Arab /'ærəb/ n **1** any of the people descended from the original inhabitants of the Arabian Peninsula, now living in the Middle East and N Africa generally. **2** a type of horse originally bred in Arabia.
▶ **Arab** adj of Arabia or the Arabs: *the Arab countries.*

arabesque /ˌærə'besk/ n **1** [C, U] (in art) an elaborate design of leaves, branches, etc winding round each other. **2** [C] (in ballet) a position in which the dancer is balanced on one leg with the other lifted and stretched backwards parallel to the ground.

Arabian /ə'reɪbiən/ adj of Arabia or the Arabs: *the Arabian Sea.*

Arabic /'ærəbɪk/ adj of the Arabs, esp of their language or literature: *Arabic poetry.*
▶ **Arabic** n [U] the language of the Arabs.
■ ˌarabic ˈnumeral (also ˌarabic ˈfigure) n any of the symbols 0, 1, 2, 3, 4, etc. Compare ROMAN NUMERAL.

arable /'ærəbl/ adj (**a**) (of land) used or suitable for growing crops: *arable fields.* (**b**) (of crops) grown on such land. (**c**) involved in or relating to the growing of crops: *arable farms/farmers* ○ *arable cultivation.*
▶ **arable** n [U] arable land or crops: *persuade farmers to switch to arable.*

arbiter /'ɑːbɪtə(r)/ n ~ (of sth) a person who has power or influence over what will be done, accepted, etc in a particular area of activity: *the arbiters of fashion/good taste* ○ *In this instance, the Prime Minister is the final arbiter.*

arbitrage /'ɑːbɪtrɑːʒ, 'ɑːbɪtrɪdʒ/ n [U] (commerce) the practice of buying stocks, shares, currencies, etc in one place and selling them in another in order to take advantage of differences in price.

arbitrary /'ɑːbɪtrəri; US 'ɑːrbətreri/ adj **1** based on personal opinion or impulse, not on any reason or system: *arbitrary decisions* ○ *The choice of players for the team seems completely arbitrary.* **2** using power without restriction and without considering others: *an arbitrary ruler* ○ *arbitrary powers.* ▶ **arbitrarily** adv. *Plans are arbitrarily changed or reversed.* **arbitrariness** n [U].

arbitrate /'ɑːbɪtreɪt/ v to make a judgement about or settle an argument between two parties, usu when asked by them to do so: [V] *arbitrate in a dispute* [Vpr] *arbitrate between management and the unions* [V, Vn] *The elders have power to arbitrate (land disputes).* [also Vnpr].

arbitration /ˌɑːbɪ'treɪʃn/ n [U, C] the process of having a dispute settled by a person or group not involved in the dispute: *take/refer the matter to ar-*

bitration ○ *be prepared to accept independent arbitration* ○ *The union finally agreed to go to arbitration as a way of ending the strike.*

arbitrator /'ɑːbɪtreɪtə(r)/ n a person chosen to settle a dispute between two parties.

arboreal /ɑː'bɔːriəl/ adj (techn) of or living in trees: *Squirrels are arboreal creatures.*

arboretum /ˌɑːbə'riːtəm/ n (pl **arboretums** or **arboreta** /-tə/) a place where trees are grown for scientific study or for display.

arbour (US **arbor**) /'ɑːbə(r)/ n a place in the shade of trees or climbing plants, esp one in a garden made by training branches over a wooden framework for people to sit under.

arc /ɑːk/ n **1** part of a circle or some other curved line. ⇨ picture at CIRCLE. **2** (a thing with) a curved shape: *the arc of a rainbow* ○ *move in a graceful arc.* **3** an electric current passing across a gap between two terminals (TERMINAL n 3).
▶ **arc** v (pt, pp **arced** /ɑːkt/; pres p **arcing** /'ɑːkɪŋ/) [V] **1** to form an electric arc. **2** to have or move in the shape of an arc.
■ ˈarc lamp (also ˈarc light) n a lamp giving light produced by an electric arc.

arcade /ɑː'keɪd/ n a covered passage or area, esp one with arches and shops along one or both sides: *a ˈshopping arcade.* See also AMUSEMENT ARCADE.

arcane /ɑː'keɪn/ adj secret; mysterious: *arcane rituals/ceremonies/customs.*

arch¹ /ɑːtʃ/ n **1** a curved structure supporting the weight of sth above it, eg a bridge or the upper part of a building: *a bridge with three arches.* ⇨ picture at CHURCH. **2** (also **archway**) a similar structure forming a passage or an ornamental entrance: *Go through the arch and follow the path.* ○ *Marble Arch is a famous London landmark.* **3** a thing shaped like an arch, esp the raised part of the foot between the sole and the heel. ⇨ picture at FOOT¹.
▶ **arch** v **1** to form part of the body into the shape of an arch: [Vn] *The cat arched its back when it saw the dog.* **2** ~ across/over sth to form an arch over sth; to extend across sth: [Vpr] *Tall trees arched across the river.*

arch² /ɑːtʃ/ adj [usu attrib] playful and deliberately provoking: *an arch smile/glance/look.* ▶ **archly** adv.

arch- comb form **1** chief; most important: *archangel* ○ *archbishop.* **2** most disliked; extreme: *arch-enemy.*

archaeology /ˌɑːki'ɒlədʒi/ n [U] the study of ancient cultures, peoples and periods of history by scientific analysis of physical remains, esp those found in the ground: *classical/marine/industrial archaeology.*
▶ **archaeological** /ˌɑːkiə'lɒdʒɪkl/ adj of or related to archaeology: *archaeological excavations/evidence.*
archaeologist /ˌɑːki'ɒlədʒɪst/ n an expert in archaeology.

archaic /ɑː'keɪɪk/ adj **1** (infml often joc) very old-fashioned: *archaic attitudes/views/practices.* **2** (abbreviated as *arch* in this dictionary) (esp of words, etc in a language) no longer in current use: *'Thou art' is an archaic form of 'you are'.* **3** of a much earlier or an ancient period in history: *archaic and classical Greek coins.*
▶ **archaism** /'ɑːkeɪɪzəm/ n **1** [C] an archaic word or expression. **2** [U] the use or copying of what is archaic, esp in language and art.

archangel /'ɑːkeɪndʒl/ n an ANGEL(1) of the highest rank.

archbishop /ˌɑːtʃ'bɪʃəp/ n a bishop of the highest rank, responsible for all the churches belonging to a religious group in a particular district: *the Archbishop of Canterbury.*

A

▶ **archbishopric** /ˌɑːtʃˈbɪʃəprɪk/ *n* (**a**) the position of an archbishop. (**b**) a district for which an archbishop is responsible.

archdeacon /ˌɑːtʃˈdiːkən/ *n* (esp in the Anglican Church) a priest next below the rank of bishop.

archdiocese /ˌɑːtʃˈdaɪəsɪs/ *n* a district under the care of an ARCHBISHOP.

archduke /ˌɑːtʃˈdjuːk; *US* -ˈduːk/ *n* (*fem* **archduchess** /ˌɑːtʃˈdʌtʃəs/) a DUKE/DUCHESS of the highest rank, esp formerly the son of the Austrian Emperor.

arch-enemy /ˌɑːtʃ ˈenəmi/ *n* a person's chief enemy.

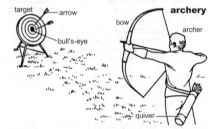

target
arrow
bow
bull's-eye
archery
archer
quiver

archer /ˈɑːtʃə(r)/ *n* a person who shoots with a bow and arrows (ARROW), esp as a sport or (formerly) in battle. ⇨ picture.
▶ **archery** /ˈɑːtʃəri/ *n* [U] the skill or sport of shooting with a bow and arrows (ARROW).

archetype /ˈɑːkɪtaɪp/ *n* (*fml*) (**a**) an original or ideal model from which others are copied: *the archetype of the wicked stepmother.* (**b**) a very typical example: *the archetype of an American film star.* ▶ **archetypal** /ˌɑːkɪˈtaɪpl/ *adj: The plot is based on the archetypal story of the wicked guardian.* ○ *He plays an archetypal bachelor.*

archipelago /ˌɑːkɪˈpeləɡəʊ/ *n* (*pl* **-os** or **-oes**) a group of many islands and the sea surrounding them: *an Indian Ocean archipelago.*

architect /ˈɑːkɪtekt/ *n* **1** a person who designs buildings and supervises the process of constructing them: *the architect's plans for the new theatre.* **2** a person who is responsible for planning or creating a particular event or situation: *an architect of economic stability* ○ *He was one of the principal architects of the revolution.*

architecture /ˈɑːkɪtektʃə(r)/ *n* **1** [U] the art and science of designing and constructing buildings. **2** [U] the style or style of a building or buildings: *the architecture of the eighteenth century* ○ *Modern architecture depresses me.* **3** [C, U] (*computing*) the nature and structure of a computer system that determines the way it operates: *disk architecture.*
▶ **architectural** /ˌɑːkɪˈtektʃərəl/ *adj* of or related to architecture: *an architectural triumph.* **architecturally** *adv: The house is of little interest architecturally.*

architrave /ˈɑːkɪtreɪv/ *n* the frame around a door or window.

archive /ˈɑːkaɪv/ *n* (often *pl*) a collection of historical documents or records of a government, a family, a place, an organization, etc: *the National Sound Archive* ○ *an archive of local history* ○ *archive material* ○ *I found this map in the family archives.*
▶ **archivist** /ˈɑːkɪvɪst/ *n* a person whose job is to develop and maintain an archive.

arch-rival /ˌɑːtʃ ˈraɪvl/ *n* a person's chief rival: *a match between Rangers and their arch-rivals Celtic.*

archway /ˈɑːtʃweɪ/ *n* = ARCH[1] **1**.

Arctic /ˈɑːktɪk/ *adj* **1** [attrib] of or occurring in the regions around the North Pole: *Arctic explorers/foxes* ○ *Arctic Norway.* **2** **arctic** (**a**) extremely cold:

arctic weather ○ *The conditions were arctic.* (**b**) [attrib] suitable for such conditions: *arctic clothing.*
▶ **the Arctic** *n* [sing] the regions around the North Pole.
■ **the ˌArctic ˈCircle** *n* [sing] the line of LATITUDE 66° 30' North. ⇨ picture at GLOBE. Compare ANTARCTIC.

-ard *suff* (with *adjs* forming *ns*) having the specified, usu negative, quality: *drunkard* ○ *dullard.*

ardent /ˈɑːdnt/ *adj* very enthusiastic or passionate about sth: *an ardent advocate of free speech* ○ *an ardent admirer/follower of sb.* ▶ **ardently** *adv.*

ardour (*US* **ardor**) /ˈɑːdə(r)/ *n* [U] great enthusiasm or passion; ZEAL: *His revolutionary ardour had inspired a new generation of followers.* ○ *Nothing could dampen (ie reduce) her ardour.*

arduous /ˈɑːdjuəs, -dʒu-/ *adj* needing much effort or energy, esp over a period of time: *an arduous journey through the Andes* ○ *The work is very arduous.*

are[1] /ə(r)/; *strong form* ɑː(r)/ ⇨ BE[1].

are[2] /eə(r), ɑː(r)/ *n* a metric unit of area, equal to 100 square metres. ⇨ App 2.

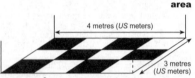

area

4 metres (*US* meters)

3 metres
(*US* meters)

area = 12m² (12 square metres, *US* -ers)

area /ˈeəriə/ *n* **1**(**a**) [C, U] the extent or measurement of a surface: *The area of the office is 35 square metres.* ○ *The kitchen is 12 square metres in area/has an area of 12 square metres.* ⇨ App 2. (**b**) [C] a particular measured surface: *Compare the areas of these two triangles.* ⇨ picture. Compare VOLUME 2. **2** [C] (**a**) a region or part of the world, a country, a city, etc: *mountainous/uninhabited/desert areas of the world* ○ *in the Bristol area* ○ *inner city areas* ○ *Do you like the area (ie district) where you're living?* (**b**) a part of a place that has a specific use: *a ˈpicnic area* ○ *the reˈception area.* (**c**) a part of a room, surface, etc: *Clean the area around the sink.* **3** [C] a subject, range of activity or interest, etc, or a specified part or aspect of it: *the area of finance/training/development* ○ *a new area of investigation* ○ *areas of concern/disagreement/controversy* ○ *The big growth area of recent years has been in health clubs.* See also GREY AREA.
■ **ˈarea code** *n* (esp in the USA) a telephone code identifying an area or a region, used before the local telephone number when calling from outside the area. See also DIALLING CODE.

arena /əˈriːnə/ *n* **1** a level area for sports, public entertainments, etc: *showjumping at Wembley Arena.* **2** a place or scene of activity or conflict: *the political arena* ○ *enter the arena of Europe.*

aren't /ɑːnt/ *short form* (*infml*) **1** are not: *They aren't here.* **2** (in questions) am not: *Aren't I clever?* ⇨ note at BE[2].

argon /ˈɑːɡɒn/ *n* [U] (*symb* **Ar**) a chemical element. Argon is present as a gas in the atmosphere. ⇨ App 7.

argot /ˈɑːɡəʊ/ *n* [C, U] a set of words and phrases used by a particular group and not easily understood by others: *the argot of the computer enthusiast.*

argue /ˈɑːɡjuː/ *v* **1** ~ (**with sb**) (**about/over sth**) to express an opposite opinion; to exchange angry words; to quarrel: *The couple next door are always arguing.* [Vpr] *Don't argue with your mother.* ○ *We had to argue with the waiter about the price of the meal.* **2** ~ (**for/against sth**) to give reasons for or against sth, esp with the aim of persuading sb to share one's own opinion: [V] *He argues convincingly.* [Vpr] *argue for the right to strike* [V.*that*] *I argued that we needed a larger office.* [Vn] *British Rail have argued the case for reducing the frequency of services.* [also V.speech]. **3** (*fml*) to suggest or indicate sth: [Vn] *This latest move argues a change in government thinking.* [also V.*that*]. **IDM** ˌargue the ˈtoss (*Brit*) to say that one disagrees about a decision, esp when it is unlikely to be changed: *It's not worth arguing the toss over such a trivial matter.* **PHRV** **argue sb into/out of doing sth** to persuade sb to do/not to do sth by giving reasons: *They argued him into withdrawing his complaint.*

▶ **arguable** /ˈɑːɡjuəbl/ *adj* **1** that can be argued or asserted: *It is arguable that we would be just as efficient with fewer staff.* **2** that can be questioned; not obviously correct: *This account contains many arguable points/statements.* **arguably** /-əbli/ *adv* (often used before a comparative or superlative adj) one could give reasons to support the view that: *It is, arguably, a more important painting than Van Gogh's 'Irises'.* ◦ *Branagh is **arguably the best** actor of his generation.*

argument /ˈɑːɡjumənt/ *n* **1** [C] ~ (**with sb**) (**about/ over sth**) a disagreement, esp an angry one; a quarrel: *get into/have an argument with the referee (about his decision).* **2** [U] ~ (**about sth**) discussion based on reasoning: *We agreed without further argument.* ◦ *Let's assume **for the sake of argument** (ie as a basis for discussion) that our subsidy is reduced by half.* **3** [C] ~ (**for/against sth**); ~ (**that…**) a reason or reasons put forward: *accept/reject an argument* ◦ *There are strong arguments for and against capital punishment.* ◦ *The government's argument is that they must first aim to beat inflation.* **4** [C] a summary of what a book, etc is about; a theme.

NOTE Compare **argument**, **row**, **quarrel**, **fight** and **altercation**. An **argument** (*over* or *about* something) is a serious verbal disagreement: *Most families have arguments over money.* ◦ *I had an argument with my neighbour about his dog.* A **quarrel** is an angry argument that may continue for a long time: *After the quarrel my sisters refused to speak to each other.*

A **row** in British English, and a **fight** in American English, is very angry and involves shouting, usually for a short time: *She had a row with her parents and left home.* ◦ *The day before the wedding they had a huge fight.*

A **row** can also be an argument between public figures or organizations: *A row has broken out over remarks made by the Minister for Education.*

A **fight** can also involve violence or weapons rather than words: *The argument soon became a fight when somebody pulled out a knife.*

Altercation is a formal word for a noisy argument.

argumentative /ˌɑːɡjuˈmentətɪv/ *adj* fond of arguing (ARGUE 1).

argy-bargy /ˌɑːdʒi ˈbɑːdʒi/ *n* [U] (*Brit infml*) noisy but usu not serious quarrelling: *What's all this argy-bargy?*

aria /ˈɑːriə/ (*pl* **arias**) *n* a song for one voice, esp in an opera or ORATORIO.

-arian /-ˈeəriən/ *suff* (forming *ns* and *adjs*) believing in; practising: *humanitarian* ◦ *disciplinarian*.

arid /ˈærɪd/ *adj* **1** (of land or a climate) having little or no rain; very dry: *the arid deserts of Africa* ◦ *Nothing grows in these arid conditions.* **2** dull; not interesting: *have long, arid discussions.* ▶ **aridity** /əˈrɪdəti/ *n* [U].

Aries /ˈeəriːz/ *n* (**a**) [U] the first sign of the ZODIAC, the Ram. (**b**) [C] (*pl* unchanged) a person born under the influence of this sign. ⇨ picture at ZODIAC. ⇨ note at ZODIAC.

aright /əˈraɪt/ *adv* (*arch or rhet*) (never used in front of the *v*) correctly: *Do I hear you aright?*

arise /əˈraɪz/ *v* (*pt* **arose** /əˈrəʊz/; *pp* **arisen** /əˈrɪzn/) **1** to appear; to occur: [V] *A new difficulty has arisen.* ◦ *Children should be disciplined **when the need** arises.* ◦ *A storm arose during the night.* **2** ~ **out of/ from sth** to occur or follow as a result of sth: [Vpr] *problems arising out of the lack of communication* ◦ *Are there any **matters arising** from the minutes of the last meeting?* **3** (*arch or fml*) to get up or stand up: [V] *They arose before dawn.*

aristocracy /ˌærɪˈstɒkrəsi/ *n* [CGp] the highest social class; people of noble birth or rank: *members of the aristocracy* ◦ (*fig*) *an aristocracy of talent* (ie the most able or talented members of a society).

aristocrat /ˈærɪstəkræt; *US* əˈrɪst-/ *n* a member of the ARISTOCRACY; a person of noble birth. Compare COMMONER.

▶ **aristocratic** /ˌærɪstəˈkrætɪk; *US* əˌrɪstə-/ *adj* belonging to or typical of the ARISTOCRACY: *an aristocratic name/family/manner/lifestyle.*

arithmetic /əˈrɪθmətɪk/ *n* [U] (**a**) the branch of MATHEMATICS that deals with the adding, multiplying, etc of numbers in sums: *He's not very good at arithmetic.* (**b**) these sums: *I did some quick **mental arithmetic** to work out which was cheaper.* ◦ *There's something wrong with the arithmetic — we can't possibly have sold that many copies.*

▶ **arithmetic** /ˌærɪθˈmetɪk/, **arithmetical** /-ˈmetɪkl/ *adjs* of or concerning arithmetic. ˌarithmetic proˈgression (also arithˌmetical proˈgression) *n* a series of numbers that increase or decrease by the same amount each time, eg 1, 2, 3, etc or 8, 6, 4. Compare GEOMETRIC PROGRESSION.

ark /ɑːk/ **the ark** (also ˌNoah's ˈark) *n* [sing] (in the Bible) the ship in which Noah, his family and animals were saved from the Flood.

■ **the ˌArk of the ˈCovenant** *n* [sing] a large wooden box or cupboard in which the writings of Jewish law were originally kept.

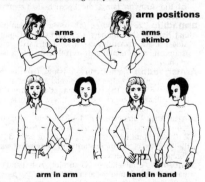

arm positions

arms crossed   arms akimbo

arm in arm   hand in hand

arm¹ /ɑːm/ *n* **1** either of the two upper limbs of the human body, from the shoulder to the hand: *She held the baby **in her arms**.* ◦ *They lay **in each other's arms**.* ◦ *He gave her his arm* (ie let her hold it for support) *as they crossed the road.* ◦ *She was carrying a book **under her arm*** (ie between her arm and her body). ◦ *She held the fish **at arm's length*** (ie as far away as possible, with the arm fully extended away from the body). ◦ *Keep your belongings **within arm's reach*** (ie where you can reach them easily). ◦ *stroll ˌarm in ˈarm* (ie with the arm of one person linked with the arm of another). ⇨ picture. ⇨ picture at HUMAN. **2 a** sleeve:

There's a tear in the arm of my jacket. **3** a thing that is shaped like or operates like an arm: *the arms of a chair* (ie the parts on which the arms can rest). ○ *The story is set at Lecco on the eastern arm of Lake Como.* ⇨ picture at GLASS. **4** a branch or division of a company or an organization: *the European arm of an engineering group* ○ *the investment banking arm.* **5** (usu *sing*) a branch or division of a country's military forces: *troops supported by the air arm.* **IDM** **the (long) arm of sb/sth** the great extent of the authority, power or influence of sb/sth: *fear the long arm of the drug cartels* ○ *He fled to Brazil trying to escape the long arm of the law.* **(with one's) arms akimbo** with one's hands on one's hips and one's elbows pointed outwards: *Aunt Eliza stood in the doorway (with her) arms akimbo.* ⇨ picture. **as long as your arm** ⇨ LONG[1]. **a babe in arms** ⇨ BABE. **chance one's arm** ⇨ CHANCE[2]. **cost/pay an ˌarm and a ˈleg** (*infml*) to cost/pay a large sum of money: *The repairs cost an arm and a leg.* **fold one's arms** ⇨ FOLD[1]. **fold sb/sth in one's arms** ⇨ FOLD[1]. **give one's right arm for sth/to do sth** ⇨ RIGHT[5]. **keep sb at arm's length** to avoid becoming too friendly or involved with sb: *keep the press at arm's length.* **a shot in the arm** ⇨ SHOT[1]. **twist sb's arm** ⇨ TWIST[1]. **with open ˈarms** ⇨ OPEN[1].

arm² /ɑːm/ *v* **1** ~ **oneself/sb (with sth)** to supply or equip oneself/sb with weapons; to prepare for war or fighting: [V] *The enemy is arming.* [Vnpr] *The mob armed themselves with sticks and stones.* [Vn] *an armed guard* ○ *Police say the man is armed and dangerous.* [Vnpr] *warships armed with nuclear weapons* ○ (*fig*) *She arrived at the interview armed with pages of statistics.* **2** [Vn] to make a bomb, etc ready to explode. Compare DISARM. See also ARMS. **IDM** **ˌarmed to the ˈteeth** having many weapons. ▶ **armed** *adj* involving the use of arms: *an armed robbery/struggle/conflict* ○ *armed neutrality* (ie remaining NEUTRAL(1a) but prepared to defend oneself against attack). **the ˌarmed ˈforces** (also **the ˌarmed ˈservices**) *n* [pl] a country's army, navy and air force.

armada /ɑːˈmɑːdə/ *n* **(a)** [C] a large fleet of ships. **(b) the Armada** [sing] the Spanish fleet sent to attack England in 1588.

armadillo /ˌɑːməˈdɪləʊ/ *n* (*pl* **-os**) a small animal that lives in the Southern USA and Central and S America. An armadillo has a shell of hard plates around its body enabling it to roll itself into a ball when attacked.

Armageddon /ˌɑːməˈgedn/ *n* [sing] **(a)** (in the Bible) the final conflict between good and evil at the end of the world. **(b)** (also **armageddon**) any similar dramatic conflict, esp one likely to cause the end of life on earth: *a nuclear armageddon.*

armament /ˈɑːməmənt/ *n* **1** [C often *pl*] weapons, esp large guns, tanks, etc: *the armaments industry.* **2** [C usu *pl*] military forces equipped for war. **3** [U] the process of equipping military forces for war. Compare DISARMAMENT.

armband /ˈɑːmbænd/ (also **armlet**) *n* a band of material worn round the arm or sleeve: *Many people at the funeral were wearing black armbands.*

armchair /ˈɑːmtʃeə(r), ˌɑːmˈtʃeə(r)/ *n* a usu low, comfortable chair with supports for the arms: *sit in an armchair.* ▶ **armchair** *adj* [attrib] without having or providing practical experience of sth: *armchair critics* ○ *an armchair traveller* (ie a person who reads or hears about travel but does not travel personally).

armful /ˈɑːmfʊl/ *n* (*pl* **-fuls**) a quantity that can be carried by one or both arms: *armfuls of flowers* ○ *carrying books by the armful.*

armhole /ˈɑːmhəʊl/ *n* an opening in a garment through which the arm is put.

armistice /ˈɑːmɪstɪs/ *n* (usu *sing*) an agreement during a war to stop fighting for a certain time; a TRUCE: *ask for/seek/sign an armistice.*

armlet /ˈɑːmlət/ *n* = ARMBAND.

armour (*US* **armor**) /ˈɑːmə(r)/ *n* [U] **1** (formerly) a protective, usu metal, covering for the body, worn when fighting: *a suit of armour* ○ (*fig*) *a stream of questions designed to pierce his mental armour.* **2(a)** metal plates covering ships, tanks, cars, etc to protect them from bullets and missiles. **(b)** a force or group of vehicles protected in this way: *an attack by infantry and armour.* **IDM** **a chink in sb's armour** ⇨ CHINK[1]. **a knight in shining armour** ⇨ KNIGHT. ▶ **armoured** (*US* **armored**) *adj* **(a)** covered or protected with armour: *an armoured car* ○ *The cruiser was heavily armoured.* **(b)** equipped with vehicles strengthened in this way: *an armoured division.*

armourer (*US* **armorer**) *n* a person who makes, repairs or supplies weapons and armour.

armoury (*US* **armory**) /ˈɑːməri/ *n* **1** a place where arms and armour are kept; an ARSENAL(2): *nuclear armouries.* **2** (*US*) a building which is the HEADQUARTERS for the National Guard or an Army Reserve Unit. **3** the resources available to sb to help them achieve sth: *the social reformers' armoury of data* ○ *A good dictionary is an important weapon in any writer's armoury.*

■ **ˌarmour-ˈplated** (*US* **armor-**) *adj* (of vehicles) fitted with sheets of metal to provide protection against bullets, etc.

armpit /ˈɑːmpɪt/ *n* the hollow place under the arm at the shoulder. ⇨ picture at HUMAN.

arms /ɑːmz/ *n* [pl] **1** weapons, eg guns and explosives, esp those available to the armed forces of a country: *arms and ammunition* ○ *a large force already under arms* (ie equipped with weapons and ready to fight) ○ *nuclear arms* ○ *arms control talks* ○ *an arms depot* ○ *Policemen on special duties may carry arms.* See also FIREARM, SMALL ARMS. **2** = COAT OF ARMS: *the King's Arms* (eg as the name of a pub). **IDM** **bear arms** ⇨ BEAR[2]. **brothers in arms** ⇨ BROTHER. **present arms** ⇨ PRESENT[3]. **take up arms (against sb)** to go to war; to begin to fight: *He called on his supporters to take up arms against the state.* **(be) up in ˈarms (about/over sth)** (to be) protesting strongly about sth: *The whole town is up in arms about the plan to build an airport nearby.*

■ **ˈarms race** *n* (usu *sing*) a contest between nations in which each tries to acquire greater military strength than the others.

army /ˈɑːmi/ *n* **1(a)** [CGp] a military force that is organized and equipped for fighting on land: *The two armies fought for control of the town.* **(b) the army** [sing] the profession of being a soldier: *go into/be in/join/leave the army* ○ *army life.* **2** [CGp] **(a)** a large number of people or animals: *an army of advisers/officials/ants* ○ *the growing army of homeless young people.* **(b)** an organized group of people formed and equipped for a purpose: *an army of volunteers/workmen* ○ *the Salvation Army.*

A-road ⇨ A².

aroma /əˈrəʊmə/ *n* (*pl* **aromas**) a distinctive, usu pleasant, smell: *give off a rich aroma* ○ *the aroma of coffee/cigars/hot chestnuts.* ▶ **aromatic** /ˌærəˈmætɪk/ *adj* having a pleasant and distinctive smell; FRAGRANT: *aromatic oils/spices.*

aromatherapy /əˌrəʊməˈθerəpi/ *n* [U] the use of sweet-smelling oils and plant extracts for healing or for rubbing into the body during MASSAGE.

arose *pt* of ARISE.

around¹ /əˈraʊnd/ *adv* **1** (*infml*) approximately: *around 100 people* ○ *He arrived (at) around five o'clock.* ○ *The work will be finished (by) around Christmas.* ○ *They were fashionable (at) around the turn of the century.* **2** on every side; in every direction: *hear laughter all around.* **3** measured in a circle: *an old tree that was six feet around.* Compare ABOUT¹.

around² /əˈraʊnd/ *adv part* For the special uses of **around** in phrasal verbs, look at the verb entries. For example, the meaning of **come around to sth** is given in the phrasal verb section of the entry for **come**. **1(a)** here and there; in many directions: *run/drive/walk/look around* ○ *travel around in Europe for six weeks.* **(b)** here and there within a particular area: *books left around on the floor* ○ *children playing around on the sand.* **(c)** doing nothing in particular: *Several young girls were sitting around looking bored.* **2** available; in existence: *There was more money around in those days.* ○ *New potatoes will be around in the supermarkets soon.* ○ *Cable television has been around for some time now.* **3(a)** in the area close to sb/sth; near: *I can't see anyone around.* ○ *See you soon, I expect — I'll be around.* **(b)** throughout an area or building: *I'll send someone to show you around.* ○ *You have 15 minutes to look around.* **4** through an angle of 180°: *Turn around* (ie so as to face in the opposite direction). Compare ABOUT². ⇨ note at ROUND². **IDM** **be around** to be active and prominent in a particular field or profession: *a new tennis champion who could be around for a long time* ○ *She's been around as a film director since the 1970s.* **have been around** to have gained knowledge and experience of the world, esp in sexual matters: *He pretends he's been around but he's really very immature.* ○ *I've been around a bit — I've learned a thing or two.*

around³ /əˈraʊnd/ *prep* (*esp US*) **1(a)** (indicating movement) here and there in a place; to many places within a larger area: *running around the playground* ○ *travel around the world.* **(b)** (indicating position) here and there in a place; at many points within a particular area: *Chairs were left scattered around the room.* ○ *Blobs of paint were dotted around the canvas.* **2** in or near a place: *It's around here somewhere.* ○ *I saw him around the office this morning.* **3(a)** surrounding sb/sth: *There was a red belt around his waist.* ○ *He put his arms around her.* **(b)** moving past all sides of sth in a circle: *run around the block* ○ *The earth moves around the sun.* **(c)** following the curve of sth: *going around the corner at 80 mph.* Compare ABOUT³.

arouse /əˈraʊz/ *v* **1** ~ **sb** (**from sth**) to wake sb from sleep: [Vn, Vnpr] *He was aroused (from his nap) by the doorbell.* **2** to provoke a particular feeling or attitude: [Vn] *Her strange behaviour aroused our suspicions.* ○ *His interest had first been aroused by a trip to the local museum.* ○ *He succeeded in arousing the nation's sympathy.* **3(a)** ~ **sb** (**from/out of sth**) to make sb become active or involved in sth: [Vnpr] *arouse sb from apathy/inactivity* [also Vn]. **(b)** [Vn] to stimulate sb sexually. See also ROUSE. ▶ **arousal** /əˈraʊzl/ *n* [U]: *sexual arousal.*

arpeggio /ɑːˈpedʒiəʊ/ *n* (*pl* **-os**) (*music*) the notes of a CHORD(1) played quickly one after the other: *practising arpeggios.*

arr *abbr* **1** arrival; arrive(s); arrived; arriving: *arr London 06.00.* Compare DEP 1. **2** (*music*) arranged by: *English folk-song, arr Percy Grainger.*

arraign /əˈreɪn/ *v* (*law*) to accuse sb formally of a crime; to bring sb to court for trial: [Vnpr] *arraign sb for/on a charge of murder* [also Vn]. ▶ **arraignment** *n* [U, C].

arrange /əˈreɪndʒ/ *v* **1** to put sth in order; to make sth tidy, neat or attractive: [Vn] *arrange the books on the shelves* ○ *arrange some flowers in a vase* ○ *She arranged all her business affairs before going on vacation.* **2(a)** to plan the details of a future event; to organize sth in advance: [Vn] *arrange a dinner to celebrate their anniversary* ○ *arrange a programme/a*

timetable/an itinerary ○ *Her marriage was arranged by her parents* (ie They chose her future husband). **(b)** ~ (**for sb/sth**) (**to do sth**) to make sure that sth happens by planning or preparing it in advance: [Vpr, Vpr.*to* inf] *I've arranged for a car (to meet you at the airport).* [V.*to* inf] *I'll arrange to be in when you call.* **3** ~ **with sb about sth**; ~ (**with sb**) **to do sth** to agree with sb about sth or to do sth: [Vpr] *I've arranged with the neighbours about feeding the cats.* [Vn] *Our staff will help you arrange a loan.* ○ *Let's arrange a time and place for our next meeting.* [V.*that*] *I arranged that we could borrow their car.* [V.*to* inf] *They arranged to meet at 7 o'clock.* **4** ~ **sth** (**for sth**) to adapt a piece of music for a particular instrument, voice, etc: [Vn, Vnpr] *He arranged many traditional folk-songs (for the piano).* ▶ **arranger** *n*: *composers and arrangers* ○ *flower arrangers.*

NOTE The verbs **arrange**, **organize** and **plan** all have two main meanings. The first is about putting things in order. The second is about making preparations.

You **arrange** things into a particular sequence or a pleasing order: *The CDs are all arranged in alphabetical order.* You **organize** things into a system so that you can use them easily: *You should organize your ideas before you write the essay.* **Plan** means to decide in advance the exact position or role of things, especially by writing or drawing your ideas first: *We planned our new kitchen on paper before buying anything.*

When you **arrange** an event such as a meeting or a party, you invite people and agree a time and place: *Could you arrange a meeting with Ms Wilson for Monday, please?* You **organize** an event by preparing and providing everything that people will need, such as transport, food, equipment, etc: *Patrick organizes the students' social programme.* When you **plan** a future event, you make decisions about what will happen and how: *We planned the meeting carefully so that nothing could go wrong.*

arrangement /əˈreɪndʒmənt/ *n* **1(a)** [U] the action of putting sth in order; the arranging of sth: *Can I leave the arrangement of the tables to you?* **(b)** [C] the result of this; a thing that has been arranged: *a plan of the seating arrangements* ○ *Her flower arrangement won first prize.* **2** [C usu *pl*] ~ (**for sth**) a plan; a preparation: *He's responsible for all the travel arrangements.* ○ *Please make your own arrangements for accommodation.* ○ *I'll make arrangements for you to be met at the airport.* **3** [C] a procedure; a method of doing sth: *new funding arrangements* ○ *There are special arrangements for people working on contracts overseas.* **4** [U, C] ~ (**with sb**) **to do sth**; ~ (**with sb**) (**about/over sth**) an agreement; a SETTLEMENT(1a): *Appointments can be made by arrangement (with my secretary).* ○ *We can come to an/some arrangement over the price.* ○ *I have an arrangement with the bank to cash cheques here.* **5** [C] a piece of music that has been adapted for a particular instrument, voice, etc: *a new arrangement of a popular dance tune.*

arrant /ˈærənt/ *adj* [attrib] (*derog*) (of a bad person or thing) to the greatest extent; complete; UTTER¹: *He's talking arrant nonsense.*

array /əˈreɪ/ *v* (*fml*) (usu passive) **1** to place a group of people or things in order, esp in a pleasing, impressive or threatening way: [Vnpr] *trophies arrayed on the mantelpiece* ○ *His soldiers were arrayed along the river bank.* **2** ~ **sb** (**in sth**) to dress sb/ oneself: [Vnpr] *be arrayed in ceremonial robes.* ▶ **array** *n* **1** [C] an impressive display or series: *an array of facts/information/statistics* ○ *an array of bottles of different shapes and sizes* ○ *a bewildering array of insurance policies.* **2** [U] (*fml*) clothes; clothing: *The guests appeared in splendid array.* **3** [C]

(*computing*) a type of data structure that has MUL-
TIPLE values.

arrears /əˈrɪəz/ n [pl] money that is owed and
should have been paid earlier: *arrears of salary* ○ *be
paid a month in arrears* (ie at the end of the period
in which work was done) ○ *rent/mortgage arrears* ○
They have fallen into arrears with the rent.

arrest /əˈrest/ v **1** ~ sb (for sth) to take and keep sb
prisoner with the authority of the law: [Vn] *After the
match three youths were arrested.* [Vnpr] *Five people
were arrested for drugs-related offences.* **2** (*fml*) to
stop a process or movement: [Vn] *arrest a decline in
share prices* ○ *Attempts are being made to arrest the
spread of the disease.* **3** (*fml*) to attract sb/sth: [Vn]
An unusual painting arrested his attention.
   ► **arrest** n [U,C] **1** the action or an instance of
arresting sb: *The police made several arrests.* ○
They were charged with resisting arrest. ○ *A warrant was issued for his arrest.* ○ *They are under
arrest* (ie being held by the police before trial) *(for
attempted burglary).* See also CITIZEN'S ARREST,
HOUSE ARREST. **2** the action or an instance of sth
stopping: *He died after suffering a cardiac arrest* (ie
when his heart stopped functioning properly).
   arresting *adj* attracting attention; striking: *an arresting smile.*

arrival /əˈraɪvl/ n **1** [U] the action of arriving:
Cheers greeted the arrival of the team. ○ *the arrival of
spring/of satellite technology* ○ **On arrival** *at the
hotel please wait for further instructions.* ○ *a party to
celebrate the arrival* (ie birth) *of their first child.* **2**
[C] a person or thing that arrives: *Late arrivals must
wait in the foyer.* ○ *We're expecting a new arrival* (ie a
new baby) *in the family soon.* Compare DEPARTURE 1.

arrive /əˈraɪv/ v **1(a)** ~ **(at/in …)** to reach a place,
esp at the end of a journey: [Vadv] *arrive home* [V]
What time did you arrive? [Vpr] *We arrived at the
station five minutes late.* ○ *They will arrive in New
York at noon.* Compare DEPART. **(b)** (of a thing) to be
brought: [V] *A parcel has arrived for you.* [Vadv] *Her
birthday card arrived late.* **2** (of an event or a
moment in time) to come: [V] *The great day/Spring
has arrived.* ○ *The baby finally arrived* (ie was born)
just after midnight. **3** (*infml*) to become well known
or successful: [V] *You know you've arrived when
you're asked to appear on TV chat shows.* **PHRV**
ar'rive at sth to reach sth: *arrive at an agreement/a
decision/a conclusion.*

arrogant /ˈærəgənt/ *adj* (*derog*) behaving in a proud
and superior manner; showing too much pride in
oneself and too little consideration for others: *an
arrogant tone of voice* ○ *He's arrogant and opinionated.* ► **arrogance** /ˈærəgəns/ n [U]: *He has a
reputation for rudeness and intellectual arrogance.*
   arrogantly *adv.*

arrogate /ˈærəgeɪt/ v **PHRV** **arrogate sth to oneself** (*fml*) to claim or take sth to which one has no
right: *arrogating all the credit to himself.*

arrow /ˈærəʊ/ n **1** a thin stick that is sharply pointed at one end and designed to be shot from a
bow¹(1): *shoot an arrow* ○ *The road continues
straight as an arrow for several miles.* ⇨ picture
at ARCHERY. **2** a mark or sign resembling an arrow
(→), used to show direction or position: *Follow the
arrows on the map.* ○ *An arrow pointed the way to the
meeting.*

arrowhead /ˈærəʊhed/ n the pointed end of an
ARROW.

arrowroot /ˈærəʊruːt/ n [U] a type of edible STARCH
prepared from the root of an American plant:
Thicken the juice with a little arrowroot.

arse /ɑːs/ (*US* **ass** /æs/) n (△ *sl*) **1(a)** the part of the
body one sits on; the bottom(3): *Get off your arse* (ie
Stop sitting around doing nothing)*!* **(b)** the ANUS. **2**
(*derog*) (usu following an *adj*) a person: *He's a fat*

lazy arse. See also SMART-ARSE. **IDM** **lick sb's arse**
⇨ LICK. **not know one's arse from one's elbow**
⇨ KNOW. **a pain in the arse/neck** ⇨ PAIN.
   ► **arse** v **PHRV** ˌarse aˈbout/aˈround (△ *Brit sl*) to
behave in a silly way: *Stop arsing about and give me
back my shoes.*
   ■ **'arse-hole** (*US* **'ass-hole**) n (△ *sl*) (often used of a
person as an insult) the ANUS.

arsenal /ˈɑːsənl/ n **1** a collection of weapons: *Britain's nuclear arsenal* ○ (*fig*) *The speaker made full
use of his arsenal of invective.* **2** a place where
weapons and explosives are made or stored.

arsenic /ˈɑːsnɪk/ n [U] an extremely poisonous
white powder used for killing rats, etc. ⇨ App 7.

arson /ˈɑːsn/ n [U] the deliberate criminal act of
setting fire to a house or other building: *an arson
attack on a school.*
   ► **arsonist** /ˈɑːsənɪst/ n a person who commits
arson.

art¹ /ɑːt/ n **1(a)** [U] the expression of human creative talent, esp in a visual form, eg painting or
SCULPTURE: *the art of the Renaissance* ○ *modern art* ○
children's art ○ *an art critic/historian/lover* ○ *the art
world.* **(b)** [U] such creative talent or skill: *Her
performance displayed great art.* ○ *This tapestry is a
work of art.* **(c)** [U] examples of the expression of
creative talent: *The walls were hung with surrealist
art.* ○ *an 'art exhibition/gallery.* **(d)** [C] a particular
form or branch of this expression: *the art of dance/
metalwork.* See also POP ART. **2** **the arts** [pl] the
creative and performing arts, eg music, poetry,
painting and dance: *sponsorship of the arts* ○ *an
appreciation of the arts* ○ *an arts centre.* Compare
FINE ART. **3** **arts** [pl] subjects of study such as languages, literature and history. Arts subjects place
greater emphasis on imaginative and creative ability than on the technical and practical skills needed
in science: *an arts degree with honours in sociology.*
Compare HUMANITIES, SCIENCE. **4** [C,U] any skill or
ability that can be developed by practice, esp contrasted with scientific technique: *the art of
appearing confident at interviews* ○ *Threading a
needle is an art in itself.* ○ *The art of letter-writing is
fast disappearing.* **IDM** **get sth down to a fine art**
⇨ FINE¹.
   ■ **'art form** n a type of artistic activity, usu involving special materials or techniques: *Photography is
now accepted as an art form.*
   ˌarts and 'crafts n [pl] activities that require both
artistic and practical skills, eg weaving, WOODWORK
and pottery (POTTER²): *an arts and crafts display.*

art² /ɑːt/ v (*arch*) (*2nd pers sing pres t* form of *be*,
used with *thou*): *'O rose, thou art sick.'*

artefact (also **artifact**) /ˈɑːtɪfækt/ n a thing made by
people, esp a tool or weapon of historical interest:
silver artefacts ○ *prehistoric artefacts made of bone.*

arteriosclerosis /ɑːˌtɪəriəʊskləˈrəʊsɪs/ n [U] a disease in which the walls of the arteries (ARTERY 1)
become harder, preventing the circulation of the
blood.

artery /ˈɑːtəri/ n **1** any of the tubes carrying blood
from the heart to all parts of the body. Compare
VEIN. See also CORONARY ARTERY. **2** an important
route for traffic or transport, eg a road, railway or
river. ► **arterial** *adj*: *arterial disease* ○ *a major
arterial highway.*

artesian well /ɑːˌtiːziən ˈwel; *US* ɑːrˈtiːʒn/ n a hole
made in the ground through which a steady supply
of water rises to the surface by natural pressure.

artful /ˈɑːtfl/ *adj* [usu attrib] **1** (of people) clever at
getting what one wants; crafty (CRAFT): *He's an artful devil.* **2** (of things or actions) designed or done
in a clever way: *an artful deception/trick/forgery.*
Compare ARTLESS. ► **artfully** /ˈɑːtfəli/ *adv.*

arthritis /ɑːˈθraɪtɪs/ n [U] a disease causing pain and

swelling in one or more joints of the body. Compare RHEUMATISM.

▶ **arthritic** /ɑːˈθrɪtɪk/ *adj* suffering from or caused by arthritis: *arthritic hands/pains.* — *n* a person suffering from arthritis.

artichoke /ˈɑːtɪtʃəʊk/ *n* **1** (also ˌglobe ˈartichoke) a round vegetable mainly composed of a mass of thick green leaves. The bottom parts of the leaves and the inside of an artichoke can be eaten when cooked. **2** (also **Jerusalem artichoke** /dʒəˌruːsələm ˈɑːtɪtʃəʊk/) a vegetable with a light brown colour that grows underground and looks like a potato.

article /ˈɑːtɪkl/ *n* **1** a particular item or separate thing, esp one of a set: *articles of clothing* (eg shirts, socks, hats, coats) ○ *toilet articles such as soap, toothpaste and shaving-cream* ○ *The articles found in the car helped the police identify the body.* **2** a piece of writing, usu dealing with a particular issue or topic, in a newspaper, magazine, etc: *an interesting article on/about education.* See also LEADING ARTICLE. **3** (*law*) a separate clause(2) or item in an agreement or a contract: *the company's articles of association* ○ *The proposal breaches article 10 of the European Convention which guarantees free speech.* ○ *After a law degree she served her articles* (ie spent an agreed period of time working and being trained) *with a firm of solicitors.* **4** (*grammar*) (abbreviated as *art* in this dictionary) either of the words 'a/an' (*the indefinite article*) or 'the' (*the definite article*). Compare DETERMINER.

▶ **article** *v* ~ **sb (to sb)** (usu passive) to employ sb under contract and provide training for a formal qualification: [Vn] *an articled clerk* [Vnpr] *articled to a firm of accountants.*

■ ˌarticle of ˈfaith *n* (a) a fundamental point of sb's religious belief. (b) any firmly held belief.

articulate¹ /ɑːˈtɪkjələt/ *adj* **1** (of a person) able to express one's ideas clearly in words: *She's unusually articulate for a ten-year-old.* **2** (of speech) clearly pronounced. Compare INARTICULATE.

articulate² /ɑːˈtɪkjuleɪt/ *v* **1** to express one's feelings, opinions, etc in words: [Vn] *Children don't always find it easy to articulate their ideas.* **2** to pronounce sth clearly and distinctly: [Vadv, Vnadv] *She's a little deaf, so articulate (your words) carefully.* [also V]. **3** (usu passive) to form a joint or connect sth by joints with sth: [Vpr, Vnpr] *bones that articulate/are articulated with others.*

▶ **articulated** *adj* (of a vehicle) with sections connected by flexible joints so that it can turn corners more easily: *an articulated lorry.* ⇨ picture at LORRY. See also TRACTOR-TRAILER.

articulation /ɑːˌtɪkjuˈleɪʃn/ *n* **1** [U] the action of expressing an idea, a feeling, etc in words: *the articulation of a belief.* **2** [U] the making of speech sounds: *As he drank more wine his articulation became worse.* **3** [U,C] a joint or connection that permits movement: *poor elbow articulation.*

artifact = ARTEFACT.

artifice /ˈɑːtɪfɪs/ *n* [U,C] the action or a means of deceiving or tricking sb in a clever way: *tell a story without artifice or guile* ○ *Pretending to faint was merely (an) artifice.*

artificer /ɑːˈtɪfɪsə(r)/ *n* a skilled worker or MECHANIC, esp one in the army or navy.

artificial /ˌɑːtɪˈfɪʃl/ *adj* **1(a)** made or produced as a copy of sth natural; not real: *artificial flowers/light/limbs/pearls.* **(b)** created by people; not existing or occurring naturally: *an artificial division into separate states* ○ *an artificial barrier/distinction/problem.* **2(a)** not what it appears; false(2a): *The outside of the house gives an artificial impression of wealth.* **(b)** insincere; not genuine: *Her artificial gaiety disguised an inner sadness.* See also FAKE. ▶ **artificiality** /ˌɑːtɪˌfɪʃiˈæləti/ *n* [U]. **artificially** /ˌɑːtɪˈfɪʃəli/ *adv*: *artificially high prices.*

■ ˌartificial insemiˈnation *n* [U] the process, esp practised on animals, by which a female is made pregnant by artificially inserting male SPERM into the VAGINA.

ˌartificial inˈtelligence (*abbr* **AI**) *n* [U] (*computing*) the development and use of computer programs (PROGRAM 1) to copy intelligent human behaviour.

ˌartificial respiˈration *n* [U] the process of forcing air into and out of the lungs to help a person who has stopped breathing begin to breathe again.

artillery /ɑːˈtɪləri/ *n* [U] **1** heavy guns, often mounted on wheels, used in fighting on land: *artillery fire* ○ *an artillery regiment.* **2** the branch of an army that uses these: *a captain in the artillery.*

artisan /ˌɑːtɪˈzæn; *US* ˈɑːrtəzn/ *n* (*fml*) a worker who is skilled at making things: *Local artisans displayed handwoven textiles.*

artist /ˈɑːtɪst/ *n* **1** a person who paints or draws pictures, produces SCULPTURE, etc: *Constable was a great English artist.* ○ *a graphic artist* ○ *It's not a photo, it's an artist's impression of what the hotel will look like.* **2** a person who does sth with great skill: *The carpenter has made this cupboard beautifully — he's a real artist.* **3** = ARTISTE: *a recording artist.*

artiste /ɑːˈtiːst/ *n* a professional entertainer, eg a singer, a dancer or an actor: *Among the artistes appearing on our show tonight we have...*

artistic /ɑːˈtɪstɪk/ *adj* **1(a)** having or showing natural skill in the arts, eg painting, music or dance: *artistic abilities/achievements.* **(b)** showing a sensitive appreciation and enjoyment of the arts: *She comes from a very artistic family.* **2** done with skill and good taste(6); beautiful: *an artistic arrangement of dried flowers* ○ *The decor is so artistic.* **3** of art and artists: *artistic freedom* ○ *an artistic temperament* (ie odd or wild behaviour thought to be typical of artists). ▶ **artistically** /ɑːˈtɪstɪkli/ *adv.*

artistry /ˈɑːtɪstri/ *n* [U] the skill of an artist: *admire the artistry of the painter's use of colour* ○ *The final movement of the concerto was played with brilliant artistry.*

artless /ˈɑːtləs/ *adj* simple and natural; without deception: *as artless as a young child* ○ *Her artless comment was mistaken for rudeness.* Compare ARTFUL.

artwork /ˈɑːtwɜːk/ *n* **1** [U] photographs and illustrations in books, newspapers and magazines. **2** [C] a work of art, esp a painting or SCULPTURE.

arty /ˈɑːti/ *adj* (*infml derog*) making an exaggerated show of being artistic or interested in art: *Joanna's arty friends* ○ *His arty clothes look out of place in the office.*

-ary *suff* (with *ns* forming *adjs* and *ns*) concerned with; of: *planetary* ○ *reactionary* ○ *budgetary* ○ *commentary.*

as /əz; *strong form* æz/ *prep* **1** so as to appear to be sb: *dressed as a policeman* ○ *They entered the building disguised as cleaners.* **2** having the function or character of sb/sth: *have a job as a packer* ○ *work as a courier* ○ *Treat me as a friend.* ○ *They accepted her as an equal.* ○ *I respect him as a writer and as a man.* ○ *use a water jug as a vase* ○ *The redundancy notice came as a real shock.* ⇨ note. **3(a)** since one is sth: *As her private secretary he has access to all her correspondence.* **(b)** when or while one is sth: *As a child she was sent to six different schools.*

▶ **as** *adv* **1 as...as** (used before *advs* and *adjs* in order to make a comparison) **(a)** (with the second *as* a *prep*) to the same extent...as; equally...as: *as tall as his father* ○ *This dress is twice as expensive as the blue one.* ○ *Her face went as white as a sheet.* ○ *He doesn't play half as well as his sister.* ○ *I haven't known him as long as you* (ie as you have known him). ○ *As often as not he's drunk.* ○ *As likely as not* (ie Very probably), *it will rain.* **(b)** (with the second *as* a *conj*) to the same extent...as; equally...as: *He* *looks as ill as he sounded on the phone.* ○ *His eyes aren't quite as blue as they look in the film.* ○ *Run as fast as you can.* ○ *He recited as much of the poem as he could remember.* ○ *She's as good an actress as she is a singer.* **2** not differently from; like: *the same as usual* ○ *As before, he remained unmoved.* ○ *The 'h' in 'honest' is silent, as in 'hour'.*

as *conj* **1** during the time when; while: *I watched her as she combed her hair.* ○ *As he grew older he lost interest in everything except gardening.* ○ *Use it as the need arises.* **2** (usu placed at the beginning of a sentence) since; because: *As you weren't there I left a message.* ○ *As she's been ill perhaps she'll need some help.* **3** (used, usu after an *adj* or *adv*, to acknowledge a fact and to indicate that, despite this, what follows is true) although; even though: *Talented as he is, he is not yet ready to turn professional.* ○ *Much as I like you, I couldn't live with you.* ○ *Try as he would/might, he couldn't open the door.* **4** in the way in which: *Do as I say and sit down.* ○ *Just as she had warned me, the shop was shut.* ○ *Leave the table as it is* (ie Do not disturb the things on it). ○ *Why didn't you take the bus as I told you to?* ○ *He became hysterical, as had happened before.* **5** a fact which: *Cyprus, as you know, is an island in the Mediterranean.* ○ *The Beatles, as many of you are old enough to remember, came from Liverpool.* **6** (usu followed by *be* or *do* + subject) and so too: *She's unusually tall, as are both her parents.* ○ *He works in advertising, as does his wife.* ⇨ note. **IDM** **as against sth** in contrast with sth: *She gets Saturdays off in her new job as against working alternate weekends in her last one.* ○ *We had twelve hours of sunshine yesterday, as against a forecast of continuous rain.* **‚as and ¹when 1** (referring to an uncertain future event or action) when: *We'll decide on our team as and when we qualify for the competition.* Compare IF AND WHEN (IF). **2** (*infml*) when possible; eventually: *I'll tell you more as and when* (ie as soon as I can). **as for sb/ sth** with regard to sb/sth: *As for you, you ought to be ashamed of yourself.* ○ *As for the hotel, it was very uncomfortable and miles from the sea.* **as from**; (*esp US*) **as of** (indicating the time or date from which sth starts): *As from next Monday you can use my office.* ○ *We will have a new address as of May 12.* **as if/as though** with the appearance of; apparently: *He behaved as if nothing had happened.* ○ *As if unsure of where she was, she hesitated and looked around.* ○ *He rubbed his eyes and yawned as though waking up after a long sleep.* ○ *As if you didn't know!* (ie You are pretending not to know.) **‚as it ¹is** taking present circumstances into account; as things are: *We were hoping to have a few days off next week — as it is, we may not be able to get away.* ○ *I thought I might be transferred but as it is I'll have to look for a new job.* **as it ¹were** (used to indicate that the speaker is giving her or his own impression of a situation and may not be using words in their exact sense): *She seemed very relaxed — in her natural setting as it were.* ○ *He'd been watching the water rising for two hours — preparing to meet his destiny, as it were — before help arrived.* **as to sth**; **as regards sth** with regard to sth; concerning sth: *As to correcting our homework, the teacher always makes us do it ourselves.* ○ *There are no special rules as regards what clothes you should wear.* **as yet** ⇨ YET. **‚as you ¹were** (used as an order to soldiers to return to their previous positions, activities, etc or informally by a speaker telling sb to ignore what he or she has just said).

NOTE When talking about the similarity between people, things and actions, you can use both **as** and **like**. **Like** is a preposition and is used before nouns and pronouns: *He has blue eyes like me.* **As** is a conjunction and is used before a clause: *She enjoys all kinds of music, as I do.* In speaking **like** is fre-

quently used as a conjunction, replacing both **as** and **as if**: *Nobody understands him as/like I do.* ○ *It looks as if/looks like we're going to be late.*

Compare the use of **as** and **like** when talking about occupations or functions: *She works as a teacher* (ie She is a teacher). ○ *She ordered us around like a teacher* (ie She is not a teacher but she behaved like one).

ASA /ˌeɪ es ¹eɪ/ *abbr* **1** (in Britain) Advertising Standards Authority. **2** (used esp of a scale of film speeds) American Standards Association: *ASA 700* ○ *a 400 ASA film.*

asap /ˌeɪ es eɪ ¹piː/ *abbr* as soon as possible.

asbestos /æsˈbestəs/ *n* [U] a soft grey mineral substance, used esp formerly in building as a protection against fire or to prevent heat loss.
▶ **asbestosis** /ˌæsbesˈtəʊsɪs/ *n* [U] a disease of the lungs caused by breathing in asbestos dust.

ascend /əˈsend/ *v* (*fml*) to go or come up: [V] *The path started to ascend more steeply at this point.* ○ *The tasks were listed* **in ascending order of** *difficulty* (ie with the easiest first). [Vn] *We ascended the path.* ○ (*fig*) *ascend the throne* (ie become king or queen) ○ *notes ascending and descending the scale.* Compare DESCEND.

ascendancy (also **ascendency**) /əˈsendənsi/ *n* [U] ~ **(over sb/sth)** the position of having dominant power or control: *economic/moral/political ascendancy* ○ *He has (gained) the ascendancy over all his main rivals.*

ascendant (also **ascendent**) /əˈsendənt/ *n* **IDM** **in the ascendant** rising in power and influence: *Though he is still very young his political career is already in the ascendant.*

ascension /əˈsenʃn/ *n* **1** [U] (*fml*) the action of going or coming up. **2 the Ascension** [sing] (in the Bible) the departure of Jesus from the earth into heaven.
■ **As¹cension Day** *n* [U, C] the day on which the Ascension is remembered in the Christian Church, ie the Thursday that is the 40th day after Easter.

ascent /əˈsent/ *n* **1** [C, U] an act of going or coming up: *the ascent of Mount Everest* ○ *the best means of ascent* ○ *Who was the first person to make an ascent in a balloon?* **2** [C usu *sing*] an upward path or slope: *The last part of the ascent is very steep.* Compare DESCENT. **3** [U] the process by which sb advances or makes progress: *the ascent of man.*

ascertain /ˌæsəˈteɪn/ *v* (*fml*) to investigate sth so that one knows and is certain; to find out sth: [Vn] *ascertain the facts* [V.that] *ascertain that the report is accurate* [V.wh] *ascertain who is likely to come to the meeting* ○ *The police are trying to ascertain what really happened.*

ascetic /əˈsetɪk/ *adj* [usu attrib] not allowing oneself pleasures and comforts; having or involving a very simple life: *the ascetic existence of monks and hermits.*
▶ **ascetic** *n* a person who leads a very simple life without basic comforts, esp for religious reasons.
asceticism /əˈsetɪsɪzəm/ *n* [U].

ASCII /¹æski/ *abbr* (*computing*) American Standard Code for Information Interchange.

ascribe /əˈskraɪb/ *v* **PHRV** **ascribe sth to sb/sth** to consider or declare sth to be caused by, written by or belonging to sb/sth: *He ascribed his failure to bad luck.* ○ *This play is usually ascribed to Shakespeare.* ○ *You can't ascribe the same meaning to both words.*
▶ **ascribable** *adj* [pred] ~ **to sb/sth** that can be ascribed to sb/sth: *His success is ascribable simply to hard work.*

ascription /əˈskrɪpʃn/ *n* [C, U] ~ **(to sb/sth)** (*fml*) the action or an instance of ascribing (ASCRIBE) sth to sb/sth.

[V.*to* inf] = verb + *to* infinitive   [Vn.inf (no *to*)] = verb + noun + infinitive without *to*   [V.*ing*] = verb + -*ing* form

ASEAN /ˈæsiæn/ **Asean** abbr Association of South East Asian Nations.

asepsis /ˌeɪˈsepsɪs; US əˈsep-/ n [U] (medical) the state of being free from harmful bacteria.

asexual /ˌeɪˈsekʃuəl/ adj **1** without sex or sex organs: asexual reproduction. **2** not involving sexual relations: an asexual relationship.

ash¹ /æʃ/ n (a) [C] a tree commonly found in forests, with grey bark and hard wood. (b) [U] its wood, used for making eg tool handles.

ash² /æʃ/ n [U] a powder that remains after sth, esp tobacco or coal, has burnt: volcanic ash ○ Don't drop cigarette ash on the carpet. Compare ASHES.
■ ˌAsh ˈWednesday n [U, C] the first day of Lent. See also SHROVE TUESDAY.

ashamed /əˈʃeɪmd/ adj [pred] **1** ~ (of sth/sb/oneself); ~ (that…); ~ (to do sth) feeling shame and embarrassment about sth/sb or because of one's own actions: She was bitterly/deeply ashamed of her behaviour at the party. ○ Behave yourself! I'm ashamed of you. ○ You should be ashamed of yourself for telling such lies. ○ He felt ashamed of having done so little work. ○ I feel ashamed that I haven't written for so long. ○ I was ashamed to be associated with such a dishonest act. **2** ~ to do sth unwilling to do sth because of shame or embarrassment: I'm ashamed to admit/say I didn't keep my promise. ○ He felt ashamed to ask for help. ○ I'm ashamed to let you see my paintings.

ashen /ˈæʃn/ adj (esp of sb's face) very pale: She heard the tragic news ashen-faced/her face ashen.

ashes /ˈæʃɪz/ n [pl] **1** the powder that remains after sth has been destroyed by burning: the ashes of a camp-fire ○ Ashes were all that remained of her books after the fire. ○ The house was burnt to ashes overnight. ○ (fig) the ashes of revolution. Compare ASH². **2** the remains of a human body after it has been cremated (CREMATE): His ashes were buried next to those of his wife. **IDM** **sackcloth and ashes** ⇨ SACKCLOTH. Compare ASH².

ashore /əˈʃɔː(r)/ adv to or on the shore or land: We went ashore when the boat reached the port. ○ The cruise includes three days ashore in Gothenburg.

ashram /ˈæʃrəm/ n a place where Hindus go for a period of time to pray and MEDITATE(1) alone.

ashtray /ˈæʃtreɪ/ n a small dish or container into which people who smoke put tobacco ash, cigarette ends, etc.

ashy /ˈæʃi/ adj of or like ashes, esp in colour or texture: His face was ashy grey.

Asian /ˈeɪʃn, ˈeɪʒn/ n a native or inhabitant of Asia.
► **Asian** adj of Asia: Asian music.

Asiatic /ˌeɪʃiˈætɪk, ˌeɪʒi-/ adj of Asia: the Asiatic plains.

aside /əˈsaɪd/ adv part **1** to one side; out of the way: pull the curtain aside ○ Stand/Step aside and let these people pass. ○ He took me aside (ie away from a group of people) to give me some advice. ○ (fig) You must put aside (ie out of your thoughts) any idea of a holiday this year. ○ Leaving aside (ie Not considering at this stage) the cost of the scheme, let us examine its benefits. ○ All our protests were brushed/swept aside (ie ignored). ○ We cannot allow such talented young people to be cast aside (ie ignored or rejected). **2** in reserve; for use later: set aside some money for one's retirement ○ Please put this jumper aside (ie reserve it) for me. **3** (following ns) being an exception; excepted: Money worries aside, things are going quite well.
► **aside** n **1** (in the theatre) words spoken by an actor on stage that are intended to be heard by the audience but not by the other characters on stage. **2** a remark that is not directly relevant to the main subject: I mention it only as an aside. **3** a remark not intended to be heard by everyone present: He kept making rude asides during the meeting.
■ **aside from** prep (esp US) = APART FROM.

ask /ɑːsk; US æsk/ v **1** ~ (sb) (about sb/sth) to request information by means of a question: [V.speech] 'Where are you going?' she asked. [Vpr] She asked about my future plans. [Vnpr] Ask him about the ring you lost — someone may have handed it in to the receptionist. [Vn] Don't be afraid to ask questions. ○ Did you ask the price? [Vnn] She asked them their names. [V.wh] He asked where I lived. [Vn.wh] I had to ask the teacher what to do next. [V.wh, Vn.wh] She asked (me) if I could drive. [V] I'm not insisting, I'm only asking. **2** ~ (sb) for sth; ~ sth (of sb) to request that sb gives sth or does sth: [Vpr] Why don't you ask for a pay increase? ○ ask for a cheese sandwich [Vn] ask sb's advice/opinion/views ○ If you want to camp in this field you must ask the farmer's permission. [Vn, Vnpr] May I ask a favour (of you)? [Vnpr] It's asking an awful lot of you to have my whole family to stay. [V.wh] I asked whether the airline would change my ticket. [Vn.wh] They asked the bank whether the loan could be increased. [V.wh, Vn.wh] She asked (me) if I would drive her home. [Vn.to inf] I asked James to buy some bread. [V.speech] 'Could you help me move the table?' she asked. **3** to request permission to do sth: [V.to inf] ask to use the car ○ ask to speak to sb (eg on the phone) [V.wh] Ask whether it's all right to park here. [Vn.wh] I asked my boss whether I could have the day off. [Vn.to inf] I must ask you to excuse me. [also V.speech] **4** ~ sb (to sth) to invite sb: [Vnpr] ask them to dinner [Vnp] He's asked me out several times already. ○ Shall we ask the neighbours in/round (ie to our house)? [Vn.to inf] She's asked him to come to the party. **5** ~ sth (for sth) to request sth as a price: [Vn] You're asking too much — you'll never sell it at that price. [Vnpr] How much are they asking for their house? **6** to expect or demand sth: [Vn.to inf] It's asking a lot to expect them to win from this position. [Vnpr] You're asking too much of him — he's already working as hard as he can. [also Vn]. **IDM** ˈask for trouble/it (infml) to behave in a way that is likely to result in trouble for oneself: Driving after drinking alcohol is asking for trouble. **for the ˈasking** if one simply asks: The job is yours for the asking (ie If you say you want it, it will be given to you). **I ˈask you** (infml) (expressing shock, annoyance, etc): I ask you! Have you ever heard anything so ridiculous in all your life? **if you ask ˈme** in my opinion: If you ask me, this is a complete waste of time. **PHR V** ˈask after sb to request information about sb's health or news about sb: He always asks after you in his letters. ˌask aˈround to ask a number of different people at different times in order to find out sth: I don't know of any vacancies in the company but I'll ask around. ˈask for sb/sth to say that one wants to see or speak to sb or to be directed to sth: ask for the manager/the bar.
■ ˈasking price n the price at which sth is offered for sale: Never offer more than the asking price for a house.

NOTE Ask is the most usual verb to describe making a request: I've asked Andrew to babysit. ○ Dial 999 and ask for an ambulance. The verb request is mainly used in formal speech and writing, for example on signs. It is often in the passive form: Customers are requested not to smoke. ○ I gave my credit card number as requested. Beg means to ask for something that is important to you in a way that shows you are very upset or worried: He begged her to forgive him for hurting her. ○ 'Please don't cry!' I begged. Entreat, implore and beseech are formal words used especially in literature meaning to ask in a very worried and serious way.

askance /ə'skæns/ *adv* **IDM** **look askance (at sb/ sth)** to look at sb/sth with suspicion or disapproval: *look askance at the price* ○ *She looked at me somewhat askance when I suggested she paid for both of us.*

askew /ə'skjuː/ *adj* [pred], *adv* not in a straight or level position: *That picture is askew.* ○ *He had his hat on askew.* ○ *The line is drawn all askew.*

asleep /ə'sliːp/ *adj* [pred] **1** sleeping: *The baby was asleep upstairs.* ○ *Don't wake her up — she's fast/ sound asleep* (ie sleeping deeply). ○ *He fell asleep during the lecture.* ○ *I've only just got up and I'm still half asleep* (ie not fully awake). **2** (of limbs) having no feeling; NUMB: *I've been sitting on my leg and now it's asleep.*

asp /æsp/ *n* a small poisonous snake found esp in N Africa.

asparagus /ə'spærəgəs/ *n* [U] a plant whose young green shoots are cooked and eaten as a vegetable: *asparagus soup* ○ *Do you like asparagus?*

aspect /'æspekt/ *n* **1** [C] **(a)** a particular part or feature of sth: *the worst aspect of the situation* ○ *examine every aspect of the policy* ○ *There was also the political aspect.* **(b)** a way in which sth may be considered; a point of view: *look at the problem from every aspect* ○ *from the financial/safety aspect.* **2** [U,sing] (*fml*) the appearance of a person or thing: *a man of enormous size and terrifying aspect* ○ (*fig*) *Events began to take on a more sinister aspect.* **3** [C usu *sing*] the side of a building that faces a particular direction: *The house has a southern aspect.* **4** [U] (*grammar*) a form of a verb that indicates the way in which an action is regarded, eg whether it happened in the past but is still continuing or relevant in some way, or whether it is completely finished: *'She has lived here for ten years' is different in aspect from 'She lived here for ten years'.*

aspen /'æspən/ *n* a type of POPLAR tree with leaves that move even in the slightest wind.

asperity /æ'sperəti/ *n* [U] (*fml*) the quality of being harsh or severe, esp in manner or tone: *reply with some asperity.*

aspersions /ə'spɜːʃnz; *US* -ʒnz/ *n* [pl] (*fml or rhet*) critical or unpleasant remarks that may damage sb's reputation: *It is unfair to cast aspersions on his performance at university.*

asphalt /'æsfælt; *US* -fɔːlt/ *n* [U] a black sticky substance used esp for making road surfaces.
▶ **asphalt** *v* [Vn] to cover a road, path, etc with asphalt.

asphyxia /æs'fɪksiə, əs'f-/ *n* [U] lack of oxygen, causing death or loss of consciousness.
▶ **asphyxiate** /əs'fɪksieɪt/ *v* (usu passive) to cause sb to lose consciousness or to die by preventing them from breathing enough oxygen; to SUFFOCATE sb: *He was asphyxiated by the smoke and poisonous fumes.* **asphyxiation** /əs,fɪksi'eɪʃn/ *n* [U]: *The cause of death was asphyxiation.*

aspic /'æspɪk/ *n* [U] a clear jelly made from meat juices and served with or around meat, fish, eggs, etc: *chicken in aspic.*

aspirant /ə'spaɪərənt, 'æspərənt/ *n* ~ (**to sth**) (*fml*) a person who is ambitious for sth: *aspirants to the presidency.* ▶ **aspirant** *adj*: *aspirant actors/politicians.*

aspirate /'æspərət/ *n* (*phonetics*) the sound of the letter 'h': *The word 'hour' is pronounced without an initial aspirate.*
▶ **aspirate** /'æspəreɪt/ *v* to pronounce sth with an 'h' sound: [Vn] *The 'h' in 'hour' is not aspirated.*

aspiration /,æspə'reɪʃn/ *n* **1** [UC often *pl*] ~ (**for sth**); ~ (**to do sth**) a strong desire or ambition: *He has serious aspirations for a career in politics.* ○ *I've*

never had any aspiration to become rich and famous. **2** [U] the action of pronouncing sth with an 'h' sound.

aspire /ə'spaɪə(r)/ *v* ~ **to sth**; ~ **to do sth** to have a strong desire or ambition to gain or achieve sth: [Vpr] *aspire to knowledge/wealth/fame* [V.*to* inf] *The film aspires to be a serious historical study.* [V] *Aspiring musicians must practise many hours a day.*

aspirin /'æsprɪn, 'æspərɪn/ *n* [U,C] a common drug used for relieving pain and reducing fever. It is usu taken in the form of tablets (TABLET 1): *Do you have any aspirin?* ○ *Take two aspirins for your headache.*

ass¹ /æs/ *n* **1** (also **donkey**) an animal with long ears related to the horse. **2** (*infml*) a stupid person; a fool: *Don't be such an ass!* ○ *I made an ass of myself at the meeting — standing up and then forgetting the question.*

ass² /æs/ *n* (*US sl* ⚠) = ARSE.

assail /ə'seɪl/ *v* ~ **sb** (**with sth**) (*fml*) to attack sb violently or repeatedly: [Vnpr] *assailed with fierce blows to the head* ○ (*fig*) *assail sb with questions/ insults* [Vn] *be assailed by worries/doubts/fears* ○ *A feeling of panic assailed him.*
▶ **assailant** *n* (*fml*) a person who attacks sb, esp physically: *He was unable to see his assailant clearly in the dark.*

assassin /ə'sæsɪn; *US* -sn/ *n* a person who murders sb, esp sb important or famous, for money or for political reasons.

assassinate /ə'sæsɪneɪt, -sən-/ *v* (often passive) to murder sb, esp sb important or famous, for money or for political reasons: [Vn] *The prime minister was assassinated by extremists.* ▶ **assassination** /ə,sæsə'neɪʃn; *US* ə,sæsə'neɪʃn/ *n* [U,C]: *an assassination attempt on the president* ○ *political assassinations.*

assault /ə'sɔːlt/ *n* **1** [C] ~ (**on/against sb/sth**) a violent attack: *make an assault on the enemy lines* ○ (*fig*) *mount a determined/sustained assault on poverty* ○ *an assault on sb's religious beliefs* ○ *The theory came/was under assault from all sides.* **2** [U,C] ~ (**on sb**) a physical attack on sb, esp when this is a crime: *an alarming increase in cases of indecent assault* (ie of a sexual nature) ○ *be charged with assault.*
▶ **assault** *v* to attack sb physically and violently, esp when this is a crime: [Vn] *He got two years' imprisonment for assaulting a police officer.* [Vnadv] *Six women have been sexually assaulted in the area recently.*
■ **as,sault and battery** *n* [U] (*law*) a crime that involves threatening and making a physical attack on sb.
as'sault course *n* an area used for training soldiers, etc consisting of obstacles which they have to climb, go through, etc.

assay /ə'seɪ/ *n* [C,U] the testing of metals, etc for quality: *make an assay of an ore.*
▶ **assay** *v* [Vn] to test the quality of a metal, etc.

assemblage /ə'semblɪdʒ/ *n* **1** [C] a collection of things or a gathering of people: *an odd assemblage of broken bits of furniture.* **2** [U] (*fml*) the process of coming together or bringing people or things together as a group.

assemble /ə'sembl/ *v* **1** to come together or bring people or things together as a group: [V] *The whole school assembled in the main hall.* [Vn] *assemble evidence/material/equipment* ○ *The director has assembled a first-rate cast.* ○ *He then addressed the assembled company.* **2** to fit together the parts of sth: [Vn] *assemble the parts of a watch* ○ *The desk is easy to assemble — all you need is a screwdriver.*

assembly /ə'sembli/ *n* **1(a)** [U] the meeting together of a group of people for a specific purpose: *deny sb the right of assembly* ○ *We'll meet at this*

assembly point at 3 o'clock. (**b**) [C, U] a gathering of the students and teachers in a school at the start or end of the day . (**c**) [CGp] a group of people meeting together, esp to discuss matters of national importance: *The motion was put to the assembly.* ○ *the legislative assemblies of the USA* ○ *The national assembly has/have met to discuss the crisis.* **2(a)** [U] the action or process of fitting together the parts of sth: *an assembly plant* (eg in a factory) ○ *The assembly of cars is often done by machines.* ○ *Each component is carefully checked before assembly.* (**b**) [C] a unit consisting of smaller manufactured parts that have been fitted together: *the tail assembly of an aircraft.*
■ as'**sembly line** *n* a sequence of machines and workers assembling sth in a factory. The product passes from one worker to another on a moving belt(2), with each one performing a particular operation on it until it is complete: *He works on the assembly line.*

assent /ə'sent/ *n* [U] ~ (**to sth**) (*fml*) agreement; approval: *give one's assent to a proposal* ○ *a murmur of assent from the crowd* ○ *The new bill passed by Parliament has received the Royal Assent* (ie been approved by the king/queen).
▶ **assent** *v* ~ (**to sth**) (*fml*) to express agreement; to give permission: [V] *I suggested we share the cost of lunch and he eventually assented.* [Vpr] *I can never assent to such a request.*

assert /ə'sɜːt/ *v* **1(a)** to make other people recognize sth by behaving firmly and confidently: [Vn] *assert one's authority/independence/rights.* (**b**) ~ **oneself** to behave in a confident manner that gains other people's attention and respect: [Vn] *You're too timid — you must try to assert yourself more.* **2** to state sth clearly and forcefully as the truth: [Vn, V.*that*] *She asserted her innocence/that she was innocent.* [V.speech] *'The effects of nuclear war vary greatly,' he asserted.*

assertion /ə'sɜːʃn/ *n* **1** [U, C] the action of claiming or stating sth forcefully: *the assertion of one's authority* ○ *frequent assertions of power.* **2** [C] a strong statement claiming the truth of sth: *the newspaper's startling/repeated assertions about his business activities* ○ *I seriously question a number of your assertions.*

assertive /ə'sɜːtɪv/ *adj* showing a strong and confident personality: *state one's opinions in an assertive tone* ○ *Len's weakness made me feel strong and assertive.* ▶ **assertively** *adv.* **assertiveness** *n* [U]: *attend an assertiveness training course.*

assess /ə'ses/ *v* **1** ~ **sth** (**as sth**) to estimate the nature, quality or value of sb/sth: [Vn] *It's difficult to assess the impact of the President's speech.* [Vn-adj] *I'd assess your chances as extremely low.* [Vnpr] *assess candidates for their suitability* [Vn-n] *assess sb as a future manager.* **2** ~ **sth** (**at sth**) to decide or fix the amount or extent of sth: [Vn] *assess sb's taxes/income* [Vnpr] *assess the damage at £3 500.* **3** to decide or fix the value of sth: [Vn] *have a house assessed by a valuer* [also Vnpr].
▶ **assessment** *n* **1(a)** [C] a carefully considered opinion or judgement: *What is your assessment of the situation?* (**b**) [U] the action of assessing sb/sth: *The judge ordered the child to be removed for assessment.* See also CONTINUOUS ASSESSMENT. **2** [C] an amount fixed for payment: *a tax assessment.*
assessor *n* a person who assesses taxes, the value of property, etc: *a report by an independent assessor.*

asset /'æset/ *n* **1** ~ (**to sb/sth**) (**a**) a valuable or useful quality or skill: *The President's greatest/chief asset is his reputation for honesty.* (**b**) a valuable or useful person or thing: *She's an enormous asset to the team.* ○ *The country's oil resources have proved a great asset.* **2** (usu *pl*) a thing, esp property owned by a person, company, etc, that has value and can be

used or sold to pay debts: *His assets included shares in the company and a house in France.* ○ *the company's net assets* ○ *add significantly to the group's asset value* ○ *asset sales/management* ○ *freeze a country's assets.* Compare LIABILITY.
■ '**asset-stripping** *n* [U] (*commerce usu derog*) the practice of buying at a cheap price a company which is in financial difficulties and then selling each of its assets (ASSET 2) separately to make a profit without any regard for the company's future.

assiduous /ə'sɪdjuəs; *US* -dʒuəs/ *adj* (*fml*) working hard and showing careful attention to detail: *be assiduous in one's duties* ○ *The book was the result of ten years' assiduous research.* ▶ **assiduously** *adv*: *She has assiduously cultivated the support of her constituents.*

assign /ə'saɪn/ *v* **1(a)** ~ **sth to sb** to give sth to sb for their use or as their share of work or responsibility: [Vnpr] *The two large classrooms have been assigned to us.* [Vnn] *I was assigned the task of checking all the equipment.* ○ *The teacher has assigned each of us a part in the school play.* [Vn] *Factory managers assign work and monitor progress.* (**b**) ~ **sb to sb/sth** to put sb under the authority of sb or into a particular official group: [Vnpr] *I was assigned to B platoon.* (**c**) ~ **sb** (**to sth/as sth**) to provide sb for a task or position; to appoint sb: [Vnpr] *They've assigned their best man to the job.* [Vn.*to* inf] *Troops were assigned to protect the visitors.* [Vn-n] *I was assigned as project manager, with a staff of ten.* **2** to name or fix a time, place, reason, etc for sth: [Vnpr] *Shall we assign Thursday morning for our weekly meetings?* ○ *It is impossible to assign an exact date to this building.* **3** ~ **sth to sb** (*law*) to transfer property, rights, etc to sb: [Vnpr] *The agreement assigns copyright to the publisher.*
▶ **assignment** *n* **1** [C] a task or duty that is assigned to sb: *homework assignments* ○ *my current assignment as a government economic adviser* ○ *I had set myself a tricky assignment.* ○ *She was sent abroad on an assignment for the Sunday Times.* **2** [U] the act of assigning sb to sth or the fact of being assigned: *her recent assignment to the commission.*

assignation /ˌæsɪg'neɪʃn/ *n* (*rhet or joc*) a meeting, esp a secret one, eg with a lover.

assimilate /ə'sɪməleɪt/ *v* **1** to absorb ideas, information, etc in the mind: [Vn] *Children need to be given time to assimilate what they have been taught.* ○ *This is not an easy concept for non-believers to assimilate.* **2(a)** to become or allow sb/sth to become part of or like another social group: [Vn] *the great American ability to assimilate other cultures* [V] *New arrivals find it hard to assimilate, and many do not wish to.* (**b**) ~ **sth to/into sth** (esp passive) to make an idea, a person's attitude, etc fit into sth: [Vnpr] *Such works were not assimilated into mainstream western art history.* ▶ **assimilation** /ə,sɪmə'leɪʃn/ *n* [U]: *cultural assimilation* ○ *the rapid assimilation of knowledge.*

assist /ə'sɪst/ *v* ~ (**sb**) **in/with sth**; ~ (**sb**) **in doing sth** (*rather fml*) to help: [Vn] *a relief fund to assist families who have lost relatives or property* [Vnpr] *Your health visitor will assist you with the procedures.* [Vpr] *We are looking for people who would be willing to assist in the group's work.* [Vn.*to* inf, Vnpr] *assist young people to make/in making their way in the world* [Vnpr] *Two men* **are assisting the police in/with their inquiries** (ie are being held by the police for questioning).

assistance /ə'sɪstəns/ *n* [U] ~ (**for/with sth**); ~ (**in doing sth / to do sth**) (*fml*) help: *Please call if you require assistance.* ○ *Can I* **be of** (*any*) *assistance, sir?* ○ *Despite his cries no one* **came to his assistance.** ○ *give/offer sb financial assistance* ○ *provide economic/military/technical assistance* ○ *I needed* *considerable assistance in finding/to find the information.* ○ *Some employers provide assistance with fees for child care.*

assistant /ə'sɪstənt/ *n* **1** a person who helps or supports sb, esp in their job: *My assistant will now demonstrate the machine in action.* See also PERSONAL ASSISTANT. **2** (*Brit*) (*US* **clerk**) a person who serves customers in a shop or behind the counter in a CAFÉ. See also SHOP ASSISTANT.
▶ **assistant** *adj* [attrib] (*abbr* **asst**) helping, and ranking below, a senior person: *the assistant manager* ○ *a senior research assistant.*
assistantship *n* (*US*) a form of financial aid awarded to a college or university student who assists a PROFESSOR while studying for a GRADUATE¹ degree.
■ as,sistant pro'fessor *n* (*US*) a college or university teacher who ranks below an associate professor (ASSOCIATE²).

assize /ə'saɪz/ *n* (usu *pl*) (formerly) a lawcourt held regularly in each county of England and Wales: *be sentenced at the assizes/at the assize court.*

Assoc (also **assoc**) *abbr* associate(d); association.

associate¹ /ə'səʊʃɪeɪt/ *v* **1** ~ sb/sth (with sb/sth) (**a**) to link people or things together in one's mind: [Vn] *You wouldn't normally associate these two writers — their styles are completely different.* [Vnpr] *Whisky is traditionally associated with Scotland.* ○ *I always associate him with fast cars.* (**b**) (usu passive) to connect people or things because they occur together, or because one produces the other: [Vnpr] *the risks associated with drugs* ○ *The new party is not associated with any existing political doctrine.* ○ *The cycle of the tides is associated with the moon.* **2** ~ with sb to meet or be involved with sb, esp sb who is not approved of: [Vpr] *I don't like you associating with such people.* **3** ~ oneself with sth to be involved in or declare that one is in agreement with sth: [Vnpr] *I have never associated myself with political extremism.* Compare DISSOCIATE.

associate² /ə'səʊʃɪət/ *adj* [attrib] **1** joined or connected with a profession or an organization: *an associate company.* **2** (used before a rank, title, etc to indicate a lower status, level of membership, etc): *an associate conductor* ○ *the associate producer of a movie* ○ *Associate members have no right to vote.*
▶ **associate** *n* **1** a partner or companion: *my closest business associates* ○ *He is consulting his associates in the bank.* ○ *The company is called Landor Associates.* **2** an associate member: *The subscription for associates is £45.*
■ as,sociate pro'fessor *n* (*US*) a college or university teacher who ranks next below a PROFESSOR.

association /ə,səʊsɪ'eɪʃn/ *n* **1** [C] a group of people joined together for a shared purpose; an organization: *Do you belong to any professional associations?* ○ *He is the chairman of the Amateur Athletic Association.* See also HOUSING ASSOCIATION. **2** [U, sing] (**a**) ~ (with sb/sth) a link or connection between people or organizations: *There has always been a close association between these two schools.* ○ *We are working in association with a number of local companies to raise money for the homeless.* ○ *His English improved enormously because of his association with native speakers.* (**b**) friendship: *She became famous through her association with several poets.* **3** [C] a mental connection between ideas; an idea or image suggested by sb/sth: *Does the sea have any strong associations for you?*
■ As,sociation 'football *n* [U] (*Brit fml*) = FOOTBALL 2.

assorted /ə'sɔːtɪd/ *adj* of different sorts; mixed: *a box of assorted chocolates.*
▶ **assortment** /ə'sɔːtmənt/ *n* a collection of different things or of different types of the same thing; a

mixture: *a wide assortment of gifts to choose from* ○ *wearing an odd assortment of clothes.*

Asst (also **asst**) *abbr* assistant: *Asst Secretary.*

assuage /ə'sweɪdʒ/ *v* (*fml*) to make sth less severe; to ease sth: [Vn] *assuage one's hunger/grief/longing.*

assume /ə'sjuːm; *US* ə'suːm/ *v* **1** to accept sth as true before there is proof: [Vn] *Why do you always assume the worst* (ie that something bad has happened)? [V.that] *I automatically/naturally assumed (that) he had told her.* ○ *It seems reasonable to assume/I think we can safely assume that the present situation is going to continue.* ○ *I hope to go to university next year, always assuming* (ie provided that) *I pass my exams.* ○ *She would, he assumed, be home at the usual time.* [V.n to inf] *We must assume him to be innocent until he is proved guilty.* **2**(**a**) (of a person, an organization, etc) to take or begin to have power, authority, etc: [Vn] *The chairman will assume office/his new responsibilities next month.* ○ *Rebel forces have assumed control of the capital.* (**b**) to begin to have a particular quality or characteristic, expression, etc: *assume a harassed look* ○ *The problem is beginning to assume massive proportions* (ie become very great). (**c**) to display sth falsely; to pretend sth: [Vn] *assume ignorance/indifference/an air of concern.*
▶ **assumed** *adj* [attrib] pretended; false: *He was living under an assumed name.*

assumption /ə'sʌmpʃn/ *n* **1** [C] a thing that is thought to be true or certain to happen, but is not proved: *an implicit/underlying assumption* ○ *What leads you to make that assumption?* ○ *The theory is based on a series of false/wrong assumptions.* ○ *We are working on the assumption that the rate of inflation will not increase next year.* **2** [C, U] ~ of sth an act of taking or beginning to have power, authority, etc: *her assumption of supreme power.*

assurance /ə'ʃʊərəns; *Brit* also -ʃɔːr-/ *n* **1** (also **self-assurance**) [U] confident belief in one's own abilities and powers: *act with/display/possess assurance* ○ *She shows remarkable assurance on stage for one so young.* **2** [C] a statement expressing certainty about sth; a promise: *seek/receive assurances on a range of issues* ○ *He gave me his personal assurance that the article would be finished by Friday.* ○ *Despite all/repeated assurances to the contrary, parents are seeing examination standards dropping.* **3** [U] (*esp Brit*) insurance, esp on sb's life.

assure /ə'ʃʊə(r); *Brit* also -ʃɔː(r)/ *v* **1**(**a**) ~ sb (of sth) to tell sb sth positively or confidently, esp because they may have doubts about it: [Vn.that] *We were assured that everything possible was being done.* ○ *They'll be perfectly safe with us, I (can) assure you .* [V.speech] *'He'll come back,' Susan assured her airily.* [Vnpr] *They assured him of their willingness to work hard.* (**b**) ~ oneself (of sth) to cause oneself to be sure or feel certain about sth: [Vnpr] *He assured himself of the child's safety.* [Vn.that] *She assured herself that the letter was still in the drawer.* Compare REASSURE. **2** (often passive) to make sth certain; to ENSURE sth: [Vn] *Victory was now assured.* [Vnn] *Her achievement has assured her a place in the history books.* **3** (*Brit*) to INSURE sth, esp against sb's death: [Vn] *What is the sum assured?* ⟐ **IDM** **rest assured** ⇨ REST¹.
▶ **assured** *adj* **1** (also **self-assured**) confident: *He spoke in a calm, assured voice.* **2** certain to happen; guaranteed: *an assured income/tenancy.* **assuredly** /ə'ʃʊərədli; *Brit* also -ʃɔːr-/ *adv* (*dated*) certainly.

aster /'æstə(r)/ *n* a garden plant similar to a DAISY with pink, purple or white flowers.

asterisk /'æstərɪsk/ *n* a symbol like a star (*) used in writing and printing to draw attention to sth, esp an additional note or a FOOTNOTE: *put an asterisk beside/next to their names.*

[V.*to* inf] = verb + *to* infinitive   [Vn.inf (no *to*)] = verb + noun + infinitive without *to*   [V.*ing*] = verb + *-ing* form

astern /əˈstɜːn/ adv **1** in, at or towards the back part of a ship or the tail of an aircraft. **2** (of a ship) backwards: *Full speed astern!*

asteroid /ˈæstərɔɪd/ n any of many small planets revolving round the sun.

asthma /ˈæsmə; US ˈæzmə/ n [U] a chest illness that causes difficulty in breathing: *asthma sufferers* ○ *a severe asthma attack.*
▶ **asthmatic** /æsˈmætɪk; US æz-/ adj of or suffering from asthma: *an asthmatic child* ○ *She is asthmatic.*
— n a person suffering from asthma.

astigmatism /əˈstɪgmətɪzəm/ n [U] a fault in the eye that prevents it seeing things clearly.

astir /əˈstɜː(r)/ adv, adj [pred] **1** in a state of excited movement: *The news set the whole town astir.* **2** (dated) out of bed: *No one was astir.*

astonish /əˈstɒnɪʃ/ v to surprise sb greatly: [Vn] *The news astonished everyone.* [Vn.that] *It astonishes me that no one has thought of this before.* [Vn.to inf] *He was genuinely astonished to be offered the job.*
▶ **astonished** adj [usu pred] very surprised: *She looked astonished when she heard the news.*
astonishing adj very surprising: *an astonishing performance/achievement* ○ *I find it absolutely astonishing that none of you liked the play.* ○ *There were an astonishing number of applicants for the job.*
astonishingly adv: *Jack took the news astonishingly well.* ○ *Astonishingly, a crowd of 50000 turned out to hear him.*
astonishment n [U] very great surprise: *Imagine my astonishment when Peter walked in!* ○ *She was watching the whole incident with astonishment.* ○ *To my astonishment I had completely disappeared.* ○ *He gaped at me in astonishment.*

astound /əˈstaʊnd/ v (usu passive) to surprise or shock sb very much: [Vn] *His arrogance astounded her.* [Vnpr] *She was astounded at his arrogance.* [Vn.to inf] *We were astounded to discover that he had left his wife.* [Vn.that] *They were astounded that anyone could survive such a crash.*
▶ **astounding** adj extremely surprising: *It was an absolutely astounding performance.*

astrakhan /ˌæstrəˈkæn; US ˈæstrəkən/ n [U] the tightly curled wool of young lambs, or material made to look like this: *an astrakhan hat.*

astray /əˈstreɪ/ adv away from the correct path or direction: *We were led astray by a misleading sign.* ○ (fig) *His friends led him astray, and he ended up in prison.* **IDM** **go aˈstray** (esp Brit) (of an object) to become lost: *Your letter seems to have gone astray.*

astride /əˈstraɪd/ adv **1** with one leg on each side. **2** with legs wide apart.
▶ **astride** prep with one leg on each side of sth: *sitting astride a horse* ○ (fig) *a village astride the main road.*

astringent /əˈstrɪndʒənt/ adj **1** harsh; severe: *astringent criticism/critics.* **2** (medical) that can make the skin tighter and stop bleeding: *an astringent cream.*

astro- comb form of the stars or outer space: *astronaut* ○ *astrology.*

astrology /əˈstrɒlədʒi/ n [U] the study of the positions of the stars and of the movements of the planets in the belief that they influence human affairs: *Do you believe in astrology?* ⇨ note at ZODIAC.
▶ **astrologer** /-ədʒə(r)/ n a person who practises astrology.
astrological /ˌæstrəˈlɒdʒɪkl/ adj: *astrological influences.*

astronaut /ˈæstrənɔːt/ n a person who is trained to travel in a spacecraft.

astronomy /əˈstrɒnəmi/ n [U] the scientific study of the sun, moon, stars, planets, etc.

▶ **astronomer** /-nəmə(r)/ n a person who studies astronomy.
astronomical /ˌæstrəˈnɒmɪkl/ adj **1** of astronomy. **2** (also **astronomic**) (infml) (of an amount, price, etc) very large: *He's been offered an astronomical salary.* ○ *The cost will be astronomical.* **astronomically** adv: *Interest rates are astronomically high.*

astrophysics /ˌæstrəʊˈfɪzɪks/ n [sing v] the branch of ASTRONOMY dealing with the physical and chemical structure of the stars, planets, etc.

astute /əˈstjuːt; US əˈstuːt/ adj clever and quick at seeing how to gain an advantage; SHREWD: *an astute lawyer/businessman/judge of character* ○ *It was an astute move to sell the shares just then.* ▶ **astutely** adv. **astuteness** n [U].

asunder /əˈsʌndə(r)/ adv (dated or fml) into pieces; apart: *families rent/torn asunder by the revolution.*

asylum /əˈsaɪləm/ n **1** (also fml **political asylum**) [U] protection given by a state to sb who has left their own country, esp for political reasons: *seek asylum in the UK* ○ *He asked the government to grant asylum to the refugees.* **2** [C] (dated) a hospital for the care of mentally ill people: *a lunatic asylum.*
▶ **aˈsylum seeker** n a person who asks for political asylum.

asymmetric /ˌeɪsɪˈmetrɪk/ (also **asymmetrical** /-ɪkl/) adj not having parts or features that correspond to each other in size, shape, function, etc; lacking SYMMETRY(1): *Most people's faces are asymmetrical.*

at /ət; strong form æt/ prep **1(a)** (indicating a point in space): *at the end of the runway* ○ *at the corner of the street* ○ *go in at the side door* ○ *change at Crewe* ○ *arrive at the airport* ○ *At the roundabout take the third exit.* ○ *I'll be at home all morning.* **(b)** (used with the name of a building, esp with reference to the activities happening inside): *She's at the theatre/cinema* (ie watching a play/film). ○ *She works at the hospital.* ○ *He's at* (ie staying at) *the Grand Hotel.* **(c)** (indicating presence at an event): *at a concert/conference/match.* **(d)** (indicating a place of employment or study): *He's been at the bank longer than anyone else.* ○ *I'm at the head office.* ○ *She's at Oxford* (ie Oxford University). (Compare: ... *spending three days in Oxford as a tourist.*) **(e)** (used with the name of a person + 's to refer to that person's home or place of work): *They're at Keith's.* ○ *I was at my father's.* ○ *They didn't have any bread at the baker's.*
2(a) (indicating an exact point in time): *She'll meet/leave at 2 o'clock* ○ *at 3.15/at a quarter past 3* ○ *at the end of the week* ○ *We woke at dawn.* ○ *I didn't know he was dead at the time of speaking to you* (ie when I spoke to you). ○ *At the moment you called I was in the bath.* **(b)** (indicating a period of time): *At night you can see the stars.* ○ *What are you doing at/* (US) *on the weekend?* ○ *take a few days off at Christmas/ Easter.* **(c)** (used to indicate the age at which sb does sth): *She got married at 55.* ○ *You can retire at 60.* ○ *He left school at (the age of) 16.* ⇨ note at TIME¹. **3(a)** in the direction of or towards sb/sth: *aim the ball at the hole* ○ *throw stones at the can in the water* (ie trying to hit it) ○ *direct one's advertising at a wider audience* ○ *The dog rushed at me, wagging its tail.* ○ *smile/stare/wave at sb* ○ *She shouted at me but I couldn't hear.* **(b)** (used after a v to show that sb tries to do sth, or partly does sth, but does not succeed or complete it): *He clutched wildly at the rope as he fell.* ○ *I could only guess at the meaning of the sign.* ○ *She nibbled at a sandwich* (ie ate only tiny bits of it). **4** (indicating the distance away from sth): *hold sth at arm's length* ○ *Can you read a car number-plate at fifty metres?* **5** (indicating a state, condition or continuous activity): *put sb at risk* ○ *Our country is now at war.* ○ *The soldiers were*

standing at ease (ie in a relaxed position). ○ *She's at work in the garden.* ○ *I think Mr Harris is at lunch.* **6(a)** (indicating a rate, price, speed, etc): *House prices rose at a higher rate than inflation.* ○ *driving at 70 mph* ○ *I bought this coat at half-price/at 50% discount.* ○ *They went into his office six at a time.* ○ *The TV was on at full volume.* (**b**) (indicating order or frequency): *at the first attempt* ○ *at two-minute intervals* (ie once every two minutes). **7** in response to sth: *attend the dinner at the chairman's invitation* ○ *at the king's command.* **8** (used with *her, his, our,* etc and a superlative *adj*): *This was Madonna at her best.* ○ *an example of local craftsmanship at its finest* ○ *The garden's at its most beautiful in June.* **9** (used after many *adjs* and *ns*): *good/clever/skilled at restoring furniture* ○ *hopeless at (playing) chess* ○ *She's a genius at doing crossword puzzles.* ○ *impatient at the delay* ○ *amused at the cartoons* ○ *delighted at the result* ○ *puzzled at her silence* ○ *his anger at being beaten.* **IDM** **at that** also; too; in addition: *He managed to buy a car after all — and rather a nice one, at that.* **where it's 'at** (*infml*) a place or an activity that is very popular or fashionable: *Judging by the crowds waiting to get in this seems to be where it's at.*

atavistic /ˌætəˈvɪstɪk/ *adj* of or relating to the behaviour of one's ancestors in the distant past: *an atavistic urge.*

ate *pt* of EAT.

-ate *suff* **1** (with *ns* forming *adjs*) full of or showing a specified quality: *affectionate* ○ *passionate* ○ *Italianate.* **2** (forming *ns*) (**a**) a specified status or function: *doctorate.* (**b**) a person or group of people with a specified status: *potentate* ○ *electorate.* (**c**) (*chemistry*) a salt(2) formed by the action of a particular acid: *sulphate* ○ *nitrate.* **3** (with *ns* and *adjs* forming *vs*) to give to sth the specified thing or quality: *hyphenate* ○ *chlorinate* ○ *activate.* ► **-ately** (forming *advs*): *affectionately.*

atelier /əˈteliei; *US* ˌætlˈjei/ *n* a room or building in which an artist works.

atheism /ˈeɪθiɪzəm/ *n* [U] the belief that God does not exist.
► **atheist** /ˈeɪθiɪst/ *n* a person who believes that there is no God: *a complete/confirmed atheist.* Compare AGNOSTIC, HEATHEN 1, PAGAN.
atheistic /ˌeɪθiˈɪstɪk/ *adj.*

athlete /ˈæθliːt/ *n* **1** a person who trains to compete in physical exercises and sports, esp running and jumping. **2** a person who has the strength and skill to perform well at sports: *She's a natural athlete.*
■ **ˌathlete's 'foot** *n* [U] (*infml*) a disease of the feet affecting the skin between the toes.

athletic /æθˈletɪk/ *adj* **1** physically strong, healthy and active: *an athletic figure* ○ *She looks very athletic.* **2** [attrib] of or relating to physical exercises and sports, esp running and jumping: *an athletic club* ○ *athletic sports.* ► **athleticism** /æθˈletɪsɪzəm/ *n* [U]: *move with athleticism and grace.*

athletics /æθˈletɪks/ *n* [sing *v*] physical exercises and competitive sports, esp running and jumping: *an athletics meeting/squad.*

-ation ⇨ **-ION**.

atishoo /əˈtɪʃuː/ (*Brit*) (*US* also **achoo**) *interj* (used in writing to indicate the noise made by sb sneezing (SNEEZE *v*)).

-ative *suff* (with *vs* forming *adjs*) doing or tending to do sth: *illustrative* ○ *imitative* ○ *talkative.* ► **-atively** (forming *advs*): *quantitatively.*

atlas /ˈætləs/ *n* a book of maps: *a road atlas of Europe.*

atmosphere /ˈætməsfɪə(r)/ *n* **1(a)** **the atmosphere** [sing] the mixture of gases that surrounds the earth: *the upper atmosphere.* (**b**) [C] a mixture of gases that surrounds any planet or star: *the moon's atmosphere* ○ *an atmosphere that supports life.* **2** [sing] the air in or around a place: *a stuffy overheated atmosphere.* **3** [sing] a feeling in the mind that is created by a group of people or a place; a mood: *a genuine pub atmosphere* ○ *a carnival atmosphere* ○ *An atmosphere of tension filled the room.* ○ *The whole atmosphere changed as soon as she walked in.* ○ *The atmosphere over dinner was relaxed and friendly.*

atmospheric /ˌætməsˈferɪk/ *adj* **1** of or relating to the earth's atmosphere: *atmospheric pollution* ○ *unusual atmospheric conditions.* **2** creating a distinctive mood: *atmospheric lighting* ○ *a highly atmospheric piece of music.*
■ **ˌatmospheric 'pressure** *n* [U] pressure at a particular point due to the weight of the column of air above it.

atoll /ˈætɒl/ *n* an island made of CORAL and shaped like a ring with a lake of salt water in the middle.

atom /ˈætəm/ *n* **1** the smallest part of an element that can be part of a chemical reaction: *the splitting of the atom* ○ *Two atoms of hydrogen combine with one atom of oxygen to form a molecule of water.* **2** an extremely small quantity or thing: *There isn't an atom of truth in the rumour.*

atomic /əˈtɒmɪk/ *adj* [usu attrib] (**a**) of an atom or atoms: *atomic physics.* (**b**) of or relating to the energy released by atoms when they are split: *US atomic capabilities* ○ *atomic energy/power* ○ *the atomic bomb* ○ *atomic warfare.* See also NUCLEAR.

atomize, -ise /ˈætəmaɪz/ *v* [Vn] to reduce sth to atoms or very small pieces.
► **atomizer, -iser** *n* a device for forcing liquid, esp perfume, out through a very small hole as a fine spray.

atone /əˈtəʊn/ *v* ~ (**for sth**) (*fml*) to act in a way that compensates for a previous wrong, error, etc: [Vpr] *atone for a crime/a sin/one's mistakes* [V] *a desire to atone.* ► **atonement** *n* [U].

atop /əˈtɒp/ *prep* (*dated or rhet*) at or on the top of sth: *a seagull perched atop the mast.*

-ator *suff* (with *vs* forming *ns*) a person or thing that performs the specified action: *creator* ○ *percolator.*

atrocious /əˈtrəʊʃəs/ *adj* **1** very wicked, cruel or shocking: *atrocious crimes/acts of brutality.* **2** (*infml*) very bad or unpleasant: *speak French with an atrocious accent* ○ *Isn't the weather atrocious?* ► **atrociously** *adv.*

atrocity /əˈtrɒsəti/ *n* (**a**) [C esp *pl*] a very wicked or cruel act: *Many atrocities have been committed against innocent people in wartime.* (**b**) [U] great wickedness or cruelty.

atrophy /ˈætrəfi/ *n* [U] the condition of losing flesh, muscle, strength, etc in a part of the body, esp because of inadequate blood supply or lack of exercise: (*fig*) *The cultural life of the country will sink into atrophy unless more writers and artists emerge.* ► **atrophy** *v* (*pt, pp* **-ied**) to suffer atrophy or cause sth to suffer atrophy: [Vn] *atrophied limbs/muscles* ○ (*fig*) *Their idealism had become totally atrophied.* [also V].

attach /əˈtætʃ/ *v* **1** ~ **sth** (**to sth**) to fasten or join sth to sth: [Vnpr] *attach a label to each piece of luggage* [Vn] *a house with a garage attached* ○ *Just complete the attached form and return it in the envelope provided.* Compare DETACH 1. **2(a)** ~ **oneself to sb/sth** to join sb/sth as a companion or member, sometimes as one who is not welcome or invited: [Vnpr] *A young man attached himself to me at the party and I couldn't get rid of him.* ○ *I attached myself to a group of tourists entering the museum.* (**b**) ~ **sb to sb/sth** (esp passive) to make sb available to a person or group for special duties: [Vnpr] *You'll be attached to this department until the end of the year.* **3(a)** ~ **sth** (**to sth**) to believe there is eg value, importance or truth, etc in sth: [Vnpr] *Do you attach any significance to what he said?* [Vn] *There is no* *mystery attached.* (**b**) ~ **to sb** (*fml*) to be connected with sb: [Vpr] *No blame attaches to you in this affair.* **IDM** **no strings attached/without strings** ⇨ STRING[1].

▶ **attached** *adj* [pred] ~ (**to sb/sth**) full of affection for sb/sth: *I've never seen two people so attached (to each other).* ○ *We've grown very attached to this house and would hate to move.*

attachment *n* **1** [U] the action of attaching or the fact of being attached: *two centuries of attachment to Britain* ○ *She's on attachment to* (ie temporarily working in) *the Ministry of Defence.* **2** [C] a thing that is or can be attached to sth: *an electric drill with a range of different attachments* ○ *a shower attachment.* **3** [U] ~ (**to/for sb/sth**) affection: *feel a strong/ deep attachment to one's friends.*

attaché /əˈtæʃeɪ; US ˌætəˈʃeɪ/ *n* a person on the staff of an AMBASSADOR, esp one who has a particular area of responsibility: *the cultural/military/press attaché.*
■ **atˈtaché case** *n* a small hard case for carrying documents.

attack /əˈtæk/ *n* **1** [C, U] ~ (**on sb/sth**) a violent attempt to hurt, overcome or defeat sb/sth: *launch/ make/mount an attack on the enemy/bridge/town* ○ *a sudden unprovoked attack* ○ *a series of racial/sex attacks* ○ *the victim of a terrorist attack* ○ *Our troops are now on the attack.* ○ *The patrol came under attack from all sides.* See also COUNTER-ATTACK. **2** [C, U] ~ (**on sb/sth**) strong criticism in speech or writing: *a scathing/fierce/powerful attack on the government's policies.* **3** [C] ~ (**on sth**) a vigorous attempt to deal with sth: *launch an all-out attack on poverty/unemployment/smoking.* **4** [C] a sudden short period of illness or discomfort: *an attack of asthma/flu/hiccups/nerves* ○ (*fig*) *I got an attack of the giggles.* See also HEART ATTACK. **5** [C usu *sing*] (*sport*) the players who are in the position of trying to score in a game, eg of football or hockey: *England's attack has been weakened by the injury of certain key players.* Compare DEFENCE 3.

▶ **attack** *v* **1** to make an attack on sb/sth: [V] *They decided to attack at night.* [Vn] *attack a neighbouring country* ○ *A woman was attacked and robbed by a gang of youths.* **2** to act harmfully on sth/sb: [Vn] *a disease that attacks the brain* ○ *Rust attacks metals.* **3** to criticize sb/sth severely: [Vn] *a newspaper article attacking the vice-president.* **4** to begin to deal with sth vigorously; to TACKLE(1) sth: [Vn] *The government is making no attempt to attack unemployment.* ○ *They attacked their meal with gusto.* **5** (*sport*) to play in order to win, esp by trying to score goals: [V] *They kept attacking and finally won a penalty.* ○ *good attacking football.* **attacker** *n* a person who attacks: *a sex attacker.*

attain /əˈteɪn/ *v* **1** to succeed in getting sth; to achieve sth, esp with effort: [Vn] *attain a position of power* ○ *attain one's goal/ambition* ○ *attain our target of $50 000.* **2** [Vn] (*fml*) to reach a particular age or condition: *attain retirement age.*
▶ **attainable** *adj* that can be attained: *These objectives are certainly/perfectly attainable.*
attainment *n* **1** [U] success in reaching or achieving sth: *The attainment of her ambitions was still a dream.* **2** [U,C usu *pl*] a thing attained, esp skill or knowledge: *raise the standard of educational attainment* ○ *attainment targets for students* ○ *a scholar of the highest attainments.*

attempt /əˈtempt/ *v* to make an effort to succeed at sth; to try to do sth: [Vn] *The prisoners attempted an escape, but failed.* ○ *All candidates must attempt Questions 1-5.* [V.to inf] *He admitted attempting to smuggle cannabis.*
▶ **attempt** *n* **1** ~ (**to do sth / at doing sth**) an act of attempting sth: *a rescue/a coup/an assassination*

attempt ○ *desperate/vain/abortive attempts* ○ *They made no attempt to escape.* ○ *My early attempts at learning to drive were unsuccessful.* ○ *Farmers are certain to resist any attempt to reduce subsidies.* **2** ~ (**at sth**) a thing produced by sb trying to do or make sth: *My first attempt at a chocolate cake tasted horrible.* **3** ~ (**on sth**) an effort to improve on sth: *the latest attempt on the world land speed record.* **4** ~ **on sth** an effort to kill sb: *They have made an attempt on her life.*
attempted *adj* [attrib] (of a crime, etc) that has not succeeded: *an attempted cover-up* ○ *The police have charged the man with attempted murder/rape.*

attend /əˈtend/ *v* **1(a)** to be present at an event: [Vn] *I was unable to attend his funeral.* [V, Vn] *They had a quiet wedding — only a few friends attended (it).* [Vnadv] *The meeting was well attended* (ie many people were there). (**b**) to go regularly to a place: [Vn] *attend school/church.* ⇨ note at SCHOOL. **2** ~ **to sb/sth** (**a**) to deal with sb/sth: [Vpr] *I have some urgent business to attend to.* (**b**) to give practical help and attention to sb/sth: [Vpr] *A nurse attends to his needs constantly.* ○ *Are you being attended to, sir* (eg said by an assistant to a customer in a shop)? **3** ~ (**to sb/sth**) (*fml*) to concentrate on sb/sth: [Vpr] *You can't have been attending properly.* [Vpr] *Attend to your work and stop talking.* **4** (*fml*) (**a**) to care for sb: [Vn] *Dr Patel attended her in hospital.* (**b**) to be with sb/sth; to accompany sb: *The Queen was attended by her ladies-in-waiting.*
▶ **attender** *n* a person who regularly to a place: *She's a regular attender at evening classes.*

attendance /əˈtendəns/ *n* **1(a)** [U] the action or time of being present: *Attendance at these lectures is not compulsory.* ○ *A nurse was in constant attendance* (ie always present or near). **2** [C] a number of people present: *They're expecting a large attendance at the meeting.* ○ *Attendances have increased/are up since we reduced the price of tickets.* **IDM** **dance attendance on/upon sb** ⇨ DANCE[2].
■ **atˈtendance allowance** *n* (*Brit*) money paid by the state to sb who cares for a severely ill or disabled (DISABLE 1) relation.

attendant /əˈtendənt/ *n* **1** a person whose job is to provide a service in a public place: *a cloakroom/car park/museum attendant.* **2** (esp *pl*) a servant or companion: *the Queen's attendants.*
▶ **attendant** *adj* [attrib] (*fml*) accompanying: *attendant circumstances/problems* ○ *famine and its attendant diseases.*

attention /əˈtenʃn/ *n* **1** [U] the action of turning one's mind to sth/sb or noticing sth/sb: *an issue which has become the focus of media/international attention* ○ *the report's attention to detail* ○ *Small children have a very short attention span.* ○ *Please pay attention* (ie listen carefully) *(to what I am saying).* ○ *She was trying to attract the waiter's attention.* ○ *It has come/been brought to my attention* (ie I have been informed) *that...* **2** [U] special care or action: *This letter is for the urgent/ personal attention of the manager.* ○ *She is in need of medical attention.* ○ *The roof needs attention* (ie needs to be repaired). **3** [C usu *pl*] (*fml*) a kind or thoughtful (THOUGHT[2]) act: *She was flattered by his many little attentions.* **4** [U] a position taken by a soldier, standing very straight with feet together and arms stretched downwards: *come to/stand at attention.* Compare EASE[1] 3. **IDM** **catch sb's attention/eye** ⇨ CATCH[1]. **call sb's attention to sth** ⇨ CALL[1]. **draw attention to sth/sb** ⇨ DRAW[1]. **give one's undivided attention; get/have sb's undivided attention** ⇨ UNDIVIDED. ▶ **attention** *interj* **1** (calling people to listen to an announcement, etc): *Attention, please! The bus will leave in ten minutes.* ○ *Attention all shipping...* **2** (also *infml* **shun** /ʃʌn/) (ordering soldiers to come to attention (4)).

attentive /ə'tentɪv/ adj ~ (to sb/sth) giving close attention to sb/sth; alert: *an attentive audience* ○ *A good hostess is always attentive to the needs of her guests.* ▶ **attentively** adv: *listening attentively to the speaker.* **attentiveness** n [U].

attenuate /ə'tenjueɪt/ v (fml) **1** to make sth/sb thin: [Vn] *attenuated limbs.* **2** to reduce the force or value of sth: [Vn] *an attenuated strain of the virus.* ▶ **attenuation** /ə,tenju'eɪʃn/ n [U].

attest /ə'test/ v (fml) **1** ~ (to) sth to be or give clear proof of sth: [V] *She is, as countless stories about her attest, deeply religious.* [Vpr] *I can attest to his tremendous energy and initiative.* [Vn] *His concern for the famine victims is an attested fact.* **2** [Vn] to declare sth to be true or genuine; to be a witness to sth: *attest a signature/will.*

attic /'ætɪk/ n a space or room immediately below the roof of a house: *furniture stored in the attic* ○ *an attic bedroom.* Compare GARRET. See also LOFT[1].

attire /ə'taɪə(r)/ n [U] (fml or rhet) clothes; dress: *wearing formal attire.*

▶ **attired** adj [pred] (fml or rhet) ~ (in sth) dressed: *suitably attired in clerical garb.*

attitude /'ætɪtjuːd; US -tuːd/ n **1** ~ (to/towards sb/ sth) a way of thinking about sb/sth or behaving towards sb/sth: *changes in public attitudes* ○ *That's a very sexist attitude.* ○ *I don't like your attitude.* ○ *What is your attitude to abortion?* ○ *She shows a very professional/positive attitude to her work.* ○ *I take the attitude that people are in control of their own destinies.* **2** (fml) a position of the body: *The photographer has caught him in the attitude of prayer* (ie kneeling). **IDM** **strike an attitude/a pose** ⇨ STRIKE[2].

attn abbr (commerce) for the attention of: *Publicity Dept, attn Mr C Biggs.*

attorney /ə'tɜːni/ n **1** (esp US) a lawyer, esp one qualified to act for clients in a lawcourt. See also DISTRICT ATTORNEY. **2** a person appointed to act for another in business or legal matters: *He was given power of attorney* (ie authority to act as an attorney) *over the funds.*

■ **At,torney-'General** n (in certain countries) the chief legal officer, appointed by the government. Compare SOLICITOR-GENERAL.

attract /ə'trækt/ v **1(a)** ~ sb (to sb/sth) (esp passive) to cause sb to feel interest, pleasure, affection, etc: [Vnpr] *Babies are attracted to bright colours.* ○ *I was always attracted to the idea of working overseas.* [Vn, Vnpr] *Her shyness was what attracted me (to her) most.* [Vn] *the need for child-care facilities to attract and keep women workers* ○ *The light attracted a lot of insects.* ○ *The dog was attracted by the smell of the meat.* **(b)** to cause a particular reaction: [Vn] *attract sb's attention/interest/support* ○ *The new play has attracted considerable criticism.* **2** to pull sth by force: [Vn] *A magnet attracts steel.*

attraction /ə'trækʃn/ n **1** [U, sing] the action or power of attracting sb/sth: *the secrets of sexual attraction* ○ *I can't see the attraction of sitting on the beach all day.* ○ *They felt a strong mutual attraction.* ○ *She felt an immediate attraction for/to him.* Compare REPULSION. **2** [C] a person or thing that attracts sb/sth: *Buckingham Palace and other major tourist attractions* ○ *One of the main attractions/An added attraction of the job is the chance to travel.* ○ *City life holds few attractions for me.*

attractive /ə'træktɪv/ adj having the power to attract; pleasing or interesting: *attractive prices* ○ *The porch is a particularly attractive feature of the building.* ○ *He's nice, but I don't find him at all attractive physically.* ○ *The company has made us a highly attractive proposition.* ⇨ note at BEAUTIFUL. ▶ **attractively** adv: *attractively arranged/displayed/ presented.* **attractiveness** n [U]: *the growing attractiveness of living abroad.*

attribute[1] /ə'trɪbjuːt/ v ~ sth to (sb/sth) to regard sth as belonging to, caused by or produced by sb/ sth: [Vnpr] *This play is usually attributed to Shakespeare.* ○ *She attributes her success to hard work and a bit of luck.* [Vn] *The committee refused to attribute blame without further information.*

▶ **attributable** /ə'trɪbjətəbl/ adj [pred] ~ to sb/sth that can be attributed to sb/sth: *Their illnesses are attributable to poor diet.*

attribution /,ætrɪ'bjuːʃn/ n [U, C]: *the mistaken attribution of 4 000 votes to the Democratic Party* ○ *It is difficult to be sure whether this attribution is correct.*

attribute[2] /'ætrɪbjuːt/ n a quality regarded as a natural or typical part of sb/sth: *Her greatest attribute was her kindness.* ○ *Patience is one of the most important attributes in a teacher.*

attributive /ə'trɪbjətɪv/ adj (grammar) (abbreviated as *attrib* in this dictionary) (of adjectives or nouns) used directly before a noun, to describe it. Compare PREDICATIVE. ▶ **attributively** adv.

attrition /ə'trɪʃn/ n [U] a gradual process of becoming or making sb/sth weaker and less confident through continual attacks, difficulties, etc. See also WAR OF ATTRITION.

attune /ə'tjuːn; US ə'tuːn/ v ~ sth/sb to sth (usu passive) to make sth/sb adjust to sth new and become familiar or in harmony with it: *become attuned to the idea of change* [Vnpr] *We/Our ears are now attuned to the noise of the new factory nearby.*

atypical /,eɪ'tɪpɪkl/ adj not representative or characteristic of its type; not typical: *atypical behaviour* ○ *a creature that is atypical of its species.*

aubergine /'əʊbəʒiːn/ (also esp US **eggplant**) n [C, U] a large dark purple vegetable with a soft white inside, usu cooked before eating.

auburn /'ɔːbən/ adj (esp of hair) reddish-brown.

auction /'ɔːkʃn, 'ɒk-/ n [C, U] a public event at which things are sold to the person who offers the most money for them: *a cattle auction* ○ *attend all the local auctions* ○ *The house is up for auction/will be sold by auction.* ○ *It should fetch* (ie be sold for) *£100 000 at auction.*

▶ **auction** v [Vn] to sell sth at an auction. **PHRV auction sth off** to sell sth at an auction, esp sth that is no longer required: *The Army is auctioning off some surplus equipment.*

auctioneer /,ɔːkʃə'nɪə(r), ,ɒk-/ n a person whose job is conducting auctions.

audacious /ɔː'deɪʃəs/ adj **1** showing a willingness to take risks; bold(1): *an audacious decision/plan/ scheme.* **2** showing a lack of respect; IMPUDENT: *an audacious remark.* ▶ **audaciously** adv. **audacity** /ɔː'dæsəti/ n [U]: *He had the audacity to tell me I was too fat.* ○ *I admire the sheer audacity of the plan.*

audible /'ɔːdəbl/ adj that can be heard clearly: *Her voice was barely/scarcely audible above the noise of the wind.* Compare INAUDIBLE. ▶ **audibility** /,ɔːdə'bɪləti/ n [U]. **audibly** /-əbli/ adv: *As the curtain rose, the audience gasped audibly.*

audience /'ɔːdiəns/ n **1** [CGp] a group of people who have gathered together to hear or watch sb/sth: *The audience was/were enthusiastic on the opening night of the play.* ○ *She has addressed audiences all over the country.* **2** [C] a number of people who watch, read or listen to the same thing: *a TV audience* ○ *An audience of millions watched the funeral on television.* ○ *His book reached an even wider audience when it was made into a film.* **3** [C] a formal interview with a ruler or an important person: *request an audience with the Pope.*

audio /'ɔːdiəʊ/ n [U, usu attrib] sound recorded and produced by electronic means: *study at home with workbooks, audio and video cassettes* ○ *audio equipment.* Compare VIDEO.

audio- comb form of hearing or sound: *audiovisual.*

[V.to inf] = verb + to infinitive   [Vn.inf (no to)] = verb + noun + infinitive without to   [V.ing] = verb + -ing form

audiovisual /ˌɔːdiəʊˈvɪʒuəl/ *adj* (*abbr* **AV**) using both sight and sound: ˌaudiovisual ˈaids for the class-room, such as video recorders and overhead projectors.

audit /ˈɔːdɪt/ *n* [C, U] **1** an official examination of the accounts of a company, etc to see that they are true and correct: an annual audit report ○ prepare accounts for audit. **2** an examination of the quality, state, efficiency, etc of sth: an environmental audit.
▶ **audit** *v* [Vn] to examine the accounts of a company, etc officially.

audition /ɔːˈdɪʃn/ *n* a short performance given by an actor, a singer, a musician, etc to test whether he or she is suitable for a particular role, job, place at college, etc: I'm going to the audition but I don't expect I'll get a part.
▶ **audition** *v* **1** ~ (**for sth**) to take part in an audition: [Vpr] Which part are you auditioning for? [also V]. **2** to watch and listen to sb at an audition: [Vn] None of the actors we've auditioned is suitable.

auditor /ˈɔːdɪtə(r)/ *n* a person who officially examines the accounts of a company, etc; a person who performs an AUDIT.

auditorium /ˌɔːdɪˈtɔːriəm/ (*pl* **auditoriums** or **auditoria** /-riə/) *n* the part of a theatre, concert hall, etc in which the audience sits.

auditory /ˈɔːdətri; *US* -tɔːri/ *adj* (*techn*) of or concerned with hearing: the auditory nerve. ⊏> picture at EAR[1].

au fait /ˌəʊ ˈfeɪ/ *adj* [pred] ~ (**with sth**) (*French*) completely familiar (with sth): It's my first week here so I'm not yet au fait with the system.

Aug *abbr* August: 31 Aug 1993.

aught /ɔːt/ *pron* (*arch*) anything. **IDM** **for aught/all one/sb cares/knows** (indicating that sth does not matter to one/sb): I might as well be dead for aught/all he cares.

augment /ɔːɡˈment/ *v* (*fml*) to make sth larger in number or size; to increase sth: [Vn] augment one's income by writing reviews. ▶ **augmentation** /ˌɔːɡmenˈteɪʃn/ *n* [U, C].

augur /ˈɔːɡə(r)/ *v* to be a sign of sth in the future; to FORETELL sth: [Vn] Does this augur victory or defeat for the government in the election? [Vadv] The quality of your work augurs well/ill for the forthcoming examinations.
▶ **augury** /ˈɔːɡjʊri/ *n* a sign of what will happen in the future; an OMEN.

august /ɔːˈɡʌst/ *adj* [usu attrib] inspiring feelings of respect; grand and impressive: an august body of elder statesmen.

August /ˈɔːɡəst/ *n* [U, C] (*abbr* **Aug**) the 8th month of the year, next after July. For further guidance on how August is used, see the examples at April.

auk /ɔːk/ *n* a northern sea bird with short narrow wings.

auld lang syne /ˌɔːld læŋ ˈsaɪn/ *n* (*Scot*) the title of a popular song sung esp at the beginning of each new year. It expresses feelings of friendship for the sake of good times long ago.

aunt /ɑːnt; *US* ænt/ *n* **1** the sister of one's father or mother or the wife of one's uncle: Aunt Mary is my mother's sister. She is the only aunt I have. ⊏> App 4. **2** (*infml*) (used by children, usu in front of a first name) a woman who is a friend of one's parents. See also AGONY AUNT.
▶ **auntie** (also **aunty**) /ˈɑːnti; *US* ˈænti/ *n* (*infml*) aunt.

au pair /ˌəʊ ˈpeə(r)/ (*French*) a person, usu a young woman from abroad, who stays free of charge with a family in return for doing work in the house, looking after the children, etc: an au pair girl ○ We've got a German au pair for six months.

aura /ˈɔːrə/ *n* a distinctive atmosphere that seems to surround and be caused by a person or thing: She always has an aura of confidence about her.

aural /ˈɔːrəl/ *adj* of or concerning the ear or hearing: aural and visual images ○ aural comprehension tests.
▶ **aurally** *adv*.

aureole /ˈɔːriəʊl/ *n* a HALO.

au revoir /ˌəʊ rəˈvwɑː(r)/ *interj* (*French*) goodbye until we meet again.

auricle /ˈɔːrɪkl/ *n* **1** the external part of the ear. ⊏> picture at EAR[1]. **2** (a small section in) each of the two upper parts of the heart. Compare VENTRICLE 1.

aurora borealis /ɔːˌrɔːrə ˌbɔːriˈeɪlɪs/ *n* [sing] (also **the northern lights** [pl]) bands of light, mainly red and green, seen in the sky at night near the North Pole and caused by electrical RADIATION(1).

auspices /ˈɔːspɪsɪz/ *n* [pl] **IDM** **under the auspices of sb/sth** with the help, support, protection, etc of sb/sth: set up a business under the auspices of a government aid scheme ○ a relief expedition under United Nations auspices.

auspicious /ɔːˈspɪʃəs/ *adj* showing signs of future success; favourable; promising: an auspicious date for the wedding ○ make an auspicious start to the new term. Compare INAUSPICIOUS.

Aussie /ˈɒzi/ *n, adj* (*infml*) (a native or inhabitant) of Australia.

austere /ɒˈstɪə(r), ɔːˈstɪə(r)/ *adj* **1** severe and morally strict; having no pleasures or comforts: My father was always a rather distant, austere figure. ○ monks leading simple, austere lives. **2** very simple and plain; without decoration: The room was furnished in austere style.
▶ **austerely** *adv*.
austerity /ɒˈsterəti, ɔː-/ *n* **1** [U] the quality of being austere: the austerity of the government's economic measures ○ War was followed by many years of austerity. **2** [C usu *pl*] a condition, an activity or a practice that is part of an austere way of life: Wartime austerities included food rationing and shortage of fuel.

Australian /ɒˈstreɪliən, ɔːˈstreɪliən/ *n, adj* (abbreviated as *Austral* in this dictionary) (a native or inhabitant) of Australia.
■ **Auˌstralian ˈRules** *n* [U] an Australian game, similar to Rugby and played by two teams of 18 players.

authentic /ɔːˈθentɪk/ *adj* known to be true or genuine: an authentic document/signature/painting ○ authentic French cheeses.
▶ **authentically** /-kli/ *adv*.
authenticity /ˌɔːθenˈtɪsəti/ *n* [U] the quality of being authentic: The authenticity of the manuscript is beyond doubt.

authenticate /ɔːˈθentɪkeɪt/ *v* to prove sth to be valid or genuine or true: [Vn] authenticate a claim ○ a historically authenticated document [Vn-n] Experts have authenticated the writing as that of Shakespeare himself. ▶ **authentication** /ɔːˌθentɪˈkeɪʃn/ *n* [U].

author /ˈɔːθə(r)/ *n* **1** the writer of a book, play, etc: Dickens is my favourite author. ○ She is the author of numerous scientific articles and books. **2** the person who creates or begins sth, esp a plan or an idea: As the author of the proposal I can't really comment.
▶ **authoress** /ˈɔːθəres/ *n* (*dated*) a woman author.
authorial /ɔːˈθɔːriəl/ *adj* [usu attrib] of an author.
authorship *n* [U] **1** the identity of the writer of a book, etc: The authorship of this poem is not known. ○ She admitted her authorship of the offending lines. **2** the occupation of being an author.

authoritarian /ɔːˌθɒrɪˈteəriən/ *adj* favouring complete obedience to authority, esp that of the state, at the expense of personal freedom: an authoritarian government/regime/doctrine ○ The school is run on authoritarian lines.

▶ **authoritarian** *n* a person who believes in complete obedience to authority: *My father was a strict authoritarian.* **authoritarianism** *n* [U].

authoritative /ɔːˈθɒrətətɪv; *US* -teɪtɪv/ *adj* **1** given with or showing authority; requiring obedience; official: *authoritative instructions/orders* ○ *an authoritative manner/tone of voice.* **2** that can be trusted; reliable: *information from an authoritative source.* ▶ **authoritatively** *adv*.

authority /ɔːˈθɒrəti/ *n* **1** [U] **(a)** the power to give orders and make others obey: *The leader must be a person of authority.* ○ *She now has authority over the people she used to take orders from.* ○ *a deep distrust of those in authority* (ie having a position of power or command) ○ *I am acting under the authority of* (ie following orders issued by) *the UN.* ○ *It was done without the manager's authority* (ie permission). **(b)** ~ **(to do sth)** the right to act in a specific way: *Only the treasurer has authority to sign cheques.* ○ *We have the authority to search this building.* **2** [C often *pl*] a person or group having the power to make decisions or take action: *He's in the care of the local authority.* ○ *a local education authority* ○ *The health authorities are investigating the matter.* ○ *I shall have to report this to the authorities.* **3(a)** [U] the power to influence people because of inspiring respect, having special knowledge, etc: *the moral authority of the Bible* ○ *have an air of authority* ○ *He can speak with authority on a great range of subjects.* **(b)** [C, U] ~ **(on sth)** a person with special knowledge: *She's an authority on phonetics.* **(c)** [C] a book, etc that can supply reliable information or evidence: *What is your authority for that statement?* ○ *I have it on good authority* (ie have reliable information) *that she's thinking of leaving her job.*

authorize, -ise /ˈɔːθəraɪz/ *v* **1** to give authority to sb: [Vn] *our authorized agent* [Vn.*to* inf] *I have authorized him to act for me while I am away.* **2** to give approval or permission for sth: [Vn] *authorize a payment* ○ *an authorized biography* ○ *Has this visit been authorized?*

▶ **authorization, -isation** /ˌɔːθəraɪˈzeɪʃn; *US* -rəˈz-/ *n* **1** ~ **(for sth / to do sth) (a)** [U] the permission or power given to sb to do sth: *enter a security area without authorization.* **(b)** [C] a document, etc giving this: *May I see your authorization for this?* **2** [U] the action of authorizing sth.

■ **the ₁Authorized ˈVersion** *n* a version of the Bible in English. It was first published in 1611 and has traditionally been used in Anglican worship.

autism /ˈɔːtɪzəm/ *n* [U] (*psychology*) a serious mental condition that develops during childhood, in which one becomes unable to communicate or form relationships with others.

▶ **autistic** /ɔːˈtɪstɪk/ *adj* (*psychology*) suffering from autism: *autistic behaviour/children.*

auto /ˈɔːtəʊ/ *n* (*pl* **-os**) (*infml esp US*) a car: *the auto industry.*

aut(o)- *comb form* **1** of oneself: *autobiography* ○ *autograph.* **2** by oneself or itself; independent(ly): *autocracy* ○ *automobile.*

autobiography /ˌɔːtəbaɪˈɒɡrəfi/ *n* **(a)** [C] the story of a person's life written by that person: *A more detailed account of the incident is given in her autobiography.* **(b)** [U] this type of writing. Compare BIOGRAPHY.

▶ **autobiographical** /ˌɔːtəˌbaɪəˈɡræfɪkl/ *adj* of or concerning autobiography: *His novels are largely autobiographical* (ie They describe many of his own experiences).

autocracy /ɔːˈtɒkrəsi/ *n* **(a)** [U] government of a country by one person with absolute power. **(b)** [C] a country governed in this way.

autocrat /ˈɔːtəkræt/ *n* **1** a ruler who has absolute power; a DESPOT. **2** a person who expects to be obeyed at all times and pays no attention to the opinions, feelings, etc of others. ▶ **autocratic** /ˌɔːtəˈkrætɪk/ *adj: an autocratic administrator/ leader* ○ *autocratic rule.* **autocratically** /-kli/ *adv*.

autocross /ˈɔːtəʊkrɒs/ *n* (*Brit*) (*US* **rally**) [U] the sport of motor racing across country.

Autocue /ˈɔːtəʊkjuː/ *n* (*propr*) a device used by speakers or performers on television. It is placed next to the camera and displays the words that are to be spoken. Compare TELEPROMPTER.

autograph /ˈɔːtəɡrɑːf; *US* -ɡræf/ *n* a person's signature or HANDWRITING, esp that of a famous person: *ask for sb's autograph* ○ *sign one's autograph* ○ *I've got lots of famous people's autographs.* ○ *an autograph book/album.*

▶ **autograph** *v* to write one's name on or in sth, esp a book one has written or a photograph of oneself: [Vn] *an autographed copy.*

automat /ˈɔːtəmæt/ *n* (*US*) a restaurant in which customers get their own food from machines operated by coins.

automate /ˈɔːtəmeɪt/ *v* (esp passive) to use machines to do work previously done by people: [Vn] *Technological advances have enabled most routine tasks to be automated.* ○ *This part of the assembly process is now fully automated.*

automatic /ˌɔːtəˈmætɪk/ *adj* **1** (of a machine) working by itself without direct human control: *an automatic washing-machine* ○ *automatic gears* (ie in a motor vehicle) ○ *an automatic rifle* (ie one that continues firing as long as the TRIGGER is pressed). **2** (of actions or thoughts) occurring or happening naturally or from habit, without conscious control: *For most of us breathing is automatic.* ○ *It was an automatic assumption.* **3** following necessarily: *A fine for this offence is automatic.*

▶ **automatic** *n* **1** an automatic machine, gun or tool: *a burst of automatic fire.* ⟹ picture at GUN. **2** a car that changes gear without direct action from the driver.

automatically /-kli/ *adv: The process was controlled automatically.* ○ *I turned left automatically without thinking.*

■ ₁**automatic ˈpilot** (also **autopilot**) *n* a device in an aircraft or a ship to keep it on a set course without human control: *The plane's on automatic pilot.* ₁**automatic transˈmission** *n* [U, C] a system in a motor vehicle that changes the gears automatically.

automation /ˌɔːtəˈmeɪʃn/ *n* [U] the use of automatic equipment and machines to do work previously done by people: *the advantages of computerization and automation* ○ *office automation* ○ *Automation meant the loss of many factory jobs.*

automaton /ɔːˈtɒmətən/ *n* (*pl* **automatons** or **automata** /-tə/) **1** = ROBOT 1. **2** a person who seems to act in a mechanical manner, without thinking. Compare ROBOT 2.

automobile /ˈɔːtəməbiːl; *US* -məʊ-/ *n* (*esp US*) a car. ⟹ picture.

automotive /ˌɔːtəˈməʊtɪv/ *adj* concerned with motor vehicles: *the automotive industry* ○ *automotive engineers.*

autonomous /ɔːˈtɒnəməs/ *adj* having control over one's own affairs; acting independently: *an alliance of autonomous states.* ▶ **autonomously** *adv*.

autonomy /ɔːˈtɒnəmi/ *n* [U] control over one's own affairs; independence: *a campaign for greater autonomy* ○ *Branch managers have full autonomy in their own areas.*

autopsy /ˈɔːtɒpsi/ *n* an examination of a dead body to discover the cause of death; a POST-MORTEM(1): *an autopsy report.* Compare BIOPSY.

auto-suggestion /ˌɔːtəʊ səˈdʒestʃən/ *n* [U] (*psychology*) a process by which a person acts according to suggestions made from within herself or himself, eg during HYPNOSIS.

autumn /ˈɔːtəm/ (US **fall**) n [U, C] the third season of the year, coming between summer and winter. Autumn lasts from September to November in the northern parts of the world: *The leaves turn brown in autumn.* ○ *in the autumn of 1980* ○ *in (the) early/late autumn* ○ *It's been one of the coldest autumns for years.* ○ *the autumn term at college* ○ *autumn colours/weather/fashions* ○ (*fig also US*) *in the autumn* (ie the later part) *of one's life.*
▶ **autumnal** /ɔːˈtʌmnəl/ adj [usu pred] of or like autumn: *autumnal mists* ○ *The weather in June was positively autumnal.*

auxiliary /ɔːgˈzɪliəri/ adj giving help or support; additional: *auxiliary troops* ○ *an auxiliary nurse* ○ *an auxiliary generator in case of power cuts.*
▶ **auxiliary** n **1** [C] a person or thing that helps: *medical auxiliaries.* **2 auxiliaries** [pl] additional, esp foreign, troops used by a country at war. **3** [C] (also **au,xiliary ˈverb**, abbreviated as *aux v* in this dictionary) a verb used with main verbs to show tense, mood², etc, and to form questions, eg 'do' and 'has' in 'Do you know where he has gone?' Compare MODAL.

AV /ˌeɪ ˈviː/ abbr audiovisual: *AV materials.*

avail /əˈveɪl/ v ~ oneself of sth (*fml*) to make use of sth; to take advantage of sth: [Vnpr] *Guests are encouraged to avail themselves of the full range of hotel facilities.*
▶ **avail** n **IDM of little/no aˈvail** not very/not at all effective or successful: *Our protests were of no avail.* **to little/no aˈvail; without aˈvail** with little/no success: *The doctors tried everything to keep him alive but to no avail.*

available /əˈveɪləbl/ adj **1** (of things) that can be obtained or used: *Tickets are available at the box office.* ○ *You will be informed when the book becomes available.* ○ *This was the only available room.* **2** (of people) free to see or talk to people: *I'm available in the afternoon.* ○ *The director was not available for comment.* ▶ **availability** /əˌveɪləˈbɪləti/ n [U]: *the availability of cheap office space* ○ *This offer is subject to availability.*

avalanche /ˈævəlɑːnʃ; US -læntʃ/ n a mass of snow, ice and rock that slides rapidly down the side of a mountain: *Yesterday's avalanche killed a party of skiers and destroyed several trees.* ○ (*fig*) *We received an avalanche of letters in reply to our advertisement.*

avant-garde /ˌævɒŋ ˈgɑːd/ adj favouring new and unusual ideas, esp in art and literature: *avant-garde writers/artists* ○ *the avant-garde movement.*
▶ **the avant-garde** n **(a)** [U] new and unusual ideas or art; books, etc expressing these: *a promoter of the avant-garde.* **(b)** [CGp] a group of people introducing such ideas, etc: *a member of the avant-garde.*

avarice /ˈævərɪs/ n [U] (*fml*) an extreme desire for wealth or gain: *be motivated by greed and avarice.* ▶ **avaricious** /ˌævəˈrɪʃəs/ adj: *an avaricious look.*

Ave abbr (in names) Avenue: *5 St George's Ave.*

avenge /əˈvendʒ/ v **(a)** to punish or hurt sb for a wrong done to sb/oneself; to take or get revenge(1): [Vn] *She avenged her father's murder.* **(b)** ~ oneself **on sb/sth** to take or get revenge(1) on sb/sth for such a wrong: [Vnpr] *She avenged herself on her father's killers.* ▶ **avenger** n.

avenue /ˈævənjuː; US -nuː/ n **1** (abbr **Ave**) a street, esp a wide one lined with trees or tall buildings. ⇨ note at ROAD. **2** a wide road or path, often lined with trees, esp one that leads to a large house. **3** a way of approaching or making progress towards sth: *an avenue to success/fame* ○ *Several avenues are open to us.* ○ *We have explored every avenue.*

aver /əˈvɜː(r)/ v (-**rr**-) (*fml*) to state sth firmly and positively; to assert sth: [V.*that*] *She averred (that) there was no risk.* [also Vn].

average /ˈævərɪdʒ/ n **1** [C] the result of adding several amounts together and then dividing this total by the number of amounts: *The average of 4, 5 and 9 is 6.* ○ *They have an average of just over two children per family.* **2** [U] a standard or level regarded as usual: *These marks are well above/below average.* ○ *Unemployment here is around the national average.* ○ *We fail about two students a year on average.*
▶ **average** adj **1** [attrib] found by calculating or estimating the average: *The average age of the students is 19.* ○ *an average wind speed of 40 mph* ○ *The average temperature in Oxford last month was 18°C.* **2** of the ordinary or usual standard: *children of average intelligence* ○ *Rainfall is about average for the time of year.* ○ (*derog*) *a fairly average game.*
average v **1** (no passive) to do or amount to sth as an average measure or rate: [Vn] *Pay rises this year averaged 2%.* ○ *This car averages 40 miles to the gallon.* ○ *The rainfall averages 36 inches a year.* **2** to find the average of sth: [Vn] *Her earnings are averaged over the whole period.* [also V]. **PHRV** ,**average ˈout (at sth)** to result in an average of sth: *Meals average out at about £10 per head.* ○ *Sometimes I pay, sometimes he pays — it seems to average out* (ie result in a fair balance) *in the end.* ,**average sth ˈout (at sth)** to calculate the average of sth: *Averaged out over a period, industrial accidents occur at least twice a week.*

averse /əˈvɜːs/ adj [pred] ~ **to sth** (*fml or rhet*) not liking sth; opposed to sth: *He seems to be averse to hard work.* ○ *I'm not averse to a drop of whisky after dinner.*

aversion /əˈvɜːʃn; US əˈvɜːrʒn/ n **1** [C, U] ~ (**to sb/sth**) a strong dislike: *I have an aversion to getting up early.* ○ *He took an immediate aversion to his new boss.* **2** [C] a thing that is strongly disliked: *Smoking is one of my pet* (ie particular, personal) *aversions.*

avert /əˈvɜːt/ v **1** ~ **sth (from sth)** to turn sth away: [Vn, Vnpr] *avert one's eyes/gaze/glance (from the terrible sight)* [Vnpr] *I tried to avert my thoughts from the subject.* **2** to prevent sth; to avoid sth: [Vn] *avert an accident/a crisis/a disaster by prompt action* ○ *He managed to avert suspicion.*

aviary /ˈeɪviəri; US -vieri/ n a large cage or building for keeping birds in, eg in a zoo.

aviation /ˌeɪviˈeɪʃn/ n [U] the design, manufacture and operation of aircraft: *civil aviation* ○ *the aviation business/industry.*
▶ **aviator** /ˈeɪvieɪtə(r)/ n (*dated*) a person who flies an aircraft as the pilot or one of the crew.

avid /ˈævɪd/ adj ~ (**for sth**) eager and enthusiastic; keen: *an avid reader/collector of old coins* ○ *avid for news of her son.*
▶ **avidity** /əˈvɪdəti/ n [U] (*fml*) eagerness: *the avidity of the press for royal gossip.*
avidly adv: *She reads avidly.*

avionics /ˌeɪviˈɒnɪks/ n [sing v] the science of electronics (ELECTRONIC) applied to the design and manufacture of aircraft.

avocado /ˌævəˈkɑːdəʊ/ n (pl **-os**) (also ,**avocado ˈpear**) a tropical fruit that has soft pale green oily flesh and is often eaten at the beginning of a meal.

avoid /əˈvɔɪd/ v **(a)** to keep oneself away from sb/sth; to try not to do sth: [Vn, Vnpr] *Try to avoid (driving in) the rush-hour.* [Vn] *I think he's avoiding me.* ○ *She avoided my eyes* (ie avoided looking into my eyes). **(b)** to stop sth happening; to prevent sth: [Vn] *Try to avoid accidents.* [V.*ing*] *I just avoided running over the cat.* **IDM avoid sb/sth like the ˈplague** (*infml*) to try very hard not to meet sb, do sth, etc: *He's been avoiding me like the plague since our quarrel.*
▶ **avoidable** adj that can be avoided: *This sort of accident is wholly avoidable.*

avoidance n [U] the action of avoiding sb/sth: *tax avoidance* (ie arranging one's affairs so as to pay the smallest amount of tax required by law).

avoirdupois /ˌævədə'pɔɪz, ˌævwɑːdjuː'pwɑː/ n [U] the system of weights based on the pound¹(1c). ⇨ App 2.

avow /ə'vaʊ/ v (*fml*) to declare sth openly; to admit: [Vn-n] *avow oneself (to be) a socialist* [Vn] *avow one's belief/faith/conviction* ○ *He's an avowed Marxist.* ○ *The avowed aim/intention of this administration is to reduce taxation.* [also V.speech, V.*that*].
▶ **avowal** n (*fml*) [C, U] a clear and open declaration: *make a passionate avowal of love.*
avowedly /ə'vaʊɪdli/ adv (*fml*) clearly and openly; as is or must be admitted: *The society is avowedly political in its aims.*

avuncular /ə'vʌŋkjələ(r)/ adj (*fml*) of or like an uncle, esp in manner, ie kind, protective, etc: *He adopts an avuncular tone of voice when giving advice to junior colleagues.*

AWACS /'eɪwæks/ abbr airborne warning and control system (a system for detecting enemy aircraft over long distances): *AWACS aircraft.*

await /ə'weɪt/ v (*fml*) **1** (of a person) to wait for sb/ sth: [Vn] *awaiting instructions/results/a reply* ○ *a long-awaited change* ○ *her eagerly awaited return.* **2** to be ready or waiting for sb/sth: [Vn] *A warm welcome awaits all our customers.* ○ *A surprise awaited us on our arrival.* Compare WAIT².

awake¹ /ə'weɪk/ v (*pt* awoke /ə'wəʊk/; *pp* awoken /ə'wəʊkən/) **1** to stop or make sb stop sleeping; to wake: [V] *She awoke when the nurse entered the room.* [Vpr] *I awoke from a deep sleep.* [Vn] *His voice awoke the sleeping child.* ⇨ note at AWAKE². **2** to make sth become active again: [Vn] *The letter awoke old fears.* **PHRV** **awake to sth** to become aware of sth; to realize sth: *awake to the dangers/the opportunities/one's surroundings.*

awake² /ə'weɪk/ adj [pred] **1** not asleep, esp immediately before and after sleeping: *They aren't awake yet.* ○ *be kept awake by the noise from next door* ○ *Are the children still awake?* ○ *They're wide* (ie fully) *awake.* ○ *She lies awake at night worrying.* **2** ~ **to sth** conscious or aware of sth: *Too few are awake to the danger facing the country.*

NOTE Compare **awake**, **awaken**, **wake up** and **waken**. When you are **awake**, you are not asleep yet, or have recently stopped sleeping: *I was awake half the night worrying.* ○ *Is the baby awake yet?* When you have finished sleeping you **wake up**: *What time do you usually wake up?*
The verb **awake** is usually only used in writing and in the past tense **awoke**: *She awoke to a day of brilliant sunshine.* Somebody or something can **wake** you **up**, or **wake** you: *The children woke me up.* ○ *I was woken (up) by the telephone.* **Waken** and **awaken** are much more formal: *She asked not to be wakened.* **Awaken** is used especially in literature: *The Prince awakened Sleeping Beauty with a kiss.*

awaken /ə'weɪkən/ v (*rather fml*) **1** (esp passive) to stop or make sb stop sleeping; to waken: [V] *We awakened to find the others had gone.* [Vn] *I was awakened by the sound of church bells.* ○ (*fig*) *They were making enough noise to awaken the dead.* ⇨ note at AWAKE². **2** to become or make sth active again: [V] *an awakening realization that all was not well* [Vn] *Her story awakened our interest.* **PHRV** **awaken (sb) to sth** to become or make sb aware of sth: *awaken society to the dangers of drugs* ○ *People have awakened to the fact that the policy is not working.*
▶ **awakening** /ə'weɪkənɪŋ/ n **1** [C usu *sing*] an act of realizing sth: *The discovery that her husband was unfaithful to her was a rude* (ie shocking) *awaken-*

ing. **2** [U, C] the beginning or early development of sth: *the awakening of religious feeling.*

award /ə'wɔːd/ v ~ **sth** (**to sb**) to make an official decision to give sth to sb, esp as a prize, payment, compensation, etc: [Vnn] *The judges awarded both finalists equal points.* ○ *The court awarded him damages of £50 000.* ○ *She was awarded a medal for bravery.* [Vnpr] *The contract was awarded to an Italian company.* [Vn] *The referee awarded a penalty.*
▶ **award** n **1** [U] the decision to give sth, made by a judge, etc: *the award of a scholarship.* **2** [C] (**a**) ~ (**for sth**) a prize, certificate, sum of money, etc given to sb in honour of their achievement: *win the award for best actor* ○ *She showed us the athletics awards she had won.* ○ *an award presentation/ceremony.* (**b**) money to be paid to sb, eg as part of their salary: *a 5% pay award* ○ *an award of £600 000 libel damages.* **3** [C] (*Brit*) an amount of money paid to a student at university, etc to help meet living costs; a GRANT n: *She is not eligible for an award.*
■ **award-winning** adj [attrib] having won or deserving to win a prize: *an award-winning play/ musician/performance.*

aware /ə'weə(r)/ adj **1** [pred] ~ **of sb/sth**; ~ **that…** having knowledge of sb/sth; realizing sth: *be fully aware of the risk/danger/threat* ○ *Are you aware of the time?* ○ *It happened without my being aware of it.* ○ *I'm **acutely/well aware that** very few jobs are available.* ○ *She became aware that something was burning.* ○ *I don't think you're aware (of) how much this means to me.* **2** interested in and knowing about sth, esp current events: *She's always been a politically aware person.* ▶ **awareness** n [U, sing]: *public awareness* ○ *political/spiritual/ecological awareness* ○ *an awareness of the project's limitations.*

awash /ə'wɒʃ; *US* ə'wɔːʃ/ adj [pred] **1** covered or flooded with water, esp sea water: *The ship's deck was awash.* ○ *The sink had overflowed and the kitchen floor was awash.* **2** ~ **with sth** (*infml*) having sth in great quantities or numbers: *The streets were awash with political leaflets.* ○ *The town was awash with reporters/rumours.*

away /ə'weɪ/ adv part For the special uses of **away** in phrasal verbs, look at the verb entries. For example, the meaning of **get away with sth** is given in the phrasal verb section of the entry for **get**. **1** ~ (**from sb/sth**) (**a**) to or at a distance from sb/sth in space or time: *The sea is two miles away from the hotel.* ○ *The station is only a few minutes' walk away.* ○ *Christmas is only a week away.* ○ *They're away on vacation for two weeks.* ○ *Don't go away.* (**b**) to a different place or in a different direction: *Have you cleared away your books from the table?* ○ *Put your toys away now.* ○ *The bright light made her look away.* ○ *a shift away from treating mental patients in hospitals.* **2** continuously: *She was still writing away furiously when the bell went.* ○ *They worked away for two days to get it finished.* ○ *After five minutes they were talking away like old friends.* **3** until disappearing completely: *The water boiled away.* ○ *The picture faded away.* ○ *The hut was swept away by the flood.* ○ (*fig*) *They danced the night away* (ie all night). **4** (of a sports team) at the opponents' ground: *Oxford United is playing away tomorrow.* [attrib] *We lost all our away matches.* Compare HOME² 3. **IDM** **away with sb/sth** (used in exclamations) remove sb/sth; make sb/sth leave: *Away with all these petty restrictions!*

awe /ɔː/ n [U] a feeling of respect combined with fear or wonder: *gaze/look with awe at sth* ○ *Her first view of the pyramids filled her with awe.* ○ *I was/lived/ stood in awe of my father until I was at least fifteen.* ○ *My brother was much older and cleverer than me so I always held him in awe.*
▶ **awe** v (usu passive) to fill sb with awe: [Vn] *awed by the solemnity of the occasion* ○ *an awed silence.*

awesome /-səm/ adj **1** causing awe: *an awesome sight/task* ○ *His strength was awesome.* **2** (*US infml*) very good; wonderful: *an awesome new car.*
awesomely adv.

■ ¹**awe-inspiring** adj causing awe: *The view from the summit is awe-inspiring.*

awestruck /ˈɔːstrʌk/ adj suddenly filled with wonder and respect or fear: *awestruck at the grandeur of the scene.*

awful /ˈɔːfl/ adj **1** extremely bad or unpleasant; terrible: *an awful accident/experience/shock* ○ *The plight of starving people is too awful to think about.* **2** (*infml*) very bad; ROTTEN(2): *What awful weather!* ○ *I feel awful.* ○ *It's an awful nuisance!* ○ *The film was awful.* **3** [attrib] (*infml*) very great: *That's an awful lot of money.* ○ *I'm in an awful hurry to get to the bank.*
▶ **awful** adv (*US infml*) very; extremely: *It was awful slow, but it got there.*
awfully /ˈɔːfli/ adv (*infml*) very; very much: *It's awfully hot.* ○ *I'm awfully sorry.* ○ *It's awfully kind of you.* ○ *I'm afraid I'm awfully late.* ○ *Thanks awfully for the present.* **awfulness** n [U]: *the sheer awfulness of the situation.*

awhile /əˈwaɪl/ adv for a short time: *Please stay awhile.* ○ *We won't be leaving yet awhile* (ie until some time later).

awkward /ˈɔːkwəd/ adj **1** badly designed; difficult to use: *The handle of this teapot has an awkward shape.* ○ *It's an awkward door — you have to bend down to go through it.* **2** causing difficulty, embarrassment or INCONVENIENCE: *an awkward series of bends in the road* ○ *ask an awkward question* ○ *You've put me in an awkward position.* ○ *Please arrange the next meeting at a less awkward time.* ○ *It's very awkward of you to arrange your holiday for next week.* ○ *Stop being so awkward!* ○ *He can be an awkward customer* (ie difficult or dangerous to deal with). **3** embarrassed: *an awkward silence/smile* ○ *I realized they wanted to be alone together so I felt very awkward.* **4** not smooth and graceful; CLUMSY: *Swans are surprisingly awkward on land.* ○ *I was always an awkward dancer.* ▶ **awkwardly** adv: *an awkwardly placed mirror* ○ *'I hope I'm not disturbing you,' Richard said awkwardly.* ○ *She fell awkwardly and broke her hip.* **awkwardness** n [U].

awl /ɔːl/ n a small pointed tool for making holes, esp in leather or wood.

awning /ˈɔːnɪŋ/ n a sheet of material stretching out from above a door or window. Awnings are used as a protection against rain or sun: *sit under the blue and white striped awning of a café.*

awoke pt of AWAKE¹.

awoken pp of AWAKE¹.

AWOL /ˈeɪwɒl/ abbr absent without leave (esp from service in the armed forces): *He's gone AWOL.*

awry /əˈraɪ/ adv **1** wrong(ly); not as expected: *Our plans went awry.* ○ *His analysis is wildly awry.* **2** out of position; untidy: *Her clothes were all awry.*

axe (*US* also **ax**) /æks/ n **1** [C] a tool with a wooden handle and a heavy metal blade used for chopping wood, cutting down trees, etc: *A man burst in wielding an axe.* ⇨ picture. **2 the axe** [sing] the complete

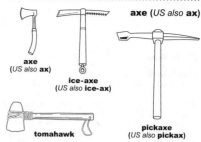

axe (*US also* **ax**)

axe
(*US also* **ax**)

ice-axe
(*US also* **ice-ax**)

tomahawk

pickaxe
(*US also* **pickax**)

loss of sth or a big reduction in the size or extent of sth, eg in the number of jobs at a company or in the amount of money available to an organization: *Community arts projects are facing the axe* (ie may not receive any more money). ○ *Clerical and office workers will not escape the axe.* **IDM** ,**have an** ¹**axe to grind** to have private reasons for being involved in sth: *She had no particular axe to grind and was only acting out of concern for their safety.*
▶ **axe** (also *esp US* **ax**) v **1** to remove sb/sth or dismiss sb from their job: [Vn] *He/His job has been axed.* **2** to reduce costs, services, etc by a large amount: [Vn] *School grants are to be axed next year.*

axiom /ˈæksiəm/ n a statement that is accepted as true without further proof or argument.
▶ **axiomatic** /ˌæksiəˈmætɪk/ adj of or like an axiom; clear and obvious without needing to be proved: *It is axiomatic (to say) that a whole is greater than any of its parts.*

axis /ˈæksɪs/ n (pl **axes** /ˈæksiːz/) **1** an imaginary line through the centre of an object, around which the object turns: *The earth's axis is the line between the North and South Poles.* ⇨ picture at GLOBE. **2** a line that divides a regular shape into two equal parts: *The axis of a circle is its diameter.* **3** a fixed reference line for measurement, eg on a GRAPH: *the horizontal (y) and vertical (x) axes* ○ *The main road is on a north-south axis.* **4** (usu *sing*) an agreement or ALLIANCE between two or more countries.

axle /ˈæksl/ n (**a**) a rod that connects a pair of wheels on a vehicle: *The back axle is broken.* ⇨ picture at CAR. (**b**) a rod on which or with which a wheel turns, eg on a bicycle.

ayatollah /ˌaɪəˈtɒlə/ n a senior Muslim religious leader in Iran.

aye (also **ay**) /aɪ/ interj (*arch or dialect*) yes: *Aye, I know what you mean.* ○ ,*Aye,* ¹*aye, sir!* (eg in reply to an order by a naval officer).
▶ **aye** (also **ay**) n **IDM** **the ayes** ¹**have it** more people have voted for sth than against it.

azalea /əˈzeɪliə/ n a bush, often grown in gardens, with large pink, purple, white or yellow flowers.

azimuth /ˈæzɪməθ/ n (*astronomy*) an angle corresponding to a distance around the earth's horizon, used to determine the position of a star, planet, etc.

azure /ˈæʒə(r); *Brit also* ˈæzjʊə(r)/ adj, n [U] (having) a bright blue colour, like the sky: *a dress of azure silk* ○ *a lake reflecting the azure of the sky.*

Bb

B¹ (also **b**) /biː/ n (pl **B's, b's** /biːz/) **1** the second letter of the English alphabet: *There are three b's in bubble.* **2 B** (*music*) the 7th note in the scale¹(6) of C major. **3 B** an academic mark of the second highest standard: *get (a) B/'B' in English.* **4 B** a second imagined or possible thing or person: *We'll have to adopt plan B.* **IDM from A to B** ⟹ A¹.

B² /biː/ symb **1** second in rank: *play for the B team.* **2** (*Brit*) (used in Britain before a number to refer to a particular secondary road): *the B1224 to York.* Compare A² 1.
■ **'B-road** n (*Brit*) a secondary road, especially one joining small towns and villages. Compare A-ROAD.

b abbr born: *Emily Jane Clifton b 1800.* Compare D 1.

BA /ˌbiː'eɪ/ abbr (US **AB**) Bachelor of Arts (a first degree awarded by universities in arts and certain other subjects): *have/be a BA in history* ○ *Jim Fox BA (Hons).* Compare BSc.

baa /bɑː/ n the cry of a sheep or lamb.
▶ **baa** v (*pres p* **baaing**; *pt* **baaed** or **baa'd** /bɑːd/) [V] to make a baa; to BLEAT v(1).

babble /'bæbl/ v **1(a)** to talk quickly and in a way that is difficult or impossible to understand: [V] *Stop babbling and tell me slowly.* [V, Vp] *tourists babbling (away) in a foreign language* [also V.speech]. **(b)** to talk continuously in a confused way; to talk nonsense: [Vpr, Vp] *What is he babbling (on) about?* **2** (of streams, etc) to make the continuous sound of water flowing: [V] *a babbling brook.*
▶ **babble** n [U] **1(a)** the sound of people talking quickly and in a way that is difficult or impossible to understand: *hear the babble of many voices.* **(b)** foolish or confused talk: *His constant babble irritates me.* **2** the gentle sound of water flowing over stones, etc.

babe /beɪb/ n **1** (*arch*) a baby. **2** (*US sl*) (used esp as a form of address expressing affection for a young woman, one's wife, husband, lover, etc). **IDM a ˌbabe in 'arms** a very young baby not able to walk or crawl.

babel /'beɪbl/ n [sing] a scene of noisy talking and confusion: *a babel of voices in the busy market.*

baboon /bə'buːn; US bæ-/ n a large African or Arabian monkey with a face like a dog's. ⟹ picture at MONKEY.

baby /'beɪbi/ n **1(a)** a very young child or animal: *Both mother and baby are doing well.* ○ *a baby boy/girl* ○ *a baby thrush/monkey/crocodile.* **(b)** (*infml*) the youngest member of a family or group: *He's the baby of the team.* **(c)** (*derog*) a person who behaves like a child or is too easily frightened or upset: *Stop crying and don't be such a baby.* **2** (*sl esp US*) (used esp as a form of address expressing affection for a young woman, one's wife, husband, lover, etc). **3** [attrib] very small of its kind: *a baby car.* **IDM be one's/sb's/sb's baby** (*infml*) to be sth that one has created and cares about or that one is responsible for: *The whole project is your baby now.* **leave sb holding the 'baby** (*infml*) to abandon sth that is one's own responsibility, usu without warning, for others to deal with: *His business partners were left holding the baby.* **throw the baby out with the 'bath water** to get rid of sth valuable or desirable at the same time as one is getting rid of sth useless or undesirable.
▶ **baby** v (*pt, pp* **babied**) to treat sb like a baby; to

give sb excessive care and attention: [Vn] *Don't baby him — he's old enough to look after himself.*

babyhood n [sing] **(a)** the state of being a baby. **(b)** the time when one is a baby.

babyish adj of, like or suitable for a baby: *Now that Ned can read he finds his early picture books too babyish.*

■ **'baby boom** n a period during which the rate of births increases greatly, eg after a war.

'baby buggy n = PRAM.

'baby carriage n (US) = PRAM.

ˌbaby 'grand n a small grand piano (GRAND).

'baby-minder n (*Brit*) a person paid to look after a baby for long periods (eg while the parents are working).

'baby-talk n [U] very simple or invented language used by or to babies before they can speak properly.

'baby tooth n (*esp US*) = MILK-TOOTH.

Babygro /'beɪbɪgrəʊ/ n (pl **-os**) (*propr*) a garment for babies, usu covering the whole body except the head and hands, made of a material that stretches easily.

babysit /'beɪbɪsɪt/ v (**-tt-**; *pt, pp* **-sat**) to look after a child for a short time while the parents are out: [V] *She regularly babysits for us.* ▶ **babysitter** (also **sitter**) n. **babysitting** n [U].

baccalaureate /ˌbækə'lɔːriət/ n **1** the last secondary school examination in France and many international schools: *sit/take/pass/fail one's baccalaureate.* **2** (US) a religious service for students who have completed high school or college.

bacchanalian /ˌbækə'neɪliən/ adj (*dated fml*) involving wild noisy behaviour and the drinking of a lot of alcohol: *bacchanalian revels.*

baccy /'bæki/ n [U] (*Brit infml*) tobacco.

bachelor /'bætʃələ(r)/ n **1(a)** a man who is not and never has been married: *He remained a bachelor all his life.* ○ *a confirmed bachelor* (ie one who has decided never to marry). Compare SPINSTER. **(b)** [attrib] of or suitable for a bachelor: *a bachelor flat.* **2** a person who holds a first university degree: *a bachelor's degree* ○ *Bachelor of Arts/Science.* See also BA, BSc. ▶ **bachelorhood** n [U].

bacillus /bə'sɪləs/ n (pl **bacilli** /bə'sɪlaɪ/) any of various types of bacteria that cause disease.

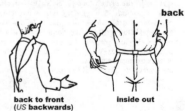

back

back to front (US **backwards**) **inside out**

back¹ /bæk/ n **1** the part or surface of an object that is furthest from the front, less visible, less used or less important: *He had a bad cut on the back of his head.* ○ *You've got a stain on the back of your shirt.* ○ *The index is at the back (of the book).* ○ *We sat in the back of the car* (ie in the seats behind the driver). ○ *I was at the back (of the cinema) and couldn't see well.* ○ *a room at the back of the house* ○ *a house with a*

[Vnn] = verb + noun + noun   [V-adj] = verb + adjective   For more help with verbs, see Study pages **B4–8**.

garden at the back ○ Write your address on the back (of the cheque). ○ the back of one's hand (ie not the palm). Compare FRONT 1. **2(a)** the part of the human body from the neck down to the buttocks (BUTTOCK); the SPINE(1): He lay on his back and looked up at the sky. ○ She broke her back in a climbing accident. **(b)** the part of an animal's body that corresponds to this: Fasten the saddle on the horse's back. ⇨ picture at HORSE. **3** the part of a chair against which one's back rests when one is sitting. **4** (in certain team games, eg football) a player whose main function is to defend. Compare FORWARD⁴. **IDM** **at the back of one's mind** in one's thoughts, but not of immediate or great concern; being sth that one is aware of but not mainly thinking about: At the back of his mind was the vague idea that he had met her before. **the ˌback of beˈyond** an isolated place, far from any centre of social and cultural activity: They live somewhere at the back of beyond. **ˌback to ˈback 1** with one back against another back: Stand back to back and let's see which of you is taller. **2** in succession; one after the other: win three tournaments back to back ○ back-to-back victories. **ˌback to ˈfront** (Brit) (US **backwards**) with the back placed where the front should be: Your sweater is on back to front. ⇨ picture. **be glad, etc to see the back of sb/sth** (infml) to be pleased, etc not to see or have contact with sb/sth again: I've never liked my boss — when he retires I'll be glad to see the back of him. **behind sb's ˈback** without sb's knowledge or agreement: They say nasty things about him behind his back. Compare TO SB'S FACE (FACE¹). **be on sb's ˈback** to annoy sb by continually demanding that they do sth they are unwilling or too busy to do: I have to finish this today — the boss is on my back about it. **break one's ˈback (to do sth)** to work very hard to achieve sth. **break the ˈback of sth** to finish the larger or more difficult part of a task: The essay's not finished yet but at least I've broken the back of it. **get/ put sb's ˈback up** to make sb angry: His rude manner put my back up. **get off sb's ˈback** (infml) to stop annoying or criticizing sb: Get off my back and let me do things my way! **have one's ˌback to the ˈwall** to be in a difficult position; to be under pressure. **have eyes in the back of one's head** ⇨ EYE¹. **know sb/sth like the back of one's hand** ⇨ KNOW. **live off sb's back** ⇨ LIVE². **make a rod for one's own back** ⇨ ROD. **on one's back** in bed because one is ill or injured. **a pat on the back** ⇨ PAT¹ n. **pat sb/oneself on the back** ⇨ PAT¹ v. **put one's ˈback into sth** to do sth with great energy or effort. **a stab in the back** ⇨ STAB n. **stab sb in the back** ⇨ STAB v. **turn one's back** to turn so that one is facing the opposite direction: He turned his back and walked away. **turn one's back on sb/sth** to reject or ignore sb/sth that one was previously involved with or close to: He turned his back on his family when he became famous. **water off a duck's back** ⇨ WATER¹. **you scratch my back and I'll scratch yours** ⇨ SCRATCH¹.
▶ **backless** adj (of a dress) cut low at the back¹(1).
■ **ˈback-breaking** adj requiring great physical effort: back-breaking work.
ˌback-to-ˈback n (Brit) any of a row of houses separated from the houses behind them by a common wall: streets of back-to-backs ○ back-to-back housing.

back² /bæk/ adj (esp attrib and in compounds; no comparative or superlative) **1** situated behind or at the back of sth: the back door. ⇨ picture at HOUSE¹: Put your bag on the back seat of the car. ○ back teeth ○ sit in the back row ○ a back room (ie one at the back of a building) ○ the back page of a newspaper. Compare FRONT adj. **2(a)** of or from a past time: back issues of a magazine. **(b)** owed for a time in the past; OVERDUE: back pay/taxes/rent. **IDM** **by/through the back door** in an unfair or indirect way: He used his

influential friends to help him get into the civil service by the back door. **on the back ˈburner** (infml) (of an idea, a plan, etc) left aside for the time being, to be done or considered later.
■ **ˌback ˈbench** n (usu pl) (Brit) any of the seats in the House of Commons for Members of Parliament who do not hold senior posts in the Government or the Opposition: He resigned as Home Secretary and returned to the back benches. ○ ˌback-bench M'Ps/ sup'port/'critics. **ˌback-ˈbencher** n.
ˌback-ˈdoor adj [attrib] using indirect or secret means in order to achieve sth: adopt a back-door approach.
ˌback ˈnumber (also **ˌback ˈissue**) n an old issue of a newspaper or magazine.
ˌback ˈroom n [esp attrib] a place where secret but important work is done: back-room staff/support/ operations.
ˈback-room boys n [pl] (infml esp Brit) scientists, engineers, etc whose work does not receive public attention but makes an important contribution to sth.
ˌback ˈseat n a seat at the back of a car, etc. **IDM** a **ˌback-seat ˈdriver** (derog) a passenger in a car who irritates the driver by constantly giving advice that is not wanted. **take a back seat** to take or to be given a less important position or status: She took a back seat in the discussion. ○ He was working so hard that his family life had to take a back seat.

back³ /bæk/ adv part, adv For the special uses of **back** in phrasal verbs, look at the verb entries. For example, the meaning of **pay sb back** is given in the phrasal verb section of the entry for **pay²**. **1(a)** away from the front or centre; behind one: I stepped back to let them pass. ○ Sit back and relax. ○ You've combed your hair back. ○ He turned and looked back. ○ She fell back towards the end of the race. Compare FORWARD² 1. **(b)** at a distance away from sth: The barriers failed to keep/hold the crowds back. ○ Our house stands back from the road. ○ Stand back and give me some room. **(c)** under control; prevented from being expressed or coming out: He could no longer hold back his tears. ○ She tends to keep her real feelings back. **2** to or into an earlier place, condition, situation or activity: Put the book back on the shelf. ○ Please give me my ball back. ○ The manager will be back (ie will return) on Monday. ○ It takes me an hour to walk there and back. ○ We came back from our holiday on the 25th. ○ This is the wrong road — we'll have to go back. ○ Could you go back to the beginning of the story? ○ He woke up briefly and then went back to sleep. ○ The party expects to be back in power after the election. ○ We had a break and then went back to work. ○ We'll come back to this subject later. **3(a)** in or into the past; ago: The village has a history going back to the Middle Ages. ○ She left back in November. ○ That was a few years back. **(b)** before a particular place; before reaching this place: We should have turned left five kilometres back. **(c)** at a place previously left or mentioned: Back at home, her parents were worried. ○ This wouldn't happen back in New York. **4** in return: If he kicks me, I'll kick him back. ○ Jane wrote him a long letter, but he never wrote back. ○ She smiled at him, and he smiled back. ○ Could you phone back later, please? **5** fashionable again: The styles of the 1960s are back (in fashion). **IDM** **ˌback and ˈforth** from one place to another and back again repeatedly: ferries sailing back and forth between the island and the mainland. **(in) back of sth** (US infml) behind sth: the houses (in) back of the church.
■ **ˌback-ˈpedal** v (-ll-; US -l-) **1** ~ (on sth) to withdraw from an earlier statement or policy; to reverse one's previous action or opinion: [Vpr] The government was back-pedalling on their election promises.

[also V]. **2** [V] to PEDAL backwards on a bicycle, etc. ꞌ**back talk** *n* [U] (*US*) = BACKCHAT.

back⁴ /bæk/ *v* **1(a)** to give help or support to sb/sth: [Vn] *Her parents backed her in her choice of career.* ○ *The revolution was backed by foreign powers.* **(b)** to give financial support to sb/sth: [Vn] *They persuaded various banks to back the project.* **2** to move or make sth move backwards: [Vpr] *back out of a parking space* ○ *He backed into the car behind.* [Vp, Vnp] *If you can't drive in forwards, try backing (it) in.* [Vnpr] *I couldn't back the car out of the mud.* [also V, Vn]. **3** to bet money on sb/sth winning sth: [Vn] *I backed four horses but won nothing.* ○ *Did anyone back the winner?* ○ *The favourite was heavily backed* (ie Much money was bet on its winning the race). **4** ~ **sth (with sth)** (usu passive) to cover the back of sth in order to support or protect it: [Vnpr] *The photograph was backed with cardboard.* [also Vn]. **5** (in music) to accompany sb: [Vn] *a singer backed by a full orchestra.* **IDM** **back sb into a corner** to put sb into a position in which it is difficult for them to defend or justify sth. ꞌ**back the wrong ꞌhorse** to support sb/sth that loses. **PHRV** ꞌ**back aꞌway (from sb/sth)** to move backwards because of fear or dislike: *The child backed away from the big dog.* ○ (*fig*) *The government said that they would not back away from* (ie be afraid to take) *tough measures.* ꞌ**back ꞌdown**; (*US*) ꞌ**back ꞌoff** to withdraw a claim, a demand or an accusation; to admit defeat: *He proved that he was right and his critics had to back down.* ꞌ**back ꞌoff** to move away from sb, esp so as to stop threatening or annoying them: *I've had enough criticism from you — back off, will you?* ꞌ**back ꞌonto sth** to face sth at the back: *Our house backs onto the river.* ꞌ**back ꞌout (of sth)** to withdraw from an agreement, a promise, etc: *It's too late to back out (of the deal) now.* ꞌ**back ꞌup** to move backwards, esp in a vehicle: *You can back up another two metres or so.* ꞌ**back sb/sth ꞌup** to support sb/sth; to say or indicate that sth is true: *His version of events is backed up by all the available evidence.* ○ *If they don't believe you, I'll back you up.* ꞌ**back sth ꞌup** (*computing*) to make a copy of a file, PROGRAM(1), etc in case the original is lost or damaged.

▶ **backer** *n* **1** a person who gives support, esp financially, to another person, a project, etc. **2** a person who bets money on a horse, etc.

backing *n* **1** help; support: *Without financial backing the project cannot succeed.* ○ *You have my backing in whatever decision you take.* **2** [U] material used to form the back of sth or to support sth: *cloth/rubber/cardboard backing.* **3** [U, C usu *sing*] (esp in pop music) the music or singing that accompanies the main singer: *vocal/instrumental backing* ○ *a backing group.*

backache /ꞌbækeɪk/ *n* [U, C] an ACHE or pain in the back.

backbiting /ꞌbækbaɪtɪŋ/ *n* [U] unkind and unpleasant talk about sb who is not present: *work in an atmosphere of backbiting and bitterness.*

backbone /ꞌbækbəʊn/ *n* **1** [C] the line of bones down the middle of the back from the SKULL to the hips; the SPINE(1). ⇨ picture at SKELETON. **2** [sing] the chief support of a system or an organization: *Such large businesses are the backbone of the economy.* **3** [U] strength of character: *He's able enough but lacks the backbone to succeed in such a competitive industry.*

backchat /ꞌbæktʃæt/ (*Brit*) (*US* **back talk**) *n* [U] (*infml*) rude or cheeky (CHEEK) remarks made in reply to sb in authority, showing lack of proper respect: *I want none of your backchat!*

backcloth /ꞌbækklɒθ/ *n* (*Brit*) **1** a printed cloth hung at the back of a stage in a theatre, as part of the scenery. **2** the background to an event or situation: *The current crisis must be seen against a backcloth of historical tensions.*

backcomb /ꞌbækkəʊm/ *v* [Vn] to comb hair from the ends back towards the SCALP(1) to give it a fuller appearance.

backdate /ˌbækꞌdeɪt/ *v* to make sth valid from an earlier date: [Vnpr] *a pay increase awarded in May and backdated to 1 January* [also Vn]. Compare POSTDATE.

backdrop /ꞌbækdrɒp/ *n* = BACKCLOTH 1.

backfire /ˌbækꞌfaɪə(r)/ *v* **1** (of a motor vehicle) to make a sudden loud noise like an explosion because of a fault in a part of the engine: [V] *The van backfired noisily.* **2** ~ **(on sb)** to have the opposite effect to the one intended; to have a result that is unpleasant for the person or people responsible for the action: [V, Vpr] *The plan to keep the party secret backfired (on us) when almost no one came.* Compare MISFIRE.

backgammon /ˌbækꞌgæmən, ꞌbækgæmən/ *n* [U] a game for two players who throw DICE and move pieces around a specially marked board.

background /ꞌbækgraʊnd/ *n* **1** [sing] the part of a picture, photograph or view behind the main objects, people, etc: *a photograph with trees in the background* ○ *a painting with a background of blues and greens.* Compare FOREGROUND a. **2** [sing] a position or function that does not attract attention or is less noticeable than that of others: *Ministers have a great many advisers in the background.* ○ *In the background, his enemies were plotting his downfall.* ○ *Throughout his wife's successful career, he stayed in the background.* ○ *background music* (eg in restaurants). Compare FOREGROUND b. **3(a)** [sing] the circumstances, facts or events that influence, cause or explain sth: *These political developments should be seen against a background of increasing civil unrest.* ○ *background information.* **(b)** [U] information concerning these: *Can you give me more background on the company's financial position?* **4** [C, U] **(a)** a person's social class, family status, level of education, etc: *He comes from a poor background.* ○ *a middle-class family background* ○ *She has friends from a variety of backgrounds.* **(b)** a person's past experience, work, type of education, training, etc: *graduates with science backgrounds* ○ *His background is in industry.*

backhand /ꞌbækhænd/ *n* [sing] (in tennis, etc) a stroke played with the back of the hand turned in the direction towards which the ball is hit: *He has a good backhand* (ie can make good backhand shots). ○ *a backhand stroke/shot/drive.* Compare FOREHAND.

backhanded /ˌbækꞌhændɪd/ *adj* **1** done with the back of the hand turned in the direction in which one is hitting: *a backhanded blow.* **2** indirect; AMBIGUOUS(1): *pay sb a ˌbackhanded ꞌcompliment* (ie one that seems to express praise, admiration, etc but could be regarded as an insult).

backhander /ꞌbækhændə(r)/ *n* **1** (*infml*) a BRIBE. **2** a blow with the back of the hand. **3** a BACKHANDED (1) stroke.

backlash /ꞌbæklæʃ/ *n* [sing] a strong reaction by a large number of people against a social or political development or event: *The fall of the fascist dictatorship was followed by a left-wing backlash.*

backlog /ꞌbæklɒg/ *n* (usu *sing*) an amount of work or a number of matters that should have been dealt with but have been allowed to accumulate: *a backlog of work/unanswered letters* ○ *After the postal strike there was a huge backlog of undelivered mail.*

backpack /ꞌbækpæk/ *n* a large bag carried on the back; a RUCKSACK. ⇨ picture at LUGGAGE.

▶ **backpack** *v* to travel or walk carrying such a bag: [V, Vpr] *go backpacking (around Europe).* **backpacker** *n*.

backscratching /ꞌbækskrætʃɪŋ/ *n* [U] (*infml*)

help or useful service given to sb in return for the same from them: *mutual backscratching.*

backside /ˈbæksaɪd/ *n* (*infml*) the part of the body on which one sits: *Get off your backside and do some work!*

backslapping /ˈbækslæpɪŋ/ *n* [U] loud and enthusiastic praise or congratulation (CONGRATULATE): *The team's victory was followed by a great deal of backslapping in the dressing-room.* ▶ **backslapping** *adj* [attrib]: *backslapping tributes/greetings.*

backsliding /ˈbækslaɪdɪŋ/ *n* [U] failure to maintain good standards of behaviour, etc or a return to one's former bad ways: *The government promised there would be no backsliding from their strong fiscal policies.*

backstage /ˌbækˈsteɪdʒ/ *adv* **1** behind the stage in a theatre: *I was taken backstage to meet the actors.* **2** not seen or known about by the public; in secret: *I'd like to know what really goes on backstage in government.* ▶ **backstage** *adj*: ˌbackstage ˈstaff ○ ˌbackstage diˈplomacy.*

backstreet /ˈbækstriːt/ *n* **1** a street in a quiet, often poor, part of a town or city, away from the main roads: *It'll be quicker if we go through the backstreets.* ○ *a backstreet bar.* **2** [attrib] operating secretly and often illegally; not official: *a backstreet abortionist* ○ *backstreet dealers.*

backstroke /ˈbækstrəʊk/ *n* [U] a swimming stroke done on one's back.

backswing /ˈbækswɪŋ/ *n* (in sport) a movement backwards of the arms before hitting a ball.

backtrack /ˈbæktræk/ *v* **1** to return by the same route along which one came: [V] *If we backtrack, we might find out where we went wrong.* **2** to withdraw from an earlier statement or policy: [V] *He quickly backtracked when he realized he had no evidence to support his accusations.*

backup /ˈbækʌp/ *n* **1** [U] support; help: *The police had military backup.* ○ *the backup team of a racing driver.* **2** [U,C] a reserve; a thing or person that can replace another if necessary: *a backup system/procedure* ○ *We can use him as a backup if another player isn't available.* **3** [U,C] (*computing*) a copy of a file, PROGRAM(1), etc for use in case the original is lost or damaged: *a backup disc.*

backward /ˈbækwəd/ *adj* **1** directed behind: *a backward glance.* **2** directed towards a past point in a way that is undesirable; RETROGRADE: *She felt that going back to live in her home town would be a backward step.* **3** having made or making less than normal progress: *a backward part of the country, with no paved roads and no electricity* ○ *John was very backward as a child; he was nearly three before he could walk.* **4** [pred] ~ (**in sth**) lacking confidence to assert oneself: *Sheila is very clever but rather backward in expressing her ideas.* Compare FORWARD[1].
▶ **backwardness** *n* [U].
backwards (also **backward**) *adv* **1** away from one's front; towards the back: *He looked backwards over his shoulder.* **2** in the REVERSE[1] direction: *It's not easy to run backwards.* ○ *The word 'star' is 'rats' backwards.* **3** to a previous point or stage: *take a journey backwards through time* (ie imagine one is going back to an earlier period in history) ○ *Instead of making progress, my work actually seems to be going backwards.* **4** (*US*) = BACK TO FRONT. ⇨ note at FORWARD[2]. **IDM** ˌbackward(s) and ˈforward(s) from one place to the other and back again repeatedly: *travelling backwards and forwards between the east coast and the west coast.* **bend/lean over ˈbackwards (to do sth)** (*infml*) to make a great effort, esp in order to be fair or helpful: *Although we bent over backwards to be kind to her,*

she still seemed to resent us. **know sth backwards** ⇨ KNOW.

backwash /ˈbækwɒʃ/ *n* [sing] **1** the backward movement of water in waves, esp behind a moving ship. **2** the results, usu unpleasant, of an action, a policy or an event: *the backwash effect of the war years.*

backwater /ˈbækwɔːtə(r)/ *n* (usu *sing*) **1** a part of a river not reached by the current, where the water does not flow. **2** an isolated place that is not affected by modern events, progress, new ideas, etc: *live in a quiet backwater.*

backwoods /ˈbækwʊdz/ *n* [pl] **1** remote forest land that has not been cleared. **2** a remote area with few inhabitants which is not influenced by modern life.

backyard /ˌbækˈjɑːd/ *n* (**a**) (*Brit*) an area with a hard surface at the back of a house or another building, often surrounded by a wall. (**b**) (*US*) the whole area behind and belonging to a house, including the lawn, garden, etc. **IDM** **in one's (own) backyard** close to where one lives; within one's own area of operation: *The villagers didn't want a new factory in their backyard.* ○ *The party leader is facing opposition in his own backyard.*

bacon /ˈbeɪkən/ *n* [U] cured (CURE[1] 3) meat from the back or sides of a pig: *a rasher* (ie a thin, flat slice) *of bacon.* Compare GAMMON, HAM 1b, PORK. **IDM** **bring home the bacon** ⇨ HOME[3]. **save one's/sb's bacon** ⇨ SAVE[1].

bacteria /bækˈtɪəriə/ *n* [pl] (*sing* **bacterium** /-iəm/) the simplest and smallest forms of plant life. Bacteria exist in large numbers in air, water and soil, and also in living and dead creatures and plants, and are often a cause of disease.
▶ **bacterial** /-riəl/ *adj* connected with or caused by bacteria: *bacterial action/growth.*
bacteriology /bækˌtɪəriˈɒlədʒi/ *n* [U] the scientific study of bacteria. **bacteriologist** /-dʒɪst/ *n.*

bad[1] /bæd/ *adj* (**worse** /wɜːs/; **worst** /wɜːst/) **1(a)** of poor quality; below an acceptable or desirable standard: *a bad lecture/harvest* ○ *bad pronunciation/eyesight* ○ *You can't take photographs if the light is bad.* (**b**) (of people) not competent; not able to do sth well or in a satisfactory way: *a bad teacher/hairdresser/poet* ○ *a bad liar/listener* ○ *a bad loser* (ie sb who complains when they lose a game, etc). **2** morally unacceptable; wicked: *It's bad to steal.* ○ *When he was old, he regretted all the bad things he had done in his life.* **3** unpleasant: *a bad smell.* ○ *In the recession, our firm went through a bad time.* ○ *What bad weather we're having!* ○ *He's had some bad news: his father has died suddenly.* **4** [usu attrib] (of undesirable things) serious; severe; terrible: *a bad mistake/accident/fracture/headache.* **5** (of food) not fit to be eaten because of decay: *bad eggs/meat* ○ *The fish will go bad if you don't put it in the fridge.* **6** [usu attrib] (of parts of the body) unhealthy, diseased or causing pain: *bad teeth* ○ *a bad back/leg* ○ *She has to take it easy because she has a bad heart.* **7** [pred] ~ **for sb/sth** causing or likely to cause damage to sb/sth; harmful: *Smoking is bad for you/for your health.* ○ *Too much rain is bad for the crops.* **8** not suitable: *Is this a bad time to ask you for a favour?* ○ *This beach is good for swimming but bad for surfing.* **IDM** Most idioms containing **bad** are at the entries for other major words in each idiom, eg **turn up like a bad penny** ⇨ PENNY. **not ˈbad** (*infml*) quite good; better than expected: *'How are you feeling?' 'Not too bad!'* ○ *That wasn't bad for a first attempt.* **too bad** (*infml*) **1** a shame; a pity: *It's too bad you can't come to the party.* **2** (*ironic*) (used when not being sympathetic) bad luck: *'My helping's rather small.' 'Too bad!' It's too bad, that's what.*
▶ **bad** *adv* (*US infml*) badly (BAD[1]): *That's what I want, and I want it bad.* ○ *Are you hurt bad?*

baddy *n* (*infml*) a bad or evil character in a film, play, book, etc: *a simple story of goodies versus baddies.*

badly *adv* (**worse, worst**) **1(a)** in an inadequate or unsatisfactory way: *play/work/sing badly* ○ *badly made/dressed.* (**b**) not successfully: *Things have been going badly at work recently.* ○ *I'm afraid our team's doing very badly.* (**c**) not favourably: *The economic crisis reflects badly on the government's policies.* **2** (with expressions connected with wanting, needing, etc) very much: *badly in need of repair* ○ *They want to see her very badly.* **3** (describing unpleasant situations or events) to a great extent; seriously: *badly wounded* ○ *a badly bruised thumb* ○ *badly beaten at football.* **IDM** **badly 'off** having little money; poor: *She's been very badly off since losing her job.* ○ *We shouldn't complain about being poor — many families are much worse off (than we are).* **be badly 'off for sth** to be in need of sth; not to have enough of sth: *The refugees are badly off for blankets, and even worse off for food.*

badness *n* [U].

■ **,bad 'debt** *n* [C, U] a debt that is unlikely to be paid.

,bad 'language *n* words that are generally considered unacceptable because they are too rude; swear-words (SWEAR): *There's no need to use bad language!*

'bad-mouth *v* [Vn] (*US infml*) to say very unpleasant things about sb.

,bad-'tempered *adj* frequently getting angry; in an angry mood: *I'm often bad-tempered early in the morning.*

bad² /bæd/ *n* **the bad** [U] bad things, people, events, etc: *She has had little experience of the bad in life.* **IDM** **take the ,bad with the 'good** to accept the bad aspects of sth as well as the good ones. **to the 'bad** (*Brit*) having made a financial loss of a specified amount: *I am £500 to the bad* (ie I have £500 less than I had).

bade ⇨ BID¹.

badge /bædʒ/ *n* (**a**) a small piece of metal or cloth with a design or words on it. A badge is attached to a piece of clothing and shows a person's membership of sth, name, support for sth, etc: *a uniform with a badge on it* ○ *He wore a badge saying 'Save the Environment'.* ⇨ picture at HAT. (**b**) any feature or sign that shows a quality or condition: *He regards his beard as a badge of masculinity.*

badger¹ /'bædʒə(r)/ *n* an animal with grey fur and black and white stripes on its head. Badgers live in holes in the ground and move about at night. ⇨ picture.

badger
snout

badger² /'bædʒə(r)/ *v* ~ **sb** (**into doing sth**) to put pressure on sb; to ask or tell sb repeatedly: [Vn, Vnpr] *Stop badgering your father (with questions).* [Vnpr] *She badgered me into doing what she wanted.* [Vn.to inf] *Tom has been badgering us to buy him a camera.*

badinage /'bædɪnɑːʒ; *US* ,bædən'ɑːʒ/ *n* [U] (*French*) friendly joking between people; BANTER.

badminton /'bædmɪntən/ *n* [U] a game for two or four people played with rackets (RACKET¹ 1) and a SHUTTLECOCK on a court with a high net.

baffle¹ /'bæfl/ *v* **1** to be too difficult or strange for sb to understand, solve or explain: [Vn] *One of the exam questions baffled me completely.* ○ *Police are baffled as to the identity of the killer.* ▶ **bafflement** *n* [U]. **baffling** *adj*: *a baffling crime.*

baffle² /'bæfl/ *n* a screen used to control or prevent the flow of sound, light or liquid.

bag¹ /bæg/ *n* **1** [C] (**a**) (often in compounds) a container made of flexible material, eg paper, plastic, cloth or leather, with an opening at the top, that is used for carrying things from place to place: *a 'shopping-bag* ○ *a 'handbag* ○ *a 'kitbag* ○ *a 'toolbag* ○ *a 'mailbag.* ⇨ picture at GOLF. (**b**) such a container with its contents; the amount it contains: *two bags of coal.* **2 bags** [pl] loose folds of skin under the eyes: *She had dark bags under her eyes from lack of sleep.* **3** [C] all the birds, animals, etc shot or caught on one occasion: *We got a good bag today.* **4** [C] (*infml derog*) an unpleasant, ugly or bad-tempered, usu older, woman: *She's an awful old bag!* **IDM** **,bag and 'baggage** with all one's possessions, often suddenly or secretly: *Her tenant left, bag and baggage, without paying the rent.* **a ,bag of 'bones** an extremely thin person or animal: *The cat had not been fed for weeks and was just a bag of bones.* **a bag/bundle of 'nerves** ⇨ NERVE. **sb's bag/box of tricks** ⇨ TRICK. **be in the 'bag** (*infml*) (of a desirable result, outcome, etc) to be certain to happen: *Her re-election is in the bag.* **let the cat out of the bag** ⇨ CAT. **pack one's bags** ⇨ PACK². **the whole bag of tricks** ⇨ WHOLE.

bag² /bæg/ *v* (-gg-) **1** ~ **sth** (**up**) to put sth into a bag or bags: [Vn, Vnp] *bag (up) wheat.* **2** (of hunters) to kill or catch sth: [Vn] *They bagged nothing except a couple of rabbits.* **3** (*Brit infml*) to take or occupy sth before sb else can do so: [Vn] *She had already bagged the most comfortable chair.* ○ *Quick – bag that empty table over there* (eg in a crowded restaurant)! **4** (of clothes) to hang loosely and out of shape: [Vpr] *jeans that bag at the knee* [also V]. **IDM** **bags (I) ...** (*Brit infml*) (said by sb wanting to claim sth first): *Bags I sit in the front seat.*

bagatelle /,bægə'tel/ *n* **1** [U] a game played on a board with small balls that are hit into holes. **2** [C] a small and unimportant thing or amount: *It cost a mere bagatelle.*

bagel /'beɪgl/ *n* a hard bread roll in the shape of a ring. ⇨ picture at BREAD.

baggage /'bægɪdʒ/ *n* [U] personal possessions packed in cases, etc for travelling; LUGGAGE: *excess baggage* (ie weighing more than the limit allowed on an aircraft) ○ *baggage handlers* (ie people employed to load and UNLOAD(1a) baggage at airports). ⇨ picture at LUGGAGE. **IDM** **bag and baggage** ⇨ BAG¹.

■ **'baggage car** *n* (*US*) = LUGGAGE-VAN.

'baggage room *n* (*US*) = LEFT-LUGGAGE OFFICE.

baggy /'bægi/ *adj* (**-ier, -iest**) (esp of clothes) hanging loosely: *baggy shirts.*

bagpipes /'bægpaɪps/ (also **pipes**) *n* [pl] a musical instrument played by blowing air into a bag held under the arm, and pressing it out through pipes: *Scottish bagpipes.* ⇨ picture.

bagpipes
bagpipe
kilt

bags /bægz/ *n* [pl] ~ (**of sth**) (*Brit infml*) plenty of sth; a lot of sth: *There's bags of room.* ○ *Don't worry about money: I've got bags.*

bah /bɑː/ *interj* (expressing disgust or contempt).

bail¹ /beɪl/ *n* [U] (**a**) money paid by or for sb accused of a crime, as a guarantee that they will return for their trial if they are allowed to go free until then: *Bail was set at $1 million.* (**b**) permission for sb to be released with such a guarantee: *The judge granted/refused him bail.* **IDM** **go/stand 'bail (for sb)** to give money to obtain sb's freedom until their trial: *His father stood bail for him.* **jump bail** ⇨ JUMP¹. **(out) on bail** free until one's trial after sb has given a guarantee to pay bail money: *The accused was released on bail (of £1 000).* ○ *He committed another crime while he was out on bail.*

▶ **bail** *v* **1** (usu passive) to release sb on bail: [V.n-

to inf] *He was bailed to appear in court on 15 March.* **PHRV** **bail sb out 1** to obtain the release of sb on bail: *Her parents bailed her out and took her home.* **2** (*infml*) to rescue sb from esp financial difficulties: *The club faced bankruptcy until a wealthy local businessman bailed them out.*

bail² (also **bale**) /beɪl/ *v* ~ (**sth**) (**out**) to throw water out of a boat with buckets, etc: [Vn, Vnp] *bailing water (out)* [Vp] *The boat will sink unless we bail out.* [also V].

bail³ /beɪl/ *n* (usu *pl*) (in cricket) either of the two small pieces of wood resting on each set of three stumps (STUMP 3).

bailiff /'beɪlɪf/ *n* **1** a law officer whose job is to take the possessions or property of people who cannot pay their debts. **2** (*Brit*) a person employed by the owner as manager of an estate or farm. **3** (*US*) an official in a lawcourt, esp one who takes people to their seats and announces the arrival of the judge.

bairn /beən/ *n* (*Scot*) a child.

bait /beɪt/ *n* [U] **1** food, or sth that looks like food, put on a hook to catch fish or placed in nets, traps, etc to attract animals or birds: *use live worms as bait* ○ *The fish nibbled at/rose to/took/swallowed the bait.* **2** a person or thing that is used to attract or tempt sb: *The police used him as bait to trap the killers.* **IDM** **rise to the bait** ➪ RISE². **swallow the bait** ➪ SWALLOW¹.
▶ **bait** *v* **1** ~ **sth** (**with sth**) to put food, or sth that looks like food, on or in sth to catch fish, animals, etc: [Vn] *bait a trap* [Vnpr] *bait a hook with a worm.* **2** [Vn] to try to annoy sb by making cruel or insulting remarks.

baize /beɪz/ *n* [U] a thick, usu green, woollen cloth used esp for covering certain types of tables, eg those on which BILLIARDS and card-games are played.

bake /beɪk/ *v* **1** ~ **sth** (**for sb**) to be cooked or cook sth by dry heat in an oven: [Vn] *bake bread/cakes* [V, Vn] *The bread is baking/being baked.* [Vnn, Vnpr] *I'm baking Alex a birthday cake/baking a birthday cake for Alex.* ○ *baked potatoes* (ie potatoes baked in their skins). ➪ note at COOK. **2** to become or to make sth become hard by heating: [Vn-adj] *The sun baked the ground hard.* [Vn] *Bricks are baked in kilns.* **3** (*infml*) to be or become very hot: [V] *It's absolutely baking today!* ○ *We sat baking in the sun.*
▶ **baker** *n* a person whose job is baking and selling bread, etc: *buy some rolls at the baker's.* **IDM** **a baker's 'dozen** 13.
baking *n* (often in compounds) the action or process of baking: *a baking tin/tray/sheet.*
bakery /'beɪkəri/ *n* a place where bread is baked for sale.
■ **baked 'beans** (*US* also **ˌBoston baked 'beans**) *n* [pl] a type of white beans cooked in TOMATO sauce and usu sold in tins.
ˌbaking-'hot *adj* (*infml*) very hot: *a ˌbaking-hot ˈday.*
'baking-powder *n* [U] a mixture of powders used to make cakes, etc rise and become light as they are baked.
'baking soda *n* [U] (*US*) = SODIUM BICARBONATE.

Bakelite /'beɪkəlaɪt/ *n* [U] (*propr*) a type of plastic: *an old-fashioned black Bakelite telephone.*

balaclava /ˌbælə'klɑːvə/ (also **ˌBalaclava 'helmet**) *n* a type of woollen hat that covers the head and neck but not the face.

balalaika /ˌbælə'laɪkə/ *n* a musical instrument like a GUITAR with a TRIANGULAR body and two, three or four strings, popular esp in the former USSR.

balance¹ /'bæləns/ *n* **1** [U, sing] (**a**) ~ (**in sth / between A and B**) the condition that exists when two opposites are equal or in correct proportions: *Try to achieve a proper balance between work and play.* ○ *This newspaper maintains a good balance in its presentation of different opinions.* (**b**) the pleasing proportion of parts in a whole: *All the parts of the building are in perfect balance.* ○ *The painting has a good balance of shapes and colours.* **2** [U] (**a**) the even distribution of weight so that sb/sth remains steady: *Skiers need a good sense of balance.* ○ *It is difficult to keep your balance on an icy pavement.* *She cycled too fast round the corner, lost her balance and fell off.* (**b**) steadiness (STEADY) of mind or feelings; SANITY: *His wife's sudden death upset the balance of his mind.* **3** [C usu *sing*] (*finance*) the difference between two columns of an account, ie money received or owing and money spent or owed: *check one's bank balance* (ie find out how much money there is in one's account). **4**(**a**) [C usu *sing*] an amount of money still owed after some payment has been made: *The balance (of $500) will be paid within one week.* (**b**) **the balance** [sing] the remaining part of sth after part has already been used, taken, etc: *The balance of your order will be supplied when we receive fresh stock.* ○ *When will you take the balance of your annual leave?* ➪ note at REST³. **5** [C] an instrument used for weighing things, esp one with a bar which is supported in the middle and has dishes hanging from each end. ➪ picture at SCALE³. **IDM** **(be/hang) in the 'balance** (of a decision, result, sb's future, etc) to be uncertain or at a critical(3a) stage: *The future of the project is (hanging) in the balance.* (**catch/throw sb) off 'balance** to find or cause sb to be in danger of falling: *I was caught off balance by the sudden wind and nearly fell.* ○ (*fig*) *The senator was clearly caught off balance by the unexpected question.* **on 'balance** (*infml*) having considered every aspect, argument, etc: *Despite some failures, our firm has had quite a good year on balance.* **redress the balance** ➪ REDRESS. **strike a balance** ➪ STRIKE². **tip the balance/scale** ➪ TIP².
■ **ˌbalance of 'payments** *n* [sing] the difference between the amount paid to foreign countries for imports and services and the amount received from them for exports, etc in a given period: *a healthy balance-of-payments position.*
ˌbalance of 'power *n* [sing] **1** a situation in which power is equally divided among rival states or groups of states. **2** (*politics*) the power held by a small group when rival larger groups are equal or almost equal in strength: *Since the two main parties each won the same number of seats, the minority party holds the balance of power.* ○ *The three branches of the government ensure a balance of power.*
ˌbalance of 'trade *n* [sing] the difference in value between exports and imports: *a ˌbalance-of-trade 'deficit* (ie when a country's exports are worth less than its imports).
'balance sheet *n* a written record of money received and paid out, showing the difference between the two total amounts.

balance² /'bæləns/ *v* **1**(**a**) to keep or put sth in a state of balance¹(2a): [Vnpr] *a clown balancing a stick on the end of his nose* [also Vn]. (**b**) to be or put oneself in a state of balance: [Vpr] *He balanced precariously on the narrow window-ledge.* ○ *How long can you balance on one foot?* [also V]. **2** (*finance*) (**a**) to compare the total amounts of money gained and money spent in an account and record the sum needed to make them equal: [Vn] *balance an account/the books* ○ *balance the budget* (ie to arrange for income and spending to be equal). (**b**) (of an account, a balance sheet, etc) to show equal totals for money received and money spent: [V] *Do the firm's accounts balance?* (**c**) to be of the same value as sth opposite; to OFFSET sth: [Vn] *This year's profits will balance our previous losses.* ○ (*fig*) *His lack of experience was balanced by a willingness to learn.* **3** ~ **A against B** to compare the value of one plan, argument, etc with that of another: [Vnpr] *She balanced the attractions of a high salary against the* *prospect of working long hours.* **4** to give equal importance to different parts of sth: [Vn] *This school aims to balance the amount of time spent on arts and science subjects.*

▶ **balanced** *adj* [usu attrib] keeping or showing a balance: *a balanced state of mind* ○ (ie one in which no single emotion is too strong) ○ *a balanced decision* (ie one reached after comparing all the arguments) ○ *a balanced diet* (ie one with the quantity and variety of food needed for good health).

■ **'balancing act** *n* a skilled way of reaching agreement without offending opposing people or groups: *A delicate balancing act is needed in order to satisfy the two sides.*

balcony /'bælkəni/ *n* **1** a platform with a wall or rail built onto the outside wall of a building and reached from an upstairs room. ➪ picture. **2** (*US*) = CIRCLE 3. Compare FIRST BALCONY.

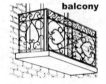
balcony

bald /bɔːld/ *adj* **1** (of people) having little or no hair on the head: *He started going bald quite young.* **2** without the expected covering: *Our dog has a bald patch* (ie a patch with no hair) *on its leg.* ○ *bald* (ie badly worn) *tyres.* **3** without any extra detail or explanation; plain or dull: *bald facts* ○ *a bald statement of the facts.* **IDM** **(as) bald as a coot** (*Brit infml*) completely bald.

▶ **balding** *adj* becoming bald: *He was already balding at the age of 25.*

baldly *adv* in plain words: *To put it baldly...* (ie If I may speak plainly, without trying to soften what I am saying ...).

baldness *n* [U].

■ **,bald 'eagle** *n* a N American eagle with a white head and white tail feathers, used as a symbol of the USA.

balderdash /'bɔːldədæʃ/ *n* [U] (*dated infml*) nonsense: *He's talking complete balderdash.*

bale¹ /beɪl/ *n* a large mass of paper, straw, goods, etc pressed together and tied with rope or wire ready to be moved, sold, etc: *bales of hay* ○ *The cloth was packed in bales.*

▶ **bale** *v* ~ sth **(up)** to make sth into or pack sth in bales: [Vn] *baling hay.*

bale² /beɪl/ *v* = BAIL². **PHRV** **bale (also bail) out (of sth)** to jump out of an aircraft that is damaged or out of control using a PARACHUTE.

baleful /'beɪlfl/ *adj* threatening evil or harm: *a baleful look/influence/presence.* ▶ **balefully** /'beɪlfəli/ *adv.*

balk ➪ BAULK.

ball¹ /bɔːl/ *n* **1(a)** a round object, either solid or hollow, used esp for kicking, hitting or throwing in games: *a 'golf ball* ○ *a 'tennis-ball* ○ *a 'cricket ball.* ➪ picture at BASKETBALL, HOCKEY, SNOOKER. **(b)** a thing or mass of material that is a round shape: *a 'meat ball* ○ *a 'snowball* ○ *a ball of 'wool/'string.* See also CRYSTAL BALL. **2(a)** (*Brit*) (in cricket) a single throw of the ball by the BOWLER¹(1) to the BATSMAN. **(b)** (in baseball) a ball that has been thrown by the PITCHER² but not played by the batter (BAT¹) because it is too wide: *two balls and one strike.* **(c)** (in football, hockey, etc) a movement of the ball by a player: *send over a high ball.* **3** a round part of sth: *the ball of the foot* (ie the part near the base of the big toe) ○ *the ball of the thumb* (ie the part near the palm). ➪ picture at HAND¹. **4** (usu *pl*) (*infml*) a TESTICLE. **IDM** **the ball is in one's/sb's 'court** one/sb must make the next move in a negotiation, etc. **a ball of 'fire** (*infml*) a person who is full of energy and enthusiasm: *He's not exactly a ball of fire, is he?* **have the ball at one's 'feet** (*Brit*) to have a good chance of

succeeding. **have something/a lot on the 'ball** (*US infml*) to be capable and efficient. **(be) on the 'ball** (*infml*) to be alert and aware of new ideas, methods, trends (TREND), etc: *The new publicity manager is really on the ball.* **play 'ball (with sb)** (*infml*) to work willingly with others; to COOPERATE(1): *How can we achieve anything if they refuse to play ball (with us)?* **set/start/keep the ball 'rolling** to begin/continue a conversation or an activity.

▶ **ball** *v* to form sth into a ball by winding, squeezing, etc: [Vn] *ball one's fists.*

■ **,ball-'bearing** *n* **(a)** a type of BEARING(4) in which a ring of small metal balls is used to enable moving parts of a machine to move smoothly. **(b)** (usu *pl*) any of these metal balls.

'ball game *n* **1(a)** any game played with a ball. **(b)** (*US*) a game of baseball. **2** (usu *sing*) (*sl*) a state of affairs: *We're into a whole new ball game.*

'ball-point (also **,ball-point 'pen**) *n* a pen that writes with a tiny ball at its point which rolls ink onto the paper. Compare BIRO.

ball² /bɔːl/ *n* a formal party for dancing. **IDM** **have (oneself) a 'ball** (*infml*) to have a very good time.

ballad /'bæləd/ *n* **1** a simple song or poem, esp one that tells a story: *a ballad singer.* **2** a slow popular song about love: *Her latest single is a ballad.*

ballast /'bæləst/ *n* [U] **1** heavy material placed in a ship or a BALLOON(2) to keep it steady. **2** stones, etc used to make a foundation for a railway, road, etc.

ballboy /'bɔːlbɔɪ/ *n* a young boy who collects balls for the players in a tennis match.

ballcock /'bɔːlkɒk/ *n* a device with a floating ball that controls the level of the water entering a water tank.

ballerina /,bælə'riːnə/ *n* a female dancer in ballet: *a prima ballerina* (ie one who takes leading parts).

ballet /'bæleɪ/ *n* **1(a)** (sometimes **the ballet**) [U] a style of dancing used to tell a story in a dramatic performance with music but without speech or singing: *I enjoy (the) classical ballet.* ○ *ballet music.* **(b)** [C] a story performed in this way: *Have you seen this ballet before?* **2** [CGp] a group of dancers who regularly perform ballet together: *members of the Bolshoi Ballet.*

■ **'ballet-dancer** *n* a person who dances in ballets.

ballgirl /'bɔːlgɜːl/ *n* a young girl who collects balls for the players in a tennis match.

ballistics /bə'lɪstɪks/ *n* [sing *v*] the study of things that are shot or fired through the air, eg bullets, missiles, etc: *a ballistics expert.*

■ **bal,listic 'missile** *n* a missile that is shot up into the air at the speed and angle required to fall on a target.

ballocks = BOLLOCKS.

balloon /bə'luːn/ *n* **1** a thin rubber bag that one blows into to fill with air. Balloons are usu brightly coloured and used as children's toys or decorations at parties: *blow up/burst/pop a balloon.* **2** (also **hot-'air balloon**) a large flexible bag filled with hot air or gas to make it rise in the air, often carrying a basket, etc for passengers. **3** (in a comic strip (COMIC)) a thing shaped like a balloon in which the words or thoughts of the characters are shown. **IDM** **when the bal'loon goes up** (*Brit infml*) when expected trouble begins: *I don't want to be around when the balloon goes up.*

▶ **balloon** *v* **1** to swell out like a balloon(1): [V, Vp] *Her skirt ballooned (out) in the wind.* **2** [V] (usu go **ballooning**) to travel in a balloon(2) as a sport.

balloonist *n* a person who travels by balloon(2), esp as a sport.

ballot /'bælət/ *n* **1(a)** [U] the system of secret voting: *elected by ballot.* **(b)** [C] an instance of this: *hold a ballot of members* ○ *We should put it to a ballot.* **2** [C] the number of votes recorded in an election, etc.

B

▶ **ballot** v ~ **sb** (**about/on sth**) to ask sb to vote secretly about sth: [Vn, Vnpr] *The union balloted its members (on the proposed changes).*

■ **'ballot-box** n a box in which people place their ballot-papers (BALLOT) after voting. (*Brit fig*) *a party worthy of your support at the ballot-box* (ie in an election).

'ballot-paper n a piece of paper on which people mark their choice in a ballot.

ballpark /'bɔːlpɑːk/ n **1** [C] (*US*) a place where baseball is played. **2** [sing] (*infml*) an area(3) or range(3): *They're simply not in the same ballpark* (ie Their ideas, ability, achievements, etc are completely different). ○ *a ballpark figure* (ie a rough estimate).

ballroom /'bɔːlruːm/ n a large room used for formal dancing. Compare DANCEHALL.

■ **,ballroom 'dancing** n [U] a formal type of dancing done usu by couples and to conventional rhythms.

balls /bɔːlz/ n (⚠ *infml*) **1** [sing v] (*Brit*) nonsense: *That's a load of balls!* ○ *What he said was all balls.* **2** [pl] courage: *She had the balls to say exactly what she thought.*

▶ **balls** *interj* (*Brit* ⚠ *infml*) nonsense: *Absolute balls!*

balls v **PHRV** **,balls sth 'up** (*US* also **,ball sth 'up**) (⚠ *infml*) to ruin sth; to make a mess of sth: *He ballsed up all my plans by being so late.*

balls-up /'bɔːlz ʌp/ (*US* also **ball-up** /'bɔːl ʌp/) n (⚠ *infml*) a mess; a bad job: *I made a proper balls-up of my exams.*

ballyhoo /,bæli'huː; *US* 'bælihuː/ n [U] (*infml derog*) excessive noise, fuss, publicity, etc.

balm /bɑːm/ n [U,C] **1** (also **balsam**) an oil that is obtained from certain trees and plants. It smells sweet and is used for healing or making skin softer: *More men are now using skin balm after shaving.* **2** a thing that calms the mind: *The gentle music was (a) balm to his ears.*

▶ **balmy** *adj* (**-ier, -iest**) **1** (of air) gentle and pleasantly warm: *a balmy summer's evening.* **2** (*esp US*) = BARMY.

baloney = BOLONEY.

balsa /'bɔːlsə/ n (**a**) [U] a type of tough light wood used for making models, etc. (**b**) [C] the tropical American tree from which this comes.

balsam /'bɔːlsəm/ n **1**(**a**) [U,C] = BALM 1. (**b**) [C] any of various trees from which BALM(1) is obtained. **2** [C] a plant, usu with pink or white flowers, grown in gardens.

baluster /'bæləstə(r)/ n any of the short pillars forming a BALUSTRADE.

balustrade /,bælə'streɪd/ n a row of upright posts or small pillars joined together along the top. Balustrades are built along the edges of balconies (BALCONY 1), bridges, etc.

bamboo /,bæm'buː/ n [C,U] (*pl* **-oos**) a tall plant of the grass family with hard hollow stems that are used for making furniture, etc: *a grove of bamboos* ○ *a bamboo chair* ○ *bamboo shoots* (ie edible young bamboo plants).

bamboozle /bæm'buːzl/ v (*infml*) to confuse sb, especially by tricking them: [Vnpr] *Kasparov bamboozled his opponent with a string of unexpected moves.* ○ *He bamboozled me into believing that he'd lost all his money.* [also Vn].

ban /bæn/ v (**-nn-**) (**a**) to forbid sth officially: [Vn] *The play was banned (by the censor).* ○ *The government has banned the use of chemical weapons.* ○ *a ban-the-bomb demonstration* (ie one protesting against the use of nuclear weapons). (**b**) ~ **sb** (**from sth / doing sth**) (esp passive) to forbid sb to do sth, esp officially: [Vnpr] *He was banned from (attending) the meeting.* ○ *She's been banned from driving for six months.*

▶ **ban** n ~ (**on sth/sb**) an order that bans: *put a ban on the import of alcohol.*

banal /bə'nɑːl/ *adj* ordinary; not interesting: *banal remarks/thoughts/sentiments.*

▶ **banality** /bə'næləti/ n **1** [U] the quality of being banal: *a play of stunning banality.* **2** [C] a banal remark: *a speech consisting mainly of banalities.*

banana /bə'nɑːnə; *US* bə'nænə/ n (*pl* **bananas**) a long curved fruit with a thick skin that is yellow when ripe. Its flesh is soft and pale in colour: *a bunch of bananas.* ⇨ picture at FRUIT. **IDM** **be/go ba'nanas** (*sl*) to be/become angry, mad or silly: *Every time he sees the neighbour's cat, our dog goes completely bananas!*

■ **ba,nana re'public** n (*derog offensive*) a small poor country, esp one in Central America, whose economy depends on foreign money.

ba'nana skin n (*Brit infml*) a cause of difficulty or embarrassment, esp to a public figure, an organization, etc: *The proposed tax changes are likely to prove a banana skin for the government.*

ba,nana 'split n a sweet dish made of a banana cut in half along its length and filled with ice-cream, fruit, nuts, etc.

band¹ /bænd/ n **1** [C] (**a**) a thin flat strip or circle of any material that is put round things to hold them together or to strengthen them: *She always ties her hair back in a band.* ○ *He rolled the paper up and put a rubber band around it.* ○ *The trunk had metal bands round it for extra safety.* See also HATBAND, WAISTBAND. (**b**) a strip of colour or material on sth that is different from that around it: *a white plate with a blue band around the edge.* **2** [C] (**a**) (also **'waveband**) a range of radio waves: *a transistor tuned to the FM band.* (**b**) a range of prices, incomes, etc.

▶ **band** v [Vn] (usu passive) to put a band¹(1a) on or round sth.

band² /bænd/ n **1** [CGp] (**a**) a group of people playing popular music, often for dancing: *a 'dance band* ○ *a 'jazz/'rock band.* Compare ORCHESTRA. (**b**) a group of people playing esp wind instruments: *a brass 'band* ○ *a military 'band.* **2** [CGp] a group of people doing sth together with a common purpose: *a band of robbers/fugitives/relief workers.* See also ONE-MAN BAND.

▶ **band** v ~ **together** to unite in a group: [Vp] *band together (to protest) against a common enemy.*

bandage /'bændɪdʒ/ n a strip of material used for tying round and protecting a wound or an injury.

▶ **bandage** v ~ **sth/sb** (**up**) (**with sth**) to tie a bandage round a part of the body: [Vn, Vnp] *bandage (up) a wound* [Vn] *a bandaged hand* [also Vnpr].

Band-aid /'bændeɪd/ n [C,U] (*US propr*) a sticking-plaster (STICK²).

bandanna /bæn'dænə/ n a piece of material, often with coloured spots, usu worn round the neck.

B and B (also **b and b**) /,biː ən 'biː/ *abbr* (*infml esp Brit*) bed and breakfast.

bandit /'bændɪt/ n a member of an armed gang that robs people: *Buses driving through the mountains have been attacked by bandits.*

▶ **banditry** n [U] the activity of bandits.

bandmaster /'bændmɑːstə(r); *US* -mæs-/ n a person who conducts a band²(1), esp a military one.

bandolier (also **bandoleer**) /,bændə'lɪə(r)/ n a belt worn over the shoulder with pockets for bullets, etc.

bandsman /'bændzmən/ n (*pl* **-men** /-mən/) a person who plays in a band²(1).

bandstand /'bændstænd/ n a covered platform for a band²(1) playing outdoors.

bandwagon /'bændwægən/ n any popular or fashionable activity: *companies cashing in on the keep-fit bandwagon.* **IDM** **climb/jump on the 'bandwagon** (*infml*) to join others in doing sth fashionable or likely to be successful: *politicians eager to jump on the environmental bandwagon.*

[V.speech] = verb + direct speech   [V.that] = verb + *that* clause   [V.wh] = verb + *who, how,* etc clause

bandy¹ /'bændi/ *adj* (*usu derog*) (of the legs) curving outwards so that the knees are wide apart.
  ■ **'bandy-legged** *adj* (of people or animals) having bandy legs.

bandy² /'bændi/ *v* (*pt, pp* **bandied**) **IDM** **bandy 'words (with sb)** (*dated*) to quarrel or speak rudely: *Don't bandy words with me, young man!* **PHR V** ,**bandy** sth **a'bout/a'round** (*usu passive*) to pass on a rumour, an idea, etc, often in a careless or casual way: *The stories being bandied about are completely false.* ◦ *Her name is being bandied around as a potential head of department.*

bane /beɪn/ *n* [sing] **the ~ of sb/sth** a cause of great trouble or annoyance: *The neighbours' children are the bane of my life.* ◦ *The poor train service has been the bane of commuters for years.*
  ▶ **baneful** /-fl/ *adj* evil or causing evil: *the baneful effects of inflation.*

bang¹ /bæŋ/ *v* **1(a)** to hit sth or put sth somewhere so as to make a loud noise: [Vpr] *He was banging on the door with his fist.* [Vnadv] *She banged the door angrily.* [Vnpr] *She banged her fist on the table.* [Vnp] *I banged the box down on the floor.* [also Vn]. **(b) ~ (sth) (down, to, etc)** to close sth or be closed with a loud noise: [V] *A door was banging somewhere* (ie opening and closing noisily): [Vn] *Don't bang the door!* [Vnp] *He banged the lid down.* [also Vp]. **2(a)** to hit sth, esp a part of the body, against sth, usu by accident: [Vn,Vnpr] *She tripped and banged her knee (on the desk).* **(b) ~ into sb/sth** to crash into sb/sth violently: [Vpr] *He ran around the corner and banged straight into a lamppost.* **3** to make a loud noise like an explosion: [V] *Suddenly something banged and all the lights went out.* **PHR V** ,**bang a'bout/a'round** to move around noisily: *We could hear the children banging about upstairs.* ,**bang 'on about sth** (*Brit infml*) to talk a lot or in a boring way about sth: *The headmaster keeps banging on about exam results.*

NOTE Compare **bang, bump, knock** and **bash**. **Bang** means to hit something hard and loudly: *A little boy was banging a drum.* It may be a deliberate action to express anger or to get attention: *He banged on the wall angrily.* ◦ *I heard voices, then a car door banging.* You may **bang** a part of the body by accident: *She banged her head when she dived into the pool.*
  Bump means to hit somebody or something suddenly by accident, but not cause serious damage: *Who's bumped into the back of my car?* ◦ *He's always bumping his head on that low ceiling.*
  Knock means to make a noise when you hit something, especially to get attention: *Someone's knocking at the door — can you answer it?* ◦ *Please come in. You don't need to knock.* **Knock** can also describe an action which breaks something by accident: *I knocked the glass off the table with my elbow.*
  Bash is informal and means to hit somebody or something hard, usually causing injury or damage: *Thieves bashed her over the head and stole her purse.* ◦ *The boat bashed into the rocks.*

bang² /bæŋ/ *n* **1** a sudden loud noise: *The door swung shut with a bang.* ◦ *The bomb exploded with an enormous bang.* See also BIG BANG. **2** a sudden painful blow: *He fell and got a nasty bang on the head.* **IDM** **go (off) with a 'bang**; (*US*) **go over with a 'bang** (*infml*) (of an event, etc) to be successful: *The party went with a bang.* **with a bang** (*infml*) suddenly and with a powerful effect: *The large bill for the meal brought us back to reality with a bang.*
  ▶ **bang** *interj* (used to imitate a loud noise): *'Bang! Bang! You're dead!' shouted the small boy.*

bang³ /bæŋ/ *adv* (*infml*) **1(a)** exactly; precisely (PRECISE): *bang in the middle of the performance* ◦

You're bang on time, as usual! **(b)** completely: *a film that is bang up to date.* See also SLAP-BANG. **2** suddenly, violently or noisily: *I tripped and fell bang on the floor.* **IDM** **bang goes sth** (*infml*) that is the (sudden) end of sth: *Bang went his hopes of promotion.* **be bang 'on** (*Brit sl*) to be exactly right: *Her criticisms were bang on every time.* ◦ *Your budget figures were bang on this year.* **go 'bang** (*infml*) **1** (of a door, etc) to shut noisily. **2** to burst or explode with a loud noise: *A balloon suddenly went bang.*

bang⁴ /bæŋ/ *n* (usu *pl*) (*US*) = FRINGE 1. ⇨ picture at HAIR.

banger /'bæŋə(r)/ *n* (*Brit infml*) **1** a SAUSAGE. **2** a noisy old car. **3** a FIREWORK(1) made to explode with a loud noise.

bangle /'bæŋgl/ *n* a large ring worn as jewellery round the arm or ankle.

banish /'bænɪʃ/ *v* **1 ~ sb (from sth)** to send sb away, esp out of a country, as a punishment: [Vn,Vnpr] *He was banished (from his native land) for life.* **2 ~ sth/sb (from sth)** to make sth/sb go away; to get rid of sth/sb: [Vn,Vnpr] *She banished all thoughts of a restful afternoon (from her mind).* [Vnpr] *The children were banished from the sitting-room and made to play in the garden.*
  ▶ **banishment** *n* [U] the state or process of being banished: *lifelong banishment.*

banister (also **bannister**) /'bænɪstə(r)/ *n* [C] (also *esp Brit* **banisters** [pl]) the posts and rail that are fixed at the side of a staircase: *hold on to the banister rail* ◦ *children sliding down the banister(s).* ⇨ picture at STAIRCASE.

banjo /'bændʒəʊ/ *n* (*pl* **-os**) a musical instrument with a long neck and a round body. It has four or more strings that are played with the fingers.

bank¹ /bæŋk/ *n* **1** the land sloping up along each side of a river or canal; the ground near a river: *Several people were fishing from the river bank.* ◦ *My house is on the south bank (of the river).* ⇨ note at COAST¹. **2** a raised slope at the edge of sth or dividing sth: *low banks of earth between rice-fields* ◦ *flowers growing on the banks on each side of the country lanes.* **3** = SANDBANK. **4** an artificial slope in a road, etc that enables cars to keep going fast round a bend. **5** a mass of cloud, snow, etc, esp one formed by the wind: *The sun disappeared behind a bank of clouds.*

bank² /bæŋk/ *v* (of an aircraft, etc) to travel with one side higher than the other, usu when turning: [V, Vpr] *The plane banked steeply (to the left).* **PHR V** **bank up** to form into piles, esp because of wind: *The snow has banked up against the shed.* **bank sth up 1** to make sth into piles: *bank the earth up into a mound.* **2** to stop the water in a river, etc from flowing by piling up earth, mud, etc: *bank up a stream.* **3** to pile coal, etc on a fire so that the fire burns slowly for a long time: *We banked up the fire before going out for a walk.*

bank³ /bæŋk/ *n* **1** an organization or a place that provides a financial service. Customers keep their money in the bank safely and it is paid out when needed by means of cheques, etc: *My salary is paid directly into my bank* (ie the bank where I keep my money). ◦ *the high street banks* (ie the major ones, with branches in most town centres) ◦ *a 'bank manager* ◦ *a 'bank account* ◦ *a 'bank loan* (ie money borrowed from a bank). **2** a supply of money or counters (COUNTER²) used in certain games for payment, etc. **3** a place where sth is stored ready for use; a supply: *build up a bank of useful addresses/references/information* ◦ *a 'blood bank* ◦ *a 'data bank.* **IDM** **break the 'bank** (*Brit*) **1** (in gambling) to win more money than is in the bank³(2). **2** (*infml*) to cost more than one can afford: *Come on! One* *evening at the theatre won't break the bank.* **laugh all the way to the bank** ⇨ LAUGH.

■ **'bank balance** *n* the amount of money that sb has in their bank account at a particular time: *My bank balance is always low at the end of the month.*
'bank-book (also **passbook**) *n* a book containing a record of a customer's bank account.
'bank card *n* = CHEQUE CARD.
'bank draft *n* (a document used for) the transferring of money from one bank to another.
,bank 'holiday *n* **1** (*Brit*) a day on which banks are officially closed and which is usu a public holiday (eg Easter Monday, Christmas Day, etc): *New Year's Day is always a bank holiday.* ⇨ note at HOLIDAY. **2** (*US*) any day on which banks are closed by law.
'bank rate *n* the rate of interest¹(5) in a country, fixed by a central bank or banks.
'bank statement *n* a printed record of all the money paid into and out of a customer's bank account within a certain period: *The bank sends me a bank statement every month.*

bank⁴ /bæŋk/ *v* **1** to place money in a bank: [Vn] *bank one's savings/takings.* ~ (**with sb/sth**) to keep one's money at a particular bank: [Vpr] *Who do you bank with?* [V] *Where do you bank?* PHRV **'bank on sb/sth** to rely on sb/sth: *I'm banking on your help/ banking on you to help me.* ○ *He was banking on the train being on time.*
▶ **banker** *n* **1** a person who owns or manages a bank³(1). **2** a person who looks after the bank³(2) in certain games. **,banker's 'order** = STANDING ORDER.
banking *n* [U] the business activity of banks (BANK³ 1): *choose banking as a career* ○ *She's in banking.*

bank⁵ /bæŋk/ *n* a row or series of similar objects, eg in a machine: *a bank of lights/switches* ○ *a bank of cylinders in an engine* ○ *a bank of oars.*

banknote /'bæŋknəʊt/ *n* = NOTE¹ 4: *forged banknotes.*

bankroll /'bæŋkrəʊl/ *v* (*US infml*) to support sb/sth financially: [Vn] *American movies bankrolled by soft drinks manufacturers.*

bankrupt /'bæŋkrʌpt/ *n* (*law*) a person judged by a lawcourt to be unable to pay her or his debts in full, whose property is then taken by the court and used to repay those debts.
▶ **bankrupt** *adj* **1** unable to pay one's debts: *go/be bankrupt.* **2** ~ (**of sth**) (*derog*) completely lacking in sth that is good: *a government bankrupt of new ideas* ○ *a society that is morally bankrupt.*
bankrupt *v* to make sb bankrupt: [Vn] *an economy bankrupted by 20 years of corrupt government.*
bankruptcy /'bæŋkrʌpsi/ *n* [U, C] the state of being bankrupt: *moral/political bankruptcy* ○ *His firm is on the verge of/is facing bankruptcy.* ○ *The company filed for bankruptcy* (ie asked to be officially declared bankrupt) *in 1992.* ○ *Forty bankruptcies were recorded in this town last year.*

banner /'bænə(r)/ *n* a large strip of cloth showing an EMBLEM or a SLOGAN, or giving information about sth. Banners are often displayed or carried, usu between two poles, during political or religious processions: *A banner stretched across the road announced the local flower show.* ○ *Two protesters unfurled a banner reading 'Save our Wildlife'.* ○ (*fig*) *Her new painting keeps the modernist banner flying high.* ⇨ picture at FLAG¹. IDM **under the banner (of sth)** **1** claiming to support a particular set of ideas: *a meeting held under the banner 'Free nursery education for all'* ○ *She fought the election under the banner of equal rights.* **2** as part of a particular group or organization: *The club now comes under the respectable banner of the Royal Yachting Association.*
■ **,banner 'headline** *n* a large newspaper HEADLINE (1), often printed across a whole page.

bannister = BANNISTER.

banns /bænz/ *n* [pl] a public announcement in church that two people intend to marry each other: *read/publish the banns.*

banquet /'bæŋkwɪt/ *n* a large formal meal, usu for a special event, at which speeches are often made: *attend a state banquet in honour of the visiting French President.*
▶ **banqueting** *adj* used for or related to banquets: *a banqueting hall/suite.*

banshee /bæn'ʃiː, 'bænʃiː/ *n* (*esp Irish*) a female spirit that cries loudly and is thought by some to warn of death: *howling/screaming/wailing like a banshee.*

bantam /'bæntəm/ *n* a type of small chicken.

bantamweight /'bæntəmweɪt/ *n* a boxer weighing between 51 and 53.5 kilograms, next above FLYWEIGHT(1).

banter /'bæntə(r)/ *n* [U] a playful friendly exchange of remarks: *the traditional congratulatory banter between the astronauts and mission control.*
▶ **bantering** *adj* playful: *a bantering remark/tone of voice.*

banyan /'bænjən/ *an* Indian FIG¹ tree whose branches hang down and take root in the ground.

baptism /'bæptɪzəm/ *n* [U, C] a ceremony marking a person's admission into the Christian Church either by dipping the person in water or by scattering a few drops of water on her or him, and often giving her or him a name or names: *There were six baptisms at our local church last week.* IDM **a ,baptism of 'fire** a difficult introduction to an experience: *a young teacher facing her baptism of fire.*
▶ **baptismal** /bæp'tɪzməl/ *adj* [attrib] of or related to baptism: *baptismal water.*

Baptist /'bæptɪst/ *n* a member of a Protestant Church that believes in BAPTISM by being dipped completely in water at an age when a person is old enough to understand what the ceremony means: *devout Baptists.*

baptize, -ise /bæp'taɪz/ *v* **1** (esp passive) to give baptism to sb; to CHRISTEN(1) sb: [Vn-n] *She was baptized Mary.* [also Vn]. **2** to admit sb into a specified church by BAPTISM: [Vn-n] *I was baptized a Catholic.*

bar¹ /bɑː(r)/ *n* **1** [C] (**a**) a building or a room in a hotel, pub, etc in which both alcoholic and other drinks are served: *The island's only licensed bar* ○ *a bar menu* ○ *a cocktail bar* ○ *I found him in the bar of the Red Lion.* ○ *They walked into the bar.* ⇨ note at INN. (**b**) a counter where drinks are served: *sitting on a stool at/by the bar* ○ *the poolside bar area* ○ *He put his beer down on the bar.* See also LOUNGE BAR, PUBLIC BAR, SALOON BAR, WINE BAR. **2** [C] (esp in compounds) a place in which light meals, cakes, etc are served, as well as tea, coffee, soft(13) drinks, etc: *a 'sandwich bar* ○ *a 'coffee bar.* See also SNACK-BAR. **3** [C] (**a**) a long straight piece of metal: *an iron bar.* (**b**) a piece of solid material made in a regular shape: *a bar of chocolate/soap.* ⇨ note at PIECE¹. (**c**) a narrow piece of wood or metal, often parallel to others in a GRID(1), designed to stop people getting through a door, window, etc: *There's a strong bar on the door.* ○ *They fitted bars to their windows to stop burglars getting in.* (**d**) (in an electric fire) a long COIL(3) of metal that becomes red and provides heat when electricity is passed through it: *Switch another bar on if you're cold.* **4** [C] any of the sections of equal value in time into which a piece of music is divided, and the notes in it: *Hum the opening bars of your favourite tune.* ⇨ picture at MUSIC. **5** [C usu sing] ~ (**to sth**) a thing that delays or stops progress; a barrier: *Poor health may be a bar to success in life.* See also COLOUR BAR. **6 the Bar** [Gp, sing] (**a**) (*Brit*) the profession of BARRISTER: *be called to the bar* (ie be received into the profession of barrister). (**b**) (*US*) the legal profession. **IDM** be‚hind 'bars (*infml*) in prison: *The murderer is now safely behind bars.*

■ '**bar chart** *n* a diagram on which narrow bands of equal width but varying height are used to represent quantities. ⇨ picture at CHART.

'**bar code** *n* a pattern of thick and thin parallel lines printed on books in a library, goods in shops, etc. It contains information in code that a computer can interpret.

bar² /bɑː(r)/ *v* (**-rr-**) **1** to fasten a door, gate, etc with a metal or wooden bar: [Vn] *barred windows*. **2** to form an obstacle across sth so as to prevent sb's progress: [Vn] *Troops barred the road so we had to turn back.* ○ (*fig*) *Poverty bars the way to progress.* **3** ~ **sb (from sth / doing sth)** to prevent sb from using sth or from doing sth; to forbid sb/sth: [Vnpr] *She was barred from (entering) the competition because of her age.* [Vn] *All visitors were barred.* **IDM** with no holds barred ⇨ HOLD 2.

bar³ /bɑː(r)/ *prep* except for sb/sth: *The whole class is here bar two that are sick.* ○ *That's the best ice-cream I've ever tasted, bar none* (ie without any exception). See also BARRING.

barb /bɑːb/ *n* **1** the point of an ARROW(1), a fish-hook (FISH), etc curved backwards to make it difficult to pull out. ⇨ picture at HOOK. **2** a remark that is intended to hurt sb's feelings: *Her barbs of sarcasm had clearly struck home.*

▶ **barbed** *adj* **1** having a barb or barbs: *a barbed hook.* **2** (of a remark, comment, etc) hurting or intended to hurt sb's feelings: *barbed criticisms.*

‚**barbed** 'wire *n* [U] wire with short sharp points along it, used to prevent people from entering or leaving an enclosed area: *a barbed wire fence to discourage intruders.*

barbarian /bɑːˈbeəriən/ *n* (*often derog*) a person who behaves in a rough or cruel manner and is ignorant of culture and good taste: *barbarian tribes* ○ *teenagers acting like barbarians.*

barbaric /bɑːˈbærɪk/ *adj* (*often derog*) of or like a BARBARIAN; cruel or wild, and not as expected of a civilized (CIVILIZE) person: *barbaric soldiers/acts of war* ○ *The way the seals are killed is barbaric.*

barbarism /ˈbɑːbərɪzəm/ *n* (*derog*) **1** [U] the state of being without education or the standards of behaviour normally associated with CIVILIZATION(1): *be transformed from barbarism.* **2** cruel or wild behaviour: *the savagery and barbarism of war.*

barbarity /bɑːˈbærəti/ *n* [U,C] extreme cruelty: *the barbarity of the Middle Ages* ○ *the barbarities of the previous regime.*

barbarous /ˈbɑːbərəs/ *adj* (*derog*) **1** cruel, wild or SAVAGE(1b); BARBARIC: *a barbarous act/country/ culture* ○ *the barbarous treatment of prisoners* ○ *The priest's murder was condemned as barbarous.* **2** lacking education, good taste, etc: *barbarous use of language.*

barbecue /ˈbɑːbɪkjuː/ *n* (**a**) [C] a metal frame for cooking meat, etc over an open fire: *put another steak on the barbecue.* (**b**) [C] an outdoor meal or party at which food is cooked in this way: *Let's have a barbecue.* (**c**) [U] food cooked in this way: *barbecue sausages.* ○ note at COOK.

▶ **barbecue** *v* to cook food on a barbecue: [Vn] *barbecued chicken.*

barber /ˈbɑːbə(r)/ *n* a person whose trade is cutting men's hair and sometimes shaving them: *I'm going to the barber's (shop) to get my hair cut.* Compare HAIRDRESSER.

■ '**barber-shop** *n* a place where a barber works. — *adj* [attrib] of a type of music for four male voices singing in harmony(3) without being accompanied by instruments: *a barber-shop quartet.*

barbiturate /bɑːˈbɪtʃʊrət/ *n* any of a group of drugs

that make people calmer or put them to sleep: *barbiturate poisoning* ○ *He died from an overdose of barbiturates.*

bard /bɑːd/ *n* (*arch*) a poet: *the Bard (of Avon)* (ie Shakespeare).

bare¹ /beə(r)/ *adj* (**-r, -st**) **1(a)** without clothing: *bare legs* ○ *walk around in bare feet* (ie without shoes or socks, etc) ○ *bare from the waist up* (ie wearing no clothes above the waist). (**b**) without the usual or expected covering or protection: *bare floors* (ie without a carpet) ○ *a bare hillside* (ie one without plants, bushes or trees) ○ *trees that are already bare* (ie that have already lost their leaves) ○ *with his head bare* (ie not wearing a hat) ○ *with one's bare hands* (ie without tools or weapons). **2** ~ **(of sth)** empty or almost empty; lacking the usual or expected contents: *a room bare of furniture* ○ *bare shelves* ○ *The shop window was bare.* **3** [attrib] only just sufficient; basic or simple: *the bare necessities/bare(st) essentials of life* (ie things needed simply to stay alive) ○ *a bare majority* (ie a very small one) ○ *the bare facts* (ie without any additional comment or detail) ○ *have the bare minimum qualifications for the job.* **IDM** the bare 'bones (of sth) the main or basic facts about sth: *These are the bare bones of the story. Jim can give you all the details.* lay sth 'bare to expose or make known sth secret or hidden: *lay bare the truth/sb's treachery/a plot.* ▶ **bareness** *n* [U].

bare² /beə(r)/ *v* to remove the covering from sth, esp from part of the body: [Vn] *bare one's chest* ○ *bare a wire* (ie cut off the covering of rubber, etc before making an electrical connection). **IDM** bare one's 'heart/'soul (to sb) (*rhet or joc*) to make one's deepest and most private feelings known to sb. bare one's/its 'teeth (of a person or an animal) to show one's/its teeth, esp when angry: *He bared his teeth at her in a grimace.*

bareback /ˈbeəbæk/ *adj, adv* on a horse without a saddle: *a bareback rider* ○ *ride bareback.*

barefaced /ˈbeəfeɪst/ *adj* [attrib] (*derog*) showing no shame despite being dishonest or clearly wrong: *a barefaced lie* ○ *He had the barefaced nerve to accuse me of cheating!*

barefoot /ˈbeəfʊt/ (also **barefooted** /ˌbeəˈfʊtɪd/) *adj, adv* without any covering on the feet: *children running barefoot in the sand.*

bareheaded /ˌbeəˈhedɪd/ *adj, adv* without a covering on the head.

barely /ˈbeəli/ *adv* **1** only just: *barely 10% of the population* ○ *barely perceptible/recognizable* ○ *We barely had time to catch the train.* ○ *He was* **barely able** to stand. ○ *He can barely read or write.* ○ *Schools got barely a mention in the report.* **2** only a very short time before: *I had barely started speaking when he interrupted me.* ○ *The policy had barely been introduced before it was abandoned.* Compare HARDLY, SCARCELY.

bargain¹ /ˈbɑːgən/ *n* ~ **(with sb) 1** an agreement in which two or more people or groups promise to do sth for each other: ***make/strike a bargain with*** *sb* ○ *If you promote our goods, we will give you a good discount as our part of the bargain.* ○ *The bargain they reached with their employers was to reduce their wage claim in return for a shorter working week.* ○ *I've done what I promised and I expect you to* **keep your side of the bargain** (ie do what you agreed in return). ○ *A bargain's a bargain* (ie When an agreement has been reached, it should be kept). **2** a thing bought or sold for less than its usual price when this is to the advantage of the buyer: *goods at bargain prices* ○ *pick up a good bargain* ○ *The car was a bargain at that price.* ○ *You must admit that I'm offering you a bargain.* **IDM** drive/strike a hard bargain ⇨ HARD¹. into the 'bargain; *US* also in the 'bargain (*infml*) (used to emphasize an addi-

tional piece of information) also; in addition: *She was a distinguished scientist — and a gifted painter into the bargain.*
■ ‚bargain 'basement *n* a part of a large shop, usu in the BASEMENT, where goods are sold at reduced prices: *bargain basement offers/prices.*
'bargain-hunting *n* [U] the activity of looking for goods at prices that are lower than usual and good value for money.

bargain² /'bɑːgən/ *v* ~ (with sb) (about/over/for sth) to discuss prices, conditions, terms of trade, etc with sb in order to reach an agreement that is favourable to oneself: [V] *Never pay the advertised price for a car — always try to bargain.* [Vpr] *Dealers bargain with growers over the price of coffee.* ○ *The unions bargained (with management) for a shorter working week.* **PHR V** ‚bargain sth a'way to give sth away and fail to get sth of equal value in return: *The leaders bargained away the freedom of their people.* 'bargain for sth; 'bargain on sth (*infml*) (often in negative sentences) to expect sth; to consider sth as likely to happen; to be prepared for sth: *The exam was more difficult than I had bargained for.* ○ *The thieves didn't bargain on the guard dogs patrolling the warehouse.* ○ *When the minister agreed to answer questions on television, he got more than he (had) bargained for.*

bargaining /'bɑːgənɪŋ/ *n* [U] discussion of prices, conditions, terms of trade, etc with the aim of making an agreement that is favourable to oneself: *establish a bargaining procedure* ○ *private sector wage bargaining* ○ *After much hard bargaining we reached an agreement.* See also COLLECTIVE BARGAINING.
■ 'bargaining counter *n* a special advantage that can be used by one side in a negotiation to make the outcome more favourable to itself: *Ownership of the land gives us a strong bargaining counter.*
'bargaining position *n* the circumstances that one is in when discussing prices, conditions, terms of trade, etc: *If people badly need your goods, you're in a strong bargaining position.*
'bargaining power *n* [U] the extent to which one can make an agreement that is favourable to oneself when discussing prices, conditions, terms of trade, etc: *Since our goods can be bought cheaper elsewhere, we have little bargaining power when dealing with customers.*

barge¹ /bɑːdʒ/ *n* a large boat with a flat bottom, used for carrying goods and people on rivers, canals, etc.

barge² /bɑːdʒ/ *v* (*infml*) to move in a rough way, pushing people out of the way or crashing into them: [Vpr] *Stop barging into people!* ○ *He barged past (me) and went to the front of the line.* [Vnpr] *They barged their way through the crowd.* [also V, Vnp]. **PHR V** ‚barge 'in (on sth) / 'into sth to enter or interrupt sth rudely and forcefully: *I tried to stop him coming through the door but he just barged (his way) in.* ○ *She barged in on our meeting without even knocking.*

bargepole /'bɑːdʒpəʊl/ *n* **IDM** not touch sb/sth with a bargepole ▷ TOUCH¹.

baritone /'bærɪtəʊn/ *n* (*music*) (**a**) a male singing voice between TENOR² and BASS¹(2). (**b**) a singer with such a voice. (**c**) a musical part written for a baritone voice.

barium /'beərɪəm/ *n* [U] a chemical element. ▷ App 7.
■ ‚barium 'meal *n* a substance containing barium that a patient takes, usu by swallowing it, before having an X-RAY because it makes internal organs more clearly visible.

bark¹ /bɑːk/ *n* [U, C] the tough outer covering of tree trunks and branches.

bark² /bɑːk/ *n* (**a**) the short sharp harsh sound made by dogs and foxes. (**b**) any similar sound, eg the sound of a gun being fired or of a cough. **IDM** sb's bark is worse than their bite (*infml*) sb is rarely as angry or as fierce as they appear or sound.
▶ **bark** *v* **1**(**a**) ~ (at sb/sth) (of dogs, etc) to give a bark or barks: [Vpr] *Our dog always barks at strangers.* [V] *I could hear a dog barking.* ○ *The barking finally stopped.* (**b**) (of people coughing, guns, etc) to make a similar sound: [V] *have a barking cough.* **2** ~ (at sb); ~ sth (out) to say sth in a sharp harsh voice: [Vpr] *When she's angry, she often barks at the children.* [Vn, Vnp] *The sergeant barked (out) an order.* [V.speech] *'Get out!' she barked.* **IDM** bark up the wrong 'tree (esp in the continuous tenses) to pursue a course of action or line of thought that is wrongly directed: *If you think that, you're barking up the wrong tree altogether.*
■ ‚barking 'mad *adj* (*Brit infml*) completely mad.

barker /'bɑːkə(r)/ *n* (*infml*) a person who stands outside or near a place and tries to attract customers to it by shouting loudly.

barley /'bɑːli/ *n* [U] (**a**) a type of grain used for food and for making beer and whisky. (**b**) the plant that produces this: *fields of winter barley.* ▷ picture at CEREAL.
■ 'barley sugar *n* a hard clear sweet²(1) made from boiled sugar.
'barley water *n* [U] (*Brit*) a drink, sometimes flavoured, made by boiling barley in water: *lemon barley water.*

barmaid /'bɑːmeɪd/ *n* a woman who serves drinks at a bar.

barman /'bɑːmən/ *n* (*pl* -men /-mən/) (*US* also **bartender**) *n* a man who serves drinks at a bar.

bar mitzvah /ˌbɑː 'mɪtsvə/ *n* a ceremony and celebration held on the 13th birthday of a Jewish boy, at which he assumes the religious responsibilities of an adult.

barmy (*esp US* **balmy**) /'bɑːmi/ *adj* (-ier, -iest) (*infml*) foolish; crazy: *That music is driving me barmy!*

barn /bɑːn/ *n* **1**(**a**) a large simple building for storing grain, HAY, etc on a farm. (**b**) a building for sheltering farm animals, eg cows or horses. **2** (*derog*) any large, apparently bare, building that is not attractive: *They live in a great barn of a house.* **3** (*US*) a building in which buses, vans, etc are kept when not in use.
■ 'barn dance *n* an informal social occasion at which traditional country dances are performed.
'barn-owl *n* a type of owl that often makes its nest in barns and other buildings. ▷ picture at OWL.

barnacle /'bɑːnəkl/ *n* a small SHELLFISH that attaches itself to objects under water, eg to rocks or the bottoms of ships.

barnstorm /'bɑːnstɔːm/ *v* (*US*) to travel quickly through an area making political speeches, presenting plays, etc: [Vn] *He'll barnstorm the southern states in an attempt to woo voters.* [also V].

barnyard /'bɑːnjɑːd/ *n* an area on a farm around a BARN(1).

barometer /bə'rɒmɪtə(r)/ *n* **1** an instrument for measuring air pressure, used esp for forecasting the weather: *The barometer is falling* (ie Wet weather is indicated). **2** a thing that indicates changes in public opinion, market prices, sb's mood, etc: *a reliable barometer of public feeling.*

baron /'bærən/ *n* **1** a nobleman of the lowest rank. In Britain barons have the title *Lord*; in other countries they have the title *Baron*. **2** a BUSINESSMAN(1) who controls a large part of a particular industry: *a 'press baron* ○ *'oil barons.*
▶ **baroness** /'bærənəs, ˌbærə'nes/ *n* **1** a woman holding the rank of baron. **2** the wife of a baron.
baronial /bə'rəʊnɪəl/ *adj* [usu attrib] of or suitable

for a baron: *a baronial hall* ○ *live in baronial splend-our.*

barony *n* the rank or title of a baron.

baronet /ˈbærənət/ *n* (*abbrs* **Bart**, **Bt**) a man holding the lowest rank of honour in Britain that can be inherited: *Sir Vivian is the eleventh baronet.*
▶ **baronetcy** /ˈbærənətsi/ *n* the rank or title of a baronet.

baroque /bəˈrɒk; *US* bəˈrəʊk/ *adj* having the highly decorated and elaborate style fashionable in the arts, esp architecture, in Europe in the 17th and 18th centuries: *baroque churches/palaces* ○ *baroque music/style.*
▶ **baroque** (often **the baroque**) *n* [U] the baroque style or baroque art: *paintings representative of the baroque.*

barque /bɑːk/ *n* a sailing ship with 3, 4 or 5 masts (MAST) and sails.

barrack /ˈbærək/ *v* **1** (*Brit*) to shout criticism or protests at players in a game, speakers at a meeting, performers, etc: [V, Vn] *The crowd started barracking (the team).* **2** (*Austral*) to cheer or shout encouragement to a person or team that one supports: [Vpr] *barrack for the Labour candidate* [also Vn].▶ **barracking** *n* [U]: *The crowd gave the visiting politician quite a barracking.*

barracks /ˈbærəks/ *n* **1** [sing or pl *v*] a large building or group of buildings for soldiers to live in: *The men marched **back to (their) barracks**.* ○ *As punishment, the men were **confined to barracks**.* ○ *There used to be a barracks in this town.* **2** [sing *v*] (*infml*) any large ugly building: *the communal barracks of the outer suburbs.*

barracuda /ˌbærəˈkjuːdə; *US* -ˈkuːdə/ *n* a large fierce tropical fish with sharp teeth.

barrage /ˈbærɑːʒ; *US* bəˈrɑːʒ/ *n* **1(a)** heavy continuous firing of a large number of guns in a particular direction, to restrict enemy movement, enable troops to advance, etc. **(b)** a continuous stream of questions, criticisms, etc delivered quickly, one after the other: *face a barrage of angry complaints.* **2** /*US* ˈbærɪdʒ/ a barrier built across a river to store water, prevent flooding, etc.

keg
barrel
barrel
milk churn
drum

barrel /ˈbærəl/ *n* **1(a)** a large round, usu wooden, container with flat ends and curved sides. ⇨ picture. **(b)** the amount that a barrel contains; the contents of a barrel: *barrels of oil.* **2** a long metal tube forming part of sth, esp a gun. ⇨ picture at GUN. **lock, stock and barrel** ⇨ LOCK[1]. **(get/ have sb) over a barrel** (*infml*) (to put/have sb) in a position in which they must do what one wants them to do: *Since we need them to lend us money, they've got us over a barrel.* **scrape the barrel** ⇨ SCRAPE[1].
■ ˈ**barrel-organ** (also **hurdy-gurdy**) *n* a mechanical instrument from which music is produced by turning a handle, usu played in the streets for money, esp formerly.

barren /ˈbærən/ *adj* **1** (of land) not good enough to produce crops. **2** (of plants or trees) not producing fruit or seeds. **3** (*dated or fml*) (of women or female animals) not able to produce children or young. **4** [usu attrib] not producing anything; without success or useful result: *a barren discussion* ○ *go through a barren period.* ▶ **barrenness** /ˈbærənnəs/ *n* [U].

barricade /ˌbærɪˈkeɪd/ *n* a barrier made from the nearest available objects and placed across sth as a defence or an obstacle: *The soldiers **stormed the barricades** erected by the rioters.*
▶ **barricade** *v* to defend or block sth with a barricade: [Vn] *They had barricaded all the doors and windows.* **PHRV barricade oneself/sb in/inside (sth)** to put a barricade in front of oneself/sb to prevent anyone from coming in or out: *They barricaded themselves in (their) rooms).*

barrier /ˈbæriə(r)/ *n* **1** a thing that prevents or controls movement from one place to another: *The crowd were kept behind barriers.* ○ *Show your ticket at the barrier.* **2(a)** ~ (**to/against sth**) a thing that prevents sth or makes sth impossible: *Poor health may be a barrier to success.* ○ *trade barriers.* **(b)** ~ (**between sb and sb**) a thing that makes communication or good relationships between people difficult or impossible: *barriers of race and religion* ○ *the language barrier* ○ *There is an ideological barrier between us.* See also SOUND BARRIER.

barring /ˈbɑːrɪŋ/ *prep* if there is/are not sth; except for sth: *Barring accidents, we should arrive on time.* ○ *Meals are available at all times, barring Sunday evenings.* Compare BAR[3].

barrister /ˈbærɪstə(r)/ *n* (in English law) a lawyer who has the right to speak and argue in higher courts of law. Compare ADVOCATE *n* 2, SOLICITOR.

barrow[1] /ˈbærəʊ/ *n* **1** = WHEELBARROW. **2** a small cart with two wheels, pulled or pushed by hand.
■ ˈ**barrow boy** *n* (*Brit*) a man or boy who sells things from a barrow in the street.

barrow[2] /ˈbærəʊ/ *n* a large pile of earth built over a burial place in ancient times. See also TUMULUS.

Bart /bɑːt/ *abbr* Baronet.

bartender /ˈbɑːtendə(r)/ *n* (*esp US*) = BARMAN.

barter /ˈbɑːtə(r)/ *v* **(a)** ~ **sth (for sth)**; ~ **sth (away)** to exchange goods, property, etc for other goods, etc without using money: [Vnpr] *barter wheat for machinery* ○ (*fig*) [Vnp] *barter away sb's rights/ honour/freedom* [also Vn]. **(b)** ~ (**with sb)** (**for sth**) to trade by exchanging sth for sth else without using money: [Vpr] *The prisoners tried to barter with the guards for their freedom.* [also V]. ▶ **barter** *n* [U]: *The islanders use a system of barter instead of money.*

basalt /ˈbæsɔːlt; *US* bəˈsɔːlt/ *n* [U] a type of dark rock of volcanic (VOLCANO) origin.

base[1] /beɪs/ *n* **1** [C usu *sing*] **(a)** the lowest part of sth, esp the part on which it rests or is supported: *the base of a pillar/column/lamp* ○ *the base of the spine.* **(b)** (*geometry*) the line or surface on which a figure stands: *the base of a triangle/pyramid.* **2** [C] a point from which sth, eg an idea or belief, starts or is developed: *She used her family's history as a base for her novel.* ○ *His arguments have a sound economic base.* **3** [C] a thing on which sth, eg an activity or a situation, is founded or built: *The party's main **power base** is in the agricultural regions.* ○ *an economy with a solid **industrial/manufacturing base**.* **4** [C usu *sing*] the first part or ingredient to which other things are added: *a drink with a rum base* ○ *Some paints have an oil base.* ○ *Put some moisturizer on as a base before applying your make-up.* **5(a)** [C, U] a place where armed forces, people on expeditions (EXPEDITION), etc keep their supplies and from which they operate: *establish a base* ○ *a* ˈ*naval base* ○ *an* ˈ*air base* ○ *After the attack, they returned to base.* ○ *a base camp* (eg when climbing a mountain). **(b)** [C] a central place in or from which sb/sth operates: *The town provides an ideal base for touring the area.* ○ *The company has its base in New York, and branch offices all over the world.* **6** [C] (*chemistry*) a substance, eg an ALKALI, that can combine with an acid to form a salt. **7** [C usu *sing*] (*mathematics*) a number on which a system of numbers is built up, eg 10 in the decimal system, 2 in the BINARY system. **8** [C] (in baseball) each of the four positions to be reached by a runner. **IDM** **not get to first base** ⇨ FIRST BASE. **off base** (*US infml*) mistaken; not accurate; wrong: *Your interpretation of the situation is way off base.* See also DATABASE.

▶ **baseless** *adj* without cause or foundation; not supported by facts or good reasons: *baseless fears/ rumours/suspicions.*

■ **'base rate** *n* (*finance*) an interest rate set by a central bank and used by individual banks as a basis for fixing the interest rates they charge on loans, etc.

base² /beɪs/ *v* **1** ~ **sth on sth** to use or have sth as the foundation for sth else or as a point from which sth else can start to develop: [Vnpr] *What exactly do you base that opinion on?* ○ *This novel is based on historical facts.* ○ *Direct taxation is usually based on income* (ie A person's income is used to calculate the amount of tax he or she has to pay). ○ *The prosecution case was based on the evidence of two witnesses.* **2** ~ **sb/oneself in/at …** (usu passive) to situate sb in a place in or from which they operate: [Vnadv] *Where is your company based?* [Vnpr] *Most of our staff are based in Cairo.* ○ *If we base ourselves in a central hotel, sightseeing will be easier.*

▶ **-based** (forming compound *adjs*) established in the specified place or way: *a Paris-based company* ○ *a broadly-based curriculum.*

base³ /beɪs/ *adj* (**-r, -st**) (*fml derog*) not honourable; without moral principles: *acting from base motives.*

▶ **basely** *adv* in a base manner.

■ **,base 'metal** *n* a metal that is not a precious metal.

cap — bat — **baseball**
batter
umpire
catcher
glove

baseball /'beɪsbɔːl/ *n* [U] a game popular in the USA, played with a bat and ball by two teams of nine players. Each player tries to hit the ball and then run round each of the four bases (BASE¹ 8) on the field before the ball is returned: *a baseball stadium.* ⇨ picture. Compare ROUNDERS.

baseline /'beɪslaɪn/ *n* **1** (*sport*) a line marking each end of the court in tennis or the boundary of the running track in baseball. ⇨ picture at TENNIS. **2** a line or level used as a base for measuring or comparing sth: *the figure used by analysts as a baseline.*

basement /'beɪsmənt/ *n* a room or rooms in a building, partly or completely below ground level: *a basement flat/car park* ○ *Kitchen goods are sold in the basement.*

bases **1** *pl* of BASIS. **2** *pl* of BASE¹.

bash /bæʃ/ *v* (*infml*) **1** to strike sb/sth heavily: [Vnpr] *bash sb on the head with a club* [also Vn]. **2** ~ **(sth) against/into sb/sth** to hit or cause sth to hit sth with great force: [Vpr] *I braked too late and bashed into the car in front.* [Vnpr] *He tripped and bashed his head against the railing.* **3** to criticize sb/sth strongly: [Vn] *She frequently gets bashed in the press.* **PHRV** **,bash a'head/a'way/'on (with/at sth)** to do or continue doing something with energy

and enthusiasm: *If we keep bashing away at the job, we might get it finished on time.* **,bash sth 'in/'down** to cause sth to collapse inwards by striking it violently: *bash in the lid of a box* ○ *They bashed the door down.* **,bash sb 'up** (*Brit infml*) to attack sb violently: *He was bashed up in the playground by some older boys.*

▶ **bash** *n* (*infml*) a violent blow: *give sb a bash on the nose.* **IDM** **have a bash (at sth)** (*infml esp Brit*) to attempt sth, esp sth one has not attempted before, without expecting to succeed: *I've never tried water-skiing before, but I'd love to have a bash at it.*

bashing *n* [U, C] (often in compounds) a violent attack or repeated attacks, physically or with words: *union-bashing* (ie repeated criticism of trade unions) ○ *give sb a bashing.* ⇨ note at BANG¹.

bashful /'bæʃfl/ *adj* shy and easily embarrassed: *Come on, don't be bashful, tell me what you want!*

▶ **bashfully** /-fəli/ *adv*: *smile bashfully.*

basic /'beɪsɪk/ *adj* **1** ~ **(to sth)** forming a base from which sth develops or on which sth is built; fundamental: *basic principles in life* ○ *His basic problem is that he lacks confidence.* ○ *the basic vocabulary of a language* ○ *These facts are basic to an understanding of the case.* **2** most simple in nature or level: *the basic requirements of the job* ○ *The camp-site provided only basic facilities.* ○ *basic pay* (ie without additions, eg for working longer hours) ○ *learn basic skills* ○ *My French is pretty basic but I can just about make myself understood.* ○ *the cost of basic foods.*

▶ **basically** /-kli/ *adv* in a general or simple sense; with regard to the main aspect or aspects of sth: *Despite her criticisms, she is basically very fond of you.* ○ *The novel is basically about human relationships.* ○ *Basically I agree with your proposals, although there are a few small points I'd like to discuss.*

basics *n* [pl] the essential facts or principles: *Let's stop wasting time on theories and get down to basics* (ie concentrate on important matters). ○ *learn the basics of computer programming.*

BASIC /'beɪsɪk/ *abbr* (*computing*) a simple programming (PROGRAM *v* 1) language using familiar English words. It is widely used on personal computers.

basil /'bæzl/ *n* [U] a sweet-smelling HERB used in cooking: *flavoured with basil.*

basilica /bə'zɪlɪkə/ *n* (*architecture*) a large church or hall with a curved end and two rows of columns inside. In ancient Rome basilicas were used as law-courts: *the Basilica of St Peter's in Rome.*

basilisk /'bæzɪlɪsk/ *n* (in myths) a reptile that was believed to be able to cause death by its look or breath: (*fig*) *He fixed me with a basilisk stare.*

basin /'beɪsn/ *n* **1** = WASH-BASIN: *a 'hand basin.* **2(a)** a usu round open bowl for holding liquids or (in Britain) for preparing food in. (*Brit*) *a 'pudding basin.* ⇨ picture at BUCKET. **(b)** the contents of or the amount contained in such a bowl: *a basin of hot water.* **3** an area of land drained by a river: *the Amazon basin.* **4** a depression in the earth's surface; a round valley: *The village lay in a peaceful basin surrounded by hills.* **5** a sheltered area of water providing a safe harbour for boats.

▶ **basinful** /-fʊl/ *n* (*pl* **-fuls**) the amount that a basin contains: *two basinfuls of water.*

basis /'beɪsɪs/ *n* (*pl* **bases** /'beɪsiːz/) **1** the thing that supports sth, esp an idea or an argument, and from which it develops; the foundation of sth: *The basis of a good marriage is trust.* ○ *There is no basis for such wild accusations.* ○ *He has been selected for the team on the basis of* (ie because of) *his recent form.* ○ *Her theories have no basis in reality.* **2** the point from which discussion, etc starts or is developed: *a basis for rational debate* ○ *No basis for negotiations has been agreed upon.* ○ *This agenda will form the basis of our next meeting.* **3** the way

B

in which sth is arranged or organized: *Payment will be made on a weekly/monthly basis.* ○ *Do you have to travel on a regular basis or only occasionally?* ○ *I don't intend to live here on a permanent basis.* ○ *conduct research on a scientific basis.*

bask /bɑːsk; *US* bæsk/ *v* ~ (**in sth**) to sit or lie, enjoying the warmth or light of sth: [Vpr] *basking in the sunshine* ○ *(fig) basking in sb's favour/in the warm glow of success* [V] *basking by the fire/on the beach.*

basket /'bɑːskɪt; *US* 'bæs-/ *n* **1(a)** a container for holding or carrying things. Baskets are made of thin strips of material that bends and twists easily, eg wood, CANE(1) or wire: *a 'shopping basket* ○ *a picnic basket* ○ *a 'clothes/'laundry basket* (ie in which dirty clothes are kept before being washed) ○ *a ˌwaste-'paper basket* ○ *a wicker basket.* ⇨ picture at BAS-KETBALL. **(b)** the contents of a basket or the amount that a basket contains: *They picked three baskets of apples.* **2** a goal scored, or the goal itself, in BAS-KETBALL. **IDM** **put all one's eggs in/into one basket** ⇨ EGG¹.
▶ **basketful** /-fʊl/ *n* (*pl* **-fuls**) = BASKET 1b.

basket — ball   **basketball**

basketball /'bɑːskɪtbɔːl; *US* 'bæs-/ *n* [U] a game played by two teams of five or six players. Goals are scored by throwing a large ball into a net with an open bottom which is fixed high on a metal ring at the opponents' end of the court. ⇨ picture.

bas-relief /ˌbæs rɪ'liːf/ *n* **(a)** [U] a form of SCULPTURE or carving in which the figure or design projects only slightly from its background. **(b)** [C] an example of this.

bass¹ /beɪs/ *n* **1** (also **bass guitar**) [C] an electric GUITAR that produces very low notes: *a bass player* ○ *bass and drums* ○ *Carol's on bass* (ie She is playing the bass guitar in the band). **2** [C] **(a)** a male singer with a voice in the lowest range. **(b)** such a voice: *Is he a bass or a baritone?* Compare TENOR², ALTO 1,2, SOPRANO, BARITONE. **3** = DOUBLE-BASS. **4** [U] the lowest part or tone in music, for voice or instruments: *He sings bass.* ○ *He always plays his stereo with the bass turned right up.*
▶ **bass** *adj* [attrib] low in tone: *a ˌbass 'voice* ○ *a ˌbass 'drum* ○ *the ˌbass 'clef* (ie the symbol in music showing that the notes following it are low in pitch¹(2)). Compare TREBLE².

bassist *n* a person who plays the bass guitar or double-bass (DOUBLE¹).

bass² /bæs/ *n* (*pl* unchanged or **basses**) an edible fish of the PERCH² family. Some types of bass live in the sea and some in rivers, etc.

basset /'bæsɪt/ (also **'basset-hound**) *n* a dog with short legs, used in hunting.

bassoon /bə'suːn/ *n* a musical instrument like a large wooden tube. It is played by blowing through a double REED(2), and produces a deep low sound: *He plays the bassoon in the school orchestra.* ⇨ picture at MUSICAL INSTRUMENT.

bastard /'bɑːstəd, 'bæs-; *US* 'bæs-/ *n* **1** (*sl*) **(a)**

(derog) an unpleasant or cruel person, usu a man: *You rotten bastard!* ○ *He's a real bastard, leaving his wife like that.* **(b)** a person, esp a man, of the specified type: *What a lucky bastard!* ○ *The poor bastard!* *He's just lost his job.* ○ *Harry, you old bastard! Fancy meeting you here!* **2** *(infml)* a thing that causes difficulty, pain, etc: *It's a bastard of a problem.* ○ *This headache's a real bastard.* **3** *(often derog)* a person whose parents are not married to each other: *a bastard daughter/son.*
▶ **bastard** *adj* [attrib] not pure or genuine; showing an odd mixture: *a bastard style/language.*

bastardize, -ise *v* to make sth less pure by mixing it with sth else: [Vn] *a bastardized form of music.*

baste¹ /beɪst/ *v* to pour fat or juices over meat, etc during cooking: [Vn] *baste the turkey.*

baste² /beɪst/ *v* [Vn] to sew pieces of material together temporarily with long loose stitches; to TACK(4) sth.

bastion /'bæstɪən/ *n* **1** a person or thing that is defending or protecting sth that is threatened: *a bastion of democracy/freedom/socialism* ○ *He believes that the last bastions of privilege are finally crumbling.* **2** a place that soldiers are defending, eg a fort, near enemy territory.

bat¹ /bæt/ *n* a piece of wood with a handle, made in various sizes and shapes and used for hitting the ball in games such as cricket, baseball and PING-PONG. ⇨ picture at BASEBALL, CRICKET¹. Compare RACKET¹ 1. **IDM** **off one's own 'bat** (*Brit infml*) without help or encouragement from anyone else: *She made the suggestions entirely off her own bat* (ie without being asked for them). **(right) off the 'bat** (*US infml*) immediately; without delay: *He answered all their questions right off the bat.*
▶ **bat** *v* (**-tt-**) **1(a)** to use a bat: [V] *He bats well.* **(b)** to have a turn with a bat: [V] *Each team batted for two hours.* **2** to hit sth with a bat: [Vnp] *batting a ball (about)* [also Vn]. **'batter** *n* (*US*) (esp in baseball) a player who bats. ⇨ picture at BASEBALL.

bat² /bæt/ *n* a small animal like a mouse with wings. Bats fly at night and feed on fruit and insects. **IDM** **blind as a bat** ⇨ BLIND¹. **have bats in the 'belfry** *(infml)* to be crazy; to have strange ideas. **like a bat out of 'hell** *(infml)* very fast: *She dashed out of the door like a bat out of hell.*

bat³ /bæt/ *v* (**-tt-**) **IDM** **not bat an 'eyelid**; *(US)* **not bat an 'eye** *(infml)* not to show any surprise or feelings: *She listened to the sad news without batting an eyelid.*

batch /bætʃ/ *n* **1** a number of people or things dealt with as a group: *a new batch of recruits for the army* ○ *a batch of letters to be answered.* **2** a quantity of bread, cakes, etc baked together: *loaves baked in batches of twenty.* **3** *(computing)* a set of jobs that are processed together by a computer: *a batch run.*
■ **,batch 'processing** *n* [U] *(computing)* the system of processing a batch of jobs together.

bated *adj* **IDM** **with bated 'breath** holding one's breath because one is anxious or excited: *We waited with bated breath for the winner to be announced.*

bath /bɑːθ; *US* bæθ/ *n* (*pl* **baths** /bɑːðz; *US* bæðz/) **1** [C] an act of washing the whole body, esp when sitting or lying in water: *I think I'll have/take a hot bath and go to bed.* ○ *(esp US) He takes a bath every morning.* **2** [C] **(a)** (also **'bath-tub, tub**) a large long container for water in which a person sits to have a bath. **(b)** this with the water in it ready for use: *Please run a bath for me.* ○ *Your bath is ready.* **3** [C] **(a)** a container for liquid in which sth is washed or dipped. Baths are used in chemical and industrial processes: *an 'oil bath* (eg for parts of machinery). **(b)** this with the liquid in it: *a bath of red dye.* **4** **baths** [pl] *(Brit)* a public building where people can go to swim in a pool or have a bath: *'swimming-*

baths ∘ Turkish ¹baths. See also BLOOD BATH. **IDM**
throw the baby out with the bath water ⇨
BABY.
▶ **bath** v (Brit) **1** to give a bath to sb: [Vn] bath the
baby. **2** to have a bath: [V] I bath every night.
■ ¹**bath mat** n a small mat for a person to stand on
after getting out of a bath.
¹**bath-tub** n = BATH 2.
Bath chair /ˌbɑːθ ¹tʃeə(r)/ n a type of chair with
wheels, for a person who is ill.
bathe /beɪð/ v **1** to apply water to sth, esp a part of
the body: [Vn] The doctor told her to bathe her eyes
twice a day. ∘ The nurse bathed the wound. **2** (US) to
give a bath to sb: [Vn] bathe the baby. **3** (esp Brit) to
go swimming in the sea, a river, a lake, etc for
enjoyment: [V] On hot days we often bathe/go bathing in the river. See also SUNBATHE.
▶ **bathe** n (usu sing) (esp Brit) an act of swimming
in the sea, etc: It was a warm sunny day, so we went
for a bathe.
bathed adj [pred] ~ **in/with sth** wet or bright all
over because covered with sth: His face was bathed
in tears. ∘ After the match, I was bathed with sweat. ∘
The countryside was bathed in brilliant sunshine.
bather /¹beɪðə(r)/ n.
bathing /¹beɪðɪŋ/ n [U] (esp Brit) the action of going
into the sea, etc to bathe: She's fond of bathing. ∘
Bathing prohibited! (ie Bathing is not allowed here,
eg because it would be unsafe.)
■ ¹**bathing-cap** n a soft, usu rubber, cap that fits
closely over the head to keep the hair dry while
swimming.
¹**bathing-costume** n (Brit becoming dated) =
SWIMMING-COSTUME.
¹**bathing-suit** n (US or dated Brit) = SWIMMING-
COSTUME.
bathos /¹beɪθɒs/ n [U] (in writing, speech or drama)
a sudden change from what is important or deeply
felt to what is foolish or absurd: a serious play with
moments of comic bathos. Compare ANTICLIMAX.
bathrobe /¹bɑːθrəʊb; US ¹bæθ-/ (also **robe**) n **1** a
loose garment worn before and after taking a bath.
2 (US) = DRESSING-GOWN.
bathroom /¹bɑːθruːm, -rʊm; US ¹bæθ-/ n **1** a room
in which there is a bath, and also usu a wash-basin
(WASH²) and a toilet: Go and wash your hands in the
bathroom. **2** (US euph) a toilet: I have to go to the
bathroom. ⇨ note at TOILET.
batik /bəˈtiːk, ¹bætɪk/ n **(a)** [U] a method of making
coloured designs on cloth by putting wax on the
parts that are not to be coloured: a batik dress. **(b)**
[C] a piece of cloth treated in this way: a range of
batiks.
batman /¹bætmən/ n (pl **-men** /-mən/) (Brit) a soldier who acts as an army officer's personal servant.
baton /¹bætɒn; US bəˈtɒn/ n **1** = TRUNCHEON: a
baton charge (ie one made by police, etc armed with
batons to force a crowd back). **2** a short thin stick
used by the person conducting a band or an ORCHES-
TRA. **3** a short stick that indicates a certain, esp
military, rank: a Field Marshal's baton. **4** a short
stick carried and handed to the next person in a
RELAY² race. **5** a stick held and waved by the person
who marches in front of a military band.
■ ¹**baton round** n a rubber or plastic bullet fired to
control a crowd that has become aggressive or violent.
batsman /¹bætsmən/ n (pl **-men** /-mən/) a player
who bats in cricket: He's a good batsman but a poor
bowler. ⇨ picture at CRICKET¹.
battalion /bəˈtæliən/ n (abbr **Bn**) a large group of
soldiers that form part of a regiment or BRIGADE(1): a
tank battalion ∘ the 2nd battalion of the Light Infantry.
batten¹ /¹bætn/ n **1** a long strip of wood, used esp to
keep other building materials in place on a wall or

roof. **2** a strip of wood or metal used to fasten down
covers over an opening in the DECK¹(1a) of a ship.
▶ **batten** v ~ **sth (down)** (esp on a ship) to fasten
sth securely with battens (BATTEN¹ 2): [Vnp] batten
down the hatches (eg when a storm is expected) [also
Vn].
batten² /¹bætn/ v **PHRV** **batten on sb** (esp derog)
to live comfortably by taking things from other
people for one's own advantage: Instead of getting a
job, she battened on her rich relatives.
batter¹ /¹bætə(r)/ v ~ **(at/on) sth** (esp passive) to hit
sb/sth hard and repeatedly: [Vpr] She battered at the
door with her fists. [Vp] He kept battering away until
I let him in. [Vn] battered babies/wives (ie ones that
suffer repeated violence from their parents/
husbands). **PHRV** ¹**batter sth** ¹**down** to hit sth repeatedly until it breaks and falls down: If they won't
let us in we may have to batter the door down.
ˌ**batter sth to** ¹**sth** to hit sth repeatedly until it
becomes damaged in the way specified: The huge
waves battered the wrecked ship to ¹pieces. ∘ The
victim's face was battered to a ¹pulp.
▶ **battered** adj damaged because of age, regular
use or frequent accidents: a battered old hat ∘ Your
car looks a bit battered.
■ ¹**battering-ram** n a large heavy log with an iron
head formerly used in war for breaking down walls,
etc.
batter² /¹bætə(r)/ n [U] a liquid mixture of flour and
eggs with milk or water, used in cooking: fish fried
in batter ∘ pancake batter.
batter³ ⇨ BAT¹.
battery /¹bætri, -təri/ n **1** [C] a device that contains
and supplies electricity, eg in a car or a clock: a
¹camera battery ∘ The car won't start because the
battery is flat (ie it can no longer supply electricity).
∘ a battery-powered lamp. ⇨ picture at CAR. **2** [C]
(a) a group of big guns on a ship or on land. **(b)** an
army unit consisting of big guns, with men and
vehicles: a battery commander. **3** [C] a large and
often confusing set of similar things that are used
together: a battery of telephones ∘ (fig) She faced a
battery of tests. **4** [C] (Brit) a series of many small
cages in which hens, etc are kept on a farm: a
battery hen. Compare FREE-RANGE. **5** [U] (law) the
criminal act of treating sb violently or threatening
them. Compare ASSAULT AND BATTERY. **IDM** **recharge one's batteries** ⇨ RECHARGE.
■ ˌ**battery** ¹**farm** n (Brit) a farm where large numbers of hens are kept in batteries (BATTERY 4).
ˌ**battery** ¹**farming** n [U].
battle /¹bætl/ n **1** [C,U] a fight between armies,
ships or planes: a fierce battle ∘ the battle of Waterloo
∘ die in battle ∘ the noise of battle. **2** [C] ~ **(for/
against sth)** any contest or struggle: a battle of
words/wits ∘ the battle for human rights ∘ Their
whole life was a constant battle against poverty. **IDM**
do ¹**battle (with sb) (over sth)** to fight or argue
fiercely. **half the** ¹**battle** an important or the most
important part of achieving sth: When you're sick,
wanting to get well again is often half the battle. **join
battle** ⇨ JOIN. **a losing battle** ⇨ LOSE.
▶ **battle** v ~ **(with/against sb/sth) (for sth)**; ~ **(on)**
to try very hard; to struggle: [Vpr] battling against
poor health ∘ They battled with the wind and the
waves. [Vp] Progress is slow but we keep battling on.
[V.to inf] The doctors are battling to save his life.
[also V].
■ ¹**battle-cruiser** n (formerly) a large ship used in
war. A battle-cruiser was faster and lighter than a
BATTLESHIP.
¹**battle-cry** n **(a)** (esp formerly) a shout given by
soldiers in battle. **(b)** a phrase used by a group of
people working together in a particular contest or
campaign: 'Equality for All' is a popular political
battle-cry.

battleaxe /ˈbætl æks/ *n* **1** (formerly) a heavy AXE with a long handle, used as a weapon. **2** (*infml derog*) an older woman who behaves in a fierce or bad-tempered way.

battledress /ˈbætldres/ *n* [U] a soldier's normal uniform.

battlefield /ˈbætlfiːld/ (also **battleground** /ˈbætlɡraʊnd/) *n* the place where a battle is or was fought.

battlements /ˈbætlmənts/ *n* [pl] (the flat roof of a tower or castle surrounded by) low walls with openings at intervals made for shooting through. ⇨ picture at CASTLE.

battleship /ˈbætlʃɪp/ *n* a large ship used in war with big guns and heavy armour.

batty /ˈbæti/ *adj* (**-ier, -iest**) (*infml*) (of people, ideas, etc) crazy; slightly mad. Compare BATS.

bauble /ˈbɔːbl/ *n* (*usu derog*) an ornament of little value.

baulk (also **balk**) /bɔːk/ *v* **1** ~ (**at sth**) to be unwilling to do or become involved in sth because it is difficult, dangerous, unpleasant, expensive, etc: [Vpr] *The horse baulked at* (ie refused to jump) *the high hedge.* ○ *His parents baulked at the cost of the guitar he wanted.* [also V]. **2** (*dated*) (**a**) to block or prevent sth deliberately: [Vn] *balk sb's plans.* (**b**) ~ **sb of sth** (usu passive) to prevent sb from getting sth: [Vnpr] *They were baulked of their prey.*

bauxite /ˈbɔːksaɪt/ *n* [U] the mineral like clay from which ALUMINIUM is obtained.

bawdy /ˈbɔːdi/ *adj* (**-ier, -iest**) dealing with sexual matters in an amusing way: *bawdy jokes/stories.* ▶ **bawdily** *adv.* **bawdiness** *n* [U].

bawl /bɔːl/ *v* ~ (**sth**) (**out**) to shout or cry loudly: [V] *That baby has been bawling for hours.* [Vpr] *He bawled at me across the street.* ○ *We bawled for help but no one heard us.* [Vn, Vnp, Vpr] *The sergeant bawled* (out) *a command* (*to his men*). [also Vp, V.speech]. **PHRV** **bawl sb 'out** (*infml esp US*) to speak angrily to sb; to SCOLD sb severely.

bay¹ /beɪ/ *n* a part of the sea, or of a large lake, enclosed by a wide curve of the shore: *the Bay of Bengal* ○ *Hudson Bay.*

bay² /beɪ/ (also **ˈbay-tree**) *n* a tree with dark green leaves and purple berries. ■ **ˈbay-leaf** *n* (*pl* **-leaves**) a dried leaf of the bay-tree used in cooking to give flavour to food.

bay³ /beɪ/ *n* **1** any of a series of sections in a building, a structure or an area, esp one designed for storing things, parking vehicles, etc: *a ˈparking/ˈloading bay* ○ *Put the equipment in No 3 bay.* See also SICKBAY. **2** a curved area of a room or building that projects outwards from the rest of the building. ■ **ˌbay ˈwindow** *n* a window, usu with glass on three sides, projecting from an outside wall. ⇨ picture at HOUSE¹.

bay⁴ /beɪ/ *n* a deep bark, esp of dogs when hunting. **IDM** **at ˈbay** (esp of a hunted animal) in a situation in which those attacking or pursuing must be faced because it is impossible to escape from them. **hold/ keep sb/sth at ˈbay** to prevent an enemy, a problem, etc from coming close or having a bad effect: *hold one's fears at bay* ○ *I'm trying to keep my creditors at bay.* ▶ **bay** *v* (esp of hunting dogs) to make a deep bark: [V] *baying hounds* ○ (*fig*) *a baying mob of spectators* [Vpr] *His opponents are baying for (his) blood* (ie eager for his ruin).

bay⁵ /beɪ/ *n, adj* (a horse) of a reddish-brown colour: *riding a big bay* ○ *a bay mare.*

bayonet /ˈbeɪənət/ *n* a long sharp blade that can be fixed onto the end of a RIFLE¹ and used as a military weapon. ▶ **bayonet** /ˈbeɪənet, ˌbeɪəˈnet/ *v* to STAB(1) sb/sth with a bayonet: [Vn] *The dead soldiers had been bayoneted.*

bayou /ˈbaɪuː/ *n* (in the southern USA) a part of a river away from the main stream that moves slowly and contains many water plants.

bazaar /bəˈzɑː(r)/ *n* **1** (in eastern countries) a group of shops or stalls. **2** (in Britain, the USA, etc) a sale of goods to raise money, esp for charity: *a church bazaar.*

bazooka /bəˈzuːkə/ *n* a weapon light enough to be carried and consisting of a long tube from which missiles are fired.

BBC /ˌbiː biː ˈsiː/ *abbr* British Broadcasting Corporation. The BBC broadcasts television and radio programmes and receives funds from the sale of television licences: *listen to the BBC* ○ *The news is on BBC1 at 9 pm.* Compare IBA, ITV.

BC /ˌbiː ˈsiː/ *abbr* before Christ: *in (the year) 2000 BC.* Compare AD.

be¹ /biː; *strong form* biː/ *v* ⇨ note at BE². **1** (used after *there* and before *a/an, no, some, etc* + *n*) (**a**) to exist: *There are no easy answers.* ○ *There are many such people.* ○ *Once upon a time there was a princess.* ○ *There have been cows in that field since my grandfather's time.* ○ *Is there a God?* ○ *For there to be life there must be air and water.* (**b**) to be present: *There's a bus-stop down the road.* ○ *There were no books on the shelf.* ○ *There are some good photographs in this exhibition.* **2** (used after *it* indicating time): *It's half past two.* ○ *It was late at night when we finally arrived.* **3** (with an *adv* or a prepositional phrase indicating position in space or time) (**a**) to be situated; to be in a place: *The lamp is on the table.* ○ *The stable is a mile away.* ○ *Mary's upstairs.* ○ *John's out in the garden.* ○ *They are on holiday in Italy.* (**b**) to happen; to occur: *The party is at work.* ○ *The election was on Monday.* ○ *The concert will be in the school hall.* ○ *The meetings are on Tuesdays and Thursdays in the main hall.* (**c**) to remain: *She has been in her room for hours.* ○ *They're here till Christmas.* ○ *The situation is the same as when I last spoke to you.* (**d**) to attend; to be present: *Were you at church yesterday?* ○ *I'll be at the party.* **4** (with an *adv* or a prepositional phrase indicating direction, place of origin, etc) to go; to come; to arrive: *I'll be on my way very soon.* ○ *She's from Italy* (ie her native country is Italy). ○ *He'll be here soon, I'm sure.* **5** (usu with an *adv* or a prepositional phrase indicating destination; in the perfect tenses only) to visit or call: [Vpr] *I've never been to Spain.* [Vadv] *She had been abroad many times.* [V] *Has the postman been* (ie called) *yet?* ⇨ note at BEEN. **6** (indicating a quality or a state) [V-adj] *Life is unfair.* ○ *The earth is round.* ○ *He is ten years old.* ○ *Be quick!* ○ *'How are you?' 'I'm quite well, thanks.'* [Vpr] *I am of average height.* [V-n] *She's a great beauty.* **7** (indicating what sth is made of) [V-n] *Is your jacket real leather?* **8** (indicating the identity, name, profession, interest, etc of the subject) [V-n] *Today is Monday.* ○ *You are the man I want.* ○ *'Who is that?' 'It's my brother.'* ○ *Susan is a doctor.* ○ *Peter is an amateur painter in his spare time.* ○ *He wants to be* (ie become) *a fireman when he grows up.* **9** (indicating possession, actual or intended): *The money's not yours, it's John's* (ie It belongs to John and not to you). ○ *This parcel is for you.* **10** (showing equivalence in value, number, etc) (**a**) to cost: [V-n] *'How much is that dress?' 'It's £50.'* (**b**) to amount to; to be equal to: [V-n] *Twice two is four.* ○ *Three and three is six.* ○ *Four threes are twelve.* ○ *How much is a thousand dollars in pounds?* (**c**) to constitute: [V-n] (*saying*) *Two is company; three's a crowd.* ○ *London is not England* (ie Do not think that all of England is like London). (**d**) to represent: [V-n] *Let x be the sum of a and b.* (**e**) to mean: [V-n] *Winning the award was everything to her.* ○ *A thousand dollars is nothing to a rich man.* **IDM** Most idioms containing **be** are at the entries for the nouns or adjectives in the idioms, eg **be the death of sb** ⇨ DEATH. **...as/ that was** ...as sb/sth used to be or be called: *Miss Brown that was* (ie before her marriage) ○ *'Where's the Concert Hall?' 'It's the Odeon Cinema as was, in the High Street.'* **the ˌbe-all and ˈend-all (of sth)** (*infml*) the most important part; all that matters: *Her boyfriend is the be-all and end-all of her existence.* **(he, she, etc has) been and ˈdone sth** (*infml*) (expressing surprise and annoyance): *Someone's been and parked in front of the entrance!* **be oneˈself** to act naturally: *Don't act sophisticated — just be yourself.* **ˌbe that as it ˈmay** despite that; nevertheless: *I accept that he's old and frail; be that as it may, he's still a fine politician.* **ˌleave/ˌlet sb/ sth ˈbe** (*infml*) to leave sb/sth alone without disturbing them or interfering: *Leave her be, she obviously doesn't want to talk about it.* ○ *Let the poor dog be* (ie Don't annoy it). **-to-ˈbe** (in compounds) future: *his ˌbride-to-ˈbe* ○ *ˌmothers-to-ˈbe* (ie pregnant women).

be² /biː; *strong form* biː/ *aux v* ⇨ note. **1** (used with a past participle to form the passive): *He was killed in the war.* ○ *Where were they made?* ○ *The thief was caught.* ○ *The house is/was being built.* ○ *You will be severely punished if you do not obey.* **2** (used with present participles to form continuous tenses): *They are/were reading.* ○ *I am studying Chinese.* ○ *I'll be seeing him soon.* ○ *What have you been doing this week?* ○ *I'm always being criticized.* **3** (with *to* + infinitive) (**a**) (expressing instructions received, duty, necessity, etc): *I am to phone them once I reach the airport.* ○ *You are to report to the police.* ○ *What is to be done about this problem?* (**b**) (expressing arrangement): *They are to be married in June.* ○ *Each participant was to pay his own expenses.* (**c**) (expressing possibility): *The book was not to be* (ie could not be) *found.* (**d**) (expressing destiny): *He was never to see his wife again* (ie Although he did not know it would be so at the time, he did not see her again). ○ *She wanted to write a successful novel but it was not to be* (ie It turned out never to happen). (**e**) (only in the form *were*, in conditionals): *If I were to tell you/Were I to tell you that I made it myself, would you believe me?* ○ *If it were to rain, we would have to cancel the match tomorrow.*

NOTE The forms of **be** (main verb and auxiliary verb)

present tense

full forms	short forms	negative short forms
I am	I'm	I'm not
you are	you're	you aren't
he	he's	he
she is	she's	she isn't
it	it's	it
we	we're	we
you are	you're	you aren't
they	they're	they

The form **'s** and **'re** can be added to other subjects: *Sally's ill.* ○ *The boys're late.*
The negative full forms are formed by adding **not**: **I am not, you are not, he is not**, etc.
Alternative negative short forms are **you're not, he's/she's/it's not, we're not, they're not**.
Questions are formed by placing the verb before the subject: **am I? aren't you? is he not?** etc.
The short negative question form for **I** is **aren't: aren't I?**

present participle: being

past tense

full forms		negative short forms
I was		I wasn't
you were		you weren't
he		he
she was		she wasn't
it		it
we		we
you were		you weren't
they		they

There are no past tense short forms of **be**.
The negative full forms are formed by adding **not**: **I was not, you were not, he was not**, etc.
Questions are formed by placing the verb before the subject: **was I? weren't you? was he not?** etc.

past participle: been

The other tenses of **be** are formed in the same way as those of other verbs: **will be, would be, has been**, etc.
The pronunciation of each form of **be** is given at its entry in the dictionary.

be- *pref* **1** (with *vs* and *adjs* ending in *-ed*) all around; all over: *besmear* ○ *bedeck* ○ *bejewelled.* **2** (with *ns* and *adjs* forming transitive *vs*) to make or treat sb/ sth as: *befriend* ○ *belittle.* **3** (with intransitive *vs* forming transitive *vs*): *bemoan* ○ *bewail.*

beach /biːtʃ/ *n* a stretch of sand or stones along the edge of the sea or a lake: *tourists sunbathing on the beach.* ⇨ picture at COAST¹. ⇨ note at COAST¹. **IDM not the only pebble on the beach** ⇨ PEBBLE.
▶ **beach** *v* to come or bring sth onto the shore from out of the water: [Vn] *a beached whale* (ie one that has come onto the shore and is unable to return to the water again) ○ *find a place to beach a boat* [also V].
■ **ˈbeach-ball** *n* a large light colourful ball used for playing games on the beach.
ˈbeach buggy *n* a small motor vehicle used for racing on beaches, waste ground, etc.

beachcomber /ˈbiːtʃkəʊmə(r)/ *n* a person without a regular job who lives by selling whatever he or she can find on beaches.

beachhead /ˈbiːtʃhed/ *n* a strong position on a beach established by an army which has just landed and is preparing to advance and attack. See also BRIDGEHEAD.

beachwear /ˈbiːtʃweə(r)/ *n* [U] clothes for wearing on the beach.

beacon /ˈbiːkən/ *n* **1** a fire lit on the top of a hill, eg as a signal. **2(a)** a light fixed on rocks or on the coast to warn or guide ships, or on a mountain, tall building, etc to warn aircraft. (**b**) a flashing light used esp to guide pilots when landing aircraft. **3** a signal station such as a LIGHTHOUSE. **4** a radio station or transmitter (TRANSMIT) whose signal helps ships and aircraft to discover their position. See also BELISHA BEACON.

bead /biːd/ *n* **1(a)** [C] a small piece of usu hard material with a hole through it, used esp for putting together with others on a string, or for sewing onto material: *a string of glass beads* ○ *a bead curtain.* (**b**) **beads** [pl] a string of beads usu worn around the neck; a NECKLACE: *She fastened the beads round my neck.* (**c**) **beads** [pl] a ROSARY. **2** [C] a drop of certain types of liquid: *beads of sweat on his forehead.*
▶ **beaded** *adj* decorated with beads: *a beaded jacket.*
beading *n* [U,C] a strip of wood, stone or plastic with a pattern on it, used for decorating the edges of furniture, doors, etc.
beady /ˈbiːdi/ *adj* (of eyes) small, round and bright, and observing everything closely or with suspicion:

keep a beady eye on sb/sth ○ *Not much escapes our teacher's beady eyes.*

beagle /'biːgl/ *n* a small dog with short legs that is kept as a pet or used for hunting.

beak¹ /biːk/ *n* the hard pointed or curved part of a bird's mouth. ⇨ picture at WOODPECKER.
▶ **beaked** /biːkt/ *adj* (usu in compounds) having a beak of the specified type: *long-beaked.*

beak² /biːk/ *n* (*Brit sl*) a judge, magistrate or head teacher: *go/be brought up before the beak* (ie be forced to appear before one for trial or punishment).

beaker /'biːkə(r)/ *n* **1(a)** a tall narrow plastic or paper cup, often without a handle, used for drinking from: *buy some paper beakers for the picnic.* (**b**) this and its contents: *a beaker of coffee from the drinks machine.* **2** an open glass container with a LIP(2), used in scientific experiments.

beam /biːm/ *n* **1** a strong ray of light or stream of electric waves or particles (PARTICLE 2): *the beam of the torch/searchlight* ○ *The car's headlights were on full beam* (ie at full capacity and not directed downwards). ○ *a laser beam* ○ *A beam of light shone across the road.* **2** a long piece of wood, metal, concrete, etc, usu supported at both ends, that bears the weight of part of a building or other structure. ⇨ picture at SCALE³. **3** a broad and happy smile: *a beam of pleasure.* **IDM** **broad in the beam** ⇨ BROAD¹. **off** '**beam** (*infml*) mistaken; wrong: *Your calculation is way off beam.*
▶ **beam** *v* **1** (of the sun, etc) to produce light and warmth: [Vp] *We sat by the pool as the sun beamed down.* [also V]. **2 ~ (sth) (at sb)** to give a broad and happy smile: [V] *The winner was beaming with satisfaction.* [Vpr] *She beamed at me in approval.* [Vn, Vnpr] *She beamed approval (at me).* **3** to broadcast a message, television programme, etc from a distant place: [Vnpr] *The President's speech was beamed live from Washington to Moscow.*
beamed *adj* having beams: *a beamed roof.*

bean /biːn/ *n* **1(a)** any of various smooth seeds that grow in long pods (POD) on several types of plant and are eaten as vegetables: ,*broad* '*beans* ○ '*kidney beans* ○ '*soya beans* ○ ,*haricot* '*beans* ○ (*US*) *navy beans.* (**b**) any of the various plants that bear these seeds. (**c**) a POD containing such seeds, which is itself eaten as a vegetable: ,*runner* '*beans.* **2** (esp in compounds) a similar seed of another plant: *coffee/cocoa beans.* **IDM** **full of beans/life** ⇨ FULL. **a hill of beans** ⇨ HILL. **not have a** '**bean** (*esp Brit infml*) to have no money: *I'd like to go out tonight but I haven't got a bean.* **spill the beans** ⇨ SPILL.
■ **bean curd** /'biːn kɜːd/ *n* [U] = TOFU.
'**bean sprouts** *n* [pl] bean seeds that are just beginning to grow, often eaten raw esp in Chinese dishes.

beanbag /'biːnbæg/ *n* a large cushion filled with tiny round pieces of plastic and used as a seat.

beanfeast /'biːnfiːst/ (also **beano**) *n* (*dated Brit infml*) a happy celebration or party.

beanpole /'biːnpəʊl/ *n* (*infml*) a tall thin person.

bear

polar bear   grizzly

1m

bear¹ /beə(r)/ *n* **1** a large heavy wild animal with thick fur: *a polar bear* ○ *a grizzly bear.* ⇨ picture. **2** (*finance*) a person who sells stocks, shares, etc, hoping to buy them back later at lower prices: *a* '*bear market* (ie a situation in which share prices are

falling rapidly and are therefore attractive to such people). Compare BULL¹ 3. See also TEDDY BEAR.
▶ **bearish** /'beərɪʃ/ *adj* (*finance*) showing, causing or expecting a fall in the prices: *a bearish view of investment prospects* ○ *The equity market is becoming increasingly bearish.* Compare BULLISH.
■ '**bear-hug** *n* an act of holding sb strongly and tightly in one's arms: *He gave me a friendly bear-hug.*

bear² /beə(r)/ *v* (*pt* **bore** /bɔː(r)/; *pp* **borne** /bɔːn/) **1** to show sth; to carry sth so that it can be seen; to display sth: [Vn] *The document bore his signature.* ○ *The insignia bear the royal coat of arms.* ○ *I saw a tombstone bearing the date 1602.* ○ *He was badly wounded in the war and still bears the scars.* ○ *She bears little resemblance to* (ie is not much like) *her mother.* ○ *The title of the essay bore little relation to the contents* (ie was not much connected with them). **2** to be known by sth; to have sth: [Vn] *a family that bore an ancient and honoured name* ○ *A married woman usually bears her husband's surname.* **3** (*dated or fml*) to carry sb/sth, esp while moving: [Vn] *to bear a heavy load* ○ *three kings bearing gifts* [Vnp, Vnpr] *The canoe was borne (along) by the current.* ⇨ note at CARRY. **4** (**a**) to support the weight of sb/sth: [Vn] *The ice is too thin to bear your weight.* (**b**) to take responsibility, etc on oneself: [Vn] *Do the bride's parents have to bear the cost of the wedding?* ○ *You shouldn't have to bear the blame for other people's mistakes.* **5(a)** (with *can/could*, in negative sentences and questions) to accept sth unpleasant without complaining; to stand sth: [Vn] *The pain was almost more than he could bear.* ○ *She couldn't bear the thought of losing him.* [V.ing] *I can't bear having cats in the house.* [V.to inf] *How can you bear to eat that stuff?* [V.to inf, V.ing] *He can't bear to be laughed at/being laughed at.* (**b**) (in negative sentences) to be suitable for sth; to allow sth: [Vn] *Modern paintings don't bear comparison with those of the old masters* (ie because they are greatly inferior). ○ *The plan won't bear close inspection* (ie It will be found not to be satisfactory when carefully examined). [V.ing] *Her joke doesn't bear repeating* (ie because it is not funny or may offend people). ○ *His sufferings don't bear thinking about* (ie because they are or were so terrible). **6 ~ sth (against/towards sb)** to keep feelings, etc in the mind: [Vnpr, Vnn] *bear a grudge against sb/bear sb a grudge* [Vnpr] *He bears no resentment towards them.* [Vnn] *She bore him no ill will.* [also Vn]. **7 ~ oneself well, etc** to move, behave or act in a specified way: [Vnadv] *He bears himself* (ie stands, walks, etc) *proudly, like a soldier.* [Vnpr] *She bore herself with dignity throughout the funeral.* **8** (*fml*) to give birth to sb: [Vn] *bear a child* [Vnn] *She has borne him six sons.* ⇨ note. **9** to produce fruit, crops, etc; to yield sth: [Vn] *trees bearing pink blossom* ○ (*fig*) *His efforts bore no result* (ie were not successful). **10 ~ (to the) north, left, etc** to go or turn in the specified direction: [Vadv, Vpr] *When you get to the fork in the road, bear (to the) right.* **IDM** **bear** '**arms** (*arch*) to serve as a soldier; to fight. **bear the** '**brunt of sth** to receive the main force, shock or impact of sth: *They bore the full brunt of the attack.* ○ *His secretary has to bear the brunt of his temper.* **bear/stand comparison with sb/sth** ⇨ COMPARISON. **bear** '**fruit** to have or bring about a result, usu a successful one: *Her efforts finally bore fruit and permission was granted.* **bear** '**hard,** '**heavily, se**'**verely, etc on sb** to be a cause of hardship or suffering to sb: *Taxation bears heavily on us all.* **bear in** '**mind (that)...** to remember that...; to take it into account that...: *I'd love to play tennis with you, but please bear in mind (that) this is only the second time I've played.* **bear/keep sb/sth in mind** ⇨ MIND¹. **bear** '**witness (to sth)** to provide evidence of the truth (of sth); to be proof (of sth): *His evidence / He bore witness to my testimony.* ○ *(fig) The new housing bears witness to the energy of the local council.* **be borne 'in on sb** to come to be realized by sb: *The terrible truth was borne in on him* (ie He became fully aware of it). ○ *It was gradually borne in on us that defeat was inevitable.* **bring pressure to bear on sb** ⇨ PRESSURE. **bring sth to bear (on sb/sth)** to apply or direct attention, influence, etc; to EXERT sth: *We must bring all our energies to bear upon the task.* ○ *Pressure was brought to bear on us to finish the work on time.* **grin and bear it** ⇨ GRIN. **PHRV** **bear 'down on sb/sth 1** (*esp Brit*) to move towards sb/sth in a determined or threatening way. **2** (*esp US*) to press or weigh down on sb/sth: *Bear down on it with all your strength so it doesn't move.* **'bear on sth** to relate to sth; to affect sth: *These are matters that bear on the welfare of the community.* **bear sb/sth 'out** to support sb; to show that a story, etc is true: *The other witnesses will bear me out/bear out what I say.* **,bear 'up (against/under sth)** to show that one is strong enough to continue during a difficult time: *Bear up! Things could be a lot worse.* ○ *He's bearing up well under the strain of losing his job.* **'bear with sb/sth** to show patience, etc towards sb/sth: *We must bear with her* (ie treat her with sympathy) *during this difficult period.* ○ *If you will bear with me* (ie be patient and listen to me) *a little longer, I'll answer your question.*

NOTE The verb **bear** when it means 'to give birth to' is formal. The past participle is **borne**: *She was not able to bear children.* ○ *She has borne (him) six children.* The usual verb is **have**: *She's had six children.* The past participle **born** is only used in the passive voice: *He was born in 1974.* ○ *Ten babies were born in this hospital today.*

bearable /'beərəbl/ *adj* that can be endured or tolerated: *The climate is quite bearable.* Compare UNBEARABLE.

beard¹ /biəd/ *n* (**a**) [U, C] hair growing on the chin and the lower cheeks of a man's face: *a week's growth of beard* ○ *a false/grey/bushy/long/white beard* ○ *He has (grown) a beard.* ⇨ picture at HEAD¹. Compare MOUSTACHE, WHISKER 2. (**b**) [C] similar hair growing on an animal: *a goat's beard.*
▶ **bearded** *adj* having a beard.
beardless *adj* (*esp Brit*)

beard² /biəd/ *v* to challenge or oppose sb openly: [Vn] *It was brave of you to beard the boss about your salary increase.* **IDM** **beard the lion in his 'den** to visit sb important in order to challenge him, obtain a favour, etc.

bearer /'beərə(r)/ *n* **1** a person who brings a letter, message, etc: *I'm the bearer of good news.* **2** a person employed to carry things, eg equipment on an EXPEDITION: *A team of African bearers came with us on safari.* See also STANDARD-BEARER, STRETCHER-BEARER. **3** a person who has a cheque, etc for the payment of money to herself or himself: *This cheque is payable to the bearer* (ie to the person who presents it at a bank).

bearing /'beəriŋ/ *n* **1** [sing] (**a**) a person's way of standing, walking, etc; DEPORTMENT(a): *a man of upright, military bearing.* (**b**) behaviour: *her dignified bearing throughout the trial.* **2** [U] ~ **on sth** the way in which sth is related or relevant to sth: *What he said had little bearing on the problem.* **3** [C] (*techn*) a direction that is measured from a fixed point, usu in degrees: *take a (compass) bearing on the lighthouse.* **4** [C] (*techn*) a device that allows part of a machine to turn smoothly: *ball-'bearings.* **IDM** **get/take one's 'bearings** to find out where one is by becoming familiar with one's surroundings. **lose one's bearings** ⇨ LOSE.

bearish ⇨ BEAR¹.

bearskin /'beəskin/ *n* **1** the fur of a bear: *a bearskin rug.* **b** a tall hat of black fur worn for ceremonies by certain British soldiers.

beast /bi:st/ *n* **1** (*dated or fml*) an animal, esp a large one with four feet: *wild beasts* ○ *The lion is sometimes called the king of beasts.* **2**(**a**) a cruel or disgusting person: *Only a beast could abuse a child.* ○ *Alcohol brings out the beast in him* (ie makes him act in a violent and cruel way). (**b**) (*infml derog*) (often used in fun) an unpleasant person or thing: *Stop tickling me, you beast!* ○ *I caught a real beast of a cold.*
▶ **beastly** *adj* **1** like a beast. **2** (*Brit infml*) unpleasant; NASTY: *What beastly weather!* ○ *That's absolutely beastly of him.* — *adv* (*Brit infml*) very; extremely: *It's beastly cold outside!* **beastliness** *n* [U].
■ **,beast of 'burden** *n* an animal, such as a DONKEY, used for carrying heavy loads on its back.

beat¹ /bi:t/ *v* (*pt* **beat**; *pp* **beaten** /'bi:tn/) **1** to hit sb/sth hard repeatedly, esp with a stick or the hand: [Vpr] *Somebody was beating at the door.* [Vnpr] *Who's beating the drum?* [Vnpr] *She was beating the dust out of the carpet* (ie removing dust from the carpet by beating it). [Vn-adj] *They beat the prisoner unconscious* (ie hit him until he became unconscious). ⇨ note at HIT¹. **2** ~ **against/on sth/sb** (of the rain, sun, wind, etc) to strike sth/sb: [Vpr] *Hailstones beat against the window.* ○ *The waves were beating on the shore.* **3** ~ **sth (up)** to mix sth with short quick movements of a fork, etc: [Vn, Vnp, Vnpr] *beat the eggs (up) (to a frothy consistency)* [Vnp] *beat the flour and milk together.* **4**(**a**) (of the heart) to expand and contract regularly; to PULSATE(1): [V] *She's alive — her heart is still beating.* (**b**) to give a regular rhythmical (RHYTHM) sound: [V] *We heard the drums beating.* (**c**) to move or make sth move up and down repeatedly; to FLAP²(1): [V] *The bird's wings were beating frantically.* [Vn] *It was beating its wings.* **5**(**a**) ~ **sb (at sth)** to defeat sb; to win against sb; to do better than sb: [Vn] *Our team was easily beaten.* [Vnpr] *He beats me at chess.* (**b**) to be better than sth; to defeat sth: [Vn] *Nothing beats home cooking.* ○ *You can't beat Italian clothes.* ○ *The government's main aim is to beat inflation.* ○ *beat the speed record* (ie go faster than anyone before) ○ *If we leave early we should beat* (ie avoid) *the rush hour traffic.* (**c**) (*infml*) to be too difficult for sb; to PERPLEX sb: [Vn] *a problem that beats even the experts* ○ *It beats me/ What beats me is* (ie I don't know) *how/why he did it.* **6** to change the shape of sth, esp metal, by striking it with a hammer, etc: [Vn] *beaten silver* [Vnpr, Vnp] *The gold is beaten (out) into thin strips.* [Vn-adj] *to beat metal flat.* **7** [V, Vn] to strike bushes, etc so as to make birds or animals come out and fly or run towards people waiting to shoot them for sport. **8** to make a path, etc by walking repeatedly or by pressing branches down and walking over them: [Vn] *a well-beaten track* (ie one worn hard by much use) [Vnpr] *The hunters beat a path through the undergrowth.* **IDM** **beat about the 'bush** to talk about sth without coming to the main point: *Stop beating about the bush and tell us who won.* **beat sb at their own 'game** to defeat or do better than sb in an activity which they have chosen or in which they think that they are strong. **beat the 'clock** to finish a task, race, etc before a particular time. **beat/knock the 'daylights out of sb** ⇨ DAYLIGHTS. **beat the 'drum (for sb/sth)** to speak enthusiastically in support of sb/sth. **beat/knock hell out of sb/sth** ⇨ HELL. **beat sb 'hollow** (*Brit*) to defeat sb totally: *Our team was beaten hollow.* **'beat it** (*sl*) (usu imperative) to go away immediately: *This is private land, so beat it!* **beat the 'rap** (*US sl*) to escape without being punished. **beat a**

(hasty) re'treat to go away or back quickly, esp to avoid sth unpleasant: *The poacher beat a hasty retreat when he saw the farmer coming.* **beat 'time (to sth)** to mark or follow the rhythm, esp of music, by waving a stick or by tapping one's foot, etc: *She beat time (to the music) with her fingers.* **can you beat that/it!** (expressing surprise or shocked amusement). **if you can't beat them, 'join them** (*catchphrase*) if a rival group, company, etc continues to be more successful than one's own, it is better to go over to their side and get any advantages one can by doing so. **,off the ,beaten 'track** in a place that is far away from other people, houses, etc: *They live miles off the beaten track.* **a rod/stick to 'beat sb with** a fact, an argument, an event, etc that is used in order to blame or punish sb. **PHRV**

,beat sth 'down 1 to hit a door, etc repeatedly until it breaks open: *The thieves had beaten the door down.* **2** to make sth flat: *The wheat had been beaten down by the rain.* **beat 'down (on sb/sth)** (of the sun) to shine with great heat: *The sun beat down (on the desert sand).* **,beat sb/sth 'down (to sth)** to persuade sb to reduce the price at which they are selling sth: *He wanted $8000 for the car but I beat him down to $6000).* ○ *I beat down the price (to $6000).* **'beat sb into/to sth** to bring sb to a specified state by hitting them repeatedly: *The prisoners were beaten into submission.* ○ *The dog was beaten to death.*

,beat sb/sth 'off to drive sb/sth back or away by fighting: *The attacker/attack was beaten off.* ○ *She beat off a challenge to her leadership of the party.*

,beat sth 'out 1 to produce a rhythm, etc by hitting sth repeatedly: *She beat out the rhythm on a tin can.* **2** to put out a fire by beating: *We beat the flames out.* **3** to remove sth by striking it with a hammer, etc: *They can beat out the dent in the car's wing.*

'beat sb out of sth (*US sl*) to cheat sb by taking sth: *Her brother beat her out of $200.*

'beat sb to ... to arrive at a place, etc before sb: *I'll beat you to the top of the hill* (ie I'll race you and get there first). **,beat sb 'to it** to achieve, reach or take sth before sb else: *Scott wanted to reach the South Pole first, but Amundsen beat him to it.* ○ *I was about to take the last cake, but he beat me to it.*

,beat sb 'up to hit or kick sb severely: *He was badly beaten up by a gang of thugs.*
▶ **beat** *adj* [pred] extremely tired: *I'm (dead) beat.*

beating *n* **1** an act of hitting sb repeatedly with a stick, etc, usu as a punishment: *give sb/get a good* (ie severe) *beating.* **2** (*infml*) a heavy defeat: *Our team got a sound beating.* **IDM take a lot of / some 'beating** to be difficult to do better than: *She will take some beating* (ie It will be difficult to do better than her). ○ *His record will take a lot of beating.*
■ **,beat-'up** *adj* [usu attrib] (*infml esp US*) worn out; damaged: *a ,beat-up old 'car.*

beat² /biːt/ *n* **1(a)** [C] a stroke on a drum, etc; the sound of this: *a single beat on the drum.* **(b)** [sing] a regular sequence of strokes on a drum, etc; the sound of this: *the steady beat of the drums.* **2** [C] the main rhythm or unit of rhythm in a piece of music, a poem, etc: *The song has a good beat.* **3** [C] the route along which sb goes regularly during their work: *a policewoman out on the/her beat.*

beater /'biːtə(r)/ *n* **1** (often in compounds) an implement used for beating things: *a 'carpet-beater* ○ *an 'egg-beater.* **2** (often in compounds) a person who often hits or hurts another person: *a wife/child beater.* **3** a person employed to drive birds and animals out of bushes, etc to be shot at in sport.

beatific /,biːə'tɪfɪk/ *adj* (*fml*) showing or giving great joy and peace: *a ,beatific 'smile/'expression.*

beatify /bi'ætɪfaɪ/ *v* (*pt, pp* **-fied**) [Vn] (of the Pope) to honour a dead person by stating officially that he

or she is specially holy. Compare BLESSED 1, CANONIZE. ▶ **beatification** /bi,ætɪfɪk'eɪʃn/ *n* [C,U].

beatitude /bi'ætɪtjuːd; *US* -tuːd/ *n* **1** [U] (*fml*) great happiness; blessedness (BLESSED). **2 the Beatitudes** [pl] (in the Bible) a series of eight statements by Christ about those who are BLESSED(2), each beginning 'Blessed are...'.

beatnik /'biːtnɪk/ *n* (*dated*) (in the 1950s and early 1960s) a person who rejected ordinary society by behaving and dressing in ways that were not conventional. Compare HIPPIE.

beau /bəʊ/ *n* (*pl* beaux or beaus /bəʊz/) **1** (*US*) a male lover; a BOYFRIEND. **2** (formerly) a rich fashionable young man; a DANDY(1).
■ **the beau monde** /,bəʊ 'mɔːd/ *n* [sing] fashionable society.

Beaujolais /'bəʊʒəleɪ; *US* ,bəʊʒə'leɪ/ *n* (*pl* unchanged) [C,U] a type of wine, usu red, from the Beaujolais district of France.

beaut /bjuːt/ *n* (*US and Austral sl*) an excellent or beautiful person or thing.
▶ **beaut** *adj, interj* (*sl esp Austral*) excellent; very good.

beauteous /'bjuːtɪəs/ *adj* (*arch*) beautiful.

beautician /bjuː'tɪʃn/ *n* a person whose job is to give treatments to the face or body as a way of improving people's physical appearance.

beautiful /'bjuːtɪfl/ *adj* **1** having beauty; giving pleasure to the senses or the mind: *a beautiful face/ baby/flower/view/voice/poem/smell/morning* ○ *beautiful weather/music.* **2** very good: *The organization was beautiful.* ○ *What beautiful timing!*
▶ **beautifully** /-fli/ *adv* **1** in a beautiful way: *She sings beautifully.* **2** very well: *That will do beautifully.* ○ *The car is running beautifully.*

NOTE When talking about people's faces, **beautiful** and **pretty** usually describe women, and **good-looking** and **handsome** usually describe men. You use **beautiful** when you think someone has unusually good physical features. **Pretty** can be used when you are not referring to sexual attractiveness and is often used to describe children. **Pretty** may also be used to describe a man or boy who looks quite feminine. A **handsome** woman has an impressive appearance. **Attractive** can describe both men and women and refers especially to sexual attractiveness. You can also say that a woman is **good-looking**.

beautify /'bjuːtɪfaɪ/ *v* (*pt, pp* **-fied**) [Vn] to make sb/ sth beautiful; to ADORN sb/sth. Compare PRETTIFY.

beauty /'bjuːti/ *n* **1** [U] a combination of qualities that give pleasure to the senses (esp to the eye or ear) or to the mind: *the beauty of the sunset/of her singing/of poetry* ○ *She was a woman of great beauty.* ○ *a beauty competition/contest* (ie one in which judges decide on the most beautiful competitor). **2** [C] **(a)** a person or thing that is beautiful: *She was a famous beauty in her youth.* ○ *Your new car is an absolute beauty.* **(b)** a fine or excellent example: *Look at these moths: here's a beauty.* ○ *His last goal was a beauty.* **(c)** a pleasing or attractive feature: *I'm always finding new beauties in Shakespeare's poetry.* ○ *The beauty of living in California is that the weather is so good.* ○ *The machine needs very little attention — that's the beauty of it.* **IDM beauty is only skin-'deep** (*saying*) outward appearance is less important than hidden or inner qualities.
■ **'beauty queen** *n* a woman judged to be the most beautiful in a beauty contest.
'beauty salon (also **'beauty parlour**) *n* a place where customers receive treatment to their face, hair, nails, etc in order to improve their physical appearance.
'beauty sleep *n* [U] (*joc*) enough sleep at night,

regarded as important for a person's beauty: *I like to go to bed early — I need my beauty sleep!*

'beauty spot *n* **1** a place famous for its beautiful scenery. **2** an artificial spot or MOLE¹ on a woman's face, once thought to add to her beauty.

beaux *pl* of BEAU.

beaver /'biːvə(r)/ *n* **(a)** [C] an animal with brown fur, a wide flat tail and strong teeth. Beavers live both on land and in water and can cut down trees with their teeth to build dams (DAM¹). See also EAGER BEAVER. **(b)** [U] the fur of this animal: *a beaver hat.*
▶ **beaver** *v* **PHR V** **beaver away (at sth)** *(infml esp Brit)* to work hard: *She's been beavering away at her homework for hours.*

bebop /'biːbɒp/ *(also* **bop)** *n* [U] a type of JAZZ music with complex, usu fast, rhythms.

becalmed /bɪ'kɑːmd/ *adj* [usu pred] (of a ship with a sail) unable to move because there is no wind.

became *pt* of BECOME.

because /'bɪ'kɒz, bɪkəz; *US also* -'kɔːz/ *conj* for the reason that: *I did it because he told me to.* ○ *Just because I don't complain, people think I'm satisfied.*
■ **because of** *prep* by reason of sb/sth; on account of sb/sth: *They are here because of us.* ○ *He walked slowly because of his bad leg.* ○ *Because of his wife('s) being there, I said nothing about it.*

beck¹ /bek/ *n* (*Brit dialect*) a small stream.

beck² /bek/ *n* **IDM** **at one's/sb's ˌbeck and 'call** always ready to obey one's/sb's orders immediately: *The king has always had servants at his beck and call.* ○ *I'm not at your beck and call, you know.*

beckon /'bekən/ *v* ~ (to) sb (to do sth) to make a gesture to sb with the hand, arm or head, usu to make them come nearer or to follow: [Vn, Vn.*to* inf] *She beckoned me (to follow).* [Vpr, Vpr.*to* inf] *I could see him beckoning to me (to join him).* ○ [V] *(fig) As I get older, the prospect of retirement beckons.* **PHR V** **ˌbeckon sb 'in, 'on, 'over, etc** to make a gesture to sb to move in a specified direction: *The policeman beckoned us over.* ○ *A girl standing at the mouth of the cave beckoned him in.* ○ *They beckoned me into the room.*

become /bɪ'kʌm/ *v* (*pt* **became** /bɪ'keɪm/; *pp* **become)** **1(a)** to come to be; to grow to be: [V-adj] *They soon became angry.* ○ *He has become accustomed to his new duties.* [V-n] *That child was to become a great leader.* ○ *They became close friends.* ○ *She became a doctor.* ○ *It has become a rule that we have coffee together every morning.* **(b)** to begin to be: [V-adj] *It's becoming dangerous to go out alone at night.* [V-n] *The traffic pollution is becoming a cause for concern.* ○ *Those boys are becoming a nuisance.* ⇨ note. **2** (*fml*) [Vn] **(a)** to be suitable for sb; to suit sb: *Her new hat certainly becomes her.* **(b)** to be fitting or appropriate for sb: *Vulgar language does not become a young lady.* ○ *It ill becomes you to criticize others when your own behaviour is just as bad as theirs.* **IDM** **what becomes of sb/sth** what is happening to sb/sth: *What will become of my children if I die?* ○ *I wonder whatever became of the people who lived next door?* ○ *What became of the dreams of our youth?* (ie What we hoped for did not actually happen.)
▶ **becoming** *adj* (*fml*) **1** (*approv*) (of clothes, etc) well suited to the person wearing them/it: *a becoming hat/hairstyle* ○ *Your outfit is most becoming.* **2** suitable; appropriate; fitting: *He behaved with a becoming modesty/with a modesty becoming his junior position.* Compare UNBECOMING. **becomingly** *adv.*

NOTE Become, get, go and turn can all be followed by an adjective to talk about a change in the state or appearance of a person or thing, either permanent or temporary. **Become** and **get** can describe changes in people's emotional or physical state. **Become** is more formal and **get** is used more in speaking: *He became/got very angry.* ○ *I'm getting*

tired. They can also describe natural or social changes: *It's starting to get dark.* ○ *Divorce is becoming more common.*
Go is used for negative changes in a person or thing: *He's going bald/deaf.* ○ *The radio's gone wrong.* ○ *The meat went bad.* **Go** and **turn** are used with colours: *Her fingers went blue with cold.* ○ *Wait till the lights turn green.* **Turn** also describes the weather changing: *It suddenly turned very cold.*

B Ed /ˌbiː 'ed/ *abbr* Bachelor of Education: *have/be a B Ed* ○ *Dilip Patel B Ed.*

bed¹ /bed/ *n* **1(a)** [C, U] a thing to sleep or rest on, esp a piece of furniture with a MATTRESS and coverings: *go to bed* ○ *be in bed* ○ *get out of/into bed* ○ *sit on the bed* ○ *a double bed* ○ *a room with two single beds/ twin beds* ○ *a four-poster bed* ○ *The tramp's bed was a park bench.* ○ *Can you give me a bed for the night?* ○ *Will you help me* **make the beds** (ie arrange them so that they are ready for sleeping in)? See also BUNK-BED, CAMP-BED, WATER-BED. **(b)** [U] being in bed; the use of a bed; sleep or rest: *I've put the children to bed.* ○ *He likes a mug of cocoa before bed.* ○ *It's time for bed.* **2** [C] the bottom of the sea, a river, a lake, etc: *explore the ocean bed.* **3** [C] (*geology*) a layer of clay, rock, etc below the soil on the surface; a STRATUM: *a bed of clay/limestone/sand.* **4** [C] a flat base on which sth rests; a foundation: *The machine rests on a bed of concrete.* ○ *a railway track laid on a bed of stones.* **5** [C] a piece of ground in a garden for growing flowers, vegetables, etc: *a 'seed-bed* ○ *'flower-beds* ○ *a bed of herbs.* **IDM** **a bed of 'roses** a life of pleasure and ease: *Working here isn't exactly a bed of roses!* **die in one's bed** ⇨ DIE¹. **go to bed with sb** (*infml*) to have sex with sb. **have got out of bed on the wrong side** to be bad-tempered for the whole day. **one has made one's bed, so one must 'lie on/in it** (*saying*) one must accept the consequences of one's own actions. **take to one's 'bed** to go to one's bed because of illness and stay there. **wet the/one's bed** ⇨ WET *v.*
■ **ˌbed and 'board** *n* [U] sleeping accommodation and meals.
ˌbed and 'breakfast (*abbrs* B and B, b and b) *n* [U] sleeping accommodation and a meal the next morning, in private houses and small hotels: *Do you do bed and breakfast?* ○ *Bed and breakfast costs £15 a night.*

bed² /bed/ *v* (**-dd-**) **1** ~ sth in sth to place or fix sth firmly; to EMBED sth: [Vnpr] *The bricks are bedded in concrete.* **2** to plant sth: [Vnpr] *Bed the roots in the compost.* [also Vn]. **3** (usu passive) to provide sb with accommodation for the night: [Vnpr] *The wounded were bedded in the farmhouse.* **4** (*infml*) to have casual sex with sb: [Vn] *He's bedded more girls than he can remember.* **PHR V** **ˌbed 'down** to settle for the night, esp in a place where one would not usu sleep: *The soldiers bedded down in a barn.* **ˌbed sth/sb 'down** to put sb to bed or provide an animal with straw, etc to rest on for the night. **ˌbed sth 'out** to transfer young plants from pots, etc to a garden bed: *bed out the seedlings/young cabbages.*
▶ **-bedded** (forming compound *adjs*) having the specified type or number of beds: *a single-/double-/twin-bedded room.*

bedding *n* [U] **1** mattresses (MATTRESS) and coverings for a bed. **2** straw, etc for animals to sleep on.
'bedding plant *n* a plant suitable for planting in a garden bed.

bedbug /'bedbʌg/ *n* an insect that is found in dirty houses and lives by biting people in their beds and sucking their blood.

bedchamber /'bedˌtʃeɪmbə(r)/ *n* (*arch*) a bedroom.

bedclothes /'bedkləʊðz/ *n* [pl] coverings for a bed, such as sheets, blankets (BLANKET 1), etc.

bedcover /ˈbedkʌvə(r)/ n a cover on a bed: *hide under the bedcovers.*

bedeck /bɪˈdek/ v ~ **sth/sb** (**with sth**) (esp passive) to decorate sth/sb with flowers, flags, jewels, etc: [Vnpr] *streets bedecked with coloured ribbons* [also Vn].

bedevil /bɪˈdevl/ v (-ll-; *US* -l-) to cause sb/sth great trouble continually; to AFFLICT sb/sth: [Vn] *an industry bedevilled with strikes* ○ *Misfortune bedevilled them throughout their lives.*

bedfellow /ˈbedfeləʊ/ n (**a**) a person with whom one shares a bed. (**b**) a companion or partner: *The fortunes of war create strange bedfellows* (ie unexpected people helping each other).

bedhead /ˈbedhed/ n (*Brit*) (*US* **headboard**) the end part of the framework of a bed, behind the head of a person sleeping in it.

bedlam /ˈbedləm/ n [U] a scene of noisy confusion: *The children had been left on their own all day and when I got back the place was absolute bedlam.*

bedlinen /ˈbedlɪnɪn/ n [U] sheets and pillowcases (PILLOWCASE).

Bedouin (also **Beduin**) /ˈbeduɪn/ n (*pl* unchanged) a member of a wandering Arab tribe living in tents in the desert: *a Bedouin tribe.*

bedpan /ˈbedpæn/ n a container for use as a toilet by a person who is ill and in bed.

bedpost /ˈbedpəʊst/ n each of the upright supports at the corners of a bed (esp the old-fashioned type).

bedraggled /bɪˈdrægld/ adj made wet, dirty or untidy by rain, mud, etc: *their bedraggled appearance/ clothes/hair* ○ *The tents looked very bedraggled after the storm.*

bedridden /ˈbedrɪdn/ adj having to stay in bed, esp permanently, because of illness or weakness.

bedrock /ˈbedrɒk/ n [U] (**a**) the solid rock beneath loose soil, sand, etc: *reach/get down to bedrock.* (**b**) basic facts or principles: *the bedrock of one's beliefs.*

bedroom /ˈbedruːm, -rʊm/ n a room for sleeping in.
▶ **bedroom** adj [attrib] concerning sexual relationships: *The play is a hilarious bedroom comedy.*
-bedroomed (forming compound adjs) having the specified number of bedrooms: *a four-bedroomed detached property.*

bedside /ˈbedsaɪd/ n [usu *sing*] the area beside a bed: *a bedside table.*
■ ˌbedside ˈmanner n [sing] a doctor's way of dealing with a patient: *a good bedside manner* (ie one that is friendly and pleasant).

bedsitting room /ˌbedˈsɪtɪŋ ruːm, rʊm/ (also *infml* ˌbedˈsitter, ˈbedsit) n (*Brit*) a room used for both living and sleeping in.

bedsore /ˈbedsɔː(r)/ n a sore place on a person's body caused by lying in bed for a long time, eg when ill.

bedspread /ˈbedspred/ n the top cover spread over a bed.

bedstead /ˈbedsted/ n a framework of wood or metal supporting the springs and MATTRESS of a bed.

bedtime /ˈbedtaɪm/ n [U] the time when sb goes to bed: *It's long past your bedtime.* ○ *a bedtime story* (ie one read to a child at bedtime).

bedwetting /ˈbedwetɪŋ/ n [U] the habit of urinating (URINE) in bed while asleep.

bee¹ /biː/ n an insect with four wings that can sting. Bees live in large groups (*colonies*) and collect NECTAR and POLLEN from plants to produce honey and wax. ⇨ picture. **the ˌbee's ˈknees** (*infml*) an excellent or the best person or thing: *She thinks she's the bee's knees* (ie has a very high opinion of herself). **the birds and the bees** ⇨ BIRD. **busy as a bee** ⇨ BUSY. **have a ˈbee in one's bonnet (about sth)** (*infml*) to think or talk about sth constantly; to be obsessed (OBSESS) with sth: *Our teacher has a bee in his bonnet about punctuation.*

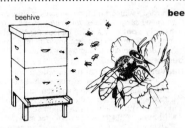

beehive · bee

bee² /biː/ n (*US*) a meeting in a group, esp of friends and people who live near each other, for work or pleasure: *a ˈsewing-bee* ○ *a ˈspelling-bee.*

beech /biːtʃ/ n (**a**) [C] a type of tree with smooth bark, shiny leaves and small nuts. (**b**) [U] the wood of this tree.

beef /biːf/ n **1** [U] the flesh of a cow, a BULL¹(1) or an OX, used as meat: *roast beef* ○ *beef cattle* (ie those bred for their meat). **2** [U] (*infml*) strength from powerful muscles: *He's got plenty of beef.* **3** [C] (*infml*) a complaint; a GRUMBLE n(1): *He came to me with a beef about the noise we'd been making.*
▶ **beef** v ~ (**about sth/sb**) (*infml*) to complain; to GRUMBLE(1): [Vpr] *What are you beefing about now?* [also V]. **ˌbeef sth ˈup** (*infml esp US*) to add force or weight to sth: *The company are taking on more staff to beef up production.* ○ *The new evidence beefed up their case considerably.*
beefy adj (-ier, -iest) (*infml*) big and strong: *beefy arms and legs.*
■ ˌbeef ˈtea n [U] (*Brit*) a drink, usu for people who are ill, made by boiling beef in water.

beefburger /ˈbiːfbɜːɡə(r)/ n a HAMBURGER(1).

beefcake /ˈbiːfkeɪk/ n [U] (*sl esp US*) (pictures of) men with big muscles, esp as seen in advertisements or sex magazines: *Hollywood starlets and aspiring beefcake.*

beefeater /ˈbiːfiːtə(r)/ n (*Brit*) a guard at the Tower of London.

beefsteak /ˈbiːfsteɪk/ n a thick piece of BEEF(1); a thick STEAK(1).

beehive /ˈbiːhaɪv/ n a container made for bees to live in. ⇨ picture at BEE.

beeline /ˈbiːlaɪn/ n **make a ˈbeeline for sth/sb** (*infml*) to go directly and quickly towards sth/sb: *As soon as he arrived at the party he made a beeline for the bar.*

been /biːn, bɪn; *US* bɪn/ *pp* of BE¹.

NOTE **Been** is the past participle of **be**: *I've never been seriously ill.* It is also the past participle of **go**: *I've never been to London.* **Gone** is also a past participle of **go**. *They've been to the cinema* means that they went but they have now returned. *They've gone to the cinema* means that they went and are still there now.

beep /biːp/ n a short high-pitched sound, such as that made by a car horn or by electronic equipment.
▶ **beep** v to make this sound: [V] *The computer beeps regularly.*

beer /bɪə(r)/ n **1(a)** [U] an alcoholic drink made from MALT and flavoured with hops (HOP 2b): *a barrel/bottle/glass of beer* ○ *a ˈbeer glass.* ⇨ picture at GLASS. (**b**) [C] a type of beer: *beers brewed in Germany.* (**c**) [C] a glass, bottle or can of beer: *Two beers, please.* **2** [U,C] (esp in compounds) any of various other fermented (FERMENT¹) drinks made from roots, etc: *ginger ˈbeer.* See also SMALL BEER. **ˌbeer and ˈskittles** (*Brit*) pleasure; amusement: *Marriage isn't all beer and skittles* (ie isn't always free of trouble).
▶ **beery** /ˈbɪəri/ adj (**a**) like or smelling of beer: *fat,*

[V.*to* inf] = verb + *to* infinitive   [Vn.inf (no *to*)] = verb + noun + infinitive without *to*   [V.*ing*] = verb + *-ing* form

beery men. (**b**) influenced by the drinking of beer, etc: *beery songs/evenings in the pub.*

■ ¹**beer-mat** *n* a small, usu cardboard, mat for putting under a beer glass on a table, etc.

beeswax /ˈbiːzwæks/ *n* [U] wax made by bees and used for making wood polish, candles, etc.

beet /biːt/ *n* [U, C] **1** a type of plant with a root which is used as a vegetable, esp for feeding animals or for making sugar. See also SUGAR BEET. **2** (*US*) = BEETROOT.

beetle /ˈbiːtl/ *n* any of several types of insect, often large and black, with hard wing-cases.
▶ **beetle** *v* **PHRV** ˌbeetle aˈlong, aˈbout, aˈway, ¹off, *etc* (*infml*) to move along, etc quickly; to hurry: *The kids beetled off home.*

beetroot /ˈbiːtruːt/ (*US* **beet**) *n* [U, C] a plant with a dark red round root which is eaten as a vegetable when cooked. **IDM** **red as a beetroot** ⇨ RED¹.

befall /bɪˈfɔːl/ *v* (*pt* **befell** /bɪˈfel/; *pp* **befallen** /bɪˈfɔːlən/) (used only in the 3rd person) (*arch*) to happen; to happen to sb: [V] *We shall never leave you, whatever befalls.* [Vn] *A great misfortune befell him.*

befit /bɪˈfɪt/ *v* (**-tt-**) (used only in the 3rd person) (*fml*) to be right and suitable for sb/sth; to be appropriate for sb/sth: [Vn] *You should dress in a way that befits a woman of your position.* ○ *a speech befitting/that befits the great occasion.*

before¹ /bɪˈfɔː(r)/ *adv* at an earlier time; in the past; already: *You should have told me so before.* ○ *It had been fine the day/week before* (ie the previous day/week). ○ *That had happened long before* (ie a long time earlier). ○ *I've seen that film before.* ⇨ note at BEFORE². Compare AFTER¹, AFTERWARDS.

before² /bɪˈfɔː(r)/ *prep* **1** earlier than sb/sth: *before lunch* ○ *the day before yesterday* ○ *two days before Christmas* ○ *The year before last he won a gold medal, and the year before that he won the silver.* ○ *She's lived there since before the war.* ○ *He arrived before me.* ○ *He taught English as his father had before him.* ○ *Something ought to have been done before now.* ○ *We'll know before long* (ie soon). ○ *Turn left just before* (ie before you reach) *the cinema.* Compare AFTER² 1. **2(a)** (with reference to position) in front of sb/sth: *They knelt before the throne.* ○ *Before you is a list of the points we have to deal with in this meeting.* Compare BEHIND¹ 1. (**b**) (with reference to order or arrangement) in front of sb/sth; ahead of sb/sth: *B comes before C in the alphabet.* ○ *Your name is before mine on the list.* ○ *ladies before gentlemen* ○ *He puts his work before everything* (ie regards it as more important than anything else). Compare AFTER² 3. (**c**) (with reference to the future) facing sb/sth; ahead of sb/sth: *The task before us is a daunting one.* **3(a)** in the presence of sb who is listening, watching, etc: *He was brought before the judge.* ○ *She said it before witnesses.* ○ *He made a statement before the House of Commons.* (**b**) to be considered or discussed by sb/sth: *The proposal went before the Board.* **4** (*fml*) under pressure from sb/sth: *They retreated before the enemy.*

NOTE Before and after relate to time and can be (**a**) adverbs: *I think we've met before.* ○ *They lived happily ever after.* (**b**) prepositions: *the day after/before my birthday.* (**c**) conjunctions: *We had dinner after/before they arrived.*
   Behind and in front of are prepositions and are opposite in meaning. They describe the relative position of people or things: *The garage is behind the house.* ○ *The baby loves hiding behind the curtains.* ○ *My dog ran in front of a bus.* ○ *John is in front of me in the photo.* Behind and in front are also adverbs: *The taxi followed on behind.* ○ *I'd like to sit in front.*
   Before and after can refer to position when this is

connected with time or the order of something in a sequence: *I was before/after you in the line.* ○ *C comes before G in the alphabet.*

before³ /bɪˈfɔː(r)/ *conj* **1** earlier than the time when: *Do it before you forget.* ○ *Did she leave a message before she went?* ○ *Before I made a decision, I thought carefully about it.* ○ *Leave your key at reception before departing.* Compare AFTER³. **2** until: *It may be many years before the economic situation improves.* ○ *How long did it take before you started to have some success?* ○ *It was some time before I realized the truth.* **3** (*fml*) rather than: *He'd starve before he stole anything* (ie He'd prefer to die of starvation rather than steal food).

beforehand /bɪˈfɔːhænd/ *adv* in advance; in preparation; earlier: *I had made enquiries beforehand.* ○ *He warned me beforehand what to expect.* ○ *We were aware of the problem beforehand.* Compare BEHIND-HAND.

befriend /bɪˈfrend/ *v* to act as a friend to or become a friend of sb, esp sb needing help: [Vn] *They befriended the young girl, giving her food and shelter.*

befuddled /bɪˈfʌdld/ *adj* made stupid; confused: *his befuddled mind* ○ *be befuddled by drink.*

beg /beg/ *v* (**-gg-**) **1** ~ (**from sb**); ~ (**for**) **sth (from/of sb**) to ask for money, food, clothes, etc as a gift or as charity: [V] *There are hundreds begging in the streets.* ○ *a begging letter* (ie one that asks for help, esp money) [Vpr] *He was so poor he had to beg for money from passers-by.* [also Vn, Vnpr]. **2** ~ **sth (of sb)**/~ (**sb**) **for sth** to ask sb for sth in an anxious or HUMBLE(1) way: [Vn] *Set him free, I beg you!* [Vpr] *Don't go, I beg of you.* [Vnpr] *May I beg a favour of you?* ○ *He begged her for forgiveness.* [V.to inf] *He begged to be allowed to come with us.* [Vn.to inf] *I beg you not to take any risks.* [V.that] *She begged that her husband (might) be released.* [V.speech] *'Help me,' he begged.* ⇨ note at ASK. **3** ~ (**for sth**) (of a dog) to sit with the front legs raised, expecting to be given sth: [V] *teach one's dog to beg* [also Vpr]. **IDM** **beg sb's ¹pardon** to tell sb one is sorry for sth one has done or said, or intends to do or say, that is not convenient for others or is considered rude in polite society. See also I BEG YOUR PARDON. **beg the ¹question 1** to assume that an argument, etc is true, even though it has not been proved: *Your proposal begs the question of whether a change is needed at all.* **2** to raise a question about sth that has not been dealt with or proved in a satisfactory manner: *This crisis begs the question of his fitness to be the country's leader.* **go ¹begging** (*Brit*) (of things) to be available because no one else wants it or is using it: *If that sandwich is going begging, I'll have it.* **I beg to differ** (used to express polite disagreement with sb): *'He's clearly the best candidate.' 'I beg to differ.'* **I beg your pardon 1** I am sorry; please excuse me : *'You've taken my seat.' 'Oh I beg your pardon!'* **2** please repeat that: *I beg your pardon — I didn't hear what you said.* **3** (expressing anger) I must object; I am offended: *I beg your pardon but the woman you're insulting happens to be my wife.* See also PARDON ME. **PHRV** ˌbeg ¹off to say that one is unable to do sth one has agreed to do: *He promised to attend but then begged off.*

began *pt* of BEGIN.

beget /bɪˈget/ *v* (**-tt-**; *pt* **begot** /bɪˈgɒt/ or, in archaic use, **begat** /bɪˈgæt/; *pp* **begotten** /bɪˈgɒtn/) **1** (*arch*) to be the father of sb: [Vn] *Abraham begat Isaac.* **2** (*dated or fml*) to cause sth; to result in sth: [Vn] *War begets misery and ruin.* ▶ **begetter** *n*.

beggar /ˈbegə(r)/ *n* **1** a person who lives by begging. **2** (*Brit infml*) (usu with an *adj*) a person: *You lucky beggar!* ○ *The cheeky beggar!* **IDM** ˌbeggars can't be ¹choosers (*infml saying*) when you have no choice, you must be satisfied with what is available: *I would have preferred a bed, but beggars can't be choosers so I slept on the sofa.*

▶ **beggar** *v* to make sb/sth very poor: [Vn] *a nation beggared by crippling taxes.* **IDM** **beggar de'scription** to be too extraordinary, bad, etc to describe: *a sunset which beggared description* ○ *His conduct is so bad it beggars (all) description.*

beggarly *adj* **1** very poor: *a beggarly existence.* **2** very small and mean; not at all generous: *a beggarly wage.*

begin /bɪ'gɪn/ *v* (**-nn-**; *pt* **began** /bɪ'gæn/; *pp* **begun** /bɪ'gʌn/) ⇨ note. **1(a)** to do the first part of sth; to start: [Vn] *begin work/a meeting* ○ *The building hasn't even been begun.* ○ *I began school* (ie attended it for the first time) *when I was five.* [Vn, Vpr] *He has begun (on)* (ie started reading or writing) *a new book.* [Vpr] *Let's begin at* (ie start from) *page 9.* ○ *He began (his talk) with an apology.* ○ *She began by telling us a story.* **(b)** to start to take place: [V] *When does the concert begin?* [Vpr] *The meeting will begin at nine.* [Vadv] *Building began last year.* [Vadv, Vpr] *The new fare will be £1, beginning (from) next month.* **(c)** be sth first, before becoming sth else: [Vn-n] *He began as an actor before starting to direct films).* ○ *What began as a minor scuffle turned into a full-scale riot.* **2(a)** (used to indicate mental or physical activities which are starting) [V.*to inf*] *She began to feel dizzy.* ○ *I'm beginning to understand.* ○ *I was beginning to think you'd never come.* ○ *He began to get dressed.* [V.*ing*] *Everyone began talking at once.* **(b)** (used to indicate a process that is starting, when the subject is a thing, not a person): [V.*to inf*] *The paper was beginning to peel off the walls.* ○ *The water is beginning to boil.* [V.*to inf*, V.*ing*] *It began to snow/began snowing.* ○ *The train has begun to slow/begun slowing down.* ⇨ note. **3** to start or make sth start for the very first time: [V] *The school began in 1920, with only 10 pupils.* [Vn] *He began a new magazine on post-war architecture.* **4** to have its STARTING-POINT; to have its nearest boundary: [Vpr] *The English alphabet begins with 'A' and ends with 'Z'.* [Vadv] *Where does Asia begin and Europe end?* **5** to be the first to do sth or to start speaking: [V] *Shall I begin?* [V.speech] *'I'm sorry,' she began.* **6** (*infml*) (usu in negative sentences) to make an attempt to do sth: [V.*to inf*] *The authorities couldn't even begin to assess the damage* (ie because it was so great). ○ *I can't begin to* (ie I don't know how) *to thank you enough.* ○ *He didn't even begin to understand my problem.* **IDM** **charity begins at home** ⇨ CHARITY. **to begin with 1** at first: *To begin with he had no money, but later he became immensely rich.* ⇨ note at HOPEFUL. **2** in the first place; firstly (FIRST¹): *I'm not going. To begin with I don't have a ticket, and secondly I don't like the play.*

▶ **beginner** *n* a person who is just beginning to learn or do sth: *a beginner's course.* **IDM** **beginner's 'luck** good luck or unexpected success at the start of learning to do sth.

beginning *n* **1(a)** the place or time at which sth starts: *Recite the poem (right) from the (very) beginning.* ○ *I've read the book from beginning to end.* ○ *Monday morning — the beginning of a new week.* **(b)** the first part: *I missed the beginning of the film.* ○ *You've made a good beginning.* **2** (often *pl*) a source; an origin: *Did democracy have its beginnings in ancient Greece?* ○ *Many big businesses start from small beginnings.* **IDM** **the beginning of the 'end** the first clear sign of a final result: *The upsurge of nationalism may prove to be the beginning of the end of/for Communism worldwide.*

***

NOTE Begin and start can often be used in the same way, though **start** is more common in speaking: *She started/began working here a year ago.* ○ *The concert starts/begins at 7.30.* ○ *As soon as everyone is quiet,*

we can *begin/start*. **Begin** is often used when you are describing a series of events: *The story begins in a London suburb.* **Start** can also mean 'to start something happening', or 'to start a machine working': *Who started the fire?* ○ *The car won't start/I can't start the car.*

Note that after continuous tenses of **begin** and **start** the *-ing* form of the verb is not normally used: *He started/began crying* or *to cry*, but *It's starting/beginning to rain* (NOT *raining*).

begone /bɪ'gɒn; *US* -'gɔːn/ *interj* (*arch*) go away immediately.

begonia /bɪ'gəʊniə/ *n* a garden plant with brightly coloured leaves and flowers.

begot *pt* of BEGET.

begotten *pp* of BEGET.

begrudge /bɪ'grʌdʒ/ *v* **1** to feel unwilling to give sth that one has to give: [Vn] *I begrudge every penny I pay in tax.* [also V.*ing*, Vn *ing*]. **2** to feel that sb does not deserve and should not have sth good: [Vnn] *Nobody begrudges you your success.*

▶ **begrudging** *adj* not generous; unwilling to give sth: *I thought you were a little begrudging in your remarks about her performance.* **begrudgingly** *adv.*

beguile /bɪ'gaɪl/ *v* (*dated or fml*) **1** to delight sb; to CHARM²(1) or amuse sb: [Vnpr] *He beguiled us with many a tale of adventure.* **2** ~ **sth (with/by sth)** to make time, etc pass pleasantly: [Vn] *They sang songs to beguile the tedium of the long journey.* [also Vnpr]. **3** ~ **sb (into doing sth)** to cheat sb; to trick sb: [Vnpr] *They were beguiled into giving him large sums of money.* [also Vn].

▶ **beguiling** *adj* attractive in a pleasant but sometimes misleading way: *beguiling advertisements.* **beguilingly** *adv.*

begun *pp* of BEGIN.

behalf /bɪ'hɑːf; *US* -'hæf/ *n* **IDM** **on behalf of sb / on sb's behalf**; (*US*) **in behalf of sb / in sb's behalf** as the representative(3) of sb; in the interests of sb: *On behalf of my colleagues and myself I thank you.* ○ *Ken is not present, so I shall accept the prize on his behalf.* ○ *The legal guardian must act on behalf of the child.* ○ *Don't be worried on my behalf* (ie about me).

behave /bɪ'heɪv/ *v* **1** ~ **well, badly, etc (towards sb)** to act or react in the specified way: [Vpr] *She behaves (towards me) more like a friend than a mother.* [Vadv] *He has behaved disgracefully towards his family.* **2** ~ **(oneself)** to act in a correct or polite way, with good manners: [V, Vn] *Children, please behave (yourselves)!* **3** (of things) to work or function well (or in a manner specified way): [Vadv] *How's your new car behaving?* ○ *This will mean a change in the way our courts behave.*

▶ **-behaved** (forming compound *adjs*) behaving in a specified way: *well-/ill-/badly-behaved children.*

behaviour (*US* **behavior**) /bɪ'heɪvjə(r)/ *n* **1** [U] the way sb behaves, esp towards other people; one's attitude and manners: *She was ashamed of her children's (bad) behaviour.* ○ *His behaviour (towards me) has been very strange recently.* **2** [U] the way sb/sth acts or functions in particular situations: *study the behaviour of infants/apes/bees/molecules.* **IDM** **be on one's best behaviour** ⇨ BEST¹.

▶ **behavioural** (*US* **-oral**) /-jərəl/ *adj* of behaviour. **be,havioural 'science** *n* [U] the study of human behaviour.

behaviourism (*US* **-orism**) /-jərɪzəm/ *n* [U] (*psychology*) the theory that all human behaviour is learnt to fit in with external conditions, and is not influenced by people's thoughts and feelings. **behaviourist** (*US* **-orist**) /-jərɪst/ *n.*

behead /bɪ'hed/ *v* to cut off sb's head, esp as a punishment: [Vn] *King Henry VIII had two of his wives beheaded.*

beheld *pt*, *pp* of BEHOLD.

***

behest /bɪˈhest/ n **IDM** **at sb's beˈhest** (dated or fml) on sb's orders; at sb's request: at the king's behest/at the behest of the king.

behind¹ /bɪˈhaɪnd/ prep **1(a)** at or towards the back of sb/sth: Who's the girl standing behind Richard? ○ Stay close behind me in the crowd. ○ The golf course is behind our house. ○ a small street behind the station ○ She glanced behind her. ○ work behind the counter (eg as a sales assistant in a shop) ○ Don't forget to lock the door behind you (ie when you leave). ○ (fig) The accident is behind you now (ie in the past), so try to forget about it. **(b)** on the other side of sb/sth, and often hidden: hide behind a tree ○ Behind the curtain she found a door. ○ The sun disappeared behind the clouds. ○ (fig) Behind his severe manner he's a very kind man. Compare IN FRONT OF. ▷ note at BEFORE². **2** making less progress than sb/sth: He's behind the rest of the class in reading. ○ Britain is behind Japan in developing modern technology. ○ be behind schedule (ie late). **3** giving support to or approval of sb/sth: My family is right behind me in my ambition to become a doctor. ○ He can't win the election with only 30% of the voters behind him. **4** responsible for starting or developing sth: the thought that was behind the suggestion ○ the man behind the plan to build a new hospital. **IDM** **be behind sth** to be the reason for sth: What's behind the smart suit and eager smile?

behind² /bɪˈhaɪnd/ adv part **1** at or towards the back of sb/sth; further back: She cycled off down the road with the dog running behind. ○ The others are a long way behind. ○ What have we left behind (ie after going away)? ○ Don't look behind or you may fall. ○ He was shot from behind as he ran away. ○ We had fallen so far behind that it seemed pointless continuing. ○ I was told to stay behind after school (ie remain in school after lessons were over). Compare IN FRONT (FRONT). ▷ note at BEFORE². **2** ~ (with/in sth) late in paying money or completing work: I'm terribly behind (with the rent) this month. ○ He's behind in handing in his homework.

behind³ /bɪˈhaɪnd/ n (infml euph) the part of the body that one sits on; the bottom(3): She fell backwards and landed on her behind. ○ He kicked the boy's behind.

behindhand /bɪˈhaɪndhænd/ adj [pred] ~ (with/in sth) late, esp in paying a debt: be behindhand with the rent ○ get behindhand in one's work. Compare BEFOREHAND.

behold /bɪˈhəʊld/ v (pt, pp beheld /bɪˈheld/) (arch or rhet) (often imperative) to look at or see sth, esp sth unusual: [Vn] The children's faces were a joy to behold. ○ Behold the king! **IDM** **lo and behold** ▷ LO. ▶ **beholder** n (saying): Beauty is in the eye of the beholder (ie Different people may not find the same things beautiful).

beholden /bɪˈhəʊldən/ adj [pred] ~ **to sb (for sth)** (dated or fml) owing thanks or having a duty towards sb because of sth they have done: We were beholden to him for his many acts of kindness.

behove /bɪˈhəʊv/ (US **behoove** /bɪˈhuːv/) v (used with it; not in the continuous and rarely in the past tenses) (dated or fml) to be right or necessary for sb: It ill behoves Anne (ie Anne ought not) to speak like that of her benefactor.

beige /beɪʒ/ adj, n [U] (of a) very light yellowish brown: a beige carpet.

being¹ /ˈbiːɪŋ/ n **1** [U] **(a)** existence: What is the purpose of our being? ○ The European Community **came into being/was brought into being** as a result of the Treaty of Rome. **(b)** one's inner nature; self: I detest violence with my whole being. **2** [C] a living creature: the rights of human beings ○ a strange being from another planet.

being² /ˈbiːɪŋ/ pres p of BE¹,².

bejewelled (US **bejeweled**) /bɪˈdʒuːəld/ adj decorated with jewels.

belabour (US **belabor**) /bɪˈleɪbə(r)/ v **1** ~ sb/sth **(with sth)** (arch) to hit sb/sth hard and repeatedly, esp with a stick: [Vnpr] (fig) The latest trade figures provide another stick for the opposition to belabour the government with. [also Vn]. **2** (fml) to stress sth too much: [Vn] I don't wish to belabour the point.

belated /bɪˈleɪtɪd/ adj coming very late or too late: a belated apology ○ the government's belated response to the official report on childcare. ▶ **belatedly** adv.

belay /bɪˈleɪ/ v [Vn] (in climbing and sailing) to fix a rope round a PEG¹(1), rock, etc in order to secure it. ▶ **belay** n an act of belaying.

belch /beltʃ/ v **1** [V] to send out gas from the stomach noisily through the mouth. **2** ~ sth **(out/forth)** to send sth out from an opening with force: [Vn, Vnpr] factory chimneys belching smoke (into the sky) [Vp] The volcano belched out smoke and ashes. ▶ **belch** n an act or a sound of belching: He gave a loud belch.

beleaguered /bɪˈliːgəd/ adj **1** surrounded by an enemy; besieged (BESIEGE 1): a beleaguered garrison. **2** worried by repeated attacks or criticism: give much needed support to the beleaguered party leaders.

belfry /ˈbelfri/ n the part of a church tower in which bells hang. ▷ picture at CHURCH. **IDM** **have bats in the belfry** ▷ BAT².

belie /bɪˈlaɪ/ v (pres p **belying**; pp **belied**) **1** to give a false idea of sth: [Vn] His cheerful manner belied a deep feeling of sadness. **2** to fail to justify or fulfil a hope, promise, etc: Practical experience belies this theory.

belief /bɪˈliːf/ n **1** [U] ~ **in sth/sb** a feeling that sth/sb is real and true; trust or confidence in sth/sb: I admire his passionate belief in what he is doing. ○ The incident has shaken my belief (ie weakened my confidence) in the police. ○ She has lost her belief in God. ○ He came to me **in the belief that** I could help him. Compare DISBELIEF, UNBELIEF. **2** [C] **(a)** a thing that one accepts as true or real; what one believes: It is my belief that (ie I believe that) she is guilty. ○ The government took no action, reinforcing the popular belief that it did not care. ○ She was imprisoned for her dissident beliefs. **(b)** a religion or sth taught as part of a religion: Christian beliefs. **IDM** **beyond beˈlief** too great, difficult, terrible, etc to be believed: I find his behaviour (irresponsible) beyond belief. **to the best of one's belief/knowledge** ▷ BEST³.

believe /bɪˈliːv/ v (not in the continuous tenses) **1(a)** to feel sure of the truth of sth: [Vn] She believed everything he told her. ○ I refuse to believe it. ○ I'll believe it/that when I see it (ie I will not believe it until I have solid evidence). ○ I'm told he's been in prison, and I can well believe it (ie it does not surprise me). ○ Don't believe what you read in the papers. **(b)** to accept the statement of sb as true: [Vn] I don't know which of them to believe. **2** to think; to suppose: [V.that] People used to believe (that) the world was flat. ○ It was widely believed that he had betrayed his country. ○ I believe I should congratulate you on becoming a father. ○ It happened on 22 February, a Monday I believe. ○ The police believed him to be guilty. ○ I genuinely believe it to have been a mistake. ○ 'Is he coming?' 'I believe so/not.' [also V.wh]. **3** to have a religious faith: [V] He thinks that everyone who believes will go to heaven. **PHRV** **beˈlieve in sb/sth** to feel sure of the existence of sb/sth: I believe in God. ○ Do you believe in ghosts? **beˈlieve in sth/sb**; **beˈlieve in doing sth** to trust sth/sb; to feel sure of the value or truth of sth: She has doubts about him, but I believe in him implicitly. ○ Do you believe in nuclear disarmament? ○ He believes in getting plenty of exercise. ˈ**believe sth**

of sb to accept that sb is capable of a particular action, etc: *If I hadn't seen him doing it I would never have believed it of him.* **IDM believe it or 'not** it may sound surprising but it is true: *Believe it or not, we were left waiting in the rain for two hours.* **be-lieve (you) 'me** I can tell you confidently: *Believe you me, this administration won't meddle with the tax system.* **don't you be'lieve it!** it is not true; it will not happen: *'He's only 34.' 'Don't you believe it — he's at least 40.'* **give sb to believe/understand** ⇨ GIVE¹. **make believe (that...)** to pretend: *The boys liked to make believe (that) they were astronauts.* See also MAKE-BELIEVE. **not believe one's 'ears/'eyes** to be unable to believe that what one hears or sees is real because one is so surprised: *I stared at her, scarcely able to believe my ears.* **seeing is be'lieving** (*saying*) one needs to see sth before one can believe that it really exists or happens. **would you be'lieve (it)?** (expressing great surprise or shock) although it is hard to believe: *Today, would you believe, she came to work in an evening dress!*
▶ **believable** *adj* that can be believed: *an entirely believable explanation/scenario* ○ *a play with believable characters.* Compare UNBELIEVABLE.
believer *n* a person who believes, esp sb with religious faith: *a message to all true believers of Islam.* Compare UNBELIEVER. **IDM be a (great/firm) be-liever in sth** to feel sure that sth is important or valuable: *I'm a great believer in (taking) regular physical exercise.*

Belisha beacon /bəˌliːʃə ˈbiːkən/ (also **beacon**) *n* (*Brit*) a post with an orange flashing light on top, marking a pedestrian crossing (PEDESTRIAN).

belittle /bɪˈlɪtl/ *v* to make a person or an action seem unimportant or of little value: [Vn] *Don't belittle yourself* (ie Don't be too modest about your abilities or achievements). ○ *She felt belittled by her hus-band's arrogant behaviour.*
▶ **belittling** *adj* making sb seem unimportant or of little value: *I find it belittling to be reprimanded by someone so much younger than me.*

bell /bel/ *n* **1(a)** a hol-low metal object, usu shaped like a cup, that makes a ringing sound when struck: *a peal of church bells* ○ *a 'hand bell* ○ *a 'bicycle bell.* ⇨ picture. ⇨ picture at BI-CYCLE. **(b)** an electrical apparatus which makes a ringing sound when a button on it is pushed: *Ring the bell to see if they're in.* **2** the sound of a bell as a signal or warning: *There's the bell for the end of the lesson.* ○ *The dinner bell sounded.* ○ *An alarm bell went off.* **3** a thing shaped like a bell(1a): *the bell of a flower.* **IDM clear as a bell** ⇨ CLEAR¹. **give sb a 'bell** (*Brit infml*) to call sb by telephone. **ring a bell** ⇨ RING². **sound as a bell** ⇨ SOUND². ■ **'bell-bottoms** *n* [pl] trousers that become gradually wider below the knee.
'bell-pull *n* a handle or cord pulled to make a bell ring.
'bell-push *n* a button pressed to operate an electric bell.
'bell-ringer *n* a person who rings church bells. See also CAMPANOLOGY.
'bell-ringing *n* [U].

bellboy /ˈbelbɔɪ/ (also **bellhop** /ˈbelhɒp/) *n* (*US*) = PAGE³ a.

belle /bel/ *n* (*rather dated*) a beautiful woman: *I'm sure you'll be the belle of the ball* (ie the most beauti-ful woman present at a dance)*!* ○ *Mary-Lou is a real Southern belle.*

belles-lettres /ˌbel ˈletrə/ *n* [sing or pl *v*] (*French*)

clapper   bell

literary studies and writings, contrasted with those on commercial, technical, scientific, etc subjects.

bellicose /ˈbelɪkəʊs; *Brit also* -kəʊz/ *adj* (*fml*) show-ing eagerness to fight; aggressive: *a bellicose nation/ nature.* ▶ **bellicosity** /ˌbelɪˈkɒsəti/ *n* [U].

-bellied ⇨ BELLY.

belligerent /bəˈlɪdʒərənt/ *adj* **1** showing an eager-ness to fight or argue; aggressive: *a belligerent person/ manner/speech.* **2** (of a country) fighting a war.
▶ **belligerence** /-əns/ *n* [U].
belligerent *n* a country, group or person fighting a war.
belligerently *adv.*

bellow /ˈbeləʊ/ *v* **1** to make a deep loud noise like a BULL¹(1); to roar, esp with pain: [V] *The bull bel-lowed.* [Vpr] *He was bellowing with pain.* **2** ~ (**sth**) (**at sb**) to say sth loudly or angrily; to shout: [Vpr] *The music was so loud we had to bellow at each other to be heard.* [V.speech] *'Get out!' he bellowed.* [Vnpr] *The sergeant bellowed orders at his platoon.* [also V, Vn]. ▶ **bellow** *n*: *He let out/gave a sudden bellow of rage.*

bellows /ˈbeləʊz/ *n* [sing or pl *v*] an apparatus for blowing air into or through sth. Its most common uses are to make a fire burn better or to make a church organ²(1) produce sound: *She picked up a pair of bellows* (ie a small bellows with two handles to be pushed together).

belly /ˈbeli/ *n* **1(a)** the part of the body between the chest and the legs, containing the stomach, bowels, etc. See also ABDOMEN 1. ⇨ picture at HORSE. **(b)** the stomach: *He went to bed with an empty belly* (ie hungry). **2** (*esp rhet*) the round part of sth: *in the belly of a ship.* ⇨ picture at MUSICAL INSTRUMENT.
▶ **-bellied** /-belid/ (forming compound *adjs*) having a belly of the specified type: *'pot-bellied.*
belly *v* (*pt, pp* **bellied**) **PHRV** ˌbelly 'out to swell out: *The sails bellied out.*
■ **'belly-button** *n* (*infml*) a NAVEL.
'belly-dance *n* a dance, originating in the Middle East, performed by a woman with EROTIC move-ments of her belly and hips. **'belly-dancer** *n.*
'belly-laugh *n* (*infml*) a deep loud laugh.
bellyache /ˈbelieɪk/ *n* [C, U] (*infml*) stomach pain.
▶ **bellyache** *v* ~ (**about sth**) (*infml*) to complain, esp repeatedly and without good reason: [V] *Stop bellyaching all the time!* [also Vpr].

bellyflop /ˈbeliflɒp/ *n* (*infml*) a bad DIVE²(1) in which the body hits the water almost flat, rather than at an angle.

bellyful /ˈbeliful/ *n* **IDM have had a 'bellyful of sb/sth** (*infml*) to have had as much as one can tolerate of sb/sth: *I've had a bellyful of your com-plaints.*

belong /bɪˈlɒŋ; *US* -lɔːŋ/ *v* (not in the continuous tenses) to have a proper place, as specified: [Vadv] *Where does this belong* (ie Where is it kept)*?* ○ *I've never felt that art and self-improvement belong to-gether.* ○ *I don't feel I belong here/I have no sense of belonging here.* [Vpr] *The hammer belongs (in the shed) with the rest of the tools.* ○ *A child belongs with* (ie should live with and be cared for by) *its mother.* ○ *These articles don't belong under this heading* (ie are wrongly classified). **PHRV be'long to sb 1** to be the property of sb: *Who does this pen belong to?* ○ *A helicopter belonging to the oil company has crashed.* ○ *The earth does not belong to man; man belongs to the earth.* **2** to be given to sb fairly: *All the credit for this belongs to our sales staff.* **3** (of a period of time) to be the most successful for sb: *Yesterday belonged al-most entirely to the Australians* (ie their team dominated the game). **be'long to sth** to be a mem-ber of a group, a family, an organisation, etc: *He has never belonged to a trade union.* ○ *Shallots belong to the onion family.*
▶ **belongings** *n* [pl] a person's movable posses-

sions, ie not land, buildings, etc: *After his death his sister sorted through his (personal) belongings.* ○ *The tourists lost all their belongings in the hotel fire.*

beloved *adj* (**a**) /bɪˈlʌvd/ [pred] ~ **by/of sb** much loved by sb: *those long brown envelopes beloved of lawyers.* (**b**) /bɪˈlʌvɪd/ [attrib] much loved: *in memory of my beloved husband.*

▶ **beloved** /bɪˈlʌvɪd/ *n* (*arch or rhet*) a much loved person.

below /bɪˈləʊ/ *prep* at or to a lower level, position, rank, etc than sb/sth: *Please do not write below this line.* ○ *Skirts must be below (ie long enough to cover) the knee.* ○ *courses below degree level* ○ *The temperature remained below freezing all day.* ○ *A sergeant in the police force is below an inspector.* ○ *The standard of his work is well below the average of his class.* ○ *You can cross the river a short distance below (ie down the stream from) the waterfall.* Compare ABOVE[1].

▶ **below** *adv part* **1** at or to a lower level, position or place: *the sky above and the sea below* ○ *They live on the floor below.* ○ *I could see cattle grazing by the lake, far below.* ○ *See below (eg at the bottom of the page) for references.* ○ *The passengers who felt seasick stayed below (ie on a lower* DECK[1](1a)*).* **2** (of a temperature) lower then zero: *The thermometer had dropped to a record 40 below (ie –40°).* Compare ABOVE[1].

belt /belt/ *n* **1** a long narrow piece of leather, cloth, etc, usu worn around the waist: *He did up/fastened/tightened his belt.* ○ *a belt buckle.* ⇨ picture at BOXING. **2** an endless moving strip of material, used to drive machinery or carry things along. See also CONVEYOR BELT, FAN BELT. **3** a sometimes narrow area or region that is distinct from those around it: *a country's* ˈcotton/ˈcorn/inˈdustrial *belt* ○ *I live in the* comˈmuter/ˈstockbroker *belt.* ○ *a belt of rain moving across the country.* See also GREEN BELT. **4** (*sl*) an act of hitting sth/sb hard: *She gave the ball a terrific belt.* **IDM** **below the** ˈ**belt** unfair or unfairly: *He know's I'm a bit deaf so his remarks about 'not paying attention' were distinctly below the belt.* ˌ**belt and** ˈ**braces** (*infml*) using extra measures to make sure that a plan, etc will succeed: *a belt-and-braces policy.* **tighten one's belt** ⇨ TIGHTEN. **under one's** ˈ**belt** (*infml*) achieved; obtained: *She already has good academic qualifications under her belt.* See also LIFEBELT.

▶ **belt** *v* **1**(**a**) ~ **sth** (**up**) to put or fasten a belt round sth: [Vn, Vnp] *Your coat looks better belted (up).* (**b**) to attach sth with a belt: [Vnp] *The officer belted his sword on.* [also Vnpr]. **2** (*sl*) to hit sb hard: [Vn, Vnn] *If you don't shut up, I'll belt you (one).* **3** (*sl esp Brit*) to move very fast in the specified direction: [Vp, Vpr] *A car came belting along (the road).* [Vpr] *He went belting up the motorway at 90 mph.* **PHRV** ˌ**belt sth** ˈ**out** (*sl*) to sing or play sth loudly and forcefully: *a radio belting out pop music* ○ *She can really belt out a tune.* ˌ**belt** ˈ**up** **1** (*infml*) fasten one's seat-belt (SEAT[1]). **2** (*Brit sl*) (usu imperative) to be quiet: *For goodness sake, belt up, will you?*

beltway /ˈbeltweɪ/ *n* (*US*) a wide road for traffic to move quickly round the edge of a city.

bemoan /bɪˈməʊn/ *v* (*fml*) to express one's sorrow or disappointment about sth: [Vn] *He bemoaned the shortage of funds available for research.*

bemused /bɪˈmjuːzd/ *adj* confused and unable to think clearly: *a bemused expression/smile* ○ *He was totally bemused by all the activity around him.*

bench /bentʃ/ *n* **1** [C] (**a**) a long seat made of wood or stone: *a park bench.* (**b**) (in the British Parliament) a seat for a certain group of politicians: *the back-/cross-/front-benches* ○ *There was cheering from the Labour benches.* **2 the bench** (**a**) [sing] a court of law: *the Queen's Bench* (ie a division of the British High Court of Justice). (**b**) [sing] a judge, or the

judge's seat in court: *The attorney turned to address the bench.* (**c**) [Gp] judges or magistrates as a group. **3** [C] a long table for a CARPENTER, scientist, etc to work at. **IDM** **on the** ˈ**bench** having being appointed as a judge or magistrate.

benchmark /ˈbentʃmɑːk/ *n* an example of sth which is used as a standard or point of reference for making comparisons: *This settlement will be seen as a benchmark for future pay negotiations.*

bend[1] /bend/ *v* (*pt, pp* **bent** /bent/) **1** to force sth that was straight into an angle or a curve: [Vnp, Vnadv] *bend the wire up/down/forwards/back* [Vn] *It's hard to bend an iron bar.* ○ *The heat of the fire has bent these old records.* ○ *Can you touch your toes without bending your knees?* [also Vnpr]. **2** (of an object) to become curved: [Vpr] *The road bends (to the right) after a few yards.* [V] *As I climbed along it, the branch bent but didn't break.* [also Vp, Vadv]. **3** to lean or cause sb to lean, esp in a specified direction: [Vp] *She bent down and picked it up.* ○ *Bend over and touch your toes.* [Vadv] *He bent forward to listen to the child.* [Vadv, Vnadv] *They (were) bent double, crouching under the table.* [Vnpr] *His head was bent over a book.* [also V, Vpr, Vn]. **IDM** **bend sb's** ˈ**ear** (*infml*) to talk to sb about a problem that one has. **bend/lean over backwards** ⇨ BACKWARDS. **bend/stretch the rules** ⇨ RULE. **on bended** ˈ**knee(s)** (as if) kneeling to pray or to beg for sth. **PHRV** **be** ˈ**bent on sth / on doing sth** to be determined on a course of action: *He is bent on winning at all costs.* See also HELL-BENT. ˈ**bend sb to sth** (*fml*) to force sb to submit to sth: *She tried to bend the others to her will.*

▶ **bendy** *adj* (*Brit infml*) (**a**) having many bends; winding: *a bendy road.* (**b**) that can be bent easily; flexible: *a bendy twig.*

bend[2] /bend/ *n* a curve or turn, esp in a road, river, etc: *a gentle/sharp bend.* **IDM** **round the bend/twist** (*infml*) crazy or very annoyed: *His behaviour is driving me round the bend.* ○ *He's gone completely round the twist.*

bender /ˈbendə(r)/ *n* (*sl*) a period of drinking a lot of alcohol: *He went on a drunken bender for three days.*

bends /bendz/ *n* **the bends** [pl] (*infml*) severe pains and difficulty in breathing experienced by people who have been diving (DIVE[1] 2) deep under water and who come to the surface too quickly.

beneath /bɪˈniːθ/ *prep* (*fml*) **1** in or to a lower position than sb/sth; under sb/sth: *They found the body buried beneath a pile of leaves.* ○ *The boat sank beneath the waves.* **2** not worthy of sb: *He considers such jobs beneath him* (ie not suited to his rank or status). ○ *They thought she had married beneath her* (ie married a man of lower social status). Compare ABOVE[2].

▶ **beneath** *adv* (*fml*) in or to a lower position; underneath: *Her careful make-up hid the signs of age beneath.*

Benedictine *n* **1** /ˌbenɪˈdɪktɪn/ [C] a monk or nun of the religious order[1](12) founded by Saint Benedict: *a Benedictine monastery.* **2** /ˌbenɪˈdɪktiːn/ [U, C] (*propr*) a LIQUEUR originally made by monks of the Benedictine order.

benediction /ˌbenɪˈdɪkʃn/ *n* [C, U] (*fml or techn*) a prayer of blessing, esp one said before a meal or at the end of a church service: *pronounce/say the benediction* ○ *confer one's benediction on sb.*

benefaction /ˌbenɪˈfækʃn/ *n* (*fml*) **1** [U] the action of giving sth for a good cause or of doing good. **2** [C] a thing given for a good cause or in order to do good; a gift or donation (DONATE).

benefactor /ˈbenɪfæktə(r)/ *n* (*fem* **benefactress** /ˈbenɪfæktrəs/) a person who gives money or other help to a school, hospital, charity, etc.

benefice /ˈbenɪfɪs/ *n* the position, in charge of a

PARISH(1), that provides a priest in the Christian Church with her or his income.

beneficent /bɪˈnefɪsnt/ adj (fml) showing active kindness; generous: a beneficent patron. ▶ **beneficence** /bɪˈnefɪsns/ n [U].

beneficial /ˌbenɪˈfɪʃl/ adj ~ (to sth/sb) having a helpful or useful effect; favourable: a beneficial result/influence ○ Fresh air is beneficial to one's health.

beneficiary /ˌbenɪˈfɪʃəri; US -ˈfɪʃieri/ n **1** a person who receives money or property when sb dies: the main beneficiary of a will. **2** a person who gains or benefits from sth: the potential beneficiaries of this medical research.

benefit /ˈbenɪfɪt/ n **1** [U,C] a thing that one gains from sth; an advantage that sth gives: She didn't get much benefit from her course. ○ I've **had the benefit of** a good education. ○ **With the benefit of** modern technology, a great deal of progress has been made. ○ The new regulations will be **of benefit to** us all. ○ A change of manager would certainly be to the club's benefit. ○ the benefits of modern medicine/science/higher education ○ Membership entitles you to many benefits. **2** [U,C] money provided, esp by the government, to those who are entitled to receive it, eg those who are unemployed, ill, etc: unemployment/sickness benefit. See also HOUSING BENEFIT. **3** [C esp attrib] a public performance or game held in order to raise money for a particular player, charity, organization, etc: a benefit match/concert ○ It's his benefit year. **IDM for sb's benefit** in order to help, guide or provide sth useful for sb: The warning sign was put there for the benefit of the public. ○ Although she didn't mention me by name, I know her remarks were intended for my benefit. **give sb the ˌbenefit of the ˈdoubt** to accept that sb has not done sth wrong, is telling the truth, etc because there is no clear evidence to support one's feeling that this may not be the case: By allowing her to go free the judge gave the accused the benefit of the doubt.

▶ **benefit** v (pt, pp **-fited**; US also **-fitted**) **1** to do good to sb/sth; to be of advantage or use to sb/sth: [Vn] The new facilities have benefited the whole town. **2** ~ **(from/by sth)** to receive benefit from sth; to gain sth from sth: [V] The new tax laws are good for some people but I won't benefit. [Vpr] I feel that I have benefited from this experience.

benevolent /bəˈnevələnt/ adj ~ (to/towards sb) **1** being or showing a desire to be kind, helpful or generous: a benevolent air/attitude/manner ○ a benevolent dictator. Compare MALEVOLENT. **2** doing good rather than making profit; CHARITABLE(2): a benevolent society/fund. ▶ **benevolence** /bəˈnevələns/ n [U]. **benevolently** adv: smiling benevolently.

benighted /bɪˈnaɪtɪd/ adj (dated) without moral or intellectual understanding; ignorant: bring hope and enlightenment to a benighted people.

benign /bɪˈnaɪn/ adj **1** (of people or actions) kind; gentle. Compare MALIGN. **2** (of climate) mild; pleasant. **3** (of a growth(4a) in the body) not likely to spread or occur again after treatment; not dangerous: a benign tumour. Compare MALIGNANT 1. ▶ **benignly** adv: smile benignly.

bent¹ /bent/ n (usu sing) ~ (for sth/ doing sth) a natural taste or interest: She has a strong musical bent. ○ He showed a literary bent from a very early age.

bent² /bent/ adj (sl esp Brit) **1** dishonest; CORRUPT¹(1): a bent copper (ie police officer). **2** (derog offensive) HOMOSEXUAL.

bent³ pt, pp of BEND¹.

bentwood /ˈbentwʊd/ n [U] wood that is artificially shaped for making furniture: bentwood chairs.

benzene /ˈbenziːn/ n [U] a colourless liquid obtained from PETROLEUM and coal tar (COAL), used in making plastics and many chemical products.

bequeath /bɪˈkwiːð, -ˈkwiːθ/ v ~ **sth (to sb)** (fml) **1** to arrange, by making a will¹(5), to give property, money, etc to sb when one dies: [Vnpr] He bequeathed £5 000 to charity. [Vnn] She has bequeathed me her jewellery. [also Vn]. **2** to pass sth on or leave sth for those who come later: [Vnpr] discoveries bequeathed to us by scientists of the last century [also Vn, Vnn].

bequest /bɪˈkwest/ n (fml) a thing that one leaves to sb else when one dies, or the act of doing this: leave a bequest of £2 000 each to one's grandchildren ○ a donation by bequest.

berate /bɪˈreɪt/ v [Vn] (fml) to speak to or criticize sb angrily.

bereave /bɪˈriːv/ v (fml) (usu passive) to cause sb to be without a relative or close friend, esp because he or she has died: [Vn] He has recently been bereaved and is off work.

▶ **bereaved** adj (fml) having lost sb, esp a relative or close friend, who has died recently: the bereaved husband/wife. **the bereaved** n (pl unchanged) (fml) a person who is bereaved: The bereaved is/are still in mourning. ○ send one's sympathy to the bereaved. **bereavement** n **(a)** [U] the state of being bereaved: experience the shock of bereavement ○ bereavement counselling. **(b)** [C] an instance of this: a recent bereavement in the family.

bereft /bɪˈreft/ adj [pred] ~ **(of sth)** (fml) **1** without or having lost a particular power or quality: be bereft of speech (ie be unable to speak) ○ bereft of hope (ie without hope) ○ bereft of reason (ie mad). **2** lacking hope, support or ideas: He was utterly bereft when his wife died. ○ She felt alone and bereft in the big city. ○ The government seems bereft in the face of the country's economic problems.

beret /ˈbereɪ; US bəˈreɪ/ n a round flat cap with no PEAK¹(3), usu made of soft cloth. ⇨ picture at HAT.

berk /bɜːk/ n (Brit sl derog) a stupid person.

berry /ˈberi/ n (often in compounds) a small juicy fruit with small seeds: blackberries ○ gooseberries ○ holly berries ○ pick berries. **IDM brown as a berry** ⇨ BROWN.

berserk /bəˈzɜːk, -ˈsɜːk/ adj [usu pred] out of control with anger: He **went berserk** and attacked me.

berth /bɜːθ/ n **1** a place to sleep on a ship, train, etc. **2** a place for a ship to be tied up in a harbour or anchored (ANCHOR v 1): find a safe berth (eg one protected from bad weather). **3** (infml) a job or place in a team, etc: She's hoping to win back her berth in the national side. **IDM give sb/sth a wide berth** ⇨ WIDE.

▶ **berth** v **1** (usu passive) to provide sb with a place to sleep on a ship, train, etc: [Vn] Six passengers can be berthed on the lower deck. **2(a)** [Vn] to tie up a ship in a harbour or at a suitable place. **(b)** [V] (of a ship) to come to a berth; to MOOR².

beseech /bɪˈsiːtʃ/ v (pt, pp besought /bɪˈsɔːt/ or beseeched) (fml) to ask in an urgent begging way; to IMPLORE: [Vn] Spare him, I beseech you. [Vn.to inf] I beseech you to think seriously about this. [also V, Vnpr]. ⇨ note at ASK.

▶ **beseeching** adj [attrib] (of a look, tone of voice, etc) appealing or begging for sth. **beseechingly** adv.

beset /bɪˈset/ v (**-tt-**; pt, pp beset) (fml) (esp passive) to trouble or threaten sb/sth constantly and from all sides: [Vn] beset by doubts ○ The voyage was beset with dangers. ○ the difficulties/pressures/temptations that beset us all.

▶ **besetting** adj [attrib] habitually affecting or troubling sb: a besetting difficulty/sin/temptation.

beside /bɪˈsaɪd/ prep **1** at the side of sb/sth; next to sb/sth: Sit beside your sister. ○ I keep a dictionary beside me when I'm doing crosswords. **2** compared with sb/sth: *Beside your earlier work this piece seems rather disappointing.* **IDM** **be'side oneself (with sth)** having lost one's control of oneself because of the intensity of the emotion one is feeling: *He was beside himself with rage when I told him what I had done.*

besides /bɪ'saɪdz/ *prep* **1** in addition to sb/sth: *There will be five of us for dinner, besides the children.* ○ *The play was badly acted, besides being far too long.* **2** (following a negative) except sb/sth; apart from sb/sth: *She has no relations besides an aged aunt.* ○ *No one writes to me besides you.*

▶ **besides** *adv* in addition; also: *I don't really like the colour and besides, it's more than I can afford.* ○ *Peter is our youngest child, and we have three others besides.*

besiege /bɪ'siːdʒ/ *v* **1** to surround a place with armed forces in order to capture it or make the people in it SURRENDER: [Vn] *Troy was besieged by the Greeks.* **2(a)** to surround sb/sth closely; to crowd round sb/sth: [Vn] *The union spokesman was besieged by reporters.* **(b)** ~ **sb with sth** (usu passive) to make so many requests, complaints, etc to sb that they are unable to deal with them all: [Vnpr] *The BBC has been besieged with phone-calls and letters of complaint.*

besmirch /bɪ'smɜːtʃ/ (also **smirch**) *v* (*fml*) to damage the reputation of sb/sth in the opinion of others: [Vn] *besmirch sb's reputation/name/honour.*

besom /'biːzəm/ *n* a brush made by tying thin sticks to a long pole.

besotted /bɪ'sɒtɪd/ *adj* [pred] ~ **(by/with sb/sth)** made silly or stupid, esp by love for sb/sth: *He is totally besotted with the girl* (ie deeply in love with her).

besought *pt, pp* of BESEECH.

bespectacled /bɪ'spektəkld/ *adj* wearing spectacles.

bespoke /bɪ'spəʊk/ *adj* [usu attrib] (*Brit*) (*US* **custom-made**) **(a)** (of clothes) made specially according to the individual customer's requirements: *a bespoke suit.* **(b)** making such clothes: *a bespoke tailor.*

best¹ /best/ *adj* (superlative of GOOD¹) of the most excellent, desirable, suitable, etc type or quality: *my best friend* ○ *the best dinner I've ever had* ○ *The best thing to do would be to apologize.* ○ *The best thing about the party was the food.* ○ *He's the best man for the job.* ○ *What is the best make of tennis-racket?* ○ *the best-looking man she had ever met* ○ *the company's best-ever results* ○ *It's best to go by bus.* See also GOOD¹, BETTER¹. **IDM** **be on one's best be'haviour** to behave in the most polite or appropriate way one can. **one's best bet** (*infml*) the action or decision most likely to have the desired result: *Your best bet would be to call again tomorrow.* **one's best bib and 'tucker** (*dated or joc*) one's best clothes, worn only on special occasions. **one's best/strongest card** ⇨ CARD¹. **the best/better part of sth** ⇨ PART¹. **make the best use of sth** to use sth in the most profitable way that one can: *She's certainly made the best use of her opportunities.* **with the ˌbest will in the 'world** even if one makes the greatest effort; even though one would very much like to: *With the best will in the world, this job cannot be done in less than a week.*

■ **ˌbest 'man** *n* a male friend or relative of a BRIDE-GROOM who assists him at his wedding. Compare BRIDESMAID.

best² /best/ *adv* (superlative of WELL²) (often in compounds) **(a)** in the most excellent manner: *the best-dressed politician* ○ *the best-kept garden in the street* ○ *He works best in the mornings.* ○ *These insects are best seen through a microscope.* ○ *She's the person best able to cope.* **(b)** to the greatest degree; most: *his*

best-known/best-loved poem ○ *I enjoyed her first novel best (of all).* **(c)** in the most suitable way: *Some things are best kept secret.* ○ *Do as you think best* (ie what you think is the most suitable thing to do). **IDM** **as ˌbest one 'can** not perfectly but as well as one is able to: *The facilities were not ideal but we managed as best we could.* **for reasons/ some reason best known to oneself** ⇨ REASON¹. **had better/best** ⇨ BETTER². **know best** ⇨ KNOW.

■ **ˌbest 'seller** *n* a product, esp a book, that sells in very large numbers: *the best-seller list.* **ˌbest-'selling** *adj* having very large sales; very popular: *a ˌbest-selling 'novel/'author.*

best³ /best/ *n* [sing] **1** that which is most excellent or pleasant; the person or thing of the highest quality: *She wants the best of everything* (ie wants her life, possessions, etc to be perfect). ○ *When you pay that much for a meal you expect the best.* ○ *He was acting from the best of motives.* ○ *They're all good players, but she's the best of the lot/bunch.* ○ *He is among the best of our workers.* ○ *We're the best of friends* (ie very close friends). **2** that which is as close as possible to what is required or desired: *£50 is the best I can offer you.* ○ *The best we can hope for is that we don't lose money on the deal.* ○ *I've only done a temporary repair because that's the best I can manage.* **IDM** **all the 'best** (*infml*) (used esp when saying goodbye) I hope everything goes well for you; my best wishes to you: *Goodbye, and all the best!* ○ *Here's wishing you all the best in the coming year.* **at 'best** taking the most hopeful or favourable view: *We can't arrive before Friday at best.* ○ *His action was at best ill-advised.* **at its/one's best** in the best state or form: *modern architecture at its best* ○ *Chaplin was at his best playing the little tramp.* ○ *I wasn't feeling at my best at the party so I didn't enjoy it.* **(even) at the 'best of times** even when circumstances are most favourable: *He's bad-tempered at the best of times — he'll be even worse now!* **be (all) for the 'best** to be good in the end, although not at first seeming to be good: *Perhaps not getting that job will turn out to be all for the best — you might get one you prefer.* **the best of 'both worlds / all possible worlds** the benefits of widely differing situations, enjoyed at the same time: *She's a career woman and a mother, so she has/gets/enjoys the best of both worlds.* **the best of British (luck) (to sb)** (*Brit often ironic*) (used when wishing sb good luck in some activity, esp when they are thought unlikely to succeed). **the best of / good luck** ⇨ LUCK. **(play) the best of 'three, etc** (to play) up to three, five, etc games, the winner being the person who wins most of them: *We were playing the best of five but we stopped after three because John won them all.* **bring out the 'best/'worst in sb** to cause sb's best/worst qualities to be revealed: *The family crisis really brought out the best in her.* **do, try, etc one's (level/very) 'best ; do the best one 'can** to try as hard as possible: *I did my best to stop her.* ○ *It doesn't matter if you don't win — just try your best.* **(do, etc sth) for the 'best** with the intention of helping sb; intended to help sb: *I'm sorry my advice offended you — I meant it for the best.* **get/have the best of sth** to gain the greatest advantage from sth: *We certainly got the best of the deal.* **hope for the best** ⇨ HOPE. **look one's/its 'best** to look as beautiful, attractive, etc as possible: *The scenery looks its best in the autumn.* **make the best of sth/it/things/a bad job** to do the best one can and be as cheerful as possible in a bad or unpleasant situation: *We decided to make the best of a bad job and have our picnic despite the awful weather.* **one's Sunday best** ⇨ SUNDAY. **to the best of one's be'lief/'knowledge** as far as one knows, although one is not certain: *To the best of my knowledge she is still living there.* **with the 'best (of them)** as well as anyone: *At sixty he* *still plays tennis with the best of them.* **with the best of in'tentions** intending only to help or do good: *It was done with the best of intentions.*

best⁴ /best/ *v* [Vn] to defeat or do better than sb.

bestial /'bestiəl; *US* 'bestʃəl/ *adj (derog)* of or like a BEAST(2); cruel: *a bestial nature/act* ○ *bestial violence.* ▶ **bestiality** /,besti'æləti; *US* ,bestʃi-/ *n* [U] **1** the quality of being bestial: *an act of horrifying bestiality.* **2** sexual activity between a human and an animal.

bestir /bɪ'stɜ:(r)/ *v* (**-rr-**) ~ **oneself** *(fml or joc)* to become active or busy: [Vn] *If I might prevail on you to bestir yourself, there is work to be done.* [also Vn.to inf].

bestow /bɪ'stəʊ/ *v* ~ **sth** (**on sb**) *(fml)* to present sth as a gift to sb: [Vnpr] *an honour bestowed on her by the king* [also Vn].

bet /bet/ *v* (**-tt-**; *pt, pp* **bet** or **betted**) **1** ~ (**sth**) (**on/against sth**) to risk money on a race or on some other event of which the result is doubtful: [V] *I don't approve of betting.* [Vpr] *He spends all his money betting on horses.* ○ *'He'll be back.' 'I wouldn't bet on it* (ie It is rather unlikely)*.'* [Vnn] *She bet me $20 that I wouldn't be able to give up smoking.* [also Vnpr, V.that, Vn.that]. See also BETTING. **IDM** **bet one's bottom 'dollar (on sth / that...)** *(infml)* to be completely certain about sth: *You can bet your bottom dollar he won't have waited for us.* **I bet (that)...** *(infml)* I am certain (that sth will happen): *I bet he arrives late — he always does.* **you 'bet** *(infml)* you can be sure (of it): *'Are you going to the match?' 'You bet (I am)!'*
▶ **bet** *n* **1(a)** an arrangement to risk money, etc on an event of which the result is doubtful: *make a bet* ○ *have an each-way bet on the Derby* ○ *win/lose a bet* ○ *'Liverpool are bound to win.' 'Do you want a bet?* (ie I disagree with you)*.'* **(b)** money, etc risked in this way: *place/put a bet on a horse* ○ *I hear you're taking bets on whether she'll agree to marry him.* ○ *People felt that investing in property was a good/sure/safe bet.* **2** *(infml)* an opinion, esp one that is formed quickly or without much thought: *My bet is they've been held up in the traffic.* ○ *That seems like a fair bet.* **IDM** **a safe bet** ⇨ SAFE¹. **one's best bet** ⇨ BEST¹. **hedge one's bets** ⇨ HEDGE.

beta /'bi:tə; *US* 'beɪtə/ *n* the second letter of the Greek alphabet (B, β), often used to show that sth is second in a series or in rank: *He got a beta for his essay.* Compare ALPHA.

bête noire /,bet 'nwɑ:(r)/ *(pl* **bêtes noires** /,bet 'nwɑ:z/) *(French)* a person or thing that one particularly dislikes.

betide /bɪ'taɪd/ *v* **IDM** **woe betide sb** ⇨ WOE.

betoken /bɪ'təʊkən/ *v (fml)* to be a sign of sth; to indicate sth: [Vn] *milder weather betokening the arrival of spring.*

betray /bɪ'treɪ/ *v* **1** ~ **sb/sth** (**to sb**) to give or show sb/sth to an enemy: [Vn] *betray state secrets* [Vnpr] *Judas betrayed Jesus to the authorities.* **2** [Vn] **(a)** to show a lack of loyalty to sb/sth: *betray one's country/one's principles/one's wife* ○ *She felt cheated and betrayed.* **(b)** to act in a way that is not worthy of the trust, confidence, etc placed in one: *He should have returned the money; he has betrayed our trust.* **3** [Vn] **(a)** to show sth without intending to do so; to be a sign of sth: *She said she was sorry, but her eyes betrayed her secret delight.* ○ *His accent betrayed the fact that he was not English.* **(b)** ~ **oneself** to show what or who one really is: *He had a good disguise, but as soon as he spoke he betrayed himself* (ie he was recognized by his voice)*.*
▶ **betrayal** /bɪ'treɪəl/ *n* **(a)** [U] the action of betraying sb/sth or the fact of being betrayed: *feel a sense of isolation and betrayal.* **(b)** [C] an instance of this: *a cowardly betrayal of his friends.*

betrothal /bɪ'trəʊðl/ *n* ~ (**to sb**) *(fml or dated)* an agreement to be married.

betrothed /bɪ'trəʊðd/ *adj (fml or dated)* engaged to be married: *the betrothed couple.* ▶ **betrothed** *n* [sing]: *dreaming of his betrothed.*

better¹ /'betə(r)/ *adj* (comparative of GOOD¹) **1(a)** more excellent or desirable: *a better worker/job/car* ○ *He was in a much/far better mood than usual.* ○ *The weather couldn't have been better.* ○ *I liked last week's programme, but this week's was even better.* ○ *Life was difficult then but things have got better and better over the years.* ○ *There's nothing better than a good hot bath before bedtime.* **(b)** more skilled: *She's better at science than me.* **(c)** more suitable; clearer: *Having talked to everyone involved I now have a better idea (of) what happened.* ○ *Can't you think of a better word than 'nice' to describe your trip?* See also BEST¹. **2** partly or fully recovered from an illness: *I'm (feeling) much better today, thanks.* ○ *His ankle is getting better.* See also WELL² 1. Compare WORSE 2. **IDM** **against one's better 'judgement** even though one feels that it may be unwise: *He agreed, much against his better judgement.* **the best/better part of sth** ⇨ PART¹. **one's better 'half** *(infml joc)* one's wife or husband. **better luck 'next time** *(saying)* (used to encourage sb after they have not succeeded at sth). **discretion is the better part of valour** ⇨ DISCRETION. **have seen/known better 'days** to be poorer or in a worse state now than formerly: *That coat has seen better days.* **(be) little/no better than** (to be) almost the same as: *He's no better than a common thief.* **prevention is better than cure** ⇨ PREVENTION. **that's better** (said to sb who is upset when they are trying to become calmer, to encourage them): *Dry your eyes. That's better.* **two heads are better than one** ⇨ HEAD.

better² /'betə(r)/ *adv* (comparative of WELL²) **1** in a more pleasant, efficient, desirable, etc way: *You would write better if you had a good pen.* ○ *She sings better than I do.* **2** to a greater degree; more: *I like him better than her.* ○ *You'll like the play better when you understand it more.* ○ *The better I know her, the more I admire her.* ○ *He's looking for a better-paid job.* **3** (used to suggest that it would be a good idea to do sth): *His advice is better ignored.* ○ *Some things are better left unsaid.* **IDM** **be better 'off 1** to be happier or more at ease in a specified state or position: *We'd be better off without him as a partner.* ○ *She'd be better off in an old people's home, really.* **2** to have more money: *We could afford a car if we were better off.* **be better off doing sth** to be wiser to do sth specified: *He'd be better off going to the police about it.* **better the devil you 'know (than the devil you 'don't)** *(saying)* it is wiser to deal with an undesirable but familiar person, situation, etc than to risk a change which may make things worse. **better late than 'never** *(saying)* **1** (used as an excuse or apology when one is late). **2** some success, however delayed or small it is, is better than none at all. **better safe than 'sorry** *(saying)* it is wiser to be very cautious and take extra care than to be in a hurry and careless, and so do sth which one may regret. **do better to do sth** to be more sensible if one does sth: *Don't buy now — you'd do better to wait for the sales.* **go one 'better (than sb/sth)** to do better (than sb/sth); to outdo sb/sth: *I bought a small boat, then he went one better and bought a yacht.* **had better/best** would be wise to: *You'd better not say that.* ○ *Hadn't we better take an umbrella?* ○ *I had better* (ie I think I should) *begin by introducing myself.* ○ *'I promise I'll pay you back tomorrow.' 'You'd better.'* (ie as a threat). ➤ note at SHOULD. **know better** ⇨ KNOW. **not know any better** ⇨ KNOW. **old enough to know better** ⇨ OLD. **think better of it / of doing st** ⇨ THINK¹. **think better of sb** ⇨ THINK¹.

better[3] /'betə(r)/ n [U] that which is better: *I ex-pected better of him* (ie I thought he would have behaved better). **IDM** **(feel/be) (all) the better for sth** (to feel/be) in a better physical or mental state because of sth: *You'll feel all the better for (having had) a holiday.* **a change for the better/worse** ⇨ CHANGE[2]. **for ,better or 'worse** whether the result is good or bad: *It's done, and, for better or worse, we can't change it now.* **get the better of sb/sth** to defeat sb/sth: *You always get the better of me at chess.* ○ *His shyness got the better of him* (ie He was so shy he could not speak, take action, etc at that moment). **get the better of sth** to win in an argument, etc: *She always gets the better of our quarrels.* **the less/least said (about sb/sth) the better** (*saying*) that person or thing is an unpleasant sub-ject and it is better not to talk about her/him/it. **so much the ,better/'worse (for sb/sth)** that is even better/worse: *The result is not very important to us, but if we do win, (then) so much the better.* **the sooner the better** ⇨ SOON. **think (all) the better of sb** ⇨ THINK[1].

better[4] /'betə(r)/ v [Vn] **1(a)** to do better than sth; to SURPASS sth: *This achievement cannot be bettered.* **(b)** to improve sth: *The government hopes to better the conditions of the workers.* **2** ~ **oneself** to get a better social position or status.
  ▶ **betterment** n [U] (*fml*) the process of becoming or making sth/sb better; improvement, esp of a person or of people generally.

better[5] /'betə(r)/ n a person who bets (BET).

betting /'betɪŋ/ n [U] the action of risking money on sth of which the result is doubtful: *illegal betting.* **IDM** **what's the betting ... ?** (*infml*) it seems likely that...: *What's the betting it'll rain tomorrow?*
  ■ **'betting-shop** n (*Brit*) the shop where one can bet. See also BOOKMAKER.

between /bɪ'twiːn/ prep **1(a)** in or into the space separating two or more points, objects, people, etc: *Q comes between P and R in the English alphabet.* ○ *Peter sat between Mary and Jane.* ○ *Switzerland lies between France, Germany, Austria and Italy.* ○ *The spoon fell between the cooker and the cupboard.* ○ *I lost my keys somewhere between the car and the house.* ○ (*fig*) *My job is somewhere between a typist and a personal assistant.* **(b)** in the period of time separating two days, years, events, etc: *It's cheaper between 6 pm and 8 am.* ○ *I'm usually free between Tuesday and Thursday.* ○ *Children must attend school between 5 and 16.* ○ *Many changes took place between the two world wars.* **2** at some point along a scale from one amount, weight, distance, etc to an-other: *cost between one and two pounds* ○ *weigh between nine and ten kilos* ○ *I'd estimate that London is between fifty and sixty miles from Oxford.* ○ *The temperature remained between 25°C and 30°C all week.* **3** (of a line) separating one place from an-other: *build a wall between my garden and my neighbour's* ○ *draw a line between sections A and B* ○ *the border between Sweden and Norway.* **4** from one place to another: *fly between Rome and Paris twice daily* ○ *sail between Dover and Calais* ○ *a good road between Tokyo and Kyoto.* **5** (indicating a connec-tion or relationship): *a clear difference/distinction/contrast between two things* ○ *an obvious link between unemployment and the crime rate* ○ *the bond between a boy and his dog* ○ *They have settled the dispute between them.* ○ *the affection/friendship/love between people.* **6(a)** shared by two people or things: *We drank a bottle of wine between us.* ○ *This is just between you and me/between ourselves* (ie It is a secret). ○ *They carried only one rucksack between them.* ○ *negotiations between management and unions.* **(b)** by the actions or contributions of a number of people or things: *They wrote the book*

between them. ○ *Between them they raised £500.* ○ *We can afford to buy a house between us.* ⇨ note at AMONG.
  ▶ **between** (also **in between**) adv **(a)** in or into the space separating two or more points, objects, people, etc: *You'd have a good view of the sea from here except for the hotels in between.* **(b)** in the period of time separating two dates, events, etc: *We have two lessons this morning, but there's some free time in between.*

betwixt /bɪ'twɪkst/ adv, prep **IDM** **be,twixt and be'tween** in a middle position; neither one thing nor the other: *It's difficult buying clothes for ten-year-olds — at that age they're betwixt and between.*

bevel /'bevl/ n **1** a slop-ing edge or surface, eg at the side of a picture frame or a sheet of glass. ⇨ picture. **2** a tool for making sloping edges or surfaces on wood or stone.
  ▶ **bevel** v (**-ll-**; *US* **-l-**) to give a sloping edge to sth: [Vn] *bevelled edges.*

bevel

bevel

beverage /'bevərɪdʒ/ n (*fml or joc*) any type of drink except water, eg milk, tea, wine, beer: *al-coholic beverages.*

bevy /'bevi/ n a large group: *a bevy of beautiful girls.*

bewail /bɪ'weɪl/ v (*fml or joc*) to express sorrow about sth; to complain about sth: [Vn] *bewailing one's lost youth/innocence* ○ *bewail the falling stand-ard of service.*

beware /bɪ'weə(r)/ v ~ (**of sb/sth**) (used only in the infinitive and imperative) to be cautious of sb/sth; to take care about sb/sth: [Vpr] *He told us to beware of pickpockets/the dog/icy roads.* [V] *Beware — wet paint!*

bewilder /bɪ'wɪldə(r)/ v to confuse sb: [Vn] *The noise and the crowds bewildered her.* ○ *I am totally bewildered by these crossword clues.*
  ▶ **bewildering** /bɪ'wɪldərɪŋ/ adj confusing: *a bewil-dering array/range/variety of dishes to choose from* ○ *fashions changing with bewildering rapidity.* **bewil-deringly** adv.
  bewilderment n [U] the state of being bewildered: *watch/listen/gape in (utter) bewilderment.*

bewitch /bɪ'wɪtʃ/ v [Vn] **1** to put a magic spell on sb: [Vn] *The wicked fairy bewitched the prince and turned him into a frog.* **2** to attract or delight sb very much: [Vn] *He was bewitched by her beauty.*
  ▶ **bewitching** adj very attractive and delightful: *a bewitching smile/girl/performance.*

beyond /bɪ'jɒnd/ prep **1** at or to the further side of sth: *The new housing project stretches beyond the playing-fields.* ○ *The road continues beyond the vil-lage up into the hills.* **2** later than a specified time: *It won't go on beyond midnight.* ○ *I know what I'll be doing for the next three weeks but I haven't thought beyond that.* ○ *We're planning for the year 2000 and beyond.* **3** more than sth; apart from sth: *Our suc-cess was far beyond what we thought possible.* ○ *I didn't notice anything beyond her rather strange ac-cent.* ○ *He's living beyond his means* (ie spending more than he earns). ○ *She's got nothing beyond her state pension.* ○ *That's (going) beyond a joke* (ie That is no longer funny). **4** without the possibility of sth: *The bicycle is beyond repair* (ie is too badly damaged to repair). ○ *After 25 years the town centre had changed beyond (all) recognition.* ○ *They're paying $75 000 for a small apartment — it's beyond belief.* ○ *The situation is beyond our control.* **IDM** **be beyond sb** (*infml*) to be impossible for sb to imagine, under-stand or do: *It's beyond me why she wants to marry*

Jeff. ○ *How people design computer games is beyond me.* ○ *Carrying all three suitcases was beyond me.*
▶ **beyond** *adv* at or to the further side; further on: *Snowdon and the mountains beyond were covered in snow.* ○ *The immediate future is clear, but it's hard to tell what lies beyond.*

bezique /bɪˈziːk/ *n* [U] a card-game for two people played with a double pack[1](7) of 64 cards.

bi- *pref* (forming *ns* and *adjs*) two; twice: *biplane* ○ *bicentenary* ○ *biannual* ○ *bilingual.* Compare DI-, TRI-.

NOTE note that **bi-** is used with certain expressions of time (eg *bimonthly*) to mean both 'every two' (months) and 'twice a' (month). There is a distinction between *biennial* (every two years) and *biannual* (twice a year).

biannual /baɪˈænjuəl/ *adj* occurring twice a year: *a biannual meeting.* Compare BIENNIAL. ▶ **biannually** *adv.*

bias /ˈbaɪəs/ *n* [U, C usu *sing*] **1** an opinion or feeling that strongly favours one side in an argument or one thing in a group, sometimes unfairly; a prejudice: *The university has a bias towards/in favour of/ against the sciences.* ○ *The committee is of a conservative bias.* ○ *A judge should be completely without bias.* **2** an edge cut diagonally (DIAGONAL) across the threads of a piece of cloth: *The skirt is cut on the bias.*
▶ **bias** *v* (**-s-, -ss-**) ~ **sb** (**towards/in favour of/ against sb/sth**) to influence sb, esp unfairly, so that they have a bias: [Vnpr] *The newspapers have bias(s)ed people against her.* [also Vn]. **biased** (also **biassed**) *adj* showing a bias: *a bias(s)ed account/ jury* ○ *He is clearly bias(s)ed in the government's favour.*

bib /bɪb/ *n* **1** a piece of cloth or plastic that is fixed under a child's chin to protect its clothes while it is eating. **2** the front part of an APRON(1), above the waist. **IDM** **one's best bib and tucker** ⇨ BEST[1].

bible /ˈbaɪbl/ *n* (**a**) (also the **Bible**) the sacred writings of the Christian Church, consisting of the Old Testament and the New Testament. (**b**) [C] a copy of these: *a leather-bound bible.* (**c**) [C] any book that a person values and often uses: *the stamp-collector's bible.*
▶ **biblical** /ˈbɪblɪkl/ *adj* of or in the Bible: *a biblical theme/expression* ○ *biblical times/language.*
■ **ˈBible-bashing** *n* [U] (*infml derog*) the vigorous expression of Christian beliefs.

biblio- *comb form* (forming *ns* and *adjs*) of books: *bibliophile* ○ *bibliographical.*

bibliography /ˌbɪbliˈɒɡrəfi/ *n* **1** [C] a list of books or articles about a particular subject or by a particular author: *There is a useful bibliography at the end of each chapter.* **2** [U] the study of the history of books and their production. ▶ **bibliographer** /-ˈɒɡrəfə(r)/ *n.* **bibliographical** /ˌbɪbliəˈɡræfɪkl/ *adj.*

bibliophile /ˈbɪbliəfaɪl/ *n* a person who loves or collects books.

bibulous /ˈbɪbjʊləs/ *adj* (*joc or rhet*) excessively fond of alcoholic drink.

bicameral /ˌbaɪˈkæmərəl/ *adj* (*techn*) having two main parts of parliament (eg in Britain the House of Commons and the House of Lords): *a bicameral system of government.*

bicarb /ˈbaɪkɑːb/ *n* [U] (*infml*) = SODIUM BICARBONATE.

bicarbonate /ˌbaɪˈkɑːbənət/ *n* [U] (*chemistry*) a salt containing a double proportion of carbon dioxide (CARBON).
■ **biˌcarbonate of ˈsoda** *n* [U] = SODIUM BICARBONATE.

bicentenary /ˌbaɪsenˈtiːnəri; US -ˈten-/ *n* a 200th anniversary; a celebration of this: *1989 was the bicentenary of the French Revolution.* ○ *bicentenary celebrations.*

bicentennial /ˌbaɪsenˈteniəl/ *adj* happening once in 200 years; marking a BICENTENARY: *a bicentennial anniversary/celebration.* ▶ **bicentennial** *n* = BICENTENARY.

biceps /ˈbaɪseps/ *n* (*pl* unchanged) the large muscle at the front of the upper arm, which bends the elbow: *His biceps are impressive.* Compare TRICEPS.

bicker /ˈbɪkə(r)/ *v* ~ (**with sb**) (**over/about sth**) to argue about unimportant things: [V, Vpr] *The children are always bickering (with each other) (over their toys).*

bicycle /ˈbaɪsɪkl/ *n* a vehicle with two wheels on which a person rides, using pedals (PEDAL 1) to drive it along: *Can you ride a bicycle?* ⇨ picture. See also BIKE 1, CYCLE 3.
▶ **bicycle** *v* to ride on a bicycle: [V] *a bicycling holiday* [Vpr] *We bicycled to town.* [also Vp].
bicyclist *n* a person who rides a bicycle.
■ **bicycle-clip** *n* each of a pair of clips (CLIP[1] 1) for holding trousers at the ankles while riding a bicycle. ⇨ picture at CLIP[1].

bicycle

1 backstays	24 reflector
2 bell	25 rim
3 brake	26 saddle (*esp US* seat)
4 brake-cable	27 spoke
5 brake lever	28 sprocket
6 carrying rack	29 tyre (*US* tire)
7 chain	30 valve
8 chain-wheel	31 wheel
9 crank	
10 crossbar	
11 dynamo	
12 forks	
13 frame	
14 front light	
15 gear-lever	
16 gears	
17 handlebars	
18 hub	
19 mud-flap	
20 mudguard	
21 pedal	
22 pump	
23 rear light	

bid¹ /bɪd/ v (-dd-; pt, pp bid; in sense 3, pt usu bade /beɪd, bæd/; pp bidden /ˈbɪdn/) **1** ~ (sth) (for sth); (esp US) ~ (sth) (on sth) (**a**) to offer a price in order to buy sth, esp at an AUCTION: [Vn, Vpr] What am I bid (for this painting)? ○ She bid £500 (for the painting). [Vnpr] We had hoped to get the house but another couple was bidding against us (ie repeatedly offering a higher price than us). [also V]. (**b**) to offer a price for doing work, providing a service, etc: [Vpr] Several firms have bid for the contract to build the new concert hall. [also V, Vn, Vnpr]. **2** (in certain card-games) to make a bid²(4): [Vn] bid two hearts [also V]. **3** (arch or fml) (**a**) to order sb; to tell sb: [Vn.inf (no to), Vn.to inf] She bade me (to) come in. [Vn] Do as you are bidden. (**b**) to invite sb: [Vnpr, Vn.to inf] guests bidden to (attend) the feast. (**c**) ~ sth to sb (no passive) to say sth as a greeting, etc: [Vnn] bid sb good morning [Vnpr] He bade farewell (ie said goodbye) to his sweetheart. **IDM** bid fair to do sth (arch or rhet) to seem likely to do sth: The plan for a new hospital bids fair to succeed.
▶ **biddable** adj ready to obey: She is a placid and biddable child.

bidder n a person or group that bids at an AUCTION: The house went to the highest bidder (ie the person who offered the most money).

bidding n [U] **1** (fml) an order or request: do sb's bidding (ie obey sb) ○ At his father's bidding (ie Because his father requested it) he wrote to his lawyer. **2** the offering of prices at an AUCTION or in business: Bidding was brisk (ie Many offers were made one after the other). ○ Several UK companies are **in the bidding** (ie offering prices). **3** (in certain card-games) the process of bidding (BID¹ 2): Can you remind me of the bidding (ie who bid what)?

bid² /bɪd/ n **1** a price offered in order to buy sth at an AUCTION or in business: make a bid of £50 for a painting ○ Any higher/further bids? ○ a **takeover bid** for the company. **2** (esp US) = TENDER² n. **3** an effort to do, obtain, achieve, etc sth; an attempt: They failed in their bid to reach the summit. ○ make a bid for power/popular support. **4** a statement of the number of tricks (TRICK 5) a player proposes to win in a card-game: 'It's your bid next.' 'No bid.'

bide /baɪd/ v (arch) = ABIDE. **IDM** bide one's ˈtime to wait for a good opportunity: His political rivals are biding their time until after the election for a chance to attack his policies.

bidet /ˈbiːdeɪ; US bɪˈdeɪ/ n a low bowl for washing the bottom and genitals (GENITAL).

biennial /baɪˈenɪəl/ adj happening every second year: a biennial film festival. Compare BIANNUAL.
▶ **biennial** n a plant that lives for two years, producing flowers in the second year.
biennially adv.

bier /bɪə(r)/ n a frame on which a COFFIN or a dead body is carried or placed before burial.

biff /bɪf/ n (infml) a sharp blow, esp with the FIST: She gave me a biff on the ear.
▶ **biff** v (infml) to hit or strike sb: [Vn] biff sb on the nose.

bifocal /ˌbaɪˈfəʊkl/ adj (esp of spectacles) having lenses (LENS) with two parts, one for looking at distant objects and one for looking at close objects.
▶ **bifocals** n [pl] spectacles that are bifocal: a pair of bifocals.

bifurcate /ˈbaɪfəkeɪt/ v [V] (fml) (of roads, rivers, branches of trees, etc) to divide into or have two branches: to FORK v(2). ▶ **bifurcation** /ˌbaɪfəˈkeɪʃn/ n [C, U].

big /bɪg/ adj (-gger, -ggest) **1** large in size, extent or intensity: a big garden/man/majority/defeat/ explosion/argument ○ the big toe (ie the largest). ⇨ picture at FOOT¹. ○ a big 'g' (ie a capital G) ○ (infml) big money (ie a lot of money) ○ the big screen (ie the cinema) ○ The bigger (ie the worse) the crime, the longer

the jail sentence. ○ He's the biggest liar (ie He tells more lies than anyone else) I know. ○ She's a big eater/spender (ie She eats/spends a lot). ○ He uses a lot of big (ie long or unusual) words. Compare SMALL. ⇨ note. **2** (more) grown up: my big sister (ie my older sister) ○ Don't cry — you're a big boy now! **3** [attrib] important: the big match ○ a big decision ○ the biggest moment of my life. **4** (infml) ambitious and grand: have big ideas/plans. **5** (infml esp US) popular with the public: Video games are big this year. ○ A lot of British bands are big in Japan. **6** ~ on sth (infml esp US) enthusiastic about sth; keen on sth: The firm is big on staff training programmes. **7** ~ of sb (esp ironic) (not) generous of sb: It's very big of you to help, now that I've almost finished! **IDM** be/get too big for one's boots (infml) to be/ become too proud of oneself; to be/become conceited (CONCEIT). a ˌbig ˈcheese (sl derog) a very important and powerful person. ˌbig ˈdeal! (infml ironic) I am not impressed: We're getting a wage increase of £40 a year, before tax. Big deal! a big fish (in a little pond) an important and influential person (in a small community). a big noise/shot/name (infml) an important person. the big stick the threat of using force, esp of great military strength. the big three, four, etc the three, four, etc most important nations, people, companies, things, etc: a meeting of the big five. the ˈbig time (infml) the highest or most successful level in a profession, etc, esp in entertainment. sb's eyes are bigger than their stomach ⇨ EYE¹. give sb/get a big ˈhand to APPLAUD(1) sb/be applauded loudly and generously: Let's all give her a big hand. have bigger / other fish to fry ⇨ FISH¹. have a big mouth to boast a lot or talk too much. in a big/small way ⇨ WAY¹.
▶ **big** adv (sl) **1** in a big or impressive way: We need to think big. ○ He likes to talk big (ie to boast). **2** successfully: a band which comes/goes over big with pop fans worldwide.

bigness n [U].

■ **the ˌBig ˈApple** n [sing] (US sl) New York City: I've worked in the Big Apple for 20 years.

ˌbig ˈbang n (usu sing) the explosion that some scientists suggest created the universe: the big bang theory.

ˌBig ˈBrother n a leader or government that has absolute control over every aspect of people's lives while pretending to act in their interests.

ˌbig ˈbusiness n [U] commerce on a very large financial scale.

the ˌBig ˈDipper n (US) = PLOUGH 2.

ˌbig ˈdipper n (Brit) a narrow railway at a FAIR³(1) with a track that rises and falls steeply. See also ROLLER-COASTER.

ˌbig ˈend n (in an engine) the end of a connecting rod that fits around the CRANKSHAFT.

ˌbig ˈgame n [U] larger animals hunted for sport.

ˈbig-head n (infml) a person who has too high an opinion of her or his own importance. **big-ˈheaded** adj.

ˌbig-ˈhearted adj very kind; generous.

ˌbig ˈtop n the main tent at a CIRCUS(1).

ˌbig ˈwheel n = FERRIS WHEEL.

NOTE You can use big or large to describe animals, objects, places, etc. Big is more common in speaking: They live in a big/large house. ○ Which is the biggest/largest desert in the world? ○ a big/large crowd of people.

Big can be used to describe people, especially children: He wasn't a very big baby. You also usually use big when talking about clothes: The skirt doesn't fit — it's too big.

Large is used for sizes of things you buy: Small, medium or large — the T-shirts are all the same price. ○ A burger and large fries, please. Large is sometimes used as a polite word for 'fat': She's rather a large woman.

B

A large number/amount/quantity of something can also be a more formal way of saying 'a lot of': *They spent a large amount of money on their daughter's wedding.*

You use **great** to describe somebody or something that is important or has an impressive quality: *a great artist* ○ *the great Pacific Ocean* ○ *Peter the Great was a Russian ruler.* **Great** can be used with uncountable nouns: *It gives me great pleasure to announce the winner.* ○ *He was in great pain.*

Great big is more informal and means 'very big': *A great big dog came running towards us.*

bigamy /ˈbɪgəmi/ *n* [U] the crime of marrying when one is still legally married to sb else.
▶ **bigamist** *n* a person who is guilty of bigamy.
bigamous /ˈbɪgəməs/ *adj* guilty of bigamy; involving bigamy: *a bigamous marriage.* **bigamously** *adv.*

bight /baɪt/ *n* a long inward curve in a coast: *the Great Australian Bight.*

bigot /ˈbɪgət/ *n* a person who has strong and unreasonable(2) beliefs and opinions, especially about religion or politics, and will not listen to or accept the opinions of anyone who disagrees: *religious bigots.*
▶ **bigoted** *adj* showing that one refuses to listen to or accept the opinions of others: *bigoted views* ○ *He is so bigoted that it is impossible to argue with him.*
bigotry *n* [U] a bigoted attitude or bigoted behaviour.

bigwig /ˈbɪgwɪg/ *n* (*infml*) an important person.

bijou /ˈbiːʒuː/ *n* (*pl* **bijoux** /ˈbiːʒuː/) (*French*) a jewel.
▶ **bijou** *adj* [attrib] (*sometimes derog or ironic*) (of a building) small and elegant: *They live in what an estate agent might refer to as a bijou residence.*

bike /baɪk/ *n* (*infml*) **1** a bicycle. **2** a motor cycle (MOTOR). Compare CYCLE 3. **IDM on your bike!** (*Brit sl*) (used as a command) go away!
▶ **bike** *v* [V] (*infml*) to ride a bicycle or motor cycle (MOTOR): [V] *Let's go biking.*

biker /ˈbaɪkə(r)/ *n* a young person who rides a motor cycle (MOTOR), often as a member of a gang: *a biker's leather jacket.*

bikini /bɪˈkiːni/ *n* a costume with two pieces worn by women for swimming and lying in the sun: *a bikini top* (ie the top half of a bikini).

bilabial /ˌbaɪˈleɪbiəl/ *n* (*phonetics*) a speech sound produced by using both lips: *In English, b, p and m are bilabials.* ▶ **bilabial** *adj.*

bilateral /ˌbaɪˈlætərəl/ *adj* having two sides; affecting or involving two groups, countries, etc: *a bilateral agreement/treaty.* Compare MULTILATERAL, UNILATERAL. ▶ **bilaterally** *adv.*

bilberry /ˈbɪlbəri; *US* -beri/ (also **whortleberry**, *Brit* **blaeberry**) *n* (**a**) a small N European SHRUB that grows on hills and in mountain woods. (**b**) its edible dark blue berry. Compare BLUEBERRY.

bile /baɪl/ *n* [U] **1** the bitter yellow liquid produced by the LIVER(1) to help the body to DIGEST²(1a) fats. **2** bad temper: *He unleashed a torrent of bile* (ie angry criticism).

bilge /bɪldʒ/ *n* **1** [C] the almost flat part of the bottom of a ship, inside or outside. **2** (also **bilge-water**) [U] dirty water that collects in a ship's bilge. **3** [U] (*sl*) worthless ideas or talk; nonsense: *Don't talk such bilge!*

bilingual /ˌbaɪˈlɪŋgwəl/ *adj* **1**(**a**) able to speak two languages equally well: *He is bilingual (in French and Spanish).* (**b**) having or using two languages: *a bilingual community.* **2** expressed or written in two languages: *a bilingual dictionary.* Compare MONOLINGUAL, MULTILINGUAL.

bilious /ˈbɪliəs/ *adj* **1** feeling sick or making one feel sick: *I feel a little bilious after last night's dinner.* ○ *a bilious attack/headache.* **2** bad-tempered. **3** of

an unpleasant colour (similar to BILE(1)): *a bilious (shade of) green.* ▶ **biliousness** *n* [U].

bill¹ /bɪl/ *n* **1** a written statement of money owed for goods or services supplied: *telephone/gas/heating bills* ○ *a bill for £5* ○ *Have you paid the bill?* **2** a written or printed notice; a POSTER(a). **3** a programme of entertainment (at a cinema, theatre, etc): *a horror double bill* (ie programme consisting of two horror films) *on TV.* **4** a written plan for a proposed new law, presented to parliament for discussion: *propose/pass/throw out/amend a bill* ○ *the Industrial Relations Bill.* **5** (*US*) = NOTE¹ 4: *a ten-dollar bill.* **IDM a clean bill of health** ⇨ CLEAN¹. **fill/fit the bill** to be adequate or suitable for a specific purpose: *If you're very hungry a double helping of spaghetti should fit the bill!* **foot the bill** ⇨ FOOT². **head/top the bill** to be the most important item or person on a list or a programme of entertainments: *She topped the bill at the London Palladium.* **pick up the bill/tab** ⇨ PICK¹.
▶ **bill** *v* **1** ~ **sb** (**for sth**) to send sb a bill for sth: [Vn, Vnpr] *I can't pay for the books now. Will you bill me (for them) later?* **2** ~ **sb/sth as sth** to announce or advertise sb/sth as sth: [Vn-n] *It is billed as the country's biggest sports event.* ○ *She was billed as 'The Queen of Comedy'.* [also Vn-adj].
■ **bill of ex'change** *n* a written order to pay money to a named person on a given date.
bill of 'fare *n* (*dated*) a list of dishes that can be ordered in a restaurant; MENU(1).
bill of 'lading *n* a list giving details of a ship's cargo.
bill of 'rights *n* a statement of the basic rights of the citizens of a country: *the Bill of Rights of the US Constitution.*
bill of 'sale *n* an official document recording the sale of personal property.

bill² /bɪl/ *n* **1** a bird's beak¹. **2** (esp in place-names) a narrow piece of land going out into the sea: *Portland Bill.*
▶ **bill** *v* **IDM bill and 'coo** (*infml*) (of lovers) to kiss and speak in a loving way to each other.

billboard /ˈbɪlbɔːd/ *n* (*esp US*) a large outdoor board for advertisements; a HOARDING(1).

billet /ˈbɪlɪt/ *n* a place, often a private house, provided for soldiers to live in temporarily, esp during a war: *The troops are all in billets* (ie not in camp or BARRACKS(1)).
▶ **billet** *v* ~ **sb** (**on/with sb**) (esp passive) to find soldiers accommodation, esp in a private house, often by ordering the owner to accept them: [Vnpr] *The soldiers were billeted with a farmer.* [also Vn].

billet-doux /ˌbɪleɪ ˈduː/ *n* (*pl* **billets-doux** /ˌbɪleɪ ˈduːz/) (*joc*) a love-letter (LOVE¹).

billfold /ˈbɪlfəʊld/ *n* (*US*) = WALLET.

billhook /ˈbɪlhʊk/ *n* a tool with a long handle and a curved blade used for cutting the small branches off trees, etc.

billiards /ˈbɪliədz/ *n* [sing *v*] a game for two people played with cues (CUE²) and three balls on a long table covered with green cloth: *have a game of billiards.*
▶ **billiard-** /ˈbɪliəd-/ (in compounds) of or used for billiards: *a billiard-cue/-room/-table.*

billion /ˈbɪljən/ *pron, det* **1** 1 000 000 000; one thousand million(s). **2** (*Brit*) (formerly) 1 000 000 000 000; one million million(s).
▶ **billion** *n* (*pl* unchanged or **billions**) **1** the number 1 000 000 000. **2** (*Brit*) (formerly) the number 1 000 000 000 000.
For further guidance on how *billion* is used, see the examples at *hundred.*

billionaire /ˌbɪljəˈneə(r)/ *n* (*fem* **billionairess** /ˌbɪljəˈneərəs/) a person who has a thousand million pounds, dollars, etc; a very rich person.

billow /'bɪləʊ/ n **1** (*arch*) a large wave²(1). **2** a moving mass of smoke, steam, etc like a wave.
▶ **billow** v to rise or roll like waves: [V] *billowing clouds* [Vpr, Vp] *sails billowing (out) in the wind* [Vpr] *Smoke billowed from the burning houses.*

billy /'bɪli/ (also **'billycan**) n a metal can with a lid and handle used by campers (CAMP¹) for cooking.

billy-goat /'bɪli gəʊt/ n a male goat. ⇨ picture at GOAT. Compare NANNY-GOAT.

billy-oh (also **'billy-o**) /'bɪli əʊ/ n **IDM** **like 'billy-oh** (*dated Brit infml*) very much, hard, strongly, etc: *go/ work/run like billy-oh* ○ *It was raining like billy-oh.*

bimbo /'bɪmbəʊ/ n (*pl* **-os** *or* **-oes**) **1** (*Brit derog*) an attractive young woman, esp one who is not very intelligent: *in the company of a glamorous bimbo half his age.* **2** (*US derog*) a foolish or stupid person: *This office is run by a bunch of bimbos.*

bimonthly /ˌbaɪ'mʌnθli/ adj produced or happening every second month or twice a month: *a bimonthly journal/event.*

bin /bɪn/ n a large container, usu with a lid, for storing bread, flour, coal, etc or for putting rubbish in: *a 'bread bin.* See also DUSTBIN.
▶ **bin** v (**-nn-**) (*Brit infml*) to throw sth away as rubbish: [Vn] *Shall I bin these old newspapers?*
■ **'bin-liner** n a (usu plastic) bag for lining a rubbish bin.

binary /'baɪnəri/ adj of or involving a pair or pairs: *binary codes/numbers/opposites.*
■ ˌbinary 'digit n either the number 0 or the number 1, as used in the binary system.
'**binary system** n a system of numbers, common in computing, using only the two numbers 0 and 1.

bind /baɪnd/ v (*pt, pp* **bound** /baʊnd/) **1** ~ **A** (**to B**); ~ **A and B** (**together**) (**a**) to tie or fasten sb/sth, eg with rope: [Vn, Vnpr] *The hostages were bound (with ropes) and gagged.* [Vn, Vnpr] *They bound his legs (together) so he couldn't escape.* [Vnpr] *He was bound to a chair.* (**b**) to make people or things together; to unite people or things: [Vnpr] *the feelings that bind him to her* [Vnp] *attempts to bind East and West Germany more closely together* [also Vn]. **2** ~ **sth** (**up**) to tie a long narrow piece of material round sth: [Vn, Vnp] *bind (up)* (ie fasten a BANDAGE so as to cover) *a wound.* **3** ~ **sth** (**in sth**) to fasten sheets of paper between covers: [Vn] *bind a book* ○ *a well-bound book* [Vnpr] *two volumes bound in leather.* **4** ~ **sth** (**with sth**) to cover the edge of sth in order to strengthen it or as a decoration: [Vnpr] *bind the cuffs of a jacket with leather* [Vn] *bind the edge of a carpet.* **5** to stick together or make sth stick together in a solid mass: [V, Vn] *Add an egg yolk to the flour and fat to make it bind/to bind the mixture.* **6** ~ **sb** (**to sth**) (esp passive) to make it a duty or legal obligation for sb to do sth: [Vnpr] *They were bound to secrecy* (ie made to promise to keep sth secret). [Vn.*to* inf] *bind sb to pay a debt* [also Vn]. **IDM** **bind/ tie sb hand and foot** ⇨ HAND¹. **PHRV** **bind sb over** (**to keep the peace**) (*law*) to warn sb that they will be made to appear in court again if they break the law: *The judge bound him over (to keep the peace) for a year.*
▶ **bind** n [sing] (*infml*) an annoying situation or restriction: *It's a hell of a bind having to stay indoors on a nice day like this.*

binder n **1** a cover for holding sheets of paper, magazines, etc together: *a ring binder.* **2** a person who puts covers on books; a BOOKBINDER. **3** a machine that binds (BIND 1) corn into sheaves (SHEAF 2) after cutting it.

binding n **1** [C] a strong covering holding the pages of a book together: *books in fine leather bindings.* **2** [C, U] fabric used for binding (BIND 4) edges, eg BRAID(1). — adj ~ (**on/upon sb**) placing a legal obligation on sb: *The agreement is binding on both parties.*

bindweed /'baɪndwiːd/ n [U] a type of wild plant that twists itself round other plants; wild CONVOLVULUS.

binge /bɪndʒ/ n (*infml*) **1** a time of wild or excessive eating and drinking: *He went on/had a three-day binge.* **2** an instance of excessive INDULGENCE(2) in anything; a SPREE: *a 'shopping binge.*
▶ **binge** v (*pres p* **bingeing**; *pp* **binged**) ~ (**on sth**) (*esp US*) to eat and drink excessively or without being able to control oneself: [Vpr] *bingeing on cakes, sweets and ice-cream.* [also V].

bingo /'bɪŋgəʊ/ n [U] a gambling game in which players cover numbers on individual cards as the numbers are called out in no special order. The winner is the first person to cover all her or his numbers: *a 'bingo hall.*

binoculars /bɪ'nɒkjələz/ n [pl] an instrument with a LENS(1) for each eye, making distant objects seem nearer: *watch the horse-race through (a pair of) binoculars.*

binomial /baɪ'nəʊmiəl/ n (*mathematics*) (in ALGEBRA), an expression consisting of two groups of numbers, letters, etc joined by + or –. ▶ **binomial** adj.

bi(o)- *comb form* of living things; of (esp human) life: *biology* ○ *biodegradable* ○ *biography.*

biochemistry /ˌbaɪəʊ'kemɪstri/ n [U] the scientific study of the chemistry of living things.
▶ **biochemical** /ˌbaɪəʊ'kemɪkl/ adj.
biochemist /ˌbaɪəʊ'kemɪst/ n an expert in biochemistry.

biodegradable /ˌbaɪəʊdɪ'greɪdəbl/ adj (of substances) that can be made to rot by bacteria: *biodegradable household cleaning products.*

biography /baɪ'ɒgrəfi/ n (**a**) [C] the story of a person's life written by sb else: *Boswell's biography of Johnson.* (**b**) [U] such writing as a part of literature: *I prefer biography to fiction.* Compare AUTOBIOGRAPHY.
▶ **biographer** /baɪ'ɒgrəfə(r)/ n a person who writes a biography.
biographic, -ical /ˌbaɪə'græfɪk, -ɪkl/ adjs.

biological /ˌbaɪə'lɒdʒɪkl/ adj of or relating to BIOLOGY: *a biological experiment/reaction* ○ *biological soap-powders* (ie ones containing substances which destroy chemical compounds from living things, attacking stains of food, blood, etc). ▶ **biologically** adv.
■ ˌbio ˌlogical 'clock n a natural mechanism in living creatures that controls their regular physical activities, eg sleeping.
ˌbio ˌlogical 'warfare (also ˌgerm 'warfare) n [U] the use of germs (GERM 1) as a weapon in war.

biology /baɪ'ɒlədʒi/ n [U] the scientific study of the life and structure of plants and animals.
▶ **biologist** /-dʒɪst/ n an expert in biology. Compare BOTANY, ZOOLOGY.

biomass /'baɪəʊmæs/ n the total quantity or weight of living creatures in a given area or volume: *the biomass of a forest.*

bionic /baɪ'ɒnɪk/ adj (in stories) having artificial parts of the body and so able to do things no normal human being can do.

biopic /'baɪəʊpɪk/ n a film about the life of a particular person.

biopsy /'baɪɒpsi/ n (*medical*) the examination of liquids or tissue taken from the body of sb who is ill in order to find out more about their disease. Compare AUTOPSY.

biorhythm /'baɪəʊrɪðəm/ n any of the repeated patterns of physical, emotional and intellectual activity believed by some people to affect human behaviour.

biotechnology /ˌbaɪəʊtek'nɒlədʒi/ n [U] (*techn*) the

use of BIOLOGICAL processes for industrial and other purposes, eg in producing ANTIBIOTIC drugs.

bipartisan /ˌbaɪpɑːtɪˈzæn; US ˌbaɪˈpɑːrtɪzn/ *adj* of or involving two political parties: *a bipartisan policy ∘ bipartisan talks.*

biped /ˈbaɪped/ *n* (*techn*) a creature with two feet. Compare QUADRUPED.

biplane /ˈbaɪpleɪn/ *n* an early type of aircraft with two sets of wings, one above the other. Compare MONOPLANE.

birch /bɜːtʃ/ *n* **1(a)** [C] (*pl* unchanged or **birches**) a type of tree, common in northern countries, with smooth bark[1] and thin branches. **(b)** (also **'birchwood**) [U] its hard pale wood. **2** [C] a bunch of birch sticks formerly used for beating people as a punishment: *the campaign to bring back the birch.*

bird /bɜːd/ *n* **1** a creature covered with feathers and with two wings and two legs. Most birds can fly: *a bird's nest with eggs in it.* **2** (*sexist sl esp Brit*) a young woman: *Terry's got a new bird* (ie GIRLFRIEND). **3** (*infml*) a person: *a queer bird ∘ a wise old bird ∘ The professional footballer who also plays cricket is a rare bird nowadays* (ie There are very few of them). **IDM** **the bird has 'flown** the wanted person has escaped. **a bird in the 'hand is worth two in the 'bush** (*saying*) it is better to be satisfied with what one has than to risk losing everything by trying to get much more. **the birds and the 'bees** (*euph*) the basic facts about sex: *tell a child about the birds and the bees.* **a ˌbird's-ˌeye 'view (of sth)** a general view from a high position looking down: *From the plane we had a bird's-eye view of Manhattan.* **birds of a 'feather (flock to'gether)** (*saying*) people of the same sort (are found together). **an early bird** ⇨ EARLY. **(strictly) for the birds** (*infml derog*) not important; worthless. **give sb / get the 'bird** (*sl*) **1** to shout at sb/be shouted at rudely as a sign of disapproval: *The comedian got the bird* (ie was shouted at by the audience). **2** (*US*) to give sb/receive a rude gesture with the middle finger. **kill two birds with one stone** ⇨ KILL.

■ **'bird-bath** *n* a small container filled with water for birds to wash themselves in, usu in a garden.

ˌbird of 'paradise *n* a bird with very bright feathers, found mainly in New Guinea.

ˌbird of 'passage *n* **1** a bird that travels regularly from one part of the world to another at different times of the year. **2** a person who passes through a place without staying there long.

ˌbird of 'prey *n* a bird that kills other creatures for food: *Eagles and owls are birds of prey.*

'bird sanctuary *n* an area where birds are protected and helped to breed.

'bird-song *n* [U] the musical sounds made by birds.

'bird-table (*US* also **bird feeder**) *n* a platform on which food for birds is placed, usu in a garden.

'bird-watcher *n* a person who enjoys regularly studying birds in their natural surroundings. **'bird-watching** *n* [U].

birdbrained /ˈbɜːdbreɪnd/ *adj* (*infml derog*) stupid; silly: *a birdbrained idea/suggestion.*

birdcage /ˈbɜːdkeɪdʒ/ *n* a cage for a domestic bird or birds.

birdie /ˈbɜːdi/ *n* **1** (*infml*) (used esp by or to children) a little bird. **2** a score of one stroke under PAR[1](1) for a hole at golf. Compare EAGLE 2.

birdseed /ˈbɜːdsiːd/ *n* [U] special seeds for feeding birds in cages.

biro /ˈbaɪrəʊ/ *n* (*pl* **-os**) (*Brit propr*) a type of ballpoint (BALL[1]).

birth /bɜːθ/ *n* **1(a)** [U] the coming of young from out of the mother's body; the process of being born: *The father was present at the (moment of) birth.* ∘ *She gave birth (to a healthy baby) last night.* ∘ *The baby weighed seven pounds at birth.* ∘ *He has been blind from birth* (ie all his life). **(b)** [C] an instance of this:

There were three births at the hospital yesterday. **2** [C] the coming into existence of sth; the beginning of sth: *the birth of capitalism/socialism/a political party/an idea ∘ Marx's ideas gave birth to communism.* **3** [U] family origin; DESCENT(2): *of noble birth ∘ She was English by birth but later took French nationality.*

■ **'birth certificate** *n* an official document giving the date and place of a person's birth.

'birth control *n* [U] the practice of controlling the number of children one has, esp by CONTRACEPTION: *The pill is one method of birth control.*

'birth rate *n* the number of births per year per thousand people of the population of a place.

birthday /ˈbɜːθdeɪ/ *n* (the anniversary of) the day of a person's birth: *Happy birthday! ∘ a 'birthday card/party/present.* **IDM** **in one's 'birthday suit** (*infml joc*) without any clothes on; naked.

birthmark /ˈbɜːθmɑːk/ *n* a red or brown mark on a person's skin from birth.

birthplace /ˈbɜːθpleɪs/ *n* the house or area where a person was born: *Mozart's birthplace is (in) Salzburg.*

birthright /ˈbɜːθraɪt/ *n* the things that sb may claim because of who they are or where they were born: *The estate is the birthright of the eldest son.* ∘ (*fig*) *Freedom is our natural birthright.*

biscuit /ˈbɪskɪt/ *n* **1** (*Brit*) (*US* **cookie**) [C] a small flat thin piece of pastry baked until it is crisp: *chocolate biscuits ∘ cheese and biscuits.* **2** [C] (*US*) a type of soft bread roll, usu eaten with GRAVY(1). **3** [U] a pale brown colour. **4** [U] (*techn*) clay pots, etc that have been fired (FIRE[2] 7) but not covered with a GLAZE. **IDM** **take the 'biscuit** (also *esp US*) **take the cake** (*infml*) to be extremely or specially amusing, annoying, surprising, etc: *He's done stupid things before, but this really takes the biscuit* (ie is the most stupid thing).

bisect /baɪˈsekt/ *v* [Vn] to divide sth into two (usu equal) parts. ▶ **bisection** /baɪˈsekʃn/ *n* [U, C].

bisexual /ˌbaɪˈsekʃuəl/ *adj* **1** sexually attracted to both men and women. Compare HETEROSEXUAL, HOMOSEXUAL. **2** having both male and female sexual organs; Compare HERMAPHRODITE. ▶ **bisexual** *n* a person who is bisexual.

bisexuality /ˌbaɪˌsekʃuˈæləti/ *n* [U].

bishop /ˈbɪʃəp/ *n* **1** a senior priest in charge of the work of the Church in a city or district: *the Bishop of Durham.* **2** a piece used in the game of CHESS, shaped like a bishop's hat. Bishops may only move diagonally (DIAGONAL). ⇨ picture at CHESS. ▶ **bishopric** /ˈbɪʃəprɪk/ *n* **1** the official position of a bishop. **2** the district under a bishop's control; a DIOCESE.

bison /ˈbaɪsn/ *n* (*pl* unchanged) either of two types of large hairy wild cattle from North America or parts of Europe.

bistro /ˈbiːstrəʊ/ *n* (*pl* **-os**) a small restaurant.

bit[1] /bɪt/ *n* **1(a)** [C] a small piece or amount of sth: *bits of bread/cheese/paper ∘ a bit of advice/help/luck/news ∘ I've got a bit of* (ie some) *shopping to do.* **(b)** [sing] **a ~ (of sth)** (*infml often ironic*) a large amount: *'How much money has he got in the bank?' 'A fair bit.' ∘ It took quite a bit of effort to paint the whole of the house. ∘ This novel will take a bit of reading* (ie a long time to read). **2** [C] (*US sl*) (usu *pl* and in phrases) 12½ cents: *two bits or a quarter (of a dollar).* See also THREEPENNY BIT. **3** [sing] (*sl*) a set of actions, ideas, etc associated with a specific group, person or activity: *She couldn't accept the whole drug-culture bit.* **IDM** **a bit** (*esp Brit*) **1** [U] rather: *'Are you tired?' 'Yes, I am a bit (tired).' ∘ This book costs a bit (too) much. ∘ These trousers are a bit tight.* **2** a short time or distance: *Wait a bit! ∘ Move up a bit.* **bit by 'bit** a piece at a time; gradually: *He assembled the model aircraft bit by bit. ∘ She saved*

---

money bit by bit until she had enough to buy a car. **a bit 'much** (*infml*) excessive; not reasonable: *The noise from the neighbours' party is getting a bit much.* ○ *It's a bit much calling me at three o'clock in the morning.* **a bit of a** (*Brit infml*) rather a: *He's a bit of a bully/coward/fool/bore.* ○ *The rail strike is a bit of a nuisance.* **a bit of all 'right** (*Brit sl*) a very attractive or pleasing person or thing: *Dave's new girlfriend is a bit of all right, isn't she?* **a bit of 'crumpet/'fluff/'skirt/'stuff** (*Brit sl sexist*) a pretty girl or woman. **,bits and 'bobs/'pieces** (*infml*) small objects or items of various kinds: *I always have a lot of bits and pieces in my coat pocket.* **a bit 'thick** (*Brit infml*) more than one can or wishes to tolerate; not fair or reasonable: *It's a bit thick expecting us to work on Sundays.* **do one's 'bit** (*infml*) to do one's share of a task: *We can finish this job on time if everyone does their bit.* **every bit as good, bad, etc (as sb/sth)** just as good, bad, etc; equally good, bad, etc: *Rome is every bit as beautiful as Paris.* ○ *He's every bit as clever as she is.* **not a 'bit**; **not one (little) 'bit** not at all; not in any way: *'Are you cold?' 'Not a bit.'* ○ *It's not a bit of use* (ie There's no point in) *complaining.* ○ *I don't like that idea one little bit.* **not a 'bit of it!** (*Brit infml*) not at all; on the contrary: *You'd think she'd be tired after such a long journey, but not a bit of it!* **not take a blind bit of notice** ⇨ BLIND[1]. **to bits** into small pieces: *pull/tear sth to bits* ○ *The parchment came/fell to bits in my hands.*

▶ **bitty** *adj* (*Brit usu derog*) composed of small bits; lacking unity: *a bitty conversation/interview/film* ○ *The play is rather bitty.*

■ **'bit part** *n* a small part in a play or film.

bit² /bɪt/ *n* **1** the metal part of a BRIDLE put in a horse's mouth as a way of controlling it. ⇨ picture at HARNESS. **2(a)** the part of a tool that cuts or grips when twisted. **(b)** a tool or part of a tool for drilling (DRILL[1] *v* 1) holes. ⇨ picture at DRILL[1]. See also DRILL[1]. **IDM** **champ at the bit** ⇨ CHAMP[1]. **get/take the bit between one's/the teeth** to deal with a difficult problem, task, etc with determination.

bit³ /bɪt/ *n* (*computing*) the smallest unit of information used by a computer, expressed as a choice between two possibilities.

bit⁴ *pt* of BITE[1].

bitch /bɪtʃ/ *n* **1** a female dog or other animal of the dog family, eg a fox: *a greyhound bitch.* Compare DOG[1] 1, VIXEN 1. **2** (*sl derog*) a woman, esp a cruel and unpleasant one: *The silly bitch has forgotten.* ○ *She can be a real bitch.* **3** (*sl*) a difficult problem or situation: *Life's a bitch* (ie Life is difficult and unpleasant). See also SON OF A BITCH.

▶ **bitch** *v* ~ **(about sb/sth)** (*infml*) to make unkind and critical comments; to complain: [Vpr] *She's always bitching about the people at work.* [also V].

bitchy *adj* (**-ier, -iest**) unkind or bad-tempered: *a bitchy remark/person.* **bitchiness** *n* [U].

bite¹ /baɪt/ *v* (*pt* **bit** /bɪt/; *pp* **bitten** /'bɪtn/) **1** ~ **(into sth)** to cut into sth with the teeth: [V] *Does your dog bite?* (ie Does it have a habit of biting people?) [Vpr] *She bit into the apple.* ○ *dogs biting at* (ie trying to bite) *each other's tails* [Vn] *That dog just bit me in the leg.* ○ *Stop biting your nails!* [Vnp] *bite off* (ie cut off by biting) *a large chunk of bread.* **2** (of an insect or a snake) to wound sb with a sting or with the teeth: *badly bitten by mosquitoes* ○ (*joc*) *We were bitten to death* (ie bitten a great deal) *by flies while we were camping.* See also FROSTBITTEN. **3** (of fish) to take or try to take the BAIT(1): [V] *The fish won't bite today.* ○ (*fig*) *I tried to sell him my old car, but he wouldn't bite* (ie he did not accept the offer). **4** to take a strong hold; to grip sth firmly: [V] *Wheels won't bite on a slippery surface.* **5** to become effective, usu in an unpleasant way: [V] *The government's economic measures are beginning to bite.* **IDM** **be**

bitten by sth to have a strong interest in or enthusiasm for sth. **bite the 'bullet** (*infml*) to accept sth unpleasant because one cannot avoid it. **bite the 'dust** (*infml*) **1** to fall down dead. **2** to be defeated or rejected: *Another of my great ideas bites the dust!* **bite the hand that 'feeds one** to harm sb who has been kind to one. **bite/snap sb's head off** ⇨ HEAD[1]. **bite one's 'lip** to grip one's lip or lips between one's teeth to prevent oneself from saying sth, showing emotion, etc. **bite off more than one can 'chew** (*infml*) to attempt to do too much or to do sth that is too difficult. **bite one's 'tongue** to try hard not to say what one thinks or feels; to blame oneself for having said sth embarrassing, etc. **once bitten, twice shy** ⇨ ONCE. **what's biting/eating him, you, etc?** (*infml*) what is worrying him, you, etc?

▶ **biting** *adj* **1** causing a sharp pain: *a biting wind.* **2** (of remarks) cruel and critical: *biting sarcasm/wit.* **bitingly** *adv*.

bite² /baɪt/ *n* **1** [C] (**a**) an act of biting: *eat sth in one bite* ○ *The dog gave me a playful bite.* (**b**) a piece cut off by biting: *a sandwich with a bite out of it.* **2** [sing] (*infml*) food: *I haven't had a bite (to eat) all day.* **3** [C] a wound made by an insect or a snake: *mosquito bites.* **4** [C] the taking of BAIT(1) by a fish: *fishermen waiting for a bite.* **5** [sing, U] sharpness (SHARP): *There's a bite in the air* (ie It's cold). ○ *a wine with real bite* (ie a strong flavour) ○ *His words had no bite* (ie were harmless or not effective). See also FROSTBITE. **6** [U] cutting power or firm grip: *This drill has no bite.* **IDM** **sb's bark is worse than their bite** ⇨ BARK². **have/get two bites at the 'cherry** to have a second opportunity to do sth; to make a second attempt at doing sth.

■ **'bite-sized** *adj* usu [attrib] small enough to be put into the mouth whole and then eaten: *cut the meat into bite-sized pieces.*

bitten *pp* of BITE[1].

bitter /'bɪtə(r)/ *adj* **1** having a sharp and often unpleasant taste; not sweet: *Black coffee leaves a bitter taste in the mouth.* ○ *bitter chocolate.* Compare SOUR. **2** causing or caused by great unhappiness: *learn from bitter experience* ○ *Failing the exam was a bitter disappointment to him.* ○ *shed bitter tears.* **3** feeling or showing great anger or dislike, esp because of sth that one thinks is unfair: *bitter quarrels/enemies/words* ○ *She feels/is very bitter about her divorce.* **4** (of weather conditions) very sharp, cold and unpleasant: *a bitter wind.* **IDM** **a bitter 'pill (for sb) (to swallow)** a fact or an event that is unpleasant to accept or very disappointing: *Defeat in the election was a bitter pill for him to swallow.* **to/until the bitter 'end** until all that is possible has been done; until the absolute end in spite of difficulties: *fight/struggle to the bitter end* ○ *stay watching the match until the bitter end.*

▶ **bitter** *n* [U,C] (*Brit*) a type of brown beer with a bitter taste: *A pint of bitter, please.*

bitterly *adv* in a bitter way: *bitterly disappointed/disappointing* ○ *He bitterly regrets all the harm he has done.* ○ *She wept bitterly.* ○ *complain bitterly* ○ *He is bitterly* (ie very strongly) *opposed to nuclear weapons.* ○ *It's bitterly cold outside today.*

bitterness *n* [U]: *The pay cut caused bitterness and resentment among the staff.*

bitters *n* [U, sing or pl *v*] a strong alcoholic liquid made from plants, used to add flavour to certain drinks: *gin with a dash of bitters.*

■ **,bitter-'sweet** *adj* **1** sweet but leaving a bitter taste. **2** causing or showing pleasure mixed with sadness: *bitter-sweet memories.*

bittern /'bɪtən/ *n* a bird related to the HERON that lives in marshy (MARSH) places and has a distinctive loud call.

B

bitumen /ˈbɪtʃəmən; US bəˈtuːmən/ n [U] a black sticky substance obtained from petrol, used for covering roads or roofs.
▶ **bituminous** /bɪˈtjuːmɪnəs; US -bəˈtuː-/ adj of or containing bitumen: *bituminous coal.*

bivalve /ˈbaɪvælv/ n any SHELLFISH with a double shell, eg a MUSSEL. Compare MOLLUSC.

bivouac /ˈbɪvuæk/ n a temporary camp without tents or any other cover, used esp by soldiers or people climbing mountains.
▶ **bivouac** v (-ck-) to stay in a bivouac, esp during the night: [V] *We bivouacked on the open plain.*

bizarre /bɪˈzɑː(r)/ adj very strange; not at all logical: *a bizarre coincidence/incident/situation* ○ *a film with a bizarre plot.* ▶ **bizarrely** adv: *behave bizarrely.*

bk abbr (pl **bks**) book: *Headway Bk 2.*

blab /blæb/ v (-bb-) **1** ~ (**to sb**) (**about sth**) (*infml*) to reveal a secret, esp by talking carelessly: [Vpr] *One of the gang blabbed to the police and they were all arrested.* [also V]. **2** [V, Vpr, Vp] = BLABBER.

blabber /ˈblæbə(r)/ (also **blab**) v (*infml*) to talk foolishly or too much: [Vpr, Vp] *What's he blabbering (on) about?* [also V].

blabbermouth /ˈblæbəmaʊθ/ n (*infml derog*) a person who reveals secrets by talking too much.

black¹ /blæk/ adj **1(a)** of the very darkest colour; the opposite of white: *black shoes* ○ *a black suit* ○ *big black clouds* ○ *The sky was as black as coal/ink/pitch.* Compare WHITE¹. (**b**) without light; completely dark: *a black night.* **2** (of tea or coffee) without milk: *Two black coffees, please.* Compare WHITE¹. **3** (also **Black**) (*sometimes offensive*) (**a**) of a race that has dark skin: *Many black people emigrated to Britain in the 1950s.* ○ *Britain's Black community.* (**b**) of black people: *black culture.* **4** very dirty; covered with dirt: *hands black with grime.* **5** without hope; very sad or depressing: *The future looks black.* ○ *black* (ie very great) *despair* ○ *black news* ○ *a black day/week* (ie one full of sad or terrible events). **6** full of anger or hatred: *give sb a black look* ○ *be in a black mood.* **7** evil or wicked: *a black deed/lie.* **8** (of humour) intended to be funny but about TRAGIC(1) or terrible things: *a black comedy* ○ *black humour.* **9** (of goods, etc) not to be handled by trade union members while others are on strike: *The strikers declared the cargo black.* **IDM** (**beat sb**) **black and blue** (hit sb until they are) covered with bruises (BRUISE): *The fall from her horse left her black and blue all over.* **not as black as it/one is painted** not as bad as it/one is said to be: *Our boss isn't really as black as he's painted.* **the pot calling the kettle black** ⇨ POT¹. ▶ **blackness** n [U].
■ **the black art** n (often pl) = BLACK MAGIC.

,**black belt** n (**a**) a black belt worn by sb who has reached the highest rank in JUDO, KARATE, etc. (**b**) a person who has achieved this rank.

,**black box** n an automatic device for recording details of the flight of a plane.

,**black cherry** n (**a**) a N American type of CHERRY (1) with a dark skin: *black cherry jam.* (**b**) the tree on which it grows.

,**black comedy** n [C, U] a play, film, etc that shows TRAGIC(1) or terrible things in a way that is intended to be funny; comedy of this type in a play, film, etc.

the Black Country n [sing] a heavily industrial area in the West Midlands of England.

the Black Death n [sing] a widespread EPIDEMIC(1) of BUBONIC PLAGUE that killed many people in Europe in the 14th century.

the black economy n [sing] business activity or work which is not official but which people are engaged in to avoid paying taxes, etc: *The growing black economy is beginning to worry the government.*

,**Black English** n [U] the form of English spoken by many black people, esp in US towns and cities.

,**black eye** n an area of dark skin that forms around sb's eye, caused by a blow: *give sb a black eye* (ie he hit sb in the eye causing a BRUISE).

,**black hole** n a region in space from which no matter¹(3a) or RADIATION(1) can escape.

,**black ice** n [U] a thin transparent layer of ice on a road surface: *The lorry skidded on a patch of black ice.*

,**black magic** n [U] a type of magic that involves calling on the powers of evil.

,**Black Maria** /məˈraɪə/ n (*infml*) a police van for transporting prisoners in.

,**black mark** n an indication that sb has done sth bad that others disapprove of; a mark of DISCREDIT²: *His outrageous behaviour earned him a black mark with his hostess.* ○ *The public scandal left a black mark on/against his career.*

,**black market** n [sing] the illegal buying and selling of goods or foreign money, esp when trade in such things is officially controlled: *buy/sell sth on the black market* ○ *black-market goods.* ,**black marketeer** n a person who trades in the black market.

,**black mass** n a ceremony like a Christian one, but in which the devil is worshipped instead of God.

,**Black Muslim** n a member of a group of black people, esp in the USA, who follow Islam and want a separate black society to be established.

,**black pepper** n [U] pepper made by crushing whole dried berries of the pepper plant, including their outer coverings.

,**Black Power** n [U] a movement supporting civil rights and political power for black people.

,**black pudding** n [U, C] (*Brit*) (US **blood sausage**) a type of large dark SAUSAGE made from dried blood, fat and grain.

,**black sheep** n a person who is strongly disapproved of by other members of her or his family: *My brother is the black sheep of the family.*

,**black spot** n (*Brit*) (**a**) a place where accidents often happen, esp on a road: *a notorious (accident) black spot.* (**b**) a place in which a particular problem is widespread: *unemployment black spots.*

,**black tie** n (**a**) a black bow-tie (BOW¹) worn with a dinner-jacket (DINNER). (**b**) [esp attrib] requiring formal dress: *a black tie dinner/affair* ○ *It's black tie* (ie Dinner-jackets should be worn).

,**black-water fever** n [U] a very severe type of MALARIA.

,**black widow** n a poisonous American SPIDER, the female of which often eats the male.

black² /blæk/ n **1** [U] the darkest colour: *Black is not my favourite colour.* **2** [U] black clothes or material: *Everyone at the funeral was dressed in black.* **3** (usu **Black**) [C] (*sometimes offensive*) a person of a race that has a dark skin: *Discrimination against Blacks is still common in many societies.* **IDM** **be in the black** to have money in one's bank account. Compare THE RED. ,**black and white** (of television, photographs, etc) showing no colours except black, white and shades of grey: *an old black and white television set* ○ *a film made in black and white* ○ *black-and-white photos.* **in black and white** in writing or in print: *I could hardly believe it but there it was in black and white on the front page.* (**in**) **black and white** (in) extreme terms, by which things or people are considered completely good or bad, completely right or wrong, etc: *see/view the issue in black and white.*

black³ /blæk/ v **1** to make sth black; to put black polish on esp shoes: [Vn] *blacked faces.* **2** (*Brit*) to refuse to handle goods or do business with sb; to BOYCOTT sth/sb: [Vn] *The lorry had been blacked by strikers and could not be unloaded.* **PHR V** ,**black out** to lose consciousness or memory temporarily: *The plane dived suddenly, causing the pilot to black out.* ,**black sth out 1** to put out lights, etc completely or cover windows, etc so that light cannot be seen from outside: *houses blacked out during an air raid.* **2** to cover (sth written or printed) with black ink, etc so that it cannot be read.

blackball /'blækbɔ:l/ *v* to prevent sb from joining a club or group by voting against them: [Vn] *blackball a candidate.*

blackberry /'blækbəri; *US* -beri/ *n* (**a**) (also **bramble**) a wild SHRUB with thorns (THORN) on its stems. (**b**) its small dark edible fruit: *blackberry and apple pie.* — *v* [V] (*pt, pp* **-ried**) (usu **go blackberrying**) to pick[1](2) blackberries.

blackbird /'blækbɜ:d/ *n* **1** a European bird of the THRUSH[1] family, the male of which is black. **2** (*US*) any of various birds with black feathers.

blackboard /'blækbɔ:d/ (*US* also '**chalkboard**) *n* a board with a smooth, usu dark, surface that is used for writing on with chalk, esp by a teacher in a school.

blackcurrant /ˌblæk'kʌrənt/ *n* (**a**) a common garden SHRUB. (**b**) its small dark edible berry.

blacken /'blækən/ *v* **1** to make sth or become black or very dark: [Vn] *hands blackened with oil* [also V]. **2** to say things that damage or destroy sb's reputation, etc: [Vn] *blacken a person's character/name.*

blackguard /'blægɑ:d/ *n* (*dated*) a man who is not honourable; a SCOUNDREL.

blackhead /'blækhed/ *n* a very small black spot on the skin, caused by dirt blocking a PORE[1].

blackjack /'blækdʒæk/ *n* **1** [C] (*esp US*) a type of club[2](1) used as a weapon, esp a metal pipe covered with leather. **2** [U] = PONTOON[1].

blackleg /'blækleg/ *n* (*derog*) a person who works when her or his fellow workers are on strike. See also STRIKEBREAKER.

blacklist /'blæklɪst/ *n* a list of people who are considered unacceptable by an organization or a government: *a blacklist of suspected terrorists.*
▶ **blacklist** *v* to put sb on a blacklist: [Vn] *He was blacklisted because of his anti-government activities.*

blackmail /'blækmeɪl/ *n* [U] **1** the act of demanding money from sb in return for not revealing secret or unpleasant information about them: *be found guilty of blackmail.* **2** the use of threats to put pressure on a person or group: *'Increase productivity or lose your jobs.' 'That's blackmail!'* ○ *moral/ emotional blackmail.*
▶ **blackmail** *v* ~ sb (**into doing sth**) to force sb to do sth by blackmail: [Vn, Vnpr] *He was blackmailed by an enemy agent (into passing on state secrets).* [Vnpr] *The strikers refused to be blackmailed into returning to work.* **blackmailer** *n* a person who commits blackmail.

blackout /'blækaʊt/ *n* **1(a)** a period when all lights must be put out or covered, esp during an air attack: *Curtains must be drawn during the blackout.* (**b**) a period of darkness caused by an electrical power failure. (**c**) (in a theatre) a moment when all the lights on stage are suddenly put out, eg at the end of a scene. **2** a temporary loss of consciousness, sight or memory: *She had a blackout and couldn't remember anything about the accident.* **3** a situation in which the release of information is officially prevented: *The government imposed a news blackout* (ie stopped the broadcasting and printing of news) *during the crisis.*

blackshirt (also **Blackshirt**) /'blækʃɜ:t/ *n* a member of a fascist (FASCISM) organization, esp one with a black shirt as part of its uniform.

blacksmith /'blæksmɪθ/ (also **smith**) *n* a person whose job is to make and repair things made of iron, esp horseshoes (HORSESHOE 1).

blackthorn /'blækθɔ:n/ *n* a prickly SHRUB with white flowers and purple fruit.

bladder /'blædə(r)/ *n* **1** a bag made of MEMBRANE(1)

in which URINE collects in human and animal bodies before being passed out. ▷ picture at REPRODUCTION. See also GALL-BLADDER. **2** a hollow bag that can be filled with air or liquid for various uses (eg the rubber bag inside a football).

blade /bleɪd/ *n* **1(a)** the flat cutting part of a knife, sword, etc: *a penknife with five blades.* ▷ picture at SWORD. (**b**) = RAZOR-BLADE. **2** the flat wide part of an OAR, a propeller (PROPEL), a SPADE[1], a bat[1], etc. ▷ picture at ROWING-BOAT. **3** the flat narrow (usu pointed) leaf of grass, wheat, etc: *a blade of grass.*

blaeberry /ˌbleɪbəri; *US* -beri/ *n* (*Brit*) = BILBERRY.

blah /blɑ:/ *n* [U] (*infml*) useless or boring talk; talk of no importance: *That's just a lot of blah.* ○ *There he goes, blah blah blah, talking nonsense as usual.*

blame /bleɪm/ *v* ~ sb (**for sth**)/~ sth **on sb** to consider or say that sb is responsible for sth bad: [Vn] *I don't blame you* (ie I think your action was justified). ○ (*saying*) *A bad workman blames his tools* (ie refuses to accept the responsibility for his own mistakes). ○ *If you fail the exam you'll only have yourself to blame* (ie it will be your own fault). [Vnpr] *She blamed him for the failure of their marriage/blamed the failure of their marriage on him.* **IDM** **be to blame (for sth)** to be responsible for sth bad; to deserve to be blamed: *She was in no way to blame.* ○ *Which driver was to blame for the accident?*
▶ **blame** *n* [U] ~ (**for sth**) **1** responsibility for sth done badly or wrongly: *bear/take/accept the blame (for sth)* ○ *Where does the blame for our failure lie?* (ie Who or what is responsible?) ○ *Don't lay/put the blame for your own mistakes on other people!* **2** criticism for doing sth wrong: *He got all the blame but it wasn't really his fault.* **blameless** *adj* deserving no blame; innocent: *a blameless life* ○ *None of us is entirely blameless in this matter.* **blamelessly** *adv.*
blameworthy *adj* deserving blame.

blanch /blɑ:ntʃ; *US* blæntʃ/ *v* **1** ~ (**with sth**) (**at sth**) to become pale because of fear, shock, etc: [V] *She blanched visibly when I told her the news.* [Vpr] *He blanched (with fear) at the sight of the snake.* **2** to prepare food, esp vegetables, by putting it briefly into boiling water: [Vn] *blanched broccoli* ○ *You blanch almonds to remove their skins.*

blancmange /blə'mɒnʒ/ *n* [C, U] a cold sweet dish like jelly, made with milk in a mould.

bland /blænd/ *adj* (**-er, -est**) **1** without features that attract attention; not interesting: *bland background music* ○ *rows of rather bland buildings.* **2** (*sometimes derog*) (of food) very mild in flavour; not having a strong or interesting taste: *a very bland wine* ○ *This cheese is too bland for my taste.* **3** gentle or casual; showing no strong emotions: *He reacted in his usual bland way.* ○ *bland comments.* ▶ **blandly** *adv.* **blandness** *n* [U].

blandishments /'blændɪʃmənts/ *n* [pl] (*fml*) pleasant talk or actions with which one tries to persuade sb to do sth: *He refused to be moved by either threats or blandishments.*

blank /blæŋk/ *adj* (**-er, -est**) **1(a)** without written or printed words, etc: *a blank sheet of paper* ○ *Fill in the amount of your payment in the blank space below.* ○ *Write on one side of the page and leave the other side blank.* (**b**) (of a tape, etc) with nothing recorded on it: *a blank cassette.* (**c**) (of a document, etc) with empty spaces for writing answers, a signature, etc: *a blank form.* (**d**) bare; empty: *a blank wall* (ie without doors, windows, pictures, etc). **2(a)** showing no feeling, understanding or interest: *She stared at me with a blank expression (on her face).* ○ *He looked blank and said he had no idea what I was talking about.* ○ *Her questions were met with blank looks all round* (ie No one seemed to know how to answer them). **(b)** (of the mind) temporarily unable to understand or remember sth: *Suddenly my mind went blank.* **3** [attrib] (of negative things) total; absolute: *a blank denial/refusal.*

▶ **blank** *n* **1(a)** an empty space in a form, document, etc for writing answers, a signature, etc: *fill in the blanks on the question paper* ○ *If you can't answer the question, leave a blank.* **(b)** a printed document with empty spaces: *I've filled in this application form incorrectly. Can I have another blank?* **2** an empty space or period of time: *My mind was a (complete) blank — I couldn't think of a single answer.* ○ *The time she spent in hospital is a complete blank for her.* **3** = BLANK CARTRIDGE. **IDM draw a blank** ⇨ DRAW¹.

blank *v* **PHR V** ,**blank sth 'out** to cover sth completely: *The person in front of me stood up, blanking out my view.* ○ *The sun had gone, blanked out by dark clouds.*

blankly *adv*: *He stared blankly into space, not knowing what to say next.* ○ *'I don't understand it,' she said blankly.*

blankness *n* [U].

■ ,**blank 'cartridge** *n* a CARTRIDGE(1) that contains explosive but no bullet: *firing blanks.*

,**blank 'cheque** (*US* ,**blank 'check**) *n* **(a)** a signed cheque on which the amount to be paid is left blank, for the person receiving the money to write in. **(b)** complete authority to do sth: *The architect was given a blank cheque to design a new city centre.*

,**blank 'verse** *n* [U] poetry that does not RHYME.

blanket /'blæŋkɪt/ *n* **1** a thick woollen covering used, esp on beds, for keeping people warm: *It's cold — I need another blanket.* **2** a thick mass or layer covering sth: *a blanket of fog/cloud/smoke/snow.* **3** [attrib] applying to all cases, classes or situations; without exceptions: *a blanket agreement/term/rule.* See also WET BLANKET. **IDM born on the wrong side of the blanket** ⇨ BORN.

▶ **blanket** *v* (usu passive) ~ **sth (in/with sth)** to cover sth completely: [Vnpr] *The countryside was blanketed with snow/fog.* [also Vn].

blankety-blank /,blæŋkəti 'blæŋk/ *adj, n* (*infml euph*) (used in spoken English in place of a rude word which the speaker does not want to say).

blare /bleə(r)/ *v* **1** ~ **(out)** to make a loud harsh sound like a TRUMPET(1): [V] *Car horns blared.* [Vp] *The trumpets blared 'out.* **2** ~ **sth (out)** to produce a loud and unpleasant noise: [Vnpr] *The radio was blaring out pop music.* [also Vn].

▶ **blare** *n* [sing] a blaring sound: *the blare of police sirens/a brass band.*

blarney /'blɑːni/ *n* [U] (*infml*) **1** pleasant or convincing talk that is intended to FLATTER(1) or persuade. **2** friendly but empty talk; nonsense.

blasé /'blɑːzeɪ; *US* blɑː'zeɪ/ *adj* ~ (**about sth**) not impressed, excited or worried by sth because one has already experienced or seen it so often: *a blasé attitude/manner* ○ *She's very blasé about exams.*

blaspheme /blæs'fiːm/ *v* ~ (**against sb/sth**) to swear or curse using the name of God; to speak in a very rude way about God or sacred things: [Vpr, Vn] *blaspheme (against) the name of God* [V] *He always swears and blasphemes when he's drunk.*

▶ **blasphemer** *n* a person who blasphemes.

blasphemous /'blæsfəməs/ *adj* showing contempt or lack of respect for God and sacred things: *Many found the film blasphemous.* **blasphemously** *adv*.

blasphemy /'blæsfəmi/ *n* **(a)** [U] blasphemous behaviour or language: *the sin of blasphemy.* **(b)** [C] an instance of this: *accused of publishing blasphemies.*

blast¹ /blɑːst; *US* blæst/ *n* **1** [C,U] an explosion or a powerful movement of air from an explosion: *a bomb blast* ○ *Several passers-by were killed by the blast.* **2** [C] a sudden strong movement of air: *the wind's icy blasts* ○ *a blast of hot air from the furnace.*

3 [C] a single loud sound made by a brass instrument, whistle, car horn, etc: *blow a blast on a bugle/ trumpet* ○ *a long blast on the referee's whistle.* **4** [C] (*infml*) a severe criticism: *I got a blast from the boss for being late.* **5** [sing] (*US*) a wild party or good time: *We had quite a blast last night.* **IDM full blast** ⇨ FULL.

■ '**blast-furnace** *n* a FURNACE into which blasts of hot air are forced in order to melt iron ORE.

blast² /blɑːst; *US* blæst/ *v* **1** to destroy sth or break sth (esp rocks) apart, using explosives: [Vn] *blast a hole in a mountain* ○ *The village was blasted by enemy bombs.* [VN] *Danger! Blasting in progress!* **2** to damage or destroy sth (esp plants) by disease, cold, heat, etc; to cause sth to WITHER: [Vn] *buds/crops blasted by frost/wind.* **3** to make or cause sth to make a loud harsh noise: [Vp] *blasting away on his trumpet* [Vn] *I blasted my horn to make him move on.* [also V]. **4** (*infml*) to criticize sb/sth severely: [Vn] *The film was blasted by the critics.* **5** to hit or kick sth with great power: *He blasted the ball past the goalkeeper.* **6** to break sth in a specified way by blasting: [Vnp] *The explosion blasted the door open/ down/in.* **PHR V** ,**blast 'off** (of spacecraft) to be launched; to take off: *The rocket blasted off at noon.*

▶ **blast** *interj* (expressing annoyance): *Damn and blast!* ○ *Blast! I've burnt the toast again.* ○ *Blast this useless car!*

blasted *adj* [attrib] (*infml*) very annoying: *What a blasted nuisance!*

■ '**blast-off** *n* the launching of a spacecraft: *Blast-off is in 30 seconds.* See also LIFT-OFF.

blatant /'bleɪtnt/ *adj* done openly and without shame; very obvious; FLAGRANT: *blatant disregard for the law* ○ *a blatant lie.* ▶ **blatancy** /'bleɪtnsi/ *n* [U]: *the sheer blatancy of the crime.* **blatantly** *adv*: *a blatantly unfair decision.*

blather /'blæðə(r)/ (also **blether** /'bleðə(r)/) *v* [V, Vpr, Vp] ~ (**on**) (**about sb/sth**) to talk foolishly. ▶ **blather** (also **blether**) *n* [U] foolish talk.

blaze¹ /bleɪz/ *n* **1** [C] **(a)** a very large fire, esp a dangerous one: *Five people died in the blaze.* **(b)** a strong bright flame or fire: *Dry wood makes a good blaze.* **2** [sing] ~ **of sth (a)** a very bright display of light, colour, etc: *The garden is a blaze of colour* (ie full of colourful flowers). ○ *The city centre is a blaze of lights in the evening.* **(b)** an impressive or striking display or show of sth: *a blaze of glory/publicity.* **(c)** a sudden explosion of a violent feeling: *a blaze of anger/passion/temper.*

blaze² /bleɪz/ *v* **1** to burn brightly and fiercely: [V] *A good fire was blazing in the fireplace.* ○ *When the firemen arrived the whole building was blazing.* **2** to shine brightly: [V] *Bright lights blazed all along the street.* [Vpr] *The sun blazed down on the desert sand.* [also Vp]. **3** ~ (**with sth**) to show a strong feeling, esp anger: [Vpr] *She was blazing with fury* (ie was extremely angry). [V] *a blazing row* (ie an argument in which people shout at each other very loudly) [Vpr] *His eyes blazed (with anger).* **PHR V** ,**blaze a'way** to fire continuously with guns: *Our gunners/ guns were blazing away at the enemy all day.* ,**blaze 'up 1** to burst into flames: *The fire blazed up when he added paraffin.* **2** to become angry suddenly: *He blazed up without warning.*

▶ **blazing** *adj* [attrib] very hot: *blazing heat.*

blaze³ /bleɪz/ *n* **1** a white mark on an animal's face. **2** a mark cut in the bark of a tree to show sb which way to go.

▶ **blaze** *v* **IDM blaze a 'trail** to be the first to do sth that others follow; to be a PIONEER(1) in sth: *blazing a trail in the field of laser surgery.* Compare TRAIL- BLAZER.

blaze⁴ /bleɪz/ (also **blazon**) *v* (usu passive) to make news, information, etc known widely: [Vnpr] *The* *story was blazed all over the daily papers* [also Vn].

blazer /ˈbleɪzə(r)/ *n* a jacket, not worn with matching trousers, often showing the colours or BADGE(1) of a club, school, team, etc.

blazes /ˈbleɪzɪz/ *n* [pl] (*sl*) (esp in expressions of anger or surprise) hell(3): *Who the blazes is that?* ○ *What the blazes are you doing?* ○ *Go to blazes!*. **IDM** **like blazes** vigorously; very fast: *run/work like blazes*.

blazon /ˈbleɪzn/ *v* [Vn, Vnpr] **1** = EMBLAZON. **2** = BLAZE⁴.

bleach /bliːtʃ/ *v* to become or cause sth to become white or pale by a chemical process or the effect of sunlight: [V] *bones of animals bleaching in the desert* [Vn] *bleach cotton/linen* ○ *hair bleached by the sun*.
▶ **bleach** *n* [U,C] a chemical that bleaches: *soak shirts in bleach to remove the stains*.

bleachers /ˈbliːtʃəz/ *n* [pl] (*US*) cheap seats at a sports ground that are not covered by a roof.

bleak /bliːk/ *adj* (**-er, -est**) **1(a)** (of an area of land) bare and exposed to the wind, etc: *bleak hills/mountains/moors*. (**b**) (of the weather) cold and miserable: *a bleak winter day*. **2** (of a situation) not hopeful or encouraging; depressing: *a bleak outlook/prospect* ○ *The future looks bleak*. ▶ **bleakly** *adv*: *bleakly lit corridors* ○ *a bleakly realistic account of urban poverty* ○ *'There seems no hope,' she said bleakly*. **bleakness** *n* [U].

bleary /ˈblɪəri/ *adj* (of eyes) not clear, esp because one is tired; seeing dimly (DIM 2).
▶ **blearily** *adv* with bleary eyes: *look blearily at sb*.
■ ˌbleary-ˈeyed *adj* having bleary eyes: *He appeared at breakfast bleary-eyed from lack of sleep*.

bleat /bliːt/ *n* (**a**) (usu *sing*) the sound made by a sheep, goat or calf. (**b**) a weak, foolish or complaining cry.
▶ **bleat** *v* **1** [V] to make a bleat. **2** ~ (**about sth**) to speak in a weak or complaining voice: [V.speech] *'What did I do wrong?' he bleated feebly*. [Vpr] *It is fashionable nowadays to bleat about the problems of industry*. [also V, Vn].

bleed /bliːd/ *v* (*pt, pp* **bled** /bled/) **1** to lose or give out blood: [V] *bleed to death* ○ *My finger's bleeding*. **2** to draw blood from sb: [Vn] *Doctors used to bleed people as a way of treating illness*. **3** ~ **sb** (**for sth**) (*infml*) to force sb to give a lot of money, esp against their will; to EXTORT money from sb: [Vnpr] *The blackmailers bled him for every penny he had*. [Vn-adj] *Poor people are being bled dry by the country's harsh taxes*. [also Vn]. **4** to remove air or liquid from sth so that it works properly: [Vn] *bleed a radiator* ○ *bleed brakes*. **IDM** **bleed sb** ˈwhite to take away all sb's money. **one's heart bleeds for sb** ⇨ HEART.

bleeder /ˈbliːdə(r)/ *n* **1** (*Brit sl derog or joc*) a person: *You stupid bleeder!* **2** (*infml*) a person who bleeds easily, esp one suffering from HAEMOPHILIA.

bleeding /ˈbliːdɪŋ/ *adj* [attrib] (*Brit sl*) = BLOODY².

bleep /bliːp/ *n* a short high-pitched sound made by an electronic device as a signal or to attract attention: *The computer gave a regular bleep*. Compare BLIP 1.
▶ **bleep** *v* **1** [V] to make a bleep or bleeps. **2** to summon sb, eg a doctor, by causing an electronic device that he or she carries to make a bleep: [Vn] *Please bleep the doctor on duty immediately*. **bleeper** *n* a device that bleeps in order to attract attention.

blemish /ˈblemɪʃ/ *n* a mark or fault spoiling sth that is otherwise beautiful or perfect: *a blemish on a pear/carpet/tablecloth* ○ *She has a small blemish above her right eye*. ○ (*fig*) *His character/reputation is without (a) blemish*.
▶ **blemish** *v* (usu passive) to spoil sth that is otherwise beautiful or perfect: [Vn] *a blemished peach* ○ *The pianist's performance was blemished by several wrong notes*.

blench /blentʃ/ *v* [V] to make a sudden movement because of fear; to FLINCH.

blend /blend/ *v* **1** to mix different types of sth in order to produce the quality required: [Vn] *blended whisky/tea/coffee/tobacco*. **2(a)** ~ **A with B**/~ **A and B** (**together**) to mix one thing with another; to mix things together: [Vnpr] *Blend the eggs with the milk*. [Vn, Vnp] *Blend the eggs and milk (together)*. (**b**) ~ (**with sth**)/~ (**together**) to form a mixture; to mix: [Vpr] *Oil does not blend with water*. [V, Vp] *Oil and water do not blend (together)*. **3(a)** ~ (**with sth**)/~ (**together**) to combine well with sth; to look or sound good together: [Vpr] *Those cottages blend perfectly with the landscape*. [V, Vp] *Their voices blend (together) well*. (**b**) ~ (**into sth**) (esp of colours) to join together so that one is not clearly separate from the other(s): [Vpr] *The sea and the sky seemed to blend into each other*. [also V]. **PHRV** ˌblend ˈin (**with sth**) to mix in harmony with sth; to look or sound good (with sth): *The new office block doesn't blend in with its surroundings*. ˌblend sth ˈin (in cooking) to add another ingredient to sth and mix the two: *Heat the butter gently and then blend in a little flour*.
▶ **blend** *n* (**a**) a mixture of different types of sth: *Which blend of coffee do you prefer?* (**b**) a mixture of different things: *The story is a blend of comedy and tragedy*.

blender *n* a machine for chopping and mixing food into a liquid, eg when making soup. See also LIQUIDIZER.

bless /bles/ *v* (*pt, pp* **blessed** /blest/) [Vn] **1** to ask for God's favour and protection for sb/sth: *They brought the children to Jesus and he blessed them*. ○ *The Pope blessed the crowd*. ○ *The priest blessed the harvest*. **2** (esp in Christian ritual) to make sth sacred or holy; to CONSECRATE sth: *The priest blessed the bread and wine*. **3** (esp in Christian services) to call God holy; to praise God: *'We bless Thy Holy Name.'* **4** (*fml*) (esp imperative in prayers) to give health, happiness or success to sb/sth: *Bless* (ie We ask God to bless) *all those who are hungry, lonely or sick*. **5** (*dated infml*) (esp in exclamations expressing surprise): *Bless me!* ○ *Well, I'm blessed!* ○ *I'm blessed if I know* (ie I don't know at all)*!* **IDM** **be blessed with sth/sb** to be fortunate in having sth/sb: *She is blessed with excellent health*. ○ *We're blessed with five lovely grandchildren*. ˈbless you (used as an *interj* to express thanks or affection, or said to sb who has sneezed): *You've bought me a present? Bless you!*

blessed /ˈblesɪd/ *adj* **1** holy; honoured in the Roman Catholic Church: *the Blessed Sacrament* ○ *the Blessed Virgin* (ie the mother of Jesus, the Virgin Mary) ○ *the blessed martyrs*. **2** (in religious language) fortunate: *Blessed are the meek*. **3** [attrib] giving pleasure; enjoyable: *a moment of blessed calm*. **4** (*infml euph*) (used to express mild anger, surprise, etc) damned (DAMN²): *It's a blessed nuisance*. ○ *I can't see a blessed thing without my glasses*. ▶ **the Blessed** *n* [pl *v*] those who live with God in heaven.
blessedly *adv*: *It's so blessedly quiet here*.
blessedness /ˈblesɪdnəs/ *n* [U].

blessing /ˈblesɪŋ/ *n* **1** (usu *sing*) (**a**) God's favour and protection: *ask for God's blessing*. (**b**) a prayer asking for this. (**c**) a short prayer of thanks to God before or after a meal: *say a blessing*. **2** (usu *sing*) good wishes; approval: *I cannot give my blessing to such a proposal*. **3** a thing that one is glad about; a thing that brings happiness: *the blessings of modern civilization* ○ *What a blessing you weren't hurt in the accident!* **IDM** **a blessing in disˈguise** a thing that seems unfortunate, but is later seen to be fortunate: *Not getting into that university may be a blessing in disguise; I don't think you'd have been happy there*.

B

count one's blessings ⇨ COUNT¹. See also MIXED BLESSING.

blether = BLATHER.

blew *pt* of BLOW¹.

blight /blaɪt/ *n* **1** [U] any plant disease: *potato blight*. **2** [C] ~ **(on sb/sth)** any force that indirectly harms or destroys sth: *The bad weather cast/put a blight on our community.* ∘ *Unemployment is a blight on our community.* **3** [U] an ugly or neglected (NEGLECT 1) state, esp of a city: *the blight of inner-city slums.* ▶ **blight** *v* [Vn] **1** to affect a plant with blight(1): *The rose bushes were blighted by mildew.* **2** to spoil or ruin sth: *a career blighted by poor health* ∘ *Modern buildings have blighted the village.*

blighter /'blaɪtə(r)/ *n* (*Brit infml often derog*) (often used as a form of address) a person (esp a man): *You lucky blighter!* ∘ *The blighter stole my purse!*

blimey /'blaɪmi/ (also **cor blimey** /ˌkɔː 'blaɪmi/) *interj* (*Brit sl*) (expressing surprise or annoyance): *Blimey, that's a funny hat!*

blimp /blɪmp/ *n* a small AIRSHIP without a rigid frame.

Blimp /blɪmp/ (also ˌColonel 'Blimp) *n* (*Brit infml derog*) an older person with extremely conservative opinions (esp an old army officer). ▶ **blimpish** *adj.*

blind¹ /blaɪnd/ *adj* **1** unable to see: *a blind person* ∘ *be blind from birth* ∘ *be blind in one eye.* **2** [attrib] of or for blind people: *a 'blind school.* **3** [pred] ~ **(to sth)** not willing or able to understand or notice sth; not aware of sth: *I must have been blind not to realize the danger we were in.* ∘ *He is completely blind to her faults.* **4** [usu attrib] (*fig*) **(a)** without reason or judgement: *blind hatred/obedience/prejudice* ∘ *be in a blind panic/rage* ∘ *love/faith that is blind.* **(b)** not ruled by purpose: *the blind forces of nature/destiny* ∘ *blind chance.* **5** [usu attrib] hidden; not plain to see: *a blind driveway/entrance* ∘ *a blind bend/corner/turning* (ie one that prevents the driver from seeing the road ahead). **6** (of flying an aircraft in cloud, FOG, etc) done with the aid of instruments only, without being able to see: *a blind landing.* **IDM** **(as) blind as a 'bat** unable to see clearly or easily: *He's as blind as a bat without his glasses.* **not take a ˌblind bit of 'notice** to take no notice at all; not to listen to sb: *I warned her, but she didn't take a blind bit of notice.* **turn a blind 'eye (to sth)** to pretend not to notice: *Teachers often turn a blind eye to minor breaches of discipline.*
▶ **the blind** *n* [pl *v*] blind people: *a school for the blind.* **IDM** **the blind leading the 'blind** (*saying*) people without enough experience or knowledge attempting to guide or advise others like them.
blind *adv* without being able to see; with the aid of instruments only: *drive/fly blind.* **IDM** **blind 'drunk** (*infml*) very drunk. **swear 'blind** ⇨ SWEAR.
blindly *adv.*
blindness *n* [U].
■ ˌblind 'alley *n* **1** a narrow street that is closed at one end; a CUL-DE-SAC. **2** (*fig*) a course of action which may seem promising in the begining but which has no satisfactory result in the end.
ˌblind 'date *n* (*infml*) an arrangement to meet socially made between two people who have not met each other before.
ˌblind-man's 'buff *n* a game in which a player whose eyes are covered with a piece of cloth tries to catch and identify the other players.
'blind spot *n* **1** the part of the RETINA in the eye that is not sensitive to light. **2** an area that a motorist cannot see: *I didn't see the car that was overtaking me — it was in my blind spot.* **3** a subject about which a person is ignorant or unable to give a balanced opinion: *History is one of her blind spots.*

blind² /blaɪnd/ *v* **1** to make sb temporarily or permanently blind: [Vn] *a blinding flash/light* ∘ *momentarily blinded by the bright sunlight* ∘ *The*

soldier was blinded in the explosion. Compare DEAFEN. **2** ~ **sb (to sth)** to make sb no longer able to use their reason, judgement or good sense: [Vn, Vnpr] *Her love for him blinded her (to his faults).* [Vn] *Don't be blinded by his lies.* **IDM** **blind sb with science** to confuse sb with a display of technical knowledge.
▶ **blinding** *adj* very intense: *a blinding headache/revelation/force.* **blindingly** *adv*: *It was blindingly obvious.*

blind³ /blaɪnd/ *n* **1** (*US* also **shade**, **window shade**) (often *pl*) a screen for a window, esp one made of a roll of cloth that is fixed at the top of the window and pulled down: *draw/lower/raise the blinds.* See also VENETIAN BLIND. **2** (usu *sing*) a thing or person used in order to deceive or mislead: *His job as a diplomat was a blind for his spying.*

blinder /'blaɪndə(r)/ *n* (*Brit infml*) an excellent performance or piece of play in a game: *play a blinder (of a shot, game, etc)* ∘ *The last goal was a blinder.*

blinders /'blaɪndəz/ *n* [pl] (*US*) = BLINKERS.

blindfold /'blaɪndfəʊld/ *v* [Vn] to cover sb's eyes with a piece of cloth, etc so that they cannot see: *The hostages were kept bound and blindfolded.*
▶ **blindfold** *n* a cloth or covering used for blindfolding sb.
blindfold *adj, adv* with the eyes blindfolded: *I could do that blindfold* (ie easily, regardless of obstacles).

blink /blɪŋk/ *v* **1** to shut and open the eyes quickly: [V] *He blinked in the bright sunlight.* [Vpr] *She just stood there blinking at them.* [V, Vn] *How long can you stare without blinking (your eyes)?* **2** to shine with an unsteady light; to flash on and off: [V] *harbour lights blinking on the horizon* ∘ *The computer controls started blinking.* See also WINK **PHR V** ˌblink sth a'way/'back to try to control tears or clear the eyes by blinking: *Though clearly upset, he bravely blinked back his tears.*
▶ **blink** *n* **1** an act of blinking. **2** a sudden quick GLEAM(1) of light. **IDM** **the blink of an 'eye** a very short time: *It all happened in the blink of an eye.* **on the 'blink** (*infml*) (of a machine) not working properly; out of order: *The washing-machine's on the blink again.*
blinker *n* a device that blinks, esp a vehicle's INDICATOR(2b): *The blinkers aren't working.*

blinkered /'blɪŋkəd/ *adj* **1** (of a horse) wearing BLINKERS. **2** (*Brit fig derog*) having or showing a narrow view of things and not prepared to consider the opinions of others; narrow-minded (NARROW): *a blinkered attitude.*

blinkers /'blɪŋkəz/ (*US* also **blinders**) *n* [pl] leather pieces fixed on a horse's BRIDLE to prevent the horse from seeing sideways. ⇨ picture at HARNESS.

blinking /'blɪŋkɪŋ/ *adj, adv* (*Brit infml euph*) = BLOODY²: *It's a blinking nuisance.*

blip /blɪp/ *n* **1** a spot of light on a RADAR screen: *a series of electrical blips.* Compare BLEEP. **2** a sudden but temporary change that does not affect the general progress of sth: *a blip on the stock market.*

bliss /blɪs/ *n* [U] perfect happiness; great joy: *a life of bliss* ∘ *living in married/wedded bliss* (ie very happily married) ∘ *What bliss! I don't have to go to work today.*
▶ **blissful** /-fl/ *adj* extremely happy; full of joy: (*ironic*) *blissful ignorance* (ie being unaware of sth unpleasant). **blissfully** /-fəli/ *adv*: *blissfully happy/ignorant/unaware.*

blister /'blɪstə(r)/ *n* **1** a swelling under the skin like a bubble filled with liquid, caused by rubbing, burning, etc: *These tight shoes have given me blisters on my heels.* **2** a similar swelling on the surface of metal, painted wood, plants, etc.
▶ **blister** *v* to form or make sth form blisters: [V] *My feet blister easily.* [Vn] *The hot sun blistered the paint.* **blistered** *adj*: *cracked and blistered skin.*

blistering /'blɪstərɪŋ/ *adj* **1** (of heat or speed) very great; extreme: *The runners set off at a blistering pace.* **2** (of criticism) severe; sharp: *blistering sarcasm/scorn/contempt* ○ *He delivered a blistering attack on the government's policies.* **blisteringly** *adv*.
■ **'blister pack** *n* (*Brit*) a packet in which goods are sold, consisting of a transparent bubble of plastic on a base of cardboard, etc.

blithe /blaɪð/ *adj* [usu attrib] happy and not anxious; careless(1): *the blithe optimism of youth* ○ *a blithe lack of concern.* ▶ **blithely** *adv*: *He was blithely unaware of the trouble he had caused.*

blithering /'blɪðərɪŋ/ *adj* [attrib] (*infml derog*) absolute: *You blithering idiot!*

B Litt /ˌbiː 'lɪt/ *abbr* Bachelor of Letters: *have/be a B Litt in English from Hull University* ○ *Sue Hill B Litt.*

blitz /blɪts/ *n* **1** [C] a sudden concentrated military attack, esp from the air: *carry out a blitz on enemy targets.* **2 the Blitz** [sing] the German air attacks on Britain in 1940. **3** [C] ~ (**on sth**) (*fig infml*) any sudden or concentrated effort: *I had a blitz on the kitchen today, and now it's really clean.*
▶ **blitz** *v* to attack or damage sth in a blitz(1): [Vn] *Many towns were badly blitzed during the war.*

blitzkrieg /'blɪtskriːɡ/ *n* a concentrated military campaign intended to win a quick victory.

blizzard /'blɪzəd/ *n* a severe SNOWSTORM with strong winds: *blizzard conditions.*

bloated /'bləʊtɪd/ *adj* swollen with fat, gas or liquid: *a bloated face* ○ *I've had so much to eat I feel absolutely bloated.* ○ (*fig*) *bloated with pride.*

bloater /'bləʊtə(r)/ *n* a HERRING that has been preserved with salt and wood smoke.

blob /blɒb/ *n* a drop of (esp thick) liquid; a small round mass or spot of colour: *a blob of paint/wax/cream.*

bloc /blɒk/ *n* a group of countries or parties united by a common interest: *the former Eastern bloc.* See also EN BLOC.

block¹ /blɒk/ *n* **1(a)** [C] a large solid piece of wood, stone, metal, etc, usu with flat surfaces: *a block of concrete/granite/marble.* ⇨ note at PIECE¹. **(b)** [C] a piece of wood for chopping or hammering on: *a 'chopping-block* ○ *a butcher's block.* **(c) the block** [sing] (formerly) a large piece of wood on which a condemned person's head was cut off: *go/be sent to the block.* **2** [C] a child's wooden or plastic toy brick; an obstacle: *a set of (building) blocks.* **3** [C] (*esp Brit*) a large building divided into separate rooms, flats or offices: *blocks of 'flats* ○ *an 'office block* ○ *a 'tower block* (ie a tall block of flats) ○ *a 'prison block.* **4** [C] **(a)** a group of buildings with streets on four sides: *go for a walk around the block.* **(b)** (*esp US*) the length of one side of such a group: *He lives three blocks away from here.* **5** [C] a large quantity of things regarded as a single unit: *a block of theatre seats* ○ *a block of shares* (ie in a business) ○ *a block booking* (ie the reserving at one time of a large number of seats). **6** [C] a pad of paper for writing or drawing on. **7** [C] a piece of wood or metal with designs on it for printing. **8** [C usu *sing*] a thing that makes movement or progress difficult or impossible; an obstacle: *a block in the pipe/gutter/drain* ○ *a roadblock* ○ (*fig*) *The government's stubborn attitude was a block to further talks.* ○ *I've got writer's block* (ie I cannot think of anything to write). ○ *My son's always had a mental block about team games.* **IDM** **a chip off the old block** ⇨ CHIP¹. **knock sb's block/head off** ⇨ KNOCK².
■ **,block and 'tackle** *n* a lifting device consisting of ropes and pulleys (PULLEY).
,block 'letter (also **,block 'capital**) *n* a separate capital letter: *fill in a form in block letters.*
,block 'vote (also **'card vote**) *n* a voting system in which each person who votes has influence in proportion to the number of people he or she represents. See also STUMBLING-BLOCK.

block² /blɒk/ *v* **1(a)** ~ **sth** (**up**) to make movement or flow difficult or impossible; to OBSTRUCT sth: [Vn, Vnp] *a drain blocked (up) by mud/dead leaves* ○ *My nose is blocked (up)* (eg because of a heavy cold). [Vn] *Heavy snow is blocking all roads into Scotland.* ○ *A large crowd blocked the corridors and exits.* ○ *There's a big tree blocking our view.* [Vnp] *They'd blocked up the windows with bricks.* **(b)** to prevent sb/sth from moving or making progress; to HINDER sb/sth: [Vn] *block an opponent's move* (eg in a game of CHESS) ○ *The accident blocked downtown traffic.* ○ *Progress in the talks was blocked by the government's intransigence.* **2** (*techn*) to limit or prevent the use of a currency or sale of investments, assets (ASSET 2), etc: [Vn] *blocked sterling.* **3** [Vn] (in cricket) to stop the ball with the bat without trying to hit it hard. **PHRV** **,block sth 'in/'out** to make a quick sketch or plan of sth: *block in the plan of a house.* **,block sth 'off** to separate one place from another using a solid barrier: *Police blocked off the street after the explosion.* **,block sth 'out 1** to stop light, noise, etc from coming in. **2** to avoid remembering or thinking about sth: *block out painful memories.*
▶ **blockage** /'blɒkɪdʒ/ *n* **(a)** a thing that blocks flow or movement: *a blockage in an artery/a drainpipe/a road.* **(b)** a state of being blocked.

blockade /blɒ'keɪd/ *n* **1** the act of surrounding or closing a place, esp a port, by an enemy to prevent people or goods getting in or out: *impose a blockade.* **2** anything that prevents access or progress: *a police blockade across the road* ○ *an economic blockade.* **IDM** **break/run a blockade** (esp of a ship) to get through a blockade(1).
▶ **blockade** *v* to close a town, port, etc with a blockade(1): [Vn] *The harbour was blockaded by enemy vessels.*

blockbuster /'blɒkbʌstə(r)/ *n* (*infml*) **1** a very successful book or film: *Her latest novel has the makings of a major blockbuster.* ○ *a blockbuster movie.* **2** a very powerful bomb.

blockhead /'blɒkhed/ *n* (*infml*) a very stupid person.

blockhouse /'blɒkhaʊs/ *n* a concrete structure strengthened to give protection against guns, and with openings for the people defending it to shoot from.

bloke /bləʊk/ *n* (*Brit infml*) a man: *He's a nice bloke.*

blond (also, esp of a woman, **blonde**) /blɒnd/ *n* a person, esp a woman, having hair of a pale golden colour: *a slim, blue-eyed blonde* ○ *Is she a natural blonde?* Compare BRUNETTE.
▶ **blond** *adj* having hair of a pale golden colour.

blood¹ /blʌd/ *n* **1** [U] the red liquid flowing through the bodies of humans and animals: *He lost a lot of blood in the accident.* ○ *a pool of congealed blood on the floor* ○ *Much blood was shed* (ie Many people were killed) *in the war.* **2** [U] (*fml*) family or race: *He is of noble blood.* ○ *Most of my family are musicians; it runs in our blood* (ie is characteristic of our family). **3** [C] (*dated Brit*) a rich and fashionable young man. **IDM** **bad 'blood (between A and B)** feelings of mutual hatred or strong dislike: *There's a lot of bad blood between their two families.* **be after/out for sb's 'blood** (*infml*) to intend to hurt or punish sb: (*usu joc*) *I was late for work again this morning, so my boss is after my blood!* **blood and 'thunder** (*infml*) violent and melodramatic (MELODRAMA) action in films, novels, etc: [attrib]: *a blood-and-thunder story.* **blood is thicker than 'water** (*saying*) family relationships are the strongest ones. **sb's 'blood is up** sb is in a fighting mood: *After being insulted like that, my blood is really up!* **(have sb's) 'blood on one's hands** (to carry) responsibility for the death of a person or people: *a dictator with the blood of thousands on his hands.* **(like getting / trying to get) blood out of / from a ¹stone** (of money, sympathy, understanding, etc) almost impossible to obtain from sb: *Getting a pay rise in this firm is like getting blood from a stone.* **draw blood** ⇨ DRAW¹. **flesh and blood** ⇨ FLESH. **one's flesh and blood** ⇨ FLESH. **freeze one's blood**; **make one's blood freeze** ⇨ FREEZE. **give blood** to allow doctors to remove blood from one's body in order to store it for use by other people. **in cold blood** ⇨ COLD¹. **make sb's ¹blood boil** to make sb very angry: *The way he treats his children makes my blood boil.* **make sb's blood run cold** to fill sb with fear and horror: *The sight of the dead body made his blood run cold.* **new / fresh ¹blood** (in a group, firm, club, etc) new members, esp young ones, with new ideas, skills or methods: *This company badly needs (some) new blood.* **of the blood** (¹royal) related to the royal family: *a prince of the blood (royal).* **spill blood** ⇨ SPILL. **stir the blood** ⇨ STIR. **sweat blood** ⇨ SWEAT *v.*

■ **¹blood bank** *n* a place where blood is stored for use in hospitals, etc.

¹blood bath *n* the killing of many people on one occasion; a MASSACRE(1): *The battle was a blood bath.*

¹blood-brother *n* a man who has sworn to treat another man as his brother, usu in a ceremony in which their blood is mixed together.

¹blood count *n* (an act of counting) the number of red and white cells in a sample of blood.

¹blood-curdling *adj* filling one with horror; very frightening: *a blood-curdling scream.*

¹blood donor *n* a person who gives some of her or his blood to be put into the bodies of other people.

¹blood feud *n* a continuous quarrel between groups or families, with each murdering members of the other; a VENDETTA.

¹blood group *n* any of the several distinct classes of human blood: *His blood group is AO.*

¹blood-heat *n* [U] the normal temperature of human blood (about 37°C, 98.4°F).

¹blood-letting *n* [U] **1** the killing or wounding of people; BLOODSHED. **2** bitter quarrelling, esp between rival groups: *This blood-letting is damaging the reputation of the party.*

¹blood-lust *n* [U] a strong desire to kill.

¹blood-money *n* [U] **1** money paid to a person hired to kill sb. **2** money paid to the family of a murdered person as compensation.

¹blood orange *n* a type of orange whose soft edible part is red.

¹blood-poisoning (also *techn* **toxaemia**) *n* [U] infection of the blood with harmful bacteria, esp through a cut or wound.

¹blood pressure *n* [C, U] the pressure of blood as it travels round the body. Blood pressure is often measured to check a person's health since it is closely related to the force and rate at which the heart beats: *have high / low blood pressure* ○ *(fig) Politicians always raise his blood pressure* (ie make him extremely angry).

¸blood-¹red *adj* having the same red colour as blood: *Her fingernails were blood-red.* ○ *a blood-red sky.*

¹blood relation (also **¹blood relative**) *n* a person related to sb by birth rather than by marriage.

¹blood sports *n* [pl] sports in which animals or birds are killed: *I'm opposed to all blood sports, but especially fox-hunting.*

¹blood test *n* an examination of a sample of blood, esp so that a doctor can make judgements about the condition of a patient.

¹blood transfusion *n* [U, C] (an occasion of) putting new blood into the body of a person or an animal.

¹blood-vessel *n* any of the tubes through which blood flows in the body: *burst a blood-vessel.*

blood² /blʌd/ *v* [Vn] **1** to give sb her or his first experience of an activity: *young soldiers not yet blooded in action.* **2** (in hunting) to allow a young dog to taste the blood of eg a fox for the first time.

bloodhound /'blʌdhaʊnd/ *n* a type of large dog with a good sense of smell, used for following human or animal tracks.

bloodied /'blʌdid/ *adj* partly covered with blood: *bloodied bandages.*

bloodless /'blʌdləs/ *adj* **1** without blood or killing: *a bloodless coup / revolution.* **2** (of a person) pale: *bloodless cheeks.* **3** lacking emotion; cold¹(3a).

bloodshed /'blʌdʃed/ *n* [U] the killing or wounding of people: *The two sides called a truce to avoid further bloodshed.* ○ *The march ended in bloodshed.*

bloodshot /'blʌdʃɒt/ *adj* (of eyes) red because of swollen or broken blood-vessels (BLOOD¹): *His eyes were bloodshot from lack of sleep.*

bloodstain /'blʌdsteɪn/ *n* a mark on sth caused by blood. ▶ **'bloodstained** *adj*: *a bloodstained shirt.*

bloodstock /'blʌdstɒk/ *n* [U] horses of pure breed, bred esp for racing.

bloodstream /'blʌdstriːm/ *n* [sing] the blood flowing through the body: *inject drugs into the bloodstream* ○ *the amount of alcohol in his bloodstream.*

bloodthirsty /'blʌdθɜːsti/ *adj* **1(a)** cruel and eager to kill: *a bloodthirsty killer / tribe.* **(b)** taking pleasure in or showing interest in killing and violence: *bloodthirsty spectators.* **2** (of a book, film, etc) describing or showing killing and violence.

bloody¹ /'blʌdi/ *adj* (**-ier**, **-iest**) **1** covered with blood; bleeding: *His clothes were torn and bloody.* ○ *give sb a bloody nose* (ie hit their nose so that it bleeds). **2** involving a lot of killing and wounding: *a bloody battle.* ▶ **'bloodily** *adv*.

bloody² /'blʌdi/ *adj* [attrib], *adv* (⚠ *Brit infml*) **1** (used to emphasize a judgement or comment) absolute(ly); extreme(ly): *bloody nonsense / rubbish* ○ *This rail strike is a bloody nuisance.* ○ *Don't be such a bloody fool!* ○ *That was a bloody good meal!* **2** (used to make a statement of anger or annoyance stronger): *What are you doing?* ○ *I don't bloody care.* **IDM** **bloody well** (*Brit infml*) (used to make an angry statement, esp an order, stronger) certainly; definitely: *'I'm not coming with you.' 'Yes you bloody well are!'*

■ **¸bloody-¹minded** *adj* (*Brit infml*) refusing to be helpful in a deliberately unreasonable way: *Everybody else accepts the decision. Why must you be so bloody-minded?* **bloody-mindedness** *n* [U].

bloom /bluːm/ *n* **1** [C] a flower, esp of plants admired mainly for their flowers (eg roses): *These chrysanthemums have beautiful blooms.* ○ *an exotic bloom.* ⇨ picture at FLOWER. Compare BLOSSOM. **2** [U] the perfect or most beautiful state of sth: *be in / have lost the bloom of youth.* **IDM** **in (full) bloom** (of plants, gardens, etc) with fully developed flowers: *The garden always looks lovely when the roses are in bloom.*

▶ **bloom** *v* [V] **1** to produce flowers: *Daffodils and crocuses bloom in the spring.* **2** to be in a very healthy condition; to FLOURISH(2): *Our sales figures are now blooming.*

bloomer /'bluːmə(r)/ *n* (*dated Brit infml*) a serious mistake: *He made a bit of a bloomer.*

bloomers /'bluːməz/ *n* [pl] **1** (*infml*) KNICKERS(1). **2** short loose trousers gathered at the knee, formerly worn by women for games, riding bicycles, etc: *a pair of bloomers.*

blooming /'bluːmɪŋ, 'blʊm-, -ɪn/ *adj* [attrib], *adv* (*Brit infml euph*) = BLOODY²: *What blooming (awful) weather!*

blooper /'bluːpə(r)/ *n* (*infml esp US*) an embarrassing public mistake.

---

blossom /'blɒsəm/ n (a) [C] a flower, esp of a fruit tree or bush. Compare BLOOM 1. (b) [U] a mass of flowers on a tree or bush: *apple/cherry blossom* ○ *The lilac trees are in (full) blossom* (ie bearing blossom).
▶ **blossom** v **1** (of a tree or bush) to produce blossom: [V] *The cherry trees blossomed early this year.* **2** ~ (**out**) (**into sth**) (**a**) to develop in a healthy or promising way; to grow or develop (into sth); to FLOURISH(1): [V] *a blossoming friendship/career* ○ *rumours of a blossoming romance with her dancing partner* ○ *Mozart blossomed (as a composer) very early in life.* [Vpr, Vp] *She has blossomed (out) into a beautiful young woman.* (**b**) to become more lively: [V, Vp] *He used to be painfully shy, but now he's started to blossom (out).*

blot /blɒt/ n **1** a spot or STAIN made by ink, etc: *a page covered in (ink) blots.* **2** ~ (**on sth**) an act or quality that spoils sb's good character or reputation: *Their handling of the economic crisis has been a serious blot on the government's record.* **IDM a blot on the landscape** an object, esp an ugly building, that spoils the beauty of a place.
▶ **blot** v (**-tt-**) **1** to make a blot or blots on paper: [Vn] *an exercise book blotted with ink.* **2**(**a**) to dry sth with blotting-paper: [Vn] *blot one's writing-paper.* (**b**) ~ **sth** (**up**) to absorb sth with blotting-paper, etc: [Vn, Vnp] *She blotted the ink (up).* **IDM blot one's copybook** (*infml*) to spoil one's good record or reputation: *She blotted her copybook by being an hour late for work.* **PHRV ,blot sth 'out 1** to cover or hide writing, etc with a blot: *Several words in the letter had been blotted out.* **2** (esp of mist, etc) to hide sth completely: *Thick cloud blotted out the view.* **3** to remove or destroy thoughts, memories, etc completely: *He tried to blot out anything that would remind him of his ordeal.*
blotter n a pad or large piece of blotting-paper.
■ **'blotting-paper** n [U] paper that absorbs wet ink.

blotch /blɒtʃ/ n a large mark, usu not regular in shape, on skin, paper, material, etc: *His face was covered in ugly red blotches.*
▶ **blotched**, **blotchy** *adjs* covered in blotches: *blotchy skin.*

blotto /'blɒtəʊ/ *adj* [pred] (*infml*) very drunk: *You were completely blotto last night.*

blouse /blaʊz; US blaʊs/ n **1** a garment like a shirt, worn by women: *a green silk blouse.* **2** a type of jacket worn by soldiers as part of their uniform.

blow¹ /bləʊ/ v (*pt* **blew** /bluː/; *pp* **blown** /bləʊn/ or, in sense 12, **blowed** /bləʊd/) **1** (often with *it* as the subject) (of the wind or a current of air) to be moving: [V, V-n] *It was blowing hard/blowing a gale* (ie There was a strong wind). [Vpr] *A cold wind blew across the river from the east.* **2** to send out a current of air, etc from the mouth: [V] *You're not blowing hard enough!* [Vpr] *It is not very polite to blow on one's food* (ie to cool it). ○ *She blew on her fingers* (ie to warm them). ○ *The policeman asked me to blow into the breathalyser.* [Vnp] *He drew on his cigarette and blew out a stream of smoke.* [also Vnpr]. **3** to be moved by the wind: [V, Vp] *hair blowing (about) in the wind.* **4** to make or shape sth by blowing: [Vn] *blow smoke-rings* ○ *blow bubbles* (eg by blowing onto a thin layer of water mixed with soap) ○ *blow glass* (ie send a current of air into melted glass to shape it). **5** to use sth to make a current of air: [Vn] *blow bellows.* **6**(**a**) to produce sound from a brass instrument, whistle, etc by blowing into it: [Vn, Vpr] *blow (on) a horn* [Vn] *The referee blew his whistle.* (**b**) (of an instrument, etc) to make a sound when blown: [V] *the noise of trumpets blowing.* **7** to melt or cause sth to melt with too strong an electric current: [V] *A fuse has blown.* [Vn] *I've blown a fuse.* **8** to break sth open with

explosives: [Vn] *The safe had been blown by the thieves.* **9** (*sl*) to make known sth that was secret: [Vn] *The spy's cover was blown.* **10** ~ **sth** (**on sth**) (*infml*) to spend a lot of money (on sth), esp in a RECKLESS way: [Vnpr] *She was left £5000 by her grandfather and blew the lot on a holiday.* [also Vn]. **11** to spoil or fail to use an opportunity: [Vn] *He blew it/blew his chances by arriving late for the interview.* **12** (*pp* **blowed** /bləʊd/) (*infml*) (used esp in the imperative in certain phrases to express anger, surprise, etc) [Vn] *Blow it! We've missed the bus.* ○ *Well, blow me (down)/I'm blowed! I never thought I'd see you again.* ○ *I'm blowed if I'm going to* (ie I certainly will not) *let him treat you like that.* ○ *Let's take a taxi and blow* (ie never mind) *the expense.* **13** (*sl esp US*) to leave a place suddenly: [V] *Let's blow!* [also Vn]. **IDM blow one's/sb's 'brains out** to kill oneself/sb by shooting in the head. **blow hot and 'cold (about sth)** (*infml*) to keep changing one's opinions about sth: *He blows hot and cold about getting married.* **blow (sb) a 'kiss** to kiss one's hand and then pretend to blow the kiss (towards sb). **blow one's/sb's 'mind** (*sl*) to produce a very strong pleasant or shocking feeling in one/sb. **blow one's 'nose** to clear MUCUS out of one's nose by breathing strongly out through it into a HANDKERCHIEF. **blow one's own 'trumpet** (*infml*) to praise one's own abilities and achievements; to boast. **blow one's 'top**; (*US*) **blow one's 'stack** (*infml*) to lose one's temper. **blow the 'whistle on sb/sth** (*infml*) to make sb suddenly stop doing sth, esp sth illegal, usu by informing people in authority: *They cheated the company for years until one of their colleagues blew the whistle on them.* **puff and blow** ⇨ PUFF². **see which way the wind is blowing** ⇨ WAY¹. **PHRV ,blow (sb/sth) 'down, 'off, 'over, etc** to move or be moved in the specified direction by the force of the wind, sb's breath, etc: *My hat blew off.* ○ *The door blew open.* ○ *Several chimneys blew down during the storm.* ○ *I was almost blown over by the wind.* ○ *The ship was blown onto the rocks.* ○ *The bomb blast blew two passers-by across the street.* ○ *He blew the dust off the book* (ie removed the dust by blowing).
,blow 'in /, blow 'into sth (*infml*) to arrive or enter a place suddenly: *Look who's just blown in!*
,blow 'out 1 (of a flame, etc) to be put out by the wind, etc: *Somebody opened the door and the candle blew out.* **2** (of an oil or gas WELL⁴) to send out gas suddenly and forcefully. **,blow itself 'out** (of a storm, etc) to lose its force finally. **,blow sth 'out** to put out a flame, etc by blowing.
,blow 'over to go away without having a serious effect: *The storm blew over in the night.* ○ *The scandal will soon blow over.*
,blow 'up 1 to explode; to be destroyed by an explosion: *The bomb blew up.* ○ *A policeman was killed when his booby-trapped car blew up.* **2** to start suddenly and with force: *A storm is blowing up.* ○ *A political crisis has blown up over the president's latest speech.* **3** (*infml*) to lose one's temper: *I'm sorry I blew up at you.* **,blow sb 'up** (*infml*) to speak to sb very severely: *She got blown up by her boss for being late.* **,blow sth 'up 1** to destroy sth by an explosion: *The police station was blown up by terrorists.* **2** to fill sth with air or gas so that it becomes firm: *The tyres on my bike need blowing up.* **3** to make a photograph bigger; to ENLARGE(1) sth: *What a lovely photo! Why don't you have it blown up?* **4** (*infml*) to exaggerate sth: *His abilities as an actor have been greatly blown up by the popular press.* ○ *The whole affair was blown up out of all proportion.*
▶ **blow** *interj* (used to express anger or annoyance): *Blow! I've forgotten my library ticket.*
blowy *adj* with strong winds blowing: *a blowy day.*
■ **'blow-dry** v (*pt, pp* **-dried**) [Vn] to put hair into a particular style while drying it with an electric

machine. — *n*: *ask the hairdresser for a wash and blow-dry*.

'blow-hole *n* **1** a NOSTRIL at the back of the head of a WHALE. **2** a hole in the ice through which seals, etc breathe. **3** an opening for air, smoke, etc to escape in a tunnel.

'blow-out *n* **1** an occasion when a tyre on a motor vehicle bursts: *have a blow-out on the motorway*. **2** an occasion when an electric FUSE¹(1) melts. **3** a sudden escape of oil or gas from a WELL⁴. **4** (*sl*) a large meal.

'blow-up *n* an enlargement (ENLARGE) of a photograph, picture or design: *Do a blow-up of this corner of the negative*.

blow² /bləʊ/ *n* an act of blowing: *Give your nose a good blow* (ie Clear it thoroughly).

blow³ /bləʊ/ *n* **1** a hard hit given with one's closed hand, a weapon, etc: *He received a severe blow on/to the head.* ○ *a knock-out blow* ○ *a flurry of blows.* **2 ~ (to sb/sth)** a sudden shock that affects sb/sth badly: *a shattering blow to one's pride* ○ *His wife's death came as a terrible blow (to him).* ○ *Is there any way we can soften the blow?* **IDM a ,blow-by-,blow ac'count, de'scription, etc (of sth)** an account giving all the details of an event in the order in which they happened: *He insisted on giving us a blow-by-blow account of the evening's events.* **come to 'blows (over sth)** to start fighting because of sth: *We almost came to blows over what colour our new carpet should be.* **deal sb/sth a blow; deal a blow to sb/sth** ⇨ DEAL¹. **strike a blow for/ against sth** ⇨ STRIKE².

blower /'bləʊə(r)/ *n* **1** [C] a device that produces a current of air. **2 the blower** [sing] (*Brit infml*) the telephone: *You can always get me on the blower*.

blowlamp /'bləʊlæmp/ (*Brit*) (*US* **torch**, **'blow-torch**) *n* a tool used for directing a very hot flame onto part of a surface, eg to remove old paint.

blown *pp* of BLOW¹.

blowzy (also **blowsy**) /'blaʊzi/ *adj* (*derog*) (of a woman) fat and untidy in appearance, with a rather red face.

blubber¹ /'blʌbə(r)/ *n* [U] the fat of whales (WHALE) and other sea animals, from which oil is obtained.

blubber² /'blʌbə(r)/ *v* (*usu derog*) to cry noisily: [V] *Stop blubbering, you big baby!*

bludgeon /'blʌdʒən/ *n* a short thick stick with a heavy end, used as a weapon.
▶ **bludgeon** *v* to hit sb repeatedly with a heavy object: [Vn] *He had been bludgeoned to death.* **PHRV 'bludgeon sb into (doing) sth** to force sb to do sth: *They tried to bludgeon me into joining their protest, but I refused.*

blue¹ /bluː/ *adj* (**bluer, bluest**) **1** having the colour of a clear sky or the sea in sunlight: *blue eyes* ○ *a blue dress/shirt* ○ *Her hands were blue with cold.* ⇨ picture at SPECTRUM. **2** [pred] (*infml esp US*) sad; depressed: *feeling blue.* **3** connected with sex in a way that may be thought offensive; OBSCENE: *a blue film/movie/joke.* **IDM between the devil and the deep blue sea** ⇨ DEVIL¹. **black and blue** ⇨ BLACK¹. **sb's ,blue-eyed 'boy** (*infml esp Brit often derog*) a person treated with special favour by sb: *He's the manager's blue-eyed boy.* **once in a blue moon** ⇨ ONCE. **scream, etc blue 'murder** (*infml*) to protest wildly and noisily: *The union yelled blue murder when one of its members was sacked.* **(do sth) till one is blue in the 'face** (*infml*) (to work, etc) as hard and as long as one possibly can, usu without success: *He can write me letters till he's blue in the face, I'm not going to reply.* ▶ **blueness** *n* [U].
■ **,blue 'baby** *n* a baby whose skin is blue at birth because of a fault in the heart.
,blue 'blood *n* [U] noble birth. **,blue-'blooded** *adj*: *a ,blue-blooded 'family*.

,blue 'cheese (*US* also **bleu cheese**) *n* [C,U] cheese showing lines of blue mould².

,blue-'chip *adj* [attrib] (*commerce*) of or offering industrial shares (SHARE¹ 3) that are thought to be a safe investment: *blue-chip stocks/companies*.

,blue-'collar *adj* [attrib] of or relating to people doing practical work or work requiring physical strength: *blue-collar workers/jobs* ○ *a blue-collar union*. Compare WHITE-COLLAR.

,blue 'pencil (*Brit*) a pencil, traditionally blue, for crossing out or altering the offensive parts of a book, play, etc before it is shown to the public.

,Blue 'Peter *n* a blue flag with a central white square, used to show that a ship is about to sail.

'blue tit *n* a small bird with a blue head, tail and wings and yellow parts underneath.

,blue 'whale *n* a type of WHALE that is the largest known living animal.

blue² /bluː/ *n* **1(a)** [C,U] a blue colour: *light/dark blue* ○ *material with a lot of blue in it.* **(b)** [U] blue clothes: *dressed in blue.* **2** [C] **(a)** (*Brit*) a distinction awarded to a person who represents either Oxford or Cambridge University at a particular sport: *get a/one's blue for hockey/football.* **(b)** a person who has won such a distinction: *an Oxford hockey blue .* **3** [sing or pl *v*] **(a) the blues** slow sad JAZZ music originating among Blacks in the southern USA: *a blues singer/melody.* **(b) blues** a song of this type: *sing a blues.* **4 the blues** [pl] (*infml*) feelings of deep sadness or depression: *have (an attack of) the blues.* **IDM a bolt from the blue** ⇨ BOLT¹. **the boys in blue** ⇨ BOY¹. **out of the 'blue** unexpected(ly); without warning: *She arrived out of the blue.* ○ *His resignation came (right) out of the blue.*

bluebell /'bluːbel/ *n* a plant with blue or white flowers shaped like bells. ⇨ picture at FLOWER.

blueberry /'bluːbəri/ *n* **(a)** a small N American bush. **(b)** its edible dark blue berry. Compare BILBERRY.

bluebottle /'bluːbɒtl/ *n* a large noisy fly with a blue body.

bluegrass /'bluːgrɑːs/ *US* -græs/ *n* [U] (*US*) traditional country music played on stringed instruments (STRING²), esp banjos (BANJO) and guitars (GUITAR).

blueprint /'bluːprɪnt/ *n* **1** a photographic print of building plans, with white lines on a blue background. **2** a detailed plan or scheme: *The government have described their manifesto as a blueprint for the future.*

bluestocking /'bluːstɒkɪŋ/ *n* (*sometimes derog*) a woman having, or pretending to have, literary tastes and learning.

bluff¹ /blʌf/ *v* to try to deceive sb by pretending to be stronger, braver, cleverer, etc than one really is: [V,Vn] *I don't believe he'd really do it — he's only bluffing (us).* **PHRV 'bluff sb into doing sth** to make sb do sth by deceiving her or him: *You'll never bluff them into letting you go.* **,bluff it 'out** to survive a difficult situation by deceiving others. **,bluff one's way 'out (of sth)** to escape from a difficult situation by deceiving others.
▶ **bluff** *n* [U,C] bluffing; a threat intended to influence sb without being carried out: *The company's threat to fire anyone who went on strike was just (a) bluff.* **IDM call sb's bluff** ⇨ CALL¹.

bluff² /blʌf/ *n* a steep cliff.

bluff³ /blʌf/ *adj* (of people or their manner, etc) direct and not very polite, though having a pleasant nature underneath: *He is kind and friendly despite his rather bluff manner.* ▶ **bluffness** *n* [U].

bluish /'bluːɪʃ/ *adj* tending towards blue; fairly blue: *eyes of bluish green*.

blunder /'blʌndə(r)/ *n* a stupid or careless mistake: *an administrative blunder* ○ *make a series of costly blunders.* ⇨ note at MISTAKE.

▶ **blunder** v to make a blunder: [V] *a blundering fool* ○ *The police blundered badly in arresting the wrong man.* **PHRV** ˌblunder aˈbout, aˈround, etc to move about in an awkward or uncertain way, as if blind: *He blundered about the room, feeling for the light switch.* ˌblunder ˈinto sth to walk into sth because of being awkward or unable to see: *In the darkness, she blundered into the hall table.* ○ *(fig) They blundered into a situation which they did not understand.*

blunderbuss /ˈblʌndəbʌs/ n an old type of gun with a wide mouth that could fire many small bullets at short range.

blunt /blʌnt/ adj (**-er, -est**) **1** without a sharp edge or a point: *a blunt knife/saw/pencil* ○ *Police said he had been battered with a **blunt instrument**, possibly a hammer.* **2** (of a person, remark, etc) frank and direct; not trying to be polite or tactful (TACT): *a blunt refusal* ○ *Let me be quite blunt (with you) — your work is appalling.*
▶ **blunt** v [Vn] **1** to make sth blunt(1) or less sharp: *a knife blunted by years of use.* **2** to cause sth to have less power or effect: *a fine mind blunted by boredom* ○ *The impact of the report will be severely blunted by this latest news.*
bluntly adv in a blunt(2) manner: *To put it bluntly, your work isn't good enough.*
bluntness n [U].

blur /blɜː(r)/ n a thing that does not appear or sound clear and distinct: *The town was just a blur on the horizon.* ○ *Everything is a blur when I take my glasses off.* ○ *(fig) My memories of childhood are only a blur.*
▶ **blur** v (**-rr-**) **1(a)** to become difficult to see through clearly: [V] *His eyes blurred with tears.* **(b)** to make sth become difficult to see clearly: [Vn] *a horizon blurred by a grey mist.* **2** to become or make sth difficult to distinguish clearly: [V] *The old ethnic boundaries have blurred now.* [Vn] *She tends to blur the distinction between family and friends.*
blurred /blɜːd/ adj **1** not clear in shape, outline, etc: *a blurred picture taken with a slow-speed camera.* **2** difficult to distinguish: *The boundaries between East and West have become blurred.*
blurry /ˈblɜːri/ adj: *blurry, distorted photographs.*

blurb /blɜːb/ n a short description of the contents of a book that is printed on the cover: *the publisher's blurb.*

blurt /blɜːt/ v **PHRV** ˌblurt sth ˈout to say sth suddenly and without careful consideration: *He blurted out the bad news before I could stop him.*

blush /blʌʃ/ v **1** ~ (with sth) (at sth) to become red in the face because of shame, embarrassment, etc: [V] *Don't tell everyone — you're making me blush!* ○ *a photograph of the **blushing bride*** [Vpr] *He blushed crimson with embarrassment when I kissed him.* ○ *She blushed at (the thought of) her stupid mistake.* **2** (fml) to be ashamed: [V.to inf] *I blush to admit/confess that…*
▶ **blush** n an example of blushing: *She turned away to hide her blushes.* ○ *betrayed by the hot blush that spread up into his face.* **IDM** **spare sb's blushes** ⇨ SPARE².
blusher n [C,U] a substance that is put on the cheeks to give them more colour.

bluster /ˈblʌstə(r)/ v ~ (on) (about sth) to talk in an aggressive, boasting, threatening or loudly protesting way, usu with little effect: [V.speech] *'But I haven't the authority,' he blustered.* [Vnpr] *His attempts to bluster his way out of trouble were not convincing.* [also V, Vp, Vpr].
▶ **bluster** n [U] blustering talk or behaviour; noisy but empty threats: *I wasn't frightened by what he said — it was just bluster.*
blustery /ˈblʌstəri/ adj (of the weather) with strong winds: *a cold blustery day.*

bn abbr billion.

BO /ˌbiː ˈəʊ/ abbr (infml esp Brit) body odour: *have BO.*

boa /ˈbəʊə/ n **1** (also **ˈboa constrictor**) a large S American snake that kills animals for food by winding its long body round them and crushing them. ⇨ picture at SNAKE. **2** = FEATHER BOA.

boar /bɔː(r)/ n (pl unchanged or **boars**) **1** a male wild pig. **2** a male domestic pig that has not been castrated (CASTRATE). Compare HOG 1, SOW².

board¹ /bɔːd/ n **1** [C,U] a long thin flat piece of a hard material, esp cut wood, used for building walls, floors, boats, etc: *He had ripped up the carpet, leaving only the bare boards.* See also CHIPBOARD, FLOORBOARD, HARDBOARD, SKIRTING-BOARD. **2** [C] (esp in compounds) **(a)** a flat piece of wood or other stiff material used for a particular purpose: *a ˈnotice-board* ○ *He put the poster up on the board.* ○ *a ˈdiving-board* ○ *She dived from the top board.* ○ *an ˈironing-board* ○ *a ˈbreadboard* (ie for cutting bread on) ○ *a ˈcircuit board* ○ *The teacher wrote some sums on the board* (ie the BLACKBOARD). See also DRAWING-BOARD. **(b)** a flat piece of a stiff material marked with patterns, etc on which particular games are played: *Let's play backgammon. Where's the board?* ○ *a chess-board.* ⇨ picture at CHESS. **3** [CGp] a group of people controlling a company or other organization; a committee or council: *a prisoner's parole board* ○ *She has a seat on/is on the board (of directors) of a large company.* ○ *The board is/are unhappy about falling sales.* ○ (US) *the board of education/elections/estimate* ○ *attend a ˈboard meeting* ○ *discussions at board level.* **4** [U] the cost of daily meals in rented accommodation: *He pays £80 a week (for) board and lodging.* See also BED AND BOARD, FULL BOARD, HALF BOARD. **IDM** **(be) above ˈboard** (esp of a business arrangement) honest and open: *Don't worry; the deal was completely above board.* **aˌcross the ˈboard 1** involving all members, groups or classes of a company, an industry, a society, etc: *This firm needs radical changes across the board.* ○ *an aˌcross-the-board ˈwage increase.* **2** (US) (of a bet) placed so that one wins if the horse, etc finishes the race in first, second or third place. **be on/tread the boards** (dated or joc) to be a professional actor; to take part in a play. ˌgo by the ˈboard (of plans, principles, etc) to be abandoned, rejected or ignored: *I'm afraid the new car will have to go by the board — we simply can't afford it.* **on ˈboard** on or in a ship or an aircraft: *Have the passengers gone on board yet?* See also BOARD² 3. **sweep the board** ⇨ SWEEP¹. **take sth on ˈboard** (infml) **1** to accept a responsibility, etc: *I'm too busy to take any new jobs on board at the moment.* **2** to understand and appreciate sth fully.
■ **ˈboard-game** n a game played on a board¹(2b).

board² /bɔːd/ v **1** ~ sth (up) to supply or cover sth with boards (BOARD¹ 1): [Vn] *boarded floors/panels* [Vnp] *All the windows of the old house are now boarded up.* **2** ~ at… /with sb to live and take meals in sb's house: [Vpr] *He boarded at my house/with me until he found a flat.* See also BOARD¹ 4. **3** to get on or into a ship, a train, an aircraft, a bus, etc: [Vn] *Please board the plane immediately.* See also ON BOARD. **IDM** **be boarding** (of a plane, etc) to be ready for passengers to get on or into it: *Flight BA193 for Paris is now boarding.* **PHRV** ˌboard ˈout to have meals away from the place where one lives. ˌboard sb ˈout to arrange accommodation for sb away from their place of work, school, etc in return for payment: *Many students have to be boarded out in the town.*
▶ **boarder** n **1** a person who boards at sb's house. **2** a pupil who lives at a boarding-school during the term: *This school has 300 boarders and 150 day pupils.*

B

■ **'boarding card** *n* a card allowing a person to board a ship or plane.

'boarding-house *n* a house whose owner provides people with meals and accommodation in return for payment.

'boarding-school *n* a school where some or all of the pupils live during the term. Compare DAY-SCHOOL.

boardroom /'bɔːdruːm, -rʊm/ *n* a room in which the meetings of the board of directors of a company are held: *a boardroom row*.

boardwalk /'bɔːdwɔːk/ *n* (*US*) a raised path, usu made of boards, along a beach.

boast /bəʊst/ *v* **1** ~ (**about/of sth**) to talk about one's own achievements, abilities, etc with too much pride and satisfaction: [V] *Stop boasting!* [Vpr] *He's always boasting about his children's success at school.* ○ *That's nothing to boast about.* ○ *She boasted of her skill at chess.* [V.that] *He boasted that he was the best player in the team.* [also V.speech]. **2** (not usu in the progressive tenses) to possess sth that one can be proud of: [Vn] *The city boasts one of the most famous art galleries in the world.* ○ *No other company can boast such a record.*

▶ **boast** *n* **1** ~ (**that...**) (*derog*) a statement showing too much pride and satisfaction: *His boast that he could drink ten pints of beer impressed nobody.* ○ *Her claim that she could beat us all was clearly* **no idle/empty boast.** **2** a good reason for being proud: *It was his* **proud boast** *that he had never missed a day's work because of illness.*

boastful /-fl/ *adj* (*usu derog*) showing too much pride in oneself: *boastful talk* ○ *He emerges from his writings as a boastful, overbearing and bumptious man.* **boastfully** /-fəli/ *adv*.

boat /bəʊt/ *n* **1** a small hollow structure for travelling in on water, moved by oars (OAR), sails or a motor: *a rowing-/sailing-boat* ○ *take a* **boat trip** ○ *The motor/fishing boat chugged along.* ○ *We crossed the river in a boat/* **by boat**. ○ *Boats for hire — £10 an hour.* ○ *the Oxford and Cambridge boat race.* See also CANAL BOAT, LIFEBOAT, PLEASURE-BOAT. **2** (*infml*) any ship: *'How are you going to France?' 'I'm going by/ taking the boat* (eg the FERRY).*' See also GRAVY-BOAT, SAUCE-BOAT.* **IDM** **be in the same boat** ⇨ SAME¹. **burn one's boats/bridges** ⇨ BURN. **miss the boat/bus** ⇨ MISS². **push the boat out** ⇨ PUSH¹. **rock the boat** ⇨ ROCK².

▶ **boating** *n* [U] the activity of using a small boat for pleasure: *We* **go boating** *on the lake every weekend.* ○ *a boating lake/holiday.*

■ **'boat-hook** *n* a long pole with a hook at one end, used for pulling or pushing boats.

'boat-house *n* a shed beside a river or lake for keeping boats in.

'boat people *n* [pl] refugees (REFUGEE) who have left a country in boats: *Vietnamese boat people.*

boater /'bəʊtə(r)/ *n* a hard straw hat with a flat top.

boatman /'bəʊtmən/ *n* (*pl* **-men**) (**a**) a man who transports people in small boats for payment. (**b**) a man who hires out small boats.

boatyard /'bəʊtjɑːd/ *n* a place where boats are kept, repaired, hired out, etc.

bob¹ /bɒb/ *v* (**-bb-**) ~ (**sth**) (**up and down**) to move or make sth move quickly up and down, esp in water: [Vpr, Vp] *boats bobbing (up and down) on the waves* [Vn] *She bobbed her head nervously.* ○ *bob a curtsy* [also Vnp, Vnpr]. **PHRV** **,bob 'up** to come to the surface quickly; to appear suddenly: *She dived below the surface, then bobbed up again like a cork a few seconds later.* ○ *He keeps bobbing up in the most unlikely places.*

▶ **bob** *n* **1** a quick movement down and up: *a bob of the head.* **2** a CURTSY. See also BOBS.

bob² /bɒb/ *n* a style in which the hair is cut short so

that it hangs loosely above the shoulders: *She wears her hair in a bob.* See also BOBBED.

bob³ /bɒb/ *n* (*pl* unchanged) (*infml*) a former British coin, the SHILLING, replaced by the 5p coin.

bob⁴ /bɒb/ *n* **IDM** **bob's your 'uncle** (*infml*) (used to express the ease with which a task can be completed successfully): *To switch the computer on, turn this, press that, and bob's your uncle!*

bobbed /bɒbd/ *adj* cut in the style of a BOB².

bobbin /'bɒbɪn/ *n* a small CYLINDER(1) round which thread, wire, etc is wound for use in a machine.

bobble /'bɒbl/ *n* a small woollen ball used as a decoration, esp on a hat.

bobby /'bɒbi/ *n* (*Brit infml*) a police officer.

bobby-pin /'bɒbi pɪn/ *n* (*US*) = HAIRGRIP.

bobs /bɒbz/ *n* [pl] ⇨ BITS AND BOBS (BIT¹).

bob-sleigh /'bɒbsleɪ/ (also **bob-sled** /-sled/) *n* a large racing SLEDGE for two or more people: *a two-/ four-man bob-sleigh.*

bod /bɒd/ *n* (*Brit infml*) a person, esp a man: *He's an odd bod.*

bode /bəʊd/ *v* **IDM** **bode 'well/'ill (for sb/sth)** to be a good/bad sign for sb/sth: *These trading figures do not bode well for the company's future.*

bodice /'bɒdɪs/ *n* the upper part of a woman's dress, down to the waist.

-bodied /-'bɒdid/ (forming compound *adjs*) having the specified type of body: *big-bodied* ○ *able-bodied* ○ *full-bodied.*

bodily /'bɒdɪli/ *adj* [attrib] of the human body; physical: *bodily needs* (eg food, warmth) ○ *bodily organs* (eg the heart, the stomach) ○ *bodily harm* (ie physical injury).

▶ **bodily** *adv* **1** as a whole or mass; completely: *The monument was moved bodily to a new site.* **2** by taking hold of the body; using force: *The prisoners were thrown bodily into the police van.*

body /'bɒdi/ *n* **1** [C] (**a**) the whole physical structure of a human being or an animal: *body tissues* ○ *body fat* ○ *the female body* ○ *My whole body ached.* (**b**) the body of a dead person or animal: *The police found a body at the bottom of the lake.* ○ *His body is being brought back to his birthplace for burial.* **2** [C] the main part of a human body, apart from the head and limbs: *He has a strong body, but rather thin legs.* ○ *She was badly burned on the face and body.* See also -BODIED. **3(a)** [sing] **the ~ of sth** the main part of sth, esp a vehicle or building: *the body of a plane/ ship/car* ○ *the body of a theatre/concert hall* (ie the central part where the seats are) ○ *The main body of the book deals with the author's political career.* (**b**) [C] **~ of sth** a large amount of sth; a mass or collection of sth: *a body of evidence/information* ○ *large bodies of water* (eg lakes or seas) ○ *There is a large body of support for nuclear disarmament.* **4** [CGp] a group of people working or acting as a unit: *a body of troops/supporters* ○ *professional bodies such as the Law Association* ○ *an independent legislative body* ○ *an elected body* ○ *The governing body of the school is/are concerned about discipline.* ○ *The protesters marched* **in a body** (ie all together) *to the White House.* **5** [C] a distinct piece of matter; an object: *heavenly bodies* (ie stars, planets, etc) ○ *I've got some kind of* **foreign body** (eg an insect or a piece of dirt) *in my eye.* **6** [U] a full strong flavour, esp of wine: *a wine with plenty of body.* **IDM** **body and 'soul** with all one's energies; completely: *love sb body and soul.* **keep body and 'soul together** to stay alive, though with some difficulty; to survive: *They scarcely have enough money to keep body and soul together.* **over my dead body** ⇨ DEAD. **sell one's body** ⇨ SELL.

■ **'body-blow** *n* a severe disappointment or setback (SET¹): *The death of their leader was/dealt a body-blow to the party.*

ˈbody-building *n* [U] the practice of strengthening the muscles of the body through exercise.

ˈbody clock *n* the natural instinct of the human body that controls its functions, eg the need to sleep: *I only arrived in London yesterday and my body clock is still on New York time.*

ˈbody language *n* [U] the process of communicating by the way one sits, stands, moves, etc rather than by words.

ˈbody odour *n* [U] (*abbr* **BO**) the smell of the human body, esp of sweat, usu regarded as unpleasant.

the ˌbody ˈpolitic *n* [sing] (*fml*) the state regarded as an organized group of citizens.

ˈbody stocking *n* a garment that fits closely over the whole body from the neck to the ankles, often including the arms, worn eg by dancers.

Actions expressing emotions

Often parts of the body are closely linked to particular verbs. The combination of the verb and part of the body expresses emotions or attitudes.

action	part of body	possible emotion or attitude expressed
clench	fist	anger, aggression
crease/furrow/knit	brow	concentration, puzzlement
drum	fingers	impatience
lick	lips	anticipation
purse	lips	disapproval, dislike
raise	eyebrows	inquiry, surprise
shrug	shoulders	doubt, indifference
stick out	tongue	disrespect
wrinkle	nose	dislike, distaste

---

bodyguard /ˈbɒdigɑːd/ *n* [C, CGp] a man or group of men whose job is to protect an important person: *The President's bodyguard is/are armed.*

bodywork /ˈbɒdiwɜːk/ *n* [U] the main outside structure of a motor vehicle: *paint/repair/damage the bodywork of a car.*

Boer /ˈbɔː(r)/ *n* (formerly) an African of Dutch origin; an Afrikaner: *the Boer War* (ie the war between the Boers and the British (1899–1902)).

boffin /ˈbɒfɪn/ *n* (*Brit infml*) a scientist, esp one doing research.

bog /bɒɡ/ *n* **1** [C, U] (an area of) wet soft ground formed of decaying plants: *a peat bog* ○ *Keep on the path — parts of the reserve are bog.* **2** [C] (*Brit sl*) a toilet.

▶ **bog** *v* (-gg-) PHRV **bog (sth/sb) down** (usu passive) **1** to sink or make sth/sb sink into mud or wet ground: *The tank (got) bogged down in the mud.* **2** to become or make sth/sb become stuck and unable to make progress: *The discussions got bogged down in irrelevant detail.*

boggy /ˈbɒɡi/ *adj* (of land) soft and wet: *boggy ground/moorland.*

bogey¹ /ˈbəʊɡi/ *n* **1** (in golf) the score of one over the standard for a hole. **2** (*dated esp Brit*) (in golf) the standard score that a good player should make for a hole or course. Compare PAR¹ 1.

bogey² (also **bogy**) /ˈbəʊɡi/ (*US* also **boogey** /ˈbuːɡi/) *n* (**a**) (also **ˈbogeyman**, **ˈbogyman** /-mæn/, *US* **boogeyman** /ˈbuːɡimæn/) an imaginary evil spirit (used to frighten children): *The bogeyman's coming!* (**b**) a thing that causes fear, often without reason: *the bogey of unemployment.*

boggle /ˈbɒɡl/ *v* ~ (**at sth**) (*infml*) to hesitate to do sth because of alarm or surprise: [Vpr] *He boggled at the thought of swimming in winter.* [also V]. IDM **boggle sb's/the ˈmind** (*US infml*) to astonish or shock sb: *The vastness of space really boggles the mind.* Compare MIND-BOGGLING. **the mind/ imagination ˈboggles (at sth)** (*infml*) one can

hardly accept or imagine a particular idea, suggestion, etc: *The mind boggles at the amount of work involved in such an undertaking.* ○ *I've heard he keeps a giraffe as a pet — the imagination boggles!*

bogus /ˈbəʊɡəs/ *adj* not genuine; false: *a bogus passport/doctor/claim.*

bohemian /bəʊˈhiːmiən/ *n, adj* (a person, esp an artist) having or displaying a very informal way of life which does not follow conventional rules of behaviour.

boil¹ /bɔɪl/ *v* **1(a)** (of a liquid) to be heated to the point where it forms bubbles and turns to steam: [V] *The kettle* (ie The water inside it) *is boiling.* ○ *Have the potatoes* (ie Has the water in which the potatoes are being cooked) *boiled yet?* ⇨ note at WATER¹. (**b**) ~ (**away**) to continue to boil: [Vp] *There's a saucepan boiling away on the stove.* [also V]. **2** to cause a liquid to boil: [Vn] *boil some water for the rice.* ~ **sth (for sb)** to cook sth in boiling water: [Vn] *boiled cabbage/carrots/potatoes* [Vnn, Vnpr] *Please boil me an egg/boil an egg for me.* [also V]. ⇨ note at COOK. **4** ~ (**over**) to be very angry: [Vpr, Vp] *He was boiling (over) with rage.* IDM **boil ˈdry** (*Brit*) (of a liquid) to boil until there is none left: *Don't let the pan boil dry.* **keep the pot boiling** ⇨ POT¹. **make sb's blood boil** ⇨ BLOOD¹. PHRV **ˌboil (sth) aˈway** to boil or make sth boil until nothing remains: *The water in the kettle had all boiled away.* **ˌboil (sth) ˈdown** to be reduced or reduce sth by boiling. **ˌboil sth ˈdown (to sth)** (*infml*) to produce a summary of sth; to leave out the parts of sth which are not important: *The original programme has been boiled down to just twenty minutes.* **ˌboil ˈdown to sth** (to be able) to be summarized (SUMMARIZE) as sth; to have sth as its basic or most important factor: *The issue really boils down to a clash between left and right.* ○ *It all boils down to money in the end.* **ˌboil ˈover 1** (of liquid) to boil and flow over the side of a pan, etc: *The milk is boiling over.* **2** (*infml*) to become very angry; to lose one's temper. **3** (of a situation, quarrel, etc) to reach a point of crisis; to explode: *The unrest could boil over into civil war.*

▶ **boil** *n* [sing] the act or process of boiling; the point at which esp liquid boils: ***Bring** the mixture **to the boil**, then let it simmer for ten minutes.* ○ *Let it **come to the boil** slowly.* ○ *Don't leave it **on the boil** for long.* IDM **off the ˈboil** having just stopped boiling: (*fig infml*) *He began by playing brilliantly but he's rather gone off the boil* (ie he has begun playing less well) *in the last few minutes.*

boiling *adj* = BOILING HOT: *You must be boiling in that thick sweater.* ■ **ˌboiled ˈsweet** *n* (*Brit*) (*US* **ˌhard ˈcandy**) a sweet made of boiled sugar. **ˌboiling ˈhot** *adj* (*infml*) very hot: *a boiling hot day.* **ˈboiling-point** *n* **1** the temperature at which a liquid begins to boil. **2** (*fig*) a condition or state of great excitement: *Racial tension has reached boiling-point.*

boil² /bɔɪl/ *n* a painful infected lump that swells under the skin and is full of PUS.

boiler /ˈbɔɪlə(r)/ *n* **1** a metal container in which water is heated, eg to produce steam in an engine. **2** a container in which hot water is kept, esp for heating a building and providing other household needs. **3** (*Brit*) a large metal container for boiling dirty clothes to get them clean.

■ **ˈboiler suit** *n* (*esp Brit*) (*US* **coveralls**) a garment which covers the body, arms and legs, worn for doing rough or dirty work. Compare OVERALLS.

boisterous /ˈbɔɪstərəs/ *adj* **1** (of people or behaviour) noisy, lively and cheerful: *a boisterous party* ○ *The children are very boisterous today.* **2** (of the sea, weather, etc) rough. ▶ **boisterously** *adv.* **boisterousness** *n* [U].

---

bold /bəʊld/ *adj* (**-er, -est**) **1** confident and brave; enterprising (ENTERPRISE): *I don't feel bold enough to ask for a pay increase.* ○ *a bold move to tackle unemployment* ○ *a bold plan to rebuild the city centre.* **2** (*dated*) without feelings of shame; IMMODEST(1): *She waited for him to invite her to dance, not wishing to seem bold.* **3** that can be clearly seen; having a strong clear appearance: *the bold outline of a mountain against the sky* ○ *bold, legible handwriting* ○ *She paints with bold strokes of the brush.* **4** printed in thick type²(b): *The headwords in this dictionary are in bold type.* **IDM** **be/make so bold (as to do sth)** (*fml*) (used esp when politely asking a question, making a suggestion, etc) to dare (to do sth): *May I make so bold as to ask what you mean by that?* (**as**) **bold as** ˈ**brass** without shame; IMPUDENT: *He walked in, bold as brass, and asked me to lend him £50.* **put on, etc a bold/brave front** ⇨ FRONT. ▶ **boldly** *adv.* **boldness** *n* [U].

bole /bəʊl/ *n* the main stem or trunk(1) of a tree.

bolero /bəˈleərəʊ/ *n* (*pl* **-os**) **1** (the music for) a type of Spanish dance. **2** /*also* ˈbɒlərəʊ/ a woman's short jacket with no fastening at the front.

boll /bəʊl/ *n* the part of the cotton plant that contains the seeds.

bollard /ˈbɒlɑːd/ *n* **1** (*Brit*) a short post used to stop cars from going onto a road or part of a road. **2** a short thick post on a ship or on land close to water, to which a ship's rope may be tied.

bollocks (also **ballocks**) /ˈbɒləks/ *n* [pl] (*Brit* ⚠ *infml*) **1** testicles (TESTICLE). **2** [U] nonsense: *What a load of bollocks!*
▶ **bollocks** *interj* (*Brit* ⚠ *infml*) (used to express contempt) nonsense.

boloney (also **baloney**) /bəˈləʊni/ *n* [U] (*infml*) nonsense; rubbish: *Don't talk boloney!*

Bolshevik /ˈbɒlʃəvɪk; *US also* ˈbəʊl-/ *n* **1** a member of the socialist (SOCIALISM) group which supported the Russian revolution in 1917 and became the Russian Communist Party in 1918. **2** (*infml often derog*) a socialist (SOCIALISM) with extreme political opinions.
▶ **Bolshevik** *adj* of or like the Bolsheviks.
Bolshevism /ˈbɒlʃəvɪzəm/ *n* [U].
Bolshevist /ˈbɒlʃəvɪst/ *n*.

bolshie (also **bolshy**) /ˈbɒlʃi/ *adj* (*Brit infml derog*) deliberately creating difficulties and refusing to be helpful: *be in a bolshie mood* ○ *be bolshie about sth.*

bolster /ˈbəʊlstə(r)/ *n* a thick PILLOW shaped like a long tube that is placed across the top of a bed under other pillows.
▶ **bolster** *v* ~ **sb/sth (up)** to give support to sb/sth; to strengthen sth: [Vn] *bolster sb's morale/courage/confidence* [Vn, Vnp] *The high interest rates helped to control inflation and bolster (up) the economy.*

bolt

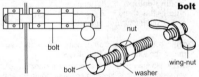

nut
bolt
bolt
bolt
washer
wing-nut

bolt¹ /bəʊlt/ *n* **1** a narrow piece of metal that slides across to lock a door, window, etc. ⇨ picture. **2** a metal pin used with a nut(2) for fastening things together. ⇨ picture. **3** (*formerly*) a short heavy ARROW(1) shot from a CROSSBOW. **4** a flash of lightning. **5** a quantity of cloth, etc wound in a roll. **IDM** **a** ˌ**bolt from the** ˈ**blue** an event which is not expected and is usu not welcome; a complete surprise: *The news of his death was (like) a bolt from the blue.* **the nuts and bolts** ⇨ NUT. **shoot one's bolt** ⇨ SHOOT¹.
▶ **bolt** *v* (**a**) to fasten sth with a bolt¹(1): [V] *The*

gate bolts on the inside.* [Vn] *Remember to bolt all the doors and windows.* (**b**) ~ **A to B**; ~ **A and B** (**together**) to fasten objects together with bolts (BOLT¹ 2): [Vnpr] *The vice is bolted to the work-bench.* [Vnp] *The various parts of the car are bolted together.* **PHRV** ˌ**bolt sb** ˈ**in/**ˈ**out** to prevent sb from leaving/entering a room, house, etc by bolting the doors, etc.

bolt² /bəʊlt/ *v* **1** [V] (**a**) (esp of a horse) to run away suddenly out of control: *The horse bolted in terror at the sound of the gun.* (**b**) (of a person) to run away quickly, esp to escape: *When the police arrived the burglars bolted.* (**c**) (*US*) to stop supporting a particular group or political party. **2** ~ **sth (down)** to swallow food quickly: [Vnp] *He had to bolt down his breakfast in order to catch the bus to work.* [also Vn]. **3** (of plants) to grow quickly upwards and stop producing flowers as seeds develop: [V] *You should pick the lettuces before they bolt.* **IDM** **lock, etc the stable door after the horse has bolted** ⇨ STABLE².
▶ **bolt** *n* [sing] an act of bolting (BOLT² 1b): *When the police arrived she made a bolt for the door* (ie to escape through it).
■ ˈ**bolt-hole** *n* (*Brit*) a place to which one can escape.

bolt³ /bəʊlt/ *adv* **IDM** **bolt** ˈ**upright** very straight; quite upright: *sitting bolt upright.*

bomb /bɒm/ *n* **1** [C] a container filled with explosive material, made to explode at a particular time or when dropped or thrown: *Enemy aircraft dropped hundreds of bombs on the city.* ○ *Terrorists planted a 50-pound bomb in the railway station.* ○ *The men were killed in a bomb attack.* **2** [C] (in compounds) an explosive device placed in or attached to a specified object: *a* ˈ*letter-bomb* ○ *a* ˈ*parcel/*ˈ*car bomb.* **3** **the bomb** [sing] the atomic bomb (ATOMIC) or hydrogen bomb (HYDROGEN) as a factor in international politics: *Anti-nuclear organizations want to ban the bomb.* **4** **a bomb** [sing] (*infml*) (**a**) (*Brit*) a lot of money: *That dress must have cost (her) a bomb!* ○ *Some company directors make* (ie earn) *an absolute bomb.* (**b**) (*US sl*) a complete failure: *Her performance was a real bomb.* **IDM** **go like a** ˈ**bomb** (*Brit infml*) **1** (of a vehicle) to go very fast: *Her new car goes like a bomb.* **2** to be very successful: *Last night's party went like a bomb.* ○ *Her new novel is going like a bomb* (ie selling well).
▶ **bomb** *v* **1** to attack sb/sth with bombs; to drop bombs on sb/sth: [Vn] *London was heavily bombed during the last war.* ○ *Terrorists bombed several police stations.* **2** ~ **(out)** (*infml esp US*) to fail: [V] *Her new play bombed after only three nights.* [Vn] *I really bombed the final exam.* [also Vp]. **PHRV** ˈ**bomb along, down, up, etc** (*infml esp Brit*) to move very fast, usu in a vehicle, in the specified direction: *bombing down the motorway at ninety miles an hour.* ˌ**bomb sb** ˈ**out** (esp passive) to destroy sb's home with bombs: *Our parents were bombed out twice during the war.*
■ ˈ**bomb-disposal** *n* [U] safely removing or blowing up bombs which have not exploded: *a bomb-disposal squad/team/officer/unit.*
ˈ**bomb-site** *n* an area in a town where all the buildings have been destroyed by bombs.

bombard /bɒmˈbɑːd/ *v* ~ **sb/sth (with sth)** **1** to attack a place with bombs or shells (SHELL 4), esp from big guns: [Vn] *Enemy positions were bombarded before our infantry attacked.* [also Vnpr]. **2** to attack sb with constant questions, criticism, etc: [Vnpr] *Reporters bombarded the President with questions about his economic policy.* ○ *We've been bombarded with letters of complaint from viewers.* ▶ **bombardment** *n* [C, U].

bombardier /ˌbɒmbəˈdɪə(r)/ *n* **1** (*Brit*) a soldier of low rank in an ARTILLERY(2) regiment. **2** (*US*) a member of the crew of a war plane who aims and releases bombs.

bombast /'bɒmbæst/ n [U] words without meaning used to impress other people and sound important: *His speech was full of bombast.* ▸ **bombastic** /bɒm'bæstɪk/ *adj*: *a bombastic speaker* ○ *bombastic language.* **bombastically** /-kli/ *adv*.

bomber /'bɒmə(r)/ n **1** a plane that carries and drops bombs. **2** a person who uses bombs, esp illegally.

bombproof /'bɒmpruːf/ *adj* strong enough to give protection against exploding bombs: *a bombproof shelter.*

bombshell /'bɒmʃel/ n (*infml*) **1** an event that causes great and usu unpleasant surprise: *The news of his death was a bombshell.* **2** a very attractive person, esp a woman: *a blond(e) bombshell.*

bona fide /ˌbəʊnə 'faɪdɪ/ *adj* genuine(ly); without deception; legal(ly): *a bona fide agreement/contract/deal.*
▸ **bona fides** /-diːz/ n [pl v] (*law*) honest and sincere intention: *establish one's bona fides* ○ *His bona fides remain unproven.*

bonanza /bə'nænzə/ n **1** a situation or event which creates a sudden increase in wealth, luck or profits: *a cash bonanza for investors* ○ *a bonanza of 10 million dollars* ○ *It's been a bonanza* (ie very profitable) *year for the tourist trade.* **2** a large or extra amount of sth desirable: *a sports bonanza* (ie on television or in a newspaper).

bond /bɒnd/ n **1** [C] a force or feeling that joins together people or groups: *the bonds of friendship/ affection* ○ *the Anglo-American bond* ○ *The trade agreement helped to strengthen the bonds between the two countries.* **2** [C] a certificate issued by a government or a company acknowledging that money has been lent to it and will be paid back with interest[5]: *National Savings bonds* ○ *government bonds.* See also JUNK BOND, PREMIUM BOND. **3** [C] **(a)** a written agreement or promise that it is against the law to break: *We entered into a solemn bond.* **(b)** a signed document containing such an agreement. **4 bonds** [pl] the ropes or chains holding sb a prisoner: (*fig*) *the bonds of oppression/tyranny/ injustice.* **IDM** **sb's word is as good as their bond** ⇨ WORD.
▸ **bond** v **1** ~ **A and B (together)** ; ~ **A to B** to join two things securely together: [Vnpr] *You need a strong adhesive to bond wood to metal.* [also Vn,Vnp]. **2** ~ **(sb) (with sb)** to establish a relationship of trust and affection with sb: [V] *They've bonded well.* [also Vpr, Vn, Vnpr].

bondage /'bɒndɪdʒ/ n [U] **1** (*dated or fml*) the state of being a slave or prisoner: *keep sb in bondage* ○ (*fig*) *freed from the bondage of time.* **2** the practice of being tied with ropes or chains in order to gain sexual pleasure.

bone /bəʊn/ n **1** [C] any of the hard parts that form the SKELETON(1) of an animal's body: *This fish has a lot of bones in it.* ○ *I've broken a bone in my arm.* ○ *Her bones were laid to rest* (ie Her body was buried). ⇨ picture at TOOTH. **2** [U] the hard substance of which bones are made: *Buttons are sometimes made of bone.* **IDM** **a bag of bones** ⇨ BAG[1]. **the bare bones** ⇨ BARE[1]. **a bone of con'tention** a subject about which there is disagreement: *The border has always been a bone of contention between the two countries.* **close to/near the 'bone** (*Brit infml*) **1** (of a remark, question, etc) revealing the truth about sb/sth in a way that is likely to cause offence: *Some of his comments about her appearance were a bit close to the bone.* **2** (of a joke, story, etc) likely to offend some people, esp because they are about sex: *Some scenes in the play are rather near the bone.* **cut, pare, etc sth to the 'bone** to reduce sth greatly: *Our budget has been pared to the bone.* **dry as a bone** ⇨ DRY[1]. **feel it in one's bones** ⇨ FEEL[1]. **have a 'bone to pick with sb** to have sth to argue or quarrel about with sb: *I've got a bone to pick with*

you. Where's the money I lent you last week? **make no bones about (doing) sth** to be frank about sth; to admit sth; not to hesitate to do sth: *He made no bones about his extreme left-wing views.* ○ *She made no bones about telling her husband she wanted a divorce.* **skin and bone** ⇨ SKIN. **work one's fingers to the bone** ⇨ FINGER[1].
▸ **bone** v to take bones out of sth: [Vn] *bone a fish/a chicken/a piece of beef.* **PHRV** ˌbone 'up on (sth) (*infml*) to study hard, usu for a specific purpose: *I must bone up on my French before we go to Paris.*
-boned (forming compound *adjs*) having the type of bones specified: *small-boned* ○ *large-boned.*
■ ˌbone 'china n [U] thin CHINA(1) made of clay mixed with animal bones which have been crushed.
ˌbone-'dry *adj* [usu pred] completely dry.
ˌbone 'idle *adj* (*derog*) very lazy.
'bone-meal n [U] crushed animal bones used for making soil richer.

bonehead /'bəʊnhed/ n (*infml derog*) a stupid person.

bonfire /'bɒnfaɪə(r)/ n a large fire made outdoors for burning rubbish or as part of a celebration: *We made a bonfire of dead leaves in the backyard.*
■ 'Bonfire Night n (in Britain) the night of 5 November when many people light bonfires and let off fireworks (FIREWORK) to celebrate the failure of the plot in 1605 to blow up the parliament buildings.

bongo /'bɒŋgəʊ/ n (*pl* **-os** or **-oes**) either of a pair of small drums played with the fingers: *bongo drums/ rhythms.*

bonhomie /'bɒnəmi; US ˌbɒnə'miː/ n [U] (*French*) cheerful friendliness (FRIENDLY).

bonk /bɒŋk/ v **1** (*sl joc*) to have sex with sb: [Vn] *He's been bonking one of his students.* [also V]. **2** (*infml*) to hit sb without causing serious harm: [Vn] *bonk sb on the head.*
▸ **bonk** n **1** [sing] (*sl joc*) an act of having sex with sb: *have a bonk (with sb).* **2** [C] (*infml*) a hit or an act of hitting: *a bonk on the head.*

bonkers /'bɒŋkəz/ *adj* [pred] (*infml*) completely mad; crazy: *You're stark raving bonkers!*

bon mot /ˌbɒn 'məʊ/ n (*pl* bons mots /ˌbɒn 'məʊz/) (*French*) a funny and clever remark.

bonnet /'bɒnɪt/ n **1** a hat tied with strings under the chin, worn by babies and (esp formerly) by women. **2** (*US* **hood**) the metal part over the front of a motor vehicle, usu covering the engine. ⇨ picture at CAR. **IDM** **have a bee in one's bonnet** ⇨ BEE[1].

bonny /'bɒni/ *adj* (**-ier, -iest**) (*esp Scot*) attractive or beautiful; fine: *a bonny lass/baby* ○ *That's a bonny idea.* ▸ **bonnily** *adv*.

bonsai /'bɒnsaɪ/ n (*pl* unchanged) **(a)** [C] a plant, esp a small tree, which is grown in a pot and is prevented from reaching its normal size. **(b)** [U] the art of growing plants or trees by this method, originally developed in Japan.

bonus /'bəʊnəs/ n (*pl* **-es**) **1** a payment added to what is usual or expected: *a productivity bonus* (ie money added to wages when workers produce more goods, etc) ○ *Company employees received a £50 Christmas bonus.* **2** anything pleasant in addition to what is expected: *The warm weather this winter has been a real bonus.*

bony /'bəʊni/ *adj* **1** of or like bone. **2** full of bones: *This fish is very bony.* **3** very thin so that the bones can be seen: *bony fingers* ○ *a tall bony man.* ⇨ note at THIN.

boo /buː/ *interj*, n **1** a sound made to show disapproval or contempt: *The candidate's speech was greeted with boos and jeers.* **2** a sound made loudly in order to give sb a surprise or a shock. **IDM** **not say boo to a goose** ⇨ SAY.
▸ **boo** v to show disapproval or contempt for sb/sth

by shouting 'boo': [V] *You can hear the crowd boo-ing.* [Vnp, Vnpr] *The actors were booed off (the stage)* (ie forced to leave by booing). [also Vn].

boob¹ /buːb/ *n* (also *esp US* **booboo** /'buːbuː/) *n* (*infml*) a stupid mistake: *I'm afraid I've made a bit of a boob.*

▶ **boob** *v* to make a boob: [V] *Oh dear, I've boobed again.*

boob² /buːb/ *n* (*sl*) (usu *pl*) a woman's breast.

booby /'buːbi/ *n* (*dated derog*) a foolish person: *You great booby!*

■ **'booby prize** *n* a prize given as a joke to the person who is last in a race or competition.

'booby trap *n* **1** a hidden trap intended to surprise sb, eg sth balanced on top of a door so that it will fall on the first person opening it. **2** a hidden bomb designed to explode when an object that seems harmless is touched: *The police did not go near the abandoned car, fearing it was a booby trap.* ∘ *a booby-trap bomb.* **booby-trap** *v* (**-pp-**) to place a booby trap in or on sth: [Vn] *The car had been booby-trapped by terrorists.*

boogie /'buːgi; *US* 'bʊgi/ (also ‚boogie-'woogie /-'wuːgi; *US* -'wʊgi/) *n* [U] a type of blues (BLUE² 3) music, played on the piano, with a strong beat²(2): *play boogie* ∘ *a boogie beat.*

boohoo /'buːhuː‚ ‚buː'huː/ *interj* (used in written English to represent the sound of sb crying noisily).

book¹ /bʊk/ *n* **1** [C] (**a**) a number of printed or written sheets fastened together within a cover so that the pages can be turned freely: *a leather-bound book.* (**b**) a written work, eg a novel, dictionary, etc: *writing/reading a book about/on Shakespeare* ∘ *a book by Stephen King.* **2** [C] a number of sheets of paper fastened together in a cover and used for writing in: *Write the essay in your (exercise-)books.* ∘ *an address book* (ie one for writing addresses in). **3 books** [pl] the written records of the financial affairs of a business; accounts (ACCOUNT¹ 1): *do the books* (ie check the accounts) ∘ *The company's books are audited every year.* **4** [C] a number of similar items fastened together in tne shape of a book: *a book of stamps/tickets/matches* ∘ *a cheque-book.* **5** [C] any of the main divisions of a large written work: *the books of the Bible.* **6** [C] a record of bets made, eg on a race: *keep/make/open a book (on sth)* (ie take bets on a match, race, etc). **7 the book** [sing] (*Brit*) the telephone directory (TELEPHONE): *Are you in the book?* **IDM** **be in sb's good/bad 'books** (*infml*) to have/not have sb's favour or approval: *You'll be in the boss's bad books if you don't work harder.* **bring sb to 'book (for sth)** to force sb to give an explanation of (their behaviour), usu because they are doing sth wrong: *bring a criminal to book.* **by the 'book** (*infml*) strictly according to the rules: *He's always careful to do things by the book.* **a closed book** ⇨ CLOSE⁴. **cook the books** ⇨ COOK. **every trick in the book** ⇨ TRICK. **(be) on the books of sb/sth 1** (to have one's name) on an official list, esp people who are available for a particular type of work: *We've got very few accountants on our books at present.* **2** (to be) employed as a player by a football club: *He's on Everton's books.* **an open book** ⇨ OPEN². **read sb like a book** ⇨ READ. **suit one's/sb's book** ⇨ SUIT². **take a leaf out of sb's book** ⇨ LEAF. **throw the 'book at sb** (*infml*) to remind sb forcefully of the correct way of doing sth (and perhaps punish them for not following it).

■ **'book club** *n* a society which sells books to its members on special terms.

'book-end *n* (usu *pl*) either of a pair of supports to keep a row of books upright.

'book-plate *n* a piece of paper, usu with a printed design, stuck in a book to show who owns it.

'book token *n* (*Brit*) a card, usu given as a gift, that

can be exchanged for books of a specified value: *a £10 book token.*

book² /bʊk/ *v* **1(a)** ~ sth (**up**) to reserve a place, accommodation, etc; to buy a ticket, etc in advance: [V] *Book early if you want to be sure of a seat.* [Vn] *book a hotel room/a seat on a plane* ∘ *I'd like to book three seats for tonight's concert.* [Vn, Vnp] *The hotel/performance is fully booked/is booked up* (ie There are no more rooms/tickets available). (**b**) ~ sb on sth to reserve a place, ticket, etc for sb on a plane, etc: [Vnpr] *We're booked on the next flight.* (**c**) to hire sb in advance: [Vn] *We've booked a magician for our Christmas party.* **2** (*infml*) to enter the name of sb in an official book or record when they have committed a crime or an offence: [Vn] *The police booked me for speeding.* ∘ *He was booked by the referee for foul play.* **PHR V** ‚**book 'in /** ‚**book 'into sth** to register at a hotel, an airport, etc. ‚**book 'in** to reserve a room at a hotel, etc for sb: *We've booked you in at the Plaza for two nights.*

▶ **bookable** *adj* **1** that can be reserved: *All seats are bookable in advance.* **2** (of an offence in football) so serious that the name of the player responsible is written down in a book by the REFEREE.

booking *n* [C,U] (*esp Brit*) (an instance of) reserving seats, etc in advance; a RESERVATION(1): *a block booking* ∘ *a booking clerk/form/office/hall* ∘ *We can't accept any more bookings.* ∘ *She's in charge of booking(s).*

bookbinder /'bʊkbaɪndə(r)/ *n* a person whose job is putting covers on books. ▶ **bookbinding** *n* [U].

bookcase /'bʊkkeɪs/ *n* a piece of furniture with shelves for books.

bookie /'bʊki/ *n* (*infml*) = BOOKMAKER.

bookish /'bʊkɪʃ/ *adj* **1** fond of reading and studying: *She was always a bookish child.* **2** having knowledge or ideas gained from reading rather than practical experience. ▶ **bookishness** *n* [U].

bookkeeper /'bʊkkiːpə(r)/ *n* a person whose job is keeping a record of the financial affairs of a business. ▶ **bookkeeping** *n* [U].

booklet /'bʊklət/ *n* a thin book, usu in paper covers.

bookmaker /'bʊkmeɪkə(r)/ (also *infml* **bookie** /'bʊki/) *n* a person whose job is taking bets on horse races, etc. ▶ **bookmaking** *n* [U].

bookmark /'bʊkmɑːk/ (also **'bookmarker** /-mɑːkə(r)/) *n* a thing such as a strip of card, etc placed between the pages of a book to mark the place where the reader has finished reading.

bookseller /'bʊkselə(r)/ *n* a person whose job is selling books.

bookshop /'bʊkʃɒp/ (*US* also **'bookstore** /'bʊkstɔː(r)/) *n* a shop which sells mainly books.

bookstall /'bʊkstɔːl/ (*US* also **'news-stand**) *n* a stall or KIOSK(1) at which books, newspapers and magazines are sold, eg at a station.

bookworm /'bʊkwɜːm/ *n* a person who is very fond of reading: *She's a bit of a bookworm.*

boom¹ /buːm/ *v* **1** to make a deep hollow sound: [V] *waves booming on the sea-shore* [V, Vp] *We could hear the enemy guns booming (away) in the distance.* ∘ *The principal's voice boomed (out) across the playground.* **2** ~ (sth) (**out**) to say (sth) in a booming voice: [V.speech] *'Get out of my sight!' he boomed.* [also V, Vp, Vn, Vnp].

▶ **boom** *n* (usu *sing*) a deep hollow sound: *the boom of the guns/the surf.* See also SONIC BOOM.

boom² /buːm/ *n* ~ (**in sth**) a sudden increase in population, trade, etc; a period of wealth and success: *a boom in car sales* ∘ *The oil market is enjoying an unprecedented boom.* ∘ *a boom year (for trade, exports, etc).*

▶ **boom** *v* to have a period of rapid economic growth: [V] *Business is booming.*

■ **'boom town** *n* a town that grows or becomes rich during a boom.

boom³ /buːm/ *n* **1** (on a boat) a long pole used to keep the bottom of a sail stretched. ⇨ picture at YACHT. **2** a long movable arm for a MICROPHONE: *a boom microphone.* **3** a floating barrier placed across a river or the entrance to a harbour, eg to prevent logs from floating away or to stop enemy ships from coming in.

boomerang /'buːməræŋ/ *n* a curved flat piece of wood which can be thrown so that it returns to the thrower. Boomerangs were first used by Australian Aborigines as weapons when hunting: (*fig*) *The plan had a boomerang effect* (ie caused unexpected harm to the person responsible for it).
▶ **boomerang** *v* ~ (**on sb**) (of a plan or remark) to cause unexpected harm to the person responsible for it; to BACKFIRE(2): [V, Vpr] *His attempt to discredit his opponent boomeranged (on him) when he was charged with libel.*

boon¹ /buːn/ *n* a thing that is good or helpful for sb; a benefit; an advantage: *Parks are a great boon to/ for people in big cities.* ○ *A thick coat is a real boon in cold weather.*

boon² /buːn/ *adj* **IDM** **a boon companion** a close friend with whom one enjoys spending time: *Bill and Bob are boon companions.*

boondocks /'buːndɒks/ **the boondocks** *n* [pl] (*US sl derog*) an area far away from cities or towns: *He lives way out in the boondocks.*

boor /bʊə(r), bɔː(r)/ *n* (*derog*) a rough or rude person: *Don't be such a boor!*
▶ **boorish** /'bʊərɪʃ, 'bɔːrɪʃ/ *adj* of or like a boor: *boorish youths/behaviour/remarks.* **boorishly** *adv.* **boorishness** *n* [U].

boost /buːst/ *v* to help or encourage sb/sth; to increase the strength or value of sth: [Vn] *boost imports/share prices/the dollar* ○ *boost production* ○ *The unexpected win helped to boost the team's morale.* ○ *boost an electric current.*
▶ **boost** *n* an increase in sth: *a boost in sales, exports, etc.* **2** help or encouragement: *give the economy/the pound a welcome boost* ○ *give sb's confidence a boost* ○ *This will be a boost for the president's popularity.*

booster *n* **1** a thing that helps or encourages sb/ sth: *a morale booster* (ie sth that makes one feel more confident). **2** a device for increasing electrical power. **3** (also **'booster rocket**) a ROCKET(2a) used to give speed to a missile or spacecraft as it takes off. **4** an extra amount of a VACCINE or drug given to increase or renew the effect of an earlier one: *a tetanus booster.*

boot

wellington

boot¹ /buːt/ *n* **1** a covering for the foot, ankle and often the leg below the knee. Boots are made of leather or rubber and worn esp outdoors: *a pair of winter boots* ○ *tough boots for walking.* ⇨ picture. ⇨ picture at SKIING. Compare SHOE 1, SANDAL. See also WELLINGTON. **2** (*Brit*) (*US* trunk) the space in a car, usu at the back, for putting cases, shopping, etc in: *Put the luggage in the boot.* ⇨ picture at CAR. See also CAR-BOOT SALE. **3** (usu *sing*) (*infml*) a blow with the foot; a kick: *He gave the ball a tremendous boot.*
IDM **be/get too big for one's boots** ⇨ BIG. **the boot is on the other 'foot** the situation is the

opposite of what it was before: *When young people become parents themselves they find that the boot is on the other foot.* **give sb/get the 'boot** (*infml*) to dismiss sb/to be dismissed from a job: *He should have been given the boot years ago.* **have one's heart in one's boots** ⇨ HEART. **lick sb's boots** ⇨ LICK. **put the 'boot in** (*infml esp Brit*) to kick sb hard; to treat sb in a cruel way. **tough as old boots** ⇨ TOUGH.
▶ **boot** *v* **1** to kick sth/sb: [Vn, Vnp] *boot a ball (about)* [Vnpr] *boot sb in the face.* **2** [V, Vp, Vn, Vnp] ~ (**sth**) (**up**) (*computing*) to prepare a computer for operation by loading an operating system (OPERATE), a PROGRAM(1), etc. **PHRV** **,boot sb 'out (of sth)** (*infml*) **1** to throw sb out by force: *His father booted him out of the house.* **2** (usu passive) to dismiss sb from a job: *He was booted out of office after three disastrous years as a minister.*

boot² /buːt/ *n* **IDM** **to boot** (*arch or joc*) in addition; as well: *She's an attractive woman, and wealthy to boot.*

bootee /buː'tiː/ *n* **1** a baby's woollen boot. **2** a woman's short boot.

booth /buːð; *US* buːθ/ *n* **1** a small, usu temporary, tent or building where one can buy things, watch shows, etc at a market, a FAIR³ or an exhibition: *In the next booth children were watching a puppet show.* **2** a small enclosed space for a specific purpose: *a telephone booth* (ie for a public telephone) ○ *a polling booth* (ie for voting at an election).

bootlace /'buːtleɪs/ *n* a string or leather strip for tying boots or shoes.

bootleg /'buːtleg/ *v* (**-gg-**) [Vn] to make or sell goods, esp alcoholic drinks, illegally. ⇨ note at SMUGGLE.
▶ **bootleg** *adj* [attrib] (*esp of alcohol*) made and sold illegally: *smuggling bootleg liquor* ○ *a bootleg cassette* (eg one recorded illegally at a concert). **bootlegger** /-legə(r)/ *n.*

bootstrap /'buːtstræp/ *n* **IDM** **pull oneself up by one's bootstraps** ⇨ PULL¹.

booty /'buːti/ *n* [U] goods that have been stolen, esp by an enemy in war; LOOT(1); PLUNDER *n*(2).

booze /buːz/ *v* (*infml*) (used esp in the continuous tenses) to drink alcohol, esp in large quantities: [V] *He likes to go out boozing with the boys.*
▶ **booze** *n* [U] (*infml*) alcoholic drink: *Her husband's been/gone on the booze* (ie drunk/started drinking too much alcohol) *again.*
boozer *n* (*infml*) **1** a person who drinks a lot of alcohol: *He's always been a terrible boozer.* **2** (*Brit*) pub.
boozy *adj* (*Brit infml*) drinking or involving a lot of alcohol: *a boozy old man* ○ *a boozy party.*
■ **'booze-up** *n* (*Brit infml*) an occasion when people drink a lot of alcohol: *The party was a real booze-up.*

bop /bɒp/ *n* **1** [U] = BEBOP. **2** [C] (*esp Brit infml*) (**a**) a dance to pop music: *Let's have a bop.* (**b**) a social occasion with dancing to such music: *There's a bop on in the village hall tonight.*
▶ **bop** *v* (**-pp-**) **1** (*Brit infml*) to dance to pop music: [V] *go bopping.* See also TEENY-BOPPER. **2** (*esp US*) to strike sb/sth with the hand, a stick, etc.

borage /'bɒrɪdʒ; *US* 'bɔːrɪdʒ/ *n* [U] a European plant with blue flowers and hairy leaves which are used in salads (SALAD) and to give flavour to drinks.

borax /'bɔːræks/ *n* [U] a white mineral powder used in making glass and as an ANTISEPTIC.

Bordeaux /bɔː'dəʊ/ *n* (*pl* unchanged) [U, C] a red or white wine from the Bordeaux district of SW France. Compare CLARET.

bordello /bɔː'deləʊ/ *n* (*pl* **-os**) (*esp US*) a BROTHEL.

border /'bɔːdə(r)/ *n* **1(a)** [C] the line dividing two countries or areas; the land near this line: *The* *terrorists escaped across/over the border.* ○ *a border town/guard/patrol* ○ border incidents (ie small fights between soldiers of two countries that are next to each other). **(b) the Border** [sing] one particular border or the area near it, esp that between England and Scotland, or the United States and Mexico. ⇨ note. **2** [C] a band or strip, usu ornamental, around or along the edge of sth: *the border of a picture/ photograph* ○ *a handkerchief/table-cloth with an embroidered border.* **3** [C] a strip of ground along the edge of a lawn or path for planting flowers, etc: *a herbaceous border* ○ *a border of tulips.* ⇨ picture at HOUSE¹.

▸ **border** *v* **1** to be a border(1) to sth; to be on the border(1) of sth: [Vn] *Our garden is bordered on one side by a stream.* ○ *How many countries border Switzerland?* **2** (esp passive) ~ **sth (with sth)** to put a border(2) on sth: [Vnpr] *a handkerchief bordered with lace* [also Vn]. **3** [Vpr] ~ **on sth (a)** to be next to sth: *The new housing estate borders on the motorway.* **(b)** to come close to being sth: *His reply to the teacher was bordering on rudeness.* ○ *Our task borders on the impossible.*

borderer *n* a person who lives near a border(1), esp the one between England and Scotland.

> **NOTE** A **border** or **frontier** is the dividing line between two countries or the area near that line: *the border/frontier between Spain and France* ○ *the Canadian border/frontier*. A **border** exists between two states or counties within a country: *We crossed the border from Victoria to South Australia at midnight.* **Frontier** (not **border**) is also used to describe more abstract things: *The frontiers of science are being pushed back all the time.* A **boundary** is a line marking the limits of an area of land: *The lane marks the boundary of our land.*

borderland /ˈbɔːdəlænd/ *n* **1** [C] the district on either side of a border(1) or boundary. **2** [sing] a state or condition between two extremes, having certain features of each of them: *the borderland between fact and fancy.*

borderline /ˈbɔːdəlaɪn/ *n* the line that divides one area, etc from another: *(fig) The borderline between informal language and slang is hard to define.*

▸ **borderline** *adj* not definitely relevant or acceptable; only just acceptable: *a borderline case* ○ *a borderline candidate* (ie sb who may or may not pass an examination, be suitable for a job, etc) ○ *a borderline pass/failure (in an examination).*

bore¹ /bɔː(r)/ *v* **1** to make a hole with a tool or by digging: [V] *boring for oil* [Vpr] *This drill can bore through rock.* ○ *(fig) His eyes seemed to bore into me.* [Vnpr] *bore a hole in wood* ○ *bore a tunnel through a mountain/under the Channel* [also Vn]. **2** to move by digging or pushing: [Vnpr] *He bored his way to the front of the crowd.* (also Vpr, Vp, Vnpl).

▸ **bore** *n* **1** (esp in compounds) the hollow part inside a gun barrel(2); the width of this part: *a twelve-bore shotgun* ○ *small-bore guns.* **2** (also **ˈbore-hole**) a deep hole made in the ground, esp to find water or oil.

bore² /bɔː(r)/ *v* to make sb lose interest or feel tired by being dull(1): [Vn] *I've heard all his stories before; they bore me/he bores me.* ○ *Stop me if I'm boring you.*

▸ **bore** *n* a person or thing that bores; an annoying situation: *Don't be such a bore!* ○ *We've run out of petrol. What a bore!* **IDM** **a crashing bore** ⇨ CRASH².

bored *adj* ~ **(with sb/sth)** feeling tired because one has nothing to do or has lost interest in sb/sth: *I get very bored with my own company* (ie with no one else to talk to, etc).

  boredom /-dəm/ *n* [U] the state of being bored: *a look of boredom on her face.*

boring /ˈbɔːrɪŋ/ *adj* not interesting; dull: *a boring conversation/job/book/party.*

bore³ /bɔː(r)/ *n* a strong high wave that moves quickly along a narrow river from the sea.

bore⁴ *pt* of BEAR².

born /bɔːn/ *v* (used only in the passive, without *by*) **be born** to come into the world by birth: *She was born in 1950.* ○ *(fig) The Trades Union movement was born* (ie founded) *in the early years of the century.* ○ *He was born to be a great writer* (ie This was his destiny from birth). ⇨ note at BEAR². **IDM** **(not) be born ˈyesterday** (not) to be foolish or easily deceived because of lack of experience: *You can't fool me. I wasn't born yesterday, you know.* **be / be born / be made that/this way** ⇨ WAY¹, **ˌborn and ˈbred** by birth, background(4a) and education: *He's Boston born and bred.* ○ *She was born and bred a Catholic.* **born of sb/sth** coming from the specified type of parents, background(4a), origin, etc: *He was born of German parents.* ○ *Her socialist beliefs were born of a hatred of injustice.* **born on the wrong side of the ˈblanket** *(dated Brit euph)* born from parents who were not married to each other; ILLEGITIMATE. **born with a silver ˈspoon in one's mouth** *(saying)* having wealthy parents. **in all one's born ˈdays** *(dated infml)* in one's whole life: *I've never heard such nonsense in all my born days!* **not know one is ˈborn** *(Brit infml)* to have an easy life without realizing how easy it is: *If you get up at 8 o'clock, you don't know you're born! I have to get up at 5!* **there's one born every ˈminute** *(saying)* there are a lot of foolish people. **to the manner born** ⇨ MANNER.

▸ **born** *adj* [attrib] being, or likely to become, the specified thing by natural ability or quality: *be a born leader/loser/writer/athlete.*

-born (forming compound *ns* and *adjs*) born in the specified order, way or place: *first-born* ○ *nobly-born* ○ *French-born* .

■ **ˌborn-aˈgain** *adj* [usu attrib] having changed one's religious beliefs, esp to a basic form of Christianity: *a ˌborn-again ˈChristian.*

borne *pp* of BEAR². ⇨ note at BEAR².

borough /ˈbʌrə; *US* -rəʊ/ *n* **1** *(Brit)* a town or district with its own representative(s) in parliament: *the London borough of Greenwich* ○ *the boroughs under Labour control* ○ *Lambeth borough council.* Compare PARISH 2. **2** *(US)* **(a)** (in certain states) a town with a legal corporation. **(b)** any of the five administrative areas of New York City.

borrow /ˈbɒrəʊ/ *v* ~ **(sth) (from sb/sth)** **1** to take and use sth that belongs to sb else, usu with their permission and with the intention of returning it: [Vpr, Vnpr] *borrow (money) from the bank/a friend* [Vn] *I've forgotten my pen. Can I borrow yours?* [Vnpr] *borrow a book from the library* [also V]. Compare LEND. **2(a)** to take and use ideas, etc as one's own; to copy sth: [Vpr] *borrow freely from other writers* [Vn] *borrow sb's style/methods* [Vnpr] *Handel borrowed music from other composers.* [also V]. **(b)** (of a language) to take a word or phrase from another language: [Vnpr] *The expression 'nouveau riche' is borrowed from French.* [also Vn, Vpr]. **IDM** **(be living on) borrowed ˈtime** (to be still alive after) a longer period of time than one might have been expected to live, eg after a serious illness.

▸ **borrower** *n* a person who borrows. Compare LENDER.

borrowing *n* **1** [U] the activity of borrowing money by people or organizations: *high interest rates which help to keep borrowing down* ○ *borrowing costs.* **2** [C] a thing borrowed, esp money or a word taken by one language from another: *The company will soon be able to repay its borrowings from the bank.* ○ *French has many borrowings from English.*

Borstal /ˈbɔːstl/ *n* [C, U] (formerly, in Britain) an

institution for reforming young criminals: *be sent to Borstal*. See also APPROVED SCHOOL, DETENTION CENTRE, REFORMATORY.

bosh /bɒʃ/ *n* [U], *interj* (*dated infml*) nonsense: *You're talking bosh!*

bosom /'bʊzəm/ *n* **1** [C] (**a**) a person's chest, esp a woman's breasts: *hold sb to one's bosom* ○ *She has a large bosom.* (**b**) each of a woman's breasts. **2** [C] the part of a dress covering the bosom: *a rose pinned to her bosom.* **3** [sing] **the ~ of sth** the loving care and protection of sth: *live in the bosom of one's family* ○ *welcomed into the bosom of the Church.*
▶ **bosomy** *adj* (*infml*) (of a woman) having large breasts.
■ **,bosom 'friend** *n* a very good friend.

boss¹ /bɒs/ *n* (*infml*) a person who controls or gives orders to workers; a manager; an employer: *ask one's boss for a pay increase* ○ *a regional party boss* ○ *Who's (the) boss in this house* (ie Who is in control)?
▶ **boss** *v* **~ sb (about/around)** (*infml derog*) to give orders to sb in an unpleasant or forceful way: [Vnp] *He's always bossing his wife about.* [also Vn].
bossy *adj* (**-ier, -iest**) (*derog*) fond of giving people orders; OVERBEARING. **bossily** *adv*. **bossiness** *n* [U].

boss² /bɒs/ *n* a round projecting piece of metal or wood, esp in the centre of a shield or as a decoration on a church ceiling.

boss-eyed /'bɒs aɪd/ *adj* (*Brit infml*) (**a**) blind in one eye. (**b**) CROSS-EYED.

botany /'bɒtəni/ *n* [U] the scientific study of plants and their structure. Compare BIOLOGY, ZOOLOGY.
▶ **botanical** /bə'tænɪkl/ *adj* of or relating to botany. **bo,tanical 'gardens** (also **bo,tanic 'gardens**) *n* [pl] a park where plants and trees are grown for scientific study.
botanist /'bɒtənɪst/ *n* an expert in botany.

botch /bɒtʃ/ *v* **~ sth (up)** to spoil sth by poor work; to repair sth badly: [Vn] *a botched rescue operation* ○ *The actor botched his lines* (ie forgot them or failed to say them properly). [Vnp] *Instead of mending my car properly, he really botched it up.*
▶ **botch** (also **botch-up**) *n* a piece of work that is badly done: *a botch job* ○ *make a botch-up of sth.*

both¹ /bəʊθ/ *adj* (with plural *ns*, which may be preceded by a *def art*, a *demonstrative det* or a *possess det*) the two; the one as well as the other: *hold sth in both hands* ○ *Both books/Both the books/Both these books are expensive.* ○ *Both (her) children are at college.* ○ *He is blind in both eyes.* ○ *There are shops on both sides of the street.* **IDM** **have/want it/things 'both ways** (to try) to combine two ways of thinking or behaving which are (or seem to be) exclusive of each other: *You can't have it both ways* (ie You must decide on one thing or the other). ⇨ note at ALL.

both² /bəʊθ/ *pron* (**a**) **~ (of sb/sth)** (referring back to a plural *n* or a *pron*) the two; not only the one but also the other: *He has two brothers: both live in Toronto.* ○ *His parents are both dead.* ○ *My sister and I both went to the party.* ○ *I like these shirts. I'll take both (of them).* ○ *I've invited them both.* (**b**) **~ of sb/sth** (referring forward to a plural *n* or a *pron*) the two; not only the one but also the other: *Both of us want to go to the party.* (Compare: *We both want to go to the party.*) ○ *Both of her children have blue eyes.* (Compare: *Her children both have blue eyes.*) ⇨ note at ALL.

both³ /bəʊθ/ *adv* **~ ... and ...** not only... but also...: *be both tired and hungry* ○ *She speaks both French and English.* ○ *Both his brother and sister are married.* ○ *She was a success both as a pianist and as a conductor.*

bother /'bɒðə(r)/ *v* **1(a)** **~ sb (about/with sth)** to cause trouble or annoyance to sb; to PESTER sb: [Vn] *I'm sorry to bother you, but could you tell me the way to the station?* ○ *Does the pain from your operation bother you much?* ○ *Does my smoking bother you?*

[Vn, Vnpr] *Don't bother your father (about it) now; he's very tired.* [Vn.to inf] *She's always bothering me to lend her money.* ○ **~ to worry sb**: [Vn] *What's bothering you?* ○ *Don't let his criticisms bother you.* ○ *It bothers me that he can be so insensitive.* ○ *She didn't seem to be bothered.* ○ *I'm not really bothered* (ie I don't care) *who wins.* **2(a)** **~ (with sth)** to take the time or trouble to do sth: [V] *'Shall I help you with the washing-up?' 'Don't bother — I'll do it later.'* [Vpr] *Don't bother with the dirty dishes.* [V.to inf] *He didn't even bother to say thank you.* [V.ing] *I didn't bother asking why.* ○ *Why bother going to the cinema when you can see so many good films on television?* (**b**) **~ about sb/sth** to concern oneself about sb/sth: [Vpr] *Don't bother about us — we'll join you later.* ○ *It's not worth bothering about.* **3** (*Brit*) (used in the imperative to express annoyance at sth) [Vn] *Bother this car! It's always breaking down.* **IDM** **bother oneself/one's head about sth** to be anxious or worried about sth: *Don't bother your pretty little head about a thing — leave it all to me!* **can't be bothered (to do sth)** will not do sth because one considers it to be too much trouble: *The grass needs cutting but I can't be bothered to do it today.* ○ *She's capable of producing excellent work but usually she can't be bothered.* **hot and bothered** ⇨ HOT.
▶ **bother** *n* **1** [U] trouble or fuss: *You seem to be in a spot of bother.* ○ *Did you have much bother finding the house?* ○ *'Thanks for your help!' 'It was no bother.'* ○ *I'm sorry to have put you to all this bother* (ie to have caused you so much trouble). ○ *They went to a lot of bother* (ie it took a lot of time or trouble). **2 a bother** [sing] an annoying thing: *What a bother! We've missed the bus.*
bother *interj* (*Brit*) (used to express annoyance): *Oh bother! I've left my money at home.*
botheration /ˌbɒðə'reɪʃn/ *interj* (*dated infml*) = BOTHER *interj*.
bothersome /-səm/ *adj* causing bother; annoying.
bothy /'bɒθi/ *n* (*Scot*) a small hut, esp one for farm workers to live in.

bottle

stopper — cork

bottle

bottle

decanter

carafe

bottle /'bɒtl/ *n* **1** [C] (**a**) a glass or plastic container, usu with a narrow neck, used esp for storing liquids: *a 'wine/beer bottle* ○ *a 'milk bottle* ○ *put the cap/top back on the bottle* ○ *Come to my party on Saturday — and remember to bring a bottle* (eg of wine). ○ *a bottle of pills.* See also HOT-WATER BOTTLE. ⇨ picture. (**b**) the amount contained in a bottle: *We drank a bottle (of wine) between us.* **2 the bottle** [sing] (*euph*) alcoholic drink: *She's a bit too fond of the bottle.* **3** [C usu *sing*] a baby's feeding-bottle (FEED¹) or milk from this (used instead of mother's milk): *brought up on the bottle* ○ *give a baby its bottle.* **4** [C] a large metal container holding gas for heating or cooking. **5** [U] (*Brit sl*) courage; confidence: *He's got (a lot of) bottle!* **IDM** **be on the 'bottle** (*infml*) to drink alcohol regularly in large quantities; to be an alcoholic (ALCOHOL): *He was on the bottle for five years.* **hit the bottle** ⇨ HIT¹.
▶ **bottle** *v* (**a**) to put sth into bottles: [Vn] *bottled beer/gas.* (**b**) (*esp Brit*) to preserve sth by storing it in glass containers with a wide neck: [Vn] *jars of bottled plums* ○ *Do you bottle your fruit or freeze it?* **PHRV** **,bottle 'out (of sth)** (*Brit infml*) to decide in

a cowardly way not to do sth: *She bottled out of telling him.* ,**bottle sth 'up** not to allow emotions to be seen; to restrain or suppress feelings: *Instead of discussing their problems, they bottle up all their anger and resentment.* ○ *'bottled-up tension.*

■ **'bottle bank** *n* a large container in a public place where empty bottles are placed so that the glass can be used again.

'**bottle-feed** *v* (*pt pp* **-fed**) to feed a baby with a bottle: [Vn] *Were you bottle-fed or breast-fed as a child?*

,**bottle-'green** *adj* dark green.

'**bottle-opener** *n* a metal device for opening bottles of beer, etc.

'**bottle party** *n* (*Brit*) a party to which guests bring bottles of wine, etc.

bottleneck /'bɒtlnek/ *n* (**a**) a narrow stretch of road which causes traffic to slow down or stop. (**b**) anything that slows down production in a manufacturing process, etc.

bottom /'bɒtəm/ *n* **1** [C usu *sing*] the lowest part or point of sth: *the bottom of a hill/mountain/slope/ valley* ○ *The telephone is at the bottom of the stairs.* ○ *There are tea-leaves in the bottom of my cup.* ○ *The book I want is (right) at the bottom of the pile.* ○ *Sign your name at the bottom of the page, please.* **2** [C usu *sing*] the part on which sth rests; the part that faces downwards: *The manufacturer's name is on the bottom of the plate.* ○ *I scraped the bottom of my car on some rocks.* **3** [C] (*esp Brit*) the part of the body on which one sits; the buttocks (BUTTOCK): *fall on one's bottom* ○ *smack a child's bottom.* **4** [sing] the farthest part or point of sth: *There's a post office at the bottom of the road.* ○ *The tool-shed is at the bottom of the garden* (ie at the end farthest from the house). **5** [sing] (**a**) the lowest position in a class, list, etc: *She started at the bottom and worked her way up to become manager of the company.* (**b**) a person or group in this position: *He was always bottom of the class in science.* ○ *Our team came/was bottom of the league last season.* **6** [sing] the ground under a sea, lake or river: *The water is very deep here — I can't touch (the) bottom.* ○ *Several enemy ships went to the bottom* (ie sank). **7** [C] a ship's HULL[1] or KEEL. **8** [C usu *pl*] the lower half of a garment in two pieces: *pyjama bottoms* ○ *track suit bottoms.* **9** [U] the lowest gear of a motor vehicle: *drive up a steep hill in bottom.* **IDM** **at bottom** in reality; really: *He seems aggressive but at bottom he is very kind and good-natured.* **be/lie at the bottom of sth** to be the basic cause or origin of sth: *Who is at the bottom of these rumours?* **the bottom (of sth) falls out** a collapse occurs: *The bottom has fallen out of the market* (ie Trade has dropped to a very low level). ○ *The bottom fell out of his world* (ie His life lost its meaning) *when his wife died.* **bottom/top of the pile** ⇨ PILE[1]. **bottoms 'up!** (*infml*) (said as a TOAST[2], esp as a way of telling people to finish their drinks). **from top to bottom** ⇨ TOP[1]. **get to the bottom of sth** to find out the real cause of sth or the truth about sth: *We must get to the bottom of this mystery.* **knock the bottom out of sth** ⇨ KNOCK[2]. **touch bottom** ⇨ TOUCH[1].

▶ **bottom** *adj* [attrib] in the lowest or last position: *the bottom line (on a page)* ○ *the bottom rung (of a ladder)* ○ *the bottom step (of a flight of stairs)* ○ *Put your books on the bottom shelf.* ○ *Our team got the bottom score.* ○ *go up a hill in bottom gear.* **IDM** **bet one's bottom dollar** ⇨ BET.

bottom *v* **PHRV** ,**bottom 'out** (*commerce*) (of prices, trade, etc) to reach the lowest level: *There is no sign that the recession has bottomed out yet.*

bottomless *adj* **1** very deep: *a bottomless pit/ gorge/chasm.* **2** (*fig*) without limit or end: *bottomless reserves of energy.*

bottommost /'bɒtəmməʊst/ *adj* [attrib] lowest: *the bottommost depths of the sea.*

■ **the ,bottom 'line** *n* [sing] (*infml*) the fundamental or deciding factor; the essential point in an argument, etc: *If you don't make a profit you go out of business: that's the bottom line.* See also ROCK-BOTTOM.

botulism /'bɒtjulɪzəm/ *n* [U] a severe illness caused by bacteria in badly preserved food.

boudoir /'bu:dwɑ:(r)/ *n* (esp formerly) a woman's bedroom or small private room.

bouffant /'bu:fɒ; *US* bu:'fɑ:nt/ *adj* (of a person's hair) in a style that makes it stand out from the head in a round shape: *a ,bouffant 'hairdo.*

bougainvillaea (also **bougainvillea**) /,bu:gən'vɪliə/ *n* a tropical climbing plant with red or purple flowers.

bough /baʊ/ *n* (esp fml) any of the main branches of a tree.

bought *pt, pp* of BUY.

bouillon /'bu:jɒn/ *n* [U] a type of thin clear soup; stock[1](8).

boulder /'bəʊldə(r)/ *n* a large rock that has been worn and shaped by water or the weather.

boulevard /'bu:ləvɑ:d; *US* 'bʊl-/ *n* **1** a wide city street, often with trees on each side. **2** (*US*) a broad main road.

bounce /baʊns/ *v* **1** to move or make sth, esp a ball, move quickly up, back or away after hitting sth: [V] *This ball doesn't bounce.* [Vpr] *The ball bounced over the fence.* ○ *light/sound bouncing off the walls* [Vn] *The goalkeeper bounced the ball twice before kicking it.* [Vnpr] *She bounced the ball against the wall.* **2**(**a**) (of a person) to jump up and down in a lively manner, esp in the specified direction: [Vpr, Vp] *The child bounced (around) on the bed.* [V] *She walked with short bouncing steps.* (**b**) to make a child go up and down like this as a game: [Vn] *He bounced his baby on his knee.* ⇨ note at JUMP[1]. **3** (*infml*) (of a cheque) to be sent back by a bank as worthless because there is not enough money in the account: [V] *I hope this cheque doesn't bounce.* **4** to move in the specified direction in a bouncing or vigorous manner: [Vpr] *The car bounced along the bumpy mountain road.* [Vp] *He came bouncing into the room.* **PHRV** ,**bounce 'back** (*infml*) to recover well after trouble, illness, hardship, etc: *Share prices bounced back this morning.* ○ *She's had many misfortunes in her life but she always bounces back.*

▶ **bounce** *n* **1** [C] an act of bouncing: *catch a ball first bounce* (ie after it has bounced once). **2** [U] (**a**) the ability to bounce: *There's not much bounce left in this football.* (**b**) liveliness: *She's so full of bounce.*

bouncer *n* **1** (*infml*) a person employed by a club, restaurant, etc to throw out people who cause trouble. **2** (also **bumper**) a ball bowled in cricket that bounces high and forcefully from the pitch: *bowl sb a fast bouncer.*

bouncing *adj* ~ (**with sth**) strong and healthy: *a bouncing baby* ○ *He was bouncing with energy.*

bouncy *adj* (**-ier, -iest**) **1** (of a ball) that bounces well. **2** (of a person) lively: *She looked bouncy and confident.*

bound[1] /baʊnd/ *v* to run with jumping movements in a specified direction: [Vnpr] *He bounded into the room and announced that he was getting married.* ○ *The dog came bounding up to us, wagging its tail.* [also Vp].

▶ **bound** *n* a high jump: *The dog cleared* (ie jumped over) *the gate in one bound.* **IDM** **by/in leaps and bounds** ⇨ LEAP.

bound[2] /baʊnd/ *v* (usu passive) to form the boundary of sth; to limit sth: [Vn] *Germany is bounded on the west by France and on the south by Switzerland.* ○ *The airfield is bounded by woods on all sides.*

bound³ /baʊnd/ adj [pred] ~ (**for...**) going or ready to go in the direction of a place: *Where are you bound (for)?* ○ *We are bound for home.* ○ *This ship is* **outward bound/homeward bound** (ie sailing away from/towards its home port).
▶ **-bound** (forming compound *adjs*) moving towards a specified place or in a specified direction: *We're Paris-bound.* ○ *Northbound traffic may be delayed because of an accident on the motorway.*

bound⁴ *pt, pp* of BIND.

bound⁵ /baʊnd/ adj [pred] ~ **to do sth 1** certain to do sth: *The weather is bound to get better tomorrow.* ○ *You've done so much work that you're bound to pass the exam.* **2** forced by law, circumstances or duty to do sth: *They are bound by the contract to deliver the goods on time.* ○ *I am bound to say I disagree with you on this point.* **IDM** **bound 'up in sth** very busy with sth; very interested or involved in sth: *She seems very bound up in her work.* **bound 'up with sth** closely connected with sth: *Most of his problems are bound up with his childhood.* **honour bound** ⇨ HONOUR¹. **I'll be bound** (*dated infml*) I feel sure: *The children are up to some mischief, I'll be bound!*
▶ **-bound** (forming compound *adjs*) **1** confined to a specified place: *I hate being desk-bound* (eg in an office) *all day.* ○ *His illness has left him completely house-bound.* **2** prevented from going somewhere or from operating normally by the specified conditions: *fog-bound/snowbound/snowbound airports* ○ *Strikebound travellers face long delays this weekend.*

boundary /'baʊndri/ n **1** a line that marks a limit; a dividing line: *The fence marks the boundary between my land and hers.* ○ *live outside the city boundary* ○ (*fig*) *Scientists continue to push back the boundaries of knowledge.* ⇨ note at BORDER. **2** (in cricket) a hit of the ball that crosses the boundary of the playing area scoring 4 or 6 runs (RUN² 9): *He scored 26 runs, all in boundaries.*

bounden /'baʊndən/ adj **IDM** **a/one's bounden 'duty** (*fml*) a duty that one feels one must carry out; a solemn responsibility: *There are certain essential services which the local authority has a bounden duty to keep going.*

boundless /'baʊndləs/ adj without limits; huge: *boundless energy/enthusiasm.* ▶ **boundlessly** adv.

bounds /baʊndz/ n [pl] the accepted or furthest limits of sth: *It is **not beyond the bounds of possibility** that he'll win the match.* ○ *Are there no bounds to his ambition?* ○ *Public spending must be kept within reasonable bounds.* **IDM** **know no bounds** ⇨ KNOW. **out of 'bounds (to sb)** (*US*) **off limits** (of a place) not allowed to be entered or visited by sb: *The town's bars and discos are out of bounds to troops.*

bounteous /'baʊntɪəs/ adj (*fml or rhet*) giving or given generously: *The earth has yielded a bounteous harvest.*

bountiful /'baʊntɪfl/ adj (*fml or rhet*) **1** in large quantities: *a bountiful supply of food.* **2** giving generously: *belief in a bountiful God.*

bounty /'baʊnti/ n [U] (*dated*) money, etc given generously as a gift or a reward; generous acts: *Royal bounty supplied the central parks of London.*

bouquet /buˈkeɪ/ n **1** a bunch of flowers for carrying in the hand, often presented as a gift: *a bride's bouquet* ○ *The soloist received a huge bouquet of roses after her performance.* **2** the characteristic smell of a wine, etc: *a red wine with a very pleasant bouquet.*
■ **bouquet garni** /'bu:keɪ gɑːˈniː/ a bunch of herbs (HERB), often in a small bag, used in cooking for giving flavour to soups, meat dishes, etc.

bourbon /'bɜːbən/ n (**a**) [U] a type of whisky mainly made in the USA. (**b**) [C] a glass of this.

bourgeois /'bʊəʒwɑː, ˌbʊəʒ'wɑː/ adj **1** (*politics*) of or relating to the middle class: *bourgeois voters.* **2** (*derog*) (**a**) mainly interested in possessions and social status: *They've become very bourgeois since they got married.* (**b**) conventional; conservative: *bourgeois tastes/attitudes/ideas.* **3** (*politics*) supporting the interests of CAPITALISM; not communist.
▶ **bourgeois** n (*pl* unchanged) [C] a bourgeois person; a capitalist (CAPITALISM).

bourgeoisie /ˌbʊəʒwɑːˈziː/ n [Gp] (*usu derog*) **1** the middle classes in society: *the rise of the bourgeoisie in the 19th century.* **2** the capitalist (CAPITALISM) class. Compare PROLETARIAT.

bourse /bʊəs/ n a stock exchange (STOCK¹), esp (**the Bourse**) the one in Paris.

bout /baʊt/ n **1** ~ (**of sth / doing sth**) (**a**) a short period of intense activity: *She has bouts of hard work followed by long periods of inactivity.* (**b**) an attack or period of an illness: *a bout of flu/bronchitis/rheumatism* ○ *He suffers from frequent bouts of depression.* **2** a boxing or wrestling (WRESTLE) contest.

boutique /buːˈtiːk/ n a small shop selling clothes or other items.

bovine /'bəʊvaɪn/ adj [usu attrib] **1** (*fml*) of or relating to cattle: *bovine diseases.* **2** (*derog*) dull and stupid: *a bovine expression/character/mentality* ○ *bovine stupidity.*

bow
bow
bow-tie

bow¹ /bəʊ/ n **1** a piece of wood bent into a curve by a tight string joining its ends, used as a weapon or in sport for shooting arrows (ARROW 1): *hunting with bows and arrows.* ⇨ picture at ARCHERY. **2** a wooden rod with strands of HORSEHAIR stretched from end to end, used for playing musical instruments with strings. ⇨ picture at MUSICAL INSTRUMENT. **3(a)** a knot made with loops: *tie shoelaces in a bow.* (**b**) a RIBBON(1b) tied in this way: *a dress decorated with bows.* ⇨ picture. **IDM** **have two strings / a second, etc string to one's bow** have a second activity, skill or resource available to one, as a replacement for or an alternative to a first: *As both a novelist and a university lecturer, she has two strings to her bow.*
▶ **bow** v [V, Vn] to use a bow¹(2) on a musical instrument with strings. **bowing** n [U] the technique of using the bow to play a VIOLIN, etc.
bowed /bəʊd/ adj bent in a curved shape: *a small man with bowed legs.*
■ **bow-legs** n [pl] legs that curve out at the knees. **bow-legged** adj: *a bow-legged cowboy.*
bow-tie n a man's tie tied in a knot with a double loop, worn esp on formal occasions. ⇨ picture.

bow² /baʊ/ v **1** ~ (**down**) (**to/before sb/sth**) to bend the head or body as a sign of respect or as a greeting: [V] *The cast bowed as the audience applauded.* [Vpr] *We all bowed to the Queen.* [Vp] *The priest bowed down before the altar.* [Vn] *The congregation bowed their heads in prayer.* **2** (usu passive) to cause sth to bend: [Vn] *His back was bowed with age.* [also Vnpl]. **IDM** **bow and 'scrape** (*derog*) to try to gain approval by excessive politeness and obedience: *The waiter showed us to our table with much bowing and scraping.* **PHRV** **bow 'out (of sth) 1** to withdraw from sth: *I'm bowing out of this scheme — I don't approve of it.* **2** to retire from or give up a position: *After thirty years in politics, he is finally bowing out.* **bow to sth** to submit to sth; to accept or obey sth: *bow to the inevitable* ○ *bow to sb's opinion/wishes/greater experience* ○ *We're tired of having to bow to authority.*
▶ **bow** n an act of bending the head or body as a sign of respect or as a greeting: *acknowledge sb with*

a bow ○ *He made a bow and left the room.* **IDM** **take a/one's 'bow** (of an actor or actors) to acknowledge APPLAUSE by bowing (BOW² 1).

bow³ /baʊ/ *n* (often *pl*) the front or forward end of a boat or ship: *The yacht hit a rock and damaged her bows.* ⇨ picture at YACHT. Compare STERN². **IDM** **a shot across the/sb's bows** ⇨ SHOT¹.

bowdlerize, -ise /'baʊdləraɪz/ *v* [Vn] (*derog*) to remove words or scenes that are considered likely to offend or shock from a book, play, etc; to EXPURGATE sth.

bowel /'baʊəl/ *n* **1** [C] (usu *pl*, except in medical use and when used attributively) one of a system of tubes below the stomach through which waste matter passes before leaving the body; INTESTINE: *a bowel complaint/disorder* ○ *cancer of the bowel* ○ *open/move one's bowels* (ie DEFECATE). **2 bowels** [pl] the deepest inner part of sth: *in the bowels of the earth* (ie deep underground). ■ **'bowel movement** *n* an act of emptying waste matter from the bowels.

bower /'baʊə(r)/ *n* (**a**) a shady place under trees or climbing plants in a wood or garden. (**b**) a summerhouse (SUMMER).

bowl¹ /baʊl/ *n* **1(a)** (esp in compounds) a deep round dish, used esp for holding food or liquid: *a sugar bowl* ○ *a fruit bowl* ○ *a soup bowl.* ⇨ picture at PLATE¹. (**b**) the amount contained in a bowl: *a bowl of soup/cereal/fruit.* ⇨ picture at BUCKET. **2** the part of certain objects that is shaped like a bowl: *the bowl of a spoon* ○ *a lavatory bowl* ○ *He filled the bowl of his pipe with tobacco.* **3** (*esp US*) a large round theatre without a roof, used for for concerts, etc in the open air: *the Hollywood Bowl.*

bowl² /baʊl/ *n* **1** [C] a heavy wooden ball that rolls in a curve, used in the game of bowls. **2** [C] a heavy ball used in skittles (SKITTLE 2) and tenpin bowling (TENPIN). **3 bowls** [sing *v*] a game played on a smooth lawn, in which players take turns to roll bowls as near as possible to a small ball: *a bowls club/match.* **4** [C] (*US*) a football game played after the regular season between the best teams: *the Rose Bowl.*

bowl³ /baʊl/ *v* **1** [V, Vn] to roll a ball in the games of bowls (BOWL²) or BOWLING. **2** (in cricket) to send the ball from one's hand towards the batsman by swinging the arm over one's head without bending one's elbow: [V] *bowl fast/slow* ○ *Well bowled!* [Vn] *bowl a couple of balls.* **3 ~ sb (out)** (in cricket) to dismiss a batsman by bowling a ball that hits the WICKET(a): [Vn] *He was bowled for 12* (ie dismissed in this way after scoring 12 runs (RUN² 9)). [also Vnp]. **4** (*Brit*) to move fast and smoothly in the specified direction: [Vp, Vpr] *We were bowling along (the motorway) at seventy miles per hour.* **PHRV** **,bowl sb 'over 1** to knock sb down. **2** to surprise sb greatly; to astonish sb: *We were bowled over by the news of her sudden marriage.*

bowler¹ /'baʊlə(r)/ *n* **1** a person who bowls (BOWL³ 2) in cricket: *a fast/slow bowler* ○ *a left-arm spin bowler.* ⇨ picture at CRICKET¹. **2** a person who plays bowls (BOWL²).

bowler² /'baʊlə(r)/ *n* (also **,bowler 'hat**, *US* **derby**) a hard, usu black, hat with a curved BRIM(2) and round top, worn esp by men in business. ⇨ picture at HAT.

bowling /'baʊlɪŋ/ *n* [U] **1** a game in which players roll heavy balls along a special track towards a group of wooden objects and try to knock over as many of them as possible: *a bowling match.* See also SKITTLE 2, TENPIN BOWLING. **2** (in cricket) sending the ball from one's hand towards the batsman: *a good piece of bowling.* ■ **'bowling-alley** *n* (**a**) a long narrow track along which balls are rolled in bowling. (**b**) a building containing several of these.

'bowling-green *n* an area of grass cut short on which the game of bowls (BOWL²) is played.

bowls ⇨ BOWL² 3.

bowman /-mən/ *n* (*pl* **-men** /-mən/) (*dated*) an ARCHER.

bow-wow /ˌbaʊ 'waʊ/ *interj* (used to imitate the bark² of a dog).
▶ **'bow-wow** *n* (used by or when speaking to young children) a dog.

box¹ /bɒks/ *n* **1** [C] (**a**) (esp in compounds) a container made of wood, cardboard, metal, etc with a flat base and sides and often a lid, used esp for holding solid things: *a tool-box* ○ *a money-box* ○ *a shoe box* ○ *a cigar box* ○ *She packed her books in cardboard boxes.* (**b**) a box of chocolates/matches/cigars. **2** [C] (**a**) a separate section or enclosed area, eg for a group of people in a theatre or for witnesses in a lawcourt: *reserve a box at the theatre* ○ *the witness box* ○ *the press box* (ie for journalists). See also HORSEBOX. (**b**) a small hut for a specific purpose: *a sentry-box* ○ *a signal-box* ○ *a telephone-box.* **3** [C] an area enclosed within straight lines on a form or page: *tick the appropriate box.* **3 the box** [sing] (*infml*) the television: *What's on the box tonight?* **4 the box** [sing] (*infml*) (in football) the penalty area: *tackled inside the box.* **5** [C] = BOX NUMBER. **6** [C] (*US* ⚠ *sl*) the VAGINA. See also BALLOT-BOX, BLACK BOX, DISPATCH-BOX, LETTER-BOX. **IDM** **sb's bag/box of tricks** ⇨ TRICK.
▶ **box** *v* to put sth into a box: [Vn] *a boxed set of records.* **PHRV** **,box sb/sth 'in** to prevent sb/sth from moving freely, esp in a race: *One of the runners got boxed in on the final bend.* **,box sb/sth 'in/'up** (usu passive) to shut sb/sth in a small space: *He feels boxed in, living in that tiny room.* ○ *She hates being boxed up in an office all day.*
boxful *n* (*pl* **-fuls**) a full box (of sth): *a boxful of books/clothes/toys.*
■ **'box junction** *n* (*Brit*) an area of road where two roads cross, marked with a pattern of yellow lines in which vehicles must not stop.
'box number *n* a number given in newspaper advertisements to which replies may be sent.
'box-office *n* the place at a theatre, cinema, etc where tickets are bought or reserved: *The box office is open from 9 am* ○ *The film was a box-office success* (ie It was financially successful because many people went to see it).

boxing

box² /bɒks/ *v* **~ (against sb)** to fight sb with the fists (FIST) as a sport: [V] *Did you box at school?* [Vn, Vpr] *He was boxing (against) a much taller opponent.* **IDM** **box sb's 'ears** to hit sb on the side of the head with one's hand in anger or as a punishment: *He boxed the boy's ears for being rude.*
▶ **boxer** *n* **1** a person who boxes, esp for a living: *a heavyweight boxer.* ⇨ picture. **2** a dog like a BULLDOG but with longer legs. **'boxer shorts** *n* [pl] men's UNDERPANTS similar in design to SHORTS worn by boxers.
boxing *n* [U] the sport of fighting with the fists (FIST): *a boxing champion/match.* **'boxing glove** *n*

either of a pair of very large thick gloves worn for boxing. ⇨ picture.

box³ /bɒks/ n **(a)** [C,U] a small EVERGREEN bush with thick dark leaves, used esp for garden hedges. **(b)** (also **'boxwood**) [U] the hard wood of this bush, used for carving, etc.

boxcar /'bɒkskɑ:(r)/ n (US) an enclosed railway goods van.

Boxing Day /'bɒksɪŋ deɪ/ n [U,C] (esp Brit) the first day after Christmas Day that is not a Sunday. Boxing Day is an official holiday in Britain.

boy¹ /bɔɪ/ n **1** [C] a young male person: He lived in Edinburgh as a boy. ○ A group of boys were playing football in the street. ○ How many boys are there in your class at school? See also OLD BOY. **2** [C] a male child; a son: The Joneses have two boys and a girl. ○ Her eldest boy is at college. **3** [C] (esp in compounds) a boy or young man who does a specified job: the paper-boy (ie the boy who delivers the newspapers). **4 the boys** [pl] (infml) a group of men who are friends and mix socially: a night out with the boys (eg at a pub or bar) ○ He plays football with the boys on Saturday afternoons. ○ He likes to feel that he's one of the boys (ie accepted as part of the group). **IDM back-room boys** ⇨ BACK-ROOM. **sb's blue-eyed boy** ⇨ BLUE¹. **the boys in 'blue** (Brit infml) the police or a group of police officers. **,boys ,will be 'boys** (saying) young boys, and also sometimes grown men, occasionally behave in a CHILDISH way, and this may be excused. **jobs for the boys** ⇨ JOB¹. **man and boy** ⇨ MAN¹. **sort out the men from the boys** ⇨ SORT².

▶ **boyhood** n [U,C usu sing] the state or time of being a boy: a happy/unhappy/lonely boyhood ○ boyhood friends.

boyish adj (usu approv) of or like a boy: boyish ambitions/hopes/enthusiasm ○ He/She has boyish good looks.

■ **,boy 'scout** n = SCOUT 2.

boy² /bɔɪ/ interj (infml esp US) (expressing surprise, pleasure, relief or contempt): Boy, am I glad to see you!

boycott /'bɔɪkɒt/ v **(a)** (usu of a group of people) to refuse to take part in sth or to have social contact or do business with a person, company, country, etc, either as a punishment or as a way of protesting about sth: [Vn] Athletes from several countries boycotted the Olympic Games. **(b)** to refuse to handle or buy goods as a punishment or in protest: [Vn] boycotting foreign imports.

▶ **boycott** n an act of boycotting sb/sth: place/put sth under a boycott.

boyfriend /'bɔɪfrend/ n a person's regular male companion with whom he or she has a romantic or sexual relationship: She had lots of boyfriends before she got married.

Br abbr **1** British. **2** (religion) Brother: Br Peter.

bra /brɑ:/ n = BRASSIÈRE.

brace¹ /breɪs/ n **1** [C] a device that holds things firmly together or holds and supports them in position: a neck brace (ie worn to support the neck after injury). **2** [C] (US **braces** [pl]) a metal device worn inside the mouth, esp by children, for making the teeth straight: My daughter has to wear a brace on her teeth. **3 braces** [pl] (US **suspenders**) straps for holding trousers up. They are fastened to the top of the trousers at the front and back and passed over the shoulders: a pair of braces. **4** [C] either of the two marks { and } used in printing or writing to show that words, etc between them are connected. Compare BRACKET 2. **IDM belt and braces** ⇨ BELT.

brace² /breɪs/ n (pl unchanged) a pair (esp of birds or animals killed in hunting): two brace of partridge(s).

brace³ /breɪs/ v **1** [Vn] to make sth stronger or firmer; to support sth. **2** ~ **sth/oneself (against sth)** to place one's hand or foot firmly in order to

balance oneself or to prepare for an impact or a violent movement: [Vnpr] He braced himself against the seat of the car as it hit a tree. [also Vn]. **3** ~ **oneself/sb (for sth)** to prepare oneself for sth difficult or unpleasant: [Vn] Brace yourself — I've got some bad news for you. [Vnpr] We braced ourselves for a bumpy landing. ○ Britain is bracing itself/is braced for another week of strikes.

▶ **bracing** adj (esp of weather conditions) cool and fresh; invigorating (INVIGORATE): bracing sea air ○ a bracing walk.

bracelet /'breɪslət/ n a piece of jewellery worn on the wrist or arm.

bracken /'brækən/ n [U] a large type of FERN that grows thickly on hills and in woods. In the autumn it turns brown: entangled in the bracken.

bracket /'brækɪt/ n **1** a wooden or metal support fixed to or built into a wall to hold a shelf, lamp, etc. **2** (usu pl) (in printing or writing) any one of the marks used in pairs for enclosing words, figures, etc to separate them from what comes before or after, eg ( ) (round brackets or parentheses), [ ] (square brackets), < > (angle brackets), { } (braces): Put your name in brackets at the top of each page. ⇨ App 3. **3** a group or category within specified limits: be in the lower/higher income bracket ○ the 20–30 age bracket (ie those people between the ages of 20 and 30).

▶ **bracket** v **1** [Vn] (in printing or writing) to enclose words, figures, etc in brackets. **2** ~ **A and B (together)**; ~ **A with B** to put things or people in the same category (to suggest that they are similar, equal or connected in some way): [Vnpr] It's wrong to bracket him with the extremists in his party — his views are very moderate. [also Vn,Vnpl].

brackish /'brækɪʃ/ adj (of water) slightly salty: plants adapted to the brackish conditions.

brae /breɪ/ n (Scot) (often in names of places) a steep slope.

brag /bræg/ v (-gg-) ~ **(about/of sth)** to talk with too much pride (about sth); to boast: [V] Stop bragging! [Vpr] He's been bragging about his new car. [V.that] She bragged that she could run faster than me.

▶ **braggart** /'brægət/ n (dated) a person who brags.

Brahmin /'brɑ:mɪn/ (also **Brahman** /-ən/) n a Hindu of the highest CASTE(1).

braid /breɪd/ n **1** [U] threads of silk, cotton, etc woven together in a narrow strip for decorating clothes and material: The general's uniform was trimmed with gold braid. **2** [C] (US) a PLAIT or PIGTAIL: She wears her hair in braids. ⇨ picture at PLAIT.

▶ **braid** v **1** [Vn] to decorate clothes or material with braid. **2** (US) = PLAIT v [Vn] She braids her hair every morning.

Braille /breɪl/ n [U] a system of reading and writing for blind people, representing the letters of the alphabet by raised dots which they can read by touching them.

brain /breɪn/ n **1(a)** [C] the organ of the body inside the head that controls thought, memory and feeling: a disease of the brain ○ The brain is the centre of the nervous system. ○ suffer brain damage ○ brain surgery ○ a brain cell. **(b) brains** [pl] the substance of the brain, used as food: calves' brains. **2** [U,C often pl] intelligence: He hasn't got much brain. ○ She has an excellent brain. ○ You need brains to become a university professor. ○ He has one of the best brains in the college. **3(a)** [C] (infml) a clever person: He is one of the leading brains in the country. **(b)** the **brains** [sing v] (infml) the cleverest person in a group: He's the brains of the family. ○ She was the brains behind the whole scheme. **IDM blow one's/ sb's brains out** ⇨ BLOW¹. **cudgel one's brains** ⇨ CUDGEL. **have sth on the brain** (infml) to think about sth all the time and be unable to forget it even if one wants to: I've had this tune on the brain all *day but I can't remember what it's called.* **pick sb's brains** ⇨ PICK¹. **rack one's brain** ⇨ RACK². **tax one's/sb's brain** ⇨ TAX.

▶ **brain** *v* to kill a person or an animal with a heavy blow on the head: [Vn] (*fig infml*) *I nearly brained myself on that low beam.*

brainless *adj* stupid; foolish: *That was a pretty brainless thing to do.*

brainy *adj* (**-ier, -iest**) (*infml*) very clever; intelligent: *Her children are all very brainy.*

■ **brain death** *n* [U] very serious damage to the brain which cannot be cured. A person in such a condition cannot breathe without the help of machines and is considered by doctors to be dead even if her or his heart is still beating. **brain dead** *adj* suffering from brain death.

brain drain *n* (usu *sing*) (*infml*) the loss to a country when skilled and clever people leave it to go and live and work in other countries.

brains trust (*US* **brain trust**) *n* [Gp] a group of experts who answer questions and give advice, eg to the government or a corporation.

brain-teaser *n* a difficult problem; a PUZZLE(2).

brainchild /ˈbreɪntʃaɪld/ *n* [sing] a person's own plan, invention or idea: *The new arts centre is the brainchild of a wealthy local businessman.*

brainpower /ˈbreɪnpaʊə(r)/ *n* [U] the ability to think; intelligence.

brainstorm /ˈbreɪnstɔːm/ *n* **1** a sudden violent mental disturbance. **2** (*Brit infml*) a moment of confusion which causes one to forget sth or behave in a strange way: *I must have had a brainstorm — I couldn't remember my own telephone number for a moment.* **3** (*US*) = BRAINWAVE.

brainstorming /ˈbreɪnstɔːmɪŋ/ *n* [U] a method of solving problems in which all the members of a group suggest ideas and then discuss them: *a brainstorming session.*

brainwash /ˈbreɪnwɒʃ/ *v* ~ **sb** (**into doing sth**) to force sb to reject old beliefs or ideas and to accept new ones by using special continuous methods to persuade them: [Vnpr] (*fig*) *I refuse to be brainwashed by advertisers into buying something I don't need.* [also Vn]. ▶ **brainwashing** *n* [U].

brainwave /ˈbreɪnweɪv/ (*US* **brainstorm**) *n* (*infml*) a sudden clever idea: *Unless someone has a brainwave soon we'll never solve this problem.*

braise /breɪz/ *v* to cook meat or vegetables slowly with very little liquid in a closed container: [Vn] *braised beef and onions* ○ *braising steak* (ie meat suitable for braising).

brake /breɪk/ *n* a device for slowing or stopping a car, bicycle, train, etc: *put on/apply/release the brake(s)* ○ *The taxi skidded to a halt **with a screech of brakes**.* ○ *His brakes failed on a steep hill.* ○ *Put your foot on the brake* (ie the brake PEDAL(1) in a car, etc). ○ (*fig*) *The government is determined to put a brake on public spending.* ⇨ picture at BICYCLE, CAR. See also HANDBRAKE, DISC BRAKE.

▶ **brake** *v* to slow down or make sth slow down using a brake: [V] *The driver braked hard as the child ran onto the road in front of him.* [also Vn].

■ **brake light** (*US* **stoplight**) *n* a red light at the back of a car, etc which lights up when the brakes are used.

bramble /ˈbræmbl/ *n* (*esp Brit*) a wild prickly bush with red or black berries; a BLACKBERRY bush.

bran /bræn/ *n* [U] the outer covering of grain which is separated from it when it is made into flour. Compare HUSK.

branch /brɑːntʃ; *US* bræntʃ/ *n* **1** a part of a tree which grows out from the trunk and on which leaves, etc grow: *He climbed up the tree and hid among the branches.* **2** a local office or shop belonging to a large firm or organization: *The bank has branches in all parts of the country.* ○ *We have*

five branch offices in the USA alone. **3** a usu smaller or less important division of a river, road, railway or mountain range: *a branch of the Rhine* ○ *a branch line* (ie a division of a main railway line, serving country areas). **4** a division of a family, a subject of knowledge, or a group of languages: *His uncle's branch of the family emigrated to Australia.* ○ *Gynaecology is a branch of medicine.* **IDM** **root and branch** ⇨ ROOT¹.

▶ **branch** *v* (of a road) to divide into branches: [V] *The road branches in a couple of miles.* **PHR V** **branch 'off** (of a vehicle or road) to turn from one road into a (usu) smaller one: *The car in front of us suddenly branched off to the left.* ○ *The road to the village branches off on the right.* **branch 'out (into sth)** to extend or expand one's activities or interests in a new direction: *The company began by specializing in radios but has now branched out into computers.* ○ *She's leaving the company to branch out on her own.*

brand /brænd/ *n* **1** a type of product manufactured by a particular company; a trade mark (TRADE¹): *Which brand of toothpaste do you prefer?* ○ *Our product is the brand leader* (ie sells better than others of the same type). ○ *brand loyalty* (ie the tendency of customers to continue buying the same brand). **2** a particular type or kind: *a strange brand of humour.* **3(a)** a mark made with a hot piece of metal esp on cattle to show who owns them. (**b**) (also **branding-iron**) the tool used for this. ⇨ picture at IRON.

▶ **brand** *v* **1** ~ **sth** (**on sth**) to mark sth with or as if with a brand(3b): [Vn] *On big farms cattle are usually branded.* [also Vnpr]. **2** (esp passive) ~ **sb** (**as sth**) to give a bad name or reputation to sb, esp unfairly: [Vn-n] *She was branded a traitor.* ○ *He was branded (as) a trouble-maker for taking part in the demonstration.* [also Vn-adj]. **branding-iron** *n* = BRAND 3b.

■ **brand name** *n* the name given to a particular product by the company that produces it for sale.

brand-'new *adj* completely new: *Come and look at our video — it's brand-new.*

> **NOTE** A **brand** is a product with a name (a **brand name**) that is made by a particular company. It is used especially of food and small household goods: *The supermarket's own brands are packaged in blue and white.* ○ *Which brand of washing powder do you buy?* The word **brand** is used a lot in advertising. **Make** usually applies to machines, equipment and cars: *What make of car do you drive?* ○ *Our washing-machine is an Italian make.*

brandish /ˈbrændɪʃ/ *v* to wave sth in order to threaten sb or because one is angry, excited, etc: [Vn] *brandish a gun/a knife/an axe* ○ *The demonstrators brandished banners and shouted slogans.*

brandy /ˈbrændi/ *n* (**a**) [U] a strong alcoholic drink usu made from wine. (**b**) [C] a type of brandy: *The finest brandies are made in Cognac.* (**c**) [C] a glass of brandy: *Two brandies and soda, please.*

■ **brandy-snap** *n* a crisp biscuit made of thin GINGERBREAD rolled into a tube and often filled with cream.

brash /bræʃ/ *adj* (*often derog*) **1** confident in a rude, noisy or aggressive way: *a brash young salesman* ○ *Her brash and abrasive style made her very unpopular.* **2** (of colours, clothing, etc) too bright: *He was wearing a rather brash tie.* ▶ **brashly** *adv*. **brashness** *n* [U].

brass /brɑːs; *US* bræs/ *n* **1** [U] (**a**) a bright yellow metal made by mixing copper and ZINC: *brass doorknobs/buttons* ○ *a brass foundry* ○ *a brass plate* (ie a brass sign outside a house or an office giving the name and profession of the person who lives or works there). (**b**) [U] objects made of brass, esp ornaments: *do/clean/polish the brass.* **2 the brass**

[Gp] the musical instruments made of brass which form a band or part of an ORCHESTRA: *The brass is/ are too loud.* ○ *The brass section consists of four trumpets and three trombones.* ⇨ picture at MUSICAL INSTRUMENT. **3** [C] (*esp Brit*) a flat piece of brass with words or a picture on it, fixed to the floor or wall of a church in memory of sb who has died. **4** [U] (*Brit sl*) money: *He's got plenty of brass.* **5** [U] (*infml*) cheek(2); impudence (IMPUDENT): *He had the brass to ask his boss for a 20% pay increase.* See also TOP BRASS. **IDM** **bold as brass** ⇨ BOLD. **get down to brass ˈtacks** (*infml*) to start to consider the basic facts or practical details of sth.
▶ **brassy** *adj* **1** like brass in colour. **2** (*usu derog*) like a brass musical instrument in sound; loud and harsh. **3** (*usu derog*) (esp of a woman) loud, bright and VULGAR in dress, manner, appearance, etc.
■ ˌbrass ˈband *n* a band of musicians playing mainly brass instruments.
ˌbrass ˈknuckles *n* [pl] (*US*) = KNUCKLEDUSTER.
ˈbrass-rubbing *n* **(a)** [U] making a copy of the design on a brass(3) by rubbing a piece of paper placed over it with chalk or wax. **(b)** [C] a picture made in this way.

brasserie /ˈbræsəri; *US* ˌbræsəˈriː/ *n* a type of restaurant serving drinks, esp beer, with food.

brassière /ˈbræsiə(r); *US* brəˈzɪər/ (also **bra** /brɑː/) *n* a garment which women wear under their other clothes to cover and support their breasts.

brat /bræt/ *n* (*derog*) a child, esp one that behaves badly.

bravado /brəˈvɑːdəʊ/ *n* [U] a display of bold talk or behaviour to impress other people: *Take no notice of his threats — they're sheer bravado.*

brave /breɪv/ *adj* (**-r, -st**) **1** (of a person) ready to face and endure danger, pain or suffering; having no fear: *brave men and women* ○ *Be brave!* ○ *It was brave of her to go into the burning building.* ○ *He was very brave about his operation.* **2** (of an action) requiring or showing courage: *a brave act/deed/speech* ○ *She put up a brave fight against her illness.* **IDM** **(a)** ˌbrave new ˈworld (*catchphrase often ironic*) a new and hopeful period in history resulting from major changes in society: *Where is the brave new world of health care promised by the government?* **put on, etc a bold/brave front** ⇨ FRONT.
▶ **brave** *n* [C] a native American WARRIOR(2).
brave *v* to endure or face sth/sb without showing fear: [Vn] *brave dangers* ○ *brave one's critics* ○ *We decided to brave* (ie go out in spite of) *the bad weather.* **PHRV** **ˌbrave it ˈout** to face anger, suspicion or blame with a refusal to change one's behaviour or accept defeat: *With no one to help him against his accusers he had to brave it out alone.*
bravely *adv.*
bravery /ˈbreɪvəri/ *n* [U] being brave; courage: *a medal for bravery in battle.*

bravo /ˌbrɑːˈvəʊ/ *interj, n* (*pl* **-os**) a shout of approval, esp to an actor, singer, etc: *Bravo! Well played!*

bravura /brəˈvjʊərə/ *n* [U] (*often used attributively*) brilliant style or technique in performing: *a bravura performance.*

brawl /brɔːl/ *n* a rough or noisy fight, esp in a public place: *a drunken brawl in a bar.*
▶ **brawl** *v* to take part in a brawl: [V] *gangs of youths brawling in the street.* **brawler** *n.*

brawn /brɔːn/ *n* [U] **1** strong muscles; strength: *a job needing brains* (ie intelligence) *rather than brawn.* **2** (*Brit*) (*US* ˈhead cheese) meat, esp from a pig's or calf's head, cooked and pressed in a pot with jelly.
▶ **brawny** *adj* (**-ier, -iest**) having or showing strong muscles: *a brawny physique* ○ *a brawny man.*

bray /breɪ/ *n* **(a)** the harsh cry of a DONKEY. **(b)** a

sound like this. ▶ **bray** *v* (*often derog*) to make a bray: [V] *a braying laugh.*

brazen /ˈbreɪzn/ *adj* **1** (*derog*) open and without shame: *brazen insolence/rudeness* ○ *an unforgivable act of brazen savagery* ○ *a brazen hussy.* **2(a)** made of brass; like brass. **(b)** having a harsh sound: *the brazen notes of a trumpet.*
▶ **brazen** *v* **PHRV** ˌbrazen it ˈout to behave, after doing wrong, as if one has nothing to be ashamed of.
brazenly *adv* without shame.

brazier /ˈbreɪziə(r)/ *n* an open metal framework for holding a coal fire: *workmen brewing tea on a burning brazier.*

breach /briːtʃ/ *n* **1** [C, U] the breaking of or failure to do what is required by a law, an agreement, a duty, etc: *a breach of loyalty/trust/protocol* ○ *a breach of confidence* (ie giving away a secret) ○ *sue sb for breach of contract* ○ *a breach of security* (ie failure to protect official secrets) ○ *They are in breach of the Official Secrets Act.* **2** [C] a break in usu friendly relations between people or groups: *a breach of diplomatic relations between two countries.* **3** [C] an opening made in a wall or barrier, eg by an attacking army: *The huge waves made a breach in the sea wall.* **IDM** **step into the breach** ⇨ STEP[1].
▶ **breach** *v* to make a gap in a wall, barrier, etc: [Vn] *Our tanks have breached the enemy defences.*
■ ˌbreach of ˈpromise *n* [U] (*law*) the breaking of a promise, esp (formerly) a promise to marry sb.
ˌbreach of the ˈpeace *n* (usu *sing*) (*law*) the crime of causing a public disturbance, eg by fighting in the street.

bread

French loaf

pitta

bagel

rolls

croissant

slice

crust

loaf

bread /bred/ *n* [U] **1** a food made of flour, water and usu YEAST mixed together and then baked: *a loaf/ slice/piece of bread* ○ *wholemeal bread* ○ *brown/white bread.* ⇨ picture. See also CRISPBREAD, GINGERBREAD. **2** (*sl*) money. **IDM** ˌbread and ˈwater (*Brit*) the plainest and cheapest possible food: *I had to live on bread and water when I was a student.* **know which side one's bread is buttered** ⇨ KNOW. **take the bread out of sb's ˈmouth** to take away sb's means of earning a living.
■ ˌbread and ˈbutter /ˌbred n ˈbʌtə(r)/ *n* [U] **1** slices of bread spread with butter. **2** (*infml*) (the way of earning) one's living: *He's trying to get work as an actor, but he earns his bread and butter as a waiter.* ○ *Jobs, pensions and housing are the bread-and-butter issues of politics* (ie the basic ones).
ˈbread bin *n* (*Brit*) (*US* **bread box**) a container for keeping bread in.

breadbasket /ˈbredbɑːskɪt; *US* -bæs-/ *n* (*US*) an area of agricultural land that provides large amounts of food, esp grain, for other areas: *We travelled across the breadbasket of America.*

breadboard /ˈbredbɔːd/ *n* a board of wood, etc for cutting bread on.

breadcrumbs /ˈbredkrʌmz/ *n* [pl] tiny pieces of bread, usu from the inner part of a LOAF[1]: *fish covered with breadcrumbs and then fried.*

breadline /'bredlaɪn/ *n* (*esp US*) a line of poor people waiting for free food to be given to them. **IDM** **on the breadline** very poor: *Millions of people are still living on or below the breadline.*

breadth /bredθ/ *n* **1** [U, C] the distance or measurement from side to side; width: *The average breadth of the reef is ten miles.* **2** [U] wide extent, eg of knowledge; range¹(2): *Her breadth of experience makes her ideal for the job.* **3** [U] freedom from prejudice and willingness to accept new or different ideas, opinions, etc: *show breadth of mind/outlook/ opinions.* **IDM** **the length and breadth of sth** ⇨ LENGTH.

breadwinner /'bredwɪnə(r)/ *n* a person who supports a family with the money he or she earns: *Mum's the breadwinner in our family.*

break¹ /breɪk/ *v* (*pt* **broke** /brəʊk/; *pp* **broken** /'brəʊkən/) **1(a)** ~ (**in/into sth**) (of a whole object) to be damaged and separated into two or more parts as a result of force or strain (but not by cutting): [V] *The string broke.* ○ *Glass breaks easily.* [Vpr] *The bag broke under the weight of the bottles inside it.* ○ *She dropped the plate and it broke into pieces/in two.* (**b**) ~ **sth** (**in/into sth**) to cause a whole object to be damaged in this way: [Vn] *break a cup/vase/window* ○ *She fell off a ladder and broke her arm.* ○ *If you pull too hard you will break the string.* [Vnpr] *He broke the bar of chocolate into two (pieces).* **2(a)** to stop working as a result of being damaged: [V] *My watch has broken.* (**b**) to damage sth and stop it from working: [Vn] *I think I've broken the washing-machine.* **3** to cut the surface of the skin so as to cause it to bleed: [Vn] *The dog bit me but didn't break the skin.* **4** to fail to follow or obey sth; to fail to keep a law, promise, etc: [Vn] *break the law/the rules/the conditions* ○ *break an agreement/a contract/a promise/one's word* ○ *break an appointment* (ie fail to come to it) ○ *He was breaking the speed limit* (ie travelling faster than the law allows). **5** ~ (**off**) to stop doing sth for a while: [V] *Let's break for lunch.* [also Vp]. **6** [Vn] (**a**) to interrupt sth: *break sb's concentration* ○ *We broke our journey (in London) at Oxford* (ie stopped in Oxford on the way to London). ○ *a broken night's sleep* (ie a night during which one keeps waking) ○ *her decision to break her career to go back to college* ○ *I broke my diet by eating a bar of chocolate.* (**b**) to cause sth to end: *She broke the silence by coughing.* ○ *Someone laughed suddenly, and the spell was broken.* (**c**) to bring sth to an end by force: *break a blockade/siege* ○ *The employers have not broken the dockers' strike.* **7** (of the weather) to change suddenly after a period without change: [V] *The fine weather/The heatwave broke at last.* **8** to show an opening: [V] *The clouds broke and the sun came out.* **9** [V] (**a**) to come into being: *Dawn/The day was breaking.* Compare DAYBREAK. (**b**) (*Brit*) to begin suddenly and violently: *The storm broke.* (**c**) to become known; to be revealed: *There was a public outcry when the scandal broke.* **10(a)** [Vn] to destroy sth or make it weaker: *break sb's morale/resistance/resolve/spirit* ○ *The government is determined to break the power of the trade unions.* ○ *The scandal broke him* (ie ruined his reputation and destroyed his confidence). (**b**) to become weak or be destroyed: [V] *Throughout the ordeal his spirit never broke.* ○ *He broke under questioning* (ie was no longer able to endure it) *and confessed to everything.* (**c**) to OVERWHELM sb with a strong emotion, eg grief: [Vn] *The death of his wife broke him completely.* **11** [V] (**a**) (of the voice) to change its tone because of emotion: *Her voice broke as she told us the dreadful news.* (**b**) (of a boy's voice) to become deeper at PUBERTY: *His voice broke when he was thirteen.* **12** to do better than the previous record¹(4) in a particular sport, event, etc: [Vn] *break the Commonwealth/World/Olympic 100 metres record.*

13 [V] (of a bowled (BOWL³ 2) ball in cricket) to change direction after hitting the ground. **14** (of the sea) to fall in waves: [V] *the sound of waves breaking on the beach* ○ *The sea was breaking over the wrecked ship.* **15** to find the meaning of sth secret: [Vn] *break a code.* **16** (*esp US*) to change a banknote (NOTE¹ 4), etc for coins: [Vn] *Can you break a twenty dollar bill?* **IDM** Idioms containing **break** are at the entries for the nouns or adjectives in the idioms, eg **break even** ⇨ EVEN²; **break sb's/one's heart** ⇨ HEART. **PHRV** ,**break a'way (from sb/sth) 1** to escape suddenly from being held prisoner: *The prisoner broke away from his guards.* **2** to leave a political party, state, etc, esp to form a new one: *Several Labour MPs broke away to join the Social Democrats.* ○ *A province has broken away to form a new state.*

,**break 'down 1** to stop working because of a mechanical, electrical, etc fault: *The telephone system has broken down.* ○ *We* (ie Our car) *broke down on the freeway.* **2** to fail; to collapse: *Negotiations between the two sides have broken down.* ○ *If law and order break down, anarchy will result.* **3** (of sb's health) to become very bad; to collapse: *Her health broke down under the pressure of work.* **4** to lose control of one's feelings: *He broke down and wept when he heard the news.* See also BREAKDOWN. ,**break (sth) 'down** (esp of money spent) to be divided or divide into parts by analysis: *Expenditure on the project breaks down as follows: wages £10m, plant £4m, raw materials £5m.* See also BREAKDOWN. ,**break sth 'down 1** to make sth collapse by hitting it hard: *Firemen had to break the door down to reach the people trapped inside.* **2** to cause sth to collapse; to overcome or destroy sth: *break down resistance/opposition* ○ *break down sb's reserve/shyness* ○ *Attempts must be made to break down the barriers of fear and hostility which divide the two communities.* **3** to change the chemical composition(3) of sth: *Sugar and starch are broken down in the stomach.*

'**break sth from sth** to remove sth from sth larger by breaking: *He broke a piece of bread from the loaf.* ,**break 'in** to enter a building by force: *Burglars had broken in while we were away.* See also BREAK-IN. ,**break sb/sth 'in** to train sb/sth: *break in new recruits/a young horse.* ,**break 'in (on sth)** to interrupt or disturb sth: *She longed to break in on their conversation but felt it would seem rude.*

break into sth 1 to enter sth by force: *Our house was broken into by burglars last week.* **2** to begin laughing, singing, etc suddenly: *As the President's car arrived, the crowd broke into loud applause.* **3** to change suddenly from a slower to a faster pace: *break into a trot/canter/gallop* ○ *The man broke into a run when he saw the police.* **4** (of an activity) to use up time that would normally be spent doing sth else: *All this extra work I'm doing is breaking into my leisure time.* **5** (*Brit*) to use a banknote (NOTE¹ 4) or coin of high value to buy sth costing less: *I can't pay you the 50p I owe you without breaking into a £5 note.* **6** to open and use sth kept for an emergency: *break into emergency supplies of food.*

,**break 'off** to stop speaking: *He broke off in the middle of a sentence.* ,**break (sth) 'off** to separate sth or become separated from sth as a result of force or strain: *The door-handle has broken off.* ○ *She broke off a piece of chocolate and gave it to me.* ,**break sth 'off** to end sth suddenly: *break off diplomatic relations (with a country)* ○ *They've broken off their engagement/broken it off.*

,**break 'out** (of violent events) to start suddenly: *Fire broke out during the night.* ○ *Rioting broke out between rival groups of fans.* ○ *War broke out in 1939.* See also OUTBREAK. ,**break 'out (of sth)** to escape from a place or a situation, esp by using force: *Several prisoners broke out of the jail.* ○ *She felt the need to break out of her daily routine and do some-*

[V.*to* inf] = verb + *to* infinitive   [Vn.inf (no *to*)] = verb + noun + infinitive without *to*   [V.*ing*] = verb + -*ing* form

thing exciting. See also BREAK-OUT. ,**break** ¹**out in sth** to suddenly become covered in sth: *Her face broke out in a rash.* ○ *He broke out in a cold sweat* (eg through fear).

,**break** ¹**through** to make new and important discoveries: *Scientists think they are beginning to break through in the fight against cancer.* See also BREAK-THROUGH. ,**break** ¹**through (sth) 1** to make a way through sth using force; to penetrate sth: *Demonstrators broke through the police cordon.* **2** (of the sun or moon) to appear from behind clouds: *The sun broke through (the clouds) at last in the afternoon.* ¹**break through sth** to overcome sth: *break through sb's reserve/shyness.*

,**break** ¹**up 1** (of members of a group) to go away in different directions: *The meeting broke up at eleven o'clock.* **2** (*Brit*) (of a school, its staff or its pupils) to begin the holidays when school closes at the end of term: *When do you break up for Christmas?* **3** (*Brit*) to become very weak; to collapse: *He was breaking up under the strain.* **4** (*US*) to be overcome with laughter: *Woody Allen makes me just break up.* ,**break (sth)** ¹**up 1** to separate or make sth separate into smaller pieces: *The ship broke up on the rocks.* ○ *The ship was broken up for scrap metal.* **2** to end sth or to come to an end: *Their marriage has broken up.* ○ *They decided to break up the partnership.* See also BREAKUP. ,**break sth** ¹**up 1** to make people leave sth or stop doing sth, esp by using force: *break up a fight* ○ *Police were called in to break up the meeting.* **2** to divide sth into smaller parts: *Sentences can be broken up into clauses.* **3** (of an activity) to make something seem less boring by adding variety: *A car radio helps to break up the monotony of a long drive.* ,**break** ¹**up (with sb)** to end a relationship with sb: *She's just broken up with her boyfriend.* See also BREAKUP.

¹**break with sb** to end a relationship with sb: *break with one's girlfriend/boyfriend.* ¹**break with sth** to give up sth; to abandon sth: *break with tradition/old habits/the past.*

▶ **breakable** /¹breɪkəbl/ *adj* easily broken. **breakables** *n* [pl] breakable objects, eg glasses and cups.

■ ¹**break-dancing** *n* [U] a very lively style of dancing, often in a competition or as a display, esp popular with young Black Americans.

¹**break-in** *n* an entry into a building using force: *Police are investigating a break-in at the bank.*

¹**break-out** *n* an escape from prison, esp one involving the use of force: *a mass break-out of prisoners.*

break² /breɪk/ *n* **1** ~ (**in sth**) (**a**) an opening made by breaking; a broken place: *a break in a fence/wall/water-pipe.* (**b**) a gap; a space: *a break in the clouds* (ie where blue sky can be seen) ○ *Wait for a break in the traffic before crossing the road.* **2**(**a**) an interval, esp between periods of work; a pause: *morning break* (eg between lessons at school) ○ *lunch-break* (eg in an office, a school or a factory) ○ *have/take an hour's break for lunch* ○ *work for five hours without a break* ○ *a break in a conversation.* (**b**) a short holiday: *a weekend break in the country* ○ *I'm in need of a break.* **3** ~ (**in sth**); ~ (**with sb/sth**) (**a**) a change or an interruption in sth continuous: *a break in a child's education* ○ *a break in the weather* (ie a change from bad to good weather) ○ *a break with tradition* (ie a change from what is accepted in art, behaviour, etc). (**b**) the end of a relationship: *a break in diplomatic relations* ○ *She's been depressed since the break with her boyfriend.* **4** (*infml*) a piece of luck, esp one that leads to further success: *a big/lucky break* ○ *a bad break* (ie a piece of bad luck) ○ *give sb a break* (ie a chance to show their ability). **5** (in cricket) a change in direction of a bowled (BOWL³ 2) ball after it hits the ground: *an off/a leg break* (ie a ball that spins to the right/left on bouncing). **6** (also **break of** ¹**service**, ¹**service break**) (in tennis)

an instance of winning a game when one's opponent is serving (SERVE 8): *Smith has had two breaks already in this set.* ○ *break point* (eg when the score is 30-40). **7** (in BILLIARDS or SNOOKER) a series of successful shots by one player; the score made by such a series: *a break of 52.* **IDM** **break of** ¹**day** (*fml*) dawn: *at break of day.* **make a** ¹**break (for it)** to escape, esp from prison. **make a clean break** ⇨ CLEAN¹.

> **NOTE** A **break** is a rest during the working day or at school: *a lunch/coffee break* ○ *the mid-morning break* ○ *10 minutes' break.* It also covers the meanings of several other words. A **pause** is usually short and often applied to speech: *a pause for breath* ○ *a pause/break in the conversation.* **Recess** is the scheduled holiday of Parliament, and in American English it is also the break between school classes. An **interval** in British English is the break between the parts of a play, etc: *We had a quick drink in the interval.* This is also called an **intermission**, especially in American English. An **interlude** may be an interval or a short event during a longer activity, often contrasting with it: *Her time in Paris was a happy interlude in a difficult career.* A **rest** is a necessary period of relaxation after an activity: *You look tired. You need a good rest.*

breakage /¹breɪkɪdʒ/ *n* (**a**) [C] the act or an instance of breaking sth: *a breakage or similar accident* ○ *All breakages must be paid for.* (**b**) [U] the action of breaking sth or the damage caused by this: *measures to reduce the risk of breakage.*

breakaway /¹breɪkəweɪ/ *n* ~ (**from sth**) **1** (often used attributively) the loss of members from a group: *a breakaway from the Republican party* ○ *a breakaway group on the left of the Labour party.* **2** a change from an established custom or tradition: *a complete breakaway from the old style of popular music.*

breakdown /¹breɪkdaʊn/ *n* **1** a mechanical failure: *Our car/We had a breakdown on the motorway.* **2** a collapse or failure: *a breakdown in the negotiations* ○ *the breakdown of a marriage.* **3** the collapse of sb's (esp mental) health: *She suffered a complete nervous breakdown.* **4** a detailed analysis of information presented in the form of numbers, etc: *a breakdown of income and expenditure.*

breaker /¹breɪkə(r)/ *n* **1** a large wave that breaks into FOAM(1a) as it moves towards the shore. **2** (usu in compounds) a person or thing that breaks sth: *a lawbreaker* ○ *a record-breaker* ○ *a circuit-breaker.* See also TIE-BREAKER.

breakfast /¹brekfəst/ *n* [C, U] the first meal of the day: *a light/big/hearty breakfast* ○ *English/continental breakfast* ○ *have bacon and eggs for breakfast* ○ *They were having breakfast when I arrived.* ○ *She doesn't eat much breakfast.* See also BED AND BREAKFAST. **IDM** **a dog's breakfast/dinner** ⇨ DOG¹.

▶ **breakfast** *v* ~ (**on sth**) (*fml*) to eat breakfast: [Vpr] *We breakfasted at 7 on toast and coffee.* [also V].

breakneck /¹breknek/ *adj* [attrib] very fast and dangerous: *drive/ride/travel at breakneck speed.*

breakthrough /¹breɪkθruː/ *n* **1** an important development or discovery, esp in scientific knowledge: *a breakthrough in negotiations* ○ *a major breakthrough in cancer research.* **2** an act of breaking through an obstacle, eg an enemy's defences.

breakup /¹breɪkʌp/ *n* **1** the end of a relationship or association: *The breakup of their marriage shocked their friends.* **2** the division of sth into smaller parts: *the breakup of large estates.*

breakwater /¹breɪkwɔːtə(r)/ *n* a wall built out into the sea to protect a coast or harbour from the force of the waves.

bream /briːm/ *n* (*pl* unchanged) (**a**) a type of fish of the CARP[1] family found in rivers and lakes. (**b**) (also **'sea bream**) a type of sea-fish similar to this.

breast /brest/ n **1** [C] either of the two parts of a woman's body that produce milk: *feeding a baby at the breast* ○ *cancer of the breast* ○ *The breasts swell during pregnancy.* **2** [C] (**a**) (*rhet*) the upper front part of the human body; the chest: *clasp/hold sb to one's breast.* (**b**) the part of a garment covering this: *a soldier with medals pinned to the breast of his coat.* **3** [C, U] the part of an animal or a bird corresponding to the human breast, esp when eaten as food: *chicken breasts* ○ *breast of lamb* ○ *a bird with a red breast.* **4** [C] (*rhet*) the source of feelings or emotions; the heart: *a troubled breast.* **IDM** **make a clean breast of sth** ⇨ CLEAN[1].
▶ **breast** v (**a**) (*dated*) to touch sth with one's breast(2a): [Vn] *The champion breasted the tape* (ie to win a race). (**b**) (*fml*) to face and move forward against sth: [Vn] *breasting the waves.*
■ **'breast-feed** v (*pt, pp* **'breast-fed**) to feed a baby with milk from the breast: [Vn] *Were her children breast-fed or bottle-fed?*
,**breast 'pocket** n a pocket on the inside or the outside of the breast of a jacket, or on the outside of a shirt.
'breast-stroke n [sing] a style of swimming with chest downwards, in which the arms are extended in front of the head and then pulled sideways and back, while the legs move in a corresponding way: *do (the) breast-stroke.*

breastbone /'brestbəʊn/ (also **sternum**) n a thin flat bone in the chest between the ribs (RIB 1). ⇨ picture at SKELETON.

breastplate /'brestpleɪt/ n a piece of armour covering the breast.

breath /breθ/ n **1(a)** [U] the air taken into and sent out from the lungs: *You can see people's breath on a cold day.* ○ *His breath smelt of garlic.* ○ *She paused for breath, then went on speaking.* (**b**) [C] a single act of taking air into the lungs: *take a deep breath* (ie fill one's lungs with air). **2** ~ **of sth** [sing] a slight movement of air: *There wasn't a breath of air/wind.* **3** ~ **of sth** [sing] a slight suggestion, feeling or sign of sth: *a breath of scandal* ○ *the first breath of spring.* **IDM** **a breath of fresh 'air 1** an opportunity to breathe clean air, esp out of doors: *I like to have a breath of fresh air during my lunch hour.* **2** a person or thing that is a welcome change: *Her smile is a breath of fresh air in this gloomy office.* **the breath of 'life (to/for sb)** a thing that sb needs or depends on: *Religion is the breath of life to/for her.* **catch one's breath** ⇨ CATCH[1]. **draw breath** ⇨ DRAW[1]. **get one's 'breath (again/back)** to start breathing normally again after physical exercise: *It took us a few minutes to get our breath back after running for the bus.* **hold one's 'breath** to stop breathing for a short time (eg during a medical examination or from fear or excitement): *How long can you hold your breath for?* ○ *The crowd held its/their breath as he ran up to take the penalty kick.* **in the same breath** ⇨ SAME[1]. **one's last / dying 'breath** the last moment of one's life. **(be) out of / short of 'breath** breathing very quickly, esp after exercise: *We were all out of breath when we got to the top of the hill.* **save one's breath** ⇨ SAVE[1]. **say sth, speak, etc under one's 'breath** to say sth, etc quietly so as not to be heard: '*Idiot!' she muttered under her breath.* **take sb's 'breath away** to surprise or delight sb very much: *The view from the top took my breath away.* **waste one's breath** ⇨ WASTE[1]. **with bated breath** ⇨ BATED.
▶ **breathy** /'breθi/ adj (of the voice) with a noticeable sound of breathing.
■ **'breath test** n a test of a driver's breath to measure how much alcohol he or she has drunk.

Breathalyser, -yzer /'breθəlaɪzə(r)/ n (*propr*) a

device used by the police for measuring the amount of alcohol in a driver's breath.
▶ **breathalyse, -yze** v [Vn] to test sb with a Breathalyser.

breathe /briːð/ v **1** to take air into the lungs and send it out again: [V] *breathing deeply* ○ *People breathe more slowly when they are asleep.* ○ *She's still breathing* (ie still alive). ○ *He was breathing hard/heavily after his exertions.* [Vn, Vnp] *It's good to breathe (in) fresh country air instead of city smoke.* [Vn] *When the danger had passed we all **breathed a sigh of relief.*** **2** ~ **in/out** to take or send out a fuller breath than normal, esp deliberately: [Vp] *The doctor told me to breathe in and then breathe out (again) slowly.* **3** to say sth quietly: [Vn] *breathe loving words in sb's ear* ○ *breathe a threat* [V.speech] '*Goodbye darling,' she breathed.* **4** to show that one is full of a feeling: [Vn] *The team breathed confidence before the match.* **5** (of wine, a material, etc) to be open to the air: [V] *It's best to allow red wine to breathe before you drink it.* **IDM** **(be able to) breathe (easily/freely) again** to feel calm or relieved after a period of stress or danger; to relax: *Now my debts are paid I can breathe again.* **breathe down sb's 'neck** (*infml*) to follow sb or to watch what sb is doing (too) closely: *I can't concentrate with you breathing down my neck.* **breathe one's 'last** (*fml euph*) to die. **(not) breathe a 'word (of/about sth) (to sb)** (not) to tell sb sth (esp a secret): *Promise me you won't breathe a word of this to anyone.* **PHR V** **'breathe sth into sb/sth** to fill a person or group with a feeling: *The new manager has breathed fresh life into the company* (ie given it new energy and enthusiasm).
▶ **breathing** n [U] the action of breathing: *heavy breathing* ○ *breathing apparatus* ○ *deep breathing exercises.* **'breathing-space** n [C, U] a time to rest between two periods of effort; a pause: *The summer break gave us a welcome breathing-space.*

breather /'briːðə(r)/ n (*infml*) **1** a short pause for rest: *take/have a breather.* **2** a short period of exercise, esp in the open air: *I must go out for a quick breather.*

breathless /'breθləs/ adj **1(a)** breathing quickly or with difficulty: *breathless after running up the stairs* ○ *Heavy smoking makes him breathless.* (**b**) making one breathless: *breathless haste/hurry/pace/speed.* **2** holding one's breath or making one hold one's breath (because of fear, excitement, etc): *breathless with terror/wonder/amazement* ○ *a breathless audience/public* ○ *a breathless hush in the concert hall* ○ *waiting in breathless anticipation.* **3** with no air or wind: *a breathless calm.* ▶ **breathlessly** adv. **breathlessness** n [U].

breathtaking /'breθteɪkɪŋ/ adj very exciting; extraordinary: *a breathtaking view/mountain range/waterfall* ○ *Her beauty was breathtaking.* ▶ **breathtakingly** adv.

bred *pt, pp* of BREED.

breech /briːtʃ/ n the back part of a gun barrel(2) where the bullet or SHELL(4) is placed: *a breech-loading gun.* Compare MUZZLE 2.
■ **'breech birth** (also ,**breech de'livery**) n a birth in which the baby's bottom or feet appear first.

breeches /'brɪtʃɪz/ n [pl] **1** short trousers fastened just below the knee, worn esp when riding a horse or as part of ceremonial dress: *a pair of breeches* ○ '*riding breeches.* **2** (*joc*) trousers.

breed /briːd/ v (*pt, pp* **bred** /bred/) **1** (of animals) to produce young ones: [V] *How often do lions breed?* **2** to keep (animals or plants) for the purpose of producing young ones, esp in a controlled way: [Vn] *breed cattle/dogs/horses* ○ *dogs bred for their aggression.* **3** to lead to sth; to cause sth: [Vn] *Dirt breeds disease.* ○ *Unemployment breeds social unrest.* **4** ~ **sb (as sth)** to train or educate sb as they grow up: [Vn]

B

a well-bred child [Vn-n] *Spartan youths were bred as warriors.* [also Vnpr, Vn.*to* infl]. ▷ BORN. **familiarity breeds contempt** ▷ FAMILIARITY.

▶ **breed** *n* **1** a particular type of animal or plant. Its members have a similar appearance and are usu developed by deliberate selection: *a breed of cattle/ sheep* ○ *What breed is your dog?* **2** a type; a kind: *a new breed of politician.*

breeder *n* a person who breeds animals: *a dog/ horse/cattle breeder* ○ *a breeder of racehorses.* **breeder reactor** *n* a type of nuclear REACTOR that produces more RADIOACTIVE material than is put into it.

breeding *n* [U] **1** the keeping of animals for breeding: *the breeding of horses* ○ *a breeding programme.* **2** the producing of young animals, plants, etc: *the breeding season.* **3** good training or family background, resulting in good manners: *a man of good breeding.* **breeding-ground** *n* **1** (*fig*) a place where sb/sth good or bad can develop: *Damp, dirty houses are a breeding-ground for disease.* ○ *Youth clubs are the best breeding-grounds for the sports stars of the future.* **2** a place where wild animals go to produce their young ones: *Some birds fly south to find good breeding-grounds.*

breeze /briːz/ *n* **1** [C, U] a light wind: *a sea breeze* ○ *A gentle breeze was blowing.* ○ *There's not much breeze today.* **2** [sing] (*infml esp US*) a thing that is easy to do or enjoy: *Some people think learning to drive is a breeze.* **IDM** **shoot the breeze** ▷ SHOOT[1].

▶ **breeze** *v* (*infml*) to move in a cheerful casual way in the specified direction: [Vp] *Look who's just breezed in!* [Vpr] *He breezes through life, never worrying about anything.*

breezy *adj* **1** having light winds: *a breezy day* ○ *breezy weather* ○ *a breezy corner/beach/hillside.* **2** having or showing a cheerful CAREFREE manner: *You're very bright and breezy today!* **breezily** /ˈbriːzɪli/ *adv.* **breeziness** /ˈbriːzinəs/ *n* [U].

breeze-block /ˈbriːz blɒk/ (*Brit*) *n* a light building block[1](1a) made of coal ashes, sand and cement.

brethren /ˈbreðrən/ *n* [pl] **1(a)** members of a male religious group; brothers (BROTHER 3). (**b**) members of the Christian Church, or certain other religious groups. **2** (*often rhet*) people having a common interest or engaged in a common activity: *We must take care to protect the weaker brethren in our society.*

breve /briːv/ *n* (*music*) a long note equal to two semibreves (SEMIBREVE).

breviary /ˈbriːviəri; *US* -ieri/ *n* a book of prayers to be said daily by Roman Catholic priests.

brevity /ˈbrevəti/ *n* [U] **1** the quality of being brief and exact in speaking or writing: *He is famous for the brevity of his speeches.* ○ (*saying*) *Brevity is the soul of wit.* **2** the fact of lasting a short time: *the brevity of human life.*

brew /bruː/ *v* **1** to make beer: [Vn] *He brews his own beer at home.* ○ *the brewing industry.* **2(a)** ~ **sth** (**up**) to prepare a hot drink, esp tea or coffee: [Vn, Vnp] *We brewed (up) a nice pot of tea.* (**b**) (esp of tea or coffee) to become ready for drinking: [V] *There's (a pot of) coffee brewing in the kitchen.* **3(a)** (of sth unpleasant) to start to develop; to seem likely to happen: [V] *There's a storm brewing.* ○ *Trouble is brewing in the factory.* ○ *In 1938 war was brewing in Europe.* (**b**) ~ **sth** (**up**) to prepare or plan sth unpleasant: [Vn] *Those boys are brewing mischief.* [Vn, Vnp] *brew (up) a wicked plot.* **PHR V** **brew 'up** (*infml*) to prepare a drink of tea or coffee: *campers brewing up outside their tents.*

▶ **brew** *n* **1(a)** a drink made by brewing, esp with regard to its quality: *home brew* (ie beer made at home) ○ *What's your favourite brew (of beer)?* ○ *I like a good strong brew* (eg of tea). (**b**) an amount of drink brewed at one time: *We'll need more than one brew (eg of tea) for twenty people.* ○ *this year's brew*

(ie of beer). **2** any mixture of circumstances, ideas, events, etc: *The film is a rich brew of adventure, sex and comedy.*

brewer *n* a person or a company that makes beer: *Most English pubs are owned by the big brewers.*

brewery /ˈbruːəri/ *n* a building in which beer is brewed. Compare DISTILLERY.

■ **'brew-up** *n* (*Brit infml*) an act of making tea: *We always have a brew-up at 11 o'clock.*

briar = BRIER.

bribe /braɪb/ *n* a sum of money, services, etc given or offered to sb in return for some, often dishonest, help: *take/accept bribes* ○ *The policeman was offered/ given a bribe of £5 000 to keep his mouth shut.*

▶ **bribe** *v* ~ **sb** (**with sth**) to give sth to sb as a bribe; to try to persuade sb to do sth with a bribe: [Vnpr] *attempt to bribe a jury with offers of money* ○ *He bribed his way past* (ie gave a bribe to) *the guard and escaped.* [Vn.*to* infl] *One of the witnesses was bribed to give false evidence.* [also Vn]. **PHR V** **'bribe sb into doing sth** to make sb do sth with a bribe: *She was bribed into handing over secret information.*

bribery /ˈbraɪbəri/ *n* [U] the giving or taking of bribes: *accuse/convict sb of bribery* ○ *a bribery scandal.*

bric-à-brac (also **bric-a-brac**) /ˈbrɪk ə bræk/ *n* [U] ornaments, small items of furniture and other objects of little value: *market stalls selling an array of cheap bric-à-brac.*

brick /brɪk/ *n* **1** [C, U] (a usu rectangular (RECTANGLE) block of) baked or dried clay used for building: *a pile of bricks* ○ *houses built/made of red brick* ○ *a brick wall.* ▷ picture at HOUSE[1]. See also REDBRICK. **2** [C] a child's usu wooden toy building block. **3** [C] a thing shaped like a brick, esp a block of ice-cream. **4** [C] (*dated Brit infml*) a person that one can rely on; a good friend: *She's been a real brick, looking after me while I've been ill.* **IDM** **bang, etc one's head against a brick wall** ▷ HEAD[1]. **drop a brick/clanger** ▷ DROP[2]. **like a cat on hot bricks** ▷ CAT. **like a ton of bricks** ▷ TON. **make bricks without 'straw** (*Brit*) to try to work without the necessary material, money, information, etc.

▶ **brick** *v* **PHR V** **brick sth 'in/'up** to fill in or block an opening with a wall of bricks: *brick up a window/doorway/fireplace to prevent draughts.*

brickbat /ˈbrɪkbæt/ *n* **1** a piece of brick, esp one thrown as a weapon. **2** (*infml*) a rude remark: *The minister's speech was greeted with brickbats.*

bricklayer /ˈbrɪkleɪə(r)/ (also *Brit infml* **brickie** /ˈbrɪki/) *n* a person who is trained or skilled in building with bricks. ▶ **bricklaying** *n* [U].

brickwork /ˈbrɪkwɜːk/ *n* [U] **1** the bricks in a wall, building, etc: *decorative/ornamental brickwork* ○ *repairing the brickwork.* **2** building with bricks: *Are you any good at brickwork?*

brickyard /ˈbrɪkjɑːd/ *n* a place where bricks are made.

bridal /ˈbraɪdl/ *adj* [attrib] of a BRIDE or a wedding: *a bridal bouquet/gown* ○ *the bridal party* (ie the bride and the people helping and accompanying her) ○ *a bridal suite* (ie a set of rooms in a hotel for a newly married couple).

bride /braɪd/ *n* a woman on or just before her wedding day; a newly married woman.

bridegroom /ˈbraɪdɡruːm/ (also **groom**) *n* a man on or just before his wedding day; a newly married man: *Let's drink (a toast) to the bride and bridegroom!*

bridesmaid /ˈbraɪdzmeɪd/ *n* a young woman or girl (usu not married and often one of several) accompanying and helping a BRIDE at her wedding. Compare BEST MAN.

bridge[1] /brɪdʒ/ *n* **1(a)** a structure of wood, iron, concrete, etc, built to provide a way across a river,

B

road, railway, etc: *a bridge over/across the stream* ○ *a railway bridge* (ie one for a railway across a river, etc). (**b**) a thing that provides a connection or contact between two or more different things: *Cultural exchanges are a way of building bridges between nations.* **2** the raised platform on a ship from which it is controlled and steered by the captain and officers. **3(a)** the hard upper part of the nose. (**b**) the part of a pair of glasses that rests on the nose. ⇨ picture at GLASS. **4** a movable piece of wood, etc on a VIOLIN, etc, over which the strings are stretched. ⇨ picture at MUSICAL INSTRUMENT. **5** a device for keeping false teeth permanently in place, fastened to natural teeth on each side. **IDM** **burn one's boats/bridges** ⇨ BURN. **cross one's bridges when one comes to them** ⇨ CROSS². **a lot of / much water has flowed, etc under the bridge** ⇨ WATER¹. **water under the bridge** ⇨ WATER¹.

▶ **bridge** *v* [Vn] to build or form a bridge over sth: *bridge a river/canal/ravine.* **IDM** **bridge a/the 'gap** **1** to fill an awkward or empty space: *bridge a gap in the conversation* ○ *A snack in the afternoon bridges the gap between lunch and supper.* **2** to reduce the distance (between two very different groups): *How can we bridge the gap between rich and poor?*
■ **'bridging loan** *n* money lent, esp by a bank, for a short time, eg to enable sb to buy a new house while they are waiting to sell their old one.

bridge² /brɪdʒ/ *n* [U] a card-game for four players developed from WHIST, in which one player's cards are exposed on the table and played by her or his partner: *make up a four at bridge.*

bridgehead /'brɪdʒhed/ *n* (**a**) a strong position captured and held in enemy territory, esp on the enemy's side of a river. Compare BEACHHEAD. (**b**) a good position from which to make progress: *This agreement will be a bridgehead for further talks.*

bridle /'braɪdl/ *n* a set of leather bands attached to a metal bit²(1) and reins (REIN 1a), which is put on a horse's head and used for controlling it.
▶ **bridle** *v* **1** [Vn] to put a bridle on a horse. **2** to keep one's feelings, etc under control; to restrain sth: [Vn] *bridle one's emotions/passions/temper/rage* ○ *bridle one's tongue* (ie be careful what one says). Compare UNBRIDLED. **3** ~ (**at sth**) to show that one is angry or offended about sth, esp by moving one's head up or back in a proud way: [Vpr] *He bridled a little at her insensitive remarks.* [also V].
■ **'bridle-path** (*Brit* also **'bridle-way**) *n* a rough path suitable for people riding horses, etc and walking, but not for cars, etc: *We followed footpaths and bridle-ways.*

Brie /briː/ *n* [U] a type of soft French cheese.

brief¹ /briːf/ *adj* (**-er, -est**) **1(a)** lasting only a short time; short: *a brief conversation/discussion/meeting/visit/delay* ○ *Mozart's life was brief.* (**b**) (of speech or writing) using few words; CONCISE: *a brief account/report/description of the accident* ○ *Please be brief* (ie say what you want to say quickly). **2** (of clothes) short or tight: *a brief skirt.* **IDM** **in brief** in a few words: *In brief, your work is most unsatisfactory.* ○ *Here is the news in brief.*
▶ **briefly** *adv* **1** for a short time: *He paused briefly before continuing.* **2** in a few words: *Briefly, the argument is as follows…*

brief² /briːf/ *n* **1** the instructions and information that a person receives about her or his job and responsibilities or a particular task, etc: *It's not part of my brief to train new employees.* ○ *I was given the brief of reorganizing the department.* ○ **stick to one's brief** (ie only do what one is required to do). **2** (*law*) (**a**) a legal case¹(5) given to a BARRISTER to argue in court: *Will you accept this brief?* (**b**) a summary of the facts of a legal case¹(5) prepared for a BARRISTER. **IDM** **hold no brief for (sb/sth)** not to

support or be in favour of sb/sth: *I hold no brief for those who say that violence can be justified.*
▶ **brief** *v* **1** ~ **sb** (**on sth**) to give sb detailed information or instructions in order to prepare them for sth: [Vn] *The President was fully briefed before the meeting.* [Vnpr] *The Air Commodore briefed the bomber crew on their dangerous mission.* Compare DEBRIEF. **2** (*law*) to give a brief²(2b) to sb: [Vn.to inf] *The company has briefed a top lawyer to defend it.* [also Vn]. **briefing** *n* (**a**) [c] a meeting for giving instructions or information to people: *a press/police/management briefing.* (**b**) [C, U] the detailed instructions and information given at such a meeting: *receive (a) thorough/full briefing* ○ *a briefing session.*

briefcase /'briːfkeɪs/ *n* a flat leather or plastic case for carrying documents. ⇨ picture at LUGGAGE.

briefs /briːfs/ *n* [pl] short PANTS(1a) or KNICKERS: *a new pair of briefs.*

brier (also **briar**) /'braɪə(r)/ *n* **1** a prickly bush, esp a wild rose bush. **2(a)** a bush with a hard root used for making tobacco pipes. (**b**) a tobacco pipe made from this.

brig /brɪg/ *n* **1** a ship with two masts (MAST 1) and square sails. **2** (*US*) a prison, esp one on a WARSHIP for members of the Navy.

Brig *abbr* Brigadier: *Brig (John) West.*

brigade /brɪˈgeɪd/ *n* **1** one of the units (UNIT 3a) that an army is divided into. **2** an organization of people working together: *the fire brigade.* **3** any group of people who are similar in some way: *More and more people are joining the health-food brigade.*
▶ **brigadier** /ˌbrɪgəˈdɪə(r)/ *n* an officer with a high rank in the British Army. ⇨ App 6.

brigand /'brɪgənd/ *n* (*dated*) a member of a gang that robs people, esp one that attacks travellers in forests and mountains.

bright /braɪt/ *adj* (**-er, -est**) **1** full of light; shining strongly: *bright sunshine* ○ *bright eyes* ○ *Tomorrow's weather will be cloudy with bright periods.* ○ *The sitting-room is brighter in the afternoons.* **2** (of a colour) strong; vivid; not pale¹(2): *a bright blue dress* ○ *The leaves on the trees are bright green in spring.* **3** clever; intelligent: *a bright idea/suggestion* ○ *He is the brightest (child) in the class.* **4** cheerful and lively: *She gave me a bright smile.* ○ *I'm not very bright early in the morning.* **5** likely to be successful; hopeful: *a child with a bright future* ○ *Prospects for the coming year look bright.* **IDM** **(be/get up) bright and 'early** very early in the morning: *You're (up) bright and early today!* **(as) bright as a 'button** very clever; quick to understand: *That little girl's as bright as a button.* **the bright 'lights** the excitement of city life: *He grew up in the country, but then found he preferred the bright lights.* **a bright 'spark** (*infml often ironic*) a lively and intelligent person (esp one who is young and promising): *Some bright spark left the tap running all night.* **look on the 'bright side** to be cheerful or hopeful about sth in spite of difficulties.
▶ **bright** *adv* brightly: *The stars were shining bright.*
brighten /'braɪtn/ *v* ~ (**sth**) (**up**) to become or make sb/sth brighter, more cheerful or more hopeful: [V] *The sky/weather is brightening.* [V, Vp] *He brightened (up) when he heard the good news.* [Vn, Vnp] *Flowers brighten (up) a room.*
brightly *adv*: *a brightly lit room* ○ *brightly coloured curtains* ○ *'Hi!' she called brightly.*
brightness *n* [U].
■ **bright-'eyed** *adj* with bright eyes; lively: *all bright-eyed and bushy-tailed* (ie looking eager and confident).

brill¹ /brɪl/ *n* (*pl* unchanged) a type of flat fish found esp in the sea.

brill² /brɪl/ *adj* (*Brit infml*) = BRILLIANT 2: *You look brill in that get-up.*

brilliant /'brɪliənt/ *adj* **1(a)** extremely clever or impressive; outstanding: *What a brilliant idea!* ○ *a brilliant achievement/exploit/career/performance* ○ *The play was a brilliant success.* (**b**) very intelligent, skilled or talented: *a brilliant scientist/musician/football player* ○ *She has a brilliant mind.* **2** (*Brit infml*) very good or enjoyable; excellent: *It was a brilliant party.* ○ *Your new hairstyle's brilliant!* **3** very bright; sparkling (SPARKLE): *brilliant sunshine* ○ *a brilliant diamond* ○ *a sky of brilliant blue.* ► **brilliance** /'brɪliəns/ *n* [U]. **brilliantly** *adv.*

brim /brɪm/ *n* **1** the top edge of a cup, bowl, glass, etc: *The mug was full to the brim.* **2** the flat edge around the bottom of a hat, that sticks out giving shade and protection against rain. ⇨ picture at HAT. ► **brim** *v* (**-mm-**) ~ (**with sth**) to be or become full of sth: [Vpr] *a mug brimming with coffee* ○ *eyes brimming with tears* ○ (*fig*) *The team were brimming with confidence before the game.* [also V.]. **PHRV** **brim 'over (with sth)** to be so full of a liquid, etc that it comes over the edge; to OVERFLOW: *a glass brimming over with water* ○ (*fig*) *brim over with excitement/happiness/joy.*

brimful (also **brim-full**) /ˌbrɪm'fʊl/ *adj* [pred] ~ (**of sth**) completely full of sth: *The basin was brim-full (of water).* ○ *She's certainly brimful of energy.*

-brimmed (forming compound *adjs*) (of a hat) having the type of brim specified: *a broad-/wide-/floppy-brimmed hat.*

brimstone /'brɪmstəʊn/ *n* **1** [C] a type of yellow BUTTERFLY. **2** [U] (*arch*) the chemical element SULPHUR.

brindled /'brɪndld/ (also **brindle** /'brɪndl/) *adj* (esp of dogs and cats) brown with markings of another colour.

brine /braɪn/ *n* [U] **1** very salty water used esp for preserving food: *herrings pickled in brine.* **2** sea water. ► **briny** *adj* salty.

bring /brɪŋ/ *v* (*pt, pp* **brought** /brɔːt/) **1** ~ **sb/sth** (**with one**); ~ **sth** (**for sb**) to come carrying sth or accompanying sb: [Vn, Vnpr] *He always brings a bottle of wine (with him) when he comes to dinner.* [Vnpr] *She brought her boyfriend to the party.* ○ (*fig*) *The team's new manager brings ten years' experience to the job.* [Vnpr, Vnp] *The secretary brought him into the room/brought him in.* [Vnn] *Take this empty box away and bring me a full one.* [Vnn, Vnpr] *Bring me a glass of water/Bring a glass of water for me.* **2(a)** to cause sb/sth to come or be present; to result in sth: [Vn] *Spring brings warm weather and flowers.* ○ *These pills bring relief from pain.* ○ *The revolution brought many changes.* [Vnpr] *Hello Simon! what brings you to London today?* ○ *The sad news brought tears to his eyes* (ie made him cry). (**b**) to produce sth as profit or income: [Vnn] *His writing brings him $10000 a year.* ○ *Her great wealth brought her no happiness.* [also Vn]. **3** ~ **sb/sth to/into sth** to make sb/sth be in a certain state or position: [Vnpr] *bring the meeting to an end/a close* ○ *His incompetence has brought the company to the brink of bankruptcy.* ○ *The mild weather will bring the trees into blossom.* ○ *The book brought him into conflict with the country's authorities.* **4** to make sb/sth move in the direction or way specified: [Vnp] *The judge brought his hammer down on the table.* [Vn.ing] *Her cries brought the neighbours running* (ie caused them to come running to her). **5** ~ **sth** (**against sb**) to make charges (CHARGE¹ 2), etc in a lawcourt: [Vnpr] *bring a charge/a legal action/an accusation against sb* [also Vn]. **6** to force or make oneself do sth: [Vn.to inf] *She could not bring herself to tell him the tragic news.* **IDM** Idioms containing **bring** are at the entries for the nouns or adjectives

in the idioms, eg **bring sb to book** ⇨ BOOK¹; **bring sth to light** ⇨ LIGHT¹. **PHRV** **bring sth a'bout 1** to make sth happen: *bring about reforms/a war/sb's ruin* ○ *The Liberals wish to bring about changes in the electoral system.* ⇨ note at CAUSE. **2** (*nautical*) to make a ship change direction: *The helmsman brought us* (ie our boat) *about.*

bring sb/sth 'back to return sb/sth: *Please bring back the book tomorrow.* ○ *He brought me back* (ie gave me a lift home) *in his car.* **bring sth 'back 1** to make one think about sth again; to recall(1) sth: *The old photograph brought back many pleasant memories.* **2** to restore to use sth that was used in the past: *Most people are against bringing back the death penalty.* **bring sb 'back sth** to return with sth for sb: *If you're going to the supermarket, could you bring me back some cigarettes?* **bring sb 'back to sth** to return sb to an earlier condition: *A week by the sea brought her back to health.*

bring sb/sth before sb to present sb/sth for discussion or judgement: *The matter will be brought before the committee.* ○ *He was brought before the court and found guilty.*

bring sb 'down 1 to make sb/sth lose power; to OVERTHROW sb: *The scandal may bring down the government.* **2** (in football) to make sb fall over by unfair play: *He was brought down in the penalty area.* **3** (in Rugby football) to tackle(2b) sb. **4** to make sb unhappy or less happy. **bring sth 'down 1** to lower or reduce sth: *bring down prices/the rate of inflation/the cost of living.* **2** to land an aircraft: *The pilot brought his crippled plane down in a field.* **3** to make an aircraft fall out of the sky: *bring down an enemy fighter.* **4** to make an animal or a bird fall over or fall out of the sky by killing or wounding it: *He brought down the antelope with a single shot.*

bring sb/sth 'forth (*dated or fml*) to give birth to sb; to produce sth: *She brought forth a son.* ○ *Trees bring forth fruit.*

bring sth 'forward 1 to move sth to an earlier date or time: *The meeting has been brought forward from 10 May to 3 May.* **2** to propose a subject, an idea, etc for discussion: *Please bring the matter forward at the next meeting.* **3** (in bookkeeping (BOOKKEEPER)) to transfer a total sum from the bottom of one page, etc to the top of the next: *A credit balance of £50 was brought forward from his September account.*

bring sb 'in 1 to get sb as an adviser, an assistant, etc: *Experts were brought in to advise the government.* **2** (of the police) to bring sb to a police station to be questioned or charged (CHARGE² 2a); to arrest sb: *Two suspicious characters were brought in for questioning.* **bring sth 'in 1** to introduce a new law: *bring in a bill to improve road safety.* **2** to pick up or cut and collect crops, fruit, etc: *bring in a good harvest.* **3** to give a decision in court: *The jury brought in a verdict of guilty.* **bring (sb) 'in sth** to make or earn a certain amount of money: *His freelance work brings (him) in £8000 a year.* ○ *The garage sale brought in about £100.* ○ *How much does she bring in now?* **bring sb 'in (on sth)** to allow or ask sb to take part in sth; to involve(2) sb in sth: *Local residents were angry at not being brought in* (ie not being asked for their opinion about) *the new housing proposal.*

bring sb 'off to rescue sb from a ship: *The passengers and crew were brought off by the Dover lifeboat.* **bring sth 'off** (*infml*) to manage to do sth diffi-cult successfully: *The goalkeeper brought off a superb save.* ○ *It was a difficult task, but we brought it off.*

bring sb 'on to help sb to develop or improve when they are learning to do sth: *The coach is bringing on some promising youngsters in the reserve team.* **bring sth 'on 1** to make sth, usu sth unpleasant, develop; to cause sth: *nervous tension brought on by overwork* ○ *He was out in the rain all day and this* *brought on a bad cold.* **2** to make crops, fruit, etc grow well: *The hot weather is bringing the wheat on nicely.* **bring sth on oneself/sb** to be responsible for sth, usu sth unpleasant, that happens to oneself/ sb else: *You have brought shame and disgrace on yourself and your family.*

,bring sb **'out 1** (*Brit*) to make sb stop work in protest about sth: *The shop stewards brought out the miners in sympathy.* ,bring sth **'out 1** to make sth appear or open: *The sunshine will bring out the blossom.* ○ (*fig*) *A crisis brings out the best in her.* **2** to make sth easy to see or understand: *The enlargement brings out the details in the photograph.* ○ *bring out the meaning of a poem.* **3** to produce sth; to publish sth: *The company is bringing out a new sports car in the spring.* ○ *bring out sb's latest novel* ○ *New personal computers are brought out almost daily.* ,bring sb **'out in sth** to make sb's skin be covered in spots, etc: *The heat brought him out in a rash.*

,bring sb **'over (to ...)** to bring sb to a place from another country over the sea: *Next summer he hopes to bring his family over from the States.* ,bring sb **'over (to sth)** to make sb change their ideas, loyalties, etc to one's own: *bring sb over to one's cause.*

,bring sb **'round**/(*US*) a**'round** (also ,bring sb **'to**) to make sb become conscious again: *Three soldiers fainted in the heat but were quickly brought round with brandy.* ,bring sth **'round**/(*US*) a**'round** (*nautical*) to make a boat face in the opposite direction. ,bring sb **'round**/(*US*) a**'round (to ...)** to bring sb to sb's house: *Bring your wife around one evening; we'd love to meet her.* ,bring sb **'round**/(*US*) a**'round (to sth)** to persuade sb, esp to one's own point of view: *He wasn't keen on the plan at first, but we managed to bring him round.* ,bring sth **'round**/ (*US*) a**'round to sth** to direct a conversation to a particular subject: *He brought the discussion round to football.*

,bring sb **'through** to help sb to recover; to save sb: *He was very ill, but the doctors managed to bring him through.*

,bring sb **'to** = BRING SB ROUND. ,bring sth **'to** (*nautical*) to make a boat stop.

,bring A and B to**'gether** to help two people or groups to end a quarrel: *The loss of their son brought the parents together.*

,bring sb **'under** to control a group of people who are causing trouble; to SUBDUE sb: *The rebels were quickly brought under.* ,bring sth **'under sth** to include sth within a category: *The points to be discussed can be brought under three main headings.*

,bring sb **'up 1** (esp passive) to look after a child, teaching it how to behave, etc, until it is an adult: *She brought up five children.* ○ *Her parents died when she was a baby and she was brought up by her aunt.* ○ *a well-/badly-brought up child* ○ *He was brought up to* (ie taught as a child to) *respect authority.* Compare UPBRINGING. **2** (*law*) to make sb appear for trial: *He was brought up on a charge of drunken driving.* ,bring sb/sth **'up** to move or call soldiers, guns, etc to the place where the fighting is: *We need to bring up more tanks.* ,bring sth **'up 1** to mention or introduce a subject for attention; to raise(4b) sth: *These are matters that you can bring up in committee.* **2** to VOMIT sth: *bring up one's lunch.* ,bring sb **'up against sth** to make sb face²(2) or realize sth: *Working in the slums brought her up against the realities of poverty.* ,bring sb/sth **'up to sth** to help sb/sth to reach an acceptable level or standard: *His work in biology needs to be brought up to the standard of the others.*

■ ,bring-and-**'buy sale** *n* (*Brit*) a sale, often for charity, at which people bring things for sale and buy those brought by others.

brink /brɪŋk/ *n* [sing] **1** the extreme edge of land, eg

at the top of a cliff or beside a river: *the brink of a precipice* ○ *He stood shivering on the brink, waiting to dive in.* **2** [sing] **the ~ of (doing) sth** (*fig*) the point or state very close to sth unknown, dangerous or exciting: *on the brink of collapse/war/disaster/ success* ○ *Scientists are on the brink of (making) a breakthrough in the treatment of cancer.* ○ *His incompetence has brought us to the brink of ruin.*

brinkmanship /'brɪŋkmənʃɪp/ *n* [U] the art or practice of following a dangerous policy as far as is safely possible before stopping: *engaged in a deadly game of political brinkmanship.*

briny ⇨ BRINE.

brio /'briːəʊ/ *n* [U] individual style and energy.

brioche /briˈɒʃ; *US* briˈəʊʃ/ *n* a small round sweet bread roll.

briquette (also **briquet**) /brɪˈket/ *n* a small hard block made from coal dust and used as fuel.

brisk /brɪsk/ *adj* (**-er, -est**) **1** quick; active; busy: *a brisk walk/walker* ○ *set off at a brisk pace* ○ *a brisk and efficient manner* ○ *Business is brisk* (ie Goods are being sold quickly) *today.* **2** (of wind and the weather) cold but pleasantly fresh: *a brisk breeze.* ► **briskly** *adv.* **briskness** *n* [U].

brisket /'brɪskɪt/ *n* [U] meat cut from the breast of an animal: *brisket of beef.*

bristle /'brɪsl/ *n* **1** a short stiff hair: *a face covered with bristles.* **2** one of the short stiff hairs in a brush: *My toothbrush is losing its bristles.*
► **bristle** *v* **1** ~ **(up)** (of an animal's fur) to stand up stiff because of fear or anger: [V] *The dog's fur bristled as it sensed danger.* [also Vp]. ~ **(with sth) (at sth)** to show anger, annoyance, etc in one's face or movements: [Vpr] *bristle with defiance/pride* ○ *She bristled (with rage) at the mention of his name.* [also V]. **PHR V** **'bristle with sth** to have a large number of sth, usu sth unpleasant; to be full of sth: *troops bristling with weapons* ○ *The problem bristles with difficulties.*

bristly /'brɪsli/ *adj* like or full of bristles; prickly; rough: *a bristly chin* ○ *She finds his beard too bristly.* ○ *dry bristly grass.*

Brit /brɪt/ *n* (*infml often derog*) a British person: *Brits behaving badly in foreign holiday resorts.* ⇨ note at BRITISH.

Britain /'brɪtn/ *n* = GREAT BRITAIN. ⇨ note at BRITISH.

British /'brɪtɪʃ/ *adj* (abbreviated as *Brit* in this dictionary) of the United Kingdom (of Great Britain and Northern Ireland) or its inhabitants: *a British passport* ○ *the British Government* ○ *He was born in France but his parents are British.* ○ *British-based/ -born/-built/-made/-owned* (ie based, etc in Britain or built, etc by British people or companies). **IDM** **the best of British** ⇨ BEST³.
► **the British** *n* [pl v] British people.
Britisher *n* (not used by British people) a British person, esp one from England.
Britishness *n* [U].
■ ,British **'English** *n* [U] English as spoken in the British Isles.
the ,British 'Isles *n* [U] Britain and Ireland with the islands near their coasts.

NOTE There is no noun in British English which is commonly used to refer to the nationality of the people of Britain. Instead the adjective **British** is used: *She's British.* ○ *The British are said to have an unusual sense of humour.* The noun **Britisher** is used in American English: *We were given a tour of London by a real live Britisher.* The noun **Briton** is used in newspapers to report incidents and give information about British people: *12 Britons were among the survivors.* ○ *61% of Britons believe that tobacco advertising should be banned.* It also describes the early inhabitants of Britain: *the ancient Britons*. **Brit** is an informal word also used in newspapers. It is often used humorously and can be derogatory.

Briton /'brɪtn/ *n* a British person. ⇨ note at BRITISH.

brittle /'brɪtl/ *adj* **1(a)** hard but easily broken; FRA-GILE(1): *The paint on the windows was brittle with age.* ○ *brittle bones/hair/nails.* (**b**) easily damaged; not secure: *brittle confidence* ○ *She was always nervous and mentally brittle.* **2** (of a sound) hard and sharp in an unpleasant way: *a brittle laugh* ○ *The tone of his voice was brittle.* ▶ **brittleness** *n* [U].

broach /brəʊtʃ/ *v* [Vn] **1** to introduce a subject for discussion; to bring sth up: *He broached the subject of a loan with his bank manager.* **2** to open a bottle or barrel, esp of alcoholic drink, in order to use the contents: *Let's broach another bottle of wine.*

B-road ⇨ B².

broad¹ /brɔːd/ *adj* (**-er, -est**) **1** large in extent from one side to the other; wide: *a broad street/avenue/ river/canal* ○ *broad shoulders* ○ *He is tall, broad and muscular.* Compare NARROW 1, THIN 1. ⇨ note at WIDE. **2** (after a phrase expressing measurement) from side to side; in breadth: *a river twenty metres broad.* **3(a)** of or including a great variety of people or things; EXTENSIVE(2): *a broad range of people/ opinions/backgrounds* ○ *a broad spectrum of interests* ○ *There is broad support for the government's policies.* (**b**) (of land or sea) covering a wide area: *a broad expanse of water* ○ *the broad plains of the American West.* **4** [attrib] general; not detailed: *the broad outline of a plan/proposal* ○ *The negotiators reached broad agreement on the main issues.* ○ *She's a feminist, in the broadest sense of the word.* **5** clear; obvious: *a broad grin/smile* ○ *The minister gave a broad hint that she intends to raise taxes.* **6** (of ideas, opinions, etc) not limited; LIBERAL(1): *a man of broad views.* **7** (of speech) having many of the sounds typical of a particular region: *a broad Yorkshire accent.* **8** rather rude, esp about sex: *broad humour.*
IDM **(in) broad 'daylight** (in) the clear light of day, when it is easy to see: *The robbery occurred in broad daylight, in a crowded street.* **broad in the 'beam** (*infml*) (of a person) rather fat round the hips. **it's as ˌbroad as it's 'long** (*infml*) it makes no real difference which of two alternatives one chooses.
▶ **broaden** /'brɔːdn/ *v* ~ (**out**) to become or make sth broader: [V, Vp] *The road broadens (out) after this bend.* [Vn] *You should broaden your experience/ mind by travelling more.*
broadly *adv* **1** in a broad¹(5) way: *smile/grin broadly.* **2** generally: *Broadly speaking, I agree with you.* ○ *The book takes a broadly historical approach.*
broadness *n* [U] = BREADTH.
■ ˌbroad-'based (also ˌbroadly-'based) *adj* having a large variety of people or things as a base; not limited: *a broad-based government/education.*
ˌbroad 'bean *n* (**a**) a type of bean with large flat edible seeds. (**b**) one of these seeds.
'broad jump *n* [sing] (*US*) = LONG JUMP.
ˌbroad-'leaved *adj* = BROADLEAF.
ˌbroad-'minded *adj* willing to listen to opinions and accept behaviour different from one's own; tolerant (TOLERATE). ˌbroad-'mindedness *n* [U].

broad² /brɔːd/ *n* (*US sl derog*) a woman.

broadcast /'brɔːdkɑːst; *US* -kæst/ *v* (*pt, pp* **broadcast**) **1** to send out programmes by radio or television: [Vn] *broadcast the news/a concert/a football game* ○ *The performance will be broadcast live* (ie at the same time as it happens). [V] *The BBC broadcasts all over the world.* **2** to speak or appear on radio or television: [V] *She broadcasts on current affairs.* **3** to make sth widely known: [Vn] *broadcast one's views.* **4** [V, Vn] to scatter seeds over a large area, esp by hand.
▶ **broadcast** *n* a radio or television programme: *a*

party political broadcast (eg before an election) ○ *a broadcast of a football match.*
broadcaster *n* a person who broadcasts (BROAD-CAST 2): *a well-known broadcaster on political/ religious affairs.*
broadcasting *n* [U] the sending out of programmes on radio and television: *work in broadcasting* ○ *the British Broadcasting Corporation* (ie the BBC).

broadleaf /'brɔːdliːf/ (also **broad-leaved**) *adj* (of a tree) that loses its leaves in winter; DECIDUOUS.

broadsheet /'brɔːdʃiːt/ *n* **1** a newspaper printed on a large size of paper. Compare TABLOID *n*. **2** a large piece of paper printed on one side only with information or an advertisement, etc.

broadside /'brɔːdsaɪd/ *n* (**a**) (*fig*) a fierce attack in words, either written or spoken: *The prime minister delivered/launched a broadside at his critics.* (**b**) the firing at the same time of all the guns on one side of a ship: *fire a broadside.* **IDM** **broadside 'on (to sth)** (esp of a ship) with one side facing sth; sideways: *The ship hit the harbour wall broadside on.*

broadsword /'brɔːdsɔːd/ *n* (formerly) a large sword with a broad blade, used for cutting rather than stabbing (STAB).

brocade /brə'keɪd/ *n* [C, U] a heavy material with a raised pattern woven into it, esp of gold or silver threads: *brocade curtains.*
▶ **brocade** *v* (usu passive) to weave material with raised patterns: [Vn] *richly brocaded fabrics/chairs.*

broccoli /'brɒkəli/ *n* [U] a vegetable similar to a CAULIFLOWER but with many small green or purple flower heads growing close together. ⇨ picture at CABBAGE.

brochure /'brəʊʃə(r); *US* brəʊ'ʃʊər/ *n* a small book or magazine containing pictures and information about sth or advertising sth: *a travel/holiday brochure* ○ *send off for a brochure* (ie write asking for one).

broderie anglaise /ˌbrəʊdəri 'ɒŋgleɪz/ *n* [U] decoration with sewing on fine white material; the material decorated in this way.

brogue¹ /brəʊg/ *n* (usu *pl*) a strong outdoor shoe, usu with a pattern in the leather: *a pair of brogues.*

brogue² /brəʊg/ *n* (usu *sing*) a way of speaking, esp the Irish way of speaking English: *a soft Irish brogue.* Compare ACCENT 3, DIALECT.

broil /brɔɪl/ *v* **1** (*esp US*) (**a**) to cook meat on a fire or over metal bars: [Vn] *broiled chicken.* ⇨ note at COOK. (**b**) [V] to be cooked in this way. ⇨ picture at PAN. **2** to become or make sb very hot: [V] *sit broiling in the sun* [Vn] *a broiling day.*
▶ **broiler** *n* a young chicken bred for broiling or roasting (ROAST 1): *a broiler house* (ie a building in which such chickens are kept).

broke¹ *pt* of BREAK¹.

broke² /brəʊk/ *adj* [pred] (*infml*) having no money: *Could you lend me £10? I'm completely broke!* ○ *During the recession thousands of small businesses went broke* (ie were ruined financially). **IDM** **flat/stony 'broke** (*infml*) completely broke. **go for 'broke** (*infml*) to risk everything in one determined attempt at sth.

broken¹ *pp* of BREAK¹.

broken² /'brəʊkən/ *adj* **1** that has been broken, damaged or injured; no longer whole or working properly: *a broken cup/glass/window* ○ *a broken leg/ arm* ○ *a broken radio/camera.* ⇨ picture at CHIP¹. **2** [usu attrib] not continuous; disturbed or interrupted: *broken sleep* ○ *broken sunshine.* **3** [usu attrib] (of an agreement, etc) not obeyed; to which sb has not been faithful: *a broken promise* ○ *a broken marriage* (ie one that has ended in separation(2) or DIVORCE¹(1)). **4** [attrib] (of a person) made weak and tired by illness or troubles: *He was a broken man after the failure of his business.* **5** [attrib] (of a language that is not one's own) spoken slowly and with many mistakes; not FLUENT(1a): *speak in broken English.* **6** (of land) having a rough surface: *an area of broken, rocky ground.* **IDM** **a ,broken 'reed** a person who is no longer reliable or effective.

■ **,broken-'down** *adj* in a very bad condition; worn out or sick: *a ,broken-down old 'car/'man/'horse.* Compare HEARTBROKEN.

,broken-'hearted *adj* feeling great sorrow; completely miserable: *He was broken-hearted when his wife died.* Compare HEARTBROKEN.

,broken 'home *n* a family in which the parents have divorced (DIVORCE²) or separated (SEPARATE² 3): *He comes from a broken home.*

broker /'brəʊkə(r)/ *n* **1** a person who buys and sells things, eg shares (SHARE¹ 3) in a business, for others: *an insurance broker.* **2** (also **'broker-dealer**) = STOCKBROKER. See also PAWNBROKER.

▶ **brokerage** /'brəʊkərɪdʒ/ *n* [U] a broker's charges or commission: *brokerage houses* (ie where brokers work).

brolly /'brɒli/ *n* (*Brit infml*) an UMBRELLA.

bromide /'brəʊmaɪd/ *n* **1** [C,U] a chemical compound used in medicine to calm the nerves. **2** [C] (*infml*) a common idea or saying that is no longer very useful or adequate in a particular situation.

bronchial /'brɒŋkiəl/ *adj* [usu attrib] (*medical*) of or affecting the two main branches of the WINDPIPE (**bronchial tubes** or **bronchi**) leading to the lungs: *bronchial asthma ∘ bronchial pneumonia.* ⇨ picture at RESPIRATORY.

bronchitis /brɒŋ'kaɪtɪs/ *n* [U] an illness that affects the BRONCHIAL tubes leading to the lungs: *suffering from chronic bronchitis.*

▶ **bronchitic** /brɒŋ'kɪtɪk/ *adj* suffering from bronchitis; like bronchitis: *a bronchitic cough.*

bronco /'brɒŋkəʊ/ *n* (*pl* **-os**) (*US*) a wild horse of the western USA: *thrown from a bucking bronco.*

brontosaurus /ˌbrɒntə'sɔːrəs/ *n* (*pl* **brontosauruses** /-'sɔːrəsɪz/) a large DINOSAUR with a long neck and tail.

Bronx cheer /ˌbrɒŋks 'tʃɪə(r)/ *n* (*US infml*) = RASPBERRY 2.

bronze /brɒnz/ *n* **1** [U] a metal made by mixing copper and tin: *a statue (cast) in bronze.* **2** [U] the colour of bronze, ie reddish-brown: *tanned a deep shade of bronze.* **3** [C] (**a**) a work of art made of bronze, eg a statue: *a fine collection of bronzes.* (**b**) = BRONZE MEDAL: *win an Olympic bronze.*

▶ **bronze** *v* (usu passive) to make sth bronze in colour: [Vn] *Her face was bronzed by the sun.*

bronze *adj* made of or having the colour of bronze: *a bronze vase/statue/bowl/axe ∘ the bronze tints of autumn leaves.*

■ **the 'Bronze Age** *n* [sing] the period in history between the Stone Age and the Iron Age, when people used tools and weapons made of bronze.

bronze 'medal *n* a MEDAL awarded as third prize in a competition or race.

brooch /brəʊtʃ/ (*US* also **pin** /pɪn/) *n* an ornament worn on women's clothes. It is fastened with a pin on the back of it.

brood /bruːd/ *n* [CGp] **1** all the young birds or other creatures that a mother produces at one time: *a hen and her brood (of chicks).* **2** (*joc*) a family of children: *There's Mrs O'Brien taking her brood for a walk!*

▶ **brood** *v* **1** [V] (of a bird) to sit on eggs to HATCH²(2) them. **2** ~ (**on/over sth**) to think for a long time about sth such as a failure or a disappointment: [V] *When he's depressed he sits brooding for hours.* [Vpr] *It doesn't help to brood on your mistakes.*

brooding *adj* sad and dark or threatening: *a bitter, brooding expression ∘ brooding music ∘ a brooding landscape.*

broody *adj* **1**(**a**) (of a hen) wanting to brood. (**b**)

(*fig*) (of a woman) wanting very much to have a baby. **2** suffering from depression, eg because of a failure or disappointment: *Why are you so broody today?* **broodily** *adv.* **broodiness** *n* [U].

■ **'brood-mare** *n* a female horse kept for breeding.

brook¹ /brʊk/ *n* a small stream.

brook² /brʊk/ *v* (*fml*) (usu with a negative) to tolerate sth; to allow sth: [Vn] *a strict teacher who brooks no nonsense from her pupils* [V.n *ing*] *I will not brook anyone interfering with my affairs.* [also V.*ing*].

broom¹ /bruːm, brʊm/ *n* a brush on the end of a long handle, used for sweeping floors. See also NEW BROOM.

broom² /bruːm/ *n* [U] a wild bush with yellow or white flowers.

broomstick /'bruːmstɪk/ *n* the handle of a BROOM¹. Witches (WITCH) were formerly said to ride through the air on broomsticks.

Bros *abbr* (*commerce*) Brothers: *Hanley Bros Ltd, Architects & Surveyors.*

broth /brɒθ; *US* brɔːθ/ *n* [U] soup made from water in which meat, fish or vegetables have been boiled; stock¹(8): *beef broth ∘ Scotch broth.* **IDM** **too many cooks spoil the broth** ⇨ COOK *n.*

brothel /'brɒθl/ *n* a house where men pay to have sex with prostitutes.

brother /'brʌðə(r)/ *n* **1** a man or boy having the same parents as another person: *my elder/younger brother ∘ Does she have any brothers or sisters? ∘ Have you invited the Baker brothers to the party? ∘ He was like a brother to me* (ie very kind). ⇨ App 4. **2** (often as a form of address) a man who is united with others by belonging to the same group, society, profession, etc: *Solidarity, brothers! ∘ We are all brothers in the fight against injustice. ∘ He was greatly respected by his brother officers.* **3** (*pl* **brethren** /'breðrən/) (**a**) a male member of a religious group, esp a monk; his title: *Brother Luke will say grace.* (**b**) a member of certain EVANGELICAL Christian groups: *The Brethren hold a prayer meeting every Thursday.* **IDM** **brothers in 'arms** soldiers serving together, esp in war. See also BIG BROTHER, BLOOD-BROTHER, HALF-BROTHER, STEPBROTHER.

▶ **brother** *interj* (*esp US*) (used to express annoyance or surprise): *Oh, brother!*

brotherhood /-hʊd/ *n* **1** [U] (**a**) the relationship of brothers: *the ties of brotherhood.* (**b**) friendship and understanding between people: *live in peace and brotherhood.* **2** [CGp] the members of an association formed for a particular purpose, eg a religious society or political organization.

brotherly *adj* [usu attrib] of or like a brother: *brotherly love/affection/feelings.*

■ **brother-in-law** /'brʌðər ɪn lɔː/ (*pl* **brothers-in-law** /'brʌðəz ɪn lɔː/) *n* **1** the brother of one's husband or wife. **2** the husband of one's sister. **3** the husband of the sister of one's wife or husband. ⇨ App 4.

brougham /'bruːəm/ *n* (formerly) a type of closed carriage with four wheels, pulled by one horse.

brought *pt, pp* of BRING.

brouhaha /'bruːhɑːhɑː/ *n* [U] (*infml*) noisy excitement or disturbance: *the brouhaha following the prime minister's resignation.*

brow /braʊ/ *n* **1** (usu *pl*) = EYEBROW. **2** = FOREHEAD: *mop one's brow.* **3** (usu *sing*) the top of a hill; the edge of a cliff: *The path disappeared over the brow of the hill.* **IDM** **knit one's 'brow** ⇨ KNIT. See also HIGHBROW, MIDDLEBROW, LOWBROW.

browbeat /'braʊbiːt/ *v* (*pt* **browbeat**; *pp* **browbeaten** /'braʊbiːtn/) ~ **sb** (**into doing sth**) to frighten sb with severe looks and words; to INTIMIDATE sb: [Vn] *The judge told the lawyer not to browbeat the witness.* [Vnpr] *I won't be browbeaten into accepting your proposals.*

[V.*to* inf] = verb + *to* infinitive   [Vn.inf (no *to*)] = verb + noun + infinitive without *to*   [V.*ing*] = verb + *-ing* form

▶ **browbeaten** adj frightened with severe looks and words: *a poor browbeaten little clerk.*

brown /braʊn/ adj (**-er, -est**) **1** having the colour of chocolate, or coffee mixed with milk: *brown eyes* ○ *dark brown shoes* ○ *a brown paper parcel* ○ *leaves turning brown in the autumn.* **2** having skin that is naturally brown or made brown by the sun: *He's very brown after his summer vacation.* **IDM** **(as) brown as a** ˈ**berry** having skin made brown by the sun or the weather. **in a brown** ˈ**study** (*Brit*) thinking deeply; in a REVERIE.
▶ **brown** n **1** [C, U] the colour brown: *leaves of various shades of brown.* **2** [U] brown clothes: *Brown doesn't suit you.*
brown v to become or make sth brown: [V] *Heat the butter until it browns.* [Vn] *a face browned by the sun.* **IDM** ˌ**browned** ˈ**off** (*infml esp Brit*) bored; without enthusiasm: *He's browned off with his job.*
brownish, **browny** adjs tending towards brown; fairly brown.
■ ˌ**brown** ˈ**ale** n [U, C] (*Brit*) a type of mild dark beer sold in bottles.
ˌ**brown** ˈ**bread** n [U] bread made with brown WHOLEMEAL flour.
ˌ**brown** ˈ**sugar** n [U] sugar with a brown colour, that is only partly pure.

brownie /ˈbraʊni/ n **1** a small friendly fairy. **2 Brownie** (also **ˈBrownie Guide**) a member of the branch of the Girl Guides (GIRL) for girls between 7 and 10. Brownies wear brown uniforms: *I used to be in the Brownies.* Compare CUB 2. **3** (*esp US*) a small rich(4) cake made with chocolate and nuts.
■ ˈ**brownie point** n (*joc*) an imaginary award that one gets for doing good deeds: *The boss is pleased — that's another brownie point!*

brownstone /ˈbraʊnstəʊn/ n (*US*) (**a**) [U] a type of SANDSTONE with a reddish-brown colour, used for building. (**b**) [C] a house with a front made of this stone: *New York brownstones.*

browse /braʊz/ v **1**(**a**) to examine books or other goods in a casual way: [V] *browse in a library/bookshop* ○ *browse among the antiques* ○ *Please feel free to browse.* (**b**) ~ **through sth** to look through a book, etc in this way: [Vpr] *browse through a magazine.* **2** (of cows, goats, etc) to feed by eating grass, leaves, etc: [V] *cattle browsing in the fields.*
▶ **browse** n [sing] an act of browsing: *have a browse among the second-hand books.*

bruise /bruːz/ n (**a**) an injury caused by a blow to the body, making a mark on the skin but not breaking it: *She was covered in bruises after falling off her bicycle.* (**b**) a similar mark on a fruit or vegetable.
▶ **bruise** v **1** to make a bruise or bruises on sth/sb: [Vn] *He fell and bruised himself/his leg.* ○ *Her face was badly bruised in the crash.* **2** to show the effects of a blow or knock: [V] *Don't drop the peaches — they bruise easily.* **bruiser** n (*infml*) a large strong tough man: *He looks a real bruiser.* **bruising** adj difficult and tiring: *a bruising meeting/game/profession.*

brunch /brʌntʃ/ n [C, U] (*infml esp US*) a late morning meal eaten instead of breakfast and lunch.

brunette /bruːˈnet/ n a white woman with dark hair. Compare BLOND.

brunt /brʌnt/ n **IDM** **bear the brunt of sth** ⇨ BEAR².

brush¹ /brʌʃ/ n **1** [C] an implement with short stiff hairs or wires set in a block of wood, etc. Brushes are used for many different jobs, such as sweeping, cleaning, painting, tidying the hair, etc: *a* ˈ*clothes-brush* ○ *a* ˈ*tooth-brush* ○ *a* ˌ*dustpan and* ˈ*brush* ○ *a* ˈ*hairbrush* ○ *a* ˈ*paintbrush* ○ *a* ˈ*brush stroke* (ie the mark left by a PAINTBRUSH). ⇨ picture. **2** [sing] an act of brushing: *give one's clothes/shoes/teeth/hair a (good) brush.* **3** [sing] a light touch made in passing sth/sb: *He knocked a glass off the table with a brush*

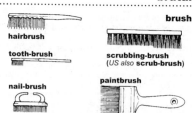

brush

hairbrush

tooth-brush

nail-brush

scrubbing-brush
(US also **scrub-brush**)

paintbrush

of his coat/arm. **4** [C] a fox's tail. **5** (also **brush-wood**) [U] land covered by small trees; UNDERGROWTH: *a brush fire.* **6** [C] ~ **with sb** a short UNFRIENDLY meeting with sb; an argument: *a brush with the law/police* ○ *She had a nasty brush with her boss this morning.* **IDM** **tarred with the same brush** ⇨ TAR v.

brush² /brʌʃ/ v **1** to use a brush on sth/sb; to clean, polish, or make sth tidy or smooth with a brush: [Vn] *brush your clothes/shoes/hair* [Vn-adj] *brush one's teeth clean.* **2** to touch sb/sth lightly in passing: [Vn] *leaves brushing one's cheek* ○ *His hand brushed hers.* **PHRV** ˌ**brush a**ˈ**gainst/**ˈ**by/**ˈ**past sb/ sth** to touch sb/sth lightly while moving close to them/it: *She brushed past him without saying a word.* ○ *A cat brushed against her leg in the darkness.*
ˌ**brush sb/sth a**ˈ**side 1** to push sb/sth to one side: *The enemy brushed aside our defences.* **2** to ignore sb/sth; to treat sb/sth as unimportant: *He brushed aside my objections to his plan.*
ˌ**brush sth a**ˈ**way/**ˈ**off** to remove sth from sth with a brush or as if with a brush: *brush mud off (one's trousers)* ○ *She brushed the fly away (from her face).*
ˌ**brush oneself/sth** ˈ**down** to clean oneself/sth by brushing thoroughly: *Your coat needs brushing down — it's covered in dust.*
ˌ**brush** ˈ**off** to be removed by brushing: *Mud brushes off easily when it's dry.* ˌ**brush sb** ˈ**off** (*infml*) to refuse to listen to sb; to ignore sb: *He's very interested in her but she's always brushing him* ˈ*off.*
ˌ**brush sth** ˈ**up /** ˌ**brush** ˈ**up on sth** to study or practise sth in order to get back a skill that one has lost: *I must brush up (on) my Italian before I go to Rome.*
■ ˈ**brush-off** n (*pl* **brush-offs**) (*infml*) a rejection; a SNUB: *He asked her for a date but she gave him the brush-off.*

brushwood /ˈbrʌʃwʊd/ n [U] **1** broken or cut branches or sticks. **2** = BRUSH¹ 5.

brushwork /ˈbrʌʃwɜːk/ n [U] the particular way in which an artist paints with a brush: *Picasso's bold brushwork.*

brusque /bruːsk, brʊsk; US brʌsk/ adj using few words in a rude or ABRUPT(2) way: *a brusque attitude/manner* ○ *He can be rather brusque at times.* ○ *His reply was typically brusque.* ▶ **brusquely** adv. **brusqueness** n [U].

Brussels /ˈbrʌslz/ adj [attrib] of or from Brussels in Belgium: *Brussels lace/carpets.*
■ ˌ**Brussels** ˈ**sprout** (also ˌ**Brussel** ˈ**sprout, sprout**) n (usu *pl*) (**a**) a plant with small edible parts like tiny cabbages (CABBAGE 1) growing on its stem. (**b**) any of these parts, eaten as a vegetable. ⇨ picture at CABBAGE.

brutal /ˈbruːtl/ adj cruel; SAVAGE(1b); without MERCY (1): *a brutal tyrant/dictator/murderer* ○ *a brutal attack/murder/punishment* ○ *the brutal* (ie harsh and direct) *truth.*
▶ **brutality** /bruːˈtæləti/ n (**a**) [U] brutal behaviour; cruelty: *police brutality.* (**b**) [C] a brutal act: *the brutalities of war.*
brutalize, **-ise** v (usu passive) to make sb unable to feel normal emotions such as pity, MERCY(1), etc: [Vn] *soldiers brutalized by a long war.*

B

brutally /-təli/ adv: *He was brutally assaulted.* ○ *Let me be brutally honest* (ie say what I think without trying to be polite).

brute /bru:t/ n **1** an animal, esp a large or fierce one: *That dog looks a real brute.* **2** (*sometimes joc*) a person who treats others in a very unkind and cruel way: *His father was a drunken brute.* ○ *You've forgotten my birthday again, you brute!* **3** an unpleasant or difficult thing: *a brute of a problem* ○ *This lock's a brute — it just won't open!*
▶ **brute** adj [attrib] (**a**) involving physical force only, and not thought or reason: *brute force/strength/instinct.* (**b**) simple and harsh: *a brute fact/necessity.*
brutish adj of or like a brute: *brutish behaviour/manners/treatment* ○ *Life for our early ancestors was nasty, brutish and short, they say.* **brutishly** adv.

BS /ˌbiː ˈes/ abbr **1** (US) Bachelor of Science. **2** (*Brit*) Bachelor of Surgery: *have/be a BS* ○ *Tom Hunt MB, BS.* **3** (on labels, etc) British Standard (showing the code number of the British Standards Institution): *produced to BS4353.* Compare ASA 2. **4** (US △ sl) bullshit: *That guy's full of BS.*

BSc /ˌbiː es ˈsiː/ (US **BS**) abbr Bachelor of Science: *have/be a BSc in Botany* ○ *Jill Ayres BSc.* Compare BA.

BSE /ˌbiː es ˈiː/ abbr (also *infml* **mad cow disease**) bovine spongiform encephalopathy, a usu fatal disease of cattle: *the spread of BSE.*

BSI /ˌbiː es ˈaɪ/ abbr British Standards Institution.

BST /ˌbiː es ˈtiː/ abbr British Summer Time. Compare GMT.

Bt abbr Baronet: *James Hyde-Stanley Bt.*

bubble /ˈbʌbl/ n **1** a floating ball formed of liquid and containing air or gas: *soap bubbles* ○ *Children love blowing bubbles.* **2** a ball of air or gas in a liquid or in a material such as glass: *Champagne is full of bubbles.* ○ *This glass vase has a bubble in its base.* **IDM** **the bubble 'bursts** a state of affairs, esp of unusual good luck, suddenly ends: *When the bubble finally burst hundreds of people lost their jobs.*
▶ **bubble** v **1** (of a liquid) to rise in bubbles or form bubbles; to boil: [V] *stew bubbling in the pot* ○ *bubbling vats of home-made beer.* **2** to make the sound of bubbles: [V] *a bubbling stream/fountain.* **3** ~ (**over**) (**with sth**) to be full of usu happy feelings: [Vpr, Vp] *be bubbling (over) with excitement/enthusiasm/high spirits* [also V]. **PHR V** **bubble a'long, 'out, 'over, 'up, etc** to move in the specified direction in bubbles or with a bubbling sound: *a spring bubbling out of the ground* ○ *Gases from deep in the earth bubble up through the lake.*
bubbly /ˈbʌbli/ adj **1** full of bubbles: *bubbly water.* **2** (*infml*) (of a person) cheerful and lively: *a bubbly personality.* — n [U] (*Brit infml*) CHAMPAGNE: *Have some more bubbly!*
■ **bubble and 'squeak** n [U] (*Brit*) cooked potato and CABBAGE that is mixed and fried.
bubble bath n (**a**) [U] liquid, crystals or powder added to a bath of water to give it lots of small bubbles on top and make it smell pleasant. (**b**) [C] a bath of water with this added.
bubble gum n [U] a type of chewing-gum (CHEW) that can be blown into bubbles.

bubonic plague /bjuːˌbɒnɪk ˈpleɪɡ/ (also **the plague**) n [U] (esp formerly) a usu fatal disease spread by rats, causing fever and swellings on the body.

buccaneer /ˌbʌkəˈnɪə(r)/ n **1** (formerly) a sailor who attacked and robbed other ships at sea; a PIRATE (1). **2** (esp in business) a person who achieves success by behaving in a dishonest or dangerous way.

buck¹ /bʌk/ n (pl unchanged or **bucks**) a male deer, rabbit or HARE. Compare STAG 1.

■ **buck-'tooth** n (pl **-teeth**) a projecting upper front tooth. **buck-'toothed** adj having buck-teeth.

buck² /bʌk/ v **1**(**a**) [V] (of a horse) to jump with the four feet together and the back bent. (**b**) [Vn, Vnp] ~ **sb** (**off**) to throw a rider to the ground by doing this. **2** (*infml*) to resist or oppose sb/sth; to avoid sth: [Vn] *Don't try to buck the system.* ○ *buck the downward trend.* **IDM** **buck one's i'deas up** (*Brit infml*) to become more alert; to take a more serious and responsible attitude. **PHR V** **buck 'up** (*dated Brit infml*) to hurry: *Buck up! We're going to be late.* **buck** (**sb**) '**up** (*infml*) to become or make sb more cheerful: *Buck up! Things aren't as bad as you think.* ○ *The good news bucked us all up.*
▶ **bucked** /bʌkt/ adj [pred] (*infml esp Brit*) pleased and encouraged: *She felt really bucked after passing her driving test.*

buck³ /bʌk/ n (US *infml*) a US dollar. **IDM** **the buck stops 'here** (*catchphrase*) the responsibility or blame is accepted here and cannot be passed on to sb else. **make a fast/quick buck** (*infml often derog*) to earn money quickly and easily: *He has a reputation for being someone who's only interested in making a quick buck.* **pass the buck** ⇨ PASS¹.

bucket **bucket** **plastic bowl** **tub**

bucket /ˈbʌkɪt/ n **1** [C] a round open container with a handle for carrying or holding liquids, sand, etc: *build sandcastles with a bucket and spade.* ⇨ picture. **2** (also **bucketful**) [C] the amount a bucket contains: *two buckets/bucketfuls of water.* **3 buckets** [pl] large amounts, esp of rain or tears: *The rain came down/fell in buckets.* ○ *She wept buckets.* **IDM** **a drop in the bucket/ocean** ⇨ DROP¹. **kick the bucket** ⇨ KICK¹.
▶ **bucket** v (*Brit*) ~ (**down**) (of rain) to pour down heavily: [Vp] *It/The rain bucketed down all afternoon.* [also V].
■ **bucket seat** n (in a car or an aircraft) a seat with a curved back, for one person.
bucket-shop n (*infml*) a travel agency (TRAVEL) that sells cheap plane tickets.

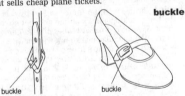

buckle **buckle** **buckle**

buckle /ˈbʌkl/ n (**a**) a metal or plastic fastening for joining the ends of a belt or strap. ⇨ picture. (**b**) a similar fastening as an ornament on a shoe. ⇨ picture.
▶ **buckle** v **1** ~ (**sth**) (**up**) to fasten sth or be fastened with a buckle: [Vn] *buckled shoes* [V] *These shoes buckle at the side.* [Vn, Vnp] *I buckled (up) my belt.* [also Vp]. **2** to become or make sth crushed or bent; to collapse: [V] *The front of the car buckled on impact.* [Vpr] *Her legs buckled under her and she fell.* ○ *buckling at the knees* ○ (*fig*) *He's beginning to buckle under the pressure of work.* [Vn] *The crash buckled the front of my car.* **PHR V** **buckle ,down to sth** (*infml*) to start sth with determination: *She's really buckling down to her new job.* **buckle sb 'in/'into sth** to fasten sb in a seat, etc with a belt: *The parachutist was buckled into his harness.* **buckle (sth) 'on** to attach or be attached with a buckle:

buckle on one's belt ○ a sword that buckles on.
ˌ**buckle 'to** (esp of a group) to make a special effort, usu in the face of difficulties: The children had to buckle to while their mother was in hospital.

buckram /'bʌkrəm/ n [U] stiff cloth used esp formerly for binding (BIND 3) books.

buckshee /ˌbʌk'ʃiː/ adj, adv (Brit sl) free of charge: buckshee tickets ○ travel buckshee.

buckshot /'bʌkʃɒt/ n [U] small pieces of lead³(1) for firing from a SHOTGUN.

buckskin /'bʌkskɪn/ n [U] a type of soft leather made from the skin of deer or goats. Buckskin is used for making gloves, bags, etc.

buckwheat /'bʌkwiːt/ n [U] dark seeds of grain used esp for making flour: buckwheat pancakes (ie made with buckwheat flour).

bucolic /bjuː'kɒlɪk/ adj (fml) of country life or the countryside; rural.

bud¹ /bʌd/ n **1** a small lump that grows on a plant and from which a flower, leaf or stem develops: Buds appear on the trees in spring. ○ The hedgerows are **in bud** (ie producing buds). **2** a flower or leaf that is not fully open. ⇨ picture at FLOWER. See also TASTE BUD. **IDM** **nip sth in the bud** ⇨ NIP.
▶ **bud** v (-dd-) to produce buds: [V] The trees are budding early this year. **budding** adj beginning to develop well: a budding novelist/actor/sportsman.

bud² /bʌd/ n (US infml) (used as a form of address) BUDDY: Listen, bud, enough of the wisecracks, OK?

Buddhism /'bʊdɪzəm/ n [U] an Asian religion founded by Gautama Siddhartha (or Buddha) in India in the fifth century BC. ▶ **Buddhist** /'bʊdɪst/ n, adj: a devout Buddhist ○ Buddhist monks ○ a Buddhist temple.

buddy /'bʌdi/ n (infml esp US) (often as a form of address) a friend: Hi there, buddy! ○ She and I were buddies at school.

budge /bʌdʒ/ v (usu in negative sentences) **1** to move or make sth/sb move slightly: [V, Vn] My car's stuck in the mud, and it won't budge/I can't budge it. **2** to change or make sb change an attitude or opinion: [V, Vn] Once he's made up his mind, he never budges/you can never budge him (from his opinion).

budgerigar /'bʌdʒərɪgɑː(r)/ n a small Australian bird of the PARROT family, often (esp in Britain) kept in a cage as a pet. Compare PARAKEET.

budget /'bʌdʒɪt/ n **1(a)** an estimate or plan of the money available to sb and how it will be spent over a period of time: a family budget ○ stay **on/within budget** (ie spend as much as/less than one planned to spend) ○ A family **on a tight budget** (ie having only a small amount of money) can't afford meat every day. **(b)** an annual government statement of a country's income from taxes and how it will be spent: The Chancellor of the Exchequer is expected to announce tax cuts in this year's budget. ○ balance the budget (ie make income equal to expenditure) ○ a budget deficit (ie when debts are greater than income). **2** an amount of money needed or provided for a specific purpose: limit oneself to a daily budget of £10 ○ a defence/science/education budget.
▶ **budget** v ~ **(sth) (for sth)** to save or provide money for a particular purpose: [V] If we spend carefully, we'll be able to afford a new car. [Vpr] budget for the coming year/for a vacation abroad/for a drop in sales [Vn] The government has budgeted £10 000 000 for education spending. [also Vn]. **budgeting** n [U].
budget adj [attrib] costing little; cheap: a budget meal/holiday.

budgetary /'bʌdʒɪtəri; US -teri/ adj of a budget: budgetary provisions/control/constraints.

■ '**budget account** (also '**budget plan**) n an account at a shop, etc into which a customer makes regular payments, receiving credit in proportion to these; a similar account at a bank, for the regular payment of bills.

budgie /'bʌdʒi/ n (infml) a BUDGERIGAR.

buff¹ /bʌf/ n [U] **(a)** a type of strong soft yellow leather. **(b)** the colour of this. **IDM** **in the 'buff** (infml) with no clothes on.
▶ **buff** adj made of or having the colour of buff: a buff envelope/uniform.
buff v ~ **sth (up)** to polish sth with a soft material: [Vn, Vnp] buff (up) one's shoes with a cloth.

buff² /bʌf/ n (preceded by a n) (infml) a person who is enthusiastic and knows a lot about a specified subject or activity: a film/computer/tennis buff. See also BLIND MAN'S BUFF.

buffalo /'bʌfələʊ/ n (pl unchanged or -oes) any of several large animals of the cow family, including the wild S African buffalo, the Asian buffalo and the N American BISON: fifty buffaloes ○ a herd of buffalo.

buffer¹ /'bʌfə(r)/ n **1** a device for reducing the effect of an impact, esp on a railway vehicle or at the end of a railway track. **2** a person or thing that reduces a shock or protects sb/sth against difficulties: His sense of humour was a useful buffer when things were going badly for him. ○ a buffer against change. **3** a country or an area between two powerful states, that reduces the risk of war between them: a buffer state/zone.
▶ **buffer** v to act as a buffer to sb or against sth: [Vn] There was little I could do to buffer the shock of the news.

buffer² /'bʌfə(r)/ n (Brit infml) a foolish old man: a silly old buffer.

buffet¹ /'bʊfeɪ; US bə'feɪ/ n **1** a counter where food and drink may be bought and eaten or drunk, esp (in Britain) in a railway station or on a train. **2** a meal at which guests serve themselves from a number of dishes; the food provided for this: Dinner will be a cold buffet, not a sit-down meal. ○ a buffet lunch/supper. **3** (US) a cupboard with drawers, for plates, knives and forks, etc; a SIDEBOARD.
■ '**buffet car** n (Brit) a railway carriage serving light meals.

buffet² /'bʌfɪt/ v ~ **sb/sth (about)** to knock or push sb/sth roughly from side to side: [Vn] flowers buffeted by the rain and wind ○ (fig) be buffeted by misfortune [Vnp] The waves buffeted the boat about.
▶ **buffet** n a blow, esp with the hand; a shock: (fig) suffer the buffets of a cruel fate.
buffeting n: The flowers took quite a buffeting in the storm.

buffoon /bə'fuːn/ n a ridiculous but amusing person; a CLOWN: play the buffoon.
▶ **buffoonery** /-əri/ n [U] ridiculous behaviour.

bug /bʌg/ n **1** [C] (esp US) any small insect. **2** [C] (infml) an infectious illness, usu fairly mild: a stomach bug ○ I think I've caught a bug. ○ He's been in bed with a bug all week. **3** (usu the bug [sing]) (infml) an enthusiastic interest in sth specified: the travel bug ○ He was never interested in cooking before, but now **he's been bitten by/he's got the bug**. **4** [C] (infml) a small hidden MICROPHONE for listening secretly to other people's conversations at a distance: search a room for bugs ○ plant a bug in the embassy. **5** [C] (infml) a fault in a machine, esp a computer: There's a bug in the system. **IDM** **snug as a bug in a rug** ⇨ SNUG.
▶ **bug** v (-gg-) **1(a)** to fit a room, telephone, etc with a hidden MICROPHONE for listening secretly to other people's conversations: [Vn] I'm sure the office is bugged. **(b)** to listen secretly to a conversation, etc with a hidden MICROPHONE: [Vn] a bugging device [Vn] Be careful what you say; our conversation may be being bugged. **2** (infml esp US) to annoy or irritate sb: [Vn] What's bugging you? ○ That man really bugs me.
■ '**bug-eyed** adj (infml) with eyes that stick out: bug-eyed with fright.

B

bugbear /ˈbʌgbeə(r)/ n a thing that is feared or disliked or that causes annoyance: *Inflation is the government's main bugbear.*

bugger /ˈbʌgə(r)/ n (△ *sl esp Brit*) **1(a)** (*derog*) an annoying person: *You stupid bugger! You could have run me over!* **(b)** a person (esp a man) of the specified type: *Poor bugger! His wife left him last week.* ○ *He's a clever bugger.* **2** a thing that causes difficulties: *This door's a (real) bugger to open.* **3** (*US*) (used to refer to a young person that one likes): *She's a cute little bugger.* **IDM** **play silly buggers** ⇨ SILLY.
▶ **bugger** v (△) **1** [Vn] to have ANAL sex with sb. **2** (*Brit sl*) (usu imperative, expressing anger or annoyance at sb/sth) [Vn] *Bugger it! I've burnt the toast.* ○ *You're always late, bugger you.* **3** ~ **sth (up)** (*Brit sl*) to break or spoil sth: [Vn] *The TV is buggered.* [Vnp] *I completely buggered up the exam.* **IDM** **,bugger 'me** (*Brit sl*) (expressing surprise or amazement): *Bugger me! Did you see that?* **PHRV** **bugger a'bout/ a'round** (*Brit sl*) to behave in a stupid or careless way: *Stop buggering about with those matches or you'll set the house on fire.* **bugger sb a'bout/ a'round** (*Brit sl*) to treat sb badly or in a casual way: *I'm sick of being buggered about by the company.* **bugger 'off** (*Brit sl*) (usu imperative) to go away: *Bugger off and leave me alone.* ○ *I was only two minutes late but they'd all buggered off.* **buggered** *adj* (*Brit sl*) [pred] very tired; exhausted: *I'm completely buggered after that game of tennis.* **IDM** **I'll be buggered** (expressing surprise or amazement): *Well, I'll be buggered! He never even said thank you!*
bugger *interj* (*Brit* △ *sl*) (expressing anger or annoyance): *Oh bugger! I've left my keys at home.*
buggery /ˈbʌgəri/ n [U] (△) ANAL sex; SODOMY.
■ **,bugger-'all** n [U] (*Brit* △ *sl*) nothing: *There's bugger-all to do in this place.*

buggy /ˈbʌgi/ n **1** a small motor vehicle, often without a roof or doors, used for a specific purpose: *a beach/golf buggy.* **2** a type of light folding PRAM. **3** (formerly) a light carriage pulled by one horse, for one or two people.

bugle /ˈbjuːgl/ n a brass musical instrument like a small TRUMPET(1), used for giving military signals. ⇨ picture at MUSICAL INSTRUMENT.
▶ **bugler** /ˈbjuːglə(r)/ n a person who blows a bugle.

build /bɪld/ v (*pt, pp* **built** /bɪlt/) **1(a)** ~ **sth (of/from/out of sth)**; ~ **sth (for sb)** to make or construct sth by putting parts or material together: [Vn] *build a house/road/railway* [Vnpr] *a house built of stone/bricks* ○ *Birds build their nests out of twigs.* ○ *They built a new room for the baby.* [Vnn] *His father built him a model aeroplane.* **(b)** to construct houses, etc: [V] *The city council intends to build on this site.* ○ *They're building over* (ie on the site of) *the old market.* **2** to develop sth; to establish sth: [Vn] *build a business from nothing* ○ *build confidence/trust* ○ *build a better future/a new career.* **IDM** **Rome was not built in a 'day** (*saying*) time and hard work are necessary for a difficult or important task. **PHRV** **,build sth 'in/,build sth 'into sth** (esp passive) **1** to make sth a permanent part of a larger structure: *build a cupboard/bookcase into a wall* ○ *We're having new wardrobes built in.* **2** (*fig*) to make sth a necessary part of sth: *build an extra clause into the contract.* **'build sth into sth** to put parts together to form sth; to create sth from sth: *build scraps of metal into a work of art* ○ *Let us build this country into a great nation.*
,build sth 'on/,build sth 'onto sth to add sth (eg an extra room) to an existing structure by building: *The new wing was built on(to the hospital) last year.* **'build on sth** to use sth as a foundation for further progress: *build on earlier achievements/success/ results.* **'build sth on sth** to base sth on sth: *build*
one's hopes on the economic strength of the country ○ *an argument built on sound logic.*
,build 'up to become greater, larger in number or more intense: *The music builds up to a rousing climax.* ○ *Traffic is building up on roads into the city.* ○ *Tension built up as the crisis approached.* **,build oneself/sb 'up** to make oneself/sb healthier or stronger: *You need more protein to build you up.* **,build sb/sth 'up** (esp passive) to speak with great praise about sb/sth, often exaggerating one's claims: *The film was built up to be a masterpiece, but I found it very disappointing.* **,build sth 'up 1** to acquire, develop or increase sth gradually: *build up a big library/a fine reputation/a thriving business* ○ *build up one's strength after an illness.* **2** (esp passive) to cover an area with buildings: *The village has been built up since I lived here.*
▶ **build** n [U, C] the shape and size of the human body: *a man of athletic/powerful/slender/average build* ○ *We are (of) the same build.* ○ *Our build is/ builds are similar.*

builder n **1** a person who builds things, esp one whose job is building houses, etc. **2** (in compounds) a person or thing that creates or develops sth: *an empire-builder* ○ *a confidence-builder.*

built (after *advs* and in compound *adjs*) made or constructed in the specified way: *a well-built man* ○ *one who is broad, with big muscles*) ○ *a solidly built wall.*
■ **'build-up** n (*pl* **build-ups**) **1(a)** a gradual increase: *a steady build-up of traffic* ○ *A build-up of enemy forces is reported.* **(b)** ~ **(to sth)** a gradual approach to an important event; a gradual preparation for sth: *the build-up to the President's visit.* **2** a favourable description, esp of a performer or spectacle, in advance: *The press has given the show a tremendous build-up.*
,built-'in (also **inbuilt**) *adj* [attrib] made to form part of a larger structure: *a bedroom with ,built-in 'wardrobes* ○ (*fig*) *,built-in guaran'tees/'weaknesses/ 'prejudice.*
,built-'up *adj* [usu attrib] covered with many buildings: *a ,built-up 'area.*

building /ˈbɪldɪŋ/ n **1** [C] (*abbr* **bldg**) a structure with a roof and walls: *Schools, churches, houses and factories are all buildings.* **2** [U] **(a)** the constructing of houses, etc: *There's building work going on next door.* ○ *building materials.* **(b)** the art or business of doing this: *the building trade.* See also BODY-BUILDING.
■ **'building block** n a basic component of sth: *Simple words are the building blocks of language.*
'building site n an area of land on which a house, etc is being built.
'building society n (*Brit*) (*US* **,savings and 'loan association**) an organization that lends money to people who wish to buy or build houses.

bulb

tulip bulb　　　　filament

light bulb

bulb /bʌlb/ n **1** the round underground part of certain plants, eg the LILY, onion and TULIP. Bulbs send roots downwards and leaves upwards. ⇨ picture. ⇨ picture at FLOWER. **2** (also **'light bulb**) the glass part that fits into an electric lamp, etc to give light when it is turned on: *change a bulb* ○ *a 60-watt light bulb.* ⇨ picture. **3** any object shaped like a bulb, eg the end of a THERMOMETER. ⇨ picture at THERMOMETER.
▶ **bulbous** /ˈbʌlbəs/ *adj* shaped like a bulb; round and fat: *a bulbous nose.*

bulge /bʌldʒ/ n **1** a round swelling; an outward curve: *What's that bulge in your pocket?* **2** (*infml*) a temporary increase in quantity: *a population bulge* ○ *After the war there was a bulge in the birth rate.*
▶ **bulge** v ~ (**out**) (**with sth**) (esp in the continuous tenses) to form a bulge: to be completely full of sth: [V] *bulging eyes* ○ *I can't eat any more — my stomach's bulging.* [Vpr] *His pockets were bulging with apples.* ○ *The lecture-hall was bulging with students.* [also Vp]. **IDM** **be bursting/bulging at the seams** ⇨ SEAM.
bulgy /ˈbʌldʒi/ adj.

bulimia /bjuːˈlɪmiə/ n [U] (*medical*) an emotional disorder, in which a person repeatedly eats too much and then suffers from depression or is physically sick.

bulk /bʌlk/ n **1** [U] size, quantity or volume, esp when great: *It's not their weight that makes these sacks hard to carry, it's their bulk.* ○ *The sheer bulk of Mozart's output is extraordinary.* ○ *a bulk order for office stationery.* **2** [C] a large shape, body or person: *She heaved her huge bulk out of the chair.* **3** [U] the part of food that contains a lot of FIBRE(1); ROUGHAGE: *You need more bulk in your diet.* **4** [sing] **the ~** (**of sth**) the main part of sth: *The bulk of the work has already been done.* ○ *The eldest son inherited the bulk of the estate.* **IDM** **in 'bulk** in large amounts: *It's cheaper to buy (goods) in bulk.*
▶ **bulk** v **IDM** **bulk 'large** (*Brit*) to seem important; to be prominent: *The war still bulks large in the memories of those who fought in it.* **PHRV** **bulk sth 'out** to make sth bigger or thicker: *add extra pages to bulk a book out.*
bulky adj (**-ier, -iest**) taking up a lot of space; awkward to move or carry: *The bulky figure of Inspector Jones appeared at the door.* ○ *a bulky parcel/crate/load.*
■ **bulk-buying** n [U] buying in large amounts, esp at a low price.

bulkhead /ˈbʌlkhed/ n a dividing wall or barrier between separate parts inside a ship or an aircraft.

bull¹ /bʊl/ n **1** the male of any animal in the cow family: *a bull neck* (ie a short thick one, like a bull's). Compare BULLOCK, COW¹ 1, OX 1, STEER². **2** the male of the elephant, the WHALE and certain other large animals. Compare COW¹ 2. **3** (*finance*) a person who buys shares (SHARE¹ 3) hoping to sell them soon afterwards at a higher price: *a bull market* (ie a situation in which share prices are rising). Compare BEAR¹ 2. **4** = BULL'S-EYE. **IDM** **a bull in a 'china shop** a person who is rough and CLUMSY(1) when skill and care are needed. **a red rag to a bull** ⇨ RED¹. **take the bull by the 'horns** to face a difficulty or danger directly and with courage.
▶ **bullish** adj (**a**) (*finance*) causing or associated with a rise in share¹(3) prices: *a bullish market/performance/outlook.* Compare BEARISH. (**b**) confident; optimistic (OPTIMISM): *The team were in bullish mood.*
■ **bull-horn** /ˈbʊl hɔːn/ n (*US*) = LOUD HAILER.
bull-'necked adj having a short thick neck.
bull-'terrier n a dog produced by crossing (CROSS² 8) a BULLDOG and a TERRIER.

bull² /bʊl/ n an official order or announcement from the POPE: *a papal bull.*

bull³ /bʊl/ n [U] (*sl*) = BULLSHIT: *That's a lot/a load of bull!*

bulldog /ˈbʊldɒg/ n a fierce powerful dog with a small body, a large head and a short thick neck. ⇨ picture at DOG.
■ **bulldog clip** n a large metal CLIP(1) for holding papers, etc together. ⇨ picture at CLIP¹.

bulldoze /ˈbʊldəʊz/ v **1** to remove sth or make sth flat with a bulldozer: [Vn] *The area is being bulldozed to make way for a new road.* **2** ~ **sb** (**into doing sth**) to force sb to do sth, esp by frightening

them: [Vnpr] *They bulldozed me into signing the agreement.* [also Vn]. **3** to push sth forcefully in the specified direction: [Vnpr] *He bulldozed his way into the room.* ○ *She bulldozed her plans past the committee.*
▶ **bulldozer** /ˈbʊldəʊzə(r)/ n a powerful motor vehicle with a broad steel blade in front, used for moving earth or clearing ground. ⇨ picture.

bullet /ˈbʊlɪt/ n a small missile with a pointed end that is fired from a gun: *He was killed by a single bullet in the heart.* ○ *a plastic bullet* ○ *There were bullet holes* (ie holes made by bullets) *in the door.* ○ *a bullet wound.* **IDM** **bite the bullet** ⇨ BITE¹.
■ **bullet-'headed** /-ˈhedɪd/ adj (*Brit usu derog*) having a small round head.

bulletin /ˈbʊlətɪn/ n **1** a short official statement of news, eg on radio or television: *a news bulletin* . **2** a printed report giving the news of an association, a group or a society.
■ **bulletin-board** n (*US*) = NOTICE-BOARD.

bulletproof /ˈbʊlɪtpruːf/ adj that can stop bullets passing through it: *a bulletproof shirt/vest/jacket.*

bullfight /ˈbʊlfaɪt/ n a traditional public entertainment, esp in Spain and S America, in which bulls (BULL¹ 1) are fought and usu killed in a BULLRING.
▶ **bullfighter** n = MATADOR.
bullfighting n [U].

bullfinch /ˈbʊlfɪntʃ/ n a small bird with a strong curved beak and a pink breast.

bullfrog /ˈbʊlfrɒg/ n a large American FROG with a loud CROAK.

bullion /ˈbʊliən/ n [U] gold or silver in large amounts, or in the form of bars: *The thieves stole £1 000 000 in gold bullion.*

bullock /ˈbʊlək/ n a BULL¹(1) that has been castrated (CASTRATE). Compare BULL¹ 1, OX 1, STEER².

bullring /ˈbʊlrɪŋ/ n a large circular outdoor theatre for bullfighting (BULLFIGHT).

bull's-eye /ˈbʊlz aɪ/ n **1** (also **bull**) (**a**) the centre of a target, having the highest value in archery (ARCHER) and darts (DART¹ 4). ⇨ picture at ARCHER, DART¹. (**b**) a shot that hits this: *scoring a bull's-eye.* **2** a large hard round sweet²(1) with a PEPPERMINT flavour.

bullshit /ˈbʊlʃɪt/ n [U] (⚠ *sl*) (also *sl* **bull**) (often as an *interj*) nonsense; rubbish: *a load/lot of bullshit* ○ *He's talking bullshit.*
▶ **bullshit** v (**-tt-**) (⚠ *sl*) to talk nonsense, esp in order to deceive sb: [V] *She's just bullshitting.* [Vn] *Don't try to bullshit me!*

bully¹ /ˈbʊli/ n a person who uses her or his strength or power to frighten or hurt weaker people: *Leave that little girl alone, you big bully!*
▶ **bully** v (*pt, pp* **bullied**) to frighten or hurt a weaker person or group: [Vn] *The older boys bullied him at school.* ○ *a small country bullied by its powerful neighbour.* **PHRV** **bully sb into doing sth** to force sb to do sth by frightening them: *The manager tried to bully his men into working harder by threatening them with dismissal.* **bullying** n [U]: *There was a lot of bullying at my school.*
■ **bully-boy** n (*Brit*) a rough violent man, esp one who is paid to frighten or injure others: *bully-boy tactics.*

bully² /'bʊli/ interj **IDM** **bully for sb** (infml esp ironic) well done: You've solved the puzzle at last! Well, bully for 'you!

bulrush /'bʊlrʌʃ/ n a type of tall plant like a REED(1) that grows in or near water.

bulwark /'bʊlwək/ n **1** a wall, esp of earth, built as a defence. **2** ~ (against sth) a person or thing that supports, defends or protects: a bulwark against political extremism ○ Democracy is a bulwark of freedom. **3** (usu pl) a ship's side above the level of the DECK¹(1).

bum¹ /bʌm/ n (infml esp Brit) the part of the body on which one sits; the buttocks (BUTTOCK). **IDM** **bums on 'seats** (used to refer to people paying to watch or take part in an entertainment): The festival organizers were chiefly concerned with **putting bums on seats**.
■ **'bum-bag** n (Brit infml) a small bag for money and other possessions, attached to a belt and worn round the waist.

bum² /bʌm/ n (infml esp US) (**a**) a person who spends his life wandering from place to place and begging for food, etc; a TRAMP n(1): bums sleeping in the streets. (**b**) a lazy or worthless person: You're just a no-good bum!
▶ **bum** adj [attrib] (infml) of bad quality; useless: a bum suggestion/idea ○ a bum deal (ie a bad BARGAIN¹).
bum v (-mm-) ~ sth (off sb) (infml) to get sth from sb by begging; to CADGE sth: [Vn] bum a lift [Vnpr] Can I bum a cigarette off you? **PHRV** **bum a'round/a'bout** to travel around or spend one's time doing nothing in particular: I bummed around (in) Europe for a year before starting my job.

bumble /'bʌmbl/ v **1** ~ (on) (about sth) to speak in a way that is confused and hard to hear or understand: [Vpr, Vp] What are you bumbling (on) about? [also V]. **2** to act or move in a specified direction in an awkward and confused way: [Vpr] The old man bumbled absent-mindedly along the road. [also Vp].
▶ **bumbling** adj [attrib] behaving in an awkward, confused way: bumbling amateurism ○ You bumbling idiot!

bumble-bee /'bʌmbl biː/ n a large hairy bee that makes a loud noise as it flies.

bumf (also **bumph**) /bʌmf/ n [U] (Brit sl joc or derog) paper, esp official documents, forms, etc: 'What's in the post today?' 'Just a lot of bumf from the insurance people.'

bummer /'bʌmə(r)/ n (sl) an unpleasant event: As a night out it was a complete bummer.

bump /bʌmp/ v **1** ~ against/into sb/sth to knock or strike sth with a short hard blow; to COLLIDE with sth: [Vpr] In the dark I bumped into a chair. ○ The car bumped against the kerb. **2** ~ sth (against/on sth) to hit or knock sth, esp a part of the body, against or on sth: [Vnpr] Be careful not to bump your head on the low beams. [also Vn]. ⇨ note at BANG¹. **3** to move across a rough surface in the specified direction: [Vp] The old bus bumped along the mountain road. [Vpr]. **PHRV** **,bump 'into sb** (infml) to meet sb by chance: Guess who I bumped into today. **,bump sb 'off** (sl) to murder sb. **,bump sth 'up** (infml) to increase or raise sth: bump up prices/salaries.
▶ **bump** n **1(a)** a short hard blow, knock or impact: He fell to the ground with a bump. ○ The passengers felt a violent bump as the plane landed. (**b**) the low dull sound made by this: I heard a bump in the next room. **2** a swelling on the body, esp one caused by a blow; a lump: covered in bumps and bruises ○ She had a nasty bump on her head after falling from her horse. **3** a part of a surface that is not flat or even: a road with a lot of bumps in it.
bump adv **IDM** **things that go bump in the night** ⇨ THING.

bumpy adj (-ier, -iest) **1** having a surface that is not even: a bumpy road/track. **2** involving sudden unpleasant movements: a bumpy ride/flight/drive.

bumper¹ /'bʌmpə(r)/ n a bar fixed to the front and back of a motor vehicle to reduce the effect of an impact. ⇨ picture at CAR.
■ **,bumper-to-'bumper** adj, adv (of vehicles) in a line, with each one close behind the one in front: We sat bumper-to-bumper in the traffic jam.

bumper² /'bʌmpə(r)/ adj [attrib] unusually and pleasantly large: a bumper crop/harvest ○ a bumper edition/issue/number (eg of a magazine).

bumph = BUMF.

bumpkin /'bʌmpkɪn/ n (derog) a person from the country who is not SOPHISTICATED.

bumptious /'bʌmpʃəs/ adj (derog) showing that one thinks one is very important in a noisy or ARROGANT way: bumptious officials. ▶ **bumptiously** adv. **bumptiousness** n [U]: His bumptiousness irritates most of his colleagues.

bun /bʌn/ n **1** a small round sweet cake: a currant bun. Compare ROLL¹ 2. **2** hair, esp a woman's, twisted into a tight knot at the back of the head: put/wear one's hair in a bun. **IDM** **have a 'bun in the oven** (Brit infml joc) to be pregnant.

bunch /bʌntʃ/ n **1** [C] a number of things, usu of the same kind, growing, fastened or in a group together: a bunch of bananas/grapes. ⇨ picture at GRAPEVINE: bunches of flowers ○ a bunch of keys. **2** [CGp] (infml) a group of people: You're behaving like a bunch of idiots! ○ I don't like any of them much, but he's **the best of the bunch**.
▶ **bunch** v ~ (sth/sb) (up) to form or cause sth/sb to form into a bunch or bunches: [V] a blouse that bunches (ie in loose folds) at the waist [Vp] Cross the road one at a time — don't bunch up. [Vnp] The runners are still all bunched up with three laps to go. [also Vn].

bundle /'bʌndl/ n **1** [C] a collection of things held or fastened together: a bundle of sticks/clothes/newspapers ○ books tied up in bundles of twenty. **2** [sing] a ~ of sth (infml) a lot of sth; a mass of sth: That child is a bundle of mischief! ○ He's not exactly a bundle of fun (ie an amusing person). **3** [sing] (infml) a large amount of money: That car must have cost a bundle. **IDM** **a bag/bundle of nerves** ⇨ NERVE. **go a bundle on sb/sth** (Brit infml) to be very keen on sb/sth: I don't go a bundle on her new husband. Do you?
▶ **bundle** v ~ sth (up) to make or tie sth into a bundle or bundles: [Vn] The firewood was cut and bundled, ready for use. [Vnp] We bundled up some old clothes for the jumble sale. **PHRV** **,bundle sth 'into sth** to put sth into a place quickly and not carefully: She bundled her clothes into the drawer without folding them. **,bundle sb 'out, 'off, 'into,** etc to cause sb to move quickly or in a rough way in the specified direction: The guards bundled him out of the building. ○ She bundled her son off to school. ○ I was bundled into a police van.

bung /bʌŋ/ n a piece of CORK(1), rubber or other material, used for closing the hole in a container, esp a barrel.
▶ **bung** v (Brit infml) to put or throw sth carelessly in the specified place or direction: [Vnadv] Bung the newspaper over here, will you? [also Vnpr, Vnp]. **PHRV** **,bung sth 'up (with sth)** (usu passive) to block sth: My nose is (all) bunged up. I've got a terrible cold. ○ The drains are bunged up with dead leaves.

bungalow /'bʌŋɡələʊ/ n a house built on one level. ⇨ picture at HOUSE¹.

bungle /'bʌŋɡl/ v to do sth badly or without skill; to fail at sth: [V] It looks as though you've bungled again. [Vn] Don't let him fix your bike. He's sure to bungle the job. ○ The gang spent a year planning the robbery and then bungled it.

▶ **bungle** n (usu *sing*) a bungled action or piece of work: *The whole job was a gigantic bungle.*
bungler /ˈbʌŋglə(r)/ n.

bunion /ˈbʌnjən/ n a painful swelling, esp on the first joint of the big toe.

bunk¹ /bʌŋk/ n **1** a narrow bed built into a wall, eg on a ship. **2** (also **ˈbunk-bed**) either of a pair of single beds, fixed one above the other as a unit, esp for children.
■ **ˈbunk-house** n a building for workers, etc to sleep in.

bunk² /bʌŋk/ n **IDM** **do a ˈbunk** (*Brit infml*) to run away or disappear suddenly and secretly: *The cashier has done a bunk with the day's takings.*

bunker /ˈbʌŋkə(r)/ n **1** a strongly built underground shelter for soldiers, guns, etc. **2** a container for storing coal, esp on a ship or outside a house. **3** (also *esp US* **trap**) an area that has been dug and filled with sand as an obstacle on a golf-course (GOLF). ⇨ picture at GOLF.
▶ **bunker** v (usu passive) (in golf) to trap a golf ball in a bunker(3): [Vn] *She/Her ball is bunkered.*

bunkum /ˈbʌŋkəm/ n [U] (*dated infml*) nonsense: *Don't believe what he's saying — it's pure bunkum.*

bunny /ˈbʌni/ (also **ˈbunny-rabbit**) n (used esp by and to small children) a rabbit.

Bunsen burner /ˌbʌnsn ˈbɜːnə(r)/ n a small gas apparatus that produces a flame, used in scientific work.

bunting¹ /ˈbʌntɪŋ/ n any of various small birds related to the FINCH and SPARROW families.

bunting² /ˈbʌntɪŋ/ n [U] coloured flags, paper, etc used for decorating streets and buildings in celebrations.

buoy /bɔɪ; *US also* ˈbuːi/ n **1** a floating object fixed to the bottom of the sea, a river, etc to mark a place that is dangerous for boats or to show where boats may go, etc. ⇨ picture at COAST¹. **2** = LIFEBUOY.
▶ **buoy** v [Vn, Vnp] ~ sb/sth (up) (esp passive) **(a)** to keep sb/sth floating: *The raft was buoyed (up) by empty petrol cans.* **(b)** to cause egp prices to be or remain at a high or satisfactory level: *Share prices were buoyed (up) by hopes of an end to the recession.* **(c)** to raise sb's hopes or spirits; to cause sb to become or remain cheerful or confident: *We felt buoyed (up) by the good news.*

buoyant /ˈbɔɪənt; *US also* ˈbuːjənt/ adj **1(a)** (of an object) that can float or continue to float: *The raft would be more buoyant if it was less heavy.* **(b)** (of a liquid) that can keep things floating in it: *Salt water is more buoyant than fresh water.* **2** (of prices, business activity, etc) tending to rise or remain at a high level, indicating success: *Share prices were buoyant today in active trading.* **3** recovering quickly from disappointment; cheerful and confident: *a buoyant disposition/personality* ∘ *Despite all the set-backs, she remained buoyant.* ▶ **buoyancy** /-ənsi/ n [U]. **buoyantly** adv.

bur (also **burr**) /bɜː(r)/ n the prickly part containing the seeds of certain plants. Burs have tiny hooks on their surface which make them stick to people's clothing or hair.

burble /ˈbɜːbl/ v **1** [V] to make a gentle bubbling (BUBBLE v) sound. **2** ~ (on) (about sth) (*Brit derog*) to speak in a confused or silly way that is difficult to hear or understand: [Vpr, Vp] *What's he burbling (on) about?* [also V].

burden /ˈbɜːdn/ n **1** [C] a thing or person that is carried; a load, esp a heavy one: *bear/carry/shoulder a heavy burden.* See also BEAST OF BURDEN. **2** [C] (*fig*) a duty, an obligation, a responsibility, etc that is not wanted or causes trouble: *the burden of heavy taxation on the taxpayer* ∘ *the burden of grief/guilt/remorse* ∘ *His invalid father is becoming a burden (to him).* **3** [sing] **the ~ of sth** the main theme of

a speech, an article, etc: *The burden of his argument was that...*
▶ **burden** v [Vn, Vnpr] ~ sb/oneself (with sth) **(a)** (usu passive) to put a heavy load on sb/oneself: *refugees burdened with all their possessions.* **(b)** to trouble sb/oneself with sth, eg a problem, a responsibility, a duty, etc: *I don't want to burden you with my problems.* ∘ *Industry is heavily burdened with taxation.* Compare UNBURDEN.

burdensome /-səm/ adj (*fml*) causing worry or hardship; hard to bear: *burdensome duties/responsibilities.*
■ **the ˌburden of ˈproof** n [sing] (*law*) the obligation to prove that what one says is true.

bureau /ˈbjʊərəʊ/ n (pl **bureaux** or **bureaus** /-rəʊz/) **1** (*Brit*) a desk with drawers, shelves and usu a sloping lid which forms a writing surface when open. **2** (*US*) = CHEST OF DRAWERS. **3** an organization or office that provides information and facts: *a travel bureau* ∘ *an information bureau.* **4** (*esp US*) a government department: *the Federal Bureau of Investigation.*

bureaucracy /bjʊəˈrɒkrəsi/ n **1(a)** [U] a system of government by departments which are managed by state officials, not by elected representatives. **(b)** [C] a country having such a system. **(c)** [CGp] the officials appointed to manage such a system, as a group. **2** [U] (*often derog*) the official rules and procedures of an organization, esp when these are seen as too complicated and not efficient: *We need to reduce paperwork and bureaucracy in the company.*

bureaucrat /ˈbjʊərəkræt/ n (*often derog*) an official working in a government department, esp one who follows administrative procedure and the rules of the department very strictly: *insensitive bureaucrats.*
▶ **bureaucratic** /ˌbjʊərəˈkrætɪk/ adj (*often derog*) of, like or relating to a BUREAUCRACY or bureaucrats: *bureaucratic government* ∘ *The report revealed a major bureaucratic muddle.* **bureaucratically** /-ɪkli/ adv.

burgeon /ˈbɜːdʒən/ v (*fml*) to begin to grow or develop rapidly; to FLOURISH(1,2): [V] *a burgeoning population* ∘ *a burgeoning talent* ∘ *His love for her burgeoned.*

burger /ˈbɜːgə(r)/ n (*infml*) = HAMBURGER 1.
▶ **-burger** (forming compound ns) (*infml*) food prepared or cooked like or with a HAMBURGER: *a ˈfishburger* ∘ *a ˈcheeseburger.*

burgher /ˈbɜːgə(r)/ n (usu pl) (*usu joc*) a citizen of a particular town, esp one who is respectable: *The pop festival has shocked the good burghers of Canterbury.*

burglar /ˈbɜːglə(r)/ n a person who enters a building, esp by force, in order to steal: *The burglars got into the house through the bedroom window.* Compare ROBBER, THIEF.
▶ **burglary** /ˈbɜːgləri/ n **(a)** [U] the crime of entering a building in order to steal: *be accused/convicted of burglary.* **(b)** [C] an instance of this: *A number of burglaries have been committed in this area recently.*
■ **ˈburglar alarm** n an automatic electronic device that rings an alarm bell when a burglar enters a building.

burgle /ˈbɜːgl/ (*US* **burglarize, -ise** /ˈbɜːgləraɪz/) v to enter a building, esp by force, and steal from it or sb: [Vn] *burgle a shop* ∘ *We were/Our house was burgled while we were away on holiday.* ⇨ note at ROB.

burgundy /ˈbɜːgəndi/ n **1** [U, C] any of various red or white wines from the Burgundy area of eastern France. **2** [U] a dark red colour: *a burgundy leather briefcase.*

burial /ˈberiəl/ n [U, C] the act or ceremony of burying sth, esp a dead body; a funeral in which the body

B

is buried: *Cremation is more common than burial in some countries.* ○ *The burial took place on Friday.* ○ *the burial service.*

■ **'burial-ground** *n* a place where dead bodies are buried; a CEMETERY: *a prehistoric burial-ground.*

burlesque /bɜːˈlesk/ *n* **1** [C,U] a comic or exaggerated IMITATION(1) or version of sth, intended to make it look ridiculous; a PARODY: *a burlesque of a novel/poem.* **2** [U] (*US*) a type of variety(4) show, often including STRIPTEASE.

▶ **burlesque** *adj* [usu attrib] of, relating to or using burlesque(1,2): *a burlesque actor* ○ *burlesque acting.*

burly /ˈbɜːli/ *adj* (**-ier, -iest**) (of a person, a body, etc) big and strong; heavily built: *a burly policeman* ○ *a burly figure.*

burn /bɜːn/ *v* (*pt, pp* **burnt** /bɜːnt/ or **burned** /bɜːnd/) **1(a)** to destroy, damage, injure or mark sb/sth by fire, heat or acid: [Vn] *burn dead leaves/waste paper/rubbish* ○ *All his belongings were burnt in the fire.* ○ *Sorry, I've burned the toast.* ○ *His face was badly burnt by the hot sun.* ○ *The soup is very hot. Don't burn your mouth.* ○ *I burnt myself while I was getting the food out of the oven.* [Vnpr] *The house was* **burnt to the ground** (ie completely destroyed by fire). **(b)** to be destroyed, damaged, injured or marked in this way: [V] *I can smell something burning in the kitchen.* ○ *Her skin burns easily.* **2** to make a hole or a mark by burning: [Vnpr] *The cigarette burnt a hole in the carpet.* [also Vn]. **3** [V] **(a)** to be on fire: *a burning building* ○ *The house burned for hours before the blaze was put out.* **(b)** to produce heat or light: *A welcoming fire was burning in the fireplace.* ○ *We could see a light burning upstairs but nobody answered the door.* **(c)** to be capable of catching fire: *Paper burns easily.* ○ *Damp wood doesn't burn well.* **4** to be killed or to kill a person or an animal by fire: [Vn, Vn-adj] *Joan of Arc was burnt (alive) at the stake.* [Vnpr] *Ten people burned to* **death** *in the hotel fire.* **5** to use sth as fuel: [Vn] *Do you burn coal as well as wood on this fire?* ○ *a furnace that burns gas/oil/coke.* **6** to be or make sb/sth so hot as to be painful: [V] *Your forehead's burning. Do you have a fever?* [Vn] *The heat from the fire was burning me so I moved away.* **7** ~ **with sth** (usu in the continuous tenses) to be filled with a strong emotion: [Vpr] *be burning with rage/desire.* **8** (usu in the continuous tenses) to have an extremely strong desire to do or have sth: [V.*to* inf] *He was burning to climb again for the sheer joy of it.* **IDM** **burn one's 'boats/'bridges** to do sth that makes it impossible to return to the previous situation later: *Think carefully before you resign — if you do that you will have burnt your boats and you might regret it.* **burn the candle at both 'ends** to become very tired by trying to do too many things and not sleeping enough. **burn one's 'fingers / get one's 'fingers burnt** to suffer as a result of doing sth without realizing the possible bad consequences for oneself: *He got his fingers badly burnt dabbling in the stock market.* **burn the midnight 'oil** to study or work until late at night: *She takes her exams next week, so she's burning the midnight oil.* **burn sth to a 'crisp** to cook sth for too long or with too much heat, so that it becomes badly burnt: *The meat was burnt to a crisp.* ○ (*fig*) *I lay in the sun all day and got burnt to a crisp.* **sb's ears are burning** ⇨ EAR¹. **feel one's ears burning** ⇨ FEEL¹. **have money to burn** ⇨ MONEY. **money burns a hole in sb's pocket** ⇨ MONEY. **PHRV burn (sth) away 1** to disappear or make sth disappear as a result of burning: *Half the candle had burnt away.* **2** to remove sth or be removed by burning: *Most of the skin on his face got burnt away in the fire.*

,**burn (sth) 'down** to destroy sth or be destroyed by fire: *The house burned down in half an hour.* ○ *Don't leave the gas on — you might burn the house down.*

,**burn sth 'off** to remove sth by burning: *Burn the old paint off before repainting the door.*

,**burn (itself) 'out** (of a fire) to stop burning by itself because there is nothing more to burn: *The fire had burnt (itself) out before the fire brigade arrived.*
,**burn (sth) 'out** to stop working or make sth stop working because of FRICTION or excessive heat: *The clutch has burnt out on my car engine.* ,**burn oneself 'out** to use up all one's energy or ruin one's health, esp by working too hard over a period of time: *If he doesn't stop working so hard, he'll burn himself out.* ○ *By the age of 25 she was completely burned out and retired from the sport.* ,**burn sb 'out** (esp passive) to force sb to leave their house by setting fire to it: *The family was burnt out (of house and home) during the race riots.* ,**burn sth 'out** (esp passive) to destroy sth completely by fire so that only the outer frame remains: *The hotel was completely burnt out.* ○ *the burnt-out wreck of a car.* **'burn (sth) to sth** to turn sth or be turned into the specified state by burning: *It burned to ashes.* ○ *You've burnt the toast to a cinder* (ie so that it is hard and black).

,**burn 'up 1** (of a fire) to produce brighter and stronger flames: *put more wood on a fire to make it burn up.* **2** (of an object entering the earth's atmosphere) to be destroyed by heat. ,**burn sb 'up** (*US infml*) to make sb very angry. ,**burn sth 'up 1** to get rid of sth by burning: *burn up all the garden rubbish.* **2** to use sth as fuel: *burn up calories.*

▶ **burn** *n* **1** an injury or a mark caused by fire, heat or acid: *He died of the burns he received in the fire.* ○ *How did that burn on the settee get there?* **2** the firing of a spacecraft's engines to change its course or make it go faster.

burner *n* the part of a cooker, heater, etc that produces a flame. **IDM on the back burner** ⇨ BACK².

burning *adj* [attrib] **1** (of feelings) intense; extreme: *a burning thirst* ○ *a burning desire for sth.* **2** very important; urgent: *one of the burning issues of the day.*

burnt *adj* marked, damaged or injured by burning: *rather burnt toast* ○ *Your hand looks badly burnt.*
,**burnt 'offering** *n* **(a)** a thing offered as a sacrifice by burning. **(b)** (*joc*) food that has been accidentally and badly burnt by the person cooking it.

■ **'burn-out** *n* [C,U] **1** physical or mental collapse caused by working too hard over a period of time: *The demands on sportsmen today can lead to burn-out at an early age.* **2** the point when a ROCKET(2), etc has used all its fuel and has no more power.

burnish /ˈbɜːnɪʃ/ *v* to make metal smooth and shiny by rubbing; to polish sth: [Vn] *burnished copper.*

burp /bɜːp/ *v* (*infml*) **1** [V] to release air from the stomach through the mouth, making a noise; to BELCH(1). **2** [Vn] to make a baby bring up air from the stomach, esp by rubbing or tapping the back.

▶ **burp** *n* (*infml*) an instance of burping; a BELCH *n*.

burr¹ = BUR.

burr² /bɜː(r)/ *n* (usu *sing*) **1** the whirring (WHIRR *v*) or humming (HUM 2) noise made eg by parts of a machine turning quickly or by a telephone. **2** strong pronunciation of the 'r' sound, typical of certain English accents (ACCENT 3); an accent with this type of pronunciation: *speak with a soft West Country burr.*

▶ **burr** *v* [V] to make a burr.

burro /ˈbʊrəʊ; *US* ˈbɜːrəʊ/ *n* (*US*) (*pl* **-os**) a small DONKEY used for carrying heavy loads.

burrow /ˈbʌrəʊ/ *n* a hole or tunnel made in the ground and used as a home or shelter by rabbits, foxes, etc.

▶ **burrow** *v* to make a hole or tunnel in the ground by digging: [V] *I saw a fox burrowing in the field.* [Vn] *Rabbits had burrowed holes in the grassy bank.* **PHRV ,burrow (one's way) 'into, 'through,**

[V.*to* inf] = verb + *to* infinitive   [Vn.inf (no *to*)] = verb + noun + infinitive without *to*   [V.*ing*] = verb + *-ing* form

¹under, etc to go in the specified direction by digging; to go deeply into sth: *The fox burrowed (its way) under the fence to reach the chickens.* ○ *The prisoners escaped by burrowing under the wall.* ○ *The child burrowed under the bedclothes.* ○ *(fig) We had to burrow through a mass of files to find the documents we wanted.*

bursar /'bɜːsə(r)/ *n* a person who manages the financial affairs of a school or college.
▶ **bursary** /'bɜːsəri/ *n* **1** a college bursar's office. **2** (*Brit*) a SCHOLARSHIP or GRANT awarded to a student.

burst¹ /bɜːst/ *v* (*pt, pp* **burst**) **1** to break or make sth break violently open or apart, esp because of pressure from inside; to explode: [V] *If you blow that balloon up any more it will burst.* ○ *The dam burst under the weight of water.* ○ *Water-pipes often burst in cold weather.* ○ *(fig) I've eaten so much I feel ready to burst!* [Vn] *The river burst its banks and flooded the town.* ○ *Don't get so angry! You'll burst a blood-vessel!* **2** ~ (**with sth**) (only in the continuous tenses) (**a**) to be very full and almost breaking open: [V] *'More pudding?' 'No thanks. I'm bursting!'* ○ *May I use your toilet — I'm bursting!* (ie I have an urgent need to urinate (URINE).) [Vpr] *a bag bursting with shopping.* (**b**) *(fig)* to be filled with a very strong emotion: [Vpr] *be bursting with happiness/pride/excitement.* **IDM** **be bursting/bulging at the seams** ⇨ SEAM. **be bursting to do sth** to be extremely eager to do sth: *She was bursting to tell him the good news.* ,**burst** (**sth**) **¹open** to open or cause sth to open suddenly or violently: *Firemen burst the door open and rescued them.* **fit to burst** ⇨ FIT¹ *adv.* **PHRV** ,**burst ¹in** to enter a room, a building, etc suddenly and noisily: *The police burst in (through the door) and arrested the gang.* ,**burst ¹in on sb/sth** to interrupt sb/sth by entering a place suddenly and noisily: *burst in on a meeting* ○ *How dare you burst in on us without knocking!* **¹burst into sth** to start producing sth suddenly and with great force: *The aircraft crashed and burst into flames* (ie suddenly began to burn). ○ *burst into tears/song* (ie suddenly begin to cry/sing) ○ *trees bursting into leaf/bloom/blossom/flower.* **¹burst into, out of, through, etc sth** to move suddenly and with great force in the specified direction: *An angry crowd burst through the lines of police and into the street.* ○ *The oil burst out of the ground.* ○ *The sun burst through the clouds.* **¹burst on/onto sth** to appear somewhere suddenly and in a striking way: *A major new talent has burst onto the literary scene.* ,**burst ¹out 1** to speak suddenly, loudly and with strong feeling; to EXCLAIM: *'I hate you!' she burst out.* **2** (with the *-ing* form) to begin doing sth suddenly: *burst ₁out ¹crying/¹laughing.*

burst² /bɜːst/ *n* **1**(**a**) an instance or the sound of bursting; an explosion: *the burst of a shell/bomb.* (**b**) a split caused by sth bursting: *a burst in a water-pipe.* **2** a brief period of strong effort: *a burst of energy/speed* ○ *work in short bursts.* **3** a sudden strong appearance or period of sth: *a burst of anger/enthusiasm* ○ *a burst of applause.* **4** a short series of shots from a gun: *several rapid bursts of machine-gun fire.*

burton /'bɜːtn/ *n* **IDM** **go for a ¹burton** (*Brit infml becoming dated*) to be lost, destroyed or killed: *It's pouring with rain, so I'm afraid our picnic's gone for a burton.*

bury /'beri/ *v* (*pt, pp* **buried**) **1** [Vn] (**a**) to place a dead body in a grave: *He was buried with his wife.* ○ *Where is George Washington buried?* ○ *He's been dead and buried for years!* (**b**) *(euph)* to lose sb by death: *She's eighty-five and has buried three husbands.* **2**(**a**) to hide sth in the ground: [Vn] *buried treasure* ○ *Our dog buries its bones in the garden.* (**b**) to cover sb/sth with soil, rocks, leaves, etc: [Vnpr] *The house*

was buried under ten feet of snow. [Vn-adj] *The miners were buried alive when the tunnel collapsed.* **3** to cover sth so that it cannot be seen: [Vnpr] *Your letter got buried under a pile of papers.* ○ *She buried her face in her hands and wept.* [Vn] *(fig) He has a tendency to bury his emotions.* **4** to dismiss sth from one's mind; to forget about sth completely: [Vn] *It's time to bury our differences and be friends again.* ○ *She wants to bury her past.* **5** ~ **sth** (**in sth**) to sink sth into sth: [Vnpr] *The lion buried its teeth in the antelope's neck.* ○ *He walked slowly, his hands buried in his pockets.* ○ *Her head was buried in the book she was reading.* **IDM** ,**bury the ¹hatchet** to end a period of being enemies or of mutual dislike and become friendly: *After not speaking to each other for years, the two brothers decided to bury the hatchet.* **bury/hide one's head in the sand** ⇨ HEAD¹. **PHRV** ¹**bury oneself in sth 1** to go to or be in a place where one will meet few people: *She buried herself (away) in the country to write a book.* **2** to involve oneself in or concentrate deeply on sth: *In the evenings he buries himself in his books.*

bus /bʌs/ *n* (*pl* **buses**, *US* also **busses**) a large vehicle that carries passengers, esp one that travels along a fixed route, stopping regularly to let people get on and off: *Shall we walk or go by bus?* ○ *a bus driver/station.* **IDM** **miss the boat/bus** ⇨ MISS².
▶ **bus** *v* (*pres p* **bussing** or **busing**; *pt, pp* **bussed** or **bused**) **1** (also **bus it**) to travel by bus: [V, Vn] *I usually bus (it) to work in the morning.* **2** [Vn] (**a**) to transport sb by bus: *They were bussed from the airport to their hotel.* (**b**) *(US)* to transport young people by bus to schools in another area so that those of different races can be educated together: *I have always been opposed to bussing.*
■ ¹**bus lane** *n* a strip of a road marked for use by buses.
¹**bus shelter** *n* a structure with a roof at a bus-stop providing shelter for people waiting for a bus.
¹**bus-stop** *n* a place where a bus regularly stops, usu marked by a sign.

busby /'bʌzbi/ *n* a tall fur hat worn by certain types of soldier for ceremonies.

bush /bʊʃ/ *n* **1** [C] (**a**) a plant that grows thickly with several stems coming up from the root; a SHRUB: *a rose-bush* ○ *gooseberry bushes.* Compare TREE. (**b**) a thing resembling this, esp an area of thick hair or fur. **2** (often **the bush**) [U] an area of wild land that is not cultivated, esp in Africa and Australia. **IDM** **beat about the bush** ⇨ BEAT¹. **a bird in the hand is worth two in the bush** ⇨ BIRD.
▶ **bushy** *adj* (**-ier, -iest**) **1** covered with bushes. **2** (of hair) growing thickly: *a bushy moustache* ○ *bushy eyebrows.*
■ ,**bush ¹telegraph** *n* [U, sing] the process by which information, news, rumours, etc spread rapidly by being passed from person to person.

bushed /bʊʃt/ *adj* [pred] *(infml esp US)* very tired.

bushel /'bʊʃl/ *n* **1** [C] a measure for grain and fruit (in the UK 8 gallons (GALLON) or about 36.4 litres). **2** **bushels** [pl] *(US infml)* a large amount: *We have bushels of the stuff.* **IDM** **hide one's light under a bushel** ⇨ HIDE¹.

Bushman /'bʊʃmən/ *n* (*pl* **-men** /-mən/) a member of various SW African tribes living and hunting in the bush(2).

busily ⇨ BUSY.

business /'bɪznəs/ *n* **1** [U] (**a**) the activity of making, buying, selling or supplying things for money; commerce; trade: *We don't do (much) business with foreign companies.* ○ *He's in (ie works in) the oil business.* ○ *She has set up in business as a bookseller.* ○ *They left their jobs to go into business on their own.* ○ *a business trip* ○ *a business lunch* ○ *business sense* (ie knowledge of or skill at commercial procedures). (**b**) the volume or rate of this

B

activity: *Business is always brisk before Christmas.*
2 [C] a commercial organization; a company or
shop: *have/own one's own business* ○ *She runs a
thriving grocery business.* ○ *Many small businesses
have gone bankrupt recently.* **3** [C,U] one's usual
occupation; one's profession: *He tries not to let (his)
business interfere with his home life.* **4** [U] a thing
that is sb's concern; a duty; a task: *It is the business
of the police to protect the community.* ○ *I shall* **make
it my business** *to find out who is responsible.* ○ *My
private life is* **none of your business/is no business of yours.** **5** [U] a thing or things that must be
dealt with; a serious matter or matters to be discussed: *The main business of this meeting is our
wages claim.* ○ *Unless there is any other business, we
can end the meeting.* **6** [sing] a matter; an affair or
an event: *an odd/a strange/a disturbing business* ○
*It's always such a business finding somewhere to
park.* ○ *I'm sick of the whole business.* ○ *That plane
crash was an awful business.* ○ *What's this business I
hear about you losing your job.* **7** [U] (*techn*) gestures, expressions on the face, etc made by actors on
stage to give extra effect to what they also say.
See also SHOW BUSINESS. **IDM** **business as** ˈusual
(*catchphrase*) things will proceed normally despite
difficulties or disturbances: *Notice to customers:
business as usual during redecoration work.* ˌbusi-
ness is ˈbusiness (*catchphrase*) in financial and
commercial matters one must not be influenced by
friendship, pity, emotion, etc. **funny business** ⇨
FUNNY. **get down to** ˈbusiness to start being serious and dealing with the matter that must be dealt
with: *OK, now we're all here, let's get down to business.* **go about one's** ˈbusiness to occupy oneself
with one's own normal activities: *streets filled with
people going about their daily business.* **go out of**
ˈbusiness to become BANKRUPT; to stop operating
through lack of funds, work, etc. **have no business to do sth/doing sth** to have no right to do
sth: *You've no business to be here — this is private
property.* **in the business of sth/doing sth** involved in or intending to do sth: *I'm not in the
business of telling other people how to run their lives.*
like ˈnobody's business (*infml*) very much, fast or
well: *My head hurts like nobody's business.* **mean
business** ⇨ MEAN¹. **mind one's own business** ⇨
MIND². **on** ˈbusiness for the purpose of doing business: *I'll be away on business next week.*
■ ˈbusiness card *n* a small card printed with sb's
name and details of their job and company.
the ˈbusiness end *n* [sing] ~ (**of sth**) (*Brit infml*)
the part of a tool, an instrument, a weapon, etc that
performs its main function: *Never hold a gun by the
business end.*
ˈbusiness park *n* an area of land specially designed
for business offices, factories, etc.
ˈbusiness studies *n* [U] the study of ECONOMICS
and management.

businesslike /ˈbɪznəslaɪk/ *adj* serious; efficient:
*Negotiations were conducted in a businesslike man-
ner.*

businessman /ˈbɪznəsmæn, -mən/ *n* (*pl* **-men**
/-mən/; *fem* **businesswoman** /-wʊmən/, *pl* **-women**
/-ˈwɪmɪn/) **1** a person working in business, esp the
manager of a company. **2** a person who is skilful in
business and financial matters: *I ought to have got a
better price for the car but I'm not a very good
businessman.* ⇨ note at GENDER.

busk /bʌsk/ *v* [V] (*Brit infml*) to perform music, etc
in a public place as a way of earning money from
people passing by. ▶ **busker** *n*: *buskers in the streets
of Paris.* **busking** *n* [U].

busman /ˈbʌsmən/ *n* **IDM** **a busman's** ˈholiday a
holiday spent doing the same thing that one does at
work.

bust¹ /bʌst/ *n* **1** a SCULPTURE of a person's head,

shoulders and chest. **2(a)** a woman's breasts; the
BOSOM(1a). (**b**) the measurement round a woman's
chest and back: *What is your bust size, madam?*
▶ **busty** *adj* (of a woman) having large breasts.

bust² /bʌst/ *v* (*pt, pp* **bust** or **busted**) (*infml*) **1** to
break or burst sth: [Vn] *I dropped my camera on the
pavement and bust it.* **2** ~ **sth/sb** (**for sth**) (of the
police) to RAID(3) and search a place or arrest sb:
[Vnpr] *Mickey's been busted for drugs.* [also Vn]. **3**
(*esp US*) to reduce sb to a lower military rank; to
DEMOTE sb: [Vn, Vnpr] *He was busted (to corporal)
for being absent without leave.* **PHRV** ˌbust ˈup
(*infml*) (esp of a couple) to quarrel and separate:
They bust up after five years of marriage. ˌbust sth
ˈup to cause sth to end by disturbing or ruining it:
bust up a meeting ○ *It was his drinking that busted
up their marriage.*
▶ **bust** *n* a RAID(3) or ARREST(1) by the police: *a
drugs bust.*
bust *adj* [pred] (*infml*) **1** broken; not working: *My
watch is bust.* ○ *I tried to make a call but the phone
was bust.* **2** (of a person or business) unable to
continue operating because of lack of money; BANK-
RUPT *adj*(1): *The way things are going, their firm will
be bust in a few months.* **IDM** **go** ˈbust (of a person
or a business) to be unable to continue operating
because of lack of money; to become BANKRUPT *adj*
(1): *He/His company went bust owing thousands of
pounds.*
■ ˈbust-up *n* (*Brit*) **1** a noisy quarrel: *They've had a
bust-up and are no longer speaking to each other.* **2**
the end of a relationship, esp between partners: *The
bust-up of their marriage was a rather nasty affair.*

buster /ˈbʌstə(r)/ *n* (*infml esp US*) **1** (*usu derog*)
(used as a form of address to a man): *Get lost,
buster!* **2** (esp in compounds) a person who breaks
sth up or stops sth: *crime busters.*

bustle¹ /ˈbʌsl/ *v* **1** to move or make sb move in a
busy or hurried way in the specified direction: [Vp]
I could hear him bustling about in the kitchen. [Vnp]
She bustled the children off to school. [also
V, Vpr, Vn, Vnpr]. **2** ~ (**with sth**) (of a place) to be
full of noise, activity, etc: [V] *a bustling street/town/
market* [Vpr] *The city centre was bustling with life.*
▶ **bustle** *n* [U] excited, intense and noisy activity:
the hustle and bustle of city life.

bustle² /ˈbʌsl/ *n* (formerly) a frame or padding (PAD¹
1) worn under a woman's skirt and used for holding
it out at the back.

busy /ˈbɪzi/ *adj* (**-ier, -iest**) **1** ~ (**at/with sth**); ~
(**doing sth**) (**a**) having much to do: *We've been
terribly busy at work recently.* ○ *Doctors are busy
people.* (**b**) occupied with sth; working on sth: *Could
I have a word with you, if you're not too busy?* ○
Please go away — can't you see I'm busy? ○ *She's busy
at/with her homework.* ○ *He was busy writing letters.*
○ *We've only got an hour to do the job, so we'd better
get busy* (ie start working). **2** full of activity: *a busy
day/life/time of year* ○ *a busy office/street/town* ○
Victoria is one of London's busiest stations. ○ *The big
stores are very busy at Christmas.* **3** (*esp US*) (of a
telephone) being used; ENGAGED(2). **4** (of a picture
or design) too full of detail: *This wallpaper is too
busy for the bedroom.* **IDM** (**as) busy as a** ˈbee very
busy (and happy to be so): *The children are busy as
bees, helping their mother in the garden.*
▶ **busily** *adv*: *busily engaged on a new project.*
busy *v* (*pt, pp* **busied**) ~ **oneself** (**with sth**); ~
oneself (**in/with**) **doing sth** to occupy oneself in an
active way or keep oneself busy with sth: [Vnpr]
busy oneself in the garden/with the housework
[Vn.ing] *He busied himself cooking the dinner.*

busybody /ˈbɪzibɒdi/ *n* (*derog*) a person who interferes in other people's affairs: *He's an interfering
busybody!*

but¹ /bət; *strong form* bʌt/ *conj* (often used to introduce a word or phrase contrasting with or qualifying what has gone before) **1** on the contrary; in contrast: *You've bought the wrong shirt. It's not the red one I wanted but the blue one.* ∘ *Tom went to the party, but his brother didn't.* ∘ *He doesn't like music but his wife does.* **2** however; in spite of this: *She cut her knee badly, but didn't cry.* ∘ *I'd love to go to the theatre tonight, but I'm too busy.* ∘ *The restaurant serves cheap but excellent food.* ∘ *He's hard-working, but not very clever.* **3** and at the same time; and on the other hand also: *He was tired but happy after the long walk.* **4** (used after an negative statement to introduce what is really the case) instead: *It isn't that he tells lies but that he exaggerates.* **5** except; otherwise than: *I had no alternative but to sign the contract.* **6** (used when expressing a sudden strong feeling, such as anger, pleasure, shock, etc): *'I'll give you ten pounds to repair the damage.' 'But that's not nearly enough!'* ∘ *'I'm getting married.' 'But that's wonderful!'* ∘ *But that's just not possible!* **7** (used before repeating a word in order to emphasize it): *Nothing, but nothing will make me change my mind.* **8** (used when expressing regret for what one is going to say): *I'm sorry but there's nothing we can do to help you.* **9** (*dated or fml*) (usu after a negative) without the result that ...; without it also being the case that ...: *I never pass my old house but I think of the happy years I spent there.* **IDM** **but then 1** on the other hand; however: *The result looks inevitable. But then, anything can happen in football.* **2** (used before a statement that explains or gives a reason for what has just been stated): *He speaks very good French — but then he did live in Paris for three years.* **not only ... but also ...** (used for emphasis) both ... and ...: *He is not only arrogant but also selfish.*

but² /bət; *strong form* bʌt/ *prep* (used after the negatives *nobody, none, nowhere,* etc, the question words *who, where,* etc, and also *all, everyone, anyone,* etc) except sb/sth; apart from sb/sth; other than sb/sth: *The problem is anything but easy.* ∘ *Everyone was there but him.* ∘ *Nobody but you could be so selfish.* ∘ *Nothing but trouble will come of this plan.* **IDM** **but for sb/sth** /bʌt fə/ except for sb/sth; without sb/sth; if it weren't/hadn't been for sb/sth: *But for the rain we would have had a nice holiday.* ∘ *But for the safety-belt I wouldn't be alive today.*

but³ /bət; *strong form* bʌt/ *adv* (*esp dated or fml*) only: *He's but a boy.* ∘ *If I had but known she was ill, I would have visited her.* ∘ *I don't think we'll succeed. Still, we can but try.* **IDM** **one cannot/could not but ...** (*fml*) one can only ...; one must ...: *It was a rash thing to do, yet one cannot but admire his courage.* ∘ *I could not but admit that he was right and I was wrong.*

but⁴ /bʌt/ *n* an objection; an argument against sth: *It's your duty to do it, so let's have no buts about it.* ∘ *There's no time for **ifs and buts** — you must decide now.*

butane /ˈbjuːteɪn/ *n* [U] a gas produced from PETROLEUM, used in liquid form as a fuel for cooking, heating, lighting, etc.

butch /bʊtʃ/ *adj* (*infml*) **1** (*often derog*) (of a woman) having a MASCULINE appearance and way of behaving; like a man. **2** (*often approv*) (of a man) MASCULINE in an exaggerated or aggressive way.

butcher /ˈbʊtʃə(r)/ *n* **1** a person whose job is cutting up and selling meat in a shop or killing animals for this: *Arthur Wilson, Family Butcher* (eg on a shop sign) ∘ *buy meat at the butcher's (shop).* **2** a person who kills people in a cruel and violent way: *a mindless butcher of innocent people.*
▶ **butcher** *v* [Vn] **1** to kill and prepare animals for meat. **2** (*derog*) to kill people in a cruel and violent way: *Women and children were butchered by the rebels.* **3** to make a mess of sth; to ruin

sth by doing it very badly: *None of the cast can act at all — they're butchering the play.*
butchery *n* [U] **1** a butcher's work. **2** cruel and violent killing.

butler /ˈbʌtlə(r)/ *n* the chief male servant of a house.

butt¹ /bʌt/ *v* **1** to hit sb/sth deliberately with the forehead or horns: [Vnpr] *butt sb in the stomach* [also Vn]. **2** to hit one's head on sth: [Vnpr] *He butted his head against the shelf as he was getting up.* **PHRV** **butt ˈin (on sb/sth)** (*infml*) to interrupt sb/sth or interfere in sth: *Don't butt in like that when I'm speaking.* ∘ *May I butt in on your conversation?*
▶ **butt** *n* a deliberate hit with the forehead or horns: *give sb a head butt.*

butt² /bʌt/ *n* a person or thing that is mocked; the target of cruel humour: *be the butt of everyone's jokes.*

butt³ /bʌt/ *n* **1** the thicker end of certain tools or weapons: *a rifle butt.* ⇨ picture at GUN. **2** the short piece at the end of a CIGAR or cigarette that is left when it has been smoked; a STUB: *an ashtray full of butts.* **3** (*infml esp US*) the buttocks (BUTTOCK); the bottom(3): *Get off your butt and do some work!*

butt⁴ /bʌt/ *n* a large barrel for storing or collecting liquid: *a water butt.*

butter /ˈbʌtə(r)/ *n* [U] **1** a pale yellow fat, made from cream, that is spread on bread, etc or used in cooking: *Would you like some more bread and butter?* ∘ *Should I use oil or butter for frying the onions?* **2** (in compounds) a similar thick food substance made from the specified material: *peanut butter.* **IDM** **(look as if / as though) butter would not melt in one's ˈmouth** to appear innocent, kind, gentle, etc although one is probably not. **like a knife through butter** ⇨ KNIFE.
▶ **butter** *v* to spread or put butter on sth, esp bread or a similar type of food; to serve sth with butter: [Vn] *(hot) buttered toast* ∘ *buttered carrots.* **IDM** **know which side one's bread is buttered** ⇨ KNOW. **PHRV** **butter sb up** (*infml*) to be extremely pleasant to sb in order to get sth from them: *I've seen you buttering up the boss!*
buttery *adj* like, containing or covered with butter.

butter-bean /ˈbʌtə biːn/ *n* a large pale yellow type of bean, often dried before being sold.

buttercup /ˈbʌtəkʌp/ *n* a wild plant with bright yellow flowers shaped like small cups. ⇨ picture at FLOWER.

butter-fingers /ˈbʌtəfɪŋgəz/ *n* (*pl* unchanged) (*infml*) (often as a form of address) a person who is likely to drop things.

the life cycle of a butterfly

antennae

butterfly

wing

caterpillar   chrysalis

butterfly /ˈbʌtəflaɪ/ *n* **1** [C] an insect with a long thin body and four usu brightly coloured wings. ⇨ picture. **2** [C] a person with a foolish or CAREFREE attitude to life: *a social butterfly.* **3** (also **ˈbutterfly stroke**) [sing] a way of swimming on one's front in which both arms are raised and lifted forwards at the same time while the legs move up and down together: *doing (the) butterfly.* **IDM** **have 'butter-flies (in one's stomach)** (*infml*) to have a nervous feeling in one's stomach before doing sth.

buttermilk /'bʌtəmɪlk/ n [U] the liquid that remains after butter has been separated from milk.

butterscotch /'bʌtəskɒtʃ/ n [U] a hard sweet made by boiling butter and sugar together.

buttock /'bʌtək/ n (esp *pl*) either of the two round parts of the body on which a person sits: *the left/right buttock* ∘ *large buttocks.* ⇨ picture at HUMAN.

button /'bʌtn/ n **1** a small, usu round, piece of metal, plastic, etc, that is sewn onto a piece of clothing. Buttons are used for fastening parts of clothes together or for decoration: *a coat/jacket/shirt/trouser button* ∘ *lose a button* ∘ *sew on a new button* ∘ *do one's buttons up.* ⇨ picture at JACKET. **2** a small part of a machine, etc that is pressed in order to operate it: *Which button do I press to turn the radio on?* See also PUSH-BUTTON. **IDM** **bright as a button** ⇨ BRIGHT. **on the 'button** (*US infml*) exactly correct: *You've got it on the button!*
▶ **button** v ~ **sth (up)** to fasten sth with buttons: [Vn, Vnp] *button (up) one's coat/jacket/shirt.* (**b**) ~ **(up)** to be fastened with buttons: [V, Vp] *This dress buttons (up) at the back.* **PHRV** **button sth 'up** (*infml*) to complete sth successfully: *The deal should be all buttoned up by tomorrow.* **button-down 'collar** n a collar with ends that are fastened to the shirt with buttons. **buttoned 'up** adj (*Brit infml*) silent and shy: *I've never met anyone so buttoned up.*
■ **button 'mushroom** n a small young MUSHROOM.

buttonhole /'bʌtnhəʊl/ n **1** a hole through which a button is passed to fasten clothing. ⇨ picture at JACKET. **2** a flower worn in the buttonhole of a coat or jacket.
▶ **buttonhole** v to make sb stop and listen, often against their will, to what one wants to say: [Vn] *He buttonholed me just as I was going for lunch.*

buttress /'bʌtrəs/ n **1** a structure, usu of stone or brick, built against a wall to support it. ⇨ picture at CHURCH. **2** a thing or person that supports or strengthens sth, or protects against sth: *The government's tight fiscal policy acts as a buttress against inflation.*
▶ **buttress** v to support or strengthen sth: [Vn] *You need more facts to buttress your argument.*

butty /'bʌti/ n (*Brit infml*) a sandwich: *jam/bacon butties.*

buxom /'bʌksəm/ adj (*usu approv*) (of women) looking fat and healthy in an attractive way, usu with large breasts.

buy /baɪ/ v (*pt, pp* **bought** /bɔːt/) **1** ~ **sth (for sb)** to obtain sth by paying money for it: [V] *House prices are low; it's a good time to buy.* [Vn] *Where did you buy that coat?* [Vn-adj] *Did you buy your car new or second-hand?* [Vnpr] *I bought this watch (from a friend) for £10.* ∘ *She's buying a present for her boyfriend.* [Vnn] *I must buy myself a new shirt.* **2** (of money) to be able to obtain sth: [Vn] *He gave his children the best education that money could buy.* ∘ *Money can't buy happiness.* ∘ *A dollar today buys much less than it did a year ago.* **3** to persuade sb to do sth, esp sth dishonest, for one in return for money, etc; to BRIBE sb: [Vn] *He can't be bought* (ie is too honest to accept money in this way). **4** (usu passive) to obtain sth by losing sth else of great value: [Vn] *His fame was bought at the expense of health and happiness.* ∘ *The victory was dearly bought* (ie Many people were killed to achieve it). **5** (*infml*) to accept sth as true; to believe sth: [Vn] *No one will buy that excuse.* **IDM** **buy a pig in a 'poke** to buy sth without seeing it or knowing if it is satisfactory. **buy 'time** to do sth in order to delay an event, a decision, etc: *The union leaders are trying to buy time by prolonging the negotiations.* **sell sb / buy a pup** ⇨ PUP. **PHRV** **buy sth 'in** to buy a good supply of sth: *buy in coal for the winter.* **buy 'into**

sth to buy shares (SHARE¹ 3) in a company: *We bought into the Xerox Company at the right time.* **buy sb 'off** to pay sb money to stop them acting against one, causing trouble, etc: *Unless he drops the charge we'll have to buy him off.* **buy sb 'out** to pay sb for their share in a business, usu in order to become the only owner of it oneself: *Having bought out all his partners he now owns the whole company.* **buy sth 'up** to buy all or as much as possible of sth: *A New York businessman has bought up the entire company.*
▶ **buy** n an act of buying sth; a thing bought or for sale: *a good buy* (ie a thing that is of good quality and not too expensive) ∘ *Best buys of the week are carrots and cabbages, which are plentiful and cheap.*
buyer n **1** a person who buys: *Have you found a buyer for your house?* **2** a person whose job is to choose and buy stock for a large shop. **buyer's 'market** n a situation in which there is a lot of sth for sale, making prices low and giving buyers an advantage.
■ **'buy-out** n an act of getting control of a company by buying enough or all of its shares (SHARE¹ 3): *a management buy-out.*

buzz /bʌz/ v **1** [V] (**a**) to make a continuous sound like that made by a bee: *flies and wasps buzzing round a jar of jam.* (**b**) (of the ears) to be filled with such a sound: *My ears began buzzing as the aeroplane rose higher.* **2** ~ **(with sth)** to be full of sth, eg excited talk, activity, ideas: [V] *The courtroom buzzed as the defendant was led in.* [Vpr] *The village was buzzing with preparations for the Queen's visit.* ∘ *The office is buzzing with rumours.* ∘ *My head was buzzing with thoughts of the day's events.* **3** ~ **(for)** sb to call sb to come with a buzzer: [Vn, Vpr] *The doctor buzzed (for) the next patient.* **4** (*infml*) to telephone sb: [Vn] *I'll buzz you at work.* **5** (of an aircraft) to fly close to sb/sth as a warning: [Vn] *Two fighters buzzed the convoy as it approached the coast.* **PHRV** **buzz a'bout/a'round (sth)** to move quickly and busily: *She buzzed around the kitchen making preparations for the party.* **buzz 'off** (*infml*) (esp imperative) to go away: *Just buzz off and leave me alone!*
▶ **buzz** n **1** [C] a continuous sound, like the one a bee makes: *the angry buzz of a bee/wasp.* **2** [C] the sound of a buzzer: *I think I heard a buzz at the door.* **3** [sing] (**a**) the low sound of a lot of people talking: *the buzz of voices in the crowded room.* (**b**) (*infml*) a rumour: *There's a buzz going round that the boss has resigned.* **4** [sing] (*infml*) (**a**) a feeling of pleasure or excitement; a THRILL: *Flying gives me a real buzz.* ∘ *She gets a terrific buzz from her new job.* (**b**) an exciting atmosphere: *There's a creative buzz about the place.* **IDM** **give sb a 'buzz** (*infml*) to make a telephone call to sb.
buzzer n an electrical device that produces a buzzing sound as a signal: *Have you set the buzzer on the cooker?*
■ **'buzz-word** n a word or phrase, esp related to a particular subject, that becomes fashionable and popular: *It was an advertising buzz-word of the eighties.* Compare VOGUE-WORD.

buzzard /'bʌzəd/ n a type of large HAWK¹(1).

by¹ /baɪ/ prep **1** near sb/sth; at the side of sb/sth; beside sb/sth: *a house by the church/river/railway* ∘ *The telephone is by the window.* ∘ *Come and sit by me.* ∘ *We had a day by the sea.* **2** (usu after a passive v, used for showing who or what does, creates or causes sth): *a play (written) by Shakespeare* ∘ *a church designed by Wren* ∘ *He was arrested by the police.* ∘ *a decision by the trade unions* ∘ *Who is that record by?* ∘ *run over by a bus* ∘ *struck by lightning.* **3**(**a**) with the action of doing sth: *Let me begin by saying ...* ∘ *He shocked the whole company by resigning.* (**b**) through the means of sth/doing sth: *The room is* *heated by gas/oil.* ○ *May I pay by cheque?* ○ *I will contact you by letter/telephone.* ○ *He earns his living by writing.* ○ *You switch the radio on by pressing this button.* ○ *By working hard he gained rapid promotion.* (**c**) (without *the*) as a result of sth; because of sth; through sth: *meet by chance* ○ *achieve sth by skill/determination* ○ *do sth by mistake/accident* ○ *The coroner's verdict was 'death by misadventure'.* **4** (indicating a means of transport or a route taken): *travel by bus/car/plane* ○ *travel by air/land/sea.* **5** not later than a specified time; before: *Can you finish the work by five o'clock/tomorrow/next Monday?* ○ *By this time next week we'll be in New York.* ○ *He ought to have arrived by now/by this time.* ○ *By the time (that) this letter reaches you I will have left the country.* **6** past sb/sth: *He walked by me without speaking.* ○ *I go by the church every morning on my way to work.* **7** (showing the route taken) passing through sth or a place: *He entered by the back door.* ○ *We travelled to Rome by Milan and Florence.* ○ *We came by country roads, not by the motorway.* **8** (usu without *the*) during sth: *travel by day/night* ○ *She sleeps by day and works by night.* ○ *The view is best seen by daylight/moonlight.* **9** to the amount or extent specified: *The bullet missed him by two inches.* ○ *House prices went up by 10%.* ○ *It would be better by far* (ie much better) *to...* **10**(**a**) from what sth shows; according to sth: *By my watch it is two o'clock.* ○ *Judging by appearances can be misleading.* ○ *I could tell by the look on her face that something terrible had happened.* (**b**) from what sth says; according to sth: *play a game by the rules* ○ *By law, you are a child until you are 18.* ○ *(fml) by your leave* (ie with your permission). **11** (indicating a part of the body, or an item of clothing touched, held, etc): *take sb by the hand* ○ *seize sb by the hair/collar/lapel* ○ *grab sb by the scruff of the neck.* **12** (with *the*, indicating a standard period or quantity): *rent a car by the day/week/month* ○ *sell eggs by the dozen/material by the yard/coal by the ton* ○ *pay sb by the day/hour* ○ *We sell ice-creams by the thousand in the summer.* **13** at the rate or in the groups specified: *improving day by day/little by little/bit by bit* ○ *The children came in two by two.* **14** (used for giving more information about sb's background(4) or character): *be German by birth/a lawyer by profession/an artist by nature.* **15** (when swearing) in the name of sb/sth: *By God!* ○ *I swear by Almighty God...* / *by all that I hold dear...* **16**(**a**) (showing the measurements of sth): *The room measures fifteen feet by twenty feet.* (**b**) (when multiplying or dividing): *6 (multiplied) by 2 equals 12.* ○ *6 (divided) by 2 equals 3.* **IDM** **by the 'by/'bye** = BY THE WAY (WAY¹). **have/keep sth by one** to have sth close to one; to keep sth where it is easy to reach: *I keep a dictionary by me when I'm doing crosswords.*

by² /baɪ/ *adv part* **1** past: *drive/go/run/walk by* ○ *He hurried by without speaking to me.* ○ *Excuse me, I can't get by.* ○ *Time goes by so quickly.* **2** near: *He lives close/near by.* **3** aside; in reserve²(1): *lay/put/set sth by* ○ *I always keep a bottle of wine by in case friends call round.* **IDM** **by and 'by** (*dated*) before long; soon: *By and by she met an old man with a beard.* **by and large** ⇨ LARGE.

by- (also **bye-**) *pref* (with *ns* and *vs*) **1** of secondary importance; INCIDENTAL: *by-product* ○ *bye-law.* **2** near: *bystander* ○ *bypass.*

bye¹ /baɪ/ *n* (*sport*) **1** (in cricket) a run²(9) scored from a ball that passes the batsman without being hit by him. **2** a situation in which a player has no opponent in one part of a contest and proceeds to the next part as if he or she had won: *She has a bye into the next round.*

bye² /baɪ/ (also **bye-bye** /ˌbaɪˈbaɪ/) *interj* (*infml*) goodbye: *Bye(-bye)! See you next week.*

bye-byes /ˈbaɪbaɪz/ (also **bye-bye** /ˈbaɪbaɪ/) *n* [U] (*Brit*) (used esp when speaking to young children) sleep: *It's time to go to/time for bye-byes!* **IDM** **go bye-bye** (*US*) (used esp when speaking to young children) **1** to go to sleep. **2** to go away; to leave.

by-election /ˈbaɪ ɪlekʃn/ *n* (*Brit*) an election of a new Member of Parliament in a single CONSTITUENCY whose previous member has died or resigned. Compare GENERAL ELECTION.

bygone /ˈbaɪɡɒn/ *adj* [attrib] past: *a bygone age* ○ *in bygone days.*
▶ **bygones** *n* [pl] **IDM** **let ˌbygones be ˈbygones** to forgive and forget past disagreements.

by-law /ˈbaɪ lɔː/ *n* **1** (also **'bye-law**) (*Brit*) a law or regulation made by a local authority(2) or council, not a central one. **2** (*US*) a regulation of a club or company.

byline /ˈbaɪlaɪn/ *n* a line at the beginning or end of an article in a newspaper, etc, giving the writer's name.

bypass /ˈbaɪpɑːs; *US* -pæs/ *n* **1** a road that passes round a city, busy area, etc so that traffic need not go through it: *If we take the bypass we'll avoid the town centre.* **2** (*medical*) a different route for blood to circulate through, eg during an operation(1) on the heart: *bypass surgery.*
▶ **bypass** *v* **1** to go round or avoid sth, using a bypass: [Vn] *We managed to bypass the shopping centre by taking side-streets.* ○ (*fig*) *bypass a difficulty/problem.* **2** to provide a town, etc with a bypass: [Vn] *a plan to bypass the town centre.* **3** to ignore a rule, procedure, etc or not ask for the usual permission, in order to get sth done quickly: [Vn] *She bypassed her colleagues on the board and went ahead with the deal.*

byplay /ˈbaɪpleɪ/ *n* [U] (in the theatre) action(2) that is less important than that of the main story, but is going on at the same time: (*fig*) *While the chairman was speaking, two committee members were engaged in heated byplay at the end of the table.*

by-product /ˈbaɪ prɒdʌkt/ *n* **1** a substance produced during the making of sth else: *Ammonia, coal tar and coke are all by-products obtained in the manufacture of coal gas.* **2** a thing that happens, often unexpectedly, as a result of sth else: *An increase in crime is one of the by-products of unemployment.*

byroad /ˈbaɪrəʊd/ (*US* also **back road**) *n* a minor road: *take the byroads.*

bystander /ˈbaɪstændə(r)/ *n* a person standing near, but not taking part, when sth happens; an ONLOOKER: *an innocent bystander* ○ *Police interviewed several bystanders after the accident.*

byte /baɪt/ *n* (*computing*) a unit of information stored in a computer, equal to eight bits (BIT³). A computer's memory is measured in bytes.

byway /ˈbaɪweɪ/ *n* **1** [C] = BYROAD: *highways and byways.* **2** **byways** [pl] the less important or well-known areas of a subject: *the byways of German literature.*

byword /ˈbaɪwɜːd/ *n* **1** ~ **for sth** a person or thing considered to be a well-known or typical example of a quality: *His name has become a byword for cruelty.* ○ *The firm is a byword for excellence.* **2** a common word or expression(3).

Byzantine /baɪˈzæntaɪn, bɪ-, -tiːn; *US* ˈbɪzəntiːn/ *adj* **1** of Byzantium or the Eastern Roman Empire. **2** of or relating to the Byzantine style of architecture. **3** (*usu derog*) like Byzantine politics, ie complicated, secret and difficult to change: *an organization of Byzantine complexity.*

[V.speech] = verb + direct speech   [V.*that*] = verb + *that* clause   [V.*wh*] = verb + *who, how*, etc clause

Cc

C¹ (also **c**) /siː/ n (pl **C's, c's** /siːz/) **1** the third letter of the English alphabet: *'Cat' starts with (a) C/'C'.* **2** **C** (*music*) the first note in the scale¹(6) of C major. **3** **C** an academic mark indicating the third highest standard: *get (a) C/'C' in physics.*

C² abbr **1** Cape: *C Horn* (eg on a map). **2** Celsius; centigrade: *Water freezes at 0°C.* Compare F² 1. **3** (also **c**) the Roman numeral (ROMAN) for 100 (Latin *centum*). **4** (also *symb* ©) copyright: *© Oxford University Press 1986.*

c abbr **1** cent(s). **2** century(1b): *in the 19th c ○ a c19 church.* Compare CENT² abbr. **3** (also **ca**) (esp before dates) about; approximately (Latin *circa*): *c1890.*

cab /kæb/ n **1** = TAXI: *We took a cab/went by cab to the hospital.* **2** the place where the driver sits in eg a train or lorry.
■ **'cab-driver** n the driver of a cab(1).

cabal /kə'bæl/ n **(a)** [C] a secret political plot. **(b)** [CGp] a group of people involved in this.

cabaret /'kæbəreɪ; US ,kæbə'reɪ/ n **1** [U,C] entertainment (esp singing or dancing) provided in a restaurant or club while the customers are eating or drinking: *a cabaret act/band/artiste.* **2** [C] a restaurant or club that provides cabaret entertainment: *a singer in a cabaret.*

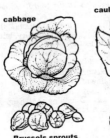

cabbage · cauliflower · cabbage · Brussels sprouts · broccoli

cabbage /'kæbɪdʒ/ n **1(a)** [C] a round vegetable with green or purple leaves. ⇨ picture. **(b)** [U] these leaves eaten as food, usu cooked. **2** [C] (*Brit infml*) **(a)** (*derog*) a dull person without interests or ambition. **(b)** (*offensive*) a person who has suffered severe brain damage and is completely dependent on others.

cabby (also **cabbie**) /'kæbi/ n (*infml*) the driver of a taxi.

caber /'keɪbə(r)/ n a long heavy wooden pole. It is thrown in the air as a trial of strength in the Scottish sport of **tossing the caber.**

cabin /'kæbɪn/ n **1(a)** a small room in a ship: *book a cabin on a boat.* **(b)** the area for passengers in an aircraft. **2** a small house or shelter, usu made of wood: *a log cabin in the woods.*
■ **'cabin-boy** n a boy who works as a servant on a ship.
'cabin class n [U] the second highest standard of accommodation on a ship.
cabin crew n [CGp] the crew members on an aircraft who attend to the passengers.
'cabin cruiser n = CRUISER 2.

cabinet /'kæbɪnət/ n **1** [C] a piece of furniture with drawers or shelves for storing or displaying things: *a 'filing cabinet ○ a 'medicine cabinet ○ a 'china cabinet.* **2** [C] a case or container for a radio, HI-FI system, television, etc. **3** (also **the Cabinet** [CGp]) a group of the most important government ministers or advisers to a president, responsible for deciding on government administration and policy: *Members of the British Cabinet are chosen by the prime minister. ○ a cabinet minister/meeting/reshuffle.*
■ **'cabinet-maker** n a person who makes fine wooden furniture.

cable /'keɪbl/ n **1(a)** [U] thick strong rope, esp of twisted wires, used for tying up ships, supporting bridges, etc. **(b)** [C] a length of this. **2** [C,U] **(a)** a set of wires for carrying electricity or electrical signals: *overhead/underground cables.* **(b)** (also **cablegram**) a message sent, usu abroad, in this way, and received in printed form: *send sb/receive a cable.* Compare TELEGRAM.
▶ **cable** v **~ (to sb) (from ...)** to send a cable(2b) to sb: [V.*that,* Vpr.*that*] *She cabled (to her husband) that she would arrive on 15 May.* [also V, Vpr]. **(b)** to inform sb by cable(2b): [Vn] *Don't forget to cable us as soon as you arrive.* [also Vn.*that*]. **(c)** **~ sth (to sb)** to send money, a message, etc by cable(2b): [Vnpr] *News of his death was cabled to his family.* [also V, Vn-n, Vnpr].
■ **'cable-car** n a vehicle supported and drawn by a moving cable(1b), usu carrying passengers up or down a mountain.
,cable 'railway n a railway on a steep slope along which cars are drawn by a moving cable(1b).
,cable 'television (also **,cable T'V**) n [U] a system of broadcasting television programmes by cable(2a) to individual paying customers.

cablegram /'keɪblgræm/ n = CABLE 2b.

caboodle /kə'buːdl/ n **IDM** **the whole caboodle** ⇨ WHOLE.

caboose /kə'buːs/ n (*US*) a guard's van, esp on a goods train.

cache /kæʃ/ n a hidden store of weapons, food, money, etc: *an arms cache.*

cachet /'kæʃeɪ; US kæ'ʃeɪ/ n [U] respect or admiration; PRESTIGE(1): *Her success in business had earned her a certain cachet in society. ○ a brand name with considerable cachet.*

cackle /'kækl/ n **1** [U] a loud noise that a hen makes, esp after laying an egg: *the cackle of hens/geese.* Compare CLUCK. **2** [C] a harsh unpleasant laugh: *The old woman gave a loud cackle.* **3** [U] noisy talk about unimportant things; CHATTER(1). **IDM** **cut the 'cackle** (*Brit infml*) (esp imperative) to stop talking about irrelevant or unimportant things.
▶ **cackle** v **1** [V] (of a hen) to make a cackle. **2** (of a person) to laugh or talk noisily: [Vp] *cackling away together for hours* [V.speech] *'Don't be ridiculous!' he cackled.* [also V].

cacophony /kə'kɒfəni/ n [U,C usu *sing*] a mixture of loud unpleasant sounds. ▶ **cacophonous** /-nəs/ adj.

cactus /'kæktəs/ n (pl **cactuses** or **cacti** /'kæktaɪ/) any of various types of plant growing in hot dry regions. Cactuses have thick, usu prickly, stems, but no leaves. ⇨ picture.

[Vnn] = verb + noun + noun   [V-adj] = verb + adjective   For more help with verbs, see Study pages **B4–8.**

cactus

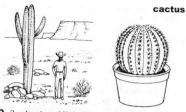

CAD /kæd, ˌsiː eɪ ˈdiː/ *abbr* computer-aided design (using computers to design manufactured goods).

cad /kæd/ *n* (*dated derog*) a man who behaves in a deceitful or dishonest way, esp towards women: *He's no gentleman, he's a cad.*

cadaver /kəˈdævə(r)/ *n* (*esp medical*) a person's dead body; a CORPSE.
▶ **cadaverous** /kəˈdævərəs/ *adj* (of a person) very pale and thin.

caddie (also **caddy**) /ˈkædi/ *n* (in golf) a person who helps a player by carrying her or his clubs during a game.
▶ **caddie** *v* ~ (**for sb**) to act as a caddie: [Vpr] *Would you like me to caddie for you?* [also V].

caddy /ˈkædi/ *n* = TEA-CADDY.

cadence /ˈkeɪdns/ *n* **1** the rise and fall of the voice in speaking: *recite poetry with slow measured cadences.* **2** (*music*) the end of a musical phrase.

cadenza /kəˈdenzə/ *n* (*music*) an elaborate passage played or sung by the soloist (SOLO) in a piece of classical music, esp near the end.

cadet /kəˈdet/ *n* a young person training to become a police officer or an officer in the armed forces: *army/naval/air force cadets* ○ *a police cadet.*

cadge /kædʒ/ *v* ~ (**sth**) (**from sb**) (*sometimes derog*) to get sth from sb by asking, often unfairly: [Vn] *Could I cadge a lift with you?* [Vpr] *He's always cadging meals from his friends.* [also V, Vpr]. ▶ **cadger** *n*.

cadmium /ˈkædmiəm/ *n* [U] (*symb* Cd) a chemical element. Cadmium is a soft bluish-white metal that looks like tin. ⇨ App 7.

cadre /ˈkɑːdə(r); US ˈkædri/ *n* (**a**) a small group of highly trained soldiers, workers, managers, etc: *a local party cadre.* (**b**) a member of such a group: *young revolutionary cadres.*

Caesarean /siˈzeəriən/ (also **Caesarian, Cae,sarean ˈsection, Caesarian section**) *n* a method of delivering a baby by cutting an opening in the mother's body: *It was a difficult birth: she had to have a Caesarean.* ○ *The baby was delivered by Caesarean section.*

caesium (*US* **cesium**) /ˈsiːziəm/ *n* [U] (*symb* Cs) a chemical element. Caesium is a soft metal with a light silver colour. ⇨ App 7.

caesura /siˈzjʊərə; US siˈzuərə/ *n* a pause near the middle of a line of poetry.

café /ˈkæfeɪ; US kæˈfeɪ/ *n* a small restaurant serving cheap meals and drinks. Alcohol is not usu sold in British cafés.

cafeteria /ˌkæfəˈtɪəriə/ *n* a restaurant (in Britain found esp in a factory or college) in which customers collect their meals on trays from a counter.

caff /ˈkæf/ *n* (*Brit sl*) a CAFÉ.

caffeine /ˈkæfiːn/ *n* [U] a drug found in tea leaves and coffee beans that stimulates the body.

caftan (also **kaftan**) /ˈkæftæn/ *n* **1** a long loose garment, usu with a belt at the waist, worn by men in the Near East. **2** a woman's long loose dress.

cage /keɪdʒ/ *n* **1** a structure made of bars or wires in which birds or animals are kept or carried: *a bird singing in a cage* ○ *a birdcage.* **2** an enclosed platform used to raise and lower people and equipment in a mine. See also RIBCAGE.

▶ **cage** *v* (usu passive) to put or keep sb/sth in a cage: [Vn] *caged animals in a zoo.* **PHR V** ˌ**cage sb ˈin** to make sb feel that they are in a cage: *I felt terribly caged in in that office.*

cagey /ˈkeɪdʒi/ *adj* (**cagier, cagiest**) ~ (**about sth**) (*infml*) cautious about giving information; secretive: *He's very cagey about his family.* ▶ **cagily** *adv*. **caginess** *n* [U].

cagoule /kəˈɡuːl/ *n* a long light jacket with a HOOD¹(1), worn to give protection from wind and rain.

cahoots /kəˈhuːts/ *n* **IDM** **be in cahoots (with sb)** (*infml*) to be planning sth, esp sth dishonest, with sb: *The two criminals were in cahoots (with each other).*

cairn /keən/ *n* a pile of rough stones built to mark a special place, eg a mountain top or sb's grave.

cajole /kəˈdʒəʊl/ *v* (**a**) ~ **sb** (**into doing sth**) to make sb do sth by cleverly persuading, deceiving or flattering (FLATTER 1) them; to COAX sb: [Vnpr] *She was cajoled into accepting a part in the play.* [also Vn]. (**b**) ~ **sth out of sb** to get information, etc from sb in this way: [Vnpr] *The confession had to be cajoled out of him.* ▶ **cajolery** *n* [U].

cake /keɪk/ *n* **1** [C,U] a sweet food of various sizes and shapes. Cakes are made from a mixture of flour, eggs, butter, sugar, etc that is baked in an oven and usu decorated, eg with cream or ICING: *a sponge cake* ○ *a chocolate cake* ○ *a fruit cake* ○ *a piece/slice of (birthday) cake* ○ *an assortment of fancy cakes* ○ *a cake tin/mix/recipe* ○ *Have some more cake!* **2** [C] any other food mixture cooked in a round flat shape: *fish cakes* ○ *poˈtato cakes.* **3** [C] a shaped or hardened mass of sth: *a cake of soap.* **IDM** **get, want, etc a slice/share of the ˈcake** to get, etc a share of the benefits or profits one has or thinks one has a right to: *The company's profits have risen, and the workers are demanding a larger slice of the cake.* **go/sell like hot cakes** ⇨ HOT. **have one's cake and ˈeat it** (*infml*) (usu in negative sentences) to enjoy the benefits from two different courses of action, etc when only one or the other is possible: *He wants a regular income but doesn't want to work. He can't have his cake and eat it!* **icing on the cake** ⇨ ICING. **a piece of cake** ⇨ PIECE¹. **take the cake** (*US*) = TAKE THE BISCUIT ⇨ BISCUIT.

▶ **cake** *v* **1** ~ **sth** (**in/with sth**) (usu passive) to cover sth thickly with sth soft that becomes hard when dry: [Vnpr] *Her shoes were caked with mud.* [also Vn]. **2** to harden into a solid mass: [V] *Blood from the wound had caked on his face.*

cal *abbr* calorie(s).

calamine /ˈkæləmaɪn/ (also **calamine lotion**) *n* [U] a pink liquid that is put on burnt skin to make it less painful.

calamity /kəˈlæməti/ *n* an event that causes great harm or damage; a disaster: *The earthquake was the worst calamity in the country's history.* ○ (*joc*) *There are worse calamities than failing your driving test.*
▶ **calamitous** /kəˈlæmɪtəs/ *adj* ~ (**to sb/sth**) involving or causing a calamity; disastrous (DISASTER 1a).

calcify /ˈkælsɪfaɪ/ *v* (*pt, pp* **-fied**) to harden or make sth harden with the addition of CALCIUM salts: [Vn] *His arteries were blocked with calcified deposits of cholesterol.* [also V].

calcium /ˈkælsiəm/ *n* [U] (*symb* Ca) a chemical element. Calcium is found as a compound in bones, teeth and chalk. ⇨ App 7.

calculabie /ˈkælkjələbl/ *adj* that can be calculated. Compare INCALCULABLE.

calculate /ˈkælkjuleɪt/ *v* to estimate sth by using numbers or one's judgement; to work sth out: [Vn, V.wh] *calculate the cost of sth/how much sth will cost* [V.wh] *The computer calculates when to switch the heating on.* [V.that] *Scientists have calculated*

C

that the world's population will double by the end of the century. ○ *I calculate that we will reach Washington at about 3 pm.* ○ *calculate that they would agree to the conditions* ○ *(US infml) I calculate* (ie suppose, think) *she's a rich woman.* **IDM** **be calculated to do sth** to be intended or designed to do sth: *This advertisement is calculated to appeal to children.* ○ *His speech was calculated to stir up the crowd.* **PHRV** ¹**calculate on sth/doing sth** to depend or rely on sth : *We can't calculate on (having) good weather for the barbecue.*

▶ **calculated** *adj* with full knowledge of what might happen; deliberate: *a calculated risk/insult/gamble/choice.*

calculating *adj* (*usu derog*) clever at planning things to one's advantage, without caring about other people: *a cold and calculating killer* ○ *a calculating businessman.*

calculation /ˌkælkjuˈleɪʃn/ *n* **1** [C,U] the act, process or result of calculating: *Our calculations show that the firm made a profit of over £1 million last year.* ○ *You're out* (ie You have made a mistake) *in your calculations.* ○ *mathematical/political/mental calculations* ○ *The use of computers in calculation.* **2** [U] (*usu derog*) careful planning for oneself without caring about other people: *an act of cold calculation.*

calculator /ˈkælkjuleɪtə(r)/ *n* a small electronic device for calculating with numbers: *a pocket calculator.*

calculus /ˈkælkjələs/ *n* (*pl* **calculi** /-laɪ/ or **calculuses** /-ləsɪz/) a branch of MATHEMATICS, divided into two parts (**differential calculus** and **integral calculus**), that deals with problems involving rates of variation.

caldron (*esp US*) = CAULDRON.

calendar /ˈkælɪndə(r)/ *n* **1(a)** a chart showing the days, weeks and months of a particular year: *Do you have next year's calendar?* (**b**) a device that can be adjusted to show the date each day: *a desk calendar.* (**c**) (*US*) a daily record of appointments. **2** (*usu sing*) a list of dates or events of a particular type: *The Cup Final is an important date in the sporting calendar.* **3** a system by which time is divided into fixed periods, showing the beginning and end of a year: *the Muslim calendar.* See also THE GREGORIAN CALENDAR.

■ ˌ**calendar** ¹**month** *n* **1** any one of the twelve months of the calendar. Compare LUNAR MONTH. **2** a period of time from a certain date in one month to the same date in the next one.

ˌ**calendar** ¹**year** (also **year**) *n* the period of time from 1 January to 31 December in the same year. See also FINANCIAL YEAR.

calf¹ /kɑːf; *US* kæf/ *n* (*pl* **calves** /kɑːvz; *US* kævz/) **1** [C] (**a**) a young cow. ⇨ picture at COW¹. Compare BULL¹ 1. ⇨ COW¹ 1. (**b**) a young animal of certain species, eg a WHALE or an elephant. Compare BULL¹ 2, COW¹ 2. **2** (also ¹**calfskin**) [U] leather made from the skin of a calf¹(1a). **IDM** (**be**) **in/with** ¹**calf** (of a cow) pregnant.

■ ¹**calf-love** *n* [U] = PUPPY-LOVE.

calf² /kɑːf; *US* kæf/ *n* (*pl* **calves** /kɑːvz; *US* kævz/) the back part of the leg below the knee: *the calf muscle.* ⇨ picture at HUMAN.

calfskin *n* = CALF¹ 2.

calibrate /ˈkælɪbreɪt/ *v* [Vn] to mark or correct the units of measurement on eg the scale of a THERMOMETER or some other measuring instrument.

▶ **calibration** /ˌkælɪˈbreɪʃn/ *n* **1** [U] the action of calibrating. **2** [C] the units of measurement marked on a THERMOMETER, etc.

calibre (*US* **caliber**) /ˈkælɪbə(r)/ *n* **1** [C] the width of the inside of a tube or the barrel(2) of a gun. **2** [U] quality; ability; distinction(2): *His work is of a pretty high/low calibre.* ○ *The firm needs more people of your calibre.*

calico /ˈkælɪkəʊ/ *n* (*pl* **-oes**; *US* **-os**) [U,C] **1** (*esp Brit*) a type of cotton cloth, esp plain white. **2** (*esp US*) a printed cotton fabric.

caliper = CALLIPER.

caliph /ˈkeɪlɪf/ *n* a title used, esp formerly, by Muslim civil and religious rulers.

▶ **caliphate** /ˈkælɪfeɪt/ *n* the position, rule or territory of a caliph.

calisthenics = CALLISTHENICS.

call¹ /kɔːl/ *v* **1** ~ (**out**) **to sb** (**for sth**); ~ (**sth**) (**out**) to say sth loudly to attract sb's attention; to shout; to cry: [V] *I thought I heard sb calling.* [V, Vp, Vn, Vnp] *Why didn't you come when I called (out) (your name)?* [Vpr] *She called to her father for help.* [Vp] *The injured soldiers called out in pain.* [Vnp] *The teacher called the children's names out* (eg to check that they were all present). [V.speech] *'Come back!' she called.* **2** [V] (of a bird or an animal) to make its characteristic cry. **3** to order or ask sb/sth to come to a specified place by shouting, writing, making a telephone call, etc; to summon sb/sth: [Vn] *call the fire department/the police/a doctor/an ambulance* [Vn, Vnp] *Call the children (in): it's time for lunch.* [Vnpr] *Several candidates were called for a second interview.* [Vnpr, Vnp] *The doctor has been called (away) to an urgent case.* [Vnp] *The ambassador was called back to London by the prime minister.* [Vn, Vnn] *I have to be at the airport in 20 minutes — please call (me) a taxi.* **4(a)** ~ (**in/round**) (**on sb/at...**) (**for sb/sth**) (*esp Brit*) to make a short visit; to go to sb's house, etc to get sth or to go somewhere with them: [Vpr, Vp] *Let's call (in) on John/at John's house.* [V, Vp, Vpr] *He was out when I called (round) (to see him).* [Vpr] *I'll call for her* (ie collect) *you at 7 o'clock.* [Vp] *Will you call in at the supermarket for some eggs and milk?* ⇨ note at VISIT. (**b**) ~ **at...** (of a train, etc) to stop at a place: [Vpr] *The train on platform 1 is for London, calling at Didcot and Reading.* **5** to make a telephone call to sb: [Vp] *I'll call again later.* [Vp] *I called in to the office to tell them I was ill.* ○ *She said she'd call back.* [Vn] *My brother called me (from Germany) last night.* **6** to order sth to happen; to announce sth: [Vn] *call a meeting/an election/a strike.* **7** to wake sb: [Vn] *Please call me at 7 o'clock tomorrow morning.* **8(a)** to describe or address sb/sth as sth; to name sb/sth: [Vn-adj] *How dare you call me fat!* [Vn-n] *His name is Richard but we call him Dick.* ○ *What was the book called?* ○ (*ironic*) *He hasn't had anything published and he calls himself a writer!* (**b**) to consider sb/sth to be sth; to regard sb/sth as sth: [Vn-adj] *I call his behaviour mean and selfish.* [Vn-n] *I would never call German an easy language.* ○ *How can you be so unkind and still call yourself my friend?* ○ *She has nothing she can call her own* (ie claim as her property). ○ *You owe me £5.04 — let's call it £5* (ie settle the sum at £5). **9** (in card-games) to declare what one proposes to win, etc; to BID²(4): [V] *Have you called yet?* [Vn] *Who called hearts?* **10** (in games) to say which side of a coin one thinks will face upwards after it is thrown: [Vn] *call heads/tails* [also Y]. **IDM** **be/feel called to (do) sth** to be/feel summoned to a particular profession: *be called to the bar* (ie become a BARRISTER) ○ *feel called to the ministry/the priesthood.* **bring/call sb/sth to mind** ⇨ MIND¹. **call sb's attention to sth** (*fml*) to invite sb to examine or think carefully about sth: *She called their attention to the lack of proper facilities.* **call sb's** ¹**bluff** to challenge sb to do what they are threatening to do (believing that they will not dare to do it). **call a** ¹**halt (to sth)** to stop work, a habit, etc: *Let's call a halt (to the meeting) and continue tomorrow.* **call sth into** ¹**play** to make use of sth; to give scope for sth: *Chess is a game that calls into play all one's powers of concentration.* **call sth into** ¹**question** to doubt sth or make others doubt sth: *His honesty has never been called into question.* **call it a 'day** (*infml*) to decide or agree to stop doing sth, either temporarily or permanently: *After forty years in politics I think it's time for me to call it a day* (ie to retire). **call it 'quits** (*infml*) to agree to stop a contest, quarrel, etc on even terms. **call sb 'names** to use insulting words about sb. **call the 'shots/'tune** (*infml*) to be in a position to control a situation. **call a spade a 'spade** to speak plainly without trying to hide one's opinion. **call sb to ac'count** (for/over sth) to make sb explain an error, a loss, etc: *His boss called him to account for failing to meet the deadline.* **call sb/sth to 'order** to ask people in a meeting to be silent so that business may start or continue. **he who pays the piper calls the tune** ⇨ PAY². **the pot calling the kettle black** ⇨ POT¹. **PHR V ,call 'by** (*infml*) to visit a place or a person briefly when passing: *Could you call by later?*

,**call sth 'down on sb** (*fml*) to cause sb to receive anger, curses, etc: *His behaviour was enough to call down the teacher's wrath on the whole class.*

'**call for sth** to require, demand or need sth: *The situation calls for prompt action.* ○ *'I've been promoted.' 'This calls for a celebration!'* ○ *That rude remark was not called for!* Compare UNCALLED-FOR.

,**call sb 'forth** (*fml*) to make sth appear or be shown; to bring sth out: *His speech called forth an angry response.*

,**call sb 'in** to ask for the services of sb: *call in a doctor/a lawyer/the police.* ,**call sth 'in** to order or request the return of sth: *Cars with serious faults have been called in by the manufacturers.*

,**call sb/sth 'off** to order dogs, soldiers, etc to stop attacking, searching, etc: *Please call your dog off — it's frightening the children.* ,**call sth 'off** to cancel or abandon sth: *call off a deal/a journey/a picnic/a strike* ○ *They have called off their engagement* (ie decided not to get married). ○ *The match was called off because of bad weather.*

'**call on/upon sb (to do sth) 1** formally to invite or request sb to speak, etc: *I now call upon the chairman to address the meeting.* **2** to ask sb urgently to do sth: *We are calling on you to help us.* ○ *I feel called upon* (ie feel that I ought) *to warn you that…*

,**call sb 'out 1** to ask sb to come, esp to an emergency: *call out the fire brigade/the troops/the guard.* **2** to order or advise workers to stop work as a protest: *Miners were called out (on strike) by union leaders.*

,**call sb/sth 'up 1** (*esp US*) to make a telephone call to sb. **2** to bring sth back to one's mind; to recall(1) sth: *The sound of happy laughter called up memories of his childhood.* **3** to use sth that is stored or kept available: *I called up his address on the computer.* ○ *She called up her last reserves of strength.* **4** to summon sb for military service; to DRAFT²(3) sb.
▶ **caller** *n* a person who makes a brief visit or a telephone call.

■ '**calling-card** *n* (*US*) = VISITING-CARD.

'**call-up** (*US* **draft**) *n* [U,C usu *sing*] an order to do military service: *receive one's call-up* ○ *young men of call-up age.*

call² /kɔːl/ *n* **1** [C] a shout; a cry: *a call for help* ○ *They came at my call* (ie when I shouted to them). **2** [C] the characteristic cry of a bird. **3** [C] a signal sounded on a horn, BUGLE, etc. **4** [C] a short visit to sb's house: *pay a call on a friend* ○ *The doctor has five calls to make this morning.* See also PORT OF CALL. **5** [C] (also '**phone call, ring**) an act of speaking to sb on the telephone: *give sb/make/receive/return a call* ○ *Were there any calls for me while I was out?* **6(a)** [C] an order, a signal or an invitation, esp to come or to meet sb; a SUMMONS: *The prime minister is waiting for a call from the Palace.* ○ *An actor's call tells him when to go on stage.* ○ *This is the last call for passengers travelling on flight BA 199 to*

Rome. ○ (*fig*) *He answered the call of duty and enlisted in the army.* ○ *a call to arms* (ie to fight, eg in the army). See also CURTAIN-CALL. (**b**) [sing] ~ (**of sth**) a strong feeling of duty to do sth, esp a job: *feel the call (of the priesthood).* (**c**) [sing] ~ **of sth** the attraction of a particular place or activity: *the call of the sea/ the wild/faraway places.* (**d**) [C] ~ **for sth** a request or demand for sth: *The President made a call for national unity.* ○ *There were calls from the Opposition parties for the prime minister's resignation.* **7** [U] ~ **for sth/to do sth** (esp in negative sentences and questions) a need or an occasion for sth: *There isn't much call for such things these days.* ○ *There was no call to be rude.* **8** [C] ~ **on sb/sth** a demand on sb/ sth: *He is a busy man with many calls on his time.* **9** [C] (in card-games) a player's bid or turn to bid: *It's your call, partner.* **IDM** **at one's/sb's beck and call** ⇨ BECK². **a call of 'nature** (*euph*) a need to go to the toilet. **a close call** ⇨ CLOSE¹. (**be) on 'call** (esp of a doctor) available for work if necessary: *Who's on call tonight?* **within 'call** near enough to hear sb shouting for help, etc.
■ '**call-box** *n* = TELEPHONE-BOX.

'**call-girl** *n* a prostitute who makes appointments by telephone.

'**call-in** *n* (*US*) = PHONE-IN.

calligraphy /kəˈlɪɡrəfi/ *n* [U] (**a**) beautiful HAND-WRITING, done with a special pen or brush. (**b**) the art of producing this. ▶ **calligrapher** *n*.

calling /ˈkɔːlɪŋ/ *n* **1** (*fml*) a profession; an occupation: *Nursing was considered a suitable calling for girls.* **2** a strong urge or feeling of duty to do a particular job; a VOCATION: *He believes it is his calling to become a priest.*

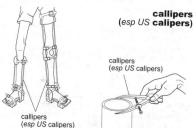

callipers
(*esp US* **calipers**)

callipers
(*esp US* calipers)

callipers
(*esp US* calipers)

calliper (also *esp US* **caliper**) /ˈkælɪpə(r)/ *n* **1 callipers** [pl] an instrument for measuring the DIAMETER(1) of tubes or round objects: *a pair of callipers.* ⇨ picture. **2** [C usu *pl*] a metal support for weak or injured legs.

callisthenics (also **calisthenics**) /ˌkælɪsˈθenɪks/ *n* [sing or pl *v*] exercises to develop strong and graceful bodies.

callous /ˈkæləs/ *adj* having or showing no sympathy for other people's feelings or suffering: *a callous person/attitude/act* ○ *the terrorists' callous disregard for human life.* ▶ **callously** *adv.* **callousness** *n* [U].

calloused /ˈkæləst/ *adj* (of the skin) hardened, eg by rough work: *calloused hands.*

callow /ˈkæləʊ/ *adj* (*derog*) not mature or experienced: *a callow youth.* ▶ **callowness** *n* [U].

callus /ˈkæləs/ *n* an area of thick hardened skin, usu caused by rubbing: *calluses on one's palms.*

calm /kɑːm; *US also* kɑːlm/ *adj* (**-er, -est**) **1** not excited, nervous or troubled; quiet: *It is important to keep/stay calm in an emergency.* ○ *The city was calm again after yesterday's riots.* ○ *his calm, authoritative voice.* **2(a)** (of the sea) without large waves; still. (**b**) (of the weather) without wind: *a calm, cloudless day.* ⇨ note at QUIET.
▶ **calm** *n* [C, U] a calm condition or period: *the calm*

of a summer evening ○ *an atmosphere of nervous/ uneasy calm after the riots.* **IDM** **the calm before the storm** a time of unusual calm immediately before an expected period of violent activity, passion, etc.

calm *v* ~ (**sb**) (**down**) to become or make sb become calm: [Vp] *Just calm down a bit!* [Vn] *The news calmed fears in the business community.* [Vn, Vnp] *Have a brandy — it'll help to calm you (down)/to calm your nerves.* ○ *a calming influence.*

calmly *adv: She reacted calmly to the news.* ○ *He walked into the shop and calmly (ie showing calm confidence) stole a pair of gloves.*

calmness *n* [U].

Calor gas /ˈkælə gæs/ *n* [U] (*Brit propr*) a type of gas stored as a liquid under pressure in containers for domestic use.

calorie /ˈkæləri/ *n* (*abbr* **cal**) **1** a unit for measuring the energy value of food: *An ounce of sugar contains about 100 calories.* ○ *Her diet restricts her to 1500 calories a day.* ○ *lose weight by reducing one's calorie intake* ○ *a high/low calorie diet.* **2** a unit for measuring a quantity of heat.
▶ **calorific** /ˌkæləˈrɪfɪk/ *adj* [usu attrib] of or producing heat: *the calorific value of gas/food* (ie the quantity of heat or energy produced by a particular amount of fuel or food).

calumny /ˈkæləmni/ *n* (*fml*) (**a**) [C] a false statement about sb, made to damage their reputation: *a victim of vicious calumnies.* (**b**) [U] the act of making such a statement; SLANDER: *accuse sb of calumny.*

calvados /ˈkælvədɒs/ *n* [U] a type of BRANDY made from apples.

calve /kɑːv; *US* kæv/ *v* to give birth to a calf: [V] *Our cows will be calving soon.*

calves *pl* of CALF[1,2].

Calvinism /ˈkælvɪnɪzəm/ *n* [U] the religious teaching of the French Protestant John Calvin (1509–64) and of his followers.
▶ **Calvinist** /ˈkælvɪnɪst/ *n* a follower of Calvinism. — *adj* (also **Calvinistic**) **1** of Calvinism. **2** (of moral attitudes) very strict.

calypso /kəˈlɪpsəʊ/ *n* (*pl* **-os**) a West Indian song in African rhythm about a subject of current interest.

calyx /ˈkeɪlɪks/ *n* (*pl* **calyxes** or **calyces** /ˈkeɪlɪsiːz/) (*botany*) a ring of leaves (called *sepals*) enclosing the BUD[1](1) of a flower. ⇨ picture at FLOWER.

cam /kæm/ *n* a projecting part on a wheel that changes the circular motion of the wheel, as it turns, into up-and-down or backwards-and-forwards motion of another part.

camaraderie /ˌkæməˈrɑːdəri; *US* ˌkɑːm-/ *n* [U] friendship and trust among people who spend a lot of time together: *He missed the old camaraderie of life in the army.*

camber /ˈkæmbə(r)/ *n* a slight upward curve on the surface of sth, esp a road.
▶ **camber** *v* to give a camber to (esp a road): [Vn] *The street is quite steeply cambered at this point.*

cambric /ˈkæmbrɪk/ *n* [U] fine white cloth made of cotton or LINEN.

camcorder /ˈkæmkɔːdə(r)/ *n* a video camera (VIDEO) that also records sound and can be carried around.

came *pt* of COME.

camel /ˈkæml/ *n* **1** [C] an animal with a long neck and one or two humps (HUMP 2a) on its back. Camels are used in desert countries for riding and for carrying goods. Compare DROMEDARY. **2** [U] a pale brown colour; FAWN[1](2).
■ **camel-hair** (also **camel's-hair**) *n* [U] **1** a soft, pale brown cloth made of camel's hair or a mixture of camel's hair and wool: *a camel-hair coat.* **2** the fine soft hair used in artists' brushes.

camellia /kəˈmiːliə/ *n* a bush, originally from

China and Japan, with shiny leaves and white, red or pink flowers.

Camembert /ˈkæməmbeə(r)/ *n* [U, C] a soft French cheese with a strong flavour.

cameo /ˈkæmiəʊ/ *n* (*pl* **-os**) **1**(**a**) a small part in a film or play, usu brief and played by a well-known actor: *a cameo performance/role.* (**b**) a short piece of writing with clever description. **2** a small piece of jewellery consisting of a hard stone with a raised design, esp one with a background of a different colour from the design: *a cameo brooch.*

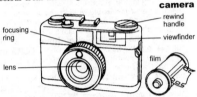
camera
rewind handle
viewfinder
film
focusing ring
lens

camera /ˈkæmərə/ *n* an apparatus for taking photographs, moving pictures or television pictures: *I've put a new film in the camera.* ○ *a video camera* ○ *The cameras clicked as he left the hotel.* ⇨ picture. **IDM** **in ˈcamera** in a judge's private room; without the press or the public being present: *The trial was held/The case was heard in camera.* **on ˈcamera** (esp of an actor) being filmed or shown on television at a particular moment.

cameraman /ˈkæmrəmæn/ *n* (*pl* **-men**) a person whose job is operating a camera for making films or in television.

camerawork /ˈkæmrəwɜːk/ *n* [U] the taking of photographs, films or television pictures: *brilliant camerawork.*

camisole /ˈkæmɪsəʊl/ *n* a short piece of clothing, usu without sleeves, worn by women on the top half of the body: *a lace/silk/cotton camisole.*

camomile (also **chamomile**) /ˈkæməmaɪl/ *n* [U] (**a**) a sweet-smelling plant with small white and yellow flowers. (**b**) its dried leaves and flowers used in medicine, etc: *camomile tea* ○ *camomile shampoo.*

camouflage /ˈkæməflɑːʒ/ *n* **1** [U] a way of hiding or disguising soldiers, military equipment, etc, eg with paint, nets or leaves, so that they look like part of their surroundings: *use the branches of trees as camouflage* ○ *camouflage jackets/trousers/uniforms* (ie covered with green and brown marks and worn esp by soldiers). **2** [C, U] the way that an animal protects itself by having a colour and shape that matches its surroundings and is not easily seen: *The polar bear's white fur is a natural camouflage.* **3** [U] the deliberate use of a situation, statement, etc to hide the truth: *The minister's reply was described as pure camouflage.*
▶ **camouflage** *v* to hide sb/sth by camouflage: [Vn] *The soldiers camouflaged themselves with leaves and branches.* ○ *The extent of the crisis has been cleverly camouflaged.*

camp[1] /kæmp/ *n* **1** a place where people live temporarily in tents or huts: *a mining/logging camp* ○ *leave/return to camp* ○ *We* **pitched/made camp** (ie put up our tents) *by a lake.* See also HOLIDAY CAMP. **2** a place where soldiers live or are trained: *an army camp.* **3** (usu in compounds) a place where people are kept in huts or tents, esp by a government and often for long periods: *a prison camp* ○ *a transit camp for refugees* ○ *a camp guard.* See also CONCENTRATION CAMP. **4** a group of people with the same, esp political or religious, ideas: *the socialist camp* ○ *bad feeling between the rival/opposing camps.* **IDM** **break/strike ˈcamp** to take down one's tent or tents and leave the camp: *We broke camp at sunrise.* **have a foot in both camps** ⇨ FOOT[1].

▶ **camp** v **1(a)** to put up a tent or tents: [V] *Where shall we camp tonight?* **(b)** ~ **(out)** to live in a tent: [V, Vp] *They camped (out) in the woods for a week.* **2** (usu **go camping**) to spend a holiday living in tents: [V] *The boys went camping in Greece last year.* **3** to live temporarily as if in a camp: [V] *I'm camping on the floor in a friend's flat for two weeks.* **camper** n **1** a person who camps. **2** (also **'camper van**) a large motor vehicle designed and equipped for people to live in while camping. **camping** n [U] living in tents on holiday: *Do you like camping?* ○ *a camping trip* ○ *camping equipment.*

■ **camp-'bed** (US **cot**) n a bed that can be folded up and moved easily (not only for use in a camp).

'camp-fire n an outdoor fire made of logs, etc by people camping: *singing round the camp-fire.*

camp-'follower n **1** a CIVILIAN who follows an army from place to place to sell goods or services. **2** (often derog) a person who shows interest in and support for a particular group, party, etc without being a member of it.

'camp-site (also **'camping site**, US **'campground**) n a place for camping, area specially equipped for people on holiday.

camp² /kæmp/ adj (infml) **1** (of a man, his manner, etc) like a woman, esp deliberately; EFFEMINATE: *a camp walk/voice/gesture.* **2** HOMOSEXUAL. **3** exaggerated in style, esp for humorous effect.

▶ **camp** n [U] camp²(3) behaviour or style: *Her performance was pure camp.*

camp v **PHR V** **camp it up** (infml) **1** to exaggerate a performance for humorous effect; to OVERACT. **2** to show that one is HOMOSEXUAL by behaving in a camp²(1) way.

campaign /kæm'peɪn/ n **1** a series of military operations with a particular aim, usu carried out in one area: *He fought in the North African campaign during the last war.* **2** a series of planned activities with a particular social, commercial or political aim: *mount/launch a campaign* ○ *organizations conducting a campaign against nuclear weapons* ○ *The company ran a successful advertising campaign to promote its new brand of washing powder.* ○ *a hard-fought election campaign* ○ *the President's campaign manager.*

▶ **campaign** v ~ **(for/against sb/sth)** to take part in or lead a campaign: [Vpr] *She spent her life campaigning for women's rights.* ○ *He has campaigned tirelessly/vigorously against corruption in the armed forces.* [V.to inf] *campaigning to save the building* [also V]. **campaigner** n a person who campaigns: *a leading human rights campaigner* ○ *an old/a seasoned campaigner* (ie sb with a lot of experience of a particular activity). **campaigning** n [U].

campanile /ˌkæmpə'niːli/ n a tower containing a bell, esp one that is not part of another building.

campanology /ˌkæmpə'nɒlədʒi/ n [U] (fml) the study of bells and the art or practice of ringing bells.

▶ **campanologist** /-ədʒɪst/ n.

camphor /'kæmfə(r)/ n [U] a strong-smelling white substance used in medicine, in making plastics and to keep insects away from clothes, etc.

campus /'kæmpəs/ n (pl **campuses**) **1** the grounds and buildings of a university or college: *He lives on (the) campus* (ie within the university grounds). **2** (US) a university or branch of a university: *campus life.*

CAMRA (also **Camra**) /'kæmrə/ abbr the Campaign for Real Ale (a British organization that aims to preserve the traditional methods of making beer): *Camra pubs.*

camshaft /'kæmʃɑːft; US -ʃæft/ n a rod with a CAM on it joining parts of machinery, esp in a motor vehicle.

can¹ /kæn/ n **1** [C] (often in compounds) a metal or plastic container for holding or carrying liquids: *an*

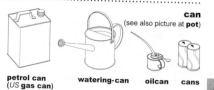

can
(see also picture at **pot**)

petrol can
(US **gas can**)   **watering-can**   **oilcan**   **cans**

'oilcan ○ *a 'petrol can/a can of 'petrol.* ⇨ picture: *a 'watering-can.* **2** [C] **(a)** (also esp Brit **tin**) a sealed metal container in which food or drink is preserved and sold: *a 'beer can.* ⇨ picture. **(b)** the contents of a can or the amount contained in a can: *a can of peaches* ○ *He drank four cans of beer.* **3** **the can** [sing] (US sl) **(a)** prison. **(b)** the toilet. **IDM** **(open up) a can of 'worms** (infml) (to create) a complicated problem: *I wish you'd never found the missing files — you've opened up a whole can of worms.* **be in the 'can** (esp of filmed or recorded material) to be completed and ready for use. **carry the can** ⇨ CARRY.

▶ **can** v (-nn-) to preserve food by putting it in a sealed can: [Vn] *canned 'fruit* ○ *a 'canning factory.* **canned** adj (infml usu derog) previously recorded: *canned laughter* ○ *I can't stand the canned music the supermarkets play these days.*

■ **'can-opener** n an apparatus for opening cans of food.

can² /kən; strong form kæn/ modal v (neg **cannot** /'kænɒt/; contracted form **can't** /kɑːnt; US kænt/; pt **could** /kəd; strong form kʊd/; neg **could not**; contracted form **couldn't** /'kʊdnt/) (used with the infinitive without to) **1(a)** (indicating ability): *I can run fast.* ○ *Can you call back tomorrow?* ○ *He couldn't answer the question.* ○ *The stadium can be emptied in four minutes.* ○ *I can't promise anything, but I'll do what I can.* **(b)** (indicating acquired knowledge or skill): *They can speak French.* ○ *Can he cook?* ○ *I could drive a car before I left school.* **(c)** (used with verbs related to perceiving things): *I can hear music.* ○ *I thought I could smell something burning.* ○ *He could still taste the garlic they'd had for lunch.* ⇨ note. **2(a)** (indicating that one is allowed to do sth): *You can take the car, if you want.* ○ *We can't wear jeans at work.* ○ *The boys could play football but the girls had to go to the library.* **(b)** (indicating requests for permission to do sth): *Can I read your newspaper?* ○ *Can I take you home?* ⇨ note at MAY¹. **3** (indicating requests for help): *Can you help me with this box?* ○ *Can you feed the cat, please?* **4(a)** (indicating possibility): *That can't be Mary — she's in hospital.* ○ *He can't have slept through all that noise.* ○ *There's someone outside — who can it be?* ⇨ note at MIGHT¹. **(b)** (used to express confusion, doubt or surprise): *What 'can they be doing?* ○ *Can he be serious?* ○ *Where 'can she have put it?* **5** (used to describe typical behaviour or a typical state): *He can be very tactless sometimes.* ○ *She can be very forgetful.* ○ *Scotland can be very cold.* ○ *It can be quite windy on the hills.* **6** (used to make suggestions): *We can eat in a restaurant, if you like.* ○ *I can take the car if necessary.* ⇨ note at SHALL.

NOTE **Can** is used to say that somebody has the ability or opportunity to do something: *Can you swim?* ○ *We can have lunch in the garden today.*

Be able to is used to form the future and present perfect tenses and the infinitive: *You'll be able to get a taxi outside the station.* ○ *I haven't been able to get much work done today.* ○ *We are pleased to be able to offer families a 10% discount.*

Could is used to talk about general ability in the past: *Hannah could walk when she was nine months old.*

Was/were able to (NOT **could**) is used when referring to the specific ability to do something on

[V] = verb used alone   [Vn] = verb + noun   [Vp] = verb + particle   [Vpr] = verb + prepositional phrase

a particular occasion in the past: *I was able to get a half price ticket with my Student Identity Card.*

Manage to is used when referring to a particular past event to say whether somebody has succeeded in doing something: *She didn't manage to answer all the questions in the exam.* ○ *Luckily we managed to get a last minute cancellation.*

Can is also used to ask for and give permission. ⇨ note at MAY[1].

canal /kəˈnæl/ *n* **1** a channel cut through land for boats or ships to travel along, or to carry water to fields for crops: *The Suez Canal joins the Mediterranean and the Red Sea.* ○ *an irrigation canal.* Compare RIVER 1. **2** a tube through which air or food passes in a plant or in an animal's body: *the alimentary canal.*

▶ **canalize, -ise** /ˈkænəlaɪz/ *v* [Vn] **1** to make a canal through an area. **2** to convert a river into a canal. **canalization, -isation** /ˌkænəlaɪˈzeɪʃn; *US* -nələˈz-/ *n* [U].

■ **caˈnal boat** *n* a long narrow boat used on canals.

canapé /ˈkænəpeɪ; *US* ˌkænəˈpeɪ/ *n* a small biscuit or piece of bread, pastry, etc spread with cheese, meat, fish, etc and usu served with drinks at a party.

canard /kæˈnɑːd, ˈkænɑːd/ *n* a false report or rumour.

canary /kəˈneəri/ *n* a small yellow bird with a beautiful song, often kept in a cage as a pet.

canasta /kəˈnæstə/ *n* [U] a card-game played with two packs of cards.

cancan /ˈkænkæn/ *n* (usu **the cancan** [sing]) a lively dance in which the legs are kicked high, performed by women in long skirts.

cancel /ˈkænsl/ *v* (**-ll-**; *US* **-l-**) **1** to say that sth which has already been arranged and decided upon will not be done or take place: [Vn] *I was ill and had to cancel all my appointments.* ○ *The match had to be cancelled because of bad weather.* Compare POSTPONE. **2** to order sth to be stopped; to make sth no longer valid: [V] *The travel brochure said we were free to cancel at any time.* [Vn] *cancel an agreement/a contract/a subscription/an order.* **3** to put a line through sth written: [Vn] *Cancel that last sentence.* **4** [Vn] to mark a ticket or a stamp[2](1) to show that it may not be used again. **PHR V** **,cancel (sth) ˈout** to be equal and opposed to sth in force and effect: *These arguments cancel (each other) out.* ○ *Her kindness and generosity cancel out her occasional flashes of temper.*

▶ **cancellation** /ˌkænsəˈleɪʃn/ *n* **1** [U] the action of cancelling or of being cancelled: *We need at least 24 hours' notice of cancellation.* ○ *a cancellation fee/charge* ○ *Heavy snow has caused the cancellation of several matches.* **2** [C] **(a)** an instance of cancelling sth: *a lot of late cancellations from holiday-makers this year* ○ *cancellations on the railways.* **(b)** a thing that has been cancelled, eg a theatre ticket: *Are there any cancellations for this evening's performance?* **3** [C] a mark used to cancel a ticket, etc.

Cancer /ˈkænsə(r)/ *n* **(a)** [U] the fourth sign of the ZODIAC, the Crab. **(b)** [C] a person born under the influence of this sign. ⇨ picture at ZODIAC. ⇨ note at ZODIAC.

cancer /ˈkænsə(r)/ *n* **1(a)** [C,U] an abnormal growth(4) of cells in the body which often causes death: *Most skin cancers are completely curable.* ○ *The cancer has spread to his stomach.* **(b)** [U] the disease in which such growths form: *The risk of lung cancer from passive smoking is small.* ○ *having radiotherapy for cancer of the liver* ○ *cancer research.* **2** [C] an evil or dangerous thing that spreads quickly: *Violence is a cancer in our society.* Compare CANKER 3.

▶ **cancerous** /ˈkænsərəs/ *adj* of, like or affected

with cancer: *cancerous cells* ○ *Is the tumour benign or cancerous?*

candelabrum /ˌkændəˈlɑːbrəm/ *n* (*pl* **candelabra** /-brə/; also *sing* **candelabra**, *pl* **candelabras** /-brəz/) a large ornamental holder with several branches for candles or lights.

candid /ˈkændɪd/ *adj* not hiding one's thoughts; frank and honest: *a candid opinion/statement* ○ *Let me be absolutely candid with you: your work is not good enough.* See also CANDOUR. ▶ **candidly** *adv*: *Candidly* (ie In my honest opinion), *David, I think you're being very unreasonable.*

candidacy /ˈkændɪdəsi/ (also *fml esp Brit* **candidature**) *n* [C,U] the fact or condition of being a candidate(1): *announce/withdraw one's candidacy* ○ *We will support him in his candidacy for president/ the presidency.*

candidate /ˈkændɪdət, -deɪt/ *n* **1** a person who applies for a job or is suggested by other people for election: *a presidential candidate* ○ *He stood/was selected as the local Labour candidate in the last general election.* ○ *The right-wing group has put up its own candidate for the post.* **2** a person taking an examination: *Most candidates passed easily.* **3** ~ **(for sth)** a person who is considered suitable for a particular position or likely to get sth: *The company is having to reduce staff and I fear I'm one of the likely candidates (for redundancy).* ▶ **candidature** /ˈkændɪdətʃə(r)/ *n* (*fml esp Brit*) = CANDIDACY.

candied /ˈkændɪd/ *adj* [attrib] (of fruit) preserved by boiling in sugar: *candied plums* ○ *candied peel* (eg of oranges).

candle /ˈkændl/ *n* a round stick of wax with a WICK through it which is lit to give light as it burns: *He blew out the flickering candle.* ⇨ picture. **IDM** **burn the candle at both ends** ⇨ BURN. **the game is not worth the candle** ⇨ GAME[1]. **not hold a candle to sb/sth** (*infml*) to be inferior to sb/sth: *She writes well enough but she can't hold a candle to the more serious novelists.*

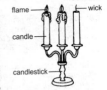

candle
flame — wick
candle
candlestick

candlelight /ˈkændl laɪt/ *n* [U] light produced by candles: *read by candlelight.*

candlelit /ˈkændl lɪt/ *adj* [attrib] lit by candles: *a romantic candlelit dinner for two.*

candlestick /ˈkændlstɪk/ *n* a holder for one or more candles: *silver candlesticks.* ⇨ picture at CANDLE.

candlewick /ˈkændlwɪk/ *n* [U] a soft cotton fabric with a raised fluffy (FLUFF) pattern: *a candlewick bedspread.*

candour (*US* **candor**) /ˈkændə(r)/ *n* [U] the quality of being frank and honest in one's behaviour or speech: *With refreshing candour, he admitted that he had lied repeatedly.*

C and W *abbr* (*music*) country-and-western.

candy /ˈkændi/ *n* (*esp US*) **(a)** [U] sweets or chocolate: *I don't like candy.* ○ *a candy bar.* **(b)** [C] a sweet or a chocolate: *a box of candies.*

candyfloss /ˈkændiflɒs/ (*Brit*) (*US* ˌcotton ˈcandy) *n* [U] a type of light fluffy (FLUFF) sweet made by spinning melted sugar. It is usu eaten on a stick.

cane /keɪn/ *n* **1(a)** [C] the hard hollow stem of certain plants, eg BAMBOO. **(b)** [U] such stems used as a material for making furniture, etc: *a cane chair.* **2(a)** [C] a length of cane, or a thin rod, used for supporting plants, as a stick to help sb walk or for beating people as a punishment: ⇨ picture at CRUTCH. **(b)** **the cane** [sing] (in some schools) the punishment in which children are beaten with a cane: *get/be given the cane* ○ *Discipline is still enforced by the cane in some schools.*

▶ **cane** v **1** to punish sb by beating them with a cane: [Vn] *The headmaster caned the boys for disobedience.* **2** (*infml esp Brit*) to defeat sb totally: [Vn] *We really caned them in the last match.* **caning** n [U, C]: *give sb a caning.*
■ **'cane-sugar** n [U] sugar obtained from the juice of sugar-cane (SUGAR).

canine /'keɪnaɪn/ adj of, like or relating to dogs.
▶ **canine** (also **'canine tooth**) n (in a human being) any of the four pointed teeth next to the incisors (INCISOR). ⇨ picture at TOOTH.

canister /'kænɪstə(r)/ n **1** a usu metal container for holding tea, coffee, etc. **2** a small container filled with shot[1](3) or gas, that bursts and releases its contents when fired from a gun or thrown.

canker /'kæŋkə(r)/ n **1** [U] a disease that destroys the wood of plants and trees. **2** [U] a disease causing sore patches on the ears of animals, esp dogs and cats. **3** [C] an evil or dangerous influence that spreads and affects people's behaviour. Compare CANCER 2.
■ **'canker sore** n (*US medical*) a painful spot inside the mouth.

cannabis /'kænəbɪs/ (also sl **dope, pot**) n [U] a drug made from the dried leaves and flowers of the HEMP(2) plant, which is smoked or chewed (CHEW) for its effect on the mind and body. Possessing and using it is illegal in many countries: *cannabis resin* ∘ *a cannabis plant.* See also HASHISH, MARIJUANA.

cannelloni /ˌkænəˈləʊni/ n [U] rolls of PASTA filled with meat or cheese.

cannery /'kænəri/ n a place where food is canned (CAN[1]).

cannibal /'kænɪbl/ n (**a**) a person who eats human flesh: *a cannibal tribe.* (**b**) an animal that feeds on the flesh of its own species.
▶ **cannibalism** /'kænɪbəlɪzəm/ n [U] **cannibalistic** /ˌkænɪbəˈlɪstɪk/ adj.
cannibalize, -ise /'kænɪbəlaɪz/ v to use a machine, vehicle, etc to provide spare parts for others: [Vn] *He cannibalized an old radio to repair his cassette-player.* **cannibalization, -isation** /ˌkænɪbəlaɪˈzeɪʃn; US -lə'z-/ n [U].

cannon /'kænən/ n (pl unchanged) **1** an old type of large heavy gun that fired solid metal balls. **2** an automatic gun firing shells (SHELL 3a) from an aircraft, a tank(2), etc: *two 20-millimetre cannon.* See also WATER-CANNON.
▶ **cannon** v PHRV **cannon against/into/off sb/ sth** (of a moving person, vehicle, etc) to hit something by accident and with force: *The ball cannoned off a defender's leg straight into the goal.*
■ **'cannon-ball** n a large metal ball fired from a cannon(1).
'cannon-fodder n [U] soldiers regarded only as material to be used up in war.

cannonade /ˌkænəˈneɪd/ n a continuous firing of heavy guns.

cannot /'kænɒt/ (*esp fml*) = CAN NOT (CAN[2]).

canny /'kæni/ adj (**-ier, -iest**) intelligent, careful and showing good judgement, esp in business matters: *a canny fellow/move.* ▶ **cannily** adv. **canniness** n [U].

canoe /kəˈnuː/ n a light narrow boat moved by one or more paddles (PADDLE[1] 1). ⇨ picture. IDM **paddle one's own canoe** ⇨ PADDLE[1].
▶ **canoe** v (pt, pp **canoed**; pres p **canoeing**) [V] (often **go canoeing**) to travel in a canoe. **canoeing** n [U] the sport of travelling in a canoe.
canoeist /kəˈnuːɪst/ n a person who travels by canoe. ⇨ picture.

canon[1] /'kænən/ n **1** a general rule, standard or principle by which sth is judged: *This play offends against all the canons of good taste.* **2**(**a**) a list of sacred books accepted as genuine: *the canon of Holy Scripture.* (**b**) a set of writings, etc accepted as the

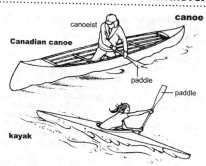

canoe

Canadian canoe

canoeist

paddle

paddle

kayak

genuine work of a particular author: *the Shakespeare canon.*
▶ **canonical** /kəˈnɒnɪkl/ adj **1** according to church law: *canonical teaching.* **2** included in the canon[1](2a).
■ **ˌcanon 'law** n [U] church law.

canon[2] /'kænən/ n a priest with special duties in a cathedral: *The Rev Canon Arthur Brown.*

canonize, -ise /'kænənaɪz/ v (usu passive) to declare officially, that sb is a saint, usu with a ceremony: [Vn] *martyrs canonized by the Pope.* ▶ **canonization, -isation** /ˌkænənaɪˈzeɪʃn; US -nə'z-/ n [C, U].

canopy /'kænəpi/ n **1** a hanging cover forming a shelter above a bed, THRONE, etc. **2** a cover for the COCKPIT of an aircraft. **3** (*fml or rhet*) any covering that hangs over sth: *the grey canopy of the sky* ∘ *a canopy of leaves* (eg in a forest).

cant[1] /kænt/ n [U] insincere talk, esp about religion or moral issues; HYPOCRISY: *cant expressions* ∘ *The report was surprisingly free of cant.*

cant[2] /kænt/ v ~ (**sth**) (**over**) to turn over or make sth turn over: [Vn] *cant a boat to repair it* [Vp] *He sat canted over to one side in his chair.* [also V, Vnp].

can't short form of CANNOT (CAN[2]).

Cantab /'kæntæb/ abbr (esp in degree titles) of Cambridge or Cambridge University (Latin *Cantabrigiensis*): *James Cox MA (Cantab).* Compare OXON 2.

cantankerous /kænˈtæŋkərəs/ adj bad-tempered and tending to argue about unimportant things: *His illness has made him increasingly cantankerous.* ▶ **cantankerously** adv.

cantata /kænˈtɑːtə/ n a short musical work, often on a religious subject. Cantatas are written to be sung by soloists (SOLO), usu with a CHOIR, and accompanied by an ORCHESTRA: *Bach's cantatas.* Compare ORATORIO.

canteen /kænˈtiːn/ n **1** (*Brit*) a place where food and drink are served in a factory, an office, a school, etc: *We went down to the canteen for lunch.* **2** a small container used by a soldier or a camper (CAMP[1]) for carrying water, etc. **3** (*Brit*) a case or box containing a set of knives, forks and spoons.

canter /'kæntə(r)/ n (**a**) [sing] a movement of a horse that is faster than a TROT but slower than a GALLOP(1a): *a light/a steady/an easy/an even canter* ∘ *The pony broke into a canter.* (**b**) a ride on a horse moving at this speed: *go for a canter.* IDM **at a canter** without much effort; easily: *She won the contest at a canter.*
▶ **canter** v (**a**) [V] (of a horse or rider) to move at a canter. (**b**) to make a horse move at a canter: [Vn] *We cantered our horses for several miles.*

canticle /'kæntɪkl/ n a religious song whose words are taken from the Bible.

cantilever /'kæntɪliːvə(r)/ n a beam, usu of metal, projecting from a wall to support a BALCONY or similar structure.

C

■ **'cantilever bridge** *n* a bridge made of two cantilevers projecting from large pillars.

canto /ˈkæntəʊ/ *n* (*pl* **-os**) any of the main divisions of a long poem.

canton /ˈkæntɒn/ *n* any of the official areas into which some countries, eg Switzerland, are divided.

cantor /ˈkæntɔː(r)/ *n* the man who leads the singing in a church or SYNAGOGUE.

canvas /ˈkænvəs/ *n* (*pl* **canvases** /-vəsɪz/) **1** [U] a strong rough type of cloth used for making tents, sails, etc and by artists for painting on: *canvas bags/chairs/shoes* ○ *sleeping **under canvas*** (ie in tents). **2** [C] **(a)** a piece of canvas for painting on. **(b)** a painting on canvas, esp in oils (OIL 4): *Turner's canvases.*

canvass /ˈkænvəs/ *v* **1** ~ **(sb) (for sth)** to go around an area asking people for political support: [V, Vpr] *go out canvassing (for votes)* [Vn] *The Democratic candidate will canvass the constituency next month.* [also Vnpr]. **2** to find out what people think about a particular issue or product by asking them: [Vn] *canvass views/opinions* ○ *canvass voters before an election.* **3** to discuss an idea thoroughly: [Vn] *The proposal has been widely canvassed.*
▶ **canvass** *n* an act of canvassing.
canvasser *n* a person who canvasses.

canyon /ˈkænjən/ *n* a very deep narrow valley, usu with a river flowing through it: *the Grand Canyon in Arizona.*

CAP /ˌsiː eɪ ˈpiː/ *abbr* Common Agricultural Policy (of the European Union).

cap /kæp/ *n* **1(a)** a type of soft hat without a BRIM(2) but often with a PEAK¹(3). Caps are worn esp by men and boys, often as part of a uniform: *in/wearing his school cap.* ⇨ picture at HAT. **(b)** (esp in compounds) any of various types of soft hat that fit closely and are worn for different purposes: *a 'bathing-cap* ○ *a 'baseball cap* ○ *a 'nurse's cap* ○ *a 'shower-cap.* ⇨ picture at BASEBALL, HAT. **2** (*sport esp Brit*) **(a)** a cap given to sb who is chosen to play for a school, county, country, etc, esp at football or cricket: *He won his first cap* (ie was first chosen to play) *for England against France.* **(b)** a player chosen for such a team: *three new caps in the side.* **3** an academic head-dress with a square flat top and a TASSEL: *wear cap and gown on graduation day.* Compare MORTARBOARD. **4** a protective cover or top for a pen, a bottle, the LENS(1) of a camera, etc. **5** = DUTCH CAP: *to fit a cap.* **6** a small amount of explosive powder in a metal container, used esp in toy guns: *a cap gun/pistol.* **IDM** **cap in 'hand** in a HUMBLE(1) way, as if begging: *come/go cap in hand to sb* (eg asking for money). **a feather in one's cap** ⇨ FEATHER¹. **if the cap fits (, wear it)**, (*US*) **if the shoe fits (, wear it)** if one feels that a remark applies to oneself (one should accept it and take it as a warning): *I have noticed some of you coming to work late recently. I shall name no names, but if the cap fits...* See also ICE-CAP.
▶ **cap** *v* (**-pp-**) **1** (usu passive) to cover the top or end of sth: [Vn] *mountains capped with snow/mist* ○ *snow-capped mountains.* **2(a)** (*esp Brit*) to set a limit to sth: [Vn] *cap the rates.* **(b)** (often passive) (esp of a government) to limit the spending of an official organization: [Vn] *Twenty councils are to be capped this year.* **3** [Vn] to follow a joke, story, etc with another that is better, bigger, funnier, etc. **4** to put an artificial top on a tooth or teeth: [Vn] *He's had his front teeth capped.* **5** (usu passive) (*sport esp Brit*) to choose a player for a major (esp football or cricket) team: [Vn] *He was capped 36 times for Wales.* **IDM** **to cap it 'all** as a final piece of bad or good luck: *I had a rotten day at the office, and to cap it all my car broke down on the way home!* See also CHARGE-CAPPING, RATE-CAPPING.

capability /ˌkeɪpəˈbɪləti/ *n* **(a)** [U, C] ~ **(to do sth /**

of doing sth); ~ **(for sth)** the ability or power to do sth: *weapons that have the capability to cause/of causing mass destruction* ○ *a nuclear capability* (ie the power or weapons necessary for fighting a nuclear war) ○ *explore the new computer's capabilities.* **(b)** **capabilities** [pl] the qualities which sb has for doing things but which may not have been fully developed: *She has great capabilities as a writer.* ○ *Age has nothing to do with a person's capabilities.*

capable /ˈkeɪpəbl/ *adj* **1** [pred] ~ **of sth / doing sth** having the ability or quality necessary for doing sth: *You are capable of better work than this.* ○ *I'm sure he is capable of running a mile in four minutes.* ○ *a new microchip that is capable of a much wider range of applications* ○ *He's quite/fully capable of lying* (ie It would not be surprising if he lied) *to get out of trouble.* **2** having (esp practical) ability; able; competent: *a very capable woman.* **3** [pred] ~ **of sth** (*fml*) (of situations, remarks, etc) open to or allowing sth: *Our position is capable of improvement.* See also CAPABILITY, INCAPABLE.
▶ **capably** *adv* in a capable(2) way: *handle a situation/manage a business capably.*

capacious /kəˈpeɪʃəs/ *adj* (*fml*) (of things) that can hold a lot; roomy (ROOM): *The car has a capacious boot.* ▶ **capaciousness** *n* [U].

capacity /kəˈpæsəti/ *n* **1** [U] the ability to hold or contain sth: *a hall with a seating capacity of 2000* ○ *The room was filled to capacity* (ie completely full). ○ *They played to a **capacity crowd/audience*** (ie one that filled all the available space). **2** [sing] **(a)** ~ **(for sth)** the ability to produce, experience, understand or learn sth: *She has an enormous capacity for hard work.* ○ *This book is within the capacity of* (ie can be understood by) *younger readers.* **(b)** ~ **to do sth** the ability to do sth: *a leader with the capacity to inspire loyalty.* **3** [sing] the power to produce sth: *factories working at full capacity.* **4** [U, C] the volume, eg of cylinders (CYLINDER 2) in a motor vehicle's engine: *What capacity is your car?* **5** a function or position; a role: ***acting in her capacity as manager/in her managerial capacity.***

caparisoned /kəˈpærɪsnd/ *adj* (*dated or fml*) (of an animal or its rider) decorated with special coverings: *finely/richly/brightly caparisoned.*

cape¹ /keɪp/ *n* **1** [C] (*abbr* **C**) (often in place names) a piece of high land sticking out into the sea: *Cape Horn.* **2 the Cape** [sing] **(a)** the Cape of Good Hope. **(b)** Cape Province.
■ **ˌCape ˈColoured** *n, adj* (a person) of the mixed White and non-White population of Cape Province in South Africa.

cape² /keɪp/ *n* a loose outer garment without sleeves, like a CLOAK(1) but usu shorter: *a bullfighter's cape.*
▶ **caped** *adj* wearing a cape.

caper¹ /ˈkeɪpə(r)/ *v* ~ **(about)** to jump or run about as though enjoying oneself: [V, Vp] *foals capering (about) in the fields.*
▶ **caper** *n* **1** (*infml*) **(a)** any activity, esp a dishonest one: *What's your little caper, then?* **(b)** (*dated*) a trick; a PRANK. **2** a playful jump or dance.

caper² /ˈkeɪpə(r)/ *n* (usu *pl*) the flower BUD of a prickly European bush, pickled (PICKLE) for use in flavouring food: *a leg of mutton with caper sauce.*

capillary /kəˈpɪləri; *US* ˈkæpəleri/ *n* any of the very narrow tubes that carry blood between the arteries (ARTERY 1) and veins in the body. ⇨ picture at RESPIRATORY.
■ **caˌpillary atˈtraction** (also **caˌpillary ˌaction**) *n* [U] (*techn*) the force that causes a liquid to be drawn along a very narrow tube.

capital¹ /ˈkæpɪtl/ *n* **1** the most important town or city of a country or region, usu its centre of government: *Cairo is the capital of Egypt.* ○ *Troops are stationed in and around the capital.* ○ *London, Paris* *and Washington DC are capital cities.* **2** a place that is associated more than any other with a particular activity, product, etc: *Liverpool, the comic capital of England.* **3** (also ,capital 'letter) a letter of the form and size used to begin a name or a sentence: *In this sentence, the word BIG is in capitals, please.* **4** the top part of a column(1). ➪ picture at COLUMN.

▶ **capital** *adj* [usu attrib] **1** involving punishment by death: *a capital offence* ○ *Do you believe in capital punishment for murder* (ie executing people who have killed others)? **2** (of letters) having the form and size used to begin a name or a sentence: *London is spelt with a capital 'L'.* **3** (*dated Brit*) excellent: *What a capital idea!* **IDM** **with a capital A, B, etc** (used to emphasize sth said or written about a person or thing): *She's a feminist with a capital F* (ie a very strong feminist (FEMINISM)).

capital² /'kæpɪtl/ *n* **1** [U] wealth or property that can be used to produce more wealth: *a business in need of a substantial injection of new capital.* **2** [sing] a sum of money used to start a business: *set up a business with a starting capital of £100 000* ○ *a good return on capital.* **3** [U] all the wealth owned by a person or a business: *capital assets.* **4** [U] people who use their money to start businesses, thought of as a group: *capital and labour.* **IDM** **make capital (out) of sth** to use a situation, etc for one's own advantage: *The Opposition parties made (political) capital out of the disagreements within the ruling party.*

■ ,capital ex'penditure *n* [U] money spent by a business on buildings, equipment, etc.
,capital 'gains *n* [pl] profits made from the sale of investments or property. ,capital 'gains tax *n* [U] (*Brit*) the tax on such profits.
'capital goods *n* [pl] goods, eg factory machines, used in producing other goods. Compare CONSUMER GOODS.
,capital-in'tensive *adj* (of industrial processes) needing the investment of very large sums of money (as contrasted with a very large number of workers). Compare LABOUR-INTENSIVE.
,capital 'levy *n* a general tax on private wealth or property. Compare INCOME TAX.
,capital 'sum *n* a single payment of money, eg by an insurance company to sb.

capitalism /'kæpɪtəlɪzəm/ *n* [U] an economic system in which a country's trade and industry are controlled by private owners for profit, rather than by the state: *the impact of Western capitalism.*

▶ **capitalist** *n* **1** a person who owns or controls a lot of capital²(1); a rich person. **2** a person who supports capitalism. — *adj* based on or supporting capitalism: *a capitalist system/economy.* **capitalistic** /,kæpɪtə'lɪstɪk/ *adj.* Compare SOCIALISM.

capitalize, -ise /'kæpɪtəlaɪz/ *v* **1** [Vn] to write or print a letter as a capital²(3). **2** [Vn] (usu passive) (**a**) to convert possessions into capital²(1) by selling them. (**b**) to provide a company, etc with capital²(1): *The company will be capitalized at £9.4 million.* ○ *The industry is under-capitalized* (ie not enough money invested in it). **PHRV** 'capitalize on sth to use sth for one's own advantage; to profit from sth: *capitalize on the government's embarrassment/on the mistakes made by a rival firm.* ▶ **capitalization, -isation** /,kæpɪtəlaɪ'zeɪʃn; *US* -lə'zeɪʃn/ *n* [U, sing]: *The deal gives the group a market capitalization of £67 million.*

capitation /,kæpɪ'teɪʃn/ *n* a tax or payment of an equal amount for each person: *a capi'tation allowance/fee/grant.*

capitulate /kə'pɪtʃuleɪt/ *v* ~ (**to sb/sth**) to stop fighting against or resisting sb/sth and agree to what they want: [V] *I will never capitulate!* [Vpr] *We*

had no choice but to capitulate to their demands. ▶ **capitulation** /kə,pɪtʃu'leɪʃn/ *n* [C].

capon /'keɪpɒn, 'keɪpən/ *n* a male chicken that has been castrated (CASTRATE) and made fat for eating.

cappuccino /,kæpu'tʃiːnəʊ/ *n* (*pl* -os) (**a**) [U] ESPRESSO coffee with hot milk added. (**b**) [C] a cup of this.

caprice /kə'priːs/ *n* (**a**) [C] a sudden change in attitude or behaviour with no obvious cause; a WHIM. (**b**) [U] the tendency to such changes.

capricious /kə'prɪʃəs/ *adj* showing sudden changes in attitude or behaviour: *a cruel, capricious and unjust system of punishment* ○ (*fig*) *a capricious climate.* ▶ **capriciously** *adv.* **capriciousness** *n* [U].

Capricorn /'kæprɪkɔːn/ *n* (**a**) the 10th sign of the ZODIAC, the Goat. (**b**) [C] a person born under the influence of this sign. ➪ picture at ZODIAC. ➪ note at ZODIAC.

capsicum /'kæpsɪkəm/ *n* the fruit of a tropical plant, containing hot-tasting seeds. Capsicums are red, green or yellow when ripe, and are eaten as vegetables, raw or cooked. Compare PEPPER 2.

capsize /kæp'saɪz; *US* 'kæpsaɪz/ *v* (**a**) (esp of a boat) to turn over: [V] *The yacht/We capsized in heavy seas.* (**b**) [Vn] to make sth, esp a boat, turn over.

capstan /'kæpstən/ *n* a thick revolving post round which a rope or cable is wound, eg to raise a ship's ANCHOR.

capsule /'kæpsjuːl; *US* also 'kæpsl/ *n* **1** a small case that contains a quantity of a drug and dissolves when swallowed: *The medicine can be taken in tablet or capsule form.* **2** an area for people or instruments in a spacecraft. See also TIME CAPSULE.

Capt *abbr* Captain: *Capt (Terence) Jones.*

captain /'kæptɪn/ *n* **1** (the title of) the person in charge of a ship or civil(2) aircraft: *The captain gave the order to abandon ship.* ○ *Captain Johnson and his co-pilot.* **2** (the title of) an army, navy or (in the USA) air force officer. ➪ App 6. **3** the leader of a group or team: *He is (the) captain of the football team.*

▶ **captain** *v* to be the captain of a football team, etc: [Vn] *Who is captaining the side today?*
captaincy /'kæptənsi/ *n* (**a**) [C,U] the position of captain: *She has recently taken over the captaincy.* (**b**) [C] a period of being captain: *during her captaincy.* (**c**) [U] the quality of a captain's actions: *showing fine captaincy.*

■ ,captain of 'industry *n* a person who manages a large industrial company.

caption /'kæpʃn/ *n* **1** words printed with a picture, photograph or CARTOON(1) in order to describe or explain it. **2** words shown on a cinema or television screen, eg to establish the scene of a story (eg 'New York 1981').

▶ **caption** *v* (usu passive) to provide sth with a caption: [Vn] *a picture captioned 'the President relaxing on holiday'.*

captivate /'kæptɪveɪt/ *v* to attract sb greatly; to CHARM²(1) sb: [Vn] *He was captivated by her beauty.*
▶ **captivating** *adj* fascinating; charming: *a captivating woman* ○ *He found her captivating.*

captive /'kæptɪv/ *adj* **1** [esp attrib] kept as a prisoner; unable to escape; not free: *a captive bird* ○ *captive breeding* (ie the catching and organized breeding of wild animals) ○ *They were taken/held captive by masked gunmen.* ○ (*fig*) *a captive balloon* (ie one that is held by a rope from the ground). **2** [attrib] having little or no freedom to go elsewhere or to make other choices: *A salesman loves to have a captive audience.* ○ *a captive market.*

▶ **captive** *n* a person or an animal that is a prisoner: *Three of the captives tried to escape.*

captivity /kæp'tɪvəti/ *n* [U] the state of being a prisoner or not free: *He was held in captivity for*

C

three years. ○ *Wild animals do not often breed well in captivity.*

captor /ˈkæptə(r)/ *n* a person who captures a person or an animal: *The hostages were well treated by their captors.*

capture /ˈkæptʃə(r)/ *v* **1** to take a person or an animal as a prisoner: [Vn] *capture an escaped convict.* **2** to take or win control of sth by force or skill: [Vn] *capture a town* ○ *capture sb's attention/public support/a large share of the votes.* **3** to succeed in representing sb/sth in a picture, on film, etc: [Vn] *capture a baby's smile in a photograph* ○ *The film captures the atmosphere of the period.* **4** [Vn] to store data in a computer.
▶ **capture** *n* [U] the action of capturing sb/sth or of being captured: *the capture of a thief* ○ *He evaded capture for three days.* ○ *data capture* (ie in a computer).

car /kɑː(r)/ *n* **1** (also ˈmotor car, *esp US* **automobile**) a road vehicle with an engine and usu four wheels. One person drives it and it can usu carry three or four passengers: *What kind/make of car do you have?* ○ *We're going (to London) by car.* ○ *get in/get out of the car* ○ *a car driver/manufacturer* ○ *a car crash.* ⇨ picture. **2** (in compound *ns*) **(a)** a carriage of a specified type on a train: *a dining-/sleeping-car.* **(b)** (*US*) any carriage or van on a train: *Several cars went off the rails.* **3** the part of a BALLOON(2), lift(2), cable railway (CABLE 1), etc that carries passengers: *a cable car.*
■ ˈ**car bomb** *n* a bomb placed to explode in or under a parked car: *a terrorist car bomb attack.*
ˌ**car-**ˈ**boot sale** *n* (*Brit*) an outdoor sale at which people sell things they no longer want from the boots (BOOT¹ 2) of their cars.
ˈ**car park** (*US* **parking-lot**) *n* an area or a building for parking cars: *a multi-storey car park.*
ˈ**car phone** *n* a radio telephone for use in a road vehicle.

carafe /kəˈræf/ *n* **(a)** a glass container in which wine or water are served at meals. ⇨ picture at BOTTLE. **(b)** the amount contained in this: *I can't drink more than half a carafe.*

caramel /ˈkærəməl/ *n* **1** [U, C] a type of hard sticky sweet made by heating butter, sugar, milk, etc: *a piece of caramel.* **2** [U] burnt sugar used for giving colour and flavour to food. **3** [U] a light brown colour.
▶ **caramelize**, **-ise** /ˈkærəməlaɪz/ *v* **(a)** [V, Vn] to turn or make sth turn into caramel. **(b)** [Vn] to cover or cook food with burnt sugar.

carapace /ˈkærəpeɪs/ *n* the hard shell on the back of certain animals, eg a TORTOISE.

carat /ˈkærət/ *n* (*abbr* **ct**) **1** a unit of weight for precious stones. It is equal to 200 milligrams (MILLIGRAM). **2** (*US* **karat**) a unit for measuring how pure gold is (the purest gold being 24 carats): *a 20-carat gold ring* ○ *a ring of 20 carats.*

caravan /ˈkærəvæn/ *n* **1(a)** (*Brit*) (*US* **trailer**) a large vehicle on wheels, equipped for living and sleeping in. Caravans are usu pulled by cars and used for holidays: *a caravan park/site.* **(b)** a covered cart used for living in and usu pulled by a horse: *a gypsy caravan.* **2** a group of people with vehicles or animals travelling together for safety, esp across the desert: *a refugee caravan.*
▶ **caravan** *v* (**-nn-**) (usu **go caravanning**) (*Brit*) to have a holiday in a caravan: [V] *We're going caravanning in Spain this summer.*

caraway /ˈkærəweɪ/ *n* [C, U] a plant with seeds that have a strong taste and are used for giving flavour to bread, cakes, etc: *Add a teaspoon of caraway seed(s).*

carbine /ˈkɑːbaɪn/ *n* a short light automatic RIFLE¹.

carbohydrate /ˌkɑːbəʊˈhaɪdreɪt/ *n* [C, U] any of several substances such as sugar or STARCH(1a) that are composed of CARBON(1), HYDROGEN and oxygen.

Carbohydrates contained in food provide the body with energy and heat. **2 carbohydrates** [pl] foods that contain a lot of carbohydrate and are thought to make people fat: *I'm trying to cut down on carbohydrates.*

carbolic /kɑːˈbɒlɪk/ (also **car**ˌ**bolic** ˈ**acid**) *n* [U] a powerful liquid used as an ANTISEPTIC and a disinfectant (DISINFECT): *carbolic soap.*

carbon /ˈkɑːbən/ *n* **1** [U] (*symb* **C**) a chemical element. Carbon is present in all living substances and occurs in its pure form as diamond and GRAPHITE. ⇨ App 7. **2** [C] = CARBON COPY: *a top copy and two carbons.* **3** [C] a piece of carbon paper.
■ ˌ**carbon** ˈ**copy** *n* **1** a copy made with carbon paper: *I keep a carbon copy of every letter I type.* **2** a person or thing that is almost or exactly the same as another: *She's a carbon copy of her sister.*
ˌ**carbon** ˈ**dating** *n* [U] a method of calculating the age of very old objects by measuring the amounts of different forms of carbon in them.
ˌ**carbon di**ˈ**oxide** *n* [U] the gas breathed out by people and animals from the lungs or produced by burning carbon.
ˌ**carbon mon**ˈ**oxide** *n* [U] a poisonous gas formed when carbon burns partially but not completely. It is produced eg when petrol is burnt in petrol engines.
ˈ**carbon paper** *n* [U] a type of thin paper covered with carbon or some other dark substance and used between sheets of plain paper for making copies of written or typed documents.

carbonated /ˈkɑːbəneɪtɪd/ *adj* containing carbon dioxide (CARBON), FIZZY: *carbonated drinks.*

carboniferous /ˌkɑːbəˈnɪfərəs/ *adj* (*geology*) **1** producing coal: *carboniferous rocks.* **2 Carboniferous** of the period in the earth's history when layers of coal were formed underground.

carboy /ˈkɑːbɔɪ/ *n* a large round glass or plastic bottle, usu protected by an outer frame of wood, etc and used for containing dangerous liquids.

carbuncle /ˈkɑːbʌŋkl/ *n* **1** a large painful swelling under the skin. **2** a bright red jewel with a round shape.

carburettor /ˌkɑːbəˈretə(r)/ (*US* **carburetor** /ˈkɑːbəreɪtər/) *n* an apparatus in a petrol engine, esp in a motor vehicle. Petrol and air are mixed together in the carburettor to make the explosive gas which provides power. ⇨ picture at CAR.

carcass /ˈkɑːkəs/ *n* **1** the dead body of an animal, esp one ready for cutting up as meat: *vultures picking at a lion's carcass.* Compare CORPSE. **2** the bones of a cooked bird: *You might find a bit of meat left on the chicken carcass.* **3** (*joc* or *derog*) a person's body: *Move your carcass!*

carcinogen /kɑːˈsɪnədʒən/ *n* (*medical*) any substance that produces CANCER.
▶ **carcinogenic** /ˌkɑːsɪnəˈdʒenɪk/ *adj* (*medical*) producing CANCER.

card¹ /kɑːd/ *n* **1** [U] thick stiff paper or thin cardboard: *a piece of card.* **2** [C] **(a)** a piece of card or plastic with information on it, used to identify a person, to record information or as proof of membership: *an identity card* ○ *a record card* ○ *a membership card.* See also CASHCARD, CHEQUE CARD, CREDIT CARD. **(b)** = BUSINESS CARD: *I'll give you my card, in case you have any further enquiries.* See also VISITING CARD. **3** [C] **(a)** a piece of card with a picture on it, for sending greetings, an invitation, etc: *a* ˈ*Christmas/*ˈ*birthday card* ○ *a get-*ˈ*well card* (ie one sent to sb who is ill). **(b)** = POSTCARD: *David sent us a card from Spain.* **4** [C] = PLAYING-CARD: *a pack of cards.* **5 cards** [pl] card-games: *win/lose at cards* ○ *Let's play cards.* **6** [C] a programme of events at a race-meeting (RACE¹), etc. **7** [C] (*dated infml*) an odd or amusing person: *Bertie's quite a card.* **IDM** **one's best/strongest** ˈ**card** one's strongest or most

car (*esp US* **automobile**)

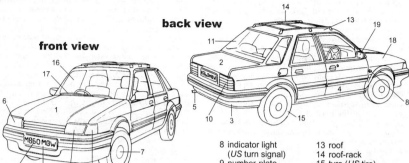

front view

back view

3 bumper	8 indicator light
4 door	(*US* turn signal)
5 exhaust-pipe	9 number-plate
1 bonnet	6 headlight *and*
(*US* hood)	sidelight
2 boot	(*US* parking light)
(*US* trunk)	7 hubcap

8 indicator light
  (*US* turn signal)
9 number-plate
  (*US* license plate)
10 tail-light
  (*US also* tail-lamp)
11 rear window
12 registration number
  (*esp US* license plate
  number)

13 roof
14 roof-rack
15 tyre (*US* tire)
16 windscreen
  (*US* windshield)
17 windscreen wiper
  (*US* windshield wiper)
18 wing (*US* fender)
19 wing mirror
  (*US* side mirror)

the interior

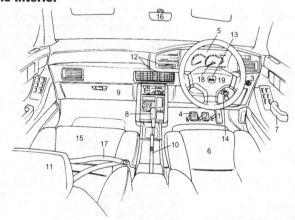

1 accelerator pedal
  (*US* gas pedal)
2 brake pedal
3 choke
4 clutch pedal
5 dashboard
6 driver's seat
7 door handle
8 gear lever
  (*US* gear shift)
9 glove compartment
10 handbrake
11 headrest
12 heater
13 horn
14 ignition switch
15 passenger seat
16 rear-view mirror
17 seat-belt
18 speedometer
19 steering wheel

the engine
and the chassis

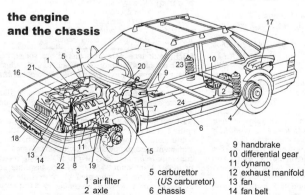

1 air filter
2 axle
3 battery
4 brake drum
5 carburettor
  (*US* carburetor)
6 chassis
7 clutch
8 dipstick

9 handbrake
10 differential gear
11 dynamo
12 exhaust manifold
13 fan
14 fan belt
15 gearbox
16 leads

17 petrol tank
  (*US* gas tank)
18 radiator
19 shock absorber
20 silencer
  (*US* muffler)
21 sparking-plug
22 ignition
23 suspension
24 transmission shaft
  (*US* drive shaft)

effective point in a discussion, etc. **(have) a card up one's** '**sleeve** (have) a useful idea, plan, etc that one keeps secret until it is needed. **get one's** '**cards / give sb their** '**cards** (*infml*) to be dismissed/dismiss sb from a job. **have the cards/ odds stacked against one** ⇨ STACK. **hold/keep one's cards close to one's** '**chest** to keep one's ideas, plans, etc secret. **lay/put one's cards on the** '**table** to be honest and open about one's own position and plans: *We can only reach agreement if we both put our cards on the table.* **on the** '**cards** (*infml*) likely or possible: *An early wedding certainly looks on the cards.* **play one's** '**cards well, right, etc** to act in the most clever and effective way to achieve sth: *You could end up running this company if you play your cards right.* **show one's hand/ cards** ⇨ SHOW².

■ '**card-carrying** adj [attrib] registered as a member of a political party or other organization: *a card-carrying member of the Communist party.*

'**card-game** n a game in which cards (CARD¹ 4) are used: *Bridge, poker and whist are card-games.*

'**card index** n = INDEX 1b.

'**card-sharp** (also '**card-sharper**) n a person who makes money by cheating at card-games.

'**card-table** n a table for playing card-games on, esp a folding one.

'**card vote** n = BLOCK VOTE.

card² /kɑːd/ n a wire brush or an instrument with teeth (TOOTH 2) for cleaning or combing wool.
▶ **card** v [Vn] to clean or comb wool with a card.

cardamom /'kɑːdəməm/ n **(a)** [C] a SE Asian plant. **(b)** [U] its seeds used as a spice.

cardboard /'kɑːdbɔːd/ n [U] **1** thick stiff paper used for making boxes, the cover of books, etc: *a cardboard box.* **2** [attrib] not strong or real; lacking depth: *a cardboard character* ∘ *cardboard emotions.*

cardholder /'kɑːdhəʊldə(r)/ n a person who has a plastic card¹(2) from a bank, shop or other organization, with which he or she can pay for goods or obtain money: *American Express cardholders.*

cardiac /'kɑːdiæk/ adj (*medical*) of or relating to the heart or heart disease: *cardiac muscles/disease/ patients* ∘ *cardiac arrest* (ie a temporary or permanent stopping of the heart).

cardigan /'kɑːdɪgən/ n a knitted woollen jacket, usu with no collar and fastened with buttons at the front.

cardinal¹ /'kɑːdɪnl/ n any of a group of senior Roman Catholic priests who elect the Pope: *Cardinal Basil Hume.*

cardinal² /'kɑːdɪnl/ adj [usu attrib] most important; chief; fundamental: *a cardinal rule/reason/virtue/ sin.*
▶ **cardinal** (also ‚cardinal '**number**) n a whole number representing quantity, eg 1, 2, 3, etc. Compare ORDINAL

■ ‚cardinal '**points** n [pl] the four main points of the COMPASS(1), ie North, South, East and West.

cardi(o)- comb form of the heart: *cardiogram* ∘ *cardiologist.*

cardiology /‚kɑːdi'ɒlədʒi/ n [U] the branch of medicine concerned with the heart and its diseases. ▶ **cardiologist** /-dʒɪst/ n.

care¹ /keə(r)/ n **1** [U] the process of looking after sb/sth; the providing of what sb/sth needs for their health or protection: *She was too young to give the child the care it needed.* ∘ *the care of the elderly in society* ∘ *medical/health care* ∘ *skin/hair care.* See also CHILD CARE. **2** [U] ~ (**over sth / in doing sth**) serious attention or thought in doing sth properly or avoiding damage to sth: *She arranged the flowers with great care.* ∘ *You should take more care over your work.* ∘ *Care is needed when crossing the road.* ∘ *Fragile — handle with care* (eg as a warning on a container holding glass). **3(a)** [U] worry; anxiety:

free from care. **(b)** [C esp pl] a cause of or reason for worry: *weighed down by the cares of a demanding job* ∘ *not have a care in the world* (ie have no worries or responsibilities). **IDM** '**care of sb** (*abbr* c/o) (esp written on envelopes) at the address of sb: *Write to him care of his lawyer.* **have a** '**care** (*dated*) (esp imperative) to be careful. **in** '**care** (*Brit*) (of children) being looked after by the local authority because the parents are dead or unable to look after them properly. **in the care of sb** being looked after by sb: *They left the child in a friend's care.* **take care (that ... /to do sth)** (esp imperative) to be careful: *Take care (that) you don't drink too much/ not to drink too much.* ∘ *Goodbye, and take care!* **take care of oneself/sb/sth 1** to make sure that one/sb is safe and well; to look after oneself/sb/sth: *My sister is taking care of the children while we're away.* ∘ *He's old enough to take care of himself.* **2** to be responsible for sb/sth; to deal with sb/sth: *Mr Smith takes care of marketing and publicity.* ∘ *Her secretary took care of all his appointments.* ⇨ note at CARE². **under the care of sb** receiving medical care from sb: *She's under the care of a specialist.*

care² /keə(r)/ v **1** ~ (**about sb/sth**) to feel that sb/ sth is important or interesting; to be worried or concerned: [V] *He failed the examination but he didn't seem to care.* [Vpr] *Don't you care about this country's future?* ∘ *She really cares about other people and their problems.* ∘ *All she cares about is her social life.* [V.wh, Vpr] *I don't think she cares (about) what happens to her children.* ⇨ note. **2** ~ **for sth** (in negative sentences or questions, esp with *would*) to like or be willing to have sth or to do sth: [Vpr] *Would you care for a drink?* ⇨ note. [V.to inf] *Would you care to go for a walk?* ∘ *If you'd care to wait here, I'll tell him you've arrived.* ⇨ note at WANT¹. **IDM for aught/all one/sb cares/knows** ⇨ AUGHT. **not care/give a damn** ⇨ DAMN⁴. **not care/give a fig** ⇨ FIG¹. **not care/give a fuck** ⇨ FUCK. **not care/ give a hoot / two hoots** ⇨ HOOT. **not care** '**less** (*infml*) not to mind or be concerned about sth at all: *I couldn't care less who wins the match.* **not care a straw / two straws (about sth/sb)** not to care at all about sth/sb: *He couldn't care a straw about my feelings.* **who** '**cares?** (*infml*) no one cares; I don't care: '*Who do you think will be the next president?'* '*Who cares?'* **PHRV** '**care for sb 1** to look after sb, esp sb who is sick or old: *care for the sick* ∘ *Who will care for him if his wife dies?* **2** to love or be very fond of sb: *He cares for her deeply.* '**care for sb/sth** (in negative or interrogative sentences) to like sb/sth; to enjoy sth: *I like him but I don't care for her.* ∘ *I don't care much/much care for opera.*
▶ **caring** /'keərɪŋ/ adj [esp attrib] showing or feeling affection and concern for other people: *caring parents* ∘ *Children need a caring environment.* ∘ *nursing and other caring professions* (ie ones that involve looking after or helping other people).

NOTE Both **take care of** somebody or something and **care for** somebody can mean 'to look after': *Who takes care of the children while you're at work?* ∘ *He's caring for his elderly parents.*

Care for is also sometimes used to mean 'to like or love somebody or something': *Steve didn't think she cared for him any more.* ∘ *I don't care for seafood.* **Care for** something and **care to do** something are quite formal and mean 'to wish' or 'to like'. These expressions are mostly used with *would* in negative statements and in offers and invitations: *I wouldn't care to be in his position.* ∘ *Would you care for a cup of coffee?* **Care about** somebody or something or **care** means 'to be interested or concerned': *She doesn't care about anybody except herself.* ∘ *Don't you care what happens to him?*

careen /kə'riːn/ v **1(a)** [Vn] to turn a ship on its

side, esp for cleaning or repairing. (**b**) [V] (of a ship) to turn or lean over. **2** (*US*) (of a vehicle) to rush forward leaning from side to side: [Vpr] *The driver lost control and the car careened down the hill.*

career /kəˈrɪə(r)/ *n* **1** [C] a job or profession, esp one with opportunities for progress or promotion: *a career in accountancy/journalism/politics* ○ *She chose an academic career.* ○ *a career diplomat* (ie a professional one) ○ *a caˈreers adviser/officer/teacher* (ie an adviser, etc whose job is to give people information about jobs and professions). **2** [C] the time that one spends and the progress one makes in a particular job, etc: *look back on a successful career* ○ *During her career she met many famous people.* ○ *My school career was not very impressive.*

▶ **career** *v* (*esp Brit*) to move about quickly and often without control: [Vpr] *careering down the road on a bicycle* ○ *The car careered off the road into a ditch.* [also Vp].

careerist /kəˈrɪərɪst/ *n* (*often derog*) a person whose main aim is to be successful in her or his career by any possible means.

■ **caˈreer girl** (also **caˈreer woman**) *n* (*esp sexist or derog*) a woman who is more interested in a professional career than in eg getting married and having children.

carefree /ˈkeəfriː/ *adj* without responsibilities or worries: *a carefree life/attitude/atmosphere.*

careful /ˈkeəfl/ *adj* **1** [pred] ~ (**about/of/with sth**); ~ (**about/in**) **doing sth** taking care, esp to avoid hurting oneself/sb or damaging sth; cautious: *Be careful not to/that you don't hurt her feelings.* ○ *Be careful with the glasses* (ie Don't break them). ○ *Be careful of the dog; it sometimes bites people.* ○ *Be careful (about/of) what you say to him.* ○ *Be careful (about/in) crossing the road.* ○ *He's very careful with his money* (ie He doesn't spend it on unimportant things). **2**(**a**) giving a lot of attention and thought to doing sth properly: *a careful worker.* (**b**) done with a lot of attention and thought: *a careful piece of work* ○ *a careful examination of the facts.* ▶ **carefully** /ˈkeəfəli/ *adv*: *Please listen carefully.* ○ *I always drive more carefully at night.* **carefulness** *n* [U].

careless /ˈkeələs/ *adj* **1** ~ (**about/of sth**) not taking care; not giving enough attention and thought: *a careless driver/worker* ○ *careless about spelling/money/one's appearance.* **2** resulting from a lack of attention and thought: *a careless error/mistake.* ▶ **carelessly** *adv.* **carelessness** *n* [U].

carer /ˈkeərə(r)/ *n* a person who looks after a sick or old person at home.

caress /kəˈres/ *n* a gentle touch, stroke or kiss, esp to show love.

▶ **caress** *v* to touch, stroke or kiss sb/sth, esp to show love: [Vn] *She caressed his hand.*

caretaker /ˈkeəteɪkə(r)/ (*Brit*) (*US* **janitor**) *n* a person who is employed to look after a house, building, etc: *the school caretaker.*

▶ **caretaker** *adj* [attrib] holding power temporarily: *a caretaker manager/government/prime minister.*

careworn /ˈkeəwɔːn/ *adj* showing signs of much worry: *She looked tired and careworn.*

carfare /ˈkɑːfeə(r)/ *n* (*US*) the money that one must pay to travel on a bus or TRAM.

cargo /ˈkɑːɡəʊ/ *n* [C,U] (*pl* **-oes**; *US* **-os**) (a load of) goods carried in a ship or an aircraft: *a cargo ship.*

NOTE Compare **cargo**, **freight** and **goods**. These words are used before the names of the different vehicles that transport things rather than people: *a cargo ship/plane* ○ *a freight/goods train.* They can also refer to what is being transported: *We watched the ship's cargo being unloaded.* ○ *freight such as coal and steel.* **Cargo** can also be countable and refer to particular products: *a cargo of cars.* **Freight** is

uncountable and can refer to a method of transporting goods: *The shipping agent also offers air freight facilities.* ○ *What is the freight charge?* It can also be used as a verb: *You can freight your belongings home by air or ship.*

caribou /ˈkærɪbuː/ *n* (*pl* unchanged or **caribous**) a N American REINDEER: *a herd of fifty caribou.*

caricature

    portrait   **caricature**

caricature /ˈkærɪkətʃʊə(r)/ *n* (**a**) [C] a picture, description or impression(5) of sb/sth that makes them look funny or ridiculous by exaggerating certain characteristics: *draw a caricature of a politician* ○ *He does very funny caricatures of all his friends.* ⇨ picture. (**b**) [U] the art of making such pictures, etc. ▶ **caricature** *v* [Vn] to make or give a caricature of sb/sth.

caricaturist *n*.

caries /ˈkeəriːz/ *n* [U] (*medical*) decay in bones or teeth: *dental caries.*

carillon /kəˈrɪljən; *US* ˈkærəlɒn/ *n* **1** a set of bells made to sound³(2) either from a KEYBOARD(2) or by a mechanism. **2** a tune played on bells.

carious /ˈkeəriəs/ *adj* (*medical*) (esp of bones or teeth) decayed; affected with CARIES.

carload /ˈkɑːləʊd/ *n* the number of people or quantity of goods that a car can carry: *a carload of shopping.*

carmine /ˈkɑːmaɪn/ *adj, n* [U] (of) a deep red colour.

carnage /ˈkɑːnɪdʒ/ *n* [U] the killing of many people: *a scene of carnage* (eg a place where there has been a battle).

carnal /ˈkɑːnl/ *adj* (*fml*) of the body; sexual or SENSUAL: *carnal desires.* ▶ **carnally** /ˈkɑːnəli/ *adv.*

■ **carnal ˈknowledge** *n* [U] (*law*) sex(2).

carnation /kɑːˈneɪʃn/ *n* (**a**) a garden plant with sweet-smelling (usu white, pink or red) flowers. (**b**) any of these flowers: *wear a carnation in one's buttonhole.* ⇨ picture at FLOWER.

carnival /ˈkɑːnɪvl/ *n* (**a**) [C, U] (a period of) public entertainment and fun that happens at a regular time of year, eg in Roman Catholic countries during the week before Lent: *Were you in Brazil during carnival?* ○ *a carnival atmosphere.* (**b**) [C] a festival of this kind, usu with a procession: *a street carnival.*

carnivore /ˈkɑːnɪvɔː(r)/ *n* an animal that eats meat. Compare HERBIVORE.

▶ **carnivorous** /kɑːˈnɪvərəs/ *adj* (of an animal) that eats meat.

carob /ˈkærəb/ *n* (**a**) [C] a southern European tree. (**b**) [U] its seeds ground into powder which is used as a substitute for chocolate.

carol /ˈkærəl/ *n* a song of joy, esp a Christmas HYMN: *a Christmas carol* ○ *carol singers* (ie singers who visit people's houses at Christmas to sing carols and collect money, usu for charity).

▶ **carol** *v* (*-ll-*; *US* *-l-*) **1** [V] to sing happily. **2** [V] (usu **go carolling**) to sing Christmas carols: *We often go carolling* (ie go from house to house, singing carols) *at Christmas.*

carotid /kəˈrɒtɪd/ *adj, n* (relating to) either of the two large blood-vessels (BLOOD¹) (**carotid arteries**) in the neck, carrying blood to the head.

carouse /kəˈrauz/ v [V] (esp fml) to drink alcohol and enjoy oneself with others in a noisy lively way.
► **carousal** /kəˈrauzl/ n [C, U].

carousel (US **carrousel**) /ˌkærəˈsel/ n **1** (US) = ROUNDABOUT² 2. **2** (esp at an airport) a belt(2) that moves round continuously so that passengers can collect their cases, etc from it.

carp¹ /kɑːp/ n (pl unchanged) a large edible fish that lives in rivers, lakes, etc.

carp² /kɑːp/ v ~ (**at/about sb/sth**) (derog) to complain continually about unimportant matters: [V] have a carping tongue ○ carping criticism [Vpr, Vp] She's always carping (on) at her children.

carpenter /ˈkɑːpəntə(r)/ n a person whose job is making or repairing wooden objects and structures. Compare JOINER.
► **carpentry** /-tri/ n [U] the art or work of a carpenter: learn carpentry ○ a fine piece of carpentry.

carpet /ˈkɑːpɪt/ n **1(a)** [U] thick woollen or artificial fabric for covering floors: a roll of carpet. **(b)** [C] a piece of this shaped to fit a particular room: lay a carpet (ie fit it to a floor) ○ We have fitted carpets (ie carpets from wall to wall) in our house. ○ We need a new bedroom carpet. Compare RED CARPET. **2** [C] a thick layer of sth on the ground: a carpet of leaves/moss/snow. **IDM on the ˈcarpet** (infml) called to see sb in authority because one has done sth wrong: The boss had me on the carpet over my expenses claim. **sweep sth under the carpet** ⇨ SWEEP¹.
► **carpet** v **1** to cover sth with or as if with a carpet: [Vn] carpet the stairs [Vnpr] a lawn carpeted with fallen leaves. **2** (infml) (esp passive) to tell sb that they have made a mistake, done sth badly, etc; to REPRIMAND sb: [Vn] be carpeted by one's boss.
■ **ˈcarpet-bag** n (formerly) a travelling bag made of carpet. **ˈcarpet-bagger** n **1** (derog) a political candidate, etc who hopes for success in an area where he or she is not known and is therefore not welcome. **2** (US) a person from the northern states who went to the South after the Civil War for private gain.
ˈcarpet-slippers (Brit) (US **house slippers**) n [pl] soft shoes with the upper part made of wool or cloth, worn indoors.
ˈcarpet-sweeper n a device with revolving brushes for sweeping carpets.

carpeting /ˈkɑːpɪtɪŋ/ n [U] carpets in general or the material used for carpets: new offices with wall-to-wall carpeting ○ plain woollen carpeting.

carport /ˈkɑːpɔːt/ n a shelter for a car, usu built beside a house. It consists of a roof supported by posts.

carriage /ˈkærɪdʒ/ n **1** (Brit also **coach**) (US **car**) [C] a separate section of a train, for carrying passengers: a first-/second-class carriage. **2** (also **coach**) [C] a vehicle, usu with four wheels, pulled by a horse or horses, for carrying people. **3(a)** (esp Brit) (US also **handling**) [U] the transporting of goods from one place to another: The goods will be sent within 14 days, but allow time for carriage. **(b)** the cost of this: £7.95 including packaging and carriage ○ carriage free/paid (ie paid by the person sending the goods). **4** [C] a moving part of a machine that supports or moves another part: a typewriter carriage. **5** [sing] (dated) the way in which sb holds and moves their head and body: have a very upright carriage.

carriageway /ˈkærɪdʒweɪ/ n (Brit) the part of a road intended for vehicles: the northbound carriageway of a motorway. See also DUAL CARRIAGEWAY.

carrier /ˈkæriə(r)/ n **1** a person or thing that carries sth. **2** a person or company that carries goods or people for payment, esp by air: an increase in flights by foreign carriers to Heathrow airport. **3** = CARRIER BAG. **4** a usu metal framework fixed to a bicycle, etc for carrying bags, etc or a small child: strap a parcel to the carrier. **5** a person or animal that can

give a disease to others without suffering from it: Mosquitoes are carriers of malaria. See also VECTOR 3. **6** = AIRCRAFT-CARRIER.
■ **ˈcarrier bag** n (Brit) a paper or plastic bag for carrying shopping, often supplied by the shop where the goods are bought.
ˈcarrier pigeon n a PIGEON(1) trained to carry messages tied to its leg or neck.

carrion /ˈkæriən/ n [U] dead and decaying flesh: crows feeding on carrion.

carrot /ˈkærət/ n **1(a)** [C] a plant with a long pointed orange root. **(b)** [C, U] this root eaten as a vegetable: boiled beef and carrots ○ Have some more carrots. ○ grated carrot. **2** [C] a reward or an advantage promised to sb to persuade them to do sth: hold out/offer a carrot to sb. **IDM the carrot and the stick** the hope of reward and the threat of punishment used together as a means of making sb try harder: a carrot-and-stick approach.
► **carroty** adj (sometimes derog) (of hair) having an orange and red colour.

carrousel (US) = CAROUSEL.

carry /ˈkæri/ v (pt, pp **carried**) **1** to support the weight of sb/sth and take them/it from place to place; to take sb/sth from one place to another: [Vn] carry shopping/a suitcase/a handbag [Vnpr] a train carrying commuters to work ○ She carried her baby in her arms. ○ Seeds can be carried for long distances by the wind. [Vnp] He broke his leg during the match and had to be carried off. ○ The injured were carried away on stretchers. **2** (of pipes, wires, etc) to contain and direct the flow of water, electricity, etc: [Vn] a pipeline carrying oil [Vnpr] The veins carry blood to the heart. [also Vnp]. **3** to have sth with one: [Vn] Police in many countries carry guns. ○ I never carry much money (with me). ○ She was arrested at the airport for carrying drugs. ○ (fig) He'll carry the memory of the experience (with him) for the rest of his life. ⇨ note at WEAR¹. **4** (of a person, an insect, etc) to be a CARRIER(5) of a disease, VIRUS(1), etc: [Vn] He's carrying the HIV virus. ○ Mosquitoes carry malaria. **5** (dated or fml) (used esp in the continuous tenses) to be pregnant with sb: [Vn] She was carrying twins. **6** (esp of sth that does not move) to support the weight of sth: [Vn] These pillars carry the weight of the roof. ○ A road bridge has to carry a lot of traffic. ○ (fig) He is carrying the department (on his shoulders) (ie It is only functioning because of his efforts and abilities). **7 (a)** to have sth as a quality: [Vn] His voice carries the ring of authority. **(b)** to have sth as a result: [Vn] Power carries great responsibility. ○ Crimes of violence carry heavy penalties. ○ The offence carries a fine of £500. **8** to take sth to a specified point or in a specified direction: [Vnpr] The war was carried into enemy territory. ○ Her ability carried her to the top of her profession. ○ He carries modesty to extremes (ie is too modest). [also Vnp]. **9** [Vn] (in adding figures) to transfer a figure to the next column. **10** (esp passive) to approve sth by a majority of votes: [Vn] The bill/motion/resolution was carried by 340 votes to 210. **11** to win the support or sympathy of sb; to persuade people to accept one's argument: [Vn] His moving speech was enough to carry the audience. ○ He stood there, defeated, and she saw she had carried her point. **12** ~ **oneself** (esp passive) to hold or move one's head or body in a specified way: [Vnadv] She carries herself well. **13(a)** (of a missile, etc) to cover a specified distance: [Vn] The full back's kick carried 50 metres into the crowd. [also Vnp]. **(b)** (of a sound, voice, etc) to be able to be heard at a distance: [V] A public speaker needs a voice that carries (well). **14** (of a newspaper or broadcast) to contain or include sth: [Vn] Today's papers carry full reports of the President's visit. **15** (of a shop) to have sth for sale as part of its regular stock: [Vn] I'm sorry, we don't carry that particular magazine. **IDM as fast as one's legs can carry one** ⇨ FAST¹ adv. **carry all/ everything be¹fore one** to be completely successful. **carry the ¹can (for sth)** (infml) to accept the responsibility or blame for sth: He left the company and I had to carry the can for all his bad decisions. **carry coals to ¹Newcastle** (Brit) to take goods to a place where there are already plenty of them; to supply sth where it is not needed. **carry/win the day** ⇨ DAY. **carry/take sth too, etc far** ⇨ FAR¹. **carry a torch for sb** to be in love with sb, esp sb who does not love one in return. **fetch and carry** ⇨ FETCH. **PHRV ¡carry sb a¹way** (usu passive) to cause sb to become very excited or to lose control of their feelings or emotions: He tends to get carried away when watching wrestling on TV.

¡carry sb ¹back (to sth) to take sb back in memory: The sound of seagulls carried her back to childhood summers by the sea.

¡carry sth ¹forward (in bookkeeping (BOOKKEEPER)) to transfer the total of figures in a column or on a page to a new column or page.

¡carry sth ¹off to win sth: She carried off most of the prizes for swimming. ¡carry it/sth ¹off to handle a difficult situation successfully: He carried the speech off well despite feeling very nervous.

carry ¹on (infml) to argue or complain noisily: He was shouting and carrying on. ○ Stop carrying on! ¡carry ¹on (with sth/doing sth), ¡carry sth ¹on to continue doing sth: Carry on (working/with your work) while I'm away. ○ They decided to carry on (eg continue their walk) in spite of the weather. ○ Carry on the good work! ¡carry ¹on (with sb) (infml derog or joc) (used esp in the continuous tenses) to have an affair(4) with sb: He's carrying on with his boss. ○ They've been carrying on for years. ¡carry ¹on sth 1 to take part in sth: carry on a conversation/ discussion/dialogue. 2 to conduct(2) or manage sth: carry on a business.

¡carry sth ¹out 1 to do sth as required or specified; to fulfil sth: carry out a promise/a threat/a plan/an order ○ We will carry out the necessary work. 2 to perform or conduct an experiment, etc: carry out an enquiry/an investigation/a survey ○ Extensive tests have been carried out on the patient.

¡carry sth ¹over 1 to delay sth until a later time. 2 = CARRY STH FORWARD.

¡carry sb ¹through (sth) to help sb to survive a difficult period: His determination carried him through (the ordeal). ¡carry sth ¹through to complete sth successfully: It's a difficult job but she's the person to carry it through.

■ ¹carry-all n (US) = HOLDALL.

¹carry-cot n (Brit) a small bed for a baby, with handles at the sides so that it can be carried.

¡carryings-¹on n [pl] (infml derog) noisy or excited behaviour: Did you hear the carryings-on next door last night?

¹carry-on n [sing] (infml derog esp Brit) a display of excitement or silly behaviour over sth unimportant: I've never heard such a carry-on!

NOTE Compare **carry**, **bear**, **cart**, **hump** and **lug**. All of these verbs share the meaning of 'to take something from one place to another'. **Carry** is the most general: Eve came in carrying an important-looking piece of paper. ○ Could you carry this box to my car for me, please? It can also refer to vehicles transporting people: The plane was carrying 250 passengers when it crashed. **Bear** describes movement and is a formal word: The ambassador arrived bearing gifts for the Queen. You **cart** something that is large or awkward away, off, around, etc: I have to cart my bicycle up and down six flights of stairs every day. It can be quite informal and suggest unwillingness: The police carted him off in a van. **Hump** suggests moving heavy and awkward things by car-

rying them on your back or shoulders: We spent all day humping furniture. ○ The members of the band hump their own gear to the gigs. **Lug** suggests carrying a heavy or awkward thing slowly, especially by pulling it behind you: I lugged my suitcases all the way to the station.

carsick /¹kɑːsɪk/ adj [usu pred] feeling ill while travelling in a car, because of its movement: Do you get carsick? ▶ **carsickness** n [U].

cart /kɑːt/ n (**a**) a vehicle with two or four wheels but no engine, used for carrying loads and usu pulled by a horse: a horse and cart. See also WAGON 2. (**b**) (also ¹**handcart**) a light vehicle with wheels that is pulled or pushed by hand. **IDM put the ¡cart before the ¹horse** to put things in the wrong order, eg by saying that sth is the cause of an event when it is really the result of what happened.

▶ **cart** v **1** to carry sth in a cart: [Vn] carting hay [Vnp] cart away the rubbish [also Vnpr]. **2** (infml) to carry sth in the hands: [Vnp] I've been carting these cases around all day. [also Vnpr]. ⇨ note at CARRY.

■ ¹**cart-horse** n a large strong horse used esp formerly for heavy work on farms, etc.

¹**cart-track** n a rough track that is not suitable for motor vehicles.

carte blanche /¡kɑːt ¹blɑːnʃ/ n [U] (French) ~ (**to do sth**) the complete freedom to act as one thinks best: give sb/have carte blanche.

cartel /kɑː¹tel/ n (usu derog) [CGp] a group of separate business firms which work together to increase profits by not competing with each other: international drug cartels.

cartilage /¹kɑːtɪlɪdʒ/ n (**a**) [U] the tough white flexible tissue attached to the bones of animals. (**b**) [C] a structure made of this: I've damaged a cartilage in my knee.

cartographer /kɑː¹tɒɡrəfə(r)/ n a person who draws maps and charts.

▶ **cartography** /kɑː¹tɒɡrəfi/ n [U] the art of drawing maps and charts.

carton /¹kɑːtn/ n a light cardboard or plastic box or pot for holding goods: a carton of milk/cream/ yoghurt/popcorn.

cartoon

YOU ARE HERE

cartoon /kɑː¹tuːn/ n **1**(**a**) an amusing drawing in a newspaper or magazine, esp one about politics or current events. ⇨ picture. (**b**) = STRIP CARTOON. **2** (also **animated cartoon**) a film made by photographing a series of gradually changing drawings, so that they look as if they are moving: a Walt Disney cartoon. **3** a drawing made by an artist as a preliminary sketch for a painting, etc.

▶ **cartoonist** n a person who draws cartoons (CARTOON 1a).

cartridge /¹kɑːtrɪdʒ/ n **1** (US **shell**) a tube or case containing explosive with a bullet, for shooting from a gun. Cartridges without bullets are also used for blasting (BLAST² 1): a cartridge belt. ⇨ picture at GUN. Compare SHELL 3, SHOT¹ 4. **2** the part of a record-player (RECORD¹) that holds the needle(6) and can be removed. **3** a sealed case containing recording tape, photographic film or ink for putting into a tape recorder (TAPE), camera or pen.

■ '**cartridge paper** n [U] thick strong paper for drawing on.

cartwheel /'kɑːtwiːl/ n **1** the wheel of a cart, usu with thick wooden spokes (SPOKE¹). **2** an acrobatic (ACROBAT) movement in which one turns over sideways putting one's hands on the ground and one's legs apart in the air like the spokes (SPOKE¹) of a wheel.
▶ **cartwheel** v (often fig) to perform a cartwheel: [V] The car hit a tree and cartwheeled across the road.

carve /kɑːv/ v **1**(a) ~ (in sth); ~ sth (out of/from/of/in sth) to form sth by cutting away material from wood or stone: [Vpr] Michelangelo carved in marble. [Vnpr] The statue was carved out of stone. [also V, Vn]. (b) ~ sth (into sth) to cut solid material in order to form sth: [Vn] carve wood [also Vnpr]. **2** to write sth by cutting on a surface: [Vnpr] carve one's initials on a tree [also Vn]. **3** ~ sth (for sb) to cut cooked meat into slices for eating: [V] Would you like to carve? [Vn] carve a joint/turkey/leg of mutton [Vnn,Vnpr] Please carve me another slice/carve another slice for me. **PHR V** ,**carve sth** '**out (for oneself)** to build one's career, reputation, etc by hard work: She carved out a name for herself as a reporter. ,**carve sth** '**up** (infml) to divide sth into parts or slices: The territory was carved up by the occupying powers.
▶ **carver** n **1** a person who carves. **2** = CARVING KNIFE.
carving n [C, U] a carved object, esp as a work of art.
■ '**carving knife** n a large knife used for carving meat. ⇨ picture at KNIFE.

caryatid /ˌkærɪ'ætɪd/ n (architecture) a statue of a female figure used as a supporting pillar in a building.

cascade /kæ'skeɪd/ n **1** a WATERFALL, esp one of several falling in stages down a steep slope with rocks. **2** a thing that falls or hangs in a way that suggests a WATERFALL: a cascade of blonde hair.
▶ **cascade** v to fall in or like a cascade: [Vpr] Water cascaded down the mountainside. ○ Her golden hair cascaded down her back. [also V, Vpl].

case¹ /keɪs/ n **1** [C] an instance of sth occurring: The company only dismisses its employees in cases of gross misconduct. ○ It's a clear case of blackmail! ○ It's a **classic case** (ie a very typical case) of bad management. **2** the **case** [sing] the situation: Is it the case (ie Is it true) that the company's sales have dropped? ○ If that is the case (ie If the situation is as stated), you will have to work much harder. **3** [C usu sing] circumstances or special conditions relating to a person or thing: In your case, we are prepared to be lenient. ○ I cannot make an exception in your case (ie for you and not for others). **4** [C] a matter that is being officially investigated, esp by the police: a murder case/a case of murder. **5** [C] (a) a question to be decided in a court of law: The case will be heard in court next week. ○ When does your case come before the court? (b) (usu sing) a set of facts or arguments supporting one side in a LAWSUIT, debate, etc: the case for the defence/prosecution ○ the case for/against the abolition of the death penalty ○ You have a very strong case. **6** [C] an instance of a disease or an injury; a person suffering from this: a case of typhoid ○ Cases of smallpox are becoming rare. **7** [C] a person having medical treatment: a hopeless case (ie a sick person who cannot be cured). **8** [U,C] (grammar) (a change in) the form of a noun, an adjective or a pronoun in certain languages, showing its relationship to another word: the nominative case ○ the accusative case ○ Latin nouns have case, number and gender. **IDM** **a case in** '**point** an example that is relevant to the matter being discussed. **as the** ,**case may** '**be** (used when describing two

or more possible alternatives) as will be determined by the circumstances: There may be an announcement about this tomorrow — or not, as the case may be. **in** '**any case** whatever happens or may have happened: There's no point complaining about the hotel room — we'll be leaving tomorrow in any case. **(just) in case (…)** because of the possibility of sth happening: It may rain — you'd better take an umbrella (just) in case (it does). **in case of sth** if sth happens: In case of fire, ring the alarm bell. **in** '**case** if that happens or has happened; if that is the situation: You don't like your job? In that case why don't you leave? **make out a** '**case (for sth)** to give arguments in favour of sth: The report makes out a strong case for increased spending on libraries.
■ ,**case** '**history** n a record of a person's background(3b), medical history, etc for use in professional treatment, eg by a doctor or social worker.
'**case-law** n [U] law based on decisions made by judges in earlier cases. Compare COMMON LAW, STATUTE LAW. See also TEST CASE.
'**case-load** n all those people for whom a doctor, social worker, etc is responsible.
'**case-study** n a detailed account of the development of a person or group of people over a period of time.

case² /keɪs/ n **1**(a) (often in compounds) any of various types of container or covering used for keeping or protecting things: a 'jewellery case ○ a 'pencil case ○ a 'packing-case (ie a large wooden box for packing goods in) ○ Exhibits in museums are often displayed in glass cases. (b) this with its contents; the amount that it contains: a case (ie 12 bottles) of champagne. **2** a SUITCASE: Could you carry my case for me?
▶ **case** v **IDM** **case the joint** (sl) to inspect a place carefully, esp before robbing it. **casing** n [U,C] a covering that protects sth: wrapped in rubber casing.

casebook /'keɪsbʊk/ n a written record kept by doctors, lawyers, etc of cases they have dealt with.

casement /'keɪsmənt/ n (also **casement window**) n a window that opens on hinges (HINGE) like a door. ⇨ picture at HOUSE¹.

casework /'keɪswɜːk/ n [U] social work involving the study of individuals or families with problems.

cash /kæʃ/ n [U] (a) money in coins or notes (NOTE¹ 4): pay (in) cash ○ I have no cash on me — may I pay by cheque? ○ I never carry much cash with me. ○ weekly cash payments of £50. (b) (infml) money in any form; wealth: I'm short of cash at the moment. ○ We need to raise some cash. **IDM** **cash** '**down** with immediate payment of cash: pay for sth cash down. ,**cash in** '**hand** the paying for goods and services in cash, esp so that the person being paid can conceal the amount that he or she earns and avoid paying tax: Can you pay me cash in hand? ○ a cash-in-hand payment of £200. ,**cash on de**'**livery** a system of paying for goods when they are delivered.
▶ **cash** v ~ sth (for sb) to exchange sth for cash: [Vn,Vnpr] cash a cheque (for sb) [also Vnn]. **PHR V** ,**cash** '**in (on sth)** to take advantage of or profit from sth: The shops are cashing in on temporary shortages by raising prices.
■ ,**cash and** '**carry** n (Brit) (a) [U] a system in which goods are sold in large quantities at lower prices than in ordinary shops, paid for in cash and taken away by the buyer. (b) [C] a shop using this system: buy food in bulk at the local cash and carry.
'**cash crop** n a crop grown for selling, rather than for use by the person who grows it. Compare SUBSISTENCE CROP.
'**cash desk** n (Brit) a desk or counter in a shop where payment is made.
'**cash dispenser** n (Brit) a machine (in or outside a

C

bank) from which cash can be obtained when a special plastic card is put in and a personal number is used.

'cash flow *n* the movement of money into and out of a business as goods are bought and sold: *a healthy cash flow situation* (eg having enough money to make payments when necessary).

'cash register *n* a machine used in shops, etc that has a drawer for keeping money in, and displays and records the price of each thing that is sold. See also TILL².

cashcard /'kæʃkɑːd/ *n* (*Brit*) a plastic card given by a bank to its customers for use in a cash dispenser (CASH).

cashew /'kæʃuː, kæ'ʃuː/ *n* **1** a tropical American tree. **2** (also **'cashew nut**) its small edible nut with a curved shape. ⇨ picture at NUT.

cashier¹ /kæ'ʃɪə(r)/ *n* a person whose job is to receive and pay out money in a bank, shop, hotel, etc.

cashier² /kæ'ʃɪə(r)/ *v* [Vn] to dismiss sb from the armed forces because he or she has done sth wrong.

cashmere /ˌkæʃ'mɪə(r)/ *n* [U] a fine soft wool, esp that made from the hair of a type of Asian goat: *an expensive ˌcashmere 'sweater*.

cashpoint /'kæʃpɔɪnt/ *n* (*Brit*) = CASH DISPENSER.

casino /kə'siːnəʊ/ *n* (*pl* **-os**) a public building or room where people play gambling games for money.

cask /kɑːsk; *US* kæsk/ *n* **(a)** a container, shaped like a barrel but smaller, used for storing liquids, esp alcoholic drinks: *an ale cask*. **(b)** the amount that it contains: *a cask of wine*.

casket /'kɑːskɪt; *US* 'kæskɪt/ *n* **1** a small, usu decorated, box for holding letters, jewels or other valuable things. **2** (*US*) a COFFIN.

cassava /kə'sɑːvə/ *n* [U] a type of flour made from the thick roots of a tropical plant.

casserole /'kæsərəʊl/ *n* **(a)** (*Brit*) [C] a dish with a lid in which meat, etc is cooked, usu in the oven, and then served at table. ⇨ picture at PAN¹. **(b)** [C,U] food cooked in a casserole: *a/some chicken casserole*.

cassette /kə'set/ *n* a small flat plastic case containing tape for playing or recording music or sound: *a cassette recorder* (ie a tape recorder (TAPE) in which cassettes are played) ○ *a video cassette* (ie for recording sound and pictures).

cassock /'kæsək/ *n* a long, usu black or red garment worn by certain members of the CLERGY, etc in church: *choirboys in red cassocks*.

cast¹ /kɑːst; *US* kæst/ *v* (*pt*, *pp* **cast**) **1** to turn or send sth in a particular direction; to direct sth: [Vn, Vnpr] *The tree cast* (ie caused there to be) *a long shadow* (*on the grass*). [Vnpr] *He cast a furtive glance at her*. ○ (*fig*) *The tragedy cast a shadow on/over their lives* (ie made them sad for a long time after it happened). ○ (*fig*) *His muddled evidence **casts doubt** on his reliability as a witness*. **2(a)** (*fml*) to throw sth, esp deliberately or with force: [Vn] *cast a stone* ○ *We cast anchor* (ie lowered it into the water) *off a small island*. [also Vnpr, Vnp]. **(b)** [V, Vn] to throw one end of a fishing-line (FISH²) out into the water. **3** to allow sth to fall or come off: [Vn] *Snakes cast their skins*. ○ *The horse cast a shoe* (ie One of its shoes came off). **4(a)** to choose actors to play parts in a play, film, etc: [V, Vn] *We're casting* (*the play*) *next week*. [Vp] ~ **as** (**sb**); ~ **sb** (**in sth**) to give sb a part in a play, etc: [Vn-n, Vnpr] *He was cast as Othello/ cast in the role of Othello*. ○ (*fig*) *Why am I always cast as a troublemaker whenever I complain?* [also Vn]. **5(a)** [Vn] to shape hot liquid metal, etc by pouring it into a mould. **(b)** ~ **sth** (**in sth**) to make an object in this way: [Vnpr] *a statue cast in bronze* ○ (*fig*) *The novel is cast in the form of a diary*. [also Vn]. **IDM cast sb adrift** (usu passive) leave sb to be

carried away on water: *When the crew mutinied he was cast adrift in a small boat without food*. **cast an eye/one's eye(s) over sb/sth** to look at or examine sb/sth quickly: *Would you cast your eye over these calculations to check that they are correct?* **cast/ shed/throw light on sth** ⇨ LIGHT¹. **cast/draw lots** ⇨ LOT⁴. **cast one's mind back** (**to sth**) to think about the past and remember things that happened: *She cast her mind back to her wedding-day*. ○ *Can you cast your mind back three months and tell me what the situation was then?* **cast one's net wide** to cover a wide field¹(4) of supply, activity, inquiry, etc: *The company is casting its net wide in its search for a new sales director*. **cast a/one's 'vote** to vote: *The votes have all been cast — they're now being counted*. **the die is cast** ⇨ DIE⁵. **PHRV** ˌcast a'bout/a'round for sth to try to find or think of sth in a hurry: *He cast about desperately for something to say*. **cast sb/sth a'side** to abandon sb/sth as useless or not wanted: *She has cast her old friends aside*. ○ *He cast aside all his inhibitions*. ○ ˌcast sb a'way (usu passive) to leave sb somewhere as a result of a SHIPWRECK: *be cast away on a desert island*. ˌcast (**sth**) 'off **1** to release a boat by freeing the ropes that hold it in position: *cast off from the shore*. **2** (in knitting) to remove stitches from the needles. ˌcast (**sth**) 'on (in knitting) to put the first line of stitches on a needle. ˌcast sb 'out (*fml*) (esp passive) to send sb away, esp using force. See also OUTCAST.

▶ **casting** *n* **1** [U] the process of choosing actors for a play, film, etc: *a strange piece of casting*. **2** [C] an object made by casting (CAST¹ 5a) hot liquid metal, etc.

■ ˌcasting 'vote *n* (usu *sing*) the vote given by a CHAIRPERSON to decide an issue when votes on each side are equal: *have the casting vote on sth*.

ˌcast 'iron *n* [U] a hard type of iron made by casting it in a mould. Compare WROUGHT IRON. ˌcast-'iron *adj* **1** made of cast iron. **2** very strong; that cannot be broken: *He has a ˌcast-iron consti'tution*. ○ *They won't find her guilty — she's got a ˌcast-iron de'fence*. **'cast-off** *adj* [attrib] (*Brit*) (esp of clothes) no longer wanted: *cast-off shoes*. — *n* (usu *pl*) a garment which the original owner will not wear again: *As a boy I often wore my elder brother's cast-offs*.

cast² /kɑːst; *US* kæst/ *n* **1** [CGp] all the actors in a play, etc: *a play with a distinguished cast* (ie with famous actors in it) ○ *a cast of thousands* (eg for a big historical film) ○ *Sir John Gielgud heads the cast* (ie is the most important actor in the film or play). ○ *a 'cast list*. **2** [C] **(a)** an object made by pouring or pressing soft material into a mould. **(b)** a mould used to make such an object. **(c)** = PLASTER CAST. **3** [C] an act of throwing sth: *the cast of the dice* ○ *make a cast with a fishing-line/net*. **4** [sing] (*fml*) a type or kind of sth: *He has an unusual cast of mind*. See also WORM-CAST.

castanets /ˌkæstə'nets/ *n* [pl] a musical instrument, used esp by Spanish dancers, consisting of two small round pieces of wood, etc which are held in the hand and hit together with the fingers to make a noise: *the clatter and whirr of castanets*.

castaway /'kɑːstəweɪ; *US* 'kæst-/ *n* a person who has been shipwrecked (SHIPWRECK) and left in a lonely place: *a castaway on a desert island*.

caste /kɑːst; *US* kæst/ *n* **1** [C] any of the Hindu social classes: *the caste system* ○ *high-caste Brahmins*. **2** [C] any exclusive social class. **3** [U] a social system based on differences in family origin, rank, wealth, etc.

castellated /'kæstəleɪtɪd/ *adj* (*techn*) built in the style of a castle with BATTLEMENTS: *castellated turrets*.

castigate /'kæstɪgeɪt/ *v* (*fml*) to criticize or punish sb severely: [Vn] *The government has been widely*

castigated in the press for its handling of the economy.
▶ **castigation** /ˌkæstɪˈgeɪʃn/ *n* [C, U].

castle /ˈkɑːsl; *US* ˈkæsl/ *n* **1** a large building or group of buildings with thick walls, towers, BATTLE-MENTS and sometimes a MOAT for defence: *a medieval castle* ∘ *Windsor Castle.* ⇨ picture. **2** (also **rook**) (in CHESS) any of four pieces placed in the corner squares of the board at the start of a game, usu made to look like a castle. ⇨ picture at CHESS. **IDM** **(build) castles in the ˈair/in ˈSpain** (to have) plans or hopes that are unlikely to be fulfilled. **an Englishman's home is his castle** ⇨ ENGLISH-MAN.

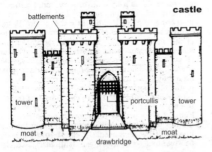

castle

battlements · tower · portcullis · tower · moat · drawbridge · moat

castor (also **caster**) /ˈkɑːstə(r); *US* ˈkæs-/ *n* any of the small wheels fixed to the bottom of a piece of furniture so that it can be moved easily.
■ **ˌcastor ˈsugar** (also **ˌcaster ˈsugar**) (*esp Brit*) (*US* **powdered sugar**) *n* [U] white sugar in fine grains (GRAIN 2).

castor oil /ˌkɑːstər ˈɔɪl; *US* ˈkæstər ɔɪl/ *n* [U] a thick yellow oil obtained from the seeds of a tropical plant and used as a type of medicine, usu as a LAXATIVE.

castrate /kæˈstreɪt; *US* ˈkæstreɪt/ *v* to remove the testicles (TESTICLE) of a male animal or person: [Vn] *A bullock is a castrated bull.* ▶ **castration** /kæˈstreɪʃn/ *n* [U].

casual /ˈkæʒuəl/ *adj* **1** [esp attrib] happening by chance: *a casual encounter/meeting/visit.* **2(a)** [usu attrib] made or done without much care or thought: *a casual remark* ∘ *a casual invitation.* (**b**) (*derog*) showing too little concern or interest; IRRESPONS-IBLE: *the company's casual attitude to office security.* (**c**) [usu attrib] not careful or thorough; not serious: *a casual inspection* ∘ *a casual glance at a book* ∘ *This may not be obvious to the casual observer.* **3** (of clothes) not formal: *a casual short-sleeved shirt.* **4** [attrib] not permanent or regular: *students looking for casual work during the holidays* ∘ *a casual la-bourer* ∘ *casual sex* (ie not involving a lasting relationship). **5** [attrib] slight; SUPERFICIAL(3a): *a casual acquaintance.*
▶ **casual** *n* **1** [C] a casual(4) worker. **2 casuals** [pl] informal clothes or shoes: *a pair of men's casuals.*
casually /ˈkæʒuəli/ *adv*: *casually dressed* ∘ *She glanced casually at the note.*
casualness *n* [U].

casualty /ˈkæʒuəlti/ *n* **1** a person who is killed or injured in war or in an accident: *Heavy casualties were reported* (ie It was reported that many people had been killed) *in the fighting.* ∘ (*fig*) *Mr Willis was the first casualty of the firm's cut-backs* (ie the first to lose his job because of them). ∘ *a casualty list.* **2** a thing that is lost, damaged or destroyed in an acci-dent: *The cottage was a casualty of the forest fire.* **3** (also **ˈcasualty ward**, **ˈcasualty department**, *US* **emergency room**) the part of a hospital where people who have been hurt in accidents are taken for urgent treatment: *After the crash she was rushed to casualty in an ambulance.*

casuistry /ˈkæzjuɪstri/ *n* [U] (*fml usu derog*) the

resolving of moral problems, esp by the use of clever but false reasoning.

cat /kæt/ *n* **1** [C] a small animal with soft fur, often kept as a pet or for catching mice: *We've got three cats and a dog.* ∘ *ˈcat food.* ⇨ picture. **2** [C] a wild animal of the cat family: *big ˈcats* (ie lions, tigers (TIGER), leopards (LEOPARD), etc). ⇨ picture. **IDM** **be the cat's ˈwhiskers/py ˈjamas** (*infml*) to be the best thing, person, idea, etc: *He thinks he's the cat's whiskers* (ie has a high opinion of himself). **not have a cat in ˈhell's chance (of doing sth)** (*infml*) to have no chance at all: *You haven't got a cat in hell's chance of winning.* **curiosity killed the cat** ⇨ CURIOSITY. **has the cat got your ˈtongue?** (said to sb, esp a child, who remains silent when expected to speak, eg after being asked a question). **let the ˈcat out of the bag** to reveal a secret carelessly or by mistake: *I wanted mother's present to be a secret, but my sister let the cat out of the bag.* **like a ˌcat on hot ˈbricks** (*infml*) very nervous: *He was like a cat on hot bricks before his driving test.* **look like sth the ˈcat brought in** (*infml*) (of a person) to look dirty or untidy. **no room to swing a cat** ⇨ ROOM. **play ˌcat and ˈmouse/play a cat-and-mouse game with sb** (*infml*) to play a cruel game with sb in one's power by constantly changing one's behaviour so that they become nervous and do not know what to expect. **put/set the cat among the ˈpigeons** (*Brit infml*) to introduce sb/sth that is likely to cause trouble or disturbance. **rain cats and dogs** ⇨ RAIN[2]. **when the cat's aˈway, the mice will ˈplay** (*saying*) people enjoy themselves more and behave with greater freedom when the person in charge of them is not there.
■ **ˈcat burglar** *n* a BURGLAR who enters houses by climbing up walls, etc.
ˌcat-o'-ˈnine-tails *n* [sing] a whip[1](1) with nine cords, formerly used for punishing prisoners.
ˌcat's ˈcradle *n* a game in which string is put round and between the fingers to form patterns.
ˈCat's-eye *n* (*Brit propr*) any one of a line of small mirrors in the centre or at the edge of a road as a guide to traffic when it is dark.

cat

leopard · tiger · lioness · lion · domestic cat

cataclysm /ˈkætəklɪzəm/ *n* a sudden violent change or disaster, eg a flood, an EARTHQUAKE or a war. ▶ **cataclysmic** /ˌkætəˈklɪzmɪk/ *adj*: *the cata-clysmic events of 1939–45.*

catacombs /ˈkætəkuːmz; *US* -kəumz/ *n* [pl] a series of underground tunnels used for burying dead people, esp in ancient Rome.

catafalque /ˈkætəfælk/ *n* a decorated platform on which the dead body of a famous person is placed before or during a funeral.

catalogue (*US* also **catalog**) /ˈkætəlɒg; *US* -lɔːg/ *n* **1** a complete list of items, usu in a special order and with a description of each: *a library catalogue* ○ *an exhibition catalogue* ○ *a mail-order catalogue* (ie a book offering goods for sale by post which is sent to people in their homes). **2** a long series of usu bad deeds, events, etc: *a catalogue of disasters/errors/crimes.*

▶ **catalogue** *v* [Vn] to list sth in a catalogue.

catalyst /'kætəlɪst/ *n* **1** a substance that makes a chemical reaction(5) happen faster without being changed itself. **2** a person or thing that causes a change: *The protests became the catalyst for political change.*

catalytic converter /ˌkætəˌlɪtɪk kən'vɜːtə(r)/ *n* (*techn*) a device used in the EXHAUST¹(2) system of motor vehicles to reduce the damage caused to the environment.

catamaran /ˌkætə-mə'ræn/ *n* a boat with two parallel hulls (HULL¹) like two boats joined together. ⇨ picture.

catamaran

hull

catapult /'kætəpʌlt/ *n* **1** (*US slingshot*) a stick shaped like a Y with a band of rubber attached to it, used esp by children for shooting stones. ⇨ picture. **2** (in ancient times) a machine for throwing heavy stones, used as a weapon in war. **3** a device for sending planes up into the air from the DECK¹(1a) of a ship.

▶ **catapult** *v* **1** [Vn, Vnpr] to shoot sth or send it up into the air using a catapult. **2** to throw sb/sth or be thrown suddenly and with force: [Vnpr] *In the crash the driver (was) catapulted through the windscreen.* ○ (*fig*) *a performance that has catapulted her from obscurity to fame overnight* [also Vpr].

catapult
(*US slingshot*)

cataract /'kætərækt/ *n* **1** a large steep WATERFALL. **2** (*medical*) a condition affecting part of the eye and causing gradual loss of sight: *an operation to remove cataracts.*

catarrh /kə'tɑː(r)/ *n* [U] a condition in which the nose and throat become full of MUCUS, as when one has a cold: *To judge from his occasional snorts, he had a severe dose of catarrh.*

catastrophe /kə'tæstrəfi/ *n* a sudden great disaster: *The earthquake was the country's worst catastrophe.* ▶ **catastrophic** /ˌkætə'strɒfɪk/ *adj: a catastrophic failure.* **catastrophically** *adv.*

catcall /'kætkɔːl/ *n* a noise or shout expressing anger or disapproval: *The senator's speech was greeted with jeers and catcalls.*

catch¹ /kætʃ/ *v* (*pt, pp* **caught** /kɔːt/) **1** to stop and hold a moving object, esp in the hands: [Vn] *I threw a ball to her and she caught it.* ○ *Our dog likes catching biscuits in its mouth.* **2** to capture sb/sth after chasing them or by trapping them, etc; to seize and hold sb/sth: [Vn] *How many fish did you catch?* ○ *I caught him* (ie met him and stopped him) *just as he was leaving the building.* [Vnpr] *catch (hold of) sb by the arm/throat/scruff of the neck.* **3** to find or discover sb doing sth; to take sb by surprise: [Vn.ing] *I caught her smoking in the bathroom.* ○ *I caught a boy stealing apples from the garden.* ○ *You won't catch me working* (ie I would never work) *on a Sunday!* ○ *I caught him staring at me.* ○ *He caught himself wondering whether he'd made a mistake.* [Vn] *The*

illness can be treated provided it's caught (ie discovered) *early enough.* [Vnpr] *You've caught me at a bad time.* **4** to be in time for (and get on) sth: [Vn] *catch a bus/plane/train* ○ *catch the post* (ie post letters before the box is emptied). **5** to be in time to find sb before they leave a place: [Vn] *I was hoping to catch you at home.* **6** (*infml esp US*) to see or hear sth; to attend sth: [Vn] *Let's eat now and maybe we could catch a movie later.* **7** to notice sth only for a moment: [Vn] *I caught a look of surprise on her face.* ○ *He caught a whiff of her perfume.* **8** ~ (**sth**) (**in/on sth**) to become stuck in or on sth, or to cause sth to become stuck: [Vpr] *Her dress caught on a nail.* [V] *The lock won't catch* (ie cannot be fastened). [Vnpr] *He caught his thumb in the door.* ○ *He caught his foot on a tree root and fell.* [also Vn]. **9** to get an illness: [V] *catch a cold* ○ *catch flu/pneumonia/bronchitis.* **10** to hear or understand sth: [Vn] *Sorry, I didn't quite catch what you said.* ○ *I don't catch your meaning.* **11** to hit sth: [Vnpr] *The stone caught him on the side of the head.* [Vnn] *She caught him a blow on the chin.* [also Vn]. **12** to begin to burn: [V] *These logs are wet: they won't catch.* **13** to reproduce(2) sth accurately: [Vn] *The artist has caught her smile perfectly.* **14** [Vn] (in cricket) to dismiss(5) a batsman by catching the ball he or she has hit before it touches the ground. **IDM** **be caught/taken short** ⇨ SHORT¹. **catch sb 'at it** = CATCH SB RED-HANDED. **catch sb's at'tention/'eye** to attract sb's attention: *Can you catch the waiter's eye?* ○ *A newspaper headline caught his attention.* **catch one's 'breath** to stop breathing for a moment, because of fear, shock, etc: *He caught his breath in surprise.* **catch one's 'death (of 'cold)** (*infml*) to catch a severe cold: *Don't go out without a coat: you'll catch your death.* **catch/take sb's fancy** ⇨ FANCY³. **catch 'fire** to begin to burn, esp by accident: *She was standing too close to the fireplace and her dress caught fire.* **'catch it** (*infml*) be punished or scolded (SCOLD): *If your father finds you here you'll really catch it!* **catch the 'light** to shine in the light. **catch sb 'napping** to gain an advantage over sb when they are not prepared; to surprise sb: *They were caught napping by the speed of the opposition.* **catch sb on the 'hop** to surprise sb by doing sth when they are not expecting it and are not ready for it: *The rush for fuel caught petrol companies on the hop.* **catch sb on the wrong 'foot** (*Brit*) to surprise sb when they are not ready or expecting sth. **catch sb red-'handed** to discover sb in the act of doing sth wrong or committing a crime. **catch 'sight of sb/sth** to see sb/sth for a moment: *She caught sight of a car in the distance.* **catch the 'sun** (of a person) to become red or brown because of spending time in the sun: *Your back looks sore — you've really caught the sun today.* **catch sb with their 'pants/'trousers down** (*infml*) to catch or trap sb when they are not prepared or expecting it. **PHRV** **'catch at sth** ⇨ CLUTCH AT STH. **ˌcatch 'on (to sth)** (*infml*) to understand sth: *He is very quick/slow to catch 'on.* **ˌcatch 'on (with sb)** (*infml*) to become popular or fashionable: *Mini-skirts first caught on in the 1960s.* **ˌcatch sb 'out** (*Brit*) **1** to show that sb is ignorant or doing sth wrong: *They tried to catch her out with a difficult question.* **2** (usu passive) to surprise sb and put them in a difficult position: *Many investors were caught out by the fall in share prices.* **ˌcatch 'up (with sb); ˌcatch sb 'up** (*Brit*) to reach (and sometimes pass by) sb who is ahead, eg in a race; to reach the same stage as sb: *Go on in front. I'll soon catch you up/catch up (with you).* ○ *After missing a term through illness he had to work hard to catch up (with the others).* **ˌcatch 'up on sth 1** to spend extra time doing sth because one has failed to do it earlier: *I've got a lot of work to catch 'up on.* **2** to find out about things that have happened: *Come over for a chat so we can catch up on*

C

---

each other's news. **be/get ˌcaught ˈup in sth** to be very interested or involved in sth: *She was caught up in the anti-nuclear movement.*

▶ **catcher** *n* (in baseball) a fielder (FIELD²) who stands behind the batter (BAT¹ *v*). ⟹ picture at BASEBALL.

catching *adj* (of a disease) easily caught; infectious.

catchy *adj* (-ier, -iest) (of a tune) pleasant and easy to remember.

■ **ˈcatch-all** *n* (*esp US*) **1** a thing for holding many small objects. **2** a word, phrase, etc that covers a range of possibilities without describing any of them exactly.

catch² /kætʃ/ *n* **1** an act of catching sth, esp a ball: *a difficult catch.* **2** (the amount of) sth caught: *a huge catch of fish* ○ (*infml*) *He's a good catch* (ie worth getting as a boyfriend or husband). **3** a device for fastening sth: *The catch on my handbag is broken.* **4** a hidden difficulty or disadvantage: *The house is very cheap. There must be a catch somewhere.* **IDM** **catch-22** /ˌkætʃ twenti 'tuː/ *n* [U] (*sl*) a difficult situation from which there is no escape, whatever action is taken, because of sth that is part of the situation itself: *the catch-22 situation facing homeless people who can't get a job without a place to live, but can't afford to pay rent without a job.* See also VICIOUS CIRCLE.

catchment area /ˈkætʃmənt eəriə/ *n* **1** (also **catchment**) (*Brit*) the area from which people are sent to a particular school, hospital, etc: *a school with a large catchment area.* **2** an area from which rain flows into a particular river, lake, etc.

catchphrase /ˈkætʃfreɪz/ *n* a well-known phrase first used by, and later associated with, an entertainer, a political leader, etc.

catechism /ˈkætəkɪzəm/ *n* a summary of the main ideas and beliefs of a religion in the form of questions and answers, used for teaching about the religion.

categorical /ˌkætə'ɡɒrɪkl; *US* -'ɡɔːr-/ *adj* (of a statement) clear and definite: *a categorical denial/ refusal.* ▶ **categorically** /-kli/ *adv*.

category /ˈkætəɡəri; *US* -ɡɔːri/ *n* a class or group of people or things regarded as having certain features, etc in common: *Job applicants normally fall into one of three categories.* ○ *The competition is divided into two categories — the first for the 10–15 age group, and the second for 15-20-year-olds.*

▶ **categorize, -ise** /ˈkætəɡəraɪz/ *v* to place sb/sth in a category: [Vn] *His work/He is difficult to categorize.* [Vn-n] *Though I sympathize with the women's movement I prefer not to be categorized as a feminist.*

cater /ˈkeɪtə(r)/ *v* **1** ~ (**for sth/sb**) to provide food and services, esp at social events: [Vpr] *cater for a party/banquet* ○ *Fifty is a lot of people to cater for!* [also V]. **2** (**a**) ~ **for sb/sth** to provide what is needed or desired by sb/sth: [Vpr] *TV must cater for many different tastes.* ○ *specially wide doors to cater for people in wheelchairs.* (**b**) ~ **to sth** to try to satisfy a particular need or demand: [Vpr] *newspapers catering to people's love of scandal.*

▶ **caterer** *n* a person whose job is providing food, etc for large social events.

catering *n* [U] the job or work of providing food, etc for social events: *Who did the catering for your son's wedding?*

caterpillar /ˈkætəpɪlə(r)/ *n* a small creature, like a worm with legs, that develops into a BUTTERFLY or a MOTH. Caterpillars feed on the leaves of plants. ⟹ picture at BUTTERFLY.

■ **ˌCaterpillar ˈtractor** *n* (*propr*) a type of heavy vehicle with an endless belt of metal plates fitted over its wheels on each side, so that it can travel over rough or very soft ground.

caterwaul /ˈkætəwɔːl/ *v* to make the loud harsh cry of a cat: [V] *Do stop caterwauling, children!*

catfish /ˈkætfɪʃ/ *n* (*pl* unchanged) a large fish found mainly in rivers, lakes, etc, with long whiskers (WHISKER 1) round its mouth.

catgut /ˈkætɡʌt/ (also **gut**) *n* [U] thin strong twisted cord made from part of the stomach of certain animals (not cats), and used for the strings of violins (VIOLIN), guitars, tennis rackets (TENNIS), etc.

Cath *abbr* Catholic.

catharsis /kə'θɑːsɪs/ *n* (*pl* **catharses** /-siːz/) [U] the process of releasing strong feelings, eg through drama or other artistic activities, as a way of providing relief from anger, suffering, etc.

▶ **cathartic** /kə'θɑːtɪk/ *adj* causing catharsis; providing relief through the open expression of strong feelings.

cathedral /kə'θiːdrəl/ *n* the main church of a district under the care of a bishop: *a cathedral city.*

Catherine wheel /ˈkæθrɪn wiːl/ (*US* also **pinwheel**) *n* a flat circular FIREWORK(1) that spins when lit.

catheter /ˈkæθɪtə(r)/ *n* (*medical*) a thin tube used for draining fluids from the body: *a urinary catheter to drain the bladder.*

cathode /ˈkæθəʊd/ *n* (*techn*) **1** the TERMINAL(3) or ELECTRODE by which electric current leaves a device. **2** the negative TERMINAL(3) of a device. Compare ANODE.

■ **ˌcathode-ˈray tube** *n* a vacuum tube, eg the picture tube of a television, in which rays from the cathode give out light and produce an image on a screen.

Catholic /ˈkæθlɪk/ *adj* **1** = ROMAN CATHOLIC: *the Catholic Church* ○ *a Catholic priest/school.* Compare PROTESTANT. **2** (also **catholic**) of or relating to all Christians or the whole Christian Church.

▶ **Catholic** *n* (*abbr* **Cath**) a member of the Roman Catholic Church: *Is she a Catholic or a Protestant?*

Catholicism /kə'θɒləsɪzəm/ *n* [U] = ROMAN CATHOLICISM.

catholic /ˈkæθlɪk/ *adj* including many or most things: *have catholic tastes/interests/views.*

catkin /ˈkætkɪn/ *n* a small thin bunch of soft flowers that grows on the branches of certain trees, eg WILLOW and BIRCH(1).

catmint /ˈkætmɪnt/ (*Brit*) (also *esp US* **catnip**) *n* [U] a plant with blue flowers whose smell is attractive to cats.

catnap /ˈkætnæp/ *n* a short sleep.

catsuit /ˈkætsuːt/ *n* a garment that fits the body closely and covers it from the neck to the feet.

cattle /ˈkætl/ *n* [pl *v*] cows and bulls (BULL 1) kept as farm animals for their milk or meat: *a herd of cattle* ○ *twenty head of cattle* (eg twenty cows) ○ *ˈcattle breeding* ○ *ˈcattle sheds* ○ *The prisoners were herded into the trucks like cattle.*

■ **ˈcattle-grid** *n* a framework with metal bars placed over a hole in the road as a barrier to stop cattle, sheep etc from passing.

catty /ˈkæti/ *adj* (-ier, -iest) deliberately unkind in what one says: *catty remarks.* ▶ **cattily** *adv.* **cattiness** *n* [U].

catwalk /ˈkætwɔːk/ *n* a long narrow raised platform or bridge, esp the platform along which models (MODEL¹6) walk in a fashion show: *The Paris catwalks were full of colour this spring.*

Caucasian /kɔː'keɪziən, kɔː'keɪʒn/ (also **Caucasoid** /ˈkɔːkəzɔɪd/) *adj* of or relating to the part of the human race with white or pale skin.

▶ **Caucasian** *n* a Caucasian person.

caucus /ˈkɔːkəs/ *n* [CGp] **1** (*derog*) (a usu secret meeting of) a small group within a larger organization or political party. **2** (*US*) (a meeting of) the members or leaders of a particular political party to choose candidates, decide policy, etc.

caught *pt, pp* of CATCH¹.

cauldron (also **caldron**) /'kɔːldrən/ *n* a large deep pot for boiling liquids or cooking food, esp over a fire: *a witch's cauldron.*

cauliflower /'kɒlɪflaʊə(r); US 'kɔːli-/ *n* [C, U] a vegetable with green leaves around a large hard white head of flowers: *Have some more cauliflower.* ⇨ picture at CABBAGE.

■ ˌcauliflower 'cheese *n* [U] (*Brit*) cauliflower cooked and served with a cheese sauce.

ˌcauliflower 'ear *n* an ear that has become swollen after being hit repeatedly, eg in boxing.

causal /'kɔːzl/ *adj* **1** of or forming a cause; relating to cause and effect: *the causal connection between events.* **2** (*grammar*) expressing or indicating a cause: *'Because' is a causal conjunction.*
▸ **causality** /kɔː'zæləti/ (also **causation**) *n* [U] (*fml*) (**a**) the relationship between cause and effect. (**b**) the principle that nothing can happen without a cause.

causation /kɔː'zeɪʃn/ *n* [U] (*fml*) **1** the causing or producing of an effect. **2** = CAUSALITY.

causative /'kɔːzətɪv/ *adj* **1** (*fml*) acting as a cause: *the causative agent in a disease.* **2** (*grammar*) (of words or forms of words) expressing a cause: *'Blacken' is a causative verb meaning 'to cause to become black'.*

cause /kɔːz/ *n* **1** [C] that which produces an effect; a person or thing that makes sth happen: *What was the cause of the fire?* ○ *Smoking is one of the main causes of heart disease.* ○ *Police are investigating the main causes of the explosion.* **2** [U] ~ (**for sth**) a reason for sth; a factor that justifies sth: *There is no cause for concern.* ○ *You have no cause for complaint/ no cause to complain.* ○ *She is never absent from work without good cause.* ⇨ note at REASON¹. **3** [C] an aim, a principle or a movement that is strongly defended or supported: *a good cause* (ie one that deserves to be supported, eg a charity) ○ *He fought for the republican cause in the civil war.* ○ *Her life was devoted to the cause of justice.* See also LOST CAUSE. **4** [C] (*law*) a matter to be resolved in a court of law: *pleading one's cause.* **IDM** **make common cause** ⇨ COMMON¹.
▸ **cause** *v* ~ **sth** (**for sb**) to be the cause of sth; to make sth happen: [Vn] *Smoking can cause lung cancer.* ○ *What caused the explosion?* [V.n *to* inf] *The cold weather caused the plants to die.* [Vnn] *He caused his parents much unhappiness.* [Vnpr] *She's always causing trouble for people.*

NOTE The verbs **cause**, **bring about** and **make** show how a certain result, situation or event happens. They are used in a variety of patterns. The direct object of **cause** or **bring about** is the result. **Bring about** is more formal and refers to a less direct cause: *Smoking can cause lung cancer.* ○ *The heavy rains brought about a plague of mosquitoes.* **Cause** can connect the result with the person who is affected: *My car has caused me a lot of trouble.* **Cause** and **make** can be used with an infinitive but not in the passive: *The pepper in the food caused me to/made me sneeze.*
When somebody **makes** you do something, they say you *must* do it. **Make** can also be used in the passive sense: *The restaurant made him pay/He was made to pay for the damage.*

causeway /'kɔːzweɪ/ *n* a raised road or path, esp across low or wet ground.

caustic /'kɔːstɪk/ *adj* **1** that can burn or destroy things by chemical action. **2** (esp of comments) deliberately unkind in a bitter unpleasant way; sarcastic (SARCASM): *caustic remarks* ○ *a caustic wit.*
▸ **caustically** /-kli/ *adv* in a caustic(2) way.
■ ˌcaustic 'soda *n* [U] a strong chemical used eg in the making of paper and soap.

cauterize, -ise /'kɔːtəraɪz/ *v* to burn the surface of the body, esp in order to destroy infection or stop a wound, etc bleeding: [Vn] *cauterize a snake-bite.*

caution /'kɔːʃn/ *n* **1** [U] being careful to avoid danger or mistakes: *Proceed with caution.* ○ *You should exercise extreme caution when driving in fog.* ○ *Such products should be treated with caution* (ie One should be very careful when using them). **2** [C] a warning, esp one given to sb who has committed a minor crime, that further action will be taken if they commit it again: *let sb off with a caution.* **IDM** **throw, fling, etc caution to the 'winds** to stop being cautious in one's actions or when deciding what to do; to decide to do sth risky.
▸ **caution** *v* (**a**) to warn sb to be careful: [Vn.*to* inf] *We were cautioned not to drive too fast.* [also Vn]. (**b**) ~ (**sb**) **against sth** to warn or advise sb against sth: [Vpr] *I would caution against undue optimism.* [also Vnpr]. **2** to give a caution(2) to sb: [Vn] *be cautioned by a judge* ○ *The players were cautioned by the referee for using bad language.*
cautionary /'kɔːʃənəri; US -neri/ *adj* giving advice or a warning: *a cautionary tale about the dangers of borrowing money.*

cautious /'kɔːʃəs/ *adj* ~ (**about/of sb/sth**) showing or having CAUTION(1); careful: *a cautious driver* ○ *cautious of strangers* ○ *cautious about spending money.* ▸ **cautiously** *adv.* **cautiousness** *n* [U].

cavalcade /ˌkævl'keɪd/ *n* a procession of people on horses, in cars, etc.

cavalier /ˌkævə'lɪə(r)/ *n* **Cavalier** a supporter of King Charles I in the English Civil War. Compare ROUNDHEAD.
▸ **cavalier** *adj* [usu attrib] showing a lack of proper concern: *display a cavalier attitude towards the feelings of others* ○ *treat sb in a cavalier manner.*

cavalry /'kævlri/ *n* (usu **the cavalry**) [Gp] soldiers fighting on horses (esp formerly) or in armoured (ARMOUR 2) vehicles: *a cavalry officer/regiment.* Compare INFANTRY.

cave /keɪv/ *n* a hollow place in the side of a cliff or hill, or underground. ⇨ picture at COAST¹.
▸ **cave** *v* (usu **go caving**) (*Brit*) to explore caves as a sport: [V] *He likes caving.* **PHRV** ˌcave 'in to fall inwards; to collapse: *The roof of the tunnel caved in* (on the workmen). ○ (*fig*) *All opposition to the proposal has caved in.*
caver *n* a person who explores caves as a sport.
■ 'cave-in *n* the sudden collapse of a roof, etc.

caveat /'kævɪæt/ *n* (*fml*) a warning that certain factors need to be considered before sth is done, accepted, etc: *I recommend the deal, but with certain caveats.*

caveat emptor /ˌkævɪæt 'emptɔː(r)/ *n* (*Latin*) the principle that the buyer is responsible for checking the quality of goods that he or she buys.

caveman /'keɪvmæn/ *n* (*pl* **-men** /-men/) **1** a person living in a cave, esp in PREHISTORIC(2) times. **2** (*infml*) a man of rough or violent feelings and behaviour.

cavern /'kævən/ *n* a cave, esp a large or dark one.
▸ **cavernous** *adj* like a cavern; large and deep: *cavernous depths* ○ *cavernous darkness/gloom.*

caviar (also **caviare**) /'kævɪɑː(r)/ *n* [U] the specially prepared eggs of a STURGEON or certain other large fish, eaten esp at the start of a meal: *a jar of finest Russian caviar.*

cavil /'kævl/ *v* (**-ll-;** *US* **-l-**) ~ (**at/about sth**) to make unnecessary complaints about sth: [Vpr] *You can hardly cavil about the odd cutlery when the meal was so delicious.* [also V].

cavity /'kævəti/ *n* an empty space within sth solid, eg a hole in a tooth: *the abdominal/nasal/oral cavity.*
■ ˌcavity 'wall *n* a wall consisting of two separate walls with a space between, designed to prevent loss of heat and to stop noise: *cavity wall insulation.*

cavort /kə'vɔːt/ v ~ (about/around) to jump or dance about in an excited way: [Vp] *Stop cavorting around and sit still!* [also V].

caw /kɔː/ n the harsh cry of a bird such as a CROW or a ROOK¹. ► **caw** v [V] *rooks cawing in the elm trees.*

cayenne /keɪ'en/ (also ,cayenne 'pepper) n [U] a type of hot-tasting red pepper.

CB /ˌsiː 'biː/ abbr **1** citizens' band: *broadcast a message on CB radio.* **2** (in Britain) Companion (of the Order) of the Bath.

CBC /ˌsiː biː 'siː/ abbr Canadian Broadcasting Corporation: *a CBC news programme* ○ *listen to (the) CBC.*

CBE /ˌsiː biː 'iː/ abbr (in Britain) Commander (of the Order) of the British Empire: *be (made) a CBE* ○ *John Adams CBE.* Compare DBE, MBE.

CBI /ˌsiː biː 'aɪ/ abbr (in Britain) Confederation of British Industry.

CBS /ˌsiː biː 'es/ abbr (in the USA) Columbia Broadcasting System: *a CBS news broadcast* ○ *listen to CBS.*

cc /ˌsiː 'siː/ abbr **1** (*commerce*) carbon copy (to): *to Luke Petersen, cc Janet Gold, Marion Ryde.* **2** cubic centimetre(s): *an 850cc engine.*

CD /ˌsiː 'diː/ abbr compact disc: *The soundtrack is available on record, tape or CD.* ○ *a CD player.*

Cdr abbr Commander: *Cdr (John) Stone.*

Cdre abbr Commodore: *Cdre (James) Wingfield.*

CD-ROM /ˌsiː diː 'rɒm/ abbr compact disc read-only memory (for displaying stored data on a computer screen).

CE abbr (in Britain) Church of England: *a CE junior school.* Compare C OF E.

cease /siːs/ v (*fml*) to come to or bring sth to an end; to stop: [V] *Hostilities* (ie Fighting) *between the two sides ceased at midnight.* [V.to inf] *That department has ceased to exist.* [Vn] *The officer ordered his men to cease fire* (ie stop shooting). [V.ing] *The factory has ceased making bicycles.* **IDM** **wonders will never cease** ⇨ WONDER.

► **ceaseless** adj not stopping; without end; continuous: *His ceaseless chatter began to annoy me.* **ceaselessly** adv.

■ **'cease-fire** n a temporary period of peace between enemies, usu while talks are taking place; a TRUCE: *negotiate/order/establish a cease-fire.*

cedar /'siːdə(r)/ n (a) [C] a tall EVERGREEN tree. (b) (also **cedarwood** /'siːdəwʊd/) [U] its hard red sweet-smelling wood, used for making boxes, furniture, pencils, etc: *a ,cedar 'chest.*

cede /siːd/ v ~ sth (to sb) (*fml*) to give up one's rights to or possession of sth, often unwillingly: [Vnpr] *cede territory to a neighbouring state* [also Vn].

ceilidh /'keɪli/ n a social occasion with music and dancing, esp in Scotland or Ireland.

ceiling /'siːlɪŋ/ n **1** the top inner surface of a room: *Mind you don't bump your head on the low ceiling.* **2** the maximum height at which a particular aircraft can normally fly: *an aircraft with a ceiling of 20 000 feet.* **3** an upper limit: *The government has set a wages and prices ceiling of 5%.* **IDM** **hit the ceiling/ roof** ⇨ HIT¹.

celebrant /'selɪbrənt/ n a priest leading a church service, esp the EUCHARIST, or a person attending it.

celebrate /'selɪbreɪt/ v **1(a)** to mark a happy or important day, event, etc with a social gathering where people can enjoy themselves: [Vn] *celebrate Christmas/sb's birthday/a wedding anniversary* ○ *celebrate a victory/success.* (b) to enjoy oneself in some way on such an occasion: [V] *It's my birthday — let's celebrate* (eg with alcoholic drink)! **2** (of a priest) to lead a religious ceremony: [Vn] *celebrate Mass/the Eucharist.* **3** (*fml*) to praise or honour sb/ sth: [Vn] *a movie celebrating the life of Martin Luther King.*

► **celebrated** adj ~ (for sth) famous: *a celebrated actor/writer/pianist* ○ *Burgundy is celebrated for its fine wines.*

celebration /ˌselɪ'breɪʃn/ n [U, C] celebrating or an occasion of celebrating: *birthday celebrations* ○ *a day of celebration.*

celebratory /ˌselə'breɪtəri; US 'seləbrətɔːri/ adj of a celebration; marking an important occasion, etc: *a celebratory mood/atmosphere* ○ *a celebratory dinner/ drink/banquet.*

celebrity /sə'lebrəti/ n **1** [C] a famous person: *celebrities of stage and screen* (ie well-known actors and film stars). **2** [U] being famous; fame.

celerity /sə'lerəti/ n [U] (*fml or rhet*) speed.

celery /'seləri/ n [U] a garden plant with crisp, pale green stems that are eaten raw or cooked as a vegetable: *a bunch/stick/head of celery* ○ *celery soup.*

celestial /sə'lestɪəl; US -tʃl/ adj **1** [attrib] of the sky: *celestial bodies* (eg the sun and the stars). **2** of heaven; DIVINE: (*fig*) *the celestial beauty of her voice.* Compare TERRESTRIAL 2.

celibate /'selɪbət/ adj (a) not married, esp for religious reasons. (b) not having sexual relations: *She decided to adopt a celibate lifestyle.*

► **celibacy** /'selɪbəsi/ n [U] the state of not being married or of not having sexual relations, esp for a long time: *Catholic priests take a vow of celibacy.*

celibate n a person who is not married; a person who does not have sexual relations.

cell /sel/ n **1** a very small room, eg for a monk in a MONASTERY or for one or more prisoners in a prison. **2** each of the small sections that together form a larger structure, eg a HONEYCOMB. **3** a device for producing an electric current, eg by the action of chemicals or light: *a photoelectric cell.* **4** a very small unit of living matter. All plants and animals are composed of cells: *red blood cells* ○ *the nucleus of a cell.* **5** a small group of people forming a centre of political activity, esp of an extreme kind: *a terrorist cell.*

cellar /'selə(r)/ n **1** an underground room for storing things: *a coal cellar.* **2** = WINE-CELLAR. See also SALT-CELLAR.

cello /'tʃeləʊ/ n (pl **-os**) a musical instrument with strings like a VIOLIN. It is held between the knees by a player sitting down. ⇨ picture at MUSICAL INSTRUMENT.

► **cellist** /'tʃelɪst/ n a person who plays the cello.

Cellophane /'seləfeɪn/ n [U] (*propr*) a thin transparent material used for wrapping things: *a Cellophane packet.*

cellular /'seljələ(r)/ adj **1** of or consisting of cells (CELL 4): *cellular tissue.* **2** of a telephone system that works by radio: *cellular phone/network/operator* ○ *cellular radio.* **3** (of cloth) loosely woven for extra warmth: *cellular blankets.*

celluloid /'seljulɔɪd/ n [U] **1** a type of transparent plastic used for making many things, esp (formerly) photographic film. **2** (*dated*) cinema films: *the celluloid heroes of one's youth.*

cellulose /'seljuləʊs/ n [U] **1** a natural substance that forms the main part of all plants and trees and is used in making plastics, paper, etc. **2** any of various compounds of this used in making paint, LACQUER, etc.

Celsius /'selsiəs/ (also **centigrade**) adj (abbr C) of or using a temperature scale where water freezes at 0° and boils at 100°: *a Celsius thermometer* ○ *20°C means twenty degrees Celsius.* ⇨ note at TEMPERATURE.

Celt /kelt, selt/ (also **Kelt** /kelt/) n (a) a member of an ancient W European people, some of whom settled in Britain before the coming of the Romans. (b) a person whose ancestors were Celts, esp one living in Ireland, Wales, Scotland, Cornwall or Brittany.

▶ **Celtic** /ˈkeltɪk, ˈseltɪk/ *adj* of the Celts or their languages.

cement /sɪˈment/ *n* [U] **1** a grey powder, made by burning clay and LIME¹(1), that sets hard after mixing with water. Cement is used in building to stick bricks together or for making very hard surfaces. Compare CONCRETE². ⇨ MORTAR¹. **2(a)** any similar soft substance that sets hard and is used for sticking things together. Compare ADHESIVE *n*, GLUE. **(b)** a substance for filling holes in teeth.
▶ **cement** *v* **1** ~ sth (over)/~ (over) sth to cover sth with cement(1): [Vnp] *They cemented over their front garden.* [also Vn]. **2** ~ A and B (together) to join things together with or as with cement: [Vnp] *Cement the two halves of the model together.* [Vnpr] *He cemented the bricks into place.* [also Vn]. **3** to establish sth firmly; to strengthen sth: [Vn] *cement a friendship.*
■ **ceˈment-mixer** *n* = CONCRETE-MIXER.

cemetery /ˈsemətri; US -teri/ *n* an area of land used for burying dead people, esp one not beside a church. Compare CHURCHYARD. ⇨ GRAVEYARD.

cenotaph /ˈsenətɑːf; US -tæf/ *n* a MONUMENT(1) in memory of people buried elsewhere, esp soldiers killed in war.

censor /ˈsensə(r)/ *n* a person officially appointed to examine books, films, plays, letters, etc and remove parts which are considered offensive, politically unacceptable or (esp in war) a threat to security: *the British Board of Film Censors.*
▶ **censor** *v* to examine or remove parts from sth, as a censor: [Vn] *censor radio/newspapers/letters* ○ *the censored version of a film.*
censorship *n* [U] the action or policy of censoring books, etc: *Strict censorship is enforced in some countries.*

censorious /senˈsɔːrɪəs/ *adj* (*fml*) tending to find faults in people or things; severely critical. ▶ **censoriously** *adv.* **censoriousness** *n* [U].

censure /ˈsenʃə(r)/ *v* ~ sb (for sth) to criticize sb severely; to show formally that one disapproves of sb: [Vn] *Two MPs were censured by the Speaker.* [also Vnpr].
▶ **censure** *n* [U] strong criticism; disapproval: *pass a vote of censure (on sb)* ○ *lay oneself open to (ie risk) public censure.*

census /ˈsensəs/ *n* (*pl* **censuses**) the official counting of sth, esp a country's population: *take a census* ○ *a traffic/wildlife census.*

cent¹ /sent/ *n* **(a)** one 100th part of a US dollar or of certain other metric units of currency. **(b)** (*abbrs* **c**, **ct**) a coin of this value. See also PER CENT, RED CENT.

> **NOTE** A hundred **cents** make up an American **dollar**: *Coffee is 90 cents a cup.* (It is also sometimes called a **penny**. See note at PENNY.) In spoken American English a **five-cent** coin is often called a **nickel** and a **ten-cent** coin is often called a **dime**. A 25-cent coin is often called a **quarter**.

cent² *abbr* century(1b): *in the 20th cent.* Compare C 2.

centaur /ˈsentɔː(r)/ *n* (in Greek myths) a creature with a man's head, arms and upper body on a horse's body and legs.

centenarian /ˌsentɪˈneərɪən/ *n* a person who is 100 years old or more.

centenary /senˈtiːnəri; US -ˈtenəri/ (US also **centennial**) *n* the 100th anniversary of sth: *The club will celebrate its centenary next year.* ○ *centenary year* ○ *centenary celebrations.*

centennial /senˈtenɪəl/ *n* (US) = CENTENARY.
▶ **centennial** *adj* **1** occurring every 100 years. **2** lasting for 100 years.

center (*US*) = CENTRE. ⇨ picture at CIRCLE.

cent(i)- *comb form* (forming *ns*) **1** hundred: *centigrade* ○ *centipede.* **2** (in the metric system) one hundredth part of: *centimetre.* ⇨ App 8.

centigrade /ˈsentɪɡreɪd/ *adj* = CELSIUS: *Boiling point is 100° centigrade.* ⇨ note at TEMPERATURE.

centigram (also **centigramme**) /ˈsentɪɡræm/ *n* one 100th part of a GRAM.

centilitre (US **centiliter**) /ˈsentɪliːtə(r)/ *n* (*abbr* **cl**) one 100th part of a litre. ⇨ App 2.

centimetre (US **centimeter**) /ˈsentɪmiːtə(r)/ *n* (*abbr* **cm**) one 100th part of a metre. ⇨ App 2.

centipede

centipede /ˈsentɪpiːd/ *n* a small crawling creature like a worm with many legs. ⇨ picture.

central /ˈsentrəl/ *adj* **1(a)** of, at, near or forming the centre of sth: *We live in central London.* ○ *Our house is very central* (ie is in or close to the centre of the town). ○ *the central plains of N America.* **(b)** easily reached from many areas; convenient: *a theatre with a very central location.* **2** most important; main; principal: *the central point of an argument* ○ *the central character in a novel* ○ *Reducing inflation is central to* (ie a major part of) *the government's economic policy.* **3** having major power or control: *central government* (ie the government of a whole country, as contrasted with local government) ○ *the central committee* (eg of a political party).
▶ **centrality** /senˈtræləti/ *n* [U] the quality of being central.
centrally /ˈsentrəli/ *adv*: *Is the house centrally heated?* (ie Does it have central heating?)
■ **ˌcentral ˈbank** *n* a national bank that does business with the government and other banks, and issues currency.
ˌcentral ˈheating *n* [U] a system for heating a building from one source by circulating hot water or hot air in pipes, etc: *central heating radiators.*
ˌcentral ˈnervous system *n* (*anatomy*) the part of the nervous system that consists of the brain and the spinal cord (SPINAL).
ˌcentral ˈprocessing unit *n*, *abbr* **CPU** the part of a computer that controls the activities of other units and performs the actions specified in the PROGRAM(1).
ˌcentral reserˈvation (*Brit*) (*US* **median**) *n* a narrow strip of land that separates the two sides of a MOTORWAY.

centralism /ˈsentrəlɪzəm/ *n* [U] the principle or practice of bringing sth, eg government or education, under the control of a single central authority.

centralize, -ise /ˈsentrəlaɪz/ *v* to come or make sth come under the control of one central authority: [Vn] *Is government becoming too centralized?* [also V]. ▶ **centralization, -isation** /ˌsentrəlaɪˈzeɪʃn; US -ləˈz-/ *n* [U]: *the centralization of power.*

centre (*US* **center**) /ˈsentə(r)/ *n* **1** [C] a point that is equally distant from all sides of sth; the middle point or part of sth: *the centre of a circle* ○ *the centre of London* ○ *a town/city centre* ○ *chocolates with soft centres.* ⇨ picture at CIRCLE. **2** [C] a point towards which people's interest is directed: *Children like to be the centre of attention.* ○ *The Prime Minister is at the centre of a political row over leaked Cabinet documents.* **3** [C] a place from which administration is organized: *a centre of power* ○ *Washington DC is a centre of government.* **4** [C] a place (eg a town or group of buildings) where certain activities or facilities are concentrated: *a centre of industry/commerce* ○ *the steel trade* ○ *a shopping/sports/leisure/community centre.* **5** (esp **the centre**) [sing] a moderate political position or party, ie one between the extremes of left and right: *This country lacks an effective party of the centre.* ○ *Are her views to the left*

C

or right of centre? ○ *a centre party.* **6** [C] (*Brit*) (in certain sports) a player whose position is in the middle of a line or group. See also CENTRE FORWARD. **7** [C] (in football, hockey, etc) a kick or hit from the side towards the middle of the pitch. **IDM** **left, right and centre; right, left and centre** ⇨ LEFT².

▶ **centre** *v* **1** to place sth in or at the centre: [Vn] *The word processor automatically centres the words on the page.* **2** [Vn] (in football, hockey, etc) to kick or hit the ball from the side towards the middle of the pitch. **PHRV** **'centre (sth) on/upon/round/ around sb/sth** to have sb/sth as its centre or main concern or theme; to concentrate or be concentrated on sb/sth: *The social life of the town centres round the local sports club.* ○ *Her research is centred on the social effects of unemployment.* ○ *Public interest centres on the outcome of next week's by-election.*

■ ,**centre** '**forward** (also **centre**) *n* (in football, hockey, etc) a player or position in the middle of the forward line: *play (at) centre forward.*

,**centre** '**half** *n* (in football, hockey, etc) a player or position in the middle of the half back (HALF²) line.

,**centre of** '**gravity** *n* the point around which the weight of an object is evenly distributed: *have a low/high centre of gravity.*

'**centre-piece** *n* **1** an ornament for the centre of a table, etc. **2** the most important item: *This agreement is the centre-piece of the international talks.*

,**centre** '**spread** *n* the two facing middle pages of a newspaper or magazine.

,**centre-**'**stage** (*US* **center-stage**) *n* [U] a prominent position, eg in current affairs: *take/move to/ occupy (the) centre-stage in world politics.*

centreboard (*US* **centerboard**) /'sentbɔːd/ *n* a movable board that can be lowered through a hole in the bottom of a sailing-boat (SAIL²) to keep it steady when sailing. ⇨ picture at DINGHY.

centrefold (*US* **centerfold**) /'sentəfəʊld/ *n* a large picture folded to form the middle pages of a magazine, etc.

centrifugal /sen'trɪfjəgl, ,sentrɪ'fjuːgl/ *adj* (*techn*) moving or tending to move away from a centre.

■ **cen,trifugal** '**force** *n* (*physics*) a force that appears to cause an object travelling round a centre to fly outwards and away from its circular path.

centrifuge /'sentrɪfjuːdʒ/ *n* a machine with a part inside that spins around to separate substances, eg milk and cream, the heavier substance being forced to the outer edge.

centripetal /sen'trɪpɪtl, ,sentrɪ'piːtl/ *adj* (*techn*) moving or tending to move towards a centre.

centrist /'sentrɪst/ *n* a person who holds moderate political views.

▶ **centrist** *adj* of moderate political views: *a centrist government/party/newspaper.*

centurion /sen'tjʊəriən; *US* -'tʊər-/ *n* (in ancient Rome) an officer commanding a unit of 100 soldiers.

century /'sentʃəri/ *n* **1(a)** a period of 100 years. **(b)** (*abbrs* **c**, **cent**) any of the periods of 100 years before or after the birth of Christ: *the 20th century* (ie AD 1901–2000 or 1900–99). **2** (in cricket) a score of 100 runs by one batsman in an INNINGS: *make/score a century* ○ *She reached her century with a boundary.* **IDM** **the turn of the year/century** ⇨ TURN².

ceramic /sə'ræmɪk/ *adj* made of clay that is permanently hardened by heat: *ceramic tiles/bowls/ bricks.*

▶ **ceramic** *n* a pot or other object made of clay: *an exhibition of ceramics by Picasso.*

ceramics *n* [sing *v*] the art of making and decorating clay pots, etc.

cereal /'sɪəriəl/ *n* **1(a)** [C] any of various types of grass producing edible grains, eg wheat, rye, BARLEY. ⇨ picture. **(b)** [U] the grain produced by such a grass: *cereal products.* **2** [C, U] food made from the

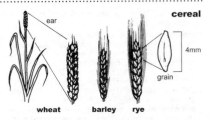

cereal

grain of cereals, often eaten for breakfast with milk: '*breakfast cereals* ○ *a bowl of cereal.*

cerebral /'serəbrəl; *US* sə'riːbrəl/ *adj* **1** of the brain: *a cerebral haemorrhage.* **2** relating to the mind rather than the feelings; intellectual: *His poetry is very cerebral.*

■ ,**cerebral** '**palsy** *n* [U] a disease that causes a person to lose control of her or his movements because of brain damage before or at birth. Compare SPASTIC.

cerebrum /sə'riːbrəm, 'serəbrəm/ *n* (*pl* **cerebra** /-brə/) (*anatomy*) the front part of the brain, concerned with feeling and thinking.

ceremonial /,serɪ'məʊniəl/ *adj* of, used for or involving a ceremony; formal: *ceremonial dress* ○ *a ceremonial occasion.*

▶ **ceremonial** *n* [C, U] a system of rules and procedures for ceremonies or formal occasions: *the ceremonials of religion* ○ *performed with due ceremonial.*

ceremonially /-niəli/ *adv.*

ceremony /'serəməni; *US* -məʊni/ *n* **1** [C] a formal act or series of formal acts performed on a religious or public occasion: *marriage/wedding/awards ceremonies.* **2** [U] formal behaviour: *There's no need for ceremony between friends.* ○ *The Queen was crowned with much (pomp and) ceremony.* **IDM** **stand on** '**ceremony** to behave formally: *Please don't stand on ceremony* (ie Please be natural and relaxed) *with me.* See also MASTER OF CEREMONIES.

▶ **ceremonious** /,serə'məʊniəs/ *adj* behaving or performed in a formal or elaborate way: *He unveiled the picture with a ceremonious gesture.* Compare UNCEREMONIOUS. **ceremoniously** *adv.*

cerise /sə'riːz, sə'riːs/ *adj*, *n* [U] (of) a light clear red colour.

CERN (also **Cern**) /sɜːn/ *abbr* European Organization for Nuclear Research (French *Conseil Européen pour la Recherche Nucléaire*).

cert¹ /sɜːt/ *n* (*Brit infml*) a thing that is sure to happen, be successful, etc; a certainty: *Black Widow is a **dead cert** for* (ie is sure to win) *the next race.*

cert² *abbr* **1** certificate. **2** certified.

certain /'sɜːtn/ *adj* **1** [pred] ~ (**that ...**); ~ (**to do sth**) sure beyond doubt; that can be relied on: *It is certain that he will agree/He is certain to agree.* ○ *One thing is certain — I'm not coming here again.* **2** [pred] ~ (**that ...**); ~ (**of/about sth**) firmly believing sth; completely sure: *I'm certain (that) she saw me.* ○ *She saw me — I'm certain of that.* ○ *I'm not certain (about) what she wants.* **3** [attrib] sure to come, happen or be effective: *There is no certain cure for this disease.* ○ *They face certain death unless they can be rescued today.* **4** [attrib] specific but not named or stated: *For certain personal reasons I will be unable to attend the meeting.* ○ *The terrorists will only release their hostages on certain conditions.* **5** [attrib] named but not known: *A certain Mr Brown telephoned while you were out.* **6** [attrib] slight; little: *There was a certain coldness in her attitude towards me.* ○ *I felt a certain reluctance to tell her the news.* **IDM** **for** '**certain** without doubt: *I couldn't say for certain when he'll arrive.* ○ *I don't yet know for certain.* **make certain (that ...)** to find out whether sth is definitely so: *I think there's a train at 8.20 but you ought to make certain.* **make certain of sth/of doing sth** to do sth in order to be sure that sth else will happen: *You'd better leave now if you want to make certain of getting there on time.*

▶ **certain** *pron* ~ **of ...** some particular members of a group of people or things: *Certain of those present had had too much to drink.*

certainly *adv* **1** without doubt; definitely: *He will certainly die if you don't call a doctor.* ○ *I'm certainly never going there again.* Compare SURELY. **2** (used in answer to questions) of course: *'May I borrow your pen for a moment?' 'Certainly.'* ○ *'Do you let your children drink alcohol?' 'Certainly not!'*

certainty /'sɜːtnti/ *n* **1** [C] a thing that is certain: *political/religious/moral certainties* ○ *Her return to the team is now regarded as a certainty.* ○ *That horse is a certainty to win the Derby.* **2** [U] the state of being certain: *I can't say with any certainty where I'll be next week.* ○ *There can be no certainty of success.*

NOTE **Certain** and **sure** are often used in the same way: *Are you sure/certain (that) you locked the door?* ○ *They're sure/certain to be late.* ○ *We must make sure/certain (that) we arrive on time.* You can say **it is certain** (NOT 'it is sure'): *It is certain that thousands of people died during the revolution.* **Sure** can often sound less strong than **certain**, especially in conversation: *I'm sure she'll come if she can* (ie I believe/hope she will). ○ *I'm 100 per cent certain she'll come* (ie I have no doubt).

certificate /sə'tɪfɪkət/ *n* an official written or printed statement that may be used as proof or evidence of certain facts: *a ˈbirth/ˈmarriage/ˈdeath certificate* ○ *an examination certificate* (ie proving that sb has passed an examination).

▶ **certificated** /-keɪtɪd/ *adj* (*esp Brit*) having the correct qualification or certificate: *a certificated teacher/trainer/consultant.*

certify /'sɜːtɪfaɪ/ *v* (*pt, pp* **-fied**) **1** ~ **sb/sth as sth** to declare sth formally, esp in writing or on a printed document: [Vn] *a document certifying sb's birth* ○ *a certified accountant/surveyor* (ie with the correct qualification for the job) [V.*that*] *He certified (that) it was his wife's handwriting.* [Vn-adj] *The doctor certified him (as) fit for work.* [also Vn-n, Vn.*to* inf]. **2** (*Brit*) (esp passive) to officially declare sb to be mad: [Vn, Vn-adj] *He was certified (insane) and sent to a mental hospital.*

▶ **certifiable** /'sɜːtɪfaɪəbl/ *adj* that can or should be certified (CERTIFY 2): (*infml*) *He's certifiable* (ie mad, crazy).

certification /ˌsɜːtɪfɪ'keɪʃn/ *n* [U] the action of certifying or state of being certified.

■ ˌ**certified** ˈ**cheque** *n* a cheque that is guaranteed by the bank.

ˌ**certified** ˈ**mail** *n* [U] (*US*) = RECORDED DELIVERY.

ˌ**certified** ˌ**public acˈcountant** *n* (*US*) = CHARTERED ACCOUNTANT.

certitude /'sɜːtɪtjuːd; *US* -tuːd/ *n* [U] (*fml*) a feeling of certainty; lack of doubt.

cervix /'sɜːvɪks/ *n* (*pl* **cervices** /-vɪsiːz/ or **cervixes** /-vɪksɪz/) (*anatomy*) the narrow part of a woman's WOMB where it joins the VAGINA. ⇨ picture at REPRODUCTION.

▶ **cervical** /'sɜːvɪkl, sə'vaɪkl/ *adj* [esp attrib] of or relating to the cervix: *cervical cancer* ○ *a cervical smear* (ie one taken from the cervix to test for CANCER(1)).

cessation /se'seɪʃn/ *n* [U,C] (*fml*) the action or act of stopping; a pause: *The bombardment continued without cessation.* ○ *a temporary cessation of hostilities.*

cesspit /'sespɪt/ (also **cesspool** /'sespuːl/) *n* **1** a covered hole or container in the ground into which

liquid waste from a building flows. **2** a dirty or CORRUPT[1] place: *a cesspool of vice.*

cf /ˌsiː'ef/ *abbr* compare (Latin *confer*). Compare CP.

CFC /ˌsiː ef 'siː/ *abbr* chloro-fluorocarbon (any of a group of gases used eg in AEROSOL containers and thought to be harmful to the OZONE layer in the earth's atmosphere).

CFE /ˌsiː ef 'iː/ *abbr* (in Britain) College of Further Education.

ch (also **chap**) *abbr* CHAPTER(1): *the Gospel of St John ch 9 v 4.*

Chablis /'ʃæbliː/ *n* [U] a dry white wine from E France.

cha-cha /'tʃɑː tʃɑː/ (also ˌ**cha-cha-**ˈ**cha**) *n* a dance performed with small steps and swinging hip movements: *dance/do the cha-cha.*

chafe /tʃeɪf/ *v* **1** ~ **(at/under sth)** to become irritated or IMPATIENT(1b) because of sth: [Vpr] *The passengers sat chafing at the long delay.* ○ *chafe under an illness* [also V]. **2** to become or make sth sore by rubbing: [V] *Her skin chafes easily.* [Vn] *His shirt collar chafed his neck.* ○ *chafed hands.*

chaff[1] /tʃɑːf; *US* tʃæf/ *n* [U] **1** the outer covering of any grain used as food, eg corn, wheat, etc. The chaff is separated from the grain by threshing (THRESH) or winnowing (WINNOW). Compare HUSK. **2** straw and HAY cut up as food for cattle. **IDM** **separate the wheat from the chaff** ⇨ SEPARATE[2].

chaff[2] /tʃɑːf; *US* tʃæf/ *v* [Vn, Vnpr] ~ **sb (about sth)** (*dated or fml*) to make a joke about sb or TEASE(1) sb in a friendly way.

chaffinch /'tʃæfɪntʃ/ *n* a small European bird of the FINCH family.

chagrin /'ʃægrɪn; *US* ʃə'grɪn/ *n* [U] a feeling of disappointment or annoyance at having failed, made a mistake, etc: *Much to his chagrin, he came last in the race.*

▶ **chagrined** *adj* affected with chagrin: *be/feel chagrined at/by sth.*

chain /tʃeɪn/ *n* **1(a)** [U,C] connected metal links or rings, used for pulling or supporting loads or for fastening or restraining things; a length of this: *keep a dog on a chain* ○ *Remember to put the chain on the door when you lock it.* ○ *The prisoners were kept in chains.* ⇨ picture. **(b)** [C] a length or loop of chain used for a specific purpose: *a bicycle chain* (ie for transmitting power from the pedals (PEDAL 1) to the wheels) ○ *The mayor wore her chain of office round her neck.* ○ *She wore a locket hanging on a silver chain.* ○ ***pull the chain*** (ie to FLUSH[2](2) the toilet). ⇨ picture at BICYCLE. **2** [C usu *pl*] (*fig*) a thing that confines or restrains: *the chains of poverty.* **3** [C] a series of connected things or people: *a chain of mountains/a mountain chain* ○ *a chain of events/circumstances/ideas* ○ *a human chain* (ie a line of people linking arms, esp as a protest). See also FOOD-CHAIN. **4** [C] a group of shops or hotels owned by the same company: *a chain of supermarkets/a supermarket chain.* **5** [C] (formerly) a unit of length (66 feet) for measuring land.

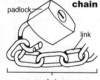

padlock

chain

link

chain

▶ **chain** *v* ~ **sb/sth (to sb/sth)**; ~ **sb/sth (up)** (esp passive) to fasten or confine sb/sth with or as if with a chain: [Vn, Vnp] *chain (up) a dog for the night* [Vnpr] *prisoners chained to a wall/each other* ○ (*fig*) *Too many women feel chained to the kitchen sink* (ie feel that they spend all their time doing household tasks).

■ ˈ**chain-gang** *n* (*US*) a group of prisoners chained together or forced to work in chains.

ˈ**chain-letter** *n* a letter sent to several people, each

of whom is asked to make copies of it and send them to other people who will do the same.

'chain-mail *n* [U] armour made of small metal rings linked together.

,chain re'action *n* (**a**) (*techn*) a chemical change forming products which themselves cause more changes so that new compounds are produced. (**b**) a series of events, each of which causes the next: *The government fear the strike may produce a chain reaction in other industries.*

'chain-saw *n* a SAW[2] with teeth set on a loop of chain and driven by a motor.

'chain-smoke *v* [V, Vn] to smoke cigarettes or cigars continuously, esp by lighting each from the one just smoked. **'chain-smoker** *n*.

'chain-store *n* any of a series of similar shops owned by the same company.

chair /tʃeə(r)/ *n* **1** [C] a movable seat with a back and sometimes with arms, for one person to sit on: *a table and chairs* ○ *Have a chair* (ie Sit down). **2** the **chair** [sing] (the function of) the person in charge of a meeting: *She takes the chair in all our meetings.* ○ *Who is in the chair today?* ○ *All remarks should be addressed to the chair.* ⇨ note at GENDER. **3** [C] the position of a university PROFESSOR; a professorship (PROFESSOR): *He holds the chair of philosophy at Oxford.* **4 the chair** [sing] (*US infml*) = THE ELECTRIC CHAIR. See also MUSICAL CHAIRS.
► **chair** *v* to act as CHAIRMAN OR CHAIRWOMAN of sth: [Vn] *Who's chairing the meeting?*
■ **'chair-lift** *n* a series of chairs hung from a moving cable for carrying people up and down a mountain, etc.

chairman /'tʃeəmən/ *n* (*pl* **-men** /-mən/; *fem* **'chairwoman** /-wʊmən/, *pl* **-women** /-wɪmɪn/) **1** the person in charge of a meeting: *We need to elect a new chairman of the committee.* **2** the permanent president of a committee, a company, etc: *He is (the) chairman of the board of governors* (eg of a school). ○ *the Conservative Party chairman* ○ *the chairman's report* (ie the annual report of a company, presented at its annual general meeting). ⇨ note at GENDER.
► **chairmanship** /'tʃeəmənʃɪp/ *n* (**a**) [C] the position of a chairman. (**b**) [U] the state of being a chairman: *under his skilful chairmanship.*

chairperson /'tʃeəpɜːsn/ *n* (*pl* **-persons**) a CHAIRMAN or CHAIRWOMAN. ⇨ note at GENDER.

chaise longue /ˌʃeɪz 'lɒŋ; *US* 'lɔːŋ/ *n* (*pl* **chaises longues** /ˌʃeɪz 'lɒŋ; *US* 'lɔːŋ/) (*French*) a long low seat with one arm, on which the person sitting can stretch out her or his legs.

chalet

chalet /'ʃæleɪ/ *n* **1**(**a**) (esp in Switzerland) a type of mountain hut or house built of wood with a roof that slopes down over the sides. ⇨ picture. (**b**) a house built in a similar style. **2** a small house or hut on a beach or in a holiday camp.

chalice /'tʃælɪs/ *n* a large cup for holding wine, esp one from which wine is drunk in the Christian communion service. ⇨ picture at CHURCH. **IDM** a **poisoned chalice** ⇨ POISON.

chalk /tʃɔːk/ *n* **1** [U] a type of soft white rock. Chalk can be burnt to make LIME[1]: *the chalk downs of*

southern England. **2**(**a**) [U] a substance similar to chalk made into white or coloured sticks for writing or drawing: *a stick of chalk* ○ *a picture drawn in chalk on the blackboard* ○ *a teacher with chalk on his jacket* ○ *chalk dust.* (**b**) [C] one of these sticks: (*a box of*) *coloured chalks.* **IDM** **different as chalk and/ from cheese** ⇨ DIFFERENT. **not by a long chalk/ shot** ⇨ LONG[1].
► **chalk** *v* ~ **sth** (**up**) (**on sth**) to write or draw sth with chalk: [Vnpr] *a message chalked on the blackboard* [Vnpr, Vnp] *dishes chalked (up) on the menuboard in a restaurant* [Vnp] *chalk up one's score* (eg when playing darts (DART[1] 4)) [also V, Vn]. **PHR V** **,chalk sth 'out** to draw the outline of sth with chalk: *The boys chalked out goalposts on the playground wall.* **,chalk sth 'up** (*infml*) to achieve or register sth: *The team has chalked up its fifth win in a row.* **,chalk sth 'up (to sb/sth)** (*Brit*) to charge drinks, etc bought in a pub to sb's account, to be paid for later: *Chalk this round up to me, please, barman.* **,chalk sth 'up to sth** (*US*) to consider that sth is caused by sth: *She was not a success in her first job but we can chalk it up to lack of experience.*

chalky *adj* (**-ier, -iest**) of or like chalk: *chalky soil* ○ *His face was chalky white.* **chalkiness** *n* [U].

chalkboard /'tʃɔːkbɔːd/ *n* (*esp US*) = BLACKBOARD.

challenge[1] /'tʃælɪndʒ/ *n* **1** ~ (**to sb**) (**to do sth**) an invitation or call to sb to take part in a game, contest, fight, etc to prove who is better, stronger, more able, etc: *issue/accept/meet a challenge.* **2** a difficult task that tests sb's ability: *She likes her job to be a challenge.* ○ *Reducing the gap between rich and poor is one of the main challenges facing the government.* **3** ~ (**to sth**) a statement or an action that questions or disputes sth: *a serious challenge to the President's authority* ○ *His statements are often* **open to challenge.** **4** an order given by a guard, etc telling sb to stop and say who they are: *The sentry gave the challenge, 'Who goes there?'*

challenge[2] /'tʃælɪndʒ/ *v* **1** ~ **sb** (**to sth**) to invite sb to do sth, esp to take part in a contest or to prove or justify sth: [Vnpr] *challenge sb to a duel/a game of tennis* [Vn.to inf] *She challenged the newspaper to prove its story.* [also Vn]. **2** to question whether sth is true, right or valid; to dispute sth: [Vn] *challenge sb's authority/right to do sth* ○ *challenge a claim/an assertion/a verdict* ○ *This new discovery challenges traditional beliefs.* **3** to test the ability of sb; to stimulate sb: [Vn] *The job doesn't really challenge him.* **4** to order sb to stop and say who they are: [Vn] *The sentry challenged the stranger at the gates.*
► **challenger** *n* a person who challenges, esp in sport: *the challenger for the heavyweight title.*

challenging *adj* offering problems that test sb's ability; DEMANDING: *a challenging assignment/job/ test.*

chamber /'tʃeɪmbə(r)/ *n* **1** [C] (formerly) a room, esp a bedroom. **2** (in compounds) a room of the specified type: *a torture/gas/burial/decompression chamber.* **3 chambers** [pl] (**a**) a judge's room for hearing cases that do not need to be taken into court. (**b**) (*Brit*) a set of rooms in a larger building, esp the offices used by barristers (BARRISTER) for seeing clients, etc. **4** [C, CGp] (the hall used by) a governing assembly, eg one of the houses of a parliament: *The members left the council chamber.* ○ *the Upper/Lower Chamber* (eg, in Britain, the House of Lords/Commons). **5** [C] (**a**) an enclosed space in the body of an animal, in a plant or in certain types of machinery: *the chambers of the heart* (ie the AURICLE(2) and the VENTRICLE) ○ *a combustion chamber.* ⇨ picture at PISTON. (**b**) an enclosed space under the ground: *The explorers discovered a vast underground chamber.* **6** [C] the part of a gun that holds the bullets.

■ **chamber concert** *n* a concert of music for a small group of instruments.

chamber music *n* [U] music written for a small group of instruments.

Chamber of Commerce *n* a group of people representing the local business community, organized to promote their interests.

chamber orchestra *n* a small group of musicians, esp one that plays early classical music.

chamber-pot *n* (esp formerly) a bowl kept in a bedroom for urinating (URINE) in, esp at night.

chamberlain /ˈtʃeɪmbəlɪn/ *n* (formerly) an official who managed the household of a king, queen or nobleman.

chambermaid /ˈtʃeɪmbəmeɪd/ *n* a woman whose job is cleaning and tidying bedrooms, usu in a hotel.

chameleon /kəˈmiːliən/ *n* **1** a small LIZARD that can change colour according to its surroundings. **2** (*often derog*) a person who changes her or his behaviour, opinions, etc to suit the situation.

chamois /ˈʃæmwɑː; *US* ˈʃæmi/ *n* (*pl* unchanged) a type of small ANTELOPE living in the mountains of Europe and Asia.

■ **chamois-leather** (also **shammy-leather** /ˈʃæmi leðə(r)/, **shammy**) *n* (**a**) [U] soft leather made from the skin of goats, sheep, deer, etc. (**b**) [C] a piece of this: *polish the car with a shammy*.

chamomile = CAMOMILE.

champ¹ /tʃæmp/ *v* **1** ~ (**at/on**) **sth** (esp of horses) to bite or eat sth noisily: [Vn] *The mare was champing hay in her stable.* [also V,Vpr]. **2** ~ (**at sth**) (used esp in the continuous tenses) to be eager or IMPATIENT(1b), esp to begin sth: [Vpr] *He was champing with rage at the delay.* [V.*to* inf] *The boys were champing to start.* [also V]. **IDM** **champ at the bit** (*infml*) to be eager or IMPATIENT(2) to start doing sth.

champ² /tʃæmp/ *n* (*infml*) = CHAMPION 1.

champagne /ʃæmˈpeɪn/ *n* [U] an expensive French white wine with bubbles in it: *a glass of champagne* ○ *champagne cocktails*.

champers /ˈʃæmpəz/ *n* [U] (*Brit infml*) = CHAMPAGNE.

champion /ˈtʃæmpiən/ (also *infml* **champ**) *n* **1** a person, a team, an animal, etc that has won a competition: *a chess champion* ○ *The English football team were world champions in 1966.* ○ *the heavyweight (boxing) champion of the world* ○ *a champion swimmer/horse/marrow.* **2** a person who fights, argues or speaks in support of sb/sth: *a champion of the poor/of women's rights.*

▶ **champion** *v* to support sb/sth; to defend sb/sth vigorously: [Vn] *champion the cause of gay rights.*

championship *n* (often *pl*) **1** a contest to decide who is the champion: *win the world championship* ○ *The European championships are being held in Rome.* ○ *a championship medal.* **2** [C] the position of being a champion: *The championship is ours.* ⇨ note at SPORT. **3** [U] strong and active support: *her lifelong championship of good causes.*

chance¹ /tʃɑːns; *US* tʃæns/ *n* **1** ~ of (doing) sth/to do sth/that... [C,U] a possibility of sth happening, esp sth desirable: *Is there any chance of getting tickets for tonight's performance?* ○ *What are the chances of his coming?* ○ *She has a good chance/no chance/not much chance/only a slim chance of winning.* ○ *What chance of success do we have?* ○ *There's a faint chance that you'll find him at home.* ○ *There's a million-to-one chance of my getting the job.* **2** [C] ~ (of doing sth/to do sth) a suitable time or occasion to do sth; an opportunity: *It was the chance she had been waiting for.* ○ *You won't get another chance of going there.* ○ *Please give me a chance to explain.* ○ *You'd be a fool to ignore a chance like that.* ○ *This is your big chance* (ie your best opportunity of success)! ⇨ note at OCCASION. **3** [C] an unpleasant or dangerous possibility; a risk: *This road may not*

be the right one — *but that's a chance we're going to have to take.* **4** [U] the way in which things happen without any cause that can be seen or understood; luck; FORTUNE(1): *Chance plays a big part in many board games.* ○ *I met her quite by chance/by sheer chance* (ie accidentally). ○ *It was (pure) chance our meeting in Paris/that we met in Paris.* ○ *Since you can't be sure what will happen you must just trust to chance.* ○ *It's important that we plan everything carefully and leave nothing to chance.* ○ *a game of chance* (ie one decided by luck, not skill) ○ *a chance meeting/encounter/occurrence/happening* (ie one that was not planned). **5** [C] an event, esp a lucky one, that was not planned: *By a happy chance a policeman was passing as I was attacked.* **IDM** **as chance would have it** although it was not planned; as it happens or happened: *As chance would have it he was going to London as well and was able to give me a lift.* **by any chance** (esp in questions) perhaps; possibly; I wonder(2c): *Would you by any chance have change for $5?* **the chances are (that)...** (*infml*) it is likely that...: *The chances are that she'll be coming.* **chance would be a fine thing** (*infml*) I would like to do sth but will never have an opportunity to do it. **an even chance** ⇨ EVEN². **fat chance** ⇨ FAT¹. **a fighting chance** ⇨ FIGHT¹. **give sb/sth half a chance** to give sb/sth some opportunity of being or doing sth: *She's very bright and I'm sure she'll succeed given half a chance.* **have/with an eye for/on/to the main chance** ⇨ EYE¹. **no chance** (*infml*) there is no possibility of that: *'Do you think we'll get a ticket for tonight's game?' 'No chance!'* **not have a cat in hell's chance** ⇨ CAT. **not have a dog's chance** ⇨ DOG¹. **not have a snowball's chance in hell / a snowball in hell's chance** ⇨ SNOWBALL. **on the (off) chance (of doing sth / that...)** because of the possibility of sth happening, although it is unlikely: *I didn't think you'd be at home, but I just called on the off chance.* **a sporting chance** ⇨ SPORTING. **stand a chance (of sth / of doing sth)** to have a possibility of (achieving) sth: *He stands a (good/fair) chance of passing the examination.* **take a chance (on sth)** to choose to do sth, knowing that it might be the wrong choice: *Although rain was forecast we decided to take a chance on it and have the party out of doors.* **take a chance / chances** to behave carelessly; to take risks: *You should never take chances when driving a car.* **take one's chances** to use one's opportunities well: *Success in life is often a question of taking one's chances when they come.*

chance² /tʃɑːns; *US* tʃæns/ *v* (usu not in the continuous tenses) **1** (*infml*) to risk sth: [Vn] *'Take an umbrella.' 'No — I'll chance it* (ie risk getting wet).' [V.*ing*] *We'll have to chance meeting an enemy patrol.* **2** (*fml*) to happen by chance: [V.*to* inf, V.*that*] *She chanced to be in/It chanced that she was in when he called.* **IDM** **chance one's arm** (*Brit infml*) to take a risk, although it is likely that one will fail. **PHR V** **chance on/upon sb/sth** (*fml*) to meet sb or find sth by chance: *Then one day I chanced upon an advertisement in the local paper.*

chancel /ˈtʃɑːnsl; *US* ˈtʃænsl/ *n* the part of a church near the ALTAR(1), where the priests and the CHOIR(1) usu sit during services. ⇨ picture at CHURCH.

chancellery /ˈtʃɑːnsələri; *US* ˈtʃæns-/ *n* **1** [C] the position, department or official residence of a CHANCELLOR: *head of the Bonn Chancellery.* **2** [Gp] the staff in the department of a CHANCELLOR. **3** [C] an office where business is done in an EMBASSY(b) or a CONSULATE.

chancellor /ˈtʃɑːnsələ(r); *US* ˈtʃæns-/ *n* **1** a senior state or law official of various kinds: *the Lord Chancellor* (ie in Britain, the highest judge (and CHAIRMAN of the House of Lords)). **2** the head of

government in certain European countries, eg Germany. **3(a)** (in Britain) the HONORARY head of certain universities. (**b**) (in the USA) the chief administrative officer in certain universities.
■ ˌChancellor of the Exˈchequer *n* (in Britain) the government minister responsible for financial affairs.

chancery /ˈtʃɑːnsəri; *US* ˈtʃæns-/ *n* **1 Chancery** (in Britain) the Lord Chancellor's division of the High Court (HIGH¹): *the Chancery Division*. **2** (*US*) a court that decides cases (CASE¹ 5) using general principles of justice and fairness (FAIR¹) not covered by the law. **3** (*esp Brit*) an office where public records are kept.

chancy /ˈtʃɑːnsi/ *adj* (**-ier, -iest**) risky; uncertain: *Finding a job can be a chancy business.*

chandelier /ˌʃændəˈlɪə(r)/ *n* a hanging light with branches for several electric bulbs (BULB 2) or candles. Chandeliers are often decorated with many small pieces of glass.

chandler /ˈtʃɑːndlə(r); *US* ˈtʃænd-/ *n* **1** (also **ship's chandler**) a person or shop that sells ropes, canvas and other supplies for ships. **2** (*US*) a person who makes or sells candles.

change¹ /tʃeɪndʒ/ *v* **1** to become or make sb/sth different; to alter: [V] *You've changed a lot since I last saw you.* ○ *Our plans have changed.* ○ *a changing world* [Vn] *change one's attitude/ideas/opinion* ○ *an event which changed the course of history* ○ *a changed man/appearance* ○ *changed circumstances.* ⇨ note. **2(a)** ~ (**sb/sth**) (**from sth**) **to/into sth** to pass or make sb/sth pass from one form to another: [Vpr] *Caterpillars change into butterflies or moths.* [Vnpr] *The witch changed the prince into a frog.* ○ *They changed the little cottage into a splendid house.* (**b**) ~ (**sb/sth**) (**from A**) (**to/into B**) to pass or make sb/sth pass from one stage to another: [V, Vpr] *The traffic lights have changed (from red to green).* [Vpr] *Britain changed to a metric system of currency in 1971.* [Vnpr] *War had changed him from a boy into a man.* **3(a)** ~ **sb/sth** (**for sb/sth**); ~ **sth** (**to sth**) to take or use another instead of sb/sth; to replace sb/sth with another: [Vn] *change one's doctor* ○ *change one's job* ○ *change one's address* (ie move to a new home) ○ *change a light bulb* ○ *change gear* (ie use a different gear in a car, etc in order to travel at a higher or lower speed) ○ *I must change my shirt* (ie put on a clean one). [Vnpr] *I'm thinking of changing my car for a bigger one.* ○ *He suddenly changed his manner to a more sympathetic one.* ○ *She changed her name to his when they got married.* (**b**) to move from one state, position, direction, etc to another: [Vn] *The leaves change colour in the autumn.* ○ *change sides* (eg in a war, debate, etc) ○ *At half-time the teams changed ends.* ○ *The ship changed course* (ie began to travel in a different direction). ○ *The wind has changed direction.* (**c**) ~ **sth** (**with sb**) (used with a plural object) (of two people) to exchange positions, places, etc: [Vn, Vnpr] *Can we change seats?/Can I change seats with you?* (**d**) ~ (**from sth to sth**) to go from one train, bus, etc to another: [Vn] *Change trains at Crewe for Stockport.* [Vpr] *This is where we change from train to bus.* [V] *All change!* (ie This train stops here; everyone must leave it.) (**e**) to put different clothes or a different covering on sb/sth: [Vn] *change* (ie put a clean NAPPY on) *the baby* ○ *change* (ie put clean sheets on) *the beds.* **4** ~ **sth** (**for/into sth**) to exchange money for the same amount in different coins or notes or in a different currency: [Vn] *Can you change a five-pound note?* [Vnpr] *I need to change my dollars into francs.* **5** ~ (**out of sth**) (**into sth**) to take off one's clothes and put others on: [V] *go upstairs to change* [Vpr] *Do you want us to change* (ie into more formal clothes) *for dinner?* ○ *Go and change out of those wet clothes into something dry.* **IDM** **change** ˈhands to pass to a

different owner: *The house has changed hands several times recently.* **change horses in mid**ˈstream to transfer one's support or trust from one person or group to another in the middle of an activity. **change one's/sb's** ˈmind to alter one's/sb's decision or opinion: *Nothing will make me change my mind.* **change/swap places** ⇨ PLACE¹. **change one's** ˈspots to make one's character or way of life different: *He's too old to change his spots now!* **change** ˈstep to alter the way one is marching so that one's feet are moving correctly with the others in the group. **change the** ˈsubject to start talking about sth different. **change one's** ˈtune (*infml*) to express a different opinion or behave differently because circumstances or one's attitude have changed: *He said he'd never get married but when he met Kathy he soon changed his tune.* **change one's** ˈways to start to live one's life differently, esp in order to suit different circumstances: *As a boy he was always in trouble with the police, but now he's completely changed his ways.* **chop and change** ⇨ CHOP³. **PHRV** ˌchange ˈback (**into sb/sth**) to return to one's earlier form, character, etc: *Do you wish you could change back to being a child again?* ˌchange ˈback (**into sth**) to take off one's clothes and put on others that one was wearing earlier: *Can I change back into my jeans now?* **change sth back (into sth**) to exchange some money for the same amount in the currency that it was in before: *change back francs into dollars.* ˌchange ˈdown (*esp Brit*) to start using a lower gear when driving a car, etc: *change down from fourth (gear) into/to third.* ˌchange ˈover (**from sth**) (**to sth**) to change from one system or position to another: *The country has changed over from military to civilian rule.* ˌchange ˈup (*esp Brit*) to start using a higher gear when driving a car, etc.
▸ **changeable** /ˈtʃeɪndʒəbl/ *adj* tending to change; often changing: *a changeable person/mood* ○ *changeable weather.*
■ ˈchange-over *n* a change from one system or situation to another: *a peaceful change-over to civilian rule* ○ *a change-over period.*

NOTE Compare **change, alter, modify** and **vary**. **Change** has a general use and describes any act of making something different: *He changed the design completely.* ○ *The name in the passport had been changed.* You **alter** something by making a difference in its appearance, character, use, etc: *Mum altered my sister's old dresses to fit me.* It can also mean that there are a lot of differences between one place or time and another: *On the last stage of our journey the scenery altered dramatically.*
  Modify is more formal. It can mean to change part of the structure or function of an object, especially a machine: *The car has been modified for racing.* It can also mean to change your behaviour, an attitude or an idea to make it more suitable for a particular situation: *Adults often modify their language when talking to young children.*
  Vary describes regularly changing something so that it remains interesting and successful: *Vegetarians can vary their diet with nuts, pulses and grains.*
  All these verbs, except **modify**, can also be intransitive: *Her expression changed when she heard the news.* ○ *This town hasn't altered since I was a child.* ○ *Political opinions vary according to wealth and family background.*

change² /tʃeɪndʒ/ *n* **1** [U, C] ~ (**in/to sth**) the action or an instance of making or becoming different: *a change in the weather* ○ *There has been a change in the programme.* ○ *The government plans to make important changes to the tax system.* ○ *Doctors say there is no change in the patient's condition.* ○ *Are you*

[Vnn] = verb + noun + noun   [V-adj] = verb + adjective   For more help with verbs, see Study pages B4–8.

for or against change? **2** [C] ~ (**from sth**) (**to sth**) (**a**) (usu *sing*) a variation in one's routine, occupation, surroundings, etc: *a welcome change from town to country life* ○ *She badly needs a change.* ○ *It certainly makes a change to read a bit of good news in the papers for once.* (**b**) an act of going from one train or bus to another: *We had to make a quick change at Crewe.* **3** [C] ~ (**of sth**) (**a**) an act of replacing one thing with another: *a change of job* ○ *Please note my change of address.* ○ *The party needs a change of leader.* ○ *This is the third change of government the country has seen in two years.* (**b**) a thing used in place of another or others: *Don't forget to take a change of* (ie a second set of) *clothes.* **4** [U] (**a**) money returned when the price of sth is less than the money used in payment: *Don't forget your change!* ○ *I paid with a £10 note and got £2.50 change.* (**b**) coins of low value; coins rather than notes: *I don't have any small change.* ○ *Have you got any change for the ticket machine?* (**c**) coins or notes of lower values that together are worth the same as a single coin or note of a higher value: *Can you give me/Have you got change for a five-pound note?* **IDM** a **change for the 'better/'worse** a person, thing, situation, etc that is better/worse than the present or previous one: *The situation is now so bad that any change is likely to be a change for the better.* **a ,change of 'air/'climate** different conditions or surroundings: *A change of air* (eg A holiday away from home) *will do you good.* **a ,change of 'heart** a great change in one's attitude or feelings, often resulting in friendlier or more helpful behaviour. **the ,change of 'life** (*euph*) = MENOPAUSE. **for a 'change** to vary one's routine; for the sake of variety: *We usually go to France for our holidays, but this year we're going to Spain for a change.* **get no change out of sb** (*infml*) to get no help, information, etc from sb. **ring the changes** ⇨ RING². **a wind / the winds of change** ⇨ WIND¹.

▶ **changeless** *adj* never changing: *a changeless God.*

changeling /ˈtʃeɪndʒlɪŋ/ *n* a child believed to have been secretly left in exchange for another, esp (in stories) by fairies.

channel /ˈtʃænl/ *n* **1**(**a**) [C] a stretch of water joining two seas: *the Bristol Channel.* (**b**) **the Channel** [sing] = THE ENGLISH CHANNEL: *The Channel crossing was very calm.* ○ *the Channel tunnel.* **2** [C] (**a**) a band¹(2a) of frequencies (FREQUENCY 2) used for broadcasting a particular set of radio or television programmes: *satellite channels.* (**b**) a particular television station(3): *What's your favourite channel?* ○ *change/switch channels* ○ *There's a good movie on Channel 4 tonight.* **3** [C] a way or system by which news, information, etc may travel: *Your complaint must be made through the proper channels.* ○ *He has secret channels of information.* **4** [C] the course in which anything moves; a direction: *The club provides a channel for local community work.* **5** [C] (**a**) the low bed¹(2) of a river, stream or canal: *dried-up channels, where once rivers flowed.* (**b**) a passage along which a liquid may flow: *Channels had been worn in the rock by the movement of the water.* **6** [C] a part of a stretch of water, deeper than the parts on either side of it, suitable for ships, boats, etc to sail on: *The channel is marked by buoys.*

▶ **channel** *v* (-**ll**-; *US* also -**l**-) **1** to carry sth in a channel; to direct sth: [Vnpr] *Water is channelled through a series of irrigation canals.* ○ (*fig*) *We must channel all our energies into the new scheme.* ○ *Funds for the project will be channelled through local government.* [also Vn]. **2** to form a channel or channels in sth: [Vn] *Deep grooves channelled the soft rock.*

chant /tʃɑːnt; *US* tʃænt/ *n* **1** words sung or shouted repeatedly, to the same rhythm: *The team's sup-*

porters sang a victory chant. **2** a religious song or prayer sung or said with syllables or words on the same note.

▶ **chant** *v* [V, Vn, V.speech] **1** to sing or shout sth repeatedly, using the same rhythm: *'We are the champions!' chanted the fans.* **2** to sing or say a religious song or prayer as a chant: *chant the liturgy.*

chanty, chantey (*US*) = SHANTY².

chaos /ˈkeɪɒs/ *n* [U] complete disorder or confusion: *The burglars left the house in (a state of) chaos.* ○ *The heavy snow has caused chaos on the roads.*

▶ **chaotic** /keɪˈɒtɪk/ *adj* in a state of chaos: *With no one to keep order the situation in the classroom was chaotic.* **chaotically** /keɪˈɒtɪkli/ *adv.*

chap¹ /tʃæp/ *v* (-**pp**-) (**a**) (of the skin) to become rough and painful; to crack: [V] *My skin soon chaps in cold weather.* (**b**) (usu passive) (esp of the weather) to make the skin rough, cracked and painful: [Vn] *chapped lips* ○ *hands and face chapped by the cold.*

▶ **chap** *n* a painful crack in the skin.

chap² /tʃæp/ *n* (*infml esp Brit*) a man or boy: *He's a nice chap.*

chap³ *abbr* chapter(1).

chapel /ˈtʃæpl/ *n* **1** [C] a separate part of a church or cathedral with its own ALTAR, used for small services (SERVICE 8) and private prayer: *a 'Lady chapel* (ie one dedicated (DEDICATE 3) to Mary, the mother of Jesus). ⇨ picture at CHURCH. **2** [C] a small building or room used for Christian worship, eg in a school, prison, large private house, etc: *a college chapel* ○ *Chapel is* (ie Services in chapel are) *at 8 o'clock.* **3** [C] (*Brit*) a place used for Christian worship by Nonconformists: *a Methodist 'chapel* ○ *She goes to/attends chapel regularly.* **4** [CGp] (the members of) a branch of a trade union in a newspaper office or printing house: *The chapel has/have voted against a strike.*

chaperon (also **chaperone**) /ˈʃæpərəʊn/ *n* (esp formerly) an older person, usu a woman, who looks after a girl or a young single(2) woman on social occasions.

▶ **chaperon** (also **chaperone**) *v* [Vn] to act as a chaperon for sb.

chaplain /ˈtʃæplɪn/ *n* a priest or other Christian minister¹(3) who works in the CHAPEL(2) of a school, prison, etc, or with the armed forces: *an army chaplain.* Compare PADRE.

▶ **chaplaincy** *n* the position, work or house of a chaplain.

chaplet /ˈtʃæplət/ *n* a circle of leaves, flowers, jewels, etc for the head.

chapter /ˈtʃæptə(r)/ *n* **1** [C] (*abbrs* **ch**, **chap**) a main division of a book, usu with a number or a title: *I've just finished Chapter 3.* ○ *in the previous/next/last chapter* ○ *Have you read the chapter on the legal system?* **2** [C] a period of time in a person's life or in history: *the most glorious chapter in our country's history.* **3** [Gp] (**a**) all the priests of a cathedral or the members of another religious community: *the dean and chapter.* (**b**) [C] a meeting of these. **4** (esp *US*) a local branch of a society, club, etc. **IDM** ,**chapter and 'verse** the exact details of sth, esp the exact place where certain information may be found: *I can't quote chapter and verse but I can give you the main points the author was making.* **a ,chapter of 'accidents** a series or sequence of unfortunate events.

■ **'chapter house** *n* a building used for the meetings of a chapter(3,4).

char¹ /tʃɑː(r)/ *v* (-**rr**-) to become or make sth black by burning; to SCORCH: [Vn] *charred wood* ○ *the charred remains of the bonfire* [also V].

char² /tʃɑː(r)/ *n* (*Brit*) = CHARWOMAN.

▶ **char** *v* (-**rr**-) [V] to work as a CHARWOMAN.

char³ /tʃɑː(r)/ n [U] (dated Brit infml) tea: a cup of char.

charabanc /'ʃærəbæŋ/ n (dated Brit) an early type of bus used esp for pleasure trips.

character /'kærəktə(r)/ n **1** [C] **(a)** all the mental or moral qualities that make a person, group, nation, etc different from others: What does her handwriting tell you about her character? ○ His character is quite different from his wife's. ○ Generosity is part of the American character. ○ She has a very strong/weak character. **(b)** all the features that make a thing, a place, an event, etc what it is and different from others: the character of the desert landscape ○ The whole character of the village has changed since I was last here. ○ The day took on the character of (ie became like) a nightmare as disaster followed disaster. **2** [U] **(a)** interesting or unusual qualities or features: You may not like her, but she's got a lot of character. ○ drab houses with no character. **(b)** the ability to handle difficult or dangerous situations; moral strength: a woman of character ○ It takes character to say a thing like that. ○ Some people think military service is character-building. **3** [C] **(a)** (infml) a person, esp an odd or unpleasant one: a suspicious-looking character. **(b)** (approv) a person who is not ordinary or typical; a very individual person: She's a real/quite a character! **4** [C] a person in a novel, play, etc: a major/minor character in the film ○ the characters in the novels of Charles Dickens. **5** [C] a person's (esp good) reputation: damage sb's character. **6** [C] a letter, sign or mark used in a system of writing or printing: Chinese/Greek/Russian characters. **IDM** ,in/,out of 'character typical/not typical of a person's character(1a): Her behaviour last night was completely out of character.
▶ **characterful** adj full of character(2a); interesting; unusual: characterful cottages.
characterless adj (derog) without character(2a); not interesting; ordinary: a characterless place.
■ 'character actor n an actor who specializes in playing odd or unusual characters.

characteristic /ˌkærəktə'rɪstɪk/ adj ~ (of sb/sth) forming part of the character(1) of a person or thing; typical: She spoke with characteristic enthusiasm. ○ Such bluntness is characteristic of him.
▶ **characteristic** n a typical feature or quality: What characteristics distinguish the Americans from the Canadians? ○ Arrogance is one of his less attractive characteristics.
characteristically adv: Characteristically she took the joke very well. ○ He made a characteristically witty speech.

characterize, -ise /'kærəktəraɪz/ v **1 (a)** to be typical or characteristic of sb/sth: [Vn] the rolling hills that characterize this part of England. **(b)** (esp passive) to give sb/sth their most noticeable quality or feature: [Vn] His work is characterized by its imagery and humour. **2** ~ sb/sth (as sth) to describe or show the character(1) of sb/sth as sth: [Vn-adj] The novelist characterizes his heroine as capricious and passionate. [Vnadv] How would you characterize the mood of the 1980s? [also Vn·n].
▶ **characterization, -isation** /ˌkærəktəraɪ'zeɪʃn/ n [U] the action or process of characterizing (CHARACTERIZE 2), esp the description of human character in novels, plays, etc: Mark Twain's skill at characterization.

charade /ʃə'rɑːd; US ʃə'reɪd/ n **1** [C] an act, an event, a situation, etc that is clearly false and absurd: Their whole marriage had been a charade: they had never loved each other. **2** charades [sing v] a game in which one team acts a series of little plays containing syllables of a word which the other team tries to guess. **3** [C] a scene in a game of charades.

charcoal /'tʃɑːkəʊl/ n **1** [U] a black substance made by burning wood slowly in an oven with a little air. Charcoal is used esp as fuel or for drawing: a stick/piece/lump of charcoal ○ barbecue charcoal ○ a charcoal sketch. **2** (also ,charcoal 'grey) [U] a very dark grey colour.

chard /tʃɑːd/ (also **Swiss chard**) n [U] a vegetable with edible white stems and green leaves, usu eaten cooked.

charge¹ /tʃɑːdʒ/ n **1** [C] a price asked for goods or services: an admission/entry charge (eg to visit a museum) ○ There is a fixed charge of £10 a week for electricity. ○ His charges are very reasonable. ○ All goods are delivered free of charge. ⇨ note at PRICE. **2** [C] a claim that a person has done wrong, esp a formal claim that he or she is guilty of a crime; an accusation: arrested on a charge of murder/a murder charge ○ The police brought a charge of theft against him. ○ I resent the charges of incompetence made against me. ○ He will be sent back to England to face a charge of (ie be tried for) armed robbery/to face charges. **3(a)** [U] responsibility for sb/sth; care¹(4) or control of sb/sth: leave a child in a friend's charge ○ He has charge of the Middle East office. ○ He assumed full charge of the firm after his father's death. ○ He was left in charge of the store while the manager was away. ○ The department was badly organized until she took charge (of it). ○ These patients are under the charge of Dr Williams. **(b)** [C] (fml) a person or thing left in sb's care¹(4): He became his uncle's charge after his parents died. **4** [C] a sudden rush or violent attack (by soldiers, wild animals, football players, etc): lead a charge ○ He made a charge for the ball. **5** [C] (fml) a task or duty: His charge was to obtain certain information regarding this. **6** [C] an amount of explosive needed to fire a gun or cause an explosion. **7** [C] an amount of electricity put into a battery or contained in a substance: a positive/negative charge. **8** [sing] a power to excite the feelings: His music carries a very strong emotional charge. ○ (infml esp US) I get quite a charge out of watching baseball. **9** [C] (fml) instructions; directions: the judge's charge to the jury (ie his advice to them about their VERDICT). **IDM** prefer/press 'charges (of sth) (against sb) (law) to accuse sb formally of a crime so that they can be tried in a court of law: We haven't enough evidence to prefer/press charges (of professional misconduct) against him. reverse the charges ⇨ REVERSE³.
■ 'charge account n (US) = CREDIT ACCOUNT.
'charge-cap v (Brit) (of the government) to set an upper limit on the amount that a local authority can charge, esp for public services: [Vn] Some boroughs have had to reduce their education budgets after being charge-capped. charge-capping n [U].
'charge card n a small, usu plastic, card provided by an organization, with which one may buy goods from various shops, etc. The full amount owed must then be paid on demand. See also CREDIT CARD, GOLD CARD.
'charge-hand n (Brit) a worker in charge of others on a particular job. See also FOREMAN 1.
'charge-nurse n (Brit) a nurse who is in charge of a hospital ward(1).
'charge-sheet n (Brit) a record kept in a police station of charges (CHARGE¹ 2) made against people.

charge² /tʃɑːdʒ/ v **1** ~ (sb/sth) for sth; ~ (sb) sth (for sth) to ask an amount as a price: [Vnpr] How much do you charge for repairing shoes? ○ As long as you've paid in advance we won't charge you for delivery. [Vn, Vn·n] I'm not going there again — they charged (me) £2 for a cup of coffee! [also V, Vpr]. **2(a)** ~ sb (with sth/doing sth) to accuse sb of sth, esp formally in a court of law: [Vnpr] He was charged with murder. ○ She charged me with neg-

lecting my work. [also Vn]. (**b**) (*fml*) to claim; to assert: [V.*that*] *It is charged* (ie in a court of law) *that on 30 November, the accused...* **3(a)** ~ ((at) sb/ sth) to rush forward and attack sb/sth: [Vn, Vpr] *The troops charged (at) the enemy lines.* [Vn] *One of our strikers was violently charged by a defender* (ie in a game of football). [also V]. (**b**) ~ **down, in, up,** etc to rush in the specified direction: [Vpr] *The children charged down the stairs.* [also Vp]. **4** (*fml*) to give sb a responsibility; to command or instruct sb: [Vn.*to* inf] *I charge you not to forget what I have said.* [Vn] *The judge charged the jury* (ie advised them about their VERDICT). **5(a)** to load sth with electricity: [Vn] *charge a battery.* (**b**) ~ sth (with sth) (esp passive) to fill sth with an emotion: [Vnpr] *a voice charged with tension* ∘ *The atmosphere was charged with excitement.* [also Vn]. **6** [Vn, Vnpr] ~ sth (with sth) (**a**) to load a gun. (**b**) (*Brit fml*) to fill a glass: *Please charge your glasses and drink a toast to the bride and groom!* **PHRV** **charge sth (up) to sb; charge sth up** to record sth as a debt to be paid by sb: *Please charge these goods (up) to my account.* **charge sb with sth/doing sth** (*fml*) (esp passive) to give sb a duty or responsibility: *She was charged with an important mission.*

chargeable /'tʃɑːdʒəbl/ *adj* **1** ~ to sb (of a sum of money) that must be paid by sb or can be demanded from sb: *Any expenses you may incur will be chargeable to the company.* ∘ *A sales tax is chargeable on most goods.* **2(a)** that can result in a legal charge¹(2): *a chargeable offence.* (**b**) that can be charged (CHARGE² 2a): *If you steal, you are chargeable with theft.*

chargé d'affaires /ˌʃɑːʒeɪ dæˈfeə(r)/ *n* (*pl* **chargés d'affaires** /ˌʃɑːʒeɪ dæˈfeə(r)/) **1** an official who takes the place of an AMBASSADOR in a foreign country when the ambassador is absent. **2** an official below the rank of AMBASSADOR who acts as the senior representative of her or his country in a minor foreign country.

charger /'tʃɑːdʒə(r)/ *n* **1** an apparatus for charging (CHARGE² 5a) a battery: *a battery charger.* **2** (*arch*) a horse ridden by a soldier in battle.

chariot /'tʃæriət/ *n* an open vehicle with two wheels, pulled by horses. Chariots were used in ancient times in battle and for racing.
▸ **charioteer** /ˌtʃæriəˈtɪə(r)/ *n* a person driving a chariot.

charisma /kəˈrɪzmə/ *n* [U] great charm or personal power that can attract, influence and inspire people: *a politician with tremendous popular charisma.*
▸ **charismatic** /ˌkærɪzˈmætɪk/ *adj* **1** having charisma: *a charismatic figure/leader/politician.* **2** (of a religious group) believing in special gifts from God, eg the power to heal the sick: *the charismatic movement.*

charitable /'tʃærətəbl/ *adj* **1** of, for or connected with a charity(1) or charities: *a charitable institution/organization/body* ∘ *a charitable venture* (ie one to raise money for charity). **2** generous in giving money, food, etc to poor people. **3** ~ (to/ towards sb) kind in one's attitude to others: *That wasn't a very charitable remark.* ∘ *You should try to be more charitable to your neighbours.* ▸ **charitably** /-bli/ *adv.*

charity /'tʃærəti/ *n* **1** [C] a society or an organization for helping people in need: *Many charities sent money to help the victims of the famine.* ∘ *The money the concert raised will go to various charities.* **2** [U] (**a**) the aim of giving money, food, help, etc to people in need: *do sth out of charity* ∘ *raise money for charity* ∘ *a charity ball/concert/garage sale.* (**b**) the money or help given in this way: *live on/off charity.* **3** [U] kindness and sympathy towards others, esp when judging them: *'It's not really his fault,' she said with great charity.* ∘ *He showed little charity towards*

his elderly parents. **IDM** **charity begins at 'home** (*saying*) a person's first duty is to help and care for her or his own family.

charlady /'tʃɑːleɪdi/ *n* = CHARWOMAN.

charlatan /'ʃɑːlətən/ *n* a person who falsely claims to have a special knowledge or skill.

Charleston /'tʃɑːlstən/ *n* (usu **the Charleston**) [sing] a fast dance, popular in the 1920s, in which the knees are turned inwards and the legs kicked sideways.

charlie /'tʃɑːli/ *n* (*Brit infml*) a foolish person: *You must have felt a proper charlie!* ∘ *He looks a real charlie in that hat.*

charm¹ /tʃɑːm/ *n* **1(a)** [U] the power of pleasing, fascinating or attracting people: *a woman of great charm* ∘ *He has a lot of charm.* ∘ *the charm of the countryside in spring.* (**b**) [C] a pleasing or attractive feature or quality: *a woman's charms* (ie her beauty or attractive manner). **2** [C] (**a**) a small ornament worn on a chain round the wrist, etc: *a 'charm-bracelet.* (**b**) an object worn because it is believed to protect the person wearing it and bring good luck: *a lucky charm.* **3** [C] an act or words believed to have magic power; a magic spell. **IDM** **,work like a 'charm** (*infml*) to be immediately and completely successful: *Those new pills you gave me worked like a charm.*

charm² /tʃɑːm/ *v* **1** to please, attract or delight sb; to FASCINATE sb: [Vn] *He charms everyone he meets.* ∘ *He was charmed by her vivacity and high spirits.* **2** (esp passive) to control or protect sb/sth by or as if by magic: [Vn] *He has led a charmed life* (ie escaped many dangers, as if protected by magic). ∘ *She has entered the charmed circle of the President's political advisers.* **PHRV** **charm sth from/out of sb/sth** to get sth from sb/sth by using charm: *She could charm the birds from the trees!*
▸ **charmer** *n* a person who charms people of the opposite sex. See also SNAKE-CHARMER.
charming *adj* very pleasing; delightful: *a charming man/village/song.* ⇨ note at NICE. **charmingly** *adv.*
charmless /'tʃɑːmləs/ *adj* lacking charm; not attractive: *a charmless town.*

charnel-house /'tʃɑːnl haʊs/ *n* (esp formerly) a place for keeping dead human bodies or bones.

chart /tʃɑːt/ *n* **1** [C] an illustration or a page of illustrations giving clear information, esp about sth that changes over a period of time; a diagram: *a weather chart* ∘ *a temperature chart* (ie showing changes in a person's temperature) ∘ *a sales chart* (ie showing the level of a company's sales). ⇨ picture. Compare MAP, PLAN 2c. See also FLOW CHART. **2** [C] a detailed map, esp for use at sea or in the air: *a naval chart.* **3** **the charts** [pl] a list, produced each week, of the most successful pop music records: *Her latest song has been in the charts for four weeks.*
▸ **chart** *v* **1** to record or follow sth on or as if on a chart: [Vn] *Scientists are carefully charting the progress of the spacecraft.* **2** to plan a course of action, etc: [Vn] *He had carefully charted his route to the top of his profession.* **3** to make a chart of sth; to MAP sth: [Vn] *charted territory.*

charter /'tʃɑːtə(r)/ *n* **1(a)** a written statement describing the rights that a certain group of people have or should have: *the European Union's Social Charter of workers' rights.* (**b**) a written statement by a ruler or a government giving certain rights and privileges to a town, company, university, etc or allowing a new organization, etc to be founded: *Certain towns were allowed to hold weekly markets, by royal charter.* ∘ *the power to grant university charters.* (**c**) a written statement of the main functions and principles of an organization or institution; a CONSTITUTION(1): *the charter of the United Nations.* **2** the hiring of an aircraft, a ship, a

chart

bar chart

months of the year

pie chart

farm land 28%

forests 43%

towns 5%

mountains 24%

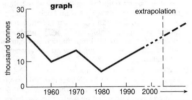

graph

extrapolation

bus, etc for a particular purpose or group of people: *low-cost charters/charter flights to Australia* ○ *a* ˈ*charter plane.*
▶ **charter** *v* [Vn] **1** to give a charter(1) to sb/sth. **2** to hire an aircraft, etc for a particular purpose: *a chartered plane.*

chartered /ˈtʃɑːtəd/ *adj* [attrib] qualified according to the rules of a professional association which has a royal charter(1b): *a chartered engineer/librarian/ surveyor.* ˌ**chartered ac**ˈ**countant** (*Brit*) (*US* ˌ**certified** ˌ**public ac**ˈ**countant**) *n* a fully trained and qualified ACCOUNTANT.

chartreuse /ʃɑːˈtrɜːz; *US* ʃɑːrˈtruːz/ *n* [U] **1** a green or yellow LIQUEUR. **2** a pale yellow or pale green colour.

charwoman /ˈtʃɑːwʊmən/ *n* (*pl* **-women** /-wɪmɪn/) (also *esp Brit* **charlady, char**) *n* a woman employed to clean a house, an office building, etc.

chary /ˈtʃeəri/ *adj* [usu pred] ~ (**of sth/doing sth**) cautious; WARY: *chary of lending money.*

chase¹ /tʃeɪs/ *v* **1** ~ (**after**) **sb/sth** to run after sb/ sth in order to catch them: [Vn] *My dog likes chasing rabbits.* [Vn, Vpr] *He chased (after) the burglar but couldn't catch him.* **2** ~ (**after**) **sb** to try to start a sexual relationship with sb, in an obvious way: [Vn, Vpr] *He's always chasing (after) women.* **3** (*infml*) to try to get or win sth: [Vn] *Several companies are chasing this particular deal.* ○ *Liverpool are chasing their third league title in four years.* **4(a)** ~ **sb** (**up**) to make contact with sb again in order to obtain information, get sth done, etc: [Vn, Vnp] *We need to chase (up) all members who have not yet paid their subscriptions.* **(b)** ~ **sth** (**up**); (*US*) ~ **sth down** to try to find sth that is needed: [Vn, Vnp] *Please chase (up) those delayed orders.* **PHR V** ˌ**chase a**ˈ**bout, a**ˈ**round, etc** to rush or hurry in the specified direction: *I've been chasing around town all morning looking for a present for her.* ˌ**chase sb/sth a**ˈ**way,** ˈ**off,** ˈ**out, etc** to force sb/sth to run away, etc; to drive¹(2) sb/sth away, etc: *chase the cat out of the kitchen.*
▶ **chase** *n* **1** [C] an act of chasing sb/sth: *The bank robbers were caught after a car chase.* ○ *We lost him in the narrow streets and had to* ***give up/abandon the chase*** (ie stop chasing him). **2 the chase** [sing]

hunting, esp as a sport: *enjoy the thrill of the chase.* **3** (usu **Chase**) [C] a STEEPLECHASE 1: *The Jockeys Handicap Chase.* See also PAPER-CHASE, WILD-GOOSE CHASE. **IDM** **give** ˈ**chase** to begin to run after sb/ sth: *After the robbery the police immediately gave chase.*

chase² /tʃeɪs/ *v* (*techn*) to cut patterns or designs on metal: [Vn] *chased silver.*

chaser /ˈtʃeɪsə(r)/ *n* **1** a horse for STEEPLECHASE racing. **2** (*infml*) a drink taken after another of a different kind, eg a weaker alcoholic drink after a strong one.

chasm /ˈkæzəm/ *n* **1** a deep crack or opening in the ground. **2** a very wide difference between people, groups, etc, esp one that is unlikely to change; a GULF(2): *the vast chasm separating rich and poor.*

chassis /ˈʃæsi/ *n* (*pl* unchanged /ˈʃæsiz/) the framework on which the body and working parts of a vehicle, radio or television are built. ⇨ picture at CAR.

chaste /tʃeɪst/ *adj* **1(a)** not having sex except with the person to whom one is married. See also CHASTITY. **(b)** (*dated*) not having had sex with anyone. **2** (of behaviour, speech, etc) pure; DECENT: *a chaste kiss on the cheek.* **3** (of artistic, etc style) simple; not elaborate: *chaste designs.* ▶ **chastely** *adv.*

chasten /ˈtʃeɪsn/ *v* (esp passive) to make sb behave better, esp as the result of being punished or having a bad experience: [Vn] *a chastening experience* ○ *He was greatly chastened by his failure.*

chastise /tʃæˈstaɪz/ *v* [Vn] **1** to criticize sb for having done sth wrong; to SCOLD sb: *The newspapers were chastised for their treatment of the incident.* **2** (*dated*) to punish sb severely, esp by beating. ▶ **chastisement** /tʃæˈstaɪzmənt, ˈtʃæstɪzmənt/ *n* [C, U].

chastity /ˈtʃæstəti/ *n* [U] the state of being CHASTE (1): *vows of chastity* (eg those taken by a priest).

chasuble /ˈtʃæzjʊbl/ *n* a loose garment worn over all other clothes by a priest at certain religious services.

chat /tʃæt/ *n* [C, U] ~ (**about sb/sth**) a friendly informal conversation: *I had a long chat with her (about her job).* ○ *That's enough chat — get back to work.* ⇨ note at TALK².
▶ **chat** *v* (**-tt-**) ~ (**away**); ~ (**to/with sb**) (**about sth/ sb**) to have a chat: [V, Vpl] *They were chatting (away) in the corner.* [Vpr] *What were you chatting to him about?* **PHR V** **chat sb up** (*Brit infml*) to talk to sb in a friendly way because you find them attractive or you want to gain sth from them: *Who was that girl I saw you chatting up last night?*

chatty *adj* (**-ier, -iest**) **1** fond of chatting; easy to talk to. **2** like lively conversation; informal: *a chatty description/style/letter.*
■ ˈ**chat show** (*esp US* **talk show**) *n* a television or radio programme in which people, esp well-known people, are invited to talk in an informal way about various topics: *a chat-show host.*

château /ˈʃætəʊ; *US* ʃæˈtəʊ/ *n* (*pl* **châteaux** /-təʊz/) a castle or large country house in France.

chattel /ˈtʃætl/ *n* **IDM** **sb's goods and chattels** ⇨ GOODS.

chatter /ˈtʃætə(r)/ *v* **1** ~ (**away/on**) (**to sb**) (**about sth**) to talk quickly, continuously or foolishly, usu about unimportant matters: [V] *chattering crowds of sightseers* [Vp] *I left them chattering away to each other about their favourite television programmes.* ○ (*fig*) *The machine was switched on and chattered away to itself in the corner.* [also Vpr]. **2** ~ (**away**) (of birds and monkeys) to make quick short sounds that are high in pitch¹(2) and rapidly repeated: [V] *sparrows chattering in the trees* [also Vp]. **3** [V, Vp] ~ (**together**) (of the teeth) to knock together repeatedly with a short sharp sound because of cold or fear.
▶ **chatter** *n* [U] **1** continuous rapid talk: *I've had*

enough of your constant chatter. **2** chattering sound: *the chatter of monkeys/typewriters.*

chatterbox /'tʃætəbɒks/ *n* a person who talks a lot, esp about unimportant matters.

chauffeur /'ʃəʊfə(r); US ʃəʊ'fɜːr/ *n* a person employed to drive a car, esp for sb rich or important.
▶ **chauffeur** *v* [Vn] to drive sb as a chauffeur.

chauvinism /'ʃəʊvɪnɪzəm/ *n* [U] **1** an aggressive and unreasonable belief that one's own country is better than all others. **2** = MALE CHAUVINISM.
▶ **chauvinist** /'ʃəʊvɪnɪst/ *n, adj* (a person) showing or feeling chauvinism: *Don't be such a (male) chauvinist!* ○ *chauvinist attitudes.* **chauvinistic** /ˌʃəʊvɪ'nɪstɪk/ *adj.* **chauvinistically** /-kli/ *adv.*

ChB /ˌsiː eɪtʃ 'biː/ *abbr* Bachelor of Surgery (Latin *Chirurgiae Baccalaureus*): *have/be a ChB* ○ *Philip Watt MB, ChB.*

cheap /tʃiːp/ *adj* (**-er, -est**) **1(a)** low in price; costing (relatively) little money: *cheap tickets/fares* ○ *the cheap seats in a theatre* ○ *Cauliflowers are very cheap at the moment.* (**b**) worth more than the cost; offering good value: *These wool carpets are cheap at £10.99 a metre.* ○ *$3 is very cheap for a hard-cover book.* ○ *immigrant workers, used as a source of cheap labour* (ie labour that is paid very little, esp unfairly). **2** charging (CHARGE² 1) low prices: *a cheap hairdresser/restaurant.* **3** of poor quality; inferior: *cheap furniture/jewellery/shoes* ○ *a **cheap and nasty** bottle of wine.* **4** (of people, words or actions) unpleasant and mean²(2); not clever or worthy of respect: *a cheap gibe/joke/remark/retort* ○ *That was a cheap trick to play on her.* ○ *He's just a cheap crook.* ○ *His treatment of her made her feel cheap.* **5** (*US infml derog*) extremely careful with one's money; mean²(1). **IDM cheap at the 'price**; (*US*) **cheap for the 'price** so well worth having that the price, however high it is, does not seem too much: *The holiday will be very expensive but if it helps to make you fit and healthy again it will be cheap at the price.* **on the 'cheap** (*infml*) without paying or asking the usual, or a fair, price: *buy/sell/get sth on the cheap.*
▶ **cheap** *adv* (*infml*) for a low price: *get sth cheap* ○ *sell sth off cheap.* **IDM ,go 'cheap** (*infml*) to be offered for sale at a low price: *The local shop has some radios going cheap.* **not come 'cheap** to cost a lot of money: *High quality electronic equipment doesn't come cheap.*
cheaply *adv* **1** for a low price: *buy/sell/get sth cheaply.* **2** in a cheap(1a,3) manner: *The room was cheaply furnished.* **IDM get off lightly/cheaply** ⇨ LIGHTLY.
cheapness *n* [U].

cheapen /'tʃiːpən/ *v* **1** to make oneself/sb less worthy of respect; to DEGRADE(1) oneself/sb: [Vn] *I felt cheapened by working for an employer I knew was dishonest.* **2** to become or make sth cheap or cheaper: [Vn] *cheapen the cost of sth* ○ *The recession is cheapening local currencies in relation to international currencies.* [also V].

cheat /tʃiːt/ *v* **1** to trick or deceive sb/sth: [Vn] *Many people are cheated by shop signs offering 'bargains'.* ○ *The employees feel cheated by their low pay rise.* ○ *cheat the taxman* (ie avoid paying one's taxes) ○ (*fig*) *cheat death* (ie come close to dying but stay alive by luck or intelligence). **2** ~ (**at sth**) to act dishonestly or unfairly in order to win an advantage, esp in a game or an examination: [Vpr] *accuse sb of cheating at cards* [also V]. **3** ~ (**on**) **sb** (*esp US*) to be sexually UNFAITHFUL(1) to one's wife, husband or lover. **PHRV 'cheat sb ('out) of sth** to prevent sb from having sth, esp in an unfair or dishonest way: *He was cheated (out) of his rightful inheritance.*
▶ **cheat** *n* **1** a person who cheats, esp in a game: *You little cheat!* **2** a dishonest trick.

check¹ /tʃek/ *v* **1(a)** to examine sth in order to make sure that it is correct, safe, satisfactory or in good condition: [Vn] *check the oil* (ie make sure there is enough oil in a car engine) ○ *check the tyres* (ie make sure there is enough air in a car's tyres) ○ *check the items against the list* (ie to see that they are all on it) ○ *You must check your work more carefully — it's full of mistakes.* (**b**) ~ (**up**) (no passive) to make sure of sth by examining or investigating it: [V, Vp, V.*that*] *I think I remembered to turn the oven off but you'd better check (up) (that I did).* [V.*wh*] *Could you go and check if the baby's asleep?* ○ *I'd better check with Jane* (ie ask her) *what time she's expecting us.* See also CROSS-CHECK, DOUBLE-CHECK. **2(a)** to make sb/sth stop or go more slowly; to control sb/sth: [Vn] *check the enemy's advance* ○ *check the flow of blood from a wound* ○ *The government is determined to check (the growth of) public spending.* (**b**) to prevent a feeling, etc from showing; to restrain sth/oneself: [Vn] *unable to check one's laughter/tears/anger.* **3** to stop suddenly: [V] *She went forward a few yards, checked and turned back.* **4** [Vn] (*US*) (**a**) to leave hats, coats, etc to be stored for a short period: *You can check your coats at reception.* (**b**) to leave cases, etc ready to be transported. **PHRV ,check 'in (at…)**; **'check into…** to register as a guest at a hotel or as a passenger at an airport, etc: *Passengers should check in for flight BA 125 to Berlin.* **,check sth 'in** to leave or accept sth that is to be transported by train or by air: *check in one's luggage.* **,check sth 'off** to mark items on a list as correct or as having been dealt with: *As I packed my case I checked everything off on my list.* **'check ('up) on sb** to investigate sb's behaviour, background, etc: *The police are checking up on him.* **'check ('up) on sth** to examine sth to discover if sth is true, safe, correct, etc: *The doctor checked up on his patient's records.* **,check 'out (of…)** to pay one's bill and leave a hotel. **,check sth 'out** (*esp US*) **1** = CHECK (UP) ON STH. **2** to register sth as having been borrowed: *The book was checked out of the library in your name.* **,check 'over/'through sth** to examine sth to make sure that it is correct: *Check over/through your work before you give it to the teacher.*
▶ **checker** *n* a person who checks things, esp stores, orders, etc.
■ **'check-in** *n* **1** an act of checking in at an airport: *the check-in desk* ○ *one's check-in time.* **2** a place where one checks in at an airport before a flight.
'checking account *n* (*US*) = CURRENT ACCOUNT.
'check-list *n* a list of items to be marked as present or having been dealt with: *a check-list of things to take on holiday.*
'check-up *n* a thorough examination, esp a medical one: *go for/have a check-up.*

check² /tʃek/ *n* **1** [C] ~ (**on sth**) an examination or a method of testing to make sure that sth is correct, safe, satisfactory or in good condition: *security checks* ○ *Could you give the tyres a check, please?* ○ *We conduct regular checks on the quality of our products.* ○ *Factory workers are advised to keep a check on whether the machines are functioning properly.* **2** [C] ~ (**on sb**) an investigation: *The police ran a check on all the victim's friends.* **3** [C] (**a**) a slowing down or stopping; a pause: *a check in the rate of production.* (**b**) ~ (**on sth**) a thing that restrains or stops sth: *The presence of the army should act as a check on civil unrest.* **4** [U] (in CHESS) a situation in which a player's king(4) is directly threatened by one or more of her or his opponent's pieces: *'Check!' she announced proudly, 'You're in check.'* See also CHECKMATE. **5** [C] (*US*) = CHEQUE. **6** [C] (*US*) = BILL¹ 1: *I'll ask the waiter for the check.* **7** [C] (*US*) a ticket used to identify and claim clothes or property left in a CLOAKROOM(1) or left-luggage office (LEFT¹). **8** [C] (*US*) = TICK¹ 3. **IDM hold/keep sth in 'check** to prevent sth from advancing or increasing; to control sth: *keep one's temper in check* ○ *The epidemic was held in check by widespread vaccination.* **take a rain check** ⇨ RAIN CHECK. ► **check** *interj* (*US*) (indicating that one agrees with what has been said).

check³ /tʃek/ n (**a**) [C] a pattern of crossed lines (often in different colours) forming squares: *Which do you want for your new dress, stripes or checks?* (**b**) [U] cloth with this pattern: *a check skirt/jacket/table-cloth.*

► **checked** /tʃekt/ *adj* having a check pattern: *checked material.* ⇨ picture at PATTERN.

checkbook /'tʃekbʊk/ n (*US*) = CHEQUE-BOOK.

checkerboard /'tʃekəbɔːd/ n (*US*) = DRAUGHT-BOARD.

checkered (*esp US*) = CHEQUERED.

checkers /'tʃekəz/ n (*sing v*) (*US*) = DRAUGHTS.

checkmate /'tʃekmeɪt/ (also **mate**) n [U] **1** (in CHESS) a situation in which one player cannot prevent her or his king(4) being captured and the other player therefore wins the game. See also CHECK² 4. **2** total defeat.

► **checkmate** v [Vn] **1** (in CHESS) to defeat one's opponent by putting her or him in checkmate(1). **2** to defeat sb/sth totally.

checkout /'tʃekaʊt/ n **1** a place where customers pay for goods in a shop: *a huge supermarket with 40 checkouts* ○ *checkout counters/points/queues.* **2** an act of checking out (CHECK¹5).

checkpoint /'tʃekpɔɪnt/ n a place, eg on a border, where travellers are stopped and their vehicles and documents inspected.

checkroom /'tʃekruːm, -rʊm/ n (*US*) a room in a hotel, theatre, etc where hats, coats, etc may be left temporarily.

Cheddar /'tʃedə(r)/ n [U] a type of firm yellow cheese.

cheek /tʃiːk/ n **1** [C] either side of the face below the eye: *healthy pink cheeks* ○ *with tears rolling down her cheeks* ○ *dancing cheek to cheek* (ie with the cheek of one partner touching that of the other). ⇨ picture at HEAD¹. **2** [U, sing] (*esp Brit*) talk or behaviour that is rude and lacking in respect: *That's enough of your cheek!* ○ *He had the cheek to ask me to do his work for him.* ○ *What (a) cheek!* **3** [C] (*infml*) either of the buttocks (BUTTOCK). **IDM** ,**cheek by** '**jowl (with sb/sth)** close together: *live/lie cheek by jowl.* **turn the other** '**cheek** to do nothing in return when one has been attacked or insulted. **with tongue in cheek** ⇨ TONGUE.

► **cheek** v (*Brit*) to speak to sb in a rude way, or a way that shows a lack of respect: [Vn] *punished for cheeking the teacher.*

-**cheeked** (forming compound *adjs*) having the specified type of cheeks: *a rosy-cheeked boy.*

cheeky *adj* (**-ier, -iest**) showing lack of respect, esp in a bold or cheerful way: *a cheeky boy/remark.* **cheekily** *adv.* **cheekiness** n [U].

■ '**cheek-bone** n the bone below the eye.

cheep /tʃiːp/ v to make the weak high cry that certain (esp young) birds make: [V] *sparrows cheeping in the garden.* ► **cheep** n.

cheer¹ /tʃɪə(r)/ v **1** to give shouts of joy, praise, support or encouragement to sb: [V] *The crowd cheered loudly as the Pope appeared.* [Vn] *The winning team were cheered by their supporters.* **2** to give comfort, hope, or encouragement to sb: [Vn] *He was greatly cheered by the news.* **PHRV** ,**cheer sb** '**on** to encourage sb to make greater efforts by cheering: *The crowd cheered the runners on as they started the last lap.* ,**cheer (sb)** '**up** to become or make sb happier or more cheerful: *Try and cheer up a bit; life isn't that bad!* ○ *You look as though you need cheering up.* ○ (*fig*) *Flowers always cheer a room up.*

► **cheering** *adj* encouraging: *cheering news* ○ *It is*

cheering to know that one's efforts are appreciated. — n [U]: *The cheering could be heard half a mile away.*

cheer² /tʃɪə(r)/ n **1** [C] a shout of joy, praise, support or encouragement: *the cheers of the crowd* ○ ***Three cheers for*** (ie Shout 'HURRAH!' three times for) *the bride and groom!* **2** [U] (*dated or fml*) a mood of happiness: *Christmas should be a time of good cheer.*

■ '**cheer-leader** n (*esp US*) a person, usu a young woman, who leads the cheers of a crowd, esp a sporting event.

cheerful /'tʃɪəfl/ *adj* **1**(**a**) in a good mood; happy: *a cheerful smile/disposition* ○ *You're very cheerful today.* (**b**) causing happiness; pleasant: *The news isn't very cheerful, I'm afraid.* **2** pleasant and bright: *cheerful colours* ○ *a cheerful room.* **3** helpful and enthusiastic: *a cheerful worker.* ► **cheerfully** /-fəli/ *adv*: *accept sth cheerfully* ○ *smile/whistle/work cheerfully.* **cheerfulness** n [U].

cheerio /ˌtʃɪəri'əʊ/ *interj* (*Brit infml*) goodbye.

cheerless /'tʃɪələs/ *adj* dull and depressing: *a cold, cheerless day* ○ *a damp, cheerless room.*

cheers /tʃɪəz/ *interj* (*infml*) **1** used for expressing good wishes before drinking esp alcohol. **2** (*Brit*) goodbye: *Cheers! See you tomorrow night.* **3** (*Brit*) thank you.

cheery /'tʃɪəri/ *adj* (**-ier, -iest**) lively and cheerful: *a cheery smile/wave* ○ *a cheery 'Good morning'.* ► **cheerily** *adv.* **cheeriness** n [U].

cheese /tʃiːz/ n (**a**) [U] a food made from milk which can be either firm or soft and of which there are many different types: *Cheddar cheese* ○ *a lump/piece/slice of cheese* ○ *a cheese sandwich.* See also BLUE CHEESE, COTTAGE CHEESE, CREAM CHEESE. (**b**) [C] a particular type of this food: *a selection of French cheeses.* **IDM** **a big cheese** ⇨ BIG. **different as chalk and/from cheese** ⇨ DIFFERENT.

► **cheese** v **PHRV** ,**cheese sb** '**off** (*infml*) (esp passive) to make sb annoyed, bored or frustrated (FRUSTRATE): *He's cheesed off with his job.*

cheesy *adj* **1** like cheese in taste or smell. **2** (*infml esp US*) of poor quality; cheap: *The decor looks pretty cheesy.*

■ '**cheese-board** n **1** a board from which cheese is served during a meal. **2** a range of different cheeses served during a meal: *Dinner ended with a marvellous cheese-board.*

'**cheese-paring** n [U], *adj* (*derog*) (the practice of) being excessively careful about spending money.

cheeseburger /'tʃiːzbɜːgə(r)/ n a HAMBURGER with a slice of cheese on or in it.

cheesecake /'tʃiːzkeɪk/ n [C, U] a type of cake made with cream cheese (CREAM), eggs, sugar, etc on a base of pastry or crushed biscuits: *a cherry cheesecake* ○ *Have some more cheesecake.*

cheesecloth /'tʃiːzklɒθ; *US* -klɔːθ/ n [U] a thin, loosely woven, cotton fabric: *a cheesecloth shirt.*

cheetah /'tʃiːtə/ n an African wild animal of the cat family with black spots and long legs. Cheetahs can run very fast.

chef /ʃef/ n a professional cook, esp the chief cook in a restaurant. Compare COOK.

chef-d'oeuvre /ʃeɪ 'dɜːvrə/ n (*pl* **chefs-d'oeuvre** /ʃeɪ 'dɜːvrə/) (*French*) a very fine piece of work, esp the best done by a particular artist; a MASTERPIECE.

chemical /'kemɪkl/ *adj* **1** of or relating to chemistry: *the chemical industry* ○ *the chemical elements.* ⇨ App 7. **2** produced by or using chemistry or chemicals: *a chemical experiment* ○ *a chemical reaction.*

► **chemical** n a substance obtained by or used in a chemical process.

chemically /-kli/ *adv*: *The raw sewage is chemically treated.*

■ ,**chemical engi**'**neering** n [U] ENGINEERING that deals with processes involving chemical changes and with the equipment needed for these. ‚**chemical engi'neer** n.

‚**chemical 'warfare** n [U] the use of poisonous gases and other harmful chemicals as weapons in war.

chemise /ʃə'miːz/ n a loose dress that hangs straight from the shoulders, worn by women.

chemist /'kemɪst/ n **1** (*US* **druggist**) a person who prepares and sells medicines, and usu also sells cosmetics (COSMETIC), etc: *buy aspirin at the chemist's* (ie chemist's shop) *on the corner*. Compare PHARMACIST. **2** a scientist who is trained in chemistry.

chemistry /'kemɪstri/ n [U] **1** the scientific study of the structure of substances, how they react when combined or in contact with one another, and how they behave under different conditions: *Chemistry was her favourite subject at school.* ○ *a chemistry lesson.* **2** the chemical structure and behaviour of a particular substance, etc: *the chemistry of copper* ○ *We do not fully understand the chemistry of genes.* **3** any mysterious or complex change or process: *the strange chemistry that causes two people to fall in love.*

chemotherapy /ˌkiːməʊ'θerəpi/ n [U] the treatment of disease, esp CANCER, by drugs and other chemical substances.

cheque (*US* **check**) /tʃek/ n a special printed form on which one writes an order to a bank to pay a sum of money from one's account¹(2) to another person: *write (sb)/sign a cheque for £50* ○ *Are you paying in cash or by cheque?* See also BLANK CHEQUE. ⇨ EUROCHEQUE, TRAVELLER'S CHEQUE.
  ■ '**cheque-book** (*US* '**checkbook**) n a book of printed cheques. ‚**cheque-book 'journalism** n [U] (*derog*) the practice of paying people large sums of money for the exclusive right to print stories about their personal affairs in a newspaper.
  '**cheque card** (also **banker's card**) n (*Brit*) a card given by a bank to sb who has an account¹(2) with it, guaranteeing that the bank will pay the money written on their cheques up to a specified amount.

chequered (*US* **checkered**) /'tʃekəd/ adj [esp attrib] **1** marked by periods of good and bad luck: *a chequered career/history/past.* **2** having a pattern consisting of squares of different colours: *a chequered blanket.*

cherish /'tʃerɪʃ/ v **1** to love and want to protect sb/ sth: [Vn] *Children feel the need to be cherished.* ○ *a country where people cherish their independence.* **2** to keep a feeling or an idea in one's mind or heart and think of it with pleasure: [Vn] *cherish the memory of one's dead mother* ○ *cherish the hope of winning an Olympic medal* ○ *He cherishes the illusion that she's in love with him.*

cheroot /ʃə'ruːt/ n a CIGAR with both ends open.

cherry /'tʃeri/ n **1** [C] A small soft round fruit with a stone(5) in the middle. Cherries are red or black when ripe. ⇨ picture at FRUIT. **2(a)** (also '**cherry-tree**) [C] a tree on which cherries grow: *a flowering cherry* ○ '**cherry blossom.** **(b)** [U] the wood of this tree. **3** (also ‚**cherry 'red**) [U] a bright red colour: *cherry lips.* **IDM** **have/get two bites at the cherry** ⇨ BITE².

cherub /'tʃerəb/ n **(a)** (in art) a small PLUMP naked child with wings. **(b)** a child who looks sweet or innocent: *What a little cherub!*
  ► **cherubic** /tʃə'ruːbɪk/ adj (esp of a child) with a round and innocent face.

chervil /'tʃɜːvɪl/ n [U] a garden HERB whose leaves are used for giving flavour to soups, etc: *dried chervil.*

chess /tʃes/ n [U] a game for two people, played on a board marked with black and white squares, on which pieces are moved according to certain rules.

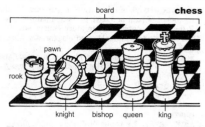

The aim is to CHECKMATE(1) the opponent's king(4). ⇨ picture.

chessboard /'tʃesbɔːd/ n a board with 64 black and white squares on which CHESS and draughts (DRAUGHT 4) are played. ⇨ picture at CHESS.

chessman /'tʃesmæn/ n (pl **-men** /-men/) any of the pieces used in the game of CHESS. ⇨ picture at CHESS.

chest /tʃest/ n **1** a large strong usu wooden box for keeping or moving things in: *a* '**tea chest** ○ *a* '**medicine chest** ○ *a* '**tool chest.** **2** the upper front part of the body from the neck to the stomach: *a hairy chest* ○ *What size are you round the chest?* ○ '**chest pains** ○ *a* '**chest cold** (ie one that affects the lungs (LUNG)). ⇨ picture at HUMAN. **IDM** ‚**get sth off one's chest** (*infml*) to talk about a problem or say sth that one has wanted to say for a long time, so that one has a feeling of relief: *You're obviously worried about something; why not get it off your chest?* **hold/keep one's cards close to one's chest** ⇨ CARD¹.
  ► **-chested** (forming compound adjs) having the specified type of chest: ‚**broad-'chested** ○ ‚**bare-'chested** ○ *She's* ‚**flat-'chested** (ie She has very small breasts).
  chesty adj (*infml*) suffering from or showing signs of chest disease: *My cold's much better but I'm still a bit chesty.* ○ *a chesty cough.*
  ■ ‚**chest of 'drawers** (*US* also **bureau**) n a piece of furniture with drawers for keeping clothes in.

chestnut /'tʃesnʌt/ n **1(a)** (also '**chestnut tree**) [C] any of various types of tree producing smooth brown nuts inside prickly cases. **(b)** the wood of a chestnut tree: *a chestnut* '**table.** **2** [C] a nut of a chestnut tree, some types of which can be eaten: *roast chestnuts.* ⇨ picture at NUT. **3(a)** [U] a deep reddish-brown colour: *chestnut* '**hair** ○ *a chestnut* '**mare.** **(b)** [C] a horse of this colour. **4** [C] (*infml*) an old joke or story that is so familiar that it is no longer amusing: *Oh no, not that old chestnut!*

chevron /'ʃevrən/ n **(a)** (*Brit*) a bent line in the shape of a V used as a road marking, esp to warn of danger. **(b)** a piece of cloth in the shape of a V or Λ, worn on the sleeve by police officers or soldiers as a mark of rank.

chew /tʃuː/ v ~ (**at/on/through sth**); ~ **sth** (**up**) to work food between the teeth, esp to make it easier to swallow: [Vn] *cows chewing the cud* [Vpr] *The dog was chewing at a large bone.* ○ (*fig*) *She sat chewing on the end of a pencil, waiting for inspiration.* [also V, Vnp]. **IDM** **bite off more than one can chew** ⇨ BITE¹. ‚**chew the 'fat/'rag** (*infml*) to have a long friendly talk about different things; to CHAT. **PHR V** ‚**chew sth 'over** (*infml*) to think about sth slowly and carefully: ‚*chew over a* '**problem** ○ *I'll give you till tomorrow to* ‚*chew it* '**over.**
  ► **chew** n **1** an act of chewing. **2** a hard sweet that can be chewed.
  ■ '**chewing-gum** (also **gum**) n [U] a sweet sticky substance made to be chewed for a long time but not swallowed. See also BUBBLE GUM.

Chianti /ki'ænti/ n [U] a dry red or white wine from central Italy.

chiaroscuro /ki͟ˌɑːrəˈskʊərəʊ/ *n* [U] (*art*) **1** the treatment of light and dark parts in a painting, etc. **2** the use of contrast in literature, music, etc.

chic /ʃiːk/ *adj* fashionable and elegant: *She always looks so chic.*
▶ **chic** *n* [U] the quality of being fashionable and elegant: *her casual chic* ○ *wear matching earrings for a touch of chic.*

chicanery /ʃɪˈkeɪnəri/ *n* [U] the use of clever but misleading talk in order to trick sb; false argument: *political chicanery* ○ *lead a life of deceit and chicanery.*

chick /tʃɪk/ *n* **1** a young bird, esp a young chicken, just after coming out of its egg: *a hen with her chicks.* **2** (*dated sexist*) a young woman.

chicken /ˈtʃɪkɪn/ *n* (**a**) [C] a large domestic bird commonly kept for its eggs or meat: *keep chickens* ○ *free-range chickens* ○ *a chicken run.* Compare COCK[1], HEN. (**b**) [U] its flesh eaten as food: *slices of roast chicken* ○ *chicken breast* ○ *a chicken wing/thigh.* See also SPRING CHICKEN. **IDM** **a ˌchicken-and-ˈegg situation** (*infml*) a situation in which it is difficult to tell which one of two things was the cause of the other. **count one's chickens** ⇨ COUNT[1].
▶ **chicken** *v* **PHRV** **ˌchicken ˈout (of sth)** (*infml*) to decide not to do sth because one is afraid: *He had an appointment to see the dentist but he chickened out (of it) at the last moment.*
chicken *adj* [pred] (*infml*) cowardly.
■ **ˈchicken-feed** *n* [U] **1** food for chickens and other such birds. **2** (*infml*) a small amount, esp of money: *Your salary is chicken-feed compared to what you could earn in America.*

chickenpox /ˈtʃɪkɪnpɒks/ *n* [U] a disease, esp of children, with a mild fever and a lot of red spots on the skin: *catch/get chickenpox.*

chick-pea /ˈtʃɪk piː/ *n* a pale yellow seed, similar in size to a PEA(1a), which is cooked as a vegetable.

chicory /ˈtʃɪkəri/ *n* [U] (**a**) (also **endive**) (*Brit*) a plant with bitter leaves which are eaten as a vegetable, raw or cooked. (**b**) the root of this plant, which is dried and used with or instead of coffee.

chide /tʃaɪd/ *v* (*pt* **chided** /ˈtʃaɪdɪd/ or **chid** /tʃɪd/; *pp* **chided** or **chidden** /ˈtʃɪdn/) **~ sb/oneself (for sth/doing sth)** (*dated or fml*) to criticize or blame sb/oneself for doing sth wrong: [Vnpr] *She chided him for not telling the truth.* [also Vn].

chief /tʃiːf/ *n* **1** (often as a title) a leader or ruler, esp of a tribe: *Chief Buthelezi.* **2** the person with the highest rank in an organization, a department, etc: *a chief of police* ○ *army chiefs.* **IDM** **(there are) too many chiefs and not enough Indians** (*infml saying*) (there are) too many people giving orders and not enough people carrying out the work, because everybody wants to be in charge.
▶ **chief** *adj* **1** [esp attrib] most important; main; principal: *the chief rivers of India* ○ *The chief thing to remember is…* ○ *Smoking is one of the chief causes of lung cancer.* **2** [attrib] having the highest rank or authority: *the chief priest.* **chiefly** *adv* (**a**) above all; mainly: *The government is chiefly concerned with controlling inflation.* (**b**) mostly; mainly: *Air consists chiefly of nitrogen.*
■ **ˌChief ˈConstable** *n* (*Brit*) the head of the police force in a particular area.
ˌChief of ˈStaff *n* the most senior officer serving under and advising the person who commands (COMMAND[1]) each of the armed forces.
-in-ˈchief (forming compound *ns*) highest in rank: *editor-in-chief* ○ *commander-in-chief.*

chieftain /ˈtʃiːftən/ *n* the leader of a tribe or CLAN: *a Highland chieftain.*

chiffon /ˈʃɪfɒn; *US* ʃɪˈfɒn/ *n* [U] a thin, almost transparent, fabric made of silk, nylon, etc: *a chiffon scarf.*

chignon /ˈʃiːnjɒn/ *n* a twisted mass of hair worn at the back of the head by women.

chihuahua /tʃɪˈwɑːwə; *US* -ˈwɑːwɑː/ *n* a very small dog with smooth hair, originally from Mexico.

chilblain /ˈtʃɪlbleɪn/ *n* (usu *pl*) a painful red swelling, esp on the hand or foot, caused by cold or by bad circulation of the blood.

child /tʃaɪld/ *n* (*pl* **children** /ˈtʃɪldrən/) **1**(**a**) a young person from birth to the age of full physical development; a boy or girl: *a child of six* (ie one who is six years old) ○ *a child actor.* See also ONLY CHILD. (**b**) a son or daughter of any age: *When he retired his children took over the business.* ○ *She is married with three children.* ⇨ App 4. (**c**) a baby: *She is expecting* (ie is pregnant with) *her first child.* ○ *laws to protect the unborn child* (ie to protect babies before they are born). **2**(**a**) (*derog*) a person who behaves like a child and is not mature or responsible: *You wouldn't think a man of forty could be such a child.* (**b**) a person without experience in sth: *She's a child in financial matters.* ○ *He's a child where women are concerned* (ie in his relationships with women). **3 ~ of sth** a person or thing strongly influenced by a period, place or person: *She's a real child of the (19)60s.* **IDM** **be with ˈchild** (*arch*) to be pregnant. **ˈchild's play** (*infml*) a thing that is very easy to do: *It's not a difficult climb — it should be child's play for an experienced mountaineer.* **spare the rod and spoil the child** ⇨ SPARE[2].
▶ **childhood** /ˈtʃaɪldhʊd/ *n* [U,C] the condition or period of being a child: *the joys of childhood* ○ *She had an unhappy childhood.* ○ *childhood memories.* **IDM** **a/one's second ˈchildhood** (*often joc*) a period in later life when one acts as one did as a child, either for fun or because one's mind becomes weak: *He's in his second childhood, playing with his grandson's toy trains.*
childless *adj* having no children: *a childless couple/marriage.*
■ **ˈchild abuse** *n* [U] cruel treatment of children, esp by adults, involving violence or sexual activity: *victims of child abuse* ○ *laws to prevent child abuse.*
ˈchild-bearing *n* [U] the process of giving birth to children: *She's past child-bearing age.*
ˌchild ˈbenefit *n* [U] (in Britain) regular payment made by the government to parents of children up to a certain age.
ˈchild care *n* [U] the care of children, esp by sb who is paid to look after them: *The company provides child care facilities.*
ˈchild-minder *n* (*esp Brit*) a person who is paid to look after children, esp those whose parents are both at work.

childbirth /ˈtʃaɪldbɜːθ/ *n* [U] the process of giving birth to a child: *She died in childbirth.*

childish /ˈtʃaɪldɪʃ/ *adj* (**a**) of or typical of a child: *childish handwriting.* (**b**) (*derog*) (of an adult) like or behaving like a child; not mature or responsible; silly: *Don't be so childish!* ○ *a childish attitude/ action.* Compare CHILDLIKE. ▶ **childishly** *adv*: *behave childishly.* **childishness** *n* [U].

childlike /ˈtʃaɪldlaɪk/ *adj* (*esp approv*) like or typical of a child; innocent: *childlike enjoyment/trust/ honesty.* Compare CHILDISH.

childproof /ˈtʃaɪldpruːf/ *adj* (of equipment, etc) that cannot be operated, opened, damaged, etc by a young child: *Most car doors are now fitted with childproof locks.*

chili (*US*) = CHILLI.

chill /tʃɪl/ *n* **1** [sing] an unpleasant coldness (COLD[1]) in the air, in the body, in water, etc: *There's quite a chill in the air this morning.* ○ (*fig*) *a chill in the country's relations with Britain* (ie a period of time when they are less friendly). **2** [C] an illness caused by cold and damp, with fever and shivering (SHIVER[1]); a cold[2](2): *catch a chill.* **3** [sing] (**a**) a feeling of depression: *The news of the disaster cast a*

C

chill over the party. (**b**) a sudden feeling of the type specified: *a chill of fear/apprehension/disgust.* **IDM** **take the 'chill off sth** to warm food slightly.

▶ **chill** *v* **1** (usu passive) to make sb/sth cold: [Vn] *We were chilled by the icy wind.* ○ *Come by the fire — you must be* **chilled to the bone/marrow** (ie very cold)*!* ○ *(fig) They were chilled* (ie frightened) *at the prospect of a long and bitter war.* **2(a)** to become or make sth cool, eg in a refrigerator (REFRIGERATE): [V] *Let the pudding chill for an hour.* [Vn] *This wine is best served chilled.* (**b**) (in a shop, etc) to preserve food at a low temperature without freezing it: [Vn] *our range of chilled products.*
chill *adj* = CHILLY: *a chill wind.*
chilling /'tʃɪlɪŋ/ *adj* frightening: *a chilling ghost story.*
chilly /'tʃɪli/ *adj* (**-ier**, **-iest**) **1** rather cold and unpleasant: *a chilly day/morning/room* ○ *feel chilly.* **2** not friendly: *a chilly welcome/reception/stare* ○ *chilly politeness.* **chilliness** *n* [U].

chilli (*US* **chili**) /'tʃɪli/ *n* (*pl* **chillies**; *US* **chilies**) [C, U] the small POD of a type of pepper plant, often dried or made into powder and used to give a hot taste to food: *How much chilli did you put in the curry?* ○ *chilli peppers* ○ *'chilli powder.*
■ ,**chilli con 'carne** /kɒn 'kɑːni/ *n* [U] a dish of BEEF(1) and beans, with chillies or chilli powder added to give flavour.

chime /tʃaɪm/ *n* (**a**) the series of notes sounded by a set of bells: *ring the chimes* ○ *the chime of church bells/of the clock.* (**b**) a set of bells rung to make a tune: *a chime of bells.*
▶ **chime** *v* **1(a)** (of bells) to sound a chime; to ring: [V] *cathedral bells chiming.* (**b**) [Vn] to cause bells to ring. **2** (of bells or a clock) to show the time by ringing: [V, Vn] *The clock chimes every quarter/ chimes the quarters* (ie rings every quarter of an hour). **PHRV** **chime in (with sth)** to join or interrupt a conversation: *He kept chiming in with his own opinions.* **chime (in) with sb/sth** to be in agreement with sth: *This view chimes with government reports on spending.*

chimera (also **chimaera**) /kaɪ'mɪərə/ *n* **1** an imaginary creature composed of the parts of several different animals. **2** a wild or impossible idea.
▶ **chimerical** /kaɪ'merɪkl/ *adj* not realistic; imaginary: *a chimerical notion/claim.*

chimney /'tʃɪmni/ *n* **1** a structure through which smoke or steam is carried away from a fire, FURNACE(2), etc and through the roof or wall of a building: *a blocked chimney* ○ *factory chimneys.* ▷ picture at HOUSE¹. **2** (*techn*) a narrow opening in a rock or cliff up which a person may climb. ▷ picture at MOUNTAIN.
■ '**chimney-breast** *n* the part of the wall of a room that encloses the bottom of the chimney and the fireplace.
'**chimney-piece** *n* (*Brit*) = MANTELPIECE.
'**chimney-pot** *n* (*Brit*) a short pipe fitted to the top of a chimney on the roof of a building. ▷ picture at HOUSE¹.
'**chimney-stack** *n* **1** (*Brit*) a group of chimneys standing together, esp on a roof. **2** (*US*) a very tall chimney, esp on the roof of a factory.
'**chimney-sweep** (also **sweep**) *n* a person whose job is removing SOOT, etc from inside chimneys.

chimp /tʃɪmp/ *n* (*infml*) a CHIMPANZEE.
chimpanzee /,tʃɪmpæn'ziː/ *n* a type of small African APE(1). ▷ picture at APE.
chin /tʃɪn/ *n* the front part of the face below the mouth: *His scarf was knotted under his chin.* ○ *a double chin* (ie a fold of fat under the chin). ▷ picture at HEAD¹. **IDM** **chuck sb under the chin** ▷ CHUCK¹. **keep one's 'chin up** (*infml*) to remain cheerful in difficult circumstances.
▶ **chinless** *adj* having a small chin, regarded as a sign of a weak character. **IDM** **a chinless 'wonder**

(*Brit infml derog*) a young upper-class (UPPER) man with a weak character.
■ '**chin-wag** *n* (*Brit infml*) a friendly conversation: *have a good chin-wag with the neighbours.*

china /'tʃaɪnə/ *n* [U] (**a**) a fine baked white clay used in making cups, plates, etc; PORCELAIN: *made of china* ○ *a china vase.* (**b**) objects made of this, eg cups and plates: *household china* ○ *Shall we use the* (ie our) *best china?* ○ *a china cupboard/cabinet.* **IDM** **a bull in a china shop** ▷ BULL¹.
■ ,**china 'clay** *n* [U] = KAOLIN.
Chink /tʃɪŋk/ *n* (⚠ *sl offensive*) a Chinese person.
chink¹ /tʃɪŋk/ *n* a narrow opening; a crack: *He peeped through a chink in the fence.* ○ *There was only a chink of light showing under the door.* **IDM** **a chink in sb's 'armour** a weak point in sb's argument, character, etc.
chink² /tʃɪŋk/ *n* ~ (**of sth**) the light ringing sound made by coins, glasses, etc striking together: *the chink of ice-cubes in cold drinks.*
▶ **chink** *v* ~ (**A and B**) (**together**) to make or cause sth to make this sound: [V] *Voices chattered and cups chinked on saucers.* [Vn] *We chinked glasses and drank to each other's health.* [also Vp, Vnp].
chintz /tʃɪnts/ *n* [U] a type of cotton cloth with a printed design (esp of flowers), used for curtains, cushions, etc and for covering furniture.
▶ **chintzy** *adj* **1** of, like or decorated with chintz. **2** (*derog*) too bright and colourful; lacking in taste¹(6): *chintzy jewellery.*

chip
chip
chip   crack
chipped   **cracked**   **broken**

chip¹ /tʃɪp/ *n* **1** a small or thin piece cut or broken off from wood, stone, glass, etc: *a chip of wood* ○ *chocolate chip cookies* (ie biscuits containing small pieces of chocolate). **2** the place from which a small piece has been broken: *This mug has a chip in it.* ▷ picture. **3** (*US* **French fry**) (usu *pl*) a long thin piece of potato fried in deep fat: *a plate of chips* ○ ,*fish and* '*chips* (ie fish in BATTER², fried and served with chips). ▷ picture at POTATO. **4** (*US*) = CRISP *n* 1. **5** a round flat piece of plastic used to represent money, esp in gambling: *(fig) The deal is being used as a* **bargaining chip** (ie offered in return for sth else). **6** = MICROCHIP. **7** (also '**chip shot**) (esp in golf and football) a shot or kick in which the ball goes high in the air and then lands within a short distance. **IDM** **a ,chip off the old 'block** (*infml usu approv*) a person who is like her or his mother or father in character. **have a 'chip on one's shoulder** (*infml*) to be bitter(3) and easily offended because one thinks that one has been unfairly treated or that one is regarded as inferior by other people: *She's got a chip on her shoulder about not having gone to university.* **have had one's 'chips** (*Brit sl*) to be dead, dying or defeated. **when the chips are 'down** (*infml*) when one has reached a very important point in one's affairs and realizes what must be done: *When the chips were down he found the courage to carry on.*
■ '**chip shop** (also *sl* **chippy**, **chippie**) *n* (*Brit infml*) a shop selling fish and chips and certain other esp fried foods for people to take home and eat.

chip² /tʃɪp/ *v* (**-pp-**) **1(a)** to break or cut sth at the edge or surface: [Vn] *a badly chipped cup* ○ *chip a tooth/a bone* ○ *He chipped one of my best glasses.* ○ *chipped nail varnish.* ▷ picture at CHIP¹. (**b**) to break at the edge or surface: [V] *Be careful with these plates — they chip very easily.* ○ *The paint is chipping badly.* **2(a)** ~ sth **from/off** sth; ~ sth **off** to break or cut a small piece from the edge or surface of sth: [Vnpr] *A piece was chipped off the piano when we moved house.* ○ *We chipped the old plaster (away)* (ie removed it in small pieces) *from the wall.* [also Vnp]. (**b**) ~ **off** (**sth**) to be broken off in small pieces: [Vp] *The paint has chipped off where the table touches the wall.* [also Vpr]. **3** (esp in golf and football, etc) to hit or kick the ball so that it goes high in the air and then lands within a short distance: [Vp, Vnp] *He chipped (the ball) in* (ie into the hole) *from forty yards.* [also V, Vn]. **PHR V** ,**chip a**'**way at sth** to break off small pieces from sth continuously: *chipping away at a block of marble with a chisel* ○ (*fig*) *He kept chipping away at the problem until he had finally solved it.* ,**chip** '**in** (**with sth**) (*infml*) **1** to contribute or interrupt a conversation: *She chipped in with some interesting remarks.* **2** to contribute money: *If everyone chips* '*in we'll be able to buy her a really nice present.*

▶ **chippings** *n* [pl] (*Brit*) small pieces of stone, etc used for making a road surface: *Danger! Loose chippings* (eg as a warning to drivers).

chipboard /'tʃɪpbɔːd/ *n* [U] a building material made of small pieces of wood pressed and stuck tightly together in flat sheets.

chipmunk /'tʃɪpmʌŋk/ *n* a small N American animal similar to a SQUIRREL but with black and white markings along its back.

chipolata /ˌtʃɪpə'lɑːtə/ *n* (*esp Brit*) a small thin SAUSAGE.

chippy (also **chippie**) /'tʃɪpi/ *n* (*Brit sl*) = CHIP SHOP.

chiropodist /kɪ'rɒpədɪst/ (*US* **podiatrist**) *n* a person whose job is the care and treatment of people's feet.

▶ **chiropody** /kɪ'rɒpədi/ (*US* **podiatry**) *n* [U] the work of a chiropodist.

chiropractor /'kaɪərəʊpræktə(r)/ *n* a person whose job is treating disorders in people's joints, esp those of the SPINE(1), by using her or his hands to press and move the bones.

▶ **chiropractic** /ˌkaɪərəʊ'præktɪk/ *n* [U] the work of a chiropractor.

chirp /tʃɜːp/ (also **chirrup** /'tʃɪrəp/) *n* a short sharp sound made by small birds or certain insects: *the chirp of a sparrow.*

▶ **chirp** (also **chirrup**) *v* to make a chirp: [V, Vp] *birds chirping (away) merrily in the trees.*

chirpy /'tʃɜːpi/ *adj* (**-ier, -iest**) (*Brit infml*) lively and cheerful: *You seem very chirpy today!* ▶ **chirpily** *adv*: *whistle chirpily.* **chirpiness** *n* [U].

chisel

mallet

chisel

chisel /'tʃɪzl/ *n* a tool with a sharp flat edge at the end, for shaping wood, stone or metal. ➪ picture.

▶ **chisel** *v* (**-ll-**; *US* also **-l-**) (**a**) ~ **sth** (**into sth**) to cut or shape sth with a chisel: [Vpr] *masons chiselling at the church stonework* [Vnpr] *lettering chiselled into the stone* ○ *The sculptor chiselled the lump of marble into a fine statue.* ○ (*fig*) *a woman with (finely) chiselled* (ie very sharp and clear) *features* [also V]. (**b**) ~ **sth** (**out of sth**) to form sth using a chisel: *a temple chiselled out of solid rock.*

chit¹ /tʃɪt/ *n* (*usu derog*) a small young woman or girl, esp one who is thought to have no respect for older people: *a mere chit of a girl.*

chit² /tʃɪt/ *n* **1** a short written note or letter. **2** a note showing an amount of money owed, eg for

drinks at a hotel: *Can I sign a chit for the drinks I've ordered?*

chit-chat /'tʃɪt tʃæt/ *n* [U] (*infml*) conversation about things which are not important; CHAT: *They spent the afternoon in idle chit-chat.*

chivalry /'ʃɪvəlri/ *n* [U] **1** polite and helpful behaviour, esp by men towards women. **2(a)** (in the Middle Ages) the ideal qualities expected of a KNIGHT(2), such as courage, honour and concern for weak and helpless people. (**b**) the religious, moral and social system of the Middle Ages, based on these qualities: *the age of chivalry.*

▶ **chivalrous** /'ʃɪvlrəs/ *adj* **1** (of men) polite and helpful towards women: *a chivalrous old gentleman.* **2** (in the Middle Ages) showing the qualities of a perfect KNIGHT(2). **chivalrously** *adv.*

chive /tʃaɪv/ *n* [C usu *pl*] a plant with long thin leaves like grass which taste similar to onions and are used to add flavour to food: *chopped parsley and chives* ○ *a chive and garlic dressing.*

chivvy (also **chivy**) /'tʃɪvi/ *v* (*pt, pp* **chivvied, chivied**) ~ **sb** (**into sth / along / up**) (*Brit*) to ask sb repeatedly to do sth, often in an annoying way: [Vn.to inf] *His mother kept on chivvying him to get his hair cut.* [Vnp] *If you don't chivvy the others along/up, we'll never get there on time.* [also Vn, Vnpr].

chloride /'klɔːraɪd/ *n* [U] a compound(1b) of CHLORINE and one other element(4): *sodium chloride.*

chlorine /'klɔːriːn/ *n* [U] (*symb* Cl) a chemical element(4). Chlorine is a poisonous gas with a strong smell, used for making water pure and in the manufacture of other chemicals. ➪ App 7.

▶ **chlorinate** /'klɔːrɪneɪt/ *v* to treat sth, esp water, with chlorine: [Vn] *Is the swimming-pool chlorinated?* **chlorination** /ˌklɔːrɪ'neɪʃn/ *n* [U]: *a chlorination plant.*

chloroform /'klɒrəfɔːm; *US* 'klɔːr-/ *n* [U] a colourless liquid used in medicine, etc to make people unconscious, eg before an operation.

▶ **chloroform** *v* [Vn] to make sb unconscious with chloroform.

chlorophyll /'klɒrəfɪl; *US* 'klɔːr-/ *n* [U] the green substance in plants that absorbs light from the sun to help them grow. See also PHOTOSYNTHESIS.

choc /tʃɒk/ *n* (*Brit infml*) (usu *pl*) a chocolate: *a box of chocs.*

■ '**choc-ice** (also '**choc-bar**) *n* (*Brit*) a small block of ice-cream with chocolate on the outside.

chock-a-block /ˌtʃɒk ə 'blɒk/ *adj* [pred] ~ (**with sth/sb**) (*Brit*) completely full; full of people or things pressed close together: *The town centre was chock-a-block (with traffic).*

chock-full /ˌtʃɒk 'fʊl/ *adj* [pred] ~ (**of sth/sb**) completely full: *an essay chock-full of spelling mistakes.*

chocolate /'tʃɒklət/ *n* **1** [U] a brown edible substance in the form of powder or a solid block, made from the seeds of a tropical tree. **2** [U,C] a sweet made of or covered with this substance: *a bar of (milk/plain) chocolate* ○ *a box of chocolates* ○ *Have another chocolate.* **3** [U] a drink made by mixing chocolate powder with hot water or milk: *a mug of hot chocolate.* **4** [U] the colour of chocolate; dark brown.

▶ **chocolate** *adj* **1** made or covered with chocolate: *chocolate* '*sauce* ○ *a chocolate* '*biscuit* ○ '*chocolate cake.* **2** having the colour of chocolate; dark brown: *a chocolate carpet.*

choice /tʃɔɪs/ *n* **1** [C] ~ (**between A and B**) an act of choosing between two or more possibilities: *women forced to make a choice between family and career* ○ *We are faced with a difficult choice.* ○ *What influenced you most in your choice of car?* **2** [U] the right or possibility of choosing: *If I had the choice, I would stop working tomorrow.* ○ *He had no choice but to leave* (ie This was the only thing he could do).

○ *the choice of fish or meat as a main course* ○ *I think you're making a mistake, but it's your choice!* **3** [C] one of two or more possibilities from which sb may choose: *You have several choices open to you.* **4** [C] a person or thing chosen: *She wouldn't be my choice as manager.* ○ *She's **the obvious choice** for the job.* ○ *I don't like his choice of* (ie the people he chooses as his) *friends.* ○ *The film was the critics' choice at Cannes this year.* ○ *The colour wasn't my first choice.* **5** [U] the number or range of different things from which to choose: *There's not much choice in the stores.* See also HOBSON'S CHOICE. **IDM** **be spoilt for choice** ⇨ SPOIL. **by 'choice** because one has chosen: *I wouldn't go there by choice.* **of one's 'choice** that one chooses: *First prize in the competition will be a meal for two at the restaurant of your choice.*

▶ **choice** *adj* (**-er, -est**) **1** [esp attrib] (esp of fruit, vegetables and meat) of very good quality. **2** carefully chosen: *She summed up the situation in a few choice phrases.* ○ (*joc*) *He used some pretty choice* (ie rude or offensive) *language!*

choir /'kwaɪə(r)/ *n* **1** [CGp] an organized group of singers, esp one that performs in public, or in church services, etc: *She sings in the school choir.* **2** [C] the part of a church where the choir sits during services: *choir-stalls.* ⇨ picture at CHURCH.

choirboy /'kwaɪəbɔɪ/ *n* a boy who sings in a church CHOIR.

choirmaster /'kwaɪəmɑːstə(r)/ *n* a person who trains a CHOIR(1).

choke /tʃəʊk/ *v* **1** ~ (**on sth**) to be unable to breathe because the passage to one's lungs is blocked by sth: [Vpr] *She choked (to death) on a fish bone.* [also V]. **2** to cause sb to stop breathing by squeezing or blocking the passage to their lungs; (of smoke, etc) to make sb unable to breathe easily: [Vnpr] *choke the life out of sb* [Vn] *The fumes almost choked me.* **3** ~ (**with sth**) to become or make sb become unable to speak: [Vpr] *She was choking with emotion.* [Vn] *Anger choked his words.* ○ *He spoke in a choked voice, barely concealing his grief.* [also V]. **4** ~ **sth** (**up**) (**with sth**) to block or fill a passage, space, etc: [Vn, Vnp] *dead leaves choking (up) the drains* [Vnpr] *The garden is choked with weeds.* **PHRV** **,choke sth 'back** to restrain or suppress sth: *choke back one's tears/anger/indignation.* **,choke sth 'down** to swallow sth with difficulty. **,choke sth 'off** (*infml*) to prevent or stop sth: *High interest rates have choked off industrial growth.*

▶ **choke** *n* **1** an act or sound of choking. **2** a KNOB(1b) that operates the device controlling the flow of air into a petrol engine: *Won't your car start? Try giving it a bit more choke* (ie reducing the flow of air into the engine by pulling out the choke). ⇨ picture at CAR.

choked *adj* [pred] ~ (**about sth**); (*US*) ~ (**up about sth**) (*sl*) upset; angry: *He was pretty choked about being dropped from the team.*

choker /'tʃəʊkə(r)/ *n* a NECKLACE or band of material worn closely round the throat by women: *a pearl choker.*

cholera /'kɒlərə/ *n* [U] an infectious and often fatal disease, common in hot countries, causing severe DIARRHOEA and vomiting (VOMIT): *an outbreak of cholera* ○ *a cholera epidemic.*

choleric /'kɒlərɪk/ *adj* (*fml*) easily made angry; bad-tempered: *a choleric old man.*

cholesterol /kə'lestərɒl/ *n* [U] a substance found in most tissues of the body and in blood, where too much can cause damage to the arteries (ARTERY 1): *A high cholesterol level can cause heart disease.*

chomp /tʃɒmp/ *v* ~ (**at/on sth**) (*esp Brit*) to CHEW or bite noisily: [Vn, Vpr] *chomping (on) a bar of chocolate* [also V]. Compare CHAMP[1] 1.

choose /tʃuːz/ *v* (*pt* **chose** /tʃəʊz/; *pp* **chosen**

/'tʃəʊzn/) **1** ~ (**between A and/or B**); ~ (**A**) (**from B**); ~ **sb/sth as sth** to pick out or select sb/sth that one prefers or considers the best, most suitable, etc from a number of alternatives: [V] *be free to choose* [Vpr] *She had to choose between giving up her job or hiring a nanny.* ○ *We offer a wide range of excursions to choose from.* [Vn] *choose a carpet/career/chairman* ○ *choose your words carefully* ○ *She was allowed to retire at a time **of her own choosing**.* [Vnpr] *We have to choose a new manager from a short list of five candidates.* [V.wh] *Have you chosen what you want for your birthday?* [V.to inf] *We chose to go by train.* [Vn-n, Vn.to inf] *The Americans chose Bill Clinton as president/to be president.* **2** to like; to prefer: [V] *You may do as you choose.* [V.to inf] *The author chooses to remain anonymous.* **IDM** **pick and choose** ⇨ PICK[1]. **there is nothing, not much, little, etc to choose between A and B** there is very little difference between two or more things or people.

▶ **chooser** *n* **IDM** **beggars can't be choosers** ⇨ BEGGAR. See also CHOICE.

NOTE Compare **choose, select, pick** and **opt for**. You **choose** when you decide which thing you want: *You may choose up to seven library books.* ○ *I can't decide which wine to have — you choose.* You can **choose** between two things: *She chose the red sweater rather than the pink one.* You **select** something by choosing very carefully: *Our shops select only the best produce.* You **pick** something without thinking very carefully: *Every time you get a question right you can pick a card.* You **opt for** a particular course of action after examining its advantages and disadvantages: *Most people in Britain opt for buying a house rather than renting.*

choosy /'tʃuːzi/ *adj* (**-sier, -siest**) (*infml*) careful in choosing; difficult to please: *She's very choosy about who she goes out with.*

chop[1] /tʃɒp/ *v* (**-pp-**) **1** ~ **sth** (**up**) (**into sth**) to cut sth into pieces with an AXE(1), a knife, etc: [Vn] *chopping wood for the fire* ○ *a chopping board/block* (ie used for chopping food) ○ *finely chopped onions/carrots/parsley* [Vnpr, Vnp] *He chopped the logs (up) into firewood* (ie into sticks). [Vnpr] *Chop the meat into cubes before frying it.* ⇨ note at CUT[1]. **2** [Vn] to hit sth, esp a ball, with a short downward stroke or blow. **3** (*Brit infml*) (esp passive) to stop or greatly reduce sth: *Bus services in this area have been chopped.* **PHRV** **,chop at sth** to aim blows at sth with an AXE(1), a knife, etc. **,chop sth 'down** to make sth fall down by cutting it at the base: *chop down a dead tree.* **,chop sth 'off** (**sth**) to remove sth from sth by cutting with an AXE(1), etc: *He chopped a branch off the tree.* ○ (*infml*) *King Charles I had his head chopped off.* **,chop a/one's way 'through sth** to make a path through sth by chopping branches, etc.

chop[2] /tʃɒp/ *n* **1** [C] (**a**) a cutting stroke, esp one made with an AXE(1): *She cut down the sapling with one chop.* (**b**) a chopping blow, esp one made with the side of the hand: *a karate chop.* **2** [C] a thick slice of meat, usu including a RIB(2): *lamb/pork chops.* **3** **the chop** [sing] (*sl esp Brit*) an act of dismissing sb from a job; an act of killing sb or ending sth: *She got/was given the chop after ten years with the company.* ○ *It looks as though he's **for the chop*** (ie He is likely to be dismissed). ○ *The public spending cuts will mean the chop for several hospitals.*

chop[3] /tʃɒp/ *v* (**-pp-**) **IDM** **,chop and 'change** (*Brit*) to keep changing one's plans, opinions, etc.

chop-chop /,tʃɒp 'tʃɒp/ *interj* (*Brit infml*) hurry up; do sth quickly: *Chop-chop! We haven't got all day!*

chopper /'tʃɒpə(r)/ *n* **1** a chopping tool, esp a short AXE(1) or a heavy knife with a large blade. **2** (*infml*) a HELICOPTER.

choppy /ˈtʃɒpi/ *adj* (**-ier, -iest**) (of the sea) moving in short broken waves; slightly rough. ▶ **choppiness** *n* [U].

chopstick /ˈtʃɒpstɪk/ *n* (usu *pl*) either of a pair of thin sticks made of wood, plastic, etc, used in China, Japan, etc for lifting food to the mouth.

chopsuey /ˌtʃɒpˈsuːi/ *n* [U] a Chinese dish of small pieces of meat fried with rice and vegetables.

choral /ˈkɔːrəl/ *adj* of, composed for or sung by a CHOIR(1): *a choral society* ○ *choral evensong* ○ *Beethoven's Choral Symphony.*

chorale /kɒˈrɑːl/ *n* **1** a piece of music with a grand but simple tune, composed to be sung in church. **2** (*esp US*) a group of singers; a CHOIR(1).

chord /kɔːd/ *n* **1** (*music*) a combination of notes sounded together in harmony: *play a chord on the piano/guitar.* **2** (*mathematics*) a straight line that joins two points on the edge of a circle or the ends of an ARC(1). ▷ picture at CIRCLE. **IDM** **strike/touch a 'chord (with sb)** to cause other poeple to feel sympathy with what one is saying; to mention sth that others have in common: *The speaker had obviously struck a chord with his audience.* **touch the right chord** ▷ TOUCH².

chore /tʃɔː(r)/ *n* **1** a task done as part of a routine: *doing the household/domestic chores* (ie cleaning the rooms, making the beds, etc). **2** an unpleasant or boring task: *She finds shopping a chore.*

choreograph /ˈkɒriəgrɑːf, -græf; US ˈkɔːriəgræf/ *v* to design and arrange the steps and movements for dancers in a show, etc: [Vn] (*fig*) *Everyone stood up with a choreographed smoothness.*

choreography /ˌkɒriˈɒgrəfi; US ˌkɔːri-/ *n* [U] (the art of designing and arranging) the steps and movements in dances, esp ballet. ▶ **choreographer** /ˌkɒriˈɒgrəfə(r); US ˌkɔːri-/ *n*. **choreographic** /ˌkɒriəˈgræfɪk; US ˌkɔːri-/ *adj*.

chorister /ˈkɒrɪstə(r); US ˈkɔːr-/ *n* a person, esp a boy, who sings in a CHOIR(1).

chortle /ˈtʃɔːtl/ *n* a loud laugh of pleasure or amusement.
▶ **chortle** *v* to make a chortle: [V] *chortle with delight at a joke* [also V.speech].

chorus /ˈkɔːrəs/ *n* **1** [CGp] a usu large group of singers; a CHOIR(1): *the Bath Festival Chorus.* **2** [C] a piece of music, usu part of a larger work, composed for a CHOIR(1): *the Hallelujah Chorus.* **3** [C] a part of a song that is sung after each verse, esp by a group of people: *Bill sang the verses and everyone **joined in the chorus.*** **4** [C] a thing said or shouted by many people together: *a chorus of boos/cheers/laughter* ○ *The proposal was greeted with a chorus of approval.* **5** [CGp] a group of performers who sing and dance in a musical comedy: *a chorus line.* **6** [CGp] (in ancient Greek drama) a group of singers and dancers who comment on the events of the play. **7** [C] (esp in Elizabethan drama) an actor who speaks the opening and closing words of a play. **IDM** **in chorus** all together; in UNISON: *act/speak/answer in chorus.*
▶ **chorus** *v* to sing or say sth all together: [Vn] *The crowd chorused their approval (of the decision).* [V.speech] *'Bravo, bravo!' chorused the audience.*
■ **'chorus girl** *n* a girl or young woman who sings or dances in a CHORUS(5).

chose *pt* of CHOOSE.

chosen *pp* of CHOOSE.

chow¹ /tʃaʊ/ (also **chow-chow** /ˈtʃaʊ tʃaʊ/ *n* a breed of dog with a thick coat of hair, originally from China.

chow² /tʃaʊ/ *n* [U] (*sl*) food.

chowder /ˈtʃaʊdə(r)/ *n* [U] (*US*) a thick soup made with fish and vegetables: *clam chowder.*

chow mein /ˌtʃaʊ ˈmeɪn/ *n* [C] a Chinese dish of fried noodles (NOODLE) with meat and vegetables.

Christ /kraɪst/ *n* (**a**) (also **Jesus, Jesus Christ** /ˌdʒiːzəs ˈkraɪst/) the man who founded the Christian religion and who Christians believe is the son of God. (**b**) an image or picture of Christ.
▶ **Christ** *interj* (also **Jesus, Jesus Christ**) (△ *infml*) (expressing anger, annoyance, surprise, etc): *Christ! Look at the time — I'm late!*

christen /ˈkrɪsn/ *v* **1** to give a name to a baby at her or his BAPTISM as a sign of admission to a Christian Church: [Vn-n] *The child was christened Mary.* [also Vn]. Compare BAPTIZE. **2** to give a name to sb/sth: [Vn-n] *Because of his tough policies he has been christened 'the Man of Iron' by the popular press.* ○ *They christened the boat 'The Aurora'.* [also Vn]. **3** (*infml*) to use sth for the first time: [Vn] *Let's have a drink to christen our new wine glasses.*
▶ **christening** /ˈkrɪsnɪŋ/ *n* a ceremony in which sb is christened; a BAPTISM: *a christening service.*

Christendom /ˈkrɪsndəm/ *n* [sing] (*dated*) all the Christian people and countries of the world: *famed throughout Christendom.*

Christian /ˈkrɪstʃən/ *adj* **1** of or based on the teachings of Christ or Christianity: *the Christian Church/faith/religion* ○ *a Christian upbringing.* **2** believing in the Christian religion: *a Christian country.* **3** of Christians: *the Christian sector of the city.* **4** showing the qualities of a Christian; kind and fair: *That's not a very Christian way to behave.*
▶ **Christian** *n* a person who believes in the Christian religion: *born-again Christians.*
Christianity /ˌkrɪstiˈænəti/ *n* [U] **1** the religion based on the belief that Christ was the son of God, and on his teachings: *She was converted to Christianity.* **2** being a Christian: *He derives inner strength from his Christianity.*
■ **'Christian name** (also **first name, forename,** *US* **given name**) *n* a name given to sb when they are christened (CHRISTEN); a first name: *Do you know her well enough to call her by her Christian name?* ▷ note at NAME¹.

Christlike /ˈkraɪstlaɪk/ *adj* like Christ in character or action: *showing Christlike humility.*

Christmas /ˈkrɪsməs/ *n* **1** (also ˌChristmas ˈDay) an annual public holiday on 25 December. It is celebrated by Christians as the date of Christ's birth: *Christmas dinner/presents.* See also BOXING DAY. **2** (also ˈChristmastime) the period that includes Christmas Day and several days before and after it: *spend Christmas with one's family* ○ *the Christmas holidays.* See also FATHER CHRISTMAS.
▶ **Christmassy** /ˈkrɪsməsi/ *adj* (*infml*) typical of Christmas; with a lot of Christmas decorations, etc.
■ **'Christmas box** *n* (*Brit*) a small gift, usu of money, given at Christmas, esp to sb who provides a service throughout the year, eg a POSTMAN or a MILKMAN.
'Christmas cake *n* [C, U] (*Brit*) a rich decorated fruit cake eaten at Christmas.
'Christmas card *n* a greetings card sent to friends at Christmas.
ˌChristmas ˈcracker *n* = CRACKER 2b.
ˌChristmas ˈEve *n* the day before Christmas Day, 24 December; the evening of this day.
ˌChristmas ˈpudding *n* [C, U] (*Brit*) a rich sweet PUDDING made with dried fruit and eaten (usu hot) at Christmas.
'Christmas tree *n* an EVERGREEN or artificial tree decorated with lights, coloured ornaments, etc in people's homes at Christmas.

chromatic /krəˈmætɪk/ *adj* **1** (*music*) of the **chromatic scale**, a series of musical notes that rise or fall in semitones (SEMITONE). Compare DIATONIC. **2** of colour; having colour.

chrome /krəʊm/ *n* [U] a shiny metal used esp as a protective covering for other metals; CHROMIUM:

chrome polish (eg for use on the parts of a car covered with chrome) ○ *glittering modern buildings of chrome and steel and glass.*

chromium /ˈkrəʊmiəm/ *n* [U] (*symb* **Cr**) a metallic chemical element used as a protective covering for other metals. Chromium is also mixed with other metals to make alloys (ALLOY²): *chromium plating* (eg on a car BUMPER¹) ○ *chromium-plated.* ⇨ App 7.

chromosome /ˈkrəʊməsəʊm/ *n* (*biology*) any of the tiny parts like threads in animal and plant cells, carrying GENETIC information on the particular characteristics that each animal or plant will have. ▶**chromosomal** /-əl/ *adj*: *chromosomal abnormalities.*

chronic /ˈkrɒnɪk/ *adj* **1** (esp of a disease) lasting for a long time; happening continually: *chronic bronchitis/arthritis/asthma* ○ *the country's chronic unemployment problem.* Compare ACUTE 3. **2** having had a disease or a habit for a long time: *a chronic alcoholic/depressive.* **3** (*Brit sl*) very bad: *The film was absolutely chronic.* ▶ **chronically** /ˈkrɒnɪkli/ *adv*: *a hospital for the chronically ill.*

chronicle /ˈkrɒnɪkl/ *n* (often *pl*) a record of historical events in the order in which they happened: *He consulted the chronicles of the period.*
▶ **chronicle** *v* to record sth in a chronicle: [Vn] *chronicling the events of a war.* **chronicler** /ˈkrɒnɪklə(r)/ *n*.

chron(o)- *comb form* of or relating to time: *chronology* ○ *chronometer.*

chronological /ˌkrɒnəˈlɒdʒɪkl/ *adj* arranged in the order in which they occurred: *a chronological list of Shakespeare's plays* (ie in the order in which they were written). ▶ **chronologically** /-kli/ *adv.*

chronology /krəˈnɒlədʒi/ *n* **1** [U] the science of fixing the dates of historical events. **2** [C] an arrangement or list of events in the order in which they occurred: *a chronology of Mozart's life.*

chronometer /krəˈnɒmɪtə(r)/ *n* a very accurate clock, esp one used at sea.

chrysalis /ˈkrɪsəlɪs/ *n* (*pl* **chrysalises**) (**a**) the form of an insect (esp a BUTTERFLY or MOTH) while it is changing into an adult and is enclosed in a hard case; a PUPA. ⇨ picture at BUTTERFLY. (**b**) this hard case.

chrysanthemum /krɪˈsænθəməm, krɪˈzæ-/ *n* (*pl* **-mums**) a garden plant with brightly coloured flowers. ⇨ picture at FLOWER.

chub /tʃʌb/ *n* (*pl* unchanged) a small fish with a thick body, living in rivers, etc.

chubby /ˈtʃʌbi/ *adj* (**-ier, -iest**) round and slightly fat: *chubby cheeks* ○ *a chubby child.* ⇨ note at FAT¹.
▶**chubbiness** *n* [U].

chuck¹ /tʃʌk/ *v* **1** (*infml esp Brit*) to throw sth carelessly or casually: [Vnpr] *Chuck it in the bin!* [Vnp] *chuck old clothes away/out* [Vnn] *Chuck me (over) the newspaper if you've finished reading it.* [also Vn]. **2** ~ **sb/sth (in / up)** (*infml*) to give up or abandon sth: [Vn,Vnp] *He chucked (in) his job last week.* **IDM** **chuck sb under the chin** to touch sb gently under the chin in a friendly or playful way.
PHRV **‚chuck sb ˈoff (sth); ‚chuck sb ˈout (of sth)** (*infml*) to force sb to leave a place: *They were chucked out of the disco for being too rowdy.* ○ *The conductor chucked them off the bus.*

chuck² /tʃʌk/ *n* a part of a tool, eg a DRILL¹(1), that can be adjusted to grip sth tightly. ⇨ picture at DRILL¹.

chuck³ /tʃʌk/ *n* [U] a piece of meat, esp BEEF, cut from the part of the animal between the neck and the ribs (RIB 1).

chuckle /ˈtʃʌkl/ *v* to laugh quietly or to oneself: [V,Vpr] *He chuckled (to himself) as he read the newspaper.* [Vpr] *What are you chuckling about?* [also V. speech].
▶ **chuckle** *n* a quiet laugh: *She gave a chuckle of delight.*

chuffed /tʃʌft/ *adj* [pred] ~ (**about/at sth / doing sth**) (*Brit infml*) very pleased: *look/feel chuffed* ○ *She was really chuffed at/about getting a pay rise.*

chug /tʃʌg/ *v* (**-gg-**) **1** [V] to make the regularly repeated dull sound of an engine running slowly. **2** (*US sl*) to drink sth completely, without stopping: [Vn] *He chugged a whole bottle of beer.* **PHRV** **chug along, down, up, etc** to move steadily in the specified direction while making a chugging sound: *The boat chugged along the canal.*
▶ **chug** *n* the sound made by a chugging engine.

chum /tʃʌm/ *n* (*infml*) a good friend: *an old school chum.*
▶ **chum** *v* (**-mm-**) **PHRV** **chum up (with sb)** (*dated infml*) to become very friendly with sb.
chummy *adj* (*infml*) very friendly. **chummily** *adv.* **chumminess** *n* [U].

chump /tʃʌmp/ *n* (*dated infml*) a foolish person: *Don't be such a chump!*

chunk /tʃʌŋk/ *n* **1** a thick solid piece that has been cut or broken off sth: *a chunk of bread/meat/ice/wood.* ⇨ note at PIECE¹. **2** (*infml*) a fairly large amount of sth: *I've already written a fair chunk of my article.*

chunky /ˈtʃʌŋki/ *adj* (**-ier, -iest**) **1** having a short strong body: *a chunky football player.* **2** thick and solid: *chunky jewellery/furniture.* **3** (of food) containing thick pieces: *chunky marmalade.* **4** (*Brit*) (of clothes) made of thick, usu woollen, material: *a chunky sweater.*

church /tʃɜːtʃ/ *n* **1** [C] a building used for public Christian worship: *The procession moved into the church.* ○ *a church steeple* ○ *church services.* ⇨ picture. **2** [U] a service(8) in a church; public worship: *Church begins/is at 9 o'clock.* ○ *How often do you go to church?* ○ *They're in/at church* (ie attending a service). ⇨ note at SCHOOL¹. **3 the Church** [sing] all Christians regarded as a group: *The Church has a duty to condemn violence.* **4 Church** [C] a particular group of Christians; a DENOMINATION(1): *the Anglican Church* ○ *the Catholic Church* ○ *the Free Churches.* **5 the Church** [sing] the ministers of the Christian religion, esp the Church of England; the CLERGY: *the conflict between (the) Church and (the) State* ○ *go into/enter the Church* (ie become a Christian minister).
■ **the ‚Church of ˈEngland** *n* [sing] the Anglican Church in England, recognized by the state and having the queen or king as its head.

churchgoer /ˈtʃɜːtʃɡəʊə(r)/ *n* a person who goes to church services regularly.
▶ **churchgoing** *n* [U] the practice of going regularly to church services.

churchman /ˈtʃɜːtʃmən/ *n* (*pl* **-men** /-mən/; *fem* **churchwoman** /-wʊmən/, *pl* **-women** /-wɪmɪn/) **1** a Christian minister¹(3). **2** a member or supporter of the Church.

churchwarden /tʃɜːtʃˈwɔːdn/ *n* (in a Church of England PARISH) one of usu two elected officials responsible for church money and property.

churchyard /ˈtʃɜːtʃjɑːd/ *n* an enclosed area of land round a church, often used for burials. Compare GRAVEYARD, ⇨ CEMETERY.

churlish /ˈtʃɜːlɪʃ/ *adj* rude or bad-tempered: *It seems churlish to refuse such a generous offer.* ▶ **churlishly** *adv.* **churlishness** *n* [U].

churn /tʃɜːn/ *n* **1** a machine in which milk or cream is shaken to make butter. **2** (*Brit*) a large, usu metal, container in which milk is carried from a farm. ⇨ picture at BARREL.
▶ **churn** *v* **1** [Vn] (**a**) to shake milk or cream to make butter. (**b**) to make butter in this way. **2** (**a**) ~ **sth (up)** to make sth move violently; to stir or disturb sth: [Vn,Vnp] *motor boats churning (up) the peaceful waters of the bay* [Vnp] *The earth had been churned up by the wheels of the tractor.* ○ (*fig*) *The bitter argument left her feeling churned up* (ie upset

C

C

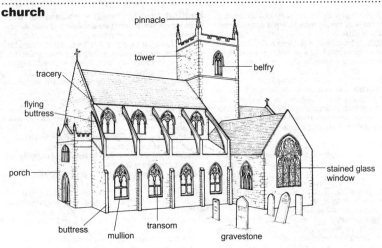

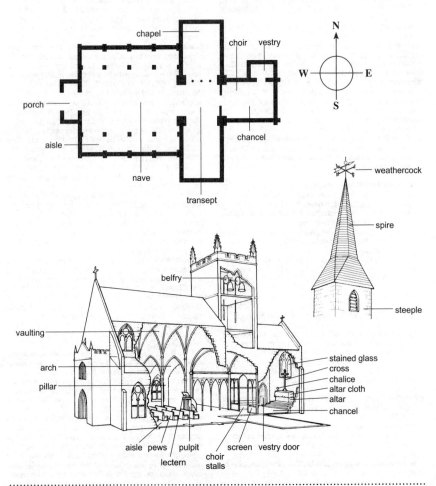

and emotional) *inside*. (**b**) (esp of liquids) to move about violently: [V] *the churning waters of a whirlpool* ○ *His stomach churned with nausea.* **PHRV** **churn sth 'out** (*infml often derog*) to produce sth quickly and in large amounts: *She churns out novels at the rate of three a year.*

chute /ʃuːt/ *n* **1** a tube or passage down which people can drop or slide things: *a laundry/rubbish chute* (eg from the upper floors of a high building). **2** a structure down which people can slide into a swimming-pool (SWIM). **3** (*infml*) = PARACHUTE.

chutney /'tʃʌtni/ *n* [U] a mixture of fruit or vegetables, sugar, spices and VINEGAR, eaten with cold meat, cheese, etc: *green tomato chutney* ○ *mango chutney*.

CIA /ˌsiː aɪ 'eɪ/ *abbr* (in the USA) Central Intelligence Agency: *working for the CIA.* Compare FBI.

cicada /sɪ'kɑːdə; *US* sɪ'keɪdə/ *n* a small jumping insect common in hot countries. Male cicadas make a continuous high-pitched sound by rubbing their legs together.

CID /ˌsiː aɪ 'diː/ *abbr* (in Britain) Criminal Investigation Department (the department of the police force responsible for solving crimes): *an inspector from the CID.*

-cide *comb form* (forming *ns*) **1** an act of killing sb: *genocide* ○ *patricide.* **2** a person or thing that kills: *insecticide* ○ *fungicide.*

▶ **-cidal** *comb form* (forming *adjs*) of or related to killing: *homicidal.*

cider /'saɪdə(r)/ (*US* **hard cider**) *n* (**a**) [U] an alcoholic drink made from the juice of apples: *dry/sweet cider* ○ *cider apples* ○ *a 'cider-press* (ie for squeezing the juice from apples). Compare PERRY. (**b**) [C] a glass of this: *Two ciders, please.*

cigar /sɪ'gɑː(r)/ *n* a roll of dried tobacco leaves for smoking: *the smell of cigar smoke.*

cigarette /ˌsɪgə'ret; *US* 'sɪgəret/ *n* a roll of tobacco enclosed in thin paper for smoking: *a packet/pack of cigarettes* ○ *light a cigarette.*

■ **ciga'rette-case** *n* a small flat, usu metal, box for holding cigarettes.

ciga'rette-holder *n* a tube in which a cigarette may be held for smoking.

ciga'rette-lighter (also **lighter**) *n* a device that produces a small flame for lighting cigarettes, etc.

ciga'rette-paper *n* a piece of thin paper in which tobacco is rolled to make cigarettes: *a packet of cigarette-papers.*

C-in-C /ˌsiː ɪn 'siː/ *abbr* Commander-in-Chief.

cinch /sɪntʃ/ *n* (*infml*) **1** an easy task: *'How was the exam?' 'It was a cinch!'* **2** a sure or certain thing: *He's a cinch to win the race.*

cinder /'sɪndə(r)/ *n* [C usu *pl*] a small piece of ash or partly burnt coal, wood, etc that is no longer burning but may still be hot: *There was nothing left but cinders.* ○ *a cinder track* (ie a track for runners made with finely crushed cinders). **IDM** **burn, etc sth to a 'cinder** to cook or burn sth, esp food, until it is hard and black: *The cakes were burnt to a cinder.*

■ **'cinder block** *n* (*US*) = BREEZE-BLOCK.

Cinderella /ˌsɪndə'relə/ *n* a person or thing that has been constantly ignored, and deserves to receive more attention: *This department has been the Cinderella of the company for far too long.*

cine- *comb form* of the cinema: *cine-projector.*

cine-camera /'sɪni kæmərə/ (*Brit*) (*US* **motion-picture camera**) *n* a camera used for taking moving pictures.

cinema /'sɪnəmə/ *n* (*esp Brit*) **1** [C] (*US* **movie house**, **movie theatre**) a building in which films (FILM[1] 1) are shown: *our local cinema.* **2 the cinema** [sing] (also *Brit infml* **the pictures**, *US* **the movies**) films generally: *go to the cinema.* **3** (also **the cinema**) [sing] (*esp Brit*) (*US* also **the movies**) films as

an art or an industry: *She's interested in (the) cinema.* ○ *He works in the cinema.*

▶ **cinematic** /ˌsɪnə'mætɪk/ *adj* of or relating to cinema: *cinematic techniques.*

cinematography /ˌsɪnəmə'tɒgrəfi/ *n* [U] the art or science of making cinema films. **cinematographer** /ˌsɪnəmə'tɒgrəfə(r)/ *n*.

cinnamon /'sɪnəmən/ *n* [U] a spice made from the inner bark of a SE Asian tree, used esp to give flavour to sweet foods: *a stick of cinnamon* ○ *cinnamon cakes.*

cipher (also **cypher**) /'saɪfə(r)/ *n* **1(a)** [C, U] a secret way of writing, esp one in which a set of letters or symbols is used to represent others: *a message in cipher.* (**b**) [C] a message written in such a way. (**c**) [C] a key[5](5b) to such a secret message. Compare CODE 1. ⇨ DECIPHER. **2** [C] the symbol 0, representing zero or no amount. **3** [C] (*derog*) a person or thing of no importance: *He's a nobody — a mere cipher.*

circa /'sɜːkə/ *prep* (*Latin*) (*abbrs* **c**, **ca**) (used with dates) about: *born circa 150 BC.*

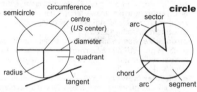

circle

circle /'sɜːkl/ *n* **1(a)** a round space enclosed by a curved line, every point on the line being the same distance from the centre. (**b**) the line enclosing a circle: *Use your compasses to draw a circle.* ⇨ picture. **2** a thing shaped like a circle; a ring: *a circle of trees/hills/spectators* ○ *standing in a circle.* **3** (*US* **balcony**) a group of seats in curved rows raised above the floor level of a theatre, cinema, etc: *We've booked seats in the circle.* **4** a group of people who are connected by having the same interests, professions, etc: *be well known in business/political/ theatrical circles* (ie among people connected with business, politics, the theatre) ○ *move in fashionable circles* ○ *She has a large circle of friends.* **IDM** **come full circle** ⇨ FULL. **go round in 'circles** to work at a task without making any progress. **run round in (small) circles** (*infml*) to be actively busy with (often) unimportant matters while achieving little or nothing. **square the circle** ⇨ SQUARE[3]. **a vicious circle** ⇨ VICIOUS. See also THE ARCTIC CIRCLE.

▶ **circle** *v* **1** ~ (**about/around/round**) (**above/over sb/sth**) to move in a circle, esp in the air: [Vpr, Vp] *vultures circling (round) over a dead animal* [also V]. **2(a)** to move in or form a circle round sb/sth: [Vn] *The plane circled the airport twice before landing.* ○ *The moon circles the earth every 28 days.* ○ *a town circled by hills.* (**b**) to draw a circle round sth: [Vn] *spelling mistakes circled in red ink.*

circlet /'sɜːklət/ *n* a circular band made of precious metal, flowers, etc, worn round the head as an ornament: *a circlet of daisies round her forehead.*

circuit /'sɜːkɪt/ *n* **1** a line, route or journey round a place: *The circuit of the city walls is three miles.* ○ *The earth takes a year to make a circuit of* (ie go round) *the sun.* ○ *She ran four circuits of the track.* **2(a)** a complete path along which an electric current flows: *There must be a break in the circuit.* (**b**) an apparatus through which an electric current flows: *a circuit diagram* (ie one showing the connections in such an apparatus). **3** a regular journey made by a judge round a particular area to hear cases in court: *go on circuit* (ie make this journey) ○ *a circuit judge.* **4** (in sport) a series of games or matches in which the same players regularly take part: *the American* *golf circuit.* **5** a series of places where performances, exhibitions, etc take place: *the lecture/comedy/cabaret circuit.* See also CLOSED-CIRCUIT TELEVISION, SHORT CIRCUIT. ·

▶ **circuitry** /'sɜːkɪtri/ *n* [U] a system of electrical circuits or the equipment forming this.

■ **'circuit board** *n* a board that holds electrical circuits and their components, used inside electrical equipment.

'circuit-breaker *n* an automatic device for interrupting an electric current.

'circuit training *n* [U] (in sport) a method of training using a series of different exercises.

circuitous /səˈkjuːɪtəs/ *adj* (*fml*) going a long way round; indirect; ROUNDABOUT¹: *a circuitous route.* ▶ **circuitously** *adv.*

circular /'sɜːkjələ(r)/ *adj* **1** shaped like a circle; round. **2** moving round in a circle: *a circular tour* (ie one taking a route that brings travellers back to the point where they started). **3** (of reasoning) using the point it is trying to prove as evidence for its conclusion: *a circular argument.* **4** [usu attrib] sent to a large number of people: *a circular letter.*

▶ **circular** *n* a printed letter, notice or advertisement sent to a large number of people.
circularity /ˌsɜːkjəˈlærəti/ *n* [U].
circularize, -ise /'sɜːkjələraɪz/ *v* to send a circular to sb: [Vnpr] *All our branch offices have been circularized with details of the changes in the company.* [also Vn].

■ **ˌcircular 'saw** *n* a SAW² driven by a motor and used for cutting wood, etc. It consists of a revolving metal disc with sharp teeth on its edge.

circulate /'sɜːkjəleɪt/ *v* **1(a)** to go round or make sth go round continuously: [Vpr] *Blood circulates through the body.* [also V, Vn, Vnpr]. **(b)** to move about freely: [V] *open a window to allow the air to circulate.* **2** to pass or make sth pass from one place, person, etc to another: [V] *The news of her death circulated* (ie spread) *quickly.* [V, Vpr] *The host and hostess circulated* (*among their guests*). [Vn] *circulate a letter* [V, Vn] *Some unpleasant rumours are circulating/being circulated at Westminster.* [also Vnpr]. **3** to inform sb by means of a CIRCULAR: [Vnpr] *Has everyone been circulated with details of the conference?* [also Vn].

circulation /ˌsɜːkjəˈleɪʃn/ *n* **1** [C, U] the movement of blood round the body and from and to the heart: *have (a) good/bad circulation.* **2** [U] **(a)** the passing or spreading of sth from one person or place to others: *the circulation of news/information/rumours.* **(b)** the state of circulating or being circulated: *Police say a number of forged banknotes are in circulation.* ○ *Dollar bills have been withdrawn from circulation.* ○ (*fig*) *She's been ill but now she's back in circulation* (ie going out and meeting people again). **3** [C] the number of copies of a newspaper, magazine, etc regularly sold to the public: *a newspaper with a (daily) circulation of more than one million* ○ *circulation figures.*

circulatory /ˌsɜːkjəˈleɪtəri; *US* 'sɜːrkjələtɔːri/ *adj* of or relating to the circulation of blood: *circulatory disorders.*

circumcise /'sɜːkəmsaɪz/ *v* [Vn] **(a)** to cut off the FORESKIN of a boy or man for religious or medical reasons. **(b)** to cut off all or part of the external sex organs of a girl or woman.

▶ **circumcision** /ˌsɜːkəmˈsɪʒn/ *n* [U, C] the action or ceremony of circumcising sb.

circumference /səˈkʌmfərəns/ *n* **(a)** a line that marks out a circle or that goes round any other curved shape. ⇨ picture at CIRCLE. **(b)** the length of this line: *The circumference of the earth is almost 25 000 miles/The earth is almost 25 000 miles in circumference.* Compare PERIMETER.

circumflex /'sɜːkəmfleks/ (also ˌcircumflex 'ac-cent) *n* a mark (ˆ) put over a vowel in French and some other languages to show how it is pronounced, as in *rôle* or *fête.*

circumlocution /ˌsɜːkəmləˈkjuːʃn/ *n* [U, C] (*fml usu derog*) the use of many words to say sth that could be said in a few words, esp when one does not wish to speak clearly and directly. ▶ **circumlocutory** /ˌsɜːkəmˈlɒkjʊtəri, ˌsɜːkəmləˈkjuːtəri; *US* -ˈlɒkjətɔːri/ *adj.*

circumnavigate /ˌsɜːkəmˈnævɪɡeɪt/ *v* (*fml*) to sail round sth, esp the world: [Vn] *Who was the first person to circumnavigate the globe?* ▶ **circumnavigation** /ˌsɜːkəmˌnævɪˈɡeɪʃn/ *n* [C, U].

circumscribe /'sɜːkəmskraɪb/ *v* [Vn] **1** (*fml*) to restrict sth within limits; to confine sth: *a life circumscribed by poverty* ○ *laws passed to circumscribe the power of the government.* **2** (*techn*) to draw a circle round another shape so that it touches all the outside points or corners: *circumscribe a square.* ▶ **circumscription** /ˌsɜːkəmˈskrɪpʃn/ *n* [U].

circumspect /'sɜːkəmspekt/ *adj* [usu pred] (*fml*) considering everything carefully before acting; cautious. ▶ **circumspection** /ˌsɜːkəmˈspekʃn/ *n* [U]: *proceeding with great circumspection.* **circumspectly** *adv.*

circumstance /'sɜːkəmstəns, -stɑːns, -stæns/ *n* **1** [C usu *pl*] a condition or fact connected with an event or action: *What were the circumstances of/surrounding her death?* (ie Where, when and how did she die?) ○ *She was found dead in suspicious circumstances* (ie She may have been murdered). ○ *He was a victim of circumstance(s)* (ie What happened to him was beyond his control). ○ *Force of circumstance caused us* (ie Circumstances forced us) *to leave London.* **2** circumstances [*pl*] (*fml*) a person's financial position: *What are his circumstances?* ○ *She was widowed and living in reduced/straitened circumstances* (ie with very little money). **IDM in/under the 'circumstances** since this is the case; since the state of affairs is as it is: *Under the circumstances* (eg Because the salary offered was too low) *he felt unable to accept the job.* ○ *She coped well in the circumstances* (eg even though she was feeling ill). **in/under no circumstances** in no case; never: *Under no circumstances should you lend him any money.* **pomp and circumstance** ⇨ POMP.

circumstantial /ˌsɜːkəmˈstænʃl/ *adj* **1** (of evidence) consisting of details that strongly suggest sth but do not prove it: *You can't convict a man of a crime on circumstantial evidence alone.* **2** (of a description) giving full details.

circumvent /ˌsɜːkəmˈvent/ *v* (*fml*) to find a way of overcoming or avoiding sth: [Vn] *circumvent a law/rule/problem/difficulty.* ▶ **circumvention** /ˌsɜːkəmˈvenʃn/ *n* [U].

circus /'sɜːkəs/ *n* **1(a)** [C] a travelling company of people and trained animals that entertain the public with clever, daring or amusing acts: *circus performers/acrobats/clowns* ○ *circus elephants.* **(b)** the circus [sing] a public performance given by such a company, usu in a large tent called a *big top*: *go to the circus.* **2** [C] (*infml*) a group of people involved in the same activity, often in a lively or noisy way: *the media circus* (ie a gathering of journalists, etc). **3** [C] (*Brit*) (in place names) an open space in a town where several streets meet: *ˌPiccadilly 'Circus.* Compare ROUNDABOUT² 1. **4** [C] (in ancient Rome) a place like a big outdoor theatre for public games, races, etc.

cirrhosis /səˈrəʊsɪs/ *n* [U] an often fatal disease of the LIVER(1), suffered esp by people who drink too much alcohol.

cirrus /'sɪrəs/ *n* (*pl* cirri /'sɪraɪ/) [U] a type of light cloud that forms high in the sky: *cirrus clouds.*

cissy = SISSY.

cistern /ˈsɪstən/ *n* a water tank, esp one connected to a toilet or in the roof of a house supplying water to the rooms below.

citadel /ˈsɪtədəl, -del/ *n* (**a**) a fort on high ground, built to protect a city. (**b**) ~ (**of sth**) a centre of power that is strongly defended by those within it and difficult to enter for those outside or opposed to it: *a citadel of government/culture/free thought.*

cite /saɪt/ *v* (*rather fml*) **1**(**a**) to speak or write words taken from a passage, a book, an author, etc; to quote sth/sb: [Vn] *She cited (a verse from) (a poem by) Keats.* (**b**) to mention sth as an example or to support an argument; to refer to sth: [Vn-n] *She cited the high unemployment figures as evidence of the failure of government policy.* [also Vn]. **2** to praise sb by officially mentioning an outstanding act or achievement, esp courage in war: [Vn] *He was cited in dispatches.* **3** (*law*) to summon sb to appear in a court of law: [Vn] *be cited in divorce proceedings.*
▶ **citation** /saɪˈteɪʃn/ **1**(**a**) [U] an action of citing sth/sb. (**b**) [C] a passage cited (CITE 1a); a QUOTATION (1,2): *Some dictionary writers use citations to show what words mean.* **2** [C] an official report recognizing an outstanding act or achievement, esp courage in war: *receive a citation for bravery.*

citizen /ˈsɪtɪzn/ *n* **1** a person who has full rights as a member of a country, either by birth or by being given such rights: *an American citizen* ○ *She is German by birth but is now a French citizen.* **2** a person who lives in a town or city: *the citizens of Rome.* **3** (*esp US*) = CIVILIAN.
▶ **citizenry** /ˈsɪtɪzənri/ *n* [Gp] (*fml*) the citizens of a town, country, etc.
citizenship *n* [U] being a citizen, esp of a particular country, with the rights and duties that involves: *apply for/be granted British citizenship.*
■ **ˌcitizen's arˈrest** *n* an ARREST(1) made by a member of the public (allowed in certain cases under common law).
ˈcitizens' band *n* [U] (*abbr* **CB**) a range of radio frequencies (FREQUENCY 2) used by members of the public, esp drivers of lorries and cars, for communicating with each other over short distances.

> **NOTE** Citizen, subject and national all mean a person who has the rights given by a state to the people, eg the right to vote. **Citizen** is used in all types of states: *a French/Norwegian citizen.* **Subject** can be used when the state is ruled by a king or queen: *a British subject.* **National** is often used when somebody is living in another country: *Many Turkish nationals work in Germany.*

citric acid /ˌsɪtrɪk ˈæsɪd/ *n* [U] (*chemistry*) an acid found in the juice of oranges and other sour fruits.

citrus /ˈsɪtrəs/ *n* any of a group of related trees that have fruits, including the orange, LEMON, LIME and GRAPEFRUIT: *citrus fruit.*

city /ˈsɪti/ *n* **1** [C] a large and important town: *Which is the world's largest city?* ○ *the city ˈcentre* (ie the central area of a city). See also INNER CITY. **2** [C] (**a**) (*Brit*) a town with special rights given by a king or queen and usu containing a cathedral: *the city of York.* (**b**) (*US*) a town given special rights by the State. **3** [CGp] all the people living in a city: *The city turned out to welcome back its victorious team.* **4** **the City** [sing] (*Brit*) the oldest part of London, now its commercial and financial centre: *She works in the City* (eg in the head office of a bank). ○ *a City stockbroker* ○ *The City reacted sharply to the fall in oil prices.* **IDM the freedom of the city** ⇨ FREEDOM.
■ **ˈcity desk** *n* **1** (*Brit*) the department of a newspaper dealing with financial news. **2** (*US*) the department of a newspaper dealing with local news.
ˌcity ˈeditor *n* **1** (*Brit*) a journalist responsible for financial news in a magazine or newspaper. **2** (*US*)

a journalist responsible for local news in a newspaper or magazine.
ˌcity ˈhall *n* [C, U] (*esp US*) (a building used for) the administrative offices of a city council: *leading a march to (the) City Hall to protest at local housing conditions.*
ˌcity-ˈstate *n* (esp formerly) an independent state consisting of a city and the area around it (eg Athens in ancient times).

civet /ˈsɪvɪt/ *n* **1** (also **ˈcivet-cat**) [C] a small animal like a cat living in central Africa and S Asia. **2** [U] a strong-smelling substance obtained from a civet and used in making PERFUME(1).

civic /ˈsɪvɪk/ *adj* [usu attrib] **1** of a town or city; MUNICIPAL: *civic buildings/administration.* **2** of citizens: *civic pride* (ie citizens' pride in their town) ○ *civic duties/responsibilities.*
▶ **civics** /ˈsɪvɪks/ *n* [sing *v*] the study of the rights and responsibilities of citizens.
■ **ˌcivic ˈcentre** *n* (*Brit*) an area in which the public buildings of a town (eg the town hall, library, etc) are situated.

civil /ˈsɪvl/ *adj* **1** of or relating to the citizens of a country: *civil disorder* (eg violent protest) ○ *civil strife* (eg fighting between different political or religious groups within a country). **2** of or relating to ordinary citizens rather than the armed forces or the Church: *civil government.* **3** polite and helpful: *How very civil of you!* **4** involving civil law rather than criminal law: *civil cases* ○ *a civil court.* Compare CRIMINAL 2.
▶ **civility** /səˈvɪləti/ *n* (**a**) [U] polite behaviour: *Staff are trained to treat customers with civility at all times.* (**b**) [C usu *pl*] a polite act or remark.
civilly /ˈsɪvəli/ *adv*: *She greeted him civilly but with no sign of affection.*
■ **ˌcivil deˈfence** (*US* **civil defense**) *n* [U] the organization and training of people to protect themselves from air attacks or other dangers during war.
ˌcivil disoˈbedience *n* [U] refusing to obey certain laws, pay taxes, etc, as a peaceful means of esp political protest: *a campaign of civil disobedience.*
ˌcivil engiˈneering *n* [U] the design and building of roads, railways, bridges, canals, etc. **ˌcivil engiˈneer** *n*.
ˌcivil ˈlaw *n* [U] law dealing with the private rights of citizens, rather than with crime.
ˌcivil ˈliberty *n* [U, C usu *pl*] a person's right to say or do what he or she wants provided it is within the law.
the ˈcivil list *n* [sing] (*Brit*) an allowance of money made each year by Parliament for the household expenses of the British royal family.
ˌcivil ˈmarriage *n* a marriage that does not involve a religious ceremony but is recognized by law.
ˌcivil ˈrights *n* [pl] the rights of each citizen to be free and equal to others, eg in voting and employment, regardless of sex, race or religion: *a civil rights campaigner* ○ *the civil rights movement* (eg for black people in the USA).
ˌcivil ˈservant *n* (esp *Brit*) a person who works in the civil service.
the ˌcivil ˈservice *n* (**a**) [sing] all government departments other than the armed forces: *the French civil service* ○ *She works in the civil service* (eg in the Home Office). (**b**) [Gp] all the people employed in these departments: *The civil service is/are threatening to strike.*
ˌcivil ˈwar *n* [C, U] a war between groups of citizens of the same country: *the Spanish Civil War* ○ *the outbreak of civil war.*

civilian /səˈvɪliən/ *n* a person not serving in the armed forces or the police force: *Two soldiers and one civilian were killed in the explosion.* ○ *He left the army and returned to civilian life.*

civilization, -isation /ˌsɪvəlaɪˈzeɪʃn; *US* -ələˈz-/ *n*

C

1 [U] an advanced and organized state of human social development: *the technology of modern civilization* ○ *bring civilization to backward peoples.* **2** [C, U] a society, its culture and its way of life during a particular period of time or in a particular part of the world: *the civilizations of ancient Egypt and Babylon* ○ *western civilization.* **3** [U] the human race: *environmental damage that endangers the whole of civilization.* **4** [U] the comfortable conditions of a modern society: *live far from civilization* (ie far from a large town or city) ○ *(joc) It's good to get back to civilization after living in a tent for two weeks!* **5** [U] the process of becoming or making sb civilized (CIVILIZE).

civilize, -ise /ˈsɪvəlaɪz/ v [Vn] **1** to cause sb/sth to improve from a primitive stage of human society to a more developed one: *civilize a primitive tribe.* **2** to improve sb's behaviour or manners: *His wife has had a civilizing influence on him.*
▶ **civilized, -ised** /ˈsɪvəlaɪzd/ adj **1** having an advanced and organized state of human social development: *all countries in the civilized world.* **2** having high moral standards: *No civilized country should permit such terrible injustice.* **3** having or showing good behaviour or manners: *They were brought up to behave in a civilized way in public.*

civvies /ˈsɪviz/ n [pl] (*sl*) ordinary clothes, ie not military uniform: *It'll be good to get back into civvies when I'm on leave.*

Civvy Street /ˈsɪvi striːt/ n [U] (*dated Brit sl*) life outside the armed forces, ie not military life.

cl abbr (pl unchanged or **cls**) centilitre: *75 cl.*

clack /klæk/ n a short sharp sound made by hard objects hitting each other, often repeatedly: *the clack of high heels on a stone floor* ○ *the clack of knitting needles/a typewriter.*
▶ **clack** v to make or cause sth to make a clack: [V] *The wooden rattle clacked noisily.* ○ *(fig) Pay no attention to clacking tongues* (ie to people's gossip). [also Vn].

clad /klæd/ adj **1** (used after an adv, with in and a n, or in compounds) (*dated or fml*) dressed: *warmly/scantily clad* ○ *motor cyclists clad in leather/leather-clad motor cyclists.* **2** (*fml*) (in compounds) covered: *an ivy-clad tower* ○ *ironclad battleships.*

cladding /ˈklædɪŋ/ n [U] a protective covering put on the surface of a material or the outside walls of a building: *metal/plastic/timber cladding.*

claim¹ /kleɪm/ v **1** to state or declare that sth is a fact or is the case but not to prove this: [Vn] *After the battle both sides claimed victory.* [V.that] *She claims (that) she is related to the author.* [V.to inf] *He claimed to have been abroad when the crime was committed.* **2** to demand or request sth because it is or one believes it is one's legal right or one's property: [Vn] *claim diplomatic immunity/the protection of the law* ○ *After the Duke's death, his eldest son claimed the title.* ○ *She claims ownership* (ie says she is the real owner) *of the land.* ○ *claim an item of lost property.* **3(a)** to demand or request money from one's insurance company for sth lost, stolen or damaged: [V, Vn] *Have you claimed (the insurance) yet?* [Vpr] *You can always claim on the insurance.* **(b)** to demand money as compensation for sth: [Vnpr] *They claimed damages for the company's failure to honour the contract.* [Vn] *claim a refund.* **(c)** to apply or ask for money from a government, a company, etc because one is entitled to it: [Vn] *claim unemployment benefit* ○ *claim expenses for a business trip.* **4** to require or deserve sth: [Vn] *important matters claiming one's attention.* **5** (of a disaster, an accident, etc) to cause the loss of sth or the death of sb: [Vn] *The earthquake claimed thousands of lives/victims.* [PHRV] **claim sth 'back** to ask or demand that sth be returned because one believes it is one's

legal right to have it: *You can claim your money back if the goods are damaged.*

claim² /kleɪm/ n **1** [C] a statement that sth is true or a fact, esp one which others may not accept or agree with: *Despite his claims of innocence, he was found guilty.* **2** [C, U] ~ (**to sth**); ~ (**on sb/sth**) a right that sb has or believes that they have: *His claim to ownership of the land was contested in court.* ○ *I make no claim to expertise in such matters.* ○ *You have no claim on me* (ie no right to demand anything from me). ○ *His only claim to fame* (ie The only thing in his life which makes him unusual) *is that he was at school with the prime minister.* **3** [C] (**a**) ~ (**for sth**) a demand for a sum of money that one is or believes one is entitled to: *make a claim on an insurance policy* ○ *put in a claim for a pay rise.* (**b**) a sum of money demanded in such circumstances: *The insurance company paid the full claim.* [IDM] **lay claim to sth 1** to state that one has a right to sth: *lay claim to an inheritance/an estate/a property.* **2** (usu negative) to state that one has knowledge, understanding, a skill, etc: *I lay no claim to being an expert economist.* **stake a/one's claim** ⇨ STAKE v. See also NO CLAIMS BONUS.
▶ **claimant** /ˈkleɪmənt/ n a person who claims sth because they are or believe they are entitled to it: *claimants for state benefits* ○ *insurance claimants.*

clairvoyance /kleəˈvɔɪəns/ n [U] the power of seeing in the mind either future events or things that exist or are happening out of sight. ▶ **clairvoyant** /kleəˈvɔɪənt/ n, adj: *She goes to a clairvoyant regularly.* ○ *You don't have to be clairvoyant to predict the outcome of the election.*

clam /klæm/ n a large edible SHELLFISH that lives in sand or mud. It has a shell in two parts which can open and close: *clam soup* ○ *Whenever I raised the question of his childhood he shut up like a clam and refused to discuss it.* ⇨ picture at SHELLFISH.
▶ **clam** v (**-mm-**) [PHRV] **clam 'up** (*infml*) to become silent; to refuse to speak: *He always clams up when we ask him about his family.*

clamber /ˈklæmbə(r)/ v to climb with difficulty or effort, using the hands and feet: [Vpr] *The children clambered over the rocks.* [also Vp].

clammy /ˈklæmi/ adj (**-ier, -iest**) damp, sticky and unpleasant: *clammy hands* ○ *a face clammy with sweat* ○ *clammy weather.*

clamour (*US* **clamor**) /ˈklæmə(r)/ n [C, U] **1** a loud confused noise, made esp by many people shouting: *the clamour of the busy market.* **2** ~ (**for sth**) a loud demand or protest: *a clamour for revenge.*
▶ **clamorous** /ˈklæmərəs/ adj: *the clamorous cawing of crows* ○ *clamorous protests.*
clamour (*US* **clamor**) v **1** (of many people) to make a loud confused noise: [V] *The press clamoured around the car as the President left the meeting.* **2** ~ (**for/against sth**) to make a loud demand or protest: [Vpr] *The public are clamouring for a change of government.* [V.to inf] *The baby clamoured to be fed.*

clamp /klæmp/ n **1** a device for holding things tightly together, usu by means of a screw. ⇨ picture. **2** a device for attaching to a car that has been parked illegally, so that it cannot be driven away.

clamp

▶ **clamp** v **1** (**a**) to hold sth tightly with a clamp: [Vn] *Clamp both ends of the wood before you saw it.* (**b**) to grip or hold sth very tightly: [Vn] *He kept his pipe clamped between his teeth.* **2** ~ **A and B** (**together**); ~ **A to B** to fasten one thing to another with a clamp(1): [Vnp] *clamp two boards together* [also Vn, Vnpr]. **3** to fix a clamp(2) to a car so that it cannot be driven away: [Vn] *Oh, no — I've been* *clamped!* **PHRV** **clamp down on sb/sth** (*infml*) to become suddenly very strict about sth; to use one's authority against sb or to prevent or suppress sth: *The government intends to clamp down on soccer hooliganism.*

■ **'clamp-down** *n* a sudden policy of being very strict and using one's authority to prevent or suppress sth: *a government clamp-down on tax evasion.*

clan /klæn/ *n* [CGp] **1** a group of families, esp in Scotland, descended from a common ancestor: *the* '*Campbell clan/the clan* '*Campbell.* **2** (*infml*) a large family forming a close group. **3** a group of people closely connected by similar aims, interests, etc.

▶ **clannish** *adj* (*often derog*) (of members of a group) associating closely with each other and showing little interest in other people.

clandestine /klæn'destɪn, -taɪn, 'klændəstaɪn/ *adj* (*fml*) done secretly; kept secret: *a clandestine meeting.*

clang /klæŋ/ *n* a loud ringing sound of metal being struck: *the clang of the school bell.*

▶ **clang** *v* to make or cause sth to make a clang: [Vadv] *The prison gates clanged shut.* [also V, Vn].

clanger /'klæŋə(r)/ *n* (*Brit infml*) an obvious and embarrassing mistake: *Mentioning her ex-husband was a real clanger.* **IDM** **drop a brick/clanger** ⇨ DROP[2].

clangour (*US* **clangor**) /'klæŋgə(r), 'klæŋə(r)/ *n* [U] (*fml*) a continuous loud ringing noise or disturbance. ▶ **clangorous** /'klæŋgərəs, 'klæŋərəs/ *adj*.

clank /klæŋk/ *n* a loud sound made by pieces of metal moving or hitting each other: *the clank of heavy chains.*

▶ **clank** *v* [V, Vn] to make or cause sth to make a clank.

clansman /'klænzmən/ *n* (*pl* **-men** /-mən/; *fem* '**clanswoman** /-wʊmən/, *pl* **-women** /-wɪmɪn/) a member of a CLAN(1).

clap[1] /klæp/ *v* (**-pp-**) **1(a)** to strike the inner surface of one's hands together: [Vn] *She clapped her hands in delight.* ∘ *They clapped their hands in time to the music.* (**b**) to do this repeatedly as a way of showing approval of sb/sth; to APPLAUD sb/sth: [V] *The audience clapped enthusiastically.* [also Vn]. **2** ~ **sb on sth** to strike sb lightly with an open hand, usu in a friendly way: [Vnpr] *clap sb on the back.* **3** to put sb/sth somewhere quickly and strongly: [Vnpr] *The police officer clapped the handcuffs on him and took him away.* ∘ *clap sb in prison* ∘ *'Oh, dear!' she cried, clapping a hand to her forehead.* **IDM** **clap/lay/set eyes on sb/sth** ⇨ EYE[1]. **PHRV** **,clap sth 'on (sth)** (*infml*) to add sth to the price of sth, esp when this seems unfair: *The government has clapped an extra ten pence on a packet of cigarettes.*

▶ **clap** *n* **1** [sing] an act of clapping the hands or the sound this makes: *The audience gave her a big clap at the end of the performance.* **2** [C] ~ **on sth** a friendly hit with an open hand: *give sb a clap on the back.* **3** [C] a sudden loud noise: *a clap of thunder.*

■ **,clapped 'out** *adj* (*Brit infml*) **1** (of things) completely worn out and useless: *a clapped-out old bicycle.* **2** (of people) extremely tired: *She was clapped out by the end of the day.*

clap[2] /klæp/ (also **the clap**) *n* [U] (*sl*) a disease caught by having sex with an infected person; GONORRHOEA.

clapboard /'klæpbɔːd; *US* 'klæbərd/ *n* [U] (*US*) = WEATHERBOARDING: *clapboard cottages.*

clapper /'klæpə(r)/ *n* a piece of metal that is fixed loosely inside a bell and makes the bell sound by striking its side. ⇨ picture at BELL. **IDM** **like the** '**clappers** (*Brit infml*) very fast or hard; vigorously: *go/run/work like the clappers.*

clapperboard /'klæpəbɔːd/ *n* a device used during the making of films. It consists of a pair of con-

nected boards that are hit together sharply to help the matching of the sound and the picture.

claptrap /'klæptræp/ *n* [U] worthless, insincere or stupid talk; nonsense: *He talked a lot of pompous claptrap about the sanctity of press freedom.*

claret /'klærət/ *n* (**a**) [C, U] any of various types of dry red wine, esp from the Bordeaux area of France: *I prefer Burgundy to claret.* (**b**) [U] the colour of this. Compare BORDEAUX.

▶ **claret** *adj* dark red.

clarify /'klærəfaɪ/ *v* (*pt, pp* **-fied**) **1** to become or make sth clearer or easier to understand: [Vn] *clarify a remark/a statement* ∘ *I hope that what I say will clarify the situation.* [also V]. **2** to make sth, esp a fat, pure by heating it: [Vn] *clarified butter.* ▶ **clarification** /ˌklærɪfɪ'keɪʃn/ *n* [U, C]: *The whole issue needs clarification.* ∘ *make further clarifications to the contract.*

clarinet /ˌklærə'net/ *n* a musical instrument of the WOODWIND group. The player blows through a single REED(2) while pressing keys (KEY[1] 4) or covering holes with the fingers. ⇨ picture at MUSICAL INSTRUMENT.

▶ **clarinettist** (also **clarinetist**) *n* a person who plays the clarinet.

clarion /'klærɪən/ *adj* [attrib] loud, clear and stimulating: *a **clarion** call to action.*

clarity /'klærəti/ *n* [U] the state or quality of being clear: *clarity of expression/thought/vision.*

clash[1] /klæʃ/ *v* **1(a)** ~ **(with sb)** to come together and fight: [V] *The two armies clashed.* [Vpr] *Demonstrators clashed with police.* (**b**) ~ **(with sb)** (**on/over sth**) to disagree seriously: [Vpr, V] *The Government clashed with the Opposition/The Government and the Opposition clashed on the question of unemployment.* **2** ~ **(with sth)** to happen at the same time in a way that is not convenient: [V] *It's a pity the two concerts clash; I wanted to go to both of them.* [Vpr] *Your party clashes with a wedding I'm going to.* **3** ~ **(with sth)** (of colours, designs, etc) to fail to match or look good together: [Vpr, V] *The (colour of the) wallpaper clashes with (the colour of) the carpet/The wallpaper and the carpet clash.* **4** ~ **(sth and sth)** (**together**) to strike together or make things strike together with a loud harsh noise: [V] *Their swords clashed.* [Vn, Vnp] *She clashed the cymbals (together).*

clash[2] /klæʃ/ *n* **1(a)** ~ **(with sb/sth);** ~ **(between A and B)** a violent contact; a fight: *Clashes broke out between police and demonstrators.* (**b**) ~ **(with sb/sth)** (**on/over sth);** ~ **(between sb and sb)** (**on/over sth**) a serious disagreement; an argument: *a head-on clash between the prime minister and the leader of the Opposition on defence spending.* (**c**) a serious difference; a conflict: *a clash of interests/personalities* ∘ *a culture clash.* **2** ~ **(between A and B)** a situation in which events or dates are at the same time, in a way which is not convenient: *a clash between two classes.* **3** an example of colours, designs, etc not matching or looking good together. **4** a loud harsh noise made by metal objects striking together: *a clash of cymbals/swords.*

clasp[1] /klɑːsp; *US* klæsp/ *n* **1** a device for fastening things together, eg the ends of a belt or a NECKLACE, together: *The clasp of my brooch is broken.* **2(a)** a firm hold with the hand; a grip: *He held her hand in a firm clasp.* (**b**) a firm hold in the arms; an EMBRACE(1).

■ '**clasp-knife** *n* a folding knife with a device for holding the blade open.

clasp[2] /klɑːsp; *US* klæsp/ *v* **1(a)** to hold sb/sth tightly in the hand; to GRASP or grip sb/sth: [Vn] *clasping the microphone in both hands* ∘ *They clasped hands (ie held each other's hands) briefly before saying goodbye.* [Vnp] *His hands were clasped together in prayer.* (**b**) to hold sb tightly with the arms; to EMBRACE(1) sb: [Vnpr] *He clasped her to his*

C

chest. ○ *They stood clasped in each other's arms.* [also Vn]. **2** to fasten sth with a CLASP[1](1): [Vnpr] *clasp a bracelet round one's wrist.*

class /klɑːs; *US* klæs/ *n* **1(a)** [CGp] a group of people at the same social or economic level: *the working/middle/upper class* ○ *the professional class(es).* **(b)** [U] a system that divides people into such groups: *class differences/distinctions/divisions.* **(c)** [U] a person's position in a society with such a system: *a society in which class is more important than ability.* **2(a)** [CGp] a group of students taught together: *top of the class* ○ *We were in the same class at school.* ○ *The remedial class is/are difficult to teach.* **(b)** [C] an occasion when this group meets to be taught; a lesson: *I have a history class at 9 o'clock.* **(c)** [CGp] (*US*) a group of students who finish their studies at school or university in a particular year: *the class of '82.* **3** [C] a category of people, animals or things that are grouped together, esp because they have similar characteristics or qualities: *different classes of nouns/insects/vehicles.* ○ *Dickens was in a different class from* (ie was much better than) *most of his contemporaries.* ○ *a top-class athlete* (ie an excellent one). **4** [U] **(a)** high quality; excellence: *The team tries hard but it lacks class.* **(b)** elegant or superior style(3): *From the way she dresses you can see that she has class.* **5** [C] (esp in compounds) each of several different levels of comfort, etc available to travellers in a train, plane, bus, etc: *first class* ○ *tourist class* ○ *a second-class compartment* (eg on a train). **6** [C] (*Brit*) (esp in compounds) each of several grades of achievement in a university degree examination: *a first-/second-/third-class (honours) degree.* **7** [C] (*biology*) the second highest group into which animals and plants are divided, below a PHY-LUM and including several orders (ORDER[1] 10). Compare FAMILY 4, GENUS 1, SPECIES 1. **IDM** **in a class of one's/its ˈown; in a class by oneˈself/ itˈself** better than everyone/anything else of the same kind: *Pele was in a class of his own as a footballer.*
▶ **class** *adj* [attrib] excellent; of high quality: *a class player/performer.*
class *v* ~ **sb/sth (as sth)** to place sb/sth in a category; to consider that sb/sth is one of a particular type: [Vn-n] *Immigrant workers were classed as resident aliens.* ○ *Is architecture classed as an art or a science?* [also Vn-adj, Vn].

classless *adj* [usu attrib] **1** without social classes: *a classless society.* **2** not clearly belonging to any particular social class: *a classless accent.*

classy /ˈklɑːsi; *US* ˈklæsi/ *adj* (**-ier, -iest**) (*infml*) of high quality; expensive and stylish (STYLE): *a classy hotel.*

■ ˈ**class-conscious** *adj* aware of belonging to a particular social class or of the differences between social classes. ˈ**class-consciousness** *n* [U].

ˌ**class ˈstruggle** (also ˌ**class ˈwar**) *n* [U, sing] (*polit-ics*) conflict and disagreement between the different classes in a society, esp between the rich ruling classes and the poor working classes.

classic[1] /ˈklæsɪk/ *adj* [usu attrib] **1** deserving to be considered one of the best or most important of its type: *a classic novel/comment/goal.* **2** very typical: *This is a classic example/case of bureaucratic inefficiency.* ○ *She displays the classic symptoms of pneumonia.* **3(a)** simple and elegant in form or style; classical(4): *a classic design.* **(b)** (esp of clothes) having a simple traditional style that is not affected by changes in fashion: *a classic dress.*

classic[2] /ˈklæsɪk/ *n* **1** [C] a writer, an artist or a work of art recognized as being of high quality and lasting value: *This novel may well become a classic.* ○ *She enjoys reading the classics* (ie the great works of literature). **2** [C] an outstanding example of its kind: *The football match was a classic.* **3 Classics**

[sing *v*] the study of ancient Greek and Roman language and literature: *She did/read Classics at university.*

classical /ˈklæsɪkl/ *adj* [usu attrib] **1** of, relating to or influenced by the art and literature of ancient Greece and Rome: *classical studies* ○ *a classical scho-lar* (ie an expert in Latin and Greek) ○ *a classical education* (ie one based on the study of Latin and Greek) ○ *classical architecture.* **2** (of music) serious and traditional in style: *the classical music of India.* Compare POP[2]. **3** established and widely accepted; traditional: *the classical Darwinian theory of evolu-tion* ○ *classical and modern dance.* **4** simple and elegant in form or style: *a classical elegance.* ▶ **classically** /ˈklæsɪkəli/ *adv.*

classicism /ˈklæsɪsɪzəm/ *n* [U] **1** the style and principles of classical(1) art and literature. Compare IDEALISM 2, REALISM 3, ROMANTICISM. **2** SIMPLICITY and harmony of style or form.
▶ **classicist** /ˈklæsɪsɪst/ *n* **1** a person who follows classicism in art or literature. **2** an expert in or student of ancient Greek and Latin.

classification /ˌklæsɪfɪˈkeɪʃn/ *n* **1** [U] the action or process of classifying sth or of being classified: *a style of music that defies classification* (ie is like no other). **2** [C] a group or class(3) into which sth is put. **3** [U] (*biology*) the placing of animals and plants into groups according to their structure, ori-gin, etc. **4** [C] (in libraries, etc) a system of arranging books, magazines, etc in groups accord-ing to their subject.

classify /ˈklæsɪfaɪ/ *v* (*pt, pp* **-fied**) **1(a)** to arrange sth in categories or groups: [Vn] *The books in the library are classified by/according to subject.* **(b)** ~ **sb/sth (as sth)** to place sb/sth in a particular cat-egory: [Vn-n] *Would you classify her novels as ser-ious literature or as mere entertainment?* [also Vn-adj, Vn]. **2** [Vn] to declare information, docu-ments, etc to be officially secret and available only to certain people.
▶ **classifiable** /ˈklæsɪfaɪəbl/ *adj* that can be classi-fied.
classified *adj* [usu attrib] **1** arranged in groups: *a classified directory* (ie one in which the names of firms, etc are entered in sections with titles, eg engineers, doctors, car repairs, etc). **2** declared officially secret and available only to certain people: *classified information/documents.* ˌ**classi-fied adˈvertisements** (also ˌ**classified ˈads, ˈsmall ads** /ˈædz/, **classifieds**, *esp US* ˈ**want ads**) *n* [pl] small advertisements placed in a newspaper, etc by people wishing to buy or sell sth, employ sb, find a job, etc.

classmate /ˈklɑːsmeɪt; *US* ˈklæs-/ *n* a person who was or is in the same class as oneself at school: *We were classmates at school.*

classroom /ˈklɑːsruːm, -rʊm; *US* ˈklæs-/ *n* a room where a class of pupils or students is taught.

clatter /ˈklætə(r)/ *n* [sing] a continuous noise like that of hard objects falling or knocking against each other: *the clatter of cutlery/horses' hoofs/a type-writer.*
▶ **clatter** *v* to make or cause sth to make a clatter: [Vn] *Don't clatter your knives and forks.* [also V, Vpr]. **PHR V** **clatter across, down, in, etc** to move across, etc, making a clatter: *The children clattered* (ie ran noisily) *downstairs.* ○ *The cart clat-tered over the cobblestones.*

clause /klɔːz/ *n* **1** (*grammar*) a group of words that includes a subject[1](6) and a verb, forming a sentence or part of a sentence: *In the sentence 'He often visits Spain because he likes the climate', 'He often visits Spain' is a main clause and 'because he likes the climate' is a subordinate clause.* **2** a paragraph or section in a legal document stating a particular obligation, condition[1](3b), etc: *There is a clause in*

....

the contract forbidding tenants to sublet. ○ clause 23(b) of the treaty.

claustrophobia /ˌklɔːstrəˈfəʊbiə/ n [U] an abnormal fear of being in an enclosed space.

▶ **claustrophobic** /ˌklɔːstrəˈfəʊbɪk/ adj suffering from or causing claustrophobia: feel claustrophobic ○ a claustrophobic little room.

clavichord /ˈklævɪkɔːd/ n an early type of musical instrument like a piano with a very soft tone.

clavicle /ˈklævɪkl/ n (anatomy) the collar-bone (COLLAR). ⇨ picture at SKELETON.

claw /klɔː/ n **1** any of the pointed nails on the feet of some animals and birds: Cats have sharp claws. ○ The eagle held a mouse in its claws. **2** either of two parts that certain SHELLFISH have for catching and gripping things; a PINCER(2): a lobster's claw. ⇨ picture at SHELLFISH. **3** a mechanical device like a claw, used for gripping and lifting things. **IDM** **get one's claws into sb** (infml) **1** to criticize sb severely or attack sb with words: After four defeats in a row the press have really got their claws into the England team. **2** (derog) (esp of a woman) to attach oneself to and control a partner: She's really got her claws into him!

▶ **claw** v ~ (at) sb/sth to scratch or tear sb/sth with a claw or claws or with one's fingernails: [Vpr] The cats clawed at each other. ○ The prisoner clawed at the cell door in desperation. [Vn] His face was badly clawed. **IDM** **claw one's way across, through, up, etc** to move across, etc by using the claws or the hands: They slowly clawed their way up the cliff. ○ (fig) She clawed her way to the top of her profession by hard work and ruthless determination.
PHRV ˌclaw sth ˈback (of a government) to recover money paid to certain groups of people, esp by taxing them.
■ ˈclaw-back n an act of clawing money back, or the money recovered in this way.
ˈclaw-hammer n a hammer with one end of its head bent and divided for pulling out nails. ⇨ picture at HAMMER.

clay /kleɪ/ n [U] a type of stiff sticky earth that becomes hard when baked and is used for making bricks, pots, etc: clay modelling ○ clay tiles. **IDM** **have feet of clay** ⇨ FOOT¹.

▶ **clayey** /ˈkleɪi/ adj like, containing or covered with clay: Clayey soils are impervious to water.
■ ˈclay court n a type of tennis court with a surface of clay: a clay-court player.
ˌclay ˈpigeon n a disc thrown in the air as a target for shooting at: clay ˈpigeon shooting.
ˌclay ˈpipe n a tobacco pipe made of hardened clay.

claymore /ˈkleɪmɔː(r)/ n a large sword with two sharp edges, formerly used in Scotland.

clean¹ /kliːn/ adj (-er, -est) **1(a)** free from dirt: clean hands ○ clean air (ie free from smoke, etc) ○ a clean wound (ie one that is not infected) ○ wash/wipe/scrub/brush sth clean ○ I want this whole house squeaky clean (ie very clean). **(b)** free from substances that are unpleasant, harmful or not wanted; pure: clean air/water. **(c)** that has been washed since it was last worn or used: a clean dress/towel/knife ○ He wears clean socks every day. ○ put clean sheets on a bed. **(d)** having clean habits: Cats are clean animals. **2** not yet used; not marked: a clean sheet of paper. **3(a)** not sexually offensive; not OBSCENE: Keep it clean (ie Do not tell dirty jokes)! **(b)** innocent; morally pure: good clean fun. **4(a)** showing or having no record of offences: a clean driving-licence ○ a clean police record. **(b)** (sl) not possessing or containing anything illegal, eg drugs, stolen goods, etc: The police raided her flat but she/it was clean. **5** played or done within the rules; fair: a hard-fought but clean match ○ a clean tackle (eg in a game of football). **6** with a smooth edge or surface; regular; even: A sharp knife makes a clean cut. ○ a

clean break (eg the breaking of a bone in one place). **7** (esp in sport) skilfully and accurately done: a clean hit/stroke/blow. **8** having a simple and pleasing shape: a car with clean lines. **9** (infml) (of a nuclear weapon) producing relatively little RADIOACTIVE material. **IDM** **(as) clean as a ˈwhistle** (infml) **1** very clean. **2** quickly and skilfully: The dog jumped through the hoop as clean as a whistle (ie without touching it). **a clean bill of ˈhealth** a report showing that a person's health is good, esp after an illness, or that an organization, etc has been found to be in good condition: The doctor gave him a clean bill of health. **a clean ˈsheet/ˈslate** a record of work or behaviour that does not show any wrongdoing in the past: He came out of prison hoping to start (life) again with a clean sheet (ie with his previous offences forgotten). **keep one's nose clean** ⇨ NOSE¹. **make a clean break (with sth)** to change one's previous manner of living entirely: He's made a clean break with the past. **make a clean ˈbreast of sth** to tell the truth about sth after not doing so; to confess sth: He made a clean breast of it and told the police everything. **make a clean sweep (of sth) 1** to remove things or people that are thought to be unnecessary: The new manager made a clean sweep of the department. **2** to win all of a group of similar or related competitions, games, etc: The Chinese made a clean sweep of (the medals in) the gymnastics events. **show a clean pair of heels** ⇨ SHOW². **wipe the slate clean** ⇨ WIPE.

▶ **clean** adv simply and completely: The bullet went clean through his shoulder. ○ The thief got clean away. ○ I clean forgot about it. ○ The batsman was clean bowled (ie without the ball hitting the bat or the pads first). **IDM** **come clean (with sb) (about sth)** (infml) to confess fully: I've got to come 'clean (with you) — I was the one who broke the kitchen window.
■ ˌclean-ˈcut adj **(a)** having a clear outline: ˌclean-cut ˈfeatures. **(b)** (approv) looking neat and respectable: a ˌclean-cut ˈstudent.
ˌclean-ˈshaven adj (of men) not having any hair on the lower part of the face: Beards and moustaches are out of fashion — men prefer the clean-shaven look.

clean² /kliːn/ v **1(a)** to make sth clean or free of dirt, etc: [V] Spend all day cooking and cleaning [Vn] clean the windows/one's shoes/one's teeth ○ The cat sat cleaning itself. **(b)** to become clean: [V] This floor cleans easily (ie is easy to clean). **2** to remove the internal organs of a fish or a chicken, etc before one cooks it: [Vn] cleaning poultry. **PHRV** ˌclean sth ˈdown to clean sth thoroughly by wiping or brushing it: clean down the walls. **ˌclean sth from/off sth** to remove sth from sth by brushing, scraping, wiping, etc: She cleaned the dirt from her fingernails. **ˌclean sth ˈout** to clean the inside of sth thoroughly: clean out the stables. **ˌclean sb/sth ˈout (of sth)** (infml) **1** to use up or take all sb's money: I haven't a penny left — buying drinks for everyone has cleaned me out completely. **2** to steal everything from a person or place: The burglars cleaned her out of all her jewellery. **ˌclean (oneself)** (infml) to make oneself clean, esp by washing: My hands are filthy — I'd better go and clean (myself) up. **ˌclean (sth) ˈup 1** to remove dirt, rubbish, etc from a place to clean it: The workmen cleaned up (the mess) before they left. ○ I seem to spend all my time cleaning up after my family! ○ clean up beaches after an oil spillage. **2** (infml) to gain or win a lot of money: He cleaned up (a small fortune) when he sold the business. ○ clean up at cards. **ˌclean sth ˈup** to remove criminals, harmful influences, etc from sth: The new mayor is determined to clean up the city. ○ a campaign to clean up television (ie reduce the amount of sex and violence shown).

▶ **clean** *n* [sing] an act of cleaning: *The house needs a good clean.*

■ **¹clean-up** *n* (**a**) the removal of dirt, etc from a person or place. (**b**) the removal of criminals, harmful influences, etc.

cleaner /ˈkliːnə(r)/ *n* **1** (esp in compounds) a person or thing that cleans: *an ¹office cleaner* (ie sb employed to clean offices) ○ *a ¹floor cleaner* (ie a substance that removes dirt from floors) ○ *a vacuum cleaner.* **2 cleaners** [pl] (also **cleaner's**) a shop where clothes and fabrics are cleaned, esp with chemicals: *send a suit to the cleaner's* ○ *pick up shirts from the cleaners.* **IDM take sb to the ¹cleaners/ ¹cleaner's** (*infml*) **1** to rob or cheat sb of all their money, possessions, etc. **2** to criticize sb harshly.

cleaning /ˈkliːnɪŋ/ *n* [U] the work of making the inside of a house, etc clean: *do the cleaning.*

■ **¹cleaning lady** (also **¹cleaning woman**) *n* a woman who is employed to clean the inside of a building, esp an office.

cleanliness /ˈklenlinəs/ *n* [U] the habit of being clean or of keeping things clean: *He is meticulous about his appearance and obsessive about cleanliness.*

cleanly /ˈkliːnli/ *adv* easily; smoothly: *Blunt scissors don't cut cleanly.* ○ *catch a ball cleanly.*

cleanse /klenz/ *v* ~ **sb/sth (of sth)** to make sb/sth thoroughly clean: [Vn] *a cleansing cream* (ie one that cleans the skin) [Vnpr] (*fig fml*) *She felt cleansed of her sins after confession.*

▶ **cleanser** *n* a substance that cleanses: *a skin cleanser* ○ *a household cleanser.*

clear¹ /klɪə(r)/ *adj* (**-er, -est**) **1(a)** easy to see or hear: *a clear photograph* ○ *a clear reflection in the water* ○ *a clear voice/speaker/sound.* (**b**) easy to understand; not causing confusion: *a clear statement/explanation/article/meaning* ○ *You'll do as you're told, is that clear?* ○ *This behaviour must stop — do I make myself clear* (ie express myself clearly)? ○ *I hope I made it clear (to him) that he was no longer welcome here.* **2** ~ **(about/on sth)** having or feeling no doubt or confusion: *a clear thinker* ○ *a clear understanding of the problems* ○ *My memory is not clear on that point.* ○ *Are you quite clear about what the job involves?* **3** ~ **(to sb) (that ...)** obvious: *a clear case of cheating* ○ *have a clear advantage/lead* (eg in a contest) ○ *It is quite clear to me that she is not coming.* ○ *It is not clear what they want us to do.* **4** definite; leaving no doubt: *She made a clear statement of her intentions.* ○ *a clear majority.* **5(a)** that one can see through; transparent: *clear glass* ○ *the clear water of a mountain lake* ○ *clear soup* (ie without solid ingredients). (**b**) without cloud or mist: *a clear sky/day* ○ *clear weather.* (**c**) (of skin) without spots (SPOT¹ 2) or marks: *clear skin* ○ *a clear complexion.* (**d**) (of eyes) bright; showing that sb is alert. **6** ~ **(of sth)** (**a**) free from obstacles, difficulties, etc: *a clear view of the stage* ○ *Wait until the road is clear (of traffic) before crossing.* (**b**) (of a time) without anything having been arranged or having to be done: *I want to keep next weekend clear so that I can do some gardening.* (**c**) free from guilt: *have a clear conscience.* (**d**) free from sth undesirable: *clear of debt* ○ *You are now clear of all suspicion.* **7** [pred] ~ **(of sb/sth)** not touching sth; away from sth: *The plane climbed until it was clear of the clouds.* ○ *Park (your car) about nine inches clear of the kerb.* **8** [attrib] complete; whole: *Allow three clear days for the letter to arrive.* **9** [attrib] (of a sum of money) after deductions (DEDUCTION 2b), eg taxes, expenses, etc; NET²: *a clear profit.* **IDM (as) clear as a ¹bell** very clearly and easily heard. **(as) clear as ¹day** easy to see or understand; obvious. **the coast is clear** ⇨ COAST¹. **in the ¹clear** (*infml*) no longer in danger or suspected of sth: *She was*

very ill for a few days but the doctors say she's now in the clear.

▶ **clearly** *adv* **1** in a clear manner, so that sth is easy to hear, see or understand: *speak clearly* ○ *It is too dark to see clearly.* **2** obviously; without doubt: *Clearly, that cannot be true.*

clearness *n* [U] the state of being clear; CLARITY: *the clearness of the atmosphere* ○ *clearness of vision.*

■ **‚clear-¹headed** *adj* thinking or understanding clearly; sensible. **‚clear-¹headedly** *adv.* **‚clear-¹headedness** *n* [U].

‚clear-¹sighted *adj* seeing, understanding or thinking clearly; able to make good decisions and judgements.

clear² /klɪə(r)/ *adv* **1** clearly; distinctly: *I can hear you loud and clear.* **2** ~ **(of sth)** out of the way of or away from sth; no longer near or touching sth: *Stand clear of the doors.* ○ *She managed to leap clear of* (ie out of) *the burning car.* ○ *He jumped three inches clear of* (ie above) *the bar.* **3** completely: *The prisoner got clear away.* **4** ~ **to sth** (*esp US*) all the way to sth: *He climbed clear up to the top of the tree.* **IDM keep/stay/steer clear (of sb/sth)** to avoid contact with sb; to avoid becoming involved in sth, going near a place or using sth: *We all keep clear of the boss when she's in a bad mood.* ○ *Try to steer clear of trouble.* ○ *I prefer to stay clear of town during the rush-hour.* ○ *His doctor advised him to steer clear of alcohol.*

■ **‚clear-¹cut** *adj* definite; not VAGUE(1): *‚clear-cut ¹plans/pro¹posals/di¹stinctions.*

clear³ /klɪə(r)/ *v* **1(a)** (of a liquid) to become transparent: [V] *The muddy water slowly cleared.* (**b**) (of the sky or the weather) to become free of cloud or rain: [V] *The sky cleared after the storm.* (**c**) ~ **(away)** (of FOG, smoke, etc) to disappear: [V, Vp] *It was a fine day once the mist had cleared (away).* **2(a)** ~ **A (of B) / ~ B (from/off A)** to remove sth that is not wanted or is no longer needed from a place: [Vn] *clear the table* (eg take away dirty plates, etc after a meal) [Vnpr] *The land was cleared of snow.* ○ *clear papers off a desk.* (**b**) to remove an obstacle from sth: [Vn] *clear one's throat* (ie make a sound like a small COUGH(1) in order to be able to speak clearly) ○ *The cars blocking the motorway have now been cleared out of the way and traffic is flowing again.* [Vnpr] *clear the streets of snow/clear snow from the streets* ○ (*fig*) *clear one's mind of doubt.* (**c**) [Vn] to remove data that is no longer required from the memory of a computer, etc. **3** ~ **sb (of sth)** to show sb to be innocent: [Vn] *Throughout his imprisonment, he fought to clear his name.* [Vnpr] *She was cleared of all charges.* **4** to get past or over sth without touching it: [Vn] *The horse cleared the fence easily.* ○ *The car only just cleared* (ie avoided hitting) *the gatepost.* **5(a)** to get permission for or allow a ship, plane or cargo to leave or enter a place: [Vnpr] *clear goods through customs* ○ *clear a plane for take-off* [also Vn]. (**b**) (of goods) to pass through sth after satisfying official requirements: [Vn] *Our baggage has cleared customs.* **6(a)** ~ **sth (with sb/sth)** to give or get official approval for sth to be done: [Vn] *clear an article for publication* [Vnpr] *I'll have to clear it with the manager before I can return your money.* (**b**) to decide officially after investigating sb that they can be given special or important work or allowed access to secret information: [Vn] *She's been cleared by security.* **7** to pass a cheque through a clearing house (CLEAR³) so that the money is put into the account of the person to whom it is written: [Vn] *Cheques take 3 working days to clear.* **8** to gain or earn a sum of money as profit after deductions (DEDUCTION 2b), eg tax, expenses, etc: [Vn] *clear £1 000 on a deal* ○ *How much do you clear a month in that job?* **9** to pay back fully a sum of money owed: [Vn] *clear one's debts.* **10** [V, Vn] (in football,

hockey, etc) to kick or hit the ball away from the area near the goal that is being defended. **IDM** **clear the ¹air** to remove tension, suspicion, anger, etc from a situation by discussing it openly: *A frank discussion can help to clear the air.* **clear the ¹decks** (*infml*) to prepare for a particular activity, event, etc by removing anything that is not essential to it. **clear the way** to remove an obstacle or obstacles so that progress or movement is possible: *talks to clear the way for a wage agreement* ○ *Could you clear the way, please? People are trying to get through.* **PHRV** **clear (sth) away** to remove sth because it is not wanted or no longer required, or in order to leave a clear space: *clear away the dishes.* **¦clear ¹off** (*infml*) (esp imperative) to go or run away: *You've no right to be here. Clear off!* ○ *He cleared off as soon as he saw the policeman coming.* **¦clear ¹out (of...)** (*infml*) to leave a place quickly: *He cleared out before the police arrived.* ○ *Clear out!* **¦clear sth ¹out 1** to make sth empty or tidy by removing what is inside it: *clear out a cupboard/the attic.* **2** to throw away things that are not wanted: *clear out old clothes.* **¦clear ¹up 1** (of the weather) to become fine or bright: *I hope it clears up this afternoon.* **2** (of an illness, infection, etc) to disappear as good health returns: *Has your rash cleared up yet?* **¦clear (sth) ¹up** to make sth tidy: *Please clear up (the mess in here).* **¦clear sth ¹up** to solve or explain sth: *clear up a mystery/difficulty/misunderstanding.* ■ **¹clearing bank** *n* (*Brit*) any bank belonging to a clearing-house (CLEAR³).
¹clearing-house *n* a central office at which banks exchange cheques and then pay in cash the amount they still owe each other.

clearance /'klɪərəns/ *n* **1** [C, U] an act or the process of clearing, removing or getting rid of sth: *land clearance* ○ *'slum clearance* (ie knocking down houses in SLUM areas) ○ *a 'clearance sale* (ie one in which all the stock in a shop is sold at reduced prices before the shop closes permanently). **2** [C] (in football, hockey, etc) an act of kicking or striking the ball away from the goal that is being defended: *a fine clearance by the full back.* **3** [C, U] a space left clear when one object moves past or under another: *a clearance of only two feet* (eg for a ship moving through a canal) ○ *There is not much clearance for tall vehicles passing under this bridge.* **4(a)** [C, U] a document giving permission for a ship or plane to leave a place or for goods to pass through CUS-TOMS(2): *get clearance for take-off* ○ *How long will customs clearance take?* **(b)** [U] official permission for sb to work with secret information, etc: *give sb security clearance.* **(c)** [U] official approval for sth to go ahead or be done: *get clearance from Head Office.* **5** [C, U] the process of clearing cheques at a clearing-house (CLEAR³ 7).

clearing /'klɪərɪŋ/ *n* an open space from which trees have been cleared in a forest.

clearway /'klɪəweɪ/ *n* (*Brit*) a main road other than a MOTORWAY on which vehicles may not normally stop or park.

cleat /kliːt/ *n* **1** a small wooden or metal bar fastened to sth, on which ropes may be fastened by winding. **2** (usu *pl*) a strip of rubber, wood, etc fastened to the sole of a boot, shoe, etc to prevent slipping.

cleavage /'kliːvɪdʒ/ *n* **1** [C, U] (*infml*) the division between a woman's breasts that can be seen above a dress which does not completely cover them: *That gown shows a large amount of (her) cleavage!* **2** [C] **(a)** a split or division: *There is a deep cleavage between rich and poor in our society.* **(b)** a line along which material such as rock or wood splits.

cleave¹ /kliːv/ *v* (*pt* **cleaved** /kliːvd/, **clove** /kləʊv/ or **cleft** /kleft/; *pp* **cleaved**, **cloven** /'kləʊvn/ or **cleft**) **1** (*dated or fml*) to split sth by chopping it

with sth sharp and heavy: [Vnpr] *cleave a block of wood in two* [Vn-adj] *cleave a man's head open with a sword.* **2** ~ **through sth** / ~ **sth (through sth)** (*dated or fml*) to make a way through sth, esp by splitting it: [Vn, Vpr] *The ship's bows cleaved (through) the waves.* [Vnpr] *cleave a path through the jungle* ○ (*fig*) *cleaving one's way/a path through the crowd.* **IDM** **be (caught) in a cleft ¹stick** to be in a difficult situation, when any action one takes will have bad consequences.
■ **¦cleft ¹palate** *n* an abnormal condition in which the roof of sb's mouth is split at birth, making them unable to speak properly.

cleave² /kliːv/ *v* (*pt* **cleaved** /kliːvd/ or **clave** /kleɪv/; *pp* **cleaved**) ~ **to sb/sth** (*arch*) to remain attached, faithful or stuck to sb/sth: [Vpr] *cleave to old ways of life.*

cleaver /'kliːvə(r)/ *n* a heavy knife with a broad blade used for chopping meat.

treble clef   bass clef   clef

staff

clef /klef/ *n* (*music*) a symbol at the beginning of a line of printed music (or *stave*) showing the pitch¹(2) of the notes on it: *the treble/bass clef.* ⇨ picture.

cleft¹ /kleft/ *n* a crack or split occurring naturally, eg in the ground or in rock.

cleft² *pt*, *pp* of CLEAVE¹.

clematis /'klemətɪs, klə'meɪtɪs/ *n* [U, C] a climbing plant with white, purple or pink flowers.

clement /'klemənt/ *adj* (*fml*) **1** (esp of weather) mild. **2** showing MERCY.
▶ **clemency** /'klemənsi/ *n* [U] (*fml*) **1** MERCY, esp when punishing sb: *He appealed to the judge for clemency.* **2** a mild quality, esp of weather.

clementine /'klemənti:n/ *n* a type of small orange.

clench /klentʃ/ *v* **1** to close sth tightly or press sth firmly together, showing determination, anger, pain, etc: [Vn] *clench one's fist/jaws/teeth* ○ *a clenched-fist salute.* **2** ~ **sb/sth (in/with sth)** to hold sb/sth tightly and firmly: [Vn, Vnpr] *clench the railings (with both hands)* [Vnpr] *money clenched tightly in one's fist.*

clerestory /'klɪəstɔːri/ *n* the upper part of a wall in a large church, with a row of windows in it, above the lower roofs.

clergy /'klɜːdʒi/ *n* [*pl* *v*] the people who have been officially made priests or ministers (MINISTER¹3), esp in a Christian Church: *All the local clergy attended the ceremony.* ○ *The new proposals affect both clergy and laity.* Compare LAITY.

clergyman /'klɜːdʒimən/ *n* (*pl* **-men** /-mən/) a priest or minister¹(3) in a Christian Church.

cleric /'klerɪk/ *n* **1** a CLERGYMAN. **2** a religious leader in any religion.

clerical /'klerɪkl/ *adj* **1** of or done by a CLERK(1) or clerks: *'clerical work* ○ *¦clerical 'error* (ie one made in copying or calculating sth). **2** of the CLERGY: *a ¦clerical 'collar* (ie one that fastens at the back, worn by priests, etc).

clerk /klɑːk; *US* klɜːrk/ *n* **1** a person employed in an office, a bank, etc to keep records, accounts, etc: *a 'bank clerk* ○ *a 'filing clerk.* **2** an official in charge of the records of a council, court, etc: *the Town 'Clerk* ○ *the Clerk of the 'Court* ○ *clerk of (the) 'works* (ie the person responsible for materials, etc for building work done by contract). **3** (*US*) **(a)** (also **'desk clerk**) a receptionist (RECEPTION) in a hotel. **(b)** (also **'salesclerk**) an assistant in a shop.
▶ **clerk** /klɜːrk/ *v* (*US*) [V] to work as a CLERK(1), esp in a shop.

clever /'klevə(r)/ adj (-er, -est) **1(a)** quick at learning and understanding things; intelligent: *clever at arithmetic* ○ *a clever student* ○ *Clever girl!* **(b)** skilful: *be clever with one's hands* ○ *be clever at making excuses.* **2** (of things, ideas, actions, etc) showing intelligence or skill; INGENIOUS: *a clever scheme/invention* ○ *What a clever idea!* **3** (*infml derog*) quick and sharp with words, in a way that is considered annoying or does not show respect: *Do as you're told and don't get clever with me!* **IDM** **too clever by** '**half** (*infml derog esp Brit*) too confident of being clever, in a way that is considered annoying or that causes one to fail at sth. ▶ **cleverly** adv. **cleverness** n [U].
■ '**clever Dick** (*Brit* also '**clever clogs**) n (*infml derog*) a person who thinks he or she is always right or knows everything: *She's such a clever Dick — you can't tell her anything.*

cliché /'kliː.ʃeɪ; US kliːˈʃeɪ/ n **(a)** [C] a phrase or an idea which is used so often that it is no longer interesting, effective or relevant: *a cliché-ridden style* ○ *In the words of the old cliché, I'm 'over the moon'.* **(b)** [U] the use of such phrases.
▶ **clichéd** (also **cliché'd**) /'kliːʃeɪd; US kliːˈʃeɪd/ adj full of clichés.

click /klɪk/ n a short sharp sound, like that of a key turning in a lock: *the click of a switch* ○ *He saluted with a click of his heels.*
▶ **click** v **1** to make or cause sth to make a click: [V] *What's that clicking noise?* [V-adj] *The door clicked shut.* [Vpr] *The bolt clicked into place.* [Vn] *click one's tongue/heels/fingers.* **2** (*infml*) (esp with *it*) to become clear or understood suddenly: [V] *I puzzled over it for hours before it finally clicked.* **3** (*infml*) **(a)** to become friendly at once: [V] *We met at a party and just clicked immediately.* **(b)** ~ (**with sb**) to become popular with sb: [V, Vpr] *The TV series has really clicked (with young audiences).*

client /'klaɪənt/ n **1** a person who uses the services of a professional person or organization, eg a lawyer or a bank. **2** a customer in a shop.

clientele /ˌkliːɒnˈtel; US ˌklaɪənˈtel/ n [Gp] **1** customers or clients as a group: *an international clientele* ○ *Our clientele come/comes mainly from the film industry.* **2** the people who go, esp regularly, to a theatre, restaurant, etc: *the pub's clientele.*

cliff /klɪf/ n a steep, usu high, face¹(3) of rock, esp at the edge of the sea: *The sign said, 'Keep away from the cliffs.'* ○ *the cliff edge/top* ○ *a cliff path.* ⇨ picture at COAST¹.
■ '**cliff-hanger** n a story or situation which is very exciting because it is not clear what will happen next or in the end: *The first part of the film ended with a real cliff-hanger.*

climactic /klaɪˈmæktɪk/ adj forming a CLIMAX; very exciting; most important: *a climactic scene in a play* ○ *climactic moments in history.*

climate /'klaɪmət/ n **1(a)** the regular pattern of weather conditions (temperature, amount of rain, winds, etc) of a particular place: *Britain has a temperate climate.* ○ *changes in the earth's climate.* **(b)** an area or a region with certain weather conditions: *She moved to a warmer climate.* **2** a general attitude or feeling; an atmosphere: *a climate of suspicion* ○ *the present political climate* ○ *the current climate of opinion* (ie the general or fashionable attitude to an aspect of life, policy, etc). **IDM** **a change of air/climate** ⇨ CHANGE².
▶ **climatic** /klaɪˈmætɪk/ adj of climate: *climatic changes/conditions/trends.* **climatically** /-klɪ/ adv.
climatology /ˌklaɪməˈtɒlədʒi/ n [U] the science or study of climate.

climax /'klaɪmæks/ n **1(a)** the most exciting or important event or point in time: *the climax of his political career* ○ *The climax of the celebration was a firework display.* ○ *Fighting in the capital reached a*
new climax today. **(b)** the most intense or exciting part, esp of a play, piece of music, etc: *The music approached a climax.* ○ *His intervention brought their quarrel to a climax.* **2** the highest point of sexual pleasure; an ORGASM.
▶ **climax** v **1** ~ (**sth**) (**in/with sth**) to bring sth to or come to a climax(1a): [V] *The play climaxes in the third act.* [Vpr] *Her career climaxed with the award of an Oscar.* [also Vn, Vnpr]. **2** [V] to have an ORGASM.

climb /klaɪm/ v **1(a)** to go up or over sth by effort, esp using one's hands and feet: [Vn] *climb a wall/a mountain/a tree/a rope/the stairs* ○ *The car slowly climbed the hill.* **(b)** to go or come in the specified direction, esp upwards, by effort: [Vpr] *climb up/down a ladder/along a ridge/into a car/out of bed/over a gate/through a hedge* ○ *climb into/out of one's clothes* (ie put them on/take them off) [V] *This is where we start climbing* (ie upwards). [Vadv] *Monkeys can climb well.* **2** [V] **(a)** to go up mountains, etc as a sport: *He likes to go climbing most weekends.* **(b)** (of aircraft, the sun, etc) to go higher in the sky: *The plane climbed to 20000 feet.* **(c)** to slope upwards: *The road climbs steeply for several miles.* **(d)** (of plants) to grow up a wall or some other support: *a climbing rose.* **3** to make progress or rise in social rank, etc by one's own effort: [V] *In a few years he had climbed to the top of his profession.* **4** (of currency, temperature, etc) to increase in value or level: [V] *The dollar has been climbing steadily all week.* ○ *Interest rates began to climb.* **IDM** **climb/jump on the bandwagon** ⇨ BANDWAGON. **PHR V** **climb down** (**over sth**) (*infml*) to admit a mistake or withdraw from a position in an argument, etc: *As new facts became known, the government was forced to climb down over its handling of the spy scandal.* See also CLIMB-DOWN.
▶ **climb** n **1** an act or instance of climbing: *an exhausting climb* ○ *a rapid climb to stardom.* **2** a place or distance climbed or to be climbed: *It's an hour's climb to the summit.*
climber n **1** a person who climbs (esp mountains) or an animal that climbs. **2** a climbing plant. ⇨ picture at HOUSE¹. **3** (*infml*) a person who tries to improve her or his status in society: *a social climber.*
climbing n [U] the activity of climbing rocks or mountains as a sport.
■ '**climb-down** n an act of admitting one was wrong or of withdrawing from a position in an argument, etc: *The announcement represents an embarrassing climb-down by the government.*
'**climbing-frame** n (*Brit*) a structure of joined bars, etc for children to climb.

clime /klaɪm/ n (usu pl) (*arch or joc*) a country; a climate(1): *seeking sunnier climes.*

clinch /klɪntʃ/ v **1** (*infml*) to confirm or settle sth finally; to FINALIZE sth: [Vn] *clinch a deal/an argument/a bargain/a victory* ○ *The score was level until a last-minute goal clinched it for us.* **2** (esp of boxers) to hold each other tightly with the arms: [V] *The boxers clinched and the referee had to separate them.* ○ (*infml*) *The scene ended as the lovers clinched.*
▶ **clinch** n **(a)** (in boxing) an act of clinching (CLINCH 2): *get into/break a clinch.* **(b)** (*infml*) an EMBRACE.
clincher n (usu *sing*) (*infml*) a point, remark, event, etc that settles an argument, a decision, etc.

cling /klɪŋ/ v (*pt, pp* **clung** /klʌŋ/) **1** ~ (**on**) **to sb/sth**; ~ **onto sb/sth**; ~ **on**; ~ **together** to hold on tightly to sb/sth: [Vpr] *survivors clinging to a raft* ○ *The children were clinging onto their mother.* [Vpr, Vp] *They clung to each other/clung together as they said goodbye.* [Vp] *Cling on tight!* **2** ~ (**to sth**) to become attached to sth; to stick to sth: [V, Vpr] *The smell of smoke clings (to one's clothes) for a long* *time.* [Vpr] *a dress that clings to* (ie fits closely so as to show the shape of) *the body.* **3** ~ **(on) to sth** to want to keep sth, esp without good reason; to refuse to abandon sth: [Vpr] *cling to a belief/an opinion/a theory* ○ *politicians who cling to power/office* ○ *cling on to one's possessions* ○ *She clung to the hope that he was still alive.* **4** ~ **(to sb)** to be emotionally dependent on sb; to stay too close to sb: [Vpr] *Small children cling to their mothers.* ○ *He clung to me like a leech all evening.* [also V]. **5** ~ **to sb/sth** to stay close to sb/sth: [Vpr] *The ship clung to the coastline.* ○ *Don't cling to the curb when you're driving.*

▶ **clinging** (also **clingy**) *adj* **1** (of clothes) sticking to the body and showing its shape. **2** (*usu derog*) emotionally dependent: *a clinging child.*

■ **'cling film** *n* [U] thin transparent plastic material used for wrapping food, etc. See also SHRINK-WRAPPED.

clinic /'klɪnɪk/ *n* **1** a special place or time at which specialized medical treatment or advice is given to visiting patients: *a dental/diabetic/fracture clinic* ○ *She is attending the antenatal clinic.* ○ *The family planning clinic is on Wednesday evenings.* **2** (*esp Brit*) a private or specialized hospital: *He is being treated at a private clinic.* **3** an occasion in a hospital when students learn by watching how a specialist examines and treats his patients. **4** (*US*) a group of doctors sharing the same building and working together.

clinical /'klɪnɪkl/ *adj* **1** [attrib] of or for the direct examination and treatment of patients and their illnesses: *clinical research* (ie not THEORETICAL) ○ *clinical trials* ○ *clinical training* (ie the part of a doctor's training done in a hospital). **2** without feeling; cold¹(3a): *He watched her suffering with clinical detachment.* **3** (of a room, building, etc) very plain; without decoration: *The office was bare and clinical, painted white throughout.* ▶ **clinically** *adv*: *clinically dead* (ie judged to be dead from the condition of the body).

clink¹ /klɪŋk/ *n* a sharp ringing sound like that made by small pieces of metal or glass knocking together: *the clink of coins/keys/glasses.*

▶ **clink** *v* to make or cause sth to make a clink: [V] *coins clinking in his pocket* [Vn] *They clinked glasses and drank to each other's health.*

clink² /klɪŋk/ *n* [sing] (*sl*) prison: *be (put) in (the) clink.*

clinker /'klɪŋkə(r)/ *n* [C, U] (a piece of) the hard rough material left after coal has burnt at a high temperature.

clinker-built /'klɪŋkə bɪlt/ *adj* (of a boat) made with the outside boards or metal plates (PLATE¹ 4) overlapping (OVERLAP 1) downwards.

clip

bulldog clip   bicycle-clip   paper-clip

clip¹ /klɪp/ *n* **1** (esp in compounds) any of various plastic or metal devices used for holding things together: *a 'paper-clip* ○ *a 'bicycle-clips.* ⇨ picture. **2** a piece of jewellery fastened to clothes by a clip: *a diamond 'clip.* **3** a set of bullets in a metal holder which is placed in or attached to a gun, etc for firing.

▶ **clip** *v* (-pp-) ~ (sth) (on)to sth; ~ (sth) on; ~ (A and B) together to fasten sth or be fastened to sth else with a clip: [Vnp, Vp] *Do you clip those earrings on/Do those earrings clip on?* [Vnpr] *There was a*

cheque clipped to the back of the letter. [Vnp] *clip documents together.*

■ **'clip-on** *adj* fastened to sth with a clip: *clip-on earrings* ○ *a clip-on bow-tie.*

clip² /klɪp/ *v* (-pp-) **1** ~ **sth (off sth)** to cut sth with SCISSORS or SHEARS, esp in order to make it shorter; to trim sth: [Vn] *clip a hedge/one's fingernails* ○ *clip a sheep* (ie cut off its hair for wool) [Vn-adj] *The dog's fur was clipped short for the show.* [Vnpr] (*fig*) *Australia clipped two seconds off the old record.* **2** [Vn] (*Brit*) to make a hole in a bus or train ticket to show that it has been used. **3** (*infml*) to hit sb/sth sharply: [Vn] *The car clipped the pavement as it turned.* [Vn, Vnpr] *clip sb's ear/clip sb on the ear.* **4** [Vn] to omit parts of words when speaking. **IDM** **clip sb's 'wings** to prevent sb from being active or from doing what they are ambitious to do: *Having a new baby to look after has clipped her wings a bit.* **PHR V** **₁clip sth 'out of sth** to cut sth from sth else with SCISSORS, etc: *clip an article out of the newspaper.*

▶ **clip** *n* **1** an act of clipping: *The edge of the lawn needs a clip.* **2** (*infml*) a sharp blow: *She gave him a smart clip round the ear.* **3** a short piece of a film, shown separately: *Here is a clip from his new film.*

clipped *adj* with a short clear pronunciation: *his clipped military tones.*

clipping *n* **1** (usu *pl*) a piece cut off: *hair/nail/ hedge clippings.* **2** (*esp US*) = CUTTING¹ 1.

■ **'clip-joint** *n* (*sl derog*) a place of entertainment, esp a NIGHTCLUB, which regularly charges its customers prices that are too high.

NOTE Compare **clip, shave, trim** and **prune**. These verbs all refer to cutting off a part of something that is no longer wanted, in order to make it smaller, shorter or tidier. The direct object can be either the thing you cut a part from, or the part you remove.

Clip can mean cutting off a part that you do not want: *He clipped the hedge with a pair of shears.* It can also mean 'to remove a part in order to keep it': *For more information just clip the coupon below.* You **shave** hair from your face or body, or **shave off** hair so that the skin is smooth: *The monks shave their heads.* ○ *He shaves off his beard in summer.*

To **trim** means to cut a small amount off something to make it tidy: *I asked the hairdresser to trim my hair.* ○ *Trim any excess fat off the meat before cooking.* You **prune** plants to make them grow better and stronger: *You should prune roses at the end of the winter.* ○ *I've pruned all the dead branches off the tree.*

clipboard /'klɪpbɔːd/ *n* a small board with a clip at the top for holding papers. It provides support for sb who wants to write while standing or moving around.

clipper /'klɪpə(r)/ *n* **1 clippers** [pl] an instrument for cutting small pieces off things: *hair/hedge clippers* ○ *(a pair of) nail clippers.* ⇨ picture at SCISSORS. **2** a fast ship with sails.

clique /kliːk/ *n* [CGp] (*sometimes derog*) a small group of people, often with shared interests, who spend their time together and do not readily allow others to join them: *The club is dominated by a small clique of intellectuals.*

▶ **cliquy** /'kliːki/ (also **cliquey, cliquish**) *adj* (*derog*) (**a**) (of people) tending to form a clique. (**b**) dominated by a clique or cliques: *Our department is very cliquey.*

clitoris /'klɪtərɪs/ *n* a small part of the female sex organs which becomes larger when the female is sexually excited. ▶ **clitoral** /'klɪtərəl/ *adj.*

Cllr *abbr* (*Brit*) Councillor: *Cllr Michael Booth.*

cloak /kləʊk/ *n* **1** [C] a type of coat that has no sleeves, fastens at the neck and hangs loosely from the shoulders. ⇨ picture. **2** [sing] a thing that hides or covers: *They left under the cloak of darkness.*

○ *The author prefers to hide behind a cloak of anonymity.*
▶ **cloak** *v* ~ **sth** (**in sth**) to cover or hide sth with or as if with a cloak: [Vn] *A tall cloaked figure entered the room.* [Vnpr] *The negotiations are cloaked in mystery/secrecy.*
■ **,cloak-and-'dagger** *adj* [attrib] (esp of a story, film, etc) involving mystery, adventure and secret plots.

cloakroom /'kləʊkruːm, -rʊm/ *n* **1** a room, usu in a public building, where coats, hats, etc may be left for a time. **2** (*Brit euph*) a toilet: *the ladies' cloakroom.*

clobber¹ /'klɒbə(r)/ *v* (*infml*) **1** to strike sb/sth heavily and repeatedly; to treat sb/sth roughly: [Vn] *I'll clobber that dog if it doesn't stop barking.* ○ (*fig*) *The new tax laws will clobber small businesses* (ie harm them financially). **2** (esp passive) to defeat sb/sth completely: [Vn] *Our team got clobbered on Saturday.*

clobber² /'klɒbə(r)/ *n* [U] (*Brit infml*) clothing or equipment, esp for a specific activity: *You should see the clobber he takes when he goes climbing!*

cloche /klɒʃ/ *n* **1** (*esp Brit*) a movable glass or plastic cover used for protecting outdoor plants. **2** a woman's hat, shaped like a bell and fitting close to the head.

clock¹ /klɒk/ *n* **1** an instrument for measuring and showing time (not carried or worn like a watch): *The kitchen clock says* (ie shows) *it's ten past six.* ○ *The clock struck twelve/noon/midnight.* ○ *What time is it by the church clock?* ○ *a clock face with numbers on.* See also ALARM CLOCK, BODY CLOCK, GRANDFATHER CLOCK. **2** (*infml*) an instrument, eg a taxi METER or a MILOMETER, for measuring and recording things other than time: *a second-hand car with 20 000 miles on the clock.* IDM **around/round the 'clock** all day and all night: *Surgeons are working round the clock to save his life.* ○ *Doctors must provide a round-the-clock service.* **beat the clock** ⇨ BEAT¹. **put/turn the 'clock back** to return to a past age or to old-fashioned ideas, laws, customs, etc: *The new censorship law will put the clock back (by) 50 years.* **put the clock/clocks forward/back** (in certain countries) to change the time officially, usu by one hour, at the beginning/end of summer: *Remember to put your clocks back (one hour) tonight.* **watch the clock** ⇨ WATCH¹. **,work against the 'clock** to work fast in order to finish a task before a certain time.
■ **,clock 'radio** *n* a combined radio and alarm clock (ALARM 4).
'clock tower *n* a tall tower, usu forming part of a building, with a clock at the top.
'clock-watcher *n* (*usu derog*) a worker who is always checking the time to know when he or she may stop working.

clock² /klɒk/ *v* **1** ~ **sth** (**up**) to achieve or register a specified time, distance, speed, etc: [Vn] *He clocked 9.6 seconds in the 100 metres.* [Vnp] *My car has clocked up 50 000 miles.* ○ *The company clocked up sales of over £2 million last year.* **2** to record the time of sb/sth, eg with a STOPWATCH; to time²(3) sb/sth: [Vn] *The police often clock motorists on this stretch of road.* PHRV **,clock (sb) 'in/'on; ,clock (sb) 'out/'off** (*Brit*) **,punch (sb) 'in/'out** (*US*) to record the time at which one (or sb else) arrives at or leaves work, esp by means of an automatic device: *Workers usually clock off at 5.30.* ○ *What is 'clock-in/clocking-'in time at your office?*

clockwise /'klɒkwaɪz/ *adv, adj* moving in a curve

cloak

in the same direction as the hands of a clock: *turn the key clockwise/in a clockwise direction.* Compare ANTICLOCKWISE.

clockwork /'klɒkwɜːk/ *n* [U] machinery with wheels and springs (SPRING¹ 1), like that in a mechanical clock: *a clockwork toy* (ie one that is wound up with a key) ○ *working with clockwork* (ie absolute) *precision* ○ *He's in the pub by six o'clock every day, regular as clockwork* (ie very regularly). IDM **like 'clockwork** smoothly; according to plan: *The operation went like clockwork.*

clod /klɒd/ *n* a lump of earth or clay.

clodhopper /'klɒdhɒpə(r)/ *n* (*infml*) **1** (*derog*) (esp as a form of address) an awkward or CLUMSY(1) person. **2** (usu *pl*) (*joc*) a large heavy shoe.

clog¹ /klɒg/ *n* a shoe made entirely of wood or with a wooden sole.
■ **'clog-dance** *n* a dance performed by people wearing clogs.

clog² /klɒg/ *v* (**-gg-**) ~ (**sth**) (**up**) (**with sth**) to block sth or become blocked with thick or sticky material: [Vp] *The pipes are clogging up.* [Vnpr] *pores clogged with dirt* [Vnpr, Vnp] *a drain clogged (up) with dead leaves* ○ (*fig*) *Don't clog (up) your memory with useless facts.* [Vn] *That heavy oil will clog up the machinery* (ie prevent it from working properly). [Vn] (*fig*) *The road was clogged* (ie with traffic) *in both directions.* [also V, Vpr].

cloister /'klɔɪstə(r)/ *n* **1** [C often *pl*] a covered passage round an open court¹(5) or square²(2a), forming part of a college, cathedral or CONVENT. A cloister usu has solid walls round its outer sides and rows of arches with columns along its inner sides. **2** [sing] life in a CONVENT or MONASTERY: *the calm of the cloister.*
▶ **cloistered** *adj* kept or keeping oneself away from the outside world; sheltered: *a cloistered life* ○ *cloistered academics.*

clone /kləʊn/ *n* **1** (*biology*) any of a group of plants or animals produced artificially from the cells (CELL 4) of a single ancestor and therefore exactly the same as it. **2** a person or thing that seems to be an exact copy of sb/sth else: *She's almost a clone of her mother, isn't she?* **3** (*computing*) a computer designed to copy the functions of another, usu more expensive, model: *an IBM clone.*
▶ **clone** *v* to produce a plant or an animal as a clone: [Vn] *genetic cloning.*

clonk /klɒŋk/ *n* (*infml*) a short loud sound of heavy things hitting each other: *the clonk of machinery.*
▶ **clonk** *v* [V, Vn] (*infml*) to make or cause sth to make a clonk.

close¹ /kləʊs/ *adj* (**-r, -st**) **1** [pred] ~ (**to sb/sth**); ~ (**together**) near in space or time : *The church is close to the school.* ○ *The two buildings are close together.* ○ *This supermarket is our closest* (ie the nearest one to our home). ○ *be in close proximity* (ie almost touching) ○ *The children are close to each other in age.* ○ *Their birthdays are very close together.* ○ *Christmas is getting close.* ○ *The policeman was shot at close range* (ie from nearby). ○ *He was close to tears* (ie almost crying). **2(a)** near in relationship: *a close relative.* **(b)** ~ (**to sb**) well-known, understood and liked by sb: *a close friend* ○ *She is very close to her father/She and her father are very close.* **(c)** deeply involved, esp in the work or activities of sb/sth: *the Queen's closest advisers* ○ *The two companies have close links with each other.* ○ *She maintains close contact with the school.* **3** ~ (**to sth**) almost exact; very similar: *There's a close resemblance/similarity* (ie They are very much alike). ○ *His feeling for her was close to hatred.* **4** [attrib] careful; thorough; detailed: *On closer examination/inspection the painting proved to be a fake.* ○ *pay close attention to sth* ○ *close reasoning* (ie showing each step clearly). **5** (of a competition, game, etc) won by only a small amount or distance: *a close contest/match/election* ○

a close finish ○ *The game was closer than the score suggests.* **6** with little or no space between; DENSE: *close print* ○ *The soldiers advanced in close formation.* **7** (of a danger) threatening directly; only just avoided: *We caught the train in the end, but it was close* (ie we nearly missed it). **8** near to the surface; very short: *A new razor gives a close shave.* **9** [attrib] carefully guarded; strict: *in close confinement* ○ *be (kept) under close arrest* ○ *keep sth a close secret.* **10** (*esp Brit*) (**a**) (of the weather) still and heavy, as it is before a storm; HUMID: *It's very close and thundery today.* (**b**) (of a room) without fresh air; STUFFY(1): *a close atmosphere* ○ *Open a window — it's very close in here.* **11** [pred] ~ (**about sth**) unwilling to give certain information; SECRETIVE: *She's always been a bit close about their relationship.* **12** [pred] ~ (**with sth**) mean²(1); STINGY: *He's very close with his money.* **13** (*phonetics*) (of vowels) pronounced with the tongue raised near to the roof of the mouth: *The English vowels /iː/ and /uː/ are close.* **IDM at/from ¦close ¦quarters** very near: *fighting at close quarters.* **a ¦close ¦call/¦shave** (*infml*) a situation in which one only just manages to avoid an accident, a disaster, etc: *We didn't actually hit the other car, but it was a close call.* **a close/near ¦thing** ⇨ THING. **close/dear/near to sb's heart** ⇨ HEART. **close/ near to home** ⇨ HOME¹. **keep a close ¦eye/ ¦watch on sb/sth** to watch sb/sth carefully. ▶ **closely** *adv*: *listen closely* (ie carefully) ○ *follow an argument closely* ○ *a closely contested election* ○ *She closely resembles her mother.* ○ *The two events are closely connected.* **closeness** *n* [U].

■ **¦close season** (also *esp US* **¦closed season**) *n* [sing] the time of the year when it is illegal to kill certain animals, birds and fish because they are breeding.

close² /kləʊs/ *adv* near; with little space between; in a close position: *They sat close to each other/close together.* ○ *hold sb close* (ie tightly in one's arms) ○ *follow close behind sb* ○ *She stood close (up) against the wall.* **IDM close ¦by (sb/sth)** at a short distance (from sb/sth): *We lived close by the sea.* ○ *Our friends live close by* (ie near here). **close on** almost; nearly: *She is ¦close on ¦sixty.* ○ *It's ¦close on ¦midnight.* **close up (to sb/sth)** very near in space to sb/sth: *She snuggled close up to him.* **come close (to sth/ doing sth)** to almost reach or do sth: *He'd come close to death.* ○ *We didn't win, but we came close (to winning).* **hold/keep one's cards close to one's chest** ⇨ CARD¹. **run sb/sth ¦close** to be nearly as good, fast, successful, etc as sb/sth else: *We run our competitors close for price and quality.* **sail close/ near to the wind** ⇨ SAIL².

■ **¦close-¦cropped** (also **¦close-¦cut**) *adj* (of hair, grass, etc) cut very short.

¦close-¦fitting *adj* (of clothes) fitting close to the body.

¦close-¦fought, ¦close-¦run *adjs* [usu attrib] (of a race, contest, etc) won by a very small amount or distance: *The election was a ¦close-run ¦thing.*

¦close-¦knit *adj* (of a group of people) strongly united by shared beliefs, interests, activities, etc: *the ¦close-knit com'munity of a small village.*

¦close-¦set *adj* very close together: *¦close-set ¦eyes/ ¦teeth.*

¦close-up *n* [C,U] a photograph or film taken very close to sb/sth so that it shows a lot of detail: *a close-up of a human eye* ○ *a television scene filmed in close-up* ○ *close-up pictures of the planet.*

close³ /kləʊs/ *n* (*Brit*) **1** (esp in street names) a street, usu of private houses, that is closed at one end or has not much traffic: *Brookside Close.* See also CUL-DE-SAC. **2** the grounds and buildings surrounding and belonging to a cathedral, etc.

close⁴ /kləʊz/ *v* **1** to move or make sth move so as to cover an opening; to shut sth: [Vn] *close a door/a*

window/the curtains ○ *If you close your eyes, you can't see anything.* [V] *The door closed quietly.* ○ *This box/The lid of this box doesn't close properly* (ie the lid does not fit well). **2** ~ **sth** (**to sb/sth**) to be not open; to declare sth or be declared not open, esp for public use: [V] *The shops close* (ie stop trading) *at 5.30.* ○ *The theatres have closed for the summer.* [Vn] *They closed our local station years ago.* [Vn, Vnpr esp passive] *The museum is closed (to visitors) on Mondays.* ○ *This road is closed to traffic at the moment.* See also EARLY CLOSING. **3** to bring sth or come to an end: [V] *The debate is now in its closing stages* (ie has nearly finished). [V, Vn] *The speaker closed (the meeting) with a word of thanks to the chairman.* [Vn] *As far as I am concerned the matter is closed* (ie will not be discussed further). ○ *I hope to close the deal* (ie complete it) *within the next two days.* [Vpr] *Steel shares closed at £15* (ie This was their value at the end of the day's business on the stock exchange (STOCK 1)). ⇨ note. **4** to become or make sth smaller or narrower: [V] *The gap between the two runners is beginning to close* (ie One runner is catching up with the other). [Vn] *He's closing the gap on his rivals.* **IDM be¦hind closed ¦doors** without the public being allowed to attend or know what is happening; in private: *The meeting was held behind closed doors.* **a closed ¦book (to sb)** a subject about which one knows nothing: *Nuclear physics is a closed book to most of us.* **close/shut the door on sth** ⇨ DOOR. **close one's ¦mind to sth** to be unwilling to consider sth as a possibility: *He's closed his mind to the idea of moving to the States.* **close (the/one's) ¦ranks 1** (of members of a group) to forget disagreements and unite in order to protect or defend common interests: *In times of crisis party members should close ranks.* **2** (of soldiers) to come closer together in a line or lines. **shut/close one's eyes to sth** ⇨ EYE¹. **with one's eyes shut/closed** ⇨ EYE¹. **PHRV ¦close around/round/over sb/sth** to surround and hold sb/sth: *His hand closed over the money.* ○ *She felt his arms close tightly around her.* **¦close ¦down** (of a radio or television station) to stop broadcasting: *It is midnight and we are now closing down.* **¦close (sth) ¦down** to stop or make sth stop operating or providing a service, usu permanently: *Many businesses have closed down because of the recession.* **¦close ¦in** (of days) to become gradually shorter: *The days are closing in now that autumn is here.* **¦close ¦in (on sb/sth) 1** to surround sb/sth: *Darkness was gradually closing in.* **2** to come nearer to sb/sth, esp in order to attack from several directions: *The enemy is closing in (on us).* **¦close ¦up** (of a wound) to heal: *The cut took a long time to close up.* **¦close (sth) ¦up 1** to shut sth, esp temporarily: *Sorry, madam, we're closing up for lunch.* ○ *He closes the store up at 5.30.* **2** to come or bring sth closer together: *The sergeant-major ordered the men to close up (ranks).* **¦close with sb** (*dated*) (of soldiers) to come together and start fighting: *close with the enemy.*

■ **¦close-down** *n* **1** the stopping of work, esp permanently, in an office, a factory, etc. **2** the end of broadcasting on television or radio, usu until the next day.

¦closing date *n* the last date by which sth must be done, esp applying for a job: *The closing date for applications is 25 May.*

¦closing-time *n* the time when a shop, pub, bar, etc ends business for the day.

NOTE Close and shut often have the same meaning although **close** can be a quieter action: *Close/shut the door behind you.* ○ *The door shut/closed behind me.* ○ *I shut/closed my eyes and fell asleep immediately.* You usually **shut** a container such as a box: *My suitcase was so full I couldn't shut it.*

When referring to the time when a shop, office, etc

is no longer open, you can use both **shut** and **close**: *What time do the banks shut/close?* **Close** is used in connection with public places such as museums and theatres: *Museums are closed on Mondays.* ○ *The gallery will close in 10 minutes.*

Close can also mean 'to finish or make something finish': *The meeting closed at 10 pm.* ○ *The chair closed the meeting at 10 pm.* When a road or railway is **closed** you cannot use it: *They've closed the road because of an accident.* **Lock** means to close a door, box, etc with a key: *Don't forget to lock the back door.*

close⁵ /kləʊz/ *n* [sing] (*esp fml*) the end of a period of time or an activity: *at the close of the day* ○ *towards the close of the 17th century* ○ *The day had reached its close.* ○ *at close of play* (ie at the end of the day's play in a cricket match) ○ *The ceremony **was brought to/came to/drew to a close** with the singing of the national anthem.*

closed /kləʊzd/ *adj* **1(a)** not communicating with or influenced by others: *a closed society/economy.* **(b)** [usu attrib] limited to certain people; not open to everyone: *a closed membership* ○ *a closed scholarship.* **2** not willing to accept new ideas: *He has a closed mind.*

■ ₁closed-₁circuit ¹television *n* [U] a television system in which signals are sent by wires to a limited number of receivers (RECEIVER 2): *The bank uses closed-circuit television for security.*

¹closed season *n* [sing] (*esp US*) = CLOSE SEASON.

₁closed ¹shop *n* [sing] a factory, business, etc in which employees must all be members of a specified trade union: *a ₁closed-shop a¹greement.*

closet /¹klɒzɪt/ *n* (*esp US*) a cupboard or small room for storing things. **IDM come out of the closet** to announce sth openly about oneself that one has previously kept secret, esp because of fear or shame or embarrassment.

▶ **closet** *adj* [attrib] secret: *a closet homosexual* ○ *I suspect he's a closet fascist.*

closet *v* ~ **A and B (together); ~ A with B** (usu passive) to shut sb away in a room for a private meeting: [Vpr, Vp] *He was closeted with the manager/He and the manager were closeted together for three hours.* [also Vn].

closure /¹kləʊʒə(r)/ *n* [C, U] an act or the process of closing sth or of being closed: *factory closures* ○ *The threat of closure affected the workers' morale.*

clot /klɒt/ *n* **1** a lump formed from a liquid, eg from blood when it is exposed to the air. **2** (*Brit infml joc*) a stupid person; a fool: *You silly clot!*

▶ **clot** *v* (-tt-) to form or cause sth to form clots: [V] *A haemophiliac's blood will not clot properly.* [also Vn].

■ ₁clotted ¹cream *n* [U] (*Brit*) a very thick cream made by slowly heating milk: *scones and jam with clotted cream.*

cloth /klɒθ; *US* klɔːθ/ *n* (*pl* **cloths** /klɒθs; *US* klɔːðz/) **1** [U] fabric made by weaving cotton, wool, silk, etc: *enough cloth to make a suit* ○ *good-quality woollen cloth* ○ *three metres of cloth.* **2** [C] (esp in compounds) a piece of cloth used for a special purpose: *a ¹dishcloth* ○ *a ¹floorcloth* ○ *a ¹tablecloth.* **3 the cloth** [sing] (*fml or joc*) the clothes worn by the CLERGY, seen as a symbol of their profession: *the respect due to his cloth* ○ *a man of the cloth* (ie a priest). **IDM cut one's coat according to one's cloth** ⇨ COAT.

■ ₁cloth ¹cap *n* (*Brit*) a soft, usu leather, cap with a PEAK¹(3), regarded as a symbol of working men: *a cloth-cap mentality.*

clothe /kləʊð/ *v* **(a)** ~ **sb/oneself (in sth)** (*rather fml*) (usu passive) to put clothes on sb/oneself; to dress sb/oneself: [Vnpr] *They were clothed from head to foot in white.* [Vn] *warmly clothed* ○ *They threw her fully clothed* (ie wearing all her clothes) *into the*

swimming-pool. **(b)** to provide clothes for sb: [Vn] *He can barely feed and clothe his family.* **(c)** ~ **sth in sth** (*fml*) to cover sth as if with clothes: [Vnpr] *a landscape clothed in mist.*

clothes /kləʊðz, kləʊz/ *n* [pl] (not used with numerals) the things worn to cover a person's body; garments: *warm/fashionable/expensive clothes* ○ *put on/take off one's clothes.*

■ ¹clothes-brush *n* a brush for removing dust, hair, etc from clothes.

¹clothes-hanger *n* = HANGER.

¹clothes-horse *n* **1** a frame on which clothes are hung to dry after they have been washed. **2** (*derog joc*) a person, esp a woman, who cares a lot about wearing fashionable clothes.

¹clothes-line *n* a rope stretched between posts, usu outside, on which clothes are hung to dry after they have been washed. ⇨ picture at HOUSE¹.

¹clothes-peg (*Brit*) (*US* ¹clothes-pin) *n* a small wooden or plastic device for fastening clothes to a clothes-line. ⇨ picture at PEG¹.

clothing /¹kləʊðɪŋ/ *n* [U] clothes: *articles/items of clothing* ○ *waterproof clothing* ○ *the clothing industry.* **IDM a wolf in sheep's clothing** ⇨ WOLF.

cloud¹ /klaʊd/ *n* **1** [C, U] (any of) the grey or white masses of very small drops of water which can be seen floating in the sky: *a thick bank of clouds* ○ *black clouds appearing from the west* ○ *There wasn't a cloud in the sky.* ○ *The top of the mountain was covered in cloud.* **2** [C] **(a)** a mass of smoke, dust, etc in the air. **(b)** a mass of insects moving together in the sky: *a cloud of locusts.* **3** [C] a thing that causes sadness, concern, etc: *A cloud of suspicion is hanging over him.* ○ *Her arrival **cast a cloud** (of gloom) over the party.* ○ *The only **cloud on the horizon** (ie cause for worry) is their lack of money.* **IDM every cloud has a silver ¹lining** (*saying*) there is always a comforting or more hopeful side to a sad or difficult situation. **have one's head in the clouds** ⇨ HEAD¹. **on cloud ¹nine** (*infml*) very happy: *He was on cloud nine after winning the competition.* **under a ¹cloud** in DISGRACE¹ or suspected of doing sth bad: *She left the company under a cloud.*

▶ **cloudless** *adj* without clouds; clear: *a cloudless sky.*

cloudy *adj* (-ier, -iest) **1** covered with clouds: *a cloudy sky.* **2** (esp of liquids) not clear or transparent: *The water looked cloudy and not fit to drink.* **cloudiness** *n* [U].

■ ₁cloud-¹cuckoo-land (*Brit*) (*US* ¹cloud-land) *n* [U] (*derog*) an ideal place or situation that exists only in the mind of a person and not in real life: *You're in cloud-cuckoo-land if you think they'll pay you any more money.*

cloud² /klaʊd/ *v* **1** to become or make sth dull or not clear: [V] *Her eyes clouded with tears.* [Vn] *Tears clouded her eyes.* ○ *Steam clouded the mirror.* ○ *(fig) Old age has clouded his judgement.* ○ *Don't cloud the issue* (ie Don't try to take attention away from what is important). **2** ~ **(over)** (of sb's face) to show sadness, worry or anger: [V, Vp] *His face clouded (over) when he heard the news.* **3** to spoil sth: [Vn] *cloud sb's enjoyment/happiness.* **PHRV cloud ¹over** (of the sky) to become covered with clouds: *It started to cloud over in the afternoon.*

cloudburst /¹klaʊdbɜːst/ *n* a sudden and violent fall of rain.

clout /klaʊt/ *n* (*infml*) **1** [C] a heavy blow with the hand or a hard object: *get a clout across the back of the head* ○ *He gave the ball a terrific clout.* **2** [U] power or influence: *This union hasn't much clout with the government.*

▶ **clout** *v* [Vn] (*infml*) to hit sb/sth heavily with the hand or a hard object.

clove¹ /kləʊv/ *n* the dried flower BUD¹(2) from a tropical tree, used as a spice: *ground cloves.*

clove² /kləʊv/ n any of the small separate sections of certain types of BULB(1): *a clove of garlic.* ⇨ picture at ONION.

clove³ pt of CLEAVE¹.

cloven pp of CLEAVE¹.

■ ˌcloven ˈhoof (also ˌcloven ˈfoot) n the divided foot of certain types of animal, eg cows, sheep and goats. ˌcloven-ˈhoofed adj.

clover /ˈkləʊvə(r)/ n [U] a small plant with (usu) three leaves on each stem, and purple, pink or white flowers, grown as food for cattle, etc: *(a) four-leaf/ -leaved ˈclover* (ie a rare type of clover with four leaves, thought to bring good luck to anyone who finds it). **IDM** **in clover** (*infml*) in great ease or comfort: *be/live in clover.*

clown /klaʊn/ n **1** an entertainer, esp in a CIRCUS(1), who paints her or his face, dresses in a ridiculous way and performs funny or foolish tricks in order to make people laugh. **2** (*sometimes derog*) a stupid, foolish or playful person: *Stop it, you clown!* ○ *He likes **playing the clown**, but can be serious when he wants to be.*
▶ **clown** v ~ (*about/around*) (*often derog*) to act in a foolish playful way, like a clown: [V, Vp] *Stop clowning (around)!*
clownish adj of or like a clown: *clownish dress/ antics.*

cloying /ˈklɔɪɪŋ/ adj (of food, etc) too sweet or rich(4): (*fig*) *a cloying smile/manner* ○ *cloying whimsy.*

cloze test /ˈkləʊz test/ n a test in which the person being tested tries to fill in words that have been left out of a text, in order to show that he or she understands it.

club¹ /klʌb/ n (esp in compounds) **1(a)** [C] a group of people who meet together regularly, esp for a particular activity such as a sport: *a golf/football/ hockey club* ○ *a film club* ○ *a working men's club* ○ *a youth club.* (**b**) [C] the building or rooms used by a club: *have a drink at the golf club* ○ *the club bar.* **2** [CGp,C] (esp in Britain) an organization owning a building where elected, usu male, members may stay temporarily, have meals, read the newspapers, etc; such a building: *The club has/have decided to increase subscriptions.* ○ *He's a member of several London clubs.* ○ *a gentlemen's club.* **3** [C] a business organization offering benefits to members who agree to make regular payments of money: *a book club.* **4** [C] = NIGHTCLUB. **IDM** **in the club** (*Brit sl*) pregnant. **join the club** ⇨ JOIN.
▶ **club** v (-bb-) **PHR V** **club together (to do sth)** (of the members of a group) to make separate contributions of money, etc so that the total can be used for a specific purpose: *They clubbed together to buy the chairman a present.*
■ ˌclub ˈsandwich n (*esp US*) a sandwich consisting of three slices of bread and two layers of meat, LETTUCE, TOMATO, etc.

club² /klʌb/ n **1** a heavy stick with one end thicker than the other, used as a weapon. **2** a stick with a specially shaped end for hitting the ball in golf. ⇨ picture at GOLF.
▶ **club** v (-bb-) to hit or beat sb/sth with a club or heavy object: [Vnpr] *be clubbed to death* ○ *Many of the demonstrators were clubbed to the ground and kicked.* [also Vn].
■ ˌclub-ˈfoot n a foot that is badly shaped from birth. ˌclub-ˈfooted adj.

club³ /klʌb/ n (**a**) **clubs** [sing or pl v] one of the four suits (SUIT¹ 2) in a pack of cards. The cards in this suit have a black design with three leaves on them: *the ace of clubs.* ⇨ picture at PLAYING-CARD. (**b**) [C] a card of this suit¹(2): *play a club.*

clubhouse /ˈklʌbhaʊs/ n the building used by a sports club, esp a golf club.

clubland /ˈklʌblænd/ n [U] (*Brit*) an area of a town

or city, esp London, where there are many clubs (CLUB¹ 2): *a well-known figure in London's clubland.*

cluck /klʌk/ n the noise that a hen makes.
▶ **cluck** v **1** [V] to make a cluck. **2** (of people) to express annoyance, etc by making a similar noise. [V, Vn] *She clucked (her tongue) in disapproval.* [also V.speech].

clue /kluː/ n **1** ~ (**to sth**) a fact or piece of evidence that helps to solve a problem or reveal the truth in an investigation: *The only clue to the identity of the murderer was a half-smoked cigarette.* ○ *We have no clue as to where she went after she left home.* **2** a word or words indicating the answer to be inserted in a CROSSWORD. **IDM** **not have a ˈclue** (*infml*) **1** to know nothing about sth or how to do sth: *'When does the train leave?' 'I haven't a clue.'* **2** (*derog*) to be stupid or lacking in ability: *'Don't ask him to do it — he hasn't a clue.'*
▶ **clue** v **PHR V** **clue sb ˈin (about/on sth)** (*US infml*) to give sb the latest information about sth: *Can you clue me in on the facts of the case?* ˌ**clue sb ˈup (about/on sth)** (*infml esp Brit*) (usu passive) to give sb a lot of information (about sth): *She's really clued up on politics* (ie She knows a lot about politics).
clueless /ˈkluːləs/ adj (*infml derog*) stupid or lacking in ability: *He's absolutely clueless.*

clump¹ /klʌmp/ n a group of things or people together, esp trees or plants: *a small clump of oak trees* ○ *a clump of spectators.*

clump² /klʌmp/ v ~ **about**, **around**, **etc** to walk in the specified direction putting the feet down heavily: [Vp, Vpr] *clumping about (the room) in heavy boots.*
▶ **clump** n [sing] the sound made by sb putting their feet down heavily: *the clump of boots.*
clumpy adj (esp of shoes) heavy and awkward.

clumsy /ˈklʌmzi/ adj (-ier, -iest) **1** not graceful in movement or shape; awkward: *You clumsy oaf — that's the second glass you've broken today!* **2** done without skill or in a way that offends people: *a clumsy apology/reply/speech* ○ *a clumsy forgery* (ie one that is easy to detect). **3** (of tools, furniture, etc) difficult to use or move; not well designed: *a clumsy old wooden cupboard* ○ *It's not easy walking in these clumsy shoes.* ▶ **clumsily** adv. **clumsiness** n [U].

clung pt, pp of CLING.

clunk /klʌŋk/ n a dull sound made by or as if by heavy metal objects striking together.
▶ **clunk** v [V] to make a clunk.

cluster /ˈklʌstə(r)/ n (**a**) a number of things of the same kind growing closely together: *a cluster of berries/flowers/curls.* (**b**) a close group of people, animals or things: *a cluster of houses/spectators/ islands/bombs/stars.*
▶ **cluster** v **PHR V** **cluster / be clustered (to-gether) round/around sb/sth** to form a cluster round sb/sth; to surround sb/sth closely: *roses clus-tering round the window* ○ *The village clusters around the church.* ○ *Reporters (were) clustered round the newly-wed stars.*

clutch¹ /klʌtʃ/ v (**a**) to seize sb/sth eagerly: [Vn] *He clutched the rope we threw to him.* (**b**) to hold (sb/ sth) tightly: [Vnpr] *clutch a baby in one's arms* ○ *Mary was clutching her doll to her chest.* [also Vn]. **IDM** **clutch/grasp at straws** ⇨ STRAW. **PHR V** ˈ**clutch/ˈcatch at sth** to try to seize sth, esp sud-denly: *He clutched at the branch but couldn't reach it.*
▶ **clutch** n **1** [C] (**a**) a device that connects and disconnects (DISCONNECT) working parts in a ma-chine, esp the engine and gears in a motor vehicle: *let out the clutch* (ie when changing gear) ○ *She released the clutch and the car began to move.* ⇨ picture at CAR. (**b**) the PEDAL¹(1) that operates this device: *take one's foot off the clutch.* ⇨ picture at CAR. **2** **clutches** [pl] power or control: *be in sb's*

clutches ∘ *fall into the clutches of sb/sth* ∘ *have sb in one's clutches* ∘ *escape from sb's clutches*. **3** [sing] the act of holding sth in the fingers or the hands.

clutch² /klʌtʃ/ *n* (**a**) a set of eggs that a hen sits on and that HATCH² together. (**b**) a group of young chickens that are born from these eggs. (**c**) a small group of people, animals or things: *a clutch of reporters/companies*.

clutter /ˈklʌtə(r)/ *n* (*derog*) (**a**) [U] things lying about in disorder, esp unnecessary things: *How can you work with so much clutter on your desk?* (**b**) [sing] a state of disorder: *My room is always in a clutter*.

▶ **clutter** *v* ~ *sth* (**up**) (**with sth**) (esp passive) to fill or cover sth with a lot of things so that it is untidy: [Vnpr] *a room cluttered with unnecessary furniture* [Vnp] *Don't clutter up my desk — I've just tidied it.* ∘ (*fig*) [Vnpr, Vnp] *His head is cluttered (up) with useless facts.* [also Vn].

cm *abbr* (*pl* unchanged or **cms**) centimetre: *600 cm × 140 cm* (ie as a measure of area).

CND /ˌsiː en ˈdiː/ *abbr* (in Britain) Campaign for Nuclear Disarmament.

co- *pref* (used fairly widely with *adjs*, *advs*, *ns* and *vs*) together: *co-produced* ∘ *co-operatively* ∘ *co-author* ∘ *coexist*.

CO /ˌsiː ˈəʊ/ *abbr* Commanding Officer: *report to the CO.*

Co *abbr* **1** (*esp commerce*) company: *Pearce, Briggs & Co* ∘ *the Stylewise Furniture Co* ∘ (*infml*) *Were Jane and Mary and Co* /ˈmeəri ən kəʊ/ *at the party?* **2** county: *Co Down, Northern Ireland* ∘ *Niagara Co, New York.*

c/o /ˌsiː ˈəʊ/ *abbr* (on letters, etc addressed to a person staying at sb else's house) care of: *Mr Peter Brown, c/o Mme Marie Duval...*

coach¹ /kəʊtʃ/ *n* **1** [C] (*esp Brit*) a comfortable bus, usu with a single DECK¹(1b), for carrying passengers over long distances: *travel by overnight coach to Scotland* ∘ *a coach station* ∘ *a coach tour of Italy.* **2** [C] = CARRIAGE 2. **3** [C] a large carriage with four wheels, pulled by horses and used, esp formerly, for carrying passengers. See also STAGECOACH. **4** [U] (*US*) the cheap class or seats in an aircraft: *If you travel by coach you have less leg-room.*
■ ˈcoach-house *n* a building where coaches (COACH¹ 3) are or were kept: *He lives in a converted coach-house.*
ˈcoach station *n* a place where coaches (COACH¹ 1) start and finish their journeys: *Victoria coach station.*

coach² /kəʊtʃ/ *n* **1** a person who trains people in sport: *a tennis/football/swimming coach.* **2** a teacher who gives private lessons to prepare students for examinations: *a mathematics coach.*
▶ **coach** *v* (**a**) ~ *sb* (**for/in sth**) to teach or train sb, esp for an examination or in a sport: [Vnpr] *coach a swimmer for the Olympics* ∘ *coach sb in French* [Vn] *She has talent but she will need coaching.* ∘ *a coaching programme/session.* (**b**) to work or act as a coach: [V] *She'll be coaching all summer.* ⇨ note at TEACH.

coachload /ˈkəʊtʃləʊd/ *n* a group of people travelling in a coach¹(1): *a coachload of schoolchildren/holiday-makers.*

coachman /ˈkəʊtʃmən/ *n* (*pl* **-men** /-mən/) a driver of a carriage pulled by horses.

coachwork /ˈkəʊtʃwɜːk/ *n* [U] the main outside structure of a road or railway vehicle.

coagulate /kəʊˈægjuleɪt/ *v* to change or to make sth change from a liquid to a thick and partly solid state; to CLOT: [V] *Blood coagulates in air.* [Vn] *Air coagulates blood.* ▶ **coagulation** /kəʊˌægjuˈleɪʃn/ *n* [U].

coal /kəʊl/ *n* (**a**) [U] a hard black mineral found below the ground, used for burning to supply heat and to make coal gas and coal tar: *put more coal on the fire* ∘ *a sack/lump of coal* ∘ *a coal fire* ∘ *coal dust* ∘ *the coal industry.* (**b**) [C] a piece of this material, esp one that is burning: *A hot coal fell out of the fire and burnt the carpet.* ⇨ CARRY. **haul sb over the coals** ⇨ HAUL.
■ ˌcoal-ˈblack *adj* very dark: ˌcoal-black ˈeyes.
ˌcoal-ˈfired *adj* heated or made to work by coal: ˌcoal-fired ˈpower stations.
ˈcoal gas *n* [U] a mixture of gases produced from coal, used for lighting and heating.
ˈcoal-hole *n* (*Brit*) a small cupboard or room, usu underground, for storing coal.
ˈcoal-scuttle (also scuttle) *n* a container for coal, usu kept beside the fireplace.
ˈcoal tar *n* [U] a thick black sticky substance produced when gas is made from coal.

coalesce /ˌkəʊəˈles/ *v* (*fml*) to come together and form one group, substance, mass, etc; to unite: [V] *The views of party leaders coalesced to form a coherent policy.* ▶ **coalescence** /ˌkəʊəˈlesns/ *n* [U].

coalface /ˈkəʊlfeɪs/ (also face) *n* an exposed mass of coal in a mine: *work at the coalface.*

coalfield /ˈkəʊlfiːld/ *n* a large area where there are layers of coal underground.

coalition /ˌkəʊəˈlɪʃn/ *n* **1** [CGp] a temporary union of separate political parties, usu in order to form a government: *form a coalition* ∘ *a left-wing coalition* ∘ *a coalition government.* **2** [U] the action of uniting into one body or group: *the coalition of forces.*

coalman /ˈkəʊlmən/ *n* (*pl* **-men** /-mən/) a man whose job is to deliver coal to people's houses.

coalmine /ˈkəʊlmaɪn/ (also pit) *n* a place underground where coal is dug.
▶ **coalminer** *n* a person whose job is digging coal in a coalmine.

coaming /ˈkəʊmɪŋ/ *n* a raised border round a ship's hatches (HATCH¹ 1b) to keep water out.

coarse /kɔːs/ *adj* (**-r**, **-st**) **1**(**a**) rough or loose in texture: *bags made from coarse linen* ∘ *a coarse complexion/skin.* (**b**) consisting of large grains or thick pieces; not fine: *coarse sand/salt* ∘ *coarse grass/hair.* **2**(**a**) not polite or refined; VULGAR: *coarse manners/laughter/tastes* ∘ *A coarse, red-faced man yelled something across the street.* (**b**) rude; OBSCENE: *coarse jokes/humour/language.* **3** (of food, wine, etc) of low quality; inferior.
▶ **coarsely** *adv*: *chop onions coarsely* (ie into large pieces).
coarsen /ˈkɔːsn/ *v* to become or make sth coarse: [Vn] *The sea air had coarsened her skin.* [also V].
coarseness *n* [U].
■ ˌcoarse ˈfish *n* (*pl* unchanged) (*Brit*) any fish, other than SALMON and TROUT, that lives in rivers, lakes, etc rather than the sea. ˌcoarse ˈfishing *n* [U] trying to catch coarse fish as a sport.

coast¹ /kəʊst/ *n* the land beside or near to the sea: *The ship was wrecked on the Florida coast.* ∘ *islands off the Scottish coast* ∘ *a village on the south coast* (eg of England) ∘ *spend a day by the coast* (ie the SEASIDE) ∘ *a coast road* (ie one that follows the line of the coast). ⇨ picture. **IDM the ˌcoast is ˈclear** (*infml*) there is no danger of being seen or caught: *They waited until the coast was clear before loading the stolen goods into the van.*
▶ **coastal** *adj* [usu attrib] of or near a coast: *coastal waters* ∘ *a coastal town/area.* Compare INLAND.

NOTE Coast and shore both describe land that is next to large areas of water. The **shore** is the edge of the land next to the sea or a lake: *They camped on the shore of Lake Bala.* ∘ *The survivors swam to the shore.* The land at the edge of a river or a stream is a **bank**. Coast can also refer to a wider area of land or a long stretch of land next to the sea or ocean: *We live at/on the coast.* ○ *Genoa is on Italy's Mediterranean coast.* In American English, **coast** also describes the land along the Atlantic (or east) and the Pacific (or west) coast of the United States and Canada: *Don and Sally relocated to the west coast last year.* The **beach** is the part of the shore which the sea covers at high tide. It is used by people for walking, relaxing, etc: *We spent the day at the beach.* ○ *The beach was crowded with people sunbathing.* In British English the **seaside** is an area on the coast where people go on holiday: *Brighton is a famous British seaside town.* ○ *The kids love going to the seaside.*

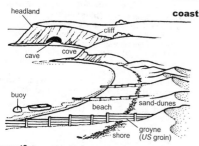

coast

coast² /kəʊst/ v **1(a)** to move, esp down a hill, in a car, on a bicycle, etc, without using power: [Vadv] *coast downhill* (ie in NEUTRAL *n*(2) *to save petrol* [Vp] *coasting along on a bicycle* (ie without using one's legs) [also V]. **(b)** to make progress without much effort: [Vpr, Vadv] *The Democrats are coasting to victory/coasting home* (ie winning easily) *in the election.* [also V]. **2** to sail from port to port along a coast: [V] *coasting vessels.*

coaster /ˈkəʊstə(r)/ n **1** a small mat or tray put under a glass or a bottle to protect a polished table, etc from marks. **2** a ship that sails from port to port along a coast. See also ROLLER-COASTER.

coastguard /ˈkəʊstgɑːd/ n **(a)** [CGp] an organization whose job is to watch the sea near a coast in order to get help for people or ships in trouble and to prevent smuggling (SMUGGLE): *a coastguard station/vessel.* **(b)** [C] a member of this organization.

coastline /ˈkəʊstlaɪn/ n the shape or appearance of a coast: *a rugged/rocky/indented/beautiful coastline.*

coat /kəʊt/ n **1** a long piece of clothing with sleeves and usu buttons at the front, that is worn over other clothes, esp to keep warm, dry, etc: *a waterproof/ fur/leather coat* ○ *You'll need a coat if you're going for a walk.* See also RAINCOAT, OVERCOAT. **2** a jacket. **3** the fur, hair or wool that covers an animal's body: *a dog with a smooth/shaggy coat* ○ *animals in their winter coats* (ie grown long for extra warmth). **4** a layer of paint or some other substance covering a surface: *give the walls a second coat of paint.* IDM ,cut one's 'coat ac,cording to one's 'cloth (*saying*) to do only what one can manage to do or has enough money to do and no more: *We wanted to buy a bigger house than this but it was a case of cutting our coat according to our cloth.*
▶ **coat** v ~ **sb/sth (in/with sth)** (usu passive) to cover sb/sth with a layer of sth: [Vnpr] *coat fish in batter* ○ *peanuts coated in/with chocolate* ○ *furniture coated with dust* [Vn] *a coated tongue.* **coating** n a thin layer or covering: *a coating of wax/chocolate/ paint.*
■ **'coat-hanger** n = HANGER
,**coat of 'arms** n [C] (*pl* **coats of arms**) (also **arms** [pl]) a design on a shield used by a family, city, university, etc as its own special symbol. ▷ picture.

'**coat-tails** n [pl] IDM **on sb's coat-tails** using another person's success, progress, etc to benefit oneself: *He only got where he is today (by riding) on the coat-tails of more able men.*

coax /kəʊks/ v ~ **sb (into/out of (doing) sth)** to persuade sb gently or gradually: [Vnpr] *He coaxed her into letting him take her to the theatre.* ○ *She coaxed him out of his bad temper.* [Vn.to inf] *coax a child to take its medicine* ○ (*fig*) [Vn] *coax a fire with* (ie make it burn) *paraffin.* PHRV **coax sth out of/from sb** to get sth from sb by gently persuading them: *I had to coax the information out of him.* ○ *She coaxed a smile from the baby.*
▶ **coaxing** n [U] gentle attempts to make sb/sth do sth: *It took a lot of coaxing before he agreed.* ○ *With a little coaxing I got the engine started.* **coaxingly** adv: *speak coaxingly.*

cob /kɒb/ n **1** [C] (*Brit*) a round LOAF¹ of bread: *a wholemeal cob.* **2** [C] = CORN-COB: *corn on the cob.* **3** (also '**cob-nut**) [C] a large type of HAZELNUT. **4** [C] a strong horse with short legs. **5** [C] a male SWAN. **6** [U] (*Brit*) a mixture of clay and straw used, esp formerly, for building houses: *cob and thatch cottages.*

cobalt /ˈkəʊbɔːlt/ n [U] a chemical element. Cobalt is a hard silvery (SILVER) white metal often mixed with other metals, and used to make a blue colouring material for glass, etc: ,*cobalt 'blue.* ▷ App 7.

cobber /ˈkɒbə(r)/ n (*Austral or NZ infml*) (used esp as a form of address between men) a friend or companion.

cobble¹ /ˈkɒbl/ (also '**cobblestone**) n (usu *pl*) a round stone formerly used for covering the surfaces of roads, etc: *The cart clattered over the cobbles.*
▶ **cobble** v (usu passive) to cover the surface of a road with cobbles: [Vn] *cobbled streets.*

cobble² /ˈkɒbl/ v [Vn] (*dated*) to repair shoes. PHRV **cobble sth together** to put sth together or make sth quickly or carelessly: *He hastily cobbled together an essay from some old lecture notes.*

cobbler /ˈkɒblə(r)/ n **1** (*becoming dated*) a person who repairs shoes. **2** (*esp US*) a fruit pie with thick pastry on top. **3** (*esp US*) a cold drink made with wine, LEMON, sugar and ice.

cobblers /ˈkɒbləz/ n [sing v] (*Brit sl*) nonsense(2); rubbish(2): *What a load of (old) cobblers!*

COBOL /ˈkəʊbɒl/ n [U] (*computing*) a programming (PROGRAM *v*) language designed for use in commerce.

cobra /ˈkəʊbrə/ n a poisonous snake found in India and Africa. ▷ picture at SNAKE.

cobweb /ˈkɒbweb/ n **(a)** a fine net of threads made by a SPIDER, used to trap insects, etc. **(b)** a single thread of this. See also WEB 1.

Coca-Cola /ˌkəʊkə ˈkəʊlə/ (also *infml* **Coke**) n (*propr*) **(a)** [U] a popular type of COLA drink that does not contain alcohol. **(b)** [C] a bottle, can or glass of this.

cocaine /kəʊˈkeɪn/ n [U] a drug which some people take illegally for pleasure and may become addicted (ADDICT) to. Doctors sometimes use it as an anaesthetic (ANAESTHESIA).

coccyx /ˈkɒksɪks/ n (*pl* **coccyxes** or **coccyges** /ˈkɒksɪdʒiːz/) (*anatomy*) a small bone at the bottom of the SPINE(1) in humans. ▷ picture at SKELETON.

cochineal /ˌkɒtʃɪˈniːl/ n [U] a bright red substance used for giving colour to food.

cock¹ /kɒk/ n **1** (*US* **rooster**) [C] an adult male chicken: *The cock crowed.* Compare HEN 1. **2** [C] (esp in compounds) a male of any other bird: *a ,cock*

coat of arms

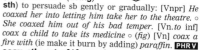

shield

unicorn

C

'**pheasant** o a ¡cock '**robin**. Compare HEN 2. **3** [U] (*Brit* △ *sl*) nonsense: *He's talking cock!* **4** [C] = STOPCOCK. **5** [sing] (*dated Brit sl*) (used as a friendly form of address between men). **6** [C] (△ *sl*) a PENIS. **IDM** ¡cock of the '**walk** (*often derog*) a person who dominates others within a group. **go off at ¡half** '**cock** (*infml*) to start before preparations are complete, so that the effect or result is not satisfactory: *We didn't have copies of the book for the launch party so it went off very much at half cock.*

■ **cock-a-doodle-doo** /¡kɒk ə ¡duːdl 'duː/ *n* the noise made by a cock[1](1).

¡**cock-a-'hoop** *adj* [usu pred] very pleased, esp about being successful: *She's cock-a-hoop about getting the job.*

¡**cock-and-'bull story** *n* an absurd and unlikely story, esp one used as an excuse or explanation: *He told us some cock-and-bull story about having lost all his money down a drain.*

'**cock crow** *n* [U] dawn: *wake at cock crow.*

'**cock-fight** *n* a fight between two cocks, watched as a sport. '**cock-fighting** *n* [U].

cock² /kɒk/ *v* **1** ~ sth (**up**) to cause sth to be upright or to point upwards; to raise sth: [Vn, Vnp] *The horse cocked (up) its ears when it heard the noise.* [Vn, Vnpr] *The dog cocked its leg (against the lamp-post)* (ie in order to urinate (URINE)). **2** to make sth turn at an angle; to TILT sth: [Vnpr] *She cocked her hat at a jaunty angle.* o *The bird cocked its head to one side.* **3** [Vn] to make a gun ready for firing by raising the hammer[1](2). **IDM** **cock an ear/eye for/ at sth/sb** to listen/look carefully for/to/at sth/sb: *He cocked an eye at the ceiling.* o *She kept her ears cocked for the sound of the postman coming up the drive.* **cock a snook at sb/sth** (*Brit*) to show contempt for or resistance to sb/sth, esp in a bold or cheerful way: *cocking a snook at authority.* **knock sb/sth into a cocked hat** ⇨ KNOCK². **PHR V** ¡**cock sth 'up** (*Brit infml*) to spoil or ruin sth because of lack of efficiency; to BUNGLE sth: *The travel agent completely cocked up the arrangements for our holiday.* o *Trust him to cock it/things up!*

■ '**cock-up** *n* (*Brit infml*) an act of ruining sth because of lack of efficiency; a mess: *She made a complete cock-up of the arrangements.* o *What a monumental cock-up it all is!*

cockatoo /¡kɒkə'tuː/ *n* (*pl* **-oos**) a type of PARROT(1) with a large row of feathers standing up on its head.

cocker /'kɒkə(r)/ (also ¡cocker '**spaniel**) *n* a small type of SPANIEL with soft brown fur. ⇨ picture at DOG[1].

cockerel /'kɒkərəl/ *n* a young COCK[1](1).

cock-eyed /'kɒk aɪd/ *adj* (*infml*) **1** not straight or level; CROOKED(1): *That picture on the wall looks cock-eyed to me.* **2** not at all practical; absurd: *a cock-eyed scheme.*

cockle /'kɒkl/ *n* a small edible SHELLFISH. **IDM** **warm the cockles** ⇨ WARM².

cockney /'kɒkni/ *n* (*pl* **-eys**) **1** [C] a native of London, esp the East End (EAST). **2** [U] the way of speaking typically used by cockneys: *a cockney accent* o *cockney rhyming slang.*

cockpit /'kɒkpɪt/ *n* an enclosed area in an aircraft, a racing car or a boat where the pilot, driver, etc sits to steer from. ⇨ picture at AIRCRAFT, YACHT.

cockroach /'kɒkrəʊtʃ/ *n* a large brown insect with wings, commonly found in dirty houses.

cocksure /¡kɒk'ʃʊə(r); *Brit also* -ʃɔː(r)/ *adj* ~ (**about/of sth**) (*infml*) very confident, in a way that annoys other people: *He's so cocksure — I'd love to see him proved wrong.*

cocktail /'kɒkteɪl/ *n* **1** [C] an alcoholic drink consisting of a spirit, or several spirits, mixed with fruit juice, etc: *a cocktail bar/cabinet/lounge* o *a cocktail party.* **2** [C, U] a dish of small pieces of food, usu served cold at the beginning of a meal: *(a) prawn/shrimp cocktail* o *(a) fruit cocktail.* **3** [C]

(*infml*) any mixture of substances: *a lethal cocktail of drugs.* See also MOLOTOV COCKTAIL.

■ '**cocktail dress** *n* a dress that is suitable for cocktail parties and other formal occasions.

'**cocktail stick** *n* a small sharp piece of wood on which small pieces of food are served, eg at cocktail parties.

cocky /'kɒki/ *adj* (**-ier, -iest**) (*infml*) too proud of oneself, esp in a bold and cheerful way that annoys other people: *unbearably cocky.* ▶ **cockiness** *n* [U].

cocoa /'kəʊkəʊ/ *n* (**a**) [U] dark brown powder made from the crushed seeds of a tropical tree; chocolate powder. (**b**) [C, U] a hot drink made from this with milk or water, drunk esp in the evening before going to bed: *Two cocoas, please.* o *a mug of cocoa.*

coconut /'kəʊkənʌt/ *n* (**a**) [C] the large brown seed of a tropical tree. It consists of a hard shell containing edible white flesh, which surrounds a hollow area containing juice (called MILK): *a row of coconut palms.* (**b**) [U] the edible white flesh of this, often used to give flavour to cakes, biscuits, etc: *shredded coconut* o *coconut flakes.*

■ '**coconut 'matting** *n* [U] a floor covering material made from the tough FIBRE(1) that forms the outer covering of coconut shells.

'**coconut shy** *n* (*Brit*) a stall at a FAIR³(1) where people try to knock coconuts off stands by throwing balls at them.

cocoon /kə'kuːn/ *n* **1** a fine covering like silk threads made by an insect LARVA to protect itself while it is a CHRYSALIS. **2** any soft protective covering: *wrapped in a cocoon of blankets.*

▶ **cocoon** *v* ~ sb/sth (**in sth**) (**from sth**) (usu passive) to wrap sb/sth in a protective covering: [Vnpr] *cocooned from the outside world in her warm bed* [also Vn].

cod /kɒd/ *n* (*pl* unchanged) (**a**) [C] a large sea fish. (**b**) [U] its flesh eaten as food.

■ ¡**cod-liver 'oil** *n* [U] oil obtained from the LIVER of cod. It is rich in VITAMIN A and vitamin D and is often taken as a medicine, esp by children.

COD /¡siː əʊ 'diː/ (**a**) *abbr* (*Brit*) cash on delivery. (**b**) (*US*) collect (payment) on delivery.

coda /'kəʊdə/ *n* (*music*) the final passage of a piece of music.

coddle /'kɒdl/ *v* (*sometimes derog*) to treat sb with great care and sympathy: [Vn] *He'll never be coddled after his illness.* o *International sportsmen are cosseted and coddled as never before.* Compare MOLLYCODDLE.

code /kəʊd/ *n* **1** [C, U] (often in compounds) a system of words, letters, symbols, etc that represent others, used for secret messages or for presenting or recording information briefly: *a letter in code* o *We'll break/crack their code* (ie discover how to read it) *somehow!* o *What tax code are you on?* See also BAR CODE, MORSE CODE, POSTCODE. **2** [C] = DIALLING CODE: *What's the code for Bristol?* **3** [C] (**a**) a set of laws or rules arranged in a system: *the penal code* o *a disciplinary code.* See also GENETIC CODE, HIGHWAY CODE. (**b**) a set of moral principles accepted by society or a group of people: *a strict code of conduct/honour* o *a code of dress.*

▶ **code** *v* to put or write sth in code: [Vn] *coded messages* o *data coded in binary form.*

■ '**code-name** *n* a name used for sb/sth when it is necessary to keep their real name secret, eg as part of a SPY operation: *Her code-name was Tulip.* **code-named** *adj* [pred].

¡**code of 'practice** *n* (*pl* **codes of practice**) a set of professional standards agreed on by members of a particular profession: *the broadcasting code of practice.*

codeine /'kəʊdiːn/ *n* [U] a drug used to relieve pain.

[Vnn] = verb + noun + noun   [V-adj] = verb + adjective   For more help with verbs, see Study pages **B4–8**.

codger /ˈkɒdʒə(r)/ n (infml) a man, esp an old one who has strange habits: *He's a funny old codger.*

codicil /ˈkəʊdɪsɪl; US ˈkɒdəsl/ n (law) a later addition to a will'(5), esp one that changes part of it: *She added a codicil to her will just before she died.*

codify /ˈkəʊdɪfaɪ; US ˈkɒdəfaɪ/ v (pt, pp **-fied**) [Vn] to arrange laws, rules, etc according to a system. ▶ **codification** /ˌkəʊdɪfɪˈkeɪʃn; US ˌkɒd-/ n [U].

codswallop n [U] (Brit infml) nonsense: *He's talking (a load of) codswallop.*

coed /ˌkəʊˈed/ n (infml esp US) a female student at a COEDUCATIONAL school or college.
▶ **coed** adj (infml) COEDUCATIONAL: *a ˌcoed ˈschool.*

coeducational /ˌkəʊedʒuˈkeɪʃənl/ adj of or relating to the system of educating girls and boys together: *a coeducational school.*

coefficient /ˌkəʊɪˈfɪʃnt/ n **1** (mathematics) a number placed before and multiplying another quantity: *In 3xy, 3 is the coefficient of xy.* **2** (physics) a number that measures a particular property(3) of a substance under specified conditions: *the coefficient of friction.*

coerce /kəʊˈɜːs/ v ~ sb (into sth / doing sth) (fml) to make sb do sth by using force or threats: [Vn] *an attempt to coerce the government* [Vnpr] *coerce sb into submission* ∘ *We were coerced into signing the contract.*
▶ **coercion** /kəʊˈɜːʃn; US also -ʒn/ n [U] the action of coercing sb or the process of being coerced: *our concern about the use of coercion* ∘ *He paid the money under coercion.*
coercive /kəʊˈɜːsɪv/ adj using force or threats: *coercive measures/tactics.*

coexist /ˌkəʊɪɡˈzɪst/ v [V, Vpr] ~ (with sb/sth) (a) to exist together at the same time or in the same place. (b) (of opposing countries or groups) to exist together without fighting.
▶ **coexistence** n [U] the state of coexisting: *peaceful coexistence.*

C of E /ˌsiː əv ˈiː/ abbr Church of England: *Are you C of E?* Compare CE.

coffee /ˈkɒfi; US ˈkɔːfi/ n **1** [U] the seeds (called **coffee beans**) of a tropical bush, or a powder made from them: *half a pound of coffee* ∘ *decaffeinated coffee* ∘ *I never buy **instant** coffee* (ie coffee powder that dissolves in boiling water). ∘ *coffee ice-cream.* **2(a)** [U] a drink made by adding hot water to coffee powder or coffee beans that have been ground up. Coffee may be drunk with milk and/or sugar added: *a cup of coffee* ∘ *make/percolate some coffee* ∘ *install a coffee machine in the office.* (b) [C] a cup of this drink: *'Tea or coffee?' she asked.* ∘ *Two strong **black** coffees, please* (ie without milk). **3** [U] the colour of coffee mixed with milk; light brown: *a coffee carpet.*
■ ˈ**coffee bar** n (Brit) (also ˈ**coffee-house**) a place serving coffee as well as other drinks and simple meals.
ˈ**coffee break** n a short period of time when people stop working and drink coffee, etc, eg in an office.
ˈ**coffee-morning** n (Brit) a social gathering in the morning, usu at sb's house and often to raise money for charity.
ˈ**coffee-shop** n (esp US) a small restaurant, esp in a hotel or shop, serving coffee as well as other drinks and simple meals.
ˈ**coffee-table** n a small low table. ˈ**coffee-table book** n a large expensive illustrated book, esp considered as one that is only intended to be read casually.

coffer /ˈkɒfə(r); US ˈkɔː-/ n **1** [C] a large strong box for holding money or other valuable items; a chest. **2 coffers** [pl] (fml) a store of money; a supply of funds: *The nation's coffers are empty.*

coffin /ˈkɒfɪn; US ˈkɔː-/ n a box in which a dead body

is buried or cremated (CREMATE). **IDM** **a nail in sb's/sth's coffin** ⇨ NAIL.

cog-wheel
cogs
cog-wheel

cog /kɒg/ n each of a series of teeth on the edge of a wheel that fit between those of a similar wheel, so that each cog can cause the other one to move. ⇨ picture. **IDM** **a cog in the maˈchine** (infml) a person who plays only a small part in a large organization or process.

cogent /ˈkəʊdʒənt/ adj (of arguments, reasons, etc) convincing; strong: *cogent evidence* ∘ *He produced cogent reasons for the change of policy.* ▶ **cogency** /ˈkəʊdʒənsi/ n [U]. **cogently** adv: *Her case was cogently argued.*

cogitate /ˈkɒdʒɪteɪt/ v ~ (about/on/over sth) (fml or joc) to think deeply about sth: [V] *He sat cogitating for several minutes before replying.* [also Vpr]. ▶ **cogitation** /ˌkɒdʒɪˈteɪʃn/ n [U].

cognac /ˈkɒnjæk; US ˈkəʊ-/ n (a) [U] a type of fine BRANDY made in W France. (b) [C] a glass of this.

cognate /ˈkɒgneɪt/ adj ~ (with sth) (linguistics) (of a word or language) having the same source or origin as another one: *The German word 'Haus' is cognate with the English word 'house'.* ∘ *German and Dutch are cognate languages.*
▶ **cognate** n (linguistics) a word that is cognate with another: *'Haus' and 'house' are cognates.*

cognition /kɒgˈnɪʃn/ n [U] (psychology) the action or process of acquiring knowledge and understanding through thought, experience or the senses.
▶ **cognitive** /ˈkɒgnətɪv/ adj of or relating to cognition: *a child's cognitive development.*

cognizance /ˈkɒgnɪzəns/ n [U] **1** (fml) knowledge; awareness: *have cognizance of sth.* **2** (esp law) the scope or extent of sb's knowledge or concern: *These matters fall within/go beyond the cognizance of this court.* **IDM** **take cognizance of sth** (esp law) to acknowledge or consider sth: *take cognizance of new evidence.*
▶ **cognizant** adj [pred] ~ of sth (fml) having knowledge of sth; aware of sth.

cognoscenti /ˌkɒnjəˈʃenti/ n [pl] (Italian) people who have a lot of knowledge or experience of sth, esp art, food, wine, etc: *a restaurant favoured by the cognoscenti.*

cohabit /kəʊˈhæbɪt/ v ~ (with sb) (fml) (usu of a man and a woman) to live together without being married: [V, Vpr] *They were cohabiting/He was cohabiting with her for three years before their marriage.* ▶ **cohabitation** /ˌkəʊˌhæbɪˈteɪʃn/ n [U].

cohere /kəʊˈhɪə(r)/ v **1** to stick together in a mass or group to form a whole: [V] *Parts of the book are brilliant but it fails to cohere as a whole.* Compare COHESION 1. **2** ~ (with sth) (of ideas, reasoning, etc) to have a logical connection; to be consistent: [Vpr] *This view does not cohere with their other beliefs.* [also V].
▶ **coherent** /kəʊˈhɪərənt/ adj **1** (of ideas, thoughts, speech, reasoning, etc) logical or consistent; easy to understand; clear: *a coherent analysis/argument/ description* ∘ *The government lacks a coherent economic policy.* **2** (of a person) able to talk clearly: *He was not very coherent on the telephone.* **coherence** /-rəns/ n [U]: *narrative coherence* ∘ *His arguments lack coherence.* **coherently** adv: *express one's ideas coherently.* Compare INCOHERENT.

cohesion /kəʊˈhiːʒn/ n [U] **1** the state of sticking together; unity: *the cohesion of the family unit* ∘

social/political/economic cohesion. Compare COHERE 1. **2** (*chemistry*) the force that causes molecules (MOLECULE) to stick together.

▶ **cohesive** /kəʊˈhiːsɪv/ *adj* (**a**) sticking together easily or well: *a cohesive social unit*. (**b**) causing or helping things or people to stick together: *cohesive forces such as religion or sport*. **cohesively** *adv*. **cohesiveness** *n* [U].

cohort /ˈkəʊhɔːt/ *n* [CGp] **1** a group of people united in supporting an idea, a person, etc. **2** (*esp US often derog*) a companion; a COLLEAGUE. **3** (in the army of ancient Rome) each of the ten units forming a LEGION(1b).

COI /ˌsiː əʊ ˈaɪ/ *abbr* (in Britain) Central Office of Information.

coiffure /kwɑːˈfjʊə(r)/ *n* (*French*) the way in which (esp a woman's) hair is arranged; a HAIRSTYLE. ▶ **coiffured** *adj*: *carefully coiffured hair*.

coil /kɔɪl/ *v* ~ (**oneself/sth**) **round sth / up** to wind or twist oneself/sth round and round in circles or loops: [Vpr, Vnpr] *The snake coiled (itself) round the branch.* [Vn, Vnp] *coil (up) a length of rope/flex/wire* [Vn] *a coiled spring* [also Vp].

▶ **coil** *n* **1** a length of rope, etc wound into a series of loops: *a coil of flex*. **2** a single ring or loop of rope, etc: *the thick coils of a python* ∘ *a coil of hair*. **3** (*techn*) a length of covered wire wound in continuous circles, through which an electric current can pass. **4** = INTRA-UTERINE DEVICE.

coin /kɔɪn/ *n* (**a**) [C] a piece of metal used as money: *a 20p coin* ∘ *a handful of coins*. (**b**) [U] money made of metal: *£5 in coin*. **IDM** **the other side of the coin** ⇨ SIDE¹.

▶ **coin** *v* **1** to invent a new word or phrase: [Vn] *As a writer he coined many terms now in common use.* **2** [Vn] to make coins or make metal into coins. **IDM** **ˈcoin it/money** (*infml*) (esp in the progressive tenses) to earn a lot of money easily or quickly: *Her new chain of fast-food restaurants must be really coining it.* **to coin a ˈphrase 1** (*ironic*) (used to apologize for using a well-known ordinary expression rather than an original one). **2** (used to introduce a new expression, or a well-known expression that one has changed slightly).

coinage /ˈkɔɪnɪdʒ/ *n* **1** [U] (**a**) coins: *silver coinage* ∘ *medieval coinage*. (**b**) the process of making coins: *techniques of coinage*. **2** [U] the system of coins in use: *the introduction of decimal coinage*. **3**(**a**) [C] a newly invented word or phrase: *I haven't heard that expression before — is it a recent coinage?* (**b**) [U] the inventing of a new word or phrase: *the clever coinage of advertising slogans*.

coincide /ˌkəʊɪnˈsaɪd/ *v* ~ (**with sth**) **1** (of events) to happen at the same time or during the same period of time as sth else: [Vpr] *Her arrival coincided with our departure.* [V] *Our holidays don't coincide.* **2** to be exactly the same as or very similar to sth else: [V] *Their stories coincided.* [Vpr, V] *Her taste in music coincides with her husband's/Their tastes in music coincide.* **3** (of two or more objects or places) to occupy the same space: [Vpr] *The position of the manor coincides with that of an earlier dwelling.* [also V].

coincidence /kəʊˈɪnsɪdəns/ *n* **1** [C, U] (a surprising instance of) similar events or circumstances happening at the same time by chance: *'I'm going to Paris next week.' 'What a coincidence! So am I.'* ∘ *By a strange coincidence we happened to be travelling on the same flight.* ∘ *The plot of the novel relies too much on coincidence to be convincing.* ∘ *By coincidence, both letters arrived on the same day.* **2** [U] the fact or state of two or more things being exactly the same: *the coincidence of their ideas*.

coincident /kəʊˈɪnsɪdənt/ *adj* ~ (**with sth**) (*fml*) **1** happening in the same place or at the same time: *changes coincident with volcanic activity*. **2** of a cor-

responding type: *A child's performance is often coincident with her social class or background*.

▶ **coincidental** /kəʊˌɪnsɪˈdentl/ *adj* [usu pred] resulting from (a) COINCIDENCE: *The similarity between these two essays is too great to be coincidental* (ie One must have been copied from the other). ∘ *a coincidental meeting*. **coincidentally** *adv*.

coir /ˈkɔɪə(r)/ *n* [U] rough material made from the outer part of coconuts (COCONUT), used for making ropes, mats, etc: *coir matting*.

coitus /ˈkəʊɪtəs, ˈkɔɪtəs/ (also **coition** /kəʊˈɪʃn/) *n* [U] (*medical or fml*) sex(2a). ▶ **coital** /ˈkəʊɪtl, ˈkɔɪtl/ *adj*.

Coke /kəʊk/ *n* [C, U] (*propr infml*) = COCA-COLA.

coke¹ /kəʊk/ *n* [U] a solid black substance produced from coal and burnt as a fuel: *a coke furnace*.

coke² /kəʊk/ *n* [U] (*sl*) COCAINE.

cola (also **kola**) /ˈkəʊlə/ *n* [U] a popular FIZZY drink that does not contain alcohol. Its flavour comes from the seeds of a W African tree.

Col *abbr* Colonel: *Col (Terence) Lloyd*.

col¹ /kɒl/ *n* a low point or pass²(4) in a mountain range.

col² *abbr* column(3).

colander *n* /ˈkʌləndə(r)/ a metal or plastic bowl with many small holes in it, used to drain water from vegetables, etc, esp after cooking.

cold¹ /kəʊld/ *adj* (**-er, -est**) **1** of or at a low or lower than usual temperature, esp of when compared to the temperature of the human body: *feel cold* ∘ *have cold hands/feet/ears* ∘ *a cold bath/climate/day/house/ room/wind/winter* ∘ *cold weather/water* ∘ *It/The weather is getting colder.* Compare HOT, WARM¹. **2** (of food or drink) not heated; having cooled after being heated or cooked: *Would you like coffee or a cold drink?* ∘ *have cold meat and salad for supper* ∘ *Don't let your dinner get cold* (ie Eat it while it is still warm). **3**(**a**) (of a person's manner, etc) not kind, friendly or enthusiastic; without emotion: *a cold look/stare/welcome/reception* ∘ *cold fury* (ie violent anger kept under control). (**b**) unable to respond sexually; FRIGID(1). **4** giving an impression of being cold: *a cold grey colour* ∘ *cold skies*. **5** (of the smell or trail of an animal or a person being hunted) no longer easy to follow: *The police tracked the stolen goods to a deserted warehouse but there the trail went cold.* **6** (in children's games) not close to finding sb/ sth hidden, guessing the correct answer, etc. **7** [pred] (*infml*) unconscious: *knock sb (out) cold.* **8** [pred] dead. **IDM** **blow hot and cold** ⇨ BLOW¹. **ˌcold ˈcomfort** a thing that offers little or no comfort or compensation: *After losing my job it was cold comfort to be told I'd won the office raffle*. **ˌcold ˈturkey** (*sl*) **1** (*Brit*) a frank statement of the truth, often about sth unpleasant: *talk cold turkey to/with sb.* **2** (*esp US*) a way of treating a drug ADDICT by suddenly stopping her or him taking the drug altogether instead of gradually reducing the amount taken. **get/have cold ˈfeet** (*infml*) to become/be afraid of or nervous about doing sth, esp sth risky or dangerous: *He got cold feet at the last minute.* **give sb / get the cold ˈshoulder** to treat sb/be treated in a way that is deliberately not friendly. See also COLD-SHOULDER. **go hot and cold** ⇨ HOT. **in cold ˈblood** deliberately and without feeling pity or regret: *kill/murder/shoot sb in cold blood.* **leave sb ˈcold** to fail to affect, interest or impress sb: *Her entreaties left him cold.* **make sb's blood run cold** ⇨ BLOOD¹. **pour/throw cold ˈwater on sth** to discourage or say that one is not in favour of sth: *pour cold water on sb's plans/ideas/hopes.*

▶ **coldly** *adv* in a way that is not friendly or enthusiastic: *stare coldly at sb* ∘ *'I don't need your help,' she said coldly*. **coldness** *n* [U] the state of being cold: *She was hurt*

[V.*to* inf] = verb + *to* infinitive   [Vn.inf (no *to*)] = verb + noun + infinitive without *to*   [V.*ing*] = verb + *-ing* form

by his coldness (ie lack of friendly behaviour) *towards her.*

■ ,cold-'blooded /-'blʌdɪd/ *adj* **1** (*biology*) having a blood temperature which varies with the temperature of the surroundings: *Reptiles and fish are cold-blooded.* **2** (*derog*) (of people or actions) without emotion or pity; cruel: *a cold-blooded murderer/murder.*

,cold 'chisel *n* a CHISEL used for cutting metal.

'cold cream *n* [U] a smooth thick liquid for cleaning and softening the skin.

'cold cuts *n* [pl] (*esp US*) cooked meat, cut in slices and served cold.

'cold frame *n* a small wooden frame covered with glass and used to protect young plants.

,cold-'hearted /-'hɑːtɪd/ *adj* without sympathy or kindness; unkind.

,cold-'shoulder *v* [Vn] to treat sb in a way that is deliberately not friendly.

'cold snap *n* a sudden short period of cold weather.

,cold 'storage *n* [U] the storing of things in a very cold place, eg a refrigerator (REFRIGERATE), in order to preserve them: (*fig*) *put a plan/an idea into cold storage* (ie to decide not to use it immediately but to reserve it for later).

,cold 'sweat *n* [sing] a state in which sb sweats and feels cold at the same time, caused by fear or illness: *be in a cold sweat (about sth).*

,cold 'war *n* [U, sing] a state of hostility between nations without actual fighting: *cold-war attitudes/diplomacy/rhetoric.*

cold² /kəʊld/ *n* **1** [U] a lack of heat or warmth; a low temperature, esp in the atmosphere: *shiver with cold* ○ *the heat of summer and the cold of winter* ○ *Don't stand outside in the cold.* ○ *She doesn't seem to feel the cold.* **2** [C, U] a common illness affecting the nose or throat or both. Colds make one SNEEZE, cough, etc and are passed easily to other people: *a bad/heavy/slight cold* ○ *have a cold in the head/on the chest* ○ *catch (a) cold.* **IDM** (**leave sb/be**) **,out in the 'cold** not part of a group or an activity; ignored: *When the coalition was formed, the Communists were left out in the cold.*

■ 'cold sore *n* (*infml*) a number of painful spots (SPOT 3) near or in the mouth, caused by a VIRUS.

coleslaw /'kəʊlslɔː/ *n* [U] raw CABBAGE(1) and carrots (CARROT 1), etc chopped and mixed with MAYONNAISE and eaten as a SALAD.

colic /'kɒlɪk/ *n* [U] a severe pain in the stomach, suffered esp by babies.

▶ **colicky** *adj* of, like or suffering from colic.

colitis /kə'laɪtɪs/ *n* [U] (*medical*) an illness in which the COLON² becomes inflamed (INFLAME) and sore.

collaborate /kə'læbəreɪt/ *v* **1** ~ (**with sb**) (**on sth**) to work together with sb, esp to create or produce sth: [Vpr] *She collaborated with her sister/She and her sister collaborated on a biography of their father.* [also V]. **2** ~ (**with sb**) (*derog*) to help enemy forces occupying one's country: [V, Vpr] *He was suspected of collaborating (with the enemy).*

▶ **collaboration** /kə,læbə'reɪʃn/ *n* [U] **1** ~ (**with sb**) (**on sth**); ~ (**between A and B**) the action of collaborating (COLLABORATE 1): *She wrote the book in collaboration with her sister* (ie They wrote it together). **2** ~ (**with sb**) the action of helping enemy forces occupying one's country.

collaborative /kə'læbərətɪv; *US* -reɪt-/ *adj* [attrib] done or made by two or more people, groups, etc working together: *a collaborative project/effort.* **collaboratively** *adv.*

collaborator /kə'læbəreɪtə(r)/ *n* a person who collaborates.

collage /'kɒlɑːʒ; *US* kə'lɑːʒ/ *n* **1(a)** [U] a form of art in which pieces of paper, cloth, photographs, etc are arranged and stuck to a surface. **(b)** [C] a picture made in this way. **2** [C] a collection of things that

may or may not be related: *an interesting collage of 1960s songs.*

collapse /kə'læps/ *v* **1** to fall down or fall in suddenly, often after breaking apart: [V] *The whole building collapsed.* ○ *The roof collapsed under the weight of snow.* ○ *The wind caused the tent to collapse.* **2(a)** (of a person) to fall down (and usu become unconscious, esp because one is very ill: [V] *He collapsed (in the street) and died on the way to the hospital.* **(b)** to sit or lie down and relax, esp after working hard, etc: [V] *When I get home I like to collapse on the sofa and listen to music.* **3 (a)** to fail suddenly or completely; to break down: [V] *His health collapsed under the pressure of work.* ○ *The enterprise collapsed through lack of support.* ○ *Talks between management and unions have collapsed.* **(b)** to be defeated or destroyed: [V] *All opposition to the scheme has collapsed.* **4** (of prices, currencies, etc) to decrease suddenly in value: [V] *Share prices collapsed after news of poor trading figures.* **5** to fold sth or be folded into a shape that uses less space: [V] *a chair that collapses for easy storage* [also Vn]. **6** (*medical*) **(a)** [V] (of a lung or blood-vessel (BLOOD¹)) to fall inwards and become flat and empty. **(b)** [Vn] to make a lung or blood-vessel (blood¹) do this.

▶ **collapse** *n* [sing] **1** a sudden fall: *the collapse of the building/roof/bridge.* **2** a failure; a BREAKDOWN: *the collapse of negotiations/sb's health/law and order* ○ *The economy is in a state of (total) collapse.* ○ *a state of physical/mental/nervous collapse.* **3** a sudden drop in value: *the collapse of share prices/the dollar/the market.*

collapsible *adj* that can be folded into a shape that uses less space: *a collapsible bicycle/boat/chair.*

collar /'kɒlə(r)/ *n* **1** a band round the neck of a shirt, coat, dress, etc, either upright or folded over: *turn one's collar up against the wind* (ie to keep one's neck warm) ○ *grab sb by the collar* ○ *What is your collar size?* ⇨ picture at JACKET. See also DOG-COLLAR. **2** a band of leather, metal, etc put round an animal's (esp a dog's) neck: *Our dog has its name on its collar.* **3** a metal band or ring joining two pipes or rods, esp in a machine. **IDM** **hot under the collar** ⇨ HOT. See also BLUE-COLLAR, WHITE-COLLAR.

▶ **collar** *v* (*infml*) to seize sb by the collar; to capture sb: [Vn] *The policeman collared the thief.* ○ *She collared me* (ie stopped me in order to talk to me) *as I was leaving the building.*

■ 'collar-bone *n* the bone joining the BREASTBONE and the shoulder-blade (SHOULDER). ⇨ picture at SKELETON.

collate /kə'leɪt/ *v* **1** to collect and combine information from two or more different books, sources, etc: [Vn] *collate all the available data.* **2** [Vn] to collect together and arrange the pages of a book, etc in the correct order.

▶ **collation** /kə'leɪʃn/ *n* **1** [C] (*fml or rhet*) a light meal, esp at an unusual time: *a cold collation.* **2** [U] the action or process of collating things.

collateral /kə'lætərəl/ *adj* **1** connected but less important; additional: *collateral benefits* ○ *a collateral aim.* **2** descended from the same ancestor, but by a different line: *a collateral branch of the family.*

▶ **collateral** *n* [U] property offered by sb as a guarantee that they will pay back a loan: *The bank will insist on collateral for a loan of that size.*

colleague /'kɒliːg/ *n* a person with whom one works, esp in a profession or business: *the Prime Minister's Cabinet colleagues* ○ *David is a colleague of mine/David and I are colleagues.*

collect¹ /kə'lekt/ *v* **1** ~ **sth** (**up/together**) to bring or gather sth together: [Vn, Vnp] *collect (up) the empty glasses/dirty plates/waste paper* [Vnp] *collect together one's belongings* [Vn] *information collected by satellite* ○ *the collected works of Dickens* (ie a series of books containing everything he wrote) ○ *No* one uses the computer — *it just sits there collecting dust.* **2** to come together; to assemble or accumulate: [V] *A crowd soon collected at the scene of the accident.* ○ *Dust had collected on the window-sill.* **3** to obtain money, contributions, etc from a number of people or places: [V, Vn] *We're collecting (money) for famine relief.* [Vn] *The Internal Revenue is responsible for collecting income tax.* **4** (*infml*) to receive sth: [Vn] *She collected first prize/a cheque for £1 000.* **5** to obtain and keep examples of sth as a HOBBY or for study: [Vn] *collect stamps/old coins/matchboxes/first editions* ○ *Record collecting can be an expensive pastime.* **6** (*esp Brit*) to come for and take away sb/sth; to FETCH sb/sth: [Vn] *The dustmen collect the rubbish once a week.* ○ *collect a child from school* ○ *collect a suit from the cleaners.* **7** to regain or recover control of oneself, one's thoughts, etc: [Vn] *collect oneself after a shock* ○ *collect one's thoughts before an interview.*

▶ **collect** *adj, adv* (*US*) (of a telephone call) to be paid for by the person being called: *a collect call* ○ *call sb collect* (ie transfer the charge).

collectable *adj* worth collecting (COLLECT[1] 5).

collected *adj* [pred] in control of oneself; calm: *She always stays cool, calm and collected in a crisis.*

collect[2] /ˈkɒlekt/ *n* (in the Anglican or the Roman Catholic Church) a short prayer, usu read on a particular day.

collection /kəˈlekʃn/ *n* **1** [C, U] an act or the process of collecting (COLLECT[1] 5) sth: *There are two collections a day from this letter-box* (ie It is emptied twice a day). ○ *The council is responsible for refuse collection.* **2** [C] a group of objects that have been collected (COLLECT[1] 5): *a stamp/coin/record collection* ○ *This painting comes from his private collection.* **3** a group of poems, stories, etc published in one volume: *a collection of critical essays.* **4** [C] a range of new clothes, etc designed or made as a group and offered for sale: *You are invited to view our autumn collection.* **5** [C] (**a**) the collecting (COLLECT[1] 3) of money during a church service or a meeting: *The collection will be taken (up)/made after the sermon.* ○ *a collection for famine relief.* (**b**) a sum of money collected in this way: *a large collection.* **6** [C] a group of objects or people: *a collection of junk/rubbish* ○ *There was an odd collection of guests at the party.*

collective /kəˈlektɪv/ *adj* of a group or society as a whole; joint[2](1); shared: *collective action/effort/guilt/responsibility/wisdom* ○ *collective leadership* (ie government by a group rather than an individual). Compare INDIVIDUAL *n* 2.

▶ **collective** *n* (**a**) [C] an organization or enterprise, esp a farm, owned and controlled by the people who work in it: *a workers' collective.* (**b**) [CGp] these people as a group.

collectively *adv*: *They were known collectively as the 'Gang of Four'.*

collectivism /-ɪzəm/ *n* [U] the social and economic system in which all land, business, industry, etc is owned by the community or by the state, for the benefit of everyone. **collectivist** *n, adj.*

collectivize, -ise /kəˈlektɪvaɪz/ *v* [Vn] to transfer farms, industries, land, etc from private ownership to ownership by the state. **collectivization, -isation** /kəˌlektɪvaɪˈzeɪʃn; *US* -vəˈz-/ *n* [U].

■ **col‚lective ˈbargaining** *n* [U] negotiation about pay, working conditions, etc between a trade union and an employer.

col‚lective ˈfarm *n* a farm or group of farms owned by the state and run by the workers.

col‚lective ˈnoun *n* (*grammar*) a noun that is SINGULAR(1) in form but can refer to a number of people or things and, esp in British English, agree with a PLURAL(1) verb: *'Flock' and 'committee' are collective nouns.*

collector /kəˈlektə(r)/ *n* (esp in compounds) a person who collects (COLLECT[1] 3,5) things: *a ˈstamp-collector* ○ *a ˈtax-collector* ○ *a ˈticket-collector* (eg at a railway station).

■ **colˈlector's item** (also **colˈlector's piece**) *n* a thing worth putting in a collection because it is very beautiful, rare, etc.

colleen /ˈkɒliːn/ *n* (*Irish*) a girl or young woman.

college /ˈkɒlɪdʒ/ *n* **1** [C, U] an institution for higher education or professional training: *a college of further education* (ie providing education and training for people over 16) ○ *the Royal College of Art* ○ *a secretarial college* ○ *Our son is going to college* (ie starting a course of study at a university or a college) *next year.* ○ *She's at* (ie studying at) *college.* ⇨ note at SCHOOL[1]. **2** [C] (**a**) (in Britain) any of a number of independent institutions within certain universities, each having its own teachers, students and buildings: *the Oxford and Cambridge colleges* ○ *New College, Oxford.* (**b**) (in the USA) a university, or part of one, offering UNDERGRADUATE courses. **3** [C, U] the building or buildings of a college(2): *Are you living in college?* ○ *a college chapel.* **4** [C] (*esp Brit*) (in names) a school: *Eton College* ○ *a sixth-form college.* **5** [C] an organized group of professional people with particular aims, duties or privileges: *the Royal College of Surgeons* ○ *the College of Cardinals* (ie as a group, when electing or advising the Pope).

collegiate /kəˈliːdʒiət/ *adj* [usu attrib] **1** of or relating to a college or its students: *collegiate life.* **2** consisting of or having colleges: *Oxford is a collegiate university.*

collide /kəˈlaɪd/ *v* ~ (**with sb/sth**) **1** (of moving objects or people) to strike violently against sth or each other: [Vpr] *As the bus turned the corner, it collided with a van.* [V] *The bus and the van collided.* ○ *The particles are accelerated and collide at high speed.* ○ *We collided on the pavement.* **2** (of people, aims, opinions, etc) to be in disagreement or opposition: [V] *The interests of the two countries collide.* [also Vpr]. See also COLLISION.

collie /ˈkɒli/ *n* a dog with long hair and a long pointed nose. Collies are often used for guarding and tending sheep. ⇨ picture at DOG[1].

collier /ˈkɒliə(r)/ *n* (*dated esp Brit*) a coalminer (COALMINE).

colliery /ˈkɒliəri/ *n* (*esp Brit*) a COALMINE with its buildings.

collision /kəˈlɪʒn/ *n* [C, U] ~ (**with sb/sth**); ~ (**between A and B**) **1** (an instance of) one object or person striking against another violently: *a (head-on) collision between two cars* ○ *The liner was in collision with an oil-tanker.* ○ *The two ships were in/came into collision.* **2** strong disagreement; a conflict of opposing aims, ideas, opinions, etc: *a collision between rival ideologies* ○ *Her political activities brought her into collision with the law.*

■ **colˈlision course** *n* a course of action that is certain to lead to a collision with sb/sth: *The government and the unions are on a collision course.*

collocate /ˈkɒləkeɪt/ *v* ~ (**with sth**) (*linguistics*) (of words) to be used regularly together in a language; to combine: [Vpr] *'Weak' collocates with 'tea' but 'feeble' does not.* [V] *'Weak' and 'tea' collocate.*

▶ **collocation** /ˌkɒləˈkeɪʃn/ *n* **1** [U] the action of collocating. **2** [C] a regular combination of words: *'Resounding victory' and 'crying shame' are English collocations.*

colloquial /kəˈləʊkwiəl/ *adj* (of words, phrases, etc) used in normal conversation but not formal speech or writing. See also INFORMAL 3, SLANG.

▶ **colloquialism** *n* a colloquial word or phrase: *'On the blink'* (ie not working) *is a colloquialism.*

colloquially /-kwiəli/ *adv.*

colloquy /ˈkɒləkwi/ *n* [C, U] (*fml*) (a) conversation.

collude /kəˈluːd/ *v* ~ (**with sb**) (**in sth/doing sth**) to plan with sb to deceive or cheat others: [Vpr] *His sisters colluded in keeping it secret.* [also V].

collusion /kə'luːʒn/ *n* [U] ~ **(with sb)**; ~ **(between sb and sb)** *(fml)* secret agreement or understanding between two or more people with the aim of deceiving or cheating others: *There was collusion between the two witnesses* (eg They gave the same false evidence). ○ *The police were acting in collusion with the drug traffickers.* ▸ **collusive** /kə'luːsɪv/ *adj*.

collywobbles /'kɒliwɒblz/ *n* [pl] *(Brit infml)* a feeling of fear or anxiety, sometimes causing pain in the stomach: *have an attack of (the) collywobbles.*

cologne /kə'ləʊn/ *n* [U] = EAU-DE-COLOGNE.

colon¹ /'kəʊlən/ *n* the mark (:) used in writing and printing. A colon shows that what follows is an example, a list or a summary of what precedes it, or a contrasting idea. ⇨ App 3. Compare SEMICOLON.

colon² /'kəʊlən/ *n* (*anatomy*) the lower part of the large INTESTINE. ⇨ picture at DIGESTIVE SYSTEM.

colonel /'kɜːnl/ *n* (**a**) an army officer, commanding a regiment. (**b**) an officer of similar rank in the US air force. ⇨ App 6.
■ **Colonel 'Blimp** *n* = BLIMP.

colonial /kə'ləʊnɪəl/ *adj* [esp attrib] **1** of, relating to or possessing a colony(1a) or colonies: *France was once a colonial power.* ○ *Kenya was under (British) colonial rule for many years.* **2** (of a style of architecture or furniture) typical of a former period of colonial rule: *colonial residences in New England* ○ *a colonial-style ranch.*
▸ **colonial** *n* a person living in a colony(1a) who is not a member of the native population.
colonialism *n* [U] the policy of acquiring colonies (COLONY 1a) and keeping them dependent.
colonialist *n, adj*: *European colonialists* ○ *colonialist oppression.*

colonist /'kɒlənɪst/ *n* a person who settles in an area that has been made a colony.

colonize, -ise /'kɒlənaɪz/ *v* to establish a colony in an area: [Vn] *Britain colonized many parts of Africa.*
▸ **colonization, -isation** /ˌkɒlənaɪ'zeɪʃn; US -nə'z-/ *n* [U]: *the colonization of N America by the British and French.*

colonnade /ˌkɒlə'neɪd/ *n* a row of columns, usu with equal spaces between them and often supporting a roof, etc.
▸ **colonnaded** /ˌkɒlə'neɪdɪd/ *adj* having a colonnade.

colony /'kɒləni/ *n* **1(a)** [C] a country or an area settled and controlled by people from another country, sometimes by force: *a former British colony* (eg Australia). Compare PROTECTORATE. (**b**) [CGp] a group of people who settle in a colony. **2** [CGp] (**a**) a group of people from a foreign country living in a particular city or country: *the American colony in Paris.* (**b**) a group of people with the same occupation, interest, etc living together in the same place: *an artists' colony* ○ *a nudist colony.* **3** [CGp] (*biology*) a group of animals or plants living or growing in the same place: *a colony of ants* ○ *a seal colony.*

color (*US*) = COLOUR.

coloratura /ˌkɒlərə'tʊərə; US ˌkʌl-/ *n* [U] complicated ornamental passages for a singer, eg in opera: *a coloratura soprano* (ie one who specializes in singing such passages).

colossal /kə'lɒsl/ *adj* very large; huge; IMMENSE: *a colossal building/man/price/amount.* ▸ **colossally** *adv*.

colossus /kə'lɒsəs/ *n* (*pl* **colossi** /-'lɒsaɪ/ *or* **colossuses** /-'lɒsəsɪz/) a person or thing of very great size, importance, ability, etc: *Mozart is a colossus among composers.*

colour¹ (*US* **color**) /'kʌlə(r)/ *n* **1(a)** [U] a visible quality that objects have, produced by the way they reflect light: *The garden was a mass of colour.* ○ *You*

need more colour in this room. ○ *The leaves are changing colour.* (**b**) [C] a particular type of this: *Red, orange, green and purple are all colours.* ○ *'What colour is the sky?' 'It's blue.'* ○ *a sky the colour of lead* (ie a grey sky). See also PRIMARY COLOUR. **2(a)** [C, U] a substance used to give colour to sth, eg paint or dye: *use plenty of bright colour in a painting* ○ *She paints in water-colour(s).* (**b**) [U] the use of all colours, not only black and white: *Is the film in colour or black and white?* ○ *colour photography/television/printing.* **3** [U] redness (RED) of the face, usu regarded as a sign of good health: *He has very little colour* (ie is very pale). ○ *lose colour* (ie become paler) ○ *She has a high colour* (ie a very red face). ○ *The fresh air brought colour to their cheeks.* **4** [U] the colour of the skin, esp as showing the race sb belongs to: *be discriminated against on account of one's colour/on grounds of colour* ○ *colour prejudice.* **5 colours** [pl] a BADGE, an item of clothing, etc of a particular colour, worn to show that one is a member of a particular team, school, political party, etc: *He is racing in the royal colours* (ie to show that the horse he is riding is owned by the king or queen). **6 colours** [pl] (*Brit*) an award given to a regular or outstanding member of a sports team, esp in a school: *get/win one's (football) colours.* **7 colours** [pl] the flag or flags of a ship or regiment: *salute the colours.* **8** [U] (**a**) interesting and vivid detail or qualities: *Her description of the area is full of colour.* (**b**) the distinctive quality of sound in music; tone: *orchestral colour* ○ *His playing lacks colour.* **IDM** **give/lend 'colour to sth** to make sth seem true or probable: *The scars on his body lent colour to his claim that he had been tortured.* **nail one's colours to the mast** ⇨ NAIL *v*. **off 'colour** (*infml*) not in very good health; ill: *feel/look/seem a little off colour.* **see the colour of sb's 'money** to make sure that sb has enough money to pay for sth: *Don't let him have the car until you've seen the colour of his money.* **troop the colour** ⇨ TROOP. **one's true colours** ⇨ TRUE. **with flying colours** ⇨ FLYING.
▸ **colourful** (*US* **colorful**) /-fl/ *adj* **1** full of colour; bright: *a colourful dress/scene* ○ *colourful material.* **2** interesting or exciting; vivid: *a colourful character/life/story/period of history.*
colourless (*US* **colorless**) *adj* **1** without colour; pale: *a colourless liquid* (eg water) ○ *colourless cheeks.* **2** not interesting; dull: *a colourless character/existence/style.*
■ **'colour bar** (*US* **'color line**) *n* a social system in which people without a white skin are not given the same rights as those with a white skin.
'colour-blind *adj* unable to see the difference between certain colours, esp red and green. **'colour-blindness** *n* [U].
'colour code *n* a system of marking things with different colours to help people to distinguish between them. Colour codes are used to mark electrical wires, office files, etc. **'colour-coded** *adj*.
'colour-fast *adj* (of a fabric) having a colour that will not change or fade when it is washed.
'colour scheme *n* an arrangement of colours, esp in the decoration and furniture of a room: *I don't like the colour scheme in their sitting-room.*
'colour supplement *n* a magazine printed in colour and issued with a newspaper.

colour² (*US* **color**) /'kʌlə(r)/ *v* **1** to put colour on sth, eg with coloured pencils, paint, etc: [Vn] *colour a picture* [Vn-adj] *Lucy drew a nice picture but she coloured the sky green.* **2(a)** to become coloured; to change colour: [V] *It is autumn and the leaves are beginning to colour* (ie turn brown). (**b**) ~ **(at sth)** to become red in the face; to BLUSH: [Vpr] *She coloured (with embarrassment) at his remarks.* [also V]. **3** (esp passive) to affect sth, esp in a negative way; to distort sth: [Vn] *His attitude to sex is coloured by his* strict upbringing. ○ *Don't allow personal loyalty to colour your judgement.* ○ *She gave a highly coloured* (ie exaggerated) *account of the incident.* **PHR V** ˌ**colour sth** ¹**in** to fill a particular area, shape, etc with colour: *The child coloured in all her drawings with a crayon.*

▶ **coloured** (*US* **colored**) *adj* **1** (often in compounds) having colour; having the specified colour: *coloured chalks* ○ ¹*cream-coloured* ○ ¹*flesh-coloured*. **2(a)** (*dated often offensive*) (of people) of a race that does not have a white skin. (**b**) **Coloured** (*S African*) (of people) of mixed race. — *n* (**a**) (*offensive*) a person from a race that does not have a white skin. (**b**) **Coloured** (*S African*) a person of mixed race.

colouring *n* **1(a)** [U] the action of putting colour on sth: *Children enjoy colouring.* ○ *a colouring book.* (**b**) [U] a way or style in which sth is coloured, or in which an artist uses colour in paintings, etc. **2** [U] the colour of a person's skin; a person's COMPLEXION: *She has (a) very fair colouring.* **3** [C, U] a substance used to give a particular colour to sth, esp to food: *This yoghurt contains no artificial flavouring or colouring.*

colt /kəʊlt/ *n* **1** a young male horse up to the age of 4 or 5. Compare FILLY, GELDING, STALLION. **2** (*Brit*) a member of a sports team consisting of young players: *He plays for the England Rugby Union Colts.*
▶ **coltish** /ˈkəʊltɪʃ/ *adj* (usu of young people) behaving in a lively but slightly awkward way.

columbine /ˈkɒləmbaɪn/ *n* a garden plant with flowers that have thin pointed petals (PETAL).

column

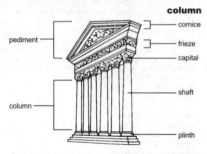

- cornice
- frieze
- capital
- shaft
- plinth

pediment

column

column /ˈkɒləm/ *n* **1** a tall pillar, usu round and made of stone, either supporting part of the roof of a building or standing alone as a MONUMENT: *The temple is supported by massive columns.* ○ *Nelson's Column is a famous landmark in London.* ⇨ picture. **2** a thing shaped like a column: *a column of smoke* (ie smoke rising straight up) ○ *the* ˌ*spinal* ¹*column* (ie the BACKBONE(1)) ○ *a column of mercury* (ie in a THERMOMETER). **3** (*abbr* **col**) one of two or more sections of printed material arranged beside each other on a page of a book, newspaper, etc: *Each page of this dictionary has two columns of text.* **4** a part of a newspaper regularly dealing with a particular subject or written by the same journalist: *the* ¹*fashion/*¹*gossip/fi*¹*nancial column* ○ *the correspondence columns of 'The Times'* ○ *I always read her column in the local paper.* See also PERSONAL COLUMN, AGONY COLUMN. **5(a)** a long line of vehicles, ships, etc following one behind the other. (**b**) a large group of soldiers, tanks (TANK 2), etc moving forward in short rows. **6** a series of numbers arranged one under the other: *add up a long column of figures.* See also FIFTH COLUMN.
▶ **columnist** /ˈkɒləmnɪst/ *n* a journalist who regularly writes an article commenting on politics, current events, etc for a newspaper or magazine: *a gossip/political/cookery columnist.*

coma /ˈkəʊmə/ *n* (*pl* **comas**) a deep unconscious

state, usu lasting a long time and caused by severe injury or illness: *go into a coma* ○ *He was in a coma for several weeks.*
▶ **comatose** /ˈkəʊmətəʊs/ *adj* **1** in a coma; deeply unconscious. **2** feeling very tired or drained of energy: *feeling comatose after a large meal.*

comb /kəʊm/ *n* **1** [C] (**a**) a piece of plastic, metal, etc with teeth, used for tidying and arranging the hair. (**b**) a small piece of plastic, metal, etc with teeth, worn by women to hold the hair in place or as an ornament. **2** [C usu *sing*] an act of tidying the hair with a comb: *Your hair needs a (good) comb.* **3** [C] a thing shaped or used like a comb, esp a device for preparing wool, cotton, etc for manufacture. **4** [C, U] = HONEYCOMB. **5** [C] the soft red part on the head of a domestic FOWL, esp a COCK¹. **IDM** **with a fine-tooth comb** ⇨ FINE¹.
▶ **comb** *v* **1** to pass a comb through the hair in order to tidy or arrange it: [Vn] *Don't forget to comb your hair before you go out!* **2** [Vn] to prepare wool, cotton, etc for manufacture with a comb(3). **3** ~ (**through**) **sth** (**for sb/sth**) to search sth thoroughly: [Vpr] *He combed through the files looking for evidence of fraud.* [Vnpr] *Police are combing the woods for the missing children.* [also Vn]. **PHR V** **comb sth out (of sth)** to tidy the hair with a comb or remove knots, dirt, etc from it: *Long hair is often difficult to comb out.* ○ *She combed the mud out of the dog's fur.*

combat /ˈkɒmbæt/ *n* [C, U] a fight or fighting between two people, armies, etc: *armed/unarmed combat* (ie with/without weapons) ○ *The troops were exhausted after months of fierce combat.* ○ *a combat jacket/mission/zone.* See also SINGLE COMBAT.
▶ **combat** *v* (**a**) to fight or struggle against sb/sth: [Vn] *combat the enemy.* (**b**) to try to reduce or destroy sth: [Vn] *combating disease/inflation/terrorism.*
combatant /ˈkɒmbətənt/ *n* a person involved in fighting in a war: *As many civilians as combatants have died in the war.* Compare NON-COMBATANT.
combative /ˈkɒmbətɪv/ *adj* eager or ready to fight or argue: *in a combative mood.* **combatively** *adv.*

combination /ˌkɒmbɪˈneɪʃn/ *n* **1** [U] the joining or mixing together of two or more things or people; the state of being joined or mixed together: *It is the combination of wit and political analysis that makes his articles so readable.* ○ *The firm is working on a new product in combination with several overseas partners.* **2** [C] a number of things or people joined or mixed together; a mixture or BLEND: *Pink is a combination of red and white.* ○ *A combination of factors led to her decision to resign.* ○ *The architecture in the downtown area is a successful combination of old and new.* ○ *What an unusual combination of flavours!* **3** [C] a sequence of numbers or letters used to open a combination lock. **4** **combinations** [pl] a single garment covering the body and legs, worn (esp formerly) next to the skin as UNDERWEAR.
■ **combi**¹**nation lock** *n* a type of lock, eg on a safe, that can only be opened with a particular sequence of numbers or letters.

combine¹ /kəmˈbaɪn/ *v* **1** ~ (**with sth**); ~ **A and B / A with B** to join or make things join together to form a whole: [V, Vpr] *Hydrogen and oxygen combine/Hydrogen combines with oxygen to form water.* [V. to inf] *Circumstances have combined to ruin our plans for a holiday.* [Vnpr] *Combine the eggs with a little flour and heat the mixture gently.* [Vn usu passive]: *a kitchen and dining-room combined* (ie one room used as both) ○ *Success was achieved by the combined efforts of the whole team.* **2** ~ **A and B / A with B** to do two or more things at the same time; to have two or more different characteristics: [Vnpr] *combine business with pleasure* [Vn] *He combines arrogance and incompetence in his dealings with the staff.*
■ **com**¹**bining form** *n* (*linguistics*) (abbreviated as

comb form in this dictionary) a form of a word which can combine with another word or another combining form to make a new word, eg *Anglo-*, *-philia*.

combine² /'kɒmbaɪn/ *n* **1** a group of people or firms acting together in business. **2** (also ‚combine ˈharvester) an agricultural machine that harvests (HARVEST *v*) a crop and separates the grains from the rest of the plant. Compare HARVESTER 2.

combo /'kɒmbəʊ/ *n* (*pl* **-os**) (*infml*) a small band that plays JAZZ or dance music.

combustible /kəm'bʌstəbl/ *adj* that can catch fire and burn easily: *Petrol is (highly) combustible.*
▶ **combustible** *n* (usu *pl*) a combustible substance or material.

combustion /kəm'bʌstʃən/ *n* [U] **1** the process of burning. **2** a chemical process in which substances combine with oxygen in air, producing heat and light: *an internal-combustion engine.*
■ com'bustion chamber *n* an enclosed space in which COMBUSTION(2) takes place, eg in an engine.

come /kʌm/ *v* (*pt* came /keɪm/; *pp* come) **1(a)** ~ (to...) (from...) to move to, towards, into, etc a place where the speaker or writer is, or a place being referred to by her or him: [Vpr] *She came into the room and shut the door.* ○ *She came slowly down the stairs.* ○ *He has come all the way from Leeds to be with us today.* ○ *She comes to work by bus.* ○ *Strange noises were coming from his room.* [Vp] *Are you coming out for a walk?* [Vadv] *Our son is coming home for Christmas.* ○ *Come here!* ○ *Come (and visit us) again soon!* [V] *There's a storm coming* (ie approaching). ⇨ note at AND, VISIT. **(b)** ~ (to...) to arrive at a place where the speaker or writer is or at a place being referred to by her or him: [Vpr] *They came to a river.* ○ *They came* (eg arrived at my house) *at 8 o'clock.* [Vadv] *What time will you be coming?* ○ *Spring came late this year.* ○ *The road comes within a mile of the farm.* [V] *Have any letters come for me?* ○ *I've come to collect my book/come for my book.* ○ *Help has come at last.* ○ *The time has come* (ie Now is the moment) *to act.* **(c)** ~ (to sth) (with sb) to move in order to be with sb at a particular place or be present at an event: [Vpr] *I've only come for an hour.* ○ *Are you coming (to the cinema) with us tonight?* ○ *'Would you like to come to dinner next Friday?' 'I'd love to.'* ○ *Are you coming to my party?* ○ *Who are you coming with?* ○ *I'll be coming with Keith.* [also V]. **(d)** to take part in the specified activity, esp a sport, usu with other people: [V.ing] *Why don't you come ice-skating (with us) tonight?* **2** to travel a specified distance: [Vn] *We've come fifty miles since lunch.* ○ (*fig*) *This company has come a long way* (ie made a lot of progress) *in the last five years.* **3** (used with a present participle to show that sb/sth moves in the way specified or that sb is doing sth while moving) [V.ing] *He came hurrying to see her as soon as he heard she was ill.* ○ *The children came running to meet us.* ○ *She came sobbing* (ie was crying as she came) *into the room.* ○ *Sunlight came streaming through the window.* **4** (not in the continuous tenses) to occupy a particular position in space or time; to occur: [V-adj] *She came first* (ie received the highest mark) *in English.* ○ (*fig*) *His family comes first* (ie is the most important thing in his life). [Vpr] *May comes between April and June.* ○ *'A' comes before 'B' in the alphabet.* [V-n] *Her death came as a terrible shock (to us all).* ○ *Her resignation came as a surprise/It came as a surprise when she resigned.* **5** ~ **in sth** (not in the continuous tenses) (of goods, products, etc) to be available: [Vpr] *This dress comes in three sizes.* ○ *Do these shoes come in black?* [V-adj] *New cars don't come cheap* (ie They are expensive). **6** to become; to prove to be: [V-adj] *My shoelaces have come undone.* ○ *This envelope has come unstuck.*

○ *The handle has come loose.* ○ *Everything will come right in the end.* **7** to reach a point at which one realizes, understands, believes, etc sth: [V.to inf] *She had come to see the problem in a new light.* ○ *In time he came to love her.* ○ *I have come to believe that the government's economic policy is misguided.* **8** (used in questions after *how* to ask for an explanation or a reason for sth) [V.to inf] *How did he come to break his leg?* ○ *How do you come to be so late?* Compare HOW COME. **9** ~ **sth** (with sb) (*Brit infml*) to behave in the specified way: [V-n] *Don't come the bully with me!* ○ *She tried to come the innocent but I was not deceived.* **10** (*infml*) (used only in the form **come** before an expression of time) when the specified time comes: *We'll have been married for two years come Christmas.* ○ *Come* (ie By) *next week she'll have changed her mind.* **11** [V] (*infml*) to have a sexual ORGASM. **12** (used with *to* or *into* + *n* in many expressions to show that the state or condition indicated by the *n* has been reached, eg *At last winter came to an end*, ie ended; *The trees are coming into leaf*, ie starting to grow leaves; for similar expressions, see entries for *ns*, eg **come to grief** ⇨ GRIEF).

IDM Most idioms containing **come** are at the entries for the nouns or adjectives in the idioms, eg **come a cropper** ⇨ CROPPER. **be as ‚clever, ˌstupid, etc as they ˈcome** (*infml*) to be very clever, stupid, etc. ‚**come aˈgain?** (*infml*) (used to ask sb to repeat sth because one does not understand it or can hardly believe it): *'She's an entomologist.' 'Come again?' 'An entomologist — she studies insects.'* ‚**come and ˈgo** to exist or be present in a place for a short time and then stop or depart: *The pain in my leg comes and goes* (ie Sometimes my leg is painful and sometimes it is not). ○ *Governments come and go* (ie One government is replaced by another) *but does anything really change?* **come ˈeasily, ˈnaturally, etc to sb** (of an activity, a skill, etc) to be easy, natural, etc for sb to do: *Acting comes naturally to her.* ˈ**come it** (*Brit sl*) to behave rudely or without respect towards sb: *Don't come it with me, young man!* ‚**come over ˈfaint, ˈdizzy, ˈgiddy, etc** (*Brit infml*) to feel suddenly faint¹(2b), etc: *I suddenly came over (all) funny/queer and had to lie down.* **come to ˈnothing; not ˈcome to anything** to have no useful or successful result; to be a complete failure: *How sad that all his hard work should come to ˈnothing.* ○ *Her plans didn't ˈcome to anything.* **come to ˈthat; if it comes to ˈthat** (*infml*) (used to introduce sth that is connected with and in addition to what has just been mentioned): *He looks just like his dog — come to that, so does his wife!* ‚**come what ˈmay** despite any problems or difficulties that may occur: *He promised to support her come what may.* **how ˈcome (...)?** (*infml*) how does/did it happen (that...)?; what is the explanation (of sth)?: *If she spent five years in Paris, how come she can't speak a word of French?* ○ *You were an hour late this morning — how ˈcome?* **not ˈcome to much** not to be, become or do anything of importance: *He'll never come to much* (ie have a successful career) *— he's too lazy.* ○ *I don't think her idea of becoming a journalist ever came to much.* **to ˈcome** (used after a *n*) in the future: *in years to come* ○ *for some time to come* (ie for a period of time in the future). **when it comes to sth / doing sth** when it is a case, matter or question of sth/doing sth: *I'm as good a cook as she is except when it comes to (making) pastry.* **PHRV** ‚**come aˈbout** (of a boat) to change direction. ‚**come aˈbout (that...)** to happen: *Can you tell me how the accident came about?* ○ *How did it come about that he knew where we were?*

‚**come aˈcross** (also ‚**come ˌover**, ‚**come ˈthrough**) **1** to be understood or communicated: *He spoke for a long time but his meaning didn't really come across.* **2** to make an impression of the specified type: *She comes across well/badly in interviews.* ○ *He*

came over as sympathetic/as a sympathetic person.
'**come across sb/sth** to meet or find sb/sth by chance: *I came across an old school friend in Oxford Street this morning.* ○ *She ˌcame across some old ˈphotographs in a drawer.*
'**come after sb** to chase or pursue sb: *We only realized it was private land when the owner came after us with a big stick.*
ˌ**come aˈlong 1** to arrive; to appear: *When the right opportunity comes along, she'll take it.* ○ *'Is she married?' 'No. She says she's waiting for the right man to come along.'* **2** = COME ON 3. **3** = COME ON 4.
ˌ**come aˈpart** to break or fall into pieces: *The book just came apart in my hands.*
ˌ**come aˈround (to ...)** = COME ROUND (TO ...).
ˌ**come aˈround (to sth)** = COME ROUND (TO STH).
'**come at sb** (also '**come for sb**) to attack sb: *She came at me with a rolling-pin.* '**come at sth** to discover facts, the truth, etc: *The truth is often difficult to 'come at.*
ˌ**come aˈway (from sth)** to become detached from sth: *The plaster had started to come away from the wall.* ˌ**come aˈway with sth** to leave a place with a feeling, an impression, etc: *We came away with the distinct impression that all was not well with their marriage.*
ˌ**come ˈback 1** to return: *You came back* (ie came home) *very late last night.* ○ *The colour is coming back to her cheeks.* **2** to become popular, successful or fashionable again: *Miniskirts are starting to come back.* **3** (of a rule, law or system) to be restored or put back into operation: *Some people would like to see the death penalty come back.* ˌ**come ˈback at sb** to reply to sb forcefully or angrily: *She came back at the speaker with some sharp questions.* ˌ**come ˈback (to sb)** to return to sb's memory: *It's all coming back to me now* (ie I'm beginning to remember everything). ○ *Once you go to France, your French will soon come back.* ˌ**come ˈback to sb (on sth)** to reply to sb about sth after a period of time: *Can I come back to you on that one* (ie on that subject) *later?* ˌ**come ˈback to sth** to return to a subject, idea, etc: *Let's come back to the point at issue.* ○ *It all comes back to a question of money.*
'**come before sb/sth 1** to be presented to sb/sth for discussion, decision or judgement: *The case ˌcomes before the ˈcourt next week.* **2** to have greater importance than sb/sth else: *Fighting poverty and unemployment should come before all other political considerations.*
'**come between sb and sb** to disturb or harm a relationship between two people: *It's not a good idea to come between a man and his wife.* ○ *I'd hate anything to come between us.* '**come between sb and sth** to prevent sb from doing or having sth: *He never lets anything come between him and his evening pint of beer.*
ˌ**come ˈby** = COME ROUND (TO ...). '**come by sth 1** to obtain sth, usu by effort: *Jobs are hard to come by these days.* **2** to receive sth: *How did you come by that scratch on your cheek?*
ˌ**come ˈdown 1** to collapse: *The ceiling came down with a terrific crash.* **2** (of rain, snow, etc) to fall: *The rain came down in torrents.* **3** (of an aircraft) to land or fall from the sky: *We were forced to come down in a field.* ○ *Two of our fighters came down inside enemy lines.* **4** (of prices, the temperature, etc) to become lower; to fall: *The price of petrol is coming down/Petrol is coming down in price.* **5** to reach a decision in favour of/against sth: *The committee came down in support of his application.* ○ *come down against the proposal.* ˌ**come ˈdown (from ...)** (*Brit*) to leave a university (esp Oxford or Cambridge) after finishing one's studies: *When did you come down (from Oxford)?* ˌ**come ˈdown (from ...) (to ...)** to come from one place to another, esp (in Britain) from the North of England to London, or from a city or large

town to a smaller place: *We hope to come down to London next week.* ○ *They've recently come down from New York to live in the country.* ˌ**come ˈdown on sb** (*infml*) **1** to criticize sb severely: *Don't come down too hard on her.* **2** to punish sb: *The courts are coming down heavily on young offenders.* ˌ**come ˈdown on sb for sth** (*infml*) to demand payment or money from sb: *His creditors came down on him for prompt payment of his bills.* ˌ**come ˈdown to sb** to be passed from one generation to another: *stories that came down to us from our ancestors.* ˌ**come ˈdown to sth 1** to reach as far down as a specified point: *Her hair comes down to her waist.* **2** to be a simple matter of sth: *It comes down to two choices: either you improve your work, or you leave.* ○ *The whole dispute comes down to a power struggle between management and trade unions.* ˌ**come ˈdown with sth** to become ill with a specified illness: *I came down with the flu and was unable to go to work.*
come for sb = COME AT SB.
ˌ**come ˈforward** to offer one's help, services, etc: *come forward with help/information/money* ○ *Police have asked witnesses of the accident to come forward.*
'**come from ...** (not used in the continuous tenses) to have as one's place of birth or place of residence: *She comes from London.* ○ *Where do you come from?* '**come from ... /sth** to be a product of or originate from a place or a thing: *Much of the butter eaten in Britain comes from New Zealand.* ○ *Milk comes from cows and goats.* ○ *This poem comes from his new book.* ○ *Where does all her hostility come from?* '**come from sth** (also **come of sth**) to have certain people as one's ancestors: *She comes from/of a long line of actors.* **come from doing sth** = COME OF STH/DOING STH.
ˌ**come ˈin 1** (of the tide) to move towards the land; to rise: *The tide was coming in fast.* **2** to finish a race in a particular position: *Which horse came in first?* **3** to become fashionable: *Long hair for men came in in the sixties.* **4** to become available at a particular time of the year: *Strawberries usually come in in late June.* **5** to be received as income: *She has over a thousand pounds a month coming in from her investments.* **6** to have a part in sth: *I understand the plan perfectly, but I can't see where I come in.* **7** (of news, a report, etc) to be received by a television station, the offices of a newspaper, etc: *News is coming in of a serious train crash in Scotland.* **8** to contribute to a discussion: *Would you like to come in at this point, bishop?* ˌ**come ˈin for sth** to receive sth; to be the object of sth, esp sth unpleasant: *The government's economic policies have come in for a lot of criticism in the newspapers.* ˌ**come ˈin on sth** to have a part or share in sth; to join sth: *If you want to come in on the scheme, you must decide now.* ˌ**come ˈin with sb** (*infml*) to join sb in a scheme, project, etc.
ˌ**come ˈinto sth** to inherit sth: *She came into a fortune when her uncle died.* **2** to be important or relevant to sth: *If he's the best person for the job, the colour of his skin shouldn't come into it.*
'**come of sth** = COME FROM STH. **come of sth / doing sth** (also **come from doing sth**) to be the result of sth: *He promised to help, but I don't think anything will come of it.* ○ *This is what comes of being over-confident.* ○ *No harm can come from trying.*
ˌ**come ˈoff 1** to be able to be removed: *'Does this knob come off?' 'No, it's fixed on permanently.'* ○ *These stains won't come off, I'm afraid.* **2** (*infml*) to take place; to happen: *When's the wedding coming off?* ○ *Did your proposed trip to Rome ever come off?* **3** (*infml*) (of a plan, scheme, etc) to be successful; to have the intended effect or result: *Her attempt to break the world record nearly came off.* ○ *The play doesn't quite come off.* **4** (*infml*) (followed by an *adv*) to have the specified result after a fight, contest, etc: *He always comes off badly in his fights with other boys.* ○ *Who came off best in the debate?* ˌ**come ˈoff**

(sth) 1 to fall from sth: *come off one's bicycle/horse.*
2 to become detached or separated from sth: *When I tried to lift the jug, the handle came off (in my hand).* ○ *Lipstick often comes off on wine glasses.* ○ *A button has come off my coat.* ¦**come ˈoff it** (*infml*) (used in the imperative to tell sb to stop saying things that one thinks or knows are not true): *Come off it! We don't have a chance of winning.* ¦**come ˈoff sth 1** (of an amount of money) to be removed from a price: *I've heard that ten pence a gallon is coming off the price of petrol.* **2** to stop taking medicine, a drug, etc: *come off the pill/drugs/drink.*

¦**come ˈon 1** (of an actor) to walk onto the stage. **2** (of a player) to join a team during a match: *Robson came on in place of Wilkins ten minutes before the end of the game.* **3** (also ¦**come aˈlong**) (esp with an *adv*) to make progress; to grow; to improve: *The garden is coming on nicely.* ○ *Her baby is coming on well.* ○ *His French has come on a lot since he joined the conversation class.* **4** (also ¦**come aˈlong**) (used in the imperative to encourage sb to do sth, eg to hurry, try harder, be more sensible, etc): *Come on, we'll be late for the theatre.* ○ *Come along now, someone must know the answer.* ○ *Come on, you don't really believe that.* **5** (esp in the continuous tenses) to begin: *I've got a cold coming on.* ○ *I think there's rain coming on.* ○ *It's getting colder: winter is coming on.* **6** (of a film, play, etc) to be shown or performed: *There's a new play coming on at the local theatre next week.* ○ *What time does the news come on?* ¦**come on/ upon sb/sth** (*fml*) to meet or find sb/sth by chance: *I came upon a group of children playing in the street.* ¦**come ˈon to sth** to start talking about a subject: *I'd like to come on to that question later.*

¦**come ˈout 1** (of the sun, moon or stars) to become visible; to appear: *The rain stopped and the sun came out.* **2** (of plants) to begin to appear or produce flowers: *The crocuses came out late this year because of the cold weather.* **3** to be produced or published: *When is her new novel coming out?* **4** (of news, the truth, etc) to become known; to be told or revealed: *The full story came out at the trial.* ○ *It came out that he'd been telling a pack of lies.* **5** (of photographs) to be developed (DEVELOP 3): *Our holiday photos didn't come out* (eg because the film was faulty). **6** to be revealed or shown clearly: *The bride comes out well* (ie looks attractive) *in the photographs.* ○ *His arrogance comes out in every speech he makes.* ○ *Her best qualities come out in a crisis.* ○ *The meaning of the poem doesn't really come out in his interpretation.* **7** (of words, a speech, etc) to be spoken: *I tried to say 'I love you,' but the words wouldn't come out.* **8** to say publicly whether one agrees or disagrees with sth: *In her speech, the minister came out in favour of a change in the law.* ○ *He came out against the plan.* **9** to stop work; to strike¹(1): *The miners have come out (on strike).* **10** (of a young girl) to be formally introduced to high society: (*dated*) *Fiona came out last season.* ○ *a coming-out ball.* **11** (of a sum, problem, etc) to be solved: *I can't make this equation come out.* **12** to declare openly that one is a HOMOSEXUAL: *She's been much happier since she came out.* **13** to have a specified position after doing sth: *She came out first in the examination.* ¦**come ˈout (of sth) 1** (of an object) to be removed from a place where it is fixed: *The little girl's tooth came out when she bit into the apple.* ○ *I can't get this screw to come out of the wall.* **2** (of dirt, etc) to be removed from sth by washing, cleaning, etc: *These ink stains won't come out (of my dress).* ○ *Will the colour come out* (ie fade or disappear) *if the material is washed?* ¦**come ˈout at sth** to amount to a particular cost or sum: *The total bill comes out at £500.* ¦**come ˈout in sth** (of the skin) to become partially covered in spots, etc: *Hot weather makes her come out in a rash.* ¦**come ˈout of one-self** to relax and become more confident and friendly with others: *You need to come out of yourself*

a bit more! ¦**come ˈout of sth 1** to originate in or develop from sth: *The book he wrote came out of his experiences in India.* ○ *Rock music came out of the blues.* **2** to be in a specified state as a result of sth: *They came out of the deal considerably poorer.* ¦**come ˈout with sth** to say sth; to express sth: *He came out with a stream of abuse.* ○ *She sometimes comes out with the most extraordinary remarks.*

¦**come ˈover** = COME ACROSS. ¦**come ˈover (to ...)** = COME ROUND (TO ...). ¦**come ˈover (to ...) (from ...)** to travel from one, usu distant, place to another: *Why don't you come over to England for a holiday?* ○ *Her grandparents came over* (eg to America) *from Ireland during the famine.* ¦**come ˈover (to sth)** to change from one side, opinion, etc to another: *a Labour MP who came over to the Liberals.* ¦**come ˈover sb** (of a feeling) to affect sb: *A fit of dizziness came over her.* ○ *I can't think what came over me* (ie I do not know what caused me to behave in that way).

¦**come ˈround** (also *esp US* **come aˈround**) **1** to come by a longer route than usual: *The road was blocked so we had to come round by the fields.* **2** (of a regular event) to occur again: *Christmas seems to come round quicker every year.* **3** (also ¦**come ˈto**) to regain consciousness, esp after fainting (FAINT²): *Throw some water on his face — he'll soon come round.* ○ *Your husband hasn't yet come round after the anaesthetic.* **4** (*infml*) to become happy again after being in a bad mood: *Don't scold the boy; he'll come round in time.* ¦**come ˈround/aˈround (to ...)** (also ¦**come ˈover (to ...**), ¦**come ˈby**) to visit sb or a place, usu within the same town, city, etc: *Do come round and see us some time.* ○ *Why don't you come around (to my apartment) this evening?* ¦**come ˈround (to sth)** (also ¦**come aˈround (to sth)**) to be converted to sb else's opinion or view: *She will never come round (to our way of thinking).*

¦**come ˈthrough 1** = COME ACROSS. **2** (of news, a message) to arrive by telephone, radio, etc or through official channels: *A message is just coming through.* ○ *Your posting has just come through: you're going to Hong Kong.* ¦**come ˈthrough (sth)** to recover from a serious illness or avoid serious injury; to survive sth: *He's very ill but doctors expect him to come through.* ○ *With such a weak heart she was lucky to come through (the operation).* ○ *She came through without even a scratch* (eg was not even slightly injured in the accident). ○ *He has come through two world wars.* ¦**come ˈthrough with sth** to give sb sth that is owed to them or that they are waiting for: *The bank finally came through with my new cheque-book.*

¦**come ˈto** = COME ROUND 3. ¦**come to oneˈself** to return to one's normal state: *The shock made her hesitate for a moment but she quickly came to herself again.* ˈ**come to sb (that ...)** (of an idea) to occur to sb: *The idea came to me in my bath.* ○ *It suddenly came to her that she had been wrong all along.* ˈ**come to sb (from sb)** (of money, property, etc) to be inherited by sb: *The farm came to him on his father's death.* ○ *He has a lot of money coming to him when his uncle dies.* ˈ**come to sth 1** to amount to sth; to be equal to sth: *The bill came to $30.* ○ *I never expected those few items to come to so much.* **2** (used esp with *this*, *that* or *what* as object) to reach a particular (usu bad) situation or state of affairs: *The doctors will operate if it proves necessary — but it may not come to that.* ○ *'There's been another terrorist bomb attack.' 'Really? I don't know what the world is coming to.'* ○ *Things have come to such a state in the company that he's thinking of resigning.* ○ *Who'd have thought things would come to this* (ie become so bad or unpleasant)?

ˈ**come under sth 1** to be included within a certain category: *What heading does this come under?* **2** to be the target of sth: *The head teacher came under a lot of criticism from the parents.*

C

,come 'up 1 (of plants) to appear above the soil: *The daffodils are just beginning to come up.* 2 (of the sun) to rise: *We watched the sun come up.* 3 to occur, esp unexpectedly: *We'll let you know if any vacancies come up.* ○ *I'm afraid something urgent has come up; I won't be able to see you tonight.* 4 to be mentioned or discussed: *The subject came up in conversation.* ○ *The question is bound to come up at the meeting.* 5 (of a specified event or time) to be about to happen: *Her birthday is coming up soon.* 6 to be dealt with by a court of law: *Her divorce case comes up next month.* 7 (of a ticket, number, etc in betting games) to be drawn; to win: *My number came up and I won £100.* ,come 'up (to ...) (*Brit*) to begin one's studies at a university, esp at Oxford or Cambridge: *She came up (to Oxford) in 1994.* ,come 'up (to ...) (from ...) to come to one place from another, esp (in Britain) from a smaller place to London or from the South to the North of England: *She often comes up to London* (eg from Oxford) *at weekends.* ○ *Why don't you come up to Scotland for a few days?* ,come 'up (to sb) to approach sb, eg to talk: *He came up (to me) and asked for a light.* ,come 'up against sb/sth to be faced with or opposed by sb/sth: *We expect to come up against a lot of opposition to the scheme.* ,come 'up for sth to be considered as a candidate for sth: *She comes up for re-election next year.* ,come 'up to sth 1 to reach up as far as a specified point: *The water came up to my neck.* 2 to reach an acceptable level or standard: *His performance didn't really come up to his usual high standard.* ○ *Their trip to France didn't come up to expectations.* ,come 'up with sth to find or produce an answer, a sum of money, etc: *She came up with a new idea for increasing sales.* ○ *How soon can you come up with the money?*

'come upon sb/sth = COME ON/UPON SB/STH.

▶ **come** *interj* (used to encourage sb to be sensible or reasonable, or to show slight disapproval): *Oh come (now), things aren't as bad as that.* ○ *Come, come, Miss Jones, be careful what you say.*

■ ,come-'hither *adj* [attrib] (*dated infml*) (of a look or manner) suggesting that one would like to have sex with sb; flirtatious (FLIRT): *a ,come-hither 'glance/'smile.*

'come-on *n* (*usu sing*) (*infml*) a gesture, remark, description, etc that is intended to attract one or persuade one to do sth: *the come-on of holiday brochures* ○ *She gave him the come-on* (ie tried to attract him sexually).

comeback /'kʌmbæk/ *n* 1 a return to a former successful position: *an ageing pop star trying to make/stage a comeback.* 2 (*infml*) a quick reply to a critical remark.

comedian /kə'miːdiən/ *n* (*fem* **comedienne** /kə,miːdi'en/) 1 an entertainer on stage, television, etc who makes people laugh by telling jokes, etc: *a stand-up comedian* ○ (*fig*) *He seems to regard himself as the office comedian.* 2 an actor who plays comic parts.

comedown /'kʌmdaʊn/ *n* (*usu sing*) (*infml*) a loss of importance or social position: *Having to work as a clerk is a real comedown for him after running his own business.*

comedy /'kɒmədi/ *n* 1(a) [C] a light or amusing play or film, usu with a happy ending: *a musical comedy.* (b) [U] plays or films of this type: *I prefer comedy to tragedy.* Compare TRAGEDY 2. 2 [U] an amusing aspect of sth; humour: *He didn't appreciate the comedy of the situation.* ○ *the slapstick comedy of silent films.* See also BLACK COMEDY, SITUATION COMEDY.

comely /'kʌmli/ *adj* (-lier, -liest) (*dated or fml*) (esp of a woman) pleasant to look at; attractive.

comer /'kʌmə(r)/ *n* 1 (*usu pl*) a person who comes: *The race is open to* ***all comers*** (ie Anyone may take

part in it). 2 (*infml esp US*) a person who is likely to be successful.

comet /'kɒmɪt/ *n* an object that moves round the sun and looks like a bright star with a tail.

comeuppance /kʌm'ʌpəns/ *n* [sing] (*infml*) a punishment or fate that one deserves: *I'd like to see him* ***get his comeuppance.***

comfort /'kʌmfət/ *n* 1 [U] the state of being free from suffering, pain or worry; feeling at ease: *live in comfort.* ○ *They did everything for our comfort.* 2 [U] help or kindness to sb who is suffering; CONSOLATION: *a few words of comfort* ○ *draw/take comfort from sb's words* ○ *The news brought comfort to all of us.* 3 [sing] a person or thing that brings relief or CONSOLATION: *Her children are a great comfort to her.* ○ *It's a comfort to know that she is safe.* 4 [C esp pl] a thing that brings physical comfort: *The hotel has all modern comforts/every modern comfort* (eg central heating, hot and cold water, etc). ○ *He likes his comforts.* See also CREATURE COMFORTS. **cold comfort** ▷ COLD[1].

▶ **comfort** *v* to give comfort(2) to sb: [Vn] *comfort a dying man* ○ *The child ran to its mother to be comforted.* **comforting** *adj* giving comfort(2): *a comforting smile* ○ *It is comforting to know we have your support.* **comfortingly** *adv.*

comfortless *adj* without comforts (COMFORT 4): *a comfortless room.*

comfortable /'kʌmftəbl, -fət-/ *adj* 1(a) allowing one to relax pleasantly: *a comfortable bed/position/room.* (b) relaxing pleasantly: *She made herself comfortable in a big chair.* ○ *The patient is comfortable* (ie is not in pain) *after his operation.* 2 free from difficulty, fear or worry: *a comfortable life/job* ○ *I never feel very comfortable in his presence.* ○ *He's still not entirely comfortable with the idea.* 3 [pred] (*infml*) quite wealthy: *They may not be millionaires but they're certainly very comfortable.* 4 more than adequate; quite large: *a comfortable income* ○ *She won by a comfortable margin.*

▶ **comfortably** /-təbli/ *adv* 1 in a comfortable way: *All the rooms were comfortably furnished.* 2 by a clear margin: *The favourite won the race comfortably.* **comfortably 'off** having enough money to live in comfort.

comforter /'kʌmfətə(r)/ *n* 1 a person or thing that comforts. 2 (*Brit*) (*US* **pacifier**) = DUMMY 3. 3 (*US*) a QUILT.

comfy /'kʌmfi/ *adj* (-ier, -iest) (*infml*) comfortable.

comic /'kɒmɪk/ *adj* 1 [usu attrib] making people laugh; funny: *a comic song/performance* ○ *His accident with the hose brought some welcome* ***comic relief*** *to a very dull party.* 2 [attrib] of comedy: *comic opera* ○ *a comic actor.*

▶ **comic** *n* 1 a COMEDIAN(1): *a popular TV comic.* 2 (*US* 'comic book) a magazine, esp for children, containing stories told mainly in pictures.

comical /'kɒmɪkl/ *adj* amusing, often because odd or absurd: *He looked highly comical wearing that tiny hat.* **comically** /-kli/ *adv*: *clothes that were almost comically inappropriate.*

■ 'comic strip (also ,strip car'toon) *n* a sequence of drawings telling a story, printed in newspapers, etc.

coming /'kʌmɪŋ/ *n* [sing] an arrival: *the coming of the space age.* ,**comings and 'goings** (*infml*) arrivals and departures: *the constant comings and goings at a hotel* ○ *With all the comings and goings* (eg of visitors) *I haven't been able to do any work at all.*

▶ **coming** *adj* [attrib] approaching; next: *in the coming week* ○ *This coming Sunday is her birthday.*

comma /'kɒmə/ (*pl* **commas**) *n* the mark (,) used in writing and printing to indicate a slight pause or break between parts of a sentence. See also INVERTED COMMAS. ▷ App 3.

command¹ /kəˈmɑːnd; US -ˈmænd/ v **1** (of sb in authority) to tell sb that they must do sth; to order: [V, Vn] *Do as I command (you).* [Vn] *(rhet) I am yours to command* (ie Tell me what you want me to do)*!* [V.*that*] *(fml) The tribunal has commanded that all copies of the book (must) be destroyed.* [Vn. *to* inf] *The officer commanded his men to fire.* ⇨ note at ORDER². **2** to have authority over sb/sth; to be in control of sb/sth: [V] *Does seniority give one the right to command?* [Vn] *The ship's captain commands all the officers and men.* **3** (no passive) to deserve and get sth: [Vn] *Great men command our respect.* ∘ *The plight of the famine victims commands everyone's sympathy.* **4** (no passive) (of a place, fort, etc) to be placed so as to control sth: *The castle commanded the entrance to the valley.* ∘ *(fig) The house commands a fine view.* **5** *(fml)* (no passive) to have sth ready to use: [Vn] *command funds/skill/resources* ∘ *She commands a six-figure salary.*

▶ **commanding** *adj* **1** [attrib] having the authority to give formal orders: *one's commanding officer.* **2** [usu attrib] in a position to control or dominate: *The fort occupies a commanding position.* ∘ *One team has already built up a **commanding lead**.* **3** [usu attrib] seeming to have authority; impressive: *a commanding voice/tone/look.*

command² /kəˈmɑːnd; US -ˈmænd/ n **1** [C] **(a)** an order: *Her commands were quickly obeyed.* ∘ *Give your commands in a loud, confident voice.* **(b)** *(computing)* an instruction to a computer. **2** [U] *(esp military)* control; authority: *to have/take command of a regiment* ∘ *He should not be given command of troops.* ∘ *Who is **in command** (ie in charge) here?* ∘ *The army is **under the command** of General Smith.* ∘ *He has twenty men under his command.* See also SECOND IN COMMAND. **3** Command [C] a part of an army, air force, etc organized and controlled separately: *Western Command* ∘ *Bomber Command.* **4** [U, sing] ~ **(of sth)** the ability to use or control sth: *He has (a) good command of the French language* (ie can speak it well). ∘ *She has enormous funds at her command.* ∘ *He has no command over himself* (ie cannot control his feelings, temper, etc).

IDM at/by sb's comˈmand *(fml)* having been ordered by sb: *I am here at the King's command.* **be at sb's comˈmand** to be ready to obey sb. **your wish is my command** ⇨ WISH *n.*

■ **comˌmand perˈformance** *n* a performance of a play, film, etc given at the request of a head of state (who usu attends).

commandant /ˈkɒməndænt/ n (often as a title) the officer in charge of a particular military force or institution: *the refugee camp commandant* ∘ *Commandant Macdonald.*

commandeer /ˌkɒmənˈdɪə(r)/ v to take possession or control of vehicles, buildings, etc by force or for official, esp military, purposes: [Vn] *commandeering private cars to transport troops.*

commander /kəˈmɑːndə(r); US -ˈmæn-/ n **1** a person who is in charge of sth: *the commander of the expedition.* **2(a)** (the title of) a senior officer in the British or American Navy. ⇨ App 6. **(b)** (in Britain) a London police officer of high rank.

■ **comˌmander-in-ˈchief** n (pl **commanders-in-chief**) the commander of all the armed forces of a country.

commandment /kəˈmɑːndmənt; US -ˈmænd-/ n (in the Bible) any of **the Ten Commandments**, ten laws given by God to the Jews: *keep/break God's commandments.*

commando /kəˈmɑːndəʊ; US -ˈmæn-/ n (pl **-os**) (a member of) a group of soldiers specially trained for carrying out quick attacks in enemy areas.

commemorate /kəˈmeməreɪt/ v **(a)** to keep a great person, event, etc in people's memories: [Vn] *We commemorate the founding of our nation with a public holiday.* **(b)** (of a statue, etc) to remind people of sb/sth: [Vn] *This memorial commemorates those who died in the war.*

▶ **commemoration** /kəˌmeməˈreɪʃn/ n [C, U] (an act of or ceremony for) commemorating sb/sth: *a statue **in commemoration of** a national hero.*

commemorative /kəˈmemərətɪv; US -ˈmemərett-/ adj helping to commemorate sb/sth: *commemorative stamps/medals.*

commence /kəˈmens/ v *(fml)* to begin or make sth begin; to start: [V, Vn] *Shall we commence (the ceremony)?* [V.*ing*] *The new trains will commence running next month.* [also V.*to* inf].

▶ **commencement** n [UC usu *sing*] **1** *(fml)* beginning. **2** *(esp US)* a ceremony at which academic degrees are officially given.

commend /kəˈmend/ v **1** ~ **sb (on/for sth)**; ~ **sb/ sth (to sb)** to praise or recommend sb/sth: [Vn] *Her work was highly commended.* ∘ *The book has much to commend it.* [Vnpr] *The journalist was commended for his reporting of the case.* ∘ *His reputation does not commend him to me.* **2** ~ **oneself/itself to sb** *(fml)* to be acceptable to sb; to be liked by sb: [Vnpr] *a plan which is unlikely to commend itself to the public.* **3** ~ **sb/oneself/sth to sb** *(fml)* to put sb/ oneself/sth into the care of sb: [Vnpr] *Almighty God, we commend to Your loving care all who suffer* (ie as a prayer).

▶ **commendable** /-əbl/ adj deserving praise: *The police showed commendable restraint in the face of great provocation.* **commendably** /-əbli/ adv.

commendation /ˌkɒmenˈdeɪʃn/ n **(a)** [U] praise; approval. **(b)** [C] ~ **(for sth)** an award involving the giving of special praise: *a commendation for bravery* ∘ *Her painting won a commendation from the teacher.*

commensurate /kəˈmenʃərət/ adj ~ **(with sth)** *(fml)* in the right proportion (to sth); appropriate: *Her low salary is not commensurate with her abilities.*

comment /ˈkɒment/ n [C, U] ~ **(on sth)** a written or spoken remark giving an opinion on, explaining or criticizing an event, a person, a situation, etc: *Have you any comment(s) to make on the recent developments?* ∘ *His behaviour has aroused much comment* (ie caused a lot of talk, gossip, etc). ∘ *In the next hour we shall be presenting news and comment from around the world.* **IDM** ˌno ˈcomment (said in reply to a question) I have nothing to say about that: *'Will you resign, sir?' 'No comment!'*

▶ **comment** v ~ **(on sth)** to make comments; to give one's opinion: [V, Vpr] *He refused to comment (on the case) until after the trial.* [V.*that*] *Asked about the date of the election, the prime minister commented that no decision had yet been made.*

commentary /ˈkɒməntri; US -ˈteri/ n **1** [C, U] ~ **(on sth)** a spoken description of an event as it happens: *a broadcast commentary on a football game* ∘ *Our reporters will give us **a running commentary** on the election results as they are announced.* **2** [C] ~ **(on sth)** a set of notes explaining the text of a book, etc: *a Bible commentary.*

commentate /ˈkɒmənteɪt/ v ~ **(on sth)** to describe, an event as it happens, esp on television or radio: [Vpr] *commentate on an athletics meeting* [also V].

▶ **commentator** /ˈkɒmənteɪtə(r)/ n ~ **(on sth)** **1** a person who commentates: *a sports commentator.* **2** a person who writes or speaks on current affairs: *an informed commentator on political events.*

commerce /ˈkɒmɜːs/ n [U] trade, esp between countries; the buying and selling of goods: *leaders of industry and commerce* ∘ *commerce with foreign nations.* See also CHAMBER OF COMMERCE.

commercial /kəˈmɜːʃl/ adj **1** [usu attrib] engaged in or concerned with commerce: *commercial law* ∘ *commercial activities such as finance* ∘ *doing a commercial course at the local college.* **2(a)** [attrib]

[V.speech] = verb + direct speech   [V.*that*] = verb + *that* clause   [V.*wh*] = verb + *who, how,* etc clause

making or intended to make a profit: *The play was a commercial success* (ie made money). ○ *Oil is present in commercial quantities* (ie There is enough to make it profitable). (**b**) (*often derog*) intended to make a profit, esp without regard to quality, etc: *His later paintings are far too commercial.* **3** (of television or radio) paid for by the money charged for broadcasting advertisements: *I work for a commercial radio station.*
▶ **commercial** *n* an advertisement on television or radio.

commercialism /kə'mɜːʃəlɪzəm/ *n* [U] (*derog*) practices and attitudes that are too concerned with the making of profit: *excessive commercialism in the theatre.*

commercialize, -ise /kə'mɜːʃəlaɪz/ *v* (*often derog*) (esp passive) to make money or try to make money out of sth: [Vn] *Sport has become much more commercialized in recent years.* ○ *Christmas is far too commercialized.*

commercially /-ʃəli/ *adv*: *The product is not yet commercially available.* (ie You cannot buy it in the shops yet.) ○ *Commercially, the play was a failure, though the critics loved it.*

■ **com,mercial 'art** *n* [U] art used in advertising, selling, etc.

com,mercial 'break *n* a planned interruption of a television or radio programme for advertisements.

com,mercial 'traveller (also **travelling salesman**) *n* a person who travels over a large area visiting shops, etc with samples of goods, trying to obtain orders.

com,mercial 'vehicle *n* a van, lorry, etc for transporting goods.

commiserate /kə'mɪzəreɪt/ *v* ~ (**with** *sb*) (**for / on / over** *sth*) to feel or say that one feels sympathy: *I commiserated with her on the death of her pet dog.* [also V, V.speech].
▶ **commiseration** /kə,mɪzə'reɪʃn/ *n* [C usu *pl*, U] ~ (**for/on/over** *sth*) (an expression of) sympathy for sb: *We offer our congratulations to the winner and commiserations to the gallant losers.*

commission /kə'mɪʃn/ *n* **1** [C] ~ (**to do** *sth*) an action, task or piece of work given to sb to do: *She has received many commissions to design public buildings.* **2** [C, U] (an amount of) money paid to sb for selling goods which increases with the quantity of goods sold: *You get (a) 10% commission on everything you sell.* ○ *earn £2 000 (in) commission* ○ *She is working for us **on commission*** (ie is not paid a salary, but receives a part of the value of the things she sells). **3** (often **Commission**) [C] (**a**) a group of important officials chosen for a particular responsibility: *the European Commission.* (**b**) ~ (**on** *sth*) a group of people officially chosen to investigate sth and write a report: *a Royal Commission on gambling* ○ *set up a commission to look into the matter.* **4** [U] ~ (**of** *sth*) (*fml*) doing sth wrong or illegal: *the commission of a crime.* **5** [C] the rank of an officer in the armed forces: *He resigned his commission to take up a civilian job.* **IDM** **in/out of com'mission** available/not available for use: *Some wartime vessels are still in commission.* ○ *With several of their planes temporarily out of commission, the airline is losing money.* ○ (*fig*) *I got flu and was out of commission for a week.*
▶ **commission** *v* **1**(**a**) to give a commission(1) to sb: [Vn.to inf] *commission an artist to paint a picture* [also Vn]. (**b**) to give sb the job of making sth: [Vn] *He commissioned a statue of his wife.* **2** ~ *sb* **as** *sth* (usu passive) to appoint sb officially by means of a commission(5): [Vn-n] *She was commissioned (as a) lieutenant in the Women's Army Corps.*
■ **com,missioned 'officer** *n* an officer in the armed forces who holds a commission(5), esp one who has been specially trained as an officer.

commissionaire /kə,mɪʃə'neə(r)/ *n* (*becoming*

dated esp Brit) a person in uniform at the entrance to a cinema, theatre, hotel, etc whose job is to open the door for people, find them taxis, etc.

commissioner /kə'mɪʃənə(r)/ *n* **1** (usu **Commissioner**) a member of a commission(3), esp one with particular duties: *the Church Commissioners* (ie the group of people responsible for managing the financial affairs of the Church of England) ○ *European Commissioners.* **2** a public official of high rank: *a police commissioner.*

commit /kə'mɪt/ *v* (-**tt**-) **1** to do sth illegal or wrong: [Vn] *commit murder/suicide/theft.* **2** [Vnpr] (**a**) ~ **sb to** *sth* to order sb to be sent to a place for treatment, punishment, etc: *commit a patient to a psychiatric hospital* ○ *commit a man to prison.* (**b**) ~ **sth to** *sth* to transfer sth to a state or place so as to be kept for future use: *commit sth to paper/to writing* (ie write sth down) ○ *commit a list to memory.* **3** ~ **sb/oneself (to** *sth***/to doing** *sth***)** to promise sth or to promise to do sth in a way that makes it impossible to change one's plans: [Vn] *I can't come on Sunday: I'm already committed* (ie I have arranged to do sth else). [Vnpr] *commit oneself to a course of action* ○ *Signing this form commits you to buying the goods.* ○ *The company has committed funds to an advertising campaign.* [Vn.to inf] *He has committed himself to support his brother's children.* **4** ~ **oneself (on** *sth***)** to give one's opinion openly so that it is difficult to change it: [Vn] *I asked her what she thought, but she refused to commit herself.* [also Vnpr]. Compare NON-COMMITTAL. **5** ~ **sb for** *sth* to send sb for a trial in a higher court: [Vnpr] *The magistrates committed him for trial at the Old Bailey.*
▶ **committal** /kə'mɪtl/ *n* [U] the action of committing (COMMIT 2a) sb, esp to prison: *At the committal proceedings the police withdrew their case.*
committed *adj* (*usu approv*) caring a lot about a cause(3), one's job, etc or loyal to a particular ideal: *a committed Christian/doctor/teacher/communist.* Compare UNCOMMITTED.
commitment *n* **1** [C] ~ (**to** *sth* **/ to do** *sth*) a thing one has promised to do: *I will honour my existing commitments but am reluctant to make any more work at present.* ○ *a commitment to pay £100 to charity.* **2** [U] ~ (**to** *sth*) (*approv*) the state of being willing to give a lot of time, work, energy, etc to sth: *We're looking for someone with a real sense of commitment to the job.* **3** [U] ~ (**to** *sth*) the action of committing sb/sth or of being committed (COMMIT 2,3): *the commitment of a patient to a mental hospital* ○ *the commitment of funds to medicine.*

committee /kə'mɪti/ *n* [CGp] a group of people appointed, usu by a larger group, to deal with a particular matter: *a committee meeting/member* ○ *be/sit on a committee* ○ *The committee has/have decided to dismiss him.* ○ *the transport committee* ○ *This was discussed in committee* (ie by the committee).

commode /kə'məʊd/ *n* **1** a piece of furniture like a chair or a small cupboard used to hold a chamberpot (CHAMBER). **2** a chest of drawers (CHEST).

commodious /kə'məʊdiəs/ *adj* (*fml*) having a lot of space available for use: *a commodious house/room/armchair.*

commodity /kə'mɒdəti/ *n* **1** a useful or valuable thing: *household commodities* (eg pots and pans) ○ (*fig*) *She possesses that increasingly rare commodity, a truly independent mind.* **2** (*finance*) an article, a product or a material that is bought and sold, esp between countries: *basic commodities like sugar and cocoa* ○ *Trading in commodities was brisk.* ○ *the commodity/commodities market.*

commodore /'kɒmədɔː(r)/ *n* (the title of) a senior officer in the British or US Navy. ⇨ App 6.

common¹ /'kɒmən/ *adj* (-**er**, -**est**) **1** usual or familiar; happening or found often and in many places: *a common flower/sight/occurrence* ○ *Doctors are still* *trying to find a cure for* **the common cold.** ○ *Is this word in common use?* (ie Is it commonly used?) ○ *Smith is a common English surname.* ○ *Robbery is not common in this area.* ○ *Car thefts are becoming increasingly common.* Compare UNCOMMON. **2** [attrib] ~ **(to sb/sth)** shared by or belonging to two or more people, or most of a group or society: *common property/ownership* ○ *We share a common purpose.* ○ *He and I have a common interest: we both collect stamps.* ○ *He is French and she is German, but they have English as a common language* (ie they can both speak English). ○ *measures taken for the common good* (ie for the benefit of everyone) ○ *A fruity quality is common to all wine made from this grape.* **3** [attrib] without special rank or quality; ordinary: *He's not an officer, but a common soldier.* ○ *the common people* (ie the average citizens of a country) ○ *He's nothing less than* **a common criminal.** **4** (*derog*) showing a lack of good taste¹(6); regarded as being typical of the lower classes; VULGAR(1): *She's so common, shouting like that so all the neighbours can hear!* **5** (*mathematics*) belonging to two or more quantities: *a common factor/multiple.* See also COMMON DENOMINATOR. **IDM** **be common/public knowledge** ⇨ KNOWLEDGE. **¡common or ¹garden** ordinary; not unusual: *It isn't a rare bird, just a common or garden sparrow.* **the ¡common ¹touch** the ability, esp of sb of high rank, to deal with and talk to ordinary people in a friendly way and be liked by them: *A politician needs the common touch.* **make common ¹cause (with sb)** (*fml*) to unite in order to achieve a shared aim: *The rebel factions made common cause (with each other) to overthrow the regime.*

▶ **commonly** *adv* **1** usually; very often: *It's a commonly held opinion.* ○ *Thomas, commonly known as Tom* ○ *The disease is less rare than commonly supposed.* **2** (*derog*) in a common¹(4) manner.

■ **¡common ¹decency** *n* [U] polite behaviour to be expected from a reasonable person: *You'd think he'd have the common decency to apologize for what he said.*

¡common de¹nominator *n* **1** (*mathematics*) a number that can be divided exactly by all the numbers written below the line in a group of fractions. **2** an idea, a quality or an attitude that is shared by all the members of a group: *have difficulty finding a common denominator between them in terms of style.* See also LOWEST COMMON DENOMINATOR (LOW¹).

¡common ¹ground *n* [U] shared opinions, interests, aims, etc: *The two rival parties have no common ground between them.*

¹common land *n* [U] land that belongs to or may be used by the community, esp in a village. Compare COMMON².

¡common ¹law *n* [U] (in England) a system of laws developed from old customs and from decisions made by judges, ie not created by parliament. Compare CASE-LAW, STATUTE LAW. **¡common-law ¹wife**, **¡common-law ¹husband** *ns* a person with whom a man or woman has lived for some time and who is recognized as a wife or husband under common law, without a formal marriage ceremony.

the ¡Common ¹Market *n* [sing] = THE EUROPEAN UNION.

¡common ¹noun *n* (*grammar*) a word that can refer to any member of a class of similar things (eg *book, dog, house* or *knife*).

¹common-room *n* (*Brit*) a room for use of the teachers or students of a school, college, etc when they are not teaching or studying: *the sixth-form common-room.*

¡common ¹sense *n* [U] practical good sense gained from experience of life, not by special study: *It's common sense to keep medicines away from children.* ○ *I like her common-sense approach to everyday problems.*

common² /ˈkɒmən/ *n* an area of open land which anyone may use, usu in or near a village: *cows grazing on the common* ○ *go for a walk on the common.* Compare COMMON LAND. **IDM** **have sth in common (with sb/sth)** to share interests, characteristics, etc: *Jane and I have nothing in common.* ○ *I have nothing in common with Jane.* **in common** for or by all of a group: *land owned in common by the residents.* **in common with sb/sth** together with sb/sth; like sb/sth: *In common with many others, she is finding it hard to get a job.*

commoner /ˈkɒmənə(r)/ *n* one of the common people, not a nobleman. Compare ARISTOCRAT, NOBLEMAN.

commonplace /ˈkɒmənpleɪs/ *adj* **1** (*often derog*) ordinary; not interesting: *a commonplace little man.* **2** not unusual: *Western clothes are now commonplace in Beijing.*

▶ **commonplace** *n* **1** a remark, etc that is ordinary and not new or interesting: *a conversation consisting largely of commonplaces* ○ *The book's 'revelations' are no more than commonplaces.* **2** an event, topic, etc that is ordinary or usual: *Air travel is a commonplace nowadays.*

Commons /ˈkɒmənz/ *n* **the Commons** [pl] = THE HOUSE OF COMMONS.

commonwealth /ˈkɒmənwelθ/ *n* **1** [C] (**a**) an independent state or community: *measures for the good of the commonwealth.* (**b**) (usu **Commonwealth**) a group of states that have chosen to be politically linked: *the Commonwealth of Australia.* **2** **the Commonwealth** [sing] the association consisting of the United Kingdom and various independent states and dependencies (DEPENDENCY) which used to be part of the British Empire.

commotion /kəˈməʊʃn/ *n* [U, C] (an instance of) noisy confusion or excitement: *The children are making a lot of commotion.* ○ *Suddenly, there was a great commotion next door.*

communal /ˈkɒmjənl, kəˈmjuːnl/ *adj* **1(a)** for the use of all; shared: *communal land/facilities/property* ○ *The apartment has four separate bedrooms and a communal kitchen.* (**b**) of or for a community: *communal life/living.* **2** involving different groups in a community: *communal violence/riots between religious factions.* ▶ **communally** *adv.*

commune¹ /kəˈmjuːn/ *v* **PHRV** **commune with sb/ sth** (*fml*) to feel close to sb/sth, esp by talking about personal things: *commune with one's friends* ○ *commune with God in prayer* ○ *walking in the woods, communing with nature.*

commune² /ˈkɒmjuːn/ *n* [CGp] **1** a group of people, not all of one family, living together and sharing property and responsibilities: *a hippy commune.* **2** the smallest division of local government in France and certain other countries.

communicable /kəˈmjuːnɪkəbl/ *adj* that can be communicated or passed on to others: *communicable diseases.*

communicant /kəˈmjuːnɪkənt/ *n* a person who receives COMMUNION(1).

communicate /kəˈmjuːnɪkeɪt/ *v* **1** ~ sth (to sb/ sth) (**a**) to make sth known: [Vn] *This poem communicates the author's despair.* [Vnpr] *The officer communicated his orders to the men by radio.* (**b**) to pass sth on; to transmit sth: *communicate a disease (to others).* **2(a)** ~ (**with sb**) to exchange information, news, ideas, etc with sb: [V] *Although he was once a close friend of mine, we haven't communicated for years.* ○ *Deaf people communicate by sign language.* [Vpr] *The police communicate with each other by radio.* (**b**) to make one's ideas, feelings, etc clear to others: [V] *A politician must be able to communicate.* **3** ~ (**with sb**) to have a good relationship because of shared feelings and understanding: [V, Vpr] *Something must be wrong*

----

with our marriage — we don't seem to communicate (with each other) any more. **4 ~ (with sth)** to be connected with sth: [V] *communicating rooms* (ie rooms with a connecting door) [also Vpr].

communication /kə₁mjuːnɪˈkeɪʃn/ *n* **1** [U] the action or process of communicating (COMMUNICATE 1b,2a,2b,3): *the communication of disease* ○ *The language difficulties make communication very difficult.* ○ *Good communication is important in any relationship.* ○ *We are in regular communication with each other by telephone or letter.* **2** [C] (*usu fml*) a thing that is communicated; a message: *to receive a secret communication.* **3** [U] (also **communications** [pl]) the means of communicating, eg roads, railways, telephone lines between places, or radio and television: *Telephone communications between the two cities have been restored.* ○ *The heavy snow has prevented all communication with the highlands.* ○ *a communication satellite/link* ○ *a world communications network.*

■ **com₁muni'cation cord** *n* a cord that passes along the length of a train inside the coaches, and that passengers can pull to stop the train in an emergency.

communicative /kəˈmjuːnɪkətɪv; *US* -keɪtɪv/ *adj* ready and willing to talk and give information: *I don't find Peter very communicative.* Compare RESERVED.

communicator /kəˈmjuːnɪkeɪtə(r)/ *n* a person who is able to describe her or his ideas, feelings, etc clearly to others: *She's a born communicator.*

communion /kəˈmjuːniən/ *n* **1 Communion** (also **Holy Communion**) [U] (in the Christian Church) a religious ceremony during which people eat bread and drink wine in memory of the death of Christ: *go to Communion* (ie attend church for this celebration). See also EUCHARIST. **2** [C] a group of people with the same religious beliefs: *We belong to the same communion.* **3** [U] ~ (**with sb/sth**) (*fml*) the state of sharing or exchanging the same thoughts or feelings: *poets who are in communion with nature.*

communiqué /kəˈmjuːnɪkeɪ; *US* kə₁mjuːnəˈkeɪ/ *n* an official announcement, esp to newspapers, etc: *The leaders attending the summit conference have issued a joint communiqué.*

communism /ˈkɒmjunɪzəm/ *n* [U] **1** a social and economic system in which the state owns and controls the means of production on behalf of the people. Its aim is to create a society in which everyone is paid and works according to their needs and abilities. **2 Communism (a)** a political movement or set of ideas that aims to establish communism. **(b)** the system of government by a ruling Communist Party, such as the government of the former Soviet Union.

▶ **communist** /ˈkɒmjənɪst/ *n* **1** a supporter of communism. **2 Communist** a member of a Communist party or movement. — *adj*: *have communist ideals* ○ *a Communist country/government/regime* ○ *Communist leaders.*

■ **the 'Communist Party** *n* **1** a political party supporting Communism. **2** (in Communist countries) a single official ruling party of the state.

community /kəˈmjuːnəti/ *n* **1 the community** [sing] the people living in one place, district or country, considered as a whole: *work for the good of the community* ○ *community service.* **2** [CGp] a group of people of the same religion, race, occupation, etc, or with shared interests: *the British community in Paris* ○ *a community of monks.* **3** [U] the condition of sharing, having things in common or being alike in some way: *community of interests* ○ *a community spirit* (ie a feeling of sharing the same attitudes, interests, etc). **4** [C] (*techn*) a group of animals or plants living or growing in the same place.

■ **com'munity centre** *n* a place where the people

from the same part of a town, etc can meet for sporting activities, education classes, social occasions, etc.

commute /kəˈmjuːt/ *v* **1** to travel regularly by bus, train or car between one's place of work (usu in a city) and one's home (usu at a distance): [Vpr] *She commutes from Oxford to London every day.* [V, Vp] *She lives in the country and commutes (in).* **2 ~ sth (to sth)** to replace one punishment by another that is less severe: [Vnpr] *commute a death sentence to one of life imprisonment* [Vn] *She was given a commuted sentence.* **3 ~ sth (for/into sth)** to change sth, esp a form of payment, for or into sth else: [Vn] *commute one's pension* [Vnpr] *commute an annuity into a lump sum.*

▶ **commutable** /kəˈmjuːtəbl/ *adj* ~ (**for/into sth**) that can be made, paid, etc in a different form: *A pension is often commutable into a lump sum.*

commutation /₁kɒmjuˈteɪʃn/ *n* (*fml*) **1** [C,U] the replacement of one punishment by another that is less severe: *He appealed for (a) commutation of the death sentence to life imprisonment.* **2(a)** [U] replacing one method of payment by another. **(b)** [C] a payment made in this way.

commuter *n* a person who commutes (COMMUTE 1): *The five o'clock train is always packed with commuters.* ○ *the commuter belt* (ie the area around a large city, from which people commute to work).

compact¹ /kəmˈpækt/ *adj* **1** closely packed together: *a compact mass of sand* ○ *Stamp the soil down so that it's compact.* **2** small and neat; made to use little space: *a compact flat/car* ○ *The computer looks compact and functional.*

▶ **compact** *v* (usu passive) to press sth firmly together: [Vn] *Loosen the compacted soil surface with a rake.*

compactly *adv.*

compactness *n* [U].

■ **₁compact 'disc** *n* (*abbr* **CD**) a small disc on which information or sound is recorded. Compact discs are played on special machines that contain lasers (LASER).

compact² /ˈkɒmpækt/ *n* a formal agreement between two or more people, countries, etc: *The two states have made a compact to cooperate in fighting terrorism.*

compact³ /ˈkɒmpækt/ *n* **1** a small flat box containing a mirror and powder, etc for the face, with a pad or brush for putting it on. **2** (*esp US*) a small car.

companion /kəmˈpæniən/ *n* **1(a)** a person or an animal that goes with, or spends much time with, another: *my companions on the journey* ○ *A dog is a faithful companion.* ○ (*fig*) *Fear was the hostage's constant companion.* **(b)** a person who shares in the work, pleasures, sadness, etc of another: *companions in arms* (ie soldiers serving together) ○ *companions in misfortune* (ie people suffering together). **(c)** a person with similar tastes, interests, etc to one's own and whose company one enjoys; a friend: *She's an excellent companion.* ○ *They're 'drinking companions* (ie They often go out drinking together). ○ *His brother is not much of a companion for him.* **2** a person employed to live with and help another, esp sb old or ill: *to take a post as a ₁paid com'panion.* **3** one of a matching pair or set of things: *The companion volume will soon be published.* **4** (used in book titles) a book giving useful facts and information on a particular subject: *the ₁Gardener's Com'panion.*

IDM a boon companion ⇨ BOON².

▶ **companionable** *adj* friendly.

companionship *n* [U] the relationship between friends or companions: *the companionship of old friends* ○ *She turned to me for companionship.*

companion-way /kəmˈpæniən weɪ/ *n* a staircase to a CABIN(1) on a ship.

company /'kʌmpəni/ n **1** (often **Company**) [CGp] a group of people working together for business or commercial purposes; a business organization: *a manufacturing company* ○ *an insurance company* ○ *I get a company car with my new job.* Compare FIRM². **2** [U] being together with another or others: *I enjoy his company* (ie I like being with him). ○ *be good/bad company* (ie be pleasant/unpleasant to be with) ○ *I hate going out alone — I take my daughter for company* (ie as a companion). **3** [U] a group of people together; a number of guests: *She told the assembled company what had happened.* ○ *We're expecting company* (ie guests or visitors) *next week.* ○ *It's bad manners to whisper in company* (ie in the presence of others). **4** [CGp] a group of people, esp entertainers, working together: *a theatrical company* (ie a number of actors regularly performing together) ○ *the ship's company* (ie the crew). **5** [CGp] a part of a BATTALION of INFANTRY, usu commanded by a captain or a MAJOR². **IDM the 'company one keeps** the type of people with whom one spends one's time: *(saying)* *You may know a man by the company he keeps* (ie judge his character by his friends). **get into / keep bad 'company** to associate with bad people or people that others disapprove of. **in company with sb** together with sb: *I, in company with many others, feel this decision was wrong.* **in good 'company** *(joc)* in the same situation as sb else, esp sb more important: *'I'm late again!' 'Well, you're in good company. The boss isn't here yet.'* **keep sb 'company** to remain with sb so that they are not alone: *I'll stay here and keep you company.* **part company** ⇨ PART². **present company excepted** ⇨ PRESENT¹. **two's 'company (, three's a 'crowd)** *(saying)* (used esp of people in love) it is better for two people to be alone with each other and without others present.

comparable /'kɒmpərəbl/ adj ~ **(to/with sb/sth)** able or suitable to be compared with sb/sth else: *The achievements of an athlete and a writer are not comparable.* ○ *His work is comparable with the very best in modern fiction.*

comparative /kəm'pærətɪv/ adj **1** involving comparison or comparing: *comparative linguistics/ religion* ○ *a comparative study of the social systems of two countries.* **2** measured or judged by comparing; relative: *living in comparative comfort* (eg compared with others, or with one's own life at an earlier period) ○ *In a poor country, owning a bicycle is a sign of comparative wealth.* **3** *(grammar)* of adjectives and adverbs that express a greater degree or 'more', eg *better, worse, slower, more difficult.* Compare POSITIVE 10, SUPERLATIVE 2.
▶ **comparative** n *(grammar)* the form of adjectives and adverbs that expresses a greater degree: *'Better' is the comparative of 'good'.*
comparatively adv as compared to sth or sb else: *comparatively wealthy/small/good/old.*

compare /kəm'peə(r)/ v **1** ~ **A and B**; ~ **A with/to B** to examine people or things to see how they are alike and how they are different; to judge one thing and measure it against another thing: [Vn] *Compare (the style of) the two poems.* [Vnpr, Vn] *If you compare her work with his/If you compare their work, you'll find hers is much better.* [Vnpr] *Compared to many people she's quite rich.* See also CF. **2** ~ **A to B** to show that a particular person or thing is similar to sb/sth else: [Vnpr] *Poets have compared sleep to death.* **3** ~ **with sb/sth** to be compared with or be worthy to be compared with sb/sth: [Vpr] *This cannot compare with that* (ie No comparison is possible because they are so different). ○ *He cannot compare with* (ie is not nearly as great as) *Shakespeare as a writer of tragedies.* ○ *Our prices compare very favourably with those of our competitors.* [also V]. **IDM compare 'notes (with sb)** to exchange ideas or opinions: *We saw the play separately and compared notes afterwards.*
▶ **compare** n **IDM beyond com'pare** *(fml)* to such an extent that no comparison can be made with anything or anyone else: *a diamond beyond compare in its beauty.*

comparison /kəm'pærɪsn/ n **(a)** [U] the action of comparing: *He showed us a good tyre for comparison (with the worn one).* **(b)** [C] ~ **(of A and/to/with B)**; ~ **(between A and B)** an instance of comparing: *the comparison of the heart to/with a pump* ○ *comparisons between Britain and the rest of Europe* ○ *It's an interesting comparison.* ○ *You shouldn't draw unfair comparisons — the two are completely different.* **IDM bear/stand comparison with sb/sth** to be able to be compared favourably with sb/sth: *That's a good dictionary, but it doesn't bear comparison with this one.* **by/in comparison (with sb/sth)** when compared: *The tallest buildings in London are small in comparison with those in New York.* **there's no com'parison** (used to emphasize the difference between two people or things being compared): *'Is he as good as her at chess?' 'There's no comparison (ie She is much better).'*

compartment /kəm'pɑːtmənt/ n any of the sections into which a larger area or enclosed space, esp a railway carriage, is divided: *The first-class compartments are in front.* ○ *a case with separate compartments for shoes, jewellery, etc.*
▶ **compartmentalize, -ise** /ˌkɒmpɑːt'mentəlaɪz/ v ~ **sth (into sth)** to divide sth into compartments or categories: [Vnpr] *Life today is rigidly compartmentalized into work and leisure.* [also Vn].

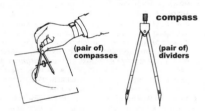

compass
(pair of) compasses
(pair of) dividers

compass /'kʌmpəs/ n **1** (also **magnetic compass**) [C] a device for finding direction, with a needle that always points to the north: *the points of the compass* (ie N, NE, E, SE, S, SW, W, NW, etc). **2** [C] (also **compasses** [pl]) an instrument with two movable legs joined together at the top, used for drawing circles, measuring distances on a map or chart, etc: *a pair of compasses.* ⇨ picture. **3** [C usu *sing*] scope; a range¹ (3): *beyond the compass of the human mind* ○ *the compass of a singer's voice* (ie the range from the lowest to the highest sound that he or she can sing).

compassion /kəm'pæʃn/ n [U] ~ **(for sb)** pity for the sufferings of others, making one want to help them: *be filled with compassion* ○ *a woman of great compassion.* ○ *The plight of the refugees arouses our compassion.* ○ *Out of* (ie Because of) *compassion for her terrible suffering they allowed her to stay.*
▶ **compassionate** /kəm'pæʃənət/ adj showing or feeling compassion: *They allowed her to stay on compassionate grounds* (ie out of compassion). **compassionately** adv. **compassionate leave** n [U] *(Brit)* a period of time that sb is allowed to be away from his job because of special personal circumstances: *She was allowed compassionate leave from work to attend her father's funeral.*

compatible /kəm'pætəbl/ adj ~ **(with sb/sth)** **(a)** (of people, ideas, principles, etc) suited; that can exist together without problems or conflict: *We decided to separate when we realized we were not really compatible.* ○ *driving a car at a speed compatible with* safety (ie at a safe speed). (**b**) (of pieces of equipment) that can be used together: *This printer is compatible with most microcomputers.*

▶ **compatibility** /kəmˌpætə'bɪləti/ *n* [U] ~ (**with sb/sth**); ~ (**between A and B**) the state of being compatible.

compatibly /-əbli/ *adv*.

compatriot /kəm'pætriət; *US* -'peɪt-/ *n* a person who was born in, or is a citizen of, the same country as another: *The Australians claimed their compatriots worked harder than the British.* ○ *Steffi Graf's German compatriot, Anke Huber.*

compel /kəm'pel/ *v* (**-ll-**) **1** (*fml*) to make sb do sth; to force sb: [Vn.to inf] *We cannot compel you to (do it), but we think you should.* ○ *I was compelled to* (ie I had to) *acknowledge the force of his argument.* ○ *If the board approved the proposal I should feel compelled to resign.* Compare IMPEL. **2** [Vn no passive] (*fml*) (**a**) to get sth by force or pressure; to make sth necessary: *You can compel obedience, but not affection.* ○ *Circumstances have compelled a change of plan.* (**b**) (not in the continuous tenses) to inspire sth strongly: *His courage compels universal admiration.* ○ *music that compels an audience's attention.*

▶ **compelling** *adj* (**a**) extremely interesting and exciting, so that one has to pay attention: *a compelling novel/account/story.* (**b**) that one must accept or agree with: *a compelling reason/argument.* Compare COMPULSION.

compendium /kəm'pendiəm/ *n* (*pl* **compendiums** or **compendia**) ~ (**of sth**) **1** a collection of detailed items of information, esp in a book: *The book is an invaluable compendium of ideas, facts and figures.* **2** (*Brit*) a collection of different games sold in one box.

compensate /'kɒmpenseɪt/ *v* ~ (**sb**) **for sth** to provide sth good to balance or reduce the bad effect of damage, loss, injury, etc: [Vpr] *Nothing can compensate for the death of a loved one.* ○ *A dog's good sense of smell compensates for its poor eyesight.* [Vnpr] *She was compensated by the insurance company for her injuries.* [also Vn]. ▶ **compensatory** /ˌkɒmpen'seɪtəri; *US* kəm'pensətɔːri/ *adj*: *The court awarded her compensatory damages.*

compensation /ˌkɒmpen'seɪʃn/ *n* ~ (**for sth**) (**a**) [U] the action of compensating: *Compensation of injured workers has cost the company a lot.* ○ *Have you considered the matter of compensation?* (**b**) [U,C] a thing, esp an amount of money, given to compensate for sth: *receive £5000 in compensation/by way of compensation/as a compensation for injury* ○ *My job is hard, but it has its compensations* (ie pleasant aspects that make it less bad).

compère /'kɒmpeə(r)/ *n* (*Brit*) a person who introduces the performers in a variety(4) show, etc, esp on radio or television.

▶ **compère** *v* [Vn] (*Brit*) to act as a compère for a show.

compete /kəm'piːt/ *v* ~ (**against/with sb**) (**in sth**) (**for sth**) to try to win sth by defeating others who are trying to do the same: [Vpr] *a horse that has competed in the Kentucky Derby four times* [Vpr, V.to inf] *Several companies are competing (against/with each other) for the contract/to gain the contract.* [V] *Physics is a set of competing theories about the nature of the universe.*

competence /'kɒmpɪtəns/ *n* [U] **1** ~ (**as/in sth**); ~ (**in doing sth/to do sth**) being able to do sth well: *No one doubts her competence as a teacher.* ○ *Many have begun to doubt the government's competence in managing/to manage the economy.* **2** (*law*) the authority of a court, judge, etc to deal with a matter: *matters within/beyond the competence of the court* (ie ones that it can/cannot legally deal with).

competent /'kɒmpɪtənt/ *adj* **1** ~ (**to do sth**) (of people) having the necessary ability, authority, skill, knowledge, etc: *a highly competent driver* ○

competent at/in one's work ○ *She's not competent to look after young children.* Compare INCOMPETENT. **2** quite good, but not excellent: *I'd call it a competent piece of work rather than an outstanding one.* ▶ **competently** *adv*.

competition /ˌkɒmpə'tɪʃn/ *n* **1** [C] an event in which people compete; a contest: *boxing/chess/beauty competitions* ○ *He came first in the poetry competition.* ⇨ note at SPORT. **2** [U] ~ (**between/with sb**) (**for sth**) the action of competing; activity in which people compete: *Competition between bidders for this valuable painting has been keen.* ○ *We're in competition with* (ie competing against) *several other companies for the contract.* **3** the competition [Gp] those competing against sb: *She had a chance to see the competition* (ie the other people who were trying to get the same job as she was) *before the interview.*

competitive /kəm'petətɪv/ *adj* **1** involving people competing against each other: *competitive examinations for government posts* ○ *competitive sports.* **2** ~ (**with sb/sth**) as good as or better than others: *This would make teachers' pay competitive with that of other professions.* ○ *Our firm is no longer competitive in world markets.* ○ *a store offering very competitive prices* (ie as low as in any other shop) ○ *This should give us a competitive edge* (ie an advantage). **3** (of people or their attitude) having a strong urge to be more successful than others: *You have to be highly/intensely/fiercely competitive to do well in sport nowadays.* ○ *The trouble is, you've just no competitive spirit.* ▶ **competitively** *adv*: *competitively priced goods.* **competitiveness** *n* [U]: *declining British competitiveness in world markets.*

competitor /kəm'petɪtə(r)/ *n* **1** a person or an organization that competes against others, esp in business; a rival: *our main/leading competitors* ○ *The firm has better products than its competitors.* **2** a person who competes in a sporting contest: *competitors in the last Olympic Games.* Compare CONTESTANT.

compile /kəm'paɪl/ *v* **1**(**a**) to collect information and arrange it in a book, list, report, etc: [Vn] *The police are compiling statistics for a report on traffic accidents.* (**b**) (often passive) to produce a book, list, or report in this way: [Vn] *a guidebook compiled from a variety of sources* ○ *They compiled a complete catalogue of Rembrandt's paintings.* **2** [Vn] (*computing*) to use a computer PROGRAM to translate instructions from one programming (PROGRAM *v*) language into another so that a particular computer can understand them.

▶ **compilation** /ˌkɒmpɪ'leɪʃn/ *n* (**a**) [U] the action of compiling sth. (**b**) [C] a group or set that is compiled from items previously separate: *Her latest album is a compilation of all her best singles.*

compiler /kəm'paɪlə(r)/ *n* **1** a person who compiles. **2** (*computing*) a computer PROGRAM that compiles (COMPILE 2) instructions.

complacency /kəm'pleɪsnsi/ *n* [U] (*usu derog*) a calm feeling of satisfaction with oneself, one's work, etc: *These are very good sales figures, but there's no room/cause for complacency.* ○ *There's an air of complacency in his behaviour which I dislike.*

complacent /kəm'pleɪsnt/ *adj* ~ (**about sb/sth**) (*usu derog*) showing calm satisfaction with oneself, one's work, etc: *a complacent smile/manner/tone of voice* ○ *We are all much too complacent about the quality of our water-supply.* ▶ **complacently** *adv*.

complain /kəm'pleɪn/ *v* **1** ~ (**to sb**) (**about/of sth**) (*often derog*) to say that one is annoyed, unhappy or not satisfied: [V.that] *Holiday-makers complained bitterly that the resort was filthy.* [Vpr] *They have complained (to the council) about the noise.* [V.speech] *'I can't see a thing,'* she complained. [V] *You're always complaining!* ○ (*infml*) *'What was the weather like on your vacation?' 'Oh, I can't complain* (ie It was not bad).' [also Vpr.*that*]. **2** ~ **of sth** to say one is suffering from a pain, etc: [Vpr] *The patient is complaining of acute earache.* ▶ **complainingly** *adv:* '*Why me?*' *he asked complainingly.*

complainant /kəm'pleɪnənt/ *n* (*law*) = PLAINTIFF.

complaint /kəm'pleɪnt/ *n* **1** [C] ~ (**about sth**); ~ (**against sb**); ~ (**that...**) (**a**) a reason for not being satisfied: *a common complaint* ○ *I have a number of complaints about the service in this hotel.* (**b**) a statement that one is annoyed or not satisfied about sth: *submit a formal complaint* ○ *complaints against the police* ○ *complaints about/of bad workmanship* ○ *The management ignored our complaints that washing facilities were inadequate.* ○ *investigate/lodge/make/ reject/uphold a complaint* ○ *You must follow the official* **complaints procedure.** **2** [U] the action of complaining: *You have no cause/grounds for complaint.* **3** [C] (*sometimes euph*) an illness; a disease: *suffering from a heart complaint* ○ *chickenpox and other childhood complaints.*

complaisance /kəm'pleɪzəns/ *n* [U] (*fml*) willingness to do what pleases other people.
▶ **complaisant** /-zənt/ *adj* (*fml*) ready to please other people or to accept what they say or do without arguing: *a complaisant husband.*

complement /'kɒmplɪmənt/ *n* **1** ~ (**to sth**) a thing that contributes new or contrasting features or qualities which improve sth or make it complete: *Rice makes an excellent complement to a curry dish.* **2** the complete number or quantity needed or allowed: *We've taken on our* **full complement** *of new trainees for this year.* ○ *the ship's complement* (ie all the officers and other sailors). **3** (*grammar*) a word or words, esp adjectives and nouns, used after linking verbs such as *be* and *become*, and describing the subject of the verb: *In the sentence 'I'm angry,' 'angry' is a complement.*
▶ **complement** /'kɒmplɪment/ *v* to add new or contrasting features which show the best qualities of sth or which improve it: [Vn] *His business skill complements her flair for design.* ○ *Use herbs that complement each other.* Compare COMPLIMENT.

complementary /ˌkɒmplɪ'mentri/ *adj* ~ (**to sth**) combining well to form a balanced or attractive group or whole: *complementary colours and patterns* ○ *They have complementary personalities* (ie Each has qualities which the other lacks). ○ *Successful policies had to be complementary to sound environmental practice.* ˌcomplementary ˈangle *n* either of two angles which together make 90°. **complementary medicine** *n* [U] (*esp Brit*) = ALTERNATIVE MEDICINE.

complete¹ /kəm'pliːt/ *adj* **1**(**a**) having all necessary or appropriate parts; whole: *a complete set/ collection/holiday package* ○ *a complete dinner service* ○ *a complete edition of Shakespeare's works* (ie one that includes all of them). (**b**) ~ **with sth** (following *ns* or predicative) having sth as an additional part or feature: *a radio* **complete with** *a carrying case* ○ *It* **comes complete with** *all fittings.* ○ (*joc*) *a stage pirate complete with eye patch and cutlass.* **2** [pred] finished; ended: *When will the building work be complete?* **3** [usu attrib] (often used for emphasis) to the greatest extent or degree possible; in every way: *a complete stranger/idiot/nonentity* ○ *a complete ban on tobacco advertising* ○ *It came as a complete surprise to me.*
▶ **completely** *adv* (often used for emphasis) in every way possible; totally: *completely innocent/ happy* ○ *We were completely and utterly lost.*
completeness *n* [U]: *For (the sake of) completeness I have included everyone's addresses.*

complete² /kəm'pliːt/ *v* **1**(**a**) (often passive) to finish making or doing sth: [Vn] *15 students have completed the course.* ○ *When will the railway be*

completed? (**b**) to make sth whole or perfect: [Vn] *I only need one volume to complete my set of Dickens's novels.* ○ (*fig*) *A few words of praise from her would have completed his happiness.* **2** (*sometimes more fml*) to write all the required information on a form, etc: [Vn] *Complete your application in ink.* ○ *a completed questionnaire.*

completion /kəm'pliːʃn/ *n* **1** [U] (**a**) the action or process of completing sth: *Completion of the new building is taking longer than expected.* (**b**) the state of being complete: *The film is nearing completion.* ○ *the completion date.* **2** [U,C] (*commerce*) the formal completing of a contract of sale: *You may move into the house on completion.* ○ *Completions fell by more than 50% last month.*

complex¹ /'kɒmpleks; *US* kəm'pleks/ *adj* (**a**) having many parts connected together in a particular pattern: *a complex system/network* ○ *brains as large and as complex as ours.* (**b**) difficult to understand or explain because there are many different aspects or people involved: *a complex argument/system/ problem/subject* ○ *highly/enormously complex relationships* ○ *The situation was more complex than we realized.* Compare COMPLICATED.
▶ **complexity** /kəm'pleksəti/ *n* (**a**) [U] the state of being complex: *a problem of great/fantastic/ increasing complexity.* (**b**) [C usu *pl*] a complex thing: *the complexities of higher mathematics.*
■ ˌcomplex ˈsentence *n* (*grammar*) a sentence which has a main part and at least one extra part: *a complex sentence containing three subordinate clauses.*

complex² /'kɒmpleks/ *n* **1** (esp following an *adj* or *n* that specifies type) a group of similar buildings or facilities on one site: *a big industrial complex* (ie a site with many factories, etc) ○ *a sports/leisure complex.* **2**(**a**) (*psychology*) (esp in compounds) an abnormal mental state resulting from past experience or suppressed desires: *suffering from a persecution complex* ○ *an inferiority complex.* (**b**) (*infml*) an extremely strong concern or fear: *a weight complex* ○ *He has a bit of a complex about his nose.*

complexion /kəm'plekʃn/ *n* **1** the natural colour and appearance of a person's skin, esp of the face: *a good/dark/sallow complexion.* **2** (usu *sing*) the general character or aspect of sth: *the political complexion of Eastern Europe* ○ *Her resignation puts a different complexion on things.* ○ *a victory that changed the whole complexion of the war* (ie made the probable result different, gave hopes of an early end, etc).

compliance /kəm'plaɪəns/ *n* [U] ~ (**with sth**) **1** (*fml*) obedience to a command, rule or request: *her reluctant compliance* ○ *deterrent fines, sufficient to secure/ensure compliance with the law* ○ *The move is* **in compliance with** *the European agreement on pesticides.* **2** (*usu derog*) the tendency to agree (too readily) to do what others want: *ready compliance with all her wishes.* See also COMPLY.

compliant /kəm'plaɪənt/ *adj* (*usu derog*) (too) willing to agree with other people, to obey rules, etc: *a more compliant attitude* ○ *The government, compliant as ever, gave in to their demands.*

complicate /'kɒmplɪkeɪt/ *v* to make sth more difficult to do, understand or deal with: [Vn] *Her refusal to help complicates matters.* ○ *several complicating factors* ○ *The issue is further complicated by class.*
▶ **complicated** *adj* (**a**) (often less formal than *complex*) having many parts connected together in a particular pattern: *complicated wiring/machinery* ○ *The price structure is complicated.* (**b**) (often used to describe sth that one cannot understand or does not want to say more about) difficult to understand or explain because there are many different parts, aspects or people involved: *a very complicated*

situation/process/matter ○ *a ridiculously complicated plot* ○ *He's married to her, and she's in love with his brother-in-law, and...oh, it's too complicated to explain!* Compare COMPLEX[1].

complication /ˌkɒmplɪˈkeɪʃn/ *n* **1** [C] a thing that makes a situation more complex or difficult: *a serious/common complication* ○ *A further complication was Fred's refusal to travel by air.* **2** complications [pl] (*medical*) a new illness, or further development of an illness, that makes treatment more difficult: *Complications set in after the operation, and the patient died.*

complicity /kəmˈplɪsəti/ *n* [U] ~ (**in sth**) (*law or fml*) the action of taking part with another person in a crime, plot or other wrongdoing: *barely suppressed looks of complicity and amusement* ○ *He was suspected of complicity in her murder.*

compliment /ˈkɒmplɪmənt/ *n* **1** [C] an expression of praise, admiration, approval, etc: **pay sb a compliment** (ie praise them) ○ *She's always fishing for compliments* (ie trying to obtain them indirectly). ○ *'What an amazing hat!' 'Hmm... I'll take that as* (ie regard it as) *a compliment.'* ○ *'Don't bother to return the compliment* (ie do the same for me).' (*fig fml*) *These beautiful flowers are a compliment to the gardener's skill* (ie show how skilful he or she is). **2** compliments [pl] (*fml*) greetings, usu as part of a message: *My compliments to your wife* (ie Please give her a greeting from me). ○ *Compliments of the season* (eg said at Christmas or the New Year). ○ *The flowers are with the compliments of* (ie are a gift from) *the management.*

▸ **compliment** /ˈkɒmplɪment/ *v* ~ **sb** (**on sth**) to express praise or admiration of sb: [Vnpr] *I complimented her on her English.* [also Vn]. Compare COMPLEMENT.

■ ˈ**compliment slip** *n* a small printed piece of paper sent by a firm or organization with a free sample, information sheet, etc.

complimentary /ˌkɒmplɪˈmentri/ *adj* **1** expressing admiration, praise, etc: *a complimentary remark/review* ○ *She was highly complimentary about my paintings.* **2** given free of charge: *a complimentary seat/ticket/copy of a book* ○ *Wine is complimentary.*

comply /kəmˈplaɪ/ *v* (*pt, pp* **complied**) ~ (**with sth**) to obey a command, rule, request, etc: [V] *There are stiff penalties for failing/refusing to comply.* [Vpr] *The Courts ordered them to comply fully with EC directives on equal treatment for women.* ○ *Certain conditions have to be complied with.* See also COMPLIANCE.

component /kəmˈpəʊnənt/ *n* any of the parts of which sth is made: *the components of an engine/a camera* ○ *a factory supplying electronic components for the car industry* ○ (*fig*) *Surprise is an essential component of my plan.* ▸ **component** *adj* [attrib]: *analysing the component parts of a sentence.*

compose /kəmˈpəʊz/ *v* **1**(**a**) to write music, opera, poetry, etc: [Vn] *songs composed by Schubert* [V] *She began to compose at an early age.* See also COMPOSER, COMPOSITION 1. (**b**) (*fml*) to write a letter, speech, etc with great care and thought: [Vn] *I'm composing a formal reply to the letter.* **2**(**a**) **be composed of sth** (not usu in the continuous tenses) to be made of or formed from the specified parts, elements or people: *a committee composed largely of lawyers* ○ *Water is composed of hydrogen and oxygen.* (**b**) (*fml*) (no passive; not in the continuous tenses) (of parts or elements of sth) to form a whole: [Vn] *the ten short scenes that compose the play.* ⇔ note at COMPRISE. See also COMPOSITION 3. **3** (no passive) to bring oneself or one's feelings or expression under control: [Vn] *His mind was in such a whirl that he could hardly compose his thoughts.* ○ *She had to sit down a*

moment and compose herself before going on. See also COMPOSURE.

▸ **composed** *adj* having one's feelings or expression under control: *a composed manner/look* ○ *He remained perfectly composed.*

composer /kəmˈpəʊzə(r)/ *n* a person who composes esp music: *Beethoven and other great composers.*

composite /ˈkɒmpəzɪt/ *adj* [attrib] having or made of different parts or materials: *a composite substance* ○ *a composite illustration* (ie one made by putting together two or more separate pictures). ▸ **composite** *n*: *The play is a composite of reality and fiction.*

composition /ˌkɒmpəˈzɪʃn/ *n* **1**(**a**) [C] a thing composed, eg a piece of music or a poem: *'Swan Lake' is one of Tchaikovsky's best-known compositions.* (**b**) [U] the action of composing this: *He played a piano sonata of his own composition* (ie that he himself had composed). (**c**) [U] the art of composing music: *studying composition at music school.* **2** [C] a short piece of writing done as a school or college exercise; an essay. **3** [U] the parts or elements of which sth is made: *analyse the exact composition of the soil* ○ *the ethnic composition of the town's society.* **4** [U] (*art*) the arrangement of people or things in a painting, photograph, etc: *Her drawing is competent, but her composition is poor.*

compositor /kəmˈpɒzɪtə(r)/ *n* a skilled person who arranges type[2](1) for printing.

compos mentis /ˌkɒmpəs ˈmentɪs/ *adj* [pred] (*Latin infml or joc*) having full control of one's mind: *I had only just woken up and wasn't yet fully compos mentis.* Compare NON COMPOS MENTIS.

compost /ˈkɒmpɒst; *US* -pəʊst/ *n* [U, C] a mixture of decayed plant matter, MANURE, etc added to soil to improve the growth of plants.

▸ **compost** *v* [Vn] (**a**) to make sth into compost: *composting the kitchen waste.* (**b**) to put compost on or in sth.

composure /kəmˈpəʊʒə(r)/ *n* [U] the state of being calm in mind or behaviour: *keep/lose/regain one's composure* ○ *He showed great/remarkable composure in a difficult situation.* See also COMPOSE 3.

compote /ˈkɒmpɒt; *US* ˈkɒmpəʊt/ *n* [C, U] (a dish of) fruit cooked with sugar.

compound[1] /ˈkɒmpaʊnd/ *n* **1**(**a**) a thing composed of two or more separate things combined together: *The play was an odd mixture, a compound of humour and appalling insensitivity.* (**b**) (*techn*) a substance consisting of two or more elements (ELEMENT 4) in a chemical combination in fixed proportions: *Common salt is a compound of sodium and chlorine.* Compare MIXTURE 1, ELEMENT 4. **2** (*grammar*) a noun, an adjective, etc composed of two or more words or parts of words, written as one or more words, or joined by a HYPHEN: *'Travel agent', 'dark-haired' and 'policeman' are compounds.*

▸ **compound** *adj* [attrib] composed of two or more parts: *compound words* ○ *an insect's compound eye.*

■ ˌ**compound ˈfracture** *n* the breaking of a bone in which part of the bone comes through the skin.

ˌ**compound ˈinterest** *n* [U] interest[1](5) paid on both the original capital[2](2) and the interest added to it. Compare SIMPLE INTEREST.

compound[2] /kəmˈpaʊnd/ *v* **1** to make sth bad worse by causing further harm: [Vn] *Initial planning errors were compounded by the careless way in which the plan was carried out.* **2**(**a**) (*fml or techn*) to mix sth together: [Vn] *the vat in which the chemicals are compounded.* (**b**) ~ **sth** (**of/from sth**) (*fml*) (usu passive) to make sth by mixing: [Vnpr] *a medicine compounded from* (ie made of) *various herbs* ○ (*fig*) *Her character was compounded in equal parts of meanness and generosity.* [also Vn].

compound[3] /ˈkɒmpaʊnd/ *n* an area enclosed by a

fence, etc, in which a house, factory or other building stands: *a prison compound*.

comprehend /ˌkɒmprɪˈhend/ *v* (*fml*) (often in negative sentences) to understand sth fully: [Vn] *failing to comprehend the seriousness of the situation* ○ *victims of forces they can't begin to/can barely comprehend* [V.*wh*] *The committee can't seem to comprehend what limited mobility means.* [V] *He stood staring at the dead body, unable to comprehend.* [also V.*that*].

comprehensible /ˌkɒmprɪˈhensəbl/ *adj* ~ (**to sb**) that can be understood fully by sb: *a book that is comprehensible only to specialists.* ▶ **comprehensibility** /ˌkɒmprɪˌhensəˈbɪləti/ *n* [U].

comprehension /ˌkɒmprɪˈhenʃn/ *n* **1** [U] the power of understanding: *How anyone could behave like that is beyond my comprehension* (ie I cannot understand it.). **2** [U, C] an exercise aimed at improving or testing one's understanding of a language (written or spoken): *a French comprehension test.*

comprehensive /ˌkɒmprɪˈhensɪv/ *adj* **1** that includes everything or nearly everything: *the most comprehensive description/guide/report I have read* ○ *Come and see our comprehensive selection of furnishing fabrics.* ○ *She took out a comprehensive insurance policy* (ie one covering most risks). **2** (*Brit*) (of education) for pupils of all abilities in the same school.

▶ **comprehensive** (also **compreˈhensive school**) *n* (*Brit*) a large secondary school at which children of all abilities are taught: *Our children go to the local comprehensive.*

comprehensively *adv*: *Our team was comprehensively* (ie thoroughly) *defeated.*

comprehensiveness *n* [U].

compress¹ /kəmˈpres/ *v* ~ **sth** (**into sth**) **1** to press or squeeze sth into a smaller space: [Vn] *compressed air* [Vnpr] *compressing straw into blocks for burning.* **2** to express ideas, etc in a shorter form: [Vnpr] *compress an argument into just a few sentences* ○ *The movie compresses several years into half an hour.* [also Vn].

▶ **compression** /kəmˈpreʃn/ *n* [U]: *gases under compression* ○ *data compression.*

compressor /kəmˈpresə(r)/ *n* a machine that compresses air or other gases.

compress² /ˈkɒmpres/ *n* a pad or cloth pressed onto a part of the body to stop bleeding, reduce fever, etc: *a cold/hot compress.*

comprise /kəmˈpraɪz/ *v* (not in the continuous tenses) (**a**) to have sb/sth as parts or members; to be composed of sb/sth: [Vn] *a committee comprising people of widely differing views* ○ *The living accommodation comprises three bedrooms, a kitchen and a bathroom.* (**b**) to be the parts or members that form sth: [Vn] *Two small boys and a dog comprised the street entertainer's only audience.*

> **NOTE** Note the use of **comprise**. It can mean **consist of** or **be composed of** (ie be formed of): *The British Parliament comprises/consists of/is composed of the House of Commons and the House of Lords.* It can also mean **compose** or **constitute** (ie form): *The House of Commons and the House of Lords comprise/compose/constitute the British Parliament.* This use of **comprise** is less common, and careful speakers avoid **be comprised of** in the first sense.

compromise /ˈkɒmprəmaɪz/ *n* (**a**) [U] the giving up of particular demands by each side in a dispute, so that an agreement may be reached which satisfies both sides to some extent: *There is no prospect of compromise in sight.* ○ *They worked out a compromise agreement.* ○ *a compromise candidate.* (**b**) [C] ~ (**between A and B**) a settlement reached in this way: *Can the two sides ever arrive at/reach a com-*

promise on this issue? ○ *The final proposals were a rather unsuccessful compromise between the need for profitability and the demands of local conservationists.*

▶ **compromise** *v* **1** ~ (**on sth**) to settle a dispute, etc by making a compromise: [V] *show a willingness/refusal to compromise* [Vpr] *I wanted to go to Greece, and my husband wanted to go to Spain, so we compromised on* (ie agreed to go to) *Italy.* **2** to bring sth/sb/oneself into danger or under suspicion by foolish behaviour: [Vn] *He has irretrievably compromised himself by accepting money from them.* **3** to weaken a belief, standard, etc by adapting it: [Vn] *She refused to compromise her principles.* ○ *The aim is to improve the factory's efficiency, without compromising safety.*

compromising *adj*: *The photographs showed the couple in highly compromising* (ie suspicious or embarrassing) *circumstances.*

compulsion /kəmˈpʌlʃn/ *n* ~ (**to do sth**) **1** [U] strong force or pressure making sb do sth they do not want to do: *There should be no compulsion on a single mother to name the father of her child.* **2** [C] an urge that one cannot resist, esp one that makes one behave in a way that is unreasonable: *a compulsion to destroy things.* Compare COMPEL.

compulsive /kəmˈpʌlsɪv/ *adj* **1** extremely interesting; fascinating: *The new TV drama is compulsive viewing.* **2**(**a**) driven by a desire that is impossible to control: *compulsive gambling/eating.* (**b**) (of people) not able to control one's desire or need to do sth: *a compulsive eater/liar/gambler.* ▶ **compulsively** *adv*: *a compulsively readable book.*

compulsory /kəmˈpʌlsəri/ *adj* that must be done; required by the rules, etc: *Is military service compulsory in your country?* ○ *English is a compulsory subject.* ○ *compulsory drug tests.* ▶ **compulsorily** /kəmˈpʌlsərəli/ *adv.*

compunction /kəmˈpʌŋkʃn/ *n* [U] ~ (**about doing sth**) (*fml*) (usu in negative sentences) a feeling of guilt or regret for one's action: *without the slightest compunction* ○ *If I thought that my superiors had made a bad decision, I would have no compunction about saying so.*

computation /ˌkɒmpjuˈteɪʃn/ *n* [C, U] (*fml*) an act or the process of calculating: *A quick computation revealed that we would not make a profit.* ○ *It will cost £5 000 by my computations.*

▶ **computational** *adj* [usu attrib] (**a**) using computers: *computational linguistics.* (**b**) of computers: *the demand for computational power.*

compute /kəmˈpjuːt/ *v* ~ **sth** (**at sth**) to calculate sth, esp with a computer: [Vn] *Scientists can accurately compute the course of the rocket.* [Vnpr] *He computed his losses at £5 000.*

▶ **computing** *n* [U] the operation of computers: *a course in computing* ○ *the firm's computing capacity.*

computer

monitor

screen

mouse

floppy disk

keyboard

disk drive

computer /kəmˈpjuːtə(r)/ *n* an electronic device for storing and analysing information fed into it, for calculating, or for controlling machinery automatically: *Is the new information available on* (the) *computer yet?* ○ *The accounts are processed by computer.* ○ *a laptop/personal computer* ○ *a computer error* ○ *a computer programmer* ○ *computer science/software/graphics* ○ *computer-aided design.* ⇨ picture.

▶ **computerize, -ise** /-təraɪz/ v (**a**) to provide a computer to do the work of or for sth: [Vn] *The accounts section has been completely computerized.* (**b**) to store information in a computer: *The firm has computerized its records.* ○ *a computerized image/ sewing-machine/ticket system.* **computerization, -isation** /kəmˌpjuːtəraɪˈzeɪʃn; US -rəˈz-/ n [U].

comrade /ˈkɒmreɪd; US -ræd/ n **1** a person who is a member of the same trade union as oneself, or of the same socialist (SOCIALISM) or Communist political party, etc: *We must fight for our rights, comrades!* ○ *the Chinese leader, Comrade Deng Xiaoping.* **2** (also **comrade-in-arms**) (*dated*) a companion who shares one's activities, esp a trusted one: *encouraging his frightened comrades.* ▶ **comradely** /ˈkɒmreɪdli/ adj: *give some comradely advice.* **comradeship** /ˈkɒmreɪdʃɪp/ n [U].

Con abbr = CONS.

con¹ /kɒn/ n [sing] (*sl*) a trick; an instance of cheating sb: *This so-called bargain is just a big con!* ○ *a con trick* ○ *He's a real con artist* (ie a person who regularly cheats others).
▶ **con** v (**-nn-**) (*infml*) (**a**) to deceive sb: [Vn] *You can't con me — you're not really sick!* (**b**) ~ sb (**into doing sth / out of sth**) to persuade sb to do sth or to give one sth after dishonestly gaining their trust. [Vnpr] *I was conned into buying a useless car.* ○ *She conned me out of $100.*
■ **con man** /ˈkɒn mæn/ n (pl **con men** /ˈkɒn men/) (*infml*) a man who tricks others into giving him money, etc.

con² /kɒn/ n (*sl*) = CONVICT n.

con³ /kɒn/ n **IDM** **the pros and cons** ⇨ PRO¹.

concatenation /kənˌkætəˈneɪʃn/ n ~ (**of sth**) (*fml*) a series of things or events linked together: *an unfortunate concatenation of mishaps.*

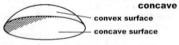
concave
convex surface
concave surface

concave /kɒnˈkeɪv/ adj (of an outline or a surface) curved inwards like the inner surface of a ball. ⇨ picture. Compare CONVEX.
▶ **concavity** /ˌkɒnˈkævəti/ n (**a**) [U] the quality of being concave. (**b**) [C] a concave surface.

conceal /kənˈsiːl/ v ~ sth/sb (**from sb/sth**) to keep sth/sb from being seen or known about; to hide sth/sb: [Vn] *Pictures concealed the cracks in the walls.* ○ *They could barely conceal their glee.* [Vnpr] *The microphone was cunningly concealed in a bunch of flowers.* ○ *He did his best to conceal his heavy drinking from his family.* See also ILL-CONCEALED.
▶ **concealment** n [U] the action of concealing or state of being concealed: *without any attempt at concealment* ○ *Fear of discovery forced him into concealment.*

concede /kənˈsiːd/ v **1** ~ sth (**to sb**) to admit that sth is true, valid, proper, etc: [Vnpr] *concede a point to sb in an argument* [Vn] *She grudgingly had to concede defeat* (ie admit that she had lost). [V.speech] *'OK, I might have been wrong,' he conceded.* [V.that] *I was forced to concede that she might be right.* [Vnn] *I concede you that point, but it doesn't disprove my argument.* **2** ~ sth (**to sb**) to give sth away; to allow sb else to have sth: [Vn] *We must not concede any of our territory* (ie allow another country to have it). [Vnpr] *England conceded a goal to their opponents in the first minute.* **3** to admit that one has lost a game, an election, etc: [V, Vn] *After losing her queen she was forced to concede (the game).* See also CONCESSION 1.

conceit /kənˈsiːt/ n **1** [U] excessive pride in oneself or in one's powers, abilities, etc: *The conceit of the man — comparing his own work with Picasso's!* **2** [C] (*techn*) a clever expression or idea, esp in a work of literature: *The plot is based upon a fanciful conceit.*
▶ **conceited** adj full of conceit; VAIN(1): *insufferably conceited.* **conceitedly** /-ɪdli/ adv.

conceive /kənˈsiːv/ v **1** ~ of sth; ~ sth (**as sth**) to form an idea, a plan, etc in the mind; to imagine sth: [Vn] *It was then that I conceived the notion of running away.* [V.that] *I cannot conceive* (ie I do not believe) *that he would wish to harm us.* [V.wh] *I cannot conceive why you allowed the girls to go alone* (ie I think you were very foolish to allow it). [Vn-n, Vpr] *The ancients conceived (of) the world as (being) flat* (ie They thought it was flat). **2** to become pregnant with a child: [V] *She was told she couldn't conceive.* [Vn] *The child was conceived on the night of their wedding.*
▶ **conceivable** /-əbl/ adj that can be conceived or believed: *I suppose it is just conceivable that she might have helped him escape.* ○ *a hotel that offers every conceivable luxury.* **conceivably** /-əbli/ adv: *He couldn't conceivably have* (ie I don't believe he could have) *intended this to happen.*

concentrate /ˈkɒnsntreɪt/ v **1**(**a**) ~ (**sth**) (**on sth/ doing sth**) to direct one's attention, effort, etc intensely on sth, not thinking about other less important things: [V, Vpr] *I can't concentrate (on my work) with all that noise going on.* [Vnpr] *We must concentrate our efforts on improving education.* [Vn] *Painting concentrates the/one's mind wonderfully.* (**b**) ~ on sth to do one particular thing and no other: [Vpr] *Having failed my French exams, I decided to concentrate on science subjects.* ○ *a firm which concentrates on the European market.* **2** to come together or bring sth together at one place: [Vadv] *Troops are concentrating south of the river.* [Vnpr] *The government's plan is to concentrate new industries in areas of high unemployment.* ○ *Power is largely concentrated in the hands of the ruling classes.* [also Vpr]. **3** [Vn] (*techn*) to increase the strength of a substance or solution by reducing its volume, eg by boiling it.
▶ **concentrate** n [C, U] a substance or solution made by concentrating (CONCENTRATE 3): *an orange concentrate which you dilute with water* ○ *copper in concentrate.*
concentrated adj **1** intense: *concentrated study/ effort* ○ *concentrated fire* (ie the firing of guns all aimed at one point). **2** increased in strength or value by concentrating (CONCENTRATE 3): *a concentrated solution* ○ *concentrated fruit juice.*

concentration /ˌkɒnsnˈtreɪʃn/ n **1** [U] ~ (**on sth**) the ability to concentrate(1): *Stress and tiredness often result in a lack of concentration.* ○ *a book that requires great powers of concentration* ○ *I found it hard to keep my concentration with so much noise going on.* ○ *a rare lapse of concentration* ○ *intense/ complete concentration.* **2** [C] ~ (**of sth**) a close gathering of people or things: *heavy concentrations of enemy troops/industrial buildings.* **3** [C] (*techn*) the amount of a substance in a liquid or in another substance: *high mecury concentrations in the water.*
■ **concenˈtration camp** n a prison consisting usu of a set of buildings inside a fence, where political prisoners, prisoners taken during a war, etc are kept in very bad conditions: *Nazi concentration camps.*

concentric /kənˈsentrɪk/ adj ~ (**with sth**) (of circles) having the same centre: *concentric rings.* Compare ECCENTRIC 2.

concept /ˈkɒnsept/ n ~ (**of sth / that…**) an idea or principle relating to sth abstract: *The concept of community care is not new.* ○ *He can't grasp the basic concepts of mathematics.* ○ *the concept that everyone should have an equal opportunity* ○ *a whole new concept in English language teaching.*

▶ **conceptual** /kən'septʃuəl/ *adj* of or based on concepts: *establish a conceptual framework within which to consider the issues.* **conceptually** *adv.*

conception /kən'sepʃn/ *n* **1** [U,C] conceiving (CONCEIVE 1) or being conceived: *the moment of conception ○ an unplanned conception.* **2(a)** [U] the forming of a basic idea: *The plan, brilliant in its conception, failed because of inadequate funding.* **(b)** [C] ~ (**of sth / that...**) an idea, a plan or an intention: *Marx's conception of social justice ○ He has no conception of* (ie does not know) *how difficult it is to be with a baby all day.*

conceptualize, -ise /kən'septʃuəlaɪz/ *v* [Vn] to form an idea of sth in one's mind.

concern¹ /kən'sɜːn/ *v* **1** [Vn] **(a)** to be relevant to sb; to affect sb: *Don't interfere in what doesn't concern you. ○ The loss was a tragedy for all concerned* (ie all those affected by it). *○ Where the children are concerned* (ie In matters where one must think of the children)... *○ To whom it may concern...* (eg at the beginning of a public notice or of a job reference about sb's character, ability, etc). **(b)** to be about sth; to have sth as a subject: *a report that concerns drug abuse.* **2** ~ **oneself with/in/about sth** to interest oneself in sth: [Vnpr] *There's no need to concern yourself with this matter; we're dealing with it.* **3** to worry sb: [Vn] *The company's losses are beginning to concern the shareholders.* [Vn.*that*] *It concerns me that you no longer seem to care.* See also CONCERNED. **IDM** **as/so far as sb/sth is concerned** ⇨ FAR¹. **be concerned in sth** (*fml*) to have a connection with or responsibility for sth: *Everyone who was directly concerned in the incident has now resigned.* **be concerned to do sth** to regard it as important to do sth. **be concerned with sth** to be about sth: *Her latest documentary is primarily/exclusively concerned with youth unemployment.*

▶ **concerned** *adj* ~ (**about/for sth**); ~ (**that...**) worried; troubled: *Concerned parents held a meeting. ○ The President is deeply/genuinely concerned about this issue. ○ He didn't seem in the least concerned for her safety. ○ I'm concerned that they may have got lost.* **concernedly** /-'sɜːnɪdli/ *adv.*

concerning *prep* (*rather fml*) about sth/sb; on the subject of or in connection with sth/sb: *allegations concerning police methods.*

concern² /kən'sɜːn/ *n* **1(a)** [U] ~ (**about/for/over sth/sb**); ~ (**that...**) worry; anxiety: *There is no cause for concern. ○ widespread public concern about corruption ○ There is now growing/considerable concern for their safety. ○ They expressed their concern that little was being done to help the homeless.* **(b)** [C] a cause of anxiety: *Our main concern is that they are not receiving enough help. ○ economic/environmental concerns.* **2** [C] a thing that is important or interesting to sb: *What are your main concerns as a writer? ○ It's no concern of mine* (ie I am not involved in it or I have no responsibility for it). *○ What concern is it of yours?* (ie Why do you take an interest in it or interfere with it?) **3** [C] a company; a business: *a huge industrial concern.* **4** [C] ~ (**in sth**) a share: *He has a concern in* (ie owns part of) *the business.* **IDM** **a going concern** ⇨ GOING.

concert /'kɒnsət/ *n* a musical entertainment given in public by one or more performers: *a pop concert ○ the Bach concert ○ give a concert for charity ○ a concert pianist/hall/tour.* Compare RECITAL. **IDM** **in ¹concert** giving a live public performance rather than a recorded one: *see Michael Jackson in concert.* **in concert (with sb/sth)** (*fml*) working together with sb/sth: *a plan devised in concert with local businesses.*

■ **¹concert-goer** *n* a person who attends concerts, esp of classical music.

¹**concert 'grand** *n* a piano of the largest size, used esp for concerts.

¹**concert-master** *n* (*esp US*) = LEADER 2.

concerted /kən'sɜːtɪd/ *adj* [usu attrib] arranged or done together with sb: *European Union governments will now have to make a concerted effort to combat pollution. ○ a concerted attack/campaign.*

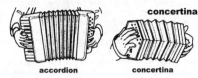

accordion   concertina

concertina /ˌkɒnsə'tiːnə/ *n* a musical instrument like a small ACCORDION. It is held in the hands and played by pressing the ends together to force air past reeds (REED 2). ⇨ picture.

▶ **concertina** *v* (*pt, pp* **concertinaed**; *pres p* **concertinaing**) to fold up by being pressed together from each end: [V] *The truck crashed into the tree and concertinaed.*

concerto /kən'tʃɜːtəʊ/ *n* (*pl* **-os**) a musical composition for one or more SOLO instruments playing with an ORCHESTRA: *a ¹piano concerto ○ a concerto for two violins.*

concession /kən'seʃn/ *n* **1** ~ (**to sb/sth**) **(a)** [C] a thing agreed or given, esp after discussion, an argument, etc: *The company was finally forced to make important concessions to the workers. ○ Her sole concession to fashion was her wide-brimmed hat.* **(b)** [U] the action of conceding (CONCEDE): *a settlement made without concession to local nationalism.* **2** [C] (*Brit*) a reduction in price for particular categories of people: *special concessions on all bus fares for old people.* **3** [C] ~ (**to do sth**) a right given or sold to sb by the owner of sth, allowing them to use or operate it: *mining/oil concessions* (ie allowing minerals or oil to be taken out of the ground) *○ a concession to drill for oil.* **4** [C] (*esp US*) a space or privilege within certain premises for providing a service or running a small business: *a hot-dog concession at Yankee Stadium.*

▶ **concessionary** /kən'seʃənəri; *US* -neri/ *adj* involving a CONCESSION(2): *concessionary rates/fares.*

conch /kɒntʃ/ *n* **(a)** a type of SHELLFISH. **(b)** the large shell of this creature.

conciliate /kən'sɪlieɪt/ *v* to make sb less angry or more friendly, esp by being kind and pleasant or by giving them sth: [Vn] *The government are mainly concerned to conciliate public opinion.*

▶ **conciliation** /kənˌsɪli'eɪʃn/ *n* [U]: *She ignored his attempts at conciliation. ○ A conciliation service helps to settle disputes between employers and workers.* **conciliator** /kən'sɪlieɪtə(r)/ *n* a person who tries to conciliate.

conciliatory /kən'sɪliətəri; *US* -tɔːri/ *adj* intended or likely to conciliate: *a conciliatory gesture/smile/tone.*

concise /kən'saɪs/ *adj* giving a lot of information in few words; brief: *a concise summary ○ clear and concise instructions ○ His observations were concise and to the point.* ▶ **concisely** *adv.* **conciseness** *n* [U].

conclave /'kɒŋkleɪv/ *n* a private and secret meeting: *a conclave of judges/cardinals ○ sit/meet in conclave.*

conclude /kən'kluːd/ *v* **1** ~ **sth (from sth)**; ~ (**from sth) that...** (not in the continuous tenses) to reach a decision about what one believes as a result of reasoning: [Vnpr] *What do you conclude from that?* [Vpr.*that*] *We must conclude from these remarks that all hope of a settlement is dead.* [V.*that*] *The jury concluded that she was guilty. ○ The public might be forgiven for concluding that* (ie It looks as though) *the government does not care about this*

[V] = verb used alone   [Vn] = verb + noun   [Vp] = verb + particle   [Vpr] = verb + prepositional phrase

C

issue. [also Vn]. **2** ~ (**sth**) (**with sth**) (*usu fml*) to come to an end or bring sth to an end: [V] *The meeting concluded at 8 o'clock.* ○ *a few concluding remarks* [Vpr] *The story concludes with the hero's death.* ○ *He concluded by saying that...* [Vnpr] *She concluded her talk with a funny story.* [also Vn, V.speech]. **3** ~ **sth** (**with sb**) to arrange and settle an agreement formally and finally: [Vnpr] *The USA have concluded a new trade agreement with China.* [Vn] *Once the price had been agreed, a deal was quickly concluded.*

conclusion /kən'kluːʒn/ *n* **1** [C] ~ (**that...**) a belief or an opinion that is the result of reasoning: *a summary of the main conclusions and recommendations of the report* ○ **I came to the conclusion** *that he'd been lying.* ○ *What conclusions do you draw from the evidence you've heard?* ○ *I reached the inescapable/unavoidable conclusion that...* **2** [C usu sing] the end of sth: *at the conclusion of his speech* ○ *bring sth to a speedy conclusion* ○ **In conclusion** (ie Lastly) *I'd like to say that...* **3** [U] the formal and final arranging or settling of sth: *Hostilities ended with the successful conclusion of a peace treaty.* **IDM** **a foregone conclusion** ⇨ FOREGONE. **jump/leap to con'clusions / to the con'clusion that...** to make a decision about sb/sth too quickly, before one has learned or thought about all the facts: *She was seen having lunch with him one day and everyone jumped to the wrong conclusion.*

conclusive /kən'kluːsɪv/ *adj* (of facts, evidence, etc) convincing; ending doubt: *Her fingerprints on the gun were conclusive proof of her guilt.* ○ *The temperature data we had was not totally conclusive.* ▶ **conclusively** *adv*: *show/demonstrate/prove sth conclusively.*

concoct /kən'kɒkt/ *v* **1** to make sth by mixing ingredients (esp ones that do not usu go together): [Vn] *He concocted a surprisingly tasty supper of pasta and vegetables.* **2** (*derog*) to invent a story, an excuse, etc: [Vn] *She'd concocted some unlikely tale about the train being held up by cows on the line.* ▶ **concoction** /kən'kɒkʃn/ *n* a thing that is concocted; a mixture: *Do you expect me to drink this vile concoction?*

concomitant /kən'kɒmɪtənt/ *adj* ~ (**with sth**) (*fml*) accompanying; happening at the same time as sth else: *travel and its concomitant discomforts.* ▶ **concomitant** *n* ~ (**of sth**) (*fml*) a thing that typically happens at the same time as sth else: *the infirmities that are the concomitants of old age.*

concord /'kɒŋkɔːd/ *n* [U] **1** ~ (**with sb**) (*fml*) peace and harmony between people; absence of quarrelling: *living in concord (with neighbouring states).* Compare DISCORD 1, HARMONY. **2** ~ (**with sth**) (*grammar*) agreement between words in GENDER, number(8), etc, so that eg a PLURAL noun is followed by a plural form of a verb.

concordance /kən'kɔːdəns/ *n* an alphabetical (ALPHABET) list of the words used by an author or in a text or set of texts. Concordances also show how often and where each word is used: *a 'Bible concordance* ○ *a concordance to Shakespeare.*

concordat /kɒn'kɔːdæt/ *n* an agreement, esp between a state and the Church on matters relating to church affairs.

concourse /'kɒŋkɔːs/ *n* **1** an open area forming part of a building or large group of buildings, where people can walk about: *The ticket office is at the rear of the station concourse* (ie its main hall). **2** (*fml*) a gathering of people or things; a crowd: *a vast concourse of pilgrims.*

concrete¹ /'kɒŋkriːt/ *adj* **1** existing in a form that can be touched, felt, seen, etc; real or solid: *Physics deals with the forces acting on concrete objects.* Compare ABSTRACT¹ 1. **2** definite; positive: *concrete*

proposals/evidence/facts ○ *The police have nothing concrete to go on.* ▶ **concretely** *adv*.

concrete² /'kɒŋkriːt/ *n* [U] building material made by mixing cement with sand, small stones and water: *a slab of concrete* ○ *modern buildings made of concrete* ○ *a concrete path/floor* ○ *life in the **concrete jungle** of the big city.* ▶ **concrete** *v* ~ **sth** (**over**) to cover sth with concrete: [Vn, Vnp] *concrete a road (over).* ■ **'concrete mixer** (also **ce'ment-mixer**) *n* a machine with a container that revolves and is used to mix sand, cement, etc into concrete.

concubine /'kɒŋkjubaɪn/ *n* (in countries where a man can legally have more than one wife) a woman who lives with a man, often as well as his wife or wives, but with lower status: *The sultan's wives and concubines live in the harem.*

concupiscence /kən'kjuːpɪsns/ *n* [U] (*fml often derog*) strong sexual desire; LUST.

concur /kən'kɜː(r)/ *v* (**-rr-**) ~ (**with sb/sth**) (**in sth / that...**) (*fml*) to agree; to express agreement: [V, Vpr] *She has expressed her opposition to the plan, and I fully concur (with her) (in this matter).* [also Vpr.*that*, V.*that*]. ▶ **concurrence** /kən'kʌrəns/ *n* (*fml*) **1** [U, sing] agreement: **With your concurrence** (ie If you agree), *I will confirm the arrangement.* ○ *a concurrence of ideas/views.* **2** [sing] an instance of two or more things happening at the same time: *an unfortunate concurrence of events.*

concurrent /kən'kʌrənt/ *adj* ~ (**with sth**) existing, happening or done at the same time: *developments concurrent with this.* **concurrently** *adv*: *He was given two prison sentences, to run concurrently.*

concuss /kən'kʌs/ *v* (usu passive) to cause damage to sb's brain, usu temporarily, so that they become unconscious or confused: [Vn] *He was badly concussed in the collision.*

concussion /kən'kʌʃn/ *n* [U] damage to sb's brain caused by a blow, violent shaking, etc, making them become temporarily unconscious: *The patient is suffering from severe concussion following his fall.*

condemn /kən'dem/ *v* **1** ~ **sb/sth** (**for/as sth**) to say that one disapproves strongly of sb/sth; to criticize sb/sth: [Vn] *We all condemn cruelty to children.* [Vnpr] *The papers were quick to condemn him for his mistake.* [Vn-adj] *She is often condemned as uncaring.* **2(a)** ~ **sb** (**to sth/to do sth**) (*law*) to say what sb's punishment is to be: [Vnpr] *condemn sb to death/hard labour* [Vn.to inf] *He was found guilty and condemned to be shot.* (**b**) to show or suggest that sb is guilty: [Vn] *His nervous looks condemned him.* **3** ~ **sb to sth/to do sth** (usu passive) to make sb endure or accept a situation, etc that they do not like or want: [Vnpr] *an unhappy worker, condemned to a job he hates* [Vn.to inf] *As an old person, one is often condemned to live alone.* **4** ~ **sth** (**as sth**) to say officially that sth is dangerous or not fit for use: [Vn-adj] *The meat was condemned as unfit for human consumption.* [Vn] *a condemned building* [also Vn-n]. ▶ **condemnation** /ˌkɒndem'neɪʃn/ *n* (**a**) [U] the action of condemning sb/sth or of being condemned: *The incident attracted/aroused widespread condemnation.* (**b**) [C] an instance of this: *many condemnations of her action.* ■ **con,demned 'cell** *n* a prison cell where a person who is to be punished by death is kept.

condensation /ˌkɒnden'seɪʃn/ *n* **1** [U] drops of water that form on a cold surface when steam or water VAPOUR(1) touches it: *His shaving mirror was covered with condensation.* **2(a)** [U] changing or being changed from a gas or a solid to a liquid: *the condensation of steam to water.* (**b**) [C,U] an act or a product of making sth shorter: *The report is a brilliant condensation of several years' work.*

condense /kən'dens/ *v* **1(a)** ~ (**sth**) (**into/to sth**) to

change or make sth change from gas or VAPOUR(1) to a liquid: [V, Vpr, Vn, Vnpr] *steam that condenses/is condensed (into water) when it touches a cold surface.* ⇨ note at WATER[1]. (**b**) (of a liquid) to become or be made thicker or stronger, by losing some of the water: [V] *Soup condenses when boiled.* [also Vn]. **2** ~ **sth (into sth)** to put sth into fewer words: [Vnpr] *condense a long report into a brief summary* [Vn] *a condensed version of the original novel.*
■ **con,densed 'milk** *n* [U] milk that has been made thicker by evaporation (EVAPORATE) and sweeter by adding sugar. It is usu sold in tins.

condenser /kən'densə(r)/ *n* **1** a device for cooling VAPOUR(1) and making it change into a liquid. **2** a device for receiving and storing electricity, esp in a car engine.

condescend /ˌkɒndɪ'send/ *v* **1** (*often derog*) to do sth that one clearly thinks is below one's dignity or level of importance: [V.*to* inf] *She actually condescended to say hello to me in the street today.* ○ (*ironic*) *Perhaps your father would condescend to help with the washing-up!* **2** ~ **to sb** (*derog*) to behave in a kind or polite way, but so as to show that one feels one is better than other people: [Vpr] *I do wish he wouldn't condescend to the junior staff in his department.* ▶ **condescending** *adj: a condescending person* ○ *condescending behaviour* ○ *She's so condescending!* **condescendingly** *adv.* **condescension** /ˌkɒndɪ'senʃn/ *n* [U]: *He gave me some friendly advice without a trace of condescension.*

condiment /'kɒndɪmənt/ *n* [C esp *pl*, U] a substance like salt or pepper that is used to give flavour to food.

condition[1] /kən'dɪʃn/ *n* **1** [sing, U] (**a**) the present state of a thing: *be in good/poor/excellent/perfect condition* ○ *The ship is not in a condition/is in no condition* (ie is not fit) *to make a long voyage.* (**b**) a state of health or being physically fit: *He's in excellent condition for a man of his age.* ○ *I've had no exercise for ages; I'm really out of condition* (ie not fit). ○ *She's in no condition* (ie is not well enough) *to travel.* **2 conditions** [pl] circumstances, esp those that affect the way people live, work, etc: *under existing conditions* ○ *poor working conditions* ○ *climatic conditions* ○ *fire-fighters having to operate in very difficult conditions.* **3** [C] (**a**) a thing that is necessary to make sth else possible; a thing on which another thing depends: *One of the conditions of the job is that you should be able to drive* (ie In order to get the job you must be able to drive). ○ *He was allowed to go out, but his parents made it a condition that he should be home before midnight.* ○ *I'll let you borrow it on one condition: (that) you lend me your bicycle in return.* ○ *You can go out on condition (that)* (ie only if) *you wear an overcoat.* (**b**) a thing that forms part of an agreement, a contract, etc: *the terms and conditions of the lease.* **4** [sing] a particular state of existence: *the human condition* ○ *the condition of slavery* (ie being a slave). **5** [C] an illness; a medical problem: *have a heart/liver/brain condition* ○ *What is the treatment for this condition?* ⇨ note at ILLNESS. **6** [C] (*dated*) a position in society; a rank: *people of every condition/of all conditions.* **IDM** **in mint condition** ⇨ MINT[2]. **on no condition** (*fml*) in no situation; under no circumstances: *You must on no condition tell him what happened.*

condition[2] /kən'dɪʃn/ *v* **1** (often passive) to have an important effect on sb/sth; to determine(5) sth: [Vn] *The pace of change is conditioned by the health of the economy.* **2** ~ **sb/sth (to sth/to do sth)** (usu passive) to train sb/sth to behave in a certain way or to become used to certain circumstances: [Vn] *We have all been conditioned by our upbringing.* [Vnpr] *It didn't take them long to become conditioned to the new environment.* [Vn.*to* inf] *Animals can be conditioned to expect food at certain times.* **3** to make or keep sth healthy or in a good state for use: [Vn]

leather conditioned by a special process ○ *a lotion that conditions the skin.* See also AIR-CONDITIONED.
▶ **conditioner** /kən'dɪʃənə(r)/ *n* [C, U] a thing or substance that conditions (CONDITION[2] 3) sth, esp a liquid that keeps the hair healthy and shiny: *a shampoo and conditioner.*
conditioning /kən'dɪʃənɪŋ/ *n* [U] training or experience that leads sb/sth to behave in a certain way or to become used to certain circumstances: *The animal's conditioning had made it aggressive.* See also AIR-CONDITIONING.
■ **con,ditioned 'reflex** *n* a response that a person or an animal is trained to make to a particular STIMULUS, even if it is not a normal or natural response.

conditional /kən'dɪʃənl/ *adj* (**a**) ~ **(on/upon sth)** depending on sth: *conditional approval/acceptance* ○ *Payment of the money is conditional upon delivery of the goods* (ie If the goods are not delivered, the money will not be paid). ○ *He was found guilty of the offence and given a conditional discharge* (ie allowed to go free on certain conditions). (**b**) (*esp grammar*) containing or implying a condition(3a) or qualification(3): *a conditional clause* (ie one beginning with *if* or *unless*). ▶ **conditionally** /-ʃənəli/ *adv.*

condolence /kən'dəʊləns/ *n* [U, C often *pl*] (an expression of) sympathy: *a letter of condolence* ○ *Please accept my condolences on your father's death.*

condom /'kɒndɒm/ *n* a rubber CONTRACEPTIVE worn on the PENIS during sex(2); a SHEATH(2).

condominium /ˌkɒndə'mɪnɪəm/ *n* (*pl* **condominiums**) **1** [C] (*US*) (a flat in) a block of flats, each of which is owned by the person who lives in it. **2(a)** [U] the governing of a country by two or more states together. (**b**) [C] a country governed in this way.

condone /kən'dəʊn/ *v* to accept wrong behaviour or to treat it as if it were not serious; to ignore sth: [Vn] *condone violence/adultery/fraud* ○ *Foul play can never be condoned.* ○ *Not punishing them amounts to condoning their crime.* [also V.*ing*, V.*n* ing].

condor /'kɒndɔː(r)/ *n* a type of large VULTURE(1) found mainly in S America.

conducive /kən'djuːsɪv; US -'duːs-/ *adj* [pred] ~ **to sth** helping sth to happen or making it likely: *The noisy surroundings were hardly conducive to concentrated study.*

conduct[1] /'kɒndʌkt/ *n* [U] **1** a person's behaviour, esp its moral aspect: *observe the rules of conduct* ○ *The prisoner was released early because of good conduct.* **2** ~ **of sth** the action or manner of directing or managing a business, campaign, etc: *There was growing criticism of the government's conduct of the war.*

conduct[2] /kən'dʌkt/ *v* **1(a)** to direct or manage sth: [Vn] *conduct business/a meeting/negotiations* ○ *She was appointed to conduct the advertising campaign.* ○ *These findings emerge from a survey conducted by the Sunday Times.* (**b**) to direct the performance of a group of people playing or singing music: [Vn] *a concert by the Philharmonic Orchestra, conducted by Sir Colin Davis* [also V]. **2** to lead or guide sb: [Vnpr] *A guide conducted us round the museum.* [also Vp]. **3** ~ **oneself well, badly, etc** (*fml*) to behave in the specified way: [Vnadv] *How did the prisoner conduct himself?* [Vnadv, Vnpr] *conduct oneself honourably/with dignity/like a gentleman.* **4** (of a substance) to allow heat, electricity, etc to pass along or through it: [Vn] *Copper conducts electricity better than other materials do.*
■ **con,ducted 'tour** *n* a tour in which a guide takes visitors round a building, town, etc, often giving them information about it.

conduction /kən'dʌkʃn/ *n* [U] the passing of electricity along wires or of heat by contact.

conductive /kən'dʌktɪv/ *adj* that can conduct(4)

heat, electricity, etc. ▶ **conductivity** /ˌkɒndʌk-ˈtɪvəti/ *n* [U]: *the low conductivity of lead.*

conductor /kənˈdʌktə(r)/ *n* **1** a person who directs the performance of a group of people playing or singing music, etc, esp by standing in front of them and making gestures with her or his arms: *the conductor's baton.* **2(a)** a person who collects fares on a bus. **(b)** (*US*) (*Brit* **guard**) a person in charge of a train. **3** a substance that conducts (CONDUCT 4) heat or electricity: *a 'lightning-conductor* ○ *Wood is a poor conductor.*

▶ **conductress** /kənˈdʌktrəs/ *n* (*Brit*) a woman conductor(2a) on a bus.

conduit /ˈkɒndjuɪt; *US* -du-/ *n* **(a)** a pipe or channel along which liquids flow. **(b)** a tube for protecting insulated (INSULATE) electric wires.

cone /kəʊn/ *n* **1** (*geometry*) a solid figure that slopes up to a point from a circular flat base. ⇨ picture at SOLID. **2** a solid or hollow thing that has the shape of a cone: *the cone of the volcano* ○ *We had chips out of a paper cone.* **3** a plastic object in the shape of a cone that is used with others to separate off or close sections of a road: *There were cones all along the motorway where roadworks were in progress.* **4** an edible container for an ice-cream, in the shape of a cone; an ice-cream in such a container: *Two vanilla cones, please.* **5** the hard dry fruit of a tree that has leaves like needles, eg a PINE[1] or a FIR. ⇨ picture at PINE[1].

▶ **cone** *v* PHRV ˌ**cone** ˈ**off** to mark or separate sth with cones (CONE 3): *cone off a section of motorway during repairs* ○ *cone off parking spaces that must not be used.*

coney = CONY.

confection /kənˈfekʃn/ *n* **1** (*fml*) a dish, etc made with sweet ingredients. **2** an imaginative and skilful mixture of things, esp an elaborate piece of clothing: *a pale pink confection of silk and lace.*

▶ **confectioner** *n* a person who makes or sells sweets, cakes, etc: *I bought it at the confectioner's (shop).* **confectionery** /kənˈfekʃənəri; *US* -ʃəneri/ *n* **(a)** [U] sweets, chocolates, cakes, etc. **(b)** [C] a business or shop selling these.

confederacy /kənˈfedərəsi/ *n* **1** [C] a union or association, esp of states; an ALLIANCE. **2 the Confederacy** [sing] the Confederate States (CONFEDERATE).

confederate /kənˈfedərət/ *adj* joined together by an agreement or a TREATY(1): *the Confederate States of America.*

▶ **confederate** *n* **1** a person one works with, esp in sth illegal or secret; an ACCOMPLICE: *his confederates in the crime.* **2 Confederate** a supporter of the Confederate States.

■ **the Conˌfederate ˈStates** *n* [pl] the eleven states that separated from the USA in 1860–61, causing the American Civil War.

confederation /kənˌfedəˈreɪʃn/ *n* an organization consisting of countries, businesses, etc that have joined together for mutual benefit: *the Confederation of British Industry.*

confer /kənˈfɜː(r)/ *v* (-rr-) **1** ~ **sth** (**on sb**) to give a degree, title, privilege, etc to sb: [Vnpr] *The Queen conferred knighthoods on several distinguished men.* [Vn] *He behaves as if high rank automatically confers the right to be obeyed.* **2** ~ (**with sb**) (**on/about sth**) to have discussions, esp in order to exchange opinions or get advice: [Vpr] *She said she wished to confer with her advisers before announcing a decision.* [also V].

▶ **conferment** *n* [C, U] (*fml*) the action or an instance of awarding a degree, an honour, etc.

conference /ˈkɒnfərəns/ *n* a meeting for discussion or an exchange of views, esp one held regularly: *Many international conferences are held in Geneva.* ○ *The director is in conference* (ie at a

meeting) *and cannot be disturbed.* See also PRESS CONFERENCE.

confess /kənˈfes/ *v* **1(a)** ~ (**to sth / doing sth**); ~ (**sth**) (**to sb**) to say or admit, often formally, that one has done wrong, committed a crime, etc: [V, Vn] *The prisoner refused to confess (his crime).* [Vpr] *She finally confessed to having stolen the money.* [V.that] *He confessed that he had not been telling the truth.* [also Vnpr]. **(b)** to admit sth, often unwillingly, eg because one feels slightly ashamed: [Vpr] *She confessed to (having) a dread of spiders.* [V.that] *I am fairly bored, I must confess.* [Vn-adj, V.n to inf] *He confessed himself (to be) totally ignorant of their plans.* [also V.speech]. See also SELF-CONFESSED. **2(a)** ~ (**sth**) (**to sb**) (esp in the Roman Catholic Church) to tell one's sins formally to a priest: [V.that, Vpr.that] *He confessed (to the priest) that he had sinned.* **(b)** (of a priest) to hear the sins of sb in this way: [Vn] *The priest confessed the criminal.*

▶ **confessedly** /-ədli/ *adv* by sb's own admission(1).

confession /kənˈfeʃn/ *n* **1** [C, U] **(a)** (a formal statement) admitting that one is guilty of a crime, etc: *to make a full confession of one's crimes* ○ *The prisoner was finally brought to confession.* **(b)** (a statement) admitting sth that one is slightly ashamed of, etc: *I'm afraid I have a confession to make — I lost the pen you lent me.* **2** [C, U] (in the Roman Catholic Church) a formal admission(1) of one's sins to a priest: *The priest will hear confessions in English and French.* ○ *I always go to confession on Fridays.* **3** [C] a declaration of one's religious beliefs, principles, etc: *a confession of faith.*

confessional /kənˈfeʃənl/ *n* a private, usu enclosed, place in a church where a priest sits to hear confessions (CONFESSION 2): *the secrets of the confessional.*

confessor /kənˈfesə(r)/ *n* a priest who hears sb's confessions (CONFESSION 2).

confetti /kənˈfeti/ *n* [sing *v*] small pieces of coloured paper that people traditionally throw over a man and woman who have just got married, or (in the USA) at other special events.

confidant /ˈkɒnfɪdænt, ˌkɒnfɪˈdɑːnt/ *n* (*fem* **confidante**) a person that one trusts enough to speak to about one's private affairs or secrets.

confide /kənˈfaɪd/ *v* ~ **sth to sb** to tell a secret to sb, while trusting them not to tell others: [Vnpr] *She confided her troubles to a friend.* [V.that, Vpr.that] *He confided (to me) that he had applied for another job.* [also V.speech]. PHRV **confide in sb** to trust sb enough to tell a secret to them: *There's no one here I can confide in.*

▶ **confiding** *adj* [usu attrib] trusting; not suspicious: *He was a practised swindler and took advantage of the old woman's confiding nature.* **confidingly** *adv*.

confidence /ˈkɒnfɪdəns/ *n* **1** [U] **(a)** ~ (**in sb/sth**) a feeling or belief that one can firmly trust or rely on sb, sb's ability or sth that is said, reported, etc: *to have/lose confidence in sb* ○ *I have little confidence in him.* ○ *Don't put too much confidence in what the papers say.* ○ *There is a lack of confidence in the current government.* **(b)** a feeling of certainty; trust in one's own ability: *He answered the questions with confidence.* ○ *You are too shy: you should have more confidence (in yourself).* **2** [C] a secret told to sb: *The two girls sat in a corner exchanging confidences.* IDM **in sb's confidence** trusted with sb's secrets: *He's said to be very much in the President's confidence.* **take sb into one's confidence** to tell sb one's secrets, etc: *I'm sure I could help him if only he'd take me into his confidence.*

■ **'confidence trick** (also *infml* **'con trick**, *US* **'confidence game**) *n* an act of tricking or cheating sb by first gaining their trust.

confident /ˈkɒnfɪdənt/ adj **1** feeling or showing confidence(1b) in oneself or one's ability: *a confident smile/manner/speech* ○ *He's more socially confident than his brother.* See also SELF-CONFIDENT. **2** ~ (**of sth / that ...**) feeling or showing certainty about sth: *feel confident of succeeding/that one will succeed* ○ *The team is confident of victory.* ○ *Are you confident that this information is correct?* ▶ **confidently** adv.

confidential /ˌkɒnfɪˈdenʃl/ adj **1** to be kept secret; not to be made known to others: *confidential information/files/letters.* **2** (of a way of speaking) indicating that what one says is private or secret: *speaking in a confidential tone.* **3** [attrib] trusted with private information or secrets: *a confidential secretary.* ▶ **confidentiality** /ˌkɒnfɪˌdenʃɪˈælətɪ/ n [U]. **confidentially** /-ʃəlɪ/ adv: *He told me confidentially that he's thinking of retiring early.* ○ *Confidentially, what do you think of the new managing director?*

configuration /kənˌfɪɡəˈreɪʃn; US kənˌfɪɡjəˈreɪʃn/ n (*usu techn*) an arrangement of the parts of sth; the form, shape or figure resulting from such an arrangement: *the configuration of a computer system/the earth's surface/the vocal tract/the solar system.*

configure /kənˈfɪɡə(r); US kənˈfɪɡjər/ v [Vn] (*esp computing*) to arrange sth for a particular purpose, usu so that it can be used with other equipment.

confine /kənˈfaɪn/ v **1** ~ **sb/sth to sth** to restrict or keep sb/sth within certain limits: [Vnpr] *I wish the speaker would confine himself to the subject.* ○ *Confine your criticism to matters you understand.* **2** ~ **sb/sth** (**in/to sth**) to keep a person or an animal in a small or enclosed space: [Vnpr] *Isn't it cruel to confine a bird in a cage?* ○ *After her operation, she was confined to bed for a week.* ○ *I would hate to be confined in an office all day.* [also Vn].
▶ **confined** adj (of space) small and enclosed: *It was difficult to work efficiently in such a confined space.*
confinement n **1** [U] the state of being confined: *to be placed in confinement* (ie in a prison, mental hospital, etc) ○ *He was sentenced to three months' solitary confinement* (ie kept apart from other prisoners). **2** [U,C] the time during which a woman is giving birth to a child: *Her confinement was approaching.* ○ *a home confinement* (ie a birth taking place at the mother's home rather than in hospital).
confines /ˈkɒnfaɪnz/ n [pl] (*fml*) limits; borders; boundaries: *beyond the confines of human knowledge* ○ *within the confines of family life.*

confirm /kənˈfɜːm/ v **1** to provide evidence or state that a report, an opinion, etc is true or correct; to establish the truth of sth: [Vn] *The rumours of an attack were later confirmed.* ○ *The announcement confirmed my suspicions.* ○ *Please write to confirm your reservation* (ie say that it is definite). [V.that] *When asked, she confirmed that she was going to retire.* [also V.wh]. **2(a)** ~ **sth**; ~ **sb** (**in sth**) to make sb feel or believe sth even more strongly: [Vn,Vnpr] *The incident confirmed (him in) his dislike of dogs.* **(b)** to make power, a position, an agreement, etc more definite or official; to establish sth more firmly: [Vn-n] *He has been confirmed as captain for the rest of the season.* [Vn] *After a six-month probationary period, her appointment was confirmed.* [also Vnpr]. **3** (usu passive) to admit sb to full membership of the Christian Church: [Vn] *She was baptized when she was a month old and confirmed when she was thirteen.*
▶ **confirmed** adj [attrib] firmly established in a particular habit or state: *a confirmed bachelor* (ie a single man who is unlikely to marry) ○ *a confirmed drunkard/gambler.*
confirmation /ˌkɒnfəˈmeɪʃn/ n [U,C] **1** (a statement, letter, piece of information, etc) confirming that sth is true, correct or definite: *The evidence*

appeared to provide confirmation of his guilt. ○ *She nodded her head in confirmation.* ○ *Please send us written confirmation of your holiday dates.* **2** a religious ceremony at which a person is admitted as a full member of the Christian Church: *The bishop conducted a number of confirmations at the service.*

confiscate /ˈkɒnfɪskeɪt/ v to take sb's property away from them by the use of one's authority, usu as a punishment: [Vn] *The teacher confiscated Ian's catapult.* ○ *If you are caught smuggling goods into the country, they will probably be confiscated.* ▶ **confiscation** /ˌkɒnfɪˈskeɪʃn/ n [U,C].

conflagration /ˌkɒnfləˈɡreɪʃn/ n (*fml*) a great fire that destroys a lot of property, etc.

conflate /kənˈfleɪt/ v (*fml*) to combine two sets of information, texts, etc into one: [Vn] *The results of the two experiments were conflated.* ▶ **conflation** /kənˈfleɪʃn/ n [U,C].

conflict /ˈkɒnflɪkt/ n [C,U] ~ (**between A and B**) **1(a)** a serious disagreement; an argument: *a long and bitter conflict between employers and workers* ○ *Many people came/were brought into conflict with the authorities over the new tax.* **(b)** a struggle; a fight: *soldiers involved in armed conflict.* **2** a serious difference of opinions, wishes, etc; a CLASH²(1b): *the conflict between one's duty and one's desires* ○ *a conflict of interests* (ie between the achievement of one aim and that of another) ○ *Your statement is in conflict with the rest of the evidence.*
▶ **conflict** /kənˈflɪkt/ v ~ (**with sth**) to be very different (to sth); to be in opposition; to CLASH¹(1b): [V] *conflicting evidence/interests/views* ○ *The statements of the two witnesses conflict.* [Vpr] *Their account of events conflicts with ours.*

confluence /ˈkɒnfluəns/ n (*usu sing*) **1** a place where two rivers flow together and become one: *the confluence of the Blue Nile and the White Nile.* **2** (*fml*) a coming together: *a strange confluence of circumstances.*

conform /kənˈfɔːm/ v **1** ~ (**to/with sth**) to follow generally accepted rules, standards, etc; to COMPLY: [V, Vpr] *her refusal to conform (to the normal social conventions)* [Vpr] *The building does not conform to/with safety regulations.* **2** ~ **with/to sth** to agree or be consistent with sth: [Vpr] *His ideas do not conform with mine.*
▶ **conformist** /kənˈfɔːmɪst/ n a person who conforms to accepted behaviour, the established religion, etc: *She's too much of a conformist to wear silly clothes.* See also NONCONFORMIST.
conformity /kənˈfɔːmətɪ/ n [U] ~ (**to/with sth**) (*fml*) behaviour, etc that conforms to established rules, customs, etc: *intellectual/social/religious conformity.*

conformation /ˌkɒnfɔːˈmeɪʃn/ n [U,C] (*fml*) the way in which sth is formed; the shape or structure of sth: *a horse with (a) good conformation.*

confound /kənˈfaʊnd/ v **1** (*fml*) to confuse and surprise sb; to PUZZLE(1) sb: [Vn] *The sudden rise in share prices has confounded the City.* **2** (*fml*) to defeat sb or prevent sth; to prove sb/sth wrong: [Vn] *confound an enemy/a rival/a critic* ○ *confound a plan/an attempt* ○ *His extraordinary success had confounded all our expectations.* **3** (*dated infml*) (used as an *interj* to express anger): [Vn] *Confound it!* ○ *Confound you!*
▶ **confounded** adj [attrib] (*infml*) (used to emphasize one's annoyance): *You're/It's a confounded nuisance!* **confoundedly** adv (*dated infml*) very: *It's confoundedly hot in here.*

confront /kənˈfrʌnt/ v **1 (a)** (of a difficulty, etc) to face sb so that they cannot avoid it: [Vn] *the problems confronting us* ○ *Confronted by an angry crowd, the police retreated.* **(b)** to face and deal with a problem, difficulty, etc: [Vn] *confront danger/fear/grief* ○ *She knew she'd have to confront her parents when she got home.* **2** ~ **sb with sb/sth** to make sb face or consider sb/sth unpleasant, difficult, etc: [Vnpr] *They confronted the prisoner with his ac- cusers.* ○ *When confronted with the evidence of her guilt, she confessed.*

▶ **confrontation** /ˌkɒnfrʌn'teɪʃn/ *n* [C, U] (an in- stance of) angry disagreement or opposition: *a confrontation between the government and the unions.*

confuse /kən'fjuːz/ *v* **1** to make sb unable to think clearly; to BEWILDER sb: [Vn] *They confused me by asking so many questions.* **2** ~ **A and/with B** to mistake one person or thing for another: [Vn] *I always confuse the sisters: they look so alike.* [Vn, Vnpr] *Don't confuse Austria and/with Austra- lia.* [Vnpr] *'Flaunt' should not be confused with 'flout'.* **3** to make sth less clear; to MUDDLE sth: [Vn] *Don't confuse the issue* (eg by introducing irrelevant topics). **4** to put sth into disorder; to upset sth: [Vn] *Her unexpected arrival confused all our plans.*

▶ **confused** *adj* **1** unable to think clearly; bewil- dered (BEWILDER): *All your changes of plan have made me totally confused.* ○ *The old lady easily gets confused.* **2** mixed up; not clear: *a confused account of what happened.* **confusedly** /-ədli/ *adv.*

confusing *adj* difficult to understand; not clear: *a most confusing speech* ○ *The instructions on the box are very confusing.* **confusingly** *adv.*

confusion /kən'fjuːʒn/ *n* **1** [U, C] a state of uncer- tainty about what is happening, intended, required, etc; an instance of this: *There is some confusion about what the correct procedure should be.* ○ *doubt caused by various confusions in policy.* **2** [U] the mistaking of one person or thing for another: *There has been some confusion of names.* **3** [U] a lack of control or order; PANIC: *Her unexpected arrival threw us into total confusion.* ○ *Fighting had broken out and the centre of the city was in a state of confusion.* **4** [U, C] a state of being not clear in one's mind because of lack of understanding, embarrassment, etc: *gazing in confusion at the strange sight* ○ *the confusions of adolescence.*

confute /kən'fjuːt/ *v* [Vn] (*fml*) to prove a person or an argument to be wrong.

conga /'kɒŋgə/ *n* (the music for) a lively dance in which the dancers follow a leader linked together in a long winding line.

congeal /kən'dʒiːl/ *v* to become or make sth thick or solid, esp by cooling: [V] *The blood had congealed round the cut on her knee.* [Vn usu passive]: *Use hot water to rinse the congealed fat off the dinner plates.*

congenial /kən'dʒiːniəl/ *adj* **1** (of people) pleasing because of having a personality, interests, etc that are similar to one's own: *a congenial companion.* **2** ~ **(to sb)** pleasant because suited to one's nature or tastes: *a congenial climate/environment/hobby* ○ *I find this aspect of my job particularly congenial.*

congenital /kən'dʒenɪtl/ *adj* **1** (of diseases, etc) present from or before birth: *congenital defects/ blindness.* **2** [attrib] (of people) born with a certain illness or condition: (*fig*) *a congenital liar* (ie sb who always tells lies).

conger /'kɒŋgə(r)/ (also ˌconger **'eel**) *n* a large type of EEL living in the sea.

congested /kən'dʒestɪd/ *adj* **1** ~ **(with sth)** too full; too crowded: *streets heavily congested with traf- fic.* **2(a)** (of parts of the body, eg the lungs) abnormally full of blood. **(b)** (of the nose) blocked with MUCUS: *He had a cold and was very congested.*

congestion /kən'dʒestʃən/ *n* [U] the state of being crowded, blocked or too full of sth: *traffic congestion* ○ *congestion of the lungs.*

conglomerate /kən'glɒmərət/ *n* **1** (*commerce*) a large corporation formed by joining together different firms: *a mining/a chemical/an airline con- glomerate.* **2** a number of things or parts put together: *The new ensemble was a conglomerate of three different bands.* **3** (*geology*) a type of

rock made of small stones held together by dried clay, etc.

▶ **conglomeration** /kənˌglɒmə'reɪʃn/ *n* **1** [C] (*infml*) a number of different things gathered to- gether or found in the same place: *a conglomeration of rusty old machinery.* **2** [U] the process of becom- ing, or state of being, a conglomerate(1).

congratulate /kən'grætʃuleɪt/ *v* **1** ~ **sb (on sth)** to tell sb that one is pleased about their good luck or achievements: [Vnpr] *congratulate sb on their marriage/new job/good exam results* [also Vn]. **2** ~ **oneself (on sth/doing sth)** to consider oneself for- tunate or successful; to be proud of sth: [Vnpr] *You can congratulate yourself on having done an excellent job.* [also Vn].

▶ **congratulation** /kənˌgrætʃu'leɪʃn/ *n* **1** [U] the action of congratulating sb or of being congratu- lated: *a speech of congratulation for the winner.* **2** **congratulations** [pl] **(a)** words of congratulation: *offer sb one's congratulations on his success.* **(b)** (also *infml* **congrats**) (used as an *interj*): *Congratulations on passing your driving test!*

congratulatory /kənˌgrætʃu'leɪtəri; *US* kən'grætʃə- lətɔːri/ *adj* [usu attrib] intended to congratulate: *a congratulatory messsage/telegram.*

congregate /'kɒŋgrɪgeɪt/ *v* to come together in a crowd: [V, Vpr] *A crowd quickly congregated (round the speaker).*

congregation /ˌkɒŋgrɪ'geɪʃn/ *n* [CGp] **1** a group of people gathered together for religious worship, usu excluding the priest and CHOIR(1). **2** a group of people who regularly attend a particular church, etc.

▶ **Congregational** *adj* of a union of Christian Churches in which individual congregations are responsible for their own affairs.

congress /'kɒŋgres; *US* -grəs/ *n* [CGp] **1** a formal meeting or series of meetings for discussion be- tween representatives: *a medical/international/ party congress* ○ *the Trades Union Congress.* **2** **Congress** a governing body that makes laws, esp that of the USA: *Congress is/are expected to veto the proposals.* Compare SENATE 1, HOUSE OF REPRESENTA- TIVES.

▶ **congressional** /kən'greʃənl/ *adj* of a congress or Congress: *a congressional investigation/committee.*

Congressman /'kɒŋgresmən/ *n* (*pl* **-men** /-mən/; *fem* **Congresswoman** /-wʊmən/, *pl* **-women** /-wɪmɪn/) a member of the US Congress, esp the House of Representatives.

congruent /'kɒŋgruənt/ *adj* **1** (*geometry*) having the same size and shape: *congruent triangles.* **2** ~ **(with sth)** (*fml*) suitable or fitting for sth: *measures congruent with the seriousness of the situation.* ▶ **congruence** /'kɒŋgruəns/ *n* [U].

conic /'kɒnɪk/ *adj* (*geometry*) of a CONE(1): *a conic section* (ie the shape formed when a plane¹(2) passes through a CONE(1)).

▶ **conical** /'kɒnɪkl/ *adj* with a shape like a CONE(1): *a conical hat/shell/hill.*

conifer /'kɒnɪfə(r), 'kəʊn-/ *n* a type of tree that bears cones (CONE 5). Most conifers keep their leaves all through the year: *pines, yews and other conifers.* ▶ **coniferous** /kəʊ'nɪfərəs/ *adj*: *coniferous trees/ forests.* Compare EVERGREEN.

conjecture /kən'dʒektʃə(r)/ *v* (*fml*) to form (and express) an opinion not based on firm evidence; to guess: [V] *It was just as I had conjectured.* [V.that] *He conjectured that the population might double in ten years.* [also V.wh].

▶ **conjecture** *n* (*rather fml*) **(a)** [C] a guess: *I was right in my conjectures.* **(b)** [U] guessing: *What the real cause was is open to conjecture.* ○ *Your theory is pure conjecture.* **conjectural** /kən'dʒektʃərəl/ *adj*: *a conjectural hypothesis.*

---

conjoin /kən'dʒɔɪn/ v [V, Vn] (*fml*) to join or make sb/sth join together; to unite.

conjugal /'kɒndʒəgl/ adj (*fml*) of marriage or the relationship between a husband and a wife: *conjugal life/bliss/rights*. Compare CONNUBIAL.

conjugate /'kɒndʒəgeɪt/ v (*grammar*) (**a**) [Vn] to give the different forms of a verb, as they vary according to number, TENSE², etc. (**b**) (of a verb) to have different forms showing number, TENSE², etc: [V] *How does this verb conjugate?*
▶ **conjugation** /,kɒndʒu'geɪʃn/ n (*grammar*) (**a**) [U, C] the way in which a verb conjugates: *a verb with an irregular conjugation*. (**b**) [C] a class of verbs that conjugate in the same way: *Latin verbs of the second conjugation*.

conjunction /kən'dʒʌŋkʃn/ n **1** [C] (*grammar*) (abbreviated as *conj* in this dictionary) a word that joins words, phrases or sentences, eg *and*, *but*, or. **2** (*fml*) (**a**) [C] a combination of events, etc: *an unusual conjunction of circumstances*. (**b**) [U] the action of joining or condition of being joined together: *the conjunction of workmanship and artistry in making jewellery* ○ *The British police are working* **in conjunction with** (ie together with) *the FBI on the investigation*. **3** [C, U] (*techn*) the appearance of coming close to each other of certain stars, planets, etc as observed from the earth: *I was born when Mars was in conjunction with Neptune*.

conjunctivitis /kən,dʒʌŋktɪ'vaɪtɪs/ n [U] a painful swelling of the thin transparent layer which covers the EYEBALL.

conjure /'kʌndʒə(r)/ v to do clever tricks which seem magical, esp with quick movements of the hands: [V] *learn how to conjure*. **PHRV** **,conjure sth a'way** to make sth disappear as if by magic: *conjure the pain away*. **,conjure sth 'up 1** to make sth appear as a picture in the mind: *a tune which conjures up pleasant memories*. **2** to ask a spirit or ghost to appear, esp by using a magic ceremony: *conjure up the spirits of the dead*. **,conjure sth 'up; conjure sth (up) from/out of sth** to make sth appear suddenly or unexpectedly, as if by magic: *I had lost my pen, but she conjured up another one for me from somewhere*. ○ *conjuring a delicious meal out of a few unpromising leftovers*.
▶ **conjurer** (also **conjuror**) /'kʌndʒərə(r)/ n (*esp Brit*) a person who performs conjuring tricks. Compare MAGICIAN.
conjuring /'kʌndʒərɪŋ/ n (*esp Brit*) [U] the performance of clever tricks which seem magical, esp involving quick movements of the hands: *a 'conjuring trick*.

conk¹ /kɒŋk/ n (*Brit sl*) a person's nose.

conk² /kɒŋk/ v [Vn] (*infml esp US*) to hit sb hard, esp on the head. **PHRV** **conk out** (*infml*) **1** (of a machine) to stop working: *The car conked out halfway up the hill.* **2** (of people) to become tired and stop; to fall asleep or die: *Grandpa usually conks out* (ie sleeps) *for an hour or so after lunch.*

conker /'kɒŋkə(r)/ n (*infml esp Brit*) **1** [C] the nut of the horse chestnut (HORSE) tree. ⇨ picture at HORSE CHESTNUT. **2 conkers** [sing v] (*Brit*) a children's game played with conkers on strings, in which two players take turns to try to hit and break each other's conker.

con man ⇨ CON¹.

connect /kə'nekt/ v **1** ~ (sth) (up) (to/with sth) to come or bring sth together or into contact; to join: [Vn] *The two towns are connected by an excellent bus service.* [Vn, Vnpr] *A railway connects Oxford and/with Reading.* [Vnpr, Vnp] *Connect the fridge (up) to the electricity supply.* [Vnpr] *The thigh-bone is connected to the hip-bone.* [V, Vp] *The wires connect (up) under the floor.* [Vpr] *Where does the stove connect with the gas-pipe?* [V] *The two rooms have a connecting door* (ie so that you can go straight from one

room into the other). **2(a)** ~ sb (with sb/sth) (usu passive) to associate or link sb with sb/sth: [Vnpr] *We're connected by marriage.* [Vnpr] *a man connected with known criminals* ○ *She is connected with a noble family.* See also WELL-CONNECTED. (**b**) ~ sb/sth (with sb/sth) to think of different things or people as having a relationship to each other: [Vn] *I was surprised to hear them mentioned together: I've never connected them before.* [Vnpr] *People connect Vienna with waltzes and coffee-houses.* **3** ~ (with sth) (of a train, plane, etc) to arrive just before another train, plane, etc leaves, so that passengers can change from one to the other: [V] *These two planes connect.* ○ *There's a connecting flight at midday.* [Vpr] *The 9.00 am train from London connects with the 12.25 pm from Crewe.* **4** ~ sb (with sb) to put sb into contact by telephone: [Vn, Vnpr] *Hold on, I'll just connect you (with Miss Jones).* **5** ~ (with sb/sth) (*infml*) (of a blow, etc) to strike or touch sb/sth: [V, Vpr] *I took a wild swing which failed to connect (with his chin).*
■ **con'necting-rod** n a rod linking the PISTON and the CRANKSHAFT in an engine.

connection (*Brit also* **connexion**) /kə'nekʃn/ n **1(a)** [C] ~ between sth and sth; ~ with/to sth a point where two things are connected; a thing that connects: *There's a faulty connection in the fuse-box.* ○ *What is the connection between the two ideas?* (ie How are they linked?) ○ *Is there a connection between smoking and lung cancer?* ○ *His dismissal has no connection with* (ie is not due to) *the quality of his work.* (**b**) [U] connecting or being connected: *How long will the connection of my new phone take?* **2** [C] a train, plane, etc that leaves a station, an airport, etc soon after another arrives, enabling passengers to change from one to the other: *The flight was late so I missed my connection.* **3** [C usu *pl*] a person or organization that one knows socially or through business, esp one that has influence or can give help, advice, etc: *I heard about it through one of my business connections.* **4 connections** [pl] people to whom one is connected by a family relationship: *She is British but also has German connections.* **IDM** **in connection with sb/sth** with reference to sb/sth: *I am writing to you in connection with your recent job application.* ○ *He is wanted by the police in connection with two murders.* **in this/that connection** (*fml*) with reference to this/that.

connective /kə'nektɪv/ adj (*esp medical*) that connects things: *connective tissue.*

conning tower /'kɒnɪŋ taʊə(r)/ n a raised structure on a SUBMARINE containing the PERISCOPE.

connive /kə'naɪv/ **1** v (*derog*) ~ at/in sth to ignore or seem to allow a wrong action: [Vpr] *By not protesting you are conniving at the destruction of the environment.* **2** ~ (with sb) (to do sth) to work together with sb in order to do sth wrong or illegal: [V.to inf, Vpr.to inf] *They had connived (with the mayor) to get funds secretly allocated to the project.* [also V].
▶ **connivance** /kə'naɪvəns/ n [U] ~ (at/in sth) conniving at a wrong action: *a crime carried out with the connivance of/in connivance with the police.*
conniving adj acting in a deceitful or unpleasant way so as to harm others: *You conniving bastard!*

connoisseur /,kɒnə'sɜː(r)/ n an expert on matters in which appreciation of beauty is needed, esp the fine arts: *a connoisseur of painting/old porcelain/antiques/wine.*

connote /kə'nəʊt/ v (of words) to suggest sth in addition to the main meaning: [Vn] *a term connoting disapproval.* Compare DENOTE.
▶ **connotation** /,kɒnə'teɪʃn/ n an idea suggested or implied by a word in addition to its main meaning: *The word 'hack' means 'journalist' but has derogatory connotations.*

connubial /kə'njuːbɪəl; US -'nuː-/ adj (*fml or joc*) of marriage; of husband and wife: *connubial life/bliss.* Compare CONJUGAL.

conquer /'kɒŋkə(r)/ *v* **1** to take possession and control of a country, city, etc by force: [Vn] *The Normans conquered England in 1066.* **2** to defeat an enemy, a rival, etc: [Vn] *England conquered their main rivals in the first round of the competition.* **3** to overcome an obstacle, emotion, etc: [Vn] *The mountain was not conquered* (ie successfully climbed) *until 1953.* ○ *Smallpox has finally been conquered.* ○ *You must conquer your fear of driving.* **4** to gain the admiration, love, etc of sb/sth: [Vn] *He set out to conquer the literary world of New York.* ○ *She has conquered the hearts of many men* (ie they have fallen in love with her).
▶ **conqueror** /'kɒŋkərə(r)/ *n* a person who conquers: *William the Conqueror* (ie King William I of England).

conquest /'kɒŋkwest/ *n* **1(a)** [U] the action or an instance of conquering (CONQUER) sb/sth; defeat: *the Norman Conquest* (ie of England in 1066) ○ *the conquest of cancer.* **(b)** [C] a thing gained by conquering: *the Spanish conquests in South America.* **2** [C] (*usu joc*) a person whose admiration or (esp) love has been gained: *He is one of her many conquests.* ○ *You've made quite a conquest there* (ie He or she likes you)!

Cons *abbr* (*Brit politics*) Conservative: *James Crofton (Cons).*

consanguinity /ˌkɒnsæŋ'gwɪnəti/ *n* [U] (*fml*) relationship by being descended from the same family: *close ties of consanguinity.*

conscience /'kɒnʃəns/ *n* [C,U] a person's awareness of right and wrong with regard to his or her own thoughts and actions: *have a clear/guilty conscience* (ie feel one has done right/wrong) ○ *My conscience was troubled by the unkind things I had said to her.* ○ *She cheerfully cheats and lies; she has no conscience at all.* ○ *I must go. It's a matter of conscience* (ie I think it would be morally wrong not to go). ○ *He has a strong social/political conscience.* IDM **in (all/good) conscience** honestly; fairly: *You cannot in all conscience regard that as fair pay.* ○ *I could not in conscience refuse to help.* **on one's 'conscience** making one feel guilty for doing or failing to do sth: *It's still on my conscience that I didn't warn her in time.* ○ *I must write to him about his wife's death — I've had it on my conscience for weeks now.*
■ **'conscience money** *n* [U] money that one pays in order to make one feel less guilty.
'conscience-stricken /-strɪkn/ *adj* filled with a feeling of guilt for what one has done.

conscientious /ˌkɒnʃi'enʃəs/ *adj* (of people or their actions) showing that one cares about doing things well and thoroughly: *a conscientious worker/student/attitude* ○ *This essay is a most conscientious piece of work.* ▶ **conscientiously** *adv.* **conscientiousness** *n* [U].
■ **ˌconscientious ob'jector** *n* a person who refuses to serve in the armed forces because he or she thinks it is morally wrong. Compare PACIFIST.

conscious /'kɒnʃəs/ *adj* **1** knowing what is going on around one because one is able to use one's senses and mental powers: *He was in a coma for days, but now he's (fully) conscious again.* ○ *She spoke to us in her conscious moments.* **2** ~ **of sth/that ...** aware; noticing: *be conscious of being watched/conscious that one is being watched* ○ *Are you conscious (of) how people will regard such behaviour?* **3** (of actions, feelings, etc) realized or controlled by oneself: *One's conscious motives are often different from one's subconscious ones.* ○ *I had to make a conscious effort not to be rude to him.* **4** being particularly aware of and interested in the thing mentioned: *trying to make the workers more politic-*

ally conscious ○ *Teenagers are often very 'fashion-conscious.* ▶ **consciously** *adv.*

consciousness /'kɒnʃəsnəs/ *n* [U] **1** the state of being conscious(1): *The blow caused him to lose consciousness.* ○ *recover/regain consciousness after an accident.* **2** the state of being aware; awareness: *my consciousness of her needs.* **3** all the ideas, thoughts, feelings, etc of a person or people: *attitudes that are deeply ingrained in the child's consciousness.*
■ **'consciousness-raising** *n* [U] the activity of making people become more aware of important social and political issues: *a consciousness-raising campaign/crusade.*

conscript /kən'skrɪpt/ *v* ~ **sb** (**into sth**) to force sb by law to serve in the armed forces: [Vnpr] *conscripted into the army* ○ (*fig*) *I got conscripted into the team when our top player was injured.* [also Vn]. Compare DRAFT² 3.
▶ **conscript** /'kɒnskrɪpt/ *n* a person who has been conscripted: *conscript soldiers* ○ *a conscript army.* Compare VOLUNTEER 2.
conscription /kən'skrɪpʃn/ *n* [U] the conscripting of people into the armed forces.

consecrate /'kɒnsɪkreɪt/ *v* **1** to bring sth into religious use or admit sb into a religious office(5) by a special ceremony: [Vn] *The new church was consecrated by the Bishop of Chester.* ○ *consecrated bread and wine* (ie made into the body and blood of Christ, according to Christian belief) [Vn-n] *He was consecrated Archbishop last year.* **2** ~ **sth/sb to sth** to reserve sth/sb for or devote sth/sb to a special, esp religious, purpose: [Vnpr] *consecrate one's life to the service of God/to the relief of suffering.* Compare DEDICATE 3. ▶ **consecration** /ˌkɒnsɪ'kreɪʃn/ *n* [C,U]: *the consecration of a bishop* (ie the ceremony at which a priest is made a bishop).

consecutive /kən'sekjətɪv/ *adj* coming one after the other without interruption; following continuously: *on three consecutive days, Monday, Tuesday and Wednesday.* ▶ **consecutively** *adv.*

consensus /kən'sensəs/ *n* [U, sing] ~ (**on sth / that ...**) a general agreement about a matter of opinion: *The two parties have reached (a) consensus.* ○ *There is a broad consensus (of opinion) in the country on this issue.* ○ *consensus politics* (ie the practice of proposing policies which will be given support by all or most parties).

consent /kən'sent/ *v* ~ (**to sth**) to give agreement or permission: [V] *When she told me what she wanted I readily consented.* ○ *sex between consenting adults* (ie who both agree to it) [Vpr] *She won't consent to him staying out late/to his staying out late.* [V.to inf] *They finally consented* (ie agreed) *to go with us.*
▶ **consent** *n* [U] ~ (**to sth**) agreement; permission: *Her parents refused (to give) their consent to the marriage.* ○ *He gave his consent for the project to get under way.* ○ *She was chosen as leader by common consent* (ie Everyone agreed to the choice). ○ *Such action is only permitted with the prior consent of the committee.* See also AGE OF CONSENT.

consequence /'kɒnsɪkwəns; *US* -kwens/ *n* **1** [C esp *pl*] a result or an effect of sth else: *He invested heavily in the property market just before the recession, with disastrous consequences.* ○ *be ready to take/suffer/bear the consequences of one's actions* (ie accept the bad things which happen as a result). ○ *He fell ill, and they had to cancel the trip as a consequence (of this).* **2** [U] (*fml*) importance: *It is of no consequence.* ○ *a man of consequence* (ie an important man or man of high rank). IDM **in consequence (of sth)** (*infml*) as a result of sth: *The child was born deformed in consequence of an injury to its mother.*

consequent /'kɒnsɪkwənt/ *adj* ~ (**on/upon sth**) (*fml*) following sth as a result or an effect: *his resig-*

nation and the consequent public uproar ○ *the rise in prices consequent upon the failure of the crops.*
▶ **consequently** *adv* as a result; therefore: *My car broke down and consequently I arrived rather late.*

consequential /ˌkɒnsɪˈkwenʃl/ *adj* (*fml*) following as a direct result or effect of sth: *She was injured and suffered a consequential loss of earnings.* ▶ **consequentially** /-ʃəli/ *adv.*

conservancy /kənˈsɜːvənsi/ *n* (often **Conservancy**) [CGp] (*Brit*) a group of officials controlling a port, a river, an area of land, etc: *the Thames Conservancy* ○ *the Nature Conservancy Council.*

conservation /ˌkɒnsəˈveɪʃn/ *n* [U] **1** the prevention of loss, waste, damage, destruction, etc: *the conservation of forests/water resources/old buildings* ○ *wildlife conservation* ○ (*physics*) *the conservation of energy* (ie the principle that the total quantity of energy in the universe never varies). **2** the care and management of the natural environment: *She is very interested in conservation.*
▶ **conservationist** /-ʃənɪst/ *n* a person who is interested in conservation(2).
■ **conser'vation area** *n* (*Brit*) an area protected by law from changes that would damage its natural character or architecture.

conservatism /kənˈsɜːvətɪzəm/ *n* [U] **1** the tendency to resist great or sudden change, esp in politics: *people's innate conservatism.* **2** (usu **Conservatism**) the principles of the Conservative Party in British politics.

conservative /kənˈsɜːvətɪv/ *adj* **1** opposed to great or sudden social or political change; having traditional attitudes and values: *Old people are usually more conservative than young people.* ○ *a conservative style of dress* ○ *conservative tastes in music.* **2** (usu **Conservative**) of the British Conservative Party: *Conservative principles/candidates/voters.* **3** (of an estimate, etc) cautious; deliberately low: *There must have been a thousand people there, at a conservative guess.*
▶ **conservative** *n* **1** a conservative person. **2** (usu **Conservative**) a member of the British Conservative Party.
conservatively *adv.*
■ **the Con'servative Party** *n* one of the main British political parties, which supports free enterprise and private ownership of industry. Compare THE LABOUR PARTY, THE LIBERAL DEMOCRATS.

conservatoire /kənˈsɜːvətwɑː(r)/ *n* (esp in names) a school of music, drama, etc, esp in Europe: *She studied at the Paris Conservatoire.*

conservatory /kənˈsɜːvətri; *US* -tɔːri/ *n* a room with glass walls and a glass roof built on the side of a house. Conservatories are used to protect plants from cold weather. ⇨ picture at HOUSE¹.

conserve¹ /kənˈsɜːv/ *v* to prevent sth from being changed, lost or destroyed: [Vn] *conserve one's strength/health/resources* ○ *new laws to conserve wildlife in the area.* Compare PRESERVE¹.

conserve² /ˈkɒnsɜːv/ *n* [U, C often *pl*] jam, usu with quite large pieces of fruit in it. Compare PRESERVE² 2.

consider /kənˈsɪdə(r)/ *v* **1** ~ sb/sth (for/as sth) to think about sb/sth, esp in order to make a decision: [Vn] *We have considered your application carefully, but cannot offer you the job.* ○ *a carefully considered decision/statement/proposal* [Vnpr, Vn-n] *consider sb for a job/as a candidate* [V.wh] *Have you considered how to get there?* [V.ing] *We are considering going to Canada* (ie we may go there). [also V]. **2** ~ sb/sth (as) sth to think or have the opinion; to regard sb/sth as sth: [V.that] *We consider that you are not to blame.* [Vn-adj] *We consider this (to be) very important.* ○ *Consider yourself lucky you weren't fired!* ○ *Do you consider it wise to interfere?* ○ *The painting was once considered (as) worthless, but it now turns out to*

be very valuable. [Vn-n] *He will be considered a weak leader.* [V.n to inf] *He's generally considered to have the finest tenor voice in the country.* **3** to take sth into account; to make allowances for sth: [Vn] *We must consider the feelings of other people.* ○ *In judging him you should consider his youth.* **4** (*fml*) to look carefully at sb/sth: [Vn] *He stood considering the painting for some minutes.* **IDM** **one's con,sidered o'pinion** one's opinion formed after some thought: *It's my considered opinion that you should resign.*

considerable /kənˈsɪdərəbl/ *adj* great in amount or size: *a considerable quantity/sum/distance* ○ *brought here at considerable expense.*
▶ **considerably** /-əbli/ *adv* much; a lot: *It's considerably colder this morning.*

considerate /kənˈsɪdərət/ *adj* ~ (**towards sb**) careful not to hurt or trouble others; thoughtful (THOUGHT²): *a considerate person/act/attitude* ○ *She's always very considerate towards her employees.* ○ *It was considerate of you not to play the piano while I was asleep.* Compare INCONSIDERATE, CONSIDERATION 3. ▶ **considerately** *adv.*

consideration /kənˌsɪdəˈreɪʃn/ *n* **1** [U] the action of considering (CONSIDER 1) or thinking about sth: *Please give the matter your careful consideration.* ○ *The proposals are still under consideration* (ie being considered). **2** [C] a thing that must be thought about or taken into account; a reason: *Time is an important consideration in this case.* ○ *Several considerations have influenced my decision.* **3** [U] ~ (**for sb/sth**) the quality of being sensitive or considerate towards others, their feelings, etc: *He has never shown much consideration for his wife's needs.* ○ *The papers did not print the story out of consideration for the bereaved family's feelings.* **4** [C] (*fml*) a reward; a payment: *I will do it for you for a small consideration* (of £50). **IDM** **in consideration of sth** (*fml*) in return for sth; because of sth: *a small payment in consideration of sb's services.* **take sth into consideration** to take account of sth; to make allowances for sth: *I always take fuel consumption into consideration when buying a car.* ○ *Taking everything into consideration, the event was remarkably successful.*

considering /kənˈsɪdərɪŋ/ *prep, conj* taking sth into consideration; taking sth into account: *She's very active, considering her age.* ○ *Considering he's only just started, he knows quite a lot about it.* ○ *You've done very well, considering* (eg in view of the difficult circumstances).

consign /kənˈsaɪn/ *v* **1** (*fml*) (**a**) ~ sb/sth to sb/sth to give sb/sth up to sb/sth; to deliver sb/sth to sb/sth: [Vnpr] *consign a child to its uncle's care* ○ *consign one's soul to God* ○ (*fig*) *The body was consigned to the flames* (ie burned). (**b**) ~ sth to sth (*often joc*) to put away sth that is not wanted: [Vnpr] *an old chair that had been consigned to the attic* ○ *consign the food to the dustbin.* **2** ~ sth (**to sb**) to send goods, etc, esp to a buyer: [Vn, Vnpr] *The goods have been consigned (to you) by rail.*
▶ **consignment** *n* **1** [C] a quantity of goods consigned (CONSIGN 2) together: *a consignment of wheat bound for Europe.* **2** [U] the action of consigning sb/sth. **IDM** **on consignment** (of goods) supplied to a shop, etc for sale but only paid for after being sold: *take/send/ship/supply goods on consignment.*

consist /kənˈsɪst/ *v* (not in the continuous tenses) **PHRV** **consist in sth/doing sth** (*fml*) to have the specified thing as its main or only element or feature: *The beauty of the poem consists in its imagery.* ○ *Respecting people consists in giving due weight to their interests.* **consist of sth** to be composed of sth: *The committee consists of ten members.* ○ *a mixture consisting of flour and water* ○ note at COMPRISE.

consistency /kənˈsɪstənsi/ *n* **1** [U] (*approv*) the quality of being consistent(1a): *She has played with* *great consistency all season.* ○ *You may disagree with his political views but they do at least have the merit of consistency.* **2** [C, U] the degree of thickness, or solidity (SOLID), esp of thick liquids or of sth made by mixing with a liquid: *Mix flour and milk to a firm consistency.* ○ *It should have the consistency of thick soup.*

consistent /kənˈsɪstənt/ *adj* **1(a)** (*approv*) (of a person, behaviour, views, etc) always following the same pattern or style; not changing: *You're not very consistent: first you condemn me, then you praise me.* (**b**) always present or the same: *consistent interference/opposition* ○ *consistent results/ standards.* **2** [pred] ~ (**with sth**) in agreement or harmony with sth: *What you say now is not consistent with what you said last week.* ○ *The pattern of injuries is consistent with* (ie could have been caused by) *an attack with a knife.* ○ *I left as early as was consistent with politeness.* Compare INCONSISTENT. ▶ **consistently** *adv*.

consolation /ˌkɒnsəˈleɪʃn/ *n* **1** [U] comfort or compensation: *a few words of consolation* ○ *Money is no consolation when you don't like your work.* **2** [C] a person or thing that comforts: *Your friendship has been a great consolation to me.* ○ *At least you weren't hurt — that's one consolation* (ie one good aspect of an otherwise bad situation).

■ **conso'lation prize** *n* a prize given to sb who has just missed winning or has come last.

consolatory /kənˈsɒlətəri; *US* kənˈsəʊlətɔːri/ *adj* tending or intended to CONSOLE[1]; comforting: *a consolatory letter/remark.*

console[1] /kənˈsəʊl/ *v* ~ **sb/oneself** (**with sth**) to give comfort or sympathy to sb who is unhappy, disappointed, etc: [Vn] *Nothing could console him when his pet dog died.* ○ *It is a consoling thought that there are others in a much worse position.* [Vnpr] *He consoled himself with the thought that it might have been worse.*

console[2] /ˈkɒnsəʊl/ *n* **1** a panel for the switches, controls, etc of electronic or mechanical equipment. **2** a radio or television CABINET(2) designed to stand on the floor. **3** a frame containing the KEYBOARD(1b) and other controls of an organ[2].

consolidate /kənˈsɒlɪdeɪt/ *v* **1** to become or make sth more solid, secure or strong: [V] *The time has come for the firm to consolidate after several years of rapid expansion.* [Vn] *With his new play he has consolidated his position as the country's leading dramatist.* **2** (*esp commerce*) to unite or combine things into one: [Vn] *All the debts have been consolidated.* [V] *The two companies consolidated for greater efficiency.* ▶ **consolidation** /kənˌsɒlɪˈdeɪʃn/ *n* [U]: *the consolidation of the party's position at the top of the opinion polls.*

■ **the Conˌsolidated 'Fund** *n* [sing] (in Britain) a government fund into which money from taxes is paid, used esp to pay interest[1](5) on the national debt.

consommé /kənˈsɒmeɪ; *US* ˌkɒnsəˈmeɪ/ *n* [U] a clear soup made with the juices from meat.

consonance /ˈkɒnsənəns/ *n* [U] **1** ~ (**with sth**) (*fml*) agreement: *a policy that is popular because of its consonance with traditional party doctrine.* **2** [U, C] (*techn*) a pleasing harmony of musical notes.

consonant[1] /ˈkɒnsənənt/ *n* (*phonetics*) (**a**) a speech sound produced by completely or partly stopping the air being breathed out through the mouth. (**b**) a letter of the alphabet or PHONETIC symbol for such a sound, eg *b, c, d, f,* etc. Compare VOWEL b.

consonant[2] /ˈkɒnsənənt/ *adj* [pred] ~ **with sth** (*fml*) in agreement or harmony with sth: *behaving with a dignity consonant with his rank.*

consort[1] /ˈkɒnsɔːt/ *n* **1** a husband or wife, esp of a ruler: *the prince consort* (ie the queen's husband). **2** (*music*) a group of instruments or players playing

esp early music. **IDM** **in consort with sb** (*fml*) together with sb: *acting in consort with persons unknown.*

consort[2] /kənˈsɔːt/ *v* ~ **with sb/together** (*fml often derog*) to spend time with sb / together; to associate with sb: *He'd been consorting with known criminals.* ○ *They have been seen consorting together.*

consortium /kənˈsɔːtiəm/ *n* (*pl* **consortiums** or **consortia** /-tiə/) a temporary association of several countries, companies, banks, etc for a common purpose: *the Anglo-French consortium that built the Channel Tunnel.*

conspicuous /kənˈspɪkjuəs/ *adj* ~ (**for sth**) (**a**) easily seen; noticeable: *If you're walking along a badly-lit road at night you should wear conspicuous clothes.* ○ **make oneself conspicuous** (ie attract attention by unusual behaviour, wearing unusual clothes, etc). (**b**) remarkable; NOTABLE: *Her first play was a conspicuous success.* ○ (*ironic*) *She wasn't exactly conspicuous for her helpfulness* (ie She was not helpful). **IDM** **conˌspicuous by one's 'absence** obviously absent when one ought to be present: *When it came to cleaning up afterwards, the boys were conspicuous by their absence.* ▶ **conspicuously** *adv*: *conspicuously absent.* **conspicuousness** *n* [U].

■ **conˌspicuous conˈsumption** *n* [U] the buying of expensive goods simply in order to impress people and improve one's social status.

conspiracy /kənˈspɪrəsi/ *n* [C, U] a secret plan by a group of people to do sth illegal or harmful: *a conspiracy to overthrow the government* ○ *a conspiracy of silence* (ie an agreement not to talk publicly about sth which should not remain secret) ○ *accused of conspiracy to murder* ○ *face conspiracy charges.* Compare PLOT[2] 2.

conspire /kənˈspaɪə(r)/ *v* **1** ~ (**with sb**) (**against sb**); ~ (**together**) (**against sb**) to make secret plans with others, esp to do sth illegal or harmful: [Vpr] *conspire with others against one's leader* [V.to inf] *They were charged with conspiring to pervert the course of justice.* [also V, Vp]. **2** ~ **against sb/sth** (of events) to seem to act together; to combine in an unfortunate way for sb/sth: [Vpr] *circumstances conspiring against our success* [V.to inf] *events that conspired to bring about his downfall.*

▶ **conspirator** /kənˈspɪrətə(r)/ *n* a person who conspires: *political conspirators.*

conspiratorial /kənˌspɪrəˈtɔːriəl/ *adj*: *talking in conspiratorial whispers* ○ *She handed the note to me with a conspiratorial air.*

constable /ˈkʌnstəbl; *US* ˈkɒn-/ *n* (*Brit*) = POLICE CONSTABLE: *Constable Johnson.* See also CHIEF CONSTABLE.

constabulary /kənˈstæbjələri; *US* -leri/ *n* [CGp] the police force of a particular area, town, etc, esp in Britain: *the Royal Ulster Constabulary.*

constancy /ˈkɒnstənsi/ *n* [U] (*approv fml*) **1** the quality of being firm and not changing: *constancy of purpose.* **2** the quality of being faithful: *a husband's constancy.*

constant /ˈkɒnstənt/ *adj* **1** [usu attrib] going on all the time; happening again and again: *constant chattering/complaints/interruptions* ○ *This entrance is in constant use: do not block it.* **2** not changing; fixed: *a constant speed/value* ○ *Pressure in the container remains constant.* **3** [usu attrib] (*approv*) firm; faithful: *a constant friend/companion/supporter.*

▶ **constant** *n* (*mathematics or physics*) a number or quantity that does not vary. Compare VARIABLE *n*.

constantly *adv* continuously; frequently: *We drove through constantly changing scenery* ○ *She worries constantly.*

constellation /ˌkɒnstəˈleɪʃn/ *n* **1** a named group of stars (eg *the Great Bear*). **2** a group of associated or similar people or things, esp famous ones: *a constellation of Hollywood talent.*

consternation /ˌkɒnstəˈneɪʃn/ *n* [U] great surprise, anxiety or mental confusion: *cause/create/spread consternation among people* ○ *filled with consternation* ○ *To her consternation, she was then asked to make a speech.*

constipated /ˈkɒnstɪpeɪtɪd/ *adj* unable to empty the bowels: *If you're constipated you should eat more vegetables and fruit.*
▶ **constipation** /ˌkɒnstɪˈpeɪʃn/ *n* [U] the state of being constipated.

constituency /kənˈstɪtjuənsi/ *n* (**a**) [C] a district that has its own elected representative in government. (**b**) [CGp] the people who vote in such a district: *constituency opinion.* (**c**) [CGp] a group of people with the same interests who are expected to support sb, esp politically: *Mr Jones has a natural constituency among steel workers.*

constituent /kənˈstɪtjuənt/ *adj* [attrib] forming or helping to make a whole: *Analyse the sentence into its constituent parts.*
▶ **constituent** *n* **1** a member of a CONSTITUENCY(a). **2** any of the parts that make a whole: *the chemical constituents of a substance.*
■ **con‚stituent as'sembly** *n* [CGp] an assembly that has the power to make or alter a political CONSTITUTION(1).

constitute /ˈkɒnstɪtjuːt; *US* -tuːt/ *v* **1** (not in the continuous tenses) to be or be equivalent to: [V-n] *My decision does not constitute* (ie should not be regarded as) *a precedent.* ○ *The defeat constitutes a major set-back for the government.* **2** (*fml*) (not in the continuous tenses) to be or form a whole; to be the components of sth: [Vn] *Women constitute more than sixty per cent of the company's workforce.* ⇨ note at COMPRISE. **3** (esp passive) to give formal authority to a group of people; to establish sth: [Vn] *The committee had been improperly constituted, and therefore had no legal power.*

constitution /ˌkɒnstɪˈtjuːʃn; *US* -ˈtuːʃn/ *n* **1** [C] a system of laws and principles according to which a state or other organization is governed: *According to/Under the US Constitution…* ○ *In one article/clause of the constitution…* ○ *A two-thirds majority is needed to amend the club's constitution.* **2(a)** [U] (*fml*) the action or manner of forming or establishing sth: *the constitution of an advisory group.* (**b**) [C] (*fml*) the general structure of a thing: *the constitution of the solar spectrum.* **3** [C] the condition of a person's body or mind with regard to health, strength, etc: *have a robust/weak constitution* ○ *our physical/mental constitutions* ○ *Only people with a strong constitution should go climbing.*

constitutional /ˌkɒnstɪˈtjuːʃənl; *US* -ˈtuː-/ *adj* **1** of a CONSTITUTION(1): *constitutional government/reform* ○ *a constitutional issue/crisis.* **2** consistent with, allowed by or limited by a CONSTITUTION(1): *one's constitutional rights* ○ *They claimed that the new law was not constitutional.* ○ *a constitutional monarchy/ruler.* **3** of a person's CONSTITUTION(3): *constitutional weakness/robustness.*
▶ **constitutional** *n* (*dated or joc*) a short walk taken to improve or maintain one's health: *go for/take a constitutional.*
constitutionalism /-ˈʃənəlɪzəm/ *n* [U] constitutional government, or a belief in the practice of such a system.
constitutionally /-ˈʃənəli/ *adv.*

constrain /kənˈstreɪn/ *v* (*fml*) **1** (esp passive) to force sb to act or behave in a particular way, often when they would prefer not to: [Vn.*to* inf] *With some embarrassment she felt constrained to point out his mistake.* [Vn] *Men and women are becoming less constrained by stereotyped roles.* **2** to restrict sb/sth or to limit their scope: [Vn] *Work has been con-* *strained by insufficient space and poor facilities.* ○ *constrain sb's potential/sth's development.*
▶ **constrained** *adj* (of voice, manner, etc) not natural; forced or embarrassed.

constraint /kənˈstreɪnt/ *n* **1** [C] ~ (**on sth**) a thing that limits or restricts: *constraints of time/money/space* ○ *There are no constraints on your choice of subject for the essay* (ie You can choose whatever subject you like). **2** [U] strong pressure; tight control: *act under constraint* (ie because one has little or no choice). **3** [U, sing] (*fml*) a manner that is not natural or relaxed; restrained behaviour: *I was aware of a certain constraint in his dealings with me.*

constrict /kənˈstrɪkt/ *v* to make sth tight, smaller or narrower: [Vn] *a tight collar that constricts the neck* ○ *administering a drug that constricts the blood-vessels.* ▶ **constricted** *adj*: *Our way of life is rather constricted* (ie We cannot do so many things) *now that our income is so reduced.* **constriction** /kənˈstrɪkʃn/ *n* [U, C]: *a constriction in the chest* ○ *the constrictions of life on a low income.*

construct /kənˈstrʌkt/ *v* ~ **sth** (**from/out of/of sth**) to build sth; to put or fit sth together; to form sth: [Vn] *construct a factory/an aircraft/a model* ○ *construct a sentence/a theory* ○ *a well-constructed novel* [Vnpr] *a hut constructed (out) of branches.* **2** (*geometry*) to draw a line, figure, etc in agreement with certain rules: [Vn] *construct a triangle.*
▶ **constructor** *n* a person who constructs things: *racing-car constructors.*

construction /kənˈstrʌkʃn/ *n* **1** [U] the action or manner of constructing sth: *the construction of new roads* ○ *The new road is still **under construction*** (ie being built). ○ *The wall is of very solid construction.* ○ *the construction industry* (ie the building of roads, bridges, buildings, etc). **2** [C] a thing constructed; a structure or building: *a complex construction of wood and glass* ○ *The shelter is a brick construction.* **3** [C] (*fml*) a sense in which words, statements, etc are to be understood; a meaning: *What construction do you put on this letter?* (ie What do you think it means?) See also CONSTRUE. **4** [C] the way in which words are put together to form a phrase, clause or sentence: *This dictionary gives the meanings of words and also illustrates the constructions they can be used in.*

constructive /kənˈstrʌktɪv/ *adj* having a useful purpose; helpful: *constructive criticism/proposals/remarks* ○ *I'm trying to be constructive.* Compare DESTRUCTIVE. ▶ **constructively** *adv.*

construe /kənˈstruː/ *v* ~ **sth** (**as sth**) (*fml*) (usu passive) to understand or interpret the meaning of words, sentences, actions, etc in a particular way: [Vnadv] *Her remarks were wrongly construed* (ie were not properly understood). [Vn-n] *Such action may be construed as unfair pressure and resented.* [also Vn-adj]. See also CONSTRUCTION 3.

consul /ˈkɒnsl/ *n* **1** an official appointed by a state to live in a foreign city. A consul's job is to help people from her or his own country who are travelling or living there, and to protect their interests: *the British Consul in Marseilles.* Compare AMBASSADOR, HIGH COMMISSIONER. **2** either of the two magistrates elected each year to rule in ancient Rome before it became an empire. ▶ **consular** /ˈkɒnsjələ(r); *US* -səl-/ *adj: consular officials/duties.*

consulate /ˈkɒnsjələt; *US* -səl-/ *n* the offices of a CONSUL(1): *the American consulate in Poznan.* Compare EMBASSY 1, HIGH COMMISSION.

consult /kənˈsʌlt/ *v* **1** ~ **sb/sth** (**about sth**) to go to a person, book, etc for information, advice, etc: [Vn] *consult one's lawyer/a map/a dictionary/one's watch* ○ *If the pain continues, you should consult a doctor.* [V] *a consulting engineer* (ie one who has expert knowledge and gives advice). **2** ~ (**with**) **sb** to discuss matters with sb; to CONFER(2) with sb: [Vpr]

consult with one's partners [Vn] You must consult your manager before taking a decision on this.
■ con'sulting room n a room where a doctor talks to and examines patients.

consultancy /kən'sʌltənsi/ n a company that gives expert advice in business, law, etc: a management/recruitment/design consultancy ○ consultancy fees.

consultant /kən'sʌltənt/ n 1 ~ (on sth) a person who gives expert advice in business, law, etc: a firm of management consultants ○ the president's consultant on economic affairs. 2 ~ (in sth) (Brit) a hospital doctor of senior rank: a consultant in obstetrics ○ a consultant surgeon. Compare REGISTRAR 3.

consultation /ˌkɒnsl'teɪʃn/ n 1 [U] the action or process of consulting (CONSULT) sb/sth: acting in consultation with the director (ie with his advice and agreement) ○ consultation of a dictionary. 2 [C] (a) a meeting for discussion: top-level consultations on trade matters between the American and Chinese delegations. (b) a meeting to discuss or ask for advice about a sick person.

consultative /kən'sʌltətɪv/ adj giving advice or making suggestions; ADVISORY: a consultative committee/document.

consume /kən'sjuːm; US -'suːm/ v [Vn] 1(a) to use sth: consume resources/time/stores/services ○ The car consumes a lot of fuel. See also TIME-CONSUMING. (b) to destroy sb/sth, esp by fire: The fire quickly consumed the wooden hut. ○ (fig) be consumed (ie filled) with envy/hatred/greed. 2 (fml) to eat or drink sth. See also CONSUMPTION 1a.
▶ **consuming** adj [attrib] that takes all sb's time, energy, interest, etc: Building model trains is his consuming interest/passion.

consumer /kən'sjuːmə(r); US -suː-/ n a person who buys goods or uses services: Consumers are encouraged to complain about faulty goods. ○ electricity consumers ○ consumer demand/rights/protection ○ We live in a consumer society. Compare PRODUCER 1.
▶ **consumerism** /-ɪzəm/ n [U] (esp derog) the belief that a society or individual benefits from using a large quantity of goods and services: damage to the environment caused by mass consumerism.
consumerist adj [attrib]: a consumerist attitude/culture.
■ con,sumer 'durables n [pl] goods expected to last for a long time after they have been bought, eg a FREEZER.
con'sumer goods n [pl] GOODS bought and used by individual customers, eg food, clothing, domestic appliances. Compare CAPITAL GOODS.

consummate¹ /kən'sʌmət/ adj [attrib] (fml) highly skilled; perfect: a consummate artist/performance/piece of work ○ She dealt with the problem with consummate skill. ○ (derog) a consummate liar.

consummate² /'kɒnsəmeɪt/ v (fml) 1 to make a marriage legally complete by having sex: [Vn] The marriage lasted only a week and was never consummated. 2 to make sth complete or perfect: [Vn] His work as an artist was never consummated by public recognition.
▶ **consummation** /ˌkɒnsə'meɪʃn/ n [C, U] the action or moment of completing, making perfect, or fulfilling sth: the consummation of one's life's work/one's ambitions/a marriage.

consumption /kən'sʌmpʃn/ n [U] 1(a) the using up of food, energy, resources, etc: Gas and oil consumption always increases in cold weather. ○ The meat was declared unfit for human consumption. ○ (fig) The material was considered unsuitable for public consumption (ie It was decided not to publish it). See also CONSPICUOUS CONSUMPTION. (b) an amount used: a car with low/high fuel consumption. 2 (dated) TUBERCULOSIS of the lungs.

consumptive /kən'sʌmptɪv/ n, adj (dated) (a person) suffering from CONSUMPTION(2).

cont abbr 1 contents. 2 (also **contd**) continued: cont on p 74.

contact /'kɒntækt/ n 1 [U] ~ (with sb/sth) (a) the state of touching: The two substances are now in contact (with each other), and a chemical reaction is occurring. ○ His hand came into contact with (ie touched) a hot surface. ○ The label sticks on contact (ie when it touches a surface). ○ (fig) The troops came into contact with (ie met) the enemy. ○ (fig) Pupils must be brought into contact with (ie exposed to) new ideas. (b) communication: in constant radio/telephone contact (with sb) ○ Beyond a certain distance we are out of contact with our headquarters. ○ She's lost contact with her son (ie no longer hears from him, knows where he is, etc). ○ two people avoiding eye contact (ie avoiding looking directly at each other) ○ Here's my contact number (ie temporary telephone number) while I'm on holiday. 2 [C] an instance of meeting or communicating: have extensive contacts with firms abroad. 3 [C] a person that one knows, esp one who can be helpful in business, etc: I have a useful contact in New York. 4 [C] (a) an electrical connection: There's a poor contact that causes power to fail occasionally. (b) a device that makes an electrical connection: The switches close the contacts and complete the circuit. 5 [C] (medical) a person who may be infectious because he or she has recently been near to sb with a CONTAGIOUS(1a) disease. **IDM** make contact (with sb/sth) to succeed in speaking to or meeting sb/sth: They made contact with headquarters by radio. ○ I finally made contact with her in Paris.
▶ **contact** /'kɒntækt/ v to reach sb/sth by telephone, radio, letter, etc; to communicate with sb/sth: [Vn] Where can I contact you tomorrow?
■ 'contact lens n a small round piece of thin plastic placed on the surface of the eye to help a person see better.

contagion /kən'teɪdʒən/ n 1 [U] the spread of disease by close contact with other people. 2 [C] a disease that can be spread by contact: (fig) the contagion of political extremism. Compare INFECTION.

contagious /kən'teɪdʒəs/ adj 1(a) (of a disease) spreading by contact: Scarlet fever is highly contagious. (b) (of a person) having a disease that can be spread to others by contact. 2 spreading easily from one person to another: contagious laughter/enthusiasm ○ Yawning is contagious. Compare INFECTIOUS. ▶ **contagiously** adv.

contain /kən'teɪn/ v (not in the continuous tenses) 1 to have or hold sth within itself: [Vn] The atlas contains forty maps. ○ Whisky contains a large percentage of alcohol. ○ What does that box contain? ○ Her statement contained several inaccuracies. ○ This barrel contains (ie can hold) 50 litres. 2 to control oneself or one's feelings; to hold sth back: [Vn] I was so furious I couldn't contain myself (ie had to express my feelings). ○ Please contain your enthusiasm for a moment. ○ She could hardly contain her excitement. 3 to prevent sth from spreading in a harmful way or becoming more serious: [Vn] Government forces have failed to contain the rebellion.
▶ **containment** n [U] the keeping of sth within limits, so that it cannot spread in a harmful way: the containment of a fire/a radioactive leak ○ the containment of aggressive military regimes ○ Knowing they were unlikely to win, the team concentrated on containment (ie limiting the other team's chances of scoring).

container /kən'teɪnə(r)/ n 1 a box, bottle, etc in which sth is kept, transported, etc: Food will last longer if stored in an airtight container. 2 a large metal box of standard size for transporting goods by road, rail, sea or air: a 'container train/ship/lorry (ie one designed to transport such containers).

contaminate /kən'tæmɪneɪt/ v to make sth/sb IM-PURE(1) by adding substances that are dangerous or carry disease: [Vn] *contaminated drinking-water* ○ *a river contaminated by chemicals* ○ *Flies contaminate food.* ○ *(fig) They are contaminating the minds of our young people with these subversive ideas.*
▶ **contaminant** /kən'tæmɪnənt/ n a substance that contaminates things: *environmental contaminants.*
contamination /kən,tæmɪ'neɪʃn/ n [U]: *radioactive contamination.*

contd *abbr* = CONT 2.

contemplate /'kɒntəmpleɪt/ v **1** to consider the possibility of sth: [Vn] *The consequences of a nuclear war are too awful to contemplate.* ○ *She is contemplating a visit to* (ie may visit) *America.* [V.ing] *I'm not contemplating retiring* (ie I do not intend to retire) *yet.* [V.n ing] *No one would contemplate such a thing happening.* **2(a)** to look at or consider sb/sth in a calm/careful way: [Vn] *She stood contemplating the painting.* [V.wh] *He contemplated what the future would be like without the children.* **(b)** to think deeply about sth, esp as a religious practice; to MEDITATE(1): [V] *a few quiet minutes in the middle of the day to sit and contemplate* [Vn] *contemplating the death of Our Lord* [also V.wh].
▶ **contemplation** /,kɒntəm'pleɪʃn/ n [U] **1** the action of looking at sth/sb in a calm/careful way: *He stood in silent contemplation of the scene before him.* **2** deep thought; meditation (MEDITATE 1): *a life of prayer and contemplation* ○ *He sat there deep in contemplation.* **3** *(fml)* consideration; intention: *New and desperate measures to deal with the crisis are in contemplation.*
contemplative /kən'templətɪv, 'kɒntəmpleɪtɪv/ adj **1** fond of contemplation; showing careful thought: *a contemplative person/manner/look.* **2** engaging in religious meditation (MEDITATE 1): *a contemplative order of nuns.*

contemporaneous /kən,tempə'reɪniəs/ adj ~ **(with sb/sth)** *(fml)* existing or happening at the same time: *contemporaneous events/developments.* ▶ **contemporaneously** adv.

contemporary /kən'temprəri; US -pəreri/ adj **1** ~ **(with sb/sth)** of the time or period being referred to; belonging to the same time: *Many contemporary writers condemned the emperor's actions.* ○ *a contemporary record of events* (ie one made by sb living at that time) ○ *Dickens was contemporary with Thackeray.* **2** of the present time; modern: *contemporary events/fashions/dance/theatre* ○ *furniture in a contemporary style.* ⇨ note at NEW.
▶ **contemporary** n a person who lives or lived at the same time as another, usu being roughly the same age: *She and I were contemporaries at college.*

contempt /kən'tempt/ n [U] **1** ~ **(for sb/sth)** the feeling that sb/sth is completely worthless and cannot be respected: *I feel nothing but contempt for people who treat children so cruelly.* ○ *Such behaviour is beneath contempt* (ie so bad that it is not worth feeling contempt for). ○ *I shall treat that suggestion with the contempt it deserves.* ○ *opinions which are generally held in contempt.* **2** ~ **(for sb/sth** lack of regard for rules, danger, etc: *His remarks betray a staggering contempt for the truth* (ie completely false). **IDM** **familiarity breeds contempt** ⇨ FA-MILIARITY.
▶ **contemptible** /kən'temptəbl/ adj deserving contempt; DESPICABLE: *contemptible cowardice.*
contemptuous /kən'temptʃuəs/ adj ~ **(of sth/sb)** feeling or showing contempt: *a contemptuous person/attitude* ○ *He threw it away with a contemptuous gesture.* ○ *She has always shown herself to be contemptuous of public opinion.* **contemptuously** adv.
con,tempt of 'court (also **contempt**) n [U] the refusal to obey an order made by a court of law; lack

of respect for a court or judge: *They were jailed for contempt (of court).*

contend /kən'tend/ v **1** ~ **with/against sb/sth**; ~ **for sth** to struggle in order to overcome a rival, competitor or difficulty: [Vpr] *Several teams are contending for* (ie trying to win) *the prize.* ○ *She's had a lot of problems to contend with.* [V] *A struggle between contending* (ie rival) *groups.* **2** (no passive) to give sth as one's opinion; to assert: [V.that] *I would contend that unemployment is our most serious social evil.*
▶ **contender** n a person who tries to win sth in a contest: *the two contenders for the heavyweight title.*

content¹ /kən'tent/ adj [pred] ~ **(with sth)**; ~ **(to do sth)** feeling satisfaction with what one has; not wanting more; happy: *Now that she has apologized, I am content.* ○ *Are you content with your present salary?* ○ *He is content to stay in his present job for the time being.* ○ *Not content with simply protesting to the management, the unions are threatening all-out strike action.* Compare CONTENTED.
▶ **content** n [U] the state of being content; contentment: *a look of utter content on his face.* **IDM** **to one's heart's content** ⇨ HEART.
content v **1** ~ **oneself with sth** to accept sth, even though one would have liked more or better: [Vnpr] *As there was no milk, we had to content ourselves with black coffee.* **2** *(fml)* to satisfy sb; to make sb content: [Vn] *My apology appeared to content her.*
contented adj showing or feeling happiness or satisfaction: *a contented person/cat/smile.* Compare DISCONTENTED. **contentedly** adv.
contentment n [U] the state of being content: *a warm feeling of security and contentment.*

content² /'kɒntent/ n **1** **contents** [pl] the things contained in sth: *the contents of a room/box/bottle/pocket* ○ *The drawer had been emptied of its contents.* ○ *She hadn't read the letter and so was unaware of its contents.* ○ *At the front of the book is a table of contents, giving details of what is in it.* **2** [sing] the things written or spoken about in a book, an article, a programme, a speech, etc: *The content of your essay is excellent, but it's not very well expressed.* ○ *a journal of mainly technical content.* **3** [sing] (preceded by a n) the amount of sth contained in sth else: *the silver content of a coin* ○ *food with a high fat content.*

contention /kən'tenʃn/ n **1** [U] ~ **(for sth / to do sth)** competing for sth, esp with a good chance of succeeding: *After a series of defeats, the team is no longer in contention for the title/to win the title* (ie competing for it). **2** [U] *(fml)* angry disagreement; dispute: *This is not a time for contention.* **3** [C] ~ **(that...)** *(fml)* a statement of belief or opinion: *It is my contention that you are wrong, and I shall try to prove it.* **IDM** **a bone of contention** ⇨ BONE.

contentious /kən'tenʃəs/ adj *(fml)* **1** likely to cause disagreement: *a contentious issue/matter* ○ *a contentious clause in a treaty.* **2** fond of arguing or quarrelling.

contest /kən'test/ v to claim that sth is wrong or not proper; to dispute sth: [Vn] *contest a statement/point* ○ *contest a will* (ie try to show that it was not properly made in law). **2** to take part in and try to win sth: [Vn] *As a protest, the party has decided not to contest this election.* ○ *contest a seat in Parliament* ○ *a hotly contested game* (ie one in which the players try very hard to win and the scores are close).
▶ **contest** /'kɒntest/ n **1** an event in which people compete against each other for a prize; a competition: *a boxing/archery/dancing/beauty contest* ○ *The election was so one-sided that it was really no contest* (ie only one side was likely to win). ⇨ note at SPORT. **2** ~ **(for sth)** a struggle to gain control of sth: *a contest for the leadership of the party.*

contestant /kən'testənt/ n ~ (**for sth**) a person who is in a contest; a competitor. Compare COMPETITOR.

context /'kɒntekst/ n [C,U] **1** words that come before and after a word, phrase, statement, etc, helping to show what its meaning is: *Can't you guess the meaning of the word from the context?* ∘ *Don't quote my words out of context* (eg so as to mislead people about what I mean). **2** circumstances in which sth happens or in which sth is to be considered: *In the context of the present economic crisis it seems unwise to lower taxes.* ∘ *You have to see these changes in context: they're part of a larger plan.*
▶ **contextual** /kən'tekstʃuəl/ adj of or according to context: *Contextual clues can help one to find the meaning.* **contextually** adv.

contiguous /kən'tɪgjuəs/ adj ~ (**to/with sth**) (fml or techn) touching; near: *contiguous circles* ∘ *The bruising was not contiguous to the wound.* ▶ **contiguity** /ˌkɒntɪ'gjuːəti/ n [U].

continent¹ /'kɒntɪnənt/ n **1** [C] each of the main land masses of the Earth, ie Europe, Asia, Africa, N and S America, Australia, Antarctica. **2 the Continent** [sing] (Brit) the MAINLAND of Europe: *holidaying on the Continent.*

continent² /'kɒntɪnənt/ adj **1** (medical) able to control one's BLADDER and bowels. **2** (fml) having control of one's feelings and esp sexual desires. ▶ **continence** n [U]. Compare INCONTINENT.

continental /ˌkɒntɪ'nentl/ adj **1** belonging to or typical of a continent: *continental movements over millions of years.* **2** (also **Continental**) (Brit) of the MAINLAND of Europe: *ˌcontinental 'countries/'rivals/ 'markets* ∘ *continental Europe* ∘ *a continental holiday* ∘ *continental-style beers.*
▶ **continental** n (Brit often derog) an inhabitant of the MAINLAND of Europe.
■ **ˌcontinental 'breakfast** n a light breakfast typically consisting only of coffee and bread rolls with butter and jam. Compare ENGLISH BREAKFAST.
ˌcontinental 'drift n [U] (techn) the slow movement of the continents towards and away from each other during the history of the Earth.
ˌcontinental 'quilt n (Brit) = DUVET.
ˌcontinental 'shelf n [sing] an area of land under the sea where it is shallow, between the shore of a continent and the deeper ocean.

contingency /kən'tɪndʒənsi/ n an event that may or may not occur; a possibility: *Be prepared for all contingencies* (ie for whatever may happen). ∘ *contingency plans/arrangements.*

contingent¹ /kən'tɪndʒənt/ adj ~ **on/upon sth** (fml) dependent on sth that may or may not happen: *Our success is contingent upon your continued help.*

contingent² /kən'tɪndʒənt/ n [CGp] **1** a number of troops supplied to form part of a larger force: *a small British contingent in the UN peace-keeping force.* **2** a group of people attending a gathering and sharing particular characteristics, eg place of origin: *A large contingent from Japan was present at the conference.* ∘ *There were the usual protests from the anti-abortion contingent.*

continual /kən'tɪnjuəl/ adj (esp derog) occurring repeatedly all the time; always happening: *continual rain/talking/interruptions* ∘ *The company receives continual complaints about the quality of its products.* ▶ **continually** /-juəli/ adv: *They're continually arguing.* ∘ *I continually have to remind him of his responsibilities.*

> **NOTE** Compare **continual** and **continuous**. **Continual** describes an action which is repeated again and again: *Please stop your continual questions!* ∘ *He was continually late for work.* **Continuous** describes things or actions which continue without stopping or interruption: *There is a continuous flow of traffic*

on this road. ∘ *Stir the mixture continuously until the sugar has dissolved.*

continuance /kən'tɪnjuəns/ n [U] (fml) the state of continuing to exist or operate: *During the continuation of an agreement* ∘ *We can no longer support the President's continuance in office.*

continuation /kənˌtɪnju'eɪʃn/ n **1** [sing, U] an instance or the action of continuing: *He argued for a continuation of the search.* ∘ *Continuation of play after the tea interval was impossible because of rain.* **2** [C] a thing that continues or extends sth else: *This road is a continuation of the motorway.*

continue /kən'tɪnjuː/ v **1** to go or move further; to make sth go or move further: [Vadv] *How far does the road continue?* ∘ *The desert continued as far as the eye could see.* [Vpr] *We continued up the mountain on horseback.* [Vn, Vnpr] *They are continuing the new road (to the coast)* (ie building more of it until it reaches the coast). [also V, Vp]. **2** ~ (**with sth**) to go on existing, happening or doing sth without stopping: [V-adj, V.to inf] *The circumstances continue (to be) favourable.* [V] *Wet weather is likely to continue for a few more days.* [Vn, Vpr] *We will continue (with) the payments for another year.* [V.to inf, V.ing] *How can you continue to work/continue working with all that noise going on?* **3** ~ (**as sth**) to stay; to remain: [V-n] *He is to continue as manager.* [Vpr] *continue at school/in one's job.* **4(a)** to start again after stopping; to RESUME(1): [V, Vn] *The story continues/is continued in our next issue.* [V.to inf, V.ing] *We continued to rehearse/continued rehearsing the chorus after the break.* **(b)** [V] to speak or say sth again after stopping: *Please continue; I didn't mean to interrupt.* [V.speech] *'And what's more,' he continued, 'they wouldn't even let me in!'*
▶ **continued, continuing** adjs [attrib] going on without stopping: *continued opposition/resistance/ concern* ∘ *continuing success/uncertainty/discussions.*

continuity /ˌkɒntɪ'njuːəti; US -'nuː-/ n **1** [U] the state of being continuous: *We must ensure continuity of fuel supplies.* **2** [U, C] the logical connection between the parts of sth: *His article lacks continuity; he keeps jumping from one subject to another.* ∘ *There are obvious continuities between diet and health.* **3** [U] (in cinema or television) the correct sequence of action in a film, etc: *Continuity is ensured by using the same props in successive scenes.* ∘ *a conti'nuity girl/man* (ie one who makes sure the correct sequence is kept). **4** [U] (broadcasting) the connecting comments, announcements, etc made between broadcasts: *a continuity announcer.*

continuous /kən'tɪnjuəs/ adj going on without stopping or being interrupted: *Education is a continuous process.* ∘ *Our political institutions are in continuous evolution.* ∘ *A continuous belt feeds components into the machine.* ⇨ note at CONTINUAL. ▶ **continuously** adv.
■ **conˌtinuous asˈsessment** n [U] a system for assessing a student's progress throughout a course of study as well as or instead of by examinations.
conˈtinuous tense (also **proˈgressive tense**) n (grammar) the form of a verb, eg 'I am waiting' or 'It is raining', that is made from a part of *be* and a present participle. It is used to express an action that continues for a period of time.

continuum /kən'tɪnjuəm/ n (pl **continuums** or **continua** /-juə/) a sequence of things of a similar type, in which the ones next to each other are almost the same, but the ones at either end are quite distinct: *Historians see the past, the present and the future as forming some kind of continuum.*

contort /kən'tɔːt/ v ~ (**sth**) (**with sth**) (esp passive) to become or make sth twisted out of its natural shape: [Vpr, Vnpr] *Her face contorted/was contorted with pain.* [V] *His face contorted, then relaxed.*

▶ **contorted** *adj*: *contorted branches/limbs* ○ *(fig) The statement is a highly contorted version of the truth.*
contortion /kən'tɔ:ʃn/ *n* (**a**) [U] a twisted state, esp of the face or body. (**b**) [C] an instance or a result of this: *perform a series of yoga contortions.* **contortionist** /-ʃənɪst/ *n* a person who is skilled in contorting her or his body, esp one who does this to entertain others. ⇨ picture.

contortionist

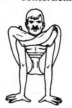

contour /'kɒntʊə(r)/ *n* **1** the outline or outer edge of sth, representing its shape or form: *The road follows the natural contours of the coastline.* ○ *the smooth contours of a sculpture.* **2** (also **'contour line**) a line on a map joining points that are the same height above the level of the sea: *a contour map* (ie one showing these lines). ⇨ picture at MAP.
▶ **contoured** *adj* having clearly defined or specially designed contours: *the elegantly contoured lines of a new car.*

contra- *comb form* **1** (with *vs* and *ns*) opposite to; against: *contradistinction* ○ *contraceptive.* **2** (with *ns*) (*music*) having a pitch[1](4) an OCTAVE below: *contrabassoon.*

contraband /'kɒntrəbænd/ *n* [U] goods brought into or taken out of a country illegally: *contraband tobacco* ○ *contraband trade.*

contraception /ˌkɒntrə'sepʃn/ *n* [U] the practice of or methods used in deliberately preventing a woman becoming pregnant as a result of having sex.
▶ **contraceptive** /ˌkɒntrə'septɪv/ *n* a device or drug used to prevent a woman becoming pregnant: *oral contraceptives.* — *adj*: *a contraceptive pill/sheath* ○ *contraceptive methods/precautions.*

contract[1] /'kɒntrækt/ *n* ~ (**with sb**) (**for sth/to do sth**) an official legal agreement, usu written: *You shouldn't enter into/make a contract until you have studied its provisions carefully.* ○ *We have a contract with the government for the supply of vehicles/to supply vehicles.* ○ *When the legal formalities have been settled, the buyer and seller of a house can exchange contracts* (ie to complete their agreement legally). ○ *He has agreed salary terms and is ready to sign a new contract* (ie of employment). ○ *I'm not a permanent employee; I'm working here on a fixed-term contract.* ○ *the contract price/date* (ie the price/date agreed to) ○ *a contract worker* (ie one employed on a contract). **IDM** **be under contract (to sb)** to have made a contract to work for sb: *a pop group that is under contract to one of the big record companies.*
▶ **contractual** /kən'træktʃuəl/ *adj* of or contained in a contract: *contractual liability/obligations.*

contract[2] /kən'trækt/ *v* **1**(**a**) to make a legal agreement with sb for them to work for one, provide one with a service, etc: [Vpr] *They had contracted with a local firm for the supply of fuel* (ie agreed to buy fuel from it). [Vn.to inf] *They were contracted to do the job.* [Vnpr] *He is contracted to Everton for the next two seasons.* (**b**) to make a legal agreement to work for sb, provide sb with a service, etc: [V.to inf] *The company had contracted to do the repairs by the end of the month.* **2** ~ **sth** (**with sb**) (*fml*) to make a legal or formal agreement to have a particular relationship: [Vn] *She had contracted a most unsuitable marriage.* [Vnpr] *hoping to contract an alliance with a neighbouring state.* **3** (*fml*) to develop or catch an illness: [Vn] *He contracted measles/AIDS.* **4** (*fml*) to acquire sth, esp sth unpleasant: [Vn] *debts/obligations/bad habits contracted in his youth.* **5**(**a**)

to become less in extent or amount: [V] *contracting health service budgets* ○ *Business has contracted a lot recently.* (**b**) to become or make sth become smaller, tighter, etc: [V] *Metals contract as they get cooler.* [Vn] *Try not to contract your leg muscles.* [Vpr] *The tunnel contracts to a narrow passageway.* Compare EXPAND. (**c**) ~ **sth** (**to sth**) (*grammar*) (esp passive) to make a shorter form of a word or words by joining them together or omitting certain letters: [Vn] *contracted forms* [Vnpr] *'He will' is often contracted to 'He'll'.* **PHRV** **ˌcontract 'out (of sth)** (*Brit*) to withdraw from, or not enter into, an agreement or contract: *Few employees have so far contracted out of the pension scheme.* **ˌcontract sth 'out (to sb)** to arrange for work to be done by another firm rather than one's own: *Catering services were contracted out.*
▶ **contraction** /kən'trækʃn/ *n* **1** [U] the action of contracting sth or of being contracted (CONTRACT[2] 5): *more signs of contraction in the service industries* ○ *the contraction of a muscle.* **2** [C] (*medical*) the tightening of a woman's WOMB that occurs at intervals in the hours before she gives birth to a child. **3** [C] a short form of a word: *'Can't' is a contraction of 'cannot'.*

contractor /kən'træktə(r)/ *n* a person or firm that does jobs or provides goods or services under contract: *a building contractor* ○ *a firm of defence contractors* (ie who make weapons, etc) ○ *Who were the contractors on/for the new motorway?* (ie Who built it?)

contradict /ˌkɒntrə'dɪkt/ *v* **1** to say that sth a person has said or written is wrong, and that the opposite is true: [Vn] *Don't you dare contradict me!* ○ *Why do you always contradict everything I say?* ○ *The speaker had got confused, and started contradicting himself.* **2** (of facts, evidence, etc) to be contrary to sth or to give opposite information: [Vn] *The two statements contradict each other.* ○ *The report contradicts what we heard yesterday.*
▶ **contradiction** /ˌkɒntrə'dɪkʃn/ *n* **1**(**a**) [U] the action of contradicting (CONTRADICT 1) sb/sth: *She will permit no contradiction.* ○ *I think I can say, without fear of contradiction, that…* (**b**) [C] an instance of contradicting sb or sth they have said: *That's a flat contradiction of what you said before.* **2** ~ (**between sth and sth**) (**a**) [U] lack of agreement between statements, facts, actions, etc, so that at least one must be false: *I find no contradiction between his publicly expressed opinions and his private actions.* ○ *His evidence is in direct contradiction to* (ie directly contrary to) *that of the other witnesses.* (**b**) [C] an instance of this: *It's a contradiction to say you love animals and yet wear furs.* **IDM** **a ˌcontradiction in 'terms** a statement containing two words which contradict each other's meaning: *'A generous miser' is a contradiction in terms.*

contradictory /ˌkɒntrə'dɪktəri/ *adj* containing information which contradicts (CONTRADICT 2) other information: *contradictory statements/reports/evidence.*

contradistinction /ˌkɒntrədɪ'stɪŋkʃn/ *n* **IDM** **in contradistinction to sth/sb** (*fml*) by contrast with sth/sb; as opposed to (OPPOSE) sb/sth: *I refer specifically to permanent residents, in contradistinction to temporary visitors.*

contraflow /'kɒntrəfləʊ/ *n* (*Brit*) a transferring of traffic from its usual half of the road to the other half, so that it shares it with traffic coming in the other direction: *A contraflow system is in operation on this section of the motorway.*

contraindication /ˌkɒntrəˌɪndɪ'keɪʃn/ *n* (*medical*) a sign that a drug may be harmful in particular circumstances: *Contraindications listed include high blood pressure.*

contralto /kən'træltəʊ/ (also **alto**) *n* (*pl* **-os**) (*music*)

(a) a singing voice of the lowest range for a woman: *a contralto voice.* (b) a musical part written for such a voice. (c) a female singer with such a voice. Compare SOPRANO.

contraption /kən'træpʃn/ n (*infml*) a machine or device, esp an unusual or complicated one: *a peculiar contraption for removing the peel from oranges.*

contrapuntal /ˌkɒntrə'pʌntl/ adj (*music*) having two or more tunes played together to form a whole: *contrapuntal variations.* See also COUNTERPOINT.

contrariwise /'kɒntreəriwaɪz/ adv **1** (used at the beginning of a clause or sentence to introduce a contrast with the previous one) on the contrary; on the other hand. **2** in the opposite direction: *I work from left to right, he works contrariwise.*

contrary¹ /'kɒntrəri; US -treri/ adj [usu attrib] opposite in nature, tendency or direction: *contrary beliefs/opinions/ideas/views/advice* ○ *traffic moving in contrary directions* ○ *The results were contrary to all expectation.*
■ **contrary to** *prep* in opposition to sth; against sth: *Such practices as these are contrary to the law/rules.* ○ *Contrary to popular belief/opinion, the administration is highly centralized.* ○ *Contrary to his doctor's orders, he had gone back to work.*

contrary² /'kɒntrəri; US -treri/ n **the contrary** [sing] the opposite: *I've never opposed it. The contrary is true: I've always supported it.* **IDM** **on the 'contrary** (used at the beginning of a clause or sentence to emphasize that what follows is true, and is the opposite of what was said previously): *It doesn't seem ugly to me; on the contrary, I think it's rather beautiful.* **quite the contrary** (used at the end of a sentence or by itself to emphasize that the opposite of what has been said is true): *There's no complacency among Labour leaders, quite the contrary.* **to the 'contrary** indicating or proving the opposite: *I will come on Monday unless you write to the contrary* (ie telling me not to come). ○ *proof/evidence to the contrary* (ie that sth is not true).

contrary³ /kən'treəri/ adj (*derog*) refusing to behave well or to obey sth; OBSTINATE: *He's an awkward, contrary child.* ▶ **contrarily** adv. **contrariness** n [U].

contrast¹ /kən'trɑːst; US -'træst/ v **1** ~ (A and/with B) to compare two people or things and show the differences between them: [Vn] *It is interesting to contrast the two writers.* [Vn, Vnpr] *contrasting his attitude and/with hers.* **2** ~ (with sb/sth) to show a clear difference when close together or when compared: [Vpr] *Her actions contrasted sharply with her promises.* [Vadv] *Her actions and her promises contrasted sharply* (ie She did not do as she had promised).
▶ **contrasting** adj [usu attrib] very different in style, colour, etc: *contrasting examples/ideas/patterns.*

contrast² /'kɒntrɑːst; US -træst/ n ~ (to/with sb/sth); ~ (between A and B) **1** [U] the action or process of contrasting (CONTRAST¹ 1) two or more things or people: *Careful contrast of the two plans shows up some key differences.* ○ *In contrast with their system, ours seems very old-fashioned.* **2(a)** [U] the state of one thing being very different from sth else: *The paper is in stark contrast to an earlier report.* ○ *The contrast of light and shade is important in photography.* ○ *His white hair was in sharp contrast to* (ie was very clearly different from) *his dark skin.* **(b)** [C *usu sing*] a difference that is clearly seen when things are compared or put close together: *The white walls make a contrast with the black carpet.* ○ *There is a remarkable contrast between the two brothers.* **(c)** [sing] a thing that shows such a difference: *The work you did today is quite a contrast to* (ie is very much better/worse than) *what you did last week.* **IDM** **by/in 'contrast** (used to

emphasize that sth is clearly different from sth else): *This generation has, by contrast, made the environment a focus of attention.* ○ *In contrast, Sargent's film is more of a documentary.*

contravene /ˌkɒntrə'viːn/ v (*fml*) to act or to be contrary to a law, principle, etc: [Vn] *You are contravening the Data Protection Act.* ▶ **contravention** /ˌkɒntrə'venʃn/ n [U, C]: *He acted in direct contravention of* (ie against) *my wishes.* ○ *a blatant contravention of the treaty.*

contretemps /'kɒntrətɒ̃/ n (*pl* unchanged) (*French fml or joc*) an unfortunate event or disagreement: *There was a minor contretemps with one of the passengers.*

contribute /kən'trɪbjuːt; Brit also 'kɒntrɪbjuːt/ v **1** ~ (sth) (to/towards sth) to give sth, esp money or goods, to help a person or an organization: [Vpr] *contribute to a charity collection* [Vnpr] *contribute aid for refugees* [Vn] *We contributed £10.* [V] *Everyone should contribute if they possibly can.* **2** ~ **to sth** to increase sth or add to sth: [Vpr] *Her work has contributed enormously to our understanding of this difficult subject.* **3** ~ **to sth** to help to cause sth: [V] *a contributing factor* [Vpr] *Does smoking contribute to lung cancer?* **4** ~ (sth) (to sth) **(a)** to speak during a meeting or conversation, esp to give one's opinion: [Vpr] *The chairman encouraged everyone to contribute to the discussion.* [also V, Vn, Vnpr]. **(b)** to write material for a publication, radio or television programme: [Vnpr] *She has contributed several poems to literary magazines.* [Vpr] *He contributes regularly to New Scientist.* [also V,Vn].
▶ **contributor** /kən'trɪbjətə(r)/ n ~ (to sth) **1** a person who contributes (CONTRIBUTE 1,2,4) sth: *Contributors include Ted Hughes and George Melly.* **2** a thing that helps to cause a disease or situation: *a major contributor to pollution.*

contribution /ˌkɒntrɪ'bjuːʃn/ n ~ (to/towards sth) **1** [C] a thing, esp money, that is given to a person or an organization: *a small contribution* (ie gift of money) *to the church collection* ○ *Europe's contribution to the international space station* ○ *National Insurance contributions.* **2** [C] an item to be included in a publication, broadcast, discussion, etc: *a powerful contribution to the debate* ○ *The editor is short of contributions for the May issue.* **3** [C *usu sing*] a factor or course of action that helps to cause sth: *He made a very positive contribution to the project.* ○ *Britain's contribution to the greenhouse effect* ○ *The signing of such a treaty would be a major contribution towards world peace.* **4** [U] the action of contributing (CONTRIBUTE 1,4) sth: *the contribution of money to charity.*

contributory /kən'trɪbjətəri; US -tɔːri/ adj [usu attrib] **1** helping to cause sth: *a contributory factor/cause* ○ *contributory negligence* (eg that has helped to cause an accident). **2** paid for by contributions: *a con,tributory 'pension plan* (ie paid for by both employers and employees).

contrite /'kɒntraɪt, kən'traɪt/ adj (*fml*) filled with or showing deep regret for having done wrong: *a contrite apology/manner* ○ *Gloria looked contrite, even distressed.* ▶ **contritely** adv. **contrition** /kən'trɪʃn/ n [U]: *tears of contrition.*

contrivance /kən'traɪvəns/ n (*fml*) **1** [C] a clever or complicated device or tool, esp one made for a particular purpose: *a contrivance for cutting curved shapes.* **2** ~ **(a)** the capacity to do or achieve sth: *Some things are beyond human contrivance.* **(b)** the process of planning or making sth: *the contrivance of an effective method.* **3(a)** [C] an elaborate or deceitful plan: *an ingenious contrivance to get her to sign the document without reading it.* **(b)** [U] clever and deceitful behaviour: *Honesty rather than contrivance is what we expect here.*

contrive /kən'traɪv/ v (*fml*) **1** to design or make a

plan, machine, etc in a clever or elaborate way or in order to deceive sb: [Vn] *contrive a device/an experiment/a means of escape* ○ *contrive a way of avoiding paying tax* [V.*that*] *We contrived that she should leave early that day.* **2** to manage to do sth in spite of difficulties: [V.*to* inf] *contriving to live on a small income* ○ (*ironic*) *He contrived to make matters worse* (ie accidentally made them worse by what he did).
▶ **contrived** *adj* (*derog*) (**a**) planned in advance rather than being genuine or SPONTANEOUS: *a contrived outburst* ○ *a contrived incident intended to mislead the newspapers.* (**b**) obviously invented; not true to life: *a novel with a very contrived plot.*

control¹ /kən'trəʊl/ *n* **1** [U] ~ (**of/over sb/sth**) the power or authority to direct, order or manage: *children who lack parental control* (ie are not kept in order by their parents) ○ *In the latest elections our party has got/gained /lost control of the council.* ○ *She managed to keep control of her car on the ice.* ○ *A military government took control (of the country).* ○ *The city is in/under the control of enemy forces.* ○ *The pilot lost control of the plane.* ○ *Due to circumstances beyond/outside our control, we cannot land here.* **2** [U] the ability to remain calm and not to get upset or angry: *He got so angry he lost control (of himself)* (ie started to behave wildly). ○ *It was some time before she regained control.* **3(a)** [U] management or restriction of sth: *traffic control* ○ *control of foreign exchange* ○ *She argued for import control* (ie the restricting of imports). ○ *stock control* ○ *arms-control talks.* (**b**) [C] ~ (**on sth**) a means of limiting or regulating sth: *government controls on trade and industry* ○ *The arms trade should be subject to rigorous controls.* **4** [C] (*techn*) a standard of comparison for checking the results of an experiment: *One group was treated with the new drug, and a second group was given a sugar pill as a control.* ○ *a con'trol group.* **5** [C usu *pl*] the switches, buttons, etc by which a machine is operated or regulated: *the controls of an aircraft* ○ *a control panel/board/lever* ○ *The pilot is at the controls.* ○ *the volume control of a radio* (ie the one which regulates how loud it is). **6** [sing] a place from which orders are issued or at which checks are made: *Mission control ordered the spacecraft to return to earth.* ○ *We went through passport control and into the departure lounge.* See also BIRTH CONTROL, REMOTE CONTROL. ⇨ SELF-CONTROL. **IDM** **be in control (of sth)** to direct, manage or rule sth: *She may be old, but she's still very much in control (of all that is happening).* ○ *Who's in control of the project?* ○ *Enemy forces are in control of the city.* **be/get out of con'trol** to be/ become impossible to manage: *The children are out of control.* ○ *Inflation has got out of control.* **bring/ get sth/be under con'trol** to succeed in managing or regulating sth/to be managed or regulated successfully: *You must get your spending under control.* ○ *The fire has been brought under control.* ○ *Don't worry; everything's under control* (ie all difficulties are being dealt with).
■ **con'trol tower** *n* a building at an airport from which the movements of aircraft are controlled.

control² /kən'trəʊl/ *v* (**-ll-**) **1** to have power or authority over sb/sth: [Vn] *a dictator who controlled the country for over 30 years* ○ *Can't you control that child* (ie make it behave properly)? ○ *companies controlled by his father* ○ *a car which is hard to control at high speeds* ○ *I was so furious I couldn't control myself* (ie remain calm) *and I hit him.* **2** to limit or regulate sth: [Vn] *control traffic/ immigration/supplies/prices* ○ *This knob controls the volume.* ○ *regular inspections to control product quality* ○ *government efforts to control inflation* (ie stop it getting worse) ○ *Use of photocopiers is strictly con-*

trolled. ○ *The bomb was detonated in a controlled explosion.*
▶ **controllable** *adj* that can be controlled: *Drugs can make violent patients controllable.*
controlled *adj* remaining calm and not getting angry or upset: *his quiet and controlled manner* ○ *She remained quite calm and controlled.*
controller *n* a person who manages or directs sth, esp a department or division of a large organization: *the controller of BBC Radio 4* ○ *an air traffic controller.*
■ **con,trolling 'interest** *n* (*finance*) the possession of enough stock¹(5b) of a company to make one able to control its decisions: *have a controlling interest in a company.*

controversial /ˌkɒntrə'vɜːʃl/ *adj* causing or likely to cause CONTROVERSY: *a controversial figure/ decision/book.* ▶ **controversially** /-ʃəli/ *adv.*

controversy /'kɒntrəvɜːsi; *Brit also* kən'trɒvəsi/ *n* [U, C] ~ (**about/over/surrounding sth**) public discussion or argument, often rather angry, about sth which many people disagree about or are shocked by: *The appointment of the new director aroused a lot of controversy.* ○ *a bitter controversy about/over the siting of the new airport* ○ *the controversy surrounding the minister's decision to resign.*

controvert /ˌkɒntrə'vɜːt/ *v* (*fml*) to deny the truth of sth; to argue about sth: [Vn] *a fact that cannot be controverted.*

contusion /kən'tjuːʒn; *US* -'tuː-/ *n* [C, U] (*medical*) (an) injury to part of the body that does not break the skin; a BRUISE.

conundrum /kə'nʌndrəm/ *n* **1** a question, usu involving a trick with words, that is asked for fun; a RIDDLE¹(1). **2** a confusing problem that is difficult to solve: *an issue that is a real conundrum for the experts.*

conurbation /ˌkɒnɜː'beɪʃn/ *n* a large area consisting of various towns that have expanded and joined together.

convalesce /ˌkɒnvə'les/ *v* to regain one's health and strength over a period of time after an illness: [V] *She went to the mountains to convalesce after leaving hospital.*
▶ **convalescence** /ˌkɒnvə'lesns/ *n* [sing, U] the process of convalescing, or a period of time spent convalescing: *an operation that requires a long convalescence.*
convalescent /ˌkɒnvə'lesnt/ *adj* connected with convalescence: *a convalescent home* (ie a type of hospital where people convalesce). — *n* a person who is recovering from an illness.

convection /kən'vekʃn/ *n* [U] the transfer of heat in a liquid or gas as the hotter part rises and the cooler, heavier part sinks: *convection currents.*

convector /kən'vektə(r)/ (also **con,vector 'heater**) *n* an appliance that warms air in a room by passing it over hot surfaces and then circulating it.

convene /kən'viːn/ *v* (*fml*) **1** to summon people to come together; to arrange a meeting, etc: [Vn] *convene the members/a conference.* **2** to come together for a meeting, etc: [V] *The committee will convene at 9.30 tomorrow morning.*
▶ **convener** (also **convenor**) *n* (**a**) a person who convenes meetings. (**b**) (*Brit*) a senior trade union official in a factory or other place of work: *the works convenor.*

convenience /kən'viːniəns/ *n* **1** [U] the quality of being convenient or suitable; freedom from trouble or difficulty: *a transport system planned for the passengers' convenience* ○ *I keep my reference books near my desk for convenience.* See also MARRIAGE OF CONVENIENCE, FLAG OF CONVENIENCE. **2** [C] (**a**) a situation, appliance or device that is useful, helpful or suitable: *It was a great convenience to have the shops so near.* ○ *The house has all the modern con-*

veniences (eg central heating, hot water supply, etc).
(**b**) (*Brit euph*) a toilet for the use of the general public: *There is a **public convenience** on the corner of the street.* **IDM** **at one's con'venience** when or where it suits one: *On a camping holiday you can stop at your own convenience; you're not dependent on hotels.* **at your earliest con'venience** ⇨ EARLY.

■ **con'venience food** *n* [U] food, eg in a tin, packet, etc, that needs very little preparation after being bought.

con'venience store *n* (*US*) a shop that sells food, household items, etc and stays open longer than other shops.

convenient /kən'viːniənt/ *adj* ~ (**for sb/sth**) **1** suiting sb's needs or plans; giving no trouble or difficulty; suitable: *I can't see him now; it's not convenient.* ○ *Will it be convenient for you to meet me at 8 tomorrow morning?* ○ *We must arrange a convenient time and place for the meeting.* **2** situated nearby; easily accessible: (*infml*) *a house that is convenient for* (ie is near) *the shops.* **3** saving time and effort: *We took the most convenient route.* ○ *A bicycle is often more convenient than a car in busy cities.* Compare INCONVENIENT. ▶ **conveniently** *adv*: *The hotel is conveniently situated close to the beach and the shops.*

convent /'kɒnvənt/ *n* a building in which a community of nuns live: *enter a convent* (ie become a nun) ○ *a convent school* (ie one run by nuns). Compare MONASTERY, NUNNERY.

convention /kən'venʃn/ *n* **1** [C] a conference of members of a profession, political party, etc: *a teachers'/dentists' convention* ○ *hold a convention* ○ *the US Democratic Party Convention* (ie to elect a candidate for President). **2(a)** [U] what is generally believed or expected about how people should act or behave in certain circumstances: *Convention dictates that a minister should resign in such a situation.* ○ *By convention the deputy leader is always a woman.* ○ *defy convention by wearing outrageous clothes* ○ *a slave to convention* (ie sb who always follows accepted ways of doing things). (**b**) [C] a way in which sth is usu done: *the conventions which govern stock-market dealing* ○ *diplomatic conventions.* **3** [C] an agreement between states, rulers, etc that is less formal than a TREATY(1): *the Geneva Convention* (ie about the treatment of prisoners of war, etc).

conventional /kən'venʃənl/ *adj* **1(a)** (*often derog*) tending to follow what is done or considered acceptable by society in general: *conventional clothes/behaviour* ○ *She's very conventional in her views.* *The conventional wisdom* (ie the generally accepted view) *is that high wage rises increase inflation.* (**b**) following what is traditional or the way that sth has been done for a long time: *a conventional design/method.* **2** (esp of weapons) not nuclear: *conventional missiles/warfare* ○ *a conventional power station* (ie using oil or coal as fuel, rather than nuclear power). ▶ **conventionally** /-ʃənəli/ *adv*: *conventionally dressed/designed.*

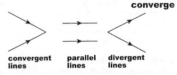

converge

| convergent lines | parallel lines | divergent lines |

converge /kən'vɜːdʒ/ *v* **1** ~ (**on/at** ...) (of two or more things) to move towards the same place; to move towards and meet at the same place: [V] *We worked in the same industry but our paths never converged* (ie we never met). [Vpr] *armies converging on the capital city* ○ *Enthusiasts from around the world converge on* (ie come to) *Le Mans for the*

annual car race. **2** to become similar or the same: [V] *The policies of the main political parties have started to converge.* Compare DIVERGE. ▶ **convergent** /kən'vɜːdʒənt/ *adj*: *convergent lines/opinions.* ⇨ picture. **convergence** *n* [U].

conversant /kən'vɜːsnt/ *adj* [pred] ~ **with sth** (*fml*) having knowledge of sth; familiar with sth: *You need to be fully conversant with the rules of the game.*

conversation /ˌkɒnvə'seɪʃn/ *n* ~ (**with sb**) (**about sth**) (**a**) [C] a usu informal talk, esp one involving a small group of people or only two: *having a quiet conversation with a friend* ○ *She tended to monopolize the conversation.* ○ *It's time we had a serious conversation about your career.* (**b**) [U] the activity of talking in this way: *He was deep in conversation with his accountant.* ○ *I hate having to make polite conversation* (ie to speak merely in order to appear polite) *at a party.* ⇨ note at TALK[2]. ▶ **conversational** /-ʃənl/ *adj* (**a**) [attrib] connected with talking to others, esp in an informal way: *conversational skills.* (**b**) appropriate to conversation; COLLOQUIAL; not formal: *adopt a conversational tone/manner/style.*

conversationalist /-ʃənəlɪst/ *n* a person who is good at talking to others, esp in an informal way: *a fluent conversationalist.*

converse[1] /kən'vɜːs/ *v* ~ (**with sb**) (**about sth**); ~ (**together**) (*fml*) to talk to sb, esp in an informal way: [Vpr, Vp] *I watched them conversing quietly with each other/together in a corner.* [also V].

converse[2] /'kɒnvɜːs/ *n* **the converse** [sing] **1** the opposite: *He thinks he's attractive to women, though in fact the converse is the case.* **2** a statement that reverses another statement: *'He is happy but not rich' is the converse of 'He is rich but not happy'.* ▶ **converse** *adj* [usu attrib] opposite to sth: *They hold converse opinions.*

conversely *adv* in a way that reverses or is opposite to sth: *You can add the fluid to the powder or, conversely, the powder to the fluid.*

conversion /kən'vɜːʃn; *US* kən'vɜːrʒn/ *n* ~ (**from sth**) (**into/to sth**) (**a**) [U] the action or process of converting sth/sb or of being converted: *the conversion of a barn into a house/of pounds into dollars* ○ *the conversion of the Anglo-Saxons by Christian missionaries* ○ *Conversion to gas central heating will save you a lot of money.* ○ *a metric conversion table* (ie showing how to change metric amounts into or out of another system). (**b**) [C] an instance of this: *a building firm which specializes in house conversions* (eg converting large houses into several smaller ones) ○ *her conversion to Catholicism* ○ *He kicked a penalty goal and two conversions* (ie in Rugby football). ○ *She began by supporting monetarist economics, but later underwent quite a conversion* (ie completely changed her opinion) *when she saw how it increased unemployment.*

convert[1] /kən'vɜːt/ *v* **1(a)** ~ (**sth**) (**from sth**) (**into/to sth**) to change from one form or use to another: [Vpr] *Britain converted to a decimal currency system in 1971.* [Vn] *a ferry that was converted to carry troops during the war* ○ *a converted flat* (ie made by dividing up a large house) [Vnpr] *convert rags into paper/a house into flats/dollars into francs* ○ *The room was converted from a kitchen to a lavatory.* [also V]. (**b**) ~ **into/to sth** to be able to be changed from one form or use to another: [Vpr] *a sofa that converts (in)to a bed.* **2** ~ (**sb**) (**from sth**) (**to sth**) to change sb's beliefs, eg one's religion; to persuade sb to change their beliefs: [Vpr] *He has converted to Catholicism.* [Vnpr] *convert sb from Christianity to Islam* [also V, Vn]. **3** [Vn] (in Rugby football) to gain extra points after scoring a TRY[2](2) by kicking a goal. **IDM** **preach to the converted** ⇨ PREACH. ▶ **converter** (also **convertor**) *n* **1** (*physics*) (**a**) a device for converting alternating current (ALTERN-

ATE²) to direct current (DIRECT¹) or direct current to alternating current. (**b**) a device that changes the WAVELENGTH of a radio signal. **2** a container used in turning melted metal into steel. See also CATALYTIC CONVERTER.

convert² /ˈkɒnvɜːt/ *n* ~ (**to sth**) a person who has converted or been converted to a different belief, eg a different religion: *converts to the Jewish faith* ○ *a convert to socialism* ○ (*fig*) *The new newspaper is already winning/gaining converts* (ie people who used to read other newspapers).

convertible /kənˈvɜːtəbl/ *adj* ~ (**into/to sth**) that can be converted to a different form or use: *a sofa that is convertible (into a bed)* ○ *convertible currencies* (ie that can be exchanged for those of other countries).
▶ **convertibility** /kənˌvɜːtəˈbɪləti/ *n* [U].
convertible *n* a car with a roof that can be folded down or removed.

convex /ˈkɒnveks/ *adj* with a curved surface like the outside of a ball: *a convex lens/mirror*. ⇨ picture at CONCAVE. Compare CONCAVE. ▶ **convexity** /kɒnˈveksəti/ *n* [U].

convey /kənˈveɪ/ *v* **1** ~ **sb/sth** (**from...**) (**to...**) (*fml*) to take, carry or transport sb/sth; to transmit sth: [Vnpr] *Pipes convey hot water from the boiler to the radiators.* [Vn] *This train conveys both passengers and goods.* ○ *a message conveyed by radio.* **2** ~ **sth** (**to sb**) to make ideas, feelings, etc known to another person; to communicate sth to sb: [Vn] *a poem that perfectly conveys the poet's inner longing* [V.wh] *Words cannot convey how delighted I felt.* [Vnpr] *Please convey my best wishes to your mother.* [also Vpr.wh]. **3** [Vn, Vnpr] ~ **sth** (**to sb**) (*law*) to transfer full legal rights to the ownership of land, property, etc to sb.
▶ **conveyor** (also **conveyer**) *n* a person or thing that conveys sb/sth: *one of the largest conveyors of passenger traffic.* **conˈveyor belt** (also **conveyor**) *n* a continuous moving belt or band used for transporting loads, eg products in a factory or cases, etc at an airport.

conveyance /kənˈveɪəns/ *n* **1** [U] (*fml*) the process of taking sb/sth from one place to another: *the conveyance of goods by rail.* **2** [C] (*fml*) a vehicle: *old-fashioned conveyances* ○ *a public conveyance.* **3** (*law*) (**a**) [U] the legal process of transferring the ownership of property: *an expert in conveyance.* (**b**) [C] a legal document confirming this process: *draw up a conveyance.*
▶ **conveyancer** *n* an expert in conveyance(3a).
conveyancing *n* [U] the branch of law concerned with transferring the ownership of property.

convict /kənˈvɪkt/ *v* ~ **sb** (**of sth**) (of a JURY(1) or judge) to decide and declare in a lawcourt that sb is guilty of a crime: [Vn] *a convicted murderer* ○ *There wasn't enough evidence to convict him.* ○ *She has twice been convicted of fraud.* Compare ACQUIT 1.
▶ **convict** /ˈkɒnvɪkt/ (also *infml* **con**) *n* a person who has been convicted of a crime or crimes and is in prison: *an escaped convict.*

conviction /kənˈvɪkʃn/ *n* **1** ~ (**for sth**) (**a**) [U] the action of finding sb guilty of or being found guilty of a crime in a lawcourt: *an offence which carries, on conviction, a sentence of not more than five years' imprisonment.* (**b**) [C] an instance of this: *She has had six previous convictions for theft.* **2** [U, C] ~ (**that...**) a firm opinion or belief: *It's my conviction that complacency is at the root of our troubles.* ○ *Do you always act in accordance with your convictions?* **3** [U] the appearance of being sincere, firmly believed or truly meant: *His arguments are forcefully put, but they lack conviction.* ○ *The leader's speech in defence of the policy didn't* **carry much conviction.**
IDM **have/lack the courage of one's convictions** ⇨ COURAGE.

convince /kənˈvɪns/ *v* **1** ~ **sb** (**of sth**) to cause sb to believe that sth is the case: [Vn, Vnpr] *How can I convince you (of her honesty)?* [Vn.that] *What she said convinced me that I had been wrong.* **2** to persuade sb to do sth: [Vn.to inf] *What convinced you to vote for them?*
▶ **convinced** *adj* **1** [pred] ~ (**of sth/that ...**) completely sure about sth: *I am convinced of her innocence/convinced that she is innocent.* **2** [attrib] firm in one's belief: *a convinced Christian.*
convincing *adj* that makes sb believe sth or persuades sb: *a convincing speech/argument/liar* ○ *a convincing victory* (ie an easy one). **convincingly** *adv*: *Her case was convincingly argued.*

convivial /kənˈvɪviəl/ *adj* (*esp fml*) **1** (of a person) cheerful and friendly; fond of the company of others: *convivial companions.* **2** (of an event or a situation) pleasant, friendly and socially enjoyable: *a convivial evening/atmosphere* ○ *convivial surroundings* ▶ **conviviality** /kənˌvɪviˈæləti/ *n* [U].

convocation /ˌkɒnvəˈkeɪʃn/ *n* **1** [CGp] a large formal assembly, esp of church officials or of members of a university. **2** [U] (*fml*) the action of calling together such an assembly.

convoke /kənˈvəʊk/ *v* (*fml*) to call together or summon a large assembly: [Vn] *convoke Parliament.*

convoluted /ˈkɒnvəluːtɪd/ *adj* **1** extremely complicated and difficult to follow: *a convoluted argument/explanation* ○ *a book with a convoluted plot.* **2** (*fml*) having many twists or curves: *the convoluted folds of the brain.*

convolution /ˌkɒnvəˈluːʃn/ *n* (usu *pl*) **1** a twist or curve, esp one of many: *an ornate carving with many convolutions.* **2** a thing that is very complicated and difficult to follow: *the bizarre convolutions of the story.*

convolvulus /kənˈvɒlvjələs/ *n* (*pl* unchanged) [C, U] a climbing plant with flowers shaped like a TRUMPET(2).

convoy /ˈkɒnvɔɪ/ *n* [CGp] a group of vehicles or ships travelling together, esp one that is accompanied by armed troops, other vehicles, etc for protection: *The convoy was attacked by submarines.* ○ *a convoy of lorries/armoured personnel carriers.* **IDM** **in ˈconvoy** (of travelling vehicles) as a group; together: *We decided to drive in convoy because I didn't know the route.*

convulse /kənˈvʌls/ *v* (often passive) to make or cause sb/sth to make sudden violent movements that cannot be controlled: [Vn] *be convulsed with laughter/anger* ○ *a country convulsed by earthquakes* [V] *Her shoulders convulsed in helpless mirth.*

convulsion /kənˈvʌlʃn/ *n* **1** [C usu *pl*] a sudden violent body movement that cannot be controlled, caused by muscles contracting: *The child reacted to the drug by going into convulsions.* **2** [C] a severe or violent disturbance: *political convulsions threatening the stability of new democracies.* **3** **convulsions** [pl] laughter that cannot be controlled: *The story was so funny it had us in convulsions.*

convulsive /kənˈvʌlsɪv/ *adj* **1** having, producing or consisting of body movements that cannot be controlled: *a convulsive movement/attack.* **2** violently disturbing: *The French Revolution was a convulsive historical event.* ▶ **convulsively** *adv*: *weeping convulsively.*

coo¹ /kuː/ *v* (*pt, pp* **cooed** /kuːd/; *pres p* **cooing**) **1** to make the soft cry that a DOVE(1) or PIGEON makes: [V] *The baby was cooing happily.* **2** to say sth in a gentle voice, esp when showing affection: [V.speech] *'It will be all right,' she cooed soothingly.* [also V]. **IDM** **bill and coo** ⇨ BILL². ▶ **coo** *n* (*pl* **coos**).

coo² /kuː/ *interj* (*Brit infml*) (used for expressing surprise): *Coo, look at him!*

cook /kʊk/ *v* **1(a)** ~ **sth** (**for sb**) to prepare food by heating it, eg by boiling, baking, frying, etc: [V]

Where did you learn to cook? [Vpr] *I'm cooking for some friends tonight.* [Vn] *These potatoes aren't (properly) cooked!* ◦ *a cooked breakfast* [Vnn] *He cooked me my dinner.* [Vnpr] *I like to cook Chinese dishes for my family.* (**b**) to be prepared in this way: [V] *The vegetables are cooking.* ◦ *This kind of meat tastes better if it cooks for at least two hours.* ⇨ note. **2** (*infml derog*) to alter sth dishonestly or illegally; to FALSIFY sth: *cook the accounts/figures.* **3** (*infml*) (used in the continuous tenses) to be planned; to happen as a result of a plot: [V] *What's cooking?* ◦ *Everybody is being very secretive — there's something cooking.* **IDM** **cook the 'books** (*infml*) to alter facts or figures dishonestly or illegally: *He cooked the books to avoid paying tax.* **cook sb's 'goose** (*infml*) to make sure that sb fails: *When the police found his fingerprints he knew his goose was cooked* (ie knew that he would be caught). **PHRV** **,cook sth 'up** (*infml*) to invent sth, esp in order to deceive: *cook up an excuse/a story/a theory.*

▶ **cook** *n* a person who cooks food, esp as a job: *employed as a cook in a hotel* ◦ *I'm not much of a cook* (ie I don't cook well). ◦ *Were you the cook?* (ie Did you cook this food?) Compare CHEF. **IDM** **too many cooks spoil the 'broth** (*saying*) if too many people are involved in doing sth, it will not be done well.

cooking *n* [U] (**a**) the process of preparing food by heating: *She does all the cooking.* ◦ *Chinese 'cooking.* (**b**) food that is prepared by heating: *He missed his mother's cooking when he left home.* — *adj* suitable for cooking rather than eating raw or drinking: *'cooking apples/sherry.*

■ **'cook-chill** *adj* (of food) prepared by being cooked, kept at a low temperature and then heated again: *,cook-chill 'meals* ◦ *,cook-chill 'processes.*

NOTE There are several ways of cooking: with water, oil or in dry heat.

You can **boil** vegetables, eggs, rice, etc by covering them with water and heating to a high temperature.

You can **steam** fish, vegetables, puddings, etc by placing the food above boiling water and covering it.

You can **fry** meat, fish, eggs, etc in a shallow pan of hot oil. Chips, etc can be completely covered in very hot oil and **deep-fried.**

You can **sauté** small pieces of vegetables, etc very quickly in a little oil.

You can **roast** large pieces of meat, potatoes, etc in some oil in the heat of an oven.

You can **bake** bread, cakes, biscuits, etc in the heat of an oven.

You can **grill** (also **broil** in American English) flat pieces of meat or fish, etc by placing them under direct heat.

You can **barbecue** pieces of meat, etc outside on a special grill that is heated by an open fire.

cookbook /'kʊkbʊk/ *n* = COOKERY BOOK.

cooker /'kʊkə(r)/ *n* (*esp Brit*) **1** an appliance for cooking, consisting of an oven, a heating surface and often also a GRILL(1a). Most cookers use gas or electricity for producing heat: *a 'gas cooker* ◦ *an e,lectric 'cooker.* Compare STOVE[1]. See also PRESSURE-COOKER. **2** a fruit, esp an apple, that is suitable for cooking rather than eating raw: *These apples are good cookers.* Compare EATING APPLE.

cookery /'kʊkəri/ *n* [U] the skill or practice of cooking: *a cookery course* ◦ *learn cookery at school.*
■ **'cookery book** (*Brit*) (also **'cookbook**) *n* a book that gives instructions on cooking and how to cook individual dishes.

cookhouse /'kʊkhaʊs/ *n* (*pl* /-haʊzɪz/) an outdoor kitchen, eg in a camp.

cookie (also **cooky**) /'kʊki/ *n* (*pl* -**kies**) (*US*) **1** a sweet biscuit: *Mom made some more peanut butter cookies!* **2** (*infml*) a person of a specified type: *He's a*

tough cookie. **IDM** **that's the way the cookie crumbles** ⇨ WAY[1].

cookware /'kʊkweə(r)/ *n* [U] equipment for cooking, eg pans, etc.

cool[1] /ku:l/ *adj* (**-er, -est**) **1(a)** fairly cold; not hot or warm: *a cool breeze/day/surface* ◦ *cool autumn weather* ◦ *Let's sit in the shade and keep cool.* ◦ *The coffee's not cool enough to drink.* ◦ *find a cool spot to sit in.* (**b**) giving a feeling of not being too warm: *cool clothing.* (**c**) (of colours) suggesting the quality of being cool: *a room painted in cool greens and blues.* **2** calm; not excited, angry or emotional: *Keep cool!* ◦ *She always remains* **cool, calm and collected** *in a crisis.* ◦ *He has a cool head* (ie doesn't get agitated). **3** ~ (**about sth**); ~ (**towards sb**) not friendly, interested or enthusiastic: *She was decidedly cool about the proposal.* ◦ *He has been rather cool towards me ever since we had that argument.* ◦ *They gave the Prime Minister* **a cool reception.** **4** bold in a calm confident way: *You should have seen the cool way she took my radio without even asking!* **5** [attrib] (*infml*) (used esp about a sum of money, for emphasizing how large it is): *The car cost a cool thirty thousand.* **6** (*sl*) excellent; impressive: *You look pretty cool in that new outfit.* **IDM** (**as**) **,cool as a 'cucumber** very calm and controlled, esp in difficult circumstances. **play it 'cool** (*infml*) to deal with a situation in a deliberately calm way: *I decided to play it cool rather than letting her know my real feelings.*

▶ **cool** *n* **the cool** [sing] cool air or a cool place; the quality of being cool[1](1): *step out of the sun into the cool* ◦ *the pleasant cool of the evening.* **IDM** **keep/lose one's cool** (*infml*) to remain calm/to become angry, excited, etc: *She kept her cool while everyone else panicked.* ◦ *I lost my cool and shouted at them.*

coolly /'ku:lli/ *adv* in a way that is not friendly, interested or enthusiastic: *He received my suggestion coolly.*

coolness *n* [U] the quality of being cool: *the pleasant coolness of the sea* ◦ *I admire her coolness under pressure.* ◦ *I noticed a certain coolness* (ie lack of friendly feeling) *between them.*

■ **,cool-'headed** *adj* calm; not getting excited or nervous: *a cool-headed judgement.*

cool[2] /ku:l/ *v* ~ (**sth/sb**) (**down/off**) to become or make sb/sth cool or cooler: [V] *My enthusiasm for the idea is beginning to cool.* [V, Vp] *The hot metal contracts as it cools* (*down*). ◦ *Let the pie cool* (*off*) *a bit before serving it.* [Vn] *A cooling drink is welcome on a hot day.* [Vn, Vnp] *A swim in the sea should cool you* (*down*). **IDM** **cool it** (*infml*) (esp imperative) to calm down: *Cool it! Don't get so excited!* **,cool one's 'heels** to be kept waiting: *Let him cool his heels for a while; that'll teach him to be so rude.* **PHRV** **,cool (sb) 'down/'off** to become or make sb calm, less excited or less enthusiastic: *She's very angry; don't speak to her until she's cooled down a bit.* ◦ *A day in jail cooled him off.*

■ **,cooling-'off period** *n* (in industrial disputes) a compulsory delay before a strike, during which it may be possible for the two sides to reach an agreement.

'cooling tower *n* a large tall structure used in industry for cooling water before it is used again.

coolant /'ku:lənt/ *n* [C,U] a liquid that is used for cooling an engine, a nuclear REACTOR, etc.

cooler /'ku:lə(r)/ *n* **1** [C] a container in which things are cooled: *Put the beer for the picnic in the cooler.* **2** [C] (*esp US*) a long drink with ice in: *a wine cooler.* **3 the cooler** [sing] (*sl*) prison: *two years in the cooler.*

coolie /'ku:li/ *n* (*dated* ⚠ *offensive*) (in Eastern countries) a worker with no special skill or training.

coon /ku:n/ *n* (⚠ *sl derog offensive*) a black person.

coop /ku:p/ *n* a cage for chickens, etc.

C

▶ **coop** v PHRV ,coop sb/sth ¹up (in sth) (usu passive) to confine sb/sth in a small space; to keep sb/sth inside, restricting their/its freedom: *I've been cooped up indoors all day.*

co-op /ˈkəʊɒp/ n (*infml*) a COOPERATIVE(3) shop, society or business: *a wine produced by the local growers' co-op.*

cooper /ˈkuːpə(r)/ n a person who makes barrels.

cooperate (also **co-operate**) /kəʊˈɒpəreɪt/ v 1 ~ (with sb) (in doing/to do sth) to work or act together with another or others for a common purpose: [Vpr] *cooperate with one's friends in raising/to raise money* [V] *The two schools are cooperating on the project.* 2 to be helpful by doing what one is asked to do: [V] *The police told him they would release him if he cooperated (eg by telling them everything he knew).*

cooperation (also **co-operation**) /kəʊˌɒpəˈreɪʃn/ n [U] 1 ~ (with sb) (in doing sth / on sth); ~ (between A and B) (in doing sth / on sth) doing sth or working together for a common purpose: *a report produced by the government in cooperation with the chemical industry* ◦ *cooperation between the police and the public in catching the criminal.* 2 willingness to be helpful and do as one is asked: *We should be grateful for your cooperation in clearing the hall as quickly as possible.*

cooperative (also **co-operative**) /kəʊˈɒpərətɪv/ adj 1 [usu attrib] involving acting or working together with another or others for a common purpose; joint: *a cooperative venture.* 2 helpful by doing what one is asked to do: *The bank has been very cooperative in helping me sort out my late husband's finances.* Compare UNCOOPERATIVE. 3 [usu attrib] (*commerce*) owned and run by the people involved, with profits shared by them: *a cooperative farm/venture* ◦ *The cooperative movement started in Britain in the 19th century; cooperative societies set up shops to sell low-priced goods to poor people.*

▶ **cooperative** (also **co-operative**) n a cooperative(3) business or other organization: *agricultural cooperatives in India and China* ◦ *The bicycle factory is now a workers' cooperative.* ◦ *a housing cooperative* (ie a house or group of houses of which those who live there have joint ownership).

cooperatively (also **co-operatively**) adv.

co-opt /kəʊˈɒpt/ v ~ sb (onto/into sth) (of the members of a committee) to vote for the appointment of sb as an extra member of the committee: [Vn, Vnpr] *co-opt a new member (onto the executive).*

coordinate¹ (also **co-ordinate**) /kəʊˈɔːdɪnət/ n 1 either of two numbers or letters used to fix the position of a point on a GRAPH or map: *the x and y coordinates on a graph* ◦ *coordinates of latitude and longitude.* ⇨ picture at MAP. 2 **coordinates** [pl] matching pieces of esp women's clothing.

■ **co,ordinate ¹clause** n (*grammar*) each of two or more clauses in a sentence that make separate parallel statements, have similar patterns and are often joined by *and, or, but*, etc. Compare SUBORDINATE CLAUSE.

coordinate² (also **co-ordinate**) /kəʊˈɔːdɪneɪt/ v to make things, people, parts, etc function together efficiently and in an organized way: [Vn] *coordinate one's movements when swimming* ◦ *We must coordinate our efforts* (ie work together) *to help the flood victims.* ◦ *The plan was not* (ie Its parts or the people involved were not) *very well coordinated.* ◦ *a coordinating committee* ◦ *a search coordinated with other police forces.*

▶ **coordination** (also **co-ordination**) /kəʊˌɔːdɪˈneɪʃn/ n [U] 1 the action of coordinating: *the coordination of the work of several people* ◦ *a pamphlet produced by the government in coordination with* (ie working together with) *the Sports Council.* 2 the ability to control one's movements properly:

have good/poor coordination ◦ *You need good coordination of hand and eye to play ball games.*

coordinator n: *The campaign needs an effective coordinator.*

coot /kuːt/ n a black water bird with a white spot on the forehead. ⇨ picture. IDM **bald as a coot** ⇨ BALD.

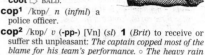
coot

cop¹ /kɒp/ n (*infml*) a police officer.

cop² /kɒp/ v (**-pp-**) [Vn] (*sl*) 1 (*Brit*) to receive or suffer sth unpleasant: *The captain copped most of the blame for his team's performance.* ◦ *The heavy rain missed the north of the country altogether, and the south copped the lot.* 2 to catch or arrest sb in the act of doing sth wrong: *He was copped for speeding.* 3 (*Brit*) to take hold of sth: *'Cop this,' he said, throwing me the magazine.* IDM **cop hold of sth** (*Brit sl*) to take hold of sth: *Here, cop hold of the screwdriver while I use the hammer.* ¹**cop it** (*sl*) 1 to be punished: *When he finds out you broke his hi-fi, you'll really cop it!* 2 to be killed. PHRV ,cop ¹out (of sth) (*sl derog*) to avoid or withdraw from doing sth one ought to do, because of being afraid, lazy, etc: *He kept boasting about taking part in the race and then copped out at the last moment.* ◦ *She copped out of the cleaning and left it all to me.*

▶ **cop** n IDM **not much ¹cop** (*Brit sl*) not very good: *He's not much cop as a singer.*

■ ¹**cop-out** n (*sl derog*) an act of or excuse for copping out: *The TV debate was a cop-out: it didn't tackle any of the real issues.*

cope¹ /kəʊp/ v (**a**) ~ (with sth) (of a person) to deal successfully with sth difficult; to manage: [V] *Her husband's left her and the kids are running wild, so it's not surprising that she can't cope.* [Vpr] *cope with problems/difficulties/misfortune.* (**b**) ~ with sth to have the capacity to deal with sth successfully: [Vpr] *There was too much work for our computer to cope with.* ◦ *The roads simply can't cope with all the traffic now using them.*

cope² /kəʊp/ n a long loose garment worn by priests on special occasions.

copilot /ˈkəʊpaɪlət/ n the assistant pilot in an aircraft.

coping /ˈkəʊpɪŋ/ n (*architecture*) the top row of bricks or stones, usu sloping, on a wall: *coping-stones.*

copious /ˈkəʊpiəs/ adj produced in large quantities; ABUNDANT: *copious flowers/tears* ◦ *She supports her theory with copious evidence.* ◦ *I took copious notes.* ▶ **copiously** adv: *weeping/writing copiously.*

copper¹ /ˈkɒpə(r)/ n 1 [U] (*symb* Cu) a chemical element. Copper is a common, fairly soft, reddish brown metal through which heat passes easily: *the mining of copper in central Africa* ◦ *Is the pipe copper or lead?* ◦ *a copper pipe/wire/alloy* ◦ *her copper-coloured hair.* ⇨ App 7. 2 [C] (*esp Brit*) a brown coin of low value made from copper or a similar metal: *It only costs a few coppers* (ie is cheap).

▶ **coppery** /ˈkɒpəri/ adj similar to or having the colour of copper: *coppery leaves.*

■ ,**copper-¹bottomed** adj safe in every way; certain not to fail: *a copper-bottomed guarantee/ assurance/deal.*

copper² /ˈkɒpə(r)/ n (*infml*) a police officer.

copperplate /ˈkɒpəpleɪt/ n [U] a neat old-fashioned way of writing with sloping letters that are joined to each other with loops: *written in copperplate (script).*

coppice /ˈkɒpɪs/ n (*esp Brit*) = COPSE.

copse /kɒps/ (also **coppice**) n a small area of trees or bushes growing close together.

copula /ˈkɒpjələ/ n (*pl* **copulas**) (*grammar*) a type of verb that connects a subject with its COMPLE-MENT(3): *In 'George became ill', the verb 'became' is a copula.*

copulate /ˈkɒpjuleɪt/ *v* ~ **(with sb/sth)** *(fml)* to have sex: [Vpr] *The male bird performs a sort of mating dance before copulating with the female.* [also V]. ▶ **copulation** /ˌkɒpjuˈleɪʃn/ *n* [U].

copy¹ /ˈkɒpi/ *n* **1** [C] a thing that is made to look like sth else, eg a picture, document, etc: *Is this the original drawing or is it a copy?* ○ *a perfect copy* ○ *Make three carbon copies of the letter.* **2** = PHOTOCOPY *n.* **3** [C] a single example of a book, newspaper, record, etc of which many have been made: *Have you a copy of yesterday's 'Times', please?* ○ *If you can't afford a new copy of the book, perhaps you can find a second-hand one.* ○ *You receive the top copy of the receipt, and we keep the carbon.* **4** [U] written material that is to be printed, esp in a newspaper or an advertisement: *She has handed in her copy to the editor.* ○ *The government crisis will make good copy.* ○ *prepare copy for a brochure.*

copy² /ˈkɒpi/ *v* (*pt, pp* **copied**) **1(a)** ~ **sth (down/out) (from/off sth) (in/into sth)** to write sth exactly as it is written elsewhere: [Vnp] *The teacher wrote the sums on the board, and the children copied them down in their exercise books.* ○ *copy out a letter* (ie write it out again completely) [Vnpr] *copy notes (from a book, etc) into a notebook* [also Vn]. **(b)** to make a copy of sth on a machine: [Vn] *copy documents on a photocopier.* **2** to behave or do sth in the same way as sb else: [Vn] *She's a good writer: try to copy her style.* ○ *Don't always copy what the others do; use your own ideas.* **3** ~ **(from/off sb)** to cheat by writing or doing the same thing as sb else: [V, Vpr] *She was punished for copying (off one of her friends) during the examination.*
▶ **copier** *n* = PHOTOCOPIER.

copybook /ˈkɒpibʊk/ *n* a book containing models of how to write for pupils to follow. **IDM** **blot one's copybook** ⇨ BLOT.
▶ **copybook** *adj* [attrib] done exactly according to established beliefs about how sth should be done: *It was a copybook operation by the police; all the criminals were arrested and all the stolen property quickly recovered.*

copycat /ˈkɒpikæt/ *n* (*infml derog*) (often used as a form of address, esp by children) a person who copies other people because he or she admires them or has no individual ideas: (*fig*) *copycat crimes* (ie ones that are similar to and seen as copying a well-known earlier crime).

copyist /ˈkɒpiɪst/ *n* **1** a person who makes copies, esp written ones. **2** a person who copies the styles of others, esp in art.

copyright /ˈkɒpiraɪt/ *n* [U,C] ~ **(in/on sth)** the legal right, held for a certain number of years, to print, publish, sell, broadcast, perform, film or record an original work or any part of it: *Copyright expires fifty years after the death of the author.* ○ *The poem is still under copyright, so you have to pay to quote it.* ○ *sued for breach of copyright/for infringing copyright* ○ *Who owns the copyright in/on this song?*
▶ **copyright** *v* [Vn] to obtain copyright for sth.
copyright *adj* protected by copyright; not allowed to be reproduced without permission from the owner of copyright: *This material is copyright.*

copywriter /ˈkɒpiraɪtə(r)/ *n* a person who writes advertising or publicity material.

coquetry /ˈkɒkɪtri/ *n* [U] (*fml*) behaviour that is typical of a COQUETTE.

coquette /kɒˈket/ *n* (*fml often derog*) a woman who behaves in a playful way that is intended to be attractive to men; a FLIRT(1). ▶ **coquettish** /kɒˈketɪʃ/ *adj*: *a coquettish smile/manner.* **coquettishly** *adv*.

cor /kɔː(r)/ (also **cor blimey**) *interj* (*Brit infml*) (used

for expressing surprise, admiration, pleasure, etc): *Cor! Look at that view!*

coracle /ˈkɒrəkl/ *n* a small light boat made of a framework of sticks covered with WATERTIGHT(1) material, eg skins. Coracles are used by people catching fish in Wales and Ireland.

coral /ˈkɒrəl; US ˈkɔːrəl/ *n* **1** [U] a red, pink or white hard substance formed on the bottom of the sea from the bones of tiny creatures: *a necklace made of coral* ○ *a coral island/reef.* **2** [C] a creature that produces coral; a POLYP.
▶ **coral** *adj* like coral in colour; pink or red: *coral lipstick.*

cor anglais /ˌkɔːr ˈɒŋgleɪ; US ɔːŋˈgleɪ/ (*pl* **cors anglais** /ˌkɔːr ˈɒŋgleɪ/) (*Brit*) (*US* **English horn**) *n* (*music*) a WOODWIND instrument similar to the OBOE but larger and playing lower notes.

corbel /ˈkɔːbl/ *n* (*architecture*) a piece of stone or wood that projects from a wall to support sth, eg an arch.

cord /kɔːd/ *n* **1** [U,C] a long thin flexible material made of twisted strands, thicker than string and thinner than rope; a piece of this: *parcels tied with stout cord.* **2** [C] a part of the body that is like a cord because it is long, thin and flexible: *the spinal cord* ○ *the vocal cords.* **3** [C,U] wire, or a piece of wire, with a protective covering; FLEX(1). **4(a)** [U] CORDUROY: *cord trousers/skirts.* **(b)** **cords** *pl* CORDUROY trousers: *a man wearing blue cords.*
▶ **cordless** /ˈkɔːdləs/ *adj* (of an electrical tool or a telephone) having its own internal power supply; used without a plug into a power supply: *a cordless drill/phone.*

cordial¹ /ˈkɔːdiəl; US ˈkɔːrdʒəl/ *adj* pleasant and friendly: *a cordial smile/welcome/handshake.*
▶ **cordiality** /ˌkɔːdiˈæləti; US ˌkɔːrdʒi-/ *n* [U]: *I was greeted with a show of cordiality.*
cordially /-diəli; US -dʒəli/ *adv* **1** in a cordial manner: *You are cordially invited to a party for Michael Brown on his retirement.* **2** (esp with *vs* indicating dislike) thoroughly: *They cordially detest each other.*

cordial² /ˈkɔːdiəl; US ˈkɔːrdʒəl/ *n* [U,C] a sweet drink that is not alcoholic, made from fruit juice or having the flavour of fruit: *lime juice cordial.*

cordite /ˈkɔːdaɪt/ *n* [U] an explosive substance used in bullets, shells, bombs, etc.

cordon /ˈkɔːdn/ *n* **1** a line or ring of police officers, soldiers, etc guarding sth or preventing people from entering or leaving a place: *Demonstrators tried to break through the police cordon.* **2** a fruit tree with all its side branches cut off so that it grows as a single stem, usu against a wall or along wires.
▶ **cordon** *v* **PHRV** **cordon sth off** to block or enclose sth by forming a line or ring round it: *Police cordoned off the area until the bomb was defused.*

cordon bleu /ˌkɔːdɒ̃ ˈblɜː/ *adj* [usu attrib] (*French*) (of a cook, dish, etc) of the highest standard of skill in cooking, esp classical French cooking: *a cordon bleu chef* ○ *cordon bleu cuisine.*

corduroy /ˈkɔːdərɔɪ/ *n* **1** [U] a strong cotton cloth covered with parallel soft raised ridges: *a corduroy jacket.* **2** **corduroys** *pl* trousers made of corduroy: *a pair of blue corduroys.*

CORE (also **Core**) /kɔː(r)/ *abbr* (in the USA) Congress of Racial Equality.

core /kɔː(r)/ *n* **1** the hard centre of certain fruits, eg apples, containing the seeds. ⇨ picture at FRUIT. **2** the central part of an object: *the core of a nuclear reactor* ○ *the Earth's core.* **3** the most important part of sth: *one of his core beliefs/activities/areas* ○ *Let's get to the core of the argument.* ○ *This concept is at the very core of her theory.* ○ *English is a subject on the core curriculum* (ie one which all the students have to do). **IDM** **to the ˈcore** right to the centre: *rotten to the core* (ie completely bad) ○ *He is American to the*

core (ie completely American in attitudes, beliefs, etc). See also HARD CORE.
▶ **core** v [Vn] to take out the core of a fruit, esp an apple.

co-respondent /ˌkəʊ rɪˈspɒndənt/ n (law) a person accused of committing ADULTERY with the husband or wife of sb who is seeking a DIVORCE1: cite (ie name) sb as co-respondent.

corgi /ˈkɔːgi/ n (pl **corgis**) a breed of small dog.

coriander /ˌkɒriˈændə(r); US ˌkɔːr-/ n [U] **(a)** a plant whose fresh leaves are used in cooking. **(b)** its dried seeds used as a spice.

cork /kɔːk/ n **1** [U] a light flexible substance that is the thick bark of a type of OAK tree growing around the Mediterranean: Cork is often used for insulation. ○ cork tiles/table-mats. **2** [C] a small round object made of cork or plastic, used for closing bottles, esp wine bottles: draw/pull out the cork ○ The champagne corks were popping (ie People were celebrating). ⇨ picture at BOTTLE.
▶ **cork** v ~ **sth (up)** to close or seal a bottle, barrel, etc with a cork or sth similar: [Vnp] cork it up for tomorrow [also Vn]. **PHR V** ,**cork sth ˈup** (infml) to keep one's feelings private and not express them: Don't cork it all up: if you feel angry, show it.
corked adj (of wine) made bad by a decayed cork(2).

corkage /ˈkɔːkɪdʒ/ n [U] a charge made by a restaurant for opening wine a customer has bought elsewhere.

corker /ˈkɔːkə(r)/ n [usu sing] (dated infml) an excellent or astonishing person or thing: It was his first goal of the season, and an absolute corker (ie a very good one).

corkscrew /ˈkɔːkskruː/ n a device for pulling corks (CORK 2) from bottles.

corm /kɔːm/ n (botany) a small round underground part of certain plants, similar in appearance to a BULB(1), from which the new plant grows each year. ⇨ picture at FLOWER.

cormorant /ˈkɔːmərənt/ n a large black bird with a long neck which lives near water, esp the sea, and eats fish.

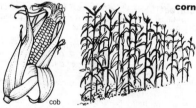

corn

cob

corn1 /kɔːn/ n [U] **1** (esp Brit) **(a)** any plant that produces grain, esp wheat, OATS, RYE and MAIZE: a field of corn ○ a ˈcornfield ○ a sheaf of corn. ⇨ picture. **(b)** (esp US) the seeds of these plants; MAIZE: grinding corn to make flour ○ corn-fed chickens. **2** (esp US) MAIZE. See also SWEET CORN.
■ **corn circle** n = CROP CIRCLE.
ˈ**corn-cob** (also **cob**) n the long hard part at the top of a MAIZE plant, on which the grains grow. ⇨ picture.
ˈ**corn exchange** n a place where corn is bought and sold.
,**corn on the ˈcob** n [U] MAIZE cooked with all the grains still attached to the head of the plant.
ˈ**corn pone** (US also **pone**) n /pəʊn/ [U] baked or fried bread made from MAIZE.

corn2 /kɔːn/ n a small, often painful, area of hardened skin on the foot, esp on the toe.

cornea /ˈkɔːniə/ n (anatomy) the transparent protective outer covering of the eye. ⇨ picture at EYE1.
▶ **corneal** /ˈkɔːniəl/ adj of the cornea: a corneal transplant.

corned beef /ˌkɔːnd ˈbiːf/ n [U] BEEF preserved in salt: a tin of corned beef.

cornelian /kɔːˈniːliən/ n a dull red, brown or white stone, used in jewellery.

corner1 /ˈkɔːnə(r)/ n **1(a)** a place where two or three lines, sides, edges or surfaces meet: A square has four corners; a cube has eight. ○ standing at a street corner ○ the shop on the corner ○ the traffic-lights at the corner of Lansdowne Road ○ When I turned the corner (of the street) he had disappeared. ○ He hit his knee on the corner of the table. **(b)** a sharp bend in a road: The van took the corner too fast. **(c)** the area near where two or three edges or surfaces meet: In the corner of the room stood a big old chair. ○ The address is in the top right-hand corner of the letter. **2** a region or an area, esp one that is hidden or remote: She lives in a quiet corner of rural Yorkshire. ○ He knew every corner of the old town. ○ They flocked to the royal wedding from **all corners of/ the four corners of** the earth (ie from every country). **3** (usu sing) a difficult or awkward situation: She'll need luck to get out of a **tight corner** like that. ○ The interviewer had driven/forced her into a corner. **4** (usu sing) ~ **(in/on sth)** (commerce) complete ownership or control of supplies of sth, enabling one to decide its price: a company with a corner in tin ore/on the tin market. **5** (also ˈ**corner-kick**) (in football) a kick from the corner of the field, given to a team when an opposing player kicks the ball over his own goal-line (GOAL 1a): The referee awarded a corner. **6** (in boxing and wrestling (WRESTLE)) any of the four corners of the ring: And in the blue corner, Buster Smith. ⇨ picture at BOXING. **IDM** (**just**) **around/round the ˈcorner** very near: Her house is (just) round the corner. ○ (fig) Good times are just around the corner (ie will soon happen). **back sb into a ˈcorner** ⇨ BACK4. **cut ˈcorners** to do sth in the easiest, quickest or cheapest way, often by ignoring rules or omitting sth: We've had to cut a few corners to get his order ready in time. **cut (off) a ˈcorner** (esp Brit) to go across a corner1(1a) and not round the sides of it: a path cutting off the corner ○ The lawn is damaged here because people cut (off) the corner. **out of the corner of one's ˈeye** by looking at sth from the side of one's eye and not straight at it: I caught sight of her out of the corner of my eye. **turn the ˈcorner** to pass a critical point in an illness or a period of difficulty and begin to improve.
▶ -ˈ**cornered** (in compound adjs) **1** with the specified number of corners: a ,three-cornered ˈhat. **2** with the specified number of people, groups, etc involved: The election was a three-cornered fight between the Conservatives, Labour and the Liberal Democrats.
■ ,**corner ˈshop** n (Brit) a small shop selling different goods, esp one near people's houses.

corner2 /ˈkɔːnə(r)/ v (often passive) **1** to get a person or an animal into a place or situation from which it is hard to escape: [Vn] The escaped prisoner was cornered at last. ○ a cornered fox ○ She felt cornered: there was no way out now. **2** to approach sb in a determined way, because one wants to speak to them: [Vn] As a financial writer, I am frequently cornered for advice. **3** (Brit) (of a vehicle or driver) to go round a corner1(1a,1b): [Vadv] The car corners well (ie remains steady on curves). **4** (commerce) to gain complete ownership or control of sth: [Vn] corner the market in silver.

cornerstone /ˈkɔːnəstəʊn/ n **1** a stone that forms the base of a corner of a building, often laid in position at a special ceremony. **2** an important feature or quality on which sth is based or on which it depends; a foundation: traditions which are the cornerstone of Western civilization.

cornet /ˈkɔːnɪt/ n **1** a brass musical instrument, like a TRUMPET(1) but smaller. **2** (also **cone**) (Brit) a container for ice-cream in the shape of a CONE(2). Cornets are made of thin crisp biscuit.

cornflakes /'kɔːnfleɪks/ n [pl] small crisp yellow pieces of MAIZE made by crushing and heating the grains. Cornflakes are usu eaten with milk and often sugar for breakfast.

cornflour /'kɔːnflaʊə(r)/ (US **cornstarch**) n [U] finely ground flour made esp from MAIZE or rice.

cornflower /'kɔːnflaʊə(r)/ n a small plant with blue flowers, often growing wild.

cornice /'kɔːnɪs/ n (architecture) an ornamental border, eg in stone or PLASTER(1), round the top of the walls of a room or outside walls of a building: a lofty corridor with a moulded cornice. ⇨ picture at COLUMN.

Cornish /'kɔːnɪʃ/ adj of Cornwall in SW England.
■ **Cornish 'pasty** n a small pie consisting of pastry filled with meat and vegetables.

cornstarch /'kɔːnstaːtʃ/ n [U] (US) = CORNFLOUR.

cornucopia /ˌkɔːnjuˈkəʊpiə/ n **1** (fml or joc) a very large supply of sth: The book is a cornucopia of information. **2** (also ˌhorn of 'plenty) an ornamental animal's horn shown in art as completely full of flowers, fruit and corn.

corny /'kɔːnɪ/ adj (-ier, -iest) (infml) (a) too often heard or repeated; not original in any way: a corny joke ○ It sounds a little corny, but as soon as I saw her I knew she was the one for me. (b) (derog) too sentimental: a corny song.

corollary /kəˈrɒləri; US 'kɔːrəleri/ n ~ (of/to sth) (fml) a natural or logical consequence or result: The substance is not specifically banned, and the corollary of that is that the police cannot take any action against users unless some other offence is committed.

corona /kəˈrəʊnə/ n (pl coronas /-nəz/ or coronae /-niː/) (also **halo**) (astronomy) a ring of light seen round the sun or moon, eg during an ECLIPSE(1).

coronary /'kɒrənri; US 'kɔːrəneri/ adj (anatomy) of the heart: a coronary care unit.
■ ˌcoronary 'artery n (anatomy) an ARTERY(1) that supplies blood to the heart.
ˌcoronary 'heart disease n [U] (medical) disease resulting from damage to the coronary arteries.
ˌcoronary throm'bosis n (pl thromboses /-siːz/) (also infml coronary) (medical) the blocking of a coronary artery by a CLOT(1) of blood, damaging the heart and possibly causing death: a near-fatal coronary. Compare HEART ATTACK.

coronation /ˌkɒrəˈneɪʃn; US ˌkɔːr-/ n a ceremony at which a crown is formally put on the head of a new king or queen: the coronation of Elizabeth II ○ coronation robes.

coroner /'kɒrənə(r); US 'kɔːr-/ n an official who investigates any violent or suspicious death by holding an INQUEST(1).

coronet /'kɒrənet; US 'kɔːr-/ n (a) a small crown worn on formal occasions by a member of the peerage (PEER¹). (b) a circular decoration for the head, esp one made of flowers.

Corp abbr (US) Corporation: West Coast Motor Corp.

corporal¹ /'kɔːpərəl/ n (abbr Cpl) an officer of low rank in the army, air force, marines (MARINE²) or police force. ⇨ App 6.

corporal² /'kɔːpərəl/ adj (fml) of or affecting the human body. Compare CORPOREAL.
■ ˌcorporal 'punishment n physical punishment, eg by whipping or beating.

corporate /'kɔːpərət/ adj **1** of or relating to a corporation(1a,b): corporate planning/finance/borrowing/loyalty ○ our corporate identity (ie the idea people have of us as a company) ○ the increasing importance of corporate hospitality (ie the entertaining of clients by companies to help develop good business relationships). **2** [attrib] united in a single group: a corporate body/organization. **3** [attrib] of

or shared by all the members of a group: corporate responsibility/action.

corporation /ˌkɔːpəˈreɪʃn/ n [CGp] **1** (abbr **corp**) (a) a group of people having authority to operate as a single unit with a separate legal existence, eg for business purposes: urban development corporations. (b) a business company: large multinational corporations ○ the Mitsubishi Trust and Banking Corporation. **2** (esp Brit) a group of people elected to govern a town; a council: the Lord Mayor and Corporation of the City of London ○ corporation refuse collection.
■ ˌcorpo'ration tax n [U] (esp Brit) a tax paid by business companies on their profits.

corporeal /kɔːˈpɔːriəl/ adj (fml) **1** of or for the body: corporeal needs (eg food and drink). **2** that can be touched; physical rather than spiritual: his corporeal presence. Compare CORPORAL².

corps /kɔː(r)/ n (pl unchanged /kɔːz/) [CGp] **1**(a) a military force composed of two or more divisions: the 6th Army Corps. (b) one of the technical branches of an army: the ˌRoyal ˌArmy 'Medical Corps. **2** a group of people involved in a particular activity: the Diplo'matic Corps (ie all the people representing foreign states in a particular country) ○ the 'press corps (ie foreign journalists).
■ **corps de ballet** /ˌkɔː də 'bæleɪ; US bæ'leɪ/ n [CGp] (French) dancers in a ballet company who dance together as a group.

corpse /kɔːps/ n a dead body, esp of a human being: The corpse was barely recognizable. Compare CARCASS.

corpulent /'kɔːpjələnt/ adj (fml esp euph) (of a person) fat.

corpus /'kɔːpəs/ n (pl corpora /'kɔːpərə/ or corpuses /-sɪz/) a collection of written and/or spoken texts: analyse a corpus of spoken dialect ○ the entire corpus of Milton's works.

corpuscle /'kɔːpʌsl/ n (anatomy) any of the red or white cells in the blood.

corral /kəˈraːl; US -'ræl/ n (esp US) an enclosure for horses, cattle, etc on a farm or RANCH.
▶ **corral** v (-ll-) [Vn] to drive cattle, etc into a corral.

correct¹ /kəˈrekt/ adj **1** true; right; accurate and without mistakes: the correct answer/approach/procedure ○ Do you have the correct time? ○ The description is correct in every detail/absolutely correct. ○ 'Am I correct in thinking that you are a writer?' 'Yes, that's correct.' **2** (of behaviour, etc) following accepted standards or convention; proper: a very correct young lady ○ Such casual dress would not be correct for a formal occasion. ▶ **correctly** adv: forecast/guess correctly ○ He believed, perhaps correctly, that... ○ behave very correctly. **correctness** n [U]: question the correctness of the court's decision.

correct² /kəˈrekt/ v **1** (a) to make sth right or accurate, eg by changing it or removing mistakes: [Vn] correct sb's spelling ○ Please correct my pronunciation if I go wrong. ○ Spectacles correct faulty eyesight. ○ 'It was in April — no, May,' he said, correcting himself. (b) (of a teacher, etc) to mark the errors in sth: [Vn] correct an essay/a test. **2** to tell sb they have made a mistake: [Vn] 'Correct me if I'm wrong, but isn't this last year's brochure?' ○ Yes, you're right — **I stand corrected** (ie I accept that I made a mistake).

correction /kəˈrekʃn/ n **1** [U] the action or process of correcting sth: Your work still contains mistakes which need correction. **2** [C] (a) a change that makes sth more accurate than before: She made a few small corrections to the minutes of the meeting. (b) a mark on paper showing where sth was wrong: an exercise with corrections all over it in red ink. **3** (infml) (used when one wants to correct sth one has just said): Why do you dislike me? Correction — why do you *make such a show of disliking me?* **4** [U] (*dated euph*) punishment: *the correction of young offenders.*

corrective /kəˈrektɪv/ *adj* designed to correct²(1a) sth: *take* **corrective action** ∘ *corrective training* (ie to improve the behaviour of young criminals) ∘ *corrective surgery for a deformed leg.*
▶ **corrective** *n* ~ (**to sth**) a thing that helps to give a more accurate or fairer view of sb/sth: *Experiences of this kind provide a useful corrective to the popular myth about modern technology.*

correlate /ˈkɒrəleɪt; US ˈkɔːr-/ *v* (**a**) ~ (**with sth**) to have a mutual relationship or connection, in which one thing affects or depends on another: [Vpr] *The results of this experiment do not correlate closely with those of earlier ones.* [V] *The data do not seem to correlate.* (**b**) ~ **A and/with B** to show such a relationship or connection between two or more things: [Vn] *Researchers are trying to correlate the two sets of figures.* [Vnpr] *We can often correlate age with frequency of illness.*
▶ **correlation** /ˌkɒrəˈleɪʃn; US ˌkɔːr-/ *n* [C, U] ~ (**with sth**); ~ (**between A and B**) a mutual relationship: *a direct/clear correlation between bans on tobacco advertising and a reduction in the number of smokers.* ∘ *complete lack of correlation.*

correspond /ˌkɒrəˈspɒnd; US ˌkɔːr-/ *v* **1** ~ (**to/with sth**) to be the same as or to agree: [Vpr] *Your account of events corresponds with hers.* [V] *Your account and hers correspond.* [Vpr] *correspond broadly/closely/exactly with their requirements* ∘ *The written record of our conversation doesn't correspond to* (ie is different from) *what was actually said.* **2** ~ (**to sth**) to be equivalent or similar: [Vpr] *The American Congress corresponds to the British Parliament.* [also V]. **3** ~ (**with sb**) to exchange letters: [V, Vpr] *We've corresponded (with each other)* (ie written to each other) *for years but I've never actually met him.*
▶ **corresponding** *adj* equivalent or related: *a decline in profits and a corresponding reduction of the workforce* ∘ *Imports in the first three months have increased by 10 per cent compared with the corresponding period last year.* **correspondingly** *adv*: *The new exam is longer and correspondingly more difficult to pass.*

correspondence /ˌkɒrəˈspɒndəns; US ˌkɔːr-/ *n* **1** [C, U] ~ (**with sth/between sth and sth**) a state of being related or similar; an instance of this: *very little correspondence with reality* ∘ *a close correspondence between the two accounts.* **2** [U] ~ (**with sb**) (**a**) the letters a person receives: *sb's personal/private correspondence* ∘ *She has a lot of correspondence to deal with.* (**b**) the action or activity of writing letters: *I refused to enter into any correspondence* (ie exchange letters) *with him about it.*
■ **corre'spondence course** *n* a course of study, often done at home, using books and exercises sent by post.

correspondent /ˌkɒrəˈspɒndənt; US ˌkɔːr-/ *n* **1** a person who contributes news or comments regularly to a newspaper, radio station, etc, esp from abroad: *our Hong Kong correspondent* ∘ *a foreign/war/sports correspondent.* **2** a person who writes letters to another person: *He's a poor correspondent* (ie He does not write regularly).

corridor /ˈkɒrɪdɔː(r); US ˈkɔːr-/ *n* **1** a long narrow passage, from which doors open into rooms: *Go along/down the corridor, turn left, and you'll see his office in front of you.* **2** a long narrow strip of land belonging to one country that passes through the land of another country. **IDM** **the corridors of 'power** (*often joc*) the senior levels of government or administration, where important decisions are made: *an issue much discussed in the corridors of power.*

corroborate /kəˈrɒbəreɪt/ *v* (often passive) to confirm or give support to a statement, belief, theory,

etc: [Vn] *a diagnosis corroborated by further tests* ∘ *Independent witnesses have corroborated her account.*
▶ **corroboration** /kəˌrɒbəˈreɪʃn/ *n* [U]: *In corroboration of his story* (ie to give support to it) *he produced a signed statement from his employer.*
corroborative /kəˈrɒbərətɪv; US -reɪtɪv/ *adj* [usu attrib] tending to corroborate sth: *corroborative evidence* ∘ *corroborative reports/accounts.*

corrode /kəˈrəʊd/ *v* (**a**) to destroy sth slowly, esp by chemical action: [Vn] *Acid corrodes metal.* ∘ *badly corroded copper pipes* ∘ *the corroding effects of salt* ∘ (*fig*) *A bitter envy had corroded their friendship.* (**b**) to be destroyed slowly in this way: [V] *The metal has corroded because of rust.*
▶ **corrosion** /kəˈrəʊʒn/ *n* [U]: *signs/evidence of corrosion* ∘ *Clean off any corrosion before applying the paint.*
corrosive /kəˈrəʊsɪv/ *adj* tending to corrode: *Rust and acids are corrosive.* ∘ (*fig*) *the corrosive effects of these measures on everyone's civil liberties.*

corrugated /ˈkɒrəgeɪtɪd; US ˈkɔːr-/ *adj* shaped into a series of regular folds: *corrugated cardboard* (ie used for packing goods that break easily) ∘ *a roof made of sheets of corrugated iron.* ⇨ picture.

corrugated
corrugated iron

corrupt¹ /kəˈrʌpt/ *adj* **1** (*derog*) (esp of people with authority or power) willing to act dishonestly or illegally in return for money or personal gain: *corrupt officials accepting bribes* ∘ *a brutal and corrupt regime* ∘ *corrupt practices.* **2** not following accepted standards of behaviour, esp sexually: *their corrupt leisure industry.* **3** (*techn*) (of languages, texts, data, etc) containing errors or changes and no longer in the original state: *a corrupt manuscript.* ▶ **corruptly** *adv.*

corrupt² /kəˈrʌpt/ *v* (*derog*) [Vn] **1** to make sb/sth CORRUPT¹(1): *young people whose morals have been corrupted* ∘ *the corrupting influence/effect of television.* **2** (often passive) to change sth, so that it is no longer in its original state: *corrupted data* ∘ *a corrupted form of Buddhism.* ▶ **corruptible** *adj.*

corruption /kəˈrʌpʃn/ *n* **1** [U] dishonest or wicked behaviour: (*esp law*) *allegations of widespread corruption in high places* ∘ *cases of bribery and corruption.* **2** [U] the act of corrupting (CORRUPT²) or the process of being corrupted: *officials who are open to corruption* (ie will accept offers of money, etc) ∘ *He claimed that sex and violence on TV led to the corruption of young people.* **3** [C usu *sing*] the form of a word, etc which has been changed from its original form in an unusual way: *a corruption of the Gaelic word.*

corsage /kɔːˈsɑːʒ/ *n* a small bunch of flowers worn on the upper part of a woman's dress.

corset /ˈkɔːsɪt/ *n* a tightly fitting garment worn under the outer garments to shape the body, or to support it in case of injury.

cortege (also **cortège**) /kɔːˈteʒ; *Brit* also -ˈteɪʒ/ *n* [CGp] a solemn procession, esp for a funeral.

cortex /ˈkɔːteks/ *n* (*pl* **cortices** /ˈkɔːtɪsiːz/) (*medical*) the outer layer of an organ of the body, esp the brain: *the cerebral cortex.*

cortisone /ˈkɔːtɪzəʊn, -səʊn/ *n* [U] (*medical*) a HORMONE(b) used in the treatment of ARTHRITIS and some allergies (ALLERGY).

cos¹ /kɒs/ (also ˌ**cos** ˈ**lettuce**) (*Brit*) (*US* **romaine**) *n* [C, U] a type of LETTUCE with long crisp leaves.

cos² (also **'cos**) /kɒz/ *conj* (*infml*) (esp in spoken English) because: *I can't see her at all, cos it's too dark.*

cos³ /kɒs/ *abbr* (*mathematics*) cosine. Compare SIN².

cosh /kɒʃ/ n (esp Brit) a short heavy piece of metal or solid rubber used as a weapon.
▶ **cosh** v [Vn] (esp Brit) to hit sb hard with a cosh or sth similar.

co-signatory /ˌkəʊˈsɪɡnətəri; US -tɔːri/ n ~ (of/to sth) a person or state signing a formal document that is also signed by others: co-signatories of/to the treaty.

cosine /ˈkəʊsaɪn/ n (abbr cos) (mathematics) (of an angle) the RATIO of the shorter side next to this angle in a right-angled TRIANGLE(1) to the longest side. Compare SINE, TANGENT 2.

cosmetic /kɒzˈmetɪk/ n (usu pl) a substance for putting on the body, esp the face, to make it beautiful: a bag full of cosmetics ○ the cosmetics industry ○ cosmetic companies.
▶ **cosmetic** adj 1 (usu derog) intended to improve only the appearance of sth and not its fundamental character: The reforms he claims to have made are in fact purely/merely cosmetic. 2 involving or concerned with treatment to restore or improve a person's outward appearance rather than for health reasons: cosmetic surgery/dental work ○ a cosmetic surgeon. **cosmetically** /-kli/ adv.

cosmic /ˈkɒzmɪk/ adj [usu attrib] 1 of the whole universe: Physics is governed by cosmic laws. 2 very great and important: a disaster of cosmic proportions.
■ **cosmic 'rays** n [pl] rays (RAY¹ 1a) that reach the earth from outer space.

cosmology /kɒzˈmɒlədʒi/ n [U] the scientific study of the universe and its origin and development.

cosmonaut /ˈkɒzmənɔːt/ n an ASTRONAUT, esp one from the former Soviet Union.

cosmopolitan /ˌkɒzməˈpɒlɪtən/ adj 1 containing or influenced by people from all over the world: a cosmopolitan city/resort/society ○ a cosmopolitan atmosphere. 2 (approv) having a broad view or experience of the world and free from national prejudice: a cosmopolitan person/outlook.

cosmos /ˈkɒzmɒs/ n the cosmos [sing] the universe, seen as an ordered system.

cosset /ˈkɒsɪt/ v (derog) to give sb/sth a lot of care and protection from harm; to PAMPER sb/sth: [Vn] His mother flattered and cosseted him. ○ (fig) an industry cosseted by government subsidies.

cost¹ /kɒst; US kɔːst/ v (pt, pp cost or, in sense 3, costed) 1 to require payment of a particular amount of money in order to be bought, made, done, etc: [Vn] These chairs cost £40 each. [Vnn] The meal cost us about £30. ○ The scheme is costing the taxpayer 10 billion pounds a year. [Vadv] How much does it cost? ○ It costs too much. [Vn.to inf] The hospital will cost an estimated £2 million to build. 2(a) to result in the loss of sth: [Vnn] Dangerous driving could cost you your life. ○ The scandal cost her her career (ie resulted in her having to resign or being dismissed). (b) to require a particular effort or sacrifice: [Vnn] All this is costing me a great deal of time. ○ Her irresponsible behaviour cost her father many sleepless nights. 3 (pt, pp costed) (commerce) to estimate how much money will be needed or the price to be charged for sth: [Vn] The project has only been roughly costed. [Vnpr] Their accountants have costed the scheme at $8.1 million. [also Vn]. See also COST-ING. 4 (infml) to be expensive for sb: [Vn] You can have the de luxe model if you like, but it'll cost you.
IDM **cost/pay an arm and a leg** ⇨ ARM¹. **cost sb 'dear** to cause sb to suffer serious loss or injury: That one little mistake cost him dear and he went on to lose the game. **PHRV** **cost sth 'out** to estimate in detail how much money one will need for sth.
▶ **costing** n [C] (commerce) an estimate of how much money will be required for sth: a detailed costing of the project ○ long-term costings.

cost² /kɒst; US kɔːst/ n 1(a) [U] the price to be paid

or amount of money needed for sth: the high cost of car repairs ○ bear the full cost of the damage ○ I was forced to abandon the project on the grounds of cost. ○ We made a small charge for parking to **cover the cost** of hiring the hall. ○ A new computer system has been installed at a cost of £80 000. ○ a low-cost scheme ○ a **cost-conscious** business ○ make **cost-saving** cutbacks. ⇨ note at PRICE. (b) [C usu pl] an amount of money needed for a particular activity or purpose, esp in business: the costs involved in starting a business ○ labour/operating costs ○ The industry will have to pass its increased costs on to the consumer (ie charge more for its product). 2 **costs** [pl] (law) the expense of having a case decided in a lawcourt: pay a £1 000 fine and £300 costs. 3 [U, sing] the effort, loss or sacrifice necessary in order to do or obtain sth: the cost in time and labour ○ the environmental cost of nuclear power ○ The battle was won at (a) great cost in human lives. ○ She saved him from drowning but **at the cost of** her own life (ie she died). **IDM** **at 'all cost/costs** as the most important consideration, regardless of how much time, money, etc is necessary to achieve sth: We must prevent them from finding it at all costs. **at any cost** under any circumstances: They are determined to succeed at any cost. **at 'cost** for the amount of money needed to produce or obtain sth: goods sold at cost. **count the cost** ⇨ COUNT¹. **to one's 'cost** to one's loss or disadvantage: He's an excellent tennis player, as I know to my cost (ie as I know because I have been beaten by him).
■ **cost-'benefit** n [U] (economics) the relating of the cost of sth to the benefit it gives: cost-benefit analysis.
'cost-cutting n [U] reduction in the money spent on sth, esp because of financial difficulty: a cost-cutting exercise/measure ○ Emphasis on efficiency and cost-cutting has resulted in greater centralization.
cost-ef'fective adj giving enough profit, benefit, etc in relation to money spent: It isn't cost-effective to build cars in such small quantities. **cost-ef'fectiveness** n [U].
the cost of 'living n [sing] the level of prices, esp for food, clothing and accommodation of an average standard: a rise in the cost of living ○ the high cost of living in the capital.
cost 'price n [U] (commerce) the cost of producing sth or the price at which it is sold without profit. Compare SELLING PRICE.

co-star /ˈkəʊ stɑː(r)/ v (-rr-) (a) (of a film, etc) to have a star(3) who is equal in status to another or others: [Vn] The movie co-starred Robert Redford (and Paul Newman). (b) ~ (with sb) to appear as a star with sb: [V, Vpr] Maggie Smith co-stars (with Laurence Olivier).
▶ **co-star** /ˈkəʊ stɑː(r)/ n a person who co-stars: Her co-star was Jeremy Irons.

costly /ˈkɒstli; US ˈkɔːst-/ adj (-ier, -iest) costing a lot; expensive: It would be too costly to repair the car. ○ a costly mistake/failure (ie one involving great loss).

costume /ˈkɒstjuːm; US -tuːm/ n 1 [C,U] (a) clothes worn by people from a particular place or during a particular historical period: dressed in the costume of a French nobleman/in Welsh national costume ○ People wore sixteenth-century costumes for the parade. (b) clothes worn by actors during a play: a clown costume ○ five costume changes ○ That jacket is part of the Professor's costume. Compare UNIFORM¹. 2 [C] = SWIMMING-COSTUME.
▶ **costumed** adj [usu attrib] wearing a costume.
■ **'costume jewellery** n [U] bright or expensive-looking jewellery made with cheap materials.

cosy (US **cozy**) /ˈkəʊzi/ adj (-ier, -iest) (approv) 1(a) comfortable and usu warm and secure because of being small or enclosed: *a cosy room/chair/feeling* ○ *I felt all cosy tucked up in bed.* (**b**) private and friendly: *a cosy chat by the fireside* ○ *cosy evenings in the pub.* **2** (*often derog*) a little too comfortable and convenient, and not always honest or right: *a cosy arrangement/deal/relationship* ○ *The danger is that things get too cosy.* ○ (*infml*) *He's had it too cosy in that job.* ▶ **cosily** *adv*: *sitting cosily in an armchair by the fire.* **cosiness** *n* [U].

cot

cot (*US* **crib**)　　　　**cradle**

cot /kɒt/ *n* **1** (*Brit*) (*US* **crib**) a bed for a young child, usu with sides to prevent the child falling out. ⇨ picture. **2** (*US*) a simple narrow bed, eg a camp-bed (CAMP¹).
■ **cot-death** (*Brit*) (*US* **crib-death**) *n* [C, U] the sudden death of a sleeping baby who had not been ill.

coterie /ˈkəʊtəri/ *n* [CGp] (*often derog*) a small group of people with shared activities, interests, tastes, etc, esp one that tends to be exclusive: *a literary coterie* ○ *a coterie of friends and advisers.*

cottage /ˈkɒtɪdʒ/ *n* a small simple house, esp in the country in Britain or in a holiday resort in the USA: *farm labourers' cottages* ○ *a charming little thatched cottage with roses round the door* ○ *a summer cottage.* ▶ **cottager** /ˈkɒtɪdʒə(r)/ *n* a person who lives in a cottage.
■ ˌ**cottage** ˈ**cheese** *n* [U] a soft white cheese with small lumps in, which is made from sour skimmed milk (SKIM).
ˌ**cottage** ˈ**hospital** *n* (*Brit*) a small hospital in a country area.
ˌ**cottage** ˈ**industry** *n* a business that is run at home, esp one involving skilled work such as weaving or knitting.
ˌ**cottage** ˈ**loaf** *n* (*Brit*) a round mass of bread with a smaller round piece on top.
ˌ**cottage** ˈ**pie** *n* [U, C] (*Brit*) = SHEPHERD'S PIE.

cotton¹ /ˈkɒtn/ *n* **1** [U] a plant with soft white hairs round its seeds which are used for making thread, cloth, etc: *working in the cotton fields.* **2** cloth made from the white hairs of the cotton plant: *a cotton dress* ○ *pure cotton.* **3** (*esp Brit*) thread that is used for sewing: *a needle and cotton.*
■ ˌ**cotton** ˈ**candy** *n* [U] (*US*) = CANDYFLOSS.
ˌ**cotton** ˈ**wool** *n* [U] (*esp Brit*) a soft mass of usu white material, used esp for cleaning the skin or a wound: *cotton wool balls* ○ (*fig*) *You shouldn't wrap your children in cotton wool* (ie protect them too much from the world).

cotton² /ˈkɒtn/ *v* **PHR V** **cotton on (to sth)** (*infml*) to begin to understand or realize sth without being told: *She's finally cottoned on to why he's promoting her faster than anyone else.* **cotton to sb** (*US infml*) to begin to like sb.

couch¹ /kaʊtʃ/ *n* **1** a long comfortable seat; a SOFA: *He slept on the couch.* **2** a long piece of furniture like a bed, esp in a doctor's examination room: *on the psychiatrist's couch.*
■ ˌ**couch po**ˈ**tato** *n* (*joc or derog*) a person who spends a lot of time at home watching television.

couch² /kaʊtʃ/ *v* ~ **sth (in sth)** (*fml*) to express a thought or an idea in a particular style or manner: [Vnadv] *a carefully couched reply* [Vnpr] *His letter was couched in conciliatory* **terms**.

cougar /ˈkuːɡə(r)/ *n* (*esp US*) = PUMA.

cough /kɒf; *US* kɔːf/ *v* **1** to push out air violently

and noisily through the throat, esp when one has a cold or a sore throat: [V] *He was coughing and sneezing/wheezing/spluttering.* ○ *have a* **coughing fit** [V, Vp] *She was coughing (away) all night.* **2** ~ **sth (up)** to force sth out of the throat or lungs by coughing: [Vn, Vnp] *He'd been coughing (up) blood.* **3** (of a machine) to make a sudden harsh noise: [V] *The engine coughed and spluttered into life.* **PHR V** **cough (sth) up** (*infml*) to say or produce sth unwillingly: *He owes us money, but he won't cough (it) up.*
▶ **cough** *n* **1** [C] an act or sound of coughing: *She gave a little/gentle/polite cough to attract my attention.* **2** [sing] an illness, infection, etc that causes a person to cough often: *My cough's nearly better now.* ○ *He developed a dry irritating cough.* ○ ˈ**cough medicine/mixture** (ie taken to relieve a cough). See also WHOOPING COUGH.

could¹ /kəd; *strong form* kʊd/ *modal v* (*neg* **could not**; *contracted form* **couldn't** /ˈkʊdnt/) **1** (used in asking permission): *Could I use your phone, please?* ○ *Could I borrow your bicycle?* ○ *Could we come round next week?* ⇨ note at MAY¹. **2** (used in making polite requests): *Could you babysit for us on Friday?* ○ *Could you just type one more letter before you go?* ○ *Do you think I could have a glass of water?* Compare WOULD. **3** (used to indicate possibility): *You could be right, I suppose.* ○ *My wife's in labour — the baby could arrive at any time.* ○ *Don't worry — they could have just forgotten to phone.* ○ *You couldn't have left it on the bus, could you?* ○ *'Have some more chocolate mousse.' 'Oh, I couldn't, thank you* (ie I'm too full).' ⇨ note at MIGHT¹. **4** (used in making suggestions): *We could write a letter to the director.* ○ *You could always try his home number.* **5** (used to indicate annoyance): *They could have let me know they were going to be late!* **6** (*infml*) (used to emphasize how strongly one wants to express one's feelings): *I'm so fed up I could scream!*

could² *pt* of CAN². ⇨ note at CAN².

council /ˈkaʊnsl/ *n* [CGp] **1** a group of people elected to manage affairs in a city or county: *work for/on the council* ○ *She's a member of the town council.* ○ *Essex County Council* ○ *a Labour-controlled council* ○ *council workers/services/elections* ○ *The local council is/are in charge of repairing roads.* ○ (*Brit*) *a council flat/house* (ie one built by a local council and rented to the people who live in it). **2** a group of people appointed or elected to give advice, make rules, manage affairs, etc: *a council of elders* ○ *the Food Research Council* ○ *In Britain, the Arts Council gives grants to theatres.* See also PRIVY COUNCIL.
■ ˈ**council-chamber** *n* a large room in which a council meets.
ˈ**council estate** *n* (*Brit*) an area of houses built by a local council(1): *a run-down council estate.*
ˌ**council of** ˈ**war** *n* (*pl* **councils of war**) a meeting to discuss how to deal with an urgent and difficult situation: *Senior managers had/held a council of war.*
ˈ**council tax** *n* [C, U] (in Britain) a tax charged by local authorities, based on the value of a person's house, etc.

councillor (*US* also **councilor**) /ˈkaʊnsələ(r)/ *n* a member of a COUNCIL(1): *Councillor Jones* ○ *an independent councillor.*

counsel¹ /ˈkaʊnsl/ *n* **1** [U] (*fml*) advice, esp that given by older people or experts: *wise counsel* ○ *Listen to the counsel of your elders.* **2** [C] (*pl* unchanged) ~ (**for sb**) (*law*) a BARRISTER or group of lawyers conducting a law case: *instruct the counsel for the defence/prosecution* ○ *defence counsel* ○ *The court then heard counsel for the dead woman's father.* See also KING'S/QUEEN'S COUNSEL (KING). **IDM** **keep one's own** ˈ**counsel** (*fml*) to keep one's opinions, plans, etc secret. **take counsel with sb/together** (*fml*) to meet in order to discuss a problem or ask advice.

counsel² /'kaʊnsl/ v (**-ll-**; *US* also **-l-**) **1** to give professional advice to sb who has a problem: [Vn] *a psychiatrist who counsels alcoholics*. **2** (*fml*) (**a**) to give the specified advice: [Vn] *I would counsel caution in such a case.* (**b**) (*fml*) to recommend a particular course of action: [Vn.*to* inf] *He counselled them to give up the plan.* ○ (*fig*) *She longed to go but the voice of reason counselled her to stay.*

▶ **counselling** /-səlɪŋ/ n [U] professional advice about a problem: *offer psychiatric/financial counselling* ○ *a student counselling service.*

counsellor (*US* also **counselor**) /'kaʊnsələ(r)/ n **1** an adviser, esp one who has professional training: *his economic counsellor* ○ *a marriage guidance counsellor.* **2** (*US or Irish*) a lawyer.

count¹ /kaʊnt/ v **1** ~ (**from sth**) (**to sth**) to say or name numbers in order: [V] *Billy can't count yet.* [Vpr] *She can count from 1 to 20 in French.* ○ *I can count (up) to 100.* **2** ~ **sth** (**up**) to calculate the total of sth: [Vn] *Don't forget to count your change.* ○ *I counted 47 boats moored near to the bridge.* [Vnp] *Have the votes been counted up yet?* [V.*wh*] *Count how many glasses we have, will you?* **3** to include sb/sth when one calculates a total: [Vn] *fifty people,* **not counting** *the children* ○ *The list was long, because he counted every project costing over ECU 1 million.* **4(a)** ~ (**for sth**) to be of value or importance: [V] *First impressions of people do count.* ○ *We have only a few bullets left, so make each one count* (ie use it effectively). [Vpr] *Knowledge without common sense counts for little.* (**b**) ~ (**as sth**) to be acceptable or valid: [V] *You didn't shut your eyes before you made the wish, so it doesn't count!* [V-n] *This must surely count as one of the team's finest victories.* **5** ~ **sb/ oneself/sth** (**as**) **sb/sth** to consider sb/sth to have a particular characteristic or to be of a particular type or quality: [Vn-adj] *I count myself lucky to have a job.* [Vn-n] *We count her as one of our oldest friends.* **IDM** **count one's 'blessings** to be grateful for the good things one has: *Don't complain! Count your blessings!* **count one's 'chickens (before they are 'hatched)** to be too confident that sth will be successful. **count sheep** to imagine sheep jumping over a fence and count(2) them, in order to help oneself go to sleep. **count the cost (of sth)** to suffer the consequences of a careless or foolish action: *The town is now counting the cost of its failure to provide adequate flood protection.* **stand up and be 'counted** to say publicly that one agrees with sth, supports sb, etc: *The campaign needs all the support it can get on this, so now is the time to stand up and be counted!* **PHRV** ,**count a'gainst sb**; ,**count sth a'gainst sb** to be considered/to consider sth to be to the disadvantage of sb: *Your criminal record could count against you in finding a job.* ○ *He is young and inexperienced, but please don't count that against him.*

'**count sb/sth among sb/sth** to regard sb/sth as one of the specified group: *I no longer count him among my friends.*

,**count 'down** to signal the approach of a specific day or moment: *They've been counting down to the royal wedding.* See also COUNTDOWN.

,**count sb/sth 'in** to include sb/sth: *If you're all going to the party, you can count me in too* (ie I will come with you).

'**count on sb/sth** to rely on sb/sth with confidence: *I'm counting on you to talk to Aunt Emma.* ○ *Don't count on a salary increase this year* (ie You may not get one). ○ *'I'm sure Jack will help me.' 'I wouldn't count on it* (ie He may not).'

,**count sb/sth 'out 1** to count(2) things one by one, esp slowly: *The old lady counted out thirty cents and*

gave it to the beggar. **2** (of a REFEREE in boxing) to count(1) up to ten over a boxer who has been knocked down. The boxer has then lost the fight: *The referee counted him out in the first round.* **3** (*infml*) to exclude sb from an activity or arrangement: *If there are going to be drugs at the party, you can count me out.*

,**count to'wards sth** to be included in or relevant to sth not yet obtained or decided: *These marks will count towards your final grade.*

▶ ,**countable 'noun** n = COUNT NOUN.

count² /kaʊnt/ n **1** [C] an act of counting (COUNT¹ 1,2): *a second count of the votes* ○ *The company had a total of 650 shareholders,* **at the last count.** ○ *Start on a count of 5* (ie after I have counted up to 5). ○ *By my count that's five cakes you've had already.* ○ *The teacher did a quick count of the pupils present.* See also HEADCOUNT. **2** [C usu *sing*] the total number of things reached by counting (COUNT¹ 2): *Do you accept the official government count of the unemployed?* ○ *The body count is 62* (ie 62 people have died). ○ *A creamy sauce will boost the calorie count.* See also BLOOD COUNT, POLLEN COUNT. **3** (usu **the count**) [sing] (in boxing) an act of counting up to ten seconds by the REFEREE when a boxer has been knocked down: *He survived a count of eight and went on to win the fight.* **4** [C] (*law*) any of a group of offences of which a person is accused: *charged with two counts of forgery and one of fraud* ○ *She was found guilty on all counts.* **5** [C usu *pl*] any of a set of points made in a discussion or an argument: *I disagree with you on both counts.* **IDM** **keep (a) count (of sth)** to remember or record a series of numbers or amounts over a period of time: *I find it hard to keep count of the score.* ○ *It helps to keep a count of what you drink.* **lose count** ⇨ LOSE. **out for the count 1** (in boxing) unable to get up again within ten seconds of being knocked down. **2** defeated or tired out.

■ '**count noun** (also '**countable noun**) n (*grammar*) a noun that can be used in the PLURAL and with such words as *many* and *few: This dictionary uses the code [C] for count nouns.*

count³ /kaʊnt/ n (the title of) a nobleman in certain countries, eg France and Italy, equal in rank to a British EARL: *Count Almaviva* ○ *His father is a count, I believe.* See also COUNTESS.

countdown /'kaʊntdaʊn/ n ~ (**to sth**) **1** [C] the act of counting seconds backwards to zero, eg before launching a spacecraft: *The countdown was stopped with only 7 minutes to go.* **2** [sing] the period immediately before sth important happens: *the countdown to the local election.*

countenance /'kaʊntənəns/ n (*fml*) **1** [C] the expression on a person's face: *his troubled/impassive/ warlike countenance.* **2** [U] support; approval: *I would not give/lend countenance to such a plan.*

▶ **countenance** v (*fml*) to support or approve sth: [Vn] *Such behaviour will not be countenanced.* [V.*ing*] *They refused to countenance supplying inferior equipment.* [V.n *ing*] *He wouldn't countenance our staying out after 11 pm.*

counter¹ /'kaʊntə(r)/ n **1** a long flat surface over which goods are sold or business is done in a shop, bank, etc: *chocolate displayed on the counter* ○ *the ticket reservation counter.* **IDM** **over the 'counter 1** (of medicines) that can be bought without a PRE-SCRIPTION(1a): *These tablets are available over the counter.* **2** without a special licence or arrangement: *buying guns over the counter.* **under the 'counter** (of goods bought or sold) secretly and sometimes illegally: *Pornography is no longer sold under the counter in many countries.*

counter² /'kaʊntə(r)/ n **1** a small disc used for playing or scoring in certain board games. **2** (esp in compounds) an electronic device for counting sth: *an engine's rev counter* ○ *You need to reset the counter.* See also BARGAINING COUNTER.

counter³ /ˈkaʊntə(r)/ *adv* ~ **to sth** in the opposite direction to sth; in opposition to sth: *act counter to one's wishes* ○ *Economic trends are **running counter** to the forecasts.*

counter⁴ /ˈkaʊntə(r)/ *v* ~ **(with sth)**; ~ **sb/sth (with sth)** to respond to sb/sth with an opposing view, an attack, etc: [Vpr] *Linda countered with a joke of her own.* [V.speech] *'A Scotsman might not agree with that,' she countered.* [Vn] *Such arguments are easily countered.* [Vnpr] *The senator countered his critics with a strong speech defending his policies.* [V.*that*] *I pointed out the shortcomings of the scheme, but he countered that the plans were not yet finished.*
▶ **counter** *n* ~ **(to sb/sth)** (*fml*) a response to sb/sth that opposes or challenges their ideas, position, situation, etc: *The employers' association was seen as a counter to union power.*

counter- *comb form* (forming *ns, vs, adjs* and *advs*) **1** opposite in direction or effect: *counter-productive* ○ *counterbalanced.* **2** made in response to, or so as to defeat sb/sth: *counter-attack* ○ *counter-argument* ○ *counter-demonstration.* **3** corresponding: *counterpart.*

counteract /ˌkaʊntərˈækt/ *v* to act against and reduce the force or effect of sth: [Vn] *counteract (the effects of) a poison* ○ *counteracting sb's influence* ○ *This trend towards extremism in the party must be counteracted.*

counter-attack /ˈkaʊntər ətæk/ *n* **(a)** a response to an argument or accusation: *For the sake of party morale, it was clearly necessary to launch some sort of counter-attack.* **(b)** an attack made in response to an enemy's attack: *the Russian counter-attack.*
▶ **counter-attack** *v* to make a counter-attack on sb/sth: [V] *Government forces counter-attacked.* [also Vn].

counterbalance /ˈkaʊntəbæləns/ *n* a weight or force that balances another by having the opposite effect: *a vital counterbalance to the powers of the police.*
▶ **counterbalance** /ˌkaʊntəˈbæləns/ *v* to act as a counterbalance to sb/sth: [Vn] *The 4% fall in the pound is counterbalanced by the 1% rise in bank base rates.*

counterblast /ˈkaʊntəblɑːst; US -blæst/ *n* ~ **(to sth)** a powerful reply: *Her article was a counterblast to her critics.*

counter-claim /ˈkaʊntə kleɪm/ *n* a claim made in opposition to another claim: *Amongst all the claims and counter-claims it was hard to say who was telling the truth.*

counter-clockwise /ˌkaʊntə ˈklɒkwaɪz/ *adv* (*US*) = ANTICLOCKWISE.

counter-espionage /ˌkaʊntər ˈespiənɑːʒ/ *n* [U] secret action taken against the activities of an enemy's spies (SPY).

counterfeit /ˈkaʊntəfɪt/ *adj* (esp of money) deliberately made so as to be exactly like sth, in order to deceive; not genuine: *counterfeit coins/banknotes* ○ *This ten-dollar bill is counterfeit.* Compare FORGERY.
▶ **counterfeit** *v* to copy coins, writing, etc in order to deceive: [Vn] *a gang of criminals counterfeiting £10 notes.* Compare FORGE² 2.
counterfeiter *n* a person who counterfeits money, etc. Compare FORGER.

counterfoil /ˈkaʊntəfɔɪl/ *n* (*Brit*) the part of a cheque, ticket, etc which can be detached and kept as a record; a STUB(2).

counter-insurgency /ˌkaʊntər ɪnˈsɜːdʒənsi/ *n* [U] action taken against a group of people trying to take control of a country by force: *counter-insurgency units.*

counter-intelligence /ˌkaʊntər ɪnˈtelɪdʒəns/ *n*

[U] measures intended to prevent an enemy country from finding out one's secrets, eg by giving them false information: *the counter-intelligence service.*

countermand /ˌkaʊntəˈmɑːnd; US ˈkaʊntərmænd/ *v* (*fml*) to cancel an order that has already been given, esp by giving a new and opposite one: [Vn] *The instruction was immediately countermanded.*

countermeasure /ˈkaʊntəmeʒə(r)/ *n* (often *pl*) a course of action to remove, prevent, or protect against sth undesirable or dangerous: *devise/ implement countermeasures against the threatened strike.*

counterpane /ˈkaʊntəpeɪn/ *n* (*dated*) = BEDSPREAD.

counterpart /ˈkaʊntəpɑːt/ *n* a person or thing that corresponds to or has the same function as sb/sth else: *a traditional gypsy caravan and its modern counterpart* ○ *the Syrian Foreign Minister and his Egyptian counterpart* ○ *The sales director phoned her counterpart in the other firm* (ie the other firm's sales director).

counterpoint /ˈkaʊntəpɔɪnt/ *n* (*music*) **1** [U] the art or practice of combining two or more tunes to be played together according to fixed rules: *The melodies are played in counterpoint.* **2** [C] ~ **(to sth)** a tune played in combination with another one: *the solo violin counterpoint to the main tune.*

counter-productive /ˌkaʊntə prəˈdʌktɪv/ *adj* [usu pred] having the opposite effect to that intended: *Increases in taxation would be counter-productive.*

counter-revolution /ˌkaʊntə ˌrevəˈluːʃn/ *n* [C,U] violent opposition to or action against a government established as a result of a revolution, in order to destroy and replace it: *stage a counter-revolution* ○ *the forces of counter-revolution.*
▶ **counter-revolutionary** /-ˈluːʃənəri; US -neri/ *n, adj* (a person) involved in a counter-revolution: *a counter-revolutionary rebellion* ○ *denounced as counter-revolutionaries.*

countersign /ˈkaʊntəsaɪn/ *v* to sign a document already signed by another person, esp in order to confirm that it is valid: [Vn] *All cheques must be countersigned by one of the directors.*

counter-tenor /ˌkaʊntə ˈtenə(r)/ *n* (*music*) **(a)** a man's singing voice higher than TENOR²(a). **(b)** a man with such a voice; a male ALTO(1b). **(c)** a musical part written for a singer with such a voice.

countervailing /ˈkaʊntəveɪlɪŋ/ *adj* [attrib] (*fml*) acting as a COUNTERBALANCE to sth: *all the disadvantages without any of the countervailing advantages.*

countess /ˈkaʊntɪs, -es/ *n* **1** (the title of) a woman who has the rank of a COUNT³ or an EARL. **2** the wife or widow of a COUNT³ or an EARL.

countless /ˈkaʊntləs/ *adj* [esp attrib] very many; too many to be counted or mentioned: *I've told her countless times.*

countrified /ˈkʌntrɪfaɪd/ *adj* (*often derog*) like or made like the countryside or the people who live there, in appearance, behaviour, etc: *quite a countrified part of the city.*

country /ˈkʌntri/ *n* **1(a)** [C] an area of land that forms a politically independent unit; a nation; a state: *European countries* ○ *leading industrial countries* ○ *There will be rain over all parts of the country.* **(b) the country** [sing] the people of a country(1a); the nation as a whole: *The whole country is on holiday.* ⇨ note. **2 the country** [sing] any area outside large towns and cities, typically with villages, fields, woods, etc: *live in the country* ○ *spend a pleasant day in the country* ○ *country cottages/ roads/life.* See also COUNTRYSIDE. **3** [U] (often with a preceding *adj*) an area of land, esp with regard to its physical features: *rough/marshy country* ○ *We passed through miles of wooded country.* **IDM across country** directly across fields, etc or not by a main

C

road: *walking/riding across country*. See also CROSS-COUNTRY. **go to the ˈcountry** (*Brit*) (of a government) to decide to hold an election to choose a new parliament: *He went to the country over the issue and lost the general election.*

■ ˌcountry-and-ˈwestern *n* [U] *abbr* **C and W** (also ˈcountry music) a type of music that originates from the traditional music of the southern and western USA: *a country-and-western singer.*

ˈcountry club *n* a club in the country(2) which has sports and social facilities.

ˌcountry ˈdance *n* (*esp Brit*) a traditional type of dance, esp one in which couples in groups face each other in two long lines.

ˌcountry ˈhouse *n* a large house in the country(2) surrounded by woods, fields, etc, usu owned either by a rich person or by an organization formed to preserve such places.

ˌcountry ˈseat *n* = SEAT¹ 5.

ˌcountry-ˈwide *adj, adv* over the whole of a country(1a): *a country-wide mail-order service* ○ *The film will be released in London in March and country-wide in May.*

NOTE Country is the most usual and neutral word for an independent geographical area with its own government: *We passed through four countries on our way to Greece.*
The word **state** emphasizes the political organization of the area under an independent government, and it can refer to the government itself: *the member states of the EU* ○ *a one-party state* ○ *The State provides free education and health care.* **Nation** refers to a political unit and is more formal than **state**: *the United Nations* ○ *How many countries are there in the Association of South East Asian Nations?*
A **state** may also be a part of a larger country but have some level of control over its own affairs: *There are 13 states in Malaysia.*
Nation and **country** can also mean 'all the people in a country': *The President will address the nation on television this evening.* ○ *The whole country was outraged by the bombing.* In addition, **nation** can suggest a community of people who share a culture and language: *the Zulu nation.*
Land is used especially in literature to mean 'country': *He left the land of his birth twenty years ago.* ○ *the most magnificent castle in all the land.*

countryman /ˈkʌntrimən/ *n* (*pl* **-men** /-mən/; *fem* **countrywoman** /-wʊmən/, *pl* **-women** /-wɪmɪn/) **1** a person living in or born in the same country(1a) as sb else: *He is partnered by Peter Blake, a fellow countryman of his.* **2** a person living in or born in the country(2).

countryside /ˈkʌntrisaɪd/ *n* (usu **the countryside** [U]) fields, woods, etc outside towns and cities: *the surrounding countryside* ○ *narrow roads meandering through open countryside* ○ *the preservation of the countryside.* See also COUNTRY 2.

county /ˈkaʊnti/ *n* **1** an administrative division of Britain, the largest unit of local government: *the county of Kent* ○ *a county boundary* ○ *county cricket.* Compare PROVINCE 1, STATE¹ 3. **2** (in the USA and other countries) the largest administrative division of a state.
▶ **county** *adj* (*Brit infml usu derog*) having a high social status and a way of life thought to be typical of English upper class people.
■ ˌcounty ˈclerk *n* (*US*) an elected county official who keeps records of property ownership, etc.
ˌcounty ˈcouncil *n* a group of people elected to govern a county: *a member of Lancashire County Council.* ˌcounty ˈcouncillor *n.*
ˌcounty ˈcourt *n* **1** (in Britain) a local lawcourt where civil(4) cases are dealt with. **2** (in the USA)

an administrative body in counties in certain states. Compare CROWN COURT.
ˌcounty ˈtown *n* (*Brit*) (*US* ˌcounty ˈseat) the main town of a county, the centre of its administration.

coup /kuː/ *n* (*pl* **coups** /kuːz/) **1** a sudden, illegal and often violent, change of government: *put down/foil a coup attempt* ○ *The army mounted/staged a coup (d'état).* ○ *The Prime Minister was overthrown in a military coup.* **2** a surprising and successful action: *an attempted boardroom coup* ○ *This contract represents a brilliant marketing coup for IBM.*
■ **coup de grâce** /ˌkuː də ˈgrɑːs; *US* ˈgræs/ *n* (*pl* **coups de grâce** /ˌkuː ˈgrɑːs/) (*French*) a blow that kills a person or an animal, esp to end their suffering when they are badly injured: (*fig*) *Poor exam results dealt the coup de grâce to* (ie ended) *his university career.*
coup d'état /ˌkuː deɪˈtɑː/ *n* (*pl* **coups d'état** /ˌkuː deɪˈtɑː/) = COUP 1.

coupé /ˈkuːpeɪ; *US* kuːˈpeɪ/ (*US* also **coupe** /kuːp/) *n* a car with two doors and a sloping back.

couple¹ /ˈkʌpl/ *n* **1** two people who are seen together or are associated, esp a man and woman together: *married couples* ○ *a young/an elderly couple* ○ *Several couples were on the dance floor.* **2** [sing] (**a**) ~ (**of sth**) two people or things: *I saw a couple of men get out.* ○ *I'll have a couple of dozen eggs.* ○ *Could I ask just a couple more questions?* (**b**) a small number of people or things, a few: *a couple of minutes/hours/days/weeks/months/years* ○ *She jogs a couple of miles every morning.* **IDM in two/a couple of shakes** ⇨ SHAKE².

couple² /ˈkʌpl/ *v* **1** ~ sb/sth **with** sb/sth to link or associate sb/sth with sb/sth: [Vnpr] *The name of Mozart is forever coupled with the city of Salzburg.* ○ *The bad light, coupled with* (ie together with) *the wet ground, made play very difficult.* **2** ~ **A on** (**to B**); ~ **A and B** (**together**) to fasten or link together two things, pieces of equipment, etc: [Vnp] *two computers coupled together* [Vn, Vnp, Vnpr] *The dining-car was being coupled (on) (to the last coach).* **3** [V] (*rhet or euph*) (of two people or animals) to have sex.
▶ **coupling** /ˈkʌplɪŋ/ *n* **1** [U, C] the action of joining or linking two things or an instance of this: *an unusual coupling of Mozart and Grieg concertos on a cassette.* **2** [C] a link connecting two parts of sth or two pieces of equipment.

couplet /ˈkʌplət/ *n* two lines of verse of equal length one after the other: *rhyming couplets.*

coupon /ˈkuːpɒn/ *n* **1** a small piece of paper that gives the holder the right to do or receive sth, eg goods, in exchange: *food coupons* ○ *money-off coupons* ○ *This coupon entitles you to 50p off your next purchase.* **2** a printed form, often cut out from a newspaper, that is used to enter a competition, to order goods, etc: *an entry coupon* ○ *Fill in/Complete and return the attached coupon.*

courage /ˈkʌrɪdʒ/ *n* [U] (*approv*) the ability to control fear when facing danger, pain, opposition, etc; bravery (BRAVE): *He showed great courage and determination in battle.* ○ *I want to ask for more money but I haven't yet plucked up/summoned (up) enough courage to do it.* ○ *moral courage* ○ *She didn't have the courage to refuse.* See also DUTCH COURAGE. **IDM have/lack the courage of one's conˈvictions** to be/not to be brave enough to say or do what one feels to be right. **screw up one's courage** ⇨ SCREW. **take courage (from sth)** to begin to feel happier and more confident because of sth. **take one's ˌcourage in both ˈhands** to make oneself do sth that one is afraid of.
▶ **courageous** /kəˈreɪdʒəs/ *adj* without fear; brave: *a courageous action/decision* ○ *These women are resourceful and courageous.* **courageously** *adv*: *He has spoken out courageously on several occasions.*

courgette /kʊəˈʒet; *Brit* also kɔːˈʒet/ *n* (*Brit*) (*US*

zucchini) a small green MARROW² eaten as a vegetable, usu cooked. ⇨ picture at MARROW².

courier /'kʊriə(r)/ n **1** a person employed to guide and assist a group of tourists. **2** a messenger who transports parcels or important papers: *We sent the documents by courier.*

course¹ /kɔːs/ n **1** [C usu *sing*] a direction or route followed by a ship or an aircraft, or by a river, boundary line, etc: *The plane was on/off course* (ie going/not going in the intended direction). ○ *The ship's course was due north.* ○ *The captain set a course for* (ie directed the ship/plane towards) *New York.* ○ *trace the course of the Charles River.* **2** [C usu *sing*] **(a)** a direction in which sth is progressing: *His arguments suddenly changed course and he began to attack the government.* ○ *The company is on course to achieve its projected turnover for the year.* See also COLLISION COURSE. **(b)** (also **course of action**) [C] a way of acting or proceeding: *What course of action would you recommend?* ○ *There are various courses open to us.* ○ *The wisest course would be to ignore it.* **3** [sing] ~ **of sth** continuous forward movement through time: *In the course of* (ie during) *my long life I've seen many changes.* ○ *the course of history* ○ *I didn't sleep once during the entire course of the journey.* **4** [C] ~ (**in/on sth**) (*education*) a series of lessons, lectures, etc: *a 'French/a 'chemistry/an 'art course* ○ *take/do a two-year postgraduate course in accountancy* ○ *go on an intensive 'training course* ○ *The college runs/offers specialist 'language courses.* See also CORRESPONDENCE COURSE, FOUNDATION COURSE, REFRESHER COURSE, SANDWICH COURSE. **5** [C] ~ (**of sth**) (*medical*) a series of treatments, pills, etc: *prescribe a course of antibiotics/injections/X-ray treatment.* **6** [C] any of the separate parts of a meal, eg soup, DESSERT: *a five-course dinner* ○ *The main course was a vegetable stew.* **7** [C] **(a)** an area of land for playing golf: *He set a new course record.* ⇨ picture at GOLF. **(b)** a stretch of land or water for races: *a five-mile 'rowing course.* See also ASSAULT COURSE, RACECOURSE. **8** [C] a continuous layer of brick, stone, etc in a wall: *damp-proof course.* **IDM** **be par for the course** ⇨ PAR¹. **in course of sth** (*fml*) experiencing the specified process: *a house in course of construction* (ie being built). **in the course of 'time** when enough time has passed; eventually: *Be patient: I'm sure you will be promoted in the course of time.* **in due course** ⇨ DUE¹. **in the ordinary, normal, etc course of events, things, etc** as things usually happen; normally: *In the ordinary course of events, I visit her once a week.* **a matter of course** ⇨ MATTER¹. **a middle course** ⇨ MIDDLE. **of course** (used as well as or instead of 'yes' or 'no' to emphasize one's answer: *'Do you like my mother?' 'Of course I do.'* ○ *'Did she go back to him?' 'No, of course not!'* **2** (used as a polite way of saying 'yes' to a request or of agreeing with sb): *'May I try one of your cakes?' 'Of course — help yourself.'* ○ *'He will be remembered as a great President.' 'Of course, but not with affection.'* **3** (used to indicate that what one is saying is generally understood or accepted): *That was 40 years ago, but of course you wouldn't remember it.* **run/take its 'course** to develop in the usual way; to proceed to the usual end: *We can't cure the disease; it must run its course.* ○ *The decision cannot be reversed; the law must take its course* (ie the punishment must be carried out). **stay the course** ⇨ STAY¹.
■ **,course of 'action** n (*pl* **,courses of 'action**) = COURSE¹ 2b.
'course-work n [U] essays, projects, etc completed by a student during a course¹(4): *Course-work accounts for 40% of the total marks.*

course² /kɔːs/ v (*esp rhet*) (esp of liquids) to move or flow freely: [Vpr] *Tears coursed down her cheeks.* [also Vp].

court¹ /kɔːt/ n **1(a)** [C] a place where trials or other law cases are held; a lawcourt: *the civil courts* ○ *a 'magistrate's court* ○ *initiate court proceedings* ○ *attend a court hearing* ○ *She had to appear in court to give evidence.* ○ *This case will never get/go to court.* ○ *The case was settled out of court* (ie was settled without the need for it to be heard in court). ○ *an out-of-court settlement.* **(b)** **the court** [sing] the people present in a lawcourt, esp those directly involved in a trial: *The court rose* (ie stood up) *as the judge entered.* ○ *the court's ruling/decision* ○ *Please tell the court all you know.* See also CONTEMPT OF COURT, COUNTY COURT, CROWN COURT, HIGH COURT, KANGAROO COURT, SUPREME COURT. **2** (often **Court**) **(a)** [C] the official residence of a king or queen: *attend a ceremony at court.* **(b)** **the court** [sing] the king or queen and all his or her advisers, officials, family, etc: *The court moves to the country in the summer.* See also COURTIER. **3** [C] (*sport*) a space marked out for tennis or similar games, either indoors or outdoors: *a 'tennis/'squash court* ○ *They've been on court now for 3 hours.* ⇨ picture at TENNIS. **4** [C] (*Brit*) (*abbr* Ct) (used in the names of short enclosed streets or of blocks of flats): *She lives at 23, Waverley Court.* **5** [C] = COURTYARD. **IDM** **the ball is in one's/sb's court** ⇨ BALL¹. **hold 'court** to entertain and receive attention from people who admire one: *There's a movie star holding court in the hotel lobby.* **laugh sb/sth out of court** ⇨ LAUGH. **out of 'court** not appropriate, suitable or worthy of consideration: *The sheer cost of the scheme puts it right out of court.* ○ *His remark was ruled out of court.* **pay court to sb** ⇨ PAY². **take sb to 'court** to make a charge against sb, to be settled in court: *He was taken to court over an alleged breach of contract.*
■ **'court-card** (*Brit*) (*US* **face-card**) n a card¹(4) that has on it a picture of a king, queen or JACK.
'court-house n **(a)** a building containing courts of law. **(b)** (*US*) the administrative offices of a county.
,court of ap'peal n (*pl* **courts of appeal**) (also **appeal court**) n a court to which one can appeal(4b) against a judgement one disagrees with.
,court of in'quiry n (*pl* **courts of inquiry**) (*law*) a special court that investigates a particular matter.
,court of 'law n (*pl* **courts of law**) = LAWCOURT.
,court 'order n a legal order made by a judge in court, telling sb to do or not do sth.
'court shoe n a light formal type of shoe with a high narrow heel, worn by women.

court² /kɔːt/ v **1** (*dated*) **(a)** (of a man) to try to win the affections of a woman, esp with the idea of marrying her: [Vn] *He had been courting Jane for six months.* **(b)** (of a man and woman) to spend time together, esp with the idea of marrying: [V] *a courting couple* ○ *The two have been courting for a year.* See also COURTSHIP 1a. **2(a)** to try to gain the favour of a rich or influential person: [Vn] *He has been assiduously/blatantly courting the director in the hope of getting the leading part in the play.* [Vnn] *He is being courted as a possible buyer for the company.* **(b)** (*fml often derog*) to try to win or obtain sth: [Vn] *court sb's approval/support.* **3** (usu not passive) to do sth that might lead to sth unpleasant; to take a risk: [Vn] *Once again he has courted controversy/disapproval.* ○ *To go on such an expedition with inadequate supplies would be to court disaster.*

courteous /'kɜːtiəs/ adj having or showing good manners; polite: *unfailingly courteous* ○ *I was courteous, but did not encourage conversation.* See also COURTESY. ► **courteously** adv: *He courteously stood aside to let us pass.*

courtesan /,kɔːtɪ'zæn; US 'kɔːtɪzn/ n (formerly) a prostitute with wealthy or noble clients.

courtesy /'kɜːtəsi/ n **1** [U] polite behaviour; good manners: *We were treated with great/the utmost courtesy.* ○ *They didn't even have the courtesy to*

C

apologize. ○ *As a matter of courtesy you should tell her you won't be able to attend the meeting.* ○ *It would only have been* **common courtesy** *to say thank you.* ○ **Do me the courtesy** *of listening* (ie Please listen) *to what I have to say.* ○ *We were just paying a courtesy call/visit.* **2** [C] (*fml*) a polite remark or act: *exchange courtesies.* **IDM (by) courtesy of sb** by the permission, kindness or favour of sb: *These photographs have been reproduced by courtesy of the British Museum.*

▶ **courtesy** *adj* [attrib] (esp of vehicles) provided free, eg by a hotel, to transport guests to or from an airport, a station, etc: *a courtesy car/coach/minibus.*

■ **'courtesy light** *n* a small light inside a car which is automatically switched on when sb opens the door.

courtier /ˈkɔːtɪə(r)/ *n* (formerly) a companion or adviser of a king or queen at court.

courtly /ˈkɔːtli/ *adj* (*fml*) polite and refined; showing dignity: *the old gentleman's courtly manners.*

court martial /ˌkɔːt ˈmɑːʃl/ *n* (*pl* **courts martial**) trial by a special court for dealing with offences against military law: *Four officers were yesterday sentenced at a court martial.* ○ *All now face court martial.*

▶ **court-martial** *v* (**-ll-**; *US* **-l-**) ~ **sb** (**for sth**) (often passive) to hold a trial of sb in a court martial: [Vn, Vnpr] *be court-martialled (for neglect of duty).*

courtroom /ˈkɔːtruːm, -rʊm/ *n* a room in which trials or other legal cases are held: *the crowded courtroom* ○ *a courtroom drama.*

courtship /ˈkɔːt ʃɪp/ *n* [U,C] **1(a)** the process of developing a close relationship with a person of the opposite sex, esp with the idea of marrying: *They married after a brief courtship.* **(b)** special behaviour by animals and birds to attract a MATE[1](4a): *the courtship rituals of the peacock.* **2** ~ **of sb** the process of gaining a person's favour or support: *the courtship of political minorities.*

courtyard /ˈkɔːtjɑːd/ (also **court**) *n* a space without a roof but enclosed by walls, esp forming part of a castle, large house, hotel, etc.

cousin /ˈkʌzn/ *n* **1(a)** (also **first cousin**) a child of one's uncle or aunt: *She is my cousin.* ○ *We are cousins* (ie children of each other's aunts/uncles). **(b)** a person of one's own age or generation to whom one is not closely related: *She's a distant cousin of mine, I believe.* See also SECOND COUSIN. ⇨ App 4. **2** (usu *pl*) a person, usu in a different country, with whom one has ideas, customs, etc in common: *our American cousins.*

couture /kuˈtjʊə(r); *US* -ˈtʊər/ *n* [U] **(a)** (also **haute couture**) the design and manufacture of fashionable clothes: *Chanel's couture house* ○ *the way forward for couture in the nineties.* **(b)** such clothes: *the wives of pop stars buying couture* ○ *couture accessories.*

▶ **couturier** /kuˈtjʊərieɪ; *US* -ˈtʊər-/ *n* a person who designs or makes fashionable clothes, esp for women.

cove[1] /kəʊv/ *n* a small BAY[2]: *lazing on the sand in a quiet cove.* ⇨ picture at COAST[1].

cove[2] /kəʊv/ *n* (*dated Brit sl*) a man.

coven /ˈkʌvn/ *n* a meeting or group of witches (WITCH).

covenant /ˈkʌvənənt/ *n* **1** a formal promise to pay money regularly to a charity, trust[1](3a), etc. See also DEED OF COVENANT. **2** (*law*) a formal legal agreement or contract.

▶ **covenanted** *adj* [attrib] promised through a covenant: *covenanted donations.*

Coventry /ˈkɒvəntri, ˈkʌv-/ *n* **IDM send sb to Coventry** ⇨ SEND.

cover[1] /ˈkʌvə(r)/ *v* **1** ~ **sth** (**up/over**) (**with sth**) to place sth over or in front of sth in order to hide or protect it: [Vnpr] *Cover the chicken loosely with foil.* ○

She covered her face with her hands. ○ *He covered the cushion with new material.* [Vn, Vnp, Vnpr] *He covered (up) the body (with a sheet).* [Vnpr, Vnp] *She covered her knees (up) with a blanket.* [Vn, Vnp] *The hole was quickly covered (over).* [Vn] (*fig*) *He laughed to cover* (ie hide) *his nervousness.* **2** to lie or extend over the surface of sth: [Vn] *Snow covered the ground.* ○ *Flood water covered the fields near the river.* ○ *Much of the country is covered by forest.* **3** ~ **sb/sth in/with sth** to put or scatter a layer of liquid, dust, etc on sb/sth: [Vnpr] *The players were soon covered in/with mud.* ○ *The wind blew in from the desert and covered everything with sand.* **4** to include sth; to deal with or apply to sth: [Vn] *Her lectures covered the subject thoroughly.* ○ *The survey covers all aspects of the business.* ○ *a report covering the years 1984 to 1994* ○ *the salesman covering the northern part of the country* (ie selling to people in that region) ○ *Do the rules cover* (ie Can they be made to apply to) *a case like this?* ○ *The scheme will not be covered by any EU directives.* See also COVERAGE 2. **5(a)** (of money) to be enough for sth: *£50 should cover your expenses.* **(b)** to give or make enough money for sth: *Your parents will have to cover your tuition fees.* ○ *The show barely covered its costs.* **6(a)** to travel a specified distance: [Vn] *By sunset we had covered thirty miles.* **(b)** to extend over a specified area: [Vn] *The reserve covers an area of some 1140 square kilometres.* **7** (of a journalist) to report on an event such as a trial or an election: [Vn] *She's covering the Labour Party's annual conference.* See also COVERAGE 1. **8** ~ (**for sb**) to do sb's work, duties, etc during their absence: [Vpr] *I'll cover for Jane while she's on vacation.* [also V, Vn]. **9** ~ **sb/sth** (**against/for sth**) to protect sb/sth against loss, etc by insurance: [Vnpr] *Are you fully covered against/for fire and theft?* [V.n to inf] *Does this policy cover my husband to drive?* **10** **(a)** to protect sb by threatening to shoot or by shooting at anyone who tries to attack them: [Vn] *Cover me while I move forward.* ○ *The artillery gave us covering fire* (ie shot to protect us). **(b)** (of guns, forts, etc) to be in a position to shoot at and therefore control an area, a road, etc: [Vn] *The artillery is covering every approach to the town.* **(c)** to continue aiming a gun at sb, so that they cannot shoot or escape: [Vn] *Cover her while I phone the police.* ○ *Keep them covered!* **IDM cover/hide a multitude of sins** ⇨ MULTITUDE. **PHRV ,cover sth 'in** to put a protective covering or roof over an open space: *We're having the yard/passage/terrace covered in.* **,cover sth 'up** (*derog*) to make efforts to hide a mistake, sth illegal, etc: *The government is trying to cover up the full extent of the scandal.* **,cover 'up for sb** to hide sb's mistakes, crimes, etc in order to protect them.

▶ **covered** *adj* **1** ~ **in/with sth** [pred] having a large number or amount of sth: *trees covered in/with blossom/fruit* ○ *The furniture was all covered in dust.* ○ *Not so long ago the country was covered with windmills.* ○ *His hands were covered in blood.* ○ (*fig*) *I was covered in/with confusion/embarrassment* (ie very confused and embarrassed). **2** having a cover, esp a roof: *covered seating* ○ *a covered market.*

covering /ˈkʌvərɪŋ/ *n* **(a)** a thing that is used to cover[1](1) sth else: *a protective covering* ○ *vinyl floor covering* ○ *Melt the cake covering.* **(b)** a thing that is covering sth else, esp temporarily: *a light covering of snow on the ground.*

■ **,covering 'letter** (*Brit*) (*US* **'cover letter**) *n* a letter sent with a document or with goods, usu explaining the contents.

'cover-up *n* (usu *sing*) (*derog*) an act of concealing a mistake, sth illegal, etc: *An army spokesman said there had been no cover-up.*

cover[2] /ˈkʌvə(r)/ *n* **1** [C] **(a)** a thing that covers sth: *a plastic cover for a personal computer* ○ *a 'cushion/*

¹duvet cover ○ *Some chairs are fitted with velvet/ floral covers.* See also LOOSE COVERS, DUST-COVER. **(b)** a top or lid: *a manhole cover.* **2** [C] either or both of the thick protective outer pages of a book, magazine, etc, esp the front one: *a book with a leather cover* ○ *the front cover of the December issue* ○ *read a book from cover to cover* (ie from beginning to end) ○ *The magazine had a picture of a horse on the cover* (ie the front cover). **3 the covers** [pl] the sheet, BLANKET(1), DUVET, etc that one has over one in bed; the BEDCLOTHES: *She crept under the covers and was soon asleep.* **4** [U] a place or an area giving shelter or protection: *The land was flat and treeless and gave no cover to the troops.* ○ *As soon as the rain started we ran for cover.* ○ *There was nowhere we could take cover* (ie go for protection) *from the storm.* ○ *The bicycles are kept under cover* (ie in a shelter or shed). **5** [U] support and protection from attack: *Artillery gave cover* (ie fired at the enemy to stop them firing back) *while the infantry advanced.* ○ *The operation will not be possible without air cover* (ie protection by military aircraft). **6** [C usu *sing*] **(a)** ~ **(for sth)** a means of concealing sth illegal, secret, etc: *His business was a cover for drug dealing.* **(b)** a false identity or reason for doing sth: *Several agents had to leave the country when their cover was blown* (ie revealed). **7** [U] ~ **(against sth)** insurance against loss, injury, etc: *take out a policy that gives extra cover against fire* ○ *have fully comprehensive cover.* **8** [U] ~ **(for sb)** the performance of another person's work, duties, etc during her or his absence: *a midwife who provides emergency cover (for sick colleagues).* **9** [C] an envelope or a packet in which sth is sent: *under plain cover* (ie in an envelope or a parcel that does not show who sent it, what its contents are, etc) ○ *(commerce) Your order is being dispatched under separate cover* (ie in a separate envelope or parcel). **IDM** **break ¹cover** to leave a place where one has been hiding. **under (the) cover of sth 1** concealed by sth: *We travelled under cover of darkness.* **2** with the pretence of sth: *under cover of anonymity.* See also UNDERCOVER.

■ **¹cover charge** *n* an amount of money to be paid in some restaurants in addition to the cost of each customer's food and drink.

¹cover girl *n* a girl whose photograph appears on the cover of a magazine.

¹cover story *n* **1** the main article in a magazine, usu advertised or begun on the front cover: *The issue generated more letters than any previous cover story.* **2** a story invented to conceal sth, esp a person's identity or reasons for doing sth: *You need a good cover story in case anyone asks you what you're doing there.*

coverage /ˈkʌvərɪdʒ/ *n* [U] **1** ~ **(of sth)** the reporting of news, events, etc: *extensive TV/press/ media coverage of the election campaign* ○ *There's not much coverage of foreign news in the newspaper we get.* **2** the extent to which sth is covered (COVER¹ 3,4): *a dictionary with good coverage of American words.*

coveralls /ˈkʌvərɔːlz/ *n* [pl] *(US)* = OVERALLS.

coverlet /ˈkʌvələt/ *n* a decorative cover spread over the top of a bed; a BEDSPREAD.

covert¹ /ˈkʌvət, ˈkəʊvɜːt/ *adj* concealed or secret; not open: *a covert glance/threat/operation* ○ *Their relationship became more and more covert.* ► **covertly** *adv*: *She watched him covertly.* Compare OVERT.

covert² /ˈkʌvət/ *n* an area of thick low bushes or trees among which animals, esp hunted animals, hide.

covet /ˈkʌvɪt/ *v* *(fml)* to want very much to possess sth, esp sth that belongs to sb else: [Vn] *covet sb's job* ○ *He had long coveted the chance to work with a* famous musician. ○ *this year's winners of the coveted trophy* (ie which everyone would like to win).

► **covetous** *adj (usu derog)* having or showing a strong desire to possess sth, esp sth that belongs to sb else: *a covetous look/glance.* **covetously** *adv.* **covetousness** *n* [U].

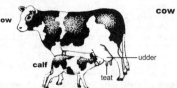

cow¹ /kaʊ/ *n* **1** a large female animal kept on farms to produce milk or BEEF¹(1): *milking the cows* ○ *a large herd of dairy cows grazing in the meadow.* ⇨ picture. Compare BULL¹ 1, CALF. See also CATTLE, HEIFER. **2** a female of certain types of animal, eg a female elephant, WHALE or SEAL¹. Compare BULL¹ 2. **3** [usu *sing*] *(derog sl offensive)* a woman: *You stupid cow!* See also SACRED COW. **IDM** **till the ¹cows come home** *(infml)* for a very long time; for ever: *You can talk till the cows come home — you'll never make me change my mind.*

■ **¹cow-pat** *n* a flat round mass of cow DUNG on the ground.

cow² /kaʊ/ *v* ~ **sb (into sth/doing sth)** (esp passive) to make sb do as one wants by frightening them; to INTIMIDATE sb: [Vnpr] *The men had been cowed into total submission.* [also Vn].

► **cowed** *adj* made to feel inferior and afraid: *silent, cowed obedience* ○ *She is not cowed but defiant.*

coward /ˈkaʊəd/ *n (derog)* a person who lacks courage when facing a dangerous or unpleasant situation and tries to avoid it: *Don't be such a coward — jump!* ○ *I'm a terrible coward when it comes to dealing with sick people* (ie It upsets me and I avoid it).

► **cowardice** /ˈkaʊədɪs/ *n* [U] the fear of and desire to avoid dangerous or unpleasant situations: *He felt ashamed of his cowardice in not coming forward to support his friend.* ○ *She accused the censors of moral cowardice.*

cowardly *adj (derog)* lacking courage; typical of a coward: *cowardly lies/behaviour* ○ *a cowardly and brutal attack* ○ *It was cowardly of you not to admit your mistake.*

cowboy /ˈkaʊbɔɪ/ *n* **1** a man who looks after cattle in the western parts of the USA. Cowboys are usu skilled riders: *a cowboy movie* (ie one showing adventures in the American West) ○ *small boys playing a game of cowboys and Indians.* **2** *(Brit infml derog)* a dishonest or careless person in business, esp one who has no qualifications: *The people who did our double glazing were just cowboys/cowboy operators.*

cower /ˈkaʊə(r)/ *v* to bend down and/or move backwards with your head lowered because of fear or distress: [V] *People would cower as he passed.* ○ *The dog was cowering in a corner of the room.* [Vp] *He cowered away/back as she raised her hand.*

cowhand /ˈkaʊhænd/ *n* a person who looks after cows.

cowhide /ˈkaʊhaɪd/ *n* [U] leather made from the skin of a cow.

cowl /kaʊl/ *n* **1** a large loose covering for the head, worn esp by monks. **2** a cap for a chimney, etc, usu made of metal. Cowls often revolve with the wind and are designed to improve the flow of air or smoke. ⇨ picture at HOUSE¹.

► **cowling** *n* a metal covering for an engine, esp on an aircraft. ⇨ picture at AIRCRAFT.

[V] = verb used alone   **[Vn]** = verb + noun   **[Vp]** = verb + particle   **[Vpr]** = verb + prepositional phrase

cowman /ˈkaʊmən/ n (pl **-men** /-mən/) a man who is employed to look after cows.

cowrie /ˈkaʊri/ n a small shell formerly used as money in parts of Africa and Asia.

cowshed /ˈkaʊʃed/ n a farm building where cows are kept when not outside, or where their milk is taken.

cowslip /ˈkaʊslɪp/ n a small wild plant with sweet-smelling yellow flowers.

cox /kɒks/ (also **coxswain** /ˈkɒksn/) n a person who steers a boat that is rowed by other people, esp in races.
▶ **cox** v to act as cox for sb: [Vn] coxed pairs ○ She coxed the Oxford boat.

coy /kɔɪ/ adj (**-er**, **-est**) (usu derog) **1** pretending to be shy or modest, although really liking the attention one is receiving: a coy smile ○ Don't be so coy about your achievements. **2** unwilling to give information, answer questions, etc in a rather annoying way: He was a little coy when asked where the money had come from. ○ Officials are coy about the details. ▶ **coyly** adv: They giggled coyly. ○ a sack-like dress that coyly hinted at pregnancy. **coyness** n [U].

coyote /kaɪˈəʊti; Brit also kɔɪ-/ n a small WOLF(1) that lives on the plains of western N America.

cozy (US) = COSY.

cp /ˌsiː ˈpiː/ abbr compare. Compare CF.

Cpl abbr Corporal.

crab /kræb/ n **1(a)** [C] a sea creature that has a hard shell and ten legs, two of which are pincers (PINCER 2). Crabs move sideways on land. ⇨ picture at PINCER, SHELLFISH. **(b)** [U] the flesh of this eaten as food: dressed crab (ie prepared for eating). **2** the **Crab** [sing] the fourth sign of the ZODIAC; Cancer.
▶ **crabwise** /ˈkræbwaɪz/ adv sideways, often in a stiff or awkward way: shuffle crabwise across the floor.

crab-apple /ˈkræb æpl/ n **(a)** a tree with fruit like small hard sour apples. **(b)** this fruit, often used in making jam: crab-apple jelly.

crabbed /ˈkræbɪd, kræbd/ adj **1** (of sb's writing) small and difficult to read. **2** = CRABBY.

crabby /ˈkræbi/ adj (**-ier**, **-iest**) (infml) bad-tempered and miserable.

crack¹ /kræk/ v **1** to break or make sth break without dividing into separate parts: [V] The ice cracked as I stepped onto it. ○ Ominous cracking noises came from the roof. [Vn] You can crack this toughened glass, but you can't break it. ○ She has cracked a bone in her arm. ○ Her lips were dry and cracked. **2** to break sth open or into pieces: [Vn] crack a nut ○ crack a safe (ie open it to steal from it) [Vn-adj] crack an egg open. **3** ~ sth (on/against sth) to hit sth sharply: [Vnpr] I cracked my head on the low ceiling. **4** (no passive) to make a sharp sound or cause sth to make a sharp sound: [V] The hunter's rifle cracked and the deer fell dead. [Vn] crack a whip/one's knuckles. **5** (of the voice) to change in depth, loudness, etc suddenly and in a way that cannot control: [V] In a voice cracking with emotion, he told us of his son's death. **6(a)** to be unable to resist pressure or change any longer: [V] Sooner or later he'll crack under questioning. ○ The old institutions are cracking. **(b)** [V] = CRACK UP. **7** (infml) to find the solution to a problem, puzzle, etc; to defeat sth: [Vn] His new computer game was a tricky one, but we finally cracked it. ○ crack the enemy's code ○ crack a smuggling ring ○ The firm has cracked the private car market (ie discovered how to obtain a large share of it). **8** [Vn] (infml) to open a bottle, esp of alcoholic drink, and drink its contents. **9** (infml) to tell a joke: [Vn] chatting and cracking jokes. **IDM** get ˈcracking/ˈweaving (infml esp Brit) to begin immediately and work quickly: There's a lot to

be done, so let's get cracking. **not all/everything it's/one's/they're cracked ˈup to be** (infml) not as good as people say: He's not such a good writer as he's cracked ˈup to be. **PHRV** ˌcrack ˈdown (on sb/sth) to try harder to prevent an illegal activity or to stop people from becoming involved in it and deal more severely with those who are caught doing it: Police are cracking down on drug dealers. See also CRACK-DOWN. ˌcrack ˈon (with sth) (infml) to make good progress: If we keep cracking on (with the painting), we'll be finished by tea-time. ˌcrack ˈup (infml) to lose one's physical or esp mental health; to collapse under the strain: You'll crack up if you carry on working so hard.
▶ **cracked** /krækt/ adj **1** having cracks (CRACK¹): a cracked and dirty mug ○ cracked walls ○ He suffered broken ribs and a cracked skull. ○ Her lips were dry and cracked. ⇨ picture at CHIP¹. **2** [pred] (infml) crazy: I think he's a bit cracked, don't you?
cracking /ˈkrækɪŋ/ n [U] lines on a surface where it is damaged or beginning to break: a lot of discoloration and cracking. — adj [usu attrib] (Brit infml) excellent: cracking bargains ○ She's in cracking form at the moment. ○ We set off **at a cracking pace** (ie very quickly). — adv (infml) (used esp before good for emphasis): a cracking good (ie extremely good) dinner.
■ ˈcrack-down n ~ (on sb/sth) severe measures to restrict or discourage undesirable or criminal people or actions: a government crack-down on student demonstrations.

crack² /kræk/ n **1** [C] ~ (in sth) **(a)** a line along which sth has broken, but not into completely separate parts: dangerous cracks in the ice ○ a china cup covered in small/fine cracks ○ Cracks were beginning to develop/appear in the walls of the house. ○ (fig) The cracks (ie faults) in the Government's economic policy are beginning to show. ⇨ picture at CHIP¹. **(b)** a narrow space or opening: She peeped through a crack in the curtains. ○ Open the door a crack (ie open it very slightly). **2** [C] a sudden sharp noise: the crack of a pistol shot ○ a loud crack of thunder. **3** [C] ~ (about sth) a sharp blow, usu one that can be heard: give sb/get a crack on the head. **4** [C] ~ (about sth) (infml) a clever and amusing remark, often a critical one; a joke: She made a rather mean crack about his fatness. **5** [C] ~ at sth/doing sth (infml) an attempt at sth: She hopes to have a crack at the world record soon. ○ Let's have a/another crack at solving this puzzle. **6** [U] a powerful drug which is a form of COCAINE: Crack is now widely available in Britain. ○ a crack addict. **IDM** at the crack of ˈdawn (infml) very early in the morning: get up at the crack of dawn. **a fair crack of the whip** ⇨ FAIR¹. **paper over the cracks** ⇨ PAPER.
▶ **crack** adj [attrib] very clever or expert; excellent: a crack regiment ○ He's a **crack shot** (ie an expert at shooting).
■ ˈcrack-brained adj (infml) crazy; very foolish: a crack-brained idea/scheme.

cracker /ˈkrækə(r)/ n **1** (also **cream cracker**, US also **soda cracker**) a thin dry biscuit, typically eaten with cheese. **2(a)** a small FIREWORK that explodes with a sharp sound. **(b)** (Brit also **Christmas cracker**) a party toy consisting of a cardboard tube wrapped in paper that makes a sharp explosive sound as its ends are pulled apart. Crackers usu contain a small gift, a paper hat and a joke: a box of crackers. **3** (Brit infml) a person or thing that one admires: That was a cracker of a shot!

crackerjack /ˈkrækədʒæk/ n (US sl) an exceptionally fine person or thing: Joe is a real crackerjack in science and math.

crackers /ˈkrækəz/ adj [pred] (Brit infml) mad; crazy: That noise is driving me crackers ○ You must be absolutely/completely crackers!

crackle /'krækl/ v to make small sharp sounds, like those made when dry sticks burn: [V] *a crackling camp-fire* ○ *The frost crackled under our feet as we walked.* ○ *(fig) The atmosphere crackled with tension/anticipation as the two boxers stepped into the ring.*
▶ **crackle** n [U,C] a series of small sharp sounds: *the distant crackle of machine-gun fire* ○ *Can you get rid of the crackles on my radio?*
crackling /'kræklɪŋ/ n **1** [sing, U] a series of sharp sounds: *There was a crackling in the bushes and suddenly a large bird appeared.* **2** [U] the crisp skin on roast PORK.

crackpot /'krækpɒt/ n (*infml*) a person with strange or crazy ideas: *He's a complete crackpot!* ○ *a crackpot notion/scheme.*

-cracy comb form (forming ns) government or rule of: *democracy* ○ *bureaucracy.* See also -CRAT.

cradle /'kreɪdl/ n **1** a small bed for a baby, usu shaped like an open box, which can be pushed from side to side: *She rocked the baby to sleep in its cradle.* ⇨ picture at COT. **2** ~ **of sth** (usu *sing*) the place where sth begins: *Greece, the cradle of Western culture.* **3** a platform that can be moved up and down the outside wall of a building, etc, used by people cleaning windows, painting, etc. **4** the part of a telephone on which the RECEIVER(1) rests. See also CAT'S-CRADLE. **IDM** **from the ˌcradle to the ˈgrave** from birth to death.
▶ **cradle** v ~ **sb/sth (in sth)** to hold sb/sth gently in a hollow made with one's hands or arms, often moving them/it slightly from side to side: [Vnpr] *cradle a baby in one's arms* ○ *He cradled his injured hand in the other.* [also Vn].

craft /krɑːft; US kræft/ n **1(a)** [C] an activity involving a special skill at making things with the hands: *an emporium of African arts and crafts* ○ *traditional crafts like basket-weaving* ○ *a ˈcraft exhibition/fair.* **(b)** [U] the skills required for a particular activity: *chefs who learned their craft in top hotels* ○ *A writer only becomes a true writer by practising his craft.* **2** [U] (*fml derog*) skill in deceiving people: *He achieved by craft and guile what he could not manage by honest means.* **3** [C] (*pl* unchanged) **(a)** a boat or ship: *Hundreds of small craft surrounded the liner as it steamed into the harbour.* **(b)** an aircraft or spacecraft: *The astronauts piloted their landing craft down to the moon's surface.*
▶ **craft** v (usu passive) to make sth skilfully, esp by hand: [Vn] *a carefully crafted speech* ○ *a beautiful hand-crafted silver goblet.*
crafty adj (-**ier**, -**iest**) (*usu derog*) clever in using indirect or deceitful methods to get what one wants: *a crafty politician* ○ *schoolchildren having a crafty smoke in the corridor* ○ *John's a crafty old fox.* **craftily** adv. **craftiness** n [U].

craftsman /'krɑːftsmən; US 'kræfts-/ n (*pl* -**men** /-mən/) **1** a skilled man, esp one who makes beautiful things by hand: *rugs handmade by local craftsmen* ○ *It is clearly the work of a master craftsman.* **2** a person who does sth very well and with great attention to detail: *a craftsman of the written word.* **craftsmanship** n [U] **(a)** the degree of skill involved in an activity: *the superb craftsmanship of the Ming dynasty.* **(b)** the quality of design and work shown by a finished product: *the chest's elegant craftsmanship.*

crag /kræg/ n a high steep rough mass of rock.
▶ **craggy** adj **1** having many crags: *a craggy coastline.* **2** (*usu approv*) (of esp a man's face) having strong prominent features and deep lines: *his handsome craggy face.*

cram /kræm/ v (-**mm**-) **1(a)** ~ **sth into sth/in/to** push or force too much of sth into a place: [Vnpr] *cram food into one's mouth/papers into a drawer* [Vnp] *The room's full already — we simply can't cram any more people in.* **(b)** ~ **sth (with sth)** (usu passive) to make sth too full: [Vn-adj] *The car was* crammed full. [Vn] *Supporters crammed the streets.* [Vnpr] *The streets were crammed with people waving flags.* **2** ~ **(for sth)** **(a)** (*infml*) to learn a lot of facts in a short time, esp for an examination: [Vpr] *cram for a chemistry test* [V] *She passed after just three weeks' cramming.* **(b)** to teach sb in this way: [Vn] *cram pupils.*

cramp¹ /kræmp/ n **1** [U,C] a sudden and painful tightening of the muscles, usu caused by cold or too much exercise, making movement difficult: *After swimming for half an hour I started to get cramp in my legs.* See also WRITER'S CRAMP. **2 cramps** [pl] (*esp US*) severe pain in the stomach.

cramp² /kræmp/ v to prevent or delay the movement or development of sb/sth: [Vn] *All these difficulties cramped his progress.* ○ *I feel cramped by the limitations of my job.* **IDM** **be cramped for ˈroom/ˈspace** be without enough room, etc: *We're a bit cramped for space in this attic.* **cramp sb's ˈstyle** (*infml*) to prevent sb from doing sth freely, or as well as they can: *It cramps my style to have you watching over me all the time.*
▶ **cramped** adj **1(a)** (of space) narrow and restricted: *cramped, uncomfortable conditions* ○ *Our accommodation is rather cramped.* **(b)** (of people) not having room to move freely: *We're all a bit cramped (for space) in here!* **2** (of sb's writing) with small letters close together, and therefore difficult to read.

crampon /'kræmpɒn/ n (usu *pl*) a metal plate with pointed pieces of metal on one side, worn on shoes for walking or climbing on ice and snow.

cranberry /'krænbəri; US -beri/ n a small red sour berry, used for making sauce and in cooking: *roast turkey with cranberry jelly.*

crane¹ /kreɪn/ n **1** a machine with a long arm which is used to lift and move heavy weights. ⇨ picture at OIL RIG. **2** a large bird with long legs and a long neck.

crane² /kreɪn/ v to stretch one's neck: [Vn] *crane one's neck to see sth* [V, Vp] *craning (forward) to get a better view* [also Vnpr, Vnp].

cranium /'kreɪniəm/ n (*pl* **craniums** or **crania** /'kreɪniə/) (*anatomy*) the hard part of the head enclosing the brain; the SKULL. ▶ **cranial** /'kreɪniəl/ *adj: cranial nerves.*

crank¹ /kræŋk/ n (*derog*) a person with strange fixed ideas, esp on a particular subject: *a health-food crank* (ie one who insists on eating unusual food for health reasons) ○ *I don't care if people think I'm a crank.*
▶ **cranky** adj (-**ier**, -**iest**) (*infml derog*) **1** strange; ECCENTRIC(1): *a cranky notion.* **2** (of machines, etc) not reliable: *a rattling, cranky old engine.* **3** (*US*) bad-tempered.

crank² /kræŋk/ n a bar and handle in the shape of an L for converting movement backwards and forwards into circular movement: *The pedals of a bicycle are attached to a crank.* ⇨ picture at BICYCLE.
▶ **crank** v ~ **sth (up)** to cause sth to turn or start by means of a crank: [Vn, Vnp] *crank (up) an engine.*

crankshaft /'kræŋkʃɑːft/ n (*techn*) a rod or SHAFT(2) that turns or is turned by a CRANK².

cranny /'kræni/ n a very small hole or opening, esp in a wall: *spiders in all the cracks and crannies.* **IDM** **every nook and cranny** ⇨ NOOK.

crap /kræp/ v (-**pp**-) (⚠ *sl*) to push out waste matter from the body; to DEFECATE: [V] *a dog crapping on the lawn.*
▶ **crap** n (⚠ *sl*) **1** [U] waste matter from the body; EXCREMENT. **2** [sing] an act of defecating (DEFECATE): *have a crap.* **3** [U] nonsense; rubbish: *You do talk a load of crap!*
crap adj (*sl*) bad; worthless: *a crap band/photograph.*
crappy adj (*sl*) bad; worthless: *a crappy book/programme.*

crape /kreɪp/ = CREPE.

craps /kræps/ n [sing v] (US) a gambling game played with two dice: *shoot craps* (ie play this game).
▶ **crap** adj [attrib] of or for craps: *a crap game.*

crash¹ /kræʃ/ n **1** an accident in which a vehicle hits sth, eg another vehicle, usu causing damage, and often injury or death to passengers: *a crash involving two cars and a lorry* ○ *a 'car/'plane crash.* **2** (usu *sing*) a sudden loud noise made eg by sth falling or breaking: *the crash of dishes being dropped* ○ *The tree fell with a great crash.* ○ *His words were drowned in a crash of thunder.* **3** a sudden/serious fall in the price or value of sth, or the collapse of a business: *the 1987 stock market crash.*
▶ **crash** adj [attrib] involving hard work or considerable effort over a short period of time in order to achieve quick results: *a crash course in computer programming* ○ *a crash diet.*
crash adv with a crash: *The vase fell crash onto the tiles.*
■ '**crash barrier** n (a) a strong low fence at the side of a road to prevent vehicles from driving off the edge, or in the middle of a dual carriageway (DUAL). (b) a fence or rail to restrain crowds.
'**crash-helmet** n a hat made of very strong material and worn eg by motor cyclists (MOTOR) to protect the head.
'**crash-land** v to land or land an aircraft roughly in an emergency, usu causing damage: [V] *The plane crash-landed on a golf course.* [Vn] *The pilot crash-landed the plane after engine failure.* ,**crash-'landing** n: *make a crash-landing.*

crash² /kræʃ/ v **1** ~ (sth) (into sth) (a) (of a vehicle or its driver) to hit or cause a vehicle to hit sth, usu causing damage, and often injury or death to passengers: [V, Vpr] *The plane crashed (into the mountain).* [Vn, Vpr] *He crashed his car (into a wall).* [Vn] *a crashed lorry/plane.* (b) to move or cause sth to move noisily or violently: [Vp, Vpr] *an enraged elephant crashing about/through the undergrowth* [Vnpr] *He crashed the trolley through the doors.* **2** to fall or strike sth noisily or violently: [Vpr, Vp] *Rocks came crashing (down) onto the car.* [Vpr] *The brick crashed through the window.* ○ *The dishes crashed to the floor.* [Vnpr, Vnp] *She crashed the plates (down) on the table.* **3** to make a loud noise: [V] *The thunder crashed overhead.* **4** (of a business, financial institution, government, etc) to fail suddenly; to decrease suddenly and considerably in value: [V] *The company crashed with debts of £2 million.* ○ *Prices crashed.* **5** (of a machine or system) to fail suddenly: [V] *The computer system keeps crashing.* **6** [Vn] (*infml* = GATECRASH: *crash a party.* **7** ~ (out) (sl) to sleep somewhere temporarily: [Vpr, Vp] *Mind if I crash (out) on your floor tonight?* **IDM** **a crashing** '**bore** a very boring person.

crass /kræs/ adj (*fml*) **1** very stupid and/or not at all sensitive: *the crass questions that all disabled people get asked.* **2** [attrib] (of a bad quality) extreme; very great: *crass stupidity/ignorance.* ▶ **crassly** adv. **crassness** n [U].

-crat comb form (forming ns) a member or supporter of a type of government, rule or SYSTEM(3): *democrat* ○ *bureaucrat.* ▶ **-cratic** (forming adjs): *aristocratic.*

crate /kreɪt/ n (a) a large wooden container for transporting goods: *a crate of bananas.* (b) a container made of metal or plastic divided into small individual units, for transporting or storing bottles: *a crate of milk/wine.*
▶ **crate** v ~ sth (up) to put sth in a crate: [Vn, Vnp] *crating (up) books and furniture.*

crater /'kreɪtə(r)/ n **1** a large hole in the top of a VOLCANO. ⇨ picture at VOLCANO. **2** a large hole in the ground made by the explosion of a bomb, etc or by sth large hitting it: *a meteorite crater.*

cravat /krə'væt/ n a short wide strip of material worn by men round the neck, folded inside the collar of a shirt.

crave /kreɪv/ v **1** ~ (for) sth to have a strong desire for sth: [Vn] *give her the admiration she craves* [Vpr] *Some people worship the past, others crave for change and novelty.* **2** (*arch*) to ask for sth eagerly; to beg for sth: [Vn] *crave sb's forgiveness.*
▶ **craving** n ~ (for sth) a strong desire: *She developed a craving for oranges.* ○ *a desperate craving to be loved.*

craven /'kreɪvn/ adj (*fml derog*) cowardly: *admit to a craven fear of spiders.*

crawl /krɔːl/ v **1(a)** to move slowly, with the body on or close to the ground, or on hands and knees: [Vpr] *a beetle crawling along a leaf* ○ *The wounded man crawled painfully to the phone.* [V]. *A baby crawls before it can walk.* [also Vp]. (b) (of vehicles) to move very slowly: [Vpr] *The traffic crawled over the bridge.* [also V, Vp]. See also KERB-CRAWLING. **2** ~ (to sb) (*infml derog*) to try to gain sb's favour by praising them, doing what will please them, etc: [V, Vpr] *I don't like crawling (to my boss).* **IDM** **make one's/sb's flesh crawl/creep** ⇨ FLESH. **PHR V** '**crawl with sth** (esp in the continuous tenses) to be covered or filled with things that crawl or with people: *The ground was crawling with ants.* ○ *The place is crawling with* (ie is full of) *police.*
▶ **crawl** n [sing] **1** (*derog*) a very slow pace: *traffic moving at a crawl* ○ *We slowed to a crawl.* See also PUB CRAWL. **2** (often **the crawl**) a fast swimming stroke that involves moving each arm in turn over one's head while kicking rapidly with the feet: *Can you do the crawl?*
crawler n (*infml derog*) a person who crawls (CRAWL 2).

crayfish /'kreɪfɪʃ/ n (*pl* unchanged) **1** an animal like a small LOBSTER that lives in rivers and lakes. **2** (also **crawfish**) a large LOBSTER that lives in the sea.

crayon /'kreɪən/ n a coloured pencil or stick of coloured chalk or wax, used for drawing: *a blue crayon* ○ *a crayon drawing.*
▶ **crayon** v [V, Vn] to draw sth with crayons.

craze /kreɪz/ n (a) ~ (for sth) an enthusiastic but usu brief interest in sth that is shared by many people: *the craze for exercising at all hours of the day and night* ○ *the current/latest teenage dance craze that is sweeping Europe.* (b) an object of such an interest: *Pet pigs are the latest craze.*

crazed /kreɪzd/ adj ~ (with sth) wild and lacking control; mad: *a crazed look in his eyes* ○ *She was crazed with grief.* ○ *drug-crazed hippies.*

crazy /'kreɪzi/ adj (-**ier**, -**iest**) **1** (*infml*) (a) very foolish; not sensible: *a crazy person/idea/suggestion* ○ *You must be crazy to go walking in such awful weather.* ○ *She's absolutely crazy to lend him the money.* (b) mad: *He's crazy — he ought to be locked up.* ○ (*fig*) *That noise is driving me crazy* (ie annoying me very much). **2** [pred] ~ (about sth/sb) (*infml*) wildly excited; enthusiastic: *The kids went crazy when Michael Jackson appeared.* ○ *I'm crazy about steam-engines.* ○ *She's crazy about him* (ie loves him a lot). **IDM** **like** '**anything/'crazy/'mad** (*infml*) very fast, hard, much, etc: *I had to run like anything to catch the bus.* ○ *We worked like crazy to get it done on time.* ▶ **crazily** adv. **craziness** n [U].
■ ,**crazy** '**paving** n [U] (*esp Brit*) pieces of stone that are not regularly shaped, fitted together on the ground to make a path or PATIO. ⇨ picture at HOUSE¹.

creak /kriːk/ v to make a harsh sound: [V] *She heard a floorboard creak upstairs.* ○ *a creaking bed/staircase* [V-adj] *The garden gate creaked open.* [Vpr] (*fig*) *The new system is already creaking under the strain* (ie unable to meet the demands placed upon it).

▶ **creak** *n* such a sound: *hear a series of creaks and groans.*

creaky *adj* that creaks: *a creaky floor-board* ○ *a creaky old lift* ○ (*fig*) *the country's creaky legal system.*

cream¹ /kriːm/ *n* **1** [U] the thick white or pale yellow liquid that rises to the top of milk and contains the fat: *a bowl of peaches and cream* ○ *a carton of cream* ○ *put cream in one's coffee* ○ *whipped cream* ○ *cream buns/cake* (ie containing cream). See also CLOTTED CREAM, DOUBLE CREAM, SINGLE CREAM, SOUR CREAM. **2** [C,U] (in compounds) any type of food containing cream or a substance similar to cream: *ice-cream* ○ *chocolate creams* (ie soft chocolate sweets). See also SALAD CREAM. **3** [C,U] a smooth soft mixture or thick liquid used as a COSMETIC, in medicine, for polishing, etc: *soothing creams and lotions* ○ *shaving cream* ○ *antiseptic cream.* See also COLD CREAM. **4 the cream** [sing] ~ (**of sth**) the best part of a group or set: *the cream of this year's graduates.*

▶ **cream** *adj* pale yellow, almost white: *a cream dress.*

creamery /ˈkriːməri/ *n* (**a**) a place where butter and cheese are made. (**b**) a place where milk, cream, butter, etc are sold.

creamy *adj* (**-ier, -iest**) **1** thick and smooth like cream, or containing a lot of cream: *creamy soup/ yoghurt* ○ *paint of a creamy, smooth consistency* ○ *a creamy taste.* **2** pale yellow, almost white, in colour: *a creamy skin.*

■ ˌcream ˈcheese *n* [U] soft white cheese containing a lot of cream.

ˌcream ˈcracker *n* (*Brit*) = CRACKER 1.

ˌcream ˈtea *n* (*Brit*) a meal consisting of tea with scones (SCONE), jam and thick cream.

cream² /kriːm/ *v* (**a**) to crush cooked vegetables, esp potatoes, and mix them with milk or butter until they are soft and smooth: [Vn] *creamed parsnip.* (**b**) to mix sth together into a soft smooth paste: [Vn, Vnp] *Cream the butter and sugar (together).* **PHRV** ˌcream **sb/sth** ˈoff to take away the best people or things: *The most able pupils are creamed off and put into special classes.*

crease /kriːs/ *n* **1** a line made on cloth, paper, etc by crushing, folding or pressing: *iron a crease into one's trousers* ○ *crease-resistant cloth* (ie that does not easily get creases in it). **2** a line in the skin, esp on the face: *the tired creases around her eyes.* **3** (in cricket) a white line made at each end of the pitch to mark the positions of the BOWLER¹(1) and batsman. ⇨ picture at CRICKET¹.

▶ **crease** *v* **1** to develop creases or make sth develop creases: [V] *material that creases easily* [Vpr] *Her face creased into a smile.* [Vn] *Pack the clothes carefully so that you don't crease them.* ○ *A slight frown creased her brow.* **2** ~ **sb** (**up**) (*Brit infml*) to amuse sb greatly: [Vn, Vnp] *Her jokes really creased me (up).*

create /kriˈeɪt/ *v* **1** to cause sth to exist; to make sth new or original: [Vn] *God created the world.* ○ *a ballet created by Kenneth MacMillan* ○ *an organization created in 1991* ○ *a newly created holiday resort* ○ *The government plans to create more jobs/ opportunities for young people.* **2** to have sth as a result; to produce a feeling, situation, etc: [Vn] *create confusion* ○ *His shabby appearance creates a bad impression.* ○ *Her last book created a sensation.* ○ *The scheme probably created more problems than it solved.* ○ *The firm's closure created a feeling of unease and sadness in the town.* **3** to give sb a particular rank: [Vn] *create eight new peers* [Vn-n] *He was created Baron of Banthorp.*

creation /kriˈeɪʃn/ *n* **1** [U] the action or process of creating sth: *the creation of the world* ○ *a job creation scheme* ○ *encourage the creation of new markets over-*

seas ○ *He proposed the creation of a travelling library service.* **2** [C] (**a**) a thing made, esp by means of special skill or talent: *a literary/artistic creation* ○ *The chef had produced one of his most spectacular creations, a whole roasted swan.* (**b**) a new type of garment or hat: *the latest stunning creations from London's fashion houses.* **3**(**a**) (usu **the Creation**) [sing] the making of the world, esp by God as told in the Bible. (**b**) (often **Creation**) [U] all created things: *respect all God's creation.*

creative /kriˈeɪtɪv/ *adj* **1** [attrib] of or involving the skilful and imaginative use of sth to produce eg a work of art: *her creative use of light and colour* ○ *He teaches creative writing* (ie teaches people to write fiction, plays, etc). **2** able to create things, usu in an imaginative way: *She's very creative; she writes poetry and paints.* ○ *creative energy/ideas.* ▶ **creatively** *adv.* **creativity** /ˌkriːeɪˈtɪvəti/ *n* [U]: *hamper sb's creativity* ○ *Creativity and originality are more important than technical skill.*

creator /kriˈeɪtə(r)/ *n* **1** [C] a person who creates sth: *Walt Disney, the creator of Mickey Mouse.* **2 the Creator** [sing] God.

creature /ˈkriːtʃə(r)/ *n* **1** a living being, esp an animal: *octopuses and other marine creatures* ○ *That dog's a ferocious creature!* ○ *strange creatures from Mars.* **2** (esp following an *adj*) a person, considered in a particular way: *She was a charming young creature.* ○ *a poor creature* (ie a person for whom one feels pity) ○ *It's 12.00, so he'll be at lunch now — he's a creature of habit* (ie a person whose daily life follows a fixed routine). **IDM** **sb's creature/the creature of sb** (*fml derog*) a person who is totally dependent on sb else, and does whatever they want. ■ ˌcreature ˈcomforts *n* [pl] all the things needed for a person's comfort, eg good food, a nice home.

crèche /kreʃ/ *n* (*Brit*) a place where babies are looked after while their parents work, play sports, shop, etc: *set up a company crèche.*

credence /ˈkriːdns/ *n* [U] (*fml*) (**a**) belief in or acceptance of sth as true: *I give/attach little credence to such rumours.* (**b**) the quality that makes people likely to believe sth: *a theory gaining credence in Whitehall* ○ *The evidence gives/lends credence to his arguments.*

credentials /krəˈdenʃlz/ *n* [pl] **1** ~ (**for/as sth**); ~ (**to do sth**) qualities, achievements, qualifications, etc that make a person suitable: *She has the perfect credentials for the job.* ○ *He will have first to establish his leadership credentials.* **2** documents showing that a person is what he or she claims to be, can be trusted, etc: *examined sb's credentials.*

credible /ˈkredəbl/ *adj* that can be believed; convincing: *a credible witness* ○ *Her story seems barely credible* (ie seems almost impossible to believe). ○ *Is there a credible alternative to the nuclear deterrent?* Compare CREDITABLE.

▶ **credibility** /ˌkredəˈbɪləti/ *n* [U] **1** the quality of being generally accepted and trusted: *a book which restored/bolstered his academic credibility* ○ *After the recent scandal the government has lost all credibility.* **2** the quality of being credible: *beyond credibility.*

credibly /-əbli/ *adv*: *I am credibly informed that* (ie I have been told by sb who can be believed)...

■ ˌcrediˈbility gap *n* [sing] the difference between what sb says and what is generally thought to be true.

credit¹ /ˈkredɪt/ *n* **1** [U] permission to delay payment for goods and services until after they have been received; the system of paying in this way: *refuse/grant sb credit* ○ *I bought it on credit* (ie did not have to pay for it until some time after I got it). ○ *give/offer sb six months' interest-free credit* (ie allow sb to pay within six months, without any extra* charge) ○ *a credit period/agreement/limit* ○ *the increase in consumer credit.* Compare HIRE PURCHASE. **2(a)** [U] the status of being trusted to pay money back to sb who lends it to one: *How's your credit these days?* **(b)** [C, U] a sum of money lent by a bank, etc; a loan: *The bank refused further credit to the company.* See also CREDIT RATING, CREDITWORTHY. **3(a)** [U] the state of having money in one's bank account: *Your account is in credit* (ie There is money in it). ○ *I'm about £400 in credit at the moment.* ○ *You have a credit balance of £250.* **(b)** [C, U] a sum of money paid into an account, esp a bank account: *a credit of £35* ○ *You'll be paid by direct credit into your bank account.* **(c)** [C] a record of such a payment: *the credit column.* Compare DEBIT. **4** [U] ~ **(for sth)** praise; approval; respect: *a player who rarely seems to get the credit he deserves* ○ *I can't take any of the credit — the others did all the work.* ○ *I was furious when she was given the credit for my idea.* ○ *At least give him credit for trying* (ie praise him, even though he did not succeed). ○ *His courage has brought great credit to/reflects credit on* (ie gives a good reputation to) *his regiment.* Compare DISCREDIT[2]. **5 the credits** [pl] a list of the actors, the director and all the other people who worked on a film, television programme, etc, shown at the beginning or end of it. **6** [sing] ~ **to sb** a person or thing that, because of their qualities or achievements, brings honour or respect to sb/sth else, causing people to respect them/it: *She is a credit to her teachers.* **7** [C] (*esp US*) an entry(3a) on a record showing that a student has completed a course: *have three credits each in Math and English.* **IDM do sb credit**; **do credit to sb/sth** to make sb worthy of praise or respect: *Your honesty does you credit.* ○ *His improved performance does great credit to his trainer.* **have sth to one's credit** to have achieved sth: *He is only thirty, and already he has four films to his credit* (ie he has made four films). **on the 'credit side** (used to introduce the good points about sth, esp when the bad points are also mentioned): *On the credit side, he's always willing to work after hours.* **to sb's credit** making sb worthy of praise or respect: *Jack, to his credit, refused to get involved.* ○ *It was to her credit that she managed not to get angry.*

■ **'credit account** (*US* **charge account**) *n* an account[1](2) with a shop that allows one to pay for goods at fixed intervals, eg every month, rather than paying the full price immediately.

'credit card *n* a small plastic card that allows its holder to buy goods and services on credit[1](1) and to pay at fixed intervals: *credit-card transactions.* Compare CHARGE CARD, CHEQUE CARD.

'credit note *n* (*commerce*) a note given to a customer who has returned goods, allowing her or him to have other goods with a value equal to those returned.

'credit rating *n* a judgement by other people of how reliable sb is likely to be in paying for goods bought on credit[1](1).

'credit transfer *n* a transfer of money direct from one bank account to another, without using a cheque.

credit[2] /'kredɪt/ *v* **1** ~ **sb/sth with doing sth**;~ **sth to sb/sth** (usu passive) to acknowledge that sb/sth is responsible for doing sth, esp sth good: [Vnpr] *She was wrongly credited with being the author of the piece.* ○ *The invention of the electric guitar is credited to him.* **2** ~ **sb/sth with sth**; ~ **sth to sb/sth (a)** to believe that sb/sth has a particular good quality or feature: [Vnpr] *Until now I've always credited you with more sense.* ○ *The relics are credited with miraculous powers.* ○ *Miraculous powers are credited to the relics.* **(b)** ~ **sb/sth as sth** (usu passive) to believe sb/sth to be sb/sth of a particular type or quality: [Vn-n] *The cheetah is generally credited as*

the world's fastest animal. **3** (used mainly in questions and negative sentences) to believe sth, esp sth surprising or unexpected: [Vn] *And, would you credit it, he won first prize!* ○ *I can barely credit what she said.* **4** ~ **sb/sth with sth**; ~ **sth to sb/sth** to record an amount as having been paid into sb's bank account: [Vnpr] *credit a customer with $80* ○ *credit $80 to a customer/an account.*

creditable /'kredɪtəbl/ *adj* (*fml*) good and deserving praise but not outstanding; bringing credit[1](4): *a creditable attempt* ○ *explaining it in a way creditable to himself* ○ *She won a creditable 16 per cent of the vote.* Compare CREDIBLE. ▶ **creditably** /'kredɪtəbli/ *adv*: *She performed very creditably in the exam.*

creditor /'kredɪtə(r)/ *n* a person, company, etc to whom money is owed: *His creditors are demanding to be paid.* ○ *Japan is one of the world's leading creditor countries.*

creditworthy /'kredɪtwɜːði/ *adj* (of people, business firms, etc) accepted as safe to lend money to, because of being reliable in paying money back. ▶ **creditworthiness** *n* [U].

credo /'kriːdəʊ, 'kreɪdəʊ/ *n* (*pl* **credos**) a set of beliefs: *her political credo.*

credulity /krɪ'djuːləti; *US* -'duː-/ *n* [U] a tendency to believe things too willingly or readily: *a statement which stretches/strains one's credulity to the limit* (ie is almost impossible to believe).

credulous /'kredjələs; *US* -dʒə-/ *adj* too ready to believe things. Compare INCREDULOUS.

creed /kriːd/ *n* **1** [C] a set of beliefs or opinions, esp religious beliefs: *people of all races, colours and creeds* ○ *What is your political creed?* **2 the Creed** [sing] a short summary of Christian belief, esp as said or sung as part of a church service(8).

creek /kriːk; *US also* krɪk/ *n* **1** (*Brit*) a narrow stretch of water flowing in from a coast; an INLET(1). **2** (*US*) a small river; a stream. **IDM up the 'creek** (*infml*) in serious difficulties: *I'm really up the creek without my car.*

creel /kriːl/ *n* a basket for holding fish that one has just caught.

creep /kriːp/ *v* (*pt, pp* **crept**) **1(a)** (of people or animals) to move slowly, quietly and carefully, esp bending down so as not to be seen: [Vpr] *The cat crept silently towards the bird.* [Vadv] *They crept downstairs, anxious not to wake the baby.* [also Vp]. ⇨ note at PROWL. **(b)** to move or develop very slowly: [Vpr] *watching the sunlight creep across the window* ○ *A feeling of drowsiness crept over him.* [Vp] *creeping along at 10 miles per hour.* **2** (of plants) to grow along the ground, up walls, etc by means of long stems or roots: [Vpr] *Ivy had crept up the castle walls.* [V] *a creeping vine.* See also CREEPER. **IDM make one's/sb's flesh crawl/creep** ⇨ FLESH. **PHRV ˌcreep 'in/into sth** to begin to occur or happen: *A number of mistakes had crept in.* ○ *New ideas are creeping slowly into the firm.* **ˌcreep 'up** to increase in amount, price, etc: *House prices are creeping up again.* **ˌcreep 'up on sb** **1** to move slowly nearer to sb without being seen: *She crept up on him from behind.* **2** to begin to affect sb, esp before they realize it: *Old age soon creeps up on you.*

▶ **creep** *n* (*infml derog*) a person who tries to win sb's favour by always agreeing with them or doing things for them: *He's a prize/real creep!* **IDM give sb the 'creeps** (*infml*) **1** to make sb afraid and cause an unpleasant sensation in their skin, as if things are creeping over it: *This old house gives me the creeps.* **2** to make sb feel extreme dislike: *I can't stand him — he gives me the creeps.*

creeping *adj* [attrib] (of sth bad) gradual and not easily noticed: *creeping inflation in the housing market* ○ *The disease results in creeping paralysis.*

creeper /'kriːpə(r)/ *n* a plant that grows along the

ground, up walls, etc, often winding itself round other plants.

creepy /ˈkriːpi/ *adj* (**-ier, -iest**) (*infml*) **1** causing an unpleasant feeling of fear or horror: *a creepy ghost story* ○ *It's sort of creepy down in the cellar!* **2** strange in a disturbing way: *That was a really creepy coincidence.*

creepy-crawly /ˌkriːpi ˈkrɔːli/ *n* (*infml esp Brit*) an insect, a worm, etc thought of as unpleasant or frightening.

cremate /krəˈmeɪt/ *v* (often passive) to burn a dead body to ashes, esp in a ceremonial way at a funeral: [Vn] *He wants to be cremated, not buried.*

▶ **cremation** /krəˈmeɪʃn/ *n* (**a**) [U] the action of cremating sb: *the cost of cremation.* (**b**) [C] a funeral at which a body is cremated: *She attended John's cremation last Tuesday.*

crematorium /ˌkreməˈtɔːriəm/ *n* (*pl* **crematoriums** or **crematoria** /-ˈtɔːriə/) a building in which bodies are cremated.

crème de la crème /ˌkrem də lɑ ˈkrem/ **the crème de la crème** *n* [sing] (*French fml or joc*) the best people or things from a group: *'This school takes only the crème de la crème,' she said.*

crenellated (*US* **-elated**) /ˈkrenəleɪtɪd/ *adj* having BATTLEMENTS: *a crenellated castle/wall.* ➪ picture at CASTLE.

creole /ˈkriːəʊl/ *n* **1** [U, C] a language formed by a mixing of two other languages, and used as the main language in the community in which it is spoken. Compare PIDGIN. **2** (*usu* **Creole**) [C] (**a**) a person of mixed European and African race, esp one living in the West Indies. (**b**) a person who has among her or his ancestors one of the first European people who settled in the West Indies or Spanish America, or one of the French or Spanish people who settled in the southern states of the USA: *Creole cookery.*

creosote /ˈkriːəsəʊt/ *n* [U] a thick brown oily liquid used to preserve wood.

▶ **creosote** *v* [Vn] to treat sth with creosote.

crepe (also **crêpe**, **crape**) /ˈkreɪp/ *n* [U] **1** a light thin fabric whose surface looks as though it has been repeatedly folded and crushed: *a black crepe dress.* **2** a type of tough rubber used for the soles of shoes: *crepe-soled shoes.*

■ ˌ**crepe ˈpaper** *n* [U] a type of thin paper whose surface looks like that of crepe(1). It is used esp for making decorations.

crept *pt, pp* of CREEP.

crescendo /krəˈʃendəʊ/ *n* (*pl* **crescendos**) **1** [C, U] (**a**) (*music*) a gradual increase in how loudly a piece of music is played or sung. Compare DIMINUENDO. (**b**) a gradual increase in any noise: *Voices rose in a crescendo and drowned him out.* **2** [C *usu sing*] (*infml*) (**a**) the loudest point of a period of continuous noise: *The children's shrieks suddenly reached a crescendo.* (**b**) the busiest, most intense moment in a period of activity or excitement: *The advertising campaign reached a crescendo just before Christmas.*

crescent /ˈkresnt; *Brit* also ˈkreznt/ *n* **1** [C] a narrow curved shape that is at its widest in the middle and becomes narrow and pointed at each end, like the new moon. ➪ picture. **2** (often in names) a curved street with a continuous row of houses on it: *I live at 11, Park Crescent.* ➪ picture. **3** the Crescent [sing] the religion of Islam: *the Cross (ie Christianity) and the Crescent.*

crescent

cress /kres/ *n* [U] any of various small plants with hot-tasting leaves used in sandwiches and salads (SALAD).

crest /krest/ *n* **1**(**a**) the top of a slope or hill. (**b**) the white top of a large wave. ➪ picture at SURFING. **2** a design representing a family, an organization, etc, esp one that has a long history: *a cap with the school crest and motto on it.* **3** a small group of feathers standing up on a bird's head. **IDM the crest of a/ the ˈwave** the point of greatest success, happiness, etc: *After its election victory, the party is on the crest of a wave.* ○ *He was riding the crest of a new wave of popular fame.*

▶ **crested** *adj* **1** having a crest(2): *crested note-paper.* **2** (used esp in names of birds or animals) having a crest(3): *the great-crested grebe.*

crestfallen /ˈkrestfɔːlən/ *adj* sad because of unexpected failure, disappointment, etc: *He returned empty-handed and crestfallen.*

cretin /ˈkretɪn; *US* ˈkriːtn/ *n* (*offensive*) a very stupid person: *Why did you do that, you cretin?* ▶ **cretinous** /ˈkretɪnəs; *US* ˈkriːtnəs/ *adj*.

crevasse /krəˈvæs/ *n* a deep open crack, esp in ice.

crevice /ˈkrevɪs/ *n* a narrow opening or crack in a rock or wall.

crew /kruː/ *n* [CGp] **1**(**a**) all the people working on a ship, an aircraft, etc: *The ship had a crew of 60.* ○ *All the passengers and crew survived the crash.* (**b**) all these people except the officers: *the officers and crew of the SS Neptune.* (**c**) a rowing team: *a member of the Cambridge crew.* **2** a group of people working together: *a camera/film crew* ○ *an ambulance crew.* **3** (*usu derog*) a group of people: *The people she'd invited were a pretty **motley crew**.*

▶ **crew** *v* ~ (**for sb/on sth**) to act as a member of a crew(1,2) esp on a ship: [Vnpr] *A group of friends agreed to crew for him on the trip.* [Vn] *Ambulances will be crewed by military personnel.*

■ ˈ**crew cut** *n* a very short HAIRSTYLE for men.

ˌ**crew ˈneck** *n* a narrow band round the neck of a JERSEY(1). ➪ picture at NECK.

crewman /ˈkruːmən/ *n* (*pl* **-men** /-mən/) a member of a crew(1,2).

crib¹ /krɪb/ *n* **1** [C] (*esp US*) = COT 1. ➪ picture at COT. **2** [C] a wooden framework for holding food for animals. **3** [C] a model, eg in a church at Christmas, representing the scene at Christ's birth. **4** [U] = CRIBBAGE.

crib² /krɪb/ *n* (*infml*) **1** a thing used to help one understand or remember sth, eg a version of a foreign text one is studying translated into one's own language. **2** a thing copied dishonestly from the work of another person, eg in an examination.

▶ **crib** *v* (**-bb-**) ~ (**sth**) (**from/off sb**) (*infml*) to copy another student's written work dishonestly: [Vnpr, Vpr] *In the exam, I cribbed (an answer) from the girl next to me.* [V] *She's always cribbing.* [also Vn].

cribbage /ˈkrɪbɪdʒ/ (also **crib**) *n* [U] a card-game in which the score is kept by putting small pegs (PEG¹ 1) in holes in a board.

crick /krɪk/ *n* [sing] a painful stiff feeling in one's muscles, esp in the neck: *to have/get a crick in one's neck/back.*

▶ **crick** *v* [Vn] to cause a crick in one's neck.

cricket¹ /ˈkrɪkɪt/ *n* [U] a game played on grass with bats and ball by two teams of 11 players each. Each member of one team tries to score runs by hitting the balls bowled to them by members of the other team. Players are out when the balls bowled to them hit the WICKET(a), or in other ways. The team scoring the most runs wins: *a cricket match/ball/team.* ➪ picture. **IDM not ˈcricket** (*infml esp Brit*) unfair; not honourable: *You can't do it without telling him; it just isn't cricket.*

▶ **cricketer** *n* a cricket player.

cricketing *adj* [attrib] of or for cricket; playing cricket: ˈcricketing boots ○ *a* ˌcricketing ˈnation.

cricket² /ˈkrɪkɪt/ *n* a small brown jumping insect

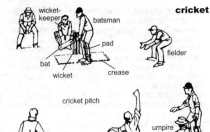

cricket

wicket-keeper, batsman, pad, fielder, bat, wicket, crease

cricket pitch

umpire, bowler

that makes a high-pitched sound by rubbing its front wings together: *the chirping of crickets.*

cried *pt, pp* of CRY¹.

crier /ˈkraɪə(r)/ *n* = TOWN CRIER.

cries /kraɪz/ **1** *3rd pers sing pres t* of CRY¹. **2** *pl* of CRY².

crikey /ˈkraɪki/ *interj* (*Brit infml*) (used to express surprise, fear, etc): *Crikey! What a big dog!* ◦ *Oh crikey! I've forgotten to buy her a present.*

crime /kraɪm/ *n* **1(a)** [C] an offence for which one may be punished by law: ***commit a (serious) crime*** ◦ *a minor crime like shoplifting* ◦ *convicted of crimes against humanity* ◦ ***war crimes.*** (**b**) [U] activities that involve breaking the law: *an increase in crime* ◦ *the spread of organized crime* ◦ *the police role in preventing and detecting crime* ◦ *crime prevention* ◦ *crime fiction/novels* (ie stories dealing with crime) ◦ *He took to a life of crime* (ie became a criminal). **2** (usu **a crime**) [sing] an act that is foolish or morally wrong: *It's a crime to waste money like that.* ◦ *It's a crime the way he bullies his children.*

criminal /ˈkrɪmɪnl/ *adj* **1** [usu attrib] of or involving crime: *criminal offences/damage/negligence.* **2** [attrib] concerned with crime: *criminal law* ◦ *a criminal lawyer.* Compare CIVIL 4. **3** morally wrong; DISGRACEFUL: *a criminal waste of public money* ◦ *It's criminal the way she lies and cheats to get what she wants.*
▶ **criminal** *n* a person who commits a crime or crimes: *petty criminals* ◦ *a war criminal.*
criminality /ˌkrɪmɪˈnæləti/ *n* [U] criminal acts; the state of being involved in crime.
criminalize, -ise /ˈkrɪmɪnəlaɪz/ *v* **1** to make sth illegal by passing a new law: [Vn] *criminalize abortion.* **2** to treat sb as a criminal: [Vn] *We believe we are being criminalized and persecuted.*
criminally /-nəli/ *adv* as defined by criminal(2) law: *criminally insane* ◦ *Not a single officer has been found criminally liable.*

criminology /ˌkrɪmɪˈnɒlədʒi/ *n* [U] the scientific study of crime and criminals. ▶ **criminologist** /-dʒɪst/ *n*.

crimp /krɪmp/ *v* [Vn] (**a**) to press cloth, paper, etc into small folds or ridges. (**b**) to make waves in sb's hair by pressing with a hot iron¹(2).

crimson /ˈkrɪmzn/ *adj, n* [U] (of) a deep red: *crimson flowers* ◦ *Jane went bright crimson* (ie Her face became red with embarrassment).

cringe /krɪndʒ/ *v* **1** ~ (**at sth**) to move back or lower one's body in fear; to cower: [V] *a child cringing in terror* [Vpr] *The dog cringed at the sight of the whip.* ◦ (*fig*) *I cringe with embarrassment* (ie feel very embarrassed) *when I reread those first stories I wrote.* **2** ~ (**to/before sb**) (*derog*) to show excessive respect to sb who is more powerful than oneself in

an attempt to gain favour from them: [Vpr] *She's always cringing to the boss.* [also V].

crinkle /ˈkrɪŋkl/ *n* a thin fold or WRINKLE(1,2), eg in paper, cloth or skin.
▶ **crinkle** *v* to develop crinkles; to produce crinkles in sth: [V, Vp] *The paper blackened, crinkled (up) and turned to ashes.* [Vn] *the dead plant's crinkled leaves* [also Vnp].
crinkly /ˈkrɪŋkli/ *adj* (**a**) having crinkles: *crinkly plastic packing material.* (**b**) (of hair) having tight curls.

crinoline /ˈkrɪnəlɪn/ *n* a light framework covered with fabric, formerly worn under a long skirt to make it stand out.

cripple /ˈkrɪpl/ (*sometimes offensive*) *n* a person who is unable to walk or move properly because of disease or injury to the back or legs: (*fig*) *a psychological cripple.* Compare DISABLED.
▶ **cripple** *v* (usu passive) **1** to make sb a cripple: [Vn] *crippled by polio* ◦ *crippled with rheumatism* ◦ *their crippled daughter.* **2** to damage or harm sb/sth seriously: [Vn] *a ship crippled by a storm* ◦ *The business has been crippled by the recession.* ◦ *The country has crippling* (ie extremely large) *debts.*

crisis /ˈkraɪsɪs/ *n* (*pl* **crises** /-siːz/) [C,U] a time of great difficulty or danger or when an important decision must be made, eg in an illness, sb's life, history, etc: *financial/economic/political/domestic crises* ◦ *a crisis in southern Africa* ◦ *come to/reach a crisis* ◦ *a government in crisis* (ie going through a difficult period) ◦ *In times of crisis it's good to have a friend to turn to.* ◦ *The fever has passed its crisis* (ie its most dangerous point). ◦ *The government is holding crisis talks with the unions.* See also CRITICAL 3.

crisp /krɪsp/ *adj* (**-er, -est**) (*usu approv*) **1(a)** (esp of food) hard, dry and easily broken: *a crisp cracker/biscuit* ◦ *crisp pastry/toast* ◦ *The snow was crisp underfoot.* (**b**) (esp of fruit or vegetables) firm and fresh: *a crisp apple/lettuce.* (**c**) (esp of paper or cloth) slightly stiff: *a crisp new $5 bill* ◦ *a crisp white shirt.* **2** (of the air or the weather) dry and cold: *a crisp winter morning* ◦ *the crisp air of an autumn day.* **3** (of hair) tightly curled. **4** (of pictures, designs, etc) clear and distinct: *crisp architectural lines* ◦ *in crisp focus.* **5** (*sometimes derog*) (of sb's manner, way of speaking, etc) quick and confident, often suggesting one is busy or not interested; sharp; BRISK: *a crisp order* ◦ *Her response was crisp and unfriendly.* ◦ *His answer was crisp and clear.*
▶ **crisp** (also **poˌtato ˈcrisp**, *US* **poˈtato chip, chip**) *n* a thin slice of potato, fried and dried, often with different flavours and sold in packets. ⇨ picture at POTATO. **IDM** **burn sth to a crisp** ⇨ BURN.
crisp *v* ~ (**sth**) (**up**) (*Brit*) to become or make sth crisp: [Vnp] *crisp the bread up in the oven* [Vp] *The top of the pie is crisping up nicely.* [also Vn].
crisply *adv*: *crisply fried* ◦ *'Take a seat,' she said crisply.*
crispness *n* [U].
crispy *adj* (*infml approv*) = CRISP *adj* 1a,b: *crispy bacon.*

crispbread /ˈkrɪspbred/ *n* [C,U] a thin crisp biscuit usu made from RYE and eaten esp with cheese: *a lunch of crispbreads and cottage cheese.*

criss-cross /ˈkrɪs krɒs; *US* krɔːs/ *adj* [attrib] with lines or paths crossing each other: *a criss-cross pattern/design.*
▶ **criss-cross** *v* to form a criss-cross pattern on sth: [V] *railway lines criss-crossing in a complex network* [Vn] *Drainage canals criss-cross the landscape.* [Vnpr] *a wooded area criss-crossed with tracks.*

criterion /kraɪˈtɪəriən/ *n* (*pl* **criteria** /-riə/) a standard or principle by which sth is judged: *Success in making money is not always a good criterion of success in life.* ◦ *What are the criteria for deciding* (ie How do we decide) *who gets the prize?*

critic /ˈkrɪtɪk/ n **1** a person who expresses a low opinion of sb/sth, shows faults in sb/sth, etc: *I am my own severest critic.* ○ *She confounded her critics by breaking the record* (ie They said she would not be able to do so, but she did). **2** a person who judges the quality of sth, esp works of art, literature and music: *a music/theatre/literary/critic* ○ *a play much praised by the critics.*

critical /ˈkrɪtɪkl/ adj **1** ~ (of sb/sth) indicating the faults in sb/sth or one's disapproval of sb/sth: *a critical remark/report* ○ *The inquiry was critical of her handling of the affair.* ○ *(derog) Why are you always so critical?* **2** [attrib] of or relating to the judgement or analysis of sth, esp literature, art, etc: *In the current critical climate her work is not popular.* ○ *The movie has received critical acclaim* (ie praise from the critics). ○ *Try to develop a more critical attitude, instead of accepting everything at face value.* **3(a)** of or at a crisis: *We are at a critical time in our country's history.* ○ *The patient's condition is critical* (ie He is very ill and may die). **(b)** of the greatest importance; CRUCIAL: *The depth of the foundations is critical.* ○ *The growing undercurrent of public protest proved a critical factor.* ▶ **critically** /-ɪkli/ adv: *speak critically of sb* ○ *He is critically ill.*

criticism /ˈkrɪtɪsɪzəm/ n **1(a)** [U] the action or process of indicating the faults of sb/sth or one's disapproval of sb/sth: *a scheme that is open to criticism* ○ *The bank's actions* **attracted heavy/strong/ widespread criticism**. ○ *He hates/can't take criticism* (ie being criticized). **(b)** [U,C] a remark that indicates a fault or faults: *in response to the* **criticism levelled** *at senior officers* ○ *I have two main criticisms of your plan.* **2(a)** [U] the art of making judgements on literature, art, etc: *literary criticism.* **(b)** [C] such a judgement.

criticize, -ise /ˈkrɪtɪsaɪz/ v **1** ~ sb/sth (for sth) to indicate the faults of sb/sth: [V,Vn] *Stop criticizing (my work)!* [Vnpr] *He was criticized by the committee for failing to report the accident.* [V.n ing] *He criticized my taking unnecessary risks.* **2** to form and express a judgement on a work of art, literature, etc: [Vn] *teaching students how to criticize poetry.*

critique /krɪˈtiːk/ n a critical(2) analysis: *The book presents a critique of the government's economic policies.*

croak /krəʊk/ n a deep harsh sound, like that made by a FROG.
▶ **croak** v **1** [V] (of a bird, FROG, etc) to make a croak or croaks. **2** (of a person) to speak or say sth with a deep harsh voice: [V] *Because of her sore throat all she could do was croak.* [V,Vnp] *He croaked (out) a few words.* [also V.speech]. **3** [V] (*sl*) to die.

crochet /ˈkrəʊʃeɪ; US krəʊˈʃeɪ/ n [U] **(a)** a method of making clothes, mats, etc from wool or thread by using a special needle with a hook at the end to make a pattern of connected loops. **(b)** fabric made in this way: *a beige crochet sweater.*
▶ **crochet** v (*pt, pp* **crocheted** /-ʃeɪd/; *pres p* **crocheting** /-ʃeɪɪŋ/) to make sth in this way: [Vn] *a crocheted skirt* [also V].

crock¹ /krɒk/ n **1** [C] (*dated*) a large pot or JAR¹(1) made of baked clay, eg for containing water: *a bread crock* ○ (*US △ sl*) *That's a crock of shit* (ie That's completely false). **2** crocks [pl] = CROCKERY.

crock² /krɒk/ n (*Brit infml*) **1** a vehicle that is old or in bad condition. **2** an old person: *What does a young girl like you want with an old crock like me?*

crockery /ˈkrɒkəri/ n (also **crocks** [pl]) cups, plates, dishes, etc, esp ones made of baked clay.

crocodile /ˈkrɒkədaɪl/ n **1** a large reptile that lives esp in rivers and lakes in hot parts of the world. Crocodiles have a hard skin, a long tail, and very big jaws. Compare ALLIGATOR. **2** (*Brit infml*) a long line of people, esp children, walking in pairs. **IDM**

¹crocodile tears the insincere expression of sorrow: *She shed crocodile tears* (ie pretended to be sorry) *when she dismissed him from his job.*

crocus /ˈkrəʊkəs/ n (pl **crocuses** /-sɪz/) a small plant that produces yellow, purple or white flowers early in spring. ⇨ picture at FLOWER.

croft /krɒft; US krɔːft/ n (*Brit*) a small farm or the house on it, esp in Scotland.
▶ **crofter** n (*Brit*) a person who rents or owns a small farm, esp in Scotland.

croissant /ˈkrwæsɒ̃; US krwɑːˈsɒ̃/ n (*French*) a roll with a curved shape made of light pastry, eaten esp at breakfast. ⇨ picture at BREAD.

crone /krəʊn/ n (*usu derog*) an ugly old woman.

crony /ˈkrəʊni/ n (*infml often derog*) a close¹(2b) friend or companion: *He spends every evening drinking in the pub with his cronies.*

crook /krʊk/ n **1** (*infml*) a dishonest person; a criminal: *The crooks got away with most of the money.* ○ *That used-car salesman is a real crook.* **2** a bend or curve in sth, esp at one's elbow or knee: *carrying a rifle* **in the crook of his arm** (ie at the inside of his elbow with the arm bent). **3(a)** a long stick with a large hook at one end, used esp formerly for catching sheep: *a shepherd's crook.* **(b)** (*infml*) = CROSIER. **IDM by hook or by crook** ⇨ HOOK¹.
▶ **crook** v to bend esp one's finger or arm: [Vn, Vnpr] *She crooked a finger (at me) and beckoned me to follow her.*
crook adj [usu pred] (*Austral infml*) ill: *I'm feeling a bit crook.*

crooked /ˈkrʊkɪd/ adj **1** not straight or level; twisted, bent or curved: *a crooked lane/branch/table* ○ *a crooked smile* (ie one in which the mouth slopes down at one side) ○ *You've got your hat on crooked.* **2** (*infml*) (of people or actions) dishonest; illegal: *a crooked businessman/deal* ○ *All the officials are crooked.* ▶ **crookedly** adv. **crookedness** n [U].

croon /kruːn/ v ~ (sth) (to sb) to sing or say sth quietly and gently: [V,Vn] *croon soothingly (to a child)* [Vn] *croon a sentimental tune* [Vnpr] *croon a baby to sleep* [V.speech] 'What a beautiful little baby,' she crooned.
▶ **crooner** n (*becoming dated*) a singer who sings sentimental songs.

crop /krɒp/ n **1(a)** [C] an amount of grain, fruit, etc grown or collected in one year or season: *the potato crop* ○ *a good crop of rice* ○ *a bumper* (ie very large) *crop* ○ *suffering severe drought and crop failure.* **(b)** [C] a plant that is grown in large quantities: *a root crop, such as carrots* ○ *The main crops are maize and coffee.* **(c)** crops [pl] agricultural plants in the fields: *spray/treat the crops with chemicals/pesticides.* See also CASH CROP. **2** [sing] ~ of sth a group of people or quantity of things appearing or produced at the same time: *this year's crop of students* ○ *The programme brought quite a crop of complaints from viewers.* **3** [C] a very short HAIRCUT. **4** [C] a part of a bird's throat like a bag, where food is stored before passing into the stomach. **5** (also **¹hunting-crop**) [C] a whip with a short loop, used by riders.
▶ **crop** v (-pp-) **1(a)** to cut sth very short, esp sb's hair: [Vn, Vn-adj] *with hair cropped (short).* **(b)** to cut the edges of a picture or photograph: [Vn] *crop a photo so it fits in the frame.* **(c)** (of animals) to bite off and eat the tops of plants: [Vn, Vn-adj] *Sheep had cropped the grass (short).* **2(a)** (of plants, fields, etc) to bear a crop(1a): [Vadv] *The beans cropped well this year.* **(b)** (usu passive) to pick or gather a crop(1a): [Vn] *Lemons are cropped three times a year.* **(c)** to use land to grow crops (CROP 1b,c): [Vn] *The river valley is intensively cropped.* **PHRV ¹crop ¹up** to appear or occur, esp unexpectedly: *All sorts of difficulties have cropped up.* ○ *The subject cropped up quite naturally as we talked.*

■ **'crop circle** (also **'corn circle**) *n* a usu circular area in a field of crops that has suddenly become flat. There are several theories about how crop circles are formed.

cropper /'krɒpə(r)/ *n* **IDM** **come a 'cropper** (*infml*) **1** to fall over. **2** to fail; to suffer a disaster: *Foreign investors came a cropper.*

croquet /'krəʊkeɪ; *US* krəʊ'keɪ/ *n* [U] a game played on a lawn, in which each player uses a wooden MALLET(2) to knock wooden balls through a series of hoops (HOOP 3).

croquette /krəʊ'ket/ *n* a ball of soft potato, fish, etc covered with BREADCRUMBS and cooked in fat.

crosier (also **crozier**) /'krəʊzɪə(r); *US* 'krəʊʒər/ (also *infml* **crook**) *n* a long ceremonial stick, usu with a hook at one end, carried by a bishop.

   cross

swastika   **Maltese cross**   **Latin cross**

cross¹ /krɒs; *US* krɔːs/ *n* **1** [C] a mark made by drawing one line across another, eg × or +: *The place is marked on the map with a cross.* ○ *The teacher put a cross next to my name.* See also NOUGHTS AND CROSSES. ⇨ picture. **2(a)** [C] a wooden frame made of a long piece of wood with a shorter piece fixed across it near the top. In ancient times people were hung on crosses and left there to die as a punishment. **(b) the Cross** [sing] (in Christianity) the cross on which Christ died. **(c)** [C] anything having the shape of this cross and used as a Christian symbol: *There were gold crosses embroidered on the altar cloth.* ○ *She wore a small silver cross on a chain round her neck.* ○ *We met at the stone cross on the village green.* ⇨ picture at CHURCH. **(d)** [C usu *sing*] a sign in the shape of a cross made with the right hand as a Christian religious act: *The priest made a cross over her head.* **(e) the Cross** [sing] the Christian religion: *the Cross and the Crescent* (ie Christianity and Islam). See also RED CROSS. **3** (usu **Cross**) [C] a small piece of metal in the shape of a cross given as a MEDAL for courage, etc: *the Victoria Cross* ○ *the Distinguished Service Cross.* **4** [C usu *sing*] ~ **(between A and B) (a)** an animal or a plant that is produced from different breeds or varieties: *A mule is a cross between a horse and a donkey.* **(b)** a mixture of two different things: *a play that is a cross between farce and tragedy.* See also HYBRID. **5** [C] a source of sorrow, worry, etc; a problem: *We all have our crosses to bear.*

cross² /krɒs; *US* krɔːs/ *v* **1** ~ **(over) (from sth/to sth)** to go across; to pass or extend from one side to the other side of sth: [V, Vp] *The river is too deep; we can't cross (over).* [Vpr] *He crossed to the bookcase in the corner.* ○ *cross from Dover to Calais* ○ *cross into China* [Vn] *cross a road/a river/a bridge/a desert/ the sea/the mountains* ○ *cross France by train* ○ *Electricity cables cross the valley.* ○ (*fig*) *A look of annoyance crossed her face.* ○ (*fig*) *It was the type of film that crossed all social barriers* (ie that appealed to people of all ages, classes, races, etc). **2(a)** (no passive) (of people travelling or letters in the post) to pass each other going in opposite directions: [Vn] *We crossed a young couple on the way.* [V] *Our letters crossed in the mail* (ie Each was sent before the other was received). **(b)** to pass across each other: [V] *The roads cross just outside the town.* [Vp] *The straps cross over at the back and are tied at the waist.* ○ [V] (*fig*) *Our paths crossed* (ie We met by chance) *several times.* **3** to put or place sth across or over sth else: [Vn] *cross one's legs* (ie place one leg over the other) ○ *sit with one's legs crossed* ⇨ picture at CROSS-LEGGED. ○ *cross one's arms on one's chest* ○ *a flag with a design of two crossed keys* ○ (*fig*) *We seem*

to have got a crossed line (ie a telephone call that interrupts another call because of a wrong connection). **4** (in football, etc) to kick or pass a ball sideways across the pitch: [V, Vpr] *Wilson crossed (to Bates).* **5** to draw a line across sth: [Vn] *cross the t's* ○ *cross a cheque* (ie, in Britain, draw two lines across it so that it can only be paid through a bank account) ○ *a crossed cheque* (ie a cheque marked in this way). **6** ~ **oneself** (no passive) to make the sign of the cross¹(2d) on one's chest: [Vn] *He crossed himself as he passed the church.* **7** to oppose or speak against sb or their plans or wishes: [Vn] *She doesn't like to be crossed.* ○ *to be crossed in love* (ie fail to win the love of sb one loves). **8** ~ **(sth with sth)** to cause two different types of animal or plant to breed together: [Vnpr] *to cross a horse with an ass* [Vn] *Varieties of roses can be crossed to vary their colour.* **IDM** **,cross one's 'bridges when one 'comes to them** to worry about a problem when it actually occurs and not before: *We'll cross that bridge when we come to it.* **cross one's 'fingers** to hope that one's plans will be successful: *I'm crossing my fingers that my proposal will be accepted.* ○ *Keep your fingers crossed!* **cross my 'heart (and hope to die)** (*infml saying*) (used to emphasize the honesty of what one says or promises): *I saw him do it — cross my heart.* **cross one's 'mind** (of thoughts, etc) to come into one's mind: *It never crossed my mind that she might lose* (ie I confidently expected her to win). **,cross sb's 'palm with 'silver** to give sb some money so that they will do one a favour, esp tell one's FORTUNE(3). **,cross sb's 'path** to meet sb, usu by chance: *I hope I never cross her path again.* **,cross the 'Rubicon** to take an action or start a process which is important and which cannot be reversed: *The chairman and I have crossed swords before over this issue.* **dot one's/the i's and cross one's/the t's** ⇨ DOT. **get, etc one's lines crossed** ⇨ LINE¹. **get one's wires crossed** ⇨ WIRE. **PHRV** **,cross sb/sth 'off (sth)** to draw a line through a person's name or an item on a list because he, she or it is no longer required or involved: *We can cross his name off (the list), as he's not coming.* **,cross sth 'out/'through** to draw a line through a word, usu because it is wrong: *Two words have been crossed out.* **,cross 'over** to move or change from one type of culture, music, political party, etc to another: *reggae crossing over into soul* ○ *films becoming popular in the core 16–25 age range before crossing over to mass appeal.* See also CROSS-OVER 2.

cross³ /krɒs; *US* krɔːs/ *adj* (**-er, -est**) **1** ~ **(with sb) (about sth)** (*infml esp Brit*) annoyed and rather angry: *I was cross with him for being late.* ○ *What are you so cross about?* ○ *She gave me a cross look.* **2** [attrib] (of currents or winds) moving in opposite directions; contrary: *Strong cross breezes make it difficult for boats to leave harbour.* See also CROSS-WIND. **IDM** **at cross 'purposes** not understanding or having the same aims, etc as each other: *I realized we had been (talking) at cross purposes.* ○ *ministries working at cross purposes.* ► **crossly** *adv*: *'Well, what did you expect?' she said crossly.*

cross- *comb form* (forming *ns*, *vs*, *adjs* and *advs*) involving movement or action from one thing to another or between two things: *'cross-current* ○ *,cross-'fertilize* ○ *,cross-'cultural* ○ *,cross-'country* ○ *,cross-Channel 'ferries.*

crossbar /'krɒsbɑː(r); *US* 'krɔːs-/ *n* a bar that goes across and between two things, eg the bar joining the two upright posts of a football goal, or the front and back of a bicycle frame. ⇨ picture at BICYCLE.

cross-benches /'krɒs bentʃɪz; *US* 'krɔːs/ *n* [pl] the seats in the British parliament (now only the House of Lords) occupied by those members who do not regularly support a particular political party.

▶ **cross-bencher** n a Member of Parliament who usu occupies the cross-benches.

crossbones /ˈkrɒsbəʊnz; US ˈkrɔːs-/ n [pl] ⇨ SKULL AND CROSSBONES.

cross-border /ˈkrɒs bɔːdə(r); US ˈkrɔːs/ adj [attrib] involving movement or action across a border(1a): *cross-border attacks.*

crossbow /ˈkrɒsbəʊ; US ˈkrɔːs-/ n a small powerful bow¹(1) fixed across a wooden support where the ARROW(1) is held and then released by pulling a TRIGGER. Compare LONGBOW.

cross-breed /ˈkrɒs briːd; US ˈkrɔːs/ n an animal or a plant produced by the breeding of different species or varieties.

▶ **cross-breed** v (pt, pp **cross-bred**) to breed or cause an animal or a plant to breed in this way: [Vn] *cross-bred sheep* [V] *improve crops by cross-breeding.* See also INTERBREED.

cross-check /ˌkrɒs ˈtʃek; US ˌkrɔːs/ v ~ sth (against sth) to make sure that information, figures, etc are correct, eg by using a different method or system to check them: [Vn] *Cross-check your answer by using a calculator.* [Vnpr] *He cross-checked the names against a list.* [also V]. ▶ ˈcross-check n.

cross-country /ˌkrɒs ˈkʌntri; US ˌkrɔːs/ adj [usu attrib], adv across fields or open country rather than on main roads, tracks, etc: *a ˌcross-country ˈrun/ˈrace/ˈroute* ∘ *cross-country skiing* ∘ *travel cross-country.* ⇨ picture at SKIING.

▶ **cross-country** n a cross-country race: *enter for the mile and the cross-country.*

cross-cultural /ˌkrɒs ˈkʌltʃərəl; US ˌkrɔːs/ adj involving, or containing ideas or elements from, two or more different cultures: *cross-cultural understanding/studies.*

cross-current /ˈkrɒs kʌrənt; US ˈkrɔːs/ n **1** a current in the sea or a river that crosses another. **2** a set of beliefs, views, etc contrary to others, esp those of the majority: *a cross-current of opinion against the prevailing view.*

cross-dressing /ˌkrɒs ˈdresɪŋ; US ˌkrɔːs/ n [U] the practice of wearing clothes usu worn by a person of the opposite sex; transvestism (TRANSVESTITE). ▶ ˌcross-ˈdresser n.

cross-examine /ˌkrɒs ɪgˈzæmɪn; US ˌkrɔːs/ v **1** (esp law) to question sb carefully in order to test whether answers given to previous questions are correct: [Vn] *The prosecution lawyer cross-examined the defence witness.* [also V]. **2** to question sb aggressively or in great detail: [Vn] *Whenever he comes in late his wife cross-examines him about where he's spent the evening.* Compare EXAMINE 3. ▶ **cross-examination** /ˌkrɒs ɪgˌzæmɪˈneɪʃn; US ˌkrɔːs/ n [U, C]: *He broke down under/during cross-examination* (ie while being cross-examined) *and admitted the truth.*

cross-eyed /ˈkrɒs aɪd; US ˈkrɔːs/ adj with one eye or both eyes turned permanently inward towards the nose: *a ˌcross-eyed ˈgirl* ∘ *The photograph makes him look cross-eyed.*

cross-fertilize, -ise /ˌkrɒs ˈfɜːtəlaɪz; US ˌkrɔːs/ v [Vn] **1** (botany) to FERTILIZE a plant by using POLLEN from a different type of plant. **2** to stimulate the development of sb/sth in a useful or positive way with ideas from a different area: *Literary studies have been cross-fertilized by new ideas in linguistics.* ▶ **cross-fertilization, -isation** /ˌkrɒs ˌfɜːtəlaɪˈzeɪʃn; US ˌkrɔːs ˌfɜːrtləˈzeɪʃn/ n [U, C].

crossfire /ˈkrɒsfaɪə(r); US ˈkrɔːs-/ n [U] **1** (military) the firing of guns from two or more points so that the bullets, etc cross each other: *Doctors who went to help the wounded were caught in the crossfire.* **2** a situation in which two people or groups are arguing or competing with each other and in which another becomes involved against their will: *When two industrial giants clash, small companies can get caught*

in the crossfire (ie become involved and suffer as a result).

cross-hatch /ˈkrɒs hætʃ; US ˌkrɔːs/ v to mark or colour sth with sets of parallel lines crossing each other: [Vn] *cross-hatch an area on a map/graph.* ▶ **cross-hatching** n [U].

crossing /ˈkrɒsɪŋ; US ˈkrɔːs-/ n **1** a place where two roads, two railways, or a road and a railway cross: *The accident happened at a dangerous crossing.* Compare JUNCTION, LEVEL CROSSING. **2(a)** a place, esp on a street, where people can cross safely: *The car slowed down as it approached the crossing.* Compare PEDESTRIAN CROSSING, PELICAN CROSSING, ZEBRA CROSSING. **(b)** a place where people can cross from one country to another: *arrested by guards at the border crossing.* **(c)** a place where a river can be crossed: *The next crossing point is several miles downstream.* **3** a journey across a sea, wide river, etc: *a ferry crossing* ∘ *a rough crossing from Dover to Calais.*

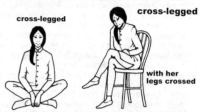

cross-legged   **cross-legged**

with her legs crossed

cross-legged /ˌkrɒs ˈlegd; US ˌkrɔːs/ adv with one leg over the other, esp at the ankles, and the knees apart: *sitting cross-legged on the floor.* ⇨ picture.

crossover /ˈkrɒsəʊvə(r); US ˈkrɔːs/ n **1** [C] a bridge or other structure for crossing a river, a main road, etc. **2** [U] the process of developing or changing from one type of culture, music, political party, etc to another.

crosspiece /ˈkrɒspiːs; US ˈkrɔːs-/ n a piece of a structure, tool, etc that lies or is fixed across another piece.

cross-ply /ˈkrɒsplaɪ; US ˈkrɔːs/ adj (of tyres) having layers of fabric with cords lying across them to strengthen them. Compare RADIAL n.

cross-question /ˌkrɒs ˈkwestʃən; US ˌkrɔːs/ v [Vn] to question sb thoroughly and often aggressively; to CROSS-EXAMINE(2) sb.

cross-reference /ˌkrɒs ˈrefrəns; US ˌkrɔːs/ n ~ (to sth) a note directing a reader to another part of a book, file, etc for further information: *follow up all the cross-references.*

▶ **cross-reference** v [Vn, Vnpr] ~ sth (to sth) (usu passive) to provide a book, etc with cross-references.

crossroads /ˈkrɒsrəʊdz; US ˈkrɔːs-/ n (pl unchanged) [sing v] a place where two roads meet and cross: *We came to a crossroads.* **IDM** at a/the ˈcrossroads at an important point in one's life, career, etc: *The business is at the crossroads: our future depends on the success of this merger.*

cross-section /ˈkrɒs sekʃn, ˌkrɒs ˈsekʃn; US ˈkrɔːs/ n **1** [C, U] a surface formed by cutting through sth, esp at right angles (RIGHT¹): *examining a cross-section of the kidney under the microscope* ∘ *The girder is square in cross-section.* **2** [C usu sing] a typical or representative sample: *a cross-section of the electors/population* ∘ *a broad cross-section of opinion.*

cross-stitch /ˈkrɒs stɪtʃ; US ˈkrɔːs/ n **(a)** [C] a stitch formed by two stitches crossing each other. **(b)** [U] sewing in which this stitch is used.

crosswalk /ˈkrɒswɔːk; US ˈkrɔːs/ n (US) = PEDESTRIAN CROSSING.

crosswind /ˈkrɒswɪnd; US ˈkrɔːs-/ n a wind blowing across the direction in which cars, aircraft, etc are travelling: *Strong crosswinds blew the plane off course.*

crosswise /ˈkrɒswaɪz; US ˈkrɔːs-/ *adj* [attrib], *adv* **1** across, esp diagonally (DIAGONAL): *a yellow flag with a red band going crosswise from top left to bottom right.* **2** in the form of a cross.

crossword /ˈkrɒswɜːd; US ˈkrɔːs-/ (also ˈcrossword puzzle) *n* a game in which words have to be fitted across and downwards in a pattern of numbered spaces within a usu square diagram. The words are found by solving clues CLUE(2): *the 'Daily Telegraph' crossword* ○ *I've done the crossword, except for 3 across and 10 down.* ⇨ picture.

crossword

crotch /krɒtʃ/ (also **crutch**) *n* the place where a person's legs, or trouser legs, join.

crotchet /ˈkrɒtʃɪt/ (US ˈquarter note) *n* (*music*) a note(5b) equal to half a MINIM. ⇨ picture at MUSIC.

crotchety /ˈkrɒtʃəti/ *adj* (*infml*) bad-tempered; easily made angry: *He felt tired and crotchety.*

crouch /kraʊtʃ/ *v* **1** to lower the body, esp by bending the knees and keeping the body close to them, eg in fear or to hide: [V] *The cat crouched, ready to pounce.* ○ *I crouched behind the sofa.* [Vp] *She crouched down and held her frozen hands towards the fire.* [Vadv] *He crouched low.* ⇨ picture at KNEEL. **2** ~ **over sb/sth** to bend over sb/sth so that you are very close to them: [Vpr] *He crouched over the papers on his desk.*
▸ **crouched** *adj*: *She sat crouched in a corner.*
crouch *n* [sing] a crouching position: *drop down into a crouch.*

croup¹ /kruːp/ *n* [U] a disease of children that causes coughing and difficulty in breathing.

croup² /kruːp/ *n* the round part, covered with flesh, above the back legs of certain animals, esp horses. ⇨ picture at HORSE.

croupier /ˈkruːpieɪ; US -piər/ *n* a person in charge of a gambling table who deals (DEAL¹ 1) cards, collects and pays out money, etc.

croûton /ˈkruːtɒn/ *n* a small piece of TOAST¹ or fried bread, usu served on or with soup.

crow¹ /krəʊ/ *n* a large black bird with a harsh cry. **IDM** as the ˈcrow flies in a straight line: *It's only a mile to my house as the crow flies, but over four miles by road.* stone the crow ⇨ STONE *v*.
■ ˈcrow's-feet *n* [pl] lines in the skin around the outer corner of the eye.
ˈcrow's-nest *n* (esp formerly) a platform fixed to the top of a ship's MAST(1) from which sb can see a long way and watch for land, danger, etc.

crow² /krəʊ/ *v* **1** [V] (of a COCK¹(1)) to make repeated loud high sounds, esp early in the morning. **2** [V] (of a baby) to make sounds showing pleasure. **3** ~ (**about/over sb/sth**) (*often derog*) to express great pride and satisfaction, esp about one's own success: [V, Vpr] *He was crowing with pleasure (about winning our golf match).* [also V.speech].
▸ **crow** *n* [sing] a crowing sound. See also COCK CROW.

crowbar /ˈkrəʊbɑː(r)/ *n* a straight iron bar, usu with a curved end, used to force open boxes, move heavy objects, etc.

crowd¹ /kraʊd/ *n* **1** [CGp] (**a**) a large number of people gathered together, esp outside: *A crowd was already collecting outside the embassy gates.* ○ *He pushed his way through the crowd.* ○ *Police had to break up the crowd.* ○ *crowd control.* (**b**) a mass of spectators; an audience: *The match attracted a large*

crowd/a crowd of over 50 000. ○ *The crowd cheered the winning hit.* **2** [CGp] (*infml often derog*) a particular group of people: *the media crowd* ○ *I don't associate with that crowd.* **3** **the crowd** [sing] (*sometimes derog*) ordinary people, not special or unusual in any way: *move with/follow the crowd* (ie do as everybody else does) ○ *He prefers to be one of the crowd.* ○ *Her linguistic ability sets her apart from and superior to everyone else).* **IDM** crowds/a (whole) crowd (of) very many (people): *It was easy to escape the crowds.* ○ *There were crowds of people waiting to get in.* ○ *A whole crowd of us arrived at the party uninvited.* follow the crowd ⇨ FOLLOW.
■ ˈcrowd-puller *n* (*infml*) a person or thing that attracts a large audience.

crowd² /kraʊd/ *v* **1** ~ **about/around/round (sb/sth)** to gather closely around sb/sth: [Vp, Vpr] *We all crowded round (the table) to get a better view.* **2** to fill a space completely so that there is little room to move: [Vn] *Tourists crowded the pavement.* **3** (*infml*) to put pressure(4) on sb, eg by standing close and watching them or making them rush: [Vn] *Don't crowd me — I need time to think!* **PHRV** ˌcrowd ˈin on sb (of thoughts, questions, etc) to come in large numbers and occupy all one's attention: *Memories crowded in on me.* ○ *Social problems were crowding in on the country.* ˌcrowd ˈinto/ˈonto sth; ˌcrowd ˈin to move in large numbers into a small space: *We'd all crowded into Harriet's small sitting-room.* ○ *Spectators crowded onto the terraces.* ○ *There's room for everyone if we crowd in a bit.* ˌcrowd sb/sth ˈinto/ˈonto sth; ˌcrowd sb/sth ˈin to put many people or things into a small space or period of time: *They crowd people into/onto the buses.* ○ *Guests were crowded into the few remaining rooms.* ○ *She crowds too much detail into her paintings.* ˌcrowd sb/sth ˈout (of sth) **1** to keep sb/sth out of a space by filling it oneself: *The pub's regular customers are being crowded out by tourists.* **2** to prevent sb/sth from operating successfully: *Small shops are being crowded out by the big supermarkets.*
▸ **crowded** *adj* ~ (**with sth**) **1** having (too) many people: *crowded buses/streets/rooms/hotels* ○ *London was very crowded.* ○ *In spring the place is crowded with skiers.* **2** full of sth: *a house crowded with paintings* ○ *days crowded with activity* ○ *We have a very crowded schedule.*

crown¹ /kraʊn/ *n* **1**(**a**) [C] a circular head-dress usu made of gold and jewels and worn by a king or queen on official occasions. (**b**) (usu **the Crown**) [sing] a king or queen representing the institution governing a country: *land owned by the Crown* ○ *a minister of the Crown* ○ *Who appears for the Crown in this case?* (ie Who is bringing the criminal charge¹(2) against the accused person on behalf of the state?) (**c**) **the crown** [sing] the position or power of a king or queen: *She refused the crown* (ie refused to become queen). **2** [C] a circle of flowers, leaves, etc worn on the head, esp as a sign of victory, or as an award: *Christ's crown of thorns* ○ (*fig*) *two boxers fighting it out for the world heavyweight crown* (ie to become CHAMPION). **3** (usu **the crown**) [sing] (**a**) the top of the head or of a hat: *His hair is rather thin on the crown.* (**b**) the highest part of sth: *the crown of a hill* ○ *drive on the crown of the road.* **4** [C] (**a**) the part of a tooth that is visible, rather than its root. (**b**) an artificial replacement for this or part of this. **5** [C] anything in the shape of a crown(1a), esp an ornament or a BADGE: *A major has a crown on the shoulder of his uniform.* **6** [C] a former British coin worth 5 shillings (SHILLING) (now 25p). **IDM** the jewel in the crown ⇨ JEWEL.
■ ˌcrown ˈcolony *n* a colony ruled directly by the British government.
ˌCrown ˈCourt *n* (in England and Wales) a lawcourt

in which criminal cases are tried (TRY[1] 3a) by a judge and JURY. Compare COUNTY COURT.

,crown 'jewels *n* [pl] the crown and other royal ornaments worn or carried by a king or queen on formal occasions.

,Crown 'prince *n* a prince who will become king when the present king or queen dies.

,Crown prin'cess *n* **1** the wife of a Crown prince. **2** a princess who will become queen when the present king or queen dies.

crown[2] /kraʊn/ *v* **1** to put a crown on the head of a new king or queen as a sign of royal power: [Vn, Vn-n] *She was crowned (queen) in 1953.* ○ *the **crowned heads** (ie kings and queens) of Europe.* **2** ~ **sth (with sth)** (often passive) (*rhet*) to form or cover the top of sth: [Vnpr] *hills crowned with trees* [Vn] *Beautiful fair hair crowns her head.* **(b)** to make sth complete or perfect: [Vn] *The award of this prize has crowned a glorious career.* [Vnpr] *Their efforts were finally crowned with success.* **3** (*infml*) to hit sb on the head: [Vn] *Shut up or I'll crown you.* **4** [Vn] (also **cap**) to put an artificial top on a tooth. ⇨ CROWN[1] 4b. **IDM** **to crown it 'all** as the final event in a series of fortunate or unfortunate events: *It was cold and raining, and, to crown it all, we had to walk home.*

▶ **crowning** *adj* [attrib] making perfect or complete: *The performance provided the **crowning touch** to the evening's entertainments.* ○ *the crowning moment of her career* ○ *Her **crowning glory** is her hair.*

crozier = CROSIER.

crucial /ˈkruːʃl/ *adj* ~ **(to/for sth)** very important, esp for its effect on sth: *a crucial decision/issue/factor* ○ *at the crucial moment* ○ *Winning this contract is crucial to the future of our company.* ▶ **crucially** /-ʃəli/ *adv*: *It is crucially important that we keep together at all times.*

crucible /ˈkruːsɪbl/ *n* **1** a pot in which metals are melted. **2** (*rhet*) a severe test or trial: *an alliance forged in the crucible of war.*

crucifix /ˈkruːsəfɪks/ *n* a model of the Cross[1](2b) with the figure of Jesus on it.

crucifixion /ˌkruːsəˈfɪkʃn/ *n* [C, U] the killing of sb by fastening them to a cross[1](2a), sometimes with nails: *the Crucifixion* (ie of Jesus).

cruciform /ˈkruːsɪfɔːm/ *adj* having the shape of a cross: *a cruciform church.*

crucify /ˈkruːsɪfaɪ/ *v* (*pt, pp* **-fied**) **1** [Vn] to kill sb by fastening them to a cross[1](2a), sometimes with nails. **2** [Vn] (*infml*) to treat or punish sb very severely: *The minister was crucified* (ie very severely criticized) *in the press for his handling of the affair.*

crud /krʌd/ *n* (*infml*) [U] any dirty or unpleasant substance: *all the crud in the bottom of the saucepan.*

crude /kruːd/ *adj* (**-r, -st**) **1** [usu attrib] in the natural state; not refined: *crude oil/ore.* **2(a)** not skilfully made; not prepared and completed in much detail; rough[1](3): *a crude sketch/method/approximation* ○ *I made my own crude garden furniture.* **(b)** not showing good taste[1](6) or education; COARSE: *crude manners* ○ *He told some rather crude* (ie sexually offensive) *jokes.*

▶ **crudely** *adv*: *a crudely assembled bookcase* ○ *express oneself crudely.*

crudeness *n* [U].

crudity /ˈkruːdəti/ *n* [U,C] **1** the state or quality of being crude(2a), or an example of this: *the crudity of his drawing* ○ *the novel's structural crudities.* **2** crude(2b) behaviour or remarks: *The crudity of his language offended her.*

crudités /ˈkruːdɪteɪ; *US* ˌkruːdɪˈteɪ/ *n* [pl] (*French*) pieces of raw vegetables, usu served with a sauce into which they are dipped.

cruel /ˈkruːəl/ *adj* (**-ller, -llest**) **1** (*derog*) ~ **(to sb/sth)** having or showing a desire to cause pain and suffering: *a cruel boss/master/dictator* ○ *Don't be*

C

cruel to animals. ○ *His eyes were cruel and hard.* ○ *Sometimes you have to **be cruel to be kind*** (ie make sb suffer because they will benefit from this later). **2** causing pain or suffering: *a cruel blow/punishment/joke/fate* ○ *cruel* (ie bad) *luck* ○ *War is cruel.* ▶ **cruelly** /ˈkruːəli/ *adv*: *The dog had been cruelly treated.* ○ *I was cruelly deceived.*

cruelty /ˈkruːəlti/ *n* **1** [U] ~ **(to sb/sth)** behaviour that causes pain or suffering to others, esp intentionally: *his cruelty to his children* ○ *cruelty-free products* (ie not involving the use of animals in testing them). **2** [C usu *pl*] a cruel act: *the cruelties of life.*

cruet /ˈkruːɪt/ *n* **(a)** a small container for salt, pepper, oil, etc for use on the table at meals. **(b)** a set of these.

cruise /kruːz/ *v* **1** to sail about in an area, either for pleasure visiting different places, or, in war, looking for enemy ships: [Vn] *They spent a year cruising the Indian Ocean.* [Vpr] *a destroyer cruising around the Baltic Sea* [V, Vp] *We spent several days cruising (about).* **2(a)** (of a motor vehicle or an aircraft) to travel at a steady and moderate speed, esp so as to use fuel efficiently: [Vpr] *cruising at 10 000 ft/350 miles per hour* [V] *a cruising speed of 50 miles per hour* [Vp] *The car was just cruising along slowly.* **(b)** (of a motor vehicle or its driver) to travel with no particular destination, esp slowly: [Vp] *Taxis cruised about, hoping to pick up late fares.* [Vpr] *She cruised round the block looking for a parking space.* **3** to achieve an aim easily, without much effort: [Vpr] *cruise to a victory/into the lead/past the winning-post* [Vp] *He's just cruising along, doing the minimum amount of work.* [Vadv] *The favourite cruised home in the first race.* **4** [Vp] (*sl*) (esp of a HOMOSEXUAL person) to go about in public places looking for sb to have sex with.

▶ **cruise** *n* a voyage by sea, stopping at various places, esp as a holiday: *go on/for a cruise* ○ *a round-the-world cruise.*

cruiser /ˈkruːzə(r)/ *n* **1** a large WARSHIP. **2** (also **'cabin cruiser**) a motor boat with sleeping accommodation, used for pleasure trips.

■ **'cruise control** *n* [U] a device in a motor vehicle that allows it to maintain the speed that the driver has chosen: *The new model has cruise control.*

,cruise 'missile *n* a missile, usu with a nuclear WARHEAD, which flies low and is guided by its own computer.

crumb /krʌm/ *n* **1** [C] a very small piece, esp of bread, cake or biscuit, which has fallen off a larger piece: *sweep the crumbs off the table.* ⇨ note at PIECE[1]. **2** [C] a small piece or amount: *a few crumbs of information* ○ *I failed my exam, and my only **crumb of comfort** is that I can take it again.* **3** [U] the soft inner part of a LOAF[1](1) of bread. Compare CRUST 1a.

crumble /ˈkrʌmbl/ *v* **1** ~ **(sth) (into/to sth)**; ~ **(sth) (up)** to break or break sth into very small pieces: [Vn, Vnp] *crumble one's bread (up)* ○ *crumbling walls* (ie that are breaking apart) [Vpr] *buildings crumbling into rubble* [also Vnpr, Vp]. **2** ~ **(into/to sth)** to begin to fail or lose strength; to come slowly to an end: [V] *The great empire began to crumble.* [Vpr] *hopes that crumbled to dust* [Vp] *His power was crumbling away.* **IDM** **that's the way the cookie crumbles** ⇨ WAY[1].

▶ **crumble** *n* [U,C] (*Brit*) a dish of fruit covered with a rough mixture of flour, butter and sugar and cooked in the oven: *apple/rhubarb crumble.*

crumbly /ˈkrʌmbli/ *adj* that crumbles easily: *crumbly bread/cheese/soil* ○ *a dry crumbly texture.*

crumbs /krʌmz/ *interj* (*Brit infml*) (used to express surprise, uncertainty, etc): *Crumbs, look at the time!*

crummy /ˈkrʌmi/ *adj* (*infml*) of very bad quality; unpleasant: *a crummy little street in the worst part of town* ○ *Most of his records are pretty crummy.*

crumpet /'krʌmpɪt/ n **1** [C] (*esp Brit*) a small flat round cake. Crumpets are not sweet and are usu eaten hot with butter: *toasted crumpets*. **2** [U] (*Brit sl sexist*) attractive women, regarded only as sexually desirable objects: *We both had the same idea: have a few drinks and chat up the local crumpet.* **IDM** **a bit of crumpet/fluff/skirt/stuff** ⇨ BIT[1].

crumple /'krʌmpl/ v **1** ~ (**sth**) (**into sth**); ~ (**sth**) (**up**) to become crushed or crush sth into folds or creases (CREASE): [V] *material that crumples easily* ○ *The front of the car crumpled on impact.* [Vnpr] *He crumpled the paper into a ball.* [Vnp] *crumpling the note up in his fist* [Vp] (*fig*) *His face crumpled up and he began to cry.* [also Vpr]. **2** to become weak suddenly; to collapse: [V] *All resistance to the proposal has crumpled.* ▶ **crumpled** *adj*: *a crumpled suit/envelope/£10 note* ○ *The letter was a bit crumpled at the edges.* ○ *She was lying in a crumpled heap* (ie with her body bent forward) *on the floor.*

crunch /krʌntʃ/ v **1** ~ **sth** (**up**) to crush sth noisily with the teeth when eating: [Vn] *crunch peanuts/ biscuits* [Vn, Vnp] *The dog was crunching (up) a bone.* **2** to make or cause sth to make a harsh crushing noise: [V] *The frozen snow crunched under our feet.* [Vn] *The wheels crunched the gravel.* Compare SCRUNCH. **3** (*computing*) [Vn] to process large amounts of data very rapidly. See also NUMBER CRUNCHING. ▶ **crunch** *n* **1** [C usu *sing*] a noise made by crunching; an act of crunching: *He bit into the apple with a crunch.* ○ *The car hit the tree with a loud crunch.* **the crunch** [*sing*] an important and often unpleasant point, situation or piece of information: *The crunch is that we can't afford to have a holiday this year.* ○ **The crunch came** *when she returned from America.* ○ *He always says he'll help,* **but when it comes to the crunch** (ie when it is time for action or decision), *he does nothing.*
crunchy *adj* (*approv*) firm and crisp, and making a sharp sound when broken or crushed: *crunchy biscuits/salads/snow.*

crusade /kruːˈseɪd/ n **1** (usu *pl*) any one of the wars fought by European Christian countries to recover the Holy Land (HOLY) from the Muslims in medieval times. **2** ~ (**for/against sth**); ~ (**to do sth**) any struggle or campaign for sth believed to be good, or against sth believed to be bad: *a crusade against corruption* ○ *a private crusade to preserve the valley's wild flowers.* ▶ **crusade** *v* ~ (**for/against sth**) to take part in a crusade(2): [Vpr] *crusading for fairer treatment of minorities* [V] *crusading fervour.*
crusader *n* a person taking part in a crusade: *a crusader against world hunger.*

crush[1] /krʌʃ/ v **1** to press or squeeze sth/sb hard, causing damage, injury or loss of shape: [Vn] *Don't crush the box — it has flowers in it.* ○ *Wine is made by crushing grapes.* ○ *a crushed mudguard* [Vnpr] *Several people were* **crushed to death** *by falling rocks.* **2** ~ **sth** (**up**) to break sth firm or hard into small pieces or into powder by pressing: [Vn, Vnp] *Huge hammers crush (up) the rocks.* [Vn] *First crush the biscuits, then mix them with the butter.* **3** to become or make sth full of small folds or creases (CREASE[1] 1): [Vn] *The clothes were badly crushed in the suitcase.* [V] *Some synthetic materials do not crush easily.* **4** to defeat or destroy sb/sth completely: [Vn] *The rebellion was crushed by government forces.* ○ *Her refusal crushed all our hopes.* ○ *He felt completely crushed* (ie shocked and upset) *by her unkind remark.* **PHRV** **crush (sb/sth) into, past, through, etc sth** to push or press sb/sth into a small space or an awkward position: *A large crowd crushed past (the barrier).* ○ *You can't crush twenty people into such a tiny room.* ○ *The postman tried to crush the packet through the letter-box.* ,**crush sth** '**out (of sth)** to

remove sth by pressing or squeezing: *crush the juice out of oranges.*
▶ **crushing** *adj* [usu attrib] **1** complete; severe: *a crushing defeat/blow* ○ *The expense was crushing.* **2** intended to embarrass sb or make them feel inferior: *a crushing look/remark.* **crushingly** *adv.*

crush[2] /krʌʃ/ n **1** [C usu *sing*] a crowd of people pressed close together in a small space: *a big crush in the theatre bar* ○ *I couldn't get through the crush.* **2** [C] ~ (**on sb**) (*infml*) a strong but often brief feeling of love for sb: *He's got a crush on his history teacher.* **3** [U] (*Brit*) a drink made from fruit juice: *lemon crush.*
■ '**crush barrier** *n* (*Brit*) a usu temporary fence put up to restrain crowds.

crust /krʌst/ n **1**(**a**) [C, U] the hard outer surface of bread: *a white loaf with a crisp brown crust* ○ *Cut the crusts off when you make sandwiches.* ⇨ picture at BREAD. (**b**) [C] (*esp rhet*) a slice of bread, esp a thin dry one: (*fig*) *earn one's crust* (ie one's living) ○ *He'd share his last crust with you* (ie He is very generous). **2** [C usu *sing*] a layer of pastry, esp on top of a pie: *Bake until the crust is golden.* **3** [C, U] a hard layer or surface, esp above or round sth soft or liquid: *a thin crust of ice/frozen snow* ○ *feet covered with a brown, scaly crust* ○ *the earth's crust* (ie the part nearest its surface). See also THE UPPER CRUST.
▶ **crusted** *adj* [usu pred] ~ (**with sth**) having a hard layer or covering: *pork crusted in breadcrumbs* ○ *walls crusted with dirt* ○ *He washed the crusted blood from his face.*

crustacean /krʌˈsteɪʃn/ n any of various types of animal that have a hard outer shell and live mostly in water: *Crabs, lobsters and shrimps are crustaceans.*

crusty /'krʌsti/ *adj* **1** having a crisp outer layer: *crusty French bread* ○ *a crusty pizza base* ○ *the crusty bark of old willows.* **2** (*infml*) (esp of older people or their behaviour) quickly and easily irritated: *a* **crusty old** *soldier.*

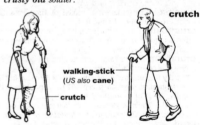

crutch

walking-stick
(*US also* cane)

crutch

crutch /krʌtʃ/ n **1** a support in the form of a pole, placed under the arm to help a person who has difficulty in walking: *a pair of crutches* ○ *go about on crutches.* ⇨ picture. **2** a person or thing that provides help or support: *High interest rates are merely a crutch for the country's ailing economy.* **3** = CROTCH.

crux /krʌks/ n [*sing*] the most important or difficult part of a problem, an issue, etc: *Now we come to the crux of the matter.*

cry[1] /kraɪ/ v (*pt, pp* **cried**) **1** ~ (**for/over sth/sb**); ~ (**with sth**) (no passive) to produce tears; to WEEP(1): [V] *He cried because he had hurt his knee.* ○ *It's all right — don't cry.* [Vpr] *cry for joy* (ie because one is happy) ○ *The child was crying for* (ie because it wanted) *its mother.* ○ *cry with pain/hunger* [Vn] *cry bitter tears* ('V.speech) *'Oh mummy!' she cried.* ⇨ note. **2**(**a**) ~ (**out**) (of people or animals) to make loud sounds without words, expressing fear, pain, etc: [V] *The monkeys cry shrilly when they see danger.* [Vpr, Vp] *She cried (out) in pain after accidentally cutting herself.* ⇨ note at SHOUT. (**b**) ~

(out) **(for sth)** to call out loudly in words, esp in fear, anger or surprise: [Vpr, Vp] *He cried (out) for mercy.* [V.speech] *'Help, help!' he cried.* **IDM** **cry one's 'eyes/'heart out** to cry with great sadness, esp for a long time. **cry over spilt 'milk** to feel sad about sth that has happened and cannot be changed: *You've broken it now — it's no use crying over spilt milk! cry/sob oneself to sleep* ⊳ SLEEP¹. **cry 'wolf** to pretend there is danger and call for help when it is not needed. **for ,crying out 'loud** (used to express annoyance or surprise): *For crying out loud! Why did you do that?* **laugh till/until one cries** ⊳ LAUGH. **a shoulder to cry on** ⊳ SHOULDER. **PHRV ,cry sth 'down** (*esp Brit*) to say that sth is not very good, important or valuable: *Don't cry down her real achievements.* **,cry 'off** (*Brit*) to withdraw from sth one has promised to do: *I said I would play, but had to cry off at the last moment.* **,cry 'out for sth** (esp in the continuous tenses) to demand sth; to require that sth is done: *People are crying out for free elections.* ○ *The system is crying out for reform* (ie badly needs to be reformed).

NOTE Compare **cry, weep, sob, whimper** and **wail.** These verbs all describe the way people express emotions with tears. **Cry** has the widest use. People may **cry** because of unhappiness, joy or pain: *The little girl was crying because she was lost.* ○ *Babies cry when they are hungry.* **Weep** is more formal than **cry** and suggests stronger emotions: *She sat down and wept when she heard her father was dead.* ○ *The hostages wept for joy on their release.*

Sob means to cry noisily with irregular breathing: *He sobbed for hours when he found out she had gone.* People **whimper** when they make unhappy, frightened or complaining noises: *'Don't take me to hospital,' she whimpered.* **Wail** describes crying and complaining with great sadness: *Mourners were wailing loudly at the funeral.* Note that all these verbs are used instead of 'say' to describe a way of speaking: *'I've lost my daddy,' the little boy cried/wept/sobbed/whimpered/wailed.*

cry² /kraɪ/ *n* **1** [C] **(a)** a loud sound without words, expressing grief, pain, joy or fear: *a cry of terror* ○ *the cry of an animal in pain.* **(b)** a loud call or shout using words: *angry cries from the mob* ○ *A cry of 'Help!' was heard coming from the river.* **(c)** (*usu sing*) the characteristic call of an animal or a bird: *the cry of the rook.* **2** [sing] an act or period of crying (CRY¹ 1): *Have a good cry — it'll make you feel better.* **3** [C] **a ~ (for sth)** an urgent demand or appeal: *a cry for freedom* ○ *Her suicide attempt was a clear cry for help.* **(b)** (esp in compounds) a word or phrase that expresses a group's principles or calls people to action: *a 'battle-cry* ○ *a 'war cry* ○ *His speech attacking the government has proved a rallying cry for party dissidents.* **4** [C] (*dated*) words shouted to give information: *the old street cries of London.* **IDM** **a far cry from sth/doing sth** ⊳ FAR². **hue and cry** ⊳ HUE². **in full cry** ⊳ FULL.
■ **'cry-baby** *n* (*infml derog*) a person, esp a child, who cries too often or without good reason: *He's a dreadful cry-baby.*

crying /'kraɪɪŋ/ *adj* [attrib] **(a)** great and urgent: *There is **a crying need** for more funds.* **(b)** (esp of sth bad or wrong) extremely bad and shocking: *It's a crying shame to waste all that food.*

cryogenic /ˌkraɪə'dʒenɪk/ *adj* (*techn*) involving the use of very low temperatures: *a cryogenic storage system.*

crypt /krɪpt/ *n* a room beneath the floor of a church, used esp for worship or as a place of burial.

cryptic /'krɪptɪk/ *adj* with a meaning that is hidden or not easily understood; mysterious: *a cryptic remark/message/smile* ○ *a cryptic crossword clue* (ie one with an indirect solution). ▶ **cryptically** /-klɪ/ *adv*: *'Yes and no,' she replied cryptically.*

crypt(o)- *comb form* (forming *ns*) hidden; secret: *cryptogram* ○ *a ˌcrypto-'communist* (ie sb who has communist sympathies but keeps them secret).

cryptography /krɪp'tɒɡrəfi/ *n* [U] the art of writing or solving codes.

crystal /'krɪstl/ *n* **1(a)** [U] a clear transparent mineral, such as QUARTZ. **(b)** [C, U] a piece of this, esp when polished and used as an ornament: *a necklace of sparkling crystals* ○ *a crystal bracelet* ○ *a belt inlaid with crystal.* **2** [U] glass of very high quality made into bowls, glasses, etc: *The dining-table shone with silver and crystal.* ○ *a crystal vase/chandelier.* **3** [C] a small shape with many regular sides, formed when a substance becomes solid: *sugar/salt crystals* ○ *snow/ice crystals* ○ *Diamond is a carbon crystal.* **4** [C] a piece of glass or plastic covering the face of a watch. See also LIQUID CRYSTAL DISPLAY.
■ **ˌcrystal 'ball** *n* a clear glass ball used by people who claim that they can predict what will happen in the future by looking into it.
ˌcrystal 'clear *adj* **1** (of glass, water, etc) entirely clear and bright. **2** very easy to understand; completely obvious: *I want to make my meaning crystal clear.*
'crystal-gazing *n* [U] the practice of attempting to predict future events.

crystalline /'krɪstəlaɪn/ *adj* **1** made of or resembling crystals: *crystalline structure/minerals.* **2** (*fml*) very clear; transparent: *water of crystalline purity.*

crystallize, -ise /'krɪstəlaɪz/ *v* **1** (of thoughts, plans, etc) to become clear and definite; to make thoughts, plans, etc become clear and definite: [Vpr] *His vague ideas crystallized into a definite plan.* [Vn] *Reading your book helped to crystallize my views.* [also V, Vnpr]. **2** [Vn] to form or make sth form into crystals.
▶ **crystallization, -isation** /ˌkrɪstəlaɪ'zeɪʃn; *US* -ləˈz-/ *n* [U].
crystallized, -ised *adj* (esp of fruit) preserved in and covered with sugar: *a box of crystallized oranges.*

CS gas /ˌsiː es 'ɡæs/ *n* a gas that irritates the eyes, producing tears and making it difficult to breathe. CS gas is sometimes used to control crowds. See also TEAR-GAS.

CST /ˌsiː es 'tiː/ *abbr* (in the USA) Central Standard Time.

Ct *abbr* (written as part of an address) court¹(4): *30 Willow Ct.*

ct *abbr* (*pl* **cts**) **1** carat: *an 18 ct gold ring.* **2** cent: *50 cts.*

cu *abbr* cubic: *a volume of 2 cu m* (ie 2 cubic metres).

cub /kʌb/ *n* **1** [C] a young fox, bear, lion, etc. **2(a) the Cubs** [pl] a branch of the Scout Association (SCOUT 2) for boys between 7 and 10: *join the Cubs.* **(b) Cub** (also **'Cub Scout**) [C] a member of this. Compare BROWNIE 2.
■ **ˌcub re'porter** *n* a young newspaper reporter without much experience.

cubby-hole /'kʌbɪ həʊl/ *n* a small enclosed space or room: *My office is a cubby-hole in the basement.*

cube /kjuːb/ *n* **1(a)** (*geometry*) a solid figure with six equal square sides. ⊳ picture at SOLID. **(b)** a piece of sth, esp food, with six sides: *an ice cube* ○ *Cut the meat into cubes.* ⊳ note at PIECE¹. See also STOCK-CUBE. **2** (*mathematics*) the result of multiplying a number by itself twice: *The cube of 5 (5^3) is 125 ($5 \times 5 \times 5 = 125$).*
▶ **cube** *v* **1** (*mathematics*) (usu passive) to multiply a number by itself twice: [Vn] *10 cubed is 1 000.* **2** [Vn] to cut food into cubes.
■ **ˌcube 'root** *n* a number which, when multiplied by itself twice, produces the specified number: *The cube root of 64 ($^3\sqrt{64}$) is 4 ($4 \times 4 \times 4 = 64$).*

cubic /'kjuːbɪk/ *adj* **1** [attrib] **(a)** (in measuring the volume of sth) of three dimensions: *one cubic metre* (ie a volume equal to that of a CUBE(1) with sides that are one metre long) ○ *cubic inches/centimetres.* (**b**) measured or expressed in cubic units: *the cubic capacity of a car's engine.* **2** having the shape of a CUBE(1): *a cubic figure.*

cubicle /ˈkjuːbɪkl/ *n* a small room made by separating off part of a larger room. Cubicles are used eg for dressing or sleeping in: *a lavatory/shower cubicle.*

cubism /ˈkjuːbɪzəm/ *n* [U] a modern style of art, esp in painting, in which objects are represented as if they are composed of geometrical (GEOMETRY) shapes.
▶ **cubist** /ˈkjuːbɪst/ *adj* in the style of cubism. — *n* a cubist artist.

cuckold /ˈkʌkəʊld/ *n* (*arch usu derog*) a man whose wife has sex with another man.
▶ **cuckold** *v* [Vn] (*arch*) (**a**) (of a man) to make another man a cuckold by having sex with his wife. (**b**) (of a woman) to make her husband a cuckold by having sex with another man.

cuckoo¹ /ˈkʊkuː/ *n* a bird with a call that sounds like its name. Cuckoos leave their eggs in the nests of other birds.
■ **ˈcuckoo clock** *n* a clock that strikes the hours with sounds like a cuckoo's call, sometimes with a toy bird appearing from inside at the same time.

cuckoo² /ˈkʊkuː/ *adj* [usu pred] (*infml*) foolish; mad: *He has gone absolutely cuckoo.*

cucumber /ˈkjuːkʌmbə(r)/ *n* [C, U] a long vegetable with a green skin. It is usu eaten raw, eg in sandwiches or SALAD: *Slice the cucumber thinly.* ○ *Have some cucumber.* ⇨ picture at SALAD. **IDM** **cool as a cucumber** ⇨ COOL¹.

cud /kʌd/ *n* [U] the food that cattle bring back from the stomach into the mouth to chew again.

cuddle /ˈkʌdl/ *v* to hold sb/sth/each other close in one's arms as a way of showing love or affection: [V] *Sharon and her boyfriend were kissing and cuddling on the sofa.* [Vn, Vnpr] *The child cuddled her doll (to her chest).* [also Vnadv]. **PHRV** **cuddle up (to/against sb/sth)**; **cuddle up (together)** to lie or sit close and comfortably: *She cuddled up to her mother.* ○ *They cuddled up (together) under the blanket.*
▶ **cuddle** *n* [sing] an act of cuddling; a HUG(1): *give sb a cuddle.*
cuddly /ˈkʌdli/ (**-ier, -iest**) *adj* (*infml approv*) pleasant to cuddle; designed to be cuddled: *a cuddly toy* ○ *a cuddly* (ie close and comfortable) *relationship.*

cudgel /ˈkʌdʒl/ *n* a short thick stick or club²(1). **IDM** **take up (the) cudgels for / on behalf of sb/sth** to start to defend or support sb/sth strongly.
▶ **cudgel** *v* (**-ll-**; *US* also **-l-**) to hit sb with a cudgel: [Vnpr] *He had been cudgelled to death.* [also Vn]. **IDM** **cudgel one's brains** (*Brit*) to think very hard: *Though we cudgelled our brains for hours, the crossword finally defeated us.*

cue¹ /kjuː/ *n* **1 ~ (for sth / to do sth)** a few words or an action that give sb the signal to say or do sth, esp in a play: *Actors have to learn their cues* (ie the last words of the speeches just before their own speeches) *as well as their own lines.* ○ *When I nod my head, that's your cue to interrupt the meeting.* ○ (*fig*) *And they all lived happily ever afterwards — which sounds like the cue* (ie an appropriate moment) *for a song.* **2** an example of how to behave, what to do, etc: *Investors are **taking their cue from** the big banks and selling sterling.* **IDM** **(right) on cue** at exactly the moment that one expects or that is appropriate: *'I'm a bit worried about the weather,' he said, and right on cue it started to rain.*
▶ **cue** *v* (*pres p* **cueing**) **~ sb (in)** to give a cue(1) to sb to do sth: *I'll cue you in* (ie give you a signal to start) *by nodding my head.* [also Vn].

cue² /kjuː/ *n* a long wooden stick with a leather tip, used for striking the ball in games such as SNOOKER or BILLIARDS. ⇨ picture at SNOOKER.

cuff¹ /kʌf/ *n* **1** [C] the end of a coat or shirt sleeve at the wrist: *frayed cuffs.* ⇨ picture at JACKET. **2** (*US*) [C] = TURN-UP. **3 cuffs** [pl] (*sl*) HANDCUFFS. **IDM** **off the ˈcuff** without previous thought or preparation: *make a remark off the cuff* ○ *an ˌoff-the-cuff ˈjoke/ˈcomment/ˈspeech.*
■ **ˈcuff-link** *n* (usu *pl*) either of a pair of fastenings for shirt cuffs: *a pair of gold cuff-links.*

cuff² /kʌf/ *v* [Vn] to give sb a light blow with the open hand, esp on the head. ▶ **cuff** *n.*

cuisine /kwɪˈziːn/ *n* [U] (*French*) a style of cooking; food cooked in a certain style: *French/Italian cuisine* ○ *a restaurant where the cuisine is excellent.* See also HAUTE CUISINE.

cul-de-sac /ˈkʌl də sæk/ *n* (*pl* **cul-de-sacs**) (*French*) a street that is closed at one end: *live in a quiet cul-de-sac* ○ (*fig*) *This particular brand of socialism had entered a cul-de-sac* (ie could make no further progress).

culinary /ˈkʌlɪnəri; *US* -neri/ *adj* (*fml*) of or for cooking: *culinary skills/implements* ○ *a culinary triumph* (ie a very well cooked dish or meal).

cull /kʌl/ *v* **1** to kill a certain number of usu weaker animals in a group, in order to reduce its size: [Vn] *Deer are culled by hunters.* ○ *The herd must be culled.* **2 ~ sth (from sth)** to select or obtain sth from various different sources: [Vnpr] *information culled from a number of reference books* [also Vn].
▶ **cull** *n* (**a**) [C] an act of culling (CULL 1) sth: *an annual seal cull.* (**b**) [sing] an animal or animals that have been culled (CULL 1): *sell the cull as meat.*

culminate /ˈkʌlmɪneɪt/ *v* **PHRV** **culminate in sth** (*fml*) to reach the highest point or specified conclusion or result: [Vpr] *a long struggle that culminated in success* ○ *a series of border clashes which culminated in full-scale war* ○ *Her career culminated in her appointment as director.*
▶ **culmination** /ˌkʌlmɪˈneɪʃn/ *n* [sing] the highest point or the conclusion or result of sth, usu happening after a long time: *the successful culmination of a long campaign.*

culottes /kjuːˈlɒts/ *n* [pl] women's wide short trousers made to look like a skirt: *a pair of red culottes.*

culpable /ˈkʌlpəbl/ *adj* (*fml*) responsible and deserving blame for having done sth wrong: *culpable officials* ○ *I cannot be held culpable (for their mistakes).* ▶ **culpability** /ˌkʌlpəˈbɪləti/ *n* [U]: *debate the degree of culpability of the former prime minister.* **culpably** /ˈkʌlpəbli/ *adv.*

culprit /ˈkʌlprɪt/ *n* **1** a person who has done sth wrong or against the law: *The whole class would be punished unless the culprit was found.* ○ *Police are searching for the culprits.* **2** a person or thing responsible for causing a problem: *A faulty light switch was the culprit.*

cult /kʌlt/ *n* **1** a system of religious worship, esp one that is expressed in rituals: *the mysterious nature-worship cults of these ancient peoples.* **2** (usu *sing*) **~ (of sb/sth)** (*sometimes derog*) great admiration, love or concern for sb/sth: *the cult of physical fitness* ○ *a personality cult* (ie great admiration for a person, esp a leader). **3** a popular fashion or CRAZE: *the current cult for comic-book heroes* ○ *a ˈcult movie/book/figure/hero* (ie one that is fashionable among members of a particular, usu small, group) ○ *an artist with **cult status** a cult following* (ie one who is admired by such a group).

cultivable /ˈkʌltɪvəbl/ *adj* that can be cultivated (CULTIVATE 1a): *cultivable land/soil.*

cultivate /ˈkʌltɪveɪt/ *v* **1** [Vn] (**a**) to prepare and use land, soil, etc for growing crops. (**b**) to grow crops. **2**(**a**) (*sometimes derog*) to try to acquire or develop a relationship, an attitude, etc: [Vn] *cultivat-*

ing the friendship of influential people ○ *cultivate an air of indifference.* (**b**) (*sometimes derog*) to try to win the friendship or support of sb: [Vn] *You must cultivate people who can help you in business.* (**c**) to make the mind, feelings, etc more educated and sensitive: [Vn] *reading the best authors in an attempt to cultivate her mind.*

▶ **cultivated** *adj* (of people, manners, etc) having or showing education and good taste¹(6): *a cultivated young woman* ○ *His voice was pleasant and cultivated.*

cultivation /ˌkʌltɪˈveɪʃn/ *n* [U]: *the cultivation of the soil* ○ *land that is under cultivation* (ie is being cultivated) ○ *cultivation of the mind* ○ *the cultivation of a better relationship between the two countries.*

cultivator /ˈkʌltɪveɪtə(r)/ *n* **1** a person who cultivates the land. **2** a machine for breaking up soil, destroying weeds (WEED 1a), etc.

cultural /ˈkʌltʃərəl/ *adj* [usu attrib] of or involving culture: *cultural differences/activities/change* ○ *cultural studies* (eg of art, literature, etc) ○ *a cultural desert* (ie a place with few cultural activities). ▶ **culturally** /-rəli/ *adv.*

culture /ˈkʌltʃə(r)/ *n* **1** [U] (**a**) art, literature, music and other intellectual expressions of a particular society or time: *a society without much culture* ○ *a period of high/low culture* ○ *Universities should be centres of culture.* (**b**) an understanding or appreciation of this: *She is a woman of considerable culture.* (**c**) (*often derog*) art, literature, etc in general: *tourists coming to Venice in search of culture.* **2** [C, U] the customs, arts, social institutions, etc of a particular group or nation: *people from different cultures* ○ *Western culture* ○ *working-class culture* ○ *twentieth-century popular culture.* **3** [U] development through regular training, exercise, treatment, etc: *physical culture* (ie becoming fit and strong by doing exercises) ○ *The culture of the mind is vital.* **4** [U] the growing of plants or breeding of certain types of animal to obtain a crop or improve the species: *the culture of bees/silkworms.* **5** [C] (*biology*) a group of bacteria grown for medical or scientific study: *a culture of cholera germs.*

▶ **cultured** *adj* (of people) appreciating art, literature, music, etc; well educated; cultivated (CULTIVATE).

■ ˈ**culture shock** *n* [U] a feeling of confusion and anxiety caused by contact with another culture.

culvert /ˈkʌlvət/ *n* a drain that passes under a road, railway, etc.

cum /kʌm/ *prep* (used for linking two *ns*) also used as; as well as: *a bedroom-cum-sitting-room* ○ *a barman-cum-waiter.*

cumbersome /ˈkʌmbəsəm/ *adj* **1** heavy and difficult to carry, wear, etc: *a cumbersome parcel/costume.* **2** slow and not very efficient: *the university's cumbersome administrative procedures.*

cumin /ˈkʌmɪn/ *n* [U] (**a**) a plant with seeds that are used as a spice in cooking. (**b**) these seeds, often ground into a powder.

cummerbund /ˈkʌməbʌnd/ *n* a wide band of cloth worn round the waist, esp under a dinner-jacket (DINNER).

cumulative /ˈkjuːmjələtɪv; US -leɪtɪv/ *adj* gradually increasing in amount, force, etc by one addition after another: *the cumulative total sales for 1993* ○ *the cumulative effect of several illnesses.* ▶ **cumulatively** *adv.*

cumulus /ˈkjuːmjələs/ *n* (*pl* **cumuli** /-laɪ/) [U, C] a type of cloud formation consisting of round, usu white, masses on a flat base.

cuneiform /ˈkjuːnɪfɔːm/ *n* an ancient system of writing used eg in old Persia and Assyria: *written in cuneiform* ○ *cuneiform characters.*

cunnilingus /ˌkʌnɪˈlɪŋɡəs/ *n* [U] the practice of stimulating a woman's outer sexual organs with the mouth or tongue: *perform cunnilingus on sb.*

cunning /ˈkʌnɪŋ/ *adj* **1** (*often derog*) clever at deceiving people: *a cunning liar/spy/cheat* ○ *a cunning trick/plot* ○ *She gave a cunning smile.* **2** (of an invention, a solution to a problem, etc) clever; INGENIOUS: *a cunning device for cracking nuts.*

▶ **cunning** *n* [U] (*often derog*) cunning behaviour or thought: *When he couldn't get what he wanted openly and honestly, he resorted to low cunning.*

cunningly *adv*: *cunningly concealed.*

cunt /kʌnt/ *n* (△ *sl offensive*) **1** a woman's VAGINA and outer sexual organs. **2** (*derog*) an unpleasant person: *You stupid cunt!*

cup and saucer   mug   cup   tankard

cup¹ /kʌp/ *n* **1** [C] (**a**) a small container shaped like a bowl, usu with a handle, used for drinking tea, coffee, etc: *a* ˈ*teacup* ○ *a* ˌ*cup and* ˈ*saucer* ○ *a paper cup.* ⇨ picture. (**b**) its contents; the amount it will hold: *She drank the whole cup.* ○ *Come and have a* ˌ*cup of* ˈ*coffee.* ○ *Use two cups of flour for the cake* (ie as a measure in cooking). **2** [C] (**a**) a cup, usu gold or silver and often with two handles, awarded as a prize in a competition: *teams competing for the World Cup* (eg in football) ○ *He's won several cups for shooting.* (**b**) (usu **Cup**) such a competition: *We got knocked out of the Cup in the first round.* **3** [C] a thing shaped like a cup: *an* ˈ*egg-cup* ○ *the cup in which an acorn grows* ○ *the cups of a bra.* **4** [C, U] a drink made from wine, CIDER, etc mixed with other ingredients, eg fruit juice, and usu served cold: *a* ˈ*claret-cup.* Compare PUNCH³. **IDM (not) sb's cup of** ˈ**tea** (*infml*) (not) what sb likes, is interested in, etc: *Skiing isn't really my cup of tea.* **in one's** ˈ**cups** (*dated or rhet*) drunk.

▶ **cupful** /ˈkʌpfʊl/ *n* (*pl* **cupfuls**) the amount that a cup will hold: *3 cupfuls of water.*

■ ˈ**cup-cake** *n* a small cake baked in a paper container shaped like a cup, often with ICING on top.

ˈ**cup final** (usu **Cup Final**) *n* (*Brit*) a final match to decide the winner of a series of matches, esp in football.

ˈ**cup-tie** *n* (*Brit*) a match between teams competing for a cup, esp in football.

cup² /kʌp/ *v* (**-pp-**) (**a**) to form one's hands into the shape of a cup: [Vnpr] *She cupped her hands round her mouth and shouted.* [Vn] *holding the berries in cupped hands.* (**b**) ~ *sth* (**in/with sth**) to hold sth having one's hands in the shape of a cup: [Vnpr] *cup one's chin in one's hands.* [also Vn].

cupboard /ˈkʌbəd/ *n* a set of shelves with a door or doors in front, either built into the wall of a room or as a separate piece of furniture. Cupboards are used for storing food, clothes, dishes, etc: *a* ˌ*kitchen* ˈ*cupboard* ○ *a* ˈ*linen cupboard* ○ *a* ˈ*broom cupboard* ○ *not enough cupboard space* ○ (*fig*) *They ask for more funds, but the cupboard is bare* (ie there is no money to give them). **IDM a skeleton in the cupboard** ⇨ SKELETON.

■ ˈ**cupboard love** *n* [U] (*Brit*) affection that is shown, esp by a child, in order to gain sth: *It's only cupboard love — he wants you to give him some sweets!*

Cupid /ˈkjuːpɪd/ *n* **1** the Roman god of love. **2 cupid** [C] a picture or statue of a beautiful boy with wings and a bow and arrows (ARROW), representing love.

cupidity /kjuːˈpɪdəti/ *n* [U] (*fml*) greed, esp for money or possessions.

cupola /ˈkjuːpələ/ *n* a small DOME(1) forming a roof or part of a roof.

cuppa /ˈkʌpə/ n (Brit infml) a cup of tea: *Let's sit down and have a nice cuppa.*

cur /kɜː(r)/ n (dated derog) an aggressive dog, esp a MONGREL.

curable /ˈkjʊərəbl/ adj that can be cured: *Some types of cancer are curable.*

curacy /ˈkjʊərəsi/ n the job or position of a CURATE: *a curacy at a church in Oxford* ○ *during his curacy.*

curate /ˈkjʊərət/ n (in the Church of England) an assistant to the priest of a PARISH. Compare VICAR.

curative /ˈkjʊərətɪv/ adj that can cure illness, etc: *the curative properties of a herb.*

curator /kjʊəˈreɪtə(r)/ n a person in charge of a museum, an art gallery, etc.

curb /kɜːb/ n **1** ~ (on sth) a thing that restrains or controls sth: *put/keep a curb on one's anger/feelings* ○ *government curbs on spending.* **2** (esp US) = KERB.
▶ **curb** v to prevent sth from getting out of control; to restrain sth: [Vn] *curb one's anger/feelings* ○ *curb spending/waste.*

curd /kɜːd/ n [U] (also **curds** [pl]) a thick soft substance formed when milk turns sour, used in making cheese: ˌcurds and ˈwhey ○ *curd ˈcheese.* See also LEMON CURD.

curdle /ˈkɜːdl/ v to form or make sth form into curds (CURD): [V] *The milk has curdled* (ie become sour). [Vn] *Lemon juice curdles milk.* [Vn, V] (fig) *His screams were enough to curdle one's blood/make one's blood curdle* (ie fill one with horror). See also BLOOD-CURDLING.

cure¹ /kjʊə(r)/ v **1(a)** ~ sb (of sth) to make sb healthy again: [Vn, Vnpr] *The doctors cured her (of cancer).* **(b)** to treat an illness, etc successfully: [Vn] *This illness cannot be cured easily.* **2(a)** to find a solution to sth; to put an end to sth: [Vn] *Officials hoped that import controls might cure the economy's serious inflation.* **(b)** ~ sb of sth to stop sb from behaving in a bad or unpleasant way: [Vnpr] *That nasty shock cured him of his inquisitiveness for ever.* **3** to treat meat, fish, tobacco, etc with salt, smoke, etc in order to preserve it: [Vn] *well-cured bacon.*

cure² /kjʊə(r)/ n **1** an act of curing or the process of being cured: *The doctor cannot guarantee a cure.* ○ *Her cure took six weeks.* ○ *effect/work a cure.* **2** ~ (for sth) a substance or treatment that cures; a REMEDY(1): *Is there a certain cure for cancer yet?* ○ *a disease with no known cure* ○ *He has tried all sorts of cures, but without success.* ○ (fig) *What is the cure for the plight of the homeless?* **IDM** **prevention is better than cure** ⇨ PREVENTION.

curfew /ˈkɜːfjuː/ n a signal or time after which people must stay indoors until the next day: *impose a dusk-to-dawn curfew* (eg during military rule) ○ *lift/end a curfew* ○ *You mustn't go out after curfew.*

curio /ˈkjʊəriəʊ/ n (pl -os) a small object that is rare or unusual: *his valuable collection of curios.*

curiosity /ˌkjʊəriˈɒsəti/ n **1** [U] ~ (about sth / to do sth) a strong desire to know or learn; being CURIOUS (1a): *satisfy/arouse sb's curiosity* ○ *curiosity about other cultures* ○ *intellectual curiosity* ○ *The letter wasn't addressed to me but I opened it out of curiosity.* **2** [C] a strange or unusual thing or person: *As an example of modern design it is something of a curiosity.* **IDM** **curiosity killed the ˈcat** (saying) (said to sb to stop them being too CURIOUS(1b)).

curious /ˈkjʊəriəs/ adj **1** ~ (about sth / to do sth) **(a)** (usu approv) eager to know or learn: *curious about the origin of mankind/the structure of atoms* ○ *I'm curious to know what she said.* ○ *He is a curious boy, always asking questions.* **(b)** (derog) having or showing too much interest in the affairs of others: *curious neighbours* ○ *She's always so curious about my work.* ○ *Hide it where curious eyes won't see it.* Compare INCURIOUS. **2** strange; unusual: *What a curious thing to say.* ○ *Isn't he a curious-looking little*

man? ○ *It's curious that he didn't tell you.* ▶ **curiously** adv: *He peered curiously at the two newcomers.* ○ *She was there all day but, curiously (enough), I didn't see her.* ○ *The party was a curiously boring affair.*

curl¹ /kɜːl/ n **[C]** a thing that curves round and round, esp a small bunch of hair: *curls (of hair) falling over her shoulders* ○ *hair falling in curls over her shoulders* ○ *the little boy's golden curls* (ie curling hair) ○ *a curl of smoke rising from a cigarette* ○ *'Of course not,' he said, with a curl of his lip* (ie expressing contempt).
▶ **curly** adj (-ier, -iest) having or arranged in curls: *curly hair* ○ *a curly pattern* ○ *a ˌcurly-headed ˈgirl.* ⇨ picture at HAIR.

curl² /kɜːl/ v **1** ~ (sth) (up) **(a)** to form or make sth form into a curl or curls: [Vn, Vnp] *She has curled (up) her hair.* [V] *Does your hair curl naturally?* **(b)** to form or make sth form into a curved shape, esp so that the edges are rolled up: [V, Vp] *The frost made the leaves curl (up).* [Vn, Vnp] *The heat curled the paper (up).* [Vn] *He lay curled in the corner.* **2** to wind round and round; to COIL: [Vadv] *The smoke curled lazily upwards.* [Vpr] *The plant's tendrils curled up the stick.* [also Vp]. **IDM** **curl one's ˈlip** to SNEER or show contempt by raising a corner of one's lip. **PHRV** **ˌcurl ˈup** to lie or sit with one's back curved and one's legs drawn up close to the body: *curl up on the sofa with a good book* ○ *The dog lay curled up in front of the fire.* **ˌcurl (sb) ˈup** (Brit infml) to become or make sb very embarrassed: *My father's bad jokes always make me curl up.*
▶ **ˈcurler** n a short, usu plastic, tube around which wet or warm hair is wound to make it curl.

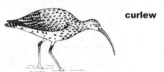
curlew

curlew /ˈkɜːljuː/ n a water bird with a long thin beak that curves downwards. ⇨ picture.

curling /ˈkɜːlɪŋ/ n a game played on ice, esp in Scotland, with heavy flat round stones which players slide along the ice towards a mark.

curmudgeon /kɜːˈmʌdʒən/ n (dated) a bad-tempered person, esp an old one. ▶ **curmudgeonly** adj.

currant /ˈkʌrənt/ n **1** a small sweet dried GRAPE used in cooking: *a currant bun.* **2** (usu in compounds) **(a)** a small black, red or white berry that grows in bunches on certain bushes: *blackcurrants* ○ *redcurrants.* **(b)** the bush on which this grows.

currency /ˈkʌrənsi/ n **1** [C, U] the system of money used in a country: *gold/paper currency* ○ *decimal currency* ○ *trading in foreign currencies* ○ *supporters of a single European currency* ○ *a currency crisis/deal.* See also HARD CURRENCY. **2** [U] the state of being in common or general use: *ideas which had enjoyed a brief currency* (ie were briefly popular) *during the 18th century* ○ *The rumour soon gained currency* (ie became widespread). ○ *Newspaper stories gave currency to the scandal* (ie spread it).

current¹ /ˈkʌrənt/ adj **1** [usu attrib] of the present time; happening now: *current issues/problems/prices* ○ *the current issue of a magazine* ○ *the current year* (ie this year) ○ *current events in India* ○ *her current boyfriend.* **2** in common or general use; generally accepted: *current opinions/beliefs* ○ *words that are no longer current* ○ *a rumour that is current* (ie widely known about) *in the city.* ⇨ note at PRESENT¹.
▶ **currently** adv at the present time: *our director, who is currently in Japan.*

■ **¹current account** (*esp Brit*) (*US* also **checking account**) *n* a bank account from which money can be withdrawn without previous notice. Current account holders are usually given a cheque-book (CHEQUE) and a plastic card to guarantee cheques or withdraw money. Compare DEPOSIT ACCOUNT, SAVINGS ACCOUNT.

,**current af'fairs** *n* [pl] events of political importance happening in the world at the present time.

current² /ˈkʌrənt/ *n* **1** [C] a movement of water or air flowing in a certain direction through a larger body of water or air: *The swimmer was swept away by the current.* ○ *She had to swim against the current.* ○ *Currents of warm air keep the hang-gliders aloft.* **2** [U, sing] the flow of electricity through sth or along a wire or cable: *a 15-amp current* ○ *turn on the current* ○ *A sudden surge in the current made the lights fuse.* See also ALTERNATING CURRENT, DIRECT CURRENT. **3** [C] the course of events, opinions, etc: *Nothing disturbed the peaceful current of life in the village.* ○ *Ministers are worried by the present current of anti-government feeling.*

curriculum /kəˈrɪkjələm/ *n* (*pl* **curricula** /-lə/) the subjects included in a course of study or taught at a particular school, college, etc: *Is Spanish on the curriculum at your school?* Compare SYLLABUS.

■ **curriculum vitae** /kəˌrɪkjələm ˈviːtaɪ/ (*abbr* **cv**) (*US* also **résumé**) *n* (usu *sing*) a brief account of sb's previous career, usu submitted with an application for a job.

curry¹ /ˈkʌri/ *n* [C, U] a dish of meat, fish, vegetables, etc cooked with certain hot-tasting spices. Curry is often eaten with rice: *a chicken/beef curry* ○ *Do you like curry?*

▶ **curried** *adj* [usu attrib] cooked with certain hot-tasting spices: *curried chicken/beef.*

■ **curry powder** *n* [U] a mixture of various spices ground to a powder and used in making curry.

curry² /ˈkʌri/ *v* (*pt, pp* **curried**) IDM **curry 'favour (with sb)** (*derog*) to try to gain sb's favour by giving them help, praise, etc.

curse¹ /kɜːs/ *n* **1** [C] a rude or offensive word or phrase used to express violent anger: *muttering obscene curses.* **2** [sing] a magical word or phrase spoken with the aim of punishing, injuring or destroying sb/sth: *The witch put a curse on him* (ie used a curse against him). ○ *be under a curse* (ie suffer as a result of a curse). Compare BLESSING 1. **3** [C] a cause of evil, harm, destruction, etc: *the curse of poverty* ○ *People who drive in the middle of the road are a curse!* **4 the curse** [sing] (*infml euph*) menstruation (MENSTRUATE): *I got the curse today.*

curse² /kɜːs/ *v* (**a**) to say rude or offensive things about sb/sth in an angry or violent way: [V] *to curse and swear* [Vn] *He cursed his bad luck.* [Vnpr] *I cursed her for spoiling my plans.* ○ *I cursed myself for my stupidity.* (**b**) to use a CURSE¹(2) against sb/sth: [Vn] *The witch-doctor has cursed our cattle.* Compare BLESS 1. PHRV **be 'cursed with sth** to have the stated bad thing, esp habitually: *be cursed with ill health/a violent temper/bad luck.*

▶ **cursed** /ˈkɜːsɪd/ *adj* [attrib] (*infml*) (used to show annoyance) unpleasant: *This work is a cursed nuisance.*

cursive /ˈkɜːsɪv/ *adj* (of writing) done with letters joined together.

cursor /ˈkɜːsə(r)/ *n* (*computing*) a movable dot on a computer screen that indicates a particular position.

cursory /ˈkɜːsəri/ *adj* (*often derog*) done quickly and not thoroughly; not detailed: *give sth a cursory glance/look/inspection* ○ *The book is cursory in its treatment of his early life.* ▶ **cursorily** /ˈkɜːsərəli/ *adv.*

curt /kɜːt/ *adj* (*derog*) rudely brief; ABRUPT(2): *a curt answer/rebuke* ○ *She's rather curt when she's angry.*

○ *I was a little curt with him* (ie spoke sharply to him). ▶ **curtly** *adv.* **curtness** *n* [U].

curtail /kɜːˈteɪl/ *v* to make sth shorter or less; to reduce sth: [Vn] *curtail a speech/one's holidays* ○ *We must try to curtail our spending.* ○ *Illness has curtailed her sporting activities.* ▶ **curtailment** *n* [U]: *the curtailment of one's rights.*

curtain /ˈkɜːtn/ *n* **1** [C] (**a**) (*US* **drape**) a piece of material hung to cover a window, and usu movable sideways: *Please draw the curtains* (ie pull them across the window(s)). ○ *lace curtains.* (**b**) a similar piece of material hung up as a screen: *Pull the curtains around the patient's bed.* ○ *a shower curtain.* **2** [sing] (**a**) a screen of heavy material that can be raised or lowered at the front of a stage: *The curtain rose/went up* (ie The play/act began). ○ *The curtain fell/came down* (ie The play/act ended). ○ (*fig*) *The curtain has fallen on her long and distinguished career* (ie Her career has ended). See also SAFETY CURTAIN. (**b**) the raising or lowering of such a curtain: *Tonight's curtain is at 7.30* (ie The play begins at 7.30). ○ *After the final curtain* (ie After the play had ended) *we went backstage.* **3** [C *esp sing*] a thing that screens, covers, protects, etc: *a curtain of fog/mist* ○ *A curtain of rain swept over the valley.* ○ *the curtain of secrecy that hides the government's intentions.* **4 curtains** [pl] ~**s (for sb/sth)** (*infml*) a situation without hope or from which one cannot escape; the end: *When I saw he had a gun, I thought it was curtains (for me).*

▶ **curtain** *v* to provide a window, etc with a curtain or curtains: [Vn] *curtained windows* ○ *enough material to curtain all the rooms.* PHRV ,**curtain sth 'off** to separate or divide sth with a curtain or curtains: *curtain off part of a room.*

■ **'curtain-call** *n* the appearance of the actors on stage after the end of a play to receive APPLAUSE: *The performers took several curtain-calls* (ie came onto the stage repeatedly).

'curtain-raiser *n* ~ **(to sth)** (**a**) a short piece performed before the main play. (**b**) a thing that precedes a similar but larger or more important event: *border incidents that were curtain-raisers to a full-scale war.*

curtsy (also **curtsey**) /ˈkɜːtsi/ *n* a woman's or girl's formal greeting, made by bending the knees with one foot in front of the other: *make/drop/bob a curtsy to the Queen.*

▶ **curtsy** (also **curtsey**) *v* (*pt, pp* **curtsied, curtseyed**) ~ **(to sb)** to make a curtsy: [Vpr] *curtsy to the Queen* [also V]. Compare BOW².

curvaceous /kɜːˈveɪʃəs/ *adj* (*approv infml esp sexist*) (of a woman) having an attractive curved figure.

curvature /ˈkɜːvətʃə(r); *US* -tʃʊər/ *n* [U] (*techn*) the state of being curved; curved shape: *the curvature of the earth's surface* ○ *suffer from curvature of the spine.*

curve /kɜːv/ *n* a line or surface that bends round; a bend: *a curve on a graph* ○ *a curve in the road* ○ *a pattern full of curves and angles* ○ *her attractive curves* (ie pleasantly curving figure).

▶ **curve** *v* (**a**) to form or make sth form a curve: [V] *The road curved suddenly to the left.* [Vn] *a knife with a curved blade.* (**b**) to move in a curve: [Vpr] *The spear curved through the air.* [also Vp, Vadv].

curvy *adj* (**-ier, -iest**) (*infml*) having many curves: *curvy lines* ○ *He likes big curvy women.*

cushion /ˈkʊʃn/ *n* **1** a small bag filled with soft material, feathers, etc. Cushions are used to make a seat more comfortable, to kneel on, etc. **2** a mass of sth soft: *a cushion of moss on the rock* ○ *a 'pincushion* ○ *A hovercraft rides on a cushion of air.* ○ (*fig*) *The three goals they scored in the first half give them a useful cushion* (ie make it easier for them to avoid being beaten). **3** the soft inside edge along each side of a table used for playing BILLIARDS, off which the balls bounce. ⇨ picture at SNOOKER.

▶ **cushion** v **1** (esp passive) to provide or protect sth with a cushion(1): [Vn] *a stool with a cushioned seat.* **2** to soften the effect of an impact: [Vn] *Powerful shock absorbers cushion our landing.* **3** ~ sb/sth (**against**/**from sth**) to protect sb/sth from sth harmful, sometimes excessively: [Vnpr] *a child who has been cushioned from unpleasant experiences* ○ *Wage increases have cushioned us against the effects of higher prices.* [also Vn].

cushy /ˈkʊʃi/ adj (**-ier, -iest**) (*infml often derog*) (esp of a job) not requiring much effort: *Her job's so cushy: she does next to nothing and earns a fortune.* ○ *It's a cushy life for the rich.* **IDM** **a cushy ˈnumber** (*infml*) a job or situation in life that is pleasant and requires little effort: *He's got himself a very cushy little number.*

cusp /kʌsp/ n **1** a pointed end where two curves meet: *the cusp of a crescent/a leaf.* **2** the time when one sign of the ZODIAC is seen as ending and the next beginning: *I was born on the cusp between Virgo and Libra.*

cuss /kʌs/ n (*dated infml*) (preceded by an *adj*) a person of the specified type: *He's an awkward/a queer old cuss.*

cussed /ˈkʌsɪd/ adj (*infml derog*) (of people) unwilling to agree or to be helpful; OBSTINATE: *She's so cussed she always does the opposite of what you ask.*

▶ **cussedly** adv. **cussedness** n [U]: (*fig*) *It rained, with the usual cussedness of the English weather.*

custard /ˈkʌstəd/ n [U] **1** (*esp Brit*) a thick sweet yellow liquid usu eaten hot with cooked fruit, pastry, etc: *apple pie and custard.* **2** a thick sweet dish made with eggs, milk and sugar that is baked or boiled: *egg custard.*

■ ˌcustard ˈpie n a flat round mass of soft wet matter, intended to look like a pie with custard in, which performers throw at each other to make people laugh.

custodian /kʌˈstəʊdiən/ n a person who takes responsibility for or who looks after sth: *a self-appointed custodian of public morals.*

custody /ˈkʌstədi/ n [U] **1** the action, right or duty of caring for sb/sth: *leave one's valuables in safe custody* (eg in a bank) ○ *When his parents died, he was placed in the custody of his aunt.* ○ *The court gave the mother custody of the child* (eg after a DIVORCE¹(1)). ○ *parents involved in a battle over custody* (ie disputing who should have the right to look after the children). **2** the state of being in prison while awaiting trial: *The judge remanded him in custody for two weeks.* ○ *be held in custody* ○ *take sb into police custody* (ie arrest them).

▶ **custodial** /kʌˈstəʊdiəl/ adj [usu attrib] involving custody: *The court imposed a short custodial sentence on him.*

custom /ˈkʌstəm/ n **1(a)** [C, U] a traditional and generally accepted way of behaving or doing things: *It takes time to get used to another country's customs.* ○ *the custom of giving presents at Christmas* ○ *holidays established by local/ancient custom.* **(b)** [C] a thing that sb habitually does; a practice: *It is my custom to rise early.* **2** [U] (*fml esp Brit*) regular dealings with a shop, etc by customers: *We would like to have your custom* (ie would like you to buy our goods). ○ *We've lost a lot of custom* (ie Fewer goods have been bought from us) *since our prices went up.*

■ ˌcustom-ˈbuilt (also ˌcustom-ˈmade) adj built or made as the buyer specifies: *a ˌcustom-built ˈcar* ○ *ˌcustom-made ˈclothes/ˈshoes.*

customary /ˈkʌstəməri; US -meri/ adj according to custom(1); usual: *Is it customary to tip waiters in your country?* ○ *She gave the customary speech of*

thanks to the chairman. ▶ **customarily** /ˈkʌstəmərəli; US ˌkʌstəˈmerəli/ adv.

customer /ˈkʌstəmə(r)/ n **1** a person or organization that buys sth from a shop or business: *one of the shop's best/most regular customers* ○ *The firm has excellent customer relations.* **2** (*infml*) (following an *adj*) a person of the specified type: *a queer/awkward/rum/tough customer* ○ *an ugly customer* ○ *a cool customer* (eg one who remains calm in a crisis).

customize, -ise /ˈkʌstəmaɪz/ v [Vn] (usu passive) to make or alter sth according to the buyer's or owner's wishes.

customs /ˈkʌstəmz/ n [pl] **(a)** the taxes that must be paid to the government on goods brought in from other countries: *pay customs on sth.* **(b)** (also **the Customs**) the government department that collects these taxes: *The Customs have seized large quantities of smuggled heroin.* ○ *How long does it take to get through customs* (ie have one's bags, etc examined by customs officers at a port, airport, etc)? ○ *a customs officer/search/check* ○ *customs duty/formalities.* Compare EXCISE¹.

cut¹ /kʌt/ v (**-tt-**; *pt, pp* **cut**) **1** to make an opening or wound in sth, esp with a sharp tool such as a knife or SCISSORS: [Vn] *He cut himself/his face shaving.* ○ *She cut her finger on a piece of broken glass.* ○ *cut sb's throat* (ie kill sb with a deep wound in the throat) [Vpr] *You need a powerful saw to cut through metal.* ○ (*fig*) *The canoe quickly cut through the water.* [Vn-adj] *The old lady had fallen and cut her head open* (ie suffered a deep wound to the head). **2(a)** ~ sth (**from sth**); ~ (**for sb**) to remove sth from sth larger using a knife, etc: [Vn] *cut some flowers* ○ *The wheat has been cut.* ○ *How many slices of bread should I cut?* [Vnpr] *She cut a slice of beef from the roast.* [Vnn, Vnpr] *Please cut me a piece of cake/cut a piece of cake for me.* **(b)** ~ sth (**in/into sth**) to divide sth into smaller pieces with a knife, etc: [Vn] *Will you cut the cake?* ○ *If you cut the bread* (ie into slices) *we'll make some toast.* [Vnpr] *She cut the meat into cubes.* ○ *cut apples into halves/thirds/quarters* ○ *The bus was cut in half/in two by the train.* **(c)** to separate sth into two pieces; to divide sth: [Vn] *cut a rope/cable/thread* ○ *Don't cut the string, untie the knots.* **(d)** to make sth shorter by cutting; to trim sth: [Vn] *cut one's hair/one's nails/a hedge* ○ *cut* (ie MOW) *the grass* [Vn, Vn-adj] *He's had his hair cut (short).* **(e)** to make or form sth by removing material with a cutting tool: [Vn] *cut a diamond* [Vnpr] *The climbers cut steps in the ice.* ○ *cut a hole in a piece of paper* ○ *cut one's initials on a tree.* ⇨ note. **3(a)** to be capable of being cut: [Vadv] *Sandstone cuts easily.* **(b)** to be capable of cutting: [V] *This knife won't cut.* [also Vadv]. **4** (*geometry*) (of a line) to cross another line: [Vn] *The line cuts the circle at two points.* **5** to lift and turn up part of a pack of cards (CARD¹ 4) in order to decide who is to play first, etc: [Vn] *cut the cards/pack* [V] *Let's cut for dealer.* **6(a)** to reduce sth by removing a part of it: [Vn] *cut prices/taxes/spending/production* [Vnpr] *His salary has been cut by ten per cent.* ○ *The new bus service cuts the travelling time by half.* ○ *Could you cut your essay from 5 000 to 3 000 words?* **(b)** ~ sth (**from sth**) to remove sth from sth; to leave out or omit sth: [Vn, Vnpr] *Two scenes were cut (from the film) by the censor.* **(c)** (*infml*) to stop sth: [Vn] *Cut the chatter and get on with your work!* **7(a)** [Vn] to prepare a film or tape by removing parts of it or putting them in a different order; to EDIT(1b) sth. **(b)** (usu imperative) to stop filming or recording: [V] *The director shouted 'Cut!'* **(c)** ~ (**from sth**) **to sth** (in films, radio or television) to move quickly from one scene to another: [Vpr] *The scene cuts from the bedroom to the street.* **8** [Vn] to switch off a light, car engine, etc. **9** (*infml*) to stay away from a lesson, meeting, etc; to

fail to attend sth: [Vn] *cut a class/lecture/tutorial.*
10 to cause physical or mental pain to sb: [Vn] *His cruel remarks cut her deeply.* **11** (*infml*) to insult sb by refusing to recognize them: [Vn, Vn-adj] *She cut me (dead) in the street the other day.* **12** to have a new tooth beginning to appear through the GUM¹: [Vn] *Our baby cut her first tooth today.* **13** to make a recording of music on a record¹(3), etc: [Vn] *The Beatles cut their first disc in 1962.* **IDM** Most idioms containing **cut** are at the entries for the nouns or adjectives in the idioms, eg **cut it/things fine** ⇨ FINE². **cut and 'run** (*sl*) to make a quick or sudden escape. **PHRV** ,cut a'cross sth not to correspond to the usual divisions between groups: *Opinion on this issue cuts across traditional political boundaries.* ,cut a'cross, a'long, 'through, etc (sth) to go across, etc sth, esp in order to make one's route shorter: *I usually cut across/through the park on my way home.*
'cut at sb / sth to try to cut or wound sb/sth with a knife, etc: *His attacker cut at him with a razor.* ∘ *She cut at the rope in an attempt to free herself.*
,cut sth a'way (from sth) to remove sth from sth by cutting: *They cut away all the dead branches from the tree.*
,cut sth 'back to make a bush, etc smaller by cutting off shoots and branches; to PRUNE²(1) sth: *cut back a rose bush.* ,cut sth 'back; ,cut 'back (on sth) to reduce sth: *cut back on spending* ∘ *If we don't sell more goods, we'll have to cut back (on) production.* See also CUT-BACK.
,cut sb 'down (*fml*) **1** to kill or injure sb by striking them with a sword or some other sharp weapon. **2** (usu passive) to kill sb: *He was cut down by pneumonia at an early age.* ,cut sth 'down **1** to make sth fall down by cutting it at the base: *cut down a tree.* **2** to make sth shorter: *cut down a pair of trousers* ∘ *Your article's too long — please cut it down to 1000 words.* ,cut sth 'down; ,cut 'down (on sth) to reduce the amount or quantity of sth; to reduce the amount one spends, eats, smokes, etc: *cut down one's expenses* ∘ *The doctor told him to cut down on his drinking.* ∘ *I won't have a cigarette, thanks — I'm trying to cut down* (ie smoke fewer).
'cut sb / sth from sth to remove sb/sth from a larger object by cutting: *cut a branch from a tree* ∘ *The injured driver had to be cut from the wreckage of his car.*
'cut 'in (on sb/sth) (of a vehicle or driver) to move suddenly in front of another vehicle, leaving little space between the two vehicles: *The sports car overtook me and then cut in (on me).* ,cut 'in (on sb/sth) to interrupt sb speaking: *She kept cutting in on our conversation.* ,cut sb 'in (on sth) (*infml*) to give sb a share of the profit in a business or an activity: *I can cut you in on the deal.*
,cut sb 'off **1** to interrupt sb and stop them speaking: *My explanation was cut off by loud protests.* **2** (often passive) to interrupt sb speaking on the telephone by breaking the connection: *We were cut off in the middle of our conversation.* ∘ *Operator, I've just been cut off.* **3** (*Brit*) (*US* ,cut sb 'out) to reject sb as one's HEIR; to DISINHERIT sb: *He cut his son off without a penny.* **4** (usu passive) to make sb die sooner than is normal: *a young man cut off in his prime.* ,cut sb/sth 'off (often passive) to stop the supply of sth to sb: *If you don't pay your gas bill soon you may be cut off.* ∘ *Our water supply has been cut off.* ∘ *Her father cut off* (ie stopped paying) *her allowance.* ,cut sth 'off to block or OBSTRUCT sth: *cut off the enemy's retreat* ∘ *cut off an escape route* ∘ *The new factory cuts off our view of the sea.* ,cut sth 'off (sth) to remove sth from sth larger by cutting: *Be careful you don't cut your fingers off!* ∘ *King Charles I had his head cut off.* ∘ *He cut off a metre of cloth from the roll.* ∘ *The winner cut ten seconds off* (eg ran the distance ten seconds quicker than) *the world record.* ,cut sb/sth 'off (from sb/sth) (often passive) to prevent sb/sth

from leaving or reaching a place or communicating with people outside a place: *an army cut off from its base* ∘ *The children were cut off* (eg trapped on a rock) *by the incoming tide.* ∘ *The village was cut off (from the outside world) by heavy snow for a month.* ∘ *She feels very cut off* (ie isolated) *living in the country.*
,cut 'out to stop functioning: *One of the plane's engines cut out.* ,cut sb 'out (*US*) = CUT SB OFF 3. ,cut sth 'out **1** to make sth by cutting: *cut out a path through the jungle* ∘ *cut out a dress from some old material* ∘ (*fig*) *He's cut out a niche* (ie found a suitable job) *for himself in politics.* **2** (*esp imperative*) to stop doing or saying sth annoying: *I'm sick of you two squabbling — just cut it out!* **3** (*infml*) to leave sth out; to omit sth: *You can cut out the unimportant details.* **4** (*infml*) to stop doing, using or eating sth: *You should cut out chocolate if you want to lose weight.* **5** to block sth, esp light: *Thick overhanging branches cut out the sunlight.* ,cut sth 'out (of sth) to remove sth from sth larger by cutting: *cut an article out of the newspaper.* be ,cut 'out for sth; be ,cut 'out to be sth (*infml*) to have the qualities and abilities needed for sth; (of two people) to be well matched: *He's not cut out for teaching/to be a teacher.* ∘ *Sally and Michael seem to be cut out for each other.*
,cut sth 'through sth to make a path or passage through sth by cutting: *The prisoners cut their way through the barbed wire and escaped.*
,cut sb 'up **1** (*infml*) to injure sb by cutting or hitting them: *He was badly cut up in the fight.* **2** to destroy sb completely: *cut up the enemy's forces.* **3** (*infml*) (usu passive) to upset sb emotionally: *He was badly cut up by the death of his son.* ,cut sth 'up to divide sth into small pieces with a knife, etc: *cut up vegetables.*
■ 'cut-back *n* a reduction: *cut-backs in public spending.*
,cut 'glass *n* [U] glass with patterns cut in it: *a ,cut-glass 'vase.*
'cut-off *n* a point at which sth is ended; a limit: *reach the cut-off point* ∘ *What is the cut-off date for registration?*
'cut-out *n* **1** a shape cut out of paper, wood, etc: *a cardboard cut-out.* **2** a device that turns off an electric current or breaks a circuit.
,cut-'price (*US* ,cut-'rate) *adj* [esp attrib] (**a**) sold at a reduced price: *,cut-price 'goods* ∘ *I bought it cut-price.* (**b**) selling goods at reduced prices: *a ,cut-price 'store.*

NOTE Compare **cut**, **saw**, **chop**, **hack**, **slash** and **tear**. Note that they can be used with a variety of prepositions and particles. **Cut** has the widest use: *She cut her finger on some broken glass.* ∘ *He cut the advertisement out of the newspaper.* ∘ *I want to have my hair cut.* ∘ *Cut two holes in the mask for the eyes.*
You **saw** wood with a special instrument called a *saw*, and **chop** it using a heavy sharp instrument called an *axe*: *We can saw off any dead branches and chop them for firewood.* **Hack** suggests hitting something with violent blows in order to cut, destroy or remove it: *When are they going to stop hacking down all the rainforests?*
Slash means to damage or injure somebody or something by cutting in long lines with a knife: *Vandals went through the train slashing seats.* You **tear** paper, etc by pulling it into pieces with your fingers: *Can I tear this article out of your magazine?* ∘ *She tore up the letter in disgust.*

cut² /kʌt/ *n* **1** a wound or an opening made with a knife, SCISSORS, etc: *She bandaged the deep cut in his leg.* ∘ *cuts and bruises on her face* ∘ *Make a small cut in the edge of the cloth.* **2** an act of cutting sth: *Your hair could do with a cut* (ie is too long). **3** ~ (in sth) a reduction in size, length, amount, etc: *announce a cut in unemployment benefit* ○ *He had to take a further cut in (his) salary.* ○ *price/job/tax cuts.* See also POWER CUT. **4** ~ (**in sth**) an act of removing part of a play, film, book, etc, eg because it is thought to be offensive: *The censor has made several minor cuts in the film.* **5** a piece of meat cut from an animal: *a lean cut of pork* ○ *cheap cuts of stewing lamb.* **6** (*infml*) a share of the profits from sth, esp sth dishonest: *Your cut will be £200.* See also SHORT CUT. **IDM** **a cut above sb/sth** (*infml*) rather better than sb/sth: *Her work is clearly a cut above that of the others.* **the cut and 'thrust (of sth)** the lively argument or activity involved in sth: *enjoy the cut and thrust of parliamentary debate.*

cute /kjuːt/ *adj* (**-r, -st**) (*sometimes derog*) **1** attractive; pretty and charming: *Isn't she a cute baby?* ○ *unbearably cute paintings of little furry animals.* **2** (*infml esp US*) clever, esp in a rather annoying way: *I have had enough of your cute remarks.* ○ *Don't be so cute!* ▶ **cutely** *adv*. **cuteness** *n* [U].

cuticle /'kjuːtɪkl/ *n* the piece of hard skin at the base of a nail on a person's finger or toe. ⇨ picture at HAND[1].

cutlass /'kʌtləs/ *n* a short sword with a slightly curved blade, used formerly by sailors. ⇨ picture at SWORD.

cutlery /'kʌtləri/ *n* [U] knives, forks and spoons used for eating and serving food: *a cutlery drawer/set.*

cutlet /'kʌtlət/ *n* **1** a thick slice of meat or fish typically cooked by frying or on a GRILL(1): *lamb cutlets.* **2** small pieces of meat or other food shaped together to look like a cutlet: *a nut cutlet.*

cutter /'kʌtə(r)/ *n* **1** (esp in compounds) (**a**) a person or thing that cuts: *a 'pastry cutter.* (**b**) **cutters** [pl] a cutting tool: *a pair of 'wire-cutters.* **2**(**a**) a small fast ship with sails. (**b**) a ship's boat, used for trips between ship and shore.

cutthroat /'kʌtθrəʊt/ *adj* [usu attrib] (of a competitive activity) fierce and intense; involving the use of extreme measures: *rival companies engaged in cutthroat competition* ○ *the cutthroat world of professional tennis.*

cutting[1] /'kʌtɪŋ/ *n* **1** (*US* **clipping**) an article, story, etc cut from a newspaper or magazine and kept for reference. **2** a piece cut off a plant to be used to grow a new plant: *chrysanthemum cuttings* ○ *take a cutting (from a rose).* **3** (also **cut**) a narrow open passage dug through high ground for a road, railway or canal. ■ ,**cutting 'edge** *n* (usu *sing*) **1** ~ (**of sth**) the latest, most advanced stage in the development of sth: *working at the cutting edge of computer technology.* **2** an advantage over sb: *We're relying on him to give the team a cutting edge.*

cutting[2] /'kʌtɪŋ/ *adj* **1** [attrib] (of wind) cold in a sharp and unpleasant way. **2** unkind and likely to hurt sb's feelings: *cutting remarks.*

cuttlefish /'kʌtlfɪʃ/ *n* a sea animal with ten arms.

cv (also **CV**) /ˌsiː 'viː/ *abbr* a record of a person's education and employment (Latin *curriculum vitae*): *send a full cv with your job application.*

-cy (also **-acy**) *suff* **1** (with *adjs* and *ns* forming *ns*) the state or quality of being: *accuracy* ○ *supremacy* ○ *infancy.* **2** (with *ns* forming *ns*) having the status or position of: *baronetcy* ○ *chaplaincy.*

cyanide /'saɪənaɪd/ *n* [U] a highly poisonous chemical compound.

cybernetics /ˌsaɪbə'netɪks/ *n* [sing *v*] the science of communication and control, esp concerned with comparing human and animal brains with machines and electronic devices. ▶ **cybernetic** *adj*.

cyclamen /'sɪkləmən; *US* 'saɪk-/ *n* a plant with pink, purple or white flowers, often grown indoors.

cycle /'saɪkl/ *n* **1** a series of events that are regularly repeated in the same order: *the cycle of the seasons* ○ *the cycle of economic booms and slumps.* See also LIFE CYCLE. **2** a complete set or series, eg of movements in a machine: *operate at a speed of 80 cycles per second.* **3** a bicycle or motor cycle (MOTOR): *a cycle shop/race.* See also BIKE.
▶ **cycle** *v* to ride a bicycle: [V] *I like to go cycling at weekends.* [Vpr] *He cycles to work every day.* [Vp, Vpr] *She cycled along (the street).* See also CYCLIST. **cycling** *n* [U] the sport or activity of riding a bicycle: *Cycling is Europe's second most popular sport.* ○ *cycling shorts.*

cyclic /'saɪklɪk, 'sɪk-/ (also **cyclical** /'sɪklɪkl, 'saɪk-/) *adj* occurring in cycles (CYCLE 1); regularly repeated: *the cyclical nature of economic activity.* ▶ **cyclically** *adv*.

cyclist /'saɪklɪst/ *n* a person who rides a bicycle.

cyclone /'saɪkləʊn/ *n* a violent storm in which strong winds move over the ground in a circle. Compare HURRICANE, TYPHOON.

cygnet /'sɪɡnət/ *n* a young SWAN.

cylinder /'sɪlɪndə(r)/ *n* **1**(**a**) (*geometry*) a solid or hollow curved figure with circular ends and straight sides. ⇨ picture at SOLID. (**b**) an object shaped like this: *a hot-water/gas cylinder* (ie one containing hot water/gas) ○ *The string is wound round a cardboard cylinder.* **2** the hollow part inside which the PISTON moves in an engine: *a six-cylinder engine/car.* ⇨ picture at PISTON. **3** **IDM** **working/firing on all 'cylinders** using all one's energy.
▶ **cylindrical** /sə'lɪndrɪkl/ *adj* shaped like a cylinder: *cylindrical columns.*

cymbal /'sɪmbl/ *n* (usu *pl*) a round brass plate used as a musical instrument. It is hit with a stick or a pair of them are struck together: *the clash of the cymbals.* ⇨ picture at MUSICAL INSTRUMENT.

cynic /'sɪnɪk/ *n* (*often derog*) **1** a person who believes that people do not do things for good, sincere or noble reasons, but only for their own advantage: *'What does he want from you in return?' 'Don't be such a cynic!'* **2** a person who questions whether sth will really happen, whether sth is important, etc: *Already one can hear the cynics saying: 'Who cares, anyway?'*
▶ **cynical** /'sɪnɪkl/ *adj* (*often derog*) **1** of or like a cynic: *a cynical remark/attitude/smile* ○ *They've grown rather cynical about democracy* (ie no longer believe that it is an honest system). **2** concerned only with one's own interests: *a cynical disregard for the safety of others* ○ *footballers who bring down their opponents with deliberate and cynical fouls.* **cynically** /-kli/ *adv*. **cynicism** /'sɪnɪsɪzəm/ *n* [U].

cypher = CIPHER.

cypress /'saɪprəs/ *n* a type of tall thin EVERGREEN tree.

cyst /sɪst/ *n* a hollow growth(4a) in the body, containing liquid matter: *a small operation to remove a cyst.*

cystic fibrosis /ˌsɪstɪk faɪ'brəʊsɪs/ *n* [U] (*medical*) a serious disease that can be passed on from parents to children. It usu affects young children and causes infection of the organs of breathing.

cystitis /sɪ'staɪtɪs/ *n* [U] (*medical*) a disease of the BLADDER affecting esp women. It is painful and the person suffering from it has to urinate (URINE) frequently.

czar = TSAR.

czarina = TSARINA.

Dd

D¹ (also **d**) /diː/ n (pl **D's**, **d's** /diːz/) **1** the fourth letter of the English alphabet: *'David' begins and ends with (a) 'D'/D.* **2 D** (*music*) the second note in the scale¹(6) of C major. **3 D** an academic mark indicating a low standard of work.

D² abbr (*US politics*) Democrat. Compare R² 3.

D³ (also **d**) symb the Roman NUMERAL for 500. See also D-DAY.

d abbr **1** died: *Emily Jane Clifton, d 1865.* Compare B. **2** (in former British currency) penny; pennies or pence : *a 2d stamp.* Compare P 2.

-d ⇨ -ED.

DA abbr (*US*) District Attorney.

dab /dæb/ v (-bb-) **1** ~ (**at**) sth (**with** sth) to press against sth lightly and gently several times: [Vn, Vnpr] *She stopped crying and dabbed her eyes (with a tissue).* [Vpr] *She dabbed at the cut with a wet cloth.* **2** ~ sth **on/off** (sth) to put on/remove sth with light quick strokes: [Vnpr] *dab paint on a picture* [Vnp] *dab off the excess water.*
▶ **dab** n [C] **1** a small quantity of paint, etc put on a surface. **2** an act of lightly touching or pressing sth without rubbing: *One dab with blotting-paper and the ink was dry.*
■ **,dab 'hand** n (*Brit infml*) a person who is very skilled at sth: *He's a dab hand at cooking spaghetti.* ○ *a dab hand with a golf club.*

dabble /'dæbl/ v **1** ~ sth (**in** sth) to put one's hands, feet, etc into water and move them around a little: [Vnpr] *She dabbled her fingers in the fountain.* [also Vn]. **2** ~ (**in/at/with** sth) to take part in sth without serious intentions: [Vpr] *He just dabbles in politics.* ○ *dabbling with drink and drugs* [also V].

dachshund /'dækshnd; US 'dɑːkshʊnd/ n a small dog with a long body and short legs. ⇨ picture at DOG¹.

dad /dæd/ n (*infml*) (often as a form of address) father: *That's my dad over there.* ○ *Hello, Dad! Where's Mum?*

daddy /'dædi/ n (used esp by and when speaking to young children) father.
■ **,daddy-'long-legs** n (pl unchanged) (*infml*) **1** (*esp Brit*) a flying insect with very long legs. **2** (*US*) a SPIDER with very long legs.

dado /'deɪdəʊ/ n (pl **-os**; US also **-oes**) the lower part of the wall of a room, when it is different from the upper part in colour or material.

daemon /'diːmən/ n a spirit that inspires sb to do or create things: *one's creative daemon.* Compare DEMON.

daffodil /'dæfədɪl/ n a yellow flower with a tall stem that grows from a BULB(1). ⇨ picture at FLOWER.

daft /dɑːft; US dæft/ adj (-er, -est) (*infml esp Brit*) foolish; silly: *Don't be so daft!* ○ *The idea isn't as daft as it sounds.* ▶ **daftness** n [U].

dagger /'dægə(r)/ n a short pointed knife used as a weapon. ⇨ picture at KNIFE. See also CLOAK-AND-DAGGER. **IDM** **at daggers 'drawn (with sb)** showing strong dislike for sb; HOSTILE(1a) towards sb: *He and his partner are at daggers drawn.* **look daggers at sb** to look very angrily at sb: *He looked daggers at me when I told him he was lazy.*

dago /'deɪɡəʊ/ n (pl **-os**) (⚠ sl offensive) a foreign person with dark skin, esp a person from Italy, Spain or Portugal.

dahlia /'deɪlɪə; US 'dælɪə/ n a garden plant with brightly coloured flowers.

daily /'deɪli/ adj [attrib], adv done, produced or happening every day: *a daily routine/visit/newspaper* ○ *events affecting the daily lives of millions of people* ○ *The machines are inspected twice daily.*
▶ **daily** n **1** a newspaper published every day except Sunday: *The story appears in all the national dailies.* **2** (also **daily help**) (*Brit infml*) a person who is employed to come to sb's house each day to clean it and do other jobs.

dainty /'deɪnti/ adj (-ier, -iest) **1** (of things) small and pretty: *dainty porcelain/lace.* **2(a)** (of people) neat and delicate(1) in build or movement: *a dainty child* ○ *dainty feet.* **(b)** (of people) having refined taste¹(6) and manners; hard to please, esp about food: *a dainty eater.* ▶ **daintily** adv: *daintily dressed* ○ *She bit daintily into the scone.* **daintiness** n [U].

dairy /'deəri/ n **1** a place where milk is kept and milk products are made. **2** a shop where milk, butter, eggs, etc are sold.
▶ **dairy** adj [attrib] **1** made from milk: *dairy products.* **2** concerned with producing milk, not meat: *the dairy industry* ○ *dairy cattle* ○ *dairy farmers.*

dairymaid /'deərimeɪd/ n (*dated*) a woman who works in a DAIRY(1).

dairyman /'deərimən/ n (pl **-men** /-mən/) a man who works in a DAIRY(1).

dais /'deɪɪs/ n [sing] a raised platform, esp at one end of a room, for sb to make a speech from.

daisy /'deɪzi/ n **(a)** a small white flower with a yellow centre, usu growing wild. ⇨ picture at FLOWER. **(b)** any of many larger types of plant with similar flowers. **IDM** **push up daisies** ⇨ PUSH¹.
■ **'daisy wheel** n a small wheel used in a printer (PRINT²) or an electric TYPEWRITER, with letters, etc arranged around its edge.

dale /deɪl/ n a valley, esp in Northern England: *the Yorkshire Dales.* **IDM** **up hill and down dale** ⇨ HILL.

dalliance /'dæliəns/ n [U] (*dated*) behaviour that involves dallying (DALLY) with sb/sth.

dally /'dæli/ v (pt, pp **dallied**) to move or act slowly: [V] *Come on — this is no time for dallying!* **PHR V** **dally with sb/sth** to treat sb/sth in a casual way, and not seriously: *She was merely dallying with him/his affections.*

Dalmatian /dæl'meɪʃn/ n a large dog with short white hair marked with dark spots. ⇨ picture at DOG¹.

dam¹ /dæm/ n a barrier made of concrete, earth, etc, built across a river to hold back the water and form a RESERVOIR(1), to prevent flooding, etc: *The dam burst.* ○ *the Hoover Dam on the Colorado River.*
▶ **dam** v [Vn, Vnp] ~ sth (**up**) to build a dam across a river, valley, etc. **PHR V** **dam sth up** to hold back one's emotions, etc: *You shouldn't dam up your feelings like this.*

dam² /dæm/ n the mother of an animal. Compare SIRE 1.

damage /'dæmɪdʒ/ n **1** [U] ~ (**to** sth) **(a)** harm caused to sth, making it less attractive, useful or valuable: *millions of dollars' worth of storm damage* ○ *brain damage* ○ *The vandals did a lot of damage to the car.* ○ *This could cause serious damage to the country's economy/to her reputation.* ○ *extensive/irreparable/permanent damage* ○ *Please let me pay*

[V.speech] = verb + direct speech   [V.*that*] = verb + *that* clause   [V.*wh*] = verb + *who*, *how*, etc clause

for the damage. (**b**) the condition of sth which has suffered this: *Let's take a look at the damage.* **2 damages** [pl] money paid or claimed as compensation for damage(1a), loss or injury: *He sued the company and won £5 000 (in) damages.* **IDM** **what's the 'damage?** (*infml*) what does/did sth cost?: *Thanks for fixing the car — what's the damage?*

▶ **damage** *v* to cause damage to sth: [Vn] *damage a fence/a car/furniture* ○ *damage sb's career* ○ *Relations between the two countries have been badly/ severely damaged by this incident.* ○ *a damaged pipeline/tendon.* **damaging** *adj* ~ (**to sth**) having a bad effect on sth: *damaging chemicals* ○ *make potentially damaging allegations* ○ *How damaging do you think this will be to the Democratic Party?*

,**damage limi'tation** *n* [U] the process of trying to stop sth, esp a political SCANDAL(1), from causing much more damage than it has already.

damask /'dæməsk/ *n* [U] silk or LINEN(1) material, with a pattern woven into it that is visible on both sides: *a damask tablecloth.*

dame /deɪm/ *n* **1** (*US sl*) (used esp by men) a woman: *Gee! What a dame!* **2 Dame** (the title of) a woman who has been awarded a special honour, similar to a knighthood (KNIGHT) for a man: *an interview with Dame Judi Dench.* **3** = PANTOMIME DAME.

damn¹ /dæm/ (also **dammit** /'dæmɪt/, **damn it**) *interj* (*infml*) (used to express annoyance, anger, etc): *Damn (it)! I've lost my pen.*

damn² /dæm/ (also **damned**) *adj* [attrib] (*infml*) (expressing disapproval, anger, impatience, etc): *Where's that damn book?*

▶ **damn** (also **damned**) *adv* (*infml*) (**a**) (expressing disapproval, anger, etc) very: *Don't be so damn silly!* ○ *You know damn well what I mean!* (**b**) (used to make a remark more forceful): *damn good/clever* ○ *As soon as the fire started, we got out pretty damn fast!* **IDM** **damn 'all** (*infml*) nothing at all.

damn³ /dæm/ *v* **1** [Vn] (**a**) (of God) to condemn sb to suffer in hell. (**b**) (used when swearing at sb/sth) *Damn you all!* ○ *Damn this computer — what's the matter with it?* **2** to criticize sth severely: [Vn] *The play was damned by the reviewers.* ○ *This is a classic case of the council being damned if they do spend money, and damned if they don't* (ie they cannot satisfy everyone). **IDM** **as near as damn it / dam-mit** ⇨ NEAR². **damn the consequences, expense, etc** do not consider the difficulties: *Let's enjoy ourselves, and damn the consequences!* **damn sb/sth with faint 'praise** to praise sb/sth only a little, suggesting that really one does not like them/ it. **I'll be damned!** (*infml*) (used as an expression of surprise): *Well, I'll be damned: she won after all!* **I'm damned if ...** (*infml*) **1** I certainly will not ...; I absolutely refuse to ...: *I'm damned if I'm going to let her get away with that!* **2** (used to make a remark more forceful) I do not: *I'm damned if I know!*

▶ **damning** *adj* very unfavourable: *damning criticism/evidence* ○ *a damning conclusion/report* ○ *She said some pretty damning things about him.*

damn⁴ /dæm/ *n* **IDM** **not care/give a 'damn (about sb/sth)** (*infml*) not to care at all: *I don't give a damn what you say, I'm going.*

damnable /'dæmnəbl/ *adj* (*dated infml*) extremely bad: *damnable weather.* ▶ **damnably** /'dæmnəbli/ *adv: damnably expensive.*

damnation /dæm'neɪʃn/ *n* [U] **1** the state of being damned (DAMN³ 1a): *suffer eternal damnation.* **2** (*dated*) (used as an *interj* to express annoyance, anger, etc): *Damnation! Somebody's taken my umbrella!*

damned /dæmd/ *adj, adv* = DAMN².

▶ **the damned** *n* [pl *v*] people who suffer in hell: *the torments of the damned.*

damnedest /'dæmdɪst/ **IDM** **the damnedest...** (*infml*) the most surprising...: *It was the damnedest thing; I could have sworn the statue moved.* **do/try one's 'damnedest** to do/try one's best: *She did her damnedest to get it done on time.*

damp¹ /dæmp/ *adj* (**-er, -est**) not completely dry; slightly wet: *damp clothes* ○ *a cold damp wind* ○ *damp, dark corridors* ○ *Don't use those sheets — they're still damp.* **IDM** **a damp 'squib** (*infml*) an event, etc that is much less impressive than expected: *The party was a bit of a damp squib.*

▶ **damp** *n* [U] the state of being damp: *Air the clothes to get the damp out.* ○ *a smell of damp in the old house.* See also RISING DAMP.

damply *adv.*

dampness *n* [U].

■ '**damp course** (also '**damp-proof course**) *n* a layer of material near the bottom of a wall to stop damp rising from the ground.

damp² /dæmp/ *v* **1** [Vn] = DAMPEN 1. **2** ~ **sth (down)** (**a**) to reduce noise, etc: [Vnp] *Soft material damps down vibrations.* [also Vn]. (**b**) [Vn, Vnp] = DAMPEN 2.

dampen /'dæmpən/ *v* **1** to make sth damp: [Vn] *She dampened his hair to make it lie flat.* **2** (also **damp**) ~ **sth (down)** to make sth less strong: [Vn,Vnp] *dampen (down) sb's spirits/enthusiasm/expectations.*

damper /'dæmpə(r)/ *n* **1** a movable metal plate that controls the flow of air to a fire. **2** a device that reduces shock or noise. **IDM** **put a damper on sth** (*infml*) to make an event, atmosphere, etc less cheerful, excited, etc: *Their argument put a real damper on the party.*

damsel /'dæmzl/ *n* (*arch*) a young woman who is not married: (*joc or rhet*) *How could I ignore a damsel in distress* (ie a woman needing help)?

damson /'dæmzn/ *n* (**a**) a tree that produces a small purple fruit like a PLUM(1a). (**b**) the fruit of this tree: *damson jam.*

dance¹ /dɑːns; *US* dæns/ *n* **1(a)** [C] a series of movements and steps that match the speed and rhythm of music: *learn new dance steps/routines.* (**b**) [C] a particular series of such movements and steps: *The rumba is a Latin-American dance.* See also COUNTRY DANCE, FOLK-DANCE, TAP-DANCE. (**c**) [C] music for a dance: *a gipsy dance played on the violin* ○ *a dance band.* (**d**) [U] dancing as an art form: *She has written a book on dance.* ○ *a student of modern dance.* **2** [C] an act of dancing: *May I have the next dance?* ○ *He did a little dance of triumph.* **3** [C] a social gathering at which people dance: *hold a dance in the village hall.* **IDM** **lead sb a dance** ⇨ LEAD¹. **a song and dance** ⇨ SONG.

■ '**dance-floor** *n* the part of the floor of a large room in a hotel, etc on which people dance.

dance² /dɑːns; *US* dæns/ *v* **1(a)** to move in a series of steps, alone or with a partner or in a group, usu in a way that matches the speed and rhythm of music: [V] *Would you like to dance?* ○ *We danced to some disco music.* ○ *I danced with her all night.* (**b**) to perform a particular dance: [Vn] *dance a waltz/the cha-cha* ○ *We danced a little jig around the table.* **2** to move in a lively way, usu up and down: [Vpr] *dance for joy* ○ *leaves dancing in the wind* ○ *eyes dancing with delight* [Vp] *a boat dancing about on the waves* [also V]. **IDM** **dance attendance on/upon sb** (*fml*) to follow sb around, attending to their wishes: *She loves to have men dance attendance on her.* **dance to sb's tune** to do what sb demands.

▶ **dancer** (**a**) a person who dances: *He's a good dancer.* (**b**) a person whose occupation is dancing: *She's a dancer.* ○ *ballet dancers.*

dancing *n* [U] moving in a way that matches the speed and rhythm of music: *'tap-dancing* ○ *streets alive with music and dancing* ○ *dancing lessons/ shoes.*

dancehall /'dɑ:nshɔ:l/ *n* a hall for public dances, which one pays to enter. Compare BALLROOM.

dandelion /'dændɪlaɪən/ *n* a small wild plant with a bright yellow flower. ⇨ picture at FLOWER.

dandified /'dændɪfaɪd/ *adj* (*usu derog*) (of a man) showing great concern about his clothes and appearance; like a DANDY¹.

dandle /'dændl/ *v* [Vn] to move a young child up and down on one's knee or in one's arms.

dandruff /'dændrʌf/ *n* [U] small pieces of dead skin from the top of the head, usu seen in the hair: *This shampoo will cure your dandruff.*

dandy¹ /'dændi/ *n* (*dated usu derog*) a man who cares too much about his clothes and appearance.

dandy² /'dændi/ *adj* (**-ier, -iest**) (*infml esp US*) very good; excellent: *all fine and dandy* ○ *That's just dandy!*

Dane /deɪn/ *n* a native of Denmark.

danger /'deɪndʒə(r)/ *n* **1** [U] **(a)** ~ **(of sth)** a chance of suffering damage, loss, injury, etc: *There's a lot of danger involved in rock climbing.* ○ *Danger — thin ice!* (eg on a sign) ○ *Is there any danger of fire?* ○ *The police said his life was in danger* (ie at risk). ○ *She was very ill, but is now out of danger* (ie not likely to die). **(b)** ~ **of sth / that…** a possibility of sth bad; a risk of sth: *After his death there was some danger that his personal papers would be destroyed.* ○ *'Nicky won't find out, will she?' 'Oh no, there's no danger of that!'* **2** [C] ~ **(to sb/sth)** a person or thing that may cause damage, loss, injury, etc: *the hidden dangers associated with exercising too much* ○ *Smoking is now recognized as a serious danger to health.* ○ *That woman is a danger to society!*

■ **the 'danger list** *n* [sing] a list of people who are very ill and near to death, esp in a hospital: *be on/ off the danger list.*

'danger money *n* [U] extra pay for dangerous work.

dangerous /'deɪndʒərəs/ *adj* ~ **(for sb/sth)** likely to cause danger or be a danger: *a dangerous bridge/ journey/illness* ○ *The river is highly dangerous for swimmers.* ○ *a potentially dangerous fall in sb's blood pressure* ○ *teenagers experimenting with dangerous drugs.* ▶ **dangerously** *adv*: *driving dangerously* ○ *dangerously ill* (ie so ill that one might die) ○ *Nationalism can be dangerously close to racism.*

dangle /'dæŋgl/ *v* **(a)** to hang or swing loosely: [Vpr] *a bunch of keys dangling at the end of a chain* [also V]. **(b)** to hold sth so that it swings loosely: [Vnpr] *He dangled his watch in front of the baby.* [also V]. **PHR V dangle sth before / in front of sb** to offer sth to sb in order to tempt them to do sth: *The prospect of promotion was dangled before him.*

Danish /'deɪnɪʃ/ *n* [U], *adj* (the language) of Denmark and its people.

■ **,Danish 'blue** *n* [U] a soft white cheese with blue veins (VEIN 1).

,Danish 'pastry (also **Danish**) *n* a sweet pastry cake containing apple, nuts, etc.

dank /dæŋk/ *adj* (**-er, -est**) damp and cold: *a dark dank cellar/cave.*

dapper /'dæpə(r)/ *adj* (*approv*) (usu of a small man) neat and elegant in appearance and often quick in movement.

dappled /'dæpld/ *adj* marked with spots or round patches of different colour or of shade: *a dappled deer/horse* ○ *trees giving dappled shade.*

Darby and Joan /,dɑ:bi ən 'dʒəʊn/ *n* [pl] (*Brit*) an old and loving married couple: *members of the local Darby and Joan club.*

dare /deə(r)/ *v* **1** (not usu in the continuous tenses) to be brave enough to do sth. ⇨ note. **2** to suggest to sb that they try to do sth dangerous or difficult; to challenge sb: [Vn] *Throw it at him! I dare you!* [Vn.to inf] *I dare you to tell your mother!* ○ *Somebody*

dared me to jump off the bridge into the river. **IDM don't you dare (do sth)** you must not or I will be very angry: *Don't you dare touch that vase.* ○ *'I'm going to tell your mother about the drugs.' 'Don't you dare!'* **how 'dare you, he, she, etc** (used to express INDIGNATION at the actions of others): *How dare you suggest that I copied your notes!* ○ *How dare he take my bicycle without even asking!* **I dare say** (*esp Brit*) I expect that; it is probable that: *I dare say you are British, but you still need a passport to prove it.*

▶ **dare** *n* (usu *sing*) a challenge to do sth dangerous or difficult: *'Why did you climb onto the roof?' 'It was a dare.'* ○ *He only entered the competition for a dare* (ie because he was challenged to do it).

NOTE Dare in sense **1** is sometimes called a *semimodal* verb because it behaves like a modal verb in some ways but also has forms which are like those of an ordinary verb. It is used especially in negative sentences and questions, after *if/whether*, or with *hardly, never, no one, nobody.* In positive sentences **dare** is not very common. A phrase like *not be afraid to* is often used instead: *She's not afraid to say what she thinks.*

Dare has certain features which are like those of modal verbs. It can form the third person singular present tense without -s (though this use is uncommon), and questions and negatives without *do* or *did.* When **dare** is used as a modal verb, it is followed by an infinitive without *to.* The negative is **dare not** (*short form* **daren't** /deənt/). The negative of the past tense is **dared not**. The forms **dare not** and **dared not** are very formal but **daren't** is quite common: *I daren't ask my boss for a day off.* ○ *Churchill dared not go against the Americans.*

Dare can also be used like an ordinary verb, forming the third person singular with *-s*, and questions and negatives with *do* and *did.* The negatives are **do not / don't dare**, **does not / doesn't dare** and **did not / didn't dare**. When used like an ordinary verb, **dare** can be followed by an infinitive with or without *to*: *Nobody dares (to) criticize his decisions.* ○ *They didn't dare (to) disobey.* ○ *We hardly dared (to) breathe as somebody walked past the door.*

daredevil /'deədevl/ *n* [often attrib] a person who is foolishly bold and seems not to care about danger: *a ,daredevil 'pilot* ○ *Don't try any daredevil stunts.*

daring /'deərɪŋ/ *n* [U] courage and willingness to take risks: *the skill and daring of the mountain climber* ○ *an ambitious plan of great daring.*

▶ **daring** *adj* **1** brave: *a daring exploit/attack.* **2** bold in a new or unusual way: *a daring plan/ innovation* ○ *a daring new art form* ○ *She said some daring* (ie bold and possibly shocking) *things.* **daringly** *adv*: *daringly modern ideas.*

dark¹ /dɑ:k/ *adj* (**-er, -est**) **1** with no or very little light: *a dark room/street* ○ *It's rather dark in here — can we have the light on?* ○ *It's too dark to play outside.* **2(a)** (of a colour) not reflecting much light; closer in shade to black than to white: *dark green/ grey/red* ○ *a dark suit.* **(b)** (of hair or eyes) brown or black. **(c)** (of skin) not fair in colour: *a dark complexion.* **(d)** (of a person) having dark hair, eyes and/or skin: *a tall, dark, handsome stranger.* Compare LIGHT¹ *adj.* **3** hidden; mysterious: *a dark secret/mystery* ○ *I'm thinking of leaving the company, but keep it dark — I don't want anyone else to know.* **4** sad; offering no hope; depressing: *dark predictions about the future* ○ *Don't always look on the dark side of things.* **5** evil: *dark powers/influence* ○ *a book which dwells on the darker side of the emperor's nature.* **IDM a dark 'horse** a person who hides facts about her or his life, esp special personal qualities or abilities: *He's a dark horse if ever there was one!*

▶ **darkly** adv **1** in a threatening or frightening way: *She hinted darkly at strange events.* **2** in a depressing or threatening way: *talk darkly of the possibility of job losses.*

darkness n [U] the state of being dark: *The room was suddenly plunged into complete darkness.* ○ *during the hours of darkness* (ie at night).

■ **the 'Dark Ages** n [pl] the period of European history between the end of the Roman Empire and the 10th century AD.

,**dark 'glasses** n [pl] glasses that have dark lenses (LENS 1), worn esp to protect the eyes from strong sunlight.

dark² /dɑːk/ n **the dark** [sing] the absence of light: *All the lights went out and we were left in the dark.* ○ *Are you afraid of the dark?* Compare LIGHT¹. **IDM** **before/after dark** before/after the sun goes down: *Try to get home before dark.* ○ *I'm afraid to go out after dark.* **in the 'dark (about sth)** not knowing about sth: *We were kept completely in the dark about the plan to sell the company.* **a leap/shot in the 'dark** an action, answer, etc that is risked in the hope that it is correct: *It's hard to know exactly what to do — we'll just have to take a shot in the dark.* ⇨ WHISTLE.

darken /'dɑːkən/ v to become dark or cause sth to become dark: [V] *The sky darkened as the storm approached.* [Vn] *He stumbled in the darkened hallway.* **IDM** **darken sb's 'door** (*joc or rhet*) to come to sb's house: *Go! And never darken my door again!*

darkroom /'dɑːkruːm, -rʊm/ n a room that can be made completely dark, used for processing photographs.

darling /'dɑːlɪŋ/ n (**a**) a person or thing that is much liked or loved: *She's a little darling!* ○ *He's the darling* (ie favourite subject) *of the media at the moment.* (**b**) (as a friendly or loving form of address): *Did you have a good day, darling?*

▶ **darling** adj [attrib] **1** much loved: *my darling daughter.* **2** (*infml*) (used esp by women) charming; pleasing: *What a darling little room!*

darn¹ /dɑːn/ v to mend a garment by passing long threads through the material and weaving other long threads across and between them to fill in the hole: [Vn] *darn a hole in my sock* [also V].

▶ **darn** n a place mended by darning.

darning n [U] **1** the action of darning: *I hate darning.* **2** things that need to be darned: *I had a pile of darning to do.*

darn² /dɑːn/ v (*infml euph*) = DAMN³ 1 [Vn] *Well, I'll be darned!* ○ *Darn those blasted kids!*

▶ **darn** (also **darned** /dɑːnd/) adj (*infml euph*) (used to express annoyance, etc): *That darn(ed) cat has eaten my supper!*

darn (also **darned**) adv (*infml euph approv or derog*) extremely; very: *a darn(ed) good try* ○ *What a darn stupid thing to say!*

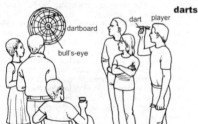

darts

dart player

dartboard

bull's-eye

dart¹ /dɑːt/ n **1** [C] a small pointed missile, often with feathers to help it fly, used as a weapon or in the game of darts. ⇨ picture. **2** [sing] a sudden fast movement: *She made a dart for the exit.* **3** [C] a pointed fold sewn in a garment to make it fit better. **4 darts** [sing v] a game in which darts are thrown at a target marked with numbers for scoring. Darts is often played in English pubs. ⇨ picture.

dart² /dɑːt/ v **1** to move suddenly and quickly in the specified direction: [Vp] *The mouse darted away when I approached.* [Vpr] *Swallows are darting through the air.* ○ *She darted into the doorway to hide.* ⇨ note at WHIZZ. **2** to send sth out suddenly and quickly: [Vnp] *The snake darted out its tongue.* [Vnpr] *She darted an angry look at him.*

dartboard /'dɑːtbɔːd/ n a circular board used as the target in the game of darts (DART¹ 4). ⇨ picture at DART¹.

dash¹ /dæʃ/ n **1** [sing] ~ (**for sth**) a sudden run or forward movement: *make a dash for freedom/shelter* ○ *We jumped into the car and made a dash for the ferry.* ○ *Mother said lunch was ready and there was a mad dash for the table.* **2** [C usu sing] (esp US) a short running race; a SPRINT n(1): *the 100-metre dash.* **3** [C esp sing] **a** ~ (**of sth**) a small amount of sth added or mixed: *a dash of lemon juice* ○ *The flag adds a dash of colour to the grey building.* **4** [C] a short level line (—) used in writing, printing and Morse Code. ⇨ App 3. **5** [sing] ~ (**of sth**) liquid striking sth or the sound this makes: *the dash of waves on the rocks* ○ *A dash of water in his face will revive him.* **6** [U] energy and confidence; style(3): *an officer famous for his skill and dash.* **7** [C] (*infml*) = DASHBOARD. **IDM** **cut a 'dash** (*Brit*) to be exciting and stylish (STYLE), in appearance or behaviour: *He really cuts a dash in his new uniform.*

dash² /dæʃ/ v **1** to move suddenly and quickly; to rush: [V] *I must dash* (ie leave quickly), *I'm late.* [Vp] *He dashed off with the money before I could stop him.* [Vpr] *She dashed into the shop.* ○ *An ambulance dashed to the scene of the accident.* **2** to strike or throw sth forcefully: [Vpr] *Waves dashed against the harbour wall.* [Vnpr] *He dashed the glass to the ground.* ○ *The boat was dashed against the rocks.* ○ *A passing car dashed mud all over us.* [also Vnp]. **IDM** **dash (it)!; (*Brit*) dash it all!** (*infml euph*) (used as a milder way of saying *damn*): *Dash it! I've broken my pen.* **PHRV** ,**dash sth 'off** to write or draw sth quickly: *She dashed off a letter to her mother.*

▶ **dashing** adj attractive in a lively or stylish (STYLE) way: *a dashing rider/officer* ○ *a dashing uniform/hat.* **dashingly** adv: *dashingly dressed.*

dashboard /'dæʃbɔːd/ (also *infml* **dash**) n the board or panel that faces the driver of a motor vehicle, carrying its instruments and controls. ⇨ picture at CAR.

dastardly /'dæstədli/ adj (*dated*) wicked or cowardly: *a dastardly act/deed* ○ *a dastardly character.*

data /'deɪtə, 'dɑːtə; US 'dætə/ n (**a**) [U or pl] facts or information used in deciding or discussing sth: *Very little data is available.* ○ *The data is/are still being analysed.* (**b**) [usu sing v] (*computing*) information prepared for or stored by a computer: *data analysis/capture/retrieval* ○ *data protection* (ie legal restrictions on access to data stored in a computer). ⇨ note at PLURAL.

■ '**data bank** n = DATABASE.

,**data 'processing** n [U] the performing of computer operations on data to analyse it, solve problems, etc.

database /'deɪtəbeɪs/ (also **data bank**) n a large store of data held in a computer and easily accessible to a person using it.

date¹ /deɪt/ n **1** (**a**) a specific numbered day of the month, or a specific year, usu given to show when sth happened or is to happen: *Today's date is the 23rd of June/June 23rd.* ○ *'What's the date?' 'The 10th.'* ○ *Has the date of the next meeting been fixed/set?* ○ *I can't come on that date.* ○ *Please give your age, sex and date of birth.* ○ *at an earlier/a later date* (ie at some time in the past/future). See also CLOSING DATE. **(b)** a written, printed or stamped statement (on a letter, coin, etc) of the time when it was written, made, etc: *There's no date on this cheque.* ○ *The manuscript bears the date 10 April 1937.* ⇨ note. **2** a period of time in history, eg one to which a work of art, etc belongs: *This vase is of an earlier date* (ie is older) *than that one.* **3** (*infml*) **(a)** an appointment to meet sb at a particular time: *We made a date to go to the theatre together.* **(b)** a meeting with a person of the opposite sex: *I have a date (with my girlfriend) tonight.* See also BLIND DATE. **(c)** (*esp US*) a person with whom one has arranged such a meeting: *My date is meeting me at seven.* **IDM** **(be/go) ¦out of ¦date 1** no longer fashionable: *Will denim jeans ever go out of date?* ○ *¦out-of-date ¦clothes/¦ideas/¦slang.* **2** no longer valid: *My passport is out of date.* **to date** until now: *To date, we have not received any replies.* ○ *This is the biggest donation we've had to date.* **¦up to ¦date 1** modern; fashionable: *She wears clothes that are right up to date.* **2** including or satisfying what is now known or required: *The list is fully up to date now that we've added the new members' names.* ○ *¦up-to-date ¦styles/¦methods/¦reference books.*

■ **'date-line** *n* **1** (also **international date-line**) [sing] the imaginary line running from north to south through the Pacific Ocean, east and west of which the date differs by one day. The line is 180° from Greenwich in England. **2** [C] a line in a newspaper above an article, etc showing when and where it was written.

NOTE When writing the date in British English, the day comes before the month. Either the cardinal number (1, 2, 3, etc), or the ordinal number (1st, 2nd, 3rd, etc) can be used: *22/22nd June 1996.* ○ *22.6.96.* In speaking **the** and **of** are used: *'When's your birthday?' 'The sixteenth of March.'* In American English the month is given first. Cardinal numbers are used in writing: *June 22 1996* ○ *6.22.96.* **The** and **of** are not used in speaking: *Her birthday is March sixteenth.*

A year is usually said as two numbers: *He was born in 1989 = nineteen eighty-nine.* ○ *Queen Elizabeth I reigned from 1558–1603 = fifteen fifty-eight to sixteen o three.* (It is also possible to say *fifteen hundred and fifty-eight* but this is less common.) ○ *AD 55 = AD fifty-five* (AD = since the beginning of Christian history) ○ *1000 BC = one thousand BC* (Before Christ). **Hundred** is used for the first year of a century: *1900 = nineteen hundred.*

date² /deɪt/ *v* **1** to write a date¹(1) on sth: [Vn] *Don't forget to date your cheque.* ○ *His last letter was dated 24 May.* **2** to work out or determine the age of sth: [Vn] *modern methods of dating rocks/fossils/tools/paintings.* **3** to seem or make sb/sth seem old-fashioned: [V] *Young people's clothes date quickly nowadays.* [Vn] *Your taste in pop music really dates you.* **4** ~ **back to... / from...** to have existed since...: [Vpr] *This castle dates from the 14th century* (ie was built then). ○ *Our partnership dates back to* (ie We have been partners since) *1960.* **5** (*infml esp US*) to go on a date¹(3b) with sb, once or regularly: [V] *They've been dating for a long time.* [Vn] *I only dated her once.*

▶ **datable** *adj* that can be dated (DATE² 2) to a particular time: *This pottery is datable to about 250 BC.*

dated *adj* old-fashioned; no longer in use: *His clothes look awfully dated.* ○ *She uses a lot of dated words.*

date³ /deɪt/ *n* a sweet brown sticky fruit that grows on a palm tree (the **date-palm**) common in N Africa and SW Asia.

dative /'deɪtɪv/ *n* (*grammar*) (in certain languages) the special form of a noun, a pronoun or an adjective used to indicate or describe esp the person who

receives sth or benefits from an action. ▶ **dative** *adj*.

daub /dɔːb/ *v* **1** ~ **A on (B)**; ~ **B (with A)** to put a soft substance on a surface in a rough or careless way: [Vnp, Vnpr] *He daubed some red paint on (the canvas).* [Vn, Vnpr] *She daubed her face (with thick make-up).* [Vnpr] *trousers daubed* (ie made dirty) *with mud.* **2** (*infml*) to paint pictures without skill or care: [Vn] *children daubing yellow circles with their fingers* [also V].

▶ **daub** *n* **1** [C, U] a soft sticky material, eg clay, for covering the surface of a wall, etc. See also WATTLE AND DAUB. **2** [C] a badly painted picture.

daughter /'dɔːtə(r)/ *n* one's female child. ⇨ App 4.

■ **daughter-in-law** /'dɔːtər ɪn lɔː/ *n* (*pl* **daughters-in-law** /'dɔːtəz ɪn lɔː/) the wife of one's son. ⇨ App 4.

daunt /dɔːnt/ *v* (usu passive) to discourage or frighten sb: [Vn] *I was rather daunted by the thought of addressing such an audience.* **IDM** **nothing 'daunted** (*fml or joc*) not at all discouraged: *Their guides deserted them, but, nothing daunted, they pressed on into the jungle.*

▶ **daunting** *adj*: *a daunting task* ○ *The prospect of meeting the President is quite daunting.* **dauntingly** *adv*.

dauntless /'dɔːntləs/ *adj* not easily discouraged or frightened: *dauntless bravery.*

dauphin /'dɔːfɪn/ *n* (formerly) the title of the king of France's eldest son.

dawdle /'dɔːdl/ *v* **(a)** to be slow; to waste time: [V] *Stop dawdling and hurry up — we're late.* ○ *She doesn't get her work done because she's always dawdling.* ○ *We dawdled over our meal for two or three hours.* **(b)** to move slowly in the specified direction: [Vpr, Vp] *We dawdled (along/back/on) towards the city centre.*

dawn¹ /dɔːn/ *n* **1** [U, C] the time of day when light first appears; DAYBREAK: *We must start at dawn.* ○ *He works from dawn till dusk.* ○ *It's almost dawn.* ○ *Dawn broke over the small town.* **2** [sing] ~ **(of sth)** the beginning or first signs of sth: *the dawn of civilization* ○ *since the dawn of time* ○ *the dawn of a new age* ○ *Peace marked a new dawn in our nation's history.* **IDM** **at the crack of dawn** ⇨ CRACK².

■ **¦dawn 'chorus** *n* (usu *sing*) the sound of birds singing in the early morning.

dawn² /dɔːn/ *v* **1** (often with *it* as subject) to begin to grow light: [V] *Day was dawning as we left.* ○ *When day dawned, we could see the damage the storm had caused.* **2** ~ **(on/upon sb)** to become (gradually) clear to sb's mind; to become obvious to sb: [V, Vpr] *It finally dawned (on me) that he had been lying all the time.* [Vpr] *The truth began to dawn on him.*

day /deɪ/ *n* **1(a)** [U] the time between the sun's rising and setting: *He has been working all day.* ○ *When I woke up, it was already day.* **(b)** [C] a period of 24 hours: *There are seven days in a week.* ○ *I saw Tom three days ago.* ○ *I'll be seeing Mary in a few days' time* (ie a few days from now). ○ *'What day of the week is it?' 'It's Monday.'* ○ *Christmas day/market day.* **(c)** [C] the hours of the day when one works: *I've done a good day's work.* ○ *Have you had a hard day at the office?* ○ *Her working day is seven hours.* ○ *The employees are demanding a six-hour day and a five-day week.* See also OPEN DAY. **2** [C usu *pl*] a particular period of time: *in his younger days I was much happier in those days* (ie at that time). ○ *in the days of Queen Victoria/in Queen Victoria's day* ○ *in days of old/in the old days* (ie in former times) ○ *present-day thought/opinion.* **IDM** **all in a day's 'work** part of the normal routine: *Injecting animals is all in a day's work for a vet.* **any day now** within a few days; soon: *The letter should arrive any day now.* **at the end of the day** ⇨ END¹. **break of day** ⇨ BREAK². **by day/night** during the day(1a)/after dark: *The fugitives travelled by night and rested by day.* **call it a day** ⇨ CALL¹. **carry/win the 'day**

(*infml*) to be successful against sb/sth: *Despite strong opposition, the ruling party carried the day.* **clear as day** ⇨ CLEAR¹. **day after 'day** for many days; continuously: *Day after day she waited in vain for him to telephone her.* **the day after to'morrow**: *If today is Wednesday, the day after tomorrow will be Friday.* **the day before 'yesterday**: *If today is Wednesday, the day before yesterday was Monday.* **day by 'day** as time goes by: *Day by day she learnt more about her job.* **day 'in, day 'out** every day without exception: *Day in, day out, no matter what the weather is like, she walks ten miles.* **a day of 'reckoning** (*fml*) a time when sth that is wrong or bad will be punished or paid for: *Critics of the government's housing policy think the day of reckoning cannot be far away.* **sb's/sth's days are 'numbered** sb/sth is soon going to die, fail, lose favour, etc: *His disease is incurable — I'm afraid his days are numbered.* ○ *This factory is no longer profitable, so its days are numbered* (ie it will soon close). **early days** ⇨ EARLY. **end one's days/life** ⇨ END². **every dog has his/its day** ⇨ DOG¹. **from day to 'day; from ‚one day to the 'next** within a short period of time: *Things change from day to day.* ○ *You don't know what his mood will be from one day to the next.* **the good/bad old days** ⇨ OLD. **have had one's 'day** to be no longer successful, powerful, etc: *He was a great singer once but now he's had his day.* ○ *Colonialism has had its day* (ie is over). **have seen/known better days** ⇨ BETTER¹. **high days and holidays** ⇨ HIGH¹. **if he's, she's, etc a 'day** (in speaking of sb's age) at least: *He's eighty if he's a day!* **in all one's born days** ⇨ BORN. **in one's 'day** during one's life; in a period of success, wealth, power, etc: *In his day, he was a very influential politician.* ○ *She was a great beauty in her day* (ie when she was young). **in 'this day and age** in modern times; NOWADAYS. **it's not sb's 'day** (*infml*) sb is having a day of very bad luck: *My car broke down, and then I locked myself out — it's just not my day!* **late in the day** ⇨ LATE². **the livelong day** ⇨ LIVELONG. **make sb's 'day** (*infml*) to make sb very happy: *If she wins, it'll make her day.* **make a day of it** (*infml*) to spend the whole day rather than part of it doing sth: *We took a picnic lunch and made a day of it.* **night and day; day and night** ⇨ NIGHT. **a ‚nine days' 'wonder** (*Brit*) a person or thing that attracts attention for a short time but is soon forgotten: *As a pop star she was a nine days' wonder — she only made one successful record.* **'one day** at some time in the future: *One day I'll get my revenge.* **'one of these days** before very long: *One of these days he'll realize what a fool he's been.* **one of those 'days** a day when a lot of things go wrong: *I've had one of those days: my train was late, and I lost my wallet.* **the order of the day** ⇨ ORDER¹. **the other day/morning/evening/week** ⇨ OTHER. **pass the time of day** ⇨ PASS¹. **the present day** ⇨ PRESENT¹. **Rome was not built in a day** ⇨ BUILD. **one's salad days** ⇨ SALAD. **save, etc sth for a rainy day** ⇨ RAINY. **'some day** at some time in the future: *Some day I'll be famous.* **'that'll be the day** (*ironic*) that's very unlikely: *'He says he'll do the ironing.' 'That'll be the day!'* **'these days** at the present time; NOWADAYS. **'those were the days** that was a happier, better, etc time: *Do you remember when we were first married? Those were the days!* **the time of day** ⇨ TIME¹. **to the 'day** exactly: *It's three years to the day since we met.* **to this 'day** even now: *To this day, I still don't know why she did it.*

■ **'day-boy, 'day-girl** *ns* (*Brit*) a pupil who lives at home but goes to a school where other pupils live during the term.

'day care *n* [U] care for small children away from home, during the day: *Day care is provided by the company she works for.* ○ *a 'day-care centre.*

'day centre *n* (*Brit*) a place that provides care for old, unemployed, etc people during the day.

'day-dream *n* pleasant thoughts that distract one's attention from the present: *She stared out of the window, lost in a day-dream.* — *v* ~ (**about sb/sth**) [V, Vpr] *He sat there day-dreaming (about his girlfriend).*

'day nursery (*Brit*) (*US* **'day care center**) *n* a place where small children are looked after while their parents are at work.

‚day 'off *n* a day on which one does not have to work: *I work from Tuesday to Saturday, and Sunday and Monday are my days off.*

‚day 'out *n* a trip or visit somewhere for a day: *The schoolchildren had a day out at the seaside.*

‚day re'lease *n* (*Brit*) [U] a system of allowing employees days off work for education.

‚day re'turn *n* (*Brit*) a ticket at a reduced price for a journey to a place and back again in the same day.

'day-room *n* a room in a hospital or other institution where people can sit, relax, watch television, etc during the day.

'day-school *n* a school attended daily by pupils living at home. Compare BOARDING-SCHOOL.

‚day-to-'day *adj* [attrib] (**a**) planning for only one day at a time: *I have organized the cleaning on a ‚day-to-'day basis, until the usual cleaner returns.* (**b**) involving daily routine: *She has been looking after the ‚day-to-day admini'stration.*

'day-trip *n* (*esp Brit*) a trip or visit completed in one day: *a day-trip to France.* **'day-tripper** *n*.

daybreak /'deɪbreɪk/ *n* [U] dawn: *leave at daybreak.*

daylight /'deɪlaɪt/ *n* [U] the light that there is during the day(1a): *before daylight* (ie before dawn) ○ *The colours look different when viewed in daylight.* ○ *I haven't seen your house in daylight before.* **IDM** **broad daylight** ⇨ BROAD¹. **‚daylight 'robbery** (*infml*) charging too much money: *Four pounds for two sandwiches? It's daylight robbery!* **see 'daylight** to understand sth that was not previously clear: *I struggled with the problem for hours before I saw daylight.*

■ **‚daylight 'saving** *n* [U] a way of making darkness fall later during summer by setting clocks an hour ahead of the standard time. **‚daylight 'saving time** (*US* also **'daylight time**) *n* [U] a period when this is in effect. Compare SUMMER TIME.

daylights /'deɪlaɪts/ *n* [pl] **IDM** **beat/knock the (living) 'daylights out of sb** (*infml*) to beat sb very severely: *If I catch you stealing again, I'll beat the daylights out of you!* **frighten/scare the (living) 'daylights out of sb** (*infml*) to frighten sb very much.

daylong /'deɪlɒŋ/ *adj* [attrib], *adv* lasting for the whole day: *a daylong meeting.*

daytime /'deɪtaɪm/ *n* [U] the time between the sun's rising and setting: *You hardly ever see owls in the daytime.*

daze /deɪz/ *v* (usu passive) to make sb unable to think or react properly because of shock, surprise, etc: [Vn] *He was dazed for a moment by the blow to his head.* ○ *They are still dazed by the extraordinary events of the last few days.*

▶ **daze** *n* **IDM** **in a daze** in a confused state: *I've been in a complete daze since hearing your sad news.* **dazed** /deɪzd/ *adj*: *a dazed expression.*

dazzle /'dæzl/ *v* (often passive) (**a**) to make sb unable to see properly for a while, because of too much light: [Vn] *I was momentarily dazzled by my headlights.* (**b**) to impress sb greatly through beauty, knowledge, skill, etc: [Vn] *She was dazzled by her first sight of the ancient city.*

▶ **dazzle** *n* [U, sing] **1** bright confusing light: *shade one's eyes from the dazzle of the midday sun.* **2** impressive brightness or spectacle: *She appeared unaffected by the dazzle of publicity.*

---

dazzling adj: a dazzling display of sporting skill.

DBE /ˌdiː biː ˈiː/ abbr (in Britain) Dame Commander (of the Order) of the British Empire: be made a DBE ○ Dame Susan Peters DBE. Compare CBE, MBE.

DC /ˌdiː ˈsiː/ abbr **1** (also **dc**) direct current. Compare AC 2. **2** District Commissioner: DC Clark. **3** District of Columbia: Washington, DC.

DD /ˌdiː ˈdiː/ abbr Doctor of Divinity: have/be a DD ○ Colin Green DD.

D-day /ˈdiː deɪ/ n [sing without the] **1** the day (6 June 1944) on which British, American and other forces landed in N France during the Second World War. **2** a date on which something important is due to happen: As D-day approached we still weren't ready to move house.

DDT /ˌdiː diː ˈtiː/ abbr [U] dichlorodiphenyltrichloroethane (a colourless chemical that kills insects and is also harmful to animals).

de- pref (with vs and related adjs, advs and ns) **1** opposite or negative of: defrost ○ decentralization. **2** removal of: defuse ○ derailment.

deacon /ˈdiːkən/ n **1** (in some Christian Churches, eg the Church of England) a minister¹(3) ranking below a priest. **2** (in Nonconformist Churches) a person who is not a minister¹(3), but who helps with church business affairs.

▶ **deaconess** /ˌdiːkəˈnes; US ˈdiːkənəs/ n a woman with duties similar to those of a deacon.

dead /ded/ adj **1(a)** no longer alive: a dead person/ animal ○ dead flowers/cells ○ He was shot dead by masked gunmen. ○ The tiger fell dead. **(b)** never having been alive; INANIMATE: dead matter (eg rock) ○ a dead planet (ie one with no life on it). **2** (infml) extremely tired; not well: You look completely dead. Are you all right? **3** [pred] **(a)** unable to feel because of cold, etc; NUMB: I couldn't unlock the door because my fingers had gone dead. **(b)** ~ to sth unable to feel or understand emotions, ideas, etc; INSENSITIVE(2): He was dead to all feelings of pity. **4** unable to work or be used because of lack of power: a dead match (ie one that has been struck) ○ a dead battery ○ The telephone went dead (ie produced no more sounds). **5** no longer in use or operation; finished: This debate is now dead. ○ My love for him is dead. ○ a dead language (eg Latin). **6(a)** (infml) without interest and liveliness; dull: What a dead place this is! ○ The acting was pretty dead. **(b)** without movement or activity: The town is dead now the factory has closed. ○ in the dead hours of the night (ie when everything is quiet). **7** [attrib] complete; absolute: dead calm/ silence ○ come to a dead stop (ie stop suddenly) ○ dead centre (ie exact centre) ○ He's a dead cert/certainty for (ie He will certainly win) the 100 metres. **8** [usu attrib] **(a)** (of sounds) dull in tone; not sharp or lively: a dead voice. **(b)** (of colours) dull; not bright: The walls were a dead brown colour. **9** (sport) **(a)** (of a ball) outside the playing area. **(b)** (esp Brit) (of the ground) tending to make balls rolling on it stop quickly: Rain had made the pitch rather dead. **IDM** **be a dead ˈringer for sb** (sl) to be very like sb in appearance: She's a dead ringer for a girl I used to know. **be the dead ˈspit of sb** (Brit infml) to look exactly like sb else. **cut sb dead** to pretend not to have seen sb; to refuse to greet sb. **(as) ˌdead as a/ the ˈdodo** (infml) completely dead; no longer effective, valid, interesting, etc: Last year's plans to reform the company are now as dead as the dodo. **(as) ˌdead as a ˈdoornail** (infml) completely dead: It lay there with its eyes closed, dead as a doornail. a ˌdead ˈduck (infml) a scheme, etc which has failed or is certain to fail: The plan is a dead duck: there's no money. **the dead hand of sth** the controlling or restricting influence of sth: delayed by the dead hand of bureaucracy. ˌdead to the ˈworld fast asleep. **drop dead** ⇨ DROP². **flog a dead horse** ⇨ FLOG. **over ˌmy dead ˈbody** (used to express one's strong

opposition to sth): They'll demolish this house over my dead body. ○ 'I'm inviting my mother to stay.' 'Over my dead body!' **wouldn't be seen ˈdead in, at, with, etc sth / doing sth** (infml) would refuse to be in, at, with, etc sth: I wouldn't be seen dead in a dress like that.

▶ **dead** adv **1** completely; absolutely; thoroughly: dead tired/drunk ○ dead sure/certain ○ dead level/ straight ○ You're dead right! ○ The train was dead on time. ○ The sight made him **stop dead (in his tracks)**. ○ dead slow (ie as slowly as possible) ○ dead ahead (ie directly ahead) ○ be dead against (ie absolutely opposed to) sth ○ She's **dead set on** getting (ie determined to get) this new job. **2** (infml) very: The instructions are dead easy to follow.

dead n the dead [pl v] those who have died: We carried the dead and (the) wounded off the battlefield. ○ She was screaming enough to **wake the dead**. **IDM** **in the / at ˌdead of ˈnight** in the quietest part of the night: They escaped at dead of night, when the guards were asleep. **in the ˌdead of ˈwinter** in the coldest part of winter.

■ **ˈdead-beat** n (infml) **1** a person who has no job and no money and has lost the will to live an active life. **2** (US) a boring person.

ˌdead ˈbeat adj [pred] (infml) very tired: You look dead beat.

ˌdead ˈend n **1** a road, passage, etc that is closed at one end: The first street we tried was a dead end. **2** a point at which one can make no further progress in work, a scheme, etc: be at/come to a dead end ○ We had reached a dead end in our research. ○ a ˌdead-end ˈjob/caˈreer (ie one that offers no chance of promotion).

ˌdead ˈheat n a result in a race when two competitors finish at exactly the same time.

ˌdead ˈletter n (usu sing) a law or practice that is generally ignored: The treaty turned out to be a dead letter from the start.

ˌdead ˈloss n (usu sing) (infml) a person or thing of no help or use to anyone: He was a very creative designer but as a manager he's a dead loss.

ˌdead ˈweight n (usu sing) a heavy mass that is difficult to lift or move: The drunken man was a dead weight in my arms. ○ (fig) cast off the dead weight of outmoded beliefs.

ˌdead ˈwood n [U] useless or unnecessary people, material, papers, etc: There's too much dead wood among the teaching staff. ○ The new manager wants to cut out the dead wood and streamline production.

deaden /ˈdedn/ v to make sth less strong or intense: [Vn] drugs to deaden the pain ○ My thick clothing deadened the blow. ○ Constant criticism has deadened their enthusiasm. ○ the deadening effect of too much violence on television. **PHRV** **deaden sb to sth** to make sb unable to be sensitive to sth: Her own unhappiness had deadened her to the suffering of others.

deadhead /ˈdedhed/ n **1** (Brit) a faded flower. **2** (infml) a dull or stupid person.

▶ **deadhead** v [Vn] to remove deadheads from a plant.

deadline /ˈdedlaɪn/ n a point in time by which sth must be done: meet/miss a deadline ○ The deadline expires at midnight tonight. ○ I prefer working to a deadline.

deadlock /ˈdedlɒk/ n [C, U] a complete failure to reach agreement or to settle a dispute: The negotiations have reached deadlock. ○ We can only make minor concessions, but it might **break the deadlock**.

deadly /ˈdedli/ adj (-ier, -iest) **1** causing or likely to cause death: deadly poison ○ deadly weapons. **2** [attrib] extreme; complete: deadly seriousness ○ I'm **in deadly earnest**. **3** extremely effective, so that no defence is possible: His aim is deadly (ie so accurate that he can kill easily). ○ *She uses wit with deadly effect.* **4** [attrib] like that of death; DEATHLY: *deadly paleness/coldness/silence.* **5** (*infml*) very boring: *the deadly monotony of her life* ○ *The concert was absolutely deadly.* **6** [attrib] filled with hate: *They are deadly enemies.*

▶ **deadly** *adv* (**a**) as if dead: *deadly pale/cold.* (**b**) (*infml*) extremely: *deadly serious/boring/dull.*

■ ˌdeadly ˈnightshade *n* [U] a poisonous plant with red flowers and black berries.

ˌdeadly ˈsin *n* (in Christianity) a sin that is regarded as leading to DAMNATION(1): *the seven deadly sins.*

deadpan /ˈdedpæn/ *adj* with no expression or emotion: *a ˌdeadpan ˈface/exˈpression* ○ *ˌdeadpan ˈcomedy/ ˈhumour* (ie when the speaker pretends to be very serious).

deaf /def/ *adj* (**-er**, **-est**) **1** unable to hear at all or to hear well: *go deaf* ○ *be deaf in one ear* ○ *She was born completely deaf.* ○ *He's getting deafer in his old age.* See also STONE-DEAF, TONE-DEAF. **2** [pred] ~ **to sth** not willing to listen or pay attention to sth: *be deaf to all advice/requests/entreaties.* **IDM** (**as**) ˌdeaf **as a ˈpost** (*infml*) very deaf. **fall on deaf ˈears** to be ignored or not noticed by others: *All her appeals for help fell on deaf ears.* **turn a deaf ˈear (to sb/sth)** to refuse to listen to sb/sth: *She turned a deaf ear to our warnings.*

▶ **deaf** *n* **the deaf** [pl *v*] deaf people: *television subtitles for the deaf.*

deafness *n* [U].

■ ˈdeaf-aid *n* (*Brit*) = HEARING-AID.

ˌdeaf ˈmute *n* a person who is deaf and DUMB(1).

deafen /ˈdefn/ *v* [Vn] (**a**) to make sb feel that they cannot hear sounds around them by making a very loud noise: *We're being deafened by next door's stereo.* (**b**) to make sb DEAF(1): *The head injury deafened her for life.*

▶ **deafening** *adj* very loud: *deafening applause* ○ *Please turn the radio down — the noise is deafening.* ○ (*joc or ironic*) *a deafening silence.* **deafeningly** *adv*: *deafeningly loud.*

deal¹ /diːl/ *v* (*pt, pp* **dealt** /delt/) ~ **sth (out)**; ~ **sth (to sb)** to distribute cards in a game: [Vnp] *Deal out ten cards each.* [V,Vn] *Whose turn is it to deal (the cards)?* [Vnn] *She dealt me four cards.* [also Vnpr]. **IDM** **deal sb/sth a ˈblow; deal a blow to sb/sth** (*fml*) **1** to hit sb/sth: *She dealt him a tremendous blow with the poker.* **2** to give sb a shock; to cause problems for sb/sth: *Her death dealt us a terrible blow.* **wheeling and dealing** ⇨ WHEEL *v*. **PHR V** ˈdeal in sth to sell sth; to trade in sth: *My bank deals in stocks and shares now.* ○ *We deal in computer software.* ˌdeal sb ˈin **1** to give cards to a new player in a game. **2** to include sb in an activity. ˌdeal sth ˈout to give sth out to a number of people; to distribute sth: *The profits will be dealt out among the investors.* ○ *The judge dealt out harsh sentences to the convicted robbers.* ˈdeal with sb to treat a particular situation involving the person specified; to handle sb: *How would you deal with an armed burglar?* ○ *They try to deal politely with angry customers.* ˈdeal with sb/sth to have social, business, etc relations with sb: *I hate dealing with large impersonal companies.* ˈdeal with sth **1** to attend to a problem, task, etc; to manage sth: *You dealt with an awkward situation very tactfully.* ○ *Haven't you dealt with* (ie replied to) *that letter yet?* **2** to take or have sth as a subject; to discuss sth: *The next chapter deals with verbs.* ○ *I'll deal with decimals in the next lesson.*

deal² /diːl/ *n* **1** an agreement, esp in business, on certain terms for buying or doing sth: *to make/ conclude/close/finalize a deal (with sb)* ○ *We did a deal with the management on overtime.* ○ *The workers are hoping for a better pay deal.* ○ *It's a deal* (ie I agree to your terms)! ○ *The deal fell through* (ie No

agreement was reached). See also NEW DEAL, PACKAGE DEAL. **2** (in games) the distribution of cards to the players: *It's your deal* (ie your turn to deal the cards). **IDM** **big deal!** ⇨ BIG. ⇨ **deal fair/square** fair treatment or terms: *We aim to give customers a fair deal.* **a good/great deal (of sth)** much; a lot: *spend a good deal of money* ○ *take a great deal of trouble* ○ *be a good deal better* ○ *see sb a great deal* (ie often). **a raw/rough ˈdeal** (*infml*) unfair treatment or terms: *If she lost her job for being late once, she got a pretty raw deal.*

deal³ /diːl/ *n* [U] (*esp Brit*) FIR or PINE¹ wood, esp boards of this for making things: *a deal table/floor.*

dealer /ˈdiːlə(r)/ *n* **1** ~ (**in sth**) a person who trades in sth: *a used-car dealer* ○ *a furniture dealer* ○ *a dealer in* (ie sb who buys and sells) *stolen goods.* See also WHEELER-DEALER. **2** the person who distributes the cards in a card-game.

▶ **dealership** *n* (**a**) the position, business or privileges of a DEALER(1). (**b**) a company with the authority to trade in sth.

NOTE Dealers, traders and merchants are all people who earn money from selling things. **Dealers** buy and sell individual objects which they know a lot about: *She's an antique dealer/a car dealer.* A **dealer** can also be somebody who buys and sells illegal or stolen things: *a drug dealer.* A **market/ street trader** sells things in an informal situation such as a market. A **trader** can also be a person or company that buys things from one country and sells them to another: *He's an international currency trader on Wall Street.* A **merchant** sells particular goods in large quantities: *tea/wine merchants.*

dealing /ˈdiːlɪŋ/ *n* **1** dealings [pl] contacts or deals (DEAL² 1), esp in business: *share dealings.* **2** [U] a way of behaving, esp in business: *Our company is proud of its reputation for fair dealing.* **IDM** **have dealings (with sb)** to have relations with sb, esp in business: *I'll have no further dealings with him.* ○ *We haven't had any previous dealings with this company.*

dealt *pt, pp* of DEAL¹.

dean /diːn/ *n* **1** a priest who supervises the other priests in a cathedral. **2** (*also* ˌrural ˈdean) (*esp Brit*) a priest who is responsible for a number of parishes (PARISH 1). **3**(**a**) (in some universities) a person who is responsible for discipline. (**b**) the head of a university department of studies: *dean of the faculty of law.*

▶ **deanery** /ˈdiːnəri/ *n* (**a**) the office or house of a DEAN(1,2). (**b**) a group of parishes (PARISH 1) under a rural dean.

dear /dɪə(r)/ *adj* (**-er**, **-est**) **1** ~ (**to sb**) loved by sb; greatly valued: *my dear wife* ○ *his dearest possessions/friends* ○ *My daughter is very dear to me.* ○ *He lost everything that was dear to him.* **2** (used before *ns* as a form of address in letters, and in a polite or IRONIC way in speech): *Dear Sir/Madam* ○ *Dear Mr Bond* ○ *My dear fellow, it's no trouble at all!* **3** (used before *ns* with *little* and *old* to show affection): *What a dear little child!* ○ *Dear old Paul!* **4** (usu dearest [attrib]) sincere; deeply felt: *It is my dearest wish/hope to see you again.* **5** [usu pred] (*Brit*) expensive: *Clothes are getting dearer.* ○ *That shop is too dear for me* (ie Its prices are too high). **IDM** **close/dear/near to sb's heart** ⇨ HEART. **cost sb dear** ⇨ COST¹. **for dear life/ for one's life** ⇨ LIFE. **hold sth/sb ˈdear** (*rhet*) to care greatly for sb/sth; to value sb/sth highly: *the ideals we hold dear.* **one's nearest and dearest** ⇨ NEAR¹.

▶ **dear** *adv* at a high cost: *If you want to make money, buy cheap and sell dear.* **IDM** **cost sb dear** ⇨ COST¹.

dear *n* **1** a nice or sweet person: *Isn't she a dear?* ○ *Be a dear and* (ie Please) *give me that book.* **2** (used to address sb with affection): *Yes, dear, I'll write to mother.* ○ *Come here, my dear.*

dear *interj* (used in expressions of surprise, annoyance, pity): *Oh dear! I think I've lost it!* ○ *Dear me! What a mess!* ○ *Oh dear! You poor thing!*

dearest /'dɪərɪst/ *n* (used to address sb one likes very much): *Come, (my) dearest, let's go home.*

dearly *adv* **1** very much: *He loves his mother dearly.* ○ *She would dearly like to get that job.* **2** with great loss, damage, etc: *She paid dearly for her mistake* (ie It caused her many problems). ○ *Victory was dearly bought* (eg because many soldiers died).

dearie /'dɪəri/ *n* (*infml*) (used to address sb in a friendly or superior way) DEAR *n*(2).

dearth /dɜːθ/ *n* [sing] ~ (**of sth**) a lack or SHORTAGE of things or people: *There seems to be a dearth of good young players at the moment.*

death /deθ/ *n* **1** [C] an act of dying or being killed: *a sudden/horrible/peaceful death* ○ *Her death was a shock to him.* ○ *There have been more deaths from drowning.* ○ *A bad driver was responsible for their deaths.* **2** [U] the end of life; the state of being dead: *Food poisoning can cause death.* ○ *burn/starve/stab sb to death* (ie until they are dead) ○ *sentenced to death* (ie to be executed) ○ *He's drinking himself to death.* ○ *One mistake could mean death* (ie could result in sb being killed). **3** [U] ~ **of sth** the ending or destruction of sth: *the death of one's plans/hopes* ○ *the death of capitalism.* **4** (also **Death**) [U] the power that destroys life, imagined as a person: *Death is often shown in paintings as a human skeleton.* **IDM** (**be**) **at death's 'door** (*often ironic*) so ill that one may die: *Stop groaning! You're not at death's door!* **be the 'death of sb** (*often joc*) to worry or upset sb very much: *Those kids will be the death of me, coming home late every night.* **be ¸in at the 'death** to be present when sth fails, comes to an end, etc: *The TV cameras were in at the death and filmed the arrest.* **catch one's death** ⇨ CATCH[1]. **dice with death** ⇨ DICE. **die the death** ⇨ DIE[1]. **¸do sth to 'death** to perform or use sth so often that people become tired of seeing or hearing it: *That idea's been done to death.* **flog sth to death** ⇨ FLOG. **frighten/scare sb to 'death** to frighten sb very much: *She was frightened to death by the thought of a visit to the dentist's.* **the kiss of death** ⇨ KISS. **a matter of life and death** ⇨ MATTER[1]. **put sb to death** to execute sb; to kill sb: *The prisoner was put to death (by firing squad) at dawn.* **sudden death** ⇨ SUDDEN. **to death** extremely; to the extreme limit: *be bored/frightened/scared/worried to death* ○ *I'm sick to death of your endless criticism.* **to the death** until sb is dead: *a fight to the death.*

■ **'death certificate** *n* an official form that states the cause and time of sb's death.

'death duty *n* (usu *pl*) (*Brit*) (formerly) a tax paid on property after the owner's death, now called *inheritance tax.*

'death-knell *n* an event indicating that the end or destruction of sth is near: *Further education cuts may sound/toll the death-knell of many small schools.*

'death-mask *n* a cast[2](2a) taken from the face of a person who has just died.

the 'death penalty *n* [sing] the punishment of being executed for a crime: *abolish the death penalty.*

'death rate *n* the number of deaths per 1 000 people in a particular group during a year.

'death-rattle *n* [sing] a sound sometimes heard in the throat of a dying person.

¸death 'row *n* (*US*) a group of prison cells for criminals condemned to death: *waiting on death row.*

'death sentence *n* the punishment of being executed for a crime, given by a judge: *receive/be given the death sentence.*

'death's head *n* a human SKULL(1) as a symbol of death.

'death-toll *n* the number of people killed, eg in a war or a natural disaster.

'death-trap *n* a dangerous place, vehicle, etc that has caused or could cause many deaths: *That sharp bend is a death-trap for motorists.* ○ *The cars blocking the exits could turn this place into a death-trap.*

'death-warrant *n* (**a**) a written order that sb should be executed. (**b**) an act, a decision, etc that causes the end of sth: *The tax is a death-warrant for small businesses.* **IDM** **sign sb's / sign one's own death-warrant** ⇨ SIGN[2].

¸death-watch 'beetle *n* a small beetle that digs into old wood making a sound like a watch ticking (TICK[1] *v* 1).

'death-wish *n* [sing] an often unconscious desire for one's own or sb else's death.

deathbed /'deθbed/ *n* a bed in which a person is dying or dies: *He forgave her on his deathbed* (ie as he lay dying). ○ *a deathbed confession.*

deathblow /'deθbləʊ/ *n* an event, act, etc that destroys or puts an end to sth: *The cutting of grants was a deathblow to many provincial drama companies.*

deathless /'deθləs/ *adj* (*fml*) never to be forgotten; never dying: (*ironic*): *The letter was written in his usual deathless* (ie bad) *prose.*

deathly /'deθli/ *adj* (**-lier, -liest**) like or suggesting death: *a deathly stillness/hush/silence/pallor.* ▸ **deathly** *adv*: *deathly pale/quiet.* Compare DEADLY.

deb /deb/ *n* (*infml*) = DÉBUTANTE.

débâcle /der'bɑːkl/ *n* a sudden and complete failure or collapse; a FIASCO: *a political/a bureaucratic/an economic débâcle* ○ *the débâcle of the summit talks.*

debar /dɪ'bɑː(r)/ *v* (**-rr-**) ~ **sb** (**from sth / doing sth**) (usu passive) (**a**) to prevent sb officially from exercising a right, etc: [Vnpr] *Convicted criminals are debarred from voting in elections.* [also Vn]. (**b**) to shut sb out of a place: [Vn, Vnpr] *People in jeans were debarred (from the club).*

debase /dɪ'beɪs/ *v* **1** to lower the quality, status or value of sth/sb/oneself: [Vn] *Sport is being debased by commercialism.* ○ *You debase yourself by telling such lies.* **2** to lower the value of coins by using less valuable metal in them: [Vn] *debase the currency.* ▸ **debasement** *n* [U].

debatable /dɪ'beɪtəbl/ *adj* not certain; open to discussion; arguable (ARGUE): *a debatable point/claim* ○ *It's debatable whether or not the reforms have improved conditions.*

debate /dɪ'beɪt/ *n* [C, U] (**a**) a formal argument or discussion of a question, eg at a public meeting or in Parliament or Congress, with two or more opposing speakers, and often ending in a vote: *After a long debate, the House of Commons approved the bill.* ○ *a debate on abortion/capital punishment* ○ *to open the debate* (ie be the first to speak) ○ *the motion under debate* (ie being discussed). (**b**) argument or discussion in general: *After much debate, we decided to move to Philadelphia.* ○ *We had long debates at college about politics.* ○ *The importance of this development has been the subject of much/some debate.*

▸ **debate** *v* **1** ~ (**about sth**) to have a debate about sth; to discuss sth: [Vpr] *What are they debating about?* [Vn] *The issue/motion was first debated in the House 25 years ago.* [V.wh] *We're just debating what to do next.* [V.ing] *They debated closing the factory.* [V] *a debating society* (ie a club or group that meets to debate things). **2** to think about sth before deciding what to do: [Vn] *I debated it for a while, then decided not to go.* [V.wh] *I'm debating where to go on holiday.* ○ *She debated whether or not to tell him the news.* [V.ing] *He debated buying a new car, but didn't in the end.* **debater** *n* a person who debates (DEBATE 1).

debauch /dɪˈbɔːtʃ/ v to make sb behave in an IM-MORAL way, esp sexually, by using bad influence: [Vn] *He debauched many innocent girls.*
▶ **debauch** n an occasion of excessive drinking or IMMORAL behaviour, usu involving several people: *go on a drunken debauch.*
debauched adj: *a debauched life/man.*
debauchee /ˌdebɔːˈtʃiː/ n a debauched person.
debauchery /dɪˈbɔːtʃəri/ n [U] IMMORAL behaviour, esp in sexual matters: *a life of debauchery.*

debenture /dɪˈbentʃə(r)/ n a certificate given by a business company, etc as a RECEIPT(2) for money lent at a fixed rate of interest¹(5) until the loan is paid back: *debenture shares.*

debilitate /dɪˈbɪlɪteɪt/ v to make a person's body very weak: [Vn] *a debilitating illness/climate* ○ *She has been debilitated by dysentery.* ○ *(fig) Huge debts are debilitating their economy.*

debility /dɪˈbɪləti/ n [U] physical weakness, esp as a result of illness: *high fever and general debility.*

debit /ˈdebɪt/ n *(finance)* **(a)** a written note in an account¹(1) of a sum owed or paid out: *on the debit side of an account* ○ *(fig) Environmental pollution is seen as the debit side of industrial development.* **(b)** a sum withdrawn from an account¹(2): *My bank account shows two debits of $5 each.* Compare CREDIT¹ 3. See also DIRECT DEBIT.
▶ **debit** v ~ **sth (against/to sb/sth)**; ~ **sb/sth (with sth)** to record a sum of money owed or withdrawn by sb: [Vnpr] *Debit £5 against my account.* ○ *Debit $50 to me.* ○ *The money will be debited from your account.* [also Vn].

debonair /ˌdebəˈneə(r)/ adj (usu of men) confident and charming: *He strolled about, looking very debonair in his elegant new suit.*

debrief /ˌdiːˈbriːf/ v *(esp military)* to question a soldier, an ASTRONAUT, etc about a task that he or she has just completed: [Vn] *The defectors were debriefed at the airport by immigration officials.* [Vnpr] *Pilots were debriefed on the bombing raid.* Compare BRIEF² v 1. ▶ **debriefing** n [C, U]: *a debriefing for the released hostages* ○ *undergo debriefing.*

debris /ˈdebriː, ˈdeɪ-; US dəˈbriː/ n [U] scattered pieces, esp of sth that has been destroyed: *searching among the debris after the explosion* ○ *After the crash, debris from the plane was spread over a large area.*

debt /det/ n **1(a)** [C] a sum of money owed to sb: *If I pay all my debts I'll have no money left.* **(b)** [U] owing money, esp when one cannot pay: *third world debt* ○ *I'm in debt to the tune of £5 000.* ○ *We were poor, but we never got/ran into debt.* See also BAD DEBT. **2** [C usu *sing*] an obligation to sb for their help, kindness, etc: *owe sb a debt of gratitude* ○ *I'm happy to acknowledge my debt to my teachers.* **IDM** **be in sb's debt** *(fml)* to feel grateful to sb for their help, kindness, etc: *You saved my life: I am forever in your debt.*
▶ **debtor** /ˈdetə(r)/ n a person who owes money to sb: *receive payment from one's debtors* ○ *a debtor country/nation.*
■ **debt of honour** n a debt that one feels morally that one must pay even though one is not required by law to do so.

debug /ˌdiːˈbʌɡ/ v (**-gg-**) *(infml)* **1** [Vn] to find and remove faults in a computer PROGRAM(1), machine, etc. **2** to find and remove hidden microphones (MICROPHONE) from a room, house, etc: [Vn] *The place has been completely debugged.*

debunk /ˌdiːˈbʌŋk/ v to show that the reputation of a person, an idea, an institution, etc is false or not deserved: [Vn] *debunking the myths that have come to be regarded as historical facts.*

début (also **debut**) /ˈdeɪbjuː, ˈdebjuː; US deɪˈbjuː/ n a person's first appearance in public as a performer on stage, etc: *She's making her New York début at Carnegie Hall.*

débutante /ˈdebjutɑːnt/ (also *infml* **deb**) n a young woman making her first appearance in fashionable society.

deca- *comb form* ten: *decathlon.* ⇨ App 8.

Dec abbr December: *5 Dec 1909.*

decade /ˈdekeɪd, dɪˈkeɪd/ n a period of ten years: *the first decade of the 20th century* (ie 1901–1910 or 1900–1909).

decadence /ˈdekədəns/ n [U] *(derog)* (a state or behaviour that shows) a fall to a lower level in morals, art, literature, etc, esp after a period at a high level: *the decadence of modern society/of late Victorian art.* ▶ **decadent** /ˈdekədənt/ adj: *a decadent society/style* ○ *decadent behaviour.*

decaffeinated /ˌdiːˈkæfɪneɪtɪd/ adj with most or all of the CAFFEINE removed: *decaffeinated coffee.*

decamp /dɪˈkæmp/ v ~ **(from…)** **(to…)** to go away suddenly and often secretly: [V] *She had decamped with all our money.* [Vpr] *They suddenly decided to decamp from their London home to a cottage in the country.*

decant /dɪˈkænt/ v [Vn, Vnpr] ~ **sth (into sth)** to pour wine, etc from a bottle into another container, esp slowly so that any SEDIMENT(1) is left behind.
▶ **decanter** n a usu decorated glass bottle into which wine, etc may be decanted before serving. ⇨ picture at BOTTLE.

decapitate /dɪˈkæpɪteɪt/ v [Vn] to cut the head off esp a person or an animal. ▶ **decapitation** /dɪˌkæpɪˈteɪʃn/ n [U, C].

decathlon /dɪˈkæθlɒn/ n a sports contest in which each competitor must take part in all of ten events. See also PENTATHLON.
▶ **decathlete** /dɪˈkæθliːt/ n a competitor in a decathlon.

decay /dɪˈkeɪ/ v **1** to become or make sth bad¹(5); to rot; to DECOMPOSE: [V] *decaying teeth/vegetables* ○ *(fig) decaying buildings* [Vn] *Sugar decays your teeth.* **2** to lose power, vigour, influence, etc: [V] *a decaying culture/society/regime* ○ *Our powers decay* (ie We become less strong, alert, etc) *in old age.*
▶ **decay** n [U] the process of decaying or the state reached by decaying: *tooth decay* ○ *radioactive decay* ○ *urban/economic/spiritual decay* ○ *The feudal system slowly fell into decay* (ie stopped working).

decease /dɪˈsiːs/ n [U] *(law or fml)* the death of a person.
▶ **deceased** adj *(law or fml)* dead: *one's deceased father/uncle/spouse* ○ *Both her parents are deceased.*
the deceased n *(pl unchanged)* *(law or fml)* a person who has died, esp recently.

deceit /dɪˈsiːt/ n **1** [U] the action of deliberately trying to make sb believe sth that is not true, usu so as to get sth for oneself; deceiving sb: *He is accused of fraudulence and deceit.* **2** [C] a dishonest act or statement: *Her account of the affair was shown to be full of lies and deceits.*
▶ **deceitful** /dɪˈsiːtfl/ adj **(a)** often deceiving people; dishonest: *a deceitful child.* **(b)** intended to mislead: *deceitful words/behaviour.* **deceitfully** /-fəli/ adv. **deceitfulness** n [U].

deceive /dɪˈsiːv/ v **1** ~ **sb/oneself (into doing sth)** to make sb believe sth that is not true, esp so as to persuade them to do sth; to mislead sb deliberately: [Vn] *His friendly manner did not deceive us for long.* [Vn, Vnpr] *You can't pass exams without working, so don't deceive yourself (into thinking you can).* **2** ~ **sb (with sb)** to have sex with sb who is not one's wife, husband or partner; to be UNFAITHFUL: [Vn, Vnpr] *He's been deceiving his wife (with another woman) for months.* ▶ **deceiver** /-və(r)/ n.

decelerate /ˌdiːˈseləreɪt/ v to become or make sth become slower: [V, Vn] *Progress may have (been) decelerated because of events in Eastern Europe.* Compare ACCELERATE. ▶ **deceleration** /ˌdiːseləˈreɪʃn/ n [U, sing].

December /dɪˈsembə(r)/ n [U,C] (abbr **Dec**) the 12th and last month of the year, next after November.
For further guidance on how *December* is used, see the examples at *April*.

decency /ˈdiːsnsi/ n **1** [U] the quality of being or appearing respectable and polite: *an offence against common decency* ○ *You could at least have the decency to apologize for what you did!* **2 the decencies** [pl] the standards of respectable behaviour in society: *We must observe the decencies and attend the funeral.*

decent /ˈdiːsnt/ adj **1(a)** proper; acceptable; satisfactory: *We must provide decent housing for the poor.* ○ *The hospital has no decent equipment.* ○ *He's done the decent thing and resigned.* ○ *earn a decent wage/living.* **(b)** good; above average: *That was quite a decent lunch.* ○ *They're a decent firm to work for* (ie They treat their employees well). ○ *He's a thoroughly decent* (ie honourable) *man.* **2** not likely to shock or embarrass others; respectable: *That dress isn't decent.* ○ (infml) *Are you decent?* (ie Are you properly dressed?) ○ *She ought to have waited for a decent interval before marrying again.* Compare INDECENT.
▶ **decently** adv in a decent manner: *They're paid fairly decently.* ○ *decently dressed.*

decentralize, -ise /diːˈsentrəlaɪz/ v **(a)** to transfer power, authority, etc from central government to local government: [Vn] *decentralize planning decisions to the regions.* **(b)** to move the departments, etc of a large organization away from a single administrative centre to other places around the country: [Vn] *decentralize the building industry.* ▶ **decentralization, -isation** /ˌdiːˌsentrəlaɪˈzeɪʃn; US -lə'z-/ n [U].

deception /dɪˈsepʃn/ n **1** [U] the action of deceiving or state of being deceived: *obtain sth by deception* ○ *practise deception on the public.* **2** [C] a trick intended to deceive: *It was an innocent deception, meant as a joke.*

deceptive /dɪˈseptɪv/ adj likely to deceive; misleading: *Appearances are often deceptive* (ie Things are not always what they seem to be). ○ *Her simple style is deceptive: what she has to say is very profound.* ▶ **deceptively** adv: *The tank is deceptively small: it actually holds quite a lot.*

deci- comb form (in the metric system) one tenth part of: *decilitre* ○ *decimetre.* ⇨ App 8.

decibel /ˈdesɪbel/ n a unit for measuring the relative loudness of sounds, or for measuring power levels in electrical communications.

decide /dɪˈsaɪd/ v **1(a)** ~ (**between sth/sb**); ~ (**on/against sth/sb**) to consider sth and come to a conclusion; to make a decision: [V, V.wh] *With so much choice, it's hard to decide* (what to buy). [Vpr] *It's difficult to decide between the two.* ○ *After seeing all the candidates we've decided on* (ie chosen) *this one.* ○ *decide against changing one's job* [V.that] *It has been decided that the book should be revised.* [V.to inf] *She decided not to go alone.* **(b)** to settle a dispute, an issue or a case; give a judgement on sth: [V, Vn] *The judge will decide (the case) tomorrow.* ○ *Her argument decided the issue in his favour.* [Vpr] *The judge decided for/against the plaintiff.* **2** (of events, actions, etc) to have an important and definite effect on sth: [Vadv] *I wanted to be a painter, but circumstances decided otherwise* (ie forced me to be something else). [Vn] *A chance meeting decided my career.* [V.wh] *This last game will decide who is to be champion.* [V] *The higher salary was the deciding factor.* **3** to make sb reach a decision: [Vnpr] *What finally decided you against it?* [V.n to inf] *That decided me to leave my job.* [also Vn].
▶ **decided** adj **1** [attrib] clear; definite: *a person of decided views* ○ *He walks with a decided limp.* **2** ~

(**about sth**) firmly intending to do sth; determined: *He won't go: he's really decided about it.* **decidedly** adv definitely; thoroughly: *I feel decidedly unwell this morning.*
decider n a game, race, etc to settle a contest between competitors who have finished equal.

deciduous /dɪˈsɪdʒuəs; Brit also dɪˈsɪdjuəs/ adj (of a tree) that loses its leaves every year, usu in autumn: *deciduous forests.* Compare EVERGREEN.

decilitre /ˈdesiliːtə(r)/ n a unit of capacity in the metric system, equal to one tenth of a litre.

decimal /ˈdesɪml/ adj based on or counted in tens or tenths: *decimal coinage/currency* ○ *the decimal system.*
▶ **decimal** (also ˌdecimal ˈfraction) n a fraction expressed in tenths, hundredths (HUNDRED), etc: *The decimal 0.61 stands for 61 hundredths.* ○ *The figure is accurate to two decimal places* (ie shows two figures after the decimal point). ⇨ App 2.
decimalize, -ise /-məlaɪz/ v to change a system of currency or measurements to a decimal system: [Vn] *The country has decided to decimalize its coinage.* **decimalization, -isation** /ˌdesiməlaɪˈzeɪʃn; US -lə'z-/ n [U].
■ ˌdecimal ˈpoint n a dot or point placed after the unit figure in the writing of decimals, eg in 15.61.

decimate /ˈdesɪmeɪt/ v **(a)** to kill or destroy a large part of sth: [Vn] *Disease has decimated the population.* **(b)** (infml) to reduce sth by a lot: [Vn] *Student numbers have been decimated by cuts in grants.* ▶ **decimation** /ˌdesɪˈmeɪʃn/ n [U]: *the decimation of the rain forests.*

decimetre /ˈdesimiːtə(r)/ n a unit of length in the metric system, equal to one tenth of a metre.

decipher /dɪˈsaɪfə(r)/ v to succeed in understanding sth such as a code, an old document, sb's writing, etc: [Vn] *I can't decipher the inscription on the pillar.* ○ (infml) *Can you decipher her handwriting?* Compare INDECIPHERABLE.

decision /dɪˈsɪʒn/ n **1** ~ (**on/against sth**); ~ (**to do sth**) **(a)** [U] the action of deciding: *The moment of decision has arrived* (ie It is time to decide). **(b)** [C] a conclusion reached; a judgement: *arrive at/come to/make/reach/take a decision* ○ *his decision against going on the trip* ○ *Her decision to retire surprised us all.* ○ *give a decision on an issue* ○ *The judge's decision was to award damages to the defendant.* ○ *Discussion should be part of the decision-making process.* **2** [U] the ability to decide quickly: *This is not a job for someone who lacks decision.* Compare INDECISION.

decisive /dɪˈsaɪsɪv/ adj **1** producing a particular or definite result or conclusion: *a decisive victory/battle/moment* ○ *The injury to their key player was a decisive factor in the game.* **2** having or showing the ability to decide quickly: *a decisive person/answer/manner* ○ *Be decisive — tell them exactly what you think should be done!* Compare INDECISIVE. ▶ **decisively** adv: *act/answer decisively.* **decisiveness** n [U].

deck¹ /dek/ n **1(a)** any of the floors of a ship, esp the top open floor covering all of its length (the *main deck*): *My cabin is on E deck.* ○ *go for a stroll on deck* (ie on the main deck) ○ *be/go below deck(s)* (ie in/into the space under the main deck). ⇨ picture at YACHT. **(b)** any similar area, eg the floor of a bus: *the top deck of a double-decker bus.* Compare FLIGHTDECK. **2** (esp US) a pack of cards (CARD¹ 4). **3(a)** a platform on which the TURNTABLE(1) of a record-player (RECORD¹) rests. **(b)** a device for holding and playing CASSETTE tapes, discs, etc in HI-FI equipment. **IDM clear the decks** ⇨ CLEAR³. **hit the deck** ⇨ HIT¹.
▶ **-decker** (forming compound ns and adjs) having a specified number of decks or layers: *a ˌdouble-/ˌsingle-decker ˈbus* ○ *a ˌtriple-decker ˈsandwich* (ie one with three layers of bread).
■ ˈdeck-chair n a folding chair with a seat

D

made of a length of canvas or plastic hung on a usu wooden frame. Deck-chairs are often used out of doors, eg in parks or on the beach. ⇨ picture at HOUSE¹.

'deck-hand *n* a member of a ship's crew who works on deck.

deck² /dek/ *v* ~ **sb/sth** (**out**) (**in/with sth**) to decorate sb/sth: [Vnpr] *streets decked with flags* [Vnp] *She was decked out in her finest clothes.* [also Vn].

declaim /dɪ'kleɪm/ *v* (*sometimes derog*) to express sth loudly, forcefully or with great feeling to, or as if to, an audience: [Vn] *declaim poetry* [Vpr] *A preacher was declaiming against the ills of modern society.* [also V, V.speech].

declamation /ˌdeklə'meɪʃn/ *n* (**a**) [U] (the art of) declaiming: *the declamation of poetry.* (**b**) [C] a formal speech, esp one made with great feeling. ▸ **declamatory** /dɪ'klæmətəri; *US* -tɔːri/ *adj*: *her high-flown declamatory style.*

declaration /ˌdeklə'reɪʃn/ *n* **1**(**a**) [U] declaring; formally announcing : *He was in favour of the declaration of a truce.* (**b**) [C] a formal announcement, either spoken or written: *a declaration of war* ○ *the Declaration of Human Rights* (ie by the United Nations, stating an individual's basic rights) ○ *the Declaration of Independence.* **2** [C] a written statement giving information about sth: *a declaration of income* (ie made to the tax authorities) ○ *a customs declaration* (ie giving details of goods being brought into a country).

declare /dɪ'kleə(r)/ *v* **1**(**a**) to announce sth formally or officially; to make sth known clearly: [Vn] *declare an election/amnesty/armistice* [Vn, Vnpr] *declare war (on an enemy)* [V.that] *declare that the war is over* [Vn-n] *They declared him (to be) the winner.* [Vn-adj] *The food was declared unfit for human consumption.* ○ *I declare the meeting closed.* (**b**) to say sth firmly or with emphasis; to assert: [V.speech] *'I'm not coming with you — and that's final!' declared Mary.* [V.that] *He declared that he was innocent.* [Vn] *She declared her intention to resign.* [Vn-adj] *The experts declared themselves baffled.* **2** ~ **for/against sth/sb** (*fml*) to say that one is/is not in favour of sth/sb: [Vpr] *The commission declared against the proposed scheme.* **3** to tell the tax authorities about one's income, or CUSTOMS officers about goods brought into a country: [Vn] *You must declare all you have earned in the last year.* ○ *Do you have anything to declare?* **4** (in cricket) to choose to end one's team's INNINGS before all ten wickets (WICKET) have fallen: [V] *The captain declared at a score of 395 for 5 wickets.*

▸ **declared** *adj* [attrib] that sb has openly admitted: *He's a declared atheist.* ○ *Her declared ambition is to become a politician.*

declassify /ˌdiː'klæsɪfaɪ/ *v* (*pt, pp* **-fied**) to declare that certain information is no longer secret: [Vn] *Plans for nuclear plants have been declassified.* ▸ **declassification** /ˌdiːˌklæsɪfɪ'keɪʃn/ *n* [U].

decline¹ /dɪ'klaɪn/ *v* **1** to say 'no' to sth; to refuse sth offered, usu politely: [V, Vn] *I invited her to join us, but she declined (my invitation).* [V.to inf] *He declined to comment on the proposals.* **2** to become smaller, weaker, fewer, etc; to DIMINISH(1): [V] *Her influence declined after she lost the election.* ○ *a declining birth-rate* ○ *declining sales* ○ *He spent his declining years* (ie those at the end of his life) *in the country.*

decline² /dɪ'klaɪn/ *n* ~ (**in sth**) a gradual and continuous loss of strength, power, numbers, etc: *the decline of the Roman Empire* ○ *a decline in population/prices/output* ○ *Manufacturing output is in decline.* ○ *The industry fell/went into (a) decline soon after the war.* ○ *The number of robberies in the area is on the decline.*

decode /ˌdiː'kəʊd/ *v* [Vn] (**a**) to find the meaning of sth, esp sth written in code; to interpret sth: *decode*

the symbolism of her paintings. (**b**) to receive and interpret an electronic signal. Compare ENCODE.

▸ **decoder** *n* (**a**) a person or device that changes a code into language that can be understood. (**b**) a device that decodes an electronic signal: *a satellite TV decoder.*

décolleté /deɪ'kɒlteɪ; *US* -kɒl'teɪ/ *adj* (*French*) (of a dress, etc) with a low top that shows the upper part of the chest and usu the shoulders.

decolonize, -ise /ˌdiː'kɒlənaɪz/ *v* [Vn] to give independent status to a colony. ▸ **decolonization, -isation** /ˌdiːˌkɒlənaɪ'zeɪʃn; *US* -nə'z-/ *n* [U].

decommission /ˌdiːkə'mɪʃn/ *v* to withdraw sth from regular use; to close sth down: [Vn] *decommission a nuclear power station.*

decompose /ˌdiːkəm'pəʊz/ *v* to become bad¹(5) or ROTTEN(1); to decay: [V] *a decomposing corpse.* ▸ **decomposition** /ˌdiːˌkɒmpə'zɪʃn/ *n* [U].

decompression /ˌdiːkəm'preʃn/ *n* [U] a reduction in air pressure, esp on sb who has been experiencing high pressure, eg under water: *a decompression chamber* (ie one in which divers (DIVE¹) may return to normal pressure).

decongestant /ˌdiːkən'dʒestənt/ *n* (*medical*) a substance that helps sb with a cold to breathe more easily.

deconstruct /ˌdiːkən'strʌkt/ *v* (*techn*) to analyse the language of literature and philosophy, esp so as to show that parts of it may not be consistent with each other: [Vn] *deconstruct Shakespeare.* ▸ **deconstruction** *n* [U]. **deconstructionism** *n* [U] (*techn*) the theory and practice of deconstructing. **deconstructionist** *n, adj*: *a deconstructionist critic/approach.* Compare STRUCTURALISM.

decontaminate /ˌdiːkən'tæmɪneɪt/ *v* [Vn] to remove harmful, esp RADIOACTIVE, substances from a building, clothes, an area, etc. ▸ **decontamination** /ˌdiːkənˌtæmɪ'neɪʃn/ *n* [U].

décor /'deɪkɔː(r); *US* deɪ'kɔːr/ *n* [C, U] the furniture and decoration of a room, stage, etc: *a stylish/modern décor* ○ *Who designed the décor?*

decorate /'dekəreɪt/ *v* **1** ~ **sth** (**with sth**) to make sth more beautiful by adding ornaments to it: [Vnpr] *decorate a Christmas tree with coloured lights* ○ *The building was decorated with flags.* [Vn] *Bright posters decorate the streets.* **2** to put paint, WALLPAPER, etc on a room, house, etc: [V] *tips on interior decorating* [Vn] *We're decorating the kitchen again this summer.* **3** ~ **sb** (**for sth**) (usu passive) to give a MEDAL or some other award to sb: [Vn, Vnpr] *Several soldiers were decorated (for bravery).*

▸ **decorator** *n* a person whose job is painting and decorating rooms, houses, etc.

decoration /ˌdekə'reɪʃn/ *n* **1** [U] decorating or being decorated: *When will they finish the decoration of the bathroom?* **2** [U,C] a thing used for decorating: *the carved decoration around the doorway* ○ *Christmas decorations.* **3** [C] a MEDAL, etc given and worn as an honour: *military decorations.*

decorative /'dekərətɪv; *US also* 'dekəreɪtɪv/ *adj* that makes sth look more beautiful: *decorative icing on the cake* ○ *The coloured lights are very decorative.*

decorous /'dekərəs/ *adj* (*fml*) polite and socially acceptable: *decorous behaviour/speech.* ▸ **decorously** *adv*.

decorum /dɪ'kɔːrəm/ *n* [U] polite and socially acceptable behaviour: *maintain a proper sense of decorum.*

decoy /'diːkɔɪ/ *n* (**a**) a bird or an animal, or a model of one, used to attract others so that they can be shot or trapped. (**b**) a person or thing used to trick sb into a position of danger.

▸ **decoy** /dɪ'kɔɪ/ *v* to lead sb/sth away from their intended course by using a decoy: [Vn, Vnpr] *The* *thieves had decoyed customers (from the building) by means of a false fire alarm.*

decrease /dɪˈkriːs/ *v* to become or make sth smaller or fewer: [V] *Student numbers have decreased by 500.* ○ *Interest in the sport is steadily decreasing.* [Vn] *The government have decreased the size of grants.*

▶ **decrease** /ˈdiːkriːs/ *n* ~ **(in sth) (a)** [U] the process of decreasing; a reduction: *some decrease in the birth rate* ○ *Certain types of crime seem to be* **on the decrease.** **(b)** [C] an amount by which sth decreases: *a decrease of 3% in the rate of inflation* ○ *There has been a decrease in imports.*

decree /dɪˈkriː/ *n* **1** an order given by a ruler or an authority and having the force of a law: *issue a decree* ○ *rule by decree* (ie without asking advice from others). **2** a judgement or decision made by certain lawcourts.

▶ **decree** *v* (*pt, pp* **decreed**) to order sth by decree or as if by decree: [Vn] *The governor decreed a day of mourning.* ○ [V.that] (*fig*) *Fate decreed that they would not meet again.*

■ **de,cree ˈabsolute** *n* (*pl* **decrees absolute**) an order of a lawcourt giving a final DIVORCE[1](1) to two people.

de,cree ˈnisi /ˈnaɪsaɪ/ (*pl* **decrees nisi**) *n* an order of a lawcourt that two people will be given a DIVORCE[1](1) after a fixed period, unless good reasons are given why they should not.

decrepit /dɪˈkrepɪt/ *adj* made weak by age or hard use: *a decrepit person/horse/bicycle.* ▶ **decrepitude** /dɪˈkrepɪtjuːd; *US* -tuːd/ *n* [U] (*fml*): *The house had a forlorn air of decrepitude.*

decry /dɪˈkraɪ/ *v* (*pt, pp* **decried**) ~ **sb/sth (as sth)** (*fml*) to speak in a critical way about sb/sth; to condemn sb/sth: [Vn, Vn-n] *He decried her efforts (as a waste of time).* [also Vn-adj].

dedicate /ˈdedɪkeɪt/ *v* **1** ~ **oneself/sth to sth / doing sth** to give or devote oneself, time, effort, etc to a good cause(3) or purpose: [Vnpr] *dedicate oneself to one's work* ○ *She dedicated her life to helping the poor.* **2** ~ **sth to sb** to address sth one has written, eg a book or a piece of music to sb as a way of showing respect: [Vnpr] *She dedicated her first book to her teacher* (eg by putting his name at the front). ○ *That song was dedicated to Lynette from her husband Peter.* **3** ~ **sth (to sb/sth)** to devote a church, etc with solemn ceremonies to a sacred purpose, to the memory of sb/sth, etc: [Vn] *The chapel was dedicated in 1880.* [Vnpr] *A memorial stone was dedicated to those who lost their lives.* Compare CONSECRATE.

▶ **dedicated** *adj* ~ **(to sth)** giving time, effort and loyalty to an aim, a job, etc; committed (COMMIT): *a dedicated worker/priest/teacher* ○ *She's totally dedicated to her work.*

dedication /ˌdedɪˈkeɪʃn/ *n* ~ **(to sth) 1** [U] the state of being devoted to a cause(3) or an aim: *I admire your dedication to your work.* **2** [C] the words used in dedicating (DEDICATE 2) a book, piece of music, etc to sb. **3** [C] a ceremony for dedicating (DEDICATE 3) a church, etc.

deduce /dɪˈdjuːs; *US* dɪˈduːs/ *v* ~ **sth (from sth)** to arrive at facts, a theory, etc by reasoning; to INFER(1) sth: [V.that] *If a = b and b = c, we can deduce that a = c.* [Vnpr] *Forensic scientists can deduce a great deal from the victim's remains.* [Vpr.that] *It would be unwise to deduce from these figures that the economy is recovering.* [also Vn, V.wh, Vpr.wh]. ▶ **deducible** /dɪˈdjuːsəbl; *US* dɪˈduːsəbl/ *adj.*

deduct /dɪˈdʌkt/ *v* ~ **sth (from sth)** to take away an amount or a part: [Vnpr] *Tax is deducted from your salary.* [also Vn]. Compare SUBTRACT, ADD.

▶ **deductible** /dɪˈdʌktəbl/ *adj* that may be deducted from one's income before paying tax, or from tax to be paid: *tax deductible expenses.*

deduction /dɪˈdʌkʃn/ *n* ~ **(from sth) 1(a)** [U] the process of reasoning from general principles to a particular case; deducing (DEDUCE): *a brilliant piece of deduction* ○ *arrive at a solution by a process of deduction.* **(b)** [C] a conclusion reached by reasoning: *From what we know of her life it seems a reasonable deduction.* Compare INDUCTION 3. **2(a)** [U] the action of taking away an amount or a part; deducting (DEDUCT): *Salaries are shown without deduction of tax.* **(b)** [C] an amount or part taken away: *deductions from pay for insurance and pension.*

▶ **deductive** /dɪˈdʌktɪv/ *adj* of or using deduction (1a): *deductive reasoning.*

deed /diːd/ *n* **1** (*esp fml*) an act; a thing done intentionally: *be rewarded for one's good deeds* ○ *deeds of heroism* ○ *Deeds are better than words when people need help.* ⇨ note at ACT[1]. **2** (often *pl*) (*law*) a signed agreement, esp about the ownership of property or legal rights. See also TITLE-DEED.

■ **,deed of ˈcovenant** *n* a signed promise to pay a regular amount of money every year to a charity, an individual, etc. A deed of covenant enables the person or group receiving the money to claim in addition the tax that would normally be paid on the amount.

ˈdeed poll *n* a legal deed made by one person only, esp to change her or his name.

deem /diːm/ *v* (*fml*) (not in the continuous tenses) to consider; to regard: [Vn-n] *I deem it a great honour to be invited to address you.* ○ *She was deemed (to be) the winner.* [Vn-adj] *These measures are deemed advisable in the circumstances.*

deep[1] /diːp/ *adj* (**-er, -est**) **1(a)** extending a long way from top to bottom: *a deep well/river/trench/box.* Compare SHALLOW. ⇨ note at DIMENSION. **(b)** extending a long way from the surface or edge: *a deep wound/cleft/border/shelf* ○ (*joc*) *They live in deepest Wales* (ie in a remote part of Wales). **(c)** (after *ns*, with words specifying how far) extending down, back or in: *water six feet deep* ○ *People stood ten deep* (ie in lines of ten people one behind the other) *to see her go past.* **2(a)** [attrib] taking in or giving out a lot of air: *a deep sigh/breath.* **(b)** going a long way down, along or into sth: *a deep thrust/dive* ○ *Bradley made a deep pass into the centre of the field.* **3** (of sounds) low; not high-pitched: *a deep voice/note/rumbling.* **4** (of sleep) from which one is not easily woken. **5** (of colours) strong; vivid: *a deep red.* **6** [pred] ~ **in sth (a)** far down in sth: *with his hands deep in his pockets* ○ *rocks deep in the earth.* **(b)** thinking hard about sth; concentrating on sth: *deep in thought/study/a book.* **(c)** very involved in sth; overwhelmed (OVERWHELM 2) by sth: *deep in debt/difficulties.* **7** [usu attrib] **(a)** difficult to understand or find out: *a deep mystery/secret.* **(b)** showing intelligent awareness; PROFOUND(2): *a person with deep insight* ○ *a deep discussion* ○ *a deep* (ie intense) *stare.* **(c)** concealing one's real feelings, opinions, etc; SECRETIVE: *He's a deep one.* **8(a)** extreme(1); serious(3): *be in deep disgrace/trouble* ○ *deep divisions in the party.* **(b)** fundamental; not SUPERFICIAL(3a): *deep significance/implications.* **9** (of emotions) strongly felt; intense: *deep outrage/shame/sympathy* ○ *our deepest thanks.* **IDM** **between the devil and the deep blue sea** ⇨ DEVIL[1]. **go off the ˈdeep end** (*infml*) to become extremely angry or emotional: *When I said I'd broken it, she really went off the deep end.* **in deep ˈwater(s)** in trouble or difficulty: *Losing your passport could land you in deep water.* **throw sb in at the ˈdeep end** (*infml*) to introduce sb to the most difficult part of an activity, esp one for which they are not prepared.

▶ **-deep** (forming compound *adjs*) as far as a specified point: *They stood knee-deep in the snow.* ○ *The grass was ankle-deep.*

deepen /ˈdiːpən/ *v* to become or make sth deep or

---

deeper (most senses): [V] *The lake deepened after the dam was built.* ○ *The mystery deepens* (ie becomes harder to understand). ○ *the deepening colours of the evening sky* ○ *a deepening recession/dispute/crisis* [Vn] *deepen one's understanding of sth.*

deeply *adv* **1** a long way down or through sth: *dig deeply.* **2** greatly; intensely: *deeply interested/indebted/impressed* ○ *habits that are deeply ingrained* ○ *She felt her mother's death deeply.*

deepness *n* [U].

■ **¦deep-'sea**, **¦deep-'water** *adjs* [attrib] of or in the deeper parts of the sea, away from the coast: *¦deep-sea 'fishing* ○ *a ¦deep-sea 'diver.*

¦deep-'set *adj* (esp of eyes) set deeply back: *deep-set eyes under overhanging brows.*

the ¦Deep 'South *n* [sing] the southern states of the USA, esp Georgia, Alabama, Mississippi, Louisiana and South Carolina.

deep² /di:p/ *adv* (**-er**, **-est**) far down or in: *We had to dig deeper to find water.* ○ *They dived deep into the ocean.* ○ *They penetrated deep into enemy territory.* ○ *He went on studying deep into the night.* ○ *She gazed deep into my eyes.* **IDM** **deep 'down** (*infml*) in reality; in spite of appearances: *She seems indifferent, but deep down she's very pleased.* **go/run 'deep** (of attitudes, beliefs, etc) to be strongly and naturally held or felt: *Her faith goes very deep.* ○ *Your maternal instincts go deeper than you think.* **still waters run deep** ⇨ STILL¹.

■ **¦deep-'freeze** *v* (*pt* **¦deep-'froze**; *pp* **¦deep-'frozen**) to freeze food quickly in order to preserve it for long periods: [Vn] *¦deep-frozen 'fish.* — *n* = FREEZER.

¦deep-'fry *v* (*pt, pp* **¦deep-'fried**) [Vn] to fry food in hot fat that completely covers it. ⇨ note at COOK.

¦deep-'rooted, **¦deep-'seated** *adjs* (of attitudes, feelings, etc) not easily removed; firmly established: *¦deep-rooted 'hatred dis'like/¦prejudice/su'spicion* ○ *The causes of the trouble are deep-seated.*

deep³ /di:p/ *n* **the deep** [sing] (*dated or fml*) the sea.

antlers
deer
stag
doe

deer /dɪə(r)/ *n* (*pl* unchanged) any of several types of animal with long legs and a graceful appearance that eat grass, leaves, etc and can run quickly. Male deer usu have horns on their heads called *antlers.* ⇨ picture.

deerstalker /'dɪəstɔ:kə(r)/ *n* a cap with two peaks (PEAK³ 3), one in front and the other behind, and two pieces of cloth which are usu tied together on top but can be folded down to cover the ears. ⇨ picture at HAT.

de-escalate /ˌdi: 'eskəleɪt/ *v* [Vn] to reduce the level or intensity of a war, dispute, etc. ▶ **de-escalation** /ˌdi: ˌeskə'leɪʃn/ *n* [U].

deface /dɪ'feɪs/ *v* to spoil the appearance of sth by damaging its surface or by drawing or writing on it: [Vn] *It is an offence to deface library books.* [Vnpr] *The wall had been defaced with slogans.* ▶ **defacement** *n* [U].

de facto /ˌdeɪ 'fæktəʊ/ *adj, adv* (*Latin*) existing or doing sth in actual fact, whether or not it is justified: *a de facto ruler/government/right* ○ *Though his kingship was challenged, he continued to rule de facto.* Compare DE JURE.

defame /dɪ'feɪm/ *v* to attack the good reputation of sb; to say bad things about sb: [Vn] *The article is an attempt to defame an honest man.*
▶ **defamation** /ˌdefə'meɪʃn/ *n* [U]: *sued for defamation of character.*
defamatory /dɪ'fæmətri; *US* -tɔ:ri/ *adj* intended to defame: *a defamatory statement/book.*

default¹ /dɪ'fɔ:lt/ *n* (*esp law*) (**a**) [U] failure to do sth, esp to pay a debt or appear in court. (**b**) [C] an instance of this: *a rise in mortgage defaults* ○ *win a case/a game by default* (ie because the other party, team, etc has not taken part). **IDM** **in default of sth** (*fml*) because or in case sth is absent: *He was acquitted in default of strong evidence of his guilt.*

default² /dɪ'fɔ:lt/ *v* (**a**) to fail to do what one is supposed to do, eg to appear in a lawcourt: [V] *A party to the contract defaulted.* (**b**) ~ (**on sth**) to fail to pay a debt, etc: [Vpr] *default on a loan* [also V]. ▶ **defaulter** *n*: *mortgage defaulters.*

defeat /dɪ'fi:t/ *v* **1** to win a victory over sb; to overcome sb: [Vn] *The enemy was defeated in a decisive battle.* ○ *We will defeat the government at the next election.* ○ *He has been soundly defeated at chess.* **2** (*infml*) to be difficult for sb to understand: [Vn] *I've tried to solve the problem, but it defeats me.* ○ *Why you stay indoors on a beautiful day like this defeats me.* **3**(**a**) to stop hopes, aims, etc from becoming reality: [Vn] *By not working hard enough you defeat your own purpose.* (**b**) to prevent an attempt, a proposal, etc from succeeding: [Vn] *We've defeated moves to build another office block.*
▶ **defeat** *n* (**a**) [U] the action of defeating sb or of being defeated: *suffer/admit defeat* ○ *I never consider the possibility of defeat.* (**b**) [C] an instance of this: *We've had six wins and two defeats this season.*
defeatism /-ɪzəm/ *n* [U] a way of thinking, speaking or behaving that shows one expects not to succeed: *Not bothering to vote is a sure sign of defeatism.* **defeatist** /-ɪst/ *n, adj.*

defecate /'defəkeɪt, 'di:-/ *v* [V] (*fml*) to push out waste matter from the body through the ANUS. ▶ **defecation** /ˌdefə'keɪʃn, ˌdi:-/ *n* [U].

defect¹ /'di:fekt, dɪ'fekt/ *n* a fault or lack that spoils a person or thing: *a defect of character* ○ *genetic defects* ○ *mechanical defects in a car* ○ *defects in the education system.* ⇨ note at MISTAKE¹.

defect² /dɪ'fekt/ *v* ~ (**from sth**) (**to sth**) to leave a political party, cause(3), country, etc, and go to another: [Vpr] *She defected from the Liberals and joined the Socialists.* [V, Vpr] *One of our spies has defected (to the enemy).* ▶ **defection** /dɪ'fekʃn/ *n* [C, U] ~ (**from sth**): *Discontent will lead to further defections from the party.* ○ *Some dissidents are considering defection.* **defector** *n*: *a high-ranking defector seeking political asylum.*

defective /dɪ'fektɪv/ *adj* ~ (**in sth**) having a DEFECT¹ or defects; not perfect or complete; faulty: *a defective machine/method/theory* ○ *Her hearing was found to be slightly defective.* ○ *a defective verb* (ie one without the full range of endings that other verbs have, eg *must*). ▶ **defectively** *adv.* **defectiveness** *n* [U].

defence (*US* **defense**) /dɪ'fens/ *n* **1** [U] ~ (**against sth**) (**a**) the action of defending sb/sth from attack or of fighting against attack: *fight in defence of one's country* ○ *come/leap/rush/spring to sb's defence* ○ *weapons of offence and defence* ○ *They planned the defence of the town.* (**b**) [C] a weapon, barrier, etc used for defending or protecting: *The high wall was built as a defence against intruders.* ○ *The country's defences are weak.* ○ *coastal defences* (ie against attack from the sea) ○ *Antibodies are the body's defence against infection.* (**c**) [U] military measures for protecting a country: *The Ministry of Defence* ○ *the defence budget* ○ *civil defence.* **2**(**a**) [C, U] ~ (**against sth**) an esp legal argument used to answer an accusation or support an idea: *counsel for*

the defence ○ *The lawyer produced a clever defence of her client.* ○ *The book is a brilliant defence of* (ie argues in favour of) *their policies.* ○ *It must be said in her defence that she was only obeying instructions.* (**b**) **the defence** [Gp] a lawyer or lawyers acting for an accused person: *The defence argue/argues that the evidence is weak.* Compare PROSECUTION 2. **3** (*sport*) (**a**) [U] the protection of a goal(1a) or part of the playing area from opponents' attacks: *She plays in defence/(US) on defense.* (**b**) (usu **the defence** [Gp]) the members of a team involved in this: *He has been brought in to strengthen the defence.* Compare ATTACK 5, OFFENSE. (**c**) [C] a sports contest in which a previous winner is challenged: *his third successful defence of the title.*
▶ **defenceless** *adj* having no defence; unable to defend oneself: *a defenceless child/animal/city.* **defencelessly** *adv.* **defencelessness** *n* [U].

defend /dɪˈfend/ *v* **1** ~ **sb/sth (from/against sb/sth)** (**a**) to protect sb/sth from harm; to guard sb/sth: [Vn] *When the dog attacked me, I defended myself with a stick.* [Vnpr] *defend sb from attack/an attacker/injury* ○ *defend one's country against enemies.* (**b**) to act, speak or write in support of sb/sth: [Vn] *defend one's actions/cause/ideas/leader* ○ *defend a lawsuit* (ie fight against it in court) ○ *You'll need stronger evidence to defend your claim to the inheritance.* ○ *He's fighting to defend his seat in Congress* (ie trying to get elected again). [Vnpr] *The newspaper defended her against the accusations.* **2** (*sport*) (**a**) to protect the goal(1a), etc from one's opponents: [V] *Some players are better at defending.* [Vn, Vnpr] *They had three players defending the goal (against attack).* (**b**) (of a previous winner) to take part in a contest to keep one's position: [Vn] *the defending champion* ○ *She's running to defend her 400 metres title.* ▶ **defender** *n*: *an outspoken defender of human rights* ○ *He had to beat several defenders to score.* ⇨ picture at FOOTBALL.

defendant /dɪˈfendənt/ *n* a person accused in a legal case. Compare PLAINTIFF.

defenseman /dɪˈfensmæn/ *n* (*pl* **-men** /-men/) (*US*) a player in certain games, eg football and hockey, who plays in a defensive position. ⇨ picture at FOOTBALL.

defensible /dɪˈfensəbl/ *adj* that can be defended: *a defensible castle/position/theory.* Compare INDEFENSIBLE.

defensive /dɪˈfensɪv/ *adj* **1** used for or intended for defending: *defensive warfare/measures* ○ *a defensive weapon system to destroy incoming missiles* ○ *a team that plays a very defensive game.* **2** ~ (**about sb/sth**) showing anxiety to avoid criticism or attack: *When asked to explain her behaviour, she gave a very defensive answer.* ○ *She's very defensive about her part in the affair.* Compare OFFENSIVE 2.
▶ **defensive** *n* **IDM** **on the defensive** expecting to be attacked or criticized: *The team was thrown on(to) the defensive as their opponents rallied.* ○ *Talk about boyfriends always puts her on the defensive.*
defensively *adv.*
defensiveness *n* [U].

defer¹ /dɪˈfɜː(r)/ *v* (**-rr-**) ~ **sth (to sth)** to delay sth until a later time; to POSTPONE sth: [Vn] *deferred payment* (ie made later in separate parts after an item has been sold) [Vnpr] *defer one's departure to a later date* [V.ing] *defer making a decision.* ▶ **deferment**, **deferral** /dɪˈfɜːrəl/ *ns* [U, C].

defer² /dɪˈfɜː(r)/ *v* (**-rr-**) ~ **to sb/sth** to yield to sb or their wishes, judgement, etc, usu because of respect; to show respect: [Vpr] *On technical matters, I defer to the experts.* ○ *I defer to your greater experience in such things.*

deference /ˈdefərəns/ *n* [U] ~ (**to sb/sth**) yielding to the views, wishes, etc of others, usu because of respect; respect: *treat one's elders with due deference*

○ *show deference to a judge* ○ **Out of/In deference to** *our host I avoided all mention of his recent divorce.* ▶ **deferential** /ˌdefəˈrenʃl/ *adj* **deferentially** /-ʃəli/ *adv.*

defiance /dɪˈfaɪəns/ *n* [U] open refusal to obey authority; strong resistance to opposition; action or behaviour that defies (DEFY 1a): *In an act of defiance they continued to play their music loud.* ○ *The decision to strike was taken **in defiance of** (ie despite) the union's recommendation.*

defiant /dɪˈfaɪənt/ *adj* openly refusing to obey or resisting sb/sth; showing DEFIANCE: *a defiant manner/look/speech.* ▶ **defiantly** *adv.*

deficiency /dɪˈfɪʃnsi/ *n* ~ (**in/of sth**) **1**(**a**) [U] the state of lacking sth necessary: *Vitamin deficiency can lead to illness.* (**b**) [C] an instance of this; a lack: *suffering from a deficiency of iron* ○ *deficiency diseases* (ie those caused by the lack of some important element in diet). **2** [C] a lack of a necessary quality; a fault: *Her deficiencies as a writer are all too clear.*

deficient /dɪˈfɪʃnt/ *adj* (**a**) [usu pred] ~ (**in sth**) lacking in sth necessary: *be deficient in skill/experience/knowledge* ○ *a diet deficient in iron.* (**b**) (*fml*) inadequate : *deficient funds/supplies* ○ *Our knowledge of the universe is still extraordinarily deficient.*

deficit /ˈdefɪsɪt/ *n* (**a**) the amount by which sth, esp a sum of money, is too small: *We've raised $100, and we need $250: that's a deficit of $150.* (**b**) the amount by which money spent or owed is greater than money earned in a particular period: *a budget deficit* ○ *a huge balance of payments deficit.* Compare SURPLUS.

defied *pt, pp* of DEFY.

defile¹ /dɪˈfaɪl/ *v* (*fml or rhet*) **1** to make sth dirty or no longer pure: [Vn] *rivers defiled by pollution* ○ *Does pornography defile the minds of its readers?* **2** deliberately to damage sth holy or sacred; to DESECRATE sth: [Vn] *The altar had been defiled by vandals.* ▶ **defilement** *n.*

defile² /dɪˈfaɪl, ˈdiːfaɪl/ *n* a narrow way through mountains.

define /dɪˈfaɪn/ *v* **1** ~ **sth (as sth)** to state exactly the meaning of a word or phrase: [Vn] *Writers of dictionaries try to define words as accurately and clearly as possible.* [also Vn-n]. **2** to state or describe exactly the nature or extent of sth: [Vn] *The powers of a judge are defined by law.* [V.wh] *It's hard to define exactly how I felt.* **3** to show a line, a shape, a feature, an outline, etc clearly: [Vn] *When boundaries between countries are not clearly defined, there is usually trouble.* ○ *The mountain was sharply defined against the eastern sky.* ▶ **definable** /-əbl/ *adj.*

definite /ˈdefɪnət/ *adj* (**a**) clear; that cannot be doubted: *a definite decision/opinion/result/change* ○ *I have no definite plans for tomorrow.* ○ *I want a definite answer, 'yes' or 'no'.* (**b**) [pred] ~ (**about sth/that…**) sure; certain: *He was quite definite about when it happened.* ○ *It's now definite that she's going to be promoted.*
▶ **definitely** /ˈdefɪnətli/ *adv* **1** (used for emphasis) certainly; without doubt: *That is definitely correct.* ○ *'Are you coming?' 'Definitely!'* ○ *The film is definitely not suitable for young children.* **2** in a definite manner; clearly: *She states her views very definitely.*
■ **definite article** *n* (*grammar*) (abbreviated as *def art* in this dictionary) the word 'the'. Compare INDEFINITE ARTICLE.

definition /ˌdefɪˈnɪʃn/ *n* **1**(**a**) [C] a statement giving the exact meaning of a word or phrase: *Definitions should not be more difficult to understand than the words they define.* (**b**) [U] the action or process of stating the exact meanings of words or phrases: *Dictionary writers must be skilled in the art of definition.* ○ *Fiction-writing is, almost by definition, a lonely profession.* **2** [U] (of an image, an outline, a shape, etc) the quality of being clear: *The photograph has poor definition.* ○ *high definition television pictures.* **3** [C, U] a clear statement of the nature or extent of sth: *My duties require clearer definition.* ○ *The book attempts a definition of his role in world politics.*

definitive /dɪˈfɪnətɪv/ *adj* **1** firm, final, done with authority and not to be questioned or changed: *a definitive answer/solution/verdict.* **2** considered to be the best of its kind and unlikely to be improved upon: *the definitive biography of Churchill* ○ *His will surely be seen as the definitive Hamlet of our time.* ▶ **definitively** *adv*.

deflate *v* **1** /ˌdiːˈfleɪt, dɪ-/ **(a)** [Vn] to let air or gas out of a tyre, etc. **(b)** [V] (of a tyre, etc) to be emptied of air or gas. **2** /dɪˈfleɪt/ to make sb feel less confident than they were or less important than they thought they were: [Vn] *I felt really deflated by your nasty remark.* ○ *Nothing could deflate his ego.* **3** /ˌdiːˈfleɪt/ to reduce the amount of money being used in a country, in order to lower prices or keep them steady: [V, Vn] *The government were forced to deflate (the economy).* Compare INFLATE 3, REFLATE. ▶ **deflation** /-ˈeɪʃn/ *n* [U] the act or process of deflating or being deflated. **deflationary** /ˌdiːˈfleɪʃnəri; US -neri/ *adj: a deflationary policy/measure.*

deflect /dɪˈflekt/ *v* **1** to change or make sth change direction, esp after hitting sth: [Vpr] *The bullet deflected from the wall.* [Vnpr] *One of the defenders accidentally deflected the ball into the net.* [Vn] *(fig) The chairman tried to deflect the shareholders' criticism.* **2** ~ sb **(from sth)** to cause sb to stop pursuing a course of action: [Vnpr] *She will not be easily deflected from her purpose.* [also Vn]. ▶ **deflection** /dɪˈflekʃn/ *n* **1(a)** [U] the action of changing or causing sth to change direction, esp after hitting sth. **(b)** [C] an instance of this or the amount by which sth changes direction in this way: *The smallest deflection of the missile could bring disaster.* ○ *The ball took a huge deflection and beat the goalkeeper.* **2** [C, U] the movement or amount of movement of a pointer or needle on a measuring device from its zero position.

deflower /ˌdiːˈflaʊə(r)/ *v* [Vn] *(fml euph)* to have sex with a woman who has not had sex before.

defoliate /ˌdiːˈfəʊlieɪt/ *v* to destroy the leaves of trees or plants: [Vn] *forests defoliated by chemicals in the air.* ▶ **defoliation** /ˌdiːˌfəʊliˈeɪʃn/ *n* [U].

deforest /ˌdiːˈfɒrɪst; US -ˈfɔːr-/ (also **disafforest**) *v* [Vn] to remove trees or forests from a place. ▶ **deforestation** /ˌdiːˌfɒrɪˈsteɪʃn; US -ˌfɔːr-/ *n* [U].

deform /dɪˈfɔːm/ *v* [Vn] to spoil the shape or appearance of sth; to cause sb/sth to have a shape that is not natural: *A crippling disease had deformed his hands.* ▶ **deformation** /ˌdiːfɔːˈmeɪʃn/ *n* **(a)** [U] the process of deforming sb/sth or of being deformed: *structural deformation.* **(b)** [C] a result of this: *a deformation of the spine.* See also MALFORMATION.

deformed *adj* (of a person or part of the body) badly or not naturally shaped: *facially deformed babies* ○ *She was born with a badly deformed foot.*

deformity /dɪˈfɔːməti/ *n* **(a)** [U] the state of being deformed (DEFORM): *Drugs taken during pregnancy can lead to deformity in children.* **(b)** [C] a deformed (DEFORM) part, esp of the body: *deformities caused by poor diet* ○ *He was born with a slight deformity of the foot.*

defraud /dɪˈfrɔːd/ *v* ~ sb **(of sth)** to get sth, esp money, from sb by deception and illegally: [Vn, Vnpr] *She was defrauded (of her savings) by a dishonest accountant.*

defray /dɪˈfreɪ/ *v* *(fml)* to provide the money needed to pay for sth: [Vn] *defray costs/expenses.*

defrost /ˌdiːˈfrɒst; US -ˈfrɔːst/ *v* **1** to remove ice or frost from a refrigerator (REFRIGERATE): [Vn] *The fridge needs defrosting.* **2** to become or make sth, esp food, no longer frozen: [V] *A frozen chicken should be allowed to defrost completely before cooking.* [Vn] *How long will it take to defrost this meat?* ▷ note at WATER¹. Compare UNFREEZE 1, THAW 1a, DE-ICE, MELT 1.

deft /deft/ *adj* skilful and quick in one's movements, esp the hands: *With deft fingers she untangled the wire.* ○ *music played with deft strokes/touches* ○ *deft footwork* ○ *(fig) a deft political operator.* ▶ **deftly** *adv*. **deftness** *n* [U].

defunct /dɪˈfʌŋkt/ *adj (fml)* no longer existing or in use or effective: *a largely defunct railway network* ○ *He belonged to a now defunct political party.*

defuse /ˌdiːˈfjuːz/ *v* [Vn] **1** to remove or make useless the device that causes sth to explode: *defuse a bomb.* **2** to reduce the tension or possible danger in a difficult situation: *defuse public hostility towards the government* ○ *defuse a crisis.*

defy /dɪˈfaɪ/ *v* (*pt, pp* **defied**) **1** [Vn] **(a)** to refuse to obey or show respect for sb/sth: *She defied her parents and got married.* ○ *defy the government/the law.* **(b)** to resist sb/sth strongly: *The garrison defied enemy attacks for several days.* **2** to make sth impossible; to present difficulties that cannot be overcome: [Vn] *The door defied all attempts to open it.* ○ *The problem seems to defy solution.* ○ *a scene that defies description.* **3** to challenge sb to do sth one believes they cannot or will not do: [Vn.to inf] *I defy you to prove I have cheated.*

deg *abbr* (also *symb* °) degree(s): *42 deg/42° Fahrenheit.*

degenerate /dɪˈdʒenəreɪt/ *v* ~ **(from sth) (into sth)** to pass into a worse physical, mental or moral state than one which is considered normal or desirable: [V] *His health is degenerating rapidly.* [Vpr] *The march degenerated into a riot.* ▶ **degenerate** /dɪˈdʒenərət/ *adj* having lost the physical, mental or moral qualities that are considered normal or desirable: *degenerate art/behaviour.* **degeneracy** /dɪˈdʒenərəsi/ *n* [U]. **degenerate** *n* /dɪˈdʒenerət/ a degenerate person. **degeneration** /dɪˌdʒenəˈreɪʃn/ *n* [U] **(a)** the process of degenerating: *the slow degeneration of his mental faculties.* **(b)** the state of being degenerate.

degenerative /dɪˈdʒenərətɪv/ *adj* (of a medical condition) getting or likely to get worse: *degenerative diseases.*

degrade /dɪˈgreɪd/ *v* **1(a)** to cause sb/oneself to be less respected or have a lower status: [Vn] *degrade oneself by cheating and telling lies* ○ *Pornography degrades human dignity.* **(b)** to cause sth to become worse in quality: [Vn] *Pollution is degrading the environment.* **2** (*techn*) to become or make sth become less complex in structure: [Vn] *Many materials will degrade if buried, but this can take a long time.* [also Vn]. ▶ **degradable** *adj (techn): degradable plastics.* See also BIODEGRADABLE. **degradation** /ˌdegrəˈdeɪʃn/ *n* [U]: *living in utter degradation (eg extreme poverty)* ○ *Being sent to prison was the final degradation.*

degrading *adj (derog)* causing sb to lose their dignity and SELF-RESPECT: *their humiliating and degrading treatment of prisoners.*

degree /dɪˈgriː/ *n* **1** [C] a unit of measurement for angles: *an angle of ninety degrees (90°)* ○ *one degree of latitude* (ie about 69 miles). **2** [C] (*abbr* **deg**) a unit of measurement for temperature: *Water freezes at 32 degrees Fahrenheit (32° F) or zero/nought degrees Celsius (0° C).* **3** [C, U] amount; extent: *She shows a high degree of skill in her work.* ○ *He was not in the slightest degree interested* (ie was completely uninterested). ○ *I agree with you* **to a/to some/to a certain degree.** ○ **To what degree** (ie To what

extent/How much) *was he involved in the affair?* ○
She has also been affected, but to a lesser degree. **4**
[C] an academic title or qualification, usu with a
grade, given by a university or college to sb who has
successfully completed a course: *get* (ie be awarded)
a degree in law/a law degree ○ *the degree of Master of
Arts (MA).* **5** [C] (esp in compounds with *first, second*, etc) a grade in a scale of how serious sth is:
murder in the ˌfirst deˈgree (ie in US, of the most
serious kind) ○ ˌfirst-degree ˈmurder ○ ˌthird-degree (ie
very serious) ˈburns. **IDM** **by deˈgrees** gradually; in
stages: *By degrees their friendship grew into love.*

dehumanize, -ise /ˌdiːˈhjuːmənaɪz/ *v* to take the
human qualities away from sb: [Vn] *Torture always
dehumanizes both the torturer and the victim.* ▶
dehumanization, -isation /diːˌhjuːmənaɪˈzeɪʃn; *US*
-nəˈz- / *n* [U].

dehydrate /diːˈhaɪdreɪt/ *v* **1** (esp passive) to remove water from sth, esp food, in order to preserve
it: [Vn] *dehydrated milk in powdered form.* **2** (of the
body, tissues, etc) to lose a large amount of water:
[V] *Her body had dehydrated dangerously in the
extreme heat.* ▶ **dehydration** /ˌdiːhaɪˈdreɪʃn/ *n* [U]:
be treated for acute dehydration.

de-ice /ˌdiː ˈaɪs/ *v* to remove ice from or prevent ice
forming on sth: [Vn] *de-ice a windscreen.* Compare
DEFROST.
  ▶ **de-icer** *n* [C, U] a substance put on a surface, esp
by spraying, to remove ice or stop it forming.

deify /ˈdeɪfaɪ, ˈdiːɪfaɪ/ *v* (*pt, pp* **-fied**) to make a god
of sb/sth; to worship sb/sth as a god: [Vn] *Primitive
peoples deified the sun.*
  ▶ **deification** /ˌdeɪfɪˈkeɪʃn, ˌdiːɪfɪˈkeɪʃn/ *n* [U] the
act of making sb/sth a god or the state of being a
god: *the deification of a Roman emperor.*

deign /deɪn/ *v* (*sometimes derog or ironic*) to do sth
in a way that shows one thinks one is too important
to do it; to CONDESCEND(1): [V.to inf] *He walked past
me without even deigning to look at me.*

deity /ˈdeɪəti, ˈdiːəti/ *n* (**a**) [C] a god or GODDESS(1):
Roman deities. (**b**) **the Deity** [sing] God.

déjà vu /ˌdeɪʒɑː ˈvuː/ *n* [U] (*French*) the feeling that
one remembers an event or a scene that one has not
experienced or seen before: *I had an odd sense of
déjà vu just as you said that.*

dejected /dɪˈdʒektɪd/ *adj* depressed; sad: *dejected-
looking campers in the rain* ○ *Repeated failure had
left them feeling very dejected.* ▶ **dejectedly** *adv.*

dejection /dɪˈdʒekʃn/ *n* [U] a sad or depressed state:
The loser sat slumped in dejection.

de jure /ˌdeɪ ˈdʒʊəri/ *adj, adv* (*Latin techn*) by right;
according to law : *the de jure king* ○ *be king de jure.*
Compare DE FACTO.

dekko /ˈdekəʊ/ *n* **IDM** **have a dekko (at sth)** (*dated
Brit sl*) to look.

delay /dɪˈleɪ/ *v* **1** to be slow or late or make sb slow
or late: [V] *Don't delay! Book your trip today!*
[Vn, Vpr] *She delayed (for) two hours and missed the
train.* [Vn] *The train has been delayed due to snow on
the line.* ○ *Opponents of the bill are threatening to use
delaying tactics to prevent it becoming law.* **2** to
leave doing sth until later; to POSTPONE sth: [Vn]
*We'll have to delay our journey until the weather
improves.* ○ *Why have they delayed opening the
school?*
  ▶ **delay** *n* **1** [U] delaying or being delayed: *We must
inform them without delay.* **2** [C] the amount of
time for which sb/sth is delayed: *unexpected/slight/
long delays* ○ *There was a delay of two hours/a
two-hour delay before the plane took off.*

delectable /dɪˈlektəbl/ *adj* (*fml or rhet*) delightful;
very pleasant: *a delectable meal/performance.*

delectation /ˌdiːlekˈteɪʃn/ *n* [U] (*fml or joc*) enjoyment; entertainment.

delegate[1] /ˈdelɪɡət/ *n* a person chosen or elected by
others to express their views, eg at a meeting or
conference: *The symposium was attended by delegates from all the major hospitals.*

delegate[2] /ˈdelɪɡeɪt/ *v* **1** ~ sth (to sb) to give
duties, rights, etc to sb in a lower position or grade :
[V, Vn] *A boss must know how to delegate (work).*
[Vnpr] *The job had to be delegated to an assistant.* **2**
to choose sb to perform duties, a task, etc: [Vn.to
inf] *The new manager was delegated to reorganize
the department.* [also Vn].

delegation /ˌdelɪˈɡeɪʃn/ *n* **1** [CGp] a group of delegates (DELEGATE[1]): *The prime minister refused to meet
the union delegation.* **2** [U] the action of delegating
or of being delegated: *the delegation of authority to
junior staff.*

delete /dɪˈliːt/ *v* ~ sth (from sth) to remove or
deliberately omit sth written or printed: [Vnpr] *The
editor deleted the last paragraph from my article.*
[Vn] *Please debit my Access/Visa Card (delete as
appropriate).* ▶ **deletion** /dɪˈliːʃn/ *n* [U, C]: *make
deletions to a manuscript.*

deleterious /ˌdeləˈtɪəriəs/ *adj* ~ (to sb/sth) (*fml*)
harmful: *have a deleterious effect on a child's development.*

deli /ˈdeli/ *n* (*infml*) a DELICATESSEN.

deliberate[1] /dɪˈlɪbərət/ *adj* **1** done intentionally:
the deliberate killing of unarmed civilians ○ *a deliberate and cynical lie/ploy.* **2** not hurried; careful: *She
has a slow, deliberate way of talking.* ▶ **deliberately** *adv*: *She said it deliberately to provoke me.* ○
moving slowly and deliberately.

deliberate[2] /dɪˈlɪbəreɪt/ *v* ~ (about/on/over sth)
(*fml*) to think or talk carefully: [V, Vpr] *She deliber-
ated (on my question) for a moment and then spoke.*
[V.wh] *deliberate what action to take* ○ *deliberate
whether to leave or not.*

deliberation /dɪˌlɪbəˈreɪʃn/ *n* **1** [U, C usu *pl*] careful consideration or discussion: *After long
deliberation, they decided not to buy it.* ○ *What was
the result of your deliberations?* **2** [U] the quality of
being slow and careful in speaking or doing sth: *take
aim with great deliberation.*

delicacy /ˈdelɪkəsi/ *n* **1** [U] the quality of being
delicate: *the delicacy of the fabric/of her features/of
the craftsmanship* ○ *Her approach showed great delicacy and tact.* **2** [C] a food that is highly regarded,
esp in a particular place: *The local people regard
these crabs as a great delicacy.*

delicate /ˈdelɪkət/ *adj* **1**(**a**) very carefully made or
formed; fine: *a delicate mechanism/structure* ○ *the
delicate beauty of a snowflake.* (**b**) made of sth fine or
thin: *as delicate as silk* ○ *a baby's delicate skin.* **2**(**a**)
easily injured or damaged; FRAGILE(1): *delicate china*
○ *delicate pink flowers* ○ *upset the delicate ecological
balance of the rain forest.* (**b**) becoming ill easily; not
strong: *a delicate child/constitution.* **3**(**a**) needing
or needing much skill or careful treatment: *the delicate craftsmanship of a fine watch* ○ *a delicate surgical
operation.* (**b**) showing or needing TACT and good
judgement in human relations; sensitive: *I admired
your delicate handling of the situation.* ○ *We're conducting some very delicate negotiations.* **4** (of the five
senses, or of instruments) able to detect or show
very small changes or differences; sensitive: *a delicate sense of smell/touch* ○ *Only a very delicate
thermometer can measure such tiny changes in temperature.* **5**(**a**) (of colours) not intense; soft: *a
delicate shade of pink.* (**b**) (of food or its taste) pleasing and not strongly flavoured: *the delicate flavour of
salmon.* (**c**) (of smell) pleasing and not strong: *a
delicate aroma.* ▶ **delicately** *adv*: *a delicately
phrased compliment.*

delicatessen /ˌdelɪkəˈtesn/ (*also infml* **deli**) *n* a
shop or part of a shop selling prepared foods, often
unusual or brought from other countries, that are
ready for serving, eg cooked meats or cheeses.

D

delicious /dɪˈlɪʃəs/ adj **1** giving pleasure to the senses of taste and smell: *a delicious meal/cake* ○ *This dish is absolutely delicious with sour cream.* ○ *It smells delicious!* **2** delightful: *a delicious thrill/contentment.* ▸ **deliciously** adv: *a deliciously creamy soup.*

delight¹ /dɪˈlaɪt/ n **1** [U] a feeling of great pleasure: *give delight to sb* ○ *His face lit up with surprise and delight.* ○ *To our great delight, the day turned out fine.* ○ *He takes (great) delight in* (ie enjoys) *proving others wrong.* **2** [C] a cause or source of pleasure: *It's always a delight to hear such people talk.* ○ *the delights of living in the country.*
▸ **delightful** /-fl/ adj ~ **(to sb)** giving delight; very pleasant: *a delightful holiday/melody/setting.* ⇨ note at NICE. **delightfully** /-fəli/ adv.

delight² /dɪˈlaɪt/ v to give great pleasure to sb: [Vn] *Her singing delighted everyone.* **PHRV delight in sth/doing sth** (no passive) to take great pleasure in sth: *He delights in shocking people.*
▸ **delighted** adj ~ **(at sth/to do sth/that...)** very pleased; showing delight: *a delighted smile/look/child* ○ *I'm delighted at your success/to hear of your success/that you succeeded.* ○ *'Will you come to the party?' 'I'd be delighted (to)!'* **delightedly** adv.

delimit /diˈlɪmɪt/ v [Vn] (*fml*) to fix the limits or boundaries of sth.

delineate /dɪˈlɪnieɪt/ v (*fml*) to show sth by drawing or describing it in detail: [Vn] *delineate one's plans.*
▸ **delineation** /dɪˌlɪniˈeɪʃn/ n [U,C].

delinquency /dɪˈlɪŋkwənsi/ n [U,C] crime, usu not of a serious kind, esp as committed by young people: *bored teenagers who drift into delinquency.*

delinquent /dɪˈlɪŋkwənt/ adj (esp of young people) showing a tendency to commit crimes, esp not of a serious kind: *delinquent teenagers.*
▸ **delinquent** n a delinquent young person. See also JUVENILE DELINQUENT.

delirious /dɪˈlɪriəs, -ˈlɪəriəs/ adj **1** in an excited state and unable to think or speak clearly, usu because of illness: *He's feverish and delirious, and doesn't know where he is.* **2** very excited and happy: *a crowd of cheering, delirious fans.* ▸ **deliriously** adv: *raving deliriously* ○ *deliriously happy.*

delirium /dɪˈlɪriəm, -ˈlɪəriəm/ n [U] **1** mental disturbance caused by illness, often resulting in wild talk: *exhausted by the fever and fits of delirium.* **2** excited happiness.
■ **deˌlirium ˈtremens** /ˈtriːmenz/ n [U] (*fml*) = DT.

deliver /dɪˈlɪvə(r)/ v **1** ~ **(sth) (to sb/sth)** to take letters, parcels, goods, etc to the places or people they are addressed to: [V,Vn] *Should I collect the goods, or do you deliver (them)?* [Vnpr] *A courier delivered the parcels to our office.* ○ *Did you deliver my message to my father?* [also Vpr]. **2** to give a lecture, a speech or any other formal spoken statement: [Vn] *deliver an ultimatum* ○ *The jury finally delivered its verdict.* [Vnpr] *She is due to deliver a talk on Hungary to the society on Monday.* **3** ~ **(sth) on sth)** (*infml*) to give what is expected or promised: [V,Vpr] *They promise to finish the job in June, but can they deliver (on that)?* [Vn] *If you can't deliver improved sales figures, you're fired!* **4** ~ **sth (up/over) (to sb)** (*fml*) to give sth to sb: *deliver (up) a fortress to the enemy* ○ *deliver over one's property to one's children.* **5(a)** to help a mother to give birth to a child: [Vn] *Her baby was delivered by her own doctor.* **(b)** (*fml*) be ~ed of sb to give birth to a child: [Vnpr] *She was delivered of a healthy boy.* **6** to throw or aim sth: [Vn] *In cricket, the ball is delivered overarm.* ○ *delivering punches of great power* [also Vnpr]. **7** [Vn,Vnpr] ~ **sb (from sth)** (*arch*) to rescue sb from sth. **IDM come up with/deliver the goods** ⇨ GOODS.

deliverance /dɪˈlɪvərəns/ n [U] ~ **(from sth)** (*fml*)

being freed or rescued: *Her death was a merciful deliverance from further suffering.*

delivery /dɪˈlɪvəri/ n **1(a)** [U,C] the delivering of letters, goods, etc to sb or an instance of this: *a delivery boy/van* ○ *a delivery note* (ie sent with goods delivered and signed by the person receiving them) ○ *Your order is ready for delivery.* ○ *When can you take delivery of* (ie be available to receive) *the car?* ○ *Please pay on delivery* (ie when the goods are delivered). ○ *We have two postal deliveries a day.* **(b)** [C] letters, goods, etc delivered: *We had a big delivery of bricks today.* ○ *a special/recorded delivery.* **2** [sing] a manner of speaking in lectures, etc: *Her poor delivery spoilt an otherwise excellent speech.* **3** [C,U] the process of birth: *an easy/difficult delivery* ○ *a delivery room/suite* (ie in a hospital). **4** [C] a ball that is thrown, esp in cricket or baseball: *a fast delivery.* **IDM cash on delivery** ⇨ CASH.

dell /del/ n a small valley, usu with trees on its sides.

delphinium /delˈfɪniəm/ n a tall garden plant with blue flowers.

delta /ˈdeltə/ n **1** the fourth letter of the Greek alphabet (Δ, δ). **2** an area of land at a river's mouth, shaped like a TRIANGLE(1) and crossed by branches of the river going into the sea: *the Nile Delta.*

delude /dɪˈluːd/ v ~ **sb/oneself (with sth/into doing sth)** to mislead sb deliberately; to deceive sb: [Vn] *a poor deluded fool* ○ *You're deluding yourself if you think things will get better.* [Vnpr] *delude sb with empty promises* ○ *Don't be deluded into believing such nonsense.* See also DELUSION.

deluge /ˈdeljuːdʒ/ n **1(a)** a great flood of water: *When the snow melts, the mountain stream becomes a deluge.* **(b)** a heavy fall of rain. **2** a great quantity of sth that comes all at once: *a deluge of complaints/criticism/inquiries.*
▸ **deluge** v [Vn,Vnpr] **1** ~ **sb/sth (with sth)** (usu passive) to send or give sb/sth a very large quantity of sth: *I was deluged with phone calls.* ○ *We advertised the job and were absolutely deluged with applications.* **2** ~ **sth (with sth)** (usu passive) to flood sth, esp with water.

delusion /dɪˈluːʒn/ n **1** [U] the act of deluding or the state of being deluded. **2** [C] a false opinion or belief, esp one that may be a symptom of madness: *He is suffering under the dangerous delusion that his policies are actually working.* ○ *Her extraordinary lifestyle is inspired by delusions of grandeur* (ie a false belief in her own importance). Compare ILLUSION.

delusive /dɪˈluːsɪv/ adj not real; misleading: *a delusive belief/impression.*

de luxe /dəˈlʌks; Brit also -ˈlʊks/ adj [esp attrib] of a very high quality, high standard of comfort, etc: *a de luxe hotel/car* ○ *the de luxe edition of a book* (eg with a leather cover).

delve /delv/ v ~ **in/into sth 1** to try very hard to find information about sth: [Vpr] *The inquiry will delve very deeply into security arrangements at the airport.* **2** to search in sth: [Vpr] *She delved in her bag for a pen.*

Dem abbr (*US*) Democrat; Democratic. Compare REP 2.

demagogue /ˈdeməgɒg/ n a political leader who tries to win people's support by using arguments which are emotional and often not reasonable.
▸ **demagogic** /ˌdeməˈgɒgɪk/ adj of or like a demagogue.
demagogy /ˈdeməgɒgi/ (also **demagoguery** /ˌdeməˈgɒgəri/) n [U] the principles and methods of a demagogue.

demand¹ /dɪˈmɑːnd; US dɪˈmænd/ n **1** [C] ~ **(for sb to do sth)**; ~ **(for sth/that...)** an act of asking for sth strongly; a very determined request: *receive a tax demand* ○ *It is impossible to satisfy all their demands.* ○ *The workers' demands for higher pay were refused/rejected by the employers.* ○ *There have*

309 **demonstrable**

been fresh/renewed demands for the president to resign. ○ demands for reform/that there should be reform ○ Our organization is not in favour of abortion **on demand** (ie whenever it is asked for). ○ The new aircraft **makes** tremendous **demands of/on** pilots (ie requires them to use a lot of skill, strength, etc). **2** [U] ~ **(for sth/sb)** the desire of customers for goods or services which they wish to use or use: a sudden upsurge in **consumer demand** ○ Poor overseas demand is blamed for the car's failure. ○ Demand for fish this month has exceeded supply. ○ Good secretaries are always **in demand** (ie much wanted). ○ She is in great demand as a singer. See also SUPPLY AND DEMAND.

demand² /dɪˈmɑːnd; US dɪˈmænd/ v **1** to ask for sth very strongly, or as if one has a right to do so: [Vn] demand reform/justice/compensation ○ The workers are demanding better pay. ○ She demanded an immediate apology/explanation. [V.that] He demands that he be told everything. [V.to inf] They demanded to know what I was doing in their home. [V.speech] 'Why did you do it?' she demanded angrily. **2** [Vn] (of a process or an activity) to require or need sth: This sort of work demands great patience/one's full attention.

demanding /dɪˈmɑːndɪŋ; US dɪˈmændɪŋ/ adj **(a)** (of a task, etc) needing much patience, skill, effort, etc: a demanding schedule ○ The work is physically/intellectually demanding. **(b)** (of a person) making others work hard, meet high standards, etc: a demanding boss/father ○ Children are so demanding: they need constant attention.

demarcate /ˈdiːmɑːkeɪt/ v (fml) to mark or fix the limits of sth: [Vn] The playing area is demarcated by a white line.

demarcation /ˌdiːmɑːˈkeɪʃn/ n [U,C] a limit or boundary, esp between types of work considered by trade unions to belong to workers in different trades: a line of demarcation ○ a strike over a **demarcation dispute** in the factory.

demean /dɪˈmiːn/ v [Vn] **(a)** ~ oneself to lower oneself in dignity: I wouldn't demean myself by asking for favours from people like that. **(b)** to reduce the respect given to sb/sth: images which are considered to demean women.
▶ **demeaning** adj lowering sb's dignity: He found it very demeaning to have to work for his former employee.

demeanour (US **-nor**) /dɪˈmiːnə(r)/ n [U] (fml) a way of behaving; conduct: maintain a professional demeanour.

demented /dɪˈmentɪd/ adj **(a)** mad: a poor, demented creature. **(b)** extremely upset and excited because of worry, anger, etc: When her child was two hours late, she became quite demented. ▶ **dementedly** adv.

dementia /dɪˈmenʃə/ n [U] (medical) a serious disorder of the mind caused by brain disease or injury. See also SENILE DEMENTIA.

demerara /ˌdeməˈreərə/ (also ˌdemerara ˈsugar) n [U] a type of rough sugar, pale brown in colour.

demerit /diːˈmerɪt/ n (usu pl) (fml) a fault: consider the ˌmerits and ˈdemerits of a system.

demi- pref (with ns) half; partly: demigod.

demilitarize, -ise /ˌdiːˈmɪlɪtəraɪz/ v (usu passive) to remove military forces or buildings from an area by agreement: [Vn] a demilitarized zone. ▶ **demilitarization, -isation** /ˌdiːˌmɪlɪtəraɪˈzeɪʃn; US -rəˈz-/ n [U].

demise /dɪˈmaɪz/ n [sing] **1** (fml or joc) death. **2** the end or failure of an enterprise, institution, idea, etc: the demise of the country's communist regime.

demist /ˌdiːˈmɪst/ v [Vn] (Brit) (US defog) to remove the covering of mist from sth: demist a car windscreen.

dem(o)- comb form of people or population: demagogue ○ democracy ○ demographic.

demo /ˈdeməʊ/ n (pl **-os**) (infml esp Brit) a DEMONSTRATION(2,3).

demob /ˌdiːˈmɒb/ v (**-bb-**) [Vn] (Brit infml) to DEMOBILIZE sb.

demobilize, -ise /dɪˈməʊbəlaɪz/ v [Vn] to release sb from military service. ▶ **demobilization, -isation** /ˌdɪˌməʊbəlaɪˈzeɪʃn; US -ləˈz-/ n [U].

democracy /dɪˈmɒkrəsi/ n **1(a)** [U] a system of government by all the people of a country, usu through representatives whom they elect, thought of as allowing freedom of speech, religion and political opinion: parliamentary democracy ○ the student-led democracy movement. **(b)** [C] a country having such a system: the Western democracies. Compare DICTATORSHIP. **2** [U] control of an organization by its members, who take part in the making of decisions: industrial democracy. **3** [U] fair and equal treatment of each other by citizens, without social class divisions: Is there more democracy in Australia than in Britain?

democrat /ˈdeməkræt/ n **1** a person who believes in or supports democracy. **2 Democrat** (abbr **Dem**) a member or supporter of the Democratic Party, one of the two main political parties of the USA. Compare REPUBLICAN 2b. See also LIBERAL DEMOCRAT.

democratic /ˌdeməˈkrætɪk/ adj **1** based on the principles of DEMOCRACY(1a): democratic rights/elections ○ democratic government/rule/accountability ○ aiming to make the institutions of the EU truly democratic. **2** of or supporting control of an organization by its members: democratic involvement/participation. **3** of or supporting DEMOCRACY(3); paying no or little attention to class divisions based on birth or wealth: a democratic society/outlook. ▶ **democratically** /-kli/ adv: democratically elected/decided.
■ **the Demoˈcratic Party** n one of the two main political parties in the USA. See also THE REPUBLICAN PARTY.

democratize, -ise /dɪˈmɒkrətaɪz/ v (fml) to make a country or an institution democratic: [Vn] democratize the administration of an organization. ▶ **democratization, -isation** /dɪˌmɒkrətaɪˈzeɪʃn; US -təˈz-/ n [U]: calls for greater democratization.

demography /dɪˈmɒɡrəfi/ n [U] the study of the changing numbers of births, deaths, diseases, etc in a community over a period of time. ▶ **demographic** /ˌdeməˈɡræfɪk/ adj: demographic and social trends.

demolish /dɪˈmɒlɪʃ/ v **1(a)** to pull or knock down a building: [Vn] They've demolished the slum district. ○ The church has been partially demolished. **(b)** to destroy a theory, etc: [Vn] Her article brilliantly demolishes his whole argument. **2** (joc) to eat sth greedily: [Vn] She was busy demolishing a huge box of popcorn. ▶ **demolition** /ˌdeməˈlɪʃn/ n [U,C]: houses scheduled for demolition ○ demolition plans/work/contractors ○ His speech did a very effective demolition job on the government's policies.

demon /ˈdiːmən/ n **1** a wicked or cruel spirit: medieval carvings of demons. **2** (infml) **(a)** a person thought to be wicked, MISCHIEVOUS, etc: Your son's a little demon! **(b)** ~ **(for sth)** an energetic or aggressive person: She's a demon for work (ie She works very hard). ○ a demon bowler. **IDM** **the demon ˈdrink** (Brit joc) alcoholic drink, esp when it is the cause of wild noisy behaviour: He doesn't mean to offend anyone; it's just the demon drink talking! ▶ **demonic** /dɪˈmɒnɪk/ adj: demonic forces/energy.

demonstrable /dɪˈmɒnstrəbl; Brit also ˈdemənstrəbl/ adj that can be shown or proved: a demonstrable lie/inaccuracy ○ There is no demonstrable link between the two events. ▶ **demonstrably** /-blɪ/ adv.

[V] = verb used alone   [Vn] = verb + noun   [Vp] = verb + particle   [Vpr] = verb + prepositional phrase

D

demonstrate /ˈdemənstreɪt/ v **1(a)** ~ sth (to sb) to show sth clearly by giving proof or evidence: [V.that] *The first six months' results demonstrate convincingly that the scheme works.* [Vn] *The new president is not afraid to demonstrate his power in public.* [Vnpr] *Let me demonstrate to you the truth of what I'm saying.* [V.wh] *His sudden departure demonstrates how unreliable he is.* **(b)** to express sth by one's actions: [Vn] *Workers have already demonstrated their opposition to the plans.* **2** ~ sth (to sb) to show and explain how sth works or a way of doing sth: [Vn, Vnpr] *An assistant was demonstrating the washing-machine (to customers).* [V.wh] *She demonstrated how best to defend oneself.* **3** ~ **(against / in favour of sb/sth)** to take part in a public meeting, march, etc, usu as a protest or to show support for sth: *Police dispersed a crowd demonstrating against job cuts.* [also V]. See also DEMONSTRATOR.

demonstration /ˌdemənˈstreɪʃn/ n **1(a)** [C, U] an act of showing sth by giving proof or evidence: *convinced by scientific demonstration* ○ *a demonstration of the laws of physics.* **(b)** [C] a sign or an example of sth: *The two men embraced in a public demonstration of good will.* ○ *They gave a clear demonstration of their intentions/commitment.* **2** [C] an instance of sb showing and explaining how sth works or is done: *a cookery demonstration* ○ *She gave us a brief demonstration of the computer's functions.* ▷ note at EXHIBITION. **3** (also *infml* **demo**) [C] ~ **(against / in favour of sb/sth)** a public, often organized, meeting or march protesting against or supporting sb/sth: *take part in/go on a student demonstration* ○ *a mass demonstration.*

demonstrative /dɪˈmɒnstrətɪv/ adj **1** (of people) showing feelings, esp affection, readily: *Some people are more demonstrative than others.* **2** (*grammar*) (of a DETERMINER or pronoun) indicating the person or thing referred to: *In 'This is my bike', 'this' is a demonstrative pronoun.*

demonstrator /ˈdemənstreɪtə(r)/ n **1** a person who takes part in a public meeting, march, etc, usu as a protest or to show support for sth: *the demonstrators were dispersed by the police.* **2** a person who teaches or explains by showing how sth works, eg in a LABORATORY.

demoralize, -ise /dɪˈmɒrəlaɪz; *US* -ˈmɔːr-/ v (usu passive) to cause sb to lose confidence or hope: [Vn] *The team were not demoralized by their defeat.* ▶ **demoralized, -ised** adj: *feel very demoralized.* **demoralizing, -ising** adj: *a demoralizing experience.* **demoralization, -isation** /dɪˌmɒrəlaɪˈzeɪʃn; *US* -ˌmɔːrələ'z-/ n [U].

demote /ˌdiːˈməʊt/ v ~ sb (from sth) (to sth) to reduce sb to a lower rank or grade: [Vn, Vnpr] *He was demoted (from sergeant to corporal).* Compare PROMOTE 3. ▶ **demotion** /ˌdiːˈməʊʃn/ n [C, U].

demotic /dɪˈmɒtɪk/ adj (*fml*) (esp of language) typical of or used by ordinary people: *television, that most demotic of forces.*

demur /dɪˈmɜː(r)/ v (-rr-) ~ **(at/from sth)** (*fml*) to express a doubt about sth or an objection to sth: [Vn] *I suggested putting the matter to a vote, but the chairwoman demurred.* [also Vpr]. ▶ **demur** n IDM **without de'mur** (*fml*) without objecting or hesitating: *They accepted my proposal without demur.*

demure /dɪˈmjʊə(r)/ adj **(a)** (esp of women or children) quiet, serious and modest(2), or pretending to be so: *a very demure young lady.* **(b)** suggesting that one is demure: *a demure smile/reply.* ▶ **demurely** adv.

demystify /ˌdiːˈmɪstɪfaɪ/ v (*pt, pp* **-fied**) to make sth clear or less mysterious: [Vn] *We are trying to demystify the workings of government.* ▶ **demystification** /ˌdiːˌmɪstɪfɪˈkeɪʃn/ n [U].

den /den/ n **1** an animal's hidden home, eg a cave: *a bear's/lion's den.* **2** (*derog*) a place where people meet in secret, esp for some illegal activity: *a den of thieves* ○ *He thought of New York as* **a den of iniquity.** **3** (*infml*) a room in a home where a person can work or study without being disturbed: *retire to one's den.* IDM **beard the lion in his den** ▷ BEARD².

denationalize, -ise /ˌdiːˈnæʃnəlaɪz/ v [Vn] to put a state industry into private ownership, usu by selling shares (SHARE¹ 3) in it; to PRIVATIZE sth. Compare NATIONALIZE. ▶ **denationalization, -isation** /ˌdiːˌnæʃnəlaɪˈzeɪʃn; *US* -lə'z-/ n [U].

denial /dɪˈnaɪəl/ n **1** [C] ~ **(of sth / that...)** a statement that sth is not true: *the prisoner's repeated denials of the charges against him* ○ *an official denial that there would be an election in May.* **2** [C, U] **(a)** ~ **of sth** a refusal to give or allow sth that sb has a right to expect: *the denial of basic human rights/ freedoms.* **(b)** ~ **(of sth)** a refusal of a request, etc: *the denial of his request for leave.*

denier /ˈdeniə(r)/ n a unit for measuring how fine threads of nylon, silk, etc are: *15 denier stockings.*

denigrate /ˈdenɪgreɪt/ v to criticize sb/sth unfairly; to claim that sb/sth is inferior, worthless, etc: [Vn] *denigrate sb's character/achievements.* ▶ **denigration** /ˌdenɪˈgreɪʃn/ n [U].

denim /ˈdenɪm/ n **1** [U] a strong cotton cloth, usu blue in colour, used for making JEANS, etc. **2** **denims** [pl] JEANS made of denim.

denizen /ˈdenɪzn/ n (*fml or joc*) a person, an animal or a plant that lives, grows or is often found in a particular place: *polar bears, denizens of the frozen north* ○ (*joc*) *the denizens of the local pub.*

denomination /dɪˌnɒmɪˈneɪʃn/ n **1** a religious group or SECT: *The Protestant denominations include the Methodists, the Presbyterians and the Baptists.* **2** a class of units within a range or sequence of money, numbers, etc: *The US coin of the lowest denomination is the cent.* **3** (*fml*) a name, esp of a general class or type: *agreed denominations for various species of fish.* ▶ **denominational** /-ˈneɪʃənl/ adj of a particular denomination(1): *denominational education.*

denominator /dɪˈnɒmɪneɪtə(r)/ n (*mathematics*) the number below the line in a fraction, showing how many parts the whole is divided into, eg 4 in ¾. Compare NUMERATOR. See also COMMON DENOMINATOR.

denote /dɪˈnəʊt/ v **(a)** to be a sign or symbol of sth; to indicate sth: [Vn] *In algebra, the sign x usually denotes an unknown quantity.* [V.that] *The mark /\ denotes that a word has been left out.* **(b)** to be the name for sth; to mean sth: [Vn] *What does the term 'organic' denote?* [also V.that].

denouement (also **dénouement**) /deɪˈnuːmɒ̃; *US* ˌdeɪnuːˈmɑː/ n the last part, esp of a book, play, etc, in which everything is settled or made clear: *a surprising/satisfactory denouement.*

denounce /dɪˈnaʊns/ v ~ **sb/sth (as sth)** to criticize strongly and publicly sb/sth that one thinks is wrong, illegal, etc: [Vn] *She denounced the government's handling of the crisis.* [Vn-n] *Union officials have denounced the action as a breach of the agreement.* ○ *They were denounced to the authorities as counter-revolutionaries.* See also DENUNCIATION.

dense /dens/ adj (-r, -st) **1** (of people and things) crowded together in great numbers: *a dense crowd/ forest.* **2** (of VAPOUR(1)) not easy to see through; thick: *dense fog/smoke.* **3** (*infml*) stupid: *How can you be so dense?* ▶ **densely** adv: *a densely populated country* ○ *densely wooded* (ie covered with trees growing close together).

density /ˈdensəti/ n **1** [U] the quality of being DENSE (1,2) or the degree to which sth is dense: *crowd/ population density* ○ *low density housing.* **2** [C, U] (*physics*) the relation of weight to volume(2).

[V.*to* inf] = verb + *to* infinitive   [Vn.inf (no *to*)] = verb + noun + infinitive without *to*   [V.*ing*] = verb + *-ing* form

Linking words together

This dictionary is not just a list of words and their meanings. It contains much more information that can help you to speak and write good, natural English.

In order to use a word correctly, you need to know how to link it to other words in a sentence. The dictionary gives you information about the grammar of a word and about the structures that often follow it. It also tells you whether a word is formal or informal, helping you to choose what is appropriate for a particular context.

The dictionary also helps you to learn a word as part of a larger unit of language, for example as one element of a compound or in a common phrase.

Compounds

A COMPOUND is a noun, an adjective or a verb that has been created from two or more simple words. The second word of a compound may follow the first after a space, or it may be linked more closely to it with a hyphen:

● *car park*
● *swimming-pool*
● *daughter-in-law*
● *middle-of-the-road*

You will often find a compound spelt by different people in different ways, and sometimes you may find it spelt as a single word with no space or hyphen. This dictionary gives you the most common form of each compound and lists them after the symbol ■, near the end of the entry for the first of the words they are created from. Those normally spelt as a single word are listed separately as headwords.

Noun + noun

In English, you often find two nouns next to each other without any linking word or apostrophe s ('s). These noun groups are not compounds and do not have their own entries in the dictionary. The first noun is used like an adjective and describes the noun that follows it:

● *the chair back* (the back of the chair)
● *a family holiday* (a holiday for the family)
● *garden flowers* (flowers grown in a garden)

Where a noun is often used in this way, examples are given at the dictionary entry.

Verb + noun phrase

Another common feature of English is the use of a verb like **have**, **make**, **take** or **do** followed by a noun, for example:

● *have a shower*
● *take a rest*
● *make arrangements*
● *do the washing*

The verb by itself has little meaning; it has become part of a common phrase, a single unit of language. Sometimes, more than one verb is possible. You can say:

● *make a decision*
● *take a decision*

and

● *have a bath*
● *take a bath*

Example sentences at the entry for a noun show you which constructions you can use.

Other units of language

Where a verb is always linked to an adverb or a preposition, it is known as a PHRASAL VERB and is listed in this dictionary after the symbol **PHR V**. Its meaning must most often be learned separately from the simple verb it is derived from. Common phrasal verbs include **look after sb** and **hold sb/sth up**:

● *She **looks after** her elderly mother.*
● *Traffic **was held up** for over two hours.*

For help with phrasal verbs, ⇨ **A2–3**.

IDIOMS often have meanings that are not easy to guess and they must be learned as individual units of language. What, for instance, do you think these idioms mean?

● *push the boat out*
● *push one's luck*
● *push up daisies*

Look at **push²** to find out. For help with idioms, ⇨ **A6–7**.

Phrases such as:

● *burst into tears*
● *pay attention*

are not idioms but are simply the way that a particular idea is expressed in English. This close, almost fixed, association of words is called COLLOCATION. Example sentences at an entry show these phrases in **dark type** to help you learn them. For help with collocation, ⇨ **A4–5**.

Phrasal verbs

Look at the verbs in the sentences below:
- Jan **turned down** the offer of a lift home.
- Buying that new car has really **eaten into** my savings.
- I don't think I can **put up with** his behaviour much longer.

Phrasal verbs (sometimes called multi-word verbs) are verbs which consist of two, or sometimes three, words. The first word is a verb and it is followed by an adverb (turn **down**) or a preposition (eat **into**) or both (put **up with**). These adverbs or prepositions are sometimes called PARTICLES.

In this dictionary, phrasal verbs are listed at the end of the entry for the main verb in a section marked **PHR V**. They are listed in alphabetical order of the particles following them.

Look at the entry for **fight¹**, where the phrasal verbs come after the idioms:

> **PHR V** ˌfight ˈback to fight with new force and strength; to show resistance: *After a disastrous first half we fought back to level the scores.* ○ *Don't let them bully you. Fight back!* ˌfight sth ˈback/ˈdown to suppress feelings, etc: *fight back tears/a sense of disgust.* ˈfight for sth to try very hard to obtain or achieve sth: *fight for one's freedom/independence/rights* ○ *She is now fighting for her life in hospital.* ˌfight sb/sth ˈoff to resist sb/sth by fighting against them/it: *They had to fight off repeated enemy attacks.* ○ *fight off a cold/feeling of tiredness.* ˌfight sth ˈout to settle an argument, a dispute, etc by fighting: *I can't help them to resolve their quarrel — they must fight it out between them.*

Some verbs, for example **bring**, **come** and **take**, have many phrasal verbs associated with them. To help you find a particular phrasal verb more easily, the **PHR V** section of such verbs is divided into paragraphs, so that all the phrasal verbs using a particular particle are grouped together.

If you look at the entry for **come**, you will see that the phrasal verbs using the particle **across** are in a separate paragraph from those using the particle **about** and from those with the particle **after**.

Look at the following sentence:
- Sue **fell down** and hurt her knee badly.

The meaning of some phrasal verbs, such as **fall down**, is easy to guess because the verb and the particle keep their usual meaning. However, many phrasal verbs have idiomatic meanings that you need to learn. The separate meanings of **put**, **up** and **with**, for example, do not add up to the meaning of **put up with** (tolerate).

Some particles have particular meanings which are the same when they are used with a number of different verbs. Look at **around** in the sentences below:
- I didn't see the point of **hanging around** waiting for him, so I went home.
- We spent most of our holiday **lounging around** beside the pool.

Around adds the meaning of 'with no particular purpose or aim' and is also used in a similar way with many other verbs, such as **play**, **sit** and **wait**.

The meaning of a phrasal verb can sometimes be explained with a one-word verb. However, phrasal verbs are frequently used in informal spoken English and, if there is a one-word equivalent, it is usually much more formal in style. Look at the following sentences:
- I wish my ears didn't **stick out** so much.
- The garage **projects** 5 metres beyond the front of the house.

Both **stick out** and **project** have the same meaning – 'to extend beyond a surface' – but they are very different in style. **Stick out** is used in informal contexts, and **project** in formal or technical contexts.

Phrasal verbs can be TRANSITIVE (they take an object) or INTRANSITIVE (they have no object). Some phrasal verbs can be used in both ways:
- He told me to **shut up**. (intransitive)
- For heaven's sake **shut her up**! She's said far too much already. (transitive)

INTRANSITIVE phrasal verbs are written in the dictionary without **sb** (somebody) or **sth** (something) after them. This shows that they do not have an object.

Look at the entry below:

> ¡**eat** ¹**out** to have a meal in a restaurant, etc rather than at home: *I'm too tired to cook tonight — let's eat out.*

Eat out is intransitive, and the two parts of the verb cannot be separated by any other word. You cannot say, for example:

● ~~Shall we eat tonight out?~~

In order to use TRANSITIVE phrasal verbs correctly, you need to know where to put the object. Because of the way it lists phrasal verbs, the dictionary can help you with this.

With some phrasal verbs (often called SEPARABLE verbs), the object can go either between the verb and the particle or after the particle:

● She **tore** the letter **up**.
● She **tore up** the letter.

When the object is a long phrase, it usually comes after the particle:

● She **tore up** all the letters that he had ever sent her.

When the object is a pronoun (for example, **it** standing for 'the letter'), it must always go between the verb and the particle:

● She read the letter and then **tore** it **up**.

In the dictionary, verbs that are separable are written like this:

> **tear sth up**

When you see **sth** or **sb** between the two parts of the phrasal verb, you know that they can be separated by an object:

> ¡**call** sth ¹**off** to cancel or abandon sth: *call off a deal/a journey/a picnic/a strike* ○ *They have called off their engagement* (ie decided not to get married). ○ *The match was called off because of bad weather.*

You can say:

● They **called** the deal **off**.
and They **called off** the deal.

With other phrasal verbs (sometimes called INSEPARABLE verbs), the two parts of the verb cannot be separated by an object:

● John's **looking after** the children.
not ~~John's looking the children after.~~

● John's **looking after** them.
not ~~John's looking them after.~~

In the dictionary, verbs that are inseparable are written like this:

> **look after sb**

When you see **sb** or **sth** after the two parts of a phrasal verb, you know that they cannot be separated by an object:

> ¡**go** ¹**off sb/sth** (*Brit infml*) to lose interest in sb; to lose one's taste for sth: *Jane seems to be going off Peter.* ○ *I've gone off beer.*

You can say:

● I've **gone off** chocolate.
not ~~I've gone chocolate off.~~

When you look up a phrasal verb in the dictionary, note the position of **sb** or **sth**. It will show you where you should put the object of the verb.

Some transitive phrasal verbs can be made passive:

● The deal **has been called off**.

When this is common, you will usually find an example at the dictionary entry.

Related nouns

A particular phrasal verb may have a noun related to it. This is often listed in the compounds section of the entry, below the phrasal verbs. Look, for example, at the nouns **break-in** and **break-out** in the entry for **break¹**:

> ■ ¹**break-dancing** *n* [U] a very lively style of dancing, often in a competition or as a display, esp popular with young Black Americans.
> ¹**break-in** *n* an entry into a building using force: *Police are investigating a break-in at the bank.*
> ¹**break-out** *n* an escape from prison, esp one involving the use of force: *a mass break-out of prisoners.*

A noun is often related in meaning to only one or two of the phrasal verbs using a particle. **Break-in** is related to **break in** and **break into sth**, but not to **break sb/sth in** or **break in** (**on sth**). **Break-out** is related to **break out** (**of sth**), whereas the noun **outbreak** relates to **break out**.

There is also a noun **breakup** which is related in meaning to two phrasal verbs: **break up** (**with sb**), and to sense (**b**) of **break sth up**. In this case, the verb and particle have become joined together and form a single word, listed in this dictionary as a headword.

Collocation

What is collocation?

When we learn a language, we learn how individual words combine together in phrases and sentences.

Does the following sentence sound right?

- *Meals will be served outside on the terrace, weather allowing.*

It seems to be an acceptable English sentence, and the meaning is not very difficult to understand:

- *They'll give us our meals outside if the weather is good enough.*

However, it will sound odd to a native speaker of English, because the common combination is not, in fact, **weather allowing** but **weather permitting**. This is something that the native speaker knows but which the learner, unfortunately, has to learn. It does not help that **allow** and **permit** have very similar meanings. Only one of them, **permit**, is right in this particular context.

The way in which words belong together as **weather** and **permitting** do is known as COLLOCATION.

We can talk about both:

- *thick fog and dense fog*
- *thick smoke and dense smoke*
- *a thick forest and a dense forest*

The meaning is the same.

But we do not talk about a person having

- *~~dense hair~~*

This combination just does not sound right, even though it would easily be understood. **Dense** does not COLLOCATE with **hair**. We can only talk about somebody having **thick hair**.

It is now possible to analyse real spoken and written texts by computer and to find out which words are typically used with which other words. The collection of texts which the computer examines is called a CORPUS. If we ask the computer to search the corpus and make a list for us of which words are most often used with **hair**, it produces:

- long   black   dark   brown   cut   grey   blonde   short   red   fair   curly   dry   white   thick ...

The corpus shows us that the noun **hair** combines with a range of adjectives describing its colour, length and texture. It also shows us that **thick** is most often used with another adjective after it and the most common adjective is **black**.

There are also close associations between certain adjectives and intensifiers (adverbs which make an adjective stronger). The most common intensifier is 'very', which is used before many adjectives. Sometimes, however, a special intensifier collocates with a particular adjective.

Look at the following lists. On the left there are seven intensifiers and on the right seven adjectives. See if you can link the pairs that collocate strongly with each other.

vitally	successful
acutely	popular
heartily	serious
deadly	important
supremely	aware
highly	sick
immensely	confident

(The answers are at the bottom of **A5**.)

Types of collocation

In order to write and speak natural and correct English, you need to know, for example, which adjectives are used with a particular noun:

- *Can you say **pink** wine?*

which nouns a particular adjective is used with:

- *What sort of thing does the adjective **plush** describe?*

which verbs are used with a particular noun:

- *You know the word **brake** and that brakes are used to stop cars, etc, but which verbs are used with **brake**?*

which adverbs are used with a particular verb:

- *Do you complain **strongly** or **bitterly** about something?*

You also need to know which prepositions are used after particular verbs, adjectives and nouns:

- *Do you get compensation **for** something or **of** something?*

Collocation in this dictionary

To discover which adjectives to use with a particular noun, look at the examples at the entry for the noun. Typical adjectives used with the noun are separated by a slash (/):

● *pink wine?*

> **wine** /waɪn/ *n* **1** [U, C] an alcoholic drink made from the juice of grapes (GRAPE) that has been left to FERMENT[1]: *open a bottle of wine* ○ *dry/sweet wine* ○ *a glass of red/white/rosé/sparkling wine* ○ *vintage wines.* **2** [U, C] an alcoholic drink made from plants or fruits other than grapes (GRAPE): *apple/cowslip/rice wine.*

(No, rosé)

If you look up an adjective, you will see what nouns it commonly describes:

● *plush what?*

> ▶ **plush** (also **plushy**) *adj* (*infml*) extremely comfortable and expensive; SMART[1](4): *a plush hotel/restaurant.*

(hotel, restaurant)

Look at the examples in a noun entry to find out what verbs can be used with it:

● *using brakes?*

> **brake** /breɪk/ *n* a device for slowing or stopping a car, bicycle, train, etc: *put on/apply/release the brake(s)*

(put on, apply, release)

If you look up a verb, you will see the adverbs commonly used with it:

● *complain strongly or bitterly?*

> **complain** /kəmˈpleɪn/ *v* **1** ~ (**to sb**) (**about/of sth**) (*often derog*) to say that one is annoyed, unhappy or not satisfied: [V.*that*] *Holiday-makers complained bitterly that the resort was filthy.*

(bitterly)

Grammatical collocations like prepositions are shown in **dark type** at the beginning of an entry, before the definition. Where the pattern is optional, it is given in brackets. Look at the example sentences to see how the patterns are used:

> **compensation** /ˌkɒmpenˈseɪʃn/ *n* ~ (**for sth**) (**a**) [U] the action of compensating: *Compensation of injured workers has cost the company a lot.* ○ *Have you considered the matter of compensation?* (**b**) [U, C] a thing, esp an amount of money, given to compensate for sth: *receive £5 000 in compensation/by way of compensation/as a compensation for injury.* ○ *My job is hard, but it has its compensations* (ie pleasant aspects that make it less bad).

Important collocations are printed in **dark type** within the examples to help you learn and use them.

Look at the entry for **hope** shown below. At the beginning of the entry you can see all the grammatical collocations in brackets before the definition, like **hope of/for sth**. The example sentences show you these patterns in a typical context. The words or phrases in **dark type** within the examples are all frequently used with **hope**. If the meaning of the collocation is not obvious there is a short explanation after it in brackets.

The entry shows how you can express the idea of:

● *a little hope*
● *a hope that will not succeed*
● *destroying hope*
● *a lot of hope*
● *increasing hope*
● *basing your hope on something*

> **hope** /həʊp/ *n* **1** [C, U] ~ (**of/for sth**); ~ (**of doing sth/that**) a belief that sth desired will happen: *Don't raise his hopes too high or he may be very disappointed.* ○ *There is still a ray/glimmer of hope* (ie a slight hope). ○ *He pinned* (ie based) *all his hopes on getting that job.* ○ *All our hopes were dashed/shattered by the announcement.* ○ *It is our hope that you will find this offer satisfactory.* ○ *She still cherished a forlorn hope of seeing him again.* ○ *She has high hopes* (ie is very confident) *of winning.* ○ *They have given up all hope of finding any more survivors of the crash.*

> The answers to the linking pairs on **A4** are: *vitally important; acutely aware; heartily sick; deadly serious; supremely confident; highly successful; immensely popular.*

Idioms

What are idioms?

An idiom is a phrase whose meaning is difficult or sometimes impossible to guess by looking at the meanings of the individual words it contains. For example, the phrase **be in the same boat** has a literal meaning that is easy to interpret, but it also has a common idiomatic meaning:

● *I found the job quite difficult at first. But everyone was in the same boat; we were all learning.*

Here, **be in the same boat** means 'to be in the same difficult or unfortunate situation'.

Some idioms are colourful expressions, such as proverbs and sayings:

● *A bird in the hand is worth two in the bush.*
(It is better to be content with what one has than to risk losing everything by trying to get much more.)
● *Too many cooks spoil the broth.*
(If too many people are involved in something, it will not be done well.)

If the expression is well-known, part of it may be left out:

● *Well, I knew everything would go wrong – it's the usual story of too many cooks!*

Other idioms are short expressions that are used for a particular purpose:

● *Hang in there!*
(used for encouraging somebody to remain firm in difficult circumstances)
● *On your bike!*
(used to tell somebody to go away)

Other idioms make comparisons:

● *as light as air*
● *as hard as nails*

Many idioms, however, are not vivid in this way. They are considered as idioms because their form is fixed:

● *for certain*
● *in any case*

Looking up idioms

In this dictionary, idioms are defined at the entry for the first 'full' word (a noun, a verb, an adjective or an adverb) that they contain. This means ignoring any grammatical words such as articles or prepositions.

Idioms follow the main senses of a word, in a section marked **IDM**. Look at the entry for **depth** and the idioms connected with it:

● *in depth*
● *out of one's depth*

The words **in**, **out**, **of** and **one's** do not count as 'full' words, and so the idioms are not listed at the entries for these words.

Deciding where idioms start and stop is not always easy. If you hear the expression:

● *I dropped a clanger when I mentioned her ex-husband*

you might think that **clanger** is the only word you do not know, and look that up. In fact, **drop a clanger** is an idiomatic expression and it is defined at **drop**. A cross-reference at **clanger** directs you to **drop**[2], so you will still find the meaning.

Sometimes, one 'full' word of an idiom can be replaced by another. For instance, in the idiom **hit home**, **hit** can be replaced by **strike**. In the dictionary this is shown as:

● *hit/strike home*

and the idiom is defined at the first fixed word, **home**. If you look up the phrase at either **hit** or **strike**, cross-references direct you to **home**[3]:

hit/make/reach the headlines ⇨ HEADLINE.
hit/strike home ⇨ HOME[3].

In some idioms, many alternatives are possible. In the expression **live to tell the tale**, you could substitute **be around**, **be here** or **be still alive** for the word **live**. In the dictionary this is shown as **live, etc to tell the tale**, indicating you can use other words with a similar meaning to **live** in the idiom. Since the first 'full' word of the idiom is not fixed, the expression is defined at **tell**, with a cross-reference only at **tale**.

If you cannot find an idiom in the dictionary, look it up at the entry for one of the other main words in the expression.

The adjectives **bad** and **good** are very common in idioms, and so also are the following verbs:

be	get	leave	see
break	give	let	set
bring	go	look	stand
come	have	make	take
cut	hold	play	throw
do	keep	put	turn
fall	lay	run	work

If all the idioms in which these words occur were listed at **bad**, **be**, **break**, etc, there would be many idioms at these entries. Instead, there is a note at each telling you to look at the entry for the next noun, verb, adjective, etc in the idiom. This means that you will find **break sb's heart** at **heart**, not at **break**, and (**not**) **have a good word to say for sb/sth** at **word**, not at **have** or **good**.

Some idioms consist only of grammatical words such as **one**, **it** or **in**. These idioms are defined at the first word that occurs in them. For example, the idiom **one up on sb** is defined at the entry for **one¹**. Where an idiom consists only of one of the common words listed above and grammar words, it is defined at the common word.

Idioms are given in alphabetical order within the idioms section. Grammatical words such as **a/an** or **the**, **sb/sth**, and the possessive forms **one's**, **sb's**, **his**, **her**, etc, as well as words in brackets ( ) or after the symbol (**/**), are ignored.

Using idioms

The dictionary helps you to use idioms, as well as to understand them. It shows you if you can add any other words to an idiom. For greater emphasis you can, for example, add either **straight** or **right** to the idiom **hit sb in the eye**. Optional words such as **straight** and **right** are shown in brackets:

> **hit sb (straight/right) in the 'eye** to be very obvious or noticeable to sb: *The mistake hit me straight in the eye.*

The dictionary also shows you which parts of an idiom you can change. In the phrase **any/every Tom**, **Dick and Harry** (any ordinary person), you can use either **any** or **every**, but you cannot change the names or their order:

● *This information isn't available to any Tom, Dick and Harry.*
not ~~This information isn't available to any Pete, Joe and Harry.~~
not ~~This information isn't available to any Harry, Dick and Tom.~~

In many idioms, you can vary the pronoun or the tense of the verb to suit the sentence. For instance, **be in the same boat** can be used in different tenses:

● *We **are** all in the same boat.*
● *We **were** all in the same boat.*

However, it is not possible to replace **boat** with **ship** and keep the idiomatic meaning.

Look at the idioms in the entry for **distance**:

> **IDM** **go the (full) 'distance** (esp in sports) to continue to run, fight, etc until the end of a contest: *Nobody thought he'd last 15 rounds, but he went the full distance.* **in/into the 'distance** far away: *I could just see them in the distance.* ○ *She stood looking into the distance.* **keep sb at a 'distance** to refuse to be friendly to sb or let sb become friendly. **keep one's 'distance (from sb/sth) 1** to avoid getting too close to sb/sth: *The police kept their distance during the students' demonstration.* **2** to avoid becoming friendly with a person or involved with a cause, etc: *The president has been advised to keep his distance from the organization.* **within striking distance** ⇨ STRIKE².

● *go the (full) distance*
The example sentence shows you that you can change the tense of **go**, and that you can add the word **full**.

● *in/into the distance*
The symbol (**/**) shows you that either **in** or **into** is possible. Example sentences illustrate the use of both forms of the idiom.

● *keep sb at a distance*
You replace **sb** in an idiom with a person or a group of people. In this case, you could write as an example: *She always kept her colleagues at work at a distance.*

● *keep one's distance (from sb/sth)*
This idiom has two senses. **One's** stands for any possessive form, and in the example sentences **their** and **his** are used, agreeing with the subject of each sentence. The brackets round **from sb/sth** show you that a prepositional phrase with **from** can be added to the idiom, but that it can be complete without one. You replace **sb/sth** with either a person or a group of people, or with a thing or an activity. In the example at sense **2**, **sth** is replaced by the word **organization**.

● *within striking distance*
This idiom is not defined here but is cross-referenced to **strike²**, the first 'full' word in the idiom.

Polite expressions

In order to be polite when you are speaking English, you need to use these phrases correctly.

Excuse me ...

You say **Excuse me** when you want to go past somebody. You also say **Excuse me** to somebody you do not know when you want to attract their attention:

- *Excuse me, could you tell me the way to the station?*
- *Excuse me, is anyone sitting here?*

Sorry ...

You say **Sorry** when you need to apologize for something small:

- *Sorry I'm late.*

I beg your pardon is a formal expression:

- *I beg your pardon! I must have picked up the wrong bag by mistake.*

Sorry or **I'm sorry** is used frequently in British English:

- *I'm sorry, but do you think you could move your car? (I apologize in advance for any inconvenience.)*

In American English **Pardon me** and **Excuse me** are used for apologies:

- *Excuse me / Pardon me, I didn't see you there.*

In British English you say **Pardon?** or **Sorry?** and in American English **Pardon me?** or **Excuse me?** when you did not hear or understand what somebody said and want them to repeat it:

- *Pardon, could you say that again?*

It is not polite to say **What?** if you have not heard or understood something.

I'm afraid ...

You use the phrase **I'm afraid ...** when you want to apologize because you have to tell somebody something that they may not like:

- *I'm afraid there's been an accident.*
- *Nina's not here at the moment, I'm afraid. Can I take a message?*
- *'Do you have any decaffeinated coffee?' 'I'm afraid not.'*
- *'Has the last bus gone?' 'I'm afraid so.'*

I wonder if ...

You use expressions which show hesitancy when you are asking somebody to do something or asking for a favour:

- *Could you just help me move this box, please?*
- *I wonder if I could have a copy of that letter.*
- *Would you mind if I left a few minutes early today?*
- *Do you think I could borrow your car this evening?*

Please ...

You say **Please** when you ask for something. In British English it introduces or ends a request, but in American English it always ends a request:

- *Please could I have the menu?*
- *Could I have the menu, please?*

You also use **Please** when you ask somebody to do something:

- *Could you post this letter for me, please?*
- *Please could you post this letter for me?*

Thank you ...

When somebody gives you something, or when you buy something or receive information, you are expected to say **Thank you** or **Thanks**. Some people may be offended if you say nothing.

It is not usual to say anything in response to **Thank you** in British English, although some people may say **That's all right**, **That's okay** or **Don't mention it**. In American English **You're welcome** is common.

You say **Thank you** or **Yes, please** when you want to accept something:

- *'How about another cup of coffee?' 'Thank you.' / 'Thanks.' / 'Yes, please.'*

You say **No, thank you** or **No, thanks** when you want to refuse something:

- *'Would you like some more cake?' 'No, thank you.' / 'No, thanks.'*

Cheers ...

Cheers is often used in informal British English to mean **Thank you**:

- *'Here's that £5 I owe you.' 'Oh, cheers.'*

You also say **Cheers** before you have a drink when you are with other people.

dent /dent/ n a hollow place in a hard even surface made by a blow or pressure: *His bike hit the side of my car and made quite a dent in it.* ○ (*fig*) *The lawyer's fees will* **make a** nasty **dent in** (ie have a serious effect on) *our finances.*

▶ **dent** v to make a dent or dents in sth: [Vn] *The back of the car was badly dented in a collision.* ○ (*fig*) *The event has severely dented their image.*

dental /'dentl/ adj of or for the teeth: *dental decay/ care/health/treatment.*

■ **'dental floss** n [U] a soft thread used for cleaning between the teeth.

'dental surgeon n a DENTIST.

dentist /'dentɪst/ n a person who has been trained to treat and look after people's teeth.

▶ **dentistry** /'dentɪstri/ n [U] the work of a dentist.

denture /'dentʃə(r)/ n (usu pl) a plate¹(8) holding one or more artificial teeth: *a set of dentures.*

denude /dɪ'njuːd; US -'nuːd/ v ~ **sth (of sth)** (usu passive) to make sth bare; to take the covering off sth: *trees denuded of leaves* ○ *hillsides denuded of trees.*

denunciation /dɪˌnʌnsi'eɪʃn/ n [C, U] (an instance of) denouncing (DENOUNCE) a person, policy, etc: *her fierce denunciation(s) of her enemies.*

deny /dɪ'naɪ/ v (pt, pp **denied**) **1** to say that sth is not true: [Vn] *deny a statement/a claim/an accusation/a charge* ○ **There is no denying** (the fact) **that** … (ie Everyone must admit that …) [V.ing] *She denied knowing anything about it.* [V.that] *He denied that he had been involved.* Compare AFFIRM. **2** ~ **sth (to sb)** to refuse to give sb/sth, or to prevent sb from having, sth they want or ask for: [Vnpr] *deny help to sb* [Vnn] *Many women were denied the opportunity of having a career.* ○ *They were denied access to the information.* **3** to say that one knows nothing about sth; to refuse to acknowledge sth: [Vn] *He denied all knowledge of the affair.* ○ *The government denies responsibility for the disaster.*

deodorant /di'əʊdərənt/ n [U,C] a substance that removes or hides unpleasant smells, esp those of the body. See also ANTIPERSPIRANT.

dep abbr **1** depart(s): *dep Paris 23.05 hrs.* Compare ARR 1. **2** deputy.

depart /dɪ'pɑːt/ v ~ **(for…) (from…)** (*fml*) to go away or leave, esp when starting a journey: [Vpr] *We departed for Athens at 10 am.* ○ *The 10.15 to Leeds departs from platform 4.* [V] *I thought this a fitting moment to depart.* Compare ARRIVE 1. **IDM** **depart this 'life** (*euph*) to die. **PHRV** **de'part from sth** to behave in a way that is different from what is usual: *depart from routine/tradition* ○ *depart from* (ie not tell) *the truth.*

departed /dɪ'pɑːtɪd/ adj [esp attrib] (*fml or euph*) dead: *your dear departed brother.*

▶ **the departed** n (pl unchanged) the person who has died: *Let us pray for the soul(s) of the departed.*

department /dɪ'pɑːtmənt/ n **1** (abbr **Dept**) a division of a large organization such as a government, business, shop, university, etc: *the Department of the Environment* ○ *the Education Department* ○ *the export sales department* ○ *the men's clothing department.* **2** an area of activity or responsibility: *Don't ask me about our finances: that's my wife's department.*

▶ **departmental** /ˌdiːpɑːt'mentl/ adj of a department, rather than the whole organization: *a departmental manager/meeting.*

■ **de'partment store** n a large shop where many types of goods are sold in different departments.

departure /dɪ'pɑːtʃə(r)/ n **1(a)** [U] ~ **(from…)** the action of departing; going away : *time of departure* ○ *Their departure was totally unexpected.* ○ *the departure lounge* (ie in an AIRPORT). **(b)** [C] an instance of this: *notices showing arrivals and departures of trains.* Compare ARRIVAL. **2** [C] ~ **(from sth)** an action or a course of action different from what is usual: *a departure from tradition/the standard procedure* ○ *Working on a farm is a new departure for him.* **IDM** **a point of departure** ⇨ POINT¹.

depend /dɪ'pend/ v **IDM** **that de'pends; it (all) de'pends** (used alone, or at the beginning of a sentence) the result will be decided by sth mentioned or implied: *'Can I come?' 'That depends: there might not be room in the car.'* ○ *I don't know if we'll be able to play — it all depends what the weather's like.* **PHRV** **de'pend on/upon sb/sth 1** to be sure or expect that sth will happen: *You can never depend on his arriving on time.* ○ (*ironic*) *You can depend on her to be* (ie She always is) *late.* ○ *Depend on it* (ie You can be sure): *we won't give up.* **2** to rely on sb/ sth: *You can't depend on the train arriving on time.* ○ *She was the sort of person who could be depended on.* **de'pend on sb/sth (for sth)** (usu not in the continuous tenses) **1** to need sb/sth for a particular purpose: *I don't have a car, so I have to depend on the buses.* ○ *We depend on the radio for news.* **2** to get money or other help from sb/sth: *This area depends on the mining industry.* ○ *Children depend on their parents for food and clothing.* **de'pend on sth** to be decided by sth: *A lot will depend on how she responds to the challenge.* ○ *How much is produced depends on how hard we work.*

▶ **dependable** adj that may be relied on: *a dependable friend/car.* **dependability** /dɪˌpendə'bɪləti/ n [U].

dependant (also esp US **dependent**) /dɪ'pendənt/ n a person who depends on others for a home, food, money, etc: *an unmarried male without dependants.* Compare DEPENDENT.

dependence /dɪ'pendəns/ n [U] ~ **on/upon sb/sth** **(a)** the state of needing the help and support of others: *his dependence on his parents* ○ *Our relationship was based on mutual dependence.* Compare INDEPENDENCE. **(b)** the state of needing sth regularly: *medical treatment for drug/alcohol dependence.*

dependency /dɪ'pendənsi/ n **1** a country governed or controlled by another: *The Hawaiian Islands are no longer a dependency of the USA.* **2** ~ **on sb/sth** **(a)** the state of relying on sb/sth for sth: *financial dependency* ○ *their dependency on the welfare state.* **(b)** the state of needing sth regularly: *drug/chemical dependency.*

dependent /dɪ'pendənt/ adj **1(a)** ~ **(on/upon sb/ sth)** needing sb/sth in order to live or survive: *a woman with several dependent children* ○ *be dependent on one's parents* ○ *The charity is totally dependent upon money from the public.* **(b)** [pred] ~ **on/upon sth** needing sth physically: *be dependent on drugs/ alcohol.* **2** [pred] ~ **on/upon sth** affected or decided by sth: *A child's development is dependent on many factors.* ▶ **dependent** n (esp US) = DEPENDANT.

■ **de,pendent 'clause** n = SUBORDINATE CLAUSE.

depict /dɪ'pɪkt/ v **(a)** to show or represent sb/sth as a picture: [V.n ing] *The artist/painting depicts her lying on a bed.* [also Vn]. **(b)** to describe sth in words: [Vn] *Her novel depicts life in Victorian London.* [Vn-n] *The general is depicted as a corrupt dictator.* [also Vn-adj]. ▶ **depiction** /dɪ'pɪkʃn/ n [U, C]: *the film's depiction of adolescent love.*

depilatory /dɪ'pɪlətri; US -tɔːri/ n, adj (of) a product used esp by women for removing body hair: *depilatory creams.*

deplete /dɪ'pliːt/ v to reduce greatly the quantity, size, power or value of sth: [Vn] *Stocks of vaccines are seriously depleted.* ○ *The election has severely depleted the party's funds.* ▶ **depletion** /dɪ'pliːʃn/ n [U]: *the depletion of the ozone layer.*

deplore /dɪ'plɔː(r)/ v to be shocked or offended by sth; to condemn(1) sth: *The president said he deplored the killings.* ○ *I deplore the fact that there are so few women in top jobs.*

▶ **deplorable** /dɪ'plɔːrəbl/ adj that is, or should be,

D

condemned: *a deplorable episode/incident* ○ *The acting was deplorable* (ie very bad)! **deplorably** /-əbli/ *adv*.

deploy /dɪˈplɔɪ/ *v* **1** to move or cause troops to move into position for military action: [V] *The infantry began to deploy at dawn.* [Vn] *a reduction in the UN forces deployed in the Middle East.* **2** to use sth effectively: [Vn] *deploy one's arguments/resources.* ▶ **deployment** *n* [U].

depopulate /ˌdiːˈpɒpjuleɪt/ *v* to reduce the number of people living in a place: [Vn] *an island depopulated by disease.* ▶ **depopulation** /ˌdiːˌpɒpjuˈleɪʃn/ *n* [U].

deport /dɪˈpɔːt/ *v* ~ **sb** (**from** ...) to force sb to leave a country, usu because they have broken the law or because they have no legal right to be there: [Vn] *He was convicted of drug offences and was deported.* [also Vnpr]. ▶ **deportation** /ˌdiːpɔːˈteɪʃn/ *n* [C, U]: *a deportation order* ○ *illegal immigrants facing deportation.*

deportment /dɪˈpɔːtmənt/ *n* [U] (*fml*) (**a**) (*Brit*) a person's way of standing and walking: *Young ladies used to have lessons in deportment.* (**b**) (*US*) behaviour.

depose /dɪˈpəʊz/ *v* to remove sb, esp a ruler, from power: [Vn] *The king was deposed in a military coup.*

deposit¹ /dɪˈpɒzɪt/ *v* **1**(**a**) to lay or put sth/sb down in a specified place: [Vnpr] *Please deposit litter in the bin.* ○ *The bus deposited them near the station.* [also Vn, Vnadv]. (**b**) (esp of liquids or a river) to put down and leave sth, esp gradually and over a period of time: [Vnpr] *The Nile floods the fields and deposits mud on them.* [also Vn]. **2**(**a**) [Vn] to put money into a bank, esp so that it can gain interest¹(5). (**b**) ~ **sth** (**in sth** / **with sb**) to put sth valuable or important where it will be safe: [Vnpr] *We deposited our jewellery in the hotel safe.* [also Vn]. **3** [Vn] (**a**) to pay part of a larger sum, the rest of which is to be paid later: *I had to deposit 10% of the price of the house.* (**b**) to pay money as a guarantee in case one damages or loses sth one is renting. This money is returned if no damage is caused: *We were required to deposit $500 as well as the first month's rent.*

deposit² /dɪˈpɒzɪt/ *n* **1** a sum of money paid into a bank, etc: *She made two deposits of £500 last month.* ○ *The money is being kept* **on deposit** (ie in a deposit account). **2** ~ (**on sth**) (usu *sing*) (**a**) the payment of a part of a larger sum, the rest of which is to be paid later: *put a deposit on a new house* ○ *The shop promised to keep the goods for me if I paid a deposit.* (**b**) the sum that sb pays in advance, in case they damage or lose sth they are renting: *I had to pay a £500 deposit to the landlord.* **3**(**a**) a layer of matter laid down by a river, etc: *The floods left a thick deposit of mud on the fields.* (**b**) (usu *pl*) a layer of matter, often deep under the earth, that has formed naturally: *rich mineral deposits.* ■ **deˈposit account** *n* (*esp Brit*) an account¹(2), usu at a bank, in which money is left to gain interest¹(5). Compare CURRENT ACCOUNT, SAVINGS ACCOUNT.

deposition /ˌdepəˈzɪʃn/ *n* **1** [U] removing sb, esp a ruler, from power. **2** [U, C] (*law*) (the action of making) a formal, usu written, statement to be used in a lawcourt, eg as evidence: *take a sworn deposition from a witness.*

depositor /dɪˈpɒzɪtə(r)/ *n* a person who deposits money in a bank.

depository /dɪˈpɒzɪtri; *US* -tɔːri/ *n* a place where things are stored.

depot /ˈdepəʊ; *US* ˈdiːpəʊ/ *n* **1**(**a**) a place where large amounts of food, equipment, etc are stored. (**b**) a place where vehicles, eg buses, are kept when they are not being used. **2** (*US*) a railway or bus station.

deprave /dɪˈpreɪv/ *v* to make sb morally bad: [Vn] *a film likely to deprave and corrupt young people.*

▶ **depraved** /dɪˈpreɪvd/ *adj* morally bad; evil: *This is the work of a depraved mind.*

depravity /dɪˈprævəti/ *n* [U] the state of being depraved (DEPRAVE); wickedness: *a life of depravity.*

deprecate /ˈdeprəkeɪt/ *v* (*fml*) to feel and express disapproval of sth: [Vn] *The article deprecates their negative attitude.* ▶ **deprecating** *adj*: *a deprecating look/smile.* **deprecatingly** *adv*. **deprecatory** /ˈdeprəkeɪtəri; *US* -tɔːri/ *adj*: *deprecatory remarks.*

depreciate /dɪˈpriːʃieɪt/ *v* **1** to become less valuable: [V] *New cars depreciate quickly.* **2** (*fml*) to state that sth is not valuable, important, etc: [Vn] *I have no desire to depreciate your efforts.* ▶ **depreciation** /dɪˌpriːʃiˈeɪʃn/ *n* [U]: *currency depreciation.*

depredation /ˌdeprəˈdeɪʃn/ *n* [U, C usu *pl*] (*fml*) damage caused by an attack, accident, etc: *suffer the depredations of time.*

depress /dɪˈpres/ *v* **1** to make sb sad and without enthusiasm or hope: *Wet weather always depresses me.* **2** to make sth, esp trade, less active: *depress sales* ○ *The rise in oil prices will depress the car market.* **3** (*fml*) to press, push or pull sth down: *depress the clutch* (ie when driving).

▶ **depressed** *adj* sad and without enthusiasm or hope: *He felt deeply depressed, even suicidal at times.* **depressing** *adj* making one feel depressed: *a depressing sight/film.* **depressingly** *adv*: *The crime rate is depressingly high.*

■ **deˌpressed ˈarea** *n* a part of a country where there are too few jobs and many people are poor.

depression /dɪˈpreʃn/ *n* **1** [U] the state of being depressed: *a woman suffering from post-natal depression* ○ *He committed suicide during a fit of depression.* **2** [C] a period when there is little economic activity, and many people are poor or without jobs. See also RECESSION. **3** [C] a hollow place on the surface of sth, esp the ground. **4** [C] a weather condition in which the pressure of the air becomes lower, often causing rain: *a depression over Iceland.* Compare ANTICYCLONE.

depressive /dɪˈpresɪv/ *adj* causing depression(1); of depression: *a depressive illness.*

▶ **depressive** *n* a person who often suffers from depression(1).

deprive /dɪˈpraɪv/ *v* **PHRV** **deprive sb/sth of sth** to take sth away from sb/sth; to prevent sb/sth from enjoying or using sth: *be deprived of one's civil rights* ○ *It's wrong suddenly to deprive your body of certain foods.*

▶ **deprivation** /ˌdeprɪˈveɪʃn/ *n* **1** [U] (**a**) the action or process of depriving sb or of being deprived of sth: *sleep deprivation.* (**b**) the state of not having the benefits that most people have, such as a home and enough food, money, etc: *widespread deprivation caused by unemployment.* **2** [C] a thing of which one is deprived: *Loss of hearing is a great deprivation.*

deprived *adj* without the benefits of adequate food, houses, money, education, health care, etc: *a deprived childhood/background/area* ○ *The poorest and most deprived people will receive special government help.*

Dept *abbr* department(1): *Linguistics Dept* (eg of a university).

depth /depθ/ *n* **1** [C, U] (**a**) the distance from the top down: *the depth of the well/mine/box* ○ *Water was found at a depth of 30 feet underground.* ○ *What's the depth of the water here?* ○ (*fig*) *the depth of the current economic recession.* ⇨ picture at DIMENSION. ⇨ note at DIMENSION. (**b**) the distance from the front to the back: *shelves with a depth of 8 inches.* (**c**) the distance from the surface down: *the depth of a wound/crack.* **2** [C usu *pl*] the deepest, most extreme, most serious, etc part of sth: *explore the ocean depths* ○ *be in the depths of despair* ○ *live in the depths of the country* (ie a long way from a town) ○ *His perform-*

*ance reveals **hidden depths**. ○ in the depth of winter.*
3 [U] strength of colours, etc. **4** [U] **(a)** strength and power of feelings, etc: *the depth of her love.* **(b)** the ability to understand or explain complex ideas: *a writer of great depth and wisdom.* **(c)** having or showing this ability: *His ideas lack depth.* **IDM** ˌ**in** ˈ**depth** thoroughly: *study a subject in depth* ○ *an ˌin-depth ˈstudy.* **out of one's ˈdepth 1** in water too deep to stand in: *If you can't swim, don't go out of your depth.* **2** unable to understand a subject or topic because it is too difficult, complicated, etc: *When they start talking about economics, I'm totally out of my depth.* **plumb the depths of sth** ⇨ PLUMB¹.

deputation /ˌdepjuˈteɪʃn/ *n* [CGp] a group of people given the right to act or speak on behalf of others.

depute /dɪˈpjuːt/ *v* (*fml*) **1** to give sb else authority to act or speak on one's behalf: [Vn.*to* inf] *They were deputed to put our views to the assembly.* **2** ~ sth to sb [Vnpr] to give one's work, authority, etc to sb else.

deputize, -ise /ˈdepjətaɪz/ *v* ~ (**for sb**) to act or speak on sb's behalf: [V, Vpr] *Dr Mitchell's ill so I'm deputizing (for her).*

deputy /ˈdepjəti/ *n* a person who is next in authority after the head of a business, school, etc and who does the head's job when the head is away: *the Director General and his deputy* ○ *the deputy sheriff* ○ *I'm acting as deputy till the manager returns.*

derail /dɪˈreɪl/ *v* to cause a train to leave the railway line: [Vn] *The engine was derailed by a tree lying across the line.* ▶ **derailment** *n* [C, U].

deranged /dɪˈreɪndʒd/ *adj* unable to act and think normally, esp because of mental illness: *She's completely deranged.* ○ *a deranged attacker/mind/laugh.*
▶ **derangement** *n* [U].

derby¹ /ˈdɑːbi; *US* ˈdɜːrbi/ *n* **1** [C] an important sports contest: *a local football derby* (ie between teams from the same area or town). **2** (*US*) any of several horse races which happen every year: *the Kentucky Derby.*

derby² /ˈdɜːrbi/ *n* (*US*) = BOWLER².

deregulate /ˌdiːˈregjuleɪt/ *v* to free a trade, a business activity, etc from certain rules and controls: [Vn] *deregulate bus services/the price of oil.* ▶ **deregulation** *n* [U].

derelict /ˈderəlɪkt/ *adj* not used or cared for and in bad condition: *a derelict building* ○ *derelict land.*
▶ **derelict** *n* a person without a home, a job or property: *derelicts living on the streets.*
dereliction /ˌderəˈlɪkʃn/ *n* **1** [U] being derelict: *a house in a state of dereliction.* **2** [U, C usu *sing*] (*fml*) the deliberate failure to do what one ought to do: *Police officers found guilty of **a** serious **dereliction of duty**.*

deride /dɪˈraɪd/ *v* ~ sb/sth (**as sth**) to treat sb/sth as funny and not worthy of serious attention; to mock sb/sth: [Vn, Vn-adj] *They derided his efforts (as childish).* [also Vn-n].

de rigueur /də rɪˈɡɜː(r)/ *adj* [pred] (*French*) required by social custom: *Evening dress is de rigueur at the Casino.*

derision /dɪˈrɪʒn/ *n* [U] mocking words, behaviour or laughter: *Her proposal was greeted/met with howls of derision.* ○ *He became an object/target of universal derision.*

derisive /dɪˈraɪsɪv/ *adj* unkind and mocking: *derisive laughter/jeers.* ▶ **derisively** *adv.*

derisory /dɪˈraɪsəri/ *adj* **1** too small or inadequate to be considered seriously: *Union leaders rejected the pay offer as derisory.* **2** = DERISIVE.

derivation /ˌderɪˈveɪʃn/ *n* [U, C] the development or origin, esp of words; the process of being derived (DERIVE 2) from sth: *a word of French derivation.*

derivative /dɪˈrɪvətɪv/ *adj* (*usu derog*) copied from

sth else; not new or original: *a derivative design/style.*
▶ **derivative** *n* a word or thing derived (DERIVE 2) from another word or thing: *'Assertion' is a derivative of 'assert'.*

derive /dɪˈraɪv/ *v* **1** ~ sth from sth (*fml*) to get or obtain sth from sth: [Vnpr] *derive great pleasure from art* ○ *She derived no benefit from the course of drugs.* **2(a)** ~ from sth to have sth as its source or origin: [Vpr] *Many English words derive from Latin.* **(b)** ~ sth from sth to find the source of sth: [Vnpr] *The word 'politics' is derived from a Greek word meaning 'city'.*

derm- *comb form* of skin: *dermatology* ○ *dermatitis.*

dermatitis /ˌdɜːməˈtaɪtɪs/ *n* [U] (*medical*) a condition of the skin in which it becomes red, swollen and sore.

dermatology /ˌdɜːməˈtɒlədʒi/ *n* [U] the medical study of the skin and its diseases.
▶ **dermatologist** /ˌdɜːməˈtɒlədʒɪst/ *n* an expert in dermatology.

derogatory /dɪˈrɒɡətri; *US* -tɔːri/ *adj* (abbreviated as *derog* in this dictionary) showing a critical attitude to sb's reputation, etc; insulting: *derogatory expressions like 'the rat race'* ○ *derogatory remarks.*

derrick /ˈderɪk/ *n* **1** a large CRANE¹(1) for moving or lifting heavy weights, esp on a ship. **2** a framework over an oil well for holding the DRILL¹(1).

derring-do /ˌderɪŋˈduː/ *n* [U] (*arch or joc*) bold or brave deeds.

derv /dɜːv/ *n* [U] (*Brit*) fuel oil for DIESEL engines.

dervish /ˈdɜːvɪʃ/ *n* a member of one of various Muslim groups, esp one that performs a wild religious dance: *He threw himself around the stage like a whirling dervish.*

DES /ˌdiː iː ˈes/ *abbr* **1** (formerly in Britain) Department of Education and Science. **2** (in the USA) Department of Employment Security.

desalination /ˌdiːˌsælɪˈneɪʃn/ *n* [U] the process of removing salt from sea water: *a desalination plant.*

descale /ˌdiːˈskeɪl/ *v* to remove scale²(2) from sth: [Vn] *descale a kettle.*

descant /ˈdeskænt/ *n* (*music*) a tune that is sung or played at the same time as, and usu higher than, the main tune.

descend /dɪˈsend/ *v* **1** (*fml*) **(a)** to come or go down: [V] *The lift began to descend.* ○ *Put the eight points in **descending order** of importance.* [Vn] *Slowly she descended the stairs.* **(b)** (of a hill, etc) to lead downwards; to slope: [V] *At this point the path descends steeply.* Compare ASCEND. **2** (*fml*) (of night or darkness) to fall: [V] *Night descends quickly in the tropics.* **PHRV be desˈcended from sb** to have sb as an ancestor: *She is descended from royalty, on her mother's side of the family.* **desˈcend on/upon sb/sth** to visit sb/sth in large numbers unexpectedly or at a time that is not convenient: *My sister's family is descending on us this weekend.* ○ *In summer tourists descend on the place in their thousands.* **desˈcend to sth** (no passive) to do or say sth that is mean and not worthy of one: *He wouldn't descend to that sort of trick.*
▶ **descendant** /-ənt/ *n* a person or an animal that has another as an ancestor: *She claims to be a direct descendant of Napoleon.* Compare ANCESTOR 1.

descent /dɪˈsent/ *n* **1(a)** [C usu *sing*] a coming or going down: *The plane began its descent towards Luton airport.* ○ (*fig*) *the country's swift descent into anarchy.* **(b)** [C] a slope: *Here there is a gradual descent to the sea.* Compare ASCENT. **2** [U] ~ (**from sb**) family origins; ancestry (ANCESTOR): *be of French descent* ○ *He traces his (line of) descent from the Stuart kings.*

describe /dɪˈskraɪb/ *v* **1** ~ sb/sth (**to/for sb**); ~ sth **as sth** to say what sb/sth is like: [Vn] *Words cannot describe the beauty of the scene.* [Vnpr] *She described* *her attacker to the police.* [V.wh] *Can you briefly describe how you spend a typical day?* [Vn·adj] *She describes the experience as the most painful of her life.* [also Vn·n]. **2 ~ sb as sth** to say that sb/sth is sth; to call sb sth: [Vn·n] *She describes herself as an inventor.* [Vn·adj] *He is described by his colleagues as thoughtful and sensitive.* **3** (*fml or techn*) to make a movement which has a particular shape: [Vn] *describe a perfect circle on the ice.*

description /dɪˈskrɪpʃn/ *n* **1(a)** [U] saying in words what sb/sth is like: *This writer is not very good at description.* ○ *The scenery was beautiful beyond description* (ie utterly beautiful). **(b)** [C] a picture in words: *give a vivid/detailed/graphic description of what had happened* ○ *The man fits our description of the thief.* **2** (*infml*) (after *of* + *some, all, every*, etc) a type; a sort: *boats of every description/ all descriptions* ○ *Their money came from trade of some description.* ○ *medals, coins and things of that description.* **IDM** **answer the description** ⇨ ANSWER². **beggar description** ⇨ BEGGAR.

descriptive /dɪˈskrɪptɪv/ *adj* **1** giving a picture in words; describing sth, esp without expressing feelings or judging: *a descriptive passage in a novel.* **2** (*techn*) describing how language is actually used, without giving rules for how it ought to be used: *descriptive linguistics.* Compare PRESCRIPTIVE.

desecrate /ˈdesɪkreɪt/ *v* to treat a sacred thing or place badly or without respect: [Vn] *desecrate a grave/church/temple.* ▶ **desecration** /ˌdesɪˈkreɪʃn/ *n* [U]: *desecration of a holy shrine* ○ (*fig*) *I deplore the desecration of our countryside by new roads.*

desegregate /ˌdiːˈsegrɪgeɪt/ *v* to end the policy of keeping different races separate in sth: [Vn] *desegregate schools/public transport.* ▶ **desegregation** /ˌdiːˌsegrɪˈgeɪʃn/ *n* [U].

deselect /ˌdiːsɪˈlekt/ *v* (*Brit*) (of a local branch of a political party) to reject the existing Member of Parliament as a candidate at the next election. ▶ **deselection** *n* [U].

desert¹ /dɪˈzɜːt/ *v* **1** **(a)** to go away from a place without intending ever to return: [Vn] *The village had been hurriedly deserted as the tanks drew nearer.* **(b)** to leave sb without help or support; to abandon sb: [Vn] *He deserted his wife and children and went abroad.* ○ *His popularity declined and even his friends started deserting him.* ○ *Members are deserting the party in droves.* **(c)** (of a quality) to leave sb when needed: [Vn] *At this point his presence of mind/ courage deserted him.* **2** to leave or run away from military service without authority or permission: [V, Vn] *A soldier who deserts (his post) in time of war is punished severely.*
▶ **deserted** *adj* **(a)** having no one present: *a deserted street/area* ○ *The office was completely deserted.* **(b)** abandoned: *a deserted hut/house* ○ *a deserted wife* (ie one whose husband has left her).
deserter *n* a person who deserts (DESERT¹ 2).
desertion /dɪˈzɜːʃn/ *n* [U, C]: *Is desertion grounds for divorce?* ○ *Desertion from the army is punishable by death.* ○ *mutinies and mass desertions in the forces.*

desert² /ˈdezət/ *n* [C, U] a large area of land that has very little water and very few plants growing on it. Many deserts are covered by sand: *Somalia is mostly desert.* ○ *cross the Sahara Desert* ○ *arid desert wastes/ sands.*
■ ˌ**desert ˈisland** *n* a tropical island where no people live: *shipwrecked on a desert island.*

desertification /dɪˌzɜːtɪfɪˈkeɪʃn/ *n* [U] the process of becoming or making sth a DESERT².

deserts /dɪˈzɜːts/ *n* [pl] what one deserves: *be rewarded/punished according to one's deserts* ○ *get/ meet with one's just deserts.*

deserve /dɪˈzɜːv/ *v* (not used in the continuous tenses) to have a quality or character, or to have

done sth, that is worthy of reward, special treatment, etc: [Vn] *much deserved praise* ○ *She deserves some reward for her efforts.* ○ *He richly deserved all that happened to him.* ○ *The article deserves careful study.* [V.to inf] *They deserve to succeed.* **IDM** **one good turn deserves another** ⇨ TURN².
▶ **deservedly** /dɪˈzɜːvɪdli/ *adv* according to what is deserved; correctly: *They are proud of their achievement, and deservedly so.*

deserving /dɪˈzɜːvɪŋ/ *adj* **~ (of sth)** (*fml*) worthy of help, praise, a reward, etc: *give money to a deserving cause* ○ *be deserving of sympathy* ○ *This family is a very deserving case.*

desiccated /ˈdesɪkeɪtɪd/ *adj* (esp of food) dried, esp in order to preserve it: *desiccated coconut.*

design /dɪˈzaɪn/ *n* **1(a)** [C] **~ (for sth)** a drawing or an outline from which sth may be made: *designs for a dress/a kitchen/an aircraft* ○ *create new and original designs.* **(b)** [U] the art of making such drawings, etc: *a design studio* ○ *study textile design* ○ *computer-aided design* ○ *a famous Italian car design firm.* **2** [U] the general arrangement or planning of a building, book, machine, etc: *special new design features* ○ *The machine's unique design prevents it from ever overheating.* See also INTERIOR DESIGN. **3** [C] an arrangement of lines, shapes or figures as decoration; a pattern: *floral/abstract designs* ○ *a bowl with a striking geometric design around the rim.* **4** [U, C] a plan or an intention: *We don't know if it was done by accident or by design* (ie deliberately). **IDM** **have designs on sb/sth** (*fml or joc*) to intend to harm sb/sth or take sb/sth for oneself: *She has designs on my money.*
▶ **design** *v* **1(a)** to decide how sth will look, work, etc, esp by making plans, drawings or models of it: [Vn] *design a car/a dress/a tool/an office* ○ *We design kitchens for today's cooks.* [Vnn] *They've designed us a superb new studio.* [also V]. **(b)** to think of and plan a system, procedure, etc: [Vn] *We need to design a new curriculum for the third year.* See also DESIGNING. **2 ~ sth for sb/sth; ~ sth as sth** (usu passive) to be made, planned or intended for a particular purpose or use: [Vnpr] *The gloves were specifically designed for use in very cold climates.* [Vn·n] *This course is primarily designed as an introduction to the subject.* [Vn.to inf] *The route is designed to improve the flow of traffic.* ○ *The programme is deliberately designed to shock people.*

designate¹ /ˈdezɪgnət, -nət/ *adj* (following *ns*) appointed to a job but not yet having officially started it: *an interview with the director/archbishop designate.*

designate² /ˈdezɪgneɪt/ *v* **1** to mark or indicate sth clearly; to specify sth: [Vn] *designate the boundaries of sth* ○ *a designated no-smoking area.* **2 ~ sb/sth (as) sth** (*fml*) (usu passive) to choose or name sb/sth for a special purpose or to hold a special title or position: [Vn·n] *The town has been designated (as) a development area.* [Vn] *The chairman is allowed to designate his own successor.*

designation /ˌdezɪgˈneɪʃn/ *n* (*fml*) **1** [U] **~ (as sth)** the appointing of sb to an office or the choosing of sth for a special purpose. **2** [C] a name, title or description: *Her official designation is Financial Controller.*

designer /dɪˈzaɪnə(r)/ *n* **1** a person whose job is designing things: *an industrial designer* ○ *a talented young jewellery designer* ○ *We attended the fashion show of a leading New York designer.* **2** [attrib] (of clothes, etc) made by a famous designer: *designer jeans/sunglasses.*
■ deˌsigner ˈstubble *n* [U] (*joc*) a slight beard, thought to look fashionable and so deliberately not shaved off.

designing /dɪˈzaɪnɪŋ/ *n* [U] the art of making designs for machinery, clothes, etc.

D

desirable /dɪˈzaɪərəbl/ adj **1** ~ (that)... to be wished for: *The house has many desirable features.* ○ *Such measures are desirable if not essential.* ○ *It is clearly desirable that the proposals receive support.* **2** (of a person) causing others to feel sexual desire: *She found him highly desirable.* ► **desirability** /dɪˌzaɪərəˈbɪləti/ n [U]: *No one questions the desirability of cheaper rail fares.*

desire¹ /dɪˈzaɪə(r)/ n **1** [U, C] ~ (for sth / to do sth) a strong wish to have or do sth: *They had little desire for wealth/to become wealthy.* ○ *enough money to satisfy all your desires* ○ *He expressed a desire to see his sons again.* ○ *She experienced a sudden/intense/overwhelming desire to return home.* **2** [U, C] ~ (for sth / to do sth) a strong feeling of wanting sb sexually: *my desire for her/to make love with her* ○ *passionate/burning desires.* **3** [C usu sing] a person or thing that is wished for: *When she agreed to marry him he felt he had achieved **his heart's desire.***

desire² /dɪˈzaɪə(r)/ v (not used in the continuous tenses) **1** (*rather fml*) to wish for sth; to want sth: [Vn] *We all desire happiness and health.* ○ *I've been taking the medicine regularly but it doesn't seem to be having **the desired effect**.* [V.to inf] *In those days women desired only to please their husbands.* **2** to be sexually attracted to sb: *He still desired her, and she him.* **IDM** **leave a lot, much, something, etc to be deˈsired** to be not satisfactory.

desirous /dɪˈzaɪərəs/ adj [pred] ~ of sth/doing sth; ~ that... (*fml or rhet*) having a wish for sth; wanting sth: *a politician desirous of getting his name in the papers.*

desist /dɪˈzɪst/ v ~ (from sth/doing sth) (*fml or rhet*) to stop sth/doing sth: [Vpr] *I wish he'd desist from entertaining his friends at all hours of the day and night.* [also V].

desk /desk/ n **1** a piece of furniture with a flat or sloping top and often with drawers, at which one can read, write or work: *an office desk* ○ *children sitting at their desks* ○ *He used to be a pilot, but now he has a desk job.* **2** a table or counter where customers are served in a public building: *the check-in desk at the airport* ○ *Ask the clerk on the enquiry/information desk.* ○ *Leave a message at the desk of the hotel.* ○ *the desk sergeant in the police station.*
■ ˈdesk clerk n (*US*) = CLERK 3.

desktop /ˈdesktɒp/ n the top of a desk.
■ ˌdesktop comˈputer n a computer that fits on a desk.
ˌdesktop ˈpublishing n [U] the use of a small computer and a printer (PRINT²) to produce printed material of high quality.

desolate /ˈdesələt/ adj **1** (of a place) deserted and causing one to feel sad or frightened: *a desolate industrial landscape* ○ *a desolate, windswept moor.* **2** miserable and without friends; lonely and sad: *a desolate person/existence* ○ *We all felt absolutely desolate when she left.*
► **desolate** /ˈdesəleɪt/ v (usu passive) **1** to leave a place ruined and deserted: [Vn] *a city completely desolated by civil strife.* **2** to make sb sad and without hope: [Vn] *a family desolated by the loss of a child.*
desolation /ˌdesəˈleɪʃn/ n [U] **1(a)** a ruined deserted condition of a place, offering no joy or hope to people: *a scene of utter desolation.* **(b)** the act of making a place like this: *the desolation of the environment.* **2** misery combined with a feeling of being lonely: *His wife's death left him with a sense of complete desolation.*

despair /dɪˈspeə(r)/ n [U] the state of having lost all hope: *a cry of despair* ○ *He gave up the struggle in despair.* ○ *The general mood is one of complete and utter despair.* ○ *His stupidity is **driving me to despair**.* See also DESPERATE 1. **IDM** **be the despair of sb** (*fml*) to make sb stop hoping: *Your son is the*

despair of all his teachers (ie They no longer expect to be able to teach him anything).
► **despair** v **1** ~ (of sth/doing sth) to stop having any hope at all: [V] *Don't despair! We'll think of a way out of this!* [Vpr] *Months passed, and we began to despair of ever hearing from her again.* **2** ~ **of sb** to have lost all hope that sb will improve: [Vpr] *I despair of him; he can't keep a job for more than six months.*
despairing /dɪˈspeərɪŋ/ adj showing or feeling despair: *a despairing cry/sigh.* **despairingly** adv: *She looked despairingly at the mess.*

despatch = DISPATCH¹,².

desperado /ˌdespəˈrɑːdəʊ/ n (pl **-oes**; *US* also **-os**) (*dated*) a man who commits dangerous, esp criminal, acts without worrying about himself or other people: *a gang of armed desperadoes.*

desperate /ˈdespərət/ adj **1(a)** feeling or showing great despair and ready to do anything, without worrying about danger: *The prisoners grew increasingly desperate.* ○ *She wrote me a desperate letter.* ○ *a last desperate attempt to avoid capture.* **(b)** [attrib] (of a person) violent and dangerous: *a desperate criminal.* **2** [usu pred] ~ (for sth / to do sth) in great need: *He was so desperate for a job that he would have done anything.* ○ (*infml*) *Have you got a cigarette? I'm desperate (for one).* ○ *I was absolutely desperate to see her.* **3** extremely serious or dangerous: *a desperate situation/shortage/illness* ○ *The state of the economy is now desperate.* **4** [usu attrib] giving little hope of success; tried when everything else has failed: *a desperate bid for freedom* ○ *a desperate remedy/measure.*
► **desperately** adv: *struggling/trying desperately* ○ *desperately keen/anxious/ill.*
desperation /ˌdespəˈreɪʃn/ n [U] the state of being desperate(1,2): *driven to desperation* ○ *In desperation I went to a psychiatrist for help.*

despicable /dɪˈspɪkəbl; *rarely* ˈdespɪkəbl/ adj (*fml*) very unpleasant or evil: *a despicable action/crime.* ► **despicably** /-əbli/ adv: *behave despicably.*

despise /dɪˈspaɪz/ v [Vn] (not in the continuous tenses) to feel contempt for sb/sth; to consider sb/sth to be worthless: *despise sb's hypocrisy/meanness* ○ *Strikebreakers are often despised by their fellow workers.*

despite /dɪˈspaɪt/ prep without being affected by the factors mentioned: *They had a wonderful holiday, despite the bad weather.* ○ *Despite wanting to see him again, she refused to reply to his letters.* See also IN SPITE OF (SPITE).

despoil /dɪˈspɔɪl/ v ~ sth (of sth) (*fml*) to rob a place of sth valuable: [Vnpr] *Foreigners have despoiled the country of many priceless treasures.* [also Vn].

despondent /dɪˈspɒndənt/ adj ~ (about sth/doing sth) having or showing loss of hope: *a despondent loser/mood* ○ *She's despondent about losing her bracelet.* ► **despondency** /dɪˈspɒndənsi/ n [U]: *a general air/mood of despondency.* **despondently** adv.

despot /ˈdespɒt/ n a ruler with great power, esp one who uses it in a cruel way; a TYRANT: *an enlightened despot.*
► **despotic** /dɪˈspɒtɪk/ adj of or like a despot: *despotic rule.*
despotism /ˈdespətɪzəm/ n [U] the rule of a despot.

dessert /dɪˈzɜːt/ n **(a)** [C] any sweet food eaten at the end of a meal: *a pineapple dessert* ○ *the dessert trolley* (eg in a restaurant). See also SWEET² 2, AFTERS, PUDDING 1. **(b)** [U] the course in which this dish is served: *What's for dessert?* ○ *a dessert apple/wine.*

dessertspoon /dɪˈzɜːtspuːn/ n **(a)** a spoon of medium size, used for eating DESSERT. ⇨ picture at SPOON. **(b)** the amount held by this.

destabilize, -ise /ˌdiːˈsteɪbəlaɪz/ v to make a system, country, group, etc become less firmly established or fixed: [Vn] *The President accused the*

USA *of trying to destabilize his regime.* ○ *a danger-ously destabilizing event/factor.* ▶ **destabilization, -isation** /ˌdiːˌsteɪbəlaɪˈzeɪʃn; *US* -ləˈz-/ *n* [U]: *a campaign of destabilization.*

destination /ˌdestɪˈneɪʃn/ *n* a place to which sb/sth is going or being sent: *this year's popular holiday destinations* ○ *Tokyo was our final/ultimate destina-tion.* ○ *arrive at/reach one's destination safely.*

destined /ˈdestɪnd/ *adj* [pred] (*fml*) **1** ~ **for sth / to do sth** having a future which has been decided or planned at an earlier time, esp by fate: *Coming from a theatrical family, I was destined for a career on the stage* (ie I was expected to be an actor). ○ *We seem destined never to meet.* **2** ~ **for...** on the way to or intended for a place: *food aid destined for Central Africa.*

destiny /ˈdestənɪ/ *n* **1** [U] the power believed to control events; fate: *Destiny drew us together.* **2** [C] what happens to particular people: *events which shape the destinies of nations* ○ *He wants to be in control of his own destiny.*

destitute /ˈdestɪtjuːt; *US* -tuːt/ *adj* **1** without money, food and the other things necessary for life: *When he died, his family was left completely destitute.* **2** [pred] ~ **of sth** (*fml*) lacking sth: *They seem desti-tute of ordinary human feelings.* ▶ **destitution** /ˌdestɪˈtjuːʃn; *US* -ˈtuːʃn/ *n* [U]: *live in complete desti-tution.*

destroy /dɪˈstrɔɪ/ *v* **1** to damage sth so badly that it no longer exists, works, etc: [Vn] *a house destroyed by bombs/fire* ○ *They've destroyed all the evidence.* ○ *Vandals had virtually/effectively destroyed the bus.* ○ *The rain forest is being systematically destroyed.* ○ *She was intent on destroying everything he had worked for.* ○ (*fig*) *destroy sb's hopes/career/ reputation.* See also DESTRUCTION. **2** (*euph*) to kill an animal deliberately, usu because it is sick or not wanted: [Vn] *The injured horse had to be destroyed.* ▶ **destroyer** *n* **1** (*fml*) a person or thing that des-troys: *Drought is a major destroyer of crops.* **2** a small fast ship used in war, eg for protecting larger ships.

destruction /dɪˈstrʌkʃn/ *n* [U] (**a**) the action of destroying sth or of being destroyed: *weapons of mass destruction* ○ *a tidal wave bringing death and destruction in its wake* ○ *the destruction of the rain forests* ○ *Such a policy may unwittingly contain the seeds of* (ie elements which will lead to) *its own destruction.* (**b**) (*fml*) a thing that destroys or ruins: *Gambling was his destruction.*

destructive /dɪˈstrʌktɪv/ *adj* (**a**) causing destruc-tion or serious damage: *the destructive force of the storm* ○ *the destructive effects of anxiety on his life.* (**b**) wanting or tending to destroy: *destructive urges/ emotions* ○ *Are all small children so destructive?* Com-pare CONSTRUCTIVE. ▶ **destructively** *adv*. **destructiveness** *n* [U].

desultory /ˈdesəltrɪ; *US* -tɔːrɪ/ *adj* going from one thing to another, without a definite plan or purpose and without enthusiasm: *wander around in a desul-tory fashion* ○ *keep up a desultory conversation.* ▶ **desultorily** *adv*.

Det *abbr* Detective: *Det Insp* (ie Inspector) *(Tim) Cox.*

detach /dɪˈtætʃ/ *v* **1**(**a**) ~ **sth/itself (from sth)** to remove sth from sth larger or longer: [Vnpr] *detach a wagon from a train* ○ *He jumped as a dark shape detached itself from the wall.* [Vn] *To place your order, simply complete, detach and return the coupon.* (**b**) ~ **oneself from sb/sth** leave or separate oneself from sb/sth: [Vnpr] *She detached herself from the group and came over to join me.* Compare ATTACH 1. **2** (*military*) to send a group of soldiers, ships, etc away from the main force, esp to do special duties: [Vn] *A number of men were detached to guard the right flank.*

▶ **detached** *adj* **1** not influenced by other people

or by one's own feelings; IMPARTIAL: *a detached assessment/judgement/observer* ○ *She tried to remain completely detached.* **2** (of a house) not joined to another on either side. ⇨ picture at HOUSE[1].

detachable /-əbl/ *adj* that can be detached: *a de-tachable lining in a coat.*

detachment /dɪˈtætʃmənt/ *n* **1** [U] (**a**) the state of being not influenced by other people: *show detach-ment in one's judgements.* (**b**) a lack of emotion; INDIFFERENCE: *He answered with an air of detach-ment.* **2** [C] a group of soldiers, ships, etc sent away from a larger group, esp to do special duties: *a detachment of artillery.* **3** [U] the act or process of detaching sth or of being detached: *suffer detach-ment of the retina.*

detail¹ /ˈdiːteɪl; *US* dɪˈteɪl/ *n* **1** [C] a small individual fact or item: *an expedition planned down to the last detail* ○ *Please write to us for further details of this offer.* ○ *He refused to give precise details of how the law would be changed.* ○ *The costumes are authentic in every detail.* ○ *'It was a fantastic party.' 'Spare me the sordid details* (ie Don't tell me any more), *please!'* **2** [U] (**a**) the small particular aspects of sth: *A good organizer pays attention to detail.* ○ *a novelist with an eye for detail* (eg one who includes many small, realistic facts) ○ *She described everyth-ing in detail* (ie fully). ○ *I won't go into detail* (ie explain fully what happened) *just now.* (**b**) the smaller or less important parts of a picture, pattern, etc: *The overall composition of the picture is good but some of the detail is distracting.* Compare DETAILING. **3** [C] (*military*) a group of soldiers given special duties.

detail² /ˈdiːteɪl; *US* dɪˈteɪl/ *v* **1** to give a full list of sth, item by item; to describe sth fully: [Vn] *The computer's features are detailed in our brochure.* ○ *an inventory detailing all the goods in a shop.* **2** ~ **sb (for sth)** (*esp military*) to choose or appoint sb for special duties: [Vnpr, Vn.to inf] *detail soldiers for guard duty/to guard a bridge.*

▶ **detailed** *adj* having many details or paying great attention to details; thorough: *a detailed description/ account/analysis* ○ *detailed instructions.* **detailing** *n* [U] small details put on a building, garment, etc, esp for decoration.

detain /dɪˈteɪn/ *v* **1** to keep sb in an official place, eg a police station: [Vn] *emergency powers allowing the government to detain political prisoners without charge* ○ *The police detained him for questioning.* See also DETENTION. **2** (*fml*) to prevent sb from leaving or doing sth; delay: [Vn] *There is little to detain the visitor in these churches.* ○ *This question need not detain us long* (ie can be settled quickly).

▶ **detainee** /ˌdiːteɪˈniː/ *n* a person who is detained by police, etc: *political detainees.*

detect /dɪˈtekt/ *v* to discover or recognize sth present: [Vn] *Opticians can detect various cancers.* ○ *instruments that can detect minute amounts of radi-ation* ○ *Do I detect a note of irony in your voice?*

▶ **detectable** *adj*: *detectable signs of unease among government ministers.* **detector** *n* a device for detecting metals, explos-ives, changes in pressure or temperature, etc: *All homes should be fitted with smoke detectors.*

detection /dɪˈtekʃn/ *n* [U] the action or work of detecting sth; the process of being detected: *the de-tection of radioactivity* ○ *crime detection rates* ○ *try to escape/avoid detection by disguising oneself.*

detective /dɪˈtektɪv/ *n* a person, esp a police officer, whose job is to investigate and solve crimes: *Detect-ive Inspector (Roger) Brown* ○ *detectives from the anti-terrorist squad* ○ *employ a private detective* ○ *detective fiction/stories/novels.*

détente /deɪˈtɑːnt/ *n* [U] (*French*) the reduction of dangerous tension, esp between countries: *a period of détente.*

detention /dɪˈtenʃn/ n [U] **(a)** the act of detaining sb or the state of being detained, esp in prison: *detention without trial* ○ *deaths in detention* ○ *a detention camp for illegal immigrants.* **(b)** the punishment of being kept at school after it has closed: *be given two hours' detention.*
■ **deˈtention centre** (*Brit*) (*US* **deˈtention home**) n a place where young people who have committed offences are kept in detention for a short time.

deter /dɪˈtɜː(r)/ v (**-rr-**) ~ **sb** (**from doing sth**) to make sb decide not to do sth: [Vn] *Stiffer penalties are needed to deter crime/criminals.* [Vnpr] *What is the best way to deter young people from taking up smoking?* See also DETERRENT.

detergent /dɪˈtɜːdʒənt/ n [U,C] a substance that removes dirt, eg from the surface of clothes or dishes: *dishwasher detergents.*

deteriorate /dɪˈtɪəriəreɪt/ v ~ (**into sth**) to become worse in quality or condition: [V] *The flight has been cancelled due to deteriorating weather conditions.* ○ *His health deteriorated rapidly and he died two weeks later.* [Vpr] *The discussion quickly deteriorated into a slanging match.* ▶ **deterioration** /dɪˌtɪəriəˈreɪʃn/ n [U]: *a rapid/progressive deterioration in relations between the two countries.*

determinant /dɪˈtɜːmɪnənt/ n (*fml*) a thing that decides whether or how sth happens: *Interest rates are a major determinant of currency trends.*

determination /dɪˌtɜːmɪˈneɪʃn/ n [U] **1** ~ (**to do sth**) the quality of being firmly committed to doing sth: *a leader of courage and determination* ○ *with an air of fierce determination* ○ *You have to admire her single-minded/dogged determination to learn English.* **2(a)** the process of fixing sth exactly: *factors influencing the determination of future policy.* **(b)** the act of finding out or calculating sth: *the determination of a ship's position/of the exact composition of a substance.* See also DETERMINE.

determine /dɪˈtɜːmɪn/ v **1** (*fml*) to cause sth to happen in a particular way or be of a particular type: [Vn] *This may determine the outcome of the match.* ○ *A chance meeting determined his future.* ○ *The exam results could determine your career.* **2** (*fml*) to find out or fix sth exactly and without doubt; to calculate sth: [Vn] *determine the meaning of a word/the speed of light* [V.wh] *determine exactly what happened/how high the mountain is.* **3** (*fml*) to decide sth firmly: [Vn] *determine a date for a meeting* [Vnpr, V.that] *We determined on an early start/(that) we'd make an early start.* [V.to inf] *He determined to learn Greek.*
▶ **determined** /dɪˈtɜːmɪnd/ adj ~ (**to do sth**) having made a firm decision and having no intention of changing it: *a determined fighter/look/attitude* ○ *I'm determined to succeed.* **determinedly** adv.

determiner /dɪˈtɜːmɪnə(r)/ n (abbreviated as *det* in this dictionary) (*grammar*) a word, eg *the, some, my,* that comes before a noun to show how the noun is being used.

determinism /dɪˈtɜːmɪnɪzəm/ n [U] (*philosophy*) the belief that one is not free to choose the sort of person one wants to be, or how one behaves, because these things are decided by one's background, surroundings, etc.

deterrent /dɪˈterənt; *US* -ˈtɜː-/ n a thing that deters or is meant to deter sb: *nuclear deterrents* ○ *His punishment will be a deterrent to others.* ▶ **deterrence** /dɪˈterəns; *US* -ˈtɜː-/ n [U]: *nuclear deterrence* (ie having nuclear weapons in order to make an enemy too frightened to attack). **deterrent** adj: *have a deterrent effect.*

detest /dɪˈtest/ v (not used in the continuous tenses) to have a strong feeling of dislike for sb/sth: [Vn] *detest dogs* [V.ing] *He detests having to get up early.* [V.n ing] *I detest people complaining.*

▶ **detestable** /-əbl/ adj that one detests: *a detestable habit/child.*
detestation /ˌdiːteˈsteɪʃn/ n [U] very strong dislike.

dethrone /ˌdiːˈθrəʊn/ v to remove a ruler from power: [Vn] (*fig*) *the man who dethroned the champion.*

detonate /ˈdetəneɪt/ v to explode or cause sth to explode: [V] *The bomb failed to detonate.* [Vn] *an explosive charge detonated by remote control.*
▶ **detonation** /ˌdetəˈneɪʃn/ n [C,U] an explosion; the action of causing sth to explode.
detonator /ˈdetəneɪtə(r)/ n a device for making sth, eg a bomb, explode.

detour /ˈdiːtʊə(r)/ n a route, usu a longer one, that avoids a problem, eg a blocked road, or is taken in order to visit a place: *We had to make a detour round the floods.* ○ *It's well worth making a detour to see this charming village.* See also DIVERSION 2.

detract /dɪˈtrækt/ v ~ **from sth** to make sth seem less good or of lower value: [Vpr] *detract from the merit/value/worth/excellence of sth* ○ *No amount of criticism can detract from her achievements.* ○ *The poor service detracted from my enjoyment of the evening.*
▶ **detractor** n a person who tries to make sb/sth seem less good or valuable by criticizing it: *The scheme is better than its detractors suggest.*

detriment /ˈdetrɪmənt/ n **IDM** **to the detriment of sb/sth**; **without detriment to sb/sth** (*fml*) causing/not causing harm to sb/sth: *He works long hours, to the detriment of his health.* ○ *This tax cannot be introduced without detriment to the economy.*
▶ **detrimental** /ˌdetrɪˈmentl/ adj ~ (**to sth/sb**) harmful: *activities detrimental to our interests* ○ *The recession has **had a detrimental effect on** on business.* **detrimentally** /-təli/ adv.

detritus /dɪˈtraɪtəs/ n [U] **1** (*techn*) material such as sand or GRAVEL produced by the wearing away (WEAR[1]) of rocks, etc. **2** rubbish of any kind: *sweeping up the detritus in the city streets.*

de trop /də ˈtrəʊ/ adj [pred] (*French*) not wanted; not welcome: *Their intimate conversation made me feel distinctly de trop.*

deuce[1] /djuːs; *US* duːs/ n (in tennis) a score of 40–40, after which either side must gain two successive points to win the game.

deuce[2] /djuːs; *US* duːs/ n (*dated infml euph*) **the deuce** [sing] (used in questions to express annoyance): *Who/What/Where the deuce is that?* ○ *What the deuce is going on?* **IDM** **the deuce of a sth** a very bad case of sth: *I had the deuce of a time getting here.*

Deutschmark /ˈdɔɪtʃmaːk/ n (abbr **DM**) the unit of money in Germany.

devalue /ˌdiːˈvæljuː/ v **1** ~ (**sth**) (**against sth**) to reduce the value of a currency in relation to other currencies or to gold: [Vn] *devalue the dollar/pound/lira* [V] *Economists believe that the best solution is to devalue.* [Vpr, Vnpr] *The pound has (been) devalued against the yen.* Compare REVALUE. **2** to reduce the value or worth of sth; to give a lower value to sth: [Vn] *People must not devalue her achievement.* ○ *I would not wish to devalue your contribution to the project.* ▶ **devaluation** /ˌdiːvæljuˈeɪʃn/ n [C,U]: *There has been a further devaluation of the dollar.*

devastate /ˈdevəsteɪt/ v **(a)** to destroy sth completely; to ruin sth: [Vn] *a country devastated by war* ○ *Bombs had devastated the town.* **(b)** (*infml*) (often passive) to cause sb extreme distress; to OVERWHELM (3) sb with grief or shock: [Vn] *She was devastated by (the news of) his death.*
▶ **devastating** /ˈdevəsteɪtɪŋ/ adj **1** causing great destruction: *a devastating war/famine/storm.* **2** causing severe shock, grief or distress: *devastating*

D

criticism/news. **3** (*infml*) very impressive or effective: *devastating wit* ○ *She looked devastating* (ie very beautiful). ○ *He played with devastating effect.* **devastatingly** *adv.*

devastation /ˌdevəˈsteɪʃn/ *n* [U] great destruction: *The storm left scenes of utter devastation.*

develop /dɪˈveləp/ *v* **1** ~ (**sth**) (**from sth**) (**into sth**) to grow or cause sb/sth to grow gradually; to become or make sth larger, more advanced or more organized: [V] *The child is developing well.* ○ *The plot for the novel gradually developed in my mind.* [Vpr] *The argument developed into a bitter quarrel.* ○ *The place has developed from a small fishing village into a thriving tourist centre.* [Vnpr] *We've developed the project from an original idea by Stephen.* [also Vn]. **2** to start or cause sth to start to exist and then become greater: [V] *Symptoms of malaria developed* (ie appeared). [Vn] *The car developed engine trouble and wouldn't start.* ○ *He's developed a fondness for jazz.* **3** to treat an exposed film with chemicals so that the pictures can be seen: [Vn] *take a film to be developed.* **4** to build or change property on an area of land, esp for profit: [Vn] *The site is being developed by a local property company.*

▶ **developed** *adj* **1** advanced; mature: *a highly developed system of agriculture* ○ *She is well developed for her age.* **2** (of a country, an area, etc) having a highly organized economy and political system: *one of the less developed countries* ○ *the developed nations of the world.*

developer *n* **1** [C] a person or company that develops (DEVELOP 4) land: *property developers.* **2** [U] a substance used for developing (DEVELOP 3) films.

developing *adj* (of a country, an area, etc) trying to have more advanced political and economic systems: *a developing country* ○ *the developing world.*

development /dɪˈveləpmənt/ *n* **1** [U] the action or process of developing or being developed: *the healthy development of children* ○ *encourage the development of small businesses* ○ *land that is ripe for development* (ie ready to be built on). **2** [C] (**a**) a new stage or event: *the latest development in the continuing crisis* ○ *We must await further developments.* (**b**) a new product or invention: *Our electrically-powered car is an exciting new development.* **3** [C] a piece of land with new buildings on it: *a commercial development on the outskirts of the town.*

▶ **developmental** /dɪˌveləpˈmentl/ *adj* **1** in a state of developing or being developed: *a product at a developmental stage.* **2** connected with development: *developmental psychology.*

■ **deˈvelopment area** *n* (*Brit*) a poor area where new industries are encouraged in order to create jobs.

deviant /ˈdiːviənt/ *n, adj* (*often derog*) (a person who is) different in moral or social standards from what is considered normal or acceptable: *a sexual deviant* ○ *deviant behaviour.* ▶ **deviance** /-viəns/ *n* [U].

deviate /ˈdiːvieɪt/ *v* ~ (**from sth**) to change from a course of action or from what is normal or usual: [Vpr] *deviate from one's plan/the norm/the subject under discussion* ○ *The plane was forced to deviate from its usual route.* ○ *He never deviated from what he believed to be right.* [also V].

deviation /ˌdiːviˈeɪʃn/ *n* ~ (**from sth**) **1**(**a**) [U] the action of deviating (DEVIATE): *There was little deviation from his usual routine.* ○ *sexual deviation.* (**b**) [C] an instance of this: *a deviation from the rules.* **2** [U] (*politics*) the action of moving away from the beliefs held by the group to which one belongs: *Party ideologists accused her of deviation.* **3** [C] (*techn*) the amount by which a single measurement differs from the average: *a compass deviation of 5°* (ie from true north).

device /dɪˈvaɪs/ *n* **1** a thing made or adapted for a particular purpose: *a device for measuring pressure* ○ *a labour-saving device* ○ *an explosive device* ○ *a nuclear device* (eg a nuclear bomb or missile). ⇨ note at MACHINE. **2** a plan, scheme or trick intended to produce a special effect: *a stylistic device commonly used by the author.* **IDM** **leave sb to their own deˈvices / to themˈselves** to allow sb to do as they wish without attempting to direct or control them: *Pupils were left to their own devices while the teacher was looking for the missing book.*

devil¹ /ˈdevl/ *n* **1**(**a**) **the Devil** (*religion*) the greatest evil being; Satan: *The Devil tempted Adam and Eve.* (**b**) a wicked spirit: *He believes in devils and witches.* **2** (*infml*) (**a**) a wicked or badly behaved person: *My niece is a little devil.* ○ *He's a devil with the ladies.* (**b**) (used for emphasis when expressing an opinion of sb) a person: *The poor/lucky devil!* ○ *Which silly devil left the lights on all day?* **IDM** **be a ˈdevil** (*infml joc*) (used for encouraging sb to do sth they are hesitating to do): *Go on, be a devil — tell me what they said.* **better the devil you know** ⇨ BETTER². **between the ˌdevil and the ˌdeep blue ˈsea** in a situation where there are two equally unacceptable alternatives. **the devil** (used for emphasis in questions, esp to show annoyance): *What/Who/Why/Where the devil is that?* **the (very) ˈdevil** a very difficult or unpleasant thing: *These pans are the (very) devil to clean.* **a devil of a sth** (*infml*) a very difficult or unpleasant thing: *I had a devil of a job/time persuading them to come.* **the ˌdevil take the ˈhindmost** everybody should look after herself or himself and not care about others: *In this business you have to be tough, and the devil take the hindmost.* **go to the ˈdevil!** (*dated*) DAMN³(1b) you!; go away! **like the ˈdevil** (*infml*) very hard; with great energy: *run/work like the devil.* **speak/talk of the ˈdevil** (*infml saying*) (said when sb one has been talking about appears): *Oh, talk of the devil — here he comes now.* **there will be / was the devil / hell to pay** ⇨ PAY².

■ **ˌdevil-may-ˈcare** *adj* [esp attrib] careless and cheerful; RECKLESS: *a devil-may-care attitude to life.*

ˌdevil's ˈadvocate *n* a person who speaks against sb/sth simply to encourage discussion or to make sb justify a view or an argument: *play devil's advocate.*

devil² /ˈdevl/ *v* (**-ll-**; *US* **-l-**) to cook sth in a thick liquid with spices in it: [Vn] *devilled kidneys.*

devilish /ˈdevəlɪʃ/ *adj* wicked; cruel: *a devilish plan* ○ *devilish cunning.*

▶ **devilish** *adv* (*dated infml*) very; extremely: *a devilish hot day.*

devilishly *adv*: *devilishly cruel/difficult.*

devilment /ˈdevlmənt/ (also **devilry** /ˈdevlri/) *n* [U] wildly playful behaviour that often causes trouble; MISCHIEF(1,2): *I'm sure he's up to some devilment or other.* ○ *She played a trick on him out of sheer devilry.*

devious /ˈdiːviəs/ *adj* **1** not honest, direct or STRAIGHTFORWARD(1); CUNNING(1): *a devious lawyer/scheme/trick* ○ *get rich by devious means.* **2** (of a road, path, etc) winding; not straight: *The main road was blocked so we came by a rather devious route.* ▶ **deviously** *adv.* **deviousness** *n* [U].

devise /dɪˈvaɪz/ *v* to create or invent a plan, a system, an object, etc by careful thought: [Vn] *devise a scheme for redeveloping the city centre* ○ *devise a teaching syllabus/a new computer program.*

devoid /dɪˈvɔɪd/ *adj* [pred] ~ **of sth** without sth; completely lacking in sth: *an argument devoid of logic.*

devolution /ˌdiːvəˈluːʃn; *US* ˌdev-/ *n* [U] the transfer of power or authority from a central body to smaller ones, esp from central government to regional authorities.

devolve /dɪ'vɒlv/ v **PHRV** **devolve on/upon sb/sth** (*fml*) (of work or duties) to be transferred or passed to sb/sth at a lower level: *When the President is ill, his duties devolve upon the Vice-President.* **devolve sth to/on/upon sb/sth** (*fml*) to transfer work, duties, etc to sb/sth at a lower level: *More power is to be devolved to regional government.*

devote /dɪ'vəʊt/ v **PHRV** **devote oneself/sth to sb/ sth** to give one's time, energy, etc to sb/sth: *She devoted herself to her career.* ○ *He seems to devote all his efforts to his sporting activities.*
▶ **devoted** *adj* ~ (**to sb/sth**) constantly loving or loyal: *a devoted son/friend/supporter* ○ *She is devoted to her children.* **devotedly** *adv*.

devotee /ˌdevə'tiː/ *n* ~ (**of sth**) (**a**) a person who is extremely keen on sth: *a devotee of sports/jazz/crime fiction.* (**b**) a person who believes strongly in a particular religion, theory, etc: *Catholic devotees* ○ *devotees of alternative medicine.*

devotion /dɪ'vəʊʃn/ *n* **1** [U] ~ (**to sb/sth**) constant strong love for or loyalty to sb/sth: *a mother's devotion to her children* ○ *His devotion to the cause never wavered.* **2** [U] ~ (**to sb/sth**) the action of giving one's time, energy, etc to sb/sth: *devotion to duty* ○ *Her devotion to the job left her with little free time.* **3**(**a**) [U] religious worship; enthusiastic religious activity: *a life of devotion.* (**b**) **devotions** [pl] prayers or other religious practices: *a priest at his devotions* (ie praying).
▶ **devotional** /-ʃənl/ *adj* of or used in religious worship: *devotional literature.*

devour /dɪ'vaʊə(r)/ v **1** to eat sth completely and quickly, esp because of hunger: [Vn] *In no time at all they had devoured the entire loaf.* ○ *an animal devouring its prey.* **2** to read or look at sth eagerly and quickly: [Vn] *In his enthusiasm he devoured everything she had ever written.* **3** to destroy sth: [Vn] *Fire devoured a huge area of forest.* **IDM** **be devoured by sth** to be filled with a strong emotion: *She was devoured by the desire to succeed.*

devout /dɪ'vaʊt/ *adj* **1** believing strongly in and always obeying the rules of a particular religion: *a devout Muslim.* **2** sincere; deeply felt: *a devout hope/ wish.* ▶ **devoutly** *adv*: *devoutly Christian* ○ *I devoutly hope he does come.* **devoutness** *n* [U].

dew /djuː; *US* duː/ *n* [U] tiny drops of water that form on cool surfaces outdoors when the air is damp, esp at night: *The grass was wet with dew.*
▶ **dewy** *adj* wet with dew. ˌ**dewy-**'**eyed** *adj* **1** innocent and trusting: *He's far too dewy-eyed to succeed in business.* **2** sentimental: *She goes all dewy-eyed when she talks about her early days in show business.*

dexterity /dek'sterəti/ *n* [U] (**a**) skill in using one's hands: *A juggler needs great dexterity.* (**b**) the ability to do sth skilfully and cleverly: *mental/verbal/ political/musical dexterity.*

dexterous (also **dextrous**) /'dekstrəs/ *adj* (**a**) skilful with one's hands. (**b**) skilfully and cleverly done: *a dextrous move/flick of the wrist.* ▶ **dexterously** (also **dextrously**) *adv*.

dextrose /'dekstrəʊz, -əʊs/ *n* [U] (*chemistry*) a form of GLUCOSE.

DFE /ˌdiː ef 'iː/ *abbr* (in Britain) Department for Education.

di- *pref* **1** (with *ns*) two; double. **2** (*chemistry*) (with *ns* in names of chemical compounds) containing two atoms or groups of the specified type: *dioxide*. Compare BI-, TRI-.

diabetes /ˌdaɪə'biːtiːz/ *n* [U] a disease in which sugar and STARCH are not properly absorbed from the blood.

diabetic /ˌdaɪə'betɪk/ *adj* **1** having or related to DIABETES: *His father is diabetic.* ○ *a diabetic problem.* **2** suitable for a person who has diabetes: *a diabetic diet.*

▶ **diabetic** *n* a person who has diabetes.

diabolic /ˌdaɪə'bɒlɪk/ *adj* (**a**) of or like a devil. (**b**) clever and evil; wicked: *a diabolic plan/trick* ○ *diabolic cunning.*

diabolical /ˌdaɪə'bɒlɪkl/ *adj* **1** (*infml esp Brit*) very bad or annoying: *The film was diabolical.* ○ *What diabolical weather!* **2** = DIABOLIC. ▶ **diabolically** /-kli/ *adv*.

diadem /'daɪədem/ *n* a crown, worn as a sign of royal power.

diagnose /'daɪəgnəʊz; *US* -nəʊs/ *v* ~ **sth** (**as sth**) to identify the nature of a problem, esp an illness: [Vn] *The mechanic quickly diagnosed the fault.* ○ *The doctor diagnosed measles.* [Vn-n] *Her illness was diagnosed as a mild form of pneumonia.*

diagnosis /ˌdaɪəg'nəʊsɪs/ *n* (*pl* **diagnoses** /-siːz/) [C, U] the act of identifying the nature of a problem, esp an illness: *We are still waiting for the doctor's diagnosis.* ○ *accurate diagnosis of an electrical fault.* Compare PROGNOSIS.

diagnostic /ˌdaɪəg'nɒstɪk/ *adj* [usu attrib] connected with identifying the nature of a problem, esp an illness: *diagnostic skill/tests* ○ *symptoms that were of little diagnostic value* (ie that did not help to identify the patient's disease).
▶ **diagnostic** *n* **1** [C] (*computing*) a PROGRAM used for identifying a computer fault. **2** **diagnostics** [sing *v*] the study of diagnosing (DIAGNOSE) diseases.

diagonal /daɪ'ægənl/ *adj* (**a**) (of a straight line) joining two sides of sth at an angle. ▷ picture at VERTICAL. See also HORIZONTAL. (**b**) (of a line) straight and at an angle: *diagonal stripes.*
▶ **diagonal** *n* a straight line that joins two sides of sth at an angle; a straight line that is at an angle. **diagonally** /-nəli/ *adv*.

diagram /'daɪəgræm/ *n* a drawing or plan that uses simple lines rather than realistic details to explain or illustrate a machine, a structure, a process, etc: *a diagram of a gear-box/rail network.* ▶ **diagrammatic** /ˌdaɪəgrə'mætɪk/ *adj*: *a diagrammatic map.* **diagrammatically** /-kli/ *adv*.

dial /'daɪəl/ *n* **1** the face of a clock or watch. See also SUNDIAL. **2** a similar face or flat plate with a scale and a pointer for indicating a measurement of weight, volume, pressure, the amount of gas used, etc: *the dial of an electricity meter.* **3**(**a**) a plate or disc, etc on a radio or television that is used for selecting programmes, etc. (**b**) a similar device on other types of equipment, eg a washing-machine. **4** a disc with numbered holes on a telephone that is turned when making a call.
▶ **dial** *v* (**-ll-**; *US* **-l-**) to use a telephone by turning the dial or pushing buttons to call a number: [Vn] *Dial 0171 first for central London.* ○ *dial the operator* [also V]. '**dialling code** (*Brit*) (*US* '**area code**) *n* the numbers for an area or a country that are dialled before the number of the person one wants to speak to: *The dialling code for inner London is 0171.* '**dialling tone** (*Brit*) (*US* '**dial tone**) *n* the sound made by a telephone showing that one can begin to dial the number wanted.

dialect /'daɪəlekt/ *n* [C, U] the form of a language used in a part of a country or by a class of people with grammar, words and pronunciation that may be different from other forms of the same language: *the Yorkshire dialect* ○ *a play written in dialect* ○ *dialect words/pronunciations.* Compare ACCENT 3. ▶ **dialectal** /ˌdaɪə'lektl/ *adj*: *dialectal differences between two areas.*

dialectic /ˌdaɪə'lektɪk/ *n* [U] (also **dialectics** [sing *v*]) (*philosophy*) the art of discovering and testing truths by discussion and logical argument. ▶ **dialectical** /-kl/ *adj*: *dialectical method.*

dialogue (*US* also **dialog**) /'daɪəlɒg; *US* -lɔːg/ *n* **1** [U, C] spoken or written conversation or talk: *Most*

plays are written in dialogue. ○ *a novel with long descriptions and little dialogue* ○ *a long dialogue in the opening scene.* Compare MONOLOGUE, SOLILOQUY.
2 [C,U] a discussion between people in which opinions are exchanged: *a constructive dialogue on common problems* ○ *More dialogue between world leaders is needed.*

dialysis /daɪˈæləsɪs/ *n* (*pl* **-lyses** /-ləsiːz/) [U,C] (*medical*) the process of making blood pure by passing it through a MEMBRANE(2), used esp for treating people with damaged kidneys (KIDNEY 1): *renal dialysis* ○ *a dialysis machine.*

diamanté /ˌdiːəˈmɒnteɪ; *US* -mɒnˈteɪ/ *adj* decorated with crystal in powder form or some other substance that sparkles (SPARKLE 1): *diamanté earrings.*

diameter /daɪˈæmɪtə(r)/ *n* **1** a straight line connecting the centre of a circle or any other round object to two points on its sides: *the diameter of a tree-trunk.* ⇨ picture at CIRCLE. Compare RADIUS 1. **2** (*techn*) a measurement of how much larger sth appears when seen through a particular instrument: *a lens that magnifies 20 diameters* (ie makes an object look 20 times longer, wider, etc than it is).

diametrically /ˌdaɪəˈmetrɪkli/ *adv* completely; entirely: *We hold diametrically opposed/opposite views.*

diamond /ˈdaɪəmənd/ *n* **1(a)** [U,C] a transparent precious stone of pure CARBON(1) in crystal form, the hardest substance known, used esp in jewellery: *a ring with a diamond in it* ○ *a diamond ring/necklace.* See also ROUGH DIAMOND. **(b)** [C] a piece of this, often artificially made, used in industry, esp for cutting glass. **2** [C] a figure with four equal sides and with angles that are not right angles (RIGHT[1]). **3(a)** diamonds [sing or pl *v*] one of the four suits (SUIT[1] 2) in a pack of cards. The cards in this suit are marked with red diamond shapes: *the five of diamonds.* ⇨ picture at PLAYING-CARD. **(b)** [C] a card of this suit: *play a diamond.* **4** [C] (in baseball) the space inside the lines connecting the bases (BASE[1] 8).
■ **diamond jubilee** *n* (usu *sing*) the 60th anniversary of sth, or a celebration of it. Compare GOLDEN JUBILEE, SILVER JUBILEE.
diamond wedding *n* (usu *sing*) the 60th anniversary of a wedding. Compare GOLDEN WEDDING, SILVER WEDDING.

diaper /ˈdaɪəpə(r); *US* ˈdaɪpər/ *n* **1** [C] (*US*) = NAPPY. **2** [U] a LINEN(1) or cotton fabric with a pattern of small diamonds on it.

diaphanous /daɪˈæfənəs/ *adj* (of fabric) light, very fine and almost transparent: *a diaphanous veil.*

diaphragm /ˈdaɪəfræm/ *n* **1** the wall of muscle, between the chest and the stomach, that helps to control breathing. ⇨ picture at RESPIRATORY. **2** (*Brit* also **Dutch cap, cap**) a thin piece of plastic or rubber that is fitted over the narrow part of the WOMB to prevent SPERM entering it during sex(2a). **3** any thin sheet of material used to separate the parts of a machine, etc.

diarrhoea (*US* **diarrhea**) /ˌdaɪəˈrɪə; *US* -ˈriːə/ *n* [U] an illness in which waste matter is emptied from the bowels frequently and in a liquid form: *have a bad attack of diarrhoea* ○ *sickness and diarrhoea.*

diary /ˈdaɪəri/ *n* **1** a book, sometimes with spaces for each day of the year, in which one writes about one's daily experiences, records one's private thoughts, etc: *Old diaries tell us much about social history.* ○ *Do you keep a diary* (ie write in one regularly)? **2** (*US* **calendar**) a book with spaces for each day of the year, in which one can write down appointments, things to be done in the future, etc: *a desk diary* ○ *Make a note of the next meeting in your diary.*
▶ **diarist** /ˈdaɪərɪst/ *n* a person who writes a diary, esp one that is later published.

diaspora /daɪˈæspərə/ *n* [sing] (*fml*) the process by which people of a particular nation become scattered and settle in other countries, esp (**the Diaspora**) the Jews who left ancient Palestine in this way.

diatonic /ˌdaɪəˈtɒnɪk/ *adj* (*music*) using the notes of the appropriate major or minor scale.

diatribe /ˈdaɪətraɪb/ *n* ~ (**against sb/sth**) a long and angry attack in speech or writing: *launch a diatribe against the government.*

dice /daɪs/ *n* (*pl* unchanged) **(a)** [C] a small cube(1) of wood, plastic, etc used in games of chance. Each side of a dice has a different number of spots on it, from one to six. The side that faces upwards after the dice is thrown represents the player's score: *a pair of dice* ○ *shake/roll/throw the dice.* ⇨ picture. **(b)** [U] any game played with dice: *play dice.* **load the dice** ⇨ LOAD[2]. **no dice** (*sl esp US*) no agreement to sth requested: *I asked him if he'd lend us the money — no dice* (ie he refused), *I'm afraid.*
▶ **dice** *v* to cut meat, vegetables, etc into small cubes (CUBE 1): [Vn] *diced cucumber/cheese/beef.* **dice with death** (*infml*) to risk one's life.

dicey /ˈdaɪsi/ *adj* (**dicier, diciest**) (*infml*) risky; dangerous: *The fog made driving a bit dicey.*

dichotomy /daɪˈkɒtəmi/ *n* ~ (**between A and B**) (*fml*) a separation between two groups or things that are opposite, entirely different, etc: *the dichotomy between good and evil* ○ *They set up a false dichotomy between working and raising a family* (ie wrongly claimed that one cannot do both).

dick /dɪk/ *n* (△ *sl*) **1** a man's PENIS. **2** (also **dickhead**) (*derog*) a stupid or worthless person. See also CLEVER DICK.

dickens /ˈdɪkɪnz/ *n* **the dickens** (*dated infml euph*) (used instead of *the devil* to give emphasis, esp in questions): *Who/What/Where the dickens is that?* ○ *We had the dickens of a job finding the place.*

Dickensian /dɪˈkenziən/ *adj* of or like the novels of Charles Dickens, which often describe odd characters and bad social conditions: *a Dickensian slum.*

dicky /ˈdɪki/ *adj* (**-ier, -iest**) (*dated Brit infml*) not strong or healthy: *have a dicky heart.*

dicky-bird /ˈdɪki bɜːd/ *n* (used by or when speaking to young children) a bird. **not say, hear, etc a dicky-bird** (*Brit infml*) to say, hear, etc nothing: *'Did he say anything?' 'Not a dicky-bird.'*

dictate /dɪkˈteɪt; *US* ˈdɪkteɪt/ *v* **1** ~ (**sth**) (**to sb**) to say or read aloud words to be typed, written down or recorded on tape: [Vn,Vnpr] *dictate a letter* (*to one's secretary*) [Vnpr] *The teacher dictated a passage to the class.* [V] *I dictate and he takes it down in shorthand.* [also Vpr]. **2** ~ **sth** (**to sb**) to state or order sth with the force of authority: [Vnpr] *dictate terms to a defeated enemy* [V.that] *The law dictates that everyone be treated equally.* [also Vn]. **3** to control the outcome of sth; to determine sth: [Vn] *The size of the building is dictated by the strength of the foundations.* [V.wh] *Your job generally dictates where you live.* **PHRV dic'tate to sb** (esp passive) to give orders to sb, esp in a way that is not acceptable: *I refuse to be dictated to by you.* ○ *You can't dictate to people how they should live.*
▶ **dictate** *n* /ˈdɪkteɪt/ (usu *pl*) a command, esp one that reason, conscience, etc urges one to obey: *It is best to follow the dictates of common sense* (ie do what seems sensible).

dictation /dɪkˈteɪʃn/ *n* **1** [U] the action of speaking so that sb can write what one says: *He spoke at dictation speed.* **2** [C,U] a test in which people have to write down a passage that is read aloud, as a way of helping them to learn a language: *Our teacher gave us an English dictation.* ○ *I'm good at dictation.*

dictator /dɪkˈteɪtə(r); *US* ˈdɪkteɪtər/ *n* **1** a ruler who has total power over his country, esp one who has obtained it by force and uses it in a cruel way. **2** a person who insists that people do what he or she wants: *Our boss is a real dictator.*
▶ **dictatorial** /ˌdɪktəˈtɔːrɪəl/ *adj* of or like a dictator: *dictatorial government/powers* ○ *a dictatorial teacher/manner/tone.* **dictatorially** /-əli/ *adv.*
dictatorship *n* (**a**) [C, U] (a period of) government by a dictator. (**b**) [C] a country ruled by a dictator.

diction /ˈdɪkʃn/ *n* [U] (**a**) a style or manner of speaking: *Clarity of diction is vital for a public speaker.* (**b**) the choice and use of words: *the simple diction of her poetry.*

dictionary /ˈdɪkʃənri; *US* -neri/ *n* (**a**) a book that gives the words of a language in alphabetical (ALPHABET) order and explains their meaning, or translates them into another language: *an English dictionary* ○ *a German-French dictionary.* (**b**) a similar book that explains the terms of a particular subject: *a dictionary of architecture.*

dictum /ˈdɪktəm/ *n* (*pl* **dicta** /-tə/ or **dictums**) a short, often well-known, statement; a saying (SAY): *the famous dictum of Descartes: 'I think, therefore I am.'*

did *pt* of DO[1,2]. ⇨ note at DO[1].

didactic /daɪˈdæktɪk/ *adj* (*fml*) **1** designed for the purpose of teaching sth: *didactic poetry/methods.* **2** (*usu derog*) seeming to treat the reader, audience, etc like a child in school: *I don't like her didactic way of explaining everything.* ▶ **didactically** /-kli/ *adv.*

diddle /ˈdɪdl/ *v* ~ **sb** (**out of sth**) (*infml esp Brit*) to cheat sb, esp in small matters: [Vn] *I've been diddled! Half of these tomatoes are bad!* [Vnpr] *They tried to diddle me out of my share of the money.*

didn't /ˈdɪdnt/ *short form* did not. ⇨ note at DO[1].

die¹ /daɪ/ *v* (*pt, pp* **died**; *pres p* **dying**) **1**(**a**) to stop living; to come to the end of one's life: [Vpr] *die of cancer/hunger/grief* ○ (*fig infml*) *I almost died of embarrassment.* ○ *die from a wound* ○ *die by violence* ○ *die by one's own hand* (ie kill oneself) ○ *die for one's country* ○ *die in battle* [V] *I'll love you till the day I die.* ○ *Flowers soon die without water.* (**b**) to be sth when one dies: [V-adj] *die happy/young* [V-n] *die a beggar/martyr.* (**c**) to have a particular kind of death: [Vn] *die a lingering/natural/violent death.* **2** to stop existing; to disappear: [V] *love that will never die* ○ *dying traditions/customs* ○ *His secret died with him* (ie He died without telling it to anyone). ○ *The flame flickered and died* (ie went out). See also DYING². **⬛ be dying for sth / to do sth** (*infml*) to want sth or want to do sth very much: *I'm dying for a drink.* ○ *We're dying to know where you've been.* **die the ˈdeath** (*joc*) to end suddenly and completely: *After getting bad reviews the play quickly died the death.* **die ˈhard** to change or disappear very slowly: *Old habits die hard.* **die in one's ˈbed** to die of old age or illness. **die/fall/drop like flies** ⇨ FLY². **never say die** ⇨ SAY. **PHRV ˌdie aˈway** to become so faint or weak as to be no longer noticeable: *The noise of the car died away in the distance.* ○ *The breeze has died away.* **ˌdie ˈdown** to become gradually less strong, loud, noticeable, etc: *The flames/ storm/pain finally died down.* ○ *These rumours will soon die down.* **ˌdie ˈoff** to die one after another: *The members of the family had all died off.* **ˌdie ˈout 1** (of a family, species, etc) to have no members left alive: *The moth has nearly died out because its habitat is being destroyed.* **2** (of a custom, practice, etc) to be no longer common: *The old traditions are dying out.*
■ **ˈdie-hard** *n* a person who strongly opposes change and new ideas: *A few die-hards are trying to stop the reforms.* ○ *die-hard Communists.*

die² /daɪ/ *n* a block of hard metal with a design, etc cut into it. Dies are used for shaping other pieces of metal, eg coins, or for stamping designs on paper, leather, etc.

die³ /daɪ/ *n* (*dated*) = DICE. **⬛ the die is cast** (*saying*) a decision has been made and cannot be changed.

diesel /ˈdiːzl/ *n* **1** [C] (also **ˈdiesel engine**) an engine that burns oil as fuel, used eg for buses and trains: *a diesel lorry/truck/train.* **2** (also **ˈdiesel fuel**, **ˈdiesel oil**) [U] a heavy fuel oil used in diesel engines: *diesel-powered boats.* **3** [C] a train, motor vehicle or ship that uses diesel fuel.

diet /ˈdaɪət/ *n* **1** [C, U] the food that a person, community, etc habitually eats and drinks: *the Japanese diet of rice, vegetables and fish* ○ *eat a balanced diet* (ie a variety of healthy foods) ○ *illnesses caused by poor diet.* **2** [C] a limited variety or amount of food that a person is allowed to eat and drink, eg for medical reasons or in order to lose weight: *a salt-free diet* ○ *diet drinks* ○ *The doctor has told me to go on a diet* (eg to lose weight). **3** [sing] ~ **of sth** a regular occupation or series of activities to which one is restricted: *Children nowadays are brought up on a constant diet of television soap operas and quiz shows.*
▶ **diet** *v* to eat only some foods or a little food, esp to lose weight: [V] *You ought to diet and get more exercise.* ○ *a magazine article about dieting.*
dietary /ˈdaɪətəri; *US* -eri/ *adj* [usu attrib]: *dietary advice/habits/requirements.*
dieter *n* a person who diets.
dietetics *n* [sing *v*] the science of diet and NUTRITION.
dietician (also **dietitian**) /ˌdaɪəˈtɪʃn/ *n* an expert in the study of diet and NUTRITION.

differ /ˈdɪfə(r)/ *v* **1** ~ (**from sb/sth**) to be not the same as sb/sth; to be UNLIKE(1) sb/sth: [V] *have differing opinions/views* ○ *My parents differ widely in their tastes.* ○ *Tastes differ* (ie Different people like different things). [Vpr, V] *In this respect, French differs from English/French and English differ.* **2** ~ (**with/from sb**) (**about/on/over sth**) to disagree; not to share the same opinion: [Vpr] *I have to differ with you on that.* ○ *We differ over many things.* [also V]. **⬛ agree to differ** ⇨ AGREE. **I beg to differ** ⇨ BEG.

difference /ˈdɪfrəns/ *n* **1** [C] ~ (**between A and B**) the state or way in which two people or things are not the same, or in which sb/sth has changed: *There are marked differences between the two children.* ○ *Have you noticed a difference in her recently?* ○ *It's easy to **tell the difference** (ie distinguish) between butter and margarine.* **2** [C, U] ~ (**in sth**) (**between A and B**) the amount or degree to which two things are not the same or sth has changed: *There's an age difference of six years between them* (ie One of them is six years older than the other). ○ *I'll lend you 90% of the money and you'll have to find the difference* (ie the other 10%). ○ *We measured the difference(s) in temperature.* ○ *There's not much difference in price between the two computers.* **3** [C] ~ (**between A and B**) (**over sth**) a disagreement, often involving an argument: *Why don't you **settle your differences** and be friends again?* ○ *There was a **difference of opinion** over who had won.* **⬛ as near as makes no difference** ⇨ NEAR². **for all the ˈdifference it/sth makes** taking into account how little difference it/sth makes. **make a, no, some, etc difference (to sb/sth) 1** to have an, no, some, etc effect on sb/sth: *The rain didn't make much difference (to the game).* ○ *The sea air has made a big difference to* (ie greatly improved) *her health.* ○ *A hot shower makes all the difference* (ie makes you feel better) *in the morning.* **2** to be important, not important, etc to sb/sth; to matter: *It makes no difference (to me) what you say: I'm not going.* ○ *It* *won't make much difference whether you go today or tomorrow.* ○ *Does that make any difference* (ie Is it important, need we consider it)*?* ○ *Yes, it makes all the difference* (ie it is very important). **sink one's differences** ⇨ SINK¹. **split the difference** ⇨ SPLIT. **with a ˈdifference** (following *ns*) special; unusual: *She's an opera singer with a difference: she can act as well!*

different /ˈdɪfrənt/ *adj* **1** ~ (**from/to sb/sth**); (*esp US*) ~ (**than sb/sth**) not the same as sb/sth: *the same product with a different name* ○ *The room looks different with the furniture gone.* ○ *Their tastes are different from/to mine.* ○ *She is wearing a different dress every time I see her.* **2** separate; distinct: *I called on three different occasions, but he was out.* ○ *They are sold in different colours* (ie in a variety of colours). **3** unusual; new(2): *The flavour was really different.* ○ *I'm bored with going to the pub — let's do something different.* **IDM** (**as**) ˌdifferent as ˌchalk and/from ˈcheese (*Brit*) completely different. **a (very) different kettle of fish** (*infml*) a completely different person or thing from the one previously mentioned. **know different/otherwise** ⇨ KNOW. **on a different / the same wavelength** ⇨ WAVELENGTH. **sing a different song/tune** ⇨ SING. ▶ **differently** *adv*.

<hr>

NOTE American and British English differ in their use of prepositions after **different**.

Before a noun or an adverbial phrase, both **different from** and **different to** are used in British English: *Paul's very different from/to his brother.* ○ *This visit is very different from/to last time.* In American English people also say **different than**. **To** is not used: *Your trains are different than/from ours.* ○ *You look different than before.*

People also say **different than** instead of **different from** before a clause, especially in American English: *She looked very different from what I'd expected/than what I'd expected.*

differential /ˌdɪfəˈrenʃl/ *adj* [attrib] of, showing or depending on a difference: *differential treatment of prisoners.*
▶ **differential** *n* **1** (*esp Brit*) a difference between amounts of sth, esp pay or money: *pay/tax/price differentials* ○ *a dispute about the differential between men and women workers.* **2** (also ˌdifferential ˈgear) a gear that makes it possible for a vehicle's back wheels to turn at different speeds when going round corners. ⇨ picture at CAR.

differentiate /ˌdɪfəˈrenʃieɪt/ *v* **1**(a) ~ between A and B; ~ A (from B) to see or show that two things are different: [Vpr] *Can you differentiate between the two varieties?* [Vnpr] *you have to differentiate between those who can't pay and those who won't.* ○ *Can you differentiate one variety from the other?* [also Vn]. (b) ~ sth (from sth) to be a mark of difference between people or things: [Vn, Vnpr] *The male's orange beak differentiates it (from the female).* **2** ~ between A and B to treat people or things in a different way, esp unfairly; to DISCRIMINATE(1): [Vpr] *It is wrong to differentiate between people according to their family background.* ▶ **differentiation** /ˌdɪfərenʃiˈeɪʃn/ *n* [U].

difficult /ˈdɪfɪkəlt/ *adj* **1**(a) ~ (**to do sth**) requiring effort or skill to solve, understand, etc; not easy: *a difficult problem/language/translation* ○ *She finds it difficult to stop smoking.* ○ *This mountain is difficult to climb/It is difficult to climb this mountain.* (b) causing problems or trouble: *Their refusal puts us in a difficult position.* ○ *They made it difficult for me to see her.* ○ *Thirteen is a difficult age* (ie Children have problems then). **2** (of people) not easy to please or satisfy; not willing to COOPERATE(2): *a difficult child/customer/boss* ○ *Don't take any notice of her — she's just being difficult.*

difficulty /ˈdɪfɪkəlti/ *n* **1** [U] ~ (**in sth/in doing sth**) the state or quality of being difficult; the trouble or effort that sth involves: *the sheer difficulty of the task* ○ *Bad planning will lead to difficulty later.* ○ *do sth with/without difficulty* ○ *She got the door open, but only with some difficulty.* ○ *be working under some difficulty* (ie in difficult circumstances) ○ *I had the greatest difficulty in persuading her.* ○ *We had no difficulty (in) finding the house.* **2** [C usu *pl*] a difficult thing to do, understand or deal with: *the difficulties of English syntax* ○ *children with learning difficulties* ○ *financial difficulties* (ie problems about money) ○ *We got into difficulty/difficulties with the rent* (ie found it hard to pay).

diffident /ˈdɪfɪdənt/ *adj* ~ (**about sth**) not having or showing much confidence in one's own abilities; shy: *an able but diffident young student.* ▶ **diffidence** /-dəns/ *n* [U]: *She overcame her natural diffidence and spoke with great frankness.* **diffidently** *adv*.

diffract /dɪˈfrækt/ *v* [Vn] (*techn*) to break up a beam of light into a series of dark and light bands or into the different colours of the SPECTRUM(1). ▶ **diffraction** /dɪˈfrækʃn/ *n* [U].

diffuse¹ /dɪˈfjuːz/ *v* **1** to spread sth or become spread widely in all directions: [Vn] *On a cloudy day, sunlight is diffused and shadows are paler.* ○ *Social planning has led to greater equality and a more diffused prosperity.* [also V]. **2** (*techn*) (of gases and liquids) to become slowly mixed with sth: [V] *The milk diffused in the water, making it cloudy.* ▶ **diffusion** /dɪˈfjuːʒn/ *n* [U]: *the diffusion of information/power/wealth* ○ *the diffusion of gases and liquids.*

diffuse² /dɪˈfjuːs/ *adj* **1** widely spread out; not concentrated; general: *diffuse light* ○ *diffuse opinions.* **2** not clear or easy to understand; not CONCISE: *a diffuse writer/style* ○ *The evidence is too diffuse.* ▶ **diffusely** *adv*. **diffuseness** *n* [U].

dig¹ /dɪɡ/ *v* (**-gg-**; *pt, pp* **dug** /dʌɡ/) **1**(a) to use one's hands, a SPADE¹, a machine, etc to break up and move earth, etc; to make one's way by doing this: [V] *I spent the morning digging.* [Vp] *They are digging through the hill to make a tunnel.* [Vp] *dig down into the soil* [Vn] *It is difficult to dig the ground when it is frozen.* [Vnp] *dig the soil away (from the roots)* [Vnpr] *dig the manure into the soil.* ⇨ picture at SPADE¹. (b) to make a hole, etc by doing this: [Vn] *dig a pit/tunnel/shaft.* (c) ~ **for sth** to search for sth by doing this: [Vpr] *dig for mineral deposits.* **2** (*dated infml*) to enjoy, appreciate or understand sth: [Vn] *I don't dig modern jazz.* **IDM** **dig one's ˈheels/ˈtoes in** to resist sth in a STUBBORN(1) way; to refuse to change one's ideas or plans. **dig sb in the ribs** to push or PROD(1) sb in the side, eg to attract their attention. **dig (deep) in/into one's pocket(s)** to spend (more of) one's own money on sth. **dig one's own ˈgrave** to do sth which causes one to fail or be ruined. **PHRV** ˌdig ˈin; ˌdig ˈinto sth (*infml*) **1** to begin to eat sth enthusiastically: *The food's ready, so dig in!* **2** to push or POKE¹(1) into sth: *The stiff collar dug into my neck.* ˌdig sth ˈin; ˌdig sth ˈinto sth **1** to mix sth with soil by digging: *The manure should be well dug in.* **2** to push sth into sth: *She dug a spoon into the vegetables and put a large helping on her plate.* ○ *The rider dug his spurs into the horse's flank.* ○ *The dog dug its teeth in.* ˌdig oneself ˈin **1** (*military*) (of soldiers) to dig a TRENCH, etc for protection against attack. **2** (*infml*) to establish oneself securely in a place, job, etc.

ˌdig sb/sth ˈout (of sth) **1** to get sb/sth out by digging: *They dug the potatoes out (of the ground).* ○ *He was buried by an avalanche and had to be dug out.* **2** to get sth by searching or study: *dig information out of books and reports* ○ *dig out the truth.* **3**

<hr>

[V.*to* inf] = verb + *to* infinitive   [Vn.inf (no *to*)] = verb + noun + infinitive without *to*   [V.*ing*] = verb + *-ing* form

(*infml*) to take out sth that is difficult to find or get at: *I dug out this old photo (from my desk).*

,dig sth 'over to prepare ground thoroughly by digging: *dig the garden over.*

,dig sth 'up **1** to break up soil, etc by digging: *dig up land for a new garden.* **2** to remove sth from the ground by digging: *We dug up the tree by its roots.* ○ *An old Roman coin was dug up here last month.* **3** to discover information, etc; to reveal sth: *Newspapers love to dig up scandal.*

dig² /dɪg/ **1(a)** a push or POKE¹ with one's finger, etc: *give sb a **dig in the ribs.*** (**b**) ~ (**at sb**) a remark that is meant to irritate or upset sb: *She's always making mean little digs at him.* **2(a)** an act of digging. (**b**) the exploring of a place for the purpose of ARCHAEOLOGY: *go on (ie take part in) a dig.*

digest¹ /'daɪdʒest/ *n* a brief account; a summary: *a digest of the week's news.*

digest² /daɪ'dʒest, dɪ-/ *v* **1(a)** to change food in the stomach and bowels so that it can be used by the body: [Vn] *Some foods take longer to digest.* (**b**) (of food) to be changed in this way: [V] *It takes hours for a meal to digest.* **2** to take information in mentally; to understand sth fully: [Vn] *Have you digested the report yet?*

▶ **digestible** /daɪ'dʒestəbl, dɪ-/ *adj* that can be digested (DIGEST² 1a).

digestion /daɪ'dʒestʃən, dɪ-/ *n* (**a**) [U] the process of digesting (DIGEST² 1a) food: *Drink tea with your meal as an aid to digestion.* (**b**) [C usu *sing*] the ability to (DIGEST² 1) food: *have a good/poor digestion.*

the digestive system

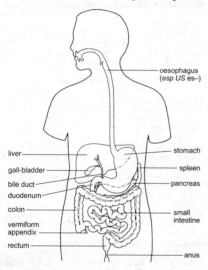

oesophagus
(*esp US* es–)

liver
gall-bladder
bile duct
duodenum
colon
vermiform
appendix
rectum

stomach
spleen
pancreas
small
intestine
anus

digestive /daɪ'dʒestɪv, dɪ-/ *adj* [usu attrib] of the DIGESTION of food: *the digestive process/juices* ○ *suffer from digestive trouble.*

■ di'gestive biscuit (also **digestive**) *n* (*Brit*) a biscuit made from WHOLEMEAL flour.

di'gestive system *n* the organs of the body that DIGEST²(1a) food. ⇨ picture.

digger /'dɪgə(r)/ *n* **1** a person who digs. **2** a large machine used for digging.

digit /'dɪdʒɪt/ *n* **1** (*mathematics*) any of the ten numbers from 0 to 9: *The number 57306 contains five digits.* **2** (*anatomy*) a finger, thumb or toe.

digital /'dɪdʒɪtl/ *adj* **1** showing amounts by means of numbers. **2** of fingers or toes.

■ ,digital 'clock, ,digital 'watch *ns* a clock or watch that shows the time by numbers rather than hands .

,digital com'puter *n* a device that calculates, etc with data represented as a series of 0s and 1s. Compare ANALOGUE 2.

,digital re'cording *n* (**a**) [C] a recording in which sounds are represented by a series of digits indicating the presence or absence of an electronic signal. (**b**) [U] the process of making such a recording.

dignify /'dɪgnɪfaɪ/ *v* (*pt, pp* -**fied**) (*fml*) **1** to make sth seem worthy or impressive; to give dignity to sth: [Vn] *The ceremony was dignified by the presence of the ambassador.* **2** ~ **sb/sth** (**with sth**) to give an impressive name to sb/sth that is not very important or valuable: [Vnpr] *Is it not a misnomer to dignify such works with the term Art?* [also Vn].

▶ **dignified** *adj* having or showing dignity: *a dignified person/manner/voice* ○ *Throughout his trial he maintained a dignified silence.*

dignitary /'dɪgnɪtəri; *US* -teri/ *n* (*fml*) a person with a high rank or position: *local dignitaries* (eg the MAYOR, council members, etc).

dignity /'dɪgnəti/ *n* **1** [U] a calm or serious manner or style: *She kept her dignity despite the booing.* **2** [U] the quality of being worthy of honour or respect: *the dignity of labour* ○ *Only a truly free person has human dignity.* **3** [C] (*fml*) a high or honourable rank or position: *The Queen conferred the dignity of a peerage on him.* **IDM** be,neath one's 'dignity (*often ironic*) below one's social, moral, etc standards: *Some husbands still think it beneath their dignity to do the shopping.* ,stand on one's 'dignity to insist on behaving or being treated in a special way because one thinks that one is important: *She never stands on her dignity with those who work for her, but treats them as friends and colleagues.*

digress /daɪ'gres/ *v* ~ (**from sth**) to leave the main subject temporarily in speech or writing: [V, Vpr] *If I may digress (from my theme) for a moment, the following story may interest you.* ▶ **digression** /daɪ'greʃn/ *n* [U, C]: *The book can be enjoyed for its digressions.*

digs /dɪgz/ *n* [pl] (*Brit infml*) a room or rooms rented in sb else's house; lodgings: *leave home and go into digs* ○ *living in digs.*

dike¹ (also **dyke**) /daɪk/ *n* **1** a ditch for allowing water to flow away from land. **2** a long wall of earth, etc to keep back water and prevent flooding.

dike² (also **dyke**) /daɪk/ *n* (*sl usu offensive*) a LESBIAN.

diktat /'dɪktæt/ *n* [C, U] (*derog*) an order, given eg by a ruler or a foreign power, that people are forced to obey: *another EU diktat from Brussels* ○ *law by diktat.*

dilapidated /dɪ'læpɪdeɪtɪd/ *adj* (of furniture, buildings, etc) falling to pieces; in a bad state of repair: *a dilapidated chair/bed* ○ *a dilapidated-looking car.* ▶ **dilapidation** /dɪ,læpɪ'deɪʃn/ *n* [U]: *in a dreadful state of dilapidation.*

dilate /daɪ'leɪt/ *v* to become or make sth wider, larger or further open: [V] *The pupils of your eyes dilate when you enter a dark room.* ○ *The horse reared up, its nostrils dilated with fear.* **PHRV dilate on sth** (*fml*) to speak or write about sth for a long time. ▶ **dilation** /daɪ'leɪʃn/ *n* [U].

dilatory /'dɪlətəri; *US* -tɔːri/ *adj* (*fml*) ~ (**in doing sth**) slow in acting; causing delay: *The government has been dilatory in condemning the outrage.* ○ *dilatory behaviour/actions.*

dilemma /dɪ'lemə, daɪ-/ *n* a situation in which one has to choose between two undesirable things or courses of action: *be in/place sb in a dilemma* ○ *a moral/ethical dilemma.* **IDM** on the horns of a dilemma ⇨ HORN.

dilettante /,dɪlə'tænti/ *n* (*pl* dilettanti /-tiː/ or dilettantes) (*usu derog*) a person who studies or does sth, but without serious interest or understanding: *a musical dilettante* ∘ *a dilettante attitude.*

diligence /'dɪlɪdʒəns/ *n* [U] steady effort; careful hard work: *She shows great diligence in her school work.*

diligent /'dɪlɪdʒənt/ *adj* showing care and effort in one's work or duties: *a diligent worker/student* ∘ *The letter was found after a diligent search in the files.* ► **diligently** *adv.*

dill /dɪl/ *n* [U] a HERB used in cooking whose seeds have a strong taste: *dill pickles.*

dilly-dally /'dɪli dæli/ (*pt, pp* **-dallied**) *v* (*infml*) to waste time; to hesitate about doing sth: [V] *Stop dilly-dallying and make up your mind!*

dilute /daɪ'luːt; *Brit also* -'ljuːt/ *v* **1** ~ sth (with sth) to make a liquid or colour thinner or weaker by adding water or another liquid: [Vn, Vnpr] *Dilute the wine (with a little water).* **2** to make sth weaker in force, effect, etc: [Vn] *Parents are worried that standards in our schools are being diluted.* ► **dilute** *adj* (of a liquid) made weaker by diluting: *dilute sulphuric acid.*

dilution /daɪ'luːʃn; *Brit also* -'ljuːʃn/ *n* [U, C usu *sing*]: *the dilution of industrial waste* ∘ *Critics see this as a further dilution of the party's policy.*

dim /dɪm/ *adj* (**-mmer**, **-mmest**) **1(a)** (of a light or an object) not easy to see; not bright: *in the dim glow of an oil-lamp* ∘ *the dim outline of the house in the moonlight.* **(b)** (of a place) where one cannot see well: *a dim corridor with no windows.* **2** (of the eyes) not able to see well: *His eyesight is getting dim.* **3** not clearly remembered; faint: *a dim memory/ recollection* ∘ (*joc*) *Once, in the **dim and distant** past, I was a student here.* **4** (*infml*) (of people) stupid. **IDM** **take a dim view of sth** (*infml*) to disapprove of sth: *She took a dim view of my suggestion.* ► **dim** *v* (**-mm-**) to become or make sth dim: [V, Vn] *The stage lights (were) dimmed as the curtain rose.* [Vn] *Old age hasn't dimmed her memory.* **dimly** *adv*: *a dimly lit room* ∘ *Dimly, across the surface of the lake, she saw a black figure.* ∘ *I can dimly (ie only just) remember my fourth birthday.* **dimness** *n* [U].
■ **'dim-wit** *n* (*infml*) (esp as a form of address) a stupid person. **dim-'witted** *adj* (*infml*) stupid.

dime /daɪm/ *n* a coin of the USA and Canada worth ten cents. ⇨ note at CENT¹. **IDM** **a dime a 'dozen** (*infml*) nearly worthless or very common: *Novels like this one are a dime a dozen.*

dimension /daɪ'menʃn, dɪ-/ *n* **1** [C, U] a measurement of any sort, eg breadth, length, thickness, height, etc: *What are the dimensions of the room?* ∘ *It is 120 cubic metres in dimension.* See also THE FOURTH DIMENSION (FOUR). ⇨ App 2. ⇨ picture. **2** **dimensions** [pl] size; extent: *a creature of huge dimensions* ∘ *I hadn't realized the dimensions of the problem.* **3** [C] an aspect of a situation, problem, etc: *There is a further dimension to this issue that we have not yet discussed.* ► **-dimensional** /-'ʃənəl/ (forming compound *adjs*) having the specified number of dimensions (DIMENSION 1): *A square is two-dimensional and a cube is three-dimensional.*

NOTE You measure some things to find out how **long**, how **wide**, and how **deep** they are: *The garage is 6 metres long and 3 metres wide.* ∘ *How deep is your freezer?* The measurement of the longer sides of a room, a rectangular area or an object is the **length**, and that of the shorter sides is the **width**. When describing a piece of furniture that has a front and a back, you can use either **length** or **width** to describe the longer sides and **depth** to describe the measurement from front to back. ⇨ note at WIDE.

diminish /dɪ'mɪnɪʃ/ *v* **1** to become or make sth smaller or less; to decrease: [V] *the world's diminishing resources* ∘ *His strength has diminished over the years.* ∘ *We'd got to the stage where our efforts were producing **diminishing returns** (ie we achieved less in proportion to the amount of time, money, etc spent).* [Vn] *Nothing could diminish her enthusiasm for the project.* **2** to make sb/sth seem less important than they really are: [Vn] *The opposition is trying to diminish our achievements.*
■ **di,minished responsi'bility** *n* [U] (*law*) mental illness or weakness because of which an accused person cannot be held fully responsible for a crime: *He was acquitted on the grounds of diminished responsibility.*

diminuendo /dɪ,mɪnju'endəʊ/ *n* (*pl* **-os**) (*music*) a gradual DECREASE in how loudly a piece of music is played or sung: *played with a diminuendo.* Compare CRESCENDO.

diminution /,dɪmɪ'njuːʃn; *US* -'nuːʃn/ *n* ~ (of/in sth) **(a)** [U] decreasing or being decreased; reduction: *Any diminution of freedom reduces the quality of life.* **(b)** [C usu *sing*] an amount of this; a reduction: *We are hoping for a small diminution in taxes.*

diminutive /dɪ'mɪnjətɪv/ *adj* extremely or unusually small: *She was a diminutive figure beside her tall husband.* ► **diminutive** *n* **(a)** a word or an ending of a word indicating that sb/sth is small, eg *piglet* (= a young pig), *kitchenette* (= a small kitchen): *a diminutive suffix.* **(b)** a short form of a word, esp a name: *'Jo' is a diminutive of 'Joanna'.*

dimmer /'dɪmə(r)/ (also **'dimmer switch**) *n* a device for varying the brightness of an electric light.

dimple /'dɪmpl/ *n* a small hollow place in the flesh, esp of the chin or cheek. Dimples are either permanent, or appear eg when a person smiles. ► **dimpled** /'dɪmpld/ *adj* having dimples: *dimpled cheeks.*

din /dɪn/ *n* [sing, U] a continuing loud unpleasant noise: *make/kick up a din* ∘ *They're making so much din that I can't hear you.* ► **din** *v* (**-nn-**) **PHRV** **,din sth 'into sb/sth** (*Brit*) to tell sb sth again and again in a forceful way: *These rules were dinned into me/my head when I was at school.*

dinar /'diːnɑː(r)/ *n* a unit of money. Dinars are used in many countries, esp in the Middle East and N Africa.

dine /daɪn/ *v* ~ (on sth) (*fml*) to eat dinner: [Vpr] *We dined at a seaside restaurant on the excellent local fish.* [also V]. **IDM** **wine and dine** ⇨ WINE *v*. **PHRV** **dine out** to dine away from one's home, eg at a restaurant or in the home of friends. **dine out on sth** to tell other people about an interesting or unusual experience one has had, esp in order to make them admire one: *She's been dining out on her visit to Buckingham Palace for weeks.*
■ **'dining-car** *n* a railway carriage in which meals are served. **'dining-room** *n* a room in which meals are eaten. **'dining-table** *n* a table used for eating on.

diner /'daɪnə(r)/ *n* **1** a person eating dinner. **2** a dining-car (DINE) on a train. **3** (*US*) a small restaurant, usu beside a main road.

ding-dong /'dɪŋ dɒŋ/ *n* **1** [U] (used to represent the sound of bells). **2** [C] (*infml*) a fierce argument or

dimensions

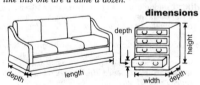

depth

height

depth

length

width

depth

contest: *The two of them were having a bit of a ding-dong about something.* ∘ *a ding-dong battle.*

dinghy

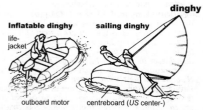

Inflatable dinghy   **sailing dinghy**

life-jacket

outboard motor   centreboard (*US* center-)

dinghy /'dɪŋi, 'dɪŋgi/ *n* (**a**) a small open boat: *a sailing dinghy.* (**b**) a rubber boat filled with air, used esp for rescuing passengers from ships and aircraft. ⇨ picture. Compare YACHT.

dingo /'dɪŋgəʊ/ *n* (*pl* **-oes**) a wild Australian dog.

dingy /'dɪndʒi/ *adj* (**-ier**, **-iest**) dirty and dark; not cheerful or bright: *a dingy room in a cheap hotel* ∘ *a dingy manufacturing town.* ▶ **dinginess** *n* [U].

dinky /'dɪŋki/ *adj* (*infml Brit*) small and neat in an attractive way: *What a dinky little hat!*

dinner /'dɪnə(r)/ *n* **1** [C,U] the main meal of the day, whether eaten in the early afternoon or in the evening: *It's time for dinner.* ∘ *When's dinner-time?* ∘ *Have you had dinner yet?* ∘ *She didn't eat much dinner.* ∘ *I never eat a big dinner.* ∘ *school dinners* ∘ *a three-course dinner* ∘ *Christmas dinner* ∘ *Shall we ask him to dinner?* ⇨ note. **2** [C] (**a**) a usu large formal social gathering at which dinner is eaten: *The prime minister attended a dinner given in his honour.* (**b**) (also '**dinner-party**) a private social gathering at which dinner is eaten: *give a dinner for friends.* **IDM** **a dog's breakfast/dinner** ⇨ DOG¹.
■ '**dinner-jacket** (*Brit*) (*US* **tuxedo**) *n* a jacket, usu black, worn with a bow-tie (BOW¹) and usu matching trousers at formal occasions in the evening.
'**dinner service** *n* a set of matching plates, dishes, etc for serving a meal.

NOTE The use of the words **dinner**, **lunch**, **supper** and **tea** varies from one English-speaking country to another, and in Britain between different areas of the country. A meal eaten in the middle of the day is usually called **lunch**. In British English this can also be called **dinner**. A meal eaten in the evening, especially a formal one, may also be called **dinner**.

Supper is usually an informal meal eaten at home in the evening. It can also be a late meal or something to eat and drink before going to bed.

Tea is a light meal of sandwiches, cakes, etc eaten with a cup of tea, in the afternoon: *Come for afternoon tea.* In British English **tea** can also be a main meal eaten early in the evening, especially by children: *What time do the kids have their tea?* In Britain children have **school dinner** at midday or they may take a **packed lunch** with them from home.

dinosaur

dinosaur /'daɪnəsɔː(r)/ *n* **1** an animal, now extinct, that lived long ago. Dinosaurs were often very large. ⇨ picture. **2** (*derog*) a person or thing that is old-fashioned and cannot adapt to changing conditions: *the bureaucratic dinosaurs of the business world.*

dint /dɪnt/ *n* **IDM** **by dint of sth** by means of sth: *He succeeded by dint of hard work.*

diocese /'daɪəsɪs/ *n* a district for which a bishop is responsible. ▶ **diocesan** /daɪ'ɒsɪsn/ *adj* [attrib].

dioxide /daɪ'ɒksaɪd/ *n* [U] (*chemistry*) a chemical formed by combining two atoms of oxygen and one atom of another element: *carbon dioxide.*

dioxin /daɪ'ɒksɪn/ *n* a chemical used in industry and agriculture. Most dioxins are poisonous.

dip¹ /dɪp/ *v* (**-pp-**) **1** ~ **sth (into sth)**; ~ **sth (in)** to put or lower sth into a liquid: [Vnpr] *Dip your pen into the ink.* [Vnp] *Dip your fingers in to see how hot the water is.* [Vn] *dip sheep* (ie put them in a liquid that protects them from infection or kills insects). **2** to go or make sth go below a surface or level: [V] *The birds rose and dipped in flight.* ∘ *Profits dipped again this year.* [Vpr, Vp] *The sun dipped (down) below the horizon.* [Vn] (*Brit*) *dip the headlights of a car* (ie lower their beams to make it easier for other drivers to see ahead) ∘ *I had to dip my head going through the doorway.* **3** to slope downward: [V, Vp] *The land dips (down) gently to the south.* **PHRV** ,**dip** '**into sth 1** to put one's hand, etc into a container to take sth out: *He dipped into his bag and took out a notebook.* **2** to take money from sth, eg an amount saved: *We had to dip into our savings to pay for this holiday.* **3** to read parts of sth briefly: *I've only had time to dip into the report.*

dip² /dɪp/ *n* **1** [C] an act of dipping. **2** [C] (*infml*) a quick BATHE(3) in the sea: *have/take/go for a dip.* **3** [U] a liquid for dipping sheep in to protect them from infection or insects. **4** [C, U] a thick mixture into which biscuits or pieces of raw vegetable are dipped before being eaten, eg at parties: *a/some cheese dip.* **5** [C] a downward slope: *a dip in the road* ∘ *a dip among the hills.* See also LUCKY DIP.

diphtheria /dɪf'θɪəriə/ *n* [U] a serious infectious disease of the throat causing difficulty in breathing.

diphthong /'dɪfθɒŋ; *US* -θɔːŋ/ *n* a union of two vowel sounds or vowel letters, eg the sounds /aɪ/ in *pipe* /paɪp/ or the letters *ou* in *doubt.*

diploma /dɪ'pləʊmə/ *n* a certificate awarded for passing an examination, completing a course of study, etc: *take/have a diploma in management studies* ∘ *a two-year diploma course.*

diplomacy /dɪ'pləʊməsi/ *n* [U] **1** the management of relations between countries, esp by each country's representatives abroad; skill in this: *International problems must be solved by diplomacy, not war.* **2** the art of or skill in dealing with people; TACT.

diplomat /'dɪpləmæt/ *n* **1** a person whose job is to represent her or his country abroad, eg an AMBASSADOR. **2** a person who is clever at dealing with people; a tactful (TACT) person.

diplomatic /,dɪplə'mætɪk/ *adj* **1** of DIPLOMACY(1): *settle disputes by diplomatic means* ∘ *break off/establish/restore diplomatic relations with a country.* **2** having or showing DIPLOMACY(2): *a diplomatic answer/move* ∘ *be diplomatic in dealing with people.* ▶ **diplomatically** /-kli/ *adv.*
■ ,**diplo,matic** '**bag** *n* a container for official letters, goods, etc sent to or from an EMBASSY.
,**diplo**'**matic corps** *n* [CGp] all the diplomats (DIPLOMAT 1) representing other countries in a city or country.
,**diplo,matic im**'**munity** *n* [U] a privilege given to diplomatic staff working abroad, by which they may not be arrested, taxed, etc.
the ,**diplo**'**matic service** *n* [sing] (*Brit*) the branch of public service concerned with the representation of a country abroad.

diplomatist /dɪ'pləʊmətɪst/ *n* (*fml*) a DIPLOMAT(1).

dipper /'dɪpə(r)/ *n* a bird that lives beside rivers. See also BIG DIPPER.

dipsomaniac /,dɪpsə'meɪniæk/ *n* a person with a desire for alcoholic drink that he or she cannot control.

[V] = verb used alone   [Vn] = verb + noun   [Vp] = verb + particle   [Vpr] = verb + prepositional phrase

D

dipstick /ˈdɪpstɪk/ n a rod for dipping into a tank or some other container to measure the depth of the liquid in it, esp oil in an engine. ⇨ picture at CAR.

dire /ˈdaɪə(r)/ adj **1** (fml) terrible; very serious or urgent: a dire situation ○ dire warnings of impending disaster ○ The firm is **in dire straits** (ie in a very difficult situation) and may go bankrupt. ○ Such action may have dire consequences. **2** (infml) extreme: We're **in dire need** of your help.

direct¹ /daˈrekt, dɪ-, daɪ-/ adj **1** [esp attrib] going in a straight line or by the shortest route, without turning aside: follow a direct course/route ○ a direct flight (ie without stopping) ○ There's a direct train from London to Leeds (ie It may stop at other stations but one does not have to change trains). ○ a direct hit/shot (ie not hitting sth else first) ○ the direct rays of the sun (ie not reflected from or blocked by sth in between). **2(a)** going straight to the point; frank: a direct person/manner/answer ○ She has a direct way of speaking. ○ He is very direct, so you always know what his real views are. **(b)** easy to see or understand; clear: direct evidence/proof ○ This information has **a direct bearing** on the case. **3(a)** with nothing or no one in between: a direct result/link/connection ○ I'm in direct contact with the hijackers. **(b)** (of family relationships) passing continuously through parent to child, rather than through brothers, sisters, cousins (COUSIN 1), etc: She is descended in a direct line from the country's first President. **4** [attrib] exact; complete: That's the direct opposite of what you told me yesterday. Compare INDIRECT.

▶ **direct** adv **1** without interrupting a journey; using a straight route: You don't have to change trains. The 10.40 goes direct. **2** with no one in between; personally: I prefer to deal with him direct.
directness n [U].

■ **diˌrect ˈaccess** /also ˌdaɪ-/ n [U] (computing) the facility of getting data immediately from any part of a computer file. See also RANDOM ACCESS.

diˌrect ˈaction /also ˌdaɪ-/ n [U] the use of strikes, protest, etc instead of negotiation to achieve one's demands.

diˌrect ˈcurrent /also ˌdaɪ-/ n [U] (abbr DC) an electric current flowing in one direction. Compare ALTERNATING CURRENT.

diˌrect ˈdebit /also ˌdaɪ-/ n [U, C] an order to a bank that allows sb else to withdraw amounts of money from one's account on agreed dates, esp to pay bills. Compare STANDING ORDER.

diˌrect ˈobject /also ˌdaɪ-/ n (grammar) a noun, pronoun phrase or noun clause which is directly affected by the action of a verb. See also OBJECT¹ 4.

diˌrect ˈspeech /also ˌdaɪ-/ n [U] a speaker's actual words or the use of these in writing. Compare INDIRECT SPEECH.

direct² /daˈrekt, dɪ-, daɪ-/ v **1(a)** to manage or control sth/sb: [Vn] She directed the planning of the festival. ○ direct a group of workers. **(b)** (esp passive) to be in charge of actors, a film, a play, etc: [V] I'd rather act than direct. [Vn] The film is directed by Steven Spielberg. **2** ~ sth to/towards...; ~ sth at sth (rather fml) to turn or aim sth in a particular direction: [Vnpr] The guide directed our attention to another picture. ○ We directed our steps towards home. ○ direct a blow at sb's head ○ Our efforts should be directed towards greater efficiency. **3** ~ sb (to...) to tell or show sb how to get somewhere: [Vn, Vnpr] Can you direct me (to the station)? **4(a)** ~ sth at/to sb (fml) to intend that a particular person or group should notice what one says or does: [Vnpr] advertising directed mainly at women ○ Let me direct these remarks to the younger students. **(b)** ~ sth to... (fml) to address a letter, parcel, etc: [Vnpr] Shall I direct the letter to his business address or to his home address? **5** (fml) to give a formal order or command:

[Vn.to inf] The officer directed his troops to advance. [V.that] The court directed that he should pay a substantial fine. ⇨ note at ORDER².

direction /daˈrekʃn, dɪ-, daɪ-/ n **1** [C,U] **(a)** a course that a person or thing moves along; a point that a person or thing looks towards: Tom went off in one direction and Harry in another. ○ The aircraft was flying in a northerly direction. ○ We looked in the direction of the sea. ○ When the police arrived, the crowd scattered in all directions. ○ Has the wind changed direction? ○ I've no **sense of direction** — I'm always getting lost. **(b)** a way in which sb/sth develops or is aimed: new directions in current research ○ That is the present direction of government thinking. ○ We're making changes in various directions (ie of various types). ○ We need a government with a clear **sense of direction** (ie that knows exactly what it wants to achieve). ○ We've raised £200 for the project. It's not much but it's **a step in the right direction**. **2** [U] management; guidance: He did the work under my direction. ○ She was entrusted with the direction of the project. ○ He feels the need for firm direction (ie wants sb to guide and advise him). **3** [C usu pl] information or instructions about what to do, where to go, how to do sth, etc: I couldn't find the hotel so I asked a policeman for directions. ○ Simple directions for assembling the model are printed on the box.

▶ **directional** /-ʃənl/ adj of direction in space: a directional aerial (ie one that transmits or receives radio signals in one direction only).

directive /daˈrektɪv, dɪ-, daɪ-/ n an official instruction: an EU directive on pollution of drinking-water.

directly /daˈrektli, dɪ-, daɪ-/ adv **1** in a direct line or manner; straight; exactly: He looked directly at us. ○ She's directly responsible to the boss. ○ It's directly opposite the church. **2(a)** at once; immediately: She didn't answer directly but sat silently for a few moments. **(b)** in a short time; soon: Tell them I'll be there directly.

▶ **directly** conj as soon as: I went home directly I had finished work.

director /daˈrektə(r), dɪ-, daɪ-/ n **1(a)** a person who directs or controls a group of people working together or an institution, a college, etc: the orchestra's musical director ○ our director of computer operations. **(b)** a member of the senior group of people that manages the affairs of a business company: the managing director ○ She's on the board of directors. **2** a person in charge of a film, play, etc who supervises and instructs the actors, camera crew and other staff. Compare PRODUCER 2a.

▶ **directorial** /ˌdaɪrekˈtɔːriəl/ adj relating to directors or their work: The film marks her directorial debut.

directorship n the position of a company director or the period during which this is held.

■ **diˌrector-ˈgeneral** n the chief ADMINISTRATOR(1) of a large, esp public, organization.

directorate /daˈrektərət, dɪ-, daɪ-/ n **1** a board¹(3) of directors. **2** a section of a government department in charge of one particular thing: a new food safety directorate. **3** the position or office of a director.

directory /daˈrektəri, dɪ-, daɪ-/ n a book giving a list, usu in alphabetical (ALPHABET) order, eg of people's names and telephone numbers, or the members of a profession, or the business firms in an area, etc: a telephone directory ○ The Directory of British Associations.

■ **diˌrectory enˈquiries** n [U] (Brit) a telephone service that one can use to find out a person's telephone number: If she's not in the telephone book, ring directory enquiries.

dirge /dɜːdʒ/ n **(a)** a song sung at a burial or for a dead person. **(b)** (infml derog) any slow sad song or piece of music.

dirk /dɜːk/ n a long DAGGER worn esp formerly by Scotsmen.

dirndl /ˈdɜːndl/ n (a) a very full wide skirt, pulled together tightly at the waist. (b) a dress with a skirt like this and a closely fitting top.

dirt /dɜːt/ n [U] **1** any substance that is not clean, eg dust, soil, mud, esp when it is where it is not wanted (eg on the skin, on clothes, in buildings): *His clothes were covered with dirt.* ○ *Remove the dirt by soaking in cold water.* **2** loose earth or soil: *a pile of dirt beside a newly dug trench.* **3** (*infml*) unpleasant, unkind or harmful talk or words: *He likes to hear all the dirt about his colleagues.* **4** (*infml*) EXCREMENT: *I've got some dog dirt on my shoe.* **IDM** **treat sb like dirt / a dog** ⇨ TREAT.
■ ˌdirt ˈcheap adj, adv (*infml*) very cheap(ly): *It was dirt cheap.* ○ *I got it dirt cheap.*
ˈdirt farmer n (*US*) a farmer who does all his own work, without paid help.
ˌdirt ˈroad n a rough country road, made of earth or GRAVEL that has been pressed down.
ˈdirt-track n a track made of cinders (CINDER), etc: *motor-cycle dirt-track racing.*

dirty¹ /ˈdɜːti/ adj (-ier, -iest) **1(a)** not clean; covered with dirt: *dirty hands/clothes/floors.* **(b)** causing one to be dirty: *a dirty job* ○ *dirty work.* **2** concerned with sex in an offensive way: *a dirty book/joke* ○ *You've got a dirty mind.* **3** [usu attrib] (*infml*) unfair; dishonest: *That's a dirty lie!* ○ *You dirty rat!* **4** (of the weather) wild and unpleasant: *I'm glad I don't have to go out on such a dirty night.* **5** [attrib] (of colours) not bright or clear: *a dirty brown sofa.* **IDM** **(be) a dirty ˈword** a thing or idea that is disliked or not respected: *Profit is not a dirty word.* **(do sb's) ˈdirty work** (to do) the tasks that sb else does not like or cannot face: *I had to tell them they'd lost their jobs — I always have to do the boss's dirty work (for him).* **do the ˈdirty on sb** (*Brit infml*) to cheat or betray sb. **give sb / get a dirty ˈlook** to look at sb with annoyance or disgust. **wash one's dirty linen in public** ⇨ WASH².
▶ ˈdirtily adv.
dirty adv (*Brit infml*) (used to emphasize the large size of sth) very: *He was carrying a dirty great box.*
■ ˌdirty old ˈman n (*infml*) an older man who takes an offensive interest in sex, or in young girls as sexually attractive.
ˌdirty ˈtrick n **1** an unkind or dishonest act: *What a dirty trick! Did he really do that?* **2** (usu *pl*) a dishonest or secret political activity, esp one to harm one's opponent's reputation: *a dirty tricks campaign.*
ˌdirty ˈweekˈend n (*esp joc*) a WEEKEND spent, esp secretly, with a sexual partner.

dirty² /ˈdɜːti/ v (*pt, pp* **dirtied**) to become or make sth dirty: [V] *White gloves dirty easily.* [Vn] *Don't dirty your new shirt.*

dis- *pref* (with adjs, advs, ns and vs) the negative or opposite of: *dishonest* ○ *disagreeably* ○ *disagreement* ○ *disengage.* ⇨ note at UN-.

disability /ˌdɪsəˈbɪləti/ n **(a)** [U] the state of being disabled (DISABLE 1): *people who cannot work because of illness or disability.* **(b)** [C] a thing that disables (DISABLE 1); a lack of sth necessary: *disabilities of sight, hearing and speech* ○ *people with learning disabilities* ○ *disability benefits.*

NOTE A **disabled** person has a permanent illness or injury that makes it difficult for her or him to move about easily: *The Dolphin Centre has a top class pool and excellent facilities for disabled swimmers.* The condition is called (a) **disability.** It may exist from birth, or be caused by an accident or illness: *Services the State can provide depend on the degree of disability.* A **disability** may not be physical: *More than a million people in Britain have some sort of learning disability.*

A **handicapped** person has severe difficulty in using a part of the body or mind normally. The condition is called a **handicap. Handicap** and **handicapped** (especially in the phrases **physically/mentally handicapped**) were used a lot in the past but many people now feel these words are offensive and prefer to use expressions with **disabled** and **disability.** The term **disabled people** rather than **the disabled** is also often preferred, because it is more personal.

If somebody's ability to hear, speak or see has been damaged but not destroyed completely, they have **impaired hearing/speech/sight** (or **vision**). People can also be described as **visually/hearing impaired** or **partially sighted:** *Books in large print are available for the partially sighted.*

disable /dɪsˈeɪbl/ v **1** (*esp* passive) to injure or affect sb so that they are unable to use their body properly: [Vn] *He was disabled after a car accident.* ○ *a progressively disabling disease.* **2** ~ **sb/sth (from sth / doing sth)** to make sb/sth unable to do sth or function properly: [Vnpr] *This choice disables you from pursuing a career in medicine.* [also Vn].
▶ **disabled** adj unable to use one's body properly because of disease, injury, etc: *a disabled child in a wheelchair.* **the disabled** n [pl v] people who are disabled: *parking spaces for the disabled.* Compare CRIPPLED. ▶ **disablement** n [U]. ⇨ note at DISABILITY.

disabuse /ˌdɪsəˈbjuːz/ v ~ **sb (of sth)** (*fml*) to free sb of false ideas: [Vnpr] *I must disabuse you of the notion that there are no very poor people in our society.*

disadvantage /ˌdɪsədˈvɑːntɪdʒ; *US* -ˈvæn-/ n a negative point or condition; a thing that tends to prevent sb succeeding, making progress, etc: *The other candidate's main disadvantage is her age.* ○ *The lack of decent public transport is a great/major/serious disadvantage.* ○ *His inability to speak French puts him at a disadvantage.* ○ *The new Common Market regulations could be/work to the disadvantage of British farmers.*
▶ **disadvantaged** adj having a poor social, educational, etc background(4); deprived (DEPRIVE): *more state help for the disadvantaged sections of the community.* **the disadvantaged** n [pl v] people who are disadvantaged: *appeals on behalf of the disadvantaged.*
▶ **disadvantageous** /ˌdɪsædvænˈteɪdʒəs/ adj ~ **(to sb)** causing a disadvantage: *in a disadvantageous position.*

disaffected /ˌdɪsəˈfektɪd/ adj not satisfied with one's situation, friends, etc and therefore lacking loyalty: *Some disaffected members left to form a new party.* ▶ **disaffection** /ˌdɪsəˈfekʃn/ n [U]: *There are signs of growing disaffection among his followers.*

disagree /ˌdɪsəˈɡriː/ v (*pt, pp* **-reed**) **(a)** ~ **(with sb/sth) (about/on/over sth)** to have a different opinion from sb; to argue slightly: [Vn] *Even friends sometimes disagree.* [Vpr] *disagree with sb/with what sb says/with sb's decision* ○ *We disagreed on the best course to follow.* Compare AGREE 2. **(b)** ~ **(with sth)** to be different; to fail to correspond: [Vpr] *The reports from Rome disagree with those from Milan.* [also V]. Compare AGREE 4. **PHRV** **disaˈgree with sb** (of food or the weather) to have a bad effect on sb; to cause sb to feel ill: *I feel sick — that fish obviously disagreed with me.* **disaˈgree with sth/ doing sth** to believe that sth is wrong; to disapprove of sth: *I disagree with spending so much money on the project.*

disagreeable /ˌdɪsəˈɡriːəbl/ adj unpleasant: *a disagreeable person/smell/experience.* ▶ **disagreeably** /-əbli/ adv.

disagreement /ˌdɪsəˈɡriːmənt/ n **1** [U] ~ **(about/on/over sth)** disagreeing; lack of agreement or approval: *Many people expressed disagreement with the*

D

D

whole idea. ○ *Experts are in total disagreement on how to proceed.* **2** [C] a difference of opinion; an argument or dispute: *disagreements between colleagues* ○ *a silly disagreement with our neighbours.*

disallow /ˌdɪsəˈlaʊ/ v to refuse to accept sth as valid: [Vn] *disallow a claim/goal.* Compare ALLOW 4a.

disappear /ˌdɪsəˈpɪə(r)/ v (**a**) to become no longer visible: [V] *The plane disappeared behind a cloud.* ○ *My spots have all disappeared.* (**b**) to stop existing: [V] *His anger soon disappeared.* ○ *The problem won't just disappear.* (**c**) to be lost or impossible to find, esp without explanation: [V] *My passport has disappeared — it was in my pocket a moment ago.* ○ *The child disappeared from his home around 4 o'clock.* ○ (*euph*) *Things tend to disappear when he's around* (ie He steals them). **IDM do a disapˈpearing act** to disappear, esp when needed or being looked for: *It's typical of Bob to do a disappearing act just when there's work to be done!* ▶ **disappearance** /-ˈpɪərəns/ n [U, C]: *At first nobody noticed the child's disappearance.* ○ *We are facing the possible disappearance of most of our rain forests.* ○ *Many disappearances are the result of terrorist activity.*

disappoint /ˌdɪsəˈpɔɪnt/ v [Vn] **1** to fail to be or do sth as good, interesting, etc as was hoped for or desired or expected by sb: *His decision to cancel the concert will disappoint his fans.* ○ *I'm sorry to disappoint you, but I can't come after all.* ○ *I've often been disappointed in love* (ie not been loved in return by sb I have loved). **2** to prevent a hope, plan, etc from becoming reality: *My expectations were not disappointed.*

▶ **disappointed** *adj* ~ (**by/about/at sth**); ~ (**in/with sb/sth**); ~ (**to do sth / that…**) sad or not pleased because one/sb has failed, some desired event has not happened, etc: *be deeply disappointed by/at sb's failure* ○ *I was very disappointed with my performance.* ○ *I'm disappointed in you — I really thought I could trust you.* ○ *He was disappointed to hear they were not coming.* ○ *I was disappointed not to be chosen.* ○ *a disappointed candidate.*

disappointing *adj* causing sb to be disappointed; not pleasing: *a disappointing game* ○ *The weather this summer has been very disappointing.* **disappointingly** *adv*: *Disappointingly, he had nothing new to show us.* ○ *The audience was disappointingly small.*

disappointment /ˌdɪsəˈpɔɪntmənt/ n **1** [U] the state of being disappointed: *To our great disappointment, it rained on the day of the picnic.* ○ *The Treasury expressed disappointment at the latest signs of wage inflation.* **2** [C] ~ (**to sb**) a thing that disappoints: *Not getting the job was a bitter/major disappointment.* ○ *His children are a disappointment to him.*

disapprobation /ˌdɪsˌæprəˈbeɪʃn/ n [U] (*fml*) disapproval.

disapprove /ˌdɪsəˈpruːv/ v ~ (**of sb/sth**) to consider sb/sth to be bad, wrong, foolish, etc: [V, Vpr] *She wants to be an actress, but her parents disapprove (of the idea).*

▶ **disapproval** /-ˈpruːvl/ n [U] not approving of sb/sth: *There is widespread disapproval of his methods.* ○ *She looked at his long hair with disapproval.* ○ *He shook his head in disapproval* (ie to show that he disapproved).

disapproving *adj* showing disapproval: *a disapproving look/frown.* **disapprovingly** *adv*: *When I suggested a drink, she coughed disapprovingly.*

disarm /dɪsˈɑːm/ v **1** to take weapons away from sb: [Vn] *Most of the rebels were captured and disarmed.* ○ (*fig*) *to disarm criticism/one's critics* (ie to do sth that prevents people from criticizing one). **2** (of a country) to reduce or ABOLISH its armed forces; to stop having weapons, esp nuclear weapons: [V] *The superpowers are unlikely to disarm unilaterally.* **3** to

make sb less suspicious, angry, HOSTILE(1), etc: [Vn] *I felt annoyed with her, but her smile disarmed me.*

▶ **disarmament** /dɪsˈɑːməmənt/ n [U]: *nuclear disarmament* (ie giving up nuclear weapons) ○ *a disarmament conference.*

disarming *adj* that disarms (DISARM 3) people: *her disarming smile/frankness/honesty.* **disarmingly** *adv*: *disarmingly frank.*

disarrange /ˌdɪsəˈreɪndʒ/ v (*fml*) to make sth untidy; to put sth in disorder: [Vn] *disarrange sb's papers/hair.*

disarray /ˌdɪsəˈreɪ/ n [U] a state in which people or things are no longer properly organized: *After their disastrous election result, the opposition parties are in some disarray.* ○ *With three teachers off sick the timetable has been thrown into complete disarray.*

disassociate = DISSOCIATE.

disaster /dɪˈzɑːstə(r); US -ˈzæs-/ n **1**(**a**) [C] a very bad accident, eg a crash or a fire, that causes great damage or loss of life; a CATASTROPHE: *an air/sea/train disaster* ○ *Thousands died in the disaster.* ○ *Then disaster struck.* ○ *a natural disaster* (ie an accident, such as an EARTHQUAKE or a flood, that is not caused by human beings) ○ *After the devastation caused by the hurricane, the President officially declared the region a **disaster area**.* (**b**) [C, U] an event that causes suffering or unfortunate consequences; a MISFORTUNE(2): *Losing your job needn't be such a disaster.* ○ *If I forget to telephone her it will be a disaster!* ○ *We all had a sense of impending disaster.* **2** [C, U] (*infml*) a person or thing that is a complete failure: *As a teacher, he's a disaster.* ○ *The play's first night was a disaster.* ○ *His career is a story of utter disaster.*

▶ **disastrous** /dɪˈzɑːstrəs; US -ˈzæs-/ *adj* being or causing a disaster: *a disastrous flood/marriage/decision* ○ *Lowering interest rates could have disastrous consequences for the economy.* **disastrously** *adv.*

disavow /ˌdɪsəˈvaʊ/ v (*fml*) to say one does not know of, is not responsible for, or does not believe in sth: [Vn] *She disavowed all knowledge of the document.* ▶ **disavowal** /-ˈvaʊəl/ n [C, U].

disband /dɪsˈbænd/ v to stop sth operating as an organization; to separate or break up: [V, Vn] *The regiment (was) disbanded soon after the war.* ▶ **disbandment** n [U].

disbar /dɪsˈbɑː(r)/ v (-**rr**-) [Vn, Vnpr] ~ **sb** (**from sth/doing sth**) (esp passive) to take away the right of a BARRISTER to practise.

disbelieve /ˌdɪsbɪˈliːv/ v **1** to refuse or be unable to believe sb/sth: *He says it's true, and I have no reason to disbelieve him.* **2** ~ **in sth** to refuse to accept the existence of sth; to have no faith in sth: [Vpr] *I gradually came to disbelieve in Christianity as a divine revelation.*

▶ **disbelief** /ˌdɪsbɪˈliːf/ n [U] lack of belief; inability to believe: *He shook his head in disbelief.* ○ *There were cries/gasps/groans of disbelief as the winners were announced.* Compare UNBELIEF.

disburse /dɪsˈbɜːs/ v (*fml*) to pay out money, esp from a fund collected for a purpose: [Vn] *cash disbursed for travelling expenses.* ▶ **disbursement** n [U, C] (*fml*): *the disbursement of loans* ○ *aid disbursements.*

disc (also *esp US* **disk**) /dɪsk/ n **1** a flat thin round object, eg a coin: *He wears an identity disc round his neck.* **2** a round surface that appears to be flat: *the moon's disc.* **3** = RECORD[1] 3: *recordings on disc and cassette.* See also COMPACT DISC. **4** = DISK 2. **5** (*anatomy*) a layer of CARTILAGE between the bones of the SPINE(1): *a **slipped disc*** (ie one that is slightly out of its proper position).

■ **ˈdisc brake** n (usu *pl*) a BRAKE that works by pressing pads against a rotating plate at the centre of eg a car wheel.

¹**disc drive** n = DISK DRIVE.

¹**disc jockey** n (abbr **DJ**) a person who plays and talks about popular music, esp on radio or television.

discard /dɪsˈkɑːd/ v **1(a)** to throw sth out or away: [Vn] *The grass was littered with discarded cans and cardboard boxes.* **(b)** to stop using, wearing, etc sth that is no longer useful: [Vn] *discard one's winter clothes in spring* ○ *(fig) discard outdated beliefs.* **2** (in card-games) to put aside a card that one does not want: [Vn] *She discarded a four, and picked up a king.* [also V].
▶ **discard** /ˈdɪskɑːd/ n a thing that is discarded, esp a card in a card-game.

discern /dɪˈsɜːn/ v (fml) (not in the continuous tenses) **(a)** to perceive, know or find out sth: [Vn] *discern sb's true intentions* [V.that] *We soon discerned that there was no easy solution.* [V.wh] *It's hard to discern what the market will do.* **(b)** to see, taste, notice, etc sth but not without effort: [Vn] *In the gloom I could just discern the outline of a building.*
▶ **discernible** adj: *discernible signs of economic recovery.*
discerning adj (approv) showing good judgement: *a fine range of tours for the discerning traveller.*
discernment n [U] (approv) the ability to judge well; INSIGHT(1a): *a woman of taste and discernment.*

discharge¹ /dɪsˈtʃɑːdʒ/ v **1** (esp passive) to give official permission for sb to leave, eg after they have carried out a duty: [Vn] *discharge a patient from hospital* ○ *The accused man was found not guilty and discharged.* **2** (esp passive) to dismiss sb from their job or position: [Vn] *He was discharged from the police force for bad conduct.* **3** [Vn] (fml) **(a)** to perform a duty: *She discharged her responsibilities with great efficiency.* **(b)** to pay a debt. **4** to give or send out liquid, gas, electric current, etc: [Vpr] *The Nile discharges* (ie flows) *into the Mediterranean.* [Vnpr] *The sewers discharge their contents into the sea.* [Vn] *Lightning is caused by clouds discharging electricity.* [V, Vn] *The wound is discharging (pus).* **5** to fire or shoot a gun, etc: [Vn] *The rifle was discharged accidentally.*

discharge² /ˈdɪstʃɑːdʒ/ n **1** [U] the action of discharging sth or of being discharged: *After his discharge from the army, he went to Canada.* ○ *the conscientious discharge of one's duties* ○ *money accepted in full discharge of a debt* ○ *the accidental discharge of a rifle.* **2** [U, C] a substance or liquid that is discharged (DISCHARGE¹ 4): *nasal/vaginal discharge.*

disciple /dɪˈsaɪpl/ n **1** a follower of a religious, political, artistic, etc leader or teacher. **2** any of the twelve close followers of Christ during his life. See also APOSTLE 1.

disciplinarian /ˌdɪsəplɪˈneəriən/ n a person who believes in or maintains strict discipline: *a good/ strict/poor disciplinarian* ○ *He's no disciplinarian* (ie He does not or cannot keep order).

discipline¹ /ˈdɪsəplɪn/ n **1(a)** [U] training or control, often using a system of punishment, aimed at producing obedience to rules, SELF-CONTROL, etc: *school discipline* ○ *Strict discipline is imposed on army recruits.* **(b)** [U] the controlled, ordered behaviour resulting from such training: *The soldiers showed perfect discipline in battle.* ○ *The children are happy at the school, but they lack discipline.* **2** [C] **(a)** a method by which training may be given: *Yoga is a good discipline for learning to relax.* **(b)** set rules for conduct: *While abroad he felt free from the normal disciplines of his own culture.* **3** [C] a branch(4) of knowledge; a subject of instruction: *scientific disciplines.*
▶ **disciplinary** /ˈdɪsəplɪnəri, ˌdɪsəˈplɪnəri; US ˈdɪsəplənəri/ adj concerning discipline: *disciplinary action/measures/charges* ○ *a disciplinary committee/*

tribunal ○ *a disciplinary hearing* (eg of a soldier accused of an offence).

discipline² /ˈdɪsəplɪn/ v **1** to train oneself/sb in obedience, SELF-CONTROL, skill, etc: [Vn] *Parents should discipline their children.* [Vn.to inf] *You must discipline yourself to finish your work on time.* **2** to punish sb: [Vn] *Anyone who breaks the law will be severely disciplined.* ▶ **disciplined** adj: *a disciplined team/mind.*

disclaim /dɪsˈkleɪm/ v to say that one does not have sth; to deny(3): [Vn] *They disclaimed all responsibility for the explosion* (ie said they did not cause it).
▶ **disclaimer** n a statement that disclaims: *The novel carries the usual disclaimer about the characters bearing no relation to living persons.*

disclose /dɪsˈkləʊz/ v ~ **sth** (**to sb**) (fml) **(a)** to make sth known, esp in public: [Vn] *refuse to disclose one's name and address* [V.that] *The government disclosed that another diplomat has been arrested for spying.* [Vnpr] *She refused to disclose her friend's whereabouts to the police.* [also V.wh, Vpr.that, Vpr.wh]. **(b)** to allow sth to be seen: [Vn, Vnpr] *He opened the box, disclosing its contents* (to the audience).
▶ **disclosure** /dɪsˈkləʊʒə(r)/ n **(a)** [U] the action of making sth known: *the magazine's disclosure of defence secrets.* **(b)** [C] a thing, esp a secret, that is made known: *startling disclosures about the minister's private life.*

disco /ˈdɪskəʊ/ n (pl **-os**) (also **discotheque** /ˈdɪskətek/) n **1** a club, party, etc, usu with flashing lights, where people dance to pop music: *disco music/dancing* ○ *Is there a good disco around here?* ○ *a Saturday night disco in the village hall.* **2** the equipment that produces the sound and lighting effects of a disco: *We're hiring a disco for the party.*

discolour (US **discolor**) /dɪsˈkʌlə(r)/ v **(a)** to change or spoil the colour of sth: [Vn] *Smoking discolours the teeth.* **(b)** to change colour: [V] *Plastic tends to warp and discolour with age.*
▶ **discoloration** /ˌdɪsˌkʌləˈreɪʃn/ n **(a)** [U] the process of discolouring: *some discoloration of the paintwork.* **(b)** [C] a discoloured spot; a STAIN n(1).

discomfit /dɪsˈkʌmfɪt/ v (fml) to confuse or embarrass sb: [Vn] *She was not in the least discomfited by the large number of press photographers.* ▶ **discomfiture** /dɪsˈkʌmfɪtʃə(r)/ n [U]: *He persisted with his questions despite her obvious discomfiture.*

discomfort /dɪsˈkʌmfət/ n **1(a)** [U] lack of comfort; slight pain: *He still suffers considerable discomfort from his injury.* **(b)** [C] a thing that causes this: *the discomforts of travel.* **2** [U] slight worry or embarrassment: *His presence caused her considerable discomfort.*
▶ **discomfort** v to cause sb discomfort: [Vn] *He looks as though nothing has ever discomforted him in his life.*

disconcert /ˌdɪskənˈsɜːt/ v (often passive) to confuse, upset or embarrass sb: [Vn] *He was disconcerted to find the other guests formally dressed.*
▶ **disconcerting** adj: *She has the disconcerting habit of addressing younger women as 'Girlie'.* **disconcertingly** adv.

disconnect /ˌdɪskəˈnekt/ v ~ **A** (**from B**) to detach sth from sth; to undo a connection: [Vn] *If you don't pay your bills they'll disconnect your electricity/gas.* ○ *Operator, I've/we've been disconnected* (ie I have lost contact with the person I was telephoning). [Vnpr] *disconnect a TV from the power supply* (ie take the plug out).
▶ **disconnected** adj (of speech or writing) lacking in logical order; INCOHERENT(2): *the disconnected ramblings of an old man.*
disconnection n [U, C].

disconsolate /dɪsˈkɒnsələt/ adj unhappy, eg because one is lonely or disappointed about sth: *You*

---

looked so disconsolate, sitting there alone in the rain.
▶ **disconsolately** *adv*.

discontent /ˌdɪskən'tent/ (also **discontentment** /ˌdɪskən'tentmənt/) *n* (**a**) [U] ~ **(with sth)** lack of satisfaction: *The strikes are a sign of growing/widespread popular discontent (with government policies).* (**b**) [C] a cause of this: *regional discontents.*

▶ **discontented** *adj* ~ **(with sth)** not satisfied: *discontented with one's job.* **discontentedly** *adv*.

discontinue /ˌdɪskən'tɪnju:/ *v* (*fml*) to stop doing or providing sth, esp sth that has been done or provided regularly for some time: [Vn] *The local rail service was discontinued in 1988.* ○ *We don't sell those jackets any more — they're a discontinued line.*

▶ **discontinuity** /ˌdɪsˌkɒntɪ'nju:əti/ *n* (*fml*) **1** [U] the quality of not being continuous. **2** [C] a break in a continuous process: *There is no discontinuity between the past and the present.*

discontinuous /ˌdɪskən'tɪnjuəs/ *adj* not continuous; INTERMITTENT.

discord /'dɪskɔ:d/ *n* (*fml*) **1** [U] disagreement; quarrelling: *A note of discord crept into their relationship.* Compare CONCORD 1, HARMONY. **2** (*music*) [C,U] a lack of harmony between notes sounded together. Compare REBATE.

▶ **discordant** /dɪs'kɔ:dənt/ *adj* **1** [usu attrib] not in agreement; in conflict: *discordant views* ○ *The attitude of the female workers struck a particularly discordant note.* **2** (of sounds) not in harmony; harsh.

discotheque ⇨ DISCO.

discount¹ /'dɪskaʊnt/ *n* [U,C] an amount of money taken off the usual cost of sth: *special discount deals available* ○ *We offer/give a 10% discount for cash (ie for immediate payment).* ○ *The shop was selling everything off **at a discount** (ie at reduced prices).* ○ *a discount shop/store (ie one that regularly sells goods at less than the usual price).* Compare REBATE.

discount² /dɪs'kaʊnt; US 'dɪskaʊnt/ *v* [Vn] **1** to offer a DISCOUNT¹ on sth: *discounted air fares.* **2** to regard sth as unimportant or not true: *discount fears/claims* ○ *You can completely discount what Jack said — he's a dreadful liar.* ○ *I don't discount the possibility that I may be wrong.*

discourage /dɪs'kʌrɪdʒ/ *v* **1** ~ **sb (from doing sth)** to take away sb's confidence or sb's hope of doing sth: [Vn] *Don't discourage her — she's doing her best.* [Vnpr] *Don't let this discourage you from trying again.* **2**(**a**) to try to stop sth by showing disapproval or creating difficulties: [Vn] *Parents should discourage smoking.* ○ *new measures to discourage car use in favour of public transport.* (**b**) ~ **sb from doing sth** to try to persuade sb not to do sth: [Vnpr] *Parents should discourage their children from smoking.*

▶ **discouraged** *adj*: *Mark felt very discouraged after losing the match.*

discouragement *n* (**a**) [U] the action of discouraging or the state of feeling discouraged: *a shrug of discouragement.* (**b**) [C] a thing that discourages: *Despite all these discouragements, she refused to give up.*

discouraging *adj*: *a discouraging result/reply.* **discouragingly** *adv*.

discourse /'dɪskɔ:s/ *n* **1** [C] (*fml*) a long and serious treatment of a subject in speech or writing. **2** [U] (*linguistics*) spoken or written language: *analyse the structure of discourse* ○ *discourse analysis.*

▶ **discourse** /dɪs'kɔ:s/ *v* [Vpr] ~ **on/upon sth** (*fml*) to give a long talk or lecture about sth.

discourteous /dɪs'kɜ:tɪəs/ *adj* (*fml*) having or showing bad manners; IMPOLITE: *It was discourteous of you to arrive late.*

▶ **discourteously** *adv*.

discourtesy /dɪs'kɜ:təsi/ *n* [U,C] (*fml*) discourteous behaviour or a discourteous act.

discover /dɪ'skʌvə(r)/ *v* **1**(**a**) to find or learn about

a place, object, etc for the first time: [Vn] *Columbus discovered America.* ○ *She was delighted to discover a very good restaurant nearby.* ○ *The microfilm was discovered hidden in a tomato.* Compare INVENT 1. (**b**) to learn or find out a piece of information: [V.*wh*] *Did you ever discover who did it?* [V.*that*] *We discovered that our luggage had been stolen.* [V.n *to* inf] *He was later discovered to have been a spy.* [also Vn]. (**c**) to be the first person to realize that sb has a particular talent, esp for acting, singing, etc, and to help them to become successful: [Vn] *Who discovered Marilyn Monroe?* **2** to find sb/sth unexpectedly: [Vn.*ing*] *I discovered him kissing my wife.* [also Vn]. ▶ **discoverer** *n*.

discovery /dɪ'skʌvəri/ *n* **1**(**a**) [U] the process of discovering sth: *a voyage of discovery* ○ *the discovery of Australia* ○ *the discovery by Franklin that lightning is electricity.* (**b**) [C] an act of discovering: *an accidental/unexpected discovery* ○ *Researchers have recently made some important new discoveries.* ○ *He buried the treasure to prevent its discovery.* **2** [C] a thing or person that is discovered: *Like many discoveries, nuclear power can be used for good or evil.* ○ *a successful singing debut by a sensational new discovery.*

discredit¹ /dɪs'kredɪt/ *v* **1** to damage the good reputation of sb/sth: [Vn] *an attempt to discredit the President.* **2** to cause sb/sth not to be believed: [Vn] *His theories were largely discredited by other scientists.* **3** to refuse to believe sb/sth: [Vn] *There is no reason to discredit what she says.*

discredit² /dɪs'kredɪt/ *n* [U] loss of reputation or respect: *Violent football fans bring discredit on the teams they support.* ○ *It is greatly **to our discredit** that we should treat a defeated enemy like this.*

▶ **discreditable** /-əbl/ *adj* (*fml*) causing a loss of reputation: *discreditable methods/tactics.*

discreet /dɪ'skri:t/ *adj* careful or showing good judgement in what one says or does; not too obvious: *We must be extremely discreet — my husband suspects something.* ○ *I should make a few discreet inquiries about the firm before you sign anything.* ○ *(fig) a discreet perfume.* See also DISCRETION 1. Compare INDISCREET. ▶ **discreetly** *adv*: *I saw him glance discreetly at his watch.*

discrepancy /dɪs'krepənsi/ *n* ~ **(in sth / between A and B)** [C,U] a difference; failure to agree: *There is discrepancy in the range of pay rises awarded.* ○ *There were many serious/slight discrepancies between the witnesses' accounts.*

discrete /dɪ'skri:t/ *adj* (*fml* or *techn*) separate; distinct: *a series of discrete events.*

discretion /dɪ'skreʃn/ *n* [U] **1** the quality of being DISCREET; good judgement: *She acted with considerable discretion.* ○ *This is a secret, but I know I can rely on your discretion (ie being completely certain you will not tell anyone).* **2** the freedom to decide for oneself what should be done: *Don't keep asking me what to do — use your own discretion.* ○ *An extra grant may be awarded in a few cases, **at the discretion of** the committee.* **IDM** **di,scretion is the ,better part of ¹valour** (*saying usu joc*) there is no point in taking unnecessary risks.

▶ **discretionary** /dɪ'skreʃənəri; US -neri/ *adj* (*esp attrib*) used, given, etc when considered necessary: *discretionary powers/measures* ○ *discretionary payments to old people in winter.*

discriminate /dɪ'skrɪmɪneɪt/ *v* **1** ~ **(between A and B);** ~ **A from B** to recognize a distinction between people or things: [Vnpr] *discriminate one case from another* [Vpr] *The law discriminates between accidental and intentional killing.* [V] *It doesn't matter how old you are — the rules don't discriminate.* **2** ~ **(against sb/in favour of sb)** to treat one person or group worse/better than others: [Vpr] *Society still discriminates against women/in* *favour of men.* [V] *We do not discriminate on grounds of age, sex or race.*

▶ **discriminating** *adj* able to judge the quality of sth: *a discriminating collector/customer* ○ *She has an artist's discriminating eye.*

discriminatory /dɪˈskrɪmɪnətəri; US dɪˈskrɪmɪnətɔːri/ *adj* discriminating against sb/sth: *discriminatory measures/practices/policies.*

discrimination /dɪˌskrɪmɪˈneɪʃn/ *n* **1** [U] ~ (**against/in favour of sb**) treating a person or group differently (usu worse) than others: *widespread racial/sexual discrimination* ○ *This is a clear case of discrimination against foreign imports.* See also POSITIVE DISCRIMINATION. **2** [U] good judgement in sth: *show discrimination in one's choice of friends/clothes.* **3** (*fml*) (**a**) [U] the ability to recognize a difference between one thing and another: *learn discrimination between right and wrong.* (**b**) [C] such a difference.

discursive /dɪsˈkɜːsɪv/ *adj* (of the way a person speaks or writes) wandering from one point to another: *The play is discursive in style.*

discus /ˈdɪskəs/ *n* (**a**) [C] a heavy disc thrown as a sport. ⇨ picture. (**b**) **the discus** [sing] the event in which this is done: *I see Britain did well in the discus.*

discus

discuss /dɪˈskʌs/ *v* ~ **sth** (**with sb**) to talk or write about sth: [Vn] *discuss the implications/merits of sth* ○ *I refuse to/I am not prepared to discuss the matter any further.* ○ *Her latest book discusses the problems of the disabled.* [Vnpr] *Please discuss it with your father and tell me what you decide.* [V.wh] *We discussed when to go/when we should go.* [V.ing] *They discussed selling the house.* [V.n ing] *We're here to discuss Ann's joining the club.*

▶ **discussion** /dɪˈskʌʃn/ *n* (**a**) [U] the process of discussing sth: *The matter will be dealt with in open discussion.* ○ *After considerable discussion they decided to accept our offer.* ○ *The plans have been* **under discussion** (ie being talked about) *for a year now.* (**b**) [C] an instance of this: *have a lively/heated discussion* ○ *hold informal/preliminary discussions on sth.* ⇨ note at TALK².

disdain /dɪsˈdeɪn/ *n* [U] ~ (**for sb/sth**) the feeling that sb/sth is not good enough to deserve one's respect; contempt: *a look of disdain* ○ *She treated his attempts to please her with cool disdain.* ○ *He has/shows a cynical disdain for popular culture.*

▶ **disdain** *v* (*fml*) to refuse sth or refuse to do sth because of one's pride: [Vn] *disdain an offer of help* [V.to inf] *He disdains to sit with people like us.*

disdainful /-fl/ *adj* ~ (**of sb/sth**) showing disdain: *a disdainful air* ○ *He's disdainful of anyone from America.* **disdainfully** /-fəli/ *adv.*

disease /dɪˈziːz/ *n* (**a**) [U] illness of the body, of the mind or of plants, caused by infection or internal disorder: *prevent/spread disease* ○ *one of the major causes of chronic heart disease.* (**b**) [C] a type or case of this: *serious/infectious/incurable diseases* ○ *a rare disease of the nervous system* ○ *check the spread of sexually transmitted diseases.* See also PARKINSON'S DISEASE, VENEREAL DISEASE. ⇨ note at ILLNESS.

▶ **diseased** *adj* suffering from a disease: *diseased kidneys* ○ (*fig*) *a diseased society.*

disembark /ˌdɪsɪmˈbɑːk/ *v* (**a**) ~ (**from sth**) (of people) to leave a ship or an aircraft: [V, Vpr] *Passengers may disembark (from the plane) by the front or rear doors.* (**b**) [Vn, Vnpr] ~ **sb/sth** (**from sth**) to cause goods or people to leave a ship or an aircraft.

▶ **disembarkation** /ˌdɪsˌembɑːˈkeɪʃn/ *n* [U]: *After disembarkation, we went through passport control.*

disembodied /ˌdɪsɪmˈbɒdid/ *adj* [usu attrib] **1** (of a soul or spirit) separated from the body. **2** (of sounds) lacking any obvious source: *a disembodied voice* (eg of sb who cannot be seen).

disembowel /ˌdɪsɪmˈbaʊəl/ *v* (**-ll-**; *US* also **-l-**) [Vn] to remove the bowels of a person or an animal.

disenchanted /ˌdɪsɪnˈtʃɑːntɪd; *US* -ˈtʃænt-/ *adj* ~ (**with sb/sth**) having lost one's good opinion of sb/sth: *disenchanted Communists* ○ *I'm becoming increasingly disenchanted with my current job.* ▶ **disenchantment** *n* [U]: *a growing sense/feeling of disenchantment with the present government.*

disenfranchise /ˌdɪsɪnˈfræntʃaɪz/ *v* to take away rights from sb, esp the right to vote for a representative in parliament: [Vn] *disenfranchised minorities.*

disengage /ˌdɪsɪnˈɡeɪdʒ/ *v* **1** ~ **sth/sb** (**from sb/sth**) (*fml*) to free sth/sb from sth/sb that holds it/them firmly: [Vn] *disengage the clutch* (ie in a car) [Vnpr] (*joc*) *She finally managed to disengage himself from her embrace.* **2** ~ (**sb/sth**) (**from sth**) (*military*) to stop fighting and withdraw, or to cause sb to do this: [V] *The fighter planes quickly disengaged.* [Vn, Vnpr] *We must disengage our troops (from the conflict).* [also Vpr]. ▶ **disengagement** *n* [U]: *begin the process of disengagement.*

disentangle /ˌdɪsɪnˈtæŋɡl/ *v* **1** ~ **sth/sb** (**from sth**) to free sth/sb from sth that has become twisted around it/them: [Vn, Vnpr] *He tried to disentangle himself (from the bushes into which he had fallen).* [Vnpr] (*fig*) *I wish I could disentangle myself from Jill* (ie from my relationship with her). ○ *disentangle the truth from the official statistics.* **2** [Vn] to make wool, string, hair, etc straight and free of knots: *disentangle the garden hose.*

disequilibrium /ˌdɪsˌiːkwɪˈlɪbriəm, -ˌekw-/ *n* [U] (*fml*) a loss or lack of balance: *the disequilibrium between savings and investment.*

disestablish /ˌdɪsɪˈstæblɪʃ/ *v* to end the official status of a national Church: [Vn] *those who want to disestablish the Church of England.* ▶ **disestablishment** *n* [U].

disfavour (*US* **disfavor**) /dɪsˈfeɪvə(r)/ *n* [U] (*fml*) dislike; disapproval: *The proposal has met with widespread disfavour.* ○ *He fell into disfavour with the prime minister and was sacked from the Cabinet.*

disfigure /dɪsˈfɪɡə(r); *US* -ɡjər/ *v* to spoil the appearance of sb/sth: [Vn] *The accident disfigured him for life.* ○ *a beautiful landscape disfigured by a power station.* ▶ **disfigurement** *n* [U, C]: *She suffered permanent physical disfigurement.*

disgorge /dɪsˈɡɔːdʒ/ *v* to pour people or things out in a great mass: [Vn, Vnpr] *The boat disgorged a crowd of passengers (onto the quay).* ○ *The pipe is disgorging sewage (into the river).*

disgrace¹ /dɪsˈɡreɪs/ *n* **1** [U] the state in which one has lost honour or the respect of others, esp because of sth one has done; shame: *His behaviour has brought disgrace on himself and on his family.* ○ *There is no disgrace in being poor.* ○ *Her father has found out about the missing money, so she's* **in disgrace** (ie regarded with great disapproval). **2** [sing] **a** ~ (**to sb/sth**) a thing or person that is so bad that one feels or should feel ashamed: *Your homework is a disgrace. You'll have to do it again.* ○ *Corrupt lawyers are a disgrace to the legal profession.* ○ *The state of our roads is a national disgrace.*

▶ **disgraceful** /-fl/ *adj* causing disgrace; very bad: *disgraceful manners/behaviour* ○ *It's disgraceful that a town of this size should not have a single decent hotel.* **disgracefully** /-fəli/ *adv.*

disgrace² /dɪsˈɡreɪs/ *v* **1** to behave so as to bring shame on oneself or sb else: [Vn] *He got drunk and disgraced himself at the wedding.* **2 be disgraced** to fall from favour, usu also losing a position of power and honour: [Vn] *After the defeat two generals were publicly disgraced.*

disgruntled /dɪsˈgrʌntld/ *adj* ~ **(at/about sth)**; ~ **(with sb)** feeling rather bitter or angry because sth has happened to upset one: *a disgruntled look* ○ *She's still feeling a little disgruntled about missing the party.*

disguise¹ /dɪsˈgaɪz/ *v* **1** ~ **sb/sth (with sth)**; ~ **sb/ sth (as sb/sth)** to make sb/sth look or sound different from normal; to give sb/sth a false appearance: [Vn] *be heavily/thinly disguised* ○ *She disguised her voice very cleverly.* [Vnpr] *Scratches on the surface can be disguised with polish.* [Vn-n] *The thieves disguised themselves as security guards.* **2** to hide sth, eg one's real feelings or aims: [Vn] *I did not attempt to/couldn't disguise my anger.* ○ *There's* **no disguising the fact** (ie It is obvious) *that he's a liar.*

disguise² /dɪsˈgaɪz/ *n* **1** [C, U] a thing worn or used for making sb/sth look or sound different from normal: *put on a disguise* ○ *grow a beard as a disguise* ○ *I didn't recognize him — he was* **in disguise**. **2** [U] the art of making sb/sth look or sound different from normal: *He's a master of disguise.* **IDM a blessing in disguise** ➪ BLESSING.

disgust¹ /dɪsˈgʌst/ *n* [U] ~ **(at sth) (for/with sb)** strong dislike for sth/sb that one feels is not right or sth that looks, smells, etc unpleasant: *She expressed disgust at the government's failure to act.* ○ *The idea of smoking fills me with disgust.* ○ *She turned away* **in disgust**.

disgust² /dɪsˈgʌst/ *v* to cause disgust in sb: [Vn] *It disgusts me to see him abusing his wife in public.* ▶ **disgusted** *adj* ~ **(at/by/with oneself/sb/sth)** feeling disgust: *We were shocked and disgusted by their living conditions.* ○ *I felt rather disgusted with myself.* **disgustedly** /dɪsˈgʌstɪdli/ *adv.*

disgusting *adj* causing disgust: *disgusting personal habits* ○ *The food at school is disgusting.* **disgustingly** *adv* **1** in a disgusting way. **2** (*joc*) extremely: *be disgustingly fit/well-read/successful.*

dish¹ /dɪʃ/ *n* **1(a)** [C] a container for holding or serving food. Dishes are usu shallow and flat on the bottom: *a glass dish* ○ *an ovenproof dish* ○ *Cover the casserole dish.* ➪ picture at PLATE¹. **(b) the dishes** [pl] the plates, bowls, cups, etc used for a meal; CROCKERY: *wash/dry/put away the dishes* ○ *I'll* **do the dishes** (ie wash them). **2** [C] **(a)** (also **dishful**) the food served in a dish: *a big dish of curry on the table.* **(b)** food prepared in a particular way as part of a meal: *a restaurant specializing in Indonesian/ vegetarian dishes* ○ *one of my favourite pasta dishes.* **3** [C] any object shaped like a dish or bowl. See also SATELLITE DISH.

dish² /dɪʃ/ *v* **PHRV** **dish sth out 1** (*infml*) to put the food on the plates for a meal: *Can you dish everything out for me?* **2** to give a lot of sth to sb: *There were students dishing out leaflets to passers-by.* ○ *dish out compliments/abuse.* **dish sth** ˈ**up 1** to put food on plates; to serve sth: *dish up another helping of spaghetti.* **2** (*derog*) to present or offer sth: *They're just dishing up the same old arguments.*

disharmony /dɪsˈhɑːməni/ *n* [U] lack of harmony between people; disagreement: *There was almost no disharmony in their marriage.*

dishcloth /ˈdɪʃklɒθ; *US* -klɔːθ/ *n* a cloth for washing dishes, etc.

dishearten /dɪsˈhɑːtn/ *v* to cause sb to lose hope or confidence: [Vn] *Don't be disheartened by this failure.* ▶ **disheartened** *adj: feel a bit disheartened* ○ *a disheartened attitude.* **disheartening** /-hɑːtnɪŋ/ *adj: dishearyening news* ○ *a rather disheartening piece of interest.*

dishevelled /dɪˈʃevld/ (*US* **disheveled**) *adj* (of the hair, clothes or appearance) very untidy: *They arrived back tired, dishevelled and bleeding.*

dishonest /dɪsˈɒnɪst/ *adj* **1** (of a person) not hon-

est: *a dishonest trader/partner* ○ *It would be dishonest of me to pretend that I enjoyed the evening.* **2** [attrib] **(a)** intended to deceive or cheat: *dishonest behaviour/goings-on/competition.* **(b)** (of money) not honestly obtained: *dishonest earnings/gains.* ▶ **dishonestly** *adv.* **dishonesty** *n* [U]: *He has a reputation for dishonesty.*

dishonour /dɪsˈɒnə(r)/ (*US* **dishonor**) *n* [U, sing] (*fml*) loss of honour or respect: *bring dishonour on one's family/regiment.*
▶ **dishonour** *v* (*fml*) to bring dishonour on sb/sth: [Vn] *Such behaviour dishonours a great tradition.* ○ *dishonour an agreement* (ie fail to keep it).
dishonourable /-nərəbl/ *adj* not honourable: *a dishonourable discharge from the army* ○ *dishonourable motives.* **dishonourably** /-nərəbli/ *adv.*

dishtowel /ˈdɪʃtaʊəl/ *n* (*US*) = TEA TOWEL.

dishwasher /ˈdɪʃwɒʃə(r); *US* -wɔː-/ *n* a machine or person that washes dishes: *dishwasher detergent.*

dishwater /ˈdɪʃwɔːtə(r)/ *n* [U] water used for washing dishes: (*joc*) *This coffee tastes like dishwater* (ie It is weak and unpleasant).

dishy /ˈdɪʃi/ *adj* (*dated infml*) (of a person) physically attractive.

disillusion /ˌdɪsɪˈluːʒn/ *v* to destroy the pleasant but mistaken beliefs or ideals of sb: [Vn] *I hate to disillusion you but most people are not as honest as you.*
▶ **disillusioned** *adj* ~ **(with sb/sth)** disappointed in sb/sth that one had admired or believed in: *Disillusioned voters want an alternative to the two main parties.* ○ *She's disillusioned with life in general.*
disillusionment (also **disillusion**) *n* [U] the state of being disillusioned: *her disillusion at being messed around by her doctors* ○ *the deep/growing disillusionment with the government's policies.*

disincentive /ˌdɪsɪnˈsentɪv/ *n* [C] ~ **(to sth)** a thing that discourages an action or effort: *Fixed wages acted as/proved to be a major disincentive to employees.*

disinclination /ˌdɪsˌɪnklɪˈneɪʃn/ *n* [sing] ~ **(to do sth)** (*fml*) lack of enthusiasm for sth; unwillingness (UNWILLING) or reluctance (RELUCTANT) to do sth: *a disinclination to travel at night.*

disinclined /ˌdɪsɪnˈklaɪnd/ *adj* [pred] ~ **(to do sth)** not willing; RELUCTANT: *I am disinclined to believe his story.*

disinfect /ˌdɪsɪnˈfekt/ *v* to clean sth by destroying the bacteria that cause disease: [Vn] *disinfect a wound/a surgical instrument/a hospital ward.*
▶ **disinfectant** /ˌdɪsɪnˈfektənt/ *n* [U, C] a substance that disinfects: *a strong smell of disinfectant.*

disinformation /ˌdɪsˌɪnfəˈmeɪʃn/ *n* [U] deliberately false information, esp from government organizations.

disingenuous /ˌdɪsɪnˈdʒenjuəs/ *adj* (*fml*) insincere, esp in pretending that one knows less about sth than one really does: *He dismissed as 'disingenuous' reports that no weapons had left the country.* ▶ **disingenuously** *adv.*

disinherit /ˌdɪsɪnˈherɪt/ *v* to prevent sb from inheriting one's property by naming another person as one's HEIR: [Vn] *He disinherited his eldest son.*

disintegrate /dɪsˈɪntɪgreɪt/ *v* **(a)** to break or cause sth to break into small parts or pieces: [V] *The plane flew into a mountain and disintegrated on impact.* [also Vn]. **(b)** to become much less strong or united: [V] *The family is starting to disintegrate.* ▶ **disintegration** /dɪsˌɪntɪˈgreɪʃn/ *n* [U]: *the gradual disintegration of traditional values.*

disinter /ˌdɪsɪnˈtɜː(r)/ *v* **(-rr-)** (*fml*) to dig up sb/sth that was buried: [Vn] *permission to disinter the body* ○ (*fig*) *disinter an old scandal.*

disinterest /dɪsˈɪntrəst/ *n* [U] lack of interest: *The drivers watched them with disinterest.*

disinterested /dɪsˈɪntrəstɪd/ *adj* **1** not influenced by personal feelings or interests: *a disinterested act of kindness* ○ *My advice is completely disinterested.* **2** (*infml*) not interested. ⇨ note at INTEREST². ▶ **disinterestedly** *adv*.

disinvestment /ˌdɪsɪnˈvestmənt/ *n* [U] (*finance*) the process of reducing or disposing of one's investment in a place, company, etc.

disjointed /dɪsˈdʒɔɪntɪd/ *adj* (of talk, writing, etc) not clear and logical in its sequence of ideas, and therefore difficult to understand: *The film was so disjointed that I couldn't tell you what the story was about.* ▶ **disjointedly** *adv*.

disk /dɪsk/ *n* **1** (*esp US*) = DISC. **2** (*computing*) a circular plate on which data can be recorded in a form that can be used by a computer: *Load the disk.* ○ *laser disk technology.* See also FLOPPY DISK (FLOP). See also HARD DISK. ▶ **diskette** /dɪsˈket/ *n* = FLOPPY DISK (FLOP).
■ '**disk drive** *n* a device that transfers data from a disk to the memory of a computer, or from the memory to the disk. ⇨ picture at COMPUTER.

dislike /dɪsˈlaɪk/ *v* to consider sb/sth unpleasant; not to like sb/sth: [Vn] *I like cats but dislike dogs.* ○ *a policy greatly disliked by the health organizations* [V.ing] *My mother dislikes seeing me with you.* [V.n ing] *Much as I dislike you whistling* (ie Though I do not like it at all), *I have to admit you do it very well.*
▶ **dislike** *n* (**a**) [U,sing] ~ (of/for sb/sth) a feeling of not liking sb/sth: *I have a strong/hearty dislike of modern music.* ○ *I took a strong/an instant dislike to him as soon as I met him.* (**b**) [C usu *pl*] a thing that one dislikes: *He soon got to know her likes and dislikes.*

dislocate /ˈdɪsləkeɪt; *US* -ləʊk-/ *v* **1** to put a bone out of its proper position in a joint: [Vn] *a dislocated shoulder.* **2** (*fml*) to stop a system, plan, etc from working as it should; to DISRUPT sth: [Vn] *Flights have been dislocated by the fog.* ▶ **dislocation** /ˌdɪsləˈkeɪʃn; *US* -ləʊ-/ *n* [C,U]: *She was treated for a dislocation and muscle strain.* ○ *These policies will cause severe economic and social dislocation for future generations.*

dislodge /dɪsˈlɒdʒ/ *v* ~ sb/sth (from sth) to move or force sb/sth from a previously fixed position: [Vnpr] *The wind dislodged some tiles from the roof.* [Vn] *There's something between my teeth and I can't dislodge it.* ○ (*fig*) *She became champion in 1992 and no one has been able to dislodge her since.*

disloyal /dɪsˈlɔɪəl/ *adj* ~ (to sb/sth) not loyal; not faithful: *be disloyal to a cause/one's country/one's friends.* ▶ **disloyalty** /-ˈlɔɪəlti/ *n* [U]: *He has been accused of disloyalty to the party.*

dismal /ˈdɪzməl/ *adj* **1** causing or showing sadness; miserable; gloomy (GLOOM): *dismal weather/surroundings* ○ *a dismal tone of voice* ○ *The news was as dismal as ever.* **2** (*infml*) less good than expected; very poor: *The team gave a dismal performance.* ○ *Their attempt to form a new party was a dismal failure.* ▶ **dismally** /-məli/ *adv*: *He tried to look cool, but failed dismally* (ie completely).

dismantle /dɪsˈmæntl/ *v* **1** to take sth apart so that it is in pieces: [Vn] *dismantle and repair a faulty motor* ○ *dismantle an exhibition.* **2** to end an organization, a system, etc in a gradual and planned way: [Vn] *We should dismantle our inefficient tax system.* ▶ **dismantling** *n* [U]: *preside over the dismantling of the Communist system.*

dismay /dɪsˈmeɪ/ *n* [U] a feeling of shock and of being discouraged: *She expressed dismay at what had occurred.* ○ *To his utter dismay, she told him that she had lost her job.*
▶ **dismay** *v* (usu passive) to fill sb with dismay: [Vnpr,Vn] *We were all dismayed at/by his refusal to cooperate.* [Vn] *Local people are dismayed that the station is to close.*

dismember /dɪsˈmembə(r)/ *v* [Vn] **1** to cut or tear off the limbs of a person or an animal: *The victim's dismembered body was found in a trunk.* **2** to divide a country, etc into parts. ▶ **dismemberment** *n* [U].

dismiss /dɪsˈmɪs/ *v* **1** ~ sb (from sth) to remove sb, esp an employee, from a position: [Vn,Vnpr] *workers who have been unfairly dismissed (from their jobs).* **2**(**a**) ~ sth (from sth) to put thoughts, feelings, etc out of one's mind: [Vnpr] *He tried to dismiss the suspicions from his mind.* [also Vn]. (**b**) ~ sb/sth (as sth) to consider sb/sth not worth thinking or talking about: [Vn-n] *She was dismissed as a mere dreamer.* [Vn-adj] *Allegations of corruption were dismissed as ridiculous.* [Vn] *I think we can safely dismiss their objections.* **3** ~ sb (from sth) to send sb away; to allow sb to leave: [Vn] *The class was dismissed at 4 o'clock.* ○ (*fml*) *The duchess dismissed her servant.* [also Vnpr]. **4** (*law*) to reject a case, etc: [Vn] *The court/judge dismissed his appeal.* **5** [Vn] (in cricket) to end the INNINGS of the other team or one of its batsmen.
▶ **dismissal** /dɪsˈmɪsl/ *n* (**a**) [U] the action of dismissing sb/sth: *The workers accused the company of unfair dismissal.* ○ *his scornful dismissal of the evidence as inadequate.* (**b**) [C] an instance of sb being dismissed: *The dismissals led to a strike.*

dismissive *adj* ~ (of sb/sth) showing in a rude, brief and casual way that sth is not considered worth thinking or talking about: *a dismissive gesture/tone of voice/shrug of the shoulders* ○ *Don't be so dismissive of her talent.* **dismissively** *adv*.

dismount /dɪsˈmaʊnt/ *v* ~ (from sth) to get off a bicycle, horse, etc: [V, Vpr] *He helped Sara dismount (from her pony).*

disobedient /ˌdɪsəˈbiːdiənt/ *adj* not showing obedience: *a disobedient child* ○ *I was very disobedient to my father.*
▶ **disobedience** /-iəns/ *n* [U] failure or refusal to obey: *He was punished for his disobedience.* See also CIVIL DISOBEDIENCE.
disobediently *adv*.

disobey /ˌdɪsəˈbeɪ/ *v* [V, Vn] to fail to obey a person, a law, an order, etc.

disorder /dɪsˈɔːdə(r)/ *n* **1** [U] a confused or untidy state; a lack of order: *My papers/financial affairs were in (complete) disorder.* ○ *Everyone began shouting at once and the meeting broke up in disorder.* **2** [U] disturbance of public order: *The capital is calm, but continuing disorder has been reported elsewhere.* **3** [C,U] a disturbance of the normal processes of the body or mind: *people suffering from severe mental disorders* ○ *a rare disorder of the liver.*
▶ **disordered** *adj* [usu attrib] suffering from lack of order or control: *a disordered existence/version of events.*
disorderly *adj* [usu attrib] **1** untidy: *a disorderly heap of clothes.* **2** (of people or behaviour) showing a lack of control; disturbing public order: *a disorderly demonstration/meeting* ○ *He was arrested for being drunk and disorderly.*

disorganize, -ise /dɪsˈɔːɡənaɪz/ *v* to spoil the organized way sb/sth is supposed to work: [Vn] *disorganize a schedule/routine.*
▶ **disorganization, -isation** /dɪsˌɔːɡənaɪˈzeɪʃn; *US* -nəˈz-/ *n* [U].
disorganized, -ised *adj* badly organized or planned: *She's so disorganized she never gets anything done.* ○ *a disorganized lesson/household.*

disorientate /dɪsˈɔːriənteɪt/ (also *esp US* **disorient** /dɪsˈɔːriənt/) *v* **1** to cause sb to lose all sense of direction: [Vn] *We were disorientated by the maze of streets.* **2** to confuse sb: [Vn] *It was a voice I had not heard before and it disorientated me.* ▶ **disorientated** (also **disoriented**) *adj*: *She felt shocked and totally disorientated.* **disorientation** /dɪsˌɔːriənˈteɪʃn/ *n* [U].

disown /dɪsˈəʊn/ v to refuse to be connected with sb/sth or to accept them as one's own: [Vn] *There are times when my children behave so badly I'd happily disown them!* ○ *He has never sought to disown responsibility for what happened.*

disparage /dɪˈspærɪdʒ/ v to suggest, esp unfairly, that sb/sth is of little value or importance: [Vn] *disparage sb's achievements/character.* ▶ **disparagement** n [U]. **disparaging** adj: *disparaging remarks/comments.* **disparagingly** adv: *speak disparagingly of sb/sb's efforts.*

disparate /ˈdɪspərət/ adj (fml) (of two or more things) so different from each other that they cannot be compared: *He is trying to bring together the disparate elements of three cultural viewpoints.*

disparity /dɪˈspærəti/ n [U,C] (fml) a difference: *There is a big disparity in their ages.* ○ *marked disparities between the countries of the EU.*

dispassionate /dɪsˈpæʃənət/ adj (approv) not influenced by emotion; IMPARTIAL: *a dispassionate view/observer.* ▶ **dispassionately** adv: *She listened dispassionately to both arguments.*

dispatch¹ (also **despatch**) /dɪˈspætʃ/ v 1 [Vn, Vnpr] ~ **sb/sth (to ...)** (fml) **(a)** to send sb/sth to a destination for a special purpose: *American warships have been dispatched to the area.* **(b)** to send a letter, message, etc. 2 [Vn] (fml) **(a)** to deal with sb who is a problem or threat: *The challenger was comprehensively despatched in two quick sets.* **(b)** (euph) to kill a person or an animal.
▶ **dispatcher** n (US) a person whose job is to supervise the departure of trains, planes, buses, etc.

dispatch² (also **despatch**) /dɪˈspætʃ/ n 1 (fml) [U] the action of dispatching (DISPATCH¹ 1) sb/sth: *The government welcomed the dispatch of the peace-keeping force.* 2 [C] **(a)** an official message or report sent quickly: *He was* **mentioned in despatches** *for bravery in battle.* **(b)** a special report sent to a newspaper by one of its writers, esp from abroad.
■ **di'spatch-box** (Brit) (US **di'spatch-case**) n **(a)** [C] a container for carrying official documents. **(b)** **the Di'spatch Box** [sing] a box in the British Parliament next to which Ministers stand when speaking. **di'spatch-rider** n a messenger who travels by motor cycle (MOTOR).

dispel /dɪˈspel/ v (-ll-) to make sth go away: [Vn] *dispel sb's doubts/fears/worries* ○ *The company is trying to dispel rumours about a take-over.*

dispensable /dɪˈspensəbl/ adj not necessary: *Hodgson's work is good, but he is dispensable.*

dispensary /dɪˈspensəri/ n **(a)** a place in a hospital, school, etc where medicines are prepared and given to people. **(b)** a place where patients are treated; a CLINIC(2). See also PHARMACY.

dispensation /ˌdɪspenˈseɪʃn/ n 1 [U] (fml) the action of distributing sth or the way in which sth is distributed: *the dispensation of global power.* 2 [C, U] (esp religion) permission to do sth that is not normally allowed: *She needs a special dispensation to marry her cousin.* ○ *The sport's ruling body gave him dispensation to compete in national competitions.* 3 [C] (religion) a religious system which is the strongest at a certain period: *the Christian dispensation.*

dispense /dɪˈspens/ v 1 ~ **sth (to sb) (a)** to distribute sth: [Vnpr] *On Saturday morning my father solemnly dispensed pocket money to each of the children.* [Vn] *a machine dispensing paper towels.* **(b)** (fml) to provide a service for people: [Vn, Vnpr] *dispense free health care (to the poor).* 2 to prepare medicine and give it to people: [Vn] (Brit) *a dispensing chemist.* PHRV **dispense with sb/sth** to manage without sb/sth; to get rid of sth: *Let's dispense with the formalities* (ie speak openly and naturally to each other)*!* ○ *Automation has largely dispensed with the need for manual checking* (ie made it unnecessary).

▶ **dispenser** n a device from which money, towels, liquid soap, paper cups, etc can be obtained: *a cash dispenser.*

disperse /dɪˈspɜːs/ v to go in different directions or make sb/sth do this: [V] *The crowd soon dispersed.* [Vn] *Security forces tried to disperse the crowds with tear-gas.* ○ *The wind dispersed the clouds.*
▶ **dispersal** /dɪˈspɜːsl/ n [U] the action or process of dispersing sb/sth: *crowd dispersal* ○ *sites for the safe dispersal of treated sewage.*
dispersion /dɪˈspɜːʃn; US dɪˈspɜːrʒn/ n [U] (fml) the process by which people or things are spread over a wide area: *population dispersion* ○ *the dispersion of light.*

dispirit /dɪˈspɪrɪt/ v to discourage sb; to depress sb: [Vn] *She refused to be dispirited by her long illness.*
▶ **dispirited** adj [usu attrib]: *a dispirited air/expression.* **dispiriting** adj: *a rather dispiriting account of office life.*

displace /dɪsˈpleɪs/ v 1 to take the place of sb/sth: [Vn] *Moderates have displaced the extremists on the committee.* ○ *Weeds tend to displace other plants.* 2(a) to remove sb/sth from the usual or correct place: [Vn] *attempts to displace or dislodge the prime minister.* **(b)** to remove sb from their home to another place, esp by force: [Vn] *families displaced by the fighting.*
displacement /dɪsˈpleɪsmənt/ n 1 [U] the action of displacing (DISPLACE) sb/sth or the process of being displaced. 2 [C usu sing] (techn) the weight of water moved out of place by a ship floating in it, used as a measure of the ship's size: *a vessel with a displacement of 10 000 tons.*

display¹ /dɪˈspleɪ/ v ~ **sth (to sb)** 1 to put sth in a place where people can see it easily: [Vn] *display a notice/goods for sale/one's wealth* ○ *His medals were now prominently displayed in the hall.* ○ *The new VDU screens display information even more clearly.* [Vnpr] *Alex proudly displayed his tattoo to his friends.* 2 to show signs of having a quality or emotion, etc: [Vn] *display one's ignorance/fear* ○ *Her writing displays considerable talent.*

display² /dɪˈspleɪ/ n 1(a) [C, U] an act of displaying sth: *a spectacular firework display* ○ *a public display of karate/of military strength* ○ *a display of courage/strength* ○ *an appalling display of prejudice/greed* ○ *A collection of family photographs is currently* **on display** *in the hall.* ○ *They put the documents on permanent display in the British Museum.* **(b)** [C] goods, works of art, etc being displayed: *The impressive/elaborate window displays in Harrods are one of the sights of London.* ⇨ note at EXHIBITION. 2 [C] a set of words, pictures, etc shown on a computer screen: *a visual display unit.* See also LIQUID CRYSTAL DISPLAY.

displease /dɪsˈpliːz/ v to make sb feel upset or angry; to annoy sb: [Vn] *He'd do anything rather than displease his parents.* ○ *Her insolence greatly displeased the judge.* ▶ **displeased** adj ~ **(with sb/sth)**: *Linda did not sound displeased to hear him.* ○ *I was most displeased with the children for waking me in the middle of the night.* **displeasing** adj ~ **(to sb/sth)**: *The overall effect is not displeasing to the eye.*
displeasure /dɪsˈpleʒə(r)/ n [U] annoyance: *The crowd showed their displeasure by booing loudly.* ○ *She was very angry and did nothing to hide her displeasure.*

disposable /dɪˈspəʊzəbl/ adj [esp attrib] 1 made to be thrown away after use: *disposable razors/nappies/syringes/plates.* 2 (finance) available for use: *disposable assets/capital/resources* ○ *These days people have less* **disposable income** (ie money that can be spent on themselves after paying tax and making other essential payments).

disposal /dɪˈspəʊzl/ n 1 [U] the action of getting rid of sth: *a bomb disposal squad* ○ *sewage disposal* systems ○ *The safe disposal of nuclear waste is a major international problem.* **2** [C] (*commerce*) the sale of part of one's business, a property, etc: *Further asset disposals are expected soon.* **IDM** **at one's/ sb's disposal** available for one to use as one wishes: *The students have a well-stocked library at their disposal.* ○ *The firm put a secretary at my disposal.*

dispose /dɪˈspəʊz/ v (*fml*) to arrange things or people in a particular way or position: [Vnpr] *Various objects were disposed on the desk in front of her.* [also Vnadv]. **PHRV** **dispose of sb/sth 1** to get rid of sb/sth that one does not want or cannot keep: *a better way of disposing of household waste* ○ *We will take away your old cooker and dispose of it for you.* **2** to deal or finish with sb/sth that is a problem or threat: *She disposed of the champion in straight sets.* ○ *The president ruthlessly disposed of his rivals* (eg dismissed them or had them killed). ○ *Their objections were easily disposed of* (ie successfully argued against).

disposed /dɪˈspəʊzd/ adj [pred] (*fml*) **1** ~ (**to do sth**) wanting or prepared to do sth: *I'm not disposed to meet them at the moment.* ○ *You're most welcome to join us if you feel so disposed.* **2** (following an adv) ~ **to/towards sb/sth** thinking that sb/sth is/is not good or valuable: *feel well/ill disposed towards sb/ sth* ○ *She's favourably disposed to new ideas.*

disposition /ˌdɪspəˈzɪʃn/ n [C usu sing] **1** a person's natural qualities of mind and character: *have a cheerful/friendly/sunny disposition* ○ *The film is not recommended to people of a nervous disposition.* **2** ~ **to sth/to do sth** (*fml*) a tendency: *have/show a disposition to violence.* **3** (*fml*) the way sth is placed or arranged: *a diagram showing the disposition of the rooms in the building.*

dispossess /ˌdɪspəˈzes/ v ~ **sb** (**of sth**) to take away property, land, a house, etc from sb: [Vn, Vnpr] *The nobles were dispossessed (of their estates) after the revolution.*
▶ **the dispossessed** n [pl v] people who have been dispossessed.
dispossession /ˌdɪspəˈzeʃn/ n [U].

disproportion /ˌdɪsprəˈpɔːʃn/ n [C,U] ~ (**between sth and sth**) (an instance of) being too great or too small when compared with sth else; being out of proportion: *the disproportion between her low salary and her many responsibilities* ○ *an area with a high disproportion of skilled to unskilled workers.*
▶ **disproportionate** /ˌdɪsprəˈpɔːʃənət/ adj relatively too large or small, etc; out of proportion: *You spend a disproportionate amount of your time* (ie too much time) *on sport.* **disproportionately** adv: *Babies often seem to have disproportionately large heads.*

disprove /ˌdɪsˈpruːv/ v to show that sth is wrong or false: [Vn] *The allegations have been completely disproved.*

disputable /dɪˈspjuːtəbl/ adj that may be questioned or argued about: *a disputable claim.* Compare INDISPUTABLE.

disputation /ˌdɪspjuˈteɪʃn/ n [C,U] (*fml*) (an instance of) disputing; an argument.

disputatious /ˌdɪspjuˈteɪʃəs/ adj (*fml*) fond of arguing.

dispute¹ /dɪˈspjuːt, ˈdɪspjuːt/ n **1** [U] argument and discussion: *There has been much dispute over the question of legalized abortion.* ○ *It is a matter of dispute whether they did the right thing.* ○ *Their conclusions are* **open to dispute**. ○ *Her courage is* **beyond dispute** (ie certain). ○ *The exact cause of the accident is still* **in dispute** (ie being argued about). **2** [C] ~ (**about/over sth**) a disagreement: *a dispute over fishing rights* ○ *industrial/pay disputes* ○ *resolve/settle a dispute* ○ *a border dispute that could*

easily become a war ○ *The union is* **in dispute with** *management about overtime rates.*

dispute² /dɪˈspjuːt/ v **1(a)** to argue about sth: [Vn] *disputed territory* (ie claimed by more than one country) [V.*wh*] *They disputed at great length what they should do.* **(b)** to question whether sth is true or valid: [Vn] *dispute a statement/decision* ○ *Their claims were* **hotly disputed** *by their rivals.* [Vn, V.*that*] *There is no disputing the importance of the treaty/that the treaty is important.* **2** ~ (**with sb**) to argue and discuss: [Vpr] *It was no use disputing with him.* [also V]. **3** to try to stop sb winning sth from one; to fight for sth: [Vn] *Several drivers are currently disputing the lead.*

disqualify /dɪsˈkwɒlɪfaɪ/ v (*pt, pp* -**fied**) ~ **sb** (**from sth/doing sth**) to prevent sb from doing sth, usu because they have broken a rule: [Vnpr] *The judge disqualified her from driving for six months.* ○ *The team has been disqualified from next year's competition.* [Vn] *Two players were disqualified for cheating.*
▶ **disqualification** /dɪsˌkwɒlɪfɪˈkeɪʃn/ n [C,U]: (*a*) *disqualification for driving while drunk.*

disquiet /dɪsˈkwaɪət/ n [U] anxiety; worry: *There is considerable public disquiet about the safety of the new trains.*
▶ **disquiet** v (*fml*) (usu passive) to make sb anxious; to worry sb: [Vn] *Government ministers are greatly disquieted by the fall in public support.* **disquieting** adj causing disquiet: *disquieting news* ○ *The rising crime figures are certainly disquieting.*

disquisition /ˌdɪskwɪˈzɪʃn/ n ~ (**on sth**) a long or elaborate spoken or written report.

disregard /ˌdɪsrɪˈɡɑːd/ v to pay no attention to sth; to treat sth as unimportant; to ignore sth: [Vn] *disregard a warning* ○ *His argument completely disregards the facts.*
▶ **disregard** n [U] ~ (**for/of sb/sth**) lack of attention or care: *She shows a total disregard for other people's feelings.*

disrepair /ˌdɪsrɪˈpeə(r)/ n [U] bad condition caused by lack of care: *be in a state of disrepair* ○ *The building* **was in/had fallen into disrepair**.

disreputable /dɪsˈrepjətəbl/ adj (**a**) having a bad reputation: *The Bronx is one of New York's more disreputable areas.* (**b**) not respectable or looking respectable: *a disreputable appearance* ○ *He has been accused of using disreputable business methods.*

disrepute /ˌdɪsrɪˈpjuːt/ n [U] the state of having a bad reputation: *As a result of their behaviour in the match both teams have been charged with* **bringing the game into disrepute**.

disrespect /ˌdɪsrɪˈspekt/ n [U] ~ (**to/towards sb/ sth**) lack of respect; being rude: *I meant no disrespect by that remark* (ie did not mean to be rude). ○ *She shows a healthy disrespect for tradition.* ○ *No disrespect (to you), but I think you are wrong.* ▶ **disrespectful** /-fl/ adj ~ (**to/towards sb/sth**). **disrespectfully** /-fəli/ adv.

disrobe /dɪsˈrəʊb/ v [V] (**a**) (*fml or joc*) to take one's clothes off. (**b**) to take off clothes worn for an official occasion or ceremony.

disrupt /dɪsˈrʌpt/ v to make it difficult for sth to proceed, eg by causing noise, problems, interruptions, etc: [Vn] *Demonstrators succeeded in disrupting the meeting.* ○ *Fog has seriously disrupted traffic.*
▶ **disruption** /dɪsˈrʌpʃn/ n [U,C]: *violent disruption caused by rioters* ○ *Officials warn of possible disruptions to rail services over the holiday weekend.*
disruptive /dɪsˈrʌptɪv/ adj causing disruption: *disruptive behaviour* ○ *A few disruptive students can easily ruin a class.*

dissatisfaction /ˌdɪsˌsætɪsˈfækʃn/ n [U] ~ (**with/at sb/sth**) lack of satisfaction: *Many viewers have written to express their dissatisfaction with current programmes.*

D

dissatisfied /dɪsˈsætɪsfaɪd, dɪˈsæt-/ adj ~ (**with sb/ sth**) not satisfied or happy: *a dissatisfied customer* ○ *I'm thoroughly dissatisfied with your work.* ○ *Many women feel dissatisfied with their appearance.*

dissect /dɪˈsekt, daɪ-/ v [Vn] **1** to cut up a dead body, a plant, etc in order to study it. **2** to examine and discuss sth in great detail: *Commentators are still dissecting the election results.* ○ *The film has been minutely dissected by the critics.* ▶ **dissection** /dɪˈsekʃn, daɪ-/ n [U]: *anatomical dissection.*

dissemble /dɪˈsembl/ v [V, Vn] (*fml*) to hide or disguise one's true thoughts and feelings.

disseminate /dɪˈsemɪneɪt/ v to spread ideas, beliefs, etc widely: [Vn] *The mass media are used to disseminate information.* ▶ **dissemination** /dɪˌsemɪˈneɪʃn/ n [U]: *the dissemination of knowledge.*

dissension /dɪˈsenʃn/ n [U, C] angry disagreement: *dissension among government ministers.*

dissent¹ /dɪˈsent/ n [U] holding opinions which differ from common or officially held ones: *their public dissent from official party policy* ○ *In those days, religious dissent was not tolerated.*

dissent² /dɪˈsent/ v ~ (**from sth**) (*fml*) to have or express opinions which are opposed to common or officially held ones or to official religious teaching, etc: [V] *There were many **dissenting voices** among the students.* [Vpr] *The committee dissented from the report's conclusions.*
▶ **dissenter** n (**a**) a person who dissents. (**b**) **Dissenter** a Protestant who refuses to accept the teachings of the Church of England: *Presbyterians and other Dissenters.* Compare NONCONFORMIST.

dissertation /ˌdɪsəˈteɪʃn/ n ~ (**on sth**) a long essay on a particular subject, esp one written for a higher university degree: *her doctoral dissertation on Arabic dialects.* Compare THESIS 2.

disservice /dɪsˈsɜːvɪs, dɪˈsɜː-/ n [U, sing] ~ (**to sb/ sth**) a harmful action: *She did her cause a great disservice by concealing the truth.*

dissident /ˈdɪsɪdənt/ n a person who strongly disagrees with or opposes official opinions and policies: *A number of dissidents have been arrested.* ○ *dissident groups.* ▶ **dissidence** /ˈdɪsɪdəns/ n [U].

dissimilar /dɪˈsɪmɪlə(r)/ adj ~ (**from/to sb/sth**) not the same; not like: *These wines are not dissimilar* (ie quite similar). ▶ **dissimilarity** /ˌdɪsɪmɪˈlærəti/ n [C, U].

dissimulate /dɪˈsɪmjuleɪt/ v [V, Vn] (*fml*) to hide or disguise one's thoughts and feelings. ▶ **dissimulation** /dɪˌsɪmjuˈleɪʃn/ n [U]: *Dissimulation and compromise are inevitable in politics.*

dissipate /ˈdɪsɪpeɪt/ v **1** to disappear or cause sth to disappear: [V] *The mist quickly dissipated as the sun rose.* [Vn] *Her son's letter dissipated all her fears and anxiety.* **2** to waste sth foolishly: [Vn] *dissipate one's efforts/energies/fortune.*
▶ **dissipated** adj (*derog*) showing enjoyment of harmful pleasures, eg drinking too much alcohol, gambling, etc: *a dissipated life.*
dissipation /ˌdɪsɪˈpeɪʃn/ n [U] **1** living a life of harmful pleasures and waste: *Years of dissipation had ruined his health.* **2** the process of dissipating sth or of being dissipated: *the dissipation of gas and petrol vapours* ○ *dissipation of the company's assets/ capital.*

dissociate /dɪˈsəʊʃieɪt, -əʊsi-/ v **1** (also **disassociate** /ˌdɪsəˈsəʊʃieɪt, -əʊsi-/) ~ **oneself from sb/sth** to say that one does not agree with or support sb/sth: [Vnpr] *I wish to dissociate myself from the views expressed by my colleagues.* **2** ~ **sb/sth from sth** to separate people or things in one's thoughts or feelings: [Vn, Vnpr] *dissociate two ideas/one idea from another.* ▶ **dissociation** /dɪˌsəʊsiˈeɪʃn/ n [U].

dissolute /ˈdɪsəluːt/ adj (*derog*) showing enjoyment of harmful pleasures and IMMORAL behaviour: *lead a dissolute life* ○ *a dissolute and worthless young man.*

dissolution /ˌdɪsəˈluːʃn/ n [U] ~ (**of sth**) the breaking up or dissolving (DISSOLVE 4) of sth: *the dissolution of a marriage/a business partnership* ○ *the dissolution of the Roman Empire.*

dissolve /dɪˈzɒlv/ v **1(a)** (of a liquid) to make a solid become liquid: [Vn] *Water dissolves salt.* (**b**) ~ (**in sth**) (of a solid) to become part of a liquid: [Vpr] *Salt dissolves in water.* [V] *Wait for the tablet to dissolve.* (**c**) ~ **sth** (**in sth**) to cause a solid to dissolve: [Vnpr] *Dissolve the salt in water.* [also Vn]. **2** to remove or destroy sth: [Vn] *a washing-powder that dissolves stains.* **3** ~ (**in sth**) to disappear: [V] *All her fears dissolved when she heard his reassuring voice.* ○ *The distant outlines of the hills appear to dissolve in the mist.* **4(a)** to cause an organization or arrangement to end officially: [Vn] *dissolve a marriage/business partnership.* (**b**) to bring the activity of an assembly to a formal end: [Vn] *Parliament will be dissolved before the run-up to the election.* **5** ~ **in/into sth** to express strong feelings or emotions which cannot control: [Vpr] *dissolve in(to) tears/laughter/giggles.*

dissonance /ˈdɪsənəns/ n **1** [U] (*fml*) lack of agreement. **2** [C, U] (*music*) a combination of musical notes that sound harsh together; a lack of harmony. ▶ **dissonant** /ˈdɪsənənt/ adj: *dissonant voices/ chords.*

dissuade /dɪˈsweɪd/ v ~ **sb** (**from sth/doing sth**) to persuade or to try to persuade sb not to do sth: [Vn] *None of their warnings could dissuade her.* [Vnpr] *He tried to dissuade me from going to live abroad.*

distaff /ˈdɪstɑːf; US ˈdɪstæf/ n **IDM** **on the distaff side** on the woman's side of the family.

distance¹ /ˈdɪstəns/ n **1** [C, U] the amount of space between two points or places: *a short/long/great distance* ○ *a distance of 20 miles* ○ *What's the distance between Oxford and Cambridge/from Oxford to Cambridge?* ○ *In the USA distance is measured in miles, not kilometres.* ○ *The beach is within **walking distance** of my house* (ie near enough to be reached easily on foot). ○ *Some birds are able to fly very long distances.* ○ (*fig*) *at a distance of fifty years.* ⇨ App 2. **2** [C, U] a distant place or point: *He won't hit the target from/at that distance.* **3** [U] being separated in space or by time: *Distance is no problem with modern telecommunications.* **4** [U] lack of friendly feelings in personal relationships: *There was a growing distance between them.* Compare THE MIDDLE DISTANCE. **IDM** **go the (full) ˈdistance** (esp in sports) to continue to run, fight, etc until the end of a contest: *Nobody thought he'd last 15 rounds, but he went the full distance.* **in/into the ˈdistance** far away: *I could just see them in the distance.* ○ *She stood looking into the distance.* **keep sb at a ˈdistance** to refuse to be friendly to sb or let sb become friendly. **keep one's ˈdistance** (**from sb/sth**) **1** to avoid getting too close to sb/sth: *The police kept their distance during the students' demonstration.* **2** to avoid becomingfriendly with a person or involved with a cause, etc: *The president has been advised to keep his distance from the organization.* **within striking distance** ⇨ STRIKE².

distance² /ˈdɪstəns/ v ~ **oneself/sb** (**from sb/sth**) to make oneself/sb become or feel separated or far away from sb/sth: [Vnpr] *She needs to distance herself from some of her more extreme supporters.* ○ *Her wealth and success have distanced her from her old friends.* [also Vn].

distant /ˈdɪstənt/ adj **1** far away in space or time: *travel to distant parts of the world* ○ *a distant land* ○ *the sound of a distant aeroplane* ○ *The airport is about ten miles distant (from the city).* ○ *I hope we'll* *meet again in the not-too-distant future.* ○ *It's only a dim and distant memory now.* ○ *World peace still seems a distant prospect.* **2** (of people) not closely related: *a distant cousin.* **3(a)** not very friendly: *He seems distant until you get to know him.* **(b)** appearing to be thinking about sth else: *She had a distant look in her eyes and obviously wasn't listening.* ▶ **distantly** *adv*: *We're distantly related.* ○ *She smiled distantly (at us).* ○ *Somewhere, distantly, he could hear the sound of the sea.*

distaste /dɪsˈteɪst/ *n* [U, sing] ~ **(for sb/sth)** a feeling that sb/sth is unpleasant or unacceptable; dislike: *wrinkle one's nose in distaste* ○ *have a distaste for violent sports.*
▶ **distasteful** /dɪsˈteɪstfl/ *adj* unpleasant: *I find his use of bad language extremely distasteful.*

distemper¹ /dɪˈstempə(r)/ *n* [U] a paint that is mixed with water and glue and used on walls, etc.

distemper² /dɪˈstempə(r)/ *n* [U] a disease of certain animals, esp dogs, causing coughing and weakness.

distend /dɪˈstend/ *v* to swell or cause sth to swell because of pressure from inside: [Vn] *starving children with huge distended bellies* [also V]. ▶ **distension** /dɪˈstenʃn/ *n* [U].

distil /dɪˈstɪl/ (*US* **distill**) *v* (**-ll-**) **1** ~ **sth (from sth)** **(a)** to turn a liquid to VAPOUR(1) by heating, then collecting the drops of liquid that form when the vapour cools: [Vnpr] *distil fresh water from sea water* [also Vn]. **(b)** to make sth, esp spirits, in this way: *whisky distilled in Scotland* [Vnpr] *Vodka is distilled from grain.* **2** ~ **sth (from/into sth)** to extract the essential meaning or most important part of an idea, etc to form sth: [Vnpr] *The notes I made will be distilled into a book.* [also Vn]. ▶ **distillation** /ˌdɪstɪˈleɪʃn/ *n* [C, U]: *a distillation of his philosophy in one paragraph* ○ *chemical distillation.*

distiller /dɪˈstɪlə(r)/ *n* a person or company that distils (DISTIL 1b) spirits.
▶ **distillery** /dɪˈstɪləri/ *n* a place where spirits are distilled. Compare BREWERY.

distinct /dɪˈstɪŋkt/ *adj* **1** easily heard, seen, felt or understood; definite: *distinct footprints in the snow* ○ *A national strike is now a distinct possibility.* ○ *I had the distinct impression that I was being watched.* ○ *She had a distinct advantage over her opponent.* **2** ~ **(from sth)** different in kind; separate: *We can separate these people into three distinct types.* ○ *Mozart's musical style is quite distinct from Beethoven's.* ○ *Rural areas, as distinct from major cities, have very different transport problems.* ▶ **distinctly** *adv*: *Economic prospects are distinctly gloomy.* ○ *I distinctly remember you promising to phone me.* ○ *Every picture in the exhibition is distinctly different.* **distinctness** *n* [U].

distinction /dɪˈstɪŋkʃn/ *n* **1** [C, U] ~ **(between A and B)** a difference or contrast between people or things: *draw a distinction between serious and popular literature.* **2(a)** [U] the separation of people or things into different groups according to quality, grade, etc: *provide social and political freedom without distinction* (ie based on race, sex, class, etc). **(b)** [C] a quality, etc that separates people or things in this way: *distinctions of birth and wealth.* **3** [U] the quality of being excellent or distinguished: *a writer/novel of distinction* ○ *She had the distinction of being the first woman to swim the Channel.* **4** [C] a mark of honour; a title, decoration, etc: *win the highest distinction for bravery* ○ *I got a distinction in my geography exam.*

distinctive /dɪˈstɪŋktɪv/ *adj* that distinguishes sth by making it different from others: *a distinctive appearance/feature/style/flavour* ○ *She was dressed in a highly distinctive black and white coat.* ▶ **distinctively** *adv*: *a distinctively nutty flavour.*

distinguish /dɪˈstɪŋgwɪʃ/ *v* **1** ~ **(between) A and B**; ~ **A from B** to recognize the difference between people or things: [Vn] *Sometimes reality and fantasy are hard to distinguish.* [Vnpr] *The twins are so alike that I can't distinguish one from the other.* [Vpr] *People who are colour-blind cannot distinguish between green and red.* **2** ~ **A (from B)** **(a)** to show the difference between people or things: [Vn, Vnpr] *The male is distinguished (from the female) by its red beak.* **(b)** to be a characteristic mark or property of sb/sth; to make sb/sth different: [Vnpr] *The power of speech distinguishes human beings from animals.* **3** to manage to see, hear, etc sth: [Vn] *I could hardly distinguish the car in front because of the fog.* **4** ~ **oneself** to make oneself noticed and admired by others by doing sth very well: [Vn] *She distinguished herself by her coolness and bravery.*
▶ **distinguishable** /dɪˈstɪŋgwɪʃəbl/ *adj* ~ **(from sb/sth)**: *The coast was barely distinguishable in the mist.* ○ *Vipers are easily distinguishable from grass snakes by their markings.*
distinguished *adj* **1** very successful and admired by other people: *a distinguished career/writer.* **2** showing dignity in appearance or manner: *I think grey hair makes you look very distinguished.*

distort /dɪˈstɔːt/ *v* **1** to pull or twist sth out of its usual shape: [Vn] *a face distorted by pain.* **2** to make sth look or sound strange and UNNATURAL(1): [Vn] *The airport announcements were so distorted that I couldn't understand what was said.* **3** to give a false account of sth: [Vn] *Foreigners are often given a distorted view of this country.* ○ *Newspapers often distort facts.* ▶ **distortion** /dɪˈstɔːʃn/ *n* [C, U]: *a distortion of the facts* ○ *modern alloys that are resistant to wear and distortion.*

distract /dɪˈstrækt/ *v* ~ **sb/sth (from sth)** to take sb's attention away from sth: [Vn] *Please be quiet! You're distracting me.* [Vnpr] *European economic recovery should not distract attention from the pressing needs of the poorer nations.*
▶ **distracted** *adj* ~ **(with/by sth)** unable to concentrate because of being worried or thinking about sth else: *She looked distracted.* **distractedly** *adv*: *He paced up and down distractedly.*
distracting *adj*: *a distracting noise.*

distraction /dɪˈstrækʃn/ *n* **1** [C] a thing that prevents sb from concentrating on what they are doing or thinking about: *I find it hard to work at home because there are too many distractions.* **2** [C] a thing that helps sb to forget their worries and problems; a thing that amuses or entertains: *TV can be a welcome distraction after a hard day's work.* **3** [U] distracting or being distracted: *To minimize distraction, I work with my back to the window.* **IDM to di'straction** so that one is in a state of mental distress: *bored to distraction* ○ *The children are driving me to distraction.*

distraught /dɪˈstrɔːt/ *adj* very sad or upset: *His mother's death left him distraught.*

distress¹ /dɪˈstres/ *n* [U] **1(a)** great pain, sorrow, suffering, etc: *Her death was the cause of great distress to all the family.* **(b)** suffering caused by lack of money, food, etc: *Rescue workers attempted to relieve the widespread distress caused by the earthquake.* **2** the state of being in danger or difficulty and needing help: *a ship in di'stress* ○ *send out a di'stress signal.*

distress² /dɪˈstres/ *v* (usu passive) to cause distress to sb/sth: [Vn] *She was too distressed to speak.* ○ *Please don't distress yourself* (ie do not worry).
▶ **distressing** *adj* causing distress: *distressing news* ○ *I found it very distressing when my parents divorced.* **distressingly** *adv*.

distribute /dɪˈstrɪbjuːt; *Brit also* ˈdɪstrɪbjuːt/ *v* **1** ~ **sth (to/among sb/sth)** to give or sell things to a

number of people; to separate sth into parts and supply the parts to various people or places: [Vn] *goods distributed and sold world-wide* [Vnpr] *The demonstrators distributed leaflets to passers-by.* **2** to spread sth or different parts of sth over an area: [Vn] *Make sure the weight is evenly distributed.* ○ *Such birds are widely distributed in Africa and Asia.*
▶ **distribution** /ˌdɪstrɪˈbjuːʃn/ *n* **1** [C,U] the giving of sth to a number of people: *distributions of food parcels to the refugees.* **2** [U, sing] the way sth is shared out or spread over an area: *a map to show the seasonal distribution of rainfall* ○ *problems caused by an uneven distribution of wealth.* **3** [U] the transport and supply of goods, etc to various people or places: *reduce manufacturing and distribution costs* ○ *a distribution company/system.* **distributional** *adj*.
▶ **distributor** /dɪˈstrɪbjətə(r)/ *n* **1** a person or company that transports and supplies goods to shops, etc in a certain area: *a major distributor of electrical goods.* **2** a device that passes electric current to the spark-plugs (SPARK) in an engine.

distributive /dɪˈstrɪbjətɪv/ *adj* [usu attrib] concerned with distribution (DISTRIBUTE): *the distributive trades.*

district /ˈdɪstrɪkt/ *n* **1** a part of a country or town having a particular quality: *mountainous/ agricultural/residential districts* ○ *the 'Lake District.* See also RED-LIGHT DISTRICT. **2** an area of a country or town treated as an administrative unit: *a 'postal/ 'tax district* ○ *rural/urban districts* (ie units of local government) ○ *district councils.*
■ ˌdistrict atˈtorney *n* (*US*) (*abbr* **DA**) a public official who represents a State or the Federal government in court in a particular district.
ˌdistrict ˈnurse *n* (*Brit*) a nurse who visits patients in their homes.

distrust /dɪsˈtrʌst/ *n* [U, sing] lack of trust; suspicion: *mutual distrust* ○ *have a distrust of strangers* ○ *She eyed him with distrust.*
▶ **distrust** *v* to have no confidence or belief in sb/ sth: [Vn] *She distrusted his motives for wanting to see her again.*
distrustful /-fl/ *adj*: *be distrustful of authority.*

disturb /dɪˈstɜːb/ *v* **1** to break the rest, concentration or calm of sb/sth: [Vn] *I'm sorry if I disturbed you.* ○ *'Exam in Progress — Do Not Disturb.'* ○ *Keep the noise down! You'll disturb the neighbours.* **2** to move sth from a settled or usual position or place: [Vn] *Don't disturb the papers on my desk.* ○ *The strike continued to disturb international air traffic all day.* **3** to cause sb to worry: [Vn] *He does not usually let criticism disturb him.*
▶ **disturbed** *adj* (*psychology*) mentally ill: *She teaches children who are emotionally disturbed.*
disturbing *adj* worrying or alarming: *a realistic but disturbing film* ○ *The news was extremely disturbing.*
disturbingly *adv*: *The project's costs remain disturbingly high.*

disturbance /dɪˈstɜːbəns/ *n* **1** [U] the action of disturbing sb/sth or the process of being disturbed: *Hedges are cut in winter to prevent disturbance to nesting birds.* **2** [sing] a person or thing that interrupts the calm concentration of others: *He was sent out of the room for causing a disturbance in class.* **3** [C] an instance of social trouble and violence: *Further disturbances occurred in the town after dark.*

disunite /ˌdɪsjuˈnaɪt/ *v* to cause sb/sth to split or become separate: [Vn] *Opposing views on health care are threatening to disunite the party.*
disunity /dɪsˈjuːnəti/ *n* [U] lack of unity; disagreement: *growing signs of disunity within the party.*

disuse /dɪsˈjuːs/ *n* [U] the state of not being used: *machinery rusty from disuse* ○ *words that have fallen into disuse.*
▶ **disused** /ˌdɪsˈjuːzd/ *adj* no longer used: *a disused 'railway line.*

ditch /dɪtʃ/ *n* a long narrow channel dug at the edge of a field, road, etc to hold or carry away water: *The car swerved and ended up in the ditch.* **IDM** **the last ditch** ⇨ LAST¹.
▶ **ditch** *v* **1** (*infml*) to get rid of or leave sb/sth: [Vn] *I hear she's ditched her boyfriend* (ie stopped seeing him). ○ *We had to ditch the car and walk home.* **2** to land an aircraft in the sea in an emergency: [V] *Sudden engine failure forced the pilot to ditch (in the Channel).* [also Vn].

dither /ˈdɪðə(r)/ *v* ~ (**about**) to hesitate about what to do; to be unable to decide: [V, Vp] *Stop dithering (about) or we'll be late!* [also Vpr].
▶ **dither** *n* a state of dithering: *He's in a terrible dither/all of a dither over whether to accept this new job offer.*

ditto /ˈdɪtəʊ/ *n* (*abbr* **do**, *symb* „) (used esp in lists to avoid repetition) the same thing again. When the symbol (") is used it means that the word above it is repeated: *1 doz bottles white wine @ £2.15 a bottle; ditto red @ £3.* ○ (*infml*) *She came in late last night and ditto the night before.*

ditty /ˈdɪti/ *n* (*often joc*) a short simple song.

diuretic /ˌdaɪjʊˈretɪk/ *n, adj* (*medical*) (a substance) causing an increase in the flow of URINE.

diurnal /daɪˈɜːnl/ *adj* **1** (*biology*) (of animals) active during the day: *Unlike most other bats, this species is diurnal.* Compare NOCTURNAL. **2** (*astronomy*) taking one day to complete: *the diurnal rotation of the earth.*

Div *abbr* division(3b): *Oxford United, League Div 1.*

diva /ˈdiːvə/ *n* (*pl* **divas**) a great or famous female singer, esp in opera.

divan /dɪˈvæn; US ˈdaɪvæn/ *n* (**a**) a long low seat without a back or arms. (**b**) (also diˌvan ˈbed) a low bed resembling this.

dive¹ /daɪv/ *v* (*pt, pp* **dived**; *US* also *pt* **dove** /dəʊv/) **1** ~ (**from/off sth**) (**into sth**); ~ (**off/in**) to jump head first into water: [Vpr] *He dived from the bridge to rescue the drowning child.* [also V, Vp]. **2** ~ (**for sth**) to go under water or to a deeper level under water: [Vpr] *dive for pearls* [V] *The whale dived as the harpoon struck it.* ○ *The submarine dived to avoid being seen.* [also Vp]. **3** [V, Vpr, Vp] (of birds or aircraft) to go steeply downwards. **4** ~ **into, under, etc sth** to move quickly in a specified direction: [Vpr] *dive under the bed* ○ *It started to rain, so we dived into a café.* **PHRV** '**dive for sth** to move quickly towards or in search of sth: *dive for the phone/the gun* ○ *We had to dive for cover when the storm started.* '**dive into sth** (*infml*) to move one's hand quickly into sth: *dive into one's pocket/ briefcase.*
▶ **diver** *n* a person who dives, esp one who works under water using a special suit.
diving /ˈdaɪvɪŋ/ *n* [U] the sport of diving into water or of swimming and exploring under water: *go diving* ○ *a diving-suit* ○ *diving lessons.* See also SKIN-DIVING.
■ '**dive-bomb** *v* [V, Vn] (of an aircraft, a pilot, etc) to drop bombs on a target after diving steeply downwards.
'**diving-board** *n* a raised board for diving from, eg at a swimming-pool (SWIM).

dive² /daɪv/ *n* **1** an act of diving: *The goalkeeper made a spectacular dive to catch the ball.* **2** (*infml*) a bar, gambling club, etc that is badly kept or not very respectable.

diverge /daɪˈvɜːdʒ/ *v* **1** ~ (**from sth**) (**a**) (of lines, roads, etc) to separate and go in different directions: [Vpr] *The coastal road diverges from the freeway just north of Santa Monica.* [fig] *our paths diverged and I never saw her again.* ⇨ picture at CONVERGE. (**b**) (*fml*) (of opinions, etc) to differ: [V]

Our views diverged so greatly that we could never agree on anything. [also Vpr]. Compare CONVERGE. **2** ~ **from sth** to turn away from a plan, standard, etc: [Vpr] *diverge from the truth/norm/usual procedure.*
▶ **divergence** /daɪˈvɜːrdʒəns/ *n* [C, U]: *the divergence between theory and practice.* **divergent** /-dʒənt/ *adj: divergent paths/opinions.*

divers /ˈdaɪvəz/ *adj* [attrib] (*dated or fml*) various; several: *a collection of essays on divers subjects.*

diverse /daɪˈvɜːs/ *adj* of different kinds; varied: *people from diverse cultures* ○ *Her interests are very diverse.*

diversify /daɪˈvɜːsɪfaɪ/ *v* (*pt, pp* **-fied**) **1** to give variety to sth; to vary sth: [Vn] *diversify one's skills/ interests* ○ *a range of diversified degree courses.* **2** ~ **(into sth)** (*commerce*) (esp of a business) to vary the range of products, investments, etc in order to be more competitive or reduce risk: [V] *The choice facing the company is simple: diversify or go bankrupt.* [Vpr] *Some publishers are now diversifying into computer software.* ▶ **diversification** /daɪˌvɜːsɪfɪˈkeɪʃn/ *n* [U].

diversion /daɪˈvɜːʃn; *US* -vɜːrʒn/ *n* **1** [C, U] (an instance of) the action of turning sth aside or changing its direction: *the diversion of a stream/one's energies* ○ *the diversion of funds* ○ *the diversion of flights because of fog.* **2** [C] (*esp Brit*) (*US* **detour**) a different route for use by traffic when the usual road is temporarily closed: *Sorry I'm late — there was a diversion.* **3** [C] an entertaining activity, esp one that turns the attention from work, study, etc: *the diversions of city life* ○ *It's difficult to concentrate when there are so many diversions.* **4** [C] a thing designed to draw attention away from sth one does not want to be noticed: *One of the gang created a diversion in the street while the others robbed the bank.* ▶ **diversionary** /daɪˈvɜːʃənəri; *US* -ˈvɜːrʒəneri/ *adj: diversionary action/tactics/raids.*

diversity /daɪˈvɜːsəti/ *n* [U, sing] the state of being varied; variety: *a wide diversity of opinion* ○ *measures to protect biological diversity.*

divert /daɪˈvɜːt/ *v* **1** ~ **sb/sth (from sth) (to sth)** (**a**) to turn sb/sth from one course to another: [Vn, Vnpr] *divert traffic (from one road to another)* ○ *divert a ship (from its course)* ○ *divert resources (to other projects).* (**b**) to take attention away from sth; to distract sb/sth: [Vnpr] *By concentrating on the sensational aspects of the case the newspapers are diverting (our) attention from the real issues.* [also Vn]. **2** to entertain or amuse sb: [Vn] *Children are easily diverted.*
▶ **diverting** *adj* entertaining.

divest /daɪˈvest/ *v* (*fml*) **1** ~ **sb/sth of sth** to take away power, rights, authority, etc from sb/sth: [Vnpr] *Many feel that local councils should be divested of their public health responsibilities* ○ *The editorial cuts have divested the book of any meaning.* **2** ~ **oneself of sth** to rid oneself of a feeling, an idea, etc: [Vnpr] *He could not divest himself of the suspicion that his wife was being unfaithful.*

divide¹ /dɪˈvaɪd/ *v* **1** ~ **(sth) (up) (into sth)** to separate or make sth separate into parts: [V] *Cells multiply by dividing.* [Vnpr, Vnp] *divide a novel (up) into chapters* ○ *The children were divided (up) into small groups.* [also Vpr, Vp, Vn]. **2** ~ **sth (out/up) (between/among sb)** to separate sth into parts and give a share to each of a number of individuals: [Vn, Vnp] *divide (out/up) the money/food/reward* [Vpr] *We divided the work between us.* **3** ~ **sth (between A and B)** to use different parts of sth, esp one's time, for different activities, etc: [Vnpr] *He divides his energies between politics and business.* [also Vn]. **4** [Vnpr] ~ **A from B** (**a**) to separate two people or things: *divide a mother from her baby.* (**b**) to be the boundary between two people or things: *The English Channel divides England from France.*

5 to make two or more people disagree: [Vn] *This issue has divided the government.* ○ *The government is divided (on this issue).* ○ *The article claims we are living in a divided society.* **6** (*mathematics*) (**a**) ~ **sth by sth** to find out how many times one number is contained in another: [Vnpr] *30 divided by 6 is 5.* (**b**) ~ **into sth** to be able to be multiplied to give another number: [Vpr] *5 divides into 30 6 times.* **7** (esp of a parliament) to separate into groups in order to vote: [V] *After a long debate the House divided.*
▶ **divider** *n* a thing that divides sth: *a ˈroom divider* (ie a screen, etc that divides a room into two parts). Compare DIVIDERS.
■ **diˌvided ˈhighway** *n* (*US*) = DUAL CARRIAGEWAY.
diˈviding line *n* a distinction made between two things that are or seem similar: *the dividing line between opinion and fact.*

divide² /dɪˈvaɪd/ *n* **1** ~ **(between A and B)** a separation or division between two groups that are very different from each other or have a strong dislike for each other: *the North/South divide in Britain* ○ *the divide between Catholics and Protestants.* **2** (*esp US*) a line of high land separating two river systems; a WATERSHED: *the Continental/Great Diˈvide* (ie that formed by the Rocky Mountains).

dividend /ˈdɪvɪdend/ *n* (*commerce*) a share of profits paid to people who own parts of a company, or to winners in the football pools (FOOTBALL): *The company has announced a dividend of 3.5 pence per share.* **IDM** **pay dividends** ⇨ PAY².

dividers /dɪˈvaɪdəz/ *n* [pl] an instrument used for measuring lines, angles, etc: *a pair of dividers.* ⇨ picture at COMPASS.

divination /ˌdɪvɪˈneɪʃn/ *n* [U] (the skill of) saying what will happen in the future or discovering hidden knowledge.

divine¹ /dɪˈvaɪn/ *adj* **1** [usu attrib] of, from or like God or a god: *divine wisdom/justice.* **2** (*dated infml*) wonderful, beautiful, etc: *You look simply divine, darling!* ▶ **divinely** *adv.*

divine² /dɪˈvaɪn/ *v* **1** (*fml*) to sense sth by guessing or INTUITION: [Vn] *divine sb's thoughts/intentions* ○ *divine the truth* [also V.*that*]. **2** to reveal sth hidden, esp the future, by magical means: [V.*wh*] *Astrologers claim to be able to divine what the stars hold in store for us.* [also Vn, V.*that*].

divinity /dɪˈvɪnəti/ *n* **1** [U] the quality of being DIVINE¹(1): *the divinity of Christ.* **2** [C] a god or GODDESS(1): *the Roman/Greek/Egyptian divinities.* **3** [U] the study of religion; THEOLOGY(1): *a doctor of divinity.*

divisible /dɪˈvɪzəbl/ *adj* [usu pred] ~ **(by sth)** (*mathematics*) that can be divided, usu with nothing remaining: *8 is divisible by 2 and 4, but not by 3.* Compare INDIVISIBLE.

division /dɪˈvɪʒn/ *n* **1** [U] (**a**) dividing or being divided: *the division of labour/wealth.* (**b**) (*mathematics*) the process of dividing one number by another: *Are you any good at division?* See also LONG DIVISION. **2** [sing] (often following an *adj*) the result of dividing: *a fair/unfair division of money.* **3**(**a**) [C] each of the parts into which sth is divided. (**b**) [CGp] (*abbr* **Div**) a major unit or section of an organization: *the ˈsales division of our company* ○ *Our team plays in the first diˈvision/division one (of the football league).* ○ *the ˈparachute division.* **4** [C] a line that divides sth; a border: *A hedge forms the division between her land and mine.* **5** [C, U] (an instance of) disagreement or difference in thought, way of life, etc: *a division of opinion* ○ *the deep/widening divisions in society today.* **6** [C] the separation of members of a parliament into groups to vote for or against sth: *The Bill was read without a division.*

▶ **divisional** /dɪˈvɪʒənl/ *adj* [attrib] of a division(3): *the diˌvisional comˈmander/headˈquarters.*

■ **diˈvision sign** *n* the sign (÷) placed between two numbers, showing that the first is to be divided by the second.

divisive /dɪˈvaɪsɪv/ *adj* causing disagreement among people: *a divisive influence/policy/effect.* ▶ **divisively** *adv.* **divisiveness** *n* [U].

divorce¹ /dɪˈvɔːs/ *n* **1** [C, U] ~ (**from sb**) (an instance of) the legal ending of a marriage: *ask/sue for a divorce ○ get/obtain a divorce ○ grounds* (ie legal reasons) *for divorce ○ start diˈvorce proceedings ○ Divorce is on the increase.* **2** [C] ~ (**between A and B**) the ending of a connection; a separation: *the divorce between religion and science.*

divorce² /dɪˈvɔːs/ *v* **1** to end one's marriage to sb by legal means: [Vn] *They're divorcing each other/ getting divorced.* [V] *He divorced and later remarried.* **2** ~ **sb/sth from sth** (often passive) to separate sb/sth from sth, esp in a false way: [Vnpr] *You can't divorce science from ethical questions. ○ a politician who is totally divorced from* (ie unable to understand or deal with) *the real needs of the country.*
▶ **divorcee** /dɪˌvɔːˈsiː/ *n* a divorced person, esp a woman.

divot /ˈdɪvət/ *n* a piece of grass and earth cut out, esp by a golf club when making a stroke.

divulge /daɪˈvʌldʒ/ *v* ~ **sth** (**to sb**) to make sth known, esp a secret: [Vn] *divulge a confidential report/sb's identity/one's age* [V.wh] *I cannot divulge how much it cost.* [also Vnpr].

Diwali /diːˈwɑːliː/ *n* a Hindu festival with lights, held between September and November.

DIY /ˌdiː aɪ ˈwaɪ/ *abbr* (*Brit infml*) do it yourself: *a DIY kit ○ DIY enthusiasts.*

dizzy /ˈdɪzi/ *adj* (**-ier, -iest**) **1(a)** (of a person) feeling as if everything is spinning round; unable to balance; confused: *dizzy with happiness/exhaustion ○ After my second glass of whisky I began to feel rather dizzy.* (**b**) of or causing this feeling: *suffer from ˈdizzy spells ○ a dizzy ˈheight/ˈspeed.* **2** (*infml esp US*) (esp of women) silly; foolish.
▶ **dizzily** *adv.*
dizziness *n* [U].
dizzying *adj* [attrib] making one feel dizzy: *the dizzying pace of events.*

DJ /ˌdiː ˈdʒeɪ/ *abbr* **1** (*Brit infml*) dinner-jacket. **2** disc jockey: *He's a radio DJ.*

DLitt /ˌdiː ˈlɪt/ (also **Litt D**) *abbr* Doctor of Letters: *have/be a DLitt in English ○ Jane Pearce DLitt.*

DM (also **D-mark**) *abbr* the main unit of money in Germany (German *Deutsche Mark*): *DM 650.*

DNA /ˌdiː en ˈeɪ/ *abbr* (*chemistry*) deoxyribonucleic acid (the chemical in the cells of animals and plants which carries GENETIC information).

do¹ /də, du; *strong form* duː/ *aux v.* ⇨ note. **1(a)** (used before a full *v* to form negative sentences and questions): *I don't like fish. ○ They didn't go to Paris. ○ Don't forget to write. ○ Does she speak French?* (**b**) (used to make tag questions): *You live in London, don't you? ○ He married his boss's daughter, didn't he? ○ She doesn't work here, does she?* **2** (used to avoid repeating a full *v*): *He plays better than he did a year ago. ○ She works harder than he does. ○ 'Who won?' 'I did.'* **3** (used when no other *aux v* is present to emphasize that a verb is positive): *He ˈdoes look tired. ○ She ˈdid write to say thank you. ○ Do shut up!* **4** (used to reverse the order of the subject and *v* when an *adv* or adverbial phrase is moved to the front): *Not only does she speak Spanish, (but) she also knows how to type. ○ Only rarely did he visit us.*

NOTE The forms of **do** (auxiliary verb)
present tense

full forms		negative short forms	
I you	do	I you	don't
he she it	does	he she it	doesn't
we you they	do	we you they	don't

The negative full forms are formed by adding **not**: **I do not, you do not, he does not**, etc.
Questions are formed by placing the verb before the subject: **do I? don't you? does he not?** etc.

present participle: doing

past tense
The past tense for all persons is **did** (negative **did not/didn't**)
Questions are formed by placing the verb before the subject: **did I? didn't you? did he not?** etc.

past participle: done

Do as a main verb forms negatives and questions with **do/does** or **did**: *How did you do it? ○ I don't do any teaching now.*
The other tenses of **do** are formed in the same way as those of other verbs: **will do, would do, have done**, etc.
The pronunciation of each form of **do** is given at its entry in the dictionary.

do² /də, du; *strong form* duː/ *v* (*3rd pers sing pres t* **does** /dʌz/; *pt* **did** /dɪd/; *pp* **done** /dʌn/)

● **Indicating an activity 1** (used esp with *what, anything, nothing* and *something*, to refer to actions which are not specified or not yet known about): [Vn] *'What are you doing this evening?' ○ Are you doing anything tomorrow evening? ○ We will do what we can to help you. ○ The company ought to do something about the poor service. ○ What does she want to do* (ie What career does she want) *when she leaves school? ○* **What do you do?** (ie What is your job?) *○ There's nothing to do in this place* (ie no means of passing one's time in an enjoyable way). *○ 'It's so unfair that she's lost her job.' 'I know, but there's nothing we can do about it* (ie we can't change the situation).' *○ 'What can I do for you?' 'I'd like a pound of apples, please.'* **2** to act; to behave: [Vadv] *Do as you wish/please. ○ Why can't you do as you're ˈtold* (ie obey instructions)? **3** to work at or perform an activity or a task: [Vn] *do a university degree ○ I'm doing some research on the subject. ○ I have a number of important things to do today. ○ She does aerobics once a week.* **4** (used esp with *the + n* or *my, his, one's + n*, to refer to tasks such as cleaning, washing, arranging, mending, etc): *do* (ie brush) *one's teeth ○ do* (ie wash) *the dishes ○ do* (ie polish) *the silver ○ do* (ie arrange) *the flowers ○ We'll have to get someone to do* (ie mend) *the roof. ○ I like the way you've done your hair.* **5** (used with *the, my, some, much*, etc + the *-ing* form of a *v* to refer to a wide range of actions) [Vn] *do the ironing/cooking/ washing/shopping ○ She did a lot of acting* (ie acted in a lot of plays) *when she was at university. ○ He does some writing* (eg writes poems, novels, etc) *in his spare time.* **6** (*US infml*) to arrange to take part in sth: [Vn] *Let's do* (ie meet for) *lunch some time.*

● **Studying or solving sth 7** to learn or study sth: [Vn] *do accountancy/engineering/law ○ She did economics at Harvard University. ○ Have you done any* (ie studied anything by) *Shakespeare?* **8** to find the answer to sth; to solve sth: [Vn] *I can't do this sum. ○ Can you do crosswords?*

● **Making, producing or performing sth 9** ~ sth **(for sb)** to produce or make sth: [Vn] *do a drawing/painting/sketch* ○ *She did five copies of the agenda.* ○ *Does this pub do* (ie provide) *lunches?* ○ *Who's doing* (ie organizing and preparing) *the food at the wedding reception?* [Vnpr, Vnn] *I'll do a translation for you/do you a translation.* **10** to perform or produce a play, an opera, etc: [Vn] *The local dramatic society are doing 'Hamlet' next month.* **11** to play the part of a character, etc; to IMITATE(2) sb: [Vn] *I thought she did Ophelia superbly.* ○ *He does Elvis Presley rather well/does a rather good Elvis Presley.* **12** (used in the perfect tense or the passive) to finish or complete sth: [V] (*infml*) *Have you done* (ie finished what you were doing)? [V.ing] *I've done talking — let's get started.* [Vn] *Did you get your article done in time?*

● **Completing an activity or a journey 13 (a)** to travel a distance: [Vn] *How many miles did you do during your tour?* ○ *My car does 40 miles to the gallon* (ie uses one GALLON of petrol to travel 40 miles). **(b)** to complete a journey: [Vn] *We did the journey (from London to Oxford) in an hour.* **(c)** to travel at or reach a speed: [Vn] *The car was doing 90 miles an hour.* **14** (*infml*) to visit a place as a tourist: [Vn] *We did Tokyo in three days.* **15** to spend a period of time: [Vn] *She did a year at university, but then decided to give up the course.* ○ *He did six years (in prison) for armed robbery.*

● **Other meanings 16** to deal with or attend to sb/ sth: [Vn] *The barber said he'd do me* (ie cut my hair) *next.* **17** ~ **(for sb/sth)**; ~ **(as sth)** to be suitable or good enough for sb/sth: [V] *'Can you lend me some money?' 'Certainly — will £10 do?'* [Vpr] *These shoes won't do* (ie are not strong enough) *for climbing.* [V-n] *This log will do fine as a table for our picnic.* [Vadv, Vnadv] *This room will do (me) nicely, thank you* (ie It has everything I need). **18** (used with *advs*, or in questions after *how*) to make progress; to perform: [Vadv] *She's doing very well at school* (ie Her work is good). ○ *How is the business doing?* ○ *Both mother and baby are doing well* (ie after the birth of the baby). ○ (*infml*) ***How are you doing?*** (ie How are you?) ○ *She did well out of* (ie made a big profit from) *the deal.* **19** to cook sth: [Vn] *Shall I do the casserole in the oven?* ○ *How would you like your steak done?* **20 (a)** (*infml*) (usu passive) to cheat sb: [Vn] *This table isn't a genuine antique; I'm afraid you've been done* (ie you have paid a lot of money for an object of little value). **(b)** (*sl*) to rob a place: [Vn] *The gang did a warehouse and a supermarket.* **21** (*Brit*) ~ **sb (for sth)** (usu passive) to arrest or CONVICT sb (for a crime): [Vnpr] *He got done for speeding.* [also Vn].

IDM Most idioms containing **do** are at the entries for the nouns or adjectives in the idioms, eg **do a bunk** ⇨ BUNK². **be/have to do with sb/sth** to be about or connected with or sb/sth: *'What do you want to see me about?' 'It's to do with that letter you sent me.'* **have (got) something, nothing, a lot, etc to do with sb/sth** to be connected with sb/sth to the extent specified: *Her job has something to do with computers.* ○ *'How much do you earn?' 'What's it got to do with you?'* ○ *Hard work has a lot to do with* (ie has contributed greatly towards) *her success.* ○ *We don't have very much to do with our neighbours* (ie We do not meet them socially). ○ *I'd have nothing to do with him, if I were you.* ˌ**how do you 'do?** (used as a formal greeting when one meets sb for the first time. The usual reply is also *How do you do?*) **it/that will never/won't 'do** (used to indicate that a situation is not satisfactory and should be changed or improved): *This is the third time you've been late for work this week; it simply won't do, I'm afraid.* ˌ**nothing 'doing** (*sl*) (used to refuse a request): *'Could you lend me $10?' 'Nothing doing!'* **that** ˈ**does**

it (*infml*) (used to show that one will not tolerate sth any longer): *That does it! I've had enough of your sarcasm. I'm leaving.* **that's** ˈ**done it** (*infml*) (used to express DISMAY or anger that an accident, a mistake, etc has spoiled or ruined sth): *That's done it. We've run out of petrol and I left the spare can at home.* **that will** ˈ**do** (used esp to order sb to stop doing or saying sth): *That'll do, children — you're getting far too noisy.* **what is sb/sth doing …?** why is sb/sth in the specified place?: *What's this pair of shoes doing on my desk?* (ie Who put them there, and why?)

PHR V ˌ**do a**ˈ**way with sth** (*infml*) to stop doing or having sth; to cause sth to end: *She thinks it's time we did away with the monarchy.* ○ *The death penalty has been done away with in many European countries.* ˌ**do a**ˈ**way with oneself/sb** (*infml*) to kill oneself/sb: *She tried to do away with herself.*

ˌ**do sb/sth** ˈ**down** (*Brit infml*) to speak of sb/sth in a critical or unkind way; to criticize sb/sth: *It has become fashionable to do down traditional moral values.*

ˈ**do for sb** (*Brit infml*) to clean sb's house: *Old Mrs Green has done for us for over 20 years.* ˈ**do for sb/ sth** (*infml*) (usu passive) to ruin, destroy or kill sb/ sth: *Unless the government provides more cash, the steel industry is* ˈ*done for.* ˈ**do for sth** (*infml*) (used in questions with *what*) to manage to obtain: *What do you do for fuel during the winter months?* ˈ**do sth for sb/sth** (*infml*) to improve the appearance of sb/ sth: *Her new hairstyle really does something/a lot for her.*

ˌ**do sb/oneself** ˈ**in** (*infml*) **1** to kill sb/oneself: *She was so depressed she felt like doing herself in.* **2** (usu passive) to make sb very tired: *Come in and sit down — you look done in.* ˌ**do sth** ˈ**in** (*infml*) to injure a part of the body: *He did his back in lifting heavy furniture.*

ˌ**do sth** ˈ**out** (*Brit infml*) to clean or tidy a room, cupboard, etc by removing things from it: *Your desk drawer needs doing out.* ˌ**do sb** ˈ**out of sth** (*infml*) to prevent sb from having sth they ought to have, esp in an unfair or dishonest way: *She was done out of her promotion.*

ˌ**do sb** ˈ**over** (*infml esp Brit*) to attack and beat sb severely: *He was done over by a gang of thugs after a football match.*

ˌ**do sth** ˈ**over 1** to clean or decorate sth again: *The paintwork will need doing over/need to be done over soon.* **2** (*US*) to do sth again: *This is no good — you'll have to do it over.*

ˈ**do sth to sth** (esp in questions with *what*) to cause sth to happen to sb/sth: *What have you done to the television? It's not working properly.* ○ *What have you done to your sister? She's very upset.*

ˌ**do** ˈ**up** to be fastened: *The skirt does up at the back.* ˌ**do oneself** ˈ**up** (*infml*) to make oneself more attractive by putting on make-up (MAKE¹), attractive clothes, etc. ˌ**do sth** ˈ**up 1** to fasten a coat, skirt, etc: *He never bothers to do his jacket up.* ○ *She asked me to do up her dress for her at the back.* **2** to make sth into a parcel; to wrap sth: *She was carrying a parcel of books done up in brown paper.* **3** (*Brit*) to repair and decorate a house, room, etc: *He makes money by buying old houses and doing them up.* ○ *We're having the kitchen done up.*

ˈ**do with sth 1** (used with *can* and *could* to express a need or desire for sth): *You look as if you could do with a good night's sleep.* ○ *I could do with a drink!* **2** (*dated Brit*) (used in the negative with *can* and *could*) to tolerate sth: *I can't do with/can't be doing with his insolence.* ˈ**do sth with sb/sth** (used in questions with *what*): *What have you done with* (ie Where have you put) *my umbrella?* ○ *Tell me what you did with yourselves* (ie how you passed the time) *on Sunday.* ○ *What are we going to do with*

D

(ie How are we going to use) *the food left over from the party?*

,do with'out (sb/sth) (used esp with *can* and *could*) to manage without sb/sth: *She can't do without a secretary.* ○ *If we can't afford a car, we'll just have to do without (one).* ○ (ironic) *I could have done without being* (ie I wish I had not been) *woken up at 3 o'clock in the morning.*

■ ,do-'gooder *n* (*infml derog*) a person who performs or tries to perform good deeds, esp by interfering in a way which annoys other people.

,do it your'self (*abbr* DIY) *n* [U] (*esp Brit*) the activity of making, repairing or decorating things in the home oneself instead of paying sb to do it: *The materials you need are available from any good ,do-it-your'self shop.*

do³ /duː/ *n* (*pl* dos *or* do's /duːz/) (*Brit infml*) a party: *I hear the Newtons are having a big do to-night.* [IDM] do's and don'ts /,duːz ən 'dəʊnts/ rules: *If you want to lose weight, here are some do's and don'ts.* fair dos/do's ⇨ FAIR¹.

do⁴ = DOH.

do⁵ *abbr* ditto.

doc /dɒk/ *n* (*infml*) (often as a form of address) doctor.

docile /'dəʊsaɪl; *US* 'dɒsl/ *adj* (of a person or an animal) easy to control: *a docile child/horse/personality.* ► docilely /-saɪlli; *US* -səli/ *adv.* docil-ity /dəʊ'sɪləti/ *n* [U].

dock¹ /dɒk/ *n* **1** [C] a part of a port, etc where ships go to have cargoes put on or taken off them, or to be repaired: *go into/be in dock* ○ *dock workers* ○ *a dock strike.* **2** docks [pl] a group of docks and the build-ings around them used for storing cargoes, etc: *London docks* ○ *He works at the docks.*
► docker *n* a person whose job is to move cargoes on and off ships.

dock² /dɒk/ *v* **1(a)** [V] (of a ship) to come into a DOCK¹(1). **(b)** [Vn] to bring a ship into a DOCK¹(1). **2(a)** (of two or more spacecraft) to be joined to-gether in space¹(5): [V] *docking manoeuvres/procedures.* **(b)** [Vn] to join two or more spacecraft together in space¹(5).

dock³ /dɒk/ *n* the part of a criminal court where the person accused of a crime stands or sits during the trial: *He's been in the dock* (ie on trial for crimes) *a few times already.*

dock⁴ /dɒk/ *v* **1** [Vn] to cut short an animal's tail. **2** ~ sth (from/off sth) to take away a part of sth, esp an amount of money: [Vnpr] *dock 15% from/off sb's earnings* [Vn] *They've docked my salary.* [Vnn] *They docked me £20.*

dock⁵ /dɒk/ *n* [U, C] a common wild plant with large leaves.

docket /'dɒkɪt/ *n* (*commerce*) a document or label listing goods delivered, jobs done, the contents of a parcel, etc.
► docket *v* [Vn] to label sth with a docket.

dockland /'dɒklænd/ *n* [U,C] the district near docks (DOCK¹ 2).

dockyard /'dɒkjɑːd/ *n* an area with docks (DOCK¹ 2) and equipment for building and repairing ships.

doctor /'dɒktə(r)/ *n* (*abbr* Dr) **1** (the title of) a person who has been trained in and practises med-ical science: *You'd better see a doctor about that cut.* ○ *Doctor Thompson.* **2** (the title of) a person who has received the highest university degree: *Doctor of Philosophy.*
► doctor *v* **1** (*infml*) to change sth in order to deceive; to FALSIFY(1) sth: [Vn] *doctor evidence/accounts/a report.* **2** (*infml*) to add sth harmful to food or drink: [Vn] *They doctored her fruit juice with vodka and she got very drunk.* **3** to treat an animal so that it is unable to reproduce: [Vn] *The cat's been doctored.*

doctoral /'dɒktərəl/ *adj* [attrib] of or relating to a doctorate: *a doctoral thesis.*

doctorate /'dɒktərət/ *n* the highest university de-gree: *She's studying for her doctorate.*

doctrinaire /,dɒktrɪ'neə(r)/ *adj* (*derog*) strictly ap-plying or insisting on a theory in all circumstances, regardless of practical problems or disagreement: *a doctrinaire Marxist* ○ *doctrinaire attitudes/beliefs/policies.*

doctrine /'dɒktrɪn/ *n* [C, U] a belief or set of beliefs held and taught by a church, a political party, a group of scientists, etc: *Catholic doctrines* ○ *Marxist doctrine* ○ *Progress has swept many of the old doc-trines away.*
► doctrinal /dɒk'traɪnl; *US* 'dɒktrənl/ *adj* of or related to a doctrine or doctrines: *doctrinal contro-versy* ○ (*derog*): *a rigidly doctrinal approach.*

document /'dɒkjumənt/ *n* an official or formal pa-per, form, book, etc giving information about sth, evidence or proof of sth, or a record of sth: *legal documents* ○ *documents of ownership* ○ *travel docu-ments* ○ *Documents detailing government meetings were leaked to the press.*
► document /'dɒkjument/ *v* [Vn] **1** to record sth in a document: *document a sale/a transaction* ○ *a film documenting peasant life during the 19th century* ○ *The story of her life is well documented* (ie There are many records of it). **2** to prove or support sth with documents: *Can you document these claims?*
documentation /,dɒkjumen'teɪʃn/ *n* [U] **1** the act of documenting or the state of being documented: *the documentation of an agreement.* **2** documents required for sth or providing evidence or proof of sth: *I couldn't enter the country because I didn't have the proper documentation.*

documentary /,dɒkju'mentri/ *adj* [attrib] **1** con-sisting of documents: *documentary evidence/proof/sources.* **2** giving a record or report of the facts of sth, esp by using pictures, recordings, etc of people involved: *a documentary account of the Vietnam war* ○ *documentary films showing the lives of working people.*
► documentary *n* a film or radio or television programme giving facts about sth: *a documentary on/about drug abuse.*

dodder /'dɒdə(r)/ *v* (*infml*) to move or act in a slow unsteady way because of old age or weakness: [Vp, Vpr] *doddering along (the pavement)* [also V].
► doddering /'dɒdərɪŋ/ (also doddery /'dɒdəri/) *adj* weak, slow and unsteady in movement, etc: *a group of doddery old men* ○ *He spoke in a low dodder-ing voice.*

doddle /,dɒdl/ *n* [sing] (*Brit infml*) a task or an activity that is easily performed: *That hill's an abso-lute doddle (to climb).*

dodge¹ /dɒdʒ/ *v* **1** to move quickly and suddenly to one side or out of the way in order to avoid sb/sth: [Vpr] *She dodged round the corner and out of sight.* [Vn] *They managed to dodge the bullets and escape unhurt.* [also V,Vp]. **2(a)** (*infml*) to avoid sth dis-honestly: [Vn] *dodge military service* [V.ing] *dodge paying one's taxes.* **(b)** to avoid facing or doing sth unpleasant: [Vn] *dodge awkward questions* ○ *She al-ways manages to dodge the housework.* [also V.ing].
► dodger *n* (*infml*) a person who avoids sth dishon-estly: *a fare dodger* (ie sb who deliberately does not pay their fare on public transport). See also DRAFT-DODGER.

dodge² /dɒdʒ/ *n* **1** (*usu sing*) a quick movement to avoid sb/sth. **2** (*infml*) a trick or dishonest act, esp a clever one, in order to avoid sth: *a 'tax dodge* ○ *When it comes to getting off work, he knows all the dodges.*

dodgems /'dɒdʒəmz/ (also 'dodgem cars) *n* [pl] (*Brit*) small electric cars ridden in an enclosure at a FAIR³(1). Drivers try to hit other cars while avoiding those that try to hit them: *have a go on the dodgems.*

dodgy /'dɒdʒi/ *adj* (-ier, -iest) (*infml esp Brit*) **1**

likely to be dishonest; suspicious: *He's a dodgy bloke — I wouldn't trust him an inch.* ○ *The scheme sounds rather dodgy to me.* **2** risky or dangerous: *Cycle across America? Sounds a bit dodgy to me.* **3** not good or reliable: *dodgy reasoning* ○ *My French is pretty dodgy.* ○ *I can't play, I've got a dodgy knee.*

dodo /ˈdəʊdəʊ/ *n* (*pl* **-os** or **-oes**) a large bird, now extinct, that was unable to fly. **IDM** **dead as a/the dodo** ⇨ DEAD.

DOE /ˌdiː əʊ ˈiː/ *abbr* (in Britain) Department of the Environment.

doe /dəʊ/ *n* a female deer, REINDEER, rabbit or HARE. ⇨ picture at DEER. Compare BUCK[1], FAWN[1] 1, HIND[2], STAG 1.

doer /ˈduːə(r)/ *n* (*approv*) a person who does things rather than thinking or talking about them: *We need fewer organizers and more doers.*

does /dʌz/ ⇨ DO[1,2]. ⇨ note at DO[1].

doesn't /ˈdʌznt/ *short form* does not ⇨ note at DO[1].

doff /dɒf; *US* dɔːf/ *v* [Vn] (*fml*) to take off one's hat. Compare DON[2].

dog[1] /dɒg; *US* dɔːg/ *n* **1** [C] (**a**) a common animal with four legs. Dogs are often kept by human beings as pets, or trained for work, hunting, guarding, etc. They may also be wild: *take the dog for a walk* ○ *guard dogs* ○ *dogs barking.* ⇨ picture. See also GUN DOG. (**b**) the male of this animal, or of the WOLF or fox. Compare BITCH 1. (**c**) **the dogs** [pl] (*Brit infml*) GREYHOUND racing: *I won £50 on the dogs.* **2** [C] (usu following an *adj*) (*infml*) a male person, esp one who has done sth unpleasant or wicked: *You dirty dog!* **3** [C] (*US sl*) a thing of poor quality; a failure: *Her last film was an absolute dog.* See also TOP DOG. **IDM** (**a case of**) ˌdog eat ˈdog (esp in business, politics, etc) a situation of fierce competition in which people are willing to harm each other in order to succeed. **a ˌdog in the ˈmanger** a person who stops others enjoying sth he or she cannot use or does not want: *Don't be such a/so dog in the manger!* **a dog's ˈbreakfast/ˈdinner** (*Brit infml*) a mess; a thing done

badly: *He's made a real dog's breakfast of these accounts.* **a ˈdog's life** an unhappy life, full of problems or unfair treatment. **every dog has his/its ˈday** (*saying*) everyone enjoys good luck or success at some point. **give a dog a bad ˈname** (*saying*) it is very difficult to lose a bad reputation. **go to the ˈdogs** (*infml*) to fall into a very bad state: *This firm's gone to the dogs since the new management took over!* **a/the hair of the dog** ⇨ HAIR. **let sleeping dogs lie** ⇨ SLEEP[2]. **not have a ˈdog's chance** to have no chance at all: *He hasn't a dog's chance of passing the exam.* **rain cats and dogs** ⇨ RAIN[2]. **the tail wagging the dog** ⇨ TAIL. **teach an old dog new tricks** ⇨ TEACH. **treat sb like dirt / a dog** ⇨ TREAT.

■ **ˈdog-biscuit** *n* a small hard biscuit fed to dogs.
ˈdog-collar *n* **1** a collar for a dog. **2** (*infml*) a stiff white collar fastened at the back and worn by a priest.
ˈdog days *n* [pl] the hottest period of the year.

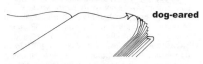

dog-eared

ˈdog-eared *adj* (of a book) having the corners of many pages turned down through use. ⇨ picture.
ˌdog-ˈend *n* (*Brit*) the end of a cigarette that has been smoked.
ˈdog-leg *n* a sharp bend, esp on a golf-course (GOLF).
ˈdog-paddle (also **ˈdoggie-paddle**) *n* [U] a simple swimming stroke, with short quick movements of the arms and legs.
ˌdog-ˈtired *adj* [usu pred] very tired.

dog[2] /dɒg; *US* dɔːg/ *v* (**-gg-**) (**a**) to follow sb closely for a long time: [Vn] *dog sb's footsteps.* (**b**) (of sth unpleasant) to be with sb all the time: [Vn] *Her career was dogged by misfortune.*

dogfight /ˈdɒgfaɪt/ **1** a fight between aircraft in

breeds of dog

All the drawings are to scale and represent the average size reached.

greyhound

cocker spaniel

collie

Dalmatian

Pekinese

Alsatian
(*US* German shepherd)

poodle

Labrador

bulldog

dachshund

40 cms

Irish setter

Scotch terrier

which they fly around close to each other. **2** a fight between dogs organized for public entertainment.

dogfish /'dɒgfɪʃ; US 'dɔːg-/ n (pl unchanged) a small SHARK(1).

dogged /'dɒgɪd; US 'dɔːgɪd/ adj [usu attrib] (approv) with determination; not giving up (GIVE¹) readily: *their dogged defence of the city* ○ *dogged persistence/refusal to admit defeat.* ▶ **doggedly** adv. **doggedness** n [U].

doggerel /'dɒgərəl; US 'dɔːgərəl/ n [U] verse that, intentionally or not, is badly written or ridiculous.

doggo /'dɒgəʊ; US 'dɔːg-/ adv **IDM** **lie doggo** ⇨ LIE².

doggone /'dɒgɒn; US 'dɔːgɒːn/ adj [attrib], adv, interj (US infml) (used for expressing annoyance or surprise): *Where's the doggone key?* ○ *Don't drive so doggone fast!* ○ *Well, doggone (it)!*

doggy (also **doggie**) /'dɒgi; US 'dɔːgi/ n (infml) (used by and to children) a dog.
▶ **doggy** adj **1** of or like a dog: *a ˌdoggy 'smell.* **2** fond of dogs: *We're not really doggy people.*
■ **'doggy bag** n a bag given to a customer in a restaurant or a guest at sb's house for taking home food that remains after a meal, a party, etc.

doghouse /'dɒghaʊs; US 'dɔːg-/ n **IDM** **in the doghouse** (infml) made to feel sb's disapproval because of sth one has done; out of favour: *I'm in the doghouse with my wife because I forgot her birthday.*

dogma /'dɒgmə; US 'dɔːgmə/ n [C,U] a belief or set of beliefs held by an authority or group, which others are expected to accept without argument: *political/social/economic dogma* ○ *She started to question the dogmas of the Church.*

dogmatic /dɒg'mætɪk; US dɔːg'mætɪk/ adj (derog) insisting that one's beliefs are right and that others should accept them, without paying attention to evidence or to other opinions: *You can't be dogmatic in matters of taste.* ○ *a dogmatic attitude/approach/view.* ▶ **dogmatically** /-klɪ/ adv: *state sth dogmatically.*

dogmatism /'dɒgmətɪzəm; US 'dɔːgmətɪzəm/ n [U] (derog) the tendency to be DOGMATIC: *religious/political dogmatism.*

dogsbody /'dɒgzbɒdi; US 'dɔːg-/ n (Brit) a person who is given boring or unpleasant jobs to do for others.

dogwood /'dɒgwʊd; US 'dɔːg-/ n [U,C] a wild bush that produces flowers.

doh (also **do**) /dəʊ/ n (music) the first and 8th note of any major scale¹(6).

doily /'dɔɪli/ n a small ornamental mat of lace, paper, etc placed under a dish or under a cake, etc on a plate.

doing /'duːɪŋ/ n **1** [C usu pl, U] a thing done or caused by sb: *I've been hearing a lot about your doings recently.* ○ *He was convinced that the whole problem was my doing* (ie I caused it). **2** [U] hard work; effort: *Getting the job finished by tomorrow will take a lot of doing.*

doings /'duːɪŋz/ n (pl unchanged) (Brit infml) a thing or things whose name one does not know or has forgotten: *Where's the doings for mending punctures?*

doldrums /'dɒldrəmz/ n **the doldrums** [pl] parts of the ocean near the EQUATOR where there is little or no wind and ships with sails cannot move. **IDM** **in the 'doldrums 1** feeling depressed; in low spirits: *He's been in the doldrums ever since she left him.* **2** not active or improving: *Despite these measures, the economy remains in the doldrums.*

dole¹ /dəʊl/ v **PHRV** **ˌdole sth 'out (to sb)** to distribute sth: *allowances doled out to the elderly* ○ *She seldom doles out praise to people who work for her.*

dole² /dəʊl/ n **the dole** [sing] (Brit infml) payment made by the state to unemployed people: *be/go on*

the dole (ie receive/register for such payments) ○ *claim the dole* ○ *lengthening dole queues.*

doleful /'dəʊlfl/ adj sad; miserable: *a doleful face/manner/expression/prospect.* ▶ **dolefully** /-fəli/ adv.

doll¹ /dɒl; US dɔːl/ n **1** a model of a human figure, esp a baby or a child, for a child to play with. **2** (dated sexist sl esp US) a pretty or attractive female: *She's quite a doll!*
■ **'doll's house** n a toy house used for playing with dolls.

doll² /dɒl; US dɔːl/ v (infml) **PHRV** **ˌdoll sb/oneself 'up** to dress sb/oneself in an attractive way: *I'm going to get dolled up for the party.*

dollar /'dɒlə(r)/ n **1** [C] (symb $) the unit of money in the USA, Canada, Australia and certain other countries: *paid in dollars* ○ *get dollar traveller's cheques.* **2** [C] a BANKNOTE or coin worth one dollar: *I have 10 dollars in my pocket.* ⇨ note at CENT. **3 the dollar** [sing] (finance) the value of the US dollar on international money markets: *The dollar closed two cents down.* **IDM** **bet one's bottom dollar** ⇨ BET. **(feel, look, etc) like a million 'dollars** (infml) (to feel, etc) wonderful.
■ **ˌdollar diˈplomacy** n [U] government policy aimed at promoting a country's business interests abroad.

dollop /'dɒləp/ n (infml) a lump of sth soft, esp food, with no particular shape: *a dollop of cream/jam/mashed potato.*

dolly /'dɒli; US 'dɔːli/ n **1** (used by and when speaking to children) a DOLL¹(1). **2** (esp US) a low platform with small wheels for moving things that are too heavy to carry. ⇨ picture at TROLLEY.
■ **'dolly-bird** (also **dolly**) n (dated Brit infml sexist) a pretty girl or woman, esp one who is dressed in an attractive way and is not considered intelligent.

dolmen /'dɒlmen/ n a group of upright stones with a large flat stone on top, used in ancient times to mark a burial place.

dolorous /'dɒlərəs; US 'dəʊlərəs/ adj [usu attrib] (fml) feeling or showing sorrow.

dolphin

dolphin /'dɒlfɪn/ n a sea animal that looks like a large fish with a pointed mouth part. Dolphins sometimes jump above the surface of the water. ⇨ picture. Compare PORPOISE.

dolt /dəʊlt/ n (derog) a stupid person.
▶ **doltish** adj stupid; foolish.

-dom suff **1** (with vs and adjs forming ns) a condition or state of: *boredom* ○ *freedom.* **2** (with ns) **(a)** the rank of; an area ruled by: *dukedom* ○ *kingdom.* **(b)** a group of: *officialdom.*

domain /də'meɪn, dəʊ-/ n **1** lands owned or ruled by a nobleman, government, etc: *trespass on the King's domain* ○ *(fig) The kitchen is my wife's domain; she doesn't like me interfering there.* **2** a field of knowledge or activity: *Military history is really outside my domain.* ○ *information that is in the public domain* (ie known by or available to the public, not secret).

dome /dəʊm/ n **1** a round roof with a circular base: *the dome of St Paul's Cathedral.* **2** a thing shaped like a dome: *the dome of a hill/of sb's forehead.*
▶ **domed** adj [usu attrib] having or shaped like a dome: *a domed forehead.*

domestic /də'mestɪk/ adj **1** [attrib] of the home, household or family: *domestic water/gas/electricity supplies* ○ *a domestic help* (ie a servant, esp one who

cleans) ○ *domestic bliss/unrest/upheavals/comforts.*
2 fond of home life; enjoying or good at cooking,
cleaning the house, etc: *I'm not a very domestic sort
of person.* **3** [usu attrib] of or inside a particular
country, not foreign or international: *domestic
trade/imports/production* ○ *domestic flights* (ie to
and from places within a country). **4** (of animals)
kept on farms or as pets; not wild.
▶ **domestic** *n* a servant in sb's house, esp one who
cleans.
domestically /-klɪ/ *adv.*
■ do₁mestic ˈscience *n* [U] = HOME ECONOMICS.

domesticate /dəˈmestɪkeɪt/ *v* [Vn] **1** to make sb
used to or fond of home life and doing jobs around
the house. **2** to make an animal used to living with
or working for humans. ▶ **domesticated** *adj: He's
become more domesticated since getting married.* ○
domesticated cattle. **domestication** /də₁mestɪˈkeɪʃn/
n [U].

domesticity /₁dəʊmeˈstɪsəti, ₁dɒm-/ *n* [U] home or
family life: *a scene of cosy domesticity.*

domicile /ˈdɒmɪsaɪl/ *n* (*fml or law*) a person's place
of residence, esp as established for official or legal
purposes.
▶ **domiciled** *adj* [pred] (*fml or law*) having one's
domicile in a place: *be domiciled in Britain/New
York.*

domiciliary /₁dɒmɪˈsɪliəri; *US* -ieri/ *adj* [attrib]
(*fml*) of, to or at sb's home: *a domiciliary visit* (eg by
a doctor or a priest).

dominant /ˈdɒmɪnənt/ *adj* most important, powerful or prominent; dominating: *the dominant
personality in a group* ○ *The castle stands in a dominant position above the town.* ▶ **dominance**
/ˈdɒmɪnəns/ *n* [U]: *assert/establish dominance over
sb* ○ *the absolute dominance of the governing party.*

dominate /ˈdɒmɪneɪt/ *v* **1(a)** to have control or
power over or a very strong influence on sb/sth: [V]
He has authority, but he doesn't try to dominate. [Vn]
*She dominated the meeting by sheer force of charac-
ter.* **(b)** to be the most obvious or important person
or thing in sth: [Vn] *She has dominated the championships for the last few years.* ○ *The election
dominated TV news coverage for over a month.* **2** (of
a building, a high place, etc) to be large, impressive
and above sth: [Vn] *The Acropolis dominates the city
of Athens.* ▶ **domination** /₁dɒmɪˈneɪʃn/ *n* [U]: *under
foreign domination* ○ *His defeat ended American domination of the sport.*

domineering /₁dɒmɪˈnɪərɪŋ/ *adj* behaving in a
forceful way without considering the wishes,
opinions or feelings of others: *a domineering
husband/manager/personality.*

Dominican /dəˈmɪnɪkən/ *n, adj* (a member) of a
religious order¹(12) founded by St Dominic.

dominion /dəˈmɪniən/ *n* **1** [U] ~ (**over sb/sth**) (*fml*)
authority to rule; control: *under foreign dominion* ○
*Man's dominion over the rest of creation is almost
complete.* **2** [C] an area controlled by one government or ruler: *the vast dominions of the Chinese
Empire.* **3** (often **Dominion**) [C] (formerly) any of
the territories of the British Commonwealth that
had their own government.

domino effect

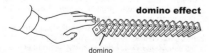

domino

domino /ˈdɒmɪnəʊ/ *n* (*pl* **-oes**) **(a)** [C] a small flat
block, often of wood, marked on one side with two
groups of dots representing numbers, used for playing games. ⇨ picture. **(b)** **dominoes** [sing *v*] a game
played with a set of these, in which players take
turns to put them onto a table.

■ ˈ**domino effect** *n* a situation in which one event
causes a series of similar events to occur one after
the other: *Employers fear a domino effect if the strike
is successful* (ie that there will be many other strikes
as a result). ⇨ picture.

don¹ /dɒn/ *n* **1** (*Brit*) a teacher at a university, esp
at an Oxford or a Cambridge college. **2** Don a title
used before a man's Christian name in Spanish-
speaking countries: *Don Felipe.*
▶ **donnish** /ˈdɒnɪʃ/ *adj* (*esp Brit*) of or like sb who
is concerned with academic rather than practical
matters; like a don: *He has a somewhat donnish air
about him.*

don² /dɒn/ *v* (**-nn-**) (*fml*) to put on clothes, etc: [Vn]
*Donning coats and gloves they set off for a brisk
stroll.* Compare DOFF.

donate /dəʊˈneɪt; *US* ˈdəʊneɪt/ *v* ~ **sth** (**to sb/sth**) to
make a gift of money, clothes, food, etc for a good
cause(3), esp to a charity: [Vnpr] *donate large sums
to relief organizations.* [also Vn].
▶ **donation** /dəʊˈneɪʃn/ *n* **(a)** [C] a thing that is
donated: *make a donation to charity/to an appeal
fund.* **(b)** [U] the act of donating sth: *organ donation*
(ie allowing doctors to use an organ from one's body
after one's death, eg to save a sick person's life).

done¹ /dʌn/ *pp* of DO¹'². ⇨ note at DO¹.

done² /dʌn/ *adj* [pred] **1** (of food) cooked enough:
The meat isn't quite done yet. ○ *a well-done steak.* **2**
(*infml*) socially acceptable, esp among people who
have a strict set of social rules: *Smoking between
courses simply isn't done.* **3** ~ (**with**) finished; completed: *When you're done, perhaps I can say
something.* ○ *Let's get the washing-up done with and
then we can relax.* **IDM** be the ˌdone ˈthing to be
conventional or acceptable behaviour: *For most
people it is still the done thing to get married.* **be/
have ˈdone with sth** to have finished dealing with
sb or doing or using sth: *When the police were done
with him, he was free to go home.* ○ *If you've done
with that magazine, can I have a look at it?* ˈ**done
for** in a situation so bad that it is impossible to get
out of it: *Unless we get some money soon, we'll be
ˈdone for.* ○ *When he pointed the gun at me, I thought
I was ˈdone for* (ie about to die). **done ˈin** extremely
tired. **hard done by** ⇨ HARD². **have ˈdone with
sth** to complete or finish dealing with sth unpleasant, esp as quickly as possible: *Let's spend another
half an hour painting and have ˈdone with it.* **over
and ˈdone with** completely finished: *I'll be glad
when the exams are over and done with.* ▶ **done**
interj (used for showing that one accepts an offer):
'I'll give you £800 for the car.' 'Done!'

Don Juan /₁dɒn ˈdʒuːən/ *n* (*infml*) a man who has
great sexual success with women: *Despite his looks
he's said to be something of a Don Juan.*

donkey /ˈdɒŋki/ *n* (*pl* **-eys**) an animal of the horse
family, with short legs and long ears. **IDM** ˈ**donkey's years** (*Brit infml*) a very long time: *It's
donkey's years since we've seen each other.* ○ *The new
motorway won't be ready for donkey's years.* **talk the
hind legs off a donkey** ⇨ TALK¹.
■ ˈ**donkey jacket** *n* (*Brit*) a thick, short, usu dark
blue coat, worn esp by workers.
ˈ**donkey-work** *n* [U] the hard dull part of a job or
task: *Typical — we do all the donkey-work and he
takes the credit!*

donor /ˈdəʊnə(r)/ *n* **1** a person who donates (DO-
NATE) sth: *He is one of the charity's main donors.* ○
donor countries (ie those which contribute money,
goods, etc to help other countries). **2** (*medical*) a
person who gives blood or a part of her or his body
to be used by doctors to help sick people: *a blood
donor* ○ *The heart transplant will take place as soon
as a suitable donor can be found.* ○ *donor organs.*

don't /dəʊnt/ *short form* do not. ⇨ note at DO¹.

doodle /ˈduːdl/ *v* to draw lines, figures, shapes, etc

casually while doing or thinking about sth else or because one is bored: *doodling in the margin of his notebook.* ▶ **doodle** *n*: *a page covered in doodles.*

doom¹ /duːm/ *n* [U] death or ruin; any terrible fate: *meet/go to one's doom* ∘ *send a man to his doom.* **IDM** ˌ**doom and** ˈ**gloom**; ˌ**gloom and** ˈ**doom** a general feeling of despair and PESSIMISM: *The chairman stressed that despite the recession the past year had not been all doom and gloom.*

doom² /duːm/ *v* ~ **sb/sth (to sth)** (usu passive) to cause sb/sth to suffer inevitable death, destruction, failure, etc: [Vn, Vn.*to* inf] *The plan was doomed (to fail) from the start.* [Vnpr] *Are whales doomed to extinction?*

doomsday /ˈduːmzdeɪ/ *n* [U] the last day of the world, when Christians believe that everyone will be judged by God. **IDM** **till** ˈ**doomsday** for ever; a long time: *This job's going to take me till doomsday.*

door /dɔː(r)/ *n* (**a**) a flat movable barrier that is fitted into and closes the entrance to a building, room, cupboard, car, etc: *knock on the door* ∘ *open/ shut/close/lock/bolt the door* (ie go and open it because sb has knocked on it or rung the bell) ∘ *the door-frame* ∘ *the front/back door* (ie the entrance at the front/back of a building) ∘ *a four-door saloon car.* ⇨ picture at CAR, HOUSE¹. (**b**) the area close to the entrance of a building; a DOORWAY: *I'll meet you at the theatre door.* (**c**) a building or home that is a particular number of buildings or homes away from another: *the family that lives three doors (up/down/along) from us* ∘ *Our other branch is just a few doors down the road.* **IDM** **at death's door** ⇨ DEATH. **behind closed doors** ⇨ CLOSE⁴. **be on the door** (*infml*) to perform some duty at the entrance to a theatre, club, etc, eg collecting tickets from people as they enter. **by/through the back door** ⇨ BACK². **close/shut the** ˈ**door on sth** to make it unlikely that sth will happen: *She was careful not to close the door on the possibility of further talks.* **darken sb's door** ⇨ DARKEN. ˌ**door to** ˈ**door** from building to building: *The journey takes about an hour, door to door.* ∘ *He went from door to door, selling encyclopedias.* ∘ *a* ˌ*door-to-door* ˈ*salesman.* (**open**) **the door to sth** (to provide) the means of getting or reaching sth; (to create) the opportunity for sth: *The agreement will open the door to greatly increased international trade.* ∘ *Our courses are the door to success in English.* **get/have a foot in the door** ⇨ FOOT¹. **keep the wolf from the door** ⇨ WOLF. **lay sth at sb's** ˈ**door** to say that sb is responsible for sth that has gone wrong: *The blame for the disaster has been laid firmly at the government's door.* **leave the** ˈ**door open** to allow for the possibility of further discussion or negotiation. **lock, etc the stable door after the horse has bolted** ⇨ STABLE². **out of** ˈ**doors** in the open air; outdoors: *eat out of doors* ∘ *You should spend more time out of doors in the fresh air.* **show sb the door** ⇨ SHOW². **shut/slam the door in sb's face** to refuse to talk to or have any dealings with sb. **shut the door on sth** ⇨ SHUT. ■ ˈ**door-keeper** *n* a person who guards the entrance to a large building, esp to check on people going in.

doorbell /ˈdɔːbel/ *n* a bell inside a building that visitors outside can ring to attract the attention of sb inside. ⇨ picture at HOUSE¹.

doorknob /ˈdɔːnɒb/ *n* a usu round handle on a door that is turned to open it.

doorman /ˈdɔːmən/ *n* (*pl* **-men** /-mən/) a man employed to stand at the entrance to a large building, eg a hotel or a theatre, and assist visitors: *The doorman got us a taxi.*

doormat /ˈdɔːmæt/ *n* **1** a mat placed near a door, for people to wipe dirt from their shoes on. **2** (*infml*) a person who allows others to treat her or him badly

or unfairly without complaining: *Stand up for yourself a bit — don't be such a doormat!*

doornail /ˈdɔːneɪl/ *n* **IDM** **dead as a doornail** ⇨ DEAD.

doorstep /ˈdɔːstep/ *n* a step leading to an outer door: *empty milk bottles left on the doorstep.* ⇨ picture at HOUSE¹. **IDM** **on one's** ˈ**doorstep** very near to where one is living: *In our holiday villas you'll have both the beach and the mountains on your doorstep.*

doorstop /ˈdɔːstɒp/ *n* a device to prevent a door from closing or from hitting a wall, etc when it is opened.

doorway /ˈdɔːweɪ/ *n* an opening into a building or room, containing a door: *standing in the doorway* ∘ *We sheltered from the rain in a hotel doorway.*

dope /dəʊp/ *n* **1** [U] (*sl*) (**a**) an illegal drug, esp one that is smoked, eg MARIJUANA: *peddle dope* ∘ *a dope dealer.* (**b**) a medicine or drug, esp one that causes sleep or a tired feeling: *The doctor gave her some dope which knocked her out straight away.* (**c**) a drug taken by an ATHLETE(1) or given to an animal to affect performance in a race: *fail a* ˈ*dope test* (ie be found in a medical test to have taken such a drug). **2** [C] (*infml*) a stupid person: *You're holding the picture upside down, you dope!* **3** [U] ~ (**on sb/sth**) (*sl*) information about sb/sth that is not generally known.
▶ **dope** *v* (**a**) to give a drug to a person or an animal in order to affect their performance in a race, etc: [Vn] *Tests revealed that the winning horse had been doped.* (**b**) to put a drug into sb's food or drink, esp in order to make them unconscious: [Vn] *The kidnappers had doped him and tied him up.* (**c**) ~ **sb (up)** (usu passive) to cause sb to be under the influence of drugs and unable to think or speak clearly or act normally: [Vnp] *They spend all their time getting doped up and listening to pop music.* [also Vn].
dopey /ˈdəʊpi/ *adj* (**-pier, -piest**) **1** (*infml*) feeling or appearing to be almost asleep, as if having taken a drug: *I'm feeling really dopey this morning.* **2** (*sl*) stupid.

dorm /dɔːm/ *n* (*infml*) a DORMITORY.

dormant /ˈdɔːmənt/ *adj* not active or growing, though able to become active or grow at a later time: *a dormant volcano* ∘ *Many plants lie dormant throughout the winter.* ∘ *The virus can lie dormant for many years.*

dormer /ˈdɔːmə(r)/ (also ˌ**dormer-**ˈ**window**) *n* an upright window built in a sloping roof. ⇨ picture at HOUSE¹.

dormitory /ˈdɔːmətri; *US* -tɔːri/ *n* **1** a room for several people to sleep in, esp in a school or other institution. **2** (*US*) a building at a college, university, etc containing students' rooms for living and sleeping.
■ ˈ**dormitory town** *n* (*Brit*) a small town from which people travel to work in a big town or city not far away.

dormouse /ˈdɔːmaʊs/ *n* (*pl* **dormice** /ˈdɔːmaɪs/) a small animal like a MOUSE(1) with a tail covered in fur.

dorsal /ˈdɔːsl/ *adj* [attrib] (*anatomy*) of or on the back of an animal or a plant: *a shark's dorsal fin.* ⇨ picture at FISH¹.

dosage /ˈdəʊsɪdʒ/ *n* (usu *sing*) the amount of a medicine or drug to be taken at one time or over a period: *Do not exceed the recommended dosage.*

do's and don'ts ⇨ DO³.

dose /dəʊs/ *n* **1** an amount of a medicine or drug to be taken at one time: *give/administer the correct dose.* **2** (*infml*) an amount or period of sth, esp sth unpleasant: *a dose of flu* ∘ *I can only stand her in small doses* (ie for a short time). ∘ *a lethal dose of radiation* ∘ *A large dose of sunshine and relaxation* *would do me a lot of good.* **IDM** **like a dose of 'salts** (*dated infml*) very fast and easily: *She gets through the housework like a dose of salts.*

▶ **dose** *v* ~ **sb/oneself** (**up**) (**with sth**) to give sb/ oneself an amount of a medicine or drug: [Vnpr] *be heavily dosed with pain-killing drugs* [Vnp] *He dosed himself up with aspirin and went to bed.* [also Vn].

doss /dɒs/ *v* **PHRV** **doss down** (*Brit sl*) to lie down to sleep, esp when one has not got a proper bed: *We dossed down on Tony's floor after the party.*

▶ **dosser** *n* (*Brit sl*) a person without a home who sleeps in the open or in cheap lodgings.

■ **'doss-house** *n* (*Brit sl*) a cheap lodging house for poor people who have no home.

dossier /'dɒsɪeɪ/ *n* ~ (**on sb/sth**) a collection of documents containing information about a person, an event or a subject; a file[1](1b).

dot /dɒt/ *n* **1** a small round mark: *Join the dots up to complete the drawing.* **2** such a mark used as a symbol in writing (eg above the letters i and j), in MATHEMATICS (eg the decimal point), in music, or to represent a short sound in Morse Code. ⇨ App 3. **3** a tiny distant object: *The island was just a dot on the horizon.* **IDM** **on the 'dot** (*infml*) exactly on time, or at the time specified: *He's very punctual — always arrives on the dot.* ○ *leave at 5 o'clock on the dot/on the dot of 5 o'clock.* **the year dot** ⇨ YEAR.

▶ **dot** *v* (**-tt-**) **1** [Vn] to mark sth with a dot. **2** (esp passive) to spread things or people in various separate places over an area: [Vnpr] *The sky was dotted with stars.* ○ *There are several small parks dotted about the town.* [also Vnp]. **IDM** **dot one's/the ,i's and cross one's/the 't's** to complete the final details of a task.

■ **,dot 'matrix printer** *n* (*computing*) a machine that prints letters, numbers, etc formed from tiny dots.

,dotted 'line *n* a line of dots showing where sth is to be written on a document, form, etc. **IDM** **sign on the dotted line** ⇨ SIGN[2].

dotage /'dəʊtɪdʒ/ *n* **IDM** **in one's dotage** old and weak in one's mind.

dote /dəʊt/ *v* **PHRV** **'dote on/upon sb/sth** to feel or show great or too much affection for sb/sth: *She dotes on her grandchildren.* ○ *They seem to dote on that dog of theirs.*

▶ **doting** *adj* [attrib] showing great or too much affection: *a doting husband/son/parent.*

dotty /'dɒti/ *adj* (**-ier, -iest**) (*infml esp Brit*) **1** strange; silly; ECCENTRIC(1): *Not another of your dotty ideas for making money!* ○ *He's getting a bit dotty in his old age.* **2** [pred] ~ **about sb/sth** very fond of or keen on sb/sth: *She's dotty about her latest boy-friend.*

double[1] /'dʌbl/ *adj* [usu attrib] **1** twice as much or as many as is usual: *a double helping* ○ *two double whiskies* ○ *a new bleach with double strength for killing germs.* **2** having or made of two things or parts that are equal or similar: *You're not supposed to park on double yellow lines.* ○ *double doors* ○ *a double-page advertisement* ○ *'Otter' is spelt with a double t.* **3** made for two people or things: *a double 'bed* ○ *a double 'room* (eg in a hotel). **4** combining two things or qualities: *a double meaning/purpose/ aim* ○ *It has the double advantage of being both easy and cheap.*

■ **'double act** *n* a pair of entertainers who perform together.

,double 'agent *n* a person who spies (SPY *v*) for two rival countries at the same time.

,double-'bass *n* the largest instrument of the VI-OLIN family and the lowest in pitch[1](2). ⇨ picture at MUSICAL INSTRUMENT.

,double 'bill *n* two films, plays, etc presented to an audience one after the other in the same pro-gramme.

,double 'bluff *n* an act of trying to deceive sb by telling them the truth while hoping that they will assume you are lying.

,double 'chin *n* a fold of fat below the chin.

,double 'cream *n* [U] (*Brit*) thick cream that con-tains a lot of milk fat.

,double-'dealer *n* (*derog*) a person who says one thing and means another; a dishonest person who deceives others. **,double-'dealing** *n* [U].

,double-'decker *n* **1** (*esp Brit*) a bus with two floors, one above the other. **2** (*esp US*) a sandwich with two layers of filling.

,double 'Dutch *n* [U] (*Brit infml*) speech or writing that makes no sense at all: *This article's so full of jargon it's just double Dutch to me.*

double entendre /,du:bl ɒ̃'tɒ̃drə/ *n* (*French*) a word or phrase that can be understood in two ways, one of which is usu sexual.

,double 'figures *n* [pl] a number that is not less than 10 and not more that 99: *The inflation rate is into double figures* (ie at or above 10% a year). **double-figure** *adj* [attrib]: *double-figure pay rises* (ie of 10% or more).

,double 'life *n* a life lived by sb who appears re-spectable to most people but at the same time is secretly engaged in another, usu immoral, activity: *The world learnt of his extraordinary double life when his mistress sold her story to the newspapers.*

,double 'standards *n* a moral principle that is applied strictly to one situation, person or group but not to another: *He seems to adopt a double standard: it's apparently all right for him to have affairs but not for her.*

,double 'take *n* a delayed reaction to a situation, remark, etc, esp for comic effect: *He did a double take when I said I was getting married.*

'double-talk *n* [U] talk that can be understood in more than one way or cannot be understood at all: *He gave us no real reasons, just the usual politician's double-talk.* — *v*: [Vnpr] *double-talk one's way out of trouble* [also V].

,double 'time *n* [U] twice the usual wage, paid for working outside normal working hours.

double[2] /'dʌbl/ *det* twice as much or as many as: *His income is double hers.* ○ *He earns double what she does.* ○ *We need double the amount we already have.*

double[3] /'dʌbl/ *adv* in twos or in two parts: *When I saw her and her twin sister I thought I was **seeing double**.* ○ *fold a blanket double* ○ *I had to **bend double** to get under the table.*

■ **,double-'barrelled** *adj* **1** (of a gun) having two barrels. **2** (*Brit*) (of a family name) having two parts, usu joined by a HYPHEN (as in *Day-Lewis*): *a double-barrelled surname.*

,double-'book *v* [Vn] to reserve the same seat in a theatre, room in a hotel, etc for two different cus-tomers at the same time. Compare OVERBOOK.

,double-'breasted *adj* (of a coat or jacket) made so that one part at the front comes across the other part when it is fastened and two rows of buttons can be seen.

,double-'check *v* to check sth for a second time or with great care: [Vn] *double-check the figures/ arrangements* [also V]. — *n: a system of checks and double-checks.*

,double-'cross *v* (*derog*) to cheat or betray sb after getting their trust: [Vn] *He double-crossed the rest of the gang and disappeared with all the stolen money.* — *n: a thriller about a double-cross that goes wrong.*

,double-'edged *adj* **1** (of a knife, etc) having two cutting edges. **2** (of a remark) having two possible meanings; AMBIGUOUS(1): *a double-edged comment/ compliment/reply.* **3** having two different, and often contrasting, elements: *a double-edged problem/ aspect.*

,double-'glaze *v* tc fit two layers of glass to the

D

windows of a room, etc to reduce heat loss, noise, etc: [Vn] *The house is double-glazed throughout.*

ˌdouble-ˈglazing *n* [U]: *have double-glazing installed.*

ˌdouble-ˈjointed *adj* [usu pred] having very flexible joints that allow the fingers, arms or legs to bend backwards as well as forwards.

ˌdouble-ˈpark *v* (usu passive) to park a car, etc beside one that is already parked in a street: [Vn] *I can't stay long — I'm double-parked.* [also V].

ˌdouble-ˈquick *adj, adv* (*infml*) very quick or quickly: *We finished the job in double-quick time.*

double⁴ /ˈdʌbl/ *n* **1** [U] twice the number or amount: *He gets paid double for doing the same job I do.* **2** [C] **(a)** a person or thing that looks exactly like another: *She's the double of her mother at the same age.* **(b)** (in a film) an actor who replaces a star in dangerous scenes. **3** [C] a glass of a spirit containing twice the usual amount: *Two Scotches, please — and make those doubles, will you?* **4** **doubles** [pl] a game, esp of tennis, in which one pair plays another: *mixed doubles* (ie in which each pair consists of a man and a woman). **5** **the double** [sing] (*sport*) the act of winning two important competitions or beating the same player or team twice, in the same season or year: *She's going for the double this year — the Olympics and the World Championship.* **6** [C] (in the game of darts (DART¹ 4)) a hit on the outer ring of the board, scoring double the number of that section. **IDM** **at the ˈdouble**; (*US*) **on the ˈdouble** (*infml*) quickly; hurrying: *The boss wants you — you'd better get upstairs at the double.* **ˌdouble or ˈquits** a risk taken, when gambling with money, to determine whether the amount a player owes or has lost will be doubled (DOUBLE⁵ 1) or reduced to nothing.

double⁵ /ˈdʌbl/ *v* **1** to become or cause sth to become twice as much or as many: [V] *The price of houses has virtually doubled over the past few years.* [Vn] *If you double all the quantities in the recipe it will be enough for eight people.* **2** to bend or fold sth into two layers: [Vn] *double a blanket for extra warmth.* **3** **~ as sth** to have a secondary function or use as sth: [V-n] *When we have guests, the sofa doubles as an extra bed.* **PHRV** **ˌdouble ˈback** to turn back in the opposite direction, esp suddenly: *The road ahead was flooded so we had to double back.* **ˌdouble (sb) ˈup** to bend or cause sth to bend the body: *be doubled up with laughter/pain.* **ˌdouble ˈup (on sth / with sb)** (*infml*) to form a pair or pairs in order to share sth: *double up on books in a class* ○ *We've only one room left: you'll have to double up with Peter.*

doublet /ˈdʌblət/ *n* a short, tightly fitting jacket worn by men in former times: *in doublet and hose.*

doubly /ˈdʌbli/ *adv* (used before *adjs*) **1** to twice the extent or amount: *Make doubly sure* (ie Check twice) *that all the doors are locked.* **2** in two ways: *She is doubly gifted: as a writer and as a painter.*

doubt¹ /daʊt/ *n* **1** [U, C] **~ (about / as to sth)**; **~ (as to) whether...** a feeling of not being certain or not believing sth: *There is (no) room for doubt.* ○ *The latest scientific discoveries cast doubt on earlier theories.* ○ *Some people have expressed/raised doubts about her honesty.* ○ *I gave him the job despite lingering/nagging doubts about his suitability.* ○ *She's sure she'll pass her exams, but personally I have my doubts.* ○ *She was without doubt* (ie definitely) *the finest ballerina of her day.* ○ *His right to the title has been established beyond (reasonable) doubt.* **2** **~ about sth/that...** (used after negatives to emphasize that one is convinced of sth) reason for not believing sth: *There's not much doubt about it* (ie It is almost certain). ○ *I have no doubt that you will succeed.* **IDM** **give sb the benefit of the doubt** ⇨ BENEFIT. **in ˈdoubt** uncertain: *The*

contract is still in doubt. ○ *If in doubt, don't* (ie Don't act unless you're certain)*!* **ˌno ˈdoubt** very probably: *No doubt he means to help, but in fact he just gets in the way.*

doubt² /daʊt/ *v* to feel uncertain about sth; to question the truth of sth: [Vn] *We have no reason to doubt her story.* ○ *'I'm telling the truth.' 'I don't doubt it (for a minute).'* [V.that] *I don't doubt that he'll come* (ie I'm sure he will). ○ *Even if he had told the police, which she doubted, why should they believe him?* [V.wh] *I doubt whether he'll come.* ○ *I doubt if that was what he wanted.* ▶ **doubter** *n*.

■ **ˌdoubting ˈThomas** *n* a person who refuses to believe sth until he or she has clear proof: *She's a real doubting Thomas — I'm sure she won't believe you're back till she sees you.*

doubtful /ˈdaʊtfl/ *adj* **1** [usu pred] **~ (about sth/ doing sth)** (of a person) feeling doubt; not sure: *She looked rather doubtful.* ○ *I feel doubtful about going/ about whether to go or not.* **2** **~ (whether/if/that...)** not likely or probable: *It is extremely/increasingly doubtful that anyone survived the explosion.* **3** causing doubt; uncertain: *The weather looks rather doubtful.* ○ *The horse is a doubtful runner/starter* (ie may not take part in the race). **4** [attrib] probably dishonest, unpleasant or not genuine: *a witness of doubtful character/honesty* ○ *a joke in doubtful taste.* ▶ **doubtfully** /-fəli/ *adv.*

doubtless /ˈdaʊtləs/ *adv* almost certainly; very probably: *He was doubtless breathing a sigh of relief yesterday.*

dough /dəʊ/ *n* [U] **1** a thick mixture of flour, water, etc ready to be baked into bread, pastry, etc: *Knead the dough well.* **2** (*sl*) money.

doughnut (also *esp US* **donut**) /ˈdəʊnʌt/ *n* a small cake, usu in the shape of a ring or a ball, made from sweet DOUGH cooked in fat. ⇨ picture at BREAD.

doughty /ˈdaʊti/ *adj* [usu attrib] (*arch or rhet*) brave and strong: *a doughty champion/performance.*

dour /dʊə(r), ˈdaʊə(r)/ *adj* severe and threatening; gloomy (GLOOM): *a dour expression* ○ *the dour Edinburgh sky.* ▶ **dourly** *adv.*

douse /daʊs/ *v* **~ sb/sth (in/with sth)** to put sb/sth into a liquid, esp water, or to throw a liquid over sb/ sth: [Vn] *douse the flames/a fire* [Vnpr] *As a joke, they doused him with a bucket of water.*

dove¹ /dʌv/ *n* **1** a bird of the PIGEON family. The white dove is often used as a symbol of peace: *The dove cooed softly.* ○ *a dove-grey carpet.* **2** a person, esp a politician, who favours peace and negotiation rather than war. Compare HAWK¹ 2.

dove² (*US*) *pt* of DIVE¹.

dovecote /ˈdʌvkɒt, ˈdʌvkəʊt/ *n* a building providing shelter for pigeons (PIGEON).

dovetail /ˈdʌvteɪl/ *n* a joint for fixing two pieces of wood together, with one piece cut in the shape of a WEDGE(1a) fitting into a GROOVE(1) of the same shape in the other. ⇨ picture.

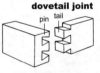

dovetail joint

▶ **dovetail** *v* **~ (sth) (with sth)** to fit together; to combine neatly: [Vpr] *My plans dovetailed nicely with hers.* [also V, Vn, Vnpr].

dowager /ˈdaʊədʒə(r)/ *n* **1** a woman who holds a title or property because of her dead husband's position: *the dowager duchess.* **2** (*infml*) an impressive, usu wealthy, old woman.

dowdy /ˈdaʊdi/ *adj* (**-ier, -iest**) (*derog*) **1** (of clothes, etc) dull; not fashionable: *wearing a dowdy grey dress.* **2** (of a person) dressed in dowdy clothes.

down¹ /daʊn/ *adv part* For the special uses of **down** in phrasal verbs, look at the verb entries. For example, the meaning of **climb down** is given in the phrasal verb section of the entry for **climb. 1(a)** from a higher to a lower level: *pull down a blind* ○ *fall/climb/jump down* ○ *He looked down at her.* ○ *The sun went down below the horizon.* ○ *The ship went down* (ie sank). **(b)** in or into the body: *The baby's sick and can't keep her food down.* **(c)** (moving) from an upright position to a HORIZONTAL one: *knock sb down* ○ *lay sth down* ○ *go and lie down* ○ *cut/burn/ break sth down.* **(d)** (moving) from an upright position to a lower level: *sit/kneel/crouch down* ○ *He bent down to pick up his gloves.* Compare UP¹ 1. **2** (indicating a lower place or state): *Mary is not down yet* (ie She is still in an upstairs room). ○ *The level of unemployment is down.* ○ *The bread is on the third shelf down* (ie from the top). ○ *We're two goals down already* (ie The other team has scored two goals and we have scored none). Compare UP¹ 2. **3** (of a CLUE(2) or an answer in a CROSSWORD) to be read from top to bottom, not from side to side: *I can't go 3 down.* Compare ACROSS¹ 5. **4(a)** away from an important place, esp a large city: *move from London down to the country.* **(b)** to or in the south of the country: *living down south.* **(c)** (*Brit*) away from a university, esp Oxford or Cambridge: *going down at the end of the year.* Compare UP¹ 6. **5** (indicating a reduction in volume, activity or quality): *Please turn the radio down a bit.* ○ *calm/quieten/settle down* ○ *The fire burned down.* ○ *The noise was dying down.* ○ *The wine was watered down for the children.* ○ *The heels of these shoes are quite worn down.* **6(a)** on paper: *write it down* ○ *copy/note/put/take sth down.* **(b)** ~ **(for sth)** added to a list: *Do you have me down for the team?* **7** ~ **(to sb/sth)** (indicating the upper and/or lower limits in a range): *Everyone played well, from the captain down.* ○ *Nobody was free from suspicion, from the head girl down to the youngest pupil.* ○ *I could see everything now, down to the pattern on the teacups.* **8(a)** (with a specified amount of money) spent or lost: *After paying all the bills, I found myself £5 down.* **(b)** as a partial payment: *Pay me $50 down/ as a down payment and the rest at the end of the month.* **9** (*infml*) (used in measuring one's progress through a series of individual people, things, etc): *'How many candidates have you seen so far?' 'Ten down, four to go* (ie four left to see).' **IDM be down to sb** (*infml*) to be the responsibility of sb: *It's down to you now to look after the family business.* **be down to sth** to have only a little money left: *be down to one's last penny/dollar* ○ *I'm afraid I can't buy you a drink — I'm down to my last 50p.* **be/go down with sth** to have or catch an illness: *Peter can't play tomorrow, he's (gone) down with flu.* **down through sth** throughout a considerable period of time: *Down through the years this town has seen many changes.* **down ¹under** (*infml*) in Australia: *Down under they speak their own kind of English.* **down with sb/sth** (used to express a wish that the existence of a person, a group or an institution should be ended): *Down with the government!* ○ *Down with school uniforms!*

■ ¡**down-and-¹out** *n* a person who has no home, money, etc.

¡**down at ¹heel** *adj* looking less attactive, SMART (1,2), etc than before, usu because of lack of money: *The car was getting rather down at heel.* ○ *a down-at-heel seaside resort.*

¡**down-to-¹earth** *adj* practical; sensible and realistic: *a down-to-earth person* ○ *a refreshingly down-to-earth approach to the problem.*

down² /daʊn/ *prep* **1** from a high or higher point on sth to a lower one: *The stone rolled down the hill.* ○ *Tears ran down her face.* ○ *Her hair hung down her back to her waist.* **2** at or to a lower part of a river or stream, nearer the sea: *There's a bridge a mile down the river from here.* **3** (of flat surfaces or areas) along; towards the direction in which one is

facing: *He lives just down the street.* ○ *Go down the road till you reach the traffic lights.* ○ *There it is, halfway down the page.* **4** throughout a period of time: *an exhibition of costumes down the ages* (ie from all periods of history).

down³ /daʊn/ *v* [Vn] (*infml*) **1** to finish a drink quickly: *We downed our beer and left.* **2** to shoot sth, esp a plane, down. **IDM ¡down ¹tools** (*Brit*) (of workers) to stop working, usu suddenly.

down⁴ /daʊn/ *adj* [pred] **1** (*infml*) sad; depressed: *feeling a bit down at the moment.* Compare UP³. **2** (of a computer, etc) not operating: *You'll have to wait — the system's down this morning.*

■ ¹**down time** *n* [U] the time during which a computer is not operating.

down⁵ /daʊn/ *n* **IDM have a down on sb/sth** (*Brit infml*) to disapprove of or feel HOSTILE(1) towards sb/ sth: *She's got a ¹down on me — I don't know why.* **ups and downs** ⇨ UP⁵.

down⁶ /daʊn/ *n* [U] **1** very fine soft feathers: *pillows filled with down.* **2** fine soft hair: *The first down was beginning to appear on the young man's face.*

downbeat /¹daʊnbiːt/ *adj* (*infml*) **1** dull or miserable; low-key (LOW¹): *The meeting was a rather downbeat affair.* Compare UPBEAT. **2** deliberately relaxed and not showing strong feelings.

downcast /¹daʊnkɑːst; *US* -kæst/ *adj* **1** (of eyes) looking downwards. **2** (of a person, an expression, etc) depressed; sad: *He seemed very downcast at the news.*

downer /¹daʊnə(r)/ *n* (*sl*) **1** a drug that has the effect of depressing the user, esp a BARBITURATE. Compare UPPER *n* 2. **2** a depressing experience, person, etc.

downfall /¹daʊnfɔːl/ *n* [sing] **(a)** a fall from a position of advantage, wealth or power: *Greed led to his downfall.* **(b)** a thing that causes this: *His vanity was his downfall.*

downgrade /¡daʊnˈɡreɪd/ *v* ~ **sb/sth (from sth)** (to sth) to reduce sb/sth to a lower grade, rank or level of importance: [Vnpr] *She's been downgraded (from principal) to deputy.* [also Vn]. Compare UPGRADE. ► **downgrading** *n* [C,U]: *He criticized the recent downgrading of welfare provision by the government.*

downhearted /¡daʊnˈhɑːtɪd/ *adj* depressed; in low spirits: *Don't be too downhearted; things will get better.*

downhill /¡daʊnˈhɪl/ *adv* towards the bottom of a hill; in a downward direction: *run downhill.* **IDM ¡go down¹hill** to get worse in health, quality, social status, etc; to DETERIORATE: *This part of the town used to be fashionable, but it's starting to go downhill.*
► **downhill** *adj* **1** [attrib] going or sloping towards the bottom of a hill: *a ¡downhill ¹race.* **2** (*infml*) easy compared to what came before: *The difficult part is learning the new computer codes — after that it's all downhill/it's downhill all the way.*

Downing Street /¹daʊnɪŋ striːt/ *n* the British prime minister or the British government (from the name of the street in London where the prime minister's official residence is): *Downing Street has so far refused to comment on these reports.*

download /¡daʊnˈləʊd/ *v* [Vn, Vnpr] (*computing*) to transfer data, a PROGRAM(1), etc from a large storage system to a smaller one.

down-market /¡daʊn ¹mɑːkɪt/ *adj* (*usu derog*) (of products, services, etc) designed to be cheap or to appeal to people in the lower social classes: *Home shopping by catalogue was once a rather down-market activity.* ► **down-market** *adv*: *going down-market.* Compare UP-MARKET.

downplay /¡daʊnˈpleɪ/ *v* [Vn] to make sth appear to be less important than it actually is.

[V] = verb used alone   [Vn] = verb + noun   [Vp] = verb + particle   [Vpr] = verb + prepositional phrase

downpour /ˈdaʊnpɔː(r)/ n a heavy, usu sudden, fall of rain: *be caught in a torrential downpour.*

downright /ˈdaʊnraɪt/ adj [attrib] (of sth undesirable) thorough; complete: *a downright lie* ○ *downright stupidity.*

▶ **downright** adv thoroughly: *He wasn't just slow, he was downright lazy.*

downs /daʊnz/ n **the downs** [pl] an area of open land with low hills, esp the chalk hills of S England: *the North/South/Sussex Downs.*

downside /ˈdaʊnsaɪd/ n (usu sing) a negative aspect; a disadvantage or set of disadvantages: *All good ideas have a downside.* ○ *the downside risk of investments.*

Down's syndrome /ˈdaʊnz sɪndrəʊm/ n [U] an abnormal condition in which a person is born with a broad, rather flat face, sloping eyes and a mental ability that is below average.

downstairs /ˌdaʊnˈsteəz/ adv **1** down the stairs: *He fell downstairs and broke his wrist.* **2** on or to a lower floor: *They're waiting for us downstairs.* ○ *the people downstairs* (ie who live on the floor below). Compare UPSTAIRS.

▶ **downstairs** adj [attrib]: *the downstairs toilet.*

downstairs n [sing v] the lower floor of a building, esp the floor at ground level: *The whole downstairs needs repainting.*

downstream /ˌdaʊnˈstriːm/ adv in the direction in which a river flows: *drift/float downstream.* Compare UPSTREAM.

downtown /ˌdaʊnˈtaʊn/ adv (esp US) to or in the centre of a city, esp the main business and commercial district: *go/live downtown* ○ *ˌdowntown Chiˈcago* ○ *a ˌdowntown hoˈtel.* Compare UPTOWN.

downtrodden /ˈdaʊntrɒdn/ adj treated badly and without respect by people in authority, so that one no longer has the will to fight back: *a downtrodden minority.*

downturn /ˈdaʊntɜːn/ n ~ (**in sth**) a reduction in economic or business activity: *hit by a downturn in consumer spending.*

downward /ˈdaʊnwəd/ adj [usu attrib] moving, leading or pointing to what is lower or less important: *a downward movement/slope* ○ *a downward trend in prices* ○ (fig) *on the downward path* (ie getting worse).

▶ **downwards** (also **downward**) adv towards what is lower: *She was lying face downwards on the grass.* ○ *The garden sloped gently downwards towards the river.* ○ (fig) *a policy welcomed by world leaders from the US president downwards.* ▷ note at FORWARD².

downwind /ˌdaʊnˈwɪnd/ adj, adv in the direction in which the wind is blowing: *sailing downwind* ○ *just downwind of the fox's den.*

downy /ˈdaʊni/ adj like or covered with DOWN⁶.

dowry /ˈdaʊri/ n [C, U] property or money brought by a BRIDE to her husband when they marry: *the dowry system.*

dowse /daʊz/ v [V, Vpr] ~ (**for sth**) to look for underground water or minerals by using a special rod that dips or shakes when it comes near water, etc.

doyen /ˈdɔɪən/ (US usu **dean** /diːn/) n (fem **doyenne** /dɔɪˈen/) a senior and greatly respected member of a group, profession, etc: *Michael Seely, the doyen of racing journalists.*

doz abbr dozen: *3 doz eggs.*

doze /dəʊz/ v to sleep lightly: [V] *dozing fitfully.*
PHRV **doze ˈoff** to begin sleeping lightly: *I dozed off during the film.*

▶ **doze** n (usu sing) a short light sleep: *I had a little doze on the train.*

dozen /ˈdʌzn/ n (pl **dozens** or unchanged when counting sth) (abbr **doz**) a set of twelve: *Eggs are sold by the dozen.* ○ *They're 70 cents a dozen.* ○ *Pack them in dozens.* ○ *Half a dozen* (ie 6) *eggs, please.* ○ *We need three dozen boxes.* **IDM** **a baker's dozen** ▷ BAKER. **a dime a dozen** ▷ DIME. **dozens of** (infml) lots of: *She's had dozens of boyfriends.* **talk, etc nineteen to the ˈdozen** talk, etc continually: *They were chatting away nineteen to the dozen.*

dozy /ˈdəʊzi/ adj (**-ier, -iest**) **1** ready to go to sleep; not very alert: *I'm feeling very dozy this afternoon.* **2** (Brit infml) stupid: *Come on, you dozy lot — use your heads!*

DPhil /ˌdiː ˈfɪl/ abbr Doctor of Philosophy: *have/be a DPhil in History* ○ *Hugh Benson DPhil.* Compare PHD.

Dr abbr **1** Doctor: *Dr (James) Walker.* **2** (in street names) Drive: *21 Elm Dr.*

drab /dræb/ adj (**-bber, -bbest**) dull; not interesting: *a drab existence* ○ *dressed in drab clothes/colours.* ▶ **drabness** n [U].

drabs /dræbz/ n **IDM** **in dribs and drabs** ▷ DRIBS.

drachma /ˈdrækmə/ n the unit of money in Greece.

draconian /drəˈkəʊniən/ adj (fml) very harsh: *giving the government draconian powers* ○ *draconian measures/laws.*

draft¹ /drɑːft; US dræft/ n **1** [C] a rough preliminary written version of sth: *This is only an early/the first draft of my speech, but what do you think of it?* ○ *a draft amendment/proposal/report.* **2** [C] (finance) a written order to a bank to pay money to sb: *a draft on an American bank.* **3 the draft** [sing] (esp US) = CONSCRIPTION. **4** [C] (US) = DRAUGHT.

■ **ˈdraft-dodger** n (esp US) a person who tries to avoid the draft¹(3) illegally.

draft² /drɑːft; US dræft/ v **1** to make a preliminary written version of sth: [Vn] *draft a contract/parliamentary bill/treaty* ○ *I'll draft the letter for you.* ○ *I'm still drafting the first chapter.* **2** to choose people and send them somewhere for a special task: [Vnp] *Extra police are being drafted in to control the crowds.* [also Vn, Vnpr]. **3** ~ **sb** (**into sth**) (US) to order sb to serve in the armed forces: [Vnpr] *be drafted into the Navy* [also Vn]. Compare CONSCRIPT.

▶ **draftee** /ˌdrɑːfˈtiː; US ˌdræfˈtiː/ n (US) a person who is drafted.

drafter n a person who drafts a law, etc.

draftsman (esp US) = DRAUGHTSMAN.

drafty (US) = DRAUGHTY.

drag¹ /dræg/ v (**-gg-**) **1** to pull sb/sth along with effort and difficulty: [Vnpr] *I heard the sound of something being dragged across the floor.* ○ *They dragged him from his bed.* ○ *We dragged the fallen tree clear of the road.* [Vnp] *dragging the bundle along* [also Vn]. ▷ picture at PULL¹. ▷ note at PULL¹. **2** to move oneself slowly and with effort: [Vadv] *She always drags behind.* [Vnpr] *She dragged herself out of bed, still half asleep.* [also Vpr, Vnp]. **3** to persuade sb to come or go somewhere unwillingly: [Vnp, Vnpr] *I could hardly drag the children away (from the party).* **4** to move with sth partly on the ground: [Vpr] *Your coat's dragging in the mud.* [also V, Vnpr]. **5** ~ (**on**) (of sth boring or irritating) to go on too long: [V] *The film dragged terribly.* [Vp] *How much longer is this meeting going to drag on?* **6** to search the bottom of a river, lake, etc with nets, hooks, etc: [Vn] *They dragged the canal for the missing child.* **IDM** **drag one's ˈfeet/ˈheels** to be deliberately slow in doing sth or in making a decision: *I want to sell the house, but my husband is dragging his feet.* **PHRV** **drag sb ˈdown** to make sb feel weak or depressed: *Hot weather always drags me down.* **drag sb/sth ˈdown (to sth)** (infml) to bring sb/sth to a lower level, standard of behaviour, etc: *I'm afraid the children will all be dragged down to his level.* ○ *Wall Street's uncertainty dragged shares down today.* **drag sth ˈin/ˈinto sth** to introduce into a conversation a subject which has nothing to do with what is being talked about: *Must* *you drag politics into everything?* ,**drag sth** '**out** to make sth longer than necessary: *Let's not drag out this discussion; we need to reach a decision.* ,**drag sth** '**out (of sb)** to make sb reveal or say sth, etc unwillingly: *drag a confession/concession out of sb.* ,**drag sth** '**up** to introduce a fact, story, etc that is considered unpleasant into a conversation: *She dragged up that incident just to embarrass me.*

drag² /dræg/ *n* **1** [sing] ~ **on sb/sth** (*infml*) a person or thing that makes progress difficult: *She loves her family, but knows they're a drag on her career.* **2** [sing] (*sl*) a boring person or thing: *Walking's a drag — let's go by car.* **3** [C] (*sl*) an act of breathing in smoke from a cigarette, etc: *Can I have a drag of your cigarette?* **4** [U] (*sl*) women's clothes worn by a man: *perform in drag.* **5** [U] (*techn*) resistance of the air to the movement of an aircraft. Compare LIFT *n* 3.

dragon /'drægən/ *n* **1** an imaginary animal like a large LIZARD with wings and claws (CLAW 1) and able to breathe out fire. ⇨ picture. **2** (*derog*) a fierce person, esp a woman: *The woman in charge of the accounts department is an absolute dragon! ∘ bossed about by her dragon of a sister.*

dragon

dragonfly /'drægənflaɪ/ *n* an insect with a long thin body and two pairs of transparent wings.

dragoon /drə'gu:n/ *n* (formerly) a soldier in European armies trained to fight on a horse, armed with a gun.
▶ **dragoon** *v* **PHR V** dra'**goon sb into sth / doing sth** to force sb to do sth: *I didn't want to be on the committee but got dragooned into it.*

drain¹ /dreɪn/ *n* **1** [C] a pipe or channel that carries away dirty water or other liquid waste: *We had to call in a plumber to unblock the drains.* ⇨ picture at HOUSE¹. **2** [C] (*US*) = PLUG-HOLE. **3** [sing] ~ **on sb/sth** a thing that continuously uses up sb's strength, time, money, etc: *Military spending is a huge drain on the country's resources.* **IDM** (**go) down the** '**drain** (*infml*) (to be) wasted or spoilt: *A single mistake, and all that time and money would go down the drain.* See also BRAIN DRAIN.

drain² /dreɪn/ *v* **1** ~ (**sth**) (**from sth**); ~ (**sth**) (**away/off**) to flow away or make a liquid flow away: [Vpr] *All the blood drained from his face* (eg on hearing bad news). [Vp] *The bath-water slowly drained away.* [Vn, Vnpr] *A mechanic drained the oil (from) the engine.* [also V, Vnpl]. **2(a)** to become dry as liquid flows away: [V] *Leave the dishes to drain.* (**b**) to make sth dry or drier by removing liquid from it: [Vn] *drain swamps/marshes ∘ good, well-drained soil/land.* **3** to empty a glass, etc by drinking everything in it: [Vn, Vn-adj] *drain one's glass (dry).* **4** ~ **sb/sth** (**of sth**) to make sb/sth weaker, poorer, etc by gradually using up their/its strength, money, etc: [Vnpr] *feel drained of energy* [Vn] *The experience left her emotionally drained.* **PHR V** ,**drain a**'**way** to disappear or fade gradually: *Her life was slowly draining away* (ie She was slowly dying).
■ '**draining-board** (*US* '**drainboard**) *n* a sloping surface beside a sink on which washed dishes, etc are put to drain.

drainage /'dreɪnɪdʒ/ *n* [U] **1** the action of draining or the process of being drained: *land drainage schemes.* **2** a system of drains.

drainpipe /'dreɪnpaɪp/ *n* a pipe used in a system of drains. ⇨ picture at HOUSE¹.

drake /dreɪk/ *n* a male duck. See also DUCK¹ 1, DUCKS AND DRAKES.

dram /dræm/ *n* (*esp Scot*) a small amount of alcoholic drink, esp WHISKY: *He's fond of his wee dram.*

drama /'drɑːmə/ *n* **1(a)** [C] a play for the theatre, radio or television: *a historical drama ∘ drama awards.* (**b**) [U] the art of writing and presenting plays: *a masterpiece of Elizabethan drama ∘ a* '*drama critic/school/group.* **2** [C] a series of exciting events: *a real-life hospital/courtroom drama ∘ A powerful human drama was unfolding before our eyes.* **3** [U, C] excitement: *Her life was full of drama.* **IDM** **make a drama out of sth** to exaggerate a small problem or incident: *He makes a drama out of a simple visit to the dentist.*

dramatic /drə'mætɪk/ *adj* **1** [attrib] of or in the form of drama: *a dramatic society ∘ a dramatic representation of a real event.* **2** (of an event, a change, etc) sudden and very noticeable: *dramatic results/developments/news ∘ a dramatic increase in the unemployment figures ∘ a dramatic impact/contrast.* **3** exciting or impressive: *dramatic pictures on TV.* **4** exaggerated for special effect: *He flung out his arms in a dramatic gesture.*
▶ **dramatically** /-klɪ/ *adv*: *His attitude changed dramatically. ∘ 'You can die having babies,' Jenny announced dramatically. ∘ a dramatically new situation.*

dramatics *n* [usu sing *v*] **1** the study or practice of acting and producing plays: *amateur dramatics.* **2** (*derog*) behaviour that is exaggerated or too emotional: *I've had enough of your dramatics.*

dramatis personae /,dræmətɪs pɜː'səʊnaɪ/ *n* [pl] (*fml*) all the characters in a play.

dramatist /'dræmətɪst/ *n* a writer of plays.

dramatize, -ise /'dræmətaɪz/ *v* **1** to make sth such as a novel or an event into a play: [Vn] *a dramatized documentary* (ie a play based on a report of real events). **2** to make an incident, etc seem more dramatic than it really is: [V] *Don't believe everything she tells you; she tends to dramatize.* [Vn] *The affair was dramatized by the press.* ▶ **dramatization, -isation** /,dræmətaɪ'zeɪʃn, -tə'z-/ *n* [U, C]: *a TV dramatization of the trial.*

drank *pt* of DRINK².

drape /dreɪp/ *v* **1(a)** ~ **sth round/over sth** to hang cloth, curtains, clothing, etc loosely on sb/sth: [Vnpr] *She had a shawl draped round her shoulders.* (**b**) ~ **sb/sth in/with sth** to cover or decorate sb/sth with cloth, etc: [Vnpr] *He appears on stage draped in a huge cloak. ∘ walls draped with tapestries.* **2** ~ **sth around/round/over sth** to allow sth to rest loosely on sth: [Vnpr] *She draped her arms around his neck.* ▶ **drape** *n* [C usu *pl*] (*US*) a long curtain.

draper /'dreɪpə(r)/ *n* (*Brit*) (esp formerly) a shopkeeper selling cloth and clothing.
▶ '**drapery** *n* **1** [U] (*US* also **dry goods** [pl]) a draper's trade or goods. **2** [U] (also **draperies** [pl]) cloth or clothing hanging in loose folds: *a cot swathed in draperies and blue ribbon.*

drastic /'dræstɪk/ *Brit* also '**drɑːs-** / *adj* **1** having a strong or violent effect: *drastic measures ∘ take drastic action ∘ They've suggested a few changes, but nothing too drastic.* **2** very serious: *a drastic shortage of food.* ▶ **drastically** /-klɪ/ *adv*: *Expenditure has been drastically reduced.*

drat /dræt/ *interj* (*infml*) (used to express annoyance): *Drat (it)! My watch has stopped.* ▶ **dratted** *adj* [attrib] (*dated infml*): *This dratted pen won't work.*

draught /drɑːft/ (*US* **draft** /dræft/) *n* **1** [C] a flow of cool air in a room or other enclosed space: *Can you close the door? There's an awful draught in here.* **2** [C] (**a**) (*fml*) one continuous process of swallowing liquid; the amount swallowed: *He emptied his glass in one long draught. ∘* (*fig*) *He took a deep draught of air into his lungs.* (**b**) (*esp arch*) a drink with some powerful or magical property: *a draught of poison ∘ a* '*sleeping draught* (ie one that sends sb to sleep). **3** **draughts** (*Brit*) (*US* **checkers**) [sing *v*] a game for two players using 24 round pieces on a board with black and white squares. Compare DRAFT¹. **IDM** **on** **'draught** drawn from a large container, esp of beer from a barrel: *This beer is not available on draught (ie It is available only in bottles or cans).*

▶ **draught** *adj* [attrib] served on draught: *draught bitter/cider/lager.*

draught *v* = DRAFT² 1.

'draughty *adj* allowing cold air in: *draughty corridors.*

■ **'draught-horse** *n* a horse used for pulling heavy loads.

draughtboard /'drɑːftbɔːd/ (*Brit*) (*US* **'checker board**) *n* a board with black and white squares, used for playing draughts (DRAUGHT 3).

draughtsman /'drɑːftsmən/ (*US* **draftsman** /'dræfts-/) *n* (*pl* **-men** /-mən/) a person whose job is to make plans and drawings of machinery or buildings.

draw¹ /drɔː/ *v* (*pt* **drew** /druː/; *pp* **drawn** /drɔːn/) **1** to make pictures, or a picture of sth, with eg a pencil or chalk, but not paint: [Vadv] *You draw beautifully.* [Vn] *draw a picture/diagram/graph* ○ *She drew a house.* ○ *He drew a circle in the sand with a stick.* ○ (*fig*) *The report drew a grim picture of inefficiency and corruption.* [also V]. **2** to move in the specified direction: [Vpr, Vp] *The train drew into the station/drew in.* [Vadv] *The figures in the distance seemed to be drawing nearer/closer.* ○ (*fig*) *Christmas is drawing near.* [Vpr] *The meeting was drawing to a close.* **3(a)** to pull or move sth into a new position, esp with a smooth controlled movement: [Vnpr] *draw the cork out of a bottle* [Vnadv] *I drew my chair up closer to the fire.* **(b)** to make sb come with or towards one: [Vnpr] *She drew me onto the balcony.* [Vnadv] *I tried to draw him aside* (eg where I could talk to him privately). **4** (of horses, etc) to pull a vehicle, eg a carriage or a cart: [Vn] *The Queen's coach was drawn by six horses.* ○ *a horse-drawn carriage/plough* [also Vnp, Vnpr]. ⇨ note at PULL¹. **5** to open or close curtains, etc: [Vn] *The blinds were drawn.* [Vnpr, Vnp] *She drew (back) a curtain across the doorway.* **6** to take out a weapon, eg a gun or a sword, from its holder, esp in order to attack sb: [Vnpr] *She drew a revolver on me.* [Vn] *He came towards me with his sword drawn.* [also V]. **7(a)** ~ **sth (from sth)** to have a particular idea after study, experience, thought or observation: [Vn, Vnpr] *What conclusions did you draw (from the report)?* [Vnpr] *draw a moral from a story* ○ *We can draw some lessons for the future from this accident.* **(b)** to express a comparison or a contrast: [Vn] *draw an analogy/a comparison/a parallel/a distinction between two events.* **8** ~ **sth from sth/sb** to take or obtain sth from sth/sb: [Vnpr] *draw information from many different sources* ○ *draw support/comfort/ strength from one's family* ○ *She drew (her) inspiration from her childhood experiences.* ○ *The army draws its recruits from all classes of society.* **9(a)** ~ **sb (to sth)** to attract or interest sb: [Vnpr] *The fire is drawing large audiences.* [Vnpr] *Her screams drew passers-by to the scene.* ○ *I felt drawn to this mysterious stranger.* ○ *The course draws students from all over the country.* **(b)** ~ **sth (from sb)** to produce a reaction or response: [Vnpr] *The announcement drew loud applause from the audience.* [Vn] *The scheme has drawn much criticism.* **10** ~ **sb (about/ on sth)** (esp passive) to make sb say more about sth: [Vn, Vnpr] *The interviewer asked about possible tax increases, but the minister refused to be drawn (on that).* **11** ~ **(for sth)**; ~ **sth (from sth)**; ~ **sb (against sb)** to decide sth by picking eg cards, tickets or numbers by chance and without conscious choice: [Vpr] *draw for partners* (eg in a card-game) [Vn] *draw the winner/the winning ticket in a raffle* [Vnpr] *draw names from a hat* [Vnpr, Vn.*to* inf] *Italy have been drawn against/drawn to play*

Spain in the World Cup. **12** ~ **(with/against sb)** to finish a game without either team winning: [V] *England and Spain drew.* [Vpr] *England drew with/ against Spain.* [Vadv] *draw three all* [Vn] *a drawn match.* **13(a)** ~ **sth (from sth)**; ~ **sth out (of sth)** to take money from a bank account: [Vnpr] *Can I draw $80 from/out of my account?* [Vnp] *I drew out £200.* [also Vn]. **(b)** ~ **sth on sth** to cause eg a cheque to be paid out of a certain account: [Vnpr] *The cheque was drawn on his personal account.* **(c)** to receive regular payments: [Vn] *She went to the post office to draw her pension.* **14(a)** ~ **sth (from sth)**; ~ **sth (off)** to take some liquid from a larger supply: [Vn, Vnpr] *draw water (from a well)* [Vnp] *He drew off a pint of beer.* **(b)** to make a liquid or gas go in a particular direction by pumping or sucking: [Vnpr, Vnp] *The device draws water along the pipe/ up into the tank.* **(c)** ~ **at/on sth**; ~ **sth in** to breathe sth in, eg smoke from a cigarette: [Vpr] *He drew thoughtfully on his pipe.* [Vnp] *She breathed deeply, drawing in the fresh mountain air.* **15** (*nautical*) (of a ship) to require a certain depth of water in which to float: [Vn] *a ship drawing 20 feet.* **IDM** **at daggers drawn** ⇨ DAGGER. **cast/draw lots** ⇨ LOT⁴. **draw (sb's) attention to sth/sb** to cause sth/sb to be noticed: *She drew my attention to an error in the report.* ○ *She's very shy and hates drawing attention to herself.* **draw a 'blank** to get no response or result: *So far, the police investigations have drawn a blank.* **draw 'blood 1** to cause sb to bleed. **2** to succeed in upsetting or harming sb: *His taunts clearly drew blood.* **draw 'breath 1** to breathe in, esp deeply after an effort: *She talks all the time and hardly stops to draw breath.* **2** (*rhet*) to live; to be alive: *as kind a man as ever drew breath.* **draw sb's 'fire** to make sb direct their anger, criticism, etc at oneself, so that others do not have to face it. **draw in one's 'horns** to become less ambitious or aggressive: *Pressure grew on the US to draw in its military horns.* **draw the 'line (at sth/doing sth)** to refuse to do or to tolerate sth any further; to set a limit: *I don't mind helping, but I draw the line at doing everything myself.* ○ *A line has to be drawn somewhere — I can't go on lending you money for ever.* **draw the 'line (between sth and sth)** to distinguish eg between two closely related ideas: *Where do you draw the line between genius and madness?* **'draw the short 'straw** to be the person in a group who is chosen or forced to perform an unpleasant duty or task: *I drew the short straw and had to clean the toilet.* **draw oneself 'up/rise to one's full height** ⇨ FULL. **draw a 'veil over sth** to choose not to say anything about sth, eg to avoid embarrassment: *I propose to draw a veil over the appalling events that followed.* **PHRV** **,draw 'back (from sth/doing sth)** to choose not to take action, esp because one feels cautious or nervous: *draw back from a declaration of war/from declaring war.* **,draw 'in** to become dark earlier in the evening as winter approaches: *The nights/days are drawing in.* **'draw sb into sth/doing sth**; **,draw sb 'in** to involve sb or make sb take part in sth, often against their will: *youngsters drawn into a life of crime* ○ *The book starts slowly, but it gradually draws you in.* **,draw 'on** (of a time or season) to approach: *Night was drawing on.* **'draw on/upon sth** to use a resource or supply: *I'll have to draw on my savings.* ○ *The novelist draws heavily on her personal experiences.* **,draw sb 'on** to attract or tempt sb: *They drew investors on with visions of instant wealth.* **,draw 'out** (of days) to become longer in spring. **,draw sb 'out** to encourage sb to talk or express themselves freely: *He's very shy and needs to be drawn out.* **,draw sth 'out** to make sth last longer than usual or necessary: *She drew the interview out to over an hour.* ○ *a long-drawn-out discussion/ struggle/process.*

[Vnn] = verb + noun + noun   [V-adj] = verb + adjective   For more help with verbs, see Study pages **B4–8**.

,**draw** ¹**up** (of a vehicle) to arrive and stop: *The taxi drew up outside the house.* ,**draw sth** ¹**up** to make or write sth that requires careful thought or planning: *draw up a contract/list* ○ *draw up a set of plans/ rules/accounts.*
■ ¹**draw-string** *n* a string that can be pulled tighter, eg to close a bag or tighten a garment: *a draw-string bag.*

draw² /drɔː/ *n* **1(a)** (usu *sing*) ~ (**for sth**) the act of selecting sth, eg the winner of a prize or matches to be played in a sports competition, by chance: *the draw for the second round of the European Cup* ○ *The draw for the raffle takes place on Saturday.* (**b**) a competition in which the winner or winners are chosen this way: *Enter our £1 million prize draw!* Compare RAFFLE, LOTTERY 1. (**c**) a sports match chosen in this way, to be played as part of a competition: *Liverpool have a home/an away draw against Manchester United.* (**d**) (usu *sing*) a set of matches decided in this way: *The champion has some difficult opponents in her half of the draw.* **2** a completed game in which neither player or side wins: *The match ended in a 2–2 draw.* Compare TIE¹ 6. **3** (usu *sing*) a person or thing that attracts people: *A live band is always a good draw at a disco.* **4** an act of breathing in the smoke from a cigarette, etc. **IDM the luck of the draw** ⇨ LUCK. **quick/slow on the** ¹**draw 1** (*infml*) quick/slow to understand or react: *He's a nice lad, but a bit slow on the draw.* **2** quick/ slow at pulling out one's gun.

drawback /ˈdrɔːbæk/ *n* ~ (**of/to sth/doing sth**) a disadvantage or problem: *The main drawback to such a holiday is the cost.*

drawbridge /ˈdrɔːbrɪdʒ/ *n* (esp formerly) a bridge across the MOAT of a castle that can be pulled up to stop people crossing: *lower/raise the drawbridge.* ⇨ picture at CASTLE.

drawer *n* **1** /drɔː(r)/ a container, similar to a box, with one or more handles but no lid, that slides in and out of a piece of furniture: *You'll find the envelope in the middle drawer of my desk.* See also CHEST OF DRAWERS, TOP DRAWER. **2** /ˈdrɔːə(r)/ (**a**) a person who writes a cheque. (**b**) a person who draws pictures: *I'm not a very good drawer.*

drawers /drɔːz/ *n* [pl] (*dated*) KNICKERS(1) or UNDER- PANTS, esp ones that cover the upper part of the legs.

drawing /ˈdrɔːɪŋ/ *n* (**a**) [C] a picture, plan or diagram made using eg a pencil or chalk, but not paint: *a collection of children's/Picasso's drawings.* (**b**) [U] the art or skill of making such pictures, etc: *classes in architectural/engineering/technical drawing.*
■ ¹**drawing-board** *n* a flat board to which paper is fixed while a drawing is made. **IDM** (**go**) **back to the** ¹**drawing-board** to prepare a completely new plan for sth because an earlier one has failed: *They've rejected our proposal, so it's back to the drawing-board, I'm afraid.* **on the** ¹**drawing-board** in preparation: *a new project on the drawing-board.*

drawing-pin /ˈdrɔːɪŋ pɪn/ (*Brit*) (*US* **thumb-tack**) *n* a short pin with a flat round head, used esp for fastening paper to a board or wall.

drawing-room /ˈdrɔːɪŋ ruːm, -rʊm/ *n* (*fml*) a room in a private house, in which people relax and guests are received and entertained. Compare LIVING-ROOM.

drawl /drɔːl/ *v* to speak or say sth in a slow lazy manner, with long vowels: [V.speech] *'Well, hi there!' he drawled.* [Vn] *He drawled a few words of apology.* [V] *a drawling voice.*
▶ **drawl** *n* [sing] a drawling manner of speaking: *He spoke in a broad Texan drawl.*

drawn¹ /drɔːn/ *adj* looking very tired or worried: *She/Her face was pale and drawn after weeks of sleepless nights.*

drawn² *pp* of DRAW¹.

dray /dreɪ/ *n* (esp formerly) a low flat cart for carrying heavy loads, esp barrels of beer.

dread /dred/ *n* (**a**) [U, sing] great fear, esp of sth that may or will happen in the future: *The prospect of growing old fills me with dread.* ○ *She has an irrational dread of hospitals.* (**b**) [sing] a thing that is greatly feared: *My constant/greatest dread is that my parents will find out.*
▶ **dread** *v* to fear sth greatly: [Vn, V.ing] *dread illness/being ill* [V.n ing] *I dread my parents finding out.* [V.to inf] *We all dread to think what will happen if the factory closes.* [also V.that]. **dreaded** (also *fml* **dread**) *adj* [attrib] greatly feared: *a dreaded disease* ○ (*joc*) *I heard the dreaded word 'homework'.*

dreadful /ˈdredfl/ *adj* **1** (*infml*) (**a**) very bad or unpleasant: *What dreadful weather!* ○ *a dreadful play/man/meal/country* ○ *The noise was dreadful.* (**b**) [attrib] (used for emphasis): *I'm afraid it's all a dreadful mistake.* ○ *He's a dreadful snob.* **2** [esp attrib] causing great fear or suffering; shocking: *a dreadful accident/disease/nightmare* ○ *He has to live with the dreadful knowledge that he caused their deaths.*
▶ **dreadfully** /-fəli/ *adv* **1** (*infml*) very; very much: *I'm dreadfully sorry.* ○ *I miss you dreadfully.* **2** in a very bad, unpleasant or shocking way: *They suffered dreadfully during the war.*

dreadlocks /ˈdredlɒks/ *n* [pl] hair twisted into long tightly curled strands, a style used esp by Rastafarians. ⇨ picture at PLAIT.

dream¹ /driːm/ *n* **1** [C] a sequence of scenes and feelings occurring in the mind during sleep: *a vivid/ disturbing dream* ○ *I have a recurrent dream that I'm acting in a play and I forget all my lines.* ○ *Good night — sweet dreams!* Compare NIGHTMARE 1. **2** [sing] a state of mind in which the things happening around one do not seem real: *be/live/go around in a (complete) dream.* **3** [C] an ambition or ideal, esp when it is not very realistic: *an impossible dream* ○ *achieve/realize/fulfil one's lifelong dream* ○ *the car/ holiday of your dreams* ○ *If I win the tournament, it will be a dream come true* (ie something I wanted very much, but did not expect to happen). **4** [sing] (*infml*) a beautiful or wonderful person or thing: *The meal she'd prepared was an absolute dream.* ○ *a dream house/kitchen.* See also DAY-DREAM, WET DREAM. **IDM a bad** ¹**dream** a situation that is so unpleasant one cannot believe it is real: *You can't be leaving me — this is a bad dream!* **beyond one's wildest dreams** ⇨ WILD. **go, etc like a** ¹**dream** (*infml*) to work very well: *My new car goes like a dream.*
▶ **dreamless** *adj* [usu attrib] (of sleep) without dreams; deep and peaceful.
■ ¹**dream world** *n* a state in which sb imagines everything is the way they would like it to be: *He lives in a dream world.*

dream² /driːm/ *v* (*pt, pp* **dreamt** /dremt/ or **dreamed** /driːmd/) **1(a)** to have a dream while asleep: [V] *She claims she never dreams.* (**b**) ~ (**of sth/doing sth**); ~ **about sb/sth/doing sth** to imagine that one sees sb/sth or experiences sth in a dream: [Vpr] *I dreamt about you last night.* [Vn] *Was it real or did I dream it?* [V.that] *I dreamt (that) I could fly.* **2** ~ (**of/about sth/doing sth**) to imagine sth: [V] *I never promised to lend you my car: you must be dreaming!* [Vpr] *He dreams of one day becoming a famous violinist.* ○ *It was the kind of home most of us only dream of.* [Vn] *Who'd have dreamt it? They're getting married!* [V.that] *I never dreamt (that) I'd see you again.* **IDM not dream of sth/ doing sth** to refuse to consider doing sth under any circumstances: *I'd never dream of allowing my child to do that.* **PHR V** ,**dream sth a**¹**way** to spend time in a lazy way, not thinking much about anything:

She dreamt her life away, never really achieving anything. ¡**dream** ˈ**on** (*infml ironic*) (used in the imperative to tell sb that a plan, etc is not practical or realistic): *So you want a pay increase? Dream on!* ¡**dream sth** ˈ**up** (*infml*) to have an idea, esp an imaginative or foolish one: *Trust you to dream up a crazy scheme like this!*

▶ **dreamer** *n* **1** a person who dreams. **2** (*usu derog*) (**a**) a person with ideas or plans that do not seem practical or realistic: *People who said man would land on the moon used to be called dreamers.* (**b**) a person who does not concentrate on what happens around her or him, but thinks about other things instead: *Don't rely on him — he's a real dreamer.*

dreamland /ˈdriːmlænd/ *n* [U] (*derog*) a pleasant but not very realistic situation imagined by sb: *You must be living in dreamland if you think he'll pay that much!*

dreamlike /ˈdriːmlaɪk/ *adj* as in a dream: *The place has an almost dreamlike quality.*

dreamy /ˈdriːmi/ *adj* (**-ier, -iest**) **1** (of a person) with thoughts far away from her or his present surroundings, work, etc: *a dreamy look in her eyes.* **2** not clear; VAGUE(1b): *I only have a dreamy recollection of what happened.* **3** (*infml*) pleasantly gentle; helping one to relax: *dreamy music.* **4** (*infml*) wonderful: *What a dreamy little house!* ▶ **dreamily** /-ɪli/ *adv*: *'He was gorgeous,' she said dreamily.* **dreaminess** *n* [U].

dreary /ˈdrɪəri/ *adj* (**-ier, -iest**) (also *arch* **drear** /drɪə(r)/) **1** that makes one sad or depressed; gloomy (GLOOM): *a dreary winter day.* **2** (*infml*) boring; dull: *dreary people leading dreary lives.* ▶ **drearily** /ˈdrɪərəli/ *adv.* **dreariness** *n* [U]: *the dreariness of the landscape.*

dredge¹ /dredʒ/ *v* (**a**) to clear mud, etc from the bottom of a river, canal, etc using a special machine or boat: [Vn] *They have to dredge the canal so that ships can use it.* (**b**) ~ **sth** (**up**) (**from sth**) to bring sth up with such a machine or boat: [Vpr] *dredge for oysters* [Vn, Vnp, Vnpr] *We're dredging (up) mud (from the river bed).* [also V]. **PHRV** ¡**dredge sth** ˈ**up** (*usu derog*) to mention sth that has been forgotten, esp sth that is unpleasant or embarrassing: *The papers keep trying to dredge up details of his early love affairs.*

▶ **dredger** *n* a boat or machine used for dredging.

dredge² /dredʒ/ *v* ~ **A** (**with B**); ~ **B over/on A** to scatter flour, sugar, etc over food: [Vnpr] *dredge a cake with icing sugar/icing sugar over a cake* [also Vn].

dregs /dregz/ *n* [pl] **1** the solid matter that sinks to the bottom of certain liquids, esp wine and beer: *tip out the coffee dregs* ∘ *He drank/drained it to the dregs* (ie all of it). **2**(**a**) the last parts of sth that remain: *with the dregs of their energy.* (**b**) the worst and most useless part of sth: *the dregs of society.*

drench /drentʃ/ *v* (esp passive) to make sb/sth completely wet: [Vn, Vnp, Vnpr] *We were caught in the storm and got drenched (through/to the skin).* [Vnpr] *Their faces were drenched with sweat.* ∘ (*fig*) *drench oneself in perfume.*

dress¹ /dres/ *n* **1** [C] a garment for a woman or girl made in one piece and covering the body down to the legs, knees or ankles according to length: *a long/short dress* ∘ *a pink chiffon dress* ∘ *a wedding dress.* **2** [U] clothes for either men or women: *wear casual/formal dress* ∘ *traditional Scottish dress* ∘ *He's got no dress sense* (ie idea of how to dress well). See also EVENING DRESS, FANCY DRESS, MORNING DRESS.

■ ¡**dress** ˈ**circle** (*Brit*) (*US* **first balcony**) *n* the first level raised above the ground floor in a theatre.

¡**dress re**ˈ**hearsal** *n* the final rehearsal (REHEARSE) of a play, with the costumes, lights, etc as they would be in a real performance: (*fig*) *The earlier*

revolts had just been dress rehearsals for full-scale revolution.

dress² /dres/ *v* **1**(**a**) to put clothes on sb/oneself: [V] *He takes ages to dress.* [Vn] *Is she old enough to dress herself yet?* (**b**) to put on formal clothes: [Vpr] *Do they expect us to dress for dinner?* [also V]. (**c**) ~ (**sb**) **in/as/for sth** to put a particular type or style of clothing on: [Vpr] *She often dresses in black.* ∘ *He was dressed as a woman* (ie wearing women's clothes). ∘ *We were dressed for cold weather.* [also Vnpr]. (**d**) to provide sb/oneself with clothes: [Vadv] *dress well/badly/fashionably* [Vn] *The princess is dressed by a talented young designer.* **2** to decorate sth: [Vn] *dress a shop window* (ie arrange a display of goods in it) [Vnpr] *dress a street with flags* ∘ *dress a Christmas tree with lights.* **3** [Vn] to clean, treat and cover a wound, etc. **4** to prepare food for cooking or eating: [Vn] *dress a chicken* (ie clean it ready for cooking) ∘ *dress a salad* (ie add a DRESSING(3) to it before serving). **IDM** **mutton dressed as lamb** ⇨ MUTTON. **PHRV** ¡**dress sb** ˈ**down** to show one's anger with sb publicly; to SCOLD sb. ¡**dress** ˈ**up** to wear one's best clothes: *Don't bother to dress up — come as you are.* ¡**dress** (**sb**) ˈ**up** (**in sth/as sb/sth**) to put on special clothes or costumes: *dress (up) as a fairy/bandit/pirate* ∘ *dressing-ˈup clothes* ∘ *Children love dressing up.* ∘ *They were dressed up in Edwardian costume.* ¡**dress sth** ˈ**up** to present sth in a way that makes it seem better or different: *rumours dressed up as hard news* ∘ *The facts are quite clear; it's no use trying to dress them up.*

▶ **dressed** *adj* [pred] wearing clothes, and not naked or wearing PYJAMAS(2), etc: *Aren't you dressed yet?* ∘ *Alison, now fully dressed, went into the hall.* ∘ *He was smartly/impeccably dressed, as usual.* **IDM** **dressed to** ˈ**kill** (*infml*) dressed so as to attract attention and admiration, esp from the opposite sex. **dressed up to the** ˈ**nines** (*infml esp Brit*) dressed in very elegant clothes; looking very SMART(1). ¡**get** ˈ**dressed** to put one's clothes on: *She got dressed and went downstairs.*

dressage /ˈdresɑːʒ/ *n* [U] (**a**) the practice of training a horse to perform various movements that show its obedience to its rider. (**b**) a display of such actions in a competition.

dresser¹ /ˈdresə(r)/ *n* **1** (*esp Brit*) a large piece of kitchen furniture with shelves for dishes and cupboards below. See also WELSH DRESSER. ⇨ picture. **2** a chest of drawers (CHEST) with a mirror on top.

dresser

Welsh dresser

dresser² /ˈdresə(r)/ *n* **1** (used with an *adj*) a person who dresses in a specified way: *a smart/ scruffy/snappy dresser.* **2** (in a theatre) a person who helps actors to put on their costumes.

dressing /ˈdresɪŋ/ *n* **1** [U] the action of putting on clothes, treating wounds, etc: *Dressing always takes her such a long time.* **2** [C, U] a thing used for treating a wound, esp a BANDAGE: *apply/change a dressing.* **3** [C, U] a sauce for food, esp a mixture of oil and VINEGAR for SALAD(1a): *salad dressing.* **4** [U] (*US*) = STUFFING 1. See also WINDOW-DRESSING.

■ ¡**dressing-**ˈ**down** *n* [sing] an act of scolding (SCOLD) sb severely: *give sb/get a (good) dressing-down.*

ˈ**dressing-gown** (*US usu* **bathrobe, robe**) *n* a long loose garment, usu with a belt, worn indoors and usu over night clothes, eg when first getting out of bed.

ˈ**dressing-room** *n* a room for changing one's clothes in, esp one for sports players or actors.

'dressing-table (*US* also **vanity**) *n* a piece of bedroom furniture with a mirror and drawers, used esp by women: *She sat at the dressing-table combing her hair.*

dressmaker /ˈdresmeɪkə(r)/ *n* a person, esp a woman, who makes women's clothes. ▶ **dress-making** *n* [U].

dressy /ˈdresi/ *adj* (**-ier, -iest**) (*infml*) (of clothes) very elegant or elaborate; to be worn on special occasions: *You can't wear that — it's much too dressy!*

drew *pt* of DRAW¹.

dribble /ˈdrɪbl/ *v* **1** to allow SALIVA to run from the mouth: [Vpr] *Take care the baby doesn't dribble over your suit.* [also V]. **2(a)** to fall in drops or a thin stream: [Vp, Vpr] *Water was dribbling out (of the tap).* ○ *Marmalade dribbled down the side of the jar.* **(b)** to pour or release sth in drops or a thin stream: [Vnpr] *Dribble the oil into the beaten egg yolks.* [also V, Vn]. **3** (in football, hockey, BASKETBALL, etc) to move the ball forward with repeated slight touches or bounces: [Vpr, Vnpr] *He dribbled (the ball) past the goalie to score.* [also V, Vn].
▶ **dribble** *n* **1** [C] a thin stream of sth liquid: *a dribble of oil.* **2** [U] SALIVA running from the mouth: *There was dribble all down her front.*

dribs /drɪbz/ *n* [pl] **IDM** **in ˌdribs and ˈdrabs** (*infml*) in small amounts or numbers: *She paid me in dribs and drabs, not all at once.*

dried *pt, pp* of DRY².

drier¹ *comparative* of DRY¹.

drier² *n* ⇨ DRY².

drift¹ /drɪft/ *n* **1** [U] **(a)** a continuous slow movement, eg of wind or water: *the drift of the tide/current* ○ *the drift of people from the country into the towns.* **(b)** the movement of a ship from a set course, due to currents, winds, etc. **2** [C] a steady movement or tendency towards sth, esp sth bad: *a slow drift into debt/war/crisis* ○ *a drift away from traditional values.* **3** [sing] the general meaning or sense of speech, writing, etc; the GIST: *My German isn't very good, but I got the drift of what she said.* ○ *I don't think I quite* ***catch your drift.*** **4** [C] a mass of sth, esp snow or sand, piled up by the wind: *deep* ˈ*snow-drifts* ○ *spring flowers in beautiful drifts.* See also CONTINENTAL DRIFT.

drift² /drɪft/ *v* **1** to be carried along gently, esp by a current of air or water: [V, Vp] *We switched off the motor and started to drift (along).* [Vpr] *The boat drifted down the river.* ○ (*fig*) *Voices drifted across the garden.* [Vp] *Time drifted past.* ○ *My thoughts drifted back to my childhood.* **2(a)** (of people) to move or go somewhere in a slow casual way: [Vpr] *The crowds drifted away from the stadium.* [Vp] *She finally drifted in two hours after everyone else.* **(b)** to progress without a clear plan or course of action: [V] *I'm happy to let things drift for now.* [Vp] *The talk drifted back to politics.* [Vpr] *I didn't mean to be a teacher — I just drifted into it.* **3** (of snow, sand, etc) to be piled into large masses by the wind: [V] *Some roads are closed because of drifting.* [also Vpr, Vp]. **4** to make sth drift²(1): [Vnadv] *The logs are drifted downstream to the mill.* [Vnpr] *The wind drifted the snow into a high bank.* [also Vnp]. **PHRV** **ˌdrift ˈoff** to fall asleep: *It was 3 o'clock before I finally drifted off (to sleep).*
▶ **drifter** *n* (*usu derog*) a person who moves from place to place and has no fixed home or job.
■ **ˈdrift-net** *n* a large net into which fish move with the tide.

driftwood /ˈdrɪftwʊd/ *n* [U] wood floating on the sea or washed onto the shore.

drill¹ /drɪl/ *n* **1** [C] a tool or machine with a pointed end for making holes: *a dentist's drill* ○ *a pneumatic drill.* See also BIT² 2b. ⇨ picture. **2** [U] training in military exercises: *New recruits have three hours of*

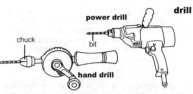

drill

power drill

chuck

bit

hand drill

drill a day. **3(a)** [U] thorough training in sth, esp by means of repeated exercises: *practise rifle drill.* **(b)** [C] such an exercise: *pronunciˈation drills.* **4(a)** [U] procedures to be followed in an emergency: *ˈlifeboat drill.* **(b)** [C] an occasion when these are practised: *There'll be a* ˈ*fire-drill this morning.* **5 the drill** [sing] (*Brit infml*) the correct or normal procedure for doing sth: *What's the drill for claiming expenses?* ○ *learn/know/teach sb the drill.*
▶ **drill** *v* **1** to make a hole in sth, using a drill: [Vpr] *drill for oil* [Vnpr] *They're drilling a new tunnel under the Thames.* [also V, Vn]. **2** to be trained or train sb thoroughly by means of regularly repeated exercises, etc: [Vn] *a well drilled team of fire-fighters.* [also V].
PHRV **ˈdrill sth into sb** to make sb learn sth by regular training: *We had the basic rules of grammar drilled into us at school.*

drill² /drɪl/ *n* a shallow FURROW(1) for sowing seeds in.

drill³ /drɪl/ *n* [U] a strong cotton cloth: *white drill shorts.*

drily = DRYLY (DRY¹).

drink¹ /drɪŋk/ *n* **1(a)** [U, C] a liquid for drinking: *food and drink* ○ *soft drinks.* **(b)** [C] an amount of a liquid drunk or served: *have a drink of water* ○ *She took a drink and put the glass down.* **2(a)** [U] (*Brit*) liquid containing alcohol for drinking: *Isn't there any drink in the house?* ○ *get the drink for a party* ○ *I'm afraid he's rather* ***the worse for drink*** (ie drunk). **(b)** [C] an amount of this drunk or served: *How about a quick drink?* ○ *Drinks are on me* (ie I will pay for them). ○ *He's had one drink too many* (ie He is slightly drunk). **3** [U] the habit of drinking too much alcohol: *Drink is a growing problem among the young.* ○ *She* ***took to drink*** *after the failure of her marriage.* ○ (*joc*) *Working here is enough to* ***drive one to drink!*** **4 the drink** [sing] (*sl*) the sea. **IDM** **be the worse for drink** ⇨ WORSE *n.* **the demon drink** ⇨ DEMON.

drink² /drɪŋk/ *v* (*pt* **drank** /dræŋk/; *pp* **drunk** /drʌŋk/) **1(a)** to take liquid into the mouth and swallow: [Vpr] *Some horses were drinking at/from a trough.* [Vn] *We sat around drinking coffee and chatting.* [also V]. **(b)** to take an amount of a liquid in this way: [Vn] *How many cups of tea do you drink in a day?* **2** to drink alcohol: [V] *He never drinks.* ○ *They drink too much.* ○ *Don't* ***drink and drive*** (ie drive a car, etc after drinking alcohol)*!* **3** to put oneself into a particular state as a result of drinking alcohol: [Vnpr] *He's drinking himself to death.* [Vnadj] (*infml*) *They drank themselves stupid.* **4** [Vn, Vnp] ~ **sth (in/up)** (of plants, the soil, etc) to take in or absorb liquid, usu water. **IDM** **drink sb's** ˈ**health** (*fml*) to express one's respect or good wishes for sb, by raising one's glass and drinking a small amount of the liquid in it. **drink like a** ˈ**fish** (*infml*) to drink a lot of alcohol regularly. **drink a toast to sb/sth** to express one's respect, good wishes, congratulations (CONGRATULATE) by raising one's glass and drinking a small amount of the liquid in it: *drink a toast to the happy couple.* **drink sb under the** ˈ**table** (*infml*) to drink more alcohol than sb else without becoming as drunk. **PHRV** **ˌdrink (sth)** ˈ**up** to drink the whole or the rest of sth, esp quickly: *I know the medicine tastes nasty, but drink it up.* ○ *Come on, drink up. It's time to go.* ○ (*Brit*) *drinking-* ˈ*up time* (ie time allowed for finishing drinks before* a pub closes). ˌdrink sth ˈin to watch or listen to sth with great pleasure or interest: *They stood drinking in the beauty of the landscape.* ˈdrink to sb/sth to express good wishes to sb/sth by raising a glass and drinking a small amount of the liquid in it; to drink a toast (DRINK²) to sb: *drink to sb's health/happiness/ prosperity* ○ *Let's drink to the success of your plans.* ○ *I'll drink to that (ie I agree)!*

▶ **drinkable** *adj* suitable or safe for drinking: *Is this water drinkable?* ○ *The wine is very drinkable* (ie pleasant to drink).

drinker *n* **1** a person who drinks alcohol, usu excessively: *a heavy drinker.* **2** a person who habitually drinks a particular drink: *a 'coffee drinker* ○ *'beer drinkers.*

drinking *n* [U] the action of drinking alcohol: *Drinking is known to be harmful.* ○ *a heavy drinking session* ○ *tough penalties for drinking and driving.* ˈdrinking-fountain *n* a device supplying water safe for drinking. ˈdrinking-water *n* [U] water that is safe for drinking.

■ ˌdrink-ˈdriver (*Brit*) (*US* ˌdrunk ˈdriver) *n* a person who drives a vehicle after drinking too much alcohol.

ˌdrink-ˈdriving (*Brit*) (*US* ˌdrunk ˈdriving) *n* [U].

drip¹ /drɪp/ *v* (**-pp-**) (**a**) to fall in small drops: [Vpr, Vp] *Rain was dripping (down) from the trees.* (**b**) to produce falling drops: [V] *Is that roof still dripping?* ○ *a dripping tap* [Vn, Vnpr] *He was dripping blood (down on the floor).*

▶ ˈdripping *adj* ~ (**with sth**) very wet: *Her clothes were still dripping wet.* ○ *Their faces were dripping with sweat.* ○ (*fig*) *dripping with jewels.* Compare WRINGING WET.

■ ˌdrip-ˈdry *adj* (of a garment) that dries quickly when hung up to drip: *a ˌdrip-dry 'shirt/'fabric.*

┌───┐
NOTE Drip, leak, ooze, run and seep all describe the way liquid escapes from a container, tap, etc. Most (not seep) also describe the way a container, tap, etc allows liquid to escape from it.
   Drip means to fall in regular drops: *Water was dripping from the pipe.* ○ *The pipe is dripping.* Liquid **leaks** from a container or machine through a hole or opening: *Water leaks through our ceiling every time it rains.* ○ *Every time it rains, the roof leaks.*
   Ooze describes thick liquids such as blood or oil which flow slowly: *My feet sank into the soft earth and wet mud oozed up between my toes.* ○ *The wound was oozing blood.*
   Water **runs** from a tap when it flows continuously: *Add the bath oil while the water is running.* ○ *Don't leave the tap running.*
   Seep means to flow very slowly so that you do not notice it immediately: *Fertilizers are seeping into our water supplies.* ○ *Oil had seeped from the engine.*
└───┘

drip² /drɪp/ *n* **1**(**a**) [sing] liquid falling in continuous drops: *the steady drip of water from a leaky tap.* (**b**) [C] any one of these drops: *The roof is leaking again — get a bucket to catch the drips.* **2** (also **drip-feed**) [C] (*medical*) a device that passes liquid food, medicine, etc directly into a patient's vein: *put sb on a drip* (ie fit such a device to a patient). **3** [C] (*sl*) a weak/dull person who lacks strength of personality: *Don't be such a drip! Come and join in the fun.*

dripping /'drɪpɪŋ/ *n* [U] fat produced by cooked meat.

drive¹ /draɪv/ *v* (*pt* **drove** /drəʊv/; *pp* **driven** /'drɪvn/) **1**(**a**) to operate, control and direct the course of a vehicle: [V] *Can you drive?* [Vn] *He drives a taxi* (ie that is his job). ○ *I drive* (ie own) *a Renault.* (**b**) to come or go somewhere by doing this: [V] *Did you drive or go by train?* [Vpr] *I drive to work.* [Vp] *Don't stop — drive on!* ⇨ note at TRAVEL. (**c**) to take sb somewhere in a car, taxi, etc: [Vnadv, Vnpr] *Could you drive me home/to the air-*

port? [also Vn, Vnpr]. **2** to force sb/sth to move in a particular direction: [Vnpr] *drive sheep into a field* ○ *Poor harvests have driven the farmers off the land.* [Vnp] *The enemy was driven back.* ○ (*fig*) *economic factors that drive inflation up.* **3** (of wind or water) to carry sth along: [Vnpr] *dead leaves driven along by the wind* [Vnpr] *Huge waves drove the yacht onto the rocks.* **4** (of rain, water, etc) to fall or move sideways rapidly and with great force: [Vpr] *The waves drove against the shore.* **5** (**a**) to force sth to go in a specified direction or into a specified position by applying pressure to it, pushing it, hitting it, etc: [Vnpr] *drive a nail into wood/a stake into the ground.* (**b**) to make an opening in or through sth by use of force: [Vnpr] *They drove a tunnel through the solid rock.* **6**(**a**) to force sb to act: [Vn] *A man driven by jealousy is capable of anything.* [Vnp] *The urge to survive drove them on.* (**b**) to cause or force sb to go into a specified unpleasant state or to do a specified thing: [Vn-adj, Vnpr] *drive sb crazy/to insanity/out of their mind* [Vn. to inf] *Hunger drove her to steal.* (**c**) to make sb/oneself work very hard or too hard: [Vn] *Unless he stops driving himself like this he'll have a breakdown.* ○ *He drives the team relentlessly.* **7** (*sport*) to hit a ball with force, sending it forward: [Vpr, Vnpr] *drive (the ball) into the rough* (ie in golf) [Vadv] *He drives beautifully* (ie plays this stroke well). [also V]. **8** (esp passive) to provide the power that causes a machine to work: [Vn] *a steam-driven locomotive.* **IDM** be ˈdriving at (always with *what* as the object) to be trying to say: *What are you 'driving at?* ○ *I wish I knew what they were really 'driving at.* **drive/strike a hard bargain** ⇨ HARD¹. **drive sth ˈhome (to sb)** make sb understand or accept sth, esp by saying it often, loudly, angrily, etc: *drive one's point home* ○ *The financial crisis has at last driven home (to the government) the need for a change in policy.* **drive a ˈwedge between sb and sb** to make people quarrel with or start disliking each other. **PHRV** ˌdrive ˈoff **1** (of a driver, car, etc) to leave: *The robbers drove off in a stolen vehicle.* **2** (in golf) to hit the ball to begin a game. ˌdrive ˈoff to take sb away in a car, etc. ˌdrive sb/sth ˈoff to force sb/sth away: *drive the enemy off.* ˌdrive sb/ sth ˈout (of sth) to force sb/sth to leave or disappear: *The supermarkets are driving small shopkeepers out of business.*

■ **drive-in** (also **drive-through, drive-thru**) *n* (*US*) a place, eg a cinema or restaurant, where one is entertained, served, etc without leaving one's car: *drive-in movies* ○ *a drive-thru bank.*

drive² /draɪv/ *n* **1** [C] a journey or trip in a car, van, etc: *Let's go for a drive in the country.* ○ *He took me out for a drive.* ○ *a forty minute/an hour's/a fifteen mile drive.* **2** (also **driveway**) [C] a private road or area between a house and the street for the use of vehicles. ⇨ picture at HOUSE¹. **3** [C] (*sport*) a stroke made by hitting a ball with force, sending it forward: *a forehand/backhand drive* (eg in tennis). **4** [U] the desire and determination to get things done or to achieve sth; energy: *She's certainly not lacking in drive.* **5** [C, U] a desire to satisfy a need: *(a) strong sexual drive.* **6** [C] (**a**) an organized effort or campaign to achieve sth: *plan a sales/a recruiting/an export drive.* (**b**) a series of military attacks. **7** (*Brit*) a social gathering to play card-games: *a 'bridge/'whist drive.* **8** [C, U] the apparatus for transmitting power to machinery: *front-/rear-/ four-wheel drive* (ie where the engine makes the front, back, or all four wheels turn) ○ *a car with left-hand drive* (ie with the steering-wheel (STEER¹) and other controls on the left) ○ *the 'drive shaft.* See also DISK DRIVE. **9** **Drive** (used in the names of roads): *ˌRodeo 'Drive.*

drivel /'drɪvl/ *n* [U] silly nonsense: *Don't talk drivel!*
▶ **drivel** *v* (**-ll-**; *US* **-l-**) ~ (**on**) (**about sth**) (esp in the

continuous tenses) to talk or write drivel: [Vp] *He was drivelling on about the meaning of life.* [also V, Vpr].

driven *pp* of DRIVE¹.

driver /'draɪvə(r)/ *n* **1** a person who drives a vehicle: *a bus/lorry/taxi driver* ○ *a learner driver* (ie sb who has not yet passed their driving test). **2** (in golf) a club²(2) with a wooden head used for hitting the ball from the TEE(1a). **IDM a back-seat driver** ⇨ BACK SEAT.
■ **'driver's license** *n* (*US*) = DRIVING-LICENCE.

driveway /'draɪvweɪ/ *n* = DRIVE² 2.

driving /'draɪvɪŋ/ *n* [U] the ability to drive or a way of driving: *His driving has improved.* ○ *Careless driving costs lives.*
▶ **driving** *adj* [attrib] **1** having great influence in causing sth to happen: *He was the **driving force** behind the band's success.* **2** having great force, esp sideways: *driving rain/sleet/snow.* **IDM (be) in the 'driving seat** in control of a situation: *What will become of the company when the new manager is in the driving seat?*
■ **'driving-licence** (*US* **'driver's license**) *n* a licence to drive a motor vehicle.
'driving school *n* a school for teaching people to drive motor vehicles.
'driving test *n* a test that must be passed to obtain a driving-licence.

drizzle /'drɪzl/ *v* (with *it* as subject) to rain lightly, with many fine drops: [V] *It had been drizzling all day.*
▶ **drizzle** *n* [U, sing] light fine rain: *A steady/thin drizzle was falling.* **drizzly** /'drɪzli/ *adj*: *a cold, drizzly day.*

drogue /drəʊg/ (also **,drogue 'parachute**) *n* a small PARACHUTE used to pull a larger one from its pack.

droll /drəʊl/ *adj* amusing: *a droll story* ○ (*ironic*) *So he thinks I'm going to apologize? How very droll!*

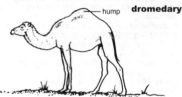

dromedary
— hump

dromedary /'drɒmədəri; *US* -deri/ *n* an animal of the CAMEL(1) family with only one HUMP(2a). ⇨ picture.

drone¹ /drəʊn/ *n* a male bee. Compare WORKER 3.

drone² /drəʊn/ *v* **1** to make a continuous low sound; to HUM(2): [V] *An aircraft droned overhead.* [also Vp]. **2** to talk or sing with a continuous MONOTONOUS sound: [V] *a droning voice* [Vp] *The chairman droned on for hours (about the company's performance).* [also V.speech].
▶ **drone** *n* (usu *sing*) **1** a continuous low sound: *the drone of bees* ○ *the drone of a distant aircraft.* **2** continuous MONOTONOUS talk: *The drone of the lecturer sent us all to sleep.* **3** (*music*) a continuous low sound made by certain instruments, eg BAGPIPES, over which other notes are played or sung.

drool /dru:l/ *v* **1** to have SALIVA coming out of the mouth: [V] *drool at the mouth.* **2** ~ (**over sb/sth**) (*infml derog*) to show in a ridiculous or excessive way how much one enjoys or admires sb/sth: *drooling over a photo of a pop star.*

droop /dru:p/ *v* to bend or hang downwards, esp through weakness or lack of energy: [V] *flowers drooping for lack of water* ○ *Her head drooped sadly.* ○ (*fig*) *His spirits drooped visibly at the news* (ie He became sad). ▶ **droop** *n* [sing]: *the exhausted droop*

of her shoulders. **droopy** *adj*: *He had a long droopy moustache.*

drop¹ /drɒp/ *n* **1** [C] a small round mass of liquid: *drops of rain/dew/sweat/condensation* ○ *tear-drops.* **2** [C esp *sing*] a small quantity of a liquid: *Could I have a drop more milk in my coffee, please?* ○ *I haven't **touched a drop** (ie drunk any alcohol) all day.* **3** drops [pl] liquid medicine poured a drop at a time into the ears, eyes or nose: *Take the drops three times a day.* **4** [sing] a reduction; a fall: *a drop in prices/temperature* ○ *a big drop in the number of people out of work.* **5** [sing] a distance straight down from a high point to the bottom: *There was a sheer drop of five hundred feet to the rocks below.* **6** [C] a delivery from a vehicle or an aircraft: *Drops of supplies are being made to villages still cut off by the snow.* **7** [C] a small round sweet of a specified flavour or type: *pear drops.* **IDM at the ,drop of a 'hat** without delay or HESITATION or without good reason: *You can't expect me to move my home at the drop of a hat.* **(only) a ,drop in the 'bucket/'ocean** a quantity too small to make any improvement or difference: *Aid to the Third World is at present little more than a drop in the ocean.*

drop² /drɒp/ *v* (**-pp-**) **1** to fall or allow sth to fall by accident: [V] *The bottle dropped and broke.* ○ *The climber slipped and dropped to his death.* [Vn] *Be careful not to drop that plate on the stone floor.* [also Vpr, Vp, Vnpr, Vnp]. **2** to fall or make sth fall deliberately: [Vpr] *She dropped to safety from the burning building.* ○ *He staggered in and dropped into a chair.* [Vnpr] *Medical supplies are being dropped to the stricken area.* [Vn] *He dropped his trousers* (ie undid them and let them fall). [also Vp, Vnp]. **3** (of people and animals) to collapse from being extremely tired: [V] *I feel ready to drop* (ie very tired). ○ *She expects everyone to work till they drop.* **4** to become or make sth weaker, lower or less: [V] *The temperature/wind/water level/has dropped considerably.* ○ *His voice dropped to a whisper.* ○ *The rate of inflation seems set to drop for the third month in succession.* ○ *The Dutch team have dropped to fifth place.* [Vn] *She dropped her eyes* (ie looked downwards). **5** to slope steeply downwards: [V, Vp, Vpr] *The ground drops sharply (away) (to the sea).* **6** ~ **sb/sth (off)** to stop so that sb can get out of a car, etc; to deliver sth on the way to somewhere else: [Vn, Vnp] *Could you drop me (off) near the post office?* **7** (*infml*) to send a letter, etc to sb: [Vnn] *drop sb a postcard.* **8** ~ **sb/sth (from sth)** to omit sb/sth by accident or deliberately: [Vn] *She's been dropped from the team because of injury.* [Vnpr] *Many dated expressions are being dropped from the new dictionary.* **9** (**a**) to stop seeing sb socially: [Vn] *She's dropped most of her old friends — or they've dropped her!* (**b**) to stop doing or discussing sth: [Vn] *Drop everything and come at once!* ○ *Let's drop the formalities — please call me Mike.* ○ *The police decided to drop the charges against her.* ○ *Look, can we just drop the subject?* **IDM die/fall/drop like flies** ⇨ FLY². **drop one's 'aitches** to omit the 'h' sound, esp from the beginning of words. In Britain dropping one's aitches is often thought to be a sign that the speaker belongs to a low social class. **drop a 'brick/'clanger** (*Brit infml*) to say or do sth that causes offence or embarrassment without realizing that it does. **drop 'dead 1** (*infml*) to die suddenly and unexpectedly. **2** (*sl*) (used to tell sb forcefully and rudely to stop annoying one, interfering, etc). **drop a 'hint (to sb)/drop sb a 'hint** to make a suggestion indirectly or with TACT. **drop sb 'in it** (*sl*) to put sb in an embarrassing situation. **drop/dump sth in sb's lap** ⇨ LAP¹. **drop/fall in/into sb's lap** ⇨ LAP¹. **drop sb a 'line** to write a (usu short) letter to sb: *Drop me a line to say when you're coming.* **drop 'names** (*infml*) to mention famous or powerful people one is supposed to know, so as to impress others. See also NAME-DROPPING. **drop a 'stitch** (in knitting) to let a stitch slip off the needle. **hear a pin drop** ⇨ HEAR. **one's jaw drops** ⇨ JAW. **let sb/sth 'drop** to do or say nothing more about sb/sth: *I suggest we let the matter drop.* **the penny drops** ⇨ PENNY. **PHRV** ,**drop 'back**; ,**drop 'behind (sb)** to move or fall into position behind sb else: *We cannot afford to drop behind our competitors.* ,**drop 'by/'in/'over/'round**; ,**drop 'in on sb**; ,**drop 'into sth** to pay a casual visit to a person or place: *Drop 'round some time.* ○ *I thought I'd drop 'in on you while I was passing.* ○ *Sorry we're late — we dropped into the pub on the way.* ⇨ note at VISIT. ,**drop 'off** (*infml*) **1** to fall into a light sleep: *I dropped off and missed the end of the film.* **2** to become fewer or less: *Traffic in the town has dropped off since the bypass opened.* ,**drop 'out (of sth) 1** to withdraw from an activity, a contest, regular use, etc: *drop out of politics* ○ *a word that is dropping out of use.* **2** to leave school, university, etc without finishing one's courses: *She started doing an engineering degree but dropped out after only a year.* **3** to withdraw from conventional society.

▶ **dropper** *n* an instrument consisting of a short glass tube with a rubber BULB(3) at one end. It is used for measuring out drops of medicine or other liquids.

droppings *n* [pl] the waste matter left by animals or birds.

■ **'drop-out** *n* a person who withdraws from conventional society or from a course of education: *a college drop-out* ○ *a university with a high drop-out rate.*

droplet /'drɒplət/ *n* a small drop of a liquid.

dross /drɒs; *US* drɔːs/ *n* [U] material without value or worth; the least valuable, attractive, etc part of sth: *The best players go off to the big clubs, leaving us the dross.*

drought /draʊt/ *n* [C, U] (a period of) continuous dry weather, esp when there is not enough water for people's needs: *areas of Africa affected by drought.*

drove¹ *pt* of DRIVE¹.

drove² /drəʊv/ *n* (usu *pl*) a moving crowd of people; a large number of things: *droves of sightseers* ○ *Letters of protest arrived* **in droves.**

▶ **drover** *n* a person who drives cattle or sheep to market.

drown /draʊn/ *v* **1(a)** to die in water or other liquid because one is unable to breathe: [V] *rescue a drowning man.* (**b**) to kill a person or an animal in this way: [Vn] *He fell overboard and was drowned.* **2** ~ **sth (in sth)** to make sth very wet; to DRENCH sth: [Vn] *a drowned valley* [Vnpr] *He drowned his meal in gravy.* **3** ~ **sb/sth (out)** (of a sound) to be louder than another sound and prevent it being heard: [Vn, Vnpr] *She turned up the radio to drown (out) the noise of the traffic.* **IDM** **drown one's 'sorrows (in drink)** (*esp joc*) to get drunk in order to forget one's troubles.

drowsy /'draʊzi/ *adj* (**-ier, -iest**) **1** half asleep; feeling SLEEPY(1): *I'd just woken up and was still drowsy.* ○ *This drug can make you drowsy.* **2** making one feel SLEEPY(1): *drowsy summer weather.* ▶ **drowsily** /-əli/ *adv: murmur sth drowsily.* **drowsiness** *n* [U].

drubbing /'drʌbɪŋ/ *n* (*infml*) (in a game or contest) a total defeat: *give sb/get a good 'drubbing.*

drudge /drʌdʒ/ *n* a person who has to do long hard boring jobs.

▶ **drudgery** /-əri/ *n* [U] hard boring work: *Women were rebelling against domestic drudgery.*

drug /drʌg/ *n* **1** a substance used as a medicine or in a medicine: *a pain-killing drug* ○ *The doctor has put me on these new drugs* (ie prescribed them for me). **2** a substance that stimulates the nervous system, esp one that is addictive (ADDICT), eg alcohol, COCAINE or HEROIN. Many drugs are illegal: *hard/soft drugs* ○ *take/use/be on drugs* ○ *peddle/push*

drugs ○ *'drug dealers* ○ *a 'drug addict* ○ *'drug-taking/-smuggling/-trafficking* ○ ,**drug-related 'crimes.**

▶ **drug** *v* (**-gg-**) to give a drug(1,2) to sb, esp to make them lose consciousness: *in a drugged state.*

druggist /'drʌɡɪst/ *n* (*esp US*) = CHEMIST¹.

drugstore /'drʌɡstɔː(r)/ *n* (*US*) a shop that sells many types of goods including drugs and medicines, and often serves light meals.

Druid /'druːɪd/ *n* a priest of an ancient Celtic religion.

drum¹ /drʌm/ *n* **1** (*music*) a musical instrument consisting of a hollow round frame with plastic or skin stretched tightly across one or both ends. It is sounded by striking with sticks or the hands: *a bass drum* ○ *a roll on the drums* ○ *play the drum(s) in a band.* ⇨ picture at MUSICAL INSTRUMENT. **2** a thing shaped like a drum, eg a barrel for oil or the container for clothes in a washing-machine (WASHING). ⇨ picture at BARREL. **3** = EARDRUM. **IDM** **beat the drum** ⇨ BEAT¹.

■ **'drum machine** *n* an electronic device that produces sounds like drums being played.

,**drum 'major** *n* an army SERGEANT(1) who leads a military band when it plays in a procession, etc.

,**drum majo'rette** /meɪdʒə'ret/ *n* (*esp US*) a girl in a short, brightly coloured costume who marches in front of a band as it plays, waving a long stick.

drum² /drʌm/ *v* (**-mm-**) **1** [V] to play a drum or drums. **2** ~ **(sth) on sth** to make a sound like a drum by tapping or beating sth continuously: [Vpr] *drum on the table with one's fingers* [Vnpr] *drum one's feet on the floor* [also Vn]. **PHRV** ,**drum sth into sb/into sb's 'head** to make sb remember sth by repeating it often: *Our teacher drummed multiplication tables into us till we knew them by heart.* ,**drum sb 'out (of sth)** to force sb to leave a group, an organization, etc as a punishment for doing sth wrong: *drummed out of the club/the regiment.* ,**drum sth 'up** to try hard to get support, customers, etc: *Manufacturers are offering big discounts to drum up business.*

▶ **drummer** *n* a person who plays a drum or drums.

drumming *n* [U, sing] a continuous sound like a drum being played: *the steady drumming of the rain on the tin roofs.*

drumbeat /'drʌmbiːt/ *n* a stroke on a drum or the sound this makes.

drumstick /'drʌmstɪk/ *n* **1** a stick for playing a drum. ⇨ picture at MUSICAL INSTRUMENT. **2** the lower part of the leg of a cooked chicken, TURKEY(1), etc.

drunk /drʌŋk/ *adj* **1** [usu pred] feeling the effects of alcoholic drink: *get drunk on cider* ○ *They put vodka in her fruit juice to get her drunk.* ○ *He was arrested for being* **drunk and disorderly.** **2** [pred] ~ **with sth** behaving in a strange, often unpleasant, way because of the excitement of sth: *drunk with joy/success.* **IDM** **blind drunk** ⇨ BLIND¹. (**as) drunk as a 'lord** (*Brit*); (*US*) (**as) drunk as a 'skunk** (*infml*) very drunk.

▶ **drunk** *n* a person who is drunk or who often gets drunk.

drunkard /-əd/ *n* a person who often gets drunk; an alcoholic (ALCOHOL).

drunken /'drʌŋkən/ *adj* [attrib] **1** drunk or often getting drunk: *a drunken reveller* ○ *her drunken boss/father.* **2** caused by or showing the effects of drink: *a drunken argument/brawl/rage/stupor/sleep* ○ *drunken laughter/voices/singing* ○ *drunken driving.* ▶ **drunkenly** *adv: stagger about drunkenly.* **drunkenness** *n* [U].

dry¹ /draɪ/ *adj* (**drier, driest**) **1** not wet, damp or sticky; without MOISTURE: *Is the washing dry yet?* ○ *Don't use this door until the paint is dry.* ○ *This pastry is too dry — add some water.* ○ *My mouth/throat feels dry.* ○ *I've got a dry cough* (ie without PHLEGM). **2** with little rain: *a dry spell/climate/*

country ○ *I hope it stays dry for our picnic.* **3** not supplying liquid: *The wells ran dry.* ○ *The cows are dry* (ie not producing milk). **4** (*infml*) (making one) thirsty: *I'm a bit dry.* ○ *This is dry work.* **5** [attrib] without butter: *dry bread/toast.* **6** (of wines, etc) not sweet: *a crisp dry white wine* ○ *a dry sherry.* **7** (of a country or region) where it is illegal to buy or sell alcoholic drink: *Some towns in Massachusetts are dry on Sundays.* **8** (of humour) pretending to be serious; IRONIC: *a dry wit.* **9** without emotion; cold[1](3a): *a dry manner/greeting/tone of voice.* **10** dull; boring: *Government reports tend to make rather dry reading.* **IDM** **boil dry** ⇨ BOIL[1]. **(as) dry as a ˈbone** completely dry. **high and dry** ⇨ HIGH[1]. **home and dry** ⇨ HOME[3]. **keep one's powder dry** ⇨ POWDER. **milk/suck sb/sth ˈdry** to obtain from sb all the money, help, information, etc they have, usu giving nothing in return. ▶ **dryly** (also **drily**) /ˈdraɪli/ *adv*: *'They're not famous for their hospitality,' he remarked dryly.* **dryness** *n* [U].
■ **dry-ˈclean** *v* [Vn] to clean clothes, etc without water, using special chemicals. **ˌdry-ˈcleaner** *n*: *My suit is at the dry-cleaner's.* **ˌdry-ˈcleaning** *n* [U].
ˌdry ˈdock *n* an enclosure for the building or repairing of ships, from which water may be pumped out: *a ship in dry dock for repairs.*
ˌdry-ˈeyed *adj* not crying (CRY[1] 1): *She remained dry-eyed thoughout the trial.*
ˌdry ˈice *n* [U] solid carbon dioxide (CARBON) used for keeping food, etc cold and for producing special effects in the theatre, etc.
ˌdry ˈland *n* [U] land as distinct from sea, etc: *I hate sailing and I couldn't wait to reach dry land.*
ˈdry law *n* (*US*) a law that forbids the selling of alcoholic drinks.
ˌdry ˈrot *n* [U] (**a**) wood that has decayed and turned to powder. (**b**) any FUNGUS(1) that causes this.
ˌdry ˈrun *n* (*infml*) a complete practice of a performance, procedure, etc before the real one: *Tonight's performance is a dry run for their big concert next week.*
ˈdry wall *n* [U] (*US*) = PLASTERBOARD.

dry² /draɪ/ *v* (*pt, pp* **dried**) **1** to become dry or make sth dry: [V,Vp] *Leave the dishes to dry (off).* [Vn,Vnp] *Dry your hands (on this towel).* **2** [V] (*infml*) (of an actor) to forget one's lines. **PHRV** **ˌdry (sb) ˈout** (*infml*) to treat sb or be treated for being dependent on alcohol. **ˌdry (sth) ˈout** to become or make sth completely dry: *Your clothes will take ages to dry out.* **ˌdry ˈup 1** (of rivers, lakes, etc) to become completely dry: *a dried-up well.* **2** (of any source or supply) to become no longer available: *If foreign aid dries up the situation will be desperate.* **3** to be unable to continue talking, esp because one has forgotten what one was going to say. **4** (*infml*) (usu imperative) to stop talking. **ˌdry (sth) ˈup** to dry dishes, etc with a towel after washing them: *Who's going to do the drying up?* See also BLOW-DRY.
▶ **drier** (also **dryer**) /ˈdraɪə(r)/ *n* (esp in compounds) a machine that dries: *a ˈclothes drier* ○ *a ˈhair-drier* ○ *a ˈtumble-drier.*

drystone /ˈdraɪstəʊn/ *adj* (of a stone wall) built without MORTAR[1] between the stones.

DSO /ˌdiː es ˈəʊ/ *abbr* (in the UK) Distinguished Service Order: *win/be awarded the DSO for bravery* ○ *Robert Hill DSO.*

DT /ˌdiː ˈtiː/ (also **DTs** /ˌdiː ˈtiːz/) *abbr* delirium tremens (a state in which people who have drunk too much alcohol feel their body shaking and imagine they can see things which are not really there): *have (an attack of) the DT's.*

DTI /ˌdiː tiː ˈaɪ/ *abbr* (in the UK) Department of Trade and Industry: *work for the DTI.*

dual /ˈdjuːəl; *US* ˈduːəl/ *adj* [attrib] having two parts or aspects; double: *his dual role as composer and*

conductor ○ *She has dual nationality* (ie is a citizen of two different countries).
▶ **dualism** /ˈdjuːəlɪzəm; *US* ˈduː-/ *n* [U] (*philosophy*) the theory based on the existence of two opposite principles, eg good and evil, in all things.
duality /djuːˈæləti; *US* duː-/ *n* [U] the condition of having two main parts or aspects.
■ **ˌdual ˈcarriageway** (*Brit*) (*US* **divided highway**) *n* a road with a central strip that divides streams of traffic moving in opposite directions.
ˌdual-ˈpurpose *adj* serving two purposes: *a dual-purpose vehicle for carrying passengers or goods.*

dub /dʌb/ *v* (**-bb-**) **1** to give sb a particular name: [Vn-n] *The papers dubbed the Beatles 'The Fab Four'.* ○ *Anorexia has been dubbed the 'slimming disease'.* **2** ~ **sth** (**into sth**) to replace the original SOUNDTRACK(a) of a film with one in a different language: [Vn] *a dubbed version* [Vnpr] *a German film dubbed into English.* Compare SUBTITLE *v*.

dubious /ˈdjuːbiəs; *US* ˈduː-/ *adj* **1** [esp pred] ~ (**about sth/doing sth**) (of a person) not certain and slightly suspicious about sth; doubtful: *I remain dubious about her motives.* ○ *Toby looked highly dubious.* **2** (*derog*) probably dishonest or risky: *a rather dubious character* ○ *a dubious business venture* ○ *His background is a little dubious, to say the least.* **3** (*esp ironic*) of which the value is doubtful: *She had the dubious honour of being the last woman to be hanged in England.* ▶ **dubiously** *adv*.

ducal /ˈdjuːkl; *US* ˈduːkl/ *adj* [usu attrib] of or like a DUKE: *the ducal palace in Rouen.*

duchess /ˈdʌtʃəs/ *n* (often titles **Duchess**) **1** the wife or widow of a DUKE: *the Duchess of Kent.* **2** a woman who holds the rank of DUKE in her own right.

duchy /ˈdʌtʃi/ *n* (also **dukedom** /ˈdjuːkdəm; *US* ˈduːk-/) *n* the territory of a DUKE or DUCHESS.

duck¹ /dʌk/ *n* (*pl* unchanged or **ducks**) **1**(**a**) [C] any of various types of common waterbird, domestic or wild: *the sound of ducks quacking nearby.* ⇨ picture. (**b**) [C] a female duck. Compare DRAKE. (**c**) [U] the flesh of the duck as food: *roast duck.* **2** [C usu *sing*] (also **ducky, ducks**) (*Brit infml*) (used as a form of address) DEAR *n*(2). **3** [C] (in cricket) a batsman's score of NOUGHT(1): *be out for a duck.* **IDM** **a dead duck** ⇨ DEAD. **(take to sth) like a ˌduck to ˈwater** (to become used to sth) very easily, without any fear or difficulty: *She's taken to teaching like a duck to water.* **water off a duck's back** ⇨ WATER[1]. See also DEAD DUCK, LAME DUCK, SITTING DUCK.

duck

▶ **duckling** /-lɪŋ/ *n* (**a**) [C] a young duck. (**b**) [U] its flesh as food. See also UGLY DUCKLING.
■ **ˌducks and ˈdrakes** *n* [U] a game in which flat stones are bounced across the surface of water.

duck² /dʌk/ *v* **1**(**a**) to move one's head or upper body down quickly so as to avoid being seen or hit: [Vpr] *I saw the gun and ducked under the table.* [Vp] *Quick! Duck down!* [V] *A plate flew across the room and he automatically/instinctively ducked.* [Vn] *He ducked his head to avoid a low branch.* [also Vnpr, Vnp]. (**b**) to avoid something thrown or aimed at one: [Vn] *duck a punch.* **2** to go or push sb under water for a short time: [Vnpr] *Her sisters ducked her in the river.* [also Vn, V]. **3** ~ (**out of**) **sth** (*infml*) to avoid a duty, responsibility etc: [Vpr] *It's his turn to wash the car but he'll try and duck out of it.* [Vn] *The government is ducking the issue.*

duct /dʌkt/ *n* **1** a tube or channel carrying liquid, gas, electric or telephone wires, etc: *One of the airducts has become blocked.* ○ *a heating duct.* **2** a tube in the body or in plants through which fluid, etc passes: *the bile duct.* ⇨ picture at DIGESTIVE SYSTEM.

dud /dʌd/ n a thing that fails to work properly: *Two of the fireworks in the box were duds.*
▶ **dud** adj faulty; worthless: *This battery is dud.* ○ *a dud cheque.*

dude /djuːd; US duːd/ n (US) **1** a city person, esp sb from the eastern USA spending a holiday on a western cattle farm: *a dude ranch* (ie one used as a holiday centre). **2** (*sl*) a man: *Who's that dude over there?*

dudgeon /ˈdʌdʒən/ n **IDM** **in high dudgeon** ⇨ HIGH[1].

due[1] /djuː; US duː/ adj **1(a)** [pred] ~ **(to do sth)** arranged or expected: *When's the baby due?* ○ *His book is due to be published in October.* ○ *The train is due (in)* (ie should arrive) *in five minutes.* **(b)** [usu pred] (of a sum of money) requiring immediate payment: *fall/become due* ○ *My rent isn't due till Wednesday.* ○ *Payment should be made on or before the due date.* **2** ~ **to sth/sb** caused by sb/sth; because of sb/sth: *absent due to illness* ○ *The team's success was partly/largely/entirely due to her efforts.* ⇨ note. **3** [attrib] suitable; right; proper: *after due consideration* ○ *make due allowance for sth.* See also DULY. **4** [pred] **(a)** ~ **(to sb)** owed as a debt or an obligation: *Have they been paid the money due to them?* ○ *I'm still due fifteen days' leave.* **(b)** ~ **for sth** owed sth; deserving sth: *She's due for promotion soon.* **IDM** **in ˌdue ˈcourse** at the appropriate time; eventually: *Your request will be dealt with in due course.* **with (all) due reˈspect** (used when one is about to disagree, usu quite strongly, with sb): *With all due respect, the figures simply do not support you on this.*

NOTE Some speakers are careful to use **due to** only after the verb *be*: *Our late arrival was due to the heavy traffic.* But many people also use it in the same way as **owing to**: *We were late owing to/due to the heavy traffic.* ○ *Due to/owing to the heavy traffic, we were late.* **Due to** can be used immediately after a noun: *Accidents due to drinking and driving increased over Christmas.*

due[2] /djuː; US duː/ n **1** one's/sb's **due** [U] a thing that should be given to sb by right: *He received a large reward, which was no more than his due* (ie at least what he deserved). ○ *She's a slow worker but, to give her her due* (ie to be fair to her), *she does try very hard.* **2** **dues** [pl] charges or fees (FEE), eg for membership of a club: *trade union dues* ○ *I haven't paid my dues yet.*

due[3] /djuː; US duː/ adv (before *north, south, east* or *west*) exactly: *sail due east* ○ *walk three miles due north.*

duel /ˈdjuːəl; US ˈduːəl/ n **1** (formerly) a formal fight between two men, using swords or guns, esp to settle a point of honour: *fight a duel* ○ *challenge sb to a duel.* **2** a contest or struggle between two people, groups, etc: *engage in a duel of words/wits* ○ *a complex legal duel.*
▶ **duelling** (US **dueling**) n [U] the fighting of duels: *duelling pistols.*

duet /djuˈet; US duˈet/ (also **duo**) n a piece of music for two players or singers: *a duet for violin and piano* ○ *We sang a duet.*

duff /dʌf/ adj (*Brit infml*) worthless or useless: *He sold me a duff radio.*

duffer /ˈdʌfə(r)/ n (*dated infml*) a person who is stupid or unable to do anything well: *I was always a bit of a duffer at maths.*

duffle bag (also **duffel bag**) /ˈdʌfl bæg/ n a canvas bag shaped like a tube and closed by a string around the top. It is usu carried over the shoulder.

duffle-coat (also **duffel-coat**) /ˈdʌfl kəʊt/ n a coat made of heavy woollen cloth, usu with a HOOD[1](1), fastened with toggles (TOGGLE[1]).

dug *pt, pp* of DIG[1].

dugout /ˈdʌɡaʊt/ n **1** (also ˌdugout caˈnoe) a CANOE

made by cutting out a long hollow space in a log. **2** a rough covered shelter, usu for soldiers, made by digging in the earth.

duke /djuːk; US duːk/ n (in titles **Duke**) **1** a nobleman of the highest rank: *He's a duke.* ○ *the Duke and Duchess of Gloucester.* See also DUCHESS. **2** (in some parts of Europe, esp formerly) a male ruler of a small independent state.
▶ **dukedom** /-dəm/ n **1** the position or rank of a duke. **2** = DUCHY.

dulcet /ˈdʌlsɪt/ adj [attrib] (*fml or joc*) sounding sweet; pleasing to the ear: (*ironic*) *I thought I recognized your dulcet tones* (ie the sound of your voice).

dulcimer /ˈdʌlsɪmə(r)/ n a musical instrument played by striking metal strings with two hammers.

dull /dʌl/ adj (-er, -est) **1** lacking interest or excitement; boring: *a rather dull diet* ○ *his dull suburban existence* ○ *The conference was deadly dull.* ○ *There's never a dull moment when John's around.* **2** not bright or clear: *a dull colour/glow* ○ *dull-looking hair* ○ *The day began grey and dull.* ○ *He heard a dull thud upstairs.* **3** slow in understanding; stupid: *a dull pupil/class/mind.* **4** (of pain) not felt sharply: *a dull ache.* **5** (of trade) not busy; slow: *There's always a dull period after the January sales.*
▶ **dull** v to become or make sth dull: [V] *The gleam of the ivory had dulled.* [Vn] *She took drugs to dull the pain.* ○ (*fig*) *Time had dulled the edge of his grief.*
dullness n [U]. **dully** /ˈdʌlli/ adj: *'I suppose so,' she said dully.* ○ *His leg ached dully.*

duly /ˈdjuːli; US ˈduːli/ adv (*fml*) **1** in a correct, proper or expected manner: *I declare that Bill Clinton has been duly elected President of the United States.* ○ *She duly won the top prize.* **2** at the expected and proper time: *I duly knocked on his door at 3 o'clock.*

dumb /dʌm/ adj (-er, -est) **1** unable to speak: *She's been dumb from birth.* **2** [usu pred] temporarily not speaking or refusing to speak: *He stood looking around him, baffled and dumb.* ○ *We were all struck dumb with amazement.* **3** (*infml*) stupid: *That was a pretty dumb thing to do.* ○ *If the police question you, act dumb* (ie pretend you do not know anything). ▶ **dumbly** adv: *She was staring dumbly into the fireplace.* **dumbness** n [U].
■ ˌdumb ˈanimals n [pl] animals, esp when regarded as helpless or deserving pity.
ˌdumb ˈblonde n (*derog*) a pretty but stupid woman with BLONDE hair: *In her early films she regularly played dumb blonde parts.*
ˌdumb ˈwaiter n a small lift for carrying food, etc from one floor to another, esp in a restaurant.

dumb-bell /ˈdʌm bel/ n **1** a short bar with a weight at each end, used for exercising the muscles, esp those of the arms and shoulders. **2** (US *infml*) a stupid person.

dumbfounded /dʌmˈfaʊndɪd/ adj (also **dumbstruck** /ˈdʌmstrʌk/) not able to speak because of surprise; astonished: *We were completely dumbfounded by her rudeness.*

dummy /ˈdʌmi/ n **1** [C] a model of the human figure, used esp for displaying or fitting clothes, etc: *a tailor's dummy* ○ *a ventriloquist's dummy.* **2** [C] a thing that appears to be real but is only an IMITATION(1): *The bottles of whisky on display are all dummies.* **3** [C] (*esp Brit*) (*Brit* also **comforter**) (*US* **pacifier**) a rubber TEAT(2) that is not attached to a bottle, for a baby to suck. **4** [sing] (in card-games, esp bridge[2]) the cards which are placed facing upwards on the table and used in turn by the partner of the player to whom they were originally given: *She played a jack from dummy.* **5** [C] (US *infml*) a stupid person.
■ ˌdummy ˈrun n a practice attack, performance, etc before the real one.

dump /dʌmp/ v **1** to put sth that is not wanted in a

place and leave it as rubbish: [Vnpr] *Some people just dump their rubbish in the river.* ○ *Forty sealed containers of nuclear waste have been dumped in the sea off Harwich.* [also Vn]. **2** to put sth down carelessly, heavily or in a mass: [Vnpr] *They've dumped a load of gravel by the garage and I can't get the car out.* [Vn] *Just dump everything over there — I'll sort it out later.* **3** (*infml often derog*) to leave or abandon sb: [Vn, Vnpr] *She dumped the kids (at her mother's) and went to the theatre.* **4** [Vn] (*commerce derog*) to sell goods abroad at a very low price because they are not wanted in the home market. **5** [Vn] (*computing*) to transfer data, etc from one part of a system to another or from one storage system to another. **IDM** **drop/dump sth in sb's lap** ⇨ LAP¹.

▸ **dump** *n* **1(a)** a place where a lot of rubbish is taken and left in a heap, sometimes without permission: *We have to take our own rubbish to the council rubbish dump.* Compare TIP² *n*. **(b)** (usu in compounds) a place where a particular dangerous substance is taken and left: *a toxic/nuclear waste dump.* **2** a temporary store of military supplies: *an ammu'nition dump.* **3** (*infml derog*) a dirty or unpleasant place: *How can you live in this dump?* See also DUMPS.

dumper *n* (also **'dumper truck**, *US* **'dump truck**) a vehicle for carrying earth, stones, etc in a container which can be raised at one end to dump its load.

dumping *n* [U] the practice of dumping sth, esp dangerous substances: *recent large-scale dumping at sea.* **'dumping ground** *n* (usu *sing*) a place where sth that is not wanted is dumped: *We are treating the atmosphere as a dumping ground for pollutants.*

dumpling /'dʌmplɪŋ/ *n* **1** a small ball of cooked DOUGH(1), eg in a stew. **2** a sweet food made of dough filled with fruit and baked: *apple dumplings.*

dumps /dʌmps/ *n* [pl] **IDM** **(down) in the 'dumps** (*infml*) depressed; feeling unhappy.

dumpy /'dʌmpi/ *adj* (**-ier, -iest**) (esp of a person) short and fat.

dun /dʌn/ *adj* of a dull greyish-brown colour: *dun leather boots.*

dunce /dʌns/ *n* a person, esp a school student, who is stupid or slow to learn.
■ **'dunce's cap** *n* a pointed paper hat formerly given to dull pupils to wear in class as a punishment.

dune /djuːn/; *US* duːn/ (also **'sand-dune**) *n* a small hill of loose dry sand formed by the wind.
■ **'dune buggy** *n* = BEACH BUGGY.

dung /dʌŋ/ *n* [U] animal waste, esp when used as MANURE: *cow dung.*

dungarees /ˌdʌŋɡə'riːz/ *n* [pl] a garment, made of strong cloth, that consists of trousers with an extra piece of cloth covering the chest, held up by straps over the shoulders: *a pair of dungarees* ○ *His dungarees were covered in grease.*

dungeon /'dʌndʒən/ *n* a dark underground room used as a prison, esp in a castle: *Throw him into the dungeons!*

dunk /dʌŋk/ *v* ~ **sth/sb (in/into sth)** **1** to dip food in liquid before eating it: [Vnpr] *dunk a doughnut in one's coffee.* [also Vn,Vnpr]. **2** to put sb/sth briefly in water: [Vnpr] *They dunked her in the swimming-pool as a joke.* [also Vn,Vnpr].

dunno /də'nəʊ/ *v* (*sl*) (I) do not know: *'Where's your mother?' I asked. 'Dunno,' he said.*

duo /'djuːəʊ; *US* 'duːəʊ/ *n* (*pl* **-os**) **1** a pair of performers: *a comedy duo.* **2** = DUET.

duodenal ulcer /ˌdjuːə,diːnl 'ʌlsə(r); *US* ˌduː-/ *n* an ULCER in part of the small INTESTINE.

duopoly /djuː'ɒpəli; *US* duː-/ *n* (*commerce*) a right to trade in a particular product or service, held by only two companies or organizations.

dupe /djuːp; *US* duːp/ *v* ~ **sb (into doing sth)** to deceive or trick sb into doing sth: [Vn] *They realized they had been duped.* [also Vnpr].

duplex /'djuːpleks; *US* duː-/ *n* (*esp US*) **1** a building divided into two homes. ⇨ picture at HOUSE¹. **2** a flat²(1) on two floors: *a duplex apartment.*

duplicate¹ /'djuːplɪkət; *US* 'duː-/ *adj* [attrib] **1** exactly like sth else; IDENTICAL(2): *a duplicate set of keys.* **2** having two parts that are similar in every detail: *a duplicate receipt/form.*
▸ **duplicate** *n* one of two or more things that are exactly alike; a copy: *Is this a duplicate or the original?* **IDM** **in duplicate** (of documents, etc) as two copies exactly alike in every detail: *prepare a contract in duplicate.*

duplicate² /'djuːplɪkeɪt; *US* 'duː-/ *v* [Vn] **1** (esp passive) to make an exact copy of sth. **2** to do sth again, esp when it is unnecessary; to repeat sth: *This research merely duplicates work already done elsewhere.* ▸ **duplication** /ˌdjuːplɪ'keɪʃn; *US* ˌduː-/ *n* [U]: *We must avoid wasteful duplication of effort.*

duplicity /djuː'plɪsəti; *US* duː-/ *n* [U] (*fml*) deliberate deception.

durable /'djʊərəbl; *US* 'dʊə-/ *adj* likely to last for a long time: *a durable peace/friendship/settlement* ○ *trousers made of durable material.* ▸ **durability** /ˌdjʊərə'bɪləti; *US* ˌdʊə-/ *n* [U]: *The fabric has a special backing for extra durability.* See also CONSUMER DURABLES.

duration /dju'reɪʃn; *US* du-/ *n* [U] the time during which sth lasts or continues: *of short/long/three years' duration* ○ *for the duration of this government.* **IDM** **for the duration** (*infml*) until the end of sth: *The war means there are no flights out of the country, so I'm stuck here for the duration* (ie until the war is over).

duress /dju'res; *US* du-/ *n* [U] threats or force used to make sb do sth: *sign a confession under duress.*

during /'djʊərɪŋ; *US* 'dʊər-/ *prep* **1** throughout a period of time: *during the 1980s* ○ *There are extra flights to Colorado during the winter.* ○ *During his lifetime his work was never published.* **2** within a specified period of time: *They only met twice during the whole time they were neighbours.* **3** at a particular time while sth progresses: *The phone rang during the meal.* ○ *Her husband was taken to the hospital during the night.*

dusk /dʌsk/ *n* [U] the time of day when the light is going but before night: *The street lights come on at dusk and go off at dawn.* ○ *Dusk was falling, so they went in.*

dusky /'dʌski/ *adj* (**-ier, -iest**) **1** not bright; DIM(1): *the dusky light inside the cave.* **2(a)** dark in colour: *dusky blue.* **(b)** (*often offensive*) having dark skin.

dust¹ /dʌst/ *n* [U] fine dry powder consisting of tiny pieces of earth, dirt, etc: *a speck of dust* ○ *clouds of dust blowing in the wind* ○ *gold/chalk dust* (ie gold/chalk powder) ○ *The furniture was covered in a thick layer of dust.* ○ *You might as well have these books; they're only gathering dust here* (ie they are not being used). ○ *The old parchment crumbled into dust when I touched it.* See also DUSTY. **IDM** **bite the dust** ⇨ BITE¹. **when the dust has settled** when the present uncertainty, unpleasant situation, etc is over.
■ **'dust cover** (also **'dust-jacket**) *n* a paper cover put around a book to protect it.
'dust-sheet *n* a sheet used for covering furniture that is not in use, to protect it from dust.
'dust-up *n* (*infml*) a noisy quarrel or fight: *There was a bit of a dust-up at the pub last night.*

dust² /dʌst/ *v* **1** ~ (**a**) to remove dust from sth by wiping or brushing, or with a quick light movement of one's hand, a cloth, etc: [Vn] *dust the furniture/books/living-room.* **(b)** ~ **sth/oneself down/off** (*Brit*) to remove dust from sb/oneself by brushing or with a quick light movement of one's hand: [Vnpr] *Dust yourself down — you're covered in chalk.* **PHRV**

D

,**dust sth 'off** to begin to use sth again, esp sth that one has not used for a long time: *For the office party I dusted off a song I'd written as a student years ago.* **'dust sth onto, over, etc sth** to put an even layer of a powder over sth: *dust sugar onto a cake.* **'dust sth with sth** to cover sth with a powder: *Lightly dust the cake with icing sugar.*

▶ **duster** *n* a cloth for dusting furniture, etc.

dustbin /'dʌstbɪn/ (*Brit*) (*US* **garbage can, trash-can**) *n* a container for household rubbish, usu kept outside: *a dustbin lid/liner.*

dustcart /'dʌstkɑːt/ (*Brit*) (*US* **garbage truck**) *n* a vehicle for collecting rubbish from outside houses, shops, etc.

dustman /'dʌstmən/ *n* (*pl* **-men** /-mən/) (*Brit*) (*US* **garbage man**) *n* a person employed by a local authority to remove rubbish from outside houses, shops, etc.

dustpan /'dʌstpæn/ *n* a small container with a wide mouth into which dust is brushed from the floor.

dusty /'dʌsti/ *adj* (**-ier, -iest**) (**a**) full of dust; covered with dust: *the dusty haze of a late summer day* ∘ *This room's awfully dusty, I'm afraid.* (**b**) (of a colour) dull: *a dusty pink.*

Dutch /dʌtʃ/ *adj* of the Netherlands (Holland), its people or their language. **IDM** **go Dutch (with sb)** to share the expenses of sth: *You mustn't pay for us all — why don't we go Dutch?*
▶ **Dutch** *n* (**a**) **the Dutch** [pl *v*] the people of the Netherlands. (**b**) [U] the language of the Dutch. See also DOUBLE DUTCH.
■ ,**Dutch 'barn** *n* a farm building consisting of a roof supported on poles, without walls, used as a shelter for HAY, etc.
,**Dutch 'cap** *n* (*Brit*) = DIAPHRAGM 2.
,**Dutch 'courage** *n* [U] (*infml*) the false courage that comes from drinking alcohol.

dutiful /'djuːtɪfl/ *US* 'duː-/ *adj* (*fml*) showing respect and obedience; doing everything that is expected of one: *a dutiful son* ∘ *She wrote a dutiful postcard to her mother.* ▶ **dutifully** /-fəli/ *adv*: *The audience applauded dutifully (ie because they were expected to rather than because they wanted to).*

duty /'djuːti/ *US* 'duːti/ *n* **1** [C,U] a moral or legal obligation: *do one's duty* ∘ *It's the duty of a doctor to try to keep people alive.* ∘ *It's not something I enjoy. I do it purely out of **a sense of duty**.* ∘ *I'll have to go, I'm afraid — **duty calls**.* **2** [C,U] a task or action that sb must perform: *routine administrative duties* ∘ *guard duty* ∘ *What are the primary duties of a traffic warden?* See also HEAVY-DUTY. **3** [C,U] ~ (**on sth**) a tax charged on particular goods, esp on imports: *customs/excise duties.* Compare TARIFF 2, DEATH DUTY, STAMP-DUTY. **IDM** **a/one's bounden duty** ⟹ BOUNDEN. **do duty for sth** to serve as or act as a substitute for sth else: *An old wooden box did duty for a table.* **in the line of duty** ⟹ LINE¹. **on/off duty** (of nurses, police officers, etc) engaged/not engaged in one's regular work: *I arrive at the hospital at eight o'clock, but I don't go on duty until nine.* ∘ *off-duty activities/hours.*
■ ,**duty-'bound** *adj* [pred] obliged (OBLIGE 1) by duty: *I'm duty-bound to help him.*
,**duty-'free** *adj, adv* (of goods) that can be imported without payment of duty(3): *duty-free cigarettes* ∘ *You're allowed 1½ litres of spirits duty-free.* ,**duty-'free shop** *n* a shop selling duty-free goods, eg at an airport.

duvet /'duːveɪ/ *n* a large cloth bag filled with soft feathers, etc, used on a bed instead of a top sheet and blankets (BLANKET 1): *a single/double duvet* ∘ *She put a new duvet cover on.*

dwarf /dwɔːf/ *n* (*pl* **dwarfs** or **dwarves**) **1** a person, an animal or a plant that is much smaller than the normal size: *a dwarf conifer.* **2** (in fairy stories) a creature like a very small man with magic powers.

▶ **dwarf** *v* to make sb/sth seem small by contrast or distance: [Vn] *Our little dinghy was dwarfed by the big yacht.*

dwell /dwel/ *v* (*pt, pp* **dwelt** /dwelt; *US* **dwelled**) [Vpr] ~ **in, at, etc** … (*arch or fml*) to live in or at a place. **PHRV** **dwell on/upon sth** to think, speak or write a lot about sth: *Let's not dwell on your past mistakes.*
▶ **dweller** *n* (esp in compounds) a person or an animal living in the place specified: '*town-/* '*city-dwellers* ∘ '*flat-dwellers* ∘ '*cave-dwellers.*
dwelling *n* (*fml or joc*) a place of residence; a house, flat, etc: *a desirable family dwelling.*

dwindle /'dwɪndl/ *v* ~ (**away**) (**to sth**) to become gradually less or smaller: [V] *dwindling hopes/popularity/profits* [Vpr, Vp] *Their savings have dwindled (away) to almost nothing.*

dye¹ /daɪ/ *v* (*3rd pers sing pres t* **dyes**; *pt, pp* **dyed**; *pres p* **dyeing**) to colour sth, esp by dipping it in a liquid: [Vn] *I'm sure she dyes her hair.* [Vn-adj] *dye a white dress blue.*
■ ,**dyed-in-the-'wool** *adj* [usu attrib] (*usu derog*) completely fixed in one's ideas, beliefs, etc: *He's a dyed-in-the-wool Marxist.*

dye² /daɪ/ *n* [C, U] a substance used to change the colour of things: *blue dye* ∘ *food containing vegetable dyes* ∘ *a tin of wood dye.* Compare STAIN.

dying¹ /'daɪɪŋ/ *pres p* of DIE¹.

dying² /'daɪɪŋ/ *adj* [attrib] occurring at or connected with the time when sb dies: *I will remember him **to my dying day**.* **IDM** **one's last/dying breath** ⟹ BREATH.
▶ **the dying** *n* [pl *v*] people who are dying: *Nurses comforted the dying.*

dyke = DIKE¹,².

dynamic /daɪ'næmɪk/ *adj* **1** (of power or a force) that produces movement. Compare STATIC 2. **2** (of a person or an organization) forceful and having a lot of energy: *a dynamic personality.*
▶ **dynamic** *n* a force that produces change, action or effects: *the inner dynamic of a historical period/ social movement/work of art.*
dynamically *adv*.

dynamics /daɪ'næmɪks/ *n* [sing *v*] the branch of PHYSICS dealing with movement and force.

dynamism /'daɪnəmɪzəm/ *n* [U] (in a person or an organization) the quality of being dynamic: *the freshness and dynamism of her approach.*

dynamite /'daɪnəmaɪt/ *n* [U] **1** a powerful explosive: *a stick of dynamite.* **2(a)** a thing likely to cause violent reactions: *The abortion issue is political dynamite.* (**b**) (*infml approv*) an extremely impressive person or thing: *Their new album is dynamite.*
▶ **dynamite** *v* [Vn] to blow sb/sth up with dynamite.

dynamo /'daɪnəməʊ/ *n* (*pl* **-os**) **1** a device for converting mechanical energy into electricity; a GENERATOR. ⟹ picture at BICYCLE. **2** (*infml*) a person who has extraordinary energy: *a human dynamo.*

dynasty /'dɪnəsti; *US* 'daɪ-/ *n* (**a**) a series of rulers all belonging to the same family: *the founder of the Tudor dynasty.* (**b**) a period during which a particular dynasty rules: *during the Ming dynasty.*
▶ **dynastic** /dɪ'næstɪk; *US* daɪ-/ *adj* [usu attrib]: *dynastic conflict.*

dysentery /'dɪsəntri; *US* -teri/ *n* [U] an infection of the bowels that causes severe DIARRHOEA.

dyslexia /dɪs'leksiə/ *n* [U] (*medical*) a slight disorder of the brain that causes difficulty in reading and spelling.
▶ **dyslexic** /dɪs'leksɪk/ *adj* suffering from dyslexia.

dyspepsia /dɪs'pepsiə; *US* dɪs'pepfə/ *n* [U] (*fml*) = INDIGESTION.
▶ **dyspeptic** /dɪs'peptɪk/ *adj* (*fml*) typical of a person suffering from dyspepsia; bad-tempered.

dystrophy /'dɪstrəfi/ *n* [U] = MUSCULAR DYSTROPHY.

[V.*to* inf] = verb + *to* infinitive   [Vn.inf (no *to*)] = verb + noun + infinitive without *to*   [V.*ing*] = verb + *-ing* form

Ee

E¹ (also **e**) /iː/ n (pl **E's**, **e's** /iːz/) [C,U] **1** the fifth letter of the English alphabet: *'Eric' begins with (an) E/'E'.* **2 E** (*music*) the third note in the scale¹(6) of C major.
■ **'E-number** n (*Brit*) a code number, beginning with the letter E, used for indicating the chemicals, artificial colours, etc that are added to food and drink, according to European Union regulations.

E² *abbr* East; Eastern: *E Asia* ∘ *London E10 6RL* (ie as a POSTCODE).

each /iːtʃ/ *indef det* (used with singular countable *ns* and singular *vs*) (of two or more) every person, thing, group, etc considered separately: *in each corner of the room* ∘ *a ring on each finger* ∘ *Each day passed without any news.* Compare EITHER.
▶ **each** *indef pron* every individual member of a group: *each of the boys/books/buildings* ∘ *Each of them phoned to thank me.* ∘ *Each of us has a company car.* (Compare: *We each have a company car.*) ∘ *I'll see each of you separately.* ∘ *He gave us an ice-cream each.*
each *indef adv* every one separately: *The cakes are 20p each.*
■ **each 'other** *pron* (used only as the object of a *v* or *prep*) the other one or ones: *Paul and Linda helped each other* (ie Paul helped Linda and Linda helped Paul). ∘ *We all write to each other regularly.* ∘ *We enjoy each other's company* (ie being with the other or the others). Compare ONE ANOTHER.
ˌ**each 'way** *adv* (*Brit*) (of a bet) placed so that one wins if the horse, etc comes first, second or third in a race: *I've put £10 each way on the favourite.* ∘ *an ˌeach-way 'bet.*

> **NOTE** Compare **each** and **every**. **Each** is used when you are talking about the items in a group individually. It is followed by a singular verb: *Each child has a coat peg with* (formal) *his or her name on.* ∘ *Each child has a coat peg with* (informal) *their name on.* **Each** can follow a plural subject: *We each have a different point of view.* You use **every** when you are talking about all the items in a group together. It is followed by a singular verb and can be modified by some adverbs: *Every/Nearly every child in the school passed the swimming test.*
> **Each of / each one of** and **every one of** come before plural nouns or pronouns, but the verb is still singular: *Each of the houses was slightly different.* ∘ *I bought a dozen eggs and every one of them was bad.* ∘ *She gave each one of/each of her grandchildren ten dollars.* **Each** can also be a pronoun on its own: *I asked all the children and each had a different excuse for being late.*

eager /'iːgə(r)/ *adj* ~ (**for sth/to do sth**) full of interest or desire; keen: *eager for success* ∘ *eager to please* ∘ *His eyes were alive and eager.* ▶ **eagerly** *adv: his eagerly awaited new production of 'Othello'* ∘ *'Who's coming?' she asked eagerly.* **eagerness** n [U, sing]: *I was surprised at his eagerness to return.*
■ ˌ**eager 'beaver** n (*infml*) a keen and enthusiastic person who works very hard.

eagle /'iːgl/ n **1** a large strong bird that hunts and eats small animals. It has a sharp curved beak and very good sight. ⇨ picture. **2** (in golf) a score of two strokes less than average. Compare BIRDIE 2, PAR¹ 1.
▶ **eaglet** /'iːglət/ n a young eagle.

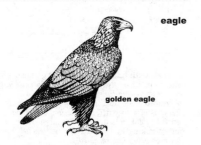

eagle

golden eagle

■ ˌ**eagle 'eye** n (usu *sing*) keen and close attention, esp to small details: *Nothing escaped our teacher's eagle eye* (ie He or she noticed everything). ˌ**eagle-'eyed** *adj.*

ear¹ /ɪə(r)/ n **1** [C] the organ of hearing; its outer visible part: *The doctor looked into my ears.* ∘ *Rabbits have large ears.* ∘ *She has an 'ear infection.* ⇨ picture. ⇨ picture at HEAD¹. **2** [sing] **an ~ (for sth)** a sense of hearing; an ability to recognize and reproduce sounds, esp in music and language: *She has a good ear for the rhythm of the language.* **3** [C usu *sing*] a willingness to listen and give attention to what sb is saying: *She's always got an ear for other people's problems.* ∘ *He has the ear of the Prime Minister.* **IDM** **(be) all 'ears** (*infml*) listening eagerly and with great interest: *Tell me your news — I'm all ears.* **bend sb's ear** ⇨ BEND¹. **box sb's ears** ⇨ BOX². **cock an ear/eye for/at sb/sth** ⇨ COCK². **sth comes to / reaches sb's 'ears** sb hears or learns about sth, eg news or gossip: *If this news ever reaches her ears, she'll be furious.* **sb's 'ears are burning** sb suspects that they are being talked about, esp in an unkind way: *All this gossip about Sarah — her ears must be burning!* **easy on the ear/eye** ⇨ EASY¹. **fall on deaf ears** ⇨ DEAF. **feel one's ears burning** ⇨ FEEL¹. **give sb / get a thick ear** ⇨ THICK. **go in 'one ear and out the 'other** to be heard but either ignored or quickly forgotten: *You never remember to do any of the things I say. Everything I tell you goes in one ear and out the other.* **have/keep an/one's ear to the 'ground** to know everything that is happening and being said: *Peter'll know — he always keeps his ear to the ground.* **have a word in sb's ear** ⇨ WORD. **keep one's ears/eyes open** ⇨ OPEN¹. **lend an ear** ⇨ LEND. **make a pig's ear of sth** ⇨ PIG. **music to one's ears** ⇨ MUSIC. **not believe one's ears/ eyes** ⇨ BELIEVE. **(be) out on one's 'ear** suddenly dismissed, forced to leave, etc. **play (sth) by 'ear** to play music by remembering how it sounds, ie without seeing a printed copy. **play it by 'ear** (*infml*) to act without detailed preparation but responding to a situation as it develops: *I've had no time to prepare for this meeting, so I'll have to play it by ear.* **prick up one's ears** ⇨ PRICK¹. **shut one's ears to sth/ sb** ⇨ SHUT. **smile, etc from ear to 'ear** to give a broad smile, etc showing that one is very pleased or happy. **turn a deaf ear** ⇨ DEAF. **(be) up to one's/ the ears/eyes/eyebrows/neck in sth** very busy with or deeply involved in sth: *I'm up to my ears in work at the moment.* **walls have ears** ⇨ WALL. **wet behind the ears** ⇨ WET. **with a flea in one's ear**

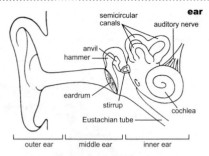

ear

semicircular canals
auditory nerve
anvil
hammer
eardrum
stirrup
cochlea
Eustachian tube

| outer ear | middle ear | inner ear |

E

⇨ FLEA. **with half an ˈear** without giving one's full attention: *I was listening to the radio with half an ear while getting lunch ready.*

▶ **-eared** /ɪəd/ (usu forming compound *adjs*) having ears of a specified type: *a ˌlong-eared ˈowl.*

earful /ˈɪəfʊl/ *n* [sing] (*infml*) a large amount of esp angry talking by sb: *He got a real earful from his boss for being late repeatedly.*

■ **ˈear-drop** *n* (usu *pl*) liquid medicine dropped into the ears.

ˈear-splitting *adj* extremely loud: *an ear-splitting crash.*

ear² /ɪə(r)/ *n* the top part of a grain plant, eg wheat, which contains the seeds. ⇨ picture at CEREAL.

earache /ˈɪəreɪk/ *n* [U, sing] pain inside the ear: *have earache.*

eardrum /ˈɪədrʌm/ (also **drum**) *n* a thin MEMBRANE(1) in the inner part of the ear that sound waves cause to VIBRATE(1). ⇨ picture at EAR¹.

earl /ɜːl/ *n* the title of a British nobleman of high rank. See also COUNTESS.

early *adj* /ˈɜːli/ (**-ier, -iest**) **1** happening or done before the usual time or the time expected: *early potatoes* (ie ones that are ready to eat early in the season) ○ *an early breakfast* (eg at 5 am) ○ *an early riser.* Compare LATE¹ 2. **2** happening or done near the beginning of a day or some other period of time: *the early morning* ○ *in early spring* ○ *He's in his early twenties* (ie aged between 20 and 23 or 24). ○ *one of Mozart's early works* (ie those written at the beginning of his career) ○ *in the early days of space exploration* (ie when it was only just beginning). Compare LATE¹ 2. **at your earliest conˈvenience** (*fml esp commerce*) as soon as possible: *Please telephone at your earliest convenience.* **an ˈearly bird** (*joc*) a person who arrives, gets up, etc early: *You're an early bird this morning!* **early ˈdays (yet)** (*esp Brit*) too soon to be sure how a situation, etc will develop: *I'm not sure if our book will be a success — it's early days yet.* **the early ˈhours** very early in the morning, ie after midnight and before dawn: *They were dancing till the early hours.* See also THE SMALL HOURS. **an early / a late night** ⇨ NIGHT.

▶ **earliness** *n* [U].

early *adv* **1** before the usual or expected time: *I got up early today.* ○ *The bus arrived five minutes early.* Compare LATE² 1. **2** near the beginning of a period of time: *Two players were injured earlier in the season.* ○ *I knew quite early (on) in the course that I wasn't going to enjoy it.* Compare LATE² 2.

■ **ˌearly ˈclosing** *n* [U] (*Brit*) the practice of closing shops on a particular afternoon every week: *It's early closing (day) today.*

ˌearly ˈwarning *n* [U, sing] advance indication of a serious or dangerous situation: *provide early warning of attack* ○ *a famine early warning system* ○ *an early warning of heart disease.*

earmark /ˈɪəmɑːk/ *v* ~ **sb/sth (for sth/sb)** (often passive) to keep sb/sth in reserve for a special purpose: [Vn, Vnpr] *earmark a sum of money (for*

research) [Vnpr] *Peter has already been earmarked for the job.*

earmuff /ˈɪəmʌf/ *n* (usu *pl*) either of a pair of coverings for the ears connected by a band across the top of the head, and worn to protect the ears, esp from the cold: *a pair of green earmuffs.*

earn /ɜːn/ *v* **1(a)** to get money by working: [Vn] *earned income* ○ *He earns £15000 a year.* ○ *She earned her living by singing in a nightclub.* **(b)** to get money as profit or interest¹(5) on a loan or an investment: [Vn] *Money earns more in a high interest account.* **2** to gain or deserve sth in return for one's achievements, behaviour, etc: [Vn] *You've certainly earned your retirement.* ○ *take a well-earned rest* [Vnn] *His honesty earned him great respect.* ○ *His bad manners earned him a sharp rebuke.*

▶ **earner** *n* **(a)** a person who earns money: *high / low wage earners.* **(b)** an activity or business that makes a profit: *Tourism is the country's biggest foreign currency earner.* ○ (*infml*) *Their shop is a nice little earner.*

earnings *n* [pl] money earned: *I've spent all my earnings.* **ˌearnings-reˈlated** *adj* (of payments, etc) linked to and changing with one's earnings: *an ˌearnings-related ˈpension plan.*

earnest¹ /ˈɜːnɪst/ *adj* intensely serious or sincere: *a terribly earnest young woman* ○ *an earnest conversation/expression.*

▶ **earnest** *n* **IDM** **in (deadly) ˈearnest 1** to a greater extent; with more determination and energy: *The publicity campaign will begin in earnest next month.* ○ *It's beginning to snow in earnest* (ie heavily). **2** serious(ly); not joking: *I knew he spoke in earnest.* ○ *You may laugh, but I'm in deadly earnest.*

earnestly *adv*: *He spoke very earnestly.* ○ *I earnestly beg you to reconsider your decision.*

earnestness *n* [U].

earnest² /ˈɜːnɪst/ *n* [sing] (*fml*) a thing meant as a sign or promise of what will follow: *The weapons were ceremoniously destroyed as an earnest of their avowed intention.*

earphones /ˈɪəfəʊnz/ *n* [pl] = HEADPHONES.

earpiece /ˈɪəpiːs/ *n* the part of a telephone, etc that is held next to the ear during use.

earplug /ˈɪəplʌg/ *n* (usu *pl*) a piece of soft material put into the ear to keep out air, water or noise.

earring /ˈɪərɪŋ/ *n* (often *pl*) a piece of jewellery worn on the LOBE(1) or edge of the ear.

earshot /ˈɪəʃɒt/ *n* **IDM** **(be) out of / within ˈearshot** where one cannot/can hear or be heard.

earth /ɜːθ/ *n* **1** (also **Earth**) [U, sing] this world; the planet on which we live: *The moon goes round the earth.* ○ *the planet Earth* ○ *depletion of the earth's ozone layer* ○ *I must be the happiest woman on earth!* **2** [U, sing] land; the surface of the world contrasted with the sky or sea: *After a week at sea, it was good to feel the earth under our feet again.* ○ *The balloon burst and fell to earth.* **3** [U] soil: *a clod/lump of earth* ○ *fill a hole with earth* ○ *cover the roots of a plant with earth.* ⇨ note. **4** [C] the hole of a wild animal, esp a fox. **5** [C usu *sing*] (*esp Brit*) (*US* **ground**) a wire that provides a connection with the ground and completes an electrical circuit. See also FULLER'S EARTH. **IDM** **charge, cost, pay, etc (sb) the ˈearth** (*Brit infml*) to charge, etc a lot of money: *I'd love that bike, but it costs the earth.* **come back/down to ˈearth (with a ˈbang/ˈbump)** (*infml*) to think about one's situation as it is and not how one would like it to be; to return to reality: *When his money ran out, he came down to earth (with a bump).* See also DOWN-TO-EARTH. **the ends of the earth** ⇨ END¹. **go/run to ˈearth/ˈground** (*Brit*) to hide oneself, eg to avoid being captured. **how, why, where, who, etc on ˈearth / in the ˈworld** (*infml*) (used for emphasis) how ever, why ever, etc: *What on* *earth are you doing?* ○ *How on earth did she manage that?* **(be, feel, look, etc) like nothing on ¹earth** (*infml*) very bad; ill; strange: *He looks like nothing on earth in those weird clothes.* **move heaven and earth** ⇨ MOVE¹. **promise the earth/moon** ⇨ PROMISE². **run sb/sth to ¹earth** to find sb/sth by searching long and carefully: *The police eventually ran him to earth in Paris.* **the salt of the earth** ⇨ SALT. **wipe sb/sth off the face of the earth / off the map** ⇨ WIPE.

▶ **earth** *v* (esp passive) to connect an electrical appliance, etc with the ground: [Vn] *Is this plug earthed?*

earthy *adj* (**-ier, -iest**) **1** of or like earth or soil: *earthy colours/smells.* **2** (of people, jokes, etc) concerned with basic physical functions; not intellectual or refined: *an earthy sense of humour* ○ *a very earthy character.* **earthiness** *n* [U].

■ **¹earth science** *n* any of various sciences, such as GEOGRAPHY(1) or GEOLOGY, concerned with the earth or part of it.

¹earth-shattering *adj* having a powerful effect, esp a surprising or shocking one: *earth-shattering news.*

NOTE Compare **earth, land, ground, floor** and **soil**. The **earth** (also **the Earth**) is the name of the planet on which we live. **Earth** can also refer to the world in contrast to the sky above: *The parachute floated gently down to earth.*

Land is the surface of the earth that is not sea: *We did not see land again until the ship reached Australia.* **Land** is also a large area which people buy, live on or grow food on: *They bought some land and built their own house.* ○ *farmland.* **The ground** is the solid surface under your feet when you are outside: *It had been raining and the ground was still wet.* The surface under your feet inside a building is **the floor**: *He dropped his coat on the floor.* Trees and plants grow in **soil** or **earth**: *The soil in this garden is very good for growing roses.* ○ *We filled a few trays with earth and planted the seeds.* **Ground** is an area of **earth/soil**: *soft ground* ○ *a piece of ground where the kids play.*

earthbound /ˈɜːθbaʊnd/ *adj* **1** attached or restricted to the earth: *earthbound forms of life* (ie unable to fly) ○ (*fig*) *an earthbound imagination.* **2** moving or directed towards the earth: *an earthbound meteorite.*

earthen /ˈɜːθn/ *adj* [attrib] made of earth: *earthen walls.*

earthenware /ˈɜːθnweə(r)/ *n* [U] pots, dishes, etc made of baked clay: *an earthenware bowl.* See also PORCELAIN.

earthling /ˈɜːθlɪŋ/ *n* a person who lives on the earth, esp as regarded in fiction by creatures from other planets.

earthly /ˈɜːθli/ *adj* **1** of this world; not spiritual: *earthly joys/possessions.* **2** (*infml*) (usu in negative sentences for emphasis) possible; remote: *There's no earthly reason why you shouldn't go.* ○ *You've no earthly hope of winning.* ○ *This book is (of) no earthly use to anybody.* **IDM** **not have/stand an ¹earthly** (*Brit infml*) not have the slightest chance, hope or idea: *'Why isn't it working?' 'I haven't an earthly* (ie I don't know at all).' ○ *With Myers competing, Davis didn't stand an earthly.*

earthquake /ˈɜːθkweɪk/ (also **quake**) *n* a sudden violent movement of the earth's surface: *The earthquake struck shortly after 5 pm.*

earthwork /ˈɜːθwɜːk/ *n* (often *pl*) (formerly) a large artificial bank¹(2) of earth used as a defence: *the remains of ancient earthworks.*

earthworm /ˈɜːθwɜːm/ *n* a common type of worm that lives in the soil. ⇨ picture at WORM.

earwig /ˈɪəwɪɡ/ *n* a small harmless insect with pincers (PINCER 2) at the back end of its body.

ease¹ /iːz/ *n* [U] **1** lack of difficulty: *the ease with which he understood the situation* ○ *He passed the exam with ease.* ○ *We've put the files here for ease of access.* **2** freedom from work, pain or anxiety; comfort: *a life of ease* ○ *ease of mind* ○ *The injection brought him immediate ease.* Compare EASY¹ 2. **IDM** **(stand) at ¹ease** (as a military command) (stand) with the feet apart and the hands behind the back. Compare ATTENTION 4. **(be/feel) at (one's) ¹ease** (to be/feel) comfortable and free from worry or embarrassment; completely relaxed: *I never feel completely at ease with him/in his company.* **ill at ease** ⇨ ILL¹. **put/set sb at (their) ¹ease** to make sb feel comfortable, free from embarrassment, etc: *He had been dreading their meeting but her warm welcome soon put him at his ease.* **put/set sb's mind at ease/rest** ⇨ MIND¹.

ease² /iːz/ *v* **1** to become or make sth less unpleasant or serious: [Vn] *the need to ease traffic congestion in the city centre* ○ *ease the burden of debt* ○ *the demand for new measures to ease the housing crisis* ○ *the easing of censorship* [V] *The situation is beginning to ease.* **2(a)** to make sth less painful, severe, worrying, etc: [Vn] *The aspirins eased my headache.* ○ *Talking eased his anxiety.* ○ *It would ease my mind to know what happened to him.* [V, Vp] *The pain will soon ease (away/off).* **(b)** ~ **sb of sth** to free sb from pain or suffering: [Vnpr] *Walking helped to ease him of his pain.* **3** to move or move sb/sth carefully and gently: [Vadv] *She eased slowly forwards.* [Vnpr] *easing her way along the ledge to reach the terrified boy* ○ *He eased himself into a chair.* [Vnp] *Ease the cake out when it has cooled.* **4** to make sth looser or less tight: [Vn] *ease the steering* ○ *The coat needs to be eased under the armpits.* **5** to become or make sth lower in price or value: [V] *Interest rates have eased since December.* [Vp] *Share prices eased back from afternoon levels.* [Vn] *There was pressure to ease taxation.* **PHR V** **¹ease (oneself/sb) into sth** to learn or become familiar with sth gradually; to help sb to do sth: *ease oneself into a new job.* **¸ease ¹off** to become less severe, urgent, etc: *The tension between us has eased off a little.* ○ *The flow of traffic eased off.* **¸ease sb ¹out (of sth)** to make sb leave their job, eg by reducing their responsibilities or making difficulties for them: *He was gradually eased out of his position as chairman.* **¸ease ¹up 1** to reduce speed: *The car eased up before the bend.* **2** to become less severe, urgent, etc: *I'm very busy just now — can it wait until things have eased up a little?* **¸ease ¹up (on sb/sth)** to become more moderate about or with sb/sth: *I would ease up on the cigarettes if I were you.*

easel /ˈiːzl/ *n* a wooden frame for holding a BLACKBOARD or a picture while it is being painted.

east /iːst/ *n* [U, sing] (*abbr* **E**) **1** (usu **the east**) the direction from which the sun rises; one of the four main points of the COMPASS(1): *The wind is blowing from the east.* ○ *He lives to the east of* (ie further east than) *Boston.* Compare NORTH, SOUTH, WEST. **2 the East** the countries of Asia, esp China and Japan: *Yoga originated in the East.* See also THE MIDDLE EAST, THE NEAR EAST, THE FAR EAST. **3 the East** (*US*) the eastern side of the USA: *I was born in the East, but now live in Los Angeles.*

▶ **east** *adj* [attrib] **1** in or towards the east: *East Africa* ○ *He lives on the east coast.* **2** coming from the east: *an east wind.* See also EASTERLY 2.

east *adv* towards the east: *two miles east of here* ○ *My window faces east.* ○ *We are travelling east.*

eastward /ˈiːstwəd/ *adj* going towards the east: *in an eastward direction.*

eastwards /ˈiːstwədz/ (also **eastward**) *adv*: *firms looking eastward for new markets* ○ *travel eastwards.* ⇨ note at FORWARD².

■ **the ¸East ¹End** *n* (*Brit*) a part of East London containing many flats, houses and factories, and

traditionally associated with the working class
(WORKING). Compare THE WEST END.

eastbound /ˈiːstbaʊnd/ *adj* travelling towards the
east: *Is this the eastbound train?* ∘ *the eastbound
section of the freeway.*

Easter /ˈiːstə(r)/ *n* an annual Christian festival that
occurs on a Sunday in March or April and celebrates the resurrection (RESURRECT) of Christ; the
period about this time: ˌEaster ˈDay ∘ ˌEaster ˈSunday ∘ ˈEaster week (ie the week beginning on Easter
Sunday) ∘ *the* ˌEaster ˈholidays.
  ▪ ˈEaster egg *n* an egg made of chocolate, or a
hen's egg with a painted shell, given as a present,
esp to children, at Easter.

easterly /ˈiːstəli/ *adj* [usu attrib], *adv* **1** in or towards the east: *in an easterly direction.* **2** (of winds)
blowing from the east: *an easterly wind.*

eastern /ˈiːstən/ (also **Eastern**) *adj* [attrib] of, from
or living in the east part of the world or of a
specified region: *Eastern customs/religions* ∘ *the eastern seaboard of the USA.*
  ▶ **easternmost** /ˈiːstənməʊst/ *adj* situated furthest
east: *the easternmost city in Europe.*

easy¹ /ˈiːzi/ *adj* (**-ier, -iest**) **1** not difficult; done or
obtained without great effort: *an easy exam* ∘ *It is an
easy place to reach.* ∘ *within easy reach* ∘ *The place is
easy to reach.* ∘ *It's easy (for you) to say that but what
do you propose to do about it?* ∘ *Finding a suitable
house is no easy matter/task.* **2** comfortable; free
from hard work, pain, anxiety, trouble, etc: *lead an
easy life* ∘ *feel easy about letting children go out alone*
∘ *My mind is easier now.* See also EASE¹ 2. **3** [attrib]
pleasant and friendly; not stiff(4) or awkward(3):
have an easy manner ∘ *be on easy terms with sb.* **4**
[attrib] open to attack, bad treatment, etc: *Half-
starved already, they were easy victims of disease.* ∘
become easy prey. **IDM** **as** ˌeasy as ˈanything / as
ˈpie / as ABˈC / as falling off a ˈlog / as ˈwinking
(*infml*) very easy or easily. ˌeasy ˈmoney money
obtained either dishonestly or for little work. ˌeasy
on the ˈear/ˈeye (*infml*) pleasant to listen to or look
at: *This music's easy on the ear late at night.* **(on)**
ˈeasy street (*US*) (enjoying) a comfortable way of
life. **an easy / a soft touch** ⇨ TOUCH². **free and
easy** ⇨ FREE¹. **have an easy ˈtime (of it)** to experience no difficulty or problems. **I'm ˈeasy** (*infml*)
(said when a choice has been offered) I do not mind:
'Would you like to walk or go by car?' 'I'm easy.' **of
easy ˈvirtue** (of a woman) willing to have sex with
anyone; having loose morals (MORAL² 1). **take the
easy way ˈout** to escape from a difficult or awkward situation by choosing the simplest, and
possibly not the most honourable, course of action.
  ▶ **easily** /ˈiːzəli/ *adv* **1** without difficulty: *I can
easily finish it tonight.* **2** (used before a superlative
adj) without doubt; by far: *It's easily the best film I've
seen this year.* **3** very probably; very likely: *That
could easily be the answer we're looking for.* **4**
quickly; more quickly than is usual: *I get bored
easily.* ∘ *He's easily upset.*
  ▪ ˌeasy ˈchair *n* a large comfortable chair.

easy² /ˈiːzi/ *adv* (**-ier, -iest**) (as a command) be careful: *Easy with that chair — one of its legs is loose.*
IDM ˌeasier ˈsaid than ˈdone more difficult to do
than to talk about: *'Why don't you get yourself a job?'
'That's easier said than done.'* ˌeasy ˈcome, ˌeasy
ˈgo (*saying*) money, possessions, etc obtained without difficulty are not considered to be very
important and may be quickly lost or spent without
regret: *I often win money at cards but never save a
penny — 'easy come, easy go' is my motto.* ˌeasy/
ˌgently ˈdoes it (*infml*) this job, etc should be done
slowly and carefully: *Take your time — easy does it.*
go ˈeasy on sb (*infml*) (usu in the imperative) to be
less severe with or critical of sb: *Go easy on the child
— he's still very young.* **go ˈeasy on sth** (*infml*)

(usu in the imperative) not to use too much of sth:
Go easy on the cornflakes; we all want some. ˌstand
ˈeasy (as a military command) stand with more
freedom of movement than when standing at ease
(EASE¹). ˌtake it/things ˈeasy to relax; to avoid
working too hard or doing too much: *I like to take
things easy when I'm on holiday.*

easygoing /ˌiːziˈɡəʊɪŋ/ *adj* (of people) happy to
accept things without worrying or getting angry: *My
mother doesn't mind who comes to stay, she's very
easygoing.*

eat /iːt/ *v* (*pt* **ate** /et/; *US* eɪt/; *pp* **eaten** /ˈiːtn/) **1** ~
(up)/~ (up) to put food into the mouth, CHEW it
and swallow it: [V] *He was too ill to eat.* [Vp] *Eat up*
(ie Finish eating) *now.* [Vnp] *Eat up* (ie Eat all) *your
dinner.* [Vn] *Lions eat meat* (ie Meat is their diet). **2**
to have a meal: [V] *Where shall we eat tonight?* **3**
(*infml*) (esp in the continuous tenses) to worry or
annoy sb: [Vn] *Tom's very quiet tonight — what's
eating him?* **IDM** **dog eat dog** ⇨ DOG¹. ˌeat sb
aˈlive (*infml*) **1** to be able to dominate or exploit sb:
That woman will eat him alive. **2** (often passive) (of
insects, etc) to bite sb many times: *I was eaten alive
by mosquitoes.* **eat one's ˈheart out (for sb/sth)** to
feel very unhappy, esp because one wants sb/sth
one cannot have: *Since he left, she's been sitting at
home eating her heart out.* **eat (like) a ˈhorse**
(*infml*) to eat a lot: *She's very thin but she eats like a
horse.* ∘ *I'm so hungry I could eat a horse!* **eat
humble ˈpie** to say one is very sorry for a mistake
one has made: *When he realizes that I am telling the
truth, he'll have to eat humble pie.* **eat out of one's/
sb's ˈhand** to be willing to be controlled or guided
by sb: *She soon had the class eating out of her hand.*
eat sb out of ˌhouse and ˈhome (*infml often joc*)
(of people) to eat a lot of sb else's food: *I hope your
brother won't stay much longer, he's eating us out of
house and home!* **eat oneself ˈsick (on sth)** (*infml*)
to eat so much (of sth) that one feels or is sick: *The
children would eat themselves sick on chocolate if I let
them.* **eat one's ˈwords** to admit that what one said
was wrong. **have one's cake and eat it** ⇨ CAKE.
I'll eat my ˈhat (*infml*) (an expression used by sb
who believes that sth is extremely unlikely to happen): *Well, if that car starts, I'll eat my hat!* **what's
biting/eating him, etc?** ⇨ BITE¹. **PHRV** ˌeat sth
aˈway / ˌeat aˈway at sth to reduce or destroy sth
gradually; to ERODE sth: *The river is eating away at
the bank.* ∘ *new buildings eating away the character
of this historic town.* ˈeat into sth **1** to penetrate
and destroy sth gradually; to dissolve or CORRODE
sth: *acid rain eating into the stone walls.* **2** to use up
a part of the available money, time, etc: *Paying for
the new carpet has eaten into my savings.* ˌeat ˈout to
have a meal in a restaurant, etc rather than at
home: *I'm too tired to cook tonight — let's eat out.*
ˌeat sb ˈup (usu passive) (of a feeling) to dominate
sb's thoughts so that their attitude to life is affected:
be eaten up with curiosity/anger/envy ∘ *Jealousy was
eating him up.* ˌeat sth ˈup to use sth in large
quantities: *This car really eats up petrol.* ∘ *The project is eating up a third of the organization's entire
research budget.*
  ▶ **eatable** *adj* fit to be eaten; good to eat: *Our school
lunches are hardly eatable.* See also EDIBLE.
  eater *n* **1** a person or an animal that eats a particular thing or eats in a particular way: *We're not great
meat-eaters.* ∘ *He's a big eater* (ie He eats a lot). **2**
(*Brit*) = EATING APPLE.
  eats *n* [pl] (*infml*) food ready to be eaten, esp at a
party: *There were plenty of eats, but not enough to
drink.*
  ▪ ˈeating apple *n* a type of apple that is suitable for
eating raw. Compare COOKER 2.

eatery /ˈiːtəri/ *n* (*infml esp US*) a restaurant or other
place that serves food.

[V.*to* inf] = verb + *to* infinitive   [Vn.inf (no *to*)] = verb + noun + infinitive without *to*   [V.*ing*] = verb + -*ing* form

eau-de-Cologne /ˌəʊ də kəˈləʊn/ (also **cologne**) n [U] a type of light PERFUME(1).

eaves /iːvz/ n [pl] the lower edges of a roof that project over the walls: *birds nesting under the eaves.* ⇨ picture at HOUSE¹.

eavesdrop /ˈiːvzdrɒp/ v (**-pp-**) ~ (**on sb/sth**) to listen secretly to a private conversation: [V] *You've been eavesdropping again!* ○ *electronic eavesdropping devices* [Vpr] *He admitted eavesdropping on his wife's phone calls.* ▶ **eavesdropper** n.

ebb /eb/ v **1** [V] (of the tide) to go out; to flow away from the land. Compare FLOW 5. **2** ~ (**away**) to grow less; to become slowly weaker or fainter: [Vp] *Daylight was ebbing away.* [V] *Our enthusiasm soon began to ebb.*
▶ **ebb** n (usu **the ebb**) [sing] the period when the tide is flowing away from the land: *an ebb tide* ○ *The tide is on the ebb* (ie is going out). **IDM at a low ebb** ⇨ LOW¹. **the ebb and flow of sth/sb**) a constant change of direction, style, etc; a regular rise and fall in intensity, numbers, etc: *the ebb and flow of conversation/workers changing shifts.*

ebony /ˈebəni/ n [U] the hard black wood of a tropical tree.
▶ **ebony** adj **1** made of ebony: *an ebony carving.* **2** black: *ebony skin.*

ebullient /ɪˈbʌliənt, -ˈbʊl-/ adj full of energy and excitement: *the ebullient director of a local firm.* ▶ **ebullience** /-əns/ n [U]: *She has an infectious ebullience that inspires all who work with her.*

EC /ˌiː ˈsiː/ abbr **1** East Central: *London EC1 4PW* (ie as a POSTCODE). **2** (usu **the EC**) European Community (the Common Market): *countries applying to join the EC* ○ *the EC Council of Ministers.* See also EU.

eccentric /ɪkˈsentrɪk/ adj **1** (of people or their behaviour) unusual; not conventional or normal; slightly odd: *his eccentric habits* ○ *an eccentric old lady.* **2** (of circles) not having the same centre. Compare CONCENTRIC.
▶ **eccentric** n an eccentric person: *The club seemed to be full of eccentrics.*
eccentrically /-kli/ adv.
eccentricity /ˌeksenˈtrɪsəti/ n **1** [U] the quality of being eccentric; unusual or strange behaviour, taste, etc: *eccentricity of style/clothing/manners/ideas.* **2** [C] an unusual or strange act or habit: *One of his eccentricities is sleeping under the bed instead of on it.*

ecclesiastic /ɪˌkliːziˈæstɪk/ n a priest or CLERGYMAN in the Christian Church.
▶ **ecclesiastical** /-kl/ adj [usu attrib] of or relating to the Christian Church: *ecclesiastical history.*

ECG /ˌiː siː ˈdʒiː/ (also US **EKG**) abbr (*medical*) electrocardiogram: *have an ECG test.*

echelon /ˈeʃəlɒn/ n **1** (often pl) a level of authority or responsibility; a rank in an organization: *the higher/upper/top echelons of the Civil Service.* **2** a formation of troops, aircraft, ships, etc each behind and to the side of the one in front: *aircraft flying in echelon* (ie in a line stretching backwards to the left or right).

echo¹ /ˈekəʊ/ n (pl **-oes**) **1(a)** the reflecting of sound waves off a wall or inside an enclosed space so that a cry, shout, etc appears to be repeated: *The cave has a wonderful echo.* **(b)** a sound repeated in this way: *If you shout loudly, you'll hear the echo.* ○ *The echoes of the cheering finally died away.* **2** a thing that resembles another so that one is reminded of it: *Echoes of his music can be heard in many rock bands.* ○ *Her speech evoked echoes of the past.*

echo² /ˈekəʊ/ v **1** (of sounds) to be reflected and repeated after the original sound has stopped: [Vpr] *His footsteps echoed in the empty hall.* ○ *Their shouts echoed through the forest.* [also V]. **2** ~ (**to/with sth**); ~ sth (**back**) (of places) to send back and repeat a

sound: [V] *The whole house began to echo.* [Vpr] *The hills echoed to/with the sound of their laughter.* [Vn, Vnp] *The valley echoed (back) his song.* **3(a)** to copy or repeat sb/sth, esp to show that one is in agreement: [Vn] *They echoed their leader's every word.* ○ *This view is echoed by many foreign businessmen.* [V.speech] *'Rome!' she echoed.* **(b)** to resemble sth so that one is reminded of it: [Vn] *His painting echoes the long hot summer days.*

éclair /ɪˈkleə(r), eɪ-/ n a small long thin cake made of soft pastry that is filled with cream and has chocolate on top.

éclat /eɪˈklɑː/ n [U] (*French*) brilliant effect: *perform with éclat.*

eclectic /ɪˈklektɪk/ adj (*fml*) (of people, beliefs, etc) not following only one style, set of ideas, etc but choosing from or using a wide range: *He has an eclectic taste in music.* ▶ **eclectically** /-tɪkli/ adv. **eclecticism** /ɪˈklektɪsɪzəm/ n [U].

eclipse /ɪˈklɪps/ n **1** [C] the blocking of the light of the sun when the moon is between it and the earth, or of the light of the moon when the earth's shadow falls on it: *a total/partial eclipse of the sun.* **2** [C,U] a loss of importance, fame, power, etc: *His reputation has suffered something of an eclipse in recent years.* ○ *He remained in eclipse for many years after his death.*
▶ **eclipse** v (often passive) **1** (of the moon, the sun, a planet, etc) to cause an eclipse: [Vn] *The sun is partly eclipsed (by the moon).* **2** to make sb/sth appear dull or unimportant by comparison; to OUTSHINE sb/sth: [Vn] *Though a talented player, he was completely eclipsed by the brilliance of his brother.*

eco- comb form (usu forming ns) of or relating to ECOLOGY or the environment: *ecosystem* ○ *eco-friendly.*

ecology /iˈkɒlədʒi/ n [U] the relation of plants and living creatures to each other and to their environment, or the study of this: *Chemicals in the factory's sewage system have changed the ecology of the whole area.*
▶ **ecological** /ˌiːkəˈlɒdʒɪkl/ adj: *an ecological catastrophe/disaster* (ie altering the whole ecological balance of the community). **ecologically** /-kli/ adv. **ecologist** /iˈkɒlədʒɪst/ n an expert in ecology.

NOTE Compare **ecology**, **ecological**, **environment** and **environmental**. These words are sometimes used in the same way although they have different meanings. **Ecology** is the natural relationship (or study of the relationship) between plants, animals and people, and the places in which they live: *The dumping of waste at sea is disrupting marine ecology.* The adjective connected with **ecology** is **ecological**.
 Environment refers to the places or situations in which plants, animals and people live: *Climbers in Nepal are damaging the environment by leaving their rubbish on the mountains.* The adjective is **environmental**.
 Sometimes **ecological** and **environmental** are used with the same nouns: *The oil spill was an ecological disaster for thousands of birds.* ○ *The oil spill caused an environmental disaster on this usually clean and beautiful island.* The adverbs **ecologically** and **environmentally** are also often confused but they do not have the same meaning: *ecologically sustainable* (ie keeping the natural balance of plants, animals and people) ○ *environmentally sound products* (ie products which help keep the world around us in good condition).

economic /ˌiːkəˈnɒmɪk, ˌekə-/ adj **1** [attrib] of or relating to trade, industry and the development of wealth: *the government's economic policy* ○ *regional economic and political affairs* ○ *economic growth/ cooperation/development/reform* ○ *a slow-down in economic activity* ○ *the current economic climate* ○

impose/lift economic sanctions (ie the action of reducing or stopping trade with a particular country) ○ *economic history/geography.* **2** profitable: *It is not always economic for buses to run on Sundays.*

economical /ˌiːkəˈnɒmɪkl, ˌekə-/ *adj* (*approv*) **1** providing good service or value in proportion to the amount of money, time, etc spent: *an economical car to run* (eg one that does not use a lot of petrol) ○ *Larger tubes of toothpaste are more economical.* **2** using no more of sth than is necessary: *an economical style of writing* (ie one that does not waste words) ○ *She was economical in her movements.* ○ (*ironic*) *Her statement was somewhat economical with the truth* (ie omitted certain important facts). ▶ **economically** /-kli/ *adv*: *His proposal is not economically sound.* ○ *use one's resources economically.*

economics /ˌiːkəˈnɒmɪks, ˌekə-/ *n* [sing *v*] (**a**) the principles of the production and distribution of goods and services and the development of wealth: *Marxist/monetarist economics* ○ *a lecturer in economics.* See also HOME ECONOMICS. (**b**) the application of these principles to a particular country or region, or to a particular area of business: *the economics of publishing* ○ *agricultural economics.*

economist /ɪˈkɒnəmɪst/ *n* an expert in ECONOMICS.

economize, -ise /ɪˈkɒnəmaɪz/ *v* ~ (**on sth**) to save money, time, resources, etc; to spend less than before: [Vpr] *economize on fuel/manpower* [V] *We're spending far too much money — we must economize.*

economy /ɪˈkɒnəmi/ *n* **1** (often **the economy**) [C] the relationship between production, trade and the supply of money in a particular country or region: *the economies of Japan and the USA* ○ *a market economy* (ie one in which the price of goods is fixed according to both cost and demand) ○ *The state of the economy is very worrying.* **2** [C, U] use of available resources in a way that saves money, time, etc or avoids waste: *practise economy* ○ *We must all make substantial economies.* ○ *It's a false economy to buy a milder, cheaper cheese for cooking* (ie It seems cheaper but it is not because one uses more). ○ *economy of language* (ie using few words) ○ *We're having an e'conomy drive* (ie making a special effort to avoid waste or wrong use of resources) *at school.* ○ *an e'conomy pack* (ie a large amount of a product offered for sale at a reduced price) ○ *travelling e'conomy class* (ie by the cheapest class of air travel).

ecosystem /ˈiːkəʊsɪstəm/ *n* all the plants and living creatures in a particular area considered together with their physical environment: *Overfishing is damaging the delicate marine ecosystem.*

ecstasy /ˈekstəsi/ *n* **1** [U,C] a feeling or state of great joy or happiness: *be in / go into / be thrown into ecstasy/ecstasies (over sth)* ○ *religious/sexual ecstasy.* **2** [U] a drug taken for pleasure, esp by young people: *a tablet of ecstasy.*
▶ **ecstatic** /ɪkˈstætɪk/ *adj* showing ecstasy; very excited and enthusiastic: *ecstatic praise/applause* ○ *She's ecstatic about her new job.* **ecstatically** /-kli/ *adv.*

-ectomy *comb form* (forming *ns*) indicating removal of part of the body by a SURGICAL operation: *a tonsillectomy* ○ *an appendectomy.*

ectoplasm /ˈektəplæzəm/ *n* [U] a substance that is thought by some to flow from a medium(3) during a TRANCE(1).

ECU (also **Ecu, ecu**) /ˈekjuː/ *abbr* (*pl* unchanged, **Ecus** or **ecus**) European Currency Unit (the unit of money of the European Union): *a budget of two million ECU.*

ecumenical /ˌiːkjuːˈmenɪkl, ˌekjuː-/ *adj* (**a**) involving members of several Christian Churches: *an ecumenical committee.* (**b**) promoting unity of the various Christian Churches throughout the world: *the ecumenical movement.*

▶ **ecumenism** /ɪˈkjuːmənɪzəm/ *n* [U] the principle or aim of uniting all Christian Churches.

eczema /ˈeksmə; *US* ɪgˈziːmə/ *n* [U] a disease that causes the skin to become red, rough and extremely sore.

ed *abbr* edited (by); edition; editor: *'Eighteenth Century Women Poets', Ed Roger Lonsdale.*

-ed (also **-d**) *suff* (with *ns* forming *adjs*) having, or having the characteristics of: *talented* ○ *bigoted* ○ *diseased* ○ *quick-witted.*

eddy /ˈedi/ *n* a circular movement of water, air, dust, etc: *The flower was caught in an eddy and floated off downstream.* ○ *Eddies of dust swirled in the road.*
▶ **eddy** *v* (*pt, pp* **eddied**) to move in or like an eddy: [V] *eddying currents* [Vpr] *The wind was eddying around the deserted stands.* [also Vp].

Eden /ˈiːdn/ *n* (also **the ˌgarden of 'Eden**) *n* [sing] the beautiful garden where, according to the Bible, Adam and Eve lived in great happiness before they rejected God: (*fig*) *The whole continent seemed an immense, wild Eden to be tamed and mastered.*

edge¹ /edʒ/ *n* **1** [C] the outside limit or boundary of an object, a surface or an area: *He stood on the edge of the cliff.* ○ *Don't put that glass so near the edge of the table.* ○ *We went down to the water's edge.* ○ *He lives at the edge of the forest.* ○ *She tore the page out roughly, leaving a jagged/ragged edge in the book.* See also LEADING EDGE. **2** [C] (**a**) the narrow part along or around a thin flat object: *Stand the coin on its edge.* (**b**) the sharp part of a blade, knife, sword, etc that is used for cutting: *a knife with a sharp edge.* **3** (usu **the edge**) [sing] the point or state immediately before something unpleasant, dangerous or exciting occurs: *species on the edge of extinction* ○ *The country was brought to the edge of war.* See also CUTTING EDGE. **4** [sing] a slight advantage over sb/sth: *The company needs to improve its competitive edge.* ○ (*infml*) *The younger man definitely had the edge (on his opponent).* **5** [sing] a strong, sharp and often exciting quality: *a hard political edge* ○ *The tart fruit gives the sauce a fresh edge.* **6** [sing] a sharp, slightly threatening tone of voice, often showing anger or annoyance: *a slight edge of cynicism* ○ *She was trying to remain calm, but there was a distinct edge to her voice.* **IDM** (**be**) **on 'edge** nervous, excited or bad-tempered: *She was a little on edge till she heard he had passed.* **on the edge of one's 'seat** very excited and giving one's full attention to sth: *The final scene had the audience on the edge of their seats.* **set sb's teeth on edge** ⇨ TOOTH. **take the 'edge off sth** to reduce or soften sth: *The sandwich took the edge off my appetite.*
▶ **-edged** /edʒd/ (forming compound *adjs*) having an edge or edges of a specified type: *a ˌblunt-edged 'razor* ○ *a ˌlace-edged 'cloth.*

edge² /edʒ/ *v* **1** ~ **sth (with sth)** (usu passive) to supply sth with a border: [Vnpr] *a road edged with grass* ○ *The handkerchief is edged with white lace.* **2** (**a**) to move or move sth slowly and carefully in a particular direction: [Vpr] *The climber edged carefully along the narrow rock ledge.* [Vpr, Vnpr] *I edged (my chair) towards the door.* [Vnadv] *The crowd gradually edged its way forward.* [also Vadv, Vp]. (**b**) to increase or decrease gradually: [Vp] *Share prices edged up by 1.5% over the year.* **PHR V** **ˌedge sb/sth 'out (of sth)** to cause sb/sth gradually to lose their position or power: *The new model has edged all the competitors out of the market.*
▶ **edging** /ˈedʒɪŋ/ *n* [U,C] a thing that forms the border or edge of sth: *a/some lace edging on a dress.*

edgeways /ˈedʒweɪz/ (*esp US* **edgewise** /ˈedʒwaɪz/) *adv* with the edge upwards or forwards; on one side: *You'll only get the desk through the door if you turn it edgeways.* **IDM** **get a word in edgeways** ⇨ WORD.

edgy /ˈedʒi/ *adj* (**-ier, -iest**) (*infml*) nervous; easily upset or annoyed: *After the recent unrest there is an edgy calm in the capital.* ○ *He gave an edgy laugh.* ► **edgily** *adv.* **edginess** *n* [U, sing].

edible /'edəbl/ *adj* fit or suitable to be eaten: *This food is scarcely edible.* ○ *edible fungi/snails.*

edict /'i:dɪkt/ *n* [U, C] an order or official statement issued by an authority: *The Pope issued an edict annulling the marriage.*

edification /ˌedɪfɪ'keɪʃn/ *n* [U] (*fml or joc*) the improvement of the mind or character: *political propaganda written for the edification of the masses.*

edifice /'edɪfɪs/ *n* (*fml or joc*) a large impressive building: *an imposing sixteenth-century edifice* ○ *They have bought some dreadful turreted edifice near Derby.* ○ (*fig*) *the whole complex edifice of the European Union.*

edify /'edɪfaɪ/ *v* (*pt, pp* **-fied**) [Vn] (*fml*) to improve the mind or character of sb. ► **edifying** *adj*: *edifying works of literature* ○ (*joc*) *The President's appearance on a TV talk show was not an edifying spectacle.*

edit /'edɪt/ *v* [Vn] **1(a)** to prepare a piece of writing, often another person's, for publication, eg by correcting it, commenting on it, or removing parts of it: *finish editing the Annual Report* ○ *edit a Shakespeare play for use in schools* ○ *This version of Casanova's memoirs has been severely edited* (ie parts have been removed). **(b)** to prepare a film, tape, radio or television programme, or book by arranging separate items or parts in a suitable sequence: *a collection of essays edited by Chris Michaels* ○ *I didn't see the whole match, just the edited highlights.* ○ *Two scenes were cut from the film during editing.* **2** to be responsible for planning, directing and publishing a newspaper, magazine, etc. **PHRV** ˌ**edit sth** ˈ**out (of sth)** to remove words, phrases or scenes that are not wanted from a book, film, etc: *They edited out most of the interview before broadcasting it.*

edition /ɪ'dɪʃn/ *n* **1** a form in which a book is published: *a paperback/hardback/de luxe edition* ○ *She collects first editions of Victorian novelists.* **2** a particular newspaper or magazine, or radio or television programme, esp one of a regular series: *an interview with the prime minister in tonight's edition of 'Panorama'* ○ *The story was in Tuesday's edition of the 'Guardian'.* **3** the total number of copies of a book, newspaper, etc issued at one time: *produce a limited edition of 500* ○ *The news was announced in time for the evening edition of the paper.* See also IMPRESSION 6, REPRINT *n.*

editor /'edɪtə(r)/ *n* **1** a person who is in charge of a newspaper or of part of a newspaper: *the editor of the 'Washington Post'* ○ *letters to the editor* ○ *the* ˈ*sports/fiˈnancial/*ˈ*fashion editor.* **2** a person who edits (EDIT 1) books, films, etc. **3** a facility for changing text or data stored in a computer. ► **editorship** *n* [U]: *She has been offered the editorship of 'The Times'.*

editorial /ˌedɪ'tɔ:riəl/ *adj* [usu attrib] of or relating to an EDITOR: *editorial policy* ○ *have full editorial control.*
► **editorial** *n* a special article in a newspaper, usu written by the EDITOR(1), giving her or his opinion on an issue of current importance.

educate /'edʒukeɪt/ *v* **1** (often passive) to train the mind and character of sb; to teach sb over a period of time at school, university, etc: [Vn] *She was educated in France.* ○ *He was educated at Winchester and Oxford.* [V] *The function of our universities is not just to educate.* **2** ~ **sb (in sth)** to teach sb about sth or how to do sth: [Vnpr] *The public should be educated in how to use energy more effectively.* [Vn.to inf] *the task of educating people to respect the environment* [also Vn]. ⇨ note at TEACH.
► **educated** /'edʒukeɪtɪd/ *adj* **(a)** having been educated, esp at a particular place or in the specified way: *a highly educated woman* ○ *self-educated.* **(b)** resulting from a good education: *an educated voice.*
educator *n* a person who educates, esp as her or his profession.
■ ˌ**educated** ˈ**guess** *n* a guess that is based on a certain degree of knowledge or experience, and is therefore probably correct.

education /ˌedʒu'keɪʃn/ *n* **1** [U, sing] a process of training and instruction, esp of children and young people in schools, colleges, etc, which is designed to give knowledge and develop skills: *students in full-time education* ○ *the state education system* ○ *a good all-round education* ○ *nursery/primary/secondary education* ○ *adult education classes* ○ *health/religious education.* **2** [U] the field of study dealing with how to teach: *a college of education* ○ *a lecturer in education.* See also FURTHER EDUCATION, HIGHER EDUCATION. **3** [U] the process of teaching sb about sth or how to do sth: *an AIDS education programme* ○ *User education is vital if the new computer system is to gain acceptance.*
► **educational** /-ʃənl/ *adj* of, about or providing education: *educational standards/psychologists/ magazines* ○ *children with special educational needs* ○ *I found the visit most educational.* **educationally** /-ʃənəli/ *adv.*
educationist /ˌedʒu'keɪʃənɪst/ (also **educationalist** /ˌedʒu'keɪʃənəlɪst/) *n* a specialist in education.

-ee *suff* **1** (with *vs* forming *ns*) a person affected by an action: *employee* ○ *payee.* Compare -ER, -OR. **2** (with *adjs*, *vs* and *ns* forming *ns*) a person described as or concerned with: *absentee* ○ *refugee.*

EEC /ˌi: i: 'si:/ *abbr* (*dated*) European Economic Community (now usu known as the European Union).

eel /i:l/ *n* a long thin fish that resembles a snake: *He was as slippery as an eel.*

-eer *suff* **1** (with *ns* forming *ns*) a person concerned with: *auctioneer* ○ *mountaineer.* **2** (with *ns* forming *vs*) (*often derog*) to be concerned with: *commandeer* ○ *profiteer.*

eerie /'ɪəri/ *adj* causing a feeling of mystery and fear: *an eerie yellow light* ○ *a strange and eerie silence.* ► **eerily** /'ɪərəli/ *adv.*

efface /ɪ'feɪs/ *v* (*fml*) to rub sth out; to cause sth to fade: [Vn] *Time and weather had long since effaced the inscription on the monument.* ○ (*fig*) *Time alone will efface those unpleasant memories.* See also SELF-EFFACING.

effect /ɪ'fekt/ *n* **1** [C, U] ~ **(on sb/sth)** a change produced by an action or a cause; a result or an outcome: *the effects of heat on metal* ○ *dramatic/ far-reaching effects* ○ *the beneficial effects of exercise* ○ *The experience had a profound effect on her.* ○ *The recent increase in burglaries has had the effect of pushing up house insurance premiums.* ○ *Despite her ordeal she seems to have suffered no ill effects.* ○ *I tried to persuade him, but with little or no effect.* See also GREENHOUSE EFFECT, SIDE-EFFECT. **2** [C, U] an impression created in the mind of a spectator, reader, etc while watching a play, listening to music or looking at a painting: *The overall effect of the sculpture is overwhelming.* ○ *The stage lighting gives the effect of a moonlit scene.* ○ *She only dresses like that for effect* (ie in order to impress people). ○ '*Jurassic Park' contains some amazing special effects.* **3** **effects** [pl] (*fml*) personal property; possessions: *The army sent her his personal effects.* **IDM bring/put sth into ef**'**fect** to cause sth to come into use: *The new system will soon be put into effect.* **come/go into ef**'**fect** (esp of laws, rules, etc) to come into use; to begin to apply: *New seat-belt regulations came into effect last week.* **in ef**'**fect 1** for practical purposes; in fact: *The two systems are, in effect, identical.* See also EFFECTIVELY 2. **2** (of a law, rule, etc) in use: *Some ancient laws are still in effect.*

take ef'fect 1 to produce the result intended or required: *The aspirins soon took effect.* **2** to come into use; to begin to apply: *The new law takes effect from tomorrow.* **to the effect that...** with the meaning, or giving the information, that...: *He left a note to the effect that he would not be returning.* **to good, etc ef'fect** producing a good, etc result or impression: *use money to good effect* ○ *The room shows off her paintings to excellent effect.* **to no ef'fect** not having the result intended or hoped for: *We warned them, but to no effect.* **to this/that ef'fect** with this/that meaning or information: *She told me to get out, or words to that effect.* **with immediate effect/with effect from...** *(fml)* starting now/starting from...: *The government has announced a rise in interest rates with effect from 5 April.*
▶ **effect** *v (fml)* to cause sth to occur; to achieve sth: [Vn] *effect a cure/change/.* ⟹ note at AFFECT¹.

effective /ɪ'fektɪv/ *adj* **1(a)** having the desired effect; producing the intended result: *seeking to make the health service as effective as possible* ○ *a simple but highly effective treatment.* See also COST-EFFECTIVE. **(b)** making a strong or pleasing impression: *a very effective colour scheme* ○ *an effective speech.* **2** [attrib] having a role or position, even though not officially appointed to it: *the effective, if not the actual, leader of the party* ○ *He has now taken effective control of the country.* **3** happening or coming into use: *Effective from 1st April, the interest rate will be increased by 1%.*
▶ **effectively** *adv* **1** in an effective(1a) way: *They do their job very effectively.* **2** for practical purposes; in effect: *They could not leave the city and were effectively being held hostage by the authorities.*
effectiveness *n* [U]: *check/test the effectiveness of the security arrangements.*

effectual /ɪ'fektʃuəl/ *adj (fml)* (not of people) producing the intended result: *take effectual action.*

effeminate /ɪ'femɪnət/ *adj (derog)* (of a man or his behaviour) having characteristics considered to be typical of a woman: *an effeminate manner/voice/walk.* ▶ **effeminacy** /ɪ'femɪnəsi/ *n* [U].

effervescent /,efə'vesnt/ *adj* **1** (of people or their behaviour) lively, excited and enthusiastic: *a warm, effervescent personality.* **2** (of a liquid) releasing bubbles of gas; FIZZY.

effete /ɪ'fiːt/ *adj (derog)* **(a)** weak, having lost power: *an effete civilization/government.* **(b)** lacking liveliness and strength; FEEBLE: *an effete young man.*

efficacious /,efɪ'keɪʃəs/ *adj (fml)* (not of people) producing the desired result; effective: *She decided it would be more efficacious to remain silent.*
▶ **efficacy** /'efɪkəsi/ *n* [U] *(fml)* the state or quality of being efficacious: *test/question/prove the efficacy of a new drug.*

efficient /ɪ'fɪʃnt/ *adj* **(a)** (of people) able to work well and without wasting time or resources; competent: *an efficient secretary/teacher/administrator* ○ *He revealed himself to be surprisingly practical and efficient.* **(b)** (esp of tools, machines, systems, etc) producing a satisfactory result without wasting time or resources: *efficient database software/heating equipment* ○ *more efficient use of energy* ○ *We offer a fast, efficient and friendly service.* ▶ **efficiency** /ɪ'fɪʃnsi/ *n* [U]: *improvements in energy efficiency at the factory* ○ *I was impressed by the efficiency with which she handled the crisis.* **efficiently** /-li/ *adv*: *a very efficiently organized event* ○ *get industry running more efficiently.*

effigy /'efɪdʒi/ *n* [C] a carved figure or model representing a person or an animal: *stone effigies of Buddha* ○ *a crude effigy of the Prime Minister.* **IDM** **burn, etc sb in effigy** to make a model of sb and burn it, etc to show one's hatred, anger, etc.

effing /'efɪŋ/ *adj* [attrib] *(sl euph)* fucking (FUCK): *It's an effing nuisance!*
■ **,effing and 'blinding** *n* [U] *(infml)* using very rude words; swearing.

effluent /'efluənt/ *n* [U, C] liquid waste matter, SEWAGE, etc, that pours out of a factory into a river, the sea, etc: *an effluent treatment plant* ○ *industrial effluent.*

effort /'efət/ *n* **1** [U] the use of much physical or mental energy to do sth: *a waste of time and effort* ○ *A lot of effort has gone into/has been put into making this event a success.* ○ *Their players attack with an economy of effort which few sides will be able to match.* **2** [C] **(a)** ~ (to do sth) an attempt that requires a lot of energy; a struggle: *make a special/determined/real effort to finish on time* ○ *It was a group effort.* ○ *Don't bother trying to persuade her; it's not worth the effort.* ○ *The local clubs are making every effort/making a concerted effort to interest more young people.* ○ *Union leaders have been invited to a meeting in an effort to head off any further disputes.* **(b)** an attempt or an action directed towards a particular cause: *the Russian space effort* ○ *the success of the government's publicity effort.* **3** [C] a result of an attempt: *I was quite pleased with my efforts.* ○ *That's a good effort* (ie That has been well done).
▶ **effortless** *adj* needing little or no effort: *She plays with seemingly effortless skill.* **effortlessly** *adv*: *He talked on smoothly and effortlessly.*

effrontery /ɪ'frʌntəri/ *n* [U, sing] bold or rude behaviour without any feeling of shame: *He had the effrontery to accuse me of lying.*

effusion /ɪ'fjuːʒn/ *n (fml)* [C, U] a heavy flow, esp of liquid: *an effusion of blood* ○ *(fig) His effusions of second-rate verse embarrassed his family.*

effusive /ɪ'fjuːsɪv/ *adj (often derog)* showing much or too much feeling or emotion: *effusive thanks* ○ *an effusive welcome* ○ *He was effusive in his praise.* ▶ **effusively** *adv*.

EFL /,iː ef 'el/ *abbr* (the teaching, learning or studying of) English as a foreign language. Compare ESL.

EFTA (also **Efta**) /'eftə/ *abbr* European Free Trade Association: *EFTA countries* ○ *In 1972 Britain left EFTA and joined the EC.*

eg /,iː 'dʒiː/ *abbr* for example; for instance (Latin *exempli gratia*): *popular pets, eg dogs, cats and rabbits.*

NOTE The abbreviations **eg** and **ie** are mostly used in written English. Instead of **eg** people say **for example.** The abbreviation **ie** is used to explain a statement or phrase that may be unclear by rephrasing it: *He admitted being 'economical with the truth' (ie lying).* When people are speaking they say **that is,** or **that is to say** instead of ie. In this dictionary we often use **ie** and **eg** after examples to give further explanation of what the examples mean.

egalitarian /i,gælɪ'teəriən/ *adj* showing or holding a belief in equal rights, benefits and opportunities for everybody: *egalitarian principles* ○ *an egalitarian society.* ▶ **egalitarianism** /-ɪzəm/ *n* [U].

egg¹ /eg/ *n* **1(a)** [C] a small OVAL object with a thin hard shell, esp one produced by a female bird and containing a young bird in the early stages of its development. Other creatures, eg reptiles, fish and insects, also produce eggs like birds: *The eggs were about to hatch.* ○ *The hen laid a large brown egg.* ○ *The blackbird's nest contained four eggs.* ○ 'crocodile eggs ○ 'ants' eggs. ⟹ picture. **(b)** [C, U] an egg, esp of a hen, or its contents, used as food: *fried/poached*

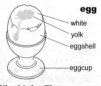

egg
white
yolk
eggshell
eggcup

---

eggs for breakfast ○ *a plate of scrambled eggs/of bacon and egg* ○ *You've got some egg* (ie a bit of cooked egg) *on your shirt.* ○ *Whisk the egg-whites until stiff.* ○ *free-range eggs* ○ '*ducks' eggs.* See also EASTER EGG. **2** [C] (in female mammals (MAMMAL)) the cell from which a new young creature is formed; an OVUM: *The male sperm fertilizes the female egg.* ○ *egg donors.* ⇨ picture at REPRODUCTION. **IDM** a **chicken-and-egg situation** ⇨ CHICKEN. **get, have, etc 'egg on / all over one's face** (*infml*) to appear foolish: *He was left with egg all over his face when his forecast was proved wrong.* **kill the goose that lays the golden eggs** ⇨ KILL. **put all one's eggs in/into one 'basket** to risk everything one has on the success of one plan, eg by putting all one's money into one business. **sure as eggs is eggs** ⇨ SURE. **teach one's grandmother to suck eggs** ⇨ TEACH.
■ **'egg-timer** *n* a device for measuring the time required for eggs to boil.

egg² /eg/ *v* **PHRV** **,egg sb 'on (to do sth)** to urge or strongly encourage sb to do sth: *I didn't want to do it but Peter kept egging me 'on.*

eggcup /'egkʌp/ *n* a small cup for holding a boiled egg. ⇨ picture at EGG¹.

egghead /'eghed/ *n* (*infml usu derog*) a very intellectual person.

eggplant /'egplɑːnt/ *n* [C,U] (*esp US*) = AUBERGINE.

eggshell /'egʃel/ *n* [C,U] the hard thin outer part of an egg. ⇨ picture at EGG¹.

ego /'iːgəʊ, 'egəʊ/ *n* an individual's idea of herself or himself, esp in relation to other people or to the outside world; SELF-ESTEEM: *a bruised/fragile ego* ○ *Losing the match made quite a dent in his ego.* See also ALTER EGO.
■ **'ego-trip** *n* (*sl*) an activity done for one's own pleasure or satisfaction, and usu to make one feel more important, etc than others: (*derog*) *If you ask me, her charity work is just one big ego-trip.*

egocentric /,iːgəʊ'sentrɪk, ,eg-/ *adj* considering only oneself; SELFISH: *a woman portrayed as egocentric and self-indulgent.*

egotism /'egəʊtɪzəm, 'iːg-/ (also **egoism** /'iːgəʊɪzəm, 'eg-/) *n* [U] (*usu derog*) the practice of thinking and talking too often or too much about oneself: *his childish egotism.*
▶ **egotist** /-tɪst/ (also **egoist** /-ɪst/) *n* a person who practises or shows egotism; a SELFISH person.
egotistic /,egə'tɪstɪk, ,iːg-/, **egotistical** /,egə'tɪstɪkl, ,iːg-/ *adjs*: *I had always thought him to be egotistical and attention-seeking.* **egotistically** /-kli/ *adv.*

egregious /ɪ'griːdʒiəs/ *adj* [usu attrib] (*fml*) (usu of sth/sb bad) exceptional; outstanding: *egregious incompetence* ○ *a most egregious error of judgement.*

eh /eɪ/ *interj* (*esp Brit* US also **huh**) (*infml*) (used to express surprise or doubt, to invite agreement, or to ask for sth to be repeated): *'Look at this. Not bad, eh?'* ○ *'I want to go home!' 'Eh?' 'I said I want to go home!'*

eiderdown /'aɪdədaʊn/ *n* a covering for a bed filled with soft feathers or other material and usu placed on top of a sheet and blankets (BLANKET 1) & QUILT. Compare DUVET.

eight /eɪt/ *n, pron, det* the number 8. See also FIGURE OF EIGHT.
▶ **eight-** (in compounds) having eight of the thing specified: *an eight-man crew.*
eighth /eɪtθ/ *pron, det* 8th. — *n* each of eight equal parts of sth.
For further guidance on how *eight* and *eighth* are used, see the examples at *five* and *fifth.*

eighteen /,eɪ'tiːn/ *n, pron, det* the number 18.
▶ **eighteenth** /,eɪ'tiːnθ/ *n, pron, det* 18th.
For further guidance on how *eighteen* and *eighteenth* are used, see the examples at *five* and *fifth.*

eighty /'eɪti/ **1** *n, pron, det* the number 80.

2 the eighties *n* [pl] the range of numbers, years or temperatures from 80 to 89. **IDM** **in one's eighties** between the ages of 80 and 90.
▶ **eightieth** /'eɪtiəθ/ *n, pron, det* 80th.
For further guidance on how *eighty* and *eightieth* are used, see the examples at *fifty, five* and *fifth.*

eisteddfod /aɪ'steðvɒd/ *n* an annual festival in Wales at which poets and musicians compete.

either /'aɪðə(r), 'iː:ðə(r)/ *indef det, indef pron* **1** one or the other of two: (**a**) (*det*) *You can park on either side of the street.* ○ *Keep either one of the photos — I don't mind which.* (**b**) (*pron*) (used with a *sing v*): *I've bought two cakes — you can have either.* ○ *Read from one of the books on the table — either of them will do.* **2** (*det*) each of two: *The offices on either side were empty.* ○ *There's a staircase at either end of the corridor.* Compare BOTH¹. ▶ **either** *indef adv* **1** (used after negative phrases to emphasize that a feeling or situation is similar to one mentioned previously, or to add extra information): *I don't like the red shirt and I don't like the green one either* (ie I DISLIKE both the red shirt and the green one). ○ *Mary won't go and Peter won't (go) either.* (Compare: *...and neither will Peter.*) ○ *He can't hear and he can hardly speak either.* ○ *I know a good Italian restaurant. It's not far from here, either.* ⇨ note at ALSO. **2 either ... or ...** (used to show a choice of two alternatives): *She's either French or Spanish.* ○ *I left it either on the table or in the drawer.* ○ *You can either write or phone to order a copy.* ○ *He either could not come or did not want to.*

ejaculate /ɪ'dʒækjuleɪt/ *v* [V] (of a man) to discharge SEMEN rapidly through the PENIS.
▶ **ejaculation** /ɪ,dʒækju'leɪʃn/ *n* **1** [C,U] a sudden release of SEMEN: *premature ejaculation.* **2** [C] (*fml*) a sudden expression of anger, surprise, etc; an EXCLAMATION.

eject /ɪ'dʒekt/ *v* **1** ~ **sb/sth (from sth)** (*fml*) to force sb to leave a place: [Vn] *eject an invading army* [Vnpr] *Police ejected a number of violent protesters from the hall.* **2** ~ **sth (from sth)** to force sth out, usu violently or suddenly: [Vnpr] *lava ejected from a volcano* ○ *Cartridges are ejected from the gun after firing.* [Vn] *Press 'Eject' to release the cassette from the recorder.* **3** to cause oneself to be thrown quickly from an aircraft in an emergency: [V] *The pilot had to eject.* [also Vpr]. ▶ **ejection** /ɪ'dʒekʃn/ *n* [U,C].

ejector seat /ɪ'dʒektə siːt/ (*US* also **ejection seat**) *n* a seat in an aircraft that allows a pilot to EJECT(3) in an emergency.

eke /iːk/ *v* **PHRV** **,eke sth 'out 1** to make a small supply of sth last longer by adding sth else to it or by using it very carefully: *eke out a student grant.* **2** to manage to make a living by doing this: *eking out a meagre existence on the barren soil.*

EKG /,iː keɪ 'dʒiː/ *abbr* (*US*) = ECG.

elaborate /ɪ'læbərət/ *adj* very detailed and complicated; carefully prepared and finished: *elaborate explanations/rituals/structures* ○ *devise an elaborate plan* ○ *take elaborate precautions* ○ *an elaborate five-course meal.*
▶ **elaborate** /ɪ'læbəreɪt/ *v* (*fml*) **1** ~ **(on sth)** to describe or explain sth in greater detail: [V] *You understand the situation; I needn't elaborate.* [Vpr] *She declined to elaborate on her argument.* **2** to make a plan, etc more detailed and complicated: [Vn] *She greatly elaborated the simple plot of the original comic poem.* **elaboration** /ɪ,læbə'reɪʃn/ *n* [U,C]: *the elaboration of a theory* ○ *The importance of this needs no further elaboration.*
elaborately *adv*: *an elaborately decorated room.*

élan /eɪ'lɒn/ *n* [U] (*French*) enthusiasm and energy; VERVE: *performing with great élan.*

eland /'iːlənd/ *n* a type of large African ANTELOPE.

elapse /ɪ'læps/ *v* (*fml*) (of time) to pass: [V] *Three years elapsed before they met again.*

E

elastic /ɪˈlæstɪk/ *adj* **1** that can be stretched, returning to its original size or shape after being released: *a bra with elastic straps* ○ *The dough should be smooth and elastic.* **2** that can be altered; not fixed; flexible: *Our plans are fairly elastic.*
▸ **elastic** *n* **1** [U] elastic cord or material, usu made with rubber thread: *The elastic in my socks has gone* (ie has broken or become weak). **2** [C] (*US*) = RUBBER BAND.
elasticated /ɪˈlæstɪkeɪtɪd/ *adj* made using elastic material: *a dress with an elasticated waist* ○ *an elasticated belt.*
elasticity /ˌiːlæˈstɪsəti, ˌelæ-, ˌiˌlæ-/ *n* [U] the quality of being elastic.
■ **e͵lastic ˈband** *n* = RUBBER BAND.
elated /iˈleɪtɪd/ *adj* ~ **(at/by sth)** very happy, excited or proud: *an elated smile* ○ *She was elated at/by the news.*
▸ **elatedly** /iˈleɪtɪdli/ *adv.*
elation /iˈleɪʃn/ *n* [U] great happiness, excitement or pride: *a look of sheer elation* ○ *share in the general mood of elation.*
elbow /ˈelbəʊ/ *n* **1(a)** the joint where the arm bends, or the outer part of this: *He sat with his elbows on the table.* ○ *He stood quietly at her elbow* (ie close beside her). ⇨ picture at HUMAN. **(b)** the part of the sleeve of a coat, jacket, etc that covers this: *a jacket patched at the elbows.* **2** a sharp bend in a pipe, chimney, etc that is shaped like an elbow.
IDM **give sb / get the ˈelbow** (*infml*) to dismiss or reject sb/to be dismissed or rejected: *She gave me the elbow when she started going out with Roger.* **more power to sb's elbow** ⇨ POWER. **not know one's arse from one's elbow** ⇨ KNOW.
▸ **elbow** *v* **PHRV** ͵**elbow sb ˈout, aˈside, etc** to push sb roughly with the elbows in the specified direction: *He elbowed me out of the way.* ͵**elbow one's way ˈin, ˈthrough, etc** to force one's way in the specified direction by using one's elbows: *He elbowed his way through (the crowd).*
■ ˈ**elbow-grease** *n* [U] (*infml*) hard physical work, esp vigorous polishing or cleaning: *If you used a bit more elbow-grease you could really make those boots shine.*
ˈ**elbow-room** *n* [U] space in which one can move freely: *Stand back — I need more elbow-room.*
elder¹ /ˈeldə(r)/ *adj* **1(a)** [attrib] (of people, esp two closely related members of a family) older; senior: *my elder brother* ○ *her elder daughter* (ie the older one of her two daughters). **(b)** **the elder** (used without an immediately following *n* to refer to the older of two people mentioned previously or soon after): *He is the elder of my two brothers.* ○ *These are my two sons. Can you guess which is the elder?* **2 the elder** (*fml*) (used before or after sb's name to distinguish them from another person with the same name): *Pitt the elder* ○ *the elder Pitt.* Compare SENIOR 3, THE YOUNGER.
▸ **elder** *n* **1** my, etc elder [sing] a person older than me, etc: *He is her elder by several years.* **2 elders** [pl] people of greater age, experience and authority: *party elders* ○ *the village elders* (ie the old and respected people of the village) ○ *Traditions were passed on by the elders of the tribe.* **3** [C] an official in a Presbyterian church. **IDM** **one's (elders and) betters** ⇨ BETTER³ 2.
■ ͵**elder ˈstatesman** *n* an old and respected politician; a person, usu retired, whose advice is still valued because of her or his long experience.

NOTE The usual comparative and superlative forms of **old** are **older** and **oldest**: *My brother is older than me.* ○ *The cathedral is the oldest building in the city.* You can also use **elder** and **eldest** as adjectives and nouns, when comparing the ages of people, especially members of a family. They are only used before a noun and you cannot say *elder than*: *My*

elder sister lives in Canada. ○ *the elder of their two children* ○ *I'm the eldest in the family.*

elder² /ˈeldə(r)/ *n* type of small tree with sweet-smelling white flowers (**elderflowers**) and bunches of small red or black berries.
elderberry /ˈeldəberi/ *n* the fruit of an ELDER² tree.
elderly /ˈeldəli/ *adj* (*often euph*) (of people) rather old; past middle age: *He's very active for an elderly man.*
▸ **the elderly** *n* [pl *v*] (*often euph*) elderly people: *care for the elderly.* ⇨ note at OLD.
eldest /ˈeldɪst/ *adj* [attrib], *n* (of people, esp three or more closely related members of a family) oldest: *Jill is my eldest daughter.* ○ *Jill is the eldest of my three children.* ○ *Jill is the eldest of three* (ie the oldest child in a family with three children). ○ *Jill is my eldest.* ⇨ note at ELDER¹.
elect /ɪˈlekt/ *v* **1** ~ **sb (to sth)**; ~ **sb (as sth)** to choose sb by voting: [Vn] *an elected assembly/representative/leader* ○ *They elected a new president.* ○ *He failed to get elected.* [Vnpr] *She was elected to parliament last year.* [Vn-n, Vn.to inf] *We elected James (to be) chairman.* [Vn-n] *He was elected as MP for Oxford East.* **2** (*fml*) to choose or decide to do sth: [V.to inf] *She elected to work overtime on Mondays.*
▸ **elect** *adj* (following *ns*) chosen for a position but not yet occupying it: *the president elect.*
the elect *n* [pl *v*] (*fml*) people specially chosen as the best.
election /ɪˈlekʃn/ *n* [U,C] the action or an instance of choosing by vote one or more of the candidates for a position, esp a political office: *In America, presidential elections are held every four years.* ○ *They are having/holding an election in Hungary next month.* ○ *He's standing for election.* ○ *her election as leader* ○ *an election campaign* ○ *the election results.* See also BY-ELECTION, GENERAL ELECTION.
▸ **electioneering** /ɪˌlekʃəˈnɪərɪŋ/ *n* [U] the activity of trying to influence people to vote for a particular candidate in an election, eg by visiting their houses or making speeches.
elective /ɪˈlektɪv/ *adj* **1** [usu attrib] having the power to elect: *an elective assembly.* **2** chosen or filled by election: *an elective office.*
▸ **elective** *n* (*esp US*) a course or subject at school or college that a student may choose as he or she wishes: *She is taking French as an elective next year.*
elector /ɪˈlektə(r)/ *n* a person who has the right to vote in an election: *Many electors didn't vote today because of the bad weather.*
▸ **electoral** /ɪˈlektərəl/ *adj* [attrib] of or relating to elections or electors: *his electoral defeat* ○ *the electoral register/roll* (ie the list of the electors in an area). **electorally** /ɪˈlektərəli/ *adv*: *an electorally damaging revelation.* **e͵lectoral ˈcollege** *n* **1** (in the USA) a group of people, including representatives from each state, who elect the President and Vice-President. **2** a group of people chosen to represent members of a party or union in the election of a leader.
electorate /ɪˈlektərət/ *n* [CGp] all the electors considered as a group: *the party favoured by the majority of the electorate.*
electric /ɪˈlektrɪk/ *adj* **1** [attrib] **(a)** using electrical power: *an electric oven/iron/guitar/razor* ○ *an electric car/train/motor.* **(b)** used for carrying an electric current to an appliance, etc: *an electric plug/socket* ○ *electric flex.* **(c)** produced by electricity: *an electric current.* **(d)** producing electricity: *an electric generator.* **2** causing sudden excitement, esp in a group of people: *The atmosphere was electric.* ○ *The news had an electric effect.*
▸ **electrics** *n* [pl] (*infml*) the system of electrical wires and components in a machine, car, house, etc:

Before buying a house make sure you have the electrics properly checked.
■ e₁lectric 'blanket *n* a BLANKET(1) that is warmed by means of an electric current passing through it.
the e₁lectric 'chair *n* [sing] (in the USA) a chair in which criminals are executed by means of an electric current.
e₁lectric 'fence *n* a wire fence through which an electric current can be passed.
e₁lectric 'field *n* (*physics*) a region of electrical influence.
e₁lectric 'shock (also shock) *n* the effect of an electric current suddenly passing through the body: *I got an electric shock from that faulty light switch.*
e₁lectric 'storm *n* a violent disturbance in the atmosphere that produces electricity.

electrical /ɪ'lektrɪkl/ *adj* of or concerned with electricity: *electrical engineering ○ electrical goods/appliances ○ The machine has an electrical fault.* ▶ **electrically** /-klɪ/ *adv: an electrically powered drill.*

electrician /ɪ,lek'trɪʃn/ *n* a person whose job is to connect, repair, etc electrical equipment: *The washing-machine has broken down — I'll phone the electrician. ○ We need an electrician to install an alarm system.*

electricity /ɪ,lek'trɪsəti/ *n* [U] the energy of charged elementary particles (ELEMENTARY), supplied as electric current for lighting, heating, driving machines, etc: *Don't leave the lights on — it wastes electricity. ○ an electricity bill ○ About 60% of the country's electricity is produced from coal.* See also STATIC *n* 2.

electrify /ɪ'lektrɪfaɪ/ *v* (*pt, pp* -fied) [Vn] 1 (esp passive) to make electricity flow through sth: *an electrified fence.* 2 (esp passive) to convert a railway, etc to the use of electric power. 3 to stimulate and greatly excite sb: *Her speech electrified the audience.* ▶ **electrification** /ɪ,lektrɪfɪ'keɪʃn/ *n* [U] the process of converting sth to the use of electric power: *the electrification of the railways.*
electrifying *adj* very exciting: *an electrifying performance ○ The effect was electrifying.*

electr(o)- *comb form* of or relating to electricity: *electromagnetic ○ electrolysis.*

electrocute /ɪ'lektrəkju:t/ *v* (often passive) to kill or injure a person or an animal by passing an electric current through them: [Vn] *In this State convicted murderers are usually electrocuted. ○ She electrocuted herself trying to change a light-bulb.* ▶ **electrocution** /ɪ,lektrə'kju:ʃn/ *n* [U].

electrode /ɪ'lektrəʊd/ *n* (often *pl*) either of two points by which an electric current enters or leaves a battery, etc; a TERMINAL(3). Compare ANODE, CATHODE.

electrolysis /ɪ,lek'trɒləsɪs/ *n* [U] 1 the destruction of hair roots by an electric current as a beauty treatment. 2 (*chemistry*) the separation of a substance into its chemical parts by an electric current.

electrolyte /ɪ'lektrəlaɪt/ *n* a liquid that an electric current can pass through, esp in an electric cell or battery.

electromagnetic /ɪ,lektrəʊmæg'netɪk/ *adj* (*physics*) having both electrical and MAGNETIC properties: *X-rays, radio waves and light waves are all types of electromagnetic radiation.* ▶ **electromagnetism** /-'mægnətɪzəm/ *n* [U].

electron /ɪ'lektrɒn/ *n* (*physics*) a tiny piece of matter with a negative electric charge, found in all atoms. Compare NEUTRON, PROTON.
■ e₁lectron 'microscope *n* a very powerful MICROSCOPE that uses beams of electrons instead of light rays.

electronic /ɪ,lek'trɒnɪk/ *adj* [usu attrib] (a) having, or operating with the aid of, many small components, eg microchips (MICROCHIP), that control and

direct an electric current: *an electronic calculator/keyboard ○ This dictionary is available in electronic form. ○ electronic music* (ie produced by processing natural or artificial sounds with electronic equipment). **(b)** concerned with such components or equipment: *an electronic engineer* (ie one whose job is to design, repair, etc electronic equipment). ▶ **electronically** /-klɪ/ *adv: process data electronically* (ie using a computer).

electronics *n* 1 [sing *v*] (a) the branch of science and technology that deals with the behaviour of electric currents in electronic equipment. **(b)** the application of this, esp in developing equipment: *He's an expert in electronics. ○ the electronics industry.* 2 [pl] the circuits and components used in electronic equipment: *There may be a fault in the electronics.*
■ ₁electronic 'mail (also email, e-mail) *n* [U] the system of sending text, pictures, etc to other people by means of computers linked to a network; information sent by this method.

electroplate /ɪ'lektrəpleɪt/ *v* (often passive) to cover sth with a thin layer of metal, usu silver, by ELECTROLYSIS(2): [Vn] *electroplated spoons.*

elegant /'elɪgənt/ *adj* 1 graceful and attractive in appearance or manner: *an elegant woman/coat/style ○ elegant manners.* 2 (of a plan, method, etc) fitting the circumstances in a clever and simple way: *an elegant solution.* ▶ **elegance** /'elɪgəns/ *n* [U]: *sartorial elegance ○ She writes with great elegance and economy.* **elegantly** *adv: He always dresses elegantly.*

elegiac /,elɪ'dʒaɪək/ *adj* (*fml*) expressing sorrow, esp about the past: *Her poetry has an elegiac quality.*

elegy /'elədʒi/ *n* a poem or song expressing sorrow, esp for the dead.

element /'elɪmənt/ *n* 1 [C] ~ (in/of sth) a necessary or characteristic part of sth: *a key element in the decision ○ Justice is an important element of good government. ○ What a sensational story! It has all the elements of a soap opera.* 2 [C usu *sing*] ~ of sth a small amount of sth; a suggestion or trace of sth: *There's an element of truth in his story. ○ There's always an element of danger in mountain-climbing.* 3 [C usu *pl*] a group of people within a larger group or society: *moderate/radical elements within the party ○ a neo-fascist element.* 4 [C] (*chemistry*) any of about 100 chemical substances which cannot be split by ordinary chemical methods into simpler substances: *Water is composed of the elements hydrogen and oxygen.* Compare COMPOUND¹ 1b. 5 [C] (according to ancient and medieval philosophy) any of the four substances, earth, air, fire and water, of which the universe was believed to be composed. 6 the elements [pl] the weather, esp bad weather: *exposed to (the fury of) the elements.* 7 [C usu *sing*] a natural or suitable environment, esp for an animal: *Water is a fish's natural element.* 8 elements [pl] the basic principles of a subject being studied; the parts that must be learnt first: *Legal training may include the elements of economics and political science.* 9 [C] the part of an electric fire, etc that gives out heat: *The kettle needs a new element.* IDM in/out of one's 'element in/not in one's usual or preferred surroundings; doing/not doing what one is good at and enjoys: *I feel out of my element in political discussions. ○ The children are really in their element playing on the beach.*
▶ **elemental** /,elɪ'mentl/ *adj* [esp attrib] 1 (*fml*) powerful and wild; like the forces of nature: *the elemental fury of the storm.* 2 basic and fundamental: *an elemental truth/concept.*

elementary /,elɪ'mentri/ *adj* 1 [attrib] (a) of or in the early stages of a course of study: *an elementary class.* **(b)** dealing with simple or basic matters, ideas, etc: *elementary mathematics* ○ *elementary human rights.* **2** easy to solve or answer: *The questions were so elementary that he easily passed the test.*

■ ₁**elementary** ˈ**particle** *n* (*physics*) any of the different types of tiny pieces of matter smaller than an atom.

₁**ele**ˈ**mentary school** *n* (*US*) a school at which elementary subjects, eg reading and writing, are taught to children between the ages of about 6 and 11. See also PRIMARY SCHOOL.

elephant /ˈelɪfənt/ *n* (*pl* unchanged or **elephants**) the largest land animal now living, with two curved tusks (TUSK), thick skin, and a long TRUNK(4): *a herd of elephant* ○ *an Indian/African elephant.*

▶ **elephantine** /ˌelɪˈfæntaɪn; *US* -tiːn/ *adj* (*derog or joc*) large and awkward like an elephant: *Their daughter is quite plump but their son is positively elephantine.*

elevate /ˈelɪveɪt/ *v* ~ **sb/sth** (**to sth**) (*fml*) **1** to raise sb/sth to a higher place or rank: [Vnpr] *She's been elevated to the post of trade minister.* ○ (*fig*) *The film elevates bad taste to new heights.* [also Vn]. **2** to make the mind, morals, etc better or more educated: [Vn] *She hoped to elevate the minds of her young students by reading them religious stories.* [also Vnpr].

▶ **elevated** *adj* **1** (*fml*) fine or noble; LOFTY(2): *elevated language/sentiments/thoughts.* **2** higher than the area around: *The town occupies an elevated position overlooking the lake.* ○ *an elevated road/railway* (ie built on supports, eg above the streets of a town).

elevating *adj* (*fml or joc*) improving the mind or morals: *elevating literature* ○ *The experience wasn't terribly elevating.*

elevation /ˌelɪˈveɪʃn/ *n* **1** [C, U] (*fml*) the process of elevating sb/sth or of being elevated: *his elevation to the peerage* ○ *the elevation* (ie noble quality) *of thought that gives poetry its value.* **2** [C] (**a**) the height of a place, esp above the level of the sea: *The city is at an elevation of 2 000 metres.* (**b**) (*fml*) a hill or high place: *a small elevation of the ground.* **3** [C] (*architecture*) one side of a building, or a drawing of this by an ARCHITECT(1): *the front/rear/side elevation of a house.*

elevator /ˈelɪveɪtə(r)/ *n* **1** (*esp US*) = LIFT *n* 1. **2** a movable part in the tail of an aircraft that is used to make it climb or dive. **3** a machine like a continuous belt with buckets along it, used for raising grain, goods, etc.

eleven /ɪˈlevn/ *n, pron, det* **1** the number 11. **2** a team of eleven players for football, hockey or cricket.

▶ **eleventh** /ɪˈlevnθ/ *n, pron, det* **1** 11th. **2** each of eleven equal parts of sth. **IDM** **at the eleventh hour** ⇨ HOUR.

■ e₁**leven-**ˈ**plus** *n* [sing] (formerly in Britain) an examination taken at the age of eleven, to decide which type of secondary school a child should go to. For further guidance on how *eleven* and *eleventh* are used, see the examples at *five* and *fifth*.

elevenses /ɪˈlevnzɪz/ *n* [usu sing *v*] (*Brit infml*) a very light meal, eg biscuits with tea or coffee, taken at about eleven o'CLOCK in the morning.

elf /elf/ *n* (*pl* **elves** /elvz/) a small fairy that is said to play tricks on people.

▶ **elfin** /ˈelfɪn/ *adj* of or like an elf: *an elfin grin/girl* ○ *She had the elfin figure of a child gymnast.*

elicit /ɪˈlɪsɪt/ *v* ~ **sth** (**from sb**) (*fml*) to draw facts, a response, etc from sb, sometimes with difficulty: [Vn] *elicit a reply* [Vnpr] *At last we've elicited the truth from him.*

elide /ɪˈlaɪd/ *v* (*linguistics*) to leave out the sound of part of a word when pronouncing it: [Vn] *The 't' in 'often' may be elided.* [also V]. See also ELISION.

eligible /ˈelɪdʒəbl/ *adj* ~ (**for sth / to do sth**) suit-

able or fit to be chosen; having the right or proper qualifications: *eligible for a pension/a job/an award* ○ *eligible for promotion/membership* ○ *eligible to join a club* ○ *an eligible young man* (eg one who is thought to be a satisfactory choice as a husband). Compare INELIGIBLE. ▶ **eligibility** /ˌelɪdʒəˈbɪləti/ *n* [U]: *Her qualifications and experience confirm her eligibility for the job.*

eliminate /ɪˈlɪmɪneɪt/ *v* **1** ~ **sb/sth** (**from sth**) to remove sb/sth, esp sb/sth that is not wanted or needed; to get rid of sb/sth: [Vn] *eliminate drug trafficking* [Vnpr] *The police have eliminated two suspects (from their enquiry)* (ie no longer consider that they may be guilty). [Vnpr] *eliminate mistakes from one's writing.* **2** (*infml*) to kill sb, esp a potential opponent, enemy, etc: [Vn] *The dictator had eliminated all his political rivals.* **3** ~ **sb** (**from sth**) (esp passive) to exclude sb from further stages in a competition, eg by defeating them: [Vn, Vnpr] *He was eliminated (from the contest) in the fourth round.*
▶ **elimination** /ɪˌlɪmɪˈneɪʃn/ *n* [U].

elision /ɪˈlɪʒn/ *n* (*linguistics*) [U, C] the leaving out of the sound of part of a word in pronunciation, as in *we'll, don't* and *let's.*

élite (also **elite**) /eɪˈliːt, ɪˈliːt/ *n* [CGp] (*often derog*) a group considered to be the best or most important because of their power, talent, wealth, etc: *a member of the ruling/intellectual élite* ○ *an élite force/regiment.*

▶ **élitism** /eɪˈliːtɪzəm, ɪ-/ *n* [U] (*often derog*) (**a**) the belief that a system, society, etc should aim at developing an élite: *Many people believe that private education encourages élitism.* (**b**) the attitude or behaviour of sb who considers they belong to an élite: *I find her élitism offensive.* **élitist** *n, adj.*

elixir /ɪˈlɪksɪə(r), -sə(r)/ *n* [U, C] **1** an imaginary substance with which medieval scientists hoped to change metals into gold or make people live for ever: *the elixir of life.* **2** an imaginary cure for any disease or illness.

Elizabethan /ɪˌlɪzəˈbiːθn/ *adj* [usu attrib] of the time of Queen Elizabeth I of England (1558–1603): *Elizabethan drama* ○ *The Elizabethan age was a time of exploration and discovery.*

▶ **Elizabethan** *n* a person who lived during the reign of Queen Elizabeth I: *Shakespeare was an Elizabethan.*

elk /elk/ *n* (*pl* unchanged or **elks**) one of the largest types of deer, found in N Europe, N Asia and N America. See also MOOSE.

ellipse /ɪˈlɪps/ *n* a regular OVAL, like a circle with its sides pressed inwards.

▶ **elliptic** /ɪˈlɪptɪk/ (also **elliptical** /ɪˈlɪptɪkl/) *adjs* shaped like an ellipse.

ellipsis /ɪˈlɪpsɪs/ *n* (*pl* **ellipses** /-siːz/) [C, U] **1** (*grammar*) the leaving out of a word or words from a sentence when the meaning can be understood without it/them: *The sentence 'He is dead and I alive' contains an ellipsis, ie of the word 'am'.* **2** three dots (…) used to indicate that a word or words have been omitted. ⇨ App 3.

▶ **elliptical** /ɪˈlɪptɪkl/ *adj* containing ellipsis: *an elliptical style of writing* (ie one that implies more than is actually said). **elliptically** /-kli/ *adv.*

elm /elm/ *n* [C] (**a**) (also ˈ**elm tree**) a tall tree with broad leaves which it loses in winter: *an elm forest.* (**b**) [U] its hard heavy wood: *This bench is made of elm.*

elocution /ˌeləˈkjuːʃn/ *n* [U] the art or style of speaking clearly and effectively, esp in public: *elocution lessons.*

elongate /ˈiːlɒŋɡeɪt; *US* ɪˈlɔːŋɡ-/ *v* [Vn] to make sth longer.

▶ **elongated** /ˈiːlɒŋɡeɪtɪd; *US* ɪˈlɔːŋɡ-/ *adj* long and thin; stretched out: *the elongated stone figures of saints decorating the church front.*

elongation /ˌiːlɒŋˈgeɪʃn; US -lɔːŋ-/ n [U]: *the elongation of certain vowel sounds.*

elope /ɪˈləʊp/ v ~ **(with sb)** to run away with one's lover, esp to get married: [V] *The young couple eloped because their parents wouldn't let them marry.* [Vpr] *He eloped with one of his students.* ▶ **elopement** n [C, U].

eloquence /ˈeləkwəns/ n [U] (the skilful use of) expressive language, esp to impress or persuade an audience: *a speech of passionate eloquence* ○ *The crowd were swayed by his eloquence.* ○ (fig) *There was eloquence in her silent gaze.*
▶ **eloquent** /-ənt/ adj (fml) having or showing eloquence: *an eloquent speaker/speech.* **eloquently** adv.

else /els/ adv (used after words like *how* or *why* to make questions, or after *nothing, nobody, something, anything, little, much,* etc) in addition to or apart from sth already mentioned: *Did you see anybody else* (ie any other person or people)? ○ *Have you anything else to do?* ○ *Ask somebody else to help you.* ○ *That must be somebody else's* (ie some other person's) *coat — it isn't mine.* ○ *Nothing else* (ie I want nothing more), *thank you.* ○ *We went to the park and nowhere else* (ie to no other place). ○ *I've tried to phone her six times today; what else can I do?* ○ *Who else was at the party?* ○ *How else* (ie In what other way) *would you do it?* ○ *I promised to do whatever else was needed.* ○ *We have some bread and little/not much else* (ie not much more). **IDM** **or else 1** otherwise; if not: *Run, or else you'll be late.* ○ *He must be joking, or else he's crazy.* **2** (infml) (used to express a threat or warning): *Give me the money or else!*

elsewhere /ˌelsˈweə(r)/ adv in, at or to some other place: *Our favourite restaurant was full, so we had to go elsewhere.*

ELT /ˌiː el ˈtiː/ abbr English Language Teaching (to students who are not native speakers of English).

elucidate /ɪˈluːsɪdeɪt/ v (fml) to make sth clear; to explain sth: [V] *You have not understood; allow me to elucidate.* [Vn] *elucidate a problem/mystery* ○ *The notes help to elucidate the difficult parts of the text.* ▶ **elucidation** /ɪˌluːsɪˈdeɪʃn/ n [U]: *The statement needs further elucidation.*

elude /ɪˈluːd/ v **1** to escape sb/sth, esp by a clever trick; to avoid sb/sth: [Vn] *elude one's enemies* ○ *He eluded capture for weeks by hiding underground.* ○ (fig) *After many attempts, success still eluded us.* **2** to be forgotten or not understood by sb: [Vn] *I recognize her face, but her name eludes me* (ie I can't remember it).

elusive /ɪˈluːsɪv/ adj **(a)** tending to escape or disappear; difficult to find or capture: *a most elusive criminal* ○ *that elusive quality that only truly great artists possess.* **(b)** difficult to remember: *an elusive perfume.* Compare ILLUSORY.

elves pl of ELF.

'em /əm/ pron (infml) = THEM: *Don't let 'em get away!*

em- ⇨ EN-.

emaciated /ɪˈmeɪsieɪtɪd/ adj thin and weak: *an emaciated child.* ○ *he looks very emaciated after his long illness.* ⇨ note at THIN. ▶ **emaciation** /ɪˌmeɪsiˈeɪʃn/ n [U].

email (also **e-mail**) /ˈiːmeɪl/ /ˈiːmeɪl/ n [U] = ELECTRONIC MAIL.

emanate /ˈeməneɪt/ v (fml) **1** ~ **from sth/sb** to come or flow from sth/sb or from a place: [Vpr] *Many of these ideas originally emanated from California.* ○ *Delicious smells were emanating from the kitchen.* **2** to produce and give sth out from oneself; to EMIT sth: [Vn] *His whole body seemed to emanate energy and confidence.* ▶ **emanation** /ˌeməˈneɪʃn/ n [C, U]: *The place gave off a strong emanation of evil.*

emancipate /ɪˈmænsɪpeɪt/ v (fml) ~ **sb (from sth)** to set sb free, esp from political, legal or social restrictions: [Vnpr] *be emancipated from colonialist*

rule [Vn] *In many countries women are still struggling to be fully emancipated* (ie to be given the same rights, opportunities, etc as men). ▶ **emancipation** /ɪˌmænsɪˈpeɪʃn/ n [U]: *the emancipation of women.*

emasculate /ɪˈmæskjuleɪt/ v (fml) to cause sb/sth to have less force or strength; to make sth weaker or less effective: [Vn] *His report is free of the legal restraints that make so many others appear emasculated.* ▶ **emasculation** /ɪˌmæskjuˈleɪʃn/ n [U].

embalm /ɪmˈbɑːm/ v to preserve a dead body from decay by using spices or chemicals: [Vn] *The Egyptians used to embalm the bodies of their dead kings and queens.* ▶ **embalmer** /ɪmˈbɑːmə(r)/ n.

embankment /ɪmˈbæŋkmənt/ n a wall or ridge of earth, stone, etc made esp to keep water back or to carry a railway or road over low ground: *A coach crashed down an embankment on the motorway.*

embargo /ɪmˈbɑːgəʊ/ n (pl **-oes**) [C] ~ **(on sth)** an official order that forbids sth, esp trade, the movement of ships, etc: *an oil/arms embargo* (ie one that restricts or forbids the buying or selling of oil/arms) ○ *lift/raise/remove an embargo on sth* (ie start trading in sth again) ○ *a trade/economic embargo against another country.*
▶ **embargoed** /-gəʊd/ adj officially forbidden or restricted: *embargoed goods.*

embark /ɪmˈbɑːk/ v ~ **(for...)** to go or be taken on board a ship or an aircraft: [V] *Passengers with cars must embark first.* [Vpr] *We embarked for Anchorage at midday.* Compare DISEMBARK. **PHR V** **em'bark on/upon sth** to start or engage in sth new or difficult: *embark on a long journey* ○ *embark on the task of improving the party's image* ○ *He embarked on a new career.*
▶ **embarkation** /ˌembɑːˈkeɪʃn/ n [U] the action or process of embarking: *the port of embarkation.*

embarrass /ɪmˈbærəs/ v (esp passive) **(a)** to make sb feel awkward, ashamed or SELF-CONSCIOUS: [Vn] *I was embarrassed by his comments about my clothes.* ○ *Are you trying to embarrass me?* **(b)** to cause difficulties for sb: [Vn] *embarrassed by lack of money* ○ *be financially embarrassed* ○ *a speech designed to embarrass the government.*
▶ **embarrassed** adj ~ **(about/at sth)** (of people or their behaviour) shy, awkward or ashamed: *He felt slightly embarrassed at being the centre of attention.* ○ *An embarrassed Clarissa nervously sipped her wine.* ○ *There was an embarrassed silence.*
embarrassing adj causing one to feel awkward, ashamed, etc: *an embarrassing incident/question/mistake* ○ *The latest rise in unemployment has proved extremely embarrassing to the government.* **embarrassingly** adv.
embarrassment n **(a)** [U] shy, awkward or guilty feelings: *He suffered a good deal of embarrassment in his youth.* ○ *She was overcome with embarrassment at the idea.* ○ *Much to the embarrassment of ministers, the proposals were leaked to the press.* **(b)** [C] a person or thing that embarrasses sb: *financial embarrassments* ○ *He's an embarrassment to his family.*

embassy /ˈembəsi/ n **(a)** an AMBASSADOR and her or his staff representing their country in a foreign country: *inform the embassy of the situation* ○ *embassy officials* ○ *the American embassy in London* ○ *He is with* (ie a member of) *the French embassy.* **(b)** the building where they work: *outside the Russian Embassy.* Compare CONSULATE, HIGH COMMISSION.

embattled /ɪmˈbætld/ adj **(a)** constantly surrounded by problems or difficulties: *an embattled party leader.* **(b)** (of an army, city, etc) ready for or involved in war: *embattled troops.*

embed /ɪmˈbed/ v (**-dd-**) ~ **sth (in sth)** (often passive) to fix sth deeply and firmly in a mass of sth: [Vnpr] *stones embedded in concrete* ○ *The arrow embedded itself in the wall.* ○ (fig) *The idea became*

---

embedded in his mind. [Vn, Vnadv] *Feelings of hatred are (deeply) embedded.*

embellish /ɪmˈbelɪʃ/ *v* ~ **sth (with sth)** **1** to make sth beautiful by adding decorations, etc: [Vnpr] *a dress embellished with lace and ribbons* [also Vn]. **2** to improve a story, statement, etc by adding interesting or amusing details, often not true: [Vn] *He admits that he embellished the account of events originally given to him.* [also Vnpr]. ► **embellishment** *n* [U,C]: *the embellishment of a building/a speech* ○ *a 16th-century church with 18th-century embellishments.*

ember /ˈembə(r)/ *n* (usu *pl*) a small piece of burning or glowing wood or coal in a dying fire: *Only the embers of the bonfire remained.* ○ *(fig) keep the embers of revolution alight.*

embezzle /ɪmˈbezl/ *v* to use money placed in one's care wrongly, esp so as to benefit oneself: [Vn] *embezzle the company's pension fund* ○ *The treasurer embezzled $2 000 of the club's money.* ► **embezzlement** *n* [C,U]: *petty embezzlements* ○ *He was found guilty of embezzlement.* **embezzler** /ɪmˈbezlə(r)/ *n*.

embitter /ɪmˈbɪtə(r)/ *v* (usu passive) to fill sb/sth with deep feelings of disappointment, envy, hatred, etc: [Vn] *She became embittered by repeated failures.* ► **embittered** *adj*: *an embittered manager* ○ *embittered relations between states.*

emblazon /ɪmˈbleɪzn/ *v* ~ **A with B/~ B on A** (usu passive) to decorate sth with a striking design or piece of writing: [Vnpr] *a T-shirt emblazoned with the band's logo* ○ *a slogan emblazoned on the back.*

emblem /ˈembləm/ *n* an object that represents sth; a symbol: *a club emblem* ○ *The dove is an emblem of peace.* ○ *The thistle is the national emblem of Scotland.* ► **emblematic** /ˌembləˈmætɪk/ *adj* (*fml*) serving as an emblem; symbolic (SYMBOL): *His work is now regarded as emblematic of recent British fiction.*

embody /ɪmˈbɒdi/ *v* (*pt, pp* **-died**) (*fml*) **1** to express or give visible form to ideas, feelings, etc: [Vn] *To me he embodies all the best qualities of a teacher.* ○ *the principles embodied in the Declaration of Human Rights.* **2** to include or contain sth: [Vn] *The latest computer model embodies many new features.* ► **embodiment** /ɪmˈbɒdimənt/ *n* a person or thing that represents or is a typical example of sth: *She's the embodiment of kindness.*

embolden /ɪmˈbəʊldən/ *v* (dated or *fml*) (often passive) to give courage or confidence to sb: [Vn] *She felt emboldened by the wine and a new feeling of intimacy.* [Vn.to inf] *His success emboldened him to expand the business.*

embossed /ɪmˈbɒst/ *adj* ~ **(with sth)** having a design on a piece of writing raised above the surface: *embossed stationery* ○ *an embossed pattern* ○ *a leather briefcase embossed with one's initials.*

embrace /ɪmˈbreɪs/ *v* **1** to hold a person, etc in one's arms as a sign of affection: [V, Vn] *They embraced (each other) warmly.* [Vn] *She embraced her son before leaving.* **2** (*fml*) to accept or believe an idea, etc willingly and enthusiastically: [Vn] *embrace Christianity* ○ *She was quick to embrace the offer/opportunity.* **3** (of things) to include sth: [Vn] *The term 'mankind' embraces all men, women and children.* ► **embrace** *n*: *He held her in a warm embrace.* ○ *She tried to avoid his embraces.*

embrasure /ɪmˈbreɪʒə(r)/ *n* (*architecture*) an opening in a wall for a door or window, wider on the inside than on the outside.

embrocation /ˌembrəˈkeɪʃn/ *n* [U] a liquid for rubbing on the body to ease sore muscles, etc; LINIMENT.

embroider /ɪmˈbrɔɪdə(r)/ *v* **1** ~ **A (on B)/~ B (with A)** to decorate cloth by sewing patterns onto it, esp using thread of various colours: [Vn] *an embroidered blouse* [Vnpr] *She embroidered flowers on the cushion (in gold thread).* ○ *She embroidered the*

cushion with flowers. [also V]. **2** (*fig*) to add details that are not true to a story, to make it more interesting: [Vn] *He's inclined to embroider the facts.* ► **embroidery** /-dəri/ *n* **1(a)** [U,C] cloth decorated with patterns sewn in thread of various colours: *a beautiful piece of embroidery* ○ *Indian embroideries.* **(b)** [U] the art or activity of decorating cloth in this way: *He's good at embroidery.* **2** [U] details that are not true, but are added for effect: *One needs to strip away the embroidery from the official statement.*

embroil /ɪmˈbrɔɪl/ *v* ~ **sb/oneself (in sth)** (often passive) to involve sb/oneself deeply in an argument or a difficult situation: *I don't want to become/get embroiled in their quarrels.* ○ *They are embroiled in a war against their will.* [Vn] *This embarrassing affair is now threatening to embroil some of the major banks.*

embryo /ˈembriəʊ/ *n* (*pl* **-os**) a young animal or plant in the very early stages of its development before birth, or before coming out of its egg or seed: *human embryos* ○ *predetermine the sex of embryos* ○ *(fig) an embryo of an idea.* Compare FOETUS. **IDM in embryo** existing but not yet developed: *My plans are still very much in embryo at this stage.* ► **embryology** /ˌembriˈɒlədʒi/ *n* [U] the scientific study of the formation and development of embryos. **embryologist** /ˌembriˈɒlədʒɪst/ *n*.

embryonic /ˌembriˈɒnɪk/ *adj* [usu attrib] in an early stage of development: *When should the embryonic cells be considered a human being?* ○ *(fig) The scheme is still in embryonic form/at an embryonic stage.*

emend /iˈmend/ *v* to remove errors from a text, esp before printing: [Vn] *emend a passage in a book.* ► **emendation** /ˌiːmenˈdeɪʃn/ *n* **(a)** [C] a letter, word, etc that is emended: *minor emendations to the official statement.* **(b)** [U] the action of emending a text.

emerald /ˈemərəld/ *n* a bright green precious stone: *a brooch of diamonds and emeralds* ○ *an emerald ring.* ► **emerald** (also ˌemerald ˈgreen) *adj* of a bright green colour: *cream and emerald tiles.* ■ **the ˌEmerald ˈIsle** *n* [sing] (*rhet*) Ireland.

emerge /iˈmɜːdʒ/ *v* **1** ~ **(from sth)** to come out of a place or up from under water: [Vpr] *The swimmer emerged from the lake.* ○ *The moon emerged from behind the clouds.* ○ *She finally emerged from her room at about ten.* [V] *When she emerged he hardly recognized her.* **2(a)** ~ **(as sth)** to develop and become noticeable, important or prominent: [V-n] *He emerged as leader at the age of thirty.* [V] *Opposition groups began to emerge.* **(b)** (often used in past tenses with *it*) (of facts, ideas, etc) to become known: [V.*that*] *It emerged that officials had taken bribes.* [V] *No new evidence emerged during the inquiry.* **3** ~ **(from sth)** to survive a difficult situation with the specified result: [Vpr] *They emerged from the election with a reduced majority.* [also V]. ► **emergence** /-dʒəns/ *n* [U]: *her emergence as a major artist* ○ *witness the emergence of a new champion.*

emergent /-dʒənt/ *adj* [usu attrib] new and still developing: *the emergent democracies of Eastern Europe.*

emergency /iˈmɜːdʒənsi/ *n* **1** [C, U] a sudden serious event or situation requiring immediate action: *This door should only be used in an emergency.* ○ *the emergency exit* ○ *The government has declared a state of emergency* (eg because of war, a natural disaster, etc). ○ *the emergency services* (ie the police, fire, AMBULANCE and COASTGUARD services) ○ *The pilot had to make an emergency landing in a field.* **2** [U] (*US*) = CASUALTY 3: *the emergency ward.*

emeritus /iˈmerɪtəs/ *adj* (often following *ns*, and having a capital in titles) (of a university teacher, esp a PROFESSOR(1)) having retired, but keeping her or his title as an honour: *the Emeritus Professor of Biology* ∘ *a professor emeritus.*

emery /'eməri/ *n* [U] a hard mineral used esp in the form of a powder for polishing and grinding.
■ '**emery-board** *n* a small strip of wood or cardboard covered in emery, used for shaping the fingernails.
'**emery-paper** *n* [U] paper covered in emery, used esp for polishing metal.

emetic /ɪ'metɪk/ *n, adj* (a medicine) causing one to bring food back up from the stomach and through the mouth: *He was given an emetic after eating poisonous berries.*

emigrate /'emɪɡreɪt/ *v* ~ (**from...**) (**to...**) to leave one's own country and go to live permanently in another: [Vpr] *emigrate from Poland to Australia to find work* [also V].
▶ **emigrant** /'emɪɡrənt/ *n* a person who emigrates: *emigrants to Canada* ∘ *emigrant labourers.* Compare IMMIGRANT.
emigration /ˌemɪ'ɡreɪʃn/ *n* [U, C]: *the mass emigration of refugees from the war* ∘ *emigration laws/officials.* Compare IMMIGRATION 1.

émigré /'emɪɡreɪ; *US* ˌemɪ'ɡreɪ/ *n* a person who has left her or his own country, usu for political reasons: *the son of Russian émigrés.*

eminence /'emɪnəns/ *n* **1** [U] (*fml*) the state of being famous or respected in one's profession: *rise to/achieve/reach eminence as a doctor.* **2** [C] (*dated or fml*) a hill: *a fortress on a rocky eminence.* **3 Eminence** [C] the title of a Roman Catholic CARDINAL¹: *His/Your Eminence* ∘ *Their/Your Eminences.*

eminent /'emɪnənt/ *adj* **1** (of people) famous and respected in a profession: *an eminent architect* ∘ *His son is only slightly less eminent.* **2** [usu attrib] (*fml*) (of qualities) remarkable; outstanding: *a man of eminent good sense.*
▶ **eminently** *adv* very; obviously: *She seems eminently suitable for the job.*

emir /e'mɪə(r), 'eɪmɪə(r)/ *n* the title of various Muslim rulers: *the Emir of Kuwait.*
▶ **emirate** /'emɪəreɪt, 'emɪrət/ *n* the position, period of rule(3) or lands of an emir: *the United Arab Emirates.*

emissary /'emɪsəri/ *n* a person sent to deliver a message, esp from one nation to another, or to conduct negotiations: *a Swedish emissary sent by the UN.*

emission /ɪ'mɪʃn/ *n* (**a**) [U] (*fml*) the production or release of sth, eg light, heat, gas, matter, etc: *the emission of carbon dioxide from vehicles* ∘ *emission controls/laws.* (**b**) [C] a thing that is produced or released by sth; a thing that is discharged: *clean up emissions from power stations.*

emit /ɪ'mɪt/ *v* (-**tt**-) **1** (of people) to produce a noise, smell, etc; to discharge sth: [Vn] *Most of the lava was emitted during the first few hours of the eruption.* ∘ *The cheese was emitting a strong smell.* ∘ *She emitted a cry of pain.*

emollient /ɪ'mɒlɪənt/ *adj* (*fml*) reducing anger, opposition, etc and promoting peace or good relations: *an emollient stance/statement/tone* ∘ *Mr Major himself could not have been more emollient.*

emolument /ɪ'mɒljumənt/ *n* (usu *pl*) (*fml or rhet*) a salary or FEE: *Her emoluments amounted to very little.*

emotion /ɪ'məʊʃn/ *n* **1** [C] a strong feeling of any kind: *Love, joy, hate, fear and jealousy are all emotions.* ∘ *The speaker appealed to our emotions rather than to our minds.* **2** [U] excitement or disturbance of the feelings: *overcome by/with emotion* ∘ *show no emotion* ∘ *He spoke of his dead wife with deep emotion.* ∘ *She answered in a voice filled/trembling with emotion.*
▶ **emotional** /-ʃənl/ *adj* **1** [attrib] of the emotions:

emotional problems. **2**(**a**) causing emotion: *emotional music/language* ∘ *Her departure was an emotional affair.* (**b**) showing emotion: *an emotional outburst/response* ∘ *She could not face another emotional scene with her father.* **3** (*sometimes derog*) having emotions that are easily excited and displayed: *an emotional man/actor/character/nature* ∘ *She is embarrassingly emotional in public.* ∘ *People get very emotional about issues like animal welfare.*
emotionally /-ʃənəli/ *adv*: *emotionally disturbed.*
emotionless *adj*.

emotive /ɪ'məʊtɪv/ *adj* (of words, etc) tending to affect the emotions: *an emotive speech* ∘ *Capital punishment is a highly emotive issue.*

empathize, -ise /'empəθaɪz/ *v* ~ (**with sb/sth**) to imagine and share the feelings, problems, etc of another person: [Vpr] *He found it difficult to empathize with a working mother of three small children.* [also V].

empathy /'empəθi/ *n* [U] ~ (**with sb/sth**) the ability to imagine and share another person's feelings, experience, etc: *The writer's imaginative empathy with his subject is clear.* ∘ *There is a natural love and empathy between them.*

emperor /'empərə(r)/ *n* (*fem* **empress** /'emprəs/) the ruler of an empire: *the Roman emperors* ∘ *the Emperor Napoleon.*

emphasis /'emfəsɪs/ *n* (*pl* **emphases** /-siːz/) [C,U] **1** the force or stress(3a) given to a word or words when spoken, esp in order to make the meaning clear or to show importance: *give special emphasis to a phrase.* **2** ~ (**on sth**) special meaning, value or importance, or the placing of this on sth: *Some schools put/lay/place great emphasis on language study.* ∘ *There has been a shift of emphasis from manufacturing to service industries.* ∘ *The emphasis is on hard work, not enjoyment.*
▶ **emphasize, -ise** /'emfəsaɪz/ *v* to put emphasis on sth; to give emphasis to sth; to stress sth: [Vn] *Which word should I emphasize?* [Vn, V.that] *He emphasized the importance of careful driving/emphasized that careful driving was important.* [also V.speech].

emphatic /ɪm'fætɪk/ *adj* **1** (abbreviated as *emph* in this dictionary) having, showing or using emphasis(1): *an emphatic denial* ∘ *He was most emphatic that I go with him.* **2** definite and clear: *an emphatic victory.* **emphatically** /-kli/ *adv*: *'Certainly not,' he replied emphatically.* ∘ *She is emphatically opposed to the proposals.*

empire /'empaɪə(r)/ *n* **1**(**a**) [C] a group of countries or states that have a single ruler or ruling power: *the Roman Empire.* (**b**) [U] (*dated or fml*) power over several countries, states, etc: *the responsibilities of empire.* See also IMPERIAL 1. **2** [C] a large commercial organization controlled by one person or group: *a publishing empire.*
■ '**empire-building** *n* [U] (*often derog*) the process of deliberately acquiring extra territory, authority, etc to increase one's power or position.

empirical /ɪm'pɪrɪkl/ *adj* based on observation or experiment, not on theory: *empirical evidence/knowledge.*
▶ **empirically** /-kli/ *adv*.
empiricism /ɪm'pɪrɪsɪzəm/ *n* [U] the belief in or use of empirical methods.
empiricist /-sɪst/ *n, adj*.

emplacement /ɪm'pleɪsmənt/ *n* a prepared position or platform for a heavy gun or guns.

employ /ɪm'plɔɪ/ *v* **1** ~ **sb** (**as sth**) to give work to sb, usu for payment: [Vn] *She hasn't been employed* (ie has not had a job) *for six months now.* ∘ *We employ a firm of management consultants.* ∘ *The company employs mainly women.* [Vnpr] *He's employed on the oil rigs.* [Vn-n] *She's employed as a shop assistant.* [Vn.to inf] *They employed him to look* *after the baby.* **2** ~ **sth** (**as sth**) (*fml*) to make use of sb/sth; to occupy time, attention, etc: [Vn] *I feel that my time could be better employed.* [Vnpr] *He was busily employed in cleaning his shoes.* [Vn-n] *He employed his knife as a lever.* [Vn.to inf] *The police had to employ force to enter the house.*

▶ **employ** *n* [U] (*fml*) service or employment: *How long has she been in your employ* (ie employed by you)?

employable /-əbl/ *adj* [usu pred] fit to be employed: *training schemes to make more people employable.*

employee /ɪm'plɔiːi:/ *n* a person who works for sb or for a company in return for wages: *The firm has over 500 employees.*

employer *n* a person or company that employs people: *They're not good employers* (ie They treat their workers badly).

employment /ɪm'plɔimənt/ *n* [U] **1(a)** the action of employing sb: *The expansion of the factory will mean the employment of sixty extra workers.* (**b**) the state of being employed: *be in/out of regular employment.* **2** work, esp in return for regular payment: *give employment to sb* ○ *find employment* ○ *The government is aiming at full employment* (ie jobs for everyone). ⇨ note at JOB.
■ **em'ployment agency** *n* a private business that helps people to find work and employers to find workers.

emporium /em'pɔːriəm/ *n* (*pl* **emporiums** or **emporia** /-riə/) (*often joc*) a shop selling a variety of goods: *an arts and crafts emporium.*

empower /ɪm'paʊə(r)/ *v* (*fml*) (often passive) to give sb the power or authority to act: [Vn.to inf] *The lawyer was empowered to pay all her client's bills.* ○ *The new laws empower the police to stop anybody in the street.* [also Vn]. ▶ **empowerment** *n* [U].

empress /'emprəs/ *n* (**a**) the female ruler of an empire. (**b**) the wife or widow of an EMPEROR.

empty¹ /'empti/ *adj* (**-ier, -iest**) **1(a)** having nothing inside: *an empty box* ○ *an empty lorry* (ie one without a load) ○ *empty hands* (ie not holding anything) ○ *Your glass is empty.* ○ *It's not good to drink alcohol on an empty stomach* (ie having eaten nothing). (**b**) with no one in it: *an empty house/room/chair/bus* ○ *empty streets* ○ *The cinema was half empty.* **2(a)** having no value; without sense or purpose: *empty threats/words/promises/dreams* ○ *My life feels empty now the children have left home.* (**b**) [pred] ~ **of sth** (*fml*) without or lacking in a quality: *words empty of meaning.* **3** (*infml*) hungry: *I feel really empty.* Compare FULL.

▶ **empties** *n* [pl] (*infml*) empty bottles, boxes, etc: *Take your empties to the bottle bank.*
emptily *adv.*
emptiness /'emptinəs/ *n* [U, sing]: *the emptiness of their lives* ○ *There was an emptiness in her heart.* ○ *He stared out at the vast emptiness of the sea.*
■ **,empty-'handed** *adj* [usu pred] bringing back or taking away nothing: *return empty-handed from an unsuccessful shopping trip* ○ *The robbers fled empty-handed.*
,empty-'headed *adj* (of people) foolish and without common sense (COMMON¹): *a silly ,empty-headed 'youth.*

> **NOTE** **Empty** and **full** have wide uses. Any container, room, or building, etc can be **empty** or **full**: *The theatre was almost empty last night.* ○ *This bottle was full yesterday and now it's empty.* **Vacant** and **occupied** refer to buildings: *There are some vacant offices on the third floor.* ○ *All the apartments are occupied now.* They can also refer to the use of a room, etc for a short time: *The toilet is vacant.* ○ *All the seats in this compartment are occupied.*

empty² /'empti/ *v* (*pt, pp* **emptied**) **1(a)** ~ **sth** (**out**);

~ **sth** (**of sth**) to make sth empty: [Vn] *empty one's glass* ○ *We have to empty the hall before ten o'clock.* [Vnp] *empty out a drawer* [Vnpr] *He emptied his pockets of their contents.* (**b**) to become empty: [V, Vpr] *The streets soon emptied (of people) when the rain started.* [V] *The cistern empties in five minutes.* **2(a)** ~ **sth** (**into/onto sth**) to remove the contents of sth and put them somewhere else: [Vn] *Have you emptied the rubbish?* [Vnpr] *She emptied the milk into the pan.* [Vnpr, Vnp] *We emptied (out) the waste paper onto the floor.* (**b**) ~ (**from/out of sth**) (**into/onto sth**) to flow or pour out: [V, Vpr] *The water slowly emptied (from the cistern).* [Vpr] *The Rhone empties into the Mediterranean.* ○ *The rubbish from the cart emptied onto the street.*

EMS /ˌiː em 'es/ *abbr* European Monetary System (a financial arrangement linking the currencies of some EU countries to the ECU). See also ERM.

EMU /ˌiː em 'juː/ *abbr* Economic and Monetary Union (of the European Union, a programme to achieve full economic unity in the EU, including use of the ECU as a common currency): *make progress towards EMU.*

emu /'iːmjuː/ *n* a large Australian bird that runs quickly but cannot fly.

emulate /'emjuleɪt/ *v* **1** (*fml*) to try to do as well as or better than sb: [Vn] *She is keen to emulate her sister's sporting achievements.* **2** (*computing*) (of a device or PROGRAM(1)) to operate in all respects like a different type of device, program, etc: [Vn] *Our new model emulates several common laser printers.*
▶ **emulation** /ˌemjuˈleɪʃn/ *n* [U].
emulator *n* (*computing*) a device or piece of SOFTWARE that enables a PROGRAM(1) or an item of equipment intended for one type of computer to be used with exactly the same results with another type of computer.

emulsion /ɪ'mʌlʃn/ *n* [C, U] **1** (also **emulsion paint**) a type of paint that dries without forming a glossy surface, used eg on the walls of a room: *Emulsion can be mixed with water to make it thinner.* **2** a substance on the surface of photographic film that is sensitive to light. **3** any thick liquid in which tiny drops of oil or fat are evenly distributed.

en- (also **em-**) *pref* **1** (with *ns* and *vs* forming *vs*) to put into or on: *encase* ○ *endanger* ○ *embed.* **2** (with *adjs* or *ns* forming *vs*) to make into; to cause to be: *enlarge* ○ *enrich* ○ *empower.*

-en *suff* **1** (with *ns* forming *adjs*) made of: *golden* ○ *wooden.* **2** (with *adjs* forming *vs*) to make or become: *blacken* ○ *sadden.*

enable /ɪ'neɪbl/ *v* **1** to make sb able to do sth by giving them the necessary authority or means: [Vn.to inf] *This pass enables me to travel half-price on trains.* ○ *A rabbit's large ears enable it to hear the slightest sound.* **2** to make sth possible: [Vn] *a conference to enable greater international cooperation.* **3** (*computing*) [Vn] to make a particular device, function, signal, etc start to operate. Compare DISABLE.

enact /ɪ'nækt/ *v* **1** (*fml*) (esp passive) to perform a part, play, etc on, or as if on, the stage of a theatre: [Vn] *a one-act drama enacted by children* ○ *A strange ritual was being enacted before our eyes.* **2** (*fml or law*) (esp passive) to make or pass a law: [Vn] *a bill enacted by Parliament* [Vn.that] *It was enacted that offenders be brought before Council.*
▶ **enactment** *n* **1** [U] (*fml or law*) the action or process of enacting sth: *the enactment of the drama/ of legislation.* **2** [C] a law: *a civil enactment dealing with private rights.*

enamel /ɪ'næml/ *n* [U] **1** a substance used to cover the surface of metal, pots, etc for decoration or as protection: *Enamel is applied when hot, and cools to give a hard glossy surface.* ○ *Some of the enamel on this pan has chipped off.* ○ *an enamel bowl* ○ *enamel paint* (ie paint that dries to make a hard shiny* surface). **2** the hard outer covering of teeth. ⇨ picture at TOOTH.

▶ **enamel** v (**-ll-**; US also **-l-**) to cover or decorate sth with enamel: [Vn] *enamelled jewellery*.

enamoured (US **enamored**) /ɪˈnæməd/ adj [pred] ~ **of/with sth** (*fml or joc*) (often in negative sentences) fond of or delighted by sth: *He was less than enamoured of the music.* ○ *She's enamoured with the boy next door* (ie in love with him). ○ *I'm not too enamoured with the idea of spending a whole day with them.*

en bloc /ˌɒ̃ ˈblɒk/ adv (*French*) all together; all at the same time: *There are reports of teachers resigning en bloc.*

encamp /ɪnˈkæmp/ v to settle in a camp: [Vn] *The soldiers are encamped in the forest.* ○ (*fig*) [V] *The strikers encamped outside the factory.*

▶ **encampment** n a place where soldiers, etc are encamped: *a gypsy encampment.*

encapsulate /ɪnˈkæpsjuleɪt/ v (*fml*) **1** ~ **sth** (**in sth**) to express the essential facts, ideas, etc of sb/sth in a brief and simple way; to SUMMARIZE sth: [Vn] *The chairwoman's short statement encapsulates the views of the committee.* [Vnpr] *The whole miserable holiday is encapsulated in that one photograph.* **2** to isolate and preserve the memory of sth: [Vn] *The poem encapsulates a moment of intimacy between the lovers.* ▶ **encapsulation** n [U].

encase /ɪnˈkeɪs/ v ~ **sth** (**in sth**) (*fml*) (often passive) to surround or cover sth closely, esp in order to protect it: [Vn] *The disease affects the membranes encasing the spinal cord.* [Vnpr] *His broken leg was encased in plaster.* ○ (*fig*) *Encased in the little black car I felt warm and safe.*

encash /ɪnˈkæʃ/ v (*fml*) to obtain money in return for a cheque, credit note, etc: [Vn] *Banks may impose a small charge for encashing cheques.* ▶ **encashment** n [U, C]: *the encashment of a life assurance policy.*

-ence ⇨ -ANCE.

-ance, -ence suff (with vs forming ns) an action or a state of: *assistance* ○ *resemblance* ○ *confidence.*

enchant /ɪnˈtʃɑːnt; US -ˈtʃænt/ v to fill sb with great delight: [Vn, Vnpr] *be enchanted by/with the singing of the children.*

▶ **enchanted** /-ɪd/ adj (**a**) filled with delight: *their enchanted faces.* (**b**) placed under a magic spell: *an enchanted garden* (eg in a fairy story).

enchanter n a person who uses magic spells, eg in fairy stories.

enchanting adj delightful: *We found the scenery enchanting.* ○ *They have enchanting children.* **enchantingly** adv.

enchantment n **1**(**a**) [U] delight: *Music seemed to have lost its enchantment for her* (ie She no longer enjoyed it). (**b**) [U] the process or state of being enchanted. **2** [C] a thing that enchants: *the enchantments of European cities.*

enchantress /-trəs/ n (**a**) a very attractive and charming woman. (**b**) a woman who uses magic spells, eg in fairy stories.

encircle /ɪnˈsɜːkl/ v (esp passive) to form a circle round sth; to surround sth: [Vn] *a lake encircled by trees* ○ *enemy troops encircling the town.* ▶ **encirclement** n [U].

encl abbr (*commerce*) (eg at the end of a letter sent together with a price list, report, etc) enclosed; enclosure.

enclave /ˈenkleɪv/ n a small territory belonging to one state or group of people surrounded by that of another: *Lebanon's Christian enclave* ○ (*fig*) *The bay is a tranquil enclave on a rugged coast.*

enclose /ɪnˈkləʊz/ v **1** ~ **sth** (**with sth**) to put sth in an envelope, letter, parcel, etc: [Vnpr] *I'll enclose your application with mine.* [Vn] *My cheque for £10.50 is enclosed.* ○ (*fml or commerce*) *Please find enclosed our current price list.* ○ *Please sign the enclosed registration card and return it to us.* **2**(**a**) (also **inclose**) ~ **sth** (**in/with sth**) to put a wall, etc round sth: [Vnpr] *enclose an area of open moor with fences* ○ *exhibits enclosed in glass cases* [also Vn]. (**b**) to surround sth: [Vn] *The walls enclose a small courtyard.*

▶ **enclosed** adj isolated from outside influence and contact: *an enclosed order of monks.*

enclosure /ɪnˈkləʊʒə(r)/ n **1**(**a**) (also **inclosure**) [C] a piece of land that is enclosed by a fence, etc: *an enclosure for horses.* (**b**) [U] the enclosing of land in this way: *opposed to the enclosure of common land.* **2** [C] a thing that is enclosed with a letter: *There were several enclosures in the envelope.*

encode /ɪnˈkəʊd/ v [Vn] (**a**) to put a message, etc into code: *encoded documents.* (**b**) (*computing*) to translate instructions or data into a form or language that can be processed by a computer: *Flight data is encoded in a magnetic strip on the boarding card.* Compare DECODE.

encompass /ɪnˈkʌmpəs/ v (*fml*) **1** to include sth: [Vn] *The general arts course encompasses a wide range of subjects.* ○ *Her knowledge encompasses all aspects of the business.* **2** to surround or cover sth completely: [Vn] *a lake encompassed by mountains.*

encore /ˈɒŋkɔː(r)/ interj (called out by an audience to ask for a further performance of sth by sb) again!; more!

▶ **encore** n (a call for) a further performance of sth by sb: *The group got/took three encores.* ○ *She played a Chopin waltz as an encore.*

encounter /ɪnˈkaʊntə(r)/ v (*fml*) **1** to find or be faced with sth, esp sth new, strange, unpleasant, difficult or dangerous: [Vn] *I encountered many problems when I first started this job.* ○ *We encountered very little traffic.* ○ *I've never encountered his novels before.* ○ *When did you first encounter Buddhism?* **2** to meet sb unexpectedly: *He was fascinated by the woman he had encountered in the airport lounge.*

▶ **encounter** n ~ (**between A and B**); ~ (**with sb/sth**) a meeting, esp a sudden or HOSTILE(1) one: *the famous encounter between Stanley and Livingstone* ○ *Three officers were killed in the encounter.* ○ *a brief encounter with an angry client* ○ *a sexual encounter.*

encourage /ɪnˈkʌrɪdʒ/ v **1** to give support, confidence or hope to sb: [Vnpr] *Her parents always encouraged her in her studies.* [Vn] *He felt encouraged by the progress he'd made.* [Vn.to inf] *She encouraged him to lose weight.* **2** to help sth to develop or increase; to stimulate sth: [Vn] *encourage exports* [Vnpr] *Don't encourage bad habits in a child.* Compare DISCOURAGE.

▶ **encouragement** n ~ (**to sb**) (**to do sth**) (**a**) [U] the action of encouraging sb/sth: *shouts of encouragement* ○ *People need encouragement to try something new.* (**b**) [C] a thing that encourages sb: *The teacher's words were a great encouragement to him.*

encouraging adj: *encouraging words/news/signs* ○ *This year's sales figures are very encouraging.* **encouragingly** adv: *She smiled/nodded encouragingly.*

encroach /ɪnˈkrəʊtʃ/ v ~ (**on/upon sth**) to go beyond the limit of what is right or natural or desirable; to INTRUDE: [Vpr] *encroach on sb's property* ○ *encroach on the liberty of the individual* [V] *The sea is gradually encroaching* (ie washing the land away). ○ *signs of encroaching madness/middle age.* ▶ **encroachment** n [U, C] ~ (**on/upon sth**): *measures to protect against encroachment by property developers* ○ *the encroachment of the desert* ○ *encroachments on freedom of speech.*

encrustation = INCRUSTATION.

encrusted /ɪnˈkrʌstɪd/ adj ~ (**with sth**) covered with or forming a layer or thin hard coat(4) of sth,

E

sometimes for decoration: *a gold crown encrusted with diamonds* ○ *a blood encrusted wound* ○ *thick grey encrusted mud.*

encumber /ɪnˈkʌmbə(r)/ *v* ~ **sb/sth (with sth)** (usu passive) to prevent sb/sth from moving or acting freely and easily: [Vnpr] *Travelling is difficult when you're encumbered with two small children and a heavy suitcase.* ○ *encumbered with debts* [Vn] *She was encumbered by her heavy costume.*

▶ **encumbrance** /ɪnˈkʌmbrəns/ *n* (*fml*) a person or thing that encumbers sb: *I knew I was an encumbrance to them.*

encyclical /ɪnˈsɪklɪkl/ *n* a letter written by the Pope to all the Roman Catholic bishops so that its contents may become widely known.

encyclopedia (also **-paedia**) /ɪnˌsaɪkləˈpiːdiə/ *n* a book or set of books giving information about every branch of knowledge, or about one particular subject. The information in encyclopedias usually consists of articles or short notes arranged in order from A to Z: *a children's encyclopedia* ○ *an encyclopedia of music.*

▶ **encyclopedic** (also **-paedic**) /ɪnˌsaɪkləˈpiːdɪk/ *adj* dealing with or having knowledge of a wide variety of subjects: *She has an en,cyclopedic ˈknowledge of natural history.*

end¹ /end/ *n* **1** an extreme point of sth; the furthest or last part of sth: *the end of a road/stick/line* ○ *the room at the end of the corridor* ○ *join the end of the queue* ○ *The end of the cat's tail was trapped in the door.* ○ *the west/east end* (ie the parts in the west/east) *of a town* ○ *We've travelled from one end of Mexico to the other.* ○ *They live in the end house.* See also BIG END, TAIL-END. **2** the final part of a story, an event, an activity, a period of time, etc; the finish; the conclusion: *at the end of the day/month/year/century* ○ *see a film from beginning to end* ○ *the end of an era* ○ *an end-of-semester party* ○ *There's no end in sight to the present crisis.* ○ *The war was finally at an end* (ie over). ○ *At last the meeting came to an end* (ie finished). ○ *The coup brought an end to / brought to an end his corrupt regime.* **3** a small piece that is left after sth has been used: *a cigarette-end* ○ *candle ends.* See also FAG-END. **4** (usu *sing*) (*often euph*) a person's death: *He's nearing his end* (ie is dying). ○ *She came to an untimely end* (ie died young). **5** an aim or a purpose: *do anything to achieve this end* ○ *further/pursue one's own ends* ○ *for commercial/political ends* ○ *with this end in view/to this end.* **6** the half of a sports pitch, etc that is defended or occupied by one team or player: *At halftime the teams changed ends.* **7** (usu *sing*) a part or share, esp of a business, with which a person is concerned: *We need someone to handle the marketing end of the business.* ○ *Are there any problems at your end?* **8** (usu *sing*) either of two places linked by a telephone call: *I answered the phone but there was no one at the other end.* **IDM** **at the ˌend of the ˈday** (*esp Brit*) when everything is taken into consideration: *At the end of the day what matters is having a good product to sell.* **(be) at the end of sth** having no more of sth: *at the end of his patience* ○ *at the end of their food supply.* **at the ˌend of one's ˈtether;** (*US*) **at the ˌend of one's ˈrope** having no patience or energy left: *I've been looking after four young children all day and I really am at the end of my tether!* **at a loose end** ⇨ LOOSE¹. **at one's wits' end** ⇨ WIT. **be at/on the receiving end** ⇨ RECEIVE. **be the ˈend** (*infml*) to be the limit of what one can tolerate; to be very bad, annoying, etc: *This is the ˈend — I'm never coming to this hotel again.* ○ *They really are the end!* **the beginning of the end** ⇨ BEGINNING. **burn the candle at both ends** ⇨ BURN. **come to a bad/sticky ˈend** to be led by one's actions to ruin, punishment, an unpleasant death, etc: *He'll come to a bad end one of these days.* **an**

ˌend in itˈself a thing that is considered important in its own right, though it may originally have had another purpose: *He began wood carving as a kind of therapy, but it soon became an end in itself.* **the end justifies the ˈmeans** (*saying*) even wrong or unfair methods may be allowed if the result or purpose of the action is good. **(reach) the end of the ˈline/ ˈroad** (*infml*) (to reach) the point at which one does not wish, or cannot bear, to continue in the same way: *It's sad that they got divorced but they had just about reached the end of the line.* **(not) the end of the ˈworld** (*infml*) (not) a complete disaster for sb: *You must realize that failing one exam is not the end of the world.* **ˌend ˈon 1** with the ends meeting or touching: *The two ships collided end on* (ie The front or back of one struck the front or back of the other). **2** with the end facing forwards: *push the bookcase end on through the door.* **(go to) the ˌends of the ˈearth** (to go to) the most remote parts of the world: *I'd go to the ends of the earth to see her again.* **ˌend to ˈend** in a line, with the ends touching: *arrange the tables end to end.* **get the wrong end of the stick** ⇨ WRONG. **go off the deep end** ⇨ DEEP¹. **in the ˈend 1** at last; finally: *He tried various different jobs and in the end he became an estate agent.* **2** when everything is taken into consideration: *You can try your best to impress the interviewers but in the end it's often just a question of luck.* **keep one's ˈend up** (*Brit infml*) to continue to be cheerful despite difficulties. **light at the end of the tunnel** ⇨ LIGHT¹. **make (both) ends ˈmeet** to earn enough money to live without getting into debt; to balance one's income and expenditure: *Being out of work and having two young children, they found it impossible to make ends meet.* **make one's hair stand on end** ⇨ HAIR. **a means to an end** ⇨ MEANS. **no ˈend** (*infml*) very much: *It saddened me no end to hear they'd split up.* **no ˈend of sth** (*infml*) very many or much; very great: *I've had no end of problems recently.* ○ *We had no end of trouble getting them to agree.* **not/never hear the end of sth** ⇨ HEAR. **on ˈend 1** upright rather than lying flat: *He placed the box on (its) end and sat on it.* **2** continuously: *It lasted for hours/days/weeks on end.* **put an ˈend to one's life/ oneself/it all** to kill oneself. **put an end / a stop to sth** to stop sth from happening any more: *The government is determined to put an end to terrorism.* **the sharp end** ⇨ SHARP. **the thin end of the wedge** ⇨ THIN. **throw sb in at the deep end** ⇨ DEEP¹. **to/until the bitter end** ⇨ BITTER.

■ **ˈend-product** *n* the final product of eg a manufacturing process.

ˌend reˈsult *n* [sing] the final outcome: *We couldn't find a taxi anywhere, so the end result was that we had to walk home.*

ˌend-ˈuser *n* (*esp computing*) a person who actually uses a product and for whom it is usu designed: *manuals geared to the end-user.*

end² /end/ *v* to finish or make sth finish: [V] *The road ends here* (ie goes no further). ○ *How does the story end?* [Vn] *They decided to end their relationship.* [Vnpr] *They ended the play with a song.* [Vpr] *Her note ended with the words: 'Sorry, I just can't go on.'* [also V.speech]. **IDM** **the be-all and end-all** ⇨ BE¹. **ˈend it all; ˌend one's ˈlife** to kill oneself: *He was so miserable that he seriously thought about ending it all.* **ˌend one's ˈdays/ˈlife (in sth)** to spend the last part of one's life in a particular state or place: *He ended his days in poverty.* **PHRV** **ˈend in sth 1** to have sth as its tip or ending: *The word ends in '-ous'.* **2** to have sth as a result or conclusion: *Their long struggle ended in failure.* ○ *The argument ended in tears.* ○ *The debate ended in uproar.* **ˌend ˈup** to reach or come to a certain place, state or action, esp by a long route or process: *If you go on like this you'll end up in prison.* ○ *After much discus-*

[Vnn] = verb + noun + noun   [V-adj] = verb + adjective   For more help with verbs, see Study pages **B4–8**.

sion about trips abroad we ended up in Cornwall. ○ At first he refused to accept any responsibility but he ended up apologizing. ○ If he carries on driving like that, he'll end up dead.
▶ **ending** n the end, esp of a story, film, play, etc or of a word: a story with a happy ending.

endanger /ɪnˈdeɪndʒə(r)/ v to cause danger to sb/sth; to put sb/sth in danger: [Vn] Smoking endangers your health. ○ Britain's economic interests could be endangered. ○ The giant panda is **an endangered species** (ie is in danger of becoming extinct).

endear /ɪnˈdɪə(r)/ v ~ **sb/oneself to sb** (fml) to make sb/oneself loved or liked by sb: [Vnpr] Her kindness to my children greatly endeared her to me. ○ He managed to endear himself to everybody.
▶ **endearing** adj causing or resulting in affection: an endearing remark/smile/habit. **endearingly** adv: an endearingly shy personality.
endearment n [C,U] a word or expression of affection: They were whispering endearments to each other. ○ 'Darling' is a term of endearment.

endeavour (US -**vor**) /ɪnˈdevə(r)/ n (fml) [U,C] an attempt or effort: Please make every endeavour to arrive punctually. ○ advances in every sphere of human endeavour ○ His endeavours should be fairly rewarded.
▶ **endeavour** v (fml) to try to do sth: [V.to inf] They endeavoured to make her happy, but in vain.

endemic /enˈdemɪk/ adj regularly found in a particular country or area, or among a particular group of people: Malaria is endemic in/to many hot countries. ○ an attitude endemic among senior members of the profession ○ the violence endemic in the city ○ plants endemic to (ie growing only in) Madagascar. Compare EPIDEMIC, PANDEMIC.

endive /ˈendaɪv, -dɪv/ n [C,U] **1** a plant with curled leaves which are eaten raw. **2** (US) = CHICORY.

endless /ˈendləs/ adj without end, or seeming to be without end: endless patience ○ endless opportunities for making money ○ an endless list of things to do ○ walking down endless corridors ○ The hours of waiting seemed endless. ○ I have to go to endless (ie very many) meetings. ▶ **endlessly** adv: talk endlessly about one's problems ○ notes endlessly repeated.

endorse /ɪnˈdɔːs/ v [Vn] **1** to give one's approval or support to a claim, statement, course of action, etc: The proposal was endorsed by the committee. ○ I am afraid I can't endorse (ie I disagree with) your opinion of the government's record. **2** to say in an advertisement that one uses and approves of a product: Well-known sportsmen can earn large sums of money from manufacturers by endorsing clothes and equipment. **3** to write one's name on the back of sth, esp a cheque. **4** (Brit) to record details of a driving offence on a driving-licence: He's had his licence endorsed for dangerous driving. ▶ **endorsement** n [U,C]: official endorsement of the scheme ○ an overwhelming endorsement of his policies ○ make money from endorsements and interviews on television ○ the endorsement of a cheque ○ He's had two endorsements for speeding.

endow /ɪnˈdaʊ/ v **1** ~ **sth (with sth)** to give money, property, etc to provide a regular income for a school, college, etc: [Vn] endow a bed in a hospital [Vnpr] endow the hospital with a bed. **2** ~ **sb/sth with sth** (esp passive) to provide sb/sth with a good quality, ability, feature, etc: [Vnpr] She's endowed with intelligence as well as good looks. ○ endow sb with authority/responsibility ○ a city endowed with numerous small parks.
▶ **endowment** n **1** [U] the action of endowing: the endowment of many schools by rich former pupils. **2** [C usu pl] money, property, etc given to provide an income: The Oxford and Cambridge colleges have numerous endowments. **3** [C usu pl] a natural talent, quality or ability: Few people are born with endow-

ments like his. **enˈdowment mortgage** n a type of MORTGAGE in which regular payments are made into an endowment policy and the loan is paid back on a specified date from the money that has accumulated.
enˈdowment policy n a form of life insurance in which a certain sum is paid to sb on a specified date or, if they die before this date, is paid to another specified person.

endurance /ɪnˈdjʊərəns; US -ˈdʊər-/ n [U] the ability or willingness to suffer patiently and without complaining or to tolerate a difficult situation for a long time: He showed remarkable endurance throughout his illness. ○ His treatment of her was **beyond endurance** (ie impossible to endure any longer). ○ reach the limits of human endurance ○ Jane's party was more of an **endurance test** (ie an occasion to suffer patiently) than anything else.

endure /ɪnˈdjʊə(r); US -ˈdʊər/ v **1** to suffer patiently sth that is painful or uncomfortable: [Vn] endure toothache ○ He endured three years in prison for his religious beliefs. **2** (esp in negative sentences) to tolerate a person, an event, etc: [Vn] I can't endure that woman a moment longer. [V.to inf, V.ing] He can't endure to be left alone/being left alone. **3** to continue in existence; to last: [V] fame that will endure for ever ○ as long as life endures ○ These traditions have endured for centuries.
▶ **endurable** /-rəbl/ adj that can be endured or tolerated: He found the boredom scarcely endurable.
enduring adj continuing in existence; lasting for a long time: enduring memories ○ an enduring peace/relationship ○ What is the reason for the game's enduring appeal? **enduringly** adv.

enema /ˈenəmə/ n the putting of liquid into the RECTUM by means of a SYRINGE, eg to clean out the bowels before an operation: give a patient an enema.

enemy /ˈenəmi/ n **1** [C] a person who strongly dislikes or wants to injure or attack sb/sth: Jane and Sarah used to be friends but now they are bitter enemies (ie of each other). ○ His arrogance made him many enemies (ie made many people hate him). **2(a)** **the enemy** [Gp] (the armed forces of) a country, side, etc with which one's country, side, etc is at war: The enemy was/were forced to retreat. ○ enemy forces/aircraft/ships ○ enemy propaganda. **(b)** [C] a member of such a force. **3** [C] anything that harms sb/sth or makes sb/sth weaker: Poverty and ignorance are the enemies of progress. **IDM** **be one's own worst enemy** ⇨ WORST.

energetic /ˌenəˈdʒetɪk/ adj full of or done with energy(1): an energetic child ○ take some energetic exercise. ▶ **energetically** /-kli/ adv: New overseas markets for the product are being energetically pursued.

energize, -ise /ˈenədʒaɪz/ v [Vn] **(a)** to give energy to sb/sth: motivate and energize workers. **(b)** to make electricity flow to a device.

energy /ˈenədʒi/ n **1** [U] the ability to put effort and enthusiasm into an activity, one's work, etc: She's full of energy. ○ His work seemed to lack energy. ○ It's a waste of time and energy. **2 energies** [pl] a person's physical and mental powers available for work or other activities: apply/devote all one's energies to a task. **3** [U] (physics) the ability of matter or RADIATION(1) to do work because of its motion, its mass, or its electric charge, etc. **4** [U] fuel and other sources of power used for operating machinery, etc: nuclear/electrical/solar energy ○ It is important to conserve energy. ○ energy efficiency ○ energy-saving measures ○ an energy crisis (eg when fuel is not freely available).

enervate /ˈenəveɪt/ v to make sb lose strength or energy: [Vn] an enervating argument/climate/illness. ▶ **enervation** /ˌenəˈveɪʃn/ n [U].

enfant terrible /ˌɒ̃fɒ̃ teˈriːbl/ n (pl **enfants terribles** /ˌɒ̃fɒ̃ teˈriːbl/) (French often joc) a usu young person whose behaviour, ideas, etc annoy, shock or embarrass those with more conventional attitudes: *Her advanced ideas have made her the enfant terrible of the art world.*

enfeeble /ɪnˈfiːbl/ v (*fml*) (esp passive) to make sb/ sth weak or FEEBLE: [Vn] *be enfeebled by a long illness* ○ *an enfeebled political system.*

enfold /ɪnˈfəʊld/ v ~ **sb/sth** (**in/with sth**) (*fml*) to enclose sb/sth, esp in one's arms; to surround sb/ sth closely: [Vnpr] *Enfolded in her arms, he felt warm and secure.* [Vn] *As night fell, the forest enfolded him, dark and protective.*

enforce /ɪnˈfɔːs/ v **1** ~ **sth** (**on/against sb**) to make sure that a law, rule, etc is obeyed; to make sth effective: [Vn] *a body set up to enforce pollution controls* [Vnpr] *enforce sanctions on/against a country.* **2** to make sth happen by force or necessity: [Vn] *enforced silence/discipline/idleness.* ▶ **enforceable** /-əbl/ *adj*: *Such a strict law is not easily enforceable.* **enforcement** *n* [U]: *law enforcement* ○ *the US Drug Enforcement Administration/Agency* ○ *strict enforcement of regulations.*

enfranchise /ɪnˈfræntʃaɪz/ v (*fml*) (esp passive) to give sb political rights, esp the right to vote at elections: [Vn] *In Britain women were enfranchised in 1918.* Compare DISENFRANCHISE. ▶ **enfranchisement** /ɪnˈfræntʃɪzmənt/ *n* [U].

Eng *abbr* **1** engineer(ing): *Tim Dale BSc (Eng).* **2** England; English.

engage /ɪnˈɡeɪdʒ/ v **1** (*fml*) to arrange to employ sb; to hire sb: [Vn] *engage a new secretary* [Vn.*to* inf] *He's been engaged to conduct a series of concerts at the Albert Hall.* [Vn-n] *She was engaged as an interpreter.* **2** (*fml*) to occupy or attract sb's thoughts, interest, etc: [Vn] *Nothing engages his attention for long.* ○ *We failed to engage any active support for the project.* **3** (*fml*) to begin fighting with sb: [V, Vn] *Our orders are to engage (the enemy) immediately.* [Vn] *Battle was engaged.* Compare DISENGAGE 2. **4** ~ (**with sth**) to establish contact with sb/sth in an attempt to understand them: [Vpr] *engage with modern art* ○ *A good politician must engage with people's real concerns.* [also V]. **5(a)** ~ (**with sth**) (of parts of a machine, etc) to fit or lock together: [V] *The two cog-wheels engaged and the machine started.* [Vpr] *One cog-wheel engages with another.* (**b**) to make parts of a machine, etc fit or lock together: [Vn] *engage the clutch/first gear* (eg in a car, when driving). Compare DISENGAGE 1. **PHRV** **enˈgage (sb) in sth** to take part in sth or make sb take part in sth: *I have no time to engage in gossip.* ○ *be engaged in politics/business* ○ *They are currently engaged in lengthy trade negotiations.* ○ *I engaged him in conversation.*

engaged *adj* [usu pred] **1** ~ (**on/upon sth**); ~ (**with sb/sth**) (of a person) busy; occupied: *I can't come to dinner on Tuesday; I'm otherwise engaged* (ie I have already arranged to do something else). ○ *The manager is engaged with a client at the moment.* ○ *He is now engaged on his first novel.* **2** (*Brit*) (*US* **busy**) (of a telephone line) in use: *Sorry! That number's engaged.* ○ *the engaged tone/signal* (ie the sound that indicates that a telephone line is engaged). **3** ~ (**to sb**) having agreed to marry: *She's engaged to Peter.* ○ *They're engaged (to be married)* (ie to each other). ○ *We're getting engaged.* ○ *an engaged couple.* **4** (esp of a toilet) occupied; already in use. Compare VACANT 1. ▶ **engaging** *adj* likely to attract or occupy the attention; charming: *an engaging smile/manner/ person.* **engagingly** *adv.*

engagement /ɪnˈɡeɪdʒmənt/ *n* **1** [C] an agreement that two people will marry: *Their engagement was announced in the local paper.* **2** [C] an arrangement to go somewhere, meet sb or do sth at a fixed time; an appointment: *I have very few engagements (for*

next week. ○ *The orchestra has several concert engagements.* **3** [C, U] (*fml*) a battle: *The general tried to avoid (an) engagement with the enemy.* **4** [U, sing] contact with or concern for sb/sth in an attempt to understand: *his engagement with theology* ○ *a continuing engagement with the problems of the inner city.* **5** [U] an arrangement to employ sb; the process leading to the employment of sb: *the engagement of three new assistants.* **6** [U] the action or result of engaging parts of a machine, etc: *after engagement of the clutch.* ■ **enˈgagement ring** *n* a ring, usu containing precious stones, that a man gives to a woman when they agree to marry.

engender /ɪnˈdʒendə(r)/ v (*fml*) to be the cause of a situation or condition: [Vn] *Some people believe that poverty engenders crime.*

engine /ˈendʒɪn/ *n* **1** a machine with moving parts that converts energy such as heat or electricity into motion: *a steam/diesel/petrol engine* ○ *My car had to have a new engine.* **2** (also **locomotive**) a machine that pulls or pushes a railway train: *I prefer to sit* (ie in a railway carriage) *facing the engine.* ▶ **-engined** (forming compound *adjs*) with the specified type or number of engines: *a twin-engined speedboat.* ■ **ˈengine-driver** (*Brit*) (*US* **engineer**) *n* a person who drives a railway engine.

engineer /ˌendʒɪˈnɪə(r)/ *n* **1** a skilled person who designs, builds or maintains engines, machines, bridges, railways, etc: *a mining/electrical/ mechanical engineer* ○ *a sound/lighting engineer* (eg in theatre or television) ○ *a software engineer.* See also CIVIL ENGINEER. **2** a skilled person who controls an engine or engines, esp on a ship or an aircraft: *a flight engineer* ○ *the chief engineer on a cruise liner.* **3** (*US*) = ENGINE-DRIVER. **4** a soldier trained to design and build military structures: *He's in the Royal Engineers* (ie a branch of the British Army). ▶ **engineer** *v* **1** (*often derog*) to arrange or cause sth, esp secretly for personal or political gain: [Vn] *engineer a plot/scheme/revolt* ○ *His enemies engineered his downfall.* **2** to build or control sth as an engineer: [Vn] *a brilliantly engineered recording.*

engineering /ˌendʒɪˈnɪərɪŋ/ *n* [U] (**a**) the practical application of scientific knowledge in the design, building and control of machines, roads, bridges, electrical apparatus, chemicals, etc: *electrical/ software/mechanical engineering* ○ *The new bridge is a triumph of engineering.* See also CHEMICAL ENGINEERING, CIVIL ENGINEERING, GENETIC ENGINEERING. (**b**) the work, science or profession of an engineer: *an engineering degree* ○ *She's studying engineering at Stanford University.*

English /ˈɪŋɡlɪʃ/ *n* [U] (**a**) the language of England, used in Britain, most countries in the British Commonwealth, the USA and some other countries: *He speaks excellent English.* ○ *I must work to improve my English.* (**b**) the study of this: *On Monday mornings we have English and History* (ie lessons in these subjects). **2 the English** [pl *v*] the people of England (sometimes wrongly used to mean the British, ie to include the Scots, the Welsh and the Irish). **IDM** **in plain English** ⇨ PLAIN¹. **the ˌKing's/ˌQueen's ˈEnglish** (in Britain) correct standard English. ▶ **English** *adj* **1** of England or its people: *the English countryside* ○ *English characteristics* ○ *He is very English in his attitudes.* **2** [attrib] of, written in or spoken in the English language: *an English translation* ○ *He's studying English literature.* ■ **ˌEnglish ˈbreakfast** *n* [C, U] a breakfast usu consisting of cooked bacon and eggs, TOAST¹ and MARMALADE, and tea or coffee. Compare CONTINENTAL BREAKFAST.

the ₁**English** ¹**Channel** (also **the Channel**) n [sing] the area of the sea between England and France.

Englishman /'ɪŋglɪʃmən/ n (pl **-men** /-mən/; fem **Englishwoman** /-wʊmən/, pl **-women** /-wɪmɪn/) a person born in England or one whose parents are English or one who has settled in England. **IDM an** ₁**Englishman's** ₁**home is his** ¹**castle** (Brit saying) an English person's home is a place where he or she may be private and safe and do as he or she wishes.

engrave /ɪn'greɪv/ v **1** ~ **B on A**/~ **A (with B)** to cut or carve words, designs, etc on a hard surface: [Vnpr] His name was engraved on the trophy. ○ The trophy was engraved with his name. [Vn] an engraved silver box. **2** ~ **sth on sth** (esp passive) to impress sth deeply on the memory or mind: [Vnpr] Memories of that terrible day are forever engraved on my mind.
▶ **engraver** n a person who engraves designs, etc on stone, metal, etc.
engraving /ɪn'greɪvɪŋ/ n **1** [U] the art of cutting or carving designs on metal, stone, etc. **2** [C] a picture printed from an engraved metal plate: I bought an old engraving of the cathedral.

engross /ɪn'grəʊs/ v ~ **sb/oneself (in sth)** to occupy all the time or attention of sb: [Vn] The subject continues to engross her. ○ It makes an engrossing story. [Vnpr] be engrossed in one's work/a book.

engulf /ɪn'gʌlf/ v ~ **sb/sth (in sth)** (of the sea, flames, etc) to surround sb/sth, esp so that they are completely covered: [Vn] a boat engulfed in/by the waves ○ Lava threatened to engulf the village. ○ She was engulfed in a crowd of reporters.

enhance /ɪn'hɑːns; US -'hæns/ v to increase or improve further the good quality, value or status of sb/sth: [Vn] enhance the reputation/position of sb ○ enhanced efficiency/importance ○ his enhanced power and influence ○ Those clothes do nothing to enhance her appearance. ▶ **enhancement** n [U,C]: computer enhancement of a photograph ○ implement a number of modifications and enhancements to a product.

enigma /ɪ'nɪgmə/ n (pl **enigmas**) a question, person, thing, circumstance, etc that is difficult to understand; a mystery: I've known him for many years, but he remains a complete enigma to me.
▶ **enigmatic** /ˌenɪg'mætɪk/ adj difficult to understand; mysterious: an enigmatic character/smile/statement. **enigmatically** /-klɪ/ adv.

enjoin /ɪn'dʒɔɪn/ v (fml) (often passive) to give instructions or advice to sb: [Vn,Vnpr] He enjoined obedience (on his followers). [Vn.to inf] We were enjoined not to betray the trust placed in us.

enjoy /ɪn'dʒɔɪ/ v **1** to get pleasure from sth: [Vn] I enjoyed the evening enormously. [V.ing] She enjoys playing tennis. **2** to have sth as an advantage or a benefit: [Vn] enjoy good health/a high standard of living/great prosperity ○ Men and women should enjoy equal rights. **IDM** ₁**en**¹**joy oneself** to experience pleasure; to be happy: He thoroughly enjoyed himself at the party. ○ The children seem to be enjoying themselves.
▶ **enjoyable** /-əbl/ adj giving pleasure; bringing happiness: an enjoyable weekend ○ The play was immensely/tremendously enjoyable. ⇨ note at NICE. **enjoyably** /-əbli/ adv.
enjoyment /ɪn'dʒɔɪmənt/ n **1(a)** [U] pleasure; satisfaction: He spoiled my enjoyment of the film by talking all the time. ○ She lives only for enjoyment. **(b)** [C] (fml) a thing that gives pleasure or satisfaction: Gardening is one of her chief enjoyments. **2** [U] (fml) the possession and use of sth: the enjoyment of equal rights/status.

enlarge /ɪn'lɑːdʒ/ v **1(a)** to become or make sth larger: [Vn] The building has been considerably enlarged. ○ enlarge one's understanding of sth ○ an enlarged heart/gland [also V]. **(b)** to reproduce a

document or photograph on a larger scale: [Vn] The police had the photograph of the missing girl enlarged. **2** ~ **(on sth)** to say or write more about sth; to add detail: [V,Vpr] Can you enlarge (on what has already been said)?
▶ **enlargement** n **1** [U] the action or process of enlarging sth or of being enlarged: the enlargement of the company's overseas activities. **2** [C] a thing that has been enlarged, esp a photograph: If you like the picture I can send you an enlargement of it. Compare REDUCTION 2.

enlighten /ɪn'laɪtn/ v to give sb greater knowledge or understanding: [Vn] I don't know how to dial a number in Athens — could you enlighten me? ○ The report makes enlightening reading.
▶ **enlightened** adj [esp attrib] (approv) free from prejudice, false beliefs, etc; having or showing an understanding of what the current situation requires, rather than following conventional thought: in these enlightened days ○ enlightened opinions/attitudes/ideas ○ an enlightened approach to teaching.
enlightenment n [U] (fml): The book adds little to our knowledge or enlightenment.

enlist /ɪn'lɪst/ v **1** ~ **(sb) (in/into/for sth)**; ~ **(sb) (as sth)** to enter or cause sb to enter the armed forces: [V] He enlisted at the age of 17. [Vpr,V-n] enlist in the Army/as a soldier [Vn] They enlisted four hundred new recruits. [also Vnpr]. **2** ~ **sth/sb (in sth/doing sth)** to obtain sth as help, support, etc; to get sb to provide help, support, etc: [Vn] a demonstration designed to enlist public sympathy [Vnpr] Can I enlist your help in collecting money for the appeal? [Vn] We've enlisted a few extra volunteers. [Vn.to inf] Sarah has been enlisted to organize the party.
▶ **enlistment** n [U] **1** the action of enlisting or being enlisted in the armed forces: voluntary enlistment. **2** the use of sb/sth to provide help, support, etc.
■ **en**₁**listed** ¹**man** n (esp US) a male member of the armed forces whose rank is below that of an officer.

enliven /ɪn'laɪvn/ v to make sb/sth more lively, cheerful or interesting: [Vn] His jokes enlivened an otherwise dull evening. ○ Try some unusual spices to enliven your cooking.

en masse /ˌɒ̃ 'mæs/ adv (French) in a mass or crowd; all together: Individually the children are delightful; en masse they can be unbearable. ○ The guests arrived en masse.

enmesh /ɪn'meʃ/ v ~ **sb/sth (in sth)** (usu passive) to involve sb/sth in a situation from which they are unable to escape: [Vnpr] He soon became enmeshed in a world of crime. [also Vn].

enmity /'enmɪti/ n [U,C] a state of or feelings of hostility towards sb: I don't understand his enmity towards his parents. ○ traditional enmities between tribes.

ennoble /ɪ'nəʊbl/ v (fml) **1** to make sb a member of the NOBILITY(2): [Vn-n] He was later ennobled as the first Baron Aldington. [also Vn]. **2** to give sb/sth greater dignity: [Vn] In a strange way she seemed ennobled by the grief she had experienced. ▶ **ennoblement** n [U].

ennui /ɒn'wiː/ n [U] the state of being bored and not satisfied because nothing interesting is happening: a sad play about middle-aged ennui.

enormity /ɪ'nɔːməti/ n **1** [U] the great size, extent or scale of sth: the enormity of a task/challenge/decision ○ People are still coming to terms with the enormity of the disaster. ○ The enormity of the crime has shocked the whole country. **2** [C usu pl] (fml) a very serious crime or sin: the enormities of the Hitler regime.

enormous /ɪ'nɔːməs/ adj very large; huge; IMMENSE: an enormous amount of money/effort ○ an enormous house ○ enormous interest/pressure/

E

responsibility ○ *The implications of the decision are enormous.*

▶ **enormously** *adv* to a very great extent: *enormously rich/influential* ○ *I enjoyed the evening enormously.* ○ *I'm enormously grateful for your help.*

enough¹ /ɪˈnʌf/ *indef det* (usu used in front of plural or uncountable *ns*) ~ **sth (for sb/sth)**; ~ **sth (for sb) to do sth** as many or as much of sth as necessary or desirable; sufficient: *Have you made enough copies?* ○ *Is there enough room for me in the car?* ○ *We have enough problems already.* ○ *I haven't got enough money to pay for a taxi.* ○ *Surely 15 minutes is enough time for you to have a bath.* ○ (dated) *There is time enough to get to the airport.* Compare SUFFICIENT.

▶ **enough** *indef pron* as many or as much as necessary or desirable: *Six bottles of wine should be enough.* ○ *Is $500 enough for your expenses?* ○ *I think I got enough of the questions right to pass.* ○ *That's enough of my problems. Let's talk about something else.* **IDM** **e,nough is eˈnough** (*saying*) it is not necessary or desirable to say or do more. **have had eˈnough (of sth/sb)** to be unable or unwilling to tolerate sth/sb any more: *After three years without promotion he decided he'd had enough and resigned.* ○ *I've had enough of your continual complaints!* ○ *I've had enough of you and I don't want to see you again!*

enough² /ɪˈnʌf/ *adv* (used after *vs, adjs* and *advs*) **1** ~ **(for sb/sth) (to do sth)** to a necessary, desirable or acceptable extent: *You're not improving because you don't practise enough.* ○ *The house wasn't big enough for us.* ○ *She's old enough to make her own decisions.* ○ *The instructions weren't clear enough for me to understand.* ○ *The government did not act swiftly enough.* **2** to a certain but not very great extent: *She plays well enough for a beginner.* ○ *He's nice enough but he doesn't particularly impress me.* **IDM** **,curiously, ,oddly, ,strangely, etc enough** it is very strange, etc that...: *Curiously enough, I said the same thing to my wife only yesterday.* **,enough ˈsaid** there is no need to say any more because I understand what you mean and accept the position. **fair enough** ⇨ FAIR². **funnily enough** ⇨ FUNNILY. **sure enough** ⇨ SURE.

en passant /ˌɒ̃ ˈpæsɒ̃/ *adv* (*French*) briefly and while talking about sth else; in passing: *He mentioned en passant that he was going away.*

enquire = INQUIRE.

enquiry = INQUIRY.

enrage /ɪnˈreɪdʒ/ *v* (esp passive) to make sb very angry: [Vnpr] *be enraged at/by sb's stupidity* [Vn] *His arrogance enraged her.*

enrapture /ɪnˈræptʃə(r)/ *v* (esp passive) (*fml*) to fill sb with great delight or joy: [Vn] *an enraptured audience* ○ *We were enraptured by the view.*

enrich /ɪnˈrɪtʃ/ *v* **1** to make sb/sth rich or richer: [Vn] *a nation enriched by oil revenues* ○ *There seemed no reason why he should not also enrich himself.* **2** to improve the quality, flavour, value, etc of sth: [Vnpr] *soil enriched with fertilizer* [Vn] *experiences which enrich our lives.* ▶ **enrichment** *n* [U].

enrol (also *esp US* **enroll**) /ɪnˈrəʊl/ *v* (**-ll-**) ~ **(sb) (in/on sth)**; ~ **(sb) (as sth)** to become or make sb a member of a group, a student on a course, etc; to register: [Vpr] *enrol in evening classes* [V] *You need to enrol before the end of August.* [Vn] *The society is hoping to enrol new members.* [also Vnpr, Vn-n].

▶ **,Enrolled ˈNurse** *n* (*Brit*) (*US* **,Licensed Practical ˈNurse**) a person who has trained as a nurse and passed examinations that allow her or him to practise most areas of nursing.

enrollee /ɪnˌrəʊˈliː/ *n* (*esp US*) a person who has enrolled in a class, school, etc.

enrolment (also *esp US* **enrollment**) *n* (**a**) [U] the action of enrolling: *enrolment fees* ○ *The aim of the school's advertisement is to increase enrolment.* (**b**)

[C] a number of people enrolled: *School enrolments are currently falling.*

en route /ˌɒn ˈruːt/ *adv* ~ **(from...)** **(to...)**; ~ **(for...)** (*French*) on the way; while travelling: *stop for a picnic en route* ○ *We stopped at Paris en route from Rome to London.* ○ *They passed through Paris en route for Rome.*

ensconce /ɪnˈskɒns/ *v* ~ **oneself/sb at, by, in, etc sth** (*fml or joc*) (esp passive) to establish or settle oneself in a safe, comfortable or pleasant place: [Vnpr] *happily ensconced by the fire with a good book* ○ *They ensconced themselves in the most beautiful villa in the South of France.*

ensemble /ɒnˈsɒmbl/ *n* **1** a small group of musicians, dancers or actors who perform together: *a woodwind ensemble.* **2** a set of clothes worn together; an OUTFIT(1): *A pair of pink shoes completed her striking ensemble.* **3** a number of things viewed as a whole: *The arrangement of the furniture formed a pleasing ensemble.*

enshrine /ɪnˈʃraɪn/ *v* (*fml*) ~ **sth (in sth)** (usu passive) to preserve sth in a place or form so that it will be remembered and respected: [Vn] *enshrine a belief/a right/a truth* [Vnpr] *a commitment enshrined in the constitution.*

enshroud /ɪnˈʃraʊd/ *v* (*fml*) (often passive) to cover sth so that it cannot be seen: [Vn] *Heavy clouds enshrouded the city.*

ensign /ˈensən/ *n* **1** a flag flown by a ship, esp one that indicates which country it belongs to: *the white ensign* (ie the flag of the British Royal Navy). **2** (*US*) an officer of the lowest rank in the navy. ⇨ App 6.

enslave /ɪnˈsleɪv/ *v* to make sb a slave: [Vn] *Early colonists enslaved and oppressed the natives.* ○ (*fig*) [Vnpr] *We have become enslaved to the motor car.* ▶ **enslavement** *n* [U]: *the enslavement of whole villages.*

ensnare /ɪnˈsneə(r)/ *v* ~ **sb/sth (in sth)** (esp passive) to catch sb/sth in, or as if in, a trap: [Vn] *ensnare an animal* [Vnpr] *He became ensnared in the complexities of the legal system.*

ensue /ɪnˈsjuː; *US* -ˈsuː/ *v* to happen afterwards or as a result; to follow: [V] *Chaos/Panic ensued.* ○ *in the ensuing* (ie following) *years.*

en suite /ˌɒ̃ ˈswiːt/ *adv, adj* (*French*) (of rooms, etc) forming a single unit: *Each bedroom in the hotel has a bathroom en suite / an en suite bathroom.*

ensure /ɪnˈʃʊə(r)*; Brit also* -ˈʃɔː(r)/ *v* to make sure of sth or make sb sure of sth; to guarantee sth: [Vn] *The book ensured his success.* [V.that] *Please ensure that all the lights are switched off at night.* [Vnn] *These pills should ensure you a good night's sleep.*

-ent ⇨ -ANT.

entail /ɪnˈteɪl/ *v* to involve sth as a necessary or inevitable part or consequence: [Vn] *This job entails a lot of hard work.* ○ *I dread moving house and all that it entails.* ○ *That will entail an early start tomorrow morning.*

entangle /ɪnˈtæŋgl/ *v* (often passive) **1** ~ **sb/sth/oneself (in/with sth)** to cause sb/sth/oneself to become twisted together with or caught in sth: [Vnpr] *The bird was entangled in the wire netting.* ○ *a fishing-line entangled with weeds* ○ *Her long hair entangled itself/got entangled in the rose-bush.* [also Vn]. **2** ~ **sb/oneself in sth/with sb** to involve sb/oneself in difficulties or complicated circumstances: [Vnpr] *become entangled in money problems* ○ *She would not let herself become entangled* (ie have a close emotional relationship) *with him.*

▶ **entanglement** *n* **1** [U] the action of entangling or the state of being entangled: *many dolphins die from entanglement in fishing-nets.* **2** [C often *pl*] a complicated or difficult relationship or situation: *entanglements with the police* ○ *emotional entanglements* ○ *an entanglement that destroyed his career.*

---

entente /ɒn'tɒnt/ n [U, sing] a friendly understanding, esp between countries: *bring about/strengthen an entente.*
■ ˌentente ˌcordi'ale /ˌkɔːdi'ɑːl/ n an entente between two countries, esp that between Britain and France.

enter /'entə(r)/ v **1(a)** to come or go in or into sth: [V] *Don't enter without knocking.* [Vn] *enter a room* ○ *The train entered the tunnel.* ○ *Where did the bullet enter the body?* ○ *A note of defiance entered her voice.* ○ *It never entered my head/mind* (ie I never thought) *that she would tell him about me.* **(b)** to come or go onto a stage during a play: [V] *Enter Hamlet/Hamlet enters* (eg as stage directions in a printed play). **2** (no passive) to become a member of sth, esp an institution or a profession: [Vn] *enter a school/college/university* ○ *enter the Army/Navy/Air Force* ○ *enter politics/the legal profession* ○ *enter Parliament* (ie become an MP) ○ *enter the Church* (ie become a priest). **3** to begin or become involved in an activity, a situation, etc: [Vn] *enter a relationship/conflict/war* ○ *The investigation has now entered a new phase.* ○ *The strike is entering its fourth week.* **4** ~ (**for sth**); ~ **sb** (**in/for sth**) to declare that one/sb/sth will take part in a competition, etc: [Vn] *enter a race/an examination* ○ *Several new firms have now entered the market* (ie are competing to sell their products with those already involved). [Vnpr] *enter a horse in a race* [V, Vpr] *Only four British players have entered (for the tournament).* **5** ~ **sth** (**up**) (**in/into/on sth**) to record names, details, etc in a book, computer, etc; to register sth: [Vn] *I haven't entered your name and occupation yet.* [Vnpr] *All sales must be entered in the ledger.* ○ *enter data into a computer* ○ *enter figures on a spreadsheet* [Vnp] *Enter up all the items purchased.* **6** (*fml*) to present sth officially: [Vn] *enter a plea of not guilty* (ie at the beginning of a court case) ○ *enter a protest.* **IDM** **enter one's name/put one's name down** ⇨ NAME[1]. **PHRV** **'enter into sth** to begin to deal with sth: *Let's not enter into details at this stage.* **2** to take an active part in sth: *enter into the spirit of an occasion* (ie begin to enjoy and feel part of it). **3** (not passive) to form part of or have an influence on sth: *This possibility never entered into our calculations.* ○ *Your personal feelings shouldn't enter into this at all.* **'enter into sth (with sb)** to begin or become involved in sth: *enter into a contract* ○ *enter into negotiations/conversation/correspondence.* **'enter on/upon sth** (*fml*) to make a start on sth; to begin sth: *enter on a new career* ○ *The President has just entered upon his second term of office.*

enterprise /'entəpraɪz/ n **1** [C] a project or an activity, esp one that is difficult or requires effort: *his latest business enterprise* ○ *a joint enterprise* ○ *The music festival is a new enterprise which we hope will become an annual event.* See also VENTURE. **2** [U] (*approv*) the ability, imagination and desire to create or carry out new projects or activities: *a job in which enterprise is rewarded* ○ *Throughout his business career he showed considerable enterprise and flair.* **3(a)** [U] business activity developed and managed by individuals rather than the state: *creating an economic environment to encourage enterprise* ○ *a network of enterprise agencies* (ie organizations created to encourage the development of small businesses). See also FREE ENTERPRISE, PRIVATE ENTERPRISE. **(b)** [C] a business company or firm: *local/large-scale/state-owned enterprises.*
▶ **enterprising** *adj* (*approv*) having or showing enterprise(2): *an enterprising company/economy* ○ *an enterprising idea/move* ○ *Peru has become increasingly popular with the more enterprising tourist.*

entertain /ˌentə'teɪn/ v **1** ~ **sb** (**to sth**) to receive sb as a guest; to provide food and drink for sb, esp in one's home: [V] *I don't entertain very often.* ○ *They do a lot of entertaining* (ie often give parties, have guests for meals, etc). [Vnpr] *Bob and Liz entertained us to dinner last night.* [Vn] *They entertain a stream of visitors throughout the summer.* **2** ~ **sb** (**with sth**) to provide sth interesting or enjoyable for sb; to amuse sb: [Vn] *Could you entertain the children for an hour, while I make supper?* [Vnpr] *He entertained us for hours with his stories and jokes.* **3** (*fml*) (not in the continuous tenses) to consider or give attention to an idea, a suggestion, a feeling, etc: [Vn] *He refuses even to entertain the notion that he might be wrong.* ○ *I have for some time entertained doubts about the wisdom of government policy.*
▶ **entertainer** n a person whose job is entertaining (ENTERTAIN 2) people, eg by singing, telling jokes or dancing: *a well-known television entertainer.*
entertaining *adj* interesting and enjoyable; amusing: *a most entertaining speech* ○ *The film was very entertaining.* **entertainingly** *adv.*
entertainment n **1** [U] the action of entertaining or the process of being entertained: *a budget for the entertainment of clients* ○ *a place of entertainment* ○ *He fell in the water, much to the entertainment of the children.* **2** [C] a thing that entertains; a public performance to entertain people: *The local entertainments are listed in the newspaper.*

enthral (also *esp US* **enthrall**) /ɪn'θrɔːl/ v (**-ll-**) (esp passive) to capture the whole of sb's attention; to interest or entertain sb greatly: [Vn] *enthralled by her beauty* ○ *a book to enthral readers of all ages.* ▶ **enthralling** *adj: an enthralling performance.*

enthrone /ɪn'θrəʊn/ v (*fml*) (esp passive) to place a king, queen or bishop on a THRONE(1), esp during a special ceremony to mark the beginning of their rule: [Vn] *The new archbishop was enthroned in York Minster.* ▶ **enthronement** n [U, C].

enthuse /ɪn'θjuːz; *US* -θuːz/ v (**a**) ~ (**about/over sth/sb**) to show or speak with great excitement, admiration or interest: [Vpr] *He hasn't stopped enthusing about his holiday since he returned.* ○ *They all enthused over the new baby.* [V] *Although the critics enthused, I thought it was a mediocre play.* [also V.speech]. (**b**) to make sb feel very interested and excited: [Vn] *As a speaker he had the ability to enthuse audiences.*

enthusiasm /ɪn'θjuːziæzəm; *US* -ˌθuː-/ n ~ (**for/about sth**) **1** [U] a strong feeling of excitement, admiration or interest; great eagerness: *The news was greeted with lack of enthusiasm in the City.* ○ *I can't say I share your enthusiasm for/about the idea.* ○ *He has the ability to generate enthusiasm in others.* **2** [C] a thing causing this feeling: *Gardening is one of her many enthusiasms.*
▶ **enthusiast** /ɪn'θjuːziæst; *US* -'θuː-/ n ~ (**for sth**) a person who habitually enjoys or feels enthusiasm for sth: *a railway enthusiast* ○ *I'm not a great enthusiast for this form of exercise.*
enthusiastic /ɪnˌθjuːzi'æstɪk; *US* -ˌθuː-/ *adj* ~ (**about sb/sth/doing sth**) feeling or showing enthusiasm: *enthusiastic applause* ○ *He doesn't know much about the subject, but he's very enthusiastic.* ○ *She's very enthusiastic about singing.* **enthusiastically** /-klɪ/ *adv: He talks enthusiastically about buying a villa in Italy.*

entice /ɪn'taɪs/ v ~ **sb** (**away**) (**from sth**) (**to sth**); ~ **sb** (**into sth/doing sth**) to tempt or persuade sb to move from one place or activity to another, usu by offering them sth pleasant or valuable: [Vnpr] *Advertisements are designed to entice people into the shops/into spending money.* ○ *He was enticed away from the firm by an offer of higher pay elsewhere.* ○ *He enticed his victim to a remote spot.* [Vn.to inf] *The prospectus enticed over 3 million people to buy shares.* [also Vnp].
▶ **enticement** n [C, U]: *I was unable to resist the enticements offered by the new job.*

enticing adj attractive or tempting: *The offer was too enticing to refuse.* ○ *An enticing smell came from the kitchen.* **enticingly** adv.

entire /ɪnˈtaɪə(r)/ adj [attrib] with no part left out; whole; complete: *The entire village was destroyed.* ○ *I've wasted an entire day on this.* ○ *We are in entire agreement with you.*
▶ **entirely** adv completely: *entirely unnecessary* ○ *Although they are twins, they look entirely different.* ○ *I'm not entirely happy about the proposal.*
entirety /ɪnˈtaɪərəti/ n (fml) **1** [U] the state of being entire or complete: *We must examine the problem in its entirety* (ie as a whole, not in parts only). **2** [sing] ~ **of sth** the whole of sth: *His string quartets span the entirety of his creative life.*

entitle /ɪnˈtaɪtl/ v **1** (usu passive) to give a title to a book, play, etc: [Vn-n] *She read a poem entitled 'The Apple Tree'.* **2** ~ **sb to sth / to do sth** (esp passive) to give sb a right to have or do sth: [Vnpr] *You are not entitled to unemployment benefit if you have never worked.* ○ *After a hard day's work one feels entitled to a rest.* [V.n to inf] *This ticket does not entitle you to travel first-class.* ▶ **entitlement** n [U,C] ~ **(to sth):** *I am writing to confirm your entitlement to housing benefit.* ○ *Have you claimed your full holiday entitlement?* ○ *All leave entitlements are equally available to men and women.*

entity /ˈentəti/ n a thing with distinct and independent existence: *a separate legal/political entity.*

entomb /ɪnˈtuːm/ v (fml) (usu passive) to place sb/sth in, or as if in, a TOMB; to bury sb/sth in or under sth: [Vn] *the site where ancient kings were entombed* [Vnpr] *Many people were entombed in the rubble of the collapsed buildings.*

entomology /ˌentəˈmɒlədʒi/ n [U] the scientific study of insects.
▶ **entomologist** /-dʒɪst/ n an expert in entomology.

entourage /ˌɒntuˈrɑːʒ/ n [CGp] all those who accompany and assist or serve an important person: *the President and his (immediate) entourage* ○ (fig) *the band's entourage of adoring fans.*

entrails /ˈentreɪlz/ n [pl] the internal organs of a person or an animal, esp the intestines (INTESTINE): *The dish was made from the entrails of a sheep.*

entrance¹ /ˈentrəns/ n **1** [C] ~ **(to sth)** an opening, a gate, a door, a passage, etc through which one enters sth: *the entrance to a cave* ○ *There is a front and a back entrance to the house.* ○ *an entrance hall/lobby* ○ *I'll meet you at the main entrance to the theatre.* **2** [C usu sing] ~ **(into/onto sth)** the act of coming or going in; the act of entering or becoming involved in sth: *His sudden entrance took everyone by surprise.* ○ *The company made a dramatic entrance into the export market.* ○ *The hero makes his entrance (onto the stage) in Scene 2.* Compare EXIT 1. **3** [U] ~ **(to sth)** the right, means or opportunity to enter a place or be a member of sth; admission: *They were refused entrance to the club.* ○ *Police officers gained entrance to the building and searched it.* ○ *a university entrance examination* ○ *an entrance fee* (ie money paid so that one may enter an exhibition, etc or join a club or society). Compare ENTRY.

entrance² /ɪnˈtrɑːns; US -ˈtræns/ v (usu passive) to fill sb with wonder or delight: [Vn] *They were completely entranced by the music.* ○ *We sat/watched/listened entranced.* ▶ **entrancing** adj: *an entrancing voice* ○ *The view was quite entrancing.*

entrant /ˈentrənt/ n **1** a person or an animal that enters a race, a competition or an examination: *the winning entrants* ○ *There are fifty entrants for the dog show.* **2** ~ **(to sth)** a person who enters a profession or an institution: *university entrants* ○ *an entrant to the diplomatic service* ○ *new women entrants to the police force.*

entrap /ɪnˈtræp/ v (-pp-) (fml) (esp passive) **1** to catch sb/sth in a trap or place from which they cannot escape: [Vn] *The entrapped water expands on freezing.* **2** ~ **sb (into doing sth)** to trick or deceive sb so that they find themselves in a difficult, embarrassing, etc situation: [Vnpr] *He felt he had been entrapped into marrying her.* [also Vn].
▶ **entrapment** n [U] **1** (fml) the action of entrapping sb/sth or the process of being entrapped. **2** (law) the action of tempting sb to commit a crime so that they can be caught while doing so.

entreat /ɪnˈtriːt/ v (fml) to ask sb sth in a very anxious or serious manner; to beg: [Vn] *Please don't go, I entreat you.* [Vn.to inf] *He entreated the king to grant him one wish.* ⇨ note at ASK.

entreaty /ɪnˈtriːti/ n [C,U] (fml) a very HUMBLE(1) or serious request: *He was deaf to all her entreaties.*

entrée /ˈɒntreɪ/ n (fml) **1** [U,C] ~ **(into/to sth)** a right of or means of gaining admission to a social group, an institution, an area of activity, etc: *Her wealth and reputation gave her an entrée into upper-class circles.* **2** [C] (a) a dish served between the fish and meat courses at a formal dinner. (b) the main course of a meal: *choose from the entrées on the menu.*

entrench (also **intrench**) /ɪnˈtrentʃ/ v (usu passive) **1** ~ **oneself/sb/sth (in sth)** (sometimes derog) to establish sb/sth very firmly with the result that change is very difficult or unlikely: [Vn] *entrenched ideas/habits* ○ *entrenched rights* (ie those that are guaranteed by law) [Vnpr] *She is deeply/firmly/thoroughly entrenched in her views.* ○ *The firm has entrenched itself in the markets of Eastern Europe.* **2** to surround or protect sb/sth with a TRENCH or trenches: [Vn] *The enemy was strongly entrenched on the other side of the river.*
▶ **entrenchment** n **1** [U] the action of entrenching sb/sth or the state of being entrenched. **2** [C] a system of trenches (TRENCH¹) made for defence.

entrepreneur /ˌɒntrəprəˈnɜː(r)/ n a person who starts or organizes a commercial enterprise, esp one involving financial risk: *local business entrepreneurs* ○ *The role of theatrical entrepreneur excited him.* ▶
entrepreneurial /-ˈnɜːriəl/ adj: *entrepreneurial flair/skills/spirit* ○ *Some investors have become more entrepreneurial.* **entrepreneurship** n [U]: *the need to encourage entrepreneurship.*

entrust /ɪnˈtrʌst/ v ~ **A to B / ~ B with A** to give responsibility for sb/sth to sb: [Vnpr] *entrust an assistant with the task/entrust the task to an assistant* ○ *They entrusted their children to him/to his care for the day.*

entry /ˈentri/ n **1(a)** [C usu sing] ~ **(into sth)** an act of coming or going in: *make an entry* ○ *The children were surprised by the sudden entry of their teacher.* ○ *The thieves had forced an entry into the building.* (b) [U] ~ **(to/into sth)** the right, means or opportunity to enter a place or be a member of sth: *We can't go along that road because the sign says 'No Entry'.* ○ *He finally gained entry to the hotel by giving some money to the doorman.* ○ *museums that charge for entry* ○ *seek entry into/to the EU* ○ *be granted/refused entry to a country* ○ *an entry visa* (ie a stamp or signature on a PASSPORT(1) allowing sb to enter a particular country). **2** (US also **entryway** /ˈentriweɪ/) [C] (a) an entrance, esp a passage or small entrance hall: *the entry to a block of flats* ○ *You can leave your umbrella in the entry.* (b) (Brit) a narrow passage between buildings. **3(a)** [C] ~ **(in sth)** an item written or printed in a list, an account book, a reference book, etc: *entries in a dictionary/an encyclopedia* ○ *There is no entry in his diary for that day.* ○ *I'll have to check the entries in the ledger.* (b) [U] the act of recording such an item: *More keyboarding staff are required for data entry.* **4** ~ **(for sth)** (a) [C] a person or thing competing in a contest, race, etc: *fifty entries for the 800 metres* ○ *a last-minute entry for the pony race* ○ *This painting is my entry for the art competition.* ○

Entries must arrive by 31 March. (**b**) [U] the action of entering a contest, race, etc: *an entry form/fee* ○ *Entry is open to anyone over the age of 18.* (**c**) [sing] a list of or the total number of people, etc entered in a contest, race, etc: *There's a large entry for the flower show this year.* Compare ENTRANCE¹.

Entryphone /'entrɪfəʊn/ *n* (*propr*) a type of telephone placed on the wall by the entrance to a building, esp a block of flats, through which visitors speak to sb inside before being allowed to enter.

entwine /ɪn'twaɪn/ *v* ~ sth (**with/in/round sth**) (esp passive) to twist or wind sth in or around sth else: [Vn] *They walked along with (their) arms entwined.* ○ (*fig*) *Their lives were closely entwined.* [Vnpr] *a mirror entwined with gilt roses.*

E-number ⇨ E¹.

enumerate /ɪ'njuːməreɪt; *US* ɪ'nuː-/ *v* (*fml*) to name things on a list one by one: [Vn] *She enumerated her objections to the proposals.*

enunciate /ɪ'nʌnsɪeɪt/ *v* **1** to say or pronounce words or sounds clearly: [V] *An actor must learn to enunciate.* [Vn] *She enunciated each word slowly for her students.* **2** (*fml*) to express a theory, an idea, etc clearly or distinctly: [Vn] *an opinion first enunciated in a letter to his father.* ▶ **enunciation** /ɪˌnʌnsɪ'eɪʃn/ *n* [U].

envelop /ɪn'veləp/ *v* ~ sth/sb (**in sth**) to wrap sth/sb up in sth; to cover or surround sth/sb completely: [Vnpr] *mountains enveloped in cloud* ○ *a baby enveloped in a blanket* ○ (*fig*) *a country enveloped in political violence* [Vn] *The coat was far too big — it completely enveloped him.*

envelope /'envələʊp, 'ɒn-/ *n* a flat paper container that can be sealed and in which letters, etc are sent: *writing-paper and envelopes* ○ *an airmail envelope* ○ *a stamped addressed envelope.*

enviable /'enviəbl/ *adj* (of people or things) causing envy; desirable enough to cause envy: *an enviable achievement/position/salary* ○ *lead an enviable life.* ▶ **enviably** /-bli/ *adv.*

envious /'enviəs/ *adj* ~ (**of sb/sth**) feeling or showing envy: *I'm so envious — I wish I had your talent.* ○ *She cast envious eyes/glances at her sister's dress.* ○ *He was envious of his brother's success.* ▶ **enviously** *adv:* *look enviously at sb.*

environment /ɪn'vaɪrənmənt/ *n* **1** [C usu *sing*] the conditions, circumstances, etc affecting a person's life: *live in a polluted environment* ○ *a competitive environment* ○ *An unhappy home environment can affect a child's behaviour.* ○ *A noisy smoke-filled room is not the best environment to work in.* **2** the **environment** [sing] the natural conditions, eg land, air and water, in which people, animals and plants live: *measures to protect the environment* ○ *Many people are concerned about the pollution of the environment.* ▶ **environmental** /ɪnˌvaɪrən'mentl/ *adj* (**a**) of or relating to the natural environment: *the environmental impact of pollution* ○ *environmental issues/problems.* (**b**) of or relating to a person's environment: *environmental health.* **environmentalist** /ɪnˌvaɪrən'mentəlɪst/ *n* a person who is concerned about and wants to improve or protect the environment: *Environmentalists are calling for the new pesticide regulations to be strictly enforced.* **environmentally** /-təli/ *adv: a policy that is environmentally sound* ○ *an environmentally sensitive area* (ie one that is easily damaged or that contains rare species) ○ *environmentally friendly products* (ie those which do not damage the environment). ⇨ note at ECOLOGY, USER-FRIENDLY.

environs /ɪn'vaɪrənz/ *n* [pl] (*fml*) the region surrounding a place, esp a town: *Berlin and its environs.*

envisage /ɪn'vɪzɪdʒ/ (also *esp US* **envision** /ɪn'vɪʒn/) *v* to imagine sth as a future possibility; to form a mental picture of sth: [Vn] *Nobody can envis-*

age the consequences of total nuclear war. [V.*ing*] *We don't envisage living in this area for very long.* [V.n ing] *I can't envisage the plan working* [V.*that*] *It is envisaged that the motorway will be completed by next spring.* [also V.*wh*].

envoy /'envɔɪ/ *n* a messenger or representative, esp one sent to deal with a foreign government: *send a United Nations envoy* ○ *a special envoy of the Swedish government.*

envy¹ /'envi/ *n* **1** [U] ~ (**of sb**); ~ (**at/of sth**) the feeling of wishing to have what sb else has or to be like sb else: *He couldn't conceal his envy of me/envy at my success.* ○ *Her colleagues were green with envy* (ie extremely full of envy). ○ *They only say such unkind things about you out of envy* (ie because they are full of envy). **2** the **envy** [sing] ~ of sb/sth a thing or person that causes feelings of envy: *a garden which is the envy of all our neighbours* ○ *He's the envy of all his rivals.* Compare JEALOUSY.

envy² /'envi/ *v* (*pt, pp* **envied**) to wish one had the same qualities, possessions, opportunities, etc as sb else: [Vn] *I really envy you — I wish I was going to Japan as well.* [Vn] *I have always envied her easygoing attitude to life.* [Vnn] *I don't envy him his money problems* (ie I am happy I do not have them). [V.n ing] *I don't envy them/their having to live in such an awful place.*

enzyme /'enzaɪm/ *n* (*biology or chemistry*) **1** a chemical substance that occurs naturally in living creatures and assists in performing chemical changes, eg in processing food in the stomach, without being changed itself. **2** a similar substance produced artificially, eg for use in detergents (DETERGENT): *Washing-powders containing enzymes are said to remove stains more efficiently.*

eon = AEON.

epaulette (also *esp US* **epaulet**) /'epəlet/ *n* a decoration on the shoulder of a coat, jacket, etc, esp on a uniform.

ephemera /ɪ'femərə/ *n* [pl] things that are used, enjoyed, etc for only a short time and then forgotten.

ephemeral /ɪ'femərəl/ *adj* lasting for a very short time: *ephemeral pleasures* ○ *Journalism is important but ephemeral.*

epic /'epɪk/ *n* **1**(**a**) a long poem about the deeds of great men and women, or about a nation's past history: *an epic poem* ○ *Homer's 'Iliad' is a famous epic.* (**b**) a long film, story, etc dealing with brave deeds and exciting adventures: *an epic about the Roman Empire.* **2** (*infml or joc*) a task, activity, etc that takes a long time, is full of difficulties and deserves notice and admiration when successfully completed: *Their four-hour match on the centre court was an epic.* ▶ **epic** *adj* [usu attrib] **1** worthy of notice and admiration because of the scale and nature of the difficulties involved: *an epic encounter/struggle/achievement* ○ *their epic journey through the mountains.* **2** on a grand scale; huge: *a tragedy of epic proportions.*

epicentre (*US* **epicenter**) /'episentə(r)/ *n* (**a**) the point at which an EARTHQUAKE reaches the earth's surface. (**b**) the central point of sth, esp of a difficult situation: *The issue lies at the epicentre of the problem of change and stability in Europe.*

epicure /'epɪkjʊə(r)/ *n* a person who takes a special interest in and gets great pleasure from food and drink of high quality: *a cookery book for real epicures.*

epicurean /ˌepɪkju'riːən/ *adj* relating to or intended for special pleasure and enjoyment: *an epicurean feast.*

epidemic /ˌepɪ'demɪk/ *n* **1** the rapid spread of a disease among many people in the same place: *a cholera/flu epidemic.* **2** a sudden rapid increase in

the extent of an undesirable activity: *an epidemic of crime in our major cities.*
▶ **epidemic** *adj* like an epidemic in extent: *Car theft is now reaching epidemic proportions.* Compare ENDEMIC, PANDEMIC.

epidemiology /ˌepɪˌdiːmiˈɒlədʒi/ *n* [U] the scientific study of the spread and control of disease.
▶ **epidemiological** /ˌepɪˌdiːmiəˈlɒdʒɪkl/ *adj.* **epidemiologist** /ˌepɪˌdiːmiˈɒlədʒɪst/ *n.*

epidermis /ˌepɪˈdɜːmɪs/ *n* [U, sing] (*anatomy*) the outer layer of the skin.

epidural /ˌepɪˈdjʊərəl/ *n* (*medical*) an anaesthetic (ANAESTHESIA) put into the lower part of the back so that no pain is felt below the waist. Epidurals are sometimes given to women who are giving birth.

epiglottis /ˌepɪˈɡlɒtɪs/ *n* (*anatomy*) a piece of tissue at the back of the tongue that closes during swallowing to prevent food or drink from entering the lungs.

epigram /ˈepɪɡræm/ *n* a short poem or phrase expressing an idea in a clever and amusing way: *The playwright Oscar Wilde was noted for his epigrams.*
▶ **epigrammatic** /ˌepɪɡrəˈmætɪk/ *adj* expressing sth, or expressed, in a brief, clever and amusing way: *an epigrammatic style.*

epigraph /ˈepɪɡrɑːf; *US* -ɡræf/ *n* a line or lines of writing on a statue, building, etc; a short phrase at the beginning of a book or part of a book.

epilepsy /ˈepɪlepsi/ *n* [U] a disease of the nervous system that causes a person to fall unconscious, often with violent movements of the body: *suffer from epilepsy.*
▶ **epileptic** /ˌepɪˈleptɪk/ *adj* of or relating to epilepsy: *an epileptic fit.* — *n* a person who suffers from epilepsy.

epilogue /ˈepɪlɒɡ/ (*US* **epilog** /-lɔːɡ/) *n* a section added at the end of a book, play, film, television programme, etc as a comment on or conclusion to what has happened in it: *Fortinbras speaks the epilogue in Shakespeare's 'Hamlet'.* Compare PROLOGUE 1.

Epiphany /ɪˈpɪfəni/ *n* a Christian festival held on 6 January, in memory of the coming of the Magi to the baby Jesus at Bethlehem.

episcopal /ɪˈpɪskəpl/ (also **episcopalian** /ɪˌpɪskəˈpeɪliən/) *adj* (*religion*) of or governed by a bishop or bishops: *episcopal duties* ○ *the Episcopal Church* (ie esp the Anglican Church in the USA and Scotland). Compare PRESBYTERIAN.
▶ **episcopalian** (usu **Episcopalian**) /ɪˌpɪskəˈpeɪliən/ *n* a member of an episcopal church.

episode /ˈepɪsəʊd/ *n* **1** an event or a situation occurring as part of a long series of events: *That's an episode in my life I'd rather forget.* ○ *One of the funniest episodes in the book occurs in Chapter 6.* **2** any one part of a continuing story that is broadcast or published in a number of parts at different times: *the final episode of a TV series.*
▶ **episodic** /ˌepɪˈsɒdɪk/ *adj* (**a**) (of a story, novel, etc) containing or consisting of a series of separate events: *the play's episodic structure.* (**b**) occurring occasionally and not at regular intervals: *episodic fits of depression.*

epistle /ɪˈpɪsl/ *n* **1** (*usu joc*) a letter: *Her mother sends her a long epistle every week.* **2** **Epistle** (*Bible*) any of the letters included in the New Testament, written by the Apostles: *the Epistle of St Paul to the Romans.*
▶ **epistolary** /ɪˈpɪstələri; *US* -leri/ *adj* (*fml*) of, expressed in or written in the form of letters: *an epistolary novel/style.*

epitaph /ˈepɪtɑːf; *US* -tæf/ *n* words written or said about a dead person, esp words on a GRAVESTONE.

epithet /ˈepɪθet/ *n* an adjective or a phrase, esp one used to describe the character or most important quality of sb/sth, eg Peter *the Great*, Attila *the Hun*: *The crowd hurled abusive epithets at him.*

epitome /ɪˈpɪtəmi/ *n* [sing] **the ~ of sth 1** a person or thing that is a perfect example of a quality, type, etc: *the absolute/very epitome of a modern politician* ○ *She's the epitome of kindness.* **2** a thing that shows on a small scale all the characteristics of sth much larger: *The divisions we see in this community are the epitome of those occurring throughout the whole country.*
▶ **epitomize, -ise** /ɪˈpɪtəmaɪz/ *v* to be a perfect example of sth: [Vn] *He epitomizes everything I dislike.* ○ *a lack of sensitivity epitomized by their handling of the dispute.*

epoch /ˈiːpɒk; *US* ˈepək/ *n* a period of time in history, a person's life, the history of the earth, etc, esp one marked by important events or special characteristics: *Einstein's theories marked a new epoch in mathematics.*
■ **ˈepoch-making** *adj* (*fml or joc*) important and remarkable enough to change the course of history and begin a new epoch: *the epoch-making discovery of America.*

equable /ˈekwəbl/ *adj* not easily upset or annoyed; always calm and reasonable: *an equable temperament* ○ *His parents are remarkably equable.* ▶ **equably** /ˈekwəbli/ *adv.*

equal /ˈiːkwəl/ *adj* **1 ~ (to sb/sth)** the same in size, quantity, quality, extent, level, status, etc: *They are of equal height.* ○ *Equal amounts of flour and sugar should be added to the mixture.* ○ *An area of forest equal to the size of Wales has been destroyed.* ○ *In intelligence, the children are about equal (to each other).* ○ *He speaks Arabic and English with equal fluency.* ○ *Women are demanding equal pay for equal work* (ie equal to that of men). ○ *equal rights/ treatment* ○ *an equal opportunities programme* (ie giving the same opportunity for employment to any person, regardless of sex, race, etc). **2** [pred] **~ to sth** having the strength, courage, ability, etc for sth: *She doesn't feel equal to the task.* ○ *He proved equal to* (ie able to deal with) *the occasion.* **IDM** **all/other things being equal** ⇨ THING. **on ˌequal ˈterms (with sb)** with neither side having an advantage over the other or being superior to the other: *be able to trade on equal terms with overseas companies.*
▶ **equal** *n* a person or thing equal to another or others in some way, esp in quality or status: *She's the equal of her brother as far as intelligence is concerned.* ○ *Our products are the equal of those produced anywhere in the world.* ○ *He treats the people who work for him as his equals.*
equal *v* (**-ll-**; *US* **-l-**) **1** to be equal to sth in amount or number: [V-n] *x plus y equals z* (ie x + y = z). **2 ~ sb/sth (as/in sth)** to be equal to, or do sth to the same level or standard as, sb/sth else: [Vn] *equal the world record* ○ *My shock was only equalled by my disgust.* [Vnpr] *Nobody else can equal him in ability.* [Vn-n] *Few politicians can equal her as a public speaker.*

equality /ɪˈkwɒləti/ *n* [U] the state of being equal, esp in status, rights, etc: *equality of opportunity* ○ *greater equality in health care* ○ *a campaign for racial equality.*

equalize, -ise /ˈiːkwəlaɪz/ *v* **1** to become or make sth equal throughout a place or group: [Vn] *a policy to equalize the distribution of resources throughout the country* [also V]. **2** (esp in football) to score a goal that makes the score of both teams equal: [V] *Germany equalized ten minutes later.* **equalization, -isation** /ˌiːkwəlaɪˈzeɪʃn; *US* -ləˈz-/ *n* [U]. **equalizer, -iser** *n* (usu *sing*) (esp in football) a goal that makes the score of both teams equal: *Chapman scored the equalizer for Liverpool.*

equally /ˈiːkwəli/ *adv* **1(a)** to an equal extent: *They are equally clever.* ○ *Both aspects are equally important.* (**b**) in an equal manner; in the same or a similar way: *treat every member of staff equally.* **2** in equal parts or amounts: *The money was equally*

divided among her four children. ○ They share the
housework equally between them. **3** in addition and
of equal importance: We must try to think about
what is best for him; equally, we must consider what
he himself wants to do.

equanimity /ˌekwəˈnɪmətɪ/ n [U] the quality or
state of being calm in mind or temper, esp in difficult situations: She is facing the prospect of her
operation with cheerful equanimity.

equate /ɪˈkweɪt/ v **1** ~ sth (with sth) to consider sth
as equal or equivalent to sth else: [Vnpr] You can't
equate the education system of Britain with that of
Germany. ○ He equates success with material wealth.
[also Vn]. **2** ~ to sth to be equal or equivalent to sth
else: [Vpr] Do my qualifications equate to any in your
country? ○ Production costs equate to around 30% of
income.

equation /ɪˈkweɪʒn/ n **1** [C] (mathematics) a statement that two amounts or values, connected by the
sign =, are equal, eg $2x + 5 = 11$. **2** [U, sing] the action
of making sth equal or considering sth as equal: The
equation of wealth with happiness can be dangerous.
3 [C usu sing] a problem or situation in which
several factors must be considered and dealt with:
When children enter the equation further tensions
may arise in a marriage.

equator /ɪˈkweɪtə(r)/ n an imaginary line, or one
drawn on a map, etc, around the earth at an equal
distance from the North and South Poles: It is often
very hot near the equator. ⇨ picture at GLOBE.

▶ **equatorial** /ˌekwəˈtɔːrɪəl/ adj of or near the
equator: an equatorial climate ○ equatorial forests.

equerry /ɪˈkweri, ˈekwəri/ n ~ (to sb) (in Britain)
an officer attending the king, the queen or a member of the royal family: He is equerry to the Prince of
Wales.

equestrian /ɪˈkwestrɪən/ adj [usu attrib] of or
involving riding a horse: equestrian skill ○ equestrian events at the Olympic Games ○ an equestrian
statue (ie one of a person on a horse).

equi- comb form equal; equally: equinox ○ equidistant.

equidistant /ˌiːkwɪˈdɪstənt, ˌek-/ adj [pred] ~ (from
sth) (fml) equally far from two or more places: Our
house is equidistant from the two pubs in the village.

equilateral /ˌiːkwɪˈlætərəl, ˌek-/ adj (geometry) having all sides equal: an equilateral triangle. ⇨
picture at TRIANGLE.

equilibrium /ˌiːkwɪˈlɪbrɪəm, ˌek-/ n [U] **1(a)** a situation in which opposing forces, influences, etc are
balanced and under control: the need to keep supply
and demand in equilibrium. **(b)** the state of being
physically balanced: He can't maintain enough equilibrium to ride a bike. **2** a state of mind in which
feelings and emotions are under control: He sat
down for a while to recover his equilibrium.

equine /ˈekwaɪn/ adj of or like a horse or horses:
equine sports ○ (fig) He has a long equine face.

equinox /ˈiːkwɪnɒks, ˈek-/ n either of the two occasions in the year (around 21 March and 22
September) when the sun crosses the EQUATOR and
day and night are of equal length: the spring and
autumn equinoxes. Compare SOLSTICE.

equip /ɪˈkwɪp/ v (-pp-) ~ oneself/sb/sth (with sth)
(for sth) **1** to supply or provide oneself/sb/sth with
what is needed for a particular purpose: [Vn] the
need for money to equip and pay an army [Vnpr]
They equipped themselves for the expedition. ○ All
students should be equipped with a pocket calculator.
2 to prepare sb mentally for a particular activity,
task, etc: [Vnpr] His wide experience ensures he is
well equipped for the challenge ahead. [Vn.to inf]
Her training has equipped her to act decisively in a
crisis.

▶ **equipment** n [U] **1** the things needed for a
particular purpose: office equipment ○ sports equipment ○ a factory with modern packaging equipment.

2 the process of equipping sb/sth: The equipment of
the photographic studio was expensive.

equitable /ˈekwɪtəbl/ adj (fml) fair and just; reasonable: an equitable distribution of wealth ○ the most
equitable solution to the dispute. ▶ **equitably** /-blɪ/
adv.

equity /ˈekwətɪ/ n **1(a)** [U] the value of the shares
issued by a company: He controls 7% of the equity.
(b) equities [pl] ordinary stocks and shares that
carry no fixed interest: invest in equities ○ the equities market. **2** [U] the money value of a property
after all charges on it, eg those relating to a MORT-
GAGE, have been paid. **3** [U] (law esp Brit) the
application of the principles of natural justice in
particular circumstances where the existing laws
would not allow a fair or reasonable result.

equivalent /ɪˈkwɪvələnt/ adj ~ (to sth) equal in
value, amount, meaning, importance, etc: £5 is
roughly equivalent to 40 French francs. ○ 250 grams
or an equivalent amount in ounces ○ The new regulation was seen as equivalent to censorship.

▶ **equivalence** /-ləns/ n [U]: the moral equivalence
between human beings and animals.

equivalent n a thing, amount, word, etc that is
equivalent: the metric equivalent of two miles ○ Is
there a French word that is the exact equivalent of the
English word 'home'?

equivocal /ɪˈkwɪvəkl/ adj (fml) not clear or definite
in meaning or intention; that can be interpreted in
more than one way; AMBIGUOUS(1): He gave an equivocal answer, typical of a politician. ○ The position of
the Liberals was more equivocal.

▶ **equivocate** /ɪˈkwɪvəkeɪt/ v (fml) to talk about sth
in a way that is deliberately not clear in order
to hide the truth or mislead people: [V.speech]
'There are no objections that we are aware of,' the
Minister equivocated. [also V, Vpr]. **equivocation**
/ɪˌkwɪvəˈkeɪʃn/ n [U, C] the use of equivocal statements to mislead people: They were criticized for
equivocation and unwillingness to commit themselves.

er /ɜː(r)/ interj (used to express the sound made when
one hesitates in a conversation): 'Will you call me?'
'Er, yes, I suppose so.' ○ I'm, er, I'm working on that.

-er suff **1** (with vs forming ns) a person or thing that
does: lover ○ computer. Compare -EE, -OR. **2** (with ns
forming ns) **(a)** a person concerned with: astronomer ○ philosopher. **(b)** a person belonging to: New
Yorker ○ villager ○ sixth-former. **(c)** a thing that has:
three-wheeler ○ double-decker. **3** (forming comparative adjs and advs): taller ○ softer ○ heavier ○ faster.

era /ˈɪərə/ n a period in history starting from a
particular time or event or having particular characteristics: This marks the beginning of a new era
in medical research. ○ the postwar era ○ the era of
glasnost.

eradicate /ɪˈrædɪkeɪt/ v to destroy sth completely;
to put an end to sth: [Vn] Smallpox has now been
eradicated. [Vnpr] a commitment to eradicate racism
from the police force. ▶ **eradication** /ɪˌrædɪˈkeɪʃn/ n
[U].

erase /ɪˈreɪz; US ɪˈreɪs/ v **1** ~ sth (from sth) to
remove all traces of sth: [Vn] erase sb's anxieties/
doubts/fears [Vnpr] He has tried to erase from his
mind all memories of the disaster. **2** to rub or scrape
sth out: [Vn] erase pencil marks. **3** to remove a
recording from a tape or information from a computer's memory: [Vn] I've erased the wrong file!

▶ **eraser** /ɪˈreɪzə(r); US ɪˈreɪsər/ n (US) (Brit fml)
(Brit also **rubber**) a piece of rubber, plastic, etc for
removing pencil marks.

erasure /ɪˈreɪʒə(r)/ n (fml) [U] the action of erasing
sth: the erasure of the incident from her memory.

ere /eə(r)/ conj, prep (arch or rhet) before: Ere long
they returned.

erect¹ /ɪˈrekt/ adj **1** in an upright position; standing on end; straight: *hold oneself/stand erect* ○ *Sit comfortably with your head erect.* ○ *The dog's ears were erect and alert.* **2** (of the PENIS or nipples (NIPPLE 1)) swollen and stiff from sexual excitement.

erect² /ɪ'rekt/ v (*fml*) **1** to build sth, eg a house or wall: [Vn] *They plan to demolish the house next door and erect a block of flats in its place.* [Vnpr] *A statue/ monument was erected to* (ie to honour the memory of) *Queen Victoria.* **2** to put sth in position and make it stand upright: [Vn] *erect a tent/sign/screen* ○ (*fig*) *erect a new charter of social values.*
▶ **erection** /ɪ'rekʃn/ n **1** [U] (*fml*) the action of erecting sth or the state of being erected: *The erection of the building took almost a year.* **2** [C] the hard swollen state of the PENIS caused by sexual excitement: *get/have an erection.*

ergo /'ɜːɡəʊ/ adv (*Latin usu joc*) therefore: *Change from within will take too long. Ergo change must come from outside.*

ergonomics /ˌɜːɡə'nɒmɪks/ n [sing v] the study of work and working conditions in order to improve people's efficiency.
▶ **ergonomic** adj designed to improve people's working conditions and efficiency: *ergonomic features.* **ergonomically** adv: *The layout is hard to fault ergonomically.*

ERM /ˌiː ɑː 'em/ abbr (*finance*) Exchange-Rate Mechanism (a means of linking the currencies of certain EU countries to the ECU): *join/leave the ERM.* See also EMS.

ermine /'ɜːmɪn/ n [U] the white winter fur of a STOAT, used esp on the ceremonial dress of judges, etc: *a gown trimmed with ermine* ○ *ermine robes.*

erode /ɪ'rəʊd/ v (esp passive) (of acids, rain, wind, etc) to destroy sth or to wear sth away gradually: [Vn] *Metals are eroded by acids.* ○ *The sea has eroded the cliff face over the years.* ○ (*fig*) *Standards in our schools/The rights of the individual are being steadily eroded.* [Vp] *The sides of the volcano are eroding away year by year.* [also V]. ▶ **erosion** /ɪ'rəʊʒn/ n [U]: *the erosion of the coastline by the sea* ○ *attempts to reduce soil erosion* ○ (*fig*) *the steady erosion of the President's credibility.*

erogenous /ɪ'rɒdʒənəs/ adj (of areas of the body) particularly sensitive to being sexually stimulated: *e‚rogenous 'zones.*

erotic /ɪ'rɒtɪk/ adj used or intended to cause sexual desire: *erotic art/verse* ○ *erotic fantasies* ○ *The photographs are profoundly erotic.*
▶ **erotica** /ɪ'rɒtɪkə/ n [pl] books, pictures, etc intended to cause sexual desire: *a collection of erotica.*
erotically /-kli/ adv.
eroticism /ɪ'rɒtɪsɪzəm/ n [U] the quality of stimulating sexual desire: *the film's blatant eroticism.*

err /ɜː(r); *US* eər/ v ~ (**in sth/doing sth**) (*fml*) to make a mistake or mistakes: [Vpr] *The judge erred in refusing permission to cross-examine the witness.* [also V]. **IDM** **err on the side of sth** to show too much of a (usu good) quality: *It's better to err on the side of tolerance* (ie be too gentle rather than too severe) *when dealing with young offenders.*

errand /'erənd/ n a short journey to take a message, buy or deliver goods, etc: *work as an errand boy* ○ *He was tired of running errands for his sister.* ○ *I've come on a special errand.* See also FOOL'S ERRAND.

errant /'erənt/ adj [attrib] (*fml or joc*) (**a**) doing wrong; not behaving or functioning properly: *errant fathers who refuse to provide maintenance for their children* ○ (*fig*) *trying to recover an errant handkerchief* (ie one that is lost). (**b**) (of a husband or wife) not sexually faithful.

erratic /ɪ'rætɪk/ adj (*usu derog*) not regular or even in movement, quality or behaviour; not reliable: *erratic eating habits* ○ *a gifted but erratic player* ○ *the company's somewhat erratic performance on the stock market* ○ *Deliveries of goods are erratic.* ▶ **erratic-**

ally /-kli/ adv: *Being out of practice the team played very erratically.*

erratum /e'rɑːtəm/ n (pl **errata** /-tə/) (usu pl) (*fml*) an error in a printed book: *a list of errata.*

erroneous /ɪ'rəʊniəs/ adj (*fml*) not correct; wrong: *erroneous ideas/conclusions/statements.* ▶ **erroneously** adv: *a poem erroneously attributed to Shakespeare.*

error /'erə(r)/ n **1** [C] ~ (**in sth/doing sth**) a thing done wrongly; a mistake: *riddled with serious/minor/silly spelling errors* ○ *a computer error* ○ *a government/clerical error in calculating unemployment benefit* ○ *make a tactical/a fundamental/an unforced error* ○ *an error of judgement* (ie a mistake in the way one assesses a situation). **2** [U] the state of being wrong in belief or behaviour: *enormous scope for error* ○ *The letter was sent to you in error* (ie by mistake). ○ *The accident was the result of pilot error.* ○ *Rising costs have left us very little margin of error* (ie scope to make any mistakes without serious consequences). ⟹ note at MISTAKE¹. **IDM** **see, realize, etc the ‚error of one's 'ways** to realize that aspects of one's behaviour are wrong and should be changed. **trial and error** ⟹ TRIAL.

ersatz /'eəzæts; *US* 'eɑːsɑːts/ adj (*often derog*) used as a substitute for and usu inferior to the original item or product: *ersatz 'fruit juices'.*

erstwhile /'ɜːstwaɪl/ adj [attrib] (*fml*) former: *His erstwhile friends turned against him.*

erudite /'eruːdaɪt/ adj (*fml*) having or showing great learning: *an erudite lecture* ○ *a witty and immensely erudite man.*
▶ **erudition** /ˌeruː'dɪʃn/ n [U] (*fml*) learning: *a work of great erudition and originality.*

erupt /ɪ'rʌpt/ v **1** (of a VOLCANO) to throw out burning rocks, LAVA, etc suddenly and with great force: [V] *It's many years since Mount Vesuvius last erupted.* [Vn] *An immense volume of rocks and molten lava was erupted.* **2** ~ (**into sth**) to begin or occur suddenly and have a great effect or impact: [V] *The crisis/scandal erupted only days before the election.* ○ *Violence has erupted between the two communities.* [Vpr] *The fighting may erupt into full-scale confrontation.* **3** ~ (**in sth**) to express one's feelings, etc very strongly, esp by shouting loudly: [V] *When Davis scored for the third time the crowd finally erupted.* ○ *The whole place erupted.* [Vpr] *erupt in tears/fits of laughter.* **4** (of spots, etc) to appear on the skin: [V] *A rash has erupted all over his back.* ▶ **eruption** /ɪ'rʌpʃn/ n [C,U]: *a major volcanic eruption* ○ *the eruption of Krakatoa* ○ *an eruption of violent protest.*

-ery (also **-ry**) *suff* **1** (with *vs* and *ns* forming *ns*) (**a**) a place where sth happens or is made: *bakery* ○ *brewery.* (**b**) the art or practice of: *cookery* ○ *pottery.* **2** (with *ns* and *adjs* forming usu uncountable *ns*) (**a**) the state or character of: *snobbery* ○ *bravery* ○ *rivalry.* (**b**) a group or collection of: *machinery* ○ *greenery* ○ *gadgetry.*

escalate /'eskəleɪt/ v to increase or develop by successive stages; to become or make sth greater or more intense: [V] *The steadily escalating costs of research* [Vpr] *These local troubles could soon escalate into civil war.* [Vn] *The government is deliberately escalating the war for political reasons.*
▶ **escalation** /ˌeskə'leɪʃn/ n [C,U] ~ (**in sth**): *an escalation in food prices* ○ *try to prevent any further escalation of the conflict.*

escalator /'eskəleɪtə(r)/ n a moving staircase carrying people up or down between floors or different levels, eg in a shop or an underground railway.

escalope /'eskəlɒp, e'skæləp/ n a thin slice of meat with no bones in it, usu covered in egg and BREADCRUMBS and fried: *escalopes of veal.*

escapade /ˌeskə'peɪd, 'eskəpeɪd/ n an incident that involves excitement or adventure, usu one that is

---

disapproved of or that one later regrets: *a foolish/childish escapade* ○ *an amorous escapade* ○ *She alone knew the real truth of his Paris escapade.*

escape¹ /ɪˈskeɪp/ *v* **1** ~ **(from sb/sth)** to become free; to get away from a place where one has been a prisoner or has felt like a prisoner: [V] *Two prisoners have escaped.* ○ *an escaped convict* [Vpr] *A lion has escaped from its cage.* ○ *She longed to escape from her mother's domination.* ○ *(fig) As a child he would often escape into a dream world of his own.* **2** (no passive) to avoid sth unpleasant or undesirable: [V, Vn] *Two of the gang were caught but their leader escaped (capture/arrest).* [Vn] *Where can we go to escape the crowds?* ○ *You can't escape the fact that you're overweight.* [Vn, V.ing] *escape criticism/being criticized for sth.* **3** (of gases, liquids, etc) to get out of a container, etc; to LEAK(1): [V] *There's gas escaping somewhere — can you smell it?* [Vpr] *heat escaping through a window* [Vn] *(fig) No sound escaped his lips.* **4** ~ **(with sth)** to suffer no harm or less harm than would normally be expected: [Vpr] *escape with a warning* [Vadv] *escape very lightly* [V-adj, Vpr] *The driver of the other car escaped unscathed/escaped with minor cuts and bruises.* [also V]. **5** (no passive) to be forgotten or not noticed by sb/sth: [Vn] *Her name escapes me* (ie I can't remember it). ○ *The fault escaped observation* (ie was not noticed) *for months.* ○ *Nothing escapes him/his attention* (ie He notices everything). ○ *(ironic) It might have escaped your notice that I've been unusually busy recently.*

escape² /ɪˈskeɪp/ *n* **1** [C, U] ~ **(from sth)** (**a**) an act or the action of escaping from a place or from a difficult or dangerous situation: *There was little possibility of escape.* ○ *three recent successful escapes/escape bids from this prison* ○ *She made her escape when the guard's back was turned.* ○ *We had a miraculous/narrow/lucky escape.* (**b**) a means of escaping: *seek escape from the noise* ○ *There was no escape from her disastrous marriage.* ○ *our escape route* ○ *The police have just found the escape vehicle.* ○ *He got out through the escape hatch* (eg on a ship or an aircraft). See also FIRE-ESCAPE. **2** [sing] a thing that distracts one temporarily from reality or from a dull routine: *He listens to music as an escape from the pressures of work.* **3** [C] a LEAK(1): *an escape of gas.* **IDM** **make ˌgood one's eˈscape** to manage to escape completely and satisfactorily.

escapee /ɪˌskeɪˈpiː/ *n* a person who has escaped, esp from prison.

escapism /ɪˈskeɪpɪzəm/ *n* [U] (*often derog*) the habit of trying to forget unpleasant realities by seeking entertainment, imagining oneself in an exciting situation, etc: *the James Bond brand of harmless escapism* ○ *For him books are a form of escapism from the real world.* ▶ **escapist** /-pɪst/ *adj*: *escapist fantasies* ○ *escapist literature* (eg romantic fiction).

escarpment /ɪˈskɑːpmənt/ *n* a long steep slope or cliff separating an area of high ground or PLATEAU(1) from the plain below: *walk along the top of the escarpment.*

eschew /ɪsˈtʃuː/ *v* (*fml*) to keep away from sth deliberately; to avoid sth: [Vn] *eschew political discussion.*

escort¹ /ˈeskɔːt/ *n* **1** [CGp, U] a person or group of people, ships, vehicles, etc accompanying sb/sth to guard or protect them or as an honour: *provide an armed escort for a visiting head of state* ○ *The convoy had an escort of ten destroyers.* ○ *soldiers on escort duty* ○ *The prisoners were transported under police/military escort.* **2** [C] (*dated or fml*) a person, esp a man, who accompanies a member of the opposite sex on a particular social occasion.

escort² /ɪˈskɔːt/ *v* ~ **sb (to sth)** to accompany sb as an ESCORT¹: [Vn] *The princess was escorted by a number of attendants.* [Vnpr] *Several large men es-* corted *him to the gate.* [Vnadv] *Her brother's friend escorted her home.*

-ese *suff* **1** (with proper *ns* forming *adjs* and *ns*) (an inhabitant or the language) of a country or city: *(a/the) Chinese* ○ *(a/the) Milanese.* **2** (with *ns* forming *ns*) (esp derog) the style of language of: *journalese* ○ *officialese.*

Eskimo /ˈeskɪməʊ/ (*pl* unchanged or **-os**) *n* a member of a race living in the Arctic regions of N America and E Siberia: *the Inuit Eskimos of Canada* ○ *Eskimo art.*

ESL /ˌiː es ˈel/ *abbr* (the teaching, learning or studying of) English as a Second Language. Compare EFL.

esophagus (*US*) = OESOPHAGUS.

esoteric /ˌesəʊˈterɪk, ˌiːsəʊ-/ *adj* (*fml*) likely to be understood only by people with a special knowledge or interest; mysterious; OBSCURE(1): *esoteric poetry/language* ○ *His tastes in music are somewhat esoteric.*

ESP /ˌiː es ˈpiː/ *abbr* **1** (the teaching, learning or studying of) English for Special/Specific (eg scientific or technical) Purposes. **2** extrasensory perception.

esp *abbr* especially.

espalier /ɪˈspæliə(r)/ *n* (a tree or SHRUB whose branches are trained on) a wooden or wire frame in a garden.

especial /ɪˈspeʃl/ *adj* (**a**) exceptional; outstanding; special: *take especial care* ○ *a matter of especial interest.* (**b**) for or belonging mainly to one person or thing; particular: *for your especial entertainment.* Compare SPECIAL.
▶ **especially** /ɪˈspeʃəli/ *adv* (abbreviated as *esp* in this dictionary) particularly; specially: *especially important/true/useful* ○ *He was well-built, but not especially tall.* ○ *This is especially for you.* ○ *I love the country, especially in spring.* ○ *She wanted to go to the mountains, especially as the weather was beginning to improve.* ○ *Old people should keep warm, especially if they find it difficult to move about.*

NOTE Especially and specially are often used in the same way. You cannot always hear the difference clearly when people are speaking: *She made the dress especially/specially for the party.* ○ *He wrote the song especially/specially for his daughter.* But especially is more common than specially and usually means 'in particular': *She loves all sports, especially swimming.* ○ *The hotel food wasn't very good, especially if you're vegetarian.* It can also mean 'to a particular degree': *I don't especially like sweet things.* Specially usually means 'for a particular purpose' and is often followed by a past participle: *The swimming-pool has been specially designed for children.* ○ *She had her clothes specially made in Paris.*

espionage /ˈespiənɑːʒ/ *n* [U] the practice of spying (SPY *v*) or using spies to obtain secret information: *found guilty of espionage* ○ *engage in/commit espionage* ○ *involved in industrial espionage* (ie spying on the secret plans of rival companies).

esplanade /ˌespləˈneɪd/ *n* a level area of open ground where people can walk, ride or drive for pleasure, esp by the sea: *a stroll along the esplanade.*

espouse /ɪˈspaʊz/ *v* (*fml*) to give one's support to a movement, theory, etc: [Vn] *espousing feminism* ○ *political causes espoused by liberals over the centuries.* ▶ **espousal** /ɪˈspaʊzl/ *n* [U] ~ **(of sth)** (*fml*): *his recent espousal of monetarism.*

espresso /eˈspresəʊ/ *n* (*pl* **-os**) (**a**) [U] coffee made by forcing boiling water under pressure through ground coffee. (**b**) [C] a cup of this: *'Two espressos, please.'*

esprit de corps /eˌspriː də ˈkɔː(r)/ *n* [U] (*French*)

[V.speech] = verb + direct speech   [V.*that*] = verb + *that* clause   [V.*wh*] = verb + *who, how*, etc clause

loyalty and other feelings uniting the members of a group.

Esq *abbr* (*fml becoming dated esp Brit*) Esquire (a polite title written after a man's name, instead of *Mr* before it, on a letter addressed to him): *Edgar Broughton, Esq.*

-esque *suff* (used with *ns* to form *adjs*) in the style or manner of: *statuesque* ○ *Kafkaesque.*

-ess *suff* (with *ns* forming *ns*) female: *lioness* ○ *actress.* ⇨ note at GENDER.

essay /'eseɪ/ *n* **1** ~ (**on sth**) a piece of writing, usu short, on any one subject: *a brilliant essay on Italian art* ○ *I handed in my history essay two days late.* **2** ~ (**in sth**) (*fml*) an attempt: *His first essay in economic reform was a disaster.*

▶ **essayist** /-ɪst/ *n* a writer of essays, esp for publication.

essence /'esns/ *n* **1** [U] that which makes a thing what it is; the most important quality, feature or characteristic of sth: *The essence of his argument is that capitalism cannot succeed.* ○ *Her art captures the essence of our times.* ○ *The two arguments are* **in essence** *the same.* **2** [C, U] an extract of a plant, drug, etc, containing all its important qualities in concentrated form: *vanilla essence.* **IDM** **of the ¹essence** necessary and very important: *Speed is of the essence in dealing with an emergency.*

essential /ɪ'senʃl/ *adj* **1** [esp pred] ~ (**to/for sth**) absolutely necessary; extremely important; VITAL(1): *an essential part/ingredient/component of sth* ○ *carry out essential repairs on the car* ○ *The government is proposing a ban on strikes in essential services.* ○ *Is money essential to happiness?* ○ *This alliance is essential for the stability of Europe.* ○ *It's essential that you attend all the meetings.* ○ *Secretary wanted: previous experience essential.* **2** [attrib] relating to the basic nature of sb/sth; fundamental: *the essential artificiality of art* ○ *the essential weakness of their negotiating position.*

▶ **essential** *n* (usu *pl*) a necessary basic element or thing: *learn the essentials of English grammar* ○ *We only had time to pack a few essentials.*

essentially /ɪ'senʃəli/ *adv* in the true and fundamental nature of sth: *an essentially political movement* ○ *It is an amusing book, but essentially a work of propaganda.*

■ **es,sential ¹oil** *n* an oil extracted from a plant and used in making PERFUME(1), producing concentrated flavours, etc.

-est *suff* (forming superlative *adjs* and *advs*): *widest* ○ *biggest* ○ *happiest* ○ *soonest.*

establish /ɪ'stæblɪʃ/ *v* **1** to begin sth on a firm or permanent basis: [Vn] *This business was established in 1860.* ○ *a newly-established company* ○ *attempt to establish a close relationship with sb* ○ *The report sets out to establish a new framework of rights and responsibilities.* **2** ~ **sb/oneself** (**in sth**) (**as sth**) to place or settle sb/oneself in a position, an office, etc, usu on a permanent basis: [Vn] *We moved into our new house last week but it will take time to get established.* [Vn-n] *They are rapidly establishing themselves as the market leaders.* [Vn-n, Vnpr] *She's now firmly established (in business) as an art dealer.* **3** to cause people to accept a belief, custom, claim, etc: [Vn] *Established practices are difficult to change.* [Vn-n, Vn] *His second novel established him/his reputation as a writer.* **4** to show sth to be true or certain; to prove sth: [Vn, V.*that*] *We've established his innocence/that he's innocent.* [V.*wh*] *The police are trying to establish where he was at the time of the incident.*

▶ **established** *adj* [attrib] (of a Church or religion) made official for a country: *Anglicanism is the established religion in England.*

establishment /ɪ'stæblɪʃmənt/ *n* **1** [U] the action of creating or founding sth on a firm or permanent

basis: *announce/support the establishment of a new college* ○ *the establishment of cultural values.* **2** [C] (*fml or joc*) an organization, a hotel or a large institution: *a research establishment* ○ *a comfortable and well-run establishment near Salzburg.* **3** (usu **the Establishment** [Gp]) (*often derog*) a group of powerful people who influence or control policies, ideas, taste, etc and usually support what has been traditionally accepted: *the military/political Establishment* ○ *orthodox Establishment views* ○ *an Establishment figure* ○ *young people rebelling against the Establishment.*

estate /ɪ'steɪt/ *n* **1** [C] an area of land, esp in the country, with one owner: *He owns a large/a 3 000-acre estate in Massachusetts.* **2** [C] (*esp Brit*) a large area of land developed for a specific purpose, eg for houses or factories: *an industrial estate* ○ *live on an estate.* See also COUNCIL ESTATE, HOUSING ESTATE. **3** [U, C] (*law*) all the money and property that a person owns, esp that which is left at her or his death: *Her estate was divided between her four children.* See also REAL ESTATE.

■ **es¹tate agent** (*Brit*) (*US* **realtor, real estate agent**) *n* a person whose job is to sell houses and land for others.

es¹tate car (*Brit*) (*US* **station-wagon**) *n* a car with a large area for cases, etc behind the seats and a door or doors at the back for easy loading. ⇨ picture at HATCHBACK.

esteem /ɪ'stiːm/ *n* [U] (*fml*) high regard; a favourable opinion: *She is held in high esteem by those who know her well.* ○ *The changes provide an opportunity for the prime minister to recapture public esteem.*

▶ **esteem** *v* (*fml*) (not used in the continuous tenses) **1** (usu passive) to have a high opinion of sb/sth; to respect sb/sth greatly: [Vnadv] *two highly esteemed professional scientists* [Vn] *an esteemed colleague* [Vn-n] *Pearls were greatly esteemed as personal ornaments.* **2** to consider sth in a particular way: [Vn-n] *I esteem it a privilege to address such a distinguished audience.*

esthete (*US*) = AESTHETE.

esthetic (*US*) = AESTHETIC.

estimable /'estɪməbl/ *adj* (*dated or fml*) worthy of great respect. See also INESTIMABLE.

estimate¹ /'estɪmət/ *n* **1** a judgement or calculation (CALCULATE), not necessarily detailed or accurate, of the size, cost, value, etc of sth: *I can only give you a rough estimate of the number of bricks you will need.* ○ *the original/earlier/latest/most recent estimate of their value* ○ *according to official government estimates* ○ *It will cost at least 10 billion dollars and that's a conservative estimate.* ○ *Flight timings are based on our best estimate and wide experience.* **2** a judgement of the character or qualities of sb/sth: *I don't know her well enough to form an estimate of her abilities.* **3** a formal statement by a builder (BUILD), etc of the price he or she will probably charge for doing specified work: *We got estimates from three different contractors and accepted the lowest.* Compare QUOTATION 3.

estimate² /'estɪmeɪt/ *v* ~ **sth** (**at sth**) (often passive) to form a rough or general idea of sth; to calculate roughly the cost, size, value, etc of sth: [Vn] *estimate the silver content of ore samples* ○ *at an estimated cost of $8 million* ○ *An estimated 15 million trees were blown down.* [Vnpr, V.n *to inf*] *We estimated his income at/to be about £35 000 a year.* [V.*that*] *Council officials estimated that the work would take three months.* [V.*wh*] *Try to estimate how much you will have to pay out over the coming year.*

estimation /ˌestɪ'meɪʃn/ *n* [U] (*fml*) judgement; opinion: *In my estimation, he's the more suitable candidate.* ○ *She has certainly gone up in my estim-*

ation (ie is more highly regarded by me) *since she told the boss what she thought of him.*

estrange /ɪ'streɪndʒ/ *v* to make sb who was formerly friendly towards one become distant or HOSTILE(1a): [Vn] *He had estranged the party leadership.*
▶ **estranged** *adj* ~ (**from sb**) (**a**) (of a husband or wife) no longer living with the other partner: *an attempt at reconciliation with her estranged husband.* (**b**) (of people, groups, etc) no longer friendly with or loyal to sb: *their estranged supporters* ○ *She felt estranged from her sister.*
estrangement *n* [U, C]: *a sense of loneliness and estrangement* ○ *The misunderstanding had caused a seven-year estrangement between them.*

estuary /'estʃuəri; *US* -ueri/ *n* a wide area of water where a river flows into the sea: *the Thames estuary.*

et al /et 'æl/ *abbr* (used esp after a name) and other people or things (Latin *et alii/alia*): *The book includes studies by Westman et al.*

et cetera /et 'setərə, ɪt-/ (*usu abbr* **etc**) and other similar things; and the rest; and so on: *all the keys to rooms, cupboards, garages, etc* ○ *She kept going on about how we'd behaved badly, let her down, etc, etc.*

etch /etʃ/ *v* **1** ~ **A** (**in/on/onto B**); ~ **B** (**with A**) to make a strong clear mark or pattern on sth: [Vnpr] *a glass tankard with his initials etched on it* ○ (*fig*) *a woman whose faced was etched* (ie deeply lined) *with suffering* ○ *trees etched* (ie having a clear outline) *against the sunset* ○ *The incident remained etched in/ on her memory for years.* [also Vn]. **2** [V, Vn] to use a needle and acid to make a picture on a thin flat sheet of metal from which copies can be printed.
▶ **etching** *n* (**a**) [U] the art of making etched prints. (**b**) [C] a copy printed from an etched piece of metal: *Hanging on the wall was a fine etching of the church.*

eternal /ɪ'tɜːnl/ *adj* **1** without beginning or end; lasting or existing for ever: *eternal life* (ie life after the death of the body) ○ *an eternal optimist* (ie sb who always expects that the best will happen) ○ *To his eternal credit, he did not mention it to anyone.* **2** [attrib] seeming never to stop; (too) frequent: *Stop this eternal chatter!* ○ *I am tired of your eternal arguments.* ▶ **eternally** /ɪ'tɜːnəli/ *adv*: *The status of women was seen as eternally fixed.* ○ *For that I'll be eternally grateful to you.* ○ *He's eternally optimistic.*
■ **e,ternal 'triangle** *n* a situation in which two people are both in love with the same person of the opposite sex.
e,ternal 'verity *n* (usu *pl*) a fundamental moral principle.

eternity /ɪ'tɜːnəti/ *n* **1** [U] (*fml*) (**a**) time without end: *Egyptian mummies preserved for all eternity.* (**b**) endless life after death: *spend eternity in a far better place.* **2 an eternity** [sing] (*infml*) a very long time that seems endless: *It seemed an eternity before the police arrived.*

ethanol /'eθənɒl/ (also **ethyl alcohol**) *n* [U] the base of alcoholic drinks, also used as a fuel or SOLVENT.

ether /'iːθə(r)/ *n* [U] **1** a colourless liquid made from alcohol, used in industry as a SOLVENT and, esp formerly, in medicine as an anaesthetic (ANAESTHESIA). **2** (*arch or joc*) the upper air: *Today's news disappears into the ether and is soon forgotten.*

ethereal /ɪ'θɪəriəl/ *adj* extremely delicate and light, and seeming to be too spiritual or perfect for this world: *ethereal music/beauty.*

ethic /'eθɪk/ *n* **1** [sing] a system of moral principles or rules of behaviour: *the Puritan ethic* ○ *a strongly defined* **work ethic**. **2 ethics** (**a**) [pl] moral principles that govern or influence a person's behaviour: *draw up a code of ethics* ○ *medical ethics* (ie those approved by the medical profession) ○ *The ethics of his decision are doubtful.* ○ *It's a question of*

professional ethics. (**b**) [sing *v*] the branch of philosophy that deals with moral principles.
▶ **ethical** /-kl/ *adj* **1** of or relating to moral principles or questions: *largely an ethical issue/ dilemma/problem* ○ *rules which govern ethical standards* ○ *draw up an ethical framework.* **2** morally correct: *His behaviour has not been strictly ethical.* **ethically** /-kli/ *adv.*

ethnic /'eθnɪk/ *adj* **1** [attrib] (**a**) of or involving a nation, race or tribe that has a common cultural tradition: *ethnic minorities/groups/communities* ○ *ethnic unrest/clashes.* (**b**) (of a person) belonging to the specified country or area by birth or family history rather than by NATIONALITY(1): *ethnic Turks.* **2** (*approv*) typical of a particular cultural group, esp one from outside Europe or the USA: *ethnic clothes/ food/music* ○ *an ethnic restaurant.* ▶ **ethnically** /-kli/ *adv*: *an ethnically divided/troubled region.*
■ ,**ethnic 'cleansing** *n* [U] (*euph*) the policy or practice of killing or driving out of an area the people of one race or religion by those of another.

ethnocentric /ˌeθnəʊ'sentrɪk/ *adj* making judgements about another race and culture using the standards of one's own: *ethnocentric assumptions.*

ethnography /eθ'nɒɡrəfi/ *n* [U] the scientific description of different races and cultures.
▶ **ethnographer** /eθ'nɒɡrəfə(r)/ *n* an expert in ethnography.
ethnographic /ˌeθnə'ɡræfɪk/ *adj*: *ethnographic research/studies.*

ethos /'iːθɒs/ *n* [sing] (*fml*) the characteristic spirit, moral values, ideas or beliefs of a group, community or culture: *a new sexual ethos* ○ *the prevailing self-help ethos* ○ *a message in tune with the post-war ethos.*

ethyl alcohol /ˌeθɪl 'ælkəhɒl, ˌiːθaɪl/ = ETHANOL.

etiolated /'iːtiəʊleɪtɪd/ *adj* pale and weak, esp because of lack of light: *an etiolated rose.*

etiquette /'etɪket, -kət/ *n* [U] the formal standards or rules of correct and polite behaviour in society or among members of a profession: *a book of etiquette* ○ *medical/legal etiquette* ○ *It is simply not etiquette.*

-ette *suff* (with *ns* forming *ns*) **1** small: *cigarette* ○ *kitchenette.* **2** artificial: *flannelette.* **3** female: *usherette.* ⇨ note at GENDER.

etymology /ˌetɪ'mɒlədʒi/ *n* (**a**) [U] the study of the origin and history of words and their meanings. (**b**) [C] the origin and history of a particular word. ▶ **etymological** /ˌetɪmə'lɒdʒɪkl/ *adj*: *an etymological dictionary.*

EU /ˌiː 'juː/ *abbr* (usu **the EU**) European Union (the Common Market). See also EC.

eucalyptus /ˌjuːkə'lɪptəs/ *n* (*pl* unchanged or **eucalyptuses**) a tall tree with green leaves throughout the year. Eucalyptus trees are grown, esp in Australasia, to provide wood and the oil from their leaves, which is used in medicine.

eucharist /'juːkərɪst/ *n* **the Eucharist** [sing] the Christian ceremony based on Christ's last supper; the bread and wine taken at this. See also COMMUNION 1.

eugenics /juː'dʒenɪks/ *n* [sing *v*] the science of producing healthy intelligent children with the aim of improving the general characteristics of the human race.

eulogize, -ise /'juːlədʒaɪz/ *v* ~ (**on/over sb/sth**) (*fml*) to praise sb/sth highly in speech or writing: [Vn, Vpr] *She's always eulogizing (over) her children's achievements.* [also V]. ▶ **eulogistic** /ˌjuːlə'dʒɪstɪk/ *adj.*

eulogy /'juːlədʒi/ *n* [C, U] ~ (**on/of/for/to sb/sth**) (*esp fml*) a speech or piece of writing containing high praise of a person or thing: *a graveside eulogy on his dead friend* ○ *Fellow actors delivered gushing eulogies at her memorial service.*

eunuch /ˈjuːnək/ *n* a man who has been castrated (CASTRATE), esp one employed in former times to guard the women's living areas in some eastern courts.

euphemism /ˈjuːfəmɪzəm/ *n* ~ (**for sth**) an expression that is gentler or less direct than the one normally used to refer to sth unpleasant or embarrassing: *'Pass away' is a euphemism for 'die'.* ○ *The government admitted there were 'problems' — a slight euphemism, given the thousands of people without food, water or shelter.* ▶ **euphemistic** /ˌjuːfəˈmɪstɪk/ *adj* (abbreviated as *euph* in this dictionary): *euphemistic language/expressions/terms.* **euphemistically** /-kli/ *adv.*

euphoria /juːˈfɔːrɪə/ *n* [U] an intense feeling of happiness and pleasant excitement: *a week of alternating euphoria and gloom* ○ *the euphoria of recent independence* ○ *She was still in a state of euphoria hours after her victory.* ▶ **euphoric** /juːˈfɒrɪk; US -ˈfɔːr-/ *adj*: *The mood/atmosphere was almost euphoric.*

eureka /juːˈriːkə/ *interj* (*joc*) (used as a cry of triumph at making a discovery) I have found it!: *Eureka — a job at last!*

Eur(o)- *comb form* of Europe or the European Community: *Euro-MP* ○ *Eurocrat.*

eurocheque /ˈjʊərəʊtʃek/ *n* a cheque issued under an arrangement between European banks which allows customers in one country to exchange cheques for cash, pay bills, etc in another.

Eurocrat /ˈjʊərəkræt/ *n* (*usu derog*) a person, esp one in a senior position, who works in the administration of the European Union: *the Brussels Eurocrats.*

Euro-election /ˈjʊərəʊ ɪlekʃn/ *n* an election of Members of the European Parliament.

Euro-MP /ˈjʊərəʊ empiː/ *abbr* Member of the European Parliament: *Euro-MPs of all parties.*

Europe /ˈjʊərəp/ *n* [U] **1** the continent next to Asia in the east, the Atlantic Ocean in the west, and the Mediterranean Sea in the south: *western/eastern/central Europe.* **2** (*Brit*) all Europe except Britain: *British holiday-makers in Europe.* **3** the European Union: *Britain went into Europe in 1973.*

European /ˌjʊərəˈpiːən, ˌjɔː-/ *adj* **1** of Europe: *European languages.* **2** of or relating to the European Community: *a single European market* ○ *our European partners.* ▶ **European** *n* **1** a native of Europe: *young Europeans.* **2** (*Brit*) a person who supports the principles and aims of the European Union: *a good European.* ■ the ˌEuropean ˈUnion (also the ˌEuropean Community, the Common Market) *n* [sing] an economic and political association established in 1958 and now including Austria, Belgium, Britain, Denmark, Finland, France, Germany, Greece, Ireland, Italy, Luxembourg, the Netherlands, Portugal, Spain and Sweden.

euthanasia /ˌjuːθəˈneɪzɪə; US -ˈneɪʒə/ *n* [U] the practice of killing without pain a person who is suffering from a disease that cannot be cured or from extreme old age, so that he or she can die with dignity: *calls for the law to be altered to allow euthanasia* ○ *She is in favour of voluntary euthanasia* (ie people being able to ask for euthanasia for themselves).

evacuate /ɪˈvækjueɪt/ *v* (**a**) ~ sth; ~ sb (from...) remove sb from a place of danger to a safer place: [Vn] *help evacuate flood victims* ○ *Police evacuated a nearby cinema.* [Vn, Vnpr] *The police had ten minutes to evacuate 300 people (from the store) after the bomb warning was given.* (**b**) to leave a place, esp because of danger: [Vn] *Families in the area were urged to evacuate their homes immediately.* ▶ **evacuation** /ɪˌvækjuˈeɪʃn/ *n* [U, C]: *the emergency evacuation of thousands of people after an earthquake* ○ *orderly evacuation from the danger area.*

evacuee /ɪˌvækjuˈiː/ *n* a person who is evacuated from a place: *wartime evacuees.*

evade /ɪˈveɪd/ *v* **1** to escape or avoid meeting sb/sth: [Vn] *evade capture by the police* ○ *evade an attack/an enemy/the press* ○ (*fig*) *He evaded my eye* (ie avoided looking into my eyes). **2** to find a way of not doing sth, esp sth that legally or morally ought to be done: [Vn] *evade military service/taxes/restrictions.* **3** to avoid dealing with sth or accepting sth fully or honestly: [Vn] *She managed to evade all the difficult questions.* ○ *Come on now, I think you're evading the issue.* ○ *He cannot evade responsibility for his actions.* **4** (*fml*) (of a quality, condition, etc) not to come or happen to sb: [Vn] *Sleep evaded him that night.* ○ *The exact figure evades me* (ie I cannot remember it). See also EVASION, EVASIVE.

evaluate /ɪˈvæljueɪt/ *v* to assess or form an idea of the amount, quality or value of sb/sth: [Vn] *evaluate the possibility/the effects/the significance of sth* ○ *attempt to evaluate the strength of European competition* ○ *Several other proposals are still being evaluated.* ▶ **evaluation** /ɪˌvæljuˈeɪʃn/ *n* [C, U]: *a preliminary evaluation of the health care system* ○ *a framework for the evaluation process.*

evanescent /ˌiːvəˈnesnt; US ˌev-/ *adj* (*fml*) quickly fading; soon disappearing from sight or memory: *as evanescent as snowflakes.*

evangelical /ˌiːvænˈdʒelɪkl/ *adj* (also **Evangelical**) **1** of a Protestant group which believes that the soul can be saved only by faith in Christ and his sacrifice: *an evangelical church.* **2** of or according to the teachings of the Christian Gospel or the Christian religion. **3** very keen to spread one's ideas about sth: *evangelical fervour.* ▶ **evangelical** *n* a member of an evangelical group.

evangelist /ɪˈvændʒəlɪst/ *n* **1** a person who tries to convert people to Christianity, esp one who travels around holding religious meetings: *converted to Christianity by a fervent American evangelist.* **2** any one of the four writers (Matthew, Mark, Luke, John) of the Gospels in the Bible: *St John the Evangelist.* ▶ **evangelism** *n* [U]. **evangelistic** /ɪˌvændʒəˈlɪstɪk/ *adj*: *evangelistic zeal.*

evangelize, -ise /ɪˈvændʒəlaɪz/ *v* [V, Vn] to try to convert people to Christianity.

evaporate /ɪˈvæpəreɪt/ *v* **1** to change or make sth change into steam and disappear: [V] *The water soon evaporated in the sunshine.* [Vn] *This process gets the oil hot enough to evaporate any remaining moisture.* ⇨ note at WATER¹. **2** to be lost or stop existing: [Vpr] *His hopes/confidence evaporated into thin air.* [V] *Their 70% majority evaporated overnight.* ▶ **evaporation** /ɪˌvæpəˈreɪʃn/ *n* [U]: *the evaporation process.* ■ eˌvaporated ˈmilk *n* [U] thick milk, usu bought in tins, which has had some of the liquid removed by evaporation.

evasion /ɪˈveɪʒn/ *n* **1** [C,U] the act or process of avoiding sb or of avoiding sth that is legally or morally required: *the burglar's evasion of the police* ○ *her deliberate/systematic evasion of responsibility* ○ *He's been charged with tax evasion.* **2** [C] a statement, an excuse, etc made to avoid dealing with sth directly or honestly: *His speech was full of evasions and half-truths.*

evasive /ɪˈveɪsɪv/ *adj* **1** intentionally not direct or completely honest: *an evasive answer* ○ *The doctors were somewhat evasive when describing his condition.* **2** (of an action) done in order to avoid a dangerous or unpleasant situation: *The ship had to take evasive action in order to avoid a collision.* ▶ **evasively** *adv.* **evasiveness** *n* [U]: *Politicians are often accused of evasiveness.*

eve /iːv/ *n* the day or evening before an event, esp a religious festival or holiday: *on Christmas Eve* (ie 24 December) ○ *a New Year's Eve party* (ie on 31 December) ○ *on the eve of the race/election/summit.*

[V.*to* inf] = verb + *to* infinitive   [Vn.inf (no *to*)] = verb + noun + infinitive without *to*   [V.*ing*] = verb + -*ing* form

even¹ /'iːvn/ *adv* **1** (used to emphasize sth unexpected or surprising in what one is saying or writing): *He never even 'opened the letter* (ie so he certainly didn't read it). ○ *He didn't answer even 'my letter* (ie so he certainly didn't answer any others). ○ *It was cold there even in 'summer* (ie so it must have been very cold in winter). ○ *Even a 'child can understand it* (ie so adults certainly can). **2** (used to emphasize a comparison, esp with sth great or extreme) still; yet: *You know even less about it than I do.* ○ *Sally drives fast, but Jane drives even faster.* ○ *She's even more intelligent than her sister.* **3** (used to add force to a more exact or PRECISE(2) version of a word, phrase, etc): *It's an unattractive building, even ugly/ ugly even.* **IDM** **even as** (*fml*) (used as a compound *conj*) just at the same time as sb does sth or as sth else happens: *Even as he shouted the warning the car skidded.* **even if/though** (used as *conjs*) in spite of the fact or belief that; no matter whether: *I'll get there, even if I have to walk all the way.* ○ *I like her even though she can be annoying at times.* **even 'now/'then 1** in spite of what has/had happened: *I've shown him the photographs but even now he won't believe me.* ○ *Even then he would not admit his mistake.* **2** (*fml*) (with continuous tenses only, often between the auxiliary and the main *v*) at this or that exact moment: *The troops are even now preparing to march into the city.* **even 'so** (used as a *conj*) in spite of that; nevertheless: *There are a lot of spelling mistakes; even so, it's quite a good essay.*

even² /'iːvn/ *adj* **1** level; smooth; flat: *The footpath is not very even.* Compare UNEVEN 1. **2** with little change or variation in quality; regular; steady: *an even colour* ○ *even breathing* ○ *Her stitches weren't very even.* ○ *This wine cellar stays at an even temperature all year round.* Compare UNEVEN 2. **3(a)** (of amounts, distances or values) equal: *Our scores are now even.* **(b)** (of two people or things) equally or closely balanced or matched: *an even game* ○ *I'd say the two players are pretty even.* Compare UNEVEN 3. **4** (of numbers) that can be divided by two: *an even number of people* ○ *4, 6, 8, 10, etc are even numbers.* Compare ODD 2. **5** (of character, mood, etc) not easily upset; calm: *of an even disposition* ○ *an even-tempered baby* ○ *She tried to keep her voice quiet and even* (ie not showing any emotion). **IDM** **be/get 'even (with sb)** (*infml*) to inflict similar trouble, harm, injury, etc on sb as they have inflicted on oneself: *He swore he'd get even with his brother.* **break 'even** to complete a piece of business, etc without making a loss: *We should begin to break even later in the year.* **an even 'chance (of doing sth)** an equally balanced chance (of sth happening or not): *I'd say she has an even chance of winning the match.* ○ *He's got a less than even chance.* **even 'money; evens** (in betting) the chance to win or lose the same amount; an equal chance that sth will or will not happen: *The evens favourite is 'Will he win?' 'It's even money.'* **honours are even** ⇨ HONOUR¹. **on an even 'keel** leading a normal life, esp emotionally, after a period of difficulty: *It took him a long time to get back on an even keel after his wife died.* ▸ **evenly** *adv: evenly balanced/matched* ○ *evenly divided/distributed* ○ *Breathe slowly and evenly.* ○ *'I shan't be coming next week,' she said evenly.* **evenness** /'iːvənnəs/ *n* [U]. ■ **,even-'handed** *adj* fair and without prejudice: *an even-handed approach* ○ *,even-handed 'justice.*

even³ /'iːvn/ *v* to make sth equal: [Vn] *Chelsea evened the score just after half-time.* **PHRV** **,even 'out** to become level or steady: *The path rose steeply for a while and then evened out.* ○ *House prices keep rising and falling but they should eventually even out.* **,even sth 'out** to spread sth evenly over a period of time or among a number of people: *Payments can be evened out on a monthly basis over the year.* ○ *He tried to even out the distribution of work*

among his employees. **,even (sth) 'up** to become or make sth more regular or evenly or equally balanced: *Moving John and Michael to the back row will even things up a bit* (ie make a more balanced group).

evening /'iːvnɪŋ/ *n* **1** [C, U] the part of the day between the afternoon and the time one goes to bed: *I'll come and see you tomorrow evening.* ○ *We were at home yesterday evening.* ○ *One warm summer evening…/On a warm summer evening… ○ the long winter evenings ○ In the evening I usually read. ○ Let's meet on Sunday evening. ○ the evening performance.* ⇨ note at MORNING. **2** [C] an occasion of a specified type, happening in the evening: *A theatre evening* (ie an evening at the theatre) *has been arranged.* ○ *musical evenings* (ie evenings especially for listening to or playing music). **IDM** **good 'evening** (used as a polite greeting or reply to a greeting when people first see each other in the evening): *'Good evening, sir.' 'Good evening.'* (In informal use the greeting *Good evening* is often shortened to just *Evening.*) **the other day/morning/evening/week** ⇨ OTHER.

▸ **evenings** *adv* (*esp US*) in the evening; every evening: *He works evenings.*

■ **'evening class** *n* a lesson for adults held at a school, college, etc in the evening: *I'm doing French evening classes this year.* See also NIGHT SCHOOL.
'evening dress *n* **1** [U] elegant clothes worn for formal occasions in the evening: *Everyone was in (full) evening dress.* **2** [C] a woman's usu long formal dress.
,evening 'paper *n* a newspaper published in the afternoon or early evening: *I saw the advert in the local evening paper.* Compare VESPERS.

evensong /'iːvnsɒŋ/ *n* [U] the service of evening prayer in the Church of England: *We attended evensong as well as morning prayer.* Compare MATINS. See also VESPERS.

event /ɪ'vent/ *n* **1** a thing that happens, esp sth important; an incident: *The American election was one of the main events of 1992.* ○ *recent dramatic events taking place in Europe ○ In the normal course of events, he would have been home by then.* ○ *By the time it was actually published, his report had been overtaken by events* (eg many of the things he predicted had actually happened). ○ *an unfortunate series of events ○ The police have reconstructed the chain of events that led to the murder.* ⇨ note at OCCURRENCE. **2(a)** a planned public or social occasion: *a fund-raising event ○ the social event of 1995.* **(b)** any of the races or competitions in a sports programme: *Which events have you entered for? ○ The 800 metres is the fourth event of the afternoon.* See also FIELD EVENTS, TRACK EVENTS. **IDM** **at 'all events / in 'any event** whatever happens; in any case: *I think she'll be interested, but in any event, the worst that she can do is say 'no'.* **be wise after the event** ⇨ WISE¹. **a happy event** ⇨ HAPPY. **in the e'vent** (*fml*) when the situation in fact came about: *I was worried about the hotel bill, but in the event I had enough money to pay.* **in the event of sth / that sth happens** (*fml*) if sth happens: *In the unlikely event of an accident, contact us at this number. ○ Sheila will inherit the money in the event of his death.* **in 'that event** if that happens: *You could be right, and in that event they'll have to give you a refund.*

▸ **eventful** /-fl/ *adj* full of interesting or exciting events: *an eventful year ○ He's had an eventful life.*

eventing /ɪ'ventɪŋ/ *n* [U] (*esp Brit*) the sport of taking part in competitions riding horses. These are often held over three days and include riding across country, jumping and DRESSAGE.

eventual /ɪ'ventʃʊəl/ *adj* [attrib] happening at last as a result: *the possibility of an eventual reunion ○ History will record their eventual acceptance of the treaty. ○ He may take eventual control of the company.*

[V.speech] = verb + direct speech   [V.*that*] = verb + *that* clause   [V.*wh*] = verb + *who, how*, etc clause

▶ **eventuality** /ɪˌventʃuˈæləti/ n (fml) a possible event or result: *We must make arrangements to cover any/every eventuality.* ○ *The money had been kept in reserve for (just) such an eventuality.*

eventually /-tʃuəli/ adv in the end; at last: *There was a long delay before she eventually agreed to see us.* ○ *He had a poor third round and eventually finished tenth.* ○ *Eventually, after looking at about forty houses, they bought the one in Russell Street.*

ever /ˈevə(r)/ adv **1** (usu in negative sentences and questions, or sentences expressing doubt or condition; usu placed before the v) at any time: *Nothing ever happens in this place.* ○ *Don't you ever wish you were rich?* ○ *If you ever visit this country, you must come and stay with us.* ○ *She seldom, if ever* (ie perhaps never), *goes to the cinema.* ○ *I hardly ever* (ie rarely) *see them nowadays.* ○ *All he ever does is complain.* ○ (infml) *I'm never ever going to speak to her again!* **2** (with the perfect tenses in questions) at any time up to the present: *'Have you ever been in a helicopter?' 'No, never.'* ○ *'Have you ever seen an elephant?' 'Yes, I have.'* (*Ever* is rarely used in the answer: say either *'Yes, I have'* or *'No, never'*, etc.) **3** (with comparatives after *than* or with superlatives) at any time before/up to now: *It's raining harder than ever.* ○ *This is the best work you've ever done.* ○ *her best ever score* ○ *He loved her more than ever.* **4** (**a**) always: *Paul, ever the optimist, agreed to give it one last try.* ○ *Her novels are **as popular as ever*** (ie as popular as they have always have been). ○ *They rode off into the sunset and **lived happily ever after*** (ie for the rest of their lives). ○ *'Who won?' 'She did, as ever.'* ○ *He told me he would love me **for ever (and ever).*** (**b**) (with comparatives) constantly; increasingly: *His debts grew ever larger.* See also FOREVER. **5** ever- (in compounds) continuously: *the ever-growing problem* ○ *an ever-present threat* ○ *the ever-increasing cost of food.* **6** (used after *when, where,* etc to emphasize one's surprise or doubt): *When/Where/How ever did you lose it?* ○ *What ever do you mean?* ⓘⓓⓜ **did you 'ever (...)!** (infml) (used as part of a question that one does not expect an answer to, or used alone to express surprise, disbelief, etc): *Did you ever hear such nonsense!* ○ *Opening the palace to the public — well, I mean, did you ever!* **'ever more** (fml) increasingly; more and more: *She became ever more nervous as the interview continued.* **ever since (...)** (used as a compound conj, prep or adv) continuously since a specified time: *I've known him ever since we were at school together.* ○ *She has been depressed since her sister's death.* ○ *He was bitten as a toddler and has been afraid of dogs ever 'since.* **'ever so / 'ever such (a)** (infml esp Brit) very; to a very great degree: *ever such a handsome man* ○ *He's ever so rich.* **if ˌever there 'was (one)** (infml) (used for emphasis) without doubt; that is certainly true: *That was a fine result if ever there was one!* ○ *If ever there was an idiotic idea, this was it!* **yours 'ever / ever 'yours** (sometimes used at the end of an informal letter, before the signature).

evergreen /ˈevəgriːn/ n a tree or bush that has green leaves throughout the year: *Few plants grow under the dense shade cast by the evergreens.* Compare DECIDUOUS, CONIFEROUS. ▶ **evergreen** adj: *evergreen hedges* ○ (fig) *a new production of Rossini's evergreen* (ie always popular) *comedy.*

everlasting /ˌevəˈlɑːstɪŋ; US -ˈlæst-/ adj **1** continuing or lasting for ever: *everlasting fame/life.* **2** (infml derog) repeated too often; lasting too long: *I'm tired of her everlasting complaints.* ▶ **everlastingly** adv.

evermore /ˌevəˈmɔː(r)/ adv (fml or rhet) always: *The land will remain part of our national heritage for evermore.*

every /ˈevri/ indef det **1**(**a**) (used with singular countable ns to refer to individual people or things

belonging to groups of three or more) each individual: *Every child in the class passed the examination.* ○ *I've got every record she has ever made.* ○ *I could hear every word they said.* ○ *He examined every item in the set carefully.* (**b**) (used with singular countable ns to emphasize the importance of each separate unit) each individual: *He enjoyed every minute of his stay.* ○ *I had to work for every single penny I earned.* ○ *They were watching her every movement.* ○ *Every time he phones I always seem to be in the shower.* ⇨ note at EACH. **2** (used with abstract ns) all possible (ones): *He tried every conceivable combination of numbers.* ○ *We have every reason to think he may still be alive.* ○ *You were given every opportunity to object at the time.* ○ *I wish you every success.* **3** (used to indicate that sth happens or is done at specified intervals) once in each: *The buses go every 10 minutes.* ○ *Prune the hedge every six or eight weeks.* ⓘⓓⓜ **every other 1** all the other people or things: *Every other girl except me is wearing jeans.* **2** every second (one); each ALTERNATE[1] (one): *They visit us every other week.*

everybody /ˈevribɒdi/ (also **everyone**) indef pron every person; all people: *The police questioned everybody in the room.* ○ *I'll never remember everybody's name.* ○ *You eat the olives; everybody else hates them.* ⇨ note at GENDER.

everyday /ˈevrideɪ/ adj [attrib] used or happening daily or regularly; familiar: *everyday objects* ○ *everyday life* ○ *a compact dictionary for everyday use.*

everyone /ˈevriwʌn/ indef pron = EVERYBODY: *Everyone was tired and irritable.* ○ *She ignored everyone else.* ○ *I've talked to nearly everyone concerned.* ⇨ note at GENDER.

everyplace /ˈevripleɪs/ indef adv (US infml) = EVERYWHERE.

everything /ˈevriθɪŋ/ indef pron **1** all things: *Everything was destroyed.* ○ *I'll tell you everything I know.* ○ *written exams on everything from chemistry to accountancy.* **2** the current situation; life generally: *Everything in the capital is now quiet.* ○ *'How's everything with you?' 'Fine, thanks.'* **3** the most important thing: *Money isn't everything.* ○ (infml) *'Keep Sarah out of this, she's got nothing to do with the situation.' 'She's got everything to do with it!'* (ie She is the central and most important part of it).

everywhere /ˈevriweə(r)/ (also **everyplace** (US infml) indef adv in or to every place: *I've looked everywhere* ○ *He follows me everywhere.*

evict /ɪˈvɪkt/ v **~ sb (from sth)** (esp passive) to remove sb from a house or land, esp with the support of the law: [Vn, Vnpr] *The tenants were evicted (from their house) for not paying the rent.* [Vnpr] *A group of protesters were evicted from the meeting.* ▶ **eviction** /ɪˈvɪkʃn/ n **~ (from sth)** [U, C]: *face eviction from one's home* ○ *the eviction of a widow and her two children* ○ *an eviction order* (ie a legal order to leave a place).

evidence /ˈevɪdəns/ n **1** [U] **~ (for sth / to do sth / that ...)** information that gives a strong reason for believing sth or proves sth: *not a scrap/shred of evidence* ○ *There is now fresh/further scientific evidence for this theory.* ○ *The medical/forensic evidence suggests (that) he is guilty.* ○ *There is no evidence that the meeting actually took place.* ○ *Have you any evidence to support this allegation?* ○ *His statement to the police was **used in evidence against** him.* **2** [U, C] signs; indications: *The room bore evidence of a struggle.* ○ *On the evidence of their recent matches it's unlikely the Spanish team will win the cup.* ○ *The cave produced evidences of prehistoric settlement.* ⓘⓓⓜ **(be) in 'evidence** clearly seen or noticed: *The police were much in evidence at today's demonstration.* **give (one's) 'evidence** to give answers to questions, describe an event at which one was present, etc in a lawcourt or at an inquiry: *give evidence for*

---

the defence. **turn King's/Queen's** ¹**evidence** (*Brit*); (*US*) **turn State's** ¹**evidence** (of a criminal) to give information in court against one's partners in order to receive a less severe punishment oneself. Compare PLEA BARGAINING.

▶ **evidence** *v* (*fml*) to prove sth by evidence; to be evidence of sth: [Vn] *Trading by big institutions continues to rule Wall Street, as evidenced by the New York Stock Exchange's own statistics.*

evident /ˈevɪdənt/ *adj* ~ (**to sb**) (**that...**); ~ (**in/from sth**) obvious to the eye or mind; clear: *It must be evident to all of you that a mistake has been made.* ○ *It is evident from this that something needs to be done.* ○ *The orchestra went about their task with evident relish.*

▶ **evidently** *adv* obviously; it appears that: *The President evidently assumes that he will still be in power next year.* ○ *Evidently they had already tried but failed to unblock the pipe.*

evil /ˈiːvl, ˈiːvɪl/ *adj* **1** morally bad; wicked: *evil thoughts/deeds* ○ *evil spirits.* **2** very unpleasant or harmful: *an evil smell* ○ *He has an evil temper.* **IDM** **the evil** ¹**day,** ¹**hour, etc** the time when sth unpleasant that one would like to avoid will happen: *I know I need to go to the dentist but I've been putting off the evil day as long as possible.*

▶ **evil** *n* (*fml*) **1** [U] wrongdoing or wickedness: *the eternal struggle between good and evil* ○ *the forces of evil* ○ *You cannot pretend there's no evil in the world.* **2** [C usu *pl*] a wicked or harmful thing: *the evils of drink/slavery* ○ *social evils.* **IDM** **the lesser of two evils; the lesser evil** ⇨ LESSER. **a necessary evil** ⇨ NECESSARY.

evilly /ˈiːvəli/ *adv* in an evil manner: *He eyed her evilly.*

■ **the ₁evil ¹eye** *n* [sing] a look believed to cause harm to the person at whom it is directed: *protection against the evil eye* ○ *an incantation to ward off the evil eye* ○ *give sb the evil eye.*

evince /ɪˈvɪns/ *v* (*fml*) to show clearly that one has a feeling, quality, etc: [Vn] *He evinced a strong desire to be reconciled with his family.*

eviscerate /ɪˈvɪsəreɪt/ *v* [Vn] (*fml*) to remove the internal organs of a body.

evocative /ɪˈvɒkətɪv/ *adj* ~ (**of sth**) that brings strong images, memories, feelings, etc of sth into one's mind: *an evocative account of his life as a coalminer* ○ *evocative smells/sounds.*

evoke /ɪˈvəʊk/ *v* to bring an image, a feeling, a memory, etc into one's mind: [Vn] *evoke admiration/surprise/sympathy* ○ *the sensations evoked in the crowd by his speech* ○ *The music evoked memories of her youth.* ▶ **evocation** /ˌiːvəʊˈkeɪʃn/ *n* [C, U] (*fml*): *a flood of childhood evocations* ○ *The play was a brilliant evocation of life in the 1930s.*

evolution /ˌiːvəˈluːʃn, ˌev-/ *n* [U] **1** (*biology*) the gradual development of the characteristics of plants and animals over many generations, esp the development of more complicated forms from earlier, simpler forms: *play an important part in human evolution* ○ *Darwin's theory of evolution.* **2** the process of gradual development: *the evolution of farming methods* ○ *In politics Britain has preferred evolution to revolution* (ie gradual development to sudden violent change).

▶ **evolutionary** /ˌiːvəˈluːʃənri, ˌev-; *US* ˌevəˈluːʃəneri/ *adj* (*fml*) of or resulting from evolution; developing: *evolutionary changes/processes.*

evolve /ɪˈvɒlv/ *v* **1** ~ (**from sth**) (**into sth**) to develop naturally and usu gradually: [Vn] *He has evolved a new theory after many years of research.* [V] *The information system can be adapted to meet evolving needs.* [V-n] *The novel evolves as an elegy for a lost way of life.* [Vpr] *The idea evolved from a drawing I discovered in the attic.* **2** (*biology*) (of plants,

animals, etc) to develop gradually from a simple form to a more complex one: [Vpr] *The three species evolved from a single ancestor.* [V] *An extraordinary system of sexual reproduction evolved.* [Vn] *The dolphin has evolved a highly developed jaw.*

ewe /juː/ *n* a female sheep. ⇨ picture at SHEEP. Compare LAMB 1, RAM¹ 1.

ewer /ˈjuːə(r)/ *n* a large JUG used esp formerly for carrying water for sb to wash in: *a basin and ewer.*

ex¹ /eks/ *n* (*pl* **exes, ex's**) (*infml*) one's former wife, husband or other partner in a relationship: *Her ex shares custody of the children.*

ex² /eks/ *prep* excluding sth; not included: *Prices quoted are ex VAT.*

ex- *pref* (used widely with *ns*) former: *ex-wife* ○ *ex-President* ○ *ex-convict.*

exacerbate /ɪɡˈzæsəbeɪt/ *v* (*fml*) to make a pain, a disease or a situation worse; to AGGRAVATE(1) sth: [Vn] *Scratching exacerbates a skin rash.* ○ *Her mother's interference only exacerbated the difficulties in their marriage.*

exact¹ /ɪɡˈzækt/ *adj* **1** correct in every detail; accurate; PRECISE(2): *an exact copy/replica of the painting* ○ *the exact time/date/figure/location/size* ○ *What were his exact words?* ○ *They elected a leader who was almost the exact opposite of the previous one.* ○ *He's in his mid-fifties — well, fifty-six to be exact.* **2(a)** capable of being accurate and careful about minor details: *She's a very exact person.* **(b)** (of a science) relying on measurements and fixed laws : *Bringing up children is not an exact science, you know!*

▶ **exactitude** /ɪɡˈzæktɪtjuːd; *US* -tuːd/ *n* [U] (*fml*) the quality or state of being exact: *scholarly exactitude.*

exactly *adv* **1** (used for emphasis) in every way; precisely (PRECISE); just²(1): *That's exactly what I expected.* ○ *I know exactly how she felt.* ○ *You've arrived at exactly the right moment.* ○ *It happened almost exactly a year ago.* ○ *His words had exactly the opposite effect.* **2** in every detail: *Your answer is exactly right.* ○ *Where exactly were you in France?* **3** (as a reply confirming what sb has just said) you are quite right: *'So she wants to sell the house and move to Berlin.' 'Exactly.'* **IDM** **not exactly** (*infml*) **1** (ironic) not at all: *He wasn't exactly pleased to see us; in fact he refused to open the door.* **2** not really; no: *'Do you have an appointment, sir?' 'Not exactly, but I know he'll see me.'*

exactness *n* [U].

exact² /ɪɡˈzækt/ *v* ~ **sth** (**from sb**) to demand and obtain sth, esp a payment: [Vnpr] *The kidnappers exacted a ransom of £50 000 from the family.* [Vn] *He exacted a terrible revenge for their treatment of him.*

▶ **exacting** *adj* making great demands; requiring great effort and attention to detail: *products designed to meet the exacting standards of today's international market-place* ○ *His work schedule is exacting.* **exaction** /ɪɡˈzækʃn/ *n* (*fml*) [U, C].

exaggerate /ɪɡˈzædʒəreɪt/ *v* to make sth seem larger, better, worse, etc than it really is: [V] *He always exaggerates to make his stories more amusing.* [Vn] *You're exaggerating the difficulties.* ○ *It would be easy to exaggerate the importance/significance of these new laws.* ○ *I'm sure he exaggerates his Irish accent.*

▶ **exaggerated** *adj* **(a)** made to seem larger, better, worse, etc than it really is: *make greatly/wildly/grossly exaggerated claims* ○ *He has an exaggerated sense of his own importance.* **(b)** produced, stated, etc in a false or elaborate way: *an exaggerated laugh* ○ *with exaggerated politeness.* **exaggeratedly** *adv.* **exaggeration** /ɪɡˌzædʒəˈreɪʃn/ *n* **1** [U] the action of exaggerating sth: *He told his story simply and*

E

without exaggeration. **2** [C] an exaggerated description or statement: *It would be an exaggeration to say he knew her well — they met only two or three times.*

exalt /ɪgˈzɔːlt/ *v* (*fml*) **1** to make sb higher in rank or greater in power: [Vn] *The poor will be exalted.* **2** to praise sb/sth highly: [Vn-n] *He was exalted as a pillar of the community.* [also Vn].

▶ **exaltation** /ˌegzɔːlˈteɪʃn/ *n* [U] **1** a state of extreme spiritual happiness: *a feeling of exaltation and delight.* **2** (*fml*) the action of exalting sb/sth: *his exaltation of their culture.*

exalted *adj* **1** (*fml or joc*) having a high rank or status: *She occupies an exalted position in the firm.* ○ *No leader, however exalted, was allowed to speak from a platform.* **2** in a state of extreme spiritual happiness: *I felt exalted and newly alive.* Compare EXULT.

exam /ɪgˈzæm/ *n* = EXAMINATION 1: *pass/fail one's exams* ○ *The teachers set and mark our school exams.* ○ *a maths exam* ○ *an exam paper* ○ *When do you take your final exams?* ○ *I got my exam results today.*

examination /ɪgˌzæmɪˈneɪʃn/ *n* **1** (*fml*) (also **exam**) [C] a formal test of sb's knowledge or ability in a particular subject, esp by means of written questions or practical exercises: *sit an examination in Human Biology* ○ *successful candidates in GCSE examinations* ○ *an ˈoral examination* ○ *an ˈentrance examination* (eg to test the ability of sb wishing to enter a school or college). **2(a)** [U] the action of inspecting sth/sb in detail: *Careful examination of the ruins revealed an even earlier temple.* ○ *On closer/further examination it was found that the signature was not genuine.* **(b)** [C] a close inspection of sth/sb or an inquiry into sth: *undergo a medical examination* ○ *an examination of business accounts* ○ *The proposals are still under examination.*

examine /ɪgˈzæmɪn/ *v* **1** ~ **sth/sb** (**for sth**) to look at sth/sb carefully and in detail in order to learn sth about or from it/them; to inspect sth/sb closely: [Vn] *The team examined the wreckage thoroughly/minutely.* ○ *examine facts/evidence/possible solutions* ○ *examine the impact of aid programmes* ○ *The doctor was examining a patient.* [Vnpr] *Detectives examined the room for fingerprints.* [V.wh] *The book examines how attitudes have changed since the war.* **2** ~ **sb** (**in/on sth**) (*fml*) to test the knowledge or ability of sb, esp by asking them questions or setting them practical tasks: [Vnpr] *examine students in mathematics/on their knowledge of mathematics* [also Vn]. **3** (*law*) to question sb formally, esp in a lawcourt: [Vn] *be examined under oath.* See also CROSS-EXAMINE. **IDM** **need, etc one's head examined** ⇨ HEAD¹.

▶ **examiner** /ɪgˈzæmɪnə(r)/ *n* a person who tests knowledge or ability: *The papers are sent to external examiners* (ie ones not connected with the students' school or college).

example /ɪgˈzɑːmpl; *US* -ˈzæmpl/ *n* **1** a fact, event, etc that illustrates or represents a general rule: *Can you give me/cite a specific example of what you mean?* ○ *This dictionary has many examples of how words are used.* ○ *It was a typical example of his generosity.* **2** a thing that is considered representative or typical of a particular group or set: *This is a good/fine example of Shelley's lyric poetry.* ○ *This church is a striking/an outstanding example of Norman architecture.* ○ *a perfect/prime example of bad manners* ○ *It is a classic example of how not to design a new city centre.* **3** ~ (**to sb**) a thing, person or quality that is worthy of being copied: *Her bravery should be an example to us all.* ○ *a shining example of moral strength* ○ *She sets an excellent example to the rest of the students.* ○ *Don't be tempted to follow his example.* ○ *He is a captain who leads by example.* **IDM** **for example** (*abbr* **eg**) as a typical case or representative: *Consider, for example, the effect that*

the new measures will have on small businesses. ○ *I know many women who have a career and a family* — *Alison, for example.* ○ *The report is incomplete; for example, it does not include sales in France.* Compare SAMPLE. **make an example of sb** to punish sb as a warning to others: *The headteacher decided to make an example of him by expelling him from the school.*

exasperate /ɪgˈzæspəreɪt; *Brit also* -ˈzɑːsp-/ *v* to irritate or annoy sb greatly: [Vn] *His constant whistling exasperated her.*

▶ **exasperated** *adj* ~ (**at/with sb/sth**) extremely annoyed, esp by a situation that one can do nothing to improve: *'Now who can that be?' said Mr Norris, exasperated.* ○ *She was thoroughly exasperated at/with her mother's attitude.*

exasperating *adj* extremely annoying: *He's probably the most exasperating man I've ever met.* ○ *It's really exasperating to run for a train and then miss it by seconds.*

exasperation /ɪgˌzæspəˈreɪʃn; *Brit also* -ˈzɑːsp-/ *n* [U]: *She sat back with a sigh of exasperation.* ○ *We eventually had to give up in exasperation.*

excavate /ˈekskəveɪt/ *v* **1** to reveal or take out sth that has been buried in the ground, as a result of digging: [Vn] *excavate a buried city/a Greek vase.* **2** (*fml*) to make a hole or channel by digging the ground: [Vn] *excavate a trench.*

▶ **excavation** /ˌekskəˈveɪʃn/ *n* **1** [U,C] the activity of excavating sth: *recent excavations at Pompeii* ○ *Excavation of the site has proved difficult.* **2** [C usu pl] a place that is being or has been excavated: *visit the excavations.*

excavator *n* (**a**) a person involved in excavating sth. (**b**) a machine used for excavating.

exceed /ɪkˈsiːd/ *v* (**a**) to be greater in number or size than sth, esp than a quantity or number: [Vn] *The price will not exceed £100.* ○ *The number admitted must not exceed 200.* ○ *Births far exceed deaths at the moment.* ○ *Their success exceeded (all) expectations* (ie was greater than anyone expected). (**b**) to go beyond what is allowed or necessary: [Vn] *exceed one's instructions/authority* (ie do more than one has permission to do) ○ *You should not exceed the speed limit* (ie drive faster than is allowed).

▶ **exceedingly** *adv* (*rather fml*) extremely; to a great or unusual degree: *an exceedingly difficult problem* ○ *They played exceedingly well.*

excel /ɪkˈsel/ *v* (**-ll-**) ~ (**in/at sth / at doing sth**) to be exceptionally good at sth: [Vpr] *excel in foreign languages* ○ *The firm excels at producing cheap radios.* [V] *Throughout her life she felt the need to excel.* **IDM** **exˈcel oneself** to do better than one has ever done before: *His meals are always very good, but this time he's really excelled himself.*

excellence /ˈeksələns/ *n* [U] ~ (**in sth**) the quality of being extremely good or outstanding: *The university's reputation for academic excellence* ○ *set high standards of excellence in the fine arts.* See also PAR EXCELLENCE.

Excellency /ˈeksələnsi/ *n* a title given to a high-ranking official, eg an AMBASSADOR: *Good evening, Your Excellency.* ○ *His Excellency the French Ambassador.*

excellent /ˈeksələnt/ *adj* **1** very good; of very high quality: *an excellent meal* ○ *provide excellent service/facilities* ○ *At $300 the bike is excellent value (for money).* ○ *She speaks excellent French.* **2** (used to indicate approval or pleasure): *You can all come? Excellent!* ▶ **excellently** *adv*.

except¹ /ɪkˈsept/ *prep* ~ (**for sb/sth**); ~ (**that…**) not including sb/sth; but not sb/sth: *The restaurant is open every day except Monday.* ○ *We'll invite everyone, except perhaps Martin.* ○ *I understand everything except why she killed him.* ○ *He could answer all the questions except for the last one.* ○ *The room was empty except for an old piano in the corner.* ○ *She*

─────────────────

[V.*to* inf] = verb + *to* infinitive   [Vn.inf (no *to*)] = verb + noun + infinitive without *to*   [V.*ing*] = verb + *-ing* form

remembered nothing about him except that his hair was black. ○ *The two books are the same except (for the fact) that this one has an answer key at the back.*

except² /ɪkˈsept/ v ~ **sb/sth (from sth)** (*fml*) (often with a negative) to exclude sb/sth: [Vnpr] *Children under five are excepted from the survey.* [Vn] *The whole staff, not excepting the art teacher, had to take part in the pantomime.* ○ *Spain excepted, the most popular European holiday destination is Greece.* **IDM** **present company excepted** ⇨ PRESENT¹.

exception /ɪkˈsepʃn/ n **1(a)** [C] a person or thing that is not included: *Most of the buildings in this town are rather unattractive, but this church is a notable exception.* ○ *The children did well, the only exception being Jo, who failed.* ○ *Freedom of choice is at the heart of all our policies, and transport is no exception.* **(b)** [U] the action of excluding sb/sth or the state of being excluded: *All students without exception must take the English examination.* ○ *I enjoyed all his novels* **with the exception of** (ie except/not including) *his last.* **2** [C] a thing that does not follow a rule: *an exception to a rule of grammar* ○ *Such community spirit is unfortunately* **the exception rather than the rule** (ie not usual). ○ *Children are not normally allowed in, but in your case I'm prepared to* **make an exception** (ie to allow you in). **IDM** **the exception proves the** ˈ**rule** (*saying*) the fact that some cases do not follow a rule proves that the rule exists, or that it applies to all other cases: *All his family have red hair except him. He is the exception that/which proves the rule.* **take** **ex**ˈ**ception to sth** to object strongly to sth; to be offended by sth: *He took great exception to what I said.* ○ *She took exception to having to wait outside in the corridor.*

▶ **exceptionable** /-ʃənəbl/ adj (*fml*) that sb may object to; likely to cause offence: *There are no exceptionable scenes in the play.*

exceptional /ɪkˈsepʃənl/ adj very unusual; outstanding: *show exceptional musical ability* ○ *This weather is exceptional for June.* ○ *I could only condone violence* **in exceptional circumstances.** Compare UNEXCEPTIONAL. ▶ **exceptionally** /-ʃənəli/ adv: *an exceptionally beautiful child.*

excerpt /ˈeksɜːpt/ n [C] ~ **(from sth)** a passage or extract from a book, film, piece of music, etc: *excerpts from a novel* ○ *I've seen a short excerpt from the movie on television.*

excess¹ /ɪkˈses/ n **1** [sing] **an ~ of sth** (*derog*) more than a reasonable or moderate degree or amount of sth: *an excess of enthusiasm/anger/emotion/zeal* ○ *An excess of fat in one's diet can lead to heart disease.* **2** [U] going beyond the normal or accepted limits: *He's drinking* **to excess.** ○ *He was driving at speeds* **in excess of** *120 mph.* **3** [C] an amount by which sth is larger than sth else: *She was charged an excess of $4 over the amount stated on the bill.* **4 excesses** [pl] (*fml*) acts that are beyond the limits of good or reasonable behaviour: *the excesses of popular journalism* ○ *His excesses at parties are well known.* ○ *One is reminded of the worst excesses (eg acts of cruelty) of the French Revolution.*

▶ **excessive** /ɪkˈsesɪv/ adj greater than what is normal or necessary; extreme: *excessive prices* ○ *an excessive amount of alcohol* ○ *an excessive enthusiasm for football.* **excessively** adv: *excessively high prices.*

excess² /ˈekses/ adj [attrib] extra or additional to the necessary or permitted amount: *excess sugar in one's diet* ○ *pay an excess fare* (eg for travelling further than is allowed by one's ticket).

■ ˌ**excess** ˈ**baggage** (also ˌ**excess** ˈ**luggage**) n [U] an amount of LUGGAGE that is over the weight that may be carried free on an aircraft.

ˌ**excess** ˈ**postage** n [U] an amount charged to a

person who receives a letter sent without stamps of sufficient value.

exchange¹ /ɪksˈtʃeɪndʒ/ n [C, U] **1(a)** the action or an instance of giving one thing or person of the same type or of equal value in return for another: *Is five apples for five eggs a fair exchange?* ○ *a house-exchange* (eg for a holiday) ○ *The exchange of prisoners during a war is unusual.* ○ *She's giving him French lessons* **in exchange for** *his teaching her English.* **(b)** the action or an instance of giving sth to another person and receiving sth in return: *the exchange of contracts* (ie when buying or selling a house) ○ *an exchange of glances* ○ *an exchange of gunfire.* **2** [C] a conversation or an argument, esp an angry one: *bitter exchanges between MP's in parliament.* **3** [U] the relation in value between the money used in different countries: *What is the* **exchange rate/rate of exchange** *between the dollar and the pound?* See also ERM, FOREIGN EXCHANGE. **4** (often **Exchange** [C]) a place where business people meet to do financial deals: *the London* ˈ*Metal Exchange* ○ *the* ˈ*Stock Exchange.* **5** [C] = TELEPHONE EXCHANGE. **6** [C] a visit or visits in which two people or groups from different countries stay with each other or do each other's jobs: *be on/do/organize an exchange* ○ *exchange teachers* ○ *Sarah is going on an exchange to Paris to stay with Pierre, and he is coming to stay with her here in Scotland next year.*

exchange² /ɪksˈtʃeɪndʒ/ v **(a)** ~ **A for B**; ~ **sth** **(with sb)** to give or receive sth/sb of the same type or of equal value in return for another: [Vnpr] *He exchanged the blue sweater for a red one.* ○ *Ali exchanged seats with Ben.* [Vn] *The warring factions exchanged hostages/prisoners.* **(b)** to give sth to another person and receive sth in return: [Vn] *exchanging blows* (ie hitting each other) ○ *They exchanged glances* (ie looked at each other). ○ *The two men exchanged greetings* (ie Each greeted the other). ○ *I heard them exchanging angry words* (ie quarrelling).

▶ **exchangeable** /-əbl/ adj that can be exchanged: *Goods bought in the sale are not exchangeable.*

exchequer /ɪksˈtʃekə(r)/ n [sing] **(a)** **the Ex-** **chequer** (formerly in Britain) the government department in charge of public money: *The Chancellor of the Exchequer is the minister in charge of finance in Britain.* Compare TREASURY 1. **(b)** the public or national supply of money: *This resulted in a considerable loss to the exchequer.*

excise¹ /ˈeksaɪz/ n [U] a government tax on certain goods manufactured, sold or used within a country: *the excise on beer/spirits/tobacco* ○ *the Board of Customs and Excise* ○ *excise duties* ○ *an excise officer* (ie an official employed in collecting excise). Compare CUSTOMS.

excise² /ɪkˈsaɪz/ v ~ **sth (from sth)** (*fml*) to remove sth completely: [Vn] *excise all references to the USSR* [Vnpr] *A lump was excised from her breast.*

▶ **excision** /ɪkˈsɪʒn/ n (*fml*) **(a)** [U] the action of excising sth: *the excision of a tumour.* **(b)** [C] a thing that is excised: *The numerous excisions have destroyed the literary value of the text.*

excitable /ɪkˈsaɪtəbl/ adj (of a person or an animal) easily excited: *an excitable and hyperactive child* ○ *She has an excitable temperament.* ▶ **excitability** /ɪkˌsaɪtəˈbɪləti/ n [U].

excite /ɪkˈsaɪt/ v **1** to cause strong feelings of eagerness and enthusiasm, esp for sth that is about to happen: [Vn] *The children were very much excited by the news.* ○ *The prospect of going to India for a year greatly excited her.* ○ *Don't excite yourself* (ie Keep calm). **2(a)** ~ **sth (in sb)** to make sb feel a particular emotion, response, or reaction: [Vn, Vnpr] *excite envy/admiration/greed (in sb)* [Vn] *excite public suspicion* ○ *Recent discoveries have excited great interest*

E

among doctors. (**b**) to make sb feel sexual desire: [Vn] *Some people are (sexually) excited by pornographic magazines.* **3** (*fml*) to make part of the body active; to stimulate sth: [Vn] *drugs that excite the nervous system.*

▶ **excitation** /ˌeksɪˈteɪʃn, ˌeksaɪ/ *n* [U] (*fml or techn*) the process of becoming or the state of being excited: *sexual excitation.*

excited /ɪkˈsaɪtɪd/ *adj* ~ (**about/at sth**); ~ (**to do sth**) feeling or showing eagerness and enthusiasm: *the children's excited faces* ○ *He was terribly excited to be asked to play for Wales.* ○ *be excited about going on holiday* ○ *It's nothing to get excited about.* **excitedly** *adv*: *The girls danced around excitedly.*

exciting *adj* causing great interest or enthusiasm: *an exciting story/discovery* ○ *A trip in a hot-air balloon sounded very exciting.* **excitingly** *adv*.

excitement /ɪkˈsaɪtmənt/ *n* **1** [U] a happy feeling of eagerness and enthusiasm: *The news of Julia's engagement caused great excitement.* ○ *The excitement soon wore off.* ○ *They were jumping about in excitement at the discovery.* ○ *His eyes were wide with excitement.* **2** [C] (*fml*) a thing that excites; an exciting incident: *After all the excitements of last month's election campaign, the papers are now rather dull.*

exclaim /ɪkˈskleɪm/ *v* to cry out suddenly and loudly, esp from pain, anger or surprise: [V.speech] *'I don't understand you,' he exclaimed angrily.* [Vpr] *I could not help exclaiming at how much his son had grown.* [V.that] *He exclaimed that he had never even met her.*

exclamation /ˌekskləˈmeɪʃn/ *n* a short sound, word or phrase expressing sudden surprise, pain, etc. *Oh!, Look out!* and *Ow!* are exclamations: *Mrs Davis gave an exclamation of disgust.*

■ **excla'mation mark** (*US* **excla'mation point**) *n* the mark (!) written after an exclamation. ⇨ App 3.

exclude /ɪkˈskluːd/ *v* **1** ~ **sb/sth** (**from sth**) (**a**) to prevent sb from entering somewhere or being involved in sth; to keep sb out: [Vnpr] *exclude a person from membership of a society* ○ *Women are still often excluded from positions of authority.* [also Vn]. (**b**) to prevent sth from entering a place; to keep sth out: [Vn, Vnpr] *All air must be excluded (from the bottle) if the experiment is to work.* **2** to reject sth as a possibility; to ignore sth as a consideration: [Vn.n] *The police have excluded robbery as a motive for the murder.* [Vn] *We must not exclude the possibility that the child has run away.* **3** to leave sth out; not to include sth: [Vn] *Lunch costs £10 per person, excluding drinks.* ○ *Buses run every hour, Sundays and public holidays excluded.* Compare INCLUDE.

exclusion /ɪkˈskluːʒn/ *n* (**a**) [U] ~ (**of sb/sth**) (**from sth**) the action of excluding sb/sth: *the exclusion of women from the temple* ○ *the exclusion of robbery as a motive* ○ *an exclusion zone around the islands* (eg excluding enemy ships). (**b**) [C] a person or thing that is excluded: *exclusions on account of age* ○ *The insurance policy contains several exclusions.* Compare INCLUSION. **IDM** **to the exclusion of sb/sth** so as to exclude other people, activities, etc: *He spent his spare time gardening, to the exclusion of all other interests.*

exclusive /ɪkˈskluːsɪv/ *adj* **1**(**a**) (of a group, society, etc) not readily admitting new members, esp if they are thought to be socially inferior: *He belongs to an exclusive club.* (**b**) expensive and not commonly bought or used by the majority of people; SMART[1](4): *exclusive styles/designs/articles* ○ *an exclusive restaurant/private school/shop.* **2** reserved for or limited to the person or group concerned: *have exclusive rights to televise the World Cup* ○ *We granted them an exclusive agency for the sale of our books in Spain.* ○ *The interview is exclusive to this magazine.* **3** not admitting sth else; that cannot

exist or be true if sth else exists or is true: *The two plans are **mutually exclusive** (ie If you accept one you must reject the other).* **4** [pred] ~ **of sb/sth** not including sb/sth; not counting sb/sth: *The ship has a crew of 57 exclusive of officers.* ○ *The price of the excursion is exclusive of accommodation.*

▶ **exclusive** *n* a newspaper or magazine story given to and published by only one newspaper: *a Daily Mirror exclusive.*

exclusively *adv*: *an area that relies almost exclusively on tourism* ○ *This special offer has been exclusively designed for readers of 'Home' magazine.* **exclusiveness, exclusivity** /ˌekskluːˈsɪvəti/ *ns* [U] the quality of being exclusive: *the resort's exclusivity* ○ *The shop was proud of its exclusiveness.*

excommunicate /ˌekskəˈmjuːnɪkeɪt/ *v* [Vn] to exclude sb as a punishment from membership of the Christian (esp Roman Catholic) Church. ▶ **excommunication** /ˌekskəˌmjuːnɪˈkeɪʃn/ *n* [U, C]: *They were threatened with excommunication.*

excoriate /ˌeksˈkɔːrieɪt/ *v* (*fml*) to criticize sb severely: [Vn] *excoriate the government for its failure to act.* ▶ **excoriation** *n* [U, C].

excrement /ˈekskrɪmənt/ *n* [U] (*fml*) solid waste matter passed from the body through the bowels; FAECES: *The lawn was covered in dogs' excrement.* ▶ **excremental** *adj*.

excrescence /ɪkˈskresns/ *n* (*fml*) an abnormal growth(4a) on an animal's body or on a plant: (*fig*) *The new office block is an excrescence* (ie It is very ugly).

excreta /ɪkˈskriːtə/ *n* [U] (*fml*) waste matter passed from the body, esp FAECES and URINE: *human excreta.*

excrete /ɪkˈskriːt/ *v* [Vn] (*fml*) (of an animal or a plant) to pass out waste matter from its body or system. ▶ **excretion** /ɪkˈskriːʃn/ *n* [U, C].

excruciating /ɪkˈskruːʃieɪtɪŋ/ *adj* (of physical or mental pain) intense; severe; very bad: *excruciating misery* ○ *Backache can be excruciating.* ○ (*joc*) *an excruciating concert* ○ *He's an excruciating bore.* ▶ **excruciatingly** *adv*: *an excruciatingly painful experience* ○ *The evening was excruciatingly dull.*

exculpate /ˈekskʌlpeɪt/ *v* [Vn, Vnpr] ~ **sb/oneself** (**from sth**) (*fml*) to say or show that sb cannot be blamed for sth or is not guilty of sth. ▶ **exculpation** *n* [U].

excursion /ɪkˈskɜːʃn; *US* -ɜːrʒn/ *n* (**a**) a short journey, esp one made by a group of people together for pleasure: *Your tour includes a one-day excursion to the Grand Canyon by air.* ○ *All the excursions had been arranged by the travel company.* ○ *an excursion ticket* (ie one issued at a reduced fare) ○ (*fig*) *a writer who made occasional excursions into the realm of science fiction.* (**b**) a short journey made for a particular purpose: *a shopping excursion.* ⇨ note at JOURNEY.

excuse[1] /ɪkˈskjuːs/ *n* **1** ~ (**for sth / doing sth**) a reason, either true or invented, given to explain or defend one's bad behaviour: *He's always making excuses for being late.* ○ *Late again? What's your excuse this time?* ○ *There's no excuse for such behaviour.* ○ *He made his excuses* (ie He said sorry and gave his reasons for leaving early) *and left.* **2** ~ (**for sth / doing sth**); ~ (**to do sth**) a reason for doing sth; an opportunity: *a good excuse for a party* ○ *The party gave me an excuse to wear my new dress.*

excuse[2] /ɪkˈskjuːz/ *v* **1** ~ **sth**; ~ **sb** (**for sth/doing sth**) to forgive a fault or wrongdoing; to PARDON[2](1) sb/sth: [Vn] *Please excuse my late arrival.* [Vnpr] *Excuse me for being late.* ○ *The audience could be excused for thinking it was an amateur production.* [V.n ing] *Excuse my interrupting you.* **2**(**a**) ~ **sth**; ~ **sb/oneself for sth/doing sth** to give reasons that justify, or are intended to justify, sb's or one's own actions or behaviour: [Vn] *Nothing can excuse such rudeness.* [Vnpr] *He excused himself for being late by* *saying that his car had broken down.* (**b**) ~ **oneself** to say in a polite way that one has to leave: [Vn] *She excused herself hurriedly, and ran out of the room.* **3** ~ **sb** (**from sth**) (esp passive) to free sb/oneself from a duty, requirement, punishment, etc: [Vnn, Vnpr] *He was excused (from) piano practice.* [Vnpr] *She excused herself from the walk saying she didn't feel well.* [Vn] *Only pregnant women can be excused.* **IDM** **be ex'cused** (*often euph*) (used esp by children at school) to be allowed to leave a room, etc, eg to go to the toilet: *Please can I be excused?* **ex'cuse me 1** used to get the attention of sb one does not know: *Excuse me, do you have the right time?* **2** (used as an apology when one interrupts, disagrees, or has to behave in a way that is not polite): *Please excuse me while I answer the telephone.* ○ *Excuse me, but I don't think that's quite true.* **3 excuse me?** (*esp US*) please repeat what you said.

▶ **excusable** /ɪkˈskjuːzəbl/ *adj* that may be excused: *Their mistake was excusable.* Compare INEXCUSABLE.

ex-directory /ˌeks dəˈrektəri/ (*US* **unlisted**) *adj* (of a person or a telephone number) not listed in the telephone DIRECTORY, at the wish of the owner of the telephone. The telephone company will not reveal ex-directory numbers to people who ask for them: *an ex-directory number* ○ *go ex-directory* ○ *She's ex-directory.*

execrable /ˈeksɪkrəbl/ *adj* (*fml*) very bad; terrible: *execrable manners/poetry.*

execute /ˈeksɪkjuːt/ *v* **1** to kill sb, esp as a legal punishment: [Vn] *execute suspected rebels* [Vnpr] *He was executed for treason.* **2** (*fml*) to do or perform what one is asked or told to do: [Vn] *execute sb's commands* ○ *execute a plan/a piece of work* ○ *The crime had been cleverly executed.* **3** (*fml*) to perform sth on the stage, at a concert, etc: [Vn] *execute a dance step* [Vnadv] *The whole sonata was superbly executed.* **4** (*law*) (**a**) to put sth into effect: [Vn] *execute a will.* (**b**) to make sth legally valid: [Vn] *execute a legal document* (ie by having it signed in the presence of witnesses, sealed and delivered).

execution /ˌeksɪˈkjuːʃn/ *n* **1** [U, C] the killing of sb, esp as a legal punishment: *condemn sb to execution by hanging* ○ *Over 200 executions take place/are carried out in the country each year.* **2** [U] the action of doing a piece of work, performing a duty, etc or putting a plan, design, etc into effect: *His original idea was good, but the execution of it was disastrous.* ○ *The plans were finally put into execution.* **3** [U] (*fml*) skill in performing eg music: *Her execution of the difficult finale was faultless.* **4** [U] (*law*) the action of fulfilling the instructions written in a will[4](5): *The solicitors are proceeding with the execution of my mother's will.* **IDM** **a stay of execution** ⇨ STAY[1] *n.*

▶ **executioner** /ˌeksɪˈkjuːʃənə(r)/ *n* a public official who executes people condemned to death.

executive /ɪgˈzekjətɪv/ *adj* [usu attrib] **1** (esp in business) relating to the management of an organization and to putting plans, decisions, etc into effect: *executive duties* ○ *a woman of considerable executive ability.* **2** having power to put important decisions, laws, etc into effect: *executive authority/power* ○ *the executive committee of a political party* ○ *the executive head of State* (eg the President of the USA).

▶ **executive** *n* **1** [C, CGp] a person or group working in administration or management in a business organization, trade union, etc: *a sales executive* ○ *She's the chief executive of a computer company.* ○ *The union executive has/have yet to reach a decision.* ○ *an executive briefcase/suite.* **2 the executive** [Gp] the branch of a government that is concerned with putting decisions, laws, etc into effect.

executor /ɪgˈzekjətə(r)/ *n* a person who is ap-

pointed by a person making a will[4](5) to carry out the instructions in it.

exegesis /ˌeksɪˈdʒiːsɪs/ *n* (*pl* **exegeses** /-siːz/) [U, C] (*fml*) the explaining and interpreting of a written work, esp the Bible.

exemplar /ɪgˈzemplɑː(r)/ *n* (*fml*) a person or thing that serves as a good or typical example; a model[1](5): *an exemplar of theatre at its most challenging.*

exemplary /ɪgˈzempləri/ *adj* **1** serving as a good example; suitable to be copied: *exemplary behaviour* ○ *an exemplary student.* **2** (*law or fml*) serving as a warning: *exemplary damages/punishment.*

exemplify /ɪgˈzemplɪfaɪ/ *v* (*pt, pp* **-fied**) **1** to be a typical example of sth: [Vnpr, Vn] *Her style exemplifies modern Italian cooking at its best.* **2** (*fml*) to give an example of sth; to illustrate sth by giving an example: [Vn] *exemplify the problems involved.* ▶ **exemplification** /ɪgˌzemplɪfɪˈkeɪʃn/ *n* [U, C].

exempt /ɪgˈzempt/ *adj* [pred] ~ (**from sth**) free from an obligation, duty or payment; not LIABLE(1,2): *exempt from military service* ○ *exempt from working overtime* ○ *goods exempt from tax* ○ *In the UK children under 16 are exempt from prescription charges.*

▶ **exempt** *v* ~ **sb/sth** (**from sth**) (*fml*) to make sb/ sth exempt: [Vnpr] *His bad eyesight exempted him from military service.* [also Vn]. **exemption** /ɪgˈzempʃn/ *n* [U, C] ~ (**from sth**): *claim/seek tax exemption* ○ *exemptions from planning restrictions.*

exercise[1] /ˈeksəsaɪz/ *n* **1**(**a**) [U] use of the body or the mind that involves effort or activity: *The doctor advised him to take more exercise.* ○ *Jogging is a healthy form of exercise.* ○ *Doing crosswords gives the mind some exercise.* (**b**) [C] an activity or a task that trains the body or the mind: *vocal/gymnastic/ keep-fit/deep-breathing exercises* ○ *exercises for the piano/flute/harp* ○ *The teacher gave her class a mathematics exercise for homework.* ○ *an exercise book* (ie a book for writing school work, notes, etc in). **2** [U] ~ **of sth** the use or application of sth: *the exercise of one's civil rights* ○ *The exercise of patience is essential in diplomatic negotiations.* ○ *His stories showed considerable exercise of the imagination.* **3** [C] ~ (**in sth**) an activity or process involving a particular skill or quality and designed to achieve a result: *an exercise in public relations* ○ *In the end it proved a pointless exercise.* **4** [C often *pl*] a series of movements or operations for training troops, etc: *military exercises.* **5 exercises** [pl] (*US*) ceremonies: *graduation exercises* ○ *opening exercises* (eg speeches at the start of a conference).

exercise[2] /ˈeksəsaɪz/ *v* **1** to perform some kind of physical exercise: [V] *He exercises twice a day.* **2** to involve sb/sth in physical or mental effort or activity: [Vn] *Horses get fat and lazy if they are not exercised.* ○ *Swimming exercises the whole body.* **3** to use or apply sth: [Vn] *exercise patience/tolerance/ power/control* ○ *exercise one's rights as a citizen* [Vnpr] *Teachers exercise authority over their pupils.* **4** (*fml*) to worry sb or occupy their thoughts: [Vn] *This problem is exercising our minds a good deal at the moment.* [Vnpr] *I am greatly exercised about my son's education.*

exert /ɪgˈzɜːt/ *v* **1** ~ **sth** (**on sb/sth**) to use or apply a quality, skill, pressure, etc: [Vn] *He exerted all his influence to make them accept his plan.* [Vnpr] *She exerted a lot of pressure on her children to succeed.* **2** ~ **oneself** (no passive) to make an effort: [Vn] *You'll have to exert yourself more if you want to pass your exam.* ○ *He doesn't have to exert himself on my behalf.*

exertion /ɪgˈzɜːʃn/ *n* [C, U] (an instance of) exerting oneself or sth; effort: *strenuous physical exertion* ○ *Now that I'm 90, I find the exertions of travel too much for me.* ○ *It requires no great exertion of the imagination to recognize that.*

exeunt /ˈeksiʌnt/ *v* (*Latin*) (as a printed stage direction in plays) they leave the stage: *Exeunt Antony and Cleopatra.* Compare EXIT *v* 2.

ex gratia /ˌeks ˈgreɪʃə/ *adv, adj* (*Latin*) done or given as a favour; not from (esp legal) obligation: *an ex gratia payment.*

exhale /eks'heɪl/ *v* to breathe out or breathe sth out: [Vnpr] *exhale air from the lungs* [Vn] *exhale smoke* [Vadv] *She exhaled very slowly to show her annoyance.* [also V]. Compare INHALE. ▶ **exhalation** /ˌeksho'leɪʃn/ *n* [U, C].

exhaust¹ /ɪgˈzɔːst/ *n* **1** [U] waste gases, steam, etc that are released from an engine or a machine, esp a vehicle: *the smell of the exhaust* ○ *exhaust fumes/ emissions.* **2** (also **ex'haust-pipe**) [C] a pipe through which exhaust gases are released: *My car needs a new exhaust.* ⇨ picture at CAR.

exhaust² /ɪgˈzɔːst/ *v* **1** to make a person or an animal very tired: [Vn] *The long cycle ride exhausted her.* ○ *She was exhausted by the trip.* ○ *He exhausted himself trying to rescue the trapped animal.* **2** to use sth until it is completely finished: [Vn] *exhaust one's strength* ○ *My patience was finally exhausted.* ○ *exhaust a money supply* ○ *exhaust a well.* **3** to talk about, write about or study a subject fully: [Vn] *I think we've exhausted that particular topic.*
▶ **exhausted** *adj* very tired: *I'm absolutely/ completely exhausted!* ○ *She felt exhausted at the end of the climb.* ○ *The exhausted troops surrendered.*
exhausting *adj* making one feel very tired: *It had been an exhausting day.*
exhaustion /ɪgˈzɔːstʃən/ *n* [U] **1** the state of being extremely tired; total loss of strength: *They were in a state of exhaustion after climbing for ten hours.* ○ *She was overcome by nervous exhaustion.* **2** (*fml*) the action of using sth until it is completely finished: *the exhaustion of the earth's natural resources.*
exhaustive /ɪgˈzɔːstɪv/ *adj* very thorough; complete: *conduct an exhaustive enquiry/search.* ▶ **exhaustively** *adv.*

exhibit¹ /ɪgˈzɪbɪt/ *n* **1** an object or a collection of objects displayed for the public, eg in a museum: *a priceless exhibit* ○ *The upper gallery contains some interesting new exhibits from Mexico.* ○ *Do not touch the exhibits.* **2** a document or other object produced as evidence in a lawcourt: *The first exhibit was a knife which the prosecution claimed was the murder weapon.* **3** (*US*) = EXHIBITION 1.

exhibit² /ɪgˈzɪbɪt/ *v* **1(a)** to show or display sth for the public, eg for pleasure or for information: [Vn] *exhibit flowers at a flower show* ○ *documents exhibited in a lawcourt.* **(b)** ~ (**at/in ...**) (of an artist) to present works of art for the public, esp in an art gallery: [V, Vn] *He has exhibited (his work) in several galleries.* **2** (*fml*) to show clearly that one possesses a quality or feeling: [Vn] *She exhibited great powers of endurance throughout the climb.* ○ *He exhibited a total lack of concern for the child.*
▶ **exhibitor** *n* a person who displays pictures, flowers, etc at a show: *Nearly fifty exhibitors have provided photographs for the display.*

exhibition /ˌeksɪˈbɪʃn/ *n* **1** (also *US* **exhibit**) [C] a collection of things shown publicly, eg works of art, goods for sale, etc: *one of the exhibition halls at the book fair* ○ *Have you seen the Picasso exhibition* (ie the exhibition of paintings, etc by Picasso)? **2(a)** [sing] ~ **of sth** an act of showing a quality or feeling: *an appalling exhibition of bad manners.* **(b)** [C] a public demonstration of a skill: *a dancing exhibition* ○ *an exhibition of pottery-making* ○ *The West Indies team gave a superb exhibition of clean, powerful hitting.* ⇨ note. **IDM** **make an exhi'bition of one-self** (*derog*) to behave foolishly or badly in public: *I'm afraid Frank got drunk and made an exhibition of himself.*
▶ **exhibitionism** /-ʃənɪzəm/ *n* [U] **1** (*often derog*) the tendency to behave in a way intended to attract attention to oneself: *the vein of exhibitionism that*

runs through all his writings. **2** (*psychology*) the mental condition that makes sb want to expose their sexual organs in public. **exhibitionist** /-ʃənɪst/ *n* a person who likes to attract attention to herself or himself: *Children are natural exhibitionists.*

NOTE Compare **exhibition, show, fair, display** and **demonstration**. An **exhibition, a show** or **a fair** is a temporary event at which different companies can show their products in an **exhibition hall/centre**: *The exhibition lasts five days.* ○ *the Frankfurt Book Fair* ○ *the Motor Show.* You can also see an **exhibition** of paintings, rare objects, etc at an art gallery or museum: *Did you see the Turner exhibition?* ○ *an exhibition of old photographs.* At a **demonstration** you see how something works or how to do something: *a cookery demonstration.* A **display** is often for public information or entertainment: *The anti-smoking display will be on for two weeks.* ○ *a fireworks display* ○ *The fashion students put on a display of their work at the end of the year.*

exhilarate /ɪgˈzɪləreɪt/ *v* (usu passive) to make sb feel very happy, lively or excited: [Vn] *exhilarated by the news* ○ *We felt exhilarated by our walk along the beach.*
▶ **exhilarating** *adj* very exciting; causing happiness: *My first parachute jump was an exhilarating experience.*
exhilaration /ɪgˌzɪləˈreɪʃn/ *n* [U]: *the sheer exhilaration of sailing single-handed.*

exhort /ɪgˈzɔːt/ *v* ~ **sb** (**to sth / to do sth**) (*fml*) to advise sb strongly; to urge sb: [Vnpr] *The chairman exhorted the party workers to action.* [Vn.to inf] *The teacher kept exhorting us to work harder.* [also Vn, V.speech]. ▶ **exhortation** /ˌegzɔːˈteɪʃn/ *n* [C, U]: *All his father's exhortations were in vain.*

exhume /eks'hjuːm, ɪgˈzjuːm; *US* ɪgˈzuːm/ *v* to take a dead body from the ground for examination: [Vn] *After exhuming the corpse the police discovered traces of poison in it.* ▶ **exhumation** /ˌekshjuːˈmeɪʃn/ *n* [U, C].

exigency /ˈeksɪdʒənsi, ɪgˈzɪd3-/ *n* [C often *pl*, U] (*fml*) an urgent need or demand; an emergency: *prepare oneself for all exigencies* ○ *the harsh exigencies of war.*

exiguous /egˈzɪgjuəs/ *adj* (*fml*) very small in size or amount; MEAGRE: *an exiguous diet* ○ *the last of the old man's exiguous savings.*

exile /ˈeksaɪl, ˈegz-/ *n* **1** [U] the state of being sent away from one's native country or home, esp for political reasons or as a punishment; forced absence: *be/live in exile* ○ *go/be sent into exile* ○ *a place of exile.* **2** [C] a long stay away from one's country or home: *After an exile of ten years her uncle returned to Britain.* **3** [C] a person who lives away from her or his own country from choice or because forced to do so: *a tax exile* (ie a rich person who moves to another country where the rate of income tax is lower) ○ *There were many French exiles in England after the Revolution.*
▶ **exile** *v* ~ **sb** (**from ...**) (esp passive) to send sb into exile: [Vn] *be exiled for life* ○ *the party's exiled leaders* [Vnpr] *She was exiled from her country because of her part in the uprising.*

exist /ɪgˈzɪst/ *v* **1(a)** to be real or actual; to have being: [V] *laws that have existed for hundreds of years* ○ *Do you believe fairies exist* (ie that there are really fairies)? ○ *Does life exist on Mars?* **(b)** to be found; to occur: *This plant exists only in Australia.* [V] *Without conservation many species would cease to exist.* **2** ~ (**on sth**) to continue living, esp with difficulty or with very little money; to survive: [V] *We cannot exist without food and water.* [Vpr] *He exists on rice and little else.* ○ *I can hardly exist on the wages I'm getting.*
▶ **existence** /-əns/ *n* **1** [U] the state or fact of existing: *Do you believe in the existence of ghosts?* ○

This is the oldest Hebrew manuscript **in existence** (ie that exists). ○ *When did the world* **come into existence** (ie begin to exist)? ○ *I was unaware of his existence until today.* **2(a)** [sing] a manner of living, esp when this is difficult, boring, etc: *living a miserable existence miles from the nearest town* ○ *We led a happy enough existence as children.* **(b)** [sing, U] continuing to live; SURVIVAL(1): *The peasants depend on a good harvest for their* **very existence** (ie simply in order to survive). ○ *They eke out a bare existence* (ie hardly manage to live) *on her low salary.*

existent /-ənt/ *adj* (*fml*) existing; actual. Compare NON-EXISTENT.

existing *adj* [attrib] found now; present[1](2): *existing rates of pay* ○ *No changes need be made to the existing rules.*

existentialism /ˌegzɪˈstenʃəlɪzəm/ *n* [U] (*philosophy*) the theory that human beings are free and responsible for their own actions in a world without meaning or God.

▸ **existential** /ˌegzɪˈstenʃəl/ *adj* **1** (*fml*) of or relating to human existence. **2** (*philosophy*) of or relating to the theory of existentialism.

existentialist /-ʃəlɪst/ *n, adj*: *She's an existentialist.* ○ *She holds existentialist views.*

exit /ˈeksɪt, ˈegzɪt/ *n* **1** an act of leaving; a departure, esp that of an actor from the stage: *The heroine makes her exit (from the stage).* ○ *To avoid meeting her he made a swift exit* (ie he left quickly). ○ *an exit visa* (ie a stamp or signature on a passport giving sb permission to leave a particular country). **2** a way out of a public building, passenger vehicle, etc: *There are four fire exits in the department store.* ○ *The emergency exit is at the back of the bus.* ○ *The exit signs in hospitals are usually illuminated.* **3** a point at which a road, etc turns off from a MOTORWAY or ROUNDABOUT[2](1), allowing vehicles to leave: *At the roundabout, take the third exit.* ○ *Get off the freeway at the exit for Encinitas.* ○ *We leave the autoroute at the next exit.*

▸ **exit** *v* **1** to go out; (esp of an actor) to leave the stage: [V] *She exits in the middle of the third scene.* [Vpr] *Scotland exited from the World Cup after their defeat by Germany.* **2** (*3rd pers sing only*) (*Latin*) (as a printed stage direction in plays) he or she leaves the stage: [V] *Exit Macbeth.* Compare EXEUNT.

■ **'exit poll** *n* a poll based on interviews with voters immediately after they have voted.

exodus /ˈeksədəs/ *n* [sing] (**from...**) (**to...**) (*fml or joc*) a departure of many people at one time: *the mass exodus of people to the seaside for the summer holidays* ○ *The play was so awful that there was a general exodus from the theatre at the interval.*

ex officio /ˌeks əˈfɪʃiəʊ/ *adj, adv* (*fml*) because of one's position, office or rank: *an ex officio member of the committee* ○ *He was present at the meeting ex officio.*

exonerate /ɪgˈzɒnəreɪt/ *v* ~ **sb** (**from sth**) to declare sb free from blame: [Vn, Vnpr] *A commission of inquiry exonerated him (from all responsibility for the accident).*

exorbitant /ɪgˈzɔːbɪtənt/ *adj* (*fml*) (of a price, demand, etc) much too high or great; unreasonable: *exorbitant rents* ○ *The price of food here is exorbitant.*

▸ **exorbitantly** *adv*: *exorbitantly expensive.*

exorcize, -ise /ˈeksɔːsaɪz/ *v* ~ **sth** (**from sb/sth**) to drive out or rid sb of an evil spirit by prayers or magic: [Vnpr] *A priest exorcized the ghost from the house.* ○ [Vn] (*fig*) *She can never exorcize the memory of her childhood sufferings.*

▸ **exorcism** /ˈeksɔːsɪzəm/ *n* [U, C] the action of exorcizing sb, or an instance of this. **exorcist** /ˈeksɔːsɪst/ *n* a person who exorcizes.

exotic /ɪgˈzɒtɪk/ *adj* **1** introduced from another country; not native: *exotic houseplants* ○ *monkeys and other exotic animals.* **2** striking or attractive

because colourful or unusual: *exotic plumage/ clothes.*

exotica /ɪgˈzɒtɪkə/ *n* [pl] strange or rare objects: *a sale of antiques and exotica.*

expand /ɪkˈspænd/ *v* **1** ~ (**sth**) (**into sth**) to become or make sth greater in size, number or importance: [V] *Metals expand when they are heated.* ○ *A tyre expands when you pump air into it.* [Vpr] *His modest business eventually expanded into a supermarket empire.* [Vn] *We have greatly expanded our foreign trade in recent years.* [Vnpr] *Why don't you expand your story into a novel?* **2** to spread out; to UNFOLD(1a): [V] *The petals of the flowers expanded in the sunshine.* ○ *His face expanded in a smile of welcome.* Compare CONTRACT[2] 5b. **3** (of a person) to become more friendly; to relax and talk more: [V] *She expanded considerably after a glass or two of wine.* **PHR V ex'pand on sth** to develop or give more of a story, an argument, etc: *You mentioned the need for extra funding. Could you expand on that?*

expanse /ɪkˈspæns/ *n* ~ (**of sth**) a wide and open area of land, sea, etc: *wide expanses of flat, open farmland* ○ *Her short skirt exposed a large expanse of thigh.*

expansion /ɪkˈspænʃn/ *n* [U, C] the action or an instance of expanding; the state of being expanded: *the expansion of gases when heated* ○ *the expansion of his business interests* ○ *expansions of the school system under successive governments.*

▸ **expansionism** /-ʃənɪzəm/ *n* [U] the belief in, or practice of, expansion, esp of one's territory or business: *the cultural and economic expansionism of Europe and America.* **expansionist** /-ʃənɪst/ *adj, n*: *Hitler's expansionist policies* ○ *a ruthless expansionist.*

expansive /ɪkˈspænsɪv/ *adj* **1** able or tending to expand: *He greeted us with an expansive gesture* (eg he stretched his arms wide) *and a wide smile.* **2** friendly and willing to talk a lot: *He was clearly relaxed and in an expansive mood.* ▸ **expansively** *adv.* **expansiveness** *n* [U].

expatiate /ɪkˈspeɪʃieɪt/ *v* **PHR V expatiate on/upon sth** (*fml*) to write or speak at great length or in detail about a subject: *He was expatiating eloquently on the state of the economy.*

expatriate /ˌeksˈpætriət; US -ˈpeɪt-/ *n* a person living outside her or his own country: *American expatriates in Paris* ○ *expatriate Englishmen in Spain.*

expect /ɪkˈspekt/ *v* **1(a)** ~ **sth** (**from sb/sth**) to think or believe that sth will happen or that sb/sth will come: [Vn, Vnpr] *This is the parcel we've been expecting (from New York).* [V.*that*] *I expect (that) I'll be back on Sunday.* [V.*to* inf] *You can't expect to learn a foreign language in a week.* [Vn, V.n *to* inf] *We expected him (to arrive) yesterday.* [V.n *to* inf] *House prices are expected to rise sharply.* ○ *You would expect there to be some disagreement on this point.* **(b)** ~ **sth** (**from sb**) to hope and feel confident that one will receive sth from sb: [Vn, Vnpr] *I was* **half expecting** *a present (from her) and was rather disappointed when I didn't get one.* ○ *I'm still learning the job so please don't expect too much (from me).* [Vnpr] *Don't expect any sympathy from me!* ⇨ note at WAIT[1]. **2** ~ **sth** (**from sb**) to require sth from sb, esp as a right or duty: [Vnpr, V.*that*, V.n *to* inf] *An officer expects obedience from his men/expects that his men will obey him/expects his men to obey him.* [V.n *to* inf] *I expect you to be punctual.* ○ *You will be expected to work on Saturdays.* [also Vn]. **3** (*infml esp Brit*) (not in the continuous tenses) to suppose sth; to assume sth: [Vn, V.*that*] *'Who has eaten all the cake?' 'Tom, I expect/I expect (that) it was Tom.'* [Vadv] *'Will you be late?' 'I expect so.'* **IDM** **be expecting (a baby/child)** (*infml*) to be pregnant: *I hear Sally's expecting again.* **(be only) to be ex'pected**

(to be) likely to happen; to be quite normal: *A little tiredness after taking these drugs is to be expected.* ○ *It is only to be expected your son will leave home eventually.* **PHRV** ex'**pect sth of sb/sth** to believe or hope that sb will act in a certain way or that sth will happen: *I expected better of him* (ie that he would behave better). ○ *People expect courtesy of the police.* Compare UNEXPECTED.

▸ **expectancy** /ɪkˈspektənsi/ *n* [U] the state of expecting or hoping: *There was an air/a sense of expectancy among the waiting crowd.* See also LIFE EXPECTANCY.

expectant /ɪkˈspektənt/ *adj* **1** expecting sth, esp sth good; hopeful: *children with expectant faces waiting for the pantomime to start.* **2** [attrib] (of mothers or fathers) expecting a baby. **expectantly** *adv.*

expectation /ˌekspekˈteɪʃn/ *n* **1** [U] ~ (**of sth**) the firm belief that sth will happen; the action of expecting sth: *He has little expectation of winning a prize.* ○ *A few fans waited for a glimpse of the star, but more in hope than in expectation.* ○ *In the twentieth century people's expectation of life has been greatly increased.* **2** [C usu *pl*] confident feelings about sth: *His parents have great expectations for his future.* ○ *She had high expectations of what university had to offer.* ○ *The holiday was **beyond all our expectations** (ie better than we had hoped for).* **IDM** **a,gainst/,contrary to (all) expec'tation(s)** quite different from what was expected: *a gold medal that was against all expectations.* **fall short of sb's / not come up to (sb's) expec'tations** to be less good than was expected: *Unfortunately the restaurant we recommended fell far short of our expectations.* ○ *His performance didn't come up to expectations.*

expectorant /ɪkˈspektərənt/ *n* (*techn*) a medicine that helps one to cough up PHLEGM, etc from the lungs: *The cough medicine contains an expectorant.*

expedient /ɪkˈspiːdiənt/ *adj* [usu pred] (of an action) useful or convenient for a particular purpose, though not necessarily fair or moral: *His action is seen as expedient rather than principled.* ○ *The government has clearly decided that a cut in interest rates would be politically expedient.*

▸ **expedience** /-əns/ (also **expediency** /-ənsi/) *n* [U]: *He acted from expediency, not from principle.*

expedient *n* a means of achieving an aim, which may not be fair or moral: *She gets quicker results by the simple expedient of telephoning customers rather than writing to them.*

expedite /ˈekspədaɪt/ *v* (*fml*) to help the progress of work, business, etc; to make sth happen more quickly: [Vn] *rapid order processing to expedite delivery to customers.*

expedition /ˌekspəˈdɪʃn/ *n* (**a**) an organized journey or voyage with a particular aim: *plan/go on an expedition to the North Pole* ○ *a hunting expedition* ○ (*joc*) *a shopping expedition.* (**b**) the people, vehicles, ships, etc making such a journey: *members of the Mount Everest expedition.*

▸ **expeditionary** /-ʃənri; *US* -neri/ *adj* [attrib] of or forming an expedition: *an expeditionary force* (eg an army sent to take part in a war abroad).

expeditious /ˌekspəˈdɪʃəs/ *adj* (*fml*) done with speed and efficiency: *an expeditious response.* ▸ **expeditiously** *adv*: *The work will be carried out as expeditiously as possible.*

expel /ɪkˈspel/ *v* (**-ll-**) ~ **sb** (**from sth**) **1** to force sb to leave a place, esp a country, school or club: [Vnpr] *Two members of the embassy staff were expelled from the country.* [Vn] *Following reports of drug-taking at the school, several senior boys have been expelled.* **2** to send or drive sth out by force: [Vnpr] *expel air from the lungs* [Vn] *a fan in the kitchen for expelling cooking smells.* See also EXPULSION.

expend /ɪkˈspend/ *v* ~ **sth** (**in/on sth / doing sth**)

(*fml*) to use or spend resources in doing sth: [Vn, Vnpr] *expend time, effort and money* (*on a project*) [Vnpr] *He had already expended large sums in pursuing his claim through the courts.*

▸ **expendable** *adj* (*fml*) that may be used up or destroyed in the process of achieving sth; not worth keeping or saving: *Former allies were considered expendable.*

expenditure /ɪkˈspendɪtʃə(r)/ *n* **1(a)** [C,U] an amount of money spent: *an increase in defence/capital/public expenditure* ○ *an expenditure of £1 000 on new furniture* ○ *a programme to reduce expenditure* ○ *Limit your expenditure to what is essential.* Compare INCOME. (**b**) [U] the action of spending or using money: *the expenditure of money on weapons.* **2** the use of effort or resources: *a huge expenditure of time and energy.*

expense /ɪkˈspens/ *n* **1(a)** [U] the spending of resources, esp money; the cost of sth: *the expense of time, energy and cash* ○ *He hired a plane, **regardless of expense.*** ○ *Most children in Britain are educated at public expense.* ○ *The garden was transformed **at great/considerable/vast expense.*** ○ *She **spared no expense** (ie spent as much money as was needed) to make the party a success.* (**b**) [C usu *sing*] a cause of spending money: *Running a car is a big expense.* **2 expenses** [pl] money spent in doing a specific job, or for a specific purpose: *travelling expenses* ○ *House repairs, new furniture and other expenses reduced her bank balance to almost nothing.* ○ *Who's meeting* (ie paying for) *the expenses of your trip?* ○ *She's just returned from an all-expenses-paid trip to Sweden* (ie paid for by her employer). **IDM** **at sb's expense 1** with sb paying: *We were entertained at the company's expense.* **2** so as to make sb appear foolish, feel less important, etc: *They had a good laugh at Sam's expense.* **at the expense of sth** with loss or damage to sth: *He built up a successful business but at the expense of his health.* **go to / put sb to the expense of sth / doing sth; go to / put sb to a lot of, etc expense** to spend/make sb spend money on sth: *It's stupid to go to the expense of taking music lessons if you never practise.* ○ *Their visit has put us to a great deal of expense.* **no expense(s) 'spared** with no regard for the cost: *I'm going to take you out to dinner, no expense spared.*

■ ex'**pense account** *n* a record of money spent by an employee in the course of her or his work, which is later paid back by the employer: *Whenever he entertains clients, he puts it on/charges it to his expense account.*

expensive /ɪkˈspensɪv/ *adj* costing a lot of money: *an expensive car* ○ *Houses are very expensive in this area.* ○ *It's too expensive for me to buy.* Compare INEXPENSIVE. ▸ **expensively** *adv*: *an expensively dressed woman.*

experience /ɪkˈspɪəriəns/ *n* **1** [U] the process of gaining knowledge or skill over a period of time through seeing and doing things rather than through studying: *We all learn by experience.* ○ *Not many people have had experience of real hunger.* ○ *Does she have much teaching experience?* ○ *He hasn't had enough previous experience* (ie experience of work) *for us to give him the job.* ○ *Our next speaker is a person with **long experience** of this problem.* ○ *I know from experience that he'll arrive late.* **2** [C] an event or activity that affects one in some way: *an unpleasant/a trying/an unusual experience* ○ *You must try some of her home-made wine — it's quite an experience* (ie it is very unusual)! ○ *He had many interesting experiences while travelling in Africa.*

▸ **experience** *v* to have experience of sth; to feel sth: [Vn] *experience pleasure/pain/difficulty/hardship* ○ *The child had never experienced kindness.* ○ *I experienced a brief moment of panic.* **experienced** *adj* having experience in a particular field or activity;

---

activity; having knowledge or skill as a result of experience: *an experienced nurse* ○ *He's experienced in looking after children.*
experiential /ɪkˌspɪəri'enʃl/ *adj* (*fml*) involving or based on experience: *experiential knowledge.*

experiment /ɪk'sperɪmənt/ *n* [C, U] (**a**) a scientific test done carefully in order to study what happens and to gain new knowledge: *perform/carry out/conduct an experiment* ○ *The researchers are repeating the experiment on rats.* ○ *prove a theory by experiment.* (**b**) ~ (**in sth**) any new activity used to find out what happens or what effect it has: *an experiment in communal living* ○ *The play was staged as an experiment.*
▶ **experiment** *v* ~ (**on sb/sth**); ~ (**with sth**) to make an experiment; to try sth new: [V] *We experimented until we succeeded in mixing the right colour.* [Vpr] *experiment on animals* ○ *experiment with different hairstyles.* **experimenter** *n* a person who experiments.
▶ **experimentation** /ɪkˌsperɪmen'teɪʃn/ *n* [U] (*fml*) the activity, process or practice of making experiments: *experimentation with a new brand of socialism* ○ *Many people object to experimentation on embryos.*

experimental /ɪkˌsperɪ'mentl/ *adj* using or based on new ideas or methods and not yet firmly established: *an experimental farm* ○ *an experimental physicist* ○ *experimental theatre* ○ *The technique is still at the experimental stage — it hasn't been fully developed yet.* ○ *Doctors stress that this type of treatment is still experimental.* ▶ **experimentally** /-təli/ *adv*: *The new measures were introduced experimentally in 1993.*

expert /'ekspɜːt/ *n* ~ (**at/in/on sth / doing sth**) a person with special knowledge, skill or training in a particular field: *an agricultural expert* ○ *an expert in psychology* ○ *get the advice of the experts* ○ *an expert at getting his own way* ○ *an expert on Japan/Mozart/ancient Greek vases.*
▶ **expert** *adj* ~ (**at/in sth / doing sth**) done with, having or involving great knowledge or skill: *take expert advice* ○ *an expert rider* ○ *have expert knowledge* ○ *He's expert at/in cooking good cheap meals.* ○ *She glanced down the page with an expert eye.* Compare INEXPERT. **expertly** *adv*: *expertly applied theatrical make-up.*
■ ˌ**expert** '**system** *n* (*computing*) a computer PROGRAM(1) containing knowledge and practical experience gathered from experts in a particular field. The program asks users a series of questions about their problem and gives them appropriate advice based on its store of knowledge: *an expert system to aid medical diagnosis.*

expertise /ˌekspɜː'tiːz/ *n* [U] ~ (**in sth / doing sth**) expert knowledge or skill, esp in a particular field: *professional/scientific/technical expertise* ○ *They have considerable expertise in dealing with oil spills.* ○ *We were amazed at his expertise on the ski slopes.*

expiate /'ekspieɪt/ *v* (*fml*) to accept punishment for a wrongdoing and do sth to show one is sorry: [Vn] *expiate one's guilt.* ▶ **expiation** /ˌekspi'eɪʃn/ *n* [U].

expire /ɪk'spaɪə(r)/ *v* **1** (of sth that lasts for a period of time) to finish or come to an end; to be no longer valid: [V] *Our present lease on the house expires next month.* ○ *When does your driving licence expire?* ○ *His term of office as Chairman expires at the end of June.* **2** [V] (*esp medical*) to breathe out air. **3** [V] (*dated fml*) to die.
▶ **expiration** /ˌekspə'reɪʃn/ *n* [U] (*fml*) **1** the ending of the period when an agreement, a contract, etc is in force or is valid: *the expiration of a lease/tenancy/share offer.* **2** (*esp medical*) the breathing out of air.

expiry /ɪk'spaɪəri/ *n* ~ (**of sth**) an ending of the period when an agreement, a contract, etc is in force

or is valid: *the expiry of a driving licence/lease/credit card* ○ *What is the expiry date?*

explain /ɪk'spleɪn/ *v* **1** ~ **sth** (**to sb**) to give or be a reason for sth; to account for sth: [Vn] *That explains his absence.* [V.that] *He explained that his train had been delayed.* [V.speech] *'I had to wait over an hour at the dentist's,' he explained.* [V.wh] *They explained what had happened.* ○ *Please explain why you are late.* [Vnpr] *She explained her conduct to her boss.* [Vpr.that] *She explained to the children that the school had been closed.* [Vpr.wh] *The manager has explained to customers why the goods were late.* **2** ~ **sth** (**to sb**) to make sth plain or clear; to describe sth in detail so that it can be more easily understood: [Vn] *A dictionary explains the meaning of words.* [Vnpr] *He explained his plan to us.* [V.wh, Vpr.wh] *Can you explain (to me) how it works?* [V] *Let me explain.* **ɪᴅᴍ** **ex'plain oneself** to make one's meaning clear: *I don't understand your argument — could you explain yourself a bit more?* **2** (*fml*) to give reasons for one's behaviour: *Last week you were late for work every day — please explain yourself.* **ᴘʜʀᴠ** **ex,plain sth a'way** to give excuses why one should not be blamed for a fault, mistake, etc, or why sth is not important: *Government ministers will not find it easy to explain away their poor performance in recent by-elections.*

explanation /ˌeksplə'neɪʃn/ *n* **1** [U] the action or process of explaining sth: *He left the room **without (further) explanation**.* ○ *These developments need a word of explanation.* ○ *'I had to see you,' he said by way of explanation.* **2** [C] a statement, fact, circumstance, etc that explains sth: *a plausible/satisfactory explanation of the mystery* ○ *That's not an adequate explanation.* ○ *The most likely explanation is that his plane was delayed.* ○ *I can think of no other explanation for his absence.*

explanatory /ɪk'splænətri; *US* -tɔːri/ *adj* [usu attrib] giving, serving or intended as an explanation: *explanatory notes at the back of a book.*

expletive /ɪk'spliːtɪv; *US* 'eksplətɪv/ *n* (*fml*) a word, esp a rude word, that expresses one's anger, pain, etc; a swear-word (SWEAR): *'Damn!' is an expletive.* ○ *She dropped the iron on her foot and uttered several vigorous expletives.*

explicable /ɪk'splɪkəbl, 'eksplɪkəbl/ *adj* (*fml*) that can be explained: *His behaviour is explicable in the light of his recent illness.* Compare INEXPLICABLE.

explicate /'eksplɪkeɪt/ *v* (*fml*) to explain and analyse sth, esp an idea, a principle or a work of literature, in detail: [Vn] *explicate one's moral values.* ▶ **explication** /ˌeksplɪ'keɪʃn/ *n* [U, C]: *give a long explication of a theory.*

explicit /ɪk'splɪsɪt/ *adj* **1**(**a**) (of a statement, etc) clearly and fully expressed: *He gave me explicit directions (on) how to get there.* ○ *They gave explicit reasons for leaving.* (**b**) (of a person) saying sth clearly, exactly and openly: *She was quite explicit about why she had left.* Compare IMPLICIT 1. **2** openly portrayed or described and not left to the imagination: *The film contains a number of explicit sex scenes.* ▶ **explicitly** *adv*: *a novel dealing explicitly with incest* ○ *He was explicitly forbidden to see the children.* **explicitness** *n* [U]: *sexual explicitness in the arts.*

explode /ɪk'spləʊd/ *v* **1** to burst or make sth burst loudly and violently; to blow up: [V] *The boiler exploded, injuring several people.* ○ *The firework exploded in his hand.* [Vn] *They exploded the bomb by remote control.* Compare IMPLODE. **2**(**a**) ~ (**with/into sth**) (of people) to show sudden violent emotion: [V.speech] *'Something wrong!' he exploded, 'You ask me if there's something wrong!'* [Vpr] *explode with rage/fury/joy* ○ *Everyone exploded into laughter.* [also V]. (**b**) (of feelings) to burst out suddenly: [V] *At last his anger exploded.* **3** ~ (**into sth**) to change or develop suddenly and violently: [Vpr] *The protest march exploded into a riot.* ○ *In spring the resort explodes into life.* **4** (esp of a population) to increase suddenly or quickly: [V] *the exploding world population.* **5** to show that a theory, an idea, etc is false: [Vn] *explode a superstition* ○ *The myth that eating carrots improves your eyesight was exploded years ago.* See also EXPLOSION.

▶ **exploded** *adj* (used of a drawing or diagram) showing the parts of a structure in their relative positions but slightly separated from each other: *exploded drawings of aircraft.*

exploit¹ /ˈeksplɔɪt/ *n* [C usu *pl*] a brave, exciting or interesting act: *He describes his exploits as a war correspondent in his new autobiography.* ○ *(joc) I'm not interested in hearing about Bill's amorous exploits.* ⇨ note at ACT¹.

exploit² /ɪkˈsplɔɪt/ *v* **1** to use, work or develop sth, esp natural resources, fully: [Vn] *exploit oil reserves/ water power/solar energy* ○ *exploit an opportunity.* **2** (*derog*) to use or treat sb/sth in an unfair and SELFISH manner for one's own advantage or profit: [Vn] *child labour exploited in factories* ○ *exploit a situation for one's own advantage* ○ *They exploited her generosity shamelessly.*

▶ **exploitation** /ˌeksplɔɪˈteɪʃn/ *n* [U] (*sometimes derog*): *full exploitation of oil wells* ○ *the exploitation of cheap labour.*

exploitative /ɪkˈsplɔɪtətɪv/ *adj* (*derog*) using sb/sth in an unfair and SELFISH manner: *the exploitative role of multinational companies.*

exploiter *n*: *exploiters of anti-government feelings.*

explore /ɪkˈsplɔː(r)/ *v* **1(a)** to travel into or around in a place, esp a country, in order to learn about it: [Vn] *explore the Arctic regions* ○ *Columbus discovered America but did not explore it.* [Vnpr] *explore the sea bed for* (ie in the hope of finding) *oil* [V] *As soon as they arrived in the town they went out to explore.* **(b)** to feel sth thoroughly with one's hands or another part of one's body: [Vn] *explore the dark recesses of the cupboard.* **2** to examine sth thoroughly in order to test it or find out about it: [Vn] *explore one's conscience* ○ *We explored several solutions to the problem.* ○ *The biological effects of radiation are still being explored.*

▶ **exploration** /ˌekspləˈreɪʃn/ *n* [U,C]: *the exploration of space* ○ *a voyage of exploration* ○ *oil/gas exploration* (ie looking for natural oil/gas reserves) ○ *a detailed exploration of the subject* ○ *the film's explorations of human character* ○ *Her explorations led her into the deserts of central Asia.*

exploratory /ɪkˈsplɒrətri; *US* -tɔːri/ *adj* happening or being conducted for the purpose of learning more about the state or nature of sth: *exploratory medical tests* ○ *an exploratory expedition up the Amazon.*

explorer /ɪkˈsplɔːrə(r)/ *n* a person who explores: *cave explorers* ○ *Marco Polo was one of the great explorers.*

explosion /ɪkˈspləʊʒn/ *n* **1(a)** a sudden loud violent release of energy caused eg by a bomb exploding: *gas explosions* ○ *The explosion was heard over a mile away.* **(b)** a sudden violent expression of anger, laughter, etc: *an explosion of rage.* **2** a great and sudden increase: *a population explosion* ○ *an explosion of interest in learning Japanese* ○ *the explosion of oil prices.*

explosive /ɪkˈspləʊsɪv, -zɪv/ *adj* **1** easily able or likely to explode: *an explosive mixture of chemicals* ○ *explosive materials* ○ *Hydrogen is highly explosive.* **2** likely to cause violence, arguments or strong feelings, esp of anger and hatred: *an explosive situation/ issue* ○ *an explosive temper* ○ *Politics can be an explosive subject.*

▶ **explosive** *n* [C,U] a substance that is able or likely to explode: *secret stores of arms and explosives* ○ *The bomb was packed with several pounds of high* *explosive* (ie a substance that explodes with great force).

explosively *adv.*

exponent /ɪkˈspəʊnənt/ *n* **1** a person who supports and promotes a theory, belief, cause(3), etc: *a leading exponent of free trade* ○ *Huxley was an exponent of Darwin's theory of evolution.* **2** a person who is able to perform a particular activity with skill: *the most famous exponent of the art of mime.* **3** (*mathematics*) a figure or symbol that shows how many times a quantity must be multiplied by itself: *In a^3, the figure ^{3} is the exponent.*

▶ **exponential** /ˌekspəˈnenʃl/ *adj* (*mathematics*) **1** of or indicated by an exponent(3): 2^4 *is an exponential expression.* **2** produced or indicated by multiplying a set of numbers by themselves: *an exponential curve/function* ○ (*fig*) *exponential* (ie more and more rapid) *growth.* **exponentially** /-ʃəli/ *adv*: *increase exponentially.*

export¹ /ɪkˈspɔːt/ *v* **1** ~ (**sth**) (**to ...**) to sell and transport goods to a foreign country: [Vn] *Currently only 5% of their output is exported.* ○ *steel-exporting countries* [Vnpr] *Much of the fruit is exported to Europe.* ○ *India exports tea and cotton to many different countries.* [also V, Vpr]. **2** to spread an idea, a belief, a system, etc to another country or region: [Vn] *The powerful dance rhythm has been exported across the world.* Compare IMPORT¹.

▶ **exportation** /ˌekspɔːˈteɪʃn/ *n* [U] the exporting of goods: *He manufactures paper for exportation only.*

exporter *n* a person, company or country that exports goods: *Britain is no longer a net exporter of vehicles.* ○ *Argentina is the world's biggest/leading exporter of beef products.*

export² /ˈekspɔːt/ *n* **1** [U] the business or action of selling and transporting goods to a foreign country: *a ban on the export of gold* ○ *an 'export licence* ○ *launch an 'export drive* ○ *'export duties* (ie tax paid on goods sent abroad for sale). **2** [C usu *pl*] a thing that is sold to a foreign country: *a system of export quotas* ○ *calls for the government to support industry and promote exports* ○ *a rise/fall in exports* ○ *What are the country's chief exports?* Compare IMPORT².

expose /ɪkˈspəʊz/ *v* **1** to make sth visible; to display sth: [Vn] *His trousers were too short, exposing his white ankles.* ○ *She lifted the leaves to expose a lovely row of radishes.* **2** ~ **sth/sb/oneself** (**to sth**) to leave sb/sth/oneself no longer covered or protected: [Vn] *The soil was washed away by the flood, exposing the bare rock.* [Vnpr] *expose employees to unnecessary risks* ○ *Don't expose babies to strong sunlight.* ○ (*fig*) *expose oneself to criticism/ridicule* ○ *He believes in regularly exposing his pupils to great works of art.* **3** to make known sth that was secret; to reveal sth: [Vn] *expose a plot/a fraud/an injustice/a weakness* ○ *an unfortunate remark which exposed his ignorance of the subject* [Vn-n] *She was exposed as an impostor.* **4** to allow light to reach film, esp by using a camera: [Vn] *expose a reel of film.* **5** [Vn] ~ **oneself** to show one's sexual organs in public. See also EXPOSURE.

▶ **exposed** *adj* **1** (of a place) not sheltered from wind or weather: *The cottage is in a very exposed position at the top of the hill.* **2** open to attack or criticism while having very little support or protection: *She was left feeling exposed and vulnerable.*

exposé /ekˈspəʊzeɪ; *US* ˌekspəʊˈzeɪ/ *n* an account of the facts of a situation, esp when these are shocking or have been deliberately kept secret: *a damning exposé of corruption within the government.*

exposition /ˌekspəˈzɪʃn/ *n* (*fml*) **1** [C,U] an explanation of a theory, plan, etc: *a brilliant exposition of the advantages of nuclear power.* **2** [C] an exhibition of goods or works of art.

expostulate /ɪkˈspɒstʃuleɪt/ *v* (*fml*) to protest to sb about sth; to argue with sb, esp to persuade them not to do sth: [Vpr] *They expostulated about the financial risks involved in his plan.* [also V]. ▶ **ex-postulation** /ɪkˌspɒstʃuˈleɪʃn/ *n* [U, C].

exposure /ɪkˈspəʊʒə(r)/ *n* **1** [U] ~ **(to sth)** the action of exposing sth or the state of being exposed: *brief/prolonged exposure to radiation* ○ *the exposure of currency frauds* ○ *the benefits of constant exposure to a bilingual environment.* See also INDECENT EXPOSURE. **2** [U] the medical condition caused when sb has been exposed to severe weather conditions: *Two climbers were brought in suffering from exposure.* **3** [U] publicity on television, in newspapers, etc: *seeking maximum exposure* ○ *Her new film has had a lot of exposure in the media.* **4** [C] **(a)** a photograph: *take/make four exposures.* **(b)** the length of time that light is allowed to reach a film when taking a photograph: *We used long exposures.* ○ *an exposure meter.*

expound /ɪkˈspaʊnd/ *v* ~ **sth (to sb)**; ~ **on sth** (*fml*) to explain or make sth clear by giving details: [Vn] *expound a theory* [Vnpr] *He expounded his views on education to me at great length.* [Vpr] *We left him still expounding on the last act of the play.*

express¹ /ɪkˈspres/ *v* **1** to show or make known a feeling, an opinion, etc by words, looks or actions: [Vn] *express one's doubts/reservations/fears about sth* ○ *express one's emotions/views/interest/surprise* ○ *Words cannot express my gratitude to all those who have supported me.* [V.wh] *I still can't express how I feel.* **2** ~ **oneself** to speak, write or communicate in some other way what one thinks and feels: [Vnpr] *He is still unable to express himself in English.* ○ [Vnadv] *Dramatic gestures were how she often chose to express herself.* **3** ~ **sth as/in sth** (*esp mathematics*) to represent sth in a particular way, eg by symbols: [Vnpr] *The prices are expressed in local currency.* [Vn-n] *The figures are expressed as percentages.*

express² /ɪkˈspres/ *adj* [attrib] **1** (*esp Brit*) going or delivered quickly: *an express delivery service* ○ *an express letter* ○ *an express bus/coach.* **2** clearly and definitely stated: *It was his express wish that you should have his gold watch after he died.* ▶ **express** *adv* (*esp Brit*) by a special fast delivery: *The parcel was sent express.* **expressly** *adv* **1** clearly; definitely: *You were expressly told not to touch my papers.* **2** with a special purpose: *a dictionary expressly written for foreign students of English.*

express³ /ɪkˈspres/ *n* **1** (also **express train**) [C] a fast train that stops at few places: *the 0800 express to Edinburgh* ○ *the Baltimore express.* **2(a)** (also *esp US* **special delivery**) [U] a service for sending or transporting goods quickly: *send goods by express.* **(b)** [C] (*US*) a company that delivers goods quickly.

expression /ɪkˈspreʃn/ *n* **1** [C] a look on a person's face that shows a mood or feeling: *He didn't notice her expression.* ○ *Her face wore a worried/pained/peculiar expression.* ○ *'I don't understand,' he said, (with) an expression of complete surprise on his face.* **2(a)** [U] the action or process of making known one's feelings, opinions, ideas, etc: *the expression of grief* ○ *The school encourages free expression in art, drama and creative writing.* ○ *The poet's anger finds expression* (ie expresses itself) *in the last verse of the poem.* **(b)** [C] (*fml*) an instance of this: *expressions of concern/interest/support* ○ *I have not heard a single expression of regret.* **3** [C] a word or phrase: *He has an irritating habit of using outdated English expressions to show his familiarity with the language.* ○ *'Shut up' (meaning 'Stop talking') is not a polite expression.* **4** [U] a strong show of feeling for the meaning when playing music or speaking: *recite a poem with expression* ○ *She puts great expression into her violin playing.* ▶ **expressionless** *adj* not showing feelings,

thoughts, etc: *an expressionless face/voice/tone.* Compare EXPRESSIVE.

expressionism /ɪkˈspreʃənɪzəm/ *n* [U] a style of painting, music, drama, film, etc that tries to express the artist's or writer's emotional experience rather than to show the physical world in a realistic way. ▶ **expressionist** /-ʃənɪst/ *adj, n*: *of the expressionist school* ○ *expressionist art.*

expressive /ɪkˈspresɪv/ *adj* **1** showing or able to show one's feelings or thoughts: *an expressive gesture* ○ *an expressive piece of music* ○ *He has a wonderfully expressive face.* Compare EXPRESSIONLESS. **2** [pred] ~ **of sth** (*fml*) showing sth: *architecture expressive of the modern age* ○ *His every word and gesture is expressive of a powerful sincerity.* ▶ **expressively** *adv.* **expressiveness** *n* [U].

expressway /ɪkˈspreswei/ (also **thruway, freeway**) *n* (*US*) = MOTORWAY: *a major accident on the expressway.* ⇨ note at ROAD.

expropriate /eksˈprəʊprieɪt/ *v* (*fml or law*) (of a government or an authority) to take away property, etc from its owner for public use without payment: [Vn] *an expropriated landless labouring class* ○ *The new regime expropriated his estate for military purposes.* ▶ **expropriation** /ˌeksprəʊpriˈeɪʃn/ *n* [U, C].

expulsion /ɪkˈspʌlʃn/ *n* ~ **(from...)** [U, C] the action of forcing sb/sth to leave a place or an institution; the action of expelling (EXPEL) sb: *The headteacher threatened him with expulsion.* ○ *These clubs face expulsion from the league.* ○ *the expulsions of senior diplomats.*

expunge /ɪkˈspʌndʒ/ *v* ~ **sth (from sth)** (*fml*) to remove words or names completely from a list, book, etc: [Vnpr] *Her name was permanently expunged from the records.* [Vn] (*fig*) *He found it hard to expunge the memory of those dreadful times.*

expurgate /ˈekspəgeɪt/ *v* to remove from a book, etc parts that may cause offence: [Vn] *an expurgated edition of a novel.*

exquisite /ɪkˈskwɪzɪt, ˈekskwɪzɪt/ *adj* **1** extremely beautiful or delicate; finely or skilfully made or done: *an exquisite little painting/piece of lace* ○ *exquisite workmanship.* **2** (*fml*) **(a)** (of an emotion) strongly felt; ACUTE(2a): *exquisite pleasure/pain.* **(b)** (*approv*) (of a quality) delicate; sensitive: *exquisite tact/taste* ○ *an exquisite sense of timing.* ▶ **exquisitely** *adv*: *exquisitely tailored clothes.*

ex-serviceman /ˌeks ˈsɜːvɪsmən/ *n* (*pl* **-men** /-mən/; *fem* **ex-servicewoman** /-wʊmən/, *pl* **-women** /-wɪmɪn/) (*esp Brit*) a person who was formerly in one of the armed services: *an organization for ex-servicemen.*

ext *abbr* (as part of a telephone number) extension: *ext 4299.*

extant /ekˈstænt, ˈekstənt/ *adj* (esp of documents) still in existence: *the earliest extant account of the Arab conquests.*

extempore /ekˈstempəri/ *adj, adv* spoken or done without previous thought or preparation: *an extempore speech.* ▶ **extemporize, -ise** /ɪkˈstempəraɪz/ *v* (*fml*) to speak or perform without previous preparation: [V] *He forgot his words and had to extemporize.* **extemporization, -isation** /ɪkˌstempəraɪˈzeɪʃn; *US* -rəˈz-/ *n* [U, C].

extend /ɪkˈstend/ *v* **1** to make sth longer or larger in space or time: [Vn] *extend a fence/road/garden* ○ *There are plans to extend the no-smoking area.* ○ *extend a deadline/visa* ○ *The government voted to extend the state of emergency for another six months.* ○ *Careful maintenance can extend the life of your car by several years.* **2** to make a business, an idea, an influence, etc cover or operate in a wider area: [Vnpr] *The company plans to extend its operations into Europe.* [Vn] *extend one's repertoire on the piano* ○ *aiming to extend the technology.* **3** to relate to or

include sb/sth; to operate in a particular area or situation: [Vpr] *The argument does not extend to politicians.* ○ *His willingness to help did not extend beyond making a few phone calls.* **4 ~ sth to sb** (*fml*) (**a**) to give or make sth available to sb, esp in order to help them: [Vnpr] *organizations which extend credit to people* ○ *extend citizenship to the immigrant community.* (**b**) to offer sth to sb: [Vnpr] *extend hospitality to overseas students* ○ *extend an invitation/a warm welcome to sb* [also Vnn]. **5**(**a**) (of space, land, time, etc) to reach or stretch for a particular distance: [V-n, Vpr] *The track extends (for) many miles into the desert.* [Vpr] *My backyard extends as far as the river.* ○ *His writing career extended over a period of 40 years.* (**b**) to make sth reach or stretch: [Vnpr] *extend a rope between two posts* [also Vn]. (**c**) to stretch part of the body, esp an arm or leg, away from oneself: [Vnpr] *He extended his hand to* (ie offered to shake hands with) *the new employee.* [also Vn]. **6** (esp passive) to use or stretch the abilities or powers of sb/sth/oneself to the greatest possible degree: [Vn] *Jim didn't really have to extend himself in the examination.* ○ *Hospitals were already fully extended because of the epidemic.*
▶ **extendable** *adj* that can be extended: *an extendable ladder* ○ *extendable credit.*
extended *adj* [attrib] long; wider or longer than usual or expected: *go on extended leave/an extended holiday* ○ *the cost of extended hospital treatment.*
ex,tended 'family *n* a family structure in which uncles, aunts (AUNT) and cousins (COUSIN) are regarded as close relatives and everyone has an obligation to help and support each other.

extension /ɪkˈstenʃn/ *n* **1** [U] the action or process of making sth longer or larger, or of making sth cover a wider area or larger group of people: *The extension of the subway will take several months.* ○ *the extension of new technology into developing countries* ○ *the extension of credit facilities.* **2** [C] (**a**) ~ (**to sth**) an added part; an addition to sth: *build a 160-bed extension to a hospital* ○ *Our extension* (ie the extension to our house) *is nearly finished.* ○ (*fig*) *The characters she plays are only extensions of herself.* (**b**) ~ (**of sth**) an additional period of time: *The Chairman was voted a two-year extension of office.* ○ *He's been given an extension to finish writing his thesis.* **3** [C] a line leading from the main telephone to another room or office in a building. In an office building each extension usu has its own number: *She has an extension in the kitchen and in the bedroom.* ○ *Phone me at the office — I'm on extension 326.* **⬛** **by ex'tension** taking the argument or situation one stage further: *He criticized senior doctors, and by extension hospital administrators, for opposing the changes.*
▪ **ex'tension lead** *n* an electrical cable with a plug at one end and a SOCKET(2) at the other to which an appliance can be connected if its own cable is too short to reach a socket in a wall.

extensive /ɪkˈstensɪv/ *adj* **1** large in area; extending far: *The house has extensive grounds.* **2** large in amount or scale: *cause extensive damage* ○ *an extensive programme of reform* ○ *make extensive alterations to a building* ○ *Choose from our extensive range of bedroom furniture.* ○ *Her knowledge of the subject is extensive.* ▶ **extensively** *adv*: *a spice used extensively in Eastern cookery* ○ *He has travelled extensively in Europe.*

extent /ɪkˈstent/ *n* [U] the size, range or scale of sth: *I was amazed at the extent of his knowledge.* ○ *He had not anticipated the full extent of the violence.* **⬛** **to some, what, such an, a certain, etc extent** to the degree specified: *To some extent we are all responsible for what has happened.* ○ *To what extent can he be believed?* ○ *The carpet was badly stained, to such an extent that* (ie so much that) *you couldn't tell*

its *original colour.* ○ *I agree with you to a certain/a limited extent, but...*

extenuating /ɪkˈstenjueɪtɪŋ/ *adj* [attrib] providing grounds for a wrong or illegal act to be excused or judged less serious: *The charge was reduced from murder to manslaughter because of* **extenuating circumstances**.

exterior /ɪkˈstɪəriə(r)/ *adj* [usu attrib] on or coming from the outside; outer: *the exterior walls of a house.* Compare INTERIOR 1, EXTERNAL.
▶ **exterior** *n* **1** [sing] the outward appearance of sb: *Underneath that hard exterior, says his wife, he is just a big softy.* **2** [C] the outside of sth, esp a building: *pub exteriors* ○ *The house has a Georgian exterior.*

exterminate /ɪkˈstɜːmɪneɪt/ *v* to destroy completely a race or group of people or animals: [Vn] *The indigenous population was virtually exterminated by settlers.* ○ *What exterminated the dinosaur?* ▶ **extermination** /ɪkˌstɜːmɪˈneɪʃn/ *n* [U].

external /ɪkˈstɜːnl/ *adj* **1** of, for or situated on the outside of sth: *the external walls of the building* ○ *an external television aerial* ○ *for external use only* (eg on the label of a pot of skin cream) ○ *All his injuries are external* (ie He has not been injured inside his body). **2** happening or coming from outside a place, a group, sb's mind, etc: *a tribe hardly affected by external influences* ○ *a company's external financing* ○ *external trade* (ie with foreign countries) ○ *Canada's Minister for External Affairs* ○ *an external examination* (ie one set by an organization other than one's own school, etc) ○ *an external student* (ie one registered with a university but studying privately and not attending a course there). Compare INTERNAL, EXTERIOR.
▶ **externalize, -ise** /-nəlaɪz/ *v* [Vn] (*fml*) to express one's thoughts or feelings in words or actions.
externally /ɪkˈstɜːnəli/ *adv*: *The building has been carefully restored externally.*
externals *n* [pl] (*fml*) outward features or appearances: *Do not judge people by externals alone.*

extinct /ɪkˈstɪŋkt/ *adj* (**a**) (of a type of animal, plant, etc) no longer in existence: *an extinct species* ○ *The red squirrel is now virtually extinct in England.* ○ (*fig*) *a wire-cage lift of a type that is almost extinct* ○ *The old use of the word 'gay' to mean 'happy' is almost extinct.* (**b**) (of a VOLCANO) no longer active. ▶ **extinction** /ɪkˈstɪŋkʃn/ *n* [U, C]: *a tribe threatened with extinction* ○ *a species thought to be on the edge/point/verge of extinction* ○ *save a plant from extinction* ○ *the extinction of his youthful hopes.*

extinguish /ɪkˈstɪŋgwɪʃ/ *v* (*fml*) (**a**) to cause sth to stop burning: [Vn] *A sign flashed up telling them to extinguish their cigarettes.* ○ *They tried to extinguish the flames.* (**b**) to end the existence of a feeling, condition, etc: [Vn] *This defeat effectively extinguished all hopes of independence.* ○ *His behaviour extinguished the last traces of affection she had for him.*
▶ **extinguisher** *n* = FIRE EXTINGUISHER.

extirpate /ˈekstəpeɪt/ *v* (*fml*) to remove or destroy completely sth undesirable or bad: [Vn] *extirpate terrorism/ illiteracy.* ▶ **extirpation** /ˌekstəˈpeɪʃn/ *n* [U].

extol /ɪkˈstəʊl/ *v* (**-ll-**) ~ **sb** (**as sth**) (*fml*) to praise sb/sth highly: [Vn] *a report extolling the merits of small businesses* ○ *Government ministers began to extol the virtues of British technology.* [Vn-n] *He was extolled as a hero.*

extort /ɪkˈstɔːt/ *v* ~ **sth** (**from sb**) to obtain sth by violence, threats, etc: [Vnpr] *extort money/bribes from sb* [also Vn]. ▶ **extortion** /ɪkˈstɔːʃn/ *n* [U]: *obtain money by extortion.*

extortionate /ɪkˈstɔːʃənət/ *adj* (*derog*) (of demands, prices, etc) much too great or high; excessive: *offer* *loans at extortionate rates of interest* ○ *The price of perfume is extortionate.*

extra /ˈekstrə/ *adj* more than or beyond what is usual, expected or necessary; additional: *demand extra pay for extra work* ○ *order an extra pint of milk* ○ *The bus company provided extra buses because there were so many people.* ○ *We need an extra £5 million a year to cover the costs of research.* ○ *place an extra burden on the taxpayer* ○ *Take extra care.*
▶ **extra** *adv* **1** more than usually: *an extra large helping of rice* ○ *extra fine quality.* **2** in addition: *earn a bit extra this month* ○ *charge/pay 20% extra* ○ *price $6.30, postage and packing extra.*
extra *n* **1** an extra thing; a thing that costs extra: *a new car with all the extras* ○ *The price you pay for your excursion is the complete price; there are no hidden extras.* ○ *School fees are £550 a term; music and dancing are* **optional extras.** **2** (esp in making films) a person employed to play a very small part, eg in a crowd scene: *We need hundreds of extras for the battle scenes.*
■ **ˌextra ˈtime** *n* [U] (*sport*) a further period of play at the end of a football match, etc when the scores are equal at the end of the normal period.

extra- *pref* (with *adjs*) **1** outside; beyond: *extramarital* ○ *extracurricular.* **2** (*infml*) very; to an exceptional degree: *extra-thin* ○ *extra-special.*

extract /ɪkˈstrækt/ *v* ~ **sth** (**from sb/sth**) **1(a)** to take or get sth out, usu with effort or by force: [Vnpr] *manage to extract a cork from a bottle* ○ *He extracted a crumpled note from his pocket.* [Vn] *have a tooth extracted.* (**b**) to obtain money, information, etc, usu from a person who is unwilling to give it: [Vnpr] *extract a contribution from everyone* ○ *It took me days to extract the truth/the information/a confession from her.* [also Vn]. **2** to obtain sth from sth else by a particular process: [Vnpr] *extract juice from oranges/oil from olives* ○ *extract energy from the waves* [also Vn]. **3** to select and present passages, examples, words, etc from a book, speech, etc: [Vn] *She extracted passages for the students to translate.* [also Vnpr].
▶ **extract** /ˈekstrækt/ *n* **1** [U,C] a substance that has been extracted (EXTRACT 2): ˈ*beef extract* ○ ˈ*herbal extracts* ○ ˌ*extract of* ˈ*malt.* **2** [C] ~ (**from sth**) a passage selected from a poem, book, piece of music, etc: *a short/brief extract from a piano sonata* ○ *an extract from 'Oliver Twist' by Charles Dickens* ○ *She read out extracts from his letters.*
extraction /ɪkˈstrækʃn/ *n* **1(a)** [U] the action or process of removing sth with effort or by force: *the extraction of a tooth* ○ *the extraction of information* ○ *the mineral extraction process at a mine.* (**b**) [C] an instance of extracting a tooth: *He needs two extractions.* **2** [U] (*fml*) the origin of a person's family: *an American of Hungarian extraction.*
exˈtractor (also **exˈtractor fan**) *n* an electric fan, usu fitted in a window or a wall, that removes bad air or smells from a room. ⇨ picture at FAN¹.

extracurricular /ˌekstrəkəˈrɪkjələ(r)/ *adj* [usu attrib] outside the regular course of work or studies at a school or college: *She's involved in many* **extracurricular activities,** *including music, sport and drama.*

extradite /ˈekstrədaɪt/ *v* ~ **sb** (**to…**) (**from…**) to send back sb accused or found guilty of a crime to the country where the crime was committed: [Vn] *The government has refused to extradite a man wanted for a bank robbery in France.* [also Vnpr]. ▶
extradition /ˌekstrəˈdɪʃn/ *n* [C,U]: *seek the extradition of a suspected drug trafficker* ○ *an extradition agreement/treaty* ○ *start extradition proceedings.*

extramarital /ˌekstrəˈmærɪtl/ *adj* (of a married person's sexual relationships) occurring outside marriage: *have extramarital affairs.*

extramural /ˌekstrəˈmjʊərəl/ *adj* [usu attrib] **1** (*esp*

Brit) (of university courses, etc) arranged for people who are not full-time members of a university: *extramural studies/lectures.* **2** additional to one's work, course of study, etc and often not connected with it: *Some of our research students have extramural commitments.*

extraneous /ɪkˈstreɪniəs/ *adj* ~ (**to sth**) (*fml*) not belonging to or directly connected with the subject or matter being dealt with: *cut out all extraneous information/material/details.*

extraordinaire /ɪkˌstrɔːdɪˈneə(r)/ *adj* (*approv often joc*) (following *ns*) outstanding; remarkable: *an opera for children from the musician extraordinaire Daryl Runswick.*

extraordinary /ɪkˈstrɔːdnri; *US* -dəneri/ *adj* **1** not normal or ordinary; very unusual; remarkable: *extraordinary weather for this time of year* ○ *a most extraordinary story/achievement/spectacle* ○ *a child born in extraordinary circumstances* ○ *It seems quite extraordinary that the Prime Minister can claim these figures as a triumph.* **2** [attrib] (*fml*) (of arrangements, meetings, etc) additional to what is usual or ordinary: *hold an* **extraordinary general meeting.** **3** (following *ns*) (*techn*) (of an official) specially employed; additional to the usual staff: *an ambassador extraordinary.* ▶ **extraordinarily** /ɪkˈstrɔːdnrəli; *US* -dənerəli/ *adv*: *extraordinarily beautiful/diverse/difficult/effective* ○ *Extraordinarily, the referee took no action.*

extrapolate /ɪkˈstræpəleɪt/ *v* ~ (**sth**) (**from sth**) (*fml*) to estimate sth unknown from facts or information that are available: [Vn,Vnpr] *They extrapolate a figure of at least 8 000 vacant teaching posts (from responses to their questionnaire).* [Vpr] *We can extrapolate to some extent from present trends (to the future).* ▶ **extrapolation** /ɪkˌstræpəˈleɪʃn/ *n* [U,C]: *Extrapolations from results obtained in developed countries are invalid.* ⇨ picture at CHART.

extraterrestrial /ˌekstrətəˈrestriəl/ *adj* of or from outside the planet Earth and its atmosphere: *extraterrestrial life/beings.*

extravagant /ɪkˈstrævəgənt/ *adj* **1** (*sometimes derog*) (**a**) (of a person or an organization) willing to use more of sth, esp money, than is necessary or appropriate: *I only buy chocolates when I'm feeling extravagant.* ○ *She's rather extravagant when it comes to buying perfume.* (**b**) (of things) showing or resulting from this tendency: *an extravagant five-course meal* ○ *have extravagant tastes* ○ *an extravagant use of natural resources.* **2** (of ideas, speech or behaviour) beyond what is reasonable, usual or necessary: *extravagant praise/claims/promises* ○ *pay extravagant compliments.*
▶ **extravagance** /-gəns/ *n* **1** [U] the action or habit of being extravagant: *The government slashed public spending to make up for its past extravagance.* **2** [C] an extravagant item, act, statement, etc: *He can ill afford such extravagances.*
extravagantly *adv*: *extravagantly dressed.*

extravaganza /ɪkˌstrævəˈɡænzə/ *n* an entertainment with elaborate and colourful costumes, scenery, etc: *He's planning a multi-million dollar musical extravaganza.*

extreme /ɪkˈstriːm/ *adj* **1(a)** very great: *suffering from extreme anxiety* ○ *a period of extreme coolness in diplomatic relations* ○ *show extreme flexibility.* (**b**) not ordinary or usual; serious or severe: *take extreme measures* ○ *The child will be removed from its parents only in* **extreme cases.** ○ *He promised he would not resort to anything as extreme as plastic surgery.* (**c**) (*often derog*) (of people and their opinions) far from moderate: *an extreme nationalist organization* ○ *hold extreme left-wing/right-wing views* ○ *His ideas are too extreme for me.* **2** [attrib] as

E

far away as possible, esp from the centre or beginning; remote: *in the extreme north of a country* ○ *at the extreme edge of the forest.*

▶ **extreme** *n* [C usu *pl*] **1** a feeling, condition, etc as far apart or as different from another as possible: *dealing with her extremes of mood* ○ *The truth lies somewhere between these two extremes.* ○ *She was once terribly shy but now she's gone to the opposite/other extreme.* **2** the greatest or highest degree of sth: *He could not tolerate the extremes of heat in the desert.* **IDM** **go, etc to ex'tremes** to act or be forced to act in a way that is far from moderate or normal: *In the jungle, they were driven to extremes in order to survive.* **in the ex'treme** (*fml*) to the highest degree; extremely: *I found his remarks about the cooking offensive in the extreme.*

extremely *adv* (usu with *adjs* and *advs*) to a very high degree: *extremely complicated/dangerous/useful* ○ *That's extremely unlikely.* ○ *I'm extremely sorry for the delay.* ○ *He behaved extremely badly.* ○

extremist *n* (*usu derog*) a person who holds extreme views, esp in politics or religion: *assassinated by extremists* ○ *extremist policies.* **extremism** *n* [U] the holding of extreme views: *the dangers of political extremism.*

extremity /ɪkˈstremətɪ/ *n* (*fml*) **1(a)** [C] any one of the furthest points, ends or limits of sth: *at the camp's northern extremity.* **(b) extremities** [pl] the furthest parts from the centre of the human body, esp the hands and feet: *Cold affects the extremities first.* **2** [C, U] an extreme degree of sadness, suffering, despair, etc: *reach an extremity/the extremities of pain* ○ *observe how people react **in** extremity or under pressure.*

extricate /ˈekstrɪkeɪt/ *v* ~ **oneself/sb/sth (from sth)** (*fml*) to free or release oneself/sb/sth from sth; to DISENTANGLE(1) oneself/sb/sth: [Vnpr] *The bird had to be extricated from the netting.* ○ *extricate oneself from an unhappy love affair* [also Vn].

extrinsic /eksˈtrɪnsɪk, -trɪnzɪk/ *adj* ~ **(to sth)** (*fml*) not belonging to or part of the real nature of a person or thing; coming from outside: *extrinsic evidence* ○ *factors extrinsic to his work.* Compare INTRINSIC.

extrovert /ˈekstrəvɜːt/ *n* a lively cheerful person who likes to be with others and to attract attention: *She's a good person to invite to a party because she's such an extrovert.* Compare INTROVERT.

▶ **extrovert** *adj* of or typical of an extrovert: *extrovert behaviour.*

extrude /ɪkˈstruːd/ *v* **1** (*fml*) to force or squeeze sth into or out of sth by pressure; to be forced or squeezed in this way: [Vnpr] *extrude glue from a tube* [Vpr] *If pressure is applied, the seal will extrude into the gap.* **2** (*techn*) to shape metal, plastic, etc by forcing it through a DIE²: [Vn] *nylon extruded as very thin fibres.* ▶ **extrusion** /ɪkˈstruːʒn/ *n* [C, U].

exuberant /ɪgˈzjuːbərənt; *US* -ˈzuː-/ *adj* **1** (esp of people and their behaviour) filled with or showing great happiness and excitement; very lively and cheerful: *All evening she was witty and exuberant.* ○ *an exuberant comic style* ○ *an exuberant imagination.* **2** (of plants, etc) growing vigorously: *exuberant foliage.* ▶ **exuberance** /-rəns/ *n* [U]: *We can excuse his behaviour as youthful exuberance.* **exuberantly** *adv.*

exude /ɪgˈzjuːd; *US* -ˈzuːd/ *v* **1** (of a liquid or smell) to come out slowly; to give out a liquid or smell from the body, etc: [Vpr, Vn] *Sweat exuded from him/He exuded sweat.* [Vn] *creatures that exude scents* [also Vnpr]. **2** to display a feeling openly and strongly: [Vn] *She exudes confidence/optimism.*

exult /ɪgˈzʌlt/ *v* ~ **(at/in sth)** (*fml*) to show or feel great joy because of sth that has happened; to get great pleasure from sth: [V] *Crowds exulted when victory was announced.* [Vpr] *The nation exulted at*

the team's success. ○ *He exulted in his role as national hero.* [also V.speech, V.*that*].

▶ **exultant** /-ənt/ *adj* ~ **(at sth)** exulting: *an exultant shout/mood* ○ *The fans were exultant at their team's victory.* **exultantly** *adv.*

exultation /ˌegzʌlˈteɪʃn/ *n* [U] ~ **(at sth)** great joy or pleasure, esp because of sth that has happened: *carried along on a tide/wave of exultation.*

-ey ⇨ -Y¹.

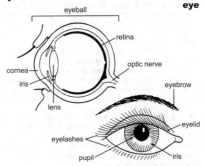

eye

eyeball

retina

optic nerve

eyebrow

cornea

iris

lens

eyelid

eyelashes

pupil

iris

eye¹ /aɪ/ *n* **1(a)** each of the two organs on the face that are used for seeing: *I can't see out of this eye.* ○ *She opened/closed her eyes.* ○ *He is blind in one eye.* ○ *He lost an eye in the war.* ○ *I have something in my eye.* ○ *have an eye operation* ○ *His eyes fell upon* (ie He suddenly noticed) *an advertisement in the magazine.* ⇨ picture. ⇨ picture at HEAD¹. **(b)** the visible coloured part of this: *have blue eyes.* **2(a)** [often *pl*] the power of seeing; the ability to see: *You must have sharp eyes to be able to spot such a tiny detail.* ○ *The eyes often deteriorate as one gets older.* **(b)** [usu *sing*] the ability to make good judgements about sth one sees: *To her expert eye, the painting was clearly a fake.* ○ *She has a good eye for a bargain.* **3** a thing like an eye: *the eye of a needle* (ie the hole for the thread to go through) ○ *a hook and eye* (ie a fastening with a hook and loop for a dress, etc) ○ *the eye of a potato* (ie a point from which a shoot will grow). **IDM** **the apple of sb's eye** ⇨ APPLE. **as far as the eye can see** ⇨ FAR¹. **be all 'eyes** to be watching eagerly: *The children were all eyes as we slowly unwrapped the parcel.* **before sb's very eyes** ⇨ VERY². **the blink of an eye** ⇨ BLINK. **cast an eye / one's eye(s) over sb/sth** ⇨ CAST¹. **catch sb's attention/eye** ⇨ CATCH¹. **clap/lay/set eyes on sb/sth** (*infml*) to see sb/sth: *I disliked the place the moment I clapped eyes on it.* ○ *I hope I never set eyes on him again.* **cock an ear/eye for/at sb/sth** ⇨ COCK². **cry one's eyes/heart out** ⇨ CRY¹. **easy on the ear/eye** ⇨ EASY¹. **an ˌeye for an 'eye (and a ˌtooth for a 'tooth)** it is right to give sb a punishment that is as serious as the offence they have committed: *The death penalty for murder works on the principle of an eye for an eye.* **the eye of the 'storm** a relatively calm spot in the centre of a storm, esp a HURRICANE. **sb's eyes are bigger than their 'stomach** (*saying*) sb is too greedy because they have asked for or taken more food than they can eat. **feast one's eyes** ⇨ FEAST. **for sb's eyes 'only** to be seen, read, etc only by the person specified: *The top secret file was marked 'for the President's eyes only'.* **get one's 'eye in** (*Brit*) (in ball games) to become able, through practice, to follow with one's eyes the movement of the ball: *Once I'd got my eye in, I started to play better.* **have/with an eye for/on/to the main 'chance** (*Brit*) to look/looking for an opportunity for personal gain, esp to make money. **have one's 'eye on sb** to watch sb and keep checking what they are doing,

---

[V.*to* inf] = verb + *to* infinitive   [Vn.inf (no *to*)] = verb + noun + infinitive without *to*   [V.*ing*] = verb + *-ing* form

what progress they are making, etc: *I've got my eye on you, so you'd better behave.* **have one's 'eye on sth** to have a desire for sth: *I'm thinking of buying a car — there's a nice new model I've got my eye on.* **have/with an eye to sth/doing sth** to have sth/having sth as one's aim or purpose: *He always has an eye to business* (ie looks for a chance of doing business). ○ *He kept the customer talking with an eye to selling him something else.* **have eyes in the back of one's 'head** to observe everything, including things that are difficult to see: *How did you know I was behind you? You must have eyes in the back of your head.* **have/with half an / one eye on sth** to give/giving partial attention to sth: *I only had half an eye on the programme because I was reading the paper.* **have a roving eye** ⇨ ROVE. **hit sb in the eye** ⇨ HIT[1]. **in the eyes of the 'law, 'world, etc** from the point of view of the law, etc; as the law, etc sees it: *In the eyes of the law she is guilty though few ordinary people would think so.* **in the eyes of 'sb / in 'sb's eyes** in the opinion or judgement of sb: *In the eyes of the critics, he can do no wrong.* **in one's mind's eye** ⇨ MIND[1]. **in the public eye** ⇨ PUBLIC. **in the twinkling of an eye** ⇨ TWINKLE. **keep a close eye/watch on sb/sth** ⇨ CLOSE[1]. **keep one's ears/eyes open** ⇨ OPEN[1]. **keep an eye on sb/sth** to watch or check sb/sth to make sure they are safe, etc; to look after sb/sth: *Could you keep an eye on my suitcase for a moment?* **keep an eye open/out (for sb/sth)** (*infml*) to watch for sb/sth; to be careful to notice sb/sth: *I've lost my ring — could you keep an eye out for it when you clean the house?* **keep one's 'eyes peeled/skinned (for sb/sth)** to watch constantly and carefully; to be very careful to notice sb/sth: *She walked along slowly, keeping her eyes peeled/skinned for any unusual flowers.* **keep a weather eye on sth** ⇨ WEATHER[1]. **look sb in the 'eye(s)/'face** to look at sb steadily without shame or embarrassment: *Can you look me in the eye and tell me you're not lying? ○ He couldn't bear to look her in the face.* **make 'eyes at sb** to look at sb in a way that shows that one finds them attractive: *He made eyes at her across the room.* **make sheep's eyes at sb** ⇨ SHEEP. **meet sb's eye** ⇨ MEET[1]. **my 'eye** (*infml*) (used to indicate that one does not agree with sth or believe sth) nonsense; rubbish: *She said she was only twenty-two — twenty-two my eye!* **the naked eye** ⇨ NAKED. **never/not (be able to) take one's 'eyes off sb/sth** to watch sb/sth constantly; to be unable to stop watching sb/sth: *She never took her eyes off him the whole evening.* **not bat an eyelid/eye** ⇨ BAT[3]. **not believe one's ears/eyes** ⇨ BELIEVE. **one in the eye (for sb/sth)** (*infml*) a defeat or disappointment, esp one that is deserved: *If she gets the job, it'll be one in the eye for Peter: he thought he was bound to get it.* **only have eyes for / have eyes only for sb** to be interested in or in love with the specified person only: *It's no use asking Kim to go out with you; she only has eyes for Mark.* **open one's/sb's eyes (to sth)** ⇨ OPEN[2]. **out of the corner of one's eye** ⇨ CORNER[1]. **pull the wool over sb's eyes** ⇨ PULL[1]. **(not) see eye to 'eye with sb** (not) to agree fully with sb; (not) to have similar views or attitudes to sb: *Jim and I have always seen eye to eye on politics. ○ She left because she didn't see eye to eye with her boss.* **see, look at, etc sb's/sth's eyes** to view or consider sth from sb else's point of view: *If you saw the situation through my eyes, you'd realize why I'm so angry.* **shut/close one's eyes to sth** to refuse to see or notice sth: *The government shuts its eyes to poverty. ○ She closed her eyes to her husband's infidelities.* **a sight for sore eyes** ⇨ SIGHT[1]. **there is more in/to sb/sth than meets the eye** ⇨ MEET[1]. **turn a blind eye** ⇨ BLIND[1]. **up to one's/the ears/eyes/eyebrows/neck in sth** ⇨ EAR[1]. **with one's 'eyes open** fully aware of possible difficulties involved in

or consequences of what one is doing: *I moved to this country with my eyes open, so I'm not complaining.* **with one's 'eyes shut/closed 1** without effort; easily: *He's cooked that meal so often he can do it with his eyes closed.* **2** without paying attention to what is going on around one: *If you go around with your eyes shut, you never learn anything about life.*

▶ **-eyed** (forming compound *adjs*) having an eye or eyes of the specified kind: *a blue-eyed girl ○ a one-eyed man.* See also BLACK EYE, PRIVATE EYE.

■ **'eye-catching** *adj* striking and noticeable, esp because of being pleasant to look at: *an eye-catching dress/poster.*

'eye-level *adj* [usu attrib] level with a person's eyes when looking straight ahead: *The oven has an eye-level grill.*

'eye-liner (also **liner**) *n* a COSMETIC applied as a line round the eye or part of it.

'eye-opener *n* an event, etc that reveals an unexpected fact or causes surprise: *My trip to India was quite an eye-opener.*

'eye-shadow *n* [C, U] a type of COSMETIC applied to the eyelids (EYELID).

'eye strain *n* [U] a tired condition of the eyes caused eg by a long period of reading or looking at a computer screen.

'eye-tooth *n* (*pl* **'eye-teeth**) either of the two pointed teeth in the upper human jaw, under the eye. Compare CANINE *n*. **IDM** **give one's eye-teeth for sth** to wish to possess or obtain sth very much: *I'd give my eye-teeth for a new car like that.*

eye² /aɪ/ *v* (*pres p* **eyeing** or **eying**) to look at or watch sb/sth, esp with curiosity, suspicion or desire: [Vn] *He eyed me curiously/warily. ○ The children were eyeing the sweets hungrily.* **PHRV** **,eye sb 'up** (*infml*) to look at sb in a way that shows that one has a special interest in them: *I could see that she was eying me up as a potential customer.*

eyeball /'aɪbɔːl/ *n* the whole round part of the eye, like a ball. ⇨ picture at EYE[1]. ⇨ note at BODY. **IDM** **,eyeball to 'eyeball (with sb)** face to face with sb, esp in an angry way: *They confronted each other eyeball to eyeball.*

eyebrow /'aɪbraʊ/ *n* the line of hair above the human eye: *pluck one's eyebrows.* ⇨ picture at EYE[1]. ⇨ note at BODY. **IDM** **raise one's eyebrows** ⇨ RAISE. **up to one's/the ears/eyes/eyebrows/neck in sth** ⇨ EAR[1].

eyeful /'aɪfʊl/ *n* (*pl* **-fuls**) **1** a thing thrown or blown into one's eye: *get an eyeful of sand.* **2** (*infml*) an interesting or attractive sight: *She's quite an eyeful!* **IDM** **have/get an eyeful (of sth)** (*infml*) to have a long look at sth interesting, remarkable, unusual, etc: *Come and get an eyeful of this — there's a giraffe in the garden!*

eyeglass /'aɪglɑːs; *US* -glæs/ *n* a LENS(1) for one eye to help sb to see sth more clearly: *The old man wore an eyeglass attached to a piece of ribbon.*

eyelash /'aɪlæʃ/ (also **lash**) *n* each of the hairs growing on the edge of the EYELID: *She was wearing false eyelashes* (ie artificial ones stuck to the eyelids). ⇨ picture at EYE[1].

eyelet /'aɪlət/ *n* a hole with a metal or leather ring round it in a piece of material, for passing a rope or string through.

eyelid /'aɪlɪd/ (also **lid**) *n* the upper or lower of two folds of skin that close to cover the EYEBALL: *His eyelid is swollen.* ⇨ picture at EYE[1]. **IDM** **not bat an eyelid/eye** ⇨ BAT[3].

eyepiece /'aɪpiːs/ *n* a LENS(1) at the end of a TELESCOPE or MICROSCOPE through which one looks. ⇨ picture at MICROSCOPE.

eyesight /'aɪsaɪt/ *n* [U] the power of seeing; the ability to see: *have good/bad/poor eyesight.*

eyesore /'aɪsɔː(r)/ *n* an ugly object; a thing that is

unpleasant to look at: *That old factory is a real eyesore!*

eyewash /'aɪwɒʃ; US -wɔːʃ/ n [U] (*infml*) insincere talk; nonsense: *His story may sound convincing enough but it's all complete eyewash.*

eyewitness /'aɪwɪtnəs/ n a person who has person-ally seen sth happen and can give evidence about it: *an eyewitness account of a crime.*

eyrie (also **eyry**) /'ɪəri, 'eəri, 'aɪəri/ n **1** a nest of a bird of prey (BIRD), esp an EAGLE(1), built high up among rocks. **2** a high place in which sb lives or from which sb can observe what is below.

Ff

F¹ (also **f**) /ef/ *n* (*pl* **F's, f's** /efs/) **1** the 6th letter of the English alphabet: *'Fabric' starts with an 'F'/F.* **2** **F** (*music*) the fourth note in the scale¹(6) of C major.

F² *abbr* **1** degree or degrees Fahrenheit: *Water freezes at 32°F.* Compare C² 2. **2** (*Brit*) (in academic degrees) Fellow of: *FRCM* (ie Fellow of the Royal College of Music). Compare A¹ 3. **3** (of lead³(2) used in pencils) fine.

f *abbr* **1** (also **fem**) female. **2** (also **fem**) (*grammar*) feminine. **3** (*music*) loudly (Italian *forte*). Compare P3.

fa = FAH.

fab /fæb/ *adj* (*Brit sl*) marvellous; FABULOUS(1).

fable /'feɪbl/ *n* **1(a)** [C] a short story that is intended to teach a moral lesson. Fables are not based on fact and often have animals as characters: *Aesop's fables.* **(b)** [U] such stories considered as a group: *a land famous in fable.* See also LEGEND 1, MYTH 1. **2** [C, U] a statement or an account that is not true: *have difficulty distinguishing fact from fable.* See also FICTION 2, MYTH 2.

▶ **fabled** /'feɪbld/ *adj* told of or famous in fables: *a fabled monster.*

fabric /'fæbrɪk/ *n* **1** [C, U] a type of cloth, esp one that is woven: *woollen/silk/cotton fabrics* ○ *a striped fabric.* **2** [sing] **the ~ (of sth) (a)** the walls, floors and roof of a building, etc: *The entire fabric of the church needs renovation.* **(b)** the structure of sth: *The whole fabric of society was torn apart by the war.*

fabricate /'fæbrɪkeɪt/ *v* [Vn] **1** to invent false information, a false account of events, etc: *fabricate evidence* ○ *The reason he gave for his absence was obviously fabricated.* **2** to make or manufacture sth from various materials: *a specially fabricated container.* ▶ **fabrication** /ˌfæbrɪ'keɪʃn/ *n* [U, C]: *alleged fabrication of evidence* ○ *The newspaper story turned out to be a complete fabrication.*

fabulous /'fæbjələs/ *adj* **1** (*infml*) wonderful; marvellous: *a fabulous performance* ○ *The food is fabulous.* **2** very great: *fabulous wealth.* **3** [attrib] (*fml*) appearing in fables (TABLE 1): *fabulous heroes.* ▶ **fabulously** *adv* extremely: *fabulously rich.*

façade /fə'sɑːd/ *n* **1** (*fml*) the front of a building: *a classical façade.* **2** an outward appearance, esp one that creates a false impression: *maintain a façade of indifference* ○ *They seem happy together, but it's all a façade.* ○ *Squalor and poverty lay behind the city's glittering façade.*

face¹ /feɪs/ *n* **1** the front part of the head from the forehead to the chin: *a pretty/handsome face* ○ *Go and wash your face.* ○ *He was so ashamed that he hid his face in his hands.* ○ *The ball hit him in the face.* ○ *I saw many familiar/strange faces* (ie people whom I recognized/did not recognize). **2** an expression shown on the face: *a sad face* ○ *smiling faces* ○ *She had a face like thunder* (ie She looked very angry). **3(a)** a surface or side of sth: *A cut diamond has many faces.* ○ *They disappeared from/off the face of the earth* (ie totally disappeared). ○ *The team climbed the north face of the mountain.* See also COALFACE. **(b)** the front or main side of sth: *the face of a clock* ○ *a clock-face* ○ *He put the cards face up/down on the table* (ie with their faces visible/not visible). **4** an aspect of sth: *the many faces of crim-inal activity.* **5** the outward appearance of sth: *preserve the face of an old town.* **6** the nature of sth: *developments that have changed the face of society.* **7** = TYPEFACE. **IDM** **be staring sb in the face** ⇨ STARE. **be written all over sb's face** ⇨ WRITE. **cut off one's nose to spite one's face** ⇨ NOSE¹. **one's 'face falls** one's expression changes to one of disappointment, sadness, etc: *Her face fell when she heard the news.* **ˌface to 'face (with sb/sth)** close to and looking at sb/sth: *I've always admired her acting and would love to meet her face to face.* ○ *He turned the corner and found himself face to face with a policeman.* ○ *The two came/were brought face to face in a TV interview.* **fly in the face of sth** ⇨ FLY¹. **get, etc egg on / all over one's face** ⇨ EGG¹. **have the 'face (to do sth)** (*Brit infml*) to be bold enough; not to be too ashamed to do sth: *I don't know how you have the face to ask for more money when you do so little work.* **in the face of 'sth 1** in spite of sth: *succeed in the face of danger* ○ *continue in the face of criticism.* **2** when opposed by sb/sth: *We are powerless in the face of such a threat.* **keep a straight face** ⇨ STRAIGHT¹. **laugh in sb's face** ⇨ LAUGH. **laugh on the other side of one's face** ⇨ LAUGH. **a long face** ⇨ LONG¹. **look sb in the eye/ face** ⇨ EYE¹. **lose face** ⇨ LOSE. **not just a pretty face** ⇨ PRETTY. **on the 'face of it** (*infml*) judging by how sth appears: *On the face of it, he seems to be telling the truth though I suspect he's hiding something.* ○ *It's a wonderful offer on the face of it.* **plain as the nose on one's face** ⇨ PLAIN¹. **pull / make 'faces / a 'face (at sb)** to produce an expression on one's face that shows dislike, disgust, etc or that is intended to be amusing: *He pulled a funny face behind the teacher's back.* ○ *Don't make a face like that — it's lovely soup!* **put a bold, brave, good, etc 'face on sth** to act as if sth unpleasant or upsetting is not as bad as it really is: *Her exam results were disappointing but she tried to put a brave face on it.* **save face** ⇨ SAVE¹. **set one's face against sb/sth** to be determined to oppose sb/sth: *The government appears to have set its face against any reduction in taxes.* **show one's face** ⇨ SHOW². **shut/slam the door in sb's face** ⇨ DOOR. **shut your mouth/face!** ⇨ SHUT. **a slap in the face** ⇨ SLAP¹. **stuff one's face** ⇨ STUFF². **till one is blue in the face** ⇨ BLUE¹. **to sb's 'face** openly and directly so that sb can hear: *I was very angry and said so to his face.* ○ *They called their teacher 'Fatty', but never to his face.* Compare BEHIND SB'S BACK (BACK¹). **wipe sb/sth off the face of the earth / off the map** ⇨ WIPE. See also ABOUT-FACE, VOLTE-FACE.

▶ **faceless** *adj* not known by name; with no clear character or identity: *faceless bureaucrats.*

■ **'face-card** *n* (*esp US*) = COURT-CARD.
'face-cloth *n* = FLANNEL 2.
'face-cream *n* [U,C] cream used to soften or clean the skin of the face.
'face-lift *n* **1** an operation to make the face look smoother and younger by tightening the skin: *She only looks young because she's had a face-lift.* **2** a process of improving the appearance of sth, esp a building or part of one: *The court-house certainly needs a face-lift.*
'face-pack *n* a substance put on the face to clean and improve the quality of the skin and then removed.

'face-saving adj [usu attrib] intended to avoid embarrassment or loss of dignity for sb: *a face-saving compromise/exercise/formula.*

,face 'value n [U,C] the value printed on money or stamps. **IDM** **take sth at (its) face 'value** to assume that sth is really what it appears to be: *Taken at face value, the figures look very encouraging.* ○ *You shouldn't take anything she says at face value.*

face² /feɪs/ v **1** to have or turn the face or front towards sb/sth; to be opposite sb/sth: [Vn] *Turn round and face me.* ○ *They sat facing each other.* ○ *The garden faces south.* **2** to be willing to see sb or deal with sth: [Vn] *He couldn't face his mother after he'd crashed the car.* ○ *I can't face work today — I feel too ill.* **3** to accept that sth is real or true, even if it is unpleasant: [Vn] *You must face (the) facts — there's nothing you can do.* ○ *She refuses to face the truth.* **4** to need attention from sb: [Vn] *Several problems face the government.* ○ *The company is facing heavy losses.* **5** to force sb or be forced to deal with a difficult or unpleasant situation: [Vnpr] *We are faced with a tricky decision.* ○ *The directors face charges of fraud.* **6** ~ sth (with sth) to cover sth with a layer of different material: [Vnpr] *face a wall with plaster* ○ *face the neckline of a blouse.* **IDM** **face the 'music** (*infml*) to accept the criticisms, unpleasant consequences, etc that follow a decision or action of one's own: *You've been caught cheating — now you must face the music.* **let's 'face it** (*infml*) we must accept it as true: *Let's face it, we won't win whatever we do.* **PHRV** **face 'up to sth** to accept and deal with sth unpleasant or difficult: *He must face up to the fact that he is no longer young.* ○ *You've got to face up to your responsibilities.*

► **-faced** (forming compound *adjs*) with the specified type of face: *red-faced* ○ *baby-faced.*

facet /'fæsɪt/ n **1** a particular part or aspect of sth: *Photographers have recorded every facet of our society.* ○ *Now let's look at another facet of the problem.* **2** any of the many sides of a cut stone or jewel. ⇨ picture.

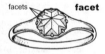

facets   **facet**

facetious /fə'si:ʃəs/ adj (*usu derog*) trying to be amusing but in a way or at a time that is not considered appropriate: *a facetious young man* ○ *She kept making facetious remarks.* ► **facetiously** adv.

facia = FASCIA.

facial /'feɪʃl/ adj of or for the face: *a facial expression* ○ *a facial massage.*
► **facial** n a beauty treatment for the face: *I've made an appointment for a facial next week.*
facially /'feɪʃəli/ adv: *She may resemble her father facially, but in other respects she's not at all like him.*

facile /'fæsaɪl; US 'fæsl/ adj (*usu derog*) (**a**) (of speech or writing) produced without effort or careful thought; SUPERFICIAL(3a): *a facile remark.* (**b**) [attrib] easily obtained or achieved, but of little value: *a facile success/victory.*

facilitate /fə'sɪlɪteɪt/ v (*fml*) to make sth, esp an action or a process, easy or easier: [Vn] *It would facilitate matters if you were more cooperative.*
► **facilitation** /fə,sɪlɪ'teɪʃn/ n [U].
facilitator n a person or thing that makes sth happen more easily: *The teacher acts as a facilitator of learning.*

facility /fə'sɪləti/ n **1** [U, sing] the ability to learn or do things easily; ease: *have (a) great facility for (learning) languages* ○ *He plays the piano with surprising facility.* Compare FACULTY 2. **2** [C usu *pl*] a piece of equipment, a building, a service, etc that is provided for a particular purpose: *'sports facilities* ○ *'washing/'postal/'shopping/'banking facilities* ○ *facilities for study* (eg libraries). **3** [C] an extra feature of a machine, service, etc: *a word processor with a facility for checking spelling* ○ *a bank account with an overdraft/credit facility.*

facing /'feɪsɪŋ/ n **1** [C] an outer layer or covering of sth: *the stone facing of a building.* **2(a)** [C] a layer of material sewn on the inside of esp the neck and armholes (ARMHOLE) of a garment to strengthen it: *cut the facings out of thinner material.* (**b**) **facings** [pl] parts of a garment, eg the collar or pockets, made in a different colour or material: *a brown jacket with green facings.*

facsimile /fæk'sɪməli/ n **1** [C] an exact copy of a piece of writing, a picture, etc: *a facsimile edition* ○ *reproduced in facsimile.* **2** [U,C] = FAX n: *send a letter by facsimile.*

fact /fækt/ n **1** [C] a thing that is known or can be proved to have happened, to be true or to exist: *No one can deny the fact that fire burns.* ○ *Poverty and crime are facts.* ○ *I know for a fact* (ie I know that it is really true) *that he's involved in some illegal activities.* ○ *I won't come here again, and that's a fact!* ○ *The judge instructed both lawyers to stick to the facts of the case.* **2** [C] a situation or set of circumstances that exists: *The fact that I couldn't speak the language made things very difficult for me.* ○ *In spite of the fact that he had never played the game before, he played well.* ○ *In view of the fact that it's getting late, we'll end the meeting now.* **3** [C] a piece of information on which a belief or an argument is based: *If you're going to make accusations, you'd better get your facts right* (ie make sure they are correct). **4** [U] what is true; reality: *The story is founded on fact.* ○ *It's important to distinguish fact from fiction.* **IDM** **accessory before/after the fact** ⇨ ACCESSORY. **as a matter of fact** ⇨ MATTER¹. **the fact (of the matter) is (that)** ... the truth is that ...: *A new car would be wonderful but the fact of the matter is (that) we can't afford one.* ○ *I agree that he tried hard. Nevertheless, the fact remains that he has not finished the job on time.* **,facts and 'figures** accurate and detailed information: *Before we make a decision, we need more facts and figures.* **a ,fact of 'life** a true thing that cannot be ignored, even if it is unpleasant: *We must all die some time — that's just a fact of life.* **the ,facts of 'life** (*euph*) the details of sexual behaviour and reproduction, esp as told to children. **the facts speak for them'selves** what is known to be true about sth is enough to allow conclusions to be reached, without further explanation. **in (actual) fact** (used for emphasizing that sth is true) really; actually: *I thought the work would be difficult. In fact, it's quite easy.* ○ *In actual fact, he's much nicer than he seems.* **in point of fact** ⇨ POINT¹.

■ **'fact-finding** adj [attrib] done or established in order to discover the truth about a situation: *go on a fact-finding mission/tour.*

'fact-sheet n a piece of paper giving information about a subject, esp one discussed on a television or radio programme: *For further details, write in for our free fact-sheet.*

faction /'fækʃn/ n **1(a)** [C] a small group within a larger one that opposes some of its beliefs or activities: *rival factions within the government.* (**b**) [U] the opposition or activities of such a group: *a party divided by faction and intrigue.* **2** [U] films, programmes, plays, books, etc that combine real events with fiction.
► **factional** adj relating to or caused by faction(1b): *factional disputes.*

factitious /fæk'tɪʃəs/ adj (*fml*) deliberately created or developed; not genuine; artificial: *an atmosphere of factitious and self-conscious frivolity.*

factor /'fæktə(r)/ n **1** [C] any of the things that cause or influence sth: *environmental/economic factors* ○ *Soil and climate are two key factors that affect vegetation growth.* ○ *The result will depend on a number of different factors.* **2** [C] (*mathematics*) any number, except 1, by which a larger number can be divided: *2, 3, 4 and 6 are factors of 12.* **3** [sing] (**a**) the amount by which sth increases or decreases: *a growth factor of 3%.* (**b**) a grade in a system of measurement: *a suntan lotion with a high protection factor* ○ *The wind-chill factor will make it seem colder today.*

factorial /fæk'tɔːriəl/ *n* (*mathematics*) the product of a whole number and all those whole numbers below it: *factorial 5 (represented as 5!)* (ie the product of 5 × 4 × 3 × 2 × 1).

factory /'fæktri, -təri/ *n* a building or group of buildings where goods are manufactured or assembled: *a car factory* ○ '*factory workers.*
■ '**factory farm** *n* a farm where animals are kept and bred in a way designed to produce the maximum yield of meat, milk, eggs, young, etc. '**factory farming** *n* [U]. See also BATTERY FARM.

───────────────

NOTE Factory, works, plant and mill are all industrial buildings, but they involve different processes or produce different kinds of things. A **factory** is a building where products are made or put together: *a shoe/chocolate factory.* A **works** is a large group of buildings and machinery which produces materials needed in industry: *an engineering works* ○ *the old ironworks/gasworks.* **Plant** describes a large building or group of buildings in which complex industrial processes are carried out: *the new hi-tech desalination plant* ○ *a nuclear-power plant.* It can also refer to a large factory which produces vehicles or other large machines: *Rolls Royce's Glasgow plant.* A **mill** processes certain raw materials: *a paper/cotton/steel mill.*

───────────────

factotum /fæk'təʊtəm/ *n* (*fml or joc*) a person employed to do all types of work: *a general factotum.*

factual /'fæktʃʊəl/ *adj* based on or containing facts: *give a factual account of events.* ▶ **factually** /-tʃʊəli/ *adv: factually correct.*

faculty /'fæklti/ *n* **1** [C] any of the powers of the body or mind: *the faculty of sight* ○ *one's mental faculties* (ie the power of reason) ○ *be in full possession of one's faculties* (ie be able to see, hear, speak, understand, etc). **2** [sing] ~ **of/for doing sth** a particular ability for doing sth: *have a great faculty for learning languages.* Compare FACILITY 1. **3**(**a**) [C] a department or group of related departments in a university, etc: *the Faculty of Law* ○ *the Engineering Faculty.* (**b**) [CGp] all the teachers in one of these: *a faculty meeting.* (**c**) [CGp] (*US*) the whole teaching staff of a university, etc.

fad /fæd/ *n* a fashion, an interest, a preference, an enthusiasm, etc that is not likely to last: *Will Tom go on collecting stamps or is it only a passing fad?*
▶ **faddy** *adj* (*infml derog*) having a lot of unusual likes and dislikes, esp concerning food: *a faddy eater.*

fade /feɪd/ *v* **1** to lose or make sth lose colour, strength or freshness: [V] *Jeans fade when you wash them.* ○ *the fading light of evening* ○ *flowers fading at the end of summer* [Vn] *The sun has faded these curtains.* **2** ~ (**away**) to disappear gradually from sight, hearing, memory, etc: [Vp] *The sound of the cheering faded away in the distance.* ○ *The crowd began to fade away.* [Vpr] *All memory of her childhood had faded from her mind.* ○ *As evening came, the coastline faded into darkness.* [V] *Hopes of reaching an agreement are fading (fast).* **PHRV** **fade a'way** (of people) to become weaker, thinner, etc; to die: *In the last weeks of her life she simply faded away.* ,**fade (sth)** '**in/'out** (*cinema or broadcasting*) to become or make sth gradually more/less clear or loud: *Fade out the music at the end of the scene.*
■ '**fade-in** *n* (*cinema or broadcasting*) the process or an instance of making a picture or sound gradually clearer or louder.

'**fade-out** *n* [U, C] (*cinema or broadcasting*) the process or an instance of making a picture or sound gradually less clear or loud.

faeces (*US* **feces**) /'fiːsiːz/ *n* [pl] (*fml*) waste matter that is passed from the body through the bowels. ▶ **faecal** (*US* **fecal**) /'fiːkl/ *adj* (*fml*).

fag /fæg/ *n* **1** [C] (*Brit infml*) a cigarette. **2** [sing] (*infml esp Brit*) a boring or tiring task: *I've got to tidy my room. What a fag!* **3** [C] (*esp US*) = FAGGOT 3.
■ '**fag-'end** *n* (*Brit infml*) **1** the end of a cigarette after it has been smoked: *The floor was littered with fag-ends.* **2** the last or inferior part of sth: *He only heard the fag-end of their conversation.* ○ *the fag-end of the day.*

fagged /fægd/ (also ,**fagged** '**out**) *adj* (*Brit infml*) very tired.

faggot (*US* **fagot**) /'fægət/ *n* **1** a ball of chopped meat and bread that is baked or fried: *faggots and chips.* **2** a bunch of sticks tied together for burning. **3** (also *esp US* **fag**) (*dated infml offensive*) a male HOMOSEXUAL.

fah (also **fa**) /fɑː/ *n* (*music*) the fourth note of any major scale¹(6).

Fahrenheit /'færənhaɪt/ *adj* (*abbr* **F**) of or using a temperature scale on which water freezes at 32° and boils at 212°: *Temperatures tomorrow will rise to around seventy degrees Fahrenheit.* ⇨ note at TEMPERATURE.

fail /feɪl/ *v* **1**(**a**) ~ (**in sth / to do sth**) not to succeed in sth: [Vpr] *I seem to fail in everything I do.* [V.to inf] *The letter failed to arrive in time.* [Vn] *He failed his driving test.* (**b**) to decide that sb/sth has not passed an examination, a test, etc: [Vn] *The examiners failed over half the candidates.* **2** to forget or fail to do sth: [V.to inf] *He never fails to write* (ie always writes) *to his mother every week.* ○ *She failed to keep* (ie did not keep) *her appointment.* **3** (of things) not to continue to develop or to last as long as needed: [V] *The power failed as soon as I switched on the machine.* ○ *The crops have failed again.* **4**(**a**) (of people) to disappoint sb; to be absent or lacking when needed: [Vn] *He felt he had failed his family by being unemployed.* ○ *She promised that she wouldn't fail him.* (**b**) to be inadequate: [Vn] *My courage failed me at the last minute.* ○ *Words fail me* (ie I cannot express how I feel). **5**(**a**) (of health, sight, etc) to become weak: *Her eyesight is failing.* ○ *His last months in office were marked by failing health.* (**b**) to stop working properly: [V] *The brakes failed on the hill, but I managed to stop the car.* **6** (of a business, etc) to be unable to continue: [V] *Several banks failed during the recession.*
▶ **fail** *n* a failure in an examination: *I got three passes and one fail.* **IDM** **without** '**fail** definitely; always: *I'll be there at two o'clock without fail.* ○ *He is late for every meeting without fail.*
■ '**fail-safe** *adj* [attrib] (of equipment, machinery, etc) designed so that it does not become dangerous if it goes wrong: *a fail-safe device/mechanism/system.*

failing¹ /'feɪlɪŋ/ *n* a weakness or fault, esp of character: *acknowledge failings in the judicial system* ○ *A common failing amongst politicians is to cling to power for far too long.*

failing² /'feɪlɪŋ/ *prep* if sth does not happen or is not possible; without sth: *Ask a friend to recommend a doctor or, failing that* (ie if this is not possible), *ask for a list in your local library.*

failure /'feɪljə(r)/ *n* **1**(**a**) [U] lack of success in doing or achieving sth: *Failure in this examination should not stop you trying again.* ○ *The enterprise was doomed to failure.* ○ *All my efforts ended in failure.* (**b**) [C] a person, an attempt or a thing that fails: *My attempt to make friends with her mother was a disastrous/dismal/total failure.* ○ *He was a failure as a teacher.* ○ *Success came after many failures.* **2** [U, C] the state or an instance of being inadequate or

───────────────
[V. speech] = verb + direct speech   [V. *that*] = verb + *that* clause   [V. *wh*] = verb + *who, how*, etc clause

of not functioning as is expected or required: *a case of* ¹*heart failure* ○ *me*¹*chanical failure* ○ *a series of* ¹*crop failures* ○ *A* ¹*power failure plunged everything into darkness.* **3** [C, U] ~ **to do sth** (an instance of) not doing sth or forgetting to do sth: *repeated failures to appear in court* ○ *the failure of the United Nations to maintain food supplies* ○ *failure to comply with the regulations.*

faint¹ /feɪnt/ *adj* (**-er**, **-est**) **1** that cannot be clearly perceived by the senses; not intense in colour, sound or smell: *a faint glow/glimmer* ○ *a faint smell of perfume* ○ *We saw the faint outline of the mountain through the mist.* ○ *The sounds of music grew fainter and fainter.* **2(a)** (of physical abilities) lacking strength: *in a faint voice* ○ *His breathing became faint.* (**b**) [pred] (of people) likely to lose consciousness; GIDDY(1a): *She suddenly felt faint.* (**c**) [pred] (of people) weak and tired; lacking physical strength: *The explorers were faint from hunger and cold.* **3** (of ideas, etc) possible but unlikely; VAGUE(1a): *There is still a faint hope/chance that she may be cured.* **4** (of actions, etc) unlikely to have much effect; not enthusiastic: *a faint show of resistance.* **IDM** **damn sb/sth with faint praise** ⇨ DAMN³. **not have the** ¹**faintest/**¹**foggiest (idea)** (*infml*) not to know at all: *'Do you know where she is?' 'Sorry, I haven't the faintest.'* ▶ **faintly** *adv*: *She smiled faintly.* ○ *I was faintly alarmed to hear this.* **faintness** *n* [U].

■ ¹**faint-**¹**hearted** *adj* not brave; TIMID. **the faint-hearted** *n* [pl v]: *The 130-mile ride is **not for the faint-hearted**.*

faint² /feɪnt/ *v* to lose consciousness because of heat, shock, loss of blood, etc: [V] *Do not bend over suddenly because this can cause fainting or dizziness.* [Vpr] *He fainted from hunger.*

▶ **faint** *n* [sing] the state of fainting or having fainted: *She fell to the ground in a (dead) faint.*

fair¹ /feə(r)/ *adj* **1(a)** ~ (**to sb**) treating each person, side, etc equally and according to the rules or law: *the fairest solution* ○ *be scrupulously fair* ○ *promise a fairer distribution of wealth* ○ *We have to be fair to both players.* ○ *She deserves a fair trial.* (**b**) ~ (**to/on sb**) reasonable and just or appropriate in the circumstances: *a fair deal/share/wage/price* ○ *The punishment was quite fair.* ○ *Was it fair to her friends to take her children with her?* ○ *It's not fair to give him the prize/not fair that he should be given the prize.* ○ *It seems only fair to add that ...* ○ *She shouldn't keep changing the timetable — it's not fair on the students.* ○ *'How often do you actually see such cases in practice?' 'That's a fair question, and it deserves an answer.'* **2(a)** average; quite good: *There's a fair chance that we might win this time.* ○ *His knowledge of French is only fair.* (**b**) [attrib] (*infml*) quite large, long, etc: *A fair number of people came along.* ○ *a fair-sized town* ○ *We've still got a fair bit* (ie quite a lot) *to do.* **3** (of the skin or the hair) pale; light in colour: *a fair complexion* ○ *All her children are fair.* **4(a)** (of the weather) good; dry and fine: *a fair and breezy day* ○ *The weather looks set fair for the weekend.* (**b**) (of winds) favourable: *They set sail with the first fair wind.* **5** (*arch or rhet*) beautiful: *a fair maiden* ○ *This fair city.* **IDM** **by fair means or** ¹**foul** somehow, whether by honest or dishonest methods: *She's determined to win, by fair means or foul.* **a fair crack of the** ¹**whip** (*infml*) a reasonable chance to share in sth, to be successful, etc: *I felt we weren't getting a fair crack of the whip.* **a fair/square deal** ⇨ DEAL². **fair** ¹**dos/**¹**do's** (*Brit infml*) (used esp as an *interj*) fair treatment; fair shares: *Come on, fair dos — you've had a long ride, now it's my turn.* (**give sb / get) a fair** ¹**hearing** (to give sb/to get) the opportunity to be listened to without prejudice, usu in a lawcourt. **fair's fair** (*infml*) (used as a protest or to remind sb that sb else should be dealt with fairly): *'Come on, Sarah. Give me some more — fair's fair!'* **have, etc (more than) one's fair share of sth** to have, etc (more than) a usual or an expected amount of sth: *He's had (more than) his fair share of problems.* ▶ **fairness** *n* [U]: *the need for fairness and balance in the new law* ○ *In (all) fairness, it must be said that he's done a splendid job.*

■ ¹**fair** ¹**game** *n* [U] a person or thing that it is considered reasonable to chase, mock, criticize, etc: *The younger teachers were fair game for playing tricks on.*

¹**fair-**¹**haired** *adj* with light or BLOND hair.

¹**fair-**¹**minded** *adj* fair in judgement.

¹**fair** ¹**play** *n* [U] respect for the rules, or the equal treatment of both or all sides, eg in an argument or a sports contest: *ensure fair play in take-over bids* ○ *As the referee, I was determined to **see fair play**.*

the ¹**fair** ¹**sex** (also **the fairer sex**) *n* [Gp] (*dated or joc*) women.

¹**fair-weather** ¹**friend** *n* a person who stops being a friend when one is in trouble.

fair² /feə(r)/ *adv* according to the rules, or to what is just or reasonable: *Come on, you two, fight fair!* ○ *They'll respect you as long as you play fair (with them).* **IDM** **bid fair to do sth** ⇨ BID¹. **fair and** ¹**square 1** exactly on target: *I hit it fair and square.* **2** with no uncertainty or possibility of error, etc: *The blame rests fair and square on my shoulders.* **fair e**¹**nough** (*infml*) (used esp as an *interj*), sometimes to show unwilling agreement) all right; I accept what you say. **one can't say fairer** ⇨ SAY. **set fair (to do sth / for sth)** likely to do or achieve sth: *She seems set fair to win the championship.*

fair³ /feə(r)/ *n* **1** a collection of outdoor entertainments, stalls, etc, usu on a large piece of open ground: *take the children to the fair* ○ *all the fun of the fair.* **2** a market and show, esp of farm animals and farm products, held regularly in a particular place, often with entertainments: *the Appleby Horse Fair* ○ *a county fair.* **3** an exhibition of commercial and industrial goods: *a world trade fair* ○ *a craft fair.* ⇨ note at EXHIBITION.

fairground /¹feəɡraʊnd/ *n* an outdoor area where a FAIR³(1) is held: *fairground attractions.*

fairly /¹feəli/ *adv* **1** in a fair manner; honestly: *You're not treating us fairly.* ○ *His attitude could fairly be described as hostile.* **2** (before adjs and advs) to a certain extent; quite: *I'm fairly certain/confident.* ○ *a fairly typical reaction* ○ *a fairly easy book* ○ *We must leave fairly soon* (ie before very long). **3** (*Brit rhet*) completely; actually: *I fairly jumped for joy.* ○ *The time fairly raced by.* **IDM** **fairly and squarely** = FAIR AND SQUARE.

NOTE The adverbs **fairly**, **quite**, **rather** and **pretty** can all mean 'not very' and are used to change the strength of adjectives and adverbs. The effect they have often depends on the intonation of the speaker's voice. **Rather** is the most formal and is used in British English: *It will feel rather cold today with temperatures around 2°C.* **Pretty** is the strongest and is used mostly in speaking: *That was a pretty good game, wasn't it?* **Fairly** is the weakest and is usually used with positive qualities: *The room is fairly tidy/spacious.* ○ *She's fairly friendly/happy.*

Rather and **pretty** can sound enthusiastic when used with positive qualities: *The food at the party was rather/pretty good.* They sound unenthusiastic when used with negative or variable qualities: *The room is rather untidy/small.* ○ *She's rather unfriendly/unhappy.*

Only **rather** can be used with comparative expressions and with **too**: *The holiday house was rather bigger than we expected.* ○ *These shoes are rather too small.* **Rather** and **quite** can come before *a/an* when this is followed by an adjective + noun: *It was quite/*

rather a hot day. ○ *It was a fairly/rather/pretty hot day.*

fairway /ˈfeəweɪ/ *n* the area on a golf-course (GOLF) between the TEE(a) and the GREEN²(4) where the grass is kept short. ⇨ picture at GOLF. Compare ROUGH³ 1.

fairy /ˈfeəri/ *n* **1** a small imaginary being, esp a female one, with magical powers: *a wicked fairy* ○ *fairy wings/voices.* **2** (*sl derog*) a male HOMOSEXUAL. ■ ˈfairy cake *n* (*Brit*) a small soft light cake, usu with ICING, for one person. ˌfairy ˈgodmother *n* a person who provides unexpected help. ˈfairy lights *n* [pl] small coloured electric lights used as decoration, esp on a Christmas tree (CHRISTMAS). ˈfairy story *n* **1** (also ˈfairy tale) a story about fairies, magic, etc, usu for children: *He's like the prince in a fairy story.* ○ *fairy-tale castles* ○ *This is the stuff of which fairy tales are made.* **2** a story that is not true; a lie: *Now tell me the truth: I don't want any more of your fairy stories.*

fairyland /ˈfeərilænd/ *n* **1** [U] the home of fairies. **2** [sing] a beautiful or magical place: *The toy-shop is a fairyland for young children.*

fait accompli /ˌfeɪt əˈkɒmpliː; *US* əkɒmˈpliː/ *n* (usu sing) (*pl* **faits accomplis** /ˌfeɪz əˈkɒmpliː; *US* əkɒmˈpliː/) (*French*) a thing already done, that cannot be changed and is therefore not worth arguing about: *The sale of the factory was presented to the workers as a fait accompli.*

faith /feɪθ/ *n* **1** [U] ~ (in sb/sth) trust; complete confidence: *put one's faith in God* ○ *I haven't/don't put much faith in this medicine.* ○ *I've lost faith in the government's promises.* **2** [U, sing] strong religious belief: *blind/unquestioning faith* ○ *lose one's faith* ○ *Faith is stronger than reason.* **3** [C] a religion: *spread the faith* ○ *the Jewish and Muslim faiths.* **IDM** break/keep faith with sb to break/keep one's promise to sb; to stop being/continue to be loyal to sb. in good ˈfaith with honest intentions: *She signed the letter in good faith, not realizing its implications.* ○ *He bought the painting in good faith (eg not realizing that it had been stolen).* ■ ˈfaith-healing *n* [U] a method of treating sick people that depends on faith and prayer rather than on medicines or other treatment.

faithful /ˈfeɪθfl/ *adj* **1** ~ (to sb/sth) (a) loyal to sb/sth over a long period of time: *a faithful friend/servant/dog* ○ *He remained faithful to his beliefs.* (b) (of a husband, wife or partner) never having a sexual relationship with anyone else: *She was always faithful to her husband.* **2** [attrib] able to be trusted: *a faithful worker* ○ *a faithful correspondent* (ie one who writes letters regularly). **3** true to the facts; accurate: *a faithful copy/description/account.* ▶ the faithful *n* [pl *v*] true believers, esp in a religion or political ideal: *The President will keep the support of the party faithful.* faithfully /-fəli/ *adv* (a) in a faithful manner: *The old nurse had served the family faithfully for thirty years.* (b) carefully; accurately: *I followed the instructions faithfully.* ⇨ note at YOUR. **IDM** yours faithfully ⇨ YOURS. faithfulness *n* [U]: *faithfulness to tradition* ○ *She was touched by his faithfulness.*

faithless /ˈfeɪθləs/ *adj* that cannot be trusted; not loyal: *a faithless friend/wife/ally.*

fake /feɪk/ *n* (a) an object, eg a work of art, that seems genuine but is not: *a clever/cheap fake* ○ *spot/detect a fake* ○ *It's not a real diamond necklace, it's just a fake!* See also COUNTERFEIT, FORGERY. (b) a person who tries to deceive others by pretending to be what he or she is not. ▶ **fake** *adj* not genuine, though intended to appear so: *fake furs/jewellery* ○ *a fake tan.* Compare ARTIFICIAL.

fake *v* **1** to make sth false appear to be genuine: [Vn] *He faked his father's signature.* ○ *She faked her own death.* ○ *Sally's whole story had been faked (ie None of it was true).* **2** to pretend to experience a feeling or condition: [Vn] *fake surprise/grief/illness.* faker *n*.

fakir /ˈfeɪkɪə(r); *US* fəˈk-/ *n* **1** a Hindu religious beggar regarded as a holy man. **2** a member of a Muslim holy sect who lives by begging.

falcon /ˈfɔːlkən; *US* ˈfælkən/ *n* a bird of prey (BIRD) that has long pointed wings. ▶ **falconer** *n* a person who trains falcons to hunt and kill other birds or animals for sport . **falconry** /-ri/ *n* [U] the art of breeding and training falcons.

fall¹ /fɔːl/ *v* (*pt* **fell** /fel/; *pp* **fallen** /ˈfɔːlən/) **1(a)** to become no longer balanced or supported and drop suddenly: [V, Vn] *He slipped and fell (ten feet).* [Vpr] *The book fell off the table onto the floor.* ○ *He fell into the river.* [Vp] *She fell over and banged her head.* ○ *The baby was trying to walk but kept falling down.* ○ *I need a new bicycle lamp — my old one fell off and broke.* ○ *The roof of the tunnel fell in, burying six miners.* (b) to drop suddenly from an upright position and lie flat or broken; to collapse: [V] *Many trees fell in the storm.* ○ (*fig*) *Six wickets fell (ie Six batsmen in cricket were dismissed) before lunch.* [Vpr] *Part of the hotel fell into the sea.* [Vp] *The old abbey is falling down.* **2** to come down towards the ground; to descend: [V] *The rain was falling steadily.* ○ *The leaves fall in autumn.* **3** (of hair or material) to hang down: [Vpr] *Her hair fell over her shoulders in a mass of curls.* **4** ~ (away/off) to slope downwards: [V, Vp] *Beyond the hill, the land falls (away) sharply towards the river.* **5** to decrease in amount, number or intensity: [Vpr] *Their profits have fallen by 30 per cent.* [Vn] *Share prices fell 30p.* [V] *Prices continued to fall on the stock market today.* ○ *falling birth rates* ○ *The temperature fell sharply in the night.* **6(a)** to lose one's position, office or power; to be defeated: [V] *The coup failed but the government fell shortly afterwards.* (b) ~ (to sb) (of a fort, city, etc) to be captured: [V, Vpr] *Troy finally fell (to the Greeks).* [Vpr] *The constituency has now fallen to the Democrats.* **7** to die in battle; to be shot: [V] *a memorial to those who fell (in battle).* **8** ~ (into sth) to pass into a specified state; to begin to be sth: [V-adj] *fall asleep* ○ *He fell silent.* ○ *Has she fallen ill again?* ○ *The book fell open (ie opened by chance) at a page of illustrations.* [V-n] *She fell an easy prey to his charm.* [Vpr] *fall under the influence of sb* ○ *He fell into a doze.* ○ *We fell easily into conversation.* ○ *The house fell into decay.* **9** ~ (on sb/sth) to come quickly and suddenly; to descend: [V] *A sudden silence fell.* ○ *Darkness falls quickly in the tropics.* [Vpr] *An expectant hush fell on the guests.* **10** to happen or occur: [Vadv] *Easter falls early this year.* [Vpr] *Christmas Day falls on a Monday.* **11** to belong to a particular class, group or area of responsibility: [Vpr] *Out of over 400 staff there are just 7 that fall into this category.* ○ *This case falls outside my jurisdiction.* ○ *This falls under the heading of scientific research.* **12** to move in the direction or occur in the position specified: [Vpr] *Which syllable does the stress of this word fall on?* ○ *My eye fell on (ie I suddenly saw) a curious object.* ○ *A shadow fell across her face.* **13** to be spoken: [V] *I guessed what was happening from a few words she let fall (ie from what she said).* ○ (*rhet*) *Not a word fell from his lips.* **IDM** Idioms containing **fall** are at the entries for the nouns or adjectives in the idioms, eg **fall in love** ⇨ LOVE¹. **PHRV** ˌfall aˈbout (*infml*) to laugh so much that one loses control of oneself: *We all fell about (laughing/*

with laughter) when he did his imitation of our English teacher.

,fall ˈapart **1** to break into pieces: *My car is falling apart.* **2** to stop existing or functioning effectively: *Their marriage finally fell apart.* ○ *The deal fell apart when we failed to agree on a price.*

,fall ˈaway **1** to leave; to DESERT¹: *His supporters fell away as his popularity declined.* **2** to decrease gradually; to disappear: *The market for their products fell away to almost nothing.* ○ *All our doubts fell away.*

,fall ˈback **1** to move or turn back; to RETREAT(1): *The enemy fell back as our troops advanced.* **2** to decrease in value or amount: *Share prices fell back after brisk early trading.* ,fall ˈback on sb/sth to go to sb for support or have sth to use when in difficulty: *We can always fall back on candles if the electricity fails.* ○ *She's completely homeless — at least I have my parents to fall back on.*

,fall ˈbehind (sb/sth) to fail to keep level with sb/sth: *She soon fell behind the leaders.* ○ *France has fallen behind (Germany) in coal production.* ,fall ˈbehind with sth to fail to pay for sth or to do sth when it is due: *Don't fall behind with the rent, or you'll be evicted.* ○ *I've fallen behind with my work again.*

,fall ˈdown to be shown to be false or inadequate: *Where the proposal falls down is in not taking enough account of the feelings of local people.*

ˈfall for sb (*infml*) to be strongly attracted to sb; to fall in love with sb: *They fell for each other instantly.* ˈfall for sth (*infml*) to allow oneself to be persuaded by sth and to make an unwise decision or judgement: *The salesman said the car was in good condition, and I was foolish enough to fall for it.*

,fall (sb) ˈin to form or make sb form a military formation: *The sergeant ordered his men to fall in.* ,fall ˈin with sb/sth **1** to meet sb by chance; to become involved with sb/sth: *He fell in with bad company.* **2** (*Brit*) to agree to sth: *She fell in with my idea at once.*

ˈfall into sth **1** to be caught by sb's trap: *They fell right into our trap.* **2** to be able to be divided into sth: *My talk falls naturally into three parts.*

,fall ˈoff to decrease in quantity or quality: *Attendance at my lectures has fallen off considerably.* ○ *It used to be my favourite restaurant but the standard of cooking has fallen off recently.*

,fall on/upon sb/sth **1** to attack sb/sth fiercely: *They fell on the retreating army and routed them.* ○ *The children fell on the food and ate it greedily.* **2** to be the responsibility of sb: *The full cost of the wedding fell on me.*

,fall ˈout to become loose and drop: *His hair is falling out.* ○ *My tooth fell out.* ,fall (sb) ˈout to leave or make sb leave a military formation. ,fall ˈout (with sb) to quarrel (with sb): *They fell out with each other just before the wedding.* ˈfall out of sth to lose a habit or state gradually: *fall out of love/fashion.*

,fall ˈover sb/sth to hit one's foot against sth when walking and fall, or almost fall: *I rushed for the door and fell over the dog in the hallway.* ,fall ˈover oneself to do sth (*infml*) to be specially eager to do or achieve sth: *People were falling over themselves to be introduced to the star of the film.*

,fall ˈthrough to fail to be completed: *Our plans fell through because of a sudden death in the family.*

ˈfall to (doing sth) to begin to do sth, esp sth unpleasant or unwise: *She fell to brooding about what had happened to her.* ˈfall to sb (to do sth) (*fml*) to become the duty or responsibility of sb: *It fell to me to inform her of her son's death.*

▶ **the fallen** *n* [pl] (*dated or fml*) people, esp soldiers, killed in war.

■ ˈfall-back *adj* [attrib] (esp of a plan or course of action) ready for use in an emergency: *establish a fall-back position.*

,falling ˈstar *n* = SHOOTING STAR.

ˈfall-off *n* [usu *sing*] a reduction in quantity or quality: *a recent fall-off in sales.*

fall² /fɔːl/ *n* **1** [C] an act or instance of falling: *I had a fall (from a horse) and broke my arm.* ○ *That was a nasty fall.* **2** ~ (of sth) (**a**) [C] an amount of sth that falls or has fallen: *a heavy fall of snow/rain* ○ *a fall of rock(s).* (**b**) [sing] the way in which sth falls or happens: *the fall of the cards/dice.* **3** [C] ~ (in sth) a reduction in value, quantity, intensity, etc: *a steep fall in prices/profits* ○ *a fall in the numbers attending.* **4** [sing] ~ (of sth) a defeat, esp a political one; a collapse: *the fall of the Roman Empire/of Singapore* ○ *events leading to the fall of the last Labour government.* **5** [C] (*US*) = AUTUMN: *in the fall of 1970* ○ *last fall.* **6** the Fall [sing] (*Bible*) the occasion when Adam and Eve did not obey God and had to leave the Garden of Eden. **7** falls [pl] (esp in names) a large amount of water falling down from a height; a WATERFALL: *The falls upstream are full of salmon.* ○ *Niagara Falls.* **IDM** pride comes/goes before a fall ⇨ PRIDE. ride for a fall ⇨ RIDE².

■ ˈfall-off *n* [sing] ~ (in sth) a reduction in numbers, quality, etc: *There has been a slight fall-off in attendance since last week.*

fallacy /ˈfæləsi/ *n* **1** [C] a false or mistaken belief: *It is a common fallacy that a heavy tax on cars will solve all London's transport problems.* **2** [C,U] false reasoning or a false argument: *a statement based on fallacy.*

▶ **fallacious** /fəˈleɪʃəs/ *adj* (*fml*) misleading; based on error: *fallacious arguments.*

fallen *pp* of FALL¹.

fall guy /ˈfɔːl gaɪ/ *n* (esp *US*) (**a**) a person who is blamed or punished for the wrongdoing of sb else; a SCAPEGOAT. (**b**) a person who is easily tricked or made to look foolish.

fallible /ˈfæləbl/ *adj* capable of making mistakes: *The President has proved he is fallible after all.* ▶ **fallibility** /ˌfæləˈbɪləti/ *n* [U]: *human fallibility.*

Fallopian tubes /fəˌləʊpɪən ˈtjuːbz; *US* ˈtuːbz/ *n* [pl] (*anatomy*) the two tubes along which a woman's egg cells move to the WOMB. ⇨ picture at REPRODUCTION.

fallout /ˈfɔːlaʊt/ *n* [U] **1** RADIOACTIVE waste carried in the air after a nuclear explosion. **2** bad results of a situation: *the current crisis and its political fallout.*

fallow /ˈfæləʊ/ *adj* **1** (of farm land) that has been dug but then left without crops being planted on it, in order to allow essential chemical elements, etc to increase in it: *allow land to lie fallow.* **2** (of a period of time) not creative or successful.

false /fɔːls/ *adj* **1** wrong; not correct: *sing a false note* ○ *A whale is a fish. True or false?* ○ *Predictions of an early improvement in the housing market proved false.* **2**(**a**) not genuine; artificial: *false hair/teeth/eyelashes.* (**b**) deliberately made in order to deceive: *false scales/dice* ○ *a false passport* ○ *a suitcase with a false bottom.* (**c**) pretended: *false modesty* ○ *false tears.* (**d**) [usu attrib] misleading; not what it appears to be: *give a false impression of great wealth* ○ *a false sense of security* (ie feeling safe when one is really in danger) ○ *Buying a cheap computer is a false economy* (ie will not actually save you money). **3** deliberately meant to deceive: *false evidence* ○ *give a false name* ○ *present false claims to an insurance company.* **4** ~ (to sb) not faithful; not loyal: *a false friend/lover.* **IDM** under false preˈtences pretending to be sb else or to have certain qualifications, etc in order to deceive people: *obtaining money under false pretences.*

▶ **false** *adv* **IDM** play sb ˈfalse to deceive or cheat sb: *Is my memory playing me false or did she win Wimbledon once in the 60s?*

F

falsely adv: be falsely accused of sth.
■ ¡false a'larm n a warning or fear about sth which does not happen: Rumours of a bread shortage turned out to be a false alarm.
¡false 'move n an unwise or forbidden action that may have unpleasant consequences: One false move could jeopardize the whole operation.
¡false 'start n (a) (sport) a start made before the signal for a race has been given. (b) an attempt to begin sth which does not succeed: After several false starts, she became a successful journalist.

falsehood /'fɔːlshʊd/ n (fml) (a) [C] a statement that is not true; a lie. (b) [U] the state of being false: test the truth or falsehood of her claims.

falsetto /fɔːl'setəʊ/ n (pl -os) [C,U] an unusually high voice, esp when singing: sing falsetto ∘ in a falsetto wail.

falsies /'fɔːlsɪz/ n [pl] (infml) pads of material to make a woman's breasts seem larger.

falsify /'fɔːlsɪfaɪ/ v (pt, pp -fied) **1** to alter a document, etc falsely: [Vn] falsify the records/accounts. **2** to present sth falsely: [Vn] falsify an issue/the facts. ▶ **falsification** /ˌfɔːlsɪfɪ'keɪʃn/ n [U,C]: an inquiry into falsification of evidence by the police.

falsity /'fɔːlsəti/ n [U] (a) the condition of not being true. (b) the action of lying.

falter /'fɔːltə(r)/ v **1** to start to lose strength or stop making progress: [V] The success of these reforms faltered in the late 1980s. [Vpr] For a moment he faltered in his purpose. **2** to move, walk or act in a way that shows lack of confidence: [V] Jane walked boldly up to the platform without faltering. **3(a)** to speak in a way that is not confident: [V] Halfway down the first page he faltered and dried up. [also V.speech]. **(b)** [V] (of the voice) to become unsteady; to WAVER: [V]. ▶ **faltering** /'fɔːltərɪŋ/ adj: signs of faltering confidence in the government ∘ a baby's first faltering steps ∘ She tried to explain in her faltering English.

fame /feɪm/ n [U] the condition of being known or talked about by many people: achieve instant/ overnight fame and fortune ∘ Her fame quickly grew/ spread. ∘ He first rose/came to fame in the 1940s. ∘ Her main claim to fame is that she once went out with Mick Jagger. See also FAMOUS. ▶ **famed** adj [pred] ~ (for sth): the fairy-tale castles for which Austria is famed ∘ staying near the famed Waikiki Beach.

familial /fə'mɪliəl/ adj [attrib] (fml) occurring in or characteristic of a family: a protective familial environment.

familiar /fə'mɪliə(r)/ adj **1** ~ (to sb) well known; often seen or heard: familiar faces/surroundings/ images/themes ∘ facts that are familiar to every schoolboy ∘ There was something vaguely familiar about him. ∘ Such accounts of environmental pollution are now depressingly familiar. **2** ~ with sth having a good knowledge of sth: facts with which every schoolboy is familiar ∘ By now you will be familiar with the layout of the house. **3** ~ (with sb) friendly and informal: You seem to be on very familiar terms with your bank manager. ∘ (derog) The children are too familiar with their teacher. See also FREE¹ 9.
▶ **familiarly** adv in an informal manner: William, familiarly known as Billy.

familiarity /fəˌmɪli'ærəti/ n [U] **1** ~ with sth a good knowledge of sth: His familiarity with the local languages surprised me. **2** ~ (to/towards sb) (sometimes derog) a friendly informal manner: You should not address your teacher with such familiarity. **IDM** familiarity breeds con'tempt (saying) knowing sb/sth very well may lead to a loss of respect, etc for them/it.

familiarize, -ise /fə'mɪliəraɪz/ v **PHR V** familiarize sb/oneself with sth to get or give sb a thorough knowledge of sth: familiarize oneself with the rules

of the game ∘ familiarize the trainees with the equipment. ▶ **familiarization, -isation** /fəˌmɪliəraɪ'zeɪʃn; US -rə'z-/ n [U].

family /'fæməli/ n **1(a)** [CGp] a group consisting of one or two parents and their children: help for families on low incomes ∘ Almost every family in the country owns a television. ∘ All (the members of) my family enjoy skiing. ∘ The new tax will cost the average British family of four an extra £10 a week. ∘ He's a friend of the family (ie He is known and liked by the parents and their children). ∘ a family tradition ∘ the family car ∘ your family doctor. **(b)** [CGp] a group consisting of one or two parents, their children and close relations: All our family came to our grandfather's eightieth birthday party. ∘ the Royal Family (ie the children and close relations of the king or queen) ∘ a family-owned company ∘ a family-run hotel ∘ have no family ties. See also EXTENDED FAMILY, NUCLEAR FAMILY. **(c)** [attrib] suitable for all members of this group to enjoy together, regardless of age: a family show ∘ family entertainment. **2(a)** [CGp] a person's husband or wife and children: prisoners and their families ∘ the victim's family and friends. **(b)** [CGp,U] a person's children, esp young children: Address the letter to Mr and Mrs Jones and family. ∘ They have a large family. **3(a)** [CGp] all the people descended from a common ancestor: Some families have farmed in this area for hundreds of years. ∘ She comes from a famous family. ∘ the family silver. **(b)** [U] a line of ancestors: a man of good family. **4** [C] a group of related animals, plants, etc: Lions belong to the cat family. ∘ the Germanic family of languages. **IDM** (put sb / be) in the 'family way (infml) (to make sb/be) pregnant. **run in the 'family** to be a feature that occurs repeatedly in different generations of a family: Red hair runs in his family. **start a family** ⇨ START².
■ ¡family 'credit n [U] (in Britain) a regular payment by the government to a family with an income below a certain level.
'family man n (pl men) a man who has a wife and children, and enjoys home life.
'family name n a SURNAME. ⇨ note at NAME¹.
¡family 'planning n [U] the process of planning the number of children, intervals between births, etc in a family by using birth control (BIRTH): go along to the family planning clinic.
¡family 'tree n a diagram that shows the relationship between different members of a family. ⇨ App 4.

famine /'fæmɪn/ n [C,U] a time when there is very little food in a region: a famine in Ethiopia ∘ raise money for famine relief ∘ The long drought was followed by months of severe famine. ⇨ note at HUNGER.

famished /'fæmɪʃt/ adj [usu pred] (infml) very hungry: When's lunch? I'm famished!

famous /'feɪməs/ adj ~ (for sth) known to very many people: an internationally famous actor ∘ He became rich and famous almost overnight. ∘ New York is famous for its skyscrapers. ∘ She is more famous as a writer than as an actress. See also WORLD-FAMOUS.
▶ **famously** adv in a way that is known to many people: When Calvin Coolidge was said to be dead, she famously asked, 'How can they tell?' **IDM** get on/ along 'famously (infml) to have an extremely good relationship, esp at a first meeting: The two children got on famously.

fan¹ /fæn/ n a person who admires or supports sb/ sth very strongly: 'jazz fans ∘ visiting 'football fans ∘ a Pavarotti fan ∘ I'm a big 'fan of yours. ∘ She's his greatest 'fan/his number one 'fan.
■ 'fan club n an organized group of a person's fans: the Madonna fan club.

F

¹fan mail *n* [U] letters from fans to the person they admire.

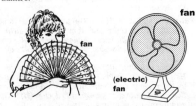

fan

fan

(electric) fan

fan² /fæn/ *n* **1** an object that is held in the hand and waved to create a current of cool air. ⇨ picture. **2** a device with blades that are operated mechanically to create a current of cool air: *She turned the electric fan on.* ⇨ picture at CAR.
■ **¹fan belt** *n* a belt(2) driving the fan that cools the RADIATOR(2) of a car, etc. ⇨ picture at CAR.

fan³ /fæn/ *v* (-nn-) **1** to make a current of air blow onto sb/sth with a fan, one's hand, etc: [Vn] *He sat fanning himself/his face with a newspaper.* ○ *fan a fire* (ie to make it burn more strongly). **2** to make an emotion, a rumour, etc stronger, sometimes deliberately: [Vn] *Public anxiety is being fanned by the media.* **3** ~ (**sth**) **out** to spread from a central point: [Vp] *The main railway lines fan out from the capital.* ○ *The army fanned out across the city.* [Vnp] *He fanned out the cards in his hand.* **IDM** **fan the ¹flames (of sth)** to make emotions, etc stronger or activity more intense: *Her wild behaviour merely fanned the flames of his jealousy.*

fanatic /fə'nætɪk/ *n* (*often derog*) a person who is too enthusiastic about sth: *a religious/political fanatic* ○ *a fitness fanatic* ○ *model train fanatics.* ▶ **fanatical** /-kl/ *adj*: *a fanatical Catholic* ○ *a gardener with an almost fanatical devotion to the perfect lawn* ○ *She's fanatical about keeping fit.* **fanatically** /-kli/ *adv*: *fanatically loyal/tidy.* **fanaticism** /-tɪsɪzəm/ *n* [U]: *religious fanaticism.*

fancier /'fænsiə(r)/ *n* (esp in compounds) a person with a special interest in and love for sth: *a ¹dog-fancier* ○ *a ¹pigeon-fancier.*

fanciful /'fænsɪfl/ *adj* **1** using or relying on the imagination rather than reason: *The scheme/notion is not as fanciful as it sounds.* ○ *It is not wholly fanciful to suggest that…* **2** (of things) designed or decorated in an odd but creative manner.

fancy¹ /'fænsi/ *v* (*pt, pp* fancied) **1** (*Brit infml*) to have a desire or wish for sth; to want sth: [Vn] *I fancy a cup of tea.* ○ *What do you fancy for supper?* [V.ing] *I didn't fancy living by the sea.* **2** to think or believe sth; to imagine sth: [V.that] *He fancied (that) he heard footsteps behind him.* **3** (*infml esp Brit*) to find sb attractive: [Vn] *I think she fancies me.* **4** to think that sb/sth will win or be successful in sth: [Vn] *Which horse do you fancy in the next race?* ○ *She thinks she's certain to get the job but I don't fancy her chances myself.* [V.n to inf] *Australia are strongly fancied to retain the trophy.* **5** (*esp Brit*) [Vn] *Fancy that!* [V.n ing] *Well, fancy her being so rude!* [V.ing] *Fancy never having seen the sea!* [also V]. **IDM** **¹fancy oneself** (*Brit infml often derog*) to have a very high opinion of oneself; to be too proud of oneself. **¹fancy oneself as sth** to like the idea of being sth: *She rather fancies herself as a singer.*

fancy² /'fænsi/ *adj* (-ier, -iest) **1(a)** not plain or ordinary; unusual, esp in being complicated or highly decorated: *That's a very fancy calculator!* ○ *a fancy piece of footwork.* **(b)** [attrib] (esp of small things) brightly coloured; made to please the eye or taste: *fancy cakes/goods.* **2** exaggerated: *Don't start getting any fancy ideas.* ○ *Top designer labels tend to*

come with fancy price tags to match. **3** (*US*) (of food, etc) above average quality: *fancy vegetables.*
■ **¹fancy ¹dress** *n* [U] unusual or amusing clothes worn esp at parties to make sb look like another person, an animal, etc: *I'm going to the fancy dress ball as Mickey Mouse.*

fancy³ /'fænsi/ *n* **1** [C] a thing imagined: *silly teenage fancies* ○ *evil fancies that returned to plague him at night.* **2** [U] the power of the mind to imagine things, esp things that are not real. **3** [C usu *pl*] (*Brit*) a small decorated cake: *a box of iced fancies.* **IDM** **catch/take sb's ¹fancy** to attract or please sb: *She looked in all the shops but there was nothing that caught her fancy.* **take a ¹fancy to sb/sth** (*esp Brit*) to become fond of sb/sth, often without an obvious reason: *I've suddenly taken a fancy to ghost stories.* **take/tickle sb's ¹fancy** to please or attract sb immediately: *The idea tickled his fancy.* **when/ whenever the fancy ¹takes one** when one feels like doing sth: *She seems to flit across the Atlantic whenever the fancy takes her.*
■ **¹fancy-¹free** *adj* not emotionally involved with anyone: *She's footloose and fancy-free.*

fanfare /'fænfeə(r)/ *n* **1** a short ceremonial piece of music: *A fanfare of trumpets sounded as the queen entered.* **2** [U,C] an elaborate welcome: *The new policy was introduced amid much fanfare/ accompanied by a fanfare of publicity.*

fang /fæŋ/ *n* a long sharp tooth, esp of a dog or snake: *The wolf bared its fangs.*

fanlight /'fænlaɪt/ *n* a small window above a door or another window.

fanny /'fæni/ *n* **1** (*Brit △ sl*) the female sex organs. **2** (*sl esp US*) a person's bottom(3).

fantasize, -ise /'fæntəsaɪz/ *v* ~ (**about sth**) to imagine; to create a FANTASY: [V] *I'm only fantasizing.* [Vpr] *idly fantasizing about the Prince* [V.that] *He sometimes fantasized that he had won a gold medal.*

fantastic /fæn'tæstɪk/ *adj* **1** (*infml*) extremely good; excellent: *win a fantastic new car* ○ *a fantastic opportunity* ○ *She's a fantastic swimmer.* ○ *You passed your test? Fantastic!* **2** (*infml*) very large; extraordinary: *receive absolutely fantastic support* ○ *a fantastic range of possibilities* ○ *Their wedding cost a fantastic amount of money.* **3(a)** (also **fantastical**) wild and strange: *fantastic dreams/stories.* **(b)** impossible to carry out; not practical: *fantastic schemes/proposals.* ▶ **fantastically** /-kli/ *adv*: *fantastically expensive.*

fantasy /'fæntəsi/ *n* **1** [U] imagination, esp when it has no connection at all with reality: *live in a ¹fantasy world* ○ *These calculations are pure/mere fantasy.* **2** [C] an idea that is wild or not realistic; a product of the imagination: *his recurring fantasy of/ about becoming a movie star* ○ *have sexual fantasies* ○ *She has written a romantic escapist fantasy.* See also FANTASIZE.

fanzine /'fænziːn/ *n* a magazine for fans (FAN¹): *a pop music fanzine.*

far¹ /fɑː(r)/ *adv* (**farther** /'fɑːðə(r)/ or **further** /'fɜːðə(r)/; **farthest** /'fɑːðɪst/ or **furthest** /'fɜːðɪst/) **1** (usu in questions and negative sentences) (of space) at or to a great distance: *'How far is it to the bank from here?' 'It's not very far.'* ○ *'How far have we walked?' 'A long way — about ten miles.'* ○ *We didn't go far.* **2** (followed by particles and preps) **(a)** (of space) by a great distance: *far above the clouds* ○ *countries as far apart as Japan and Brazil* ○ *There's a stream not far from here.* ○ *Call me if you need me; I won't be far away/off.* **(b)** (of time) a long way: *far back in history* ○ *as far back as 1902* ○ *We danced far into the night.* **(c)** to a great extent: *live far beyond one's means* ○ *He's fallen far behind in his work.* **3** (followed by comparative adjs and advs) very much: *a far more reliable car* ○ *a far better solution* ○ *He runs far faster than his brother.* **IDM** **as far as** to the place mentioned, but no further: *I've read as far as the third chapter.* ○ *I'll walk with you as far as the post office.* ○ *We'll go by train as far as London, and then take a coach.* **as/so far as 1** the same distance as: *We didn't go as far as the others.* **2** to the extent that; as much as: *So far as I know/As far as I can see, that is highly unlikely.* ○ *His parents supported him as far as they could.* **3** (of progress) up to a specified point but not beyond: *She managed to crawl as far as the door.* ○ *We've got as far as collecting our data but we haven't analysed it yet.* **as/so far as it, etc 'goes** to a limited extent, usu less than desirable: *Your plan is a good one as far as it goes, but there are several points you've not considered.* **as/so far as sb/sth is concerned** to the extent that sb/sth is involved or affected: *The rise in interest rates will be disastrous as far as small firms are concerned.* ○ *The car is fine as far as the engine is concerned, but the bodywork needs a lot of attention.* ○ *As far as I'm concerned you can do what you like.* **as far as the eye can 'see** to the horizon: *The prairies stretch on all sides as far as the eye can see.* **by 'far** (used with comparative or superlative *adjs* or *advs*) by a great amount: *It is quicker by far to go by train.* ○ *She is the best by far/She is by far the best.* **carry/take sth too, etc 'far** to continue doing sth beyond reasonable limits: *Don't be such a prude — you can carry modesty too far!* ○ *It's time to be serious; you've carried this joke far enough.* **far/ farther/further afield** ⇨ AFIELD. **far and a'way** (followed by comparative or superlative *adjs*) by a very great amount; very much: *She's far and away the best actress in the movie.* **far and 'near/'wide** everywhere; from or to a large area: *They searched far and wide for the missing child.* **far be it from me to do sth (but...)** (*infml*) I certainly don't want you to think I would do sth (but...): *Far be it from me to interfere in your affairs but I would like to give you just one piece of advice.* **far from doing sth** instead of doing sth that is expected: *Far from enjoying dancing, he loathes it.* **far from sth / from doing sth** not at all; almost the opposite of sth: *The problem is far from easy* (ie is very difficult). ○ *Your account is far from (being) accurate.* **far 'from it** (*infml*) certainly not; almost the opposite: *'Are you happy here?' 'No, far from it; I've never been so miserable in my life.'* **few and far between** ⇨ FEW[1]. **go as/so far as to do sth / as that, etc** to be willing to go to extreme limits in dealing with sth: *I won't go so far as to say that he is dishonest* (ie I won't actually accuse him of being dishonest, even though I might suspect him of it). **go 'far 1** (of money) to buy many goods, etc: *A pound doesn't go very far* (ie You can't buy very much for a pound) nowadays. **2** (of food, supplies, etc) to be enough for what is needed; to last: *Four bottles of wine won't go far among twenty people.* **go / a long 'way** (of people) to be very successful: *Someone as intelligent as her should go far.* **go far / a long way towards sth / doing sth** to make a considerable contribution towards sth: *concessions which go a long way towards satisfying his critics* ○ *The new legislation does not go far enough towards solving the problem.* **go too 'far** to behave in a way that is beyond reasonable limits: *He's always been pretty crude but this time he's gone too far.* **in so 'far as** to the extent that: *That's the truth, in so far as I know it.* **not be far 'off/'out/'wrong** (*infml*) to be almost correct: *Your guess wasn't far out.* **'so far; 'thus far** until now; up to this/that point, time, etc: *The results have been encouraging, so far.* **,so 'far** (*infml*) only to a limited extent: *I trust him only so far (and no further).* **,so far, so 'good** (*saying*) up to now everything has been successful. **so near and yet so far** ⇨ NEAR[2].

■ **'far-away** *adj* [attrib] **1** distant; remote: *visit far-away places.* **2** with one's thoughts far away from

one's present surroundings, etc: *You have a far-away look in your eyes.*

,**far-'fetched** *adj* (*usu derog*) **1** (of a comparison) not natural; forced. **2** (*infml*) (of a story, an account, etc) exaggerated; INCREDIBLE: *The film's plot is interesting but rather far-fetched.*

,**far-'flung** *adj* [usu attrib] **1** spread over a wide area; distributed widely: *a far-flung network of contacts.* **2** distant: *Her fame has reached the most far-flung corners of the globe.*

,**far 'gone** *adj* [attrib] (*infml derog*) in an advanced state of eg illness, madness or drunkenness (DRUNKEN): *She was too far gone to understand anything we said to her.*

'**far-off** *adj* [attrib] remote: *a far-off country/galaxy.*

,**far-'reaching** *adj* likely to have a wide influence or many results: *a far-reaching inquiry* ○ *far-reaching consequences/implications.*

,**far-'sighted** *adj* **1** (*approv*) (**a**) (also ,**far-'seeing**) seeing future problems and possibilities clearly and planning for them: *a far-sighted diplomat/ entrepreneur.* (**b**) (of ideas, etc) showing an awareness of future needs: *far-sighted changes in the organization.* **2** (*esp US*) = LONG-SIGHTED.

far² /fɑː(r)/ *adj* (**farther** /'fɑːðə(r)/; or **further** /'fɜːðə(r)/; **farthest** /'fɑːðɪst/ or **furthest** /'fɜːðɪst/) [attrib] **1** more remote: *at the far end of the street* ○ *on the far bank of the river* ○ *She is on the far right of the party* (ie holds extreme right-wing (RIGHT[5]) views). **2** (*dated or fml*) distant: *a far country* ○ *to journey into far regions.* **IDM a far cry from sth / doing sth** (*infml*) a very different experience from sth/doing sth: *Life on a farm is a far cry from what I've been used to.*

■ **the ,Far 'East** *n* China, Japan and other countries of E and SE Asia.

farce /fɑːs/ *n* **1**(**a**) [C] a funny play for the theatre based on ridiculous and unlikely situations and events. (**b**) [U] the style of writing in plays of this type: (*fig*) *The match ended in a moment of pure farce.* **2** [C] an absurd, POINTLESS or badly organized event: *The trial was a complete farce.* ○ *The meeting rapidly degenerated into a farce.*

▶ **farcical** /'fɑːsɪkl/ *adj* absurd; ridiculous: *a situation verging on the farcical.*

fare¹ /feə(r)/ *n* [C, U] money charged for a journey by bus, ship, taxi, etc: *a cab fare* ○ *He can't afford the air fare home.* ○ *travel at half/full/reduced fare* ○ *fare increases.* See also RETURN FARE.

fare² /feə(r)/ *n* [U] (*dated or fml*) food, esp when offered at a meal: *simple/wholesome fare.*

fare³ /feə(r)/ *v* (*fml*) to make progress in the way specified; to get on (GET): [Vadv] *London luxury hotels fared badly in the survey.* ○ *Clinton has fared little better than Bush in this regard.*

farewell /ˌfeə'wel/ *interj* (*arch or fml*) goodbye: *Thousands had come to bid/say farewell to the great man as he was laid to rest.*

▶ **farewell** *n* [C, U] the action or an instance of saying goodbye: *a farewell party/gift/appearance* ○ *bid sb a fond farewell* ○ *She raised a hand in farewell.*

farm¹ /fɑːm/ *n* **1** an area of land, and the buildings on it, used for growing crops or keeping animals: *a 200-acre farm* ○ *a farm labourer* ○ *farm produce* ○ *farm machinery.* **2** a FARMHOUSE and the buildings near it: *get some eggs at the farm.* **3** a place where the specified fish or animals are bred: *a trout-/ mink-/pig-farm.* See also BATTERY FARM, COLLECTIVE FARM, DAIRY FARM, FACTORY FARM, HEALTH FARM.

■ '**farm-hand** *n* a person who works for a farmer.

farm² /fɑːm/ *v* (**a**) to grow crops or keep animals: [Vn] *He farms beef cattle.* ○ *organically farmed produce* [also V]. (**b**) to use land for this: [Vn] *intensively farmed land* ○ *She farms 200 acres.* **PHR V** ,**farm sb 'out (to sb)** (*derog esp Brit*) to arrange for sb to be cared for by other people, who are paid for

F

doing this: *The children were farmed out to child-minders at an early age.* ‚**farm sth ¹out (to sb)** to send out work to be done by others: *We farm out a lot of work to freelancers.*
▶ **farmer** *n* a person who owns or manages a farm: *an or¹ganic farmer* ○ *a ¹dairy farmer* ○ *¹peasant farmers.*
farming *n* [U] the business of working on or managing a farm: *take up farming* ○ *¹pig farming* ○ *modern farming methods* ○ *a farming community.*
farmhouse /¹fɑːmhaʊs/ *n* (*pl* **-houses** /-haʊzɪz/) a farmer's house.
farmland /¹fɑːmlænd/ *n* [U] land that is cultivated or on which animals are kept: *fertile/rich farmland.*
farmstead /¹fɑːmsted/ *n* a FARMHOUSE and the buildings near it.
farmyard /¹fɑːmjɑːd/ *n* a space enclosed by or next to farm buildings.
farrago /fə¹rɑːgəʊ/ *n* (*pl* **-os**; *US* **-oes**) (*derog*) a confused collection; a mixture: *a farrago of half-baked ideas.*
fart /fɑːt/ *v* (⚠) [V] to let air from the bowels come out through the ANUS. **PHRV** ‚**fart a¹bout/a¹round** (*sl*) to waste time, esp by behaving in a foolish way: *Stop farting around and give me a hand with this!*
▶ **fart** *n* (⚠) **1** a releasing of air through the ANUS. **2** (*sl*) an unpleasant, boring or stupid person: *He's just a silly old fart.*
farther /¹fɑːðə(r)/ *adj* (comparative of FAR²) more distant in space, direction or time: *on the farther shore of the lake* ○ *The church was farther down the road than I thought.* ○ *Rome is farther from London than Paris is.*
▶ **farther** *adv* (comparative of FAR¹) at or to a greater distance in space or time: *We can't go any farther without resting.* ○ *Let us look farther forward into the next century.* **IDM** **far/farther/further afield** ⇨ AFIELD.

NOTE Farther and further both mean 'more distant'. **Further** is much more common than **farther** in British English, in both speaking and writing: *Do you want to walk a little further/farther along here?* **Farthest** and **furthest** mean 'most distant': *Which town is furthest/farthest from the sea?* In both British and American English **further** also means 'more, or additional': *Are there any further questions?* ○ *a College of Further Education.* **Farther** cannot be used with this meaning.

farthest /¹fɑːðɪst/ *adj* (superlative of FAR²) **1** most distant in space, direction or time: *Go to the farthest house in the village and I'll meet you there.* **2** longest: *The farthest distance I've ever run is ten miles.*
▶ **farthest** *adv* (superlative of FAR¹) **1** at or to the greatest distance in space or time: *Who ran (the) farthest?* ○ *It's ten miles away, at the farthest.* ⇨ note at FARTHER. **2** to the highest degree or extent; most: *She is the farthest advanced of all my students.*
farthing /¹fɑːðɪŋ/ *n* a former British coin, withdrawn in 1961, worth one quarter of an old penny.
fascia (also **facia**) /¹feɪʃə/ *n* **1** = DASHBOARD. **2** a board or panel on the front of sth, usu with control switches: *The oven switch is on the left of the fascia.* **3** a board, etc above the front entrance of a shop, with the name of the shop on it.
fascinate /¹fæsɪneɪt/ *v* to attract or interest sb greatly: [Vn] *New York has always fascinated me.* ○ *The children watched, fascinated, as the chocolate was poured onto the cakes.* [Vn.to inf] *She was fascinated to discover that he had lived in China.* [V] *a play which never fails to fascinate.*
▶ **fascinating** *adj* having great attraction or charm: *a fascinating city/story* ○ *The results of the survey make fascinating reading.* ○ *Your journey sounds absolutely fascinating.* **fascinatingly** *adv.*
fascination /‚fæsɪ¹neɪʃn/ *n* **1** [sing] a very strong

attraction: *Stamp-collecting holds a peculiar fascination for some people.* **2** [U] ~ (**for/in/with sb/sth**) the state of being fascinated by sb/sth: *He watched the snake in horrified fascination.* ○ *the public's enduring fascination with Elizabeth Taylor.*
fascism (also **Fascism**) /¹fæʃɪzəm/ *n* [U] an extreme right-wing (RIGHT⁵) political system or attitude, which favours strong central authority and does not allow freedom of speech: *the conflict between fascism and socialism* ○ *the dangers of fascism.*
▶ **fascist** (also **Fascist**) /¹fæʃɪst/ *n* (*usu derog*) a person who supports fascism. — *adj*: *a fascist state* ○ *fascist opinions/sympathies.*
fashion /¹fæʃn/ *n* **1(a)** [C,U] a popular style of clothes, hair, etc at a particular time or place: *dressed in the latest fashion* ○ *a ¹fashion show/ designer/magazine* ○ *the autumn ¹fashion lines* ○ *Long skirts have come into fashion again. Faded jeans are still in fashion too.* ○ *Some styles are never/never go out of fashion.* **(b)** [C] a popular way of behaving, doing an activity, etc: *changing fashions* ○ *Fashions in art and literature come and go.* See also OLD-FASHIONED. **2** [sing] a manner or way of doing sth: *Don't you speak to me in that fashion!* ○ *In true fairy-tale fashion, they lived happily ever after.* ○ *parading in time-honoured fashion through the town.* See also PARROT-FASHION. **IDM** **after a ¹fashion** to a certain extent, but not very well: *I can play the piano, after a fashion.* **after the fashion of sb/sth** (*fml*) like sb/sth; in the style of sb/sth: *The room was furnished after the fashion of a modern public library.* **be all the ¹fashion/¹rage** to be the latest style or activity: *Suddenly, collecting teddy bears is all the fashion.*
▶ **fashion** *v* ~ **A from/out of B**; ~ **B into A** to give form or shape to sth; to design or make sth: [Vn,Vnpr] *fashion a doll (from a piece of wood)* [Vnpr] *fashion a lump of clay into a crude bowl.*
fashionable /¹fæʃnəbl/ *adj* **1** following a style that is currently popular: *fashionable clothes/furniture/ ideas* ○ *It is becoming fashionable to have long hair again.* **2** used or visited by people following a current fashion: *a fashionable hotel/resort* ○ *The movie made black berets highly fashionable for a while.* ▶ **fashionably** /-əbli/ *adv*: *fashionably dressed.*
■ **¹fashion-conscious** *adj* aware of the latest fashions and wanting to follow them: *her fashion-conscious young secretary.*
fast¹ /fɑːst; *US* fæst/ *adj* (**-er, -est**) **1(a)** moving or able to move quickly; rapid: *a fast car/horse* ○ *the world's fastest runner* ○ *a fast bowler.* **(b)** happening quickly: *a fast journey/trip* ○ *the fastest rate of increase for many years.* **2** (of a surface) producing or allowing quick movement: *a fast road/pitch* ○ *the fast lane of the freeway.* **3** (of a watch or clock) showing a time later than the true time: *I'm early — my watch must be fast.* ○ *That clock's ten minutes fast.* **4** (of photographic film) very sensitive to light, allowing a short exposure. **IDM** **fast and ¹furious** (of games, parties, shows, etc) lively and full of rapid action. **make a fast/quick buck** ⇨ BUCK³. **pull a fast one** ⇨ PULL¹.
▶ **fast** *adv* quickly: *Don't drive so fast!* ○ *The water was rising fast.* ○ *Her heart beat faster.* ○ *Can't you run any faster than that?* ○ (*fml*) *Night was fast approaching.* ○ *a fast-flowing stream* ○ *Computer training is a fast-growing market.* **IDM** **(run, etc) as fast as one's legs can carry one** as fast as one is able to.
■ ‚**fast ¹breeder** (also ‚**fast ¹breeder reactor**) *n* (*physics*) a REACTOR(1) that produces the nuclear substance it needs as fuel.
‚**fast ¹food** *n* [U,C] food that can be cooked easily and is sold by restaurants to be eaten quickly or taken away: *hamburgers, chips and other fast foods* ○ *a ‚fast ¹food restaurant/outlet/chain.*

ˌfast-ˈforward v [V] to press a button on a machine, eg a VIDEO(2b), in order to wind a tape forward quickly. — n [U]: *Put it on fast-forward.*

fast² /fɑːst; US fæst/ adj **1** [pred] firmly fixed or attached; secure: *make a boat fast* (ie tie it securely). **2** (of colours) not likely to fade or run¹(14a). **IDM** **hard and fast** ⇨ HARD¹.

▶ **fast** adv firmly; securely; tightly: *be fast asleep* (ie sleeping deeply) ○ *The boat was stuck fast in the mud.* **IDM** **hold ˈfast to sth** to continue to believe in an idea, a principle, etc with determination, despite all difficulties. **play fast and ˈloose (with sb/sth)** to change one's attitude towards sb/sth repeatedly in an insincere way; to treat sb lightly or casually: *He's playing fast and loose with that girl's feelings.* **stand ˈfast/ˈfirm** to refuse to move back or change one's views. **thick and fast** ⇨ THICK.

fast³ /fɑːst; US fæst/ v to eat little or no food for a period of time, esp for religious reasons: [V] *Muslims fast during Ramadan.*

▶ **fast** n a period of not eating food: *a fast of three days* ○ *break one's fast* ○ ˈfast days.

fasten /ˈfɑːsn; US ˈfæsn/ v **1(a)** ~ sth (down) to secure or fix sth firmly: [Vnp] *fasten down the lid of a box* [Vn] *Please fasten your seat-belts.* ○ *Have you fastened all the doors and windows?* **(b)** ~ sth (up) to close or join sth: [Vnp] *Fasten up your coat.* [Vn] *The tent flaps should be securely fastened.* **(c)** to become closed or attached: [Vpr] *The door fastens with a latch.* [Vp] *This dress fastens up* (eg has buttons or a ZIP) *at the back.* [also V]. ~ sth (on/to sth); ~ A and B (together) to attach one thing firmly to another thing: [Vnadv] *fasten two sheets of paper together (with a pin)* [Vnpr] *He fastened a brooch on a blouse* ○ (fig) *He fastened his eyes on me.* **PHR V** ˈfasten on(to) sb/ sth to select or follow sb/sth in a determined way: *fasten onto an idea* ○ *He was looking for someone to blame and fastened on me.*

▶ **fastener** /ˈfɑːsnə(r); US ˈfæs-/ (also **fastening** /ˈfɑːsnɪŋ; US ˈfæs-/) n a device that fastens sth: *a zip-fastener* ○ *a leather handbag with strap fastenings.*

fastidious /fæˈstɪdiəs/ adj **1** selecting carefully; choosing only what is good: *a fastidious craftsman.* **2** (*sometimes derog*) hard to please; easily disgusted: *Her odd table manners embarrassed some of her more fastidious friends.* ▶ **fastidiously** adv: *He inspected his fingernails fastidiously.* **fastidiousness** n [U].

fastness /ˈfɑːstnəs; US ˈfæs-/ n (*rhet*) a usu remote place that has been strengthened against attack; a STRONGHOLD: *a mountain fastness.*

fat¹ /fæt/ adj (**-tter, -ttest**) **1** (of the body) large in size; containing too much fat²: *a big fat man/woman* ○ *If you eat too much chocolate you'll get fat.* ○ *He grew fatter and fatter.* ⇨ note. Compare THIN 2. **2** large; round: *a big fat apple.* **3** thick; well filled: *a fat book* ○ *a fat wallet* (one with a lot of money in). **4** (*infml*) large in quantity: *a fat sum/profit* ○ *He gave me a nice fat cheque* (one for a lot of money). **IDM** **(a) fat ˈchance (of sth / doing sth)** (*infml ironic*) (often as an *interj*) (there is) no chance at all: *'Maybe they'll let us in without tickets.' 'Fat chance (of that)!'* **a fat lot (of good, etc)** (*infml ironic*) very little: *A fat lot ˈyou care* (ie You don't care at all). ○ *A fat lot of good ˈthat did me* (ie It didn't help me at all). ▶ **fatness** n [U].

■ ˌfat ˈcat n (*infml esp US*) a person who is rich and powerful.

ˈfat-head n (*infml*) a stupid person.

NOTE Compare **fat, plump, chubby**, etc. When describing people who have too much fat on their bodies **fat** is the most usual and direct word: *a fat man* ○ *Does this dress make me look fat?* In English it is not polite to say to somebody that they are fat. People sometimes use **large** as a euphemism for **fat**.

You can use **plump** to suggest that somebody is slightly fat in an attractive way: *She was a plump,*

pleasant-faced woman. ○ *Tears ran down his plump cheeks.* **Plump** can also be used to describe certain types of food: *firm plump tomatoes.* **Tubby** is often used in a friendly way to describe people who are short and round. **Chubby** is used to describe children or a particular part of the body: *the baby's chubby cheeks / legs.*

Stout is often used to describe older people who have a round and heavy appearance: *He was a short stout man with a bald head.* **Podgy** is especially used to refer to hands and fingers that are fat. **Flabby** describes flesh that is fat and loose: *This exercise is good for flabby thighs and bottoms.*

Overweight is the most neutral term: *She's about 10 kilos overweight.* Doctors use **obese** to describe people who are so fat that they are unhealthy.

fat² /fæt/ n **1** [U] **(a)** a white or yellow GREASY substance in the bodies of animals and humans, under the skin: *excess body fat* ○ *This ham has too much fat on it.* **(b)** an oily substance found in certain seeds. **2** [C,U] fat from animals, plants or seeds, treated so that it becomes pure for use in cooking: *Fried potatoes are cooked in deep fat.* **3** [C,U] animal and vegetable fats, esp as part of a person's diet: *You should cut down on fats and carbohydrates.* ○ *foods which are low in fat* ○ *fat-free yoghurts.* **IDM** **chew the fat/rag** ⇨ CHEW. **the fat is in the ˈfire** (*infml*) there will be a lot of trouble now. **live off/on the fat of the land** ⇨ LIVE².

fatal /ˈfeɪtl/ adj ~ (to sb/sth) **1** causing or ending in death: *a fatal accident / blow* ○ *fatal injuries* ○ *The fall almost proved fatal.* **2** causing disaster: *a fatal mistake* ○ *There was a fatal flaw in the plan.* ▶ **fatally** adv: *fatally wounded / weakened.*

fatalism /ˈfeɪtəlɪzəm/ n [U] the belief that events are decided by fate; the acceptance of all that happens as inevitable.

▶ **fatalistic** /ˌfeɪtəˈlɪstɪk/ adj showing a belief in fate: *a fatalistic person / attitude / outlook.*

fatality /fəˈtæləti/ n **1** [C] (*fml*) a death caused by accident or in war, etc: *a campaign to reduce the number of fatalities on our roads.* **2** [U] the sense of being controlled by fate.

fate /feɪt/ n **1** [U] the power believed to control all events in a way that cannot be resisted; destiny: *We planned to marry in June, but fate decided otherwise.* ○ *By a strange turn/twist of fate, she was also at the party.* **2** [C] what will happen or has happened to sb/sth: *abandon sb to their fate* ○ *The court will decide our fate(s).* ○ *Nothing is known of the fate of the three men.* ○ *His predecessor was toppled from power and he looks likely to suffer a similar fate.* ○ (*joc*) *Having to watch their home videos all evening was a fate worse than death!* **IDM** **sure as fate** ⇨ SURE. **tempt fate/providence** ⇨ TEMPT.

fated /ˈfeɪtɪd/ adj ~ (to do sth) unable to escape a particular destiny: *As it turned out, they were fated never to meet again.* ○ *He believes that everything in life is fated.*

fateful /ˈfeɪtfl/ adj [usu attrib] having an important, often very bad, effect on future events: *the fateful moment when he first set eyes on her* ○ *a fateful decision.*

father¹ /ˈfɑːðə(r)/ n **1(a)** (also used, esp formally and by older people, as a form of address) a man in relation to a child or children born from an OVUM that he has fertilized (FERTILIZE 1): *My father died in 1992.* ○ *Ben's a wonderful husband and father.* ○ *You've been like a father to me.* ○ *Can I get you anything, father?* **(b)** any male animal in relation to its young. ⇨ App 4. **2** (usu *pl*) (*fml*) an ancestor: *the land of our fathers.* **3** a man who founds sth, first leads sb/sth, or is the most important influence in the early history of sth: *city fathers* ○ *Gillray is considered by many to be the father of the modern* *political cartoon.* See also FOUNDING FATHER. **4 Father** God: *Our (Heavenly) Father* ○ *God the Father.* **5** the title of a priest, esp in the Roman Catholic Church and the Orthodox Church: *Yes, Father* ○ *Father Dominic.* See also HOLY FATHER. **IDM** **from ˌfather to ˈson** from one generation of a family to the next: *The farm has been handed down from father to son since 1800.* **like ˌfather, like ˈson** (*saying*) a son's character, actions, etc resemble, or can be expected to resemble, his father's. **old enough to be sb's father/mother** ⇨ OLD.

▶ **ˈfatherhood** *n* [U] the state of being a father: *the responsibilities that fatherhood brings.*

ˈfatherless *adj* [usu attrib] (**a**) no longer having a father. (**b**) not seeing one's father regularly.

ˈfatherly *adj* like or typical of a father: *fatherly advice* ○ *He keeps a fatherly eye on his players.*

■ **ˌFather ˈChristmas** (*Brit*) (also **Santa Claus**) *n* an imaginary old man with a red ROBE(1) and a long white BEARD¹. Parents tell small children that he comes down the chimney at Christmas to bring them presents.

ˈfather-figure *n* an older man who is respected because he advises and protects others.

ˈfather-in-law /ˈfɑːðər ɪn lɔː/ (*pl* **fathers-in-law**) *n* the father of one's husband or wife. ⇨ App 4.

ˈFather's Day *n* a day, usu the third Sunday in June, when fathers traditionally receive gifts and cards from their children: *Happy Father's Day, dad!*

father² /ˈfɑːðə(r)/ *v* **1** to become the male parent of sb: [Vn] *father a child.* **2** to create or DEVISE sth: [Vn] *father a plan.*

fatherland /ˈfɑːðəlænd/ *n* the country where one was born, esp as a place to which one owes loyalty: *God bless our German fatherland.*

fathom /ˈfæðəm/ *n* a measure (6 feet or 1.8 metres) of the depth of water: *The harbour is four fathoms deep.* ○ *The ship sank in twenty fathoms.*

▶ **fathom** *v* ~ **sb/sth** (**out**) to understand sb/sth fully; to find a reason or an explanation for sth: [Vn] *For reasons that I have never been able to fathom, the jury found him guilty.* [Vnp] *I'm trying to fathom out the motives behind his proposal.*

fatigue /fəˈtiːg/ *n* **1** [U] (*fml*) the condition of being very tired, usu because of hard work or exercise: *a decline in performance due to fatigue* ○ *A tremendous feeling/sense of fatigue swept over him.* **2** [U] weakness in metals, etc caused by repeated stress: *The plane's wing showed signs of metal fatigue.* **3 fatigues** [pl] (*esp US*) clothes worn by soldiers for specific purposes: *combat/camouflage fatigues.*

▶ **fatigued** *adj* [pred] (*fml*) very tired: *feeling fatigued.*

fatten /ˈfætn/ *v* ~ (**sb/sth**) (**up**) to become or make sb/sth fat or fatter: [V, Vp] *The pigs are fattening (up) nicely.* [Vn] *fatten cattle for (the) market.*

▶ **fattening** *adj* (of food) that makes people fat easily: *fattening cakes* ○ *Pasta is no longer regarded as fattening.*

fatty /ˈfæti/ *adj* (**-ier, -iest**) containing a lot of fat: *fatty tissue* ○ *fatty foods/meals.*

▶ **fatty** /ˈfæti/ *n* (*infml derog*) (esp as a form of address) a fat person.

fatuous /ˈfætʃuəs/ *adj* stupid and silly; foolish: *a fatuous grin/remark.* ▶ **fatuously** *adv.*

faucet /ˈfɔːsɪt/ *n* (*esp US*) a tap.

fault /fɔːlt/ *n* **1** [C] an aspect of sth that is wrong or not perfect; a mistake or FLAW: *I like him in spite of all his faults.* ○ *The book's virtues far outweigh its faults.* ○ *a major fault in/of the machine's design* ○ *a structural/an electrical fault.* ⇨ note at MISTAKE¹. **2** [U] the responsibility for a mistake or offence: *'Whose fault was it?' 'Mine, I'm afraid.'* ○ *It's all/entirely his fault.* ○ *The fault really lies with the leadership of the movement.* **3** [C] (in tennis, etc) a mistake made when serving (SERVE 8): *She has*

served seven **double faults** *in this set.* **4** [C] (*techn*) a place where there is a break in the layers of rock of the earth's CRUST(3): *earthquakes along the San Andreas fault.* **IDM** **at ˈfault** wrong; responsible for sth bad: *It is the system which is at fault.* **find fault** ⇨ FIND¹. **to a ˈfault** (esp of good qualities) excessively so: *She is generous to a fault.*

▶ **fault** *v* to discover a fault in sb/sth: [Vn] *No one could fault his performance.*

faultless *adj*: *Their teamwork was faultless.* **faultlessly** *adv*: *The engine performed faultlessly.*

faulty *adj* having a fault or faults: *a faulty switch* ○ *faulty workmanship* ○ *faulty instructions.*

■ **ˈfault-finding** *n* [U] (*usu derog*) looking for faults in other people's work or behaviour.

faun /fɔːn/ *n* (in Roman myths) a god of the fields and woods, with a human body and a goat's horns and legs.

fauna /ˈfɔːnə/ *n* [sing *v*] all the animals of an area or of a period of time: *the unique fauna of East Africa* ○ *conservation of the local flora and fauna.* Compare FLORA.

faux pas /ˌfəʊ ˈpɑː/ (*pl* **faux pas** /ˌfəʊ ˈpɑːz/) *n* an action, remark, etc which causes embarrassment because it is not socially correct: *He committed one or two faux pas when it came to Japanese protocol.*

favour¹ (*US* **favor**) /ˈfeɪvə(r)/ *n* **1** [U] approval or support: *win sb's favour* ○ *her fall from international/royal favour* ○ *He's not in favour with the media right now.* ○ *Make-up for men seems to be going out of favour again.* ○ *The scheme found favour with the town planners.* **2** [U] treatment that is too generous to one person or group in preference to others: *As an examiner she was completely fair, showing no favour to any particular candidate.* **3** [C] an act of kindness that one does to help sb, esp when asked; a helpful act: *I had a word with her boss, as a special favour to her.* ○ *Can I ask a favour (of you)?* ○ *Do me a favour and turn the music down while I'm on the phone, will you?* ○ (*infml*) *The orchestra did Beethoven no favours* (ie played his music badly). **4 favours** [pl] the act of allowing sb, esp a man, to make love to one: *be (too) free with one's sexual favours.* **IDM** **curry favour** ⇨ CURRY². **in favour of sb/sth 1** in support of sb/sth: *He argued/voted in favour of the death penalty.* ○ *There were 247 votes in favour (of the motion) and 152 against.* ○ *Public feeling is increasingly in favour of women priests.* **2** to be replaced by sb/sth else: *She's sold her old car in favour of one that's smaller and more economical.* **in sb's favour** to the advantage of sb: *The court decided in his favour.* ○ *bend the rules in sb's favour* ○ *The exchange rate is in our favour* (ie It will benefit us when we change money).

favour² (*US* **favor**) /ˈfeɪvə(r)/ *v* **1** to support sb/sth; to prefer sb/sth: [Vn] *favour an idea/a candidate/a ban on sth* [V.ing] *Mr Baker favours changing the law on this.* **2** to give an advantage to sb/sth: [Vn] *The match schedule favours certain teams.*

▶ **favoured** /ˈfeɪvəd/ *adj* **1** having or given special advantages: *a member of the President's favoured circle of advisers.* **2** preferred: *the single most favoured option for dealing with traffic congestion.*

favourable (*US* **favorable**) /ˈfeɪvərəbl/ *adj* (**a**) pleasing; good: *show sb in a favourable light* ○ *We formed a very favourable impression of her.* (**b**) giving or showing approval: *attract favourable attention* ○ *a favourable report* ○ *The public reaction to the new tax was generally favourable.* (**c**) ~ (**to/toward sb/sth**) tending to support sb/sth : *create an environment favourable to their interests* ○ *Some think the deal is too favourable to IBM.* (**d**) ~ (**for sth**) helpful; suitable: *favourable winds* ○ *conditions favourable for skiing.* ▶ **favourably** (*US* **favor-**) /-əbli/ *adv*: *speak very favourably of a plan* ○ *These figures compare/*

contrast favourably with last year's. ○ *I was very favourably impressed by her new husband.*

favourite (*US* **favor-**) /ˈfeɪvərɪt/ *adj* [attrib] most liked: *It's one of my favourite restaurants.* ○ *It was the critics' favourite movie of the year.* ○ *Who is your favourite writer?*

▶ **favourite** (*US* **favor-**) *n* **1** a person or thing liked more than others: *She loved all her grandchildren but Ann was her favourite.* ○ *This record is my all-time favourite.* ○ *The radio was playing lots of old favourites.* ○ *These videos are great favourites with the children.* **2 the favourite** (in racing) the horse, competitor, etc expected to win: *The favourite came third.* ○ *Desert Orchid started the clear/hot favourite for the 2000 Guineas.* ○ *Faldo and Norman are joint favourites.*

favouritism (*US* **-vor-**) /-ɪzəm/ *n* [U] (*derog*) the practice of giving unfair advantages to the people that one likes best: *Our teacher is guilty of (showing) blatant favouritism.*

fawn¹ /fɔːn/ *n* **1** [C] a deer less than one year old. **2** [U] a light yellowish brown.

▶ **fawn** *adj* having the colour fawn: *a fawn rain-coat.*

fawn² /fɔːn/ *v* ~ (**on/upon sb**) (*derog*) to try to win the approval of sb, esp sb important, by praising them a lot, hurrying to do things for them, etc: [V] *fawning slaves* ○ *a fawning courtier/aide* [Vpr] *a rich but insecure person who likes to be fawned upon.*

fax /fæks/ *v* ~ **sth** (**through**) (**to sb**) to send a copy of a document, an illustration, etc by an electronic system using telephone lines: [Vnn] *Please fax me the layout for the new catalogue.* [Vnpr] *The plans were faxed to us by our New York office.* [also Vn,Vnp].

▶ **fax** *n* (**a**) [U] a system for faxing copies: *sent by fax* ○ *a fax machine* ○ *My fax number is 0171 436 4130.* (**b**) [C] a faxed copy: *receive/send faxes.*

faze /feɪz/ *v* (*infml esp US*) to upset or shock sb, esp so that they cannot continue doing sth: [Vn] *She's so calm; nothing seems to faze her.*

FBI /ˌef biː ˈaɪ/ *abbr* (*US*) Federal Bureau of Investigation: *head of the FBI* ○ *an FBI agent.* Compare CIA.

FCO /ˌef siː ˈəʊ/ *abbr* (in Britain) Foreign and Commonwealth Office.

fealty /ˈfiːəlti/ *n* [U] (*arch*) loyalty to sb: *take an oath of fealty.*

fear¹ /fɪə(r)/ *n* (**a**) [U] an unpleasant feeling caused by the possibility of danger, pain, a threat, etc: *overcome by fear* ○ *feel/show no fear* ○ *White with fear, she rose to her feet.* ○ *The local people live in constant/daily fear of violence from young hooligans.* ○ *He entered the interview room in fear and trembling* (ie feeling very frightened). (**b**) [C] this feeling caused by sth specific: *have genuine/understandable/well-founded fears* ○ *an instinctive fear of heights* ○ *The doctor's report confirmed our worst fears.* ○ *dismiss sb's fears as irrational* ○ *overcome/allay sb's fears* ○ *continuing interest-rate fears.* **IDM** **for fear of sth / of doing sth**; **for fear (that...)** to avoid the danger of sth happening: *We spoke in whispers for fear of waking the guards/for fear (that) we might wake the guards.* **in ˌfear of one's ˈlife** anxious for one's own safety. **ˌno ˈfear** (*infml*) (used when answering a suggestion) certainly not: *'Are you coming climbing?' 'No fear!'* **put the fear of ˈGod into sb** (*infml*) to make sb very frightened.

▶ **fearful** /-fl/ *adj* **1** ~ (**of sth / of doing sth**); ~ (**that**)... nervous and afraid: *fearful of waking the guards/fearful that we might wake the guards* ○ *her fearful eyes.* **2** terrible; causing horror: *a fearful road accident.* **3** (*infml*) very great; very bad: *He had a fearful row with his wife.* **fearfully** /-fəli/ *adv*: *glancing fearfully around* ○ *fearfully expensive.*

fearless *adj* not afraid: *a fearless mountaineer* ○ *supple and fearless in the water.* **fearlessly** *adv*. **fearlessness** *n* [U].

fearsome /ˈfɪəsəm/ *adj* frightening, esp in appearance: *a fearsome sight/spectacle* ○ *He has a fearsome reputation as a fighter.* ○ (*fig*) *a fearsome task* (ie one that frightens one because it is difficult).

fear² /fɪə(r)/ *v* **1**(**a**) to be afraid of sb/sth: [Vn] *fear death/illness* ○ *She fears no one.* ○ *The plague was greatly feared in the Middle Ages.* (**b**) to feel fear about doing sth: [V] *Never fear* (ie Don't worry), *everything will be all right.* [V.to inf] (*fml*) *She feared to speak in his presence.* [also V.ing]. **2** to feel that sth bad may happen: [Vn] *They feared the worst* (ie thought that the worst had happened or would happen). [Vadv] *'Are we going to be late?' 'I fear so.'* [V.that] *I fear (that) he may die.* **PHRV** **ˈfear for sb/ sth** to be anxious or troubled about sb/sth: *I fear for their safety in this weather.*

feasible /ˈfiːzəbl/ *adj* that can be done; practical(3); possible: *a feasible idea/suggestion/scheme* ○ *It is no longer feasible for one country to dominate the world.*

▶ **feasibility** /ˌfiːzəˈbɪləti/ *n* [U]: *We are carrying out a feasibility study on the proposal for a new power station.*

feast /fiːst/ *n* **1**(**a**) an unusually large or elaborate meal: *a ˈwedding feast.* (**b**) a thing that pleases the mind or the senses with its variety or rich quality: *a feast of colours/sounds.* **2** (*fml*) a religious festival celebrated as a happy occasion: *the feast of Christmas* ○ *a ˈfeast-day.*

▶ **feast** *v* ~ (**on/off sth**) to enjoy a feast(1a): [Vpr] *They feasted on goose from their own farm.* [also V]. **IDM** **feast one's ˈeyes (on sb/sth)** to enjoy the beauty of sb/sth: *We feasted our eyes on the wonderful scenery.*

feat /fiːt/ *n* an achievement needing skill, strength or courage: *brilliant feats of engineering* ○ *perform feats of daring* ○ *That was no mean feat* (ie It was a great achievement). ⇨ note at ACT¹.

feather¹ /ˈfeðə(r)/ *n* any of the many light parts that grow from a bird's skin and cover its body. A feather has a hollow stem in the centre with fine strands growing out on either side: *a feather duster* (ie one made of feathers). ⇨ picture. **IDM** **birds of a feather** ⇨ BIRD. **(be) a ˈfeather in one's ˈcap** an achievement, etc that one can be proud of: *Winning the gold medal was yet another feather in her cap.* **light as air / as a feather** ⇨ LIGHT³. **ruffle sb's feathers** ⇨ RUFFLE. **smooth sb's ruffled feathers** ⇨ SMOOTH². **you could have knocked me down with a feather** ⇨ KNOCK².

feather

▶ **feathery** /ˈfeðəri/ *adj* **1** light and soft like feathers: *feathery snowflakes.* **2** covered or decorated with feathers: *a feathery hat.*

■ **ˌfeather ˈbed** *n* a MATTRESS stuffed with feathers. **ˌfeather-ˈbed** *v* (**-dd-**) (*Brit*) to make things easy for sb, esp by helping them financially: [Vn] *The industry has been feather-bedded by government grants for too long.*

ˌfeather ˈboa (also **boa**) *n* a long thin garment like a SCARF, made of feathers and worn, esp formerly, over the shoulders by women.

ˈfeather-brained *adj* (*derog*) foolish; silly.

feather² /ˈfeðə(r)/ *v* (usu passive) to cover or fit sth with feathers: [Vn] *a feathered hat.* **IDM** **feather one's (own) ˈnest** (*usu derog*) to make oneself richer, more comfortable, etc, usu at sb else's expense. **tar and feather sb** ⇨ TAR *v*.

featherweight /'feðəweɪt/ n a boxer weighing between 53.5 and 57 kilograms, next above BANTAMWEIGHT: *the featherweight championship.*

feature /'fiːtʃə(r)/ n **1(a)** [C] one of the parts of the face, eg nose, mouth, eyes, which together form its appearance: *His eyes are his most striking feature.* ⇨ picture at HEAD. **(b) features** [pl] the whole face: *a woman of handsome/striking/delicate features.* **2** [C] a distinctive characteristic; an aspect: *an interesting feature of city life* ○ *memorable features of the Scottish landscape* ○ *The many examples of usage are a special feature of this dictionary.* **3** [C] **(a)** ~ **(on sb/sth)** in newspapers, television, etc) a special or prominent article or programme about sb/sth: *We'll be doing a special feature on education in next week's programme.* **(b)** the main film in a cinema programme: *There's sometimes a cartoon before the feature.* ○ *a 'feature film.*
▶ **feature** v **1** to give a prominent part to sb/sth; to display or advertise sth: [Vn] *a film that features a new French actress* ○ *a menu featuring many mouth-watering dishes.* **2** ~ **in sth** to have a prominent part in sth; to appear in sth: [Vpr] *Does a new job feature in your future plans?*
featureless adj without distinct features (FEATURE 2); not interesting: *a featureless landscape.*

Feb abbr /feb/ (infml) February: *18 Feb 1934.*

febrile /'fiːbraɪl/ adj (fml) nervous or excited, as if with a fever: *febrile pre-election activity.*

February /'februəri; US -ueri/ n [U, C] (abbr **Feb**) the second month of the year, next after January. For further guidance on how *February* is used, see the examples at *April.*

fecal (US) = FAECAL.

feces (US) = FAECES.

feckless /'fekləs/ adj (derog) not able to manage things properly or look after oneself; not responsible or efficient: *feckless parents with more children than they can support.* ▶ **fecklessness** n [U].

fecund /'fiːkənd, 'fek-/ adj (fml) (capable of) producing young or new living things; FERTILE(2): (fig) *a fecund imagination.* ▶ **fecundity** /fɪ'kʌndəti/ n [U].

fed pt, pp of FEED[1].

federal /'fedərəl/ adj **1** of a system of government in which several states unite but keep considerable control over their own internal affairs: *federal unity.* **2** (within a federal system) relating to central rather than local government: *The Trans-Canada highway is a federal responsibility.* **3 Federal** (US) supporting the union party in the American Civil War.
▶ **federalism** /-ɪzəm/ n [U].
federalist /-ɪst/ n a supporter of federal union or power.
federally adv by the federal government: *This development is federally funded.*
■ **the ,Federal ,Bureau of Investi'gation** n [sing] (abbr **FBI**) (in the USA) the department responsible for investigating crimes against federal law and protecting national security.

federate /'fedəreɪt/ v [V] (of states, organizations, etc) to unite under a central government, while keeping some local control.

federation /,fedə'reɪʃn/ n **1** [C] a union of states in which individual states keep control of many internal matters but in which foreign affairs, defence, etc are the responsibility of the central government. **2** [C] a group of societies, trade unions, etc organized like a federation. **3** [U] the action of forming a federation.

fed up /,fed 'ʌp/ adj [pred] ~ **(about/with sb/sth)** (infml) tired or bored; unhappy or depressed: *What's the matter? You look pretty fed up.* ○ *I'm fed up with waiting for her to telephone.* ○ *I'm fed up with people being rude to me all the time.*

fee /fiː/ n **(a)** (usu pl) an amount of money paid for professional advice or services, eg to private teachers, doctors, etc: *pay the lawyer's fees* ○ *fee-paying customers* ○ *a fee-paying school* (ie where fees must be paid). ⇨ note at INCOME. **(b)** an amount of money paid to join a club, do an examination, etc: *If you want to join, there's an entrance fee of £20 and an annual membership fee of £10.*

feeble /'fiːbl/ adj (-r /-blə(r)/; -st /-blɪst/) **(a)** weak; faint: *a feeble old man* ○ *a feeble cry* ○ *a feeble lamp.* **(b)** (derog) lacking force; not effective: *a feeble argument/attempt/excuse/joke.* ▶ **feebleness** n [U].
feebly /'fiːbli/ adv.
■ ,**feeble-'minded** adj (usu derog) having less than usual intelligence; stupid.

feed[1] /fiːd/ v (pt, pp fed /fed/) **1** ~ **sb/sth (on sth)**; ~ **sth to sb/sth** to give food to a person or an animal: [Vn] *She has a large family to feed.* ○ *I fed and watered the horses.* ○ *The baby can't feed itself yet* (ie can't put food into its own mouth). [Vnpr] *What do you feed your dog on?* [Vnn] *feed the baby some more stewed apple.* See also BREAST-FEED, FEEDER. **2(a)** ~ **(on/off sth)** (esp of animals) to eat: [Vpr] *The cows were feeding on hay in the barn.* [V] (infml) *Have you fed yet?* **(b)** to be food for a person or an animal: [Vn] *There's enough here to feed us all.* **3** ~ **A (with B) /** ~ **B into A** to supply sth with material: [Vn, Vnpr] *feed the fire (with wood)* [Vn] *The lake is fed by several small streams.* ○ *Excuse me a minute — I need to go and feed the meter* (ie put extra coins into it, eg for parking). [Vnpr] *The moving belt feeds the machine with raw material/feeds raw material into the machine.* **4** to provide advice, information, etc to sb, esp regularly: [Vnn] *Our overseas agents feed us regular information about the state of the market in their area.* [also Vnpr]. **IDM** **bite the hand that feeds one** ⇨ BITE[1]. **PHRV** ,**feed sth 'in** to supply sth, esp to a machine: *To get a ticket you need to feed another coin in.* '**feed on/off sth** to be made stronger by sth: *Hatred feeds on envy.* ,**feed sb 'up** (Brit) to give extra food to sb to make them more healthy: *You look very thin; I think you need feeding up a bit.*
■ '**feeding-bottle** n a bottle with a rubber TEAT(2) for feeding liquid foods to babies or animals.

feed[2] /fiːd/ n **1** [C] a meal, usu for animals or babies: *When is the baby's next feed?* **2(a)** [U, C] food for animals, or a type of this: *high-protein animal feeds.* **(b)** [U] material supplied to a machine. **3** [C] a pipe, channel, etc along which material is carried to a machine: *The petrol feed is blocked.*

feedback /'fiːdbæk/ n [U] **1** information about a product, etc that a user gives back to the company that made or sold it: *We need more feedback from the consumer in order to improve our goods.* **2** (techn) the return to its source of part of what a system produces, esp so as to change what it produces: *If you turn the amplifier up too much you get loud feedback.* ○ *The feedback from the computer enables us to update the program.*

feedbag /'fiːdbæg/ n (US) = NOSEBAG.

feeder /'fiːdə(r)/ n **1** (following an adj) a thing, esp an animal or a plant, that feeds in a specified way: *a messy/dainty/greedy feeder.* **2** (Brit) a baby's BIB(1) or feeding-bottle (FEED[1]). **3** a minor route or means of transport that links outside areas with the main route, service, etc: *a new feeder road for the motorway* ○ *a feeder line for the Santa Fe Railroad.* **4** a feeding apparatus in a machine.

feel[1] /fiːl/ v (pt, pp felt /felt/) **1** to explore or perceive sth by touching it or by holding it in the hands: [Vn] *feel a rock/a piece of cloth* ○ *Can you feel the bump on my head?* ○ *Can you tell what this is by feeling it?* [V.wh] *Feel how rough this is.* **2** (not usu in the continuous tenses) to be aware of or experience sth physical or emotional; to have the sensation of sth: [Vn] *We all felt the earthquake tremors.* ○ *Can you feel the tension in this room?* ○ *After the accident, she couldn't feel anything* (ie she lost the sense of touch) *in her left leg.* ○ *He seemed to feel no remorse at all.* [V.n ing] *I could feel myself falling asleep.* ○ *I can feel a nail sticking into my shoe.* [Vn.inf (no *to*), V.n ing] *I felt something crawl(ing) up my arm.* **3** to have the specified physical, emotional or moral feeling: [V-adj] *feeling cold/hungry/comfortable/sad/happy* ○ *You'll feel better after a good night's sleep.* ○ *She felt betrayed.* ○ *I feel rotten about not taking the children out.* [Vadv] *How are you feeling today?* ○ *He feels strongly about this issue.* **4** to have the impression that one is sth: [V-n] *Standing there on stage I felt a complete idiot.* **5** ~ **(to sb) (like sth/sb)** (not in the continuous tenses) to give a sensation or an impression of sth or of being sth/sb: [V-adj] *The water feels warm.* ○ *Nothing feels right in our new house.* [Vadv] *How does it feel to be alone all day?* [Vpr] *This wallet feels (to me) like leather.* ○ *It feels like rain* (ie seems likely to rain). ⇨ note. **6** ~ **as if... / as though...** (not in the continuous tenses) to have or give the impression that ...: *I feel as if I'm going to be sick.* ○ *My cold feels as though it's getting better.* ○ *It felt as though a great weight had been lifted from us.* **7** to be particularly aware of sth; to be affected by sth: [Vn] *He feels the cold a lot.* ○ *She felt her mother's death very greatly.* ○ *We all feel the force of her arguments.* ○ *The effects of the recession are being felt everywhere.* ○ *Don't you feel the beauty of the countryside?* **8** to be capable of sensation: [V] *The dead cannot feel.* **9** to have as an opinion; to consider; to think; to believe: [V.*that*] *We all felt (that) our luck was about to turn.* ○ *I felt (that) I had to write and thank you for your kindness.* [V.n to inf, Vn-n] *She felt it (to be) her duty to tell the police.* [V.n to inf, V.*that*] *He felt the plan to be unwise/felt (that) the plan was unwise.* [Vn-adj] *I felt it advisable to do nothing.* **10** ~ **(about/around) (for sb/sth)** to search with the hands, the feet, a stick, etc: [Vpr] *He felt in his pocket for some money.* ○ *She felt along the wall for the door.* [Vp] *I had to feel about in the dark for the light switch.* **IDM be/feel called to sth** ⇨ CALL[1]. **,feel one's 'age** to realize that one is growing old, as one becomes less strong or one's ideas are thought to be old-fashioned: *My children's skill with computers really makes me feel my age!* **feel one's 'ears burning** to think or imagine that others are talking about one. **feel 'free (to do sth)** (*infml*) (said when giving permission): *'May I use your phone?' 'Feel free.'* ○ *Feel free to ask questions if you don't understand.* **feel 'good** to feel happy, confident, etc: *It makes me feel good to know my work is appreciated.* **feel (it) in one's 'bones (that...)** to know or SENSE sth by INTUITION, without any direct proof: *I know I'm going to fail this exam — I can feel it in my bones.* **feel like sth / doing sth** to think that one would like (to do/have) sth; to want (to do) sth: *I feel like (having) a drink.* ○ *We'll go for a walk if you feel like it.* **feel one'self** to feel fit and healthy: *I don't quite feel my'self today.* **feel the 'pinch** (*infml*) to suffer from a lack of money: *As the level of unemployment rises, more and more families are starting to feel the pinch.* **feel one's 'way 1** to move along carefully, eg in darkness, by touching walls, objects, etc. **2** to proceed cautiously: *At this early stage of the negotiations both sides are still feeling their way.* **look/feel small** ⇨ SMALL. **make one's presence felt** ⇨ PRESENCE. **not be/feel up to the mark** ⇨ MARK[1]. **PHRV 'feel for sb** to have sympathy for sb: *I really 'felt for her when her husband died.* **,feel 'up to (doing) sth** to consider oneself capable of (doing) sth: *If you feel 'up to it, we could go for a walk after lunch.*

▶ **feelingly** *adv* with deep emotion: *He spoke feelingly about his dead father.*

NOTE There are several verbs relating to the five senses of sight, smell, hearing, taste and touch. They are often used with the verb **can** and are not usually used in the continuous tenses.

See, smell, hear, taste and **feel** describe experiencing something through one of the senses: *He saw a light in the window.* ○ *I heard an explosion last night.* ○ *I can smell gas.* These verbs can also describe somebody's physical ability to use their eyes, ears, etc: *Grandma can't see/hear very well any more.*

Look, smell, listen, taste, sound and **feel** are used to describe how somebody or something is experienced through one of these patterns: **(a)** *She looks happy* (ie She's smiling). **(b)** *The wine tastes like water* (ie It's very weak). **(c)** *The singer sounds as though she has a sore throat* (ie The sound of her voice suggests she has a sore throat).

Look, smell, listen, taste and **feel** can describe making a deliberate effort to use the particular sense: *Look! Can you see that beautiful butterfly?* ○ *'I can't hear anything.' 'Listen carefully.'* ○ *'Taste this soup. What do you think?' 'I can't taste any garlic.'*

Feel and **look** can express a person's physical or mental state. In this sense, the continuous tenses can be used: *I feel sick/nervous/disappointed.* ○ *He was feeling tired so he didn't come to the party.* ○ *You're looking happy!*

feel[2] /fi:l/ *n* **1** an act of feeling: *Let me have a feel.* **2** the **feel** the sense of touch: *rough/smooth to the feel* (ie when touched or felt). **3** the **feel (a)** the sensation that sth gives when touching or being touched: *You can tell it's silk by the feel.* ○ *She loved the feel of the sun on her skin.* **(b)** the impression created by a situation, etc: *the feel of the place/the meeting/the occasion.* **IDM** **get the feel of sth / of doing sth** (*infml*) to become familiar with sth or with doing sth: *I haven't got the feel of the gears in this car yet.* **have a feel for sth** (*infml*) to have a sensitive appreciation or an easy understanding of sth: *He certainly has a feel for languages.*

feeler /'fi:lə(r)/ *n* a long thin part on an insect's head, which it uses for testing things by touch. **IDM** **put out 'feelers** (*infml*) to check other people's opinions carefully before doing sth: *I'll try to put out some feelers to gauge people's reactions to the idea.*

feeling /'fi:lɪŋ/ *n* **1(a)** [C] ~ **(of sth)** a thing that is felt through the mind or the senses: *a feeling of hunger/well-being/discomfort/gratitude/frustration/joy* ○ *'I really resent the way he treated me.' 'I know the feeling* (ie know how you feel).*'* **(b)** [sing] ~ **(of sth / that...)** an idea or a belief that is difficult to define and not based entirely on reason: *a feeling of danger* ○ *I can't understand why, but suddenly I had this feeling that something terrible was going to happen.* **(c)** [sing] an attitude; an opinion: *The feeling of the meeting* (ie The opinion of the majority) *was against the proposal.* ○ *My own feeling is that we should buy it.* **2** **feelings** [pl] a person's emotions rather than her or his mind: *deep religious feelings* ○ *sexual feelings* ○ *The speaker appealed more to the feelings of her audience than to their reason.* ○ *You've hurt my feelings* (ie You've offended me). ○ *I kept off the subject of her divorce to spare her feelings.* **3** ~ **for sb/sth (a)** [U, sing] sensitive understanding; appreciation: *a painter with a feeling for space* ○ *He plays the piano with great feeling.* **(b)** [U] sympathy for sb/sth: *You have no feeling for the sufferings of others.* **4(a)** [U] strong emotion, esp anger, resentment (RESENT), etc: *She spoke with feeling about the plight of the homeless.* ○ *Feeling over the dismissal ran high* (ie There was much anger, etc about it). **(b)** [C] an example of this: *strong feelings.* **5** [U] the ability to feel: *I've lost all feeling in my legs.* **IDM**

F

[V.speech] = verb + direct speech [V.*that*] = verb + *that* clause [V.*wh*] = verb + *who, how,* etc clause

have mixed feelings ⇨ MIXED. **no hard feelings** ⇨ HARD[1]. **a/that sinking feeling** ⇨ SINK[1].

feet pl of FOOT[1].

feign /feɪn/ v to pretend to be affected by sth; to SIMULATE(1) sth: [Vn] *feign sleep/illness/madness/ignorance* ○ *feigned innocence.*

feint /feɪnt/ n (esp in sport) a movement made to deceive an opponent.
► **feint** /feɪnt/ v to make a feint: [V] *He feinted with his left hand and landed a solid punch with his right.*

feisty /'faɪsti/ adj (**-ier, -iest**) (*US infml approv*) (of people) showing a lot of energy or spirit(5).

feldspar /'feldspɑː(r)/ n [U] a type of white or red mineral rock.

felicitations /fə,lɪsɪ'teɪʃnz/ n [pl] (*fml or joc*) words of congratulation (CONGRATULATE).

felicitous /fə'lɪsɪtəs/ adj (*fml*) (esp of words) well chosen; APT(1): *felicitous remarks* ○ *Her choice of music is felicitous.* ► **felicitously** adv.

felicity /fə'lɪsəti/ n (*fml*) **1** [U] great happiness. **2** [U] the quality of being pleasing, well designed, well chosen, etc: *stories illustrated with great felicity.* **3** [C,U] a pleasing style or feature of speaking or writing: *Her book displays many subtle felicities of language.*

feline /'fiːlaɪn/ adj, n (of or like) an animal of the cat family: *She walks with a feline grace.*

fell[1] pt of FALL[1].

fell[2] /fel/ v [Vn] **1** to cut down a tree. **2** to knock sb to the ground by hitting them: *He felled his opponent with a single blow.*

fell[3] /fel/ n an area of hills or MOORLAND in northern England: *the Lakeland Fells.*

fell[4] /fel/ adj **IDM** **at/in one fell swoop** in a single action, esp a violent one: *If the new law is passed, it will remove press freedom at one fell swoop.*

fellatio /fə'leɪʃiəʊ/ n [U] (*fml*) stimulating the PENIS by sucking or licking.

fellow /'feləʊ/ n **1** (*infml*) (also *sl* **feller, fella** /'felə/) a man or boy; a CHAP[2]: *He's a nice fellow.* ○ *Poor fellow!* ○ (*joc*) *Where can a fellow* (ie Where can I) *get a bite to eat around here?* **2** (usu pl) a companion; a COMRADE: *fellows in good fortune/misery* ○ *Her fellows do not share her interest in computers.* See also PLAYFELLOW. **3** (*infml*) (also *sl* **feller, fella** /'felə/) the BOYFRIEND or lover of a girl or woman: *Have you met her new fellow?* **4** [attrib] of the same class, type, etc: *a fellow member* ○ *one's ,fellow-'countrymen* ○ *my fellow-travellers on the train.* **5** (*esp Brit*) a member of an academic or professional society: *Fellow of the Royal Academy.* **6** a senior member or a member of the governing body(4) of certain colleges or universities. **7** (*esp US*) a GRADUATE[1](1) student holding a FELLOWSHIP(4).
■ ,**fellow-'feeling** n [U] sympathy with sb whose experience, etc one shares.

fellowship /'feləʊʃɪp/ n **1** [U] friendly association with others; companionship (COMPANION): *live on terms of good fellowship with one's neighbours* ○ *Christian fellowship.* **2**(**a**) [C] a group or society of people sharing a common interest or aim. (**b**) [U] membership in such a group or society: *admitted to fellowship.* **3** [C] (*esp Brit*) the position of a fellow(6) of a college. **4** [C] an award of money to a GRADUATE[1](1) student in return for some teaching, research work, etc: *We give three research fellowships a year.*

felony /'feləni/ n [C,U] (*law*) a serious crime, eg murder, RAPE[1](1a) or ARSON: *a series of felonies* ○ *be convicted of felony.*
► **felon** /'felən/ n a person guilty of felony.

felt[1] /felt/ n [U] wool, hair or fur rolled flat into a thick cloth: *felt hats/slippers.*
■ ,**felt-tip 'pen** (also ,**felt-tipped 'pen**, ,**felt-'tip**) n a

pen with a tip made of felt: *Felt-tip pens are used especially for writing or drawing in different colours.*

felt[2] pt, pp of FEEL[1].

fem abbr **1** female. **2** feminine.

female /'fiːmeɪl/ adj **1**(**a**) of the sex that can give birth to children or produce eggs: *a female dog/cat/pig.* (**b**) (of plants and flowers) producing fruit: *a female fig-tree.* **2** of or typical of women: *female suffrage* ○ *the female mentality.* **3** (*techn*) (of an electrical SOCKET, etc) having a hollow part designed to receive an inserted part.
► **female** n **1** a female animal or plant. **2** (*often derog*) a woman: *Who on earth is that female he's with?* ⇨ note at GENDER.

NOTE **Female** and **male** refer to the sex of living things. They can be adjectives or nouns: *a female child/cat* ○ *the males in the herd.* The nouns **woman/man** are used to refer to people in most situations: *a brilliant woman* ○ *the man who lives next door* ○ *Men are usually taller than women.* **Male** and **female** as nouns are used in medical or scientific contexts and can be considered offensive if used in other situations.

Masculine and **feminine** are adjectives used to describe the behaviour, appearance, etc which people think of as normal or acceptable for each of the two sexes. You can use them to describe the 'opposite' sex: *He has a sensitive, feminine side to his nature.* ○ *She has quite a masculine-sounding voice.* The nouns and adjectives **masculine** and **feminine** (as well as **neuter**) show gender in grammar.

feminine /'femənɪn/ adj **1** of or like women; having the qualities or appearance considered characteristic of women: *a feminine voice/figure/appearance.* **2** (*grammar*) (**a**) (abbreviated as *fem* in this dictionary) of a class of words that refer to female persons, animals, etc and often have a special form: *'Lioness' is the feminine form of 'lion'.* ○ *The feminine equivalent of 'earl' is 'countess'.* (**b**) of the feminine GENDER(1): *The French word for 'table' is feminine.* ⇨ note at FEMALE. Compare MASCULINE, NEUTER 1.
► **feminine** n (*grammar*) (**a**) [C] a feminine word or word form. (**b**) **the feminine** [sing] the feminine GENDER(1): *French adjectives end in -e in the feminine.*
femininity /,femə'nɪnəti/ n [U] the quality of being feminine.

feminism /'femənɪzəm/ n [U] (**a**) belief in the principle that women should have the same rights and opportunities as men. (**b**) the movement(5) in support of this.
► **feminist** /'femənɪst/ n a supporter of feminism: *Suffragettes were among the first feminists in Britain and the USA.* ○ *He has strong feminist opinions.*

femme fatale /,fæm fə'tɑːl/ n (pl **femmes fatales** /,fæm fə'tɑːl/) (*French*) a woman to whom a man feels very strongly attracted, with dangerous or unhappy results: *She was his femme fatale.*

femur /'fiːmə(r)/ n (pl **femurs** or **femora** /'femərə/) (*anatomy*) the thick bone in the upper part of the leg. ⇨ picture at SKELETON. ► **femoral** /'femərəl/ adj: *the femoral artery.*

fen /fen/ n an area of low wet land with few trees, esp (**the Fens**) those in eastern England.

fence[1] /fens/ n a structure of rails, posts, wire, etc, esp one put round a field or garden to mark a boundary or to keep animals in one place. ⇨ picture at HOUSE[1]. **IDM** **come down on one side of the fence or the other** ⇨ SIDE[1]. **mend fences** ⇨ MEND. **sit on the fence** ⇨ SIT.
► **fence** v to surround, divide, etc sth with a fence: [Vn] *Farmers fence their fields.* [Vnpr] *His land was fenced with barbed wire.* **PHRV** ,**fence sb/sth 'in 1** to surround or enclose sb/sth with a fence: *The grounds are fenced in to prevent trespassing.* **2** to restrict the freedom of sb: *She felt fenced in by*

F

domestic routine. **,fence sth 'off** to separate one area from another with a fence: *One end of the garden was fenced off for chickens.*
fencing /'fensɪŋ/ *n* [U] material used for making fences, eg wood, wire, etc.

fencing

fencer   mask

foil

parrying   lunging

fence² /fens/ *v* **1** [V] to fight with a long thin sword as a sport. **2** ~ **(with sb)** to use words in a clever but indirect way when speaking to sb, esp because one is hoping to gain an advantage in the conversation: [Vpr] *We were fencing with each other, both refusing to come to the point.* [also V].
▸ **fencer** *n* a person who fences (FENCE² 1). ⇨ picture.
fencing *n* [U] the sport of fighting with swords. ⇨ picture.
fence³ /fens/ *n* a criminal who buys and sells stolen goods.
fend /fend/ *v* **PHRV** **fend for one'self** to support and care for oneself: *It is time you left home and learnt to fend for yourself.* **fend sth/sb off** to defend oneself from sth/sb; to avoid sth/sb: *fend off a blow* ○ *The minister had to fend off some awkward questions from reporters.* ○ *He tried to kiss her but she fended him off.*
fender /'fendə(r)/ *n* **1** a low metal frame placed around a fireplace to prevent burning coal from falling out. **2** a soft solid object such as a mass of rope or a rubber tyre, hung over the side of a boat to prevent damage when it comes next to another boat or to land. **3** (*US*) (**a**) a MUDGUARD over the wheel of a bicycle. (**b**) = WING 4.
fenland /'fenlænd, -lənd/ *n* [U] (in Britain) an area of low wet land with few trees.
fennel /'fenl/ *n* [U] a plant with yellow flowers, whose leaves and seeds are used in cooking. Its root can also be eaten as a vegetable.
feral /'fɪərəl, 'ferəl/ *adj* (*fml*) (of animals) living wild, esp after escaping from life as a pet, from a farm, etc: *feral cats.*
ferment¹ /fə'ment/ *v* to change or make sth change by means of a chemical reaction involving esp YEAST or bacteria: [V] *Fruit juices ferment if they are kept a long time.* ○ (*fig*) *His anger fermented inside him.* [Vn] *Yeast is used in fermenting sugar to produce alcohol.*
▸ **fermentation** /,fɜːmen'teɪʃn/ *n* [U]: *Sugar is converted into alcohol through (the process of) fermentation.*
ferment² /'fɜːment/ *n* [U] political or social excitement or uncertainty: *The country was in (a state of) ferment.*
fern /fɜːn/ *n* [C, U] a type of plant with large delicate leaves and no flowers: *ferns growing in pots* ○ *hillsides covered in fern.* ▸ **ferny** *adj.*
ferocious /fə'rəʊʃəs/ *adj* fierce, violent or SAVAGE (1): *a ferocious beast* ○ *ferocious cruelty* ○ *a ferocious onslaught* ○ *a ferocious campaign against us in the press.* ▸ **ferociously** *adv: snarling ferociously.*
ferocity /fə'rɒsəti/ *n* [U] fierce behaviour; violence: *The lion had attacked its victim with great ferocity.* ○ *She was surprised at the ferocity of his argument.*
ferret /'ferɪt/ *n* a small fierce animal kept for driving rabbits from their holes, killing rats, etc. Compare WEASEL.

▸ **ferret** *v* **1** [V] (usu **go ferreting**) to hunt rabbits, rats, etc with ferrets. ~ **(about)** **(for sth)** (*infml*) to search; to look carefully amongst a lot of things: [Vp] *I spent the day ferreting about in the attic.* [Vpr] *I was ferreting for old photographs.* **PHRV** **,ferret sth 'out** (*infml*) to discover sth by searching thoroughly or asking many questions: *ferret out a secret/the truth.*
Ferris wheel /'ferɪs wiːl/ (also **big wheel**) *n* (at a FAIR³(1), etc) a large upright revolving wheel with seats hanging from its edge for people to ride in.
ferrous /'ferəs/ *adj* [attrib] containing or relating to iron: *ferrous and non-ferrous metals.*
ferrule /'feruːl; *US* 'ferəl/ *n* a metal ring or cap placed on the end of a stick, an UMBRELLA, etc to stop it becoming damaged.
ferry /'feri/ *n* (**a**) a boat that carries people and goods across a stretch of water: *catch/take the ferry* ○ *the cross-channel ferry service.* (**b**) the place where such a service operates: *We waited at the ferry for two hours.*
▸ **ferry** *v* (*pt, pp* **ferried**) to transport people or goods by boat, aircraft, etc for a short distance, sometimes regularly over a period of time: [Vnp] *Can you ferry us across?* [Vnpr] *ferry goods to the mainland* ○ *ferry the children to and from school* [Vn, Vnpr] *planes ferrying food (to the refugees).*
■ **'ferry-boat** *n* a boat used as a ferry.
ferryman /'ferɪmən/ *n* (*pl* **-men** /-mən/) a person in charge of a FERRY, esp across a river: *shout for the ferryman.*
fertile /'fɜːtaɪl; *US* 'fɜːrtl/ *adj* **1** (of land or soil) that can produce good crops: *a fertile region of the country.* **2** (of plants or animals) that can produce fruit or young. **3** that produces or can produce good results: *a fertile partnership* ○ *The inner cities are fertile ground for army recruitment.* **4** (of a person's mind) full of new ideas; inventive (INVENT): *have a fertile imagination.* Compare INFERTILE, STERILE.
▸ **fertility** /fə'tɪləti/ *n* [U] the state or condition of being fertile: *the fertility of the soil* ○ *great fertility of mind.*
fertilize, -ise /'fɜːtəlaɪz/ *v* [Vn] **1** to introduce POLLEN into a plant so that it develops seed, or SPERM into an egg or a female animal so that a young animal, etc develops inside: *a fertilized egg/cell* ○ *Flowers are often fertilized by bees as they gather nectar.* **2** to make soil, etc more FERTILE(1) by adding a substance such as MANURE to it: *fertilize the garden.*
▸ **fertilization, -isation** /,fɜːtəlaɪ'zeɪʃn; *US* -lə'z-/ *n* [U]: *successful fertilization by the male.*
fertilizer, -iser *n* [C, U] a natural or artificial substance added to soil to make it more FERTILE(1): *chemical fertilizers* ○ *a bag of fertilizer* ○ *Get some more fertilizer for the garden.* Compare MANURE.
fervent /'fɜːvənt/ (also *fml* **fervid** /'fɜːvɪd/) *adj* showing strong or intense feelings; enthusiastic; passionate: *fervent desire/hope/wishes* ○ *a fervent admirer/believer/supporter.* ▸ **fervently** *adv: We fervently hope they will succeed.*
fervour (*US* **fervor**) /'fɜːvə(r)/ *n* [U] strength or intensity of feeling; enthusiasm: *speak with great fervour* ○ *religious/nationalistic/revolutionary fervour.*
fester /'festə(r)/ *v* **1** (of a cut or wound) to become infected and filled with yellow PUS: [V] *a festering sore.* **2** (of bad feelings, thoughts, etc) to become steadily worse, making one increasingly bitter(3) and angry: [V] *The issues raised by the controversy continue to fester.*
festival /'festɪvl/ *n* **1** a day or period of religious or other celebration: *Christmas and Easter are Christian festivals.* ○ *a festival atmosphere.* See also HARVEST FESTIVAL. **2** a series of performances of

F

music, drama, films, etc given regularly, esp once a year: *the Edinburgh Festival* ○ *a jazz festival.*

festive /ˈfestɪv/ *adj* of or suitable for a festival; bright and cheerful: *the festive season* (ie Christmas) ○ *The whole town is in festive mood.*

festivity /feˈstɪvəti/ *n* **1** [U] celebration; happiness and enjoyment: *The wedding was an occasion of great festivity.* **2 festivities** [pl] celebrations; happy and enjoyable events held in honour of sb/sth: *wedding festivities.*

festoon /feˈstuːn/ *n* a chain of flowers, coloured paper, lights, etc hung in a curve or loop, esp as a decoration.
▶ **festoon** *v* ~ sb/sth (with sth) (esp passive) to decorate or cover sb/sth with festoons of sth: [Vnpr] *a room festooned with cobwebs/paper streamers.* [also Vn].

feta (also **fetta**) /ˈfetə/ *n* [U] a white cheese made with sheep's milk, esp in Greece: *slices of feta* ○ *feta cheese.*

fetal ⇨ FOETUS.

fetch /fetʃ/ *v* **1** ~ sb/sth (for sb) (*esp Brit*) to go and find and bring back sb/sth: [Vn] *Fetch a doctor at once.* [Vnpr] *I have to fetch the children from school.* [Vnp] *The chair is in the garden — please fetch it in.* [Vnn, Vnpr] *Should I fetch you your coat/fetch your coat for you from upstairs?* **2** (of goods) to be sold for a price: [Vn] *The picture should fetch at least £2 000 at auction.* [Vn, Vnn] *Those old books won't fetch (you) much.* **3** (*infml*) to hit sb, esp with the hand: [Vnn] *She fetched him a terrific slap in the face.* **IDM fetch and ˈcarry (for sb)** to act like a servant for sb; to be busy with small duties: *He expects his daughter to fetch and carry for him all day.* **PHR V ˌfetch ˈup** (*Brit infml*) to arrive at a certain place or in a certain position, often by chance: *At lunch-time they all fetched up in the bar of the local pub.*

fetching /ˈfetʃɪŋ/ *adj* (*infml approv*) attractive: *a fetching smile* ○ *You look very fetching in that hat.* ▶ **fetchingly** *adv.*

fête /feɪt/ *n* an outdoor entertainment or sale, usu to raise money for a special purpose: *the school/village/church fête.*
▶ **fête** *v* (esp passive) to honour or entertain sb in a special way: [Vn-n] *be fêted as a great opera singer* [Vn] *The winner was fêted wherever she went.*

fetid (also **foetid**) /ˈfetɪd; *Brit also* ˈfiːtɪd/ *adj* smelling very unpleasant; stinking (STINK 1): *fetid air.*

fetish /ˈfetɪʃ/ *n* **1(a)** (*usu derog*) a thing to which more respect or attention is given than is normal or sensible: *He makes a fetish of his work.* ○ *She has a fetish about cleanliness.* (**b**) (*techn*) an object or activity that is necessary for or adds to an individual's sexual pleasure. **2** an object that certain people worship, esp because a spirit is believed to live in it. ▶ **fetishism** *n* [U] (*techn*): *magazines which cater to fetishism.* **fetishist** *n.*

fetlock /ˈfetlɒk/ *n* the part of a horse's leg above and behind the HOOF, where long hair grows out. ⇨ picture at HORSE.

fetter /ˈfetə(r)/ *n* (usu *pl*) **1** a chain put round a prisoner's feet to restrict movement: *He was kept in fetters.* **2** (*rhet*) a thing that restricts or hinders (HINDER) sb: *freed from the fetters of ignorance.*
▶ **fetter** *v* [Vn] **1** to put sb in fetters. **2** to restrict or HINDER sb in any way: *I hate being fettered by petty rules and regulations.*

fettle /ˈfetl/ *n* **IDM in fine, good, etc ˈfettle** fit and cheerful: *The team are all in excellent fettle.*

fetus ⇨ FOETUS.

feud /fjuːd/ *n* ~ (**between A and B**); ~ (**with sb**) a long and bitter quarrel between two people, families or groups: *a long-running feud between the two artists* ○ *Because of a family feud, he never spoke to his wife's parents for years.* See also BLOOD FEUD.

▶ **feud** *v* ~ (**with sb/sth**) to take part in a feud: [V] *feuding neighbours/factions* [Vpr] *The two tribes are always feuding (with each other) over land.*

feudal /ˈfjuːdl/ *adj* of or like the social system that existed during the Middle Ages in Europe. Under this system people received land and protection from a nobleman, and worked and fought for him in return: *the feudal system* ○ *feudal barons* ○ *The way some landowners treat their tenants today seems almost feudal.*
▶ **feudalism** /-dəlɪzəm/ *n* [U] the feudal system, or the attitudes and structure of this.

fever /ˈfiːvə(r)/ *n* **1** [C, U] an abnormally high body temperature, esp as a sign of illness: *He has a high fever.* ○ *Aspirin can reduce fever.* **2** [U] (esp in compounds) a specified disease in which a fever occurs: *yellow/typhoid/rheumatic/scarlet fever.* See also HAY FEVER. **3(a)** [sing] a state of nervous excitement: *He waited for her arrival in a fever of impatience.* (**b**) [U] (*infml*) (esp in compounds) great enthusiasm for or excitement about sth: *election fever* ○ *World Cup fever has gripped the country.*
▶ **fevered** *adj* [attrib] **1** affected by or suffering from a fever: *She cooled his fevered brow.* **2** highly excited: *a fevered imagination* ○ *fevered negotiations.*
feverish /ˈfiːvərɪʃ/ *adj* **1** having a fever; caused by or accompanied by a fever: *feverish dreams* ○ *The child's body felt feverish.* **2** quick or excited: *feverish activity* ○ *with feverish haste.* **feverishly** *adv* in a very quick or excited way: *searching feverishly for a cigarette.*
■ **ˈfever pitch** *n* [U] a very high level of excitement: *His anxiety reached fever pitch.* ○ *The crowd had been roused to fever pitch by the drama of the game.*

few1 /fjuː/ *indef det, adj* [usu attrib] (**-er, -est**) (used with *pl* countable *ns* and a *pl* *v*) not many: *Few people live to be 100.* ○ *a man/woman of few words* (ie one who speaks very little) ○ *There are fewer cars parked outside than yesterday.* ○ *The police have very few clues to the murderer's identity.* ○ *The few houses we have seen are in terrible condition.* ○ *There were too few people at the meeting.* ○ *The last few years have been very difficult.* ○ *I visit my parents every few days/weeks/months* (ie once in a few days, etc). ○ *Accidents at work are few.* (Compare: *There are few accidents at work.*) ⇨ note at LESS, MUCH1.
IDM ˌfew and ˌfar beˈtween not frequent, with long periods of waiting involved: *Buses in this area were few and far between.* ○ *The sunny intervals we were promised have been few and far between.*
▶ **few** *indef pron* not many people, things or places (**a**) (referring back): *Of the 150 passengers, few escaped injury.* ○ *Few can deny the impact of his leadership.* ○ *Hundreds of new songs are recorded each week but few (of them) get into the charts.* (**b**) (referring forward): *The few who came to the concert really enjoyed it.* ○ *We saw few of the sights as we were only there for two hours.* ○ *As few as five people arrived on time.* **fewer** *indef pron: Fewer than 50 students applied for the course.* ○ *She had no fewer than 13 children.*
the few *n* [pl *v*] a small group of people; the MINORITY(2): *Real power belongs to the few.* Compare THE MANY.

few2 /fjuː/ **a few** *indef det* (used with *pl* countable *ns* and a *pl* *v*) a small number of; some: *a few letters* ○ *a few days ago* ○ *He asked us a few questions.* ○ *We're having a few people for lunch.* ○ *Only a few* (ie Not many) *students were awarded distinctions.* ⇨ note at MUCH1.
▶ **a few** *indef pron* a small number of people, things or places; some (**a**) (referring back): *She's written many books but I've only read a few (of them).* (**b**) (referring forward): *A few of the seats were empty.* ○ *I recognized a few of the other guests.* **IDM a good ˈfew**; **quite a ˈfew**; (*fml*) **not a ˈfew** a considerable

number; a lot; many: *There were a good few copies sold on the first day.* ○ *Quite a few of my friends are vegetarian.* ¹**have a few** (usu in the present perfect) to drink enough alcohol to make one drunk or almost drunk: *I've had a few* (ie a few glasses of beer, wine, etc) *already, actually.* ○ *She looks as if she's* ¹*had a few.*

a few *adv* a small but important number: *a few too many mistakes* ○ *Perhaps you could give me a few more details of the scheme.*

fey /feɪ/ *adj* charming in a strange, VAGUE(1) or rather silly way: *One of the guests was a slightly fey romantic novelist.*

fez /fez/ *n* (*pl* **fezzes**) a red hat with a flat top and a TASSEL but no BRIM(2). ⇨ picture at HAT.

ff *abbr* **1** (written after the number of a page, line, etc) and the following pages, lines, etc: *See pp 10 ff.* **2** (*music*) very loudly (Italian *fortissimo*). Compare PP 3.

fiancé (*fem* **fiancée**) /fɪˈɒnseɪ; *US* ˌfiːɑːnˈseɪ/ *n* a man or woman to whom one is engaged to be married: *her fiancé* ○ *his fiancée.*

fiasco /fɪˈæskəʊ/ *n* (*pl* **-os**; *US* also **-oes**) a complete and ridiculous failure: *the Suez fiasco of 1956* ○ *The party turned into/was a complete fiasco.*

fiat /ˈfiːæt, ˈfaɪæt/ *n* [C, U] (*fml*) an official order given by sb in authority: *Prices have been fixed by government fiat.*

fib /fɪb/ *n* (*infml*) a statement that is not true, esp about sth unimportant; a lie: *Stop telling fibs.*
▶ **fib** *v* (**-bb-**) [V] to say things that are not true. **fibber** *n*: *You little fibber!*

fibre (*US* **fiber**) /ˈfaɪbə(r)/ *n* **1** [U] the part of food that one's body cannot DIGEST²(1a) but which helps the body to function well: *dietary fibre* ○ *Dried fruits are especially high in fibre.* **2** [C] a material made from a mass of thin threads: *nylon and other man-made fibres.* See also GLASS FIBRE. **3** [C] any of the thin threads of which many animal and plant tissues are formed: *cotton/wood/nerve/muscle fibres.* **4** [U] (*fml*) strong character: *a woman of strong moral fibre.*
▶ **fibrous** /ˈfaɪbrəs/ *adj* like or made of fibres: *fibrous tissue.*
■ **fibre** ¹**optics** *n* [U] the sending of information by means of INFRARED light signals along a thin glass fibre: *fibre-optic cables.*

fibreglass (*US* ¹**fiber-**) /ˈfaɪbəɡlɑːs; *US* -ɡlæs/ (also **glass fibre**) *n* [U] a material made from glass fibres (FIBRE) and RESIN(2), used for keeping heat in a building and in making cars, boats, etc: *a fibreglass racing yacht.*

fickle /ˈfɪkl/ *adj* (*usu derog*) **1** often changing: *The weather here is notoriously fickle.* ○ *the fickle world of fashion.* **2** (of a person) not faithful or loyal: *a fickle friend.* ▶ **fickleness** *n* [U]: *the fickleness of the English climate.*

fiction /ˈfɪkʃn/ *n* **1** [U] a type of literature describing imaginary events and people, not real ones: *works of popular fiction* ○ *She writes historical/romantic fiction.* ○ *Truth is often stranger than fiction.* Compare NON-FICTION. See also SCIENCE FICTION. **2** [C] a thing that is invented or imagined and is not true: *The government is trying to maintain the fiction that the country's economy is improving.*
▶ **fictional** /-ʃənl/ *adj* of fiction; told as or occurring in a story: *fictional characters* ○ *a fictional account of life on a farm.*

fictionalize, -ise /ˈfɪkʃənəlaɪz/ *v* to write about a true event as if it were fiction or in the style of a story, inventing some of the details, characters, etc: [Vn] *a fictionalized account of her childhood.*

fictitious /fɪkˈtɪʃəs/ *adj* imagined or invented; not real: *The account he gives of his childhood is quite fictitious.* ○ *All the places and characters in my novel are entirely fictitious.*

fiddle /ˈfɪdl/ *n* **1** (*infml*) a VIOLIN. **2** (*Brit sl*) a thing done dishonestly; a SWINDLE: ¹*tax fiddles* ○ *The stewardess lost her job because of an alleged* ¹*drinks fiddle.* **IDM** **be on the** ¹**fiddle** (*sl*) to behave dishonestly. **fit as a fiddle** ⇨ FIT¹. **play second** ¹**fiddle (to sb/sth)** to be treated as less important than another person, activity, etc: *I have no intention of playing second fiddle to the new director, so I've resigned.*
▶ **fiddle** *v* **1** ~ **(about/around) with sth** [Vpr] also Vp] **(a)** to move sth a little or touch sth often: *She fiddled with the things on her desk to avoid having to look at him.* **(b)** to try to make sth work by changing its controls, by moving parts of it, etc: [Vpr] *He was fiddling with the remote control.* [also Vp]. **2** to change sth dishonestly in order to get money, a position, etc for oneself: [Vn] *They won the contract by fiddling the figures.* ○ *He was accused of fiddling his expenses.* ○ ~ **about/around** to spend time in a way that does not achieve any positive results: [Vp] *Stop fiddling about and do some work.* **fiddler** /ˈfɪdlə(r)/ *n* a person who plays the VIOLIN.
¹**fiddling** /ˈfɪdlɪŋ/ *adj* [usu attrib] (*infml*) unimportant; TRIVIAL: *fiddling little details.*

fiddly /ˈfɪdli/ *adj* (*infml*) small and awkward to do or use: *Changing a fuse is one of those fiddly jobs I hate.* ○ *The dress is attractive but the buttons are far too fiddly.*

fidelity /fɪˈdeləti/ *n* [U] **1** ~ **(to sb/sth)** **(a)** loyalty; a faithful attitude towards sth: *fidelity to one's principles/religion/leader.* **(b)** loyalty towards one's husband or wife in not having any other sexual partner: *Marital fidelity is not valued as highly as it once was.* **2** (*fml*) accuracy in relation to sth else: *fidelity to the text of the play* ○ *translate sth with the greatest fidelity.* See also HIGH FIDELITY.

fidget /ˈfɪdʒɪt/ *v* ~ **(with sth)** to make constant small movements, in a way that annoys other people: [V] *Stop fidgeting and sit still!* [Vpr] *She was fidgeting anxiously with her cardigan buttons.*
▶ **fidget** *n* a person who fidgets: *You're such a fidget!*
fidgety *adj* unable to remain still or quiet; often fidgeting: *a fidgety child.*

field¹ /fiːld/ *n* **1** [C] an area of land, usu enclosed by a fence, hedge, etc, used for animals or crops: *working in the fields* ○ *a ploughed field* ○ *a field of wheat.* **2** (usu in compounds) an open space used for a specified purpose: *a* ¹*baseball/*¹*cricket field* ○ *a* ¹*landing field* ○ *men dying on the field of battle.* ⇨ picture at FOOTBALL. See also BATTLEFIELD, PLAYING-FIELD. **3** [C] (usu in compounds) **(a)** a wide area of sth: *an* ¹*ice-field* (eg around the North Pole). **(b)** (esp in compounds) an area from which minerals, etc are obtained: ¹*coalfields* ○ ¹*gold-fields* ○ *a new* ¹*oilfield.* **4** [C] the range of a subject, an activity or an interest: *in the field of politics/science/music* ○ *He's a very big name in his field.* ○ *That is outside my field* (ie not among the subjects I know about). **5** [C] an area or a space within which a specified force can be felt: *a strong magnetic* ¹*field* ○ *the earth's gravitational* ¹*field* (ie the space in which the earth's gravity has an effect). **6** [Gp] (*sport*) **(a)** all the people or animals competing in an event: *The field includes three world record holders.* ○ *She's a long way ahead of the rest of the field.* **(b)** (in cricket and baseball) the team that is not batting (BAT¹ *v* 1b), thought of with regard to their positions on the field: *bowling to a defensive field.* **IDM** **hold the** ¹**field (against sb/sth)** not to be replaced by sb/sth; to remain dominant: *Einstein's ideas on physics have held the field for years.* **play the** ¹**field** (*infml*) to avoid giving oneself completely to one person, activity, etc. **take the** ¹**field** (in sport) to go onto the playing area.
■ ¹**field-day** *n* **1** a day or period of great excitement and activity: *Whenever there's a government scandal*

the newspapers **have a field-day. 2** a day of outdoor scientific study. **3** (*US*) a sports day at a school, college, etc.

'field events *n* [pl] the sports done by athletes (ATHLETE 1) that are not races, eg jumping, throwing the JAVELIN, etc. Compare TRACK EVENTS.

'field-glasses *n* [pl] = BINOCULARS.

'field hockey *n* [U] (*US*) = HOCKEY.

,Field 'Marshal *n* (the title of) an officer of the highest rank in the British Army. ⇨ App 6.

,field of 'vision *n* (*pl* fields of vision) the total amount of space that can be seen from a particular point, without moving: *obstruct sb's field of vision.*

'field sports *n* [pl] outdoor sports, eg hunting, fishing and shooting.

'field-test *v* to test sth by using it in the conditions for which it is meant: [Vn] *The equipment has all been field-tested.* **'field test** *n*: *undergo rigorous field tests.*

'field trip *n* a journey made by a group of people in order to study sth in a practical way: *We went on a geology field trip.*

field² /fiːld/ *v* **1(a)** (in cricket and baseball) to stand ready to pick up or catch and throw back the ball: [V] *John's fielding just now, not bowling.* **(b)** (in cricket, etc) to pick up or catch and throw back the ball: [V] *He fields well.* [Vn] *She fielded the ball.* **2 (a)** to select sb to play in a game of football, hockey, cricket, etc: [Vn] *They're fielding a very strong side this season.* **(b)** (of a political party) to give official support to a candidate in an election: [Vn] *The Democrats fielded 48 fewer candidates than last time.* **3** to deal successfully with a series of questions, etc: [Vn] *The minister fielded all the questions about his personal life.* ▸ **'fielder** *n* = FIELDSMAN. ⇨ picture at CRICKET¹.

fieldsman /ˈfiːldzmən/ *n* (*pl* -men /-mən/) (in cricket, etc) a member of the team that is not batting (BAT¹ *v* 1b).

fieldwork /ˈfiːldwɜːk/ *n* [U] practical work done outside the school, office, etc. ▸ **'fieldworker** *n*.

fiend /fiːnd/ *n* **1** an evil spirit; a devil: *the fiends of hell.* **2(a)** a very cruel or unpleasant person. **(b)** a person who causes trouble or annoyance: *Stop teasing her, you little fiend!* **3** (*infml*) a person who is very fond of or interested in sth specified: *a ,fresh-'air fiend.*

▸ **fiendish** *adj* **1** fierce or cruel: *a fiendish temper.* **2** (*infml*) extremely bad, unpleasant or difficult: *a fiendish problem.* **3** (*infml*) clever and complicated: *a fiendish plot/idea.* **fiendishly** *adv* (*infml*) very; extremely: *a fiendishly difficult puzzle.*

fierce /fɪəs/ *adj* (-r, -st) **1** violent and angry: *fierce dogs/winds* ○ *the scene of fierce fighting* ○ *look fierce/ have a fierce look* ○ *launch a fierce attack on sb.* **2(a)** intense; strong: *fierce concentration/loyalty/hatred* ○ *Competition between rival companies is becoming fiercer.* ○ *His wife is his fiercest critic.* **(b)** strong in a way that is unpleasant or that cannot be controlled: *fierce heat.* ▸ **fiercely** *adv*: *fiercely competitive/ independent/proud* ○ *fiercely critical of sb.* **fierceness** *n* [U].

fiery /ˈfaɪəri/ *adj* [usu attrib] **1(a)** like or consisting of fire: *fiery red hair* ○ *a fiery glow in the sky.* **(b)** producing a burning sensation in the throat: *a fiery Mexican dish* ○ *fiery liquor.* **2(a)** quickly or easily becoming angry: *a fiery temper* ○ *He's a fiery individual.* **(b)** (of words, etc) intense; passionate: *a fiery speech.* **(c)** full of high spirits: *a fiery horse.*

fiesta /fiˈestə/ *n* a festival, esp a religious one in countries where Spanish is spoken.

fife /faɪf/ *n* a small high-pitched musical instrument like a FLUTE, used with drums in military music: *a fife and drum band.*

fifteen /ˌfɪfˈtiːn/ *n*, *pron*, *det* **1** the number 15.

2 a team of Rugby Union players: *He's in the first fifteen.* ▸ **fifteenth** /ˌfɪfˈtiːnθ/ *n*, *pron*, *det.* For further guidance on how *fifteen* and *fifteenth* are used, see the examples at *five* and *fifth.*

fifth /fɪfθ/ *pron*, *det*, *adv* 5th: *Today is the fifth (of March).* ○ *She led for most of the race, but finished fifth.* ○ *Princess Beatrice is (the) fifth in line to the throne.* ○ *the fifth book on the list* ○ *This is the fifth day of the conference.* ○ *in the fifth century BC* ○ *Edward V* (ie 'Edward the Fifth') ○ *Thailand's fifth-largest bank.*

▸ **fifth** *n* each of five equal parts of sth: *He gave her a fifth of the total amount.* ○ *They divided the money into fifths and took one fifth each.*

fifthly *adv* in the fifth position or place.

■ **,fifth 'column** *n* an organized group of people working secretly for the enemy within a country at war.

fifty /ˈfɪfti/ *n*, *pron*, *det* **1** the number 50. **2 the fifties** [pl] the numbers, years or degrees of temperature from 50 to 59: *The total amount is somewhere in the fifties.* ○ *She was born in the fifties* (ie in the 1950s). ○ *'How warm is it today?' 'It's in the (high/low) fifties.'* **IDM** **in one's 'fifties** between the ages of 50 and 60: *She's in her early/mid/late fifties.*

▸ **fiftieth** /ˈfɪftiəθ/ *n*, *pron*, *det* 50th.

■ **,fifty 'cents** (also **50¢**) *n* (*US*) [pl] a half of one dollar.

,fifty-'fifty *adj*, *adv* (*infml*) shared or sharing equally between two: *divide the profits on a fifty-fifty basis* (ie take equal shares) ○ *a fifty-fifty chance of winning* (ie an equal chance of winning or losing) ○ *We went fifty-fifty on the meal* (ie shared the cost equally).

,fifty 'pence (also **,fifty 'p, 50p**) *n* (*Brit*) **(a)** [pl] 50 new pence: *That'll be fifty pence, please.* **(b)** [C] a coin worth 50 new pence: *Put a fifty p in the machine.* For further guidance on how *fifty* and *fiftieth* are used, see the examples at *five* and *fifth*.

fig¹ /fɪɡ/ *n* a soft sweet fruit, full of small seeds and often eaten dried: *a fig-tree.* **IDM** **not care/give a 'fig (for sb/sth)** not to care at all about sth; to consider sb/sth as having no value or importance: *I don't give a fig what others think of me.*

■ **'fig-leaf** *n* a leaf of a fig-tree, traditionally used for covering the sex organs of naked bodies in drawings, statues, etc.

fig² *abbr* **1** figurative(ly). **2** figure¹(7a): *See fig 3.*

fight¹ /faɪt/ *v* (*pt*, *pp* fought /fɔːt/) **1** to struggle against sb/sth using physical force, in a war, battle, etc: [V] *soldiers training to fight* ○ *Do stop fighting, boys!* [V.to inf] *He always fights to win* (ie tries his hardest to win). ○ *She'll fight like a tiger to protect her children.* [Vpr] *The two dogs were fighting over a bone.* ○ *Britain fought with/alongside* (ie on the same side as) *France against Germany in the last war.* ○ *Have you been fighting with* (ie against) *your brother again?* [Vp] *Though heavily outnumbered they fought on bravely.* [Vn] *He fought many opponents throughout his boxing career.* **2** to take part in a battle, contest, etc: [Vn] *fight a war/a duel/an election campaign* ○ *The government has to fight several by-elections in the coming months.* **3 ~ (against)** sth to try hard to overcome, destroy or prevent sth: [Vpr, Vn] *fight (against) disease/poverty/oppression/ ignorance* [Vn] *fight a fire* ○ *We will fight the decision vigorously.* **4 ~ (about/over sth)** to quarrel or argue: [Vpr] *It's a trivial matter and not worth fighting about.* [also V]. **IDM** **a ,fighting 'chance** a small but distinct chance of success if a great effort is made: *There is a fighting chance that we can still save the old church from demolition.* **fighting 'talk/ 'words** a statement or challenge showing that one is ready to fight very hard for sth. **fight 'shy of sth** to be unwilling to do or become involved in sth; to avoid sth: *He was unhappy in his job for years but*

always fought shy of admitting it. **PHR V** ,fight
'**back** to fight with new force and strength; to show
resistance: *After a disastrous first half we fought
back to level the scores.* ○ *Don't let them bully me.
Fight back!* ,fight sth '**back**/'**down** to suppress feelings, etc: *fight back tears/a sense of disgust.* '**fight
for sth** to try very hard to obtain or achieve sth:
fight for one's freedom/independence/rights ○ *She is
now fighting for her life in hospital.* ,fight sb/sth
'**off** to resist sb/sth by fighting against them/it:
They had to fight off repeated enemy attacks. ○ *fight
off a cold/feeling of tiredness.* ,fight sth '**out** to settle
an argument, a dispute, etc by fighting: *I can't help
them to resolve their quarrel — they must fight it out
between them.*

▶ **fighter** *n* **1** a person who fights, esp in war or in
sport: *a professional fighter.* See also FIRE-FIGHTER,
FREEDOM FIGHTER. **2** (*usu approv*) a person who does
not admit defeat without a hard struggle against sth:
She won't give up easily: she's a real fighter. **3** a fast
military aircraft designed to attack other aircraft: *a
jet* '*fighter* ○ '*fighter bases/planes* ○ *a* '*fighter pilot.*
fighting *n* [U]: *outbreaks of street fighting* ○ *reports
of heavy/fierce fighting around the capital.*

fight² /fait/ *n* **1** [C] an act of fighting or struggling: *a
fight between two dogs* ○ *a world title fight* ○ *He
accidentally got into a fist fight.* ○ *continue the fight
against poverty/crime/disease* ○ *a fight for survival* ○
the fight to protect endangered species ○ *The team put
up a good fight* (ie played hard and well) *but were
finally beaten.* ⇨ note at ARGUMENT. **2** [U] the desire
or ability to fight or resist; determination: *In spite of
many defeats, they still had plenty of fight left in
them.* ○ *Losing their leader took all the fight out of
them.* **IDM** **a fight to the** '**finish** a struggle, etc that
continues until one side has clearly won. **pick a
fight/quarrel** ⇨ PICK¹.

figment /'figmənt/ *n* **IDM** **a figment of sb's
imagi'nation** a thing that is not real but only imagined: *I don't know whether she's really ill or
whether it's just a figment of her imagination.*

figurative /'figərətɪv/ *adj* **1** (abbreviated as *fig* in
this dictionary) (of a word, phrase, etc) used in an
imaginative or metaphorical (METAPHOR) way that is
different from the usual or basic meaning: *'He exploded with rage' shows a figurative use of the verb
'explode'.* Compare LITERAL 1b. **2** (of paintings, art,
etc) representing people, etc as they are: *a figurative
animal sculpture.* ▶ **figuratively** *adv*: *He was
unique, literally and figuratively a prince among
men.*

figure¹ /'figə(r); *US* 'figjər/ *n* **1** [C esp *pl*] a specific
amount, esp one given in official information, re-
ports, etc by an organization: *the latest trade/
unemployment figures* ○ *monthly sales figures* ○
*Viewing figures for the series have dropped dramatic-
ally.* **2** [C] a written symbol for a number, esp 0 to 9:
Write the figure '7' on the board. ○ *He has an income
of six figures/a six-figure income* (eg £100000 or
more). See also DOUBLE FIGURES. **3** **figures** [pl]
(*infml*) ARITHMETIC: *Are you good at figures?* ○ *I'm
afraid I have no head for figures.* **4** [C] (**a**) the
shape of the human body, esp when considered to be
attractive: *She's always had a good figure.* ○ *You need
to watch your figure* (ie take care not to get fat). (**b**)
the human body in terms of its general appearance
or what it represents: *The nurse was a reassuring
figure in her starched white uniform.* ○ *Help was at
hand in the figure of a burly police constable.* (**c**) a
person seen from a distance or not clearly: *I saw a
figure approaching through the gloom.* ○ *No one noticed the sleeping figure in the corner.* **5** [C] a person
of the specified type: *a key/leading figure in the
mining industry* ○ *a cult figure* ○ *The event was
attended by many public figures.* See also FATHER-
FIGURE. **6** [C] a representation of a person or an

animal in drawing, painting, etc: *The central figure
in the painting is the artist's daughter.* ○ *a bronze
figure of a horse.* **7** [C] (**a**) a diagram or an illustration: *The figure on page 22 shows a political map of
Africa.* (**b**) a shape enclosed by lines or surfaces: *a
five-sided figure.* **8** [C] a pattern or series of movements: *The skater executed a perfect set of figures.* ○
'*figure-skating.* **IDM** **be/become a figure of** '**fun** to
be/begin to be laughed at by other people. **cut a
fine, poor, sorry, etc** '**figure** to have a fine, etc
appearance. **facts and figures** ⇨ FACT. **in round
figures/numbers** ⇨ ROUND¹. **put a figure on sth**
to give a price or an exact number for sth: *It's
impossible to put a figure on the number of homeless
people in London.* **single figures** ⇨ SINGLE.

■ ,**figure of** '**eight** (*US* also ,**figure** '**eight**) *n* a thing
that resembles the number 8 in shape: *skating fig-
ures of eight on the ice.*

,**figure of** '**speech** *n* a word or phrase used for
vivid or dramatic effect: *I didn't mean she really has
her head in the sand — it's just a figure of speech.*

figure² /'figə(r); *US* 'figjər/ *v* **1** ~ **in/on sth** to appear
or be mentioned: [Vpr] *This character figures prominently in many of her novels.* ○ *He's figured in
countless public debates on the issue.* ○ *It doesn't
figure high on my list of priorities.* [also Vadv]. **2** (**a**)
to think sth; to calculate: [V.*that*] *I figured (that) you
wouldn't come.* [Vn] *It's what I figured.* (**b**) (used
with *it* or *that*) (*infml*) to be likely or able to be
understood: [V] *'John isn't here today.'* '*That figures, he didn't look very well yesterday.'* **PHR V**
'**figure on sth/doing sth** (*US*) to include sth in
one's plans; to rely on sth: *I figure on being in New
York in January.* ,**figure sb/sth** '**out** **1** to understand sb/sth by thinking about them/it: *I've never
been able to figure him out.* ○ *I can't figure out why he
quit his job.* ○ *Have you figured out what's wrong
with your car?* **2** to discover sth by using ARITH-
METIC; to calculate sth: *Have you figured out how
much the trip will cost?*

figurehead /'figəhed/ *n*
1 a large wooden statue,
usu representing a hu-
man figure, placed at the
front end of a ship. ⇨
picture. **2** a person in a
high position but with-
out real authority: *The
elected head of state is a
figurehead only — the
real power lies elsewhere.*

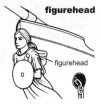
figurehead
figurehead

figurine /'figəri:n; *US* ,figjə'ri:n/ *n* a small ornamental statue, esp of a person.

filament /'filəmənt/ *n* **1** a very thin strand, like a
thread. **2** a thin wire in a light-bulb (LIGHT¹) that
glows when electricity is passed through it. ⇨ picture at BULB.

filch /filtʃ/ *v* (*infml*) to steal sth, esp sth of small
value: [Vn] *Who's filched my pencil?*

file¹ /fail/ *n* **1**(**a**) any of various types of drawer,
shelf, holder, cover, box, etc, usu with a wire or
metal rod for keeping loose papers together and in
order, so that they can be found easily: *a stack of
files* ○ *I bought a file for my letters.* (**b**) a file and its
contents: *top secret police files* ○ *a file of cuttings* ○
Where's the customer order file? ○ *have/open/keep a
confidential file on each member of staff.* **2** an organized collection of related data or material in a
computer: *I can't access/update the file on your company because I've forgotten the code.* **IDM** **on** '**file / on
the** '**files** kept in a file: *We have all your particulars
on file.*

▶ **file** /fail/ *v* **1** ~ **sth (away)** to place sth in order
in a file, so that it can be easily referred to when
needed: [Vnp] *I keep all my letters filed away in a
drawer.* [Vn] *File these contracts for me please,*

Emma. **2** to send sth so that it can be officially recorded: [Vn] *file a complaint.*

■ **¹filing cabinet** (*Brit*) (*US* **¹file cabinet**) *n* a piece of office furniture with deep drawers for storing files.

¹filing clerk (*US* **¹file clerk**) *n* a person who files letters, etc and does general office tasks.

file² /faɪl/ *n* a line of people or things one behind the other. **IDM** **(in) Indian/single ¹file** (in) one line, one behind the other: *walking in single file along the narrow path.* See also THE RANK AND FILE.

▶ **file** *v* ~ **in, out, off, past, etc** to march or walk in the specified direction in a single line: [Vpr] *The men filed onto the parade-ground and past the general.* [Vp] *The children filed silently in.*

file³ /faɪl/ *n* a metal tool with a rough surface for cutting or shaping hard substances or for making them smooth. See also NAIL-FILE.

▶ **file** *v* to cut or shape sth or to make sth smooth with a file: [Vpr] *file through one's prison bars* [Vn, Vn-adj] *file one's fingernails (smooth)* [also Vnpr]. **PHRV** **¹file sth ¹down** to make sth smooth and smaller in size by using a file. **filings** /ˈfaɪlɪŋz/ *n* [pl] the small pieces removed by a file: *iron filings.*

filial /ˈfɪliəl/ *adj* [usu attrib] of or expected from a son or daughter: *filial duty/affection.*

filibuster /ˈfɪlɪbʌstə(r)/ *n* (*esp US*) a long speech made in order to delay or prevent the making of decisions, eg in a parliament. ▶ **filibuster** *v* (*esp US*): [V] *filibustering tactics.*

filigree /ˈfɪlɪɡriː/ *n* [U] fine ornamental work using gold, silver or copper wire: *a filigree brooch.*

filings ⇨ FILE³.

fill¹ /fɪl/ *v* **1(a)** ~ **sth (with sth)**; ~ **sth (for sb)** to make sth full of sth; to occupy all of the space in sth: [Vnpr] *fill a hole with earth/a tank with petrol/a hall with people* ∘ *Please fill this glass for me.* ∘ *The tankard was filled to the brim.* ∘ *The air was filled with a high-pitched whistling.* ∘ *(fig) I was filled with admiration for his bravery.* [Vn] *Smoke filled the room.* ∘ *fill a vacuum/a void* ∘ *aim to fill a gap in the market* ∘ *The wind filled the sails* (ie made them swell out). [Vn-adj] *fill a bucket full of water* [also Vnn]. **(b)** ~ **(with sth)** to become full: [V] *The hall soon filled.* [Vpr] *Her eyes suddenly filled with tears.* ∘ *The sails filled with wind.* **2** ~ **sth (with sth)** to block a hole, gap, etc: [Vn] *The dentist filled two of my teeth.* [Vnpr] *I must fill that crack in the wall with plaster.* See also FILLING. **3 (a)** to hold a position: [Vn] *She fills the post satisfactorily* (ie performs her duties well). **(b)** to appoint sb to a position: [Vn] *The vacancy has already been filled.* **IDM** **fill/fit the bill** ⇨ BILL¹. **fill sb's shoes** to take over sb's function, duties, etc and perform them in a satisfactory way. **PHRV** **¹fill ¹in (for sb)** to take sb's place for a short time: *My partner is on holiday this week so I'm filling in (for him).* **¹fill ¹in 1** (*US* also **¹fill sth ¹out**) to add what is necessary to make sth complete: *fill in an application form* (ie write one's name and other details required) ∘ *To order, fill in the coupon on p 54.* **2** to fill sth completely: *The hole has been filled in.* **3** to spend time with waiting for sth: *He filled in the rest of the day watching television.* **¹fill sb ¹in on sth)** to give sb full details about sth: *Can you fill me in on what has been happening?* **¹fill ¹out** to become larger, rounder or fatter: *Her cheeks began to fill out.* ∘ *He used to be a very thin child but he's filled out a lot recently.* **¹fill sth ¹out** ⇨ FILL STH IN 1. **¹fill (sth) ¹up** to become or make sth completely full: *The gutter has filled up with mud.* ∘ *fill up the tank with oil.*

▶ **filler** *n* [U,C] a substance used to fill a hole in sth or to increase the size of sth. **¹filler cap** *n* a cap for covering the pipe through which petrol is put into a motor vehicle.

¹filling-station *n* = PETROL STATION.

fill² /fɪl/ *n* **1** [C] the amount needed to fill sth: *a fill of tobacco/petrol/oil.* **2** [U] one's ~ **(of sth/sb)** (*fml*) **(a)** as much as one can eat or drink. **(b)** as much as one can tolerate: *She felt she had had her fill of entertaining and needed a rest.*

fillet /ˈfɪlɪt; *US* fɪˈleɪ/ *n* [C,U] a piece of meat or fish without bones: *plaice fillets* ∘ *a/some fillet steak.*

▶ **fillet** *v* to cut meat or fish into fillets: [Vn] *grilled filleted sole.*

filling /ˈfɪlɪŋ/ *n* **1** [C] **(a)** the process of using a substance to fill a hole in a tooth: *I had to have two fillings at the dentist's today.* **(b)** this substance in one tooth: *One of my fillings came out this morning.* **2** [C,U] food put between slices of bread to make a sandwich, or between layers of cake, etc: *pie fillings* ∘ *a cake with jam filling.*

fillip /ˈfɪlɪp/ *n* a thing that stimulates or encourages sth; a BOOST *n(2)*: *an advertising campaign to give a much-needed fillip to sales.*

filly /ˈfɪli/ *n* a young female horse. Compare COLT 1, MARE 1.

film¹ /fɪlm/ *n* **1** [C] (*esp Brit*) a story, etc recorded as a set of moving pictures to be shown on television or at the cinema; a MOVIE: *Have you seen the new 'Star Trek' film?* ∘ *my favourite horror film* ∘ *an international film festival* ∘ *a film crew/producer/critic* ∘ *a feature film* ∘ *My cousin is in films* (ie works in the film industry). **2** [C,U] a roll or sheet of thin flexible plastic that is sensitive to light, for use in photography: *She put a new film in her camera.* ∘ *expose/develop 50 feet of film.* ⇨ picture at CAMERA. **3** [C usu *sing*] ~ **(of sth)** a thin covering on or over sth: *a film of dust* ∘ *a film of oil on water* ∘ *A film of mist lay over the fields.*

▶ **filmy** *adj* [usu attrib] thin and almost transparent: *a filmy cotton blouse.*

■ **¹film-maker** *n* (*esp Brit*) a person who makes films for television and the cinema.

¹film star (*esp Brit*) (also *esp US* **movie star**) *n* a well-known cinema actor.

film² /fɪlm/ *v* to make a film¹(1) of a scene, story, etc: [Vn] *They're filming a new comedy.* ∘ *A scene went wrong during the filming of 'Death Wish III'.* [Vn.ing] *The TV crew filmed the candidates speaking in the town square.* [V] *They've been filming on location for six months.* **PHRV** **¹film ¹over** to become covered with a thin layer of sth: *Her eyes filmed over with tears.*

Filofax /ˈfaɪləʊfæks/ *n* (*propr*) a DIARY with pages that can be moved around, for recording information in as well as for making notes of appointments, etc.

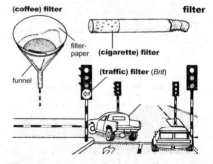

(coffee) filter   filter

filter-paper   (cigarette) filter

(traffic) filter (*Brit*)

funnel

filter /ˈfɪltə(r)/ *n* **1** a device containing paper, sand, cloth, etc that is used to hold back certain materials in a liquid or gas passed through it: *an ¹oil filter* ∘ *¹coffee filter* ∘ *filter-paper* ∘ *I only smoke cigarettes with filters.* ∘ *Change the filter in your water-filter jug every two weeks.* ⇨ picture. **2** a screen that allows light only of a particular WAVELENGTH to pass through: *I took this picture with a red filter.* **3** (*Brit*) a device that gives a signal to show that traffic may turn left while other traffic waiting to go straight ahead or turn right is still stopped by a red traffic-light (TRAFFIC). ⟶ picture.

▶ **filter** *v* **1** to pass liquid, light, etc through a filter, esp to make it pure: [Vn] *All drinking-water must be filtered.* See also FILTRATION. **2** ~ **in**, **out**, **through**, **etc** (**a**) to pass or flow slowly or in small quantities in a specified direction: [Vp, Vpr] *Light was filtering through (the curtains).* [Vpr] *The villagers filtered out of the room.* (**b**) to become known gradually: [Vp] *The news of the defeat started to filter 'through.* [also Vpr]. **3** [V] (*Brit*) (of traffic) to turn left while other traffic waiting to go straight ahead or turn right is stopped by a red traffic-light (TRAFFIC).

■ **'filter tip** *n* a cigarette with a filter for smoke at one end. **'filter-tipped** *adj*.

filth /fɪlθ/ *n* [U] **1** disgusting dirt: *the stench and filth of the prison.* **2** very rude and offensive words, literature, magazines, etc: *How can you read such filth?*

▶ **filthy** *adj* (**-ier, -iest**) **1**(**a**) dirty in a disgusting way: *a beggar dressed in filthy rags.* (**b**) very rude and offensive; OBSCENE: *filthy language.* **2** (*infml*) (esp of weather) very unpleasant: *Isn't it a filthy day?*
filthy *adv* **1** in a filthy way: *filthy 'dirty.* **2** (*infml*) very: *filthy 'rich.*

filtration /fɪl'treɪʃn/ *n* [U] the process of filtering (FILTER *v*) liquid, etc.

fin /fɪn/ *n* **1** a thin flat part of a fish that sticks out from its body, used for swimming and steering. ⟶ picture at FISH¹. **2** a part shaped like a fin on an aircraft, a car, etc for helping to keep it STABLE¹(a): *tail fins.* ⟶ picture at AIRCRAFT.

final /'faɪnl/ *adj* **1** [attrib] at the end; coming last: *the final chapter of a book* ○ *his final act as party leader* ○ *When the final whistle went, the score was 6 all.* ○ *The project is in its final stages.* **2** [usu pred] (of a decision, etc) that cannot be argued with or changed: *The referee's ruling is final.* ○ *I'm not coming, and that's final!* ○ *I'll give you $500 for it, and that's my final offer!* **IDM** **in the last/final analysis** ⟶ ANALYSIS. **say/be one's last/final word** ⟶ WORD. **the last/final straw** ⟶ STRAW.

▶ **final** *n* **1** the last of a series of contests or competitions: *the 'tennis finals* ○ *The teams met in this year's European Cup 'Final* (ie the last in a series of esp football matches). See also QUARTER-FINAL, SEMIFINAL. **2** (usu *pl*) the last set of university examinations: *sit/take one's finals* ○ *the law final(s).*
finalist /-nəlɪst/ *n* a player who is in the final part of a competition: *an Olympic finalist.*
finally /-nəli/ *adv* **1** at last; eventually: *After a long delay the performance finally started.* ○ *Finally, to avoid an unpleasant scene, his wife agreed to leave the party.* **2** as a last point: *Finally, I would like to say…* **3** in a way that ends all discussion about sth: *We must settle this matter finally.*

finale /fɪ'nɑːli; *US* -'næli/ *n* the last part of a piece of music or a drama, etc: *plan a grand finale to the evening* ○ *the rousing finale of Beethoven's Ninth Symphony.*

finality /faɪ'næləti/ *n* [U] the quality or fact of being final: *'There's nothing to explain,' she said with (an air of) grim finality.*

finalize, -ise /'faɪnəlaɪz/ *v* to put sth into its final form; to complete sth: [Vn] *finalize one's plans/ arrangements* ○ *Our route after that has not yet been finalized.*

finance /'faɪnæns, faɪ'næns, fə'næns/ *n* **1** [U] ~ (**for sth**) the money used or needed to support an activity, project, etc: *Finance for education comes from taxpayers.* **2** [U] the management of money, esp

public money: *an expert in finance* ○ *our finance director* ○ *the Minister of Finance.* **3** **finances** [pl] the money available to a person, company or country: *your partner's personal finances* ○ *Are the firm's finances sound?* ○ *The high cost of rented accommodation put a severe strain on our finances.*

▶ **finance** *v* to provide money for a project, etc; to FUND sth: [Vn] *borrow to finance the take-over bid* ○ *The plan is partly financed by a government grant.* ○ *publicly financed services.*

■ **'finance house** (also **'finance company**) *n* a company that lends money, esp for hire purchase (HIRE) arrangements.

financial /faɪ'nænʃl, fə'næ-/ *adj* concerning money and finance: *give financial support/assistance/ backing* ○ *be in financial difficulties* ○ *the President's financial advisers* ○ *Tokyo and New York are major financial centres.* ▶ **financially** /-ʃəli/ *adv*: *be financially dependent on sb* ○ *He will not benefit financially from the deal.*

■ **fi,nancial 'year** (*US* **fiscal year**) *n* a period of twelve months over which annual accounts and taxes are calculated.

financier /faɪ'nænsiə(r), fə-; *US* ˌfɪnən'sɪər/ *n* a person who provides money for businesses, etc on a large scale: *a consortium of financiers.*

finch /fɪntʃ/ *n* (often in compounds) any of several types of small bird: *a 'chaffinch* ○ *a 'goldfinch* ○ *a 'bullfinch.*

find¹ /faɪnd/ *v* (*pt, pp* **found** /faʊnd/) **1** to discover sth unexpectedly or by chance: [Vn] *Look what I've found.* [Vnpr] *I found a £5 note on the pavement.* ○ *He woke up and found himself in a hospital bed.* [Vnp] *I was disappointed to find you out* (ie that you were out) *when I called.* [Vn-adj] *We came home and found her asleep on the sofa.* **2** ~ **sth/sb (for sb)** (**a**) to discover sth/sb by searching, inquiry or effort: [Vnpr] *After months of drilling, oil was found off the coast.* [Vn] *try to find a cure for cancer* ○ *It seems impossible to find a way to stop the vandals.* ○ *I managed to find a solution to the problem.* ○ *It's hard to find/I'm having trouble finding anything new to say on this subject.* [Vnn, Vnpr] *Can you find me a hotel/find a hotel for me?* [V.that] *The report finds that 30% of the country's firms go bankrupt within a year.* (**b**) to obtain sth/sb or get sth/sb back, esp sth/sb that was lost: [Vn] *Did you find the pen you lost?* ○ *The missing child has not been found yet.* [Vnn, Vnpr] *I'll find you your shoes/find your shoes for you.* (**c**) to succeed in obtaining sth: [Vn] *I keep meaning to write, but never seem to find (the) time.* ○ *It would be nice to get a car but where would we find the money?* **3** to discover sth by experience: [V.that] *I find (that) it pays to be honest.* [Vn-adj] *He finds his new job rather boring.* ○ *You may find it hard to accept your illness.* ○ *We found the beds very comfortable.* ○ *He finds talking about his problems difficult.* [Vn-n] *We found him (to be) extremely good company.* **4** to arrive at sth naturally; to reach sth: [Vn] *Water will always find its own level.* ○ *The arrow found its mark.* ○ *The money was finding its way directly into the police chief's pocket.* **5** (used in a statement of fact, indicating that sth exists): [Vn] *You'll find* (ie There is) *a teapot in the cupboard.* ○ *These flowers are found* (ie exist, grow) *only in Africa.* **6** (*law*) to decide and declare as a VERDICT: [Vnadv] *How do you find the accused?* [Vn-adj] *The jury found him guilty (of manslaughter).* [Vpr] *The court found in her favour.* **IDM** **all 'found** (*Brit*) (of wages) with free food and lodging included. **be found 'wanting** to be shown to be not reliable enough or not capable of doing sth well enough. **find fault (with sb/sth)** to look for and discover mistakes in sb/sth; to complain about sb/sth: *She's always finding fault (with me).* **find one's 'feet** to become able to act independently and confidently: *I* only recently joined the firm so I'm still finding my feet. **(not) find it in one's heart / oneself to do sth** (usu with *can/could*) (not) to be able to do sth because of kindness or consideration: *I cannot find it in myself to condemn a mother who steals for a hungry child.* ○ *Can you find it in your heart to apologize?* **find/meet one's match** ⇨ MATCH¹. **find one's ˈvoice/ˈtongue** to be able to speak or express one's opinion: *She suddenly found her tongue again.* **find one's way (to ...)** to discover the right route (to a place): *I hope you can find your way home.* ○ *She couldn't find her way out of the building.* **take sb as one ˈfinds them** to accept sb as they are without expecting them to be well organized or to behave in a special way: *We've only just returned from holiday so you must take us as you find us.* **PHRV find for/ against sb** (*law*) to give a VERDICT in favour of/ against sb: *The jury found for the defendant.* **find sth out** to learn sth by study or inquiry: *Can you find out what time the train leaves?* ○ *Try to find out if anything's bothering her.* ○ *We found out later that he'd been lying to us.* **find sb out** to discover that sb has done sth wrong, has lied, etc: *He had been cheating the taxman but it was years before he was found out.*

▶ **finder** *n* a person who finds sth: *Lost: one diamond ring. Finder will be rewarded.*

finding *n* (often *pl*) **1** a thing that is discovered as the result of an official inquiry: *The findings of the Commission will be published today.* ○ *The report's main finding is that pensions are inadequate.* **2** (*law*) the decision or VERDICT of a court.

find² /faɪnd/ *n* a thing or person that has been found, esp one that is interesting, valuable or useful: *an important archaeological find* ○ *Our new babysitter is a real find.*

fine¹ /faɪn/ *adj* (**-r, -st**) **1(a)** of high quality: *a very fine performance* ○ *a particularly fine example of this style of decoration* ○ *fine clothes/wines* ○ *This is arguably the finest collection of paintings in Europe.* **(b)** carefully and skilfully made; delicate: *fine workmanship* ○ *fine silk/china.* **(c)** very good; beautiful or pleasing: *a fine view* ○ '*How was your skiing holiday?*' '*Fine — plenty of snow.*' ○ *a fine-looking young man* ○ (*ironic*) *This is a fine mess we're in!* **(d)** (of a person) well; in good health: '*How are you?*' '*Fine, thanks.*' ○ *My mother was feeling fine when I got home.* **(e)** (*esp Brit*) (of weather) bright; clear; not raining: *It poured all morning, but turned fine later.* **(f)** (of metals) refined; pure: *fine gold.* **2** made of very small grains or pieces: *fine powder/flour/dust* ○ *Sand is finer than gravel.* **3** thin: *fine hair/thread* ○ *a pencil with a fine point.* **4** difficult to perceive; SUBTLE(1): *You are making very fine distinctions.* ○ *There is a fine line (to be drawn) between assertiveness and aggressiveness.* **5** (of speech or writing) grand, esp in an insincere way: *His speech was full of fine words which meant nothing.* **6** (*infml*) yes; that is satisfactory: '*I'll leave these on your desk in the morning, OK?*' '*Fine.*' **IDM** **chance would be a fine thing** ⇨ CHANCE¹. **the finer points (of sth)** the details or aspects of sth which can be recognized and appreciated only by those who understand or know it well: *I don't understand the finer points of billiards but I enjoy watching it on TV.* **get sth down to a fine ˈart** (*infml*) to learn to do sth perfectly: *She's got the business of buying birthday presents down to a fine art.* **not to put too fine a ˈpoint on it** speaking plainly and honestly: *I don't much like modern music — in fact, not to put too fine a point on it, I hate it.*

▶ **finely** *adv* **1** well; in a splendid way: *finely dressed.* **2** into small grains or pieces: *finely chopped herbs.* **3** in a very delicate way: *a finely tuned engine* ○ *The match was finely balanced.*

fineness *n* [U].

■ **fine ˈart** *n* [U] (also **the fine ˈarts** [pl]) art or forms of art that appeal to one's sense of beauty, eg painting, SCULPTURE, etc: *a fine-arts course.*

the fine print *n* [U] = THE SMALL PRINT (SMALL).

fine-tooth comb *n* **IDM** **(go over, through, etc sth) with a fine-tooth comb** (to examine sth) closely and thoroughly: *Police experts are sifting all the evidence with a fine-tooth comb.*

fine² /faɪn/ *adv* **1** (*infml*) very well: *That arrangement suits me fine.* **2** (in compounds) **(a)** in a way that is difficult to detect or describe: *ˌfine-ˈdrawn distinctions.* **(b)** in a delicate way: *fine-spun cloth.* **IDM** **cut it/things ˈfine** to leave oneself only the MINIMUM(1) amount, esp of time: *If we only allow five minutes for catching our train, we'll be cutting it very fine.*

■ **ˌfine-ˈtune** *v* to adjust sth slightly and usu repeatedly, until it is as effective as it can be: [Vn] *We spent the next few weeks fine-tuning the scheme and made some useful improvements.*

fine³ /faɪn/ *n* a sum of money that must be paid as a punishment for breaking a law or rule: *parking fines* ○ *Offenders will be liable to a heavy/stiff fine.* ○ *Her escapade cost her $1000 in fines.*

▶ **fine** *v* ~ **sb (for sth / doing sth)** to punish sb by making them pay a fine: [Vnpr] *She was fined for dangerous driving.* [Vnn] *The court fined him a total of £500.* [also Vn].

finery /ˈfaɪnəri/ *n* [U] colourful and elegant clothes or decoration: *court officials dressed in/decked out in all their finery* ○ *The garden looks beautiful in its summer finery* (ie with its bright flowers, lawns, etc).

finesse /fɪˈnes/ *n* [U] skill in dealing with people or situations in a clever and SUBTLE(2) way: *a politician of great skill and finesse* ○ *He lacked his father's tact and finesse.*

finger¹ /ˈfɪŋɡə(r)/ *n* **1(a)** any of the five parts extending from each hand: *He poked at the spider with a stubby finger.* ○ *She dipped her finger into the mixture.* ○ *He counted the guests on his fingers* (ie used his fingers to help him do the sum). **(b)** any of these except the thumb: *a broken finger* ○ *a beckoning finger* ○ *She clicked her finger and thumb together.* See also FOREFINGER, INDEX FINGER, RING FINGER. ⇨ picture at HAND. ⇨ picture at BODY. **2** a part of a glove that fits over a finger. **3** a piece of bread, cake, etc shaped like a finger: *a finger of toast.* See also FISH FINGER. **IDM** **be all ˌfingers and ˈthumbs** to be awkward with one's hands: *Can you thread this needle for me? I'm all fingers and thumbs today.* **burn one's fingers / get one's fingers burnt** ⇨ BURN. **cross one's fingers** ⇨ CROSS². **get, pull, etc one's ˈfinger out** (*infml*) to stop being lazy; to work faster: *If you don't pull your finger out, you'll never get the job finished.* **have a finger in every ˈpie** (*infml*) to be involved in everything. **have/keep one's finger on the ˈpulse (of sth)** to know all the latest news, developments, etc. **have, etc one's ˈfingers in the till** (*infml*) to steal money from one's place of work: *He was caught with his fingers in the till.* **lay a ˈfinger on sb** to touch sb, esp with the intention of harming them: *If you lay a finger on that child, I'll never forgive you.* **lift/raise a finger/ hand** ⇨ LIFT. **point a/the finger** ⇨ POINT². **put one's finger on sth** to identify an error, the cause of a problem, etc exactly: *I can't quite put my finger on the flaw in her argument.* **snap one's fingers** ⇨ SNAP¹. **twist sb round one's little finger** ⇨ TWIST¹. **work one's fingers to the ˈbone** to work very hard.

■ **ˈfinger-mark** *n* a mark made by a dirty finger: *leave finger-marks all over the wall.*

finger² /ˈfɪŋɡə(r)/ *v* to touch or feel sth with the fingers: [Vn] *She fingered the knife hidden in her pocket.* ○ *He was nervously fingering his tie.* ○ *I don't like eating food that's been fingered by someone else.*

▶ **fingering** /ˈfɪŋɡərɪŋ/ *n* [U] the method of using

the fingers in playing a musical instrument: *a piano piece with tricky fingering*.

fingernail /ˈfɪŋgəneɪl/ *n* a layer of nail over the upper surface of the tip of a finger: *have/get dirt under the fingernails* ○ *Go and clean your fingernails*.

fingerprint /ˈfɪŋgəprɪnt/ *n* [C usu *pl*] a mark made by the lower surface of the tip of a finger and used for identifying people, esp criminals: *take the prisoner's fingerprints*. See also GENETIC FINGERPRINT.

fingertip /ˈfɪŋgətɪp/ *n* [C usu *pl*] the end of a finger furthest from the hand: *She held the paper lightly between her fingertips*. **IDM** **at one's ˈfingertips** easy to reach or obtain; completely familiar to one: *He has all the necessary facts at his fingertips*. **to one's ˈfingertips** in every way; completely: *She's an artist to her fingertips*.

finicky /ˈfɪnɪki/ *adj* (*derog*) **1** making too much of a fuss about what one eats, wears, etc: *a finicky eater/ dresser*. **2** showing or requiring great attention to detail: *This job is too finicky for me*.

finish /ˈfɪnɪʃ/ *v* **1(a)** to come to an end or bring sth to an end: [V] *Term/School finishes next week*. [Vn] *finish one's work* [V.ing] *finish reading a book*. **(b)** to reach the end of a task or an activity: [V] *Wait — I haven't finished yet.* ○ *We should finish at around 6.30.* ○ *Two of the runners failed to finish.* [V-adj] *She was leading for part of the race but finally finished fourth.* [V-n] *Faldo got a 72 today and finished five under par*. **2** ~ **sth (off/up)** to eat, drink or use what remains of sth: [Vn, Vnp] *We might as well finish (up) the cake — there isn't much left*. **3** ~ **sth (off)** to complete sth or make sth perfect: [Vn] *a beautifully finished wooden bowl* ○ *She's* **putting the finishing touches** *to her display*. [Vnp] *Could you finish this typing off for me?* **4** ~ **sb (off)** (*infml*) to tire sb so that they cannot do any more: [Vn, Vnp] *That bike ride absolutely finished me (off)*. **PHRV** ˌfinish **sb/ sth ˈoff** (*infml*) to destroy sth/sb: *That fever nearly finished him off.* ○ *She used her last bullet to finish off the wounded animal.* ˌfinish **ˈup** (followed by an *adj* or *n*) to be in a particular state at the end of sth: *He could finish up dead or badly injured*. ˈfinish **with sb/sth 1** to have no further need or use for sth: *Please put the saucepan away if you've finished with it.* ○ *Can you wait a minute? I haven't finished with these papers yet*. **2** (of sb in a position of authority or power) to be no longer dealing with sb: *Has Mr Glover finished with the trainees yet?* ○ *You'll be sorry by the time I've finished with you* (eg finished punishing you). **3** to end a relationship with sb or a connection with sth: *She should finish with him — he treats her very badly.* ○ *I've finished with gambling*. **finish (up) with sth** to have sth at the end: *We had a long lunch and finished up with another bottle of champagne.* ○ *To finish with, we have a Chopin waltz*.

▶ **finish** *n* **1** [C usu *sing*] the last part or the end of sth: *an exciting finish to the race* ○ *It was a close/tight finish.* ○ *the perfect finish to a meal* ○ *The story was a lie from start to finish.* ○ *The strikers wanted to battle/fight on to the finish* (ie to the last possible moment before defeat). See also PHOTO FINISH. **2(a)** [C, U] the state of being finished or perfect: *Give your furniture a professional finish.* ○ (*fig*) *His manners lack finish*. **(b)** [C] a substance or texture used for completing the surface of wood, etc: *varnishes available in a range of finishes* ○ *a gloss/matt finish*. **IDM** **a fight to the finish** ⇨ FIGHT².

finisher *n* a person or animal that finishes a race, etc: *The first four finishers qualify for the final*.

■ **ˈfinishing line** (*Brit*) (also *esp US* **ˈfinish line**) *n* the line across a sports track which marks the end of a race: *She crossed the finishing line well ahead of the others*.

ˈfinishing-school *n* a private, usu expensive, school where girls are taught how to behave in fashionable society.

finished /ˈfɪnɪʃt/ *adj* **1** [pred] ~ **(with sb/sth)** (*infml*) in a state of having completed sth or no longer dealing with sb/sth: *I won't be finished for another hour.* ○ *I'm not finished with you yet.* ○ *She decided she was finished with working for others.* **2** [pred] no longer powerful or effective; ruined: *The scandal means he's finished in politics.* ○ *Their marriage was finished.* **3** [usu attrib] made; completed: *the finished product/article*.

finite /ˈfaɪnaɪt/ *adj* **1** limited in extent: *finite global resources*. Compare INFINITE. **2** (*grammar*) (of a verb form) that has a specific tense, person and number: *'Am', 'is', 'are', 'was' and 'were' are the finite forms of 'be'; 'be', 'being' and 'been' are the non-finite forms*.

fiord (also **fjord**) /ˈfiːɔːd/ *n* a long narrow strip of sea between high cliffs, as in Norway.

fir /fɜː(r)/ (also **ˈfir-tree**) *n* a type of tree with leaves like needles that stay on throughout the year. Compare PINE¹.

■ **ˈfir-cone** *n* the fruit of the fir-tree.

fire¹ /ˈfaɪə(r)/ *n* **1** [U] a process of burning that produces light and heat and often smoke and flames: *Are you afraid of fire?* **2(a)** [U] burning that destroys buildings, vehicles, trees, etc: *The house is on fire.* ○ *an automatic fire detection system* ○ *fire-fighting equipment* ○ *a factory gutted by fire* ○ *The candle had set the curtains on fire* (ie had made them start burning). ○ *A former employee admitted setting fire to the depot.* ○ *The car overturned and caught fire*. **(b)** [C] an instance of this: *a house fire* ○ *forest fires* ○ *A fire broke out in the warehouse yesterday.* ○ *The fire raged all night long*. **3(a)** [C] fuel, eg wood or coal, burning in an area specially enclosed for this purpose, and used for cooking food or heating a room: *make/build a fire* ○ **light a fire** *in the grate* ○ *a log fire* ○ *sit in front of a blazing/ roaring fire*. See also CAMP-FIRE. **(b)** [C] an apparatus for heating rooms: *a gas/electric fire*. See also HEATER, STOVE¹. **4** [U] shooting from guns: *automatic/sniper fire* ○ *Troops came/were under (heavy) fire* (ie were being shot at). ○ *The gunmen opened fire on* (ie began to shoot) *the police.* ○ *return (sb's) fire* (ie shoot back at sb) ○ *Their officer ordered them to* **hold their fire** (ie not to shoot). ○ *The girl was in the (direct) line of fire* (ie between the person shooting and the target). **5** [U] strong emotion; angry or excited feeling; enthusiasm: *His speech lacked fire*. **IDM** **a ball of fire** ⇨ BALL¹. **a baptism of fire** ⇨ BAPTISM. **draw sb's fire** ⇨ DRAW¹. **the fat is in the fire** ⇨ FAT². **get on like a house on fire** ⇨ HOUSE¹. **hang fire** ⇨ HANG¹. **have many, etc irons in the fire** ⇨ IRON¹. **no smoke without fire** ⇨ SMOKE¹. **on ˈfire** giving one a painful burning sensation: *Her heart was on fire.* ○ *He couldn't breathe. His chest was on fire*. **out of the frying-pan into the fire** ⇨ FRYING-PAN. **play with ˈfire** to take foolish and dangerous risks. **set the world on fire** ⇨ WORLD. **under ˈfire** being criticized severely: *The government is under fire from all sides on its economic policy*.

■ **ˈfire-alarm** *n* a bell or other device that gives warning of a fire: *The fire-alarm went off just before lunch*.

ˈfire-ball *n* a bright ball of fire, esp one at the centre of an explosion.

ˈfire-bomb *n* a bomb that burns fiercely after it explodes, causing destruction by fire: *a fire-bomb attack*.

ˈfire-break *n* a strip of land cleared of trees in order to stop fire from spreading in a forest.

ˈfire brigade (usu **the fire brigade**) (*Brit*) (also **ˈfire service**, *US* **ˈfire department**) *n* (usu *sing*) a team of people trained and employed to stop fires burning: *call out the fire brigade*.

[V] = verb used alone   [Vn] = verb + noun   [Vp] = verb + particle   [Vpr] = verb + prepositional phrase

'fire door n a special type of door that can resist burning.

'fire-drill (also **'fire-practice**) n [C, U] a practice of the procedures that must be used in order to escape safely from a burning building, etc.

'fire-engine n a special vehicle carrying equipment for fighting large fires.

'fire-escape n a special staircase or apparatus by which people can escape from a burning building, etc: *leave by the fire-escape.*

'fire extinguisher (also **extinguisher**) n a metal container with water or a chemical mixture inside for putting out small fires.

'fire-fighter n a person who tries to stop a large fire burning.

'fire-guard n a protective metal frame round a fire in a fireplace.

'fire-lighter n [C, U] (a small piece of) material that burns easily, used to help start a fire in a fireplace.

'fire-power n [U] **1** the capacity to destroy, measured by the number and size of guns available. **2** financial, intellectual or emotional strength: *The Democrats lost their political fire-power.*

'fire-practice n [C, U] = FIRE-DRILL.

'fire service n = FIRE BRIGADE.

'fire station n a building for a fire brigade (FIRE[1]) and its equipment.

'fire-water n [U] (*infml joc*) strong alcoholic drink.

fire[2] /'faɪə(r)/ v **1** ~ (sth) (at sb/sth); ~ (sth) into sth; ~ (on sb/sth) **(a)** to shoot with a gun or bow[1](1) at sb/sth; to shoot a bullet from a gun or an ARROW from a bow[1](1): [V, Vpr] *The officer ordered his men to fire (at the enemy).* [Vn, Vnpr] *He fired several arrows (at the target).* [Vpr, Vnpr] *The police fired (rubber bullets) into the crowd.* ○ *She fired (a pistol) into the air.* [Vn] *Soldiers fired on the crowd, killing three people.* ○ *Our car was fired on.* **(b)** (of a gun or bow[1](1)) to shoot a bullet or an ARROW at sb/sth: [Vn] *This weapon fires anti-aircraft missiles.* [V] *The pistol suddenly fired.* [also Vpr, Vnpr]. **2** ~ **sth at sb** to address words in quick succession at sb: [Vnpr] *fire insults/questions/ideas at sb.* **3** ~ **sb (for sth / doing sth)** (*infml*) to dismiss an employee from a job: [Vn, Vnpr] *He was fired (for stealing money from the till).* **4** to set fire to sth with the aim of destroying it: [Vn] *fire a haystack.* **5** (of the explosive mixture in an engine) to burn, driving the engine: [V] *The engine isn't firing.* [Vpr] *The engine is only firing on three cylinders.* **6** ~ **sb (with sth)** to fill sb with a strong emotion; to stimulate the imagination: [Vnpr] *be fired with enthusiasm/longing* [Vn] *Adventure stories fired his imagination.* **7** to heat an object made of clay in order to harden and strengthen it: [Vn] *fire pottery/bricks in a kiln.* **IDM working/firing on all cylinders** ⇨ CYLINDER. **PHRV ,fire a'way** (*infml*) (usu imperative) to begin asking questions; to begin to speak: *'I've got a couple of questions I'd like to ask you.' 'Right, fire away.'* **,fire sth 'off** to shoot a bullet from a gun: *fire off a few rounds/all one's ammunition.* **,fire sth/sb 'up** to stimulate or excite feelings, etc: *fire up public concern* ○ *Both teams were clearly fired up for the match.*

▶ **-fired** (forming compound *adjs*) supplied by or using the specified fuel: *gas-fired central heating* ○ *a coal-fired power station.*

firing /'faɪərɪŋ/ n [U] the action of firing guns: *There was continuous firing to our left.*

■ **'firing-line** n the front line of battle, nearest the enemy. **IDM be in the 'firing-line** to receive criticism, blame, etc, esp because of one's responsibilities or position: *The Employment Secretary found himself in the firing-line over the recent job cuts.*

'firing-squad n [CGp] a group of soldiers ordered to shoot a condemned person: *He was sentenced to death by firing-squad.*

firearm /'faɪərɑːm/ n (usu *pl*) a gun that can be carried, eg a RIFLE[1] or REVOLVER: *a 'firearms certificate* ○ *'firearms offences.*

firebrand /'faɪəbrænd/ n a person who is very active in social or political affairs and is thought by others to be causing trouble: *a young right-wing firebrand.*

firecracker /'faɪəkrækə(r)/ n (*esp US*) a small FIREWORK that explodes with a loud cracking noise.

firefly /'faɪəflaɪ/ n a type of flying insect that glows in the dark.

firelight /'faɪəlaɪt/ n [U] light from a fire in a fireplace: *shadows dancing in the firelight.*

fireman /'faɪəmən/ n (*pl* **-men** /-mən/) a member of a fire brigade (FIRE[1]).

fireplace /'faɪəpleɪs/ n an open space for a fire in a room, usu made of brick or stone and set into a wall: *a huge open fireplace.*

fireproof /'faɪəpruːf/ adj that can resist great heat without burning, cracking or breaking: *a fireproof door/staircase.*

fireside /'faɪəsaɪd/ n (usu *sing*) the part of a room beside the fireplace, esp considered as a warm comfortable place: *sitting **by the fireside*** ○ *a fireside chair.*

firewood /'faɪəwʊd/ n [U] wood used for lighting fires or as fuel: *chop/gather firewood.*

firework /'faɪəwɜːk/ n **1** [C] a device containing chemicals that burn and explode, used esp at celebrations: *set off (ie explode) a few fireworks* ○ *The firework spluttered and went out.* **2 fireworks** [pl] **(a)** a display of fireworks: *Are you going to the fireworks tonight?* **(b)** (*infml*) angry or passionate words: *There'll be fireworks when your father catches those boys!*

firm[1] /fɜːm/ adj (**-er, -est**) **1(a)** not yielding when pressed; fairly hard: *firm soil* ○ *a firm cushion/mattress/sofa* ○ *firm flesh/muscles.* **(b)** strongly fixed in place; secure or solid: *firm foundations* ○ *get a firm foothold.* **2** (of a movement) steady and strong; not weak or uncertain: *a firm handshake/grip/hold.* **3** not likely to change; definite: *a firm belief/believer in socialism* ○ *a firm decision/date/offer* ○ *firm opinions/convictions/principles* ○ *We have no firm evidence.* ○ *She is now the **firm favourite** to win the championship.* **4** ~ (**with sb**) strong and consistent in attitude and behaviour; DECISIVE(2): *exercise firm leadership/control/discipline* ○ *Parents must be firm with their children.* ○ *'I don't want to be unkind,' he said in a firm voice.* **5** [usu pred] ~ (**against sth**) (of a currency, etc) not lower than another currency, etc and possibly about to rise in price: *The pound remained firm against the dollar, but fell against the yen.* **IDM be on firm 'ground** to be sure of one's facts; to be secure in one's position, esp in a discussion. **a firm 'hand** strong discipline or control: *That boy needs a firm hand to help him grow up.*

▶ **firm** v to become or make sth firm: [V] *Interest rates firmed slightly.* [Vn] *Fill the pots with firmed damp soil.* **PHRV ,firm sth 'up 1** to put sth into a final fixed form: *firm up a contract/a deal/an agreement.* **2** to make part of the body firmer and less fat: *Exercise will help to firm up your muscles.*

firm adv **IDM hold 'firm to sth** to believe consistently in a principle, theory, etc: *hold firm to one's beliefs/ideals.* **stand fast/firm** ⇨ FAST[2].

firmly adv in a firm way: *The fence posts were fixed firmly in the ground.* ○ *It is now firmly established as one of the leading brands in the country.* ○ *The suggestion was politely but firmly rejected.*

firmness n [U].

firm[2] /fɜːm/ n a business company: *a firm of accountants* ○ *a law firm.* Compare COMPANY.

firmament /'fɜːməmənt/ n **the firmament** [sing] (*arch*) the sky.

first[1] /fɜːst/ det **(a)** 1st; coming before all others in time, order, importance, etc: *the first public perform-ance of the play* ○ *his first wife* ○ *their first baby* ○ *her first job* ○ *students in their first year at college* ○ *at the first* (ie earliest) *opportunity* ○ *the first signs that winter is approaching* ○ *one's first impression/reaction* ○ *King Edward I* (said as 'King ˌEdward the ˈFirst') ○ *go back to first* (ie basic) *principles* ○ *an issue of the first importance* ○ *She won first prize in the competition.* ○ *Your first duty is to your family.* ○ *English isn't her first* (ie her native) *language.* (**b**) never having happened or been experienced before: *his first real taste of success* ○ *It was the first time they had ever met.* Compare LAST¹ 1. **IDM (the) first/last/next but ¹one, ¹two, etc** the first/last/next, not counting one, two, etc: *Take the first turning but one* (ie the second turning) *on your left.* ○ *I live in the last house but two* (ie the third house from the end) *in this street.*

▶ **firstly** *adv* (in giving a list) to begin with: *There are two reasons for this decision: firstly, ...*

■ ˌfirst ¹aid *n* [U] treatment given to an injured person before a doctor comes.

ˌfirst ¹balcony *n* (*US*) = DRESS CIRCLE.

ˌfirst ¹base *n* the first of the bases (BASE¹ 8) that must be touched in a game of baseball. **IDM not get to first ¹base (with sth/sb)** (*infml esp US*) to fail to make a successful start in a project, relationship, etc; to fail to achieve even the first step.

ˌfirst ¹class *n* [U] **1** the most comfortable accommodation in a train, ship, etc: *Smoking is not allowed in first class.* ○ *first-class carriages/compartments/seats.* **2** the class of mail that is delivered most quickly: *First class costs more.* ○ *A first-class letter should arrive the following day.* ○ *Ten first-class stamps, please.* — *adj* in the best group or highest category; excellent: *The entertainment provided was first class.* ○ *They can afford to eat at first-class restaurants.* ○ *She's got a first-class degree from Hull University.* ○ *They're first-class people — you'll like them.* — *adv* by the best or quickest form of transport or mail: *travel first class* ○ *I sent the letter first class on Monday.*

ˌfirst ¹cousin *n* = COUSIN.

ˌfirst-day ¹cover *n* (*Brit*) an envelope with a set of special stamps that have the POSTMARK of the first day of issue.

ˌfirst de¹gree *n* [U] the least serious of three categories of murder or burn: *He was charged with murder in the first degree/ˌfirst-degree ¹murder.* ○ *Hot coffee can give ˌfirst-degree ¹burns.*

¹first-ever *adj* [attrib] never having happened or been experienced before: *the first-ever woman vice-president.*

ˌfirst ¹finger *n* = INDEX FINGER.

ˌfirst ¹floor (usu **the first floor**) *n* [sing] **1** (*Brit*) the floor immediately above the floor on ground level: *a ˌfirst-floor ¹flat.* **2** (*US*) the floor on ground level. ⇨ note at FLOOR¹.

¹first-fruit *n* (usu *pl*) **1** the earliest agricultural produce, crops, etc of the season. **2** the first results of sb's work or efforts.

ˌfirst ¹gear *n* the lowest gear on a car, bicycle, etc, used when travelling slowly.

ˌfirst ¹lady *n* **1** the First Lady [sing] (*US*) the wife of the President of the USA or of a state GOVERNOR(1). **2** [C usu *sing*] the leading woman in a specified activity or profession: *recognized as the first lady of romantic fiction.*

ˌfirst ¹light *n* [U] the time when light first appears in the morning; dawn: *We left before/at first light.*

¹first name *n* a personal name given to sb at their birth, usu coming before a family name: *Mrs Williams's first names are Margaret Elizabeth.* ○ *be on first-name terms with sb* (ie call them by their first name as a sign of a friendly informal relationship). ⇨ note at NAME¹. ⇨ App 5. Compare FORENAME, GIVEN NAME, CHRISTIAN NAME.

ˌfirst ¹night *n* the first public performance of a play, film, etc: *tickets for the first night of 'Fiddler on the Roof'* ○ *suffer from ˌfirst-night ¹nerves* (ie as a performer).

ˌfirst of¹fender *n* a person who has been found guilty of a crime for the first time.

the ˌfirst ¹person *n* [sing] **1** (*grammar*) a set of pronouns and verb forms used by a speaker to refer to herself or himself: *'I am' is the first person singular of the present tense of the verb 'to be'.* ○ *'I', 'me', 'we' and 'us' are first-person pronouns.* **2** a way of writing fiction as if one of the characters is telling the story: *Hemingway often writes in the first person.*

ˌfirst-¹rate *adj* excellent; of the best quality: *a ˌfirst-rate ¹meal* ○ *The food here is first-rate.* — *adv* in very good health; very fit.

ˌfirst re¹fusal *n* [U] (*Brit*) the right of deciding whether to accept or refuse sth before it is offered to others: *If you ever decide to sell your car, I hope you'll give me (the) first refusal.*

¹first school *n* (in Britain) a school for children between the ages of 5 and 8 or 9.

¹first-time *adj* [attrib] doing or experiencing sth for the first time: *ˌfirst-time ¹house buyers.*

the ˌFirst World ¹War (also **World War I**) *n* [sing] the major international war of 1914–1918, fought mainly in Europe.

first² /fɜːst/ *adv* **1(a)** before anyone or anything else; at the beginning: *Susan came into the room first.* ○ *Who came first in the race?* (ie Who won?) ○ *He climbed out of the window feet first.* ○ *Ladies first* (said by a man, allowing a woman to enter a room, etc before he does). (**b**) before another event or time: *First I had to decide what to wear.* ○ *Think first, then act.* ○ *'Do you want a drink?' 'I'll finish my work first.'* Compare LAST². **2** for the first time: *When did you first meet him?* ○ *The play was first performed in Paris.* ○ *When he first arrived in this country, he couldn't speak any English.* **3** (in giving a list) to begin with: *This method has two advantages: first it is cheaper and second(ly) it is quicker.* ⇨ note. **4** (used to show that one is very opposed to doing sth) in preference to sth else: *He said he'd resign first* (ie rather than do what had been suggested). **IDM at ¹first** at or in the beginning; to start with: *At first I thought he was shy, but then I discovered he was just not interested in other people.* ○ *(saying) If at first you don't succeed, try, try again.* **come ¹first** to be considered as more important than anything else: *In any decision he makes, his family always comes first.* ˌfirst and ¹foremost more than anything else; most importantly: *He does a bit of writing, but first and foremost he's a teacher.* ˌfirst ¹come, ˌfirst ¹served (*saying*) people will be dealt with, seen, etc strictly in the order in which they arrive or apply. ˌfirst of ¹all **1** before (doing) anything else; at the beginning: *First of all she just smiled, then she started to laugh.* **2** most importantly: *Well, first of all we can't possibly spare the time.* ˌfirst ¹off (*infml*) before anything else: *First off, let's see how much it'll cost.* **head first** ⇨ HEAD¹. ˌput sb/sth ¹first to consider sb/sth to be more important than anyone/anything else: *put one's career/reputation/children first.*

■ ¹first-born *n, adj* [attrib] (*dated*) (a child) born before other children; (the) oldest: *their first-born son.*

NOTE When you want to order instructions, facts, etc in a sequence, you can use **first, second, third**, etc, or **firstly, secondly, thirdly** at the beginning of a sentence, followed by a comma: *She left her job for three reasons. First(ly) the low wages; second(ly), the long hours; and third(ly), there was no chance of promotion.* **At first** means 'at the beginning of a period of time': *I didn't like learning to drive at first, but after a while I started to enjoy it.*

first³ /fɜːst/ *n, pron* **1 the first** [C] (*pl* unchanged) the first person or thing mentioned or occurring: *I'm the first in my family to go to university.* ○ *Sheila and Jim were the first to arrive.* ○ *I'd be the first to admit* (ie I will most willingly admit) *I might be wrong.* ○ *The first I heard about the firm closing down* (ie The first time I became aware of it) *was when George asked me what I planned to do.* Compare LAST¹ *n* 1. **2** [C] (*infml*) an achievement, event, etc never done or experienced before: *a real first for the German team.* **3** [C] ~ (**in sth**) (*Brit*) a university degree of the highest class: *She got a first in maths at Exeter.* **4** [U] the lowest gear on a car, bicycle, etc, used when travelling slowly: *go up the hill in first.* **IDM** **from the (very) first** from the beginning: *They were attracted to each other from the first.* **from first to last** from beginning to end; throughout: *It was a splendid show from first to last.*

firsthand /ˌfɜːstˈhænd/ *adj* [attrib], *adv* gained or coming directly from the original source: ˌfirsthand inforˈmation ○ *experience sth firsthand.*

firth /fɜːθ/ *n* (esp in Scottish place names) a narrow strip of the sea when it runs a long way into the land, or a part of a river where it flows into the sea.

fiscal /ˈfɪskl/ *adj* of or relating to public money, esp taxes: *the government's fiscal policy.* ■ ˌfiscal ˈyear *n* (*US*) = FINANCIAL YEAR.

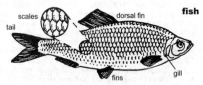
scales / dorsal fin / tail / fins / gill / **fish**

fish¹ /fɪʃ/ *n* (*pl* unchanged or **fishes**) ⇨ note. **1** [C] a creature that lives in water, breathes through gills (GILL¹), and uses fins (FIN) and a tail for swimming: *They caught several fish.* ○ *shoals of fish* ○ *There are some rare fishes lurking in the deeper British lakes.* ⇨ picture. **2** [U] the flesh of fish eaten as food: *frozen/smoked/fresh fish* ○ *boiled/fried/grilled fish* ○ *fish curry* ○ *Fish forms the main part of their diet.* **3** [U] (*infml*) a person of the specified type: *He seems a cold fish* (ie a person who shows no feelings) *to me.* ○ *He's a queer/an odd fish — he hasn't been out of his house for years.* **IDM** **a big fish** ⇨ BIG. **a different kettle of fish** ⇨ DIFFERENT. **drink like a fish** ⇨ DRINK². **a ˌfish out of ˈwater** a person who feels uncomfortable or awkward because he or she is in strange surroundings: *With my school background I feel like a fish out of water among these university people.* **have bigger/other fish to ˈfry** to have more important, interesting, etc things to do. **there are (plenty of) other fish in the ˈsea; there are (plenty) more (good) fish in the ˈsea** there are many other people/things that are as good as the one that sb has failed to get.

▶ **fishy** *adj* (**-ier, -iest**) **1** of or like a fish, esp in smell or taste: *a fishy smell.* **2** (*infml*) causing feelings of doubt or suspicion: *There's something fishy going on here.*

■ ˌfish and ˈchips (*Brit*) (*US* ˈfish fry) *n* [sing] fish fried in BATTER² and eaten with fried potato chips: *Fish and chips is very expensive these days.* ○ *a fish and chip shop.*

ˈfish cake *n* a small flat mass of cooked fish mixed with potato and usu fried.

ˌfish-eye ˈa lens *a* lens with a wide angle that gives a distorting effect.

ˈfish farm *n* an area of water used for breeding fish as a business.

ˌfish ˈfinger (*Brit*) (*US* ˌfish ˈstick) *n* a small narrow piece of fish covered with BREADCRUMBS.

ˈfish-hook *n* a sharp metal hook with its point curved back to form a BARB, used for catching fish. ⇨ picture at HOOK.

ˈfish-knife *n* a knife with a broad blade and without a sharp edge, used for eating fish.

ˈfish-slice *n* (*Brit*) a usu metal kitchen tool consisting of a broad flat blade that has narrow gaps in it and is attached to a long handle, used for turning or lifting food when cooking. ⇨ picture at KITCHEN. Compare SPATULA.

NOTE Fish as a countable noun has two plural forms: **fish** and **fishes**. Fish is the more usual form, used when you are referring to a number of them in the water: *The number of fish in coastal waters has decreased.* ○ *We caught a lot of fish during the competition.* Fishes is used to refer to different species of fish: *He studies in particular the fishes of the Indian Ocean.*

fish² /fɪʃ/ *v* **1**(a) ~ (**for sth**) to try to catch fish with hooks, nets, etc: [V] *I often fish/go fishing at weekends.* [Vpr] *fishing for salmon.* (b) to try to catch fish in an area of water: [Vn] *fish a river/lake.* **2** ~ (**for sth**) to search for sth, esp in a dark or hidden place: [Vpr, Vp] *She fished (around) in her bag for the keys.* **PHRV** ˈfish for sth to try to obtain sth by indirect methods: *fish for compliments/information.* ˌfish sth ˈout (of sth) to take or pull sth out (of sth), esp after searching for it: *Several old cars are fished out (of the canal) every month.* ○ *He fished a length of string out of his pocket.*

▶ **fishing** *n* [U] catching fish as a job or sport: *deep-sea fishing* ○ *a fishing boat* ○ *fishing grounds* ○ *Fishing is the main industry of the area.* ˈfishing-line *n* a long thread with a hook attached, used for catching fish. ˈfishing-rod (*US* also ˈfishing pole) *n* a long wooden or metal rod with a fishing-line attached to it.

fisherman /ˈfɪʃəmən/ *n* (*pl* **-men** /-mən/) a person who catches fish, either as a job or as a sport. See also ANGLER.

fishery /ˈfɪʃəri/ *n* **1** (usu *pl*) a part of the sea where fish are caught for commercial purposes: *coastal fisheries.* **2** the business or industry of fishing: *the Ministry of Agriculture, Fisheries and Food.*

fishmonger /-mʌŋgə(r)/ *n* (*Brit*) a person whose job it is to sell fish in a shop: *buy fish at the fishmonger's/from the fishmonger.*

fishnet /ˈfɪʃnet/ *n* [U] a fabric made of threads forming a pattern of small regular holes: *fishnet tights.*

fish-plate /ˈfɪʃpleɪt/ *n* a flat piece of iron joining one length of railway line to the next.

fissile /ˈfɪsaɪl; *US* ˈfɪsl/ *adj* (*physics*) capable of nuclear FISSION(1).

fission /ˈfɪʃn/ *n* [U] **1** (*physics*) the splitting of the NUCLEUS(1b) of an atom, resulting in the release of a large amount of energy: *nuclear fission.* **2** (*biology*) the division of cells into new cells as a method of reproducing the species.

fissiparous /fɪˈsɪpərəs/ *adj* reproducing by division of biological cells.

fissure /ˈfɪʃə(r)/ *n* a long deep crack in rock or in the earth. ▶ **fissured** *adj*: *fissured precipices.*

fist /fɪst/ *n* a hand when it is closed tightly with the fingers bent into the palm: *He punched me with his fist.* ○ *He clenched his fists.* ⇨ note at BODY. **IDM** **hand over fist** ⇨ HAND¹. **make a good, poor, etc fist of sth** (*infml*) to make a good, bad, etc attempt at sth: *He was making a brave fist of appearing cheerful.* **shake one's fist** ⇨ SHAKE¹.

▶ **fistful** /ˈfɪstfʊl/ *n* a number or quantity that can be held in a fist: *a fistful of ten-pound notes.*

fisticuffs /ˈfɪstɪkʌfs/ *n* [pl] (*arch or joc*) fighting with the fists (FIST): *engage in fisticuffs* ○ (*fig*) *a bout of verbal fisticuffs.*

fit¹ /fɪt/ *adj* (**-tter, -ttest**) **1** ~ (**for sth / to do sth**) in good health, esp because of regular physical exercise: *Top sportsmen have to be very fit.* ○ *He's been ill and isn't fit enough for work yet.* ○ *He keeps (himself) fit by running several miles every day.* ○ *fighting fit* (ie in very good physical condition and full of energy).* ⇨ note at HEALTHY. **2** [usu pred] ~ **for sb/sth;** ~ **to do sth** of a suitable quality or standard for sb/sth; good enough for sb/sth: *beaches fit for swimming* ○ *The food was not fit for human consumption/ not fit to eat* (ie was too bad to be eaten). **3** (*fml*) suitable and right by normal social standards: *a fit subject for discussion* ○ *It is only fit and proper that she should visit her elderly mother.* **4** [usu pred] ~ **to do sth** (*infml*) in such a condition as to be likely or ready to do or suffer sth specified: *They worked till they were fit to drop* (ie so tired they were likely to collapse). ○ *He's so angry that he's in no fit state to see anyone.* **IDM (as) ˌfit as a ˈfiddle** (*infml*) in very good physical condition. **see/think ˈfit (to do sth)** to consider it correct, convenient or acceptable to do sth; to decide or choose to do sth: *The newspaper did not see fit to publish my letter.* ○ *You must do as you think fit.*

▶ **fit** *adv* **IDM ˌfit to ˈburst** (*infml*) very much: *smile/ laugh fit to burst.*

fitness *n* [U] **1** the condition of being physically fit: *In many sports technique is as important as (physical) fitness.* **2** ~ **for sth / to do sth** the condition of being suitable for sth: *Doubts have been expressed about his fitness for office.*

fit² /fɪt/ *v* (**-tt-**; *pt, pp* **fitted**; *US* also **fit**) **1(a)** to be the right shape and size for sb: [V, Vn] *These shoes don't fit (me).* [Vadv, Vnadv] *The jacket fits (him) very well.* [Vadv] *a close-fitting dress* [Vn] *I can never get clothes to fit me.* ○ *The key doesn't fit the lock.* **(b)** ~ **sb (for sth)** (esp passive) to try clothing on sb in order to make or alter it to the right size and shape: [Vnpr] *He went to the tailor's to be fitted for a new suit.* [also Vn]. **2(a)** to be of the right size, type or number to go somewhere: [Vpr] *The dresser won't fit in/into our new kitchen.* [Vp] *The lift was so small that only three people could fit in.* **(b)** ~ **sth into sth / in** to find or have sufficient space or room for sb/sth in a place: [Vnp] *We can't fit any more chairs in.* [Vnpr] *We can fit the piano nicely into that space.* **3** ~ **A (on/to B); ~ B with A** to supply sth and fix or put it into place: [Vnpr] *fit handles on the cupboard/ fit the cupboard with handles* ○ *The room was fitted with a new carpet.* [Vn] *I fitted these shelves myself.* **4** ~ **A (on/to B); ~ A and B together** to join one thing to another to make a whole: [Vnpr] *fit a plug on the iron* [Vn] *fit a new exhaust-pipe* [Vnp] *fit the pieces of the jigsaw together.* **5** to be in agreement or harmony with sth; to match or suit sth: [V] *Something doesn't quite fit here.* [Vn] *The facts certainly fit your theory.* ○ *The punishment ought to fit the crime.* [Vpr] *His pictures don't fit into any category.* **6** ~ **sb/ oneself/sth for sth** to make sb/oneself/sth suitable for a particular role or task: [Vnpr] *Am I really fitted for the role of director?* [Vnpr, Vn.to inf] *His experience fits him for the job/to do the job.* **IDM fill/fit the bill** ⇨ BILL¹. **fit (sb) like a ˈglove 1** to be the perfect size or shape for sb: *The dress fits (me) like a glove.* **2** to be very suitable and accurate: *I like the way you described him — it fits him like a glove.* **if the cap fits** ⇨ CAP. **PHRV ˌfit sb/sth ˈin; ˌfit sb/sth ˈin/ˈinto sth** to succeed in finding time to see sb or to do sth: *I'll try and fit you in after lunch.* ○ *I had to fit ten appointments into one morning.* **ˌfit ˈin (with sb/sth)** to be a smoothly fitting part of sth; to be in harmony with sb/sth: *He's never done this type of work before; I'm not sure how he'll fit in (with the other staff).* ○ *Where do I fit in?* ○ *Do these plans fit in with your arrangements?* **ˌfit sb/sth ˈout/ˈup (with sth)** to supply sb/sth with the necessary equipment, clothes, food, etc; to equip sb/sth: *fit out a ship* before a long voyage ○ *It's expensive getting the children fitted out with clothes for their new school.*

▶ **fitted** *adj* [attrib] **1** (*esp Brit*) (of a carpet) cut and laid so that it covers a floor completely and is fixed into place. See also WALL-TO-WALL. **2** (*esp Brit*) **(a)** (of furniture) built to be fixed into a particular space; built-in (BUILD): *fitted cupboards.* **(b)** (of a room) having the appropriate units of furniture, etc linked together and fixed in place: *a fitted kitchen.*

fitter *n* **1** a person whose job is to put together, adjust and repair machinery and equipment: *a gas fitter.* **2** a person whose job is to cut, fit and alter clothes or carpets.

fit³ /fɪt/ *n* [sing] (usu with a preceding *adj*) the way in which sth, esp a garment, fits: *The coat was a good/ bad/tight/loose fit.*

fit⁴ /fɪt/ *n* **1** a sudden attack of a disease, eg EPILEPSY, involving violent movements and loss of consciousness: *have an epileptic ˈfit.* **2** a sudden, usu short, attack of a minor illness: *a fit of coughing* ○ *a ˈfainting fit.* **3** a sudden rush of laughter, activity, etc, esp one that is difficult to stop: *get a fit of hysterics/(the) giggles* ○ *We were all in fits (of laughter)* (ie laughing out of control) *at his jokes.* **4** a short period of an intense feeling: *a fit of anger/rage/frustration.* **IDM by/in ˌfits and ˈstarts** by stopping and then starting again; not continuously: *Because of other commitments I can only write my book in fits and starts.* **have/throw a ˈfit** (*infml*) to be very shocked, worried or angry: *Your mother would have a fit if she knew you were here.*

▶ **fitful** /-fl/ *adj* occurring in short periods; not regular and steady: *fitful bursts of energy* ○ *a fitful night's sleep.* **fitfully** /-fəli/ *adv: sleep fitfully.*

fitment /ˈfɪtmənt/ *n* (usu *pl*) (*Brit*) a piece of furniture or equipment, esp one forming part of a group or series: *kitchen fitments* (eg cupboards).

fitting¹ /ˈfɪtɪŋ/ *adj* suitable for the occasion; right or proper: *a fitting end to the day* ○ *It was fitting that he should be here to receive the prize in person.*

fitting² /ˈfɪtɪŋ/ *n* **1** (usu *pl*) a small part on or attached to a piece of furniture or equipment: *electrical fittings* ○ *a pine cupboard with brass fittings.* **2** (usu *pl*) any of the items, eg a COOKER or shelves, that are fixed in a building but can be removed when the owner moves to a new house. Compare FIXTURE 2, MOVABLES. **3** the process or an occasion of having a garment made or altered to one's size: *have a fitting for a wedding dress* ○ *costume fittings.*

five /faɪv/ *n, pron, det* the number 5: *a birthday card with a big five on it* ○ *Five and five make ten.* ○ *Three fives are fifteen.* ○ *Look at page five.* ○ *Everyone took the exam, but only five passed.* ○ *Five of the students passed.* ○ *There were five children at the party.* ○ *This shirt only cost five dollars* (ie \$5). ○ *He's five (years old) today.* ○ *education for the under-fives* (ie children under five years old).

▶ **five-** (in compounds) having five of the thing specified: *a five-day week* (ie working five days out of seven, usu Monday to Friday) ○ *a five-year contract* ○ *a five-sided figure.*

fiver /ˈfaɪvə(r)/ *n* **1** (*Brit infml*) a five-pound note; £5: *Can you lend me a fiver?* **2** (*US infml*) a five-dollar note; \$5.

■ **ˌfive o'clock ˈshadow** *n* [sing] (*infml*) a dark appearance on a man's chin and face caused by the slight growth of hair that has occurred since he shaved in the morning.

ˌfive ˈpence (also **ˌfive pence ˈpiece, ˌfive ˈp, 5p**) *n* (*Brit*) a coin worth five pence: *I've got a five pence somewhere.*

fivefold /ˈfaɪvfəʊld/ *adj, adv* ⇨ -FOLD.

fives /faɪvz/ *n* [sing *v*] a game, played esp in Britain, in which a ball is hit with the hands against the walls of a court. Players normally wear special gloves when playing.

fix¹ /fɪks/ *v* **1** to fasten sth firmly to sth: [Vnpr] *fix a shelf to the wall* ○ *fix a post in the ground* ○ (*fig*) *fix the blame on sb.* **2** to decide a price, date, etc definitely; to set¹(9) or specify sth: [Vn] *Has (the date of) the next meeting been fixed?* [Vnpr] *We will fix the rent at £100 a week.* **3** to discover or establish the exact nature, position, time, etc of sth: [Vn] *We can fix the ship's exact position at the time the fire broke out.* **4** ~ **sth on sb/sth** to direct one's eyes or mind towards sb/sth with steady attention: [Vnpr] *Her eyes were fixed intently on the screen.* ○ *fix one's thoughts/attention on sth.* **5** ~ **sth (up)** to arrange or organize sth: [Vn, Vnp] *I'll fix (up) a meeting.* [Vnp] *You have to fix visits up in advance with the museum.* [Vnpr] (*infml*) *Don't worry, I'll fix it with* (ie make sure the plan is convenient for) *Sarah.* **6** (*esp US*) to provide or prepare sth, esp food: [Vn] *He's just fixing a snack.* [Vnn] *Can I fix you a drink?* [Vnpr] *Let me fix supper for you.* **7** to repair or mend sth: [Vn] *The car won't start — can you fix it?* ○ *My watch needs fixing.* **8** to put sth in order; to adjust sth: [Vn] *Let me fix my hair* (ie make it look tidy) *and then I'll be ready.* **9** (*infml*) (esp passive) to influence the result of sth or a person's actions by unfair or illegal means: [Vn] *I'm sure the race was fixed.* ○ *The jury/judge had been fixed.* **10** (*infml*) to punish or kill sb, esp sb who has harmed one; to deal with sb: [Vn] *I'll fix him so that he never bothers you again.* **11** [Vn] to treat photographic film, a dye, etc with a chemical so that the colours do not change or fade. **PHRV** **'fix on sb/sth** to decide to have sb/sth; to choose sb/sth: *They've fixed on Ashby as the new chairman.* ○ *Have you fixed on a date for the wedding?* **,fix sth 'up** to repair, decorate or adapt sth: *He fixed up the cottage before they moved in.* **,fix sb 'up (with sb)** (*US infml*) to arrange for sb to go on a date¹(3b) with sb: *We fixed Ron up with Carol.* **,fix sb 'up (with sth)** (*infml*) to arrange for sb to have sth; to provide sb with sth: *I'll fix you up with a place to stay.* ○ *She's got herself fixed up with a cosy flat.* **'fix sb with sth** (*fml*) to direct one's look, attention, etc at sb: *He fixed her with an angry stare.*

▶ **fixed** /fɪkst/ *adj* **1** already arranged and decided; not changing: *fixed prices* ○ *a fixed rate of interest.* **2** (of ideas, wishes, etc) held (too) firmly; not open to discussion or easily changed: *He had the fixed idea that a woman's place was in the home.* **3** [attrib] (of an expression on sb's face) not changing; not natural: *a fixed smile/glare/stare.* **4** [pred] ~ **for sth** (*infml*) provided or supplied with sth: *How are you fixed for money/food/time?* **fixedly** /ˈfɪksɪdli/ *adv* with great interest; steadily: *stare fixedly at sb/sth.* **fixed 'assets** *n* [pl] land, buildings, equipment, etc owned by a business. **fixed 'costs** *n* [pl] business costs that do not vary with the amount of work produced.

fixer /ˈfɪksə(r)/ *n* **1** (*infml*) a person who makes (sometimes illegal) arrangements: *a fixer for a terrorist group* ○ *a political fixer.* **2** a chemical substance used to treat photographic film or dyes to prevent colours from changing or fading.

fixity /ˈfɪksəti/ *n* [U] (*fml*) the quality of being firm or steady: *She displayed great fixity of purpose.*

fix² /fɪks/ *n* **1** [C usu *sing*] (*infml*) an awkward or difficult situation: *be in/get oneself into a fix.* **2** [sing] (*infml*) a thing arranged dishonestly: *Her promotion was a fix, I'm sure.* **3** [C] (*sl*) an injection (INJECT) of a drug, eg HEROIN: *get oneself a fix.* **4** [C] (**a**) the act of finding the position of a ship, an aircraft, etc by using RADAR, a COMPASS(2), etc: *get a fix on the yacht's position.* (**b**) a position found by such means.

fixated /fɪkˈseɪtɪd/ *adj* [pred] ~ (**on sb/sth**) being attached to or interested in sb/sth to an abnormal

degree: *He is fixated on things that remind him of his childhood.*

fixation /fɪkˈseɪʃn/ *n* ~ (**on/with sb/sth**) an abnormal interest in or feeling about sb/sth; an obsession (OBSESS): *a mother fixation* ○ *He's got this fixation on/with tidiness.*

fixative /ˈfɪksətɪv/ *n* [C, U] **1** a chemical substance used to treat photographic film or dyes to prevent colours from changing or fading. **2** a substance used for sticking things together or keeping things in position.

fixture /ˈfɪkstʃə(r)/ *n* **1** a sports event, esp a match or race, on a day fixed for this: *an annual fixture* ○ *Saturday's fixture against Wigan* ○ *a fixture list.* **2** (usu *pl*) a thing, such as a bath, water tank or toilet, that is fixed in a building and is not removed when the owner moves house: *'plumbing fixtures* ○ *The price of the house includes many existing **fixtures and fittings**.* Compare FITTING² 2, MOVABLES. **3** (*infml*) a person or thing that is always present in a place or position and appears unlikely to leave it: *We were originally just looking after the cat for a friend but it seems to have become a **permanent fixture**.*

fizz /fɪz/ *v* **1** (of a liquid) to produce bubbles of gas: [Vpr] (*fig*) *Athletes fizzed with team spirit.* [also V]. **2** to HISS, like wood beginning or failing to burn: [V] *The match fizzed briefly and went out.*
▶ **fizz** *n* [U] **1** the quality of having a lot of bubbles of gas in a liquid: *This lemonade has lost its fizz.* ○ (*fig*) *put some fizz into the show* ○ (*fig*) *The fizz has gone out of the market.* **2**(**a**) a fizzing sound: *the fizz of a firework.* (**b**) (*infml*) a drink, esp CHAMPAGNE, that has a lot of bubbles of gas: *a glass of fizz.*

fizzle /ˈfɪzl/ *v* [V] to make a weak fizzing (FIZZ 2) sound. **PHRV** **fizzle out** to end or fail in a weak or disappointing way: *After a promising start, the project soon fizzled out.*

fizzy /ˈfɪzi/ *adj* (**-ier, -iest**) (of a drink) having a lot of bubbles of gas: *fizzy drinks/lemonade.*

fjord = FIORD.

flab /flæb/ *n* [U] (*infml derog*) the soft loose flesh on a person who is fat: *You need to get rid of all that flab!*
▶ **flabby** /ˈflæbi/ *adj* (**-ier, -iest**) (*derog*) **1**(**a**) soft and loose; not strong or firm: *flabby muscles/thighs/features.* (**b**) having soft loose flesh: *He's getting fat and flabby because he doesn't have enough exercise.* ⇨ note at FAT¹. **2** weak; not powerful or effective: *flabby excuses* ○ *a flabby argument/plot/speech.*

flabbergast /ˈflæbəɡɑːst; *US* -ɡæst/ *v* (*infml*) (usu passive) to astonish sb completely; to shock or surprise sb very much: [Vn] *He was flabbergasted when he heard that his friend had been accused of murder.*

flaccid /ˈflæksɪd/ *adj* (*fml*) soft and weak or loose; not firm: *a flaccid mouth* ○ (*fig*) *Their play was flaccid and uninspired.*

flag¹ /flæɡ/ *n* **1** a usu OBLONG or square piece of cloth with a particular design, which can be attached by one edge to a rope, pole, etc. A flag is used as a symbol of a country or an organization, or as a signal: *The national flag of the United Kingdom is called the Union Jack.* ○ *The ship was sailing under the Dutch flag* (ie The Dutch flag was flying from its MAST). ○ *All the flags were flying at half-mast* (ie in honour of a famous dead person). ○ *The guard waved his flag and the train pulled out of the station.* ○ *The white flag is a symbol of a truce or surrender.* ⇨ picture. **2** a small piece of paper or cloth, often attached to a stick or pin, esp one given to sb who contributes to a charity appeal: *children selling flags for cancer research.* **IDM** **fly/show/wave the 'flag** to represent or make known one's support for or loyalty to one's country, political party, movement, etc, esp in order to encourage others to do the same: *I'm not very religious but I do go to church occasionally, just to show the flag.* **keep the 'flag flying** to represent one's country, political party, etc: *Our exporters proudly kept the flag flying at the international trade exhibition.*

▶ **flag** *v* (-gg-) **1** to mark sth for particular attention with a special mark or label: [Vn] *I've flagged all the names and addresses to be printed out onto labels.* **2** (esp passive) to place a flag or flags on sth; to decorate sth with flags: [Vn] *The streets were flagged to celebrate the local team's victory.* **PHRV** **flag sth down** to signal to a moving vehicle to stop, usu by waving one's arm: *flag down a taxi.*

■ **'flag-day** *n* **1** (*US* **tag day**) a day on which money is collected in public places for a charity, and a small paper flag or STICKER(1) is given to people who contribute. **2** Flag Day (*US*) 14 June, the anniversary of the day in 1777 when the Stars and Stripes became the national flag.

flag of con'venience *n* a flag of a foreign country under which a ship registers, eg to avoid the taxes and regulations of the owner's home country.

'flag-pole *n* = FLAGSTAFF.

'flag-waving *n* [U] (*derog*) the expression of national or group feelings, esp in an exaggerated way: *I didn't think much of her speech — it was just a flag-waving exercise* (ie one that did not deal with real issues).

flag² /flæg/ *v* (-gg-) to become tired, weaker and less active or enthusiastic: [V] *My strength/interest/enthusiasm is flagging.* ○ *the flagging fortunes of the socialists* ○ *The children showed no signs of flagging.*

flag³ /flæg/ *n* = FLAGSTONE.

▶ **flagged** /flægd/ *adj* covered with flagstones (FLAGSTONE): *a flagged floor/passage/terrace.*

flag⁴ /flæg/ *n* a type of plant with very long narrow leaves and yellow flowers, usu growing near water.

flagellate /'flædʒəleɪt/ *v* [Vn] (*fml*) to whip sb or oneself as a religious punishment or for sexual pleasure. ▶ **flagellation** /ˌflædʒə'leɪʃn/ *n*.

flagon /'flægən/ *n* a large bottle or similar container, often with a handle, in which wine, CIDER, etc is sold or served.

flagrant /'fleɪgrənt/ *adj* (usu of a bad action) particularly shocking and obvious: *a flagrant breach of justice* ○ *flagrant violations of human rights.* ▶ **flagrantly** *adv*: *She flagrantly refused to apologize.*

flagship /'flægʃɪp/ *n* **1** a ship which has the COMMANDER of a fleet on board. **2** (usu *sing*) the most important of a group of products, projects, services, etc: *a flagship store* ○ *This is the flagship of our range of learners' dictionaries.*

flagstaff /'flægstɑːf; *US* -stæf/ (also **flag-pole**) *n* a long pole on which a flag is flown.

flagstone /'flægstəʊn/ (also **flag**) *n* a flat piece of stone, usu square or OBLONG, for a floor, path, etc: *grass growing up between the flagstones.*

flail /fleɪl/ *n* a tool consisting of a stick swinging from a long handle, used esp formerly to separate grains of wheat, etc from their dry outer covering by beating the wheat repeatedly.

▶ **flail** *v* **1** to wave or swing about wildly: [V, Vp] *The creature lay on its back, its legs flailing (about/around) helplessly.* [Vn] *flail one's arms/hands above one's head.* **2** [Vn] to beat sth, eg with a stick.

flair /fleə(r)/ *n* **1** [sing, U] ~ **for sth** a natural ability to do sth well: *He doesn't show much flair for the piano.* ○ *She has a real flair for languages* (ie is quick at learning them). **2** [U] an original and attractive quality; style(3) and imagination: *entrepreneurial/theatrical flair* ○ *She dresses with real flair.*

flak /flæk/ *n* [U] **1** guns shooting at enemy aircraft; fire from these guns: *run into heavy flak.* **2** (*infml*) severe criticism: *take/face plenty of flak from the hostile audience* ○ *The plans for the new tax have come in for a lot of flak* (ie have been very strongly criticized).

■ **'flak jacket** *n* a heavy protective jacket strengthened with metal.

flake /fleɪk/ *n* a small, very thin layer or piece of sth; a small loose bit: *dried onion flakes* ○ *flakes of snow* ○ *Scrape off all the loose flakes of paint before redecorating.* See also CORNFLAKES, SNOWFLAKE, SOAP FLAKES. ⇨ note at PIECE¹.

▶ **flake** *v* ~ **(off)** to come or fall off or cause sth to fall off in flakes: [V, Vp] *The paint on the walls is beginning to flake (off).* [Vnp] *He worked at it with his knife, flaking off layers of rust.* **PHRV** **flake out** (*infml*) to collapse or fall asleep because one is extremely tired: *When I got home from the airport, I flaked out in the nearest armchair.* **flaked** *adj* [attrib] (of food) cut into flakes: *flaked cod* ○ *flaked almonds.*

flaky *adj* (-ier, -iest) **1** composed of flakes; tending to break into flakes: *flaky pastry* ○ *dry flaky skin.* **2** (*US infml*) behaving in a very strange or crazy way. **flakiness** *n* [U].

flambé /'flɒmbeɪ; *US* flɑːm'beɪ/ *adj* (*French*) (following *ns*) (of food) covered with alcohol, esp BRANDY, lit and allowed to burn briefly: *steak flambé.*

flamboyant /flæm'bɔɪənt/ *adj* **1** (of people or their behaviour) tending to attract attention; very confident and noticeable: *a flamboyant young poet* ○ *flamboyant gestures.* **2** bright in colour; noticeable and unusual in style: *flamboyant clothes/designs.* ▶ **flamboyance** /-'bɔɪəns/ *n* [U]: *He lacked the flamboyance of most of his colleagues.* **flamboyantly** *adv*.

flame¹ /fleɪm/ *n* **1** [C, U] a hot glowing quantity of burning gas that comes from sth on fire: *The curtains were enveloped in a sheet of flame.* ○ *the tiny flame of a cigarette-lighter* ○ *The house was in flames* (ie was on fire, burning). ○ *An oil heater was knocked over and immediately burst into flames* (ie suddenly began to burn strongly). ○ *The whole house went up in flames* (ie was destroyed by fire). ⇨ picture at CANDLE. **2** [C] a bright light or brilliant colour, usu red or orange: *a flame-red car* ○ *The flowering shrubs were a scarlet flame.* **3** [C] (*rhet*) an intense feeling, esp love: *the flame of passion.* **4** (usu **old flame**) [C] (*infml*) a person with whom one was once in love; a former BOYFRIEND or GIRLFRIEND. **IDM** **fan the flames** ⇨ FAN³.

■ **'flame-thrower** *n* a weapon that projects a stream of burning fuel.

flame² /fleɪm/ *v* **1** to burn with a bright or brighter flame: [V] *flaming torches* ○ *a fire flaming in the grate* [V-adj] *The burning coals started to flame yellow and orange.* **2** to glow or shine with the colour of flames: [V-adj] *wooded hillsides that flame red in autumn* [V] *a flaming sunset* ○ *flaming red hair* [Vpr] *His cheeks/face flamed with anger/embarrassment.* **3** ~ **(out/up)** (of a strong feeling) to appear suddenly and violently: [V, Vp] *Hatred flamed (up) within him.* [Vp] *'Idiot!' she shouted, her anger flaming out.*

▶ **flaming** *adj* [attrib] **1** passionate or violent: *a flaming row/argument/temper.* **2** (*infml*) (used for emphasis to show annoyance) absolute; UTTER[1]: *You flaming idiot!*

flamenco /fləˈmeŋkəʊ/ *n* [C, U] (*pl* **-os**) a fast exciting Spanish dance or the music played, esp on a GUITAR, to accompany it: *flamenco dancing.*

flamingo /fləˈmɪŋgəʊ/ *n* (*pl* **-os**) a bird with long thin legs, a long neck and pink feathers.

flammable /ˈflæməbl/ *adj* easily catching fire; that can burn easily: *a sofa made from flammable materials.* Compare INFLAMMABLE, NON-FLAMMABLE. ⇨ note at INVALUABLE.

flan /flæn/ *n* an open pie made of pastry or cake and containing a filling of cheese and egg, fruit, etc: *an apple flan.* Compare PIE, QUICHE, TART[1].

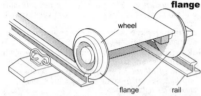

flange

wheel

flange   rail

flange /flændʒ/ *n* a projecting edge of sth, used for holding it in place or for attaching it to sth else. ⇨ picture.

flank /flæŋk/ *n* **1** the side of an animal or a person between the ribs (RIB) and the hip. ⇨ picture at HORSE. **2** the side of sth, eg a building or mountain. **3** the left or right side of an army, football team, etc: *Our orders are to attack their left flank.*
▶ **flank** *v* (often passive) to be placed on each side of or at the side of sb/sth: [Vn] *The prisoner was flanked by the two detectives.* ○ *Tall hedges flank the road for several miles.*

flannel /ˈflænl/ *n* **1(a)** [U] a type of soft loosely woven woollen cloth: *a grey flannel skirt.* **(b)** **flannels** [pl] men's trousers made of this cloth: *a pair of cricket flannels.* **2** [C] (*US* also **wash-cloth**) a small piece of cloth used for washing oneself. **3** [U] (*Brit infml*) smooth talk deliberately avoiding a particular subject or situation: *Please cut the flannel and give us a straight answer.*
▶ **flannel** *v* (**-ll-**; *US* **-l-**) (*Brit infml*) to speak or write flannel(3): [V] *Stop flannelling and answer the question!*

flannelette /ˌflænəˈlet/ *n* [U] a type of soft cotton material: *flannelette nightgowns/sheets.*

flap¹ /flæp/ *n* **1** [C] a flat piece of material that covers an opening or hangs down from sth: *the flap of an envelope* ○ *a tent flap* ○ *the flap of a table* (ie an extra section attached so that it can hang down when not in use). **2** [C] a part of the wing of an aircraft that can be lifted in flight to control upward movement. ⇨ picture at AIRCRAFT. **3** [C usu *sing*] the action or sound of a light blow or of sth moving up and down or from side to side: *He gave me a flap on my shoulder with his newspaper.* ○ *With a flap of its wings, the bird was gone.* **4** [sing] (*infml*) a state of worry, confusion, nervous excitement, etc: *I got in a real flap when I thought I'd lost my keys.*

flap² /flæp/ *v* (**-pp-**) **1** to move, swing, wave, etc up and down or from side to side, usu making a gentle noise: [V] *The sails were flapping gently in the wind.* [Vn] *The bird flapped its wings and flew away.* ○ *She flapped her hand as if shooing something away.* **2** to attempt to give a light blow to sth with a flat object: [Vpr, Vnpr] *flap at a fly with a cloth/flap a cloth at a fly.* **3** (of a bird) to fly with large and often noisy movements of its wings: [Vpr, Vp] *The heron flapped slowly (off) across the lake.* **4** (*infml*) to become anxious or excited; to worry: [V] *There's no need to flap!* [Vp] *The organizers of the event were flapping about in the hall.*

flapjack /ˈflæpdʒæk/ *n* **1** a cake made from OATS, butter and honey or SYRUP(2). **2** (*esp US*) a thick PANCAKE(1).

flapper /ˈflæpə(r)/ *n* (*dated infml*) a fashionable and lively young woman, originally in the 1920s.

flare¹ /fleə(r)/ *v* **1** to burn brightly but briefly or not steadily: [V] *The match flared in the darkness.* ○ *flaring gas jets.* **2** to burst into sudden activity or anger: [V] *Tempers flared at the conference.* [Vpr] *Discontent flared into open aggression.* **PHR V** **,flare ˈup 1** to burn suddenly more intensely: *The fire flared up as I put more logs on it.* **2** to reach a more violent state; to become suddenly angry: *Violence has flared up again.* ○ *He flares up at the slightest provocation.* **3** (of an illness) to start again: *My back trouble has flared up again.*
▶ **flare** *n* **1** (usu *sing*) a bright but brief or unsteady light or flame: *the sudden flare of a torch in the darkness.* **2** a device that produces a flaring light used esp as a signal: *The ship sent up distress flares to attract the attention of the coastguard.*
■ **ˈflare-path** (*Brit*) (also *esp US* **apˈproach lights** [pl]) *n* a line of lights on a RUNWAY to guide aircraft landing or taking off.
ˈflare-up *n* **1** a sudden expression of strong or violent feeling: *These flare-ups happen in every family.* **2** a sudden rush of light or flame.

flare² /fleə(r)/ *v* to become or make sth wider at the bottom: [V, Vp] *This skirt flares (out) at the hem.* [V] *Her nostrils flared angrily.* [Vn] *flared trousers.* Compare TAPER[1] 1.
▶ **flare** *n* **1** [C] a shape that becomes gradually wider: *a skirt with a slight flare.* **2 flares** [pl] (*infml*) trousers with wide bottoms.

flash¹ /flæʃ/ *n* **1** [C] **(a)** a sudden brief bright light or flame: *a flash of lightning* ○ *a signal flash.* **(b)** a sudden brief rush of feeling or show of humour, understanding, etc: *a flash of pity/excitement/inspiration/intuition.* **2** [C] = NEWSFLASH. **3** [C, U] a device or system that produces a brief bright light for taking photographs indoors or in poor light: *a camera with a built-in flash* ○ *I'll need flash for this shot.* **4** [C] a band or patch of cloth worn as a symbol on a military uniform, eg on the shoulder. **IDM** **a ,flash in the ˈpan** a sudden brilliant success that lasts only a short time and is not repeated: *His first novel was a flash in the pan — he hasn't written anything decent since.* **in/like a ˈflash** very quickly; at once; immediately: *The biscuits all went in a flash.* **quick as a flash** ⇨ QUICK.
▶ **flash** *adj* (*infml derog*) attracting attention by being large, bright, expensive, etc: *a big flash car.*
■ **ˈflash bulb** *n* a small BULB(2) that can be fixed into a flash¹(3): *popping flash bulbs.*
ˈflash-cube *n* a set of four flash bulbs arranged as a CUBE(1a).
ˈflash-flood *n* a sudden flood of water, usu caused by heavy rain: *Flash-floods have been reported in North Wales.*
ˈflash-gun *n* a device that holds and operates a flash¹(3).

flash² /flæʃ/ *v* **1(a)** to give or produce a brief bright light: [V] *Lightning flashed during the storm.* ○ *A lighthouse was flashing in the distance.* ○ (*fig*) *Her eyes flashed angrily.* [Vp] *lights flashing on and off.* **(b)** to make sth shine briefly or suddenly: [Vnpr] *flash a torch in sb's eyes/at sb* [also Vn]. **2(a)** to make a signal with a light: [Vn, Vnpr] *flash a warning (to sb) with one's headlights.* **(b)** to give a look, express a feeling, etc suddenly and quickly: [Vn] *Her eyes flashed anger and defiance.* [Vnn] *He flashed her a charming smile.* [also Vnpr]. **3** to move or pass very quickly: [Vp] *The train flashed by at high speed.* ○ *Our holiday flashed past.* [Vpr] *The ball flashed past the post.* ○ *An idea flashed into her mind.* **4** to send sth by radio, television, etc: [Vn] *flash a mess-*

age on the screen [Vnpr] *News of the tragedy was flashed across the country.* **5** to show or display sth briefly: [Vn] *flash an identification card* [Vnp] (*derog*) *He's flashing his money around* (ie to gain the admiration of others). **6** [V] (*infml*) (esp of a man) to show one's sexual organs briefly in public. **PHR V** **flash** ꞌ**back** (of one's thoughts) to return to an earlier time: *My mind flashed back to our previous meeting.*

▶ **flasher** /ꞌflæʃə(r)/ *n* (*infml*) **1** a person who flashes (FLASH² 6). **2** a light on a vehicle that flashes on and off and is used to indicate which way the vehicle is turning. See also INDICATOR 2b.

■ ꞌ**flash card** *n* a card with a word or words and sometimes a picture on it. Flash cards are held up for pupils as a visual aid to learning.

flashback /ꞌflæʃbæk/ *n* a part of a film, play, etc that shows a scene earlier in time than the main story: *The events that led up to the murder were shown in a series of flashbacks.*

flashing /ꞌflæʃɪŋ/ *n* a usu metal strip of material put on a roof where it joins a wall, etc, to prevent water getting through: *lead flashings around chimneys.*

flashlight /ꞌflæʃlaɪt/ *n* **1** (esp US) = TORCH 1. **2** a device that produces a brief bright light for taking photographs indoors or in poor light: *flashlight photography.*

flashpoint /ꞌflæʃpɔɪnt/ *n* [C, U] a point or place at which violence or anger cannot be controlled: *Community unrest is rapidly approaching (the) flashpoint.* ○ *The town became a flashpoint during the riots.*

flashy /ꞌflæʃi/ *adj* (**-ier, -iest**) (*usu derog*) attractive in a bright way but not of good quality or in good taste: *flashy clothes/jewellery* ○ *a flashy car.* ▶ **flashily** *adv: flashily dressed.*

flask /flɑːsk; *US* flæsk/ *n* **1(a)** a bottle with a narrow neck(3), esp one used in scientific work for mixing or storing chemicals. **(b)** a container of this shape for storing oil, wine, etc. **2** (also ꞌ**hip-flask**) a small flat bottle made of metal or glass and often covered with leather, used for carrying alcohol in one's pocket. **3** (*Brit*) = VACUUM FLASK: *a flask of tea.* Compare THERMOS.

flat¹ /flæt/ *adj* (**-tter, -ttest**) **1** having only one level; not curving or sloping: *low buildings with flat roofs* ○ *People used to think that the world was flat.* **2** smooth and even; without lumps, holes, etc: *a flat surface for writing on* ○ *The countryside is very flat here* (ie has no hills). **3** having a broad level surface but little height or depth: *a flat cap* ○ *flat dishes/ plates* ○ *flat shoes* (ie with no heels or very low ones) ○ *The cake was flat* (ie did not rise while cooking). **4** [attrib] completely definite; firm; absolute: *give sb a flat denial/refusal.* **5** dull; lacking interest or energy: *speak in a flat voice* ○ *He felt a bit flat after his friends had gone.* **6** [usu pred] (of pictures, photographs or colours) without contrast, texture or depth. **7** not having much trade or business: *The market has been very flat today.* **8** having a single price for a variety of goods or services: *The firm charges a flat fee for their services.* ○ *flat-rate* (ie standard and fixed) *contributions.* **9** (*music*) **(a)** (used following the name of a note) half a tone¹(6) lower than the specified note: *B flat is a semitone below B.* ⇨ picture at MUSIC. **(b)** below the correct pitch¹(2): *Your piano is flat; it needs tuning.* Compare SHARP 11. **10** (of a drink) no longer having bubbles in; not fresh: *The lager tastes/has gone flat.* **11** (of a tyre) not containing enough air, eg because of a PUNCTURE. **12** (of a battery) unable to supply any more electric current. **13** (of feet) not having normal raised arches (ARCH¹ 3). **IDM** **and** ꞌ**that's** ꞌ**flat** that's my final decision: *I'm not going out with you and that's flat!* **(as)** ꞌ**flat as a** ꞌ**pancake** completely flat: *The country round about is as flat as a pancake.* **in a flat** ꞌ**spin** rushing about in a state of great

alarm or confusion: *I've been in a flat spin all morning.*

▶ **flatly** *adv* **1** showing little interest or enthusiasm: *'Maybe,' he said flatly, 'I'll see.'* **2** in a very definite and firm manner; absolutely: *She flatly denies all the allegations.* ○ *Our request was flatly rejected.*

flatness *n* [U].

■ ꞌ**flat-**ꞌ**bottomed** *adj* (of a boat) having a flat bottom and used esp in shallow water.

ꞌ**flat-fish** *n* a type of sea fish with a flat body, eg PLAICE.

ꞌ**flat-**ꞌ**footed** *adj* **1** having feet without normal raised arches (ARCH¹ 3). **2** (*infml*) unable to move quickly and smoothly; awkward or CLUMSY(1): *His speed and skill make other players look flat-footed.* **3** not clever or imaginative: *Subjects need not be taught in such a flat-footed way.*

ꞌ**flat-racing** *n* [U] horse-racing over level ground without jumps. Compare STEEPLECHASE 1.

flat² /flæt/ *n* **1** [C] (*esp Brit*) (also *esp US* **apartment**) a set of rooms for living in, including a kitchen, usu on one floor of a building: *a new block of flats* ○ *They're renting a furnished flat on the third floor.* ○ *Many large old houses have now been converted into flats.* **2** [sing] **the ~** (**of sth**) the flat level part of sth: *the flat of the hand* ○ *the flat of a sword/a blade/an oar* ○ *on the flat* (ie on level ground). **3** [C usu *pl*] an area of low flat land, esp near water: ꞌ*mud-flats* ○ ꞌ*salt flats.* **4 the flat** [sing] the season of flat-racing (FLAT¹) for horses. **5** [C] (*music*) a sign (♭) indicating that a note should be played half a tone¹(6) lower; a note played half a tone lower than another named note: *play an E flat.* ⇨ picture at MUSIC. Compare NATURAL *n* 1, SHARP *n*. **6** [C] (*infml esp US*) a flat¹(11) tyre. **7** [C] a movable upright section of stage scenery.

▶ **flatlet** /-lət/ *n* (*Brit*) a very small flat²(1).

flat³ /flæt/ *adv* **1** spread out on one level in a straight position, against another surface: *She lay flat on her back.* ○ *I want the sofa there — flat against the wall.* ○ *He knocked his opponent flat.* ○ *I tripped and fell flat on my face.* ○ *The earthquake laid the city flat* (ie destroyed it, making all the buildings fall). **2** definitely and directly; completely: *My boss told me flat that I could not leave early.* ○ *I made them a reasonable offer but they turned it down flat.* **3** lower than the true or correct pitch¹(2): *She sings flat all the time.* **4** (used after a phrase with *in* indicating a period of time, to emphasize how short it is) exactly: *I can change a tyre in two minutes flat.* **IDM** **fall** ꞌ**flat** (of a joke, story, performance, etc) to fail completely to produce the effect intended or expected: *All my funny stories fell completely flat.* **flat/stony broke** ⇨ BROKE². **flat** ꞌ**out 1** as fast as possible; using all one's strength or resources: *running/working/training flat out.* **2** extremely tired: *After running in the marathon, she was flat out for a week.*

flatcar /ꞌflætkɑː(r)/ *n* (US) a railway truck without a roof or sides, used for carrying goods.

flatmate /ꞌflætmeɪt/ *n* a person who shares a flat²(1) with one or more others: *My flatmate has gone away for the weekend.* Compare ROOM-MATE.

flatten /ꞌflætn/ *v* **1** ~ (**sth**) (**out**) to become or make sth flat or flatter: [Vp] *The land flattens out near the coast.* [V, Vp] *The graph flattens (out) gradually after a steep fall.* [Vn] *a field of wheat flattened by storms* ○ *Several buildings had been flattened* (ie destroyed) *in the blast.* [Vn, Vnp] *flatten (out) a piece of metal by hammering it* [Vnpr] *He flattened himself against the wall to let the others pass.* **2** to defeat sb/sth completely; to depress or HUMILIATE sb: [Vn] *She has effectively flattened press speculation.* ○ *He was totally flattened by her sarcasm.*

flatter /ꞌflætə(r)/ *v* **1** to praise sb too much or in an

insincere way, esp in order to gain favour for one-self: [Vn] *If you flatter your mother a bit she might invite us all to dinner.* **2** (usu passive) to give a feeling of pleasure or honour to sb: [Vn] *I was very flattered by the invitation to speak at the conference.* **3** to make sb look particularly attractive or seem more attractive than they really are: [Vn] *You need a hairstyle that flatters the shape of your face.* ○ (*ironic*) *This photograph certainly doesn't flatter you* (ie It makes you look rather ugly). **4** ~ **oneself (that ...)** (no passive) to please oneself by believing sth good but usu not true about oneself or one's abilities: [Vn] *Do you really think he likes you? You flatter yourself!* [Vn.*that*] *He flatters himself that he speaks French well.*
▶ **flatterer** /ˈflætərə(r)/ *n.*
flattering /ˈflætərɪŋ/ *adj* (**a**) making sb look more attractive: *That's a very flattering dress Ann's wearing.* (**b**) giving pleasure or honour to sb: *His comments weren't very flattering.*
flattery /ˈflætəri/ *n* [U] praise that is excessive or insincere: *You're too intelligent to fall for his flattery.*

flatulent /ˈflætjʊlənt; *US* -tʃə-/ *adj* **1** causing or suffering from gas in the stomach or bowels: *feel rather flatulent.* **2** (*derog*) (of speech, etc) sounding grand but with little substance; exaggerated: *flatulent boasts.*
▶ **flatulence** /ˈflætjʊləns; *US* -tʃə-/ *n* [U] discomfort caused by having too much gas in the stomach or bowels.

flaunt /flɔːnt/ *v* (*usu derog*) to display sth one is proud of in an obvious way in order to gain the admiration of other people: [Vn] *He's always flaunting his wealth.* ○ *They openly flaunted their relationship.*

flautist /ˈflɔːtɪst/ (*US* **flutist** /ˈfluːtɪst/) *n* a person who plays the FLUTE, esp as a profession.

flavour (*US* **flavor**) /ˈfleɪvə(r)/ *n* **1** [U] taste and smell, esp of food: *Adding salt to food improves the flavour.* ○ *a watery soup without much flavour.* **2** [C] a particular type of taste: *wines with a delicate flavour* ○ *six different flavours of ice-cream.* **3** [C, U] a special quality, characteristic or atmosphere: *a room with a definite French flavour* ○ *The film captures/retains much of the book's exotic flavour.* ○ *I have tried to convey something of the flavour of the argument.* **IDM** **flavour of the ¹month** the current fashion; sth that is popular at a particular time: *Environmental issues are no longer flavour of the month.* ○ *We're not the political flavour of the month.*
▶ **flavour** (*US* **flavor**) *v* ~ **sth (with sth)** to give flavour to food or drink by adding sth with a distinct taste: [Vnpr] *flavour a cake with vanilla, orange or lemon* [Vn] *Spices are used to flavour the rice.* **-flavoured** (*US* **-flavored**) (forming compound *adjs*) having a flavour of the specified kind: *lemon-flavoured sweets.* **flavouring** (*US* **flavoring**) /ˈfleɪvərɪŋ/ *n* [C, U] a thing added to food to give it flavour: *orange flavouring* ○ *This drink contains no artificial flavourings.*
flavourless (*US* **flavorless**) *adj* having no flavour: *a flavourless meal.*

flaw /flɔː/ *n* ~ **(in sth/sth)** **1** a crack, fault or mark in an object or in material: *The vase is perfect except for a few small flaws in its base.* **2** a mistake that makes sth weaker or less acceptable: *an argument full of flaws* ○ *a flaw in a contract* ○ *the fatal flaw in the system.* **3** a weak part in sb's character: *Pride was the greatest flaw in his personality.* See also FAULT 1.
▶ **flaw** *v* (usu passive) to make sth have a flaw; to damage or spoil sth: [Vn] *The scheme is badly/ severely/obviously flawed.* ○ *a flawed argument* ○ *the film's flawed heroine.*
flawless *adj* perfect; without fault: *a flawless*

complexion/performance ○ *Her English is almost flawless.* **flawlessly** *adv.*

flax /flæks/ *n* [U] **1** a small plant with blue flowers, grown for its stem and seeds. **2** the thread got from the stem of the flax plant, used in making LINEN(1).
▶ **flaxen** /ˈflæksn/ *adj* (of hair) pale yellow: *a flaxen-haired child.*

flay /fleɪ/ *v* **1** to remove the skin from a dead animal. **2** to whip sb/sth violently: [Vn] *He nearly flayed the wretched horse alive* (ie He beat it so much that it almost died). **3** to criticize sb/sth severely: [Vnpr] *Paul flayed her with reproaches.*

flea /fliː/ *n* a small jumping insect without wings that feeds on the blood of animals and humans: *be bitten by a flea* ○ *The cat has fleas.* **IDM** **with a ¹flea in one's ear** with severe and clearly expressed anger and disapproval from sb: *He interrupted the board meeting and got sent away with a flea in his ear.*
■ **¹flea-bite** *n* **1** the bite of a flea. **2** a small and unimportant problem or cost.
¹flea market *n* (*infml*) an outdoor market that sells old and used goods at low prices.
¹flea-pit *n* (*infml derog*) an old and dirty cinema, theatre, etc.

fleck /flek/ *n* (usu *pl*) ~ **(of sth)** **1** a very small patch or spot of a colour: *His hair was dark, with flecks of grey.* **2** a small piece or grain of sth; a SPECK: *flecks of dust/foam/dandruff.*
▶ **fleck** *v* ~ **sth (with sth)** (usu passive) to cover or mark sth with flecks: [Vnpr] *The sea was flecked with foam.* [Vn] *Flakes of paint flecked the bare boards.*

fled *pt, pp* of FLEE.

fledged /fledʒd/ *adj* (of birds) having mature wing feathers for flying; able to fly. See also FULLY-FLEDGED.

fledgling (also **fledgeling**) /ˈfledʒlɪŋ/ *n* **1** a young bird that is just able to fly. **2** [usu attrib] a person, an organization, a system, etc that is new and without experience: *fledgling democracies.*

flee /fliː/ *v* (*pt, pp* **fled** /fled/) ~ **(from sb/sth)** (**a**) to run or hurry away; to escape, esp from danger: [Vpr] *The customers fled from the bank when the alarm sounded.* [V] *She burst into tears and fled.* (**b**) to leave one's home or country permanently, esp because of fear: [V] *flee in search of a better life* [Vn] *During the civil war thousands of people fled the country.* [Vpr] *Her family fled to safety from the war-torn city.*

fleece /fliːs/ *n* **1** [C] the wool coat of a sheep or goat: *fine thick fleeces.* ⇨ picture at SHEEP. **2** [U] a type of fabric with a texture like sheep's wool: *a wind-resistant jacket lined with polyester and cotton fleece.*
▶ **fleece** *v* (*infml*) to take a lot of money from sb, esp by charging them too much or tricking them: [Vn] *Some local shops are really fleecing the tourists.*
fleecy *adj* soft and light in texture, like sheep's wool, or appearing so: *a fleecy sweatshirt/towel* ○ *fleecy clouds.*

fleet¹ /fliːt/ *n* **1**(**a**) [C] a group of ships commanded by the same person, esp in war: *a fleet of destroyers.* (**b**) [C] a group of ships fishing or sailing together: *the local fishing fleet.* (**c**) (usu **the fleet**) [CGp] all the warships (WARSHIP) of a country; the navy. **2** [C] a group of aircraft, buses, taxis, etc travelling together or owned and operated by one organization: *the company's new fleet of vans* ○ *a 200-strong fleet of coaches.*
■ **¹fleet ¹admiral** *n* an officer of the highest rank in the US navy. ⇨ App 6.

fleet² /fliːt/ *adj* (*dated*) fast; light and quick in running: *fleet of foot* ○ *fleet-footed.*

fleeting /ˈfliːtɪŋ/ *adj* passing quickly; lasting only a short time: *a fleeting glimpse/smile* ○ *For a fleeting moment I thought the car was going to crash.* ○ *We* *paid a fleeting visit to Paris.* ▶ **fleetingly** *adv: smile fleetingly.*

Fleet Street /ˈfliːt striːt/ *n* [sing] a street in central London where many major newspapers formerly had their offices. It is used to refer to British, esp London, newspapers and journalists in general: *Fleet Street loves a good scandal.*

flesh /fleʃ/ *n* **1** [U] (**a**) the soft substance between the skin and bones of animal or human bodies, consisting of muscle and fat: *The trap had cut deeply into the rabbit's flesh.* (**b**) this as food: *Tigers are flesh-eating animals.* **2** [U] the skin or surface of the human body: *the pale flesh of English people on holiday abroad.* **3** the flesh [sing] the human body and its needs or desires, esp contrasted with the mind or the soul: *the pleasures/sins of the flesh* ○ (*saying*) *The spirit is willing but the flesh is weak* [ie Although sb may want to do sth, they are too lazy, tired, weak, etc actually to do it]. **4** [U] the soft part of fruits and vegetables, esp the part that is usu eaten: *the sweet flesh of a mango.* ⇨ picture at FRUIT. **IDM** ˌflesh and ˈblood the human body or human nature with its emotions, weaknesses, etc: *It was more than flesh and blood could bear.* **go the way of all flesh** ⇨ WAY[1]. **in the ˈflesh** in physical form; in person: *I've listened to all her records but I've never seen her in the flesh.* **make one's/sb's ˈflesh crawl/creep** to make one/sb feel nervous, afraid or full of disgust: *The mere sight of snakes makes my flesh creep.* **one's (ˌown) ˌflesh and ˈblood** close relations in one's family: *You can't treat her like that! She's your sister, your own flesh and blood!* **one's pound of flesh** ⇨ POUND[1]. **a thorn in sb's flesh/side** ⇨ THORN.
▶ **flesh** *v* **PHRV** ˌflesh sth ˈout to add more details or information to sth: *Your ideas will need fleshing out before you present them to the board.*

fleshly *adj* (*fml or rhet*) of the body; SENSUAL or sexual: *fleshly lusts.*

fleshy *adj* **1** of or like flesh; rather fat: *fleshy arms/lips.* **2** soft, thick and MOIST in texture: *fleshy peaches/leaves.*
■ **ˈflesh-wound** *n* a wound that breaks the skin but does not reach the bones or internal organs of the body.

fleshpots /ˈfleʃpɒts/ *n* [pl] (*joc usu derog*) places supplying things to enjoy, esp good food, drink and entertainment: *the fleshpots of the capital.*

fleur-de-lis (also **fleur-de-lys**) /ˌflɜː də ˈliː, -ˈliːs/ *n* (*pl* **fleurs-** /ˌflɜː də ˈliː, -ˈliːs/) a design representing a LILY flower with three petals (PETAL) joined together, formerly the royal coat of arms (COAT) of France.

flew *pt* of FLY[1].

flex[1] /fleks/ *n* (*esp Brit*) (*US* **cord**) [C, U] a length of flexible wire in a protective covering, used for carrying an electric current to an appliance: *an electric kettle flex.*

flex[2] /fleks/ *v* to bend or move a limb, joint or muscle, esp in order to exercise one's body before an activity: [Vn] *flex one's knee/fingers/muscles* [V] *His hand flexed on the gun.* **IDM** **flex one's ˈmuscles** to show one's strength and power, esp as a warning or to display pride in oneself: *flex one's political muscles* ○ *Shareholders need to flex their muscles on issues of principle.*

flexible /ˈfleksəbl/ *adj* **1**(**a**) easily changed to suit new conditions: *a flexible design/approach* ○ *work flexible hours* ○ *Our plans are quite flexible.* (**b**) (of people) willing and able to change to suit different circumstances: *You need to be more flexible and imaginative in your approach.* ○ *If you can be flexible, book your holiday at the last minute and save money.* **2** that can bend easily without breaking: *flexible plastic tubing.* ▶ **flexibility** /ˌfleksəˈbɪləti/ *n* [U]: *have/offer a degree of flexibility* ○ *Employing part-*

time staff gives companies greater flexibility. **flexibly** /ˈfleksəbli/ *adv.*

flexitime /ˈfleksitaɪm/ *n* [U] a system in which employees can start and finish work at different times, provided that each of them works a certain number of hours in a week or month: *She works flexitime.*

flibbertigibbet /ˌflɪbətiˈdʒɪbɪt/ *n* a silly person who talks too much and cannot be relied on.

flick /flɪk/ *n* **1** [C usu *sing*] a quick sharp blow or movement, eg with a whip or the tip of a finger: *We have electricity at the flick of a switch.* ○ *He threw the ball back with a quick flick of the wrist.* See also FLIP. **2** [C usu *sing*] a quick look through the pages of a book, magazine, etc: *I've had a quick flick through the catalogue.* See also FLIP. **3**(**a**) [C] (*dated infml*) a cinema film. (**b**) the flicks [pl] (*dated infml*) the cinema: *What's on at the flicks?*
▶ **flick** *v* **1** ~ A (with B); ~ B (at A) to strike sb/sth with a flick; to give a flick with sth: [Vnpr] *He flicked me with the wet towel/flicked the wet towel at me.* [also Vn]. **2** ~ sth (off, on, etc) to move sth with a flick: [Vn, Vnp] *flick the light switch (on)* [ie turn on the light) [Vnp] *She flicked back her hair.* [Vn-adj] *He flicked the knife open.* [Vnpr] *Cliff was ready to flick the ball into the goal.* **3** to move or move sth quickly and lightly: [Vpr] *The cow's tail flicked from side to side.* [Vn] *flick an eyelid* [Vp] *His eyes flicked away towards the door.* **PHRV** ˌflick sth aˈway; ˌflick sth from/off sth to remove sth with a quick sharp movement: *She saw him flick away a tear.* ○ *The waiter flicked the crumbs off the table.* ˌflick ˈthrough (sth) to turn the pages of a book, etc quickly, looking briefly at the contents: *Sam flicked through a magazine while he waited.*
■ **ˈflick-knife** *n* (*pl* **-knives**) (*US* **ˈswitch-blade**) a knife with a blade inside the handle that jumps out quickly when a button is pressed.

flicker /ˈflɪkə(r)/ *v* **1**(**a**) (of a light or flame) to burn or shine in an unsteady way: [V] *The candle flickered for a moment and went out.* [Vp] *Lights flickered on and off.* (**b**) (of an emotion) to be felt or seen briefly: [Vpr] *A suspicion flickered through her mind.* ○ *A faint smile flickered across her face.* **2** to move backwards and forwards lightly and quickly: [V] *flickering eyelids* [Vpr] *Shadows flickered across the garden.* ○ *The leaves flickered gently in the breeze.*
▶ **flicker** *n* (usu *sing*) (**a**) a flickering movement or light: *the flicker of images on the screen.* (**b**) a faint and brief experience, esp of an emotion: *a flicker of hope/despair/interest.*

flies /flaɪz/ *n* the flies [pl] the space above the stage of a theatre, used for lights and for storing scenery. See also FLY[3] 1.

flight[1] /flaɪt/ *n* **1** [U] (**a**) the action or process of flying through the air or space; the ability to fly: *the age of supersonic flight* ○ *flight safety* ○ *The bird had been shot down in flight* [ie while flying]. (**b**) the movement or path of a thing through the air: *the flight of an arrow/a dart/a missile.* **2** [C] (**a**) a journey made by air, esp in an aircraft: *have a smooth/comfortable/bumpy flight* ○ *All flights have been cancelled because of fog.* (**b**) an aircraft making such a journey: *We're booked on the same flight.* ○ *catch/take/board the early flight to Brussels* ○ *Flight BA 4793 will arrive in London Heathrow at 16.50.* **3** [C] a group of aircraft working as a unit: *an aircraft of the Queen's flight.* **4** [C] ~ of sth a number of birds flying together: *a flight of geese.* **5** [C] a series of steps between two floors or levels: *We had to climb six flights of stairs to the top floor.* **6** [C] ~ of sth an idea or a statement that is very imaginative but usu not practical or sensible: *wild flights of fancy/imagination.* **IDM** **in the first/top ˈflight** having a leading place; among the best of a particular group: *She's in the top flight of journalists.*
▶ **flight** *v* (in sport) to make a ball, etc move

F

through the air in a particular way: [Vn] *a well-flighted pass.*

flightless *adj* (of birds or insects) unable to fly.

■ **'flight crew** *n* [C] the people who operate and work on an aircraft.

'flight-deck *n* **1** the control room of a large aircraft, from which the pilot and crew fly the plane. **2** (on a ship that carries aircraft) a surface where aircraft take off and land.

,flight lieu'tenant *n* (in Britain) an officer in the Royal Air Force. ⇨ App 6.

'flight path *n* the direction or course of an aircraft through the air: *The flight paths of two planes crossed, with fatal results.*

'flight-recorder (also **black 'box**) *n* an electronic device in an aircraft that automatically records details of the flight.

'flight sergeant *n* (in Britain) a rank in the Royal Air Force. ⇨ App 6.

'flight simulator *n* a device used on the ground for training pilots by reproducing accurately all the conditions of flying.

flight² /flaɪt/ *n* [U, sing] the action or an instance of running away from danger: *the flight of refugees from the advancing forces* ○ (*fig*) *The financial crisis produced a flight of capital* (ie the sending of money out of a country). **IDM** **put sb to 'flight** to force sb to run away: *The enemy was quickly put to flight.* **take (to) 'flight** to run away: *The gang took (to) flight when they heard the police car.*

flighty /'flaɪti/ *adj* (**-ier, -iest**) (esp of a woman or her behaviour) constantly changing; not consistent or reliable.

flimsy /'flɪmzi/ *adj* (**-ier, -iest**) **1(a)** (of cloth or material) light and thin: *a flimsy dress.* (**b**) not strong or solid enough for the purpose for which it is used: *a flimsy cardboard box.* **2** weak; not convincing: *a flimsy excuse* ○ *The evidence against him is pretty flimsy.*

flinch /flɪntʃ/ *v* **1** ~ (**at sth**) to make a sudden automatic movement because of pain, fear or shock: [V] *He took all the blows without flinching.* [Vpr] *Paul flinched at the sight of her covered in blood.* [Vpr, Vp] *She flinched (away) from the dog.* **2** ~ **from sth/from doing sth** to avoid thinking about or doing sth unpleasant: [Vpr] *We shall never flinch from (the task of) telling the people the whole truth.*

fling /flɪŋ/ *v* (*pt, pp* **flung** /flʌŋ/) **1** to throw sth violently or angrily : [Vnpr] *fling a stone at a window* [Vnp] *He flung away the letter in disgust.* [also Vn]. **2** to put or push sb/sth somewhere quickly or roughly and forcefully: [Vnpr, Vnp] *She flung the papers (down) on the desk and stormed out.* [Vnpr] *He flung her to the ground.* ○ *He was flung into prison* (ie put into prison roughly and perhaps without trial). [Vn-adj] *He flung the door open.* **3** to move oneself or part of one's body suddenly or forcefully: [Vnpr] *She flung herself onto the sofa.* [Vnp] *He flung his arm out just in time to stop her falling.* **4** ~ **sth** (**at sb**) to say or express sth to sb aggressively: [Vnpr] *Make sure of your facts before you start flinging accusations at people.* [also Vn, Vnp]. **PHRV** **'fling oneself at sb** = THROW ONESELF AT STH/SB. **'fling oneself into sth** to start or do sth with a lot of energy and enthusiasm: *She flung herself into her new job.* **,fling sth 'off/'on** to take off or put on clothes quickly and carelessly: *She flung on her coat and ran to the bus-stop.* See also FAR-FLUNG.

▶ **fling** *n* (*infml*) (**a**) a short period of enjoyment or of wild behaviour: *a last/final fling* ○ *have a/one's fling.* (**b**) a brief casual love affair: *I had a few flings in my younger days.* See also HIGHLAND FLING.

flint /flɪnt/ *n* **1** [U, C] a very hard grey stone that can produce a SPARK(1a) of fire when struck against steel: *This layer of rock contains a lot of flint.* ○ *prehistoric flint tools* ○ (*fig*) *His eyes were cruel and*

hard as flint. **2** [C] (**a**) a piece of flint or a similar substance used to produce a SPARK(1a) eg in an old type of gun. (**b**) a small piece of hard metal used to produce a spark in a cigarette lighter (CIGARETTE).

▶ **flinty** *adj* **1** made of or containing flint; very hard, like flint. **2** cruel; without pity: *flinty eyes.*

flintlock /'flɪntlɒk/ *n* an old-fashioned gun, in which the GUNPOWDER is lit by a SPARK struck from a FLINT, causing the gun to FIRE²(1b).

flip /flɪp/ *v* (**-pp-**) **1** ~ (**over**) to turn over or make sth turn over onto its side or back with a sudden sharp movement: [Vp] *The plane crashed and flipped over.* [Vnp] *The wind will flip it over.* ○ *She flipped over the page.* **2** to switch sth on or off with a quick sharp movement; to FLICK(1) sth: [Vn] *flip the switch* [Vnp] *He flipped the light on.* **3** to send sth into the air with a sharp movement of the thumb and finger so that it turns over: [Vn, Vnpr] *flip a coin (in the air).* **4** (*sl*) to become very angry, excited or enthusiastic: [V] *My mother really flipped when I told her I was getting married.* **IDM** **,flip one's 'lid** (*sl*) to become very emotional and lose control; to go crazy; to flip(4). **PHRV** **'flip through sth** to turn the pages of sth quickly, looking briefly at the contents: *She flipped through her notes.*

▶ **flip** *n* a quick light blow or movement, causing sth to turn over: *give a coin a flip* ○ *Her heart did a flip.*

flip *adj* (*infml*) showing that one does not take sth as seriously as one should; FLIPPANT: *a flip comment* ○ *Don't be flip with me.*

flip *interj* (expressing annoyance or great surprise): *Oh, flip!*

flipping *adj, adv* (*Brit infml*) (used as a mild swearword (SWEAR) for emphasis or to express annoyance): *I hate this flipping hotel!* ○ *What flipping awful weather!*

■ **'flip chart** *n* a pad of large sheets of paper fixed to a stand and used at conferences, etc for presenting information to an audience: *prepare a flip chart in advance.*

'flip-flop (*US* **thong**) *n* a type of open SANDAL with a strap that goes between the big toe and the toe next to it: *a pair of flip-flops.* ⇨ picture at SANDAL.

'flip side *n* (*usu sing*) ~ (**of/to sth**) **1** another aspect of a situation, way of considering a problem, result of an action, etc that may not be welcome or desirable: *The flip side to our optimism on inflation is the hardship suffered by many in reducing it.* **2** (*dated*) the reverse¹ side of a record, esp the side that does not have the main song or piece of music on it.

flippant /'flɪpənt/ *adj* not showing a serious attitude or sufficient respect: *a flippant answer/remark* ○ *Don't be so flippant — this is an important matter.* ▶ **flippancy** /-ənsi/ *n* [U]: *His flippancy conceals a deep insecurity.* **flippantly** *adv.*

flipper /'flɪpə(r)/ *n* **1** each of the broad flat limbs that certain sea animals have and use for swimming: *Seals, turtles and penguins have flippers.* **2** either of a pair of pieces of flat rubber worn on sb's feet to help them to swim quickly, esp under water.

flirt /flɜːt/ *v* **1** ~ (**with sb**) to behave towards sb as if one finds them physically attractive, but without any serious intention of having a relationship: [Vpr] *He enjoys flirting with the girls in the office.* [also V]. **2** ~ **with sth** (**a**) to consider sth but not seriously: [Vpr] *In his youth he flirted with Communism.* ○ *I'm flirting with the idea of getting a job in China.* (**b**) to take a serious risk and be very close to danger or disaster: [Vpr] *flirt with danger/death.*

▶ **flirt** *n* a person who flirts with many people: *They say she's a terrible flirt.*

flirtation /flɜː'teɪʃn/ *n* **1** [U] the action of flirting. **2** [C] (**a**) ~ (**with sb**) a brief love affair that is not taken seriously: *carry on/have a flirtation with sb.*

(b) ~ **(with sth)** a brief period of being involved in sth but not seriously; a SUPERFICIAL(3a) interest in sth: *a brief and unsuccessful flirtation with the property market.*

flirtatious /flɜːˈteɪʃəs/ *adj* **(a)** tending to flirt with many people: *an attractive, flirtatious young woman.* **(b)** of or related to flirting: *flirtatious behaviour.*

flirty *adj* (*infml*) tending to flirt.

flit /flɪt/ *v* (**-tt-**) ~ **(from A to B)** to fly or move lightly and quickly from one thing or place to another: [Vp] *butterflies flitting about among the flowers* [Vpr] *She seems to spend her life flitting from one country to another.* ○ (*fig*) *A thought flitted through my mind* (ie came suddenly but then quickly disappeared).

▶ **flit** *n* (*Brit infml*) a sudden and secret departure from a place, eg in order to avoid paying debts: *do a (moonlight) flit.*

float¹ /fləʊt/ *v* **1** to stay on or close to the surface of a liquid and not sink: [V] *Wood floats.* [Vpr] *Try and float on your back.* **2** to move slowly and without resistance in air or water; to DRIFT²(1): [Vp] *The smell of new bread floated up from the kitchen.* [Vpr] *A balloon floated across the sky.* ○ *The raft was floating gently down the river.* ○ (*fig*) *Thoughts of lazy summer afternoons floated through his mind.* **3** to make sth move on or close to the surface of a liquid: [Vn] *There wasn't enough water to float the ship.* [Vpr] *float a raft of logs down the river* ○ *We waited for the tide to float the boat off the sandbank.* **4** to suggest sth for consideration: [Vn] *Let me float a couple of ideas.* **5** (*commerce*) to start a company or a business scheme; to sell shares to the public as a way of doing this: [Vn] *a company recently floated on the Stock Exchange* ○ *Shares were floated at 460p.* **6** (*techn*) **(a)** to allow the foreign exchange values of a currency to vary freely according to the value of other international currencies: [Vn] *float the pound/dollar/yen.* **(b)** [V] (of a currency) to find its own value in this way. **IDM** **float/walk on air** ⇨ AIR¹. **PHR V** **float aˈbout/aˈround** (esp in the continuous tenses) **1** (of a rumour) to circulate among people: *There's a rumour floating around that you're thinking of leaving.* **2** (of an object) to be in a place that is not known or specified: *Have you seen my keys floating about (anywhere)?* **float aˈbout/aˈround (sth)** (*infml*) (of a person) to move from place to place with no particular purpose; to do nothing in particular: *My weekend was very boring — I just floated about (the house) or watched TV.*

▶ **floating** *adj* [usu attrib] not fixed or settled permanently in a place: *floating exchange rates* ○ *a floating population* (ie one in which people are constantly moving from one place to another). See also FLOTATION.

■ **ˌfloating ˈvoter** *n* a person who has not decided which way to vote or who does not always vote for the same political party: *The outcome of this election may be decided by floating voters.*

float² /fləʊt/ *n* **1(a)** a small light object attached to a fishing-line (FISH²), which stays on the surface of the water until a fish has been caught. **(b)** a light object that keeps a fishing net, etc at or near the surface of the water. **(c)** a light object held by a person who is learning to swim and which prevents her or him from sinking. **2(a)** a lorry, cart or low platform on wheels on which people in costumes are carried in a procession or things are displayed: *The club display was mounted on a huge float and paraded through the main street.* **(b)** = MILK FLOAT. **3** a sum of money in coins of low value that is provided for sb before they start selling things, so that they can give change to customers. **4** (*commerce*) the act or process of selling shares in a company for the first time: *They lack permission for a proper share float.*

flock¹ /flɒk/ *n* [CGp] **1** ~ **(of sth)** a group of sheep, goats or birds of the same type, either kept together

or feeding and travelling together: *a flock of wild geese* ○ *flocks of sheep and herds of cattle.* **2** a large crowd of people: *People came in flocks to see the royal procession.* **3** the people in the area for which a priest is responsible or who attend her or his church: *preaching to his flock.*

▶ **flock** *v* to go or gather together in great numbers: [Vpr] *In summer, tourists flock to the museums and art galleries.* [Vp] *Huge numbers of birds had flocked together by the lake.*

flock² /flɒk/ [U] soft wool or cotton material for stuffing cushions, etc: *a flock mattress* ○ *flock wallpaper* (ie with a raised pattern made of soft material on its surface).

flog /flɒg/ *v* (**-gg-**) **1** to beat sb severely, esp with a stick or whip, as a punishment: [Vn, Vnpr] *The boy was cruelly flogged (for stealing).* **2** ~ **sth (to sb)** (*Brit infml*) to sell sth to sb: [Vn] *We should be able to flog the car for a good price.* [Vnpr] *She flogged her guitar to another student.* [Vnn] *I had a letter from a company trying to flog me insurance.* ⇨ note at SELL. **IDM** **flog a dead ˈhorse** (*infml*) to waste one's efforts on sth that has no chance of success or cannot be changed. **ˌflog sth to ˈdeath** (*infml*) to repeat sth so often or continue sth for so long that other people lose interest in it. **ˌflog oneself/sth to ˈdeath / into the ˈground** to make such heavy demands on oneself/sth that one/it becomes weak or useless: *She's flogging herself to death at work.* ○ *If you keep driving like that, you'll flog the engine into the ground.*

▶ **flogging** *n* [C, U] an instance or the action of beating or whipping sb.

flood¹ /flʌd/ *v* **1(a)** (of a place that is usu dry) to become filled or covered with water; to fill or cover a place with water: [V] *The cellar floods whenever it rains heavily.* **(b)** (of a river, etc) to OVERFLOW(1), esp because of heavy rain: [V] *damage caused when the Ganges floods* [Vn] *The river burst its banks and flooded the valley.* **2** to arrive, go or send sth somewhere in large quantities: [Vpr] *Refugees continue to flood into neighbouring countries.* [Vn] *Cheap imported goods are flooding the market.* [Vnpr] *The office was flooded with applications for the job.* [also Vp]. **3** to cover or fill sth completely; to spread into sth: [Vn, Vpr] *Sunlight flooded (into) the room.* [Vnpr] *The room was suddenly flooded with light.* **4** (of a thought or feeling) to fill sb suddenly; to flow powerfully: [Vpr] *A great sense of relief flooded over him.* [Vp] *Memories of her childhood came flooding back.* [also Vn]. **5** [Vn] to fill the CARBURETTOR of a motor engine with too much petrol so that the engine will not start. **PHR V** **ˌflood sb ˈout** to force sb to leave home because of a flood: *Several families were flooded out by a burst water main.* ▶ **flooding** *n* [U]: *Widespread flooding is affecting large areas of the south-west.*

flood² /flʌd/ *n* **1** a large quantity of water covering an area that is usu dry: *The heavy rain has caused floods in many parts of the country.* ○ *We can't get across the fields because the river is in flood* (ie has flowed over its banks and caused a flood). ○ *We had a flood in our cellar when the pipes burst.* **2** ~ **(of sth)** a great quantity or volume of sth that appears or is produced: *a flood of anger/abuse/complaints* ○ *a flood of letters/refugees* ○ *The child was in floods of tears* (ie was crying a lot).

floodgate /ˈflʌdɡeɪt/ *n* a gate that can be opened or closed to control a flow of water. **IDM** **open the floodgates** ⇨ OPEN².

■ **ˈflood-plain** *n* an area beside a river that becomes flooded regularly.

ˈflood-tide *n* a tide that rises very high at particular times of the year.

floodlight /ˈflʌdlaɪt/ *n* (esp *pl*) a large powerful light that produces a wide beam, used for lighting sports grounds, theatre stages, the outside of buildings, etc: *a match played under floodlights*. ⇨ picture at FOOTBALL.

▶ **floodlight** *v* (*pt, pp* **floodlighted** or **floodlit** /-lɪt/) (usu passive) to light sth using floodlights: *The Town Hall is floodlit in the evenings*.

floor¹ /flɔː(r)/ *n* **1** [C usu *sing*] the lower surface of a room, on which one stands, walks, etc: *There weren't enough chairs so I had to sit on the floor*. ○ *The bare concrete floor was cold on my feet*. ○ *5 000 square metres of floor space*. **2** [C usu *sing*] the bottom of the sea, an area of land, a cave, etc: *the ocean/forest/valley/cave floor*. ⇨ note at EARTH. **3** [C] all the rooms, etc on the same level in a building; a level or STOREY of a building: *Her office is on the second floor*. ⇨ note. **4 the floor** [*sing*] (**a**) the part of an assembly hall where members sit, eg in the Houses of Parliament or US Congress: *speak from the floor*. (**b**) an opportunity or the right to speak in an assembly, meeting or discussion: *The floor is yours — present your proposal*. **5** [C usu *sing*] an area in a building where a particular activity takes place: *the dance floor* (ie the part of the floor of a club, etc where people dance) ○ *the factory floor* (ie the part of a factory where goods are produced, in contrast with the offices of those who manage it) ○ *the floor of the Stock Exchange* (ie where the trading takes place). **6** [C] a minimum level for wages or prices: *Prices have gone through the floor* (ie fallen to a very low level). Compare CEILING 3. **IDM be/get in on the ground floor** ⇨ GROUND FLOOR. **hold the floor** to speak to a group of people, esp at great length or with determination, so that no one else has a chance to say anything: *She held the floor for over an hour*. **take the floor** to get up and start to dance on a dance floor: *She took the floor with her husband*. **wipe the floor with sb** ⇨ WIPE.

▶ **flooring** *n* [U] material used for making floors: *vinyl flooring*.

■ **floor show** *n* a series of performances, eg of singing and dancing, presented in a club, bar, etc.

NOTE In British English the floor of a building at street level is the **ground floor** and the floor above that is the **first floor**. In American English the street level is often called the **first floor** and the one above is the **second floor**.

floor² /flɔː(r)/ *v* **1** (*infml*) to defeat or confuse sb so that they are unable to respond: [Vn] *Tom was completely floored by two of the questions in the exam*. **2** to knock sb down by hitting them: [Vnpr] *He floored his opponent with a fine punch in the first round*. [also Vn]. **3** to provide a building or room with a floor of a particular type: [Vnpr] *The room is floored with pine*. [also Vn].

floorboard /flɔːbɔːd/ *n* (usu *pl*) any of the long wooden boards used for making floors: *bare/loose floorboards* ○ *hidden under the floorboards*.

floozie (also **floozy**) /fluːzi/ *n* (*infml derog*) a girl or woman, esp one with low moral standards.

flop /flɒp/ *v* (**-pp-**) **1** to fall, move or hang heavily, loosely or in an awkward way: [Vpr] *The pile of books flopped noisily onto the floor*. ○ *Her hair flopped over her eyes*. [Vp] *The fish we'd caught were flopping around in the bottom of the boat*. [V] *His head began to flop and seconds later he was asleep*. **2** to sit or lie down heavily and awkwardly because of being tired: [V] *I'm ready to flop*. [Vpr] *Exhausted, he flopped into the nearest chair*. [Vp] *She staggered into the room and flopped down*. **3** (*infml*) to fail totally; to be completely UNSUCCESSFUL: [V] *His first record flopped but his second was a big hit*.

▶ **flop** *n* **1** (usu *sing*) a flopping movement or sound. See also BELLYFLOP. **2** (*infml*) a total failure; a completely UNSUCCESSFUL thing: *Despite all the publicity, her latest novel was a complete flop*.

flop *adv* with a flop: *fall flop into the water*.

floppy *adj* falling or hanging loosely; soft and flexible; not stiff: *a floppy hat*. — *n* (*infml*) = FLOPPY DISK.

floppy disk (also **floppy**, **diskette**) *n* (*computing*) a flexible DISK(2) for recording and storing data in a form that a computer can read. ⇨ picture at COMPUTER. Compare HARD DISK.

flora /flɔːrə/ *n* [*sing v*] all the plants of a particular area or period of time: *the flora of the Himalayas/the Palaeozoic era*. Compare FAUNA.

floral /flɔːrəl/ *adj* [usu attrib] (**a**) made of or consisting of flowers: *floral arrangements/tributes*. (**b**) decorated with flower designs: *floral wallpaper*.

floret /flɒrət; *US* flɔːr-/ *n* each of the edible stems of certain vegetables: *cauliflower/broccoli florets*.

florid /flɒrɪd; *US* flɔːr-/ *adj* **1** (*usu derog*) elaborate or ORNATE; having or done with too much decoration: *florid music/poetry/art* ○ *a florid style of writing*. **2** (of a person's face) red in colour: *a florid complexion*.

florin /flɒrɪn; *US* flɔːr-/ *n* a former British coin worth two shillings (SHILLING 1) or one tenth of £1.

florist /flɒrɪst; *US* flɔːr-/ *n* a person who owns or works in a shop that sells flowers and plants: *order a wreath from the florist* ○ *buy a bouquet at the florist's*.

floss /flɒs; *US* flɔːs/ *n* [U] **1** silk thread used in embroidery (EMBROIDER). **2** = DENTAL FLOSS.

flotation /fləʊˈteɪʃn/ *n* [C, U] (*commerce*) the procedure of starting to sell shares in a company to the public, esp in order to raise money for it.

flotilla /fləˈtɪlə; *US* fləʊ-/ *n* a group of boats or small, esp military, ships sailing together: *a flotilla of destroyers* ○ *flotilla holidays in the Mediterranean*.

flotsam /flɒtsəm/ *n* [U] parts of a ship or its cargo found floating in the sea. Compare JETSAM. **IDM flotsam and jetsam 1** people who have no homes or work and who wander about in a helpless way. **2** an untidy collection of unimportant or useless objects.

flounce¹ /flaʊns/ *v* to move about in an exaggerated way to show that one is angry about sth or to draw attention to oneself: [Vpr] *She flounced out of the room*. [also Vp].

flounce² /flaʊns/ *n* a wide strip of cloth or lace sewn by its upper edge to a garment, eg a skirt. ▶ **flounced** *adj*: *a flounced petticoat*.

flounder¹ /flaʊndə(r)/ *v* **1** to move or struggle in a helpless or desperate manner, eg in water, mud, snow, etc: [Vp] *Ann couldn't swim and was floundering about/around in the deep end of the swimming-pool*. [Vpr] *They floundered through the snowdrifts*. [also V]. **2** to be unable to react or do sth well because of surprise, confusion or lack of knowledge: [V] *The question took him by surprise and he floundered for a while*. ○ *The new job demands considerable technical know-how and at the moment I'm floundering a bit*.

flounder² /flaʊndə(r)/ *n* a small flat edible fish that lives in the sea.

flour /flaʊə(r)/ *n* [U] a fine powder obtained by grinding grain, esp wheat, used for making bread, cakes, etc.

▶ **flour** *v* to cover sth with a thin layer of flour: [Vn] *Roll the dough on a lightly floured surface*.

floury /flaʊəri/ *adj* **1** covered with flour: *She wiped her floury hands with a damp cloth*. **2** of or like flour: *a floury texture*. **3** (of potatoes) soft and fluffy (FLUFF) when cooked.

flourish /flʌrɪʃ/ *v* **1** to be successful, active or widespread; to PROSPER: [V] *Few businesses are flourishing in the present economic climate*. ○ *In Germany the baroque style of art flourished in the 17th and 18th centuries*. **2** to grow in a healthy way; to be well: [V] *These plants flourish in a damp climate*. ○ *I'm glad to hear you're all flourishing, despite the* *awful weather.* **3** to wave sth about in order to attract attention to it: [Vn] *He rushed into the room flourishing the local newspaper excitedly.*

▶ **flourish** *n* (usu *sing*) **1** a bold sweeping movement or gesture, used esp to attract attention: *He opened the door for her with a flourish.* **2** an impressive act or way of doing sth: *The exhibition opened with a flourish — a huge firework display.* **3** a flowing curve, esp in writing or decoration.

flout /flaʊt/ *v* to show that one has no respect for sth by openly refusing to obey it: [Vn] *flout the law/ rules.*

flow /fləʊ/ *v* **1(a)** (of a liquid) to move freely and continuously: [V] *She lost control and the tears began to flow.* [Vpr] *Most rivers flow into the sea.* [Vp] *Blood suddenly started flowing out.* **(b)** to move freely and continuously within a closed system; to circulate: [V] *The traffic was flowing in a steady stream.* [Vpr] *Blood flows to all parts of the body.* [Vp] *In convection, hot currents flow upwards.* **2** to proceed or be produced smoothly, continuously and naturally: [V] *Conversation flowed freely throughout the meal.* ○ *It was a good meeting, in which ideas flowed.* [Vpr] *Confidence flows from her.* **3** (of clothing or hair) to hang loosely and freely: [V] *long flowing robes* [Vpr] *with hair flowing over her shoulders* [also Vp]. **4** to be available in large quantities; to be distributed freely: [V] *The party became livelier as the drink began to flow.* **5** (of the sea tide) to come in; to rise: [V] *The tide began to flow, covering our footprints.* Compare EBB 1. **PHRV** ,**flow 'in/into sth** to arrive or go somewhere in a steady stream: *The election results flowed in throughout the night.* ○ *Offers of help flowed into the office.* '**flow from sth** (*fml*) to come from sth; to result from sth: *Many benefits will flow from this discovery.* ,**flow 'out (of sth)** to leave somewhere in a steady stream: *Profits are flowing out of the country.*

▶ **flow** *n* (usu *sing*) **1** ~ (**of sth/sb**) the flowing movement of sth/sb; a continuous stream of sth: *a steady flow of traffic* ○ *stop the flow of blood* ○ *The government is trying to stop the flow of refugees entering the country.* **2** ~ (**of sth**) the continuous production or supply of sth: *cut off the flow of oil* ○ *the constant flow of information.* **3** smooth and continuous talk by sb: *You've interrupted my flow and now I can't remember what I was saying.* ○ *When I joined them, Bob was already in full flow* (ie busily talking). **4** a tide coming in: *the ebb and flow of the sea.* **IDM** **the ebb and flow** ⇨ EBB *n*.
■ '**flow chart** *n* a diagram showing the development of sth through different stages or processes.

flower /'flaʊə(r)/ *n* **1(a)** the part of a plant from which the seed or fruit develops, often brightly coloured and lasting only a short time: *The plant has a brilliant purple flower.* **(b)** a flower with its stem that has been picked as a decoration: *arrange some flowers in a vase.* **(c)** a plant grown for the beauty of its flowers: *plant flowers in the garden* ○ *a flower show.* ⇨ picture. **2** [sing] **the ~ of sth** (*rhet*) the finest or best part of sth: *the flower of the nation's youth.* **IDM** **in/into** '**flower** in/into the state of having the flowers open: *The roses have been in flower for a week.* ○ *The crocuses are late coming into flower.*

▶ **flower** *v* **1** to produce flowers; to BLOOM: [V] *These plants will flower in the spring.* ○ *a late-flowering chrysanthemum.* **2** to develop fully; to reach the best state: [V] *Their friendship flowered while they were at college.* **flowered** /'flaʊəd/ *adj* [usu attrib] decorated with patterns of flowers: *flowered wallpaper/cloth/curtains.* **flowering** /'flaʊərɪŋ/ *n* (usu *sing*) ~ (**of sth**) the full development of sth; the development of sth to its highest point: *the gradual flowering of modern democracy.*

flowery /'flaʊəri/ *adj* **1** covered with or decorated with a design of flowers: *flowery fields* ○ *a flowery*

scarf. **2** (*usu derog*) (esp of speech or writing) not expressed simply; elaborate: *a flowery language.*
■ '**flower-bed** *n* a piece of ground in a garden or park where flowers are grown.

'**flower children** (also '**flower people**) *n* [pl] (*dated*) people wearing or carrying flowers as a symbol of their belief in love and peace.

'**flower power** *n* [U] (*dated*) the ideas or movement of the flower children.

flowerpot /'flaʊəpɒt/ *n* a container made of plastic or clay for growing plants in. ⇨ picture at POT¹.

flown *pp* of FLY¹.

fl oz *abbr* (*pl* unchanged or **fl ozs**) fluid ounce.

Flt Lt *abbr* Flight Lieutenant: *Flt Lt (Robert) Bell.*

flu /fluː/ (also *fml* **influenza**) *n* an infectious illness like a bad cold, causing a high temperature, pains and weakness.

fluctuate /'flʌktʃueɪt/ *v* ~ (**between sth and sth**) **(a)** (of prices, numbers, rates, etc) to rise and fall; to change frequently: [V] *fluctuating temperatures* [Vpr] *Prices fluctuated between £10 and £15.* **(b)** (of feelings, attitudes or states) to change frequently in a way that is not regular: [V] *Her standard of work tends to fluctuate.* [Vpr] *He/His mood seems to fluctuate between happiness and despair.* ▶ **fluctuation** /ˌflʌktʃu'eɪʃn/ *n* [C, U] ~ (**of/in sth**): *wide fluctuations of temperature* ○ *currency fluctuation.*

flue /fluː/ *n* a channel or pipe in a chimney that takes smoke or hot air from a BOILER or an oven.

fluent /'fluːənt/ *adj* **1(a)** ~ (**in sth**) able to speak or write accurately and easily, esp in a foreign language: *a fluent speaker (of Spanish)* ○ *She's fluent in English and German.* **(b)** able to perform an action smoothly and easily: *a fluent dancer/musician.* **2(a)** (of a language, esp of a foreign language) expressed accurately and easily: *speak/write fluent Russian.* **(b)** (of an action) done smoothly and easily: *fluent movements.*

▶ **fluency** /'fluːənsi/ *n* [U] the quality or condition of being fluent: *Fluency in French and German is required for this job.*
fluently *adv.*

fluff /flʌf/ *n* [U] **(a)** small soft pieces of material, eg wool, that gather on the surface of garments, etc: *Balls of fluff and dust had collected under the bed.* **(b)** soft fur on animals or birds. **IDM** **a bit of crumpet/fluff/skirt/stuff** ⇨ BIT¹.

▶ **fluff** *v* **1** ~ **sth (out/up)** to shake sth into a soft full mass; to spread sth out lightly: [Vnp] *fluff up the pillows* ○ *The bird fluffed out its feathers.* [also Vn]. **2** (*infml*) to do sth badly; to fail at sth: [Vn] *fluff a shot* (ie in golf, tennis, etc) ○ *The leading actor fluffed his lines several times.*

fluffy *adj* **1** like fluff; covered with fluff: *a soft, fluffy kitten.* **2** (of food) soft, light and containing air: *Beat the butter and sugar until soft and fluffy.*

fluid /'fluːɪd/ *n* [C, U] any liquid substance: *You must drink plenty of fluids.* ○ *cleaning fluid.*

▶ **fluid** *adj* **1** that can flow freely, as gases and liquids do; not solid or rigid: *a fluid substance.* **2** not fixed; that can be changed: *fluid arrangements/ ideas/opinions* ○ *The situation is still fluid.* **3** (of movements) smooth and elegant: *a fluid style of piano playing.*
fluidity /flu'ɪdəti/ *n* [U] the quality or state of being fluid: *fluidity of sound/movement.*
■ **fluid ounce** *n* (*abbr* **fl oz**) a liquid measure equal to 0.05 of a British PINT or 0.0625 of an American pint. ⇨ App 2.

fluke /fluːk/ *n* (usu *sing*) a lucky thing that happens by accident, not because of planning or skill: *Passing the exam was a real fluke — he did no work at all.* ○ *The team are determined to show that their last win was no fluke.*

flummox /'flʌməks/ *v* (*infml*) to confuse sb; to make sb unable to think clearly: [Vn] (esp passive): *The*

flowers common in Britain and the United States

All the drawings are to scale and represent the average height reached.

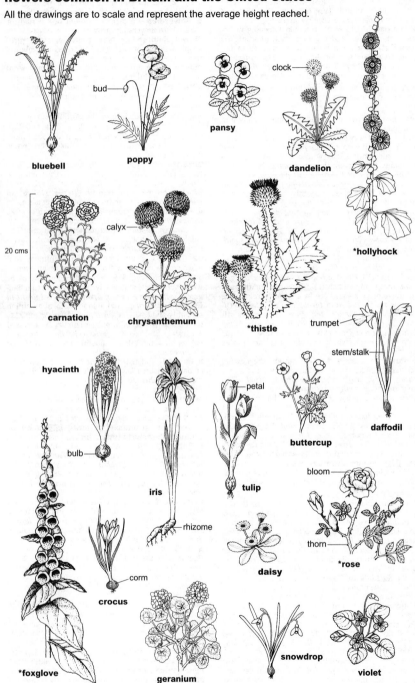

bud

clock

pansy

bluebell

poppy

dandelion

*hollyhock**

20 cms

calyx

carnation

chrysanthemum

*thistle**

trumpet

stem/stalk

hyacinth

petal

daffodil

bulb

buttercup

iris

bloom

rhizome

tulip

thorn

*rose**

corm

daisy

crocus

*foxglove**

geranium

snowdrop

violet

*The illustration shows the top third of the whole plant.

[Vnn] = verb + noun + noun   [V-adj] = verb + adjective   For more help with verbs, see Study pages **B4–8**.

first question was quite easy but the next one flummoxed me completely.

flung *pt, pp* of FLING.

flunk /flʌŋk/ *v* (*US infml*) **1** to fail an examination, academic course, etc: [Vn] *flunk biology.* [also V]. **2** to give sb a mark in an examination, etc which means that they have failed it: [Vn] *He flunked me in chemistry.* **PHRV** **,flunk 'out** (*US infml*) to be dismissed from a school, etc for failure: *flunk out of college.*

flunkey (also **flunky**) /ˈflʌŋki/ *n* (*pl* **-eys** or **-ies**) **1** a servant in uniform. **2** (*derog*) a person who tries to gain the favour of sb important or powerful by doing small unimportant tasks for them.

fluorescent /flɔːˈresnt, ˌfluəˈr-/ *adj* (of substances) that use certain forms of RADIATION in order to produce light: *a fluorescent lamp* (ie one that contains such a substance) ○ *fluorescent lighting* ○ *fluorescent clothing* (ie in bright glowing colours). Compare PHOSPHORESCENT. ▶ **fluorescence** *n* [U]: *X-ray fluorescence.*

fluoride /ˈfluəraɪd, ˈflɔːr-/ *n* a chemical compound of FLUORINE, believed to protect teeth from decay. ▶ **fluoridation** /ˌfluərɪˈdeɪʃn, ˌflɔːr-/ *n* [U] the addition of fluoride to a water supply in order to prevent tooth decay.

fluorine /ˈfluəriːn, ˈflɔːr-/ *n* [U] (*symb* F) a chemical element. Fluorine usu occurs as a pale yellow poisonous gas. ⇨ App 7.

flurry /ˈflʌri/ *n* **1** a sudden short rush of snow, rain, wind, etc: *light snow flurries/flurries of snow.* **2** ~ (**of sth**) (**a**) a sudden short period of intense activity: *a flurry of activity/excitement.* (**b**) a lot of things arriving or happening at once: *a flurry of letters/ phone calls.*

flush¹ /flʌʃ/ *n* **1** [C usu *sing*] (**a**) a flow of blood to the face that causes a red colouring: *A pink flush spread over his cheeks.* (**b**) a sudden strong feeling: *a flush of enthusiasm/anger/pride.* **2** [*sing*] an act of cleaning esp, esp a toilet, with a sudden flow of water: *Give the toilet a flush.* **3** [C] a new fresh growth(3), esp of plants: *The bush produces a second flush of flowers in the autumn.* **IDM** (**in**) **the first flush of 'sth** (in) a period when sth is fresh, new and strong: *be in the first flush of youth/manhood.*

flush² /flʌʃ/ *v* **1**(**a**) (of a person's face) to become red because of a rush of blood to the skin: [V-adj] *Her cheeks flushed crimson.* [also V]. (**b**) (of eg illness or feelings) to make the face red: [Vn] *Fever/Anger flushed his cheeks.* **2**(**a**) ~ **sth** (**out**) to clean esp a toilet or drain by causing a sudden flow of water to pass through it: [Vn] *Please flush the toilet after you've used it.* [also Vnp]. (**b**) (of a toilet) to be cleaned in this way: [V] *The toilet won't flush.* **3** ~ **sth away, down, through, etc** (**sth**) to dispose of sth with a sudden flow of water: [Vnpr] *He tore up the letter and flushed it down the lavatory.* **PHRV** **,flush sb/sth 'out** (**of sth**) to force sb/sth out of the place where they are hiding: *flush out spies/ criminals* ○ *flush out potential customers.*

▶ **flushed** *adj* ~ (**with sth**) very excited or pleased by sth; filled with a specified emotion: *be flushed with success/pride/joy/anger.*

flush³ /flʌʃ/ *adj* ~ (**with sth**) **1** completely level or even with another surface: *The door should be flush with the wall.* **2** [pred] (*infml*) having a lot of sth, esp money: *I'm feeling flush this week — I'll pay.*

flush⁴ /flʌʃ/ *n* (in card-games) a set of cards held by a player, all of which belong to the same suit¹(2): *a royal flush* (ie the five highest cards of a suit).

fluster /ˈflʌstə(r)/ *v* (esp passive) to make sb nervous and confused, esp because there is too much to do: [Vn] *Don't get flustered — there's plenty of time.*

▶ **fluster** *n* [sing] the state of being flustered: *be all in a fluster.*

flute /fluːt/ *n* a musical instrument like a thin pipe, which is held sideways and played by blowing

across a hole at one end and covering other holes with the fingers. ⇨ picture at MUSICAL INSTRUMENT. ▶ **flutist** /ˈfluːtɪst/ *n* (*US*) = FLAUTIST.

fluted /ˈfluːtɪd/ *adj* decorated with long curved grooves (GROOVE 1) cut in the surface: *fluted columns/pillars.* ▶ **fluting** *n* [U]: *wood decorated with fine fluting.*

flutter /ˈflʌtə(r)/ *v* **1**(**a**) (of wings or creatures with wings) to move lightly and quickly: [Vpr] *moths fluttering round a lamp* [V] *The bird fluttered briefly and then lay still.* [also Vp]. (**b**) to move the wings in this way: [Vn] *The bird fluttered its wings and flew away.* **2**(**a**) to move about in or through the air lightly and quickly: [V] *curtains fluttering in the breeze* [Vpr] *a flag fluttering from the masthead* ○ *The leaves fluttered to the ground.* (**b**) to move sth lightly and quickly: [Vn, Vnpr] *She fluttered her eyelashes at me.* **3** (of the heart) to beat very fast: [V] *His heart fluttered with excitement.*

▶ **flutter** *n* **1** [usu *sing*] a quick light movement: *the flutter of wings* ○ *with a flutter of her long dark eyelashes.* **2** [*sing*] a state of nervous or confused excitement: *be in a flutter/all of a flutter* ○ *feel a flutter of delight/panic.* **3** [C] an abnormally fast HEARTBEAT. **4** [U] the rapid variation in pitch¹(2) or volume of recorded sound. Compare WOW². **5** [C] ~ (**on sth**) (*Brit infml*) a small bet: *have a flutter (on a horse) at the races.*

fluvial /ˈfluːviəl/ *adj* (*techn*) of or found in rivers: *fluvial deposits of mud.*

flux /flʌks/ *n* **1** [U] continuous change; the state of not being settled: *a company/country in a state of flux.* **2** [*sing*] ~ (**of sth**) (*esp techn*) a flow or act of flowing: *a flux of neutrons* ○ *magnetic flux.*

fly¹ /flaɪ/ *v* (*pt* **flew** /fluː/; *pp* **flown** /fləʊn/) **1** (of a bird or an insect) to move through the air, using wings: [V] *watch the birds learn to fly* [Vpr] *A wasp flew into the room.* [also Vp]. **2**(**a**) (of an aircraft or a spacecraft) to move through air or space: [Vpr] *a plane flying from London to New York* ○ *fly at the speed of sound* [Vadv] *I can hear a plane flying overhead.* [also Vp]. (**b**) to travel in an aircraft or a spacecraft: [Vpr] *I'm flying to Hong Kong tomorrow.* [V] *Is this the first time that you've flown?* [also Vp]. ⇨ note at TRAVEL. **3**(**a**) to direct or control the flight of an aircraft, etc: [Vn] *a pilot trained to fly large passenger aircraft* [also V]. (**b**) to transport goods or passengers in an aircraft: [Vnp] *The stranded tourists were finally flown home.* ○ *He had flowers specially flown in for the ceremony.* [also Vnpr]. (**c**) to travel over an ocean or area of land in an aircraft: [Vn] *fly the Atlantic.* **4**(**a**) to go or move quickly; to rush: [V] *It's late — I must fly.* [Vp] *The train was flying along.* [Vpr] *The dog flew down the road after the cat.* (**b**) to move suddenly and with force: [Vpr, Vp] *A large stone came flying (in) through the window.* [V-adj] *David gave the door a kick and it flew open.* [also Vadv]. (**c**) (of time) to pass very quickly: [V] *Doesn't time fly?* [Vp] *Summer has just flown by.* **5** [Vn] (**a**) to make a KITE(1) rise and stay high in the air. (**b**) to raise a flag so that it is displayed: *fly the Union Jack/Stars and Stripes.* **6** to move about freely; to be carried about in the air: [Vpr, Vp] *hair flying (about) in the wind* [V] *be hit by flying glass.* **7** (*rhet*) to escape from sb/sth: [Vn] *Both suspects have flown the country.* [also V]. **8** (of stories, rumours, etc) to be talked about by many people; to be current: [V, Vp] *There are lots of rumours flying (around) at the moment.* **IDM** **as the crow flies** ⇨ CROW¹. **the bird has flown** ⇨ BIRD. **fly/show/wave the flag** ⇨ FLAG¹. **fly 'high** to be successful. **fly in the face of 'sth** to be contrary to sth; to oppose sth: *Such a proposal is flying in the face of common sense.* **fly into a 'passion, 'rage, 'temper, etc** to become suddenly very angry: *He always flies into a rage when he can't have his own*

[V] = verb used alone   [Vn] = verb + noun   [Vp] = verb + particle   [Vpr] = verb + prepositional phrase

way. **fly a ˈkite** (*Brit infml*) to do or say sth simply in order to see how people will react. **(go) fly a/one's ˈkite** (*US infml*) (esp imperative) go away and stop annoying sb or interfering with sb/sth. **fly/go off at a tangent** ⇨ TANGENT. **fly off the ˈhandle** (*infml*) to become suddenly and wildly angry. **fly/go out of the window** ⇨ WINDOW. **keep the flag flying** ⇨ FLAG¹. **let ˈfly (at sb/sth) (with sth)** to attack sb with words or physically: *He let fly at me with his fist.* ○ *She let fly (at him) with a stream of abuse.* **pigs might fly** ⇨ PIG.
PHRV **ˈfly at sb** to attack sb suddenly: *He flew at me without warning.*

■ **fly-away** /ˈflaɪ əweɪ/ *adj* (esp of hair) loose, soft and fine; difficult to control.
fly-by /ˈflaɪ baɪ/ *n* (*pl* **ˈfly-bys**) (*US*) = FLY-PAST.
fly-by-night /ˈflaɪ baɪ naɪt/ *adj* [usu attrib] (of a person or company) not reliable or honourable; interested only in making quick profits: *fly-by-night operators.*
ˈfly-past /-pɑːst; *US* -pæst/ (*Brit*) (*US* **ˈfly-by**, **ˈfly-over**) *n* a ceremonial flight of aircraft over or past sth in a special formation, as part of a display.

fly² /flaɪ/ *n* **1** a small flying insect with two wings. There are many different types of fly: *a house-fly* ○ *fly-spray* (ie for killing flies). ⇨ picture at INSECT. See also FRUIT-FLY. **2** a real or artificial fly used as BAIT(1) in fishing. **IDM** **die/fall/drop like ˈflies** to collapse or die in very large numbers: *People were dropping like flies in the intense heat.* **a/the fly in the ˈointment** a person or thing that spoils an otherwise satisfactory situation or occasion. **a fly on the ˈwall** a person who watches others without being noticed: *I wish I could be a fly on the wall when they discuss my future.* **(there are) no flies on ˈsb** (*infml*) sb is clever and not easily tricked. **not harm/hurt a ˈfly** to be kind and gentle and unwilling to cause unhappiness: *Our dog may look fierce but he wouldn't hurt a fly.*
■ **ˈfly-blown** *adj* in a bad condition; dirty or not fit to eat: *Everything in the shop looked rather fly-blown.*
ˈfly-fishing *n* [U] a type of fishing in which artificial flies are used as BAIT(1).
ˈfly-paper *n* [U] a strip of sticky paper for catching flies.

fly³ /flaɪ/ *n* **1** [sing] (also **flies** [pl]) (*Brit*) an opening down the front of a pair of trousers or SHORTS(1), that fastens with a ZIP or buttons and is usu covered over by a strip of material: *John, your flies are/fly is undone!* **2** [C] a piece of material, eg canvas, covering the entrance to a tent.

flyer (also **flier**) /ˈflaɪə(r)/ *n* **1(a)** a pilot of an aircraft. **(b)** a person who travels in an aircraft as a passenger: *a frequent flyer.* **2** a person who operates a model aircraft, etc from the ground: *kite flyers.* **3** a thing that flies in a specified way: *Sandflies are poor flyers.* **4** a person, an animal, a vehicle, etc that moves very quickly: *a 150 mph flyer.* **5** a small sheet of paper advertising an event, a shop, a product, etc that is widely distributed: *hand out flyers for a new café* **6** = HIGH-FLYER.

flying /ˈflaɪɪŋ/ *adj* moving by flight; able to fly: *flying insects.* **IDM** **get off to / have a ˌflying ˈstart** to begin sth well; to have an advantage at the beginning: *Our trip got off to a flying start because the weather was good and the roads were clear.* **with ˌflying ˈcolours** with great and obvious success: *She came through/passed her exams with flying colours.*
▶ **flying** *n* [U] the action of going in an aircraft, esp for travel or sport: *I'm terrified of flying — I'd rather go by sea.*
■ **ˌflying ˈbuttress** *n* (*architecture*) a structure like half of an arch that supports the outside wall of a large building, esp a church. ⇨ picture at CHURCH.
ˌflying ˈdoctor *n* (esp in Australia) a doctor who

travels in an aircraft to visit patients who live in remote places.
ˌflying ˈfish *n* a type of tropical fish that can rise and move forward above the surface of the water using its fins (FIN 1) as wings.
ˌflying ˈjump (also **ˌflying ˈleap**) *n* a forward jump made while running quickly: *take a flying leap into the air.*
ˈflying officer *n* an officer in the Royal Air Force. ⇨ App 6.
ˌflying ˈpicket *n* a worker or group of workers on strike¹(1) who are ready to travel quickly to different factories, etc to persuade other workers to join the strike.
ˌflying ˈsaucer (also **ˌunidentified ˌflying ˈobject**) *n* a spacecraft, shaped like a SAUCER or disc, that some people claim to have seen and that is believed to have come from another planet.
ˈflying squad *n* (usu **the Flying Squad**) (*Brit*) a group of police officers who are always ready to act quickly, eg when a crime has occurred.
ˌflying ˈvisit *n* a very brief visit: *pay a flying visit to Paris.*

flyleaf /ˈflaɪliːf/ *n* (*pl* **-leaves** /-liːvz/) a page at the beginning or end of a book, usu with nothing printed on it.

flyover /ˈflaɪəʊvə(r)/ *n* **1** (*Brit*) (*US* **ˈoverpass**) a bridge that carries one road or railway above another. **2** (*US*) = FLY-PAST.

flysheet /ˈflaɪʃiːt/ *n* an additional outer cover for a tent to give protection from rain.

flyweight /ˈflaɪweɪt/ *n* **1** a boxer of the lightest class, weighing between 48 and 51 kg. **2** a wrestler (WRESTLE) weighing between 48 and 52 kg.

flywheel /ˈflaɪwiːl/ *n* a heavy wheel that revolves to keep a machine operating at an even speed.

FM *abbr* /ˌef ˈem/ (*radio*) frequency modulation: *the FM band* ○ *on 102 FM.* Compare AM 1.

FO /ˌef ˈəʊ/ *abbr* (formerly in Britain) Foreign Office: *He used to work at the FO.* Compare FCO.

foal /fəʊl/ *n* the young of a horse or of a related animal, eg a DONKEY. **IDM** **in foal** (of a female horse, etc) pregnant.
▶ **foal** *v* [V] to give birth to a foal.

foam /fəʊm/ *n* [U] **1(a)** a mass of small, usu white, air bubbles formed in or on a liquid: *The breaking waves left the beach covered with foam.* **(b)** a mass of bubbles of SALIVA or PERSPIRATION: *a dog with foam at its mouth.* **2** one of various chemical substances forming a thick mass of bubbles and used for different purposes: *ˈshaving foam* ○ *a bottle of ˈbath foam/ ˈfoam bath* ○ *The fire extinguisher directs foam onto the fire.* **3** a light form of rubber or plastic similar to SPONGE(2). Foam is used to fill seats, cushions, etc: *sheets of packing foam* ○ *ˌfoam ˈrubber.*
▶ **foam** *v* to form or produce foam(1,2); to FROTH: [V] *tankards of foaming beer* [Vpr] *The dog was foaming at the mouth* ○ (*fig*) *Staff are* **foaming at the mouth** (ie very angry) *over the proposed job cuts.*
foamy *adj* full of or like foam(1,2).

fob¹ /fɒb/ *n* **(a)** a chain attached to a watch that is carried in a pocket. **(b)** an ornament, esp a watch, hung from such a chain: *a fob watch.*

fob² /fɒb/ *v* (-bb-) **PHRV** **ˌfob sb ˈoff (with sth)** (*esp Brit*) to give an excuse for not providing or doing sth for sb or to give sb sth that is inferior to what they want: *I won't be fobbed off this time — I'm determined to say what I think.* ○ *You can't fob an expert off with cheap imitations.* **ˌfob sth ˈoff on/ onto sb** to trick or deceive sb into buying or accepting sth inferior: *Don't try fobbing off last year's goods on me!*

focal /ˈfəʊkl/ *adj* [attrib] providing a FOCUS(1).
■ **ˌfocal ˈlength** (also **focal ˈdistance**) *n* the dis-

tance between the centre of a mirror or a LENS(1) and its FOCUS(2).

¹focal point *n* a place or thing that is a centre of interest or activity: *The club provides a focal point for overseas students.* ○ *Reducing unemployment is the focal point of the government's plans.*

focus /ˈfəʊkəs/ *n* (*pl* **focuses** or **foci** /ˈfəʊsaɪ/) ⇨ note at PLURAL. **1** [U,C usu *sing*] ~ (**for/on sth**) a centre of activity, interest, etc: *provide a focus for political protest* ○ *an intellectual focus* ○ *a change/ shift of focus* ○ *Her beauty makes her the focus of attention.* ○ *In tonight's programme our focus is on Germany.* ○ *The primary school acts as a focus for village life.* **2** [C] a point at which rays of light, sound, etc meet or from which they appear to come. **3** [U,C] a point or distance at which the outline of an object is most clearly seen by the eye or through a LENS(1): *The children's faces are badly out of focus* (ie not clearly defined) *in the photograph.* ○ *Don't take the picture until you've got us all in focus.* ○ (*fig*) *Let's try to bring the problem into focus* (ie define it clearly). **4** [C] an adjustment or a device on a LENS(1) to produce a clear image: *The focus on my camera is faulty.*

▶ **focus** *v* (**-s-** or **-ss-**) **1** ~ (**sth**) (**on sb/sth**) to direct attention, feelings, comments, efforts, etc to a particular problem or situation; to concentrate on sth: [Vn] *focus one's anger* [Vnadv] *The proposals need to be better focused.* [V,Vpr] *I'm so tired I can't focus* (*on anything*) *today.* [Vpr] *Researchers have focused on the short-term effects.* ○ *Suspicion focused on the company chairman.* [Vnpr] *The conference focused attention on the risk of fire.* ○ *Please focus your minds on the following problem.* **2(a)** to adapt to a particular level of light and become able to see clearly: [V] *His eyes focused slowly in the dark room.* (**b**) ~ **sth** (**on sth**) to adjust a LENS(1) or the eye in order to see sth clearly: [Vn,Vnpr] *Focus your camera* (*on those trees*). (**c**) ~ **sth** (**on sth**) to direct sth onto a point: [Vnpr] *If you focus the sun's rays through a magnifying glass on a dry leaf, it will start to burn.* [also Vn]. **focused** *adj* clearly and precisely (PRECISE) directed; having or showing clear aims: *highly focused ambitions* ○ *a more focused approach/outlook/interest.*

fodder /ˈfɒdə(r)/ *n* [U] **1** dried food, HAY, etc for horses and farm animals. **2** things or people thought of only as material for a specified use: *This story will be more fodder for the gossip columnists.* See also CANNON-FODDER.

foe /fəʊ/ *n* (*dated or fml*) an enemy.

foetus (*US* **fetus**) /ˈfiːtəs/ *n* a young human, animal, bird, etc that has developed past a certain stage within its mother's body or in an egg before birth. Compare EMBRYO 1.

▶ **foetal** (*US* **fetal**) /ˈfiːtl/ *adj* of or like a foetus: *foetal tissue* ○ *She lay curled up in a/the foetal position* (ie like that of a foetus).

fog /fɒg; *US* fɔːg/ *n* [U,C] **1** a thick cloud of tiny drops of water close to or just above land or sea; thick mist: *Dense/thick fog is affecting roads in the north and visibility is very poor.* ○ *Patches of fog will clear by mid-morning.* ○ *We get heavy fogs on this coast in winter.* ⇨ note. **IDM** **in a fog** unable to think clearly or understand sth: *be in a fog of misery* ○ *I'm in a complete fog about computer technology.*

▶ **fog** *v* (**-gg-**) **1** to cover sth or become covered with fog or steam: [V,Vp] *The windscreen has fogged* (*over/up*). [Vn,Vnp] *Steam had fogged the bathroom mirror* (*up*). **2** to confuse or PUZZLE sb: [Vn] *I'm a bit fogged by these instructions.* **3** to confuse sth being discussed; to make sth difficult to perceive: [Vn,Vnp] *obscure arguments that only fog* (*up*) *the real issues.*

foggy *adj* (**-ier, -iest**) **1** not clear because of fog: *foggy weather* ○ *a foggy day.* **2** confused; VAGUE(1):

My ideas on the subject are a little foggy. **IDM** **not have the faintest/foggiest** ⇨ FAINT¹.

■ **¹fog-bound** *adj* unable to travel or operate normally because of fog; trapped by fog: *fog-bound planes/passengers* ○ *She spent hours fog-bound in Brussels.*

¹fog-lamp (also *esp US* **¹fog-light**) *n* a powerful light on the front or back of a car, etc for use in fog.

NOTE **Fog**, **mist** and **haze** are all clouds of water vapour above the ground. **Fog** is the thickest and occurs during cold weather: *Dense fog made driving conditions hazardous.* **Haze** is thin and occurs in hot weather or because of smoke, etc: *Heat shimmered in a haze over the sea.* **Smog** is an unhealthy mixture of smoke and fog in the air of many cities.

foghorn /ˈfɒghɔːn/ *n* an instrument that makes a loud noise to warn ships of danger in FOG: (*joc or derog*) *He's got a voice like a foghorn* (ie a loud, harsh voice).

fogy (also **fogey**) /ˈfəʊgi/ *n* (*pl* **fogies** or **fogeys**) a person with old-fashioned ideas which he or she is unwilling to change: *Come to the disco and stop being such an old fogey.*

foible /ˈfɔɪbl/ *n* a small weakness or slightly unusual aspect of a person's character that is usu harmless and tolerated by others: *We all have our little foibles.*

foil¹ /fɔɪl/ *n* **1** [U] metal made into a very thin flexible sheet: *tin/aluminium foil* ○ *the gold/silver foil round a chocolate bar* ○ *Cover the dish with foil and bake for 45 minutes.* **2** [C] a person or thing that contrasts with, and so emphasizes, the qualities of another: *The pale walls provide a perfect foil for the brightly painted dishes and jars.*

foil² /fɔɪl/ *v* to prevent sb from achieving sth; to prevent a plan, etc from succeeding: [Vnpr] *He was foiled in his attempt to deceive us.* [Vn] *His attempt to deceive us was foiled.*

foil³ /fɔɪl/ *n* a long thin light sword with a protective button on the point, used in fencing (FENCE² 1). ⇨ picture at FENCING. Compare SABRE.

foist /fɔɪst/ *v* **PHRV** **¹foist sth on/upon sb** to force sb into accepting sth that is not wanted : *Although he's very religious he doesn't try to foist his beliefs on others.*

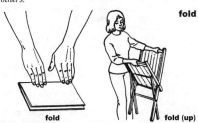

fold / fold / fold (up)

fold¹ /fəʊld/ *v* **1(a)** ~ **sth** (**up**); ~ **sth** (**back, down, over, etc**) to bend or close sth so that one part of it lies flat on another: [Vn,Vnp] *fold clothes* (*up*) *neatly* [Vnp] *fold the sheet down* ○ *The flag was folded away for another year.* ○ *The top of the bag was folded over and stapled.* [Vn] *a folded newspaper* ○ *The bird folded its wings.* [Vn,Vp] *Fold the letter* (*in two*) *before putting it in the envelope.* (**b**) ~ (**up**) to be able to be bent or made flat for storage or easy carrying: [V-adj,Vp] *The garden table folds* (*away/up*) *flat.* [V] *a folding chair/bed/bicycle.* ⇨ picture. **2** ~ **A in B**; ~ **B round A** to cover or wrap sth in sth: [Vnpr] *Fold the glass bowl in newspaper.* ○ *Fold newspaper round the glass bowl.* Compare UNFOLD. **3** ~ (**up**) (*infml*) (**a**) (of a business, project, etc) to stop trading or functioning: [V,Vp] *The company folded* (*up*) *last week.* (**b**) (of a play, etc) to stop being performed: [V] *The show folded after only a week.* [also

Vp]. **IDM** **fold one's 'arms** to bring one's arms together and cross them over one's chest. **fold sb/ sth in one's 'arms** to hold sb/sth closely: *The father folded the tiny child in his arms.* **fold one's 'hands** to bring or hold one's hands together: *She sat quite still, her hands folded in her lap.* **PHR V** **,fold sth 'in**; **,fold sth 'into sth** (in cooking) to mix one ingredient gently with another, usu with a spoon: *Fold in the beaten whites of two eggs.*

▶ **fold** *n* **1(a)** a part of sth, esp fabric, that is folded or hangs as if folded: *a dress hanging in loose folds* ○ *folds of skin.* **(b)** a mark or line made by folding; a CREASE(1). **2** a hollow place among hills or mountains. **3** (*geology*) a bend in the line of rocks below the earth's surface that has been caused by movements in the earth's CRUST(3).

fold² /fəʊld/ *n* **1** [C] an area in a field surrounded by a fence or wall where sheep are kept for safety. **2 the fold** [sing] a group of people who are seen as offering security and protection or who share the same beliefs, etc: *leave the party fold* ○ *Although he ran away from home five years ago, his family are still hoping he will **return to the fold**.*

-fold *suff* (with numbers forming *adjs* and *advs*) multiplied by; having the specified number of parts: *tenfold* ○ *twofold.*

foldaway /'fəʊldəweɪ/ *adj* [usu attrib] that can be folded flat for storage: *a foldaway bed.*

folder /'fəʊldə(r)/ *n* a cardboard or plastic cover for holding loose papers, etc.

foliage /'fəʊliɪdʒ/ *n* [U] the leaves of a tree or plant; leaves with their stems and branches: *a mass of green foliage* ○ *My flower arrangement needs more foliage.*

folio /'fəʊliəʊ/ *n* (*pl* **-os**) **(a)** a large sheet of paper folded once, making two leaves (LEAF 2) or four pages of a book. **(b)** a book of a large size made of sheets folded in this way: *We have several early folios for sale.* ○ *a folio volume.*

folk /fəʊk/ *n* **1** (also *esp US* **folks** [pl *v*]) **(a)** (often used in the plural as a friendly form of address) people ○ general: *Some old folk(s) have peculiar tastes.* ○ *Well, folks, what are we going to do today?* **(b)** people from a particular country or region, or associated with a particular way of life: 'country folk ○ 'townsfolk ○ 'farming folk. **2 folks** [pl] (*infml*) **(a)** the members of one's own family; one's relatives: *How are your folks?* **(b)** (*esp US*) one's parents: *Have you ever met my folks?* **3** [U] music or song in the traditional style of a country or community; folk music: *a folk concert.*

▶ **folk** *adj* [attrib] (of art, culture, etc) traditional; originating from ordinary people: *folk music* ○ *folk beliefs* ○ *a folk museum.*

■ **'folk-dance** *n* a traditional dance of a community or country, or the music for this.

folklore /'fəʊklɔː(r)/ *n* [U] the traditions, stories, customs, etc of a community, or the study of these.
▶ **folklorist** /'fəʊklɔːrɪst/ *n* a person who studies folklore, esp as an academic subject.
■ **,folk 'memory** *n* a memory of sth in the past that the people of a community or country never forget.
'folk-singer *n* a person who sings folk-songs.
'folk-song *n* a song in the traditional style of a country or community.
'folk-tale *n* a story passed on in spoken form from one generation to the next.

folksy /'fəʊksi/ *adj* (*infml*) **1** simple in manners and customs; friendly and informal. **2** (of art, fashions, etc) traditional in style, esp in an artificial way: *folksy pastimes like lace-making.*

follicle /'fɒlɪkl/ *n* any of the tiny holes in the skin from which hairs grow.

follow /'fɒləʊ/ *v* **1** ~ sth (by/with sth) (to cause sth) to come, go or take place after sb/sth else in space, time or order: [Vn] *Her dog follows her everywhere.* ○

I think we're being followed. [V, Vp] *You go first and I'll follow (on) later.* [Vn] *Monday follows Sunday.* ○ *One misfortune followed another.* ○ *The lightning was quickly followed by heavy thunder.* [Vnpr] *You should follow your treatment with plenty of rest in bed.* [V] *There followed a brief lull in the conversation.* **2(a)** to go along a road, path, etc: [Vn] *Follow this road until you get to the church, then turn left.* **(b)** (of a road, path, etc) to go in the same direction as sth or parallel to sth: [Vn] *The lane follows the edge of a wood for about a mile.* **3(a)** to act according to sth: [Vn] *follow the instructions* ○ *follow sb's advice* ○ *I don't want you to **follow my example** and rush into marriage.* **(b)** to accept sb/sth as a guide, a leader or an example; to copy sb/sth: [Vn] *follow the latest fashions* ○ *follow the teachings of Muhammad.* **4** to do sth as one's particular job or trade: [Vn] *follow a legal career.* **5** to understand an explanation or the meaning of sth: [V, Vn] *Sorry, I don't follow (you).* ○ *I couldn't follow his argument at all.* ○ *The plot is almost impossible to follow.* **6** to watch or listen to sth very carefully: [Vn] *The children sat enthralled, following every word intently.* **7** to take an active interest in sth: [Vn] *Have you been following the basketball tournament?* ○ *Millions of fans follow TV soap operas.* **8** to read a text while listening to the same text being spoken by sb else; to read a musical score¹(3a) while listening to the music being performed: [Vn] *Follow the passage in your books while I read it to you.* **9** (of a book, film, etc) to be concerned with the life or development of sb/sth: [Vn] *The novel follows the fortunes of a village community in Scotland.* **10(a)** ~ (on/from sth); ~ (on from sth) to result from sth; to happen as a consequence: [V] *Inevitably, an argument followed.* [Vp, Vn] *Disease often follows (on from) starvation because the body is weakened.* [also Vpr]. **(b)** ~ (from sth) (not usu in the continuous tenses; often with *it* and a *that* clause) to happen as a necessary and logical consequence: [V, Vpr] *I don't see how that follows (from what you've said).* [V. that] *If a = b and b = c it follows that a = c.* ○ *She's not in the office but it doesn't necessarily follow that she's ill.* **11** to develop or happen in a particular way: [Vn] *The day followed the usual pattern.* **IDM** **as 'follows** (used to introduce a list): *The main events were as follows: first, the president's speech, then the secretary's reply, and finally the chairman's summing-up.* **follow the 'crowd** to be happy to do what most people do: *Not wanting to make my controversial views known yet, I preferred to follow the crowd for a while.* **follow in sb's 'footsteps** to do as sb else does; to follow a similar occupation or style of life as sb else: *She works in theatre, following in her father's footsteps.* **follow one's (own) 'nose 1** to go straight forward: *The garage is a mile ahead up the hill — just follow your nose.* **2** to act according to one's instinct or what seems reasonable, rather than following any particular rules, etc: *Since you don't know the language I can only suggest that you follow your nose.* **follow 'suit** to act or behave in the way that sb else has just done: *One of the major banks has lowered its interest rates and the others are now expected to follow suit.* **to 'follow** (in a restaurant, etc) as the next course of a meal: *Soup, and then steak to follow, please.* **PHR V** **follow 'through** (in tennis, golf, etc) to complete a stroke by continuing to move the club, RACKET¹, etc after hitting the ball. **,follow sth 'through** to carry out or continue sth to the end; to complete sth: *Starting projects is one thing — following them through is another.* **,follow sth 'up 1** to take further action on sth; to develop or exploit sth: *You should follow up your phone call with a letter.* **2** to investigate sth closely: *follow up a lead/clue/ rumour.*

▶ **follower** *n* a person who follows sb/sth; a supporter of a particular person, cause(3) or belief: *the*

[Vnn] = verb + noun + noun   [V-adj] = verb + adjective   For more help with verbs, see Study pages **B4–8**.

followers of Mahatma Gandhi ○ He's a follower, not a leader. See also CAMP-FOLLOWER.

■ ˌfollow-ˈthrough n (in tennis, golf, etc) the final part of a stroke after the ball has been hit.

ˈfollow-up n (pl -ups) an action or a thing that continues or exploits what has already been started or done: The book is a follow-up to her successful television series.

following /ˈfɒləʊɪŋ/ adj [attrib] **1** next in time: It rained on the day we arrived, but the following day was sunny. **2** about to be mentioned: Answer the following questions.

▶ following n [sing] a group of supporters: Our party has a large following in the south. **2** the following [sing or pl v] what follows or comes next: The following is of the greatest importance. ○ The following are extracts from the original article.

following prep after or as a result of sth: Following his arrest there were demonstrations in many parts of the country.

folly /ˈfɒli/ n **1(a)** [U] ~ (to do sth) being foolish; lack of wisdom: an act of sheer folly ○ It's utter folly to go swimming in this weather. **(b)** [C] a foolish or unwise act, idea or practice: regret one's youthful follies. **2** [C] an ornamental building that has no practical purpose, eg a tower or an artificial ruin built in a garden.

foment /fəʊˈment/ v to create esp political trouble or to make it worse: [Vn] foment discord/ill feeling/civil disorder.

fond /fɒnd/ adj (-er, -est) **1** [attrib] kind and loving; AFFECTIONATE: a fond look/embrace/farewell ○ I have very fond memories (ie ones recalled with affection) of my childhood. ○ The children then performed a short play, watched by their fond parents. **2** [pred] ~ of sb/(doing) sth feeling affection for sb; finding sth pleasant or enjoyable: fond of music/cooking/going to parties ○ I've always been very fond of your mother. ○ John's rather too fond of his own voice (ie He talks too much). **3** [attrib] (of wishes or ambitions) hoped for, but not likely to come true; foolishly held; NAIVE(1): fond hopes of success ○ I was brought up in the fond belief that people are basically unselfish.

▶ fondly adv **1** gently; in a loving way: He held her hand fondly. **2** in a foolishly hopeful way: I fondly imagined that you cared.

fondness n [U, sing] ~ (for sb/sth): his fondness for his eldest grandchild ○ have a fondness for sweets.

fondant /ˈfɒndənt/ n [U, C] a soft sweet²(1) that melts in the mouth: fondant icing.

fondle /ˈfɒndl/ v to touch or stroke sb/sth gently, sometimes in a sexual way: [Vn] fondle a cat ○ He fondled her breasts.

fondue /ˈfɒndjuː/ n [C, U] **1** a dish¹(2) of melted cheese, usu mixed with wine and other ingredients, into which pieces of bread are dipped. **2** a dish¹(2) of hot oil or other liquid into which pieces of meat, fish, etc are dipped: a beef fondue.

font /fɒnt/ n **1** a large raised bowl in a church, usu carved from stone, that holds water for BAPTISM. **2** = FOUNT².

food /fuːd/ n **1** [U] any substance that people or animals eat or drink, or that plants absorb, to maintain life and growth: a shortage of food in some countries ○ the food industry ○ We cannot survive for long without food and drink. ○ She is a lover of good food. **2** [C, U] a specific type of food: breakfast food ○ baby/health foods ○ frozen/processed foods ○ a can of dog food. See also FAST FOOD, JUNK FOOD. **IDM** food for ˈthought an idea that is worth thinking about seriously.

■ ˈfood-chain n a series of living creatures, each of which feeds on the one below it in the series.

ˈfood poisoning n [U] an illness of the stomach caused by eating food containing harmful bacteria.

ˈfood processor n an electrical appliance that mixes or cuts up food.

ˈfood stamp n (US) a piece of paper that can be used to buy food, given by the government to poorer people.

foodstuff /ˈfuːdstʌf/ n (usu pl) any substance used as food: essential foodstuffs.

fool¹ /fuːl/ n **1** (derog) a person who acts in a stupid or foolish way; a person lacking in good sense or judgement: What fools we were not to realize he was cheating us! ○ Don't be such a fool! ○ I was fool enough (ie so stupid as) to believe him. **2** (formerly) a man employed by a king, noble, etc to amuse others with jokes and tricks; a jester (JEST). See also APRIL FOOL. **IDM** act/play the ˈfool to behave in a silly way or so as to amuse (and perhaps annoy) others. be ˌno ˈfool; be ˌnobody's ˈfool to be a wise and clever person; to be not easily deceived. make a ˈfool of oneself/sb to behave foolishly/trick sb into behaving foolishly. ˌmore fool ˈsb (used as an exclamation) the person specified is unwise in behaving in the way he or she does: 'I got up early to do some work and now I'm exhausted.' 'ˌMore fool ˈyou!' (there is) ˌno fool like an ˈold fool (saying) the foolish behaviour of an older person seems even more foolish because he or she is expected to be more sensible than a younger person. not/never suffer fools gladly ⇨ SUFFER.

▶ fool v **1(a)** ~ (about/around) to behave in a stupid or foolish way: [Vp, Vpr] Stop fooling (about) with that knife or someone will get hurt. **(b)** to joke or TEASE(1); to pretend: [V] I was only fooling when I said I'd lost your keys. **2** ~ sb (into doing sth) to trick or deceive sb, eg so as to make them do sth or so as to be able to take sth from them: [Vn] You can't/don't fool me! ○ She certainly had me fooled. [Vnpr] She fooled him into thinking the painting was genuine. **IDM** you could have fooled ˈme (infml) I find it difficult to believe: Is that really a wig? You could have fooled me! **PHR V** ˌfool aˈbout/aˈround to waste time; to be IDLE: I was meant to be working on Sunday, but I just fooled around all day. ˌfool aˈround (infml esp US) to have a casual sexual relationship, esp when married or with a married person.

fool adj [attrib] (US infml) foolish; silly: That fool husband of mine locked us out of the house.

■ ˌfool's ˈerrand n a task that has no hope of success: go/be sent on a fool's errand.

ˌfool's ˈparadise n [sing] a state of happiness that is based on a false idea, although the happy person does not know this: I realized later that I'd been living in a fool's paradise.

fool² /fuːl/ n [C, U] (usu in compounds) a cold light PUDDING or custard made of cooked fruit mixed with cream or CUSTARD(1): a/some rhubarb fool.

foolhardy /ˈfuːlhɑːdi/ adj foolishly daring or BOLD(1): foolhardy behaviour ○ It was foolhardy of him to go swimming alone. ▶ foolhardiness n [U].

foolish /ˈfuːlɪʃ/ adj **1(a)** (of people) lacking good sense or judgement; silly: She's a foolish interfering old woman! ○ I was foolish enough to believe him. ○ It would be foolish (of us) to pretend that the accident never happened. **(b)** (of actions, statements, etc) showing a lack of good sense or judgement; unwise or stupid: a foolish decision/comment/reply. **2** [usu pred] made to feel or look ridiculous and embarrassed; stupid: I felt very foolish having to stand up and give a speech. ○ He's afraid of looking foolish in front of all his friends. ▶ foolishly adv. foolishness n [U].

foolproof /ˈfuːlpruːf/ adj not capable of going wrong or of being used wrongly; reliable and easy to operate: a foolproof method/plan/scheme ○ a foolproof security system.

foolscap /ˈfuːlskæp/ n [U] (Brit) a large size of

paper for writing or printing, about 330 x 200 (or 400) mm: *a lengthy report, running to over 200 pages of foolscap/foolscap pages.*

foot

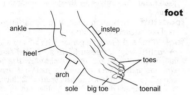

ankle · instep · heel · toes · arch · sole · big toe · toenail

foot¹ /fʊt/ *n* (*pl* **feet** /fiːt/) **1** [C] the lowest part of the leg, below the ankle, on which a person or an animal stands: *He got/rose to his feet* (ie stood up). ○ *I've been* **on my feet** (ie standing or walking around) *all day.* ○ *walking round the house in bare feet* (ie not wearing shoes or socks) ○ *a* ¹*foot switch/pump* (ie operated by one's foot, not one's hand). ⇨ picture. **2** [C usu *sing*] the part of a sock or STOCKING that covers the foot. **3** [C] (*pl* **feet** or, in measurements and attributively, **foot**) (*abbr* **ft**) a measure of length equal to 12 inches: *a 6-foot high wall* ○ *We're flying at 35 000 feet.* ○ *'How tall are you?' 'Five foot nine'* (ie five feet and nine inches). ⇨ App 2. **4** [sing] the ~ of sth (**a**) the lowest part of sth; the base or bottom of sth: *at the foot of the stairs/a ladder* ○ *at the foot of the page* ○ *They camped at the foot of the cliff/ mountain.* (**b**) the end of a bed where one's feet normally are when one is lying in it: *There were clean towels at the foot of each bed.* **5** [U] (*arch*) a manner of walking or moving: *light/swift/fleet of foot.* **6** [C] a unit of rhythm in a line of poetry containing one stressed syllable and one or more syllables without stress. Each of the four divisions in the following line is a foot: *For* ¹*men / may* ¹*come / and* ¹*men / may* ¹*go.* See also ATHLETE'S FOOT, BARE-FOOT, CLUB-FOOT. **IDM** **bind/tie sb hand and foot** ⇨ HAND¹. **the boot is on the other foot** ⇨ BOOT¹. **catch sb on the wrong foot** ⇨ CATCH¹. **cut the ground from under sb's feet** ⇨ GROUND¹. **drag one's feet/heels** ⇨ DRAG¹. **fall/land on one's** ¹**feet** to have good luck after a difficult period, a business failure, etc. **find one's feet** ⇨ FIND¹. **from head to foot/toe** ⇨ HEAD¹. **get/have a** ¸**foot in the** ¹**door** to gain/have a first introduction to a profession, an organization, etc: *He always wanted to go into publishing but it took him two years to get a foot in the door.* **get/have cold feet** ⇨ COLD¹. **have the ball at one's feet** ⇨ BALL¹. **have feet of** ¹**clay** to have some basic weakness or fault. **have both feet on the** ¹**ground; have one's** ¹**feet on the ground** to be sensible, realistic and practical. **have a foot in both** ¹**camps** to have an interest in two different parties or sides, without being committed to either. **have** ¸**one foot in the** ¹**grave** (*infml*) to be so old or ill that one is not likely to live much longer. **have two left feet** ⇨ LEFT². **in one's stocking feet** ⇨ STOCKING. **itchy feet** ⇨ ITCHY. **let the grass grow under one's feet** ⇨ GRASS¹. **my** ¹**foot!** (*infml*) (said to show that one disagrees strongly with sth that has just been said) nonsense! rubbish!: *'It's too difficult.' 'Difficult my foot! Try harder!'* **on one's** ¹**feet** completely recovered from an illness or a time of trouble: *After his wife's death it took him two years to get back on his feet.* ○ *policies that will put the country on its feet again.* **on** ¹**foot** walking, rather than using any form of transport: *They set off on foot.* **pull the rug from under sb's feet** ⇨ PULL¹. **put one's** ¹**feet up** to rest or relax in a chair or on a bed, esp with one's feet supported. **put one's** ¹**foot down 1** to be very firm in opposing sth which sb wishes to do: *You've got to put your foot down and make him stop seeing her.* **2** to drive faster: *She put her foot down and roared past them.*

put one's ¹**foot in it** to say or do sth that upsets, offends or embarrasses sb. **put a foot** ¹**wrong** (*Brit*) (esp in negative sentences) to make a mistake: *In all his years in the job I've never known him (to) put a foot wrong.* **rush/run sb (clean) off their** ¹**feet** to make sb work very hard or move about a lot, so that they become very tired: *Before Christmas the shop assistants are rushed off their feet.* **set** ¹**foot in/on sth** to enter or visit a place; to arrive: *the first man to set foot on the moon* ○ *Don't ever set foot in this house again!* **set sb/sth on their/its** ¹**feet** to make sb/sth independent or successful: *set a business on its feet.* **sit at sb's feet** ⇨ SIT. **stand on one's own (two)** ¹**feet** to be independent and able to look after oneself: *Now that you're growing up you must learn to stand on your own two feet.* **start off on the right/wrong foot** ⇨ START². **sweep sb off their feet** ⇨ SWEEP¹. **under one's** ¹**feet** disturbing one, preventing one from working, etc; in the way: *The children are under my feet all day.* **vote with one's feet** ⇨ VOTE *v*. **wait on sb hand and foot** ⇨ WAIT². **walk sb off their feet** ⇨ WALK¹.

▶ **-footer** /ˈfʊtə(r)/ (forming compounds) a person or thing of the specified length, height or width: *a six-footer* (ie a person who is six feet tall or a thing that is six feet wide or long).

■ ¸**foot-and-**¹**mouth disease** *n* [U] an often fatal disease of cattle, etc which causes sore places in the mouth and feet.

foot² /fʊt/ *v* **IDM** **foot the** ¹**bill (for sth)** (*infml*) to be responsible for paying the cost of sth: *Who's going to foot the bill for all the repairs?*

▶ **-footed** (forming compound *adjs*) having feet of the specified type or number: *bare-footed* ○ *flat-footed* ○ *four-footed.*

footage /ˈfʊtɪdʒ/ *n* [U] a length of film made for the cinema or television: *old newsreel footage* ○ *film footage of the riot.*

football

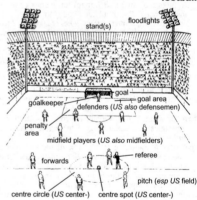

stand(s) · floodlights · goal · goal area · goalkeeper · defenders (*US also* defensemen) · penalty area · midfield players (*US also* midfielders) · forwards · referee · centre circle (*US* center-) · centre spot (*US* center-) · pitch (*esp US* field)

football /ˈfʊtbɔːl/ *n* **1** [C] a large round or OVAL ball made of leather or plastic and filled with air: *kick a football about.* **2** (also **association football**, *esp US* **soccer**) [U] a game played by two teams of eleven players, using a round ball that must not be handled during the game except by the GOALKEEPER: *boys playing football* ○ *a football stadium* ○ *football hooligans.* ⇨ picture. **3** [U] any of several outdoor games between two teams, played with a football, eg Rugby, American football and Australian Rules. **4** an issue or problem that frequently causes argument and disagreement: *Health care should not become a political football.*

▶ **footballer** *n* a person who plays football, esp as a profession.

footballing adj [attrib] of the game of football: *footballing skills*.

■ **'football pools** (also **the pools**) n [pl] a form of gambling in which people try to predict the results of football matches: *have a big win on the football pools*.

footbridge /'fʊtbrɪdʒ/ n a narrow bridge for the use of people who are walking and not for cars, etc: *cross the footbridge*.

footfall /'fʊtfɔːl/ (*fml*) n the sound of sb walking; the sound of a FOOTSTEP: *hear a light footfall*.

foothill /'fʊthɪl/ n [C usu *pl*] a hill or low mountain at the base of a higher mountain or range of mountains: *in the foothills of the Himalayas*.

foothold /'fʊthəʊld/ n **1** a place where one's foot can be supported securely when climbing. **2** (usu *sing*) a secure position in a business, profession, etc from which further progress may be made: *gain a firm foothold in the European market*.

footing /'fʊtɪŋ/ n [sing] **1** a secure grip with the feet; one's balance: *He lost his footing on the wet floor and fell*. **2** the basis on which sth is established: *This enterprise is now on a firm/sound financial footing*. ○ *Since the uprising the country has been on a war footing* (ie prepared for war). **3** the position or status of sb/sth in relation to others; the relationship between two or more people or groups: *The workers want to be on an equal footing with/on the same footing as the managers*.

footlights /'fʊtlaɪts/ n [pl] a row of lights along the front of the stage in a theatre.

footling /'fuːtlɪŋ/ adj unimportant; TRIVIAL: *Don't waste my time with such footling questions*.

footloose /'fʊtluːs/ adj free to go where one likes or do what one wants: *He's still unmarried and footloose*.

footman /'fʊtmən/ n (*pl* **-men** /-mən/) a male servant, usu in uniform, who admits visitors, serves food at table, etc.

footnote /'fʊtnəʊt/ n an additional piece of information printed at the bottom of a page in a book: (*fig*) *a footnote in racing history* ○ *a footnote to a bizarre career*.

footpath /'fʊtpɑːθ; *US* -pæθ/ n = PATH 1.

footprint /'fʊtprɪnt/ n [C usu *pl*] a mark left by a person's or an animal's foot on a surface: *leave footprints in the snow* ○ *muddy footprints on the kitchen floor*.

footrest /'fʊtrest/ n **1** (*US*) = FOOTSTOOL. **2** a support for the foot, eg on a motor cycle (MOTOR).

footsie /'fʊtsi/ n [IDM] **play 'footsie with sb** (*infml*) to touch sb's feet lightly with one's own feet, usu under a table, as a playful expression of affection or sexual interest.

footsore /'fʊtsɔː(r)/ adj having sore or tired feet, esp from walking a long way: *footsore travellers*.

footstep /'fʊtstep/ n (usu *pl*) a step taken when walking or the sound of this: *echoing footsteps* ○ *I heard his footsteps in the hall*. [IDM] **follow in sb's footsteps** ⇨ FOLLOW.

footstool /'fʊtstuːl/ (also **stool**, *US* **footrest**) n a low stool for resting the feet on when sitting in a chair.

footwear /'fʊtweə(r)/ n [U] anything worn on the feet, eg shoes and boots.

footwork /'fʊtwɜːk/ n [U] (**a**) one's manner of moving or using the feet in sports such as boxing or dancing: *deft/fancy/light/nifty footwork*. (**b**) the ability to react quickly to sudden danger, new opportunities, etc: *Her deft political footwork saved the situation*.

fop /fɒp/ n (*derog*) a man who is too concerned with his clothes and appearance; a DANDY[1]. ▶ **foppish** adj: *foppish manners*.

for[1] /fə(r); *strong form* fɔː(r)/ prep For the special

uses of **for** in phrasal verbs, look at the verb entries. For example, the meaning of **fall for sb** is given in the phrasal verb section of the entry for **fall[1]**. **1** (indicating the person intended to receive or benefit from sth): *There's a letter for you*. ○ *Are all these presents for me?* ○ *Have you made a cup of tea for Mrs Watson?* **2(a)** in order to help or benefit sb/sth: *fighting for their country* ○ *Would you please translate this letter for me?* ○ *What can I do for you?* ○ *Take some aspirin for* (ie to relieve the pain caused by) *your headache*. ○ *The assistant manager ran the business for* (ie instead of) *him while he was sick*. (**b**) as an employee of sb: *She works for a publisher*. **3** (indicating purpose or function): *go for a walk* ○ *It's a machine for slicing bread*. ○ *Are you learning English for pleasure or for your work?* ○ *For sales to* (ie In order that sales may) *increase, we must lower our prices*. ○ (*infml*) *What did you do that for* (ie Why did you do that)? **4** (indicating destination or target): *leave for home* ○ *Is this the bus for Chicago?* ○ *She knew she was destined for a great future*. ○ *a chair for visitors* ○ *bicycles for sale or for hire* ○ *It's a book for* (ie intended to be read by or to) *children*. ○ *This is the place for me* (ie I like it very much). **5** (indicating reason or cause) because of sth; on account of sth: *The town is famous for its cathedral*. ○ *Please take care of her for my sake*. ○ *I couldn't speak for laughing*. ○ *He didn't answer for fear of hurting her*. ○ *He gave me roses for my birthday*. **6** with regard to sb/sth; concerning sb/sth: *anxious for sb's safety* ○ *I'm ready for a break*. ○ *Fortunately for us, the weather changed*. **7** in defence or support of sb/sth: *Are you for or against the proposal?* ○ *Three cheers for the winner!* ○ *We're campaigning for a bypass round the town*. ○ *I'm all for pubs staying open all day*. Compare AGAINST 1. **8(a)** as a representative of sb/sth: *I am speaking for everyone in the department*. ○ *Who's the congresswoman for this district?* (**b**) meaning sth: *What's the 'S' for in A S Hornby?* ○ *Shaking your head for 'No' is not universal*. **9** (esp after a *v*) in order to obtain sth: *search for treasure* ○ *hope for a settlement* ○ *ask the policeman for directions* ○ *go to a friend for advice* ○ *There were over fifty applicants for the job*. ○ *For more information, phone this number*. **10** as the price, reward or penalty that sth carries: *buy a book for £3* ○ *She gave me their old TV for nothing*. ○ *get a medal for bravery* ○ *He was fined for dangerous driving*. **11** as the replacement of sth else: *exchange one's car for a new one* ○ *Don't translate it word for word*. **12** in return for sth; in the specified RATIO: *There's one bad apple for every three good ones*. ○ *You get a coupon for every 20 litres of petrol you buy*. **13** (after an *adj*) considering what can be expected from sb/sth: *It's quite warm for January*. ○ *She's tall for her age*. ○ *He's not bad for a beginner*. **14** (after a comparative *adj*) following sth: *You'll feel all the better for a good night's sleep*. ○ *This room would look more cheerful for a spot of paint*. **15(a)** (indicating a length of time): *I'm going away for a few days*. ○ *You said you would love me for ever*. (**b**) (indicating that sth is intended to happen at the specified time): *a reservation for the first week in June* ○ *an appointment for 12 May* ○ *We're invited for 7.30*. (**c**) (indicating the occasion when sth happens): *I'm warning you for the last time — stop talking!* **16** (indicating a distance): *He crawled on his hands and knees for 100 metres*. ○ *The road went on for miles and miles*. **17(a)** (used after an *adj* and before a *n* or *pron* + infinitive): *It's impossible for me to leave my family*. ○ *It's useless for us to continue*. ○ *It's customary for the women to sit apart*. ○ (*fml*) *For her to have survived such an ordeal was remarkable*. (**b**) (used after a *n* and before a *n* or *pron* + infinitive): *There's no need for you to go*. ○ *It's time for us to leave*. ○ *His greatest wish was for his daughter to take over the business*. (**c**) (used after *too* + *adj* or *adj* + *enough*): *The box is too heavy for me to lift*. ○ *Is it* *clear enough for you to read?* (**d**) (used before a *n* or *pron* + infinitive to show purpose or design): *letters for the manager to sign* ○ *I would give anything for this not to have happened.* ○ *It's not for me* (ie It is not my responsibility) *to say.* (**e**) (used after *more* with *than*): *Nothing would please me more than for her to win the next election.* ○ *Nothing could be more pleasant than for them both to get married.* **IDM** **be ¹for it; be ¹in for it** (*infml*) to be about to get into trouble or be punished: *You were seen stealing those apples — you're for it now.* **for ¹all 1** despite; in spite of: *For all his talk about sports cars and swimming-pools he's just an ordinary bank clerk.* **2** (used to dismiss sth as unimportant or of little interest or value): *For all I know she's still living in Boston.* ○ *You can do what you like, for all I care!* ○ *For all the good it's done we might never have bothered.*

for² /fə(r); *strong form* fɔ:(r)/ *conj* (*dated or fml*) (not usu used at the beginning of a sentence) because: *We listened eagerly, for he brought news of our families.* ○ *I believed her — for surely she would not lie to me.*

forage /ˈfɒrɪdʒ; *US* ˈfɔ:r-/ *n* [U] food for horses and cattle: *forage crops.*
▶ **forage** *v* ~ (**for sth**) to search or hunt for sth, esp food and supplies: [Vpr] *Enemy groups left the camp to forage for firewood.* [Vp] *She foraged about in her handbag, but couldn't find her keys.* [also V].
■ **¹forage cap** *n* a cap worn by a soldier that is not part of his normal uniform.

foray /ˈfɒreɪ; *US* ˈfɔ:r-/ *n* ~ (**into sth**) **1** a sudden attack, esp to obtain sth; a RAID: *make a foray into occupied territory* ○ (*fig*) *weekend shopping forays to France.* **2** a brief but vigorous attempt to become involved in a different activity, profession, etc: *the company's first foray into the computer market.*

forbade *pt* of FORBID.

forbear¹ /fɔ:ˈbeə(r)/ *v* (*pt* **forbore** /fɔ:ˈbɔ:(r)/; *pp* **forborne** /fɔ:ˈbɔ:n/) ~ (**from sth / doing sth**) (*fml*) to control one's behaviour in a patient way; to restrain angry or HOSTILE(1) feelings: [Vpr] *The workers were extremely unhappy but forbore from actually striking.* [V.*to* inf] *He forbore to mention the matter again.* [also V].
▶ **forbearance** /fɔ:ˈbeərəns/ *n* [U] (*fml*) patience; restraint; tolerance (TOLERATE): *show forbearance towards sb* ○ *exercise forbearance in dealing with people.*
forbearing *adj* (*fml*) showing forbearance: *She has a gentle and forbearing nature* ○ *Thank you for being so forbearing.*

forbear² = FOREBEAR.

forbid /fəˈbɪd/ *v* (*pt* **forbade** /fəˈbæd, fəˈbeɪd/; *pp* **forbidden** /fəˈbɪdn/) **1(a)** ~ **sb** (**from doing sth**) to order sb not to do sth: [Vn] *If you want to go, I can't forbid you.* [Vnn] *She was forbidden access to the club.* [Vn.*to* inf] *He was forbidden to talk to her.* ○ *It is forbidden (for anyone) to smoke in this room.* [Vnpr] *I can't forbid you from seeing him again.* (**b**) to order that sth is not to be done or not to happen; to refuse to allow sth: [Vn] *Her father forbade their marriage.* ○ *Photography is strictly forbidden in the museum.* ○ *Abortion is forbidden by law.* [V.*ing*] *The law forbids building on this land.* **2** (*fml*) to make sth difficult or impossible; to prevent or not to allow sth: [Vn] *Lack of space forbids further treatment of the topic here.* **IDM** **for¹bidden ¹fruit** a thing that is desired because it is disapproved of or not allowed. **God/Heaven for¹bid (that ...)** (expressing a wish that sth may not happen): *Heaven forbid (that) she's fallen down the cliff.* ○ *I dread to think what it would be like if, God forbid, there was another war.*
▶ **forbidding** *adj* looking cold and HOSTILE(1a); threatening: *a forbidding appearance/look/manner* ○ *a forbidding coastline* (ie one that looks dangerous).
forbiddingly *adv.*

forbore *pt* of FORBEAR¹.

forborne *pp* of FORBEAR¹.

force¹ /fɔ:s/ *n* **1** [U] (**a**) physical strength or power: *the force of the blow/explosion/collision* ○ *The force of his fall was broken* (ie reduced) *by the straw matting.* ○ *They used* **brute force** *to break open the door.* (**b**) violent physical action: *renounce the use of force* ○ *The rioters were taken away by force.* **2** [U] (**a**) the strength or power of sth; the influence of sth: *the full force of her argument* ○ *He gave up smoking by sheer force of will.* ○ *Through force of circumstance our plans had to be changed.* (**b**) the authority of sth: *These guidelines do not have the force of law.* **3** [C] a person, thing, belief, etc with considerable power or influence: *market* (ie economic) *forces* ○ *What is the* **driving force behind** *his writing?* ○ *the forces of evil* ○ *She's* **a force to be reckoned with** (ie a person to be treated seriously). **4** [C, U] (in scientific use) an influence tending to cause movement, that can be measured: *magnetic forces* ○ *The force of gravity pulls things towards the earth's centre.* **5** [C] the power of the wind, rain or another of the natural elements: *the forces of nature.* ⇨ note at STRENGTH. **6** [C usu *sing*] a measure of wind strength: *a force 9 gale.* **7** [CGp] a group of people organized for a specified purpose: *a sales/labour force.* **8** [CGp] an organized body of armed and specially trained people: *the police force* ○ *peace-keeping forces* ○ *the armed forces of a country* (ie its army, navy and air force). **9 the force** [sing] (*Brit*) the police force: *join the force.* **10 the forces** [pl] (**a**) (*Brit*) the army, navy and air force. (**b**) (*US*) the army. See also TASK FORCE, TOUR DE FORCE. **IDM** **bring sth / come into ¹force** to cause a law, rule, etc to become effective or come into operation: *When do the new safety rules come into force?* (**from / out of**) **force of ¹habit** (because of) the tendency to do sth in a certain way from always having done so in the past: *It's force of habit that gets me out of bed at 6.15 each morning.* **in ¹force 1** (of people) in large numbers: *Protesters turned up in force.* **2** (of a law, rule, etc) effective or in operation: *The new safety regulations are now in force.* **join forces** ⇨ JOIN.

force² /fɔ:s/ *v* **1** to make sb/oneself do sth against their/one's will; to COMPEL sb/oneself: [Vn.*to* inf] *The thief forced her to hand over the money.* ○ *He forced himself to speak to her.* [Vnpr] *force a confession out of sb* [Vnpr, Vn.*to* inf] *The president was forced into resigning/to resign.* **2** to use physical strength to achieve sth or to move sth/oneself into or through a place: [Vn] *force an entry* [Vnp] *force a way in/out/through* [Vnpr] *force one's way through a crowd* ○ *force clothes into a bag* ○ (*fig*) *The President forced the bill through Congress.* **3** to break sth open using physical strength: [Vn, Vn-adj] *force (open) a door/lock/window/safe.* **4** to act so as to make sth happen sooner, before other people are ready: [Vn] *force a decision* ○ *Be patient — we mustn't force matters.* ○ *If they still haven't made up their minds, we'll have to* **force the issue.** **5** to cause or produce sth by effort, esp when under stress: [Vn] *He forced a smile.* ○ *That argument was certainly forced* (ie not natural or convincing). **6** to make fruit, plants, etc grow or develop faster than is normal by keeping them under special conditions: [Vn] *forced rhubarb.* **IDM** **force sb's ¹hand** to make sb do sth unwillingly or sooner than they intended. **force the ¹pace** to go very fast in a race, etc in order to tire the other competitors. **PHRV** **¸force sth ¹back** to try very hard not to show an emotion: *force back one's tears.* **¸force sth ¹down 1** to make oneself swallow food and drink when one does not want to: *I didn't feel like eating but I managed to force a sandwich down.* **2** to make an aircraft land, eg because it is flying over an area without permission. **¹force sth on sb** to make sb accept sth against their will:

F

force one's ideas/company/attention on sb ∘ *Higher taxes were forced on the people.*

▶ **forced** *adj* **1** not natural, genuine or convincing: *forced laughter* ∘ *I found his reasoning rather forced.* **2** done or happening against sb's will: *forced repatriation.*

■ ˌ**forced** ˈ**labour** *n* [U] compulsory hard physical work, usu under harsh conditions. ˌ**forced** ˈ**landing** *n* an emergency landing by an aircraft. ˌ**forced** ˈ**march** *n* a long emergency march made by troops.

force-feed /ˌfɔːs ˈfiːd/ *v* (*pp, pt* **force-fed** /ˌfɔːs ˈfed/) to use force to make a person or an animal take food and drink: [Vn] *All the prisoners on hunger strike had to be force-fed.*

forceful /ˈfɔːsfl/ *adj* (*usu approv*) strong and firm; ASSERTIVE: *a forceful speaker* ∘ *a forceful argument/ speech/style of writing.* ▶ **forcefully** /-fəli/ *adv*: *argue forcefully.* **forcefulness** *n* [U].

force majeure /ˌfɔːs mæˈʒɜː(r)/ *n* [U] (*French*) unexpected circumstances, such as war, that excuse sb from keeping a promise or fulfilling a contract.

forcemeat /ˈfɔːsmiːt/ *n* [U] finely chopped meat mixed with other ingredients and used as stuffing (STUFF²), eg in a cooked chicken.

forceps /ˈfɔːseps/ *n* [pl] an instrument with two long thin parts for gripping things, used eg by doctors: *a pair of forceps* ∘ *a forceps delivery* (ie one in which the baby is delivered with the help of forceps).

forcible /ˈfɔːsəbl/ *adj* [attrib] done by or involving the use of physical force: *forcible deportation* ∘ *make a forcible entry into a building.* ▶ **forcibly** /-əbli/ *adv*: *be forcibly repatriated/restrained.*

ford /fɔːd/ *n* a shallow place in a river where one can walk or drive across. ▶ **ford** *v* [Vn] to cross a river by walking or driving across a ford.

fore /fɔː(r)/ *adj* [attrib] situated in the front part of a vehicle: *in the fore part of the ship/plane/train.* ▶ **fore** *n* **IDM** **be/come to the** ˈ**fore** be/become prominent or important: *She's always to the fore at moments of crisis.* ∘ *After the election several new Members of Parliament came to the fore.* **fore** *adv* in, at or towards the front of a ship or an aircraft. Compare AFT.

fore- *pref* (with *ns* and *vs*) **1** (of time or rank) before; in advance of: *forefather* ∘ *foreman* ∘ *foretell.* **2** (of position) in front of: *foreground* ∘ *foreshorten.*

forearm¹ /ˈfɔːrɑːm/ *n* the part of the arm from the elbow to the wrist or fingers. ⇨ picture at HUMAN.

forearm² /ˌfɔːrˈɑːm/ *v* (usu passive) to prepare oneself/sb in advance for possible danger, attack, etc: [Vn] *be forearmed against likely criticism.* **IDM** **forewarned is forearmed** ⇨ FOREWARN.

forebear (also **forbear**) /ˈfɔːbeə(r)/ *n* [C usu *pl*] a person from whom one is descended; an ancestor.

foreboding /fɔːˈbəʊdɪŋ/ *n* [C, U] a strong feeling that danger or trouble is coming: *She had* **a sense** **of foreboding** *that the plane would crash.* ∘ *The letter filled him with foreboding.*

forecast /ˈfɔːkɑːst; *US* -kæst/ *v* (*pt, pp* **forecast** or **forecasted**) to say in advance what is expected to happen; to predict sth with the help of information: [Vn] *forecast a fall in unemployment* [V.*that*] *forecast that it will rain tomorrow* [V.*wh*] *forecast what the outcome of the election will be.*

▶ **forecast** *n* a statement that predicts sth with the help of information: *forecasts of higher profits* ∘ *According to the (weather) forecast it will be sunny tomorrow.* ∘ *The forecast said there would be sunny intervals and showers.*

forecaster *n* a person who forecasts sth, esp sb whose job is to forecast the weather.

foreclose /fɔːˈkləʊz/ *v* **1** ~ (**on sb/sth**) (of a bank, etc that has lent money to sb) to take possession of sb's property, usu because they have not paid back an agreed part of the loan: [V, Vpr] *The bank foreclosed (on the mortgage).* **2** to exclude sth: [Vn] *foreclose the possibility of a divorce.*

▶ **foreclosure** /fɔːˈkləʊʒə(r)/ *n* [U, C] the action or an instance of foreclosing on a loan.

forecourt /ˈfɔːkɔːt/ *n* a large open area in front of a building, eg in front of a petrol station (PETROL).

foredoomed /fɔːˈduːmd/ *adj* ~ (**to sth**) intended as if by fate not to be successful: *Any attempt to construct an ideal society is foredoomed to failure.*

forefather /ˈfɔːfɑːðə(r)/ *n* [C usu *pl*] a person from whom one is descended; an ancestor: *the land of one's forefathers.*

forefinger /ˈfɔːfɪŋɡə(r)/ *n* the finger next to the thumb; the index finger (INDEX). ⇨ picture at HAND.

forefoot /ˈfɔːfʊt/ *n* (*pl* -**feet** /-fiːt/) either of the two front feet of an animal with four feet.

forefront /ˈfɔːfrʌnt/ *n* [sing] the ~ (**of sth**) the most forward or important position or place: *in/at the forefront of my mind* ∘ *The new product took the company to the forefront of the computer software field.*

forego = FORGO.

foregoing /ˈfɔːɡəʊɪŋ/ *adj* [attrib] (*fml*) preceding; just mentioned: *the foregoing analysis/description/ discussion.*

▶ **the foregoing** *n* [sing or pl *v*] (*fml*) what has just been mentioned: *The foregoing is a description of the plan proposed.*

foregone /ˈfɔːɡɒn; *US* -ɡɔːn/ *adj* **IDM** **a** ˌ**foregone** con**ˈclusion** a result that can be predicted with certainty: *The outcome of the vote is a foregone conclusion.*

foreground /ˈfɔːɡraʊnd/ *n* **the foreground** [sing] (**a**) the front part of a view, scene, picture, etc; the part nearest the observer: *The figure in the foreground is the artist's mother.* Compare BACKGROUND 1. (**b**) the most important or prominent position: *These teachers are keeping education in the foreground of public attention.* Compare BACKGROUND 2.

forehand /ˈfɔːhænd/ *n* [sing] (in tennis, etc) a stroke played with the palm of the hand turned towards one's opponent or towards the front of the court¹(3): *a weak forehand* ∘ *a forehand volley* ∘ *She hit the ball to my forehand.* Compare BACKHAND.

forehead /ˈfɔːhed, ˈfɒrɪd; *US* ˈfɔːred/ (also **brow**) *n* the part of the face above the eyebrows (EYEBROW) and below the hair. ⇨ picture at HEAD¹.

foreign /ˈfɒrən; *US* ˈfɔːr-/ *adj* **1**(**a**) of, in or from a country or an area other than one's own: *foreign languages/goods/students* ∘ *a foreign-owned company.* (**b**) dealing with or involving other countries: *foreign affairs/news/policy/trade* ∘ *foreign aid* (ie money, etc given by one country to another in need). **2** ~ **to sb/sth** (*fml*) not belonging naturally to sb/sth; not characteristic of sb/sth: *Dishonesty is foreign to his nature.* **3** (*fml*) coming or introduced from outside, usu by accident: *a foreign body* (eg a hair or piece of dirt) *in the eye.*

▶ **foreigner** *n* **1** a person from a country other than one's own. **2** a person who is regarded as not belonging to a particular community; a stranger or an OUTSIDER(1).

■ **the** ˌ**Foreign and** ˈ**Commonwealth Office** (*abbr* **FCO**) the British government department that deals with foreign affairs. It was formerly called, and is still sometimes referred to as, **the** ˈ**Foreign Office**. Compare THE HOME OFFICE.

ˌ**foreign ex**ˈ**change** *n* [U] money in a foreign currency: *the foreign exchange markets.*

the ˌ**Foreign** ˈ**Secretary** *n* the British government minister in charge of the Foreign and Commonwealth Office.

foreknowledge /fɔːˈnɒlɪdʒ/ *n* [U] (*fml*) knowledge of sth before it happens or exists.

foreleg /ˈfɔːleg/ *n* either of the two front legs of an animal that has four legs.

forelock /ˈfɔːlɒk/ *n* a piece of hair growing and falling over the forehead. ⇨ picture at HORSE. **IDM** **touch, tug, etc one's 'forelock** (esp formerly) to raise a hand to one's forehead when meeting sb of higher social class, as a sign of respect.

foreman /ˈfɔːmən/ *n* (*pl* -men /-mən/) **1** a worker who supervises and directs other workers. **2** a person who acts as the leader of a JURY in a lawcourt.

foremost /ˈfɔːməʊst/ *adj* [attrib] the most famous or important; the best or chief: *the foremost painter of his time.*
▶ **foremost** *adv* in the first position; mainly: *I am concerned foremost about the prosperity of the country.* **IDM** **first and foremost** ⇨ FIRST[2].

forename /ˈfɔːneɪm/ *n* (*fml*) a name preceding the family name; a person's first or Christian name. ⇨ App 5. ⇨ note at NAME[1].

forensic /fəˈrensɪk, -ˈrenzɪk/ *adj* [attrib] **1** relating to the scientific tests used to help with police investigations and legal problems: *forensic medicine/evidence/science* ∘ *forensic analysis of blood found at the scene of the crime.* **2** of, relating to or used in law or lawcourts: *forensic skills.*

foreplay /ˈfɔːpleɪ/ *n* [U] sexual activity such as touching the sexual organs and kissing before having sex.

forerunner /ˈfɔːrʌnə(r)/ *n* a person or thing that prepares the way for the coming of sb or sth else more important; a sign of what is to follow: *the forerunners of the modern diesel engine.* Compare ANCESTOR.

foresee /fɔːˈsiː/ *v* (*pt* foresaw /fɔːˈsɔː/; *pp* foreseen /fɔːˈsiːn/) to see or know that sth is going to happen in the future; to predict sth: [Vn] *These difficulties could not have been foreseen.* [V.that] *He foresaw that the job would take a long time.* [V.wh] *They could not have foreseen how things would turn out.* Compare UNFORESEEN.
▶ **foreseeable** /-əbl/ *adj* that can be foreseen: *Such an event is unlikely in/for the foreseeable future* (ie during the period of time when one knows what is going to happen).

foreshadow /fɔːˈʃædəʊ/ *v* to be a sign or warning of sth that is coming or about to happen: [Vn] *The increase in taxes had been foreshadowed in the minister's speech.*

foreshore /ˈfɔːʃɔː(r)/ *n* [U, C usu *sing*] the part of the shore between the limits of high and low tides, or between the sea and land that is cultivated or built on.

foreshorten /fɔːˈʃɔːtn/ *v* [Vn] (in drawing) to represent an object by making certain lines shorter to give an effect of distance and PERSPECTIVE(1).

foresight /ˈfɔːsaɪt/ *n* [U] the ability to see what one's future needs are likely to be; careful planning: *She had the foresight to buy land in an area scheduled for development.* ∘ *The government's policies show remarkable lack of foresight.* Compare HIND-SIGHT.

foreskin /ˈfɔːskɪn/ *n* a loose fold of skin covering the end of the PENIS. ⇨ picture at REPRODUCTION.

forest /ˈfɒrɪst; *US* ˈfɔːr-/ *n* **1(a)** a large area of land thickly covered with trees, bushes, etc: *the dense tropical forests of the Amazon basin* ∘ *forest animals/fires.* **(b)** land of this type: *Very little forest is left unexplored these days.* See also RAIN FOREST. **2** [C] a mass of tall or narrow objects that looks like a forest: *a forest of television aerials.*
▶ **forested** *adj* covered in forest: *thickly forested areas.*

forester *n* a person who looks after or works in a forest.

forestry *n* [U] the science and practice of planting, caring for and managing forests: *the Forestry Commission.*

forestall /fɔːˈstɔːl/ *v* to act before sb else so as to prevent them from doing sth: [Vn] *forestall a rival* ∘ *I started to object, but she forestalled me.* ∘ *His plans to retire were forestalled by events.*

foretaste /ˈfɔːteɪst/ *n* [sing] ~ (**of sth**) a small experience of sth before it actually happens; a sample: *Last night's street violence seems certain to be a foretaste of what is to come.*

foretell /fɔːˈtel/ *v* (*pt, pp* foretold /fɔːˈtəʊld/) (*fml*) to tell what will happen in the future; to predict sth: [Vn] *No one could have foretold such strange events.* [V.that] *The gypsy had foretold that she would never marry.* [V.wh] *It's impossible to foretell how the game will end.*

forethought /ˈfɔːθɔːt/ *n* [U] careful thought or planning for the future : *With a little more forethought we could have bought the house we really wanted.*

foretold *pt, pp* of FORETELL.

forever /fərˈevə(r)/ *adv* **1** (also **for ever**) for all time; always: *I'll love you forever!* ∘ *You'll never get your ring back — it's lost forever.* ∘ (*infml*) *It takes her forever* (ie an extremely long time) *to get dressed.* **2** (usu with *v*s in the continuous tenses) at all times; continually: *She's forever going on about how poor they are.* **3** (*infml*) (used in exclamations after the name of sb/sth, to show support): *Some fans carried a banner with 'Scotland forever!' on it.*

forewarn /fɔːˈwɔːn/ *v* ~ **sb** (**of sth**) (esp passive) to warn sb before sth happens; to advise sb of possible dangers, problems, etc: [Vnpr, Vn.that] *We had been forewarned of the risk of violence/that violence could occur.* [also Vn]. **IDM** **fore,warned is fore'armed** (*saying*) knowledge of possible dangers, problems, etc allows one to prepare for them.

foreword /ˈfɔːwɜːd/ *n* a short introduction to a book, printed at the beginning and usu written by a person other than the author. Compare PREFACE.

forfeit /ˈfɔːfɪt/ *v* to give up sth or have sth taken away as a consequence of punishment for having done sth wrong: [Vn] *Passengers who cancel their reservations will forfeit their deposit.* ∘ *He has forfeited the right to be taken seriously.*
▶ **forfeit** *n* a thing paid or given up as a penalty or punishment: *Teams that repeatedly ignore the rules must pay a forfeit.*
forfeit *adj* [pred] ~ (**to sb/sth**) (*fml*) lost, paid or given up as a forfeit: *By the Treaty of Versailles all German vessels over 1 600 tons were forfeit to the victorious powers.*
forfeiture /ˈfɔːfɪtʃə(r)/ *n* [U] ~ (**of sth**) the action of forfeiting sth or of being forfeited: *forfeiture of property.*

forgave *pt* of FORGIVE.

forge[1] /fɔːdʒ/ *n* **1** a place where metals are heated and shaped, esp one used by a BLACKSMITH. **2** (a part of a factory, etc with) a FURNACE(1) for melting metals.

forge[2] /fɔːdʒ/ *v* **1** to make a copy or an IMITATION(1) of sth in order to deceive people: [Vn] *forge a banknote/will/signature* ∘ *a forged passport.* Compare COUNTERFEIT *v*. **2(a)** to shape metal by heating it in a fire and hammering it: [Vn] *forge a sword/chain.* **(b)** to create a lasting relationship by means of much hard work: [Vn] *forge a bond/a link/an alliance* ∘ *a friendship forged in adversity.* Compare WELD.
▶ **forger** *n* a person who forges (FORGE[2] 1) money, documents, etc. Compare COUNTERFEITER.
forgery /ˈfɔːdʒəri/ *n* **1** [U] the crime of forging (FORGE[2] 1) a document, picture, signature, etc: *He spent 5 years in prison for forgery.* **2** [C] a document,

signature, etc that has been forged (FORGE² 1): *The painting was once thought to be by Van Gogh, but is now known to be a forgery.* Compare COUNTERFEIT *n*.

forge³ /fɔːdʒ/ *v* to move forward steadily or gradually: [Vadv] *forge steadily onwards* [Vpr] *forge into the lead* (ie gradually take the leading position). [also Vp]. **PHRV** **forge a'head** to advance or progress quickly; to take the leading position in a race, contest, etc: *After an uncertain start the company is now forging ahead (of its main rivals).*

forget /fə'get/ *v* (*pt* **forgot** /fə'gɒt/; *pp* **forgotten** /fə'gɒtn/) **1** ~ (**about**) **sth** (not usu in the continuous tenses) to fail to remember or recall(1) sth; to lose the memory of sth: [Vpr, Vn] *You forgot (about) my birthday* (ie did not remember it at the proper time). [Vn] *I've forgotten her name.* [V.*that*] *Did you forget (that) I was coming?* [V.*wh*] *She forgot how the puzzle fitted together.* [V.*ing*] *I'll never forget seeing my daughter dance in public for the first time.* **2(a)** to fail to remember to do sth; to NEGLECT(2) sth: [V] *'Why didn't you buy any bread?' 'Sorry, I forgot.'* [V.*to* inf] *Don't forget to feed the cat.* ○ *He forgot to pay me.* (**b**) to fail to remember to bring, buy, etc sth or look after sth/sb: [Vn] *I forgot my umbrella.* ○ *Don't forget the waiter* (ie to give him a tip³ *n*(1)). **3** ~ (**about**) **sb/sth** to stop thinking about sth/sb; to put sb/sth out of one's mind: [Vn, Vpr] *Let's forget (about) our differences.* [Vpr] *Try to forget (all) about him.* ○ *You can forget about a new car this year — I've lost my job.* [Vn] *'How much do I owe you?' 'Forget it!'* (ie Don't bother to pay me back). ○ *Cover the cake with marzipan and icing, **not forgetting** (ie and also) the roasted almonds.* [V.*that*] *I was forgetting (that) David used to teach you.* **4** ~ **oneself** (**a**) to behave without proper dignity: [Vn] *I'm afraid I rather forgot myself and kissed him wildly.* (**b**) to think about other people's needs instead of one's own: [Vn] *Forget yourself and think of someone else for a change.*

▶ **forgetful** /-fl/ *adj* **1** in the habit of forgetting; likely to forget: *Old people are sometimes forgetful.* **2** [pred] ~ **of sb/sth** not thinking about sb/sth; failing to do what one ought: *be forgetful of one's duties.*
forgetfully /-fəli/ *adv.* **forgetfulness** *n* [U].
forgettable /-əbl/ *adj* not interesting or special; easily forgotten: *various forgettable pop tunes.* Compare UNFORGETTABLE.

forget-me-not /fə'get mi nɒt/ *n* [C, U] a small plant with tiny blue flowers, or a number of these: *a clump of forget-me-not(s).*

forgive /fə'gɪv/ *v* (*pt* **forgave** /fə'geɪv/; *pp* **forgiven** /fə'gɪvn/) **1** ~ **sb**; ~ **sb** (**for sth / doing sth**) to stop being angry or bitter towards sb or about sth; to stop blaming or wanting to punish sb: [Vn] *I forgave her a long time ago.* ○ *I don't want this to spoil our friendship — let's just **forgive and forget**, shall we?* [Vnn] *She forgave him his thoughtless remark.* [Vnpr] *I cannot forgive myself for not going to see my mother before she died.* ○ **One could be forgiven for** *being* (ie it is natural that one would be) *a little suspicious.* **2** ~ **sb** (**for doing sth**) (used to make what one says more polite and less forceful, or as a mild way of saying sorry) [Vn] *Forgive my ignorance, but what exactly are you talking about?* [Vnpr, V.n *ing*] *Please forgive me for interrupting/ forgive my interrupting, but...* **3** to say that sb need not pay back a sum of money owed: [Vnn] *Won't you forgive me such a small debt?*

▶ **forgivable** /-əbl/ *adj* that can be forgiven: *His rudeness was forgivable in the circumstances.*
forgiveness *n* [U] the action of forgiving or the state of being forgiven; willingness to forgive sth/sb: *He asked/begged (my) forgiveness for what he had done.* ○ *She shows love and forgiveness for her enemies.*

forgiving *adj* ready and willing to forgive: *kind and forgiving parents* ○ *a forgiving nature.*

forgo /fɔː'gəʊ/ *v* (*pt* **forwent** /fɔː'went/; *pp* **forgone** /fɔː'gɒn; *US* -'gɔːn/) to give up or do without sth, esp sth pleasant: [Vn] *The workers agreed to forgo a pay increase for the sake of greater job security.*

forgot *pt* of FORGET.

forgotten *pp* of FORGET.

fork /fɔːk/ *n* **1** a small implement that has a handle and two or more sharp points. A fork is used for lifting food to the mouth or for holding meat, etc firmly while it is cut: *eat with a knife and fork.* ⇨ picture. **2** a tool used in farm or garden work, with a handle and long sharp metal points. **3(a)** a place where a road, river, branch of a tree, etc divides into two parts: *Go on to the fork and turn left.* (**b**) either of the two parts divided in this way: *Take the right fork.* ⇨ picture. **4** (usu *pl*) two metal supporting pieces into which a wheel on a bicycle or motor cycle (MOTOR) is fitted. ⇨ picture at BICYCLE. See also PITCHFORK, TUNING-FORK.

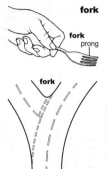

fork

fork prong

fork

▶ **fork** *v* **1** to lift, dig, move, etc sth with a fork(1,2): [Vnpr] *forking food into his mouth* [Vn, Vnp] *fork (over) the ground* [Vnpr] *Fork the manure into the soil* (ie Dig it in with a fork). **2(a)** (of a road, river, etc) to divide into two parts: [V] *The road forks just beyond the bridge.* (**b**) (of a person) to turn left or right at a fork(3): [V] *Fork left at the church.* **PHRV** **fork out (sth)** (*infml*) to pay money, usu unwillingly: *Why do I always have to fork out (money) on/ for your school trips?*

forked *adj* divided into two or more parts or branches: *the forked tongue of a snake* ○ *a bird with a forked tail* ○ *forked lightning.*

forkful /-fʊl/ *n* (*pl* **-fuls**) the amount that a fork holds: *a forkful of rice.*

■ **ˌfork-lift 'truck** *n* a vehicle with a mechanical device on the front for lifting and moving heavy objects.

forlorn /fə'lɔːn/ *adj* **1(a)** (of a person) unhappy and lonely or abandoned: *She looked very forlorn standing there in the pouring rain.* (**b**) (of places) abandoned and not cared for: *Empty houses quickly take on a forlorn look.* **2** unlikely to succeed, come true, etc: *make a forlorn attempt to lose weight* ○ *She waited **in the forlorn hope/belief** that he would come back and marry her one day.* ▶ **forlornly** *adv.*

form¹ /fɔːm/ *n* [C] **1** the external appearance of sb/ sth; the shape of sb/sth: *her slender form* ○ *The human form has changed little over the last 30 000 years.* ○ *Through the fog we could see the form of a large plane on the runway.* **2** [C] the particular way in which the parts of sth are arranged: *different forms of government* ○ *different literary forms* ○ *works for the piano in sonata form* ○ *The form of a poem is less important than its content.* **3** [C] a type or variety of sth: *different forms of transport/housing* ○ *What's the correct form of address when you talk to a bishop?* **4** [C] the particular way in which sth appears: *water in the form of ice* ○ *a generous gift in the form of £10 000* ○ *Help arrived in the form of two policemen.* ○ *The book is written in the form of letters.* ○ *This disease can take several different forms.* ○ *What form did the student protests take?* ○ *'Is', 'are' and 'were' are all forms of the verb 'to be'.* ○ *I'm opposed to censorship **in any way, shape or form**.* **5** [sing, U] the usual procedure or custom: *What's the form when you apply for a research grant?* ○ *If you have any questions about banking procedures, ask Jim. He knows the form.* ○ *Wives or husbands of employees are invited to the Christmas party* **as a matter of form.** ○ *True to form* (ie As he usually does), *he arrived an hour late.* **6** [U] the socially accepted way of doing sth: *It's considered* **good form** *to write to or phone your hostess after a dinner party.* ○ *Wearing bright colours to a funeral in Britain is* **bad form. 7** [U] **(a)** physical or mental condition: *After six months' training the whole team is in superb form.* ○ *What sort of form are you in?* ○ *She's in/on great form; I haven't seen her looking so happy and well for years.* **(b)** good physical and/or mental condition: *These exercises will keep you* **in form.** ○ *That horse looks rather* **out of form** *to me.* ○ *When he's* **on form,** *nobody plays Schubert better.* **8** [U] a record of performance in races, contests, etc: *Do you know anything about this horse's form?* ○ **On present/ current form,** *they're unlikely to win.* **9** [U] (*sl*) a record of previous crimes of which a person has been found guilty: *He's got quite a bit of form.* **10** [C] an official document containing questions and spaces for answers: *a job application form* ○ *an insurance claim form* ○ *fill in/complete and sign the necessary forms.* **11** [C] a class in a school: *He's in the sixth form; next year he's going to university.* ○ *Who's your form teacher?* **IDM** **in the shape/form of sb/sth** ⇨ SHAPE¹.

▶ **-former** (forming compound *ns*) a child or young person in the specified form¹(11) at school: *a ¹sixth-former.*

formless *adj* without a clear or definite shape or structure: *formless shadows/ideas/dreams.*

form² /fɔːm/ *v* **1(a)** to make or produce sth in a particular shape or form: [Vnpr] *Using your hands, form the dough into balls.* ○ *They form the clay into figures of animals.* [also Vn]. **(b)** to produce in its correct form: [Vn] *form the present perfect tense* ○ *She can't form her words correctly, so we think she may be a bit deaf.* **2** to have or make a particular formation, arrangement or pattern: [Vn] *The stones form a huge circle.* ○ *The mountains form a natural barrier between the two countries.* ○ *The running water had frozen and formed fantastic shapes.* **3** to move into a particular formation or pattern: [Vn] *form a line/queue* ○ *They formed a circle and started to dance.* **4(a)** to appear or develop gradually: [V] *Ice forms at 0° Celsius.* ○ *A queue for tickets started forming early in the morning.* ○ *Stormclouds had begun to form on the horizon.* ○ *Their friendship formed gradually over the years.* **(b)** to develop sth; to influence the development of sb/sth: [Vn] *form a habit* ○ *form a relationship with sb* ○ *character-forming experiences* ○ *They believed that physical hardship in childhood helped form a strong character.* **5** to bring people together in order to create a group, an organization, etc: [Vn] *form a government/ committee* ○ *form an organization to protect the environment* ○ *We're thinking of forming a new company.* **6** to be, constitute or compose sth: [V-n] *These three early paintings form the centrepiece of the exhibition.* ○ *Consultation with the public forms part of the planning process.* ○ *You and I form the only opposition to these crazy new plans.*

formal /ˈfɔːml/ *adj* (abbreviated as *fml* in this dictionary) **1** (of a style of dress, speech, writing, behaviour, etc) very correct and suitable for official or important occasions: *The parties at the US embassy are much less formal than those at the British.* ○ *She always has a very formal manner, which I find rather unpleasant.* ○ *Your letter to the bank manager needs to be more formal than that.* **2** (of a garden, house decoration, etc) arranged in a regular, classical or symmetrical (SYMMETRY) manner: *Formal*

gardens were very much in fashion in the sixteenth century. **3** official; officially recognized: *make a formal apology/complaint/request* ○ *request formal approval* ○ *comply with formal procedures* ○ *He has no formal teaching qualifications.* **4** in outward appearance but not in reality: *There is a formal resemblance between the two political systems, but in fact they function in a totally different way from each other.* ▶ **formally** /-məli/ *adv:* *The new rates of pay have not been formally agreed.* ○ *The men were taken to the police station and formally charged.* ○ *We've met each other a few times but never been formally introduced.*

formaldehyde /fɔːˈmældɪhaɪd/ *n* [U] (*chemistry*) a colourless gas with a strong smell used, esp when mixed with water as **formalin** /ˈfɔːməlɪn/, for preserving biological specimens, as a disinfectant (DISINFECT) and in making plastics.

formalism /ˈfɔːməlɪzəm/ *n* [U] (esp of art, religion, etc) excessive obedience to the correct or approved form, rules, etc rather than to feeling or meaning: *creativity reduced to an empty formalism.*

formality /fɔːˈmæləti/ *n* **1** [U] being formal(1,2): *different levels of formality* ○ *He greeted her with cool formality.* ○ *The formality of the room's furnishings was rather daunting.* **2** [C often *pl*] a formal(1) procedure in a particular social situation: *He likes to keep formalities to the minimum.* ○ *Let's skip the formalities and get down to business.* **3** [C] **(a)** (often *pl*) an official rule or procedure: *go through all the formalities to get a gun licence* ○ *comply with the formalities.* **(b)** such a procedure which is thought to be unnecessary or to have little meaning: *He knows he has the job so the interview is just a formality/a mere formality.*

formalize, -ise /ˈfɔːməlaɪz/ *v* **1** to make an arrangement, the status of sb/sth, etc official: [Vn] *formalize diplomatic relations* ○ *They decided to formalize their relationship by getting married.* **2** to give sth a fixed structure or form by establishing rules or procedures: [Vn] *The system has become highly formalized.* ▶ **formalization, -isation** /ˌfɔːməlaɪˈzeɪʃn; *US* -ləˈz/ *n* [U].

format /ˈfɔːmæt/ *n* **1** the shape and size of a book, magazine, etc: *They've changed the format of the newspaper to attract new readers.* **2** the general arrangement, plan, design, etc of sth: *There is no set format for these weekly meetings.* ○ *The talk show format is popular with viewers.* **3** the arrangement or organization of data for processing or storage by a computer. ▶ **format** *v* (**-tt-**) [Vn] (*computing*) to prepare a DISK to receive data.

formation /fɔːˈmeɪʃn/ *n* **1** [U] the action of forming sth or the process of being formed: *the formation of a new government* ○ *habit formation in children* ○ *What influences the formation of national character?* **2** [C] a thing that has been formed, esp in a particular or characteristic way: *cloud/rock formations* ○ *new word formations.* **3** [U] a particular arrangement or pattern: *aircraft flying in formation* ○ *for¹mation flying/dancing.*

formative /ˈfɔːmətɪv/ *adj* [attrib] having an important and lasting influence on the development of sb's character: *a child's formative years* ○ *formative influences in one's life.*

former /ˈfɔːmə(r)/ *adj* [attrib] **1** of an earlier period or time: *the former world champion* ○ *my former landlady* ○ *in former times* ○ *She's back to her former self again* (eg after an illness). **2** being the first of two things or people mentioned: *The former option would be more sensible.* **IDM** **a shadow of one's/its former self** ⇨ SHADOW.

▶ **formerly** *adv* in earlier times; previously: *The company formerly belonged to an international bank-*

ing group. ○ *Namibia was formerly South West Africa.*

the former [pron] the first of two things or people mentioned: *He said I had to take my holiday in June or August, so I chose the former.* Compare THE LATTER.

Formica /fɔː'maɪkə/ *n* [U] (*propr*) hard plastic that resists heat and is used for covering work surfaces.

formidable /'fɔːmɪdəbl; *Brit also* fə'mɪdəbl/ *adj* causing fear, anxiety or admiration because of size, strength, power, level of difficulty, etc: *overcome formidable political obstacles* ○ *a formidable combination of intelligence and determination* ○ *A formidable task lies ahead of us.* ○ *She was a formidable woman; no one dared to disagree with her.* ○ *He has a formidable list of qualifications.*
▶ **formidably** /-əbli/ *adv* to an impressive degree: *She's formidably well-read.*

formula /'fɔːmjələ/ *n* (*pl* **formulas** or, esp in scientific use, **formulae** /-liː/) **1** [C] (*mathematics or physics*) a rule, principle or law expressed by means of letters and symbols: *To calculate the area of a circle use the formula* πr^2. **2** [C] letters and symbols representing the parts of a chemical compound: H_2O *is the formula for water.* **3** [C] ~ (**for sth**) a particular method, form or procedure for doing or achieving sth: *They're trying to* **work out a peace formula** *acceptable to both sides in the dispute.* ○ *There's no magic formula for a perfect marriage.* ○ *Most of the detective stories on TV are made according to a similar formula.* **4** [C] a list of ingredients with which sth is made: *They use a secret formula to make Coca-Cola.* **5** [C] a fixed form of words used in a particular situation: *They've been using the same legal formulae in English lawcourts for centuries.* ○ *The governor keeps coming out with the same tired formulas.* **6** [U] (*esp US*) a type of baby food in the form of a powder to which milk or water is added. **7** [U] (used with a number for classifying different types of racing car according to engine size, etc): *the formula one champion of the world* ○ *formula two races.*
▶ **formulaic** /ˌfɔːmju'leɪɪk/ *adj* composed of set patterns of words: *Anglo-Saxon poetry is formulaic.*

formulate /'fɔːmjuleɪt/ *v* **1** to create or prepare sth carefully and with attention to detail: [Vn] *formulate a rule/policy/theory* ○ *formulate a peace agreement* [Vn.to] *Our products are carefully formulated to meet our customers' requirements.* **2** to express sth in a clear and PRECISE way, choosing one's words carefully: [Vn] *formulate one's thoughts/ideas carefully* ○ *He has lots of good ideas, but he has difficulty formulating them.* ▶ **formulation** /ˌfɔːmju'leɪʃn/ *n* [U,C]: *the formulation of policies/principles* ○ *new formulations of existing drugs.*

fornicate /'fɔːnɪkeɪt/ *v* [V,Vpr] ~ (**with sb**) (*fml usu derog*) (of people not married or not married to each other) to have sex. ▶ **fornication** /ˌfɔːnɪ'keɪʃn/ *n* [U].

forsake /fə'seɪk/ *v* (*pt* **forsook** /fə'sʊk/; *pp* **forsaken** /fə'seɪkən/) [Vn] **1** (*fml*) to give sth up completely: *forsake one's former habits/one's principles* ○ *He forsook the glamour of city life for a small cottage in the country.* **2** to abandon sb/sth: *forsake one's family and friends* ○ *a dreary forsaken spot, miles from anywhere.* See also GOD-FORSAKEN.

forswear /fɔː'sweə(r)/ *v* (*pt* **forswore** /fɔː'swɔː(r)/; *pp* **forsworn** /fɔː'swɔːn/) (*fml*) to make a promise to give up sth: [Vn] *He appears to have forsworn the wild behaviour of his younger days.* [also V.ing].

forsythia /fɔː'saɪθɪə; *US* fɑː'sɪθɪə/ *n* [U] a bush that has bright yellow flowers in the early spring.

fort /fɔːt/ *n* a building or buildings specially made or strengthened for the military defence of an area: *the remains of a Confederate fort* ○ *attack the fort at dawn.* **IDM** **hold the 'fort** to have the responsibility

or care of sth/sb while other people are away or out: *The others decided to go out for the day and left me holding the fort.*

forte¹ /'fɔːteɪ; *US* fɔːrt/ *n* (*usu sing*) a thing that sb does particularly well: *Languages were never my forte.*

forte² /'fɔːteɪ/ *adj, adv* (*abbr* **f**) (*music*) loud; (to be) played loudly. Compare PIANO².

forth /fɔːθ/ *adv part* (*arch except in certain idioms and phrasal verbs*) **1** away from a place; out: *They set forth at dawn.* ○ *And God said to them: 'Go forth and multiply.'* **2** forward; into view: *Water gushed forth from a hole in the rock.* See also HOLD FORTH. **3** (of time) forward: *From that day forth he was never seen again.* **IDM** **and so forth** ⇨ SO². **back and 'forth** ⇨ BACK³.

forthcoming /ˌfɔːθ'kʌmɪŋ/ *adj* **1** [attrib] about to happen or appear in the near future: *the forthcoming e'lections* ○ *a list of forthcoming 'books* (ie those about to be published) ○ *Among our forthcoming attractions is Walt Disney's 'The Lion King'.* **2** [pred] (often with a negative) ready or made available when needed: *The money we asked for was not forthcoming.* **3** [pred] ready to help, give information, etc: *The secretary at the reception desk was not very forthcoming.*

forthright /'fɔːθraɪt/ *adj* direct and honest in manner and speech: *condemnation in the most forthright language* ○ *He has a reputation for being a forthright critic.*

forthwith /ˌfɔːθ'wɪθ, -'wɪð/ *adv* (*fml*) immediately; at once: *The agreement between us is terminated forthwith.*

fortieth ⇨ FORTY.

fortify /'fɔːtɪfaɪ/ *v* (*pt, pp* **-fied**) **1** ~ sth (against sth/sb) (**a**) to strengthen a place against attack, eg by building high walls: [Vnpr] *fortify a town against the enemy* [Vn] *a fortified city.* (**b**) to make oneself/sb feel stronger, braver, etc: [Vn] *They went into battle fortified by prayer.* [Vnpr] *He fortified himself against the cold with a large glass of brandy.* **2** ~ sth (with sth) (usu passive) to increase the strength or quality of food or drink by adding sth to it: [Vnpr] *cereal fortified with extra vitamins* [Vn] *fortified wine* (ie wine strengthened with extra alcohol) *such as port.*
▶ **fortification** /ˌfɔːtɪfɪ'keɪʃn/ *n* **1** [C usu *pl*] a tower, wall, gun position, etc built to defend a place against attack: *impregnable fortifications.* **2** [U] the action of fortifying or strengthening sth: *plans for the fortification of the city.*

fortissimo /fɔː'tɪsɪməʊ/ *adj, adv* (*abbr* **ff**) (*music*) very loud(ly): *passages played fortissimo.*

fortitude /'fɔːtɪtjuːd; *US* -tuːd/ *n* [U] the courage to face and endure great danger or difficulties: *He bore the pain with great fortitude.*

fortnight /'fɔːtnaɪt/ *n* (*usu sing*) (*esp Brit*) two weeks: *a fortnight's holiday* ○ *a fortnight ago* ○ *in a fortnight's time* ○ *a fortnight today/tomorrow/on Tuesday* (ie two weeks after the day specified) ○ *He's had three accidents in the past fortnight.*
▶ **fortnightly** *adj, adv* (*esp Brit*) happening once a fortnight: *a fortnightly clinic/magazine* ○ *go home fortnightly.*

FORTRAN (also **Fortran**) /'fɔːtræn/ *n* [U] (*computing*) a programming (PROGRAM *v*) language used esp in scientific applications.

fortress /'fɔːtrəs/ *n* a place strengthened or well protected against attack: *fortress towns built on hilltops* ○ *Fear of terrorist attacks has transformed the conference centre into a fortress.*

fortuitous /fɔː'tjuːɪtəs; *US* -'tuː-/ *adj* (*fml*) (**a**) happening by chance: *a fortuitous meeting* ○ *The resemblance between the two books is entirely fortuitous.* (**b**) happening by a lucky chance; fortunate:

make a fortuitous choice ○ *a fortuitous set of circumstances.*

fortunate /ˈfɔːtʃənət/ *adj* having or bringing an advantage, an opportunity, a piece of good luck, etc; lucky: *I was fortunate to have/in having a good teacher.* ○ *She's fortunate enough to enjoy good health.* ○ *Remember those less fortunate than yourselves.* ○ *It was very fortunate for him that I arrived on time.* Compare UNFORTUNATE.

▶ **fortunately** *adv* (qualifying a sentence) by good luck; luckily (LUCKY): *I was late, but fortunately the meeting hadn't started.* ○ *Fortunately (for him), Mark quickly found another job.*

fortune /ˈfɔːtʃuːn/ *n* **1** [U] chance or luck, esp in the way it affects people's lives: *By a stroke of fortune he got a small part in a television play.* ○ *I had the good fortune to be chosen for a trip abroad.* ○ *Fortune smiled on him* (ie He had good luck). **2** [C usu *pl*] a thing that determines the success or progress of sb/sth: *the changing fortunes of the film industry* ○ *Britain's improving economic fortunes* ○ *a turning point in his fortunes* ○ *the fortunes of war.* **3** [C] a person's destiny or future; fate: *She tells your fortune by looking at the lines on your hand.* **4** [C usu *sing*] a large amount of money: *She inherited a huge fortune.* ○ *He made a fortune buying and selling property.* ○ (*infml*) *That ring is worth/must have cost a (small) fortune.* **IDM** **a hostage to fortune** ⇨ HOSTAGE. **seek one's fortune** ⇨ SEEK. See also SOLDIER OF FORTUNE.

■ **'fortune cookie** *n* (*US*) a thin biscuit, served in Chinese restaurants, that contains a small printed message.
'fortune-teller *n* a person who tells one's fortune (3).

forty /ˈfɔːti/ *n, pron, det* **1** the number 40. **2** **the forties** *n* [pl] numbers, years or temperatures from 40 to 49. **IDM** **in one's forties** between the ages of 40 and 50: *a man in his early forties.*

▶ **fortieth** /ˈfɔːtiəθ/ *n, pron, det* 40th.
■ **'forty 'winks** *n* [pl] (*infml*) a short sleep, esp during the day: *have forty winks.*
For further guidance on how *forty* and *fortieth* are used, see the examples at *five, fifth* and *fifty.*

forum /ˈfɔːrəm/ *n* (*pl* **forums**) **1(a)** ~ (for sth) a place where people can exchange opinions and ideas on a particular issue: *Television is now an important forum for political debate.* **(b)** a meeting organized for this purpose: *hold an international forum on drug abuse.* **2** (in ancient Rome) a public place where meetings were held.

forward¹ /ˈfɔːwəd/ *adj* **1** [attrib] **(a)** directed or moving towards the front: *forward movement.* **(b)** situated in front; near or at the front: *The forward part of the train is for first-class passengers only.* **2** appearing, developing or becoming mature earlier than usual or expected: *She's very forward for her age — she's already speaking in proper sentences.* **3** [attrib] of or relating to the future: *forward planning* ○ *forward buying* (ie buying goods at present prices for delivery later). ⇨ note at FORWARD². **4** behaving towards sb in a manner which is too familiar or confident: *He's very forward with the customers and they don't like it at all.* Compare BACKWARD.

▶ **forwardness** *n* [U] the quality of being too familiar or confident in one's manner.

forward² /ˈfɔːwəd/ *adv* **1** (also **forwards**) to the front; ahead; towards sb/sth: *He leaned forwards to hear what I was saying.* ○ *She took two steps forward.* ○ *They ran forward to welcome her.* Compare BACKWARD³ 1a. **2** towards a successful conclusion: *an important step forward* ○ *We are not getting any further forward with the discussion.* ○ *The project will go forward* (ie continue) *as planned.* **3(a)** towards the future;

ahead in time: *from this time forward* ○ *The next scene takes the story forward five years.* **(b)** earlier; sooner: *bring the meeting forward two weeks.* **IDM** **backward(s) and forward(s)** ⇨ BACKWARDS. **put the clock/clocks forward/back** ⇨ CLOCK¹.

■ **'forward-looking** *adj* having modern ideas; planning for the future: *a young forward-looking company* ○ *We need someone dynamic and forward-looking.* Compare LOOK FORWARD.

NOTE Forward, and other words ending in **-ward**, (ie in the direction of) can be adjectives, usually placed before a noun: *He performed a double forward roll on skis.* These words, such as *backward, homeward,* etc can also be adverbs: *He leaned forward so that he could see better.* **Forwards**, and other words ending with **-wards**, are adverbs following a verb: *They turned westwards (or westward) after crossing the river.*

forward³ /ˈfɔːwəd/ *v* **1(a)** ~ sth (to sb) to send a letter received at the address a person has recently moved away from, to her or his new address: [Vn, Vnpr] *Please could you forward any letters (to us in Italy).* ○ *I've written 'please forward' on the envelope.* **(b)** ~ sth (to sb) (*fml*) to send or pass goods or information to sb: [Vn] *forward a shipment of spare parts* [Vnpr] *forward a suggestion to the committee* [Vnn] *We have today forwarded you our new catalogue.* **2** to help to advance or develop sth: [Vn] *forward sb's plans/career/interests.* See also FAST FORWARD.

■ **'forwarding address** *n* a new address to which letters should be forwarded: *He didn't leave a forwarding address.*

forward⁴ /ˈfɔːwəd/ *n* an attacking player whose position is near the front of a team in football, hockey, etc. ⇨ picture at FOOTBALL. Compare BACK¹ 4. See also STRIKER 2.

forwent *pt* of FORGO.

fossil /ˈfɒsl/ *n* **1** the remains of an animal or a plant which have hardened into rock: *superbly preserved fossils over 2 million years old* ○ *the fossil record.* **2** (*infml derog*) a person who is unable to accept new ideas or adapt to new conditions: *She's a real old fossil.*

▶ **fossilize, -ise** /ˈfɒsəlaɪz/ *v* **1** (usu passive) to become or make sth become a fossil: [Vn] *fossilized bones* [also V]. **2** (of culture, ideas, etc) to become fixed; to resist change or development: [V] *He allowed his intellect and judgement to fossilize.* [also Vn]. **fossilization, -isation** /ˌfɒsəlaɪˈzeɪʃn; *US* -ləˈz-/ *n* [U]: *the long process of fossilization.*
■ **'fossil fuel** *n* [C,U] fuel, eg coal or oil, formed over millions of years from the remains of animals or plants: *What will happen when our fossil fuels run out?*

foster /ˈfɒstə(r); *US* ˈfɔː-/ *v* **1** to help the development of sth; to encourage or promote sth: [Vn] *foster an interest/attitude/impression* ○ *foster the growth of local industries.* **2** to care for a child who is not one's own but who has been formally placed in one's home for a period of time by social workers: [Vn] *They've fostered over 60 children in the last ten years.* Compare ADOPT 1. ▶ **foster-** (forming compound ns): *'foster-parents* ○ *a 'foster-child.*

fought *pt, pp* of FIGHT¹.

foul¹ /faʊl/ *adj* **1** (*infml*) very unpleasant; very bad; terrible: *I've had a foul day at work today.* ○ *She's in a foul mood.* ○ *His boss has a foul temper.* ○ *This tastes foul.* ○ *Jenny was foul to me.* **2** dirty and smelling bad: *foul water/prison air* ○ *a foul-smelling discharge.* **3** particularly evil or wicked: *a foul crime/murder.* **4** offensive; including rude words and swearing: *use foul language.* **5** rough and violent because of strong winds and rain: *a foul night/sea.* **IDM** **by fair means or foul** ⇨ FAIR¹. **fall foul**

of '**sb**/'**sth** to get into trouble with a person or an organization because of doing sth wrong or illegal: *fall foul of the* '*Companies Act* ○ *He eventually fell foul of the* '*tax authorities.*

▶ **foul** *n* (*sport*) an act or a piece of play that is against the rules of a game: *It was clearly a foul — Jones kicked him after he'd passed the ball.*

foully /'faʊlli/ *adv: swear foully.*

foulness *n* [U].

■ ,**foul-**'**mouthed** *adj* using offensive language : *a ,foul-mouthed* '*child.*

,**foul** '**play** *n* [U] **1** play that is against the rules of a sport: *He was sent off for foul play.* **2** criminal or violent activity, esp when it leads to sb's death: *The brake cable was cut and the police suspect foul play.* ○ *fresh evidence of foul play in their financial dealings.*

foul² /faʊl/ *v* **1** to make sth dirty: [Vn] *Dogs are not permitted to foul* (ie EXCRETE on) *the pavement.* **2** ~ (**sth**) (**up**) to become or make sth become caught or twisted in sth: [Vn] *The rope fouled the propeller.* [Vnpr, Vnp] *My fishing-line got fouled (up) in an old net.* [also Vp]. **3** (*sport*) to commit a foul against another player: [Vn] *He was fouled inside the penalty area.* **PHR V** ,**foul sth** '**up** (*infml*) to spoil sth: *Everything was just fine until Fred came along and fouled things up.* ○ *The weather has really fouled up my weekend plans.*

▶ '**foul-up** *n* (*infml*) a problem caused by poor organization, stupid mistakes, etc: *Whenever he's in charge of the office, there's one foul-up after another.*

found¹ *pt, pp* of FIND¹.

found² /faʊnd/ *v* **1** to start or establish an organization, institution, etc, esp by providing money for it: [Vn] *found a company/hospital/research institute* ○ *When was Oxford University founded?* **2** to begin building a town: [Vn] *The city was founded in 1157.* ○ *The ancient Greeks founded colonies in Sicily.* **3** ~ **sth on sth** (usu passive) to base sth on sth: [Vnpr] *a moral code founded on religious principles.* See also ILL-FOUNDED, WELL-FOUNDED.

■ ,**founding** '**father** *n* (*fml*) a person who starts or establishes a movement, an institution, etc: *one of the founding fathers of modern psychology.* **2 Founding Father** any member of the group of people who drew up the Constitution of the USA in 1787.

found³ /faʊnd/ *v* [Vn] to melt metal and pour it into moulds in order to make objects of a particular shape. See also FOUNDRY.

foundation /faʊn'deɪʃn/ *n* **1** [U] the action of founding an institution, organization, etc: *the foundation of the national library.* **2** [C] an organization established by a company or an individual to provide money for a particular purpose, eg for scientific research or charity: *the Ford Foundation* ○ *You may be able to get support for your training from an arts foundation.* **3** [C usu *pl*] a layer of bricks, concrete, etc forming the solid underground base of a building: *lay the foundations of a school* ○ *The explosion shook the foundations of the houses nearby.* **4** [C, U] a principle, an idea or a fact on which sth is based; a basis: *lay the foundations of one's career* ○ *provide a solid foundation for the marriage* ○ *controversies that rock the foundations of social and moral life* ○ *The rumour is totally without foundation* (ie not based on true facts). **5** (also **foun**'**dation cream**) [U] a cream put on the face before other make-up (MAKE¹) is applied.

■ **foun**'**dation course** *n* (*Brit*) a course taken at a college that usu covers a wide range of subjects and prepares students for more advanced studies: *take a foundation course in economics.*

foun'**dation-stone** *n* a large block of stone laid at a special ceremony to mark the founding of a public building.

founder¹ /'faʊndə(r)/ *n* a person who founds or establishes sth: *the founder of a city/an institution/a company.*

■ ,**founder-**'**member** *n* any of the original members of a society, an organization, etc.

founder² /'faʊndə(r)/ *v* ~ (**on sth**) **1** (of a plan, etc) to fail; to break down: [V] *The project foundered as a result of the lack of mutual trust.* [Vpr] *The talks foundered on the lack of mutual trust.* **2** (of a ship) to fill with water and sink: [Vpr] *The boat foundered on rocks near the harbour.* [also V].

foundling /'faʊndlɪŋ/ *n* (*dated*) an abandoned child of unknown parents who is found by sb.

foundry /'faʊndri/ *n* a factory where metal or glass is melted and moulded into various shapes or objects.

fount¹ /faʊnt/ *n* ~ (**of sth**) (*arch or rhet*) a source or origin of sth: *She was regarded as the fount of all wisdom.*

fount² /faʊnt/ (also **font** /fɒnt/) *n* a set of printing type of one style or size.

fountain

fountain /'faʊntən; *US* -tn/ *n* **1** an ornamental structure or statue, often in a pool or lake, from which one or more jets of water are pumped out into the air: *the fountains of Rome.* ⇨ picture. **2** a strong jet of liquid rising into the air: *A fountain of water gushed from the broken fire hydrant.* See also DRINKING-FOUNTAIN, SODA FOUNTAIN.

■ '**fountain-head** *n* an origin or source: *the fountain-head of power.*

'**fountain-pen** *n* a pen with a container from which ink flows continuously to the NIB.

four /fɔː(r)/ *n, pron, det* **1** the number 4. **2** a group of four people or things: *make up a four at tennis.* **3** (in cricket) a shot, scoring four runs, in which the ball crosses the boundary after having hit the ground. **IDM** **on all** '**fours** (of a person) supported on one's hands and knees, and usu also one's toes: *The baby was crawling about on all fours.* ⇨ picture at KNEEL.

▶ **four-** (in compounds) having four of the thing specified: *a four-sided figure.*

fourth /fɔːθ/ *pron, det* 4th. **fourthly** *adv* in the fourth position or place. **the** ,**fourth di**'**mension** *n* [sing] the dimension of time. **the** ,**fourth e**'**state** *n* [sing] (*joc*) newspapers and journalists in general. **the** ,**Fourth of Ju**'**ly** *n* [sing] the anniversary of the Declaration of Independence (1776) of the USA from Britain. — *n* each of four equal parts of sth.

■ '**four-eyes** *n* (*joc or offensive*) (used as a way of addressing a person wearing glasses).

,**four-letter** '**word** *n* any of various short words, usu referring to sexual or other body functions, that are considered rude or offensive.

,**four-**'**poster** (also ,**four-poster** '**bed**) *n* (esp formerly) a large bed with a tall post at each of the four corners to support curtains.

,**four-**'**square** *adj* **1** shaped like a square. **2** firmly based; steady or determined: *Her family stood four-square behind her* (ie supported her) *in her campaign.*

,four-wheel 'drive n [U] a system in which power is applied to all four wheels of a vehicle: *a car with four-wheel drive* ○ *four-wheel drive vehicles.* For further guidance on how *four* and *fourth* are used, see the examples at *five* and *fifth.*

fourfold /ˈfɔːfəʊld/ *adj, adv* ⇨ -FOLD.

foursome /ˈfɔːsəm/ n a group of four people, eg playing a game or taking part in a leisure activity together: *Are you free to make up a foursome at golf?*

fourteen /ˌfɔːˈtiːn/ n, pron, det the number 14. ▶ **fourteenth** /ˌfɔːˈtiːnθ/ n, pron, det 14th. For further guidance on how *fourteen* and *fourteenth* are used, see the examples at *five* and *fifth.*

fowl /faʊl/ n **1** [C] (pl unchanged or **fowls**) a bird kept on a farm, eg a chicken: *domestic fowl(s).* **2** [U] the flesh of certain types of birds, eaten for food. **3** [C] (arch) any bird: *the fowls of the air.* See also GUINEA-FOWL, WATERFOWL, WILDFOWL.

fox /fɒks/ n **1(a)** [C] (fem **vixen** /ˈvɪksn/) a wild animal of the dog family, with reddish-brown fur, a pointed face and a thick heavy tail: *Hunting foxes/ Fox-hunting is a peculiarly English sport.* ○ *The fox is known for its cleverness and cunning.* **(b)** [U] its skin and fur used to make coats, etc. **2** [C] (infml esp derog) a person who is clever and able to get what he or she wants by influencing or deceiving others: *He's a crafty/sly old fox.* ▶ **fox** v to be too difficult for sb to understand; to trick or confuse sb: [Vn] *The puzzle foxed me completely.*

foxy /ˈfɒksi/ adj **1** clever at tricking or deceiving others. **2** like a fox in appearance, ie reddish-brown in colour or having a face like a fox. **3** (sl approv esp US) (of a woman) sexually attractive: *a foxy lady.* ■ **'fox-hunting** n [U] a sport in which foxes are hunted by specially trained dogs and by people on horses. **,fox-'terrier** n a type of dog, formerly used for driving foxes out of their holes.

foxglove /ˈfɒksglʌv/ n a tall plant with purple or white flowers shaped like bells growing up its stem. ⇨ picture at FLOWER.

foxhole /ˈfɒkshəʊl/ n a hole in the ground dug by soldiers as a shelter against enemy fire and as a place to fire back from.

foxhound /ˈfɒkshaʊnd/ n a type of dog trained to hunt foxes.

foxtrot /ˈfɒkstrɒt/ n a formal dance with both slow and quick steps; the music for this.

foyer /ˈfɔɪeɪ; US ˈfɔɪər/ n an entrance hall or a large open space in a theatre, hotel, etc where people can meet or wait: *I'll meet you in the foyer at 7 o'clock.*

Fr abbr **1** (religion) Father: *Fr (Paul) Black.* **2** French.

fr abbr franc; francs: *fr18.50.*

fracas /ˈfrækɑː; US ˈfreɪkəs/ n (pl unchanged /-kɑːz/; US **fracases** /-kəsəz/) (usu sing) a noisy argument, fight or disturbance: *The police were called in to break up (ie stop) the fracas.*

fraction /ˈfrækʃn/ n **1** a small part, bit, amount, or proportion of sth: *The car missed me by a fraction of an inch.* ○ *Could you move a fraction closer?* **2** a division of a number, eg 1/3, 5/8, 0.76. See also VULGAR FRACTION. ▶ **fractional** /-ʃənl/ adj **1** very small; unimportant: *a fractional decline in earnings.* **2** (mathematics) of or in fractions: *a fractional equation.* **fractionally** /-ʃənəli/ adv to a very small degree: *One dancer was fractionally out of step.*

fractious /ˈfrækʃəs/ adj (esp of children) bad-tempered or easily irritated.

fracture /ˈfræktʃə(r)/ n **(a)** [C] an instance of breaking sth, esp a bone: *a fracture of the leg* ○ *a compound/simple fracture* (ie one in which the broken bone comes/does not come through the skin)

○ *a slight fracture in a pipe.* **(b)** [U] the breaking of sth, esp a bone: *Old people's bones are more prone to fracture.* ▶ **fracture** v to break or crack, or make sth break or crack: [V] *Her leg fractured in two places.* [Vn] *He fractured his pelvis in the accident.*

fragile /ˈfrædʒaɪl; US -dʒl/ adj **1** easily damaged or broken; delicate: *fragile china/glass* ○ *a fragile plant* ○ (fig) *a fragile economy* ○ *Human happiness is so fragile.* **2** (infml) not strong and healthy; weak, eg because one has drunk too much alcohol: *I'm feeling a bit fragile after last night's party.* Compare FRAIL. ▶ **fragility** /frəˈdʒɪləti/ n [U].

fragment /ˈfrægmənt/ n **1** a small part or piece broken off sth: *find several fragments of a Roman vase.* ⇨ note at PIECE[1]. **2** a small part of sth, not complete in itself: *I heard only a fragment of their conversation.* ▶ **fragment** /frægˈment/ v **1** to break or make sth break into small pieces or parts: [V] *The bullets fragment on impact.* [Vn] (fig) *Ownership of the large estates is increasingly fragmented* (ie divided among several people). ○ *I slept badly and had a strange, fragmented dream.* **fragmentary** /ˈfrægməntri; US -teri/ adj composed of small parts that are not connected or complete: *fragmentary evidence.* **fragmentation** /ˌfrægmenˈteɪʃn/ n [U]: *the fragmentation of the empire into small independent states.*

fragrance /ˈfreɪgrəns/ n [C, U] a pleasant or sweet smell; a PERFUME(2): *Lavender has a delicate fragrance.* ○ *They sell a wide range of fragrances.* ○ *dishes full of fragrance and flavour.*

fragrant /ˈfreɪgrənt/ adj having a pleasant or sweet smell: *fragrant herbs/flowers.* ▶ **fragrantly** adv.

frail /freɪl/ adj **1** (of a person) physically weak or delicate: *a frail child* ○ *She's nearly 90, and very frail.* **2** easily damaged or broken: *The frail vessel was pounded to pieces on the rocks.* **3** morally weak: *frail human nature.* ▶ **frailty** /ˈfreɪlti/ n **1** [U] the condition of being frail: *physical frailty* ○ (fig) *the frailty of love.* **2** [U,C] weakness in character or morals; an instance of this: *human frailty* ○ *She loved him despite his many frailties.*

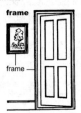

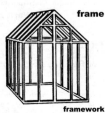

frame   frame

frame

framework

frame[1] /freɪm/ n **1** a border of wood, metal, etc in which a picture, door, piece of glass, etc is enclosed or set: *a 'picture frame* ○ *a 'window frame.* ⇨ picture. **2** the rigid structure of a piece of furniture, a building, a vehicle, etc which makes its shape and forms a support for its parts: *the frame of a cupboard/bed/rucksack* ○ *the frame of an aircraft/ car/a bicycle* ○ *a timber-frame house.* ⇨ picture at BICYCLE. See also CLIMBING-FRAME. **3** (usu pl) a structure of plastic, metal, etc that holds the glass parts of a pair of spectacles: *glasses with heavy black frames.* ⇨ picture at GLASS. **4** (usu sing) a human or animal body; its form or structure: *Sobs shook her slender frame.* **5** the general order or system that forms the background to sth: *the frame of contemporary society* ○ *It's too short a time frame* (ie period of time) *for doing the job properly.* **6(a)** any of the single photographs that a cinema film is made of. **(b)** a single picture in a comic strip (COMIC). **7** =

COLD FRAME. **8** a single round of play in the game of SNOOKER. **IDM** **in / out of the 'frame** taking part/ not taking part in sth: *We won our match, so we're still in the frame for the championship.*

■ **,frame of 'mind** *n* a particular state of one's mind or feelings; a mood: *I'm not in the right frame of mind to start discussing money.*

,frame of 'reference *n* a set of principles, standards or observations used as a basis for one's judgement, behaviour, etc: *sociological studies conducted within a Marxist frame of reference.*

frame² /freɪm/ *v* **1(a)** to put or build a frame¹(1) round sth: [Vn] *frame a photograph/painting.* **(b)** (esp passive) to serve or act as a frame¹(1) for sb/sth: [Vn] *He stood framed in the doorway.* ○ *A dense mass of black hair framed her face.* **2** to express sth in words; to compose sth: [Vn] *frame a question/an argument/a response* ○ *frame a theory/plan/set of rules.* **3** (*infml*) (esp passive) to produce false evidence against an innocent person so that he or she appears guilty: [Vn] *He maintained his innocence and claimed that he'd been framed.*

■ **'frame-up** *n* (*pl* **-ups**) (*infml*) a situation in which false evidence is produced against an innocent person so that he or she appears guilty: *Don't you see? It was all a frame-up!*

framework /ˈfreɪmwɜːk/ *n* **1** a structure giving shape and support to sth: *a bridge with a steel framework.* ⇨ picture at FRAME¹. **2** a social order or system: *civil unrest which shook the whole framework of society.* **3** a set of principles or ideas used as a basis for one's judgement, decisions, etc: *All the cases can be considered within the framework of the existing rules.*

franc /fræŋk/ *n* the unit of money in France, Belgium, Switzerland and several other countries: *The Swiss franc fell/rose against the dollar earlier today.*

franchise /ˈfræntʃaɪz/ *n* **1** [U] the right to vote at public elections: *a system of universal adult franchise* ○ *Women were not given the franchise in Switzerland until quite recently.* **2** [C] **(a)** formal permission to sell a company's goods or services in a particular area, given in exchange for a sum of money, a share of the profits, etc: *buy a fast-food/ printing franchise* ○ *grant/withdraw a franchise.* **(b)** permission given by or bought from a government to operate a particular service: *In the re-organization, Southern Television lost their franchise.* **(c)** a business, service, etc of this type: *operate a franchise.*

▶ **franchise** *v* to give or sell a franchise(2) to sb: [Vn] *sell franchised goods.*

franchisee /ˌfræntʃaɪˈziː/ a person, company, etc holding a franchise: *the company's leading franchisee in Japan.*

Franco- *comb form* French; of France: *the Franco-German alliance* ○ *a Francophile* (ie sb who likes France, French culture, etc).

francophone /ˈfræŋkəfəʊn/ *adj, n* (a person) speaking French as a main language: *the francophone countries of West Africa.*

frank¹ /fræŋk/ *adj* (**-er, -est**) open, honest and direct in speech or writing: *a frank reply/discussion/ exchange of views* ○ *To be (perfectly) frank with you, I think your son has little chance of passing the exam.*

▶ **frankly** *adv* **1** (qualifying a sentence) speaking honestly; to be truthful: *Frankly, I couldn't care less what happens to him.* ○ *Quite frankly, I'm not surprised he failed.* ⇨ note at HOPEFUL. **2** in a frank manner: *She expressed her opinions fully and frankly.*

frankness *n* [U]: *She spoke about her fears with complete/disarming frankness.*

frank² /fræŋk/ *v* [Vn] to stamp a mark on a letter, etc to show that the cost of posting it has been paid or does not need to be paid.

frankfurter /ˈfræŋkfɜːtə(r)/ (*US* also **wiener**) *n* a long thin smoked SAUSAGE, often eaten in a bread roll. See also HOT DOG.

frankincense /ˈfræŋkɪnsens/ *n* [U] a sticky substance obtained from certain trees. It is burnt to give a pleasant smell, esp in religious ceremonies. See also INCENSE¹.

frantic /ˈfræntɪk/ *adj* **1** in an extreme state of emotion, esp fear or anxiety: *frantic with worry/anger/ grief* ○ *Her parents were frantic when she did not return.* ○ *The children were driving me frantic* (ie making me very irritated). **2** hurried and excited but not well organized, usu because of the need to act quickly: *a frantic dash/search* ○ *make frantic attempts to rescue sb* ○ *frantic buying and selling on the stock market.* ▶ **frantically** /-kli/ *adv*: *shout frantically for help* ○ *work frantically to finish on time.*

fraternal /frəˈtɜːnl/ *adj* of or like a brother or brothers: *fraternal feelings* ○ *receive fraternal greetings from fellow trade unionists.*

fraternity /frəˈtɜːnəti/ *n* **1** [CGp] a group of people sharing the same profession or common interests or beliefs: *members of the medical/banking/racing fraternity.* **2** [C] (*US*) a group of male students at a university who form a social club. Compare SORORITY. **3** (*fml*) [U] a feeling of friendship, loyalty and mutual support within a group: *believe in liberty, equality and fraternity.*

fraternize, -ise /ˈfrætənaɪz/ *v* ~ (**with sb**) to have friendly social relations with people of a different status, race, group, etc: [Vpr] *We don't like lecturers fraternizing too much with the students.* [also V]. ▶ **fraternization, -isation** /ˌfrætənaɪˈzeɪʃn; *US* -nəˈz-/ *n* [U].

fratricide /ˈfrætrɪsaɪd/ *n* [U] the crime of killing one's brother.

▶ **fratricidal** /ˌfrætrɪˈsaɪdl/ *adj* fighting against or killing members of one's own family, social group or race: *be engaged in a fratricidal 'struggle.*

fraud /frɔːd/ *n* **1** [U, C] the action or an instance of deceiving sb in order to make money or obtain goods illegally: *be found guilty of fraud* ○ *a dramatic rise in computer/credit card/cheque card fraud* ○ *a £2.5 m fraud.* **2** [C] **(a)** a person who deceives others by pretending to have abilities, skills, etc that he or she does not really have; an IMPOSTOR: *She was a fraud — she had no medical qualifications at all.* **(b)** a thing that is not what it is claimed to be: *This language study method is a complete fraud.*

▶ **fraudster** a person who attempts or is guilty of fraud.

fraudulent /ˈfrɔːdjələnt; *US* -dʒə-/ *adj* **1** obtained or done by fraud; involving fraud: *make fraudulent insurance claims.* **2** deceitful or dishonest: *a fraudulent display of emotion.* **fraudulence** /ˈfrɔːdjələns; *US* -dʒə-/ *n* [U]. **fraudulently** /ˈfrɔːdjələntli; *US* -dʒə-/ *adv*: *act fraudulently.*

fraught /frɔːt/ *adj* **1** [pred] ~ **with sth** filled with sth: *a situation fraught with danger/difficulty.* **2** causing or feeling stress, anxiety, etc: *look fraught* ○ *Shopping in London seems to become more fraught every year.*

fray¹ /freɪ/ *n* **the fray** [sing] (*often joc*) a fight, a contest or an argument; an exciting or challenging activity: *ready/eager for the fray* ○ *enter/join the fray* ○ *stand above the political fray.*

fray² /freɪ/ *v* **1** to become or make sth, eg fabric, thin or worn, esp as a result of frequent use or of being rubbed against sth: [V] *This cotton frays easily.* [Vn] *Constant abrasion will fray even the thickest rope.* ○ *It's the fashion to wear frayed jeans.* **2** to show or make sth show the effects of strain: [V] *Nerves/Tempers began to fray in the heat.* [Vn] *Our relations with the neighbours have got a bit frayed recently.*

F

frazzle /ˈfræzl/ n **IDM** **beaten, burnt, worn, etc to a ˈfrazzle** completely beaten, burnt, exhausted, etc.
▶ **frazzled** adj tired and suffering from stress: *At the end of a children's party, parents always look completely frazzled.*

freak¹ /friːk/ n **1** (infml derog) a person who is considered abnormal because of her or his behaviour, appearance or ideas: *People think she's a freak just because she likes spiders.* ○ *I felt a real freak.* **2** (infml) a person with a very strong particular interest or obsession (OBSESS): ˈhealth/ˈhealth-food freaks ○ a ˈjazz freak. **3** a very unusual and unexpected event or action: *a freak accident/storm/occurrence* ○ *By some freak (of chance) he wasn't injured at all.* **4** (also ˌfreak of ˈnature) a person, an animal, a plant or a thing that is abnormal in form.
▶ **freakish** adj unusual or odd; strange: *a freakish goal* ○ *freakish behaviour.* **freakishly** adv: *a freakishly mild winter.*
freaky (infml) adj odd; strange: *that freaky friend of yours.*

freak² /friːk/ v ~ (out) (infml) to react strongly to sth which surprises, delights, shocks or frightens one: [V, Vp] *My parents really freaked (out) when they saw my purple hair.* [V] *When they told me I'd won a car, I absolutely freaked.* **PHRV** ˌfreak ˈout to behave in an excited, strange and wild manner, eg because of mental illness or drugs: *This ordinary quiet guy just freaked out and shot ten people.* ○ *John's party was really wild — everyone freaked out.* ○ (fig) *The photocopier's freaked out again.* ˌfreak sb ˈout to make sb react strongly to sth that delights, frightens, etc them: *Listening to that song always freaks me out.* ○ *Snakes really freak him out.*

freckle /ˈfrekl/ n (usu pl) a small, pale brown spot on the human skin: *Ann's face and back are covered with freckles.* Compare MOLE¹.
▶ **freckle** v to become covered with freckles: [Vadv] *He's got the sort of skin that freckles very easily.*
freckled adj: *a freckled face/schoolgirl.*

free¹ /friː/ adj (freer /ˈfriːə(r)/, freest /ˈfriːɪst/) **1(a)** (of a person) not a slave or prisoner; allowed to go where one wants: *be **as free as a bird*** ○ *After ten years in prison, he was a free man again.* ○ *Thousands of political prisoners were **set free**.* **(b)** (of an animal) not kept in a cage or tied to a post, etc: *leopards roaming free in the game reserve* ○ *The dog was chained, so how did it get free?* **2** not restricted or controlled: *free speech* ○ *a free press* ○ *the free movement of workers within the European Union* ○ *have/get free access to information* ○ *You are free to come and go as you wish.* **3** clear; not blocked: *Is the way/passage free?* ○ *a free flow of water.* **4** [pred] ~ from/of sth not containing or affected by sth unpleasant, undesirable or harmful: *soft drinks free of artificial colouring* ○ *free of typographical errors/racial prejudice* ○ *These drugs will keep her free from pain.* ○ *a holiday free from all responsibilities.* **5(a)** costing nothing: *free tickets for the theatre* ○ *a free sample* ○ *Admission is free.* **(b)** [pred] ~ (of sth) not requiring a specified payment, usu of tax or duty: *a payment of £30 000 free of tax* ○ *Delivery is free (of charge) if goods are paid for in advance.* **6(a)** not attached to sth or trapped by sth: *the free end of the rope* ○ *Let the rope run free.* ○ *One of the wheels has worked free (ie become loose).* ○ *They had to cut him free from the wreckage.* **(b)** not holding sth: *He picked up the suitcase with his free hand.* **7(a)** (of a place or piece of equipment) not occupied or being used: *Is that seat free?* ○ *The bathroom's free now.* ○ *I've tried telephoning but her line is never free.* **(b)** (of a person or time) without particular plans or arrangements; not busy: *I'm usually free in the afternoon.* ○ *Are you free for lunch?* ○ *Wednesday afternoons are free for personal study.* **8** [pred] ~ with sth ready and willing to give sth, sometimes

when this is not wanted: *He is very free with his time* (ie gives it willingly). ○ *She's always very free with pieces of advice for everybody.* **9** not showing enough respect; too familiar(3): *I don't like him — he is too free in his language and in his behaviour.* **10** (of a translation (TRANSLATE)) expressing the meaning of the original loosely, not exactly. Compare LITERAL 1a. **IDM** **feel free** ⇨ FEEL¹. **for ˈfree** without payment: *My neighbour cuts my hair for free.* **free and ˈeasy** informal; relaxed: *Life here is very free and easy.* **get, have, etc a free ˈhand** to get, have, etc permission or an opportunity to do what one chooses and make one's own decisions, esp in a job: *I was given a free hand in designing the poster.* **give, etc free/ˈrein to sb/sth** ⇨ REIN. **have one's hands free/tied** ⇨ HAND¹.
▶ **free** adv without cost or payment: *Children under five usually travel free on trains.* **IDM** **make free with ˈsb/ˈsth** to treat sb/sth without proper respect; to use sth as if it belonged to oneself: *He made free with all his girlfriend's money.*

freely /ˈfriːli/ adv **1** without anyone controlling, interfering with or trying to prevent sth: *a freely elected government* ○ *travel freely across the border.* **2** without anything blocking or restricting one/sth: *spend money freely* ○ *drugs that are freely available* ○ *Water flowed freely from the pipe.* **3** in an open and honest manner: *We are alone — you can talk quite freely.* **4** willingly; readily: *I freely admit that I made a mistake.* **5** in a willing and generous manner: *Millions of people gave freely in response to the famine appeal.*

■ ˌfree ˈagent n a person who can act as he or she pleases because he or she is not responsible to or for anyone: *No wife, no children, no debts — he's a free agent.*
ˌFree ˈChurch n a Church that does not follow the teaching or practices of established Christian Churches.
ˌfree ˈenterprise n [U] an economic system in which there is open competition in business or trade and no government control: *the party of free enterprise and market economics.*
ˌfree ˈfall n [C, U] movement through air or space without engine power or without a PARACHUTE: (fig) *Share prices went into free fall.*
▶ ˌfree ˈfloating adj not attached or linked to any particular object, group, etc: *a ˌfree-floating ˈcurrency.*

■ ˈfree-for-all n **1** a fight or an argument in which most people present take part, resulting in noise and confusion: *It started as a polite discussion but then developed into a real free-for-all.* **2** a situation in which there are no rules or controls and each person acts for her or his own advantage: *a free-for-all among exporters* ○ *a price-cutting free-for-all.*
ˌfree ˈhouse n (Brit) a pub that is privately owned and not controlled by a brewery (BREW), so that it is not restricted to selling particular types of beer: *The Swan was reopened in 1993 as a free house.* Compare TIED HOUSE.
ˌfree ˈkick n (in football) a kick taken as a penalty against the opposing team.
ˌfree ˈlove n [U] (dated) the idea or practice of having sex without being married.
ˌfree ˈmarket n an economic system in which prices are allowed to rise and fall according to supply and demand, rather than being fixed by eg the government: *a ˌfree market eˈconomy* ○ *compete in a free market.*
ˌfree ˈport n a port at which no import duty is charged on goods that have been brought there temporarily before being sent to a different country.
ˌfree-ˈrange adj (of hens or eggs) kept or produced in natural conditions where the hens can move around freely: *ˌfree-range ˈchickens.* Compare BATTERY 4.
ˌfree-ˈstanding adj **(a)** not supported by or fixed to

anything: *a ˌfree-standing ˈsculpture.* (**b**) independent and not linked to anything else: *a ˌfree-standing ˈcompany/ˈtheory.*

ˌfree ˈtrade *n* [U] a system of international trade in which there are no import restrictions, eg tax or duty: *a free trade area/zone.*

ˌfree ˈverse *n* [U] poetry without a regular rhythm or RHYME(1).

ˌfree ˈvote *n* a vote in parliament in which members do not have to follow party policy but can vote according to their own beliefs.

ˌfree-ˈwheel *v* [V] **1** to ride a bicycle without pedalling (PEDAL *v*) or drive a car without using engine power, eg when going down a hill. **2** to act without concern for rules, conventions or the consequences of what one does: *a free-wheeling economy.*

ˌfree ˈwill *n* [U] **1** the ability to decide freely what one wants to do: *I did it of my own free will* (ie I was not told or forced to do it). **2** the power to make one's own decisions without these being previously determined by eg God or fate.

free² /friː/ *v* (*pt, pp* **freed** /friːd/) **1** ~ **sb/sth (from sth)** to allow sb/sth to go free; to release sb/sth: [Vn] *freed slaves* ○ *free the prisoner* ○ *My coat caught in some barbed wire and it took me some time to free it/ myself.* [Vnpr] *free sb from captivity* ○ *free an animal from a trap* ○ *It took the firemen two hours to free the driver from the wreckage.* **2** ~ **sb/sth of/sth** to take sth that is unpleasant, not wanted, etc away from sb/sth; to get rid of sth: [Vnpr] *Relaxation exercises can free your body of tension.* ○ *The police are determined to free the town of violent crime.* **3** ~ **sb/sth for sth** to allow sth to be used for a particular purpose: [Vnpr] *The government intends to free more resources for educational purposes.* **4** to give sb the freedom to do sth they want to do: [Vn.to inf] *Winning the prize has freed him to write full-time.*

-free *comb form* (forming *adjs* and *advs*) without; free from: *fat-free* ○ *lead-free* ○ *duty-free* ○ *trouble-free.*

freebie /ˈfriːbɪ/ *n* (*infml*) a free gift: *I got these glasses as freebies at the petrol station.*

freedom /ˈfriːdəm/ *n* **1** [U] the state of not being a prisoner or a slave: *After 10 years in prison, he was given his freedom.* **2**(**a**) [U, C] ~ (**of sth**) the power or right to act, speak, etc as one wants without anyone stopping one: *freedom of speech/thought/ worship* ○ *defend press freedom* ○ *protect the freedoms of the individual.* (**b**) [U] ~ (**of sth**); ~ (**to do sth**) the state of being able to act, etc as one wants: *enjoy freedom of action/choice/movement* ○ *He enjoyed complete freedom to do as he wished.* **3** [U] ~ **from sth** the state of being without or not affected by the thing specified: *freedom from fear/pain/hunger.* **4** [sing] **the** ~ **of sth** permission to use sth without restriction: *I gave him the freedom of my house.* **IDM** **the freedom of the ˈcity** a special right or privilege given to sb, esp as an honour for public services, allowing them to use a particular city fully and freely. See also FREEMAN.

■ **ˈfreedom fighter** *n* a person belonging to a group that uses violent means to fight the government in an attempt to gain the independence of their country.

Freefone /ˈfriːfəʊn/ *n* [U] a system in Britain in which the person making a telephone call does not pay for the cost of the call: *call Freefone 0800 89216.*

freehand /ˈfriːhænd/ *adj, adv* done without the use of a ruler or COMPASS(2): *a freehand sketch* ○ *draw freehand.*

freehold /ˈfriːhəʊld/ *n* (*law*) complete ownership of property for life: *Four people can share a freehold.*
▶ **freehold** *adj, adv* held by or having the status of freehold: *freehold premises* ○ *buy a house freehold.* Compare LEASEHOLD.
freeholder *n* a person who owns property freehold.

freelance /ˈfriːlɑːns; *US* -læns/ earning one's living by selling one's services or individual pieces of work to several organizations: *a freelance writer/ designer* ○ *freelance journalism* ○ *work freelance.*
▶ **freelance** *v* to work freelance: [V] *I've freelanced for several years.*
freelance (also **freelancer**) a person who works freelance.

freeloader /ˈfriːləʊdə(r)/ *n* a person who takes advantage of free food and accommodation without giving anything in return.

freeman /ˈfriːmən/ (*pl* **freemen** /-mən/) *n* a person who has been given the freedom(5) of a city as an honour: *be made a freeman of the City of London.*

Freemason /ˈfriːmeɪsn/ *n* member of an international secret society with the aims of offering mutual help and developing friendly relations among its members.
▶ **Freemasonry** *n* [U] **1** the system, practices and rites of the Freemasons. **2** freemasonry the friendly feeling that exists between people with the same profession, interests, etc: *the freemasonry of long-distance lorry drivers.*

Freepost /ˈfriːpəʊst/ *n* [U] a system in Britain in which the cost of sending a letter is paid by the business company that receives it: *Reply to Publicity Department, FREEPOST, Oxford University Press, Oxford.*

freesia /ˈfriːzə, ˈfriːzɪə/ *n* a plant with sweet-smelling yellow, pink or white flowers.

freestyle /ˈfriːstaɪl/ *n* [U] **1** a swimming race in which any stroke may be used: *the men's 200 metres freestyle.* **2** (*sport*) a style or method that has few rules or restrictions: *freestyle skiing/wrestling.*

freethinker /ˌfriːˈθɪŋkə(r)/ *n* a person who forms her or his own ideas independently of generally accepted opinion or religious teaching. ▶
ˌfree'thinking *adj*: *freethinking artists and writers.*

freeway /ˈfriːweɪ/ *n* (*US*) = MOTORWAY. ⇨ note at ROAD.

freeze /friːz/ *v* (*pt* **froze** /frəʊz/; *pp* **frozen** /ˈfrəʊzn/)
1(**a**) to change sth or be changed from liquid to solid, esp ice, as a result of extreme cold: [V] *Water freezes at 0°C.* ○ *It's so cold that even the river has frozen.* [Vn] *The cold weather is freezing the milk outside people's back doors.* Compare THAW. ⇨ note at WATER¹. (**b**) ~ (**sth**) (**up**) become or make sth full of ice, blocked with ice or hardened with ice: [V] *The land itself freezes at such low temperatures.* [V, V-adj] *The clothes froze (solid) on the washing-line.* [Vn, Vnp] *The sudden drop in temperature froze (up) the locks on my car.* [V, Vp] *The pipes have frozen (up), so we've got no water.* **2**(**a**) (used with *it*) (of weather) to be at or below 0° Celsius: [V] *It may freeze tonight, so make sure you bring those plants inside.* [V, Vadv] *It's freezing (hard) outside.* (**b**) to be or feel very cold; to be so cold that one dies: [V] *Every time she opens the window we all freeze.* [Vpr, Vnpr] *Two men froze to death/were frozen to death on the mountain.* **3**(**a**) to keep (food) at a very low temperature in order to preserve it: [Vn] *Is this cake suitable for freezing?* ○ *I buy enough cheese for several months and freeze it* ○ *Strawberries don't taste nice if they've been frozen.* (**b**) (of food) to be able to be kept in this way: [V] *Some fruits freeze better than others.* **4**(**a**) (of a person or an animal) to stop moving suddenly because of fear, shock, etc: [V] *When she saw all the blood, she froze.* ○ *I froze with terror as the door slowly opened.* (**b**) to stop suddenly because one is ordered to, eg by the police: [V] *He shouted 'Freeze!' and I dropped the gun.* **5** to stop a film in order to look at a particular frame¹(6a): [Vn] *Freeze the action there!* **6** to hold wages, prices, etc at a fixed level for a period of time: [Vn] *Salaries have been frozen for the current year.* **7** to prevent money, a bank account, etc being used by getting a

court order which forbids it: [Vn] *freeze a society's funds* ○ *The company's assets have been frozen.* **IDM** **freeze one's ˈblood / make one's ˈblood freeze** to fill one with feelings of fear and horror: *The sight of the masked gunman made my blood freeze.* **PHR V** ˌ**freeze sb ˈout** (*infml*) to discourage sb from doing or taking part in sth by being deliberately UN-FRIENDLY, creating difficulties, etc: *I tried to talk to her about it but she just froze me out.* ˌ**freeze (sth) ˈover** (usu passive) to become or cause sth to become completely covered by ice: *The lake was frozen over until late spring.*

▶ **freeze** *n* **1** (also ˈ**freeze-up**) a period of weather during which temperatures are below 0° Celsius: *last year's big freeze* ○ *After the last freeze-up we put insulation round the pipes.* **2** the fixing of wages, prices, etc for a period of time: *a wage/price freeze.*
■ **ˈfreeze-dry** *v* (*pt, pp* **-dried**) [Vn] to preserve esp food by freezing it and then drying it in a vacuum. ˈ**freezing-point** (also **freezing**) *n* [U] the temperature at which a liquid, esp water, freezes: *The freezing-point of water is 0°C.* ○ *Tonight temperatures everywhere will be well below freezing.*

freezer /ˈfriːzə(r)/ (also ˌ**deep ˈfreeze**) *n* a large refrigerator (REFRIGERATE) or room in which food is stored for a long time at a very low temperature.

freezing /ˈfriːzɪŋ/ *adj* very cold indeed; feeling too cold: *It's freezing (cold) outside.* ○ *freezing temperatures/weather* ○ *Shut the window — it's freezing in here!* ○ *My hands are freezing.*

freight /freɪt/ *n* [U] goods or cargo transported by ships, aircraft or trains: *send goods by air freight* ○ *rail services for both passengers and freight.* ⇨ note at CARGO.

▶ **freight** *v* to transport or send sth as freight: [Vn, Vnpr] *We'll freight the order (to you) immediately.*
freighter *n* a large ship or aircraft that carries mainly freight.
■ **freight car** *n* (*US*) = WAGON 1.
ˈ**freight train** (*US*) (*Brit* **goods train**) *n* a train that carries goods only.

freightliner /ˈfreɪtlaɪnə(r)/ *n* a fast train carrying goods in special large containers.

French /frentʃ/ *n* **1 the French** [pl *v*] the people of France: *The French are renowned for their cooking.* **2** [U] the language spoken in France, parts of Belgium, Switzerland and Canada, and in certain African countries. **IDM** **take French ˈleave** to leave one's work, duty, etc without permission.

▶ **French** *adj* of France, its people or its language: *the French countryside.*
■ ˌ**French ˈbean** *n* a type of long thin green bean which is eaten whole.
ˌ**French ˈbread** *n* [U] bread in the form of long thin loaves (LOAF[1] 1). ⇨ picture at BREAD.
ˌ**French ˈdressing** *n* [U] a mixture of oil and VIN-EGAR, usu with spices, for putting on SALAD, etc.
ˌ**French ˈfries** *n* [pl] (*esp US*) long thin pieces of potato fried in oil or fat; chips (CHIP[1] 3). ⇨ picture at POTATO.
ˌ**French ˈhorn** *n* a brass wind instrument consisting of a long tube coiled in a circle with a wide opening at the end. ⇨ picture at MUSICAL INSTRU-MENT.
ˌ**French ˈkiss** *n* a kiss during which one partner's tongue is put into the other's mouth.
ˌ**French ˈletter** *n* (*infml esp Brit*) a CONDOM.
ˌ**French ˈloaf** (also ˌ**French ˈstick**) *n* a LOAF[1] of French bread. ⇨ picture at BREAD.
ˌ**French ˈpolish** *n* [U] a type of VARNISH that is painted onto wood to give a hard shiny surface.
French-polish *v* [Vn] to treat wood with French polish.
ˌ**French ˈtoast** *n* [U] bread dipped in egg and milk and then fried.
ˌ**French ˈwindow** (*US* also ˌ**French ˈdoor**) *n* a long

glass door, often one of a pair and usu opening onto a garden or BALCONY. ⇨ picture at HOUSE[1].

Frenchman /ˈfrentʃmən/ *n* (*pl* **-men** /-mən/; *fem* **Frenchwoman** /-wʊmən/, *pl* **-women** /-wɪmɪn/) a native of France.

frenetic /frəˈnetɪk/ *adj* wild and lively; using a lot of energy: *frenetic activity* ○ *a frenetic life-style* ○ *live at a frenetic pace.* ▶ **frenetically** /-klɪ/ *adv.*

frenzy /ˈfrenzi/ *n* [C usu *sing*, U] a state of extreme excitement; extreme and wild activity or behaviour: *in a frenzy of enthusiasm/violence/hate* ○ *The speaker worked the crowd up into a (state of) frenzy.* ○ *The news threw him into a frenzy.* ○ *an outbreak of patriotic frenzy.*

▶ **frenzied** /ˈfrenzid/ *adj* [usu attrib] wildly excited or out of control: *a frenzied attack* ○ *frenzied applause.* **frenziedly** *adv*: *dance/work/fight frenziedly.*

frequency /ˈfriːkwənsi/ *n* **1** [U] (**a**) the rate at which sth happens or is repeated, usu measured over a particular period of time: *Fatal road accidents have decreased in frequency over recent years.* ○ *These attacks are happening with growing/increasing frequency.* (**b**) the fact of being frequent or happening often: *the alarming frequency of computer errors* ○ *Objects like this turn up at auctions with surprising frequency.* **2** [C,U] (*techn*) (**a**) the rate at which a sound wave or radio wave vibrates (VIBRATE): *high-/low-frequency sounds* ○ *Different frequencies of sound are experienced as differences in pitch.* (**b**) a band or group of different frequencies: *change frequency on the radio* ○ *There are only a limited number of broadcasting frequencies.*

frequent[1] /ˈfriːkwənt/ *adj* happening, found, seen, etc often: *a frequent visitor to this country* ○ *make frequent trips to the States* ○ *His visits became less frequent as time passed.*

▶ **frequently** *adv* often: *Buses run frequently between the city and the airport.* ○ *His was the name most frequently mentioned.*

frequent[2] /frɪˈkwent/ *v* (*fml*) to visit a particular place often: [Vn] *A pretty village much frequented by tourists* ○ *He used to frequent the town's bars and night-clubs.*

fresco /ˈfreskəʊ/ *n* (*pl* ~**oes** or ~**os** /-kəʊz/) (**a**) [C] a picture painted on a wall or ceiling while the PLASTER[1] is still wet: *The church is famous for its frescos.* (**b**) [U] the method of painting in this way.

fresh /freʃ/ *adj* (**-er, -est**) **1**(**a**) [usu attrib] new or different: *fresh evidence* ○ *start a fresh piece of paper* ○ *make a fresh start* ○ *fresh ideas* ○ *try a fresh* (ie original) *approach* ○ *give the walls a fresh coat of paint.* (**b**) made, obtained or experienced recently and still not changed: *fresh tracks in the snow* ○ *Their memories of the wedding are still fresh in their minds.* **2** (usu of food) newly made, produced, picked or supplied; not frozen, in tins, etc: *fresh bread* (ie just baked) ○ *fresh flowers/eggs/milk* ○ *The water in this vase needs changing; I'll put some fresh in.* ○ *Which do you prefer: fresh, frozen or tinned peas?* **3** (of water) not salty: *There's a shortage of fresh water on the island.* **4** pleasantly clean, pure or cool: *a toothpaste that leaves a nice fresh taste in your mouth* ○ *a young fresh-tasting wine* ○ *Let's go for a walk and get some fresh air.* ○ *Go and put on some fresh clothes.* **5**(**a**) (of weather) rather cold, with some wind: *It's a bit fresh this morning, isn't it?* (**b**)(of the wind) cool and fairly strong: *The winds are likely to get fresher towards the end of the day.* **6** [usu attrib] clear, bright and attractive in colour or appearance: *a nice fresh green* ○ *The new paint makes the kitchen look fresh and clean.* ○ *She has a fresh* (ie healthy) *complexion.* **7** [usu pred] not tired; healthy and full of energy: *I feel **as fresh as a daisy** after my long sleep.* **8** [pred] ~ **from sth** having just come from a place or having just had a particular experience; straight from sth: *students fresh from college* ○

For more help with verbs, see Study pages **B4–8**.

fresh from her recent success at the Olympic Games.
9 ~ **(with sb)** (*infml*) too confident in behaviour or speech, esp in a sexual way, with a person of the opposite sex: *He then started to get fresh with me.* **IDM break fresh/new ground** ⇨ GROUND¹. **a breath of fresh air** ⇨ BREATH. **new/fresh blood** ⇨ BLOOD¹.

▶ **fresh** *adv* **IDM fresh out of** ˈsth (*infml esp US*) having just used all one's supplies of sth; no longer having sth: *Sorry — we're fresh out of ˈeggs.* ○ *fresh out of ˈideas.*

fresh- (forming compound *adjs*): *fresh-baked bread* ○ *fresh-cut flowers* ○ *a fresh-faced youth.*

fresher *n* (*Brit infml*) a student in her or his first year at university or college.

freshly *adv* (usu followed by a past participle) recently; newly: *freshly picked strawberries* ○ *freshly ground pepper* ○ *a freshly painted sign.*

freshness *n* [U]: *Always check the freshness of any fish you buy.* ○ *I like the freshness of his approach to the problem.*

freshen /ˈfreʃn/ *v* **1** ~ **sth (up)** to make sth cleaner, cooler, more pleasant or more attractive: [Vn] *The storm had freshened the air.* [Vnp] *A good clean will really freshen up the house.* **2** [V] (of the wind) to become strong and cool. **3** (*US*) to add more liquid, esp alcohol, to a drink: [Vn] *Can I freshen your drink?* **PHRV** ˌfreshen (oneself) ˈup to wash and make oneself look clean and tidy after a journey, before a meeting, etc: *I'll just go and freshen (myself) up before the interview.*

▶ **freshener** /ˈfreʃnə(r)/ *n* [C,U] (esp in compounds) a thing that freshens (FRESHEN 1) sth: *a ˈbreath freshener* (eg a sweet or spray) ○ *He sprayed air-freshener around the room.*

freshman /ˈfreʃmən/ *n* (*pl* -**men** /-mən/) a student in her or his first year at university or (in the USA) high school.

freshwater /ˈfreʃwɔːtə(r)/ *adj* [attrib] living in or containing fresh water; not salty or of the sea: *freshwater fish* ○ *freshwater lakes.* Compare SALT-WATER.

fret¹ /fret/ *v* (-tt-) ~ **(oneself)**; ~ **(about/over sth)** to become unhappy, bad-tempered, or anxious about sth; to worry: [V] *Her baby starts to fret as soon as she goes out of the room.* [Vn] *Don't fret yourself, we'll get there on time.* [Vpr] *Fretting about it won't help.* [also V.*that*].

▶ **fret** *n* [sing] a state of anxiety or worry: *be in a fret.*

fretful /-fl/ *adj* bad-tempered or complaining, esp because one is unhappy or worried: *a fretful child.*
fretfully *adv.*

fret² /fret/ *n* each of the bars or ridges on the neck of a guitar or similar instrument, used as a guide for the fingers to press the strings at the correct place. ⇨ picture at GUITAR.

fretsaw /ˈfretsɔː/ *n* a narrow saw fixed in a frame, used for cutting designs in thin sheets of wood.

fretted /ˈfretɪd/ *adj* (*techn*) (**a**) (esp of wood or stone) decorated with patterns made by cutting in straight lines: *an elaborately fretted border.* (**b**) fitted with frets (FRET²).

fretwork /ˈfretwɜːk/ *n* [U] ornamental patterns cut into wood and other materials, eg with a FRETSAW.

Freudian /ˈfrɔɪdiən/ *adj* (**a**) of or related to the theories of Sigmund Freud about the working of the human mind, esp his theories about SUBCONSCIOUS sexual ideas or feelings. (**b**) (of sb's speech or behaviour) possibly revealing sth about such hidden ideas or feelings: *He keeps talking about his mother. That's very Freudian!*

■ ˌFreudian ˈslip *n* a comment made accidentally by a speaker instead of what was originally intended, but which is considered to reveal her or his true thoughts.

Fri *abbr* Friday: *Fri 7 March.*

friable /ˈfraɪəbl/ *adj* (*techn*) easily broken up into small pieces: *friable soil.*

friar /ˈfraɪə(r)/ *n* a man who is a member of one of certain Roman Catholic religious orders. Friars work with people in the community rather than living permanently in a MONASTERY. Compare MONK.

▶ **friary** /ˈfraɪəri/ *n* a building in which friars live.

fricassee /ˈfrɪkəsiː/ *n* [C,U] a dish consisting of pieces of cooked meat served in a thick white sauce: *chicken fricassee.*

fricative /ˈfrɪkətɪv/ *n, adj* (*phonetics*) (a consonant) made by forcing breath out through a narrow space in the mouth with the lips, teeth, tongue, etc in a certain position. There are nine fricatives in English: /f, θ, s, ʃ, h/ are voiceless (VOICE), /v, ð, z, ʒ/ are voiced (VOICE *v*). Compare PLOSIVE.

friction /ˈfrɪkʃn/ *n* **1** [U] (**a**) the rubbing of one surface or thing against another: *Friction between moving parts had caused the engine to overheat.* (**b**) (*physics*) the resistance of one surface to another surface or substance moving over or through it: *The force of friction slows the spacecraft down as it re-enters the earth's atmosphere.* **2** [U,C] ~ (**between A and B**) disagreement or conflict between people or parties with different views: *There is a great deal of friction between the management and the workforce.* ○ *conflicts and frictions that have still to be resolved.*

Friday /ˈfraɪdeɪ, -di/ *n* [C,U] (*abbr* **Fri**) the 6th day of the week, next after Thursday.
For further guidance on how *Friday* is used, see the examples at *Monday.*

fridge /frɪdʒ/ *n* (*infml*) a refrigerator (REFRIGERATE): *Keep the milk and butter in the fridge.*

■ ˌfridge-ˈfreezer *n* an upright kitchen unit containing separate fridge and FREEZER sections.

fried *pt, pp* of FRY¹.

friend /frend/ *n* **1** a person one knows and likes, usu sb who is not a member of one's family: *He's a friend of mine/my friend.* ○ *We are good/close/old friends.* ○ *She was my best friend at school.* ○ *He had few friends among his fellow-students.* See also BOY-FRIEND, FAIR-WEATHER FRIEND, GIRLFRIEND. See also BEFRIEND. **2** ~ **of sth** a person who supports a particular cause, organization or charity, eg by contributing money or being a member: *a friend of the arts/the poor* ○ *We appeal to all friends of peace and justice around the world.* **3** a person who is of the same country or group as oneself and can be considered to have the same views or interests: *Who goes there — friend or foe?* ○ *You're among friends here — you can speak freely.* **4** a thing that is very helpful or familiar: *I've come to rely on my dictionary like an old friend.* ○ *Television can be a valuable friend for lonely people.* **5 Friend** a member of the Society of Friends; a QUAKER. **6** a person who is being talked about or addressed in public: *Our friend from China will now tell us about her research.* ○ *Friends, it is with great pleasure that I introduce our guest speaker.* ○ *my learned friend* (ie used by a lawyer of another lawyer in a lawcourt) ○ *my honourable friend* (ie used by a Member of Parliament of another Member of the same party in the House of Commons). **IDM be/make** ˈfriends **(with sb)** to be/become a friend(1) of sb: *They had a quarrel but now they're friends again.* ○ *David finds it hard to make friends (with other children).* **a** ˌfriend in ˈneed (is a ˌfriend inˈdeed)** (*saying*) a friend(1) who helps one when one needs help (is a true friend).

▶ **friendless** *adj* without any friends.

friendly /ˈfrendli/ *adj* (-**ier**, -**iest**) **1(a)** ~ **(to sb)** behaving in a kind and pleasant way; acting like a friend: *a friendly person* ○ *They were very friendly to me when I first arrived.* ○ *It wasn't very friendly of you to slam the door in his face.* (**b**) showing or expressing kindness and a helpful attitude: *a friend-ly smile/welcome/gesture/manner.* ⇨ note at NICE. **(c)** ~ **(with sb)** of a relationship in which people treat each other as friends: *friendly relations* ○ *on friendly terms with the boss* ○ *He's friendly with the girl next door.* **2(a)** not seriously competitive: *a friendly game of football* ○ *a friendly argument* ○ *friendly rivalry.* **(b)** not in conflict with each other; not enemies: *friendly nations* ○ *soldiers killed by friendly fire* (ie accidentally, by weapons fired by their own side). ▶ **friendliness** *n* [U].

-friendly (in compound *adjs*) that is of benefit to, or does not harm or damage, the thing specified: *envir-onmentally friendly products* ○ ˌozone-ˈfriendly. ⇨ note at USER-FRIENDLY.

■ ˈ**friendly match** (also **friendly**) *n* a game of foot-ball or other sports contest that is not part of a serious competitive series: *a friendly between Leeds and Liverpool.*

ˈ**Friendly Society** (also ˈ**Provident Society**) *n* an association formed to support its members, esp by giving money, when they are ill or old.

friendship /ˈfrendʃɪp/ *n* **(a)** [U] the feeling or rela-tionship that friends have; the state of being friends: *There were strong ties of friendship between them.* ○ *The aim of the conference is to promote international friendship.* **(b)** [C] ~ **(with sb)** an instance of this: *At school she formed close friendships with several other girls.* ○ *Their professional relationship developed into a lasting friendship.*

fries /fraɪz/ *n* [pl] (*esp US*) = FRENCH FRIES: *He or-dered a hamburger and fries.*

Friesian /ˈfriːʒn/ *n* a type of black and white cow that produces a lot of milk: *a herd of Friesians.*

frieze /friːz/ *n* [C] a band of painted or carved dec-oration round the top of a wall or building. ⇨ picture at COLUMN.

frigate /ˈfrɪɡət/ *n* a small fast naval ship that accom-panies other ships in order to protect them.

frigging /ˈfrɪɡɪŋ/ *adv, adj* [attrib] (△ *sl*) (used to give emphasis and usu to show annoyance, anger, etc): *It's frigging cold outside.* ○ *Mind your own frig-ging business!*

fright /fraɪt/ *n* **1(a)** [U] a sudden unpleasant feeling of fear: *trembling with fright.* See also STAGE FRIGHT. **(b)** [C usu *sing*] an instance of this: *You gave me (quite) a fright creeping up behind me like that.* ○ *I got the fright of my life* (ie I was extremely fright-ened). **2** [C usu *sing*] (*infml*) a person or thing that looks ridiculous or ugly: *She thinks that dress is pretty — I think she looks a fright in it.* **IDM** **take** ˈ**fright (at sth)** to become extremely frightened by sth: *The animals took fright at the sound of the gun.* ○ *The financial markets are taking fright at the pro-spect of a change of government.*

frighten /ˈfraɪtn/ *v* to fill sb with fear; to make sb afraid, esp suddenly: [Vn] *Sorry, I didn't mean to frighten you.* ○ *Loud traffic frightens horses.* [Vn.*that*] *It frightens me that so many countries now possess nuclear weapons.* **IDM** **frighten/scare the day-lights out of sb** ⇨ DAYLIGHTS. **frighten/scare the life out of sb** ⇨ LIFE. **frighten/scare sb to** ˈ**death** ⇨ DEATH. **PHRV** ˌ**frighten sb/sth a**ˈ**way/**ˈ**off** to force or drive a person or an animal to go away by frightening them: *The alarm frightened the burglars away.* ○ *The children's shouts frightened off the birds.* ○ *The stock market crash has frightened off investors.* ˈ**frighten sb into doing sth** to make sb do sth by frightening them: *News of the robberies frightened many people into fitting new locks on their doors.* ▶ **frightened** *adj* ~ **(of sth / of doing sth)**; ~ **(that...)** in a state of fear; afraid: *Frightened chil-dren were calling for their mothers.* ○ *He looked very frightened as he spoke.* ○ *He's frightened of spiders.* ○ *They're frightened (at the prospect) of losing power.* ○

I was frightened that the plane might crash. ⇨ note at AFRAID.

frightening /ˈfraɪtnɪŋ/ *adj* causing fear; alarming: *a frightening possibility/situation/development* ○ *It is frightening even to think of the horrors of nuclear war.* **frighteningly** *adv*: *The film was frighteningly realistic.*

frightful /ˈfraɪtfl/ *adj* **1** [attrib] (*infml*) (used for emphasis) extreme; extremely bad: *in a frightful rush* ○ *They left the house in a frightful mess.* **2** very serious, unpleasant or frightening: *a frightful acci-dent* ○ *the frightful prospect of a nuclear war.* ▶ **frightfully** /-fəli/ *adv* (*infml*) very; extremely: *I'm frightfully sorry, but I can't see you today.*

frigid /ˈfrɪdʒɪd/ *adj* **1** (of a woman) not showing any sexual desire or responses. Compare IMPOTENT 2. **2** showing no feelings of friendship or affection: *a frigid look/voice/politeness.* **3** very cold: *a frigid climate* ○ *the frigid zones near the poles.* ▶ **frigidity** /frɪˈdʒɪdəti/ *n* [U] the lack of any sexual desire or responses in a woman.

frill

frill /frɪl/ *n* **1** [C] an ornamental border on a garment or piece of cloth, esp one gathered in a number of small folds at one edge. ⇨ picture. **2** [pl] additional items that are not essential for sth but make it more attractive: *a simple meal with no frills.* ▶ **frilled** *adj* decorated with frills (FRILL 1): *a frilled dress.*

frilly /ˈfrɪli/ *adj* having many frills (FRILL 1): *a frilly petticoat.*

fringe /frɪndʒ/ *n* **1** [C] (*esp Brit*) (*US* **bangs** [pl]) the front part of sb's hair, cut so that it hangs over the forehead: *She has a fringe and glasses.* ⇨ picture at HAIR. **2** [C] an ornamental edge on a garment, carpet or piece of cloth, consisting of loose or hanging threads or cords. **3** [C often *pl*] the outer edge of an area, a group or an activity: *the fringe of the forest* ○ *on the fringes of society* ○ *on the radical fringe of the party* ○ *fringe theatre* (ie performing plays, etc that are unusual or not conventional). **4** **the fringe** [sing] events which take place during a festival or conference but are not an official part of it: *The most interesting plays are often to be found on the fringe.* ○ *a fringe meeting.* **IDM** **the lunatic fringe** ⇨ LUN-ATIC.

▶ **fringe** *v* ~ **sth (with sth)** (usu passive) to form a border around sth; to surround sth: [Vnpr] *The estate was fringed with stately elms.* **fringed** *adj* ~ **(with sth)** having a fringe(2) or fringes: *a fringed skirt* ○ *curtains fringed with gold braid.* **fringing** *n* [U] material used to make a fringe(2): *a red scarf with green fringing.*

■ ˈ**fringe benefit** *n* an extra benefit, given esp to an employee in addition to salary or wages: *The fringe benefits of the job include a car and free health insurance.*

frippery /ˈfrɪpəri/ *n* [U] (also **fripperies** [pl]) unne-cessary items of ornament or decoration, eg in clothing: *(children dressed in Victorian frippery)* ○ *(fig) He had little time for the fun and fripperies of life.*

Frisbee /ˈfrɪzbi/ *n* (*propr*) a light plastic disc, shaped like a plate, which is thrown between players in a game.

frisk /frɪsk/ *v* **1** (*infml*) to pass one's hands over sb in a search for hidden weapons, drugs or other items: [Vn] *Everyone was frisked before getting on the plane.* **2** (of animals) to run and jump in a playful way: [V, Vp] *lambs frisking (about) in the meadow.*

▶ **frisky** *adj* lively and full of energy; wanting to enjoy oneself: *a frisky puppy* ○ *I feel quite frisky this morning.*

frisson /ˈfriːsɒ̃; US friːˈsəʊn/ *n* (*French*) a sudden strong physical feeling, esp of excitement or fear: *a frisson of delight/horror/fear.*

fritter¹ /ˈfrɪtə(r)/ *v* **PHR V** ,**fritter sth aˈway (on sth)** to waste one's time, money, etc foolishly, with no clear aims: *They frittered away the entire afternoon/several opportunities.* ○ *He frittered away a fortune on gambling.*

fritter² /ˈfrɪtə(r)/ *n* (usu in compounds) a piece of fruit, meat, vegetable or other food covered in BATTER² and fried: *banana/corned-beef fritters.*

frivolous /ˈfrɪvələs/ *adj* **1** (of people, their character, etc) foolish or amusing; not serious: *frivolous comments* ○ *When we were young, we were so frivolous and carefree.* **2** having no useful or serious purpose; wasting time: *frivolous objections/criticisms/complaints* ○ *She thought that reading romantic novels was a frivolous pastime.*

▶ **frivolity** /frɪˈvɒləti/ *n* **1** [U] frivolous behaviour: *youthful frivolity.* **2** [C usu *pl*] a frivolous activity or comment: *I can't waste time on such frivolities.*
frivolously *adv.*

frizz /frɪz/ *v* to form hair into small tight curls: [Vn] *You've had your hair frizzed.*

▶ **frizz** *n* (usu *sing*) hair that is or has been tightly curled.
frizzy *adj*: *frizzy hair.*

fro /frəʊ/ *adv* **IDM** **to and fro** ⇨ TO³.

frock /frɒk/ *n* **1** (*becoming dated*) a dress worn by women or girls: *buy a new summer frock.* **2** a long loose garment with sleeves, worn by monks or priests.

■ ˈ**frock-coat** *n* a long coat worn formerly by men, now worn only on ceremonial occasions.

frog

      frog   **toad**

frog /frɒg; US frɔːg/ *n* **1** a small animal with cold blood and smooth skin that lives in or near water. It has very long back legs for jumping, and no tail. The legs of certain types of frogs are cooked and eaten as food, esp in France: *the croaking of frogs.* ⇨ picture. **2** Frog (*infml offensive*) a French person. **IDM** **have, etc a** ˈ**frog in one's throat** to lose one's voice or be unable to speak clearly for a short time.

■ **frog-spawn** /ˈfrɒgspɔːn; US ˈfrɔːg-/ *n* [U] the soft, almost transparent, jelly containing the eggs of a frog.

frogman /ˈfrɒgmən; US ˈfrɔːg-/ *n* (*pl* **-men** /-mən/) a person who swims wearing a rubber suit, flippers (FLIPPER 2) and an oxygen supply so that he or she can stay under the water: *Police frogmen searched the lake for the murder weapon.* See also DIVER.

frogmarch /ˈfrɒgmaːtʃ; US ˈfrɔːg-/ *v* to force sb to move forward with their arms held tightly together behind the back: [Vnpr] *The prisoners were frogmarched into the yard.* [also Vn, Vnp].

froing /ˈfrəʊɪŋ/ *n* **IDM** **toing and froing** ⇨ TOING.

frolic /ˈfrɒlɪk/ *v* (*pt, pp* **frolicked**) ~ (**about**) to play and move about in a lively happy way: [V, Vp] *children frolicking (about) in the swimming-pool.*

▶ **frolic** *n* [sing] a lively and enjoyable activity: *It was just a harmless frolic.*
frolicsome /-səm/ *adj* (*fml*) lively and playful: *a frolicsome kitten.*

from /frəm; *strong form* frɒm/ *prep* For the special

uses of **from** in phrasal verbs, look at the verb entries. For example, the meaning of **keep sth from sb** is given in the phrasal verb section of the entry for **keep¹**. **1** (indicating the place or direction from which sb/sth starts): *go from London to New York* ○ *a wind from the north* ○ *Has the train from Bristol arrived?* ○ *She comes home from work at 7 pm.* ○ *He fell from the seventh floor of a block of flats.* ○ *carpets stretching from wall to wall* (ie from one wall to the opposite one). **2** (indicating the time at which sth starts): *I'm on leave from June 30.* ○ *It's due to arrive an hour from now.* ○ *We lived in Scotland from 1960 to 1973.* ○ *He works from dawn till dusk.* ○ *We're open from 8 am till 7 pm every day.* ○ *He was blind from birth.* **3** (indicating who sent, gave or communicated sth): *a letter/present/phonecall from my brother* ○ *the man from* (ie representing) *the insurance company.* **4** (indicating where sb/sth originates or is stored): *I'm from New Zealand.* ○ *They come from the north.* ○ *the boy from the baker's* ○ *documents from the 16th century* ○ *famous quotations from Shakespeare* ○ *music from an opera* ○ *draw water from a well* ○ *powered by heat from the sun.* **5** (indicating distance between two places): *100 yards from the scene of the accident* ○ *It's 35 miles from Liverpool to Manchester.* ○ (*fig*) *Far from agreeing with him, I was shocked by his remarks.* **6** (indicating one limit, level or type of a range of numbers, quantities or things): *write from 10 to 15 letters daily* ○ *The temperature varies from 30 degrees to minus 20.* ○ *Our prices start from $2.50 a bottle.* ○ *The shop sells everything from shoelaces to typewriters.* **7** (indicating the state or form of sth/sb before a change): *Things have gone from bad to worse.* ○ *You need a break from routine.* ○ *translate from English to Spanish* ○ *The bus fare has gone up from 35p to 40p.* ○ *From being a librarian she is now a publisher.* **8** (indicating the material from which sth is made, the material being changed in the process): *Wine is made from grapes.* ○ *Steel is made from iron.* Compare OF 6, OUT OF 4. **9(a)** (indicating separation or removal): *separated from his mother for long periods* ○ *borrow a book from the library* ○ *release sb from prison* ○ *You can take the money from my purse.* ○ *6 from 14 leaves 8.* (**b**) (indicating that sb/sth is being protected, or that sth is being prevented): *protect children from violence* ○ *save a boy from drowning* ○ *prevent sb from sleeping* ○ *This game will stop you from getting bored.* **10** (indicating the reason for sth): *She felt sick from tiredness.* ○ *suffer from cold and hunger* ○ *She accompanied him from a sense of loyalty.* **11** (indicating the basis for making a judgement): *From the evidence we have heard so far ...* ○ *From her looks I'd say she was Scandinavian.* ○ *From what I heard last night we're going to need a new chairperson.* ○ *You can tell quite a lot from a person's handwriting.* **12** (used to make a distinction between two people, places or things): *Is Portuguese very different from Spanish?* ○ *I can't tell one twin from the other.* ○ *How do you know a fake from the original?* **13** (indicating sb's position or point of view): *Seen from above, the town covers a wide area.* ○ *From this angle it looks crooked.* ○ *From a teacher's point of view this dictionary will be very useful.* **IDM** **from ... on** starting at the specified time and continually after that: *From now on you can work on your own.* ○ *From then on she knew she would win.* ○ *She never spoke to him again from that day on.*

fromage frais /ˌfrɒmaːʒ ˈfreɪ/ *n* [U] (*French*) a type of very soft cheese, similar to YOGHURT.

frond /frɒnd/ *n* a large leaf or stem that is part of a palm² or FERN.

front /frʌnt/ *n* **1** (esp **the front**) (**a**) [C usu *sing*] the most important part or side of sth; the part or side that faces forward; the most forward part of sth: *The front of the building was covered with ivy.* ○ *Place the* *statue so that the front faces the light.* ○ *The book has the author's picture on the front.* ○ *The front of the car was badly damaged.* ○ *Several shop fronts were damaged by the explosion.* ○ *You've spilt some food down your front* (ie the clothes covering your chest). See also Y-FRONTS. (**b**) [sing] the position directly ahead of sth/sb; the most forward position or place: *Keep your eyes to the front and walk straight ahead.* ○ *The teacher made me move my seat to the front of the classroom.* ○ *There's a garden at the front of the house.* ○ *I prefer to travel in the front of the car* (ie next to the driver). Compare BACK¹ 1, REAR¹ 1. **2 the front** [sing] the road or area along the edge of the sea or a lake: *walk along the (sea) front.* See also PROMENADE. **3** [C usu *sing*] (in war) an area where fighting takes place; the furthest position that an army has reached: *be sent to/serve at the front* ○ *The army is fighting on two fronts.* **4** [sing] an outward appearance or form of behaviour that is not necessarily real or genuine: *Her rudeness is just a front (for her shyness).* ○ *put on a bold front* ○ *The prime minister stressed the need to* **present a united front** *to opposition attack* (ie act and speak as a group). **5** [C usu *sing*] ~ (**for sth**) (*infml*) a person, group or thing that serves to hide an illegal or secret activity: *The travel company is just a front for illegal drug trafficking.* **6** [C] (of weather) the forward edge of an advancing mass of warm or cold air : *A cold/warm front is moving in from the west.* **7** [C] a particular area of activity: *on the domestic/economic/education front* ○ *The government has acted swiftly on several fronts to tighten security.* **IDM back to front** ⇨ BACK¹. **in 'front before** *adv* **1** in a position further forward than but close to sb/sth: *a building with a statue in front* ○ *The children walked in twos with one teacher in front and one behind.* **2** leading or winning in a race or contest: *Car number 23 has overtaken the leader and is now in front.* Compare BEHIND². **in 'front of** *prep* **1** in a position further forward than but close to sb/sth: *The car in front of me stopped suddenly and I had to brake.* ○ *The bus stops right in front of our house.* ○ *I keep a photograph of my family in front of me on the desk.* ○ *She's entitled to put 'Professor' in front of her name.* Compare BEHIND¹. ⇨ note at BEFORE². **2** in the presence of sb: *The cheques must be signed in front of the cashier at the bank.* ○ *Please don't talk about it in front of the children.* **out 'front** in or to the part of a theatre where the audience sits. **put on, show, etc a bold/brave 'front** to try to appear brave and cheerful in order to hide one's true feelings. **up 'front** (*infml*) as payment in advance: *We'll pay you half up front and the other half when you've finished the job.*

▶ **front** *adj* [attrib] of or at the front(1): *on the front page of the newspaper* ○ *front teeth* ○ *the horse's front legs* ○ *the front wheels of the car* ○ *They keep the front room for visitors.* ○ *the front door* (ie the door that serves as the main entrance to a house) ○ *get a front seat at the theatre* (ie near and with a good view of the stage). Compare BACK² 1, REAR¹ 1, HIND¹ 1.

front *v* **1** ~ (**onto**) **sth** to have the front facing or directed towards sth; to face sth: [Vpr] *hotels that front onto the sea* [Vn] *Attractive gardens fronted the houses.* **2** (usu passive) to provide sth with a front (1a): [Vnpr] *a house fronted with Cotswold stone* ○ *a glass-fronted bookcase.* **3** (*infml*) (**a**) to act as a leader or representative of an organization: [Vn] *a company fronted by a former rock star.* (**b**) (*Brit*) to present a television programme: [Vn] *Dan Davies will front tonight's discussion on race relations.*

■ **the ˌfront 'bench** *n* [CGp] (either of the two rows of seats occupied by) the leading members of the Government and Opposition in the British Parliament: *a ˌfront-bench 'spokesman on defence.* **ˌfront-'bencher** *n* a Member of Parliament entitled to sit on the front bench. Compare THE BACK BENCH.

the ˌfront 'line *n* [sing] **1** (in war) the line of

fighting which is closest to the enemy: *Tanks are being deployed all along the front line.* ○ *ˌfront-line 'troops.* **2** the most important, advanced or responsible position: *in the front line of research.*

'front man *n* (*infml*) **1** a man who acts as the leader or representative of an organization. **2** a man who presents a television programme.

ˌfront-of-'house *n* [U] (**a**) the parts of a theatre that are used by the audience: *There was an expectant atmosphere front-of-house.* (**b**) the business of a theatre that concerns the audience, eg selling tickets and programmes: *the ˌfront-of-house 'manager.*

ˌfront-'page *adj* [attrib] interesting or important enough to be printed on the front page of a newspaper: *ˌfront-page 'news.*

ˌfront 'runner *n* the person who is leading in a race or contest, or who seems most likely to succeed or win: *He is one of the front runners in the Presidential election.*

frontage /ˈfrʌntɪdʒ/ *n* [C,U] (*fml*) the front of a building, esp a large impressive one, or in relation to the space it occupies, eg beside a road or river: *the Baroque frontage of Milan Cathedral* ○ *For sale, shop premises with frontages on two streets.* ○ *a warehouse with good river frontage.*

frontal /ˈfrʌntl/ *adj* [attrib] **1** at, from, in, or of the front: *a frontal view* ○ *a frontal attack* (ie one directed at the front or the main point) ○ *full frontal nudity* (ie showing the whole of the front of the body). **2** (*medical*) of a person's forehead: *frontal lobes.* **3** relating to a weather FRONT(6): *a cold frontal system.*

frontier /ˈfrʌntɪə(r); US frʌnˈtɪər/ *n* **1** [C] ~ (**between sth and sth**); ~ (**with sth**) the border between two countries: *the frontier between France and Switerland* ○ *a frontier zone* ○ *a frontier town* ○ *frontier disputes.* **2 the frontier** [sing] (*esp US*) the extreme limit of settled land, beyond which the country is wild and not developed: *a remote frontier settlement* ○ (*fig*) *space, the final frontier.* **3 the frontiers** [pl] the extreme limit of an area of knowledge or a particular activity: *advance the frontiers of science* ○ *expand the frontiers of legal liability.* ⇨ note at BORDER.

▶ **frontiersman** /-zmən/ *n* (*pl* **-men** /-mən/) (*US*) a man living on the frontier(2); one of the first settlers of an area.

frontispiece /ˈfrʌntɪspiːs/ *n* (usu *sing*) an illustration at the beginning of a book, on the page opposite the page with the title on it.

frost /frɒst; US frɔːst/ *n* (**a**) [U] a weather condition in which the temperature falls below freezing-point (FREEZE), accompanied by the formation of very small ice crystals: *Frost can kill young plants.* ○ *10 degrees of frost* (ie –10° Celsius). (**b**) [C] an instance or period of this: *There was a heavy/hard/sharp (ie severe) frost last night.* (**c**) [U] the small ice crystals so formed: *The car windows were covered with frost.* See also HOAR-FROST.

▶ **frost** *v* **1** ~ (**sth**) (**over/up**) to cover sth or become covered with frost: [Vnp] *The windows were all frosted up.* [V, Vp] *It was so cold that my camera lens frosted (over).* [also Vn]. **2** [Vn] (*esp US*) to decorate a cake, etc with a layer of sugar. **frosted** *adj* (esp of glass) that has been given a rough surface, so that it is difficult to see through: *frosted windows.*

frostbite /ˈfrɒstbaɪt; US ˈfrɔːst-/ *n* [U] injury, esp to the nose, fingers or toes, caused by extreme cold: *mountain climbers suffering from severe frostbite.*

▶ **'frostbitten** *adj*: suffering from frostbite.

frosting /ˈfrɒstɪŋ; US ˈfrɔːst-/ *n* [U] (*esp US*) = ICING.

frosty /ˈfrɒsti; US ˈfrɔːsti/ *adj* **1**(**a**) (of weather) very cold; cold with frost: *a frosty morning/night* ○ *The air is frosty.* (**b**) covered with frost: *frosty fields.* **2** cold and disapproving in manner; not friendly: *a* *frosty look/response/welcome.* ▶ **frostily** /-ɪli/ *adv*: *She smiled frostily.*

froth /frɒθ; US frɔ:θ/ *n* [U] **1** a mass of small bubbles, esp on the surface of a liquid: *a glass of beer with thick froth on top.* **2** (*derog*) worthless talk, ideas or activities: *the froth and gossip of TV chat shows.*
▶ **froth** *v* to have or produce froth(1): [V] *water frothing over the rocks* [Vpr] *The dog was clearly sick and **frothing at the mouth**.*
frothy *adj* **1** full of or covered with froth(1): *frothy beer* ○ *a frothy mixture of eggs and milk.* **2** (*derog*) entertaining and enjoyable, but of little value: *frothy romantic novels.* **3** (esp of clothes or fabric) light and delicate: *a frothy pink dress.*

frown /fraʊn/ *v* ~ (**at sb/sth**) to show anger, worry or deep thought by bringing one's eyebrows (EYE-BROW) together and making lines in the skin on one's forehead: [V, Vpr] *What have I done wrong? Why are you frowning (at me)?* [Vpr] *She was sitting at her desk, frowning at/over some papers.* **PHR V** **frown on/upon sb/sth** to disapprove of sb/sth: *My parents always frowned on my choice of friends.* ○ *Gambling is frowned upon by some religious groups.* ⇨ note at SMIRK.
▶ **frown** *n* a serious, angry or worried look causing lines on the forehead: *a slight frown of disapproval* ○ *She looked up with a worried frown.*

froze *pt* of FREEZE.

frozen *pp* of FREEZE: *a packet of frozen peas.*
▶ **frozen** *adj* very cold: *I feel absolutely frozen.*

fructose /ˈfrʌktəʊs, -əʊz/ *n* [U] a type of natural sugar found in eg fruit juice and honey.

frugal /ˈfruːɡl/ *adj* (**a**) using as little as possible of sth, esp money or food: *a frugal housekeeper* ○ *a very frugal existence.* (**b**) simple and plain and costing little: *a frugal meal of bread and cheese.* ▶ **frugality** /fruˈɡæləti/ *n* [U]. **frugally** /-ɡəli/ *adv*: *live frugally.*

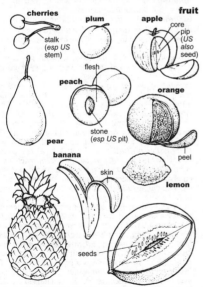

fruit

cherries

plum

apple

core
pip
(US
also
seed)

stalk
(*esp US*
stem)

flesh

peach

orange

stone
(*esp US* pit)

pear

banana

peel

skin

lemon

seeds

pineapple

melon

fruit /fruːt/ *n* **1** [C, U] the part of a plant that contains seeds and flesh and can be eaten as food; a quantity of these. Many fruits taste sweet: *tropical fruits, such as bananas and pineapples* ○ *We need to buy fruit and vegetables.* ○ *Do you prefer fresh or*

tinned fruit? ○ *dried fruit* (eg currants (CURRANT 1), etc used as food, esp in fruit cakes) ○ ˈ*fruit juice* ○ ˈ*fruit trees.* ⇨ picture. Compare VEGETABLE 1. See also KIWI FRUIT, PASSION-FRUIT. **2** [C] (*botany*) a part of a plant or tree formed after the flowers have died and in which seeds are formed. **3** [C usu *pl*] (*rhet*) any plant product used as food: *the fruits of the earth* (ie fruit, vegetables, cereals (CEREAL)). **4** (esp **the fruits** [pl]) the result or reward of some process, activity or situation: *enjoy the fruits of victory/of one's labours.* **IDM** **bear fruit** ⇨ BEAR². **forbidden fruit** ⇨ FORBID.
▶ **fruit** *v* to produce fruit: [V] *The apple trees have fruited well this year.*
■ ˈ**fruit cake** *n* [C, U] a cake containing dried fruit. **IDM** **nutty as a fruit cake** ⇨ NUT.
ˈ**fruit fly** *n* a small fly that feeds on decaying plant matter, esp fruit.
ˈ**fruit machine** (*Brit*) (also ˌone-armed ˈbandit, *esp US* ˈ**slot machine**) *n* a type of gambling machine, into which coins are inserted and which pays out money when it is operated only if certain pictures, esp of fruit, appear together.
ˌ**fruit ˈsalad** *n* [U, C] **1** a mixture of different types of fruit, cut into pieces and served as the sweet course of a meal. **2** (*US*) a dish consisting of small pieces of fruit set in jelly and served as the sweet course of a meal.

fruiterer /ˈfruːtərə(r)/ *n* (*fml esp Brit*) a person who manages a business selling fruit. Compare GREEN-GROCER.

fruitful /ˈfruːtfl/ *adj* **1** producing many good results; profitable or successful: *a fruitful experience/day's work/partnership.* **2** producing a lot of fruit. ▶ **fruitfully** /ˈfruːtfəli/ *adv*: *collaborate fruitfully with sb.* **fruitfulness** /ˈfruːtflnəs/ *n* [U].

fruition /fruˈɪʃn/ *n* [U] the successful result of a process or of sb's work, or when sb's hopes or plans are fulfilled: *After months of hard work, our plans finally **came to fruition**.*

fruitless /ˈfruːtləs/ *adj* producing little or no result; not successful: *a fruitless attempt/search* ○ *Our efforts to persuade her proved fruitless.* ▶ **fruitlessly** *adv*.

fruity /ˈfruːti/ *adj* (**-ier, -iest**) **1** like fruit in smell or taste; containing a lot of fruit: *a fruity wine* ○ *a fruity dessert.* **2** (*infml*) (of a voice) rich and deep in tone or quality. **3** (*Brit infml*) using rude language to make jokes about sex: *fruity dialogue.* **4** (*US sl*) mad; crazy.
▶ **fruitiness** *n* [U] (esp of wine) the quality of being fruity(1).

frump /frʌmp/ *n* (*derog*) a woman who wears dull old-fashioned clothes. ▶ **frumpy** (also **frumpish**) *adj*: *frumpy shoes.*

frustrate /frʌˈstreɪt; US ˈfrʌstreɪt/ *v* **1** to prevent sb from doing or achieving sth; to defeat sb: [Vn] *She had hoped to set a new world record, but was frustrated by bad weather.* ○ *He attempted to frustrate his political opponents by denying them access to the media.* **2** to upset or discourage sb: [Vn] *She was frustrated by the lack of appreciation shown of her work.*
▶ **frustrated** *adj* **1** [pred] ~ (**at/with sth**) discouraged; not satisfied: *As a nurse she got very frustrated, but being an administrator seems to suit her.* ○ *They felt angry and frustrated at/with the lack of progress.* **2** [attrib] unable to be successful in one's chosen career: *Film directors are sometimes frustrated actors.* **3** not satisfied sexually.
frustrating *adj* annoying; discouraging: *I find it frustrating that I don't speak Spanish very well.* **frustratingly** *adv*: *Progress was frustratingly slow.*
frustration /frʌˈstreɪʃn/ *n* **1** [U] the feeling of being frustrated: *mounting anger and frustration* ○ *He thumped the table **in frustration**.* **2** [C usu *pl*] a

thing that makes one feel frustrated; a disappointment: *Every job has its frustrations.*

fry¹ /fraɪ/ *v* (*pt, pp* **fried** /fraɪd/) to cook sth in very hot fat or oil: [Vn] *fried chicken* [V] *the smell of bacon frying* . ⇨ note at COOK. See also STIR-FRY. **IDM** **have bigger/other fish to fry** ⇨ FISH¹.
■ **'frying-pan** (*US* also **'fry-pan, skillet**) *n* a flat shallow pan with a long handle, used for frying food. ⇨ picture at PAN¹. **IDM** **out of the 'frying-pan into the 'fire** from a bad situation to one that is worse.
'fry-up (*Brit*) a meal of fried food, such as bacon and eggs: *We always have a fry-up for Saturday lunch.*

fry² /fraɪ/ *n* [pl] young fishes, esp ones that have just come out of their eggs. See also SMALL FRY.

fryer (also **frier**) /'fraɪə(r)/ *n* **1** a large deep pan for frying food: *deep-fat fryers.* **2** (*esp US*) a small young chicken suitable for frying.

ft *abbr* (also *symb* ') feet; foot: *11 ft × (ie by) 6 ft (11'× 6').* Compare IN⁴, YD.

fuchsia /'fju:ʃə/ *n* [C,U] a small bush with red, purple or white flowers that hang down.

fuck /fʌk/ *v* (△ *sl*) **1** [V, Vn] to have sex with sb. **2** (used as an *interj* expressing extreme anger, annoyance or disgust): [V, Vn] *Fuck (it)!* [Vn] *Fuck you — I'm leaving.* **PHRV** **,fuck a'bout/a'round** to behave foolishly or with no clear purpose; to mess about (MESS¹): *Stop fucking around and come and give me a hand.* **,fuck sb a'bout/a'round** to treat sb badly or to waste their time; to mess sb about (MESS¹): *This damn company keeps fucking me about.* **,fuck 'off** (esp imperative) to go away. **,fuck (sth) 'up** to spoil or ruin sth; to do sth wrongly.
▶ **fuck** *n* (△ *sl*) **1** [C usu *sing*] an act of sex(2). **2** **the fuck** [sing] (used for emphasis, or to express anger, annoyance or surprise): *What the fuck are you doing?!* ○ *Let's get the fuck out of here!* **IDM** **not care/give a 'fuck (about sb/sth)** to have no concern or regard for sb/sth: *He doesn't give a fuck about anyone else.*
fucker *n* (△ *sl*) (used as a general insult) a stupid person; a fool.
fucking (△ *sl*) *adj, adv* (used to add emphasis in expressions of anger or annoyance): *I'm fucking sick of the whole fucking lot of you!* **IDM** **'fucking well** (used to emphasize an angry statement, esp an order) certainly; definitely: *You're fucking well coming whether you want to or not.*
■ **,fuck 'all** *n* [U] (*Brit* △ *sl*) nothing at all: *You've done fuck 'all today.*

fuddled /'fʌdld/ *adj* confused as a result of drinking alcohol: *His mind was fuddled with gin.*

fuddy-duddy /'fʌdi dʌdi/ *n* (*infml derog or joc*) a person who has old-fashioned ideas or habits: *fuddy-duddy ideas* ○ *You're such an old fuddy-duddy!*

fudge¹ /fʌdʒ/ *n* [U] a soft sweet made from sugar, butter and milk, often with other things added to give flavour: *chocolate/walnut fudge.*

fudge² /fʌdʒ/ *v* (*infml*) to say or do sth in a VAGUE (1b) or inadequate way, usu deliberately, so as to mislead sb or to avoid making a definite choice: [V, Vn] *Politicians are quite adept at fudging (the issue).* ▶ **fudge** *n* [C, U]: *the woolly language and fudge of the policy review.*

fuel /'fju:əl/ *n* [U,C] (**a**) any material burned to produce heat or power, eg wood, coal or oil: *a car with high fuel consumption.* (**b**) a material that produces nuclear energy. See also FOSSIL FUEL. **IDM** **add fuel to the flames** ⇨ ADD.
▶ **fuel** *v* (**-ll-**; *US* **-l-**) **1** ~ (**sth**) (**up**) to supply sth or be supplied with fuel: [Vn] *an engine fuelled by paraffin* [V, Vp] *All aircraft must fuel (up) before a long flight.* [also Vnp]. **2** to increase the amount or intensity of sth: [Vn] *These reports have fuelled speculation about a royal marriage.* ○ *inflation fuelled by big wage increases.*

■ **'fuel injection** *n* [U] the direct introduction of fuel under pressure into a car engine as a way of improving the performance of the car.

fug /fʌg/ *n* (*Brit infml*) (usu *sing*) an unpleasant atmosphere in a room, etc that is hot or crowded or contains people smoking: *a fug of cigarette smoke.*

fugitive /'fju:dʒətɪv/ *n* ~ (**from sb/sth**) a person who has escaped from a place or is trying to avoid being arrested: *a fugitive from justice.*
▶ **fugitive** *adj* [attrib] **1** escaping; trying to avoid being arrested: *a fugitive offender.* **2** (*fml*) lasting only a very short time: *fugitive thoughts/images.*

fugue /fju:g/ *n* a musical composition in which one or more themes are introduced and then repeated in a complex pattern.

-ful *suff* **1** (with *ns* and *vs* forming *adjs*) full of sth; having qualities of sth; often doing sth: *beautiful* ○ *masterful* ○ *forgetful.* **2** (with *ns* forming *ns*) an amount that fills sth: *handful* ○ *mouthful* ○ *spoonful.*

fulcrum /'folkrəm, 'fʌlk-/ *n* (*pl* **fulcrums** or **fulcra** /'folkrə, 'fʌlk-/) **1** (*physics*) the point on which a LEVER(1) turns or is supported. ⇨ picture at LEVER. **2** (usu *sing*) the central or most important part of an activity, an event or a situation: *the fulcrum of the whole debate.*

fulfil (also **fulfill**) /fol'fɪl/ *v* (**-ll-**) **1** to achieve sth or correspond to sth that was expected or desired: [Vn] *fulfil sb's needs/dreams/expectations* ○ *a promising young player who never really fulfilled his potential/ ambitions.* **2** to do sth that one is expected or required to do: [Vn] *fulfil a duty/command/promise* ○ *You must fulfil the terms of your contract.* **3** to satisfy the specific requirements of sth: [Vn] *fulfil the conditions of entry to a university.* **4** ~ **oneself** to develop one's abilities and character fully: [Vn] *He was able to fulfil himself through music.*
▶ **fulfilled** *adj* satisfied; completely happy: *He doesn't feel fulfilled in his present job.*
fulfilling *adj* making sb satisfied or completely happy: *a fulfilling job/marriage.*
fulfilment *n* [U]: *find emotional/personal fulfilment.*

full /fol/ *adj* (**-er, -est**) **1** ~ (**of sth/sb**) (**a**) containing as much or as many as possible; completely filled: *a full bottle of milk* ○ *My cup is full.* ○ *The cupboard was stuffed full of old newspapers.* ○ *This bus is full — you'll have to wait for the next one.* ⇨ note at EMPTY¹. (**b**) containing much or many; crowded: *a lake full of fish* ○ *a room full of people* ○ *The book is full of interesting facts.* **2** [pred] ~ **of sth** (**a**) having a lot of a certain quality: *She's full of vitality.* ○ *The city is full of interest for tourists.* (**b**) completely occupied in thinking about sth: *She was full of the news (ie could not stop herself talking about it).* **3** having had enough to eat and drink: *No more thanks, I'm full/full 'up.* **4** [attrib] (**a**) complete; plenty of sth: *give full information/details/instructions* ○ *We need your fullest cooperation.* (**b**) (often used for emphasis) complete; maximum; to the greatest possible extent: *a full member of the club* ○ *a catalogue in full colour* ○ *pay the full cost of tuition* ○ *The roses are in full bloom.* ○ *He got full marks (ie the highest marks possible) for his essay.* ○ *What is your full name?* ⇨ note at NAME¹. (**c**) (used to emphasize an amount or quantity): *I had to wait a full hour for the bus.* ○ *Her dress was a full three inches above the knee.* **5** involving a lot of activities or interest: *lead a full life* ○ *The manager has a very full schedule.* **6** [usu attrib] rather fat and round: (*euph*) *dresses for women with a fuller figure.* **7** (of clothes) fitting loosely or made with plenty of material: *a full skirt* ○ *Please make this coat a little fuller across the back.* **8** (of a tone or voice) deep and rich. **IDM** **at full 'stretch** to the limit of one's ability or resources: *working at full stretch.* **be at full / be below strength** ⇨ STRENGTH. **come full 'circle** to return to the situation from which one started, after a series of events or experiences. **draw oneself up / rise to one's full** '**height** to stand straight and tall in order to show one's determination or superior status. **(at) full** '**blast** with maximum noise, energy or power: *a radio playing at full blast* ○ *He had the gas fire on full blast*. **full of** '**beans/'life** having a lot of energy; very lively and cheerful. **full of the joys of** '**spring** lively and cheerful. **full** '**length** with the body stretched out and flat: *lying full length on the sofa*. **full/short measure** ⇨ MEASURE². '**full of oneself** (*derog*) very proud and thinking only of oneself: *You're very full of yourself today, I must say*. **full of one's own im**'**portance** (*derog*) thinking that one is very important. **(at) full** '**pelt/full'speed** with great speed or force: *He drove full tilt into the lamppost*. **full speed/steam a'head** with as much speed and vigour as possible. **give, etc free/full rein to sb/sth** ⇨ REIN. **have, receive, etc one's/the full** '**measure** of sth to have, etc the greatest possible amount or share of sth: *achieve the full measure of freedom*. **have one's hands full** ⇨ HAND¹. **in** '**full** completely; with nothing omitted: *write one's name in full* (eg John Henry Smith, *not* J H Smith). **in full** '**cry** talking or shouting continuously and enthusiastically: *The Leeds supporters were in full cry*. **in full** '**measure** to a great extent: *She displays these qualities in full measure*. **in/under full** '**sail** (of a ship) with all the sails in position and fully spread. **in full** '**spate** completely involved in sth and likely to continue for a long time: *I arrived when the speaker was already in full spate*. **in full** '**swing** at a very busy or lively stage: *The party was in full swing when we arrived*. **in full** '**view (of sb/sth)** completely visible; in front of sb/sth: *He was savagely beaten in full view of crowds leaving the cinema*. **to the** '**full** to the greatest possible extent: *enjoy life to the full*.

▶ **full** *adv* **1** exactly; directly: *She hit/looked him full in the face*. **2** very: *as you know full well*.

fullness *n* [U, sing] the state of being full: *the fullness of life* ○ *the rounded fullness of her figure*. **IDM** **in the fullness of** '**time** at the appropriate or right time; eventually: *In the fullness of time you will marry and have children*.

fully *adv* **1** completely; entirely: *fully satisfied/developed/clothed* ○ *I was fully expecting to lose my job this month*. **2** (*fml*) (used to emphasize an amount or extent) the whole of; as much as: *The disease affects fully 30 per cent of the population*.

,**fully-**'**fledged** *adj* (*Brit*) (*US* ,**full-**'**fledged**) **1** completely developed or established: *Computer science is now a fully-fledged academic subject*. **2** (of a young bird) having grown all its feathers.

■ '**full back** *n* a defensive player in football, hockey, etc whose position is near the goal.

,**full-**'**blooded** *adj* strong, active or vigorous: *a ,full-blooded and ,passionate 'socialist*.

,**full-**'**blown** *adj* fully developed; having all the characteristics of sth: *He has some symptoms, but not yet the ,full-blown di'sease*. ○ *The border dispute has turned into a ,full-blown 'crisis*.

,**full** '**board** *n* [U] the providing of a bed and all meals, eg in a hotel: *Prices start at £60 per person per night (for) full board*. Compare HALF BOARD.

,**full-**'**bodied** *adj* rich in quality or tone: *a full-bodied red wine*.

,**full-**'**colour** *adj* printed or shown entirely in colour, using all colours, not just black and white: *a ,full-colour 'photograph/'brochure*.

,**full-**'**dress** *adj* [attrib] of major importance; on the largest possible scale: *the first ,full-dress meeting of the new* '**Cabinet**.

,**full-**'**fat** *adj* (of milk, cheese, etc) having none of the cream removed: *,full-fat 'yoghurt*.

,**full-**'**fledged** *adj* (*US*) = FULLY-FLEDGED.

,**full-**'**grown** *adj* (of a person, an animal or a plant)

having reached the maximum or mature size: *a ,full-grown 'adult*.

,**full** '**house** *n* [usu *sing*] a theatre, cinema or hall with all its seats occupied: *We have a full house tonight*.

,**full-**'**length** *adj* (**a**) of the usual length; not made shorter: *a ,full-length 'novel*. (**b**) (of a picture or mirror) showing the whole human figure. (**c**) extending to the ground: *,full length 'curtains* ○ *a ,full-length 'skirt* (ie one that reaches the ankles).

,**full** '**moon** *n* [U, C] the moon when it appears as a whole bright disc; a time when this occurs. Compare NEW MOON.

,**full** '**page** *adj* filling a complete page: *a ,full-page ad'vertisement*.

,**full-**'**scale** *adj* [attrib] **1** of the greatest importance or extent; complete and thorough: *a ,full-scale reorgani'zation of the department*. **2** not reduced in size; the same size as the object itself: *a ,full-scale 'drawing/'plan/'model*.

'**full-size** (also '**full-sized**) *adj* = FULL-SCALE.

,**full** '**stop** (*US* **period**) *n* **1** a mark (.) used at the end of a sentence. ⇨ App 3. **2** (*infml*) (used when stating a fact or an opinion to indicate that there is no need for further discussion): *I just think he is very unpleasant, full stop*. **IDM** **come to a full** '**stop** to stop completely: *The car came to a full stop at the traffic lights*.

,**full-**'**throated** *adj* shouted or sung loudly, with great force: *a ,full-throated 'roar/'cheer*.

,**full** '**time** *n* [U] the end of a game of football, etc.

,**full-**'**time** *adj* for or during the whole of the working day or week: *a ,full-time 'job*. Compare PART-TIME — *adv*: *,work full-'time*. ,**full-**'**timer** *n* a person who works full-time.

fuller's earth /,fʊləz 'ɜːθ/ *n* [U] a type of clay used for cleaning newly woven cloth and making it thicker.

fulminate /'fʊlmɪneɪt, 'fʌl-/ *v* ~ (**against sb/sth**) to protest strongly and loudly: [Vpr] *newspapers fulminating against the government's incompetence* [also V]. ▶ **fulmination** /,fʊlmɪ'neɪʃn, ,fʌl-/ *n* [C, U].

fulsome /'fʊlsəm/ *adj* (*often derog*) (esp of speech or writing) having or showing a quality, eg length, detail or praise, to a great or excessive degree: *fulsome words/compliments/explanations* ○ *be fulsome in one's praise*. ▶ **fulsomely** *adv*.

fumble /'fʌmbl/ *v* **1(a)** ~ (**for/with sth**) to use the hands in an awkward way while doing sth or looking for sth: [Vpr] *fumble in one's pocket for some coins* ○ *fumble for the light switch* ○ *She fumbled with her notes and began to speak*. ○ (*fig*) *fumble for the right thing to say* [also V]. (**b**) ~ **about/around** to move about in an awkward way while doing sth or looking for sth, esp using the hands: [Vp] *fumbling around in the dark*. **2** to fail to hold or catch sth properly: [Vn] *He fumbled the ball and dropped it*. ○ *a fumbled catch* [also V].

▶ **fumble** *n* [sing] (also **fumbling** [C usu *pl*]) an act of fumbling.

fumbling *adj* awkward, uncertain or hesitating: *our first fumbling efforts at using the computer*.

fume /fjuːm/ *n* (usu *pl*) smoke, gas or sth similar that smells strongly or is dangerous to breathe in: *petrol/diesel/exhaust fumes* ○ *The air was thick with poisonous/sulphurous fumes*.

▶ **fume** *v* **1** ~ (**at/over sb/sth**) to be very angry; to show this anger: [Vpr] *The passengers were fuming at the delay*. [V.speech] *'He should have told me!' she fumed*. [also V]. **2** to treat wood with chemical fumes to make it darker: [Vn] *fumed oak*.

fumigate /'fjuːmɪɡeɪt/ *v* to destroy infectious germs (GERM 1) or insects in sth or in a place, using the fumes (FUME) of certain chemicals: *The hospital wards were fumigated after the outbreak of typhus*. ▶ **fumigation** /,fjuːmɪ'ɡeɪʃn/ *n* [U].

fun /fʌn/ n [U] **1(a)** enjoyment; pleasure: *We had lots of fun at the fair today.* ∘ *It took all the fun out of the occasion when we heard that you were ill.* ∘ *What fun it will be when we all go camping together!* ∘ *Have fun (ie Enjoy yourself)!* ∘ *I'm teaching myself to cook, just for fun/for the fun of it.* **(b)** a source of this: *Sailing is (good/great) fun.* ∘ *It's not much fun going to a party alone.* ∘ *We didn't mean to hurt him. It was just a bit of fun.* **2** playful behaviour; good humour: *She's very lively and full of fun.* ∘ *He only said it for fun (ie as a joke) — he didn't really mean it.* **IDM** **be/ become a figure of fun** ⇨ FIGURE¹. **fun and 'games** (*infml*) amusing and enjoyable activities: *That's enough fun and games! Let's get down to work.* **make 'fun of sb/sth** to laugh at sb/sth, or to cause people to laugh at them/it, usu in an unkind way: *It's cruel to make fun of people who stammer.* **poke fun at sb/sth** ⇨ POKE¹.

▶ **fun** adj (*infml*) amusing; providing pleasure: *a fun idea* ∘ *She's really fun to be with.*

■ **'fun-loving** adj enjoying and seeking pleasure; happy and lively.

function /'fʌŋkʃn/ n **1** a special activity or purpose of a person or thing: *fulfil a useful function* ∘ *bodily functions (eg eating, sex, going to the toilet)* ∘ *The function of the heart is to pump blood through the body.* ∘ *It is not the function of this committee to deal with dismissals.* **2** an important social event or official ceremony: *Heads of state attend numerous functions every year.* **3** (*mathematics*) a quantity whose value depends on the varying values of others: (*fig*) *Salary is a function of age and experience.* **4** any of the basic operations of a computer: *function keys* ∘ *What functions can this program perform?*

▶ **function** v **1** to work; to operate: [V] *His brain seems to be functioning normally.* ∘ *This machine has stopped functioning (ie is out of order).* ∘ *the only functioning hotel in the war-torn city.* **2** ~ **as sth** to work or operate as sth; to perform the function(1) of the thing specified: [V-n] *The sofa can also function as a bed.* ∘ *Some English adverbs function as adjectives.*

functional /-ʃənl/ adj **1** practical and useful; having or providing little or no decoration: *functional furniture/clothing/architecture* ∘ *The hotel room was functional rather than luxurious.* **2** of or having a function(1) or functions: *a functional disorder (ie an illness caused when an organ of the body fails to perform its function)* ∘ *There are functional differences between the French and American presidencies.* ∘ *These units played a key functional role in the military operation.* **3** working; able to work: *The machine is now fully functional.* ∘ (*joc*) *I'm hardly functional if I don't get eight hours' sleep!* **functionality** /-'næləti/ n [U]. **functionally** /-ʃənəli/ adv.

functionalism /'fʌŋkʃənəlɪzəm/ n [U] (*esp architecture*) the principle that the purpose and use of an object should determine its shape and design. ▶ **functionalist** /-ʃənəlɪst/ n, adj.

functionary /'fʌŋkʃənəri; US -neri/ n (*often derog*) a person with official duties: *a minor functionary.*

fund /fʌnd/ n **1** [C] a sum of money saved or made available for a particular purpose: *a disaster relief fund* ∘ *the church restoration fund* ∘ *the International Monetary Fund* ∘ *a pension fund.* **2** [sing] a stock or supply of sth: *a fund of jokes/knowledge/experience.* **3 funds** [pl] financial resources: *government funds* ∘ *The hospital is trying to raise funds for a new kidney machine.* ∘ *I'm short of funds so I'll pay you back next week.*

▶ **fund** v **1** to provide sth, esp an institution or a project, with money: [Vn] *The government is funding another employment programme.* ∘ *a privately funded hospital.* See also FINANCE v. **2** (*finance*) to extend a debt over a long period at a fixed rate of interest.

funding n [U] (the providing of) funds (FUND 3) for sth: *Do you approve of state funding for the arts?*

■ **'fund-raiser** /-reizə(r)/ n **(a)** a person who seeks financial support for a cause or an organization. **(b)** a social event or an entertainment held in order to obtain such financial support.

'fund-raising n [U]: *The festival will be financed by local fund-raising.* ∘ *fund-raising activities/events/ efforts.*

fundamental /ˌfʌndəˈmentl/ adj **1(a)** very important or serious: *There are fundamental 'differences between these two government departments.* **(b)** most important; central or primary: *His fundamental concern was for her welfare.* ∘ *The fundamental question is a political one.* **(c)** that need to be known or learned first: *the fundamental rules of mathematics.* **(d)** ~ **(to sth)** essential or basic: *Hard work is fundamental to success.* **2** [attrib] (*physics*) from which everything else is made; that cannot be divided any further: *fundamental 'particles.*

▶ **fundamental** n (usu pl) a basic rule or principle; an essential part: *learn the fundamentals of geometry.*

fundamentally /-təli/ adv in the most important or essential aspects: *Her ideas are fundamentally sound, even if she sometimes says silly things.*

fundamentalism /ˌfʌndəˈmentəlɪzəm/ n [U] **1** (in Christian thought) the belief that everything in the Bible is true and should form the basis of religious thought or practice. **2** the strict following of the basic teaching of any religion. ▶ **fundamentalist** /-ɪst/ n, adj: *fundamentalist ideas/sects.*

funeral /'fju:nərəl/ n the usu religious ceremony of burying or burning a dead person: *I went to/ attended his funeral.* ∘ *'funeral rites* ∘ *a 'funeral procession* ∘ *a 'funeral march (ie a sad and solemn piece of music suitable for funerals).* **IDM** **it's/that's 'my, 'your, etc funeral** (*infml*) it's/that's my, your, etc particular and unpleasant responsibility, and no one else's: *'You're going to fail your exams if you don't work hard.' 'That's 'my funeral.'*

▶ **funerary** /'fju:nərəri/ adj [attrib] (*fml*) of or used at a funeral or funerals: *funerary rites* ∘ *a funerary urn.*

funereal /fju:ˈnɪəriəl/ adj suitable for a funeral; miserable: *a funereal expression/atmosphere* ∘ *walk at a funereal pace (ie very slowly).*

■ **'funeral director** n = UNDERTAKER.

'funeral parlour (*Brit*) (*US* **'funeral home**) n a place where dead people are prepared for burial or cremation (CREMATE) and (in the USA) where visitors can view the body.

funfair /'fʌnfeə(r)/ n = FAIR³ 1.

fungicide /'fʌŋgɪsaɪd, 'fʌndʒɪ-/ n [C, U] a substance that kills FUNGUS.

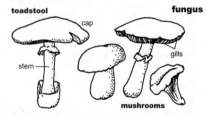

toadstool   fungus
cap
gills
stem
mushrooms

fungus /'fʌŋgəs/ n (pl fungi /'fʌŋgiː, -gaɪ, 'fʌndʒaɪ/ or funguses /'fʌŋgəsɪz/) **1** [C often pl] any of various types of plant without leaves or flowers and containing no green colouring. Fungi usually grow on other plants or on decaying matter. MILDEW and mushrooms (MUSHROOM) are examples of fungi: *The lawn was covered with fungi.* ⇨ picture. **2** [U, C] a covering or layer of MILDEW, mould or a similar

fungus, eg on a plant or wall. Fungus is often harmful: *The roses have fungus.* ○ *'fungus infections.*
▶ **fungal** /'fʌŋgl/ *adj* of, like or caused by fungus: *fungal diseases.*
fungoid /'fʌŋgɔɪd/ *adj* of or like a fungus: *fungoid growths.*

funicular /fjuː'nɪkjələ(r)/ (also **funicular railway**) *n* a railway on a steep slope, with some carriages being pulled up by a cable at the same time as others are lowered by it.

funk /fʌŋk/ *n* **1** [U] (*sl*) a type of modern dance music with a strong rhythm, sung or played mainly by black people. **2** (also ,blue 'funk) [sing] (*dated infml*) a state of fear or anxiety: *She was in a funk about changing jobs.*
▶ **funky** /'fʌŋki/ *adj* (**-ier, -iest**) (*sl*) **1** (of pop music) having a strong rhythm. **2** (*approv esp US*) very modern; fashionable.

funnel /'fʌnl/ *n* **1** a tube or pipe that is wide at the top and narrow at the bottom, used for pouring liquids or powders into a small opening: *I need a funnel to pour gasoline into the tank.* ○ picture at FILTER. **2** a metal chimney on eg a ship or an engine, through which smoke escapes.
▶ **funnel** *v* (**-ll-**; *US* **-l-**) to move or make sth move through a funnel(1) or a narrow space: [Vnpr] *funnel petrol into a can* ○ (*fig*) *The money is being funnelled through a secret bank account.* [Vpr] *The water funnelled through the gorge and out onto the plain.*

funny /'fʌni/ *adj* (**-ier, -iest**) **1** causing amusement or laughter: *funny stories* ○ *a funny man* ○ *That's the funniest thing I've ever heard.* ○ *I've been stuck in a lift myself and I can tell you, it isn't funny* (ie it is unpleasant)*!* **2** difficult to explain or understand; strange: *A funny thing happened to me today.* ○ *That's funny — he was here a moment ago and now he's gone.* ○ *It's funny how it always rains on my birthday.* ○ *The engine's making a funny noise.* **3** (*infml*) (**a**) slightly ill: *I feel a little funny today — I don't think I'll go to work.* ○ *That drink has made me feel quite funny.* (**b**) slightly ill in the mind; behaving in a strange way: *a funny old lady* ○ *She went funny after her husband died.* **IDM** 'funny business (*infml*) behaviour or activities that are illegal, suspicious or not approved of: *I want none of your funny business.*
▶ **funnily** /-ɪli/ *adv* in a strange or odd way. **IDM** funnily e'nough (used to express surprise about sth that might not have been expected): *Funnily enough* (ie It so happened that) *I met her only yesterday.*
■ 'funny-bone *n* the part of the elbow which has a very sensitive nerve, and which tingles (TINGLE 1) in an unpleasant way when it is knocked.

fur /fɜː(r)/ *n* **1** [U] soft thick hair covering the bodies of certain animals: *The kittens don't have much fur yet.* **2**(**a**) [U, C] an animal skin with fur on, esp as used for making clothes: *a coat made of fox fur* ○ *These bears are often hunted for their furs.* ○ *fur-lined boots.* (**b**) [C] a garment made of fur: *elegant ladies in furs.* (**c**) [U] a fabric made to look and feel like fur. **3** [U] a layer that forms on a person's tongue during illness. **4** [U] (*Brit*) (*US* **scale**) a hard grey layer that forms on the inside of a KETTLE or pipes, caused by water that contains LIME¹.
▶ **furred** /fɜːd/ *adj* covered with fur or sth resembling fur: *a furred tongue/kettle.*
furry /'fɜːri/ *adj* (**-ier, -iest**) **1** covered with fur: *a furry animal.* **2** like fur: *The moss was soft and furry to the touch.*

furious /'fjʊəriəs/ *adj* **1** ~ (with sb); ~ (at sth/sb) very angry: *She was absolutely furious (at his behaviour).* **2** violent; intense: *a furious storm/struggle/debate* ○ *She drove off at a furious speed.* **IDM** fast and furious ⇨ FAST¹. ▶ **furiously** *adv*: *blushing/working furiously.*

furl /fɜːl/ *v* [Vn, Vp] to roll and fasten sth, eg a sail, a flag or an UMBRELLA(1).

furlong /'fɜːlɒŋ; *US* -lɔːŋ/ *n* (esp in horse-racing) a distance of 220 yards or 201 metres; one eighth (EIGHT) of a mile. ⇨ App 2.

furlough /'fɜːləʊ/ *n* [C,U] a period of absence from duty, or permission for such absence, esp as given to civil servants (CIVIL) or soldiers working abroad: *six months' furlough* ○ *going home on furlough.*

furnace /'fɜːnɪs/ *n* **1** an enclosed space or room for heating eg metal or glass to a very high temperature: *It's like a furnace* (ie very hot) *in here — can we open a window?* See also BLAST-FURNACE. **2** an enclosed fireplace for heating the water used to heat a building by means of pipes.

furnish /'fɜːnɪʃ/ *v* **1** ~ sth (with sth) to provide sth with furniture; to put furniture in a place: *furnish a house/a room/an office* [Vnadv] *a comfortably/beautifully/sparsely furnished bedroom* [Vn] *a furnished house* (ie one rented complete with its furniture) [Vnpr] *The room was furnished with antiques.* [V] *furnishing fabric* (ie for making curtains or chair covers). **2** ~ sb/sth with sth ; ~ sth (to sb/sth) (*rather fml*) to supply or provide sb/sth with sth: [Vn] *furnish all the equipment for a major expedition* [Vnpr] *furnish a community with supplies/furnish supplies to a community* ○ *The lawyers have been furnished with all the necessary information.*
▶ **furnishings** *n* [pl] the furniture, fittings, carpets or curtains in a room or house: *soft furnishings* ○ *The wallpaper should match the furnishings.*

furniture /'fɜːnɪtʃə(r)/ *n* [U] movable articles, eg tables, chairs or beds, put into a house or an office to make it suitable for living or working in: *a piece of furniture* ○ *office/garden furniture.*

furore /fjuː'rɔːri; 'fjʊərɔː(r); *US* 'fjʊərɔːr/ (also *esp US* **furor** /'fjʊərɔːr/) *n* [sing] a display of great anger or excitement shown by a number of people, usu caused by some public event: *His novel about Jesus created/caused a furore among Christians.* ○ *once the furore over the factory closures had died down.*

furred ⇨ FUR.

furrier /'fʌrɪə(r)/ *n* a person who prepares or sells fur or fur clothing.

furrow /'fʌrəʊ/ *n* **1** a long narrow cut or channel in the earth, made esp by a plough: *furrows ready for planting.* Compare RIDGE 1. ⇨ picture at PLOUGH. **2** a deep line or fold in the skin of the face; a WRINKLE (1): *Deep furrows lined his brow.*
▶ **furrow** *v* (esp passive) to make furrows in sth: [Vn] *newly furrowed fields* ○ *She had a furrowed brow* (ie looked worried).

furry ⇨ FUR.

further /'fɜːðə(r)/ *adv* **1** at or to a greater distance in space or time; more remote; farther: *It's not safe to go any further.* ○ *Africa is further from England than France is.* ○ *The hospital is further down the road.* ○ *Can you stand a bit further away/back?* ○ *Think further back into your childhood.* **2** to a greater degree or extent: *I must enquire further into this matter.* ○ *I can offer you $50, but I can't go any further than that.* **3** in addition; also: *Further, it has come to my attention...* **IDM** far/farther/further afield ⇨ AFIELD. ○ note at FARTHER.
▶ **further** *adj* additional; more: *There are two further volumes to be published.* ○ *Have you any further questions?* ○ *There is nothing further to be said.* ○ *The museum is closed until further notice* (ie until another announcement about it is made). ,further edu'cation *n* [U] (*Brit*) formal education, but not at a university, provided for people who are older than school age.
further *v* to help the progress or development of sth: [Vn] *further sb's interests* ○ *further the cause of peace.*

furtherance /'fɜːðərəns/ *n* [U] (*fml*) the process of

helping the progress or development of sth: *a reasonable measure in the furtherance of the public interest.*

furthermore /ˌfɜːðə'mɔː(r)/ *adv* in addition; as well as what has just been said.

furthest /ˈfɜːðɪst/ *adj, adv* = FARTHEST. ⇨ note at FARTHER.

furtive /ˈfɜːtɪv/ *adj* (**a**) done secretly and quietly so as not to be noticed: *a furtive glance* ∘ *furtive movements.* (**b**) (of people or their behaviour) nervous or attracting suspicion; suggesting that one is guilty of sth or does not want to be noticed. ▸ **furtively** *adv.* **furtiveness** *n* [U].

fury /ˈfjʊərɪ/ *n* (**a**) [U] wild and often violent anger: *speechless with fury.* (**b**) [sing] an instance of this: *She flew into a fury when I refused to lend her any money.* **2** [U] the strength or violence of an activity or of the weather: *There was no shelter from the fury of the storm.* **3 the Furies** [pl] (in Greek myths) goddesses (GODDESS 1) with snakes instead of hair, sent to punish crime. **IDM** **like fury** (*infml*) with great effort, speed, etc: *He ran like fury to catch the bus.*

fuse[1] /fjuːz/ *n* **1** (in an electrical circuit) a short piece of wire that melts and breaks the circuit if the current goes above a safe level: *a 13-amp fuse* ∘ *fuse wire* ∘ *It looks as though you've blown a fuse* (ie causing an electrical appliance to stop working). **2** a piece of easily burnt material, eg rope or paper, along which a small flame moves to light eg a FIREWORK or bomb so that it explodes. **3** (*US* also **fuze** /fjuːz/) a device that makes a bomb or shell explode either when it hits sth or at a particular time: *The bomb had been set with a four-hour fuse.* **IDM** **have / be on a short fuse** ⇨ SHORT[1].
▸ **fuse** *v* **1** to stop or make sth stop working because a fuse[1](1) melts: [V] *The lights have all fused.* [Vn] *I've fused all the lights.* **2** [Vn] (usu passive) to put a fuse[1](1) in a circuit or an appliance.
■ **'fuse-box** *n* a small box or cupboard containing the fuses (FUSE[1] 1) of an electrical system.

fuse[2] /fjuːz/ *v* ~ (**sth**) **with sth**; ~ (**A and B**) (**into sth / together**) **1** to join together, or to make things join together, to form a single thing: [V, Vp] *The particles fuse (together) to form a single molecule.* [Vnpr, Vn] *a composer who fuses classical music with/and jazz.* **2** to join sth or become joined by means of heat: [Vn, Vnpr] *fuse metals (into a solid mass)* [Vnp] *fuse two pieces of wire together.*

fuselage /ˈfjuːzəlɑːʒ; *US* ˈfjuːsəlɑːʒ/ *n* the body of a plane, ie the part to which the engine, wings and tail are fitted. ⇨ picture at AIRCRAFT.

fusillade /ˌfjuːzə'leɪd; *US* -sə-/ *n* **1** a series of shots from a gun or guns fired all at once or in quick succession. **2** a series of eg explosions or things thrown in quick succession: (*fig*) *He had to face a fusillade of questions from journalists.*

fusion /ˈfjuːʒn/ *n* [U, sing] **1** the fusing (FUSE[2]) of different things into one, eg by melting: *the fusion of copper and zinc to produce brass* ∘ (*fig*) *a fusion of ideas.* **2** [U] (*physics*) the union of atomic nuclei (NUCLEUS 1b) to form a heavier nucleus, usu with energy being released: *nuclear fusion* ∘ *fusion energy.* **3** [U, sing] music that is a mixture of different styles: *The band plays rock, jazz and fusion.*

fuss /fʌs/ *n* **1**(**a**) [U] nervous excitement or activity, esp of an unnecessary kind: *Stop all this fuss and get on with your work.* ∘ *He does what he's told without any fuss.* (**b**) [sing] a display of excitement, worry or enthusiasm, esp over sth unimportant: *Don't get into a fuss about nothing.* ∘ *It's a very ordinary film — I don't know what all the fuss is about* (ie why other people think it is very good or unusual). **2** [sing] a situation in which sb gets angry or complains: *There will be a real fuss if you're caught stealing.* ∘

She's making an awful fuss about the high rent. **IDM** **make a fuss of/over sb/sth** to pay particular and often excessive attention to sb/sth: *Don't make so much fuss over details/the children.* ∘ *The cat loves being made a fuss of.*
▸ **fuss** *v* **1** ~ (**about**); ~ **about/over/with sth** to be worried or excited, esp over unimportant things; to do small, unnecessary or unimportant things: [V] *Stop fussing and eat your food!* [Vpr] *She's always fussing about some trivial matter.* [Vpr, Vp] *He kept fussing (about) with his hair.* **2** (*Brit*) (usu passive) to annoy or disturb sb: [Vn] *Children can get very fussed when adults try to help them.* **IDM** **not be fussed (about sb/sth)** (*Brit infml*) to have no preference about sth: *'Where do you want to go for lunch?' 'I'm not fussed.'* **PHR V** **fuss over sb** to pay too much attention to sb: *He's always fussing over his grandchildren.*

fusspot /ˈfʌspɒt/ *n* (*infml*) a very FUSSY(1,2) person.

fussy /ˈfʌsɪ/ *adj* (**-ier, -iest**) (*usu derog*) **1** active or excited, often in a nervous way, about unimportant things: *fussy parents* ∘ *a fussy manner.* **2** ~ (**about sth**) too concerned about detail and therefore difficult to please: *Our teacher is very fussy about punctuation.* ∘ *Don't be so fussy (about your food).* ∘ *'Where do you want to go for lunch?' 'I'm not fussy (ie I have no preference).'* **3** (of eg clothes or a design) too full of detail or decoration: *a fussy pattern.* **fussily** *adv.* **fussiness** *n* [U].

fustian /ˈfʌstɪən; *US* -tʃən/ *n* [U] **1** a type of thick rough cotton cloth: *a jacket made of fustian* ∘ *a fustian jacket.* **2** (*dated derog*) language that sounds impressive but is in fact empty and worthless.

fusty /ˈfʌstɪ/ *adj* (*derog*) **1** smelling old, damp or not fresh: *a fusty room* ∘ *This blanket smells a little fusty.* **2** old-fashioned; not having modern ideas: *a fusty old professor.*

futile /ˈfjuːtaɪl; *US* -tl/ *adj* producing no result; having no purpose: *a futile attempt/exercise* ∘ *Their efforts to revive him were futile.* ∘ *He kept making futile (ie unnecessary and silly) remarks.* ▸ **futility** /fjuː'tɪlətɪ/ *n* [U]: *the futility of war.*

futon /ˈfuːtɒn, ˈfjuː-/ *n* a Japanese MATTRESS that can be rolled out to make a low bed.

future /ˈfjuːtʃə(r)/ *n* **1**(**a**) **the future** [sing] the time that will come after the present; events that will happen then: *in the near/distant future* (ie soon/not soon) ∘ *Who knows what will happen in the future?* ∘ (*grammar*) the future tense. (**b**) [C] the condition or state of sb/sth then: *Her future is uncertain.* ∘ *The peoples of Europe are determining their own futures.* ∘ *The future of this project will be decided by the government.* (**c**) [U] the possibility of sth good, eg success or happiness, in the future: *I gave up my job because there was no future in it.* ∘ *The government will decide if there is any future for the steel industry.* **2 futures** [pl] (*finance*) goods or shares (SHARE[1] 3) bought at agreed prices but delivered and paid for later: *buy oil/coffee futures.* **IDM** **in future** (*Brit*) on every occasion after this one; from now on: *Please be more punctual in future.*
▸ **future** *adj* [attrib] of or taking place in the future: *her future husband/job/prospects* ∘ *future events/ generations.*

futurism /ˈfjuːtʃərɪzm/ *n* [U] a movement in art and literature that abandoned tradition and sought to express the energy and growth of a modern society based on machines.
▸ **futurist** *n, adj*: *The futurists worshipped motion and power.* ∘ *futurist poets.*

futuristic /ˌfjuːtʃə'rɪstɪk/ *adj* looking suitable for the future or extremely modern; not traditional: *futuristic design/furniture/housing.*

futurity /fjuː'tjʊərətɪ; *US* -'tʊər-/ *n* [U] (*fml*) future time; the future: *the contemplation of futurity.*

fuzz¹ /fʌz/ n [U] **1** short fine hair that sticks up, esp on a person's body. **2** a mass of hair in tight curls.

fuzz² /fʌz/ n **the fuzz** [Gp] (*dated sl*) the police.

fuzzy /ˈfʌzi/ adj (**-ier**, **-iest**) **1** like FUZZ¹; having a soft light hairy texture: *a fuzzy teddy bear/blanket/ sweater* ○ *fuzzy* (ie tightly curled) *hair*. **2** not clear in shape, sound, etc: *These photographs have come out all fuzzy.* ○ *The soundtrack is fuzzy in places.* ○ (*fig*) *fuzzy ideas/thinking.* ▶ **fuzzily** adv. **fuzziness** n [U].

-fy ⇨ -IFY.

Gg

G (also **g**) /dʒiː/ n (pl **G's**, **g's** /dʒiːz/) **1** the 7th letter of the English alphabet: *'Germany' begins with (a) G/'G'.* **2 G** (*music*) the fifth note in the scale¹(6) of C major.

g abbr **1** gram(s): *300g.* **2** /dʒiː/ (acceleration (ACCELERATE) due to) gravity: *Spacecraft re-entering the earth's atmosphere are affected by g forces.*

■ **G7** /ˌdʒiː'sevn/ n [Gp] the seven most important industrial countries in the world as a group: *the recent G7 summit meeting.*

gab /ɡæb/ n **IDM** **the gift of the gab** ⇨ GIFT.

gabardine (also **gaberdine**) /ˈɡæbədiːn; Brit also ˌɡæbə'diːn/ n (**a**) [U] a strong cloth used esp for making coats: *a gabardine jacket.* (**b**) [C] a garment, esp a strong RAINCOAT, made of this material.

gabble /ˈɡæbl/ v ~ (**on/away**); ~ **sth** (**out**) to say things quickly in a way that is difficult to hear clearly or understand: [V, Vn] *Take your time and don't gabble (your words).* [Vp] *They were gabbling on in a language I couldn't understand.* [Vnp] *He gabbled out some incomprehensible instructions about how to work the video.* [also V.speech].
▶ **gabble** n [U] fast speech that is difficult to understand: *the gabble of children.*

gable /ˈɡeɪbl/ n the TRIANGULAR upper part of the side or end of a building, under a sloping roof: *gable ends.* ⇨ picture at HOUSE¹.
▶ **gabled** /ˈɡeɪbld/ adj having one or more gables: *a gabled house/roof.*

gad /ɡæd/ v (**-dd-**) **PHR V** ˌgad a'bout/a'round (*infml derog*) to go around from one place to another, usu in search of pleasure and excitement: *While they gad about the world, their children are neglected at home.*

gadfly /ˈɡædflaɪ/ n **1** a fly that bites horses and cattle. **2** (*usu derog*) an annoying person, esp one who provokes others into action by criticism, etc.

gadget /ˈɡædʒɪt/ n a small mechanical device or tool: *a clever little gadget for opening tins.* ⇨ note at MACHINE.
▶ **gadgetry** n [U] a collection of gadgets: *electronic/modern gadgetry.*

Gaelic n [U], adj **1** /ˈɡeɪlɪk/ (the language) of the Celtic people of Ireland. **2** /ˈɡælɪk, ˈɡeɪlɪk/ (the language) of the Celtic people of Scotland.

gaffe /ɡæf/ n a social mistake; an embarrassing act or remark: *He didn't realize what a gaffe he'd made.*

gaffer /ˈɡæfə(r)/ n (*infml Brit sl*) a person in charge, esp of a gang of workers: *'Look out! Here comes the gaffer.'*

gag /ɡæɡ/ n **1**(**a**) a thing, esp a piece of cloth, put in or over a person's mouth to prevent her or him from speaking or shouting. (**b**) a thing placed in a patient's mouth by a DENTIST, doctor, etc to keep it open. (**c**) anything that prevents freedom of speech: (*US*) *a gag rule* (ie one that restricts discussion or debate of an issue). **2** a joke or funny story, esp one told by a professional COMEDIAN(1): *a few rather feeble gags* ∘ *a running gag* (ie one that is regularly repeated during a performance, etc).
▶ **gag** v (**-gg-**) **1** (**a**) to put a gag(1a) into or over the mouth of sb in order to stop them speaking: [Vn] *The hostages were bound and gagged.* (**b**) to prevent sb from speaking freely: [Vn] *The new censorship laws are an attempt to gag the press.* **2** ~ (**on sth**)

(*infml*) to reverse the act of swallowing: [Vpr] *gagging on a piece of raw fish* [also V].

gaga /ˈɡɑːɡɑː/ adj [usu pred] (*infml*) slightly crazy because of old age or love: *He has gone completely gaga.*

gage (*US*) = GAUGE.

gaggle /ˈɡæɡl/ n **1** a group of geese (GOOSE 1). **2** a group of noisy or talkative people: *a gaggle of tourists/schoolchildren.*

gaiety /ˈɡeɪəti/ n [U] the state of being GAY(3) and cheerful: *The colourful flags added to the gaiety of the occasion.* Compare GAYNESS.

gaily ⇨ GAY.

gain¹ /ɡeɪn/ n **1** [U] an increase in wealth; profit; advantage: *One man's loss is another's gain.* ∘ *We hope for some gain from our investment.* **2** [C] an increase in amount or power; an improvement: *a gain in weight of two pounds* ∘ *Heavy gains were recorded on the Stock Exchange today.*
▶ **gainful** /-fl/ adj [usu attrib] profitable; bringing wealth: *gainful employment.* **gainfully** /-fəli/ adv: *gainfully employed.*

gain² /ɡeɪn/ v **1**(**a**) ~ **sth** (**for sb**) to obtain or win sth, esp sth that is wanted or needed: [Vn] *gain possession of sth* ∘ *gain access to secret information* ∘ *I gained the impression that the matter had been settled.* [Vnn] *His persistence gained him victory.* [also Vnpr]. (**b**) to get more of sth, esp sth that is wanted or needed: [Vn] *gain experience/control/strength/weight* ∘ *Our campaign is gaining momentum.* ∘ *The plane rapidly gained height.* **2** ~ **by/from** (**doing**) **sth** to benefit or profit from sth/doing sth: [Vpr] *You can gain by watching how she works.* **3** (*fml*) to reach sth, usu with effort: [Vn] *After swimming for an hour, he finally gained the shore.* **4** (of a watch or clock) to go fast; to become ahead of the correct time: [Vn, Vpr] *My watch gains (by) several minutes a day.* [also V]. **IDM** **gain 'ground** (of an idea, belief, etc) to begin to have more support; to make progress: *The campaign is gaining ground.* **gain/make up ground** ⇨ GROUND¹. **gain 'time** to obtain extra time by making excuses, deliberately using slow methods, etc. **nothing venture, nothing gain/win** ⇨ VENTURE v.
PHR V 'gain in sth to obtain more of a physical or an abstract quality: *gain in beauty/height/strength/weight* ∘ *gain in confidence/influence/stature/understanding.* 'gain on sb/sth to come closer to sb/sth, esp a rival or sth pursued: *gain on the leader in a race* ∘ *The Socialists are gaining on the Conservatives in the opinion polls.*

gainsay /ˌɡeɪn'seɪ/ v (pt, pp **gainsaid** /-'sed/) (*fml*) (usu in negative sentences) to say that sth is not so; to deny sth: [Vn] *There's no gainsaying his honesty* (ie We cannot deny that he is honest).

gait /ɡeɪt/ n [sing] a way of walking: *walk with an unsteady gait.*

gaiter /ˈɡeɪtə(r)/ n a covering of cloth, leather, etc for the leg below the knee or for the ankle, worn esp formerly: *a pair of gaiters.*

gal¹ /ɡæl/ n (*dated infml*) a girl.

gal² abbr gallon(s).

gala /ˈɡɑːlə; US ˈɡeɪlə/ n a social or sporting occasion with special entertainments or performances: *a swimming gala* ∘ *a gala dinner/night.*

galactic /gə'læktɪk/ *adj* of a GALAXY or galaxies, esp the Galaxy.

galaxy /'gæləksi/ *n* **1** [C] any of the large systems of stars in outer space. **2 the Galaxy** (also **the ˌMilky ˈWay**) [sing] the system of stars that contains our sun and its planets, seen as a bright band in the night sky. **3** [C] (*fig*) a group of very famous or talented people: *a galaxy of Hollywood stars/famous intellectuals.*

gale /geɪl/ *n* **1** a very strong wind; a storm at sea: *a gale warning* ○ *gale-force winds* ○ *It's **blowing a gale** outside.* ○ *The ship lost its masts in the gale.* **2** a noisy explosion of sound, esp of laughter: *The clown's antics were greeted by **gales of laughter** from the young audience.*

gall¹ /gɔːl/ *n* [U] **1** (*infml*) bold rude behaviour; lack of respect: *Of all the gall!* (ie How rude!) ○ *Then they had the gall to complain!* **2** a bitter feeling; hatred or resentment (RESENT): *words full of venom and gall.*

■ **ˈgall-bladder** *n* (*anatomy*) an organ attached to the LIVER(1) that stores and releases BILE(1). ▷ picture at DIGESTIVE SYSTEM.

gall² /gɔːl/ *v* to annoy sb; to make sb feel shame: [Vn] *It galled him to have to ask her for a loan.*

▶ **galling** *adj* [usu pred] annoying; humiliating (HUMILIATE): *It was galling to have to apologize to a man she detested.*

gall³ /gɔːl/ *n* an abnormal growth(4b) on plants and trees produced by insects, FUNGUS(2), etc.

gall⁴ *abbr* (*pl* unchanged or **galls**) gallon(s): *petrol at £2.25 per gall.*

gallant /'gælənt/ *adj* **1** (*fml or rhet*) brave: *a gallant knight/soldier* ○ *a gallant deed/effort/struggle.* **2** fine; grand; noble: *a gallant ship.* **3** *also* /gə'lænt/ (of a man) giving special attention and respect to women.

▶ **gallant** /gə'lænt, 'gælənt/ *n* (*dated*) a fashionable young man, esp one who gives polite attention to women.

gallantly *adv.*

gallantry /'gæləntri/ *n* [U] **1** courage, esp in battle: *a medal for gallantry.* **2** polite attention given by men to women: *He won many hearts by his gallantry.*

galleon /'gæliən/ *n* a large Spanish ship with sails, used from the 15th to the 17th centuries.

gallery /'gæləri/ *n* **1** [C] a room or building for showing works of art: *an ˈart-gallery* ○ *museums and galleries.* **2(a)** [C] the highest and cheapest seats in a theatre: *Four tickets for the gallery, please.* **(b)** [Gp] the people occupying these. **3** [C] a raised covered platform or passage along an inner wall of a hall, church, etc. **4** [C] a covered walk or CORRIDOR(1) partly open at one side; a COLONNADE. **5** [C] a long narrow room, esp one used for a particular purpose: *a ˈshooting-gallery.* **IDM** **play to the ˈgallery** to behave in an exaggerated way to attract people's attention.

▶ **galleried** /'gælərid/ *adj* having or resembling a gallery(3): *a galleried bookshop/shelf.*

galley /'gæli/ *n* **1** (formerly) a long flat ship with sails, usu rowed by slaves or criminals, esp one used by the ancient Greeks or Romans in war. **2** the kitchen in a ship or an aircraft. **3** (*also* **ˈgalley proof**) a proof(2) on which text is printed in a long column before it has been divided up into pages.

Gallic /'gælɪk/ *adj* of or typical of the French people and their character: *Gallic charm* ○ *a Gallic shrug of the shoulders.*

gallivant /'gælɪvænt/ *v* (*infml derog*) (usu in the continuous tenses) to go about from one place to another, usu in search of pleasure: [V, Vpr, Vp] *They should spend less time gallivanting (about the place/about) and more with their children.*

gallon /'gælən/ *n* (*abbrs* **gal, gall**) **(a)** (*Brit*) a unit of measure for liquids, equal to about 4.5 litres. **(b)** (*US*) a similar measure, equal to about 3.8 litres. ▷ App 2.

gallop /'gæləp/ *n* **1(a)** [sing] the fastest pace of a horse, etc with all four feet off the ground at each STRIDE: *at full gallop* ○ *He rode off at a gallop.* Compare WALK¹ 1d, TROT 1, CANTER. **(b)** [C] a period of riding at this pace: *to go for a gallop.* **2** [sing] an unusually fast speed: *to work at a gallop.*

▶ **gallop** *v* **(a)** (of a horse, etc or a rider) to go at a gallop: [Vp] *The frightened mare galloped away.* [Vpr] *I enjoy galloping over the fields.* [also V, Vadv]. ▷ note at RUN¹. **(b)** (of a rider) to make a horse, etc go at a gallop: [Vnpr] *He galloped the pony along the track.* [also Vn, Vnp]. **PHRV** **gallop aˈhead (of sb)** to make rapid progress: *Japan is galloping ahead in the race to develop new technologies.* **ˈgallop through sth** to complete sth rapidly: *gallop through one's work/a lecture/a performance.* **galloping** *adj* [attrib] moving or progressing rapidly: *galloping inflation.*

gallows /'gæləʊz/ (also **the gallows**) *n* (*pl* unchanged; usu *sing* with *sing v*) a wooden framework on which criminals are killed by hanging: *send a man to the gallows* (ie condemn him to death).

■ **ˌgallows ˈhumour** (*US* **ˈhumor**) *n* [U] jokes about unpleasant things like death, disease, etc.

gallstone /'gɔːlstəʊn/ *n* a hard, often painful, mass that can form in the gall-bladder (GALL¹).

Gallup poll /'gæləp pəʊl/ *n* a way of assessing public opinion by questioning a representative sample of people, esp in order to forecast voting at an election.

galore /gə'lɔː(r)/ *adv* (following *ns*) in plenty: *have books/food/friends/money galore.*

galoshes /gə'lɒʃɪz/ *n* [pl] rubber coverings worn over shoes in wet weather: *a pair of galoshes.*

galvanic /gæl'vænɪk/ *adj* **1** producing an electric current by chemical action: *a galvanic battery* ○ *galvanic electricity.* **2** sudden and dramatic: *His appointment as manager had a galvanic effect on the team's fortunes.*

galvanize, -ise /'gælvənaɪz/ *v* **1** to cover iron, etc with ZINC in order to protect it from RUST: [Vn] *galvanized bucket* ○ *galvanized steel/wire.* **2** ~ **sb** **(into sth / doing sth)** to stir sb into action by shocking or exciting them: [Vnpr] *She has galvanized into activity an industry notoriously bad at working together.* [also Vn].

gambit /'gæmbɪt/ *n* **1** an opening move or moves in the game of CHESS, in which a player allows a piece¹(3c) to be captured in order to gain an advantage later. **2** an opening move in any situation that is calculated to gain an advantage: *a conversational gambit* ○ *His **opening gambit** at the debate was a direct attack on government policy.*

gamble /'gæmbl/ *v* ~ **sth (on sth)** to play games of chance, etc for money: [Vpr] *gamble at cards/on the horses* [V] *He spends all his time gambling in the casino.* [Vnpr] *He gambled all his winnings on the last race.* [also Vn]. **PHRV** ~ **sth away** to lose sth by gambling: *gamble away all one's money.* **ˈgamble in sth** to risk money by investing in sth: *gamble in oil shares.* **ˈgamble on sth / doing sth** to act in the hope of sth being successful, true, etc despite the risk of loss: *gamble on (having) sb's support* ○ *I wouldn't gamble on the weather being fine tomorrow.*

▶ **gamble** *n* (usu *sing*) an act of gambling; a thing that one does with a risk of loss and a chance of profit: *Setting up this business was a bit of a gamble.* ○ *The company **took a gamble** by cutting the price of their products, and it paid off* (ie was financially successful).

gambler /'gæmblə(r)/ *n*: *He's a compulsive gambler.*

gambling /'gæmblɪŋ/ *n* [U] **(a)** the practice of playing games, etc for money: *heavy gambling debts* ○ *a*

G

gambling den. (**b**) the taking of risks for possible advantage: *have a taste for gambling.*

gambol /'gæmbl/ *v* (**-ll-**; *US* also **-l-**) to jump or run about in a playful manner: [V, Vp] *children/lambs gambolling (about/around)* [also Vpr].

game¹ /geɪm/ *n* **1** [C] a form of usu competitive play or sport with rules: *popular children's games* ○ *board games like chess and Monopoly* ○ *a game of chance/skill* ○ *play a game of chess/football/hide-and-seek* ○ *Let's have a game of table tennis.* ⇨ note at SPORT. **2 games** [pl] (**a**) ATHLETICS or sport as a school activity: *Mary never played games at school.* (**b**) (also **the Games**) a meeting for ATHLETIC(2) contests: *the O₁lympic 'Games.* **3** [C] a portion of play in certain games, eg tennis or bridge², which forms a unit in scoring: *(one) game all, two games all, etc* (ie each player or team has won one game, two games, etc) ○ *Game, set and match (to Sampras)* (ie The tennis match has been won (by him)). ○ *We need another twenty points to make game* (ie in bridge). ○ *They lost the first game of the second set* (ie in tennis). **4** [C] a piece of fun: *play games with the dog.* **5** [C] (*infml*) (**a**) a secret and clever plan; a trick: *So that's his (little) game* (ie Now I know what he has been planning)! ○ *I want none of your games!* (**b**) a type of activity or business: *the 'publishing game* ○ *the game of 'politics* ○ *How long have you been in this game?* See also WAITING GAME. **6** [U] wild animals or birds hunted for sport or food: *game 'pie.* See also FAIR GAME. **IDM** **beat sb at their own game** ⇨ BEAT¹. **fun and games** ⇨ FUN. **the game is not worth the 'candle** (*saying*) the advantages to be gained from doing sth are not worth the trouble, expense, etc involved. **the game is 'up** (usu said to or by sb who has done sth wrong when they are caught) the crime, deception, etc has been discovered. **a game that 'two can play; 'two can play at 'that game** (that is) a wrongdoing or trick that sb can copy in return for the wrong done to them. **give the game away** to reveal a secret, esp by accident. **a mug's game** ⇨ MUG¹. **the name of the game** ⇨ NAME¹. (**be**) **on the 'game** (*sl esp Brit*) (to be) working as a prostitute. **play cat and mouse / play a cat-and-mouse game with sb** ⇨ CAT. **play the 'game** to behave in a fair or honourable way: *You can't leave me to amuse the children all on my own — that's not playing the game!* **play sb's 'game** to do sth which, intentionally or not, is helpful to another's plans: *She didn't realize that by complaining she was only playing Peter's game.*

■ **'game bird** *n* a bird that is hunted and killed for food or sport.

'game plan *n* a plan for success worked out in advance, esp in sport, politics or business.

'game reserve (also *Brit* **'game park**, *US* **'game preserve**) *n* an area of land reserved for the breeding and protection of game¹(6).

'game show *n* a television programme in which well-known people or members of the public compete in a game or QUIZ(1), often for prizes.

'game-warden *n* a person employed to manage a game reserve.

game² /geɪm/ *adj* ~ (**for sth / to do sth**) eager and willing to do sth risky; brave: *'Who'll climb up to get it?' 'I'm game (to try).'* ○ *He's always game for an adventure.* ▶ **gamely** *adv*: *Despite being injured he kept on gamely to the end of the match.*

game³ /geɪm/ *adj* (*dated infml*) (of a person's leg) permanently injured; LAME(1). Compare GAMMY.

gamekeeper /'geɪmkiːpə(r)/ *n* a person employed to breed and protect game¹(6) on an estate.

gamesmanship /'geɪmzmənʃɪp/ *n* [U] the art of winning games by upsetting the confidence of one's opponent(s).

gaming /'geɪmɪŋ/ *n* [U] (*dated or law*) gambling: *the*

Betting and Gaming Act ○ *spend all night at the gaming tables.*

gamma /'gæmə/ *n* the third letter of the Greek alphabet (Γ, γ).

■ **₁gamma radi'ation** *n* [U] (also **'gamma rays** [pl]) rays (RAY¹ 1a) of very short WAVELENGTH sent out by certain RADIOACTIVE substances.

gammon /'gæmən/ *n* [U] (*esp Brit*) bacon from the back leg or side of a pig: *gammon rashers/steaks.* See also BACON, HAM 1b, PORK.

gammy /'gæmi/ *adj* [usu attrib] (*infml*) (of a limb or joint) unable to function normally because of pain or stiffness (STIFF¹): *have a gammy leg/knee.* Compare GAME³.

gamut /'gæmət/ *n* **the gamut** [sing] the complete range or scale of sth: *the whole gamut of human emotions from joy to despair* ○ *In his short life he had **run the** entire **gamut** of crime, from petty theft to murder.*

-gamy *comb form* (forming *ns*) marriage or sexual union: *monogamy* ○ *polygamy.* ▶ **-gamous** (forming *adjs* and *advs*).

gamy /'geɪmi/ *adj* (of meat) having a strong flavour or smell as a result of being kept for some time before cooking.

gander /'gændə(r)/ *n* a male GOOSE(1). **IDM** **what is sauce for the goose is sauce for the gander** ⇨ SAUCE.

gang /gæŋ/ *n* [CGp] **1** an organized group of criminals: *a gang of robbers* ○ *The gang is being hunted by the police.* Compare GANGSTER. **2** a group of esp young people who go around together and often cause trouble: *a street gang* ○ *The playground was vandalized by a gang of youths.* **3** an organized group of workers: *a gang of builders.* See also CHAINGANG. **4** (*infml*) a group of people who regularly associate together: *The whole gang's here tonight.* ○ (*esp US*) *Hi, gang!*

▶ **gang** *v* **PHR V** **₁gang 'up (on/against sb)** (*derog*) to join together, esp to oppose, hurt or frighten sb: *bigger boys ganging up on smaller ones.*

gangland /'gæŋlænd/ *n* [sing] the world of criminal gangs: *gangland killings.*

gangling /'gæŋglɪŋ/ (also **gangly** /'gæŋgli/) *adj* (of a person) tall, thin and awkward in one's movements: *a gangling youth.*

ganglion /'gæŋgliən/ *n* (*pl* **ganglia** /-liə/) (*medical*) **1** a mass of nerve cells. **2** a type of CYST.

gangplank /'gæŋplæŋk/ *n* a movable wooden board for walking into or out of a boat.

gangrene /'gæŋgriːn/ *n* [U] the decay and death of body tissue when the blood supply has been stopped: *When gangrene set in, his foot had to be amputated.* ▶ **gangrenous** /'gæŋgrɪnəs/ *adj.*

gangster /'gæŋstə(r)/ *n* a member of a gang of violent criminals: *gangster movies.*

gangway /'gæŋweɪ/ *n* **1** (*Brit*) a passage between rows of seats in a theatre, an aircraft, etc. **2** a movable bridge for entering or leaving a ship. ▶ **gangway!** *interj* (used for telling people to give one room to pass).

gannet /'gænɪt/ *n* **1** a large sea bird that catches fish by diving (DIVE¹). **2** (*Brit infml*) a greedy person: *It looks as though the gannets have been at the biscuits again!*

gantry /'gæntri/ *n* a tall metal frame supporting a CRANE¹(1), railway or road signals, or a spacecraft before it is launched.

gaol ⇨ JAIL.

gaolbird ⇨ JAILBIRD.

gap /gæp/ *n* ~ (**in/between sth**) **1** an opening or a break in sth or between two things: *a gap in a fence/hedge/wall* ○ *The road goes through a gap in/between the hills.* **2** an empty interval of space or time: *a gap of five miles between towns* ○ *There were* *some unaccountable gaps in* (ie parts missing from) *his story.* ○ *a gap in the conversation* ○ *a temporary job to fill the gap between school and university* ○ *After a gap of 30 years the custom was reintroduced.* **3** a difference that separates people's opinions, development, etc: *a widening gap between the rich and poor in our society.* See also CREDIBILITY GAP, THE GENERATION GAP. **4** a lack of sth that is needed: *a gap in one's education* ○ *There was a terrible gap in her life after her husband died.* ○ *We think we've identified a gap in the market* (ie the absence of a type of article which people might wish to buy). **IDM** **bridge a/the gap** ⇨ BRIDGE[1] *v.*

gape /geɪp/ *v* **1** ~ (**at sb/sth**) (*often derog*) to stare with an open mouth, usu in surprise: [Vpr] *What are you gaping at?* [V] *The news left her gaping with astonishment.* **2** to be or become wide open: [V] *a gaping hole/wound* ○ *A huge chasm gaped before them.* [V-adj] *She reached into a large bag that gaped open on the floor.* ▶ **gape** *n*: *gapes of astonishment on the faces of the spectators.*

garage /ˈgærɑːʒ, -rɑːdʒ, -rɪdʒ; US gəˈrɑːʒ, -rɑːdʒ/ *n* **1** a building in which to keep one or more cars, vans, etc: *a house with a separate/built-in garage* ○ *a bus garage.* ⇨ picture at HOUSE[1]. **2** (*Brit*) a place where vehicles are repaired and sold and where petrol and oil may also be bought: *a garage mechanic.* See also PETROL STATION.
▶ **garage** *v* [Vn] to put a motor vehicle in a garage.
■ **ga·rage sale** *n* (*esp US*) a sale of used goods, held in the garage of a private house.

garb /gɑːb/ *n* [U] clothing, esp as worn by a particular type of person: *military/prison garb* ○ *a man in priest's garb/in the garb of a priest* ○ *students in colourful garb.*
▶ **garbed** /gɑːbd/ *adj* [pred] ~ (**in sth**) dressed in the specified way: *appropriately garbed in funereal black.*

garbage /ˈgɑːbɪdʒ/ *n* [U] **1** (*esp US*) (**a**) waste material, esp domestic waste; rubbish(1): *garbage collection/disposal* ○ *a garbage truck.* (**b**) a place or container for disposing of this: *Throw any left-over food in the garbage.* **2** (*infml*) nonsense; rubbish(2): *You do talk a load of garbage!*
■ **garbage can** *n* (*US*) = DUSTBIN.

garbled /ˈgɑːbld/ *adj* (of a message) confused or misleading: *The injured man was still groggy and could only give a garbled account of the accident.*

garden /ˈgɑːdn/ *n* **1** [C] a piece of private ground used for growing flowers, fruit, vegetables, etc, typically with a lawn or other open space for playing or relaxing: *a big house with a front and back garden* ○ *a herb/rose/vegetable garden* ○ *weeding the garden* ○ *a garden wall/shed/seat* ○ *garden flowers/plants* ○ *We've only got a small garden.* See also KITCHEN GARDEN, ROCK-GARDEN. **2 gardens** [pl] a public park: *botanical/zoological gardens.* **3** [C] (esp in compounds) a place where refreshments are served out of doors: *a beer/tea garden.* **4** [sing] a region good for growing flowers, vegetables, etc: *Kent is the garden of England.* **IDM** **common or garden** ⇨ COMMON[1]. **everything in the garden is 'lovely** (*Brit saying*) everything is very satisfactory. **lead sb up the garden path** ⇨ LEAD[1]. See also MARKET GARDEN.
▶ **garden** *v* to cultivate a garden: [V] *She's outdoors gardening every afternoon.* **gardener** /ˈgɑːdnə(r)/ *n*: *My wife's a keen gardener.* ○ *We employ a gardener two days a week.* **gardening** /ˈgɑːdnɪŋ/ *n* [U]: *organic gardening* ○ *gardening gloves/tools* ○ *I like watching the gardening programmes on television.*
■ **garden centre** *n* a place where plants, seeds, garden equipment, etc are sold.
garden 'city, garden 'suburb *ns* (*esp Brit*) a city or part of a city designed with many open spaces, parks, etc and planted with many trees.

garden party *n* a formal social event on a lawn or in a garden, usu in the afternoon.

gardenia /gɑːˈdiːniə/ *n* a tree or bush with large white or yellow flowers, usu sweet-smelling.

gargantuan /gɑːˈgæntʃuən/ *adj* huge; GIGANTIC: *a gargantuan appetite/meal/task.*

gargle /ˈgɑːgl/ *v* ~ (**with sth**) to wash one's mouth and throat with liquid kept moving there by a stream of air which is breathed out: [V, Vpr] *He always gargles (with salt water) before going to bed.*
▶ **gargle** *n* **1** [C] a liquid used for gargling: *use a gargle of salt water.* **2** [sing] an act of gargling: *have a gargle with salt water.*

gargoyle /ˈgɑːgɔɪl/ *n* an ugly carved human or animal figure, usu of stone, for carrying water away from the roof of a church, etc through its mouth.

garish /ˈgeərɪʃ/ *adj* (*derog*) bright in a harsh unpleasant way; too highly coloured or decorated: *garish clothes/colours/lights.* ▶ **garishly** *adv*: *garishly coloured/dressed/lit.*

garland /ˈgɑːlənd/ *n* a circle of flowers, leaves or ribbons (RIBBON 1b), worn esp on the head or round the neck or hung as a decoration: *a garland of victory.*
▶ **garland** *v* ~ **sb** (**with sth**) (usu passive) to put a garland or garlands on sb: [Vnpr] *garlanded with roses* [also Vn].

garlic /ˈgɑːlɪk/ *n* [U] a plant of the onion family with a strong taste and smell, used in cooking to give flavour to food: *a clove of garlic* ○ *crushed garlic* ○ *garlic butter/bread* (ie flavoured with garlic). ⇨ picture at ONION.
▶ **garlicky** *adj* smelling or tasting of garlic: *garlicky breath/food.*

garment /ˈgɑːmənt/ *n* (*fml*) an article of clothing: *a strange shapeless garment that had once been a jacket* ○ *woollen/winter/outer garments.* See also UNDERGARMENT.

garner /ˈgɑːnə(r)/ *v* ~ **sth** (**from sth**) (*fml*) to collect sth, esp in order to use it: [Vn] *garner knowledge/information* [Vnpr] *facts garnered from various sources.*

garnet /ˈgɑːnɪt/ *n* a fairly valuable stone of deep transparent red.

garnish /ˈgɑːnɪʃ/ *v* ~ **sth** (**with sth**) to decorate food for the table with small additional amounts of food: [Vnpr] *meat garnished with parsley/fresh vegetables* ○ *She garnished the fish with slices of lemon.* [also Vn].
▶ **garnish** *n* anything edible used to decorate a dish of food or add to its flavour: *a garnish of mixed herbs.*

garret /ˈgærət/ *n* a room, often small, dark and unpleasant, on the top floor of a house, esp in the roof: *a poor man living in a garret* ○ *an artist's garret.* Compare ATTIC. See also LOFT[1].

garrison /ˈgærɪsn/ *n* [CGp] soldiers living in a town or fort to defend it: *garrison duty* ○ *a garrison town* ○ *Half the garrison is/are on duty.*
▶ **garrison** *v* **1** to defend a place with or as a garrison: [Vn] *Two regiments are being sent to garrison the town.* **2** ~ **sb in...** to place soldiers as a garrison: [Vnpr] *A hundred soldiers were garrisoned in the town.*

garrotte (also **garotte**) /gəˈrɒt/ *v* [Vn] to kill sb by tightening wire or rope around their neck.
▶ **garrotte** (also **garotte**) *n* a device used for garrotting sb.

garrulous /ˈgærələs; *Brit* also -rjʊl-/ *adj* talking too much, esp about unimportant things: *becoming garrulous after a few glasses of wine.* ▶ **garrulously** *adv.*

garter /ˈgɑːtə(r)/ *n* **1** a usu elastic band worn round the leg to keep up a sock or STOCKING. **2** (*US*) = SUSPENDER.

G

gas /gæs/ n (pl **gases**) **1** [C,U] any substance like air (ie not a solid or liquid) that moves freely to fill any available space: a *gas balloon* (ie one filled with gas) ○ *Hydrogen and oxygen are gases.* ○ *Air is a mixture of gases.* **2** [U] **(a)** a gas or mixture of gases burnt as fuel for heating, cooking or (esp formerly) lighting: *butane/Calor/coal gas* ○ a *gas cooker/fire/oven/ring/stove* (ie using gas as fuel) ○ *cook on a low/medium/high gas* (ie on a gas cooker) ○ *Is your central heating gas or electricity?* ○ *Light the gas/Turn the gas on and we'll have a bowl of soup.* **(b)** a gas used to make people sleep before a medical operation: *I was given gas when the dentist pulled my tooth out.* ○ *Did you have gas or an injection?* **(c)** a poisonous gas used in war: *a gas attack.* **3** [U] (*US infml*) = PETROL. **4** [U] (*infml derog*) empty talk; boasting (BOAST 1): *Don't believe a word he says — it's all gas!* **5** [U] (*idm*) = WIND[1] 3. **IDM step on the gas** ⇨ STEP[1]. See also NATURAL GAS, TEAR-GAS.

▶ **gas** v (**-ss-**) **1** to cause a person or an animal to breathe poisonous gas: [Vn] *He was badly gassed in the war.* ○ *She committed suicide by gassing herself.* **2** ~ (**about sth**) (*infml derog*) to talk for a long time without saying much that is useful: [V, Vpr] *They sat gassing (about nothing) all morning and never did a stroke of work.*

■ **'gas chamber** n a room that can be filled with poisonous gas for killing animals or people.

gas-'cooled adj using gas to cool sth: *gas-cooled nuclear re'actors.*

gas-'fired adj using gas as fuel: *gas-fired central 'heating.*

'gas mask n a breathing apparatus worn as protection against poison gas. ⇨ picture at MASK.

'gas meter n a device for measuring the amount of gas used.

'gas station n (*US*) = PETROL STATION.

gasbag /'gæsbæg/ n (*infml derog*) a person who talks a lot. Compare WINDBAG.

gaseous /'gæsiəs, 'geisiəs/ adj of or like gas: a *gaseous mixture.*

gash /gæʃ/ n ~ (**in/on sth**) a long deep cut or wound: a *nasty gash in/on the arm* ○ *make a gash in the bark of a tree with a knife.*

▶ **gash** v ~ **sth** (**on/with sth**) to make a gash in sth: [Vn, Vnpr] *gash one's arm (on a piece of broken glass).*

gasholder /'gæshəʊldə(r)/ n = GASOMETER.

gasket /'gæskɪt/ n a soft flat sheet or ring of rubber or card used to seal a joint between two metal surfaces in order to prevent steam, gas, etc from escaping: *The engine had **blown a gasket*** (ie the gasket had suddenly let steam, etc escape).

gasman /'gæsmæn/ n (pl **-men** /-men/) (*infml*) a man employed by an organization supplying domestic gas. His job is to fit and check gas appliances and to read gas meters (METER[1]) in people's homes.

gasoline (also **gasolene**) /'gæsəliːn/ n [U] (*US*) = PETROL.

gasometer /gæ'sɒmɪtə(r)/ (also **gasholder** /'gæshəʊldə(r)/) n a very large round tank in which fuel gas is stored and from which it is distributed through pipes.

gasp /gɑːsp/ v **1** ~ (**at sth**); ~ (**for sth**) to take one or more quick deep breaths with one's mouth open, esp because of surprise, pain or lack of air: [V] *They fled gasping and choking from the burning building.* [Vpr] *We all gasped in/with astonishment at the news.* ○ *The runner was gasping for air/breath.* **2** ~ **sth** (**out**) to say sth while breathing quickly: [Vn, Vnp] *She managed to gasp (out) a few words.* [also V.speech]. **3** ~ (**for sth**) (*infml*) (used in the continuous tenses) to want sth very much, esp a drink or a cigarette: [V] *'Do you need a drink?' 'Yes, I'm gasping!'* [Vpr] *I was gasping for a cigarette.*

▶ **gasp** n a quick deep breath of pain, surprise, etc:

give a sudden audible gasp ○ *There were gasps of horror from the spectators.* **IDM at one's last gasp** ⇨ LAST[1].

gassy /'gæsi/ adj of, like or full of gas, esp in the form of bubbles in liquid: *gassy lager.*

gastric /'gæstrɪk/ adj [attrib] (*medical*) of the stomach: a *gastric ulcer.*

▶ **gastritis** /gæ'straɪtɪs/ n [U] (*medical*) an illness in which the inside of the stomach becomes swollen and painful.

gastro-enteritis /ˌgæstrəʊ ˌentə'raɪtɪs/ n [U] (*medical*) an illness in which the stomach and intestines (INTESTINE) are swollen.

gastronomy /gæ'strɒnəmi/ n [U] (*fml*) the art and science of choosing, cooking and eating good food.

▶ **gastronomic** /ˌgæstrə'nɒmɪk/ adj of gastronomy: *Lyons, the gastronomic capital of France.* **gastronomically** /-kli/ adv.

gasworks /'gæswɜːks/ n (pl unchanged) [sing or pl v] a place where gas for lighting and heating is manufactured.

gate /geɪt/ n **1(a)** a barrier, usu on hinges (HINGE), that can be pulled across or away from an opening in a wall, fence or hedge, and can be fastened shut: a *wooden/iron gate* ○ *open the garden gate* ○ a *five-bar gate* ○ *the gates of the city.* ⇨ picture at HOUSE[1]. **(b)** an opening that can be closed by this: *We drove through the palace gates.* **(c)** a similar movable barrier which controls a stream of water: a *lock/sluice gate.* **2** a means of going in or out for passengers at an airport or spectators at a sports ground: *The flight is now boarding at gate 16.* **3** the number of spectators at a sports event, esp a football match: a *gate of over 10 000.* **4** (also **'gate-money**) [U] the amount of money obtained by selling tickets for a sports event, esp a football match: *Today's gate will be given to charity.*

▶ **gated** adj [attrib] (of a road) having a gate or gates across, which need to be opened and closed by drivers using the road.

■ **'gate-money** n [U] = GATE 4.

gateau /'gætəʊ; US gæ'təʊ/ n (pl **gateaux**) [C,U] (*Brit*) a large rich cake filled with cream, often decorated with fruit, nuts or chocolate: a *slice of chocolate gateau.*

gatecrash /'geɪtkræʃ/ (also **crash**) v to enter a private social occasion without paying or being invited: [Vn] *gatecrash a party* [also V]. ▶ **'gatecrasher** n.

gatehouse /'geɪthaʊs/ n a house built at or over a gate, eg at the entrance to a park or castle.

gatekeeper /'geɪtkiːpə(r)/ n a person in charge of allowing people through a gate.

gatepost /'geɪtpəʊst/ n a post on which a gate is hung or against which it is closed. **IDM between you, me and the 'gatepost** (*infml*) (used to introduce the telling of a secret).

gateway /'geɪtweɪ/ n **1** a way in and out that can be closed by a gate or gates: *Don't stand there blocking the gateway!* **2** (usu *sing*) ~ **to sth (a)** a place through which one must go to reach somewhere else: *Dover is England's gateway to Europe.* **(b)** a means of gaining sth desired: *A good education can be the gateway to success.*

gather /'gæðə(r)/ v **1(a)** ~ **round** (**sb/sth**); ~ **sb/sth round** (**sb/sth**) to come together, or bring sb/sth together, in one place: [V] *A crowd soon gathered.* [Vp] *Gather round* (ie Form a group round me) *and listen, children!* [Vnpr] *We used to have musical evenings with the whole family gathered round the piano.* **(b)** ~ **sth** (**together/up**) to bring together objects that have been spread about: [Vn] *Give me a moment to gather my notes.* [Vnp] *She gathered together/up her scattered belongings and left.* **2(a)** ~ **sth** (**from sth**) to collect plants, fruit, etc from a wide area: [Vn] *gather wild flowers/berries/nuts* [Vnpr] (*fig*)

information gathered from various sources. (**b**) ~ **sth** (**in**) to pick or cut and collect crops for storage: [Vnp] *The harvest has been safely gathered in.* [also Vn]. **3** ~ **sth** (**from sb/sth**) to believe or understand sth: [V.that] *I gather (that) you wanted to see me.* [Vnpr] *'I'm very angry.' 'I gathered that from your letter.'* [Vpr.that] *I gathered from the way she replied that she wasn't very enthusiastic.* [Vadv] *'She won't be coming.' 'So I gather.'* **4** ~ **sth round one/sth**; ~ **sth up** to pull a garment tighter to one's body: [Vnpr] *She gathered the shawl round her/round her shoulders.* [Vnp] *She gathered up her skirts and ran.* **5** to pull sb towards one and put one's arms round them: [Vnpr] *He gathered her in his arms and kissed her.* [Vnadv] *She shivered and he gathered her close.* **6** to prepare one's mind or body to do sth that requires effort: [Vn] *He gathered all his strength and swung the axe.* ∘ *She sat trying to gather her thoughts before the interview.* **7** ~ **sth** (**in**) to draw parts of a garment together in folds and sew them in place: [Vnpr, Vnp] *a skirt gathered (in) at the waist* [also Vn]. **8** to increase or increase sth: [V] *The darkness/storm is gathering.* ∘ *in the gathering gloom of a winter's afternoon* [Vn] *The car **gathered** speed.*
▶ **gather** *n* a small fold in a garment.
gatherer /ˈgæðərə(r)/ *n* a person who collects plants, fruits, etc: *prehistoric hunters and gatherers.*
gathering /ˈgæðərɪŋ/ *n* a meeting of people, esp socially: *a small family gathering* ∘ *a gathering of friends.*

GATT /gæt/ *abbr* General Agreement on Tariffs and Trade: *GATT talks.*

gauche /gəʊʃ/ *adj* **1** socially awkward: *a gauche manner/person/remark* ∘ *I find him terribly gauche.* **2** (of literary or artistic work) not very skilled or mature: *a rather gauche style/technique.* ▶ **gaucheness** /ˈgəʊʃnəs/ *n* [U].

gaucho /ˈgaʊtʃəʊ/ *n* (*pl* **-os**) a South American COWBOY(1).

gaudy /ˈgɔːdi/ *adj* (**-ier, -iest**) (*derog*) too bright or colourful; having too much decoration, esp of a cheap kind: *gaudy jewellery/hats.* ▶ **gaudily** /ˈgɔːdɪli/ *adv.* **gaudiness** /ˈgɔːdɪnəs/ *n* [U].

gauge (*US* also **gage**) /geɪdʒ/ *n* **1** [U,C] a standard measure, esp of width or thickness: *What gauge of wire do we need?* **2** [C] the distance between rails for a train or TRAM: *standard gauge* (ie 56 ½ inches) ∘ *a narrow-gauge* (ie narrower than standard) *railway up the mountain.* **3** [C] an instrument for measuring the amount or level of sth: *a* /ˈpetrol/ˈpressure/ˈrain/ ˈspeed *gauge.* **4** [C] a fact or circumstance which one can use in estimating or judging sth; a measure: *Is a person's behaviour under stress a reliable gauge of their character?*
▶ **gauge** *v* **1**(**a**) to measure sth, esp accurately: [Vn] *precision instruments can gauge the diameter to a fraction of a millimetre.* (**b**) to make an estimate of sth: [Vn] *gauging the strength of the wind from the movement of the trees.* **2** to make a judgement about sth: [Vn] *try to gauge sb's reactions/ sympathies/sentiments* [V.wh] *It was difficult to gauge how people would respond.* [V.that] *I gauged that it was not a good moment to speak to her.*

gaunt /gɔːnt/ *adj* **1** (of a person) made exceptionally thin by hunger or suffering: *the gaunt face of a starving man.* **2** (of a place) without features or ornament; bare: *gaunt buildings.* ▶ **gauntness** *n* [U].

gauntlet /ˈgɔːntlət/ *n* **1** a metal glove worn as part of a suit of armour by soldiers in the Middle Ages. **2** a strong glove with a wide covering for the wrist, used eg when driving: *motor cyclists with leather gauntlets.* ⇨ picture at GLOVE. **IDM run the** ˈ**gauntlet** to be exposed to danger, anger or criticism: *Before getting the proposals accepted, the government had to run the gauntlet of hostility from its own sup-*

porters. **take up / throw down the** ˈ**gauntlet** to accept/offer a challenge: *The leader of the Opposition may be expected to take up the gauntlet.*

gauze /gɔːz/ *n* [U] a thin, often transparent, fabric of cotton, silk, etc: *a gauze curtain* ∘ *a wound covered with a piece of gauze.*
▶ **gauzy** *adj* of or like gauze: *a gauzy nightdress.*

gave *pt* of GIVE[1].

gavel /ˈgævl/ *n* a small hammer used by a person in charge of a meeting or an AUCTION as a signal for order or attention: *The chairman banged/rapped his gavel on the table.*

gavotte /gəˈvɒt/ *n* an old French dance or the music for it.

Gawd /gɔːd/ *n, interj* (*infml*) (used in written English to indicate a special pronunciation of *God*, esp in phrases expressing surprise, anger, annoyance, etc): *For Gawd's sake hurry up!*

gawk /gɔːk/ *v* ~ (**at sb/sth**) (*infml*) to stare in a rude or stupid way: [Vpr] *He just stood gawking at her.* [also V].

gawky /ˈgɔːki/ *adj* (esp of a tall young person) awkward in manner or movement: *a shy gawky teenager.* ▶ **gawkily** /ˈgɔːkɪli/ *adv.* **gawkiness** /ˈgɔːkinəs/ *n* [U].

gawp /gɔːp/ *v* ~ (**at sb/sth**) (*Brit infml*) to stare in a rude or stupid way: [Vpr] *crowds of onlookers gawping at the wreckage of the aircraft* [also V]. ⇨ note at LOOK[1].

gay /geɪ/ *adj* **1** HOMOSEXUAL; of or for homosexual people: *a gay person/club/bar* ∘ *the gay community* ∘ *I didn't know he/she was gay.* **2** [attrib] careless; without worries: *spending money* **with** *gay abandon.* **3** (**-er, -est**) (*becoming dated*) happy and full of fun; cheerful: *gay laughter/music.*
▶ **gaily** /ˈgeɪli/ *adv* **1** in an attractive or cheerful way: *gaily decorated buildings.* **2** without thinking of the consequences for others: *She gaily announced that she was leaving the next day.*
gay *n* a gay(1) person.
gayness /ˈgeɪnəs/ *n* [U] the state of being gay(1). See also GAIETY.

gaze /geɪz/ *v* to look long and steadily at sb/sth, usu in surprise or admiration: [Vpr] *She gazed at me in disbelief when I told her the news.* ∘ *He sat for hours just gazing into space/out of the window.* ∘ (*fml*) *She was the most beautiful woman he had ever gazed upon.* [also V, Vpl]. ⇨ note at LOOK[1].
▶ **gaze** *n* (usu *sing*) a long steady look: *She felt uncomfortable under his intense gaze.* ∘ *She dropped/ averted her gaze.*

gazebo /gəˈziːbəʊ/ *n* (*pl* **-os**) a small building designed to give a wide view of the country around.

gazelle /gəˈzel/ *n* (*pl* unchanged or **gazelles**) a small graceful ANTELOPE: *a herd of gazelle* ∘ *leap like a gazelle.*

gazette /gəˈzet/ *n* **1** an official journal with public notices and lists of government, military, legal or university appointments. **2** (used in the titles of newspapers): *the Evening Gazette.*

gazetteer /ˌgæzəˈtɪə(r)/ *an* index of place names: *a world gazetteer.*

gazump /gəˈzʌmp/ *v* (*Brit infml derog*) (usu passive) to raise the price of a house after accepting an offer from a buyer: [Vn] *We've lost the house we wanted — we've been gazumped.*
▶ **gazumping** /gəˈzʌmpɪŋ/ *n* [U] (*Brit infml derog*) the practice of gazumping buyers.

GB /ˌdʒiː ˈbiː/ *abbr* Great Britain. ⇨ note at BRITISH.

GCE /ˌdʒiː siː ˈiː/ *abbr* (formerly in Britain) General Certificate of Education: *have 9 GCEs.* Compare GCSE.

GCSE /ˌdʒiː siː es ˈiː/ *abbr* (in Britain) General

Certificate of Secondary Education: *have 8 GCSEs.* Compare A LEVEL, GCE.

Gdns *abbr* (in street names) Gardens: *7 Windsor Gdns.*

GDP /ˌdʒiː diː ˈpiː/ *abbr* gross domestic product. Compare GNP.

GDR /ˌdʒiː diː ˈɑː(r)/ *abbr* (formerly) German Democratic Republic (East Germany).

gear /ɡɪə(r)/ *n* **1** [U] equipment, clothing, etc needed for a sport, a holiday, etc: *All his camping gear was packed in the rucksack.* ○ *We're only going for two days — you don't need to bring so much gear!* ○ *She was wearing her party gear.* **2** [U] (esp in compounds) a piece of apparatus or machinery for a particular purpose: *winding-gear for lifting heavy loads.* See also LANDING-GEAR. **3(a)** [C often *pl*] a set of wheels with teeth on their edges that revolve together to transmit power from a vehicle's engine to its road wheels: *Careless use of the clutch may damage the gears.* ○ *The car started with a crashing of gears* (ie a noise made by operating them badly). ⇨ picture. ⇨ picture at BICYCLE. **(b)** [U] a particular position or setting of the gear mechanism: *engage bottom/first gear* ○ *change/shift gear* ○ *The car is in/out of gear.* **4** [U] a degree of speed or efficiency: *The party organization is moving into top gear as the election approaches.* ○ *The runner at the back suddenly changed gear* (ie got faster) *and overtook the others.*

▶ **gear** *v* **PHRV** **'gear sth to/towards/for sth** to adapt sth to a particular need or to an appropriate level or standard: *Our effort is geared to a higher level of production.* ○ *clothes geared for a particular market.* **ˌgear 'up (for/to sth); ˌgear sb/sth 'up (for/to sth)** to become or make sb/sth ready for sth: *The company's gearing (itself) up for a big export drive.* ○ *I was all geared up* (ie excited and ready) *to give a talk and now the conference has been cancelled.*

gearing /ˈɡɪərɪŋ/ *n* [U] **1** a set or an arrangement of gears: *The gearing of this machine is unusual.* **2** (*Brit finance*) the relation between money borrowed by a company from its bank and money provided by its shareholders (SHAREHOLDER).

■ **'gear-change** *n* a movement from one position of a gear mechanism to another: *a smooth gear-change.*

'gear lever (*US* usu **'gear shift**) *n* a handle used to change the setting of a vehicle's gear mechanism. ⇨ picture at BICYCLE, CAR.

gearbox /ˈɡɪəbɒks/ *n* the metal case that encloses a vehicle's gear mechanism. ⇨ picture at CAR.

gecko /ˈɡekəʊ/ *n* (*pl* **-os** or **-oes**) a small lizard that lives in people's houses in warm countries.

gee¹ /dʒiː/ (also **gee whiz**) /ˌdʒiː ˈwɪz/ *interj* (*esp US*) (expressing surprise, admiration, etc): *Gee, I like your new hat!*

gee² /dʒiː/ *v* **PHRV** **ˌgee 'up** (*infml*) (esp imperative, used for telling a horse, etc to start or go faster). **ˌgee sb/sth 'up** (*infml*) to make sb/sth work or perform more quickly or efficiently: *We need to gee them up a bit.*

gee-gee /ˈdʒiː dʒiː/ *n* (*Brit infml*) (used esp by and to small children) a horse.

geese *pl* of GOOSE.

gee-string = G-STRING.

geezer /ˈɡiːzə(r)/ *n* (*sl*) a man, esp an old one: *a funny sort of geezer.*

Geiger counter /ˈɡaɪɡə kaʊntə(r)/ *n* a device for detecting and measuring RADIOACTIVE substances.

geisha /ˈɡeɪʃə/ *n* a Japanese girl trained to entertain men with conversation, dancing or singing: *geisha girls.*

gel /dʒel/ *n* [C,U] (esp in compounds) a thick substance like jelly, used eg on the hair or skin: *'bath/'shower gel.*

▶ **gel** (also **jell**) *v* (**-ll-**) **1** to set into a jelly: [V] *This liquid gels faster in cold weather.* **2** to take definite form: [V] *My ideas are beginning to gel.*

gelatine /ˈdʒelətiːn/ (also *esp US* **gelatin** /ˈdʒelətɪn/) *n* [U] a clear substance without any taste used for making jelly as food, manufacturing photographic film, etc. ▶ **gelatinous** /dʒəˈlætɪnəs/ *adj*: *a gelatinous substance.*

geld /ɡeld/ *v* [Vn] to remove the testicles (TESTICLE) of a male animal.

▶ **gelding** /ˈɡeldɪŋ/ *n* a gelded horse. Compare STALLION.

gelignite /ˈdʒelɪɡnaɪt/ *n* [U] a powerful explosive.

gem /dʒem/ *n* **1** a precious stone or jewel, esp when cut and polished: *a crown studded with gems.* **2** a person or thing highly valued for a special quality: *This picture is the gem* (ie the best) *of the collection.* ○ *a gem of a place* ○ *She's a real gem!* Compare JEWEL 3.

Gemini /ˈdʒemɪnaɪ, -niː/ *n* **(a)** [U] the third sign of the ZODIAC, the Twins. ⇨ picture at ZODIAC. **(b)** [C] a person born under the influence of this sign. ⇨ picture at ZODIAC. ⇨ note at ZODIAC.

gemstone /ˈdʒemstəʊn/ *n* a precious stone or jewel, esp before it has been cut into shape.

Gen *abbr* General: *Gen (Stanley) Armstrong.*

gen /dʒen/ (usu **the gen**) *n* [U] ~ (**on sth**) (*dated Brit infml*) information: *Give me all the gen on the new project.*

▶ **gen** *v* (**-nn-**) **PHRV** **ˌgen (sb) 'up (on sth)** (*dated Brit infml*) to obtain information or provide sb with information about sth: *He is fully genned up on the situation.*

gendarme /ˈʒɒndɑːm/ *n* a member of the French police force.

▶ **gendarmerie** /ʒɒnˈdɑːməri/ *n* **1** [pl *v*] gendarmes as a group. **2** [C] the office from which a group of gendarmes is controlled.

gender /ˈdʒendə(r)/ *n* [C,U] **1** (*grammar*) (in certain languages) the CLASSIFICATION(1) of nouns, adjectives or pronouns as MASCULINE(2), FEMININE(2) or NEUTER(1): *In French the adjective must agree with the noun in number and gender.* **2** the condition of being male or female: *gender issues.*

NOTE When writing or speaking English it is important to use language that includes both men and women equally. The following notes give help with doing this.

The human race

Man and **mankind** have traditionally been used to mean 'all men and women'. Many people consider the use of these terms discriminates against women and prefer to use **humanity**, **the human race**, **human beings** or **people**.

Jobs

The suffix **-ess** in names of occupations such as **actress**, **authoress** and **hostess** show that the person doing the job is a woman. Many people now use the same word for both sexes because it is unnecessary to make a distinction between men and women doing the same job: **actor**, **author**, **host**.

It is also usually possible to use a neutral word like **assistant**, **worker**, **person** or **officer** instead of man/woman in the names of jobs.

salesman/saleswoman	= *sales assistant*
headmaster/headmistress	= *headteacher*
policeman/policewoman	= *police officer*
fireman/firewoman	= *fire-fighter*
chairman/chairwoman	= *chairperson* or *chair*

Many people prefer these alternatives since most jobs are now open to both sexes. They are very com-

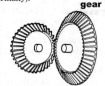
gear

---

mon in newspapers, on television and radio and in official writing, in both British and American English.

When talking about jobs that are traditionally done by the other sex, some people say: **a male secretary/nurse/model**. Or they say: **a woman doctor/ barrister/driver** (NOT **female**). Many people, especially women, feel it is offensive to mention a person's sex unnecessarily in this way.

Pronouns

Everybody, everyone, anybody, anyone, somebody, someone, etc are usually followed by the plural pronouns **they, them**, and **their**: *Does everybody know what they want?* ○ *Somebody's left their coat here.* ○ *I hope nobody's forgotten to bring their passport with them.*

You can also use **he or she, his or her**, or **him or her**, especially in more formal speech or writing: *Everyone knows what's best for him or herself.*

In writing you can also use **he/she** or **(s)he**: *If in doubt, ask your doctor. He/she can give you more information.*

Alternatively, the sentence can be rephrased, using a plural noun. Instead of saying: *A baby cries when he or she is tired* you can say *Babies cry when they are tired.*

---

gene /dʒiːn/ *n* (*biology*) a unit in a CHROMOSOME which controls inherited characteristics: *a dominant/recessive gene* ○ *genes that influence the colour of the eyes.* See also GENETIC.

genealogy /ˌdʒiːniˈælədʒi/ *n* **1** [U] the study of family history, including the study of who the ancestors of particular people were and how they were related to each other. **2** [C] a particular person's line of ancestors; a chart showing this.
▶ **genealogical** /ˌdʒiːniəˈlɒdʒɪkl/ *adj* concerned with one's ancestors and family history: *genealogical evidence/proof/records* ○ *a genealogical table/tree* (ie a chart with branches showing a family's ancestors).
genealogist /ˌdʒiːniˈælədʒɪst/ *n* an expert in genealogy.

genera *pl* of GENUS.

general¹ /ˈdʒenrəl/ *adj* **1** affecting all or most people, places or things; widespread: *a matter of general interest/concern* ○ *a general lowering of standards* ○ *The announcement met with general approval.* ○ *Once quite rare, calculators are now in general use* (ie used by most people). ○ *a general meeting/strike* ○ *The bad weather has been fairly general* (ie has affected most areas). **2** not limited to one part or aspect of a person or thing: *There is still some weakness in the legs, but her general condition is good.* ○ *The opening chapter gives a general overview of the subject.* ○ *The building was in a general state of disrepair.* **3(a)** not specialized in subject: *a general degree* ○ *general knowledge/sciences/studies* ○ *We deliberately kept the conversation/discussion fairly general.* **(b)** [attrib] not specialized or limited in range of work, use, activity, etc: *a general hospital* ○ *the general reader* ○ *the Transport and General Workers' Union.* **4** [usu attrib] normal; usual: *a general principle* (ie one true of most cases) *to which there may be several exceptions* ○ *The general practice in such cases is to apply for a court order.* ○ **As a general rule**, *the softer cheeses are less fattening.* **5** showing the chief aspects of sth; not detailed; VAGUE(1b): *speak/write in general terms* ○ *His description was too general to be of much use.* ○ *My general impression was that it was quite good.* **6** [attrib] (often in titles with a capital letter and following the *n*) chief; head: *the At,torney/ In,spector/,Governor/,Secretary* ˈGeneral ○ *the general manager.* See also POSTMASTER GENERAL. **IDM** **in** ˈgeneral **1** mainly; mostly; usually: *In general her work has been very good.* **2** as a whole: *I'm interested in European history in general.*

▶ **generalist** /ˈdʒenrəlɪst/ *n* a person competent in several different fields or activities. Compare SPECIALIST.
■ ˌGeneral Asˈsembly *n* a main meeting of representatives, eg of the United Nations.
ˌGeneral Cerˌtificate of Eduˈcation *n* (*abbr* GCE) (formerly) any of a range of examinations taken by pupils in British secondary schools. Compare A LEVEL, O LEVEL.
ˌGeneral Cerˌtificate of ˌSecondary Eduˈcation *n* (*abbr* GCSE) any of a range of examinations introduced in Britain in the late 1980s to replace both the O level GCE and the CSE.
ˌgeneral eˈlection *n* a national election to choose a government. Compare BY-ELECTION.
ˌgeneral headˈquarters *n* [sing or pl *v*] (*abbr* GHQ) a main centre of military organization and supplies.
ˌgeneral ˈpractice *n* [U] (*Brit*) the treatment by doctors of illness within the community, in contrast with work in a hospital or as a specialist in a particular area of medicine: *be/work in general practice.* ˌgeneral pracˈtitioner *n* (*abbr* GP) (*Brit*) a doctor in general practice.
the ˌgeneral ˈpublic *n* [Gp] ordinary people who are not members of a group with special privileges, experts in a particular field, etc: *The general public was/were not admitted.*
ˌgeneral-ˈpurpose *adj* [attrib] having a variety of uses: *a ˌgeneral-purpose ˈfarm vehicle.*
ˌgeneral ˈstaff (often **the general staff**) *n* [Gp] officers assisting a military leader in administration and planning.

general² /ˈdʒenrəl/ *n* (the title of) an army officer of very high rank: *a four-star general* (ie in the US army) ○ *General Roberts.* ⇨ App 6.
▶ **generalship** /ˈdʒenrəlʃɪp/ *n* [U] skill in commanding forces in battle; skill in leading people.

generalissimo /ˌdʒenrəˈlɪsɪməʊ/ *n* (*pl* **-os**) a general leading combined military, naval and air forces, or combined armies.

generality /ˌdʒenəˈræləti/ *n* **1** [C] a statement that discusses general principles or issues rather than details: *speak in bland/broad generalities* ○ *The report is full of generalities and fails to get down to specifics.* **3** **the generality** [pl *v*] (*fml*) the majority; most: *The generality of Swedes have fair hair.* **2** [U] the quality of being general: *An account of such generality is of little value.*

generalize, -ise /ˈdʒenrəlaɪz/ *v* **1** to draw a general conclusion from a particular set of examples or evidence: [Vpr] *You cannot generalize about the effects of the drug from the cases of one or two patients.* [Vn] *We are now in a position to generalize the lessons we have learnt.* [also V]. **2** ~ (**about sth**) to make general statements for which there is little evidence: [V] *Europeans, if I may generalize, are all…* [also Vpr].
▶ **generalized, -ised** *adj* **1** not specific; general¹(2): *a generalized account/comment/statement.* **2** widespread; general¹(1): *Use of this drug is now fairly generalized.*
generalization, -isation /ˌdʒenrəlaɪˈzeɪʃn; US -lə'z-/ *n* **(a)** [C] a statement that generalizes: *a speech full of broad/sweeping generalizations* ○ **make generalizations about** *sth.* **(b)** [U] the action of generalizing: *avoid generalization.*

generally /ˈdʒenrəli/ *adv* **1** by most people; widely: *He is generally popular.* ○ *The plan was generally welcomed.* **2** in general terms; without regard to details: *Let's talk first about investment generally.* ○ *Generally speaking, it's quite a fair settlement.* **3** usually: *I generally get up at 6 am.* ⇨ note at HOPEFUL.

generate /ˈdʒenəreɪt/ *v* to make sth exist or occur; to produce sth: [Vn] *generate heat/electricity/power* ○

---

generate profits/employment/enthusiasm ∘ *hatred generated by racial prejudice.*

generation /ˌdʒenəˈreɪʃn/ *n* **1** [CGp] all people born at about the same time: *the younger generation* ∘ *My generation has/have a quite different outlook from my father's and my grandfather's.* **2** [C] the average period, usu considered to be 25–30 years, in which children grow up, become adults and have children of their own: *a generation ago* ∘ *within one generation.* **3** [C,U] a single stage in a family's history: *Three generations were present — myself, my mother and my grandmother.* ∘ *stories handed down from generation to generation* ∘ *a second-/third-generation American* (ie sb whose family have lived in America for two/three generations). **4** [C usu *sing*] (**a**) a group of people of similar age involved in a particular activity: *a new generation of opera lovers/fashion designers.* (**b**) a single stage in the development of a type of product: *the new generation of airliners* ∘ *fifth-generation computing.* **5** [U] the production of sth: *nuclear power generation* ∘ *new methods of income generation* ∘ *the generation of racial hatred.* **6** (*biology*) the development of living beings: *Humans and animals were thought to have arisen by spontaneous generation.*

■ **the gene'ration gap** *n* [sing] a difference in attitude, or a lack of understanding, between young people and older people.

generative /ˈdʒenərətɪv/ *adj* **1** able to produce sth: *generative processes/programmes.* **2** (*biology*) concerned with reproducing: *generative organs.*

generator /ˈdʒenəreɪtə(r)/ *n* a machine for producing electrical energy; a DYNAMO(1): *The factory's emergency generators were used during the power cut.*

generic /dʒəˈnerɪk/ *adj* shared by or including a whole group or class of things; not specific: *The generic term for wine, spirits and beer is 'alcoholic beverages'.* ▶ **generically** /dʒəˈnerɪkli/ *adv.*

generosity /ˌdʒenəˈrɒsəti/ *n* [U] ~ (to/towards sb) the quality of being generous.

generous /ˈdʒenərəs/ *adj* **1(a)** giving or ready to give freely: *generous with one's money/in giving help* ∘ *It was generous of you to share your food with me.* (**b**) given freely; large in value or amount: *a generous gift/offer/increase* ∘ *a generous helping of potatoes.* **2** showing kindness in one's attitude to and treatment of others; noble: *a generous mind/spirit* ∘ *A wise ruler is generous in victory.* ▶ **generously** *adv*: *Please give generously.* ∘ *a dress that is generously cut* (ie uses plenty of material).

genesis /ˈdʒenəsɪs/ *n* (*pl* **geneses** /ˈdʒenəsiːz/) (*fml*) the beginning or origin of sth: *the genesis of civilization* ∘ *The genesis of the play was the author's experiences as a dock labourer.*

genetic /dʒəˈnetɪk/ *adj* of genes (GENE) or genetics: *genetic factors/information.*
▶ **genetically** /-kli/ *adv*: *genetically determined/programmed.*

geneticist /dʒəˈnetɪsɪst/ *n* a specialist in genetics.

genetics /dʒəˈnetɪks/ *n* [sing *v*] the scientific study of the ways in which different characteristics are passed from each generation of living things to the next.

■ **the ge,netic 'code** *n* [sing] the system by which genetic information is stored in chromosomes (CHROMOSOME).

ge,netic ,engi'neering *n* [U] the deliberate changing of inherited features by altering the structure or position of individual genes (GENE).

ge,netic 'fingerprinting *n* [U] the practice of analysing genetic patterns as a way of identifying individuals, esp people who have committed crimes.

genial /ˈdʒiːniəl/ *adj* friendly in a cheerful way: *a genial person/mood.* ▶ **geniality** /ˌdʒiːniˈæləti/

n [U]: *an atmosphere of warmth and geniality.*
genially /ˈdʒiːniəli/ *adv.*

genie /ˈdʒiːni/ *n* (*pl* **genies** or **genii** /ˈdʒiːniaɪ/) (in Arabian stories) a magical spirit with strange powers.

genital /ˈdʒenɪtl/ *adj* [attrib] (*medical or fml*) of animal reproduction or the sex organs: *the genital area* ∘ *genital infections/warts.*
▶ **genitals** /ˈdʒenɪtlz/ (also **genitalia** /ˌdʒenɪˈteɪliə/) *n* [pl] (*fml*) the external sex organs.

genitive /ˈdʒenətɪv/ *n* (*grammar*) (in certain languages) the special form of a noun, a pronoun or an adjective used to indicate possession or close connection. Compare POSSESSIVE *n* 2. ▶ **genitive** *adj*: *The genitive forms of the pronouns 'I', 'we' and 'she' are 'my/mine', 'our/ours' and 'her/hers'.*

genius /ˈdʒiːniəs/ *n* (*pl* **geniuses**) **1(a)** [U] an exceptionally great mental or creative ability: *a writer of genius* ∘ *It is rare to find such genius nowadays.* (**b**) [C] a person who has such ability: *Einstein was a mathematical genius.* ∘ *He is hard-working and able, but no genius.* **2** [sing] **a ~ for sth** an exceptional natural ability for doing sth; a special talent: *have a genius for languages/for making friends/for saying the wrong thing.* **IDM** **one's good/evil 'genius** a person or spirit supposed to have a strong influence on one for good or for evil: *Blame it on my evil genius!*

genocide /ˈdʒenəsaɪd/ *n* [U] the deliberate killing of a nation or race of people.

genre /ˈʒɑːnrə/ *n* a particular style or type, esp of works of art or literature: *The novel and short story belong to different literary genres.*
■ **'genre painting** *n* [C,U] a painting or style of painting that shows scenes from ordinary life.

gent /dʒent/ *n* **1** [C] (*infml or joc*) a gentleman: *This way, please, gents!* ∘ *a city/country gent* ∘ *a gents' hairdresser/outfitter.* **2** **a/the Gents** [usu sing *v*] (*Brit infml*) a public toilet for men: *Where's the nearest Gents?* ⇨ note at TOILET.

genteel /dʒenˈtiːl/ *adj* **1** (*often derog*) polite or refined, esp in an affected or exaggerated way: *She is too genteel for words!* **2** (*dated*) of the upper social classes: *living in genteel poverty* (ie trying to maintain the style of living of the upper classes, though too poor to do so). ▶ **genteelly** /dʒenˈtiːlli/ *adv.*

gentian /ˈdʒenʃn/ *n* [C,U] a plant with blue flowers that grows in mountain areas.

gentile (also **Gentile**) /ˈdʒentaɪl/ *n*, *adj* [attrib] (a person who is) not Jewish.

gentility /dʒenˈtɪləti/ *n* [U] (*usu approv*) the quality of being GENTEEL; good manners and behaviour: *He thinks fine clothes are a mark of gentility.*

gentle /ˈdʒentl/ *adj* (**-r** /ˈdʒentlə(r)/; **-st** /ˈdʒentlɪst/) **1(a)** mild; kind; careful; not rough, violent or severe: *a gentle person/manner/voice/touch* ∘ *a doctor who is gentle with his hands* ∘ *soap that is gentle on/to one's skin* ∘ *Be gentle with my best china!* (**b**) (of weather, temperature, etc) mild; not having extremes of hot or cold: *a gentle breeze* ∘ *gentle rainfall* ∘ *cook over a gentle heat.* **2** not steep or ABRUPT(1): *a gentle slope.*
▶ **gentleness** /ˈdʒentlnəs/ *n* [U].

gently /ˈdʒentli/ *adv* in a gentle(1a) manner: *handle sth gently* ∘ *speak to sb gently* ∘ *The beach slopes gently down to the sea.* **IDM** **easy/gently does it** ⇨ EASY².

gentlefolk /ˈdʒentlfəʊk/ *n* [pl *v*] (*dated*) people belonging to respected families of the higher social classes.

gentleman /ˈdʒentlmən/ *n* (*pl* **-men** /-mən/) **1** [C] (*approv*) a man who is polite and shows consideration for the feelings of other people; a man who always acts in an honourable way: *Thank you — you're a real gentleman!* ∘ *He's no gentleman!* Compare LADY 2. **2(a)** **gentlemen** [pl] (*fml*) (used as a polite form of address to men): *Gentlemen of the jury.* ○ *Ladies and gentlemen* (eg when beginning a speech),.... (**b**) [C] (used as a polite way of referring to a man): *There's a gentleman at the door.* ⇨ note at LADY. **3** [C] (*dated*) a man of wealth and social position, esp one who does not need to work for a living: *a country gentleman* ○ *a gentleman farmer* (ie one who owns a farm, but does no physical work himself). **IDM** **ladies and gentlemen** ⇨ LADY.

▶ **gentlemanly** *adj* (*approv*) of or like a gentleman (1): *gentlemanly behaviour* ○ *So far, the contest between the two candidates has been a rather gentlemanly affair.*

■ **‚gentleman's a'greement** (also **gentlemen's agreement**) *n* an agreement that has no legal force but depends on the mutual trust and good faith of those involved.

gentlewoman /ˈdʒentlwʊmən/ *n* (*pl* **-women** /-wɪmɪn/) (*arch*) a woman from a noble family; a LADY(3).

gentry /ˈdʒentri/ *n* (usu **the gentry**) [pl *v*] people of good social position: *the local gentry* ○ *a member of* **the landed gentry** (ie those that own a lot of land).

▶ **gentrify** /ˈdʒentrɪfaɪ/ *v* (*pt, pp* **-fied**) [Vn] (*infml*) to restore and improve a house, an area, etc to make it suitable for people of a higher social class than those who lived there before. **gentrification** *n* [U].

genuflect /ˈdʒenjuflekt/ *v* [V] (*fml*) to bend one's knee, esp in worship or to show respect. ▶ **genuflexion** /ˌdʒenjuˈflekʃn/ *n* [C,U].

genuine /ˈdʒenjuɪn/ *adj* **1** real; truly what it is said to be; not artificial: *a genuine Rubens* (ie a painting definitely by Rubens himself, not by sb copying his style) ○ *a genuine antique.* **2** sincere; honest: *a genuine offer of help* ○ *She seems genuine, but can I trust her?* ▶ **genuinely** *adv*: *genuinely sorry.* **genuineness** *n* [U].

genus /ˈdʒiːnəs/ *n* (*pl* **genera** /ˈdʒenərə/) **1** (*biology*) a group of animals or plants within a family(4), often itself divided into several species(1). Compare PHYLUM, CLASS 7, ORDER[1] 10. **2** (*infml*) a kind or type of person or thing.

geo- *comb form* of the earth: ‚geo'centric ○ ge'ography ○ ge'ology.

geocentric /ˌdʒiːəʊˈsentrɪk/ *adj* having the earth as its centre: *a geocentric view of the universe* .

geography /dʒiˈɒɡrəfi/ *n* **1** [U] the scientific study of the earth's surface, physical features, divisions, climate, products, population, etc: *physical/political/social geography* ○ *a geography book/student/lecture.* **2** [sing] **the ~ (of sth)** (*infml*) the arrangement of the features of a place: *getting to know the geography of a neighbourhood/house/kitchen* (ie where things in them are, in relation to each other).

▶ **geographer** /dʒiˈɒɡrəfə(r)/ *n* a student of or an expert in geography.

geographical /ˌdʒiːəˈɡræfɪkl/ *adj* of or relating to geography: *geographical features/research.* **geographically** /-kli/ *adv.*

geology /dʒiˈɒlədʒi/ *n* [U] the scientific study of the earth, including the origin and history of the rocks, soil, etc of which it is composed: *a geology course/department/lecturer.*

▶ **geological** /ˌdʒiːəˈlɒdʒɪkl/ *adj* of or relating to geology: *a geological age/fault.* **geologically** /-kli/ *adv.*

geologist /dʒiˈɒlədʒɪst/ *n* a student of or an expert in geology.

geometry /dʒiˈɒmətri/ *n* [U] a branch of MATHEMATICS dealing with the measurements and relationships of lines, angles, surfaces and solids: *a geometry set* (ie a set of the instruments needed for drawing geometric figures).

▶ **geometric** /ˌdʒiːəˈmetrɪk/ (also **geometrical** /-ɪkl/) *adj* of geometry; of or like the lines, figures,

etc used in geometry: *a geometric design.* **geo‚metric pro'gression** *n* an ordered set of numbers in which each is multiplied or divided by a fixed number to produce the next, eg 1, 3, 9, 27, 81. Compare ARITHMETIC PROGRESSION. **geometrically** /-kli/ *adv.*

geophysics /ˌdʒiːəʊˈfɪzɪks/ *n* [sing *v*] the scientific study of the earth's physical activities, eg its atmosphere, climate and oceans. ▶ **geophysical** /ˌdʒiːəʊˈfɪzɪkl/ *adj.* **geophysicist** /ˌdʒiːəʊˈfɪzɪsɪst/ *n.*

geopolitics /ˌdʒiːəʊˈpɒlətɪks/ *n* [sing *v*] the study of how politics is affected by geographical (GEOGRAPHY) factors. ▶ **geopolitical** /ˌdʒiːəʊpəˈlɪtɪkl/ *adj.*

Georgian /ˈdʒɔːdʒən/ *adj* (*Brit*) of the time of the British kings George I–IV (1714–1830): *a Georgian house* ○ *Georgian furniture.*

geranium /dʒəˈreɪniəm/ *n* a garden plant with red, pink or white flowers. ⇨ picture at FLOWER.

geriatrics /ˌdʒeriˈætrɪks/ *n* [sing *v*] a branch of medicine dealing with the diseases and care of old people.

▶ **geriatric** /ˌdʒeriˈætrɪk/ *adj* of or relating to geriatrics: *the geriatric ward of a hospital.* **geriatrician** /ˌdʒeriəˈtrɪʃn/ *n* a doctor specializing in geriatrics.

germ /dʒɜːm/ *n* **1** [C] a tiny ORGANISM(1), esp one that causes disease: *Disinfectant kills germs.* **2** [C] A portion of a living ORGANISM(1) capable of becoming a whole new organism; the EMBRYO of a seed. **3** [C usu *sing*] **~ of sth** the beginning from which sth may develop: *the germ of an idea.*

■ **‚germ 'warfare** *n* [U] = BIOLOGICAL WARFARE.

German /ˈdʒɜːmən/ *adj* of Germany, its culture, its language or its people: *German industry/traditions/grammar.*

▶ **German** *n* **1** [C] a German person. **2** [U] the language spoken in Germany, Austria and part of Switzerland.

Germanic /dʒɜːˈmænɪk/ *adj* having German characteristics: *Germanic features/attitudes* ○ *the Germanic languages* (ie the group including German, Dutch, English, etc).

■ **‚German 'measles** (also **rubella**) *n* [U] a mild infectious disease causing a sore throat and red spots all over the body. It can seriously affect babies born to women who catch it soon after they become pregnant.

‚German 'shepherd *n* (*US*) = ALSATIAN.

germane /dʒɜːˈmeɪn/ *adj* **~ (to sth)** (*fml*) connected with sth; relevant: *remarks that are germane to the discussion.*

germinate /ˈdʒɜːmɪneɪt/ *v* to start or make sth start growing: [V] *The seeds germinated within a week.* [Vn] *germinate cabbages/beans.* ▶ **germination** /ˌdʒɜːmɪˈneɪʃn/ *n* [U]: *Keep the seeds in warm damp conditions to encourage germination.*

gerontology /ˌdʒerɒnˈtɒlədʒi/ *n* [U] the scientific study of old age and the process of growing old.

gerrymander /ˈdʒerimændə(r)/ *v* [Vn] (*derog*) to fix the boundaries of or divide an area for voting in order to give unfair advantages to one party in an election. ▶ **gerrymandering** *n* [U]: *guilty of political gerrymandering.*

gerund /ˈdʒerənd/ *n* = VERBAL NOUN.

Gestapo /ɡeˈstɑːpəʊ/ *n* **the Gestapo** [Gp] (formerly) the secret police of the Nazi party in Germany.

gestation /dʒeˈsteɪʃn/ *n* **1(a)** [U] the process of carrying a young person or animal inside the mother's body for the period before birth: *Gestation in humans lasts about nine months.* (**b**) [sing] the period of time taken by this. **2** [U] the process by which an idea or a plan is developed.

gesticulate /dʒeˈstɪkjuleɪt/ *v* to move the hands or arms (usu rapidly) and expressively or to emphasize one's words: [V, Vpr] *He was gesticulating wildly (at me), but I couldn't understand what he was*

G

---

trying to tell me. ▶ **gesticulation** /dʒeˌstɪkjuˈleɪʃn/ *n* [C, U]: *wild/frantic gesticulations.*

gesture /ˈdʒestʃə(r)/ *n* **1** [C, U] a movement of a part of the body, esp the hand or head, intended to suggest a certain meaning; the use of such movements: *make a rude gesture* ○ *with a gesture of despair* ○ *communicate entirely by gesture.* **2** [C] an action done to show one's feelings or intentions: *a gesture of defiance/sympathy* ○ *The invitation was meant as a friendly gesture.*
▶ **gesture** *v* to make movements with one's hands, head, etc as a way of expressing oneself or in order to suggest some meaning: [V] *gesturing vaguely with one's hands* [Vn] *She gestured her disapproval.* [Vpr] *He gestured to/towards the door.* [V.that, Vpr.that] *He gestured (to me) that it was time to go.* [Vpr.to inf] *He gestured to them to keep quiet.* [also V.that].

get /get/ *v* (**-tt-**; *pt* **got** /gɒt/; *pp* **got**, *US* **gotten** /ˈgɒtn/)

● **Receiving or obtaining 1** (no passive) to receive sth: [Vnpr] *I got a letter from my sister this morning.* [Vn] *Did you get my postcard?* ○ *What did you get for Christmas?* ○ *He gets* (ie earns) *about £25 000 a year.* ○ *This room gets very little sunshine.* ○ *Schoolteachers get long holidays.* ○ *He got* (ie was hit by) *a bullet in the thigh.* ○ *She got a shock when she saw the telephone bill.* ○ *I got the impression that he was bored with his job.* **2** (no passive) (**a**) ~ **sth (for oneself/sb)** to obtain sth: [Vn] *Where did you get* (ie buy) *that skirt?* ○ *Did you manage to get tickets for the concert?* ○ *She opened the door wider to get a better look.* ○ *Try to get some sleep.* ○ *He doesn't look as though he gets enough exercise.* ○ *Christie got* (ie won) *the gold medal in the 100 metres.* ○ *She's just got* (ie been appointed to) *a job with a publishing company.* [Vnn] *Why don't you get yourself a car?* [Vnn, Vnpr] *Have you remembered to get your mother a birthday present/get a birthday present for your mother?* (**b**) ~ **sb/sth (for oneself/sb)** to go to a place and bring sb/sth back: [Vn] *Go and get a dictionary and we'll look the word up.* ○ *Somebody get a doctor! I think this woman's had a heart attack.* [Vnpr] *I have to go and get my mother* (ie collect her in a car) *from the station.* [Vnn, Vnpr] *Can I get you a drink/get a drink for you?* **3** ~ **sth (for sth)** (no passive) to obtain or receive an amount of money by selling sth: [Vnpr, Vn] *'How much did you get for your old car?' 'I got $800 (for it).'* **4** (no passive) to receive sth as a punishment: [Vn] *He got ten years* (ie was sentenced to ten years in prison) *for armed robbery.* **5** (no passive) (**a**) to be able to receive broadcasts from a particular television or radio station: [Vn] *We can't get Channel 4 in our area.* (**b**) to be connected with sb by telephone: [Vn] *I wanted to speak to the manager but I got his secretary instead.* **6** (no passive) to buy sth, eg a newspaper or magazine, regularly: [Vn] *Do you get the 'Telegraph' or the 'Guardian'?* **7** (no passive) to become infected with an illness; to suffer from or be affected by a pain, etc: [Vn] *get bronchitis/flu/measles* ○ *She gets* (ie regularly suffers from) *bad headaches.* **8** (no passive) to achieve or be awarded the specified examination grade, class of degree, etc: [Vn] *She got a first class degree in English at Oxford.* ○ *He got a 'C' in Chemistry.*

● **Reaching or bringing to a particular state or condition 9(a)** to reach the specified state or condition; to become: [V-adj] *get angry/bored/ hungry/worried* ○ *get fat/fit/thinner* ○ *It/The weather is getting colder.* ○ *She's getting better* (eg after her illness). ○ *You'll get wet if you go out in the rain without an umbrella.* ○ *You'll soon get used to the climate here.* ○ *We ought to go; it's getting late.* ⇨ note at BECOME. (**b**) to cause oneself to be in the specified state or condition: [V-adj] *get dressed/ undressed* (ie put one's clothes on/take one's clothes

off) ○ *They plan to get married in the summer.* ○ *She's upstairs getting ready.* (**c**) (used in place of *be* with a past participle to form passive constructions) [V-adj] *Do you think the Tories will get* (ie be) *re-elected?* ○ *I wouldn't go there after dark; you might get* (ie be) *mugged.* **10** to cause sb/sth to be or become: [Vn-adj] *She soon got the children ready for school.* ○ *I must get the dinner ready* (ie prepare it). ○ *Don't get your new dress dirty!* ○ *Do you think you'll get the work finished on time?* ○ *He got his wrist broken* (ie broke it accidentally). ○ *I couldn't get the car started this morning.* ○ *Go and get your hair cut!* ○ *She got her fingers caught in the door.* ○ *(infml) The argument at work got her upset.*

● **Making something happen 11** to bring sb/sth to the point at which they are/it is doing sth: [V.n ing] *Can you really get that old car going again?* ○ *It's not hard to get him talking; the problem is stopping him!* **12** to cause, persuade, etc sb/sth to do sth: [Vn.to inf] *I couldn't get the car to start* (ie make it start) *this morning.* ○ *He got* (ie persuaded) *his sister to help him with his homework.* ○ *You'll never get him to understand.* ○ *I can't get her to talk at all.*

● **Reaching the point where one does something 13(a)** to reach the stage at which one is doing sth; to start doing sth: [V.ing] *I got talking to her/We got talking.* ○ *We got chatting and discovered we'd been at college together.* ○ *You have an hour to clean the whole house — so get working!* (**b**) to reach the point at which one feels, knows, is, etc sth: [V.to inf] *You'll like her once you get to know her.* ○ *How did you get to know* (ie discover or learn) *that I was here?* ○ *One soon gets to like it here.* ○ *She's getting to be an old lady now.* ○ *After a time you get to realize that these things don't matter.* ○ *His drinking is getting to be a problem.* ○ *Your mother will be furious if she gets to hear of this.* **14** (*esp US*) to have the chance or opportunity to do sth; to manage to do sth: [V.to inf] *Did you get to see the Louvre while you were in Paris?* ○ *When do I get to go to a movie?*

● **Moving or causing to move 15(a)** to move to or from a specified point or in a specified direction, sometimes with difficulty: [Vpr] *The bridge was destroyed so we couldn't get across* (ie cross) *the river.* ○ *She got into bed.* ○ *She got down from the ladder.* ○ *He got into the car.* ○ *Can you get over the wall?* ○ *We didn't get* (ie go) *to bed till 3 am.* [Vp] *I'm getting off* (ie leaving the train) *at the next station.* ○ *Please let me get ¹by* (ie pass). [Vadv] *Where have they ¹got to?* (ie Where are they?) ○ *We must be getting home; it's past midnight.* (**b**) to cause sb/sth to move to or from a specified point or in a specified direction, sometimes with difficulty: [Vnpr] *The general had to get his troops across the river.* ○ *We couldn't get the piano through the door.* [Vnadv] *We'd better call a taxi and get you home.* [Vnp] *I can't get the lid on/off.* (**c**) ~ **to/into ...**; ~ **in** to arrive at or reach a place or point: [Vpr] *We got to San Diego at 7 o'clock.* ○ *The train gets into Glasgow at 6 o'clock in the morning.* [Vp] *You got in very late last night.* [Vadv] *What time did you get here?* ○ *I haven't got very far with the book I'm reading.* **16** (no passive) to travel by bus, taxi, plane, etc: [Vn] *We're going to be late; let's get a taxi.* ○ *'How do you come to work?' 'I usually get the bus.'*

● **Other meanings 17** ~ **sth (for oneself/sb)** to prepare a meal: [Vn] *Don't disturb your mother while she's getting (the) dinner.* [Vnn, Vnpr] *I have to go home and get the children their supper/get supper for the children.* **18(a)** to catch or seize sb/sth: [Vn] *He was on the run for a week before the police got him.* [Vnpr] *get sb by the arm/wrist/throat.* (**b**) to catch and harm, injure or kill sb, often in revenge for sth: [Vn] *She fell overboard and the sharks got her.* ○ *He thinks the Mafia are out to get him.* ○ *I'll get you for that, you bastard!* (**c**) to hit or wound sb: [Vnadv] *Where did the stone ¹get you?* [Vnpr] *The* *bullet got him in the neck.* ○ *I got him on the back of the head with a crowbar.* **19** (*infml*) (no passive) (**a**) to understand sb/sth: [Vn] *I don't get you/your meaning.* ○ *She didn't get the joke.* ○ *I don't 'get it — why would she do a thing like that?* (**b**) to hear sth: [Vn] *I didn't quite get what you said.* **20** (*infml*) (no passive) to confuse or puzzle sb: [Vn] *'What's the capital of Luxembourg?' 'I don't know; you've 'got me there!'* (no passive) to annoy or irritate sb: [Vn] *It really 'gets me when she bosses people around.*

IDM Most idioms containing **get** are at the entries for the nouns or adjectives in the idioms, eg **get sb's goat** ⇨ GOAT. **be getting 'on 1** (of a person) to be becoming old: *Grandma's getting on a bit and doesn't go out as much as she used to.* **2** (of time) to be becoming late: *The time's getting on; we ought to be going.* **be getting on for ...** to be near to or approaching the specified time, age or number: *It must be getting on for midnight.* ○ *He's getting on for eighty.* **sb can't/couldn't get 'over sth** (*infml*) sb is/was shocked, surprised, amused, etc by sth: *I can't get over that shirt he was wearing.* ○ *I can't get over how rude she was.* **get a'long/a'way/'on (with you)** (*Brit infml*) (used to show that one does not believe sth or to criticize sb gently): *'How old are you?' 'I'm forty.' 'Get along with you! You don't look a day over thirty-five!'* **get a'way from it all** (*infml*) to have a short holiday in a place that is totally different from where one usu lives. **get (sb) anywhere/somewhere/nowhere** (*infml*) (to cause sb) to achieve something/nothing or to make progress/no progress: *After six months' work on the project, at last I feel I'm 'getting somewhere.* ○ *This line of investigation is getting us 'nowhere.* **'get there** to achieve one's aim or complete a task by patience and hard work: *I'm sure you'll get there in the end.* ○ *Writing a dictionary is a long and difficult business but we're getting there.* **how selfish, stupid, ungrateful, etc can you 'get?** (*infml*) (used to express surprise or disapproval that sb has been so selfish, etc): *He wouldn't even lend me ten cents — how mean can you get?* **there's no getting a'way from sth; one can't get a'way from sth** one has to admit the truth of sth unpleasant: *There's no getting away from it — the economy is in a mess.*

PHR V **get a'bout/a'round** (to be able) to move from place to place: *He's getting about again after his accident.* ○ *She doesn't get around much these days.* **get a'bout/a'round/'round** (of news, a rumour, etc) to spread from person to person; to circulate: *The news of her resignation soon got about.* **get a'bove oneself** to have too high an opinion of oneself: *She's been getting a bit above herself since winning her award.* **get (sth) a'cross (to sb)** (to cause sth) to be communicated or understood: *Your meaning didn't really get across.* ○ *He's not very good at getting his ideas across.* **get a'head (of sb)** to progress (beyond sb): *She's keen to get ahead in her career.* ○ *By doing extra homework, he soon got ahead of the others in his class.* **get a'long 1** (usu in the continuous tenses) to leave a place: *It's time we were getting along.* **2** = GET ON 1. **3** = GET ON 3. **get a'long with sb; get a'long (together)** to have a comfortable or friendly relationship with sb; to get on with sb: *Do you get along with your boss?/Do you and your boss get along?* ○ *We get along just fine.* **get along with sth** = GET ON WITH STH 1. **get around 1** = GET ABOUT. **2** ⇨ GET ABOUT/AROUND/ROUND. **get around sb** = GET ROUND SB. **get around sth** = GET ROUND STH. **get around to sth / doing sth** = GET ROUND TO STH/DOING STH. **'get at sb** (*infml*) **1** (usu in the continuous tenses) to criticize sb repeatedly: *He's always getting at his*

wife. ○ *She feels she's being 'got at.* **2** to influence sb, esp unfairly or illegally: *One of the witnesses had been 'got at* (eg bribed). **'get at sb/sth** to gain access to sb/sth; to reach sb/sth: *The files are locked up and I can't get at them.* **'get at sth 1** to learn, discover or find out sth: *The truth is sometimes difficult to 'get at.* **2** (*infml*) (no passive; used only in the continuous tenses and usu in questions) to suggest sth indirectly; to imply sth: *What exactly are you 'getting at?* ○ *to imply sth: What exactly are you 'getting at?* **get a'way** to have a holiday: *We're hoping to get away for a few days at Easter.* **get away (from ...)** to succeed in leaving a place: *I won't be able to get away (from the office) before 7.* **get a'way (from sb/ ...)** to escape from sb or a place: *Two of the prisoners got away (from their captors).* **get a'way with sth 1** to steal sth and escape with it: *Thieves raided the bank and got away with a lot of money.* **2** to receive a relatively light punishment: *For such a serious offence he was lucky to get away with only a fine.* **3** (also **get a'way with doing sth**) (*infml*) to do sth wrong and not be punished for it: *If you cheat in the exam you'll never get away with it.* ○ *Nobody gets away with insulting me like that.*

get 'back to return, esp to one's home: *What time did you get back last night?* ○ *We only got back from our trip yesterday.* **get sth 'back** to obtain sth again after having lost it; to recover sth: *She's got her old job back.* ○ *I never lend books — you never get them back.* **get 'back (in)** (of a political party) to return to power after having lost it: *The Democrats hope to get back (in) at the next election.* **get 'back at sb** (*infml*) to take revenge on sb; to repay an injury or insult with a similar one: *I'll find a way of getting back at him!* **get 'back to sb** to speak or write to sb again later, esp in order to give a reply: *I hope to get back to you on the question of costs by next week.* **get 'back to sth** to return to sth: *Could we get back to the original question of funding?* **get 'behind (with sth)** to fail to proceed at the necessary rate or to produce sth at the right time: *I'm getting behind (with my work).* ○ *He got behind with his payments for the car.* **get 'by** to be considered good enough or adequate; to be accepted: *I have no formal clothes for the occasion. Perhaps I can get by in a dark suit?* ○ *He should just about get by in the exam.* **get 'by (on sth)** to manage to live, survive, etc using the specified resources: *How does she get by on such a small salary?*

get 'down (of children) to leave the table after a meal. **get sb 'down** (*infml*) to make sb feel depressed: *This wet weather is getting me down.* ○ *Don't let the incident get you down too much.* **get sth 'down 1** to swallow sth, usu with difficulty: *The medicine was so horrible I could hardly get it down.* **2** to note or record sth; to write sth down: *Did you get his telephone number down?* **get 'down to sth / doing sth** to begin to do sth; to give serious attention to sth: *get down to business* ○ *It's time I got down to some serious work.*

get 'in 1 (of a train, etc or a passenger) to arrive at a destination: *The train got in late.* ○ *What time does your flight get in?* ○ *When do you normally get in from work?* **get 'in; get 'into sth** to be elected to a political position: *The Republican candidate stands a good chance of getting in.* ○ *Labour got in* (ie won the election) *with a small majority.* ○ *She first got into Parliament* (ie became an MP) *in 1959.* **get (sb) 'in; get (sb) 'into sth** (to cause sb) to be admitted to a school, university, etc, esp after taking an examination: *He took the entrance exam but didn't get in.* ○ *She's got into Durham to read/study law.* ○ *I think we can get your son into university.* **get sb 'in** to call sb to one's house to perform a service: *We'll have to get a plumber in to replace that old pipe.* **get sth 'in 1** to collect or gather sth: *get the crops/harvest in.* **2** to buy a supply of sth: *get coal in for the winter* ○

G

Remember to get in some beers for this evening. **3** to manage to do or say sth: *I got in an hour's gardening between the showers.* ○ *She talks so much that it's impossible to get a word in.* ¡**get ¹in on sth** (*infml*) to take part in an activity: *She's hoping to get in on any discussions about the new project.* ¡**get ¹in with sb** (*infml*) (to try) to become friendly with sb, esp in order to gain an advantage: *Have you noticed how he's trying to get in with the boss?* ○ *He's got in with a bad crowd at school.*

¡**get ¹into sb** (*infml*) (of a feeling) to affect, influence or take control of sb: *I don't know what's got into him recently — he's become very bad-tempered.* ¡**get ¹into sth 1** to put on a garment, esp with difficulty: *I can't get into these shoes — they're too small.* **2** to start a career in the specified profession: *get into accountancy/journalism/publishing.* **3** to become involved in sth; to start sth: *get into an argument/a conversation/a fight (with sb).* **4** to acquire or develop sth: *get into bad habits.* **5** to become familiar with sth; to learn sth: *I haven't really got into my new job yet.* **6** (*infml*) to develop an interest in sth: *I'm really getting into jazz these days.* ○ *How did she get into* (ie start taking) *drugs?* ¡**get (oneself/sb) ¹into sth** (to cause oneself/sb) to pass into or reach the specified state or condition: *get into a fury/rage/temper* ○ *He got into trouble with the police while he was still at school.* ○ *She got herself into a real state* (ie became very anxious) *before the interview.*

¡**get (sb) ¹off 1** (to cause sb) to leave a place or start a journey: *get the children off to school* ○ *We got off immediately after breakfast.* **2** (to cause sb) to fall asleep: *I had great difficulty getting off to sleep last night.* ○ *She got the baby off (to sleep) by rocking it.* ¡**get ¹off (sth)** to leave work with permission: *Could you get off (work) early tomorrow?* ¡**get ¹off sth** to stop discussing a particular subject: *Please can we get off the subject of dieting?* ¡**get sth ¹off** to send sth by post: *I must get these letters off first thing tomorrow.* ¡**get ¹off (with sth)** to escape or nearly escape injury in an accident: *She was lucky to get off with just a few bruises.* ¡**get sth ¹off (with sth)** (*infml*) (to cause sb) to escape or nearly escape punishment: *A good lawyer might be able to get you off.* ○ *He was lucky to get off with a small fine.* ¡**get ¹off (together)** (*Brit*) (*US*) ¡**get it ¹off with sb** (*infml*) to have a sexual or romantic experience with sb: *Steve got off with Tracey/Steve and Tracey got off (together) at Denise's party.*

¡**get ¹on 1** (also ¡**get a¹long**) (esp followed by an *adv* or used in questions after *how*) to perform or succeed in a particular situation; to make progress: *Our youngest son is getting on well at school.* ○ *How did you get along in your driving test?* ○ *How are you getting along these days?* (ie Is your life enjoyable, successful, etc at the moment?) **2** to be successful in one's life or career: *Parents are always keen for their children to get on.* ○ *She's ambitious and eager to get on (in the world).* **3** (also ¡**get a¹long**) to manage or survive: *We can get on perfectly well without her.* ○ *I simply can't get along without a secretary.* ¡**get ¹on to sb 1** to contact sb by telephone or letter: *If you wish to lodge a complaint you'd better get on to the manager.* **2** to become aware of sb's presence or activities; to detect or trace sb: *He had been stealing money from the company for years before the police got on to him.* **3** to begin to discuss a new subject: *It's time we got on to the question of costs.* ¡**get ¹on with sb**; ¡**get ¹on (together)** to have a friendly relationship with sb; to get along with sb: *She's never really got on with her sister/She and her sister have never really got on.* ○ *They don't get on at all well together/get on with one another.* ○ *Our new manager is very easy to get on with.* ¡**get ¹on with sth 1** (also ¡**get a¹long with sth**) (esp followed by an *adv* or used in questions after *how*) to make progress with a task: *How's your son getting on with his*

French? ○ *I'm not getting on very fast with this job.* **2** to continue doing sth, esp after an interruption: *Be quiet and get on with your work.*

¡**get ¹out** to become known: *If this gets out there'll be trouble.* ¡**get sth ¹out 1** to produce or publish sth: *Will we get the book out by the end of the year?* **2** to say sth with difficulty: *She managed to get out a few words of thanks.* ¡**get ¹out (of sth)** to leave a place, esp in order to visit other places, meet people, etc: *You ought to get out (of the house) more.* ○ *She finds it difficult to get out now with her bad leg.* ¡**get ¹out of sth / doing sth 1** to avoid a responsibility or duty; to fail to do sth that one ought to do: *I wish I could get out of (going to) that meeting.* **2** to abandon, lose or give up a habit, routine, etc: *I can't get out of the habit of waking at six in the morning.* ¡**get sth ¹out of sb** to extract or obtain sth from sb, esp by force: *The police finally got a confession out of her* (ie made her confess). ○ *Just try getting money out of him!* (ie He is very mean.) ¡**get sth ¹out of sb/sth** to gain or obtain sth from sb/sth: *She seems to get a lot out of life.* ○ *I never get much out of his lectures.* ○ *She always gets the best out of people.*

¡**get ¹over sth** to overcome, deal with or gain control of sth: *She can't get over her shyness.* ○ *I can't get over* (ie I'm still amazed by) *how much your children have grown.* ○ *I think the problem can be got over without too much difficulty.* ¡**get ¹over sth/sb** to return to one's usual state of health, happiness, etc after an illness, a shock, the end of a relationship with sb, etc: *He was disappointed at not getting the job, but he'll get over it.* ○ *He never got over the shock of losing his wife.* ○ *I was still getting over Peter when I met and fell in love with Harry.* ¡**get sth ¹over (to sb)** to make sth clear to sb; to communicate sth to sb: *She didn't really get her meaning over to her audience.* ¡**get sth ¹over (with)** (*infml*) to complete sth unpleasant but necessary: *She'll be glad to get the exam over (and done) with.*

get round ⇨ GET ABOUT/AROUND/ROUND. ¡**get ¹round/a¹round sb** (*infml*) to persuade sb to agree to sth or to do sth which they first opposed: *She knows how to get round her father.* ¡**get ¹round/a¹round sth 1** to deal with sth successfully; to overcome sth: *Do you see a way of getting round the problem?* **2** to avoid or find a way to overcome a law, regulation, etc without acting illegally: *A clever lawyer might find ways of getting round that clause.* ¡**get ¹round/a¹round to sth / doing sth** to do sth finally after dealing with other matters; to find the necessary time to do sth: *I'm very busy at the moment but I hope to get round to answering your letter next week.*

¹**get through sth 1** to use up a large amount or quantity of sth within a specific period of time: *She gets through forty cigarettes a day.* ○ *We got through a fortune while we were in New York!* **2** (to manage) to do or complete sth: *I've got through a lot of correspondence today.* ○ *Let's start — there's a lot of work to get through/to be got through.* ¡**get (sb) ¹through (sth)** (to help sb) to be successful in or pass an examination, a test, etc: *Tom failed but his sister got through.* ○ *She got all her pupils through French A Level.* ¡**get (sth) ¹through (sth)** (to cause sth) to be officially approved or accepted: *get a proposal through a committee* ○ *Do you think the Bill will get through (Congress)?* ¡**get ¹through (to sb) 1** to reach sb: *Thousands of refugees will die if these supplies don't get through (to them).* **2** to make contact with sb, esp by telephone: *I tried ringing you several times yesterday but I couldn't get through (to you).* ¡**get ¹through (to sth)** (of a player or team) to reach the next stage of a competition: *Everton have got through to the final.* ¡**get ¹through to sb** to make sb understand the meaning of what one is saying; to communicate with sb: *I find her impossible to get through to.* ¡**get ¹through with sth** to

finish or complete a job, task, etc: *As soon as I get through with my work I'll join you.*

ˈget to sb (*infml*) to annoy, anger, or affect sb: *The pressure of work is beginning to get to him.*

ˌget sb/sth toˈgether to assemble or collect people or things: *I'm trying to get a team together for Saturday.* ○ *Could you get your things together? We're leaving in five minutes!* **ˌget toˈgether with sb**; **ˌget toˈgether** to meet with sb for social purposes or to discuss sth: *The management should get together with the union/The management and the union should get together to discuss their differences.* ○ *We must get together for a drink some time.*

ˌget ˈup 1 to stand after sitting, kneeling, etc; to rise: *The class got up when the teacher came in.* ○ *He got up slowly from the armchair.* **2** (of the sea or wind) to increase in force or strength; to become violent: *A storm was getting up.* **ˌget (sb) ˈup** (to cause sb) to get out of bed: *What time do you get up (in the morning)?* ○ *She always gets up early.* ○ *Could you get me up* (ie wake me) *at 6.30 tomorrow?* **ˌget oneself/sb ˈup** (often passive) to arrange the appearance of oneself/sb in the specified way: *She was got up* (ie dressed) *as an Indian princess.* **ˌget sth ˈup** to arrange or organize sth: *We're getting up a party for her birthday.* **ˌget ˈup to sth 1** to reach the specified point: *We got up to page 72 last lesson.* **2** to be occupied or busy with sth, esp sth surprising or undesirable: *What on earth will he get up to next?* ○ *He's been getting up to his old tricks again!*

■ **ˈget-together** *n* (*infml*) a social gathering: *We're having a little get-together to celebrate David's promotion.*

ˈget-up *n* (*infml*) a set of clothes, esp an unusual one: *She wears the most extraordinary get-ups.* ○ *He looked absurd in that get-up.*

ˌget-up-and-ˈgo *n* [U] (*infml*) the quality of being energetic and forceful: *She's got lots of get-up-and-go.*

getaway /ˈgetəweɪ/ *n* (usu *sing*) an escape, esp after committing a crime: *make a quick getaway* ○ *a getaway car* (ie one used to escape in).

geum /ˈdʒiːəm/ *n* a small garden plant with red or yellow flowers.

geyser /ˈgiːzə(r); *US* ˈgaɪzər/ *n* **1** a spring that from time to time shoots up hot water or steam from deep inside the earth. **2** (*Brit*) an apparatus used for heating large amounts of water, usu by gas, in a kitchen or BATHROOM(1).

ghastly /ˈgɑːstli; *US* ˈgæstli/ *adj* (**-ier**, **-iest**) **1** [usu attrib] causing horror or fear: *a ghastly accident/experience/fright/murder.* **2** (*infml*) very bad; unpleasant: *a ghastly error/mess/mistake* ○ *Her hairdo and make-up look positively ghastly!* ○ *What a ghastly man!* **3** [usu pred] ill; upset: *I feel ghastly — I shouldn't have drunk so much!* ○ *I felt ghastly about refusing, but I had no alternative.* **4** (*fml*) very pale in appearance, like a dead person: *She had a ghastly pallor.* ○ *His face was a ghastly white.*

ghee (also **ghi**) /giː/ *n* [U] a type of liquid butter used in Indian cooking.

gherkin /ˈgɜːkɪn/ *n* a small green CUCUMBER preserved in VINEGAR before being eaten.

ghetto /ˈgetəʊ/ *n* (*pl* **-os** or **-oes**) (*often derog*) the area of a town mainly lived in by a particular national or social group. Ghettos are usu crowded, with poor housing conditions: *Black urban ghettos.*

■ **ˈghetto blaster** *n* (*infml*) a large radio and CASSETTE player that can be carried around, esp one that is used for playing loud pop music in public.

ghost /gəʊst/ *n* **1** the spirit of a dead person appearing to sb who is still living: *Her ghost is believed to haunt the old house.* ○ *I don't believe in ghosts* (ie don't believe that they exist). ○ *He looked as if he had seen a ghost* (ie looked very frightened). **2** [sing] ~ **of sth** a very faint, slight amount or trace of sth: *The ghost of a smile* (ie A very faint smile) *played round her lips.* ○ *You haven't a ghost of a chance* (ie You have no chance). **3** a faint secondary image on a television screen, caused by a fault. **IDM give up the ˈghost 1** to die. **2** (*joc*) to stop working, usu permanently: *My car seems to have finally given up the ghost.*

▶ **ghost** *v* to act as a ghost-writer for sb: [Vn] *her ghosted memoirs* (ie written by someone else) [Vpr] *He ghosts for a number of sports personalities who 'write' newspaper columns.*

ghostly /ˈgəʊstli/ *adj* (**-ier**, **-iest**) like a ghost in appearance or sound: *ghostly shapes of bats flitting about in the dark* ○ *A ghostly voice seemed to whisper in my ear.*

■ **ˈghost story** *n* a story about ghosts, intended to frighten the reader.

ˈghost town *n* a town whose former inhabitants have all left.

▶ **ˈghost-writer** *n* a person who writes material for another person under whose name it is then published.

ghoul /guːl/ *n* **1** (in stories) a spirit that robs graves and feeds on the dead bodies in them. **2** (*derog*) a person with an abnormally great interest in death, disaster, etc: *ghouls who come and stare at road accidents.* ▶ **ghoulish** /ˈguːlɪʃ/ *adj*: *ghoulish behaviour/laughter.*

GHQ /ˌdʒiː eɪtʃ ˈkjuː/ *abbr* General Headquarters: *orders received from GHQ.*

GI /ˌdʒiː ˈaɪ/ *n* (*pl* **GIs**) a soldier in the US armed forces.

giant /ˈdʒaɪənt/ *n* (*fem* **giantess** /ˈdʒaɪəntes/) **1** (in children's stories and myths) a creature of human shape but very great size and strength. Giants are also often cruel and stupid. **2** an unusually large person, animal, plant, business organization, etc: *His son is a giant of 6 feet already.* ○ *He's the giant of* (ie the tallest person in) *the family.* ○ *What a giant of a tree!* ○ *the multinational ˈoil giants.* **3** a person of unusually great ability or talent: *Shakespeare is a giant among poets.*

▶ **giant** *adj* [attrib] unusually large: *a giant cabbage/a cabbage of giant size* ○ *a giant-size box of tissues* ○ *giant slalom races* ○ *The company has taken giant steps/strides forward.*

■ **ˈgiant-killer** *n* (esp in sport) a person who defeats an apparently much stronger opponent.

ˌgiant ˈpanda *n* = PANDA.

gibber /ˈdʒɪbə(r)/ *v* to speak quickly, making sounds that are confused or without meaning, often because of fear: [V] *a gibbering idiot* ○ *He cowered in the corner, gibbering with terror.* [also V.speech].

gibberish /ˈdʒɪbərɪʃ/ *n* [U] words that have no meaning or are impossible to understand; nonsense: *Don't talk gibberish!*

gibbet /ˈdʒɪbɪt/ *n* an upright wooden structure on which in former times condemned criminals were hung to die.

gibbon /ˈgɪbən/ *n* a small APE with long arms, found in SE Asia. ⇨ picture at APE.

gibe (also **jibe**) /dʒaɪb/ *n* ~ (**about/at sb/sth**) an insulting or mocking remark; a cruel joke: *a cruel/malicious/nasty gibe* ○ *cheap gibes about her fatness.*

▶ **gibe** (also **jibe**) *v* [V, V.speech].

giblets /ˈdʒɪbləts/ *n* [pl] the parts of a bird, including its heart and LIVER, which are usu removed before it is cooked. They are sometimes cooked separately to make soup, etc.

giddy /ˈgɪdi/ *adj* (**-ier**, **-iest**) **1(a)** [usu pred] having the feeling that everything is turning round and that one is going to fall: *I feel giddy; I must sit down.* ○ *have a giddy feeling* ○ (*fig*) *giddy* (ie happy and excited) *with success.* **(b)** [usu attrib] causing such a feeling: *travel at a giddy speed* ○ *look down from a giddy height* ○ (*fig*) *Life then was a succession of giddy triumphs.* **2** [attrib] (*dated*) (used to add emphasis to

G

certain exclamations): *Oh my giddy aunt!* ○ *That really is the giddy limit!* ▶ **giddily** /ˈgɪdɪli/ *adv*: *stagger giddily round the room.* **giddiness** /ˈgɪdɪnəs/ *n* [U]: *overcome by nausea and giddiness.*

gift /gɪft/ *n* **1** a thing given willingly without payment; a present: *a kind/generous/small gift* ○ *a birthday/Christmas/wedding gift* ○ *a gift to charity* ○ *a gift of chocolates/flowers.* **2** ~ **(for sth / doing sth)** a natural talent or ability: *I've always been able to learn languages easily; it's a gift.* ○ *He has many outstanding gifts.* ○ *the gift of making friends easily* ○ *have a gift for music* ○ (*ironic*) *a gift for doing/saying the wrong thing.* **3** (*usu sing*) (*infml*) a thing that is very easy to do or cheap to buy: *Their second goal was a real gift.* ○ *That exam question was an absolute gift!* ○ *It was a gift of a question.* ○ *At that price it's a gift!* **IDM** **the gift of the ˈgab** (*sometimes derog*) the ability to speak with an easy and expressive flow of words. **God's ˈgift to sb/sth** ⇨ GOD. **look a gift horse in the ˈmouth** (usu with negatives) to refuse or criticize sth that is given to one for nothing.
▶ **gifted** /ˈgɪftɪd/ *adj* having a lot of natural ability or intelligence: *a highly gifted artist/pianist/dancer* ○ *gifted children.*
■ **ˈgift shop** *n* a shop that specializes in selling articles suitable as gifts.
ˈgift token (*Brit* also **ˈgift voucher**, *US* **ˈgift certificate**) *n* a small piece of paper, usu attached to a greetings card, which can be exchanged in a shop for goods of a certain value.
ˈgift-wrap *v* (**-pp-**) (usu passive) to wrap sth that is to be given as a present in special attractive paper, etc: [Vn] *The store offers a free gift-wrapping service at Christmas.*

gig /gɪg/ *n* **1** (*infml*) a live performance of JAZZ or pop music: *do/play gigs in the local pubs.* **2** (esp formerly) a small light carriage with two wheels, pulled by one horse.

gigantic /dʒaɪˈgæntɪk/ *adj* of very great size or extent; huge: *gigantic mountain ranges* ○ *a gigantic person/appetite* ○ *a problem of gigantic proportions.*

giggle /ˈgɪgl/ *v* ~ **(at sb/sth)** to laugh lightly in a nervous or silly way: [V] *Stop giggling, children — this is a serious matter.* [Vpr] *giggling hysterically at one of her own bad jokes* [also V.speech].
▶ **giggle** *n* **1** [C] an act of giggling: *There was a giggle from the back of the class.* **2** [sing] (*Brit*) a thing that causes amusement; a joke: *What a giggle!* ○ *Today's lesson was a bit of a giggle.* ○ *I only did it for a giggle.* **3** **the giggles** [pl] continuous giggling that one cannot control: *get the giggles* ○ *She had a fit of the giggles.*
giggly /ˈgɪgli/ *adj* (*often derog*) often giggling: *a giggly schoolgirl.*

NOTE You can use the verb **giggle** and the noun (**the**) **giggles** to describe laughing in a childish and uncontrolled way, in response to something amusing and silly: *The children couldn't stop giggling at the clown's funny song.* ○ *We both collapsed into helpless giggles.* **Snigger**, and in American English **snicker**, means to laugh quietly in a rude way: *The kissing on stage made some of the young audience snigger.* **Titter** means to laugh quietly because of embarrassment or shyness: *The girls nervously tittered and chattered at the edge of the dance floor.*

gigolo /ˈʒɪgələʊ/ *n* (*pl* **-os**) (*usu derog*) a man who is paid by an older woman to be her companion or lover.

gild /gɪld/ *v* [Vn] **1** to cover sth with a thin layer of gold or with gold paint: *gild a picture-frame* ○ *gilded bronze statues.* **2** (*rhet*) to make sth bright as if with gold: *The trees were already gilded by the morning sun.* **IDM** **gild the ˈlily** to try to improve what is already satisfactory.
▶ **gilded** *adj* [attrib] wealthy and of the upper

classes: *the gilded youth* (ie young people) *of the Edwardian era.*
gilding /ˈgɪldɪŋ/ *n* [U] the material with which things are gilded; the surface made by such material: *the gilding on the dome of the mosque.*

gill¹ /gɪl/ *n* (usu *pl*) the opening on the side of a fish's head through which it breathes. ⇨ picture at FISH¹.
IDM **(be, look, etc) green/pale about the ˈgills** (*infml joc*) pale in the face with fear or sickness.

gill² /dʒɪl/ *n* a unit of liquid measure, equal to a quarter of a PINT.

gillie (also **ghillie**) /ˈgɪli/ *n* (*Scot*) a man or boy who assists sb shooting or fishing for sport in Scotland.

gilt /gɪlt/ *n* **1** [U] gold, or sth resembling gold, applied to a surface in a thin layer: *a gilt mirror.* **2** **gilts** [pl] (*Brit finance*) gilt-edged investments. **IDM** **take the gilt off the ˈgingerbread** (*Brit*) to do or be sth that makes a situation or achievement less attractive or impressive.
■ **ˌgilt-ˈedged** *adj* (*finance*) not risky; secure: *ˌgilt-edged seˈcurities/ˈshares/ˈstock* (ie investments that are considered safe and sure to produce interest).

gimcrack /ˈdʒɪmkræk/ *adj* [attrib] badly made and of little value: *gimcrack ornaments.*

gimlet /ˈgɪmlət/ *n* a small tool for making holes in wood to put screws in: (*fig*) *eyes like gimlets* (ie sharp eyes which seem to penetrate with their look).

gimmick /ˈgɪmɪk/ *n* (*often derog*) a trick or device whose purpose is to attract attention or to persuade people to buy sth: *a promotional/publicity/sales/marketing gimmick* ○ *a flashy expensive car with all the latest gimmicks like self-winding windows.*
▶ **gimmickry** /ˈgɪmɪkri/ *n* [U] (*derog*) (the use of) gimmicks: *I'm looking for solid workmanship rather than flashy gimmickry.*
gimmicky /ˈgɪmɪki/ *adj.*

gin /dʒɪn/ *n* [U,C] an alcoholic drink made from grain and flavoured with JUNIPER berries. Gin is usu drunk mixed with tonic water (TONIC) or fruit juice: *I'll have a gin and tonic, please.*

ginger /ˈdʒɪndʒə(r)/ *n* [U] **1** (a plant with) a hot-tasting root used as a flavouring: *crystallized ginger* ○ *ground/root/stem ginger.* **2** a light orange colour: *His hair was a bright shade of ginger.*
▶ **ginger** *adj* **1** [attrib] flavoured with ginger: *ginger biscuits.* **2** of the colour ginger: *ginger hair/whiskers/eyebrows* ○ *a ginger cat.*
ginger *v* **PHRV** **ˌginger sb/sth ˈup** to make sb/sth more vigorous or lively: *The party needs a bit of music or something to ginger it up.*
gingery /ˈdʒɪndʒəri/ *adj* like ginger in colour or flavour.
■ **ˌginger ˈale** *n* [U,C] a clear(5a) FIZZY drink with no alcohol in, flavoured with ginger.
ˌginger ˈbeer *n* [U,C] a slightly alcoholic FIZZY drink flavoured with ginger.
ˈginger group *n* (*Brit*) a group of people, esp within a political party, working to promote more active or lively policies on particular issues.
ˈginger-nut *n* a hard sweet biscuit flavoured with ginger.

gingerbread /ˈdʒɪndʒəbred/ *n* [U] a sweet cake or biscuit flavoured with GINGER(1). **IDM** **take the gilt off the gingerbread** ⇨ GILT.

gingerly /ˈdʒɪndʒəli/ *adv* in a careful or cautious manner, esp so as to avoid causing harm or making a noise: *She gingerly tested the water with her toe.* ○ *Putting his weight gingerly onto the injured ankle he tried a few steps.*

gingham /ˈgɪŋəm/ *n* [U] cotton or linen cloth with a pattern of stripes (STRIPE) or check³: *a gingham dress.*

ginseng /ˈdʒɪnseŋ/ *n* [U] (a plant with) a sweet-smelling root used in certain medicines.

gipsy = GYPSY.

giraffe /dʒə'rɑːf; US -'ræf/ n (pl unchanged or **giraffes**) an African animal with a very long neck and legs, and dark patches on its coat.

gird /gɜːd/ v **IDM** **gird (up) one's 'loins** (rhet or joc) to prepare for action. **PHRV** **gird oneself for sth** (arch or rhet) to prepare oneself for sth difficult or dangerous: Government ministers are girding themselves for a fierce election campaign. **gird sth on** (arch) to fasten sth on, esp with a belt: He girded on his sword.

girder /'gɜːdə(r)/ n a long strong iron or steel beam used for building bridges and the framework of large buildings.

girdle /'gɜːdl/ n **1** a cord or belt fastened round the waist to keep clothes in position: She untied the girdle of her dressing-gown. **2** (rhet) a thing that surrounds sth else: carefully tended lawns set in a girdle of trees ○ put a communication girdle round the earth. **3** (becoming dated) a garment worn by women to improve the figure. A girdle fits closely round the body under other clothes, and extends from the waist to the THIGH.
▶ **girdle** v (rhet) to surround sth: [Vn] belts of radiation girdling the earth ○ The mountain was girdled in mist.

girl /gɜːl/ n **1** [C] **(a)** a female child: a baby girl ○ a little girl of six (years old) ○ Good morning, girls and boys! **(b)** a daughter: Their eldest girl's getting married next week. **2** [C] **(a)** a young woman, usu one who is not married: a girl in her teens or early twenties ○ He was eighteen before he started going out with girls. **(b)** a woman of the specified type: (infml) the old girl who owns the dress shop ○ She's the new girl in the office, so give her any help she needs. See also CAREER GIRL. **3** [C] (usu in compounds) a female worker: an 'office-girl/a 'shop-girl/a 'telephone-girl. **4** a man's girlfriend: taking his girl home to meet his parents. **5** **girls** [pl] (infml often joc) (used esp as a friendly form of address and esp by women) women of any age: a night out with the girls.
▶ **girlhood** /'gɜːlhʊd/ n [U] the state or time of being a girl: She spent her girlhood in Africa. ○ my girlhood ambitions.
girlie /'gɜːli/ adj [attrib] containing pictures of naked or nearly naked young women intended to excite men sexually: girlie magazines.
girlish /'gɜːlɪʃ/ adj of or like a young girl: a girlish face/smile.
■ **ˌgirl 'Friday** n a young woman with a wide range of duties in an office.
ˌGirl 'Guide (Brit also **Guide**, US **ˌGirl 'Scout**) n a member of an organization for girls (equivalent to the Boy Scouts) which aims to develop practical skills, independence and concern for others. Compare SCOUT 2.

girlfriend /'gɜːlfrend/ n a female friend or companion, esp a man's regular (and possibly sexual) partner.

giro /'dʒaɪrəʊ/ n (pl **-os**) (Brit commerce) **1** [U,C] a system for transferring money directly from one bank account or post office (POST³) account to another: Money has been credited to your account by bank giro. ○ I'll pay by giro (ie using the giro system). ○ a (bank) giro credit/payment/transfer ○ a giro account (ie a special account for paying through the giro system). **2** (also **giro cheque**) [C] a cheque or an amount of money paid through the giro system, esp by the government to people who are sick or unemployed: My giro hasn't arrived this week.

girth /gɜːθ/ n **1** [U,C] **(a)** the distance round sth: a tree 1 metre in girth/with a girth of 1 metre. **(b)** the measurement round a person's waist or an animal's body: a man of enormous girth. **2** [C] a band of leather or cloth fastened tightly round the body of a horse, etc to keep the SADDLE(1) in place.

gist /dʒɪst/ n **the gist** [sing] the main point or general meaning of sth spoken or written: get (ie understand) the gist of an argument/a conversation/a book ○ I missed the prime minister's speech on television — can you give me the gist of what he said?

give¹ /gɪv/ v (pt **gave** /geɪv/; pp **given** /'gɪvn/)
● **Causing somebody or something to have or receive 1** ~ sth to sb to cause sb to receive, hold, have or own sth: [Vnn] I gave each of the boys an apple. [Vnpr] I gave an apple to each of the boys. [Vnn] Each of the boys was given an apple. [Vnpr] An apple was given to each of the boys. [Vnn, Vnpr] She gave her mother the tickets/gave the tickets to her mother to look after. [Vnn] Can I give you (ie Would you like) another slice of cake? ○ She was given a new heart in an eight-hour operation. ○ He gave the old lady his arm (ie allowed her to lean on his arm) as they crossed the road. ○ I've just been given a £2000 pay rise. **2(a)** ~ sth to sb to cause sb to have sth as a present: [Vnpr] What are you giving (to) your brother for his birthday? [Vnn] I'm giving all my friends books for Christmas. ○ Have you given the waiter a tip? **(b)** ~ (sth) to sth to contribute money to sth, esp a charity: [Vadv] Handicapped children need your help — please give generously. [Vpr, Vnpr] Many people regularly give (donations) to charity. **3** to allow sb/sth to have sth: [Vnn] They gave me a week to make up my mind. ○ (infml) I give their marriage six months at most (ie I think that it will last only six months). ○ She wishes that she'd been given the chance to go to college. ○ I'm sure he'll be successful, **given** (ie if he is given) half a chance. ○ She wants a job that gives her more responsibility. ○ What gives you the right to tell me what to do? **4** ~ (sb) sth for sth to pay money, etc to sb in order to have or do sth: [Vnpr] Do you mean to tell me you gave £1500 for that pile of scrap metal? [Vnn] How much will you give me for my old car? ○ I'd give anything/a lot for the chance to visit India. **5** ~ sth (to sb) to cause sb to have sth; to provide or supply sb with sth: [Vn] You may be called to give evidence at the trial. ○ He gives the impression of not caring a damn. ○ She gives private lessons to supplement her income. [Vnn] She gave me a ride as far as the station. ○ The sun gives us warmth and light. ○ Could you give me your honest opinion of the book? ○ What gave you the idea that I didn't like you? [Vnpr] They gave the name Roland to their first child. **6** ~ sth to sb/sth to devote time, thought, etc to sth: [Vnn, Vnpr] I've given the matter a lot of thought/given a lot of thought to the matter. [Vnpr] The government should give top priority to rebuilding the inner cities.
● **Causing somebody to suffer 7** ~ sth to sb to cause sb to suffer the specified punishment, esp a period of time in prison: [Vnn] The judge gave him a nine-month suspended sentence. ○ The old woman gave the boys a real scolding. [also Vnpr]. **8** ~ sth to sb to infect sb with an illness: [Vnn, Vnpr] You've given me your cold/given your cold to me.
● **Communicating 9** (used in the imperative) to offer sth to sb as an excuse or explanation: [Vnn] Don't give me that rubbish about having a headache — I know you don't want to go to the party. **10** to make a telephone call to sb: [Vnn] I'll give you a ring tomorrow. **11** to admit the truth of sth to sb; to GRANT(2) sth: [Vnn] The government has a good record on inflation, I give you that, but what is it doing about unemployment?
● **Performing or providing sth 12** to perform or present a play, concert, etc in public: [Vn] give a poetry reading/a song recital ○ The President will be giving a press conference tomorrow morning. ○ How many performances of the play are you giving? [Vnn] The play was given its first performance in June 1923. **13** to provide a meal, party, etc as a host: [Vn] I'm giving a dinner party next Friday evening —

G

G

would you like to come? **14** to carry out or perform an action: [Vn] *She gave a shrug of her shoulders.* ○ *He gave a start and woke up suddenly.* **15** to perform the specified action on sb/sth: [Vnn] *give sb a kick/push/shove* ○ *give sb a punch on the nose* ○ *She gave him a kiss.* ○ *Do give your shoes a polish before you go out.*

● **Expressing or declaring sth 16** to produce the specified sound: [Vn] *give a groan/laugh/sigh/ yell* ○ *He gave a strangled cry and fell to the floor.* **17** (used in the imperative) to ask people to drink a TOAST² to sb: [Vnn] *Ladies and gentlemen, I give you his Royal Highness, the Prince of Wales.* **18** (in certain sports) to declare that a player or the ball is in the specified condition or position: [Vn-adj] *He was given offside by the referee.* [also Vnadv].

● **Other meanings 19** to produce the specified feeling in sb: [Vnn] *All that heavy lifting has given me a pain in the back.* ○ *I must go to the dentist — my teeth are giving me hell.* ○ *Why don't you go for a walk? It'll give you an appetite for your lunch.* **20** to bend or stretch under pressure: [V] *The branch began to give under his weight.* ○ (fig) *The situation can't continue like this much longer — **something's got to give.*** **21** (combined with a *n* in many fixed expressions, where *give* and the *n* together have the same meaning as a *v* related in form to the *n*, eg *give sb a surprise = surprise sb*): *Let me give you a piece of advice* (ie advise you). ○ *Her acting has given pleasure to* (ie pleased) *millions (of people).* ○ *The news gave us a shock* (ie shocked us). ○ *I trust that you can give an explanation for* (ie explain) *your extraordinary behaviour?* ○ *We will give you all the help* (ie help you in every way) *we can.* (For other similar expressions, see the entries for the *ns* in each, eg *give one's approval to sth* ⇨ APPROVAL; *give one's permission* ⇨ PERMISSION.)

IDM Most idioms containing **give** are at the entries for the nouns or adjectives in the idioms, eg **give rise to sth** ⇨ RISE¹. **sb doesn't/couldn't give a 'damn, a 'hoot, etc (about sb/sth)** *(infml)* sb does not care at all (about sb/sth): *He couldn't give a damn whether he passes the exam or not.* **give and 'take** to be willing to make compromises within a relationship: *For a marriage to succeed, both partners must learn to give and take.* **give as good as one 'gets** to respond equally with words or blows in an argument, a fight, etc. **give it to sb** *(infml)* to attack, criticize or rebuke sb severely: *The boss will really give it to you if you miss the deadline for the job.* **give me sth/sb** *(infml)* (used to show that one prefers the thing or person specified to sth/sb mentioned previously): *I can't stand modern music; give me Bach and Mozart every time!* **give or 'take (sth)** the specified amount, time, etc more or less: *'How long will it take us to get there?' 'About an hour and a half, give or take (a few minutes).'* **give sb to believe/understand (that) ...** *(fml)* (often passive) to make sb believe/understand sth: *I was given to understand that she was ill.* **what 'gives?** *(infml)* what is happening?; what is the news?

PHR V **give sb a'way** (in a marriage ceremony) to lead the BRIDE to the BRIDEGROOM and hand her to him: *The bride was given away by her father.* **give sth a'way 1** to give sth free of charge: *He gave away most of his money to charity.* ○ *(infml) These watches are only a pound each; we're virtually giving them away.* **2** to distribute or present sth: *The mayor gave away the prizes at the school sports day.* **3** to fail to use or take a chance, an opportunity, etc carelessly: *They've given away their last chance of winning the match.* **give sth/sb a'way** to reveal sth/sb intentionally or without meaning to; to betray sth/sb: *She gave away state secrets to the enemy.* ○ *His accent gave him away* (ie revealed who he really was).

give sb 'back sth; give sth 'back (to sb) 1 to return sth to its owner: *Could you give me back my pen/give me my pen back?* **2** to allow sb to have or enjoy sth again: *The operation gave him back the use of his legs.*

give sth 'in to hand over sth to sb who has the authority to receive it: *Please give your examination papers in (to the teacher) when you've finished.* **give 'in (to sb/sth)** to allow oneself to be defeated or overcome by sb/sth: *The rebels were forced to give in.* ○ *She's a plucky player: she never gives in.* ○ *The authorities have shown no signs of giving in to the kidnappers' demands.*

give sth 'off to send out or discharge sth: *The oven is giving off a funny smell.* ○ *The fire doesn't seem to be giving off much heat.*

give on to / onto sth *(Brit)* to have a view of sth; to lead directly to sth: *The bedroom windows give on to the street.* ○ *This door gives onto the hall.*

give 'out 1 to come to an end; to be completely used up: *After a month their food supplies gave out.* ○ *Her patience finally gave out.* **2** (of an engine, a motor, etc) to stop working; to break down: *One of the plane's engines gave out in mid-Atlantic.* **give sth 'out 1** to distribute or hand out sth: *The teacher gave out the examination papers.* **2** to send out or discharge sth: *The radiator gives out a lot of heat.* **3** (often passive) to announce or broadcast sth: *The news of the President's death was given out on national radio.* ○ *It was given out that the President had been shot.*

give 'over (doing sth) *(Brit infml)* (used esp in the imperative or with a verb in the -ing form) to stop doing sth: *Give over, can't you? I can't work with you chattering away like that.* ○ *Give over complaining!* **give oneself 'over to sth** to sink into the specified state; to devote oneself completely to sth: *After his wife's death, he seemed to give himself over to despair.* ○ *In her later years she gave herself over to writing full-time.* **give sth 'over to sth** (usu passive) to use sth specifically for sth: *The village hall is given over to civic functions and meetings.* ○ *The period after supper was given over to games.*

give 'up to abandon an attempt to do sth: *They gave up without a fight.* ○ *She doesn't give up easily.* ○ *I give up — tell me what the answer is.* **give sb 'up 1** to stop hoping for or expecting sb to arrive or get better after illness: *There you are at last! We'd given you up.* ○ *The doctors had given her up but she made a remarkable recovery.* **2** to stop having a relationship with sb: *Why don't you give him up?* **give sth 'up** to stop doing or having sth: *You ought to give up smoking.* ○ *She didn't give up her job when she got married.* **give oneself/sb 'up (to sb)** to offer oneself/sb to be captured: *After a week on the run he gave himself up (to the police).* **give sth 'up (to sb)** to hand sth over to sb else: *We had to give our passports up to the authorities.* ○ *He gave up his seat to a pregnant woman* (ie stood up to allow her to sit down). **give 'up on sb** *(infml)* to stop trying to support or help sb.

■ **'give-away** *n (infml)* **1** a thing given free, usu with sth for sale, to persuade people to buy it: *There's a give-away cassette with each issue of the magazine.* **2** a look, remark, etc that reveals a secret without intending to: *The expression on her face was a (dead) give-away.* — *adj* (of prices) very low: *bargains at give-away prices.*

give² /gɪv/ *n* [U] the ability of sth to bend or stretch under pressure; elasticity (ELASTIC): *There is no give in a stone floor.* ○ *Don't worry if the shoes seem a bit tight at first; the leather has plenty of give in it.* **IDM** **give and 'take 1** willingness to make compromises in a relationship: *If the dispute is to be resolved there must be some give and take.* ○ *Marriage is a give-and-take affair.* **2** an exchange of words, etc: *encourage a lively give and take of ideas.*

---

given /ˈgɪvn/ *adj* [esp attrib] specified or stated: *all the people in a given area* ○ *They were to meet at a given time and place.* **IDM** **be given to sth / doing sth** to be in the habit of doing sth: *She's much given to outbursts of temper.* ○ *He's given to going for long walks on his own.*

▶ **given** *prep* taking sth into account: *Given the government's record on unemployment, their chances of winning the election look poor.* ○ *Given her interest in children/Given that she is interested in children, I am sure teaching is the right career for her.*

■ **'given name** *n* = CHRISTIAN NAME. See also FIRST NAME.

giver /ˈgɪvə(r)/ *n* (often in compounds) a person or organization that gives: *They are very generous givers to charity.*

gizzard /ˈgɪzəd/ *n* the part of a bird's stomach in which food is ground up before being digested (DIGEST² 1a).

glacé /ˈglæseɪ; *US* glæˈseɪ/ *adj* [attrib] (of fruits) preserved in sugar: *decorate a cake with glacé cherries.*

glacial /ˈgleɪʃl, ˈgleɪsɪəl/ *adj* **1** (*geology*) (**a**) of the Ice Age: *the glacial epoch/period* (ie the time when much of the northern HEMISPHERE(2) was covered by ice). (**b**) of or caused by glaciers (GLACIER): *glacial deposits* (ie rocks deposited by a moving glacier). **2** very cold; like ice: *glacial winds/temperatures* ○ *the glacial waters of the Arctic* ○ (*fig*) *Her manner was glacial and aloof* (ie not warm or friendly).

glacier /ˈglæsɪə(r); *US* ˈgleɪʃər/ *n* a mass of ice, formed by snow on mountains, moving slowly down a valley.

glad /glæd/ *adj* (-dder, -ddest) **1** [pred] (**a**) ~ (about sth / to do sth / that...) pleased; delighted: *'I passed the test.' 'I'm so glad (for you)!'* ○ *I'm glad about your passing the test.* ○ *I'm glad to hear he's feeling better.* ○ *I'm glad (that) he's feeling better.* (**b**) ~ (about/of sth); ~ (to do sth / that...) relieved: *I'm very glad (that) I didn't get involved in such a mad scheme.* (**c**) ~ **of sth** grateful for sth: *I'd be glad of* (ie I'd like) *your help/a cup of tea.* (**d**) ~ **to do sth** willing and eager to do sth: *I'd be glad to lend you the money.* ○ *If you'd like me to help you, I'd be only too glad to.* **2** [attrib] causing or bringing joy: *glad news/tidings.*

▶ **gladden** /ˈglædn/ *v* to make sb glad or happy: [Vn] *It **gladdened my heart** to see them all enjoying themselves.*

gladly *adv* **1** happily; with gratitude: *She suggested it, and I accepted gladly.* **2** willingly: *I would gladly pay extra for a good seat.* **IDM** **not/never suffer fools gladly** ⇨ SUFFER.

gladness *n* [U] joy; happiness.

■ **'glad rags** *n* [pl] (*Brit infml*) clothes for a special occasion or celebration: *put on one's glad rags.*

glade /gleɪd/ *n* an open space in a wood or forest.

gladiator /ˈglædieɪtə(r)/ *n* (in ancient Rome) a man trained to fight with weapons against other men or wild animals at public shows. ▶ **gladiatorial** /ˌglædiəˈtɔːriəl/ *adj: gladiatorial entertainment/combat.*

gladiolus /ˌglædɪˈəʊləs/ *n* (*pl* gladioli /-laɪ/ or gladioluses) a plant with long thin pointed leaves and brightly coloured flowers.

glamour (*US* also **glamor**) /ˈglæmə(r)/ *n* [U] **1** the attractive or exciting quality that makes certain activities, jobs, places, etc seem special: *hopeful young actors and actresses dazzled by the glamour of Hollywood* ○ *Now that she's an air hostess, foreign travel has lost its glamour for her.* **2** beauty or charm that is sexually attractive: *a girl with lots of glamour* ○ (*dated*) *a glamour girl/boy.*

▶ **glamorize, -ise** /ˈglæməraɪz/ *v* (*usu derog*) to make sth seem more attractive or exciting than it really is: [Vn] *Television tends to glamorize acts of violence.*

glamorous /-mərəs/ *adj* having glamour: *glamorous film stars.*
glamorously *adv: glamorously dressed.*

glance /glɑːns; *US* glæns/ *v* **1** to take a quick look: [Vpr] *She glanced shyly at him and then lowered her eyes.* ○ *glance at one's watch* ○ *glance round a room* [Vp] *I glanced up to see who had come in.* **2** ~ **at/ down/over/through sth** to read sth quickly or not thoroughly: [Vpr] *glance at the newspapers* ○ *glance down a list of names* ○ *glance over/through a letter.* **3** [Vn, Vnpr] (in cricket) to hit the ball with the face of the bat turned to one side. **4** (of bright objects or light) to flash or be reflected: [Vpr] *sunlight glancing on/off the water* [also V]. **PHR V** **glance 'off (sth)** to hit sth at an angle and bounce off in another direction: *The ball glanced off the goalpost into the net.* ○ *The tree was so hard that the blows of the axe simply glanced off.*

▶ **glance** *n* ~ (**at sb/sth**) a quick look: *take/have/ cast a glance at the newspaper headlines* ○ *We exchanged glances* (ie looked quickly at each other). ○ *a brief/casual/fleeting/furtive glance* ○ *She walked away **without a backward glance**.* ○ (*fig*) *Before the end of the programme, let's take a glance at* (ie refer briefly to) *the sports news.* **IDM** **at a (single) 'glance** with one look: *He could tell at a glance what was wrong with the car.* **at first 'glance/'sight** when seen or examined (often quickly) for the first time: *At first glance the problem seemed easy.* ○ *It was love at first sight/glance.*

glancing /ˈglɑːnsɪŋ; *US* ˈglænsɪŋ/ *adj* [attrib] hitting sb/sth at an angle rather than directly and with full force: *strike sb a glancing blow.*

gland /glænd/ *n* (*anatomy*) an organ that separates from the blood those substances that are to be used by or removed from the body: *a snake's poison glands* ○ *thyroid glands* ○ *sweat glands* ○ *The glands in his neck were quite swollen.*

▶ **glandular** /ˈglændjʊlə(r); *US* -dʒə-/ *adj* of or affecting a gland or glands. **ˌglandular 'fever** *n* [U] an infectious disease causing swelling of the LYMPH glands.

glare¹ /gleə(r)/ *n* **1** [U] a very bright and unpleasant light: *the glare of the sun* ○ *caught in the glare of the car's headlights* ○ (*fig*) *The hearings were conducted **in the full glare of publicity*** (ie with constant attention from newspapers, television, etc). **2** [C] an angry, fierce or fixed look: *give sb a hostile glare.*

glare² /gleə(r)/ *v* **1** to shine with a very bright and unpleasant light: [Vpr, Vp] *The sun was glaring (down) mercilessly from a clear sky.* **2** ~ (**at sb/sth**) to stare in a fierce or angry manner: [Vnpr] *He didn't shout or swear, but just glared at me silently.* [also V].

▶ **glaring** /ˈgleərɪŋ/ *adj* **1** bright in an unpleasant way: *glaring lights.* **2** angry; fierce: *glaring eyes.* **3** [usu attrib] that cannot or should not be ignored; shocking: *a glaring abuse/error/injustice/omission.*
glaringly *adv: glaringly obvious.*

glasnost /ˈglæznɒst/ *n* [U] (in the former Soviet Union) the policy of more open government and a wider spread of information in public affairs.

glass /glɑːs; *US* glæs/ *n* **1** [U] a hard, usu transparent, substance that can break easily (as used in windows): *cut oneself on broken glass* ○ *a sheet/pane of glass* ○ *as smooth as glass* ○ *glass jars* (ie made of glass). See also CUT GLASS, PLATE GLASS, STAINED GLASS, GLAZIER. **2** [C] (**a**) (often in compounds) a container for drinking from made of glass: *a 'beer/ 'brandy/'sherry/'whisky glass* ○ *a 'wineglass.* ⇨ picture. (**b**) the contents of this: *Could I have a glass of water, please?* **3** [U] containers and articles made of glass: *All our glass and china is kept in this cupboard.* ○ *There is a large area under glass* (ie covered with glasshouses (GLASSHOUSE 1) or frames filled with glass to protect growing plants). **4** [sing]

beer glass

glass

wineglass

beer mug
(*Brit also* **beer glass**)

tumbler

a protecting cover made of glass on a watch, picture or photograph frame, fire alarm, etc: *In case of emergency, break the glass and press the button.*

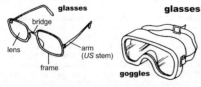

glasses

bridge

lens

arm
(*US* stem)

frame

goggles

glasses

5 glasses (also **spectacles**, *infml* **specs**) [pl] a pair of lenses (LENS1) in a frame that rests on the nose and ears. Glasses are worn to improve a person's sight or to protect the eyes from bright sunlight: *She wears glasses.* ○ *a new pair of reading glasses* ○ *dark glasses.* ⇨ picture. **6 glasses** (also ˈ**field-glasses**) [pl] = BINOCULARS. **7** [C usu *sing*] (*dated*) a mirror: *He looked in the glass to check that his tie was straight.* See also LOOKING-GLASS. **8 the glass** [sing] a BAROMETER(1): *The glass is falling* (ie It is likely to rain). See also MAGNIFYING GLASS. **IDM people in glass houses shouldn't throw stones** ⇨ PEOPLE. **raise one's glass** ⇨ RAISE.
▶ **glass** *v* **PHRV** ˌ**glass sth** ˈ**in/**ˈ**over** to cover sth with a roof or wall of glass: *a glassed-in veranda.*
glassful /-fʊl/ *n* (*pl* **-fuls**) as much as a drinking glass will hold.
■ ˈ**glass-blower** *n* a person who shapes melted glass into bottles, etc by blowing air into it through a long tube.
ˌ**glass** ˈ**fibre** *n* [U] = FIBREGLASS.

glasshouse /ˈglɑːshaʊs/ *n* (*pl* **-houses** /-haʊzɪz/) **1** a building with glass sides and a glass roof, for growing plants in; a GREENHOUSE. **2** (*Brit infml*) a military prison.

glassware /ˈglɑːsweə(r)/ *n* [U] articles made of glass, esp drinking glasses, dishes etc.

glassy /ˈglɑːsi; *US* ˈglæsi/ *adj* (**-ier, -iest**) **1** like glass: *glassy rock* ○ *a glassy sea* (ie smooth and shiny). **2** showing no interest or expression: *glassy eyes* ○ *a glassy look/stare* ○ *glassy-eyed faces.*

glaucoma /glɔːˈkəʊmə/ *n* [U] an eye disease causing gradual loss of sight.

glaze /gleɪz/ *v* **1** to fit sheets of glass into sth: [Vn] *glaze a window/house* ○ *a glazed door.* See also DOUBLE-GLAZE. ~ **sth** (**with sth**); ~ **sth** (**over**) to cover sth with a thin shiny transparent surface: [Vn] *glazed pottery/porcelain/tiles* (ie covered with a liquid which when baked gives a hard shiny surface) [Vnpr] *Glaze the pie with beaten egg.* [also Vnp]. **PHRV** ˌ**glaze** ˈ**over** (of the eyes) to show no interest or expression: *His eyes glazed over and soon he was asleep.*
▶ **glaze** *n* [C,U] (**a**) a substance used to give a thin shiny transparent surface to clay pots, PORCELAIN, etc: *The vase was sold cheaply because of a fault in the glaze.* (**b**) (beaten egg, sugar, etc used to give) a shiny attractive surface to food: *Pour the glaze over the pie.*

glazed *adj* (esp of the eyes) showing no interest or expression: *eyes glazed with boredom* ○ *the glazed faces/expressions of the survivors.*

glazier /ˈgleɪzɪə(r); *US* -ʒər/ *n* a person whose job is to fit glass into the frames of windows, etc.

gleam /gliːm/ *n* **1** [C usu *sing*] a brief or faint light, often reflected: *the sudden gleam of a match in the darkness* ○ *A few gleams of sunshine lit up the gloomy afternoon.* ○ *the gleam of moonlight on the water* ○ *the gleam of polished brassware in the firelight.* **2** [sing] a brief show of some quality or emotion: *a serious book with an occasional gleam of humour* ○ *a gleam of hope in an apparently hopeless situation* ○ *He had a nasty gleam in his eye* (ie as if planning sth unpleasant). See also GLIMMER.
▶ **gleam** *v* **1(a)** to shine with a faint or brief light: *moonlight gleaming on the water* ○ *water gleaming in the moonlight* ○ *a cat's eyes gleaming in the dark* [Vpr] (*fig*) *anticipation/excitement gleaming in their eyes.* (**b**) (of a smooth surface) to shine because it is clean: [V] *gleaming white teeth* ○ *The polished candlesticks gleamed.* **2** ~ **with sth** (esp of the face or eyes) to show the specified emotion: [Vpr] *eyes gleaming with anticipation/excitement.*

glean /gliːn/ *v* **1** ~ **sth** (**from sb/sth**) to obtain news, facts, information, etc, usu from various sources, in small quantities and with effort: [Vnpr] *glean information from overhearing other people's conversations.* **2** to gather grain left in a field after the HARVEST(1): [Vn] *glean wheat* ○ *glean a field.*

glee /gliː/ *n* [U] ~ (**at sth**) a feeling of great delight that makes one want to laugh. Glee is usu caused by sth good experienced by oneself, or sth bad that happens to sb else: *He chuckled with glee at the little joke he was about to make.* ○ *She couldn't disguise her glee at their embarrassment.*
▶ **gleeful** /-fl/ *adj* full of glee; happy: *gleeful faces/ laughter.* **gleefully** /-fəli/ *adv.*

glen /glen/ *n* a narrow valley, esp in Scotland, Ireland or the USA.

glib /glɪb/ *adj* (*derog*) speaking or spoken in a smooth clever way but not seeming sincere or honest: *a glib talker/salesman* ○ *a glib remark/speech* ○ *glib arguments/excuses* ○ *have a glib tongue.*
▶ **glibly** *adv.*

glide /glaɪd/ *v* **1** to move along smoothly and continuously, esp in the specified direction: [Vpr] *skiers gliding across the snow* ○ *a snake gliding along the ground* [Vadv] *birds gliding overhead* ○ *The boat glided silently past.* [Vp] *She glided by unnoticed.* ○ (*fig*) *The days just glided by.* [also V]. **2** to fly without engine power, either in a glider (GLIDE) or in an aircraft with engine failure: [Vp] *The pilot managed to glide down to a safe landing.*
▶ **glide** *n* **1** [sing] a continuous smooth movement: *the graceful glide of a skater.* **2** [C] (*phonetics*) a speech sound made while moving the mouth from one position to another.
glider /ˈglaɪdə(r)/ *n* a light aircraft that flies without an engine.
gliding *n* [U] the sport of flying in gliders. Compare HANG-GLIDING.

glimmer /ˈglɪmə(r)/ *v* to send out a faint unsteady light: [V] *lights glimmering in the distance.*
▶ **glimmer** *n* **1** a faint unsteady light: *a glimmer of light through the mist.* **2** a small sign of sth: *a glimmer of hope* ○ *He shows not the least glimmer of intelligence.*
glimmering /ˈglɪmərɪŋ/ *n* a glimmer: *We began to see the glimmerings of a solution to the problem.* See also GLEAM *n.*

glimpse /glɪmps/ *n* (usu *sing*) ~ (**at sb/sth**); ~ (**into sth**) a short look: *a quick glimpse at the newspaper headlines* ○ *The book provides a fascinating glimpse into the secluded life of a monastery.* ○ *He* ***caught a***

brief **glimpse** *of her in the crowd before she disappeared from view.*
▶ **glimpse** *v* to get a quick look at sb/sth: [Vn] *She glimpsed him between the half-drawn curtains.*

glint /glɪnt/ *v* **1** to give out small bright flashes of light: [V] *The ripples on the surface of the lake glinted in the sun.* **2** (of sb's eyes) to show a particular emotion: [Vpr] *eyes glinting with mischief.* [also V].
▶ **glint** *n* **1** a flash of light, esp as reflected from a hard shiny surface: *He bent down to investigate a glint of metal in the dust.* **2** an expression of the eyes indicating a particular emotion: *a glint of anger* ○ *a mischievous glint in his eye.*

glisten /ˈglɪsn/ *v* ~ (with sth) (esp of wet surfaces) to shine brightly: [V] *dew-drops glistening in the grass* [Vpr] *grass glistening with dew* ○ *eyes glistening with tears* ○ *bodies glistening with sweat.*

glitter /ˈglɪtə(r)/ *v* ~ (with sth) to shine brightly with little sharp flashes of light; to SPARKLE(1): [V] *stars glittering in the frosty sky* [Vpr] *a necklace glittering with diamonds.*
▶ **glitter** *n* [U] **1** bright light composed of many little flashes: *the glitter of decorations on a Christmas tree.* **2** an attractive, exciting or fashionable display that is sometimes false: *the superficial glamour and glitter of show business* .

glitterati /ˌglɪtəˈrɑːti/ *n* [pl] (*sl often derog*) fashionable people: *a wedding attended by the glitterati of Hollywood.*

glittering /ˈglɪtərɪŋ/ *adj* magnificent, splendid or extremely successful: *a glittering occasion attended by many well-known public figures* ○ *A glittering career has been predicted for her.*

glittery /ˈglɪtəri/ *adj* that glitters: *glittery eyes.*

glitz /glɪts/ *n* [U] (*sl usu derog*) the quality of appearing attractive and splendid, but in a SUPERFICIAL(2) or excessive way: *a resort full of glitz, gloss and high-flying celebrities.* ▶ **glitzy** *adj*: *The movie star's wedding was a glitzy affair.*

gloaming /ˈgləʊmɪŋ/ *n* **the gloaming** [sing] (*Scot or fml*) the faint light after the sun sets or before it rises; TWILIGHT.

gloat /gləʊt/ *v* ~ (about/over sth) to express or feel delight at one's own success or good luck or at sb else's failure: [V] *Though they won the election they are in no position to gloat.* [Vpr] *It's nothing to gloat about.* ▶ **gloating** *adj*: *a gloating remark/letter.*

global /ˈgləʊbl/ *adj* covering or affecting the whole world: *a global tour* ○ *global issues/problems* ○ *Pollution is a threat to the global environment.* ▶ **globally** /-bəli/ *adv*: *Eight million people globally are infected with the virus.*
■ ˌ**global** ˈ**warming** *n* [U] the increase in temperature of the earth's atmosphere, caused when certain gases, esp carbon dioxide (CARBON), trap the sun's heat. See also GREENHOUSE EFFECT.

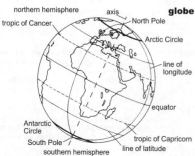

globe

northern hemisphere
axis
North Pole
tropic of Cancer
Arctic Circle
line of longitude
equator
Antarctic Circle
South Pole
tropic of Capricorn
southern hemisphere
line of latitude

globe /gləʊb/ *n* **1** [C] a model of the earth shaped like a ball and showing the countries, rivers, cities,

etc on its surface. It is usu mounted on a stand so that it can be turned round easily. **2 the globe** [sing] the earth: *travel (all) around the globe.* ⇨ picture. **3** [C] a thing shaped like a ball: *a glass lampshade in the shape of a globe* ○ *The silvery globe of the moon sank towards the horizon.*
■ ˌ**globe** ˈ**artichoke** *n* = ARTICHOKE 1.
ˈ**globe-trotting** *adj, n* [U] (*infml*) travelling in many countries throughout the world. ˈ**globe-trotter** *n.*

globule /ˈglɒbjuːl/ *n* (*fml*) a tiny drop or ball, esp of liquid or a melted solid: *globules of wax from a candle.*
▶ **globular** /ˈglɒbjələ(r)/ *adj* (*fml*) shaped like a GLOBULE(3) or ball: *a globular glass bottle.*

glockenspiel /ˈglɒkənʃpiːl/ *n* a musical instrument consisting of metal bars of varying length which produce notes when struck with two small hammers. Compare XYLOPHONE.

gloom /gluːm/ *n* [U] **1** partial darkness: *In the gathering gloom it was hard to see anything distinctly.* **2** a feeling of sadness and depression(1): *The news cast a deep gloom over the whole community.* ○ *He remained sunk in gloom for several days.* **IDM** **doom and gloom; gloom and doom** ⇨ DOOM[1].
▶ **gloomy** /ˈgluːmi/ *adj* (-ier, -iest) **1** nearly dark; not well lit: *a gloomy corner/passage/room/house* ○ *a gloomy day* (ie with dark clouds and dull light). **2** making sb feel sad and depressed: *a gloomy outlook/prospect* ○ *a gloomy face/expression/voice/person* ○ *What are you so gloomy about? Cheer up!* **gloomily** /-ɪli/ *adv.*

glorify /ˈglɔːrɪfaɪ/ *v* (*pt, pp* **-fied**) **1** (*often derog*) to make sb/sth appear better or more noble than they really are: [Vn] *a book which glorifies the horrors of war.* **2** [Vn] (**a**) to praise sb/sth highly. (**b**) to praise and worship God, eg by singing or praying.
▶ **glorification** /ˌglɔːrɪfɪˈkeɪʃn/ *n* [U]: *the glorification of violence.*
glorified *adj* [attrib] (*derog*) described in a way that makes sb/sth seem better than they are: *An air-hostess is only a glorified waitress.* ○ *The word processor is not simply a glorified typewriter.*

glorious /ˈglɔːriəs/ *adj* **1** having, worthy of or bringing great fame or GLORY(1): *a glorious deed/victory* ○ *the glorious days/years/reign of Elizabeth I* ○ *die a glorious death* (ie esp in battle for one's country). Compare INGLORIOUS 1. **2** beautiful; splendid; magnificent: *a glorious day/sunset/view* ○ *The weather was glorious.* **3** (*infml*) very pleasant; enjoyable: *have a glorious time.* ▶ **gloriously** *adv.*

glory /ˈglɔːri/ *n* **1** [U] fame and honour won by great achievements: *glory won on the field of battle* ○ *a proud father basking/bathing in his son's reflected glory* (ie sharing the fame achieved by his son) ○ *leave politics in a blaze of glory* ○ (*ironic*) *She didn't exactly cover herself with glory in the exams!* **2** [U] praise and worship of God: *'Glory to God in the highest.'* **3** [U] great beauty: *the glory of a sunset/a summer's day* ○ *the countryside in all its glory* ○ *The old house was restored to its former glory.* **4** [C] a special cause for pride, respect or delight: *the glories of nature* ○ *The temple is one of the glories of ancient Greece.* ○ *The opera was the crowning glory of his long and illustrious career.*
▶ **glory** *v* (*pt, pp* **-ied**) **PHRV** ˈ**glory in sth** to take great pleasure or pride in sth: *glory in one's freedom/success.*
■ ˈ**glory days** *n* [pl] a time in the past which people look back on as being better than the present: *the glory days of pop music* ○ *a town long past its glory days.*

gloss[1] /glɒs/ *n* **1(a)** [U, sing] a brightness or a shine on a smooth surface: *wood polished to a high gloss* ○ *the gloss on sb's hair.* (**b**) [U] (often in compounds) a

G

substance designed to give such a brightness: 'lip-gloss ○ varnishes available in gloss, satin and matt ○ a gloss finish (ie a shiny surface left after painting, processing, etc). (**c**) [U] paint which, when dry, has a hard shiny surface: a tin of gloss (paint) ○ two coats of gloss. Compare MATT. **2** [U, sing] an attractive appearance that is only SUPERFICIAL(2): the gloss and glitter of Hollywood ○ **put a** diplomatic **gloss on** the results of the enquiry ○ The affair took some of the gloss off the company's image. Compare VENEER 2.

▶ **gloss** v **PHRV** ,**gloss** '**over sth** to treat sth briefly in order to avoid giving embarrassing details: gloss over the awkward facts.

glossy adj (-ier, -iest) **1** smooth and shiny: glossy hair/photographs ○ glossy brochures/magazines (ie printed on glossy paper, with many photographs, coloured illustrations, etc and usu expensive). **2** (usu derog) making a show of being SMART¹(4) and expensive but of little real worth or importance: a glossy image ○ a glossy advertising campaign/film première.

gloss² /glɒs/ n ~ (**on sth**) (**a**) a note or comment added to a piece of writing to explain a difficult word, phrase, etc. (**b**) a way of explaining or interpreting sth: The government is trying to put an optimistic gloss on the latest trade figures.

▶ **gloss** v to give an explanation of the meaning of a word; to add a gloss to a text: [Vn] a difficult word that needs to be glossed.

glossary /'glɒsəri/ n a list of technical or special words, esp those occurring in a particular text, explaining their meanings: a glossary of financial terms. Compare VOCABULARY 3.

glove   glove   gauntlet   mitten

glove /glʌv/ n a covering made of leather, wool, etc for the hand, usu with separate parts for each finger and the thumb: a pair of gloves ○ rubber gloves for washing up ○ gardening gloves. ⇨ picture. ⇨ picture at BASEBALL. Compare MITTEN. **IDM** **fit like a glove** ⇨ FIT². **the gloves are off** sb is ready for a fight or an argument: The gloves are already off in the pre-election campaign. **hand in glove** ⇨ HAND¹. **handle, etc sb with kid gloves** ⇨ KID¹.

▶ **gloved** adj [usu attrib] wearing a glove or gloves: gloved hands/fingers.

■ '**glove compartment** n a small enclosed space or shelf facing the front seats in a car, used for holding small objects. ⇨ picture at CAR.

'**glove puppet** (Brit) (US '**hand puppet**) n a type of PUPPET worn on the hand and worked by the fingers. ⇨ picture at PUPPET.

glow /gləʊ/ v **1** to produce light and heat without flame: [V] glowing embers/charcoal ○ glowing metal in a furnace ○ A cigarette glowed in the dark. **2** ~ (**with sth**) to be, look or feel warm or red, eg after exercise or because of excitement, embarrassment, anger, etc: [V] Her cheeks glowed. [Vpr] glowing with health/pride. **3** ~ (**with sth**) to display strong or warm colour: [V] The colours glowed and deepened. [Vpr] The countryside glowed with autumn colours.

▶ **glow** n [sing] **1** a dull light: the glow of the city against the night sky ○ The fire cast a warm glow on the walls. **2** a red or warm look: cheeks with a rosy/healthy glow. **3** a feeling of pleasure and satisfaction: She felt a glow of pride in her achievement.

glowing adj [usu attrib] giving enthusiastic praise: a glowing account/report ○ describe sth in glowing

colours/terms (ie praise sth strongly). **glowingly** adv: speak/write glowingly of sb.

■ '**glow-worm** n a type of insect. The female has no wings and produces a green light at the end of her tail.

glower /'glaʊə(r)/ v ~ (**at sb/sth**) to look in an angry or aggressive way: [Vpr] He sat glowering at his opponent. [V] (fig) the glowering sky (ie with dark clouds).

glucose /'glu:kəʊs, -kəʊz/ n [U] a type of natural sugar found in fruit and easily converted to energy by the human body.

glue /glu:/ n [U, C] a sticky substance used for joining things: mend a broken cup with glue ○ a bottle/tube of glue ○ He sticks to her like glue (ie never leaves her). Compare ADHESIVE n, CEMENT 2.

▶ **glue** v ~ **A** (**to/onto B**); ~ **A and B** (**together**) to stick or join a thing or things with glue: [Vnp, Vnpr] glue the leg (back) onto the chair [Vnpr] glue two pieces of cardboard together. **IDM** '**glued to sth** (infml) continually close to or involved in sth; unwilling to leave sth: He's glued to the television (ie watching it with great interest). ○ with his ear glued to the keyhole (ie listening hard to a conversation in another room).

gluey /'glu:i/ adj sticky; like glue: a gluey mess.

■ '**glue-sniffing** n [U] the practice of breathing in the fumes (FUME) of certain types of glue as a drug, so as to become excited or to escape from reality.

glum /glʌm/ adj (infml) sad; depressed; gloomy (GLOOM): glum expressions/faces/news ○ Don't look so glum. ▶ **glumly** adv: 'Another rainy day,' he said glumly.

glut /glʌt/ v (-tt-) ~ **sth/sb** (**with sth**) (usu passive) to supply with much more than is needed: [Vn, Vnpr] The market is glutted (with cheap apples from abroad). [Vnpr] glutted with pleasure.

▶ **glut** n (usu sing) a situation in which there is more of sth than is needed or can be used; an excess: a glut of fruit/of TV quiz shows/of talent.

gluten /'glu:tn/ n [U] a sticky PROTEIN substance that is left when STARCH is removed from flour: maize gluten.

▶ **glutinous** /'glu:tənəs/ adj of or like gluten; sticky: glutinous rice.

glutton /'glʌtn/ n **1** (derog) a person who eats too much. **2** ~ **for sth** (infml) a person who is always eager for sth, esp for difficult or unpleasant tasks: He's certainly a **glutton for punishment**/work.

▶ **gluttonous** /'glʌtənəs/ adj very greedy, esp for food: a gluttonous appetite.

gluttony /-təni/ n [U] the habit or practice of eating and drinking too much.

glycerine /'glɪsəri:n, -rɪn/ (US **glycerin**) n [U] a thick sweet colourless liquid made from fats and oils. It is used in medicines, beauty products and explosives.

gm (also **gr**) abbr (pl unchanged or **gms**, **grs**) gram(s); gramme(s): 10 gm.

GMT /,dʒi: em 'ti:/ abbr Greenwich Mean Time. Compare BST.

gnarled /nɑ:ld/ adj (**a**) (of trees) twisted and rough; covered with hard lumps: a gnarled oak/branch/trunk. (**b**) (of people or their hands or fingers) twisted, with swollen joints and rough skin, esp from old age or hard work: hands gnarled with age ○ gnarled old men.

gnash /næʃ/ v to grind or strike one's teeth together as a sign of great emotion: [Vn] gnashing his teeth with/in rage. ▶ **gnashing** n [U]: (fig) There has been much **gnashing of teeth** over the proposed route for the new motorway.

gnat /næt/ n a small fly with two wings that bites.

gnaw /nɔ:/ v **1** ~ (**at**) **sth** to keep biting sth hard so that it gradually disappears: [Vn, Vpr] a dog gnaw-

ing (at) a bone [Vnp] *Rats had gnawed the lid right off.* **2** ~ **(at)** **sb/sth** to cause sb/sth continual distress or anxiety: [Vn, Vpr] *fear gnawing (at) one's heart* [V] *a gnawing sense of inadequacy* [Vpr, Vp] *Self-doubt gnawed (away) at his confidence.*

gnocchi /ˈnɒki, ˈnjɒki/ *n* [pl] an Italian dish of small cooked balls made mostly of potato or flour and served with a sauce.

gnome /nəʊm/ *n* **1(a)** (in stories) a creature, similar to a small human being, that lives under the ground and guards precious things. (**b**) a plastic or stone model of a gnome, used as an ornament in a garden. **2** (*infml usu derog*) a person with special influence, esp in financial matters: *the gnomes of Zürich.*

gnomic /ˈnəʊmɪk/ *adj* (*fml*) (of a remark, etc) wise but sometimes difficult to understand: *a gnomic phone call.*

GNP /ˌdʒiː en ˈpiː/ *abbr* gross national product: *The country's GNP has risen by 10% this year.* Compare GDP.

gnu /nuː, njuː/ *n* (*pl* unchanged or **gnus**) (also **wildebeest**) a large strong African ANTELOPE.

go¹ /ɡəʊ/ *v* (*3rd pers sing pres t* **goes** /ɡəʊz/; *pt* **went** /went/; *pp* **gone** /ɡɒn/; *US* ɡɔːn/) ⇨ note at BEEN.

● **Movement** Senses 1–6 refer esp to movement *away from* the place where the speaker or writer is or a place where they imagine themselves to be. **1(a)** to move or travel from one place to another: [Vpr] *She went into her room and shut the door behind her.* ○ *He goes to work by bus.* ○ *I have to go to Rome on business tomorrow.* ○ *We're going to Canada for our vacation this year.* ○ *She has gone to China* (ie is now in China or is on her way there). ○ *I think you should go to the doctor's.* [V] *Would you go and get me a glass of water?* [V.to inf] *She has gone to see her sister this weekend.* [Vadv] *Are you going home for Christmas?* ⇨ note at AND. (**b**) to leave one place in order to reach another; to depart: [V] *I must go/be going now.* ○ *They came at six and went at nine.* ○ *Has she gone yet?* ○ *She's been gone an hour* (ie She left an hour ago). ○ *When does the train go?* (**c**) ~ **(to sth) (with sb)** to move or travel, esp with sb else, to a particular place or in order to be present at an event: [V, Vpr] *Dave's having a party tonight; are you going (to it)?* [Vpr] *I went to the cinema with Denise last night.* ○ *Who are you going with?* ○ *I'll be going with Keith.* ○ *His dog goes everywhere with him.* **2** ~ **to sth** (**a**) (usu without *a* or *the*) to move or to travel to the place specified for the purpose associated with it: [Vpr] *go to hospital/(US) go to the hospital* (ie for medical treatment) ○ *go to prison* (ie be sent there for having committed a crime) ○ *go to market* (ie to sell one's produce). (**b**) (usu without *a* or *the*) to attend a place, esp regularly, for a particular purpose: [Vpr] *go to church/chapel/school/college* ○ *Did you go to* (ie study at) *university?* **3(a)** ~ **for sth** (also used with the *-ing* form of a *v*) to leave a place or travel to a place in order to engage in an activity or a sport: [Vpr] *go for a walk/drive/swim* ○ *Annie's not in — she's gone for a run.* ○ *Shall we go for a drink* (ie at a pub or bar) *after work?* [V.ing] *go fishing/jogging/sailing/climbing* ○ *I have to go shopping this afternoon.* (**b**) ~ **on sth** to leave a place and do sth different: [Vpr] *go on a journey/a tour/a trip/ a cruise/(a) safari* ○ *Richard has gone on leave for two weeks.* ○ *After university she went on a secretarial course.* **4** to move or travel in the specified way or over a specified distance: [Vadv] *He's going too fast.* [Vn] *We had gone about fifty miles when the car broke down.* ○ *We still have five miles to go* (ie until we reach our destination). **5** (used with the *-ing* form of a *v*) to show that sb/sth moves in the specified way or that sb/sth is doing sth while moving: *The car went skidding off the road into a ditch.* ○ *The train went chugging up the hill.* ○ *She went sobbing*

up the stairs. **6** to be sent or passed on: [V] *What time will this letter go?* [Vpr] *Such complaints must go through the proper channels.* ○ *I want this memo to go to all department managers.* **7** ~ **(from...) to...** to extend or lead from one place to another: [V-adj] *The roots of this plant go deep.* ○ (*fig*) *Differences between employers and workers go deep.* [Vadv] *Where does this road go?* [Vpr] *I want a rope that will go from the top window to the ground.* [Vp] *Our garden goes down as far as the river.*

● **Position** **8(a)** to have as a usual or proper position; to be placed: [Vpr] *This dictionary goes on the top shelf.* [Vadv] *Where do you want the piano to go* (ie be put)? ○ *'Where does this teapot go?' 'In that cupboard.'* (**b**) ~ **(in/into sth)** to fit in sth; to be able to be contained in sth: [V, Vpr] *This key won't go in* (the lock). [Vpr] *My clothes won't all go into that tiny suitcase.* [also V]. (**c**) ~ **(into sth)** (of a number) to be contained in another number, esp without any units remaining: [V-n] *3 into 12 goes 4* (ie is contained in 12 four times). [V, Vpr] *7 into 15 won't go/7 won't go into 15.*

● **Activity** **9** (used with *advs*, or in questions after *how*) to occur or happen in the way specified; to result in being; to progress: [Vadv] *'How did your interview go?' 'It went very well, thank you.'* ○ *The election went badly for the Conservatives.* ○ *Did everything go smoothly?* ○ *The meeting went better than we had expected.* [Vadv] *How's it going?/How are things going?* (ie Is your life pleasant, enjoyable, etc at the moment?) ○ *The way things are going the company will be bankrupt by the end of the year.* **10** (esp in commands) to start an activity: [V] *I'll say 'One, two, three, go!' as a signal for you to start.* **11** (of a machine, etc) to function; to work; to operate: [V] *This clock doesn't go.* ○ *Is your watch going?* [Vpr] *This machine goes by electricity.*

● **State** **12** to pass into the specified condition; to become sth: [V-adj] *go bald/blind/mad/pale/ bankrupt* ○ *Her hair is going grey.* ○ *This milk has gone sour.* ○ *Fish soon goes bad* (ie rotten) *in hot weather.* ○ *The children went wild with excitement.* ○ *Britain went Labour* (ie elected a Labour government) *in 1945.* ⇨ note at BECOME. **13** to be or live habitually in the specified state or manner: [V-adj] *She cannot bear the thought of children going hungry.* ○ *The police usually go armed in this part of the city.* **14** (used with a negative past participle to show that an action does not happen): *Her absence went unnoticed* (ie was not noticed). ○ *Police are worried that many crimes go unreported* (ie are not reported to them).

● **Sound** **15** (used esp in questions after *how*) (of a piece of music or writing) to have a certain tune or order of words: [Vadv] *How does that song go?* ○ *I forget how the next line goes.* [Vpr] *The national anthem goes like this...* [V.that, Vadv] *The story goes* (that) *she poisoned her husband/She poisoned her husband, or so the story goes* (ie It is said that she poisoned him). **16** to make the specified sound or gesture: [V-n] *The gun went 'bang'.* ○ *Cats go 'mi-aow'.* [Vpr] *She went like this with her hand.* **17** to be sounded as a signal or warning: [V] *The whistle goes at the end of the match.* ○ *No one may leave the classroom until the bell goes.*

● **Coming to an end** **18** to stop existing; to disappear: [V] *Has your headache gone yet?* ○ *I've washed it repeatedly but the stain won't go.* ○ *I left my bike outside the library and when I came out again it had gone* (ie somebody had taken or stolen it). **19** (used after *must, have to* or *can*) to be disposed of, rejected or dismissed: [V] *The old sofa will have to go.* ○ *He's incompetent — he'll have to go.* **20** to stop; to stop functioning completely; to be lost: [V] *His sight is beginning to go.* ○ *His mind is going* (ie He is

G

---

losing his mental powers). **21** to become damaged or stop functioning properly: [V] *My sweater has gone* (ie has worn into holes) *at the elbows.* ○ *I was driving into town when my brakes went.* ○ *This light bulb has gone.* ○ *The battery is going.* ○ *Her voice has gone* (ie She cannot speak properly, eg because she has a sore throat). **22** (*euph*) to die: [V] *Old Mrs Davis has gone.* **23** ~ **(on sth)** (of money) to be spent or used for sth: [Vadv] *I don't know where the money goes!* [Vpr] *All her earnings go on clothes.* ○ *Most of my salary goes on (paying) the rent.* [V.*to* inf] *The money will go to finance a new community centre.* **24** ~ **(to sb) (for sth)** to be sold: [Vadv] *The new dictionary is going well* (ie A lot of copies of it are being sold). [Vpr] *These socks are going at £1 a pair.* ○ *We won't let our house go for less than $50 000.* ○ *The antique table went to the lady in the pink hat.*

● **Commands 25** (used in negative commands with a *v* in the -*ing* form to tell sb not to do sth) [V.*ing*] *Don't go getting yourself into trouble!* **26** (*infml esp US*) (used in commands with a *v* in the infinitive without *to* to send sb away angrily): *Go jump in a lake!*

● **Other meanings 27** to contribute; to help: [V.*to* inf] *This all goes to prove my theory.* ○ *The latest unemployment figures go to show that government policy isn't working.* ○ *What qualities go to make a successful businessman?* **28** (*infml*) (only in the continuous tenses) to be available: [V] *There simply aren't any jobs going in this area.* ○ *Is there any tea going?* (ie Can I have some tea?) **29** to remain to be finished: [V] *two more exams still to go.* **30** (of time) to pass; to ELAPSE: [Vadv] *Hasn't the time gone quickly?* [V] *There are only two days to go before the election* (ie It is in two days' time). **31** to be willing to pay a certain amount of money for sth: [Vadv] *He's offered £2 500 for the car and I don't think he'll go any higher.* [Vpr] *I'll go to $3 000 but no higher.* **32(a)** (used with *to* or *into* + a *n* in many expressions to show that sb/sth has reached the state indicated by the *n*, eg *She went to sleep*, ie began to sleep; *The company has gone into liquidation*, ie become bankrupt; for similar expressions see entries for the *ns*, eg ⇨ GO TO POT). **(b)** (used with *out of* + a *n* in many expressions to show that sb/sth is no longer in the state indicated by the *n*, eg *That colour has gone out of fashion*, ie is no longer fashionable; for similar expressions see entries for the *ns*, eg ⇨ GO OUT OF USE).

IDM Most idioms containing **go** are at the entries for the nouns or adjectives in the idioms, eg **go it alone** ⇨ ALONE; **here goes** ⇨ HERE. **anything goes** (*infml*) anything that sb says or does is accepted or allowed, however shocking or unusual it may be: *Almost anything goes these days.* **as people, things, etc go** in comparison with the average person, thing, etc: *Twenty pounds for a pair of shoes isn't bad as things go nowadays* (ie considering how much shoes usu cost). **be going on (for) sth** to be near to or approaching the specified age, time or number; to be nearly sth: *He must be going on for ninety.* ○ *She's sixteen, going on seventeen.* ○ *It must be going on (for) midnight.* ○ *There were going on for* (ie nearly) *fifty people at the party.* **be going to do sth 1** (used to show what sb is intending or planning to do in the future): *We're going to spend our holidays in Wales this year.* ○ *We're going to buy a house when we've saved enough money.* **2** (used to indicate sth that is about to happen or is likely to happen in the future, for which there is some evidence already): *I think I'm going to be sick.* ○ *I'm going to be twenty next month.* ○ *If the drought continues there's going to be a famine.* **enough/ something/sth to be going 'on with** (*esp Brit*) something that is sufficient or adequate for a short time: *'How much money do you need?' '£50 should be*

enough to be going on with.' ○ *I can't lend you the whole amount now, but I can give you something to be going on with.* ○ *Here's a cup of tea to be going on with; we'll have something to eat later.* **go all 'out for sth; go all out to 'do sth** to make a very great effort to obtain sth or do sth: *The Democratic Party are going all out for victory in/going all out to win the election.* **go and do sth** (used esp to express anger or annoyance that sb has done sth foolish): *Trust him to go and mess things up!* ○ *Why did you (have to) go and upset your mother like that?* **go 'on (with you)** (used to express gentle disapproval or lack of belief): *Go on with you! Get upstairs to bed and stop monkeying around.* ○ *'How old are you?' 'I'm forty.' 'Go on (with you) — you don't look a day over thirty.'* **go 'to it** (used esp in the imperative to encourage sb to do sth) to make a special effort to do sth: *Go to it, John! You know you can beat him.* **(have) a lot, plenty, not much, nothing, etc 'going for one** (to have) many, not many, etc advantages: *You're young, intelligent, attractive: you've got a lot going for you!* ○ *The company hasn't much going for it.* **,no 'go** (*infml*) not possible or permitted: *If the bank won't lend us the money it's no go, I'm afraid.* See also NO-GO AREA. **to 'go** (*US infml*) (of cooked food sold in a restaurant or shop) for sb to take away and eat elsewhere: *Two pizzas to go!* **what/whatever ,sb says, 'goes** (*infml often joc*) the specified person has total authority and must be obeyed: *My wife wanted the kitchen painted green, and what she says, goes.* **,where does sb ,go from 'here?** (used esp about sb who is in a difficult situation) what action should sb take next, esp in order to improve the situation they are in?: *Sales are down and lay-offs are inevitable: where does the company go from here?* **,who goes 'there?** (used by a soldier on guard to order sb to say who they are): *Halt, who goes there?*

PHRV **,go a'bout 1** ⇨ GO ROUND/AROUND/ABOUT. **2** (of a boat) to change direction. **'go about sth** to continue to do sth; to keep busy with sth: *go about one's daily routine* ○ *Despite the threat of war, people went about their work as usual.* **,go a'bout sth / doing sth** to start to work at sth; to approach or TACKLE(1) sth: *You're not going about the job in the right way. How should I go about finding a job?* **,go a'bout with sb** ⇨ GO ROUND/AROUND/ABOUT WITH SB.

'go after sb to chase or pursue sb: *He went after the burglars.* **go after sb/sth** to try to get or obtain sb/sth: *He goes after* (ie tries to attract sexually) *every woman he meets.* ○ *We're both going after the same job.*

,go a'gainst sb to be not in sb's favour or not to their advantage: *The jury's verdict went against him.* **,go a'gainst sb/sth** to resist or oppose sb/sth: *Don't go against your parents/your parents' wishes.* **,go a'gainst sth** to be opposed or contrary to sth; to be in conflict with sth: *Paying for hospital treatment goes against my socialist principles.* ○ *His thinking goes against all logic.*

,go a'head 1 to travel in front of other people in one's group and arrive before them: *I'll go ahead and tell them you're on the way.* **2** to happen; to be done: *The fête went ahead despite the bad weather.* ○ *The building of the new bridge will go ahead as planned.* **,go a'head (with sth)** to begin to do sth, esp when given permission or after doubts or opposition have been expressed: *'May I start now?' 'Yes, go ahead.'* ○ *The government intends to go ahead with its tax cutting plans.*

,go a'long 1 (used esp after *as*) to proceed with an activity; to continue: *You may have some difficulty at first but you'll find it gets easier as you go along.* ○ *He made the story up as he went along.* **2** to progress; to develop: *Things are going along nicely.* **,go a'long with sb/sth** to agree with sb/sth; to accept sth: *I* *don't go along with her views on nuclear disarmament.*

go around ⇨ GO ROUND/AROUND/ABOUT. **go around with sb** ⇨ GO ROUND/AROUND/ABOUT WITH SB.

ˈ**go at sb** to attack sb: *They went at each other furiously.* ˈ**go at sth** to make great efforts to do sth; to work hard at sth: *They went at the job as if their lives depended on it.*

ˌ**go aˈway 1** to leave a place or person: *Go away!* ○ *Go away and think about it, then let me know.* **2** to leave home for a period of time, esp for a holiday: *go away on business* ○ *We're going away for a few days.* **3** to disappear; to fade: *The smell still hasn't gone away.*

ˌ**go ˈback (to...)** to return to a place where one/it was previously: *She doesn't want to go back to her husband* (ie to live with him again). ○ *This toaster will have to go back* (ie be taken back to the place where it was bought) — *it simply doesn't work* . ○ *Of course we want to go back some day* — *it's our country, our real home.* ˌ**go ˈback (to sth) 1** to remember or consider sth that happened or was said at an earlier point in time: *How far does your memory go back?* ○ *Once you have made this decision, there will be no going back* (ie you will not be able to change your mind). ○ *Can I go back to what you said at the beginning of the meeting?* ○ *To trace the origins of the Irish problem, we have to go back over three hundred years.* **2** to have existed since a specified time or for a specified period: *His family goes back to the time of the Mayflower.* ○ *How far does the tradition go back?* ˌ**go ˈback on sth** to fail to keep a promise; to change one's mind about sth: *He never goes back on his word* (ie never fails to do what he has said he will do). ˌ**go ˈback to sth / doing sth 1** to start doing sth again that one had stopped doing: *The children go back to school next week.* ○ *She's decided to go back to teaching.*

ˌ**go beˈfore** to exist or happen in an earlier time: *The present crisis is worse than any that have gone before.* ˈ**go before sb/sth** to be presented to sb/sth for discussion, decision or judgement: *go before a judge* ○ *My application goes before the planning committee next week.*

ˌ**go beˈyond sth** to be more than sth; to EXCEED sth: *This year's sales figures go beyond all our expectations* (ie are much better than we thought they would be). ○ *The matter has gone beyond a joke* (ie has become too serious to be amusing).

ˌ**go ˈby** (of time) to pass: *As time goes by my memory seems to get worse.* ○ *The weeks went slowly by.* ˈ**go by sth 1** to be guided or directed by sth: *I shall go entirely by what my solicitor says* (ie follow her or his advice). ○ *That's a good rule to go by.* **2** to form an opinion or a judgement from sth: *If past experience is anything to go by, the plane will be late.*

ˌ**go ˈdown 1** to fall to the ground: *She tripped and went down with a bump.* **2** (of a ship, etc) to disappear below the water; to sink: *Hundreds died when the ferry went down.* **3** (of the sun and moon) to disappear below the horizon; to set²(18): *We sat and watched the sun go down.* **4** (of food and drink) to be swallowed: *This pill just won't go down* (ie I can't swallow it). ○ *A glass of wine would go down very nicely* (ie I would very much like one). **5** to be reduced in size, level, etc: *The swelling has gone down a little.* ○ *The flood waters are going down.* **6** (of prices, the temperature, etc) to become lower; to fall: *The price of houses is going down/Houses are going down in price.* **7** (*infml*) to decrease in quality; to get worse: *This neighbourhood has gone down a lot recently.* See also GO DOWNHILL. **8** (*computing*) to stop working temporarily: *The system is going down in 10 minutes.* ˌ**go ˈdown (from...)** (in Britain) to leave a university, esp Oxford or Cambridge, at the end of a term or after finishing one's studies: *She went down (from Cambridge) in 1984.* ˌ**go ˈdown (in sth)** to be

written (in sth); to be recorded or remembered in sth: *It all goes down* (ie She writes it all) *in her notebook.* ○ *He will go down in history as a great statesman.* ˌ**go ˈdown (to sb)** to be defeated by sb, esp in a match or contest: *Italy went down (to Brazil) by three goals to one.* ˌ**go ˈdown (to...) (from...)** to go from one place to another, esp further south or from a city or large town to a smaller place: *They've gone down to the New Forest for a couple of days.* ˌ**go ˈdown (with sth)** (used with *advs* or in questions after *how*) (of a remark, performance, etc) to be received by sb in the specified way: *Her speech went down well (with the audience).* ○ *His plays have always gone down badly on Broadway.* ○ *Rude jokes don't go down too well with* (ie are disapproved of by) *my sister.* ˌ**go ˈdown with sth** to become ill with sth: *Our youngest boy has gone down with mumps.*

ˈ**go for sb** to attack sb: *She went for him with a carving knife.* ○ *The newspapers really went for him over his defence of terrorism.* ˈ**go for sb/sth 1** to apply to sb/sth: *What I said about Peter goes for you, too.* ○ *Britain has a high level of unemployment* — *but the same goes for many other countries.* **2** to go to a place and bring sb/sth back: *Shall I go for a doctor?* ○ *She's gone for some milk.* **3** to be attracted by sb/sth; to like or prefer sb/sth: *She goes for tall slim men.* ○ *I don't go much for modern art.* ˈ**go for sth 1** to choose sth: *I think I'll go for the fruit salad.* **2** to attempt to obtain or achieve sth: *She's going for the world record in the high jump.* ○ *Go for it!*

ˌ**go ˈin 1** to enter a room, house, etc: *Let's go in, it's getting cold.* ○ *Do go in, Mrs Brown, I'll be with you in a moment.* **2** (of the sun or moon) to disappear behind a cloud: *The sun went in and it grew colder.* **3** (in cricket) to start batting (BAT¹ *v* 1): *Who's going in next?* ˌ**go ˈin for sth 1** (in Britain) to take an examination or enter a competition: *She's going in for the Cambridge First Certificate.* ○ *Which events is he going in for at the Olympics?* **2** to choose sth as one's career: *Have you ever thought of going in for teaching?* **3** to have sth as an interest or a HOBBY: *She doesn't go in for team games.*

ˌ**go ˈinto sth** (of a vehicle) to make violent contact with sth; to hit sth: *The car skidded and went into a tree.* Compare RUN INTO STH. **2** to join an organization, esp in order to have a career in it; to enter sth: *go into the Army/the Church/Parliament* ○ *go into banking/publishing/teaching* ○ *When did Britain go into Europe* (ie join the European Union)? **3** (of a vehicle or driver) to start the specified movement: *The car went into a spin on a patch of ice.* ○ *The plane went into a nosedive.* **4** to begin to act or behave in the way specified: *He went into a long explanation of the affair.* ○ *She went into hysterics.* **5** to examine or investigate sth carefully: *We need to go into the question of costs.* ○ *I don't want to go into the minor details now.* ○ *The matter is being gone into.* Compare LOOK INTO STH. **6** (of resources, time, etc) to be spent on sth or used to do sth: *More government money needs to go into rebuilding the inner cities.* ○ *Years of work have gone into the preparation of this dictionary.*

ˌ**go ˈoff 1** to leave a place, esp in order to do sth: *She went off to fetch a drink.* ○ *He's gone off to the dentist's.* ○ *She went off in a huff.* **2** to be fired; to explode: *The gun went off by accident.* ○ *The bomb went off in a crowded street.* **3** to make a sudden loud noise: *The thieves ran away when the burglar alarm went off.* **4** (of electric power, a light, etc) to stop functioning or operating: *Suddenly the lights went off.* ○ *The heating goes off at night.* **5** (*infml*) to fall asleep: *Hasn't the baby gone off yet?* **6** (*esp Brit*) (of food) to become bad and not fit to eat: *This milk has gone off* (ie has turned sour). **7** to become worse in quality: *Her books have gone off in recent years.* **8** (used with *advs* or in questions after *how*) to happen in the way specified; to go(9): *The*

---

performance went off well. ˌgo ˈoff sb/sth (*Brit infml*) to lose interest in sb; to lose one's taste for sth: *Jane seems to be going off Peter.* ○ *I've gone off beer.* ˌgo ˈoff with sb to leave one's husband, wife, lover, etc in order to have a relationship with sb else: *He went off with his best friend's wife.* ○ *She went off with the milkman.* ˌgo ˈoff with sth to take away from a place sth that does not belong to one: *He went off with £10 000 of the company's money.* ○ *Who's gone off with my pen?*

ˌgo ˈon 1 (of a performer) to begin one's performance: *She doesn't go on till Act 2.* 2 (in sport) to join a team as a substitute during a match: *Allen went on (in place of Lineker) just before half-time.* 3 to start to function: *Why won't the heating go on?* ○ *Suddenly all the lights went on.* 4 (of time) to pass: *She became more and more talkative as the evening went on.* ○ *Things will improve as time goes on.* 5 (esp in the continuous tenses) to occur; to happen: *What's going on here?* ○ *There must be a party going on next door.* 6 (of a situation or state of affairs) to continue without changing: *This cannot be allowed to go on.* ○ *How much longer will this hot weather go on (for)?* ○ *We* (ie Our relationship) *can't go on like this — we seem to be always arguing.* 7 to continue speaking, after a short pause: *She hesitated for a moment, and then went on.* ○ *'You know,' she went on, 'I think my brother could help you.'* 8 (used to encourage or to dare sb to do sth): *Go on! Have another drink.* ○ *Go on — jump!* ˌgo ˈon (ahead) to travel in front of sb else: *You go on (ahead), I'll catch you up in a few minutes.* ˈgo on sth 1 to begin to receive payments from the State because one is unemployed: *go on social seˈcurity/the ˈdole.* 2 to start taking a drug or medicine: *go on the ˈpill* (ie start using contraceptive (CONTRACEPTION) pills). 3 (used with negatives or in questions) to base an opinion or a judgement on sth: *The police don't have much evidence to go on.* ˌgo ˈon (about sb/sth) to talk about sb/sth for a long time, esp in a boring or complaining way: *She does go on sometimes!* ○ *He went on and on about how poor he was.* ○ *I know you don't like me smoking, but there's no need to go on about it.* ˌgo ˈon (at sb) to complain to sb about their behaviour, work, etc; to criticize sb: *She goes on at her husband continually.* ˌgo ˈon (with sth) to continue an activity, esp after a pause or break: *He paused to take a sip of water, and then went on (with his story).* ○ *If we don't finish the work today, we can go on with it tomorrow.* go on doing sth to continue an activity without stopping: *He said nothing but just went on working.* ○ *If you go on drinking like this you'll make yourself ill.* ˌgo ˈon to sth to pass from one item to the next: *Let's go on to the next item on the agenda.* go on to do sth to do sth after completing sth else: *The book goes on to describe his experiences in the army.* ○ *After her early teaching career she went on to become a doctor.*

ˌgo ˈout 1 to leave one's house to go to social events: *She goes out a lot.* ○ *He goes out drinking most evenings.* 2 (of the tide) to move away from the land; to EBB(1). Compare COME IN. 3 to be sent: *Have the invitations gone out yet?* 4 (of a programme) to be broadcast on radio or television: *The first episode goes out on Friday evening at 8.00 pm.* 5 (of news or information) to be announced or published: *Word went out that the director had resigned.* 6 to stop burning or shining: *The fire has gone out.* ○ *There was a power cut and all the lights went out.* ˌgo ˈout (of sth) 1 to fail to reach the next stage of a competition, contest, etc: *She went out (of the tournament) in the first round.* 2 to be no longer fashionable or generally used: *Those skirts went out of fashion years ago.* ˌgo ˈout (to ...) to leave one's native country or state and go to a distant one: *Our daughter went out to Australia ten years ago.* ○ *We went out to California (from New York) in 1976.* ˌgo ˈout of sb/sth (of a quality or feeling) to be no longer present in

sb/sth; disappear from sb/sth: *All the fight seemed to go out of him.* ○ *The heat has gone out of the argument.* ˌgo ˈout to sb (of feelings) to be offered or extended to sb: *Our hearts/sympathies go out to relatives of the victims.* ˌgo ˈout with sb; ˌgo ˈout (together) (esp of a young person) to spend time with sb and have a romantic or sexual relationship with them: *Tom has been going out with Kate for six weeks.* ○ *Kate and Tom have been going out (together) for six weeks.*

ˌgo ˈover (used with *advs* or in questions after *how*) to be received in the specified way: *How did her speech go over?* ˌgo ˈover sth 1 to look at sth carefully; to inspect sth: *My friend's father went over the car thoroughly and advised me not to buy it.* 2 to examine the details of sth; to check sth: *You'll have to go over these figures again — they don't add up.* ○ *Go over your work carefully before you hand it in.* 3 to study sth carefully: *He went over the events of the day in his mind* (ie thought about them carefully). ○ *She likes to go over her lines before each performance.* 4 to clean sth, esp thoroughly: *She went over the room with a duster.* ˌgo ˈover (to ...) to move from one, often distant, place to another: *He went over and shook hands with his guests.* ○ *Many Irish people went over to America during the famine.* ○ *Let's go over and visit John this weekend.* ˌgo ˈover to sb/sth (*broadcasting*) to transfer to a different person or place for the next part of the broadcast: *We are now going over to the news desk for an important announcement.* ˌgo ˈover to sth to change from one side, opinion, habit, system, etc to another: *Two Conservative MPs went over to the Liberals.* ○ *She's gone over to a milder brand of cigarettes.*

ˌgo ˈround 1 to spin or revolve; to turn: *go round in a circle.* 2 to go by a longer route than usual: *The main road was flooded so we had to go round by narrow country lanes.* 3 (of a number or quantity of sth) to be enough for everyone to have one or some: *There aren't enough chairs to go round.* ○ *Is there enough food to go round?* ˌgo ˈround/aˈround/aˈbout 1 (used with an *adj*, or a *v* in the *-ing* form) to move from place to place; to behave in society: *She often goes about barefoot.* ○ *It's unprofessional to go round criticizing your colleagues.* 2 (of news, a story, etc) to pass from person to person; to circulate: *There's a rumour going round that Sue and David are having an affair.* 3 (of an illness) to spread from person to person in a group or community: *There's a lot of flu going round at the moment.* ˌgo ˈround (to ...) to visit sb or a place that is near: *go round to the post office* ○ *I'm going round to my parents' (house) later.* ˌgo ˈround/aˈround/aˈbout with sb to be often in the company of sb: *He goes round with a bunch of friends from school.*

ˌgo ˈthrough (of a law, contract, etc) to be officially approved, accepted or completed: *The bill went through* (ie was passed by Congress or Parliament). ○ *As soon as my divorce goes through, we'll get married.* ○ *The deal did not go through.* go through sth 1 to wear a hole in sth: *I've gone through the elbows of my sweater.* 2 to look at or to examine sth carefully, esp in order to find sth: *I always start the day by going through my mail.* ○ *I've gone through all my pockets but I can't find my keys.* ○ *She went through the company's accounts, looking for evidence of fraud.* 3 to discuss, study or consider sth in detail: *Let's go through the arguments again.* ○ *Could we go through (ie practise) Act 2 once more?* 4 to perform a series of actions; to follow a procedure: *Certain formalities have to be gone through before one can emigrate.* 5 to experience, endure or suffer sth: *She's been going through a bad patch* (ie a difficult or an unhappy time) *recently.* ○ *He's amazingly cheerful considering all that he's had to go through.* 6 (of a book) to be published in the specified number of printings or

G

editions: *The dictionary has gone through ten impressions.* **7** to use up or finish sth completely: *The children went through the whole packet of biscuits in five minutes.* ˌgo ˈthrough with sth to do what is necessary to complete an often difficult or unpleasant course of action: *She decided not to go through with* (ie not to have) *the operation.* ○ *He's determined to go through with the marriage despite his parents' opposition.*

ˈgo to sb/sth to be given to, awarded to or inherited by sb: *Proceeds from the concert will go to charity.* ○ *The first prize went to the youngest child in the class.* ○ *The estate went to the eldest son.*

go together ⇨ GO WITH SB, GO WITH STH.

ˈgo towards sth to be used as part of the payment for sth; to contribute to sth: *The money will go towards the new camera I'm saving up for.*

ˌgo ˈunder **1** (of sth that floats) to sink below the surface. **2** (*infml*) to become bankrupt; to fail: *The firm will go under unless business improves.*

ˌgo ˈup **1** to be built: *New office blocks are going up everywhere.* **2** (of the curtain on the stage of a theatre) to be raised or opened: *The curtain goes up on* (ie is raised to show) *a suburban living-room.* **3** to be destroyed by fire or an explosion: *The whole building went up in flames.* **4** to become higher in price, level, etc; to rise: *The price of cigarettes is going up/Cigarettes are going up (in price).* ○ *Unemployment has gone up again.* ˌgo ˈup (to ...) (*Brit*) to begin one's studies at a university, esp at Oxford or Cambridge: *She went up to Oxford in 1977.* ˌgo ˈup (to ...) (from ...) to go from one place to another, esp from a smaller place to a larger place or from the south to the north: *We went up to London last weekend.* ○ *When are you next going up to Scotland?*

ˈgo with sb (*sl*) to have a sexual or romantic relationship with sb; to have sex with sb: *He goes with a different woman every week.* See also GO OUT WITH SB.

ˌgo ˈwith sth to be included with or as a part of sth: *A new car goes with the job.* ○ *Do the carpets and curtains go with* (ie Are they included in the price of) *the house?* ˈgo with sth; ˌgo toˈgether **1** to combine well with sth; to match: *Her blouse doesn't go with her skirt/Her blouse and skirt don't go (together).* ○ *White wine goes well* (ie is suitable to drink) *with fish.* **2** to exist at the same time or in the same place as sth; to be commonly found together: *Disease often goes with poverty/Disease and poverty often go together.*

ˌgo wiˈthout (sth) (used esp after *can, could* or *have to*) to endure the lack of sth; to manage without sth: *I had to go without breakfast this morning.* ○ *How long can a human being go* (ie survive) *without food?* ○ *She went without sleep for three days.*

go² /gəʊ/ n (pl **goes** /gəʊz/) **1** [C] a person's turn to move or play in a game: *Whose go is it?* ○ *It's your go.* **2** [U] (*infml*) energy and enthusiasm: *She's full of/She's got a lot of (get up and) go!* **IDM at one ˈgo** in one single attempt: *He blew out all the candles on his birthday cake at one go.* **be all ˈgo** (*Brit infml*) to be very busy; to be full of activity: *It's all go in the office today.* **be on the ˈgo** (*infml*) to be very active or busy: *I've been on the go all week.* **first, second, etc ˈgo** (*infml*) at the first, etc attempt: *She passed her driving test first go.* **have a ˈgo (at sth / doing sth)** (*infml*) to make an attempt to do sth: *He had several goes at the high jump before he succeeded in clearing it.* ○ *I don't know if I can mend your bike but I'll have a go (at it).* **have a ˈgo at sb/sth** (*infml*) to criticize sb/sth; to complain about sb/sth: *My parents had a go at me for getting back so late.* **leave ˈgo/ˈhold (of sth)** (*infml*) to release sth: *Leave go of my arm — you're hurting me!* See also LET SB/STH GO. **make a ˈgo of sth** (*infml*) to be successful in sth: *She's determined to make a go of her new career.*

goad /gəʊd/ n **1** a pointed stick, used for making cattle move forwards. **2** a thing urging a person to

action: *offer economic help as a goad to political reform.*

▶ **goad** v ~ sb/sth (into sth / doing sth) to provoke or annoy a person or an animal continually: [Vn] *goad a mule/donkey* [Vnpr] *His persistent questions finally goaded me into answering.* ○ *I keep trying to goad these lazy fellows into action.* **PHRV ˌgoad sb ˈon** to urge and encourage sb to do sth: *goaded on by fierce ambition.*

go-ahead /ˈgəʊ əhed/ n **the go-ahead** [sing] permission to do sth: *The council have given (us) the go-ahead to start building.*

▶ **ˈgo-ahead** adj willing to try new ideas, methods, etc: *a go-ahead company/school/manager.*

goal /gəʊl/ n **1(a)** (in football, hockey, etc) a wooden framework into which the ball has to be kicked, hit, etc in order to score: *He headed the ball into an open goal* (ie one temporarily without defence). ○ *Who is in goal* (ie is GOALKEEPER) *for Arsenal?* ⇨ picture at FOOTBALL. **(b)** a point scored when the ball goes into the goal: *score a goal* ○ *the winning goal* ○ *win by three goals to one* ○ *score an own goal* (ie knock the ball by accident into the goal one's team is defending, thus giving a point to the opposing team or (*fig*) do sth that harms oneself). **2** the object of one's efforts; a target: *pursue/achieve one's goal in life* ○ *The company has set itself some long-term organizational goals.* ○ *Their goal was to eradicate malaria.*

▶ **goalless** /ˈgəʊlləs/ adj [usu attrib] with no goal scored by either team: *The match ended in a goalless draw.*

■ **ˈgoal-kick** n (in football) a kick by the defending side to start play again after the opposite side has kicked the ball over the goal-line without scoring.

ˈgoal-line n either of the pair of lines marking the two ends of a pitch.

ˈgoal-mouth n (usu *sing*) the area directly in front of a goal.

goalkeeper /ˈgəʊlkiːpə(r)/ (also *infml* **goalie** /ˈgəʊli/) n a player whose job is to prevent the other team getting the ball into her or his own team's goal. ⇨ picture at FOOTBALL, HOCKEY.

goalpost /ˈgəʊlpəʊst/ n either of the two upright posts of a goal: *a cracking shot which hit the goalpost.* ⇨ picture at RUGBY. **IDM move the goalposts** ⇨ MOVE¹.

goat
billy-goat   nanny-goat
kid

goat /gəʊt/ n **1** a small lively animal with horns and (in the male) a beard. Goats live wild in mountain areas or are kept on farms for their milk, meat or wool: *goat's cheese* ○ *climb like a mountain goat* (ie quickly and with ease). See also BILLY-GOAT, NANNY-GOAT. ⇨ picture. **2** (*sl*) an unpleasant old man, esp one who is sexually active. **IDM get sb's ˈgoat** (*infml*) to irritate or annoy sb greatly. **separate the sheep from the goats** ⇨ SEPARATE².

goatee /gəʊˈtiː/ n a man's short pointed beard.

goatherd /ˈgəʊthɜːd/ n a person who looks after a group of goats.

goatskin /ˈgəʊtskɪn/ n [U] leather made from the skin of a goat: *a goatskin bag.*

gob¹ /gɒb/ n (*infml*) a lump or drop of a thick wet substance: *a gob of butter/sauce* ○ *Gobs of spittle ran down his chin.*

gob² /gɒb/ n (*Brit sl offensive*) the human mouth: *Shut your gob* (ie Be quiet).

gobbet /ˈgɒbɪt/ n (infml) a lump or piece of sth, esp food.

gobble¹ /ˈgɒbl/ v ~ **sth** (**up/down**) to eat sth fast, and in a greedy and sometimes noisy way: [Vn, Vnp] *gobble one's food (down) in a hurry* [Vnp] *gobble up all the cakes* [also V]. **PHRV** ˌgobbie sth ˈup (infml) to use up all of sth very quickly: *The rent gobbles up half his earnings.* ∘ *Small family businesses are being gobbled up by larger firms.*

gobble² /ˈgɒbl/ v [V] (of a male turkey) to make its characteristic sound.

gobbledegook (also **gobbledygook**) /ˈgɒbldiguːk/ n [U] (infml) unnecessarily complicated language, esp in official documents, that is very difficult to understand: *forms written in gobbledegook* ∘ *It's all gobbledegook.*

goblet /ˈgɒblət/ n a cup for wine, usu of glass or metal, with a stem and base but no handle. ⇨ picture at GLASS.

goblin /ˈgɒblɪn/ n (in fairy stories) a creature resembling an ugly little man that enjoys causing trouble or hurting people.

gobsmacked /ˈgɒbsmækt/ adj (Brit infml) too surprised to be able to speak or respond: *Councillors were left gobsmacked.*

god /gɒd/ n **1** [C] a being or spirit that is believed to have power over nature and control over human affairs: *Mars was the Roman god of war.* ∘ *a river god* ∘ *a feast/sight (fit) for the gods* (ie one which is exceptionally fine). **2 God** [sing] (in various religions, esp Christianity, Judaism and Islam) the Supreme Being, CREATOR(2) and ruler of the universe: *God the Father, God the Son and God the Holy Ghost* (ie the Holy Trinity in the Christian religion) ∘ *I swear by Almighty God* (ie very solemnly) *that the evidence I shall give…* ∘ *As God is my witness* (ie I solemnly swear), *that is the truth!* ∘ *He likes to **play God*** (ie behave as if he could control people and events). ∘ *Do you believe in God?* ∘ *Good luck and God bless you.* See also ACT OF GOD. **3** [C] (**a**) a person who is admired or loved: *To her admirers she's a god.* (**b**) a thing to which too much attention is given: *Money is his god.* ∘ *the great god privatization.* **4 the gods** [pl] the gallery seats high up in a theatre: *sitting in the gods.* **IDM** God alˈmighty; God in ˈheaven; good ˈGod; (oh) (my) ˈGod (used to express surprise, horror, annoyance, etc): *God, what a stupid thing to do!* God/goodness/Heaven knows ⇨ KNOW. God/Heaven forbid ⇨ FORBID. God/Heaven help sb ⇨ HELP¹. God's gift to sb/ sth (often ironic) sb/sth that seems specially created to be useful to or enjoyed by a group of people, an industry, etc: *He seems to think he's God's gift to women.* God ˈwilling (used to express the wish that one will be able to do as one intends or plans): *I'll be back next week, God willing.* in God's ˈname (used when asking angry or surprised questions): *What in God's name was that noise?* in the lap of the gods ⇨ LAP¹. a man of God ⇨ MAN¹. please God ⇨ PLEASE. put the fear of God into sb ⇨ FEAR¹. thank God/goodness/Heaven ⇨ THANK. to ˈGod/ ˈgoodness/ˈHeaven (used after a v to express a strong hope, wish, etc): *I wish to God he'd turn that radio down!*
■ ˈgod-awful adj (infml) extremely bad; terrible: *What a god-awful day I've had!*
ˈgod-daughter n a female GODCHILD.
ˈgod-damn (also god-damned, esp US goddam /ˈgɒdæm, -dd-/) adj, adv (△ sl) (used for adding force to an expression): *Where's that god-damned pen?* ∘ *There's no need to be so goddam rude!*
ˈGod-fearing adj living a good life; very religious.
ˈGod-forsaken adj (of places) boring; miserable: *spend a year in some God-forsaken hole* ∘ *a God-forsaken little town in the middle of nowhere.*

ˈGod-given adj given or as if given, created or sent by God: *a God-given opportunity* ∘ *You've no God-given right to demand this.* Compare HEAVEN-SENT.

godchild /ˈgɒdtʃaɪld/ n (pl godchildren /ˈgɒdtʃɪldrən/) a child for whose Christian education and values one has promised to be responsible at the time of her or his BAPTISM: *Henry was his godchild.*

goddess /ˈgɒdes, -əs/ n **1** a female god, eg in Greek and Latin myths: *Diana, the goddess of hunting.* **2** a woman who is greatly loved or admired: *screen goddesses* (ie female film stars).

godfather /ˈgɒdfɑːðə(r)/ n **1** a male GODPARENT. **2** (often **Godfather**) (usu sing) a very powerful man in a criminal organization, esp the Mafia.

godhead /ˈgɒdhed/ n the Godhead [sing] (fml) God: *worshipping the Godhead.*

godless /ˈgɒdləs/ adj not respecting or believing in God; wicked.

godlike /ˈgɒdlaɪk/ adj like God or a god in some quality: *his godlike beauty.*

godly /ˈgɒdli/ adj loving and obeying God; deeply religious: *a godly society.* ▶ **godliness** n [U].

godmother /ˈgɒdmʌðə(r)/ n a female GODPARENT. See also FAIRY GODMOTHER.

godown /ˈgəʊdaʊn/ n (in Asia) a warehouse.

godparent /ˈgɒdpeərənt/ n a person who promises at a child's BAPTISM to help that child lead a Christian life.

godsend /ˈgɒdsend/ n ~ (**to sb**) an event or a thing received which is not expected but very welcome because it gives great help in time of need: *The story was a godsend to news editors on a dull bank holiday.* ∘ *Your cheque came as an absolute godsend.*

godson /ˈgɒdsʌn/ n a male GODCHILD.

goer /ˈgəʊə(r)/ n **1** (Brit sexist sl) a woman who enjoys having sex frequently, esp with different men: *She's a real goer — she'll do anything with anyone!* **2** (esp Brit infml) a person or thing that goes fast: *This new car's a real goer.*
▶ **-goer** (forming compound ns) a person who regularly goes to or attends the specified place or event: *ˈcinema-/ˈconcert-/ˈtheatre-goers* ∘ *He's a regular churchgoer.*

gofer /ˈgəʊfə(r)/ n (infml) a person whose job is to do minor administrative tasks for others; a DOGSBODY.

go-getter /ˈgəʊ getə(r)/ n (infml) a person who is aggressive and ambitious, eg in business: *He's a real go-getter!*

goggle /ˈgɒgl/ v ~ (**at sb/sth**) to stare at sb/sth with wide round eyes, esp in surprise or wonder: [Vpr] *goggle at television all day* ∘ *He goggled at the magnificent display of goods.* [V] *She just stood there goggling.*

goggles /ˈgɒglz/ n [pl] a pair of glasses that fit closely to the face to protect the eyes from wind, dust, water, etc: *wear racing/swimming/ski goggles.* ⇨ picture at GLASS.

going /ˈgəʊɪŋ/ n **1** [sing] an act of leaving a place; a departure: *We were all sad at her going.* **2** [U] the condition or state of the ground, a road, etc for walking or riding on: *The path was rough going.* ∘ *The going* (ie The surface of the course) *at Newmarket is soft today.* **3** [U] the rate of progress, travel, etc: *It was good going to reach London by midday.* ∘ *She was a company director before she was 25 — not bad going!* **IDM** comings and goings ⇨ COMING. get out, go, leave, etc while the ˌgoing is ˈgood to leave a place or stop doing sth while conditions are still favourable or while it is still easy to do so: *Life here is getting more difficult all the time — let's get out while the going's good.* heavy going ⇨ HEAVY.
▶ **going** adj **IDM** a ˌgoing conˈcern a business or activity that is making a profit and is expected to

continue to do well: *He sold the café* **as a going concern**. **the ,going 'rate (for sth)** the usual amount of money paid for goods or services at a particular time: *The going rate for freelance work is around £10 an hour.*

-going (forming compound *adjs*) going regularly to the specified place: *the ,theatre-going 'public* ○ *an ,ocean-going 'yacht.*

■ **,going-'over** *n* (*pl* **goings-over**) **1** (*infml*) an act of examining, cleaning or repairing sth thoroughly: *The document will need a careful going-over before we make a decision.* ○ *They gave the car a thorough going-over.* **2** (*sl*) a serious physical attack on sb: *The gang gave him a real going-over.*

,goings-'on *n* [pl] (*infml often derog*) unusual, surprising or morally undesirable happenings or events: *There were some strange goings-on next door last night.* ○ *I've never known such goings-on!*

goitre (*US* **goiter**) /ˈɡɔɪtə(r)/ *n* [U] a large swelling of the throat caused by disease of the THYROID.

go-kart /ˈɡəʊ kɑːt/ *n* a small low racing car with an open framework: *go-kart racing.*

gold /ɡəʊld/ *n* **1** [U] a precious yellow metal used for making coins, ornaments, jewellery, etc: *pure gold* ○ *22-carat gold* ○ *gold bars/bullion* ○ *a solid gold watch* ○ *a gold bracelet/ring/chain.* ⇨ App 7. **2** [U] (*rhet*) money in large sums; wealth: *a miser and his gold.* **3** [U, C] the colour of gold: *hair of shining gold* ○ *the reds and golds of the autumn trees* ○ *gold lettering.* **4** [C] (*sport*) a gold medal: *win a/the gold* ○ *an Olympic gold.* **IDM** **(as) good as 'gold** behaving very well: *The children were as good as gold while you were out.* **a heart of gold** ⇨ HEART. **a pot of gold** ⇨ POT[1]. **strike gold/oil** ⇨ STRIKE[2]. **worth one's/its weight in gold** ⇨ WORTH.

■ **'gold ,card** *n* a type of charge card (CHARGE[1]) issued only to people considered wealthy enough. It entitles them to a greater range of benefits and services than are offered to holders of a standard charge card.

'gold-digger *n* (*derog infml*) a woman who uses her sexual attractions to get money from men: *Young girls going out with men your age are just gold-diggers.*

'gold-dust *n* [U] gold in the form of fine powder: *Good electricians are like gold-dust* (ie are very hard to find) *round here.*

'gold-field *n* a district in which gold is found as a mineral in the ground.

,gold 'foil (also **,gold 'leaf**) *n* [U] gold beaten into a very thin sheet.

,gold 'medal *n* a MEDAL made of gold, awarded as first prize in a contest or as a mark of honour. **,gold 'medallist** *n* a winner of a gold medal.

'gold-mine *n* **1** a place where gold is dug out of the ground. **2** any source of wealth; a business that makes a good profit: *This restaurant is a potential gold-mine.*

,gold 'plate *n* [U] **(a)** dishes, etc made of gold. **(b)** material with a thin covering of gold. **,gold-'plated** *adj* having a thin covering of gold: *gold-plated earrings.*

'gold-rush *n* a rush to a region where gold has recently been discovered.

'gold standard *n* (usu **the gold standard**) [sing] an economic system in which the value of money is based on that of gold: *the abandonment of the gold standard.*

golden /ˈɡəʊldən/ *adj* **1(a)** made of gold: *a golden crown/ring.* **(b)** like gold in colour: *golden hair/ sand/light.* **2** [usu attrib] precious; fortunate: *golden memories* ○ *golden days* (ie a specially happy time or period in sb's life) ○ *This is a golden opportunity to enjoy the holiday of a lifetime.* ○ *the golden girl of Romanian sport.* **IDM** **the happy/golden mean** ⇨ MEAN[3]. **kill the goose that lays the golden egg** ⇨ KILL. **silence is golden** ⇨ SILENCE.

■ **'golden age** *n* a period in the past when commerce, the arts, etc were very successful: *looking back to a golden age of happiness and prosperity* ○ *The Elizabethan period was the golden age of English drama.*

,golden 'eagle *n* a large brownish EAGLE(1) of northern parts of the world. ⇨ picture at EAGLE.

,golden 'handshake *n* a usu large sum of money given to a senior member of a company, etc when he or she leaves.

,golden 'jubilee *n* a 50th anniversary. Compare DIAMOND JUBILEE, SILVER JUBILEE.

,golden 'rule *n* a very important principle which should be followed when performing a particular task: *The golden rule in playing tennis is to always watch the ball.*

,golden 'syrup *n* [U] (*Brit*) a very sweet sticky yellow liquid made from sugar and used in cooking, etc.

,golden 'wedding *n* the 50th anniversary of a wedding. Compare DIAMOND WEDDING, SILVER WEDDING.

goldfinch /ˈɡəʊldfɪntʃ/ *n* a small bird, common in Europe, with yellow feathers on its wings.

goldfish /ˈɡəʊldfɪʃ/ *n* (*pl* unchanged) a small orange or red fish. Goldfish are kept as pets in bowls or ponds.

goldsmith /ˈɡəʊldsmɪθ/ *n* a person who makes articles of gold.

golf course

hole　green　fairway　rough

club

bag

bunker (esp US sand trap)

trolley (US golf cart)

golf /ɡɒlf/ *n* [U] an outdoor game in which each player tries to hit a small hard ball into a series of 9 or 18 holes using as few strokes as possible: *golf balls* ○ *play a round of golf.* ⇨ picture. ▸ **golfer** *n* a person who plays golf. **golfing** *n* [U] playing golf: *We went golfing yesterday.* ○ *The hotel offers swimming, tennis and golfing.* ○ *a golfing partner/trophy/holiday.*

■ **'golf club** *n* **1** a stick used for striking the ball in golf: *a set of golf clubs.* **2(a)** a club whose members play golf. **(b)** the place where they meet and play. **'golf-course** (also **'golf-links**) *n* a large area of land where golf is played. Golf links are usu by the sea. ⇨ picture.

Goliath /ɡəˈlaɪəθ/ *n* a large or powerful person or thing: *a Goliath of a man* ○ *Arbroath are not exactly a Goliath of Scottish football.*

golliwog /ˈɡɒliwɒɡ/ (also **golly** /ˈɡɒli/) *n* a doll with a black face and thick stiff hair, usu made of cloth.

golly /ˈgɒli/ interj (infml) (used to express surprise).

goloshes = GALOSHES.

-gon comb form (forming ns) a figure with a specified number of angles: octagon/polygon. ▶ **-gonal** /-gənəl/ comb form (forming adjs): octagonal/ polygonal.

gonad /ˈgəʊnæd/ n a male or female organ (a TEST-ICLE or an OVARY) that enables a person or an animal to reproduce sexually.

gondolier   **gondola**

gondola

gondola /ˈgɒndələ/ n (pl **-las**) **1** a long boat with a flat bottom and high parts at each end, used on canals in Venice. ⇨ picture. **2** a CABIN for passengers that is suspended from an AIRSHIP or a BALLOON(2) or from a cable railway (CABLE).
▶ **gondolier** /ˌgɒndəˈlɪə(r)/ n a person who moves and steers a gondola(1). ⇨ picture.

gone¹ pp of GO¹.

gone² /gɒn; US gɔːn/ adj **1** [pred] past; departed: Gone are the days when you could buy a three-course meal for under £1. **2** (used after a phrase expressing time in weeks or months) having been pregnant for the specified period of time: She's seven months gone. **IDM** ˌgoing, ˌgoing, ˈgone (said by an auctioneer (AUCTION) to show that an item has been sold).
▶ **gone** prep past or later than a particular time: It's gone six o'clock already.

goner /ˈgɒnə(r); US ˈgɔːn-/ n (infml) a person or thing that is about to die or cannot be saved: When his parachute failed he thought he was a goner.

gong /gɒŋ/ n **1** a metal disc that makes a loud noise when struck with a stick. Gongs are used as musical instruments or to give signals, eg for meals in hotels: beat/sound a gong ∘ Do I hear the dinner gong? **2** (Brit infml) (esp in military use) a medal.

gonna /ˈgənə, ˈgɒnə/ (infml esp US) (indicating the future) going to: We're gonna win.

gonorrhoea (also **gonorrhea**) /ˌgɒnəˈrɪə; US -ˈriːə/ n [U] a disease of the sexual organs, spread by sexual contact.

goo /guː/ n [U] (infml) any sticky wet substance: a baby's face covered in goo ∘ scraping the goo from the bottom of the pan. See also GOOEY 1.

good¹ /gʊd/ adj (**better** /ˈbetə(r)/; **best** /best/) **1** of high quality; of an acceptable standard; satisfactory: a good lecture/performance/harvest/meal ∘ good pronunciation/behaviour/eyesight ∘ a good (eg sharp) knife ∘ The show is just good old-fashioned entertainment. ∘ Is the light good enough to take photographs? ∘ The car has very good brakes. ∘ I wished her good luck. ∘ Her English is very good. ∘ She has a very good (ie attractive) figure. ⇨ note at NICE. **2(a)** ~ (**at sth/doing sth**) (often used with names of occupations or with ns related to vs) able to do sth well; competent: a good teacher/ hairdresser/poet ∘ good at mathematics/languages/ describing things ∘ a good loser (ie sb who doesn't complain when they lose). **(b)** [pred] ~ **with sth/sb** capable when using, dealing with, etc sth/sb: good with one's hands (eg able to draw, make things, etc) ∘ He's very good with children (ie can look after them well, amuse them, etc). **3(a)** morally acceptable; virtuous (VIRTUE): a good deed ∘ try to lead a good life. **(b)** (esp of a child) behaving well, politely, etc:

Try to be a good girl. **4** ~ (**to sb**) willing to help others; kind: He was very good to me when I was ill. ∘ It was good of you to come. ∘ Would you be good enough to carry this for me? **5** pleasant; welcome: The firm has had good times and bad times. ∘ What good weather we're having! ∘ Have you heard the good news about my award? ∘ It's good to be home again. **6** (of food) fit to be eaten; not yet rotting: good eggs/fruit ∘ Separate the good meat from the bad. **7** [usu attrib] healthy; strong: good teeth and bones ∘ This is my good ear — I'm rather deaf in the other one. **8** (of a reason, evidence, etc) valid; strong; sound²(2): This is a good example of what I mean. ∘ I have good reason to be suspicious. ∘ Over-sleeping is hardly a good excuse for being late. **9** (of money) not false; genuine: This note is good, but that one's counterfeit. ∘ (fig) I gave good money for that camera, and it turned out to be worthless. **10** [attrib] (of clothes, etc) used only for more formal or important occasions: My one good suit is at the cleaner's. ∘ Wear your good clothes to go to church. **11** [attrib] thorough; complete; sound²(3): give sb a good beating/scolding/telling-off ∘ go for a good long walk ∘ We had a good laugh about it afterwards. **12** [usu attrib] amusing: a good story/joke ∘ 'That's a good one!' she said, laughing loudly. **13** ~ (**for sb/sth**) having a useful effect; BENEFICIAL: This cream is good for (ie helps to heal) burns. ∘ Is this kind of food good for you? ∘ Sunshine is good for your plants. **14** ~ (**for sth/to do sth**) suitable; appropriate: Now is a good time to buy a house. ∘ This beach is good for swimming but bad for surfing. ∘ She would be good for the job. **15** ~ **for sth (a)** having the necessary energy, health, strength, etc: You're good for (ie You will live) a few years yet. ∘ This car's good for many more miles. **(b)** capable of supplying or producing sth: I'll sell my bike — that's good for at least £50. ∘ This game is always good for a laugh. **(c)** (of sb or their credit) such that they will be able to pay back a sum lent: He/His credit is good for £5 000. **(d)** valid for sth: The return half of the ticket is good for three months. **16** (used in greetings, etc): Good morning/ afternoon/evening! ∘ Good night, Lynn. **17** (dated or joc) (used as a polite form of address or description): my good sir/man/friend ∘ How is your good lady (ie your wife)? **18** [attrib] (used as a form of praise): Good old Fred! ∘ Good man! That's just what I wanted. **19** [attrib] (used in exclamations): Good Heavens! ∘ Good God! **20** (used as an interj to show approval of or pleasure at sth that has been said or done, or to show that one wants to move on to a new topic of conversation: 'We hope to visit you next week.' 'Oh, good!' **21** (with a) [attrib] **(a)** great in number, quantity, etc: a good many people ∘ The kitchen was a good size. ∘ eat a good-sized meal ∘ We've come a good (ie long) way/distance. **(b)** (used with expressions of measurement, quantity, etc) not less than; rather more than: We waited for a good hour. ∘ It's a good three miles to the station. ∘ She ate a good half of the cake. **IDM** Most idioms containing **good** are at the entries for other major words in each idiom, eg **good as gold** ⇨ GOLD; **in good time** ⇨ TIME¹. **as ˈgood as** almost; nearly: He as good as called me a coward (ie suggested that I was a coward without actually using the word 'coward'). ∘ The matter is as good as settled. **good and ...** (infml) completely: I won't go until I'm good and ready. **good ˈfew** a considerable number; several: 'How many came?' 'A good few.' ∘ There are still a good few empty seats. ˌgood for ˈyou, ˌsb, ˈthem, etc; (esp Austral) **good ˈon you, etc** (infml) (used to praise sb for doing sth well): She passed the exam? Good for ˈher!
▶ **good** adv (US infml) well: Now, you listen to me good!
■ **good ˈfaith** n [U] honest or sincere intention: He acted **in good faith**.

'good-for-nothing *n, adj* [attrib] (a person who is) worthless, lazy, etc: *Where's that good-for-nothing son of yours?*

‚Good 'Friday *n* the Friday before Easter, remembered by Christians as the day of the Crucifixion of Christ.

‚good-'hearted *adj* kind.

‚good 'humour *n* [U] a cheerful mood or state of mind: *a meeting marked by good humour and friendliness* ○ *a man of great good humour.* **‚good-'humoured** *adj* cheerful; friendly. **‚good-'humouredly** *adv.*

‚good 'looks *n* [pl] the pleasing appearance of a person. **‚good-'looking** *adj* (esp of people) having a pleasing appearance: *She's terribly good-looking.* ○ *a ‚good-looking 'horse.* ⇨ note at BEAUTIFUL.

‚good 'nature *n* [U] kind and friendly feelings or behaviour towards others. **‚good-'natured** *adj* having or showing good nature: *a ‚good-natured 'person/dis'cussion.* **‚good-'naturedly** *adv.*

‚good-'neighbourliness *n* [U] friendly relations with or a friendly attitude towards one's neighbours (NEIGHBOUR).

‚good 'sense *n* [U] good or sensible judgement; practical wisdom.

‚good-'tempered *adj* not easily irritated or made angry. Compare BAD-TEMPERED.

good² /gʊd/ *n* **1** [U] that which is morally right or acceptable: *the difference between good and evil* ○ *Is religion always a force for good?* **2** [U] that which gives benefit, profit, advantage, etc: *work for the good of one's country* ○ *I'm giving you this advice **for your own good.*** ○ *Do social workers do a lot of good?* Compare DO-GOODER. **3 the good** [pl *v*] people admired for their achievements, good deeds, etc: *a gathering of the good and the great.* **IDM** **be no / not much / any / some 'good (doing sth)** to be of no, not much, etc value: *It's no good (my) talking to him.* ○ *Was his advice ever any good?* ○ *This gadget isn't much good.* ○ *What good is it asking her?* **do (sb) 'good** to benefit sb: *It will do you good to have a holiday.* ○ *This cough medicine tastes nice but it doesn't do much good* (ie is not very effective). ○ (*usu ironic*) *Much good may it do you* (ie You will not get much benefit from it). **for 'good (and 'all)** permanently; finally: *She says that she's leaving the country for good* (ie intending never to return to it). **to the 'good** (used esp to describe sb's financial state) in credit: *We are £500 to the good* (ie We have £500 more than we had). ○ *At half-time our team was one goal to the good.* **up to no 'good** (*infml*) doing sth wrong, behaving badly, etc: *Where's that child now? I'm sure he'll be up to no good wherever he is.*

goodbye /‚gʊd'baɪ/ *interj, n* (used when leaving or being left by sb): *say goodbye to sb* ○ *I waved goodbye as they drove away.* ○ *We said our goodbyes* (ie said 'Goodbye!' to each other) *and left.* ○ (*fig*) *It was hard saying goodbye to college life.* **IDM** **kiss sth goodbye / kiss goodbye to sth** ⇨ KISS.

goodish /'gʊdɪʃ/ *adj* [attrib] **1** quite good; not the best: *a goodish pair of shoes.* **2** fairly large or great: *We've walked a goodish distance today.*

goodly /'gʊdli/ *adj* (-ier, -iest) [attrib] **1** (*rhet*) large in amount: *a goodly sum of money.* **2** (*arch*) pleasant to look at.

goodness /'gʊdnəs/ *n* **1** [U] the quality of being good; kindness to sb; VIRTUE(1a): *praise God for his goodness and mercy* ○ *her goodness to her old parents* ○ *She did it entirely **out of the goodness of her heart.*** ○ *In spite of the bad things he's done I still believe in his essential goodness.* **2** [U] the quality in sth, esp food, that is good for sb/sth: *You lose a lot of the goodness in vegetables if you overcook them.* ○ *Brown bread is full of goodness.* ○ *This soil doesn't have much goodness left in it.* **3** [sing] (*euph*) (used in exclamations instead of 'God'): *Goodness, what a*

big balloon! ○ *Thank goodness* (ie expressing relief)*!* ○ *For goodness' sake* (ie expressing protest)*!* ○ *My goodness/Goodness me/Goodness gracious (me)* (ie expressing surprise)*!* **IDM** **God/goodness/Heaven knows** ⇨ KNOW. **thank God/goodness/Heaven** ⇨ THANK. **to God/goodness/Heaven** ⇨ GOD.

goods /gʊdz/ *n* [pl] **1** things for sale; MERCHANDISE: *cheap/expensive/low-quality/high-quality goods* ○ *cotton/leather/woollen goods* ○ *electrical goods.* See also CONSUMER GOODS. **2** movable property: *stolen goods.* **3** (*Brit*) (*US* **freight**) things (ie not passengers) to be transported, esp by rail: *a goods train/ wagon.* ⇨ note at CARGO. **IDM** **come up with / deliver the 'goods** (*infml*) to carry out or complete a task as expected, or fulfil a promise: *Great things were expected of the English team but on the day they simply failed to deliver the goods.*

■ **‚goods and 'chattels** *n* [pl] (*esp law*) personal possessions.

goods train *n* = FREIGHT TRAIN.

goodwill /‚gʊd'wɪl/ *n* [U] **1** friendly, helpful or COOPERATIVE(2) feelings: *a policy/spirit of goodwill in international relations* ○ *a goodwill gesture* ○ *show goodwill to/towards sb* ○ *Given goodwill on both sides I'm sure we can reach agreement.* **2** the good reputation of an established business, or the estimated financial value of this: *The name of the company for sale sarries considerable goodwill value.*

goody /'gʊdi/ *n* (*infml*) **1** (usu *pl*) (**a**) a pleasant thing to eat; a sweet, cake, etc: *a shopping basket full of goodies.* (**b**) a desirable thing: *I can now afford a new car, a video and lots of other goodies.* **2** the HERO(2) of a book, film etc; a good person: *Is he one of the goodies or one of the baddies?*

▶ **goody** *interj* (*infml*) (used esp by children, for expressing pleasure and excitement).

goody-goody /'gʊdi gʊdi/ *n* (*pl* **goody-goodies**) (*infml derog*) (used esp by and about children) a person who behaves well only in order to please or impress others: *You're such a goody-goody!*

gooey /'gu:i/ *adj* (*infml*) **1** sticky: *a gooey mess* ○ *gooey cakes.* **2** (*derog*) sentimental: *gooey remarks* ○ *Just thinking about him made her go all gooey inside.*

goof /gu:f/ *n* (*infml*) **1** a silly or stupid person. **2** a stupid mistake: *Sorry, that was a bit of a goof on my part!*

▶ **goof** *v* (*infml esp US*) to fail to do sth properly; to make a mess of sth: [V] *She had a great chance, but she goofed again.* [Vn] *It was my big chance and I goofed my lines.* **PHRV** **‚goof a'bout/a'round/'off** to behave in a way that is stupid or not responsible; to mess around (MESS¹ *v*).

goofy *adj* (*infml*) silly; stupid: *He had this really goofy grin on his face.*

googly /'gu:gli/ *n* (in cricket) a ball that is bowled as if to turn in a particular direction after bouncing, but that actually turns the opposite way.

goon /gu:n/ *n* (*infml*) **1** a stupid or crazy person. **2** (*US*) a person employed by criminals to threaten or attack people.

goose /gu:s/ *n* (*pl* **geese** /gi:s/) **1(a)** [C] a bird like a large duck with a long neck. Geese either live wild or are kept on farms. (**b**) (*masc* **gander** /'gændə(r)/) [C] the female of this bird. (**c**) [U] the flesh of the goose served as food: *goose-liver pâté.* **2** (*dated*) a foolish person. See also WILD-GOOSE CHASE. **IDM** **cook sb's goose** ⇨ COOK *v*. **kill the goose that lays the golden eggs** ⇨ KILL. **not say 'boo' to a goose** ⇨ SAY. **what is sauce for the goose is sauce for the gander** ⇨ SAUCE.

■ **'goose-flesh** *n* [U] (also **'goose-pimples** [pl]; *US* **'goose-bumps** [pl]) a condition in which the skin is temporarily raised into little lumps, caused by cold or fear.

'goose-step *n* [sing] (*often derog*) a way of marching without bending the knees.

[V] = verb used alone   [Vn] = verb + noun   [Vp] = verb + particle   [Vpr] = verb + prepositional phrase

gooseberry /ˈgʊzbəri; US ˈguːsberi/ n **1** a green, sour but edible berry that grows on a prickly bush. Gooseberries are used for making jam, pies, etc. **2** (*Brit infml*) a third person present when two people (esp lovers) wish to be alone together: *I didn't want to **play gooseberry** so I left them together.*

GOP /ˌdʒiː əʊ ˈpiː/ abbr (US) Grand Old Party (the Republican Party).

gopher /ˈgəʊfə(r)/ n a N American animal like a rat, living in holes which it digs in the ground.

Gordian knot /ˌgɔːdiən ˈnɒt/ n a difficult or apparently impossible problem or task. **IDM cut the Gordian knot** to solve a difficult problem in a direct or forceful way, rejecting gentler or more indirect methods.

gore¹ /gɔː(r)/ n [U] (esp in descriptions of fighting) blood from a cut or wound: *a movie with too much gore* (ie scenes showing violence and blood). See also GORY.

gore² /gɔː(r)/ v to wound a person or an animal with a horn or TUSK: [Vn] *He was gored to death by an angry bull.*

gorge¹ /gɔːdʒ/ n a narrow valley with steep sides, usu with a stream or river: *the Rhine gorge.* **IDM make sb's ˈgorge rise** to make sb feel sick, esp with anger or disgust: *The sight of so many starving children made his gorge rise.*

gorge² /gɔːdʒ/ v ~ (**oneself**) (**on/with sth**) to eat a lot in a greedy way; to fill oneself: [Vnpr, Vpr] *She gorged (herself) on cream-cakes.* [also V, Vn].

gorgeous /ˈgɔːdʒəs/ adj **1** (*infml*) giving pleasure and satisfaction; wonderful: *a gorgeous meal ○ gorgeous weather.* **2** (*infml*) very beautiful: *gorgeous hair.* **3** [usu attrib] with rich colours; magnificent: *walls hung with gorgeous tapestries.* ▶ **gorgeously** adv: *gorgeously dressed/decorated.*

gorgon /ˈgɔːgən/ n **1** (in Greek myths) any of three sisters with snakes instead of hair and the power to turn anyone who looked at them to stone. **2** a fierce, unpleasant or frightening woman: *Her stepmother was an absolute gorgon.*

Gorgonzola /ˌgɔːgənˈzəʊlə/ n [U] a rich strong Italian cheese with blue mould² inside.

.gorilla /gəˈrɪlə/ n (pl **-las**) a very large powerful African APE. ⇨ picture at APE.

gormless /ˈgɔːmləs/ adj (*Brit infml*) stupid; foolish: *a gormless boy ○ What a gormless thing to do!*

gorse /gɔːs/ n [U] a bush with yellow flowers and thin prickly leaves that do not fall off in winter. Gorse often grows on land that is not used or cared for.

gory /ˈgɔːri/ adj **1** covered with blood. **2** showing violence and injury: *a gory battle/fight/film/spectacle ○ (fig infml) 'Have you heard about their divorce?' 'Spare us the gory details* (ie unpleasant or shocking facts), *please.'*

gosh /gɒʃ/ interj (*infml euph*) (used as a mild alternative to 'God' to express surprise or strong feeling): *Gosh, is that the time? ○ I said I'd do it and, by gosh, I did!*

gosling /ˈgɒzlɪŋ/ n a young GOOSE(1).

go-slow /ˌgəʊ ˈsləʊ/ n (*Brit*) a type of industrial protest in which employees deliberately work more slowly than usual.

gospel /ˈgɒspl/ n **1** (*Bible*) (**a**) (usu **the Gospel**) [sing] the first four books of the New Testament, ie the life and teaching of Jesus as recorded in them: *preach the Gospel ○ the gospel message/story.* (**b**) [C] any one of these books: *the Gospel according to St John ○ St Mark's Gospel.* **2** [C usu *sing*] a set of principles: *spreading the gospel of monetarism.* **3** [U] (*infml*) the truth, esp of an unlikely story or a rumour: *Is that gospel? ○ You can take this as absolute gospel. ○ It's the **gospel truth** (ie completely

reliable information). **4** [U] a style of religious singing popular among black Americans: *a gospel choir.*

gossamer /ˈgɒsəmə(r)/ n [U] **1** the fine thread forming the webs made by small spiders. **2** any soft light delicate material: *a gown of gossamer silk ○ the gossamer wings of a fly.*

gossip /ˈgɒsɪp/ n **1** [U] (*derog*) casual talk about the affairs of other people, typically including rumour and critical comments: *Don't believe all the gossip you hear. ○ She's too fond of idle gossip. ○ It's common gossip that they're having an affair* (ie everyone is saying so). **2** [U] (*often derog*) informal writing about people and social events, eg in letters or newspapers: *the paper's gossip column ○ a gossip columnist/writer* (ie a writer of such material). **3** [C] a conversation including gossip: *have a good gossip with a friend.* **4** [C] (*derog or joc*) a person who is fond of gossip: *You're nothing but an old gossip!*
▶ **gossip** v ~ (**with sb**) (**about sth**) to talk gossip: [V] *I can't stand here gossiping all day.* [also Vpr]. ⇨ note at TALK².

gossipy /ˈgɒsɪpi/ adj: *a gossipy letter/woman.*

got pt, pp of GET. See also HAVE², HAVE TO.

Gothic /ˈgɒθɪk/ adj **1** of the Goths (Germanic people who fought against the Roman Empire). **2** (*architecture*) of or in a style common in W Europe from the 12th to the 16th centuries. Gothic architecture is noted for its pointed arches, tall thin pillars, elaborate decoration, etc: *a Gothic church/cathedral/arch/window.* **3** of or in a style of literature popular in the 18th and 19th centuries, which described romantic adventures in mysterious or frightening settings: *Gothic novels/horror.* **4** (of printing type) with pointed letters consisting of thick lines and sharp angles, as formerly used for German: *Gothic lettering.*
▶ **Gothic** n [U] the Gothic style of architecture.

gotta /ˈgɒtə/ (*infml esp US*) (have) got to: *I gotta/I've gotta go.*

gotten (*US*) pp of GET.

gouache /guˈɑːʃ, gwɑːʃ/ n [U] (**a**) a type of thick water-colour (WATER¹). (**b**) a painting done with gouache.

Gouda /ˈgaʊdə, ˈguːdə/ n [U] a type of Dutch cheese with a mild flavour.

gouge /gaʊdʒ/ n (*techn*) a sharp tool for cutting hollow areas in wood, etc.
▶ **gouge** v ~ **sth** (**in sth**) to make a hole in sth roughly or violently: [Vnpr] *Several holes had been gouged in the priceless painting.* [also Vn]. **PHRV ˌgouge sth ˈout** (**of sth**) to remove sth by digging into a surface with a sharp tool, one's fingers, etc: *gouge out a narrow groove ○ gouge a stone out of a horse's hoof ○ gouge sb's eyes out.*

goulash /ˈguːlæʃ/ n [C, U] a hot-tasting Hungarian dish¹(2) of meat boiled with vegetables and PAPRIKA.

gourd /gʊəd, gɔːd/ n (**a**) any of various types of large fruit, not normally eaten, with a hard skin and a soft inside. Gourds are often dried and used as containers. (**b**) a plant that produces these. (**c**) a bottle or bowl consisting of the dried skin of a gourd: *a wine gourd.*

gourmand /ˈgʊəmənd; US -mɑːnd/ n (*often derog*) a lover of food; a person who eats too much.

gourmet /ˈgʊəmeɪ/ n a person who knows a lot about good food, wines, etc and enjoys choosing, eating and drinking them: *gourmet restaurants* (ie serving fine food).

gout /gaʊt/ n **1** [U] a disease causing painful swelling in the joints, esp of the toes, knees and fingers. **2** [C] (*fml*) a drop or mass of thick liquid, esp blood: *gouts of lava from the volcano.*
▶ **gouty** adj suffering from gout.

Gov abbr **1** (also **Govt**) Government. **2** Governor: *Gov (Stephen) King.*

govern /ˈgʌvn/ v **1** to rule a country, etc; to control or direct the public affairs of a city, country, etc: [Vn] *The country is governed by elected representatives of the people.* [also V]. **2** to control or influence sth/sb; to determine sth: [Vn] *Everything he does is governed by self-interest.* ○ *The law of supply and demand governs the prices of goods.* ○ *There is a need for a change in the laws governing contracts between oil companies.* ○ *Since I'm unable to decide, I will be governed by you* (ie I will do as you suggest). **3** (*grammar*) (esp of a *v* or a *prep*) to have a noun or a pronoun or a case[1](8) depending on it: [Vn] *In Latin, several verbs govern the dative.*

▶ **governing** /ˈgʌvənɪŋ/ *adj* [attrib] having the power or right to govern: *the governing body of a school/college.*

governance /ˈgʌvənəns/ *n* [U] (*fml*) the activity or manner of governing; government(2): *the governance of Britain.*

governess /ˈgʌvənəs/ *n* (esp formerly) a woman employed to teach young children in their home, and usu living as a member of the household.

government /ˈgʌvənmənt/ *n* **1** (often **the Government**) [CGp] a group of people governing a country or state: *lead/form a government* ○ *the last Labour government* ○ *Foreign governments have been consulted about this decision.* ○ *She has resigned from the Government.* ○ *The Government is/are considering further tax cuts.* ○ *a government department/grant/ publication* ○ *government policies/money/ministers* ○ *government-controlled industries.* **2** [U] (**a**) the action or manner of governing: *corrupt/ineffectual/ strong government* ○ *Four years of weak government had left the economy in ruins.* ○ *The Labour Party was* **in government** *from 1964 to 1970.* (**b**) the method or system of governing: *Democratic government has now replaced military rule.* ○ *communist/ conservative/liberal/totalitarian government.* See also LOCAL GOVERNMENT.

▶ **governmental** /ˌgʌvn̩ˈmentl/ *adj* of or connected with government: *governmental institutions.*

governor /ˈgʌvənə(r)/ *n* **1(a)** (*Brit*) a person appointed to govern a province or state, esp a colony abroad: *a colonial/provincial governor.* (**b**) the elected head of each state in the USA: *the Governor of New York State.* **2** (*Brit*) (**a**) the head of an institution: *a prison governor* ○ *the governor of the Bank of England.* (**b**) a member of a governing body(4): *a school governor* ○ *the board of governors of a college/hospital.* **3** (*Brit infml*) (**a**) (also **guvnor** /ˈgʌvnə(r)/) a person who has authority over the speaker, eg an employer or a father: *I shall have to ask permission from the governor.* (**b**) (also **guv** /gʌv/, **guvnor**) (used by a man when addressing another man, esp one of higher social status): *Can I see your ticket, guvnor?*

■ **Governor-'General** *n* (*pl* **Governors-General** or **Governor-Generals**) the official representative of the British King or Queen in a Commonwealth country: *the Governor-General of Canada.*

Govt *abbr* Government.

gown /gaʊn/ *n* **1** a woman's dress, esp a long one for special occasions: *an 'evening/'wedding gown.* See also DRESSING-GOWN. **2** a loose flowing garment worn over other clothes to indicate profession or status, eg by a judge, a lawyer or a teacher: *a BA gown.* **3** a garment worn over other clothes to protect them: *a surgeon's gown.*

▶ **gowned** /gaʊnd/ *adj* wearing a gown.

GP /ˌdʒiː ˈpiː/ *abbr* general practitioner: *consult your local GP.*

Gp Capt *abbr* Group Captain: *Gp Capt (Tom) Fletcher.*

GPO /ˌdʒiː piː ˈəʊ/ *abbr* (in Britain) General Post Office: *The GPO is very busy at Christmas.*

grab /græb/ *v* (**-bb-**) **1(a)** ~ **sth (from sb/sth)** to take sth firmly and suddenly, roughly or rudely: [V]

Don't grab — there's plenty for everyone. [Vn] *He grabbed my collar and pulled me towards him.* [Vnpr] *He just grabbed the bag from my hand and ran off.* See also SMASH-AND-GRAB. (**b**) to take an opportunity, etc eagerly: [Vn] *When I gave him the chance, he grabbed it at once.* **2** ~ **at sb/sth** to try to get or catch sb/sth, not always successfully: [Vpr] *He grabbed at the boy, but could not save him from falling.* ○ (*fig*) *grabbing at any excuse to avoid having to work.* **3** (*infml joc*) to have or take sth quickly, esp when in a hurry: [Vn] *Grab a seat and make yourself at home.* ○ *Let's grab a quick sandwich before we go out.* **4** (*sl*) to interest sb; to please sb: [Vn] *I thought we might go to the disco — how does that grab you?*

▶ **grab** *n* (usu *sing*) a sudden attempt to seize sb/ sth: *He made a grab at the ball but missed.* **IDM** **up for 'grabs** (*infml*) available for anyone to take: *The job is up for grabs — why don't you apply?*

grace /greɪs/ *n* **1** [U] a quality of simple elegant beauty and smoothly controlled movement: *dance/ walk/move with grace.* **2** [U] God's mercy and favour towards the human race; the influence and result of this: *By the grace of God their lives were spared.* ○ *Did he die* **in a state of grace** (ie strengthened and inspired by God, esp after having prayed and been blessed by a priest)? ○ (*saying*) *There, but for the grace of God, go I* (ie I might have had a similar bad experience). **3** [U] extra time allowed to renew a licence, pay a bill, etc after the day when it is due: *Payment is due today, but I gave her a week's grace* (ie an extra week to pay). **4** [U] special favour or trust: *He had been the king's favourite, and his sudden* **fall from grace** *surprised everyone.* **5** [C usu *pl*] social skill: *well-versed in the social graces.* **6** [U,C] a short prayer of thanks before or after a meal: *Shall I say grace?* See also SAVING GRACE. **7 His/Her/Your Grace** (used as a title when speaking to or of an ARCHBISHOP, a DUKE or a DUCHESS): *Good morning, Your Grace!* ○ *Their Graces, the Duke and Duchess of Kent.* **IDM** **airs and graces** ⇨ AIR[1]. **be in sb's good 'graces** to have sb's favour and approval: *I'm not in her good graces at the moment.* **have the grace to do sth** to be polite enough to do sth: *He might have had the grace to say he was sorry!* **with (a) bad/good 'grace** unwillingly and rudely/willingly and happily: *She accepted his apology with (a) good grace.* ○ *He handed over the money with (a) bad grace.* **year of grace** ⇨ YEAR.

▶ **grace** *v* (*fml*) **1** to make sth more attractive; to decorate sth: [Vn] *Fine paintings graced the walls of the room.* **2** ~ **sb/sth (with sth)** to give honour or dignity to sb/sth: [Vn] *The occasion was graced by the presence of the Queen.* [Vnpr] (*ironic*) *Supper's ready — are you going to grace us with your presence?*

graceful /ˈgreɪsfl/ *adj* **1** showing a pleasing beauty of form, movement or manner: *a graceful dancer/ dance* ○ *the graceful curve of the old bridge* ○ *He was tall and graceful.* **2** pleasing in both style and attitude; polite and CONSIDERATE: *He refused in such a graceful way that we could not be offended.* ▶ **gracefully** /-fəli/ *adv.*

graceless /ˈgreɪsləs/ *adj* **1** not attractive or elegant: *The new office block is a graceless mass of glass and concrete.* **2** lacking social skill; rude: *graceless behaviour* ○ *a graceless remark.*

gracious /ˈgreɪʃəs/ *adj* **1** ~ **(to sb)** (of people or behaviour) kind, polite and generous, esp to sb of a lower social position: *a gracious lady/hostess* ○ *a gracious manner/reply/invitation/smile* ○ *He was most gracious to everyone, smiling and thanking them all.* **2** [usu attrib] showing the comfort, beauty and ease that wealth can bring: *gracious living* ○ *a gracious old mansion.* **3** [attrib] (*fml*) (used as a

G

polite term for royal people or their acts): *her gracious Majesty the Queen* ○ *by gracious permission of Her Majesty.* **4** ~ **(to sb)** (of God) showing MERCY(1). **5** *(becoming dated)* (used for expressing surprise): *Good(ness) gracious!* ○ *Gracious 'me!* ▶ **graciously** *adv.* **graciousness** *n* [U].

gradation /grə'deɪʃn/ *n* **1** [C] any of the different stages or levels into which sth is divided: *officials ranging from the very important to the unimportant, with many gradations in between.* **2** [U, C] a gradual change from one thing to another: *a painting's subtle gradation of colour.* **3** [C] a mark showing a division on a scale¹(2a): *the gradations on a thermometer.* See also GRADUATION 2.

grade¹ /greɪd/ *n* **1** a level or position of ability, quality or rank that sb/sth has: *a person's salary grade* (ie level of pay) ○ *high-/low-grade officials/ materials* ○ *the lowest grade of agricultural land.* **2(a)** a mark given in an examination or for school work: *Pupils with 90% or more are awarded Grade A.* ○ *She got excellent grades in her exams.* **(b)** a level of esp musical skill at which a pupil is tested: *He's got Violin Grade 6* (ie has passed a test at that level of skill). **3** *(US)* a class or classes in school with children of the same age and ability. Children start school in the first grade: *go up/down a grade.* **4** *(esp US)* = GRADIENT 1. **IDM** **make the 'grade** *(infml)* to reach the necessary standard; to succeed: *About 10% of trainees fail to make the grade.*
■ **'grade crossing** *n* (*US*) = LEVEL CROSSING.
'grade school *n* (*US*) = PRIMARY SCHOOL.

grade² /greɪd/ *v* **1** ~ **sth/sb by / according to sth**; ~ **sth/sb from sth to sth** (esp passive) to arrange people or things in groups according to their ability, quality, size, etc: [Vn] *graded tests for language students* [Vnpr] *The potatoes are graded by/ according to size.* ○ *Eggs are graded from small to extra-large.* [Vn-n] *a hotel graded as four-star* (ie luxury) *accommodation* [also Vn-adj]. **2** *(esp US)* to mark written work; to give a student a mark: [Vn] *The term papers have been graded.* [Vn-n] *A student who gets 90% is graded A.* **3** to make land, esp for roads more nearly level by reducing the slope: [Vn] *The trees were planted in the newly graded bank.*

gradient /'greɪdiənt/ *n* **1** the degree of slope, eg on a road, railway, etc: *a steep gradient* ○ *a hill with a gradient of 1 in 4 (or 25%).* **2** the rate at which temperature, pressure, light, etc changes between one region and another: *a strong wind gradient.*

gradual /'grædʒuəl/ *adj* **1** taking place by a series of small changes over a long period; not sudden: *gradual decline/progress* ○ *a gradual increase/ decrease/recovery* ○ *Improvements will be gradual at first.* **2** (of a slope) not steep: *a gradual incline.*
▶ **gradualism** *n* [U] a policy of gradual reform rather than sudden change or revolution. **gradualist** *n.*
gradually *adv* in a gradual way; slowly: *Things gradually improved.*

graduate¹ /'grædʒuət/ *n* **1** ~ **(in sth)** a person who holds a degree as a result of successfully completing a course at a university or college: *a graduate in law/history* ○ *a science graduate* ○ *a graduate of Yale/ a Yale graduate* ○ *a graduate student* (ie one studying for a further degree). Compare POSTGRADUATE, UNDERGRADUATE. **2** *(US)* a person who has completed a school course: *a high-school graduate* ○ *a graduate nurse* (ie one from a college that trains nurses).
■ **'graduate school** *n* (*esp US*) a department of a college or university for advanced work by graduates: *a graduate school of business.*

graduate² /'grædʒueɪt/ *v* **1** ~ **(in sth) (at/from sth)** **(a)** to get a degree, esp the first degree, from a university or college: [Vpr] *graduate in law/history at Oxford* ○ *She graduated from Harvard with a*

degree in law. [V] *When did you graduate?* **(b)** *(US)* to complete an educational course: [V, Vpr] *She's just graduated (from the School of Cookery).* **2** ~ **sb (from sth)** *(esp US)* to give a degree, DIPLOMA, etc to sb: [Vn, Vnpr] *The college graduated 50 students (from the science department) last year.* **3** ~ **(from sth) to sth** *(approv)* to make progress; to move on from sth easy or basic to sth more difficult or important: [Vpr] *Our son has just graduated from a tricycle to a bike.* **4** (esp passive) to divide sth into graded groups or levels: [Vn] *In a graduated tax scheme the more one earns, the more one pays.* **5** ~ **sth (in/into sth)** (esp passive) to mark sth into regular divisions or units of measurement: [Vnpr] *a ruler graduated in both inches and centimetres* [Vn] *a graduated measuring jug.*
▶ **graduation** /ˌgrædʒu'eɪʃn/ *n* **1** [U] **(a)** the action of graduating at a university, etc: *get a job after graduation.* **(b)** a ceremony at which degrees, etc are officially given out: *graduation day.* **2** [C] a GRADATION(3): *The graduations are marked on the side of the flask.*
■ ˌ**graduated 'pension** *n* (*Brit*) a PENSION¹ in which the amount of money paid by the employee and the size of pension received on retiring are related to the amount of salary earned: *a graduated pension scheme.*

Graeco- (also *esp US* **Greco-**) /'gri:kəʊ-/ *comb form* Greek; of Greece: ˌ*Graeco-¹Roman.*

graffiti /grə'fi:ti/ *n* [pl] drawings or writing on a wall, etc in a public place. They are usu rude, humorous or political: *The wall was covered with graffiti.*

graft¹ /grɑːft; *US* græft/ *n* **1** a piece cut from a living plant and fixed in a cut made in another plant, to form a new growth(3); the process or result of doing this: *A healthy shoot should form a strong graft.* **2** *(medical)* a healthy organ or piece of skin, bone, etc removed from a living body and attached to a damaged part of the same or another body; the process or result of doing this: *a 'skin graft.*
▶ **graft** *v* ~ **sth onto sth**; ~ **sth in/on** to attach sth as a graft: [Vn] *newly grafted tissue* [Vnpr] *graft one variety of apple onto another* [Vnp] *New skin had to be grafted on.* [Vnpr] *(fig) graft some innovations onto an outdated system.* Compare TRANSPLANT 2.

graft² /grɑːft; *US* græft/ *n* [U] **1** *(Brit)* hard work: *She reached the top only after years of **hard graft**.* **2(a)** the use of illegal or unfair means, esp bribery (BRIBE), to gain an advantage in business, politics, etc: *graft and corruption.* **(b)** profit obtained in this way.
▶ **graft** *v* ~ **(away)** *(Brit)* to work hard: [V, Vp] *grafting (away) all day.* **grafter** *n* a hard worker.

grail /greɪl/ *n* (usu **the Holy Grail**) [sing] the plate or cup used by Jesus at the Last Supper, in which one of his followers is said to have received drops of his blood at the CRUCIFIXION.

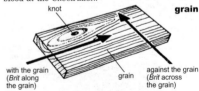

with the grain (*Brit* along the grain)   grain   against the grain (*Brit* across the grain)

grain /greɪn/ *n* **1(a)** [U] the small hard seeds of food plants such as wheat, rice, etc: *America's grain exports.* See also WHOLEGRAIN. **(b)** [C] a single seed of such a plant: *a few grains of rice.* ⇨ picture at CEREAL. **2** [C] a small hard piece of certain substances: *a grain of salt/sand/sugar.* **3** [C] a very small amount: *There isn't a grain of* (ie any) *truth in it.* **4** [C] the smallest unit of weight in various measuring systems, 0.00143 of a pound or 0.065 of a GRAM: *The analysis showed a few grains of arsenic in the solution.* ⇨ App 2. **5** [U] (a) the pattern of lines seen or felt in wood, or of layers in rock, coal, etc: *cut a piece of wood along/across the grain.* ⇨ picture. (b) the texture of wood, stone, etc: *wood of fine/medium/coarse grain.* **IDM** **(be/go) against the grain** (to be) contrary to one's nature or instinct: *It really goes against the grain to have to go into the office at weekends* (ie I do not like it).

▶ **-grained** (forming compound *adjs*) having a grain(2,5) or grains of the specified type: *coarse-grained* ∘ *fine-grained.*

grainy *adj* (esp of photographs) on which small dots of colour can be seem, producing an image that is not clear or distinct: *a grainy old black-and-white film.*

gram (also **gramme**) /græm/ *n* (*abbr* **g**) a metric unit of weight. ⇨ App 2.

-gram *comb form* (forming *ns*) **1** a metric unit of weight: *milligram* ∘ *kilogram.* **2** a thing written or drawn: *telegram* ∘ *hologram.*

grammar /ˈgræmə(r)/ *n* **1** [U] the rules in a language for changing the form of words and combining them into sentences: *a good understanding of grammar* ∘ *the principles of English grammar.* Compare MORPHOLOGY 2, SYNTAX. **2** [U] a person's knowledge and use of a language: *I'm trying to improve my grammar.* ∘ *use bad grammar* ∘ (*infml*) *Is that grammar* (ie correct use of the language)? **3** [C] a book containing a description of the rules of grammar for a particular language: *I'm writing a grammar of modern English.* ∘ *I want to buy a French grammar.*

▶ **grammarian** /grəˈmeəriən/ *n* an expert in grammar.

■ **ˈgrammar school** *n* **1** (*Brit*) (esp formerly) a type of secondary(3) school which concentrates on academic rather than technical or practical courses. **2** (*US*) = PRIMARY SCHOOL.

grammatical /grəˈmætɪkl/ *adj* of, about or conforming to the rules of grammar: *a grammatical treatise* ∘ *a grammatical error* ∘ *That sentence is not grammatical.* ▶ **grammatically** /-kli/ *adv*: *a grammatically correct sentence.*

gramme /græm/ *n* = GRAM.

gramophone /ˈgræməfəʊn/ *n* (*dated*) = RECORD-PLAYER.

gran /græn/ *n* (*Brit infml*) a grandmother: *My gran lives in Bristol.* ∘ *We're going to see Gran.* See also GRANDMA, GRANNY.

granary /ˈgrænəri/ *n* **1** a building where grain is stored: (*fig*) *The Midwest is America's granary* (ie a region producing much wheat and corn). **2** [attrib] (*Brit*) (of bread) containing whole grains of wheat: *a granary loaf.*

grand /grænd/ *adj* (**-er, -est**) **1** (sometimes in names of places or buildings) magnificent; splendid; big; of great importance : *It's not a very grand house, just a small bungalow.* ∘ *We dined in grand style.* ∘ *a grand occasion/procession* ∘ *make a grand entry/exit* (eg on the stage, in a way that attracts the attention of everyone) ∘ *Grand Canyon* ∘ *the Grand Hotel.* **2(a)** large in scope or scale; ambitious: *a grand design/plan/strategy* ∘ *operate on a grand scale.* (b) (*often derog*) proud and socially superior; intended to impress: *put on a grand air/manner* ∘ *make a grand gesture* ∘ *She loves to play the grand lady* (ie act like one). **3** (*infml*) very fine; excellent: *It's grand weather!* ∘ *I feel grand* (ie very well). ∘ *We're having a grand* (ie very enjoyable) *time.* ∘ *You've done a grand job.* **4** Grand [attrib] (used in the title of people of very high rank): *the Grand Vizier.* **IDM** **a/the ˌgrand old ˈman (of sth)** a man long and highly respected in a particular field: *the grand old man of English theatre.*

▶ **grand** *n* **1** (*pl* unchanged) (usu *pl*) (*sl*) $1 000; £1 000: *It'll cost you 50 grand.* **2** = GRAND PIANO. See also BABY GRAND, CONCERT GRAND.

grandly *adv*: *They refer to their front porch rather grandly as 'the conservatory'.* ∘ *'Dinner is served,' she announced grandly.*

grandness *n* [U].

■ ˌgrand ˈduke *n* (*fem* ˌgrand ˈduchess) a prince/princess or noble person ruling over a territory.

ˌgrand ˈjury *n* (*law esp US*) a JURY(1) that has to decide whether there is enough evidence against an accused person for a trial.

ˈgrand master *n* **1** a CHESS player of the greatest skill. **2** ˈGrand Master the head of an order of knights (KNIGHT 2) or a group of Freemasons.

ˌgrand ˈopera *n* [U, C] opera in which everything is sung and there are no spoken parts.

ˌgrand ˈpiano *n* a large piano with HORIZONTAL strings (STRING¹ 2). ⇨ picture at PIANO¹.

Grand Prix /ˌgrɑ̃ ˈpriː/ *n* (*pl* **Grands Prix** /ˌgrɑ̃ ˈpriː/) any of a series of important international races for racing cars or motor cycles (MOTOR).

ˌgrand ˈslam *n* **1** (*sport*) the winning of every single part of a contest, or all the main contests in a year. **2** (in card-games, esp bridge²) the winning of all 13 tricks (TRICK 5) in a single game.

ˌgrand ˈtotal *n* the final total when other totals have been added together: *That makes a grand total of 562.*

ˌgrand ˈtour *n* (esp formerly) a visit to the chief cities of Europe, considered as part of the education of a wealthy young person.

grand- (forming compound *ns* indicating family relationships): *grandmother* ∘ *grandchildren.*

grandad (also **grand-dad**) /ˈgrændæd/ *n* (*Brit infml*) a grandfather. See also GRANDPA.

grandchild /ˈgræntʃaɪld/ *n* (*pl* **-children**) a daughter or son of one's own child: *She has ten grandchildren.* ⇨ App 4.

granddaughter /ˈgrændɔːtə(r)/ *n* a daughter of one's own child: *a baby granddaughter.* ⇨ App 4.

grandee /grænˈdiː/ *n* **1** a person of high rank or importance: *literary/political grandees.* **2** (formerly) a Spanish or Portuguese nobleman of high rank.

grandeur /ˈgrændʒə(r)/ *n* [U] the quality of being great, magnificent and impressive in appearance or status: *the beauty and grandeur of the Swiss alps* ∘ *She clearly suffers from **delusions of grandeur*** (ie thinks she is more important than she really is).

grandfather /ˈgrænfɑːðə(r)/ *n* the father of either of one's parents: *My grandfather is over 90.* See also GRANDAD, GRANDPA. ⇨ App 4.

■ ˌgrandfather ˈclock *n* an old-fashioned type of clock in a tall wooden case that stands on the floor.

grandiloquent /grænˈdɪləkwənt/ *adj* (*fml derog*) using long words which are difficult to understand in order to impress people: *a grandiloquent speaker/speech.* ▶ **grandiloquence** /-əns/ *n* [U].

grandiose /ˈgrændiəʊs/ *adj* (*usu derog*) more elaborate than necessary; producing or meant to produce a splendid effect: *a grandiose building/style* ∘ *She had some grandiose* (ie too ambitious) *plan to start up her own company.*

grandma /ˈgrænmɑː/ *n* (*infml*) a grandmother. See also GRANNY.

grandmother /ˈgrænmʌðə(r)/ *n* the mother of either of one's parents. See also GRAN, GRANDMA, GRANNY. ⇨ App 4. **IDM** **teach one's grandmother to suck eggs** ⇨ TEACH.

grandpa /ˈgrænpɑː/ *n* (*infml*) a grandfather. See also GRANDAD.

grandparent /ˈgrænpeərənt/ *n* the father or mother of either of one's parents. ⇨ App 4.

grandson /ˈgrænsʌn/ *n* a son of one's own child: *They are very proud of their grandson.* ⇨ App 4.

G

grapevine

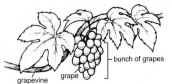

bunch of grapes

grapevine   grape

grandstand /'grændstænd/ n a large covered structure with rows of seats for spectators at races or sports meetings: *sit in the grandstand.* Compare STAND² 5.

grange /greɪndʒ/ n **1** (*Brit*) (often as part of a name) a country house with farm buildings: *ˌBiddulph ˈGrange.* **2** (*US*) a farm.

granite /'grænɪt/ n [U] hard, usu grey, stone used for building.

granny (also **grannie**) /'græni/ n (*infml*) a grandmother. See also GRANDMA.
■ **'granny flat** n (*infml*) a flat for an old person, esp in a relative's house.
'granny knot n a reef knot (REEF²) that is wrongly tied, so that it is easily undone.

grant /grɑːnt; US grænt/ v **1(a)** to agree to give or allow what is asked for: [Vn] *grant a favour/request* [Vnn] *I was granted permission to visit the palace.* **(b)** ~ sth (to sb) to give sth formally or legally to sb: [Vnpr] *These lands were granted to our family in perpetuity.* [Vnn] *She was granted a divorce.* ○ *They were granted a licence to mine in the area.* **2** (*fml*) to agree or admit that sth is true: [Vn] *grant the truth of what sb says* [Vnn] *She's a clever woman, I grant you that.* [Vn.*that*] *I grant you (that) she's a clever woman, but I wouldn't want to work for her.* [also V.*that*]. **IDM** **take sb/sth for 'granted** to be so familiar with sb/sth that one no longer appreciates their full value: *He never praises his wife: he just takes her for granted.* ○ *In this country we take freedom of speech for granted.* **take sth for 'granted** to assume sth to be true: *I take it for granted you've read this book.*
▶ **grant** n ~ **(to do sth / towards sth)** a sum of money given by an organization, esp the government, for a particular purpose: *student grants* (ie to pay for their education) ○ *award sb a research grant* ○ *provide grant aid for local forestry projects* ○ *You can get a grant to repair/towards the repair of your house.*
granted adv (used to admit the truth of a statement before introducing a contrary argument): *Granted, it's a splendid car, but have you seen how much it costs!*
■ **ˌgrant-in-ˈaid** n (pl **grants-in-aid**) an amount of money given by central government to local government or an institution.
ˌgrant-mainˈtained adj (of a school) receiving financial support from central government rather than the local authority.

granular /'grænjələ(r)/ adj **1** like, containing or consisting of small hard pieces: *a granular substance.* **2** rough to the touch or in appearance: *a granular surface/texture.*

granulated sugar /ˌgrænjuleɪtɪd 'ʃʊgə(r)/ n [U] sugar in the form of small grains.

granule /'grænjuːl/ n a small hard piece of sth; a small grain(2): *instant-coffee granules.*

grape /greɪp/ n a green or purple berry growing in bunches on a VINE, used for making wine or eaten as fruit: *pick grapes in the south of France* ○ *grape juice.* ⇨ picture at GRAPEVINE. **IDM** **sour grapes** ⇨ SOUR.

grapefruit /'greɪpfruːt/ n (pl unchanged) a large round yellow CITRUS fruit with slightly sour juicy flesh: *'grapefruit juice.*

grapeshot /'greɪpʃɒt/ n [U] (formerly) a number of small iron balls fired together from a CANNON(1).

grapevine /'greɪpvaɪn/ n **1** [C] a VINE on which grapes (GRAPE) grow. ⇨ picture. **2** (usu the **grapevine**) [sing] an informal means of passing news or rumours from person to person, eg in an office or among a group of friends: *I heard on/through the grapevine that Jill is being promoted.*

graph /grɑːf; *Brit* also grɑːf/ n (*mathematics*) a planned drawing consisting of a line or lines, sometimes curved, showing how two or more sets of numbers relate to each other: *plot crime statistics on a graph* ○ *The graph shows how house prices have risen since the 1960s.* ⇨ picture at CHART.
■ **'graph paper** n [U] paper with small squares of equal size, used esp for drawing graphs on: *a piece/ sheet of graph paper.*

-graph comb form (forming ns) **1** a thing written or drawn, etc in a specified way: *autograph* ○ *monograph* ○ *photograph.* **2** an instrument that writes or records: *telegraph* ○ *seismograph.* ▶ **-graphic(al)** comb form (forming adjs from ns ending in -*graph* or -*graphy*): *photographic* ○ *geographical.*

graphic /'græfɪk/ adj **1** [attrib] of visual art, eg printing, writing or drawing: *a graphic artist* ○ *graphic displays* ○ *a leading graphic designer.* **2** (of descriptions) giving one a clear lively picture, full of detail and easy to imagine; vivid: *a graphic account of a battle* ○ *She kept telling us about her operation, in the most graphic detail.*
▶ **graphically** /-kli/ adv **1** by writing or drawings: *We can illustrate this graphically with a bar chart.* **2** very clearly and in great detail.
graphics n [pl] designs, drawings or pictures, esp for commercial use: *computer graphics.*

graphite /'græfaɪt/ n [U] a soft black substance that is a form of CARBON(1). Graphite is used to make pencils, to LUBRICATE machinery, and in nuclear reactors (REACTOR).

-graphy comb form (forming ns) **1** indicating an art or a type of scientific study: *choreography* ○ *geography.* **2** indicating a form of writing, representation, etc: *calligraphy* ○ *photography.* ▶ **-grapher** comb form (forming ns): *geographer* ○ *photographer.*

grapnel /'græpnəl/ n (also **grappling-iron**, **grappling-hook**) a device with several hooks, attached to a rope and used for dragging sth along or for holding a boat still against sth. ⇨ picture.

grapnel

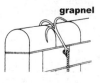

grapple /'græpl/ v **1** ~ **(with sb/sth)** to seize an opponent firmly and struggle with her or him: [Vpr] *She grappled with her assailant but he got away.* [also V]. **2** ~ **(with sth)** to work hard to overcome a difficulty: [Vpr] *He has been grappling with the problem for a long time.*
■ **'grappling-iron** (also **grappling-hook**) n = GRAPNEL.

grasp /grɑːsp; US græsp/ v **1(a)** to seize sb/sth firmly, esp with the hands: [Vn] *She grasped the rope and pulled herself up.* ○ *He grasped my hand warmly* (eg as a sign of friendship). ○ *He grasped her firmly by the arm.* **(b)** to make use of sth; to seize sth eagerly: [Vn] *grasp an opportunity.* **2** to understand sth fully: [Vn] *I don't think you've quite grasped the seriousness of the situation.* [V.*wh*] *She never could grasp how to do it.* **IDM** **clutch/grasp at straws** ⇨ STRAW. **grasp the 'nettle** (*Brit*) to deal with a difficult matter firmly. **PHRV** **'grasp at sth** to try to seize sth: *grasp at a swinging rope* ○ *He was ready to grasp at any means to defeat his opponents.*

[V.*to* inf] = verb + *to* infinitive   [Vn.inf (no *to*)] = verb + noun + infinitive without *to*   [V.*ing*] = verb + -*ing* form

▶ **grasp** *n* (usu *sing*) **1(a)** a firm hold or grip: *Take a good grasp of the handle and pull.* ○ *I grabbed him but he wriggled out of my grasp.* (**b**) power; control: *Election victory was within their grasp.* ○ *Don't let the situation slip/escape from your grasp.* **2** a person's understanding: *difficulties within/beyond one's grasp* ○ *She has a good grasp of the subject.*

grasping /ˈɡrɑːspɪŋ; US ˈɡræspɪŋ/ *adj* (*derog*) wanting a lot of money, possessions, power, etc for oneself; greedy: *a grasping landlord* ○ *She is mean and grasping.*

grass¹ /ɡrɑːs; US ɡræs/ *n* **1(a)** [U] various common wild plants with narrow green leaves and stems that are eaten by cattle, horses, sheep, etc: *a blade* (ie leaf) *of grass* ○ *grass seed* ○ *The dry grass caught fire.* (**b**) [C] any species of grass: *ornamental grasses.* **2** (usu **the grass**) [sing, U] an area of ground covered with grass¹(1), eg a lawn: *Don't walk on the grass.* ○ *cut/mow the grass* ○ *cattle put out to grass* (ie put in a field to eat the grass). **3** [U] (*sl*) MARIJUANA. **4** [C] (*Brit sl usu derog*) a person who informs the police of sb's criminal activities and plans. **IDM the grass is (always) greener on the other side (of the fence)** (*saying*) (said by or about people who never seem content and always think that others have a better situation than they have): *She writes about how much greener the grass is in America.* (**not**) **let the grass grow under one's feet** (not) to delay in getting sth done. **put sb out to ˈgrass** (*infml*) to force sb to retire, esp because of old age. **a snake in the grass** ⇨ SNAKE.

▶ **grassy** *adj* (**-ier, -iest**) covered with grass: *a grassy bank/hillside.*

■ **ˌgrass ˈcourt** *n* a tennis-court (TENNIS) with a grass surface.

ˌgrass ˈroots *n* [pl] (*esp politics*) ordinary people in society, in contrast with those who make decisions: *win support at the grass roots (level)* ○ *grass-roots opposition to the party's policy.*

ˈgrass snake *n* a small harmless type of snake.

ˌgrass ˈwidow *n* (*often joc*) a woman whose husband is temporarily absent.

grass² /ɡrɑːs; US ɡræs/ *v* **1** ~ **sth (over)** to cover an area of ground with grass: [Vn] *a small grassed area* [Vnp] *The old rose beds were levelled and grassed over.* **2** [Vn] (*US*) to feed animals with grass. **3** ~ **(on sb)** (*Brit sl usu derog*) to inform the police of sb's criminal activities or plans: [V, Vpr] *They were only caught because somebody grassed (on them).*

grasshopper /ˈɡrɑːshɒpə(r); US ˈɡræs-/ *n* an insect that jumps and makes a short high-pitched noise. **IDM knee-high to a grasshopper** ⇨ KNEE-HIGH.

grassland /-lænd/ *n* [U] (also **grasslands** [pl]) land covered with grass, esp as used for cattle, etc to feed on: *walk across open grassland.*

grate¹ /ɡreɪt/ *n* a metal frame for holding the coal or wood in a fireplace: *a fire burning in the grate.*

grate² /ɡreɪt/ *v* **1** ~ **sth (into sth)** to rub sth into small pieces, usu against a rough surface; to rub small bits off sth: [Vn, Vnpr] *Grate the carrot finely/into small pieces.* [Vn] *grated cheese/lemon rind* [Vnpr] *Grate the nutmeg into the mixture/over the pudding.* **2(a)** to make a harsh noise by rubbing: [V] *The hinges grated as the gate swung back.* [Vpr] *The wheels grated against/on the edge of the pavement.* (**b**) ~ **(on sb/sth)** to have an irritating effect: [Vpr] *His whining voice grates on my ears/nerves.* ○ *It's her ingratitude that grates on me.* [also V].

▶ **grater** *n* a device with a rough surface for grating food: *a cheese grater.*

grating *adj* irritating: *her grating voice.*

grateful /ˈɡreɪtfl/ *adj* ~ **(to sb) (for sth)**; ~ **(to do sth)**; ~ **(that …)** feeling or showing thanks and gratitude for sth being done to one or for sth fortunate that has happened: *I am deeply grateful to you for your help.* ○ *a grateful pupil* ○ *grateful thanks* ○ *We are always grateful to receive donations.* ○ *I was grateful that they didn't ask me to make a speech.* ○ (*fml*) *I would be most grateful if you could confirm your acceptance of this proposal.* **IDM grateful/thankful for small mercies** ⇨ SMALL.

▶ **gratefully** /-fəli/ *adv* with thanks and gratitude: *I offered her a lift, and she accepted gratefully.*

gratify /ˈɡrætɪfaɪ/ *v* (*pt, pp* **-fied**) (*fml*) **1** (esp passive) to give pleasure or satisfaction to sb: [Vnpr] *I was most gratified at/by/with the outcome of the meeting.* [Vn.to inf] *It gratified me to hear of your success.* [Vn.that] *I was gratified that they appreciated what I did for them.* **2** to give sb what they desire; to satisfy sb: [Vn] *gratify a person's whims* ○ *Please gratify my curiosity and tell me what it is.*

▶ **gratification** /ˌɡrætɪfɪˈkeɪʃn/ *n* (*fml*) **1** [U] the state of being pleased or satisfied: *the gratification of knowing one's plans have succeeded* ○ *sexual gratification.* **2** [C] a thing that gives one pleasure or satisfaction: *one of the few gratifications of an otherwise boring job.*

gratifying *adj* (*fml*) pleasing; causing satisfaction: *His reaction was gratifying.* ○ *It is extremely gratifying to see one's efforts rewarded.* **gratifyingly** *adv.*

grating /ˈɡreɪtɪŋ/ *n* a framework of wooden or metal bars, either parallel or crossing one another, placed across an opening, eg a window, to prevent people or animals from climbing through or to allow air to flow easily.

gratis /ˈɡrætɪs, ˈɡreɪtɪs/ *adj, adv* without payment; free of charge: *a gratis copy of a book* ○ *be admitted to the exhibition gratis.*

gratitude /ˈɡrætɪtjuːd; US -tuːd/ *n* [U] ~ **(to sb) (for sth)** the feeling of being grateful or the desire to express one's thanks: *She expressed her gratitude to all those who had supported her.* ○ *remember sb with gratitude* ○ *I owe you a debt of gratitude for what you've done.* ○ *They gave him a retirement present in gratitude for his long service.*

gratuitous /ɡrəˈtjuːɪtəs; US -ˈtuː-/ *adj* (*fml derog*) unnecessary; done, said, etc without cause or good reason: *a gratuitous insult* ○ *a gratuitous lie/liar* ○ *scenes of gratuitous violence on television.* ▶ **gratuitously** *adv.*

gratuity /ɡrəˈtjuːəti; US -ˈtuː-/ *n* **1** (*fml*) money given to sb who has done one a service(5); a tip³(1). **2** (*Brit*) money given to a employee when he or she retires.

grave¹ /ɡreɪv/ *adj* (**-r, -st**) **1** (*fml*) (of situations, etc) serious and important; giving cause for worry: *This could have grave consequences.* ○ *a grave mistake/error* ○ *grave news/danger* ○ *have grave doubts about sth* ○ *There is a grave risk of flooding.* ○ *He is in a grave condition and needs immediate medical treatment.* **2** (of people) serious or solemn in manner: *He looked grave. 'Is there anything wrong?' I asked.* ▶ **gravely** *adv: She is gravely ill.* ○ *If you think that, you are gravely mistaken.* ○ *'It's a confidential matter,' he said gravely.*

grave² /ɡreɪv/ *n* **1** [C] a hole dug in the ground for a dead body; the earth or stone placed over this: *strewing flowers on her grave* ○ *visit sb's grave.* **2** (often **the grave**) [sing] (*rhet*) death; being dead: *Is there life beyond the grave* (ie after death)? ○ *follow sb to the grave* (ie die soon after them) ○ *go to an early grave* (ie die young) ○ *He took his secret to the grave* (ie died without revealing it). **IDM dig one's own grave** ⇨ DIG¹. **from the cradle to the grave** ⇨ CRADLE. **have one foot in the grave** ⇨ FOOT¹. **turn in one's ˈgrave** (*saying*) (of a person who is already dead) likely to be shocked or angry: *His grandfather must be turning in his grave at the way he's running the company.*

grave³ /ɡrɑːv/ (also **ˌgrave ˈaccent**) *n* a mark (ˋ)

placed over a vowel to indicate how it is to be pronounced (as in French *mère*).

gravedigger /ˈɡreɪvdɪɡə(r)/ *n* a person whose job is to dig holes for people to be buried in.

gravel /ˈɡrævl/ *n* [U] small stones, often used to make the surface of paths and roads: *a load of gravel* ○ *a gravel path* ○ *a gravel pit* (ie from which gravel is dug).
▶ **gravelled** (*US* also **graveled** /ˈɡrævld/) *adj* covered with gravel: *a gravelled path.*
gravelly /ˈɡrævəli/ *adj* **1** full of or containing gravel: *a gravelly beach* ○ *gravelly soil.* **2** (of a voice) deep and rough.

gravestone /ˈɡreɪvstəʊn/ *n* a stone on top of or at the head[1](12) of a grave, with the name of the person buried there on it. ⇨ picture at CHURCH.

graveyard /ˈɡreɪvjɑːd/ *n* an area of land, often near a church, where people are buried; a CEMETERY: (*fig*) *chemicals that turn farmland into a graveyard for wildlife.*

gravitate /ˈɡrævɪteɪt/ **PHRV** **gravitate to/towards sb/sth** to move towards or be attracted to sb/sth, gradually but steadily; to turn to sb/sth: *Many young people gravitate to the city.* ○ *Their conversation usually gravitates towards sport.*
▶ **gravitation** /ˌɡrævɪˈteɪʃn/ *n* [U] a force of attraction; GRAVITY: *the effects of gravitation on bodies in space* ○ *the gravitation of holiday-makers towards Europe.* **gravitational** /-ʃənəl/ *adj: a gravitational field/force/pull.*

gravity /ˈɡrævəti/ *n* [U] **1** the force that attracts objects in space towards each other, and on the earth pulls them towards the centre of the planet, so that things fall to the ground when dropped: *the natural forces of gravity* ○ *the law of gravity.* **2(a)** extreme importance and a source of concern or worry; seriousness (SERIOUS): *I don't think you realize the gravity of the situation.* ○ *Punishment varies according to the gravity of the offence.* **(b)** serious or solemn behaviour, speech or appearance: *behave with due gravity in a court of law* ○ *The twinkle in his eye belied the gravity of his demeanour.* See also SPECIFIC GRAVITY, CENTRE OF GRAVITY.

gravy /ˈɡreɪvi/ *n* [U] **1** the juice that comes from meat while it is cooking; a sauce made from this. **2** (*sl esp US*) money or profit that is gained easily or unexpectedly.
■ **ˈgravy-boat** *n* a long low JUG used for serving and pouring gravy at a meal.
ˈgravy train *n* (*sl esp US*) a situation in which a person or group of people get a lot of money without much effort: *be/get on the gravy train.*

gray¹ /ɡreɪ/ *adj, n, v* (*esp US*) = GREY.

graze¹ /ɡreɪz/ *v* **1** (of cattle, sheep, etc) to eat growing grass: [V] *cows grazing in the fields.* **2(a)** to put cattle, etc in a field to eat grass: [Vn] *farmers grazing their herds.* **(b)** to use land to feed cattle: [Vn] *That field's being grazed this year.*
▶ **grazier** /ˈɡreɪzɪə(r)/ *n* a farmer who keeps animals that graze.
grazing *n* [U] **1** growing grass for cattle, etc to eat: *The meadow provides good/rich grazing for milk cows.* **2** (of cattle, etc) the process of eating grass: *herds led home after a day's grazing.* **3** the management of land for cattle, etc: *payments to farmers to encourage less intensive grazing.*

graze² /ɡreɪz/ *v* **1** ~ sth (**against/on sth**) to break the surface of the skin slightly by scraping it against sth: [Vnpr] *Jane one's arm against/on a rock* [Vn] *I fell and grazed my knee.* **2** to touch or scrape sth lightly while passing: [V] *Our car bumpers just grazed* (ie touched each other) *as we passed.* [Vn] *The bullet grazed his cheek.*
▶ **graze** *n* a slight injury where the skin is scraped: *have a graze on one's elbow.*

grease /ɡriːs/ *n* [U] **1** any thick oily substance, eg

that used to help machines run smoothly: *engine grease* ○ *dirty plates covered with grease* ○ *Before using varnish make sure the surface is free from grease.* ○ *Grease marks or spots can be removed with liquid detergent.* See also ELBOW-GREASE. **2** animal fat that has been softened by cooking or heating: *The grease from pork can be used for frying.*
▶ **grease** *v* to put or rub grease on or in sth: [Vn] *Pour the cake mixture into a greased tin.* **IDM** **grease sb's ˈpalm** (*infml*) to give sb money in order to persuade them to do sth dishonest for one; to BRIBE sb.
■ **ˈgrease-gun** *n* a device for forcing grease into the parts of a machine.

greasepaint /ˈɡriːspeɪnt/ *n* [U] thick make-up (MAKE¹) used by actors.

greaseproof paper /ˌɡriːspruːf ˈpeɪpə(r)/ *n* [U] paper that does not let GREASE pass through it and is used esp for wrapping food in.

greasy /ˈɡriːsi, ˈɡriːzi/ *adj* (**-ier, -iest**) **1(a)** covered with an oily substance; SLIPPERY(1): *greasy fingers/overalls* ○ *a greasy road.* **(b)** producing more oily substances than average or normal: *greasy skin/hair.* **(c)** (*derog*) containing or cooked with too much fat or oil: *greasy food/chips.* **2** (*infml derog*) (of people or their behaviour) intending to please or praise sb, but without being sincere: *He greeted me with a greasy smile.*
■ **ˌgreasy ˈspoon** *n* (*sl esp US*) a cheap dirty restaurant.

great /ɡreɪt/ *adj* (**-er, -est**) **1(a)** [usu attrib] very large; much bigger than average in size, extent or quantity: *The great ship sank below the waves.* ○ *The area of forest that has been destroyed is very great.* ○ *dive to a great depth* ○ *A great crowd had gathered.* ○ *People were arriving in great numbers.* ○ *He lives a great distance away.* ○ *She lived to a great age.* ○ *The great majority (of people)* (ie Most people) *approve.* ○ *The greater part* (ie Most) *of the area is flooded.* **(b)** [usu attrib] more than average in degree, quality or intensity; considerable; exceptional: *of great value/importance/relevance/significance* ○ *He described it in great detail.* ○ *be in great demand* (ie much wanted) ○ *Take great care of it.* ○ *It's a great relief to know you're safe.* ○ *You've been a great help.* ○ *This is a great opportunity for you.* ⇨ note at BIG. **2(a)** of excellent ability or quality; outstanding: *a great man/artist/musician* ○ *perform great deeds* ○ *the world's greatest violinist* ○ *No one would deny that Beethoven's symphonies are great masterpieces.* **(b)** of high rank or status: *a great lady* ○ *the great powers* (ie important and powerful countries) ○ *Alexander the Great.* **3** [attrib] **(a)** important; grand or exciting: *The governor was getting married, and everyone was in town for the great occasion.* ○ *As the great day approached, she grew more and more nervous.* **(b)** important; considerable: *great developments in the prevention of disease* ○ *A/The great advantage of this metal is that it doesn't rust.* **4** in a very good state of physical or mental health; fine: *in great form/shape* (ie very fit and active) ○ *in great spirits* (ie very cheerful) ○ *I feel great today!* **5(a)** (*infml*) (used to show enthusiasm) wonderful; very nice or satisfactory: *Isn't he great?* ○ *She's the greatest!* ○ *It's great that you can come!* ○ *What a great party!* ○ *He scored a great goal.* ○ *We had a great time in Majorca.* ○ *It's great to have met you!* **(b)** (*ironic*) (used to express annoyance, contempt, etc): *Oh ˈgreat, I've missed the bus again!* ○ *You've been a ˈgreat help, you have!* **(c)** ~ for (**doing**) **sth** (*infml*) very suitable for sth; ideal or useful for sth: *This little gadget's great for opening jars.* ○ *These are great shoes for muddy weather.* **(d)** [pred] ~ at (**doing**) **sth** (*infml*) clever or skilful at sth: *She's great at tennis/chess.* **6** [attrib] particularly noted for the specified characteristic, interest, etc: *We are great friends.* ○ *I've never been a great*

reader (ie I do not read much). ∘ *He's a great one for complaining* (ie He constantly complains). **7** [attrib] (*infml*) (used to emphasize an *adj* of size, etc) very: *She has four great big sons.* ∘ *He cut himself a great thick slice of cake.* **8** (added to words for relations beginning with *grand-* to show a further stage in relationship): *one's* ˌgreat ˈgrandfather (ie one's father's or mother's grandfather) ∘ *one's* ˌgreat ˈgrandson (ie the GRANDSON of one's son or daughter). ⇨ App 4. **9** (*dated infml*) (in expressions of surprise): *Great heavens!* **10 Greater** (*Brit*) (used with the name of a city) including the centre of the city and a large area all around it: ˌGreater ˈManchester ∘ ˌGreater ˈLondon. **IDM** **be no great ˈshakes** (*infml*) not to be very good, efficient, suitable, etc: *She's no great shakes as an actress.* ∘ *The film was no great shakes.* **going great ˈguns** (*infml*) proceeding quickly and successfully: *Work is going great guns now.* **a good/great deal** ⇨ DEAL². ˌgreat and ˈsmall rich and poor, powerful and weak, etc: *Everyone, great and small, is affected by these changes.* **the great sth in the ˈsky** (*joc*) a place where a particular person or thing is imagined to go after they are no longer alive or working, and similar to a place they were previously associated with on earth: *He's gone to the great ballroom in the sky.* ∘ *The car is heading for the great big garage in the sky.*
▶ **great** *n* **1** [C usu *pl*] (*infml*) a person of outstanding ability: *one of boxing's all-time greats.* **2 the great** [pl *v*] people of great wealth, status or influence: *a fashionable affair attended by **the great and the good**.*
greatly *adv* much; by much: *We were greatly amused.* ∘ *The reports were greatly exaggerated.* ∘ *He has suffered greatly.*
greatness *n* [U]: *achieve greatness in one's lifetime.*
■ ˌGreat ˈBritain (*abbr* **GB**) (also **Britain**) *n* England, Wales and Scotland.
ˌGreat ˈDane *n* a very large breed of dog with short hair.
the ˌGreat ˈWar *n* [sing] (*dated*) the world war of 1914–18.
greatcoat /ˈɡreɪtkəʊt/ *n* (*esp Brit*) a long heavy coat, esp of a type worn by soldiers, etc.
grebe /ɡriːb/ *n* a bird similar to a duck but without webbed (WEB 3) feet. Grebes live near rivers or lakes.
Grecian /ˈɡriːʃn/ *adj* of or like the styles or ideals of ancient Greece: *a Grecian urn* ∘ *his handsome Grecian profile.*
greed /ɡriːd/ *n* [U] ~ (**for sth**) (*derog*) **1** an excessive desire for food, esp when one is not hungry. **2** an excessive desire for wealth, power, etc for oneself, without consideration for the needs of other people: *the greed with which large companies swallow up their smaller competitors* ∘ *She was consumed with greed and envy.*
▶ **greedy** *adj* (**-ier, -iest**) ~ (**for sth**) full of greed or desire: *a greedy little boy* ∘ *You greedy pig!* ∘ *looking at the cakes with greedy eyes* ∘ *greedy for power* ∘ *greedy for information.* **greedily** *adv*: *He ate and drank greedily.*
Greek /ɡriːk/ *adj* of Greece or its people or language.
▶ **Greek** *n* **1** [C] a member of the people living in ancient or modern Greece. **2** [U] the language of the Greeks. **IDM** **it's all ˈGreek to me** (*infml saying*) I cannot understand it.
green¹ /ɡriːn/ *adj* (**-er, -est**) **1** of the colour of growing grass and the leaves of most plants and trees: *fresh green peas* ∘ *a dark green coat* ∘ *The gate was painted green.* ∘ *The bread was green with mould.* ⇨ picture at SPECTRUM. **2** covered with grass or other plants: *green fields/hills/suburbs.* **3** (of fruit) not yet fully ripe: *green bananas.* **4** (*infml*) lacking experience; not mature or wise: *He's still*

very green — he's bound to make mistakes. **5** [usu pred] (of the skin) pale, as if one is going to be sick: *It was a rough crossing and many of the passengers looked distinctly green.* **6** [pred] fully of envy; jealous: *What a fabulous car — I'm green with envy!* **7** (*rhet*) full of life and vigour; fresh: *keep sb's memory green* (ie not allow sb who is dead to be forgotten). **8** [usu attrib] (*esp politics*) concerned with or supporting as a political principle the protection of the environment: *green politics* ∘ *the green argument.* **IDM** **the grass is greener on the other side** ⇨ GRASS¹. **green/pale about the gills** ⇨ GILL¹.
▶ **green** *v* **1** to become or make sth green: [V] *a roof greening with moss and lichen* [Vn] *land needed for greening the cities.* **2** to become or make sth more concerned with issues related to the environment: [V] *the sudden greening of British politics* [Vn] *The review has not gone far enough in greening the party's industrial policies.*
greenish /ˈɡriːnɪʃ/ *adj* slightly green: *a greenish-yellow tinge.*
greenness *n* [U]: *All politicians profess greenness nowadays.* ∘ *Supermarkets proclaim the greenness of their products.*
■ ˌgreen ˈbelt *n* [U, C usu *sing*] an area of open land around a city, where building is strictly controlled: *Most of the area is green belt.* ∘ *New roads are cutting into the green belt.*
ˌgreen ˈfingers *n* [pl] (*infml*) skill in growing plants: *Mother has green fingers.*
ˌgreen ˈlight *n* [sing] permission to start or continue with a project: *The government has given a/ the green light to the scheme.*
ˌgreen maˈnure *n* [U] growing plants dug into the soil to make it more FERTILE(1).
ˌGreen ˈPaper *n* (in Britain) a preliminary report of government proposals, for general discussion: *issue/publish a Green Paper on the future of the universities.* Compare WHITE PAPER.
the ˈGreen Party *n* (in Britain) a political party whose main aim is the protection of the environment.
ˌgreen ˈpepper *n* = CAPSICUM.
the ˌgreen ˈpound *n* [sing] (*Brit*) the rate of exchange¹(3) for the pound in payments for agricultural produce in the European Union.
ˌgreen ˈsalad *n* [U, C] a SALAD made mainly with raw green vegetables, esp LETTUCE.
ˌgreen ˈtea *n* [U] pale tea made from leaves that have been dried but not fermented (FERMENT¹).
ˌgreen ˈvegetable *n* [C usu *pl*] a vegetable with dark green leaves, eg CABBAGE(1) or SPINACH: *Many people do not eat enough green vegetables.*
green² /ɡriːn/ *n* **1** [U, C] a green colour: *the fresh green of the countryside in spring* ∘ *curtains of bright emerald green* ∘ *a subtle combination of greens and browns.* **2** [U] green clothes: *dressed in green.* **3** [C] an area of public or common land with grass growing on it: *children playing on the village green.* **4** [C] an area with grass cut short surrounding a hole on a golf-course (GOLF): *a* ˈputting-green ∘ *the 13th* ˈgreen. ⇨ picture at GOLF. **5 greens** [pl] (*esp Brit*) green vegetables: *Eat up your greens.* **6 Green** [C usu *pl*] a member of a green¹(8) political party: *the success of the Greens in the local elections.*
greenback /ˈɡriːnbæk/ *n* (*US infml*) a US BANK-NOTE.
greenery /ˈɡriːnəri/ *n* [U] attractive growing green plants, or green leaves cut for decoration: *dry hillsides fringed with lush greenery* ∘ *The hall looks more festive with all that greenery.*
greenfield /ˈɡriːnfiːld/ *adj* [attrib] (of land) having no previous building on it, and therefore suitable for development: *a greenfield site.*
greenfly /ˈɡriːnflaɪ/ *n* (*pl* **-flies**) [C, U] any of various types of small flying insects that are harmful to plants: *The roses have got greenfly.*

greengage /'griːngeɪdʒ/ n a type of small, pale green PLUM(1a).

greengrocer /'griːngrəʊsə(r)/ n (Brit) a shopkeeper selling vegetables and fruit: *Guess who I met at the greengrocer's* (ie the greengrocer's shop) *today!* See also FRUITERER.

greenhorn /'griːnhɔːn/ n a person who lacks experience or wisdom.

greenhouse /'griːnhaʊs/ n a building with glass sides and a glass roof, in which plants are grown that need protection from cold weather: *growing tomatoes in a greenhouse.*
■ ˌgreenhouse 'gas n any of the gases that are thought to contribute to the rise in temperature of the earth's atmosphere, esp carbon dioxide (CARBON): *cut back on emissions of greenhouse gases.*
the ˈgreenhouse effect n [sing] the gradual rise in temperature of the earth's atmosphere, caused by an increase of gases, eg carbon dioxide (CARBON), in the air that trap the warmth of the sun: *The destruction of forests is contributing to the greenhouse effect.* See also GLOBAL WARMING.

greenkeeper /'griːnkiːpə(r)/ (US also **greenskeeper**) n a person whose job is to look after a golf-course (GOLF).

green-room /'griːnruːm, -rʊm/ n a room in a theatre, television studio, etc where the performers can relax when not performing.

Greenwich Mean Time /ˌgrenɪtʃ 'miːn taɪm, ˌgrɪ-, -nɪdʒ/ (abbr **GMT**) (also **Universal Time**) n [U] the time on the line of 0° LONGITUDE which passes through Greenwich, England, used as a basis for calculating time throughout the world.

greet /griːt/ v **1(a)** ~ sb (with sth) to give a sign or word of welcome or pleasure when meeting sb or receiving a guest: [Vn] *greeting her guests at the door* [Vnpr] *He greeted me with a friendly wave.* [Vnadv] *She greeted us warmly.* **(b)** ~ sth with sth (esp passive) to receive sth with a particular reaction: [Vnp] *The appointment was greeted with widespread approval.* [Vn-n] *His resignation was greeted as a clear victory for the opposition.* [Vn] *Loud cheers greeted the announcement.* **2** (of sights and sounds) to be suddenly seen or heard by sb: [Vn] *the view that greeted us at the top of the hill.*
▶ **greeting** n [C,U] the first words used when one sees sb or writes to sb; an expression or act with which sb is greeted: *exchange/send greetings* ○ *Mandy shouted a greeting.* ○ *He raised his hand in greeting.* ○ a 'greetings card (ie a card¹(3) sent at Christmas, on sb's birthday, etc). **IDM** the season's greetings ⇨ SEASON¹.

gregarious /grɪ'geəriəs/ adj **1** liking to be with other people: *She's very outgoing and gregarious.* **2** (biology) (of animals, birds, etc) living in groups or communities. ▶ **gregariously** adv. **gregariousness** n [U].

Gregorian /grɪ'gɔːriən/ adj.
■ the Greˌgorian 'calendar n [sing] the system now in general use of arranging the months in the year and the days in the month, introduced by Pope Gregory XIII (1502–85).
Greˌgorian 'chant n [C,U] a type of medieval church music named after Pope Gregory I (540–604).

gremlin /'gremlɪn/ n an imaginary wicked creature supposed to cause mechanical or other failure: *The gremlins have got into the computer again.*

grenade /grə'neɪd/ n a small bomb thrown by hand or fired from a gun: a 'hand-grenade ○ rocket-propelled grenades ○ a grenade attack.

grenadier /ˌgrenə'dɪə(r)/ n a soldier in the Grenadiers (or Grenadier Guards), a part of the British army.

grew pt of GROW.

grey (also esp US **gray**) /greɪ/ adj **1(a)** of the colour of ashes or lead: *grey eyes/hair* ○ a grey suit. **(b)** [usu pred] having grey hair: *She's gone very grey.* **(c)** dull; full of clouds and often raining: a grey day/sky ○ *The weather was grey and cold.* **(d)** (of a person) pale because tired, ill or unhappy: a face grey with pain ○ *The next morning she looked grey and hollow-eyed.* **2(a)** lacking interest or variety; depressing: a grey existence ○ *Life seemed grey and pointless after she'd gone.* **(b)** (derog) having no individual or attractive features: a government department run by grey and faceless men.
▶ **grey** (also esp US **gray**) n **1** [U,C] a grey colour: a suit of dark/light/charcoal grey. **2** [U] grey clothes: dressed in grey. **3** a grey or white horse.
grey (also esp US **gray**) v to become or make sth grey: [V] *His hair had greyed entirely.* ○ *greying curls* ○ *He was 50 and greying.* [Vn] *Worry had greyed her hair.*
greyish (also esp US **grayish**) adj slightly grey.
■ ˌgrey 'area n an area of a subject or situation that does not fit into a particular category, and is therefore difficult to deal with: *We're in a bit of a grey area.* ○ *The new rules for police procedure cleared up a lot of grey areas.*
ˌgrey-'haired adj with grey hair; old.
ˌgrey 'market n [sing] (commerce) a situation in which shares are sold before they are officially issued: *trade on the grey market.*
'grey matter n [U] (infml) intelligence; brains (BRAIN 2): *He doesn't have much grey matter, I'm afraid.*

greyhound /'greɪhaʊnd/ n a tall thin dog that can run fast and is used in racing. ⇨ picture at DOG¹.

grid /grɪd/ n **1** a framework of metal or wooden bars that are parallel or cross each other; a GRATING: *air vents covered with metal grids.* See also CATTLE GRID. **2(a)** a network of lines, esp crossing each other to form a series of squares: *New York is laid out on a grid pattern.* **(b)** a network of squares on a map, numbered for reference: *give the grid reference of a place on a map.* ⇨ picture at MAP. **3** a system of electric cables or pipes carrying gas for distributing power evenly over a large area: *the National Grid* (ie the network of electricity supply in a country). **4** a pattern of lines marking the start on a RACETRACK.

griddle /'grɪdl/ n a circular iron plate that is heated for cooking flat cakes.

gridiron /'grɪdaɪən/ n **1** a framework of metal bars used for cooking meat or fish over an open fire. **2** (US) a field for American football, the area of play being marked by a pattern of parallel lines.

grief /griːf/ n **1(a)** [U] ~ (over/at sth) deep or intense sorrow, caused esp by the death of sb: *She was overcome with grief when her husband died.* ○ the sense of grief over the loss of a child. **(b)** [C usu sing] an event causing such feelings: *His marriage to someone outside their faith was a great grief to his parents.* **IDM** come to 'grief (infml) **1** to end in total failure: *All his schemes for making money seem to come to grief.* **2** to have an accident; to fall down, crash, etc: *Several pedestrians had come to grief on the icy pavement.* good 'grief! (infml) (an exclamation of strong feeling): *Good grief! That's the most extraordinary thing I've ever seen!*
■ 'grief-stricken adj overcome by deep sorrow: *I tried to console the grief-stricken relatives.*

grievance /'griːvns/ n ~ (against sb) a real or imagined cause for complaining or protesting about sth, esp unfair treatment: *Staff were invited to air their grievances* (ie express them) *at a special meeting.* ○ *He'd been harbouring/nursing a grievance against his boss for months.* ○ *Management have set up procedures for dealing with the workers' grievances.*

grieve /griːv/ v **1** ~ (for sb); ~ (at/over/about sb/sth) to feel deep sorrow about sth that has happened, esp the death of sb: [V] *grieving families* ○

Their daughter died over a year ago, but they are still grieving. [Vpr] *grieve for a relative* ○ *grieve over the death of sb.* **2** to cause great sorrow to sb: [Vn] *The loss of such a close friend grieved her deeply.* ○ *It grieves me to have to say it, but you have only yourself to blame.*

grievous /ˈɡriːvəs/ *adj* **1** causing grief or great emotional suffering: *grievous news/losses.* **2** (*fml*) (of sth bad) severe; serious: *grievous pain/wounds* ○ *a grievous error/fault/sin/crime.* ▶ **grievously** *adv*: *Many families have suffered grievously in the current unrest.*

■ **ˌgrievous ˌbodily ˈharm** *n* [U] (*abbr* **GBH**) (*law*) serious injury done to sb in a criminal attack.

griffin /ˈɡrɪfɪn/ (also **griffon, gryphon** /ˈɡrɪfən/) *n* an imaginary creature in stories which has the head and wings of an EAGLE(1) and a lion's body.

grill /ɡrɪl/ *n* **1(a)** (*Brit*) a device on a cooker that directs heat downwards for cooking food: *an electric grill* ○ *an eye-level grill* ○ *Cook the meat under the grill for approximately 15 minutes.* ○ *a grill pan.* ⇨ picture at PAN¹. **(b)** a flat metal frame onto which food is put and cooked over a fire. See also BARBECUE. **2(a)** a dish of meat, etc cooked directly over or under great heat: *a mixed grill.* **(b)** (esp in names) a restaurant where such dishes are cooked and served: *Le Rendezvous Restaurant Grill.* **3** = GRILLE.

▶ **grill** *v* **1(a)** to cook sth over or under a grill: [Vn] *grilled steak* [Vnn] *I'll grill you some fish.* ⇨ note at COOK. **(b)** (*infml*) to expose oneself to great heat: [Vn] *sit grilling oneself in front of a fire/in the sun/ under a sun-ray lamp.* **2** (*infml*) to question sb closely and for a long time, often in an unpleasant manner: [Vn] *The police grilled him for five hours about his part in the robbery.*

grilling *n* [C]: *The minister faced a tough grilling at today's press conference.*

grille (also **grill**) /ɡrɪl/ *n* a protective screen of metal bars or wires: *The bank clerk peered at the customer through/from behind the grille.* ○ *Ensure that the grille is in place while the machinery is in operation.*

grim /ɡrɪm/ *adj* (**-mmer, -mmest**) **1** very serious in appearance; not appearing happy or relaxed: *a grim face/smile* ○ *She looked grim — I could tell something was wrong.* ○ *with a look of grim determination on his face* ○ *grim-faced policemen.* **2** unpleasant and depressing: *grim news* ○ *We face the grim prospect of still higher unemployment.* ○ *a grim little tale of torture and murder.* **3** severe; UNRELENTING: *their grim day-to-day struggle for survival.* **4** (of a place) depressing because plain, uncomfortable, not attractive, etc: *the grim walls of the prison.* **5** [pred] (*infml*) ill: *I feel pretty grim.* **6** [usu pred] (*infml*) very bad; of very low quality: *I've seen her so-called paintings and they're fairly grim, I can tell you!* ▶ **grimly** *adv*: *grimly determined.* **grimness** *n* [U].

grimace /ɡrɪˈmeɪs, ˈɡrɪməs/ *n* an ugly twisted expression on the face, expressing pain, disgust, etc or intended to cause laughter: *make/give a grimace of pain* ○ *She reacted with a grimace.*

▶ **grimace** *v* ~ (**at sb/sth**) to make a grimace or grimaces: [V] *The impact made him grimace.* [Vpr] *She grimaced at the sight of the open wound.* ⇨ note at SMIRK.

grime /ɡraɪm/ *n* [U] dirt, esp in a thick or solid layer on a surface: *the soot and grime of a big manufacturing town* ○ *a face covered with grime and sweat.*

▶ **grimy** /ˈɡraɪmi/ *adj* (**-ier, -iest**) covered with grime: *grimy hands/windows.*

grin /ɡrɪn/ *v* (**-nn-**) ~ (**at sb**); ~ (**with sth**) to smile widely, esp with the mouth open: [Vpr] *grin with delight* ○ *He grinned at me, as if sharing a secret joke.* [V] *grinning faces.* **IDM** **grin and ˈbear it** to endure pain, disappointment, etc without complaining: *It's not a situation I would have chosen but I'll just have to grin and bear it.*

▶ **grin** *n* a wide smile: *a broad/boyish/mischievous/ silly grin* ○ *Take that nasty grin off your face!*

grind /ɡraɪnd/ *v* (*pt, pp* **ground** /ɡraʊnd/) **1(a)** ~ **sth (down/up)** (**to/into sth**) to crush sth into very small pieces or powder between two hard surfaces or using an electrical or a mechanical apparatus: [Vn] *grind coffee beans/corn/pepper* [Vnp] *The elephant grinds (up) its food with/between its powerful teeth.* [Vnpr] *grind sth to dust/to a fine powder.* **(b)** ~ **sth (from sth)** to produce sth by crushing: [Vn, Vnpr] *grind flour (from corn).* **2** (*esp US*) to MINCE(1) meat: [Vn] *ground beef.* **3** ~ **sth (on/with sth)** to polish sth or make sth sharp by rubbing it on or with a rough hard surface: [Vn] *grind a knife/lens* [also Vnpr]. **4** ~ **sth (together)**; ~ **sth in/into sth** to press or rub sth firmly and often noisily: [Vn] *He grinds his teeth when he's asleep.* [Vnpr] *Dirt had become ground into the surface of the table.* ○ *grind one's heel into the fragments* (ie crush them very hard) [Vnp] *grind stones together.* **5** ~ (**away**) to make a harsh noise caused by things scraping together: [V] *grinding brakes* ○ *The old engine ground and shuddered.* [Vp] *machines grinding away in the factory.* **6** to work sth by turning a handle: [Vn] *grind a coffee-mill.* **IDM** **bring sth to a grinding halt** to cause sth to move more and more slowly and then stop completely: *The strike brought industry to a grinding halt.* **grind to a ˈhalt/ˈstandstill; come to a grinding ˈhalt** (of sth that should keep moving) to move more and more slowly and then stop completely: *The traffic ground to a halt.* ○ *There is so much traffic that the city is grinding to a halt.* **have an axe to grind** ⇨ AXE. **PHRV** **ˌgrind aˈway (at sth)** to work or study hard and for a long time: *He's been grinding away at that essay for hours.* **ˌgrind sb ˈdown** to treat sb extremely harshly; to OPPRESS sb: *people ground down by poverty/taxation/tyranny.*

ˌgrind ˈon to continue for a long time, in a way that is boring or annoying: *The speaker ground on, oblivious of his listeners' boredom.* **ˌgrind sth ˈout** (*derog*) to produce sth that is dull continuously over a period: *The jukebox ground out an incessant stream of pop music.* ○ *He grinds out cheap romantic stories at the rate of one a week.*

▶ **grind** *n* [sing] **1** (*infml*) a long dull or tiring task: *the daily grind of office work* ○ *a long uphill grind in a cycle race* ○ *Marking examination papers is a real grind.* **2** the act or an instance of grinding sth.

grinding *adj* [attrib] causing continuous hardship: *grinding poverty.*

grinder /ˈɡraɪndə(r)/ *n* a thing or person that grinds (GRIND 1): *a ˈcoffee-grinder.* See also ORGAN-GRINDER.

grindstone /ˈɡraɪndstəʊn/ *n* a stone that is shaped like a wheel and can be turned, against which one holds knives or other tools to make them sharp. **IDM** **keep one's/sb's nose to the grindstone** ⇨ NOSE¹.

grip /ɡrɪp/ *v* (**-pp-**) **1** to take and keep a firm hold of sth/sb: [Vn] *The child gripped her mother's hand tightly.* [V] *The brakes failed to grip* (ie engage with and stop the wheels) *and the car ran into a wall.* **2** (*fig*) to seize sb's attention or affect sb's feelings greatly: [Vn] *I was completely gripped by the play from start to finish.* ○ *Terror has gripped the city for days.*

▶ **grip** *n* **1** [sing] ~ (**on sb/sth**) **(a)** an act of gripping sb/sth; a firm hold: *Take a grip on the rope.* ○ *I let go/released my grip and he ran away.* ○ *The climber relaxed her grip and fell.* ○ (*fig*) *The film begins well but gradually loses its grip on one's attention.* **(b)** a way of gripping sth: *Try adjusting your grip on the club/racket.* **2** [sing] ~ (**on sb/sth**) **(a)** control or power over sb/sth: *a ruler with a powerful grip on the people/the country.* **(b)** understanding of sth: *She doesn't have much of a grip on the job.* ○ *I couldn't get a grip on what was going on.* **3** [U] the power to grip a surface: *tyres which give*

good grip on the road. **4** [sing] a force that keeps sb under its control: *the icy grip of winter* ○ *people **in** the grip of disease/despair/poverty.* **5** [C] a part that is to be gripped; a handle or a covering for it: *a tool with a wooden/metal grip.* **6** [C] = HAIRGRIP. **7** [C] (*US*) a large strong bag with handles: *a leather grip.* **IDM** **come/get to 'grips with sb** to seize sb and begin to fight them: *She was unable to get to grips with her assailant.* **come/get to 'grips with sth** to begin to deal seriously with a problem, challenge, etc: *The voters want somebody who will come to grips with the country's economic problems.* **get/keep/take a 'grip/'hold on oneself** (*infml*) to gain control of oneself and improve one's behaviour, eg after being afraid, lazy, out of control, etc: *Stop panicking and get a grip on yourself!* **lose one's grip** ⇨ LOSE.
▶ **gripping** *adj* exciting; holding the attention: *a gripping account/film/story.*

gripe¹ /graɪp/ *v* ~ (**about sb/sth**) (*infml derog*) to complain about sb/sth; to GRUMBLE(1): [Vpr] *He keeps griping about having no money.* [also V].
▶ **gripe** *n* (*infml*) a complaint: *We only had a few minor gripes about the holiday.* ○ *He always seems to have a gripe about something.*

gripe² /graɪp/ *v* to feel or cause sudden sharp pain in the stomach or intestines (INTESTINE): [V] *a griping pain in the stomach* ○ *medicine to take when your stomach gripes.*
▶ **the gripes** *n* [pl] (*infml*) sharp pain in the intestines (INTESTINE), etc.
■ **'gripe-water** *n* [U] medicine to cure stomach or intestinal (INTESTINE) pain in babies.

grisly /'grɪzli/ *adj* (**-ier, -iest**) causing horror, esp because related to physically unpleasant things: *the grisly remains of their half-eaten corpses* ○ *a grisly account of the murder.*

grist /grɪst/ *n* **IDM** **grist to the/one's/sb's 'mill** a thing that one can use for one's profit or advantage: *I never refuse odd jobs to supplement my income — it's all grist to the mill.*

gristle /'grɪsl/ *n* [U] tough tissue in meat that is difficult or unpleasant to eat; CARTILAGE in meat: *I can't eat this meat — there's too much gristle.*
▶ **gristly** /-li/ *adj* full of gristle.

grit /grɪt/ *n* [U] **1** very small hard bits of stone, sand, etc: *spread grit on icy roads* ○ *I have some grit/a piece of grit in my shoe.* **2** the courage or determination that makes it possible for sb to endure sth difficult or unpleasant: *Mountaineering in a blizzard needs a lot of grit.*
▶ **grit** *v* (**-tt-**) [Vn] to spread grit on sth, esp roads covered with ice. **IDM** **grit one's 'teeth 1** to hold one's jaws tightly together. **2** to make use of one's courage and determination when faced with a difficult or unpleasant situation: *When things get difficult, you just have to grit your teeth and persevere.*

gritty *adj* (**-ier, -iest**) **1** containing GRIT(1): *gritty vegetables.* **2** having or showing great courage or determination: *a gritty fighter.* **3** showing in a realistic way how unpleasant sth is: *a gritty description of urban violence.*

grits /grɪts/ *n* [pl] corn that has partly crushed, eaten as a breakfast food in the southern USA.

grizzle /'grɪzl/ *v* (*infml derog*) (esp of children) to keep making an unhappy or complaining noise that is similar to crying; to WHINE(2): [V] *The children grizzled throughout the journey.* ○ *Do stop grizzling, Jimmy!*

grizzled /'grɪzld/ *adj* (**a**) (of hair) grey or partly grey: *a grizzled beard.* (**b**) having grey hair.

grizzly /'grɪzli/ (also **grizzly bear**) *n* a large fierce

brown bear found in N America and parts of Russia. ⇨ picture at BEAR¹.

groan /grəʊn/ *v* **1** ~ (**at sb/sth**); ~ (**with sth**) to make a deep sad sound when in pain, or when expressing despair, disapproval or disappointment: [Vpr] *She groaned with pain.* ○ *We all groaned at his terrible jokes.* [V.speech] '*It hurts,' he groaned.* [also V]. **2** (of things) to make a deep sound caused by pressure: [V] *The timbers groaned as the ship ploughed on through the stormy sea.* **3** ~ (**about/over sth**) (*derog*) to complain: [Vpr] *She's always groaning about how much work she has to do.* [V] *Stop moaning and groaning and get on with your work.* **IDM** **,groan 'inwardly** to feel like groaning at sth but remain silent: *She groaned inwardly as she saw the fresh pile of work on her desk.* **PHRV** **'groan beneath/under sth** (*fml*) to suffer because of the pressure of sth: *For years the people here have been groaning under the weight of heavy taxes.* **'groan with sth** to be loaded with sth: *tables groaning with food.*
▶ **groan** *n* a deep sound made when in pain or when expressing despair, disapproval or disappointment: *the groans of injured men* ○ *give a groan of dismay* ○ (*fig*) *The chair gave a distinct groan as he sat down in it.*

grocer /'grəʊsə(r)/ *n* a shopkeeper who sells food in packets, tins or bottles and general small household goods: *the local grocer* ○ *Please go to the grocer's* (ie the grocer's shop) *and get me some sugar.*
▶ **groceries** *n* [pl] things sold by a grocer.
grocery *n* **1** [U] a grocer's trade: *the grocery business.* **2** [C] (*esp US*) a grocer's shop.

grog /grɒg/ *n* [U] (*infml*) **1** a drink of spirits, originally RUM¹, mixed with water and drunk esp by sailors. **2** (*Austral*) any alcoholic drink, esp beer.

groggy /'grɒgi/ *adj* weak and DIZZY(1) because of illness, shock, lack of sleep, etc: *The attack of flu left her feeling very groggy.* ○ *He's still groggy from the anaesthetic.*

groin /grɔɪn/ *n* (*anatomy*) the part of the body where the tops of the legs meet, containing the sexual organs: *She kicked her attacker in the groin.* ⇨ picture at HUMAN.

groom /gru:m/ *n* **1** a person who is employed to look after horses, eg by brushing and cleaning them. **2** = BRIDEGROOM.
▶ **groom** *v* **1(a)** [Vn] to look after or clean a horse or horses. (**b**) (of an animal) to clean the fur and skin of another or itself: [Vn] *a female ape grooming her mate* [also V]. **2** ~ **sb** (**for/as sth**) to select, prepare and train a young person for a particular career, etc: [Vnpr] *She was groomed for stardom by her ambitious parents.* [Vn-n] *He had been groomed as a future manager.* [also Vn]. **groomed** *adj* (usu following an *adv*) (of a person) caring for one's appearance in the way specified: *She is always perfectly groomed.*

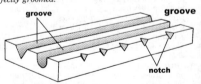

groove   groove

notch

groove /gru:v/ *n* **1** a long narrow cut or depression in the surface of hard material: *a groove for a sliding door.* ⇨ picture. **2** a track on a record into which the STYLUS fits when the record is played. **IDM** **get into/be stuck in a 'groove** to become/be fixed in a particular way of life, habit, routine, etc.
▶ **grooved** *adj* having a groove or grooves.

groovy /'gru:vi/ *adj* (*dated sl*) excellent or attractive, esp because fashionable or modern.

grope /grəʊp/ v **1** ~ (**about/around**) (**for sth**) (**a**) to try to find sth one cannot see by feeling with the hands: [Vp] *grope about in the dark* [Vpr] *grope for the door-handle/light-switch* ○ *He groped in his pocket for the keys.* [also V]. (**b**) to search for a solution to sth in one's mind, usu with difficulty: [V, Vpr] *a tricky question which left him groping (for an answer)* [also Vp]. **2** [V, Vn] (*infml derog*) to touch or FONDLE sb sexually, esp in a rough or clumsy way.
PHRV ˌgrope (**one's way**) aˈcross, aˈlong, ˈpast, etc (**sth**) to make one's way by trying to touch things as one moves, when it is difficult or impossible to see where one is going: *grope one's way along a darkened corridor.*

gross¹ /grəʊs/ n (*pl* unchanged) (*esp commerce*) a group of 144 things: *two gross of apples* ○ *sell sth by the gross.*

gross² /grəʊs/ adj (**-er, -est**) **1** very fat and ugly: *a gross person* ○ *He's not just fat, he's positively gross!* **2** not polite or refined; COARSE(2): *gross behaviour/language/manners* ○ *indulging in the grosser pleasures.* **3** [usu attrib] (*esp law fml*) very clear and very bad; FLAGRANT: *gross negligence/indecency* ○ *a gross error/injustice.* **4** [attrib] total; whole: *gross weight/profit* ○ *sb's gross income* (ie before tax, etc). Compare NET²1.
▶ **gross** v to make sth as a total amount, esp of money: [Vn] *Her last movie grossed* (ie earned) *two million dollars.*
grossly adv **1** extremely: *grossly fat/extravagant/unfair* ○ *Press reports have been grossly exaggerated.* **2** in a gross²(2) way: *behave grossly.*
grossness n [U]: *grossness of speech or conduct.*
■ ˌgross ˌnational ˈproduct n [sing] (*abbr* GNP) the annual total value of goods produced, and services provided, in a country.

grotesque /grəʊˈtesk/ adj **1** ugly or absurd in an offensive way: *a grotesque building* ○ *a grotesque distortion of the truth* ○ *It's grotesque to expect a person of her experience to work for so little money.* ○ *the grotesque sight of an old man trying to flirt with a young girl.* **2** looking strange, ugly or UNNATURAL(1) so as to cause fear or laughter: *tribal dancers wearing grotesque masks.*
▶ **grotesque** n **1** [C] a grotesque person or thing. **2** the grotesque [sing] a style of art using grotesque figures and designs.
grotesquely adv.

grotto /ˈɡrɒtəʊ/ n (*pl* **-oes** or **-os**) a cave, esp one made artificially, eg in a garden.

grotty /ˈɡrɒti/ adj (**-ier, -iest**) (*Brit infml*) unpleasant: *living in a grotty part of town* ○ *I feel pretty grotty* (ie unwell).

grouchy /ˈɡraʊtʃi/ adj (*infml*) bad-tempered or complaining: *in a grouchy mood.*

ground¹ /graʊnd/ n **1** the ground [sing] the solid surface of the earth: *sit on the ground* ○ *He slipped off the ladder and fell to the ground.* ○ *The aircraft didn't have enough power to get off the ground* (ie take off). ○ *at ground level.* **2** [U] (**a**) an area or a distance on the earth's surface; land: *have more ground than one's next-door neighbour* ○ *buy up some ground for building on* ○ *The land near the border is disputed ground.* ○ *measure the ground between two points.* (**b**) soil; earth: *solid/marshy/stony ground.* ▷ note at EARTH. **3** (esp in compounds) (**a**) [C] a piece of land, often with associated buildings, used for a particular purpose: *a* ˈpicnic/ˈcricket/ˈsports/recreˈation ground ○ *a* paˈrade-ground ○ *a* ˈplayground ○ *The cheers of the fans echoed round the ground as the teams appeared.* See also DUMPING GROUND. (**b**) grounds [pl] a large area of land or sea used for the specified purpose: ˈfishing/ˈhunting grounds. **4** grounds [pl] land or gardens round a building, often enclosed with walls, hedges or fences: *The house has extensive grounds.* ○ *the school grounds.* **5** [U] an area of interest, discussion, knowledge, ex-

perience, etc: *They managed to cover quite a lot of ground in a short programme.* ○ *Let's not go over the same ground again.* ○ *trying to find some common ground between the two sides* ○ *You're on dangerous ground* (ie saying sth likely to cause anger) *when you criticize his daughter.* ○ *I thought I'd be on safe ground* (ie talking about a suitable subject) *discussing his book with him.* **6** [C esp pl] ~ (**for sth / doing sth / to do sth**) a reason or justification (JUSTIFY) for saying, doing or believing sth: *You have no grounds for complaint.* ○ *If you continue to behave like this you will give them grounds for dismissing you.* ○ *His continued absence gives ground for concern.* ○ *Desertion is a ground* (ie a legally sufficient reason) *for divorce.* ○ *They had no grounds to arrest him.* ○ *I had to retire on medical grounds/on the grounds of ill health* (ie because I was ill). ○ *Her claim was disallowed on the grounds that she had not paid her premium.* ○ *On what grounds do you make that accusation?* ▷ note at REASON¹. **7** [C] a surface on which a design is painted, printed, cut, etc; a background: *a design of pink roses on a white ground.* **8** [U] the bottom of the sea: *The ship touched ground a few yards from the shore.* **9** grounds [pl] small pieces of solid matter that sink to the bottom of a liquid, esp coffee. **IDM** above ground above the surface of the earth. be on firm ground ▷ FIRM¹. below ground beneath the surface of the earth: *Their missile silos are below ground.* break fresh/new ˈground to make a new discovery or do sth that has not been done before: *break new ground in the field of electronics.* cut the ground from under sb's ˈfeet to spoil sb's plan, argument, defence, etc by doing or saying sth that makes it difficult for them to proceed or continue with it. flog oneself/sth to death/into the ground ▷ FLOG. gain ground ▷ GAIN². gain / make up ˈground (on sb/sth) to get gradually closer to sb/sth going in the same direction as oneself: *The police car was gaining ground on the robbers.* ○ *How can we make up ground on our competitors?* get (sth) off the ˈground to start or start sth happening or functioning successfully: *get a company off the ground* ○ *Without more money the film is unlikely to get off the ground.* give/lose ˈground (to sb/sth) **1** to RETREAT(1a). **2** to get gradually less far ahead of sb/sth going in the same direction: *The leader is losing ground as the rest of the runners accelerate.* ○ *The gas lamp gradually lost ground to* (ie was replaced by) *electric lighting.* go/run to earth/ground ▷ EARTH. have/keep a/one's ear to the ground ▷ EAR¹. have one's/both feet on the ground ▷ FOOT¹. hold/keep/stand one's ˈground to maintain one's position, claim, argument, etc despite opposition or pressure: *He held his ground in the face of close questioning.* ○ *Despite being pushed, he stood his ground.* keep both/one's feet on the ground ▷ FOOT¹. on the ˈground amongst ordinary people: *There's a lot of support for our policies on the ground.* prepare the ground ▷ PREPARE. run, drive, etc sb/oneself/sth into the ˈground (*infml*) to EXHAUST²(1) oneself/sb/sth; to wear oneself/sb/sth out (WEAR²): *By working 13 hours a day she is running herself into the ground.* ○ *We couldn't afford a new car, so we had to drive the old one into the ground.* shift one's ground ▷ SHIFT¹. suit sb down to the ground ▷ SUIT². thick/thin on the ˈground common or frequent/not common or frequent. to the ˈground (of destroying or being destroyed) completely: *The building was burned to the ground.*
■ ˈground control n [U] the staff, systems or equipment at an airport, etc concerned with making sure that aircraft or spacecraft take off or land safely.
ˈground crew n [CGp] the people at an airport who are responsible for looking after aircraft while they are on the ground.

G

,**ground** '**floor** n the floor of a building at ground level, not upstairs: *at ground-floor level* ○ *a ,ground-floor 'office.* ⇨ note at FLOOR¹. **IDM** **be/get in on the ground** '**floor** (*infml*) to join an enterprise or become involved in a project at its beginning.

'**ground-plan** n a plan of a building at ground level.

'**ground-rent** n [U, C] (in Britain) rent paid by the owner of a flat to the owner of the land on which it is built.

'**ground rule** n **1** (usu pl) a basic principle: *The new code of conduct lays down the ground rules for management-union relations.* **2** (*US*) (in baseball) a rule adapted for a particular playing field.

'**ground staff** n [CGp] **1** the people at a sports ground whose job is to maintain the condition of the grass, equipment, etc. **2** = GROUND CREW.

'**ground swell** n (usu *sing*) ~ (**of sth**) the rapid development of a feeling or an opinion in society: *Opinion polls indicate a ground swell of support for the Socialists.*

ground² /graʊnd/ v **1** ~ (**sth**) (**in/on sth**) (of a ship) to touch the sea bottom; to cause a ship to do this: [Vnpr] *Our ship was grounded in shallow water/on a sandbank.* [also V, Vpr, Vn]. **2** (esp passive) to cause or force an aircraft to stay on the ground: [Vn] *All aircraft at London Airport were grounded by fog today.* **3** [Vn] (*esp US*) = EARTH v. **4** [Vn] (*US*) to punish older children by not allowing them out of the house for a period of time. **PHRV** '**ground sb in sth** (esp passive) to give sb good teaching or basic training in sth: *I was well grounded in mathematics at school.* '**ground sth on sth** (esp passive) to base beliefs, etc on sth: *political philosophy grounded on personal experience.*

▶ **grounding** n [sing] ~ (**in sth**) the teaching of the basic elements of a subject: *get a thorough grounding in grammar.*

ground³ pt, pp of GRIND: ,*ground 'rice/'almonds* (ie reduced to a fine powder) ○ (*US*) *ground beef.*

groundless /'graʊndləs/ adj not based on any good reason: *groundless anxiety/rumours/allegations* ○ *Our fears proved groundless.* ▶ **groundlessly** adv.

groundnut /'graʊndnʌt/ n = PEANUT.

groundsel /'graʊnsl/ n [U] a wild plant with yellow flowers, sometimes used as food for animals and birds.

groundsheet /'graʊndʃiːt/ n a WATERPROOF sheet for spreading on the ground, eg in a tent.

groundsman /'graʊndzmən/ n a person whose job is to maintain a sports ground.

groundwork /'graʊndwɜːk/ n [U] ~ (**for sth**) work that provides the basis for sth: *Officials are **laying the groundwork** for a summit conference of world leaders.* Compare SPADEWORK.

group /gruːp/ n [CGp] **1** a number of people or things gathered, placed or acting together, or naturally associated: *a group of girls/trees/houses* ○ *A group of us are going to the cinema this evening.* ○ *people standing down in groups* ○ *an 'age group* (ie people of the same age or similar age) ○ *Our di'scussion group is/are meeting this week.* ○ *a 'drama group* (ie a small club for acting together) ○ *the Germanic group of languages* ○ *a group ac'tivity* (ie done by people as a group). See also BLOOD GROUP. **2** a set of business companies under joint control: *a 'newspaper group* ○ *the 'Burton Group* ○ *the group sales director.* **3** a set of musicians performing pop music together: *play in/form a (pop) group.*

▶ **group** v ~ (**sb/sth**) (**round/around sb/sth**); ~ (**sb/sth**) (**together**) to gather or form sb/sth into a group or groups: [Vpr] *The police grouped round the demonstrators.* [Vp] *Group together in fours!* [Vnp] *The teachers grouped the pupils together.* [also V, Vn, Vnpr].

groupie /'gruːpi/ n (*infml*) a person, esp a young girl, who follows around a pop group, a particular

singer or some other famous person, and tries to meet them.

grouping n a set of people acting together with a common interest or purpose, often within a larger organization: *various anti-leadership groupings within the party.*

■ ,**group** '**captain** n an officer in the British air force. ⇨ App 6.

,**group** '**practice** n a set of doctors who work together in the same premises.

,**group** '**therapy** n [U] a form of treatment in which people with similar personal problems meet together to discuss them.

grouse¹ /graʊs/ n (*pl* unchanged) (**a**) [C] a bird with a fat body and feathers on its legs, which is shot for sport and food: *grouse shooting* ○ *grouse moors.* (**b**) [U] its flesh as food: *roast grouse.*

grouse² /graʊs/ v ~ (**about sb/sth**) (*infml usu derog*) to complain regularly, esp about unimportant things; to GRUMBLE(1): [Vpr] *He's always grousing about the workload.* [also V].

▶ **grouse** n a complaint: *If you've got any grouses, you'd better tell me about them.*

grout /graʊt/ n [U] (*techn*) a substance like MORTAR¹ for filling the gaps between tiles (TILE 1) on walls, etc, esp indoors.

▶ **grout** v [Vn] to fill sth with grout. **grouting** n [U].

grove /grəʊv/ n a group of trees; a small wood: *an olive grove.*

grovel /'grɒvl/ v (**-ll-**; *US* **-l-**) ~ (**to sb**) (**for sth**) (*derog*) to speak to sb or behave in a very HUMBLE(1) manner in order to gain favour or be forgiven for sth: [Vpr] *I had to grovel to my bank manager for a loan.* [also V]. **PHRV** ,**grovel a'bout/a'round** to move about on one's hands and knees; to crawl about: *I was grovelling around under the table looking for a pin.*

▶ **grovelling** /'grɒvəlɪŋ/ adj excessively polite and HUMBLE: *a grovelling letter of apology.*

grow /grəʊ/ v (*pt* **grew** /gruː/; *pp* **grown** /grəʊn/) **1** to increase in size or quantity; to become greater: [V-adj] *How tall you've grown!* [V] *A growing child needs plenty of sleep.* ○ *She wants to let her hair grow* (ie not have it cut short). ○ *You must invest if you want your business to grow.* **2(a)** ~ (**from sth**) (**into sth**) to develop, esp into a mature or an adult form: [V] *Rice does not grow in cold climates.* [Vpr] *Plants grow from seeds.* ○ *Tadpoles grow into frogs.* (**b**) ~ **in sth** to gain a larger amount of a particular quality or feeling: [Vpr] *grow in stature/confidence/wisdom.* **3** to become over a period of time: [V-adj] *grow old(er)/rich(er)/small(er)/weak(er)* ○ *It began to grow dark.* ○ *I grew tired of waiting, and left.* **4** ~ **sth** (**from sth**) to cause or allow sth to grow: [Vn] *grow roses* ○ *grow a beard* [Vnpr] *grow onions from seed.* See also HOME-GROWN. **5** to reach the point or stage at which one does the specified thing: [V.to inf] *He grew increasingly to rely on her.* ○ *I became fonder of her as I grew to know her better.* **IDM** (**not**) **grow on** '**trees** (not) to exist in large quantities and be very easy to obtain: *You spend too much — money doesn't grow on trees, you know.* **let the grass grow under one's feet** ⇨ GRASS¹. **PHRV** ,**grow a'part (from sb**) (no passive) to stop having a close relationship with sb over a period of time: *grow apart from old schoolfriends.* ,**grow a'way from sb** (no passive) gradually to have a less close, less easy relationship with sb: *When she left school she started to grow away from her mother.* **grow into sth** (no passive) **1** to become sth gradually, as times passes: *She is growing into a beautiful young woman.* ○ *He has grown into a dreadful old bore.* **2** to become big enough to fit an item of clothing: *The coat's too big for him now, but he'll grow 'into it.* **3** to become accustomed to a new job, role or activity, and capable of doing it well: *She is a good actress, but she* *still needs time to grow into the part she is playing.* **'grow on sb** (no passive) to become attractive or pleasant to sb after not being so at first: *His music grows on you, I find.* **,grow 'out of sth 1** to become too big to wear sth: *grow out of one's clothes.* **2** to become too old for sth and stop doing it: *grow out of children's games.* **3** (no passive) to have sth as a source: *The idea for the book grew out of a brief visit to India some years ago.* **,grow 'up 1** (of people or animals) to reach the stage of full development; to become adult or mature: *She's growing up fast.* ○ *Oh, grow up* (ie Behave in a more mature way)*!* Compare GROWN UP. **2** to develop: *A close friendship gradually grew up between them.*

▶ **grower** *n* **1** a person who grows things, esp for sale: *'rose growers* ○ *I buy wine from a local grower.* **2** a plant that grows in a specified way: *a quick grower.*

growing *adj* increasing: *his growing indifference to her* ○ *a growing problem* ○ *a club with a growing membership.* **'growing pains** *n* [pl] **1** pains in the limbs of young children, sometimes thought to be caused by rapid growth. **2** problems or difficulties that occur while a new enterprise is developing but are not likely to last: *The business is still suffering from growing pains.*

growl /graʊl/ *v* **1** ~ (**at sb/sth**) (esp of animals) to make a low threatening sound, usu showing anger: [V, Vpr] *The dog growled (at the intruder).* [Vpr] (*fig*) *He's in a really bad mood today, growling at* (ie speaking angrily to) *everyone.* **2** ~ (**out**) to say sth in a low threatening voice: [V.speech] *'Keep out of this!' he growled.* [Vn, Vnp] *He growled (out) a warning.*

▶ **growl** *n* a low threatening sound or remark: *a distant growl of thunder.*

grown /grəʊn/ *adj* [attrib] adult; mature: *a grown man* ○ *a full-grown/fully grown elephant.* See also GROW 2, HOME-GROWN.

■ **grown 'up** *adj* adult; mature: *What do you want to be when you're grown up?* ○ *She has a ,grown-up 'son.* ○ *Try to behave in a more grown-up way.* **grown-up** /¹grəʊn ʌp/ *n* an adult person, not a child: *If you're good you can eat with the grown-ups.*

growth /grəʊθ/ *n* **1** [U] (**a**) the process of growing; development: *the growth of plants/hair/inflation/the economy* ○ *Lack of water will stunt the plant's growth.* ○ *a growth area/industry* (ie one that is developing faster than most others). (**b**) ~ (**in/of sth**) an increase: *the recent growth in/of violent crime.* **2** [U] an increase in economic activity, profit, etc: *The government has decided to go for growth* (ie pursue a policy of increased production, spending, etc). ○ *Japan's growth rate.* **3** [sing] a thing that grows or has grown: *a thick growth of weeds* ○ *a week's growth of beard.* **4** [C] (**a**) an abnormal or diseased formation in the body, eg a TUMOUR or CANCER(1): *a malignant growth.* (**b**) an abnormal formation on a plant.

grub¹ /grʌb/ *n* **1** [C] the LARVA of an insect. **2** [U] (*infml*) food: *Grub's up* (ie The meal is ready)*!*

grub² /grʌb/ *v* (**-bb-**) **1** ~ around/about (**for sth**) (esp in the continuous tenses) to search for sth, esp by digging or moving things around: [Vpr] *a dog grubbing for a bone* [Vp] *pigs grubbing around/ about in the dirt* ○ *He found what he wanted by grubbing around in the library.* **2** (*US sl*) to borrow sth that one is unlikely to return or replace: [Vn] *Can I grub a cigarette?* **PHRV** **,grub sth 'up/'out** dig sth up: *birds grubbing up worms* ○ *grub out a dead tree.*

grubby /¹grʌbi/ *adj* (**-ier, -iest**) **1** dirty: *grubby hands/clothes.* **2** causing moral disapproval; SORDID (2): *a grubby affair/scandal.* ▶ **grubbiness** *n* [U].

grudge /grʌdʒ/ *v* to do or give sth very unwillingly: [Vn] *He grudges every penny he has to spend.* [V.ing] *I grudge paying so much for such inferior goods.* [V.n ing] *He grudges her earning more than he*

does. [Vnn] *I don't grudge him his success* (ie I admit he deserves it).

▶ **grudge** *n* ~ (**against sb**) a feeling of intense dislike, ill will, envy or resentment (RESENT) towards sb, esp because of sth bad that they have done to one: *I bear him no grudge.* ○ *He has a grudge against me.* ○ *He has harboured/nursed a grudge against me for years.* ○ *a grudge match* (ie between two players or teams, one of which has a grudge against the other).

grudging *adj* unwilling; RELUCTANT: *a grudging admission* ○ *grudging praise.* **grudgingly** *adv*: *She grudgingly conceded that I was right.*

gruel /¹gruːəl/ *n* [U] a simple dish made of OATS, etc boiled in milk or water.

gruelling (*US* **grueling**) /¹gruːəlɪŋ/ *adj* difficult, tiring and involving great effort over a period: *a gruelling climb/race/trial/ordeal* ○ *I've had a gruelling day.*

gruesome /¹gruːsəm/ *adj* physically very unpleasant and filling one with horror or disgust: *gruesome pictures of dead bodies* ○ *a gruesome murder.* ▶ **gruesomely** *adv*.

gruff /grʌf/ *adj* (of a person's voice or behaviour) not friendly and suggesting the person is annoyed or IMPATIENT(1b): *a gruff reply* ○ *Beneath his gruff exterior he's really very kind-hearted.* ▶ **gruffly** *adv*.

grumble /¹grʌmbl/ *v* **1** ~ (**at/to sb**) (**about/at/over sth**) to complain or protest in a bad-tempered way, usu not loudly: [V] *Stop grumbling! You don't have anything to complain about.* ○ *'How are you feeling?' 'Oh, I can't/mustn't grumble, you know.'* [Vpr] *Why grumble at me about your own stupid mistakes?* [V.speech] *'Raining again,' she grumbled.* **2** to make a deep continuous sound; to RUMBLE¹(1): [V] *thunder grumbling in the distance* ○ *the sound of one's stomach grumbling.*

▶ **grumble** *n* **1** ~ (**about/at/over sth**) a complaint or protest: *My main grumble is about the lack of privacy.* **2** a deep continuous sound; a RUMBLE¹(1): *a distant grumble of thunder.*

grumbler /¹grʌmblə(r)/ *n*: *Mr White's a dreadful grumbler.*

grump /grʌmp/ *n* (*esp US*) a bad-tempered person.

grumpy /¹grʌmpi/ *adj* (**-ier, -iest**) (*infml*) bad-tempered. ▶ **grumpily** /-ɪli/ *adv*.

grunt /grʌnt/ *v* **1** [V] (**a**) (of animals, esp pigs) to make a short low rough sound from deep in the throat. (**b**) (of people) to make a similar sound expressing pain, annoyance, disapproval or lack of interest, or when making a physical effort: *He grunted as the bullet hit him.* ○ *I asked him what he thought, but he merely grunted and said nothing.* ○ *She grunted with the effort of hitting each shot.* **2** to say sth with a grunt: [Vn] *She grunted some incomprehensible reply.* [also V.speech].

▶ **grunt** *n* a short low rough sound made by an animal or a person: *give a grunt of approval/pain/ pleasure.*

gryphon /¹grɪfən/ *n* = GRIFFIN.

G-string (also **gee-string**) /¹dʒiː strɪŋ/ *n* a narrow piece of cloth, worn esp by female dancers, that covers the sexual organs and is held up by a string round the waist.

GT /¹dʒiː ¹tiː/ *abbr* a very powerful fast car (Italian *gran turismo*): *a sporting GT model* ○ *a Renault 5 Turbo GT.*

Gt *abbr* Great: *Gt Britain* ○ *Gt Yarmouth.*

guano /¹gwɑːnəʊ/ *n* [U] waste matter passed from the bodies of sea birds, used to make soil richer for growing crops, etc.

guarantee¹ /ˌgærən¹tiː/ *n* **1** a promise, usu in writing, that sth will be done or that sth is of a specified quality: *give a guarantee of good behaviour* ○ *He gave me a guarantee that it would never happen again.* ○

G

The watch comes with a year's guarantee (ie a promise to repair it free within a year of its being bought). ○ *It's still **under guarantee*** (ie The guarantee is still valid), *so the manufacturer will repair it.* ○ *provide a 5-year guarantee against rust* ○ *They are demanding certain guarantees before signing the treaty.* Compare SECURITY. **2** an item of value offered as security for carrying out the conditions in a guarantee, esp as part of a legal agreement: *We had to offer our house as a guarantee when getting the loan.* See also SECURITY 3. **3** ~ (**of sth/that...**) (*infml*) a thing that makes sth certain to happen or be the case: *Blue skies are not a guarantee of continuing fine weather.* ○ *There's no guarantee (that) she'll come* (ie She may not come).

guarantee² /ˌgærən'tiː/ *v* **1** to promise sth with certainty: [Vn] *We cannot guarantee the punctual arrival of buses in foggy weather.* [V.that] *The film's excellent — I guarantee you'll enjoy it.* [V.to inf] *We guarantee to deliver within a week.* [Vnn] *We guarantee you delivery within a week.* [Vn-adj] *This food is guaranteed free of artificial colouring.* **2** to make sth certain to happen or be the case: [Vn] *Her selection for the team should guarantee an exciting game.* ○ *Your qualifications might help you get a job but you can't guarantee that.* [also V.that]. **3** ~ sth (**against sth**) to agree to pay the cost of repairs resulting from a fault in an article which has been bought or in work done: [Vnpr] *The product is guaranteed for one year against mechanical failure or faulty workmanship.* [also Vn]. **4** to agree to be legally responsible for sth/doing sth: [Vn, V.to inf] *guarantee (to pay) sb's debts/the payment of sb's debts* [V.that] *guarantee that the debts will be paid.* **IDM** **be guaranteed to do sth** (*infml ironic*) to be certain to happen, be the case or have sth as a result: *It's guaranteed to rain just when you want to go out.* ○ *This news is not exactly guaranteed to please him.*

guarantor /ˌgærən'tɔː(r)/ *n* (*fml or law*) a person or an organization that guarantees (GUARANTEE² 3,4) sth, eg an agreement: *The United Nations will act as guarantor of the peace settlement* (ie make sure that it is observed).

guard¹ /gɑːd/ *n* **1** [U] the action or duty of watching out for attack, danger or surprise or of protecting sth/sb: *a soldier/sentry **on guard*** (ie at his post, on duty) ○ *The escaped prisoner was brought back **under close guard*** (ie closely guarded). ○ *Policemen were **keeping guard** outside the building.* ○ *guard duty* ○ *a guard dog* (ie one kept to guard a building or a place). **2** [U] a position of being ready to defend oneself, eg in boxing or fencing (FENCE² 1): *drop/keep up one's guard* ○ (*fig*) *In spite of the awkward questions the minister never let his guard fall for a moment.* **3** [C] (**a**) a person, esp a soldier or police officer, who watches over sb or sth: *The prisoner slipped past the guards on the gate and escaped.* ○ *a se'curity guard* (ie one responsible for protecting a place against entry by eg criminals) ○ *'border guards.* (**b**) (*esp US*) (*Brit* **warder**) a person who watches over prisoners in a prison. **4**(**a**) the guard [CGp] a group of soldiers who protect a building or a place: *the changing of the guard* (ie the replacing of one such group by another, eg at Buckingham Palace) ○ *The guard are/is being inspected today.* See also NATIONAL GUARD, THE OLD GUARD. (**b**) [CGp] a group of soldiers with the duty of accompanying, protecting or honouring sb: *The president always travels with an armed guard.* ○ *On her arrival the queen inspected the guard of honour.* **5** the Guards [pl] (in Britain and some other countries) regiments whose original duty was to protect the king or queen: *the ˌRoyal 'Horse Guards* ○ *The ˌScots/ˌIrish/ˌWelsh 'Guards* ○ *a Guards officer.* **6** [C] (*Brit*) a person who is in charge of a railway train and travels with it, but is not the driver. **7** [C] (often in

compounds) an object or a piece of apparatus, eg part of a machine, designed to prevent injury or loss: *Ensure the guard is in place before operating the machine.* ⇨ picture at SWORD. See also FIRE-GUARD. **IDM** **mount guard** ⇨ MOUNT². **on 'guard/off (one's) 'guard** prepared/not prepared for an attack, a surprise or a mistake: *With journalists, you always have to be on your guard against saying the wrong thing.* ○ *put sb on their guard* ○ *The lawyer's apparently innocent question caught the witness off (his) guard.* **stand 'guard (over sb/sth)** to act as a guard: *Four soldiers stood guard over the coffin.*
■ **'guard-rail** *n* a protective rail, eg to prevent people falling off a staircase or to separate them from dangerous traffic.
'guard's van (*Brit*) (*US* **caboose**) *n* the carriage in which the guard on a train travels.

guard² /gɑːd/ *v* [Vn] (**a**) to be near sb/sth in order to keep them safe, eg from danger or from being stolen; to protect sb/sth: *soldiers guarding the president* ○ *A dragon guarded the treasure.* ○ (*fig*) *a closely/ jealously guarded secret.* (**b**) to watch over sb and prevent them from escaping: *the police officers guarding the prisoners.* **PHRV** **'guard against sth/doing sth** to be careful and cautious in order to prevent sth: *guard against disease* ○ *The government must guard against introducing measures which will increase inflation.*
▶ **guarded** *adj* (of remarks, etc) cautious: *a guarded reply* ○ *You should be more guarded in what you say to reporters.* **guardedly** *adv*.

guardhouse /'gɑːdhaʊs/ *n* a building for soldiers on guard or for keeping military prisoners in.

guardian /'gɑːdiən/ *n* **1** a person who guards or protects sth: *The police are guardians of law and order.* ○ *a self-appointed guardian of public morality.* **2** a person who looks after and is legally responsible for sb unable to manage their own affairs, esp a child whose parents have died.
▶ **guardianship** *n* [U] the position or office of a guardian.
■ **ˌguardian 'angel** *n* **1** a person who protects and guides sb. **2** a spirit(2) that is believed to protect and guide a person or place.

guardroom /'gɑːdruːm, -rʊm/ *n* a room for soldiers on guard or for keeping military prisoners in.

guardsman /'gɑːdzmən/ *n* (*pl* **-men** /-mən/) a soldier in the Guards (GUARD¹ 5).

guava /'gwɑːvə/ *n* the fruit of a tropical American tree, with a light yellow skin and pink or white edible flesh.

gubernatorial /ˌguːbənə'tɔːriəl/ *adj* (*fml*) (esp in the USA) of or for the office of a state governor: *gubernatorial elections.*

gudgeon /'gʌdʒən/ *n* (*pl* unchanged) a small European fish found in rivers, lakes, etc. Gudgeon are often used as BAIT(1) to catch other fish.

guerrilla (also **guerilla**) /gə'rɪlə, ge'rɪlə/ *n* a person who is not a member of a regular army but who is engaged in fighting in small secret groups: *urban guerrillas* (ie those who fight in towns only) ○ *guerrilla war/warfare* (ie fought on one side or both sides by guerrillas) ○ *a guerrilla group/movement/ leader.*

guess /ges/ *v* **1**(**a**) ~ (**at sth**) to give an answer, form an opinion or make a statement about sth without calculating or measuring and without definite knowledge: [V] *You don't know. You're just guessing!* [Vadv] *guess right/wrong* [Vpr] *We can only guess at the murderer's real motives.* [Vn, V.wh, V.that] *'Can you guess her age/guess how old she is?' 'I'd guess that she's about thirty.'* (**b**) to find the truth or the correct answer in this way: [Vn] *She guessed the answer straight away.* ○ *The next King of France after Louis XIV was — you've guessed it — Louis XV.* [V.wh] *I knew by her smile* *that she had guessed what I was thinking.* ○ *You'll never guess how they got in!* [also V.*that*]. See also SECOND-GUESS. **2** (*infml esp US*) (no passive) to suppose sth; to consider sth likely: [V.*that*] *I guess you're feeling tired after your journey.* [Vadv] *'Will you be there?' 'I guess so.'* **3** (used in the imperative to show that one is about to say sth surprising or exciting): [V.*wh*] *Guess who I've just seen — David Bowie!* ○ *Guess what! I've just won £5 000!* **IDM** **keep sb ˈguessing** (*infml*) to keep sb uncertain about one's plans, etc.

▶ **guess** *n* ~ **(at sth)**; ~ **(that…)** an opinion formed by guessing: *have/make a guess (at sth)* ○ *If I might hazard a guess, I'd say she was about thirty.* ○ *My guess is that it will rain soon.* ○ *Your guess is as good as mine* (ie I do not know). ○ *'What's for supper?' 'I'll give you three guesses* (ie The answer is fairly obvious and you should guess it easily)*.'* See also EDUCATED GUESS. **IDM** **ˈanybody's guess** a fact or situation that no one can be sure about: *What will happen next is anybody's guess.* **at a ˈguess** making a guess: *'How old is she?' 'At a guess, about thirty.'*

guesstimate /ˈgestɪmət/ *n* (*infml*) an estimate made by combining guessing with reasoning.

guesswork /ˈgeswɜːk/ *n* [U] the process of guessing or the results got by guessing: *We got the right answer but only by pure guesswork.*

guest /gest/ *n* **1** a person who is invited to visit one's house or is being entertained at one's expense: *We are expecting guests this weekend.* ○ *He invited her to be his guest for an evening at the theatre.* ○ *an uninvited guest* ○ *the guest of honour* (ie the most important guest) *at a banquet.* **2** a person staying at a hotel or similar lodging: *This hotel has accommodation for 500 guests.* ○ *a paying guest* (ie one living in a private house, but paying as if in a hotel). **3** a visiting performer taking part in an entertainment: *tonight's guests on Terry Wogan's chat show* ○ *a guest artist/star/singer/conductor* ○ *make a guest appearance on a TV show.* **4** a person specially invited to visit a place, take part in a conference, etc: *The scientists are visiting this country as guests of the government.* ○ *a guest speaker.* **IDM** **be my ˈguest** (*infml*) (used as a response to a request) please do: *'May I see the newspaper?' 'Be my guest!'*

▶ **guest** *v* [V, Vpr] ~ **(on sth)** (*infml*) to appear as a guest(3) on a television or radio programme.

■ **ˈguest beer** *n* [U, C] (*Brit*) a beer which is not usu available in a particular pub, but which is served there for a limited period, often at a specially reduced price.

ˈguest-house *n* a small hotel.

ˈguest-night *n* an evening on which members of a club or other society may invite guests.

ˈguest-room *n* a bedroom kept for the use of guests.

ˈguest worker *n* a person who comes to live in a foreign country in order to work there: *Turkish guest workers in Germany.*

guff /gʌf/ *n* [U] (*infml*) worthless talk or ideas; nonsense: *politicians talking a lot of guff.*

guffaw /gəˈfɔː/ *v* [V, V.speech] to give a noisy laugh. ▶ **guffaw** *n*: *let out a loud guffaw* ○ *burst into guffaws.*

guidance /ˈgaɪdns/ *n* [U] **1** help or advice given to sb, eg a child or young person, esp by sb in authority: *moral/spiritual/vocational guidance.* See also MARRIAGE GUIDANCE. **2** the controlling of the direction of a moving object, eg by electronic means: *a missile guidance system.*

guide¹ /gaɪd/ *n* **1** a person who shows others the way, esp a person employed to point out interesting sights on a journey or visit: *I know the place well, so let me be your guide.* ○ *The tour guide gave a running commentary from the front of the bus.* ○ *We hired a guide to show us the way across the mountains.* **2** a

thing that helps sb, eg to form an opinion, make a decision or calculate sth: *Instinct is not always a good guide.* ○ *The essay doesn't need to be very long; as a rough guide, not more than three pages.* **3** a person who directs or influences sb's behaviour or gives sb advice: *His elder sister had been his guide, counsellor and friend.* **4** ~ **(to sth)** **(a)** (also **ˈguide-book**) a book for travellers or tourists, giving information about a place: *a guide to Italy/the British Museum.* **(b)** a book giving information about a subject: *a guide to French wines* ○ *a gardening guide.* **5** **Guide** (*Brit*) = GIRL GUIDE.

■ **ˈguide-dog** *n* a dog trained to guide a blind person.

guide² /gaɪd/ *v* **1** to show sb the way to a place, often going with them: [Vn] *If you haven't a compass, use the stars to guide you.* [Vnpr] *She guided us through the forest/to the top of the mountain.* ○ (*fig*) *This book will guide you through the maze of regulations.* [also Vnp]. **2** to direct sb's behaviour; to influence sb: [Vn] *Be guided by your sense of what is right and just.* ○ *Free enterprise is the **guiding principle** of the Conservative Party.*

▶ **guided** *adj* [usu attrib] accompanied or led by a guide: *a guided tour/visit.* **ˌguided ˈmissile** *n* a missile that can be guided to its destination while in flight by electronic devices.

guideline /ˈgaɪdlaɪn/ *n* (esp *pl*) a general rule, instruction or piece of advice: *The government has drawn up/laid down/issued guidelines on the new tax legislation.* ○ *follow the guidelines closely.*

guild /gɪld/ *n* [CGp] a society of people with similar jobs, interests or aims. Some guilds were originally associations of merchants and skilled workers in the Middle Ages: *the guild of carpenters* ○ *the Townswomen's Guild.*

guilder /ˈgɪldə(r)/ *n* the unit of money in the Netherlands.

guildhall /ˈgɪldhɔːl/ *n* a building in which members of a GUILD used to meet; a town hall (TOWN).

guile /gaɪl/ *n* [U] clever, esp deceitful, behaviour: *a man full of guile* ○ *get sth by guile.* ▶ **guileful** /-fl/ *adj.* **guileless** *adj.*

guillemot /ˈgɪlɪmɒt/ *n* a sea-bird with black and white feathers and a long narrow beak.

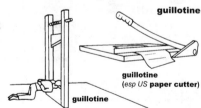

guillotine

guillotine
(*esp US* **paper cutter**)

guillotine

guillotine /ˈgɪlətiːn/ *n* **1** [C, sing] a machine of French origin for cutting people's heads off. It consists of a heavy blade which slides down a wooden frame: *sent to the guillotine.* ⇨ picture. **2** [C] (*Brit*) a device with a long blade for cutting or trimming paper. ⇨ picture. **3** [sing] (*Brit politics*) the setting of a limit to the time spent discussing a bill in Parliament so as to prevent it being held up by too much debate.

▶ **guillotine** *v* to use the guillotine(1,3) on sb/sth: [Vn] *Thousands of aristocrats were guillotined during the French Revolution.* ○ *guillotine a motion/debate/bill.*

guilt /gɪlt/ *n* **1** [U] (*law*) the condition or fact of having committed a crime: *The prosecution established his guilt beyond all doubt.* **2** [U] blame or responsibility for wrongdoing; *find out where the guilt lies* (ie who is to blame) ○ *Guilt was written all*

G

over her face (ie She obviously felt guilty). **3** [U,C] anxiety or unhappy feelings caused by the knowledge of having done wrong: *He was haunted by feelings/by a sense of guilt because he had not done enough to help his sick friend.* ○ *This is no time for guilts and misgivings.* ○ *(psychology) a guilt complex.* ▶ **guiltless** *adj: None of us is entirely guiltless in this affair.*
guilty *adj* (**-ier, -iest**) **1** ~ (**of sth**) (*esp law*) having committed a crime or done wrong; being to blame for sth: *plead guilty to a crime* ○ *The jury found the defendant guilty/not guilty.* ○ *The train driver was guilty of negligence* (eg in causing a crash). ○ *the guilty party* (ie the person to blame). **2** showing or feeling guilt: *look guilty* ○ *I feel guilty about visiting her so rarely.* ○ *have a guilty conscience* (ie be troubled by feelings of guilt). **guiltily** /-ɪli/ *adv: She looked up guiltily as I came in.*

guinea /ˈgɪni/ *n* (**a**) (esp formerly in Britain) the sum of 21 shillings (SHILLING 1) (now £1.05). Guineas are still sometimes used when stating the cost of services or the price eg of a horse. (**b**) a former British gold coin worth a guinea.

guinea-fowl /ˈgɪnifaʊl/ *n* (*pl* unchanged) a large bird of the PHEASANT family, having dark grey feathers with white spots.

guinea-pig /ˈgɪnipɪg/ *n* **1** a small animal with short ears and no tail. Guinea-pigs are often kept as pets. **2** a person or thing used in medical or other experiments: *Pupils in fifty schools are to act as guinea-pigs for these new teaching methods.*

guise /gaɪz/ *n* an outward manner or appearance, often put on in order to conceal the truth: *racialist sentiments expressed under the guise of nationalism* ○ *an ancient tale which appears in various guises in several European languages.*

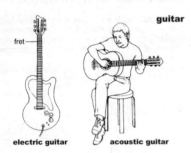

guitar

fret

electric guitar   acoustic guitar

guitar /gɪˈtɑː(r)/ *n* a musical instrument with usu six strings which is played with the fingers or a PLECTRUM: *an acoustic/a classical/an electric/a Spanish guitar* ○ *He was strumming his guitar.* ▷ picture. ▶ **guitarist** /gɪˈtɑːrɪst/ *n* a guitar player.

gulch /gʌltʃ/ *n* (US) a narrow valley with steep sides, formed by a fast stream flowing through it.

gulf /gʌlf/ *n* **1**(**a**) [C] an area of sea almost surrounded by land: *the Gulf of Mexico.* (**b**) **the Gulf** [sing] the Persian Gulf, the area of sea between the Arabian PENINSULA and Iran: *the Gulf War* (ie the one fought by the USA and other countries against Iraq in 1991) ○ *the Gulf states* (ie the countries with coasts on the Gulf). **2** ~ (**between A and B**) a large difference or division between people's feelings, opinions, etc: *The gulf between the two sides in the dispute is enormous.* **3** a wide deep crack or gap in the ground: *a yawning gulf opened up by an earthquake.*
■ **the ʹGulf Stream** *n* [sing] a warm current flowing across the Atlantic Ocean from the Gulf of Mexico towards Europe.

gull /gʌl/ (also ʹ**seagull**) *n* a large sea-bird with long wings, and usu white and grey or black feathers. There are several types of gull. ▷ picture.

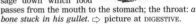

gull

gullet /ˈgʌlɪt/ *n* the passage down which food passes from the mouth to the stomach; the throat: *a bone stuck in his gullet.* ▷ picture at DIGESTIVE.

gullible /ˈgʌləbl/ *adj* willing to believe anything or anyone; easily deceived: *He must have been pretty gullible to fall for that old trick.* ▶ **gullibility** /ˌgʌləˈbɪləti/ *n* [U]: *the gullibility of the public.*

gully /ˈgʌli/ *n* **1** a small valley or channel: *a stream tumbling down a rocky gully* ○ *(fig) The child was making little gullies in his mashed potato.* **2** a deep ditch or drain.

gulp /gʌlp/ *v* **1** ~ **sth** (**down**) to swallow food or esp drink quickly or in large amounts: [Vn, Vnp] *She took the coffee, first sipping it, then gulping it (down) greedily.* [also V]. **2** to make a swallowing movement of the throat, without taking in food or drink: [V] *She gulped nervously, as if the question bothered her.* [also V.speech]. **3** ~ **sth** (**in**); ~ **for sth** to breathe, deeply and quickly, as if unable to get enough air: [V, Vpr] *She came up gulping for air.* [Vn, Vnp] *She crawled onto the river bank and lay there gulping (in) air.* **PHR V** ┌**gulp sth ʹback** to prevent the expression of emotion by swallowing: *She gulped back her tears and tried to smile.*
▶ **gulp** *n* **1** an amount swallowed or drunk: *take a gulp of cold milk* ○ *a deep gulp of sea air.* **2** an act of breathing in or swallowing sth: *sob with loud gulps* ○ *drink a glass of whisky in one gulp/at a gulp.*

gum¹ /gʌm/ *n* (usu *pl*) the firm pink flesh at the base of the teeth: *Do your gums bleed when you brush your teeth?* ▷ picture at TOOTH.

gum² /gʌm/ *n* **1** [U] (**a**) glue used for sticking light things, eg paper, together. (**b**) a sticky substance that comes out of certain trees, used for making glue. **2** [U] = CHEWING-GUM: *She chews gum all the time.* See also BUBBLE GUM. **3** [C] a transparent sweet made of a type of firm jelly: *fruit gums.*
▶ **gum** *v* (**-mm-**) ~ **A to/onto B**; ~ **A and B together**; ~ **sth** (**down**) to spread gum on the surface of sth; to stick one thing to another with gum: [Vn] *a gummed label* (ie one that is covered in glue on one side and will stick to sth when the glue is made wet) [Vnpr] *gum pictures to/onto card* [Vnp] *Gum the two edges together.* ○ *Make sure the flap is properly gummed down.* **PHR V** ┌**gum sth ʹup** (*infml*) (usu passive) to fill or cover sth with a sticky substance and stop it moving or working properly: *My eyes were so gummed up I could hardly open them.*
gummy *adj* sticky: *gummy eyes/fingers.*
■ ʹ**gum-tree** *n* a EUCALYPTUS tree. **IDM** **be up a** ʹ**gum-tree** (*infml*) be in a difficult situation.

gum³ /gʌm/ *n* **IDM** **by gum!** (*Brit infml*) (used as an expression of surprise): *By gum, you're right!*

gumbo /ˈgʌmbəʊ/ *n* [U] (US) a thick soup made with the vegetable OKRA.

gumboot /ˈgʌmbuːt/ *n* a rubber boot that extends up the leg; a WELLINGTON.

gumption /ˈgʌmpʃn/ *n* [U] (*infml*) common sense (COMMON¹) and practical intelligence, used in a manner likely to bring success: *He's a nice enough boy, but he doesn't seem to have much gumption.* ○ *He had the gumption to keep quiet.*

gun /gʌn/ *n* **1** [C] any type of weapon that fires bullets or shells (SHELL 4a) from a metal tube: *fire a gun* ○ *threaten sb with a gun* ○ *Look out, he's got a gun!* ○ *a warship with 16-inch guns* ○ *anti-aircraft guns* ○ *a toy gun* ○ *a gun battle between rival gangs.* See also AIRGUN, HANDGUN, MACHINE-GUN. ▷ picture.

G

gun

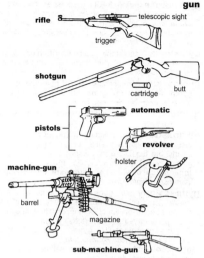

rifle — telescopic sight

trigger

shotgun

cartridge — butt

automatic

pistols

revolver

holster

machine-gun

barrel

magazine

sub-machine-gun

2 the gun [sing] the signal to begin a race, made by firing a starting PISTOL(1): *Wait for the gun!* **3** [C] (esp in compounds) a tool that forces out a substance or an object: *a 'grease-gun* ○ *a 'staple-gun.* **4** [C] (*US infml*) a person who carries a gun in order to shoot people: *a hired gun.* **IDM going great guns** ⇨ GREAT. **jump the gun** ⇨ JUMP¹. **spike sb's guns** ⇨ SPIKE *v.* **stick to one's guns** ⇨ STICK².
▶ **gun** *v* (-nn-) **PHRV be 'gunning for sb** (*infml*) be looking for an opportunity to criticize sb. **,gun sb 'down** (*infml*) (usu passive) to shoot sb, esp killing or seriously injuring them: *He was gunned down as he left his home.*
■ **'gun dog** *n* a dog trained to help in the sport of shooting, eg by collecting birds that have been shot.
'gun-metal *n* [U] a metal that is a mixture of copper and tin or ZINC: *gun-metal grey* (ie a dull, bluish-grey colour).
gunboat /'gʌnbəʊt/ *n* a small WARSHIP carrying heavy guns or missiles.
■ **,gunboat di'plomacy** *n* [U] political negotiation supported by the threat of force.
gunfire /'gʌnfaɪə(r)/ *n* [U] the firing of a gun or guns or the sound of this: *hear the crack of gunfire* ○ *A burst of gunfire came from our left.*
gunge /gʌndʒ/ *n* (*Brit* also **gunk** /gʌŋk/) *n* [U] (*infml*) an unpleasant soft or partly liquid substance: *What's this horrible gunge in the bottom of the bucket?*
gung-ho /,gʌŋ 'həʊ/ *adj* enthusiastic and eager, but not taking a situation very seriously or considering its consequences: *gung-ho soldiers* ○ *a gung-ho attitude/spirit.*
gunman /'gʌnmən/ *n* (*pl* **-men** /-mən/) a man who uses a gun to rob or kill people: *terrorist gunmen* ○ *Gunmen fired several shots at his car.*
gunner /'gʌnə(r)/ *n* a member of the armed forces trained to maintain and fire guns, esp large ones: *Its crew comprises a commander, a gunner and a driver.*
▶ **gunnery** /'gʌnəri/ *n* [U] the operation of large military guns: *improvements in naval gunnery* ○ *gunnery practice.*
gunpoint /'gʌnpɔɪnt/ *n* **IDM at 'gunpoint** while threatening sb or being threatened with a gun: *hijack a van at gunpoint* ○ *be kidnapped at gunpoint.*
gunpowder /'gʌnpaʊdə(r)/ *n* [U] explosive powder used esp in bombs or fireworks (FIREWORK 1).
gunrunner /'gʌnrʌnə(r)/ *n* a person who secretly

and illegally brings guns into a country. ▶ **gunrunning** *n* [U]: *charged with murder and gunrunning.*
gunship /'gʌnʃɪp/ *n* a heavily armed HELICOPTER or other aircraft.
gunshot /'gʌnʃɒt/ *n* [C, U] **(a)** a shot fired from a gun: *the sound of gunshots* ○ *gunshot wounds* ○ *Three people died from army gunshot.* **(b)** [U] the range of a gun: *be out of/within gunshot.*
gunsmith /'gʌnsmɪθ/ *n* a person who makes and repairs guns.
gunwale /'gʌnl/ *n* (*nautical*) the upper edge of the side of a boat or small ship.
gurgle /'gɜːgl/ *n* a sound like that made by water coming out of a bottle with a narrow neck, or by babies when they are happy: *gurgles of delight* ○ *The radiator gave a strange gurgle.*
▶ **gurgle** *v* to make a gurgle: [Vpr, V] *The water gurgled (as it ran) down the plug-hole.* [V] *The baby was gurgling happily.* ○ *The hot-water pipes were making a gurgling noise.*
guru /'guːruː/ *n* **1** a Hindu spiritual leader. **2** (*fig infml*) a respected and influential expert or person in authority: *Jean-Paul Sartre was the guru of postwar French philosophy.*
gush /gʌʃ/ *v* **1** ~ (**out**) (**of/from sth**) to flow or pour out suddenly in large quantities: [Vp, Vpr] *oil gushing out (of/from a well)* [Vpr] *blood gushing from a wound* [V] *gushing water.* **2** (*derog*) to talk or write with excessive enthusiasm or praise: [Vpr] *a young mother gushing over her baby* [V] *He has a tendency to gush when he writes about the royal family.* [V.speech] *'That's perfect!' she gushed.*
▶ **gush** *n* **1** (esp *sing*) an amount of liquid suddenly flowing or pouring out of sth: *a gush of oil/water* ○ (*fig*) *a gush of tenderness/emotion.* **2** [U] excessive praise or enthusiasm for sth: *a lot of emotional gush about family life.*
gushing *adj* (*usu derog*) expressing excessive enthusiasm or praise: *gushing compliments/letters* ○ *She was too flirtatious and gushing.* **gushingly** *adv.*
gusset /'gʌsɪt/ *n* an extra piece of cloth sewn into a garment to strengthen it or make it larger.
gust /gʌst/ *n* **(a)** a sudden strong rush of wind: *A gust of wind blew his hat off.* ○ *The wind was blowing in gusts.* **(b)** a sudden strong expression of a feeling or an emotion: *a gust of laughter/anger.*
▶ **gust** *v* (of the wind) to blow in gusts: [Vpr] *winds gusting up to 60 mph* [also V].
gusty *adj* with wind blowing in gusts: *a gusty day/wind* ○ *gusty weather/conditions.*
gusto /'gʌstəʊ/ *n* [U] enthusiasm and vigour in doing sth: *singing the choruses **with** great **gusto**.*
gut /gʌt/ *n* **1** [C] (also *infml* **guts** [pl]) **(a)** the stomach and the internal organs around it: *have a pain in the gut(s).* **(b)** this part of the body considered as the source of feelings and instincts: *She felt a thrill in her gut.* ○ *I had a feeling in my guts that something was wrong.* **2 guts** [pl] (*infml*) courage and determination, esp to do sth difficult or unpleasant: *a woman with plenty of guts* ○ (*derog*) *He disagrees with her but **doesn't have the guts** to say so.* **3** [C] **(a)** (*anatomy*) the internal part of the body through which food passes after it comes out of the stomach; the INTESTINE: *die from a ruptured gut* ○ *dissecting a frog's gut.* **(b)** (*infml*) the outward appearance of the stomach: *his huge beer gut* (ie made fat by drinking beer). **4 guts** [pl] (*infml*) the essential or most important part of sth: *remove the guts of an engine* ○ *That's basically the guts of his argument.* **5** [U] = CATGUT. **IDM hate sb's guts** ⇨ HATE. **slog/sweat one's 'guts out** (*infml*) to work very hard, to the point of collapse.
▶ **gut** *v* (-tt-) **1** to destroy the inside or contents of a building or room: [Vn] *gut the kitchen and install new units* ○ *a warehouse gutted by fire.* **2** to take out the guts of a fish or an animal, eg when preparing it

G

....
[V.speech] = verb + direct speech   [V.*that*] = verb + *that* clause   [V.*wh*] = verb + *who, how,* etc clause

as food: [Vn] *buy fish ready cleaned and gutted.*
gutted *adj* [pred] (*Brit sl*) sad or disappointed: *He felt totally gutted at being left out of the team.*
gut *adj* [attrib] based on instinct rather than thought: *a gut feeling/reaction.*
gutless *adj* cowardly; lacking spirit: *her gutless brother* ○ *gutless batting.*
gutsy /'gʌtsi/ *adj* (*infml*) (**a**) showing courage, determination and spirit: *a gutsy fighter/performance.* (**b**) full of strength and character: *a gutsy red wine* ○ *gutsy songs.*
gutter¹ /'gʌtə(r)/ *n* **1** [C] a long metal or plastic channel fixed under the edge of a roof to carry away the water when it rains: *clean out a blocked gutter.* ⇨ picture at HOUSE¹. **2**(**a**) [C] a channel or narrow area at the side of a street, next to the PAVEMENT(1): *cigarette packets thrown into the gutter.* (**b**) **the gutter** [sing] (*usu derog*) a state of life marked by poverty, bad social conditions or a lack of morals: *the language of the gutter* (ie bad language or swearing) ○ *She rose from the gutter to become a great star.*
▶ **guttering** /'gʌtərɪŋ/ *n* [U] the system of gutters under a roof.
■ **the ˌgutter ˈpress** *n* [sing] (*derog*) newspapers that print a lot of shocking stories and gossip, but not much serious news.
gutter² /'gʌtə(r)/ *v* [V] (of a candle) to burn with an unsteady flame, as if about to go out.
guttural /'gʌtərəl/ *adj* (of a sound) being or seeming to be produced in the throat; deep and rough: *guttural consonants* ○ *a low guttural growl.*
guv, guvnor ⇨ GOVERNOR 3.
guy¹ /gaɪ/ *n* **1**(**a**) [C] (*infml*) a man: *a big/nice/tough guy* ○ *a Dutch guy* ○ *At the end of the film the bad guy gets shot.* ○ *Come on, (you) guys, let's get going!* (**b**) **guys** [pl] (*US*) a group of people of either sex, esp friends or colleagues: *the guys at the office.* See also FALL GUY. **2** (in Britain) a figure in the form of a man, dressed in old clothes and burned on a BONFIRE on 5 November in memory of Guy Fawkes.
guy² /gaɪ/ (also **ˈguy rope**) *n* a rope used to keep sth steady or secured, eg to hold a tent in place: *tighten/loose the guys.*
guy³ /gaɪ/ *v* [Vn] (*Brit fml*) to mock sb/sth, esp by copying them in a funny way.
guzzle /'gʌzl/ *v* (*infml usu derog*) to eat or drink sth quickly or in large amounts: [V] *He's always guzzling.* [Vn] *guzzle beer/cakes.*
▶ **guzzler** /-zlə(r)/ *n* (*infml esp US*) a car that needs a lot of petrol: *My old Pontiac was a real (gas) guzzler.*
gybe (*US* **jibe**) /dʒaɪb/ *v* [V] (*nautical*) to change direction when the wind is behind, by swinging the sail from one side of a boat to the other.
▶ **gybe** *n* an act of gybing.

gym /dʒɪm/ *n* (*infml*) **1** [C] a GYMNASIUM: *do exercises in the gym* ○ *The new complex has squash courts, a sauna and a gym.* **2** [U] physical exercises in a gymnasium, esp at school: *I don't enjoy gym.* ○ *gym shoes* ○ *a gym teacher.*
gymkhana /dʒɪm'kɑːnə/ *n* a competition or display in which horses are ridden round a course, jump over fences, etc.
gymnasium /dʒɪm'neɪziəm/ *n* (*pl* **gymnasiums** or **gymnasia** /-ziə/) a room or hall with apparatus for physical exercise. See also GYM.
gymnast /'dʒɪmnæst/ *n* a performer of GYMNASTICS, esp as a sport.
gymnastics /dʒɪm'næstɪks/ *n* [pl] physical exercises performed as a sport or to make the body strong and flexible: *a gymnastics competition* ○ (*fig*) *mental/verbal gymnastics* (ie quick or clever thinking/use of words). ▶ **gymnastic** *adj* [attrib]: *a gymnastic display/feat.*
gynaecology (*US* **gyne-**) /ˌɡaɪnə'kɒlədʒi/ *n* [U] (*medical*) the scientific study and treatment of the diseases and disorders of women, esp those affecting the reproductive (REPRODUCTION) system.
▶ **gynaecological** (*US* **gyne-**) /ˌɡaɪnəkə'lɒdʒɪkl/ *adj*: *a gynaecological examination.*
gynaecologist (*US* **gyne-**) /ˌɡaɪnə'kɒlədʒɪst/ *n* an expert in gynaecology.
gyp¹ /dʒɪp/ *n* **IDM** **give sb ˈgyp** (*Brit dated infml*) to cause sb a lot of pain: *My rheumatism's been giving me gyp.*
gyp² /dʒɪp/ *v* [Vn] (*infml esp US*) to cheat or deceive sb, esp by taking their money.
gypsum /'dʒɪpsəm/ *n* [U] a soft white mineral like chalk that occurs naturally and is used in making plaster of Paris (PLASTER 2).
gypsy (also **gipsy, Gypsy**) /'dʒɪpsi/ *n* a member of a race of people, originally from Asia, with dark hair and skin, who move from place to place and traditionally live in caravans (CARAVAN 1): *a gypsy camp/site.* Compare TINKER 1a.
gyrate /dʒaɪ'reɪt; *US* 'dʒaɪreɪt/ *v* to move around in circles or spirals (SPIRAL *n* a); to revolve: [V] *dancers gyrating round the floor.* ▶ **gyration** /dʒaɪ'reɪʃn/ *n* [U, C usu *pl*]: *stock market gyrations* (ie rapid price changes).
gyro /'dʒaɪrəʊ/ *n* (*pl* **-os**) (*infml*) a GYROSCOPE.
gyroscope /'dʒaɪrəskəʊp/ *n* a device containing a rapidly spinning wheel, mounted in such a way that it always stays in the same PLANE¹(2) regardless of any movement of the supporting structure. Gyroscopes are often used to keep ships and aircraft steady. ▶ **gyroscopic** /ˌdʒaɪrə'skɒpɪk/ *adj*: *a gyroscopic compass.*

Hh

H (also **h**) /eɪtʃ/ n (pl **H's**, **h's** /'eɪtʃɪz/) the 8th letter of the English alphabet: *'Hat' begins with (an) H/'H'.* Compare AITCH.

ha¹ /hɑː/ interj **1** (used to express surprise, joy, triumph, suspicion, etc). **2** (also **ha! ha!**) (used in print to indicate laughter; when spoken used ironically). ▶ **ha** v **IDM** **hum and ha/haw** ⇨ HUM.

ha² abbr hectare(s).

habeas corpus /ˌheɪbɪəs 'kɔːpəs/ (law) an order requiring a person to be brought before a judge or into court, esp to investigate whether or not he or she should be released from prison: *apply for a writ of habeas corpus.*

haberdasher /'hæbədæʃə(r)/ n (dated Brit) a shopkeeper who sells small articles for sewing, eg needles, pins, cotton and buttons.
▶ **haberdashery** n **1** [U] goods sold by a haberdasher. **2** [C] a haberdasher's shop.

habit /'hæbɪt/ n **1(a)** [C] a thing that a person does often and almost without thinking, esp sth that is hard to stop doing: *eating/working habits* ○ *good/bad habits* ○ *habit-forming drugs* ○ *He has the irritating habit of biting his nails.* ○ *It's all right to borrow money occasionally, but don't let it become a habit/make a habit of it.* ○ *I'm not in the habit of staying up late* (ie I don't do it very often). ○ *I've got into the habit of turning on the TV as soon as I get home.* ○ *He's tried to give up smoking but just can't break/kick the habit.* ○ *I make a habit of never lending money to strangers.* **(b)** [U] usual behaviour: *I only do it out of habit.* **2** [C] a long garment worn by a monk or nun. **IDM** **force of habit** ⇨ FORCE¹.

habitable /'hæbɪtəbl/ adj suitable for living in: *This house is no longer habitable.*

habitat /'hæbɪtæt/ n the natural environment of an animal or a plant: *This creature's (natural) habitat is the jungle.* ○ *The marshes provide a rich habitat for water plants.*

habitation /ˌhæbɪ'teɪʃn/ n **1** [U] the process of living in a place: *houses unfit for human habitation.* **2** [C] (fml) a place to live in; a house or home: *wildlife undisturbed by human habitations.*

habitual /hə'bɪtʃuəl/ adj **1(a)** [attrib] regular; usual: *his habitual place at the table.* **(b)** done constantly or as a habit(1): *their habitual moaning.* **2** [attrib] doing sth by habit: *a habitual drunkard/liar.*
▶ **habitually** /-tʃuəli/ adv usually; regularly: *the clothes she habitually wears* ○ *Tom is habitually late for school.*

habituate /hə'bɪtʃueɪt/ v **PHRV** **habituate sb/ oneself to sth** (fml) to make sb/oneself used to sth: [Vnpr] *habituate oneself to* (ie get used to) *hard work/a cold climate.*

hack¹ /hæk/ v **1** to cut sth/sb with rough heavy blows: [Vpr, Vnp, Vp] *They hacked (away) at the undergrowth/hacked the undergrowth back to clear a path.* [Vnpr] *We had to hack our way through the jungle.* ○ *The body had been hacked in pieces/hacked to death.* ○ *Someone had hacked the legs off the carcase.* ⇨ note at CUT¹. **2** to kick sth wildly or roughly: [Vn] *hack the ball (away)/sb's legs* [also Vnp, Vnpr].
▶ **hack** n **1** an act of chopping. **2** a kick with the toe of a boot.
■ **ˌhacking ˈcough** n a short dry cough that is often repeated.

hack² /hæk/ v [V, Vpr, Vn] ~ **(into)** **(sth)** (computing infml) to gain access to the contents of a computer's memory without permission.
▶ **hacker** n (infml) a person who uses computers for enjoyment, esp in order to HACK². **hacking** n [U].

hack³ /hæk/ n **1** a person paid to do hard and often boring work, esp as a writer: *a publisher's hack* ○ *a hack journalist* ○ *'hack work* ○ *a party hack* (ie one who does the dull work for a political party). **2** a horse for ordinary riding or one that may be hired.
▶ **hack** v [V] (usu **go hacking**) (Brit) to ride on a horse at an ordinary pace, esp along roads.

hackles /'hæklz/ n [pl] the long feathers on the neck of certain birds, or the hairs on the neck of a dog, which rise when the creatures are afraid or angry. **IDM** **make sb's ˈhackles rise / raise sb's ˈhackles** to make sb angry: *Her controversial article is bound to raise a few hackles.*

hackney carriage /ˈhækni kærɪdʒ/ (also **hackney cab**) n (dated Brit) a taxi.

hackneyed /'hæknid/ adj (of a phrase, saying, etc) used so often that it has lost its impact and become dull.

hacksaw /'hæksɔː/ n a tool with a narrow blade in a frame, used for cutting metal.

had /həd, əd, d; strong form hæd/ pt, pp of HAVE¹,²,³.

haddock /'hædək/ n (pl unchanged) [C, U] a sea fish similar to a COD(1) but smaller, used for food.

hadn't /'hædnt/ short form had not. ⇨ note at HAVE.

haematology (also esp US **hem-**) /ˌhiːmə'tɒlədʒi/ n [U] the scientific study of the blood and its diseases.
▶ **haematologist** (also esp US **hem-**) n.

haem(o)- (also esp US **hem(o)-**) comb form of blood: *haematology* ○ *haemophilia.*

haemoglobin (also esp US **hem-**) /ˌhiːmə'ɡləʊbɪn/ n [U] a red substance in the blood that carries oxygen and contains iron.

haemophilia (also esp US **hem-**) /ˌhiːmə'fɪliə/ n [U] a disease, usu affecting only males though carried by females, which causes severe bleeding from even a slight injury, because the blood fails to CLOT normally.
▶ **haemophiliac** (also esp US **hem-**) /ˌhiːmə'fɪliæk/ n a person who suffers from haemophilia.

haemorrhage (also esp US **hem-**) /'hemərɪdʒ/ n **1** [C, U] (an instance of) bleeding, esp when sudden and in large amounts: *suffer a massive brain/ cerebral haemorrhage.* **2** [C] a serious loss of people, assets (ASSET 2), etc suffered by a country, an organization, etc: *The haemorrhage of party members continues.*
▶ **haemorrhage** v [V] to bleed heavily; to have a haemorrhage.

haemorrhoids (also esp US **hem-**) /'hemərɔɪdz/ (also **piles**) n [pl] painful swollen veins at or near the ANUS.

hag /hæɡ/ n (derog) an ugly or evil old woman.

haggard /'hæɡəd/ adj looking very tired and unhappy, esp from worry or lack of sleep: *a haggard face* ○ *He looks haggard.*

haggis /'hæɡɪs/ n [C, U] a Scottish dish made mainly from sheep's heart, lungs and LIVER(2) and boiled in a bag that is usu made from part of a sheep's stomach.

haggle /'hæɡl/ v ~ **(with sb)** **(about/over sth)** to argue esp about the price of sth one wants to buy: [Vpr] *It's not worth haggling over a few pennies.* [also V].

hagiography /ˌhægiˈɒgrəfi/ *n* [C,U] (a piece of) biographical writing about a person's life that is too full of praise for its subject.

hail¹ /heɪl/ *n* **1** [U] frozen rain falling as little balls of ice in a shower. **2** [sing] a large number of things coming with force, esp intended to harm sb: *a hail of bullets/stones/questions.*

▶ **hail** *v* (with *it* as subject) to fall as hail in a shower: [V] *It's started hailing.*

hail² /heɪl/ *v* **1** [Vn] (**a**) to call to a person or ship in order to attract attention: *hail a waiter* ○ *within ˈhailing distance* (ie close enough to be called to). See also LOUD HAILER. (**b**) to signal to a taxi, etc to stop. **2** ~ **sb/sth (as)** sth to acknowledge sb/sth enthusiastically as sth; to ACCLAIM sb/sth: [Vn-n] *crowds hailing him (as) king/Europe's greatest living poet* ○ *The book was immediately hailed as a masterpiece.* **3** to greet sb: [Vn] *He hailed me with a smile/wave.* **PHRV** **ˈhail from...** to originate from a place: *The band all hail* (ie come) *from Glasgow.*

hailstone /ˈheɪlstəʊn/ *n* (usu *pl*) a small ball of HAIL¹(1).

hailstorm /ˈheɪlstɔːm/ *n* a period of heavy HAIL¹(1).

hair /heə(r)/ *n* (**a**) [C] any of the fine strands that grow from the skin of people and animals: *two blonde hairs on his coat collar* ○ *There's a hair in my soup.* (**b**) [U] a mass of these, esp on the human head: *have/get's one's ˈhair cut* ○ *have long, black hair* ○ *He's losing his hair* (ie becoming BALD(1)). ○ *He's over eighty but still has a fine/full head of hair.* ⇨ picture. ⇨ picture at HEAD¹. See also CAMEL-HAIR. (**c**) [C] a soft fine strand growing on the stems and leaves of certain plants. **IDM** **get in sb's ˈhair** to annoy sb, esp by one's continual presence. **a/the hair of the ˈdog (that ˈbit you)** (*infml*) another alcoholic drink to cure the effects of the alcohol drunk previously. **hang by a hair/a thread** ⇨ HANG¹. **(not) harm, etc a hair of sb's ˈhead** (not) to injure sb, even in the slightest way. **keep your ˈhair on** (*infml catchphrase*) do not become angry; remain calm. **let one's ˈhair down** (*infml*) to behave freely or wildly after a period of being formal: *She certainly let her hair down at the office party!* **make one's ˈhair stand on end** to fill one with fear or horror. **neither hide nor hair of sb/sth** ⇨ HIDE². **not turn a ˈhair** to remain calm without displaying an expected reaction such as surprise, fear etc: *The prisoner listened to his sentence without turning a hair.* **split hairs** ⇨ SPLIT. **tear one's hair** ⇨ TEAR¹.

▶ **-ˈhaired** (in compound *adjs*) with hair of the specified kind: *a ˌwhite-haired old ˈman* ○ *a ˌcurly-haired ˈgirl.*

hairless *adj: his smooth, hairless chest.*

■ **ˈhair-drier** (also **ˈhair-dryer**) *n* a device for drying the hair by blowing hot air over it.

ˈhair-raising *adj* very frightening.

ˈhair's breadth *n* [sing] a very small amount or distance: *We won by a hair's breadth.* ○ *They came/were within a hair's breadth of being killed.* ○ *a hair's breadth escape/victory.*

ˈhair-splitting *n* [U] making small unimportant distinctions. See also SPLIT HAIRS.

hairbrush /ˈheəbrʌʃ/ *n* a brush for making the hair tidy or smooth. ⇨ picture at BRUSH¹.

haircut /ˈheəkʌt/ *n* **1** a cutting of the hair: *You need a haircut.* **2** a style in which hair is cut: *That's a nice haircut.*

hairdo /ˈheəduː/ *n* (*pl* **-os**) (*infml*) a style or process of arranging a woman's hair: *She has a new hairdo every week.*

hairdresser /ˈheədresə(r)/ *n* a person whose job is to cut and arrange hair. Compare BARBER. ▶ **ˈhairdressing** *n* [U].

hairgrip /ˈheəgrɪp/ (*Brit*) (also **grip**, *US* **bobby pin**) *n* a piece of flat wire or plastic with its ends pressed together, used for holding the hair in place.

hairline /ˈheəlaɪn/ *n* **1** the edge of a person's hair round the face. **2** a very thin line: *a ˌhairline ˈcrack/ˈfracture.*

hairnet /ˈheənet/ *n* a net for keeping the hair in place.

hair-piece /ˈheə piːs/ *n* a piece of false hair worn to increase the amount of a person's natural hair.

hairpin /ˈheəpɪn/ *n* a bent pin² for keeping long hair in position on the head.

■ **ˌhairpin ˈbend** *n* a very sharp bend in a road, esp a mountain road.

hairspray /ˈheəspreɪ/ *n* [U] a substance sprayed onto the hair to keep it in place.

hairstyle /ˈheəstaɪl/ *n* a particular way of arranging or cutting the hair. ⇨ picture.

hairy /ˈheəri/ *adj* (**-ier, -iest**) **1** having much hair: *a hairy chest* ○ *a hairy tweed coat* ○ *plants with hairy stems.* **2** (*sl*) dangerous in an exciting or unpleasant way: *Driving on icy roads can be pretty hairy.* ▶ **hairiness** *n* [U].

haj (also **hajj**) /hædʒ/ *n* (usu **the Haj** [sing]) the holy journey to Mecca made by Muslims.

hake /heɪk/ *n* (*pl* unchanged) [C,U] a fish of the COD(1) family, used as food.

halal (also **hallal**) /ˈhælæl/ *n* [U] meat from an animal killed according to Muslim law: *halal lamb.*

halcyon /ˈhælsiən/ *adj* (*dated or rhet*) peaceful and happy: *the halcyon days of one's youth.*

hale /heɪl/ *adj* (esp of an old person) strong and healthy: *At over 90, he's still hale and hearty.*

half¹ /hɑːf; *US* hæf/ *n* (*pl* **halves** /hɑːvz; *US* hævz/) **1** either of two equal or corresponding parts into which sth is or can be divided: *two and a half ounces/hours/miles* ○ *the mountainous half of the island* ○ *Mum's broken the chocolate into halves — here's your half.* ○ *John and Liz shared the prize money between them — John used his half to buy a word processor.* ○ *The second half of the book is more exciting than the first.* ⇨ note at ALL¹. **2** either of two usu equal periods of time into which a sports game, concert, etc is divided: *No goals were scored in the first half.* **3** (*Brit*) a cheaper ticket, esp for a child, on a bus or train: *Two and two halves to the city centre, please.* **4** = HALF-BACK: *playing (at) left half.* **5** (*infml esp Brit*) a half of a PINT, esp of beer: *Two halves of bitter, please.* **IDM** **and a ˈhalf** (*infml*) of more than usual importance, excellence, size, etc: *That was a game and a half!* **one's better half** ⇨ BETTER¹. **break, chop, cut, tear, etc sth in ˈhalf** to cause sth to become separated into two parts by breaking, chopping, etc: *I once saw a man tear a telephone directory in half.* **do nothing/not do anything by ˈhalves** to do whatever one does completely and thoroughly: *He's not a man who does* *things by halves — he either donates a huge sum or gives nothing.* **go half and ¦half / go ¦halves (with sb)** to share the cost of sth equally: *That was an expensive meal — let's go halves.* **the ¦half of it** (*infml*) (usu in negative sentences) the most important part: *You don't know the half of it.* **how the other half ¦lives** the way of life of a different social group, esp one much richer or poorer than oneself: *He's rich and arrogant — he couldn't care less how the other half lives.*

> **NOTE** Quarter, half and whole can all be nouns: *Cut the apple into quarters.* ○ *Two halves make a whole.* **Whole** is also an adjective: *I've been waiting here for a whole hour.* **Half** is also a determiner: *Half the work is already finished.* ○ *They spent half the time looking for a parking space.* ○ *Her house is half a mile down the road.* It can also be used as an adverb: *This meal is only half cooked.*

half² /hɑːf; *US* hæf/ *indef det* amounting to or forming a half: *half the men* ○ *half an hour/a half-hour* (ie 30 minutes) ○ *half a pint/a half-pint* ○ *half a dozen/a half-dozen* (ie 6) ○ *He has a half share in the firm.* ○ *Half the fruit was bad.* Compare ALL¹, BOTH¹. ⇨ note at ALL¹. **IDM half a ¦minute, ¦second, ¦tick, etc** (*infml*) a short time: *I'll be ready in half a minute.* **half past ¦one, ¦two, etc** 30 minutes after any hour on the clock. **half ¦one, ¦two, etc** (*Brit infml*) = HALF PAST ONE, TWO, ETC.

▶ **half** *indef pron* a quantity or amount that constitutes a half: *Half of six is three.* ○ *Half of the plums are rotten.* ○ *Half of the money is mine.* ○ *I only need half.* ○ *Out of 36 children, half passed.*

■ **¦half-and-¦half** *adj* [usu pred] being half one thing and half another: *'How do you like your coffee?' 'Half-and-half* (ie Half coffee and half milk)*, please.'*

¦half-back *n* a player between the forwards (FOR-WARD⁴) and the full backs (BACK¹ 4) in football, hockey, etc.

¦half ¦board *n* [U] the providing of bed, breakfast and one main meal at a hotel, etc. Compare FULL BOARD.

¦half-brother *n* a brother who shares only one parent with another.

¦half-caste (also **¦half-breed**) *n, adj* (*usu offensive*) (a person) of mixed race.

¦half-¦crown (also **¦half a ¦crown**) *n* (in Britain before 1971) a coin worth 2½ shillings (SHILLING 1) (now 12½ pence), or its value.

¦half ¦day *n* a day of which half, usu the afternoon, is taken as a holiday.

¦half ¦dollar *n* a US coin worth 50 cents.

¦half-¦hour (also **¦half an ¦hour**) *n* a period of 30 minutes: *He should arrive within the next half-hour.*

¦half-¦hourly *adj, adv: a half-hourly news bulletin* ○ *The buses run half-hourly.*

¦half-life *n* the time taken for the radioactivity (RA-DIOACTIVE) of a substance to fall to half its original value.

¦half-light *n* [sing] a dull light in which it is difficult to see things: *in the half-light of dawn.*

¦half-¦mast *n* **IDM at ¦half-¦mast** (of a flag) at the middle of a MAST(2), as a way of showing respect for a dead person: *Flags were (flown) at half-mast everywhere on the day of the hostage's funeral.*

¦half ¦moon *n* **1** the moon when only half of it is visible from the earth. **2** the time when this occurs. **3** an object shaped like a half moon.

¦half-note *n* (*US*) = MINIM.

¦half-¦price *adv* at half the usual price: *Children are (admitted) half-price.*

¦half-sister *n* a sister who shares only one parent with another.

¦half-¦term *n* (in Britain) a short holiday near the middle of a school term.

¦half-¦time *n* [U] an interval between the two halves

of a game of football, hockey, etc: *The score at half-time was 2–2.* ○ *the ¦half-time ¦score.*

¦half-tone *n* (*US*) = SEMITONE.

¦half-truth *n* (*usu derog*) a statement that gives only part of the truth, esp deliberately: *The newspaper reports are a mixture of gossip, lies and half-truths.*

¦half-¦yearly *adj, adv* (done or occurring) every six months: *meetings held at ¦half-yearly ¦intervals* ○ *Royalty statements are sent out half-yearly.*

half³ /hɑːf; *US* hæf/ *adv* **1** to the extent of half: *The jug was half full.* **2** partly: *half cooked* ○ *half-closed eyes* ○ *I'm half inclined to agree.* **IDM half as ¦many, ¦much, etc a¦gain** an increase of 50% of the existing number, amount, etc: *Spending on health is half as much again as it was in 1982.* **¦not ¦half** (*sl*) to the greatest possible extent: *He didn't half swear* (ie He swore violently). ○ *'Was she annoyed?' 'Not half!'* (ie She was extremely annoyed.) **not ¦half as** much less: *Her new boyfriend isn't half as good-looking (as her last one).*

■ **¦half-¦baked** *adj* (*infml*) not properly planned or considered; foolish: *a ¦half-baked i¦dea.*

¦half-¦hearted *adj* lacking enthusiasm: **make a half-hearted attempt at conversation.** **¦half-¦heartedly** *adv.*

¦half-¦timbered *adj* (of a building) having walls that consist of a wooden framework filled in with brick, stone or PLASTER(1).

halfpenny /ˈheɪpni/ *n* (*pl* usu **halfpennies** for separate coins, **halfpence** /ˈheɪpəns/ for a sum of money) (in Britain before 1984) a small coin worth half a penny, or its value.

halfway /ˌhɑːfˈweɪ; *US* ˌhæf-/ *adj, adv* situated between and at an equal distance from two points: *reach the half¦way point/stage* ○ *It's about halfway between London and Bristol.* ○ *He left halfway through the ceremony.* **IDM meet sb halfway** ⇨ MEET¹.

■ **¦halfway ¦house** *n* **1** a compromise between opposite attitudes, plans, etc. **2** a place where former prisoners, patients with mental illness, etc, can stay while preparing to return to normal life.

halfwit /ˈhɑːfwɪt; *US* ˈhæf-/ *n* (*infml or derog*) a stupid or foolish person. ▶ **¦half¦witted** *adj.*

halibut /ˈhælɪbət/ *n* [C, U] (*pl* unchanged) a large flat sea-fish that is eaten.

halitosis /ˌhælɪˈtəʊsɪs/ *n* [U] (*medical*) a condition in which the breath smells unpleasant.

hall /hɔːl/ *n* **1** (also **¦hallway**) [C] a space or passage inside the entrance or front door of a building: *Leave your coat in the hall.* **2** [C] a building or large room for meetings, meals, concerts, etc: *a 'sports hall* ○ *the ¦Royal ¦Albert ¦Hall* ○ *'dance halls.* See also MUSIC-HALL, TOWN HALL. **3** [C] = HALL OF RESIDENCE: *live in hall.* **4** [C] (*esp Brit*) (esp as part of a name) a large country house: *Haddon Hall.*

■ **¦hall of ¦residence** (*pl* **halls of residence**) (also **hall**) *n* a building for university or college students to live in.

hallelujah = ALLELUIA.

hallmark /ˈhɔːlmɑːk/ *n* **1** a mark used for indicating the origin and quality of gold, silver and PLATINUM on articles made of these metals. **2** a distinctive feature: *Attention to detail is the hallmark of a fine craftsman.* ○ *Police said the explosion bore all the hallmarks of a terrorist attack.*

▶ **hallmark** *v* [Vn] to stamp sth with a hallmark(1).

hallo = HELLO.

hallowed /ˈhæləʊd/ *adj* **1** made holy: *be buried in hallowed ground.* **2** (of things) treated with great respect, esp because of being old: *one of the theatre's most hallowed traditions.*

Hallowe'en /ˌhæləʊˈiːn/ *n* 31 October, when according to ancient tradition the spirits of dead people rise from their graves.

hallucinate /həˈluːsɪneɪt/ *v* to imagine one is seeing or hearing sb/sth when no such person or thing

---

is present; to cause sb to do this: [V] *Drug addicts often hallucinate.* [also Vn].

hallucination /həˌluːsɪˈneɪʃn/ *n* (**a**) [C, U] the belief that one is seeing or hearing sb/sth when no such person or thing is actually present: *suffer from/have hallucinations.* (**b**) [C] a thing seen or heard in this way.
▶ **hallucinatory** /həˈluːsɪnətri, həˌluːsɪˈneɪtəri; *US* həˈluːsənətɔːri/ *adj* of or causing hallucinations: *a hallucinatory experience/image/drug.*

hallucinogen /ˌhæluːˈsɪnədʒən/ *n* a drug that causes one to HALLUCINATE. ▶ **hallucinogenic** /həˌluːsɪnəˈdʒenɪk/ *adj*: *hallucinogenic drugs/effects.*

hallway /ˈhɔːlweɪ/ *n* **1** = HALL 1. **2** (*esp US*) a CORRIDOR(1).

halo /ˈheɪləʊ/ *n* (*pl* **-oes** or **-os**) (also **aureole**) **1** (in paintings, etc) a circle of light shown round or above the head of a sacred figure: *an angel with wings and a halo* ∘ (*fig*) *a halo of frizzy white hair.* **2** = CORONA.

halogen /ˈhælədʒən/ *n* (*chemistry*) any of a set of chemical elements, including FLUORINE, CHLORINE and IODINE, that form salts when combined with a metal: *halogen lamps/bulbs.*

halon /ˈheɪlɒn/ *n* (*chemistry*) any of various gases consisting of compounds of CARBON and other halogens (HALOGEN), used esp to stop fires.

halt /hɔːlt, hɒlt/ *n* **1**(**a**) [sing] a temporary stop; an interruption of progress: *Work was brought/came to a halt when the machine broke down.* ∘ *The car skidded to a halt.* (**b**) [C] a short stop during a march or journey. **2** [C] (*Brit*) a place on a railway line where local trains stop, but where there are no station buildings. IDM **bring sth to a grinding halt** ⇨ GRIND. **call a halt** ⇨ CALL¹. **come to a grinding halt** ⇨ GRIND. **grind to a halt/standstill** ⇨ GRIND.
▶ **halt** *v* to stop or make sb/sth stop temporarily: [V] *A cry rang out: 'Halt!'* [Vn] *The troops were halted for a rest.* ∘ *Production was halted by strikes.*

halter /ˈhɔːltə(r), ˈhɒlt-/ *n* a rope or leather strap put round the head of a horse for leading it.
■ **ˈhalter-neck** *n* a style of woman's dress with the top held up by a strap passing round the back of the neck, leaving the back and shoulders bare.

halting /ˈhɔːltɪŋ, ˈhɒlt-/ *adj* (*usu attrib*) slow and hesitating, as if lacking in confidence: *speak in a halting voice* ∘ *a halting reply* ∘ *a toddler's first few halting steps.* ▶ **haltingly** *adv*: *speak haltingly.*

halve /hɑːv; *US* hæv/ *v* **1** to divide sth into two equal parts: [Vn] *halve an apple.* **2** to reduce sth by a half: [Vn] *Supersonic planes halved the time needed for crossing the Atlantic.*

halves *pl* of HALF¹.

halyard /ˈhæljəd/ *n* a rope for raising or lowering a sail or flag.

ham /hæm/ *n* **1**(**a**) [C] the upper part of a pig's leg, preserved with salt or in smoke to be eaten as food: *several hams hanging on hooks.* (**b**) [U] meat from this: *a slice of ham* ∘ *a ham sandwich.* Compare BACON, GAMMON, PORK. **2** [C] the back of the leg above the knee. **3** [C] (*sl*) a person who acts or performs badly: *ham actors.* **4** [C] (*infml*) a person who sends and receives messages with radio equipment as a HOBBY: *a radio ham.*
▶ **ham** *v* (**-mm-**) ~ (**it/sth up**) (*sl*) to act in a deliberately artificial or exaggerated way: [Vnp] *The actors were really hamming it up to amuse the audience.* [also V].
■ **ˌham-ˈfisted** *adj* (*infml derog*) awkward in using the hands.

hamburger /ˈhæmbɜːɡə(r)/ *n* **1** (also **burger**) [C] a piece of finely chopped BEEF made into a flat round shape, usu fried and eaten with onions, often in a bread roll. **2** [U] (*US*) = MINCE *n*.

hamlet /ˈhæmlət/ *n* a very small village.

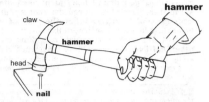
hammer

claw

hammer

head

nail

hammer¹ /ˈhæmə(r)/ *n* **1** [C] a tool with a heavy metal head used for breaking things or hitting nails: *a hammer blow* ∘ *take a hammer to sth* (ie hit sth with a hammer). ⇨ picture. **2** [C] a part of an instrument or a mechanism that hits another part to make it work. A piano has hammers which hit the strings, and a gun has a hammer which hits the bullet, etc, making the gun fire. **3**(**a**) [C] (in ATHLETICS) a metal ball attached to a wire for throwing. (**b**) **the hammer** [sing] the event in which this is thrown. IDM **be/go at it / each other ˌhammer and ˈtongs** (of two people) to argue or fight violently and noisily: *We could hear the neighbours going at each other hammer and tongs.* **come/go under the ˈhammer** to be sold at AUCTION: *This painting came under the hammer at Christie's today.*
■ **ˌhammer and ˈsickle** *n* the symbols of the industrial and agricultural worker, used esp formerly by Communist countries.

hammer² /ˈhæmə(r)/ *v* **1** to hit or beat sb/sth with or as if with a hammer: [V, Vp] *I could hear him hammering (away) next door.* [Vnp, Vnpr] *He hammered the sheet of copper (flat).* [Vnpr] *She hammered the nail in/into the wall.* [Vnpr] *She hammered him over the head with a baseball bat.* **2** to strike sth loudly: [Vpr] *hammer at the door* (ie with one's hand) ∘ *My heart was hammering against my ribs.* [Vp] *Hail was hammering down onto the roof.* [also Vnpr]. **3** (*infml*) (**a**) to defeat sb completely: [Vn] *Manchester United were hammered 5–1.* (**b**) to criticize or attack sb/sth forcefully: [Vn] *an article in which he hammers his political opponents.* PHR V **ˌhammer aˈway at sth** to work hard at sth: *I keep hammering away at this point because it's so important.*
ˌhammer sth ˈdown, ˈoff, etc to make sth fall down, off, etc by hammering it violently: *hammer the door down.*
ˌhammer sth ˈhome 1 to hammer a nail fully into sth. **2** to emphasize a point, an argument, etc so that it is fully understood.
ˌhammer sth ˈinto sb to force sb to learn sth by repeating it many times: *They have had English grammar hammered into them.*
ˌhammer sth ˈout 1 to remove a DENT in metal by hammering it from the back. **2** to develop a plan, solution, etc by great effort: *After much discussion the negotiators hammered out a compromise settlement.* **3** to play a tune, esp on the piano, loudly and with little musical skill: *Someone next door was hammering out scales.*
▶ **hammering** /ˈhæmərɪŋ/ *n* **1** [U, sing] the process or sound of sb beating or striking sth with a hammer: *hear hammering coming from next door.* **2** [C usu sing] (*infml*) a total defeat: *Our team took a terrible hammering.*

hammock /ˈhæmək/ *n* **1** a type of bed made of canvas or pieces of rope woven together, hung at each end from a wall, post, tree, etc. **2** (*US*) = HUMMOCK.

hamper¹ /ˈhæmpə(r)/ *n* **1** a large basket with a lid, esp one used to carry food, wine, etc: *a ˈpicnic hamper.* **2** (*esp Brit*) a box or parcel containing food and wine, sent as a gift: *a Christmas hamper.*

hamper² /'hæmpə(r)/ *v* (often passive) to prevent sb's free movement or activity; to restrict or HINDER sb/sth: [Vn] *Our progress was hampered by the bad weather.*

hamster /'hæmstə(r)/ *n* an animal like a large mouse, kept as a pet. Hamsters have large cheeks for storing food.

hamstring /'hæmstrɪŋ/ *n* (*anatomy*) each of the five cords at the back of the human knee, or a similar cord at the back of an animal's leg.

▶ **hamstring** *v* (*pt, pp* **hamstrung** /'hæmstrʌŋ/) **1** [Vn] to make a person or an animal unable to walk by cutting the hamstring(s). **2** to prevent sb/sth from working efficiently: [Vn] *The project was hamstrung by lack of funds.*

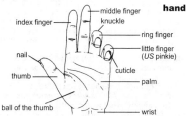

index finger
middle finger
knuckle
ring finger
little finger
(*US* pinkie)
nail
cuticle
thumb
palm
ball of the thumb
wrist
hand

hand¹ /hænd/ *n* **1** [C] the part at the end of the human arm below the wrist, including the fingers and thumb: *take/lead sb by the hand* ∘ *get down on one's hands and knees* ∘ *have one's hands in one's pockets* ∘ *two lovers holding hands* ∘ *Buckets of water were passed **from hand to hand*** (ie from one person to another in a line) *to put the fire out.* ∘ *He struck the table hard with his right hand.* ⇨ picture. See also LEFT-HAND, RIGHT-HAND. **2 a hand** [sing] (*infml*) active help: *Could you give (me) a hand with the washing-up?* ∘ *Do you want/need a hand?* **3** [sing] the part or role of sb/sth, esp in sth harmful: *I bet he had a hand in the kidnapping.* ∘ *Do I detect your hand in this?* **4** [C] (in compounds) a part that points to the numbers on a clock or DIAL(1): *the 'hour-/'minute-/'second-hand of a watch.* **5** [C] (**a**) a worker on a farm or in a factory, etc: *'farm-hands.* (**b**) a member of a ship's crew: *All hands on deck!* **6** [sing] skill in using the hands: *He has a light hand with pastry* (ie He makes it well). **7** (in compounds) done by a person, not a machine: *,hand-'built/ -'crafted/-'drawn/-'knitted/-'painted.* **8** [C] (**a**) a set of cards dealt to a player in a card-game: *have a good/bad/poor hand.* (**b**) one round in a game of cards: *Let's play one more hand.* **9** [sing] a style of HANDWRITING: *have a legible hand* ∘ *It was written in her own hand.* **10** [sing] (*dated or fml*) a promise to marry, esp one given by a woman: *He asked for her hand (in marriage).* **11** [C] a unit of measurement, about four inches or 10.16 centimetres, used for measuring the height of a horse. **IDM** **at first, second, etc 'hand** directly/indirectly; from/not from the original source: *I only heard the news at second hand.* **(close/near) at 'hand** near in place or time: *Her sister was always near at hand.* ∘ *Help was close at hand.* **at sb's hands** from sb: *I did not expect such unkind treatment at your hands.* **be a dab, an old, a poor, etc 'hand (at sth)** to have/ lack the specified skill or experience: *He's an old/a dab hand at this game* (ie very experienced). ∘ *I was never much of a hand* (ie never very good) *at cookery.* **be good with one's 'hands** to be good at practical tasks such as making or building things. **bind/tie sb hand and 'foot 1** to tie sb's hands and feet together. **2** to prevent sb from acting freely. **a bird in the hand is worth two in the bush** ⇨ BIRD. **bite the hand that feeds one** ⇨ BITE¹. **blood on one's hands** ⇨ BLOOD¹. **by 'hand 1** by a

person, not a machine: *made by hand.* **2** by a messenger, not through the post: *The note was delivered by hand.* **cap in hand** ⇨ CAP. **cash in hand** ⇨ CASH. **change hands** ⇨ CHANGE¹. **the dead hand of sth** ⇨ DEAD. **eat out of one's/sb's hand** ⇨ EAT. **fall, etc into sb's, etc 'hands** to be taken or obtained by sb, esp by an enemy: *The town fell into enemy hands.* ∘ *I would hate my diary to get into the wrong hands.* **a firm hand** ⇨ FIRM¹. **fold one's hands** ⇨ FOLD¹. **force sb's hand** ⇨ FORCE². **gain, etc the upper hand** ⇨ UPPER. **get, etc a free hand** ⇨ FREE¹. **give sb/get a big hand** ⇨ BIG. **(be) ,hand in 'glove (with sb)** (to be) working in close association: *He was found to be hand in glove with the enemy.* **,hand in 'hand 1** holding sb's hand. ⇨ picture at ARM¹. **2** closely associated; linked together: *War and suffering go hand in hand.* **,hand over 'fist** very fast and in large quantities: *The company is making money hand over fist.* **,hands 'off (sth/sb)** (*infml*) don't touch sth/sb; don't interfere: *,Hands off my 'sandwiches/my 'girlfriend!* **,hands 'up 1** (said when addressing a group of people) raise one hand, eg to answer a question: *Hands up, anyone who knows the answer.* **2** (said by a person threatening sb with a gun) raise both hands, eg to show that one is not going to fight or run away: *Hands up and don't move!* **,hand to 'hand** (of fighting) involving physical contact with one's opponent: *,hand-to-hand 'combat.* **have one's 'hands free/tied** to be/not be in a position to do as one likes. **have one's 'hands full** to be so busy that one cannot deal with anyone or anything else. **have sb in the palm of one's hand** ⇨ PALM¹. **have time on one's hands / time to kill** ⇨ TIME¹. **have, etc the whip hand** ⇨ WHIP¹. **a helping hand** ⇨ HELP¹. **hold sb's 'hand** to comfort or help sb in a sad or difficult situation: *I don't need anyone to hold my hand.* **in 'hand 1** in one's possession and available for use: *We still have some money in hand.* **2** in control: *The situation is well in hand.* **3** receiving attention and being dealt with: *the job in hand* ∘ *The work is in hand and will soon be completed.* **in one's/sb's 'hands** in one's/sb's possession, control or care: *The affair is no longer in my hands.* ∘ *Put the matter in the hands of a lawyer.* ∘ *The painting is in private hands.* **in (sb's) capable, good, etc 'hands** being well managed, etc by sb: *I've left the department in Bill's very efficient hands.* **in safe hands** ⇨ SAFE¹. **join hands** ⇨ JOIN. **keep one's 'hand in** to do an activity occasionally in order to remain skilled at it: *I like to play tennis regularly, just to keep my hand in.* **know sb/sth like the back of one's hand** ⇨ KNOW. **lay/get one's 'hands on sb/sth 1** to find or obtain sb/sth: *The book's here somewhere, but I can't lay my hands on it just now.* ∘ *I need to get my hands on a good computer.* **2** (*infml*) to catch sb/sth: *If I ever lay my hands on the thief, he'll be sorry.* **lend a hand** ⇨ LEND. **lift/raise a finger/hand** ⇨ LIFT. **lift/raise a/ one's 'hand against sb** to threaten or attack sb. **live from hand to mouth** ⇨ LIVE². **many hands make light 'work** (*saying*) a task is soon completed if many people help. **not do a hand's 'turn** to do no work: *He never does a hand's turn around the house.* **offer one's hand** ⇨ OFFER. **off one's 'hands** no longer one's responsibility: *They'll be glad to get their son off their hands financially.* **on either/ every 'hand** (*fml*) on both/all sides; in both/all directions. **on 'hand** available: *Our trained staff will be on hand to help you.* **on one's 'hands** as a responsibility; to look after: *She's got three small children on her hands.* **on the 'one hand ... on the 'other (hand) ...** (used to indicate contrasting points of view, opinions, etc): *On the one hand I want to travel abroad, but on the other I don't want to give up my job.* **out of 'hand 1** out of control: *Inflation is getting out of hand.* **2** at once; without

H

further thought or discussion: *The proposal was rejected out of hand.* ˌout of one's ˈhands no longer under one's control: *I can't help you, I'm afraid — the matter is out of my hands.* **overplay one's hand** ⇨ OVERPLAY. ˌplay into sb's ˈhands to do sth that is to an opponent's advantage. **put one's ˌhand in one's ˈpocket** to be ready to spend or give money. **putty in sb's hands** ⇨ PUTTY. **shake sb's hand**; **shake hands**; **shake sb by the hand** ⇨ SHAKE¹. **show one's hand/cards** ⇨ SHOW². **a show of hands** ⇨ SHOW¹. **sleight of hand** ⇨ SLEIGHT. **stay one's hand** ⇨ STAY¹. **take one's courage in both hands** ⇨ COURAGE. ˌtake sb in ˈhand to take control of sb in order to improve their behaviour: *Those children of his need to be taken in hand.* **take the law into one's own hands** ⇨ LAW. **take one's life in one's hands** ⇨ LIFE. **take sth into one's own ˈhands** to act oneself, esp after waiting for others to do sth which they have not done: *I decided to take matters into my own hands and inform the police.* **throw one's ˈhand in** (*infml*) to abandon an activity, a project, etc with which one is involved. **to ˈhand** within reach; readily available: *I don't have the information to hand.* **try one's hand** ⇨ TRY¹. **turn one's ˈhand to sth** to be able to do sth: *She can turn her hand to all sorts of jobs.* **wait on sb hand and foot** ⇨ WAIT². **wash one's hands of sb/sth** ⇨ WASH². **win hands down** ⇨ WIN. **wring one's hands** ⇨ WRING.

▶ **-handed** (in compound *adjs*) **1** having hands as specified: ˌempty-ˈhanded. **2(a)** using the specified hand, eg for writing or cutting things, in preference to the other: *Are you left-handed?* **(b)** made by or for the specified hand: *a one-handed catch* ○ *a right-handed glove.* See also RED-HANDED, SHORT-HANDED, SINGLE-HANDED.

handful /ˈhændfʊl/ *n* **1** [C] (*pl* **-fuls**) ~ **(of sth)** as much or as many as can be held in one hand: *pick up a handful of sand.* **2** [sing] ~ **(of sth)** a small number: *Only a handful of people came.* **3** a handful [sing] (*infml*) a person or an animal that is difficult to control: *That young lad is quite a handful* (ie is lively or often causes trouble).

■ ˈhand baggage *n* [U] (*esp US*) = HAND LUGGAGE. ˈhand-grenade *n* a GRENADE thrown by hand. ˌhand-ˈheld *adj* held in the hand: *a ˌhand-held ˈcamera/comˈputer.* ˈhand luggage (also *esp US* ˈhand baggage) *n* [U] small bags that can be carried by hand and kept with one on an aircraft. ˌhand-over-ˈfist *adv* very fast and in large amounts: *They're losing money hand-over-fist.* ˌhand-ˈpicked *adj* carefully and specially chosen. ˌhands-ˈoff *adj* [attrib] not interfering with or becoming involved in sth: *the government's hands-off approach to industrial disputes.* ˌhands-ˈon *adj* [attrib] practical(1); active: *have ˌhands-on exˈperience of a computer keyboard.*

hand² /hænd/ *v* ~ **sth** (**to sb**) to offer or give sth to sb: [Vnp] *He handed round the chocolates.* [Vnn] *Please hand me that book.* [Vnpr] *She handed it to the boy.* **IDM** ˈhand it to sb (*infml*) (always with *must* or *have (got) to*) to give sb the praise that they deserve: *You've got to hand it to her — she is extremely clever.* **PHR V** ˌhand sth ˈback (**to sb**) to return sth to the person who owns it or to where it belongs: *She handed (me) back the letter.* ○ *Control of the territory was handed back to China.* ˌhand sth ˈdown (**to sb**) **1** to give or leave sth to sb who is younger: *stories handed down from generation to generation* ○ *Most of my clothes were handed down to me by my older brother.* **2** (*esp US*) to announce sth formally or publicly: *hand down a budget/legal decision/verdict.* ˌhand sth ˈin (**to sb**) to give a piece of work, a document, etc to a person in authority: *She handed in her resignation.* ○ *A petition containing 50 000 signatures was handed in at the mayor's office.* ○ *Luckily, somebody found my keys and handed them in to the police.* ˌhand sth ˈon (**to sb**) to give sth to another person after one has finished with it: *Please hand on the magazine to your friends.* ˌhand sth ˈout (**to sb**) **1** to distribute sth: *Please hand these photocopies out (to the rest of the class) for me.* **2** to give advice, punishment, etc: *stiff sentences handed out by the courts to habitual offenders.* ˌhand (sth) ˈover (**to sb**) to transfer a position of authority or power to sb: *hand over power to an elected government* ○ *I am resigning as chairman and handing over to my deputy.* ˌhand sb ˈover to sb (esp in a news broadcast or on the telephone) to let sb listen or speak to another person: *I'm handing you over now to our home affairs correspondent.* ˌhand sb/sth ˈover (**to sb**) to deliver sb/sth formally to sb in authority: *They handed him/their weapons over to the police.*

■ ˈhand-me-downs *n* [pl] clothes that are no longer wanted and are given to another person, esp a younger brother or sister. ˈhand-out *n* **1** food, money or clothes given free to a person in need: *be dependent on hand-outs.* **2(a)** a notice, an advertisement, etc distributed to the public. **(b)** a written statement, copy of a political speech, etc that is given to the press: *election hand-outs.* **(c)** printed information given to students that contains eg a summary of a lecture or a set of exercises. ˈhand-over *n* a period during which power or responsibility is transferred from one person or group to another: *the smooth hand-over of power from the military to civilian government.*

handbag /ˈhændbæg/ (*US* also **purse**) *n* a small bag for money, keys, etc, carried esp by a woman. ⇨ picture at LUGGAGE.

handball /ˈhændbɔːl/ *n* [U] any of several games in which players throw a ball to each other or hit it with a hand against a wall.

handbill /ˈhændbɪl/ *n* a printed advertisement or announcement distributed by hand.

handbook /ˈhændbʊk/ *n* a small book giving useful facts: *a car handbook* ○ *a handbook of wild flowers.* Compare MANUAL *n* 1.

handbrake /ˈhændbreɪk/ *n* (in a motor vehicle) a BRAKE operated by hand, used when the vehicle is not moving: *Make sure the handbrake is on before leaving the vehicle.* ⇨ picture at CAR.

handcart /ˈhændkɑːt/ *n* = CART 1b.

handclap /ˈhændklæp/ *n* [sing] a clapping (CLAP¹) of the hands: *The audience started a slow handclap to show their impatience.*

handcuffs /ˈhændkʌfs/ *n* [pl] a pair of metal rings joined by a chain, for fastening round the wrists of a prisoner: *wear handcuffs* ○ *be led away in handcuffs.* ⇨ picture at SHACKLE.

▶ **handcuff** *v* ~ **sb/oneself** (**to sth/sb**) (esp passive) to put handcuffs on sb: [Vnpr] *The demonstrator had handcuffed herself to the railings.* [also Vn].

handgun /ˈhændgʌn/ *n* (*esp US*) a gun that is held and fired with one hand.

handhold /ˈhændhəʊld/ *n* a rock, etc that can be gripped by a person climbing up a steep slope.

handicap /ˈhændikæp/ *n* **1** a thing that makes progress difficult; a disadvantage: *In a job like this, lack of experience is no real handicap.* **2** a serious, usu permanent, physical or mental condition that affects one's ability to walk, see, speak, etc; a DISABILITY: *Deafness can be a serious handicap.* ○ *He strives hard to overcome his handicap.* **3** (*sport*) **(a)** a race or contest in which the stronger competitors start at a disadvantage in order to give all competitors an equal chance of success. **(b)** a disadvantage given to a competitor in such a contest, eg a weight to be

hang

carried by a horse. **4** (in golf) an advantage given to a player who is less good than others, by which strokes (STROKE 1) are deducted from her or his score at certain holes: *He's much better than I am — his handicap's 3 and I play off 11.*
▶ **handicap** *v* (-pp-) (esp passive) to make progress difficult for sb: [Vn] *be handicapped by a lack of education.* **handicapped** *adj* (*sometimes offensive*) having a handicap(2): *a mentally/visually handicapped child.* **the handicapped** *n* [pl *v*] handicapped people: *a school for the physically handicapped.* ⇨ note at DISABILITY.

handicraft /ˈhændɪkrɑːft; *US* -kræft/ *n* [U, C usu *pl*] (**a**) an activity such as sewing or weaving, done with one's hands and requiring artistic skill: *handicraft classes.* (**b**) items made in this way: *a sale of handicraft(s).*

handiwork /ˈhændɪwɜːk/ *n* [U] (**a**) work done or a thing produced with artistic skill: *She stood back to admire her handiwork.* (**b**) a thing done by a particular person, esp sth that should not have been done: *Is that drawing on the board your handiwork, Clare?*

handkerchief /ˈhæŋkətʃɪf, -tʃiːf/ *n* (*pl* **handkerchiefs** or **handkerchieves** /-tʃiːvz/) a small piece of cloth or paper tissue for blowing the nose into, wiping the face, etc.

handle /ˈhændl/ *n* **1**(**a**) the part of a door, window, etc by which it is opened: *polish the door handles.* (**b**) the part of an object, eg a bag, by which it is carried, held, etc: *The handle's broken off this cup.* ○ *There's paint all over the brush handle.* ⇨ picture at SCREWDRIVER. **2** a fact that may be taken advantage of: *His indiscretions gave his enemies a handle to use against him.* **3** (*sl*) a special name or title given to sb. **IDM fly off the handle** ⇨ FLY¹. **get a 'handle on sth** (*infml*) to understand sth: *I can't get a handle on these new tax laws.*
▶ **handle** *v* **1** to touch sth with or hold sth in the hand(s): [Vn] *Dynamite is dangerous stuff to handle.* ○ *Fragile — handle with care* (eg as a notice on a box). **2** to deal with, manage or control people, a situation, a machine, etc: [Vn] *He doesn't know how to handle old people.* ○ *This port handles 100 million tons of cargo each year.* ○ *Life is difficult but I can handle* (ie cope with) *it.* ○ *Do you think he can handle such a powerful car?* **3** (esp of a vehicle) to respond to the driver's use of the controls: [Vadv] *This car handles well.* **4** to treat a person or an animal in the way specified: [Vnadv] *be roughly handled by the police.* **5** to buy or sell sth: [Vn] *This shop does not handle foreign publications.* **6** (*fml*) to discuss or write about a subject: *a difficult topic to handle.*
handler /ˈhændlə(r)/ *n* (esp in compounds) (**a**) a person who trains and controls animals, esp dogs: *The police brought in their dog-handlers to join the hunt for the attacker.* (**b**) a person who handles or carries sth as part of her or his job: *airport baggage handlers* ○ *food handlers.*
-handled (in compound *adjs*) having a handle of the specified type: *a ˌbone-handled ˈknife* ○ *a ˌlong-handled ˈbrush.*

handlebar /ˈhændlbɑː(r)/ *n* (usu *pl*) a bar with a handle at each end, used for steering a bicycle, etc: *be thrown over the handlebars.* ⇨ picture at BICYCLE.
■ ˌhandlebar mouˈstache *n* a thick MOUSTACHE that is curved at each end.

handling /ˈhændlɪŋ/ *n* [U] **1** the cost of dealing with an order or exchanging goods, tickets, etc, that is added to the price: *a small handling charge.* Compare CARRIAGE 2. **2** the action of touching, feeling or holding sth with the hand(s): *toys that can stand up to rough handling.* **3** the action of dealing with a situation, etc: *I was impressed by your handling of the whole affair.* **4** the way in which a motor vehicle handles (HANDLE *v* 3).

handmade /ˌhændˈmeɪd/ *adj* made by hand: *ˌhandmade ˈpottery.* Compare MACHINE-MADE.
handmaid /ˈhændmeɪd/ (also **handmaiden** /ˈhændmeɪdn/) *n* (*arch*) a female servant.
handrail /ˈhændreɪl/ *n* a narrow rail that can be held for support, eg when going up or down stairs. ⇨ picture at STAIR.
handsaw /ˈhændsɔː/ *n* a SAW² used with one hand only.
handset /ˈhændset/ *n* the part of a telephone that one holds to one's ear and speaks into. Compare RECEIVER 1.
handshake /ˈhændʃeɪk/ *n* an act of shaking sb's hand with one's own, esp as a greeting. See also GOLDEN HANDSHAKE.
handsome /ˈhænsəm/ *adj* **1**(**a**) (of men) having an attractive face and figure: *a strikingly handsome doctor* ○ *He was tall, dark and handsome.* (**b**) (of women) having an attractive appearance, with large strong features: *I would describe her as handsome rather than beautiful.* (**c**) beautiful to look at: *a handsome horse/building/car.* ⇨ note at BEAUTIFUL. **2** generous: *a handsome gift/gesture/compliment.* **3** large in quantity: *make a handsome profit.*
▶ **handsomely** *adv*: *She was handsomely rewarded for her efforts.* ○ *win handsomely* ○ *His restraint paid off handsomely.* **handsomeness** *n* [U].

handstand /ˈhændstænd/ *n* an act of balancing on one's hands with one's feet in the air: *do a handstand.*
handwriting /ˈhændraɪtɪŋ/ *n* [U] (**a**) writing done with a pen or pencil, not printed or typed. (**b**) a person's particular style of writing in this way: *I can't read his handwriting.*
handwritten /ˌhændˈrɪtn/ *adj* written by hand, ie not printed or typed: *a ˌhandwritten ˈmanuscript.*
handy /ˈhændi/ *adj* (-ier, -iest) **1** useful; convenient: *a handy little gadget for taking the stones out of cherries* ○ *a handy sized torch.* **2** [pred] ~ (**for sth / doing sth**) situated or stored in a convenient place; situated near to one/sb/sth: *Our house is very handy for the schools.* ○ *Always keep a first-aid kit handy.* **3** [usu pred] skilful in using one's hands to make or repair things: *be handy about the house* ○ *handy with a sewing-machine.* **IDM** ˌcome in ˈhandy to be useful at some time in the future: *My extra earnings came in very handy.* ○ *Don't throw that cardboard box away — it may come in handy.* ▶ **handily** *adv*: *We're handily placed for* (ie within a short distance of) *the shopping centre.*
handyman /ˈhændimæn/ *n* (*pl* **-men** /-men/) a man who is good at a range of practical jobs inside and outside a house: *He had worked all his life as a handyman and gardener.*

hang¹ /hæŋ/ *v* (*pt, pp* **hung** /hʌŋ/ or, in sense 6, **hanged**) **1** to attach sth or be attached in a high position so that the lower part is free and does not touch the ground: [Vpr] *A towel hung from the rail.* ○ *a dress hanging in the wardrobe* [Vnpr, Vnp] *Hang your coat (up) on that hook.* ○ *She was hanging her washing (out) on the line.* **2** (of a thing that is attached at the top) to fall in a certain way: [Vp] *Her hair hung down almost to her waist.* [Vpr] *The curtains were hanging in folds.* [Vadv] *The dress now hung loosely on her.* **3**(**a**) to attach sth, esp a picture, or be attached, to a hook on a wall: [Vnpr] *We hung his portrait above the fireplace.* [Vpr] *Her paintings hang in the National Gallery.* [also Vn]. (**b**) ~ sth with sth (esp passive) to decorate a place by placing paintings, etc on a wall: [Vnpr] *The rooms were hung with tapestries.* **4** to stick WALLPAPER to a wall: [Vn] *He hangs wallpaper like a professional.* **5** [Vn] to attach a door or gate to a post using hinges (HINGE) so that it moves freely. **6**(**a**) to kill sb/ oneself by tying a rope around the neck and attaching the end of it to a high place before removing support from underneath: [Vn, Vnpr] *He was hanged (for murder).* [Vnpr] *She hanged herself from the rafters.* (**b**) to be killed in this way as a punishment: [V] *You can't hang for such a crime.* **7(a)** [Vn] to put meat on a hook attached eg to the ceiling and leave it until the flavour becomes stronger and it is ready for cooking. (**b**) to be left hanging in this way: [V] *Let pheasants hang for a couple of weeks.* **8** to bend or let sth bend downwards: [Vp] *The dog's tongue was hanging out.* [Vpr] *Children hung* (ie were leaning) *over the gate.* ○ *A cigarette hung from her lips.* [Vnpr] *She **hung her head** in shame.* **9** ~ (**above/ over sth/sb**) to remain, esp as sth unpleasant or threatening: [Vpr] *Smoke hung in the air above the city.* ○ *She's got those exams hanging over her.* [also V]. **10** (*infml*) (esp imperative) forget sth; do not worry about sth: *Do it and hang the expense!* **IDM** **go ˈhang** (*sl*) (used to express complete lack of concern for sb/sth): *I've had enough of my brother — he can go hang for all I care.* **hang by a ˈhair / a (single) ˈthread** (of a person's fate, etc) to be in great danger or at risk: *His life hung by a thread.* **hang ˈfire** (of a plan, etc) to be delayed or late in starting: *The project had hung fire for several years because of lack of funds.* **hang (on) ˈin there** (*infml*) to remain firm and determined in difficult circumstances. **ˈhang it (ˈall)** (*infml*) (used to express annoyance): *Hang it 'all, Mary, you can't expect me to work all weekend.* **hang on sb's ˈwords / on sb's every ˈword** to listen to sb one admires with great attention. **Iˈm hanged if I do sth** (*infml*) (used to emphasize that one cannot or will not do sth): *I'm hanged if I'm going to pay for his mistakes.* **let it and hang ˈout** (*infml catchphrase*) to express one's feelings and wishes freely. **one may/might as well be hanged/hung for a ˌsheep as (for) a ˈlamb** (*saying*) if the penalty for a more serious offence is no greater than that for a less serious one, one might as well continue to commit the more serious one. **a peg to hang sth on** ⇨ PEG¹. **(and) thereby hangs a ˈtale** there is an interesting or surprising story or piece of information connected with this. **time hangs heavy** ⇨ TIME¹. **PHRV** **ˌhang aˈbout/ aˈround (…)** (*infml*) to wait or stay near a place, with or without a particular aim or purpose: *I don't like you hanging around the streets after dark.* ○ *Stop hanging about and go and tidy your room.*

ˌhang ˈback to remain in a place after all the other people have left: *I hung back to ask the speaker a question.* **ˌhang ˈback (from sth)** to hesitate because one is nervous about doing or saying sth: *I was sure she knew the answer but for some reason she hung back.*

ˌhang ˈon 1 to grip sth firmly for support: *Hang on ˈtight — we're off!* **2** (*infml*) to wait for a short time: *Hang ˈon a minute — I'm not quite ready.* **3** (*infml*) (on the telephone) to remain connected until one is able to talk to a particular person: *The line was engaged and the operator asked if I'd like to hang ˈon.* **4** to continue doing sth in difficult circumstances: *How much longer will their troops be able to hang on in that position?* **ˈhang on sth** to depend on sth: *A lot hangs on this decision.* **ˌhang ˈon to sth 1** to hold sth tightly: *ˌHang on to that ˈrope and don't let go.* **2** (*infml*) to keep sth, not sell it or give it away: *I should ˌhang on to those old ˈphotographs — they may be valuable.*

ˌhang ˈout (*infml*) to live or spend a lot of time in a place: *She spent her time in Paris hanging out in cafés and bars.*

ˌhang toˈgether 1 (of people) to support or help one another. **2** (of statements) to be consistent: *Their accounts of what happened don't hang together.*

ˌhang ˈup (sth) to end a telephone conversation by replacing the RECEIVER(1): *Maggie hung up (the phone).* **ˌhang sth ˈup** (*infml*) to finish using sth for

the last time: *Ruth has hung up her dancing shoes.* **ˌhang ˈup on sb** (*infml*) to end a telephone call by suddenly and unexpectedly replacing the RECEIVER (1): *When I mentioned the money, he just hung up on me.* **be/get ˌhung ˈup (about/on sb/sth)** (*infml*) to be disturbed or obsessed (OBSESS) by sb/sth: *She's really hung up on that guy.*

▶ **hanging** *n* **1** [U, C] death by hanging: *sentence sb to death by hanging* ○ *public hangings.* **2 hangings** [pl] pieces of fabric placed on walls for decoration.

hang-gliding

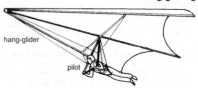

hang-glider

pilot

■ **ˈhang-gliding** *n* [U] the sport of flying while hanging from a frame like a large KITE(1) which one controls with one's body movements. See also GLIDING. ⇨ picture. **ˈhang-glider** *n* **1** a person who does hang-gliding. **2** the frame used in hang-gliding. ⇨ picture.

ˈhang-out *n* (*infml*) a place where one lives or which one visits often: *journalists' hang-outs.*

ˈhang-up *n* (*infml*) an emotional problem about sth: *She's got a real hang-up about wearing glasses.*

hang² /hæŋ/ *n* [sing] the way in which cloth, etc hangs: *the hang of a coat/skirt.* **IDM** **get the ˈhang of sth** (*infml*) to learn how to operate or do sth: *I'm still trying to get the hang of the new telephone system.* **not care/give a ˈhang (about sth/sb)** (*infml*) not to care at all.

hangar /ˈhæŋə(r), ˈhæŋɡə(r)/ *n* a large shed in which aircraft are kept.

hangdog /ˈhæŋdɒɡ/ *adj* [attrib] (of a person's look) guilty or ashamed: *his hangdog expression.*

hanger /ˈhæŋə(r)/ (also **ˈclothes-hanger**, **ˈcoat-hanger**) *n* a curved piece of wood, plastic or wire with a hook at the top, used for hanging a garment in a WARDROBE(1), etc.

hanger-on /ˌhæŋər ˈɒn/ *n* (*pl* **hangers-on** /ˌhæŋəz ˈɒn/) (*usu derog*) a person who becomes friendly with sb famous, important, etc, esp in the hope of personal gain: *The great actor was surrounded by his usual crowd of hangers-on.*

hangman /ˈhæŋmən/ *n* (*pl* **-men** /-mən/) a person whose job is to hang¹(6) criminals.

hangnail /ˈhæŋneɪl/ *n* a piece of sore broken skin near the bottom of a nail on one's finger.

hangover /ˈhæŋəʊvə(r)/ *n* **1** unpleasant physical symptoms experienced after drinking too much alcohol: *have a hangover* ○ *He's sleeping off a bad hangover.* **2** ~ (**from sth**) a practice, tradition, etc that remains after everything associated with it has been changed or lost: *This procedure is a hangover from the old system.*

hank /hæŋk/ *n* a loosely wound length of wool, etc: *wind a hank of wool into balls.*

hanker /ˈhæŋkə(r)/ *v* **PHRV** **ˈhanker after/for sth** to have a strong desire for sth: [Vpr] *hanker after one's native land* ○ *hanker for big city life.*

▶ **hankering** *n* ~ (**after/for sth**); ~ (**to do sth**) a strong desire: *have a hankering for adventure/to travel.*

hanky /ˈhæŋki/ *n* (*infml*) a HANDKERCHIEF.

hanky-panky /ˌhæŋki ˈpæŋki/ *n* [U] (*infml often joc*) behaviour that is not considered correct or acceptable, esp involving sexual activity: *There was a lot of hanky-panky going on at the party.*

Hansard /'hænsɑːd/ n [U] the official report of proceedings of the British Parliament, printed daily: *reading Hansard.*

hansom /'hænsəm/ (also ,hansom 'cab) n (formerly) a type of carriage with two wheels, pulled by a horse, with room for two passengers inside.

haphazard /ˌhæp'hæzəd/ adj without plan or order; RANDOM: *books piled on shelves in a haphazard fashion* ◦ *The government's approach to the problem was haphazard.* ▶ **haphazardly** adv.

hapless /'hæpləs/ adj [attrib] (*esp rhet*) not lucky or fortunate: *hapless passengers stranded because of the rail strike.*

happen /'hæpən/ v **1** to occur, esp as part of a series of events; to take place: [Vadv] *How did the accident happen?* ◦ *What happened next?* [V] *Whatever happens, don't let me forget to ring Jack.* ◦ *I'd stay if they promoted me, but I can't see that actually happening.* **2** to do or be sth as a result of chance: [V.*to* inf, V.*that*] *She happened to be out/It happened that she was out when he called.* [V.*to* inf] *He happens to be a friend of mine.* **IDM** **accidents will happen** ⇨ ACCIDENT. **as it happens/happened** used before saying sth surprising) actually: *We met her only yesterday, as it happens.* **in the event of sth / that sth happens** ⇨ EVENT. **it (just) so happens that...** by chance: '*You haven't got a pair of scissors in your bag, have you?' 'Well, it just so happens that I have.'* **PHRV** **'happen on sth** (*dated*) to find sth by chance. **happen to sb/sth** (esp with a pronoun as subject) to occur to sb or affect sth as the result of an action, event, etc: *I hope nothing* (ie nothing unpleasant) *has happened to them.* ◦ *What's happened to your car?*

▶ **happening** /'hæpənɪŋ/ n (**a**) (usu *pl*) a thing that happens; an event: *The book describes the day-to-day happenings of a small country town.* ◦ *There have been strange happenings here lately.* ⇨ note at OCCURRENCE. (**b**) an informal artistic performance or event.

NOTE Compare **happen**, **occur** and **take place**. **Happen** refers to accidental or unplanned events: *What happened at the meeting last night?* **Occur** is used in formal situations: *Police report that the accident occurred at about 9.30.* **Happen** is also used to talk about one event resulting from another: *What happened when you told him the news?* (ie What did he say/do?) **Take place** suggests that an event has been planned: *The funeral will take place on 24 April at 3 pm.*

happenstance /'hæpənstæns; *Brit also* -stɑːns/ [U] chance: *I found it purely by happenstance.*

happy /'hæpi/ adj (-ier, -iest) **1**(**a**) feeling or expressing pleasure, contentment (CONTENT¹), etc: *You don't look very happy today.* ◦ *a happy smile/face* ◦ *I won't be happy until I know she's safe.* (**b**) giving or causing pleasure, etc: *a happy day/marriage/ memory/ending (to a book, etc)* ◦ *spend many happy hours walking in the woods.* **2** ~ (**about/ with sb/sth**) feeling satisfied that sth is good, right, etc: *I'm not happy with his work this term.* ◦ *We liked our room, but we weren't very happy about the food in the hotel.* **3** (in greetings) full of joy: *Happy birthday!* ◦ *Happy Christmas!* **4** [pred] ~ **to do sth** (*fml*) pleased or very willing to do sth: *I am* (*more than*) *happy to be of service.* **5** fortunate; lucky: *He is in the happy position of never having to worry about money.* **6** (of words, ideas, behaviour, etc) well suited to the situation; pleasing: *not a very happy choice of words/combination of colours.* **IDM** **a ,happy e'vent** n the birth of a child. **the happy/ golden mean** ⇨ MEAN³. **many happy re'turns (of the 'day)** (used as a greeting to sb on their birthday).

▶ **happily** adv **1** in a satisfied or contented (CONTENT¹) way: *be happily married* ◦ *children playing happily on the beach.* **2** by good luck; fortunately (FORTUNATE): *Happily, the damage was only slight.* **3** in an appropriate manner: *His letter was not very happily worded.*

happiness n [U]: *find/achieve true happiness* ◦ *Their grandchildren are a constant source of happiness.*

■ **,happy-go-'lucky** adj not planning or worrying about the future: *a ,happy-go-lucky 'attitude/'person.* Compare SLAP-HAPPY.

'happy hour n (usu *sing*) (*infml*) a period during a day when one can buy alcoholic drinks in a bar more cheaply than usual.

,happy 'medium n (usu *sing*) a satisfactory balance between two extremes; a compromise: *be/provide/ strike a happy medium.*

hara-kiri /ˌhærə 'kɪri/ n [U] a ritual act of killing oneself by cutting open one's stomach with a sword, performed esp by the Samurai in Japan as an honourable way of avoiding DISGRACE¹: *commit/perform hara-kiri.*

harangue /hə'ræŋ/ n a long aggressive speech that criticizes sb/sth or tries to persuade sb to do sth: *He suddenly launched into a harangue about declining public morals.*

▶ **harangue** v to deliver a harangue to sb: [Vn] *haranguing the troops before a battle.*

harass /'hærəs, hə'ræs/ v **1** to trouble and annoy sb continually: [Vn] *be sexually harassed* ◦ *He complained of being harassed by the police.* **2** to make repeated attacks on an enemy: *aid convoys continually harassed by guerrillas.*

▶ **harassed** adj feeling or showing strain, eg because one has too much to do: *a harassed-looking waiter* ◦ *Shopping in town left her feeling tired and harassed.*

harassment n [U]: *be subject to racial/sexual/police harassment.*

harbinger /'hɑːbɪndʒə(r)/ n ~ **(of sb/sth)** (*rhet*) a sign that sth will happen soon: *The event was seen as a harbinger of things to come.*

harbour (*US* **harbor**) /'hɑːbə(r)/ n [C, U] an area of water protected from the open sea by walls or banks, in which ships can shelter: *Several boats lay at anchor in the harbour.* ◦ *We reached/entered (the) harbour at sunset.*

▶ **harbour** (*US* **harbor**) v **1** to hide and shelter in one's home sb wanted by the police, etc: [Vn] *be convicted of harbouring a wanted criminal.* **2** to keep feelings or thoughts, esp bad ones, in one's mind for a long time: [Vn] *harbour a grudge* ◦ *harbour doubts/suspicions/thoughts of revenge.* **3** to contain and allow sth to develop: [Vn] *a dirty sink harbouring germs.*

■ **'harbour-master** n an official in charge of a harbour.

harbourside /'hɑːbəsaɪd/ n [U] the area of land near a harbour: *harbourside bars.*

hard¹ /hɑːd/ adj (-er, -est) **1** firm, stiff or solid and not easily bent or broken: *ground made hard by frost* ◦ *wait for the concrete to go hard* ◦ *hard apples* ◦ *hard, muscular bodies.* Compare SOFT 1. **2** ~ (**for sb**) (**to do sth**) difficult to do, understand or answer; not easy: *a hard task/book/language/choice* ◦ *She found it hard to decide which college to apply to.* ◦ *I find his attitude very hard to take* (ie difficult to accept). ◦ *It's hard to tell whether the story is true or not.* ◦ *It's hard for old people to change their ways.* ◦ *You are hard to please/a hard person to please.* **3**(**a**) requiring a lot of physical strength or mental effort: *It's hard work shovelling snow.* ◦ *Finding the right person for a job can be hard work.* (**b**) done with a lot of strength or force: *give sb a hard kick/punch.* (**c**) (of people) putting a lot of effort, energy, etc into an activity: *She's a very hard worker.* ○ *He's **hard at work** on a new novel.* **4** full of difficulty; not easy, happy or comfortable: *have a hard day/life/childhood* ○ *Times are hard.* **5** not feeling or showing affection, pity, etc; severe; harsh: *a hard father* ○ *exchange hard words with sb* ○ *a hard smile/look.* Compare SOFT 9. **6** tough and determined to pursue one's own advantage regardless of others: *He's a hard man.* **7** involving a lot of aggressive discussion and argument in order to reach the best deal possible: *The employers and unions then entered a period of **hard bargaining**.* **8** (of the weather) severe: *a hard winter/frost.* **9** true and not able to be denied: *the hard facts of the case* ○ *have hard evidence of sth.* **10** (of sounds or colours) unpleasant to the ear or eye; harsh: *a hard voice* ○ *a very hard yellow.* **11** (of consonants) sounding sharp, not soft: *The letter 'g' is hard in 'gun' and soft in 'gin'.* Compare SOFT 15. **12** (of drinks) strongly alcoholic: *hard liquor* ○ (*joc*) *a drop of the ˈhard stuff* (ie a strong alcoholic drink, eg WHISKY). **13** (of water) containing CALCIUM and other mineral salts that are left as a layer inside pipes, etc: *a hard water area* ○ *Our water is very hard.* Compare SOFT 14. **IDM** be ˈhard on sb **1** to treat or criticize sb severely: *Don't be too hard on her — she's very young.* **2** to be unfair to sb/sth: *The new regulations are a bit hard on small businesses.* **3** to be likely to damage sth or spoil sth quickly: *These rough roads are very hard on the springs.* **drive/strike a hard ˈbargain** to argue aggressively and insist on the best possible deal or price. **give sb a hard ˈtime** to make a situation unpleasant and difficult for sb: *They gave me a hard time at the interview.* ˌhard and ˈfast (esp after a negative) (of rules, etc) that cannot be changed in any circumstances: *There are no hard and fast rules about this.* ○ *This distinction isn't hard and fast.* **(as) ˌhard as ˈnails** showing no sympathy or kindness. ˌhard ˈat it working very hard at sth: *I've been hard at it all morning.* ˌhard ˈgoing **1** difficult to understand or enjoy; boring: *I'm finding this book very hard going.* **2** difficult to make progress: *The ground was very wet so it was hard going.* ˌhard ˈlines (*Brit infml*) (used as an expression of sympathy): *You failed your driving test, I hear — hard lines!* **a hard/tough nut** ⇨ NUT. ˌhard of ˈhearing not able to hear well; rather DEAF: *TV subtitles for the hard of hearing.* **the ˈhard way 1** through having unpleasant experiences rather than by listening to what one is told: *She won't listen to my advice so she'll just have to learn the hard way.* **2** experiencing great difficulties: *He grew up the hard way — his parents didn't have a penny.* **have a hard job doing / to do sth; have a hard time doing sth** to do sth with much difficulty: *I had a hard time persuading him to come.* ○ *He had a hard job to make himself heard.* **make hard ˈwork of sth** to use more time or energy on a task than is necessary. **no hard ˈfeelings** no anger or bitterness (BITTER 3) remaining: *Now we're divorced there are no hard feelings between us.* ○ *'No hard feelings, I hope,' he said, offering me his hand.* **play hard to ˈget** (*infml*) to make oneself seem more attractive, etc by not immediately accepting an invitation to do sth: *Ask her out again — she's just playing hard to get, I'm sure.* **too much like hard ˈwork** (of an activity) requiring too much effort. ▶ **hardness** *n* [U]: *water hardness* ○ *hardness of heart.*

■ ˌhard ˈcash *n* [U] money, esp notes and coins, that is available to be spent.

ˌhard ˈcopy *n* [U] (*computing*) printed material produced by a computer, usu on paper, to be read in the ordinary way.

ˌhard ˈcore *n* **1** [Gp] the most active and committed members of an organization, etc: *a hard core of troublemakers* ○ *It's really only the hard core that bother(s) to go to meetings.* **2** [U] small pieces of

stone, brick, etc used for the foundations of roads, etc.

ˌhard-ˈcore *adj* [usu attrib] **1** following a belief or activity, etc very firmly: *hard-core supporters of the National Front.* **2** showing or describing sexual activity in a very detailed or violent way: *hard-core pornography.*

ˌhard ˈcourt *n* a tennis court with a concrete or TARMAC surface, not of grass.

ˌhard ˈcurrency *n* [U,C] a currency, eg dollars or pounds, which can be exchanged easily for another because it is not likely to lose its value: *pay in hard currency* ○ *convert roubles into hard currency.*

ˌhard ˈdisk *n* (*computing*) a sealed MAGNETIC(1) storage device, linked to or fitted inside a computer, on which large amounts of data can be recorded: *The program is stored on the hard disk.*

ˌhard ˈdrug *n* [C usu *pl*] a drug that has very strong, often dangerous, effects and can cause people to become addicted (ADDICT 1). Compare SOFT DRUG.

ˌhard-ˈfaced *adj* showing no sympathy or feeling: *hard-faced ofˈficials.*

ˌhard ˈhat *n* a special HELMET designed to protect the head, worn eg by building workers.

ˌhard-ˈheaded *adj* not allowing one's emotions to affect one's opinions or decisions: *a ˌhard-headed ˈrealist/ˈbusinessman* ○ *give a hard-headed assessment of the situation.*

ˌhard-ˈhearted *adj* lacking in feeling or sympathy; unkind.

ˌhard ˈlabour *n* [U] a prison sentence together with heavy physical labour: *be sentenced to ten years' hard labour.*

the ˌhard ˈleft *n* [Gp] the members of a left-wing (LEFT²) political party or group who hold the most extreme views.

ˌhard-ˈline *adj* (**a**) (of people) believing strongly in sth and not able or willing to change one's ideas, policies, etc: *a ˌhard-line ˈsocialist.* (**b**) (of ideas) firm and not easily changed: *a hard-line attitude/approach.* ▶ ˌhard-ˈliner *n*: *communist hard-liners.*

ˌhard-ˈluck story *n* (*often derog*) an account of one's problems told in order to gain sb's sympathy or help: *She gave me some hard-luck story about losing her job.*

ˌhard-ˈnosed *adj* (*infml*) not influenced by emotional considerations; tough: *a ˌhard-nosed ˈjournalist* ○ *hard-nosed tactics.*

ˌhard ˈporn *n* films, pictures, books, etc showing or describing sexual activity in a very detailed or violent way. Compare SOFT PORN.

the ˌhard ˈright *n* [Gp] the members of a right-wing (RIGHT⁵) political party or group who hold the most extreme views.

ˌhard ˈrock *n* [U] rock³ music with a very strong beat.

ˌhard ˈsell *n* [sing, U] an aggressive method of selling sth: *the hard sell tactics of insurance salesmen.*

ˌhard ˈshoulder *n* (*Brit*) a strip of ground with a hard surface beside a MOTORWAY where vehicles may stop in an emergency: *I pulled over onto the hard shoulder.*

ˈhard-top *n* a car with a metal roof.

hard² /hɑːd/ *adv* **1** with great effort: *work/think/pull/push hard* ○ *try hard to succeed.* **2** with difficulty; with a struggle: *Our victory was hard won.* **3** severely; heavily: *freezing/raining/snowing hard.* **4** at a sharp angle: *Turn hard left.* **IDM** be hard ˈput (to it) (to do sth) to find it very difficult to do sth: *He was hard put (to it) to explain her disappearance.* **be hard ˈup for sth** (*infml*) to have too few or little of sth: *He's hard up for ideas.* **die hard** ⇨ DIE¹. **hard ˈdone by** unfairly treated: *She feels (she's been) rather hard done by.* ˈhard on sth soon after sth: *His death followed hard on hers.* **hard on sb's ˈheels** closely following sb: *He ran ahead, with the* *others hard on his heels.* **take sth 'hard** to be very upset by sth: *When their child died they took it very hard.*

■ **,hard-'boiled** *adj* **1** (of eggs) boiled until solid inside. **2** (*infml*) not showing any feelings; tough.

,hard 'by *prep, adv* near: *,hard by the 'river* ○ *There was an inn hard 'by.*

,hard-'earned *adj* acquired with a lot of effort: *a ,hard-earned 'victory* ○ *,hard-earned 'cash.*

,hard-'fought *adj* acquired or won by competing, etc very hard: *a ,hard-fought 'battle/'contest.*

,hard-'hitting *adj* forceful and direct: *a ,hard-hitting 'speech/re'port.*

,hard-'pressed *adj* ~ (**to do sth**) experiencing difficulties or under great pressure: *hard-pressed junior doctors working long hours* ○ *They're already hard-pressed to find their rent money.*

,hard 'up *adj* having very little money: *His family has always been hard up.* ○ *hard-up students.*

,hard-'wearing *adj* lasting for a long time and remaining in good condition: *a ,hard-wearing 'carpet.*

,hard-'won *adj* gained after a hard struggle: *their ,hard-won po,litical 'freedom* ○ *,hard-won con'cessions.*

,hard-'working *adj* (of people) working with energy and care: *,hard-working 'miners* ○ *She's talented and hard-working.*

hardback /'hɑːdbæk/ *n* [C, U] a book with a stiff cover: *Hardbacks are more expensive, but they last longer.* ○ *It was published in hardback last year.* Compare PAPERBACK.

hardball /'hɑːdbɔːl/ *n* [U] (*US infml*) baseball. **IDM play 'hardball** to act aggressively in business or politics.

hardbitten /,hɑːd'bɪtn/ *adj* (of people) made hard¹(5) by experience: *a ,hardbitten de'tective.*

hardboard /'hɑːdbɔːd/ *n* [U] stiff board made from small pieces of wood that have been crushed and specially treated. It is sold in thin sheets and used instead of wood.

harden /'hɑːdn/ *v* (**a**) to become or make sth become hard, strong, firm or more fixed, etc: [V] *The varnish takes a few hours to harden.* ○ *He said nothing but I saw his face harden.* ○ *Attitudes to the strike have hardened on both sides.* [Vn] *The incident hardened his resolve to leave the company.* (**b**) (esp passive) to make sb/sth less sensitive to sth: [Vn] *a hardened criminal* (ie one who shows no regret for her or his crimes) [Vn, Vnpr] *For her own good, she must harden her heart* (against him). [Vnpr] *He became hardened to the suffering around him.* ► **hardening** *n* [U, sing]: *hardening of the arteries* ○ *a hardening of attitudes towards one-parent families.*

hardly /'hɑːdli/ *adv* **1** only just; scarcely; barely: *I hardly know her.* ○ *We had hardly begun/Hardly had we begun our walk when it began to rain.* ○ *Tom's hardly ten yet — it's too soon to think about careers!* **2** (esp after *can* or *could*) only with difficulty: *I'm so tired I can hardly stay awake.* ○ *We can hardly afford to run a car.* ○ *I could hardly believe my eyes, she looked so different.* **3** almost no; almost not: *There's hardly any milk left.* ○ *Hardly anybody* (ie Very few people) *came to the meeting.* ○ *He hardly ever* (ie very seldom) *goes to bed before midnight.* ○ *Hardly a week goes by without someone complaining* (ie Nearly every week someone complains) *about it.* ⇨ note at ALMOST. **4** (used to suggest that sth is unlikely or unreasonable): *Don't telephone yet — they'll hardly* (ie are very unlikely to) *have finished lunch.* ○ *The thieves can hardly have got very far.* **5** (used to suggest that sb is being foolish in doing or saying sth) no; not: *'Shall I invite the Hills?' 'Hardly, you know they don't get on with Liz and Simon.'* ○ *This is hardly the time to back out.* ○ *You can hardly expect me to believe that!* ○ *It's hardly surprising that she failed her exams when she did so little work.*

hardship /'hɑːdʃɪp/ *n* [U, C] suffering caused usu by a lack of money or basic necessities: *suffer years of hardship during the war* ○ *financial hardship* ○ *face appalling hardship(s).*

hardware /'hɑːdweə(r)/ *n* [U] **1** household equipment and tools, eg pans, nails, locks and brushes. **2** (*computing*) the mechanical and electronic parts of a computer. Compare SOFTWARE. **3** heavy machinery or weapons: *military hardware.*

hardwood /'hɑːdwʊd/ *n* [U] hard heavy wood from a DECIDUOUS tree, eg OAK: *hardwood doors/floors.* Compare SOFTWOOD.

hardy /'hɑːdi/ *adj* (**-ier, -iest**) **1** able to endure cold or difficult conditions; tough(2): *hardy mountain folk.* **2** (of a plant) that can survive outside through the winter. ► **hardiness** *n* [U].

hare /heə(r)/ *n* an animal like a rabbit but with longer ears and back legs and able to run very fast. **IDM mad as a hatter / March hare** ⇨ MAD.
► **hare** *v* (*Brit*) to run very fast: [Vpr, Vp] *He hared (off) down the street.* [also Vadv].
■ **'hare-brained** *adj* foolish; crazy: *a hare-brained scheme/person.*

harebell /'heəbel/ *n* a wild plant with delicate blue flowers shaped like bells and a very thin stem.

harelip /'heəlɪp/ *n* a condition in which a person's upper lip is split because it has not developed properly before birth: *be born with a harelip.*

harem /'hɑːriːm, -rəm; *US* 'hærəm/ *n* (**a**) [C] the separate part of a traditional Muslim house in which the women live. (**b**) [CGp] the women living in this.

haricot /'hærɪkəʊ/ (also ,haricot 'bean) (*Brit*) (*US* navy bean) *n* a small white bean that is usu sold dried and soaked before cooking.

hark /hɑːk/ *v* [V] (*arch*) to listen. **PHR V 'hark at sb** (*Brit infml*) (used in the imperative to draw attention to sb who has said sth foolish or who has been boasting): *Just hark at him! Who does he think he is?*
,hark 'back (to sth) (*Brit*) **1** to mention again or remember an earlier subject, event, etc: *She's always harking back to her childhood.* **2** to remind one of sth; to be like sth from the past: *paintings harking back to Turner.*

harlequin /'hɑːləkwɪn/ *n* (formerly) a comic character in PANTOMIME(1), usu wearing a mask and dressed in a costume with a diamond pattern.

harlot /'hɑːlət/ *n* (*arch derog*) a prostitute.

harm /hɑːm/ *n* [U] physical, mental or moral injury: *He meant no harm* (ie did not intend to hurt or upset anyone). ○ *A few late nights never did anyone any harm.* ○ *Don't worry, we'll make sure she comes to no harm.* ○ *I don't particularly like him but I certainly don't wish him any harm.* ○ *The treatment did him more harm than good.* **IDM ,no 'harm done** (*infml*) (used for telling sb not to worry about sth they have done because it has not caused any problem, injury, etc): *Don't worry about it, David, no harm done.* **out of harm's 'way** in a safe place: *Put that vase out of harm's way so that the children can't break it.* **there is no harm in (sb's) doing sth / it does no harm (for sb) to do sth** nothing is lost by doing sth, and some good may result from it: *He may not be able to help but there's no harm in asking him.*
► **harm** *v* to cause harm to sb/sth: [Vn] *an event which has harmed relations between the two countries* ○ *Poor exam results will harm his chances of getting into university.* **IDM not harm/hurt a fly** ⇨ FLY².

harmful /'hɑːmfl/ *adj* ~ (**to sb/sth**) causing harm: *the harmful effects of smoking* ○ *Publication of the report might be harmful to the interests of the company.*

harmless *adj* **1** without the power to harm sb/sth: *The substance is harmless to fish.* **2** unlikely to annoy or upset people: *We were just having a bit of harmless fun.* ○ *He seems a harmless enough* person to me. **harmlessly** adv: The missile exploded harmlessly in the sea. **harmlessness** n [U].

harmonic /hɑːˈmɒnɪk/ adj of or relating to harmony(3): harmonic progressions/effects.

harmonica /hɑːˈmɒnɪkə/ (also **mouth-organ**) n a small musical instrument played by passing it across the lips while blowing or sucking air through it.

harmonious /hɑːˈməʊnɪəs/ adj **1** free from disagreement or ill feeling: a harmonious community/relationship/atmosphere. **2** arranged together in a pleasing way so that each part matches the others: a harmonious group of buildings ○ harmonious colour combinations. **3** having a sweet and pleasant sound; tuneful (TUNE¹): harmonious singing. ► **harmoniously** adv.

harmonium /hɑːˈməʊnɪəm/ n a musical instrument like an organ², in which sound is produced by pumping air though metal pipes and playing a KEYBOARD(1b).

harmonize, -ise /ˈhɑːmənaɪz/ v **1** ~ (sth) (with sth) to be or make sth HARMONIOUS: [V] colours that harmonize well (ie together produce a pleasing effect) [Vpr] The cottages harmonize well with the landscape. [Vn] Care should be taken to harmonize the interests of farmers and consumers. [also Vnpr]. **2** (music) to play or sing notes that accompany the main tune and produce harmony(3). ~ (with sb/sth) [V] The group harmonizes well. [Vpr] harmonize with the lead singer [Vn] harmonize a melody. ► **harmonization, -isation** /ˌhɑːmənaɪˈzeɪʃn; US -nəˈz-/ n [U, C].

harmony /ˈhɑːməni/ n **1** [U] a state of agreement in feelings, interests, opinions, etc: working towards harmony in international affairs ○ live together **in harmony**. **2** [C,U] a pleasing combination of related things: the harmony of colour in nature ○ The designer's aim is to produce a harmony of shape and texture. **3** [U,C] (music) the way in which different notes played or sung at the same time combine to make a pleasing sound: have classes in harmony ○ study harmony ○ The two sang in harmony. ○ There are some lovely harmonies in the chorus. Compare CONCORD, DISCORD.

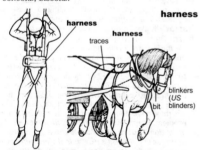

harness

harness

harness

traces

blinkers (US blinders)

bit

harness /ˈhɑːnɪs/ n **1** a set of usu leather straps and metal parts that is put round a horse's head and body so that the horse can be controlled and fastened to the cart, etc that it pulls. ⇨ picture. **2** a set of straps for fastening sth, eg a PARACHUTE, to a person's body, or for controlling a small child. ⇨ picture. **IDM** in **harness** in the routine of one's usual work: get back in harness after a holiday. **in harness (with sb)** working closely with sb in order to achieve sth: The industry is working in harness with the government to create a recovery.
► **harness** v **1** ~ sth (to sth) to put a harness on a horse, etc; to attach a horse, etc to sth by a harness: [Vnpr] harness a horse to a wagon [also Vn]. **2** to control and use a natural force to produce electrical

power, etc: [Vn] harness a river/a waterfall/the sun's rays as a source of energy [Vn.to inf] (fig) harness the skills of the workforce to achieve economic growth [also Vnpr].

harp /hɑːp/ n a large upright musical instrument with strings stretched on a frame, played with the fingers. ⇨ picture at MUSICAL INSTRUMENT.
► **harp** v **PHRV** ,harp 'on (about) sth to talk repeatedly about sth in a boring or annoying way: She's always harping on (about) how badly paid she is.

harpist n a person who plays the harp.

harpoon /hɑːˈpuːn/ n a missile like a SPEAR(1) with a rope attached. Harpoons are thrown by hand or fired from a gun, and used for catching large sea creatures, esp whales (WHALE).
► **harpoon** v [Vn] to hit sth with a harpoon.

harpsichord /ˈhɑːpsɪkɔːd/ n a musical instrument similar to a piano, but with strings that are plucked (PLUCK¹ 5) in a mechanical way.

harpy /ˈhɑːpi/ n **1** (in Greek and Roman myths) a cruel MONSTER(1a) with a woman's head and body and a bird's wings and feet. **2** a cruel greedy woman.

harridan /ˈhærɪdən/ n a bad-tempered old woman.

harrier /ˈhæriə(r)/ n **1** a type of dog used for hunting hares (HARE). **2** (used esp in the names of clubs) a CROSS-COUNTRY runner. **3** a type of small HAWK¹(1).

harrow /ˈhærəʊ/ n a heavy frame with sharp metal points or discs that is dragged over ploughed (PLOUGH v) land to break up lumps of earth, cover seeds, etc. ► **harrow** v [Vn] The field had been ploughed and harrowed.

harrowing /ˈhærəʊɪŋ/ adj very distressing: a harrowing experience/story/film.

harry /ˈhæri/ v (pt, pp **harried**) to put pressure on or annoy sb with repeated requests, questions, etc; to HARASS(1) sb: [Vn] harried by press reporters wanting a story.

harsh /hɑːʃ/ adj (**-er, -est**) **1** rough or sharp in a way that is unpleasant, esp to the senses: a harsh texture/voice/light/colour ○ be harsh to the ear/eye/touch. **2(a)** severe and without sympathy; cruel: a harsh judge/sentence/punishment ○ harsh criticisms. **(b)** (of weather or living conditions) very unpleasant and difficult to endure; severe: a harsh climate ○ harsh prison conditions ○ We have to face up to the harsh realities of life. ► **harshly** adv: be harshly treated. **harshness** n [U].

hart /hɑːt/ n (pl unchanged) an adult male deer, esp the red deer; a STAG(1). Compare HIND².

harvest /ˈhɑːvɪst/ n **1(a)** [C] the act of cutting and gathering grain and other food crops. **(b)** [C,U] the time of year when this is done: Farmers are very busy during (the) harvest. **(c)** [C] the crops or amount of crops cut and gathered at this time: gather in the harvest ○ a succession of good harvests ○ This year's wheat harvest was poor. **2** [C] the consequences of an action: We are **reaping the harvest** of (ie suffering as a result of) our past mistakes.
► **harvest** v to cut and gather a crop; to REAP(1): [Vn] The farmers are out harvesting the corn. [also V]. **harvester** n **1** a person who harvests crops. **2** an agricultural machine for cutting and gathering grain, binding (BIND) corn into bales (BALE), or threshing (THRESH) the grain. See also COMBINE² 2.
■ ,harvest 'festival n a special service held in Christian churches to give thanks for the crops after the harvest has been gathered.
,harvest 'moon n a full moon in autumn nearest to the time when day and night are of equal length (22 or 23 September).

has /həz, əz, z; strong form hæz/. ⇨ HAVE¹,²,³.

has-been /ˈhæz biːn/ n (infml derog) a person who

is no longer as famous, successful, important, popular, etc as formerly: *It's hard to be a hero one day and a has-been the next.*

hash¹ /hæʃ/ n **1** [U] a dish of cooked meat cut into small pieces and cooked again together with other ingredients. **2** [C] a mixture of old material used again. See also REHASH n. **IDM** **make a ˈhash of sth** (*infml*) to do sth badly; to make a mess of sth: *I made a real hash of the last exam.*

hash² /hæʃ/ n (*infml*) = HASHISH.

hash³ /hæʃ/ (also **ˈhash sign**) n the symbol #, esp when used before a number: *To divert a call, dial hash nine (ie #9) and the number to which you are diverting the call.*

hashish /ˈhæʃiːʃ, hæˈʃiːʃ/ (also **hash**) n [U] a drug made from the RESIN of the HEMP plant which is dried and used for smoking or chewing. Hashish is illegal in many countries. See also CANNABIS, MARIJUANA.

hasn't /ˈhæznt/ *short form* has not. ⇨ note at HAVE.

hasp /hɑːsp; US hæsp/ n part of a fastening for a door, box, etc. It consists of a hinged (HINGE v) metal strip that fits over a metal loop and is secured by a PADLOCK.

hassle /ˈhæsl/ n [C,U] (*infml*) (**a**) trouble or annoyance caused by having to do sth difficult or complicated: *Changing trains with all that luggage was a real hassle.* ○ *Organizing everything on my own was too much hassle.* (**b**) argument: *Do as you're told and don't give me any hassle!*

▶ **hassle** v ~ (**with sb**) (*infml*) to cause sb trouble or annoyance, esp by making constant demands: [Vpr] *hassling with the producer about a bigger part* [Vn] *Don't keep hassling me! I'll do it later.*

hassock /ˈhæsək/ n **1** a thick firm cushion for kneeling on, esp in church. **2** (*US*) = POUFFE.

haste /heɪst/ n [U] speed of movement or action; hurry: *Why all the haste?* ○ *In her haste to complete the work on time, she made a number of mistakes.* ○ *The letter had clearly been written **in haste**.* ○ *After his first wife died he married again with almost indecent haste.* ○ (*dated*) *We must **make haste** (ie act quickly) — there is no time to lose.* **IDM** **ˌmore ˈhaste, ˌless ˈspeed** (*saying*) one makes more real progress if one does not do things too quickly.

hasten /ˈheɪsn/ v **1** to move or act with speed; to hurry: [Vp, Vpr, Vadv] *He hastened away/to the station/home.* [V.to inf] *I have some news for you — good news, I **hasten to add**.* **2** to cause sth to be done or to happen earlier or more quickly: [Vn] *Artificial heating hastens the growth of plants.* ○ *A rise in interest rates could hasten the onset of recession.*

hasty /ˈheɪsti/ adj (**-ier, -iest**) (**a**) said, made or done quickly or too quickly; hurried: *a hasty departure/meal/farewell* ○ *hasty words that are soon regretted* ○ *I don't want to make a hasty decision.* (**b**) [usu pred] ~ (**in doing sth / to do sth**) (of a person) acting or deciding too quickly, without enough thought: *You shouldn't be too hasty in deciding to get married.* ▶ **hastily** /-ɪli/ adv: *He dressed hastily.* ○ *Perhaps I spoke too hastily.*

hat /hæt/ n **1** a covering made to fit on the head, usu with a BRIM(2) and worn out of doors: *put on/take off one's hat.* ⇨ picture. **2** (*infml*) an official or professional position or role: *wear two hats* (ie have two such roles) ○ *I'm telling you this in my lawyer's hat, you understand.* **IDM** **at the drop of a hat** ⇨ DROP¹. **I'll eat my hat** ⇨ EAT. **keep sth under one's ˈhat** to keep sth secret; not to mention sth to anyone. **knock sb/sth into a cocked hat** ⇨ KNOCK². **ˌmy ˈhat** (*Brit*) (used as an exclamation of surprise). **old hat** ⇨ OLD. **out of a/the ˈhat** picked at RANDOM from a container into which names, competition entries, etc are put: *Prizes went to the first three out of the hat.* **pass the hat round/around** ⇨

beret   bowler (US derby)   cap   hat   badge   peak   top hat   baseball cap   stetson   brim   flat cap   deerstalker   fez   skullcap   woolly hat

PASS¹. **take one's ˈhat off to sb** to acknowledge one's admiration for sb: *I must say I take my hat off to him — I never thought he would get into the first team.* **talk through one's hat** ⇨ TALK¹.

■ **ˈhat-pin** n a long pin used to fasten a hat to the hair.

ˈhat trick n three successes achieved by one person, esp in sport or a sports event. In cricket, a BOWLER¹(1) gets a hat trick when he or she gets three batsmen out with three successive balls: *win a hat trick of gold medals* ○ *score a hat trick of goals.*

hatband /ˈhætbænd/ n a band of material round a hat just above the BRIM(2), as a decoration.

hatch¹ /hætʃ/ n (**a**) an opening in a door, floor or ceiling. (**b**) (also **ˈhatchway**) an opening in a ship's DECK¹(1a) or the bottom of an aircraft, through which cargo is lowered or raised. (**c**) an opening in a wall between two rooms, esp a kitchen and a dining-room (DINE), through which dishes, etc are passed. (**d**) a door in an aircraft or a spacecraft: *an escape hatch.* **IDM** **ˌdown the ˈhatch** (*infml*) (said before a drink is swallowed) down the throat.

hatch² /hætʃ/ v **1** ~ (**out**) (**a**) (of a young bird, fish, etc) to come out of an egg: [V] *The chicks have hatched.* [Vp] *Then the caterpillar hatches out.* (**b**) (of an egg) to break open and produce a young bird, etc: [Vp] *When will the eggs hatch ˈout?* [V] *The eggs in the nest had hatched.* **2** to cause a creature to come out of an egg: [Vn] *The hen hatches her young by sitting on the eggs.* **3** ~ **sth** (**up**) to create or produce a plot, plan, etc, esp in secret: [Vnp] *What mischief are those children hatching ˈup?* [Vn] *hatch a scheme.* ▶ **hatchery** n a place for hatching eggs, esp of fish: *a ˈtrout hatchery.* Compare INCUBATOR.

hatchback /ˈhætʃbæk/ n a car with a sloping door at the back that opens upwards. ⇨ picture.

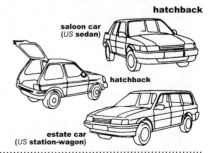

hatchback

saloon car (US sedan)   hatchback   estate car (US station-wagon)

[V] = verb used alone   [Vn] = verb + noun   [Vp] = verb + particle   [Vpr] = verb + prepositional phrase

hatchet /'hætʃɪt/ n a small AXE with a short handle. ⇨ picture at AXE. **IDM** **bury the hatchet** ⇨ BURY. ■ **'hatchet-faced** adj having a long face and sharp features.

'hatchet job n (infml esp US) a strong attack on sb in speech or writing, intended to destroy their reputation or damage them in some way: The press did a very effective hatchet job on her last film.

'hatchet man n (infml) person employed to defeat or damage sb's opponents or to carry out criminal tasks for sb.

hatchway /'hætʃweɪ/ n = HATCH[1] 1.

hate /heɪt/ v (a) to dislike sb/sth intensely; to feel hatred towards sb/sth: [Vn] My cat hates dogs. ○ her hated rival. (b) to find sth very unpleasant; to dislike sth very much: [Vn] I hate fried food. [V.to inf] He hates to be kept waiting. [V.n to inf] I hate people to take advantage of me. [V.ing] She really hates working there. ○ I hated having to disappoint them, but I had no choice. [V.n ing] She hates anyone listening when she's on the phone. (c) (infml) (no passive) to be unwilling to do sth; to regret; to be sorry: [V.to inf] I hate to trouble you but could we have a word? [V.n to inf] I would hate you to think I didn't care. **IDM** **hate sb's 'guts** (infml) to dislike sb intensely.
▶ **hate** n (a) [U] strong dislike; hatred: feel hate for sb ○ a look (full) of hate. (b) [C] (infml) a hated person or thing: men with beards are one of **my pet hates**. ○ Plastic flowers are a particular hate of mine. **hater** n.

hateful /'heɪtfl/ adj ~ (to sb) causing sb to feel hatred; very unpleasant: a hateful person/remark/deed ○ The memory of her childhood was still hateful to her.

hatred /'heɪtrɪd/ n [U,C] ~ (for/of sb/sth) very strong dislike: deep/bitter/intense hatred ○ He looked at me with hatred. ○ feel hatred for the enemy ○ She has a profound hatred of fascism. ○ an incident that revived old hatreds.

hatter /'hætə(r)/ n a person who makes and sells hats. **IDM** **mad as a hatter / March hare** ⇨ MAD.

haughty /'hɔːti/ adj (-ier, -iest) (of people or their manner) believing or showing the belief that one is superior to others; disdainful (DISDAIN): Her expression was one of haughty contempt. ▶ **haughtily** /-ɪli/ adv. **haughtiness** n [U].

haul /hɔːl/ v to pull or drag sth with effort or force: [Vpr] sailors hauling on the ropes [Vn] elephants hauling logs [Vnpr] They hauled the boat up the beach. [Vnp] I got stuck in the mud and the others had to haul me out. [also V, Vp]. ⇨ note at PULL[1]. **IDM** **haul sb over the 'coals** (infml) to criticize sb severely because they have done sth wrong: I was hauled over the coals by my boss for being late. **PHR V** **‚haul sb 'up (before / in front of sb/sth)** (infml) (usu passive) to make sb appear before a court of law or a person with the authority to punish or criticize them severely: He was hauled up before the local magistrates for dangerous driving.
▶ **haul** n **1**(a) a quantity of fish caught at one time: The fishermen had a good haul. (b) an amount gained or acquired by effort: The thieves got away with a huge haul (ie of stolen goods). ○ His haul of 40 goals in a season is a record. **2** (usu sing) a distance to be travelled: long haul flights ○ Our camp is only a short haul from here. **3** an act of hauling: With three hauls on the rope we got the boat clear of the water. **IDM** **a long haul** ⇨ LONG[1].

haulage /'hɔːlɪdʒ/ n [U] **1** the business of transporting goods by road in lorries, etc: the road haulage industry ○ a haulage contractor. **2** money charged for this: How much is haulage?

haulier /'hɔːliə(r)/ (Brit) (US **hauler** /'hɔːlə(r)/) n a person or firm whose business is transporting goods by road.

haunch /hɔːntʃ/ n **1** (usu pl) (in humans and animals) the soft part of the BUTTOCK and THIGH: crouch/sit/squat on one's haunches. **2** a leg and LOIN of deer, etc as food: a haunch of venison.

haunt /hɔːnt/ v **1** (of ghosts) to visit a place regularly: [Vn] a haunted house ○ A spirit haunts the castle. **2** (esp sth unpleasant) to return repeatedly to sb's mind; to be impossible for sb to forget: [Vn] For days he was haunted by the fear of being found out. ○ The memory of it still haunts me. **3** to visit or spend time in a place frequently: [Vn] This is one of the cafés I used to haunt.
▶ **haunt** n (often pl) a place that sb visits or spends time in frequently: revisit the haunts of one's youth ○ This pub is a favourite haunt of artists.
haunted adj (of an expression on the face) indicating that sb is very worried: His face was pale and there was a haunted look in his eyes.
haunting adj beautiful and sad, making a strong impression and remaining in the thoughts: a haunting melody/refrain. **hauntingly** adv: a hauntingly beautiful landscape.

haute couture /ˌəʊt kuːˈtjʊə(r)/ n [U] (French) the leading companies making fashionable clothes, or their products; high fashion.

haute cuisine /ˌəʊt kwɪˈziːn/ n [U] (French) cookery of a high standard.

hauteur /əʊˈtɜː(r); US hɔːˈtɜː(r)/ n [U] (fml) haughtiness (HAUGHTY).

have[1] /həv, əv, v; strong form hæv/ aux v. ⇨ note at HAVE[3]. (used with the past participle to form perfect tenses): I've finished my work. ○ He's gone home, hasn't he? ○ Have you seen it? Yes I have/No I haven't. ○ He'll have had the results by now. ○ She may not have told him yet. ○ Had they left before you got there? ○ She'd fallen asleep by that time, hadn't she? ○ If I hadn't seen it with my own eyes I wouldn't have believed it. ○ Had I known that (ie If I had known that) I would never have come. See also HAD BETTER/BEST.

have[2] /hæv/ (Brit also **have got**) v (not used in the continuous tenses). ⇨ note at HAVE[2,3].

● **Possessing 1**(a) to possess or own sth: [Vn] He has a house in Boston and a beach house on the coast. ○ Do you have any pets? ○ They've got two cars. ○ How many glasses have we got? ○ Do you have/Have you got a 50p piece? (b) to possess or show a mental quality or physical feature: [Vn] They have a lot of courage. ○ She has a good memory. ○ Giraffes have long necks. [Vnpr] You've got a cut on your chin. [Vn-adj] have a tooth loose/missing. (c) to include or contain sth as a part: [Vn] This car has a very powerful engine. ○ Does the house have central heating? [Vnpr] The hotel has TV in every room. (d) to be accompanied by sb: [Vnpr] He had some friends with him. **2** (indicating a relationship) [Vn] I have two sisters. ○ They have four children. ○ Does he have many friends? **3** to be able to use sth because it is available: [Vn] Have you got time to phone him? ○ She has no real power. ○ We don't have the resources to expand our operation. ○ I'm afraid we have no choice in the matter.

● **Experiencing 4** to feel sth; to hold sth in the mind: [Vn] I have no doubt that you're right. ○ I have the distinct feeling that something awful is going to happen. ○ She had the impression that she had seen him before. ○ Do you have any idea where he lives? ○ What reason have you got for thinking he's dishonest? **5** to experience the effects of sb's actions: [V.n ing] We've got people phoning up from all over the world. ○ They have orders coming in at the rate of 30 an hour. **6** to suffer from an illness or a disease: [Vn] She's got appendicitis. ○ He says he has a headache.

● **Showing or displaying 7** to show or demonstrate a particular quality by one's actions: [Vn.to inf] *Surely she didn't have the nerve to say that to him?* ○ *I didn't have the courage to disagree with him.* ○ *She had the confidence to take a risk.*

● **Taking or accepting somebody 8** (no passive; sometimes in the *-ing* form to indicate an intention or arrangement for the future) **(a)** to look after or care for sb/sth, esp for a limited period: [Vn] *Are you having the children tomorrow afternoon?* ○ *We've got the neighbours' dog while they're away.* ○ *We usually have my mother* (ie staying in our house) *for a month in the summer.* **(b)** to entertain sb in or invite sb to a place: [Vnpr] *How many people are you having to the party?* [Vnp] *We had some friends round for dinner last night.* [Vn.to inf] *have guests to stay for the weekend.* **9** ~ **sb as sth** to take or accept sb for a specified function: [Vn-n] *We'll have Jones as our spokesman.* ○ *Who can we have as treasurer?*

● **Other meanings 10** to hold sb/sth in a specified way: [Vnpr] *She's got him by the collar.* ○ *He had his head in his hands.* [Vnpr] *He had his head down as he walked out of the court.* **11** to place or keep sth in a specified position: [Vnpr] *Unfortunately I had my back to the camera.* ○ *We used to have that painting over the fireplace.* [also Vnp]. **12** to be in a position of needing to do sth: [Vn] *He has a lot of homework tonight.* [Vn.to inf] *I must go — I have a bus to catch.* ○ *She's got a family to feed.*

IDM ¹**have it (that) ...** to claim that it is a fact that ...; to say that ...: *Rumour has it that we'll have a new manager soon.* **have (got) it/that** ¹**coming** to be likely to suffer the unpleasant consequences of one's actions and to deserve to do so: *It was no surprise when she left him — everyone knew he had it coming (to him).* **have it** ¹**in for sb** (*infml*) to have a particular dislike of sb and to be particularly unpleasant to them: *She's had it in for him ever since he called her a fool in public.* **have it** ¹**in one (to do sth)** (*infml*) to be capable of or have the ability to do sth: *Do you think she's got it in her to be a successful dancer?* **have** ¹**nothing on sb/sth** to be not nearly as good as sb/sth: *As a player he's got nothing on the previous champion.* ○ *Your problems have nothing on mine.* **you** ¹**have me there / you've** ¹**got me there** (*infml*) **1** I admit that your argument is better than mine. **2** I don't know the answer to that.

PHRV ¸**have sth a**¹**gainst sb/sth** to dislike sb/sth for a particular reason: *What have you got against Ruth? She's always been good to you.* ¸**have sth** ¹**in** to have a supply of sth in one's home, etc: *Have we got enough food in?* ¸**have sth** ¹**on 1** to be wearing sth: *She has a red jacket on.* ○ *He's got a tie on today.* **2** to leave a piece of esp electrical equipment working: *The neighbours have their radio on all day.* **3** to have arranged to do sth: *I can't see you this week — I've got a lot on.* ¸**have sth on/with one** to be carrying sth, eg in a pocket: *I don't have any money on me.* ○ *Have you got your passport with you?* ¸**have sth** ¹**on sb** (*infml*) (no passive) to know sth bad about sb which can be used against them: *Have the police got anything on him?* ¸**have sb/sth to one**¹**self** to be able to use, enjoy, occupy etc sb/sth alone: *With my parents away I've got the house to myself.* ○ *I'd prefer to have a room to myself.*

▶ **the haves** /hævz/ *n* [pl] people who have enough money and possessions.
■ ¸**have-**¹**nots** *n* [pl] people who lack money and possessions.

NOTE In positive statements (in the present), in negative statements and in questions **have got** is the usual verb in British English to show possession, etc: *They've got a wonderful house* ○ *We haven't got a television.* ○ *'Have you got any family in America?'*

Have is also used in British English but it is more formal: *I have no objection to your request.* Some

expressions with **have** are common, even in informal language: *Honestly, I haven't a clue.* Questions and negative statements formed with **do** are now also common in British English: *Do you have any brothers and sisters?*

In the past tense **have got** is not used in positive statements, and in negatives and questions forms with **did** and **have** are often used: *We didn't have much time.* ○ *Did she have her husband with her?*

In American English **have** is the usual verb to show possession, etc in positive and negative statements and in questions: *They have a wonderful house.* ○ *We don't have a television.* ○ *Do you have any family in Europe?* **Have got** is also sometimes used in American English in positive statements: *I've got a brother in Denver and a sister in Boston.* ○ *I've got a bad cold.*

In both British and American English **have** (and forms with **do/does** and **did** in questions and negatives) are used when you are referring to a habit or routine: *In my country people usually have large families.* ○ *We don't often have time to talk.* ○ *Do you ever have headaches?*

have³ /hæv/ *v* (rarely passive except in sense 9). ➪ note.

● **Performing an action 1(a)** to perform the action indicated by the following *n* for a limited period: [Vn] *I had a swim to cool down.* ○ *Shall we have a game of cards?* ○ *(Brit)* (have a *wash/shower/bath* ○ *I'm going to have a rest now.* ○ *have a talk with sb* ○ *Let me have a try.* **(b)** to eat, drink, smoke, etc sth: [Vn] *have breakfast/lunch/dinner* ○ *I usually have a sandwich for lunch.* ○ *We have coffee at 11.* ○ *I had a cigarette while I was waiting.*

● **Receiving or undergoing 2(a)** (usu not in the continuous tenses) to receive sth from sb: [Vn] *I had a letter from my brother this morning.* ○ *What did you have for your birthday?* **(b)** to be given sth or have sth done to one: [Vn] *I'm having treatment for my back problem.* ○ *She's having an operation on her leg.* ○ *How many driving lessons have you had so far?* **3** to experience sth: [Vn] *We're having a wonderful time/holiday.* ○ *A good time was had by all* (ie Everyone enjoyed themselves). ○ *I've never had a worse morning than today.* ○ *They seem to be having some difficulty in starting the car.* ○ *She's having problems at work.* ○ *She'll have an accident one day.* ○ *I had a shock when I heard the news.*

● **Producing 4(a)** to give birth to sb/sth: [Vn] *My wife's having a baby.* ○ *Our dog has had two lots of puppies.* ➪ note at BEAR². **(b)** to produce sth: [Vn] *have a good effect/result/outcome* ○ *His paintings had a strong influence on me as a student.*

● **Causing or allowing something to happen 5** to organize or hold an event: [Vn] *Let's have a party.* ○ *We're having another meeting soon.* **6** (*fml*) to tell or arrange for sb to do sth for one: [Vn.inf (no to)] *I'll have the gardener plant some trees.* ○ *Have the driver bring the car around at 4.* **7(a)** (used with a *n* + past participle) to cause sth to be done for one by sb else: *Why don't you have your hair cut? They're going to have their house painted.* ○ *We're having our car repaired.* **(b)** (used with a *n* + past participle) to suffer the consequences of sth done to one by sb else: *He had his pocket picked* (ie Something was stolen from his pocket). ○ *She's had her wallet taken.* ○ *Charles I had his head cut off.* ○ *They have had their request refused.* **(c)** (used in negative sentences, esp after *will not, cannot,* etc) to allow or tolerate sth: [Vn] *I'm fed up with your rudeness — I won't have it any longer!* [Vn.ing] *We can't have boys arriving late all the time.* **8(a)** to cause sb to react in a particular way: [Vn.inf] *She had her audience listening attentively.* ○ *The movie had us all sitting on the edges of our seats with excitement.* **(b)** (no passive) to cause

---

[V.speech] = verb + direct speech   [V.*that*] = verb + *that* clause   [V.*wh*] = verb + *who, how,* etc clause

sb/sth to be in a certain state: [Vn-adj] *The news had me worried for a while.* ○ *They said they'd have the car ready by Tuesday.*
● **Other meanings 9** (*infml*) (esp passive) to trick or deceive sb: [Vn] *I'm afraid you've been had.* **10** [Vn] (*sl*) to have sex with sb.

IDM Most idioms containing **have** are at the entries for the nouns or adjectives in the idioms, eg **have one's eye on sb** ⇨ EYE¹; **not have the faintest/ foggiest** ⇨ FAINT¹. **have 'done with sth** (*esp Brit*) to finish sth unpleasant so that it does not continue: *Let's have done with this silly argument.* **have 'had it** (*sl*) **1** to be in a very bad condition and not capable of repair or recovery: *Let's be honest, the car's had it — we need a new one.* ○ *He felt so ill that he was sure he'd had it.* **2** to be extremely tired: *I've had it! I must get some sleep.* **3** to be unable to tolerate sth any longer: *I've had it with your constant arguing! Shut up, both of you!* **4** to be going to experience sth unpleasant: *My father saw you scratch his car — you've had it now!* **have it 'off/a'way (with sb)** (*sl*) to have sex with sb: *She was having it off with a neighbour while her husband was away on business.* **not 'having any** not willing to listen to or believe sth: *I tried to persuade her to wait for her money but she wasn't having any.* **what 'have you** (*infml*) other things, people, etc of the same kind: *There's room in the cellar to store old furniture and what have you.*

PHR V **,have sb 'back** to allow a husband, wife, etc from whom one is separated to return: *She says she'll never have him back after what he's done to her.* **,have sth 'back** to receive sth that has been borrowed, taken, etc from one: *Let me have it back soon.* ○ *You can have your files back after we've checked them.* **,have sb 'in** to employ sb to do work in one's house: *We had the builders in all last week.* **,have sb 'on** (*infml*) to try to make sb believe sth that is not true, usu to mock them or as a joke: *You really won all that money on a horse? You're having me on!* **,have sth 'out** to cause sth, esp a part of one's body, to be removed: *have a tooth/one's appendix/one's tonsils out.* **,have sth 'out (with sb)** to try to settle a dispute by discussing it or arguing about it openly: *This business with the neighbours about who owns the fence has gone on long enough — it's time we had it out (with them) once and for all.* **,have sb 'up (for sth)** (*Brit infml*) (esp passive) to cause sb to be accused of an offence in a lawcourt: *He was had up for drunken driving.*

NOTE The forms of **have** (main verb and auxiliary verb)

present tense

full forms		short forms
I	have	I've
you		you've
he		he's
she	has	she's
it		it's
we		we've
you	have	you've
they		they've

The negative full forms are formed by adding **not**: **I have not, you have not, he has not**, etc.
The negative short forms are formed by adding **n't**: **I haven't, you haven't, he hasn't**, etc.
Alternative negative short forms are formed by adding **not**: **I've not, you've not, he's not**, etc.

present participle: having

past tense
The past tense for all persons is **had** (negative **had not/hadn't**).

The short forms are formed with **'d: I'd, you'd, he'd**, etc.

past participle: had

Questions in the present and past are formed by placing the verb before the subject: **have I? hadn't you? has he not?** etc. When **have** is used as a main verb, questions and negative statements can be formed with **do/does/doesn't** and **did/didn't**: *Do you have any money on you?* ○ *We didn't have much time.*
The short forms **'ve, 's** and **'d** are not usually used when **have** is a main verb. You say *I have* (NOT *I've*) *a shower every morning.*
The other tenses of **have** are formed in the same way as those of other verbs: **will have, would have, have had**, etc.
The pronunciation of each form of **have** is given at its entry in the dictionary.

haven /ˈheɪvn/ n a place of safety or rest; a REFUGE: *Terrorists will not find a safe haven here.* See also TAX HAVEN.

haven't /ˈhævnt/ *short form* have not. ⇨ note at HAVE³.

haversack /ˈhævəsæk/ n a strong, usu canvas, bag carried on the back or over the shoulder and used for carrying food, clothes, etc when walking. See also RUCKSACK.

have to /ˈhæv tə, ˈhæf tə/ *modal v* (*3rd pers sing pres t* **has to** /ˈhæz tə, ˈhæs tə/; *pt* **had to** /ˈhæd tə, ˈhæt tə/) (in negative sentences and questions usu formed with *do*) **1** (indicating obligation or necessity): *I have to type letters and answer the phone.* ○ *He has to pass an examination before he can start work.* ○ (*fml*) *Have we to make our own way to the conference?* ○ *You don't have to knock — just walk in.* ○ *We don't have to finish this work until the end of the week.* ○ *Do they have to make so much noise all the time?* ○ *Did she have to pay a fine?* ⇨ note at MUST. **2** (used when giving advice or recommending): *You simply have to get a new job.* **3** (used when drawing a logical conclusion): *There has to be a reason for his strange behaviour.* ○ *This has to be part of the original manuscript.* **4** (*esp ironic*) (used when describing sth that happens as inevitable): *Of course, it had to start raining as soon as I'd hung all the washing out!* **IDM** **have got to** (*infml*) **1** (indicating obligation or necessity; not used in questions in US English): *I've got to pay some bills today.* ○ *How many of these tablets have you to take each day?* ○ *I haven't got to get up early tomorrow, I'm pleased to say.* **2** (used when giving advice or recommending): *You've got to try this recipe — it's delicious.*

havoc /ˈhævək/ n [U] widespread damage, destruction or disorder: *The floods created havoc throughout the area.* ○ *These insects can* **wreak havoc** *in the greenhouse.* ○ *The bad weather* **played havoc with** *our plans.*

haw¹ /hɔː/ n a red berry of the HAWTHORN bush.

haw² /hɔː/ v **IDM** **hum and ha/haw** ⇨ HUM.

hawk¹ /hɔːk/ n **1** a strong fast bird of prey (BIRD 1). **2** (*politics*) a person who favours aggressive policies in foreign affairs. Compare DOVE¹ 2.
▶ **hawkish** *adj* (*politics*) favouring aggressive policies rather than negotiation and compromise: *He is under pressure from his hawkish generals to declare war.*
■ **,hawk-'eyed** *adj* **1** having very good EYESIGHT. **2** watching closely and carefully.

hawk² /hɔːk/ v ~ **sth (about/around)** to go from place to place offering things for sale: [Vn] *The streets were full of people hawking their wares.* [Vnp]

He hawked his songs around for ages until a record company finally accepted them.

▶ **hawker** *n* a person who hawks goods.

hawser /'hɔːzə(r)/ *n* a thick rope or steel cable used on a ship.

hawthorn /'hɔːθɔːn/ *n* [C, U] a prickly bush or small tree with white, red or pink flowers and small dark red berries: *a hawthorn hedge.*

hay /heɪ/ *n* [U] grass cut and dried for use as animal food: *make hay* (ie turn it over to be dried by the sun). **IDM** **hit the hay/sack** ⇨ HIT¹. **make hay while the 'sun shines** (*saying*) to make good use of opportunities, favourable conditions, etc while they last.

■ **'hay fever** *n* [U] an illness affecting the nose, eyes and throat, caused by POLLEN breathed in from the air.

haymaking /'heɪmeɪkɪŋ/ *n* [U] the process of cutting grass and spreading it to dry. **'haymaker** *n*.

haystack /'heɪstæk/ (also **hayrick** /'heɪrɪk/) *n* a large pile of hay firmly packed for storing. **IDM** **a needle in a haystack** ⇨ NEEDLE.

haywire /'heɪwaɪə(r)/ *adj* **IDM** **be/go 'haywire** (*infml*) to be/become in a state of disorder or out of control: *Since I dropped it on the floor my watch has gone completely haywire.*

hazard /'hæzəd/ *n* ~ (**to sb/sth**) a thing that can be dangerous or cause damage; a danger or risk: *Smoking is a serious health hazard.* ○ *Wet roads are a hazard to drivers.* ○ *a fire hazard* ○ *hazard warning lights* (ie flashing lights on a car to warn other drivers). See also OCCUPATIONAL HAZARD.

▶ **hazard** *v* **1** to suggest sth while knowing that it may be wrong: [Vn] *I don't know where he is but I could hazard a guess.* [also V.speech]. **2** (*fml*) to expose sth to danger; to risk sth: [Vn] *Drink-drivers hazard other people's lives as well as their own.*

hazardous *adj* dangerous; risky: *hazardous work/conditions* ○ *The journey was hazardous.* ○ *The government has prohibited the import of hazardous wastes/chemicals.*

haze¹ /heɪz/ *n* [C, U] **1** a thin mist: *a heat haze.* ⇨ note at FOG. **2** a mental state in which one cannot think clearly and is not aware of what is happening: *I/My mind was in a complete haze.* ○ *an alcoholic haze.*

haze² /heɪz/ *v* [Vn] (*US*) to make sb, esp a new student, nervous or worried by playing tricks on them or giving them unpleasant tasks to do.

hazel /'heɪzl/ *n* a bush or small tree with small edible nuts.

▶ **hazel** *adj* (esp of the eyes) reddish-brown or greenish-brown.

hazelnut /'heɪzlnʌt/ *n* the edible nut of the HAZEL. ⇨ picture at NUT.

hazy /'heɪzi/ *adj* (**-ier, -iest**) **1** covered by a thin mist: *The mountains were rather hazy.* ○ *We couldn't see far because it was a hazy day.* **2** not clear; VAGUE(1a): *hazy memories.* **3** (of a person) rather confused; uncertain: *I'm a little hazy about what to do next.* ▶ **hazily** *adv*: *remember sth hazily.*

H-bomb /'eɪtʃ bɒm/ *n* a hydrogen bomb (HYDROGEN).

he /hi, iː, i; *strong form* hiː/ *pers pron* (used as the subject of a *v*) **1** a male person or animal mentioned earlier or being observed now: *'Where's your brother?' 'He's in Paris.'* ○ *Look! He* (ie The man we are watching) *is climbing the fence.* **2** a person, male or female, whose sex is not stated or known, esp when referring to sb previously mentioned or to a group in general: (*fml*) *If a member wishes to bring a guest into the club, he must sign the visitors' book.* ○ (*saying*) *He who* (ie Anyone who) *hesitates is lost.* See also HIM. ⇨ note at GENDER.

▶ **he** *n* [sing] a male: *What a sweet puppy! Is it a he or a she?*

he- (forming compound *ns*) male: *a 'he-goat.*

■ **'he-man** /-mæn/ *n* (*pl* **-men** /-men/) a strong man with big muscles.

HE *abbr* /ˌeɪtʃ 'iː/ Her/His Excellency: *HE the British Ambassador.* ○ *HE Governor Robert Mount.*

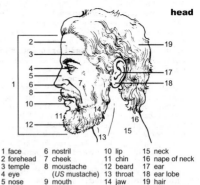

head

1 face	6 nostril	10 lip	15 neck
2 forehead	7 cheek	11 chin	16 nape of neck
3 temple	8 moustache	12 beard	17 ear
4 eye	(*US* mustache)	13 throat	18 ear lobe
5 nose	9 mouth	14 jaw	19 hair

head¹ /hed/ *n* **1(a)** [C] the part of the body containing the eyes, nose, mouth and brain: *He fell and hit his head.* ○ *The ball hit her on the head.* ○ *My head aches.* ○ *nod one's head* (ie to indicate 'yes'). ⇨ picture. ⇨ picture at HUMAN, INSECT. **(b)** **a head** [sing] this as a measure of length: *The favourite won by a head.* ○ *Tom is taller than John by a head.* **2** [C] (*infml*) a HEADACHE: *I've got a terrible head this morning.* **3** [C] the mind; the brain: *Use your head* (ie Think). ○ *The thought never entered my head.* **4** [sing] a mental or natural ability of the specified nature: *have a good head for business/figures* ○ *have no head for heights* (ie feel GIDDY(1a) and frightened in high places). **5 heads** [sing *v*] the side of a coin with the head of a person on it: *We tossed a coin* (eg to decide sth by chance) *and it came down heads.* Compare TAILS. **6 head** [pl] individual animals in a HERD(1) or FLOCK¹(1): *50 head of cattle.* **7** [C] a thing like a head in form or position, eg the striking or cutting part of a tool, the mass of leaves or flowers at the top of a stem, etc: *the head of a nail/a hammer/an axe* ○ *cut off the dead heads of the roses.* ⇨ picture at HAMMER. **8** [C usu *sing*] the FOAM(1a) on the top of poured beer, etc. **9** [C] a device on a tape recorder (TAPE) that touches the moving tape and converts the electrical signals into sound. **10** [C] the part of a spot¹(2) or BOIL² that contains PUS: *The pimple came to a head before bursting.* See also BLACKHEAD. **11** [C usu *sing*] the top or highest part of sth: *the title at the head of the page* ○ *stand at the head of the stairs* ○ *at the head of the league table* ○ *the head of the lake* (ie where a river enters it). **12** [C] the more important or prominent end of sth: *My father took his place at the head of the table.* ○ *Place the pillows at the head of the bed.* **13** [sing] **(a)** the front of a line of people: *be at the head of a queue* ○ *march at the head of the regiment.* **(b)** a leading position in sth: *be at the head of one's profession.* **14** [C] **(a)** the person in charge of a group or an organization, etc: *the head of the family* ○ *heads of department* ○ *a meeting of the heads of government* ○ *a gathering of the crowned heads* (ie kings or queens) *of Europe* ○ *a head 'teacher* ○ *the head 'waiter* ○ *head 'office* (ie a company's central place of business). **(b)** (also **Head**) (*esp Brit*) the person in charge of a school or college; a HEADMASTER or headmistress (HEADMASTER): *Report to the Head immediately!* **15** [C usu *sing*] the pressure produced by an amount of water or steam in a confined space: *They kept up a good head of steam.* **16** [C usu *sing*] (in place names) a HEADLAND: *Beachy Head.* **17** [C] a main division in a lecture, an essay, etc; a HEADING: *a speech arranged under five heads.* **IDM** **above/over sb's 'head** too

---

[V] = verb used alone   [Vn] = verb + noun   [Vp] = verb + particle   [Vpr] = verb + prepositional phrase

difficult or complicated for sb to understand: *The lecture was/went way above my head.* **a/per ˈhead** for each individual person: *The meal cost £10 a head.* **bang, etc one's head against a brick ˈwall** (*infml*) to continue without success trying to achieve sth impossible: *Don't bother trying to teach him good manners — you're only bashing your head against a brick wall!* **be/stand head and ˈshoulders above sb/sth** to be very much better than others: *She's head and shoulders above all the other players.* **bite/snap sb's ˈhead off** (*infml*) to criticize sb angrily, and often for no good reason: *I was only two minutes late but she really bit my head off.* **bother oneself / one's head about sth** ⇨ BOTHER. **bring sth / come to a ˈhead** to bring sth to/reach a point where action must be taken: *The atmosphere in the office has been tense for some time but this latest dismissal has brought matters to a head.* **bury/hide one's head in the ˈsand** (*derog*) to pretend that an obvious problem or danger does not exist. **by a short head** ⇨ SHORT¹. **drum sth into sb / into sb's head** ⇨ DRUM². **from ˌhead to ˈfoot/ˈtoe** over the whole length of one's body: *The children were covered in mud from head to toe.* See also FROM TOP TO TOE. **get it into one's ˈhead that ... 1** to understand fully ...; to realize ...: *I wish he'd get it into his head that exams are important.* **2** to begin believing that ...: *He's got it into his head that we're all against him.* **give sb their ˈhead** to let sb act freely. **go to one's ˈhead 1** (of alcoholic drink) to make one DIZZY(1) or slightly drunk: *The whisky went straight to my head.* **2** (of success or praise) to make one conceited (CONCEIT) or too confident. **harm, etc a hair of sb's head** ⇨ HAIR. **have eyes in the back of one's head** ⇨ EYE¹. **have a good ˈhead on one's shoulders** to be a sensible person; to have practical ability. **have one's head in the ˈclouds 1** to have one's thoughts far away. **2** to have ideas, aims, etc which are not realistic. **have one's ˈhead screwed on (the right way)** (*infml*) to be sensible. **have a roof over one's head** ⇨ ROOF. **have, etc a thick head** ⇨ THICK. **ˌhead ˈfirst 1** (moving, esp falling) with one's head before the rest of one's body: *She fell head first down the stairs.* **2** with too much speed and too little thought: *She plunged head first into a new career.* **ˌhead over ˈheels 1** rolling the body over in a forward direction. **2** completely: *She's head over heels in ˈlove (with him).* **heads or ˈtails?** (said when spinning a coin to decide sth by chance and asking sb to say which side will land upwards). **ˈheads will roll (for sth)** (*usu joc*) some people will be punished because of sth. **hit the nail on the head** ⇨ HIT¹. **hold one's ˈhead high** to take pride in one's achievements, worth, ability, etc; not to feel ashamed. **hold a pistol to sb's head** ⇨ PISTOL. **in one's ˈhead** in one's memory, not on paper: *How do you keep all those telephone numbers in your head?* **in over one's ˈhead** involved in sth that is too difficult or complicated for one to be able to deal with: *I lacked experience of big business and was soon in over my head.* **keep one's ˈhead** to remain calm under pressure. **keep one's ˈhead above water** to avoid becoming overwhelmed (OVERWHELM 2) by problems, esp financial ones, but only with difficulty: *I'm managing to keep my head above water, though I'm not earning much.* **keep one's ˈhead down** to avoid attracting attention. **knock sb's block/head off** ⇨ KNOCK². **knock your/their heads together** ⇨ KNOCK². **knock sth on the head** ⇨ KNOCK². **laugh, scream, etc one's ˈhead off** (*infml*) to laugh, etc very loudly: *The baby was screaming its head off but no one heard it.* **lose one's head** ⇨ LOSE. **make head or ˈtail of sth** (used with *can, be able to,* etc) to understand sth: *I can't make head (n)or tail of these instructions.* **need, etc (to have) one's ˈhead examined**

(*infml*) to show oneself to be stupid or crazy: *He swims in the sea in winter — he ought to have his head examined.* **not right in the head** ⇨ RIGHT¹. **off one's ˈhead** (*infml*) crazy; very foolish: *He's (gone) completely off his head!* **off the top of one's head** ⇨ TOP¹. **an old head on young shoulders** ⇨ OLD. **on sb's/one's (own) head be it** sb/one will be responsible for any unpleasant consequences: *You wanted to try this new route, not me, so on your head be it.* **out of one's ˈhead** (*sl*) feeling or behaving out of control, esp because of the effect of alcohol or a drug. **over sb's ˈhead** to a position of authority higher than sb: *I couldn't help feeling jealous when she was promoted over my head.* ∘ *When her boss refused to listen to her she went over his head to the managing director.* **a price on sb's head** ⇨ PRICE. **put our/your/their ˈheads together** to discuss a problem, a suggestion or an idea in order to reach a solution or plan of action: *I'm sure we can solve the problem if we all put our heads together.* **put sth into sb's ˈhead** to make sb believe sth; to suggest sth to sb: *Who's been putting such ideas into your head?* **put sth out of one's ˈhead** to stop thinking about sth; to give up a plan, etc: *You should put any idea of marriage right out of your head.* **scratch one's head** ⇨ SCRATCH¹. **shake one's head** ⇨ SHAKE¹. **(do sth) standing on one's ˈhead** (*infml*) (to do sth) very easily: *She could pass the exam standing on her head.* **stand/turn sth on its ˈhead** to reverse the order or nature of sth: *She stood my argument on its head.* ∘ *Their unexpected victory has turned the season on its head.* **take it into one's head to do sth / that ...** to decide sth suddenly, esp sth unexpected or foolish: *She suddenly took it into her head to dye her hair green.* ∘ *He's taken it into his head that I'm spreading rumours about him.* **turn sb's ˈhead** to make sb conceited (CONCEIT) or too proud: *The success of his first novel completely turned his head.* **two heads are better than ˈone** (*saying*) two people working together achieve more than one person working alone. **weak in the head** ⇨ WEAK.

▶ **headed** *adj* having a LETTERHEAD: *headed notepaper.*

-headed (in compound *adjs*) having a head or heads as specified: *a bald-headed man.*

headless *adj*: *a headless corpse.*

■ **ˈhead-butt** *n* an act of hitting sb violently and deliberately with the head. — *v*: [Vn] *He was expelled for head-butting another boy.*

ˈhead cheese *n* (*US*) = BRAWN 2.

ˈhead-dress *n* an ornamental covering or band worn on the head.

ˈhead-hunter *n* **1** a person or firm paid to find and RECRUIT(1) staff at a senior level. **2** a member of a tribe that collects the heads of dead enemies. **ˈhead-hunt** *v* to find and RECRUIT(1) sb for a senior position, esp by persuading them to leave their present position: [Vn] *Did you apply for the job or were you head-hunted?*

ˌHead of ˈState *n* (*pl* Heads of State) the chief public representative of a country, who may also be the head of government.

ˌhead-ˈon *adj, adv* (**a**) with the front parts of two vehicles crashing into each other: *a ˌhead-on colˈlision* ∘ *The cars crashed head-ˈon.* (**b**) with the front part of a vehicle hitting a fixed object: *The car hit the tree head-ˈon.* (**c**) facing sth directly and firmly: *a head-on confrontation between management and unions* ∘ *tackle a problem head-ˈon* (ie without trying to avoid it).

ˌhead ˈstart *n* an advantage already existing or gained at the beginning of sth: *Being able to read gave her a head start over the other pupils.*

ˌhead-to-ˈhead *adj, adv* facing sb/sth directly in a dispute, contest, etc: *a head-to-head confrontation with his old rival.*

ˈhead wind *n* a wind blowing from directly in front. Compare TAIL WIND.

H

head² /hed/ v **1(a)** to be at the front or top of sth: [Vn] *head a procession* ∘ *Her name headed the list.* **(b)** to lead sth: [Vn] *head a rebellion/government/ delegation.* **2** to move in the specified direction: [Vadv, Vnadv] *Where are you heading/headed?* [Vp] *We'd better be heading back now.* [Vpr] *head for/ towards the town centre* [Vpr] *(fig) Interest rates are heading towards 14%.* **3** (esp passive) to give a title or heading to an essay, etc: [Vn] *The chapter was headed 'My Early Life'.* **4** (in football) to strike the ball with one's head: [Vn, Vnpr] *head the ball (into the goal).* **IDM** **head/top the bill** ⇨ BILL¹. **PHRV** ˈhead for sth to be likely to result in a particular situation: *The talks are heading for a showdown.* ∘ *She's heading for trouble.* ˌhead sb/sth ˈoff **1** to get in front of sb/sth so as to turn them/it back or aside: *head off reporters/an angry mob.* **2** to act in order to prevent sth happening: *head off a quarrel.*

headache /ˈhedeɪk/ n **1** a continuous pain in the head: *suffer from headaches* ∘ *have a splitting headache* (ie a very bad one). **2** a person or thing that causes worry or trouble: *Their son is a constant headache to them.*

headband /ˈhedbænd/ n a strip of material worn around the head. ⇨ picture at SQUASH.

headboard /ˈhedbɔːd/ n an upright panel along the top end of a bed.

headcount /ˈhedkaʊnt/ n (an act of counting) a total number of people, eg those employed by an organization: *do a headcount* ∘ *What's the latest headcount?*

header /ˈhedə(r)/ n (in football) an act of striking the ball with the head.

headgear /ˈhedɡɪə(r)/ n [U] a hat, cap or head-dress; such things as a group.

heading /ˈhedɪŋ/ n **(a)** a word or words put at the top of a page or section of a book as a title: *chapter headings.* **(b)** the title of each of the sections into which a subject, talk, etc has been divided: *The company's aims can be grouped under three main headings.*

headlamp /ˈhedlæmp/ n = HEADLIGHT.

headland /ˈhedlənd, -lænd/ n a high piece of land that sticks out from the coast into the sea; a PROMONTORY. ⇨ picture at COAST¹.

headlight /ˈhedlaɪt/ n **(a)** (also **headlamp**) a lamp, usu one of a pair, at the front of a motor vehicle or railway engine. ⇨ picture at CAR. **(b)** the beam from this: *Driving without headlights at night is illegal.*

headline /ˈhedlaɪn/ n **1** [C] a line of words printed in large letters at the top of a page or an article, esp in a newspaper: *The scandal was in the headlines for several days.* ∘ *headline news.* **2 the headlines** [pl] a brief summary on television or radio of the most important items of news. **IDM** **hit/make/reach the** ˈheadlines to appear as an important item of news in newspapers, on television or on radio.
▶ **headline** v to provide a headline for sth: [Vn-n] *The newspaper headlined its editorial 'The beginning of the end'.* [also Vn].

headlong /ˈhedlɒŋ/ adv, adj [attrib] **1** with the head first: *fall headlong.* **2** done in a rush without considering the consequences: *a headlong gallop/ retreat/rush/stampede* ∘ *rush headlong into danger.*

headman /ˈhedmæn, -mən/ n (pl **-men** /-mæn, -men/) the chief man of a village, tribe, etc.

headmaster /ˌhedˈmɑːstə(r)/ n (fem **headmistress** /-ˈmɪstrəs/) the principal man or woman in a school (in the USA a private school), who is responsible for organizing it.

headphones /ˈhedfəʊnz/ n [pl] an apparatus that fits over the ears and is used for listening to recordings, radio broadcasts, etc: *a pair of headphones.*

headquarters /ˌhedˈkwɔːtəz/ n [sing or pl v] (abbr

HQ) a place from which an organization is controlled: *The firm's headquarters is/are in London.*
▶ **headquartered** adj having headquarters in a specified place: *News Corporation is headquartered in Sydney.*

headrest /ˈhedrest/ n a thing that supports the head of a person sitting down, eg on a seat or chair. ⇨ picture at CAR.

headroom /ˈhedruːm, -rʊm/ n [U] **(a)** the amount of space between the top of a vehicle and an object it passes under: *There is not enough headroom for buses to go under this bridge.* **(b)** the amount of space between the heads of the people in a vehicle and the roof of the vehicle.

headscarf /ˈhedskɑːf/ n (pl **-scarves**) a SCARF tied round the head, usu with a knot under the chin, worn instead of a hat.

headset /ˈhedset/ n a set of HEADPHONES, sometimes with a MICROPHONE attached.

headship /ˈhedʃɪp/ n the position of a person in charge of a school: *She's been offered the headship at the village school.*

headstone /ˈhedstəʊn/ n a piece of stone placed at one end of a grave, usu with the dead person's name, etc on it.

headstrong /ˈhedstrɒŋ; US -strɔːŋ/ adj (usu derog) determined to do things in one's own way without listening to others; SELF-WILLED.

headteacher /ˌhedˈtiːtʃə(r)/ n (esp Brit) a teacher who is in charge of a school.

headwaters /ˈhedwɔːtəz/ n [pl] a stream or streams forming the sources of a river.

headway /ˈhedweɪ/ n [U] progress, esp in difficult circumstances: *We are making little headway with the negotiations.* ∘ *The boat made slow headway against the tide.*

headword /ˈhedwɜːd/ n a word that forms a HEADING, eg in a dictionary entry.

heady /ˈhedi/ adj (**-ier, -iest**) **(a)** having a quick and exciting effect on the senses: *a heady perfume* ∘ *the heady days of one's youth* ∘ *Shares continued to make heady progress.* **(b)** (of alcoholic drinks) likely to make people drunk quickly; POTENT(1b): *a heady wine.* **(c)** (of a person) excited and acting without careful thought: *be heady with success.*

heal /hiːl/ v **1** ~ **(up) (a)** to become or make sth healthy again: [V] *The wound healed slowly.* ∘ *the healing power of sleep* [Vp] *The cut finally healed up, but it left an ugly scar.* [also Vn]. **(b)** ~ **sb (of sth)** (arch or fml) to restore sb to health; to cure sb of a disease: [Vnpr] *The holy man healed them of their sickness.* [also Vn]. **2** to cause sth to end; to make sth easier to bear: [Vn] *heal a quarrel/rift* ∘ *Time heals all sorrows.*
▶ **healer** n a person or thing that heals: *Time is a great healer.*

health /helθ/ n [U] **1** the state of being well and free from illness in body or mind: *be restored to health* ∘ *be bursting with health and vitality.* **2** the condition of a person's body or mind: *have poor health* ∘ *be in/ enjoy the best of health* ∘ *in the interests of public health* (ie the health of the general public) ∘ *Your (very) good health* (eg said before drinking to wish sb good health)! ∘ *health insurance/care* ∘ *He retired early for health reasons.* **3** the security and successful functioning of sth: *the health of one's marriage/ finances.* **IDM** **a clean bill of health** ⇨ CLEAN¹. **drink sb's health** ⇨ DRINK². **in rude health** ⇨ RUDE. **propose sb's health** ⇨ PROPOSE.
▶ **healthful** /ˈhelθfl/ adj (fml) good for the health.
■ **health centre** n (Brit) a building where a group of doctors see their patients and from where a number of local medical services operate.
ˈhealth farm n a place where people go in order to try to improve their health by eating certain food, exercising, etc.

'health food *n* [UC often *pl*] natural food, usu free of artificial substances, which is thought to be especially good for the health: *a health food restaurant/shop.*

'health service *n* a public service providing medical care. See also NATIONAL HEALTH SERVICE.

'health visitor *n* (*Brit*) a trained nurse who visits new mothers, people just out of hospital, etc in their homes and gives advice on certain areas of medical care.

healthy /'helθi/ *adj* (**-ier, -iest**) **1** having good health; well and able to resist disease: *a healthy child/animal/tree* ○ (*fig*) *a healthy bank balance.* **2** likely to produce good health: *a healthy climate/life-style/diet.* **3** indicating good health: *have a healthy appetite.* **4** normal and natural: *The child showed a healthy curiosity.* ○ *She has a healthy respect for her rival's talents.* ▶ **healthily** *adv*: *eat healthily.* **healthiness** *n* [U].

NOTE Healthy and fit both describe a person who rarely suffers from any physical illness and whose body is in good condition: *She's always been a very healthy child.* **Healthy** also refers to things that are good for your health: *This damp climate isn't very healthy.* ○ *A healthier diet means more fresh foods and less fat.* Fit suggests that your body is in very good condition, especially because you take regular exercise: *'What do you do to keep fit?' 'I swim and play tennis.'* **Well** describes somebody's health on a particular occasion: *You're looking very well.* ○ *She sent me a lovely card saying 'Get well soon.'* ○ *I think I'll go to bed. I don't feel well.* You use **well** when somebody asks you about your health: *'How are you?' 'Very well, thank you.'*

heap /hi:p/ *n* **1** a number of things or a mass of material lying in an untidy pile: *a heap of books/sand/rubbish* ○ *The building was reduced to a heap of rubble.* ○ (*fig*) *She collapsed on the floor in a heap.* See also SCRAP HEAP. **2 heaps** [pl] *~s* (**of sth**) (*infml*) a great number or amount; plenty: *There's no hurry — we've heaps of time.* ○ *I've got heaps to tell you.* **3** (*infml joc*) a motor car that is old and in poor condition. **IDM** **heaps 'better, 'more, 'older, etc** (*infml*) a lot better, etc: *Do have a second helping — there's heaps more.* ○ *He looks heaps better than when I last saw him.*

▶ **heap** *v* **1** *~* **sth** (**up**) to put things in a pile: [Vn, Vnp] *heap (up) stones to form a dam* [Vnp] (*fig*) *heap up riches* [Vn] *a heaped spoonful of flour.* **2** *~* **sth on sb/sth;** *~* **sth with sth** to place sth in a pile on sb/sth: [Vnpr] *heap food on one's plate/heap one's plate with food* ○ (*fig*) *heap praises/insults on sb.*

hear /hɪə(r)/ *v* (*pt, pp* **heard** /hɜ:d/) **1** to perceive sounds with the ears: [V] *She doesn't/can't hear very well* (ie is rather deaf). [Vn] *We listened but could hear nothing.* ○ *Have you heard her latest record?* [Vn.*in*] *I heard someone laughing.* [Vn.inf (no *to*)] *Did you hear him go out?* [Vn.to inf] *She was often heard to remark on how lonely she felt.* ○ (*fig*) *Can't you just hear her say* (ie imagine her saying) *that?* **2** to listen or pay attention to sb/sth: [Vn] *You're not to go — do you hear me!* [V.*wh*] *We'd better hear what they have to say.* [Vn.inf (no *to*)] *Be quiet — I can't hear myself think* (ie I can't concentrate)! ○ note at FEEL[1]. **3** *~* (**about sb/sth**) to be told or informed about sth: [V] *You sing very well, I hear.* [Vn] *Have you heard the news?* [V.*that*] *I heard (that) you were ill.* [Vpr] *Have you heard about his dismissal?* **4** to listen to and judge a case[1](5) in a lawcourt: [Vn] *The court heard the evidence.* ○ *Which judge will hear the case?* **IDM** ₁**hear! 'hear!** (used to express agreement and approval). **hear/see the last of sb/sth** ⇨ LAST[1]. **hear a 'pin drop** to hear the slightest noise: *The audience was so quiet you could have heard a pin drop.* **hear 'tell of sth** to hear people talking about

sth: *I've often heard tell of such things.* **'hear things** (*infml*) to imagine that one hears sth: *'Was that a knock at the door?' 'No, you must be* '*hearing things!'* **make one's voice heard** ⇨ VOICE. **not/never hear the 'end of sth** to be continually reminded of sth as a subject of discussion or cause of annoyance: *If we don't give her what she wants we'll never hear the end of it.* **PHRV** **'hear from sb** to receive a letter, telephone call, etc from sb: *How often do you hear from your sister?* **'hear of sb/sth** be told about or have knowledge of sb/sth: *I've never heard of the place.* ○ *She disappeared and was never heard of again.* **not 'hear of sth** (usu with *will* or *would*) to refuse to allow sth: *He wouldn't hear of my walking home alone.* ₁**hear sb 'out** to listen until sb has finished saying what they want to say: *I know you don't believe me but please hear me out!*

▶ **hearer** /'hɪərə(r)/ *n* a person who hears sth, esp a member of an audience.

hearing /'hɪərɪŋ/ *n* **1** [U] the ability to hear; the sense(1) with which one perceives sound: *Her hearing is poor* (ie She is rather deaf). **2** [U] the distance within which one can hear sth: *She shouldn't have said such things in/within your hearing.* **3** [C] (**a**) an opportunity to explain one's position or opinion: *be given/denied a fair hearing.* (**b**) a trial of a case[1](5) in a lawcourt, esp before a judge without a JURY: *The defendant's family were present at the hearing.* **IDM** **a fair hearing** ⇨ FAIR[1]. **hard of hearing** ⇨ HARD[1].

■ **'hearing-aid** *n* a small device that makes sounds louder and helps a deaf person to hear: *have/wear a hearing-aid.*

hearken /'hɑ:kən/ *v* [V, Vpr] *~* (**to sb/sth**) (*arch*) to listen to sb/sth.

hearsay /'hɪəseɪ/ *n* [U] things one has heard another person or other people say, which may or may not be true; rumour: *You shouldn't believe that — it's just hearsay.* ○ *hearsay evidence.*

hearse /hɜ:s/ *n* vehicle for carrying a COFFIN to a funeral.

heart /hɑ:t/ *n* **1** [C] (**a**) the hollow organ in one's chest that pumps blood through the body: *His heart stopped beating and he died.* ○ *have heart trouble/disease.* ⇨ picture at RESPIRATORY. (**b**) the part of the body where this is: *He pressed her hand against his heart.* **2** [C] the centre of a person's thoughts and emotions, esp of love; the ability to feel emotion: *I have everything my heart desires.* ○ *She knew it in her heart.* ○ *He has a kind/soft heart.* ○ *Have you no heart?* ○ *The child captured the heart of the nation.* **3** [U] enthusiasm: *I want you to put more heart into your singing.* **4** [C] (**a**) the central or most important part of sth: *in the heart of the forest/city* ○ *get to the heart of the matter/subject/mystery.* (**b**) the inner leaves of a CABBAGE(1), LETTUCE, etc. **5**(**a**) [C] a thing shaped like a heart, esp a red shape used to represent a heart, eg as a symbol of love or on a PLAYING-CARD. ⇨ picture at PLAYING-CARD. (**b**) **hearts** [sing or pl *v*] the suit[1](2) of cards marked with these: *the ten of hearts.* (**c**) [C] a card of this suit[1](2): *play a heart.* **IDM** **after one's own 'heart** of exactly the type that one likes or understands best; sharing one's tastes: *He likes good wine too — he's obviously a man after my own heart.* **at 'heart** in one's real nature, in contrast to how one may appear: *I'm a country girl at heart.* **bare one's heart/soul** ⇨ BARE[2]. **break sb's/one's 'heart** to make sb/one feel great sadness and distress: *It broke her heart when he left.* **by 'heart** from memory: *learn/know a poem by heart.* **a change of heart** ⇨ CHANGE[2]. **close/dear/near to sb's 'heart** of deep interest and concern to sb: *This subject is very close to my heart.* **cross my heart** ⇨ CROSS[2]. **cry one's eyes/heart out** ⇨ CRY[1]. **do one's 'heart good** to make one feel more positive (1b), cheerful, etc: *It does my heart good to see the* *children enjoying themselves.* **eat one's heart out** ⇨ EAT. **find it in one's heart / oneself to do sth** ⇨ FIND¹. **from the (bottom of one's) ˈheart** with sincere feeling: *This advice comes from the heart.* **give sb (fresh) ˈheart** to encourage sb; to renew sb's confidence. **give one's ˈheart to sb/sth** to begin to love sb/sth completely. **have sth at ˈheart** to be anxious to support or defend sth: *He has your interests at heart* (ie wants you to be happy and successful). **have a ˈheart** (*infml*) be sympathetic or kind; show some pity. **have the ˈheart (to do sth)** (usu in negative sentences or questions with *can* or *could*) to be cruel or unkind enough to do sth: *I hadn't the heart to refuse.* **have one's heart in one's ˈboots** to be very sad and depressed. **have one's heart in one's ˈmouth** to be very afraid or nervous about sth: *My heart was in my mouth.* **have one's heart in the right ˈplace** to be sincere and kind. **have one's heart set on sth** ⇨ SET ONE'S HEART ON STH. **heart and ˈsoul** with great energy and enthusiasm: *devote oneself heart and soul to one's work.* **one's heart ˈbleeds for sb** (*often ironic*) one feels pity or sadness for sb. **one's heart goes ˈout to sb** one feels great sympathy for sb. **one's ˈheart is in sth** one is full of determination and enthusiasm about sth: *I want her to keep learning the violin but her heart's not in it.* **a heart of ˈgold** a very kind nature: *He may seem bad-tempered but he's got a heart of gold.* **a heart of ˈstone** a cruel nature or one that shows no pity or sympathy. **one's heart ˈsinks** one has a sudden feeling of disappointment or DISMAY: *When I saw the huge pile of dirty dishes, my heart sank.* **in good ˈheart** (*Brit*) cheerful and well; in good spirits: *She seemed in good heart when I saw her.* **in one's ˈheart (of ˈhearts)** in one's deepest feelings: *He knew in his heart that he was doing the wrong thing.* **lose heart** ⇨ LOSE. **lose one's heart** ⇨ LOSE. **open / pour out one's ˈheart to sb** to express or discuss one's feelings freely. **set one's ˈheart on (having/ doing) sth** to want sth very much: *She'd set her heart on going to university.* **sick at heart** ⇨ SICK. **sob one's heart out** ⇨ SOB. **strike fear, etc into sb / sb's heart** ⇨ STRIKE². **take ˈheart (from sth)** to be encouraged or become more confident: *Industry can take heart from the most recent trade figures.* **take sth to ˈheart** to be much affected or upset by sth: *I took your criticism very much to heart.* **tear at one's/sb's heart** ⇨ TEAR¹. **tear the heart out of sth** ⇨ TEAR¹. **to one's heart's conˈtent** as much as one wishes. **wear one's heart on one's sleeve** ⇨ WEAR¹. **with all one's ˈheart / one's whole ˈheart** completely; deeply: *I hope with all my heart that you succeed.* **young at heart** ⇨ YOUNG.

▸ **-hearted** (in compound *adjs*) having feelings or a nature as specified: *kind-hearted* ○ *faint-hearted*.

heartless *adj* unkind; without pity: *a heartless woman.* **heartlessly** *adv.* **heartlessness** *n* [U].

■ **ˈheart attack** *n* a sudden illness in which the heart beats violently causing great pain and sometimes death: *have/suffer a heart attack* ○ (*joc*) *My father nearly had a heart attack when he found out how much we'd spent.* Compare CORONARY THROMBOSIS.

ˈheart failure *n* [U] the sudden failure of the heart to function properly: *die of heart failure.*

ˈheart-rending *adj* causing great sadness or distress: *a heart-rending sight/story.*

ˈheart-stopping *adj* [attrib] very exciting or tense: *a heart-stopping match/moment.*

ˌheart-to-ˈheart *n* a frank conversation about personal matters: *have a heart-to-heart with sb* ○ *a ˌheart-to-heart ˈtalk.*

ˈheart-warming *adj* causing feelings of happiness and pleasure: *a heart-warming experience/tale.*

heartache /ˈhɑːteɪk/ *n* [U,C] great sorrow or worry: *understand the heartache of women whose babies die.*

heartbeat /ˈhɑːtbiːt/ *n* [U,C] the regular movement of the heart or the sound it makes: *a rapid heartbeat.*

heartbreak /ˈhɑːtbreɪk/ *n* [U,C] very great sadness or distress: *She's had her share of heartbreak(s).* **ˈheartbreaking** *adj: heartbreaking letters/stories.*

heartbroken /ˈhɑːtbrəʊkən/ *adj* (of a person) feeling great sadness: *He was heartbroken when she left him.* Compare BROKEN-HEARTED.

heartburn /ˈhɑːtbɜːn/ *n* [U] a burning sensation in the lower part of the chest, caused by INDIGESTION.

hearten /ˈhɑːtn/ *v* (esp passive) to make sb feel cheerful and encouraged: [Vn] *We were much heartened by the news.* ▸ **heartening** *adj: heartening progress.*

heartfelt /ˈhɑːtfelt/ *adj* deeply felt; sincere: *heartfelt sympathy/thanks.*

hearth /hɑːθ/ *n* **1(a)** the bottom of a fireplace: *a fire burning in the hearth.* (**b**) the area in front of this: *slippers warming on/by the hearth.* **2** (*rhet*) home: *a longing for* **hearth and home.**

hearthrug /ˈhɑːθrʌg/ *n* a mat laid in front of a fireplace.

heartily /ˈhɑːtɪli/ *adv* **1** with obvious enjoyment and enthusiasm: *laugh/sing/eat heartily.* **2** very; greatly: *be heartily glad/pleased/relieved/upset* ○ *I'm heartily sick of this wet weather.*

heartland /ˈhɑːtlænd/ *n* the central most important part of an area: *Germany's industrial heartland.*

heartstrings /ˈhɑːtstrɪŋz/ *n* [pl] one's deepest feelings of love or pity: *play upon/pull at/tear at sb's heartstrings* (ie move them emotionally).

heartthrob /ˈhɑːtθrɒb/ *n* (*infml*) a very attractive man with whom a lot of people fall in love: *a teenage heartthrob.*

hearty /ˈhɑːti/ *adj* (**-ier, -iest**) **1** [usu attrib] showing warm and friendly feelings; enthusiastic: *a hearty welcome/reception/greeting* ○ *give one's hearty approval and support to a plan.* **2** (*sometimes derog*) loud and cheerful: *a hearty laugh/voice* ○ *a hearty and boisterous fellow.* **3** [attrib] large: *eat a hearty breakfast* ○ *have a hearty appetite.* **4** (esp of older people) strong and healthy: *She's still* **hale and hearty** *at 85.*

▸ **heartiness** *n* [U].

hearty *n* a hearty person, esp one who is fond of sport.

heat¹ /hiːt/ *n* **1** [U] (**a**) the condition of being hot; high temperature: *feel the heat of the sun's rays* ○ *The fire isn't giving out much heat.* (**b**) the level of temperature: *turn up/down the heat* ○ *What heat should I set the oven at?* (**c**) a source of heat, esp the hot part of a COOKER(1): *Remove the pan from the heat.* (**d**) hot weather: *suffer from the heat* ○ *go out in the heat* (ie at the hottest time) *of the day.* **2** [U] intense feeling, esp of anger or excitement: *in the heat of the argument* ○ *This topic generates a lot of heat.* ○ *He tried to take the heat out of the situation* (ie reduce the tension). **3** [C] a preliminary round in a contest, the winners of which take part in further rounds or the FINAL: *be eliminated in the first heat.* ▣ **be on ˈheat;** (*US*) **be in ˈheat** (of a female mammal) to be in a sexual condition ready for mating (MATE²). **in the ˌheat of the ˈmoment** while temporarily very angry, excited or upset: *His unfortunate remarks were made in the heat of the moment.*

heat² /hiːt/ *v* ~ (**sth**) (**up**) to become or make sth hot or warm: [Vp] *The room will soon heat up.* [Vn] *Heating such a big house is expensive.* [Vnp] *The pie has already been cooked* — *it just needs heating up.* [Vn] *Is it a heated swimming-pool?* [also V]. ▸ **heated** *adj* (of a person or discussion) angry;

excited: *a heated argument* ○ *She became very heated.* **heatedly** *adv*.

heater *n* a device for making a room warm or for heating water: *a gas heater* ○ *a water-heater* ○ *The heater in my car isn't working.* Compare FIRE[1] 3, STOVE[1]. ⇨ picture at CAR.

heating *n* [U] a means or system of supplying heat: *Switch the heating on — it's cold in here.* ○ *gas/oil/ solid-fuel heating.* See also CENTRAL HEATING.

heath /hi:θ/ *n* [C] an area of open wild land covered with rough grass and low plants; a small area of MOORLAND.

heathen /'hi:ðn/ *n* (*derog*) **1** (used esp by people who have a strong religious belief) a person who does not believe in any of the world's chief religions: *heathen customs.* Compare ATHEIST, PAGAN. **2** (*dated infml*) a person who lacks education or social training: *Some young heathen has vandalized the bus shelter.*

heather /'heðə(r)/ *n* [U] a low plant with small purple, pink or white flowers, common on MOORLAND.

Heath Robinson /ˌhi:θ 'rɒbɪnsən/ *adj* (*Brit joc*) (of machines and devices) very complex and clever but unlikely to work: [attrib]: *a Heath Robinson contraption.*

heatstroke /'hi:tstrəʊk/ *n* [U] a sudden illness caused by too much exposure to heat or sun.

heatwave /'hi:tweɪv/ *n* a period of unusually hot weather.

heave /hi:v/ *v* (*pt, pp* **heaved** or, in the idioms **heave in sight / into view** and the phrasal verb **heave (sth) to, hove** /həʊv/) **1(a)** to lift or drag sb/oneself or sth heavy with great effort: [Vnpr] *We managed to heave the wardrobe up the stairs.* [Vnp] *He heaved himself up onto the rock ledge.* **(b)** ~ (at/ on sth) to pull on a rope, etc: [Vpr] *heave at the anchor* [V] *We heaved as hard as we could but it didn't move.* **2** to throw sth heavy: [Vnpr] *heave a brick through a window* [Vnadv] *heave sth overboard* [also Vn]. **3** to rise and fall regularly: [V] *his heaving chest* ○ *Her shoulders heaved with emotion.* **4** to produce a sound with effort: [Vn] *heave a sigh of relief.* **5** [V, Vp] ~ (up) to be violently sick; to VOMIT. **IDM** ,heave in 'sight / into view (*esp nautical*) to become visible: *A ship hove in sight.* **PHRV** ,heave (sth) 'to (*nautical*) to stop or make a ship stop: *The vessel/We hove to.*

▶ **heave** *n* [C, U] an act of heaving; a strong pull or throw: *the steady heave of the waves* ○ *With a mighty heave he lifted the sack onto the lorry.*

heaven /'hevn/ *n* **1** [sing] (without *a* or *the*) a place believed to be the home of God and of good people after death: *go to heaven.* **2** [U, C] a place or state of very great happiness: *She was in heaven when he kissed her.* ○ *Sitting here with you is heaven.* ○ *If there's a heaven on earth, this is it!* **3** (also **Heaven**) [sing] God; Providence: *It was the will of Heaven.* **4 the heavens** [pl] the sky, as seen from the earth: *Rain fell from the heavens all day long.* **IDM God/ Heaven forbid** ⇨ FORBID. **God/Heaven help sb** ⇨ HELP[1]. **God in heaven** ⇨ GOD. **God/goodness/ Heaven knows** ⇨ KNOW. **(Good) 'Heavens!**; ,**Heavens a'bove!** (used to express surprise). **the heavens 'opened** it began to rain heavily. **move heaven and earth** ⇨ MOVE[1]. **smell, etc to high heaven** ⇨ HIGH[1]. **thank God/goodness/heaven** ⇨ THANK. **to God/goodness/Heaven** ⇨ GOD.

▶ **heavenward** /-wəd/ (also **heavenwards** /-wədz/) *adv* towards heaven: *lift/raise one's eyes heavenwards* (eg to indicate annoyance or impatience (IMPATIENT)).

■ ,**heaven-'sent** *adj* happening at a most favourable time; very lucky: *a ,heaven-sent oppor'tunity.*

heavenly /'hevnli/ *adj* [attrib] of or from heaven: *a heavenly angel/vision.* **2** [attrib] of the sky: *heav-*

enly bodies (eg the sun/moon/stars and planets). **3** (*infml*) very pleasing: *This cake is heavenly.*

heavy /'hevi/ *adj* (**-ier, -iest**) **1(a)** weighing a lot; difficult to lift or move: *The box is too heavy for me to carry.* ○ *Lead is a heavy metal.* **(b)** (used when asking how much sb/sth weighs): *How heavy is it?* **2** of more than the usual size, amount, force, etc: *heavy traffic* ○ *heavy rain* ○ *heavy seas* (ie rough, with big waves) ○ *suffer heavy casualties/losses* ○ *have heavy expenses* ○ *a heavy frost* ○ *have a heavy cold* ○ *heavy* (ie loud) *breathing* ○ *a heavy sleeper* (ie one who is difficult to wake) ○ *a heavy drinker/smoker* (ie one who drinks/smokes a lot). **3(a)** [usu attrib] full of activity; busy: *a very heavy day/programme/ schedule.* **(b)** (of work) hard, esp involving the lifting and moving of heavy objects: *employed to do the heavy work.* **4** falling or striking with force: *a heavy blow* ○ *She tripped and had a heavy fall.* **5(a)** (of food) difficult to DIGEST[2](1b): *a heavy meal.* **(b)** (of bread) solid; not risen: *a heavy loaf.* **6** [pred] ~ **on sth** (*infml*) using a lot of sth: *It's an excellent radio but very heavy on batteries.* ○ *Don't go so heavy on the sauce!* **7** (*derog*) (of a book, style, etc) serious; difficult; dull: *His article is/makes heavy reading.* **8** strict; harsh: *He tends to be rather heavy with/on his children.* **9** (of a person's appearance) large and solid; not delicate or graceful: *heavy features* ○ *the heavy mob* (ie a group of strong, often violent, people employed to help or protect sb). **10** full or loaded with sth: *trees heavy with fruit* ○ *heavy with child* (ie pregnant) ○ *heavy with sleep.* **11(a)** (of air or the weather) hot, damp and still; HUMID: *I hate this heavy weather — I wish it would rain.* **(b)** (of the sky) dark with clouds. **12** sad: *have a heavy heart.* **IDM** ,**heavy 'going** difficult or boring: *She can be rather heavy going* (ie hard to talk to in an easy, friendly way). ○ *I find the work very heavy going.* **make heavy 'weather of sth** to make a task more difficult than it really is. **take a heavy toll / take its toll** ⇨ TOLL[1].

▶ **heavily** *adv*: *a heavily loaded van* ○ *smoke/drink heavily* ○ *be heavily taxed* ○ *heavily armed terrorists* ○ *rely heavily on sb* ○ *He fell heavily and twisted his ankle.* **heaviness** *n* [U].

heavy *adv* **IDM** **lie heavy on sb/sth** ⇨ LIE[2]. **time hangs heavy** ⇨ TIME.

heavy *n* **1** (*sl*) a big strong man employed to protect a person or place, with violence if necessary: *a gangster protected by his heavies.* **2** a serious role, esp of a bad character, in a play, film, etc.

■ ,**heavy-'duty** *adj* suitable for hard use, bad weather, etc: *a ,heavy-duty 'battery/'tyre* ○ *heavy-duty clothing.*

,**heavy-'handed** *adj* **1** not sensitive to the feelings of others: *a ,heavy-handed 'manner/ap'proach/'joke.* **2** harsh; severe: *heavy-handed police methods.* **3** awkward in movements of the hands; CLUMSY.

,**heavy-'hearted** *adj* sad.

,**heavy 'industry** *n* [U, C] industry producing metal, large machines, etc.

,**heavy 'metal** *n* a type of loud rock[3] music played on electric instruments.

heavyweight /'heviweɪt/ *n* **1** a boxer of the heaviest class(3), weighing 79.5 kg or more: *a heavyweight contest.* **2** a person or thing of more than average weight. **3** a person or thing of great influence or importance: *a literary heavyweight* ○ *a heavyweight journal.*

Hebraic /hi'breɪk/ *adj* of the Hebrew language or people.

Hebrew /'hi:bru:/ *n* **1** [C] a member of a Semitic people in ancient Palestine. **2** [U] **(a)** the language of the Hebrews. **(b)** modern form of this, used esp in Israel. Compare YIDDISH. ▶ **Hebrew** *adj*: *Hebrew prophets/words.*

heck /hek/ *interj, n* (*infml euph*) (used to express

mild annoyance or surprise or for emphasis) hell(3): *Oh heck, I'm going to be late.* ∘ *We had to wait **a** heck of **a** long time.*

heckle /ˈhekl/ *v* to interrupt and annoy a speaker at a public meeting with difficult questions and rude remarks: [Vn] *He was heckled continuously during his speech.* [also V]. ▶ **heckler** /ˈheklə(r)/ *n*.

hectare /ˈhekteə(r); *Brit also* ˈhektɑː(r)/ *n (abbr* **ha**) a measure of area in the metric system, equal to 100 ares (ARE²) or 10000 square metres (2.471 acres (ACRE)). ⇨ App 2.

hectic /ˈhektɪk/ *adj* very busy; full of activity and excitement: *hectic last-minute preparations* ∘ *lead a hectic life* ∘ *Today was a bit too hectic.*

hect(o)- *comb form* a hundred: *hectare* ∘ *hectogram.* ⇨ App 8.

hector /ˈhektə(r)/ *v* to try to make sb do sth by talking or behaving aggressively; to BULLY¹ sb: [Vn] *use a hectoring tone of voice.*

he'd /hiːd/ *short form* **1** he had. ⇨ note at HAVE. **2** he would. ⇨ WILL¹, WOULD.

hedge /hedʒ/ *n* **1** a row of bushes or small trees planted close together and forming a boundary for a field, garden, etc: *a privet hedge.* ⇨ picture at HOUSE¹. **2** ~ (**against sth**) a means of defence against possible loss: *buy gold as a hedge* (ie to protect one's money) *against inflation.*

▶ **hedge** *v* **1** [Vn] to put a hedge round a field, garden, etc. **2** to avoid giving a direct answer to a question; to refuse to commit(4) oneself: [V] *Answer 'yes' or 'no' — stop hedging!* **3** ~ **sb/sth (about/ around) (with sth)** (esp passive) to surround, restrict or limit sb/sth: [Vnpr] *His belief was hedged with doubt.* [Vnp] *My life is hedged about with petty regulations.* [Vn] *We must be careful not to hedge our negotiating position.* **IDM** ˌhedge one's ˈbets to protect oneself against loss or error by supporting more than one side in a contest, an argument, etc: *hedge one's bets by backing both teams to win.* **PHR V** ˈhedge against sth to do sth to protect oneself, esp against possible loss: *ways of hedging against the exchange rate risk.* ˌhedge sb ˈin to restrict the freedom of sb.

hedging *n* [U] the work of planting or trimming hedges: *hedging implements/plants.*

hedgehog /ˈhedʒhɒg; *US* -hɔːg/ *n* a small animal with stiff spines (SPINE 2) covering its back. Hedge-hogs eat insects, move around mostly at night, and can roll into a ball to defend themselves when at-tacked.

hedgerow /ˈhedʒrəʊ/ *n* a row of bushes forming a hedge: *pick blackberries from the hedgerow.*

hedonism /ˈhiːdənɪzəm/ *n* [U] the belief that pleas-ure should be the main aim in life.
▶ **hedonist** *n* a believer in hedonism.
hedonistic /ˌhiːdəˈnɪstɪk/ *adj*.

heebie-jeebies /ˌhiːbi ˈdʒiːbiz/ *n* [pl] (*dated infml*) a feeling of nervous fear or anxiety: *Being alone in the dark gives me the heebie-jeebies.*

heed /hiːd/ *v* (*fml*) to pay attention to sth/sb: [Vn] *heed sb's advice/warning/wishes* ∘ *heed the lessons of history/the mood of the people* ∘ *He was fined for failing to heed a court order to return to work.*
▶ **heed** *n* [U] (*fml*) careful attention: *It's best to **take heed of** your doctor's advice.* ∘ *I've warned him of the risk but he **pays** little **heed** (to what I say).* **heedful** /-fl/ *adj* [usu pred] ~ (**of sth/sb**) (*fml*) careful to pay attention to sth/sb: *You should be more heedful of advice.* **heedless** *adj* [usu pred] ~ (**of sth/sb**) (*fml*) without paying attention to sth/sb: *heedless bravery* ∘ *be heedless of danger.* **heedlessly** *adv*.

hee-haw /ˈhiː hɔː/ *n* the sound made by a donkey.

heel¹ /hiːl/ *n* **1(a)** the back part of the human foot. ⇨ picture at FOOT¹. (**b**) the part of a sock, shoe, etc covering this. (**c**) the raised part under a boot or

shoe supporting this: *low/high heels.* ⇨ picture at SHOE. **2** a thing like a heel in shape or position: *the heel of the hand* (ie the front part next to the wrist). **3** (*dated sl*) an unpleasant person, esp one that cannot be trusted. **IDM** **an/one's Achilles' heel** ⇨ ACHILLES. **at/on sb's ˈheels**; **on the heels of sth** following closely after sb/sth: *The thief ran off with an angry crowd at his heels.* ∘ *These figures come (hard) on the heels of the announcement of a cut in interest rates.* **bring sb/sth to ˈheel**; **come to ˈheel 1** to accept or force sb/sth to accept discipline and control: *The rebels have been brought to heel.* **2** to make a dog come/(of a dog) to come close behind its owner: *I'm training my dog to come to heel.* **cool one's heels** ⇨ COOL². **dig one's heels/toes in** ⇨ DIG¹. **down at ˈheel 1** (of shoes) with the heels worn down (WEAR¹). **2** (of a person) untidy and badly dressed. **drag one's feet/heels** ⇨ DRAG¹. **hard on sb's heels** ⇨ HARD². **head over heels** ⇨ HEAD¹. **hot on sb's/sth's heels** ⇨ HOT. **kick one's heels** ⇨ KICK¹. **show a clean pair of heels** ⇨ SHOW². **take to one's ˈheels** to run away: *We took to our heels and ran.* **tread on sb's heels** ⇨ TREAD. **turn on one's ˈheel** to turn sharply round and go in the opposite direction. **under the ˈheel of sb** under sb's control; dominated by sb.

▶ **heel** *v* to repair the heel of a shoe, etc: [Vn] *These shoes need soling and heeling.*

-heeled (forming compound *adjs*) with heels of the specified type: *ˌhigh-heeled ˈshoes.* See also WELL-HEELED.

heel² /hiːl/ *v* **PHR V** ˌheel ˈover (esp of a ship) to lean over to one side: *The boat heeled over in the strong wind.* See also KEEL.

hefty /ˈhefti/ *adj* (**-ier, -iest**) (*infml*) **1** (of a person) big and strong. **2** [usu attrib] (**a**) (of a thing) large and heavy: *a hefty suitcase.* (**b**) (of a movement) forceful and strong: *give sb a hefty shove.* (**c**) (of an amount) large: *She earns a hefty salary.* ▶ **heftily** *adv: a heftily-built fellow.*

hegemony /hɪˈgeməni, ˈhedʒɪməni; *US* ˈhedʒə-məni, hɪˈdʒeməni/ *n* [U, C] (*fml*) control and leader-ship (LEADER), esp by one country over others within a group: *cultural/economic/military hegemony.*

heifer /ˈhefə(r)/ *n* a young cow, esp one that has not yet had a calf. Compare COW¹ 1.

height /haɪt/ *n* **1(a)** [U,C] the measurement from the bottom to the top of a person or thing: *Please state your height* (ie how tall you are). ∘ *He is 2 metres in height.* ∘ *What is the height of the moun-tain?* ∘ *The children are nearly the same height.* ⇨ App 2. ⇨ picture at DIMENSION. ⇨ note at HIGH¹. (**b**) [U] being tall or high: *She can see over the wall because of her height.* ∘ *The height of the fence makes the garden very secluded.* **2** [C, U] the distance of an object or a position above ground or sea level: *drop sth from a great height* ∘ *fly at a height of 6000 metres (above sea level)* ∘ *The aircraft was gaining/losing height.* **3** [C often *pl*] a high place or area: *be afraid of heights.* **4** [sing] the main point or highest degree of sth: *in the height of summer* ∘ *The storm was at its height.* ∘ *the height of folly* ∘ *be dressed in the height of fashion.* **IDM** **draw oneself up / rise to one's full height** ⇨ FULL.

heighten /ˈhaɪtn/ *v* to become or make sth higher or more intense: [V] *heightening tension* [Vn] *her heightened colour* (ie the increased colour in her face, caused eg by emotion) ∘ *music to heighten the dramatic effect.*

heinous /ˈheɪnəs/ *adj* very wicked: *a heinous crime/ criminal.* ▶ **heinously** *adv.* **heinousness** *n* [U].

heir /eə(r)/ *n* ~ (**to sth**) a person with the legal right to receive property or money when the owner dies: *be heir to a large fortune/a title/the throne* ∘ *She made her stepson (her) heir.*

▶ **heiress** /'eəres, -rəs/ n a female heir, esp one who inherits great wealth.

■ **heir ap'parent** n (pl **heirs apparent**) an heir whose legal right cannot be cancelled by the birth of another with a stronger claim.

ˌheir pre'sumptive n (pl **heirs presumptive**) an heir who may lose his legal right if another heir with a stronger claim is born.

heirloom /'eəluːm/ n a valuable object that has belonged to the same family for several generations: *That clock is a family heirloom.*

heist /haɪst/ n (sl esp US) a robbery (ROB): *a heist movie.*

held pt, pp of HOLD¹.

helical /'helɪkl, 'hiːl-/ adj like a HELIX.

helicopter

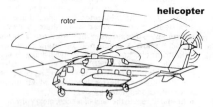

rotor —

helicopter /'helɪkɒptə(r)/ n a type of aircraft with large revolving blades but no wings. It can take off from and land in a very small area, and remain in one position in the air: *rescued from the sea by (a) helicopter* ∘ *a helicopter pilot.* ➪ picture.

heliotrope /'hiːliətrəʊp/ n **1** [C,U] a plant with small sweet-smelling purple flowers. **2** [U] a light purple colour.

heliport /'helɪpɔːt/ n a place where helicopters (HELICOPTER) take off and land.

helium /'hiːliəm/ n [U] (symb He) a chemical element. Helium is a light colourless gas that does not burn, used for filling airships (AIRSHIP) and in the freezing of food, etc. ➪ App 7.

helix /'hiːlɪks/ n (pl **helices** /'hiːlɪsiːz/) a shape like a SPIRAL or a flat COIL; an object that has this shape: *molecules in the form of a double helix.* ➪ picture at SPIRAL.

hell /hel/ n **1** [sing] (without a or the) a place believed in some religions to be the home of devils and of wicked people after death. **2** [U,C] a state or place of great suffering or wickedness; a very unpleasant experience: *endure hell on earth* ∘ *The journey was absolute/sheer hell.* ∘ *She made his life (a) hell.* **3** [U] (infml) (used to express annoyance or surprise or for emphasis): *Oh hell, I've broken it!* ∘ *Bloody hell!* ∘ *Go to hell!* ∘ *I hope to hell you're right.* ∘ *Who the hell is he?* ∘ *What the hell* (ie It doesn't matter), *I can go tomorrow instead.* **a hell of a...; a helluva** /'heləvə/ (sl) **1** (used for emphasis): *It was one hell of a fight* (eg a very violent or exciting one). **2** very: *It's a hell of a long way.* ∘ *He's a helluva (nice) guy.* **all 'hell broke / was let loose** suddenly there was great noise and confusion. **beat/ knock 'hell out of sth/sb** (infml) to hit sb/sth very hard. **be hell on sb/sth** (US infml) to be unpleasant or harmful to sb/sth: *The holes in the road are hell on the tyres.* **for the 'hell of it** (infml) just for fun: *steal a car for the hell of it.* **get the hell 'out (of ...)** (infml) to leave a place very quickly: *Let's get the hell out of this dump.* **give sb 'hell** (infml) to make life very unpleasant for sb: *The boss really gave me hell today.* ∘ *This tooth is giving me hell* (ie is very painful). **hell for 'leather** (Brit) as quickly as possible: *drive/ride/run hell for leather.* **(come) hell or high 'water** in spite of any difficulties that may occur. **like a bat out of hell** ➪ BAT². **like 'hell 1** (infml) (used for emphasis): *drive like hell* (ie very fast). **2** (sl ironic) (used before a clause) not at all:

'You can pay.' 'Like 'hell I will' (ie I certainly will not)!' **not have a cat in hell's chance** ➪ CAT. **not have a snowball's chance in hell / a snowball in hell's chance** ➪ SNOWBALL. **play 'hell with sth/sb** (infml) to affect or upset sth/sb badly: *That curry is playing hell with my insides!* **raise hell** ➪ RAISE. **sure as hell** ➪ SURE. **there will be / was the 'devil / 'hell to pay** ➪ PAY². **to 'hell with sb/sth** (used to reject sb/sth or to express great anger or dislike): *To hell with the lot of you, I'll do what I want.*

▶ **hellish** adj **1** (infml) extremely unpleasant: *His school-days were hellish.* **2** of or like hell. — adv (infml) extremely: *hellish expensive.* **hellishly** adv: *be hellishly treated* ∘ *a hellishly difficult problem.*

■ ˌhell-'bent adj [pred] ~ **on sth** completely determined to do sth whatever the result: *He seems hell-bent on drinking himself to death.*

'hell-hole n a very unpleasant place: *The hotel we were staying in was an absolute hell-hole!*

he'll /hiːl/ short form he will. ➪ WILL¹.

Hellene /'heliːn/ n a native of modern or ancient Greece.

▶ **Hellenic** /he'lenɪk, -'liːn-/ adj of the ancient or modern Greeks, their arts, culture, etc.

Hellenistic /ˌhelɪ'nɪstɪk/ adj of the Greek language and culture of the 4th–1st centuries BC.

hello interj (also **hallo, hullo**) /hə'ləʊ/ interj (used as a greeting, to answer a telephone call or to attract attention): *Hello John, how are you?* ∘ *Hello, is that Oxford 515365?* ∘ *Hullo, hullo, hullo, what's going on here?*

▶ **hello** (also **hallo, hullo**) n (pl **-os**) the cry 'hello': *He gave me a cheery hello.*

helluva ➪ HELL.

helm /helm/ n a handle or wheel for steering a ship or boat: (fig) *the helm of state* (ie government of a country). Compare TILLER. **IDM at the 'helm** leading an organization, etc; in control. **take the 'helm** to take control of an organization, etc.

■ 'helmsman /-zmən/ n (pl **-men** /-mən/) the person who steers a ship.

helmet /'helmɪt/ n a type of hard hat that protects the head, worn eg by a police officer, a soldier or a person playing certain sports. ➪ picture at AMERICAN FOOTBALL.

▶ **heimeted** adj wearing or provided with a helmet: *helmeted fire-fighters.*

help¹ /help/ v **1** ~ **(sb) (with sth)** to be useful to sb; to make it easier for sb to do sth; to assist sb: [V] *Help! I'm stuck.* [Vpr] *Can I help with the washing-up?* [V, Vn] *Your advice helped (me) a lot.* [Vn] *We must all help each other.* [Vnpr] *A man is helping the police with their enquiries.* ∘ *Can you help me up/down the stairs with this heavy case* (ie help me to carry it up/down). [Vn.to inf] *Would it help you to know* (ie if I told you) *that ...?* [Vn.to inf, Vn.inf (no to)] *This charity aims to help people (to) help themselves.* [V.to inf, Vn.to inf, Vn.inf (no to)] *I helped (him) (to) find his clothes.* [also Vnp]. **2** to improve a situation or to make sth happen: [V, Vn] *This latest development doesn't exactly help (matters).* [V.to inf] *drugs that help to take away pain.* ∘ (without to) *stiffer measures to help fight terrorism.* **3(a)** ~ **oneself/sb (to sth)** to serve oneself/sb with food, drink, etc: [Vn, Vnpr] *Help yourself (to a cigarette).* [Vnpr] *May I help you to some more meat?* **(b)** ~ **oneself to sth** to take sth without permission: [Vnpr] *He's been helping himself to my stationery.* **IDM can/could (not) help (doing) sth** can/could (not) prevent or avoid sth: *It can't/couldn't be helped* (ie There was no way of avoiding it and we must accept that). ∘ *Can I help it* (ie Is it my fault?) *if people don't read the instructions?* ∘ *He can't help having big ears.* ∘ *I wouldn't live there — well, not if I could help it.* ∘ *We can't help thinking he's still alive.* ∘ *She burst out laughing — she couldn't help it/herself* (ie could not stop herself). ∘

H

She never does more work than she can help (ie She does as little as possible). **God/Heaven** ˈ**help sb** (used when expressing fears for sb's safety): *God help you* (ie You will be in trouble) *if the teacher finds out!* **a** ˌ**helping** ˈ**hand** help: *give/lend (sb) a helping hand*. **so** ˈ**help me (God)** I swear it: *I never stole the money, so help me (I didn't)!* **PHRV** ˌ**help sb** ˈ**off/**ˈ**on with sth** to help sb to take off/put on a garment: *Can I help you on with your coat?* ˌ**help (sb)** ˈ**out** to help sb, esp in a difficult situation or a crisis: *He's always willing to help (us) out when we're short of staff.*

▶ **helper** *n* a person who helps.

helping *n* a portion of food at a meal: *have/take a second helping* ○ *She had two generous helpings of pie.*

help² /help/ *n* **1** [U] the action of helping or being helped: *Thank you for all your help.* ○ *Can I be of (any) help to you?* ○ *The map wasn't much help.* ○ *She came to our help* (ie helped us). **2** [sing] **a ~ (to sb)** a person or thing that helps: *She was more of a hindrance than a help (to me).* ○ *Your advice was a great help.* ○ (*ironic*) *You're a* ˈ*great help* (ie no help at all), *I must say!* **3** [C] a person employed to help with the cleaning, etc in a house: *The help hasn't come this morning.* See also HOME-HELP. **IDM** **there is no** ˈ**help for it** there is no way of avoiding sth or of improving an existing bad situation.

▶ **helpful** /-fl/ *adj* **~ (to sb)** giving help; useful: *a helpful person/suggestion/map* ○ *He's always very helpful to his mother.* **helpfully** /-fəli/ *adv.* **helpfulness** *n* [U].

helpless *adj* **1** unable to act without help; needing the help of others: *a helpless baby/invalid/drunkard* ○ *be helpless with laughter.* **2** without help; unable to defend oneself: *Without weapons we are helpless.* **helplessly** *adv.* **helplessness** *n* [U].

helpline /ˈhelplaɪn/ *n* a telephone service providing help with problems: *set up/run a mortgage/a suicide/an Aids helpline.*

helter-skelter /ˌheltə ˈskeltə(r)/ *adj, adv* in a disorderly (DISORDER 1) rush: *a* ˌ*helter-skelter* ˈ*dash* ○ *running helter-skelter down the road.*

▶ **helter-skelter** *n* (*Brit*) a tall tower at a FAIR³(1), with a path that winds around it from top to bottom and down which people slide on mats.

hem¹ /hem/ *n* the edge of a piece of cloth which has been turned under and sewn: *take up the hem of a dress to make it shorter.*

▶ **hem** *v* (**-mm-**) to make a hem on sth: [Vn] *hem a skirt/handkerchief.* **PHRV** ˌ**hem sb** ˈ**in** to surround and restrict the movement of sb; to confine sb: *be hemmed in by the crowd* ○ *He felt hemmed in by petty restrictions.*

hem² /hem/ (*also* **h'm** /hm/) *interj* (used in writing to indicate the slight coughing sound made when one is calling sb's attention to sth, or expressing doubt, or hesitating).

▶ **hem** *v* (**-mm-**) [V] to say *hem*; to hesitate while speaking.

hemisphere /ˈhemɪsfɪə(r)/ *n* **1** half a SPHERE(1a). **2** a half of the earth, esp as divided by the EQUATOR (**the Northern/Southern hemisphere**) or by a line passing through the poles (POLE²1) (**the Eastern hemisphere**, ie Europe, Africa, Asia, Australia, and **the Western hemisphere**, ie N and S America). ▷ picture at GLOBE. **3** (*anatomy*) either half of the brain: *the left cerebral hemisphere.*

▶ **hemispherical** /ˌhemɪˈsferɪkl/ *adj* shaped like a hemisphere.

hemline /ˈhemlaɪn/ *n* the lower edge of a dress or skirt: *lower/raise the hemline* (ie make a skirt, etc longer/shorter).

hemlock /ˈhemlɒk/ *n* (**a**) [C,U] a poisonous plant with small white flowers. (**b**) [U] the poison made from this plant.

hem(o)- ▷ HAEM(O)-.

hemp /hemp/ *n* [u] **1** a plant used for making rope and cloth: *nets made from hemp and cotton fibres.* **2** a drug made from the hemp plant. Compare CANNABIS, HASHISH, MARIJUANA.

hen /hen/ *n* **1** a female chicken often kept for its eggs or meat. **2** any female bird: *a* ˈ*guinea-hen* ○ *a hen* ˈ*pheasant.* Compare COCK¹.

■ ˈ**hen-coop** *n* a cage for keeping hens, ducks, etc in.

ˈ**hen-house** *n* a small shed for hens, ducks, etc to sleep in.

ˈ**hen-party** *n* (*infml*) a party for women only, usu held for a woman who will soon get married. Compare STAG-PARTY.

hence /hens/ *adv* **1** from this time: *a week hence* (ie in a week from now). **2** for this reason: *I fell off my bike yesterday — hence the bruises.* **3** (*arch*) from here.

henceforth /ˌhensˈfɔːθ/ (*also* **henceforward** /ˌhensˈfɔːwəd/) *adv* (*fml*) from this time on; in future: *Henceforth I expect you to be punctual for meetings.*

henchman /ˈhentʃmən/ *n* (*pl* **-men** /-mən/) (*usu derog*) a faithful follower or political supporter who always obeys the orders of his leader: *the president and his trusty henchmen.*

henna /ˈhenə/ *n* [U] a reddish dye, used esp on the hair, obtained from a tropical plant.

▶ **hennaed** /ˈhenəd/ *adj* coloured with henna.

henpecked /ˈhenpekt/ *adj* (*infml*) (of a man) dominated by a woman, usu his wife, and always doing what she tells him to do.

hepatitis /ˌhepəˈtaɪtɪs/ *n* [U] a serious disease of the LIVER(1).

heptagon /ˈheptəgən; *US* -gɒn/ *n* (*geometry*) a flat shape with seven straight sides and seven angles. ▶ **heptagonal** /hepˈtægənl/ *adj.*

her¹ /hə(r), ɜː(r), ə(r); *strong form* hɜː(r)/ *pers pron* (used as the object of *a v* or of *a prep*; also used independently and after *be*) a female person or animal mentioned earlier or being observed now: *We're going to call her Stephanie.* ○ *Please give her my regards.* ○ *The manager will be free soon — you can wait for her here.* ○ (*infml*) *That must be her now.* ○ (*fig*) *I know that ship well —I've often sailed in her.* Compare SHE. ▷ note at GENDER.

her² /hə(r), ɜː(r), ə(r); *strong form* hɜː(r)/ *possess det* of or belonging to a female person or animal mentioned earlier: *Mary's mother is dead but her father is still alive.* ○ *Jane's here, I think — isn't that her coat?* ○ *Sarah has broken her leg.*

▶ **hers** /hɜːz/ *possess pron* of or belonging to her: *This is my book so that one must be hers.* ○ *My mother has a lot of hats so I borrowed one of hers.* ▷ note at GENDER.

herald /ˈherəld/ *n* **1** a person or thing that announces or shows that sb/sth is coming: *I think of primroses as the herald of spring.* **2** (formerly) a person who made important announcements and carried messages from a ruler.

▶ **herald** *v* to announce the approach of sb/sth: [Vn] *The winning runner was heralded by a burst of cheering.* [Vn-n] *The announcement has been heralded as a breakthrough in the disarmament talks.* **heraldic** /heˈrældɪk/ *adj* of heraldry: *heraldic arms/devices.*

heraldry *n* [U] the study of the coats of arms (COAT) and the history of old families.

herb /hɜːb; *US* ɜːrb/ *n* (**a**) a plant whose leaves or seeds, etc are used to give flavour to food or for their SCENT(1) or in medicines: *Sage, mint and dill are all herbs.* ○ *a herb garden* ○ *garlic and herb cheese.* (**b**) a plant with a soft stem that dies down to the ground after flowering: *ancient meadows full of flowering herbs.*

▶ **herbal** /'hɜːbl; *US also* 'ɜːrbl/ *adj* [usu attrib] of herbs: *herbal medicine/remedies* ○ *herbal tea.* — *n* a book about herbs, esp those used in medicines.

herbalist /'hɜːbəlɪst; *US* 'ɜːrb-/ *n* a person who grows, sells or specializes in herbs for medical use.

herbaceous /hɜːˈbeɪʃəs; *US also* ɜːr-/ *adj* of or like herbs (HERB).

■ **her₁baceous** '**border** *n* a piece of ground in a garden containing plants that produce flowers year after year.

herbage /'hɜːbɪdʒ; *US also* 'ɜːr-/ *n* [U] growing plants in general, esp grass and other field plants on which cattle, etc can feed.

herbicide /'hɜːbɪsaɪd; *US also* 'ɜːr-/ *n* a substance that is poisonous to plants, used to destroy plants growing where they are not wanted.

herbivore /'hɜːbɪvɔː(r); *US also* 'ɜːr-/ *n* an animal that feeds on plants. Compare CARNIVORE. ▶ **herbivorous** /hɜːˈbɪvərəs; *US also* ɜːr-/ *adj: herbivorous mammals.*

herculean /ˌhɜːkjuˈliːən/ *adj* having or needing very great strength or effort: *a herculean task.*

herd /hɜːd/ *n* **1** [C] a number of animals, esp cattle, feeding or staying together: *a herd of cows/deer/elephant(s).* **2 the herd** [sing] (*usu derog*) a large group of people; the MOB(2): *the common herd* ○ *He preferred to stick with the herd* (ie do the same as everyone around him) *so as not to be noticed.*

▶ **herd** *v* **1** to move or drive sb/sth forward as a herd in the specified direction: [Vnpr, Vnp] *The prisoners were herded (together) onto the train.* [also Vp]. **2** to look after sheep, cattle, etc in a herd: [Vn] *a shepherd herding his flock.*

■ **the** '**herd instinct** *n* [sing] an instinct in people or animals to behave and think like the majority.

herdsman /'hɜːdzmən/ *n* (*pl* **-men** /-mən/) a person who looks after a HERD of animals.

here /hɪə(r)/ *adv* **1(a)** (with a *v* or after a *prep*) in, at or to this position or place: *I live here.* ○ *We leave here tomorrow.* ○ *Fill it up to here.* ○ *Let's get out of here.* ○ *Put the box here.* ○ *Come (over) here.* **(b)** (placed for emphasis at the beginning of a sentence and followed by the finite *v* if the subject is a *n*, but not if the subject is a *pers pron*): *Here comes the bus!* ○ *Here it comes!* ○ *Here are the others!* ○ *Here they are!* ○ *Here we are* (ie We've arrived)*!* Compare THERE¹ 1. **2** at this point (in an activity, a series of events or a situation): *Here the speaker paused to have a drink.* **3** (used for emphasis immediately after a *n*): *My friend here saw it happen.* **IDM** ₁**here and** '**there** in various places: *Cushions were scattered here and there on the floor.* ₁**here** '**goes** (*infml*) (used to announce that one is about to do something exciting, risky, etc): **here's to sb/sth** (used when drinking to a person's health or to the success of an enterprise, etc): *Here's to the bride!* ○ *Here's to your future happiness!* ₁**here, ₁there and** '**everywhere** in many different places; all around. ₁**here we go a**'**gain** (said when the same, usu undesirable, events are happening again). ₁**here you 'are** (said when giving sth to sb) this is for you; take it. **neither** '**here nor** '**there** not important; irrelevant: *The fact that I don't like your fiancé is neither here nor there — what matters is what you feel.* **sure as I'm standing here** ⇨ SURE.

▶ **here** *interj* **1** (used to attract sb's attention): *Here, let me carry it.* ○ *Here, where are you going with that ladder?* **2** (used as a reply when a list of names is being read out) I am present.

hereabouts /ˌhɪərəˈbaʊts/ *adv* (*fml*) near this place; around here: *I don't live hereabouts myself.*

hereafter /ˌhɪərˈɑːftə(r); *US* -ˈæf-/ *adv* (*fml*) **1** (in legal documents, etc) from now on; following this. **2** in future.

▶ **the hereafter** *n* [sing] the future; life after death.

hereby /ˌhɪəˈbaɪ/ *adv* (*fml*) by this means; as a result of this.

hereditary /həˈredɪtri; *US* -teri/ *adj* **1** passed on from parent to child, or from one generation to following generations: *hereditary characteristics/beliefs/factors* ○ *The disease is hereditary* **2** holding a position which has been inherited: *a hereditary ruler.*

heredity /həˈredəti/ *n* [U] **(a)** the passing on of physical or mental characteristics from parents to children: *the problem of heredity versus environment.* **(b)** such characteristics in a particular person: *part of one's heredity.*

herein /ˌhɪərˈɪn/ *adv* (*fml*) in this place or document.

hereof /ˌhɪərˈɒv/ *adv* (*fml*) of this.

heresy /'herəsi/ *n* **1** [C] a belief or an opinion that is contrary to what is generally accepted, esp in religion: *the heresies of the early Protestants.* **2** [U] the holding of such an opinion: *be guilty of heresy.*

▶ **heretic** /'herətɪk/ *n* a person who is guilty of heresy or who supports a heresy.

heretical /həˈretɪkl/ *adj* of heresy or heretics: *heretical beliefs.*

hereto /ˌhɪərˈtuː/ *adv* (*fml*) to this.

heretofore /ˌhɪətuˈfɔː(r)/ *adv* (*fml*) until now; before this time.

herewith /ˌhɪərˈwɪð, -ˈwɪθ/ *adv* (*fml*) (esp in commercial use) with this letter, etc: *Please fill in the form enclosed herewith.*

heritage /'herɪtɪdʒ/ *n* [C usu *sing*] things such as works of art, cultural achievements and customs that have been passed on from earlier generations: *our literary heritage* ○ *These ancient buildings are part of the national heritage.*

hermaphrodite /hɜːˈmæfrədaɪt/ *n* a person or an animal that has both male and female sexual organs or characteristics. Compare BISEXUAL.

hermetic /hɜːˈmetɪk/ *adj* tightly closed so that no air can escape or enter: *a hermetic seal.* ▶ **hermetically** /-kli/ *adv*: *hermetically sealed containers.*

hermit /'hɜːmɪt/ *n* a person, esp a man in early Christian times, who has withdrawn from society and lives completely alone.

▶ **hermitage** /-ɪdʒ/ *n* a place where a hermit or a group of hermits lives.

hernia /'hɜːniə/ *n* [U, C] (*medical*) a swelling caused by a part of the bowel being pushed through a weak point of the wall of the ABDOMEN(1); a RUPTURE(2b).

hero /'hɪərəʊ; *US also* 'hiːrəʊ/ *n* (*pl* **-oes**) **1** a person who is admired by others for his or her noble qualities or courage: *receive a hero's welcome* (ie such as is given to returning heroes) ○ *He died a hero/a hero's death* (ie died while doing sth very brave or noble). ○ *a local/romantic/sporting hero.* **2** the chief male character in a story, poem, play, etc: *the hero of the novel.* Compare VILLAIN. **3** (*US*) = SUBMARINE 1.

▶ **heroine** /'herəʊɪn/ *n* a female HERO(1,2).

■ '**hero-worship** *n* [U] excessive admiration for sb. — *v* (**-pp-**) to admire sb excessively: [Vn] *pop-stars hero-worshipped by their fans.*

heroic /həˈrəʊɪk/ *adj* **(a)** having the characteristics of a HERO; very brave: *heroic efforts.* **(b)** of or about heroes: *heroic myths.* ▶ **heroically** /-kli/ *adv.*

▶ **heroics** *n* [pl] **1** talk or behaviour that is excessively dramatic: *There is no need to indulge in such heroics.* **2** = HEROIC VERSE.

■ **he₁roic** '**verse** *n* [U] (also **he₁roic** '**couplets** [pl]) a verse form used in EPIC(1a) poetry, with lines that RHYME(1) in pairs and typically contain ten syllables and five stresses.

heroin /'herəʊɪn/ *n* [U] a drug made from MORPHINE, used in medicine to cause sleep or relieve pain, or by drug addicts (DRUG).

heroine ⇨ HERO.

heroism /ˈherəʊɪzəm/ n [U] brave and noble conduct; courage: *an act of great heroism.*

heron /ˈherən/ n a large bird with a long neck and long legs that lives near water. ⇨ picture.

heron

herpes /ˈhɜːpiːz/ n [U] (*medical*) a disease that causes painful patches on the skin. There are several different forms of the disease.

Herr /heə(r)/ n (pl **Herren** /ˈherən/) the German word for *Mr*; the title of a German man.

herring /ˈherɪŋ/ n (pl unchanged or **herrings**) [U,C] a N Atlantic fish, usu swimming in very large groups, used for food: *a catch of mackerel and herring* ○ *a couple of fresh herring(s)* ○ *herring fishermen.* See also RED HERRING.
■ **ˈherring-bone** n [U] a ZIGZAG pattern used in sewing and weaving. ⇨ picture at PATTERN.
ˈherring gull n a large N Atlantic GULL with black tips to its wings.

hers ⇨ HER².

herself /hɜːˈself; *weak form* həˈself/ *reflex, emph pron* (only taking the main stress in sentences when used emphatically) **1** (*reflex*) (used when the female who performs an action is also affected by it): *She ˈhurt herself.* ○ *She must be very ˈproud of herself.* **2** (*emph*) (used to emphasize the female subject or object of a sentence): *Mrs King herˈself was at the meeting.* ○ *She told me the news herˈself.* ○ *I saw Jane herˈself in the supermarket.* **IDM** (**all**) **by herˈself 1** alone: *She lives by herself.* **2** without help: *She can mend the fridge by herself.* ⇨ note at GENDER.

hertz /hɜːts/ n (pl unchanged) (*abbr* **Hz**) in radio technology, a unit of FREQUENCY(2) equal to one cycle(2) per second.

he's *short form* **1** /hiːz, his, ɪz/ he is. ⇨ note at BE². **2** /hiːz/ he has. ⇨ note at HAVE.

hesitant /ˈhezɪtənt/ *adj* tending to be slow in speaking or acting because of feeling uncertain or unwilling: *a hesitant reply/manner/voice/speaker* ○ *I'm rather hesitant about signing this.*
► **hesitancy** /-ənsi/ n [U] the state or quality of being hesitant.
hesitantly *adv.*

hesitate /ˈhezɪteɪt/ v **1** ~ (**at/about/over sth**) to be slow to speak or act because one feels uncertain or unwilling; to PAUSE in doubt: [V] *She replied without hesitating.* ○ *She hesitated before replying.* ○ (*saying*) *He who hesitates is lost.* [Vpr] *He's still hesitating about joining/over whether to join the expedition.* **2** to be worried about or shy of doing sth: [V.to inf] *I hesitate to spend that much money on clothes.* ○ *Don't hesitate to tell us if you have a problem.* ► **hesitation** /ˌhezɪˈteɪʃn/ n [U,C]: *She agreed without the slightest hesitation.* ○ *There's no time/room for hesitation.* ○ *His frequent hesitations annoyed the audience.*

hessian /ˈhesiən; *US* ˈheʃn/ n [U] a strong rough cloth made of HEMP(1) or JUTE; SACKCLOTH.

het /het/ *adj* **PHRV** (**be/get**) **het ˈup** (**about/over sth**) (*infml*) (of a person) anxious; excited: *What are you getting so het up about?*

hetero- *comb form* other; different: *heterogeneous* ○ *heterosexual.* Compare HOMO-.

heterodox /ˈhetərədɒks/ *adj* (*fml*) not conforming with accepted standards or beliefs: *a heterodox opinion/person.* Compare ORTHODOX, UNORTHODOX. ►
heterodoxy n [U,C].

heterogeneous /ˌhetərəˈdʒiːniəs/ *adj* (*fml*) composed of different kinds; varied in composition(3):

the heterogeneous population of the USA (ie consisting of many different races). Compare HOMOGENEOUS. ► **heterogeneity** /-dʒəˈniːəti/ n [U].

heterosexual /ˌhetərəˈsekʃuəl/ *adj* feeling sexually attracted to people of the opposite sex. Compare BISEXUAL, HOMOSEXUAL.
► **heterosexual** n a heterosexual person.
heterosexuality /ˌhetərəˌsekʃuˈæləti/ n [U].

heuristic /hjuˈrɪstɪk/ *adj* (*fml*) (of a method of teaching) that helps or allows learners (LEARN) to discover and learn things for themselves.
► **heuristics** n [U] (*fml*) a method of solving problems by learning from past experience and investigating practical ways of finding a solution.

hew /hjuː/ v (*pt* **hewed**; *pp* **hewed** or **hewn** /hjuːn/) **1** to chop or cut sth/sb with an AXE(1), sword, etc: [Vn] *hewing wood* [Vnp] *hew off dead branches* [also Vnpr]. **2** ~ **sth** (**down**) to make sth fall by chopping: [Vn, Vnp] *hewing (down) trees.* **3** to make or shape sth by chopping: [Vn] *roughly hewn timber* [Vnpr] *They hewed a path through the forest.* ○ *The caves are man-made, hewn out of the rock by hand.* [Vnp] (*fig*) *hew out a career for oneself.*

hex(a)- *comb form* having or consisting of six of sth: *hexagon* ○ *hexameter.*

hexagon /ˈheksəgən; *US* -gɒn/ n (*geometry*) a flat shape with six straight sides and six angles. ► **hexagonal** /heksˈægənl/ *adj.*

hexameter /hekˈsæmɪtə(r)/ n a line of verse with six METRICAL feet.

hey /heɪ/ *interj* (also **hi**) (used to call attention or express surprise or inquiry): *Hey, come and look at this!* **IDM** **hey ˈpresto** (said by a conjurer (CONJURE)) as he or she completes a trick successfully, or by sb commenting on or announcing sth that has been done very easily or quickly): *I just turned the piece of wire in the lock and hey presto, the door opened.*

heyday /ˈheɪdeɪ/ n [sing] the time of greatest success, power, influence, etc for sb/sth: *She was a great singer in her heyday.* ○ *Steam railways had their heyday in the 19th century.*

HGV /ˌeɪtʃ dʒiː ˈviː/ *abbr* (*Brit*) heavy goods vehicle, eg a lorry, bus, etc: *have an HGV licence.*

hi /haɪ/ *interj* (*infml*) **1** (used as a greeting): *Hi there!* **2** (*Brit*) = HEY.

hiatus /haɪˈeɪtəs/ n (usu *sing*) **1** a pause when nothing happens: *There will be a two-week hiatus before the talks can be resumed.* **2** a gap in a series or sequence where sth is missing.

hibernate /ˈhaɪbəneɪt/ v [V] (of animals) to spend the winter in a state like deep sleep. ► **hibernation** /ˌhaɪbəˈneɪʃn/ n [U]: *go into/come out of hibernation.*

hibiscus /hɪˈbɪskəs, haɪ-/ n [C,U] a plant or bush with large, brightly coloured flowers, grown esp in tropical countries.

hiccup (also **hiccough**) /ˈhɪkʌp/ n **1(a)** [C] a sharp, often repeated, sound in the throat caused when there is a sudden, short INVOLUNTARY stop in breathing: *give a loud hiccup.* (**b**) **hiccups** [pl] an attack of these occurring repeatedly for some time: *She laughed so much she got (the) hiccups.* **2** [C] (*infml*) a temporary small problem or delay: *There's been a slight hiccup in our mailing system.*
► **hiccup** (also **hiccough**) v [V] (*esp Brit*) to make a hiccup(1).

hick /hɪk/ n (*infml derog esp US*) an awkward or foolish country person.
► **hick** *adj* [usu attrib] (*infml derog esp US*) having a narrow view of life and the affairs of the world: *a hick town.*

hickory /ˈhɪkəri/ n (**a**) [C] a N American tree with edible nuts. (**b**) [U] its hard wood: *a hickory walking-stick.*

hide¹ /haɪd/ v (*pt* **hid** /hɪd/; *pp* **hidden** /ˈhɪdn/) **1(a)** to prevent sth/sb/oneself from being seen; to put or keep out of sight: [Vn] *The sun was hidden by the*

clouds. ○ *The trees hid the house from view.* ○ *He hid the gun in his pocket.* [Vn, Vnp] *While she's working she hides herself (away) in her room.* [also Vnpr]. (**b**) to be or get out of sight; to be or become concealed: [V] *Quick, run and hide!* ○ *The child was hiding behind the sofa.* ○ (*fig*) *She hid behind a false identity.* [Vp] *You can hide away for months in these mountains.* **2** ~ **sth (from sb)** to prevent sth from being known; to keep sth secret: [Vn] *She tried to hide her feelings.* ○ *His words had a hidden meaning.* [Vnpr] *The future is hidden from us.* **IDM** **bury/hide one's head in the sand** ⇨ HEAD¹. **cover/hide a multitude of sins** ⇨ MULTITUDE. **hide one's light under a 'bushel** to hide one's talents, abilities or good qualities because of modesty (MODEST), etc.
▶ **hide** *n* (*Brit*) a place from which people can watch wild animals or birds without being seen by them, eg in order to photograph or shoot them.
■ **,hidden a'genda** *n* (*derog*) the secret intention behind a public statement, policy, etc: *There are fears of a hidden agenda behind this decision.*
hide-and-seek /ˌhaɪd n ˈsiːk/ *n* [U] a children's game in which one player hides and the others try to find her or him.
'hide-out *n* a place for people to hide: *a guerrilla hide-out in the mountains.*

hide² /haɪd/ *n* **1** [C, U] an animal's skin, esp when bought and sold or used for making sth: *boots made of buffalo hide.* **2** [U] (*infml joc*) human skin. **IDM** **neither hide nor 'hair of sb/sth** no trace of sb/sth: *I've not seen hide nor hair of him all week.* **tan sb's hide** ⇨ TAN¹.

hideaway /ˈhaɪdəweɪ/ *n* a place where people can hide or go to be alone.

hidebound /ˈhaɪdbaʊnd/ *adj* (*derog*) not willing to consider new ideas, methods, etc; too conventional and narrow in one's views: *hidebound attitudes/conventions.*

hideous /ˈhɪdiəs/ *adj* filling the mind with horror; very unpleasant or ugly: *a hideous crime/face/noise/creature* ○ (*infml*) *I think the colour scheme they've chosen is hideous.* ▶ **hideously** *adv*: *be hideously deformed.*

hiding¹ /ˈhaɪdɪŋ/ [U] the state of being hidden: *remain in hiding* ○ *She's gone into/come out of hiding.*
■ **'hiding-place** *n* a place where sb/sth is or could be hidden.

hiding² /ˈhaɪdɪŋ/ *n* (*infml*) a beating: *His dad gave him a good hiding.* **IDM** **on a ,hiding to 'nothing** (*infml*) with no chance at all of succeeding.

hierarchy /ˈhaɪərɑːki/ *n* a system with grades of authority or status from the lowest to the highest: *She's high up in the management hierarchy.* ○ *There is a hierarchy in the classification of all living creatures.*
▶ **hierarchical** /ˌhaɪəˈrɑːkɪkl/ *adj* of or arranged in a hierarchy: *a hierarchical organization/society/structure/system.*

hieroglyph /ˈhaɪərəɡlɪf/ *n* a picture or symbol of an object, representing a word, syllable or sound, esp as used in ancient Egyptian and other writing.
▶ **hieroglyphic** /ˌhaɪərəˈɡlɪfɪk/ *adj.*
hieroglyphics *n* [pl] (writing that uses) hieroglyphs: *deciphering Egyptian hieroglyphics* ○ *His writing is so bad it just looks like hieroglyphics to me.*

hi-fi /ˈhaɪ faɪ/ *adj* [usu attrib] (*infml*) = HIGH FIDELITY: *hi-fi equipment/systems.*
▶ **hi-fi** *n* [C, U] (*infml becoming dated*) hi-fi equipment: *You must hear my new hi-fi.*

higgledy-piggledy /ˌhɪɡldi ˈpɪɡldi/ *adv*, *adj* (*infml*) without order; completely mixed up: *Files were scattered (all) higgledy-piggledy about the office.*

high¹ /haɪ/ *adj* (-er, -est) **1(a)** (of things) extending far upwards; having a relatively big distance from the base to the top: *a high fence/forehead/mountain*

○ *high heels* ○ *How high is Mt Everest?* (**b**) having a specified distance from the base to the top: *knee-high boots* ○ *The wall is six feet high.* (**c**) situated far above the ground or above the level of the sea: *a high ceiling/shelf* ○ *fly at a high altitude.* (**d**) being above the normal level: *a jersey with a high neck.* (**e**) (of a physical action) performed at or reaching a considerable distance above ground: *a high dive/kick.* ⇨ note. Compare LOW¹. **2** [usu attrib] ranking above others in importance or quality: *a high official* ○ *a man of high standing* ○ *refer a case to a higher court* ○ *high society* (ie the upper classes) ○ *She has friends in high places* (ie among people of power and influence). ○ *I have this information on the highest authority.* **3(a)** above the normal; extreme; intense: *a high price/temperature/fever/speed/wind/living standard* ○ *high voltage/blood pressure/praise* ○ *The cost in terms of human life was high.* ○ *I have high hopes of passing the exam.* ○ *A high degree of accuracy is needed.* ○ *be in high spirits* (ie be very cheerful). (**b**) of great value: *play for high stakes* ○ *My highest card is a ten.* (**c**) [usu attrib] (of aims, ideas, etc) morally good; noble: *have high ideals* ○ *a woman of high principle.* (**d**) [usu attrib] very favourable: *have a high opinion of/high regard for sb.* **4** (of a sound) at or near the top of the musical scale¹(6); not deep or low: *the high voice of a child* ○ *The note was too high for him.* **5** [attrib] (of time) fully reached: *high noon* ○ *high summer* (ie the middle of the summer). **6** (of a gear) allowing greater speed of a vehicle in relation to its engine speed: *You can change into a higher gear now you're going faster.* **7** [usu pred] (of meat, etc) beginning to go bad: *Some game-birds are kept until they are high before cooking.* **8** [pred] ~ **(on sth)** (*infml*) under the influence of esp drugs or alcohol: *be/get high on cannabis.* **IDM** **be/get on one's high 'horse** (*infml*) to act in a superior manner. **have / give sb a 'high old time** (*infml*) to enjoy oneself/entertain sb in a very cheerful or happy way. **hell or high water** ⇨ HELL. **high and 'dry** in a difficult situation, esp without help or money: *He left her high and dry in a strange country without a passport.* **high and 'mighty** (*infml*) superior in manner; ARROGANT: *There's no need to be so high and mighty with me!* **,high days and 'holidays** festivals and special occasions. **a high/low profile** ⇨ PROFILE. **high/about time** ⇨ TIME¹. **in high 'dudgeon** in an angry or offended mood: *He stalked out of the room in high dudgeon.* **smell, stink, etc to high 'heaven** (*infml*) **1** to have a strong unpleasant smell. **2** to seem to be very dishonest, not morally acceptable, etc: *The whole scheme stinks to high heaven — don't get involved in it.*
■ **,high-'born** *adj* of noble birth.
,high 'chair *n* a small child's chair with long legs and an attached tray, for use at meals.
,High 'Church *adj* of a section of the Church of England that emphasizes ritual and the authority of bishops and priests.
,high-'class *adj* **1** of high quality; excellent: *a ,high-class 'restaurant.* **2** of high social class.
,High Com'mission *n* the EMBASSY(1) of one Commonwealth country in another. Compare CONSULATE 1. **,High Com'missioner** the head of a High Commission: *the Australian High Commissioner in Ottawa.* Compare CONSUL 1.
,High 'Court (also **,High Court of 'Justice**) *n* a lawcourt at the highest level for dealing with civil(4) cases.
,higher 'animals, **,higher 'plants** *n* [pl] animals, plants, etc that are highly developed and have a complex structure.
,higher edu'cation *n* [U] education and training at universities, esp to degree level.
,high ex'plosive *n* a very powerful explosive capable of causing widespread destruction.

,high fi'delity (also 'hi-fi) n [U] the REPRODUCTION(1) of recorded sound that is of high quality and very close to the original sound.

,high-'flown adj (*usu derog*) (of language, etc) very elaborate and grand in style: ,high-flown 'rhetoric.

,high-'flyer (also **high-flier**) n a person with the ability or ambition to be very successful. ,high-'flying adj [attrib].

,high-'grade adj of high quality: ,high-grade 'petrol.

,high-'handed adj using power or authority without considering the opinions and wishes of others: *a ,high-handed 'person/'action/'manner.*

,high 'jinks n [pl] lively and playful activity; fun: *We got up to all kinds of high jinks.*

the 'high jump n a contest in which people try to jump as high as possible, over a high bar. This can be set at different heights and the person who jumps highest wins: *enter for the high jump.* **IDM** be for the 'high jump (*Brit infml*) to be likely to be severely punished: *If you're caught stealing you'll be for the high jump.*

,high-'level adj [usu attrib] (of negotiations, etc) involving very senior people: ,high-level 'talks/ 'meetings.

the 'high life n [sing] (also ,high 'living [U]) (*sometimes derog*) a style of life that involves spending a lot of money on entertainment, good food, expensive clothes, etc.

high-minded /,haɪ 'maɪndɪd/ adj having or showing a noble and moral character.

,high-'pitched adj **1** (of sounds) very high in pitch¹(2): *a ,high-pitched 'whine.* Compare LOW-PITCHED. **2** (of roofs) steeply sloping.

'high point n (usu *sing*) ~ (of sth) the best or most enjoyable moment or state reached: *It was the high point of the evening/his career.*

,high-'powered adj [usu attrib] **1** (of things) having great power: *a ,high-powered 'car/'rifle/'engine.* **2** (of people) forceful and full of energy: *high-powered business executives.*

,high 'pressure n [U] **1** a condition of the atmosphere with pressure(2) above average: *a ridge of high pressure.* **2** energetic activity and effort: *work at high pressure* ○ ,high-pressure (ie aggressive) 'salesmanship.

,high-'priced adj expensive.

,high 'priest n (*fem* ,high 'priestess) a chief priest: (*fig*) *the high priest of modern technology.*

,high-'principled adj honourable: *a ,high-principled 'person/'deed.*

,high-'ranking adj of high rank; senior: *a ,high-ranking 'army officer.*

'high-rise adj [attrib] (of a building) very tall, with many floors: *high-rise apartments.* — n: *live in a new high-rise.*

'high road n (usu *sing*) a main road: (*fig*) *take the high road* (ie the most direct way) *to happiness.*

'high school n [C, U] (*esp US*) a secondary school; a school providing more advanced education than a primary or middle school.

the ,high 'seas n [pl] the open seas beyond the legal control of any one country.

,high 'season n [U, sing] the time of year when most visitors regularly come to a resort, etc: *Hotels usually raise their prices in (the) high season.* Compare LOW SEASON.

'high-sounding adj (of language, etc) elaborate; PRETENTIOUS.

,high-'speed adj [attrib] operating at great speeds: *a ,high-speed 'rail link* ○ ,high-speed 'trains.

,high-'spirited adj lively and cheerful: *a ,high-spirited 'child.*

'high spot n ~ (of sth) (*infml*) an outstanding event, memory, etc; a most important feature: *The excursion was the high spot of the year.*

'high street n (*Brit*) (esp in names) a main street of a town, with shops, etc: ,Oxford 'High Street ○ ,high-street 'banks/'shops.

,high-'strung adj = HIGHLY STRUNG.

,high 'table n [C, U] a table on a raised platform where the most important people at a public dinner or in a college(2a) sit to eat: *dining at/on high table.*

,high 'tea n (*Brit*) a meal of cooked food, usu with tea, taken in the late afternoon or early evening.

,high-'tech adj (*infml*) **1** involving high technology. **2** (of interior design (INTERIOR 1), etc) copying styles more common in industry, etc, esp in the use of steel, glass or plastic.

,high tech'nology n [U] advanced development in technology, esp in electronics (ELECTRONIC).

,high 'tide n (**a**) [C] the sea when it has risen to its highest level. (**b**) (also **high water**) [U] the time when this occurs. Compare LOW TIDE.

,high 'treason n [U] the crime of betraying one's country or ruler.

'high-up n (*infml*) a person of high rank.

,high 'water n [U] = HIGH TIDE. ,high-'water mark n **1** a mark showing the highest level reached by the sea or by flood waters. Compare LOW-WATER MARK. **2** the highest point of achievement.

,high 'wire n (usu *sing*) a high TIGHTROPE: *a high wire trapeze artist.*

NOTE You use **high** to describe the measurement of something: *The garden wall is two metres high.* ○ *Which is the highest mountain in the world?* You also use **high** to describe the distance of something from the ground: *The room had very high ceilings.* You use **tall** and NOT **high** for people: *How tall are you?* ○ *a tall girl.* **Tall** is used for other things that are narrow such as trees: *The house was hidden by tall trees.* ○ *There was a tall bookcase against the wall.* Buildings can be **tall** or **high**: *The World Trade Center is higher/taller than the Empire State Building.*

high² /haɪ/ n **1** a high point; the highest level or number: *Profits reached a new/an all-time high last year.* **2** an area of high pressure; an ANTICYCLONE: *A high over southern Europe is bringing fine sunny weather to all parts.* **3** (*infml*) a feeling of extreme pleasure or excitement: *The drug gives you a tremendous high.* ○ *With all her recent success, she's on a real high.* **IDM** on 'high **1** in a high place: *The climbers gazed down from on high.* ○ (*fig*) *pronouncements about the company's future handed down from on high* (ie from those in the most senior positions). **2** in heaven: *The disaster was seen as a judgement from on high.*

high³ /haɪ/ adv **1** at or to a high position or level: *shelves piled high with tinned food* ○ *An eagle circled high overhead.* ○ *I can't jump any higher.* ○ *He never got very high in the company.* ○ *aim high* (ie be ambitious). **2** (of sound) at or to a high pitch¹(2): *I can't sing that high.* **IDM** fly high ➪ FLY¹. ,high and 'low everywhere: *I've searched/hunted high and low for my pen.* hold one's head high ➪ HEAD¹. ride high ➪ RIDE². run 'high (esp of feelings) to be strong and angry: *Passions ran high as the election approached.*

highball /'haɪbɔːl/ n (US) a strong alcoholic drink, eg WHISKY or GIN, served with water, etc and ice.

highboy /'haɪbɔɪ/ n (US) = TALLBOY.

highbrow /'haɪbraʊ/ adj (*sometimes derog*) dealing with or interested in serious artistic or cultural matters; intellectual: *a highbrow newspaper* ○ *highbrow drama/books/interests/tastes.* Compare LOW-BROW, MIDDLEBROW.

highfalutin /,haɪfə'luːtɪn/ adj (*infml derog*) foolishly trying to appear too grand or serious; PRETENTIOUS: *highfalutin ideas/language.*

highland /'haɪlənd/ adj [attrib] **1** of or in a region of high land, esp mountains. **2 Highland** of or in the Scottish Highlands: *Highland cattle* ○ *Highland dress.*

▶ **highland** *n* **1** [C usu *pl*] a highland region. **2 the Highlands** [pl] the highland region of Scotland. **ˈhighlander** *n* a person who lives in the Scottish Highlands.

ˌHighland ˈfling *n* a lively Scottish dance.

highlight /ˈhaɪlaɪt/ *n* **1** the best, most interesting or most exciting part of something: *The highlight of our tour was seeing the palace.* ○ *The highlights of the match will be shown at 10.25 tonight.* **2** (usu *pl*) the light or bright part of a picture or photograph. **3** (usu *pl*) an area of hair which is naturally lighter in colour than the rest or is made lighter by applying a chemical substance: *have blonde highlights put in one's hair.*

▶ **highlight** *v* **1** to give special attention to sth; to emphasize sth: [Vn] *a TV programme highlighting the problems of the unemployed* ○ *His comments do serve to highlight a major point in this discussion.* **2** to use a special coloured pen to mark part of a text: [Vn] *You don't need to read the whole report, just the bits I've highlighted.*

highlighter *n* a thick coloured pen for highlighting words in a text.

H

highly /ˈhaɪli/ *adv* **1** to an unusually great extent; very: *highly gifted/intelligent/qualified/responsible/successful people* ○ *be highly probable/likely/unlikely* ○ *The goods on display are all very highly priced.* **2** very favourably: ***think highly of sb*** (ie have a high opinion of sb) ○ ***speak highly of sb*** (ie praise sb) ○ *His films are very highly regarded.*

■ **ˌhighly-ˈstrung** *adj* (of a person) very sensitive and nervous; easily upset.

highness /ˈhaɪnəs/ *n* (usu **Highness**) a title used in speaking to or about a prince or princess: *His/Her/Your Royal Highness* ○ *Their Royal Highnesses the Duke and Duchess of Kent.*

highway /ˈhaɪweɪ/ *n* (*esp US*) **(a)** a main road, usu connecting large towns. **(b)** any public road: *The police arrested him for obstructing the highway.*

■ **the ˌHighway ˈCode** *n* [sing] (*Brit*) a small book containing the official rules for users of public roads. ⇨ note at ROAD.

highwayman /ˈhaɪweɪmən/ *n* (*pl* **-men** /-mən/) (formerly) a man, usu armed with a gun and riding a horse, who robbed travellers on public roads.

hijack /ˈhaɪdʒæk/ *v* **1** to seize control of a vehicle, esp an aircraft, in order to force it to go to a new destination or demand sth from a government in return for the safety of its passengers and crew: [Vn] *The plane was hijacked while on a flight to Delhi.* **2** (*derog*) to use an event, a meeting, etc organized by others for a particular purpose to promote one's own aims or interests: [Vn] *an attempt by a left-wing group to hijack the party conference.*

▶ **hijack** *n* an act of hijacking sth.

hijacker *n* a person who hijacks a plane, etc.

hijacking *n* [C, U]: *a recent series of hijackings.*

hike /haɪk/ *n* **1** a long walk, esp in the country, usu taken for pleasure: *go on a ten-mile hike over the moor.* See also RAMBLE *n.* **2** (*infml*) a sharp rise in prices, costs, etc: *the latest hike in interest rates.*

▶ **hike** *v* **1** (often **go hiking**) to go for a long walk, esp for pleasure: [Vpr] *We were hiking round America.* [also V]. **2** ~ **sth (up)** (*infml*) to raise prices, etc sharply: [Vn, Vnp] *Prices have been hiked (up) to unprecedented levels.* **PHRV** **ˌhike sth ˈup** (*infml*) to pull or lift sth up, esp one's clothing: *She hiked up her skirt and waded into the water.* **hiker** *n* a person who hikes (HIKE 1). **hiking** *n* [U]: *hiking boots* ○ *a hiking holiday.*

hilarious /hɪˈleəriəs/ *adj* very funny: *a hilarious account of their camping trip* ○ *Lynn found the whole situation hilarious.*

▶ **hilariously** *adv*: *be hilariously funny.*

hilarity /hɪˈlærəti/ *n* [U] great amusement; loud laughter: *scenes of hilarity* ○ *The announcement was greeted with much hilarity.*

hill /hɪl/ *n* **1** an area of land which is higher than the land around it, but not as high as a mountain: *a range of hills* ○ *an isolated hill farm* ○ *The house is on the side of a hill.* **2** a slope in a road: *push one's bike up a steep hill.* See also ANTHILL, MOLEHILL. **IDM** **a ˌhill of ˈbeans** (*US infml*) a thing of little value: *It's not worth a hill of beans* (ie It is worth very little). **old as the hills** ⇨ OLD. **ˌover the ˈhill** (*infml*) (of a person) past one's best: *Some companies think you're over the hill at 35 these days!* **up hill and down ˈdale** everywhere: *We wandered up hill and down dale in search of somewhere to eat.*

▶ **hilly** /ˈhɪli/ *adj* having many hills: *a hilly area/region* ○ *The countryside round here is very hilly.*

hill-billy /ˈhɪl bɪli/ *n* [C] (*US infml often derog*) a person from a remote country area of the southern USA: *hill-billy communities/music.*

hillock /ˈhɪlək/ *n* a small hill.

hillside /ˈhɪlsaɪd/ *n* the side of a hill: *a steep, windswept hillside* ○ *Wherever possible, the hillsides have been terraced for cultivation.*

hilltop /ˈhɪltɒp/ *n* the top of a hill: *wooded hilltops.*

hilt /hɪlt/ *n* the handle of a sword, etc. ⇨ picture at SWORD. **IDM** **(up) to the ˈhilt** to the maximum possible amount: *We're mortgaged up to the hilt.* ○ *I'll back/defend you to the hilt.*

him /ɪm; *strong form* hɪm/ *pers pron* (used as the object of a *v* or of a *prep*, and sometimes after *than* in comparative sentences) a male person or animal referred to earlier; the object form of *he*: *When did you see him?* ○ *I'm taller than him.* ○ *That's him over there.* ○ *Oh, not ˈhim again!* ⇨ note at GENDER.

himself /hɪmˈself/ *reflex, emph pron* (only taking the main stress when used as an *emph pron*) **1** (*reflex*) (used when the male subject of the verb is affected by the action described): *He ˈcut/ˈkilled/introˈduced himself.* ○ *Peter ought to be aˈshamed of himself.* **2** (*emph*) (used to emphasize the male subject or object of a sentence): *The doctor said so himˈself.* ○ *Did you see the manager himˈself?* **IDM** **be, seem, etc himˈself** be, etc in his normal state of health: *He doesn't feel quite himˈself this morning.* **(all) by himˈself 1** alone: *He lives all by himself in that large house.* **2** without help: *John managed to repair his car by himself.* See also HAVE SB/STH TO ONESELF. ⇨ note at GENDER.

hind¹ /haɪnd/ *adj* [attrib] (of the legs of an animal with four legs) situated at the back: *The horse reared up on its hind legs.* Compare FORE, FRONT. **IDM** **talk the hind legs off a donkey** ⇨ TALK¹.

hind² /haɪnd/ *n* (*pl* unchanged or **hinds**) a female deer, esp a red deer. Compare DOE, HART, STAG 1.

hinder /ˈhɪndə(r)/ *v* ~ **sb/sth (from sth / doing sth)** to prevent or delay the progress of sb/sth: [Vn] *These new laws will hinder rather than promote prison reform.* ○ *Progress has been hindered by financial difficulties.* [Vnpr] *Her shyness hinders her from getting to know her colleagues better.*

Hindi /ˈhɪndi/ *adj, n* [U] (in or of) one of the official languages of India, spoken esp in N India: *radio broadcasts in Hindi* ○ *Hindi films.*

hindmost /ˈhaɪndməʊst/ *adj* **IDM** **the devil take the hindmost** ⇨ DEVIL¹.

hindquarters /ˌhaɪndˈkwɔːtəz/ *n* [pl] the back part of an animal with four legs, including the two back legs. ⇨ picture at HORSE.

hindrance /ˈhɪndrəns/ *n* (esp *sing*) ~ **(to sth/sb)** a thing or person that restricts or hinders (HINDER) sb/sth: *The high price is a major hindrance to potential buyers.* **IDM** **without let or hindrance** ⇨ LET³.

hindsight /ˈhaɪndsaɪt/ *n* [U] understanding of a situation or an event only after it has occurred: *We* *failed, and **with (the benefit/wisdom of) hindsight** I now see where we went wrong.* Compare FORESIGHT.

Hindu /ˌhɪnˈduː; US ˈhɪnduː/ n a person, esp of N India, whose religion is Hinduism.
▸ **Hindu** adj: *a ˌHindu ˈtemple.*

Hinduism /ˈhɪnduːɪzəm/ n [U] the main religion and social system of India, which includes the worship of several gods and belief in reincarnation (REINCARNATE).

hinge /hɪndʒ/ n a small piece of metal, etc on which a lid, door or gate turns or swings as it opens and closes: *She oiled the hinges to stop the gate squeaking.* ⇨ picture.

hinge

▸ **hinge** v (esp passive) to attach sth by a hinge or hinges: [Vn] *a hinged lid* ○ *The rear door of the car is hinged at the top so that it opens upwards.* **PHRV** **ˈhinge on sth** to depend entirely on sth: *Everything hinges on the outcome of these talks.*

hint /hɪnt/ n **1** a small indication given to sb about what one is thinking, what one wants or what will happen; an indirect suggestion: *give a strong/broad/gentle/delicate hint* ○ *The opening scene gives us a hint of things to come.* ○ *He gave no hint that anything was wrong.* **2** a small sign or amount of sth: *There was more than a hint of sadness in his voice.* **3** a small piece of practical information or advice: *handy hints for home decorators.* **IDM** **drop a hint/ drop sb a hint** ⇨ DROP². **take a ˈhint** to understand and do what has been indirectly suggested: *I thought they'd never go — some people just can't take a hint!*
▸ **hint** v ~ **(at sth)** to suggest sth indirectly: [Vpr] *The possibility of an early election has been strongly hinted at.* ○ *(fig) modern furniture hinting at old-world craftsmanship* [V.that, Vpr.that] *She has already hinted (to me) that I've won the prize.* [also V].

hinterland /ˈhɪntəlænd/ n (usu sing) the often remote parts of a country away from the coast or the banks of major rivers.

hip¹ /hɪp/ n the part on each side of the human body between the top of the leg and the waist: *He stood with his hands on his hips.* ○ *the hip-bone* ○ *What is your hip measurement?*
▸ **-hipped** (forming compound adjs) having hips of the specified size or shape: *a large-/heavy-/slim-hipped girl.*
■ **ˈhip-bath** n (Brit) a bath that is large enough to sit in, but not to lie down in.
ˈhip-flask n a small metal bottle with flat or curved sides, used esp for carrying alcoholic drinks in the pocket.
ˌhip-ˈpocket n a pocket in the side of a pair of trousers just behind the hips.

hip² /hɪp/ (also **ˈrose-hip**) n the fruit of the wild rose, red when ripe.

hip³ /hɪp/ interj **IDM** **hip, hip, hurˈrah/hurˈray!** (used to express delight, approval, thanks, etc): *Three cheers for the bride and groom: Hip, hip, hurray! Hip, hip...*

hip⁴ /hɪp/ adj (infml) following or knowing about the most recent fashion in music, clothes, etc.
■ **ˈhip hop** n [U] a type of dance music similar to RAP(2), originating in the USA.

hippie (also **hippy**) /ˈhɪpi/ n a person who rejects organized society and established social habits and who joins others in leading a less conventional way of life. The hippie movement began and was most widespread in the 1960s. Compare BEATNIK.

hippo /ˈhɪpəʊ/ n (pl **-os**) (infml) = HIPPOPOTAMUS.

hippopotamus /ˌhɪpəˈpɒtəməs/ n (pl **hippopotamuses** /-məsɪz/ or **hippopotami** /-maɪ/) (also

infml **hippo**) a large African animal with short legs and thick dark skin which lives in rivers, lakes, etc.

hippy = HIPPIE.

hire /ˈhaɪə(r)/ v **1(a)** (esp Brit) to obtain the use of sth for a short time in return for payment: [Vn] *hire a car/room/costume.* Compare RENT¹ v. **(b)** (esp US) to give sb a job: [Vn] *hire a new clerk* [V] *do the hiring and firing* (ie employ and dismiss people). **(c)** to employ sb for a short time to do a particular job: [Vn] *hire a lawyer/barrister* ○ *a hired assassin* [Vn.to inf] *hire a dozen men to dig a ditch.* **2** ~ **sth (out) (to sb)** to allow the temporary use of sth, in return for payment: [Vnp] *We hire out our vans by the day.* [also Vn, Vnpr]. ⇨ note at LET².
▸ **hire** n [U] (esp Brit) the use of sth for a short time in return for payment: *bicycles for hire, £2 an hour* ○ *a car hire firm* ○ *a hire car* ○ *pay for the hire of a hall* ○ *This suit is on hire.* **IDM** **ply for hire** ⇨ PLY².
■ **ˌhired ˈhand** n (US) a person hired to work on a farm.
ˌhire ˈpurchase n [U] (Brit) (abbr **hp**) (also esp US **inˈstalment plan** [U, sing]) a system of buying an article by making regular payments for it over several months or years. The article only belongs to the buyer when all the payments have been made: *monthly hire purchase instalments* ○ *a hire-purchase agreement* ○ *We're buying a new cooker **on hire purchase**.* Compare CREDIT¹ 1.

hireling /ˈhaɪəlɪŋ/ n (usu derog) a person who is hired to work for sb.

hirsute /ˈhɜːsjuːt; US -suːt/ adj (fml or joc) (esp of a man) having a lot of hair on the face or body.

his /ɪz; strong form hɪz/ possess det of or belonging to a male person or animal referred to earlier: *James has sold his car.* ○ *He claims it was ˈhis idea.*
▸ **his** possess pron of or belonging to him: *It's not mine, it's his.* ○ *Learning to ski has always been an ambition of his.* ⇨ note at GENDER.

Hispanic /hɪˈspænɪk/ adj **1** of or from countries, esp in Latin America, in which Spanish is spoken: *Hispanic students* ○ *a Hispanic neighbourhood in New York.* **2** of Spain and Portugal.
▸ **Hispanic** n a person whose first language is Spanish, esp one from a Latin American country: *the rising population of Hispanics in the USA.*

hiss /hɪs/ v ~ **(at sb/sth) (a)** to make a sound like a long 's': [V] *The steam escaped with a loud hissing noise.* [Vpr] *The goose hissed at me angrily.* **(b)** to make this sound to show disapproval of a speaker, an actor, etc: [Vnpr] *He was hissed off the stage* (ie forced to leave it by the audience hissing). [Vn] *The crowd hissed and booed the performers.* [also V]. **(c)** to say sth with a quiet angry voice: [V.speech] *'Stay away from me!' she hissed.* [Vpr.to inf] *He hissed at them to be quiet.*
▸ **hiss** n a sound like a long 's': *the hiss of air brakes* ○ *The performers were greeted with boos and hisses.*

histamine /ˈhɪstəmiːn/ n [U] (medical) a chemical compound that is present in the body and can cause usu unpleasant reactions in certain people.

historian /hɪˈstɔːriən/ n a person who studies or writes about history: *an art historian* ○ *a military/social historian* ○ *a period long neglected by historians.*

historic /hɪˈstɒrɪk; US -ˈstɔːr-/ adj **1** important in history or likely to be considered important at some time in the future: *the preservation of historic monuments* ○ *a/an historic occasion/decision/day/visit/victory.* **2** of the period during which history has been recorded: *in historic times.* Compare PREHISTORIC.
■ **the hisˌtoric ˈpresent** n [sing] (grammar) the simple present tense used to describe events in the past in order to make the description more vivid.

historical /hɪˈstɒrɪkl; US -ˈstɔːr-/ adj [usu attrib] **1(a)** based on history; happening in the past: *a lack* of historical perspective ○ historical traditions ○ You must place these events in their historical context. (**b**) concerning past events: historical records/ documents/research. **2** (of a book, film, etc) dealing with real or imaginary people and events in the past: a historical novel. ▸ **historically** /-kli/ adv: The book is historically inaccurate. ○ Historically, powerful nations were able to protect their interests.

history /'hɪstri/ n **1** [U] the study of past events, esp the political, social and economic development of a country or nation: a student of Russian history ○ ancient/medieval/modern history ○ take a history exam. Compare NATURAL HISTORY. **2** [U] the past considered as a whole: a people with no sense of history ○ The area was inhabited long before the dawn of recorded history (ie before people wrote about events). ○ These currents changed the course of history. **3** [C] a written account of past events: the official history of the Second World War ○ writing a new history of Europe ○ Shakespeare's history plays. **4** [C usu sing] a record of what has happened to a person, family, house, etc: This house has had a long and eventful history. ○ know one's family history ○ sb's medical history ○ There is a history of heart disease in my family. ○ He has a history of violent crime. See also LIFE HISTORY. **5** [U] (infml) a fact, event, etc that is no longer relevant or important: They had an affair once, but that's **ancient/past history** now. **IDM** **make / go down in 'history** to be or do sth so important or unusual that it will be recorded in history: a discovery that made medical history.

histrionic /ˌhɪstri'ɒnɪk/ adj **1** (usu derog) (of behaviour) very dramatic and intended to attract attention: histrionic gestures. **2** (fml) of acting or the theatre: displaying her considerable histrionic talents.

▸ **histrionically** /-kli/ adv (usu derog).

histrionics n [pl] (usu derog) exaggerated dramatic behaviour intended to attract attention: Cut out the histrionics, Pete, and calm down.

hit¹ /hɪt/ v (-tt-; pt, pp hit) **1** to strike sb/sth with the hand or with an object held in the hand: [Vn] My parents never used to hit me. [Vnpr] He hit the nail with the hammer ○ She hit him on the head with her umbrella. ⇨ note. **2** to come against sth/sb with force, esp so as to cause damage or injury: [Vn] The lorry hit the lamppost. ○ I was hit by a falling stone/a stray bullet. **3** ~ **sth (on sth)** to knock part of one's body against sth: [Vnpr] He hit his head on the low ceiling. [also Vn]. **4**(**a**) to drive a ball forward by striking it with a bat, club, etc: [Vnadv] She hit it too hard and it went out. [Vnpr] hit a ball over the fence. [also Vnp]. (**b**) (sport) to score runs or points by hitting a ball: [Vn] hit a winner off the backhand ○ He's already hit two sixes. **5** to have a sudden, usu bad, effect on a person, thing or place; to affect sb/ sth: [Vn] The tax increases will certainly hit the poor. ○ His death didn't really hit me at first. [Vnadv] The recession hit the retail trade badly. ○ Rural areas have been worst hit by the strike. ○ Spain was one of the hardest hit countries. **6** (infml) to attack sb/sth: [Vn] We hit the enemy when they least expected it. **7** to reach a place: [Vn] Follow this footpath and you'll eventually hit the road. ○ We hit London at four in the morning. **8** to reach a particular level: [Vn] The yen hit a record high in trading today. ○ We **hit top form** in yesterday's match. ○ She can hit top C. **9** (infml) to experience sth difficult or unpleasant: [Vn] If you go now, you're likely to hit the rush hour. ○ hit a snag/ problem ○ Everything was going well but then we hit trouble. **10** (infml) to come suddenly into one's mind; to occur to one: [Vn] I couldn't remember where I'd seen him before, and then it suddenly hit me. **IDM** **hit the 'bottle** (infml) to drink too much alcohol over a long period: After she died, he really

hit the bottle. **hit the 'ceiling/'roof** (infml) to become suddenly very angry. Compare GO THROUGH THE ROOF (ROOF). **hit the 'deck** (infml) to fall to the ground: When the shooting started, we all hit the deck. **hit/knock sb for 'six** to affect sb very deeply: He was knocked completely for six by his sudden dismissal. **hit the 'hay/'sack** (infml) to go to bed. **hit/make/reach the headlines** ⇨ HEADLINE. **hit/ strike home** ⇨ HOME³. **hit sb (straight/right) in the 'eye** to be very obvious or noticeable to sb: The mistake hit me straight in the eye. **hit it 'off (with sb)** (infml) to have a good friendly relationship with sb: He doesn't exactly hit it off with his mother-in-law. **hit the 'jackpot** to make or win a lot of money quickly and unexpectedly. **hit/kick a man when he's down** ⇨ MAN¹. **hit/miss the mark** ⇨ MARK¹. **hit the nail on the 'head** to state the truth exactly. **hit/touch a nerve** ⇨ NERVE. **hit/strike the right/ wrong note** ⇨ NOTE¹. **hit the 'road** (infml) to start a journey. **hit sb where it 'hurts** to attack or affect sb where they will feel it most: The new tax proposals will hit the rich where it hurts. **not know what hit one** ⇨ KNOW. **PHRV** ˌhit 'back (at sb/ sth) to reply forcefully to attacks or criticism: In a TV interview she hit back at her critics. **'hit on/upon sth** to think of a good idea, etc suddenly or by chance: She hit upon the perfect title for her new novel. ˌhit 'out (at sb/sth) to attack sb/sth vigorously or violently with words or blows: I just hit out blindly in all directions. ○ In a rousing speech the President hit out at union resistance to reform.

▸ **hitter** n (esp in sport) a person who hits sth/sb: a heavy/powerful hitter.

■ ˌhit-and-'miss (also ˌhit-or-'miss) adj not done in a careful or planned way and so not likely to be effective or successful: a lot of hit-and-miss experimentation.

ˌhit-and-'run adj [attrib] **1** (derog) (**a**) (of a motorist) causing an accident and driving away immediately so as not to be identified. (**b**) (of a road accident) caused by a driver who does not stop to call an ambulance, the police, etc. **2** (of a military attack) sudden and unexpected, allowing those attacking to escape quickly: a hit-and-run raid.

'hit list n (infml) a list of people who are to be killed or against whom some action is being planned: Which industries are on the government's privatization hit list?

'hit man n (infml esp US) a person who is paid to kill another person: They hired a professional hit man.

NOTE Compare **hit**, **strike** and **beat**. Somebody can **hit** a person, an animal or a thing with their hand or with an object: I felt like hitting him! ○ Jed hit him on the shoulder with the gun. ○ She hit the nail into the wall with a hammer. **Strike** means to hit very hard, and is quite a formal word, used especially in writing and in official language: He struck her across the face. ○ He admitted striking the man repeatedly on the head with an iron bar. You also use **strike** with certain nouns: The helicopter was struck by lightning. ○ The clock struck midnight. A person or an object can **hit** or **strike** somebody or something accidentally: The car hit/struck a tree. **Beat** means to hit repeatedly and deliberately: He was beaten by his attacker. You use **beat** with certain nouns: beat eggs/a carpet/a drum.

hit² /hɪt/ n **1**(**a**) an act of hitting sb/sth: a direct hit on an enemy ship ○ That was a good hit! (**b**) (sport) a shot, etc that reaches its target: a final score of two hits and six misses. **2** a person or thing that is very popular: He's a hit with everyone. ○ hit songs/records ○ Her new movie is a **smash hit**. **IDM** **make a hit (with sb)** (infml) to make a very favourable impression on sb: You've made quite a hit with Bill.

■ **¹hit parade** *n* a list, published each week, of the most popular records.

hitch /hɪtʃ/ *v* **1** to get free rides in other people's vehicles: [Vpr] *hitch round Europe* [V] *We didn't take the train — we hitched.* [Vn, Vnpr] *Can I **hitch a lift** (with you) to the station?* See also HITCHHIKE. **2(a)** ~ **sth** (**up**) to pull one's clothes up: [Vn, Vnp] *She hitched (up) her skirt so as not to get it wet.* (**b**) ~ **oneself** to move oneself into the specified, usu higher, position: [Vn-adj] *She hitched herself upright.* [Vnpr] *He hitched himself onto the stool.* [also Vnp]. **3** to fasten sth to sth else with a loop of rope, a hook, etc: [Vnpr] *hitch a horse to a fence* [Vnp] *a car with a trailer hitched on at the back* [Vnpr] *(fig) Sweden hitched its currency to others in Europe.* **IDM** **get ¹hitched** (*infml*) to get married.
▶ **hitch** *n* **1** a difficulty or problem that delays or prevents sth happening: *The ceremony went off **without a hitch**.* ○ *Barring any last-minute hitches, we should be operational in two weeks.* **2** a type of knot: *a clove hitch.*

hitchhike /ˈhɪtʃhaɪk/ *v* to travel by getting free rides in other people's vehicles: [Vpr] *hitchhike through France to Spain* [also V]. ▶ **¹hitchhiker** *n*.

hi-tech = HIGH-TECH.

hither /ˈhɪðə(r)/ *adv* (*arch*) to or towards this place. **IDM** **¦hither and ¹thither**; **¦hither and ¹yon** in various directions; here and there: *people hurrying hither and thither.*

hitherto /ˌhɪðəˈtuː/ *adv* (*fml*) until now; until a particular time: *a hitherto unknown species of moth.*

HIV /ˌeɪtʃ aɪ ˈviː/ *abbr* human immunodeficiency virus (the virus that causes AIDS): *be ¦HIV ¹positive* ○ *How did he contract HIV?*

hive /haɪv/ *n* **1 (a)** (also beehive) [C] a box or other container for bees to live in. ▷ picture at BEE. (**b**) the bees living in a hive. **2** [C usu *sing*] a place full of busy people: *The office is **a hive of activity/ industry**.*
▶ **hive** *v* **PHRV** **hive ¹off** to become separate from a large group; to form an independent body. **¦hive sth ¹off (to/into sth)** (esp passive) to transfer work to another section or company; to make part of an organization independent: *There is talk of the railways being hived off to private ownership.*

HM *abbr* Her/His Majesty('s): *HM the Queen* ○ *HM Customs.*

h'm (also **hm**) = HEM².

HMG *abbr* (in Britain) Her/His Majesty's Government: (*infml*) *HMG should be kept informed.*

HMI /ˌeɪtʃ em ˈaɪ/ *abbr* (in Britain) Her/His Majesty's Inspector (a government official responsible for supervising standards in schools): *a visit from an HMI* ○ *an HMI report.*

HMS /ˌeɪtʃ em ˈes/ *abbr* (used before the name of a ship) (in Britain) Her/His Majesty's Ship: *HMS Apollo.* Compare USS.

HMSO /ˌeɪtʃ em es ˈəʊ/ *abbr* (in Britain) Her/His Majesty's Stationery Office.

HNC /ˌeɪtʃ en ˈsiː/ *abbr* (in Britain) Higher National Certificate (a qualification recognized by many technical and professional bodies): *have the HNC in electrical engineering* ○ *go on/do an HNC course.*

HND /ˌeɪtʃ en ˈdiː/ *abbr* (in Britain) Higher National Diploma (a qualification in technical subjects equal to a degree without honours (HONOUR¹5)): *an HND course in fashion design.*

ho /həʊ/ *interj* **1** (used to express surprise, amusement, etc): *Ho, ho! What have we here?* **2** (used to draw attention to sth): *Land ho!*

hoard /hɔːd/ *n* a store of money, food or other valued objects: *a squirrel's hoard of nuts* ○ *The farmer dug up a hoard of Roman coins.*
▶ **hoard** *v* to collect a large quantity of sth and store it secretly: [V, Vn] *People found hoarding*

(food) during the war were punished. **hoarder** *n*: *an inveterate hoarder of clothes.*

hoarding /ˈhɔːdɪŋ/ *n* **1** (*Brit*) (*US* **¹billboard**) a large board used for displaying advertisements. **2** a temporary fence of light boards, eg around a building site.

hoar-frost /ˈhɔː frɒst; *US* frɔːst/ *n* [U] white frost; very small ice crystals on grass, leaves, etc.

hoarse /hɔːs/ *adj* (**a**) (of the voice) sounding rough and harsh, eg as a result of a sore throat. (**b**) (of a person) having a hoarse voice; hardly able to speak: *He shouted himself hoarse.* ▶ **hoarsely** *adv.* **hoarseness** *n* [U].

hoary /ˈhɔːri/ *adj* **1** very old and well-known or familiar: *a hoary old joke.* **2** (also **hoar**) (esp of hair) grey or white with age.

hoax /həʊks/ *n* a lie or an act of deception, usu intended as a joke against sb: *play a hoax on sb* ○ *The fire brigade answered the emergency call but there was no fire — it was all a hoax.* ○ *a hoax phone call.*
▶ **hoax** *v* [Vn] to deceive sb as a joke. **hoaxer** *n*.

hob /hɒb/ *n* (**a**) (*Brit*) a flat heating surface for pans on the top of a COOKER(1). (**b**) (esp formerly) a flat metal shelf at the side of a fireplace, where a pan or KETTLE could be heated.

hobble /ˈhɒbl/ *v* **1** to walk with difficulty because the feet or legs hurt or are in bad condition: [Vp, Vpr] *The old man hobbled along (the road) with the aid of his stick.* [also V]. ▷ note at SHUFFLE. **2** to tie together two legs of a horse, etc to prevent it from going far away: [Vn] *(fig) The police have been hobbled by new, stricter regulations.*
▶ **hobble** *n* [sing] the awkward way sb walks when their feet or legs hurt or are in bad condition.

hobby /ˈhɒbi/ *n* a favourite activity that a person does for pleasure and not as her or his regular business: *My hobby is stamp-collecting.* ○ *I collect stamps as a hobby.*

hobby-horse /ˈhɒbi hɔːs/ *n* **1** (*Brit*) a subject that a person likes to discuss; a person's favourite topic of conversation: *get on/ride one's hobby-horse* (ie talk about one's favourite subject) ○ *You've got me onto one of my favourite hobby-horses.* **2** a toy consisting of a long stick with a horse's head on one end.

hobgoblin /hɒbˈgɒblɪn, ˈhɒbgɒblɪn/ *n* (in fairy stories) a little creature who likes to play tricks; an ugly and evil spirit(3). See also GOBLIN.

hobnail boot /ˌhɒbneɪl ˈbuːt/ (also **hobnailed boot** /-neɪld/) *n* (usu *pl*) a heavy shoe whose sole is attached to the upper part with short heavy nails.

hobnob /ˈhɒbnɒb/ *v* (**-bb-**) ~ (**with sb**); ~ (**together**) (*sometimes derog*) to spend time with sb in a friendly way; to associate with sb: [Vpr] *He likes hobnobbing with the rich and famous.* [Vadv] *They were seen hobnobbing together.*

hobo /ˈhəʊbəʊ/ *n* (*pl* **-os** or **-oes**) (*esp US*) (**a**) an unemployed worker who wanders from place to place. (**b**) a TRAMP(1).

Hobson's choice /ˌhɒbsnz ˈtʃɔɪs/ *n* [U] a situation in which a person must accept what is offered because there is no alternative other than taking nothing at all.

hock¹ /hɒk/ *n* the middle joint of an animal's back leg. ▷ picture at HORSE.

hock² /hɒk/ *v* [Vn] (*sl*) to give an object of some value as security(3) for the paying back of a loan; to PAWN² sth.
▶ **hock** *n* (*sl*) [U] the state of being pawned (PAWN²): *Her jewellery is all in hock.* ○ *get sth out of hock.* **IDM** **in ¹hock (to sb)** in debt; having financial or other obligations to sb: *I'm in hock to the tune of* (ie I owe a total of) *£5 000.* ○ *The Party has been accused of being in hock to big business.*

hock³ /hɒk/ n [U, C] (*Brit*) a German white wine: *a fine dry hock.*

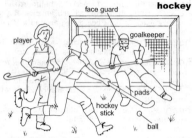

face guard   **hockey**

player   goalkeeper

pads

hockey stick

ball

hockey (*US* **field hockey**)

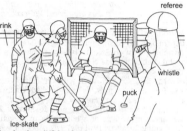

rink   referee

whistle

puck

ice-skate

ice hockey (*US* **hockey**)

hockey /'hɒki/ n [U] **1** (*Brit*) (*US* **'field hockey**) a game played on a field by two teams of eleven players each, with curved sticks and a small hard ball. ⇨ picture. **2** (*US*) = ICE HOCKEY. See also PUCK. ■ **'hockey stick** n a long stick, curved at the bottom, used to hit the ball in hockey. ⇨ picture.

hocus-pocus /ˌhəʊkəs 'pəʊkəs/ n [U] talk or behaviour designed to draw people's attention away from what is actually happening; tricks or nonsense intended to deceive.

hod /hɒd/ n a light open box attached to a pole, used by building workers for carrying bricks or heavy materials on the shoulder.

hodgepodge = HOTCHPOTCH.

hoe /həʊ/ n a garden tool with a long handle and a blade, used for breaking up the soil and removing plants which are not wanted.
▶ **hoe** v (*pres p* **hoeing**; *pt, pp* **hoed**) to use a hoe on sth: [V] *do some hoeing* [Vn] *hoe the soil/the flower beds/the weeds* [Vpr] *hoe around the roses/between the lettuces* [Vnp] *hoe out all unwanted plants.*

hog /hɒg; *US* hɔːg/ n **1** a pig bred for its meat, esp a castrated (CASTRATE) male pig. Compare BOAR, SOW². **2** (*infml derog*) a person who wants too much of sth, esp food, or thinks only of herself or himself. **IDM** **go the whole hog** ⇨ WHOLE.
▶ **hog** v (-gg-) (*infml*) to take more than one's fair share of sth; to use sth mainly for oneself excluding others: [Vn] *hog (the middle of) the road* (ie drive near the middle of the road so that others cannot get past) ∘ *hog the bathroom* (ie·spend a long time in it, preventing others from using it) ∘ *hog the fire* (ie sit in front of it so that others do not feel the heat) ∘ *an actor who likes to hog the stage/the limelight* ∘ *Stop hogging the cheese and pass it round!*

hogmanay /'hɒgmənei/ n [U] (*Scot*) the last day of the year and the celebrations that occur on it, esp in Scotland.

hogwash /'hɒgwɒʃ; *US* 'hɔːg-/ n [U] stupid talk or ideas; nonsense.

hoick /hɔik/ v (*Brit infml*) to lift or pull sth in the

specified direction, esp with a quick sudden movement: [Vnp, Vnpr] *He tried to hoick the meat out (of the tin) with a fork.*

hoi polloi /ˌhɔi pə'lɔi/ n (usu **the hoi polloi**) [pl] (*derog*) the common people; the masses.

hoist /hɔist/ v to raise sth to a higher position, often by means of ropes or special apparatus: [Vn] *hoist a flag/the sails* [Vnpr] *hoisting crates onto a ship* [Vnp] *She hoisted the boy/herself up onto the wall.* [Vn] *She hoisted her skirt to avoid getting it wet.* ∘ (*fig*) *He managed to hoist his earnings to £100 000 last year.* **IDM** **(be) hoist/hoisted by/with one's own pe'tard** (*Brit*) to be caught or injured by what one intended as a trick for others.
▶ **hoist** n an apparatus for hoisting things.

hoity-toity /ˌhɔiti 'tɔiti/ adj (*infml derog*) behaving in a proud way or showing contempt, as if one thinks one is superior to others: *a hoity-toity person/manner.*

hokum /'həʊkəm/ n [U] (*infml*) **1** films, plays or pieces of writing that are not realistic and have no artistic or literary qualities: *a piece of second-rate hokum.* **2** (*esp US*) nonsense: *He's talking complete hokum.*

hold¹ /həʊld/ v (*pt, pp* **held** /held/) **1** to keep or support sb/sth using one's arms or hands or another part of the body: [Vn] *She was holding an umbrella.* ∘ *The girl was holding her father's hand.* ∘ *They were holding hands* (ie holding each other's hands). [Vnadv] *The lovers held each other tight.* [Vnpr] *I held the rabbit by its ears.* ∘ *She was holding the baby in her arms.* ∘ *He held the knife in his teeth.* ∘ *The winning captain held the trophy in the air.* [Vadv] *Take the rope in your hands and hold tight.* **2** (**a**) to bear the weight of sb/sth: [Vn] *Is that branch strong enough to hold you/your weight?* (**b**) to restrain or control sb/sth: [Vn] *Try to hold the thief until the police arrive.* ∘ *The dam could not hold the flood waters.* **3** to keep oneself/sb/sth in the specified position or condition: [Vnpr] *The wood is held in position by a clamp.* [Vnp] *Hold your head up.* ∘ *Hold your arms out.* ∘ *It took three policemen to hold him down.* ∘ *She held out her hand to take the cup.* [Vadv, Vn-adj] *Hold (yourself) still for a moment while I take your photograph.* **4(a)** to remain secure or in position: [V] *I don't think the shelf will hold if we put anything else on it.* [Vadv] *The wooden fence held steady in spite of the strong wind.* (**b**) to continue without changing; to last: [V] *How long will this fine weather hold? ∘ If their luck holds, they could still win the championship.* (**c**) to continue to be true or valid: [V] *The offer I made to you last week still holds.* ∘ *The argument still holds.* **5(a)** to have enough space for sth/sb; to contain sth/sb: [Vn] *This barrel holds 25 litres.* ∘ *Will this suitcase hold all my clothes?* ∘ *The lift can hold up to six people.* ∘ *My brain can't hold so much information at one time.* [Vnpr] (*fig*) *Who knows what the future holds (for us)?* (**b**) to be able to drink a reasonable amount of alcohol without getting drunk: [Vn] *He's never been able to* **hold his drink**. **6** to defend sth against an attacking force; to keep possession of sth: [Vn] *hold a fort/garrison* ∘ *The town was held despite frequent enemy attacks.* ∘ *The governing party held the seat, but with a greatly reduced majority.* ∘ *The Dolphins held the lead until midway through the second half.* **7** to keep sb and not allow them to leave: [Vn] *Police are holding two men in connection with last Thursday's bank raid.* [Vn-n] *The terrorists are holding three men hostage.* ∘ *He was held prisoner for two years.* **8** (**a**) to own or possess sth; to have sth in one's possession: [Vn] *the player who holds the ace of spades* ∘ *An American conglomerate holds a major share in the company.* (**b**) to have or occupy a job or position: [Vn] *Mrs Thatcher held the post of Prime Minister longer than anyone else this century.* ∘ *How long has*

Nouns and adjectives

Nouns

We say **too much sugar** but **too many chairs**.

Nouns are of different types according to whether they have both a singular and a plural form, whether they must be used with a DETERMINER such as:

a   **both**   **each**   **the**

and whether a verb should be singular or plural in order to agree with the noun.

All nouns are marked **n** in the dictionary. Grammar information is given in square brackets [ ] to show which group each meaning of a noun belongs to. The groups are explained below.

Countable and uncountable

The two biggest groups of nouns are COUNTABLE NOUNS and UNCOUNTABLE NOUNS. Most countable nouns (or COUNT nouns) are words for separate things which can be counted, like **apples**, **books** or **teachers**. Uncountable nouns (also called UNCOUNT nouns or MASS nouns) are usually words for things which are thought of as a quantity or mass, like **water** or **time**, not as separate items.

However, there are some nouns in English which you might expect to be countable but which are not. For example, **furniture**, **information** and **equipment** are all uncountable nouns in English, although they are countable nouns in some other languages.

[C] Countable nouns

A countable noun has a singular form and a plural form. When it is singular, it must always have a determiner in front of it. Most nouns can be used with the following determiners:

any	**no**	**the**	**what**
which	**whose**		

and the possessive determiners:

my	**their**	**your** etc.

Countable nouns in the **singular** can also be used with:

a	**another**	**each**	**either**
every	**neither**	**that**	**this**

In the **plural** they can be used with:

both	**enough**	**few**	**many**
more	**most**	**other**	**several**
some	**these**	**those**	

or without a determiner at all:

- *I'm having a driving **lesson** this afternoon.*
- *She's learning to play golf – she's had **several lessons** already.*
- ***Lessons** cost £20 an hour.*

Countable nouns are the most common type of noun. If they have only one meaning, or if all their meanings are countable, they are just marked **n**. For nouns which have a number of meanings, some of which are not countable, each meaning that is countable is marked [**C**].

[U] Uncountable nouns

An uncountable noun has only one form, not a separate singular and plural. Uncountable nouns and uncountable meanings of nouns are marked [**U**]. They can be used without any determiner in front, or with one of the following determiners:

enough	**little**	**more**	**most**
much	**other**	**some**	**that**
this			

They can also be used with:

any	**no**	**the**	**what**
which	**whose**		

and the possessive determiners **my**, **their**, **your**, etc:

- *Electric fires are used to give extra **heat** in winter.*
- *There isn't **much space** in this room.*

If an uncountable noun is the subject of a verb, the verb is singular:

- *Extra **money has been made** available for this project.*
- ***Sadness is** not the same as depression.*

With nouns such as **furniture**, **information** and **equipment**, as with many other uncountable nouns, you can talk about amounts of the thing or separate parts of the thing by using phrases like **a piece of**, **three items of**, **some bits of**. Nouns like **piece**, **item** and **bit** are called PARTITIVES when used in this way:

- *I've saved up to buy **furniture** for my new house.*
- *So far, I've got **three pieces of furniture**: a chair, a table and a bed.*

There are many words for food and drink which are uncountable nouns. When you need to talk about particular amounts of them, you use partitives. Examples given at dictionary entries show the appropriate words to use. The entry for **bread** shows you that you can use **loaf**, **slice** or **piece**:

bread /bred/ n [U] **1** a food made of flour, water and usu YEAST, mixed together and then baked: *a loaf/slice/piece of bread* ○ *wholemeal bread* ○ *brown/white bread.* ▷ picture.

Some nouns also have a separate countable meaning which is used to refer to a particular amount of food or drink:

● 'How much **sugar** do you take?' [U]
'Two **sugars** (teaspoonfuls of sugar), please.' [C]
● 'How many people want **coffee**?' [U]
'Could we have four **coffees** (cups of coffee), please?' [C]

The dictionary shows the two different meanings, one labelled [U] and the other labelled [C].

Similarly, some nouns have a special countable meaning for a particular type of the thing they refer to:

● I bought some **cheese** today. [U]
● There were three small pieces of **cheese** and an apple on the plate. [U]
● I bought three different **cheeses** (different types of cheese) *today:* Cheddar, Camembert and Edam. [C]

Some nouns are marked [C, U] or [U, C]. These nouns can be countable or uncountable without changing their meaning.

Nouns + plural verbs

[pl] Plural nouns + plural verbs

A noun marked [pl] is always plural in form. It behaves like a plural countable noun and when it is the subject of a verb, the verb is in the plural.

Nouns which refer to things which have two parts joined together, for example **glasses**, **trousers** and **scissors**, behave like this. You can usually also talk about **a pair of trousers**, **a pair of scissors**, etc:

● I'm going to buy **some** new trousers.
● I'm going to buy a new **pair of trousers**.

An example is given in the entry for the noun to show that it can be used in this way.

[pl v] Nouns that look singular + plural verbs

Some plural nouns look as if they are singular. They are marked [pl v] to show that they are used with a plural verb. Nouns like this usually refer to a group of people or animals of a particular type, when they are considered together as one unit:

● **Police are** searching for a man who escaped from Pentonville prison today.
● The **cattle are** fed on barley and grass.

Adjectives that refer to a group of people of the same type or in the same situation can also be made into nouns of this type. They are always used with **the** in front of them:

● It is a myth that **the rich are** getting poorer and **the poor are** getting richer.

Nouns + singular verbs

[sing] Singular nouns + singular verbs

A noun marked [sing] is always singular in form and when it is the subject of a verb, the verb is in the singular. Many nouns like this can be used in only a limited number of ways. For example, some singular nouns must be or are often used with a particular determiner in front of them or with a particular preposition after them. The correct determiner or preposition is shown before the definition.

Look at sense 3 in the entry for **dash¹**. This sense is marked [C esp sing], indicating that **dash** in this sense is a countable noun but that it is very often singular. The pattern a ~ (of sth) shows you which determiner and preposition to use:

dash¹ /dæʃ/ n **1** [sing] ~ **(for sth)** a sudden run or forward movement: *make a dash for freedom/shelter* ○ *We jumped into the car and made a dash for the ferry.* ○ *Mother said lunch was ready and there was a mad dash for the table.* **2** [C usu sing] (esp US) a short running race; a SPRINT n(1): *the 100-metre dash.* **3** [C esp sing] a ~ **(of sth)** a small amount of sth added or mixed: *a dash of lemon juice* ○ *The flag adds a dash of colour to the grey building.* **4** [C] a short level line (—) used in writing, printing and Morse Code. ▷ App 3. **5** [sing] ~ **(of sth)** liquid striking sth or the sound this makes: *the dash of waves on the rocks* ○ *A dash of water in his face will revive him.*

[sing v] Nouns that look plural + singular verbs

Some uncountable nouns look as if they are plural. They are marked [sing v] to show that they are used with a singular verb:

- *Linguistics is a science but literature is one of the arts subjects.*
- *Darts is played in pubs in Britain.*

Nouns + singular or plural verbs

[CGp] Countable group nouns

A noun marked [CGp] is like a countable noun because it has a singular form and a plural form. However, in British English the singular form can be used with a plural verb as well as a singular one. Nouns like this usually refer to a group of people or an organization and can be thought of either as the organization or group (singular) or as many individual people (plural). In the dictionary an example is often given to show agreement with a singular and a plural verb:

- *The **committee has/have decided** to dismiss him.*
- *The **board is/are** unhappy about falling sales.*

Note that in American English a singular verb is usually used with the singular form of a countable group noun.

[Gp] Group nouns

A noun marked [Gp] is always singular but is used with either a singular or plural verb. Such nouns usually refer to a group of people who do a particular job, have a particular opinion, are of a particular type or who are represented by an official place such as the White House or the Kremlin:

- *Some of the **press has/have been criticized** for their coverage of the story.*
- *The **Vatican has/have issued** a further statement this morning.*

[sing or pl v] Plural nouns + singular or plural verbs

A noun marked [sing or pl v] looks as if it is plural but can be used with either a singular or a plural verb:

- *Turn left at the traffic lights and the army **barracks is/are** on your left.*
- *The company's **headquarters is/are located** in New York.*

Adjectives

Adjectives are labelled **adj** in this dictionary. Many can be used both before a noun:

- *a serious expression*
- *brown leaves*

and after a linking verb, for example **be**, **become**, **seem**, **turn**:

- *She looked serious.*
- *The leaves turn brown in autumn.*

[attrib]

Some adjectives, or particular meanings of adjectives, are always used before a noun, and cannot be used after a linking verb. These are labelled [attrib] (attributive). The labels [usu attrib] or [esp attrib] are used when it is rare but possible to use the adjective after a verb. Look, for example, at **sheer**[1] where senses **1** and **2** are labelled [attrib] and [usu attrib]. Sense **3** has no label because it can be used both before a noun and after a linking verb:

> **sheer**[1] /ʃɪə(r)/ *adj* **1** [attrib] (often used for emphasis) complete; nothing more than: *sheer nonsense* ○ *a sheer waste of time* ○ *The sheer size of the building was enough to impress the visitors.* ○ *Her success was due to sheer hard work.* **2** [usu attrib] (of fabrics, etc) thin, light and almost transparent: *sheer nylon.* **3** very steep: *a sheer rock face/cliff* ○ *It's a sheer drop to the sea.*

[pred]

Adjectives labelled [pred] (predicative) are used only after a linking verb, never before a noun. Look at the entry for **asleep**. Both senses must be used after a verb, and so [pred] immediately follows the **adj** label:

> **asleep** /ə'sliːp/ *adj* [pred] **1** sleeping: *The baby was asleep upstairs.* ○ *Don't wake her up — she's fast/sound asleep* (ie sleeping deeply). ○ *He fell asleep during the lecture.* ○ *I've only just got up and I'm still half asleep* (ie not fully awake). **2** (of limbs) having no feeling; NUMB: *I've been sitting on my leg and now it's asleep.*

(following *ns*)

A few adjectives, such as **designate**, always follow the noun they describe. This is indicated in the dictionary by the label (**following ns**):

> **designate**[1] /'dezɪɡneɪt, -nət/ *adj* (following *ns*) appointed to a job but not yet having officially started it: *an interview with the director/archbishop designate.*

Verbs

Look at the following sentences:

- *He sighed.*
- *She cut her hand.*
- *The soup tastes salty.*

Each sentence has a subject (**he, she, the soup**) and a verb (**sigh, cut, taste**). In the first sentence, **sigh** stands alone. Verbs like this are called INTRANSITIVE. In the second sentence, **cut** is TRANSITIVE because it requires an object (**her hand**). In the third sentence, **taste** has no object but it cannot be used alone without an adjective. An adjective like **salty** that gives more information about the subject of a verb is called a COMPLEMENT.

The following pages explain the codes used in this dictionary to show you how intransitive verbs, transitive verbs and verbs that take a complement are used. The codes for verbs which take clauses are explained on pages **B6–8**.

Compare the following sentences:

- *She can drive.*
- *She drives a fast car.*

The verb **drive** is used in both sentences. In the first it is used intransitively, without an object, and in the second it is used transitively with the noun phrase **a fast car** as the object.

In the dictionary, grammatical codes and examples show you exactly how each verb is used in each of its meanings:

> **drive¹** /draɪv/ *v* (*pt* **drove** /drəʊv/; *pp* **driven** /'drɪvn/) **1(a)** to operate, control and direct the course of a vehicle: [V] *Can you drive?* [Vn] *He drives a taxi* (ie that is his job). ○ *I drive a Renault.* (**b**) to come or go somewhere by doing this: [V] *Did you drive or go by train?* [Vpr] *I drive to work.* [Vp] *Don't stop — drive on!* ▷ note at TRAVEL. (**c**) to take sb somewhere in a car, taxi, etc: [Vnadv, Vnpr] *Could you drive me home/to the airport?* [also Vn, Vnpl].

The code in square brackets **[ ]** shows how **drive** is used in the example or examples that follow. The first code given in sense **1(a)** is **[V]**, showing that **drive** can be used without an object as an intransitive verb. This is followed by an example showing **drive** used intransitively. The next code **[Vn]** shows you that **drive** can also be a transitive verb with a noun phrase as the object. It is followed by two examples showing **drive** used transitively.

Some verbs are most typically used with a particular word after them, often an adverb or a preposition. In such cases, the adverb or preposition is shown in **dark type** before the definition:

> **behave** /bɪ'heɪv/ *v* **1** ~ **well, badly, etc** (**towards sb**) to act or react in the specified way: [Vpr] *She behaves (towards me) more like a friend than a mother.* [Vadv] *He has behaved disgracefully towards his family.*

Intransitive verbs

[V], [Vpr], [Vadv], [Vp]

Intransitive verbs do not take an object. When used alone after a subject, they are coded **[V]**:

- *A large dog* **appeared**.

Some intransitive verbs are often used with a prepositional phrase, an adverb or an ADVERBIAL PARTICLE (an adverb like **down, out** or **over**). The codes and examples show which type of word or phrase can be used with a particular verb:

- **[Vpr]** (verb + **pr**epositional phrase)
  He doesn't **care about** *other people's feelings.*
- **[Vadv]** (verb + **adv**erb)
  Well done, you **guessed right**!
- **[Vp]** (verb + **p**article)
  Sit down *and tell me all about it.*

If a particular preposition, adverb or particle must always be used with a verb, it is given in **dark type** before the definition:

> **detract** /dɪ'trækt/ *v* ~ **from sth** to make sth seem less good or of lower value: [Vpr] *detract from the merit/value/worth/excellence of sth* ○ *No amount of criticism can detract from her achievements.* ○ *The poor service detracted from my enjoyment of the evening.*

When a particular preposition, adverb or particle is usually, but not always, used with a verb, it is shown in brackets **( )**. With some verbs, any of several prepositions or particles are possible. These are shown separated by a slash (*/*):

> **boast** /bəʊst/ *v* **1** ~ (**about/of sth**) to talk about one's achievements, abilities, etc with too much pride and satisfaction: [V] *Stop boasting!* [Vpr] *He's always boasting about his children's success at school.* ○ *That's nothing to boast about.* ○ *She boasted of her skill at chess.* [V.that] *He boasted that he was the best player in the team.* [also V.speech].

Transitive verbs

[Vn], [Vnpr], [Vnadv], [Vnp]

Transitive verbs must have an object. The object can be a noun or a pronoun, a noun phrase or a clause. Pages **B6–8** explain verbs which take a clause as the object.

The code used to show a transitive verb is **[Vn]** (**v**erb + **n**oun phrase):

● *Jill's behaviour **annoyed me**.*

Most transitive verbs can be used in the PASSIVE:

● *I **was annoyed** by Jill's behaviour.*

If a transitive verb cannot be used in the passive, this is shown at the dictionary entry:

> **afford** /əˈfɔːd/ *v* **1** (no passive; usu with *can, could* or *be able to*) to have enough money, time, space, etc for a particular purpose: [Vn, V.*to* inf] *They walked because they couldn't afford (to take) a taxi.*

Like intransitive verbs, some transitive verbs are often used with a prepositional phrase, an adverb or an adverbial particle which is closely connected with the verb. The codes and examples show which type of word or phrase is used with a particular verb:

● **[Vnpr]** (**v**erb + **n**oun phrase + **pr**epositional phrase)
  *Peter **drove me to** the airport.*
● **[Vnadv]** (**v**erb + **n**oun phrase + **adv**erb)
  *That skirt **fits you** very **well**.*
● **[Vnp]** (**v**erb + **n**oun phrase + **p**article)
  *He **gathered up his papers** and left.*

If a particular preposition, adverb or particle must always be used with a verb, it is shown before the definition:

> **dedicate** /ˈdedɪkeɪt/ *v* **1** ~ oneself/sth to sth / doing sth to give or devote oneself, time, effort, etc to a good cause(3) or purpose: [Vnpr] *dedicate oneself to one's work* ○ *She dedicated her life to helping the poor.* **2** ~ sth to sb to address sth one has written, eg a book or a piece of music to sb as a way of showing respect: [Vnpr] *She dedicated her first book to her teacher* (eg by putting his name at the front). ○ *That song was dedicated to Lynette from her husband Peter.*

As with intransitive verbs, brackets **( )** are used to show that a particular preposition, adverb or particle is often, but not always, used with a verb. Look, for example, at the entry for **cover**¹. The particle **up** or **over** can be used alone after the object of the verb, or followed by a prepositional phrase using **with**. It is also possible to use a prepositional phrase without either **up** or **over**. These patterns are illustrated in the examples:

> **cover¹** /ˈkʌvə(r)/ *v* **1** ~ sth (up/over) (with sth) to place sth over or in front of sth in order to hide or protect it: [Vnpr] *Cover the chicken loosely with foil.* ○ *She covered her face with her hands.* ○ *He covered the cushion with new material.* [Vn, Vnp, Vnpr] *He covered (up) the body (with a sheet).* [Vnpr, Vnp] *She covered her knees (up) with a blanket.* [Vn, Vnp] *The hole was quickly covered (over).* ○ [Vn] (*fig*) *He laughed to cover* (ie hide) *his nervousness.*

Transitive verbs + two objects

[Vnn]

Look at the following examples:

● *I sold Jim a car.*
● *I bought Mary a book.*

Verbs like **sell** and **buy** can be used with two objects. This is indicated by the code **[Vnn]**. You can often express the same idea by using the verb as an ordinary transitive verb and adding a prepositional phrase starting with **to** or **for**:

● *I **sold** a car **to** Jim.*
● *I **bought** a book **for** Mary.*

The dictionary entry shows you, before the definition, which preposition to use:

> **buy** /baɪ/ *v* (*pt, pp* **bought** /bɔːt/) **1** ~ sth (for sb) to obtain sth by paying money for it: [V] *House prices are low; it's a good time to buy.* [Vn-adj] *Did you buy your car new or second-hand?* [Vnpr] *I bought this watch (from a friend) for £10.* ○ *She's buying a present for her boyfriend.* [Vnn] *I must buy myself a new shirt.*

Linking verbs

[V-adj], [V-n], [Vn-adj], [Vn-n]

Look at the following sentences:

● *Her voice sounds hoarse.*
● *Elena became a doctor.*

In these sentences the verb (**sound, become**) is followed by a complement, an adjective (**hoarse**) or a noun phrase (**a doctor**) which tells you more about the subject. A verb like this is called a LINKING VERB or COPULA.

Verbs which have an adjective as the complement have the code **[V-adj]**, and verbs with a noun phrase as the complement have the code [**V-n**]. If a linking verb can be used with either an adjective or a noun phrase, the dictionary entry shows both uses:

> **become** /bɪˈkʌm/ v (pt **became** /bɪˈkeɪm/; pp **become**) **1**(**a**) to come to be; to grow to be: [V-adj] *They soon became angry.* ○ *He has become accustomed to his new duties.* [V-n] *That child was to become a great leader.* ○ *They became close friends.* ○ *She became a doctor.* ○ *It has become a rule that we have coffee together every morning.* (**b**) to begin to be: [V-adj] *It's becoming dangerous to go out alone at night.* [V-n] *The traffic pollution is becoming a cause for concern. Those boys are becoming a nuisance.* ⇨ note.

There are also verbs which take both an object and a complement:

● *She considered herself lucky.*
● *They elected him president.*

The complement (**lucky**, **president**) tells you more about the object (**herself**, **him**) of the verb. The code [**Vn-adj**] shows you that a verb is transitive and takes an adjective as the complement, while the code [**Vn-n**] indicates a transitive verb that takes a noun phrase as the complement. Look, for example, at sense **8** of **call**¹:

> **8**(**a**) to describe or address sb/sth as sth; to name sb/sth: [Vn-adj] *How dare you call me fat!* [Vn-n] *His name is Richard but we call him Dick.* ○ *What was the book called?* ○ (ironic) *He hasn't had anything published and he calls himself a writer!* (**b**) to consider sb/sth to be sth; to regard sb/sth as sth: [Vn-adj] *I call his behaviour mean and selfish.* [Vn-n] *I would never call German an easy language.* ○ *How can you be so unkind and still call yourself my friend?* ○ *She has nothing she can call her own* (ie claim as her own property). ○ *You owe me £5.04 — let's call it £5* (ie settle the sum at £5).

Verbs used with clauses

Look at the following sentences:

● *George complained that it was too hot.*
● *I can't decide whether to have chocolate or strawberry ice-cream.*
● *Don't forget to lock the door.*
● *He enjoys dancing with Mary.*
● *Jane asked, 'Is the food cold?'*

All these sentences contain a verb (**complain**, **decide**, **forget**, **enjoy**, **ask**) which is used with a clause.

In this dictionary, the types of clause that can be used with verbs are called '*that* clause', '*wh*- clause', '*infinitive clause*', '*-ing* clause' and '*direct speech*'.

Verbs + *that* clause

[V.*that*], [Vn.*that*], [Vpr.*that*]

Although this type of clause is called a '*that* clause', it is not always necessary to use the word **that** itself:

● *I said that she would come.*
● *I said she would come.*

These two sentences mean the same. Both show **say** used with a '*that* clause'.

The code for a verb which takes a '*that* clause' is [**V.*that***] (verb + '*that* clause'):

● *I think I'll go swimming before lunch.*
● *I think that I'll have a rest.*

Some verbs can be used with both a noun phrase and a '*that* clause'. The code for verbs used like this is [**Vn.*that***] (verb + noun phrase + '*that* clause'):

● *Can you remind me that I need to buy some milk?*
● *I told her I would be late.*

Some verbs are followed by a prepositional phrase, often with **to**, instead of a noun phrase. These verbs have the code [**Vpr.*that***] (verb + prepositional phrase + '*that* clause'):

● *I suggested to John that he should get more exercise.*

The dictionary entry shows which types of '*that* clause' you can use:

> **whisper** /ˈwɪspə(r)/ v **1** to speak or say sth quietly, using only one's breath, so that only the people closest to one can hear: [V] *Don't you know it's rude to whisper?* [V.speech] *'Can you meet me tonight?' he whispered.* [Vnpr] *He leaned over and whispered something in her ear.* [V.that, Vpr.that] *She whispered (to me) that she was afraid.* [also Vpr, Vn, Vpr.to inf].

Verbs + *wh*- clause

[V.*wh*], [Vn.*wh*], [Vpr.*wh*]

A '*wh*- clause' is a clause beginning with one of the following words: **wh**ich, **wh**at, **wh**ose, **wh**y, **wh**ere, **wh**en, **wh**o, **wh**om, **h**o**w**, **if**, **wh**ether.

The code used in this dictionary for a verb which takes a '*wh*- clause' is [**V.*wh***] (verb + '*wh*- clause'):

● *I wonder what the new job will be like.*
● *He doesn't care how he looks.*
● *Did you see which way they went?*

Some verbs can be used with both a noun phrase and a 'wh- clause'. The code for verbs used like this is [**Vn.wh**] (verb + noun phrase + '**wh**- clause'):

- I **asked him where** the library was.
- I **told her when** the baby was due.
- He **teaches his students how** to research a subject properly.

Some verbs have a prepositional phrase, usually with **to**, instead of a noun phrase. These verbs have the code [**Vpr.wh**] (verb + prepositional phrase + '**wh**- clause'):

- Can you **explain to me why** you are so late?

Examples at an entry show you which type of 'wh- clause' you can use:

> **ask** /ɑːsk; US æsk/ v **1** ~ (sb) (about sb/sth) to request information by means of a question: [V.speech] *'Where are you going?' she asked.* [Vpr] *She asked about my future plans.* [Vnpr] *Ask him about the ring you lost — someone may have handed it in to the receptionist.* [Vn] *Don't be afraid to ask questions.* ○ *Did you ask the price?* [Vnn] *She asked them their names.* [Vn.wh] *I had to ask the teacher what to do next.* [Vwh, Vn.wh] *She asked (me) if I could drive.* [V] *I'm not insisting, I'm only asking.*

Verbs + infinitive clause

[**V.to inf**], [**Vn.to inf**], [**V.n to inf**], [**Vpr.to inf**], [**Vn.inf (no to)**]

The following examples show the infinitive form of the verb:

- eat, talk, dance
- to eat, to talk, to dance

Eat and **to eat** are both infinitives. **Eat** is called a **bare infinitive** and **to eat** is called a **to-infinitive**.

Most verbs taking an infinitive are used with the *to*-infinitive. The code for these verbs is [**V.to inf**] (verb + **to**-infinitive):

- The goldfish **need to be fed**.
- Children **learn to read** quite quickly.

Some verbs can be used with both a noun phrase and a *to*-infinitive. The noun phrase can be the object of the main verb, or the noun phrase and the infinitive clause *together* can be the object.

When the noun phrase is the object of the main verb, the code is [**Vn.to inf**], with the dot placed after the **n** to show that the noun phrase is connected more closely to the main verb than to the infinitive:

- Can you **persuade Sheila** to chair the meeting?
- She **was forced** to hand over the keys.

When the noun phrase and the infinitive clause *together* are the object of the main verb, the dot is placed between the **V** and the **n** [**V.n to inf**], to show that the noun phrase is connected closely to the infinitive:

- I expected **her to pass** her driving test first time.
- We'd love **you to come** and visit us.

Some verbs take a prepositional phrase, usually with **to**, instead of a noun phrase and have the code [**Vpr.to inf**] (verb + prepositional phrase + **to**-infinitive):

- He **shouted to Jane to ring** the police.

Only two groups of verbs are used with a bare infinitive. One is the group of MODAL VERBS (or MODAL AUXILIARIES). These are the special verbs like **can**, **must** and **will** which go before a main verb and show that an action is possible, necessary, etc. These verbs are in a separate group in the dictionary and are labelled **modal v**.

A small group of ordinary verbs, for example **see** and **hear**, can be used with a noun phrase and a bare infinitive. The code for these is [**Vn.inf (no to)**] (verb + noun phrase + **inf**initive, with a warning that the infinitive does not have **to** before it).

- Did you **hear the phone ring** just then?
- She **watched him eat** his lunch.

Verbs + -ing clause

[**V.ing**], [**Vn.ing**], [**V.n ing**]

An '-ing clause' is a clause containing a PRESENT PARTICIPLE. The present participle is the form of a verb that ends in -ing, for example **doing**, **eating** or **catching**. Sometimes, the '-ing clause' consists of a present participle on its own.

The code for a verb which takes an '-ing clause' is [**V.ing**] (verb + '-ing clause'):

- She never **stops talking**!
- I **started working** on my essay today.

Some verbs can be used with both a noun phrase and an '-ing clause'. The noun phrase can be the object of the main verb, or the noun phrase and the '-ing clause' *together* can be the object.

When the noun phrase is the object of the main verb, the code [**Vn.ing**] gives the dot after the **n** and before the '-*ing* clause' to show that the noun is connected closely with the main verb:

- *His comments* **set me** *thinking.*
- *I can* **smell something** *nice cooking.*

When the noun phrase and the '-*ing* clause' *together* are the object of the main verb, the dot is placed after the **V** and before the **n** [**V.n ing**], to show that the noun phrase is connected closely to the '-*ing* clause':

- *I hate* **him joking** (the fact that he jokes) *about serious things.*

In this pattern, you can replace **him** with the possessive pronoun **his**:

- *I hate* **his joking** *about serious things.*

The dictionary entry often shows both forms within a single example:

prevent /prɪ'vent/ *v* ~ sb/sth (from doing sth) to stop sb doing sth or to stop sth happening: [Vn] *Your prompt action prevented a serious accident.* [Vn, Vnpr] *prevent the spread of a disease/a disease from spreading* [V.n ing] *Nobody can prevent us/our getting married.*

Sentences with a possessive pronoun often sound rather formal and the object pronoun is more common. People are more likely to say:

- *I hate* **him** *joking about serious things.*

than

- *I hate* **his** *joking about serious things.*

Verbs + direct speech

[**V.speech**]

Verbs like **say**, **answer** and **demand** can be used either to report what someone has said using a '*that* clause' or to give their exact words in DIRECT SPEECH, using quotation marks (' '). Verbs which can be used with direct speech have the code [**V.speech**]. Compare:

- [**V.speech**] *'It's snowing,' she said.*

and

- [**V.that**] *She said that it was snowing.*

Writers often make a story more interesting by using verbs like **laugh** or **protest** as speech verbs so that they can show more about the way in which something is said:

- *'Oh no, not again,' Jane* **laughed**.
- *'I can't believe you did that!' he* **exploded**.

Verbs in different patterns

Many verbs, for example **watch**, can be used in a number of different ways:

- [**Vn.inf (no to)**] *I watched him eat.*
- [**Vn.ing**] *I watched him eating.*
- [**Vn**] *I watched the pianist's left hand.*
- [**V.wh**] *I watched how the pianist used her left hand.*

The dictionary entry for each verb shows the different ways in which it can be used by giving a range of example sentences. The code before each example shows what type of grammatical pattern is being used. When an example follows another one illustrating the same pattern or patterns, the code is not repeated.

Some patterns are possible after a particular verb but are less common. These are not shown in example sentences but the codes for them are given at the end of the entry or at the end of a particular sense:

promise² /'prɒmɪs/ *v* **1** ~ sth (to sb) to make a promise to sb; to tell sb that one will definitely give or do or not do sth: [V] *I can't promise, but I'll do my best.* [Vn] *The president has promised a thorough investigation into the affair.* ∘ *The promised aid was not forthcoming.* [V.to inf] *He promised to help me.* ∘ *You've got to promise not to tell anyone.* [Vnn] *I have promised myself a quiet weekend.* ∘ *She promised her grandson an ice-cream if he stopped crying.* [Vnpr] *I can't lend you my bike — I've promised it to Sally.* [Vn.that] *She promised me (that) she would be there* [V.that] *'Promise you won't forget!' 'I promise.'* [also V.speech].

he held office? ○ She held the same position in the previous company she worked for. (**c**) to have sth as sth one has gained or achieved: [Vn] She holds the world record for the long jump. ○ She holds the title of world champion. **9** to keep sb's attention or interest by being interesting: [Vn] A good teacher must be able to hold her pupils' attention. **10**(**a**) to have a belief or an opinion: [Vn] He holds strange views on religion. ○ I hold the view that the plan cannot work. (**b**) (fml) to believe, consider or regard sth to be true or the case, esp in a formal argument or an official situation: [Vn-adj] The parents will be **held responsible** for their child's behaviour. [Vn.that] (fml) I still hold that the government's economic policies are mistaken. [Vn.to inf] These vases are held to be the finest examples of Greek art. **11** to cause a meeting, conference, etc to happen: [Vn] hold a conversation with sb ○ The meeting will be held in the community centre. ○ The country is holding its first free elections for twenty years. ○ The Motor Show is usually held in October. **12** (of the wheels of a vehicle) to maintain a grip on the road: [Vn] My new car holds the road well. [also Vn]. **13** (**a**) (of a ship or an aircraft) to continue to move in a particular direction: [Vn] The ship is holding a south-easterly course. (**b**) (of a singer) to continue to sing a note: [Vn] hold a high note. **14** to wait until the person one has telephoned (TELEPHONE) is ready to speak: [V, Vn] Mr Crowther's extension is engaged at the moment; will you hold (the line)? **15** (usu in the imperative) to delay sth; to stop oneself from doing or including sth: [Vn] Hold the front page (ie Do not print it until a certain piece of news is available)! ○ Hold your fire (ie don't shoot). ○ (US infml) Give me a hot dog, but hold the (ie don't give me any) mustard.

IDM Most idioms containing **hold** are at the entries for the nouns or adjectives in the idioms, eg **hold the fort** ⇨ FORT; **hold sb/sth dear** ⇨ DEAR. **hold 'good** to remain true or valid: The same argument does not hold good in every case. **'hold it** (infml) (used to ask sb to wait, or not to move): Hold it a second — I don't think everyone's arrived yet. **there is no 'holding sb** a person cannot be prevented from doing sth: Once she gets onto the subject of politics there's no holding her. **PHRV** ˌhold sth a'gainst sb (infml) to allow sth to make one have a lower opinion of sb or feel HOSTILE(1a) towards them: He's afraid that his criminal record will be held against him when he applies for jobs. ○ He works for a rival company but I don't hold it against him.

ˌhold 'back (from doing sth) to hesitate to act or speak, eg because one is afraid or shy: She held back, not knowing how to break the terrible news. ○ She didn't hold back from telling him what she thought of him. ˌhold sb 'back to prevent the progress or development of sb: Do you think that teaching all the children together holds the brighter ones back? ˌhold sb/sth 'back to prevent sth from advancing; to control or restrain sb/sth: The police were unable to hold back the crowd. ○ The dam was not strong enough to hold back the flood waters. ˌhold sth 'back **1** to refuse or be unwilling to release sth or make sth known: hold back information ○ I think he's holding something back; he knows more than he admits. **2** to stop oneself from expressing or revealing an emotion; to control sth: She just managed to hold back her anger. ○ He bravely held back his tears.

ˌhold sb 'down to prevent sb from exercising their freedom or rights: The people are held down by a repressive military regime. ˌhold sth 'down **1** to keep sth at a low level; to keep sth down: The rate of inflation must be held down. **2** to do a job well enough to remain in it for some time: He was unable to hold down a job after his nervous breakdown.

ˌhold 'forth to speak at great length, and often in a boring way, about sth: He loves holding forth on any subject once he has an audience.

ˌhold sth 'in to restrain or control one's emotions: hold in one's feelings/temper/anger.

ˌhold 'off (of eg rain or a storm) to fail to occur; to be delayed: The rain held off just long enough for us to have our picnic. ˌhold 'off (sth / doing sth) to delay sth: Would it be better to buy a house now or hold off for a few months. ○ Could you hold off (making) your decision until next week? ˌhold sb/sth 'off to resist an attack or advance by sb: Though outnumbered, they held off (repeated attacks by) the enemy for three days.

ˌhold 'on **1** (usu imperative) to wait or stop: Hold on a minute while I get my breath back. **2** to survive in a difficult or dangerous situation: They managed to hold on until help arrived. ○ I don't think I can hold on much longer (eg I have an urgent need to go to the toilet). ˌhold sth 'on to keep sth in position: These nuts and bolts hold the wheels on. ○ This knob is only held on by sticky tape. ˌhold 'on(to sth/sb) to keep holding or gripping sth/sb; to succeed in not letting go of sth/sb: He held on(to the rock) to stop himself slipping. ○ It's very windy — you'd better hold onto your hat. ˌhold 'onto sth to decide not to give or sell sth to sb else; to keep sth: You should hold onto your oil shares. ○ I'd hold onto that house for the time being; house prices are rising sharply at the moment.

ˌhold 'out **1** to resist or survive in a dangerous or difficult situation: They held out bravely against repeated enemy bombing. **2** to continue to be sufficient; to last: We can stay here for as long as our supplies hold out. ○ I can't hold out much longer — I must find a toilet. ˌhold sth 'out to offer a chance, hope or possibility of sth: The forthcoming peace talks hold out the hope/prospect/opportunity of real progress. ○ Doctors hold out little hope of her recovering. ˌhold 'out for sth (infml) to cause a delay in reaching an agreement in the hope of gaining sth: Union negotiators are holding out for a more generous pay settlement. ˌhold 'out on sb (infml) to refuse to give sth, esp information, to sb: I'm not holding out on you — I honestly don't know where he is.

ˌhold sth 'over (often passive) to decide not to deal with sth immediately; to leave sth to be dealt with later: The matter was held over until the next meeting.

'hold to sth to refuse to abandon or change a principle, an opinion, etc; to remain loyal to sth: She always holds to this view passionately. 'hold sb to sth **1** to make sb keep a promise: 'I'll buy you a drink if we win.' 'I'll hold you to that!' ○ We must hold the contractors to (ie not allow them to charge a higher price than) their estimates. **2** to restrict sb to sth: The league leaders were held to a 0–0 draw.

ˌhold to'gether **1** to remain united: The Tory Party always holds together in times of crisis. **2** (of an argument, a theory, etc) to be logical, consistent or convincing: Their case doesn't hold together once you start examining the evidence. ˌhold sth to'gether to cause sth to remain together; to unite sth: My old radio is held together with elastic bands. ○ The country needs a leader who can hold the nation together.

ˌhold sb/sth 'up **1** to delay or block the movement or progress of sb/sth: An accident on the eastbound lane is holding up traffic. ○ My application was held up by the postal strike. ○ Our flight was held up by fog. See also HOLD-UP. **2** to use or present sb/sth as an example: She's always holding up her children as models of behaviour. ˌhold 'up sth to rob sth using the threat of force or violence: hold up a bank/post office ○ Masked men held up a security van in South London yesterday.

'hold with sth (used in negative sentences or in

questions) to agree with or approve of sth: *I don't hold with some of these modern theories on education.*
■ '**hold-up** *n* (**a**) a period in which sb is prevented from doing sth or from moving; a delay: *a hold-up on the motorway* ○ *We should arrive in half an hour, barring hold-ups.* (**b**) an act of robbing a bank, shop, etc, using the threat of force or violence: *After the hold-up, the gang made their getaway in a stolen car.*

hold² /həʊld/ *n* **1(a)** [sing] an act or manner of holding sb/sth; a grip: *She kept a firm hold of her little boy's hand as they crossed the road.* ○ *He lost his hold on the rope.* (**b**) [C] a particular way of holding an opponent, etc: '*wrestling holds.* **2** [sing] (**a**) ~ (**on/over sb/sth**) a way of influencing sb, esp one that is not open or honest: *He has some kind of sinister hold over his younger brother.* (**b**) ~ (**on sb/ sth**) power over or control of sb/sth: *The military has tightened its hold on the country.* **3** [C] a place where sb can put their hands or feet when climbing: *There are very few holds on the cliff face.* See also FOOTHOLD, TOE-HOLD. **IDM** **catch, grab, take, etc** '**hold of sb/sth** **1** to take sb/sth in the hands: *I threw the rope and he caught hold of it.* ○ *I managed to grab hold of the jug before it fell.* **2** to take control of sth: *A mood of hysteria had taken hold of the small community.* **get hold** '**of sb/sth** (*infml*) **1** to find and use sth: *Do you know where I can get hold of a second-hand carpet cleaner?* ○ *Wherever did you get hold of that idea?* **2** to reach or find sb: *I've been trying to get hold of her for days but she's never at home.* **leave go/hold** ⇨ GO². **with ,no ,holds** '**barred** with no limits, rules, etc in a fight, contest, etc, any method being allowed: *a no-holds-barred situation.*

hold³ /həʊld/ *n* the hollow part of a ship or plane, where cargo is stored.

holdall /'həʊldɔːl/ (*US* '**carry-all**) *n* a large soft bag for holding clothes, etc when travelling.

holder /'həʊldə(r)/ *n* (often forming compound *ns*) **1** a person who holds sth; a person who has sth in her or his possession: *an account-holder* ○ *a 'licence-holder* ○ *a 'ticket-holder* ○ *the current holder of the world record* ○ *holders of high office* ○ *the holder of a French passport.* **2** a thing that supports or holds sth: *a 'pen-holder* ○ *a ciga'rette-holder* ○ *a 'plant holder.*

holding /'həʊldɪŋ/ *n* **1** (often *pl*) a thing owned, such as land, shares (SHARE¹ 3), etc; an amount of personal property: *the value of their existing holdings* ○ *the museum's holdings* ○ *She has a 40% holding in the company.* **2** a piece of land held by a TENANT. See also SMALLHOLDING.
■ '**holding company** *n* a company formed to hold the shares (SHARE¹ 3) of other companies, which it then controls.
'**holding operation** *n* an action taken to control an existing situation or to prevent it becoming any worse.

hole /həʊl/ *n* **1** [C] (**a**) a hollow place in a solid mass or surface: *a hole in a tooth* ○ *dig a deep hole* ○ *The road is full of gaping holes.* (**b**) an opening through sth; a gap: *drill/punch a hole in sth* ○ *a bullet hole* ○ *The prisoners knocked a hole in the wall and escaped.* ○ *I've worn holes in my socks.* ○ *My socks are full of holes.* ○ *the hole in the ozone layer.* See also PIGEON-HOLE. **2** [C] (**a**) an animal's home; a BURROW: *a 'mouse hole* ○ *a fox's hole.* (**b**) (usu *sing*) (*infml*) a small, dark or unpleasant room, district, etc: *I don't know why you want to live here — it's a dreadful hole!* **3** [sing] (*sl*) an awkward or difficult situation: *I'm afraid I'm in a bit of a hole.* **4** [C] (*sport*) (**a**) a hollow into which a ball, etc must be hit in various games: *an ,eighteen-hole 'golf-course.* ⇨ picture at GOLF. (**b**) (in golf) a section of a golf-course between a TEE and a hole: *a short hole — win the first hole.* **IDM** **an ace in the hole** ⇨ ACE. **make a 'hole in sth** (*infml*) to use a large amount of one's money, sup-

plies, etc: *The hospital bills made a big hole in his savings.* **money burns a hole in sb's pocket** ⇨ MONEY. **pick holes in sth** ⇨ PICK¹. See also BLACK HOLE, BLOW-HOLE, WATER-HOLE.
▶ **hole** *v* **1** to make a hole or holes in sth: [Vn] *The ship was holed by an iceberg.* **2** ~ (**out**) (in golf, etc) to hit the ball into a hole: [Vp] *She holed out from forty yards.* [Vn] *He needs to hole this putt to win the hole.* **PHRV** **be ,holed 'up** (*infml*) to be hidden, esp deliberately: *The gang are holed up in the mountains somewhere.*
■ **hole in** '**one** *n* an occasion in golf when the ball is hit from the TEE directly into the hole: *do a hole in one.*

holiday /'hɒlədeɪ; *Brit also* -di/ *n* (**a**) (*esp Brit*) (also *esp US* **vacation**) (often *pl*) a period of time away from work, used esp for travel or rest: *a skiing/ walking/camping holiday* ○ *an adventure holiday* ○ *the holiday season* ○ *a holiday cottage/resort* ○ *holiday bookings/insurance* ○ *the school holidays* ○ *the Christmas holidays* ○ *My boss has gone away on holiday.* ○ *We're going to Spain for our summer holiday(s).* ○ *I'm taking a two-week holiday/two weeks' holiday.* ○ *I'm entitled to 20 days' paid holiday a year.* See also HOLS, PACKAGE HOLIDAY. (**b**) a day when people relax and no work is done: *a public holiday* ○ *Sunday is a holiday in Christian countries.* See also BANK HOLIDAY. **IDM** **a busman's holiday** ⇨ BUSMAN. **high days and holidays** ⇨ HIGH¹.
▶ **holiday** (*esp Brit*) (also *esp US* **vacation**) *v* to spend a holiday: [V] *a holidaying couple* [Vpr] *They're holidaying on the west coast of Ireland.*
■ '**holiday camp** *n* (*esp Brit*) a specially built village with accommodation and organized amusements for people on holiday, esp families.
'**holiday centre** *n* (*Brit*) a place with many facilities for tourists.
'**holiday-maker** *n* (*esp Brit*) a person who is on holiday: *The plane was packed with Dutch holiday-makers.*

NOTE **Holiday, vacation** and **leave** all describe a period of time when you are absent from your work. A (**public**) **holiday** (also **bank holiday** in Britain) is a single day without work because of a religious or national festival: *The 14th of July is a French national holiday.* ○ *The shops are closed tomorrow because it's a bank holiday.* ○ *the Martin Luther King holiday.* You use **holiday** in British English and **vacation** in American English to describe the regular periods of time when you are not at work or school each year: *Where are you going on holiday/on vacation this year?* ○ *I like to take a winter vacation.* ○ *the school summer holidays.* In British English **vacation** is used mainly for the periods when universities, courts of law, etc are closed: *I spent the summer vacations fruit picking.* **Leave** means permission to be absent from work for a special reason: *She's on maternity leave/compassionate leave.* **Leave** is also used as an official word for holiday: *How many days annual leave do you get in your job?* ○ *He's taken a month's unpaid leave.*

holier-than-thou /,həʊliə ðən 'ðaʊ/ *adj* (*infml derog*) thinking that one is morally better than others: *I can't stand his holier-than-thou attitude.*

holiness /'həʊlinəs/ *n* **1** [U] the state of being holy or sacred: *The place filled him with a sense of peace and holiness.* **2** **His/Your Holiness** a title used of or to the Pope.

holistic /həʊ'lɪstɪk/ *adj* **1** having regard to the whole of sth rather than just to parts of it: *a holistic approach to life.* **2** (*medical*) treating the whole person rather than just the symptoms of a disease: *holistic medicine.*

holler /'hɒlə(r)/ *v* (*infml esp US*) to shout sth; to YELL: [V.speech] *'Come back!' I hollered.* [also V, Vn].

[Vnn] = verb + noun + noun   [V-adj] = verb + adjective   For more help with verbs, see Study pages **B4–8**.

hollow /'hɒləʊ/ adj **1** having a hole or empty space inside; not solid: *a hollow tree/ball* ○ *I tapped the wall to see if it was hollow.* **2** deeply set, esp as a result of hunger or illness: *hollow cheeks* ○ ˌhollow-ˈeyed *from lack of sleep.* **3** [usu attrib] (of sounds) having the quality of an ECHO[1]; sounding as if coming from a hollow place: *a hollow groan* ○ *a hollow knocking sound.* **4(a)** false; not sincere: *a hollow promise* ○ *She gave a hollow laugh.* ○ *His words rang hollow.* **(b)** without real value; worthless: *hollow threats* ○ *win a hollow victory.* **IDM** **beat sb hollow** ⇨ BEAT[1].
▶ **hollow** n **(a)** a large hole in the ground: *damp/muddy hollows.* **(b)** a small valley: *a wooded/shady hollow.* **(c)** a hole or enclosed space within sth: *She held the small bird in the hollow of her hand.*
hollow v **PHRV** ˌhollow sth **'out 1** to make a hole in sth: *a canoe made from a hollowed-out log.* **2** to form sth by making a hole in sth else: *hollow out a nest in a tree-trunk* ○ *caves hollowed out (of the cliff) by the waves.*
hollowly adv: *He laughed hollowly.*
hollowness n [U]: *expose the hollowness of sb's claims.*

holly /'hɒli/ n **(a)** [C] a tree with hard prickly leaves all through the year and red berries in winter. **(b)** [U] its branches used for Christmas decorations: *a sprig of holly.*

hollyhock /'hɒlihɒk/ n a tall garden plant with brightly coloured flowers. ⇨ picture at FLOWER.

holocaust /'hɒləkɔːst/ n **(a)** [C] an occasion of great destruction, esp by fire, and great loss of human life: *fear a nuclear holocaust.* **(b) the Holocaust** [sing] the mass killing of Jews by the Nazis before and during World War II.

hologram /'hɒləgræm/ n a special photographic representation that gives a three-dimensional (THREE) image when lit in a suitable way: *Holograms are now common on credit cards.*

hols /hɒlz/ n [pl] (*Brit infml*) holidays: *during the school summer hols.*

holster /'həʊlstə(r)/ n a leather case for a PISTOL, esp one fixed to a belt or under an arm. ⇨ picture at GUN.

holy /'həʊli/ adj (-ier, -iest) **1(a)** associated with God or with religion; of God: *the ˌHoly ˈBible/ˈScriptures.* **(b)** regarded as sacred; consecrated (CONSECRATE 1): ˌholy ˈground ○ ˌholy ˈwater (ie water blessed by a priest) ○ *a holy ˈwar* (ie one fought to defend what is sacred) ○ *Islam's holiest shrine.* **2** devoted to the service of God; pure in a moral and spiritual sense: *a holy man* ○ *live a holy life.* See also HOLINESS.
■ **the ˌHoly ˈCity** n [sing] Jerusalem.
ˌHoly Comˈmunion n [U] = COMMUNION 1.
the ˌHoly ˈFather n [sing] the Pope.
the ˌHoly ˈGhost n [sing] = THE HOLY SPIRIT.
the ˌHoly ˈGrail n [sing] = GRAIL n. (*fig*) *United began their quest for the championship, the holy grail that has always eluded them.*
the ˈHoly Land n [sing] the country west of the river Jordan, held in great respect by Christians as the place where Christ lived.
the ˌholy of ˈholies n [sing] (*often joc*) a sacred place: *To the children, their father's study was the holy of holies.*
ˌholy ˈorders n [pl] the status of a bishop, priest, etc: *He decided to take holy orders.* ⇨ ORDER[1] 12.
the ˌHoly ˈSee n [sing] **1** the court of the Pope; the Vatican. **2** the office of the Pope; the PAPACY.
the ˌHoly ˈSpirit (also **the ˌHoly ˈGhost**) n [sing] the Third Person in the Trinity; God as a spirit.
ˈHoly Week n the week before Easter Sunday.
ˌHoly ˈWrit n [U] holy writings, esp the Bible: *You shouldn't treat the newspapers as if they were Holy Writ.*

homage /'hɒmɪdʒ/ n [U, C usu *sing*] ~ **(to sb/sth)** (*fml*) things said or done to show great respect; a TRIBUTE to sb or their qualities: *They stood/knelt in silent homage round her grave.* ○ *Many came to do/pay homage to the dead man.* ○ *He describes his book as 'a homage to my father'.*

home[1] /həʊm/ n **1(a)** [C, U] the place where one lives, esp with one's family: *The nurse visits patients in their homes.* ○ *He left home* (ie left his parents and began an independent life) *at sixteen.* ○ *I'll give you my home address.* ○ *home-baked bread* ○ *a quiet home-loving man* ○ *the new fashion for home-based computer-linked workers.* See also BROKEN HOME. **(b)** [C] a house, flat, etc: *a luxury home* ○ *a five-bedroom home* ○ *a rise in the number of private homes being repossessed* ○ *a home improvement grant* ○ *They have a second/a holiday home in Wales.* ○ *We spoke to Madonna at her Hollywood home.* ○ *good news for home-buyers* ○ *the growth of home-ownership.* See also MOBILE HOME, STATELY HOME. **(c)** [C] (*infml*) a place where an object is stored: *I must find a home for all these bottles.* **2** [C, U] the district or country where one was born or where one has lived for a long time or to which one feels attached: *my home town* ○ *She was born in London, but she now regards Paris as her home.* ○ *We were a long way from home.* **3** [C] an institution for people needing care or rest: *a ˈchildren's home* ○ *a home for the blind* ○ *an old ˈpeople's home.* See also NURSING HOME, REST-HOME. **4** [C] **(a)** a place where an animal or a plant lives or is most commonly found: *The tiger's home is (in) the jungle.* **(b)** a place from which sth originates: *Greece is the home of democracy.* **IDM** **at ˈhome 1** in the house, flat, etc: *Is there anybody at home?* **2** in one's own country: *the President's political standing at home and abroad.* **3** at one's ease, as if in one's own home: *Help yourself to whatever you need — just make yourself at home!* ○ *They always make us feel very much at home.* **4** (of football matches, etc) played in the town, etc to which the team belongs: *Is our next match at home or away?* ○ *a home game.* **5** (*fml*) expecting visitors and ready to receive them: *Mrs Hill is not at home to anyone except close relatives.* **charity begins at home** ⇨ CHARITY. **close/near to ˈhome** close to the point at which one is directly affected: *Her remarks about me were embarrassingly nearer to home.* ○ *The threat of war is coming steadily nearer to home.* **eat sb out of house and home** ⇨ EAT. **an Englishman's home is his castle** ⇨ ENGLISHMAN. **a ˌhome from ˈhome**; (*US*) **a home away from ˈhome** a place where one is as happy, comfortable, etc as in one's own home: *You will find our hotel a true home from home!* **one's spiritual home** ⇨ SPIRITUAL. **when he's, it's, etc at ˈhome** (*Brit joc*) (used to emphasize a question): *Who's Gloria Button when she's at home?*
▶ **homeless** adj having no home: *a hostel for homeless families.* **the homeless** n [pl v] homeless people: *provide emergency accommodation for the homeless.* **homelessness** n [U]: *to tackle the problem of homelessness.*

homeward /'həʊmwəd/ adj, adv going towards home: *the homeward journey* ○ *We were homeward bound at last.*
homewards /-wədz/ adv towards home: *travel homewards.* ⇨ note at FORWARD[2].
■ **the ˌHome ˈCounties** n [pl] the counties round London.
ˌhome ecoˈnomics n [U] the study of household management.
ˌhome-ˈgrown adj (of food, esp fruit and vegetables) grown in one's own country, garden, etc: *Are these lettuces home-grown or did you buy them in the market?* ○ (*fig*) *The team includes several foreign players because of the shortage of ˌhome-grown ˈtalent.*
ˌhome ˈhelp n (*Brit*) a person whose job is to help

others with household work, eg cooking, esp one employed by a local authority to help old or sick people in this way.

,home 'loan *n* (*infml*) = MORTGAGE.

,home-'made *adj* made at home: ,home-made 'jam ○ a ,home-made 'bomb.

the 'Home Office *n* [sing or pl *v*] the British government department dealing with law and order, IMMIGRATION, etc in England and Wales. Compare THE FOREIGN OFFICE.

,home 'rule *n* [U] the government of a country or region by its own citizens.

,home 'run *n* (in baseball) a hit that allows the person hitting the ball to run round all the bases without stopping.

,Home 'Secretary *n* (in Britain) the government minister in charge of the Home Office.

the ,home 'straight (also *esp US* the home 'stretch) *n* [sing] (a) the last part of a race, near the finish. (b) the last part of an activity, etc when it is nearly completed.

,home 'truth *n* an unpleasant fact about a person told to her or him by sb else: *It's time you listened to a few home truths about yourself.*

home² /həʊm/ *adj* [attrib] 1(a) of, belonging to or connected with one's home: *have a happy home life* ○ *home comforts* ○ *a home computer* ○ *We offer customers a free home delivery service.* (b) done or produced at home: *home cooking* ○ *home movies.* 2 in one's own country; not foreign; domestic: *the home market* ○ *home news/affairs.* 3 (*sport*) played on or connected with one's own ground: *a home match/ win* ○ *the home team* ○ *playing in front of their home crowd.*

home³ /həʊm/ *adv* 1 at, in or to one's home or country: *Is he home yet?* ○ *I got home at 7.30.* ○ *She's on her way home.* ○ *Go straight home, Billy.* ○ *We returned home.* ○ *Will the Spanish authorities send him home for trial?* ○ (*US*) *stay home* (ie stay at home). 2 to the point aimed at; as far as possible: *drive a nail home.* **IDM** bring home the 'bacon (*infml*) to achieve sth successfully. bring sth 'home to sb to make sb realize sth fully: *The television pictures brought home to us all the full horror of the famine.* come 'home (to sb) to become fully clear, often in a way that is painful: *The reality of the situation suddenly came home to him.* come home to 'roost (of wishes or words) to take effect upon the person who has said them. drive sth home ⇨ DRIVE¹. hit/strike 'home (of remarks, etc) to have the intended, often painful, effect: *I could see from her expression that his comments had hit home.* (be) home and 'dry safe and successful, esp after a difficult time. nothing to write home about ⇨ WRITE. press sth home ⇨ PRESS². ram sth home ⇨ RAM². romp home / to victory ⇨ ROMP. till the cows come home ⇨ COW¹.

■ 'home-coming *n* 1 [C, U] an arrival at home, esp of sb who has been away for a long time: *a homecoming party.* 2 [C] (*US*) an annual event at a college or university for former students.

home⁴ /həʊm/ *v* **PHRV** ,home 'in (on sth) to move directly towards sth: *The torpedo homed in on its target.* ○ *Pop fans are homing in on the concert site from miles around.*

homeland /'həʊmlænd/ *n* 1 one's native country: *forced to flee their homeland.* 2 (usu *pl*) any of the areas formerly reserved for black people in the Republic of S Africa.

homely /'həʊmli/ *adj* (-ier, -iest) 1 (*approv esp Brit*) (a) simple and plain: *homely food* ○ *a homely woman.* (b) making sb feel comfortable: *a warm and homely place/atmosphere.* 2 (*US derog*) (of a person's appearance) not attractive; plain.

homeopathy (also homoeo-) /ˌhəʊmi'ɒpəθi/ *n* [U] the treatment of a disease or condition by using

very small amounts of drugs which, if they were given to a healthy person, would produce symptoms like those of the disease, etc itself.

► **homeopath** (also homoeo-) /'həʊmiəpæθ/ *n* a person who practises homeopathy.

homeopathic (also homoeo-) /ˌhəʊmiə'pæθɪk/ *adj*: *,homeopathic 'medicines/'remedies/'treatments.*

homesick /'həʊmsɪk/ *adj* sad because one is away from home: *homesick American troops* ○ *Michael was desperately homesick for Italy.* ► **homesickness** *n* [U]: *suffering from a touch/a bout of homesickness.*

homespun /'həʊmspʌn/ *adj* plain and simple: *homespun remedies for minor ailments* ○ *a few words of homespun wisdom.*

homestead /'həʊmsted/ *n* 1 a house with the land and buildings round it, esp a farm. 2 (*US*) (formerly) an area of land given to a person by the government on condition that he or she lived on it and cultivated it. ► **homesteader** *n*.

homework /'həʊmwɜːk/ *n* [U] 1 work that a pupil is required to do away from school: *a 'homework book* ○ *The teacher gave us an essay for homework.* ○ *I haven't done my (geography) homework.* 2 (*infml*) work done in preparation for a meeting, etc: *The politicians present had clearly not done their homework* (ie found out all they needed to know about a particular topic).

homey (also homy) /'həʊmi/ *adj* pleasant and comfortable; like home.

homicide /'hɒmɪsaɪd/ *n* [C, U] the killing of one person by another; murder: *be accused of homicide* ○ *homicide cases.* See also MURDER 1. Compare MANSLAUGHTER.

► **homicidal** /ˌhɒmɪ'saɪdl/ *adj* likely, or making one likely, to kill people: *a homicidal maniac* ○ *have homicidal tendencies.*

homily /'hɒmɪli/ *n* (*often derog*) a talk, often a long and boring one, from sb giving advice on the correct way to behave, etc: *preach/give/deliver a homily.*

homing /'həʊmɪŋ/ *adj* [attrib] 1 (of a PIGEON) trained to fly home from a great distance. 2 (of a missile, etc) fitted with an electronic device that enables it to find and hit a target: *'homing devices.*

homo- *comb form* the same: *homosexual* ○ *homophone* ○ *homogeneous.* Compare HETERO-.

homoeopathy = HOMEOPATHY.

homogeneous /ˌhɒmə'dʒiːniəs/ *adj* (*fml*) formed of parts that are all of the same type: *a homogeneous group/society.* Compare HETEROGENEOUS.

► **homogeneity** /ˌhɒmədʒə'niːəti/ *n* [U] the quality of being alike.

homogenized, -ised /hə'mɒdʒənaɪzd/ *adj* (of milk) treated so that the fat in it is broken down and the cream is mixed in with the rest.

homograph /'hɒməgrɑːf; *US* -græf/ *n* a word spelt like another word but with a different meaning or pronunciation, eg *bow¹* /bəʊ/, *bow²* /baʊ/.

homonym /'hɒmənɪm/ *n* a word spelt and pronounced like another word but with a different meaning, eg *see¹*, *see²*.

homophone /'hɒməfəʊn/ *n* a word pronounced like another word but with a different meaning or spelling, eg *some, sum* /sʌm/; *knew, new* /njuː/.

Homo sapiens /ˌhəʊməʊ 'sæpienz/ *n* [U] (*Latin*) modern human beings regarded as a species.

homosexual /ˌhəʊmə'sekʃuəl, ˌhɒm-/ *adj* sexually attracted only to people of the same sex as oneself: *,homosexual 'men/'acts/re'lationships.* Compare BISEXUAL, HETEROSEXUAL.

► **homosexual** *n* a homosexual person, esp a man: *a practising homosexual.* Compare LESBIAN.

homosexuality /ˌhəʊməˌsekʃu'æləti, ˌhɒm-/ *n* [U].

Hon *abbr* 1 /ɒn/ *Honourable: the Hon Sec* (ie Honorary Secretary) ○ *the Hon Treasurer.* 2 *Honourable: the Hon Emily Smythe.* Compare RT HON.

hone /həʊn/ *v* **1** ~ sth (to sth) to develop and improve sth for a special purpose over a period of time: [Vn] *a finely honed judgement* [Vnpr] *Long practice over many years had honed his skill to perfection.* **2** to make a blade, etc sharp or sharper: [Vn].

honest /'ɒnɪst/ *adj* **1(a)** (of a person) telling the truth; not lying, cheating or stealing: *an honest witness/businessman* ○ *He was honest enough to admit that he knew nothing about the subject.* **(b)** (of a statement) frank, sincere and direct: *give an honest opinion* ○ *a refreshingly honest exchange of views* ○ *To be (quite) honest I have never been so depressed by a book in all my life.* **(c)** showing or resulting from an honest mind or attitude: *an honest face* ○ *do an honest day's work* ○ *He looks honest enough, but can we trust him?* Compare DISHONEST. **2** (of wages, etc) fairly earned: *make an honest living* ○ *try to* ***earn an honest penny.*** **IDM** **make an honest ¹woman of sb** (*dated joc*) to marry sb after having had a sexual relationship with her.
▶ **honest** *adv* (*infml*) really; and this is the truth: *It wasn't me, honest!*
honestly *adv* **1** in an honest way: *deal honestly with sb.* **2** (used for emphasis) really: *I don't honestly know.* ○ *Honestly, Helen, that's all the money I've got!* ○ *I think I can honestly say I've never smoked in my life.* ○ *Quite honestly, she isn't the sort of person we're looking for.* **3** (used to show that one disapproves of sth and is irritated by it): *Honestly! What a fuss he's making!*
■ **¹honest ¹broker** *n* a person who tries to get other people to reach an agreement, esp in industrial or international disputes.
¹honest-to-¹goodness *adj* [attrib] (*approv*) plain and simple; genuine: *a bit of honest-to-goodness hard work* ○ *There's nothing like an honest-to-goodness cup of tea!*

honesty /'ɒnəsti/ *n* [U] the quality of being honest; truthfulness (TRUTH): *a reputation for honesty* ○ *her emotional honesty* ○ *the honesty and integrity of his work.* **IDM** **in all ¹honesty** if one is being completely honest: *I can't in all honesty deny it.*

honey /'hʌni/ *n* **1** [U] a sweet sticky yellowish substance made by bees from NECTAR: *a jar/pot of honey.* **2** [C] (*infml esp US*) **(a)** (used to address a person one likes or loves): *You look great tonight, honey!* **(b)** a person or thing that is excellent or delightful: *Our baby-sitter is an absolute honey.* **IDM** **milk and honey** ⇨ MILK¹.
▶ **honeyed** /'hʌnid/ *adj* (of words) soft and intended to please: *Her honeyed tones calmed his anger.*

honeycomb /'hʌnikəʊm/ *n* [C, U] a wax structure of cells with six sides, made by bees for holding their honey and eggs. **honeycombed** *adj* ~ (**with sth**) filled with holes, tunnels, etc: *The cliffs are honeycombed with caves.*

honeydew melon /ˌhʌnidjuː 'melən; *US* -duː/ *n* a type of MELON with pale skin and sweet green flesh.

honeymoon /'hʌnimuːn/ *n* **1** a holiday taken by a newly married couple: *They went to Italy for their honeymoon.* ○ *We're on our honeymoon.* **2** a period of enthusiastic GOODWILL at the start of an activity, a relationship, etc: *The honeymoon period for the new government is over, and they must now start to tackle the country's many problems.*
▶ **honeymoon** *v* to spend a honeymoon: [Vpr] *They are honeymooning in Paris.* **honeymooner** *n*.

honeysuckle /'hʌnisʌkl/ *n* [U] a climbing plant with sweet-smelling yellow or pink flowers.

honk /hɒŋk/ *n* **1** the cry of the wild GOOSE. **2** the sound made by a car horn, esp of the old-fashioned type.
▶ **honk** *v* ~ (**sth**) (**at sb/sth**) to make or cause sth to make a honk: [V] *the honking cry of geese* [Vpr] *Why is he honking at me?* [also Vn, Vnpr].

honky-tonk /'hɒŋki tɒŋk/ *n* (*infml*) [U] a type of lively JAZZ music played on a piano.

honor (*US*) = HONOUR¹,².

honorable (*US*) = HONOURABLE.

honorarium /ˌɒnə'reəriəm/ *n* (*pl* honoraria /-riə/) a payment made for professional services for which a person is not being paid at the normal rates.

honorary /'ɒnərəri; *US* -reri/ *adj* [usu attrib] **1** (of a degree, rank, etc) given as an honour, without the usual qualification being required: *be awarded an honorary doctorate/title.* **2** (in titles **Honorary**, *abbr* **Hon**) (of a position or its holder) not paid: *the honorary (post of) President* ○ *the Honorary Secretary Mrs Hill.*

honorific /ˌɒnə'rɪfɪk/ *adj* indicating respect for the person being addressed, esp in Oriental languages: *an honorific title.*

honour¹ (*US* **honor**) /'ɒnə(r)/ *n* **1(a)** [U] great respect for sb; high public regard for sb: *the place/seat of honour* ○ *They stood in silence as a mark of honour to her.* **(b)** [U, sing] a source or feeling of pride and pleasure resulting from great respect being shown to one: *It is a great honour to be invited.* **2** [U] **(a)** good personal character; a strong sense of what is morally right: *a man of honour* ○ *Honour demands that he should resign.* See also DEBT OF HONOUR. **(b)** good reputation; respect from others: *fight for the honour of one's country* ○ *The family honour is at stake.* **3** [sing] **an** ~ **to sth/sb** a person or thing that brings credit to sth/sb: *She is an honour to her profession.* **4** [C usu *pl*] a thing given as a distinction or mark of respect, esp an official award for achievement or courage: *bury sb with full military honours* (ie with a special military ceremony) ○ *the Birthday/New Year Honours list* (ie the list of awards, titles, etc given in Britain by the King or Queen on his or her birthday or on 1 January each year). **5** honours [pl] a specialized course for a university degree or a high level of distinction reached in it: *gain an honours degree in French* ○ *graduate with first-class honours in physics.* See also HONS. **6** your/his/her Honour [sing] (used as a title of respect when addressing or referring to certain judges or people of importance): *I plead not guilty, your Honour.* **7** [C esp *pl*] any of the cards of highest value in certain card-games. **IDM** **do sb an ¹honour; do sb the ¹honour (of doing sth)** to give sb a privilege; to show great respect for sb: *You do us a great honour by attending.* ○ *Will you do me the honour of dining with me?* **do the ¹honours** (*infml*) to act as host; to perform a social duty or small ceremony for others: *The local school has asked me to do the honours on prize-giving day.* **have the ¹honour (of sth/doing sth)** (*fml*) to be given the privilege specified: *May I have the honour of the next dance?* ○ *To whom do I have the honour of speaking?* **(there is) honour among ¹thieves** (*saying*) criminals have their own standards of behaviour that they respect. **honours are ¹even** the contest is level. **(in) honour ¹bound (to do sth)** required to do sth because of one's sense of moral duty: *I feel honour bound to attend because I said I would.* **in ¹honour of sb/sth; in sb's/sth's honour** arranged as a mark of respect for sb/sth: *a ceremony in honour of those killed in the explosion* ○ *When she retired after 50 years with the company, a dinner was held in her honour.* **on my ¹honour** I swear it: *I promise I'll pay you back, on my honour.* **a point of honour** ⇨ POINT¹. **one's word of honour** ⇨ WORD.

honour² (*US* **honor**) /'ɒnə(r)/ *v* **1(a)** to show great respect for sb/sth: [Vn] *I feel highly honoured to be invited.* [Vnpr] *The President honoured us with a personal visit.* **(b)** ~ **sb** (**with sth**) (**for sth**) to give public praise or distinction to sb: [Vn] *Large crowds turned out to honour the winning team.* [Vnpr] *He was honoured with an award for his services to the* *country.* **2** to keep or fulfil an agreement, a promise, etc: [Vn] *I have every intention of honouring our contract.* **3** (*commerce*) to keep an agreement to pay sth: [Vn] *honour a cheque.*

honourable (*US* **honorable**) /ˈɒnərəbl/ *adj* **1** deserving, bringing or showing honour and respect: *a decent, honourable man* ○ *do the honourable thing by resigning* ○ *His intentions/motives are entirely honourable.* ○ *With a few honourable exceptions, software training organisations are very inadequate.* **2** (in titles **the Honourable**, *abbr* **Hon**) (**a**) a title given to certain people of high rank or office. (**b**) (in Britain) a title used by Members of Parliament when speaking about or to each other during a debate: *my Honourable friend, the member for Chester.* See also RIGHT HONOURABLE. ► **honourably** /-əbli/ *adv: act/behave honourably.*

Hons /ɒnz/ *abbr* (used after the name of a university degree) Honours (HONOUR¹ 5): *James West BSc (Hons).*

hooch /huːtʃ/ *n* [U] (*infml esp US*) alcoholic drink.

hood¹ /hʊd/ *n* **1** a covering for the head and neck, often fastened to a coat so that it can hang down at the back or be removed when not in use: *an anorak with a detachable hood.* **2** a garment of coloured silk or fur worn over a university GOWN(2) to show the degree held by the person wearing it. **3** a piece of cloth put over sb's face and head so that they cannot be recognized or so that they cannot see: *The robbers all wore hoods to hide their faces.* **4**(**a**) (*esp Brit*) a folding cover over a car, PRAM, etc: *drive with the hood down.* (**b**) a cover placed over a device or machine, eg to protect it: *a lens/cooker hood* ○ *a soundproof hood for a computer printer.* **5** (*US*) = BONNET 2. ⇨ picture at CAR.
► **hooded** *adj* **1** having a hood(1): *a hooded jacket.* **2** wearing a hood(1): *hooded monks.* **3** (of eyes) having large, partially closed, eyelids (EYELID).

hood² /hʊd/ *n* (*US sl*) = HOODLUM 2.

-hood *suff* (with *ns* or *adjs* forming *ns*) **1** the state or condition of being sth: *childhood* ○ *falsehood.* **2** a group of peole of the specified type: *priesthood.*

hoodlum /ˈhuːdləm/ *n* **1** a violent and noisy young man. **2** a violent criminal; a GANGSTER.

hoodoo /ˈhuːduː/ *n* (*pl* **-doos**) ~ (**on sb/sth**) (*esp US*) a person or thing that brings or causes bad luck.

hoodwink /ˈhʊdwɪŋk/ *v* ~ **sb** (**into doing sth**) to deceive sb; to trick sb: [Vnpr] *I was hoodwinked into believing his story.* [also Vn].

hooey /ˈhuːi/ *n* [U], *interj* (*sl*) false or foolish talk; nonsense: *That's a lot of hooey!*

hoof /huːf/ *n* (*pl* **hoofs** or **hooves** /huːvz/) the hard part of the foot of certain animals, eg horses: *hear the sound of hooves.* ⇨ picture at HORSE. **IDM** **on the ˈhoof 1** (of cattle) alive; before being killed for meat: *bought on the hoof and then slaughtered.* **2** (*infml*) while busy doing sth; without stopping to pay full attention to sth: *eat lunch/make a decision on the hoof.*

hoo-ha /ˈhuː hɑː/ (*US also* **hoop-la**) *n* [U, sing] (*infml*) a noisy or excited reaction, esp to sth unimportant; a fuss; a COMMOTION: *The publication of her memoirs caused quite a hoo-ha.*

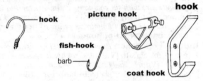
hook

hook

picture hook

fish-hook

barb

coat hook

hook¹ /hʊk/ *n* **1** a curved piece of wire or plastic attached to a rod, wall, etc, used for catching hold of

sth or hanging sth on: *a ˈcoat/ˈpicture hook* ○ *a ˈfish-hook* ○ *Hang your towel on that hook.* ⇨ picture. See also BOAT-HOOK. **2**(**a**) (in certain ball games) a shot or kick that causes the ball to go to one side instead of straight ahead. (**b**) (in boxing) a short punch with the elbow bent: *a left hook to the jaw.* **IDM** **by ˌhook or by ˈcrook** by one means or another, no matter what happens: *She was determined to get to London, by hook or by crook.* **get (sb) off the ˈhook; let sb off the ˈhook** (*infml*) to escape from or allow sb to escape from a difficult situation or punishment: *The decline of the dollar got the government off the hook.* ○ *Despite a good spell of bowling England was not let off the hook.* **hook, line and ˈsinker** entirely; completely: *What I said was untrue but he fell for it/ swallowed it* (ie believed it) *hook, line and sinker.* **off the ˈhook** (of a telephone) with the RECEIVER(3) not where is usu rests when not in use, making it impossible for the telephone to ring: *He left the phone off the hook so that he wouldn't be disturbed.* **sling one's hook** ⇨ SLING *v.*
■ **ˌhook and ˈeye** *n* (*pl* **hooks and eyes**) a small metal hook and loop which together form a fastening for clothes, etc: *do up the hook and eye of a dress.* **ˌhook-ˈnosed** *adj* having a large curved nose.

hook² /hʊk/ *v* **1**(**a**) to fasten or be fastened with or as if with a hook: [Vp] *These two pieces of the chain hook together.* [V] *a dress that hooks at the back* [Vpr] *His leg hooked round mine and tripped me up.* [Vnpr] *hook the caravan (on)to the car* [also Vn]. (**b**) to catch sth with a hook: [Vn] *hook a large fish.* **2** [Vn] to hit or kick a ball so that it goes to one side instead of straight ahead. **IDM** **be ˈhooked (on sb)** (*sl*) to be in love with sb. **be/get ˈhooked (on sth)** (*sl*) **1** to be/become completely dependent on sth: *get hooked on heroin/computer games.* **2** to be/become very keen on sth and absorbed in it: *She's completely hooked on the idea of a camping holiday.* **PHR V** **ˌhook sth/sb ˈup** to fasten a garment by means of a hook and eye (HOOK¹): *Please will you hook me up* (ie fasten my dress) *at the back?* **ˌhook (sb/sth) ˈup (to/ with sth)** to link sb/sth to electronic equipment, eg broadcasting facilities or computers: *be hooked up to a body scanner* ○ *The BBC is hooked up with Australian television.*
► **hooked** *adj* (**a**) curved like a hook: *a hooked nose/beak.* (**b**) having a hook or hooks.
■ **ˈhook-up** *n* a link between two or more pieces of electronic equipment, eg broadcasting facilities or computers: *a satellite hook-up between the major European networks.*

hookah /ˈhʊkə/ *n* a pipe used esp in Arab countries for smoking tobacco. Its long flexible tube passes through a container of water which cools the smoke as it is drawn through it.

hooker /ˈhʊkə(r)/ *n* (*sl esp US*) a prostitute.

hookey (also **hooky**) /ˈhʊki/ *n* **IDM** **play ˈhookey** (*sl esp US*) to stay away from school without permission; to play TRUANT.

hookworm /ˈhʊkwɜːm/ *n* (**a**) [C] a worm that lives in the intestines (INTESTINE) of humans and animals. (**b**) [U] a disease caused by this.

hooligan /ˈhuːlɪɡən/ *n* a young person who is violent and noisy in public places, usu with a group of such people: *football hooligans* (ie supporters who behave violently during or after a football match). ► **hooliganism** /-ɪzəm/ *n* [U].

hoop /huːp/ *n* **1** a circular band of wood, metal, etc: *a barrel bound with iron hoops.* **2** a large ring used eg at a CIRCUS for riders or animals to jump through or as a child's toy. **3** a small metal arch fixed in the ground or forming the top of a RAILING: *grow lettuces under polythene stretched over wire hoops.* **IDM** **put sb / go through the ˈhoops** to make sb/be made to endure a long, difficult and complicated test: *They really put me through the hoops at the interview.*

[Vnn] = verb + noun + noun   [V-adj] = verb + adjective   For more help with verbs, see Study pages **B4–8**.

▶ **hooped** *adj* in the shape of a hoop: *hooped earrings*.

hoop-la /'hu:p lɑ:/ *n* **1** [U] (*Brit*) a game in which players try to throw rings over objects in order to win them as prizes. **2** [U, sing] (*US infml* = HOO-HA.

hooray /hu'reɪ/ *interj* = HURRAH.

hoot /hu:t/ *n* **1(a)** (*esp Brit*) a loud laugh of delight and amusement: *She broke into hoots of laughter.* (**b**) (usu *sing*) a very amusing thing: *You should have seen her hat — it was an absolute hoot!* **2** a cry expressing disapproval or contempt: *His suggestion was greeted with hoots of derision.* **3** (*Brit*) the sound made by a vehicle's horn, a factory SIREN(1), etc. **4** the cry of an OWL. **IDM** **not care/give a 'hoot / two 'hoots** (*infml*) not to care at all.

▶ **hoot** *v* **1** to laugh loudly, showing approval: [V] *The crowd hooted and cheered.* [Vpr] *He hooted with laughter.* **2** to make noises showing disapproval or contempt: [Vn] *hoot a bad actor* [Vpr] *hoot with derision* [V] *The crowd was hooting and jeering.* [also V.speech]. **3** (*Brit*) to sound the horn of a vehicle: [V, Vn] *The driver hooted (his horn).* [Vpr] *I hooted at the car in front.* **4** to make a hoot or hoots: [V] *the eery sound of an owl hooting.* **PHRV** **,hoot sth/sb 'down** to make noises showing disapproval of what sb is saying: *The proposal was hooted down.* **,hoot sb 'off (sth)** to force sb to leave a place where they are performing, etc by making loud noises showing disapproval: *hoot a speaker off (a platform).* **hooter** *n* **1** (*esp Brit*) a SIREN(1) or whistle, used esp as a signal for work to start or stop at a factory: *The hooter sounded at dawn.* **2** (*dated esp Brit*) a car horn. **3** (*Brit sl*) the nose.

Hoover /'hu:və(r)/ *n* (*propr*) a vacuum cleaner (VACUUM).

▶ **hoover** *v* (*Brit*) to clean a carpet with a vacuum cleaner (VACUUM): [Vn] *hoover the rug/floor/bedroom.*

hooves *pl* of HOOF.

hop¹ /hɒp/ *v* (**-pp-**) **1(a)** (of a person) to move by jumping on one foot: [Vp] *He had hurt his left foot and had to hop along.* [also V, Vpr]. (**b**) (of an animal or a bird) to move by jumping with all or both feet together: [Vp] *A frog was hopping about on the lawn.* [also V, Vpr]. **2** ~ **across/over (to …)** (*infml*) to make a short quick trip to a place: [Vp] *I'm hopping over to Paris for the weekend.* **3** to change from one activity or subject to another: [Vpr] *hop from channel to channel on the TV.* **IDM** **'hop it** (*Brit sl*) to go away: *Go on, hop it!* ○ *When the burglar heard us coming he hopped it out of the window.* **,hopping 'mad** (*infml*) very angry. **PHRV** **,hop 'in / 'into sth**; **,hop 'out / 'out of sth** to move quickly and suddenly into or out of sth, esp a vehicle: *Hop in, I'll give you a lift to the station.* ○ *He hopped out of the car at the traffic lights.* **,hop 'on / 'onto sth**; **,hop 'off (sth)** to get onto or off sth, esp a vehicle, quickly and suddenly: *I hopped onto a bus and arrived ten minutes later.*

▶ **hop** *n* **1** a short jump, esp on one leg. **2** (*infml*) a short flight or one stage in a longer flight: *the long flight across the Atlantic, then the final hop from New York to Boston.* **3** (*dated infml*) an informal dance party. **IDM** **catch sb on the hop** ⇨ CATCH¹.

hop² /hɒp/ *n* (**a**) [C] a climbing plant with flowers growing in bunches. (**b**) **hops** [pl] the dried flowers of this plant, used for giving a bitter flavour to beer.

hope /həʊp/ *n* **1** [C, U] ~ **(of/for sth)**; ~ **(of doing sth / that…)** a belief that sth desired will happen: *Don't raise his hopes too high or he may be very disappointed.* ○ *There is still a ray/glimmer of hope* (ie a slight hope). ○ *He pinned* (ie based) *all his hopes on getting that job.* ○ *All our hopes were dashed/shattered by the announcement. It is our hope that you will find this offer satisfactory.* ○ *She still cherished a forlorn hope*

of seeing him again. ○ *She has high hopes* (ie is very confident) *of winning.* ○ *They have given up all hope of finding any more survivors of the crash.* **2** [C usu *sing*] a person, thing or circumstance that makes hope possible: *You are my last hope — if you can't help, I'm ruined.* ○ *We'll have to wait for someone to rescue us — that's our only hope.* **IDM** **be beyond 'hope** to have passed the point where improvement is possible: *Her condition is now beyond hope of recovery.* **hold out (some, not much, little, no, etc) 'hope (of sth / that…)** to offer some grounds for believing that sth may happen: *The doctors held out no hope of recovery/that she would recover.* **,hope against 'hope (that)…** to continue to hope for sth even though it is very unlikely. **in the hope of sth / that…** because of a wish for sth/that…: *I called in the hope of finding her at home.* **live in hope** ⇨ LIVE². **not have a 'hope (in 'hell) (of doing sth)** (*infml*) to have no chance at all: *She hasn't got a hope (in hell) of winning.* **not a 'hope**; **,some 'hope!** (*infml*) there is no chance at all that sth will happen: *'He might turn up with the cash.' 'Some hope!'*

▶ **hope** *v* ~ **(for sth)** to want sth and to consider it possible: [Vpr] *We haven't heard from him for weeks but we're still hoping for a letter.* [V.to inf] *I hope to announce the winner shortly.* [V] *All we can do now is wait and hope.* [Vadv] *'Will it rain tomorrow?' 'I hope not/so.'* [V.that] *We hope (that) you're well.* **IDM** **hope against hope** ⇨ HOPE *n.* **,hope for the 'best** to hope for a favourable result, esp when there is reason to believe that there will not be one: *I'm just going to answer all the questions I can and hope for the best.*

■ **'hoped-for** *adj* [attrib] wanted and considered possible: *They weren't given the ,hoped-for 'pay rise.*

NOTE Compare the verbs **hope** and **wish**. **Hope** (that) expresses a desire relating to the past, present or future: *I hope you weren't late.* ○ *I hope you're ready.* ○ *We hope you'll be very happy.* **Wish** (that) expresses regret about the past, present or future: *I wish I hadn't eaten so much* (but I did). ○ *I wish I had a lot of money* (but I haven't). ○ *I wish I could go with you* (but I can't).

Hope and **wish** can also be used with an infinitive, in which case the meanings are closer: *She hopes to get a job overseas* means that she would like to and there is a strong possibility that she will. In the sentence: *Many women wish to combine a career and family,* **wish** is a fairly formal way of saying 'would like' or 'want'.

hopeful /'həʊpfl/ *adj* **1** [usu pred] ~ **(of/about sth)**; ~ **(that…)** (of a person) having hope: *be hopeful of/about the outcome* ○ *I feel hopeful that we'll find a suitable house very soon.* **2** (of a thing) causing hope; likely to be favourable or successful; promising: *The latest trade figures are a hopeful sign.* ○ *The future did not seem very hopeful.*

▶ **hopeful** *n* a person who hopes to succeed at sth and may do so: *About 30 young hopefuls turned up for the audition.* **hopefully** *adv* **1** it is to be hoped; let us hope: *Hopefully, we'll arrive before dark.* **2** in a way that indicates a feeling of hope: *'I'm sure we'll find it,' he said hopefully.* **hopefulness** *n* [U].

NOTE There is a group of adverbs and adverbial phrases, (eg **frankly**, **sadly**, **to begin with**), which can be used in two different ways. **1** They can modify the whole sentence: *Frankly, I think you are completely wrong.* ○ *To begin with, these newspaper reports are not true.* ○ *Sadly, Grandfather died a few days after the accident.* **2** They can also modify the verb in the sentence: *He spoke frankly* (ie in a frank way) *about his life in prison.* ○ *I liked it in America to begin with.* ○ *Mozart wrote sadly to his wife that the concert had been a disaster.* Other examples of this

H

[V] = verb used alone　　[Vn] = verb + noun　　[Vp] = verb + particle　　[Vpr] = verb + prepositional phrase

kind of adverb are **generally, hopefully, obviously, personally, really, seriously, thankfully**. Some very careful speakers use **hopefully** only in pattern 2 to modify a verb, but its use in pattern 1 is very common.

hopeless /ˈhəʊpləs/ adj **1** not likely to improve or succeed; causing despair: *a hopeless situation/ struggle/attempt* ○ *It's hopeless trying to convince her.* ○ *Most of the students are making good progress but Jeremy seems a hopeless case.* ○ *He said that his life was a hopeless mess.* **2** feeling or showing no hope: *a sad and hopeless character* ○ *She felt lonely and hopeless.* **3** ~ **(at sth)** (*infml*) (of a person) completely lacking in ability or skill; very bad at sth: *a hopeless cook/teacher* ○ *I'm hopeless at maths.* ► **hopelessly** adv: *be hopelessly confused/outnumbered* ○ *be hopelessly in debt/in love.* **hopelessness** n [U]: *a sense/feeling of hopelessness.*

hopper /ˈhɒpə(r)/ n a structure shaped like a V, used esp for holding grain or coal. It has an opening at its base through which the contents can pass into a mill, FURNACE, etc below.

hopscotch /ˈhɒpskɒtʃ/ n [U] a game in which children HOP¹(1a) into and over squares marked on the ground in order to get a stone thrown into one of these squares.

horde /hɔːd/ n (*sometimes derog*) a very large group, esp of people; a huge crowd: *hordes of tourists/ football supporters/shoppers* ○ *Fans descended on the concert hall in their hordes* (ie in large numbers).

horizon /həˈraɪzn/ n **1 the horizon** [sing] the line at which the earth and sky appear to meet: *The sun sank below the horizon.* ○ *A ship appeared on the horizon.* **2** [C usu *pl*] the limit of a person's knowledge, experience or interest: *She wanted to travel overseas to broaden her horizons.* ○ *The company's horizons are not limited to the UK.* **IDM** **on the horizon** likely to happen soon: *There's trouble on the horizon.*

horizontal /ˌhɒrɪˈzɒntl; US ˌhɔːr-/ adj parallel to the horizon; flat; going across rather than up or down: *a horizontal line.* ⇨ picture at VERTICAL. ► **horizontal** n [C, sing] a horizontal line, surface, etc: *He shifted his position from the horizontal.* **horizontally** /-təli/ adv: *wood stacked horizontally.*

hormone /ˈhɔːməʊn/ n **(a)** a substance produced within the body and carried by the blood to an organ which it stimulates to assist growth, etc; a similar substance produced by a plant and transported in the SAP¹: *hormone deficiency/imbalance.* **(b)** an artificial substance that has a similar effect. ► **hormonal** /hɔːˈməʊnl/ adj: *hormonal changes during pregnancy.*

horn /hɔːn/ n **1(a)** [C] a hard pointed growth(3) usu curved and one of a pair, on the heads of eg cattle or deer. ⇨ picture at SHEEP. **(b)** [U] the hard substance of which this is made: *horn buttons.* **2** [C] any of various musical instruments consisting of a usu curved metal tube that is narrow at the end where one blows into it and wider at the other end: *a ʹhunting horn* ○ *a horn concerto.* See also FRENCH HORN. **3** [C] a device for sounding a warning signal: *The car swerved round the corner, its horn blaring.* See also FOGHORN. ⇨ picture at CAR. **4** [C] a thing resembling an animal's horn, eg the part projecting from the head of a SNAIL. **IDM** **draw in one's horns** ⇨ DRAW¹. **on the horns of a diʹlemma** faced with a choice between things that are equally undesirable. **take the bull by the horns** ⇨ BULL¹. ► **horned** adj having horns: *horned cattle.* **horny** adj **1** made hard and rough, eg by hard work: *horny hands.* **2** (*sl*) sexually excited: *feeling horny.* **3** made of horn(1b). ■ **ʹhorn-rimmed** adj (of spectacles) with frames made of a material like horn.

hornbeam /ˈhɔːnbiːm/ n a type of tree with smooth grey bark and hard tough wood.

hornet /ˈhɔːnɪt/ n a large WASP that can give a severe sting. **IDM** **a ʹhornet's nest** angry argument, criticism, etc involving a lot of people: *His letter to the papers has stirred up/uncovered a real hornet's nest.*

hornpipe /ˈhɔːnpaɪp/ n **(a)** a lively dance, usu performed by one person and traditionally associated with sailors. **(b)** the music for such a dance.

horoscope /ˈhɒrəskəʊp; US ˈhɔːr-/ n a forecast of sb's future based on a chart showing the relative positions of the planets, etc at a particular time, eg the time of their birth: *read the horoscopes in a magazine.* ⇨ note at ZODIAC.

horrendous /hɒˈrendəs; US hɔːˈr-/ adj (*infml*) absolutely terrible; extremely unpleasant and unacceptable: *horrendous queues/prices/problems* ○ *That colour scheme is horrendous.* ► **horrendously** adv: *horrendously expensive.*

horrible /ˈhɒrəbl; US ˈhɔːr-/ adj **1** causing horror: *a horrible crime/nightmare/death.* **2** (*infml*) very unpleasant: *horrible weather/food/people* ○ *It tastes horrible.* ○ *She's horrible (to me)!* ► **horribly** /-əbli/ adv: *She was horribly burnt.* ○ *Things began to go horribly wrong.*

horrid /ˈhɒrɪd; US ˈhɔːrɪd/ adj (*usu infml*) very bad or unpleasant; HORRIBLE: *horrid weather/food/ children* ○ *Don't be so horrid to your little sister.*

horrific /həˈrɪfɪk/ adj causing horror; horrifying (HORRIFY): *a horrific crash/murder* ○ *horrific scenes/ injuries/experiences.* ► **horrifically** /-klɪ/ adv.

horrify /ˈhɒrɪfaɪ; US ˈhɔːr-/ v (*pt, pp* **-fied**) to fill sb with horror; to shock sb greatly: [Vn] *We were horrified by what we saw.* ○ *They watched in horrified silence.*
► **horrifying** adj causing feelings of horror, shock, etc: *a horrifying sight/experience* ○ *I find their ignorance horrifying.* **horrifyingly** adv: *horrifyingly realistic.*

horror /ˈhɒrə(r); US ˈhɔːr-/ n **1** [U] a feeling of intense fear, shock and disgust: *I recoiled in horror from the snake.* ○ *His skin prickled with horror.* ○ *To her horror she saw him fall.* ○ *I have a/this horror of being trapped in a lift.* **2** [U] a feeling of intense dislike; hatred: *I have a deep horror of cruelty.* **3** [U] the extremely unpleasant nature of sth: *the full horror of life in a prison camp.* **4** [C] a thing or person that causes a feeling of horror: *the horrors of war.* **5** [attrib] (of a film, etc) designed to entertain people by causing enjoyable feelings of horror: *horror movies/stories.* **6** [C] (*infml*) a child who behaves very badly: *Her son is a little horror.* **7 the horrors** [pl] (*infml*) a feeling of intense fear or anxiety: *Public speaking gives me the horrors.* **IDM** **ʹhorror of ʹhorrors** (*usu joc or ironic*) (used to describe sth extremely unpleasant or shocking): *I got home only to discover — horror of horrors — that I'd locked myself out.*
► **horrors** interj (*usu joc*) used to express dislike or disgust: *Oh horrors! Not another invitation to one of their awful parties!*
■ **ʹhorror-struck** (also **ʹhorror-stricken**) adj filled with horror; very shocked.

hors de combat /ˌɔː də ˈkɒba/ adj (*French*) unable to take part in an activity or a sport because one is injured: *Willis is hors de combat with a twisted ankle.*

hors-d'oeuvre /ˌɔː ˈdɜːv/ n (*pl* unchanged or **-d'oeuvres** /ˈdɜːv/) small portions of different types of usu cold food served as a course at the beginning of a meal.

horse /hɔːs/ n **1** a large animal with four long legs, a MANE and a tail. Horses are used for riding on, pulling carts, etc: *mount/ride/fall off a horse.* ⇨ picture. See also COLT¹, FILLY, FOAL, GELDING, MARE, STALLION. **2** = VAULTING-HORSE. See also CLOTHES-

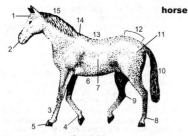

horse

1 forelock
2 muzzle
3 shank
4 pastern
5 hoof
6 belly
7 flank
8 fetlock
9 hock
10 tail
11 hindquarters
12 croup
13 back
14 withers
15 mane

HORSE, DARK HORSE, ROCKING-HORSE, SEA HORSE. **IDM**
back the wrong horse ⇨ BACK⁴. **be/get on one's
high horse** ⇨ HIGH¹. **change horses in midstream** ⇨ CHANGE¹. **a dark horse** ⇨ DARK¹. **eat a
horse** ⇨ EAT. **flog a dead horse** ⇨ FLOG.
(straight) from the horse's 'mouth (of information) given by sb who is directly involved and
therefore likely to be accurate. **hold one's 'horses**
(*infml*) (esp imperative) to wait a moment; to restrain one's enthusiasm: *Hold your horses! We need
to think first.* **lock, etc the stable door after the
horse has bolted** ⇨ STABLE². **look a gift horse in
the mouth** ⇨ GIFT. **put the cart before the
horse** ⇨ CART.
▶ **horse** *v* **PHR V** **horse a'bout/a'round** (*infml*) to
act in a noisy rough playful way.

horse chestnut

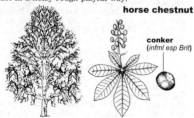

conker
(*infml esp Brit*)

■ **,horse 'chestnut** *n* **1** a large tree with widely
spreading branches and white or pink flowers. ⇨
picture. **2** the dark brown nut of the horse chestnut
tree. ⇨ picture. See also CONKER.
'horse-drawn *adj* (of a vehicle) pulled by a horse or
horses.
'horse-race *n* a race between horses with riders.
'horse-racing *n* [U].
'horse sense *n* [U] (*infml*) basic common sense
(COMMON¹).
'horse-trading *n* [U] clever BARGAINING or business
dealing: *political horse-trading.*
horseback /'hɔːsbæk/ *n* **IDM** **on 'horseback** sitting on a horse: *travel on horseback.*
▶ **horseback** *adv, adj* [attrib] (*esp US*): *ride horseback* ○ *horseback riding.*
horsebox /'hɔːsbɒks/ *n* a vehicle for transporting a
horse or horses.
horseflesh /'hɔːsfleʃ/ *n* [U] **1** the flesh of a horse,
used as food. **2** horses in general: *He's a good judge
of horseflesh.*
horsefly /'hɔːsflaɪ/ *n* a large insect that bites horses,
cattle, etc.
horsehair /'hɔːsheə(r)/ *n* [U] hair from the MANE or
tail of a horse, formerly used esp for stuffing mattresses (MATTRESS).
horseman /'hɔːsmən/ *n* (*pl* **-men** /-mən/; *fem*
'horsewoman /-wʊmən/, *pl* **-women** /-wɪmɪn/) (**a**)
a rider on a horse: *A lone horseman rode by.* (**b**) a

person who can ride a horse: *a good horsewoman.*
▶ **'horsemanship** *n* [U] skill in riding horses.
horseplay /'hɔːspleɪ/ *n* [U] rough noisy play.
horsepower /'hɔːspaʊə(r)/ *n* (*pl* unchanged) (*abbr*
hp) a unit for measuring the power of an engine,
equal to the force needed to pull 550 pounds one foot
per second: *a twelve horsepower engine.*
horseradish /'hɔːsrædɪʃ/ *n* [U] a plant with a hot-tasting root which is used for making a cold sauce:
roast beef with horseradish sauce.
horseshoe (also **shoe**) /'hɔːsʃuː, 'hɔːʃʃuː/ *n* **1** a
piece of iron in the shape of a U attached with nails
to the bottom of a horse's HOOF. A horseshoe is
regarded as a symbol of good luck. **2** anything
shaped like a horseshoe: *a horseshoe bend/desk/
ridge.*
horsewhip /'hɔːswɪp/ *n* a long whip used for driving or training horses.
▶ **horsewhip** *v* (**-pp-**) [Vn] to beat sb with a horsewhip.
horsy (also **horsey**) /'hɔːsi/ *adj* **1** of or like a horse:
He had a long, rather horsy face. **2** interested in or
involved with horses and horse-racing: *She comes
from a very horsy family.*
horticulture /'hɔːtɪkʌltʃə(r)/ *n* [U] the art, study or
practice of growing flowers, fruit and vegetables;
gardening (GARDEN): *commercial horticulture.* ▶ **horticultural** /ˌhɔːtɪ'kʌltʃərəl/ *adj*: *a horticultural
show/society/expert.* **horticulturalist, horticulturist** *n*.
hose¹ /həʊz/ (also **'hose-pipe**) *n* [C, U] a flexible
tube made of rubber, plastic or canvas, used for
directing water onto fires, gardens, etc: *a length of
hose* ○ *a garden hose* ○ *The firemen played their hoses
on* (ie directed them at) *the burning building.* ⇨
picture at HOUSE¹.
▶ **hose** *v* ~ **sth/sb (down)** to wash or water sth/sb
using a hose: [Vn] *hose the flower-beds* [Vnp] *hose
down the car.*
hose² /həʊz/ *n* [pl *v*] **1** (*dated*) (used esp in shops)
TIGHTS, stockings (STOCKING) and socks. **2** a garment
covering the body from the waist to the knees or
feet, formerly worn by men: *doublet and hose.*
hosiery /'həʊziəri; *US* 'həʊʒəri/ *n* [U] (used esp in
shops) = HOSE² 1: *the hosiery department in a store.*
hospice /'hɒspɪs/ *n* a hospital for people who are
dying: *an AIDS hospice.*
hospitable /hɒ'spɪtəbl, 'hɒspɪtəbl/ *adj* **1** ~ (**to/
towards sb**) (of a person) pleased to welcome and
entertain guests: *She is always hospitable to visitors
from abroad.* **2** pleasant to live in or visit: *a hospitable climate/place* ○ *The countryside to the north is
less hospitable.* ▶ **hospitably** /-əbli/ *adv.*
hospital /'hɒspɪtl/ *n* an institution providing medical treatment and care for ill or injured people: *go
to hospital/(US) to the hospital* (ie as a patient) ○ *be
admitted to/be taken to/be released from/be discharged from hospital* ○ *The injured were rushed to
hospital in an ambulance.* ○ *He died in hospital.* ○ *I'm
going to the hospital to visit my brother.* ○ *a hospital
nurse* ○ *receive hospital treatment.* See also COTTAGE
HOSPITAL. ⇨ note at SCHOOL¹.
▶ **hospitalize, -ise** *v* (esp passive) to send or admit
sb to hospital: [Vn] *The most severe cases may have
to be hospitalized.* **hospitalization, -isation**
/ˌhɒspɪtəlaɪ'zeɪʃn; *US* -lə'z-/ *n* [U]: *a long period of
hospitalization.*
hospitality /ˌhɒspɪ'tæləti/ *n* [U] friendly and generous treatment and entertainment of guests or
strangers, esp in one's own home: *Thank you for
your kind hospitality.* ○ *generous acts of hospitality* ○
a hospitality room/suite (ie one reserved for the use
of guests in a hotel, television studio, etc) ○ *the
hospitality industry* (ie hotels, restaurants, etc).
host¹ /həʊst/ *n* ~ **of sb/sth** a large number of people

H

or things: *He has a host of friends.* ○ *a host of other problems* ○ *I can't come, for a whole host of reasons.*

host² /həʊst/ *n* **1(a)** a person who receives and entertains other people as guests, esp in her or his home: *I was away so my son acted as host.* ○ *Mr and Mrs Hill are excellent hosts.* **(b)** a person, a place, a country or an organization that holds an event to which others are invited and makes all the arrangements for them: *the host nation* (eg for an international conference, etc) ○ *Marseille are hosts to Athens in the same competition.* ○ *The college is **playing host to** a group of visiting Russian scientists.* **2** a person who introduces a television or radio programme, a show, etc: *Your host on tonight's show is Max Astor.* **3** (*dated or joc*) a person who manages a pub. **4** an animal or a plant on which another animal or plant lives and feeds: *host organisms.* See also HOSTESS.

▶ **host** *v* to act as host at an event, on a television programme, etc: [Vn] *Which country is hosting the Olympic Games this year?* ○ *Hosting our show this evening is the lovely Gloria Monroe.*

host³ /həʊst/ *n* **the Host** [sing] the bread that is blessed and eaten at COMMUNION(1).

hostage /'hɒstɪdʒ/ *n* a person who is captured and held prisoner by one or more others who threaten to keep, harm or kill her or him unless certain demands are met: *The hijackers kept the pilot as (a) hostage on board the plane.* ○ *Three young children were taken/held hostage during the bank robbery.* **IDM** a **hostage to 'fortune** (*fml*) a person or thing that one acquires and that will cause one suffering if it is lost.

hostel /'hɒstl/ *n* a building in which cheap food and lodging are provided for students, certain groups of workers, people without homes, travellers, etc: *have a shared room in a hostel* ○ *a hostel for homeless families.* See also YOUTH HOSTEL.

hostelry /'hɒstəlri/ *n* (*arch or rhet*) a pub: *Why don't we adjourn to the local hostelry?*

hostess /'həʊstəs, -tes/ *n* **1** a woman who receives and entertains other people as guests, esp in her home. **2** a woman employed to welcome and entertain people at a NIGHTCLUB, provide information at an exhibition, etc: *a poolside hostess* ○ *The hotel has a full-time children's hostess.* **3** = AIR-HOSTESS. **4** a woman who introduces a television or radio programme, a show, etc. See also HOST² 2.

hostile /'hɒstaɪl; US -tl/ *adj* **1** ~ (**to/towards sb/sth**) **(a)** showing strong dislike; aggressive: *a hostile crowd/look/attitude* ○ *get a very hostile reception/response* ○ *She found his manner towards her distinctly hostile.* **(b)** [usu pred] showing strong rejection of sth; aggressively opposed to sth: *be hostile to reform.* **2** belonging to a military enemy: *hostile aircraft.* **3** (*commerce*) (of an offer to buy a company, etc) not welcome or wanted by the company to be bought: *a hostile take-over bid* ○ *the group's hostile £138m bid for a construction company.*

hostility /hɒ'stɪləti/ *n* **1** [U] ~ (**to/towards sb/sth**) aggressive or HOSTILE(1) feelings or behaviour: *feel no hostility towards anyone* ○ *show hostility to sb/sth* ○ *His suggestion met with some hostility.* **2** **hostilities** [pl] acts of war; fighting: *at the outbreak of hostilities* ○ *suspend hostilities* ○ *stop fighting).*

hot /hɒt/ *adj* (**-tter, -ttest**) **1(a)** having a high temperature; producing heat: *a hot day/bath* ○ *hot weather/water* ○ *Cook in a very hot oven.* ○ *This coffee is too hot to drink.* ○ *a hot (ie cooked) meal* ○ *live in a hot country* (ie one which has high average temperatures) ○ *How hot is it on the coast at this time of year?* Compare COLD¹, WARM¹. **(b)** (of a person) feeling heat, esp in an unpleasant way: *I am/feel hot.* ○ *Her cheeks were hot with embarrassment.* **(c)** causing one to feel hot: *Don't you think it's rather hot in here?* ○ *London was hot and dusty.* **2** (of food) con-

taining pepper or spices, and producing a burning sensation when tasted: *a hot curry* ○ *hot chilli/mustard.* Compare MILD. **3** intense and exciting, and involving a lot of activity, argument or strong feelings: *enter the hottest part of the election campaign* ○ *The current debate about privatization is likely to grow hotter in the coming weeks.* ○ *She found the pace too hot* (ie too fast to maintain). **4** (of a situation) difficult or dangerous to deal with and causing one to feel worried or uncomfortable: *When things got too hot the reporters left the area.* ○ *They're making life hot for her.* **5** likely to provoke anger or disapproval, eg because of being too shocking or too critical: *Some of the nude scenes were regarded as too hot for Broadway.* ○ *The report was highly critical of government policy and was considered too hot to publish.* **6** (*sl*) (of goods) stolen and difficult to dispose of because of being well-known and easily recognized: *This painting is too hot to handle.* **7** (*infml*) (of a competitor, performer, etc) very skilful, exciting or impressive: *She's one of the hottest players in the country at the moment.* ○ *They're a hot attraction.* ○ *They'll meet hotter opposition from the Australian team.* **8** (*infml*) new, exciting and in great demand: *a hot fashion accessory* ○ *one of the hottest discos in town.* **9** (of news) fresh, very recent and usu exciting: *a hot tip* ○ *hot gossip* ○ *a story that is hot off the press* (ie has just appeared in the newspapers). **10** (of feelings) very strongly felt; passionate: *have a hot temper* ○ *feel hot stirrings of desire.* **11** (of music, esp JAZZ) having a strong and exciting rhythm. **12** [pred] ~ (**at/on sth**) (*infml*) (used esp after a negative) having great skill, ability or knowledge in sth: *I'm good at history but not so hot at artithmetic.* **13** [pred] ~ **on sth** (*infml*) considering sth very important and keen that it should always happen or be done: *My boss is very hot on punctuality.* **14** [pred] (*infml*) (used esp after a negative) useful, esp for encouraging or promoting sth; good: *All this talking is great for the soul but not so hot for business.* ○ *Her exam results aren't too hot.* **15** [pred] (*infml*) (in children's games, etc) very near the object sought; very close to guessing correctly: *You're getting really hot!* See also COLD¹ 6, WARM¹ 5. **IDM** **be in / get into hot 'water** (*infml*) to be in/get into trouble. **blow hot and cold** ⇨ BLOW¹. **go hot and 'cold** to experience a sudden feeling of intense fear, anxiety or shock: *I went hot and cold when I realized that I'd lost my passport.* **go/sell like hot 'cakes** to sell quickly or in great numbers or quantity: *The new pocket computers are going like hot cakes.* **(all) hot and 'bothered** (*infml*) in a state of anxiety or confusion because of being under too much pressure, having a problem, trying to hurry, etc. **hot on sb's/sth's 'heels** following sb/sth very closely: *David burst in with Mrs Johnson hot on his heels.* ○ *The report follows hot on the heels of the Minister's statement.* **hot on sb's/sth's 'tracks/ 'trail** (*infml*) close to catching or finding the person or thing that one has been pursuing or searching for: *The police were hot on his trail.* **hot under the 'collar** (*infml*) angry or embarrassed: *He got very hot under the collar when I accused him of lying.* **in hot pur'suit (of sb)** trying with great determination to catch sb: *She dashed down the road with reporters in hot pursuit.* **like a cat on hot bricks** ⇨ CAT. **piping hot** ⇨ PIPING. **strike while the iron is hot** ⇨ STRIKE².

▶ **hot** *v* (**-tt-**) **PHRV** **hot 'up** (*Brit infml*) to become more exciting; to increase in activity; to become intense: *With only a week to go before the election things are really hotting up.*

hotly *adv* **1** in a passionate, excited or angry way: *a hotly debated topic* ○ *Recent reports in the press have been hotly denied.* ○ *'Nonsense!' he replied hotly.* **2** closely and with determination: *a hotly contested match* ○ *The pickpocket ran off, hotly pursued by the police.*

[Vnn] = verb + noun + noun   [V-adj] = verb + adjective   For more help with verbs, see Study pages **B4–8**.

H

■ ,hot 'air n [U] (*infml*) empty or excited talk that is intended to impress people.

,hot-'air balloon n = BALLOON 2.

,hot-'blooded adj (of a person) tending to become excited or angry easily; passionate: a ,hot-blooded 'lover.

'hot cake n (*US*) = PANCAKE¹.

,hot cross 'bun n a round cake, usu containing currants (CURRANT), marked with a cross and eaten esp on Good Friday.

'hot dog (*Brit also* ,hot 'dog) n a long hot SAUSAGE served in a soft bread roll, often with onions.

,hot 'favourite n the competitor widely considered most likely to win a race, etc.

,hot 'flush n a sudden sensation of being hot, caused by fear or experienced by women during the MENOPAUSE.

'hot line n **1** a direct and exclusive communication link between heads of government: a hot line to the White House. **2** a telephone link that is specially arranged and used for a particular purpose: The Foreign Office has set up a special hot line for those who fear their relatives were in the area. ○ a horoscope/mortgage hot line.

,hot po'tato n (*infml*) a thing or situation that is difficult or unpleasant to deal with: The racial discrimination issue is a political hot potato.

,hot 'property n [U, C] (*infml*) a person who is in great demand, eg as a performer: She's the hottest property since Madonna.

the 'hot seat n [sing] (*infml*) the position of a person who must take full responsibility, face criticism and justify decisions and actions.

'hot spot n (*infml*) a place where esp political trouble is likely.

,hot 'spring n a stream of naturally hot water flowing from the ground: The water in hot springs is often rich in dissolved minerals.

,hot 'stuff n [U] (*infml*) **1** a person or thing of excellent ability or quality: She's really hot stuff at tennis. **2** a sexually attractive person: She's pretty hot stuff.

,hot-'tempered adj tending to become very angry easily.

,hot-'water bottle n a container, usu made of rubber, that is filled with hot water and put in a bed to warm it. See also RED-HOT.

hotbed /'hɒtbed/ n (usu *sing*) ~ of sth a place where sth evil or undesirable is able to develop easily and freely: a hotbed of vice/intrigue/dissidents.

hotchpotch /'hɒtʃpɒtʃ/ (also *esp US* hodgepodge /'hɒdʒpɒdʒ/) n (usu *sing*) a number of things mixed together in no particular order: a hotchpotch of ideas.

hotel /həʊ'tel/ n a building where rooms and usu meals are provided for people in return for payment: staying at/in a hotel ○ a luxury/five-star hotel ○ She runs a small hotel.
▶ **hotelier** /həʊ'teliə(r), -liei; *US* ,həʊtel'jei/ n a person who owns or manages a hotel.

hotfoot /'hɒtfʊt/ adv in great haste; quickly and eagerly: He raced off with the children hotfoot in pursuit.
▶ **hotfoot** v **IDM** 'hotfoot it (*infml*) to walk or run somewhere quickly and eagerly: We hotfooted it down to the beach.

hothead /'hɒthed/ n a person who often acts too quickly, without thinking of the consequences: political hotheads. ▶ **hotheaded** /,hɒt'hedɪd/ adj: hot-headed youths going on the rampage.

hothouse /'hɒthaʊs/ n a heated building, usu made of glass, used for growing delicate plants in; a GREENHOUSE: hothouse flowers ○ (*fig*) a hothouse of cultural ideas.

hotplate /'hɒtpleɪt/ n a flat heated metal surface on

a COOKER(1), etc used for cooking food or keeping it hot.

hotpot /'hɒtpɒt/ n [C, U] a STEW of meat and vegetables cooked slowly in the oven in a dish with a lid.

hots /hɒts/ n [pl] **IDM** have the 'hots for sb (*sl esp US*) to have a strong sexual desire for sb.

hotshot /'hɒtʃɒt/ n (*infml*) a person who is exceptionally skilful, successful or respected in her or his work: a hotshot young lawyer.

hound /haʊnd/ n a dog used for hunting: The hounds picked up the scent of the fox.
▶ **hound** v to pursue sb constantly, esp in order to obtain sth; to HARASS(1) sb: [Vn] be hounded by reporters/the authorities. **PHRV** hound sb out (of sth/...) to force sb to leave sth/a place, esp by making their life there very difficult: He was hounded out of the area by rival traders.

hour /'aʊə(r)/ n **1** [C] 60 minutes; one of the 24 divisions of a day: The interview lasted half an hour. ○ a three-hour exam paper ○ an hour-long speech ○ an hour's delay ○ My attorney charges $200 an hour. ○ He was driving at about 50 miles an/per hour. ○ Paris is six hours ahead of New York. ➪ App 2. See also THE SMALL HOURS. **2** [C usu *sing*] a period of about an hour, having particular characteristics or set aside for a specified purpose: She took a long lunch hour. See also RUSH HOUR. **3** [C] the distance that can be travelled in an hour: London's only two hours away. **4** **hours** [pl] a period of time for work, use of facilities, etc: hours of business ○ opening hours ○ Office hours are from 9 am to 5 pm. ○ Doctors work long hours. **5** [C] a point in time: Who can be ringing us at this hour? See also ZERO-HOUR. **6** **hours** [pl] (*fml*) (used when calculating time according to the 24-hour clock): It's eighteen hundred hours (ie 6 pm). ○ It's twenty-one thirty hours (ie 9.30 pm). ➪ App 2. **7** [C usu *sing*] (*fml*) a moment or period of time when sth important happens: the country's finest hour ○ She helped me in my hour of need. **8** **hours** [pl] (*infml*) a long time: She spent hours preparing the meal. ○ We waited for hours. **IDM** ,after 'hours after the normal time of business: stay behind after hours to refill the shelves. at/till 'all hours at/till any time, esp when it is not usual, suitable or convenient: She stays out till all hours (ie very late). ○ He telephones me at all hours (of the day and night). at the e,leventh 'hour (*esp Brit*) at the last possible moment; only just in time: The president's visit was called off at the eleventh hour. the early hours ➪ EARLY. keep late, early, regular, etc 'hours to go to bed or go to work late, early, at the same time every day, etc. kill two, etc hours ➪ KILL. on the 'hour at exactly 1 o'clock, 2 o'clock, etc: The bus leaves every hour 'on the hour. ,out of 'hours before or after one's regular work time.
▶ **hourly** /'aʊəli/ adv every hour: Forecasts are updated hourly. — adj **1** done or occurring every hour: an hourly bus service ○ Buses leave at hourly intervals. **2** calculated according to a number of hours: be paid on an hourly basis ○ an hourly rate of $30.

■ 'hour-hand n the small hand on a clock or watch, indicating the hour.

hourglass /'aʊəglɑːs/ n a glass container holding fine sand that takes an hour to pass through the narrow gap from the upper to the lower section. ➪ picture.

hourglass

house¹ /haʊs/ n (*pl* houses /'haʊzɪz/) **1** [C] (**a**) a building for people to live in, usu for one family: He went into/came out of his house. ○ a two-bedroom house ○ Hilltop House ○ What time do you

house

row of terraced houses/terrace
(*US* **row houses**)

1 lintel
2 lamppost
3 knocker
4 doorbell
5 door
6 doorstep
7 drainpipe
8 drain
9 letter-box (*US* mailbox)
10 sash-window
11 window-sill
12 brick
13 slate
14 window-pane

semi-detached houses
(*US* **duplex**)

1 skylight
2 roof
3 pane
4 wall
5 porch
6 hanging basket
7 path (*US* front walk)
8 fence
9 bay window
10 garden gate
   (*esp US* front gate)
11 casement window

detached house
(*US* **house**)

1 chimney
2 chimney-pot
3 eaves
4 gable
5 garage
6 drive
7 border
8 hose
9 sprinkler
10 lawn
11 rockery
12 trellis
13 hedge
14 picture window
15 climber
16 gutter
17 dormer window

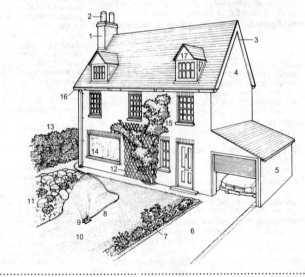

[V.*to* inf] = verb + *to* infinitive   [Vn.inf (no *to*)] = verb + noun + infinitive without *to*   [V.*ing*] = verb + *-ing* form

bungalow
(*US* ranch house)

1 cowl
2 aerial (*US* antenna)
3 conservatory
4 French window
   (*US also* French door)
5 parasol
6 clothes-line
7 crazy paving
8 deck-chair
9 vegetable garden
10 garden shed
   (*also* tool-shed)
11 back door
12 tiles

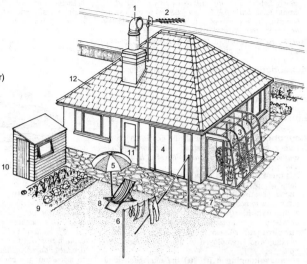

H

leave the house in the morning (ie to go to work)? ⇨ picture. (**b**) (usu *sing*) the people living in such a building; the household: *Be quiet or you'll wake the whole house!* See also COUNTRY HOUSE, MANOR HOUSE. **2** [C] (in compounds) a building made or used for some special purpose, eg for keeping animals or goods in: *a* '*hen-house* ○ *an* '*opera-house.* See also ACID HOUSE, BOARDING-HOUSE, COURT-HOUSE, DOG-HOUSE, DOLL'S HOUSE, GUEST-HOUSE, OPEN HOUSE, PUBLIC HOUSE, SUMMER-HOUSE, TIED HOUSE, WENDY HOUSE. **3** [C] (in compounds) (**a**) a restaurant: *a steak-house* ○ *a coffee-house* ○ *a bottle of house wine* (ie the cheapest wine available in a particular restaurant, not usu listed by name). (**b**) a business firm: *a fashion house* ○ *a banking house* ○ *a publishing house.* See also CLEARING-HOUSE, FINANCE HOUSE. **4** (often **House**) [C] a group of people who meet to discuss or pass laws or govern a country: *the* ˌ*House of* '*Commons* ○ *the upper house of the Japanese parliament.* **5** **the House** [sing] (*infml*) (**a**) (*Brit*) the House of Commons or the House of Lords: *enter the House* (ie become an MP). (**b**) (*US*) the House of Representatives. See also THE WHITE HOUSE. **6** a group of people discussing sth in a formal debate: *I urge the house to vote against the motion.* **7** [C] the audience in a theatre, concert hall, etc: *play to packed* (ie full) *houses* ○ *The house was transfixed.* See also FULL HOUSE, HALFWAY HOUSE. **8** [C] (*Brit*) each of several organized groups of pupils of different ages in schools, esp public schools (PUBLIC). The members of a group may live in the same building, compete against the other groups at sports, etc. **9** (usu **the House of sb/sth**) [C] an old and famous family: *the House of Windsor* (ie the British royal family). **ɪᴅᴍ** **bring the** '**house down** to make an audience laugh or CLAP¹(1b) very enthusiastically. **eat sb out of house and home** ⇨ EAT. **get on like a** '**house on fire** (*infml*) (of people) to become friends quickly and enjoy a very friendly relationship. **keep** '**house** to cook, clean and do all the other jobs around a house. **move house** ⇨ MOVE¹. **on the** '**house** paid for by the pub, firm, etc; free: *have a drink on the house.* **people in glass houses shouldn't throw stones** ⇨ PEOPLE. **put/set one's** '**house in order** to organize one's own affairs efficiently, esp before one tries to tell other people how to organize their affairs. **safe as houses** ⇨ SAFE¹. **set up** '**house** to make a place one's home.

▶ '**houseful** /-fʊl/ *n* [sing] as much or many as a house can contain: *have a houseful of guests.*

■ '**house arrest** *n* [U] the state of being a prisoner in one's own house, not in prison: *be (kept) under house arrest.*

'**house-husband** *n* a man who performs the duties around the house traditionally carried out by a woman.

the ˌ**House of** '**Commons** (also **the** '**Commons**) *n* (**a**) [Gp] the assembly of elected representatives of the British or the Canadian parliament. (**b**) [sing] the building where they meet. Compare THE HOUSE OF LORDS.

ˌ**House of** '**God** *n* (*pl* **Houses of God**) (also **House of Worship**) (*fml*) (usu *sing*) a church or CHAPEL.

the ˌ**House of** '**Lords** (also **the** '**Lords**) *n* (**a**) [Gp] the assembly of bishops and members of the NOBILITY in the British parliament. (**b**) [sing] the building where they meet. Compare THE HOUSE OF COMMONS.

the ˌ**House of** ˌ**Repre**'**sentatives** *n* [sing] the assembly of elected representatives in the central government of the USA, Australia and New Zealand. Compare CONGRESS 2, SENATE 1.

'**house party** *n* a party held at a house in the country where guests stay for a few days.

'**house-plant** *n* a plant that is grown indoors.

'**house-proud** *adj* giving great attention to the care and appearance of one's home.

the ˌ**Houses of** '**Parliament** *n* [pl] the group of buildings in London where the House of Commons and the House of Lords meet.

'**house-sit** *v* (-tt-) (*esp US*) to live in a house without paying rent, sometimes in return for payment, while the owner is away: [V] *A friend of mine needs someone to house-sit and feed her cats.* ▶ '**house-sitter** *n*.

■ ˌ**house-to-**'**house** *adj* [attrib] calling at each house in turn: *The police are making house-to-house enquiries.*

'**house-trained** (*Brit*) (*US* **housebroken**) *adj* (of pet cats or dogs) trained not to DEFECATE and urinate (URINE) inside the house.

'**house-warming** *n* a party given to celebrate moving into a new home.

house² /haʊz/ *v* **1** to provide a house or building for sb to live in or for sth to be kept in: [Vn] *The council should house homeless people.* ○ *adequately/*

[V.speech] = verb + direct speech   [V.*that*] = verb + *that* clause   [V.*wh*] = verb + *who, how*, etc clause

poorly housed ○ *an agricultural museum housed in an old farm building.* **2** (usu passive) to enclose or contain sth, esp in order to protect it: [Vn] *books housed in glass-fronted cases.*

houseboat /ˈhaʊsbəʊt/ *n* a boat that is equipped as a place to live in and usu kept at a particular place on a river.

housebound /ˈhaʊsbaʊnd/ *adj* unable to leave one's house, eg because of illness: *She's 86 and completely housebound.*

housebreaking /ˈhaʊsbreɪkɪŋ/ *n* [U] entering a building by force in order to commit a crime.

housebroken /ˈhaʊsbrəʊkn/ *adj* (*US*) = HOUSE-TRAINED.

household /ˈhaʊshəʊld/ *n* all the people living together in a house: *household bills/chores/goods/appliances* ○ *run a large household* ○ *Most households now own a television set.*

■ **ˌhousehold ˈname** (also **ˌhousehold ˈword**) *n* a name of a person or thing that has become very well known because it is so often used: *a television personality who has become a household name.*

▶ **ˈhouseholder** *n* /-həʊldə(r)/ a person who rents or who owns and occupies a house.

housekeeper /ˈhaʊskiːpə(r)/ *n* a person, esp a woman, who is employed to shop, cook, clean the house, etc.

▶ **ˈhousekeeping** *n* [U] (**a**) the management of household affairs. (**b**) money allowed for this: *save some money out of the housekeeping.*

housemaid /ˈhaʊsmeɪd/ *n* a woman servant in a large house who cleans rooms, etc. She usu lives in the house. Compare CLEANER 1.

houseman /ˈhaʊsmən/ *n* (*pl* **-men** /-mən/) (*Brit*) (*US* **intern** /ˈɪntɜːn/) a doctor with relatively low status at a hospital.

housemaster /ˈhaʊsmɑːstə(r)/ *n* (*esp Brit*) a male teacher in charge of a house¹(8).

houseroom /ˈhaʊsruːm, -rʊm/ *n* **IDM** **not give, etc sb/sth ˈhouseroom** (*derog*) not to want to have sb/sth in one's house: *I wouldn't give that table houseroom.*

housetops /ˈhaʊstɒps/ *n* **IDM** **proclaim, shout, etc sth from the ˈhousetops** to announce sth publicly so that many people know about it.

housewife /ˈhaʊswaɪf/ *n* (*pl* **-wives** /-waɪvz/) a woman whose main occupation is looking after her family, cleaning the house, etc, and who does not have regular paid work outside the home. Compare HOUSE-HUSBAND.

housework /ˈhaʊswɜːk/ *n* [U] work done in a house, eg cleaning and cooking: *do the housework.*

housing /ˈhaʊzɪŋ/ *n* **1** [U] (**a**) houses, flats, etc; accommodation: *poor housing conditions* ○ *the housing shortage* ○ *The council must improve substandard housing.* (**b**) providing accommodation for people: *the council's housing policy.* **2** [C] a hard cover that protects machinery, etc: *a car's rear axle housing.*

■ **ˈhousing association** *n* a society formed by a group of people to provide housing at a low cost and without making a profit.

ˈhousing benefit *n* [U] (in Britain) money given to certain people by local councils to help them pay for their accommodation: *apply for housing benefit.*

ˈhousing estate (*Brit*) (also *esp US* **ˈhousing development**) *n* an area in which a number of houses for living in are planned and built at the same time: *live on a housing estate.*

hove ⇨ HEAVE.

hovel /ˈhɒvl; *US* ˈhʌvl/ *n* (*derog*) a small house that is not fit to live in, esp because it is dirty, damp, etc.

hover /ˈhɒvə(r); *US* ˈhʌvər/ *v* **1** (of birds, etc) to remain in the air in one place: [Vpr] *a hawk hovering above/over its prey* [Vadv] *There was a helicopter*

hovering overhead. [also V, Vp]. **2** (of a person) to wait in a shy and uncertain manner: [Vpr] *I can't work with you hovering over me like that.* [Vp] *He hovered about outside, too afraid to go in.* [also V]. **3** to remain near sth or in an uncertain state: [Vpr] *hovering between life and death* ○ *a country hovering on the brink of war* [also V].

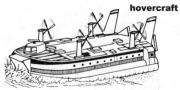
hovercraft

hovercraft /ˈhɒvəkrɑːft; *US* ˈhʌvərkræft/ *n* (*pl* unchanged) a vehicle that can move over land or water supported on a cushion of air made by jet engines. ⇨ picture.

how /haʊ/ *interrog adv* **1** in what way or manner: *How do you spell your name?* ○ *Can you show me how to use this machine?* ○ *How do you get to the town centre from here?* ○ *I don't know how I'm ever going to explain this!* **2** (used to ask about sb's health): *How are the children?* ○ *How are you feeling now?* **3** (used to ask about the condition of sth): *How was your holiday?* ○ *How is your job?* **4** (used before an *adj* or *adv* to ask about the extent, degree, age, etc of sth/sb): *How old is she?* ○ *How long did you wait?* ○ *How often do you go swimming?* ○ *How many people will be there?* ○ *How much does it cost?* ○ *I didn't know how much luggage to bring.* **5** (used to express surprise, shock, thanks, pleasure, etc): *Look how dirty that child is!* ○ *How kind of you to help!* ○ *How pale she looks!* **IDM** **ˌand ˈhow!** (*infml*) (used to agree strongly and sometimes with IRONY): *'Did you get lost?' 'And how!'* **ˌhow's ˈthat?** **1** what is the explanation for that?: *'I left work early today.' 'How's that (ie why)?'* **2** (used when asking sb's opinion of sth): *I'll tuck your sheets in for you. How's that? Comfortable?* ○ *Two o'clock on the dot! How's that for punctuality?*

▶ **how** *conj* (*infml*) (**a**) the way in which: *She described how he had run up to her and grabbed her bag.* (**b**) in any way in which: *I'll dress how I like in my own house!*

however /haʊˈevə(r)/ *adv* **1** (used before an *adj* or *adv*) to whatever extent or degree: *You won't move that stone, however strong you are.* ○ *She leaves her bedroom window open, however cold it is.* ○ *However short the journey is, you always get something to eat on this airline.* **2** (used to comment on a previously stated fact) although sth is, was or may be true; nevertheless: *She felt ill. She went to work, however, and tried to concentrate.* ○ *His first response was to say no. Later, however, he changed his mind.* ○ *I thought those figures were correct. However, I have now discovered they were not.* ⇨ note at ALTHOUGH.

▶ **however** *conj* in any way; regardless of how: *You can dress however you like.* ○ *However I approached the problem, I couldn't find a solution.*

however *interrog adv* (expressing surprise) in what way; by what means: *However did you get here without a car?* ○ *However does he manage to write music when he is so deaf?*

howitzer /ˈhaʊɪtsə(r)/ *n* a short gun for firing shells (SHELL 4a) at a high angle and at short range.

howl /haʊl/ *n* (**a**) the long loud cry of a dog, WOLF, etc: *a mournful howl.* (**b**) the loud cry of a person expressing pain, anger, amusement, etc: *let out a howl of laughter/agony/rage* ○ (*fig*) *The proposed changes caused howls of protest from the public.* (**c**) a long loud noise made eg by a strong wind: *the howl of the wind through the trees.*

▶ **howl** *v* **1** to make a howl: [Vpr] *howl with laughter/pain* ○ *The wind howled around the house.* [V] *wolves howling in the forest* ○ *a howling gale.* **2** to cry loudly: [V] *She was howling inconsolably.* **3** to say sth loudly and angrily: [V.speech] '*I hate you all!' she howled.* [Vn] *The crowd howled its displeasure.* **PHR V** **howl sb down** (of an audience, etc) to prevent a speaker from being heard by shouting angrily.

howler /ˈhaʊlə(r)/ *n* (*dated infml*) a foolish and obvious mistake, esp in the use of words: *make a real howler* ○ *The report is full of howlers.*

howling /ˈhaʊlɪŋ/ *adj* [attrib] (*infml*) very great; extreme: *a howling success* ○ *Shut the door — there's a howling draught in here!*

hp (also **HP**) /ˌeɪtʃ ˈpiː/ *abbr* **1** (*Brit*) hire purchase: *buy a new television on (the) hp.* **2** horsepower (of an engine).

HQ /ˌeɪtʃ ˈkjuː/ *abbr* headquarters: *See you back at HQ.* ○ *police HQ.*

hr *abbr* (*pl* **hrs**) hour: *Cover and chill for 1 hr.* ○ *The train leaves at 15.00 hrs.* Compare MIN 2.

HRH /ˌeɪtʃ ɑːr ˈeɪtʃ/ *abbr* Her/His Royal Highness: *HRH the Duke of Edinburgh.*

hub /hʌb/ *n* **1** the central part of a wheel. ➪ picture at BICYCLE. **2** (usu *sing*) the central point of activity, interest or importance: *the financial hub of the city* ○ *be at the hub of things* (ie where important things happen).

■ ˈ**hub-cap** *n* the round metal cover over the hub of a vehicle's wheel. ➪ picture at CAR.

hubbub /ˈhʌbʌb/ *n* [sing, U] **(a)** a loud confused noise, eg of many voices: *It was difficult to hear what he was saying over the hubbub.* **(b)** a busy situation, with a lot of noise and movement: *the day-to-day hubbub of city life.*

hubby /ˈhʌbi/ *n* (usu *sing*) (*infml*) one's husband.

hubris /ˈhjuːbrɪs/ *n* [U] (*fml*) excessive pride.

huckster /ˈhʌkstə(r)/ *n* **1** (*US*) a person who uses aggressive methods to sell things, esp one working in advertising. **2** (*dated*) a person who sells things in the streets or by going from house to house.

huddle /ˈhʌdl/ *v* to crowd together, esp in a small space and often because of cold or fear: [Vp] *sheep huddling together for warmth* [Vpr, Vnpr] *They huddled in the tent, waiting for the rain to stop.* **PHR V** ~ **up (against/to sb/sth)** to curl one's body up into a small space: *Tom was cold so he huddled up against the radiator.*

▶ **huddle** *n* a small number of people or things close together: *People standing in small huddles, sheltering from the rain.* ○ *Their clothes lay in a huddle on the floor.* **IDM** **go into a** ˈ**huddle (with sb)** (*infml*) to get close to sb, esp to talk about sth private or secret.

huddled *adj* **1** ~ **(up)** with one's body curled into a small space because of cold, fear, etc: *huddled figures in shop doorways.* **2** in an untidy group or heap: *Dirty clothes lay huddled in a corner on the floor.*

hue¹ /hjuː/ *n* (*fml*) a colour; a variety or shade of colour: *birds of many different hues* ○ *His face took on an unhealthy whitish hue.* ○ (*fig*) *politicians of every hue* (ie of every type of political belief).

hue² /hjuː/ *n* **IDM** ˌ**hue and** ˈ**cry** a general alarm or loud public protest: *Opposition politicians raised a great hue and cry when the government's plans were announced.*

huff¹ /hʌf/ *v* [V] to blow; to PUFF²(1). **IDM** ˌ**huff and** ˈ**puff** **1** to breathe heavily because one is exhausted: *When I got to the top I was huffing and puffing.* **2** to show one's annoyance in an obvious or threatening way without actually achieving anything: *After much huffing and puffing she finally agreed to help.*

huff² /hʌf/ *n* (usu *sing*) a short period of bad temper

or annoyance: *Don't talk to Michael — he's **in a bit of a huff**.* ○ *She went off/walked out in a huff.*

▶ **huffy** *adj* **(a)** in a bad temper. **(b)** easily offended: *She gets all huffy if you mention his name.* **huffily** *adv.*

hug /hʌɡ/ *v* (-**gg**-) **1** to put one's arms round sb/sth tightly, esp to show love: [Vn] *They hugged each other closely.* [Vnpr] *I hugged the books to my chest.* [also V]. **2** ~ **oneself** to feel pleased with oneself: [Vn] *She hugged herself with secret joy.* **3** (of a ship, car, etc) to keep close to sth: [Vn] *hug the shore/kerb* ○ *tyres that help a vehicle to hug the road.* **4** to fit tightly round sth: [Vn] *a figure-hugging dress.*

▶ **hug** *n* an act of hugging (HUG), esp to show love: *farewell hugs and kisses* ○ *She gave her mother an affectionate hug.* See also BEAR-HUG.

huge /hjuːdʒ/ *adj* very large in size or amount: *a huge crowd* ○ *have a huge appetite* ○ *huge debts/profits* ○ *Canada is a huge country.* ○ *He won by a huge majority.*

▶ **hugely** *adv* extremely; very much: *be hugely impressive/expensive/popular/successful* ○ *We all enjoyed the joke hugely.*

huh /hʌ/ *interj* (used to express anger, disapproval, surprise, etc, to ask a question, or to indicate that one has not heard what sb has said): *So you won't be coming tonight, huh?* ○ *You think you know the answer, huh?*

hulk /hʌlk/ *n* **1** an old ship which is no longer in use: *rotting hulks on the beach.* **2(a)** a very large and often careless person: *a great hulk of a man.* **(b)** a very large and often threatening object: *the empty hulk of the burnt out mill.*

▶ **hulking** *adj* [attrib] (*infml*) (of a person or thing) very big or heavy: *My dear little son is now a hulking teenager.*

hull¹ /hʌl/ *n* the body of a ship: *a fully-loaded tanker with its hull low in the water.* ➪ picture at CATAMARAN, YACHT.

hull² /hʌl/ *v* [Vn] to remove the outer covering of peas, beans, etc or the ring of leaves attached to strawberries (STRAWBERRY).

hullabaloo /ˌhʌləbəˈluː/ *n* (*pl* **-oos**) (usu *sing*) a continuous loud noise, esp of people shouting: *make a terrible hullabaloo* ○ *What's all this hullabaloo?*

hullo = HALLO.

hum /hʌm/ *v* (-**mm**-) **1** ~ (**sth**) (**to sb**) to sing a tune with one's lips closed: [V, Vp, Vpr] *She was humming (away) (to herself).* [Vn, Vnpr] *I don't know the words of the song but I can hum it (to you).* **2** [V] to make a low steady continuous sound like that made by bees. **3** (*infml*) to be in a state of great activity: [V, Vpr] *The whole place was humming (with excitement) when we arrived.* **IDM** ˌ**hum and** ˈ**ha/**ˈ**haw** (*Brit*); (*US*) ˌ**hem and** ˈ**haw** (*infml*) to take a long time to make a decision; to hesitate: *We hummed and hawed for ages before deciding to buy the house.*

▶ **hum** *n* (usu *sing*) a low steady continuous sound: *the murmur of bees/of distant traffic/of machines* ○ *the soft hum of conversation in the next room.*

hum *interj* (used to show that sb is hesitating or considering sth): '*Let's have a look at you. Hum, not bad, considering your age.*'

human /ˈhjuːmən/ *adj* **1** of or characteristic of people, contrasted with God, animals or machines: *a human skull* ○ *human anatomy/activity/behaviour/ happiness* ○ *a terrible loss of human life* ○ *This food is not fit for human consumption.* ○ *We must allow for* ***human error.*** ○ *I do make mistakes occasionally — I'm only human!* ➪ picture. **2** (*approv*) kind; good; having or showing the better qualities of people: *She'll understand and forgive you; she's really quite human.* **IDM** **the milk of human kindness** ➪ MILK¹.

▶ **human** *n* = HUMAN BEING: *Dogs can hear much better than humans.*

the human body

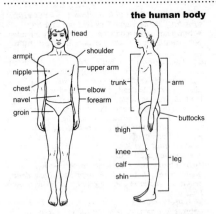

head
shoulder
armpit
upper arm
nipple
trunk
arm
chest
elbow
navel
forearm
groin
buttocks
thigh
knee
leg
calf
shin

humankind /ˌhjuːmənˈkaɪnd/ *n* [U] (*fml*) = MAN-
KIND. ➪ note at GENDER.

humanly *adj* by human means; within human ability: *The doctors did all that was **humanly possible**.*
■ **ˌhuman ˈbeing** *n* a man, woman or child; a
person.

ˌhuman ˈinterest *n* [U] the aspect of a story in a
newspaper, etc that interests people because it describes the experiences, feelings, etc of individuals:
*a personal interview with the victim to provide hu-
man interest.*

ˌhuman ˈnature *n* [U] the general characteristics
and feelings shared by all people: *You can't change
human nature.*

the ˌhuman ˈrace *n* [sing] people; MANKIND. ➪ note
at GENDER.

ˌhuman ˈrights *n* [pl] rights which it is generally
thought that every living person should have, eg the
right to freedom, justice, etc: *campaign for human
rights* ○ *the violation of human rights.*

humane /hjuːˈmeɪn/ *adj* having or showing
sympathy, kindness and understanding: *a humane
prison system* ○ *The refugees all receive fair and
humane treatment.* ○ *The animals must be reared in
humane conditions.* (**b**) causing as little pain as
possible: *the humane killing of animals.* ► **hu-
manely** *adv.*

humanism /ˈhjuːmənɪzəm/ *n* [U] a system of beliefs
that concentrates on common human needs and
seeks ways of solving human problems based on
reason rather than on faith in God.
► **humanist** /ˈhjuːmənɪst/ *n, adj* (a supporter) of
humanism: *a humanist approach.*
humanistic /ˌhjuːməˈnɪstɪk/ *adj: humanistic ideals.*

humanitarian /hjuːˌmænɪˈteəriən/ *adj* **1** concerned with or directed towards improving the lives
of people and reducing suffering: *provide humanitarian aid for the refugees* ○ *Since he is old and sick,
doctors say he should be released from prison on
humanitarian grounds.*
► **humanitarian** *n* a humanitarian person.
humanitarianism /-ɪzəm/ *n* [U].

humanity /hjuːˈmænəti/ *n* **1** [U] human beings
thought of as a group; the human race; people:
crimes against humanity. ➪ note at GENDER. **2** [U]
human nature; the quality of being human: *the humanity of Jesus.* **3** [U] the quality of being HUMANE:
*treat people and animals with warmth and human-
ity.* **4** **the humanities** [pl] the subjects of study
concerned with human culture, esp literature, language, history and philosophy.

humanize, -ise /ˈhjuːmənaɪz/ *v* [Vn] **1** to make sb
HUMANE: *the humanizing and moral effects of reading
great literature.* **2** to make sth more pleasant or

suitable for people: *humanizing prisons and public
hospitals.*

humanoid /ˈhjuːmənɔɪd/ *adj* looking like a human
being. ► **humanoid** *n.*

humble /ˈhʌmbl/ *adj* (**-r** /-blə(r)/, **-st** /-blɪst/) **1**
having or showing a low or modest opinion of one's
own importance; not proud: *Be humble enough to
learn from your mistakes.* ○ *my humble tribute to this
great man.* **2** low in rank; unimportant: *men of
humble birth/origin* ○ *a humble occupation* ○ *It affects all policemen, from the humblest traffic cop to
the head of a serious crime squad.* **3** (of a thing) not
large or elaborate; poor: *It has grown from humble
beginnings to become a multi-national company.* ○
*The humble potato is one of nature's most precious
gifts.* **IDM** **eat humble pie** ➪ EAT.
► **humble** *v* **1** to make sb/sth humble; to lower the
rank or status of sb/sth: [Vn] *a humbling experience*
○ *His resentful colleagues long to see him humbled.* **2**
(*esp sport*) (esp passive) to defeat another team,
competitor, etc: [Vn] *The champion was humbled by
a little-known outsider.* See also HUMILITY.
humbly /ˈhʌmbli/ *adv: live humbly* ○ *be humbly
born* ○ *'Sorry,' she said humbly.*

humbug /ˈhʌmbʌɡ/ *n* **1** [U] dishonest behaviour or
talk that is intended to deceive people and win their
support or sympathy: *political humbug.* **2** [C] (*Brit*)
a hard boiled sweet, usu flavoured with PEPPERMINT.

humdinger /ˌhʌmˈdɪŋə(r)/ *n* (*sl*) an excellent or
remarkable person or thing: *It's a real humdinger of
a film.*

humdrum /ˈhʌmdrʌm/ *adj* lacking excitement or
variety; dull: *the humdrum business of making
money* ○ *escape from their otherwise humdrum lives.*

humerus /ˈhjuːmərəs/ *n* (*pl* **humeri** /ˈhjuːməraɪ/)
(*anatomy*) a bone in the upper arm in humans, from
the shoulder to the elbow. ➪ picture at SKELETON.

humid /ˈhjuːmɪd/ *adj* (of the air or climate) warm
and damp: *the heavy, humid atmosphere of the Jordan valley* ○ *a hot and humid Sunday afternoon.*
► **humidifier** /hjuːˈmɪdɪfaɪə(r)/ *n* a device for keeping the air in a room, etc damp.
humidity /hjuːˈmɪdəti/ *n* [U] (**a**) the amount of
MOISTURE, esp in the air; dampness: *the low humidity
in Arizona* ○ *75 per cent humidity.* (**b**) a lot of moisture in the air: *plants that need heat and humidity.*

humiliate /hjuːˈmɪlieɪt/ *v* to make sb feel ashamed
or foolish; to injure the dignity or pride of sb: [Vn]
We didn't just win, we humiliated them! ○ *The party
was publicly humiliated in October's elections.* ○ *She
had been disappointed, hurt, even humiliated.* ► **humiliating** *adj: a deeply humiliating defeat* ○ *He faced
the humiliating possibility of his own forces disobey-
ing his orders.* **humiliation** /hjuːˌmɪliˈeɪʃn/ *n* [U, C]:
*She suffered the humiliation of having to admit she
had been wrong.* ○ *the team's final humiliation at the
hands of the Australians.*

humility /hjuːˈmɪləti/ *n* [U] a modest or low opinion
of one's own importance; modesty (MODEST 2): *true/
mock humility* ○ *His greatest quality was his humility.*

hummingbird /ˈhʌmɪŋbɜːd/ *n* a small tropical bird
that can stay in one place in the air by beating its
wings very fast, making a humming (HUM 2) sound.

hummock /ˈhʌmək/ (*US* also **hammock**) *n* a low
hill or HUMP(1) in the ground.

humorist /ˈhjuːmərɪst/ *n* a person who is known for
her or his humorous writing or talk.

humorous /ˈhjuːmərəs/ *adj* having or showing a
sense of humour; amusing; funny: *a humorous
writer/remark/touch* ○ *The day started on a humorous note.* ► **humorously** *adv: her humorously
critical outlook on life.*

humour (*US* **humor**) /ˈhjuːmə(r)/ *n* **1** [U] the quality

H

of being amusing or comic: *a story full of gentle humour* ○ *recognize the humour of a situation.* **2** [U] the ability to appreciate things, situations or people that are comic; the ability to be amused: *He has a good **sense of humour**.* ○ *a show marked by the author's own peculiar brand of humour.* **3** [U, sing] (*fml*) a person's state of mind; a mood: *be in an excellent humour* ○ *with great good humour.*

▶ **humour** (*US* **humor**) *v* to keep sb happy or CONTENT¹ by accepting or agreeing to their wishes, even if they seem unreasonable: [Vn] *It's always best to humour him when he's in one of his bad moods.*
-humoured (*US* **-humored**) (forming compound *adjs*) having or showing the specified mood: *good-humoured* ○ *ill-humoured.*
humourless (*US* **humorless**) *adj* lacking a sense of humour: *a humourless person/style.*

hump /hʌmp/ *n* **1** a round raised pile of earth, etc: *the dark hump of the mountain in the distance* ○ *a dangerous hump in the road.* **2(a)** a round projecting part on the back of a CAMEL(1) and some other creatures: *a hump-backed whale.* ⇨ picture at DROMEDARY. **(b)** a large round lump on a person's back, where the SPINE(1) is abnormally curved. **IDM** **over the 'hump** past the most difficult part of a task, etc.
▶ **hump** *v* **1** (*Brit*) to carry sth heavy: [Vnp] *I've been humping furniture around all day.* [also Vn, Vnpr]. ⇨ note at CARRY. **2** [Vn] (△ *sl*) to have sex with sb. **humped** *adj* having a hump or the shape of a hump: *a humped back.*

humpback bridge /ˌhʌmpbæk ˈbrɪdʒ/ *n* a small bridge with an arch that rises and falls steeply.

humus /ˈhjuːməs/ *n* [U] rich dark material formed by the decay of dead leaves, etc that makes the soil more FERTILE(1).

hunch /hʌntʃ/ *n* an idea based on a strong feeling that one has and not on evidence: *play/follow/back one's hunches* ○ *'How did you know that she was lying?' 'It was just/I just had a hunch.'* ○ *My hunch is that he's already left the country.*
▶ **hunch** *v* to bend the top part of one's body forward and raise one's shoulders and back: [Vn] *He hunched his shoulders* and thrust his hands deep into his pockets. [Vpr, Vp] *She hunched (forward) over the book, reading intently.* [also Vnp].
hunched *adj* ~ **(forward/over/up)**: *a hunched figure* ○ *hunched over a plate of food* ○ *She sat hunched (up) in a corner.*

hunchback /ˈhʌntʃbæk/ *n* a person who has a HUMP(2b) on her or his back.

hundred /ˈhʌndrəd/ *n, pron, det* (*pl* unchanged or **hundreds**) **1** (after *a* or *one*, a number or an indication of quantity) the number 100: *one/two/three hundred and eighty pounds* ○ *several/a few hundred* ○ *There were about a/one hundred people in the room.* ○ *I could give you a hundred reasons for not going.* ○ *This vase is worth several hundred dollars.* ○ *If I've said it once, I've said it a hundred times.* ○ *He's a hundred (years old) today.* **2 hundreds** [pl] (*infml*) a large amount: *for hundreds of years* ○ *hundreds of miles away* ○ *Her coat cost hundreds of pounds.* ○ *There are hundreds (of people)* (ie very many) *who need new housing.* ○ *Men died in their hundreds.* ⇨ App 2.
▶ **hundred-** (in compounds) having one hundred of the thing specified: *a hundred-year lease.*
hundredth /ˈhʌndrədθ, -ətθ/ *n, pron, det* 100th: *a/one hundredth of a second* ○ *her hundredth birthday.*

hundredweight /ˈhʌndrədweɪt/ *n* (*pl* unchanged) (*abbr* **cwt**) one 20th of one ton; 112 lb (in the USA, 100 lb). ⇨ App 2.

hung 1 *pt, pp* of HANG¹. **2** *adj* (of a parliament, JURY, etc) not able to reach a decision because of opinions being evenly divided.

■ **ˌhung-'over** *adj* [pred] (*infml*) having a HANGOVER (1): *I feel a bit hung-over this morning.*

hunger /ˈhʌŋgə(r)/ *n* **1** [U] **(a)** the state of not having enough to eat; lack of food: *He died of cold and hunger.* **(b)** the desire for food: *feel pangs of hunger* ○ *satisfy one's hunger.* **2** [sing] ~ **(for sth)** (*fml*) a strong desire for sth: *have an insatiable hunger for adventure.*
▶ **hunger** *v* **PHRV** **'hunger for/after sth/sb** to have a strong desire for sth/sb.
■ **'hunger march** *n* a long walk by unemployed people in order to make others aware of their sufferings. **hunger marcher** *n*.
'hunger strike *n* a refusal to take food, esp by a prisoner, as a form of protest: *be/go on (a) hunger strike.* **'hunger striker** *n*.

NOTE Compare **hunger, starvation** and **famine**. **Hunger** is the need to eat food: *She felt weak from hunger and the intense heat.* **Starvation** is a serious condition which the body suffers from when a person has not had enough food to eat for a long time: *Men, women and children are facing death by starvation in some parts of the world.* **Famine** or **a famine** occurs when large numbers of people in a country have nothing to eat and many die, for example because there has been no rain and food cannot grow: *The war has brought disease and famine to thousands of people.* ○ *There will be a terrible famine if the crops fail.*

hungry /ˈhʌŋgri/ *adj* (**-ier, -iest**) **1(a)** feeling a desire for food: *I've got a hungry family to feed.* ○ *Let's eat soon — I'm really hungry!* ○ *I don't feel very hungry.* **(b)** suffering from weakness, pain, etc because of lack of food: *the hungry masses* ○ *Thousands are going hungry because of the failure of the harvest.* **2** [pred] ~ **for sth** in need of sth; feeling a strong desire for sth: *The boy is simply hungry for affection.* ○ *The crowd was hungry for more.* **3** [usu attrib] showing hunger: *His eyes had a wild hungry look in them.* **4** [attrib] (*infml*) causing hunger: *Hay-making is hungry work.* Compare THIRSTY.
▶ **the hungry** *n* [pl *v*] hungry people: *feeding the hungry.*
hungrily /ˈhʌŋgrəli/ *adv*: *He kissed her hungrily.* ○ *She hungrily devoured two of the cakes.*

hunk /hʌŋk/ *n* **1** a large piece of sth that is cut from a larger piece: *a hunk of bread/cheese/meat.* **2** (*sl usu approv*) a big strong man, esp an attractive one: *He's a real hunk.*

hunt¹ /hʌnt/ *v* **1** to chase wild animals, esp foxes or birds, and try to kill or capture them, for food or sport: [V] *go hunting* ○ *Wolves hunt in packs.* [Vn] *eagles hunting their prey.* ○ *Porpoises are still being hunted and killed in the Arctic.* **2** ~ **(for sth/sb)** to search for sth/sb; to try to find sth/sb: [Vpr] *hunt for a lost book* [Vadv] *I've hunted everywhere but I can't find it.* [Vn] *Police are hunting an escaped criminal.* **PHRV** **ˌhunt sb/sth 'down** to pursue sb/sth until they are caught or found: *Fleeing villagers were hunted down by army helicopters.* **ˌhunt 'out** to search for sth, esp an object that has been put away or is no longer in use, until it is found: *hunt out an old diary.* **ˌhunt sth 'up** to search for sth, esp sth hidden or difficult to find: *hunt up references in the library.*
▶ **hunter** *n* **1** (often in compounds) a person who hunts: *hunters of big game in Africa* ○ *'seal hunters* ○ *'job hunters.* See also HEAD-HUNTER. **2** a horse used in hunting foxes.
hunting *n* [U] **(a)** the chasing and capturing or killing of wild animals and birds as a sport or for food: *He earned extra money by hunting and fishing.* ○ *a 'hunting knife.* **(b)** (esp in Britain) fox-hunting (FOX): *a 'hunting jacket.* See also BARGAIN-HUNTING.

H

'hunting-ground n a place where particular people may do or observe or acquire what they want: *Crowded markets are a **happy hunting-ground** for pickpockets.*

hunt² /hʌnt/ n **1** [C usu *sing*] an act of looking for sth; a search: *I had a good hunt for that key.* ○ *a murder hunt* (ie a hunt for sb who has killed sb) ○ *The hunt is on for a suitable candidate.* **2(a)** [C] (often in compounds) an act of hunting wild animals: *a 'fox-hunt.* **(b)** [CGp] (*esp Brit*) a group of people who regularly hunt foxes or deer with specially trained dogs: *a member of the Portman Hunt.*

huntsman /'hʌntsmən/ n (pl **-men** /-mən/) a person who hunts wild animals, esp foxes or deer.

hurdle /'hɜːdl/ n **1(a)** [C] (in ATHLETICS or horse-racing) each of a series of upright frames to be jumped over in a race: *five furlongs over hurdles* ○ *fall at the last hurdle.* ⇨ picture. **(b)** **hurdles** [pl] a race over these: *win the 400 metres hurdles.* **2** [C] a difficulty to be overcome; an obstacle: *economic and political hurdles standing in the way of progress* ○ *I've passed the written test; the interview is the next hurdle.*
▶ **hurdle** v ~ **(over)** sth to jump over sth while running: *hurdling (over) a barrier.* **hurdler** /'hɜːdlə(r)/ n a person or horse that runs in races over hurdles. **hurdling** n [U] the sport of racing over hurdles. ⇨ picture.

hurdling

hurdle

hurdy-gurdy /'hɜːdi ɡɜːdi/ n = BARREL-ORGAN.

hurl /hɜːl/ v **1** to throw sth/sb/oneself violently in a particular direction: [Vnpr] *rioters hurling stones at the police* ○ *He hurled the book across the room.* ○ *She hurled herself to her death over the cliff.* ○ (*fig*) *He hurled himself enthusiastically into his work.* **2** ~ sth **(at sb/sth)** to shout sth forcefully: [Vn, Vnpr] *He stood there hurling abuse/insults (at me).*

hurling /'hɜːlɪŋ/ n [U] an Irish ball game similar to hockey.

hurly-burly /'hɜːli bɜːli/ n [U] noisy, energetic and sometimes rough activity: *He enjoys the hurly-burly of political debate.*

hurrah /hə'rɑː/ (also **hurray, hooray** /hə'reɪ/) interj ~ **(for sb/sth)** (used for expressing joy, approval, etc): *Hurrah for the weekend!* **IDM hip, hip, hurrah/hurray!** ⇨ HIP³.

hurricane /'hʌrɪkən; US -keɪn/ n a violent storm with very strong winds, esp in the western Atlantic Ocean: *Hurricane Betsy is approaching the coast of Florida.* ○ *hurricane-force winds.* Compare CYCLONE, TYPHOON.
■ **'hurricane lamp** n a type of lamp with glass sides to protect the flame from the wind.

hurry /'hʌri/ n [U] the need or wish to get sth done quickly: *In his hurry to leave, he forgot his passport.* ○ *Take your time — there's no hurry.* ○ *What's the hurry/Why all the hurry? We've got plenty of time.* **IDM in a 'hurry 1** very quickly; more quickly than usual: *She dressed in a hurry.* **2** not having enough time to do sth; rushing to do sth: *I'm in rather a hurry this morning — can I speak to you later?* ○ *She's always in a tearing hurry.* **3** eager or keen to do sth: *He was in too much of a hurry to leave school.* **4** (*infml*) (usu with a negative) soon; readily: *I won't invite him again in a hurry — he behaved very badly.* **in no 'hurry / not in any 'hurry 1** having plenty of time: *I don't mind waiting — I'm not in any particular hurry.* **2** not eager or keen; unwilling: *I'm in no hurry to see him again after all the trouble he caused.*
▶ **hurry** v (pt, pp **hurried**) **1(a)** to do sth or move more quickly than usual; to rush: [V] *Don't hurry;*

there's plenty of time. [Vpr] *He picked up his bag and hurried along the platform.* ○ *She hurried after me with a letter.* [Vp] *Hurry along, children!* **(b)** to make sb do sth or move more quickly than usual or than they want: [Vn] *I'm afraid I must hurry you now — we're closing in a few minutes.* [Vnpr] *I was hurried into making an unwise decision.* **2** (esp *passive*) to do or finish sth too quickly, esp so that one spoils it: [Vn] *This work requires great care: it mustn't be hurried.* ○ *A good meal should never be hurried.* **PHR V ,hurry 'on (to do sth)** to continue speaking, etc without giving anyone else time to say anything: *He hurried on to explain why he had changed his mind.* **,hurry 'up** (*infml*) to do sth or move more quickly: *I wish the train would hurry up and arrive.* ○ *Hurry up and get ready — we're waiting!* **,hurry sb/sth 'up** to make sb/sth do sth or move more quickly; to make sth happen more quickly: *Can you do anything to hurry my order up?* **hurried** adj done quickly or too quickly: *a hurried meal* ○ *write a few hurried lines.* **hurriedly** adv: *a hurriedly arranged meeting* ○ *We had to leave rather hurriedly.*

hurt /hɜːt/ v (pt, pp **hurt**) **1(a)** to cause physical injury or pain to sb/oneself, an animal, etc: [Vn] *Did you hurt yourself?* ○ *Let go! You're hurting me.* ○ *He hurt his back when he fell.* [Vnadv] *Are you badly hurt?* **(b)** to feel pain in part of one's body: [V] *My leg/arm hurts.* ⇨ note at WOUND¹. **(c)** to cause pain: [V] *My shoes hurt — they're much too tight.* ○ *Ouch! That hurts!* ○ *It hurts when I move my leg.* [V.to inf] *It still hurts just to think of that terrible day.* **2** to cause mental suffering or distress to sb; to upset or offend sb: [Vn] *These criticisms have hurt him/his pride deeply.* ○ *I don't want to hurt your feelings but you ought to know.* **3** to have a bad effect on sth; to harm sth: [Vn] *Sales of the product have been seriously hurt by the adverse publicity.* **IDM hit sb where it hurts** ⇨ HIT¹. **it, etc won't/wouldn't 'hurt (sb/sth) (to do sth)** (esp *ironic*) sth will/would not cause harm or difficulty: *It won't hurt to postpone the meeting.* ○ *A bit of weeding wouldn't hurt (this garden).* ○ *It wouldn't hurt (you) to say sorry for once.* **not harm/hurt a fly** ⇨ FLY².
▶ **hurt** adj upset and offended: *a hurt look/expression* ○ *She was very hurt not to have been invited.*
hurt n [U, sing] mental pain or suffering: *The experience left me with a feeling of deep hurt.* **hurtful** /-fl/ adj ~ **(to sb)** causing esp mental suffering; unkind: *Her remarks were very hurtful to me.* **hurtfully** /-fəli/ adv.

hurtle /'hɜːtl/ v to move at a great or dangerous speed in the specified direction: [Vp] *During the gale, roof tiles came hurtling down.* ○ *He hurtled off in pursuit of the ice-cream van.* [Vpr] *The van hurtled round the corner.* [Vadv] *She slipped and went hurtling downstairs.*

husband /'hʌzbənd/ n a man to whom a woman is married: *She doesn't love her husband any more.* See also HOUSE-HUSBAND. ⇨ App 4. **IDM ,husband and 'wife** a married couple: *No tax is payable on gifts between husband and wife.* ○ *They lived together as husband and wife* (ie as if they were married) *for years.* ⇨ note at PARTNER.
▶ **husband** v (*fml*) to use sth very carefully and not waste it: [Vn] *husband one's strength/resources.*

husbandry /'hʌzbəndri/ n [U] (*fml*) **1** care and management of the land, crops or animals bred for food: *crop/soil/horse husbandry.* See also ANIMAL HUSBANDRY. **2** the careful management of resources.

hush /hʌʃ/ v **(a)** (often *imperative*) to be quiet; to stop talking: *Hush, you'll wake the baby!* **(b)** to make sb/sth become quieter or make sb stop talking: [Vn] *hushed conversations* ○ *speak in hushed tones* ○ *He hushed her and told her not to be foolish.* **PHR V ,hush sth 'up** (usu *derog*) to prevent sth from be-

coming generally known because of the embarrassment this might cause: *The government hushed the affair up to avoid a public outcry.*
▶ **hush** *n* [U, sing] silence, esp following a lot of noise: *There was **a sudden deathly hush**.* ○ *When she walked in, a hush fell over the room.*
■ ˌhush-ˈhush *adj* (*infml*) known only to a few people; secret: *His job is very hush-hush.*
ˈhush money *n* [U] money paid to sb to prevent them from revealing sth embarrassing about sb.

husk /hʌsk/ *n* the dry outer covering of certain nuts, fruits and seeds, esp grain: *the fibrous husk of the coconut* ○ *Brown rice has not had the husks removed.* Compare BRAN, CHAFF¹.
▶ **husk** *v* [Vn] to remove the husks from seeds, etc.

husky¹ /ˈhʌski/ *adj* **1** (of a person or voice) sounding rough as if the throat is dry; HOARSE: *a voice husky with emotion* ○ *She still sounds a bit husky after her recent cold.* **2** (*infml*) (of a man) attractive because of being big and strong: *a husky young truck-driver.* ▶ **huskily** *adv.* **huskiness** *n* [U].

husky² /ˈhʌski/ *n* a strong breed of dog with a thick coat, used in the Arctic for pulling sledges (SLEDGE): *A pack of six huskies pulled our equipment and supplies.*

hussar /həˈzɑː(r)/ *n* a CAVALRY soldier who carries light weapons.

hussy /ˈhʌsi/ *n* (*dated derog*) a girl or woman who behaves in a way that is considered shocking or morally wrong: *You brazen/insolent/shameless hussy!*

hustings /ˈhʌstɪŋz/ *n* **the hustings** [pl] the political activities, eg public meetings, that happen in the period before an election: *Most politicians will be at/on the hustings in the coming week.*

hustle /ˈhʌsl/ *v* **1** to push or move sb in a specified direction in a rough aggressive way: [Vnpr] *The spectators were hustled off the pitch.* [Vnp] *The police hustled them away very quickly.* **2** ~ **sb** (**into sth/doing sth**) to make sb act quickly and without time to consider things: [Vn] *'Why did you agree to do it?' 'They kept hustling me.'* [Vnpr] *I was hustled into (making) a hasty decision.* **3** (*infml derog esp US*) to sell or obtain sth by putting pressure on people, sometimes acting dishonestly: [Vnpr] *He hustled his script all round Hollywood but no one was interested.* [V] *They survive by hustling on the streets.* **4** [V] (*US sl*) to work as a prostitute.
▶ **hustle** *n* [U] the busy movement and activity of many people together: *I love all the hustle and bustle of the market.*
hustler /ˈhʌslə(r)/ *n* **1** (*infml esp US*) a person who hustles (HUSTLE 3). **2** (*US sl*) a prostitute.

hut /hʌt/ *n* a small, simply built house or shelter, usu made of wood, mud or metal: *a ˈbeach hut* ○ *a small mountain hut.* Compare SHED¹.

hutch /hʌtʃ/ *n* a wooden box or cage with a front made of wire, used for keeping rabbits, etc in.

hyacinth /ˈhaɪəsɪnθ/ *n* a plant with sweet-smelling white, blue or pink flowers, growing from a BULB(1) in spring. ⇨ picture at FLOWER.

hyaena ⇨ HYENA.

hybrid /ˈhaɪbrɪd/ *n* **1** an animal or a plant that has parents of different species or varieties: *A mule is a hybrid of a male donkey and a female horse.* See also CROSS-BREED. **2** a thing made by combining two different elements: *a hybrid of/between western pop and traditional Punjabi folk music.*
▶ **hybrid** *adj* **1** produced as a hybrid: *a hybrid animal/plant.* See also CROSS-BRED. **2** composed of mixed parts: *a hybrid system.*
hybridize, -ise /-aɪz/ *v* ~ (**with sth**) (**a**) (of animals or plants) to produce hybrids: [Vpr] *These species hybridize freely with the primrose.* [also V]. (**b**) [Vn] to cause animals or plants to produce hybrids. **hybridization, -isation** /ˌhaɪbrɪdaɪˈzeɪʃn/ *n* [U].

hydrangea /haɪˈdreɪndʒə/ *n* a bush with large white, pink or blue heads of flowers.

hydrant /ˈhaɪdrənt/ *n* a pipe in the street from which water can be pumped, eg to put out a fire or to clean the streets.

hydrate /ˈhaɪdreɪt, haɪˈdreɪt/ *v* to make sth absorb water: [Vn] *It protects and hydrates the skin.* ▶ **hydration** /haɪˈdreɪʃn/ *n* [U].

hydraulic /haɪˈdrɔːlɪk, -ˈdrɒl-/ *adj* (**a**) (of water, oil, etc) moved through pipes, etc usu under pressure: *hydraulic fluid.* (**b**) (of a mechanism) operated by liquid moving in this way: *hydraulic brakes* ○ *a hydraulic pump/jack/lift.* (**c**) of or relating to hydraulic systems: *hydraulic pressure* ○ *suffer complete hydraulic failure* ○ *a hydraulic engineer.*
▶ **hydraulically** /-kli/ *adv: hydraulically operated doors/brakes.*
hydraulics *n* [sing or pl *v*] the science and study of systems operating under hydraulic pressure.

hydr(o)- *comb form* **1** of water or liquid: *hydroelectricity.* **2** combined with hydrogen: *hydrochloric.*

hydrocarbon /ˌhaɪdrəˈkɑːbən/ *n* any of a group of compounds of hydrogen and carbon that are found in petrol, coal and natural gas: *a cut in hydrocarbon emissions from motor vehicles.*

hydrochloric acid /ˌhaɪdrəˌklɒrɪk ˈæsɪd; *US* -ˌklɔːr-/ *n* [U] an acid containing HYDROGEN and CHLORINE.

hydroelectric /ˌhaɪdrəʊɪˈlektrɪk/ *adj* (**a**) using the power of water that is flowing fast to produce electricity: *a hydroelectric plant/dam/turbine.* (**b**) (of electricity) produced in this way: *hydroelectric power.*

hydrofoil /ˈhaɪdrəfɔɪl/ *n* a boat equipped with a device which raises it out of the water when it is moving, enabling it to travel fast and use less fuel: *hydrofoil and ferry services.*

hydrogen /ˈhaɪdrədʒən/ *n* [U] (*symb* H) (*chemistry*) a chemical element. Hydrogen is a gas that has no colour, taste or smell and is the lightest substance known, combining with oxygen to form water. ⇨ App 7.
■ ˈhydrogen bomb (also ˈH-bomb) *n* a very powerful type of bomb that explodes when the nuclei (NUCLEUS 1) of hydrogen atoms join together.
ˌhydrogen peˈroxide *n* [U] = PEROXIDE.

hydroplane /ˈhaɪdrəpleɪn/ *n* a light boat with an engine and a flat bottom, designed to travel fast over the surface of the water.

hydroponics /ˌhaɪdrəˈpɒnɪks/ *n* [sing *v*] the practice of growing plants in water or sand, rather than in soil.

hydrotherapy /ˌhaɪdrəʊˈθerəpi/ *n* [U] the treatment of disease, etc by exercising the body in water: *undergo a course of hydrotherapy.*

hyena (also **hyaena**) /haɪˈiːnə/ *n* an animal found in Africa and Asia that eats the flesh of usu dead animals and has a cry like a wild laugh.

hygiene /ˈhaɪdʒiːn/ *n* [U] the practice of keeping oneself and one's living and working areas clean in order to prevent illness and disease: *falling standards of hygiene* ○ *Wash regularly to ensure personal hygiene.* ○ *In the interests of hygiene, please do not smoke in this shop.*
▶ **hygienic** /haɪˈdʒiːnɪk; *US* ˌhaɪdʒiˈenɪk, haɪˈdʒenɪk/ *adj* clean and not likely to cause disease: *prepare food in hygienic conditions.* **hygienically** /-kli/ *adv.*

hymen /ˈhaɪmən/ *n* (*anatomy*) the piece of skin partly covering the VAGINA of a woman who has never had sex.

hymn /hɪm/ *n* a song of praise, esp one praising God sung by Christians.
▶ **hymn** *v* [Vn] praise sb/sth, esp in hymns.

H

■ **¹hymn-book** (also *dated* **hymnal** /ˈhɪmnəl/) *n* a book of hymns.

hype /haɪp/ *n* [U] (*infml often derog*) publicity that exaggerates the good qualities or importance of sth: *media/marketing hype* ○ *It's pure hype — no skin cream could be that good.*
▶ **hype** *v* ~ **sth** (**up**) (*infml*) (esp passive) to exaggerate the good qualities or importance of sth in order to obtain maximum public attention for it: [Vn] *a holiday destination heavily hyped by the media this year* [Vnp] *The whole affair has been hyped up to a ridiculous extent.* **hyped up** *adj* (*infml*) (of a person) very excited; stimulated.

hyper- *pref* (with *adjs* and *ns*) to an excessive degree; above; over: *hypercritical* ○ *hypersensitive* ○ *hypertension.* Compare OVER-.

hyperactive /ˌhaɪpərˈæktɪv/ *adj* (esp of a child or its behaviour) excessively active; unable to relax or remain still. ▶ **hyperactivity** /ˌhaɪpərækˈtɪvəti/ *n* [U].

hyperbole /haɪˈpɜːbəli/ *n* [U, C usu *sing*] language that is deliberately and obviously exaggerated for effect: *typical travel guide hyperbole* ○ *She's not usually given to hyperbole.*

hyperinflation /ˌhaɪpərɪmˈfleɪʃn/ *n* [U] a situation in which very large and rapid price rises occur.

hypermarket /ˈhaɪpəmaːkɪt/ *n* (*Brit*) a very large shop, selling a wide range of goods, usu situated outside a town.

hypersensitive /ˌhaɪpəˈsensətɪv/ *adj* **1** having extremely sensitive feelings: *She's hypersensitive about her weight.* **2** ~ (**to sth**) abnormally physically sensitive to certain drugs, light, etc. ▶ **hypersensitivity** /ˌhaɪpəˌsensəˈtɪvəti/ *n* [U].

hypertension /ˌhaɪpəˈtenʃn/ *n* [U] (*medical*) abnormally high blood pressure.

hypertext /ˈhaɪpətekst/ *n* [U] text stored in a computer in such a way that while one is reading an article one can follow a reference to another article and read that before returning to the original article or moving to sth different: *a hypertext system.*

hyperventilate /ˌhaɪpəˈventɪleɪt/ *v* to breathe much more rapidly then normal, and so lose too much carbon dioxide (CARBON): [V] *He became so frightened that he began to hyperventilate.* ▶ **hyperventilation** /-ventɪˈleɪʃn/ *n* [U].

hyphen /ˈhaɪfn/ *n* a short line (-) used to join two words together, as in *ex-wife, co-operated* and *long-legged,* or to show that a word has been divided between the end of one line and the beginning of the next: *Lucy Hampton-Smith* ○ *Do you spell swimming-pool with a hyphen?* ⇨ App 3.
▶ **hyphenate** /ˈhaɪfəneɪt/ *v* to join or write words with a hyphen: [Vn] *Is 'ping-pong' hyphenated or not?* **hyphenation** /ˌhaɪfəˈneɪʃn/ *n* [U]: *rules of hyphenation.*

hypnosis /hɪpˈnəʊsɪs/ *n* [U] a state in which a person appears to be fully conscious but can be influenced to perform certain actions or say certain things: *put a person **under hypnosis*** ○ *undergo hypnosis in an effort to stop smoking.*
▶ **hypnotic** /hɪpˈnɒtɪk/ *adj* **1** of or producing hypnosis; making one feel very relaxed: *be in a hypnotic trance* ○ *hypnotic music/rhythms* ○ *The music had a hypnotic effect on her.* **2** (of a drug) making one sleep. — *n* a drug that makes one sleep.
hypnotism /ˈhɪpnətɪzəm/ *n* [U] the practice of hypnosis. **hypnotist** /ˈhɪpnətɪst/ *n*: *a stage hypnotist* (ie sb who practises hypnosis to entertain people).
hypnotize, **-ise** /ˈhɪpnətaɪz/ *v* **1** [Vn] to produce a state of hypnosis in sb. **2** to influence sb strongly so they can think of nothing else; to FASCINATE sb: [Vn] *He was hypnotized by her beauty.*

hyp(o)- *pref* under; beneath: *hypodermic* ○ *hypothermia.*

hypochondria /ˌhaɪpəˈkɒndrɪə/ *n* [U] abnormal and unnecessary anxiety about one's health: *suffer from hypochondria.*
▶ **hypochondriac** /-drɪæk/ *n* a person who suffers from hypochondria. — *adj* (also **hypochondriacal** /ˌhaɪpəˌkɒnˈdraɪəkl/) of or suffering from hypochondria.

hypocrisy /hɪˈpɒkrəsi/ *n* [U, C] the practice of pretending to be different from what one really is, because one wishes to appear to be a better person: *accuse sb of gross hypocrisy* ○ *This concern of his for the homeless smacks of hypocrisy.*
▶ **hypocrite** /ˈhɪpəkrɪt/ *n* (*derog*) a person who pretends to have standards or opinions which he or she does not have, or to be what he or she is not: *You're just a bunch of hypocrites!*
hypocritical /ˌhɪpəˈkrɪtɪkl/ *adj*: *I never liked my brother and it would be hypocritical of me to pretend otherwise.* **hypocritically** /-kli/ *adv.*

hypodermic /ˌhaɪpəˈdɜːmɪk/ *adj* (*medical*) (of an instrument) used for putting a drug into the body beneath the skin: *a hypodermic needle/syringe.* ⇨ picture at INJECTION.
▶ **hypodermic** *n* **1** a hypodermic needle or SYRINGE. **2** a hypodermic injection (INJECT 1): *give sb a hypodermic.*

hypotenuse /haɪˈpɒtənjuːz; *US* -nuːs/ *n* (*geometry*) the side opposite the right angle (RIGHT¹) of a right-angled triangle. ⇨ picture at TRIANGLE.

hypothermia /ˌhaɪpəˈθɜːmiə/ *n* [U] (*medical*) a dangerous condition in which the body has an abnormally low temperature: *old people dying of hypothermia in cold weather.*

hypothesis /haɪˈpɒθəsɪs/ *n* (*pl* **hypotheses** /-siːz/) an idea or a suggestion that is based on known facts and is used as a basis for reasoning or further investigation: *formulate/form a hypothesis* ○ *put sth forward as a hypothesis* ○ *refute/discuss sb's hypothesis.*
▶ **hypothesize,** **-ise** /haɪˈpɒθəsaɪz/ *v* to form a hypothesis; to assume sth as a hypothesis: [Vn] *hypothesise the existence of a hitherto unknown protein* [V.*that*] *Copernicus hypothesized that the earth and the other planets went round the sun.* [also V].
hypothetical /ˌhaɪpəˈθetɪkl/ *adj* of or based on a hypothesis; not necessarily true or real: *a hypothetical example/question* ○ *All his claims are extremely hypothetical.* **hypothetically** /-kli/ *adv.*

hysterectomy /ˌhɪstəˈrektəmi/ *n* [C, U] (*medical*) an operation for removing a woman's WOMB: *have a hysterectomy.*

hysteria /hɪˈstɪəriə/ *n* [U] **1** a nervous state in which one loses control of one's emotions, causing one to shout, laugh or cry in a wild excited way: *a crowd gripped by mass hysteria.* **2** (*derog*) an excited and exaggerated reaction to an event: *the usual media hysteria that surrounds royal visits* ○ *public hysteria about AIDS.*
▶ **hysterical** /hɪˈsterɪkl/ *adj* **1** caused by or suffering from hysteria: *hysterical laughter/weeping/screaming* ○ *He became hysterical when he saw what had happened.* ○ *hysterical fans at a rock concert.* **2** (*infml*) very amusing: *She thought that being locked out wearing only a nightdress was absolutely hysterical.* **hysterically** /-kli/ *adv: laughing/crying/shouting hysterically* ○ *The play was hysterically funny.*
hysterics /hɪˈsterɪks/ *n* [pl] **1** a fit of hysteria: *go into hysterics* ○ *She was in hysterics.* **2** (*infml*) wild laughter: *She **had** the audience **in** hysterics.* ○ *She took one look at us and fell into hysterics.* **IDM** **have hysterics** (*infml*) to be very upset and angry: *Your mother would have hysterics if she knew you were using her car.*

Hz *abbr* hertz. Compare KHZ.

I i

I¹ (also **i**) /aɪ/ *n* (*pl* **I's**, **i's** /aɪz/) the 9th letter of the English alphabet: *'Idiot' begins with an I/'I'*. **IDM** **dot one's/the i's and cross one's/the t's** ⟶ DOT.

I² /aɪ/ *pers pron* (used as the subject of a *v*) the person who is the speaker or writer: *I think I'd like a bath.* ∘ *He and I are old friends.* ∘ *When he asked me to marry him I said yes.* Compare ME¹.

I³ *abbr* (esp on a map) Island(s); Isle(s): *Stewart I.* Compare Is *abbr*.

I⁴ (also **i**) *symb* the Roman NUMERAL for 1.

-ial *suff* (with *ns* forming *adjs*) characteristic of: *dictatorial* ∘ *managerial* ∘ *editorial*. ▶ **-ially** *suff* (forming *advs*): *officially*.

iambic /aɪˈæmbɪk/ *adj* (in poetry) of or using a rhythm each part of which (an **iambus**) consists of one short or weak syllable followed by one long or strong syllable: *iambic feet* (eg I ˈsaw three ˈships come ˈsailing ˈby).

-ian (also **-an**) *suff* **1** (with proper *ns* forming *ns* and *adjs*): *Bostonian* ∘ *Brazilian* ∘ *Shakespearian* ∘ *Libran.* **2** (with *ns* ending in *-ics* forming *ns*) a specialist in: *optician* ∘ *paediatrician.*

-iana (also **-ana**) *suff* (with proper *ns* forming uncountable *ns*) a collection of objects, facts, stories, etc relating to a person, place, etc: *Victoriana* ∘ *Mozartiana* ∘ *Americana.*

-iatrics *comb form* (forming *ns*) the medical treatment of: *paediatrics.* ▶ **-iatric, -iatrical** *comb forms* (forming *adjs*).

-iatry *comb form* (forming *ns*) the healing or medical treatment of: *psychiatry.* ▶ **-iatric** *comb forms* (forming *adjs*).

IBA /ˌaɪ biː ˈeɪ/ *abbr* (in Britain) Independent Broadcasting Authority. Compare BBC, ITV.

ibex /ˈaɪbeks/ *n* (*pl* unchanged or **ibexes**) a type of mountain goat with long curved horns.

ibid /ˈɪbɪd/ *abbr* in the same book, article, passage, etc as previously mentioned (Latin *ibidem*).

-ible ⟶ -ABLE.

IBM /ˌaɪ biː ˈem/ *abbr* International Business Machines (a large computer company): *work for IBM* ∘ *IBM-compatible machines.*

-ic /-ɪk/ *suff* **1** (with *ns* forming *adjs* and *ns*) of or concerning: *poetic* ∘ *scenic* ∘ *Arabic.* **2** (with *vs* ending in *-y* forming *adjs*) that performs the specified action: *horrific* ∘ *specific.* ▶ **-ical** /-ɪkl/ *suff* (forming *adjs*): *comical.* **-ically** /-ɪkli/ *suff* (forming *advs*): *economically.*

NOTE Both **-ic** and **-ical** form adjectives from nouns: *democracy/democratic* ∘ *sociology/sociological.* Some nouns form pairs of adjectives with both **-ic** and **-ical** which have different meanings, eg *history: historic* (ie of great significance) and *historical* (ie belonging to history); *economy: economic* (ie concerned with the economy) and *economical* (ie not wasteful). Other examples are: *comic/comical, politic/political, classic/classical, poetic/poetical.* Some pairs of words have almost the same meaning: *rhythmic/rhythmical.* Note that you usually form the adverb from the adjective ending in **-ical**: *comically, poetically, rhythmically.*

IC /ˌaɪ ˈsiː/ *abbr* (*electronics*) integrated circuit.

ice¹ /aɪs/ *n* **1** [U] **(a)** water frozen so that it has become solid: *ice crystals* ∘ *pipes blocked by ice in* winter ∘ *Would you like ice in your drink?* ∘ *My hands are as cold as ice.* **(b)** a sheet or layer of this: *ice dancing* ∘ *Is the ice thick enough for skating?* ⟶ note at WATER¹. See also ICY, BLACK ICE, DRY ICE. **2** [C] (*becoming dated esp Brit*) an ice-cream: *a choc-ice* ∘ *Drinks, ices and popcorn are on sale in the foyer.* **IDM** **be skating on thin ice** ⟶ SKATE¹. **break the ˈice** to do or say sth to ease tension or an awkward situation, esp at a first meeting or at the start of a party, etc. **cut no ˈice (with sb)** to have little or no effect or influence on sb: *His excuses cut no ice with me.* **on ˈice 1** (of wine, etc) kept cold by being surrounded by ice. **2** in reserve for later use or consideration: *We put the plans for the new office on ice.* **3** (of entertainment, etc) performed by skaters (SKATE¹): *Cinderella on ice.*

■ **ˈice age** *n* any of several periods long ago when the earth's surface was covered with ice.

ˈice-axe (*US* also **ice-ax**) *n* an implement used by people climbing mountains for cutting steps, etc in ice. ⟶ picture at AXE.

ˌice-ˈblue *adj, n* [U] a very pale blue colour: ˌice-blue ˈeyes.

ˈice-bound *adj* surrounded by ice or unable to function because of ice: *an ice-bound ship/harbour.*

ˈice-breaker *n* a strong ship designed to break a passage through ice.

ˈice-cap *n* a permanent covering of ice, esp around the North and South Poles.

ˌice-ˈcold *adj* as cold as ice; very cold: ˌice-cold ˈdrinks.

ˌice-ˈcream (also *esp US* **ˈice-cream**) *n* [U, C] a cold sweet food made from frozen cream, or an artificial substance like cream, with added flavour; a portion of this: *a/some strawberry ice-cream.*

ˈice-cube *n* a small piece of ice for cooling drinks, etc.

ˈice-field *n* a large area of floating ice, esp around the North and South Poles.

ˈice-floe *n* a large area of floating ice, esp in the sea: *In spring the ice-floes break up.*

ˈice hockey (*US* **ˈhockey**) *n* [U] a form of hockey played on ice by two teams, using long sticks to hit a hard rubber disc. ⟶ picture at HOCKEY.

ˌice ˈlolly (*Brit*) (*US propr* **Popsicle**) *n* a piece of ice with a sweet flavour on a small stick.

ˈice-pack *n* a bag filled with ice, used medically to cool parts of the body, eg as a way to reduce swelling.

ˈice-pick *n* a tool with a very sharp point for breaking ice.

ˈice-rink *n* a specially prepared sheet of ice, often indoors, for skating (SKATE¹ *v* 1), playing ice hockey, etc. ⟶ picture at HOCKEY.

ˈice-skate *n* a boot with a thin metal blade on the bottom, for skating (SKATE¹ *v* 1) on ice. ⟶ picture at HOCKEY, SKATE¹ — *v* [V] to SKATE¹(1) on ice. **ˈice-skating** *n* [U].

ˈice-water *n* [U] (*esp US*) water made very cold and used for drinking.

ice² /aɪs/ *v* to cover a cake, etc with ICING: [Vn] *iced buns* ∘ *icing the Christmas cake.* **PHRV** **ˌice (sth) ˈover/ˈup** to cover sth or become covered with ice: *The pond (was) iced over during the cold spell.* ∘ *The wings of the aircraft had iced up.* **iced** /aɪst/ *adj* (of a drink) made very cold: *iced water/beer.*

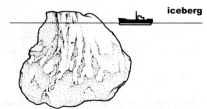

iceberg

iceberg /'aɪsbɜːg/ n a huge mass of ice floating in the sea. ⇨ picture. **IDM** **the tip of the iceberg** ⇨ TIP¹.

icebox /'aɪsbɒks/ n (dated esp US) a refrigerator (REFRIGERATE).

ICI /ˌaɪ siː 'aɪ/ abbr Imperial Chemical Industries (a large British chemical company): work for ICI.

icicle /'aɪsɪkl/ n a pointed piece of ice formed when water falling downwards, eg from a roof, freezes.

icing /'aɪsɪŋ/ (US **frosting**) n [U] a mixture of sugar, egg white, flavouring, etc used for covering and decorating cakes: chocolate icing. **IDM** **(the) icing on the 'cake** an attractive but unnecessary addition to sth that is already satisfactory.
■ **'icing sugar** (Brit) (US **powdered sugar**) n [U] white sugar in fine powder form, used esp for icing.

icon (also **ikon**) /'aɪkɒn/ n **1** (in the Orthodox Church) a painting, carving, etc, usu on wood, of a holy person. Icons are themselves regarded as sacred. **2** a person or thing that is regarded as a symbol of sth: Elvis Presley was the pop icon of the Fifties. **3** (computing) a small symbol on a computer screen representing a PROGRAM(1), etc that a user may choose.

iconoclast /aɪ'kɒnəklæst/ n a person who attacks popular beliefs or established customs. ▶ **iconoclasm** /aɪ'kɒnəklæzəm/ n [U]. **iconoclastic** /aɪˌkɒnə'klæstɪk/ adj.

-ics suff (forming ns) the science, art or activity of: aesthetics ○ athletics ○ graphics ○ acrobatics ○ dramatics.

ICU /ˌaɪ siː 'juː/ abbr intensive care unit (in a hospital).

icy /'aɪsi/ adj (-ier, -iest) **1** very cold; as cold as ice: icy winds. **2** covered with ice: icy roads. **3** (of a person's voice, manner, etc) not friendly; suggesting concealed anger: an icy glare/silence. ▶ **icily** /'aɪsɪli/ adv: 'I have nothing to say to you,' she said icily. **iciness** n [U].

ID /ˌaɪ 'diː/ abbr (esp US) identification; identity: an ID card.

id /ɪd/ n (psychology) the part of the mind relating to a person's unconscious instincts and impulses. Compare EGO.

I'd /aɪd/ short form **1** I had. ⇨ note at HAVE. **2** I would ⇨ WILL¹, WOULD.

-ide suff (chemistry) (forming ns) a compound of a particular chemical element: chloride ○ sulphide.

idea /aɪ'dɪə; US -'diːə/ n **1** [C] a plan, etc formed by thinking; a thought; a suggestion: He's full of good/ bright ideas. ○ That's an (ie a good) idea. **2** [U,sing] a mental impression: This book gives you some idea/ a good idea of life in ancient Greece. ○ Have you any idea what I mean? **3** [C] an opinion; a belief: He has some very strange ideas. **4** [sing] a belief; a feeling that sth is probable: What gave you the idea/Where did you get the idea (that) I was rich? ○ I have an idea it's going to rain. **5** the **idea** [sing] the aim or purpose: We take turns to play a card — do you **get the idea** (ie understand)? ○ The idea of the game is to get all your pieces to the other side of the board. ○ **What's the (big) idea** of turning up three hours late? **6** (used in exclamations to indicate that what has been suggested is stupid, shocking, etc): The

idea of it! ○ What an idea! **IDM** **buck one's ideas up** ⇨ BUCK². **give sb i'deas** to give sb expectations or hopes which may not be realized: Don't give her ideas — you know how difficult it is to get into show business. **have no i'dea** to be completely ignorant: 'What's the time?' 'I've no idea.' ○ He has no idea how to manage people. **not have the first idea** to know absolutely nothing about sth: Many young people today haven't the first idea how to behave! **one's idea of sth** what one thinks of as representing sth: If this is your idea of a joke, I'm not amused. **run away with the idea that...** (infml) (often used in negative sentences) to believe or accept a false impression: Don't run away with the idea that this job is going to be easy.

ideal /aɪ'diːəl/ adj **1** satisfying one's idea of what is perfect; most suitable: ideal weather for a swim ○ He's the ideal husband for her. **2** existing only in the imagination or as an idea; not realistic and so not likely to be achieved: ideal plans for reform ○ ideal happiness. ○ **In an ideal world** there would be no poverty and disease.
▶ **ideal** n **1** [C usu sing] a person or thing regarded as perfect: She's looking for a job, but hasn't found her ideal yet. **2** [C usu pl] a standard of perfection: have high ideals ○ He finds it hard to live up to his ideals.

ideally /aɪ'diːəli/ adv: She's **ideally** suited to the job. ○ Ideally, everyone should be given equal opportunities.

idealism /aɪ'diːəlɪzəm/ n [U] **1** the practice of forming, pursuing or believing in ideals (IDEAL n 2), even when this is not realistic: Idealism has no place in modern politics. **2** (philosophy) the belief that ideas are the only things that are real or about which we can know anything. Compare CLASSICISM, REALISM.
▶ **idealist** /aɪ'diːəlɪst/ n a person who has high ideals and tries to achieve them, even when this is not realistic: He is a frustrated idealist. **idealistic** /ˌaɪdɪə'lɪstɪk/ adj. **idealistically** /ˌaɪdɪə'lɪstɪkli/ adv.

idealize, -ise /aɪ'diːəlaɪz/ v to consider or represent sb/sth as perfect or ideal: [Vn] an idealized account of married life. ▶ **idealization**, **-isation** /aɪˌdiːəlaɪ'zeɪʃn; US -lə-/ n [U,C].

identical /aɪ'dentɪkl/ adj **1** [attrib] the ~ the same : This is the identical room we stayed in last year. **2** ~ (to/with sb/sth) similar in every detail; exactly alike: They're wearing identical clothes. ○ This picture is identical to one my mother has. ○ Your answers are identical with mine. ▶ **identically** /-kli/ adv.
■ **i,dentical 'twin** n either of two children or animals born from a single egg and therefore of the same sex and very similar in appearance.

identify /aɪ'dentɪfaɪ/ v (pt, pp **-fied**) **1** ~ sb/sth as sb/sth to show or prove who or what sb/sth is; to recognize sb/sth as being a particular person or thing: [Vn] Can you identify your umbrella among these? ○ There was a strange noise which Rob couldn't identify. ○ The risks are hard to identify. [Vn-adj] a factor identified as crucial to success [Vn-n] The driver was identified as Peter Harrison. ○ She identified the man as her attacker. **2** ~ sth with sth to consider sth to be the same as sth else; to EQUATE(1) two things: [Vnpr] One should not identify wealth with happiness. **PHR V** **i'dentify (oneself) with sb/ sth** to give support to sb/sth; to be associated with sb/sth: He refused to identify himself/become identified with the new political party. **i'dentify with sb** to regard oneself as sharing the same characteristics, successes, problems, etc as sb; to take sb as a model: I found it hard to identify with any of the characters in the book.
▶ **identification** /aɪˌdentɪfɪ'keɪʃn/ n [U] **1(a)** the process of identifying sb/sth or of being identified: The identification of the accident victims took some time.

(b) the action or process of identifying with sb/sth: *their identification with the struggle for independence.* **2** (*abbr* **ID**) a means of proving who one is; official papers that do this: *Can I see some identification, please?* i₁**dentifi'cation parade** *n* a number of people, including one suspected of a crime, arranged in a row to be seen by a witness or witnesses who may be able to identify the person suspected: *He had been picked out at an identification parade.*

Identikit /aɪˈdentɪkɪt/ *n* (*propr*) a set of pictures of different features that can be fitted together to form the face of a person, esp one wanted by the police, using descriptions given by people who have seen her or him: (*fig derog*) *an identikit pop star* (ie one like may others).

identity /aɪˈdentəti/ *n* **1** [C,U] who or what sb/sth is: *There is no clue to the identity of the killer.* ○ *The cheque will be cashed on proof of identity.* ○ *a case of mistaken identity* (eg when the wrong person is arrested by mistake) ○ *The British do not have a strong national identity.* ○ *She had an identity crisis when she was sixteen* (ie felt as if she lacked a personal and individual role or place in society). ○ *improve the corporate identity of a firm.* **2** [U] ~ (**between A and B**) the state of being very like or the same as sb/sth: *a feeling of identity between managers and staff.* **3** [U] ~ (**with sth**) the state of being closely involved with or part of sth: *develop a sense of identity with the organization.*

■ i'**dentity card** (also **ID card** /ˌaɪˈdiː kɑːd/) *n* a card bearing the holder's name, signature, etc, and often a photograph, carried or worn by sb to show who they are.

ideogram /ˈɪdiəgræm/ (also **ideograph** /ˈɪdiəɡrɑːf; *US* - græf/) *n* **1** a symbol used in a writing system that represents the idea, rather than the sounds forming the name, of a thing, eg in Chinese writing. **2** any sign or symbol for sth: *In this dictionary the ideogram △ is used to mean 'taboo'.*

ideology /ˌaɪdiˈɒlədʒi/ *n* [C,U] a set of ideas or beliefs that form the basis of an economic or political theory or that are held by a particular group or person: *according to Marxist/bourgeois/monetarist ideology* ○ *Our ideologies differ widely.* ▶ **ideological** /ˌaɪdiəˈlɒdʒɪkl/ *adj*: *ideological arguments/ differences* ○ *be rejected on ideological grounds.* **ideologically** /-kli/ *adv*: *ideologically correct.*

idiocy /ˈɪdiəsi/ *n* **1** [U] extremely stupid behaviour: *This is the height of idiocy.* ○ *It's sheer idiocy to go climbing in such bad weather.* **2** [C] an extremely stupid act, remark, etc: *the idiocies of bureaucracy.*

idiolect /ˈɪdiəlekt/ *n* (*linguistics*) the total amount of a particular language used by a particular person.

idiom /ˈɪdiəm/ *n* **1** [U] the style of writing, music, art, etc associated with a particular period, individual or group: *today's idiom* ○ *the popular/ religious/classical idiom.* **2** [U] the language or DIALECT of a group of people or a country: *have an ear for Irish idiom.* **3** [C] (abbreviated as *idm* in this dictionary) a phrase or sentence whose meaning is not clear from the meaning of its individual words and which must be learnt as a whole unit, eg *give way, a change of heart, be hard put to it.*

▶ **idiomatic** /ˌɪdiəˈmætɪk/ *adj* **1(a)** using or containing expressions that are natural to a native speaker of a language: *She speaks fluent and idiomatic French.* **(b)** containing an idiom(3) or idioms: *an idiomatic expression/language.* **2** appropriate to the style of writing or music associated with a particular period, individual or group: *an idiomatic rendering of a piano concerto.* **idiomatically** /-kli/ *adv.*

idiosyncrasy /ˌɪdiəˈsɪŋkrəsi/ *n* [C,U] a person's particular way of thinking, behaving, etc that is clearly different from that of others: *One of her little idiosyncrasies is always washing in cold water.* ▶

idiosyncratic /ˌɪdiəsɪŋˈkrætɪk/ *adj*: *an idiosyncratic style/approach/personality/film director.*

idiot /ˈɪdiət/ *n* **1** (*infml*) a very foolish person; a fool: *I felt a complete idiot.* ○ *No, you idiot, the other way round!* **2** a person with very low intelligence who cannot think or behave normally: *an idiot since birth* ○ *a gibbering idiot.*

▶ **idiotic** /ˌɪdiˈɒtɪk/ *adj* stupid: *an idiotic idea/ question* ○ *Don't be idiotic!* **idiotically** /-kli/ *adv.*

idle /ˈaɪdl/ *adj* **1(a)** not active or in use: *The factory machines lay idle during the workers' strike.* **(b)** not doing or having any work; not employed: *Many people were idle during the depression.* **2** (of time) not spent in doing sth particular: *We spent many idle hours just sitting in the sun.* **3** (of people) avoiding work; lazy: *an idle student* ○ *Researchers, however, have not been idle and have found new evidence to support the theory.* **4** [usu attrib] without foundation, purpose or effect; worthless or useless: *an idle boast/threat/promise* ○ *idle curiosity/speculation/ gossip* ○ *It is idle to pretend that things are getting better.*

▶ **idle** *v* **1** to do nothing; to waste time; to be IDLE(3): [V] *Stop idling and help me clean up.* [Vp, Vpr] *spend the afternoon idling around (the pool).* [V] (of an engine) to run slowly without doing any work or being in any gear. **PHRV** ₁**idle sth a'way** to waste time: *idle away the hours watching television.* **idler** /ˈaɪdlə(r)/ *n*: *a group of idlers gathered on the corner.*

idleness *n* [U]: *have/suffer six months of enforced idleness.*

idly /ˈaɪdli/ *adv* without any particular reason, purpose or foundation: *He idly stroked his beard.* ○ *'So, what next?' she said idly.* ○ *Her words were not spoken idly.* ○ *We can't sit idly by and let the countryside be destroyed* (ie do nothing to prevent it).

idol /ˈaɪdl/ *n* **1** a person or thing that is greatly loved or admired: *pop/screen/tennis idols* ○ *a fallen idol* (eg sb who has lost their popularity) ○ *He's still the idol of countless teenagers.* **2** an image of a god, often carved in stone or wood and used as an object of worship.

idolater /aɪˈdɒlətə(r)/ *n* (often *derog*) a person who worships an IDOL(2) or idols.

▶ **idolatrous** /aɪˈdɒlətrəs/ *adj* (*derog*) **(a)** worshipping idols (IDOL 2): *an idolatrous people.* **(b)** treating sb/sth as an IDOL(2): *an idolatrous love of material wealth.*

idolatry /aɪˈdɒlətri/ *n* [U] **(a)** the worship of idols (IDOL 2). **(b)** excessive love, admiration or worship of sb/sth: *He supports his local team with a fervour that borders on idolatry.*

idolize, -ise /ˈaɪdəlaɪz/ *v* [Vn] **(a)** to treat sb/sth as an idol. **(b)** to love or admire sb/sth very much: *idolize a pop group.*

idyll /ˈɪdɪl; *US* ˈaɪdl/ *n* a happy and peaceful scene or event, esp of country life, or a short piece of poetry or other writing describing this: *a rural idyll.*

▶ **idyllic** /ɪˈdɪlɪk; *US* aɪˈd-/ *adj* like an IDYLL; peaceful, beautiful and pleasant: *an idyllic setting/ cottage/island* ○ *idyllic scenery/surroundings.* **idyllically** /-kli/ *adv*: *idyllically situated in a lush green valley.*

ie /ˌaɪ ˈiː/ *abbr* that is to say; in other words (Latin *id est*): *Hot drinks, ie tea and coffee, are also available.* ⇨ note at EG.

-ie ⇨ -Y² 2.

if /ɪf/ *conj* **1** on condition that; supposing **(a)** (used with the present and present perfect tenses to introduce a likely action or situation): *If you have finished eating you may leave the table.* ○ *I'll only stay if you offer me more money.* ○ *If (it is) necessary I can come at once.* ○ *You can stay for the weekend if you like.* ○ *If anyone calls, tell them I'm not at home.* ○ *(fml) If the patient should vomit, turn him over with his head to the side.* **(b)** (used with a past tense to introduce an imaginary action or situation): *If you learned word-processing you would easily find a job.* ○ *If he were here I could explain to him myself.* ○ *If I was a man they would have given me the job.* ○ *Would she tell us the truth if we asked her?* ○ *If you liked* (ie With your approval) *I could ask my brother to look at your car.* ○ *They would have been here by now if they'd caught the early train.* ○ *I wouldn't have believed it possible, if I hadn't seen it happen.* ⇨ note at UNLESS. **2** when; whenever; every time: *If metal gets hot it expands.* ○ *She glares at me if I go near her desk.* **3** (*fml*) (used with *will* and *would* as the first part of a sentence when making a polite request): *If you will sit down for a few moments* (ie Please sit down and) *I'll tell the manager you're here.* ○ *If you would care to leave your name, we'll contact you as soon as possible.* **4** (used after *ask, know, find out, wonder*, etc to introduce one of two or more possibilities) whether: *Do you know if he's married?* ○ *I wonder if I should wear a hat.* ○ *He couldn't tell if she was laughing or crying.* ○ *Listen to the tune — see if you can remember the words.* ⇨ note. **5** (used after *vs* or *adjs* expressing feelings): *I am sorry if I disturbed you.* ○ *I'd be grateful if you would keep it a secret.* ○ *Do you mind if I turn the radio off?* **6** (also **even if**) (used when accepting that sth may be true or may happen) although: *If he said that, he didn't expect you to take it personally.* ○ *Even if you saw him pick up the money, you can't be sure he stole it.* ○ *Even if he does invite me, I still won't go.* **7** (used before an *adj* to introduce a contrast) but also; but yet: *It was thoughtless if well-meaning.* ○ *He's a real gentleman, if a little pompous at times.* **8** (used esp with a negative to express surprise, appreciation, regret, etc): *Well, if it isn't my old friend Bob Thomson — what a coincidence!* **9** (used before *you think/ask/ remember*, etc to invite sb to listen to one's opinion): *If you ask me, she's too scared to do it.* ○ *If you think about it, those children must be grown-up by now.* ○ *If you remember, Mary was always fond of animals.* **10** (used before *could, may* or *might* to introduce a suggestion or to interrupt sb politely): *If I may make a suggestion, perhaps we could begin a little earlier next week.* **IDM** **,if and** ¹**when** (used to express uncertainty about a possible event in the future): *If and when we ever meet again I hope he remembers to thank me.* **if** ¹**anything** (used to express a cautious opinion about sth, or after a negative statement to suggest that the opposite is true) if anything definite can be said, this is it: *I'd say he was more like his father, if anything.* ○ *He's not thin — if anything he's on the plump side.* **if ,I were** ¹**you** (used to introduce a piece of advice to sb): *If I were you I'd start looking for another job.* **if** ¹**not 1** (used to introduce a different suggestion or course of action after a sentence with *if* and a *v* in the present or present perfect tense) otherwise: *I'll go if you're going — if not I'd rather stay at home.* ○ *If you've finished we can have a coffee together — if not, I'll have one on my own.* **2** (used after a *yes/no* question to introduce a promise or warning): *Are you ready? If not, I'm going without you.* **3** (used to suggest that sth may be even larger, more important, etc than first indicated) perhaps even: *They cost thousands if not millions of pounds to build.* **4** (used to suggest that sb/sth is only fairly good, interesting, useful, etc) although not; but not: *It was a good if not very imaginative performance.* **if** ¹**only 1** (used to express a wish with reference to present or future time): *If only I were rich.* ○ *If only I could swim.* ○ *If only I knew her name.* ○ *If only it would stop raining.* **2** (used to express a wish that past events have been different): *If only he'd remembered to post that letter.* ○ *If only I had gone by taxi.* ¹**only if** (used at the beginning of a sentence, with the *v* in the second part of the sentence coming before its subject) only on condition that; only under the specified circumstances: *Only if a teacher*

has given permission is a student allowed to leave the room. ○ *Only if the red light comes on is there any danger to employees.*
▶ **if** *n* (*infml*) an uncertainty: *If he wins — and it's a big if — he'll be the first Englishman to win for twenty years.* ○ *Now I'm not having any ifs and buts — it's cold showers for everyone before breakfast tomorrow.*

NOTE Both **if** and **whether** are used in reporting questions which expect yes or no as the answer or offer a choice between alternatives: *She asked if/ whether I wanted a drink.* ○ *He didn't know if/ whether we should write or phone.* Before an infinitive with **to** you must use **whether**: *I'm not sure whether to buy the car or not* (NOT … *if to buy the car).*
You must use **whether** after a preposition: *It depends on whether the letter arrives in time.* **Whether** is also used to introduce a clause that is the subject of the sentence: *Whether they win or lose doesn't really matter, as long as they enjoy the game.* You can say **whether or not** but you cannot say 'if or not': *I'll be happy whether or not I get the job.*

iffy /'ɪfi/ *adj* (*infml*) doubtful; uncertain: *This year has been a bit iffy.* ○ *She's had a rather iffy relationship with some architect.*

-ify (also **-fy**) *suff* (with *ns* and *adjs* forming *vs*) to become or make sth become the thing or have the specified quality: *codify* ○ *purify* ○ *solidify.*

igloo /'ɪɡluː/ *n* (*pl* **igloos**) a small house with its roof in the shape of a dome, built by Eskimos from blocks of hard snow as a temporary shelter.

igneous /'ɪɡnɪəs/ *adj* (*geology*) (of rocks) formed when melted or liquid matter lying beneath the earth's surface becomes solid, esp after it has poured out of a VOLCANO.

ignite /ɪɡ'naɪt/ *v* to start to burn or make sth start to burn: [V] *Petrol ignites very easily.* [Vn] *He lit a match to ignite the fuse.*
▶ **ignition** /ɪɡ'nɪʃn/ *n* **1** [C usu *sing*] an electrical mechanism that makes the mixture of explosive gases in a petrol engine start to burn: *switch/turn on the ignition.* ⇨ picture at CAR. **2** [U] the action of igniting sth or being ignited.

ignoble /ɪɡ'nəʊbl/ *adj* not honourable in character or purpose; that should make one feel shame: *ignoble motives/thoughts.*

ignominy /'ɪɡnəmɪni/ *n* [U] public shame or DISGRACE¹(1): *suffer the ignominy of defeat.*
▶ **ignominious** /ˌɪɡnə'mɪnɪəs/ *adj* deserving or causing one to feel ignominy: *an ignominious defeat/failure.* **ignominiously** *adv.*

ignoramus /ˌɪɡnə'reɪməs/ *n* (*pl* **ignoramuses** /-sɪz/) an ignorant person.

ignorance /'ɪɡnərəns/ *n* [U] ~ (of sth) a lack of knowledge or information about sth: *I prefer to remain in ignorance about how you make your money.* ○ *Their fear arises out of ignorance.*

ignorant /'ɪɡnərənt/ *adj* **1** ~ (of sth) lacking education, knowledge or information: *He's ignorant but he's certainly not stupid.* ○ *I feel totally/completely ignorant of European law.* **2** (*infml*) rude through lack of knowledge of or respect for good manners: *ignorant behaviour.* ▶ **ignorantly** *adv.*

ignore /ɪɡ'nɔː(r)/ *v* **1** to pretend that sb/sth does not exist or has not happened; to pay no attention to sb/ sth: [Vn] *You've been ignoring me.* ○ *ignore advice/ criticism/feelings/regulations* ○ *You can't ignore the evidence/facts.* **2** to refuse deliberately to greet or acknowledge sb: [Vn] *I said hello to her, but she ignored me completely!*

iguana /ɪ'ɡwɑːnə/ *n* a large LIZARD of tropical America.

ikon = ICON.

il- ⇨ IN-². ⇨ note at UN-.

ilk /ɪlk/ n **IDM** **and her, his, etc ˈilk; of that / the same / her, his, etc ilk** (*infml joc*) and/of that, the same, her, etc sort or type: *pop stars and their ilk* ○ *I can't stand him, or any others of that ilk.*

ill¹ /ɪl/ adj **1** (*US usu* **sick**) [usu pred] not in full physical or mental health; sick: *He's been seriously ill for two weeks.* ○ *She fell ill/was taken ill suddenly.* ⇨ note at SICK. **2** [attrib] (**a**) not good; bad: *resign on grounds of ill health* ○ *people of ill repute* (ie with a bad reputation). (**b**) harmful; intending harm: *She suffered no ill effects from the accident.* (**c**) unkind; bad: *I don't bear her any ill will.* ○ *You ought to apologize and show there is no ill feeling between you.* **3** [attrib] not favourable: *ill luck* ○ *a bird of ill omen* (ie one thought to bring bad luck). **IDM** **bad/ill feeling** ⇨ FEELING. **ˌill at ˈease** uncomfortable; embarrassed: *be/feel ill at ease with sb.* **it's an ˌill ˈwind (that blows nobody any good)** (*saying*) few things are so bad that they do not offer some good to sb.
▶ **ill** n ⟨*fml*⟩ **1** [U] harm; evil: *I wish him no ill.* **2** [C usu *pl*] a problem; a MISFORTUNE(2): *social/financial ills* ○ *the ills of contemporary society.*

ill² /ɪl/ adv (esp in compounds) **1** badly; wrongly: *ill-advised* ○ *ill-equipped* ○ *The production is ill served by its erratic use of lighting.* ○ *It ill becomes you* (ie is not appropriate for you) *to complain.* Compare WELL¹ 1. **2** in an unkind or critical way: *speak/think ill of sb.* Compare WELL¹ 2. **3** only with difficulty; hardly: *We can ill afford the time or money for a holiday.* **IDM** **wish sb well/ill** ⇨ WISH v.

■ **ˌill-adˈvised** adj unwise; not sensible: *an ˌill-advised ˈmeeting* ○ *He was ill-advised to tell his manager.*

ˌill-asˈsorted adj badly matched; mixed: *They make an ˌill-assorted ˈcouple* (ie They do not seem well suited to each other).

ˌill-ˈbred adj badly trained from childhood; rude: *an ˌill-bred ˈchild/reˈmark.* Compare WELL-BRED.

ˌill-conˈcealed adj badly hidden: *ˌill-concealed ˈmirth.*

ˌill-conˈceived adj badly designed or planned: *an ill-conceived attempt to deny the truth.*

ˌill-conˈsidered adj not carefully or sufficiently thought about: *an ˌill-considered proˈposal/reˈsponse.*

ˌill-deˈfined adj not accurately analysed or described: *an ˌill-defined ˈrole.*

ˌill-disˈposed adj ~ (**towards sb/sth**) (*fml*) not friendly or pleasant; not favouring sb/sth: *She's very ill-disposed towards her neighbours.* Compare INDISPOSED, WELL-DISPOSED.

ˌill-eˈquipped adj ~ (**to do sth**) without the proper equipment or qualifications: *ˌill-equipped for the ˈjob* ○ *ill-equipped to deal with the increasing traffic.*

ˌill-ˈfated adj bringing or having bad luck or MISFORTUNE(1): *an ˌill-fated expeˈdition.*

ˌill-ˈfitting adj not being the right size or shape: *an ˌill-fitting ˈlid/ˈcollar.*

ˌill-ˈfounded adj not based on fact or truth: *ˌill-founded comˈplaints/ˈdoubts.*

ˌill-ˈgotten adj (*dated or joc*) obtained dishonestly: *enjoy one's ˌill-gotten ˈgains.*

ˌill-inˈformed adj having or showing little knowledge of sth: *an ˌill-informed ˈcomment* ○ *The public is remarkably ill-informed.*

ˌill-ˈjudged adj not well timed; unwise: *an ˌill-judged ˈrescue attempt.*

ˌill-ˈmannered adj having or showing bad manners; rude: *It was ill-mannered of you not to thank her.*

ˌill-preˈpared adj (**a**) not ready: *ill-prepared for the emergency.* (**b**) badly planned or organized: *an ˌill-prepared ˈtrip/ˈspeech.*

ˌill-ˈstarred adj (*rhet*) not bringing good luck: *an ˌill-starred ˈjourney/caˈreer.*

ˌill-ˈtempered adj showing the effects of a bad mood; IRRITABLE: *an ˌill-tempered ˈmatch/ˈwaiter.*

ˌill-ˈtimed adj done or happening at a time that is not appropriate: *an ˌill-timed ˈvisit* ○ *The book's publication was ill-timed.* Compare WELL-TIMED.

ˌill-ˈtreat v to treat or use sb/sth in a cruel or unkind way: [Vn] *ill-treat one's dog.* **ˌill-ˈtreatment** n [U]: *the ill-treatment of prisoners.*

I'll /aɪl/ short form **1** I shall. ⇨ SHALL. **2** I will. ⇨ WILL¹.

illegal /ɪˈliːgl/ adj against the law; not legal: *illegal immigrants/imports.*
▶ **illegality** /ˌɪlɪˈgæləti/ n **1** [U] the state of being illegal. **2** [C] an illegal act: *expose illegalities in the electoral process.*
illegally /-gəli/ adv: *an illegally parked car* ○ *cross the border illegally.*

illegible /ɪˈledʒəbl/ (also **unreadable**) adj difficult or impossible to read; not LEGIBLE: *an illegible signature.*

illegitimate /ˌɪlɪˈdʒɪtəmət/ adj **1** born of parents who are not married to each other; not LEGITIMATE (3) by birth: *an ˌillegitimate ˈchild* ○ *She's illegitimate.* **2** not allowed by the law or by the rules: *illegitimate use of company property.* ▶ **illegitimacy** /ˌɪlɪˈdʒɪtəməsi/ n [U].

illiberal /ɪˈlɪbərəl/ adj (*fml*) allowing little freedom of opinion or activity; not tolerant (TOLERATE).

illicit /ɪˈlɪsɪt/ adj (**a**) not allowed by law; illegal: *illicit alcohol/drugs.* (**b**) not approved by the normal rules of society: *illicit sex/pleasures.* ▶ **illicitly** adv.

illiterate /ɪˈlɪtərət/ adj **1** not able to read or write: *an illiterate child* ○ *an illiterate* (ie badly written) *letter.* **2** ignorant in a particular field: *be scientifically illiterate.*
▶ **illiteracy** /ɪˈlɪtərəsi/ n [U]: *tackle the problem of widespread illiteracy.*
illiterate n an illiterate person.

illness /ˈɪlnəs/ n **1** [U] the state of being ill in body or mind; lack of health: *mental illness* ○ *We've had a lot of illness in the family.* **2** [C] a type or period of illness: *serious illnesses* ○ *recovering after a long illness.*

NOTE Compare **illness, disease, ailment** and **condition**. **Illness** is a general word for a period of not being in good health: *He died unexpectedly after a short illness.* ○ *She's never had a day's illness in her life.* A **disease** is a specific illness with a name: *Measles is the most devastating of all the major childhood diseases.* It can also be used with certain organs of the body: *A healthy diet and regular exercise can help prevent heart disease.* An **ailment** is a very common illness that is not usually serious: *Common winter ailments such as colds, coughs and sore throats can usually be treated with home remedies.* A **condition** is a permanent health problem which affects a particular part of the body: *Asthma can be a very frightening condition, especially in a child.* ○ *She suffers from a heart condition.*

illogical /ɪˈlɒdʒɪkl/ adj without or contrary to logic; not sensible: *an illogical conclusion* ○ *It seems illogical to change the timetable so often.* ▶ **illogicality** /ɪˌlɒdʒɪˈkæləti/ n [C, U]. **illogically** /-kli/ adv.

illuminate /ɪˈluːmɪneɪt/ v **1** to shine light on sth: [Vn] *illuminated signs* ○ *Spotlights illuminated the courtyard.* **2** to decorate sth with bright lights for a special occasion: [Vn] *illuminate a street/building.* **3** (*fml*) to make sth clear; to help to explain sth: [Vn] *illuminate a difficult passage in a book.*
▶ **illuminated** adj (of old books, etc) decorated with gold, silver and bright colours, usu by hand: *an illuminated manuscript.*
illuminating adj helping to make sth clear or easier to understand; revealing: *an illuminating analysis/talk.*
illumination /ɪˌluːmɪˈneɪʃn/ n **1** [U, C] a source of

light: *the faint illumination of a torch.* **2 illumina-tions** [pl] (*Brit*) bright colourful lights used to decorate a town or building for a special occasion: *the Christmas illuminations in the high street.* **3** [C usu *pl*] a coloured decoration, usu painted by hand, in an old book. **4** [U] the action of illuminating sb/sth or the process of being illuminated: *the illumination of the courtyard* ○ *spiritual illumination.*

illusion /ɪˈluːʒn/ *n* **1(a)** [C] a false idea, belief or impression: *I have no illusions about my ability* (ie I know that I am not very able). ○ *She's under the illusion that* (ie believes wrongly that) *he loves her.* ○ *We're left with few illusions about the company's prospects.* **(b)** [U] a state of mind in which one is deceived in this way: *These hopes are pure/sheer illusion.* **2** [C] a thing that a person wrongly believes to exist; a false appearance: *an illusion of happiness* ○ *In the hot sun the surface of the road seems wet, but that is only an illusion.* Compare DELUSION. See also OPTICAL ILLUSION.

illusory /ɪˈluːsəri/ *adj* based on ILLUSION; not real: *Success was only illusory.* Compare ELUSIVE.

illustrate /ˈɪləstreɪt/ *v* **1** ~ **sth (with sth)** to include or use pictures, photographs or charts in a book, etc: [Vn] *an illustrated magazine/textbook* [Vnpr] *His lecture was illustrated with slides taken during the expedition.* **2** to explain or make sth clear by using examples, charts, pictures, etc: [Vn] *To illustrate my/the point I have done a comparative analysis.* ○ *The incident illustrates the need for better security.* ○ *Projected demand is illustrated in Figure 2.*
▶ **illustration** /ˌɪləˈstreɪʃn/ *n* **1** [U] the process of illustrating sth or of being illustrated: *the art of book illustration* ○ *Illustration can be more useful than definition for showing what words mean.* ○ *Let me by way of illustration quote from an article in today's 'Times'.* **2** [C] a drawing, picture or chart in a book, magazine, etc: *colour illustrations.* **3** [C] an example used to explain sth: *This is a good illustration of how prejudiced we can all be.*
illustrative /ˈɪləstrətɪv; US ɪˈlʌs-/ *adj* serving as an example or illustration: *an illustrative diagram/quotation* ○ *These materials are illustrative of a particular approach to language teaching.*
illustrator *n* a person who draws or paints pictures for books, etc.

illustrious /ɪˈlʌstriəs/ *adj* very well-known, admired and respected: *an illustrious career* ○ *illustrious figures/vistors.*

ILO /ˌaɪ el ˈəʊ/ *abbr* International Labour Organization (an organization within the United Nations concerned with working conditions and employment).

I'm /aɪm/ *short form* I am. ➪ note at BE.

im- ➪ IN-¹, IN-². ➪ note at UN-.

image /ˈɪmɪdʒ/ *n* **1** [C] a general impression that a person, an organization, a product, etc gives to the public; a reputation: *a new/youthful image* ○ *How can we improve our (public) image?* **2** [C] a mental picture or idea: *an image of refugees queuing for food* ○ *I have this image of you as always being cheerful.* **3(a)** [sing] a close copy of sb/sth: *She looks the image of her mother.* **(b)** [C] a copy of the shape of a person or thing, esp one made in stone or wood; a statue: *carved images.* **4** [C] the appearance of sb or sth when seen in a mirror or through a camera. See also MIRROR IMAGE. **5** [C] an imaginative description or comparison that produces a picture in the mind of the person reading or listening: *a poem full of startling images.* **IDM the very/living/spitting image (of sb)** a very close copy of sb: *He's the spitting image of Prince Charles.*
▶ **imagery** /ˈɪmɪdʒəri/ *n* [U] **1** imaginative language that produces pictures in the minds of people reading or listening: *poetic imagery.* **2** pictures, pho-

tographs, etc: *satellite imagery* (eg photographs of the earth taken from space).

imaginable /ɪˈmædʒɪnəbl/ *adj* that can be imagined: *The house has the most spectacular view imaginable.* ○ *They watched the match from every imaginable vantage point.*

imaginary /ɪˈmædʒɪnəri; US -dʒəneri/ *adj* existing only in the mind or imagination; not real: *imaginary fears* ○ *The story is purely/wholly imaginary.*

imagination /ɪˌmædʒɪˈneɪʃn/ *n* **1(a)** [U,C] the ability to create mental images or pictures: *a vivid imagination* ○ *He doesn't have much imagination.* ○ *Her talk captured/caught* (ie gripped and stimulated) *the imagination of the whole class.* **(b)** [C] the part of the mind that does this: *In my imagination, I thought I heard her calling me.* **(c)** [U] a thing experienced in the mind and not in reality: *Is it my imagination or have you lost a lot of weight?* **2** [U] the ability to be creative and to think of new and interesting ideas, methods, etc: *His writing lacks imagination.* ○ *Use your imagination to find an answer.* **IDM a figment of sb's imagination** ➪ FIGMENT. **the mind/imagination boggles** ➪ BOGGLE. **not by any/by no stretch of the imagination** ➪ STRETCH.
▶ **imaginative** /ɪˈmædʒɪnətɪv/ *adj* having or showing imagination: *an imaginative child/writer/idea/production.* **imaginatively** *adv*: *The exhibits were imaginatively displayed.*

imagine /ɪˈmædʒɪn/ *v* **1** to form a mental image of sth: [Vn] *Imagine a house with a big garden.* [V.that] *Imagine (that) you are on a desert island.* [V.wh] *Can you imagine what it's like to spend so much time alone?* [V.ing] *She imagined walking into the office and handing in her resignation.* [Vn-adj, V.n to inf] *Imagine yourself (to be) rich and famous.* [also V.n ing]. **2** to think of sth as probable or possible: [V.that] *I can't imagine that anyone would want such a thing.* [V.ing] *I can't imagine living anywhere else.* [V.n ing] *Would you ever have imagined him/his becoming a politician?* [also V.wh]. **3** to suppose sth; to assume sth: [V.that] *I imagine (that) John will be at the party.*

imam /ɪˈmɑːm/ *n* **1** a religious man who leads the prayers in a MOSQUE. **2 Imam** the title of various Muslim religious leaders.

imbalance /ɪmˈbæləns/ *n* (usu sing) ~ **(between A and B)**; ~ **(in sth)** a lack of balance or proportion: *an imbalance of power* ○ *an imbalance in military capability* ○ *a serious imbalance between our import and export trade.*

imbecile /ˈɪmbəsiːl; US -sl/ *n* **(a)** a person with abnormally low intelligence. **(b)** (*infml derog*) a stupid or silly person; a fool: *You imbecile!*
▶ **imbecile** *adj* [usu attrib] stupid; foolish: *an imbecile remark* ○ *imbecile behaviour.*
imbecility /ˌɪmbəˈsɪləti/ *n* **1** [U] the state of being stupid. **2** [C] a stupid act or remark.

imbibe /ɪmˈbaɪb/ *v* **1** [V,Vn] (*fml or joc*) to drink sth, esp alcohol. **2** to absorb sth: [Vn] *imbibe fresh air/knowledge/socialism.*

imbroglio /ɪmˈbrəʊliəʊ/ *n* (*pl* **-os**) (*fml*) a complicated, confused or embarrassing situation, esp a political or an emotional one: *involved in a boardroom imbroglio.*

imbue /ɪmˈbjuː/ *v* ~ **sb/sth (with sth)** (*fml*) (esp passive) to fill or inspire sb/sth with feelings, opinions or qualities: [Vnpr] *imbued with patriotism/ambition/love* ○ *politicians imbued with a desire for social change* [Vn] *attitudes and values which imbue every aspect of our lives.*

IMF /ˌaɪ em ˈef/ *abbr* International Monetary Fund (an organization within the United Nations concerned with international trade, exchange rates and the balance of payments).

imitate /ˈɪmɪteɪt/ *v* **1** to copy sb/sth; to take or

follow sb/sth as an example: [Vn] *a style imitated by more recent artists* ○ *Decide what you want to do; don't just imitate others.* **2** to copy the way a person speaks, dresses or behaves; to MIMIC sb: [Vn] *He's very clever at imitating her Irish accent.*
▶ **imitator** *n* a person who imitates other people or their ideas.

imitation /ˌɪmɪˈteɪʃn/ *n* **1** [C] a thing produced as a copy of the real thing: *That's not an original Rembrandt — it's an imitation.* ○ *a cheap/pale/poor imitation* ○ *imitation leather/fur.* **2** [U] the action of copying sb/sth: *learn sth by imitation* ○ *The house was built in imitation of a Roman villa.* **3** [C] the act of copying a person's speech or behaviour; an impersonation (IMPERSONATE): *an entertainer who does hilarious imitations of TV personalities.*

imitative /ˈɪmɪtətɪv; *US* -teɪtɪv/ *adj* copying or following a model or an example: *His style of public speaking is imitative of Kennedy's.*

immaculate /ɪˈmækjələt/ *adj* (approv) **1** perfectly clean and tidy: *an immaculate uniform/room* ○ *She always looks immaculate.* **2** right in every detail; having no mistakes: *an immaculate performance.* ▶ **immaculately** *adv*: *immaculately dressed.*

immaterial /ˌɪməˈtɪəriəl/ *adj* **1** ~ (**to sb**) not important or relevant: *The cost is immaterial.* ○ *It is immaterial (to me) whether he goes or stays.* **2** without physical form or substance: *belief in an immaterial God* ○ *the immaterial mind/soul.*

immature /ˌɪməˈtjʊə(r); *US* -ˈtʊər/ *adj* **1** not sensible in behaviour or in controlling one's feelings; less mature than one would expect: *He's very immature for his age.* **2** not fully developed or grown: *immature females/fish/plants.* ▶ **immaturity** /ˌɪməˈtjʊərəti; *US* -ˈtʊər-/ *n* [U].

immeasurable /ɪˈmeʒərəbl/ *adj* too large, wide, etc to be measured: *the immeasurable depths of the universe.* ▶ **immeasurably** /-bli/ *adv*: *Your presence has enriched our lives immeasurably.* ○ *The task seems immeasurably difficult.*

immediate /ɪˈmiːdiət/ *adj* **1(a)** happening or done at once: *I want an immediate reply.* ○ *The response of the people to the famine appeal was immediate.* ○ *take immediate action.* **(b)** [usu attrib] existing at the present time: *Our immediate concern is for the families of those who died.* **2** [attrib] nearest in time, space or relationship: *What are your plans for the immediate future?* ○ *There's no post office in the immediate neighbourhood.* ○ *his immediate predecessor* ○ *She only told her immediate family (eg her parents, husband, children, brothers and sisters).* **3** [attrib] with nothing coming in between; direct: *The immediate cause of death is unknown.* **IDM** **with immediate effect / with effect from ...** ⇨ EFFECT.
▶ **immediacy** /-əsi/ *n* [U] the quality sth has that makes it seem close and involving one directly: *the immediacy of the war, as seen on television* ○ *the immediacy of the problem.*
immediately *adv* **1** at once; without delay: *She answered almost immediately.* ○ *The point of my question may not be immediately apparent.* **2** being nearest in time or space; directly: *in the years immediately after the war* ○ *fix the lock immediately below the handle.* **3** directly or very closely: *the buildings most immediately affected by the bomb blast.* — *conj* (*esp Brit*) as soon as; the moment that: *I recognized her immediately I saw her.*

immemorial /ˌɪməˈmɔːriəl/ *adj* (*fml or rhet*) of or from a time so long ago that no one can remember it; ancient: *Farmers have been tilling these fields from/since time immemorial.*

immense /ɪˈmens/ *adj* extremely large or great: *immense power/problems/value* ○ *of immense importance.*
▶ **immensely** *adv* to a very great extent; extremely:

immensely popular/rich/successful ○ *We enjoyed the circus immensely.*
immensity /ɪˈmensəti/ *n* [U] very great size: *the immensity of the universe* ○ *It takes an effort of imagination to grasp the full immensity of the task.*

immerse /ɪˈmɜːs/ *v* **1** ~ **sth** to put sth under the surface of a liquid: [Vn, Vnpr] *Immerse the plant (in water) for a few minutes.* **2** ~ **oneself** (**in sth**) to involve oneself deeply in sth; to absorb oneself in sth: *be immersed in thought/one's business/a book* ○ *He immersed himself totally in his work.*
▶ **immersion** /ɪˈmɜːʃn; *US* -ʒn/ *n* [U] **1** the action of immersing sb/oneself/sth or the state of being immersed: *baptism by total immersion* (ie putting the whole body under water) ○ *a two-week immersion course in French* (ie in which the student will hear and use only French). **imˈmersion heater** *n* (*esp Brit*) an electric heater fitted inside a domestic water tank to provide hot water for use in the home.

immigrant /ˈɪmɪɡrənt/ *n* a person who has come to live permanently in a foreign country: *illegal immigrants* ○ *the immigrant population.*

immigration /ˌɪmɪˈɡreɪʃn/ *n* **1** [U, C] the process of coming to live in another country permanently, or an instance of this: *restrictions on immigration* ○ *immigration officers/officials* ○ *large-scale immigrations to America.* **2** (also **immiˈgration control**) [U] an area at an airport, a sea port, etc at which the passports and other documents of people wanting to come into a country are checked: *go/pass through immigration.*

imminent /ˈɪmɪnənt/ *adj* about to happen; likely to happen very soon: *The system is in imminent danger of collapse.* ○ *An announcement of further cuts in government expenditure is imminent.* ▶ **imminence** /-əns/ *n* [U]: *the imminence of death.* **imminently** *adv*.

immobile /ɪˈməʊbaɪl; *US* -bl/ *adj* **1** unable to move: *Her illness has made her completely immobile.* **2** not moving: *He sat immobile, like a statue.*
▶ **immobility** /ˌɪməˈbɪləti/ *n* [U].
immobilize, -ise /ɪˈməʊbəlaɪz/ *v* to prevent sth from moving or operating normally: [Vn] *This alarm immobilizes the car.* ○ *The firm has been immobilized by a series of strikes.*

immoderate /ɪˈmɒdərət/ *adj* (*fml*) extreme or excessive; not moderate: *immoderate eating/drinking.*
▶ **immoderately** *adv*.

immodest /ɪˈmɒdɪst/ *adj* **1** showing a lack of concern for what is considered socially acceptable, esp in matters of sexual behaviour: *an immodest dress* ○ *immodest talk/acts.* **2** showing or expressing too high an opinion of oneself or one's abilities and achievements; conceited (CONCEIT 1): *If I may be immodest for a moment, I'd like to quote from something I've just written.*

immoral /ɪˈmɒrəl; *US* ɪˈmɔːrəl/ *adj* **1** not following accepted standards of MORALITY(1); bad or wicked: *It's immoral to steal.* **2** not following accepted standards of sexual behaviour: *an immoral young man* ○ *live on/off immoral earnings* (eg as a prostitute) ○ *Some people still think it is immoral to have sex before marriage.* Compare AMORAL. ▶ **immorality** /ˌɪməˈræləti/ *n* [U, C]: *a life of immorality.* **immorally** /ɪˈmɒrəli/ *adv*.

immortal /ɪˈmɔːtl/ *adj* **1** living for ever; never dying: *The soul is immortal.* **2** famous for ever; that will be remembered for ever: *the immortal Shakespeare* ○ *In President Truman's immortal phrase/words, 'The buck stops here.'*
▶ **immortal** *n* (usu *pl*) **1** a person whose fame lasts for ever: *She is one of the Hollywood immortals.* **2** an immortal being, esp a god of ancient Greece and Rome.
immortality /ˌɪmɔːˈtæləti/ *n* [U] the state of being immortal: *belief in immortality.*

immortalize, -ise /ɪˈmɔːtəlaɪz/ v to give endless life or fame to sb/sth: [Vn] *the church immortalized in Gray's 'Elegy in a Country Churchyard'.*

immovable /ɪˈmuːvəbl/ adj **1** that cannot be moved: *an immovable object* ○ *Lock your bike to something immovable like a railing or a lamppost.* **2** not changing or yielding to argument, etc: *On this issue he is completely immovable.*

immune /ɪˈmjuːn/ adj [usu pred] **1** ~ **(to sth)** that cannot be harmed by a disease or an illness, either because of protective treatment or through the body's natural resistance: *I'm immune to smallpox as a result of vaccination.* See also AIDS. **2** ~ **(to sth)** not affected or influenced by sth: *immune to criticism/abuse/flattery.* **3** ~ **(from sth)** protected or free from sth: *immune from prosecution/recession.*
■ im'mune system n the system in the body which produces substances to help it to resist disease.
▶ **immunity** /ɪˈmjuːnəti/ n [U]: *immunity to measles/against the virus* ○ *immunity to criticism* ○ *immunity from prosecution.* See also DIPLOMATIC IMMUNITY.

immunize, -ise /ˈɪmjunaɪz/ v ~ sb **(against sth)** to make sb immune to a disease or an infection, esp by giving them a VACCINE: [Vn, Vnpr] *Have you been immunized (against smallpox) yet?* Compare INOCULATE, VACCINATE. **immunization, -isation** /ˌɪmjunaɪˈzeɪʃn; US -nəˈz-/ n [U, C]: *a worldwide immunization programme against smallpox.*

immunology /ˌɪmjuˈnɒlədʒi/ n [U] the scientific study of protection against and resistance to infection.

immure /ɪˈmjʊə(r)/ v (fml) to shut sb/oneself in a place, usu alone: [Vnpr] *immured in a convent* ○ *He immured himself in his room to work undisturbed.* [also Vn].

immutable /ɪˈmjuːtəbl/ adj (fml) that cannot be changed; that will never change: *an immutable decision* ○ *immutable principles/laws.* ▶ **immutability** /ɪˌmjuːtəˈbɪləti/ n [U].

imp /ɪmp/ n **1** a small devil or evil spirit. **2** a child that behaves badly, though not in a serious way.

impact /ˈɪmpækt/ n **1** [C usu sing] ~ **(on sb/sth)** a strong impression or effect on sb/sth: *the impact of new methods/technology on modern industry* ○ *the environmental/economic/political impact* ○ *Her speech made a tremendous impact on everyone.* ○ *Businesses around the country are beginning to feel the full impact of the recession.* **2** [C,U] the action of one object hitting another, esp with force: *craters made by meteorite impacts* ○ *the impact of a collision* ○ *The bomb exploded on impact* (ie as soon as it hit sth).
▶ **impact** /ɪmˈpækt/ v to press or fix sth firmly: [Vn] *impacted earth.* **PHRV** 'impact on sth (esp US) to have an effect on sth: *These trends are likely to impact on international financial flows.* **impacted** adj (of a tooth) held firmly in the jaw so that it cannot grow out into the mouth normally: *an impacted wisdom tooth.*

impair /ɪmˈpeə(r)/ v to damage sth or make sth weaker: [Vn] *impaired vision/growth* ○ *Too much alcohol impairs your ability to drive.* ▶ **impairment** n [U]. ⇨ note at DISABILITY.

impale /ɪmˈpeɪl/ v ~ sb/sth **(on sth)** to make a hole through sb/sth with a sharp pointed object: [Vnpr] *In trying to climb the fence he had impaled his leg/himself on the barbed wire.* [also Vn].

impalpable /ɪmˈpælpəbl/ adj (fml) **1** that cannot be touched or felt physically: *impalpable darkness/horror.* **2** not easily understood by the mind: *She was an impalpable presence lurking in his imagination.*

impart /ɪmˈpɑːt/ v **1** ~ sth **(to sth)** to give a quality to sth: [Vn, Vnpr] *Her presence imparted an air of gaiety (to the occasion).* [Vnpr] *impart spin to a ball.* **2** ~ sth **(to sb)** to make information known to

sb; to reveal sth: [Vn, Vnpr] *Teachers impart a great deal of knowledge to their pupils.*

impartial /ɪmˈpɑːʃl/ adj not favouring one person or thing more than another; fair or NEUTRAL(1a): *an impartial judge/judgement.* ▶ **impartiality** /ˌɪmˌpɑːʃiˈæləti/ n [U]: *He has a reputation for political impartiality.* **impartially** /-ʃəli/ adv.

impassable /ɪmˈpɑːsəbl; US -ˈpæs-/ adj (of a road, route, etc) impossible to travel on or over: *country lanes that are often impassable in winter* ○ *roads made impassable by fallen trees.*

impasse /ˈæmpɑːs; US ˈɪmpæs/ n (usu sing) a difficult position or situation from which there is no way out: *break/resolve the impasse* ○ *The negotiations had reached an impasse, with both sides refusing to compromise.*

impassioned /ɪmˈpæʃnd/ adj showing strong deep feeling: *an impassioned speech/appeal/plea.*

impassive /ɪmˈpæsɪv/ adj showing no sign of feeling: *an impassive expression.* ▶ **impassively** adv: *The accused sat impassively as the judge sentenced him to ten years in prison.*

impatient /ɪmˈpeɪʃnt/ adj **1(a)** ~ **(with/at sb/sth)** unable to deal calmly with sb/sth or to wait for sb/sth; easily irritated by sb/sth: *Don't be so impatient! The bus will be here soon.* ○ *You're too impatient with her — she's only a child.* **(b)** showing a lack of patience: *an impatient gesture/glance at his watch.* **2** [pred] ~ **(to do sth)**; ~ **(for sth)** very eager to do sth or for sth to happen: *young executives impatient to become managers* ○ *impatient for change/power/success.* **3** [pred] ~ **of sth** (fml) not tolerating sth: *impatient of criticism/delay.* ▶ **impatience** /ɪmˈpeɪʃns/ n [U]: *the government's growing impatience with the unions.* **impatiently** adv: *We sat waiting impatiently for the movie to start.*

impeach /ɪmˈpiːtʃ/ v **1** ~ sb **(for sth / doing sth)** to accuse a public official or politician of committing a serious crime: [Vn, Vnpr] *impeach a judge (for taking bribes).* **2** (fml) to raise doubts about sth; to question sth: [Vn] *impeach sb's motives.*
▶ **impeachable** adv (of a crime) for which a public official or politician can be impeached: *an impeachable offence.*
impeachment n [U].

impeccable /ɪmˈpekəbl/ adj perfect; without mistakes or faults: *His written English is impeccable.* ○ *impeccable behaviour/manners.* ▶ **impeccably** /-bli/ adv: *impeccably dressed.*

impecunious /ˌɪmpɪˈkjuːniəs/ adj (fml) having little or no money: *impecunious circumstances* ○ *an impecunious student.*

impedance /ɪmˈpiːdns/ n [U] (techn) the total resistance of an electric circuit to the flow of alternating current (ALTERNATE²).

impede /ɪmˈpiːd/ v (esp passive) to delay or stop the progress or movement of sb/sth: *regulations which impede imports* ○ *Completion of the building was impeded by severe weather conditions.*

impediment /ɪmˈpedɪmənt/ n **1** ~ **(to sb/sth)** a person or thing that delays or stops the progress or movement of sth: *The main impediment to growth was a lack of capital.* **2** a physical problem, esp one that makes speaking difficult: *have a speech impediment.*

impedimenta /ɪmˌpedɪˈmentə/ n [pl] (fml or joc) bags and other equipment that slow sb down, esp on a journey: *He came with his wife, six children, four dogs and various other impedimenta.*

impel /ɪmˈpel/ v (-ll-) ~ sb **(to sth)** (of a feeling, an idea, etc) to force or urge sb to do sth: [Vn] *She is impelled by a desire to change the social system.* [Vn.to inf] *I felt impelled to investigate the matter further.* Compare COMPEL.

impending /ɪmˈpendɪŋ/ adj [esp attrib] about to

happen soon; IMMINENT: *warnings of impending disaster* ∘ *his impending arrival/retirement/visit.*

impenetrable /ɪmˈpenɪtrəbl/ *adj* **1** that cannot be entered, passed through or seen through: *an impenetrable jungle/fortress* ∘ *impenetrable darkness.* **2** ~ **(to sb/sth)** impossible to understand or solve: *an impenetrable mystery* ∘ *Computer jargon is completely impenetrable to me.* ▶ **impenetrability** /ɪmˌpenɪtrəˈbɪləti/ *n* [U]. **impenetrably** /-bli/ *adv.*

imperative /ɪmˈperətɪv/ *adj* **1** [usu pred] (*fml*) very urgent or important: *It is absolutely imperative that we make a quick decision.* **2** (*fml*) expressing a command; having great authority: *an imperative tone of voice.*
▶ **imperative** *n* **1** a thing that is essential or urgent: *a moral/strategic imperative* ∘ *Survival is our first imperative.* **2** (*grammar*) a form of a verb that expresses a command: *In 'Go away!' the verb is an imperative/is in the imperative.* Compare INDICATIVE 2, INFINITIVE, SUBJUNCTIVE.

imperceptible /ˌɪmpəˈseptəbl/ *adj* that cannot be noticed or felt because of being very small, slight or gradual: *imperceptible changes in temperature* ∘ *an almost imperceptible shift of opinion.* ▶ **imperceptibly** /-əbli/ *adv*: *The light faded almost imperceptibly.*

imperfect /ɪmˈpɜːfɪkt/ *adj* **1** faulty; not perfect: *an imperfect copy* ∘ *our imperfect knowledge/ understanding of sth* ∘ *clothes sold as imperfect.* **2** [attrib] (*grammar*) of the verb tense that expresses action in the past that is not complete. It is often called the *past continuous* or *past progressive.*
▶ **imperfect** *n* the imperfect [sing] (*grammar*) the verb tense that expresses action in the past that is not complete: *In 'while I was walking home' the verb is in the imperfect.*
imperfection /ˌɪmpəˈfekʃn/ *n* [C,U] a fault that makes sb/sth imperfect: *The only slight imperfection in the painting is a scratch in the corner.* ∘ *I love him, for all (ie in spite of) his imperfections.* ∘ *There is much imperfection in nature.*
imperfectly *adv.*

imperial /ɪmˈpɪəriəl/ *adj* **1** [usu attrib] of or belonging to an empire: *the imperial palace/army* ∘ *imperial power/expansion* ∘ *the Imperial War Museum in London.* **2** [attrib] of a system of weights and measures formerly used in Britain for all goods and still used for certain goods: *an imperial pint/ gallon.* Compare METRIC.

imperialism /ɪmˈpɪəriəlɪzəm/ *n* [U] (*usu derog*) the policy of extending a country's power and influence in the world through political relations or military force, and esp in the past by acquiring colonies: *cultural/economic imperialism* ∘ *struggle against imperialism.*
▶ **imperialist** /ɪmˈpɪəriəlɪst/ *n* (*usu derog*) a person or country that supports or believes in imperialism: *imperialist forces/powers.*
imperialistic /ɪmˌpɪəriəˈlɪstɪk/ *adj.*

imperil /ɪmˈperəl/ *v* (**-ll-**; *US* also **-l-**) (*fml*) to put sb/ sth in danger: [Vn] *pollution imperilling wildlife* ∘ *We must never imperil the safety or lives of our passengers.*

imperious /ɪmˈpɪəriəs/ *adj* (*fml*) proud and expecting obedience: *an imperious look/command/gesture.*
▶ **imperiously** *adv*: *'Fetch it now,' she demanded imperiously.*

imperishable /ɪmˈperɪʃəbl/ *adj* (*fml*) that will not decay or disappear: *imperishable glory/greatness.*

impermanent /ɪmˈpɜːmənənt/ *adj* (*fml*) not permanent; temporary. ▶ **impermanence** /-əns/ *n* [U].

impermeable /ɪmˈpɜːmiəbl/ *adj* ~ **(to sth)** (of a substance) not allowing a liquid to pass through: *an impermeable membrane* ∘ *impermeable rock.*

impersonal /ɪmˈpɜːsənl/ *adj* **1** (*usu derog*) not influenced by, showing or involving human feelings : *a vast impersonal organization* ∘ *a cold impersonal*

stare ∘ *Calling the interviewees by their first names will make the meeting less impersonal.* **2** (*usu approv*) (**a**) not referring to any particular person: *Let's keep the discussion impersonal so as not to embarrass anyone.* (**b**) not influenced by personal feelings: *give an impersonal opinion.* ▶ **impersonality** /ɪmˌpɜːsəˈnæləti/ *n*: *the cold impersonality of some modern cities.*

impersonate /ɪmˈpɜːsəneɪt/ *v* (**a**) to pretend to be another person in order to entertain people: [Vn] *He can impersonate many well-known politicians.* (**b**) to copy the dress, behaviour, etc of another person in order to deceive people: [Vn] *He was caught trying to impersonate a security guard.*
▶ **impersonation** /ɪmˌpɜːsəˈneɪʃn/ *n* [C,U]: *He does impersonations of TV personalities.*
impersonator *n* a person who impersonates other people, esp as entertainment.

impertinent /ɪmˈpɜːtɪnənt/ *adj* ~ **(to sb)** not showing respect; rude: *make an impertinent remark* ∘ *a very impertinent child* ∘ *It would be grossly impertinent to tell her how the job should be done.* ▶ **impertinence** /-əns/ *n* [C usu *sing*, U]: *I've had enough of your impertinence.* **impertinently** *adv.*

imperturbable /ˌɪmpəˈtɜːbəbl/ *adj* not easily troubled or worried; calm: *She was one of those imperturbable people who never get angry or upset.* ▶ **imperturbably** /-əbli/ *adv.*

impervious /ɪmˈpɜːviəs/ *adj* ~ **(to sth)** **1** not allowing water, gas, etc to pass through: *lined with material impervious to water.* **2** not at all affected or influenced by sth: *impervious to criticism/argument/ fear.*

impetigo /ˌɪmpɪˈtaɪgəʊ/ *n* [U] an infectious disease that causes hard sore patches on the skin.

impetuous /ɪmˈpetʃuəs/ *adj* acting or done quickly, without thinking: *an impetuous young woman* ∘ *impetuous behaviour* ∘ *Don't be so impetuous!* ▶ **impetuosity** /ɪmˌpetʃuˈɒsəti/ *n* [U]. **impetuously** *adv.*

impetus /ˈɪmpɪtəs/ *n* [U, *sing*] ~ **(to sth / to do sth)** a force that encourages a process to develop more quickly: *The treaty gave fresh impetus to trade.* ∘ *What the economy needs is a new impetus.*

impiety /ɪmˈpaɪəti/ *n* [U] lack of respect, esp for God and religion. See also IMPIOUS.

impinge /ɪmˈpɪndʒ/ *v* ~ **(on/upon sth/sb)** (*fml*) to have a usu damaging or negative effect on sth/sb: [Vpr] *It is difficult to prevent problems at home impinging on your work.* [also V].

impious /ˈɪmpiəs, ɪmˈpaɪəs/ *adj* (*fml*) showing a lack of respect, esp for God and religion. See also IMPIETY.

impish /ˈɪmpɪʃ/ *adj* of or like an IMP(2); playful: *There was an impish glint in her eye.* ∘ *He takes an impish delight in shocking people.* ▶ **impishly** *adv.* **impishness** *n* [U].

implacable /ɪmˈplækəbl/ *adj* that cannot be changed or satisfied: *implacable hatred/opposition* ∘ *an implacable enemy.* ▶ **implacably** /-əbli/ *adv*: *remain implacably opposed to the plan.*

implant /ɪmˈplɑːnt; *US* -ˈplænt/ *v* ~ **sth (in/into sth)** **1** to insert tissue, etc into a part of the body: [Vn, Vnpr] *In this operation the surgeons implant a new lens (in the eye).* Compare TRANSPLANT 2. **2** to introduce or fix ideas, etc into a person's mind: [Vnpr] *implant religious beliefs in young children.* [also Vn].
▶ **implant** /ˈɪmplɑːnt; *US* -plænt/ *n* [C] a thing that is implanted in the body: *silicone breast implants.* Compare TRANSPLANT *n.*
implantation /ˌɪmplɑːnˈteɪʃn; *US* -plænt-/ *n* [U].

implausible /ɪmˈplɔːzəbl/ *adj* unlikely to be true; not convincing: *an implausible story/excuse/theory.*
▶ **implausibly** *adv.*

implement¹ /ˈɪmplɪmənt/ *v* to put sth into effect; to carry sth out: [Vn] *implement changes/policies/a*

programme of reforms. ► **implementation**
/ˌɪmplɪmenˈteɪʃn/ *n* [U]: *The government is pressing
for immediate implementation of the changes.*

implement² /ˈɪmplɪmənt/ *n* a tool; a piece of equipment: *farm implements* ○ *Man's earliest implements
were carved from stone and bone.* ⇨ note at MACHINE.

implicate /ˈɪmplɪkeɪt/ *v* ~ **sb** (**in sth**) to show that
sb is involved in sth, esp a crime: [Vnpr] *The police
are satisfied that he was not implicated in the robbery.* [Vn] *She tried to avoid saying anything that
would implicate her further.*

implication /ˌɪmplɪˈkeɪʃn/ *n* **1** [C,U] ~ (**for sb/sth**)
a thing that is suggested or implied; a thing that is
not openly stated: *Cuts in educational spending will
have far-reaching implications for the future.* ○ *They
failed to consider the wider implications of their actions.* ○ *He blames me and,* **by implication,** *my
whole family, for his unhappiness.* **2** [U] the action
of involving sb or being involved in sth, esp a crime:
She denies any implication in the affair.

implicit /ɪmˈplɪsɪt/ *adj* **1** ~ (**in sth**) implied, but not
expressed directly; not EXPLICIT(1): *implicit assumptions* ○ *an implicit threat* ○ *obligations which are
implicit in the contract.* **2** absolute; having no
doubts: *I have implicit faith in your abilities.* ►
implicitly *adv*: *She trusts him implicitly.*

implode /ɪmˈpləʊd/ *v* to burst or collapse inwards:
[V] *The windows on both sides of the room had
imploded.* Compare EXPLODE 1. ► **implosion**
/ɪmˈpləʊʒn/ *n* [C,U].

implore /ɪmˈplɔː(r)/ *v* to ask or beg for sth in a
serious way: [V.speech] *'Help me,' he implored.* [Vn]
implore sb's forgiveness/mercy [Vn.to inf] *They implored her to stay.* ⇨ note at ASK. ► **imploring** *adj*:
She gave him an imploring look.

imply /ɪmˈplaɪ/ *v* (*pt, pp* **implied**) **1** to suggest sth
indirectly rather than stating it directly: [Vn]
implied criticism/threats ○ *His silence seemed to imply agreement.* [V.that] *Are you implying that I'm
wrong?* Compare INFER. **2** to suggest sth as a logical
consequence: [Vn] *The fact that she was here implies
a degree of interest.* ○ *Increases in salaries usually
imply an increase in the number of foreign holidays
taken.*

impolite /ˌɪmpəˈlaɪt/ *adj* ~ (**to sb**) rude; not polite:
Some people think it is impolite to ask someone's age.

impolitic /ɪmˈpɒlətɪk/ *adj* (*fml*) not wise; not POL-
ITIC: *It might be impolitic to refuse his offer.*

imponderable /ɪmˈpɒndərəbl/ *adj* of which the
effect or importance cannot be measured or estimated: *The environmental impact is imponderable at
present.* ○ *an imponderable problem/question.* ► **imponderable** *n* (usu *pl*): *Whether the plan will
succeed depends on a number of imponderables.*

import¹ /ɪmˈpɔːt/ *v* ~ **sth** (**from…**); ~ **sth** (**into…**)
to bring goods, services, ideas, etc from a foreign
country into one's own country: [Vn] *The country
has to import most of its raw materials.* [Vnpr] *goods
imported from Europe into the UK* ○ *technical expertise imported from abroad.* Compare EXPORT¹.
► **importation** /ˌɪmpɔːˈteɪʃn/ *n* [U,C]: *a ban on the
importation of drugs.*
importer *n* a person, company or country that imports goods: *the world's largest importer of timber.*

import² /ˈɪmpɔːt/ *n* **1(a)** [C esp *pl*] goods, services,
ideas, etc brought from a foreign country into one's
own country: *a sharp rise in food/car imports* ○
restrict cheap foreign imports. **(b)** [U] the action of
bringing goods, etc into one's own country: *tariffs
on the import of manufactured goods* ○ *import duties/
controls.* Compare EXPORT². **2** [U] (*fml*) importance
or significance: *matters of no great import.* **3 the
import** [sing] ~ (**of sth**) (*fml*) the meaning of sth, esp
when it is not directly stated: *It is difficult to understand the full import of this statement.*

important /ɪmˈpɔːtnt/ *adj* **1** ~ (**to sb/sth**) of great

value or concern; serious: *an important decision/
announcement/meeting* ○ *Regular exercise is just as
important as eating the right type of food.* ○ *It is
important to follow the manufacturer's instructions.* ○
*It is important that students attend/for students to
attend all the lectures.* ○ *They need more money now
but, more important, they need long-term help.* ○ *It's
very/especially/vitally important to me that you
should be there.* **2** (of a person) having great influence or authority: *an important member of the
company* ○ *She likes to feel important.*
► **importance** /-tns/ *n* [U] ~ (**to/for sb/sth**) the
state of being important; having value: *the importance to the country of a healthy economy* ○ *a site of
major archaeological importance* ○ *These issues now
assume even greater importance than before.* ○ *They*
attached great **importance** to the project (ie They
considered it to be very important). ○ *State your
reasons in order of importance* (ie with the most
important one first). **IDM** **full of one's own importance** ⇨ FULL.
importantly *adv*: *strut about importantly* ○ *More
importantly, can he be trusted?*

importunate /ɪmˈpɔːtʃənət/ *adj* (*fml*) repeatedly
making requests or demands: *an importunate beggar.*

importune /ˌɪmpɔːˈtjuːn/ *v* (*fml*) ~ **sb** (**for sth**) to
ask sb repeatedly for sth, usu in an annoying man-
ner: [Vnpr] *importune sb for money* [Vn.to inf]
importune sb to increase one's allowance [also Vn].

impose /ɪmˈpəʊz/ *v* **1** ~ **sth** (**on sb/sth**) **(a)** to place
a penalty, tax, etc officially on sb/sth: [Vn] *impose a
fine/sentence* [Vnpr] *seek to impose a total ban on
strikes.* **(b)** to make sb endure sth that is not welcome or wanted; to inflict sth: [Vnpr] *impose one's
rule on a people* ○ *impose restrictions/limitations/
restraints on trade.* **2** ~ (**on sb**) to try forcefully
to make sb accept an opinion, a belief, etc: [Vnpr]
She imposed her ideas on the group. [also Vn]. **3** ~
(**oneself**) (**on sb/sth**) to take unfair advantage of sb
by expecting them to spend time with one or to do
sth for one: [Vn, Vnpr] *She'd never think of imposing
herself (on us).* [Vpr] *There are certain unscrupulous
people who are only too ready to impose on your good
nature.* [also V].
► **imposing** *adj* impressive in appearance or manner; grand: *an imposing façade/edifice* ○ *her imposing
presence.*

imposition /ˌɪmpəˈzɪʃn/ *n* ~ (**on sb/sth**) **1** [U] the
action of imposing sth: *the imposition of martial
law/of charges for eye tests.* **2** [C usu *sing*] an unfair
or unpleasant thing that sb is forced to accept: *I'd
like to stay if it's not too much of an imposition (on
you).*

impossible /ɪmˈpɒsəbl/ *adj* **1** that cannot be done
or exist; not possible: *It's impossible for me to be
there before 8.00 pm.* ○ *Teachers have found it almost/
virtually impossible to adjust to the new methods.*
2(a) very difficult to endure or deal with; HOPELESS
(1): *The decision places me in an impossible position.*
(b) (of people) badly behaved, not prepared to discuss things in a reasonable way, etc: *an impossible
child* ○ *Honestly, you're impossible at times!*
► **impossibility** /ɪmˌpɒsəˈbɪləti/ *n* [U,C usu *sing*]: *a
virtual impossibility* ○ *the logical impossibility of anyone winning a nuclear war.*
the impossible *n* [sing] a thing that cannot be
achieved: *ask for/want/attempt the impossible.*
impossibly /-əbli/ *adv*: *set impossibly high standards.*

impostor (also **imposter**) /ɪmˈpɒstə(r)/ *n* a person
who pretends to be sb else in order to deceive others.

imposture /ɪmˈpɒstʃə(r)/ *n* [U,C] (*fml*) the action or
an instance of deliberately deceiving people by pretending to be sb else.

impotent /ˈɪmpətənt/ *adj* **1** [usu pred] (*fml*) unable to take effective action; helpless: *Without the chairman's support, the committee is impotent.* **2** (of men) unable to have full sex or reach an ORGASM. ▶ **impotence** /-əns/ *n* [U]: *a feeling of impotence in the face of an apparently insoluble problem* ○ *male impotence.* **impotently** *adv.*

impound /ɪmˈpaʊnd/ *v* to take legal possession of sth: [Vn] *The police impounded his car as evidence.*

impoverish /ɪmˈpɒvərɪʃ/ *v* **1** to make sb poor : [Vn] *impoverished farmers* ○ *impoverished areas of the city.* **2** to make sth poorer or worse in quality: [Vn] *Intensive cultivation has impoverished the soil.* ▶ **impoverishment** *n* [U]: *spiritual impoverishment.*

impracticable /ɪmˈpræktɪkəbl/ *adj* impossible to put into practice; not practical: *It is impracticable to allocate a member of staff full-time to the project.* ▶ **impracticability** /ɪmˌpræktɪkəˈbɪləti/ *n* [U].

impractical /ɪmˈpræktɪkl/ *adj* **1** not sensible or realistic: *It was hopelessly impractical to think that we could finish the job in two months.* **2** not skilled at doing practical work: *an academically clever but totally impractical young man.* ▶ **impracticality** /ɪmˌpræktɪˈkæləti/ *n* [U, C].

imprecation /ˌɪmprɪˈkeɪʃn/ *n* (*fml*) a spoken curse: *mutter imprecations.*

imprecise /ˌɪmprɪˈsaɪs/ *adj* not exact or accurate; not correctly or clearly stated: *imprecise terms of reference* ○ *Parts of the account are maddeningly imprecise.* ▶ **imprecisely** *adv.* **imprecision** /ˌɪmprɪˈsɪʒn/ *n* [U].

impregnable /ɪmˈpregnəbl/ *adj* (**a**) impossible to enter or capture because of being strongly built: *an impregnable fortress.* (**b**) too strong to be overcome or defeated: *impregnable arguments* ○ *Arsenal are in an impregnable position at the top of the league.*

impregnate /ˈɪmpregneɪt; US ɪmˈpreg-/ *v* **1** ~ **sth (with sth)** (usu passive) to cause sth to be full of or soaked with a substance: [Vnpr] *a pad impregnated with insecticide* [Vn] *The smoke had impregnated their clothes.* **2** [Vn] (*fml*) to make a woman or female animal pregnant.

impresario /ˌɪmprəˈsɑːriəʊ/ *n* (*pl* **-os**) a manager or director of a ballet, a concert, a theatre or an opera company.

impress /ɪmˈpres/ *v* **1** ~ **sb (with sth)** to have a favourable effect on sb; to make sb feel admiration and respect: [Vnadv] *a critic who isn't easily impressed* [V, Vn] *The sights of the city never fail to impress (foreign tourists).* [Vnpr] *We were enormously/most impressed with/by the quality of his work.* See also IMPRESSIVE. **2** ~ **sth/itself on/ upon sb** to fix sth in sb's mind; to make sb very aware of sth: [Vnpr] *His words impressed themselves on my memory.* ○ *She impressed on her staff the importance of keeping accurate records.*

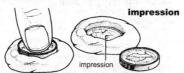

          impression

impression /ɪmˈpreʃn/ *n* **1** (esp *sing*) ~ **(of sb/ sth / of doing sth / that ...)** an idea, a feeling or an opinion about sb/sth, esp one that is formed without conscious thought or specific knowledge: *What were your first impressions of the new headmaster?* ○ *He gives the impression of being a hard worker.* ○ *My general/overall impression was that he seemed a pleasant man.* ○ *give a false/misleading impression* ○ *I had/got the distinct impression that I was being followed.* ○ *'I always thought you were a nurse.' 'I wonder how you got that impression?'* **2** ~ **(on sb)**

a deep lasting effect on the mind or feelings of sb: *create a favourable impression* ○ *His first speech as president made a strong impression on his audience.* **3** an appearance or effect that may be false: *The room's lighting conveys an impression of spaciousness.* **4** a mark left by pressing an object hard into a surface: *the impression of a leaf in a fossil.* ➪ picture. **5** ~ **(of sb)** an amusing copy of the behaviour or way of talking of a well-known person: *do a good impression of the president.* **6** a book printed with few or no changes to its contents since it was previously printed: *fifth impression 1998.* Compare EDITION 3. **IDM** **be under the imˈpression that ...** to think, usu wrongly, that sth is true or happening: *I was under the impression that you were coming tomorrow.*

▶ **impressionism** /-ʃənɪzəm/ *n* (usu **Impressionism**) [U] a style of painting developed in France in the late 19th century that creates the general impression of a subject by using effects of colour and light, without detail. **impressionist** /-ʃənɪst/ *n* **1** (usu **Impressionist**) an artist who paints in the style of Impressionism. **2** a person who entertains by doing impressions (IMPRESSION 5) of other people. — *adj* (usu **Impressionist**) of or relating to Impressionism: *Impressionist painters/landscapes.* **impressionistic** giving a general idea rather than specific facts or detailed information.

impressionable /ɪmˈpreʃnəbl/ *adj* easily influenced or affected by sb/sth: *children at an impressionable age* ○ *impressionable young people.*

impressive /ɪmˈpresɪv/ *adj* having a strong favourable effect on sb; gaining sb's admiration and respect, esp because of size, beauty or importance: *an impressive ceremony/building/speech/performance* ○ *His collection of paintings is most impressive.* ▶ **impressively** *adv.*

imprimatur /ˌɪmprɪˈmɑːtə(r)/ *n* (*fml*) official permission or approval: *give a book one's imprimatur.*

imprint /ɪmˈprɪnt/ *v* **PHRV** **imprint sth/itself in/on sth 1** to press sth hard onto a surface, leaving a mark: *tank tracks imprinted in the tarmac.* **2** to fix sth firmly in sb's mind: *The terrible scenes were indelibly imprinted on his memory/mind.*
▶ **imprint** /ˈɪmprɪnt/ *n* **1** ~ **(in/on sth)** a mark made by pressing or stamping sth onto a surface: *the imprint of a foot in the sand.* **2** (usu *sing*) ~ **(on sb/ sth)** a lasting characteristic mark or effect: *The tragedy left a lasting imprint on the community.* ○ *Her face bore the deep imprint of suffering.* **3** the name of the publisher (PUBLISH) of a book, usu printed below the title on the first page.

imprison /ɪmˈprɪzn/ *v* ~ **sb (in sth)** (esp passive) to put or keep sb in prison: [Vn] *The men were imprisoned and tortured.* [Vnpr] *be imprisoned for fraud* ○ (*fig*) *young mothers feeling virtually imprisoned in their own homes.* ▶ **imprisonment** /-mənt/ *n* [U]: *be sentenced to life imprisonment for murder.*

improbable /ɪmˈprɒbəbl/ *adj* not likely to be true or to happen; not probable: *an improbable story/ ending* ○ *It is most/highly improbable that the level of unemployment will fall.* ▶ **improbability** /ɪmˌprɒbəˈbɪləti/ *n* [U]: *the improbability of his being recaptured.* **improbably** /-əbli/ *adv.*

impromptu /ɪmˈprɒmptjuː; US -tuː/ *adj* done without advance preparation, practice or thought: *an impromptu speech/news conference/performance.*

improper /ɪmˈprɒpə(r)/ *adj* **1** wrong; not correct: *improper use of a tool/drug.* **2** not suited or appropriate to the situation or circumstances: *It was thought improper for elderly women to wear bright clothes.* **3** dishonest or morally wrong: *improper behaviour/business practices.* ▶ **improperly** *adv*: *act/behave improperly.*

impropriety /ˌɪmprəˈpraɪəti/ n (fml) [U,C] behaviour that is dishonest, morally wrong or not appropriate in the circumstances: *The investigation revealed no impropriety.*

improve /ɪmˈpruːv/ v to become or make sth better: [V] *His work is improving.* ∘ *Her health is gradually improving* (ie after an illness). [Vn] *improve one's job prospects* ∘ *a new improved washing-powder* ∘ *a much improved rail link to Southampton.* **PHRV** im'**prove on/upon sth** to achieve or produce sth of a better standard or quality than sth else: *The Kenyan girl improved on her previous best performance.*

▶ **improvement** n **1** ~ (**on/in sth**) (**a**) [U] the action or process of improving or of being improved: *There is still room for improvement in your work.* ∘ *Sales figures continue to show signs of improvement.* (**b**) [C] a positive change or effect: *see a slight/gradual/steady improvement in the weather* ∘ *The new law should produce a significant/marked improvement in working conditions.* ∘ *Their latest car is a great improvement on last year's model.* **2** [C] an addition or a change to sth that improves it or adds to its value: *home improvements* ∘ *make further improvements to the laws on racial discrimination.*

improvident /ɪmˈprɒvɪdənt/ adj (fml) not preparing for future needs, esp by wasting what one has: *improvident local councils.* ▶ **improvidence** /-əns/ n [U].

improvise /ˈɪmprəvaɪz/ *US also* ˌɪmprəˈvaɪz/ v **1** to create music, a part in a play, etc while one is playing or speaking, instead of using music or words written previously: [Vn] *an improvised speech* [V] *a talented musician able to improvise* [Vpr] *improvise on the trumpet.* **2** to make sth from whatever is available, without advanced planning: [Vn] *a hastily improvised meal* [also V]. ▶ **improvisation** /ˌɪmprəvaɪˈzeɪʃn; *US also* ˌɪmˌprɒvəˈzeɪʃn/ n [U,C]: *test one's powers of improvisation* ∘ *jazz improvisations.*

imprudent /ɪmˈpruːdnt/ adj (fml) not wise or sensible; not PRUDENT: *It would be imprudent to invest all one's money in the same company.* ▶ **imprudence** /-ns/ n [U]. **imprudently** adv.

impudent /ˈɪmpjədənt/ adj rude; not showing proper respect: *an impudent child/question.* ▶ **impudence** /-əns/ n [U]: *I've had enough of your impudence, young lady!* **impudently** adv.

impugn /ɪmˈpjuːn/ v (fml) to express doubts about sth: [Vn] *impugn sb's motives/reputation/authority.*

impulse /ˈɪmpʌls/ n **1**(**a**) [U,C usu *sing*] ~ (**to do sth**) a sudden urge to act without thinking about the results: *resist/stifle an impulse* ∘ *He felt an irresistible impulse to giggle.* ∘ *On (an) impulse, I picked up the phone and rang my sister in Australia.* (**b**) [U] the tendency to act in this way: *a man of impulse.* **2** [U,C usu *sing*] a forward movement; a STIMULUS(1): *give an impulse to industrial expansion* ∘ *His performance lost impulse in the slow movement.* **3** [C] a stimulating force in a nerve causing a muscle to react. ■ '**impulse buying** n [U] the buying of goods without having previously decided to do so.

impulsive /ɪmˈpʌlsɪv/ adj (of people or their behaviour) noted for or involving sudden action without careful thought: *an impulsive man/decision/departure.* ▶ **impulsively** adv: *'We'll all come!' Justine said impulsively.* **impulsiveness** n [U].

impunity /ɪmˈpjuːnəti/ n [U] freedom from punishment or injury: *You cannot break the law with impunity.*

impure /ɪmˈpjʊə(r)/ adj **1** not consisting entirely of one substance, but mixed with dirt or with another substance of poorer quality; not pure: *impure metals/drugs/water.* **2** (dated) morally wrong, esp in one's sexual behaviour: *impure thoughts/motives.*

▶ **impurity** /ɪmˈpjʊərəti/ n **1** [U] the state or quality of being impure. **2** [C] a substance present in another substance that makes it of poor quality: *Aluminium and lead are two of the impurities often found in tap water.*

impute /ɪmˈpjuːt/ **PHRV** **impute sth to sb/sth** (fml) to put the responsibility for sth on sb/sth; to ATTRIBUTE¹ sth to sb/sth: *impute motives/crimes/guilt to sb.* ▶ **imputation** /ˌɪmpjuˈteɪʃn/ n [U,C].

in¹ /ɪn/ adv part For the special uses of **in** in phrasal verbs, look at the verb entries. For example, the meaning of **fill in (for sb)** is given in the phrasal verb section of the entry for **fill¹**. **1**(**a**) contained within a particular area or space: *The top drawer is the one with the cutlery in.* ∘ *I'm afraid I can't drink coffee with milk in.* (**b**) into a particular area or space: *She opened the bedroom door and went in.* ∘ *The children were playing by the river when one of them slipped and fell in.* **2** (of people) at home or at a place of work: *Nobody was in when we called.* ∘ *She's usually in by seven o'clock.* ∘ *I'm afraid the manager isn't in today.* Compare OUT 2. **3** (of letters, cards, etc) delivered to the destination; received: *Applications must be in by 30 April.* **4** (of trains, buses, etc) at the place where people can get on or off, eg the station: *The coach is due in* (ie It should arrive) *at 6 o'clock.* **5** (of the tide) at or towards its highest point on land: *It's one o'clock. The tide must be in.* ∘ *Is the tide coming in or going out?* ∘ (fig) *My luck's in — I won a new car in a raffle.* **6** (of farm animals or crops) brought to the farm from the fields: *The cows will be in for milking soon.* ∘ *It's time to get the wheat in.* **7** fashionable; popular: *Short skirts are (coming) in again.* **8** elected to office: *Several new Labour councillors got in at the last election.* **9** (sport) (**a**) (of a team or a team member in cricket, baseball, etc) having a turn with the bat: *England were in first.* (**b**) (of a ball, etc in tennis, BADMINTON, etc) having landed inside the line: *Her service was in.* Compare OUT 17. **IDM** '**in for sth** (infml) to be going to experience sth soon, esp sth unpleasant: *He's in for a nasty shock/surprise!* ∘ *I'm afraid we're in for a storm.* **be/get 'in on sth** (infml) to be/become involved in sth; to have a share or knowledge of sth: *I'd like to be in on the scheme.* ∘ *Are you in on her secret?* **be (well) 'in with sb** (infml) to be (very) friendly with sb, and likely to benefit from the friendship: *He's well in with the boss.* ˌ**in and 'out (of sth)** going regularly and often to a place: *He's been in and out of hospital* (ie often ill and in hospital) *all year.*

▶ **in** adj [attrib] (infml) popular and fashionable: *the in place to go* ∘ *It's the in thing to do at the moment.*

in² /ɪn/ prep For the special uses of **in** in phrasal verbs, look at the verb entries. For example, the meaning of **deal in sth** is given in the phrasal verb section of the entry for **deal¹**. **1** (indicating place) (**a**) at a point within the area or space of sth: *the highest mountain in the world* ∘ *a country in Africa* ∘ *islands in the Pacific Ocean* ∘ *the biggest shop in town* ∘ *children playing in the street/swimming in the pool* ∘ *It's in that drawer.* ∘ *I read about it in the newspaper.* ∘ *Can you see the dog in the picture?* (**b**) within the shape of sth; enclosed by: *lying in bed* (Compare: *sitting on the bed*) ∘ *sitting in an armchair* ∘ *Leave the key in the lock.* ∘ *a cigarette in her mouth* ∘ *What have you got in your hand/pocket?* **2** (indicating movement) into sth: *He dipped his pen in the ink.* ∘ *Throw it in the fire.* ∘ *She got in her car and drove off.* **3** during a period of time: *in 1999* ∘ *in the 21st century* ∘ *in spring/summer* ∘ *in March* (Compare: *on 18 March*) ∘ *in the morning/afternoon/evening* ∘ *I'm getting forgetful in my old age.* ⇨ note at MORNING, TIME¹. **4**(**a**) after a specified length of time: *return in a few minutes/hours/days/months* ∘ *It will be ready in a week.* ∘ *She learnt to drive in three weeks*

[V.*to* inf] = verb + *to* infinitive   [Vn.inf (no *to*)] = verb + noun + infinitive without *to*   [V.*ing*] = verb + *-ing* form

(ie *After 3 weeks she could drive*). **(b)** (used after a negative or *first, last,* etc) for a period of time: *I haven't seen him in years.* ∘ *It's the first/only letter I've had in 10 days.* **5** wearing sth: *boys dressed in their best clothes* ∘ *the man in the hat* ∘ *be in uniform/mourning/disguise/armour* ∘ *She was all in black.* **6** (indicating physical surroundings, circumstances, etc): *go out in the rain* ∘ *He was sitting alone in the darkness.* **7** (indicating the state or condition of sb/sth): *I'm in love!* ∘ *His things were in order/in a complete mess.* ∘ *The house is in good repair.* ∘ *He was in a rage.* ∘ *I'm in a hurry.* ∘ *It was said in anger/in fun.* ∘ *The apple trees are in blossom.* ∘ *My son is in his early thirties.* **8(a)** (indicating sb's occupation): *He's in the army/navy/air force.* ∘ *She's in business/insurance/computers/journalism.* ∘ *He's been in politics* (ie a politician) *for twenty years.* **(b)** (indicating what sb is doing or what is happening at a particular time): *In* (ie While) *attempting to save the child from drowning, she nearly lost her own life.* ∘ *In all the commotion I forgot to tell her the news.* **9** involved in sth; taking part in sth: *be in a play/concert* ∘ *run in the 100 metres.* **10** forming the whole or part of sth; contained within sth: *There are 31 days in May.* ∘ *all the paintings in the collection/in the exhibition* ∘ *I recognize his father in him* (ie His character is partly similar to his father's). **11** (indicating form, shape, arrangement or quantities): *a novel in three parts* ∘ *stand in groups* ∘ *sit in rows* ∘ *She has her hair in a pony-tail.* ∘ *Roll it up in a ball.* ∘ *Tourists queue in* (their) *thousands to see the tomb.* **12** (indicating the medium, means, material, etc used): *speak in English* ∘ *write a message in code* ∘ *notes written in biro/ink/pencil* ∘ *printed in italics/capitals* ∘ *summarize one's ideas in a few words* ∘ *speak in a loud voice* ∘ *pay in cash* (Compare: *by cheque*) ∘ *see oneself in the mirror.* **13** with reference to sth; with regard to sth: *He's behind the others in reading but a long way ahead in maths.* ∘ *be lacking in courage* ∘ *a country rich in minerals* ∘ *three feet in length/depth/diameter* ∘ *He's blind in one eye.* **14** (used to introduce the name of a person who has a particular characteristic): *We have lost a first-rate teacher in Jim Parks.* **15** (indicating a rate or proportion): *a slope/gradient of one in five* ∘ *taxed at the rate of 15p in the pound* ∘ *One in ten said they preferred their old brand of margarine.* **IDM in that** /ɪn ðæt/ (never taking stress) for the reason that; because: *Privatization is said to be beneficial, in that it promotes competition.*

in³ /ɪn/ *n* **IDM the ˌins and ˈouts (of sth)** the details and aspects of an activity or a procedure: *know all the ins and outs of a problem* ∘ *He's been here for years — he should know the ins and outs of the job by now.*

in⁴ *abbr* (*pl* unchanged or **ins**) (also *symb* ") inch: *4 in × (ie by) 2 in (4" × 2")* ∘ *He is 6ft 2 in (tall).* Compare FT, YD.

in-¹ (also **im-**) *pref* **1** (with *vs* forming *ns* and *vs*) in; on: *intake* ∘ *imprint.* **2** (with *ns* forming *vs*) to put sb/sth into a certain state or condition: *inflame* ∘ *imperil.*

in-² (also **il-, im-, ir-**) *pref* (forming *adjs, advs* and *ns*) not: *infinite* ∘ *illogical* ∘ *immorally* ∘ *irrelevance.* ⇨ note at UN-.

-in /ɪn/ *comb form* (added to another word, usu a *v*, to indicate an activity in which many people participate): *a* ˈsit-in ∘ ˈteach-ins.

inability /ˌɪnəˈbɪləti/ *n* [U, sing] ~ **(to do sth)** lack of power, skill or ability; the state of being unable to do sth: *the inability of poor families to obtain medical treatment* ∘ *He has shown a complete inability to concentrate.*

inaccessible /ˌɪnækˈsesəbl/ *adj* ~ **(to sb)** very difficult or impossible to reach or approach; not accessible: *a remote and inaccessible region* ∘ *The temple is now inaccessible to the public.* ∘ (*fig*) *philo-*

sophical theories that are inaccessible to (ie cannot be understood by) *most of us.* ▶ **inaccessibility** /ˌɪnækˌsesəˈbɪləti/ *n* [U].

inaccurate /ɪnˈækjərət/ *adj* having errors; not correct or accurate: *an inaccurate claim/statement/description* ∘ *The maps of the area were wildly inaccurate.* ▶ **inaccuracy** /ɪnˈækjərəsi/ *n* [U, C]: *The writer is guilty of bias and inaccuracy.* ∘ *There are one or two small inaccuracies in her article.* **inaccurately** *adv.*

inaction /ɪnˈækʃn/ *n* [U] lack of action; the state of doing nothing, esp when action is appropriate or expected: *protests at official inaction.*

inactive /ɪnˈæktɪv/ *adj* **1** not active, esp physically: *Some animals are inactive during the daytime.* **2** not working or operating; not in use: *inactive station indicator boards.* ▶ **inactivity** /ˌɪnækˈtɪvəti/ *n* [U]: *political inactivity* ∘ *periods of prolonged inactivity and boredom.*

inadequate /ɪnˈædɪkwət/ *adj* **1** not sufficient or enough; not good enough for a particular purpose: *inadequate supplies/resources/preparation* ∘ *The safety precautions are totally/hopelessly/woefully inadequate.* **2** (of people) not sufficiently able or confident enough to deal with a particular situation, challenge, etc: *I felt completely inadequate to cope with the job.*

▶ **inadequacy** /ɪnˈædɪkwəsi/ *n* **1** [U] the state of being inadequate: *the inadequacy of our resources* ∘ *feel a sense of inadequacy.* **2** [C] ~ **in/of sth** a weakness: *gross inadequacies in the data* ∘ *the inadequacies of the present voting system.*

inadequately /ɪnˈædɪkwətli/ *adv*: *be inadequately prepared/insured/trained.*

inadmissible /ˌɪnədˈmɪsəbl/ *adj* that cannot be allowed or admitted, esp in a court of law: *inadmissible evidence.*

inadvertent /ˌɪnədˈvɜːtənt/ *adj* (of actions) not done deliberately or intentionally: *an inadvertent slip/omission.* ▶ **inadvertently** *adv*: *He brought back her keys which he had inadvertently put in his pocket.* **inadvertence** *n* [U].

inadvisable /ˌɪnədˈvaɪzəbl/ *adj* [usu pred] unwise; not sensible: *It is inadvisable to be too inflexible in one's travel plans.*

inalienable /ɪnˈeɪliənəbl/ *adj* [usu attrib] (*fml*) that cannot be taken away: *inalienable rights.*

inane /ɪˈneɪn/ *adj* without any meaning; silly or stupid: *an inane remark/question* ∘ *inane chatter.* ▶ **inanely** *adv*: *grin inanely.* **inanity** /ɪˈnænəti/ *n* [U, C usu *pl*].

inanimate /ɪnˈænɪmət/ *adj* not alive, esp in the way that humans and animals are: *A rock is an inanimate object.*

inapplicable /ˌɪnəˈplɪkəbl, ɪnˈæplɪkəbl/ *adj* ~ **(to sb/sth)** that is not relevant or cannot be applied to sb/sth: *The rules seem to be inapplicable to this situation.*

inappropriate /ˌɪnəˈprəʊpriət/ *adj* ~ **(to/for sb/sth)** not suitable or appropriate (for sb/sth): *an inappropriate comment/name/moment* ∘ *clothes inappropriate to the occasion* ∘ *It seems inappropriate for us to intervene at this stage.* ▶ **inappropriately** *adv*: *inappropriately dressed for a funeral.* **inappropriateness** *n* [U].

inapt /ɪnˈæpt/ *adj* not relevant, appropriate or useful: *an inapt remark/question.* ▶ **inaptly** *adv*: *an inaptly titled programme.* **inaptness** *n* [U].

inarticulate /ˌɪnɑːˈtɪkjələt/ *adj* **1** unable to express one's ideas or feelings clearly: *a clever but inarticulate person.* **2** not clearly or well expressed: *an inarticulate speech/essay* ∘ *speak in an inarticulate mumble.* **3** not expressed as spoken words: *inarticulate grunts* ∘ *Her actions were an inarticulate cry for help.* ▶ **inarticulately** *adv.*

[V.speech] = verb + direct speech   [V.*that*] = verb + *that* clause   [V.*wh*] = verb + *who, how,* etc clause

inasmuch as /ˌɪnəz'mʌtʃ əz/ *conj* (*fml*) since; because; to the extent that: *He shows an interest in other people only inasmuch as they can be useful to him.*

inattention /ˌɪnə'tenʃn/ *n* [U] ~ (**to sb/sth**) lack of attention; NEGLECT *n*: *work marred by inattention to detail.*

▶ **inattentive** /ˌɪnə'tentɪv/ *adj* ~ (**to sb/sth**) not paying attention to sb/sth; not ATTENTIVE: *an inattentive audience* ∘ *inattentive to the needs of others.* **inattentively** *adv.*

inaudible /ɪn'ɔːdəbl/ *adj* not loud enough to be heard: *speak in an almost inaudible whisper.* ▶ **inaudibility** /ɪnˌɔːdə'bɪləti/ *n* [U]. **inaudibly** /ɪn'ɔːdəbli/ *adv.*

inaugural /ɪ'nɔːgjərəl/ *adj* [attrib] of or for an inauguration (INAUGURATE): *an inaugural speech/lecture/meeting.*

inaugurate /ɪ'nɔːgjəreɪt/ *v* **1** ~ **sb** (**as sth**) to introduce a new public official or leader at a special ceremony: [Vn] *inaugurate the President* [Vn-n] *He will be inaugurated as President in January.* **2** to mark the beginning of an organization or a project, or to open a building, park, etc, with a special ceremony: [Vn] *inaugurate a scheme/a conference/ an organization* ∘ *The city library was inaugurated by the mayor.* **3** to be the beginning of sth; to introduce sth: [Vn] *The moon landing inaugurated a new era in space exploration.* ▶ **inauguration** /ɪˌnɔːgjə'reɪʃn/ *n* [U, C]: *the President's inauguration* ∘ *an inauguration speech* ∘ (*US*) *Inauguration Day* (ie when the next US President is inaugurated).

inauspicious /ˌɪnɔː'spɪʃəs/ *adj* having signs which show that future success is unlikely; not favourable: *an inauspicious occasion/event/meeting.* ▶ **inauspiciously** *adv.*

inauthentic /ˌɪnɔː'θentɪk/ *adj* not true or genuine; that cannot be believed or relied on: *an inauthentic detail/version.* ▶ **inauthenticity** /ˌɪnɔːθen'tɪsəti/ *n* [U].

inboard /'ɪnbɔːd/ *adj, adv* (situated) within the sides of or towards the centre of a boat or an aircraft: *an inboard motor.* Compare OUTBOARD.

inborn /ˌɪn'bɔːn/ *adj* existing in a person or an animal from birth; natural; INNATE: *an ˌinborn ˌtalent for 'music.*

inbred /ˌɪn'bred/ *adj* **1** existing from birth; natural: *an ˌinbred ˌsense of 'duty* ∘ *Culture is learned, not inbred.* **2** produced by INBREEDING: *The long nose on these dogs is an ˌinbred characte'ristic.*

inbreeding /'ɪnbriːdɪŋ/ *n* [U] breeding among closely related people or animals: *deformities caused by inbreeding.*

inbuilt /ˌɪn'bɪlt/ *adj* (of feelings, qualities, etc) existing as an essential part of sth; INHERENT: *inbuilt standards of behaviour* ∘ *His extra height gives him an inbuilt advantage over his opponent.* Compare BUILT-IN.

Inc (also **inc**) /ɪŋk/ *abbr* (*US*) Incorporated: *Manhattan Drugstores Inc.* Compare LTD, PLC.

inc *abbr* = INCL.

incalculable /ɪn'kælkjələbl/ *adj* **1** too large or great to be calculated; very large or great: *do incalculable harm to sb's reputation.* **2** that cannot be predicted; uncertain: *a person of incalculable moods.* ▶ **incalculably** /-əbli/ *adv.*

incandescent /ˌɪnkæn'desnt/ *adj* glowing or shining when heated: *incandescent lights* ∘ (*fig*) *She was incandescent with rage.* ▶ **incandescence** /-sns/ *n* [U].

incantation /ˌɪnkæn'teɪʃn/ *n* (**a**) [C] a series of words used as a magic spell or charm¹(3): *chant incantations to ward off evil spirits.* (**b**) [U] the saying or use of these.

incapable /ɪn'keɪpəbl/ *adj* **1** [pred] ~ **of sth /**

doing sth not able to do sth: *incapable of telling a lie* (ie too honest to do so) ∘ *incapable of sympathy* ∘ *The children seem to be totally incapable of working quietly by themselves.* **2** unable to do anything properly or to manage one's own affairs; helpless: *The patient was deemed incapable.* ∘ *He was arrested for being* **drunk and incapable.**.

incapacitate /ˌɪnkə'pæsɪteɪt/ *v* (*fml*) (usu passive) to make sb unable to do sth; to weaken (WEAK) or DISABLE(1) sb: [Vn] *be incapacitated by old age and sickness* ∘ *Persistent pain is incapacitating.*

incapacity /ˌɪnkə'pæsəti/ *n* [U] ~ (**for sth / doing sth**); ~ (**to do sth**) the lack of ability and necessary strength to do sth; weakness or inability: *a period of incapacity for work* ∘ *the incapacity to govern effectively.*

incarcerate /ɪn'kɑːsəreɪt/ *v* ~ **sb** (**in sth**) (*fml*) (esp passive) to put sb in prison: [Vn, Vnpr] *He was incarcerated (in the castle dungeon) for years.* ▶ **incarceration** /ɪnˌkɑːsə'reɪʃn/ *n* [U].

incarnate /ɪn'kɑːnət/ *adj* (following *ns*, to give emphasis) in physical human form: *The guards were sadistic beasts and their leader was the devil incarnate.* ∘ *virtue incarnate.*

▶ **incarnate** /'ɪnkɑːneɪt/ *v* (*fml*) to give real or human form to an idea, a quality, etc: [Vn] *He incarnates reform in the Communist world.*

incarnation /ˌɪnkɑː'neɪʃn/ *n* **1** [C] a person or thing that strongly displays a particular quality: *She's the incarnation of femininity.* **2** [C, U] being alive in human form, or an instance of this: *one of the incarnations of Vishnu* ∘ *He believed he had been a prince in a previous incarnation.* ∘ (*fig*) *the party's present political incarnation.* **3** **the Incarnation** [sing] (*religion*) (in Christianity) the act of God becoming a man in the person of Jesus. See also REINCARNATION.

incautious /ɪn'kɔːʃəs/ *adj* acting or done without enough care or thought; RASH². ▶ **incautiously** *adv.*

incendiary /ɪn'sendiəri; *US* -dieri/ *adj* **1** designed to set buildings, etc on fire: *an incendiary bomb/device/attack.* **2** tending to create public disturbances or violence: *incendiary words.*

▶ **incendiary** *n* a bomb that causes a fire.

incense¹ /'ɪnsens/ *n* [U] (smoke from) a substance that produces a pleasant smell when burnt, used esp in religious ceremonies.

incense² /ɪn'sens/ *v* (often passive) to make sb very angry: [Vn] *The decision to reduce pay levels has incensed the workforce.* ∘ *I feel deeply incensed by/at the way I have been treated.*

incentive /ɪn'sentɪv/ *n* ~ (**to do sth**) (**a**) [C] a thing that encourages sb to do sth: *the offer of tax incentives* ∘ *an incentive to work harder* ∘ *an incentive scheme.* Compare DISINCENTIVE. (**b**) [U] encouragement: *They don't try very hard, but then there's no incentive.*

inception /ɪn'sepʃn/ *n* [sing] (*fml*) the start or beginning of sth: *He has been director of the project since its inception.*

incessant /ɪn'sesnt/ *adj* not stopping; continual: *incessant interruptions* ∘ *a week of almost incessant rain* ∘ *an incessant stream of visitors.* ▶ **incessantly** *adv*: *quarrel incessantly.*

incest /'ɪnsest/ *n* [U] sex(2a) between people who are very closely related, eg a brother and sister or a father and daughter.

▶ **incestuous** /ɪn'sestjuəs; *US* -tʃuəs/ *adj* **1** involving incest; guilty of incest: *an incestuous relationship.* **2** (*derog*) of a group of people that have close relationships with one another and do not include people outside their group: *the incestuous atmosphere of media discourse* ∘ *Theatre people are a rather incestuous group, I find.* **incestuously** *adv.*

inch¹ /ɪntʃ/ *n* **1** (*abbr* **in**) a measure of length equal to 2.54 cm or one twelfth (TWELVE) of a foot¹(3): *I'm three inches taller than she is.* ⇨ App 2. **2** a small amount or distance: *He escaped death by an inch.* ∘ *We argued for an hour but he wouldn't budge* (ie change his attitude or ideas) *an inch.* **3** an amount of rain or snow that would cover a surface one inch deep: *Three inches of rain have fallen in Manchester in the last two days.* **IDM** by ˈinches only just: *The car missed me by inches.* **every inch 1** the whole area: *The police examined every inch of the house for clues.* **2** completely; entirely: *He looked every inch a gentleman.* **give sb an ˈinch (and they'll take a ˈmile/ˈyard)** (*saying*) if you surrender a little to sb, they will try to get a lot more: *At this stage of the negotiations, neither side is prepared to give an inch.* ˌinch by ˈinch very slowly and in small steps; by degrees: *They climbed the steep mountain inch by inch.* **within an ˈinch of sth / doing sth** very close to sth / doing sth: *He came within an inch of being killed.* ∘ *He threatened to thrash the boy within an inch of his life* (ie very severely).

inch² /ɪntʃ/ *v* ~ (sth) forward, past, through, etc (sth) to move or make sth move slowly and carefully in the specified direction: [Vnp] *inch the car forward* [Vpr, Vnpr] *He inched (his way) through the narrow passage.* [also Vp, V].

inchoate /ɪnˈkəʊət, ˈɪnkəʊeɪt/ *adj* (*fml*) just begun and therefore not fully formed or developed: *inchoate ideas.*

incidence /ˈɪnsɪdəns/ *n* [sing] **1** ~ of sth the extent to which sth happens or has an effect: *an area with a high incidence of crime/disease/unemployment.* **2** (*techn*) the way in which a ray of light strikes a surface: *the angle of incidence.*

incident /ˈɪnsɪdənt/ *n* **1** an event or a happening: *an incident in which she claimed to have seen a ghost.* **2** a military conflict between countries, opposing forces, etc: *border incidents.* **3** [U, C] public disturbance, accident or violence, or an incident of this: *The demonstration proceeded without incident.* ⇨ note at OCCURRENCE.

incidental /ˌɪnsɪˈdentl/ *adj* **1** accompanying, but not a major part of, sth; minor; SUPPLEMENTARY: *incidental expenses* ∘ *incidental music for a play.* **2** ~ (to sth) occurring by chance in connection with sth else: *an incidental discovery* ∘ *findings incidental to the main investigation.* See also COINCIDENTAL.
▶ **incidental** *n* (usu *pl*) a relatively unimportant thing that accompanies sth else: *budget for incidentals such as tips and taxi fares.*
incidentally /-tli/ *adv* **1** (used to introduce sth additional that the speaker has just thought of) by the way: *Incidentally, whatever became of Jenkins? I haven't heard of him for years.* **2** in an incidental way: *mention sth incidentally.*

incinerate /ɪnˈsɪnəreɪt/ *v* to destroy sth completely by burning; to burn sth to ashes: [Vn] *incinerate rubbish.*
▶ **incineration** /ɪnˌsɪnəˈreɪʃn/ *n* [U]: *an incineration plant.*
incinerator /ɪnˈsɪnəreɪtə(r)/ *n* a FURNACE(1) or enclosed container for burning rubbish, etc.

incipient /ɪnˈsɪpiənt/ *adj* [usu attrib] (*fml*) in its early stages; beginning to happen: *signs of incipient unrest.*

incise /ɪnˈsaɪz/ *v* to cut words, designs, etc into a surface: [Vn] *an incised letter/pattern.* Compare ENGRAVE 1.
▶ **incision** /ɪnˈsɪʒn/ *n* (**a**) [C] a cut, esp one made by a SURGEON into flesh as part of an operation(1): *make a deep incision in the thigh.* (**b**) [U] the action of cutting.

incisive /ɪnˈsaɪsɪv/ *adj* clear and PRECISE(1); direct or sharp: *incisive comments/criticism/advice* ∘ *an incisive mind.* ▶ **incisively** *adv.* **incisiveness** *n* [U].

incisor /ɪnˈsaɪzə(r)/ *n* each of the eight sharp cutting teeth at the front of the mouth. ⇨ picture at TOOTH.

incite /ɪnˈsaɪt/ *v* **1** ~ sb (to sth) to urge or persuade sb to do sth by making them very angry or excited: [Vnpr] *incite the workers to violence/against the government* [Vn.to inf] *He was accused of inciting other officers to mutiny.* **2** to create or cause sth, esp conflict or violence: [Vn] *incite a riot.*
▶ **incitement** *n* [C, U] ~ (to sth) (an) action that encourages aggressive or violent behaviour: *incitement to racial hatred.*

incivility /ˌɪnsəˈvɪləti/ *n* (*fml*) **1** [U] lack of polite behaviour. **2** [C] an act or remark that is not polite. Compare UNCIVIL.

incl (also **inc**) *abbr* including; inclusive: *total £29.53 incl tax.*

inclement /ɪnˈklemənt/ *adj* (*fml*) (of weather) cold, RAINY, etc; bad: *It's been rather inclement this week.*
▶ **inclemency** /-ənsi/ *n* [U].

inclination /ˌɪnklɪˈneɪʃn/ *n* **1** [U, C] ~ (to/for/towards sth); ~ (to do sth) a feeling that makes sb want to do sth or behave in a particular way; a DISPOSITION(2): *I have neither the time nor the inclination to go to rock concerts.* ∘ *My natural inclination is to seek a compromise solution.* ∘ *He is a doctor by profession and a musician by inclination.* ∘ *She was determined to follow her own inclinations in choosing a career.* Compare DISINCLINATION. **2** [C] a tendency: *The car has an inclination to stall on steep hills.* ∘ *He has an inclination to overdramatize.* **3**(**a**) [U] a degree of sloping. (**b**) [C] a sloping surface; a slope: *a small inclination just beyond the trees.* **4** [C usu sing] a bending or bowing movement: *with an inclination of his head.*

incline¹ /ɪnˈklaɪn/ *v* **1** to lean or slope, or cause sth to lean or slope, in a certain direction: [Vpr] *The land inclines towards the shore.* [Vnpr] *The bench is inclined at an angle of 30°.* [also Vn]. **2** to bend forward a part of the body, esp the head: [Vn] *She inclined her head in prayer.* **3** (*fml*) (**a**) ~ sb towards sth to persuade sb to do sth; to cause a certain tendency in sb; to influence sb: [Vnpr] *His love of languages inclined him towards a career as a translator.* [Vn.to inf] *His sincerity inclines me to trust him.* (**b**) ~ to/towards sth to have a physical or mental tendency towards sth; to be disposed to do sth: [Vpr] *He inclines towards laziness.* ∘ *I incline to the view that we should take no action at this stage.* [V.to inf] *The government is more effective than we incline to think.*
▶ **inclined** *adj* [pred] **1** ~ (to do sth) wanting to behave in a particular way: *I'm inclined to trust him.* ∘ *We can go for a walk, if you feel so inclined.* Compare DISINCLINED. **2** ~ to do sth having a tendency to do sth; likely to do sth: *He's inclined to be lazy.* ∘ *The car is inclined to stall on steep hills.* **3** ~ to do sth (used to make what is said sound less strong) holding a particular opinion: *I'm inclined to believe he's innocent.* ∘ *Generally speaking, I'm inclined to agree with you.* **4** having a natural ability in a specified subject: *Louise is very musically inclined.*

incline² /ˈɪnklaɪn/ *n* a sloping surface; a slope: *a gentle/steep incline.*

inclose = ENCLOSE.

inclosure = ENCLOSURE.

include /ɪnˈkluːd/ *v* **1** to have sb/sth as part of a whole: [Vn] *The conference delegates include many representatives from abroad.* ∘ *The tour included a visit to the Science Museum.* ∘ *Does the price include tax?* [V.ing] *Your duties include checking the post and distributing it.* **2** ~ sb/sth (in/among sth) to make sb/sth part of a larger group or set: [Vn] *We all went, me/myself included* (ie I was among those who went). ○ *Detailed instructions are included in the booklet.* Compare EXCLUDE.

▶ **including** /ɪnˈkluːdɪŋ/ *prep* having sb/sth as a part: *£57.50, including postage and packing* ○ *The band played a number of songs, including some of my favourites.* ○ *Sales up to and including last month amounted to £10 000.*

inclusion /ɪnˈkluːʒn/ *n* ~ (**in sth**) (**a**) [U] the action of including sb/sth or of being included: *the inclusion of the clause in the contract.* (**b**) [C] a person or thing included: *The list contains some surprising inclusions.* Compare EXCLUSION.

inclusive /ɪnˈkluːsɪv/ *adj* **1** ~ (**of sth**) including sth; including much or all: *The price is £800, inclusive of tax.* Compare EXCLUSIVE 4. **2** (following *ns*) including the limits specified: *from Monday to Friday inclusive* ○ *pages 7 to 26 inclusive.* ▶ **inclusively** *adv.*

incognito /ˌɪnkɒgˈniːtəʊ/ *adj* [pred], *adv* with one's true identity hidden, eg by using a false name: *He didn't want to be recognized, so he travelled incognito.*

incoherent /ˌɪnkəʊˈhɪərənt/ *adj* **1** talking in a way that is not clear or logical: *He was in a state of shock, sobbing and incoherent.* **2** not expressed clearly: *I had to listen to her incoherent ramblings.* ▶ **incoherence** /-əns/ *n* [U]. **incoherently** *adv.*

income /ˈɪnkʌm, -kəm/ *n* [C, U] money received over a certain period, esp as payment for work or as interest on investments: *a family with two incomes* (eg when the husband and wife both do paid work) ○ *high/low income groups* ○ *a useful source of income* ○ *Tax is payable on all income over the specified amount.* Compare EXPENDITURE.
■ **ˈincome support** *n* [U] (in Britain) money paid from government funds to people with a low income: *go on income support.*
ˈincome tax *n* [U] tax that is paid according to the level of one's income: *reduce the standard rate of income tax.* Compare CAPITAL LEVY.

> **NOTE** Your **income** is the money you receive from work, business, etc. **Pay** is a general word for money somebody receives regularly from their employer for work done. The day of the week or month when this money is received is your **pay-day**. **Wages** are paid weekly (sometimes daily) and usually in cash. They are based on an hourly, daily or weekly rate or on a certain amount of work done. Professional people such as teachers, doctors, etc, and people who work in offices, receive a **salary** every year. It is paid monthly, usually directly into a bank account: *They are offering a starting salary of £14 000 a year/per annum.* You pay a **fee** to somebody who provides a professional service: *I thought the lawyer's fees were rather high.*

incoming /ˈɪnkʌmɪŋ/ *adj* [attrib] **1** coming in: *the incoming tide* ○ *incoming telephone calls* ○ *incoming passengers.* **2** recently elected or appointed: *the incoming president.* Compare OUTGOING 2.

incommensurable /ˌɪnkəˈmenʃərəbl/ *adj* [usu pred] (also **incommensurate**) ~ (**with sth**) (*fml*) that cannot be judged or measured by the same standard as sth. ▶ **incommensurability** /-ˌmenʃərəˈbɪləti/ *n* [U, C].

incommensurate /ˌɪnkəˈmenʃərət/ *adj* [usu pred] (*fml*) **1** ~ (**with sth**) not in proportion to sth; inadequate: *His abilities are incommensurate with the demands of the job.* **2** = INCOMMENSURABLE: *The two alternatives are simply incommensurate.*

incommode /ˌɪnkəˈməʊd/ *v* [Vn] (*fml*) to trouble or bother sb.

incommunicado /ˌɪnkəˌmjuːnɪˈkɑːdəʊ/ *adj* [pred], *adv* not wanting or being allowed to communicate with other people: *The prisoner was held/kept incommunicado for six months.*

incomparable /ɪnˈkɒmprəbl/ *adj* too good, great,

etc to have an equal; beyond comparison: *the incomparable beauty of Lake Garda* ○ *He was always an incomparable showman.* ▶ **incomparability** /ɪnˌkɒmpərəˈbɪləti/ *n* [U]. **incomparably** /ɪnˈkɒmprəbli/ *adv: incomparably the greatest poet of his generation.*

incompatible /ˌɪnkəmˈpætəbl/ *adj* **1** ~ (**with sb**) not able to live or work happily with sb: *temperamentally/sexually/socially incompatible* ○ *I've never seen such an incompatible couple.* **2** ~ (**with sth**) not consistent or in logical agreement with sth: *behaviour that is totally incompatible with the aims of the society.* ▶ **incompatibility** /ˌɪnkəmˌpætəˈbɪləti/ *n* [U, C].

incompetent /ɪnˈkɒmpɪtənt/ *adj* not having or showing the necessary skills or qualifications to do sth successfully: *I suppose my application has been lost by some incompetent clerk.* ○ *He was criticized for his incompetent handling of the affair.* ○ (*fml*) *I'm incompetent to judge on such an issue.* ▶ **incompetence** /-əns/ *n* [U] the lack of skill or ability to do a task successfully: *He was dismissed for incompetence.* **incompetent** *n* an incompetent person. **incompetently** *adv.*

incomplete /ˌɪnkəmˈpliːt/ *adj* not having all its parts; not complete: *an incomplete set of figures.* ▶ **incompletely** *adv.* **incompleteness** *n* [U].

incomprehensible /ɪnˌkɒmprɪˈhensəbl/ *adj* ~ (**to sb**) that cannot be understood; not COMPREHENSIBLE: *technical expressions that are incomprehensible to most ordinary people.* ▶ **incomprehensibility** /ɪnˌkɒmprɪˌhensəˈbɪləti/ *n* [U]. **incomprehensibly** /-səbli/ *adv.*

incomprehension /ɪnˌkɒmprɪˈhenʃn/ *n* [U] failure to understand sth: *Her explanations were met with blank incomprehension.*

inconceivable /ˌɪnkənˈsiːvəbl/ *adj* very difficult to believe or imagine: *It seems inconceivable (to me) that the accident could have happened so quickly.* ○ *We are surrounded by the inconceivable vastness of space.* ▶ **inconceivably** *adv* in a way that is very difficult to believe or understand: *We are facing a crisis of almost inconceivably devastating magnitude.*

inconclusive /ˌɪnkənˈkluːsɪv/ *adj* not leading to a definite decision, conclusion or result: *inconclusive arguments/discussions/evidence.* ▶ **inconclusively** *adv: The debate ended inconclusively.*

incongruous /ɪnˈkɒŋgruəs/ *adj* strange because not in harmony with the surroundings; out of place: *Such traditional methods seem incongruous in this modern technical age.* ▶ **incongruity** /ˌɪnkɒnˈgruːəti/ *n* [U, C]: *the apparent incongruity of a scientist with a strong religious faith* ○ *cultural incongruities.* **incongruously** *adv.*

inconsequential /ˌɪnˌkɒnsɪˈkwenʃl/ *adj* unimportant or irrelevant; TRIVIAL: *inconsequential details/events/questions.* ▶ **inconsequentially** /-ʃəli/ *adv.*

inconsiderable /ˌɪnkənˈsɪdrəbl/ *adj* small in size or value; not worth considering: *a not inconsiderable* (ie a large) *sum of money.*

inconsiderate /ˌɪnkənˈsɪdərət/ *adj* (*derog*) not caring about the feelings of other people; thoughtless; (THOUGHT²); not considerate: *his inconsiderate behaviour/remarks* ○ *It is inconsiderate of people to smoke in public.* ▶ **inconsiderately** *adv.*

inconsistent /ˌɪnkənˈsɪstənt/ *adj* **1** [usu pred] ~ (**with sth**) not in harmony with sth; containing parts that do not agree with one another: *Such behaviour is inconsistent with her high-minded principles.* ○ *His account of the events was inconsistent.* **2** not staying the same; tending to change: *The team has had a very inconsistent season.* ▶ **inconsistency** /-ənsi/ *n* [U, C]: *There is much inconsistency in* *his work.* ○ *I noticed a few minor inconsistencies in his argument.* **inconsistently** *adv.*

inconsolable /ˌɪnkən'səʊləbl/ *adj* that cannot be comforted: *inconsolable grief* ○ *He was inconsolable when his wife died.* ▶ **inconsolably** /-əbli/ *adv*: *weep inconsolably.*

inconspicuous /ˌɪnkən'spɪkjuəs/ *adj* not very noticeable or obvious; not CONSPICUOUS: *a small inconspicuous crack in the vase* ○ *She tried to make herself as inconspicuous as possible* (ie tried to avoid attention). ▶ **inconspicuously** *adv.*

inconstant /ɪn'kɒnstənt/ *adj (fml)* (esp of people or their behaviour) tending to change in feelings and intentions; FICKLE: *an inconstant lover.* ▶ **inconstancy** /-ənsi/ *n* [U].

incontestable /ˌɪnkən'testəbl/ *adj* so certain that it cannot be disputed or disagreed with: *an incontestable fact.* ▶ **incontestably** /-əbli/ *adv.*

incontinent /ɪn'kɒntɪnənt/ *adj* unable to control the BLADDER(1) or bowels in passing waste matter from the body: *People often become incontinent when they get very old.* ▶ **incontinence** /-əns/ *n* [U].

incontrovertible /ˌɪnkɒntrə'vɜːtəbl/ *adj* so obvious and certain that it cannot be disputed or denied: *incontrovertible evidence/proof.* ▶ **incontrovertibly** /ˌɪnkɒntrə'vɜːtəbli/ *adv*: *incontrovertibly true.*

inconvenience /ˌɪnkən'viːniəns/ *n* (**a**) [U] trouble, difficulty or discomfort: *put sb to/suffer great inconvenience* ○ *He apologized for the inconvenience he had caused.* (**b**) [C] a person or thing that causes inconvenience: *put up with minor inconveniences* ○ *Having to change trains is a small inconvenience.*
▶ **inconvenience** *v* to cause inconvenience to sb/sth: [Vn] *The public have been greatly inconvenienced by the rail strike.*

inconvenient /ˌɪnkən'viːniənt/ *adj* causing trouble, difficulty or discomfort: *They arrived at an inconvenient time — we had just started eating.* ○ *Living such a long way from the supermarket can be very inconvenient.* ▶ **inconveniently** *adv.*

incorporate /ɪn'kɔːpəreɪt/ *v* (**a**) ~ sth (in/into sth) to make sth part of a whole; to include sth: [Vn, Vnpr] *Many of your suggestions have been incorporated (in the new plan).* (**b**) to have sth as part of a whole: [Vn] *The new car design incorporates all the latest safety features.*
▶ **incorporated** /ɪn'kɔːpəreɪtɪd/ *adj (abbr* Inc) *(US)* (following the name of a company) formed into a legal organization: *Nelson Products Inc.*
incorporation /ɪnˌkɔːpə'reɪʃn/ *n* [U]: *the incorporation of foreign words into the language.*

incorporeal /ˌɪnkɔː'pɔːriəl/ *adj (fml)* without a body or material form.

incorrect /ˌɪnkə'rekt/ *adj* **1** not correct or true; wrong: *an incorrect answer* ○ *incorrect conclusions.* **2** not according to accepted standards; not polite: *incorrect behaviour.* ▶ **incorrectly** *adv*: *answer incorrectly.* **incorrectness** *n* [U].

incorrigible /ɪn'kɒrɪdʒəbl; *US* -'kɔːr-/ *adj* (of people or their faults) that cannot be corrected or improved: *an incorrigible liar/gambler/gossip* ○ *incorrigible habits.* ▶ **incorrigibly** /ɪn'kɒrɪdʒəbli; *US* -'kɔːr-/ *adv.*

incorruptible /ˌɪnkə'rʌptəbl/ *adj* **1** that cannot be persuaded to do sth dishonest, eg by means of a BRIBE: *Judges should be incorruptible.* **2** that cannot decay or be destroyed. ▶ **incorruptibility** /ˌɪnkəˌrʌptə'bɪləti/ *n* [U]. **incorruptibly** /ˌɪnkə'rʌptəbli/ *adv.*

increase¹ /ɪn'kriːs/ *v* ~ (sth) (from A) (to B) to become or make sth greater in number, quantity, size, etc: [Vpr] *The population has increased from 1.2 million 10 years ago to 1.8 million today.* ○ *The rate of inflation has increased by 2%.* [Vn] *increased profits* ○ *He increased his speed to overtake the bus.* [also V, Vnpr]. Compare DECREASE.

▶ **increasingly** /ɪn'kriːsɪŋli/ *adv* more and more: *increasingly difficult/important/popular* ○ *People are increasingly realizing that our basic problems are not economic ones.*

increase² /'ɪnkriːs/ *n* [C, U] ~ (in sth) an amount by which sth increases: *an increase of nearly 50% over/on last year* ○ *a wage increase* ○ *Greater spending on education is expected to lead to a large increase in the number of students.* ○ *Some increase in working hours may be necessary.* Compare DECREASE *n.* **IDM** **on the ¹increase** *(infml)* increasing: *The number of burglaries in the area is on the increase.*

incredible /ɪn'kredəbl/ *adj* **1** *(infml)* difficult to believe; extraordinary: *He earns an incredible amount of money.* ○ *We had an incredible* (ie extremely good) *time.* ○ *She's an incredible actress.* **2** impossible to believe: *Her story is frankly incredible.* ▶ **incredibly** /ɪn'kredəbli/ *adv* **1** to a great degree; extremely or unusually: *incredibly hot weather.* **2** in a way that is difficult to believe; strangely (STRANGE): *Incredibly, no one had ever thought of such a simple idea before.*

incredulous /ɪn'kredjələs; *US* -dʒəl-/ *adj* not willing or able to believe; showing disbelief (DISBELIEVE): *an incredulous look/gasp* ○ *The decision was announced to an incredulous audience.* ▶ **incredulity** /ˌɪnkrə'djuːləti; *US* -'duː-/ *n* [U]: *an expression of shock and utter incredulity.* **incredulously** *adv.*

increment /'ɪŋkrəmənt/ *n* an increase, esp in money paid as a salary; an added amount: *Your salary will be £15 000 a year, with annual increments of £500.* ▶ **incremental** /ˌɪŋkrə'mentl/ *adj*: *incremental increases/benefits.* **incrementally** /-təli/ *adv.*

incriminate /ɪn'krɪmɪneɪt/ *v* to make sb appear to be guilty of wrongdoing: [V] *incriminating evidence* [Vn] *She refused to make a statement to the police in case she incriminated herself.* ▶ **incrimination** /ɪnˌkrɪmɪ'neɪʃn/ *n* [U].

incrustation /ˌɪnkrʌ'steɪʃn/ (also **encrustation** /ˌen-/) *n* [U, C] (the formation of) a hard outer covering or layer, esp one that forms gradually: *incrustations of barnacles on the hull.*

incubate /'ɪŋkjubeɪt/ *v* **1(a)** to keep eggs warm, usu by sitting on them, until they HATCH²(1b): [Vn] *a bird incubating her eggs.* (**b**) [V] (of eggs) to be kept warm until ready to HATCH²(1b). **2** *(medical or biology)* to make bacteria, etc develop; (of bacteria, etc) to develop under favourable conditions, esp heat: [Vn] *incubate germs in a laboratory* [V] *Some viruses incubate in the body very rapidly.* ○ *(fig) Plans for revolution had long been incubating in their minds.*
▶ **incubation** /ˌɪŋkju'beɪʃn/ *n* **1** [U] the hatching (HATCH² 2) of eggs: *artificial incubation* (ie using artificial warmth). **2** *(medical or biology)* (**a**) [U] the development of bacteria, etc. (**b**) (also **incubation period**) [C] the period between being infected with a disease and the appearance of the first symptoms.

incubator /'ɪŋkjubeɪtə(r)/ *n* **1** an apparatus like a box in which small weak babies are cared for, esp those born earlier than normal. **2** an apparatus like a box in which eggs can HATCH²(1b) by artificial warmth. See also HATCHERY.

incubus /'ɪŋkjubəs/ *n* (*pl* **incubuses** or **incubi** /-baɪ/) **1** *(fml)* a constantly worrying problem: *the incubus of his unpaid debts.* **2** a male evil spirit formerly supposed to have sex with a sleeping woman. Compare SUCCUBUS.

inculcate /'ɪnkʌlkeɪt; *US* ɪn'kʌl-/ *v* ~ sth (in/into sb); ~ sb with sth *(fml)* to fix ideas, principles, etc firmly in sb's mind, esp by often repeating them: [Vn, Vnpr] *inculcate (in young people) a respect for the law* [Vnpr] *inculcate young people with a respect for the law.*

incumbent /ɪn'kʌmbənt/ *adj* **1** [pred] ~ **on/upon**

sb (*fml*) necessary as part of sb's duty: *It is incumbent upon all users of this equipment to familiarize themselves with the safety procedure.* **2** [usu attrib] holding the specified official position; current[1](1): *the incumbent president.*
▶ **incumbent** *n* a person holding an official position: *the present incumbent at the White House* (ie the US President). **incumbency** /-ənsɪ/ *n* the position or period of office of an incumbent.

incur /ɪnˈkɜː(r)/ *v* (**-rr-**) to cause oneself to suffer sth bad; to bring sth upon oneself: [Vn] *incur debts/ great expense/sb's anger.*

incurable /ɪnˈkjʊərəbl/ *adj* that cannot be cured: *incurable diseases/habits* ○ (*fig*) *He's an incurable romantic.*
▶ **incurable** *n* a person with an incurable disease: *a home for incurables.*
incurably /-əblɪ/ *adv*: *be incurably ill/optimistic/ stupid.*

incurious /ɪnˈkjʊərɪəs/ *adj* (*fml*) having no curiosity; not INQUISITIVE.

incursion /ɪnˈkɜːʃn; *US* -ˈkɜːrʒn/ *n* ~ (**into sth**) (*fml*) **1** a sudden attack on or INVASION(1,2) of a place or an area of activity: *repel a sudden incursion of enemy troops (into one's territory)* ○ *foreign incursions into the domestic market.* **2** an interruption or a disturbance of sb's time, private life, etc: *I resent these incursions into my leisure time.*

Ind *abbr* (*politics*) Independent (candidate): *Tom Lee (Ind).*

indebted /ɪnˈdetɪd/ *adj* ~ (**to sb**) (**for sth**) owing money or gratitude to sb: *loans to heavily indebted countries* ○ *I am deeply indebted to you for all your advice and encouragement.* ▶ **indebtedness** *n* [U].

indecent /ɪnˈdiːsnt/ *adj* **1** (of behaviour, talk, etc) offending against accepted moral standards; not DECENT(2); OBSCENE: *That short skirt of hers is positively indecent.* **2** [usu attrib] not appropriate or proper(3): *leave a party in indecent haste* (ie too early or too soon to be polite).
▶ **indecency** /-nsɪ/ *n* **1** [U] being indecent; indecent behaviour: *arrested by the police for gross indecency* (eg showing one's sexual organs in public). **2** [C] an indecent act, gesture, expression, etc. **indecently** *adv*.
■ **in,decent exˈposure** *n* [U] the crime of intentionally showing one's sexual organs in public.

indecipherable /ˌɪndɪˈsaɪfrəbl/ *adj* that cannot be read or understood: *an indecipherable code/ signature/scribble* ○ *Her writing is completely indecipherable.*

indecision /ˌɪndɪˈsɪʒn/ *n* [U] the state of being unable to make decisions; hesitation (HESITATE): *He stood outside the door in an agony of indecision.*

indecisive /ˌɪndɪˈsaɪsɪv/ *adj* **1** unable to make decisions; hesitating: *He's too indecisive to make a good leader.* **2** not final or CONCLUSIVE: *an indecisive battle/answer/meeting.* ▶ **indecisively** *adv*.

indecorous /ɪnˈdekərəs/ *adj* (*fml*) showing a lack of dignity, good manners or good taste: *He was forced to make a hasty and indecorous departure without his clothes.*

indeed /ɪnˈdiːd/ *adv* **1(a)** (used to emphasize an affirmative reply: *'Did he complain?' 'Indeed he did/ He did indeed.'* ○ *'Do you agree?' 'Yes indeed!'* **(b)** (used to emphasize a statement, an exclamation, etc): *That is indeed remarkable/a remarkable thing!* ○ *It was bad news indeed.* ○ *So I was right — there has indeed been a conspiracy!* **2** (*esp Brit*) (used after *very* + an *adj* or *adv* to emphasize a statement, description, etc) really: *a very big parcel indeed* ○ *Thank you very much indeed!* ○ *I was very sad indeed to hear about it.* **3** (*fml esp Brit*) in fact: *I don't mind. Indeed, I am delighted to help.* ○ *I was annoyed, indeed furious, over what happened.* **4** (as a comment or response) **(a)** (*fml*) (expressing surprise, but

not disbelief): *'I saw a ghost!' 'Indeed? Where was it?'* **(b)** (expressing disbelief and even scorn): *'A ghost indeed! I've never heard anything so ridiculous!'* **(c)** (showing interest of a critical or an ironical kind): *'When will the weather improve?' 'When, indeed!'*

indefatigable /ˌɪndɪˈfætɪɡəbl/ *adj* (*fml approv*) never giving up or stopping even when tired or experiencing difficulties; tireless (TIRE[1]): *an indefatigable campaigner for civil rights.*

indefensible /ˌɪndɪˈfensəbl/ *adj* that cannot be defended, justified or excused: *indefensible behaviour/ rudeness* ○ *The government's attitude is morally indefensible.*

indefinable /ˌɪndɪˈfaɪnəbl/ *adj* that cannot be defined or adequately described: *an indefinable air of mystery.* ▶ **indefinably** /-əblɪ/ *adv*.

indefinite /ɪnˈdefɪnət/ *adj* **1** lasting an unknown length of time: *an indefinite strike* ○ *She'll be away for an indefinite period.* **2** (abbreviated as *indef* in this dictionary) not clearly defined or stated; VAGUE (1): *He gave me an indefinite answer* (ie neither 'yes' nor 'no'). ▶ **indefinitely** *adv*: *A decision has been postponed indefinitely.*
■ **in,definite ˈarticle** *n* (*grammar*) the word 'a' or 'an'. Compare DEFINITE ARTICLE.

indelible /ɪnˈdeləbl/ *adj* (of marks, ink, etc) that cannot be rubbed out or removed: *an indelible pencil* (ie one that makes such marks) ○ (*fig*) *indelible memories* ○ *She made an indelible impression on me.*
▶ **indelibly** /-əblɪ/ *adv*.

indelicate /ɪnˈdelɪkət/ *adj* (*fml often euph*) having or showing a lack of sensitive understanding or tact; rather rude or embarrassing: *indelicate remarks* ○ *It was indelicate of you to mention her marriage problems.* ▶ **indelicacy** /-kəsɪ/ *n* [U, C].

indemnify /ɪnˈdemnɪfaɪ/ *v* (*pt, pp* **-fied**) **1** ~ **sb** (**against sth**) (*law or commerce*) to promise to pay sb a sum of money for any harm they may suffer: [Vnpr] *indemnify sb against damage/injury/loss* [also Vn]. **2** ~ **sb** (**for sth**) (*fml*) to pay sb back for sth: [Vnpr] *I undertook to indemnify them for expenses incurred on my behalf.* [also Vn]. ▶ **indemnification** /ɪnˌdemnɪfɪˈkeɪʃn/ *n* [U, C].

indemnity /ɪnˈdemnətɪ/ *n* **(a)** [U] ~ (**against sth**) protection against damage or loss, esp in the form of a promise to pay for it: *an indemnity fund/ guarantee/insurance scheme.* **(b)** [C] a sum of money, etc given as payment or COMPENSATION for damage or loss: *The victorious nations are demanding huge indemnities from their former enemies.*

indent /ɪnˈdent/ *v* **1** (esp passive) to make a mark or set of marks by cutting into the edge or surface of sth: [Vn] *an indented* (ie one with a very IRREGULAR (1) shape) *coastline.* **2** to start a line of print or writing further in from the margin than the other lines: [Vn] *Please indent the first line of each paragraph.* **3** ~ **for sth** (*commerce esp Brit*) to make an official order for goods or stores: [Vpr] *indent for new equipment.*
▶ **indent** /ˈɪndent/ *n* (*commerce esp Brit*) an official order for stores or equipment.
indentation /ˌɪndenˈteɪʃn/ *n* **1** [C] **(a)** ~ (**in sth**) a mark made by indenting (INDENT 1): *She made indentations in the clay with her fingers.* **(b)** a space left at the beginning of a line of print or writing. **2** [U] the action of indenting (INDENT 1,2) sth or the process of being indented.

independence /ˌɪndɪˈpendəns/ *n* [U] ~ (**from sb/ sth**) the state of being independent: *young people who want independence from their parents* ○ *independence celebrations* (eg of a newly independent country).
■ **Indeˈpendence Day** *n* 4 July, celebrated in the USA as the anniversary of the day in 1776 when the American colonies declared themselves independent of Britain.

independent /ˌɪndɪˈpendənt/ *adj* **1** ~ (**of sb/sth**)

not dependent on other people or things; not controlled by other people or things: *old enough to be independent of one's parents* ○ *He's a very independent-minded young man.* ○ *She's a woman of independent means* (ie with a private income that is large enough for her not to have to rely financially on anyone else). ○ *Barbados was once a British colony, but now it's independent.* **2** not connected with each other; separate: *Two independent investigators have reached virtually the same conclusions.* ○ *Some independent evidence has recently come to light.* **3** financially supported by private rather than government money: *independent television* ○ *the independent sector in education* ○ *independent schools.* **4** not unfairly influenced by the people who are involved; IMPARTIAL: *an independent witness/ observer* ○ *We demand an independent inquiry into the government's handling of the affair.*
▶ **independent** *n* (*abbr* **Ind**) (*politics*) a member of Parliament, candidate, etc who does not belong to a political party: *stand as an independent.*
independently *adv*: *The couple have split up and are now living independently.* ○ *Scientists in different countries, working independently of each other, have come up with very similar results.*

in-depth /ˌɪn ˈdepθ/ *adj* [attrib] very thorough: *an ˌin-depth aˈnalysis/ˈarticle/disˈcussion/ˈinterview.*

indescribable /ˌɪndɪˈskraɪbəbl/ *adj* (esp of sth unpleasant) too extreme or unusual to be described: *indescribable squalor.* ▶ **indescribably** /-əbli/ *adv*: *indescribably beautiful/boring.*

indestructible /ˌɪndɪˈstrʌktəbl/ *adj* that cannot easily be destroyed: *an indestructible bond/ friendship* ○ *toys for young children that are virtually indestructible.*

indeterminable /ˌɪndɪˈtɜːmɪnəbl/ *adj* (*fml*) that cannot be decided or settled.

indeterminate /ˌɪndɪˈtɜːmɪnət/ *adj* not fixed or exact; VAGUE(1): *a sort of indeterminate colour, halfway between grey and brown.* ▶ **indeterminacy** /-nəsi/ *n* [U].

index /ˈɪndeks/ *n* (*pl* **indexes** or, in sense 2, **indices** /ˈɪndɪsiːz/) **1(a)** a list of names or topics referred to in a book, etc, usu arranged at the end in alphabetical (ALPHABET) order: *look sth up in the index.* **(b)** (also *Brit* **ˈcard index**, *US* ˌ**card ˈcatalog**) a set of names, book titles, etc, sometimes written on cards, usu arranged in alphabetical (ALPHABET) order: *publish an index of research/film titles* ○ *an index card.* **2(a)** a figure showing the relative level of prices or wages compared with that of a previous date: *the cost-ofˈliving index* ○ *The Dow Jones index rose/ gained/fell/slipped 15 points this morning.* **(b)** ~ (of sth) a thing that is a sign of sth else, esp because it increases or decreases in proportion to it; a measure: *The increasing sale of new cars is an index of the country's prosperity.*
▶ **index** *v* **1(a)** to make an index for sth: [Vn] *The book is not well indexed.* **(b)** to enter sth in an index: [Vnpr] *Library books are indexed by author and title.* [also Vn]. **2** ~ sth (**to sth**) to link wages, pensions (PENSION¹), etc to increases in the cost of living: [Vn] *Investors are offered a choice of indexed funds.* [also Vnpr].
indexation /ˌɪndekˈseɪʃn/ *n* [U] the linking of wages, pensions (PENSION¹), etc to increases in prices.
■ ˈ**index finger** *n* the finger next to the thumb. ▷ picture at HAND¹.
ˌ**index-ˈlinked** *adj* (of wages, pensions (PENSION¹), etc) rising in value according to increases in the cost of living.

Indian /ˈɪndiən/ *n, adj* **1** a native or an inhabitant of India: *the Indian cricket team.* **2** = NATIVE AMERICAN: *the Navajo Indians* ○ *playing cowboys and Indians.*

Compare WEST INDIAN. **IDM Indian/single file** ▷ FILE². **too many chiefs and not enough Indians** ▷ CHIEF.
■ ˌ**Indian ˈsummer** *n* **(a)** a period of calm dry warm weather in late autumn. **(b)** a pleasant period of late success or improvement, esp in sb's life.

indiarubber /ˌɪndiəˈrʌbə(r)/ *n* a piece of rubber for removing pencil or ink marks; an ERASER.

indicate /ˈɪndɪkeɪt/ *v* **1(a)** ~ **sth** (**to sb**) to show sth: [Vn] *a sign indicating a crossroads ahead* [Vpr.wh] *With a wave of his hand he indicated to me where I should sit.* [V.that] *She indicated that I should wait a moment.* [also V.wh, Vnpr, Vpr.that]. **(b)** to be a sign of sth; to suggest that sth is possible or likely: [Vn] *A red sky at night often indicates fine weather the following day.* [V.that] *Was there any evidence to indicate that he planned to return?* **(c)** to give the specified reading or measurement on a scale: [Vn] *The speedometer was indicating 95 mph.* **2** to state sth briefly or indirectly; to mention or suggest sth: [V.that] *The minister has indicated (that) he may resign next year.* [V.wh] *She has not yet indicated how she will deal with the problem.* [Vnpr] *She indicated her concern to the local council.* [also Vn, Vpr.that, Vpr.wh]. **3** (esp passive) to show that sth is necessary or would be sensible: [Vn] *a diagnosis of cancer indicating an emergency operation* ○ *With the government's failure to solve the problem of unemployment, a fresh approach is indicated.* **4** (*esp Brit*) to signal that one's vehicle is going to change direction: [V] *Why didn't you indicate?* [V.that] *He indicated (that) he was turning right.*
▶ **indication** /ˌɪndɪˈkeɪʃn/ *n* **1** [C,U] ~ (**of sth/ doing sth**); ~ (**that...**) a remark, gesture or sign that indicates sth: *She gave no indication of having heard us.* ○ *There are clear/definite indications that the situation is improving.* ○ *There is every indication that the recession is ending.* ○ *The indications are that the deal will go ahead as planned.* **2** [U] the action of indicating sth.

indicative /ɪnˈdɪkətɪv/ *adj* **1** [usu pred] ~ (**of sth**) (*fml*) showing or suggesting sth: *Their failure to act is indicative of their lack of interest.* ○ *indicative signs.* **2** (*grammar*) (of the form of a verb) stating a fact or asking questions of fact: *the indicative mood.* Compare IMPERATIVE *n* 2, INFINITIVE, SUBJUNCTIVE.

indicator /ˈɪndɪkeɪtə(r)/ *n* **1** a sign of sth; a thing that shows the state or health of sth else: *a reliable indicator of company performance.* **2(a)** a device that provides specific information, eg a DIAL on a machine showing speed or pressure: *a depth indicator.* **(b)** (*Brit*) (*US* **turn signal**) a flashing light on a vehicle showing that it is going to change direction: *His left-hand indicator is flashing.* ▷ picture at CAR.

indices *pl* of INDEX *n* 2.

indict /ɪnˈdaɪt/ *v* ~ **sb** (**for sth**) (*law*) (esp passive) to accuse sb officially of sth; to charge sb: [Vnpr] *He was indicted for/on charges of corruption.* [Vn] *They indicted people they knew to be innocent.*
▶ **indictable** *adj* for which one may be indicted: *indictable offences.*
indictment *n* **1(a)** [U] the action of indicting sb: *circumstances leading to his indictment on corruption charges.* **(b)** [C] an accusation; a written statement that indicts sb: *drop an indictment against sb.* **2** ~ **of sb/sth** a sign that sth is very bad and deserves to be condemned: *Conditions in some inner cities are a damning indictment of modern values.*

indie /ˈɪndi/ *n* (*infml*) an independent record company or band²(1a): *an indie label* ○ *the indie scene.*

indifference /ɪnˈdɪfrəns/ *n* [U] ~ (**to sb/sth**) a lack of interest, feeling or reaction towards sb/sth: *her apparent indifference to their appeals* ○ *He is angry at the indifference of the authorities to his plight.*

indifferent /ɪnˈdɪfrənt/ *adj* **1** [usu pred] ~ (**to sb/ sth**) having no interest in sb/sth; not caring about sb/sth: *indifferent to public opinion* ○ *She appeared indifferent to their sufferings.* **2** of rather low quality or ability: *an indifferent wine/meal/performance* ○ *As a reviewer I've seen hundreds of films, good, bad and indifferent.* ▶ **indifferently** *adv*: *He shrugged indifferently.*

indigenous /ɪnˈdɪdʒənəs/ *adj* ~ **(to sth)** *(fml)* belonging naturally to a place; native: *The kangaroo is indigenous to Australia.* ○ *an indigenous people/language/culture.*

indigent /ˈɪndɪdʒənt/ *adj* (*fml*) poor.

indigestible /ˌɪndɪˈdʒestəbl/ *adj* **1** difficult or impossible to eat and DIGEST²(1b): *a lumpy indigestible pudding.* **2** badly presented or expressed, and as a result difficult to understand: *indigestible statistics.*

indigestion /ˌɪndɪˈdʒestʃən/ *n* [U] pain caused by difficulty in digesting (DIGEST² 1a) food: *suffer from acute indigestion* ○ *have an attack of indigestion* ○ *Onions give me indigestion.* ○ *indigestion tablets* (ie taken to cure indigestion).

indignant /ɪnˈdɪɡnənt/ *adj* ~ **(at/over/about sth)** having or showing angry surprise because one believes that one has been treated unfairly: *an indignant look/response* ○ *Strikers are indignant at what they regard as false accusations.* ▶ **indignantly** *adv*: *'I'm certainly not asking him!' she retorted indignantly.*

indignation /ˌɪndɪɡˈneɪʃn/ *n* [U] ~ **(against sb)**; ~ **(at/over/about sth)** anger caused by sth that one considers unfair or unreasonable: *a storm/chorus of public indignation at the sudden steep rise in rail fares* ○ *arouse sb's indignation* ○ *Much* **to my indignation**, *he sat down in my seat.* ○ *feelings of* **righteous indignation** (ie indignation that one considers appropriate and justified but which others do not).

indignity /ɪnˈdɪɡnəti/ *n* **(a)** [U] treatment or circumstances that cause one to feel shame and loss of dignity or respect: *The chairman* **suffered the indignity of** *being refused admission to the meeting.* ○ *She could not bear the indignity of the disease.* **(b)** [C] an act that causes shame or embarrassment: *The hijackers subjected their captives to all kinds of indignities.*

indigo /ˈɪndɪɡəʊ/ *n* [U] a deep blue colour. ⇨ picture at SPECTRUM.

indirect /ˌɪndəˈrekt, -daɪˈr-/ *adj* **1** not direct or immediate; not obviously aimed at, caused by or resulting from sth; secondary: *an indirect cause/impact/result* ○ *find something out by indirect methods* ○ *There would be some benefit, however indirect, to the state.* **2** avoiding direct mention of a topic: *an indirect appeal for support* ○ *Their handling of the situation came under indirect attack in the press.* **3** not going in a straight line: *an indirect route.* ▶ **indirectly** *adv*: *This legislation will affect us all, directly or indirectly.* ○ *be indirectly responsible for sth.*

■ ˌindirect ˈobject *n* (*grammar*) an additional noun, noun phrase or pronoun used after certain verbs which refers to the person or thing that an action is done to or for, eg *him* in *Give him* (ie to him) *the money.* Compare OBJECT¹ 4.

ˌindirect ˈquestion (also reˌported ˈquestion) *n* (*grammar*) a question that is reported to have been asked: *In an indirect question, the question 'Where are you going?' becomes 'She asked me where I was going.'*

ˌindirect ˈspeech (also reˌported ˈspeech) *n* [U] (*grammar*) a report of what sb has said which does not reproduce their exact words: *In indirect speech, 'I'll come later' becomes 'He said he'd come later.'*

ˌindirect ˈtax *n* a tax that is not paid directly to the government but as an extra amount added to the price of particular goods.

indiscernible /ˌɪndɪˈsɜːnəbl/ *adj* that cannot be perceived: *an indiscernible difference.*

indiscipline /ɪnˈdɪsɪplɪn/ *n* [U] lack of discipline: *the growing indiscipline in schools.*

indiscreet /ˌɪndɪˈskriːt/ *adj* too open in what one says or does; too ready to reveal things that should be secret: *indiscreet love letters* ○ *One indiscreet remark could ruin the whole plan.* ▶ **indiscreetly** *adv*.

indiscretion /ˌɪndɪˈskreʃn/ *n* **(a)** [U] indiscreet behaviour: *a moment of indiscretion.* **(b)** [C] an indiscreet remark or act: *political/sexual indiscretions.*

indiscriminate /ˌɪndɪˈskrɪmɪnət/ *adj* **(a)** given or done without careful judgement, or at random: *the indiscriminate use of the oceans for dumping toxic waste* ○ *indiscriminate bombing of enemy targets* (eg that might kill ordinary people as well as damaging military sites). **(b)** ~ **(in sth)** acting without careful judgement: *be indiscriminate in one's choice of friends.* ▶ **indiscriminately** *adv*: *shooting indiscriminately into the crowd.*

indispensable /ˌɪndɪˈspensəbl/ *adj* ~ **(to sb/sth)**; ~ **(for sth / doing sth)** absolutely essential: *She concentrated on making herself indispensable to the department.* ○ *A good dictionary is indispensable for learning a foreign language.*

indisposed /ˌɪndɪˈspəʊzd/ *adj* (*fml often euph*) ill: *The soprano Sarah Walker replaces Elise Ross, who is indisposed.* Compare ILL-DISPOSED.
▶ **indisposition** /ˌɪndɪspəˈzɪʃn/ *n* [C, U] (*fml*) a slight illness; ill health: *a minor indisposition.*

indisputable /ˌɪndɪˈspjuːtəbl/ *adj* that cannot be challenged or denied: *indisputable evidence/proof/facts* ○ *The decline in manufacturing is indisputable.*
▶ **indisputably** *adv*: *indisputably the best chess player in the world.*

indissoluble /ˌɪndɪˈsɒljəbl/ *adj* (*fml*) that cannot be dissolved or broken up; firm and lasting: *indissoluble bonds/ties of friendship.* ▶ **indissolubly** /ˌɪndɪˈsɒljəbli/ *adv*: *indissolubly linked.*

indistinct /ˌɪndɪˈstɪŋkt/ *adj* not clear; VAGUE(1,3): *indistinct memories* ○ *The postmark was indistinct.* ▶ **indistinctly** *adv*.

indistinguishable /ˌɪndɪˈstɪŋɡwɪʃəbl/ *adj* ~ **(from sth)** that cannot be identified as different or distinct: *Its colour makes the moth almost indistinguishable from the branch it rests on.*

individual /ˌɪndɪˈvɪdʒuəl/ *adj* **1** [attrib] (*esp after each*) single; separate: *study the behaviour of individual cells* ○ *We interviewed each individual member of the community.* **2** [usu attrib] of or for one person: *food served in individual portions* ○ *a teacher giving individual attention to the children in her class.* **3** [usu attrib] characteristic of a single person, animal, plant or thing; particular: *an individual style of dress* ○ (*approv*) *He writes in a highly individual* (ie original) *style.*
▶ **individual** *n* **1** a single human being: *the rights of the individual compared with those of society as a whole* ○ *We welcome contact with individuals or groups interested in participating in the survey.* **2** (*infml*) a person of the specified sort: *a scruffy/an odd/a talented individual.*
individually /-dʒuəli/ *adv* separately: *individually wrapped cheeses* ○ *speak to each member of a group individually.*

individualism /ˌɪndɪˈvɪdʒuəlɪzəm/ *n* [U] **1** the feeling or behaviour of sb who likes to do things their own way, regardless of what other people do: *The arts depend on individualism, flair and eccentricity.* **2** the theory that favours complete freedom of action and belief for each individual person rather than state control: *Capitalism stresses innovation, competition and individualism.* ▶ **individualist** /-əlɪst/ *n*: *She's a complete individualist in her art.* ○

individualist *arguments/supporters.* **individualistic** /ˌɪndɪˌvɪdʒuəˈlɪstɪk/ *adj*: *highly individualistic music* ○ *individualistic capitalism.*

individuality /ˌɪndɪˌvɪdʒuˈæləti/ *n* [U] all the characteristics that belong to a particular person or thing and that make them different from others: *a performance of striking individuality* ○ *retain/lose one's individuality.*

individualized, -ised /ˌɪndɪˈvɪdʒuəlaɪzd/ *adj* (*fml*) (**a**) having an individual, a distinct or a personal character: *a highly individualized style.* (**b**) relating specifically to a particular person: *individualized financial and tax advice.*

indivisible /ˌɪndɪˈvɪzəbl/ *adj* that cannot be divided: *For her, work and leisure were indivisible.* ▶ **indivisibility** /ˌɪndɪˌvɪzəˈbɪləti/ *n* [U]. **indivisibly** /ˌɪndɪˈvɪzəbli/ *adv*.

Indo- *comb form* Indian; of India: *the Indo-Pakistan border.*
■ **Indo-European** /ˌɪndəʊˌjʊərəˈpiːən/ *adj* of the group of related languages spoken over the greater part of Europe and parts of western Asia: *Indo-European culture.*

indoctrinate /ɪnˈdɒktrɪneɪt/ *v* ~ **sb (with sth)** (*usu derog*) (often passive) to cause sb to have a particular set of beliefs, esp by giving them no opportunity to consider other points of view: [Vn, Vnpr] *indoctrinate children from an early age with strict religious beliefs* [also Vn.*to* inf]. ▶ **indoctrination** /ɪnˌdɒktrɪˈneɪʃn/ *n* [U]: *political/religious indoctrination.*

indolent /ˈɪndələnt/ *adj* (*fml*) lazy: *an indolent husband.* ▶ **indolence** /-əns/ *n* [U]: *His failure was due to indolence and lack of motivation.*

indomitable /ɪnˈdɒmɪtəbl/ *adj* (*fml approv*) that cannot be defeated or suppressed: *indomitable courage* ○ *an indomitable will/spirit* ○ *an indomitable campaigner for social justice.* ▶ **indomitably** /-əbli/ *adv*.

indoor /ˈɪndɔː(r)/ *adj* [attrib] situated, done or used inside a building: *indoor games/photography* ○ *an indoor swimming-pool* ○ *the world indoor 200 metres champion.* Compare OUTDOOR 1.

indoors /ˌɪnˈdɔːz/ *adv* in or into a building: *go/stay indoors* ○ *plants grown indoors.* Compare OUTDOORS.

indrawn /ˌɪnˈdrɔːn/ *adj* [attrib] (esp of breath) taken in: *There were indrawn breaths* (eg of shock or surprise) *at such plain speaking.*

indubitably /ɪnˈdjuːbɪtəbli; *US* -ˈduː-/ *adv* (*fml*) in a way that cannot be doubted; without question: *He was, indubitably, the most suitable candidate.*

induce /ɪnˈdjuːs; *US* -duːs/ *v* **1** to persuade or influence sb to do sth: [Vn.*to* inf] *an experience which nothing on earth would induce me to repeat* ○ *We couldn't induce him even to set foot on the boat.* **2** to cause sth: [Vn] *drugs which induce sleep* ○ *stress induced by overwork.* **3** (*medical*) to cause a woman by means of drugs to begin having her baby: [Vn] *an induced labour* ○ *We'll have to induce her.*
▶ **inducement** *n* [C, U] ~ (**to do sth**) (**a**) a thing that persuades sb to do sth; an INCENTIVE: *estate agents offering inducements to first-time buyers* ○ *There is little inducement for them to work harder.* (**b**) (*euph*) a BRIBE: *offer inducements to local officials.*

induct /ɪnˈdʌkt/ *v* ~ **sb (into sth)** to admit sb formally or with ceremony into an office or organization: [Vnpr] *be inducted into the army* [also Vn].

induction /ɪnˈdʌkʃn/ *n* [U] **1** ~ (**into sth**) the action or process of admitting sb or of being admitted to an office or organization: *the induction of new employees.* **2** the process of inducing (INDUCE 3) a woman: *the induction of labour* (ie in CHILDBIRTH). **3** a method of logical reasoning that obtains or discovers general laws from particular facts or examples. Compare DEDUCTION 1.

■ **in'duction course** *n* (*Brit*) a training course for new employees, students, etc which is designed to give them a general knowledge of their working environment, future activities, etc. Compare ORIENTATION.

inductive /ɪnˈdʌktɪv/ *adj* based on INDUCTION(3): *inductive logic/reasoning.*

indulge /ɪnˈdʌldʒ/ *v* **1** ~ **in sth** (**a**) to allow oneself to enjoy the pleasure of sth: [Vpr] *indulge in gossip/speculation/daydreams* ○ *indulge in one's favourite pastime.* (**b**) to become involved in an activity, esp one that is illegal or disapproved of: [Vpr] *indulge in profiteering/telephone tapping.* **2** to satisfy an interest, a desire, etc: [Vn] *indulge one's passion for opera/the theatre* ○ *She indulges his every whim.* **3** ~ **oneself/sb (with sth)** to allow oneself/sb to have whatever one/he/she likes or wants: [Vn] *indulge one's grandchildren* [Vnpr] *Let's indulge ourselves with a bottle of champagne.*
▶ **indulgent** /-ənt/ *adj* **1**(**a**) tending to indulge sb: *indulgent parents.* (**b**) showing that one is prepared to indulge sb: *an indulgent smile.* **2** ready to ignore faults: *take an indulgent view of the play.* See also SELF-INDULGENT. **indulgently** *adv*: *laugh indulgently.*

indulgence /ɪnˈdʌlgəns/ *n* **1** [U] (**a**) the state of being allowed whatever one wants: *a life of indulgence.* (**b**) the action or habit of satisfying one's own or other people's desires: *her indulgence in self-pity* ○ *The large menu offers a temptation to over-indulgence.* ○ *There is no limit to his indulgence for his grandchildren.* **2** [C] a thing in which a person indulges: *Treating yourself to a massage is the ultimate indulgence.*

industrial /ɪnˈdʌstriəl/ *adj* **1** [attrib] of or relating to industry : *industrial disputes/conflict/unrest* ○ *the country's industrial and commercial base* ○ *industrial development/production/output.* **2** for use in industry: *industrial diamonds/alcohol.* **3** having many well-developed industries: *an industrial society/economy* ○ *the world's leading industrial nations.*
▶ **industrialism** /-ɪzəm/ *n* [U] a social system in which large industries have an important part.
industrialist /-ɪst/ *n* a person involved in managing a large industrial firm: *prominent German industrialists.*
industrialize, -ise /-aɪz/ *v* to develop industries in a country or an area: [Vn] *the industrialized nations* [V] *Africa's need to industrialize.* **industrialization, -isation** /ɪnˌdʌstriəlaɪˈzeɪʃn; *US* -ləˈz-/ *n* [U]: *the increasing industrialization of China.*
industrially /-əli/ *adv*: *the industrially developed world.*
■ **in,dustrial 'action** *n* [U] the refusal to work normally; the interrupting of work in protest about sth: *They threaten to take industrial action.* ○ *Industrial action by train drivers seriously affected rush-hour services.*
in,dustrial archae'ology *n* [U] the study of machines, factories, bridges, etc formerly used in industry.
in,dustrial 'arts *n* [sing *v*] (*US*) the training given to students who are learning how to use tools and machines for career purposes.
in,dustrial e'state *n* a group of factories built close together, usu on the edge of a town: *a warehouse on an industrial estate.* Compare TRADING ESTATE.
in,dustrial re'lations *n* [pl] dealings between employers and employees: *foster good industrial relations.*
the In,dustrial Revo'lution *n* [sing] the development of Britain, the USA and other western nations into industrial societies in the 18th and 19th centuries.
in,dustrial tri'bunal *n* a group of officials with authority to settle disputes between employees and

employers: *The case was brought before an industrial tribunal.*

industrious /ɪnˈdʌstrɪəs/ *adj* working hard: *an industrious and inventive people.* ▶ **industriously** *adv.*

industry /ˈɪndəstri/ *n* **1** [C, U] (**a**) the making or production of things in factories: *the car/chemical/steel/nuclear industry* ○ *privatized/nationalized/state-owned industries* ○ *get a job in industry.* (**b**) a commercial activity that provides services: *the advertising/hotel/tourist/entertainment industry.* See also CAPTAIN OF INDUSTRY, COTTAGE INDUSTRY, HEAVY INDUSTRY. **2** [U] (*fml*) the quality of working hard: *praise sb for his industry.*

■ ˌindustry-ˈwide *adj* [attrib] affecting or relating to the whole of a particular industry: *engineering unions battling for an industry-wide cut in working hours.*

inebriated /ɪˈniːbrɪeɪtɪd/ *adj* [usu pred] (*fml or joc*) drunk: *become inebriated.*

inedible /ɪnˈedəbl/ *adj* (*fml*) not suitable to be eaten: *The fish was almost inedible.*

ineffable /ɪnˈefəbl/ *adj* (*fml*) too great to be described in words: *ineffable joy/beauty.* ▶ **ineffably** /-əbli/ *adv.*

ineffective /ˌɪnɪˈfektɪv/ *adj* not producing the required effect or result; not effective: *ineffective protection/controls* ○ *The anti-aircraft guns proved virtually ineffective.* ○ *The Buffalo Bills were disappointingly ineffective in the second half.* ▶ **ineffectively** *adv.* **ineffectiveness** *n* [U]: *his ineffectiveness in dealing with the situation.*

ineffectual /ˌɪnɪˈfektʃuəl/ *adj* (**a**) (of a process, etc) not producing the required effect: *an ineffectual attack/election campaign.* (**b**) (of a person) lacking the necessary skill, qualities or confidence to do a job properly: *be totally ineffectual as a leader/teacher* ○ *a well-meaning but ineffectual manager.* ▶ **ineffectually** /-tʃuəli/ *adv.*

inefficient /ˌɪnɪˈfɪʃnt/ *adj* (**a**) (of a machine, process, etc) wasting time or resources: *an inefficient fridge/heating system.* (**b**) (of a person or an organization) failing to make the best use of the available time and resources: *an inefficient management/administration.* ▶ **inefficiency** /-nsi/ *n* [U, C]: *the inefficiency of some charitable organizations* ○ *attack the local Council's inefficiencies.* **inefficiently** *adv:* *working inefficiently.*

inelegant /ɪnˈelɪɡənt/ *adj* not graceful or attractive: *an inelegant gesture/reply.* ▶ **inelegantly** *adv.*

ineligible /ɪnˈelɪdʒəbl/ *adj* ~ (**for sth/to do sth**) not qualified for or entitled to sth: *ineligible for promotion/housing benefit* ○ *ineligible to play for Wales.*

ineluctable /ˌɪnɪˈlʌktəbl/ *adj* (*fml*) that cannot be avoided: *ineluctable logic.* ▶ **ineluctably** /-əbli/ *adv.*

inept /ɪˈnept/ *adj* ~ (**at sth / doing sth**) having or showing no skill at all: *his inept handling of the crisis* ○ *a ludicrously/pitifully inept piece of journalism* ○ *I've never heard anyone so inept at making speeches.*
▶ **ineptitude** /ɪˈneptɪtjuːd; *US* -tuːd/ *n* [U] the quality of being inept: *the bungling ineptitude of the police on this occasion* ○ *sheer political ineptitude.* **ineptly** *adv.*

inequality /ˌɪnɪˈkwɒləti/ *n* [U, C] difference in size, degree, circumstances, etc, esp an unfair difference in rank, wealth or opportunity, etc: *fight against political/racial inequality* ○ *inequality of opportunity/power* ○ *enormous social/regional inequalities.*

inequitable /ɪnˈekwɪtəbl/ *adj* (*fml*) unfair: *The price charged to distributors was highly inequitable.*

inequity /ɪnˈekwəti/ *n* [U, C] (*fml*) the state of being

unfair or an instance of this: *a world in which poverty and inequity are endemic* ○ *a victim of the inequities of the legal system.*

ineradicable /ˌɪnɪˈrædɪkəbl/ *adj* (*fml*) (esp of sth bad) that cannot be removed; firmly and deeply established: *ineradicable failings/prejudices/conflicts.*

inert /ɪˈnɜːt/ *adj* **1**(**a**) without power to move or act: *She saw Laura's inert and bleeding body by the side of the road.* (**b**) (*techn*) without active chemical or other properties: *an inert gas.* **2** lacking vigour or interest: *Cynicism is soulless and inert — it changes nothing.*

inertia /ɪˈnɜːʃə/ *n* [U] **1** (*usu derog*) (**a**) lack of vigour; lack of will to move or change: *attempts to overcome our growing economic inertia* ○ *I can't seem to throw off this feeling of inertia.* **2** (*physics*) a property of matter by which it remains in a state of rest or, if in motion, continues moving in a straight line, unless acted upon by an external force.
▶ **inertial** /ɪˈnɜːʃl/ *adj* of or by inertia: *an aircraft's inertial navigation equipment.*
■ iˈnertia reel *n* a type of reel round which one end of a seat-belt (SEAT¹) is wound so that the belt will automatically lock if it is pulled suddenly, eg in an accident.
iˌnertia ˈselling *n* [U] the sending of goods to a person who has not ordered them, in the hope that he or she will not refuse them and will therefore have to pay for them later.

inescapable /ˌɪnɪˈskeɪpəbl/ *adj* impossible to avoid: *an inescapable conclusion/fact.* ▶ **inescapably** /-əbli/ *adv:* *The two factors are inescapably linked.*

inessential /ˌɪnɪˈsenʃl/ *adj* not necessary: *cut down on inessential spending.*

inestimable /ɪnˈestɪməbl/ *adj* (*fml*) too great to calculate: *be of inestimable value to sb.*

inevitable /ɪnˈevɪtəbl/ *adj* **1** impossible to avoid; certain to happen: *the inevitable consequences of the war* ○ *Defeat looks inevitable.* ○ *It is inevitable that interest rates will rise again.* **2** [attrib] (*often joc*) so frequently seen, heard, etc that it is familiar and expected: *tourists with their inevitable cameras.*
▶ **inevitability** /ɪnˌevɪtəˈbɪləti/ *n* [U, sing]: *the inevitability of death.*
the inevitable *n* [sing] that which is inevitable: *accept/bow to the inevitable* ○ *The inevitable happened — I lost my passport.*
inevitably /-əbli/ *adv* without doubt; certainly: *Inevitably, these negotiations will take time.* ○ *The fall in demand for cars will inevitably mean some workers losing their jobs.*

inexact /ˌɪnɪɡˈzækt/ *adj* not exact or PRECISE(2): *an inexact comparison.*

inexcusable /ˌɪnɪkˈskjuːzəbl/ *adj* too bad to excuse or tolerate: *inexcusable delays/rudeness.* ▶ **inexcusably** /-əbli/ *adv.*

inexhaustible /ˌɪnɪɡˈzɔːstəbl/ *adj* that will always continue; never finished: *an apparently inexhaustible supply of jokes* ○ *She seems to have inexhaustible energy.* ▶ **inexhaustibly** /-əbli/ *adv.*

inexorable /ɪnˈeksərəbl/ *adj* impossible to change or prevent: *inexorable logic* ○ *the inexorable march of progress.* ▶ **inexorably** /ɪnˈeksərəbli/ *adv:* *events that are leading inexorably towards/to a crisis.*

inexpensive /ˌɪnɪkˈspensɪv/ *adj* not costing much money; not expensive: *a relatively inexpensive meal/holiday* ○ *Window locks are inexpensive and effective.*
▶ **inexpensively** *adv.*

inexperience /ˌɪnɪkˈspɪərɪəns/ *n* [U] lack of experience: *The blunder was a sign of inexperience.*
▶ **inexperienced** *adj* ~ (**in sth**) lacking experience: *relatively inexperienced in local government* ○ *inexperienced staff/drivers.*

inexpert /ɪnˈekspɜːt/ *adj* not having particular skill

or knowledge: *To Bob's inexpert eye it looked like a camera.* ▶ **inexpertly** *adv*.

inexplicable /ˌɪnɪkˈsplɪkəbl/ *adj* impossible to explain or understand: *For some inexplicable reason, he gave up a fantastic job.* ▶ **inexplicably** /ˌɪnɪkˈsplɪkəbli/ *adv*: *inexplicably delayed/absent.*

inexpressible /ˌɪnɪkˈspresəbl/ *adj* (of a feeling) too great to be expressed in words: *To her inexpressible relief he decided not to tell the children.* ▶ **inexpressibly** /-əbli/ *adv*: *inexpressibly boring.*

inexpressive /ˌɪnɪkˈspresɪv/ *adj* showing no expression: *inexpressive eyes.*

inextinguishable /ˌɪnɪkˈstɪŋgwɪʃəbl/ *adj* (*fml*) impossible to destroy or overcome: *inextinguishable desire/loathing.*

in extremis /ˌɪn ɪkˈstriːmɪs/ *adv* (*Latin*) **1** (*religion*) (esp in the Roman Catholic Church) at the point of death. **2** (*fml*) in an emergency; as a last resort in a serious situation: *make a compromise in extremis.*

inextricable /ˌɪnɪkˈstrɪkəbl, ɪnˈekstrɪkəbl/ *adj* **1** so closely linked that separation is impossible: *Economic difficulty and political dissatisfaction are inextricable.* **2** impossible to escape from: *inextricable financial difficulties.* ▶ **inextricably** *adv*: *Our foreign policy is **inextricably bound up/linked** with that of the USA.*

infallible /ɪnˈfæləbl/ *adj* **1** not capable of making mistakes or being wrong: *None of us is infallible.* ○ *Unfortunately this guidebook is not infallible.* **2** never failing; always effective: *an infallible remedy/test.* ▶ **infallibility** /ɪnˌfæləˈbɪləti/ *n* [U]: *question of the infallibility of the Board* ○ *papal infallibility.* **infallibly** /-əbli/ *adv*.

infamous /ˈɪnfəməs/ *adj* **1** ~ (**for sth**) well-known for being bad, morally wrong, etc; NOTORIOUS: *a general infamous for his brutality* ○ *the infamous telephone tapping affair* ○ (*joc*) *The holiday wouldn't be complete without the infamous beach barbecue.* **2** (*fml*) wicked: *The way he treated his wife was infamous.*

infamy /ˈɪnfəmi/ *n* (*fml*) **1** [C, U] wickedness; morally wrong behaviour: *How could he stoop to such infamy?* ○ *the infamies of the slave trade.* **2** [U] the state of having a bad reputation or being a source of shame: *be held in infamy.*

infancy /ˈɪnfənsi/ *n* [U] **1** the state or period of being a very young child; early childhood: *die in infancy.* **2** the early stage of the development or growth of sth: *a science still in its infancy.*

infant /ˈɪnfənt/ *n* **1** a very young child, eg up to the age of two: *their infant daughter* ○ *He came to Wales 50 years ago as an infant.* ○ (*fig*) *the infant Democratic party.* **2** (in British education) a child between the ages of four and seven: *an infant school* ○ *infant teachers.*
■ ˌinfant ˈprodigy *n* an unusually talented child: *infant prodigies like Mozart.*

infanticide /ɪnˈfæntɪsaɪd/ *n* **1** [U] (**a**) the killing of a baby: *be charged with infanticide.* (**b**) the custom in some countries of killing babies that are not wanted, eg because they are girls, not boys. **2** a person who kills a baby.

infantile /ˈɪnfəntaɪl/ *adj* (**a**) [usu attrib] of or occurring among babies or very young children: *infantile diseases.* (**b**) (*derog*) (esp of the behaviour of older children or adults) typical of a small child: *infantile behaviour/jokes.*
▶ **infantilism** /ɪnˈfæntɪlɪzəm/ *n* [U] (*psychology*) the state in older children or adults of keeping the physical or mental characteristics of a very young child.

infantry /ˈɪnfəntri/ *n* [U, Gp] soldiers who fight on foot: *an infantry regiment* ○ *The infantry was/were guarding the bridge.* Compare CAVALRY.

infantryman /ˈɪnfəntrimən/ *n* (*pl* **-men**) a soldier in an INFANTRY regiment.

infatuated /ɪnˈfætʃueɪtɪd/ *adj* ~ (**with sb/sth**) (*usu derog*) having a very strong passion for sb/sth that prevents one from thinking about them/it in a balanced and sensible way: *She's clearly infatuated with the boy.*
▶ **infatuation** /ɪnˌfætʃuˈeɪʃn/ *n* [U, C] ~ (**with/for sb/sth**) the state of being infatuated; a foolish passion: *develop an infatuation for sb* ○ *It's not love; it's only a passing infatuation.*

infect /ɪnˈfekt/ *v* ~ **sb/sth** (**with sth**) **1(a)** (of harmful bacteria, etc) to enter the body of a person or an animal and cause disease: [Vn] *an infected wound* ○ *infected chickens* [Vnpr] *blood infected with HIV* ○ (*fig*) *a mind infected with racial prejudice.* (**b**) (esp passive) to cause food, water, etc to contain harmful bacteria; to CONTAMINATE sth: [Vn] *an infected reservoir.* **2** (*approv*) to spread happy and positive ideas or feelings to other people: [Vn] *Her enthusiasm and laughter infected the whole class.*

infection /ɪnˈfekʃn/ *n* **1** [U] the action or process of infecting sb or being infected with a disease: *be exposed to infection* ○ *increase the risk of infection* ○ *help your body to resist infection.* **2** [C] a disease caught esp by breathing in bacteria, etc from the air: *spread/pass on an infection* ○ *a viral infection* ○ *a chest/throat infection.* Compare CONTAGION.

infectious /ɪnˈfekʃəs/ *adj* **1(a)** (of a disease) passed from one person or animal to another, esp through the air they breathe: *Flu is highly infectious.* (**b**) [usu pred] (of a person or an animal) able to infect others with a disease: *While you are still coughing, you are infectious.* **2** quickly influencing others; likely to spread quickly: *an infectious laugh* ○ *Panic is infectious.* Compare CONTAGIOUS. ▶ **infectiously** *adv*.

infer /ɪnˈfɜː(r)/ *v* (**-rr-**) **1** ~ **sth** (**from sth**) to reach an opinion based on available information or evidence; to arrive at a conclusion: [Vn] *infer a connection between smoking and heart disease* [Vnpr] *The size of the population can be inferred from the archaeological remains.* [V.*that*] *It can be inferred that the company is bankrupt.* **2** (*infml*) to suggest indirectly that sth is true: *How dare you infer (that) she is dishonest!* Compare IMPLY 1.
▶ **inference** /ˈɪnfərəns/ *n* **1** [C] ~ (**from sth**) (**that…**) a conclusion reached on the basis of knowledge or facts: *make/draw inferences from their silence* ○ *The inference is clear — we must leave immediately.* ○ *There is a strong inference that supervision is inadequate.* **2** [U] the process of inferring sth: *If he is guilty then **by inference** so is she* (ie This conclusion follows logically from the same set of facts).

inferior /ɪnˈfɪəriə(r)/ *adj* ~ (**to sb/sth**) low or lower in rank, social position, importance, quality, etc: *be of inferior quality/status* ○ *make sb feel inferior* ○ *inferior goods/workmanship* ○ *The new terms of employment may be inferior to those they previously enjoyed.* Compare SUPERIOR.
▶ **inferior** *n* a person who is inferior in rank or status.
inferiority /ɪnˌfɪəriˈɒrəti; US -ˈɔːr-/ *n* [U] the state of being inferior: *feelings of inferiority.* **inferiˈority complex** *n* a feeling that one is less important, less clever or less admired than other people. This feeling makes some people aggressive and others shy: *She's got a real inferiority complex.* Compare SUPERIORITY COMPLEX.

infernal /ɪnˈfɜːnl/ *adj* **1** [attrib] (*infml*) (used to express annoyance): *That infernal telephone hasn't stopped ringing all day!* ○ *You're an infernal nuisance!* **2** (*fml*) of or like hell: *the infernal regions.* ▶ **infernally** /-nəli/ *adv*: *infernally rude.*

inferno /ɪnˈfɜːnəʊ/ *n* (*pl* **-os**) **1** a large dangerous

---

fire that is out of control: *Within minutes the shop was a blazing/raging/roaring inferno.* **2** a place or situation that is hot, noisy or confused: *the inferno of a hotel kitchen.*

infertile /ɪnˈfɜːtaɪl; US -tl/ *adj* **1** (of people, animals or plants) unable to reproduce: *An estimated one in ten couples is infertile.* **2** (of land) of such poor quality that little or nothing will grow in it: *infertile soil.* ▶ **infertility** /ˌɪnfɜːˈtɪləti/ *n* [U]: *offer infertility treatment to couples unable to have children.*

infest /ɪnˈfest/ *v* ~ **sth** (**with sth**) (usu passive) (of certain insects and animals) to exist in a place in large numbers, esp causing damage or disease: [Vnpr] *a cat infested with fleas* [Vn] *rat-infested slums.* ▶ **infestation** /ˌɪnfeˈsteɪʃn/ *n* [C,U]: *an infestation of cockroaches* ∘ *check for signs of infestation.*

infidel /ˈɪnfɪdəl/ *n* (*arch derog*) a person who does not believe in what is considered by the speaker to be the true religion: *wage a holy war against the infidel.*

infidelity /ˌɪnfɪˈdeləti/ *n* [C,U] the action or an instance of not being faithful to one's husband, wife or partner by having a relationship with sb else: *She tolerated her husband's frequent infidelities.*

infighting /ˈɪnfaɪtɪŋ/ *n* [U] quarrels and arguments between members of a group who are competing for power or influence: *political infighting in the Labour Party.*

infill /ˈɪnfɪl/ (also **infilling**) *n* [U] **1** the building of houses, etc in the spaces between existing ones: *infill development.* **2** material used to fill a hole or gap, eg in a wall. ▶ **infill** *v* [Vn]: *infill an old archway.*

infiltrate /ˈɪnfɪltreɪt/ *v* **1** ~ (**sb/sth**) (**into sth**) to enter or cause sb to enter a place or an organization secretly and without being noticed, esp in order to obtain information about it: [Vn] *infiltrate a drugs ring* [Vnpr] *infiltrate foreign agents into the Ministry of Defence* [Vpr] *Guerrillas have infiltrated into surrounding villages.* [also V]. **2** (of liquids or gases) to pass slowly through sth; to penetrate sth: [Vpr,Vadv] *water infiltrating (downwards) through the soil* ∘ (*fig*) [Vn] *beliefs infiltrated by new-fangled ideas.* ▶ **infiltration** /ˌɪnfɪlˈtreɪʃn/ *n* [U,C]: *infiltration of the army by drugs cartels* ∘ *guerrilla infiltration.* **infiltrator** /ˈɪnfɪltreɪtə(r)/ *n* a person who infiltrates a place or an organization: *left-wing infiltrators.*

infinite /ˈɪnfɪnət/ *adj* **1(a)** impossible to measure, calculate or imagine because of being so great; very great: *an infinite number of possibilities* ∘ *have infinite faith in sb/sth* ∘ *a painting restored with infinite care* ∘ *You need infinite patience for this job.* ∘ (*ironic*) *The company has decided,* **in its infinite wisdom,** *on group therapy sessions for all senior staff.* **(b)** without limits; without end: *Space is infinite.* ▶ **the Infinite** *n* [sing] (*rhet*) God.

infinitely *adv* **1** (esp with comparatives) very much: *infinitely better/wiser* ∘ *This wine is infinitely preferable to the others.* **2** to an infinite degree; extremely: *Human beings are infinitely flexible.*

infinitesimal /ˌɪnfɪnɪˈtesɪml/ *adj* extremely small: *an infinitesimal pause.* ▶ **infinitesimally** /-məli/ *adv.*

infinitive /ɪnˈfɪnətɪv/ *n* (*grammar*) the basic form of a verb. In English, an infinitive is used by itself, eg *read* as in *He can read*, or preceded by *to*, as in *He likes to read.* Compare IMPERATIVE *n* 2, INDICATIVE 2, SUBJUNCTIVE. **IDM split an infinitive** ⇨ SPLIT.

infinity /ɪnˈfɪnəti/ *n* **1** [U] **(a)** the state of having no end or limit: *the infinity of space.* **(b)** a point far away in space that can never be reached: *gaze into infinity* ∘ *medieval cathedrals reaching upwards to infinity.* **2** [U] (*mathematics*) a number larger than any other, expressed by the symbol ∞; infinite

quantity: *from zero to infinity.* **3** [sing] a large amount that is impossible to count: *an infinity of stars.*

infirm /ɪnˈfɜːm/ *adj* weak in body or mind, esp from old age or illness: *grow old and infirm* ∘ *mentally/physically infirm.* ▶ **the infirm** *n* [pl v] infirm people: *support for the aged and infirm.*

infirmity /ɪnˈfɜːməti/ *n* [U,C] physical or mental weakness: *fear infirmity and death* ∘ *Deafness and failing eyesight are among the infirmities of old age.*

infirmary /ɪnˈfɜːməri/ *n* **1** a hospital. **2** a special room in a school, prison, etc, for people who are ill: *the college infirmary.*

inflame /ɪnˈfleɪm/ *v* **(a)** to cause very strong feelings, esp among a lot of people, about a particular subject or person: [Vn] *inflame public opinion* ∘ *a speech guaranteed to inflame nationalist sentiments.* **(b)** to make a situation more tense, violent or hard to control: [Vn] *inflame a dispute by irresponsible remarks.* ▶ **inflamed** *adj* **1** (of a part of the body) red, sore and sometimes swollen, eg because of infection: *My eyes became red and inflamed.* **2** full of anger or violent feelings: *the inflamed mob* ∘ *inflamed passions.*

inflammable /ɪnˈflæməbl/ *adj* **1** (also **flammable**) that can very easily catch fire and burn: *inflammable material* ∘ *a dangerous accumulation of inflammable gases.* Compare NON-FLAMMABLE. ⇨ note at INVALUABLE. **2** likely to involve or cause strong or violent feelings: *a highly inflammable situation.*

inflammation /ˌɪnfləˈmeɪʃn/ *n* [C,U] a condition in which a part of the body is red, swollen and sore, esp because of infection: *(an) inflammation of the ear/lungs* ∘ *This cream will help reduce/soothe the inflammation.*

inflammatory /ɪnˈflæmətri; US -tɔːri/ *adj* **1** (*derog*) intended to cause angry or violent feelings: *an inflammatory book/remark.* **2** causing part of the body to become swollen and sore: *an inflammatory condition of the liver.*

inflate /ɪnˈfleɪt/ *v* **1** ~ (**sth**) (**with sth**) to fill sth or become filled with gas or air: [Vn] *To inflate your life-jacket pull this cord.* [also V,Vpr]. **2** (usu passive) to make sth appear more important, impressive, etc than it really is; to exaggerate sth: [Vn] *inflated egos* ∘ *He has an inflated sense of his own importance.* ∘ *inflated language* (ie full of impressive words but little meaning) ∘ *Reports of hooliganism were grossly inflated by the press.* **3** to increase the price or value of sth by a considerable amount: [Vn] *artificially inflate share prices* ∘ *inflated salaries* [also V]. Compare DEFLATE, REFLATE. ▶ **inflatable** /-əbl/ *adj* needing to be filled with air or gas before use: *an inflatable pillow/rubber dinghy.* ⇨ picture at DINGHY. — *n* **(a)** a plastic or rubber object filled with air or gas and used as a toy, for publicity, etc. **(b)** an inflatable boat.

▶ **inflation** /ɪnˈfleɪʃn/ *n* [U] **1** a rise in prices and wages caused by an increase in the money supply and demand for goods, and resulting in a fall in the value of money: *control/curb/fight against inflation* ∘ *a high/low rate of inflation.* **2** the action of filling sth with air or gas: *life-jackets with an automatic inflation device.* **inflationary** /ɪnˈfleɪʃnri; US -neri/ *adj* of, caused by or causing inflation: *inflationary wage settlements* ∘ *inflationary pressure on the pound.*

inflect /ɪnˈflekt/ *v* **1** [Vn] to make the voice higher or lower in pitch¹(2). **2** (*grammar*) to change the ending or form of a word to show its GRAMMATICAL function in a sentence: [Vn] *Russian is a highly inflected language.* [also V]. ▶ **inflection** (also **inflexion**) /ɪnˈflekʃn/ *n* **1** (*gram-*

[V.*to* inf] = verb + *to* infinitive   [Vn.inf (no *to*)] = verb + noun + infinitive without *to*   [V.*ing*] = verb + *-ing* form

mar) **(a)** [U] the changing of a word form or word ending to show its GRAMMATICAL function. **(b)** [C] such an ending or change: *Use the '-ed' inflection to indicate the past tense.* **2** [U, C] the action of inflecting the voice: *subtlety of inflection* ○ *an Irish inflection.* Compare INTONATION 1, STRESS 3a.

inflexible /ɪnˈfleksəbl/ *adj* **1** *(derog)* **(a)** unwilling to change or adapt: *hotels inflexible towards the needs of their guests* ○ *She's obstinate and inflexible.* **(b)** that cannot be changed or adapted to particular circumstances: *her inflexible will* ○ *an inflexible attitude/rule/system.* **2** difficult or impossible to bend; rigid: *inflexible plastic tiles.* ▶ **inflexibility** /ɪnˌfleksəˈbɪləti/ *n* [U]. **inflexibly** /-əbli/ *adv.*

inflict /ɪnˈflɪkt/ *v* **(a)** ~ **sth (on/upon sb/sth)** to make sb/sth suffer sth: [Vnpr] *inflict injuries/pain/suffering on sb* ○ *lasting damage inflicted on the environment* [Vn] *inflict a crushing defeat.* **(b)** ~ **sb/sth on sb** *(often joc)* to make sb accept sth that is unpleasant or not welcome: [Vnpr] *Well, I mustn't inflict my ideas/family on you any longer.* ▶ **infliction** /ɪnˈflɪkʃn/ *n* [U]: *the infliction of pain and suffering on sb.*

in-flight /ˌɪnˈflaɪt/ *adj* [usu attrib] occurring or provided during the flight of an aircraft: *ˌin-flight reˈfuelling/enterˈtainment.*

inflow /ˈɪnfləʊ/ *n* **1** the arrival of sb/sth from elsewhere; an INFLUX: *a steady inflow of capital/refugees.* **2** liquid that flows into a place: *an inflow of 25 litres per hour* ○ *an inflow pipe.* Compare OUTFLOW.

influence /ˈɪnfluəns/ *n* **1(a)** [U, sing] ~ **(on/over sb/sth)** the power to affect sb's actions, character or beliefs, esp by providing an example for them to follow, winning their admiration or making them afraid to disagree: *have a good/bad/beneficial/harmful influence on sb's behaviour/character* ○ *exert a powerful influence on sb/sth* ○ *a young ruler under the influence of his chief minister* ○ *the influence of the press and television* ○ *His parents no longer have any real influence over him.* **(b)** [C] ~ **(on sb/sth)** a person, fact, etc that exercises such power: *Those so-called friends of hers are a bad influence on her.* ○ *Religion has been an influence for good in his life.* ○ *The influences at work in this case* (ie factors affecting it) *are hard to separate out.* **2** [U] ~ **(with sb)** the ability to obtain favourable treatment from sb, eg because one knows and is respected by sb or because of one's status or wealth: *use one's influence (with sb) to obtain a job* ○ *She has great influence with the manager and could probably help you.* **3** [U, C] ~ **(on sth)** the power to affect or change the way sth functions or develops: *the influence of the moon on the tides* ○ *the influence of the climate on agricultural production* ○ *planetary/seasonal influences.* **IDM** **under the ˈinfluence** *(fml or joc)* having had too much alcohol to drink: *be charged by the police with driving under the influence (of alcohol).* ▶ **influence** *v* to have an effect or influence on sb/sth or on their/its behaviour: [Vn] *the belief of astrologers that planets influence human character* ○ *factors influencing consumer choice* ○ *I don't want to influence you either way, so I won't tell you my opinion.* ○ *As a young man, he was much influenced by Picasso.* [Vn.to inf] *Whatever influenced her to write such a letter?*

influential /ˌɪnfluˈenʃl/ *adj* ~ **(in sth / doing sth)** having a lot of influence on sb/sth: *factors that are influential in reaching a decision* ○ *an influential speech/writer* ○ *be influential in local politics.*

influenza /ˌɪnfluˈenzə/ *n* *(fml)* = FLU.

influx /ˈɪnflʌks/ *n* ~ **(into ...)** (usu *sing*) the sudden arrival of large numbers of people or large amounts of money, etc: *a huge influx of visitors* ○ *an influx of wealth.*

info /ˈɪnfəʊ/ *n* [U] *(infml)* information: *For further info phone 886521.*

inform /ɪnˈfɔːm/ *v* **1** ~ **sb (of/about sth)** to give sb facts or information about sth; to tell sb: [Vn] *If your cheque card is stolen, inform your bank immediately.* [Vnpr] *Keep me informed about the situation/of further developments.* [Vn.that] *(fml) We are pleased to inform you that you have been accepted for a place on our MBA course.* **2** ~ **against/on sb** to give evidence or make an accusation against sb, esp to the police: [Vpr] *One of the gang informed against/on the rest.* **3** *(fml)* to give sth a particular quality or character: *a sincerity which informs all her writings.* ▶ **informant** /-ənt/ *n* **(a)** a person who gives information, esp about sb's activities, to the police or a newspaper: *police informants* ○ *The journalist refused to reveal the identity of his informant.* **(b)** a person who gives information about sth, eg to sb doing research: *His informants were middle-class, professional women.*

informed *adj* having or showing relevant knowledge: *be well informed* ○ *an informed critic/member of the public* ○ *an informed choice/debate/decision.*

informer *n* a person who gives evidence or makes an accusation against a criminal, usu in return for payment.

informal /ɪnˈfɔːml/ *adj* **1(a)** not formal; relaxed and friendly: *an informal manner/tone/atmosphere.* **(b)** not official; not following established procedures: *establish informal contact with sb* ○ *an informal arrangement/meeting/visit.* **2** (of dress) casual and not particularly elegant or SMART[1](2); not for a special or official occasion. **3** (abbreviated as *infml* in this dictionary) (of language) appropriate for normal conversation and not for serious speech or writing: *an informal expression/letter.* See also COLLOQUIAL. Compare FORMAL, SLANG. ▶ **informality** /ˌɪnfɔːˈmæləti/ *n* [U]: *Great emphasis is placed on the informality of these meetings.* **informally** /ɪnˈfɔːməli/ *adv*: *dress informally* ○ *They told me informally* (ie not officially) *that I had got the job.*

information /ˌɪnfəˈmeɪʃn/ *n* (also *infml* **info**) *n* [U] ~ **(on/about sb/sth)** facts told, heard or discovered about sb/sth; knowledge: *give/provide/pass on/receive/obtain/collect information on/about sb/sth* ○ *For more/further information please write to...* ○ *a useful bit/piece of information* ○ *an information bureau/desk* ○ *According to my information* (ie what I have been told) *work was due to start last week.* ○ *A copy of the report is enclosed for your information.* **IDM** **a mine of information** ⇨ MINE[2]. ▶ **informational** *adj*: *the informational role of the media.* ■ **inforˈmation technology** *n* [U] the study or use of electronic equipment, esp computers, for storing, analysing and distributing information of all kinds, including words, numbers and pictures.

informative /ɪnˈfɔːmətɪv/ *adj* giving useful and interesting information: *an informative account of her visit* ○ *The text is interesting and informative without being too technical.*

infra- *prep* (with *adjs*) below: *infrared.* Compare ULTRA-.

infraction /ɪnˈfrækʃn/ *n* *(fml)* [U, C] the action or an instance of breaking a rule or law: *a minor infraction of the rules.*

infra dig /ˌɪnfrə ˈdɪg/ *adj* [pred] *(often joc)* not appropriate; beneath one's dignity: *dancing in the street seemed rather infra dig for a bank manager!*

infrared /ˌɪnfrəˈred/ *adj* having or using waves (WAVE[2] 6) of light which are longer than those of red in the SPECTRUM(1) and which cannot be seen: *infrared radiation* ○ *an infrared camera/lamp.* Compare ULTRAVIOLET.

infrastructure /ˈɪnfrəstrʌktʃə(r)/ *n* [C, U] the basic structures and facilities necessary for a country or an organization to function efficiently, eg buildings, transport, water and energy resources, and administrative systems: *investment in infrastructure* ○

I

improve the country's commercial/financial infra-structure. ► **infrastructural** *adj: infrastructural development.*

infrequent /ɪnˈfriːkwənt/ *adj* rare; not common: *infrequent visits/train services ○ Such cases are relatively infrequent.* ► **infrequently** *adv: This happens* **not infrequently** (ie often).

infringe /ɪnˈfrɪndʒ/ *v* **1** to break a rule, an agreement, etc: [Vn] *infringe the regulations ○ infringe copyright.* **2** ~ **(on/upon)** sth to affect sth so as to limit or restrict it; to ENCROACH on sth: [Vn] *infringe sb's liberty* [Vpr] *infringe upon the rights of other people.* ► **infringement** /-mənt/ *n* [U, C]: *anxiety about infringement of academic freedom ○ an infringement of copyright/human rights.*

infuriate /ɪnˈfjʊərɪeɪt/ *v* to make sb extremely angry and annoyed: [Vn] *Their constant criticism infuriated him.*

► **infuriating** *adj* causing anger and annoyance: *infuriating delays ○ It was infuriating to have to wait another hour.* **infuriatingly** *adv: Infuriatingly, the shop had just closed.*

infuse /ɪnˈfjuːz/ *v* **1** ~ sth into sb/sth; ~ sb/sth **with** sth to put a quality into sb/sth; to fill sb/sth with a quality: [Vnpr] *infuse new life/interest into the debate ○ infuse the debate with new life/interest.* **2(a)** to prepare a drink or medicine by soaking tea or herbs (HERB) in a liquid, esp hot water, so that the liquid absorbs the flavour: [Vn] *infuse a handful of leaves in boiling water.* **(b)** (of tea, etc) to be treated by this process: [V] *leave the tea to infuse.*

infusion /ɪnˈfjuːʒn/ *n* **1** [C usu *sing*] ~ **of** sth **(into sb/sth)** the introduction of sb/sth new that will have a positive influence: *a cash injection ○ This company needs an infusion of new blood* (ie needs new employees to give it vigour). **2(a)** [U] the act or process of soaking tea, herbs (HERB), etc in a liquid. **(b)** [C] a drink, medicine, etc prepared in this way.

ingenious /ɪnˈdʒiːniəs/ *adj* **(a)** (of a thing) original in design and well suited to its purpose: *an ingenious device/gadget.* **(b)** (of an idea) very clever and original: *an ingenious plan/method/solution.* **(c)** (of a person) clever at making or inventing sth: *She's very ingenious when it comes to finding excuses.* ► **ingeniously** *adv.*

ingénue /ˈænʒeɪnjuː; *US* ˈændʒənuː/ *n* (French) an innocent young woman, esp as portrayed in a play or film: *an ingénue role ○ She's no vulnerable young ingénue but an assured operator.*

ingenuity /ˌɪndʒəˈnjuːəti; *US* -ˈnuː-/ *n* [U] the talent for solving problems in a clever original way: *Try to use a little ingenuity.*

ingenuous /ɪnˈdʒenjuəs/ *adj* (*fml*) not attempting to deceive anyone or conceal sth: *an ingenuous smile.* Compare DISINGENUOUS. ► **ingenuously** *adv.*

ingest /ɪnˈdʒest/ *v* (*fml*) **1** to take food, etc into the body, usu by swallowing: [Vn] *ingest poison.* **2** to absorb ideas, knowledge, etc into the mind: [Vn] *ingest information.*

inglenook /ˈɪŋɡlnʊk/ *n* a space on either side of a large fireplace where one can sit.

inglorious /ɪnˈɡlɔːriəs/ *adj* (*fml*) causing shame or loss of honour: *an inglorious chapter in the nation's history.* ► **ingloriously** *adv.*

ingot /ˈɪŋɡət/ *n* a lump of metal, esp gold or silver, usu shaped like a brick.

ingrained /ɪnˈɡreɪnd/ *adj* **1** ~ **(in sb)** (of habits, attitudes, etc) deeply fixed; firmly established or held: *ingrained faults/prejudices/suspicions ○ Distrust was ingrained in her from childhood.* **2** (of dirt, marks, etc) penetrating deeply into sth, and therefore difficult to remove: *the ingrained grime of generations.*

ingratiate /ɪnˈɡreɪʃieɪt/ *v* ~ **oneself (with sb)** (*fml derog*) (no passive) to try to gain the favour of sb

by doing things that will please them, praising them, etc: [Vnpr] *She tried to ingratiate herself with the director, in the hope of getting promotion.* [also Vn]. ► **ingratiating** *adj* (*derog*) attempting to please or gain favour: *an ingratiating smile.* **ingratiatingly** *adv.*

ingratitude /ɪnˈɡrætɪtjuːd; *US* -tuːd/ *n* [U] lack of gratitude.

ingredient /ɪnˈɡriːdiənt/ *n* ~ **(for/of** sth**)** **1** any of the foods that are combined to make a particular dish: *Mix all the ingredients in a bowl.* **2** any of the things or qualities of which sth is made: *the basic ingredients of a good mystery story ○ It has all the ingredients for the ultimate holiday experience.*

ingress /ˈɪŋɡres/ *n* [U] (*fml*) the action of entering or the right to enter: *a means of ingress.*

in-group /ˈɪn ɡruːp/ *n* (usu *derog*) a group within an organization or in society that gives favoured treatment to its own members; a CLIQUE.

ingrowing /ˈɪnɡrəʊɪŋ/ *adj* [usu attrib] (of a nail on a finger or a toe) growing into the flesh: *an ingrowing toenail.*

inhabit /ɪnˈhæbɪt/ *v* to live in a place; to occupy sth: [Vn] *an island inhabited only by birds ○ the glossy television world that she imagined people like Simon inhabited.*

► **inhabitant** /-ənt/ *n* a person or an animal living in a place: *the oldest inhabitant ○ The village has fewer than 800 inhabitants.*

inhale /ɪnˈheɪl/ *v* **(a)** ~ sth **(into sth)** to breathe or breathe sth in: [V] *I want you to inhale deeply.* [Vn, Vnpr] *miners who have inhaled coal dust (into their lungs).* **(b)** ~ **(on** sth**)** to take tobacco smoke into the lungs from a cigarette, etc: [Vpr] *She* **inhaled deeply on** *her cigarette.* [also V, Vn, Vnpr]. Compare EXHALE.

► **inhaler** *n* a device that releases medicine in a fine spray to be inhaled, eg by sb with ASTHMA.

inhalation *n* [U, C]: *smoke inhalation ○ steam inhalation for colds.*

inharmonious /ˌɪnhɑːˈməʊniəs/ *adj* (*fml*) not well suited; not combining well.

inherent /ɪnˈhɪərənt; *Brit also* -ˈher-/ *adj* ~ **(in sb/ sth)** existing as a natural or permanent feature or quality of sth/sb: *an inherent distrust of foreigners ○ an inherent weakness in a design ○ the power inherent in the office of President.* ► **inherently** *adv: inherently inadequate/unfair/dishonest.*

inherit /ɪnˈherɪt/ *v* ~ sth **(from sb)** **1** to receive money, property etc as a result of the death of the previous owner: [Vn] *His son will inherit the estate.* [Vpr] *She inherited a little money from her grandfather.* Compare DISINHERIT. **2** to have features or qualities similar to those of an ancestor: [Vn] *She inherited her mother's good looks and her father's bad temper.* [also Vnpr]. **3** to be left with sth by sb who was previously in one's own position or situation: [Vn, Vnpr] *This administration has inherited many problems (from the previous one).*

► **inheritance** /-əns/ *n* **1** [U] the action of inheriting sth from sb: *The title passes by inheritance to the eldest son. ○ inheritance tax.* **2** [C] a thing that is inherited: *When she was eighteen she came into (ie received) her inheritance. ○ (fig) his artistic inheritance ○ an inheritance of a dismal trading record.* Compare LEGACY.

inheritor *n* a person who inherits: *We are the inheritors of a great cultural tradition.*

inhibit /ɪnˈhɪbɪt/ *v* **1** ~ sb **(from** sth **/ doing sth)** to make sb nervous and embarrassed and prevent them from doing sth that should be natural or easy: [Vn, Vnpr] *Shyness inhibited him (from speaking).* **2** to restrict or prevent a process or an action: [Vn] *outdated policies that inhibit economic growth ○ Cost is not an inhibiting factor in the company's plans for development.*

▶ **inhibited** *adj* (of people or their behaviour) unable to relax or express feelings in a natural way: *She's too inhibited to laugh at jokes about sex.* ○ *a nervous inhibited laugh.*

inhibition /ˌɪnhɪˈbɪʃn, ˌɪnɪˈb-/ *n* **1** [C] a feeling that makes one nervous and embarrassed, and unable to relax or behave in a natural way: *overcome one's inhibitions* ○ *She had no inhibitions about making her opinions known* (ie did so without hesitating). **2** [U] the action of inhibiting sth or state of being inhibited: *inhibition of growth.*

inhospitable /ˌɪnhɒˈspɪtəbl/ *adj* **1** (of people) not giving a friendly or polite welcome to guests: *It was inhospitable of you not to offer her a drink.* **2** (of places etc) not giving shelter; unpleasant: *an inhospitable coast/region/climate.*

in-house /ˌɪn ˈhaus/ *adj* [attrib] existing or happening within a company or an organization: *an ˌinhouse ˈlibrary/magaˈzine* ○ *ˌin-house ˈlanguage training.*

inhuman /ɪnˈhjuːmən/ *adj* **1** lacking normal human qualities of kindness, pity, etc; extremely cruel: *inhuman and degrading treatment/conditions.* **2** not human; not having or influenced by human feelings; IMPERSONAL(1): *the inhuman logic of the machine.*
▶ **inhumanity** /ˌɪnhjuːˈmænəti/ *n* [U] inhuman(1) behaviour or treatment: *man's inhumanity to man.*

inhumane /ˌɪnhjuːˈmeɪn/ *adj* not sensitive to the suffering of others; cruel: *inhumane treatment of animals/prisoners/the mentally ill.* ▶ **inhumanely** *adv.*

inimical /ɪˈnɪmɪkl/ *adj* [usu pred] ~ (**to sb/sth**) (*fml*) **1** tending to prevent or discourage sth; harmful: *Their policies are inimical to national unity.* **2** not friendly; HOSTILE(1): *politicians inimical to federalism.*

inimitable /ɪˈnɪmɪtəbl/ *adj* impossible to copy because of being too good or too typical of an individual in style: *He related, in his own inimitable way, the story of his journey through Tibet.*

iniquitous /ɪˈnɪkwɪtəs/ *adj* (*fml*) very unfair or wicked: *an iniquitous system/decision.*
▶ **iniquity** /ɪˈnɪkwəti/ *n* (*fml*) (**a**) [U] very unfair or morally unacceptable actions, behaviour, etc. (**b**) [C] an act, effect, etc that is very unfair or morally wrong: *the iniquities of the benefits system.*

initial /ɪˈnɪʃl/ *adj* [attrib] of or at the beginning; first: *an initial payment of £60 and ten monthly instalments of £25* ○ *in the initial stages* (ie at the beginning) *of the debate* ○ *My initial reaction was to refuse.*
▶ **initial** *n* (usu *pl*) the first letter of a name: *John Fitzgerald Kennedy was well-known by his initials JFK.* ○ *Just write your initials.*
initial *v* (-ll-; *US* usu -l-) to mark or sign with one's initials: [Vn] *initial a note/an agreement* ○ *The artist has initialled the picture at the bottom.*
initially /-ʃəli/ *adv* at the beginning; at first: *Initially she was very lonely, but now she has made a few friends.* ○ *The costs were not as high as we had initially feared.* ○ *My contract is initially for three years.*

initiate /ɪˈnɪʃieɪt/ *v* **1** (*fml*) to put a scheme, etc into operation; to cause sth to begin: [Vn] *initiate plans/discussions/social reforms* [Vnpr] (*law*) *initiate proceedings* (ie begin legal action) *against sb* (ie prosecute sb). **2** ~ **sb** (**into sth**) (**a**) to admit sb to membership of a group, often by means of a special ceremony: [Vnpr] *initiate sb into a secret society* [also Vn]. (**b**) to introduce sb to a particular activity or skill: [Vnpr] *an older woman who had initiated him into the mysteries of love* [also Vn].
▶ **initiate** /ɪˈnɪʃiət/ *n* a person who has been initiated into a group.
the initiated /ɪˈnɪʃieɪtɪd/ *n* [pl *v*] a group of people who share special knowledge.
initiation /ɪˌnɪʃiˈeɪʃn/ *n* [U] **1** (*fml*) the action of

starting sth: *the initiation of an investigation.* **2** ~ (**into sth**) the action of initiating sb or the process of being initiated into a group or an activity: *an initiation ceremony* ○ *her initiation into womanhood.*
initiator /ɪˈnɪʃieɪtə(r)/ *n* (*fml*) a person who starts sth: *the initiator of the project.*

initiative /ɪˈnɪʃətɪv/ *n* **1** [C] a new approach to sth; an attempt to resolve a difficulty: *a United Nations peace initiative* ○ *It is hoped that the government's latest initiative will bring the strike to an end.* **2 the initiative** [sing] the power or opportunity to act or take charge before other people do: *The company seized/took the initiative in opening up markets in Eastern Europe.* ○ *The London side lost the initiative early on in the match.* **3** [U] (*approv*) the capacity and imagination to realize what needs to be done, together with the courage and willingness to do it, esp without others' help: *He lacks the necessary initiative to be a leader.* ○ *The child showed/displayed great initiative in phoning the police.* ○ *She did it on her own initiative* (ie without anyone telling her to do it).

inject /ɪnˈdʒekt/ *v* **1** ~ **sth** (**into oneself/sb/sth**); ~ **oneself/sb/sth** (**with sth**) to insert a drug or other substance into sb/sth with a SYRINGE or similar implement: [Vnpr] *inject oneself with insulin* ○ *inject penicillin into sb/sb's arm/leg* ○ *inject foam into a cavity wall* [Vn] *inject a lethal dose.* **2** ~ **sth** (**into sth**) to introduce a new quality, element, etc into sth: [Vnpr] *inject some fresh ideas into the project* [Vn] *inject $200 m of new capital.* ▶ **injection** /ɪnˈdʒekʃn/ *n* [U, C]: *The drug was administered by injection.* ○ *a fuel-injection system* ○ *a tetanus injection* ○ *I hate having injections.* ○ *an injection of new funds.* ⇨ picture.

injection
hypodermic syringe
hypodermic needle

in-joke /ˈɪn dʒəʊk/ *n* a joke shared by a small group of people.

injudicious /ˌɪndʒuˈdɪʃəs/ *adj* (*fml*) not well judged or appropriate; unwise: *injudicious remarks.*

injunction /ɪnˈdʒʌŋkʃn/ *n* ~ (**against sb**) (*fml*) an official order, esp a written order from a lawcourt, demanding that sth must or must not be done: *be granted an injunction against sb* ○ *The government has sought an injunction preventing the paper from publishing the story.*

injure /ˈɪndʒə(r)/ *v* **1** to hurt oneself/sb/sth physically: [Vn] *He fell off his bicycle and injured himself/his arm.* ○ *She was slightly/seriously/badly injured in a road accident.* **2** to harm sth or make sth worse: [Vn] *Such malicious gossip could seriously injure her reputation.*
▶ **injured** *adj* **1** wounded; hurt: *an injured man/leg.* **2** [attrib] treated unfairly: (*esp law*) *the injured party* (ie the person who has been treated unfairly). **3** offended: *injured pride* ○ *an injured look/voice.* **the injured** *n* [pl *v*] the people injured in an accident, a battle, etc: *Ambulances took the injured to hospital.* ⇨ note at WOUND[1].

injurious /ɪnˈdʒʊəriəs/ *adj* (*fml*) ~ (**to sb/sth**) causing or likely to cause injury or harm: *Smoking is injurious to health.* ○ *injurious behaviour.*

injury /ˈɪndʒəri/ *n* ~ (**to sb/sth**) **1** [U] (**a**) physical harm to a person or an animal: *Children playing with this machine risk serious injury.* ○ *Soames is out of the match because of injury.* (**b**) damage to sb's feelings or reputation. **2** [C] an instance of harm to sb's body or feelings: *suffer severe injuries to the head and neck* ○ *a knee injury* ○ *Don't try lifting that trunk or you'll do yourself an injury!* ⇨ note at WOUND[1]. **IDM add insult to injury** ⇨ ADD.
■ **ˈinjury time** *n* [U] (*sport*) time added at the end of a game of football, hockey, etc because the game has

been interrupted, eg by injured players needing treatment.

injustice /ɪnˈdʒʌstɪs/ n **1** [U] the lack of justice: *a victim of injustice* ○ *the need to fight injustice.* **2** [C] an unfair act; an instance of unfair treatment: *expose the injustices of the system.* **IDM do oneself/sb an inˈjustice** to judge oneself/sb unfairly: *I used to think you were a selfish person but I realize now that I was doing you a grave injustice.*

ink /ɪŋk/ n [U, C] liquid for writing, drawing and printing, in various colours: *written in ink* ○ *a pen-and-ink drawing* ○ *different coloured inks.*
▶ **ink** v to cover sth with ink ready for printing: [Vn] *ink the roller of a duplicating machine.* **PHR V ink sth in** to write in ink over sth already written in pencil.
inky /ˈɪŋki/ adj **1** black like ink: *the inky blackness of the cellar.* **2** made dirty with ink: *inky fingers.*
■ **ˈink-pad** (also **stamp-pad**) n a pad soaked with ink, used with a rubber stamp²(2).
ˈink-well n a pot for holding ink that fits into a hole in a desk.

inkling /ˈɪŋklɪŋ/ n (usu *sing*) ~ (**of sth/that…**) a slight knowledge of sth secret or not previously known; a HINT(1): *He had no inkling of what was going on.* ○ *My first inkling that something was wrong was when I found the front door wide open.*

inlaid *pt, pp* of INLAY.

inland /ˈɪnlənd/ adj [usu attrib] (**a**) situated in the middle of a country, not on the coast: *inland towns/waterways.* Compare COASTAL. (**b**) (of a sea) surrounded by land or islands.
▶ **inland** /ˌɪnˈlænd/ adv in or towards the middle of a country, away from the coast: *move further inland.*
■ **the ˌInland ˈRevenue** n [sing] (in Britain) the government department responsible for collecting taxes. Compare INTERNAL REVENUE SERVICE.

in-laws /ˈɪn lɔːz/ n [pl] (*infml*) relatives by marriage: *visit one's in-laws.*

inlay /ˌɪnˈleɪ/ v (*pt, pp* inlaid /ˌɪnˈleɪd/) ~ **A** (**with B**)/ ~ **B** (**in/into A**) (esp passive) to make a design on a surface by putting pieces of wood or metal into it, so that the resulting surface is smooth; to insert pieces of wood, metal, etc in this way: [Vnpr] *ivory inlaid with gold* ○ *his initials inlaid in silver* [also Vn].
▶ **inlaid** adj decorated with inlaid designs: *a silver inlaid brass casket* (ie made of brass inlaid with silver).
inlay /ˈɪnleɪ/ n [C, U] a design or pattern made by inlaying: *a wooden jewel-box with (a) gold inlay.*

inlet /ˈɪnlet/ n **1** a strip of water extending into the land from the sea or a lake, or between islands: *a sheltered inlet.* **2** an opening to allow liquid or air to enter sth: *the fuel inlet* ○ *an inlet pipe.* Compare OUTLET 3.

in loco parentis /ɪn ˌləʊkəʊ pəˈrentɪs/ adv (*Latin fml*) acting for or instead of a parent; having the responsibility of a parent: *act/be in loco parentis.*

inmate /ˈɪnmeɪt/ n any of a number of people living together in an institution, esp a prison.

in memoriam /ˌɪn məˈmɔːriəm/ adv, prep (used esp on gravestones (GRAVESTONE)) in memory of a dead person.

inmost /ˈɪnməʊst/ adj [attrib] most private or secret: *The book reveals her inmost self/secrets.* See also INNERMOST.

inn /ɪn/ n a pub or small old hotel, now usu in the country. Compare BAR¹ 1, HOTEL, PUB.
■ **Inn of ˈCourt** n (pl **Inns of Court**) (*Brit law*) any of four law societies in London having the exclusive right of admitting people to the rank of BARRISTER in England.

NOTE Inn is an old-fashioned word used to describe

a small hotel where alcohol and meals are served. It is now used mainly as part of a name: *We stayed the night at the Bell Inn.* The usual word in British English for a place where alcoholic drink and sometimes food are served is **pub**: *The best pub around here is the King's Head.* In American English the usual word is **bar**: *We went to a bar after work and had a couple of beers.* In Britain, especially in cities, you can also go to a **wine bar** which serves wine and food.

innards /ˈɪnədz/ n [pl] (*infml*) the stomach and/or bowels: *turkey innards* ○ (*infml*) *Hunger gnawed at my innards.* ○ (*fig*) *tinkering with the innards of an ancient Citroen.*

innate /ɪˈneɪt/ adj (of a quality, feeling, etc) in one's nature; possessed from birth: *innate ability/beauty* ○ *an innate sense of style.*
▶ **innately** adv naturally: *innately dishonest.*

inner /ˈɪnə(r)/ adj [attrib] **1** inside; towards the middle of a place, not near the outside: *an inner room/door* ○ *inner London* ○ (*joc*) *I've never been inside the boss's inner sanctum* (ie private room). Compare OUTER. **2** (of feelings) private or not expressed: *his inner spiritual life* ○ *inner conflict/doubts.* **IDM the ˌinner ˈman/ˈwoman** (*rhet*) a person's mind or soul.
▶ **innermost** /-məʊst/ adj [attrib] most inward; INMOST: *express one's innermost feelings.* Compare OUTERMOST.
■ **ˌinner ˈcircle** n a small group of people controlling an organization and often working in secret.
ˌinner ˈcity n the parts of a city at or near its centre: *the problems of the inner city* ○ *ˌinner-city 'areas/'schools.*
ˈinner tube n a rubber tube filled with air inside a tyre.

innings /ˈɪnɪŋz/ n (pl unchanged) (in cricket) a time during which a team or single player is batting (BAT¹ v 1): *England made 25 runs in their first innings.* **IDM have had a good ˈinnings** (*Brit infml*) to have had a long and successful life or career: *She's had a good innings but now it's time she retired.*
▶ **inning** n (in baseball) a time during which one team is batting (BAT¹ v 1); a division of a game in which both teams have a turn to bat: *After four innings the score remained 1–1.*

innkeeper n a person who manages an INN.

innocent /ˈɪnəsnt/ adj **1** ~ (**of sth**) not guilty of wrongdoing: *be innocent of a crime/charge* ○ *They have imprisoned an innocent man.* **2** [attrib] suffering harm although not directly involved in a crime, an accident, etc: *an innocent bystander* ○ *innocent victims of the bomb blast.* **3** harmless; not intended to harm or offend: *innocent amusement/enjoyment* ○ *It was a perfectly innocent question.* **4** having little experience of deception, wrongdoing or sexual matters: *her innocent young niece* ○ *Don't be so innocent as to believe everything the politicians tell you.*
▶ **innocence** /-sns/ n [U] **1** the state of being innocent of wrongdoing: *She protested her innocence* (ie kept saying she was innocent). ○ *do sth in all innocence* (ie without knowing it to be wrong or likely to offend). **2** lack of knowledge and experience of the world: *Children lose their innocence as they grow older.*
innocent n an innocent person, esp a young child.
innocently adv: *'Is Jenny your daughter?' she asked innocently.*

innocuous /ɪˈnɒkjuəs/ adj (*fml*) **1** not intended to offend: *an innocuous remark.* **2** having no harmful effects.

innovate /ˈɪnəveɪt/ v to make changes; to introduce new ideas, methods, etc: [V] *The company collapsed because of its failure to innovate.*
▶ **innovation** /ˌɪnəˈveɪʃn/ n ~ (**in sth**) (**a**) [U] the process of innovating: *a period of innovation.* (**b**) [C]

──────────

[V.*to* inf] = verb + *to* infinitive   [Vn.inf (no *to*)] = verb + noun + infinitive without *to*   [V.*ing*] = verb + -*ing* form

a new technique, idea, etc: *recent innovations in the textile industry.*

innovative /'ɪnəveɪtɪv; *Brit also* 'ɪnəvətɪv/ (*also* **innovatory** /ˌɪnə'veɪtəri/) *adj* (*approv*) introducing or using new ideas, techniques, etc: *one of France's most innovative designers* ○ *a highly innovative approach.*

innovator /'ɪnəveɪtə(r)/ *n.*

innuendo /ˌɪnju'endəʊ/ *n* (*pl* **-os** *or* **-oes**) [C, U] (*derog*) an indirect reference to sb/sth, usu suggesting sth bad or rude: *innuendos about his private life* ○ *The play is full of sexual innuendo.*

innumerable /ɪ'njuːmərəbl; *US* ɪ'nuː-/ *adj* too many to be counted: *innumerable books/opportunities.* ⇨ note at INVALUABLE.

innumerate /ɪ'njuːmərət/ *adj* without a basic knowledge of MATHEMATICS; unable to count or do sums.

inoculate /ɪ'nɒkjuleɪt/ *v* ~ **sb** (**with sth**) (**against sth**) to INJECT(1) a person or an animal with a mild form of a disease as a way of preventing them/it catching the disease itself: [Vnpr] *inoculate sb against cholera* [also Vn]. Compare IMMUNIZE, VACCINATE. ▸ **inoculation** /ɪˌnɒkju'leɪʃn/ *n* [U, C]: *have inoculations against typhoid.*

inoffensive /ˌɪnə'fensɪv/ *adj* not causing offence; harmless: *an inoffensive remark/person.*

inoperable /ɪn'ɒpərəbl/ *adj* **1** (of CANCER(1), etc) that cannot be cured by a SURGICAL operation. **2** (*fml*) that cannot be made to work; not practical(3): *The policy was rendered inoperable.*

inoperative /ɪn'ɒpərətɪv/ *adj* not working or taking effect; not valid: *This rule is inoperative until further notice.*

inopportune /ɪn'ɒpətjuːn; *US* -tuːn/ *adj* not appropriate or convenient: *You arrived at an inopportune moment.*

inordinate /ɪn'ɔːdɪnət/ *adj* (*fml*) beyond proper or normal limits; excessive : *an inordinate amount of time/space/money* ○ *inordinate delays.* ▸ **inordinately** *adv: inordinately proud.*

inorganic /ˌɪnɔː'gænɪk/ *adj* not composed of living substances: *inorganic fertilizers* ○ *Rocks and minerals are inorganic.*

■ **inorganic 'chemistry** *n* [U] the branch of chemistry that deals with substances which do not contain CARBON(1).

in-patient /'ɪn peɪʃnt/ *n* a person who stays in hospital for a period of days while receiving treatment. Compare OUT-PATIENT.

input /'ɪnpʊt/ *n* **1** ~ (**into/to sth**) (**a**) [U] the action of putting sth into sth: *the input of additional resources into the scheme.* (**b**) [C, U] that which is put in: *agricultural inputs* ○ *the total energy input* ○ *Her input* (ie contribution) *to the project was invaluable.* **2** (*computing*) (**a**) [U] the action of putting information into a computer for processing or storage. (**b**) [C, U] information that is put in. **3** [C] a place or means through which electricity, data, etc enter a machine or system: *an input lead/device.* Compare OUTPUT.

▸ **input** *v* (**-tt-**; *pt, pp* **input** *or* **inputted**) (*computing*) to put information into a computer: [Vn] *input the monthly sales figures* [also Vnpr]. Compare OUTPUT *v.*

inquest /'ɪnkwest/ *n* ~ (**on/into sth**) **1** an official inquiry to discover facts, esp about a death which may not have happened naturally: *a coroner's inquest* ○ *The inquest heard that the car drove off after the accident.* **2** (*infml*) a discussion about sth which has not been satisfactory: *hold an inquest on the team's miserable performance.*

inquire (*also* **enquire**) /ɪn'kwaɪə(r)/ *v* (*fml*) (**a**) to ask to be told sth by sb: [Vn] *inquire sb's name* [V.wh] *inquire where to go* [V.speech] *'How long have you been with the company?' she inquired.* (**b**) ~

(**about sb/sth**) to ask for information: [Vpr] *inquire about flights to Amsterdam* [V] *'How much are the tickets?' 'I'll inquire'.* **PHRV** **in'quire after sb** to ask about sb's health or welfare: *People called to inquire after the baby.* **in'quire into sth** to try to learn the facts about sth; to investigate sth: *We must inquire further into the matter.*

▸ **inquirer** (*also* **enquirer**) /ɪn'kwaɪərə(r)/ *n* a person who inquires.

inquiring (*also* **enquiring**) /ɪn'kwaɪərɪŋ/ *adj* [usu attrib] **1** showing an interest in learning new things: *an inquiring mind.* **2** suggesting that information is needed: *an inquiring look.* **inquiringly** (*also* **enquiringly**) *adv: look at sb inquiringly.*

inquiry (*also* **enquiry**) /ɪn'kwaɪəri/ *n* **1**(**a**) [C] ~ (**about/concerning sb/sth**) a request for help or information about sb/sth: *In answer to your recent inquiry, the book you mention is not in stock.* ○ *I've been making (some) inquiries* (ie trying to find out) *about it.* ○ *an inquiry desk/office.* (**b**) **inquiries** [pl] (*Brit*) a place from which one can get information: *Ask at inquiries to find out if your bag has been handed in.* ○ *directory inquiries* (ie a service giving information about telephone numbers). **2** [U] asking; inquiring: *learn sth by inquiry* ○ *a court of inquiry* ○ *The police are following several lines of inquiry.* ○ *On inquiry* (ie Having asked) *I found it was true.* **3** [C] ~ (**into sth**) an investigation: *hold an official inquiry* ○ *call for a public inquiry into safety standards* ○ *Two men are helping the police with their inquiries.*

inquisition /ˌɪnkwɪ'zɪʃn/ *n* **1** **the Inquisition** [sing] the organization appointed by the Roman Catholic Church to suppress people who opposed its beliefs, esp from the 15th to the 17th century. **2** [C] ~ (**into sth**) (*fml or joc*) an investigation, esp one that involves a lot of personal and detailed questions: *I was subjected to a lengthy inquisition into the state of my marriage and the size of my bank balance.*

inquisitive /ɪn'kwɪzətɪv/ *adj* (*often derog*) tending to ask a lot of questions, esp about other people's affairs: *'What's that you're reading?' 'Don't be so inquisitive!'* ○ *a very inquisitive child.* ▸ **inquisitively** *adv.* **inquisitiveness** *n* [U].

inquisitor /ɪn'kwɪzɪtə(r)/ *n* a person who investigates, esp an officer of the Inquisition.

▸ **inquisitorial** /ɪnˌkwɪzɪ'tɔːriəl/ *adj* of or like an inquisitor: *act in an inquisitorial manner* ○ *an inquisitorial system of justice.* Compare ADVERSARIAL. **inquisitorially** *adv.*

inroad /'ɪnrəʊd/ *n* (usu *pl*) ~ (**into sth**) an achievement, etc, esp one made at the expense of others: *recent inroads by foreign companies into the domestic market.* **IDM** **make inroads into/on sth** to use or take more and more of sth: *Repair bills had made deep inroads into her savings.* ○ *The long illness made considerable inroads on his previously robust physique.*

inrush /'ɪnrʌʃ/ *n* (usu *sing*) the rushing in of sth; the sudden arrival of sth in large numbers: *an inrush of air/water* ○ *an inrush of tourists/visitors.*

insane /ɪn'seɪn/ *adj* **1** not sane; mad: *an insane person* ○ *Sometimes I think I'm going insane.* ○ *This job is driving me insane.* **2** (*infml*) very foolish: *an insane desire/idea/decision/policy.*

▸ **the insane** *n* [pl *v*] insane people: *an institution for the insane.*

insanely *adv: insanely jealous.*

insanity /ɪn'sænəti/ *n* [U] madness; the state of being mad: *a plea of insanity* (ie one made in a court of law on the grounds that a crime was due to a mental disorder).

insanitary /ɪn'sænətri; *US* -teri/ *adj* not clean; not free from germs: *insanitary living conditions.*

insatiable /ɪn'seɪʃəbl/ *adj* that cannot be satisfied: *an insatiable appetite/curiosity/desire/thirst* ○ *The* demand for increasingly powerful computers appears to be insatiable. ► **insatiably** /-ʃəbli/ adv.

inscribe /ɪnˈskraɪb/ v ~ A (on/in B); ~ B (with A) to write words, one's name, etc on or in sth, esp as a formal or permanent record: [Vnpr] *inscribe one's name in a book/inscribe a book with one's name* ○ *inscribe verses on a tombstone/inscribe a tombstone with verses* [Vnn] *The book was inscribed 'To Michael, with warmest regards.'* [also Vn].
► **inscription** /ɪnˈskrɪpʃn/ n words written on sth, cut in stone or stamped in metal: *There is an illegible inscription carved on the gravestone.* ○ *The inscription reads 'World Champion 1966'.*

inscrutable /ɪnˈskruːtəbl/ adj that cannot be understood or known; mysterious: *an inscrutable expression/face/gaze* (ie that does not show what sb is thinking) ○ *I find his poetry rather inscrutable.* ► **inscrutability** /ɪnˌskruːtəˈbɪləti/ n [U]. **inscrutably** /ɪnˈskruːtəbli/ adv.

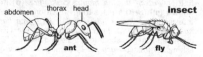

abdomen thorax head   **insect**

ant fly

insect /ˈɪnsekt/ n **1** a type of small creature having six legs and a body divided into three parts (*head, thorax* and *abdomen*). Insects usu also have wings: *Butterflies, ants, bees and flies are insects.* ○ *an insect bite.* ⇨ picture. **2** (in incorrect but common usage) any small crawling creature (eg a SPIDER). See also STICK INSECT.
► **insecticide** /ɪnˈsektɪsaɪd/ n [C,U] a substance used for killing insects: *an insecticide spray/powder* ○ *crops sprayed with insecticides.* See also PESTICIDE **insecticidal** /ɪnˌsektɪˈsaɪdl/ adj.
insectivore /ɪnˈsektɪvɔː(r)/ n an animal that eats insects: *Hedgehogs and shrews are insectivores.* **insectivorous** /ˌɪnsekˈtɪvərəs/ adj: *insectivorous birds.*

insecure /ˌɪnsɪˈkjʊə(r)/ adj **1** not secure or safe; not providing good support; that cannot be relied on: *have an insecure hold/grip on sth* (eg when climbing) ○ *This door is insecure* (ie easy to open, even when locked). ○ *(fig) an insecure job* (ie one from which one may be dismissed at any time) ○ *an insecure arrangement/plan.* **2** not feeling safe or protected; lacking confidence: *an insecure person* ○ *She feels very insecure about her marriage.* ► **insecurely** adv: *insecurely fastened.* **insecurity** /ˌɪnsɪˈkjʊərəti/ n [U]: *suffer from feelings of insecurity.*

inseminate /ɪnˈsemɪneɪt/ v to put SPERM into a female, esp a female animal, to make her pregnant. This can be done either naturally or artificially: [Vn] *inseminate a cow.* ► **insemination** /ɪnˌsemɪˈneɪʃn/ n [U]: *artificial insemination.*

insensibility /ɪnˌsensəˈbɪləti/ n [U] (*fml*) **1** the state of being unconscious: *lying in a state of drugged insensibility.* **2** ~ (**to sth**) (**a**) lack of physical feeling: *insensibility to pain/cold.* (**b**) (*derog*) lack of ability to respond emotionally: *insensibility to art/music/beauty.* (**c**) (*derog*) lack of concern about what happens to sb/sth: *He showed total insensibility to the welfare of his children.*

insensible /ɪnˈsensəbl/ adj (*fml*) **1** unconscious as the result of injury, illness, etc: *knocked insensible by a falling rock.* **2** [pred] ~ (**to sth**) not able to feel sth; having no feelings for sb/sth: *insensible to pain/cold* ○ *He seemed insensible to her needs.* Compare INSENSITIVE 2a. ► **insensibly** /-əbli/ adv.

insensitive /ɪnˈsensətɪv/ adj ~ (**to sth**) **1** not realizing or caring how other people feel, and therefore likely to hurt or offend them: *an insensitive question/manner/remark/person* ○ *She's completely*

insensitive to other people's feelings. **2** not able to feel or respond to sth: *insensitive to pain/cold* ○ *He's insensitive to criticism.* ► **insensitively** adv. **insensitivity** /ɪnˌsensəˈtɪvəti/ n [U].

inseparable /ɪnˈseprəbl/ adj ~ (**from sb/sth**) that cannot be separated: *Britain's economic fortunes are inseparable from the situation in Europe.* ○ *The two friends were inseparable — they went everywhere together.* ► **inseparability** /ɪnˌseprəˈbɪləti/ n [U]: *the inseparability of art and life.* **inseparably** /ɪnˈseprəbli/ adv: *inseparably linked/joined.*

insert /ɪnˈsɜːt/ v ~ sth (**in/into/between sth**) to put, fit or place sth into sth or between two things: [Vnpr] *insert a key into a lock* ○ *insert a new paragraph in an essay* ○ *insert a waterproof lining between two layers of material* [also Vn].
► **insert** /ˈɪnsɜːt/ n ~ (**in sth**) a thing inserted, esp an additional section in a book, newspaper, etc: *an eight-page insert.*
insertion /ɪnˈsɜːʃn/ n **1** [U] ~ (**into sth**) the action of inserting sth: *the insertion of a coin into a slot.* **2** [C] (**a**) a thing inserted, eg an announcement or advertisement put in a newspaper. (**b**) an occasion when an announcement, etc is inserted: *£10 per insertion.*

in-service /ˈɪn sɜːvɪs/ adj [attrib] carried out while actually working at a job: *in-service training for teachers.*

inset /ˈɪnset/ v (-**tt**-; pt, pp **inset**) ~ A (**with B**); ~ B (**into A**) (esp passive) **1** to put or fix sth firmly into or on the surface of sth else: [Vnpr] *a silver ring inset with pearls* ○ *a sink inset into the working surface* [also Vn]. **2** to put a small picture, map, etc within the border of a printed page or of a larger picture: [Vn] *For an explanation of the symbols see the key, inset left.* [also Vnpr].
► **inset** n an additional thing put in: *a tiled fireplace with gas fire inset* ○ *For continuation of the map, see inset.*

inshore /ˌɪnˈʃɔː(r)/ adj [usu attrib] (of sth at sea) close to the shore: *an ˌinshore ˈbreeze/ ˈcurrent* ○ *ˌinshore ˈfisheries.* ► **inshore** adv: *fishing inshore in shallow waters.* Compare OFFSHORE 1.

inside¹ /ˌɪnˈsaɪd/ n **1** (usu the **inside**) (**a**) [C usu sing] the inner part, side or surface of sth: *The inside of the box was lined with silk.* ○ *This cup is stained on the inside.* ○ *chocolates with a creamy inside* ○ *Which paint is suitable for the inside of a house?* ○ *The room had been locked from/on the inside.* ○ *The insides of the cylinders must be carefully cleaned.* (**b**) [sing] the lane or part of a road furthest from the centre: *To my surprise, the driver behind tried to overtake me on the inside.* (**c**) [sing] the side of a pavement or path that is furthest away from the road: *Walk on the inside to avoid the traffic fumes.* (**d**) [sing] the part of a curving road or track nearest to the inner or shorter side of the curve: *The favourite is coming up fast on the inside.* Compare OUTSIDE¹. **2** [sing] (also **insides** /ɪnˈsaɪdz/ [pl]) (*infml*) one's stomach and bowels: *a pain in his insides* ○ *My insides were knotted with fear.* **IDM** ˌinside ˈout with the inner surface on the outside: *wearing his socks inside out* ○ *Turn the blouse inside out before drying it.* ○ *My umbrella has blown inside out.* ⇨ picture at BACK¹. **know sb/sth inside ˈout** ⇨ KNOW. **on the inˈside** within a group or an organization and so able to obtain information not available to others: *The thieves must have had someone on the inside to help them break in.* **turn sth inside out** to search sth thoroughly by emptying it and looking through its contents: *turn a cupboard/drawer/room inside out.*
► **ˈinside** adj [attrib] **1** forming the inner part of sth; not on the outer side: *the inside pages of a newspaper* ○ *choosing to run on the inside track* ○ *He kept his wallet in an ˌinside ˈpocket.* ○ *What does your*

inside leg (ie from the CROTCH to the inner side of the foot) *measure?* **2** told or done by sb who is in a group or an organization: *Acting on* **inside information**, *the police were able to arrest the gang before the robbery occurred.* ○ *The robbery appeared to have been an* **inside job**.

insider /ɪnˈsaɪdə(r)/ *n* a person who, as a member of a group or an organization, is able to obtain information not available to others: *secret information leaked by an insider.* **in₁sider ˈdealing** (also **in₁sider ˈtrading**) *n* [U] illegal buying or selling, esp of shares (SHARE¹ 3), with the help of information known only by those connected with the business.

■ **₁inside ˈlane** *n* (usu *sing*) the section of a road or MOTORWAY that is furthest from the centre, ie nearest to the left in countries where vehicles drive on the left: *After overtaking you should move back into the inside lane.*

inside² /ɪnˈsaɪd/ (also *esp US* **inside of**) *prep* **1** on or to the inner side of sth/sb; within sth/sb: *go inside the house* ○ *put it inside its cage* ○ *Inside the box was a gold watch.* ○ *Inside the country there are severe food shortages.* ○ *You'll feel better with a good meal inside you* (ie when you have eaten a good meal). ○ *(fig) Inside most of us is a small child screaming for attention.* Compare OUTSIDE² 1. **2** (of time) in less than sth: *The job is unlikely to be finished inside (of) a year.*

▶ **inside** *adv* **1** on or to the inside: *The coat has a detachable lining inside.* ○ *She shook it to make certain there was nothing inside.* ○ *The guests had to move inside* (ie indoors) *when it started to rain.* ○ *(fig)* I *was angry inside but pretended not to care.* **2** *(sl)* in prison.

insidious /ɪnˈsɪdiəs/ *adj* (*fml derog*) spreading or acting gradually or without being noticed, but with harmful effects: *an insidious disease* ○ *Jealousy is insidious.* ▶ **insidiously** *adv*: *Cigarette advertisers work insidiously but effectively on children.*

insight /ˈɪnsaɪt/ *n* ~ (**into sth**) **1(a)** [U] (*approv*) the ability to see into the true nature of sth; deep understanding: *a person of insight* ○ *show insight into human character.* **(b)** [C] an instance of this: *a book full of remarkable insights.* **2** [C] an understanding, esp sudden, of the true nature of sth: *have/gain an insight into a problem* ○ *She was given an unpleasant insight into what life would be like as his wife.* ▶ **insightful** /-fʊl/ *adj* (*approv*) showing insight: *an insightful remark/critic.*

insignia /ɪnˈsɪɡniə/ *n* [pl] **(a)** symbols of rank or authority, eg the crown and SCEPTRE of a king or queen: *the insignia of office.* **(b)** a badge or sign that shows sb is a member of a military regiment, a club, etc: *insignia worn on the right sleeve.*

insignificant /ˌɪnsɪɡˈnɪfɪkənt/ *adj* having little or no value, use, meaning or importance: *The level of dangerous chemicals present in the river is now so low as to be insignificant.* ○ *An insignificant number of people voted against the new measures.* ○ *He was an insignificant-looking little man.* ▶ **insignificance** /-kəns/ *n* [U]: *Past conflicts* **pale into insignificance** *beside the terrible wars of the 20th century.*

insincere /ˌɪnsɪnˈsɪə(r)/ *adj* not sincere; not genuine. ▶ **insincerely** *adv.* **insincerity** /ˌɪnsɪnˈserəti/ *n* [U]: *be accused of insincerity.*

insinuate /ɪnˈsɪnjueɪt/ *v* **1** to suggest sth bad about sb/sth in an unpleasant and indirect way: [Vn] *insinuate base motives* [V.*that*] *Are you insinuating that I am a liar?* [also V,Vpr.*that*,V.speech]. **2** ~ **sth/oneself into sth (a)** (*derog*) to get oneself into a position of advantage, eg by clever talk or by gaining the favour of sb influential: [Vnpr] *He insinuated himself into my confidence.* **(b)** (*fml*) to slide sth/oneself into a position slowly and smoothly: [Vnpr] *insinuate one's body into a narrow opening.*

▶ **insinuation** /ɪnˌsɪnjuˈeɪʃn/ *n* **(a)** [U] the action of insinuating sth: *blacken sb's character by insinu-*

ation. **(b)** [C] a thing that is insinuated; an indirect suggestion, usu of sth bad: *make ugly insinuations.*

insipid /ɪnˈsɪpɪd/ *adj* (*derog*) **1** having almost no taste or flavour: *weak insipid coffee.* **2** lacking in interest or vigour: *insipid colours* ○ *an insipid performance/character.*

insist /ɪnˈsɪst/ *v* **1** ~ (**on sth**) to demand sth forcefully, not accepting a refusal: [V] *'You really must tell him!' 'All right, if you insist.'* [Vpr,V.*that*] *I insist on your taking/insist that you take immediate action to put this right.* **2** ~ **on/upon (doing) sth** to require or demand the specified thing, refusing to accept an alternative: [Vpr] *I always insist on/upon wholemeal bread.* ○ *(fig) She will insist on getting up early and playing her radio very loud* (ie She always does this, causing annoyance). **3** ~ (**on sth**) to state or declare sth forcefully, esp when other people oppose or disbelieve one: [Vpr,V.*that*] *She kept insisting on her innocence/insisting that she was innocent.* [V.speech] *'But we have the right to stay!' Laura insisted.*

▶ **insistent** /-ənt/ *adj* **1** ~ (**about/on/upon sth**); ~ (**that...**) tending to insist; not allowing refusal or opposition: *She didn't want to go but her brother was insistent.* ○ *They were insistent on having a proper contract.* ○ *He was most insistent that he never used the word 'traitor'.* **2** regular and repeated, and demanding attention: *insistent demands for higher wages* ○ *the insistent horn phrase in the third movement.* **insistence** /-əns/ *n* [U] ~ (**on/upon sth**); ~ (**that...**): *their insistence on strict standards of behaviour* ○ *At her insistence the matter was dropped.* **insistently** *adv.*

in situ /ˌɪn ˈsɪtjuː; *US* -ˈsaɪtuː/ *adv* (*Latin*) in the original or proper place: *The old fireplace is still in situ.*

insofar as /ˌɪnsəˈfɑːr əz/ = IN SO FAR AS (FAR¹).

insole /ˈɪnsəʊl/ *n* a piece of material attached to or placed on the inside of a shoe.

insolent /ˈɪnsələnt/ *adj* extremely rude and showing a lack of respect: *insolent children/behaviour.* ▶ **insolence** /-əns/ *n* [U] insolent behaviour or remarks: *dumb insolence* (ie expressed by behaviour rather than in words). **insolently** *adv.*

insoluble /ɪnˈsɒljəbl/ *adj* **1** (of substances) that cannot be dissolved; not SOLUBLE(1): *Cholesterol is insoluble in water.* **2** that cannot be solved or explained: *an insoluble problem/mystery/conflict.*

insolvent /ɪnˈsɒlvənt/ *adj* unable to pay debts; BANKRUPT(2): *He is technically insolvent.* ▶ **insolvency** /-ənsi/ *n* [U,C].

insomnia /ɪnˈsɒmniə/ *n* [U] an inability to sleep: *suffer from insomnia.* ▶ **insomniac** /ɪnˈsɒmniæk/ *n* a person who finds it difficult to go to sleep.

insouciance /ɪnˈsuːsiəns/ *n* [U] (*fml*) lack of concern or anxiety; nonchalance (NONCHALANT): *the cheerful insouciance of youth.* ▶ **insouciant** /-siənt/ *adj.*

Insp *abbr* Inspector (esp in the police force): *Chief Insp (Paul) King.*

inspect /ɪnˈspekt/ *v* **1(a)** to examine sth closely: [Vn] *Immigration officers inspected my passport.* **(b)** ~ **sb/sth for sth** to examine sb/sth in order to detect the presence of sth: [Vnpr] *inspect the boat for damage.* **2** to visit an institution officially to see that rules are obeyed, that work is done properly, etc: [Vn] *inspect a school/factory/regiment.* ▶ **inspection** /ɪnˈspekʃn/ *n* [U]: *On (closer) inspection* (ie When inspected) *the notes proved to be forgeries.* ○ *carry out regular inspections of the fire equipment.*

inspector /ɪnˈspektə(r)/ *n* **1** an official who inspects schools, factories, mines, etc. **2** (the title of) a fairly senior police officer: *Inspector Davies.* **3** an

---

official who examines bus or train tickets to check that they are valid.

▶ **inspectorate** /ɪnˈspektərət/ n [CGp] all the inspectors concerned with a particular subject or type of institution: *the primary schools inspectorate.*

■ in,spector of ˈtaxes (also ˈtax inspector) n an official who examines statements of people's income and decides the tax to be paid.

inspiration /ˌɪnspəˈreɪʃn/ n **1** [U] ~ (to do sth); ~ (for sth) the process of having one's mind or creative abilities stimulated, esp in art, music or literature: *Wordsworth found (his) inspiration in/drew (his) inspiration from the Lake District scenery.* ○ *a source of inspiration to more recent artists* ○ *The incident provided inspiration for a novel.* ○ *Her work lacks inspiration.* **2** [C usu *sing*] ~ (to/for sb) a person or thing that causes one's mind, creative abilities, interest, etc to be stimulated: *She/Her charity work is an inspiration to us all.* **3** [C usu *sing*] (*infml*) a sudden good idea: *I've just had an inspiration — why don't we try turning it the other way?*

▶ **inspirational** /-ʃənl/ adj providing inspiration: *an inspirational leader/force.*

inspire /ɪnˈspaɪə(r)/ v **1** ~ sb (to sth) to fill sb with the ability or urge to do or feel sth, esp to write, paint or compose: [Vnpr] *His success inspired the rest of us to greater efforts.* [Vn.to inf] *The Lake District scenery inspired Wordsworth to write his greatest poetry.* [Vn] *The design was inspired by a Greek vase painting.* **2** ~ sb (with sth) / ~ sth (in sb) to fill sb with thoughts, feelings or aims: [Vn] *inspire affection/loyalty/enthusiasm* ○ *Our first sight of the dingy little hotel did not inspire us with much confidence/inspire much confidence in us.*

▶ **inspired** adj (*approv*) **1** having excellent qualities, abilities or creative power: *an inspired poet/musician.* **2** showing or produced by inspiration; excellent: *an inspired piece of improvisation* ○ *an inspired guess/choice.*

inspiring /ɪnˈspaɪərɪŋ/ adj **1** that inspires sb to do sth: *an inspiring teacher/leader.* **2** (*infml*) (usu with negatives) filling one with interest and enthusiasm: *The result is less than/is hardly inspiring.*

instability /ˌɪnstəˈbɪləti/ n [U,C] the state of being not steady or STABLE¹: *mental/financial/political instability.*

install (*US* also **instal**) /ɪnˈstɔːl/ v **1** ~ sth (in sth) to fix equipment or furniture in position ready for use, esp by connecting it to an electricity or water supply: [Vnpr] *install video cameras in the city centre* [Vn] *I'm having a shower installed.* **2** to settle sb/oneself in a place: [Vnpr] *be comfortably installed in a new home* ○ *She installed herself at/behind her desk and began writing.* [also Vn]. **3** to place sb in a new position of authority, often with a ceremony: [Vn] *install a bishop* [Vn-n] *be installed as managing director.*

▶ **installation** /ˌɪnstəˈleɪʃn/ n **1** [U,C] the action or process of installing sb/sth or an instance of this: *the installation of the new vice-chancellor* ○ *installation costs* ○ *Installation of the new lift will take several days.* **2** [C] a piece of apparatus, machine, etc that is installed: *a heating installation.* **3** [C] a site containing specialist equipment or one used for a specific important purpose: *nuclear/government/military installations.*

instalment (*US* usu **installment**) /ɪnˈstɔːlmənt/ n **1** ~ (on sth) any one of the parts of a payment spread over a period of time: *pay for a car in 24 monthly instalments* ○ *keep up the instalments* (ie maintain regular payments). **2** any one of the separate but connected parts in which a story is presented over a period of time: *Don't miss next week's exciting instalment!*

■ inˈstalment plan n [U,sing] (*esp US*) = HIRE PURCHASE.

instance /ˈɪnstəns/ n ~ (of sth) a particular occurrence of sth that happens often; an example; a case: *I can quote you several instances of her being deliberately rude.* ○ *In most instances* (ie Mostly) *the pain soon goes away.* ○ *Students are not normally allowed to take dictionaries into exams, but in this instance* (ie on this occasion) *they were asked to do so.* **IDM** for ˈinstance as an example; for example: *Take, for instance, the case of Dr Biggs.* in the ˈfirst instance (*fml*) at the beginning; to begin with: *In the first instance I was inclined to refuse, but then I reconsidered.*

▶ **instance** v [Vn] to give sth as an example.

instant¹ /ˈɪnstənt/ adj **1** [usu attrib] coming or happening immediately: *instant relief from pain* ○ *instant hot water* (ie as soon as the tap is turned on) ○ *His new book was an instant success.* **2** (of food preparations) that can be made very quickly and easily: *instant coffee* (ie made by adding hot water or milk to a powder).

▶ **instantly** adv at once; immediately: *an instantly recognizable face* ○ *She caught his meaning instantly.*

instant² /ˈɪnstənt/ n (*esp sing*) **1** a single point in time: *Come here this instant* (ie immediately)! ○ *At that (very) instant the door opened.* ○ *I recognized her the instant (that)* (ie as soon as) *I saw her.* **2** a short space of time; a moment: *I'll be back in an instant.* ○ *Help came not an instant too soon.* ○ *Just for an instant I thought he was going to refuse.*

instantaneous /ˌɪnstənˈteɪnɪəs/ adj happening or done immediately: *His reaction was instantaneous.*

▶ **instantaneously** adv.

instead /ɪnˈsted/ adv as an alternative or replacement: *I've no coffee. Would you like tea instead?* ○ *Stuart was ill so I went instead.* ○ *This time there was no standing ovation. Instead, she received only a brief round of applause.*

■ instead of prep as an alternative or replacement to sb/sth: *drink tea instead of coffee* ○ *Let's play cards instead of watching television.*

instep /ˈɪnstep/ n (a) the upper part of the human foot between the toes and the ankle. ⇨ picture at FOOT¹. (b) the part of a shoe covering this. ⇨ picture at SHOE.

instigate /ˈɪnstɪgeɪt/ v to make sth begin or happen: [Vn] *instigate a strike/an attack* ○ *The police have instigated an official inquiry into the incident.*

▶ **instigation** /ˌɪnstɪˈgeɪʃn/ n [U] the action of instigating sth: *At his instigation an appeal fund was launched.*

instigator /ˈɪnstɪgeɪtə(r)/ n a person who instigates sth, esp sth considered bad: *the instigators of the rebellion.*

instil (*US* **instill**) /ɪnˈstɪl/ v (-ll-) ~ sth (in/into sb) to cause sb gradually to acquire a usu desirable quality: [Vn,Vnpr] *instilling a sense of responsibility (in/into one's children).*

instinct /ˈɪnstɪŋkt/ n ~ (for sth / doing sth); ~ (to do sth) [U,C] **1** a tendency that one is born with to behave in a certain way without reasoning or training: *a gambler by instinct* ○ *Their instinct is to run from danger.* **2** ~ (for sth) a natural feeling that makes one act or respond in a particular way: *have an instinct for survival* ○ *arouse sb's maternal instincts* ○ *I acted on instinct and threw a blanket over the flames.* ○ *Her instincts had been right.* ○ *His first instinct was to refuse.*

▶ **instinctive** /ɪnˈstɪŋktɪv/ (also **instinctual** /ɪnˈstɪŋktuəl/) adj based on instinct; not coming from training or based on reasoning: *an instinctive dislike of sb* ○ *an instinctive reaction.* **instinctively** adv: *I instinctively raised my arm to protect my face.*

institute¹ /ˈɪnstɪtjuːt; *US* -tuːt/ n (a) a society or an organization for a special, usu social, professional or educational, purpose: *a research/film institute* ∘ *the Working Men's Institute* ∘ *the Institute of Chartered Surveyors.* (**b**) a building used by an institute.

institute² /ˈɪnstɪtjuːt; *US* -tuːt/ *v* (*fml*) to establish or start sth, eg an inquiry, a custom or a rule: [Vn] *institute legal proceedings against sb* ∘ *institute a ban on the movement of livestock.*

institution /ˌɪnstɪˈtjuːʃn; *US* -ˈtuːʃn/ *n* **1** [C] (**a**) an organization established for social, educational, religious, etc purposes, eg a university: *a financial/political institution.* (**b**) an organization for helping people with special needs, eg a home for old people: *a mental institution* ∘ *living in an institution.* **2** [C] an established custom, practice(3b) or group of people, eg a society: *the institution of marriage* ∘ *Sunday lunch is a time-honoured institution in our family.* ∘ *the Institution of Environmental Health Officers.* **3** [C] (*infml usu approv or joc*) a person who is a very familiar figure in some activity or place: *When I joined the company ten years ago Mr Harris was already an institution.* **4** [U] the action or process of establishing or starting sth: *the institution of new safety procedures.*
▶ **institutional** /-ʃənl/ *adj* of, from or connected with an institution: *institutional links/control* ∘ *institutional care/food/support.* **institutionalize, -ise** /-ʃənəlaɪz/ *v* **1** to make sth into an institution (2): [Vn] *Fishing has become institutionalized, controlled by permits, licences and regulations.* **2** [Vn] to place sb in an institution(1b). **3** (esp passive) to make sb accustomed to living or working in an institution(1), esp so as to lose their ability to think or act independently: [Vn] *Staff have become institutionalized, following the same routines day after day.* **institutionalization, -isation** /ˌɪnstɪˌtjuːʃənəlaɪˈzeɪʃn; *US* -ˌtjuːʃənəˈlaɪz-/ *n* [U].

instruct /ɪnˈstrʌkt/ *v* **1** ~ **sb** (**in sth**) to teach sb a skill: [Vnpr] *instruct a group of 16 year olds in first aid* [also Vn]. ➪ note at TEACH. **2** to give orders or directions to sb: [Vn.*wh*] *They were instructed when to leave.* [Vn.*to* inf] *I've instructed them to keep the room locked.* [also V.speech]. ➪ note at ORDER². **3** (*law*) to employ a legal representative to act for one: [Vn] *It may be necessary to instruct a solicitor or debt collection agency.* **4** (*esp law*) (esp passive) to inform sb: [Vn.*that*] *We are instructed by our clients that you owe them £3 000.*
▶ **instructor** *n* (**a**) a person who instructs sb; a trainer (TRAIN²): *a driving instructor.* (**b**) (*US*) a teacher at a university.

instruction /ɪnˈstrʌkʃn/ *n* **1** [U] ~ (**in sth**) the process of teaching; knowledge or teaching given: *religious instruction* ∘ *In this course, students receive instruction in basic engineering.* **2** [C] ~ (**to do sth / that...**) (**a**) an order or direction given to sb: *leave/give detailed instructions* ∘ *carry out/ignore an instruction to fit a new switch.* (**b**) (*computing*) a word or code which, when put into a computer, makes it perform a particular operation. **3** **instructions** [pl] ~ (**to do sth / that...**) statements telling sb what they should do with sth or how sth operates: *follow the instructions on a tin of paint/in a car repair manual* ∘ *We should read the instructions first.*
▶ **instructional** /-ʃənl/ *adj* giving instruction; educational: *instructional videos.*

instructive /ɪnˈstrʌktɪv/ *adj* (*approv*) giving much useful information: *I found the visit most instructive.* ∘ *It is instructive to see how other families are tackling the problem.*

instrument /ˈɪnstrəmənt/ *n* **1** an implement or a piece of apparatus used for a particular purpose, esp for delicate or scientific work: *surgical/optical instruments* ∘ *instruments of torture.* **2** a device that measures speed, distance, etc or records information about the operation of sth, eg an engine: *a ship's instruments* ∘ *keep glancing at the instrument*

panel. ➪ note at MACHINE. **3** (also ˌmusical ˈinstrument) an apparatus for producing musical sounds, eg a piano or drum: *learning to play an instrument* ∘ *the instruments of the orchestra.* ➪ picture. **4**(**a**) ~ **for/of sth** a person or thing that makes sth happen: *an instrument of change/oppression* ∘ *The agreement was simply an instrument for regulating intergovernmental cooperation.* (**b**) ~ **of sb/sth** a person used and controlled by another person or organization, often without being aware of it: *We humans are merely the instruments of fate.* **5** a formal, esp legal, document: *a statutory instrument.*
▶ **instrumentation** /ˌɪnstrəmenˈteɪʃn/ *n* [U] **1** an arrangement of music for several instruments: *The instrumentation is particularly fine.* **2** a set of measuring instruments: *monitoring the spacecraft's instrumentation.*

instrumental /ˌɪnstrəˈmentl/ *adj* **1** [pred] ~ **in sth / doing sth** being the means of making sth happen: *He was largely instrumental in negotiating/in the negotiation of a peace settlement.* **2** of or for musical instruments: *instrumental music.*
▶ **instrumentalist** /-təlɪst/ *n* a player of a musical instrument. Compare VOCALIST.
instrumentally *adv*.

insubordinate /ˌɪnsəˈbɔːdɪnət/ *adj* (*fml*) refusing to obey instructions or show respect. ▶ **insubordination** /ˌɪnsəˌbɔːdɪˈneɪʃn/ *n* [U].

insubstantial /ˌɪnsəbˈstænʃl/ *adj* **1** not solid or real; imaginary: *an insubstantial vision/figure/creature.* **2** not strongly made or firmly based; weak: *Early aircraft were insubstantial constructions of wood and glue.* ∘ *an insubstantial argument/accusation.*

insufferable /ɪnˈsʌfrəbl/ *adj* **1** too extreme to be tolerated; impossible to bear: *insufferable smugness.* **2** (of a person) extremely annoying and unpleasant, esp because of pride: *He's an insufferable little prig!*
▶ **insufferably** /-əbli/ *adv.*

insufficient /ˌɪnsəˈfɪʃnt/ *adj* ~ (**for sth / to do sth**) not sufficient: *insufficient funds/information/time* ∘ *There was insufficient evidence to proceed with the case.* ∘ *Financial returns were insufficient to justify further expansion.* ▶ **insufficiency** /-ʃnsi/ *n* [U]. **insufficiently** *adv.*

insular /ˈɪnsjələ(r); *US* -sələr/ *adj* (*derog*) having no interest in or contact with people and ideas from outside one's own country or society; narrow(3): *insular attitudes/views.*
▶ **insularity** /ˌɪnsjuˈlærəti; *US* -səˈl-/ *n* [U] the state of being insular.

insulate /ˈɪnsjuleɪt; *US* -səl-/ *v* **1** ~ (**sth**) (**from/against sth**) to protect sth by covering it with a material that prevents sth, esp heat, electricity or sound, from passing through: [Vadv] *Plastic insulates well.* [Vn,Vpr] *insulate pipes (from loss of heat)* [also Vpr]. **2** ~ **sb/sth from/against sth** to protect sb/sth from the unpleasant effects of sth: [Vnpr] *children carefully insulated from harmful experiences* ∘ *Index-linked pensions insulate people against inflationary price increases.*
▶ **insulated** *adj* protected with a material so as to prevent loss of heat, electricity, etc: *an insulated wire* ∘ *a well-insulated house.*
insulating *adj* giving this kind of protection: *insulating materials/properties.*
insulation /ˌɪnsjuˈleɪʃn; *US* -səl-/ *n* [U] (**a**) the action of insulating sth or the state of being insulated: *Foam rubber provides good insulation.* (**b**) materials used for this: *pack the wall cavity with insulation.*
insulator /ˈɪnsjuleɪtə(r); *US* -səl-/ *n* a substance, eg rubber, or a device for insulating sth against loss of electricity, heat or sound.
■ **insulating tape** *n* [U] tape used for covering joins in electrical wires to prevent the possibility of an electric shock.

insulin /'ɪnsjəlɪn; *US* -səl-/ *n* [U] a substance, normally produced by the body itself, which controls the amount of sugar absorbed into the blood: *a diabetic relying on insulin injections.*

insult /ɪn'sʌlt/ *v* to speak or act in a way that hurts or is intended to hurt the feelings or dignity of sb: [Vn] *I felt deeply insulted by her patronizing attitude.* ▶ **insult** /'ɪnsʌlt/ *n* ~ (**to sb/sth**) a remark or an action that insults sb: *She hurled insults at the unfortunate waiter.* ○ *The questions were a real insult to our intelligence* (ie too easy). **IDM** **add insult to injury** ⇨ ADD.
insulting *adj* (**a**) causing or intended to cause offence: *insulting remarks/behaviour.* (**b**) speaking or behaving so as to cause offence: *He was most insulting to my wife.*

insuperable /ɪn'su:pərəbl; *Brit also* -'sju:-/ *adj* (*fml*) (of difficulties) that cannot be overcome: *insuperable obstacles/problems.* See also INSURMOUNTABLE.

insupportable /ˌɪnsə'pɔːtəbl/ *adj* (*fml*) impossible to bear; not to be tolerated: *Their debt had become an insupportable burden.*

insurance /ɪn'ʃʊərəns; *Brit also* -ʃɔːr-/ *n* **1** [U] (**a**) ~ (**against sth**) a contract made by a company or society, or by the state, to provide a guarantee of compensation for loss, damage, illness, death, etc in return for regular payments: *take out insurance against fire and theft* ○ *household/personal insurance* ○ *insurance premiums* (ie regular payments made for insurance) ○ *an insurance company/salesman/broker* ○ *People without insurance had to pay for their own repairs.* Compare ASSURANCE 3. See also NATIONAL INSURANCE. (**b**) [U] the business of providing such contracts: *Her husband works in insurance.* **2** [U] money paid by or to an insurance company: *When her husband died, she received £50 000 in insurance.* **3** [C, U] ~ (**against sth**) any measure taken in case of loss, failure, etc: *have a large family as (an) insurance against old age.*
■ **in'surance policy** *n* a contract between a person and an insurance company: *a medical insurance policy* ○ (*fig*) *regard nuclear weapons as an insurance policy.*

insure /ɪn'ʃʊə(r); *Brit also* -'ʃɔː(r)/ *v* **1** ~ **oneself/sb/sth** (**against sth**) to make a contract that promises to pay one/sb an amount of money in case of accident, injury, death, etc, or damage to or loss of sth: [Vn] *insure oneself/one's life for $50 000* [Vnpr] *insure one's house against fire.* **2** (*esp US*) = ENSURE.
▶ **the insured** *n* [sing or pl *v*] a person or people to whom payment will be made in the case of injury, loss, etc.
insurer /ɪn'ʃʊərə(r); *Brit also* -ʃɔːr-/ *n* a person or company agreeing to pay compensation in case of injury, loss, etc.

insurgent /ɪn'sɜːdʒənt/ *n* a person fighting against government forces in her or his own country; a REBEL(a): *an attack by armed insurgents* ○ *insurgent organizations.*

insurmountable /ˌɪnsə'maʊntəbl/ *adj* (*fml*) (of difficulties, etc) that cannot be overcome: *The problems are not insurmountable.* See also INSUPERABLE.

insurrection /ˌɪnsə'rekʃn/ *n* [C, U] a sudden, usu violent, action taken by a large part of the population to try to remove the government: *an armed insurrection* ○ *Disturbances soon turned into full-scale insurrection.*

intact /ɪn'tækt/ *adj* [usu pred] not damaged; complete; whole: *The box was recovered from the damaged vehicle with its contents intact.* ○ *He can scarcely survive this scandal with his reputation intact.*

intake /'ɪnteɪk/ *n* **1**(**a**) [U, C] the process of taking a substance into the body or a machine: *restrict one's food/salt/fluid intake* ○ *a sharp intake of breath.* (**b**) [C, U] a number of people entering an institution, etc

during a particular period: *the annual student intake* ○ *Intake in state primary schools is down by 10%.* (**c**) [C] a place where liquid, etc enters a machine: *the air/fuel intake.*

intangible /ɪn'tændʒəbl/ *adj* **1** that cannot be easily or clearly understood; difficult to define: *The old building had an intangible air of sadness about it.* **2** (*commerce*) that has no physical existence : *intangible assets/benefits.*

integer /'ɪntɪdʒə(r)/ *n* (*mathematics*) a whole number, contrasted with a fraction: *3 and 4 are integers; ¾ is not an integer.*

integral /'ɪntɪgrəl/ *adj* **1**(**a**) ~ (**to sth**) necessary to make sth complete; essential: *an integral part of American defence strategy* ○ *The moulded ceiling is integral to the design.* (**b**) [usu attrib] having or containing all parts that are necessary to be complete; whole: *an integral design.* **2** [usu attrib] included as part of the whole, rather than supplied separately: *a machine with an integral power source.*

integrate /'ɪntɪgreɪt/ *v* **1** ~ **sth** (**into/with sth**) to combine two things in such a way that one becomes fully a part of the other: [Vnpr] *integrating private schools into the state education system* [Vnadv, Vnpr] *The buildings are well integrated (with the landscape).* [also Vn]. **2** ~ (**sb**) (**into/with sth**) to become or make sb become fully a member of a community, rather than remaining in a separate group, eg because of one's race, colour etc: [V] *immigrants who try hard to integrate* [Vnpr] *integrating black people into a largely white community* [also Vn, Vpr]. Compare SEGREGATE.
▶ **integrated** /-tɪd/ *adj* with various parts or aspects linked closely together: *an integrated transport system* (eg including buses, trains and taxis) ○ *an integrated approach to pollution control.*
integration /ˌɪntɪ'greɪʃn/ *n* [U]: *progress towards closer European integration* ○ *economic/political/social integration.*
■ **integrated 'circuit** *n* a small MICROCHIP replacing several separate parts in a conventional electrical circuit.

integrity /ɪn'tegrəti/ *n* [U] **1** the quality of being honest and having strong moral principles: *personal/artistic/professional integrity* ○ *He's a man of the highest integrity.* **2** the condition of being whole and not divided: *respect/preserve a nation's territorial integrity.*

intellect /'ɪntəlekt/ *n* **1** [U] the power of the mind to think in a logical manner and acquire knowledge: *a woman with a keen intellect and exceptional qualities of leadership.* **2** [C] a person of great intelligence and powers of reasoning: *She was one of the most formidable intellects of her time.*

intellectual /ˌɪntə'lektʃuəl/ *adj* **1** [usu attrib] of or connected with a person's powers of reasoning: *intellectual development.* **2**(**a**) appealing to, needing or using sb's powers of reasoning or desire for knowledge: *intellectual interests/pursuits.* (**b**) having excellent mental abilities and enjoying activities that further develop the mind: *She's very intellectual.*
▶ **intellectual** *n* a person with a highly developed mental ability.
intellectually *adv.*
■ **intellectual 'property** *n* [U] (*law*) property such as an idea, a design, etc that has been created or invented by sb but does not exist in a physical form: *infringe intellectual property rights.* Compare COPYRIGHT.

intelligence /ɪn'telɪdʒəns/ *n* **1** [U] the power of learning, understanding and reasoning; mental ability: *a person of high/average/low intelligence* ○ *When the pipe burst, the boy had the intelligence to turn off the water at the main.* See also ARTIFICIAL INTELLIGENCE. **2** [U] information, esp of military value: *an* *intelligence-gathering agency* ∘ *intelligence sources* (ie people who provide such information) ∘ *a government intelligence service* (ie an organization that gathers such information, esp by spying (SPY *v*)).

▶ **intelligent** /-dʒənt/ *adj* **1** having or showing intelligence: *a highly intelligent child* ∘ *intelligent questions/answers/remarks*. **2** (*computing*) (of a machine or piece of SOFTWARE) that can store knowledge gained from past experience and apply it in different circumstances: *an intelligent system/workstation*. **intelligently** *adv*.
■ **in'telligence test** *n* a test to measure sb's mental ability. Compare APTITUDE TEST.

intelligentsia /ɪnˌtelɪˈdʒentsɪə/ **the intelligentsia** *n* [Gp] people within a community who are of high intelligence and are interested in culture, learning, the arts, etc.

intelligible /ɪnˈtelɪdʒəbl/ *adj* that can be easily understood: *His lecture was barely intelligible to most of the students*. Compare UNINTELLIGIBLE. ▶ **intelligibility** /ɪnˌtelɪdʒəˈbɪləti/ *n* [U]. **intelligibly** *adv*.

intemperate /ɪnˈtempərət/ *adj* (*fml*) showing a lack of control over oneself: *intemperate desires/habits/outbursts*. ▶ **intemperance** /-pərəns/ *n* [U].

intend /ɪnˈtend/ *v* **1(a)** ~ **sth** (**as sth**) to have a particular purpose or plan in mind; to mean to do sth: [V, V.*that*] *The evening didn't turn out as I intended (that it should)*. [Vn, V.to inf] *It's not what I intended (it to be)*. [V.to inf] *I hear they intend to marry.* ∘ *We may not succeed but I intend to try.* [V.ing] *I'd intended visiting you this weekend but I wasn't able to make it.* [Vn, Vnn] *He intends (you) no harm* (ie does not plan to harm you). **(b)** to have sth as a fixed plan or purpose for sb/sth: [Vn-n] *I intended it as a joke.* [V.n to inf] *The quiz is intended to be light-hearted.* [V.n to inf, V.*that*] *I intend you to take over/intend that you shall take over the business after me.* **2** ~ **sth for sth/sb** (esp passive) to plan that sth/sb should receive or be affected by sth: [Vnpr] *cars intended for the scrapyard* ∘ *I think the bomb was intended for* (ie planned to harm) *me.* **3** ~ **sth as sth** to plan that sth should be or become sth: [Vn-n] *This document is intended purely as a discussion paper.* **4** ~ **sth (by sth)** to plan that sth should have a particular meaning: [Vnpr] *What did he intend by that remark?* [Vn] *No criticism was intended.*

▶ **intended** /-dɪd/ *adj* **1** [attrib] planned; meant: *the intended meaning/result/effect/purpose.* **2** ~ **for sb/sth** [pred] planned or designed for sb/sth: *a book/course/programme intended for children/beginners* ∘ *water (not) intended for drinking.*

intense /ɪnˈtens/ *adj* **1** very great or severe; extreme: *intense pain/pressure/heat/pleasure/cold/concentration.* **2** (of emotions, etc) very strong: *feel intense interest/anger/disappointment/desire/dislike.* **3** serious and concentrated: *an intense discussion/debate* ∘ *intense activity/competition/scrutiny.* **4** (of people) feeling strongly and deeply about sth: *She gets very intense when she talks about politics.*

▶ **intensely** *adv*: *She disliked him intensely.*
intensity /-səti/ *n* [U] **1** the state or quality of being intense: *work with greater intensity.* **2** strength of emotion: *I didn't realize the intensity of people's feelings on this issue.*

intensify /ɪnˈtensɪfaɪ/ *v* (*pt, pp* **-fied**) to become or make sth become stronger or more concentrated: [V] *Her anger intensified.* [Vn] *The terrorists have intensified their bombing campaign.*
▶ **intensification** /ɪnˌtensɪfɪˈkeɪʃn/ *n* [U, sing]: *an intensification of the dispute.*
intensifier /ɪnˈtensɪfaɪə(r)/ *n* (*grammar*) a word, esp an *adj* or *adv*, eg *so, such, very,* that strengthens the meaning of another word.

intensive /ɪnˈtensɪv/ *adj* **1(a)** concentrating all one's effort on a specific area: *intensive bombard-*

ment of a town ∘ **intensive farming** (ie aimed at producing large quantities of food while concentrating resources and labour to reduce costs). See also CAPITAL-INTENSIVE, LABOUR-INTENSIVE. **(b)** involving hard work concentrated into a short time: *an intensive English course.* **2** extremely thorough: *An intensive search failed to reveal any clues.* ▶ **intensively** *adv*.
■ **in,tensive 'care** *n* [U] constant care and attention for people who are seriously ill, or the part of a hospital providing this: *The accident victims are in intensive care/in the intensive-care unit.*

intent[1] /ɪnˈtent/ *adj* **1** showing eager interest and attention: *watch with an intent gaze/look/expression.* **2** [pred] ~ **on/upon sth/doing sth** **(a)** having the specified firm intention; determined to do sth: *be intent on promotion/getting promoted.* **(b)** concentrating hard on sth: *I was so intent on my work that I didn't notice the time.* ▶ **intently** *adv*: *I listened intently to what she had to say.*

intent[2] /ɪnˈtent/ *n* [U] ~ (**to do sth**) (*fml or law*) intention; purpose: *arrest sb for loitering with intent* (ie for apparently intending to commit a crime) ∘ *His intent was to undermine their confidence.* **IDM** **to all intents and 'purposes** in all important respects: *The Warsaw Pact has to all intents and purposes ceased to exist.*

intention /ɪnˈtenʃn/ *n* [C, U] ~ (**to do sth / of doing sth / that…**) that which one proposes or plans to do; a thing intended; an aim or a plan: *It wasn't my intention to upset you.* ∘ *I came with the/every intention of staying, but circumstances have changed.* ∘ *Their intention is to make the area a public park.* ∘ *I have no intention of coming* (ie do not intend to come) *here again!* ∘ *She's full of good intentions, but unfortunately they rarely work out.* **IDM** **with the best of intentions** ⇨ BEST[3]. See also WELL-INTENTIONED.

intentional /ɪnˈtenʃənl/ *adj* done on purpose; not accidental; intended: *I'm sorry I left you off the list — it wasn't intentional.*
▶ **intentionally** /-ʃənəli/ *adv* deliberately: *I would never intentionally hurt your feelings.*

inter /ɪnˈtɜː(r)/ *v* (**-rr-**) [Vn] (*fml*) to bury a dead body. See also INTERMENT. Compare DISINTER.

inter- *pref* (with *vs, ns* and *adjs*) **1** between; from one to another: *interface* ∘ *international.* **2** together: *interconnect* ∘ *interlink.*

interact /ˌɪntərˈækt/ *v* **1** ~ (**with sth**) to act or have an effect on each other: [V] *ideas that interact* [Vpr] *Perfume interacts with the skin's natural chemicals.* **2** ~ (**with sb**) (of people) to work together or communicate: [V, Vpr] *study the complex way in which people interact (with each other) at parties.*
▶ **interaction** /-ˈækʃn/ *n* [U, C] ~ (**between sb/sth**); ~ (**with sb/sth**): *interaction between performers and audience* ∘ *the interaction of supply and demand* ∘ *classroom interactions.*
interactive /-ˈæktɪv/ *adj* **1** ~ (**with sb/sth**) (of two or more people or things) interacting: *interactive groups.* **2** (*computing*) allowing a continuous transfer of information in both directions between a computer and the person using it: *interactive media/systems.*

inter alia /ˌɪntər ˈeɪlɪə/ *adv* (*Latin fml*) among other things.

interbreed /ˌɪntəˈbriːd/ *v* ~ (**sth**) (**with sth**) to breed or make individuals of different species breed together, so producing a HYBRID(1): [V, Vpr] *Ducks don't normally interbreed (with each other) in the wild.* [also Vn, Vnpr].

intercede /ˌɪntəˈsiːd/ *v* ~ (**with sb**) (**for / on behalf of sb**) (*fml*) to act or speak on behalf of sb to another person or group in order to persuade them to show pity or act fairly, or to end a dispute: [Vpr] *We have interceded with the authorities on behalf of*

---

people unfairly imprisoned there (ie asked them to release the prisoners). [also V]. ► **intercession** /ˌɪntə'seʃn/ *n* [U].

intercept /ˌɪntə'sept/ *v* to stop sb/sth that is travelling from one place to another from reaching their/ its destination: [Vn] *intercept a missile* ○ *Reporters intercepted him as he tried to leave by the rear entrance.* ○ *The police had been intercepting his mail* (ie reading it before it was delivered).
► **interception** /ˌɪntə'sepʃn/ *n* [U, C]: *the interception of mail* ○ *a fine interception* (ie of the ball) *by the Arsenal centre forward.*
interceptor /-tə(r)/ *n* a fast military plane that attacks enemy planes carrying bombs.

interchange /ˌɪntə'tʃeɪndʒ/ *v* **1** to share or exchange sth: [Vn] *interchange ideas/information.* **2** ~ sth/sb (with sth/sb) to put each of two things or people in the other's place: [Vn] *interchange the front and rear tyres of a car* [also Vnpr].
► **interchange** /'ɪntətʃeɪndʒ/ *n* **1** [C, U] an act or the action of interchanging sth: *a regular interchange of letters.* **2** [C] a road JUNCTION(a), eg on a motorway, where vehicles leave or join a road without crossing other lines of traffic.
interchangeable /ˌɪntə'tʃeɪndʒəbl/ *adj* ~ (with sth) that can be interchanged, esp without affecting the way in which sth works: *The two words are virtually interchangeable* (ie have almost the same meaning). ○ *The product is interchangeable with sugar.* **interchangeably** *adv.*

inter-city /ˌɪntə 'sɪti/ *adj* [usu attrib] (of transport) operating between cities, usu with few stops on the way: *an ˌinter-city 'train 'service* ○ *ˌinter-city 'travel.*

intercollegiate /ˌɪntəkə'liːdʒiət/ *adj* (*esp US*) existing or done between colleges: *intercollegiate games/debates.*

intercom /'ɪntəkɒm/ *n* a system of communication by radio or telephone between or within offices, aircraft, etc: *make an announcement on/over the intercom.*

intercommunicate /ˌɪntəkə'mjuːnɪkeɪt/ (also **interconnect**) *v* (of two rooms) to have a door linking them, as well as each having a door into a CORRIDOR (1): *We had intercommunicating rooms.*

intercommunication /ˌɪntəkəˌmjuːnɪ'keɪʃn/ *n* [U]: *the process of communicating in both directions between people or groups.*

interconnect /ˌɪntəkə'nekt/ *v* to connect similar things; (of similar things) to be connected with each other: [Vn] *interconnected computers/workstations* ○ *I see these two ideas as somehow interconnected.* [V] *interconnecting hotel rooms* (ie with a door between them) ○ *It's strange how people's lives interconnect.* ►
interconnection /-'nekʃn/ *n* [C, U]: *interconnections between primary and secondary education.*

intercontinental /ˌɪntəˌkɒntɪ'nentl/ *adj* going between continents: *intercontinental travel.*

intercourse /'ɪntəkɔːs/ *n* [U] ~ (with sb); ~ (between sb and sb) (*fml*) **1** = SEX 2. **2** (*fml*) dealings with people, nations, etc: *meeting together for social intercourse.*

interdenominational /ˌɪntədɪˌnɒmɪ'neɪʃənl/ *adj* common to or shared by different religious groups: *an interdenominational school.*

interdepartmental /ˌɪntəˌdiːpɑː'tmentl/ *adj* of, concerning or done by more than one department: *an interdepartmental meeting.*

interdependent /ˌɪntədɪ'pendənt/ *adj* depending on each other: *interdependent nations/economies.* ►
interdependence /-əns/ *n* [U, sing]: *interdependence between workers and management.*

interdict /'ɪntədɪkt/ *n* (*fml*) **1** (*law*) an official court order not to do sth. **2** (in the Roman Catholic Church) an order forbidding sb to take part in church services, etc.

interdisciplinary /ˌɪntə'dɪsəplɪnəri/ *adj* of or covering more than one area of study: *interdisciplinary work/studies.*

interest¹ /'ɪntrəst, -rest/ *n* **1** [U, sing] ~ (in sb/sth) a state of wanting to learn or know about sb/sth; curiosity; concern: *feel/have/show/express (an) interest in sth* ○ *a topic that arouses/raises/stimulates a lot of interest* ○ *listen to sth with interest* ○ *do sth (just) for interest/out of interest/for interest's sake* (ie simply to satisfy a desire for knowledge) ○ *Now he's grown up he no longer takes any interest in his stamp collection.* ○ *By that stage I had lost (all) interest in the idea.* Compare DISINTEREST. **2** [U] the quality in sth that attracts sb's attention and makes them want to know more about it: *The subject holds no interest for me.* ○ *The fact that we know the people involved adds interest to the story.* ○ *There's nothing of interest in the local paper.* **3** [C] a thing with which one concerns oneself or about which one is enthusiastic: *a person of wide/varied interests* ○ *Outside her work, her main interests are music and tennis.* **4** [C usu *pl*] advantage; benefit: *look after/protect/safeguard one's own interests* (ie make sure that nothing is done to one's disadvantage) ○ *He has your best interests at heart* (ie is acting for your advantage). ○ *decide what is in the best interests of shareholders* ○ *It would be in your interest* (ie to your advantage) *to go.* **5** [U] ~ (on sth) (*finance*) money charged for borrowing money, or paid to sb who invests money: *pay interest/make interest payments on a loan* ○ *charge interest at 10%* ○ *a high/low rate of interest.* See also COMPOUND INTEREST, SIMPLE INTEREST. **6** [C usu *pl*] ~ (in sth) a legal right to share in a business, esp in its profits: *have a controlling interest in a company* (ie own enough shares to be able to say how it should be run) ○ *American interests in Europe* (eg capital invested in European countries) ○ *He has considerable business interests.* **7** [C] ~ (in sth) a personal connection with sth from which one may benefit, esp financially: *Members of Parliament wishing to speak about companies with which they are connected must first declare their interest.* See also VESTED INTEREST. **8** [C usu *pl*] a group of people engaged in the same business, etc or having sth in common which they wish to protect: *landed interests* (ie people who own land) ○ *middle-class interests* ○ *local/special interest groups.* **IDM** **in the interest(s) of sth** for the sake of sth: *In the interest(s) of safety, smoking is forbidden.* **(repay, return, etc sth) with interest 1** (*finance*) (to give back a sum of money) with interest¹(5) added. **2** (*infml*) (to respond to an action by doing the same thing to the person who did it) with added force: *return a blow with interest.*
■ **ˌinterest-'free** *adj* with no interest charged on money borrowed: *an ˌinterest-free 'loan* ○ *ˌinterest-free 'credit.*

interest² /'ɪntrəst, -rest/ *v* ~ sb/oneself (in sth) **(a)** to make sb/oneself give their/one's attention to sth or be concerned about sth: [Vn] *a topic that interests me greatly* [Vnpr] *Having lost his job, he began to interest himself in voluntary work.* **(b)** to make sb want to do, buy, eat, etc sth: [Vnpr] *Can I interest you in our latest model?*
► **interested** /-tɪd/ *adj* **1** ~ (in sth/sb); ~ (in doing sth) showing curiosity or concern about sb/sth: *an interested crowd* ○ *Are you interested in history?* ○ *The company is interested in selling its products overseas.* ○ *I tried to tell him about it, but he just wasn't interested.* ○ *I'll be interested to see what happens.* **2** in a position to obtain an advantage from sth; not IMPARTIAL: *As an interested party, I was not allowed to vote.*
interesting *adj* holding the attention; causing curiosity: *interesting ideas/features/conversation* ○ *It makes interesting reading.* **interestingly** *adv*: *Interestingly, consumer spending has increased.*

[V.*to* inf] = verb + *to* infinitive   [Vn.inf (no *to*)] = verb + noun + infinitive without *to*   [V.*ing*] = verb + -*ing* form

NOTE Interested usually means 'liking something and wanting to know about it': *She's very interested in photography.* The opposite is **not interested** or **uninterested**: *She seemed completely uninterested in hearing about my new job.* **Disinterested** does not mean **uninterested** in modern English. Somebody who is **disinterested** can be fair in judging a situation because they are not involved in it and do not expect to gain anything from it personally: *You should get advice from a disinterested third person.*

interface /ˈɪntəfeɪs/ n **1** (*computing*) **(a)** the way a computer PROGRAM(1) accepts information from or presents information to the user, eg the LAYOUT of the screen and the MENU(2) or command structure: *All the computers had different user interfaces.* **(b)** an electrical circuit, a connection or a PROGRAM(1) linking one device or system with another: *the interface between computer and printer.* **2** ~ (**between sth and sth**) a point where two subjects, systems, processes, etc meet and affect each other: *at the interface between the public and private sector* ○ *the man-machine interface.*
▸ **interface** v ~ (**sth**) (**with sth**) to connect sth or be connected by an interface: [Vnpr] *interface new systems with existing programs* [also V, Vpr].

interfere /ˌɪntəˈfɪə(r)/ v ~ (**in sth**) to concern oneself with or take action affecting sb else's affairs without needing or being invited to do so: [Vpr] *Don't interfere in matters that do not concern you!* [V] *I wish she'd stop interfering!* **PHRV** inter'**fere with sb 1** to distract sb or prevent them from doing sth: *Don't interfere with him while he's working.* **2** (*Brit euph*) to act sexually towards sb, esp a child; to MOLEST(b) sb: *She claimed that her daughter had been interfered with.* inter'**fere with sth 1** to get in the way of sth or prevent sth from being done or succeeding: *interfere with sb else's plans* ○ *Nothing is allowed to interfere with John's golf!* **2** to handle, adjust, etc sth without permission, esp so as to cause damage: *Who's been interfering with the clock? It's stopped.*
▸ **interference** /ˌɪntəˈfɪərəns/ n [U] **1** ~ (**in/with sth**) the action of interfering: *intolerable interference in another country's internal affairs* ○ *I don't want any interference from you!* **2** disturbance or interruption to a radio signal, often caused by a second signal being transmitted on a WAVELENGTH(2) close to the first: *interference from foreign broadcasting stations.*
interfering adj [attrib] (*derog*) concerning oneself in an annoying way with other people's affairs: *She's an interfering old busybody!*

interferon /ˌɪntəˈfɪərɒn/ n [U] (*biology or chemistry*) a substance produced by the body cells to prevent a harmful VIRUS(1a) developing in them.

intergalactic /ˌɪntəɡəˈlæktɪk/ adj existing or happening between galaxies (GALAXY 1).

intergovernmental /ˌɪntəɡʌvən'mentl/ adj concerning governments or happening between governments: *an intergovernmental conference.*

interim /ˈɪntərɪm/ n **IDM** **in the interim** during the time that comes between; in the MEANTIME: *'My new job starts in May.' 'What are you doing in the interim?'*
▸ **interim** adj [attrib] **(a)** intended to last or be in force only for a short time; temporary: *an interim government/report.* **(b)** (*finance*) prepared or announced after only part of a financial year has been completed; PROVISIONAL: *interim profits/dividends/results.*

interior /ɪnˈtɪəriə(r)/ n **1** [C usu sing] the inner part; the inside: *the lofty interior of a church* ○ *an interior room.* Compare EXTERIOR. **2 the interior** [sing] the part of a country or continent away from the coast: *explorers who penetrated deep into the interior.* **3 the Interior** [sing] the domestic affairs of a country, as

dealt with in the USA and certain other countries by the Department of the Interior and in the UK by the Home Office: *the Minister of the Interior* ○ *the Interior Minister.*
■ in,terior 'decorator n a person who decorates the insides of houses, etc with paint or paper.
in,terior de'sign n [U] a planned choice of style, colour, furniture, etc for the inside of a house. in,terior de'signer n.

interject /ˌɪntəˈdʒekt/ v to interrupt with eg a remark or an opinion: [Vn] *If I may interject a note of caution here ...* [V.speech] *'Oh, don't worry about the cost', he interjected.* [also V].
▸ **interjection** /ˌɪntəˈdʒekʃn/ n (*grammar*) (abbreviated as *interj* in this dictionary) a word or phrase used to express sudden surprise, pleasure, annoyance, etc, eg *Oh!, Hurray!* or *Damn!*

interlace /ˌɪntəˈleɪs/ v ~ (**sth**) (**with sth**) to weave things or be woven together; to cross or be crossed: [V] *interlacing branches* [Vnpr] *interlace sb's hair with ribbons* [also Vn, Vpr].

interleave /ˌɪntəˈliːv/ v ~ **A** (**with B**) to insert sth, eg thin layers of paper, between things: [Vn, Vnpr] *The exercise book has plain pages interleaved (with the lined pages).* [Vnpr] (*fig*) *a speech interleaved with amusing quotes.*

interlink /ˌɪntəˈlɪŋk/ v ~ (**sth**) (**with sth**) (often passive) to link things or be linked together: [Vn, V] *a series of short, interlinked/interlinking stories* [Vnpr] *rivers interlinked with the canal system* [also Vpr].

interlock /ˌɪntəˈlɒk/ v ~ (**sth**) (**with sth**) to fasten or be fastened firmly so as not to come apart accidentally: [V] *interlocking pipes/tubes* ○ (*fig*) *interlocking objectives/responsibilities* [Vn] *They walked along holding hands, their fingers interlocked.* [also Vnpr, Vpr].

interlocutor /ˌɪntəˈlɒkjətə(r)/ n (*fml*) a person taking part in a conversation or discussion.

interloper /ˈɪntələʊpə(r)/ n a person who is present in a place or situation where he or she does not belong; an intruder (INTRUDE): *She felt an interloper in her own family.*

interlude /ˈɪntəluːd/ n **1(a)** a short period of time separating the parts of a play, film, etc; an interval: *There will now be a 15-minute interlude.* **(b)** a piece performed during this: *a musical interlude.* **2** a period of time coming between two events or between two stages of sth: *a romantic interlude* ○ *a brief interlude of peace between two wars* ○ *Apart from a brief interlude in the early sixties, she's never been out of work.* ⊳ note at BREAK².

intermarry /ˌɪntəˈmæri/ v (*pt, pp* -ried) ~ (**with sb**) **1** (of national, religious, etc groups) to marry people from a different group: [Vpr] *blacks intermarrying with whites* [V] *blacks and whites intermarrying.* **2** to marry sb within one's own family or group: [V] *cousins who intermarry.* ▸ **intermarriage** /ˌɪntəˈmærɪdʒ/ n [U, C].

intermediary /ˌɪntəˈmiːdiəri; *US* -dieri/ n ~ (**between sb and sb**) a person who acts as a link or helps to make an agreement between two or more others: *act as an intermediary between the warring factions* ○ *They conducted all their business through an intermediary.* ▸ **intermediary** adj: *play an intermediary role in a dispute.*

intermediate /ˌɪntəˈmiːdiət/ adj ~ (**between A and B**) **1** situated or coming between two people or things in time, space, degree, etc: *be at an intermediate point/level/stage* ○ *The train stops at a number of intermediate stations.* **2(a)** having more than a basic knowledge or level of skill but not yet advanced: *intermediate skiers/students.* **(b)** suitable for such people: *an intermediate course book.*
▸ **intermediate** n a person or thing between two stages of experience or development.

interment /ɪnˈtɜːmənt/ n (fml) [C, U] the burying of a dead body.

interminable /ɪnˈtɜːmɪnəbl/ adj (usu derog) continuing for too long, and usu therefore annoying or boring: an interminable argument/delay/lecture. ▶ **interminably** /-əbli/ adv: The hours dragged on interminably.

intermingle /ˌɪntəˈmɪŋgl/ v ~ (sb/sth) (with sb/sth) mix or make people, ideas, substances, etc mix together: [V, Vpr] a busy trading port, where people of all races intermingle (with each other) [Vn] a book in which fact and fiction are intermingled [also Vnpr].

intermission /ˌɪntəˈmɪʃn/ n [C] a period of time during which sth stops before continuing; an interval: There will be a short intermission at the end of Act 2. ⇨ note at BREAK².

intermittent /ˌɪntəˈmɪtənt/ adj continually stopping and then starting again; not constant: intermittent rain/flashes of lightning ○ intermittent bursts of anger/energy/interest. ▶ **intermittently** adv.

intern¹ /ɪnˈtɜːn/ v ~ sb (in sth) to confine sb, esp for political or military reasons, in a prison or within a place, without allowing them to leave: [Vnpr] At the outbreak of war, German and Italian civilians living in Britain were interned in special camps. [also Vn].
▶ **internee** /ˌɪntɜːˈniː/ n a person who is interned.
internment /ɪnˈtɜːnmənt/ n [U]: demonstrate against internment without trial ○ internment camps.

intern² /ˈɪntɜːn/ n (US) = HOUSEMAN.

internal /ɪnˈtɜːnl/ adj **1** of or on the inside : the internal workings of a machine ○ internal doors/fittings. **2** (medical) of the inside of the body: internal organs/bleeding ○ She's been having some internal problems. **3** occurring in the mind, but not expressed to other people: wrestling with internal doubts. **4** existing or happening entirely within an organization and not involving people from outside: hold an internal inquiry into the dispute ○ internal divisions ○ an internal examination (ie one set and marked within a school or college). **5** of or relating to political, economic, etc activity happening entirely within a country rather than with other countries; domestic: internal affairs/trade/revenue ○ an internal flight. **6** coming from within the thing itself: a theory which lacks internal consistency (ie of which the parts do not fit together) ○ internal evidence (ie evidence contained eg within a book, showing when it was written). Compare EXTERNAL.
▶ **internalize, -ise** /-nəlaɪz/ v (psychology) to make attitudes, feelings, beliefs, etc fully part of one's personality by absorbing them through repeated experience of or exposure to them: [Vn] an analysis of how discrimination is internalized and perpetuated.
internalization, -isation /ɪnˌtɜːnəlaɪˈzeɪʃn; US -lɪˈz-/ n [U, C].
internally /-nəli/ adv: medicine taken internally (ie swallowed) ○ a theory which is not internally consistent ○ ideas generated internally within the company.
■ **in‚ternal-com'bustion engine** n an engine in which power is produced by the explosion of fuel and air inside a CYLINDER(2).
the In‚ternal 'Revenue Service n [sing] (in the USA) the government department responsible for collecting domestic taxes. Compare INLAND REVENUE.

international /ˌɪntəˈnæʃnəl/ adj of, happening or existing between two or more nations: international sport/trade/law ○ an international agreement/conference/flight ○ an international telephone call ○ a pianist with an international reputation.
▶ **international** n (sport) **(a)** a contest involving teams from two or more countries: the France-Scotland Rugby international. **(b)** a player who takes part in such a contest: a retired Welsh Rugby international.
internationalize, -ise /ˌɪntəˈnæʃnəlaɪz/ v to bring sth under the joint control or protection of many nations; to make sth international: [Vn] internationalize a conflict. **internationalization, -isation** /ˌɪntəˌnæʃnəlaɪˈzeɪʃn; US -lə'z-/ n [U].
internationally /-nəli/ adv: internationally famous pop stars.

Internationale /ˌɪntənˌæʃəˈnɑːl/ n the Internationale [sing] a socialist (SOCIALISM) song.

internationalism /ˌɪntəˈnæʃnəlɪzəm/ n [U] a belief in the need for nations to work together in a friendly spirit. ▶ **internationalist** /-ʃnəlɪst/ n.

internecine /ˌɪntəˈniːsaɪn/ adj (fml) causing destruction to both sides: internecine strife/war/conflict.

interpenetrate /ˌɪntəˈpenɪtreɪt/ v to penetrate each other, esp so as to lose individuality; to spread through (sth) thoroughly in each direction: [V, Vn] The two cultures, originally distinct, have so interpenetrated (each other) as to become virtually a single culture.
▶ **interpenetration** /ˌɪntəˌpenɪˈtreɪʃn/ n [C, U] (an instance of) interpenetrating or being interpenetrated.

interpersonal /ˌɪntəˈpɜːsənl/ adj existing or done between two people: inter‚personal 'skills.

interplanetary /ˌɪntəˈplænɪtri; US -teri/ adj between planets: interplanetary space missions.

interplay /ˈɪntəpleɪ/ n [U] ~ (of/between sth and sth) the way in which two or more things have an effect on each other: the subtle interplay of colours (ie their combined effect) in Monet's paintings ○ the interplay between generosity and self-interest.

Interpol /ˈɪntəppl/ n [Gp] an international organization through which the police forces of different countries help each other in fighting crime.

interpolate /ɪnˈtɜːpəleɪt/ v (fml) **1** to make a remark that interrupts a conversation, speech, etc: [V.speech] 'But what has this to do with me?' he interpolated. [also Vn]. **2** ~ sth (into sth) to add sth to a text, book, etc: [Vnpr] Close inspection showed that many lines had been interpolated into the manuscript at a later date. [also Vn]. ▶ **interpolation** /ɪnˌtɜːpəˈleɪʃn/ n [U, C]: the interpolation of dialogue into an account.

interpose /ˌɪntəˈpəʊz/ v (fml) **1** ~ sb/sth (between A and B) to place sb/sth between others: [Vnpr] He interposed his considerable bulk (ie body) between me and the door. [also Vn]. **2** to interrupt, esp by making a remark: [Vn] interpose an objection [V.speech] 'But how do you know that?' he interposed.

interpret /ɪnˈtɜːprɪt/ v **1(a)** to explain what sth means: [Vn] interpret data/evidence ○ interpret a difficult text/an inscription/a dream. **(b)** to perform a piece of music, a part in a play, etc in a particular way that makes clear one's ideas about its meaning: [Vn] interpret the role of Macbeth. **2** ~ sth as sth to understand sth; to decide the meaning or purpose of sth: [Vn-n] Am I to interpret your silence as acceptance or refusal? Compare MISINTERPRET. **3** ~ (for sb) to hear sth in one language and immediately translate it aloud into another: [Vpr] Will you please interpret for me? [also V].
▶ **interpretation** /ɪnˌtɜːprɪˈteɪʃn/ n **(a)** [U] the action or process of interpreting sth. **(b)** [C] a result of this; an explanation or meaning: an unusual interpretation of the play ○ The evidence suggests a rather different interpretation of events from the one you have given us. ○ What interpretation would you put/place on them (ie How would you explain them)?
interpretative /ɪnˈtɜːprɪtətɪv/ (also esp US **interpretive** /ɪnˈtɜːprɪtɪv/) adj of or providing interpretation: interpretative skills.
interpreter n a person who interprets: speak through an interpreter ○ a leading interpreter of contemporary music.

interracial /ˌɪntəˈreɪʃl/ adj existing between or involving different races (RACE³ 1): interracial violence/marriage/cooperation.

interregnum /ˌɪntəˈregnəm/ n (pl **interregnums**) (usu sing) a period when a state has no normal or legal ruler, esp after one rule ends and before the next ruler is appointed: (fig) He takes over as chairman after a lengthy interregnum.

interrelate /ˌɪntərɪˈleɪt/ v (usu passive) (of two or more things) to be connected very closely so as to have an effect on each other; to connect two or more things in this way: [Vn] a complex network of inter-related parts [V, Vn] Many would say that crime and poverty interrelate/are interrelated. [also Vpr, Vnpr].

interrelation /ˌɪntərɪˈleɪʃn/ (also **interrelationship** /-ʃɪp/) n [U, C] ~ (of/between sth and sth) a close relationship between two or more things.

interrogate /ɪnˈterəgeɪt/ v to question sb closely or aggressively and for a long time: [Vn] interrogate a prisoner ○ He refused to be interrogated.
▶ **interrogation** /ɪnˌterəˈgeɪʃn/ n [C, U]: The prisoner gave way under interrogation. ○ suffer endless interrogations about one's activities.
interrogator n a person who interrogates.

interrogative /ˌɪntəˈrɒgətɪv/ adj **1** (fml) asking or seeming to ask a question: give sb an interrogative look. **2** (grammar) (abbreviated as interrog in this dictionary) used in questions: interrogative pronouns/determiners/adverbs (eg who, which, why).
▶ **interrogative** n (grammar) an interrogative word, esp a pronoun or a DETERMINER. **interrogatively** adv.

interrupt /ˌɪntəˈrʌpt/ v **1** to stop the continuous progress of sth temporarily: [Vn] Trade between the two countries was interrupted by the war. ○ We interrupt this programme to bring you a news flash. **2** ~ (sb/sth) (with sth) (derog) to stop sb speaking or doing sth by speaking oneself or by causing some other sort of disturbance: [V, Vn] Don't interrupt (me) while I'm busy! [V.speech] 'Why is that?' Jill interrupted. [Vnpr] Hecklers interrupted her speech with jeering. [also Vpr]. **3** to break an even or continuous line, surface, etc: [Vn] a vast flat plain interrupted only by a few trees. **4** to be or get in the way of sth: [Vn] These new office buildings will interrupt our view of the park.
▶ **interrupter** n a person or thing that interrupts sb/sth.
interruption /ˌɪntəˈrʌpʃn/ n (a) [U, C] the action or an instance of interrupting sb/sth or of being interrupted: She spoke for 20 minutes without interruption. ○ Numerous interruptions have prevented me from finishing my work. (b) [C] a thing that interrupts: The birth of her son was a minor interruption to her career.

intersect /ˌɪntəˈsekt/ v **1** ~ sth (with sth) (esp passive) to divide sth by going across it: [Vn, Vnpr] a landscape of small fields intersected by/with hedges and streams. **2** (of lines, roads, etc) to meet or cross each other: [V] intersecting paths [Vn] The line AB intersects the line CD at E.
▶ **intersection** /ˌɪntəˈsekʃn/ n **1** [C] a place where two or more roads intersect: motorway intersections. **2** [C] a point where two lines, etc intersect. **3** [U] the state of intersecting sth or of being intersected: the angle of intersection.

intersperse /ˌɪntəˈspɜːs/ v ~ A with B; ~ B among/between/throughout A (esp passive) to include or scatter sth here and there among other things: [Vnpr] a day of sunshine interspersed with occasional showers ○ haunting songs interspersed between stories from the island's history.

interstate /ˌɪntəˈsteɪt/ adj [usu attrib] between states, esp in the USA: ˌinterstate ˈcommerce/ˈtensions/ˈhighways.

interstellar /ˌɪntəˈstelə(r)/ adj existing or occurring between the stars: interstellar matter/space. Compare STELLAR.

interstice /ɪnˈtɜːstɪs/ n (usu pl) ~ (of/between/in

sth) (fml) a very small gap or crack: plants growing from the interstices in the wall.

intertwine /ˌɪntəˈtwaɪn/ v ~ (sth) (with sth) to twist sth or be twisted so as to become joined: [V] Their fingers intertwined. [Vnpr] (fig) The party's history is closely intertwined with that of the union movement. [Vn] Our lives seemed inextricably intertwined. [also Vpr].

interval /ˈɪntəvl/ n **1** ~ (between sth) (a) a period of time between two events: the interval between a flash of lightning and the sound of thunder ○ She returned after an interval of about half an hour. (b) a space between two or more things: They planted trees in the intervals between the houses. **2** (Brit) a short period of time separating parts of a play, film, concert, etc: There will be an interval of 20 minutes after the second act. **3** a pause; a break in activity: an interval of silence to show respect for the dead ○ He returned to work after an interval in hospital. ⇨ note at BREAK[2]. **4** (esp pl) a short period during which sth different occurs from what is happening the rest of the time: showers and sunny intervals ○ She's delirious, but has lucid intervals. **5** (music) a difference in pitch[1](2) between two notes: an interval of one octave. **IDM** **at intervals 1** with time between: Buses to the city leave at regular intervals. ○ The runners started at 5-minute intervals. **2** with spaces between: The trees were planted at 6 metre intervals.

intervene /ˌɪntəˈviːn/ v (fml) **1** ~ (in sth / between A and B) (of people) to become involved in a situation, esp so as to prevent sth happening or to try to help sb: [V] When rioting broke out, the police were obliged to intervene. [Vpr] intervene in a dispute/quarrel ○ intervene between two people who are quarrelling ○ I intervened on her behalf to try and get the decision changed. **2** (of events or circumstances) to happen in such a way as to delay or prevent sth from being done: [V] I will come if nothing intervenes. ○ We had almost finished harvesting when a storm intervened. **3** (of time) to come or be between: [V] during the years that intervened/the intervening years.
▶ **intervention** /ˌɪntəˈvenʃn/ n ~ (in sth) [U, C]: calls for government intervention to save the ship-building industry ○ armed/military intervention ○ repeated intervention by central banks in the currency markets. **interventionism** /-ʃənɪzm/ n [U] the government policy or practice of intervening in the economic activities of one's own country or in the domestic affairs of another country. **interventionist** /-ʃənɪst/ adj: interventionist policies.

interview /ˈɪntəvjuː/ n ~ (with sb) **1** a meeting at which sb applying for a job, a place on a course, etc is asked questions to discover whether they are suitable: a job interview ○ I've got an interview with National Chemicals. ○ Applicants will be called for (an) interview in April. **2** a meeting at which a journalist asks sb questions in order to find out their views: a TV interview ○ I never give interviews. ○ In an exclusive interview with our reporter, the former prime minister condemns his party's handling of the affair. **3** a meeting between two people to discuss important matters, usu rather formally: a careers interview ○ I asked for an interview with my boss to discuss my future.
▶ **interview** v **1** ~ sb (for sth) to conduct an interview with sb, eg sb applying for a job: [Vn] interview a number of candidates [V] I'm interviewing all this afternoon. [Vnpr] We interviewed ten people for the job. **2** ~ sb (about sth) (of a journalist) to ask sb questions in an interview: [Vn, Vnpr] interview Cabinet members (about government policy).

interviewee /ˌɪntəvjuːˈiː/ n a person who is interviewed.

interviewer /ˈɪntəvjuːə(r)/ n a person who conducts an interview.

interwar /ˌɪntəˈwɔː(r)/ adj existing or happening between two wars, esp the First and Second World Wars: *the interwar period*.

interweave /ˌɪntəˈwiːv/ v (pt **-wove** /-ˈwəʊv/; pp **-woven** /-ˈwəʊvn/) ~ (**sth**) (**with sth**) (esp passive) to weave or twist two or more threads, etc together: [Vnpr] *a silk shawl interwoven with gold* ○ (fig) *dance rhythms interwoven with folk melodies* [Vn] (fig) *Their lives were interwoven* (ie closely linked). [also V].

intestate /ɪnˈtesteɪt/ adj [usu pred] (law) not having made a will before dying: *He **died intestate***.
▶ **intestacy** /ɪnˈtesəsɪ/ n [U] (law) the condition of being intestate.

intestine /ɪnˈtestɪn/ n (usu pl) a long tube in the body which helps to process food and carries the solid waste from the stomach out of the body: *worms found in the intestines of dogs and cats* ○ *Food passes from the stomach to the small intestine and from there to the large intestine*. See also ABDOMEN 1. ⇨ picture at DIGESTIVE SYSTEM. ▶ **intestinal** /ɪnˈtestɪnl, ˌɪnteˈstaɪnl/ adj: *intestinal disorders*.

intimate¹ /ˈɪntɪmət/ adj **1(a)** (of people) having a very close and friendly relationship: *intimate friends*. **(b)** (of a relationship) warm and friendly; close: *Relations with our neighbours were now cordial, even intimate*. ○ *We had been **on intimate terms*** (ie very close friends) *for some time*. **2** ~ (**with sb**) (euph) having a sexual relationship, esp outside marriage: *She was accused of being intimate with several men*. **3** likely or intended to encourage close relationships, esp sexual ones, typically by being small, quiet and private: *an intimate restaurant/setting*. **4** private and personal: *tell a friend the intimate details of one's life* ○ *an intimate conversation*. **5** [attrib] (fml) (of knowledge) detailed and obtained by deep study or long experience: *an intimate knowledge of African religions*.
▶ **intimacy** /ˈɪntɪməsɪ/ n **1** [U] **(a)** the state of being intimate; a close friendship or relationship: *family intimacy* ○ *the warm intimacy of the café* ○ *His letters had lost much of their former intimacy*. **(b)** (euph) sexual activity. **2 intimacies** [pl] intimate remarks or actions, eg touches or kisses.
intimate n an intimate friend.
intimately adv: *be intimately involved in sth* ○ *know sb intimately*.

intimate² /ˈɪntɪmeɪt/ v ~ **sth** (**to sb**) (fml) to make sth known to sb, esp privately or indirectly: [Vn] *He intimated his willingness to take part*. [V.that, Vpr.that] *She has intimated (to us) that she no longer wishes to be considered for the post*.
▶ **intimation** /ˌɪntɪˈmeɪʃn/ n (fml) **(a)** [C] ~ (**of sth / that...**) a thing intimated; a HINT(1): *He has given us no intimation of his intentions/what he intends to do*. **(b)** [U] the action of intimating sth.

intimidate /ɪnˈtɪmɪdeɪt/ v ~ **sb** (**into sth / doing sth**) to frighten sb in order to make them do sth: [Vn, Vnpr] *intimidate a witness (into silence/into keeping quiet)* (eg by threats).
▶ **intimidating** adj frightening or threatening, esp because of being very large, important or difficult: *The glen is a deep cutting between intimidating mountains*.
intimidation /ɪnˌtɪmɪˈdeɪʃn/ n [U]: *give way to intimidation*.
intimidatory /ɪnˌtɪmɪˈdeɪtərɪ/ adj intended to intimidate: *intimidatory tactics*.

into /ˈɪntə, before vowels ˈɪntu, strong form ˈɪntuː/ prep For the special uses of **into** in phrasal verbs, look at the verb entries. For example, the meaning of **lay into sb/sth** is given in the phrasal verb section of the entry for **lay¹**. **1(a)** moving or moved to a point within sth: *Come into the house*. ○ *go into town* ○ *She dived into the water*. ○ *pour tea into a cup* ○ *throw a letter into the fire* ○ *She put the money into her bank account*. ○ (fig) *He turned and walked off into the night*. Compare OUT OF. **(b)** in the direction of sth: *Speak clearly into the microphone*. ○ *Driving into the sun, we had to shade our eyes*. **(c)** to a point at which one hits or penetrates sb/sth: *The truck drove into a line of parked cars*. ○ *The wine soaked into the carpet*. **2** to a point during sth: *He carried on working late into the night*. ○ *She didn't get married until she was well into her 30s*. **3(a)** (indicating a change in form or appearance as the result of an action): *turn the spare room into a study* ○ *cut the paper into strips* ○ *translate a passage into German* ○ *collect the dirty clothes into a heap* ○ *change into a pair of jeans*. Compare OUT OF. **(b)** (indicating a change in state): *frighten sb into submission* ○ *shocked into a confession of guilt* ○ *She came into power in 1979*. **4** about or concerning sth: *an inquiry into safety procedures*. **5** (used to express division in mathematics): *3 into 24 is 8*. **IDM** be ˈinto sth (infml) to be interested in sth; to be actively involved in sth: *be (heavily) into science fiction/stamp-collecting/yoga*.

intolerable /ɪnˈtɒlərəbl/ adj too bad to be tolerated or endured: *intolerable heat/noise/behaviour* ○ *This is intolerable — I've been kept waiting for three hours!* ▶ **intolerably** /-əblɪ/ adv: *intolerably rude*.

intolerant /ɪnˈtɒlərənt/ adj ~ (**of sb/sth**) (usu derog) not willing to accept ideas, opinions, behaviour, etc different from one's own: *intolerant of opposition*. ▶ **intolerance** /-əns/ n [U]: *religious intolerance*.

intonation /ˌɪntəˈneɪʃn/ n **1** [U, C] the rise and fall of the voice in speaking, esp as this affects the meaning of what is said: *intonation patterns* ○ *In English, some questions have a rising intonation*. ○ *He thought he could detect a faint regional intonation in her voice*. Compare INFLECTION 2, STRESS 3a. **2** [U] (music) the quality of playing or singing exactly in tune: *The violin's intonation was poor*.

intone /ɪnˈtəʊn/ v to say sth in a slow, level, often solemn, voice: [Vn] *intone a prayer* [V.speech] *'We are here to pay tribute to a remarkable woman,' he intoned*.

in toto /ɪn ˈtəʊtəʊ/ adv (Latin fml) totally; altogether: *You must accept the proposal in toto or not at all*.

intoxicant /ɪnˈtɒksɪkənt/ n a substance, eg alcohol, that makes one become excited or lose control.

intoxicated /ɪnˈtɒksɪkeɪtɪd/ adj (fml) **1** drunk or under the influence of drugs: *He was arrested for driving while intoxicated*. **2** ~ (**by/with sth**) greatly excited by sth: *intoxicated by success* ○ *intoxicated with his own power*.
▶ **intoxicating** adj that can make one intoxicated: *the intoxicating effects of alcohol and drugs* ○ *the fresh, intoxicating scent of fields and woodlands*.
intoxication /ɪnˌtɒksɪˈkeɪʃn/ n [U].

intra- pref (with adjs) on the inside; within: *intravenous*.

intractable /ɪnˈtræktəbl/ adj (fml) not easily controlled or dealt with; hard to manage: *intractable children* ○ *the **intractable problem** of human greed*.
▶ **intractability** /ɪnˌtræktəˈbɪlətɪ/ n [U].

intramural /ˌɪntrəˈmjʊərəl/ adj **1** intended for full-time students living within a college: *intramural courses*. **2** (US) between teams or players from the same school: *an intramural game/league*.

intransigent /ɪnˈtrænsɪdʒənt/ adj (fml derog) unwilling to change one's views or be persuaded to agree about sth; STUBBORN(1): *Owing to their intransigent attitude we were unable to reach an agreement*.
▶ **intransigence** /-əns/ n [U].

intransitive /ɪnˈtrænsətɪv/ adj (grammar) (of verbs) not having an object: *The verb 'die' as in 'He*

---

died suddenly', is intransitive. Compare TRANSITIVE.
▶ **intransitively** *adv*.

intra-uterine /ˌɪntrə ˈjuːtəraɪn/ *adj (medical)* within the UTERUS.
■ **ˌintra-uterine deˈvice** *n (abbr* IUD) (also **coil**) a plastic or metal object inserted in the UTERUS to prevent a woman becoming pregnant.

intravenous /ˌɪntrəˈviːnəs/ *adj (medical)* into or within a vein or veins: *an intravenous injection* (ie into the blood). ▶ **intravenously** *adv*.

in-tray /ˈɪn treɪ/ *n* a tray for holding letters, etc that are waiting to be read or answered. Compare OUT-TRAY.

intrepid /ɪnˈtrepɪd/ *adj (esp rhet)* without fear; brave: *an intrepid explorer.*

intricate /ˈɪntrɪkət/ *adj* composed of many small parts put together in a complex way: *an intricate piece of machinery* ○ *a novel with an intricate plot* ○ *an intricate design/pattern.*
▶ **intricacy** /ˈɪntrɪkəsi/ *n* **(a)** **intricacies** [pl] the complicated parts or details of sth: *I was unable to follow the intricacies of the plot.* **(b)** [U] the quality of being intricate: *the intricacy of the design.*
intricately /-ətli/ *adv: intricately drawn/carved/ embroidered.*

intrigue /ɪnˈtriːg/ *v* **1** to provoke sb's interest or curiosity: [Vn] *What you say intrigues me — tell me more.* [Vn, Vpr] *The children were intrigued by/with the new toy.* [Vn.to inf] *I was thoroughly intrigued to hear what she had to say.* **2** ~ **(with sb)** to make and carry out secret plans, often with other people, with the aim of causing sb harm, doing sth illegal, etc; to PLOT² *v*: [Vpr] *He was intriguing with the leader of a rival gang.* [V.to inf] *Some of the members had been intriguing to get the secretary dismissed.* [also V].
▶ **intrigue** /ˈɪntriːg, ɪnˈtriːg/ *n* **1** [U] the making of secret plans to cause sb harm, do sth illegal, etc: *a novel of mystery and intrigue.* **2** [C] **(a)** a secret plan to cause sb harm, etc: *political/boardroom intrigues.* **(b)** a secret arrangement: *amorous intrigues.*
intriguing *adj* interesting, esp because unusual; fascinating or mysterious: *an intriguing fact/question* ○ *He found her rather intriguing.* **intriguingly** *adv: Intriguingly, the stranger kept his face hidden.*

intrinsic /ɪnˈtrɪnsɪk, -zɪk/ *adj* ~ **(to sth)** (of a value or quality) belonging naturally to sb/sth; existing within sb/sth, rather than coming from outside: *a person's intrinsic worth* (eg their personal qualities such as honour and courage, rather than wealth or social status) ○ *an intrinsic part of the plan* ○ *The concept of liberty is intrinsic to Western civilization.* Compare EXTRINSIC. ▶ **intrinsically** /-kli/ *adv: He is not intrinsically bad* (ie although circumstances might force him to behave badly sometimes).

intro /ˈɪntrəʊ/ *n (pl* **-os)** *(infml)* an introduction to sth, esp to a piece of music or writing: *There's an intro of eight bars before the singer comes in.*

introduce /ˌɪntrəˈdjuːs; *US* ˈduːs/ *v* **1** ~ **sth (into/to sth)** to bring sth into use or operation for the first time: [Vn] *The company is introducing a new range of cars this year.* ○ *a newly introduced ban on smoking in public places* ○ *New pay scales have been introduced.* [Vnpr] *introduce the latest technology into schools.* **2(a)** ~ **sth/sb (into sth)** to include sth/ sb for the first time in sth: [Vn] *A new character is introduced in Chapter 3.* [also Vnpr]. **(b)** to bring a plant, an animal or a disease to a place where it does not normally occur: [Vnpr] *Vegetation patterns changed when goats were introduced to the island.* [also Vn]. **3** ~ **oneself/sb (to sb)** to make oneself/sb known formally to sb else by giving one's/their name: [Vn] *Allow me to introduce my wife.* ○ *May I/ Let me introduce myself — I'm Helen Robinson.* [Vnpr] *I was introduced to a Greek girl at the party.* **4** ~ **sb to sth (a)** to give sb the first, most basic ideas or knowledge about sth: [Vnpr] *The first lec-*

ture introduces students to the main topics of the course. **(b)** to cause sb to start using or experiencing sth: [Vnpr] *introduce young people to alcohol/drugs* ○ *It was she who first introduced me to the pleasures of wine-tasting.* **5** to be the first or main speaker in a show, television or radio programme, etc giving details about it and presenting other artists to the audience: [Vn] *The next programme is introduced by Mary Davidson.* **6** *(esp politics)* to present sth new for discussion: [Vn, Vnpr] *introduce a Bill (before Parliament).* **7** to begin or open a piece of music or writing: [Vnpr] *A slow theme introduces the first movement.* [Vnpr] *introduce a new subject into the conversation* ○ *New players have been introduced into the team.* **8** ~ **sth (into sth)** *(fml)* to put sth into sth; to insert sth: [Vnpr] *introduce a hypodermic needle into a vein* ○ *Particles of glass had been introduced into the baby food.* [Vn] *(fig) introduce a new element of risk.*

introduction /ˌɪntrəˈdʌkʃn/ *n* **1** [U, C] the bringing of sth into use or operation for the first time: *the introduction of new manufacturing methods* ○ *problems arising from the introduction of new licensing regulations* ○ *This wine is a new introduction.* **2** [C, U] ~ **(to sb)** the act of making one person formally known to another, in which each is told the other's name: *Once the introductions were over, we got straight down to business.* ○ *a person who needs no introduction* (ie who is already well-known) ○ *a letter of introduction* (ie one which tells sb who you are, written by sb who knows both you and the person reading the letter). **3** [C, U] ~ **(to sth) (a)** the first part of eg a book or a speech, giving a general idea of what is to follow: *a short/general introduction* ○ *write an introduction to the company's annual report* ○ *By way of introduction, let me give you the background to the story.* Compare PREFACE. **(b)** a book or course for people beginning to study a subject: *'An Introduction to Astronomy'.* **(c)** [C] *(music)* a short section at the beginning of a musical composition: *an eight-bar introduction.* **4** [sing] ~ **to sth** a person's first experience of sth: *This record was his introduction to modern jazz.* **5** [C, U] the act of taking or including sth somewhere for the first time: *the introduction of disease to remote Amazon peoples.*

introductory /ˌɪntrəˈdʌktəri/ *adj* acting as an introduction(3): *introductory remarks* ○ *an introductory chapter* ○ *an introductory course in computing.*

introspection /ˌɪntrəˈspekʃn/ *n* [U] the examination of, or a concern with, one's own thoughts, feelings and motives (MOTIVE): *The election defeat led to a great deal of introspection in the party.*
▶ **introspective** /-ˈspektɪv/ *adj* tending to or showing introspection: *a thoughtful, introspective young man* ○ *introspective poetry.*

introvert /ˈɪntrəvɜːt/ *n* a person who is more interested in her or his own thoughts and feelings than in things outside herself or himself, and is often shy and unwilling to take part in activities with others. Compare EXTROVERT.
▶ **introverted** /ˈɪntrəvɜːtɪd/ *adj* having the characteristics of an introvert: *The poet became more introverted as he grew older.*
introversion /ˌɪntrəˈvɜːʃn; *US* -ˈvɜːrʒn/ *n* [U].

intrude /ɪnˈtruːd/ *v* **(a)** ~ **(into/on/upon sth/sb)** to put oneself into a place or situation where one is not welcome: [V] *I'm sorry to intrude, but could I talk to you for a moment?* [Vpr] *I felt as though I was intruding on/into their private grief.* **(b)** ~ **(in/into/ on sth)** to have an unpleasant effect; to disturb sth/ sth: *a cosy academic world where reality barely intrudes* [Vpr] *Images of his face kept intruding into my thoughts.*
▶ **intruder** *n* a person or thing that intrudes, esp sb who enters another person's property illegally.

intrusion /ɪnˈtruːʒn/ n ~ (**on/upon/into sth**) [U,C] the act of intruding (INTRUDE): *the unwelcome intrusion of politics into sport* ∘ *I am sorry for this intrusion but I need to speak to you urgently.* ∘ *This newspaper article is a disgraceful intrusion on my private life.*
▶ **intrusive** /ɪnˈtruːsɪv/ adj causing one to be disturbed: *intrusive neighbours/journalists/television cameras* ∘ *I found the noise from the roadworks very intrusive.*

intuit /ɪnˈtjuːɪt; US -ˈtuː-/ v (fml) to know sth by instinct rather than from specific facts: [Vn] (ironic) *I suppose we're meant to intuit the answer!* [also V.*that*].

intuition /ˌɪntjuˈɪʃn; US -tuː-/ n (**a**) [U] the power of understanding situations or people's feelings immediately, without the need for conscious reasoning or study: *a sudden flash of intuition* ∘ *feminine intuition* ∘ *Nobody told me where to find you — I just used my intuition.* (**b**) [C] ~ (**that...**) an idea or a piece of knowledge gained by this power: *our intuitions about what is right and wrong* ∘ *I had an intuition that something awful was about to happen.*
▶ **intuitive** /ɪnˈtjuːɪtɪv; US -ˈtuː-/ adj (**a**) of or coming from intuition: *intuitive knowledge* ∘ *an intuitive feeling about sth/approach to sth.* (**b**) possessing intuition: *Are women more intuitive than men?* **intuitively** adv: *strategies that are intuitively obvious* ∘ *Intuitively, she knew where to find him.*

Inuit /ˈɪnjuɪt, ˈɪnuɪt/ n (pl unchanged or **Inuits**) a N American Eskimo.

inundate /ˈɪnʌndeɪt/ v **1** ~ **sb** (**with sth**) (esp passive) to give or send sb so many things that they have difficulty dealing with them all; to OVERWHELM(2) sb: [Vnpr] *We were inundated with enquiries.* [also Vn]. **2** to cover an area with a very large amount of water; to flood a place: [Vn] *The river burst its banks and inundated nearby villages.* ▶ **inundation** /ˌɪnʌnˈdeɪʃn/ n [U]: *the inundation of low-lying land.*

inure /ɪˈnjʊə(r)/ v ~ **oneself/sb** (**to sth**) (fml) (usu passive) to make oneself/sb able to tolerate sth unpleasant, so that one is hardly affected by it any more: [Vnpr] *After living here for years I've become inured to the damp climate.* ∘ *Sadly, the world has grown inured to this kind of outrage.*

invade /ɪnˈveɪd/ v **1** to enter a country or territory with armed forces in order to attack or occupy it: [V] *The army invaded at dawn.* [Vn] *Alexander the Great invaded India with a large army.* **2** to enter a place in large numbers, esp so as to cause damage; to crowd into sth: [Vn] *Thousands of football fans invaded the pitch.* ∘ *The cancer cells may invade other parts of the body.* ∘ (fig) *Her mind was invaded by anxieties/nightmares.* **3** to interfere with sth; to prevent sb from fully possessing or enjoying sth that is theirs: [Vn] *invade sb's privacy/rights.*
▶ **invader** n a person or thing that invades: *repel the invader(s).* See also INVASION.

invalid¹ /ɪnˈvælɪd/ adj **1** not officially acceptable, eg because of a detail that is wrong; not legally recognized: *an invalid passport/will* ∘ *Your claim for unemployment benefit is invalid because you have a part-time job.* **2** not true or logical; not supported by reasoning: *an invalid argument/assumption/statement.*
▶ **invalidate** /ɪnˈvælɪdeɪt/ v to make sth invalid: [Vn] *false statements which invalidated the contract/her argument.* **invalidation** /ɪnˌvælɪˈdeɪʃn/ n [U].

invalid² /ˈɪnvəlɪd; Brit also ˈɪnvəliːd/ n a person made weak by illness or injury; a person who suffers from ill health for a very long time: *He has been an invalid all his life.* ∘ *her invalid mother* ∘ *an invalid chair* (ie one with wheels on for moving an invalid easily).
▶ **invalid** v ~ **sb** (**out of sth**) to make or allow sb to leave a job, esp the armed forces, because of ill health: [Vnadv] *be invalided home* [Vnpr] *He was invalided out of the army after his elbow was shattered.*

invalidity /ˌɪnvəˈlɪdəti/ n [U] the state of being an invalid: *invalidity benefit* ∘ *an invalidity pension.*

invaluable /ɪnˈvæljuəbl/ adj ~ (**to/for sb/sth**); ~ (**in sth**) extremely useful: *invaluable help/advice/information* ∘ *This book will be invaluable to/for all students of history.* ∘ *Computers have proved invaluable in the fight against crime.*

NOTE A few adjectives have meanings which you may not expect when they have the negative affixes **in-** or **-less** added. **Invaluable** means 'extremely valuable' when **valuable** means 'very useful and important': *The handbook contains over 120 pages of invaluable advice and information.* But when **valuable** means 'worth a lot of money', the opposite is **valueless** or **worthless**.
A **priceless** object, painting, jewel, etc is very old, rare or special and can never be replaced or have a price: *Priceless antiques and paintings were destroyed in the fire.* Things that are **innumerable** or **numberless** are very numerous or too many to be counted. **Inflammable** has the same meaning as **flammable** (ie that will burn). The opposite (ie that will not burn) is **non-flammable**: *Cotton is an inflammable material.*

invariable /ɪnˈveəriəbl/ (also **invariant** /ɪnˈveəriənt/) adj (fml) never changing; always the same; constant: *an invariable amount/rule* ∘ *his invariable courtesy and charm* ∘ *The invariable answer to my questions was 'No!'*
▶ **invariably** /ɪnˈveəriəbli/ adv always: *She invariably arrives late.* ∘ *'Q' is almost invariably followed by 'u' in English words.*

invasion /ɪnˈveɪʒn/ n **1** [C,U] the action of HOSTILE (2) armed forces entering a country or territory: *the invasion of Britain* ∘ *troops sent to guard against invasion.* **2** [C,U] the entry or arrival of a large number of people in a place: *an invasion of tourists.* **3** [U,C] the action of preventing sb from enjoying sth that is theirs: *an invasion of one's privacy.*

invasive /ɪnˈveɪsɪv/ adj (techn or fml) tending to spread in a harmful or unpleasant way: *invasive cancer cells/fungi* ∘ *invasive smells/noises.*

invective /ɪnˈvektɪv/ n [U] (fml) a violent attack in words; insulting language: *a speech full of invective against the government* ∘ *let out a stream of invective.*

inveigh /ɪnˈveɪ/ v **PHRV** **inveigh against sb/sth** (fml) to attack sb/sth violently in words: *inveigh against the evils of capitalism.*

inveigle /ɪnˈveɪgl/ v ~ **sb** (**into sth/doing sth**) to achieve sth or persuade sb to do sth, esp by using false praise or deception: [Vnpr] *He inveigled his way into the house.* ∘ *She inveigled him into buying a new car.* [also Vn].

invent /ɪnˈvent/ v **1** to make or design sth that has not existed before; to create sth: [Vn] *a newly invented sign language* ∘ *Laszlo Biro invented the ballpoint pen.* Compare DISCOVER 1. **2** (often derog) to give a name, reason, etc that does not exist or is not true: [Vn] *All the characters in the book are invented.* ∘ *Can't you invent a better excuse than that?*
▶ **inventive** /ɪnˈventɪv/ adj (approv) having or showing the ability to invent or create new things and think originally: *an inventive child/designer/mind* ∘ *an inventive design.* **inventively** adv. **inventiveness** n [U]: *admire the inventiveness of modern advertising.*
inventor n a person who invents sth, or whose job is inventing things: *Freud, the inventor of psychoanalysis.*

invention /ɪnˈvenʃn/ n **1**(**a**) [U] the action of inventing sth, eg a machine or a system: *the invention of radio by Marconi* ∘ *a tool of her own invention* (ie invented by herself). (**b**) [C] a thing that has been invented: *the scientific inventions of the 20th century.* (**c**) [U] the ability to invent such things; original thinking: *admire sb's artistry and invention.* **2** (*euph*) (**a**) [U] the practice of saying things that are not true, esp in order to deceive people; lying: *I'm afraid he is guilty of a good deal of invention.* (**b**) [C] a thing so invented: *The mysterious stranger she mentioned turned out to be an invention.*

inventory /'ɪnvəntri; US -tɔːri/ *n* a detailed list, eg of goods, furniture or jobs to be done: *keep/make a full inventory of the contents of a house.*

inverse /ˌɪn'vɜːs/ *adj* [usu attrib] having the opposite position, or moving in the opposite direction, in relation to sth else: *The number of copies the paper sells seems to be* **in ˌinverse proˈportion to** *the amount of news it contains* (ie The more news it contains, the fewer copies it sells).
▶ **inverse** /'ɪnvɜːs/ *n* **the inverse** [sing] the direct opposite of sth: *This is the inverse of his earlier proposition.*
inversely /ˌɪn'vɜːsli/ *adv*: *Rates are set at a level inversely related/proportional to expected demand.*

inversion /ɪn'vɜːʃn; US -'vɜːrʒn/ *n* [U, C] the action of reversing the position or order of sth, or the state of being reversed: *(an) inversion of normal word order.*

invert /ɪn'vɜːt/ *v* to put sth upside down or in the opposite order, position or arrangement: [Vn] *invert a glass* ○ *In questions, the subject and the verb are often inverted.*
■ **inˌverted ˈcommas** *n* [pl] (*Brit*) a pair of punctuation marks (PUNCTUATE), ' ' or " ", used at the beginning and end of a group of words to show that they were spoken or are being quoted. ⇨ App 3.
IDM **in inverted commas** (used to show that the speaker does not necessarily agree with a description of sb/sth): *He's a 'management consultant', in inverted commas.*
▶ **inˌverted ˈsnobbery** *n* [U] (*derog*) the attitude of finding fault with anything associated with high social status, wealth, etc so as not to appear to value these things.

invertebrate /ɪn'vɜːtɪbrət/ *n* (*biology*) an animal with no BACKBONE(1): *They feed on slugs, worms and other small invertebrates.*

invest /ɪn'vest/ *v* **1** ~ (**sth**) (**in sth / with sb**) to use money to buy eg shares or property, develop a business enterprise, etc in order to earn interest, bring profit or improve the quality of sth: [V] *Now is a good time to invest.* [Vpr] *The government has invested heavily in oil exploration/the road network.* [Vn, Vnpr] *invest £5000 in government bonds* [Vpr, Vnpr] *invest (one's savings) with a building society.* **2** ~ **sth** (**in sth / doing sth**) to give time, effort or energy to a particular task, esp for some serious purpose or useful result: [Vnpr] *invest a few hours a week in learning a new language* ○ *She's invested a lot of emotional energy in that business.* [also Vn]. **3** ~ **sb** (**with sth / as sth**) (*fml*) to give rank, office(5) or power to sb: [Vnpr] *The governor has been invested with full authority to act.* [Vn-n] *Prince Charles was invested as Prince of Wales in 1969.* [also Vn]. See also INVESTITURE. **PHRV** **inˈvest in sth** (*infml*) to buy sth expensive but useful: *I'm thinking of investing in a new car.* **inˈvest sb/sth with sth** (*fml*) to cause sb/sth to have a particular quality: *It was a match heavily invested with drama, courage and skill.*
▶ **investment** *n* **1** ~ (**in sth**) (**a**) [U] the investing of money: *The industry has declined because of a lack of (new/public/private/foreign) investment.* ○ *a company's investment plans/strategy.* (**b**) an instance of this: *Those oil shares were a good investment* (ie have been profitable). ○ *I'm hoping for a good return on my investments.* (**c**) a sum of money that is invested:

an investment of $800 in oil stocks. **2** [C] a thing that is worth buying because it may be profitable or useful in the future: *I don't really like the painting; I only bought it as an investment.* ○ *A burglar alarm is always a good investment.*
investor *n* a person or an organization that invests money: *small investors* (ie private individuals) ○ *institutional investors* (eg banks or insurance companies).

investigate /ɪn'vestɪgeɪt/ *v* **1** to discover and examine all the facts about sth, eg a crime or an accident, in order to obtain the truth: [V] *The police were baffled, and the FBI was called in to investigate.* [Vn] *investigate allegations/complaints* [Vn, V.wh] *Scientists are investigating the cause of the crash/are investigating how the crash occurred.* **2** to try to discover the facts about sb's character, background, political views, etc: [Vn] *Applicants for government posts are always thoroughly investigated before being appointed.* **3** to try to discover facts, information, etc, eg by study or research: *investigate the market for a product/for ways of increasing profits* ○ *We might be able to help you; I'll investigate the possibilities.* [also V.wh]. **4** (*infml*) to make a rapid check: [V] *'What was that noise outside?' 'I'll just go and investigate.'* [also V.wh].
▶ **investigation** /ɪnˌvestɪ'geɪʃn/ *n* [U, C] ~ (**into sth**): *The matter is* **under investigation**/*requires further investigation.* ○ *Scientists are conducting an investigation into the accident.* ○ *The police have completed their investigation(s).*
investigative /ɪn'vestɪgətɪv; US -geɪtɪv/ (also **investigatory** /ɪn'vestɪgətəri; US -gətɔːri/) *adj* of or concerned with investigating sth: *investigative journalism* (ie in which journalists try to discover important facts of public interest that have been concealed) ○ *have wide investigatory powers.*
investigator /ɪn'vestɪgeɪtə(r)/ *n* a person who investigates sth: *a private investigator* (ie a DETECTIVE) ○ *insurance investigators* ○ *Accident investigators have discovered the cause of the crash.*

investiture /ɪn'vestɪtʃə(r); US also -tʃʊər/ *n* [U, C] the ceremony at which sb is formally given an office(5), a rank or special powers: *the investiture of the Prince of Wales.*

inveterate /ɪn'vetərət/ *adj* [usu attrib] (*derog*) **1** (of people) having a certain lasting habit or interest which seems likely to continue: *be an inveterate traveller/collector/campaigner/party-goer.* **2** (of esp bad feelings or habits) having existed for a long time and likely to continue: *inveterate hostility/hatred.*

invidious /ɪn'vɪdiəs/ *adj* (*fml*) unacceptable, unfair and likely to make people feel very angry or jealous: *You put me* **in an invidious position** *by asking me to comment on my colleague's work.* ○ *It would be invidious to single out any particular person.*

invigilate /ɪn'vɪdʒɪleɪt/ *v* (*Brit*) (*US* **proctor**) to be present during an examination to make sure that it is properly conducted and that no one cheats: [Vn, Vpr] *invigilate (at) the history exam* [also V].
▶ **invigilation** /ɪnˌvɪdʒɪ'leɪʃn/ *n* [U].
invigilator /ɪn'vɪdʒɪleɪtə(r)/ (*US* **proctor**) *n* a person who invigilates.

invigorate /ɪn'vɪgəreɪt/ *v* to make sb feel more lively and healthy: [Vn] *I feel invigorated by all this fresh air!* ○ (*fig*) *New skills are needed to invigorate the country's industry.* ▶ **invigorating** *adj*: *an invigorating climate/wind/swim* ○ (*fig*) *have an invigorating effect on the region's musical life.*

invincible /ɪn'vɪnsəbl/ *adj* (*usu approv*) too strong to be overcome or defeated: *an invincible army/team* ○ *She has an invincible belief/will.* ▶ **invincibility** /ɪnˌvɪnsə'bɪləti/ *n* [U]: *confidence in their own invincibility.*

inviolable /ɪn'vaɪələbl/ *adj* (*fml*) that must always be respected and not broken or ignored: *inviolable* *rights* ○ *an inviolable oath/law/treaty* ○ *inviolable borders/frontiers* (ie that must not be changed or crossed illegally). ► **inviolability** /ɪnˌvaɪələˈbɪləti/ *n* [U].

inviolate /ɪnˈvaɪələt/ *adj* (*fml*) that has been or must be fully respected and never broken or harmed: *The treaty/The secret/Her innocence remained inviolate.*

invisible /ɪnˈvɪzəbl/ *adj* **1** ~ (**to sb/sth**) that cannot be seen; not visible: *a wizard who could make himself invisible* ○ *stars that are invisible to all but the most powerful telescopes* ○ (*fig*) *She felt invisible in such a large social gathering.* **2** [usu attrib] (*commerce*) in the form of or connected with services such as banking (BANK⁴), insurance, TOURISM, rather than goods or raw materials (RAW): *invisible earnings/exports.*
► **invisibility** /ɪnˌvɪzəˈbɪləti/ *n* [U]: *the invisibility of road signs due to the fog.*
invisibles *n* [pl] (*commerce*) invisible(2) exports and imports.
invisibly /ɪnˈvɪzəbli/ *adv*: *Birds sang invisibly in the trees.*

invitation /ˌɪnvɪˈteɪʃn/ *n* **1** [U] the action of inviting or the state of being invited: *a letter of invitation* ○ *give a concert at the invitation of the British Council* ○ *Admission is by invitation only.* ○ (*sport*) *an invitation event/tournament* (ie one in which only invited competitors may take part). **2** [C] ~ (**to sb**) (**to sth / to do sth**) a spoken or written request to go somewhere, or do sth: *send out invitations to the party* ○ *an invitation card* ○ *I accepted/declined their invitation to join the tennis club.* **3** [C usu *sing*] ~ **to sb/sth** (**to do sth**) a situation or an action that tempts or encourages sb to do sth: *An unlocked door is an (open) invitation to burglars (to walk in).*
► **invitational** /-ʃənl/ *adj, n* (*esp US sport*) (of a sports event) in which only invited competitors may take part.

invite /ɪnˈvaɪt/ *v* **1** ~ **sb** (**to/for sth**) (**a**) to ask sb in a friendly way to go somewhere or do sth, esp as a social event: [Vn] *'Are you coming to the party?' 'No, I haven't been invited.'* [Vn.to inf] *They invited me to come to their party.* [Vnpr] *invite sb to/for dinner* [Vnp] *invite sb round/in/up* (ie to or into one's house or flat) ○ *He liked the girl and decided to invite her out* (ie to come with him to an entertainment of some kind). (**b**) to ask sb formally to go somewhere or do sth: [Vnpr] *Candidates will be invited for interview early next month.* [Vn.to inf] *I've been invited to give a talk at the conference.* [Vn] *a TV discussion in front of an invited audience.* **2** ~ **sth** (**from sb**) to ask for comments, suggestions, etc: [Vn, Vnpr] *After his speech he invited questions (from the audience).* **3** to be likely to cause or attract sth, esp sth bad, often not deliberately: [Vn] *behaviour that is sure to invite criticism* [Vn, Vn.to inf] *Leaving your car unlocked is just inviting trouble/inviting someone to steal it.* ○ *The play invites comparisons with Shakespeare.*
► **invite** /ˈɪnvaɪt/ *n* (*infml*) an invitation, eg to a party: *Did you get an invite?*
inviting /ɪnˈvaɪtɪŋ/ *adj* tempting; attractive: *an inviting smell/prospect/suggestion* ○ *The sea looked really inviting.* **invitingly** *adv.*

in vitro /ɪn ˈviːtrəʊ/ *adj, adv* (*biology*) (of the fertilization (FERTILIZE) of an egg) by artificial means outside the body of the mother: *in vitro fertilization* ○ *an egg fertilized in vitro.*

invocation ⇨ INVOKE.

invoice /ˈɪnvɔɪs/ *n* ~ (**for sth**) (*commerce*) a list of goods sold or services provided together with the prices charged; a bill: *make out/send an invoice for the goods* ○ *settle/pay an invoice for £250.*
► **invoice** *v* ~ **sb** (**for sth**)/~ **sth** (**to sb**) (*commerce*) to make or send an invoice, esp as a request for payment: [Vn, Vnpr] *The company hasn't yet in-*

voiced us (for the goods we bought). [Vn] *The booking will be invoiced by your local travel agent.*

invoke /ɪnˈvəʊk/ *v* (*fml*) **1** to use sth/sb as an authority for doing or arguing sth: [Vn] *The government has invoked the Official Secrets Act in having the book banned.* ○ *She invokes several eminent scholars to back up her argument.* **2**(**a**) to refer to a person, an idea or a spirit, eg in calling for help or protection, or to inspire one: [Vn] *The new President invoked (the name/memory of) John F. Kennedy in his speech to the nation.* (**b**) to make sth appear by magic: [Vn] *invoke evil spirits.* **3** to ask, call, beg or pray for sth: [Vn] *invoke assistance in a desperate situation* [Vnpr] *invoke vengeance (up)on one's enemies.* ► **invocation** /ˌɪnvəˈkeɪʃn/ *n* [U, C] ~ (**to sb**): *the invocation of human rights* ○ *the poet's invocations of/to the Muse.*

involuntary /ɪnˈvɒləntri; *US* -teri/ *adj* **1** done without intention; done in an unconscious way or by accident: *an involuntary cry/jump/intake of breath* (eg when suddenly frightened or surprised by sth) ○ *involuntary exposure to cigarette smoke.* **2** done against sb's will; forced or compulsory: *the involuntary repatriation of immigrants.* ► **involuntarily** /ɪnˈvɒləntrəli; *US* ɪnˌvɒlənˈterəli/ *adv.*

involve /ɪnˈvɒlv/ *v* **1** (of eg a situation or an event) to have or include sth/sb as a part, an element, a condition or a result: [Vn] *a story involving pirates and buried treasure* ○ *a situation in which national security is involved* [V.ing] *The plan could involve closing several factories.* [V.n ing] *The job will involve me/my moving to Glasgow.* **2** ~ **sb** (**in sth / doing sth**) to make sb experience or take part in an activity or a situation: [Vn] *The strike involved many people.* [Vnpr] *All the students were involved in making costumes and scenery.* ○ *Schools should involve parents more in decision-making.* **3** ~ **sb in sth** to make sb suffer or experience sth: *involve sb in a lot of expense/trouble.* **4** ~ **sb** (**in sth**) to show sb to be concerned in or to have taken part in sth, esp a crime: [Vnpr] *The witness's statement involves you in the robbery.* [also Vn].
► **involved** *adj* **1**(**a**) ~ (**in sth**) (often after a *n*) taking part in or being part of sth: *be/become/get involved in politics/criminal activities/a heated argument* ○ *He knew about the robbery, but wasn't directly/actively/personally involved.* ○ *We have considered the situation and talked to the people involved/about the issues involved.* (**b**) ~ (**with sb**) closely connected with sb: *become emotionally involved with sb* ○ *He sees her often but doesn't want to get too involved.* **2** complicated in thought or form: *an involved sentence/explanation/style of writing.*
involvement *n* [U, C]: *her suspected involvement in the robbery* ○ *the doctor's emotional/romantic/sexual involvement with one of his patients* ○ *the need to avoid further military involvement.*

invulnerable /ɪnˈvʌlnərəbl/ *adj* ~ (**to sth**) **1** that cannot be harmed or damaged: *a fortification that is invulnerable to attack.* **2** that cannot be defeated or challenged; secure; safe: *Liverpool are in an invulnerable position at the top of the league.* ► **invulnerability** /ɪnˌvʌlnərəˈbɪləti/ *n* [U].

inward /ˈɪnwəd/ *adj* **1** existing in the mind and often not expressed: *inward joy/doubts/regrets* ○ *Our actions do not always reflect our inward nature.* **2** turned towards the inside: *an inward curve.* Compare OUTWARD.
► **inward** (also **inwards**) *adv* **1** into or towards the mind or soul: *an inward-looking person* (ie concerned with her or his own problems or feelings, rather than with other people) ○ *Her thoughts turned inwards.* ⇨ note at FORWARD². **2** towards the inside: *toes turned inwards.*
inwardly *adv* in the mind or spirit; without the specified thoughts or feelings being expressed to

---

[V.*to* inf] = verb + *to* infinitive   [Vn.inf (no *to*)] = verb + noun + infinitive without *to*   [V.*ing*] = verb + -*ing* form

others: *be inwardly grateful/relieved/amused* ○ *groan/sigh/smile inwardly.*
inwardness *n* [U] (*fml*) the inner nature or meaning of sth: *the inwardness of his writings.*
■ **ˌinward inˈvestment** *n* [U] (*commerce*) investment by foreign companies and organizations in one's own country.
iodine /ˈaɪədiːn; *US* -daɪn/ *n* [U] (*symb* I) (*chemistry*) a solid, but not metallic, element found in sea water. A purple solution of this is sometimes used as an ANTISEPTIC on wounds. ⇨ App 7.
ion /ˈaɪən, ˈaɪɒn/ *n* (*chemistry or physics*) an atom with a positive or negative electric charge caused by its gaining or losing one or more electrons (ELECTRON).
▶ **ionize, -ise** /ˈaɪənaɪz/ *v* [V, Vn] (esp passive) to be converted or convert sth into ions. **ionization, -isation** /ˌaɪənaɪˈzeɪʃn; *US* -nəˈz-/ *n* [U].
ionizer *n* a device used to improve the quality of air in a room by producing negative ions.
-ion (also **-ation, -ition, -sion, -tion, -xion**) *suff* (with *vs* forming *ns*) the action or condition of: *confession* ○ *hesitation* ○ *competition.*
ionosphere /aɪˈɒnəsfɪə(r)/ *n* [sing] the part of the earth's atmosphere that reflects radio waves round the earth. Compare STRATOSPHERE.
iota /aɪˈəʊtə/ *n* (esp in negative expressions) a very small amount: *There is not an/one iota of truth* (ie no truth at all) *in the story.*
IOU /ˌaɪ əʊ ˈjuː/ *n* (*infml*) (a short form of *I owe you*) a signed paper acknowledging that one owes the sum of money specified: *give sb an IOU for $20.*
IPA /ˌaɪ piː ˈeɪ/ *abbr* International Phonetic Alphabet.
ipso facto /ˌɪpsəʊ ˈfæktəʊ/ *adv* (*Latin fml*) by that very fact: *Young people tend to be regarded ipso facto as layabouts or troublemakers.*
IQ /ˌaɪ ˈkjuː/ *abbr* intelligence quotient (a measure of a person's intelligence calculated from the results of special tests): *have a high/low IQ* ○ *an IQ of 120* ○ *an IQ test.*
ir- ⇨ IN-². ⇨ note at UN-.
IRA /ˌaɪ ɑːr ˈeɪ/ *abbr* Irish Republican Army: *an IRA attack* ○ *a member of the IRA.*
irascible /ɪˈræsəbl/ *adj* (*fml*) (of a person) easily made angry. ▶ **irascibility** /ɪˌræsəˈbɪləti/ *n* [U].
irate /aɪˈreɪt/ *adj* very angry: *irate customers demanding their money back.*
ire /ˈaɪə(r)/ *n* [U] (*fml*) anger: *arouse/provoke sb's ire.*
iridescent /ˌɪrɪˈdesnt/ *adj* (*fml*) showing many bright colours which appear to change when seen from different angles: *a bird with iridescent blue-green feathers.* ▶ **iridescence** /-ˈdesns/ *n* [U].
iridium /ɪˈrɪdiəm/ *n* [U] (*symb* Ir) a chemical element. Iridium is a hard white metallic substance. ⇨ App 7.
iris /ˈaɪrɪs/ *n* **1** (*anatomy*) the coloured part round the PUPIL² of the eye. ⇨ picture at EYE¹. **2** a tall plant with long pointed leaves and large bright yellow or purple flowers. ⇨ picture at FLOWER.
Irish /ˈaɪrɪʃ/ *adj* of Ireland or its culture, language or people: *the Irish Republic* (ie Eire).
▶ **Irish** *n* **1** the **Irish** [pl *v*] the Irish people. **2** (also **Erse**) [U] the Celtic language of Ireland.
■ **ˌIrish ˈcoffee** *n* [U,C] hot coffee mixed with WHISKY and having thick cream on top.
ˌIrish ˈsetter (also **red setter**) *n* a dog with a smooth shiny reddish coat. ⇨ picture at DOG¹.
ˌIrish ˈstew *n* [U,C] a dish of MUTTON boiled with onions and other vegetables.
Irishman /ˈaɪrɪʃmən/ *n* (*pl* **-men** /-mən/; *fem* **Irishwoman** /-wʊmən/, *pl* **-women** /-wɪmɪn/) a native of Ireland.
irk /ɜːk/ *v* (esp with *it*) to annoy or irritate sb: [Vn] *It irks me to see money being wasted.*

▶ **irksome** /ˈɜːksəm/ *adj* annoying; irritating: *irksome delays* ○ *He found it irksome to have to catch a bus to work.*

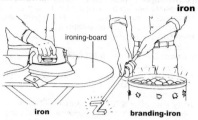

iron

iron

ironing-board

iron　　　　　　　　　branding-iron

iron¹ /ˈaɪən; *US* ˈaɪərn/ *n* **1** [U] (*symb* Fe) a chemical element. Iron is a common, very hard, metal, used esp to make steel. Iron is also found in blood and in all living things: *cast/wrought/scrap iron* ○ *as hard as iron* ○ *iron ore* (ie rock containing iron) ○ *an iron bar/gate/railing* (ie made of iron). ⇨ App 7. **2** [C] an implement with a flat base that can be heated to make clothes, etc smooth: *a* ˈ*steam-iron.* ⇨ picture. **3** [C] (esp in compounds) a tool made of iron: *a* ˈ*branding-iron* (eg for marking cattle, etc). ⇨ picture. **4** [C] a golf club with an iron or steel head. Compare WOOD 4. **5 irons** [pl] (esp formerly) chains or other fastenings put round the wrists and ankles of prisoners: *clap sb in irons.* **6** [U] a preparation of iron as a medicine: ˈ*iron tablets.* **7** [U esp attrib] (showing) physical or moral strength: *have an iron constitution* (ie very good health) ○ *an iron grip* ○ *have a will of iron/an iron will.* **IDM** **have many, etc irons in the ˈfire** to have many resources or courses of action available or be involved in many activities, areas of business, etc at the same time. **pump iron** ⇨ PUMP¹ *v.* **rule with a rod of iron** ⇨ RULE. **strike while the iron is hot** ⇨ STRIKE².
■ **the ˈIron Age** *n* [sing] the period following the Bronze Age, when iron began to be used for making tools and weapons.
the ˌIron ˈCurtain *n* [sing] (formerly) the frontier separating the former Soviet Union and other Communist countries of Eastern Europe from the West: *life behind the Iron Curtain.*
ˌiron-ˈgrey (*US* **iron-gray**) *adj* of a dark grey colour: ˌ*iron-grey* ˈ*hair.*
ˌiron ˈrations *n* [pl] a small supply of food to be used only in an emergency by soldiers, climbers (CLIMB), etc.
iron² /ˈaɪən; *US* ˈaɪərn/ *v* to make clothes, etc smooth with an iron¹(2): [Vn] *iron a shirt* [V] *She listened to the radio while she was ironing.* See also PRESS² 5. **PHRV** **ˌiron sth ˈout 1** to resolve sth that is causing difficulty, esp by discussion: *iron out misunderstandings/problems.* **2** to remove sth by ironing: *iron out creases.*
▶ **ironing** *n* [U] **(a)** the task of ironing clothes, etc: *do the ironing.* **(b)** clothes that need to be or have just been ironed: *a pile of ironing.* ˈ**ironing-board** *n* a board covered with soft material and usu with folding legs, on which clothes are ironed. ⇨ picture at IRON¹.
ironic /aɪˈrɒnɪk/ (also **ironical** /aɪˈrɒnɪkl/) *adj* **(a)** indicating that one means the opposite of what one is saying; using or expressing IRONY(1): *an ironic expression/smile/remark.* Compare SARCASM. **(b)** happening in the opposite way to what is expected, and often causing amusement because of this: *His death gave an ironic twist to the story* (eg because he died before he could enjoy the money he had stolen). ○ *It's ironic that she became a teacher, because she used to hate school when she was a girl.*
▶ **ironically** /-kli/ *adv* **1** (qualifying a whole sentence) it seems ironic that: *Ironically, she achieved*

her biggest success with what she felt was her worst book. **2** in an ironic manner: *He smiled ironically.*

ironmonger /ˈaɪənmʌŋɡə(r)/; *US* ˈaɪərn-/ (*Brit*) (*US* **ˈhardware dealer**) *n* a shopkeeper who trades in tools, household implements, etc. ▶ **ˈironmongery** /-mʌŋɡəri/ (*Brit*) (*US* **hardware**) *n* [U].

ironstone /ˈaɪənstəʊn/ *n* [U] a type of rock containing iron.

ironwork /ˈaɪənwɜːk/ *n* [U] things made of iron, eg rails or gates.

ironworks /ˈaɪənwɜːks/ *n* [sing or pl *v*] a place where iron is obtained from ORE or where heavy iron goods are made.

irony /ˈaɪrəni/ *n* **1** [U] the expression of one's meaning by saying the direct opposite of what one is thinking but using tone of voice to indicate one's real meaning. Irony is used in order to be amusing or to give sth emphasis: *'That's really lovely, that is!'* he said with heavy irony.* Compare SARCASM. **2** [U,C] a situation, an event, etc that seems deliberately contrary to what one expects, and is often amusing as a result: *the irony of fate ○ one of life's little ironies.*

irradiate /ɪˈreɪdieɪt/ *v* **1** (*techn*) to direct energy in the form of rays, esp RADIOACTIVE rays or light, onto sth: [Vn] *irradiated food* (ie food that has had RADIOACTIVE rays directed onto it to preserve it) [also Vnpr]. **2** ~ sth (**with sth**) (*fml*) (esp passive) to make sth brighter: [Vnpr] *faces irradiated with joy.* [also Vn]. ▶ **irradiation** /ɪˌreɪdiˈeɪʃn/ *n* [U]: *ultraviolet irradiation ○ Irradiation may reduce the nutritional value of food.*

irrational /ɪˈræʃənl/ *adj* not guided by reason; not logical: *irrational fears/behaviour/arguments.* ▶ **irrationality** /ɪˌræʃəˈnæləti/ *n* [U]. **irrationally** /ɪˈræʃnəli/ *adv: act/behave irrationally.*

irreconcilable /ɪˈrekənsaɪləbl, ɪˌrekənˈsaɪləbl/ *adj* ~ (**with sb/sth**) (*fml*) (**a**) (of people) not able to be persuaded to stop quarrelling. (**b**) (of ideas or actions) that cannot be brought into harmony with each other: *irreconcilable views/differences/facts.*

irrecoverable /ˌɪrɪˈkʌvərəbl/ *adj* (*fml*) that cannot be recovered or regained: *suffer irrecoverable losses* (eg in business). ▶ **irrecoverably** /-əbli/ *adv: Much of her work is now irrecoverably lost.*

irredeemable /ˌɪrɪˈdiːməbl/ *adj* (*fml*) that cannot be corrected or saved: *irredeemable mistakes ○ man's irredeemable nature.* ▶ **irredeemably** /-əbli/ *adv* (*fml*): *irredeemably wicked/evil.*

irreducible /ˌɪrɪˈdjuːsəbl; *US* -ˈduːs-/ *adj* (*fml*) that cannot be made smaller or simpler: *cut expenditure to an irreducible minimum ○ an irreducible fact.* ▶ **irreducibly** /-əbli/ *adv.*

irrefutable /ˌɪrɪˈfjuːtəbl, ɪˈrefjətəbl/ *adj* (*fml*) that cannot be proved false: *irrefutable evidence/proof/facts.* ▶ **irrefutably** /-əbli/ *adv: This cannot be irrefutably proved.*

irregular /ɪˈreɡjələ(r)/ *adj* ~ (**in sth**) **1** not regular in shape, arrangement, etc; not even²(1): *a coast with an irregular outline ○ irregular teeth.* **2** not happening, coming, going, etc regularly; varying: *an irregular pulse ○ occur at irregular intervals ○ be irregular in attending class.* **3** contrary to the rules or to what is normal or established: *an irregular practice/situation ○ keep irregular hours* (eg get up and go to bed at unusual times) *○ His behaviour is highly irregular.* **4** (*grammar*) not formed in the usual way: *irregular verbs ○ 'Child' has an irregular plural, ie 'children'.* ⇨ App 1. **5** (of troops) not belonging to the regular armed forces. ▶ **irregular** *n* (usu *pl*) a member of an irregular(5) military force.

irregularity /ɪˌreɡjəˈlærəti/ *n* **1** [U] the state or quality of being irregular: *The natural world is full of irregularity and random alteration.* **2** [C] a thing that is irregular: *the irregularities of the earth's surface ○ There were some irregularities in the ac-*

counts (eg figures that were not correct). **3** [U] (*US*) = CONSTIPATION.

irregularly *adv.*

irrelevant /ɪˈreləvənt/ *adj* ~ (**to sth**) not connected with sth; not relevant to sth: *irrelevant remarks ○ What you say is irrelevant to the matter in hand.* ▶ **irrelevance** /-əns/ (also **irrelevancy** /-ənsi/) *n* **1** [U] the state of being irrelevant: *the irrelevance of the curriculum to the children's daily life.* **2** [C usu sing] an irrelevant idea, system, etc: *If the law is no longer enforced, it becomes an irrelevance.*

irrelevantly *adv.*

irreligious /ˌɪrɪˈlɪdʒəs/ *adj* feeling no interest in, or showing a lack of respect for, religion: *an irreligious person/act.*

irremediable /ˌɪrɪˈmiːdiəbl/ *adj* (*fml*) that cannot be corrected or put right: *the irremediable destruction of the landscape.* ▶ **irremediably** /-əbli/ *adv.*

irreparable /ɪˈrepərəbl/ *adj* (of a loss, an injury, etc) that cannot be put right, restored or repaired: *cause/do irreparable damage/harm ○ His death is an irreparable loss to the nation.* ▶ **irreparably** /-əbli/ *adv.*

irreplaceable /ˌɪrɪˈpleɪsəbl/ *adj* that cannot be replaced if lost or damaged: *an irreplaceable antique vase.*

irrepressible /ˌɪrɪˈpresəbl/ *adj* that cannot be held back or controlled: *irrepressible laughter/good humour/high spirits ○ Even the irrepressible Sarah Mills was silent.* ▶ **irrepressibly** /-əbli/ *adv.*

irreproachable /ˌɪrɪˈprəʊtʃəbl/ *adj* free from blame or fault: *irreproachable behaviour.*

irresistible /ˌɪrɪˈzɪstəbl/ *adj* **1** too strong to be resisted or denied: *He felt an irresistible temptation/urge/impulse to slap her. ○ His arguments were irresistible.* **2** too delightful or attractive to be resisted: *On such a hot day, the sea was irresistible* (ie We couldn't resist the desire to swim in it). *○ She found his charms irresistible.* ▶ **irresistibly** /-əbli/ *adv: They were irresistibly drawn to each other.*

irresolute /ɪˈrezəluːt/ *adj* (*fml*) feeling or showing uncertainty; hesitating: *He paused, tense and irresolute.* ▶ **irresolutely** *adv.* **irresolution** /ɪˌrezəˈluːʃn/ *n* [U].

irrespective /ˌɪrɪˈspektɪv/ **irrespective of** *prep* not taking account of or considering sth/sb: *Candidates are assessed on merit, irrespective of race, creed or colour. ○ The weekly rent is the same irrespective of the number of occupants.*

irresponsible /ˌɪrɪˈspɒnsəbl/ *adj* (of people, actions, etc) not showing a proper sense of responsibility: *an irresponsible child ○ irresponsible behaviour ○ It was irresponsible of you to leave the car unlocked.* ▶ **irresponsibility** /ˌɪrɪˌspɒnsəˈbɪləti/ *n* [U]. **irresponsibly** /-əbli/ *adv.*

irretrievable /ˌɪrɪˈtriːvəbl/ *adj* (*fml*) that cannot be put right: *an irretrievable situation ○ the irretrievable breakdown of their marriage.* ▶ **irretrievably** /-əbli/ *adv.*

irreverent /ɪˈrevərənt/ *adj* feeling or showing no respect for sb/sth generally respected by others: *irreverent laughter/humour.* ▶ **irreverence** /-əns/ *n* [U]. **irreverently** *adv.*

irreversible /ˌɪrɪˈvɜːsəbl/ *adj* that cannot be reversed or changed back to the original state: *an irreversible change/decline ○ He suffered irreversible brain damage in the crash.* ▶ **irreversibly** /-əbli/ *adv.*

irrevocable /ɪˈrevəkəbl/ *adj* that cannot be changed or altered; final: *an irrevocable decision/judgement.* ▶ **irrevocably** /-əbli/ *adv.*

irrigate /ˈɪrɪɡeɪt/ *v* to supply land or crops with water, esp by means of specially constructed channels or pipes: [Vn] *irrigate desert areas to make them fertile.* ▶ **irrigation** /ˌɪrɪˈɡeɪʃn/ *n* [U]: *irrigation ca-*

nals ○ *Irrigation has greatly increased the area of cultivable land.*

irritable /ˈɪrɪtəbl/ *adj* easily annoyed or made angry: *The delay made everybody strained and irritable.* ▶ **irritability** /ˌɪrɪtəˈbɪləti/ *n* [U]. **irritably** /-əbli/ *adv*: *'Can't you be quiet!' his mother said irritably.*

irritant /ˈɪrɪtənt/ *n* **1** a substance that causes slight discomfort to a part of the body, eg pepper in the nose. **2** a thing that annoys sb: *The noise of traffic is a constant irritant.*
▶ **irritant** *adj* [usu attrib] causing slight discomfort to a part of the body: *exposure of the skin to irritant chemicals.*

irritate /ˈɪrɪteɪt/ *v* **1** to make sb angry, annoyed or IMPATIENT(1): [Vn, Vnpr] *be irritated by/at the delay* ○ *It irritates me to have to tidy up after others.* **2(a)** (*biology*) to cause discomfort to a part of the body: [Vn] *Acid irritates the stomach lining.* **(b)** to make sth sore: [Vn] *The smoke irritates my eyes.*
▶ **irritated** *adj* annoyed or angry: *She sounded irritated and upset.*
irritating *adj*: *an irritating habit/attitude/delay* ○ *mosquito bites which become large and irritating.* **irritatingly** *adv.*
irritation /ˌɪrɪˈteɪʃn/ *n* [U, C]: *John noted with some irritation that the gate had been left open.* ○ *a skin irritation.*

irruption /ɪˈrʌpʃn/ *n* [C] ~ (**into sth**) (*fml*) a sudden and violent entry; an act of bursting in: *the irruption of modernism into literature.*

Is *abbr* Island(s); Isle(s): *(the) Windward Is* (ie Islands) ○ *(the) British Is* (ie Isles). Compare I *abbr.*

is /s, z; *strong form* ɪz/ ⇨ BE.

ISBN /ˌaɪ es biː ˈen/ *abbr* International Standard Book Number (a number that identifies an individual book, etc and its publisher (PUBLISH)).

-ise ⇨ -IZE.

-ish *suff* **1** (with *ns* forming *adjs* and *ns*) of or from the specified country: *Turkish* ○ *Irish.* **2** (with *ns* forming *adjs*) (*often derog*) of the nature of; resembling: *childish* ○ *freakish.* **3** (with *adjs*) rather; approximately: *reddish* ○ *thirtyish.* ▶ **-ishly** (with sense 2 forming *advs*): *foolishly.*

Islam /ˈɪzlɑːm, ɪzˈlɑːm/ *n* **1** [U] the Muslim religion, based on belief in one God and revealed through the Prophet Muhammad. **2** [sing] all Muslims and Muslim countries in the world. ▶ **Islamic** /ɪzˈlæmɪk, -ˈlɑːm-/ *adj*: *Islamic law.*

island /ˈaɪlənd/ *n* **1** (*abbrs* I, Is) a piece of land surrounded by water: *a group of tropical islands* ○ *The Shetlanders are an island race.* **2** = TRAFFIC ISLAND. See also DESERT ISLAND.
▶ **islander** *n* a person living on an island, esp a small or remote one.

isle /aɪl/ *n* (*abbrs* I, Is) (esp in poetry and proper names) an island: *the Isle of Skye* ○ *the British Isles.*
▶ **islet** /ˈaɪlət/ *n* a small island.

ism /ˈɪzəm/ *n* (*usu derog*) any distinctive practice, system or philosophy: *behaviourism and all the other isms of the 20th century.*

-ism *suff* **1** (with *vs* ending in *-ize/-ise* forming *ns*): *baptism* ○ *criticism.* **2(a)** (with *ns* forming *ns*) showing qualities typical of: *heroism* ○ *Americanism.* **(b)** (with proper *ns* forming uncountable *ns*) the teaching, system or movement(5) of sth: *Buddhism* ○ *Communism.* **(c)** (with *ns*) the medical condition or disease indicated: *alcoholism.* **(d)** (with *ns*) the practice of showing prejudice on the grounds specified: *sexism* ○ *racism.*

isn't /ˈɪznt/ *short form* is not. ⇨ note at BE.

is(o)- *comb form* equal: *isobar* ○ *isometric.*

isobar /ˈaɪsəbɑː(r)/ *n* a line on a map, esp a weather chart, joining places with the same air pressure at a particular time.

isolate /ˈaɪsəleɪt/ *v* **1** ~ *oneself/sb/sth* (**from sb/**

sth) (esp *passive*) to put or keep sb/sth entirely apart from other people or things: [Vn, Vnpr] *When a person has an infectious disease, they are usually isolated (from other people).* [Vnpr] *Britain has isolated itself from other members of the Community.* [Vn] *Several villages have been isolated by heavy snowfalls.* **2(a)** to identify sth and deal with it separately: [Vn] *isolate a problem/cause.* **(b)** ~ *sth* (**from sth**) (*chemistry*) to separate a single substance, GERM(1), etc from others combined or linked with it: [Vn] *Scientists have isolated the virus causing the epidemic.* [also Vnpr].
▶ **isolated** *adj* **1** separate; single: *an isolated outbreak of smallpox* ○ *an isolated case/instance/occurrence.* **2** standing alone, esp far from others; SOLITARY(2): *an isolated building.* **3** having little contact with, or nothing in common with, other people: *feel lonely and isolated* ○ *Writers sometimes lead isolated lives.*

isolation /ˌaɪsəˈleɪʃn/ *n* [U] ~ (**from sb/sth**) the action of isolating sb/sth or the state of being isolated: *feelings of isolation in a new community* ○ *an isolation hospital/ward* (ie for people with infectious diseases). **ᴵᴰᴹ in isolation (from sb/sth)** separately; alone: *examine each piece of evidence in isolation* ○ *Looked at in isolation, these figures are not encouraging.*

isolationism /ˌaɪsəˈleɪʃənɪzəm/ *n* [U] the policy of not becoming involved in the affairs of other countries or groups. ▶ **isolationist** /-ʃənɪst/ *n, adj.*

isometric /ˌaɪsəˈmetrɪk/ *adj* (*techn*) **1** of a type of physical exercise in which muscles are made to work without much movement of the body, eg by pressing, etc. **2** of a style of drawing in three dimensions without PERSPECTIVE(1): *isometric projection.*

isosceles /aɪˈsɒsəliːz/ *adj* (*geometry*) (of a TRIANGLE (1)) having two sides equal in length. ⇨ picture at TRIANGLE.

isotope /ˈaɪsətəʊp/ *n* one of two or more forms of a chemical element with different atomic weight and different nuclear properties but the same chemical properties: *radioactive isotopes.*

issue /ˈɪʃuː; *Brit also* ˈɪsjuː, ˈɪʃjuː/ *n* **1** [C] an important topic for discussion or argument: *a vital/political/controversial issue* ○ *debate an issue* ○ *evade/avoid the issue* ○ *resolve/confuse the issue* ○ *What's at issue* (ie The point being discussed) *here is the whole future of the industry.* **2** [C] each of a regular series of publications: *the July issue of 'Yachting Monthly'.* **3(a)** [U] the supply or release of items for use or sale: *buy a set of new stamps on the day of issue* ○ *the issue of blankets to refugees* ○ *the issue of a joint statement by the French and German foreign ministers.* **(b)** [C] a number, quantity or set of items supplied and distributed at one time: *a share/rights issue* ○ *a special issue of stamps/banknotes.* **4** [sing] (*fml*) the result or outcome of sth: *bring a campaign to a successful issue.* **5(a)** [U] the action of coming, going or flowing out: *the place/point of issue of a stream.* **(b)** [sing] a flow of liquid: *an issue of blood from a wound.* **6** [U] (*law*) children of one's own: *die without issue* (ie without having had children). **ᴵᴰᴹ make an ˈissue (out) of sth** to treat a minor matter too seriously: *It's only a small disagreement — let's not make an issue of it.* **take ˈissue with sb (about/on/over sth)** to start disagreeing or arguing with sb about sth.
▶ **issue** *v* **1** ~ *sth* (**to sb**) to make sth known formally: [Vn] *issue orders/instructions* ○ *issue a challenge* ○ *The police have issued an appeal for witnesses to the accident.* **2** ~ *sth* (**to sb**)/*sb* **with sth** to supply or distribute sth to sb for their use: [Vnpr] *issue visas to foreign visitors* ○ *issue the survivors with warm clothing* [also Vn]. **3** to publish books, articles, etc; to put stamps, money, etc into

general use: [Vn] *issue a revised edition of a textbook.* **PHRV** **issue from sth** (*fml*) to come, go or flow out: *blood issuing from a wound* ∘ *smoke issuing from a chimney* ∘ *A strange noise issued from the darkness.*

-ist *suff* **1** (with *ns* ending in *-ism*) a person believing in or practising: *atheist* ∘ *journalist* ∘ *socialist.* **2** (with *ns* forming *ns*) a person concerned with: *physicist* ∘ *motorist* ∘ *violinist.* **3** (with *vs* ending in *-ize/-ise* forming *ns*) a person who does the specified action: *dramatist* ∘ *publicist.*

isthmus /ˈɪsməs/ *n* (*pl* **-es**) a narrow strip of land joining two larger areas of land that would otherwise be separated by water: *the Isthmus of Panama.*

IT /ˌaɪ ˈtiː/ *abbr* (*computing*) Information Technology.

it¹ /ɪt/ *pers pron* (used as the subject or object of a *v* or after a *prep*) **1(a)** an animal or a thing mentioned earlier or being observed now: *'Where's your car?' 'It's in the garage.'* ∘ *Did you hit it?* ∘ *Fill a glass with water and dissolve this tablet in it.* ∘ *We have $500. Will it be enough for a deposit?* **(b)** a baby, esp one whose sex is not known or not relevant: *Her baby's due next month. She hopes it will be a boy.* **2** a fact or situation already known, implied or happening: *When the factory closes, it (ie this event) will mean 500 people losing their jobs.* ∘ *Yes, I was at home on Sunday. What about/of it?* (ie Why do you ask?) ∘ *Stop it, you're hurting me!* **3** (used to identify a person): *It's the postman.* ∘ *Hello, Peter, it's Mike here.* ∘ *Was it you who put these books on my desk?* **IDM** **this/that is ˈit** **1** this/that is what is required: *We've been looking for a house for months and I think this is ˈit.* **2** this/that is the important point, reason, etc: *That's just ˈit — I can't work when you're making so much noise.* **3** this/that is the end: *I'm afraid that's ˈit — we've lost the match.*
▶ **its** /ɪts/ *possess det* of or belonging to a thing, an animal or a baby: *We wanted to buy the table but its surface was damaged.* ∘ *Have you any idea of its value?* ∘ *The dog had hurt its paw.* ∘ *The baby threw its food on the floor.*

it² /ɪt/ *pron* **1** (used in the normal subject or object position when a more specific subject or object is given at the end of a sentence or as a separate clause): *Does it matter what colour it is?* ∘ *It's impossible (for us) to get there in time.* ∘ *It's no use shouting.* ∘ *She finds it boring at home.* ∘ *It appears that the two leaders are holding secret talks.* ∘ *I find it strange that she doesn't want to travel.* **2** (used in the normal subject position to make a statement about time, distance or weather): *It's ten past twelve.* ∘ *It's our anniversary.* ∘ *It's two miles to the beach.* ∘ *It's a long time since they left.* ∘ *It was raining this morning.* ∘ *It's quite warm at the moment.* **3** circumstances or conditions; things in general: *If it's convenient I can see you tomorrow.* ∘ *It's getting very competitive in the car industry.* **4** (used to emphasize any part of a sentence): *It's ˈJim who's the clever one.* ∘ *It's ˈSpain that they're going to, not Portugal.* ∘ *It was three weeks ˈlater that he heard the news.*

italic /ɪˈtælɪk/ *adj* (of written or printed letters) sloping forwards: *write in italic script* ∘ *This sentence is in italic type.* Compare ROMAN 3.
▶ **italicize, -ise** /ɪˈtælɪsaɪz/ *v* (often passive) to print sth in italic type, eg for emphasis: [Vn] *I have italicized the words 'in my judgement'.*
italics *n* [pl] printed italic letters: *Examples in this dictionary are in italics.* ⇨ App 3.

itch /ɪtʃ/ *n* **1** [C usu *sing*] an uncomfortable feeling on the skin that causes a desire to scratch: *get/have/feel an itch.* **2** [*sing*] ~ **for sth / to do sth** (*infml*) a constant desire: *have an itch for adventure* ∘ *She cannot resist the itch to travel.* **IDM** **the seven-year ˈitch** (*infml joc*) the desire for new sexual experience that is thought to be felt after about seven years of marriage.
▶ **itch** *v* **1** to have or cause an itch: [V] *My nose is itching.* ∘ *These mosquito bites itch terribly.* **2** ~ **for sth / to do sth** (*infml*) to feel a constant desire for sth: [Vpr] *students itching for the lesson to end* [V.to inf] *I'm itching to tell you my news!*
itchy *adj* (**-ier** /ˈɪtʃiə(r)/, **-iest** /ˈɪtʃiɪst/) having or producing an itch on the skin: *an itchy nose* ∘ *feel itchy all over.* **IDM** **(get/have) itchy ˈfeet** (*infml*) (to feel) a desire to travel or move from place to place: *After a few years in one place, I get itchy feet again.*
itchiness *n* [U].

it'd /ˈɪtəd/ *short form* **1** it had. ⇨ note at HAVE. **2** it would. ⇨ WILL¹, WOULD.

-ite *suff* (with proper *ns* forming *ns*) a follower or supporter of: *Labourite* ∘ *Reaganite.*

item /ˈaɪtəm/ *n* **1** a single article or unit in a list, etc: *the first item on the agenda* ∘ *check the items in a catalogue.* **2** a single piece of news: *There's a strange news item/item of news in today's paper.*
▶ **itemize, -ise** /ˈaɪtəmaɪz/ *v* to give or write every item of sth: [Vn] *an itemized list/account/bill.*

itinerant /aɪˈtɪnərənt/ *adj* [usu attrib] (*fml*) travelling from place to place: *an itinerant musician/entertainer/worker* ∘ *lead an itinerant life.*
▶ **itinerant** *n* (*fml*) a person who travels from place to place.

itinerary /aɪˈtɪnərəri; *US* aɪˈtɪnəreri/ *n* a plan for, or record of, a journey; a route: *keep to/depart from/follow one's itinerary* ∘ *an itinerary that includes a visit to the Taj Mahal.*

-ition ⇨ -ION.

-itis *suff* (with *ns* forming uncountable *ns*) **1** (*medical*) a disease of: *appendicitis* ∘ *tonsillitis.* **2** (*infml esp joc*) an excessive interest in or exposure to: *World Cup-itis.*

it'll /ˈɪtl/ *short form* it will. ⇨ WILL¹.

its ⇨ IT¹.

it's /ɪts/ *short form* **1** it is. ⇨ note at BE². **2** it has. ⇨ note at HAVE.

itself /ɪtˈself/ *reflex, emph pron* (only taking the main stress in sentences when used for emphasis) **1** (*reflex*) (used when the animal, thing, etc causing the action is also affected by it): *The cat was ˈwashing itself.* ∘ *The company has ˌgot itself into ˈdifficulties.* **2** (*emph*) (used to emphasize an animal, a thing, etc): *The village it ˈself is pretty, but the surrounding countryside is rather dull.* **IDM** **be ˌhonesty, ˌpatience, simˌplicity, etc it ˈself** to be an example of complete honesty, etc: *The manager of the hotel was ˌcourtesy it ˈself.* **by it ˈself** **1** automatically: *The machine will start by itself in a few seconds.* **2** alone: *The statue stands by itself in the square.* **in it ˈself** considering only the thing specified; in its true nature: *In itself, the film was pretty unoriginal, but it was still very popular.*

ITV /ˌaɪ tiː ˈviː/ *abbr* (*Brit*) Independent Television: *watch (a film on) ITV* ∘ *an ITV documentary.* Compare BBC, IBA.

-ity *suff* (with *adjs* forming *ns*): *purity* ∘ *oddity.*

IUD /ˌaɪ juː ˈdiː/ *abbr* intra-uterine (contraceptive) device: *fit/use an IUD.*

I've /aɪv/ *short form* I have. ⇨ note at HAVE.

-ive *suff* (with *vs* forming *ns* and *adjs*) (a person or thing) having a tendency to or the quality of: *explosive* ∘ *captive* ∘ *descriptive.*

ivory /ˈaɪvəri/ *n* **1** [U] a substance like bone forming the tusks (TUSK) of elephants and certain other animals: *a ban on the ivory trade.* **2** [C] an object made of ivory: *a priceless collection of ivories.* **3** [U] the colour of ivory: *an ivory skin/complexion.*
■ **ˌivory ˈtower** *n* a place or situation where people retreat from the unpleasant realities of everyday life

---

[V.*to* inf] = verb + *to* infinitive   [Vn.inf (no *to*)] = verb + noun + infinitive without *to*   [V.*ing*] = verb + *-ing* form

and pretend that these do not exist: *live in an ivory tower* ○ *lead an ˌivory-tower eˈxistence.*

ivy /ˈaɪvi/ *n* [U] a climbing green plant, esp one that has dark shiny leaves with five points: *ivy-covered walls.*

■ **the ˌIvy ˈLeague** *n* [sing] a group of traditional universities in the eastern USA with a reputation for high academic standards and a high social status.

-ize, -ise *suff* (with *ns* and *adjs* forming *vs*) **1** to become or make like: *dramatize* ○ *miniaturize.* **2** to act or treat with the qualities of: *criticize* ○ *deputize.* **3** to place in: *containerize* ○ *hospitalize.* ▶ **-ization,**

-isation (forming *ns*): *immunization.* **-izationally, -isationally** (forming *advs*): *organizationally.*

NOTE In some words ending with the sound /aɪz/ **-ize** and **-ise** are equally acceptable spellings: *criticize/criticise.* In the same way both **-isation** and **-ization** are acceptable: *organization/organisation.* **-ise** is more common in British than American English. In this dictionary both spellings are shown when both are possible. There are some words which are always spelt with **-ise**, because of their origin. These include *advise, surprise, despise, exercise* and *advertise.*

Jj

J (also **j**) /dʒeɪ/ n (pl **J's**, **j's** /dʒeɪz/) the 10th letter of the English alphabet: *'John' begins with (a) J/'J'*.

jab /dʒæb/ v (**-bb-**) ~ (**at sb/sth**); ~ **sb/sth** (**with sth**) to push or POKE¹(1) at sb/sth quickly and roughly, esp with sth sharp or pointed: [Vpr] *He kept jabbing at the paper cup with his pencil.* ○ *The boxer jabbed* (ie aimed a quick blow) *at his opponent* [Vnpr] *She jabbed her finger at the papers on the desk.* [Vnp] *You nearly jabbed my eye out with your umbrella!* [also Vn]. ⇨ note at NUDGE.
▶ **jab** n **1** a sudden rough blow, usu with sth pointed: *give sb a jab in the ribs.* **2** (*Brit infml*) an injection (INJECT 1) to help prevent one catching a disease; a vaccination (VACCINATE): *Have you had your typhoid jabs yet?*

jabber /ˈdʒæbə(r)/ v (**a**) ~ (**away**) to talk rapidly in an excited manner: [V] *jabbering crowds* [Vp] *They were jabbering away in a foreign language.* (**b**) to say sth rapidly and not clearly, eg because one is embarrassed: [Vn, Vnp] *He jabbered (out) an apology.* [also V.speech].

jack¹ /dʒæk/ n **1** a device for raising heavy weights off the ground, esp one for raising a motor vehicle so that a wheel can be changed. **2** a single plug used to connect two pieces of electrical equipment, esp in a HI-FI system: *a jack plug/lead* ○ *The jacks were reversed.* **3** (also **knave**) (in a pack of cards) a card between the ten and the queen: *the jack of clubs.* **4** (in the game of bowls (BOWL² 3)) a small white ball at which players aim. See also UNION JACK. **IDM** **a jack of 'all trades** a person who can do many different types of work but not necessarily very well.
■ **Jack 'Frost** (*joc*) frost considered as a person: *Look what pretty patterns Jack Frost has painted on the windows.*
ˈ**jack-in-the-box** n (pl **-boxes**) a toy in the form of a box with a figure inside on a spring that jumps up when the lid is opened.

jack² /dʒæk/ v **PHRV** ˌ**jack sth** ˈ**in** (*Brit sl*) to abandon sth, eg a job or an attempt: *Days like this make me feel like jacking it all in.* ˌ**jack sth** ˈ**up 1** to raise sth using a JACK¹(1): *jack up a car.* **2** (*infml*) to increase sth by a considerable amount: *jack up the price/pressure.*

jackal /ˈdʒækɔːl, -kl/ n a wild animal of Africa and Asia that is related to the dog. ⇨ picture at WOLF.

jackass /ˈdʒækæs/ n (*infml esp US*) a foolish person.

jackboot /ˈdʒækbuːt/ n **1** a tall boot worn by soldiers, esp formerly. **2** harsh military rule: *be under the jackboot of a dictatorial regime.*

jacket

collar
shirt
sports jacket
button
cuff
tie
lapel
sleeve
buttonhole

jackdaw /ˈdʒækdɔː/ n a black and grey bird of the CROW¹(1) family.

jacket /ˈdʒækɪt/ n **1** a short coat with sleeves: *a denim/tweed jacket.* ⇨ picture. See also DINNER JACKET. **2** (also ˈ**dust-jacket**) a loose paper cover for a book, usu with a design or picture on it. **3** an outer cover round a tank, pipe, etc, eg to reduce loss of heat. **4** (*Brit*) the skin of a potato: *jacket po'tatoes* (ie potatoes baked without the skins being removed).

jackknife /ˈdʒæknaɪf/ n (pl **-knives**) /-naɪvz/ a large knife with a folding blade.
▶ **jackknife** v (esp of a large lorry in two parts) to bend sharply in the middle into a V-shape and go out of control: [V] *An articulated lorry has jackknifed on the M4.*

jackpot /ˈdʒækpɒt/ n (in various games) a STAKE(3) or prize that continues to be added to until it is won. **IDM** **hit the jackpot** ⇨ HIT¹.

jacks /dʒæks/ n [pl] (*esp US*) a game in which players bounce a small ball and pick up small metal objects before catching the ball.

Jacobean /ˌdʒækəˈbiːən/ adj of the reign of the English king, James I (1603–25): ˌ*Jacobean* ˈ*plays*/ˈ*dramatists.*

Jacuzzi /dʒəˈkuːzi/ n (*propr*) a large bath with jets of warm water that give a pleasant feeling to the body.

jade /dʒeɪd/ n [U] (**a**) a hard, usu green, stone from which ornaments are carved: *a jade vase/necklace* ○ *jade-green eyes.* (**b**) ornaments made of jade: *a collection of Chinese jade.*

jaded /ˈdʒeɪdɪd/ adj tired and lacking interest or pleasure in anything, usu after too much of sth: *feeling jaded with city life* ○ *a meal to tempt the most jaded palate/appetite.*

jagged /ˈdʒægɪd/ adj with rough, pointed, often sharp edges: *jagged cliffs/rocks* ○ *a piece of glass with a jagged edge.*

jaguar /ˈdʒægjuə(r)/ n a large member of the cat family with spots on its back that lives in parts of central America.

jail (*Brit* also **gaol**) /dʒeɪl/ n [C,U] a prison: *spend a year in jail* ○ *a ten-year jail sentence.*
▶ **jail** (*Brit* also **gaol**) v ~ **sb** (**for sth**) to put sb in jail: [Vnpr] *He was jailed for six years for his part in the robbery.* [also Vn].

jailer (*Brit* also **gaoler**) /ˈdʒeɪlə(r)/ n a person in charge of a jail and the prisoners in it.

jailbird /ˈdʒeɪlbɜːd/ n (*dated infml*) a person who is often sent to prison.

jalopy /dʒəˈlɒpi/ n (*infml*) an old used car.

jam¹ /dʒæm/ n [U,C] a thick sweet substance made by boiling fruit with sugar: *He spread some strawberry jam on his toast.* ○ *recipes for jams and preserves.* **IDM** **jam to'morrow** a good or pleasant thing that is always promised or expected in the future, but usu never enjoyed. **money for jam / old rope** ⇨ MONEY.
▶ **jammy** /ˈdʒæmi/ adj (*infml*) **1** covered with jam: *Don't wipe your jammy fingers on the tablecloth.* **2** (*Brit infml*) lucky, esp because sth good has happened to one without one's making any effort: *You jammy so-and-so!*

jam² /dʒæm/ v (**-mm-**) **1** ~ **sb/sth in, into, under,**

---

between, etc sth (esp passive) to squeeze sb/sth into a space so that they can hardly move: [Vnpr] *sitting on a bus, jammed between two fat men* ○ *Over 500 people were jammed into the hall.* [Vnp] *Don't park there — you'll probably get jammed in.* **2** to push sth roughly into position or a space, using force: [Vnp] *jam one's hat on* [Vnpr] *He jammed his key into the lock.* **3** ~ sth (**with sth**) to fill or crowd into an area so as to block it: [Vn, Vnp] *Weekend traffic jammed (up) the roads out of town.* [Vnpr] *The BBC switchboard was jammed with complaints.* [Vn-adj] *The terminal was jammed full of people and their luggage.* **4** to become or make sth unable to move or work: [V] *The lock jammed.* [Vn-adj] *The door was jammed open.* [Vn, Vnp] *There's something jamming (up) the photocopier.* **5** (*broadcasting*) to make a message or programme difficult to hear by sending out a signal that interferes with it: [Vn] *jam foreign radio stations.* **PHRV** **ˌjam sth ˈon** (*infml*) to operate sth, esp a BRAKE¹, suddenly and with force: *A child ran into the road and she jammed on the brakes.*

▶ **jam** *n* **1** a crowded mass of people, vehicles, etc that makes movement difficult or impossible: *a ˈtraffic jam* ○ *be stuck in a jam on the M25.* **2** (*infml*) a difficult or awkward situation: *be in/get into a jam.* **3** the failure of a system or machine caused by sth getting stuck or not working properly: *a paper jam in the photocopier* ○ *a jam in the dispatch department.*
■ **ˈjam session** *n* a performance of JAZZ given without previous preparation.

jamb /dʒæm/ *n* an upright post at the side of a door, window or fireplace.

jamboree /ˌdʒæmbəˈriː/ *n* **1** a large party; a celebration. **2** a large gathering of Scouts or Girl Guides.

jamjar /ˈdʒæmdʒɑː(r)/ *n* a glass container for jam.

jam-packed /ˌdʒæmˈpækt/ *adj* [usu pred] ~ (**with sb/sth**) (*infml*) very full or crowded: *a stadium jam-packed with spectators.*

Jan /in informal use dʒæn/ *abbr* January: *1 Jan 1996.*

jangle /ˈdʒæŋgl/ *v* **1** to make or cause sth to make a harsh metallic noise: [V] *bracelets jangling on her wrists* [Vn] *He jangled his keys.* **2** to irritate sb: [Vpr] *Her voice jangled on his ears.* [Vn] *The slow pace jangled her nerves.*
▶ **jangle** *n* [sing] a harsh, usu metallic, noise.

janitor /ˈdʒænɪtə(r)/ *n* (*US*) = CARETAKER.

January /ˈdʒænjuəri; *US* -jueri/ *n* [U, C] (*abbr* **Jan**) the first month of the year.
For further guidance on how *January* is used, see the examples at *April.*

jape /dʒeɪp/ *n* (*dated infml*) a joke played on sb.

japonica /dʒəˈpɒnɪkə/ *n* an ornamental bush with red flowers and pale green fruits.

jar¹ /dʒɑː(r)/ *n* **1(a)** a container, usu made of glass, esp one used for storing food. (**b**) this and its contents: *a jar of coffee/marmalade.* **2** (esp formerly) a tall container with a wide mouth, with or without handles: *clay water jars.* **3** (*Brit sl*) a glass of beer: *Fancy a jar after work?*

jar² /dʒɑː(r)/ *v* (**-rr-**) **1** ~ (**on sth**) to have a harsh or unpleasant effect: [Vpr] *His whistling jarred on my nerves.* **2** ~ (**with sth**) to be different in an unpleasant or annoying way; to CLASH¹(3): [V] *a jarring note of dissent* [Vpr] *His criticism jarred with the friendly tone of the meeting.* **3** to give a sudden or painful shock to sb/sth: [Vn] *He jarred his back badly when he fell.*
▶ **jar** *n* [sing] a sudden unpleasant shock: *The fall gave him a nasty jar.*

jargon /ˈdʒɑːgən/ *n* [U] (*often derog*) technical words or expressions used by a particular profession or group of people and difficult for others to understand: *banking/computer/legal jargon.*

jasmine /ˈdʒæzmɪn/ *n* [U] a plant with white or yellow sweet-smelling flowers.

jaundice /ˈdʒɔːndɪs/ *n* [U] a disease of the blood which makes the skin and the whites of the eyes become yellow.
▶ **jaundiced** *adj* affected by envy, prejudice or spite; bitter(3): *a jaundiced view of life* ○ *look at/on sth with a jaundiced eye.*

jaunt /dʒɔːnt/ *n* a short journey made for pleasure: *She's gone on a jaunt to town.*

jaunty /ˈdʒɔːnti/ *adj* feeling or showing that one is cheerful and full of confidence: *a jaunty tune/ rhythm* ○ *wear one's hat at a jaunty angle* (ie on one side). ▶ **jauntily** *adv*: *stroll jauntily down the road* ○ *'Spot of bother?' he enquired jauntily.* **jauntiness** *n* [U].

javelin /ˈdʒævlɪn/ *n* (**a**) [C] a light SPEAR(1) for throwing, usu in sport. ⇨ picture. (**b**) **the javelin** [sing] a contest in which competitors try to throw a javelin the furthest: *She came second in the javelin.*

javelin

jaw /dʒɔː/ *n* **1(a)** [C usu pl] either of the bone structures containing the teeth: *the upper/lower jaw.* (**b**) [sing] the lower part of the face; the lower jaw: *a man with a strong square jaw* ○ *The punch broke his jaw.* ⇨ picture at HEAD¹. (**c**) **jaws** [pl] the mouth with its bones and teeth: *The crocodile's jaws snapped shut.* ○ (*fig*) *escape from the jaws of* (ie likely) *death/defeat.* **2 jaws** [pl] the narrow mouth¹(2) of a valley or channel. **3 jaws** [pl] the part of a tool or machine that grips or crushes things: *the jaws of a vice.* ⇨ picture at VICE². **4** [C, U] (*infml*) a long talk or gossip: *have a jaw about old times.* **IDM** **one's ˈjaw drops** (*infml*) one shows sudden surprise or disappointment: *My jaw dropped when I saw how much lunch had cost.*

jawbone /ˈdʒɔːbəʊn/ *n* either of the two bones forming the lower jaw.

jay /dʒeɪ/ *n* a noisy bird with bright feathers.

jaywalk /ˈdʒeɪwɔːk/ *v* [V] to walk carelessly across or along town streets without paying attention to traffic.

jazz /dʒæz/ *n* [U] music of African-American origin, with strong rhythms that are freely developed by players during a performance: *traditional/modern jazz* ○ *jazz musicians.* **IDM** **and all that ˈjazz** (*sl usu derog*) and similar things: *She lectured us about the honour of the school and all that jazz.*
▶ **jazz** *v* **PHRV** **ˌjazz sth ˈup** to make sth more interesting or lively: *jazz up a party/a plain dress* ○ *Rock 'n' roll is just a jazzed up form of the blues.*
jazzy *adj* (*infml*) **1** of or like jazz: *a jazzy accompaniment.* **2** bright and likely to attract attention but usu lacking taste¹(6): *jazzy clothes/colours.*

jealous /ˈdʒeləs/ *adj* **1** ~ (**of sb/sth**) feeling or showing that one wishes one had sb else's advantages, possessions or achievements; ENVIOUS: *He was jealous of Tom/of Tom's success.* **2** feeling or showing fear and anger that sb one loves very much loves or is loved by sb else more: *a jealous husband* ○ *jealous looks.* **3** ~ (**of sth**) fiercely protective of one's rights or possessions: *keep a jealous eye on one's property* ○ *She's jealous of her privileges.*
▶ **jealously** *adv*: *a jealously guarded secret.*
jealousy /ˈdʒeləsi/ *n* (**a**) [U] the state or a feeling of being jealous: *be consumed by anger and jealousy.* (**b**) [C] an instance of this; an act or a remark that shows a person to be jealous: *She grew tired of his petty jealousies.* Compare ENVY¹.

jeans /dʒiːnz/ *n* [pl] trousers made of strong cotton,

esp DENIM(1): *a faded pair of blue jeans.* See also
DENIMS.

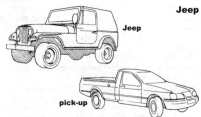

Jeep /dʒiːp/ *n* (*prop*) a small strong motor vehicle
used esp by the army for driving over rough ground.
⇨ picture.

jeer /dʒɪə(r)/ *v* ~ (**at sb/sth**) to laugh and shout rude
remarks at sb/sth; to mock sb/sth: [V] *a jeering
crowd* [Vpr] *jeer at a speaker* [Vn] *be jeered by an
angry mob.*
▶ **jeer** *n* a jeering remark: *He walked out of the
meeting to jeers and catcalls.*

Jehovah /dʒɪˈhəʊvə/ *n* (*Bible*) the name of God used
in the Old Testament.
■ **Je,hovah's 'Witness** *n* a member of a religious
organization which believes that the end of the
world is near and that everyone will be damned
(DAMN¹) except its own members.

jejune /dʒɪˈdʒuːn/ *adj* (*fml*) **1** too simple; NAIVE(1). **2**
(of ideas, writing, etc) dull; not interesting.

Jekyll and Hyde /ˌdʒekl ən ˈhaɪd/ *n* [sing] a single
person with two personalities, one good (*Jekyll*) and
one bad (*Hyde*): *a Jekyll and Hyde reputation.*

jell = GEL *v.*

jelly /ˈdʒeli/ *n* **1(a)** [U, C] (*Brit*) (*US propr* **Jello**) a
clear sweet food, usu with a fruit flavour. It is made
of liquid set¹(12) with GELATINE and shakes when
moved: *children eating jelly and ice-cream* ○ *strawberry jellies* ○ *She went into the interview, her legs
shaking like jelly* (ie because she was very nervous).
(b) [U] a substance like this made from the juices of
meat and GELATINE. **2** [U] a type of clear jam made
of fruit juice and sugar: *blackcurrant jelly* ○ *peanut
butter and jelly sandwiches.* **3** [U] any substance
with the thickness of jelly: *petroleum jelly.* See also
ROYAL JELLY.
▶ **jellied** *adj* [usu attrib] prepared or set¹(12) in
jelly; like jelly: *jellied eels.*
■ **'jelly baby** *n* [usu *pl*] (*Brit*) a small sweet in the
shape of a baby, tasting of fruit and made from
GELATINE.

jellyfish /ˈdʒelifɪʃ/ (*pl* unchanged) a sea creature
with a body like jelly and tentacles (TENTACLE 1) that
can STING²(1).

jemmy /ˈdʒemi/ (*US* **jimmy** /ˈdʒɪmi/) *n* a short
heavy steel bar used eg by a BURGLAR to force open
doors and windows.

je ne sais quoi /ˌʒə nə seɪ ˈkwɑː/ (*French often joc*)
a pleasing quality that is difficult to describe: *Their
conversation lacks a certain je ne sais quoi.*

jeopardize, -ise /ˈdʒepədaɪz/ *v* to cause sth to be
harmed, lost or destroyed; to put sth in danger of
this happening: [Vn] *The security of the whole operation has been jeopardized by their carelessness.*

jeopardy /ˈdʒepədi/ *n* **IDM in 'jeopardy** at risk:
Thousands of jobs are now in jeopardy.

jerk /dʒɜːk/ *n* **1** a sudden quick sharp movement:
*With a jerk of his head he indicated she should
follow.* ○ *The bus stopped with a jerk.* See also PHYS-
ICAL JERKS. **2** (*infml derog*) a stupid person.
▶ **jerk** *v* **1** to pull sth/sb suddenly and quickly in
the specified direction: [Vnpr] *He jerked the fishing-
rod out of the water.* [Vnp] *She jerked her hand away.*

2 to move or make sth/sb move with a short sudden
action or a series of such actions: [Vpr] *The train
jerked to a halt.* [Vp] *She jerked back in surprise.*
[Vn] *Try not to jerk the camera.* [Vnpr] *He jerked his
head towards the door.* [also V, Vnp]. **PHRV jerk sth
out** to say sth in an awkward or nervous manner:
jerk out a request/an apology.
jerky *adj* making sudden starts and stops; not moving or talking smoothly: *short jerky movements/
steps.* **jerkily** /-ɪli/ *adv.*

jerkin /ˈdʒɜːkɪn/ *n* (*Brit*) a short jacket without
sleeves fitting close to the body, worn by men or
women.

jerry-builder /ˈdʒeri bɪldə(r)/ *n* (*derog*) a person
who builds houses quickly and cheaply without concern for quality. ▶ **jerry-built** /ˈdʒeri bɪlt/ *adj*: *a
jerry-built garage.*

jerrycan /ˈdʒerikæn/ *n* a large metal or plastic container with flat sides, used for carrying petrol or
water.

Jersey /ˈdʒɜːzi/ *n* a light brown cow that produces
high quality milk.

jersey /ˈdʒɜːzi/ *n* (*pl* **-eys**) **1** (also **sweater**, *Brit* also
jumper, pullover) [C] a garment of knitted wool or
cotton without fastenings, usu worn over a shirt or
blouse: *a thick green jersey.* ⇨ picture at AMERICAN
FOOTBALL. **2** [U] a soft fine knitted fabric used for
making clothes: *made from 100% cotton jersey.*

Jerusalem artichoke ⇨ ARTICHOKE 2.

jest /dʒest/ *n* (*rather fml*) a thing said or done to
cause amusement; a joke. **IDM in 'jest** as a joke; not
seriously: *The comment was made only half in jest.*
▶ **jest** *v* (*fml*) to make jokes; to speak or act without
being serious: [Vpr] *One should not jest about such
important matters!* [also V, V.speech]. **jester** *n* (formerly) a man whose job was to make jokes to amuse
a royal court¹(2) or noble household.

Jesuit /ˈdʒezjuɪt/ *US* ˈdʒeʒəwət/ *n* a member of the
Society of Jesus, a Roman Catholic religious or-
der¹(12).

Jesus /ˈdʒiːzəs/ ⇨ CHRIST.

jet¹ /dʒet/ *n* **1** an aircraft with one or more jet
engines: *a jet fighter/airliner* ○ *The accident happened as the jet was about to take off.* **2(a)** a strong
narrow stream of gas, liquid, steam or flame, forced
out of a small opening: *The pipe burst and jets of
water shot across the room.* **(b)** a narrow opening
from which this comes: *clean the gas jets on the
cooker.*
▶ **jet** *v* (**-tt-**) (*infml*) to travel by a jet aircraft: [Vpr]
film stars jetting around the world [Vp] *jetting off to
the Seychelles* [also V].
■ **,jet 'engine** *n* an engine that gives forward movement by releasing a stream of gases at high speed
behind it. ⇨ picture at AIRCRAFT.
'jet lag *n* [U] the tired feeling and other physical
effects experienced after a long flight, esp when
there is a great difference in the local times at
which the journey begins and ends. **'jet-lagged** *adj*
affected by jet lag.
,jet-pro'pelled *adj* driven by jet engines. **,jet
pro'pulsion** *n* [U].
the 'jet set *n* [Gp] rich, successful and fashionable
people: *a resort favoured by the international jet set.*
'jet-setter *n* a member of the jet set.

jet² /dʒet/ *n* [U] a hard black mineral that can be
polished brightly and is used for jewellery: *jet beads.*
■ **,jet-'black** *adj, n* [U] (of) a deep shiny black: *,jet-
black 'hair.*

jetsam /ˈdʒetsəm/ *n* [U] things thrown away, esp
from a ship at sea. **IDM flotsam and jetsam** ⇨
FLOTSAM.

jettison /ˈdʒetɪsn/ *v* **1** to throw or drop unnecessary
goods or fuel from a ship, an aircraft, a spacecraft,
etc: [Vn] *tankers jettisoning crude oil.* **2** to abandon

[V.*to* inf] = verb + *to* infinitive   [Vn.inf (no *to*)] = verb + noun + infinitive without *to*   [V.*ing*] = verb + *-ing* form

or reject sth that is not wanted: *to jettison one's principles/responsibilities.*

jetty /'dʒeti/ *n* a wall or wooden platform built out into the sea, a river, etc, to which boats can be tied. Compare PIER 2.

Jew /dʒu:/ *n* a person of the Hebrew people or religion.
▶ **Jewess** /'dʒu:əs/ *n* a Jewish woman.
Jewish /'dʒu:ɪʃ/ *adj: the local Jewish community.*
Jewry /'dʒʊəri; *US* 'dʒu:ri/ *n* [Gp] Jewish people as a group: *world Jewry.*

jewel /'dʒu:əl/ *n* **1(a)** a precious stone, eg a diamond or a RUBY(1). **(b)** (esp *pl*) an ornament or a piece of jewellery with such a stone or stones set¹(8) in it: *wear the family jewels* ○ *a jewel box/case* (ie for keeping jewels in). See also CROWN JEWELS. **2** a small precious stone or piece of special glass used in the machinery of a watch: *a watch with 17 jewels.* **3** a person or thing that is greatly valued: *a jewel of an idea* ○ *the brightest jewel in the company's overseas operations.* Compare GEM 2. **IDM the jewel in the 'crown** the most attractive or successful part of sth: *The Knightsbridge branch is the jewel in the crown of a 500-strong chain of shops.*
▶ **jewelled** (*US* **jeweled**) *adj* decorated or set¹(8) with jewels: *a jewelled comb/dagger.*
jeweller (*US* **jeweler**) *n* a person who sells, makes or repairs jewellery or watches.
jewellery (also **jewelry**) /'dʒu:əlri/ *n* [U] ornaments, eg rings and necklaces (NECKLACE), made esp of gold or silver and set¹(8) with jewels. See also COSTUME JEWELLERY.

jib¹ /dʒɪb/ *n* **1** (*nautical*) a small sail in front of the MAINSAIL. ⇨ picture at YACHT. **2** the arm¹(3) of a CRANE¹(1), used for lifting things.

jib² /dʒɪb/ *v* (**-bb-**) ~ (**at sth / doing sth**) to refuse to continue with an action; to be unwilling to do or accept sth: [V] *He jibbed when I told him the price.* [Vpr] *She jibbed at investing any more money in the scheme.*

jibe 1 = GIBE. **2** (*US*) = GYBE.

jiffy /'dʒɪfi/ *n* [C usu *sing*] (*infml*) a moment: *I'll be with you **in a jiffy*** (ie very soon).

Jiffy bag /'dʒɪfi bæg/ *n* (*Brit propr*) a thick protective envelope for posting things in.

jig /dʒɪg/ *n* **1** a quick lively dance or the music for this: *an Irish jig.* **2** (*techn*) a device that holds a piece of work in position and guides the tools that are working on it.
▶ **jig** *v* (**-gg-**) **1** to move or make sb/sth move up and down in a series of short quick movements: [Vp] *jigging up and down in excitement* [Vn, Vnp] *to jig a baby (up and down) on one's knee* [also V]. **2** [V] to dance a jig.

jiggered /'dʒɪgəd/ *adj* [pred] (*dated infml*) surprised: *'Well, **I'll be jiggered**!' he said.*

jiggery-pokery /ˌdʒɪgəri 'pəʊkəri/ *n* [U] (*infml esp Brit*) deceitful or dishonest behaviour: *He began to suspect that there was some jiggery-pokery going on.*

jiggle /'dʒɪgl/ *v* (*infml*) to move about or shake sth lightly and quickly from side to side or up and down: [V] *jiggling in time to the music* [Vn] *jiggle a key in a lock.*

jigsaw /'dʒɪgsɔ:/ *n* **1** (also *Brit* 'jigsaw puzzle, *esp US* puzzle) a picture printed on cardboard or wood cut into various different shapes that have to be fitted together again: *do a jigsaw* ○ (*fig*) *a complex jigsaw of social and economic factors.* ⇨ picture. **2** a SAW² with a fine blade for cutting designs in thin pieces of wood or metal.

jihad /dʒɪ'hɑ:d/ *n* a holy war fought by Muslims against those who reject Islam.

jilt /dʒɪlt/ *v* to end a close emotional relationship with sb in a sudden and unkind way: [Vn] *a jilted lover.*

jimmy (*US*) = JEMMY.

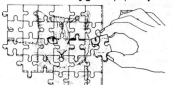
jigsaw (*esp US* **puzzle**)

jingle /'dʒɪŋgl/ *n* **1** [sing] a metallic ringing sound, like that of small bells or of coins or keys knocking against each other: *the jingle of small change in his pocket.* **2** [C] a short simple song or verse that is designed to attract attention and be easily remembered, esp one used in advertising on radio or television.
▶ **jingle** *v* to make or cause sth to make a jingle(1): [V] *jingling bracelets and bangles* [Vn] *He jingled the coins in his pocket.*

jingoism /'dʒɪŋgəʊɪzəm/ *n* [U] (*derog*) extreme and unreasonable belief that one's own country is best, together with an aggressive attitude towards other countries. ▶ **jingoistic** /ˌdʒɪŋgəʊ'ɪstɪk/ *adj: ˌjingo-istic 'patriotism.*

jink /dʒɪŋk/ *v* [V, Vpr, Vp] (*infml*) to move quickly or suddenly with sharp turns, usu to avoid being caught. ▶ **jink** *n*. See also HIGH JINKS.

jinx /dʒɪŋks/ *n* (usu *sing*) ~ (**on sb/sth**) (*infml*) bad luck, or sth/sb that is thought to bring bad luck: *There must be a jinx on this car.*
▶ **jinx** *v* (*infml*) (usu passive) to bring bad luck to sb/sth: [Vn] *a jinxed production of 'Macbeth'.*

jitters /'dʒɪtəz/ *n* (usu **the jitters**) [pl] (*infml*) feelings of being extremely nervous or uncertain about sth: *give sb the jitters* ○ *stock market jitters* ○ *I always **get the jitters** before an interview.*
▶ **jittery** /'dʒɪtəri/ *adj* (*infml*) nervous and uncertain: *jittery investors/financial markets.*

jive /dʒaɪv/ *n* [U] (often **the jive** [sing]) a fast lively form of music with a strong beat²(2); a dance done to this music.
▶ **jive** *v* [V] to dance to jive music.

Jnr (also **Jr**) *abbr* Junior: *John F Davis Jnr* (ie to distinguish him from his father with the same name). Compare SEN 2.

job /dʒɒb/ *n* **1** a paid position of regular employment: *get a part-time job as a gardener* ○ *a holiday job* ○ *Thousands of workers lost their jobs when the factory closed.* ○ *He's been **out of a job*** (ie unemployed) *for six months.* ⇨ note. **2** a particular piece of work; a task: *The shipyard is working on three different jobs* (ie building three ships). ○ *do various jobs around the house* ○ *Writing a book was a more difficult job than he'd thought.* ○ *It was/I had quite a job* (ie a difficult task) *finding this flat.* See also ODD JOBS. ⇨ note at WORK¹. **3** (usu *sing*) a responsibility, duty or function: *It's not my job to lock up!* **4** (*infml*) a thing that is completed; a product: *That car's a neat little job.* **5** (*sl*) a crime, esp stealing: *He got three years for a job he did in Leeds.* **IDM do the 'job/'trick** (*infml*) to succeed in doing what is required or desired: *This extra strong glue should do the job nicely.* **give sb/sth up as a bad 'job** (*infml*) to decide that one can no longer try to help sb or do sth because there seems no hope of success: *His parents have given him up as a bad job.* ○ *After waiting over an hour for the bus she decided to give it up as a bad job.* **a good 'job** (*infml*) (used as a comment on actions or events) a fortunate situation, event or action: *She's stopped smoking, and a good job too!* ○ *It's a good job you were there to help.* **have a hard 'job doing / to do sth** ⇨ HARD¹. **jobs for the 'boys** (*infml*) the giving of paid employment to one's supporters, friends or relations. **just the 'job/**

'ticket (*infml approv*) exactly what is wanted or needed: *Thanks for lending me your lawnmower. It was just the job for the long grass.* **make a bad, excellent, good, poor, etc job of sth** to do sth badly, well, etc: *You've certainly made an excellent job of the kitchen* (eg decorating it). **make the best of a bad job** ⇨ BEST³. **more than one's 'job's worth (to do sth)** (*Brit*) not worth doing since doing it might cause one to be dismissed from one's job: *Asking for an extra week's holiday would probably be more than my job's worth.* **on the 'job** while working; at work: *lie down/go to sleep on the job* (ie not work hard and continuously) ○ *¡on-the-job 'training* (ie training given to workers at their place of work).

▶ **jobless** *adj* unemployed: *The closure left 500 people jobless.* **the jobless** *n* [pl *v*] people who are unemployed: *training programmes for the jobless.* **joblessness** *n* [U].

■ **'job creation** *n* [U] the process of providing opportunities for paid work, esp for those who are currently unemployed: *a job-creation scheme.*

'job description *n* a written description of the exact responsibilities of a job.

'job-hunt *v* [V] (usu in the continuous tenses) to look for paid employment.

¡job 'lot *n* a collection of various different articles, esp of poor quality, offered together for sale: *We bought the equipment as a job lot.*

'job satisfaction *n* [U] satisfaction gained from doing one's job.

'job-sharing *n* [U] an arrangement by which one full-time job is done by two or more employees who share the hours of work and the pay.

NOTE Compare **job, employment, occupation, profession** and **trade**. **Employment** is a formal or official word which means the state of having paid work: *a contract of employment* ○ *Employment agencies help people to find work.* ○ *Are you in full-time employment at the moment?* **Job** means a particular type of paid work that somebody does or is trained to do: *'What's his job?' 'He's a teacher.'* ○ *I'm looking for a job.* **Occupation** is a more formal word than **job** and is used especially in written English, for example on forms and official documents: *Occupation: Teacher.* A **profession** is a job which requires higher education and specific training. A **trade** requires practical training and skill with the hands: *She's a lawyer by profession.* ○ *the medical profession* ○ *He was a gardener by trade.* ○ *the building trade.*

jobbing /'dʒɒbɪŋ/ *adj* [attrib] doing single specific pieces of work for payment: *a jobbing printer/gardener.*

jobcentre /'dʒɒbsentə(r)/ *n* (*Brit*) a government office displaying information about available jobs.

jockey /'dʒɒki/ *n* (*pl* **-eys**) a person who rides in horse races, usu as a profession.

▶ **jockey** /'dʒɒki/ *v* **PHRV** **'jockey for sth** to try by every available means to gain an advantage or a favour: *jockey for position/power/favours.*

jockstrap /'dʒɒkstræp/ *n* a garment worn by men under shorts, trousers, etc to support or protect the genitals (GENITAL), esp while playing sports.

jocose /dʒəʊ'kəʊs/ *adj* (*dated fml*) humorous; playful.

jocular /'dʒɒkjələ(r)/ *adj* (**a**) (abbreviated as *joc* in this dictionary) meant as a joke; humorous: *jocular remarks.* (**b**) fond of joking; playful: *a jocular fellow.*

▶ **jocularity** /ˌdʒɒkjə'lærəti/ *n* [U]. **jocularly** *adv*.

jodhpurs /'dʒɒdpəz/ *n* [pl] trousers that are loose above the knee and tight from the knee to the ankle, worn when riding a horse: *a pair of jodhpurs.*

jog /dʒɒg/ *v* (**-gg-**) (*often* **go jogging**) **1** to run slowly and steadily for a long time, esp for physical exercise: [Vpr] *jog around the park* [V] *He goes jogging*

every evening. ⇨ note at RUN¹. **2** to push or knock sb/sth slightly: [Vn] *He jogged my arm and made me spill my tea.* **3** to move in an unsteady way: [Vp, Vpr] *The wagon jogged along (the rough track).* **IDM** **jog sb's 'memory** to help sb to remember sth: *This photograph may jog your memory.* **PHRV** **¡jog a'long/'on** to continue in a steady manner, with little or no excitement or progress: *For years the business just kept jogging along.*

▶ **jog** *n* [sing] **1** a slow steady run, esp for exercise: *Are you coming for a jog tomorrow?* **2** a slight push or knock: *He gave her a jog with his elbow.* ○ (*fig*) *give sb's memory a jog.*

jogger /'dʒɒgə(r)/ *n* a person who jogs for exercise. **jogging** /'dʒɒgɪŋ/ *n* [U]: *take up jogging.* **'jogging suit** *n* = TRACK SUIT.

joggle /'dʒɒgl/ *v* [V, Vp, Vn, Vnp] to move or make sb/sth move or shake slightly, usu up and down.

john /dʒɒn/ *n* (*US sl*) a toilet: *go to the john.*

John Bull /ˌdʒɒn 'bʊl/ *n* (*dated*) the English nation; a typical Englishman.

joie de vivre /ˌʒwɑ də 'viːvrə/ *n* [U] (*French*) cheerful enjoyment of life: *be full of joie de vivre.*

join /dʒɔɪn/ *v* **1** ~ sth onto sth / on; ~ A to B; ~ A and B (together/up) to fasten one thing to another; to connect or combine two things: [Vnpr] *join one section of pipe to the next* [Vnp] *join two sections of pipe together* [Vnpr, Vnp] *Two extra carriages were joined onto the train/joined on at York.* [Vnpr] *The island is joined to the mainland by a bridge.* **2** ~ up with sb/sth; ~ up to meet and unite with sb/sth to form one group or thing: [V] *the place where two rivers join* [Vn] *The track joins the main road near the village.* [Vpr] *The firm joined up with a small delivery company to reduce costs.* [Vp] *The two groups of walkers joined up for the rest of the journey.* ○ *We should join together in protest.* **3** to become a member of sth; to become an employee in an organization: [V] *Membership is free, so join today!* [Vn] *join a union/choir* ○ *join the army/the EU* ○ *She joined the company last July.* ○ (*fig*) *join the growing number of unemployed.* **4** to come into the company of sb; to meet or be with sb: [Vn] *I'll join you in a minute.* ○ *Ask him to join us for lunch.* ○ *They joined* (ie got on) *the flight at Nairobi.* **5(a)** to take part in sth; to take one's place in sth: [Vn] *join a demonstration/procession/line* ○ *join the hunt for the missing boy.* (**b**) ~ sb in (doing) sth to take part with sb in an activity: [Vnpr] *Mother joins me in sending you our best wishes.* **IDM** **if you can't beat them join them** ⇨ BEAT¹. **join 'battle (with sb)** (*fml*) to begin fighting sb. **join the 'club** (said when sth bad that has already happened to oneself now happens to sb else): *You got a parking-ticket? Well, join the club!* **join 'forces (with sb)** to work together in order to achieve a common aim: *The two firms joined forces to win a major contract.* **join 'hands (with sb) 1** to hold each other's hands. **2** to work together in doing sth. **PHRV** **¡join 'in (sth / doing sth)** to take part in an activity: *Can I join in (the game)?* ○ *They all joined in singing the Christmas carols.* **¡join 'up** to become a member of the armed forces: *His grandfather joined up in 1914.*

▶ **join** *n* a place or line where two things are joined: *The two pieces were stuck together so well that you could hardly see the join.*

joiner /'dʒɔɪnə(r)/ *n* (*Brit*) a skilled worker who makes the wooden parts of a building, esp window frames and doors. Compare CARPENTER.

▶ **joinery** /'dʒɔɪnəri/ *n* [U] (**a**) the work of a joiner. (**b**) things made by a joiner.

joint¹ /dʒɔɪnt/ *n* **1** a place, line or surface at which two or more things are joined: *Check that the joints of the pipes are properly sealed.* **2** a structure in the body by which bones are fitted together and are able to move or bend: *ankle/knee/elbow joints* ○ *suffer* *from stiff joints.* **3** (*Brit*) a fairly large piece of meat, esp one cooked whole: *a joint of beef* ○ *carve the Sunday joint.* **4** (*sl*) a place where people meet to drink or for entertainment, eg a bar or club. **5** (*sl*) a cigarette containing MARIJUANA. **IDM** **case the joint** ⇨ CASE². **out of ˈjoint 1** (of bones) pushed out of the proper position; dislocated (DISLOCATE 1): *She fell and put her knee out of joint.* **2** in disorder; in a state of confusion: *His departure has thrown the balance of the team out of joint.* **put sb's nose out of joint** ⇨ NOSE¹.

▶ **joint** *v* (esp passive) **1** to provide sth with a joint¹(1,2), or joints: [Vn] *a doll with jointed limbs.* **2** to cut meat into joints: [Vn] *a jointed chicken.*

joint² /dʒɔɪnt/ *adj* [attrib] **1** shared, held or done by two or more people together: *a joint account* (ie a bank account in the name of more than one person, eg a husband and wife) ○ *joint ownership/ responsibility/consultation* ○ *a joint effort* ○ *issue a joint statement.* **2** sharing in an activity, a position or an achievement: *joint authors/owners/winners.* ▶ **jointly** *adv*: *a jointly funded project.*
■ **ˌJoint ˌChiefs of ˈStaff** *n* [pl] the military advisers to the US President.

joist /dʒɔɪst/ *n* any of the long thick pieces of wood or metal that are used to support a floor or ceiling in a building.

joke /dʒəʊk/ *n* **1** a thing said to cause amusement or laughter, eg a humorous remark or a story with a funny ending: *tell* (*sb*) *a joke* ○ *have a joke with sb* ○ *cracking jokes with one's friends* ○ *I don't get* (ie understand) *the joke.* **2** a trick played on sb for other people's amusement: *play a joke on sb* ○ *I only did it as a joke.* See also PRACTICAL JOKE. **3** [sing] a person, thing or situation that cannot be treated seriously: *His attempts at cooking are a complete joke.* **IDM** **be no ˈjoke; be/get beyond a ˈjoke** to be/become a difficult or serious matter: *Trying to find a job these days is no joke, I can tell you.* ○ *His teasing is getting beyond a joke.* **the joke's on ˈsb** (*infml*) a person who tried to make sb else look foolish now looks ridiculous instead. **make a ˈjoke about/of sb/sth** to laugh at or speak with amusement about sb/sth that may really need to be considered seriously. **take a ˈjoke** to accept playful remarks or tricks with good humour: *The trouble with Paula is she can't take a joke.*

▶ **joke** *v* ~ (**with sb**) (**about sth**) to tell jokes; to talk in a way that is not serious or sensible: [V] *I was only joking* (ie I did not mean what I said). [Vpr] *He joked about the time he fell into the river.* [also V.speech, V.*that*]. **IDM** **you are / must be / have to be ˈjoking** (used to express complete lack of belief or agreement): *'Paul's passed his driving test.' 'You must be joking — he can't even steer straight!'*
jokey *adj* joking; amusing or ridiculous: *a jokey tone of voice.*
jokingly *adv* in a joking manner.

joker /ˈdʒəʊkə(r)/ *n* **1** (*infml often derog*) a person who is fond of making jokes or playing tricks: *Some joker's been playing around with my car aerial!* **2** an extra card used in certain card-games. **IDM** **the ˌjoker in the ˈpack** a person or thing whose actions or influence cannot be predicted.

jolly /ˈdʒɒli/ *adj* (**-ier, -iest**) **1** happy and cheerful: *a jolly crowd/face.* **2** (*dated or joc infml*) lively and very pleasant; delightful or enjoyable: *a jolly party/ time.*

▶ **jollification** /ˌdʒɒlɪfɪˈkeɪʃn/ *n* [C, U] (*dated or joc*) an enjoyable activity; a celebration.
jollity /ˈdʒɒləti/ *n* [U] (*dated*) the state of being jolly.
jolly *adv* (*Brit infml*) very: *She's a jolly good teacher.* ○ *She did jolly well in the exams.* **IDM** **ˈjolly well** (*infml*) (used to emphasize a statement, esp when one is annoyed) certainly: *If you don't come now, you can jolly well walk home.*

jolly *v* (*pt, pp* **jollied**) **PHRV** **ˌjolly sb ˈalong** (*infml*) to keep encouraging sb in a friendly way: *I had to keep jollying them along to get them to finish painting the bathroom.* **ˌjolly sth ˈup** to make sth more pleasant or enjoyable: *jolly up a party.*

jolt /dʒəʊlt/ *v* **1** to disturb, push or shake sb/sth from their original or normal position, esp suddenly and roughly: [Vn] *An earthquake jolted Australia's tallest building.* [Vnadv] *He was jolted forwards by the movement of the crowd.* [Vnpr] *be jolted from one's sleep* [Vn] (*fig*) *jolt sb's assumptions/beliefs* [also Vnp, Vn-adj]. **2** (esp of a vehicle) to move with sudden movements from side to side or up and down: [Vpr] *jolt along a rough track* [also V]. **PHRV** **ˌjolt sb ˈinto / ˈout of sth** to make sb act by giving them a sudden shock: *be jolted out of one's apathy/ lethargy* ○ *be jolted into action.*

▶ **jolt** *n* (esp *sing*) **1** a sudden rough or violent movement; a JERK(1): *stop with a jolt.* **2** an unpleasant surprise; a shock: *The news of the accident gave her a nasty jolt.*

Joneses /ˈdʒəʊnzɪz/ *n* [pl] **IDM** **keep up with the Joneses** ⇨ KEEP¹.

josh /dʒɒʃ/ *v* [V, V.speech, Vn] (*infml esp US*) to make jokes or mock sb in a gentle way.

joss-stick /ˈdʒɒsstɪk/ *n* a thin stick covered with a substance that burns slowly and produces a sweet smell.

jostle /ˈdʒɒsl/ *v* **1** to push roughly against sb, usu in a crowd: [Vn, Vpr] *The youths jostled (against) her.* [V] *A lot of pushing and jostling* [Vpr, Vp] (*fig*) *All these thoughts were jostling (around) inside my mind.* **2** ~ (**for sth**) to compete with other people in a forceful manner in order to gain sth: [Vpr] *advertisers jostling (with each other) for the public's attention.*

jot¹ /dʒɒt/ *v* (**-tt-**) **PHRV** **jot sth down** to write sth down quickly and briefly: *I'll just jot down their phone number before I forget it.*

▶ **jotter** *n* a book or pad¹(3) of paper for making short notes in or on.
jottings *n* [pl] short written notes.

jot² /dʒɒt/ *n* [sing] (usu after a negative) a very small amount: *I don't care a jot for their feelings.* ○ *There's not a jot of truth in his story.*

joule /dʒuːl/ *n* (*physics*) a unit of energy or work.

journal /ˈdʒɜːnl/ *n* **1** a newspaper or magazine that deals with a particular subject or professional activity: *a medical/a scientific/an educational journal* ○ *subscribe to a trade journal* ○ *The Wall Street Journal.* **2** a daily record of news, events, activities, etc: *He kept a journal of his travels across Asia.*

▶ **journalese** /ˌdʒɜːnəˈliːz/ *n* [U] (*derog*) a style of language thought to be typical of newspapers, full of expressions that have been used so often that they have lost their force. Compare OFFICIALESE.
journalism /ˈdʒɜːnəlɪzəm/ *n* [U] the work of collecting, writing and publishing material in newspapers and magazines or on television and radio: *a career in journalism.* **journalist** /-nəlɪst/ *n* a person whose profession is journalism: *She's a journalist on the 'Independent'.* Compare REPORTER. **journalistic** /ˌdʒɜːnəˈlɪstɪk/ *adj* [attrib] of journalism; characteristic of journalism: *his journalistic background/skill.*

journey /ˈdʒɜːni/ *n* (*pl* **-eys**) **1(a)** an act of travelling from one place to another: *go on a long train journey* ○ *break one's journey* (ie interrupt it by stopping briefly at a place) ○ *the journey from Paris to Lyon* ○ *Did you have a good journey?* **(b)** the time taken in going from one place to another: *It's a day's journey by car.*

▶ **journey** *v* to go on a journey; to travel: [Vadv, Vpr] *journeying overland/across Africa.*

NOTE A **journey** can be a long or a short distance: *a 600-mile journey* ○ *How long is your journey to work?* A **voyage** is a long journey by sea or in space. Somebody's **travels** (plural) are long journeys from one place or country to another, for pleasure or interest: *He's writing a book about his travels in Central Asia.* **Travel** is an uncountable noun which describes the act of travelling: *The price includes return air travel and accommodation.*
A **tour** is a journey on which you stop and visit several places: *My parents are going on a world tour when they retire.* A **trip** is a journey to a particular place and back: *We took the kids on a trip to Disneyland.* ○ *business trips.* An **excursion** is a trip, usually made in a group, while on holiday: *There's a one-day excursion to Machu Picchu by train.*

journeyman /ˈdʒɜːnimən/ *n* (*pl* **-men** /-mən/) [often attrib] **1** a trained worker who works for an employer: *a journeyman printer.* **2** a person who is reliable but not outstanding at what he or she does for a living: *a journeyman golf professional.*

joust /dʒaʊst/ *v* [V] (of knights (KNIGHT 2) in medieval times) to fight each other with lances (LANCE¹) while riding horses, esp as a sport.

Jove /dʒəʊv/ *n* **IDM by Jove** (dated infml) (used to express surprise or to emphasize a statement).

jovial /ˈdʒəʊviəl/ *adj* very cheerful and friendly: *in a jovial mood.* ► **joviality** /ˌdʒəʊviˈæləti/ *n* [U]. **jovially** /-iəli/ *adv*.

jowl /dʒaʊl/ *n* (usu *pl*) the lower part of the face: *a man with heavy jowls* (ie having a large jaw and folds of flesh hanging from the chin). **IDM cheek by jowl** ⇨ CHEEK.

joy /dʒɔɪ/ *n* **1** [U] a feeling of great happiness or pleasure: *the sheer joy of being with her again* ○ *be overcome with joy* ○ *dance/jump/shout for joy* (ie because of feeling great joy). **2** [C] a person or thing that gives one happiness or pleasure: *the joys of fatherhood* ○ *The match was a joy to watch.* **3** [U] (*Brit infml*) (esp in questions and negative sentences) success or satisfaction: *We complained about our rooms but got no joy from the manager.* ○ *'Any joy at the shops?' 'No, they didn't have what I wanted.'* **IDM full of the joys of spring** ⇨ FULL. **sb's pride and joy** ⇨ PRIDE.
► **joyful** /-fl/ *adj* filled with, showing or causing joy(1): *joyful celebrations* ○ *on this joyful occasion.* **joyfully** /-fəli/ *adv*. *laugh joyfully.*
joyless *adj* without joy; miserable: *a joyless marriage.*
joyous /ˈdʒɔɪəs/ *adj* (*fml*) filled with, showing or causing joy(1): *a joyous occasion* ○ *in joyous anticipation.* **joyously** *adv*.

joyride /ˈdʒɔɪraɪd/ *n* (*infml*) a very fast and exciting ride in a car taken without the owner's permission: *teenagers going for joyrides round the town in stolen vehicles.* ► **joyrider** *n*. **joyriding** *n* [U].

joystick /ˈdʒɔɪstɪk/ *n* a handle in an aircraft, on a computer, etc, used for controlling direction or movement.

JP /ˌdʒeɪ ˈpiː/ *abbr* (*law*) Justice of the Peace: *Clive Small JP.*

Jr *abbr* = JNR.

jubilant /ˈdʒuːbɪlənt/ *adj* (*fml*) feeling or showing great happiness and pride, esp because of success: *jubilant crowds* ○ *be in a jubilant mood.*
► **jubilantly** *adv*.
jubilation /ˌdʒuːbɪˈleɪʃn/ *n* [U] great happiness and pride, esp because of success: *scenes of jubilation among their supporters.*

jubilee /ˈdʒuːbɪliː/ *n* a special anniversary of an event; the celebration of this. See also DIAMOND JUBILEE, GOLDEN JUBILEE, SILVER JUBILEE.

Judaism /ˈdʒuːdeɪɪzəm/; *US* -də-ɪzəm/ *n* [U] the religion of the Jewish people.

Judaic /dʒuːˈdeɪɪk/ *adj* [attrib] of Jews or Judaism: *the Judaic tradition.*

Judas /ˈdʒuːdəs/ *n* a person who betrays a friend: *They branded him a Judas.*

judder /ˈdʒʌdə(r)/ *v* to shake violently: [V] *a juddering machine* [Vpr] *The plane juddered to a halt.* [also Vp].

judge¹ /dʒʌdʒ/ *n* **1** an officer with authority to decide cases in a lawcourt: *a High Court judge* ○ *The case comes before Judge Cooper next week.* ○ *The judge sentenced him to five years in prison.* Compare MAGISTRATE. **2** a person who decides who has won a competition or contest: *a panel of judges at the flower show* ○ *The judges' decision is final* (ie It cannot be changed or challenged). **3** a person qualified or experienced in a particular field and able to give an opinion on the quality or value of sth: *a good judge of art/wine/character* ○ *The last singer was the best — not that I'm any judge* (ie I do not know much about the subject).

judge² /dʒʌdʒ/ *v* **1** ~ (**sb/sth**) **by/from/on sth** to form an opinion about sb/sth; to estimate the value, amount, etc of sth: [V] *As far as I can judge, they are all to blame.* [Vpr] *Judging from / To judge by past experience, he will be late.* [Vn] *It is difficult to judge the full extent of the damage.* [Vnpr] *Schools should not be judged only on exam results.* [V.that] *He judged that it was time to leave.* [V.wh] *I find it hard to judge how the election will go* (ie who will win). [Vn.adj] *The committee judged it advisable to postpone the meeting.* [Vn.to inf] *I judged him to be about 50.* **2(a)** to assess sb's good and bad qualities; to criticize: [V, Vn] *Who are you to judge (other people)?* **(b)** to decide a case in a lawcourt; to try¹(3) sth: [Vn] *judge a murder case.* **(c)** to decide in a lawcourt whether sb is guilty or not guilty: [Vn-adj] *He was judged guilty as charged.* **3** to decide the result or winner in a competition: [V] *The judging is about to begin.* [Vn] *judge a flower show.*

judgement (also, esp in legal use, **judgment**) /ˈdʒʌdʒmənt/ *n* **1** [U] the ability to come to sensible conclusions and make wise decisions; good sense(3): *show a lack of judgement* ○ *display/exercise/show excellent judgement* ○ *political judgement* ○ *You'll have to use your judgement and do what seems best.* ○ *We finished on time, more by luck than by judgement.* **2** [U, C] the action or process of judging (JUDGE² 1) sb/sth: *make an error of judgement* (ie make a mistake in one's analysis of a situation) ○ *I'd like to reserve judgement* (ie delay giving my opinion) *on that question.* **3** [C] ~ (**of/about/on sth**) an opinion about sth, often based on careful thought: *form/make an unfair judgement of sb's character* ○ *make a judgement on the company's export performance* ○ *In my judgement the plan is ill-conceived.* **4** [C, U] the decision of a lawcourt or judge: *The judgement was given in favour of the accused* (ie He or she was declared not guilty). ○ *The court has still to pass judgement* (ie give a decision) *in this case.* **5** [C usu *sing*] ~ (**on sb**) (*fml or joc*) an unpleasant event or situation considered to be a punishment from God for doing sth wrong. **IDM against one's better judgement** ⇨ BETTER¹. **sit in judgement** ⇨ SIT.
► **judgemental** /dʒʌdʒˈmentl/ *adj* **1** very critical: *judgemental attitudes.* **2** of or concerning judgement: *judgemental errors.*
■ **'Judgement Day** (also the **Day of 'Judgement**, the **Last 'Judgement**) *n* [sing] the day at the end of the world when God will judge everyone who has ever lived.

judicature /ˈdʒuːdɪkətʃə(r)/ *n* (*law*) **1** [U] the administration of justice. **2** [CGp] judges considered as a group.

judicial /dʒuːˈdɪʃl/ *adj* [attrib] of or by a court of law; of a judge¹(1) or of judgement(4): *a judicial inquiry/*

review/system ○ *the judicial process.* ▶ **judicially** /-ʃəli/*adv.*

judiciary /dʒuˈdɪʃəri; *US* -ʃieri/ (usu **the judiciary**) *n* [CGp] the judges of a country considered as a group: *the independence of the judiciary.*

judicious /dʒuˈdɪʃəs/ *adj* showing or having good sense(3): *a judicious choice/decision/remark.* ▶ **judiciously** *adv: a judiciously worded letter.*

judo /ˈdʒuːdəʊ/ *n* [U] a sport in which two people fight and WRESTLE(1), and try to throw each other to the ground.

jug /dʒʌg/ (*Brit*) (*US* **pitcher**) *n* (**a**) a deep container, with a handle and a lip(2), for holding and pouring liquids: *pour milk from a jug* ○ *a milk/coffee/water jug.* (**b**) the amount of liquid contained in this: *I spilt a whole jug of juice.*
▶ **jugful** /-fʊl/ *n* (*pl* **-fuls**) the amount of liquid contained in a jug.

jugged hare /ˌdʒʌgd ˈheə(r)/ *n* [U] HARE cooked in liquid in a covered dish.

juggernaut /ˈdʒʌgənɔːt/ *n* **1** (*Brit esp derog*) a very large lorry: *juggernauts roaring through country villages.* **2** a large, powerful and overwhelming (OVERWHELM) force or institution: *the juggernaut of bureaucracy.*

juggle /ˈdʒʌgl/ *v* **1** ~ (**with sth**) to throw a set of objects, eg balls, up into the air and catch them repeatedly, keeping one or more in the air at the same time: [V] *When did you learn to juggle?* [Vn, Vpr] *to juggle (with) plates/balls/hoops.* **2** ~ (**sth**) (**with sth**) to change the arrangement of sth constantly in order to achieve a satisfactory result: [Vn] *perform a delicate juggling act* [Vn] *juggling one's timetable to fit in the extra classes* [Vnpr] *juggle one's family responsibilities with the demands of one's job.*

juggling
juggler

▶ **juggler** /ˈdʒʌglə(r)/ *n* a person who juggles. ⇨ picture.

jugular /ˈdʒʌgjələ(r)/ (also **jugular ˈvein**) *n* any of several veins in the neck that carry blood from the head to the heart. **IDM go for the ˈjugular** (*infml*) to make an aggressive attack on the weakest point in an opponent's argument or character.

juice /dʒuːs/ *n* **1** [U, C] the liquid obtained from a fruit; a drink made from this: *juice squeezed from a lemon* ○ *a carton of fresh orange/pineapple juice* ○ *Two tomato juices, please.* **2** [U, C] the liquid that comes from a piece of meat when it is cooked: *Use the juices from the meat to make gravy.* **3** [C usu *pl*] the liquid in the stomach or another part of the body that helps sb to DIGEST²(1a) food: *gastric/digestive juices.* **4** [U] (*infml esp Brit*): *We ran out of juice on the motorway.* **IDM let sb stew in their own juice** ⇨ STEW.

juicer /ˈdʒuːsə(r)/ *n* a device for extracting juice from fruit.

juicy /ˈdʒuːsi/ *adj* (**-ier, -iest**) **1** containing a lot of juice and enjoyable to eat: *fresh juicy oranges.* **2** (*infml*) interesting, esp because of being exciting or shocking: *juicy gossip/details.*

ju-jitsu /dʒuːˈdʒɪtsuː/ *n* [U] the Japanese art of defending oneself from which JUDO was developed.

jukebox /ˈdʒuːkbɒks/ *n* a machine in a pub, bar, etc that automatically plays the records that one chooses when coins are inserted.

Jul *abbr* July: *21 Jul 1882.*

July /dʒuˈlaɪ/ *n* [U, C] (*abbr* **Jul**) the 7th month of the year.

For further guidance on how *July* is used, see the examples at *April.*

jumble /ˈdʒʌmbl/ *v* ~ **sth** (**up**) (usu passive) to mix things in a confused way: [Vnp] *toys, books, shoes and clothes jumbled (up) on the floor* ○ *The details of the accident were all jumbled up in his mind.* [Vn] *a jumbled collection of large and small buildings.*
▶ **jumble** *n* **1** [sing] ~ (**of sth**) a confused or untidy group of things: *a jumble of books and papers* ○ *Can you form a word from this jumble of letters?* **2** [U] (*Brit*) a mixed collection of old things that are no longer wanted, intended for a jumble sale.
■ **ˈjumble sale** (*Brit*) (*US* **ˈrummage sale**) *n* a sale of jumble(2) held in order to raise money, usu for a charity: *hold a jumble sale in aid of hospital funds.*

jumbo /ˈdʒʌmbəʊ/ *adj* [attrib] (*infml*) very large: *a jumbo(-sized) packet of washing-powder.*
▶ **jumbo** *n* (*pl* **-os**) (also ˌ**jumbo ˈjet**) a very large aircraft that can carry several hundred passengers, esp a Boeing 747.

jump¹ /dʒʌmp/ *v* **1**(**a**) to move quickly off the ground up into the air by using the force of one's legs and feet: [Vpr] *jump into the air/out of a window/over the wall/off a roof/onto the ground* [Vn] *She has jumped 2.2 metres.* [V] '*Quick, jump!' he shouted.* [Vp] *The children were jumping about/jumping up and down with excitement.* (**b**) to pass over sth by jumping: [Vn] *The horses jumped all the fences.* See also SHOWJUMPING. **2** to move quickly and suddenly: [Vpr] *He jumped to his feet as the boss came in.* [Vp] *She jumped up and ran out of the room.* ○ *Jump in, I'll give you a lift.* **3** to move suddenly in reaction to sth that causes excitement, surprise or shock: [V] *The loud bang made me jump.* ○ *Her heart jumped when she heard the news.* ⇨ note. **4** (of a device) to move suddenly and unexpectedly, esp out of the correct position: [V, Vpr] *The needle jumped (across the dial).* [also Vp]. **5** ~ (**by**) **sth** to rise suddenly by a large amount: [Vpr] *Prices jumped by 60% last year.* [Vn] *Shares jumped 27p to 666p.* **6** ~ **from sth to sth** (**a**) to change suddenly from discussing one subject to another subject: [Vpr, Vp] *I couldn't follow his talk because he kept jumping (about) from one topic to another.* (**b**) to omit part of sth and pass to a further point or stage: [Vn] *jump several steps in an argument* [Vpr] *The story then jumps from her childhood in Norfolk to her first visit to London.* **7** (*infml*) to attack sb suddenly: [Vn] *The thieves jumped him in a dark alleyway.* **8** (*infml esp US*) to travel illegally on a train, eg without paying: [Vn] *jump a freight train.* **IDM climb/jump on the bandwagon** ⇨ BANDWAGON. **jump ˈbail** to fail to appear for a trial after being released on payment of BAIL¹(1a). **jump down sb's ˈthroat** (*infml*) to respond suddenly to sb in an angry critical way. **jump the ˈgun** to do sth too soon, before the proper time: *They jumped the gun by building the garage before getting planning permission.* **jump out of one's ˈskin** (*infml*) to move violently because of a sudden shock: *I nearly jumped out of my skin when I saw this white face at the window.* **jump the ˈqueue** (*Brit*) to go to the front of a line of people without waiting for one's turn. **jump the ˈrails/ˈtrack** (of a train) to leave the rails suddenly. **jump ˈship** (of a professional sailor) to leave the ship on which one is serving, without having obtained permission. **jump/leap to conclusions/to the conclusion that...** ⇨ CONCLUSION. **jump ˈto it** (*infml*) (usu imperative) hurry and get ready: *The bus is leaving in five minutes, so jump to it!* **PHR V ˈjump at sth** to seize an opportunity, an offer, etc eagerly: *If they offered me a job in the USA, I'd jump at it/the chance.* ˌ**jump ˈin** to interrupt a conversation: *Before she could reply Peter jumped in with a further objection.* ˈ**jump on sb** (*infml*) to criticize sb/sth sharply: *My French teacher used to jump on*

(us for) mistakes like that. **jump 'out at sb** to be very obvious and easily noticed: *The mistake in the figures jumped out at me.*
■ **'jumped-up** adj [attrib] (*Brit infml*) thinking oneself to be more important than one really is: *He's not really an accountant, more a jumped-up clerk.*
,jumping-'off point n a point from which a journey, plan, campaign, etc is begun.
'jump-lead /liːd/ n (usu pl) each of two cables used to transfer electric current from a car battery to one in another car that has no power in it so that the car can be started.
'jump-off n (in SHOWJUMPING) an extra round held to decide the winner when two or more horses have the same score.
'jump rope n (*US*) = SKIPPING-ROPE
'jump-start v [Vn] to start a car by pushing it and then engaging the gears. Compare KICK-START.
'jump suit n a garment consisting of trousers and a jacket or shirt sewn together in one piece.

NOTE Compare **jump, leap, spring** and **bounce**. Leap means to jump a long way with a lot of force. You can **jump** or **leap** in any direction: *He jumped into the car/onto the platform.* ○ *I leapt down the stairs.* ○ *The dancer leapt gracefully through the air.* You also **jump** in surprise: *The sudden noise made me jump.* **Spring** usually means a short, high jump forward: *The cat sprang forward to catch a mouse.* **Bounce** means to jump up and down on a soft surface repeatedly: *The children love bouncing on the bed.*

jump² /dʒʌmp/ n [C] **1** an act of jumping: *a jump of over 6 metres* ○ *make/do a parachute jump* ○ (*fig*) *a great jump forward in technology.* **2** an obstacle to be jumped over: *The horse fell at the last jump.* See also HIGH JUMP, LONG JUMP, TRIPLE JUMP. **3** ~ (**in sth**) a sudden rise in amount, price or value: *a jump in borrowings from 24 million to 47 million dollars* ○ *The company's results show a huge/a record jump in profits.* **IDM** **be for the high jump** ⇨ THE HIGH JUMP. **keep, etc one jump ahead (of sb)** to remain one stage ahead of a rival. **take a running jump** ⇨ RUNNING.
▶ **jumpy** adj (*infml*) nervous; anxious: *Wall Street is getting jumpy.*

jumper /'dʒʌmpə(r)/ n **1** (*Brit*) = JERSEY 1: *a knitted jumper.* **2** (*US*) = PINAFORE. **3** a person, an animal or an insect that jumps: *He's a good jumper.*

Jun abbr June: *12 Jun 1803.*

junction /'dʒʌŋkʃn/ n (**a**) (*esp Brit*) (*US* also **intersection**) (often in names) a place where two or more roads or railway lines meet: *Clapham Junction* ○ *an accident near the junction of London Road and Chaucer Avenue* ○ *Join the motorway at Junction 11.* (**b**) a place where two or more things are joined: *the junction of two electric cables* ○ *a three-terminal junction box.*

juncture /'dʒʌŋktʃə(r)/ n **IDM** **at this, etc 'juncture** (*fml*) at a particular, esp important, stage in a series of events: *be at a critical juncture* ○ *It is very difficult at this juncture to predict the company's future.*

June /dʒuːn/ n [U, C] (abbr **Jun**) the 6th month of the year.
For further guidance on how *June* is used, see the examples at *April*.

jungle /'dʒʌŋgl/ n **1** [U, C] an area of land, usu in a tropical country, where trees and plants grow very thickly: *remote jungle areas* ○ *The new road was hacked out of the jungle.* **2** [sing] a confused, complicated or threatening mass of things: *a jungle of bureaucratic paperwork* ○ *the concrete jungle* (ie a typical modern city with a lot of ugly concrete buildings). **IDM** **the law of the jungle** ⇨ LAW.

junior /'dʒuːnɪə(r)/ adj **1** low in rank or status

compared with others: *a junior clerk in an office* ○ *a junior doctor/minister* ○ *at junior management level* ○ *She's junior to me.* **2** (esp in sport) of or for young people, eg up to the age of 16 or 18: *the national junior swimming championships.* **3 Junior** (abbrs **Jnr, Jr**) (*esp US*) (used after the name of a person who has the same name as his father): *Sammy Davis, Jr.* Compare SENIOR.
▶ **junior** n **1** [C] a person with a relatively unimportant job: *office juniors.* **2** [sing] (used with *her, his, your,* etc) a person who is a specified number of years younger than sb else: *He is three years her junior.* **3** [C] (in sport) a young person, eg under the age of 16 or 18: *coaching our leading juniors.* **4** [C] (*Brit*) a child who goes to junior school (JUNIOR). **5** [C] (*US*) a student in the third year of a course lasting four years at college or high school (HIGH¹).
■ **,junior 'college** n (*US*) a type of college offering students courses for two years before they complete their studies in a senior college.
,junior 'high school n (*US*) a school for young people in grades seven to nine.
'junior school n (*Brit*) a school for children from the ages of 7 to 11: *She goes to the local junior school.*

juniper /'dʒuːnɪpə(r)/ n a bush that does not lose its leaves in winter. Its purple berries are used in medicine and to give a flavour to GIN.

junk¹ /dʒʌŋk/ n [U] things that are considered useless or of little value: *I've cleared out all that old junk in the attic.* ○ *I bought these plates in a local junk shop.* ○ *You read too much junk* (ie books with no literary merit).
▶ **junk** v to reject sth that had previously been accepted: [Vn] *Plans for new offices were unceremoniously junked.*
■ **'junk bond** n (*commerce*) a BOND(2) that gives a high rate of interest but is considered to be a risky investment. Junk bonds are often issued to raise money quickly for a planned take-over (TAKE¹): *The yield on junk bonds does not compensate for the risks.*
'junk food n [U, C] (*infml derog*) food that is considered not to be good for one's health, but which many people eat because it is easy to prepare: *a diet of hamburgers, French fries and other junk foods.*
'junk mail n [U] (*derog*) advertising material for products or services that is sent to large numbers of people who have not asked for it: *The average household receives 5 items of junk mail a month.*

junk² /dʒʌŋk/ n a Chinese boat with a square sail and a flat bottom.

junket /'dʒʌŋkɪt/ n (*infml derog esp US*) a trip made esp for pleasure by a government official and paid for with government money.
▶ **junketing** n [U, C usu pl] (*often derog*) a lively celebration, esp one held to entertain visiting government officials and paid for with government money.

junkie /'dʒʌŋki/ n (*sl*) a drug ADDICT: (*fig*) *fashion junkies.*

junta /'dʒʌntə; *US* 'hʊntə/ n [CGp] (*often derog*) a group, esp of military officers, that rules a country after taking power by force in a revolution: *The coup brought a military junta to power.*

Jupiter /'dʒuːpɪtə(r)/ n (*astronomy*) the largest planet of the solar system (SOLAR), more distant from the sun than the Earth and Mars.

juridical /dʒʊə'rɪdɪkl/ adj (*fml*) of law or legal proceedings.

jurisdiction /,dʒʊərɪs'dɪkʃn/ n [U] (**a**) the official power to make legal decisions and judgements about sth: *The court has no jurisdiction over foreign diplomats.* (**b**) the limits within which legal authority can be exercised: *come within sb's jurisdiction* ○ *be beyond/fall outside sb's jurisdiction.*

jurisprudence /,dʒʊərɪs'pruːdns/ n [U] (*fml*) the

science or philosophy of law: *a professor of jurisprudence.*

jurist /'dʒʊərɪst/ *n* (*fml*) an expert in law.

juror /'dʒʊərə(r)/ *n* a member of a JURY: *select/vet the jurors.*

jury /'dʒʊəri/ *n* [CGp] **1** a group of people in a lawcourt who have been chosen to listen to the facts in a case and to decide whether the accused person is guilty or not guilty: *members of the jury* ○ *A new jury will be sworn in today.* ○ *to do/be called up for jury service* ○ *The jury returned a verdict of / found the defendant* (ie reached a decision that the person accused was) *not guilty.* **2** a group of people chosen to judge a competition: *The jury is/ are about to announce the winners.*

just¹ /dʒʌst/ *adj* **1** based on or behaving according to accepted moral principles; reasonable and fair: *a just and honourable ruler* ○ *a just decision/law/ society* ○ *be just in one's dealings with sb* ○ *The just demands of the students must be met.* **2** deserved; appropriate to the circumstances: *a just reward/ punishment* ○ *get one's just deserts* (ie get what one deserves). See also JUSTICE.
▶ **the just** *n* [pl *v*] just people.
justly *adv*: *act justly* ○ *be justly proud of sth* ○ *a justly famous poem.*

just² /dʒʌst/ *adv* **1** exactly (**a**) (before *n*s and noun phrases): *It's just two o'clock.* ○ *This gadget is just the thing for getting those nails out.* ○ *This jacket is just my size.* ○ *It's just my luck* (ie the sort of bad luck I usually have) *to be on holiday during the worst weather of the year.* (**b**) (before *adj*s, *adv*s and prepositional phrases): *The sauce tastes just right.* ○ *Put it just here/there.* ○ *You're just in time.* ○ *She looks just like her mother.* (**c**) (before clauses): *It's just what I wanted!* ○ *It was just where I expected it to be.* ○ *Just what do you think you're doing?* **2** ~ **as** (**a**) exactly as; the same as: *It's just as I thought.* (**b**) at the same moment as: *The clock struck six just as I arrived.* (**c**) (before an *adj/adv* followed by *as*) no less than; equally: *She's just as clever as her sister.* ○ *You can get there just as cheaply by air as by train.* **3** (esp after *only*) (**a**) by a small amount: *just manage to pass the entrance exam* ○ *just miss a target* ○ *I can only just reach the shelf, even when I stand on tiptoe.* ○ *She only just caught the train.* (**b**) (used before prepositional phrases of time or measurement) by a small amount; a little: *It happened just before Christmas.* ○ *He weighs just over 60 kilos.* **4** (with perfect tenses; in US English with the simple past tense) very recently; in the immediate past: *I've just seen John at the doctor's.* ○ *When you arrived he had only just left.* ○ *He has just been telling us about his trip to Rome.* ○ (*esp US*) *I just saw him a moment ago.* **5** at this/that moment; now; immediately (**a**) (esp with the present and past continuous tenses): *I'm just finishing my book.* ○ *I was just beginning to enjoy myself when we had to go home.* ○ *I'm just coming!* ○ *I'm just off* (ie I am leaving now). (**b**) ~ **about/going to do sth** (referring to the immediate future): *I was just going to tell you when you interrupted.* ○ *The potatoes are just about to boil over.* **6** simply: *just an ordinary day* ○ *Don't start worrying just because she's an hour late.* ○ *I can't just drop all my commitments.* ○ *This essay is just not good enough.* ○ *I didn't mean to upset you. It's just that I had to tell somebody.* ○ *This is not just another disaster movie: it is a masterpiece.* **7** (used, esp with the imperative, to cut short a possible argument or delay or to appeal for attention or understanding): *Just listen to what I'm saying, will you!* ○ *Just try to understand!* ○ *Just look at this!* **8** ~ (**for sth / to do sth**) only: *There is just one way of saving him.* ○ *I waited an hour just to see you.* ○ *just for fun/a laugh/a joke.* **9** (used in making a polite request, excuse, interruption, etc): *Could*

you just help me carry this table, please? ○ *I've just got a few things to do in town first.* **10** (used with *might, could,* or *may* to indicate a slight possibility of sth happening or being true) perhaps; possibly: *Try his home number — he might just/just might be in.* ○ *This could just be the deciding factor.* **11** (*infml*) (**a**) (used for emphasis) really; simply; absolutely: *The food was just wonderful!* ○ *I can just imagine his reaction.* (**b**) (used to express agreement) indeed: *'He's rather pompous.' 'Isn't he just? He's certainly is)!'* **IDM** **it is just as 'well (that...)** it is a good thing: *It's just as well that we didn't leave any later or we'd have missed the train.* **just about** (*infml*) **1** almost; very nearly: *I've met just about everyone.* ○ *'Did you reach your sales target?' 'Just about.'* **2** approximately: *He should be arriving just about now.* **just a 'minute/'moment/'second** (*infml*) to wait for a short time: *'Is Mr Schofield available?' 'Just a second, please, I'll check.'* **just like 'that** suddenly, without warning or explanation: *He left his wife and children, just like that!* **just 'now 1** at this moment: *Come and see me later — I'm busy just now.* **2** during this present period: *Business is good just now.* **3** only a short time ago: *I saw him just now.* **just on** (*infml*) (esp with numbers) exactly; having just reached: *It's just on six o'clock.* **just 'so** performed accurately or arranged very carefully: *She cannot bear an untidy desk. Everything must be just so.* **(it's/that's) just too 'bad** (*infml*) (often used to show lack of sympathy) the situation cannot be changed; one must manage as well as one can: *'I've left my purse at home.' 'That's just too bad — we're not going back now.'* Compare TOO BAD (BAD¹). **one might just as well be/do sth** one would have been in the same position if one was somewhere else, had done sth else, etc, considering how little benefit or enjoyment was received: *The weather was so bad last weekend we might just as well have stayed at home.* **not just 'yet** not at this present moment but probably quite soon: *I can't give you the money just yet.*

justice /'dʒʌstɪs/ *n* **1** [U] (**a**) right and fair behaviour or treatment: *laws based on the principles of justice* ○ *campaign for social justice.* (**b**) the quality of being fair or reasonable: *He demanded, with some justice, that he should be given an opportunity to express his views.* Compare INJUSTICE. **2** [U] the law and its administration: *the European Court of Justice* ○ *There has been a terrible **miscarriage of justice*** (ie a wrong legal decision). **3** Justice [C] (the title of) a High Court Judge: *Mr Justice Davies.* **4** [C] (*US*) a judge in a lawcourt. **IDM** **bring sb to 'justice** to arrest sb for a crime and hear their case in a court. **do oneself 'justice** to show how good or capable of doing sth one is: *He didn't do himself justice in the exams.* **do justice to 'sb/'sth; do sb/ sth 'justice 1** to treat or represent sb/sth fairly: *He didn't play as well as he can, though to do him justice it was his first game since his injury.* ○ *The photograph does not do full justice to the rich colours of the garden.* **2** to deal with sb/sth properly and in an appropriate manner: *Since we'd already eaten, we couldn't do justice to her cooking* (ie could not eat all the food she had cooked).

■ **ˌJustice of the 'Peace** *n* (*abbr* JP) a person who judges less serious cases in a local lawcourt; a MAGISTRATE.

justify /'dʒʌstɪfaɪ/ *v* (*pt, pp* **-fied**) **1(a)** to show that sb/sth is right, reasonable or just: [Vn] *Her success has clearly justified their early faith in her.* [V.n *ing*] *His present form scarcely justifies his being chosen for the team.* [also V.*ing*]. (**b**) to explain why sb/sth is right, reasonable or just: [Vn] *seek to justify a massive jump in prices* [V.*ing*, Vn] *How can they justify closing down/the decision to close down the youth club?* **2** to be a good reason or excuse for sth: [Vn]

J

Tiredness cannot possibly justify such behaviour. [also V.*ing*, V.n *ing*]. **3** to arrange lines of type so that the edges are straight: [Vn] *justified margins.* **IDM** **the end justifies the means** ⇨ END¹.

▶ **justifiable** /ˈdʒʌstɪfaɪəbl, ˌdʒʌstɪˈfaɪəbl/ *adj* that can be justified: *justifiable fear/complaints/pride* ∘ *His actions were illegal but justifiable on moral grounds.* **justifiably** /-əbli/ *adv* with good reason: *be justifiably cautious/nervous/proud* ∘ *The public can, quite justifiably, demand an explanation.*

justification /ˌdʒʌstɪfɪˈkeɪʃn/ *n* [U, C] ~ (**for sth/ doing sth**) an acceptable reason for doing sth: *I can see no possible justification for any further tax increases.* ∘ *He was getting angry — and with some justification.* ⇨ note at REASON¹. **IDM** **in justifiˈcation (for/of sb/sth)** as a defence of sb/sth: *All I can say in justification of his actions is that his children were hungry and sick.*

justified *adj* **1** ~ (**in doing sth**) having good reasons for doing sth: *She felt fully/entirely justified in asking for her money back.* **2** for which there is a good reason: *His fears proved justified.* ∘ *Their caution does not seem altogether justified.*

jut /dʒʌt/ *v* (**-tt-**) ~ (**out**) (**into, over, etc sth**) to extend outwards beyond the normal line of sth; to project: [V] *a jutting chin/jaw* [Vp] *a balcony that juts out over the garden* [Vpr, Vp] *a headland jutting (out) into the sea.*

jute /dʒuːt/ *n* [U] FIBRE(3) from the bark of a tropical plant, used esp for making rope and rough cloth: *jute mills.*

juvenile /ˈdʒuːvənaɪl; *US also* -vənl/ *n* (*fml or law*) a young person who is not yet adult: *an increase in the number of juveniles brought to court.*

▶ **juvenile** *adj* **1** [attrib] (*fml or law*) of, characteristic of, or suitable for young people who are not yet adults: *juvenile crime* ∘ *juvenile offenders.* **2** (*derog*) foolish and not mature; CHILDISH: *a juvenile sense of humour* ∘ *Don't be so juvenile!*

■ ˌjuvenile ˈcourt *n* a lawcourt that deals with cases involving young people who are not yet adults.

ˌjuvenile deˈlinquent *n* a young person, not yet an adult, who is guilty of a crime, eg damaging property. ˌjuvenile deˈlinquency *n* [U].

juxtapose /ˌdʒʌkstəˈpəʊz/ *v* ~ **A and/with B** (*fml*) to place people or things next to each other or very close together, esp to show a contrast: [Vn] *juxtapose light and shade* [Vnpr] *modern architecture juxtaposed with a Gothic cathedral.* ▶ **juxtaposition** /ˌdʒʌkstəpəˈzɪʃn/ *n* [U, C]: *the juxtaposition of narrative and descriptive passages.*

Kk

K¹ (also **k**) /keɪ/ n (pl **K's**, **k's** /keɪz/) the 11th letter of the English alphabet: *'King' begins with (a) K/'K'*.

K² /keɪ/ abbr **1** (*infml*) one thousand (Greek *kilo-*): *a salary over £40K*. **2** (*computing*) kilobyte. **3** kelvin(s).

kaftan = CAFTAN.

kale /keɪl/ n [U] a vegetable similar to CABBAGE with leaves that curl.

kaleidoscope /kə'laɪdəskəʊp/ n **1** a toy consisting of a sealed tube containing small loose pieces of coloured glass and mirrors which reflect these to form changing patterns when the tube is turned. **2** (usu *sing*) a constantly and quickly changing pattern: *The bazaar was a kaleidoscope of strange sights and sounds.* ► **kaleidoscopic** /kə,laɪdə'skɒpɪk/ adj.

kamikaze /,kæmɪ'kɑːzi/ [attrib] adj (of behaviour, etc) likely to prove dangerous or fatal to oneself; RECKLESS: *a kamikaze attack*.

kangaroo /,kæŋgə'ruː/ n (pl **-oos**) a large Australian animal with a strong tail and back legs, that moves by jumping. The female carries its young in a fold of flesh on the front of its body.

■ **,kangaroo 'court** n an illegal court formed by a group of prisoners, workers on strike, etc to settle disputes among themselves.

kaolin /'keɪəlɪn/ (also **,china 'clay**) n [U] fine white clay used in making PORCELAIN and in medicine.

kapok /'keɪpɒk/ n [U] a substance similar to cotton wool (COTTON¹), used for stuffing cushions, soft toys, etc.

kaput /kə'pʊt/ adj [pred] (*sl*) ruined; not working properly: *The entire plan's kaput*.

karaoke /,kærə'əʊkeɪ, ,kæri'əʊki/ n [U] recorded music of popular songs without the singer's voice. People use it to accompany their own performance of a song: *a karaoke night in a pub*.

karat (*US*) = CARAT 2.

karate /kə'rɑːti/ n [U] a Japanese system of fighting in which the hands and feet are used as weapons: *a karate chop* (ie a blow with the side of the hand).

karma /'kɑːmə/ n [U] (in Buddhism and Hinduism) the sum of sb's actions in one of their successive lives, believed to decide their fate in the next.

kayak /'kaɪæk/ n a small light covered CANOE, esp as used by Eskimos or in sport. ⇨ picture at CANOE.

KC /,keɪ 'siː/ abbr (*law*) (in Britain) King's Counsel. Compare QC.

kebab /kɪ'bæb/ n (often pl) small pieces of meat and vegetables cooked, and often served, on a wood or metal rod: *lamb kebabs*.

kedgeree /'kedʒəri:/ n [U, C] a cooked dish of rice, fish, eggs and sometimes onions, all mixed together.

keel /kiːl/ n a structure made of steel or wood along the bottom of a ship, on which the framework is built. **IDM** **on an even keel** ⇨ EVEN².

► **keel** v **PHR V** **,keel 'over 1** (of a ship) to turn on its side; to CAPSIZE. See also HEEL². **2** (*infml*) to fall over; to collapse: *After a couple of drinks he just keeled over on the floor.* ○ *The structure had keeled over in the high winds*.

keen¹ /kiːn/ adj (**-er**, **-est**) **1** (*Brit infml*) ~ **on sb/ sth** interested in sb/sth; fond of sb/sth: *keen on (playing) tennis* ○ *He seems very keen on my sister.* **2** (*esp Brit*) ~ **(to do sth/that...);** ~ **(on sth)** eager; enthusiastic: *a keen swimmer* ○ *keen to develop new*

trade links ○ *She's keen that we should go with her to Spain.* ○ *Her parents weren't keen on her travelling alone.* **3** (of feelings, etc) intense; strong; deep: *a keen interest/sense of loss.* **4** (of the senses) highly developed: *keen eyesight* ○ *Dogs have a keen sense of smell.* **5** quick to understand: *a keen mind/intellect.* **6** [esp attrib] (of the point or edge of a knife, etc) sharp: *a keen blade.* **7** (of a wind) extremely cold; bitter. **8** (*Brit*) (of prices) low; very competitive. **IDM** **(as) ,keen as 'mustard** (*Brit infml*) extremely eager or enthusiastic. **mad keen** ⇨ MAD. ► **keenly** adv: *be keenly aware of sth*. **keenness** n [U].

keen² /kiːn/ v (usu in the continuous tenses) (esp in Ireland) to express grief for a dead person, esp by wailing (WAIL a): [Vpr] *keening over her murdered son* [also V].

keep¹ /kiːp/ v (pt, pp **kept** /kept/) **1(a)** to continue to be in the specified condition or position; to remain or to stay: [V-adj] *keep calm in an emergency* [Vpr] *The notice said 'Keep off* (ie Do not walk on) *the grass'.* [Vp] *Keep back! The building could collapse at any moment.* **(b)** ~ **(on) doing sth** to continue doing sth; to do sth repeatedly or frequently: [V.ing] *keep smiling/walking* [Vp] *I do wish you wouldn't keep on interrupting me!* **(c)** to continue to move in the specified direction: [Vadv] *a 'keep left' sign* [Vp] *Keep on until you get to the church.* **2** to make sb/sth remain in the specified condition or position: [Vnpr] *If your hands are cold, keep them in your pockets.* ○ *Don't keep us in suspense — what happened next?* [Vn-adj] *keep sb amused/happy* ○ *These gloves will keep your hands warm.* [Vnp] *She kept her coat on.* [Vn.ing] *I'm sorry to keep you waiting.* **3** to delay or DETAIN(2) sb: [Vn] *You're an hour late — what kept you?* **4(a)** to continue to have sth; to RETAIN(1) sth: [Vn] *Here's a five dollar bill — you can keep the change.* **(b)** to continue to have sth for future use or reference: [Vn] *These jeans are hardly worth keeping.* ○ *I keep all her letters.* **(c)** ~ **sth (for sb)** to save sth for sb: [Vnpr] *Could you keep my place in the queue (for me)* (ie prevent anybody else from taking it)? [Vnn] *Please keep me a seat.* [also Vn]. **(d)** to have sth in a particular place; to store sth: [Vn] *Where do you keep the spoons?* [Vnpr] *Keep your passport in a safe place.* **5** to own and manage a shop or restaurant: [Vn] *Her father kept a grocer's shop.* **6** to own and care for animals: [Vn] *keep bees/goats/hens.* **7** to have sth regularly on sale or in stock: [Vn] *I'm sorry, we don't keep Turkish cigarettes.* **8** to know sth and not reveal it to anyone: [Vn] *Can you keep a secret?* **9** to be faithful to sth; to respect or observe(2) sth: [Vn] *keep an appointment/a promise/a treaty.* **10(a)** to make written entries in sth: [Vn] *She kept a diary for over twenty years.* **(b)** to write down sth as a record: [Vn] *keeping an account of one's expenses.* **11** to provide what is necessary for sb; to support sb financially: [Vn] *He scarcely earns enough to keep himself and his family.* **12** ~ **sb (from sth)** (*fml*) to protect sb from sth: [Vn] *May the Lord bless you and keep you* (ie used in prayers in the Christian Church). [Vnpr] *She prayed to God to keep her son from harm.* **13** (esp in sport) to guard or protect sth: *keep goal* ○ *keep wicket.* See also GOALKEEPER, WICKET-KEEPER. **14** (used esp in the continuous tenses with an *adv*, or in questions after *how*) to be in the specified state of health: [Vadv] *How is your mother keeping?* **15** (of food) to remain in good condition: [V] *Do finish off the pie; it won't keep.* ○ (*fig*) *The news will keep* (ie can be told later rather than immediately). **IDM** Most idioms containing **keep** are at the entries for the nouns or adjectives in the idioms, eg **keep house** ⇨ HOUSE¹. ‚keep 'going to make an effort to live normally when one is in a difficult situation or after experiencing great suffering: *You just have to keep yourself busy and keep going.* ‚keep 'up with the 'Joneses /'dʒəʊnzɪz/ (*infml often derog*) to try to maintain the same social and material standards as other people. **PHRV** ‚keep sb 'after (*US*) = KEEP SB BACK 1.

‚keep (sb) 'at sth to continue or make sb continue working at sth: *Come on, keep 'at it, you've nearly finished!*

‚keep (sb/sth) a'way (from sb/sth) to avoid approaching sb/sth or to prevent sb/sth from going somewhere: *Police warned bystanders to keep away from the blazing building.* ○ *In future, keep away from my wife.* ○ *Her illness kept her away from work for several weeks.*

‚keep (sb) 'back (from sb/sth) to remain or make sb remain at a distance from sb/sth: *Keep well back from the road.* ○ *Barricades were erected to keep back the crowds.* ‚keep sb 'back 1 (*Brit*) (*US* keep sb after) to make a pupil stay at school after normal hours as a punishment: *I was kept back after school for disobedience.* 2 (*US*) to make a pupil repeat a year at school because of poor marks. ‚keep sth 'back 1 to prevent a feeling, etc from being expressed; to restrain sth: *She was unable to keep back her tears.* 2 to continue to have a part of sth: *3% of your salary is kept back by your employer as an insurance payment.* ‚keep sth 'back (from sb) to refuse to tell sb sth: *I'm sure she's keeping something back (from us).*

‚keep 'down to hide oneself by not standing up straight: *Keep down! You mustn't let anybody see you.* ‚keep sb 'down to prevent a person, group, nation, etc from expressing themselves freely; to control sb: *The people have been kept down for years by a brutal régime.* ‚keep sth 'down 1 not to bring sth back through the mouth from the stomach: *The medicine was so horrid I couldn't keep it down* (ie I vomited (VOMIT)). 2 to make sth remain at a low level; to avoid increasing sth: *keep down wages/prices/the cost of living* ○ *Keep your voice down — I don't want anyone else to hear.*

'keep oneself/sb from sth / doing sth to prevent oneself/sb from doing sth: *The church bells keep me from sleeping.* ○ *I hope I'm not keeping you from your work.* 'keep (oneself) from doing sth to prevent oneself from doing sth: *She could hardly keep (herself) from laughing.* ○ *I just managed to keep myself from falling.* 'keep sth from sb to avoid telling sb sth: *I think we ought to keep the truth from him until he's better.* ○ *They don't keep anything from each other.*

‚keep 'in with sb (*infml*) to make sure that one remains friendly with sb, esp for one's own benefit: *It's best to keep in with the boss.* ‚keep sth 'in to avoid expressing an emotion, etc; to restrain sth: *He could scarcely keep in his indignation.* ‚keep oneself/sb in sth to provide oneself/sb with a regular supply of sth: *She earns enough to keep herself and all the family in good clothes.*

‚keep 'off (of rain, snow, etc) not to begin or happen: *The fête will go ahead provided the rain keeps off.* ‚keep 'off sth 1 to avoid eating, drinking or smoking sth: *keep off cigarettes/drugs/drink/fatty foods.* 2 to avoid mentioning the specified subject: *Please keep off (the subject of) politics while my father's here.* ‚keep sb/sth 'off (sb/sth) to prevent sb/sth from approaching, touching, etc sb/sth : *They*

lit a fire to keep wild animals off. ○ *Keep your hands off* (ie Do not touch) *me!*

‚keep 'on to continue: *The rain kept on all night.* ‚keep sb 'on to continue to employ sb: *He's incompetent and not worth keeping on.* ‚keep sth 'on to continue to rent a house, flat, etc: *We're planning to keep the cottage on over the summer.* ‚keep 'on (at sb) (about sb/sth) to speak to sb frequently and in an irritating way about sb/sth: *He does keep on so!* ○ *I will mow the lawn — just don't keep on at me about it!*

‚keep 'out (of sth) not to enter a place; to remain outside: *The sign said 'Ministry of Defence — Keep Out!'* ‚keep sb/sth 'out (of sth) to prevent sth from entering a place: *Keep that dog out of my study!* ○ *She wore a hat to keep the sun out of her eyes.* ‚keep (sb) 'out of sth to avoid exposing oneself/sb to sth; to avoid or prevent sb from getting involved in sth: *Try to keep out of the rain.* ○ *That child seems incapable of keeping out of mischief.*

'keep to sth 1 to avoid wandering from or leaving a path, road, etc: *Keep to the track — the land is very boggy around here.* ○ *keep to the point/subject.* 2 to remain faithful to a promise, etc; to do what has been agreed: *keep to an agreement/an undertaking/a plan.* 3 to remain in and not leave the specified place or position: *She's old and infirm and has to keep to the house/to her bed.* ‚keep (oneself) to 'oneself to avoid meeting people socially or concerning oneself with other people's affairs: *Nobody knows much about him; he keeps himself (very much) to himself.* ‚keep sth to one'self not to tell other people about sth: *I'd be grateful if you kept this information to yourself.* ○ *Kindly keep your opinions to yourself in future!*

‚keep sb 'under to control or OPPRESS(1) sb: *The local people are kept under by the army.*

‚keep 'up (of rain, snow, good weather, etc) to continue without stopping: *Let's hope the sunny weather keeps up for tomorrow's match.* ‚keep sb 'up to prevent sb from going to bed: *I do hope we're not keeping you up.* ‚keep sth 'up 1 to make sth remain at a high level: *The high cost of raw materials is keeping prices up.* 2 to prevent one's spirits, strength, etc from sinking; to maintain sth: *They sang songs to keep their morale up.* 3 to continue sth at the same, usu high, level: *The enemy kept up their bombardment day and night.* ○ *We're having difficulty keeping up our mortgage payments.* ○ *Well done! Keep up the good work/Keep it up!* 4 to continue to practise sth: *keep up old customs/traditions* ○ *Do you still keep up your Spanish?* 5 to maintain a house, garden, etc in good condition: *The house is becoming too expensive for them to keep up.* See also UPKEEP. ‚keep 'up (with sb/sth) to move or progress at the same rate as sb/sth: *Slow down — I can't keep up (with you)!* ○ *I can't keep up with all the changes in information technology.* ○ *Workers' incomes are not keeping up with inflation.* ‚keep 'up with sb to continue to be in contact with sb: *How many of your old school friends do you keep up with?* keep up with sth to learn about or be aware of the news, current events, etc: *She likes to keep up with the latest fashions.*

keep² /kiːp/ *n* **1** [U] food, clothes and other things needed for living: *It's time you got a job to earn your keep.* **2** [C] a strongly built tower of an ancient castle. **IDM** for 'keeps (*infml*) permanently; for ever: *Can I have it for keeps or do you want it back?*

keeper /'kiːpə(r)/ *n* **1** a person who cares for animals in a ZOO or a collection of items in a museum. **2** (esp in compounds) a person who is in charge of or manages sth: *a 'lighthouse-keeper* ○ *a 'gamekeeper* ○ *a 'shopkeeper.* **3** (*infml*) (**a**) = GOALKEEPER. (**b**) = WICKET-KEEPER.

K

[Vnn] = verb + noun + noun   [V-adj] = verb + adjective   For more help with verbs, see Study pages **B4–8.**

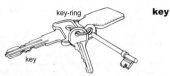

key-ring   key

key

key

keeping /ˈkiːpɪŋ/ n **IDM** **for safe keeping** ⇨ SAFE[1].
in sb's ˈkeeping in sb's care or under sb's protection: *I'll leave the keys in your keeping.* **in / out of ˈkeeping (with sth)** in/not in agreement with sth; appropriate or not appropriate: *a development wholly in keeping with what we expected* ○ *His clothes were out of keeping with the occasion.* **in safe keeping** ⇨ SAFE[1].

keepsake /ˈkiːpseɪk/ n a gift, usu small and often not very expensive, which is kept in memory of the person who gave it: *My aunt gave me one of her brooches as a keepsake.*

keg /keg/ n a small barrel, esp of beer. ⇨ picture at BARREL. See also POWDER-KEG.
■ **ˈkeg beer** n [U, C] (in Britain) beer served from metal barrels, using gas pressure.

kelp /kelp/ n [U] a type of large brown sea plant, sometimes used as MANURE.

kelvin /ˈkelvɪn/ n (abbr K) a unit of temperature equal to the Celsius degree. In the Kelvin scale 0° is fixed at absolute zero (−273.15°C). ⇨ App 8.

ken[1] /ken/ n **IDM** **beyond one's ken** not within one's range of knowledge: *The workings of the Stock Exchange are beyond my ken.*

ken[2] /ken/ v (-nn-) [Vn, V.that, V.wh] (Scot) (usu in the present tense or negative form of the past tense) to know.

kennel /ˈkenl/ n **1** (US also **doghouse**) [C] a shelter for a pet dog: *Rover lives in a kennel in the back garden.* **2 kennels** [sing or pl v] a place where dogs are bred or cared for: *We put the dog in kennels when we go away.*

kept pt, pp of KEEP[1].
■ **ˌkept ˈwoman** n (dated or joc) a woman who is given money and a home by a man in return for having sex with him regularly.

kerb (esp US **curb**) /kɜːb/ n the stone or concrete edge of a PAVEMENT(1) at the side of a road: *Stop at the kerb and look both ways before crossing the road.*
■ **ˈkerb-crawling** n [U] (Brit) the practice of driving slowly along a road in order to invite sb into one's car and have sex with them: *be arrested for kerb-crawling.* **ˈkerb-crawler** n.

kerchief /ˈkɜːtʃɪf/ n a square piece of cloth worn on the head or round the neck, esp by women.

kerfuffle /kəˈfʌfl/ n [U] (Brit infml) fuss; noise; excitement: *What's all the kerfuffle (about)?*

kernel /ˈkɜːnl/ n **1** the usu edible part inside the outer shell of a nut or the stone of a fruit. ⇨ picture at NUT. **2** the central or most important part of a subject, problem, etc: *the kernel of her argument.*

kerosene (also **kerosine**) /ˈkerəsiːn/ n [U] (esp US) = PARAFFIN: *a kerosene lamp.*

kestrel /ˈkestrəl/ n a type of small HAWK[1](1).

ketch /ketʃ/ n a small boat with two masts (MAST 1) and sails.

ketchup /ˈketʃəp/ (also esp US **catsup** /ˈkætsəp/) n [U] a thick sauce made mainly from tomatoes and spices and eaten cold: *a bottle of tomato ketchup* ○ *Do you want ketchup on your hamburger?*

kettle /ˈketl/ n a container with a lid, a handle and a SPOUT(1), used for boiling water: *an electric kettle* ○ *put/switch the kettle on* (ie start boiling some water) *and make some tea.* **IDM** **a different kettle of fish** ⇨ DIFFERENT. **the pot calling the kettle black** ⇨ POT[1].

kettledrum /ˈketldrʌm/ n a large metal drum with a round bottom and a thin plastic top that can be made tighter or looser to produce different musical notes. ⇨ picture at MUSICAL INSTRUMENT.

key[1] /kiː/ n **1** a usu small metal rod for opening or closing a lock: *turn the key in the lock* ○ *the car keys* ○ *the key to the front door* ○ *have a duplicate key cut* (ie made). ⇨ picture. **2** an instrument for turning sth, eg for winding a clock: *Where's the key for turning off the radiator?* **3** (music) a set of related notes,

based on a particular note. Pieces of music are usu written mainly by using a particular specified key: *a sonata in the key of E flat major/A minor* ○ *This piece changes key many times.* See also LOW-KEY. **4** any of the set of parts that are pressed by the fingers to operate certain machines or musical instruments: *piano/typewriter keys* ○ *function keys on a computer keyboard.* ⇨ picture at PIANO[1], SAXOPHONE. **5(a)** a set of answers to exercises or problems: *a book of language tests, complete with a key at the back.* **(b)** an explanation of the symbols used on a map or plan or in a code. **6** (usu sing) ~ (**to sth**) a thing that provides access, control or understanding: *Diet and exercise are the key (to good health).* ○ *The key to the whole affair was his jealousy.* **7** (botany) a fruit shaped like two wings around the seed of certain trees, eg ASH[1]. **IDM** **under lock and key** ⇨ LOCK[2].
▶ **key** adj [attrib] essential or very important: *a key figure in the dispute* ○ *a key industry/role/factor.*
■ **ˈkey-ring** n a ring on which keys are kept. ⇨ picture.
ˈkey signature n (music) the mark or marks shown at the beginning of a piece of music to indicate the key[1](3) in which it is written. ⇨ picture at MUSIC.

key[2] /kiː/ v ~ **sth** (**in**) (computing) to enter data by using a KEYBOARD(1): [Vn, Vnp] *Key (in) your password to gain access to the system.* **PHRV** **ˈkey sb/sth to sth** (usu passive) to make sb/sth suitable or appropriate for a particular role or job: *The farm was keyed to the needs of the local people.*
■ **ˌkeyed ˈup** adj [pred] excited, nervous or tense, esp before an important event: *We were all very keyed up before the big match.*

keyboard /ˈkiːbɔːd/ n **1(a)** a set of keys that operate a computer or TYPEWRITER. ⇨ picture at COMPUTER. **(b)** all the black and white keys on a piano, etc. **2** an electronic musical instrument that has keys like a piano and can be programmed (PROGRAM 1) to play in different styles, rhythms, etc and to sound like a range of instruments.
▶ **keyboarder** n a person who enters data into a computer using a keyboard(1a).

keyhole /ˈkiːhəʊl/ n a hole through which a key is put into a lock.

keynote /ˈkiːnəʊt/ n [C usu sing] the central theme of a speech, book, etc: *Co-operation has been the keynote of the conference.* ○ *a keynote speech* (ie one setting the tone of or introducing the theme of a meeting).

keypad /ˈkiːpæd/ n a small set of buttons for operating an electronic device, eg a telephone or CALCULATOR, or for entering data in a computer.

keystone /ˈkiːstəʊn/ n **1** (architecture) a central stone at the top of an arch locking the others into position. **2** (usu sing) the most important part of a plan, an argument, etc on which all the other parts depend: *Belief in a life after death is the keystone of her religious faith.* Compare CORNERSTONE 2.

kg abbr kilogram(s): *10 kg.*

khaki /ˈkɑːki/ n [U] a cloth of a dull brownish-yellow colour, used esp for military uniforms.
▶ **khaki** adj of the colour of khaki.

kHz abbr kilohertz. Compare Hz.

kibbutz /kɪˈbʊts/ n (pl **kibbutzim** /ˌkɪbʊtˈsiːm/) a farm in Israel in which people live together and share work, profits, decisions, etc.

kibosh (also **kybosh**) /ˈkaɪbɒʃ/ n **IDM** **put the ˈkibosh on sth** (Brit infml) (of an event, etc) to

K

prevent sth else from happening: *Breaking his leg put the kibosh on his holiday.*

kick¹ /kɪk/ v **1(a)** to strike sb/sth with the foot: [Vn, Vnpr] *Mummy, Peter kicked me (on the leg)!* **(b)** to move sth by doing this: [Vn, Vnpr] *She kicked the ball (over the hedge).* [Vnp] *Can we kick the ball around for a while?* [Vn] *(fig) He had smoked since he was 16 and found it difficult to kick the habit* (ie stop). **(c)** to make sth by kicking: [Vnpr] *He kicked a hole in the fence.* **(d)** to move the foot or feet in a sudden violent way: [V] *The child was kicking and screaming.* ○ [Vp] *(fig) She kicks out when she's angry.* **2** ~ **oneself** to be very annoyed with oneself because one has done sth stupid, missed an opportunity, etc: [Vn] *When I found I'd missed the deadline I could have kicked myself.* **3** (in football) to score sth by kicking the ball: [Vn] *kick a penalty* ○ *That's the 20th goal he's kicked this season.* **IDM** **alive and kicking** ⇨ ALIVE. **hit/kick a man when he's down** ⇨ MAN¹. **kick against the 'pricks** to hurt oneself by useless resistance or protest. **kick the 'bucket** (*sl*) to die. **kick one's 'heels** (*Brit*) to have nothing to do while waiting for sth: *She spent an hour kicking her heels waiting for the next train.* **kick over the 'traces** (of a person) to refuse suddenly to accept discipline or control from parents, etc. **kick up a 'fuss, 'row, 'shindy, 'stink, etc** (*infml*) to cause a disturbance, esp by protesting about sth. **kick sb up'stairs** (*infml*) to promote sb to a position that seems more important but in fact is less so. **PHRV** **kick a'bout/a'round** (*infml*) to exist but be forgotten or receive little notice: *My shirt is kicking about in the garden somewhere.* ○ *The idea has been kicking around for a long time.* **kick a'bout/a'round…** (*infml*) to move from place to place with no particular purpose: *He's been kicking around Europe for the past year.* **kick sb/sth a'bout/a'round** (*infml*) to treat sb/sth in a rough way or without respect: *Don't let them kick you around.* **kick sth a'bout/a'round** (*infml*) to discuss plans, ideas, etc in an informal way: *We'll kick some ideas around and make a decision tomorrow.* **kick against sth** to protest about or resist sth: *It's no use kicking against the rules.* **kick sth 'in** to break sth inwards by kicking: *kick in a door* ○ *kick sb's teeth in.* **kick 'off** to start a football match by kicking the ball: *United kicked off and scored almost immediately.* **kick (sth) 'off** (*infml*) to begin eg a meeting: *I'll ask Tessa to kick off (the discussion).* **kick sth 'off** to remove sth by kicking: *kick off one's shoes.* **kick sb 'out (of sth)** (*infml*) to dismiss sb or send them away: *They kicked him out (of the club) for fighting.*
▶ **kicker** n a person who kicks.
■ **'kick-off** n the start of a football match.

kick² /kɪk/ n **1** [C] an act of kicking: *give sb a kick on the shin* ○ *If the door won't open give it a kick.* See also FREE KICK. **2** [C] (*infml*) a strong feeling of pleasure or excitement: *I get a big kick from/out of motor racing.* ○ *do sth (just) for kicks* ○ *She gets her kicks from windsurfing and skiing.* **3** [U, sing] (*infml*) strength: *This drink has (quite) a kick (to it)* (ie is strong). **4** [C] the sudden movement made by a gun when it is fired. **IDM** **a kick in the 'teeth** (*infml*) an unpleasant or damaging action, event, etc: *The government's decision is a real kick in the teeth for the unions.*
■ **'kick-start** v to start a motor cycle (MOTOR), etc by pushing down a LEVER(2) with one's foot: [Vn] *(fig) The government's attempt to kick-start the economy has failed.* **kick-start** n a LEVER(2) used to start a motor cycle (MOTOR): *(fig) give the economy a kick-start.*

kickback /'kɪkbæk/ n (*infml*) money paid to sb who

has helped one to make a profit, often illegally: *party members accused of taking kickbacks worth millions.*

kid¹ /kɪd/ n **1(a)** [C] (*infml*) a child or young person: *How are your wife and kids?* ○ *Half the kids round here are unemployed.* **(b)** (*infml esp US*) younger: *his kid sister/brother.* **2(a)** [C] a young goat. ⇨ picture at GOAT. **(b)** [U] leather made from its skin: *kid gloves.* **IDM** **handle, treat, etc sb with kid 'gloves** to deal with sb very gently, trying not to offend or upset them.
▶ **kiddy** (also **kiddie**) n (*infml*) a child.

kid² /kɪd/ v (**-dd-**) (*infml*) **(a)** to deceive sb in a playful way; to TEASE(1) sb: [V, Vn] *You're kidding (me)* (ie I don't believe you)! [V] *I was only kidding.* ○ *No kidding! It's the honest truth.* **(b)** to deceive sb/oneself; to trick sb: [Vn] *You're kidding yourself if you think it'll be easy.* [Vn.that] *He kidded his mother that he was ill.*

kidnap /'kɪdnæp/ v (**-pp-**; US **-p-**) to take sb away by force and illegally, esp in order to obtain money in return for releasing them: [Vn] *Two businessmen have been kidnapped by terrorists.* See also ABDUCT.
▶ **kidnap** n: *a kidnap attempt/victim.* **kidnapper** n: *The kidnappers have demanded a £1 million ransom.* **kidnapping** n [C,U]: *The kidnapping occurred in broad daylight.* See also ABDUCTION.

kidney /'kɪdni/ n (pl **-eys**) **1** [C] either of a pair of organs in the body that remove waste products from the blood and produce URINE: *kidney-shaped* (ie with one side curving outwards and the other curving inwards). **2** [U,C] the kidneys of certain animals used as food: *steak and kidney pie/pudding.*
■ **'kidney bean** n a reddish-brown bean shaped like a kidney, eaten as a vegetable.
'kidney machine n (*medical*) a machine that does the work of human kidneys for people whose kidneys have become diseased or have been removed: *put a patient on a kidney machine.*

kill /kɪl/ v **1** to cause death or cause sb/sth to die: [V] *Careless driving kills!* [Vnpr] *He was killed with a knife.* [Vn] *Cancer kills thousands of people every year.* ○ *We need something to kill the weeds.* ○ *(fig infml) My mother will kill me* (ie be very angry with me) *when she finds out where I've been.* **2** (*infml*) (usu in the continuous tenses) to cause pain to sb: [Vn] *My feet are killing me.* [Vn, Vnpr] *She nearly killed herself (with) laughing.* **3** to destroy sth; to bring sth to an end: [Vn] *kill sb's affection/interest/appetite* ○ *the goal that killed Brazil's chances of winning.* **4** (*infml*) to cause sth to fail or be rejected: [Vn, Vn-adj] *kill a proposal/an idea (stone dead)* [Vn] *The play was killed by bad reviews.* **5** (*infml*) to switch or turn sth off: [Vn] *kill a light/the radio/a car engine.* **IDM** **curiosity killed the cat** ⇨ CURIOSITY. **dressed to kill** ⇨ DRESS². **have time on one's hands / time to kill** ⇨ TIME¹. **kill the goose that lays the golden 'eggs** (*saying*) to destroy sth that would have produced continuous profit in the future. **'kill oneself (doing sth / to do sth)** (*infml*) to try too hard: *The party's at eight, but don't kill yourself getting here/to get here on time.* **kill 'time; kill two, a few, etc 'hours** to spend time as pleasantly as possible but not in a useful way, esp while waiting for sth: *My flight was delayed, so I killed time/killed two hours reading a magazine.* **kill two birds with one 'stone** to achieve two aims with a single action or at the same time. **PHRV** **kill sb/sth 'off** to destroy or rid oneself of sb/sth: *He killed off all his political opponents.* ○ *Much of the local plant life has been killed off by air pollution.*
▶ **kill** n **1** an act of killing sb/sth, esp an animal: *After stalking its prey the lioness now moves in for the kill.* **2** (usu sing) an animal or animals killed: *lions feeding on their kill.* **IDM** **(be) in at the 'kill** (to be) present at the end of a dramatic struggle, series

---

[V.to inf] = verb + *to* infinitive   [Vn.inf (no *to*)] = verb + noun + infinitive without *to*   [V.ing] = verb + *-ing* form

of events, etc: *She wants to be in at the kill when his business finally collapses.*

killer *n* a person, an animal or a thing that kills: *Police are hunting her killer.* ○ *Heroin is a killer.* ○ *Sharks have the killer instinct.* See also LADY-KILLER. **'killer whale** *n* a fierce black and white WHALE that eats meat.

killing /'kɪlɪŋ/ *n* an act of killing sb deliberately: *brutal killings.* See also MERCY KILLING. **IDM** **,make a 'killing** to have a great financial success: *She's made a killing on the stock market.*

▶ **killing** *adj* (*infml*) extremely fast and tiring: *walk at a killing pace.*

killjoy /'kɪldʒɔɪ/ *n* (*derog*) a person who spoils the enjoyment of others.

kiln /kɪln/ *n* an oven for baking clay or bricks, drying wood, etc.

kilo /'ki:ləʊ/ *n* (*pl* **-os**) kilogram. ➪ App 2.

kilo- *comb form* thousand: *kilogram* ○ *kilometre.*

kilogram (also **kilogramme**) /'kɪləgræm/ *n* (*abbr* **kg**) a metric unit of weight; the basic unit of mass in the international system; 1 000 grams. ➪ App 2,8.

kilohertz /'kɪləhɜ:ts/ *n* (*pl* unchanged) (*abbr* **kHz**) a unit of measurement of radio waves.

kilometre (*US* **-meter**) /'kɪləmi:tə(r), kɪ'lɒmɪtə(r)/ *n* (*abbr* **km**) a metric unit of length; 1 000 metres. ➪ App 2.

kilowatt /'kɪləwɒt/ *n* (*abbrs* **kW, kw**) a unit of electrical power; 1 000 watts (WATT).

■ **,kilowatt-'hour** *n* a measure of electrical energy equal to the power provided by one kilowatt in one hour.

kilt /kɪlt/ *n* (**a**) a skirt of pleated (PLEAT) TARTAN wool reaching to the knees, traditionally worn by Scottish men. ➪ picture at BAGPIPES. (**b**) a similar skirt worn by women or children.

▶ **kilted** *adj* wearing a kilt.

kimono /kɪ'məʊnəʊ; *US* -nə/ *n* (*pl* **-os**) (**a**) a long loose traditional Japanese garment with wide sleeves, worn with a belt. (**b**) a European dressing-gown (DRESSING) in this style.

kin /kɪn/ *n* [pl *v*] (*dated or fml*) one's family and relations: *She's my own kin — I must help her.* Compare KINDRED *n* b. See also NEXT OF KIN. **IDM** **kith and kin** ➪ KITH.

kind¹ /kaɪnd/ *adj* (**-er, -est**) **1** ~ (**to sb/sth**) showing concern about the happiness and feelings of others in a gentle and friendly way: *a kind man/heart/face* ○ *be kind to animals* ○ *She always has a kind word for* (ie speaks kindly to) *everyone.* ➪ note at NICE. **2** (used when making polite requests or when showing appreciation of sth sb has done for one): *Would you be kind enough to help me?* (ie Please help me.) ○ *'Do sit down.' 'That's very kind of you* (ie Thank you).'

▶ **kindly** *adv* **1** in a kind manner: *treat sb kindly* ○ *He spoke kindly to them.* **2** (used when making polite requests or with IRONY(1) when ordering sb to do sth) please: *Would you kindly hold this for a moment?* ○ *Kindly leave me alone!* **IDM** **take 'kindly to sb/sth** (usu in negative sentences) to be pleased by sb/sth; to accept sb/sth willingly: *She didn't take (at all) kindly to being called plump.*

kindly *adj* [usu attrib] (**-ier, -iest**) kind or friendly in character, manner or appearance: *a kindly man* ○ *give sb some kindly advice.* **kindliness** *n* [U].

kindness *n* **1** [U] the quality of being kind: *He did it entirely out of kindness, not for the money.* **2** [C] a kind act: *It would be a kindness to ask her to stay.* ○ *I can never repay her many kindnesses to me.* **IDM** **the milk of human kindness** ➪ MILK¹.

■ **,kind-'hearted** *adj* having a kind nature; sympathetic.

kind² /kaɪnd/ *n* **1** [C] a group of people or things having similar characteristics; a particular sort, type or variety: *fruit of various kinds/various kinds*

of fruit ○ *Do you want all the same kind, or a mixture?* ○ *Don't trust him: I know his kind* (ie what sort of person he is). ○ *She's not the kind (of woman/person) to lie.* ○ *They differ in size but not in kind.* **IDM** **in 'kind 1** (of payment) in goods, produce or services, not in money: *The farmer sometimes used to pay me in kind* (eg with a sack of potatoes). **2** with something similar: *repay insults in kind* (ie by being insulting in return). **a 'kind of** (*infml*) (used to express uncertainty): *I had a kind of* (ie a VAGUE(1)) *feeling this might happen.* ○ *He's a kind of unofficial adviser.* **'kind of** (*infml*) slightly; to some extent: *I feel kind of sorry for him.* **nothing of the 'kind/'sort** not at all so: *People had told me she was very pleasant but she's nothing of the kind.* **of a 'kind 1** very similar: *They were two of a kind — both extrovert and fun-loving.* **2** (*derog*) of an inferior type: *The town offers entertainments of a kind, but nothing like what you'll find in the city.* **something of the 'kind** something like what has been said: *Did you say they're moving? I'd heard something of the kind myself.*

NOTE In formal writing there is usually a singular noun after **kind of / sort of**: *What kind of/sort of tree is that?* ○ *There are many different kinds of/sorts of snake in South America.* In informal speech people use plural nouns: *I saw all kinds of/sorts of snakes in South America.* In more formal speech the noun can begin the phrase: *Snakes of many kinds/sorts are found in South America.*

Kind of / sort of are also used informally to show that somebody or something is not certain, or to express doubt: *'Is the film based on a true story?' 'Well, kind of/sort of, but some things have been changed.'* ○ *He gave a kind of/sort of funny smile and left the room.* ○ *She kind of/sort of likes him.*

---

kindergarten /'kɪndəgɑ:tn/ *n* a school for very young children.

kindle /'kɪndl/ *v* **1** to make sb start to feel hope, anger, desire, etc: [Vn] *kindle hopes/interest/anger* ○ *She had kindled a flame within him.* **2** to set light to sth: [Vn] *kindle a fire* ○ *The sparks kindled the dry grass.*

▶ **kindling** /'kɪndlɪŋ/ *n* [U] small pieces of dry wood for lighting fires.

kindred /'kɪndrəd/ *n* (*dated fml*) (**a**) [U] a family relationship. (**b**) [pl *v*] one's family and relations: *Most of his kindred still live in Ireland.* Compare KIN 1.

▶ **kindred** *adj* [attrib] (*fml*) **1** (*dated*) having a common source; related: *kindred families.* **2** similar: *hunting and shooting and kindred activities* ○ *We immediately realized that we were kindred spirits* (ie had similar tastes, feelings, etc).

kinetic /kɪ'netɪk/ *adj* [esp attrib] (*techn*) of or produced by movement: *kinetic energy.*

king /kɪŋ/ *n* **1** (the title of) the male ruler of an independent state, usu inheriting the position by right of birth: *the King of Denmark* ○ *be made/crowned king.* Compare QUEEN 1. **2** a person, an animal or a thing thought of as best or most important in some way: *the king of comedians/of Italian red wines.* **3** (in compounds) the largest variety of a species: *a king cobra/prawn.* **4(a)** the most important piece in CHESS. ➪ picture at CHESS. (**b**) a piece in draughts (DRAUGHT 3) that has reached the opponent's side of the board and so can move backwards as well as forwards. (**c**) (in a pack of cards) a card with the picture of a king on it: *the king of spades.* **IDM** **the King's/Queen's English** ➪ ENGLISH. **a ,king's 'ransom** a very large amount of money: *That painting must be worth a king's ransom.* **turn King's/Queen's evidence** ➪ EVIDENCE. **the un-crowned king/queen** ➪ UNCROWNED.

▶ **kingly** *adj* of, like or suitable for a king; REGAL: *his kingly bearing*.

kingship /-ʃɪp/ *n* [U] the state of being, or the official position of, a king.

■ **'king-size** (also **-sized**) *adj* [esp attrib] larger than normal; extra large: *a king-size bed/cigarette* ○ *king-sized portions*.

King's/Queen's 'Bench (*abbrs* KB, QB) *n* [sing] (*law*) (in Britain) a division of the High Court of Justice.

King's/Queen's 'Counsel *n* (*abbrs* KC, QC) (*law*) (in Britain) a BARRISTER appointed to act for the government.

kingdom /'kɪŋdəm/ *n* **1** a country or state ruled by a king or queen: *the United Kingdom*. **2** any one of the three divisions of the natural world: *the animal, plant/vegetable and mineral kingdoms*. **3** an area under the control of or associated with a particular thing, person or organization: *the kingdom of the imagination* ○ *the kingdom of God/heaven*. **IDM** **till/until kingdom 'come** (*infml*) for ever: *Don't mention politics or we'll be here till kingdom come*. **to kingdom 'come** (*infml*) into the life after death: *The bomb exploded and blew them all to kingdom come*.

kingfisher /'kɪŋfɪʃə(r)/ *n* a small bird with bright colours and a long beak, which catches fish in rivers, etc. ⇨ picture.

kingfisher

kingpin /'kɪŋpɪn/ *n* a person or thing essential for success: *He's the kingpin of the whole team*.

kink /kɪŋk/ *n* **1** a sharp twist in sth that is otherwise straight, eg wire, rope or hair: *a dog with a kink in its tail*. **2** (*usu derog*) an unusual or abnormal characteristic, esp in sb's mind or personality: *straighten out the kinks in one's psyche*. ▶ **kink** *v* to form or make sth form kinks: [V] *Don't let the rope kink*. [also Vn].

kinky *adj* (*infml usu derog*) involving or suggesting unusual sexual behaviour: *kinky boots* ○ *There's lots of sex in the film, but nothing kinky*.

kinship /'kɪnʃɪp/ *n* **1** [U] a family relationship: *claim kinship with sb*. **2** [U, sing] a close feeling between people that develops as a result of common origins, attitudes, etc: *Even after meeting only once, they felt a kinship*.

kinsman /'kɪnzmən/ *n* (*pl* **-men** /-mən/; *fem* **kinswoman** /-wʊmən/, *pl* **-women** /-wɪmɪn/) (*dated or fml*) a family relation.

kiosk /'kiːɒsk/ *n* a small shop, open at the front, where newspapers, sandwiches, soft drinks, etc are sold. **2** (*Brit becoming dated*) a public telephone box.

kip /kɪp/ *n* [U, C usu sing] (*Brit sl*) sleep: *get some kip* ○ *have a kip*. ▶ **kip** *v* (**-pp-**) (*Brit sl*) to lie down to sleep: [Vpr, Vp] *kip (down) on the floor* [V] *Kip here tonight, if you like*.

kipper /'kɪpə(r)/ *n* a HERRING, split open, preserved with salt, and then dried or smoked. Kippers are often eaten cooked for breakfast.

kirk /kɜːk/ *n* (*Scot*) church: *go to (the) kirk*.

kirsch /kɪəʃ/ *n* [U] a strong alcoholic drink made from cherries (CHERRY 1).

kiss /kɪs/ *v* to touch sb/sth with the lips to show love, affection or respect, or as a greeting: [Vn] *kiss the children good night* [V] *They stood on the doorstep kissing*. [Vnpr] *She kissed him on the lips*. **IDM** **kiss sth good'bye/kiss good'bye to sth** (*sl*) to accept as certain the loss or failure of sth: *You can kiss that money goodbye — he'll never pay you back!* ▶ **kiss** *n* a touch with the lips: *give sb a kiss* ○ *greet sb with hugs and kisses*. **IDM** **blow a kiss** ⇨ BLOW¹.

the kiss of 'death (*infml esp joc*) an apparently favourable action that makes failure certain: *one of those polite lukewarm reviews that are the kiss of death for any musical*.

■ **the ˌkiss of 'life** *n* [sing] a method of restoring breathing to save the life of sb injured or rescued from drowning (DROWN 1) by putting one's own mouth on theirs and breathing into it: (*fig*) *the government's £2 million kiss of life for the ailing cotton industry*.

kit /kɪt/ *n* **1** [U] the clothing and personal equipment of a soldier, etc: *a kit allowance*. **2** [C,U] the equipment needed for a particular, esp sporting, activity, situation or trade: *a first-'aid kit* ○ *a re'pair kit* ○ *'shaving kit* ○ *'riding-kit* ○ *a 'drum kit*. **3** [C] a set of all the parts needed to assemble sth : *buy a model aeroplane kit* ○ *furniture in kit form* ○ *a kit car*.

▶ **kit** *v* (**-tt-**) **PHRV** ˌkit **sb 'out/'up (in/with sth)** (*Brit*) to equip sb: *be all kitted out in brand-new ski clothes*.

kitbag /'kɪtbæg/ *n* a long canvas bag in which soldiers, etc carry their clothes and other possessions.

rolling-pin   **kitchen implements**

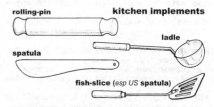

ladle

spatula

fish-slice (*esp US* **spatula**)

kitchen /'kɪtʃɪn/ *n* a room or building in which meals are cooked or prepared: *the kitchen table* ○ *kitchen units* (ie cupboards, etc forming part of a fitted kitchen). ⇨ picture. See also SOUP-KITCHEN. **IDM** **everything but the kitchen 'sink** (*infml joc*) a very large number of things, probably more than is necessary: *We seem to take everything but the kitchen sink when we go camping*.

▶ **kitchenette** /ˌkɪtʃɪ'net/ *n* a small room or part of a room used as a kitchen, eg in a flat.

■ ˌ**kitchen 'garden** *n* a garden, or part of a garden, where fruit and vegetables are grown.

kitchenware /'kɪtʃɪnweə(r)/ *n* [U] equipment used in a kitchen, eg dishes and pans.

kite /kaɪt/ *n* **1** a toy consisting of a light framework covered with paper or cloth. It flies in the air at the end of one or more long strings: *fly a kite* ○ *kite-flying*. **2** a type of HAWK(1) that catches and eats small birds and animals. **IDM** **fly a kite** ⇨ FLY¹. **fly a/one's kite** ⇨ FLY¹.

Kitemark /'kaɪtmɑːk/ *n* (in Britain) an official mark, in the form of a KITE(1), on goods approved by the British Standards Institution.

kith /kɪθ/ *n* **IDM** **kith and kin** friends and relations.

kitsch /kɪtʃ/ *n* [U] (*derog*) popular art or design that is lacking in good taste by being too bright, sentimental or PRETENTIOUS in style: *kitsch plaster dogs on the mantelpiece*.

kitten /'kɪtn/ *n* a young cat. **IDM** **have 'kittens** (*Brit infml*) to be very anxious or tense: *She's having kittens about her oral exam*.

▶ **kittenish** *adj* (*esp of women*) lively and playful.

kitty¹ /'kɪti/ *n* **1** (*infml*) a fund of money to which a group of people have contributed and in which they all share: *We each put £2 in the kitty, and then sent John to buy food for everybody*. **2** (in some card-games) a sum of money to which each player contributes and which is given to the winner.

kitty² /'kɪti/ *n* (*infml*) (used by or when speaking to young children) a cat or a KITTEN.

kiwi /ˈkiːwiː/ *n* **1** **Kiwi** (*infml*) a person from New Zealand. **2** a New Zealand bird that cannot fly, with a long beak, short wings and no tail. ▷ picture.

kiwi

■ ˈ**kiwi fruit** *n* (*pl* unchanged) a small OVAL fruit with thin brown hairy skin, soft green flesh and black seeds.

Klaxon /ˈklæksn/ *n* (*propr*) a powerful electric horn or SIREN(1).

Kleenex /ˈkliːneks/ *n* [U, C] (*pl* unchanged or **Kleenexes**) (*propr*) a sheet of soft paper used as a HANDKERCHIEF; a tissue: *a packet of Kleenex.*

kleptomania /ˌkleptəˈmeɪniə/ *n* [U] a mental condition that causes a strong desire to steal things, often with no wish to possess the things stolen.
▶ **kleptomaniac** /-niæk/ *n* a person suffering from kleptomania.

km *abbr* (*pl* unchanged or **kms**) kilometre(s): *a 10 km walk* ○ *distance to beach 2 kms.*

knack /næk/ *n* [sing] **1** ~ (**for sth/doing sth**) a skill at performing some special task; an ability: *Making pancakes is easy once you've got the knack.* ○ *lose the knack of sth* ○ *have a knack for picking winners.* **2** ~ **of doing sth** a trick or habit of doing sth: *My car has an uncanny knack of breaking down just when I need it most.* ○ *He has this unfortunate knack of always saying the wrong thing.*

knacker /ˈnækə(r)/ *v* [Vn] (*Brit sl*) to make sb very tired.
▶ **knackered** *adj* [esp pred] (*Brit sl*) extremely tired; worn-out (WORN[2]): *I was completely knackered after the game.*

knacker's yard /ˈnækəz jɑːd/ *n* [C usu *sing*] (*becoming dated*) a place where old or injured horses are taken to be killed and their flesh sold: (*fig*) *a business going nowhere except the knacker's yard.*

knapsack /ˈnæpsæk/ *n* (*dated*) = RUCKSACK.

knave /neɪv/ *n* **1** (*fml*) = JACK[1] 3: *the knave of hearts.* **2** (*arch*) a dishonest man.

knead /niːd/ *v* **1** to press and stretch DOUGH(1), wet clay, etc with the hands so that it becomes firm and smooth: [Vn, Vnpr] *Knead the dough (into a ball).* **2** [Vn] to MASSAGE(1a) muscles, etc firmly to relieve tension or pain.

knee /niː/ *n* **1(a)** the joint between the upper and lower parts of the leg, where it bends. ▷ picture at HUMAN. **(b)** the upper surface of the top part of sb's leg when they are sitting: *Come and sit on my knee.* **2** the part of a garment covering the knee: *These jeans are torn at the knee.* IDM **be/go (down) on one's ˈknees** to kneel or be kneeling, esp when praying or to show that one accepts defeat. **the bee's knees** ▷ BEE[1]. **bring sb to their ˈknees** to force sb to admit that they are defeated: *The industry was brought to its knees by the strike.* **on bended knee** ▷ BEND[1]. **weak at the knees** ▷ WEAK.
▶ **knee** *v* (*pt, pp* **kneed**) to hit or push sb/sth with the knee: [Vn, Vnpr] *knee sb (in the groin).*
■ ˌ**knee-ˈdeep** *adj* **1** deep enough to reach the knees: *The snow was knee-deep in places.* **2** ~ **in sth** deeply involved in or very busy with sth: *be knee-deep in trouble/work.* — *adv*: *He went knee-deep in the icy water.*
ˌ**knee-ˈhigh** *adj* high enough to reach the knees: ˌ*knee-high* ˈ*grass/* ˈ*boots.* IDM **knee-high to a** ˈ**grasshopper** (*joc*) (of a child) very small: *I've known him since he was knee-high to a grasshopper.*
ˈ**knee-jerk** *adj* done or produced automatically and without thought: *A knee-jerk reaction/response.*
ˈ**knee-length** *adj* long enough to reach the knee: *a* ˌ*knee-length* ˈ*skirt.*
ˈ**knees-up** *n* (usu *sing*) (*Brit infml*) a lively party, usu with dancing.

kneecap /ˈniːkæp/ *n* a small bone covering the front of the knee joint. ▷ picture at SKELETON.
▶ **kneecap** *v* (**-pp-**) [Vn] to shoot or break sb's kneecaps as a punishment. ˈ**kneecapping** *n* [C, U]: *more terrorist kneecappings.*

squatting　　　　　　　　kneel

crouching

kneeling　　　　　　on all fours

kneel /niːl/ *v* (*pt, pp* **knelt** /nelt/ or, *esp US*, **kneeled**) ~ (**down**) to take or be in a position where the body is supported by the knees, with the lower leg bent back: [V] *a kneeling figure* [V, Vp, Vpr] *They knelt (down) (on the ground) to pray.* ▷ picture.

knell /nel/ *n* (usu *sing*) the sound of a bell rung slowly after a death or at a funeral. See also DEATH-KNELL.

knew *pt* of KNOW.

knickerbockers /ˈnɪkəbɒkəz/ (*US* **knickers** /ˈnɪkəz/) *n* [pl] short trousers gathered (GATHER 1) just below the knee.

knickers /ˈnɪkəz/ *n* [pl] **1** (*Brit*) a woman's or girl's garment worn under other clothes and covering the body from the waist to the tops of the legs: *wearing only (a pair of) knickers and a bra.* **2** (*US*) = KNICKERBOCKERS. IDM **get one's ˈknickers in a twist** (*Brit sl*) to become angry, confused or nervous; to react to sth more strongly than is necessary: *There's no need to get your knickers in a twist — we've got two hours before the plane leaves.*

knick-knack (also **nick-nack**) /ˈnɪk næk/ *n* (esp *pl*) (*sometimes derog*) small ornaments on display in a house, usu of little value: *a collection of knick-knacks.*

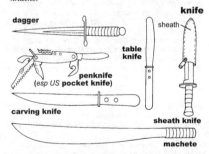

knife

dagger　　　　　　　　　　　sheath

table knife

penknife
(*esp US* pocket knife)

carving knife

sheath knife

machete

knife /naɪf/ *n* (*pl* **knives** /naɪvz/) **1** a sharp blade with a handle, used for cutting or as a weapon: *put the knives and forks on the table* ○ *He had been stabbed repeatedly with a kitchen knife.* ▷ picture. See also CARVING KNIFE, PAPER-KNIFE, PENKNIFE. **2** a cutting blade in a machine or tool. IDM **get one's ˈknife into sb/have one's ˈknife in sb** to have HOSTILE(1a) feelings and intentions towards sb one dislikes very much: *She's really got her knife into me — everything I do, she criticizes.* **the ˈknives are out (for sb)** the situation has become so bad that people are ready to destroy sb's reputation, remove sb from office, etc: *The knives were out for the chancellor.* **like a knife through ˈbutter** easily; without meeting any resistance or difficulty: *The power saw*

K

sliced the logs like a knife through butter. **turn/twist the ˈknife (in the wound)** to make sb who is already suffering suffer even more.

▶ **knife** *v* to injure or kill sb with a knife: [Vnpr] *be knifed to death* [Vn, Vnpr] *The victim had been knifed (in the chest).*

■ **ˈknife-edge** *n* (usu *sing*) the sharp edge of the blade of a knife: *(fig) have knife-edge creases in one's trousers.* **IDM** **on a ˈknife-edge 1** (of a person) very nervous about the outcome of sth: *He's on a knife-edge about his exam results.* **2** (of a situation, etc) at a critical point; very finely balanced between success and failure: *My future was poised on a knife-edge.* ○ *a knife-edge budget/victory.*

ˈknife-point *n* **IDM** **at ˈknife-point** while threatening sb or being threatened with a knife: *rob/rape sb at knife-point.*

knight /naɪt/ *n* **1** a man with a rank of honour given by the King or Queen for his services to the country, having the title 'Sir' before his name. **2** (in medieval times) a man of noble rank with a duty to fight for his King. Knights are often shown in pictures riding horses and wearing armour. **3** a chess piece, usu shaped like a horse's head. ⇨ picture at CHESS. **IDM** **a knight in shining ˈarmour** *(joc)* a person who saves one from a difficult or dangerous situation: *waiting in vain for a knight in shining armour to rescue the company.*

▶ **knight** *v* (esp passive) to make sb a knight: [Vn, Vnpr] *He was knighted by the Queen (for his services to industry).*

knighthood /-hʊd/ *n* [C, U] the rank, title or state of a knight: *be awarded/given a knighthood* ○ *receive a knighthood.*

knightly *adj* [usu attrib] *(arch)* noble and brave: *knightly chivalry.*

■ **ˌknight ˈerrant** *n* (*pl* **knights errant**) a medieval knight who wandered in search of adventure.

knit /nɪt/ *v* (**-tt-**; *pt, pp* **knitted** or, in sense 2, usu **knit**) **1(a)** to make garments, etc by creating rows of connecting loops of esp wool thread, using long metal, plastic or wooden needles: [Vn] *knit a sweater* ○ *knit 5 rows* [Vnn] *knit John a cardigan* [V] *Her favourite pastime is knitting.* [also Vpr, Vnpr]. **(b)** [Vn, Vpr, Vnpr] to perform a similar procedure using a machine. **(c)** to do the basic stitch: [Vn] *knit one, purl one* [also V]. **2** ~ (**sth**) (**together**) to join or be joined firmly or closely together: [V, Vp] *The broken bones have knit (together) well.* [Vnadv] *(fig) a tightly-/closely-knit community* ○ *a tight-/close-knit group.* **IDM** **knit one's ˈbrow(s)** to lower one's eyebrows (EYEBROW) showing concentration, disapproval, etc; to FROWN.

▶ **knit** *n* a knitted garment: *big baggy knits.*

knitter *n* a person who knits.

knitting *n* [U] material that is being knitted: *Oh dear, I've left my knitting on the bus!* **ˈknitting-needle** *n* a long thin needle used for knitting by hand.

knitwear /ˈnɪtweə(r)/ *n* [U] knitted garments.

knob /nɒb/ *n* **1(a)** a round handle, esp of a door or drawer. **(b)** a round control button for adjusting a radio, television, etc. **2** a round lump on the surface of sth, eg a tree trunk. **3** a small lump of butter, coal, etc. **IDM** **with ˈknobs on** *(Brit sl)* (used for returning and strengthening an insult): *'You're a fool!' 'And the same to you, with knobs on!'*

knobbly /ˈnɒbli/ (also *esp US* **knobby** /ˈnɒbi/) *adj* having many small hard lumps: *knobbly knees/carrots.*

knock¹ /nɒk/ *n* **1** a firm sharp sound made with the hand on a door, etc in order to attract attention: *There was a knock at the door.* ○ *If you're not up by eight o'clock I'll give you a knock (ie to wake you).* Compare TAP² *n.* **2** an injury caused by one's body hitting sth hard: *She fell off her bike and got a nasty*

knock on her leg. **3** (in an engine) the sound of metal hitting metal, indicating a mechanical problem. **IDM** **take a ˈknock** *(infml)* to be badly affected by sth; to suffer: *The dollar took a further knock today.*

knock² /nɒk/ *v* **1** to hit a door, etc firmly with the back of one's hand in order to attract attention: [V, Vpr] *knock three times (at the door/on the window).* ⇨ note at BANG¹. **2** ~ **sth** (**against/on sth**) to hit sth, often accidentally, with a sharp blow: [Vn, Vnpr] *Mind you don't knock your head (on this low beam).* [Vpr] *His hand knocked against the glass.* **3** to put sb/sth in a certain state or position by hitting them/it: [Vn-adj] *The blow knocked me flat/senseless.* [Vn.ing] *He knocked my drink flying.* **4** to make a hole in sth by hitting and breaking it: [Vnpr] *knock a hole in the wall* [Vnp] *knock the window out.* **5** [V] (of a faulty engine) to make a regular sound of metal hitting metal. **6** (of the heart or knees) to beat or shake violently, eg from fear: [V, Vp] *Her knees were knocking (together) in terror.* **7** *(infml)* to say critical or insulting things about sb/sth: [Vn] *The newspapers are always knocking the England team.* **IDM** **beat/knock the daylights out of sb** ⇨ DAYLIGHTS. **beat/knock hell out of sb/sth** ⇨ HELL. **get/knock/lick sth/sb into shape** ⇨ SHAPE¹. **hit/knock sb for six** ⇨ HIT¹. **knock sb's ˈblock/ˈhead off** *(sl)* (used esp as a threat) to hit sb in anger: *Call me that again and I'll knock your block off!* **knock the ˈbottom out of sth** to cause sth to collapse: *knock the bottom out of the coffee market* (ie cause the price of coffee to fall sharply). **knock your/their ˈheads together** *(infml)* to force people to stop quarrelling and behave sensibly: *I often feel that politicians should have their heads knocked together.* **knock sb/sth into a cocked ˈhat** to be very much better than sb/sth: *A professional photographer could knock my pathetic efforts into a cocked hat.* **knock it ˈoff** *(sl)* (esp imperative) to stop making a noise or annoying one, etc: *Knock it off, kids — I'm trying to work!* **knock sb off their ˈpedestal/ˈperch** *(infml)* to make sb lose their prominent position: *knock the market leaders off their pedestal.* **knock sth on the ˈhead** to prevent a plan, project, suggestion, etc from being taken further: *The recession knocked on the head any idea of expanding the company.* **knock on wood** = TOUCH WOOD. **knock sb ˈsideways** *(infml)* to surprise or shock sb so much that they are unable to react immediately: *The news knocked him completely sideways.* **knock ˈspots off sb/sth** *(Brit infml)* to be very much better than sb/sth: *She knocks spots off all the other candidates.* **knock the ˈstuffing out of sb** *(infml)* to make sb lose their confidence and enthusiasm; to discourage sb: *Failing the exam has knocked all the stuffing out of him.* **you could have knocked me down with a ˈfeather** *(infml)* (used to express surprise). **PHRV** **ˌknock aˈbout/aˈround (…)** *(infml)* to travel and live in various places: *spend a few years knocking about (in) Europe.* **2** to be in a place that is not remembered or not considered important: *My dictionary is knocking around here somewhere.* **ˌknock aˈbout/aˈround with sb / together** *(infml)* to be often in sb's/each other's company. **ˌknock sb/sth aˈbout/aˈround** *(infml)* to hit sb/sth repeatedly; to treat sb/sth roughly: *be badly knocked about by the police* ○ *Her husband knocks her around.*

ˌknock sb ˈback *(infml)* to cost sb a lot of money: *Buying that house must have knocked them back a bit.* **ˌknock sth ˈback** *(infml)* to drink sth eagerly and quickly: *knock back a couple of beers.*

ˌknock sb ˈdown to hit sb and make them fall to the ground: *She was knocked down by a bus.* ○ *He knocked his opponent down three times in the first round.* **ˌknock sth ˈdown** to destroy a building by breaking its walls: *These old houses are going to be knocked down.* **ˌknock sth ˈdown (to sb)** *(infml)* (at an AUCTION sale) to sell sth to a bidder (BID¹): *The* *vase was knocked down (to an American dealer) for £5 000*. ˌknock sth/sb 'down to reduce or force sb to reduce a price or charge: *I managed to knock his price/him down (from £500 to £450).*

ˌknock sth 'in; ˌknock sth 'into sth to make sth enter sth and remain firmly in place by hitting it: *knock in a few nails.*

ˌknock 'off (sth) (*infml*) to stop doing sth, esp work: *What time do you knock off (work)?* ˌknock sb 'off (*sl*) to murder sb. ˌknock sth 'off 1 to reduce the price or value of sth: *I'll knock £5 off the jug because it's chipped.* ○ *The news knocked 13% off IBM's shares today.* 2 (*infml*) to complete sth quickly and without much effort: *knock off three novels a year.* 3 (*sl*) to steal sth from a place: *knock off some watches from a shop* ○ *knock off a bank.* ˌknock sth 'off (sth) to cause sth to fall from a place: *knock sb's glass off the table.*

ˌknock sb 'out 1 (in boxing) to hit an opponent so that he cannot rise in a specified time and so loses the fight. See also KNOCKOUT 2. 2 to make sb fall asleep or become unconscious: *Don't drink too much of this — it'll knock you out!* ○ *The blow knocked her out.* 3 (*infml*) to have a strong emotional effect on sb; to astonish sb: *The movie just knocked me out — it's the best I've ever seen.* ˌknock sb/oneself 'out to make sb/oneself very tired: *Christmas shopping just knocks me out.* ˌknock sb 'out (of sth) to defeat sb so that they no longer continue competing: *France knocked Belgium out (of the World Cup).* ˌknock sth 'out (*infml*) to produce sth: *He knocks out five books a year.*

ˌknock sb/sth 'over to make sb/sth fall or spill by striking them/it: *You've knocked over my drink!*

ˌknock sth to'gether (*esp Brit*) to make or complete sth quickly and often not very well: *knock bookshelves together from old planks* ○ *knock a few scenes together to make a play.*

ˌknock 'up (in tennis, etc) to practise for a short time before the start of a game. ˌknock sb 'up 1 (*Brit infml*) to wake sb by knocking on their door: *She knocked me up at 5.30.* 2 (△ *sl esp US*) to make a woman pregnant. ˌknock sth 'up to prepare or make sth quickly and without special care: *She knocked up a fantastic meal in ten minutes.*

■ 'knock-down *adj* [attrib] (of prices) very low.

ˌknock-'kneed *adj* having legs abnormally curved so that the knees touch when standing or walking.

ˌknock-'on *adj* resulting indirectly from a previous action, etc: *create ˌknock-on em'ployment* ○ *This industrial dispute will have serious knock-on effects.*

'knock-up *n* [sing] (in tennis, etc) a short period of practice before a game: *have a quick knock-up.*

knockabout /'nɒkəbaʊt/ *adj* [usu attrib] (of a performer or a performance) amusing in a rather silly way: *knockabout comedy.*

knocker /'nɒkə(r)/ *n* 1 (also 'door-knocker) [C] a metal object attached to the outside of the door of a house, etc which is struck against the door to attract attention: *a polished brass knocker.* ➪ picture at HOUSE¹. 2 [C] (*infml*) a person who constantly criticizes. 3 **knockers** [pl] (△ *sl sexist*) a woman's breasts.

knockout /'nɒkaʊt/ *n* 1(a) a competition in which the winner continues to a further round and the loser no longer takes part: *a knockout tournament.* (b) a defeat in such a competition: *suffer a league cup knockout.* 2 a blow that causes a boxer to lose a contest: *a fifth-round knockout* ○ *a knockout punch.* 3 [sing] (*infml*) a wonderful or outstanding person or thing: *She's an absolute knockout (ie very beautiful).*

knoll /nəʊl/ *n* a small round hill.

knot¹ /nɒt/ *n* 1 a fastening made by tying a piece or pieces of string, rope, etc: *make a knot at*

knot

knot

the end of the rope* ○ *tie two ropes together with a knot* ○ *(fig) hair full of knots (ie twisted together in an untidy way).* ➪ picture. 2 a way of twisting hair into a small round shape at the back: *She wears her hair in a tight knot.* 3 a hard round spot in a piece of wood where a branch once joined the trunk or another branch. ➪ picture at GRAIN. 4 a small gathering of people: *a knot of people outside the factory gates.* **IDM** **cut the Gordian knot** ➪ GORDIAN KNOT. **tie sb/oneself into/in knots** ➪ TIE². **tie the knot** ➪ TIE².

▶ **knot** *v* (-tt-) 1 to form a knot or knots: [Vadv] *This thread knots easily.* [Vnp] *knot two ropes together.* 2 to fasten sth with a knot or knots: [Vn] *knot one's tie* [Vnpr] *a scarf knotted loosely round his neck.* 3 (of muscles, etc) to become hard and painful because of fear, excitement, tension, etc: [V, Vp] *The muscles in his neck had knotted (up).* **IDM** **get 'knotted** (*Brit sl*) (used to express contempt, annoyance, etc): *If he asks you for money again, just tell him to get knotted.*

knotty *adj* (-ier, -iest) 1 full of knots: *knotty wood* ○ *Your hair's all knotty.* 2 complex and difficult to solve: *a knotty problem/question.*

knot² /nɒt/ *n* (usu *pl*) (*nautical*) a unit of speed used by ships and aircraft; one nautical mile per hour. **IDM** **at a rate of knots** ➪ RATE¹.

know /nəʊ/ *v* (*pt* **knew** /njuː; *US* nuː/; *pp* **known** /nəʊn/) 1(a) to have sth in one's mind or memory as a result of experience, learning or being given information: [Vn] *She doesn't know your address.* [V.that] *Every child knows (that) two and two make four.* [V.wh] *I knew where he was hiding.* [V] *He did it without my knowing.* [V.to inf] *Does he know to come here (ie that he should come here) first?* [V.n to inf] *We know her to be honest.* (b) (only in the past and perfect tenses) to have seen, heard, or experienced sth: [Vn.inf (no to), V.n to inf] *I've never known it (to) snow in July before.* 2 to feel certain; to be sure: [V.that] *I know (that) it's here somewhere!* 3 to be familiar with a person or place: [Vn] *Do you know Bob Hill?* [Vadv] *I know Paris well.* [Vnpr] *I know him by sight, but not to talk to (ie I have seen him but never spoken to him).* 4 ~ sb/sth as sth (esp passive) (a) to regard sb/sth in a particular way or as having particular characteristics: [Vn-n] *It's known as the most dangerous part of the city.* [V.n to inf] *He's known to be an outstanding physicist.* (b) to give sb/sth a particular name, label, title, etc: [Vn-n] *Peter Wilson, also known as The Tiger* ○ *This area is known as the 'Cornish Riviera'.* 5 ~ sb/sth (from sb/sth) to be able to distinguish one person or thing from another; to recognize sth: [Vnpr] *know right from wrong* [Vn] *She knows a bargain when she sees one.* 6 to have learned a skill and be able to use it: [Vn] *know Japanese* [V.wh] *Do you know how to use a word processor?* 7 to have personal experience of sth: [Vn] *a man who has known both poverty and riches.* **IDM** **before one knows where one 'is** very quickly or suddenly: *We were whisked off in a taxi before we knew where we were.* **be known to sb** be familiar to sb: *He's known to the police (ie as a criminal).* **better the devil you know** ➪ BETTER². **for aught/all one/sb cares/knows** ➪ AUGHT. **for reasons / some reason best known to oneself** ➪ REASON¹. **God/goodness/Heaven knows 1** (used to emphasize that one does not know sth): *'Where are they?' 'Goodness knows.'* **2** (used to introduce evidence emphasizing the truth of a statement): *She ought to succeed; goodness knows she tries hard enough.* **have/know all the 'answers** ➪ ANSWER¹. **have/know sth off pat** ➪ PAT². **have seen/known better days** ➪ BETTER¹. **know sth as well as 'I/'you do** (used to introduce a criticism) to understand sth perfectly well: *You know as well as I do that you're being unreasonable.* **know sth 'backwards** (*infml*) to be thor-

K

oughly familiar with sth: *You've read that book so many times you must know it backwards by now!* **know 'best** to know what should be done, etc better than other people: *The doctor told you to stay in bed, and he knows best.* **know better (than that / than to do sth)** to be wiser or more sensible: *You ought to know better (than to trust her).* ○ *You left the car unlocked? You should know better than that.* **know 'different/'otherwise** (*infml*) to have information or evidence to the contrary: *He says he was at the cinema, but I know different.* **know sb/sth inside 'out; know sb/sth like the back of one's 'hand** (*infml*) to be thoroughly familiar with a person, place, subject, etc: *He's a taxi driver, so he knows the city like the back of his hand.* **know no 'bounds** (*fml*) to be very great or too great: *Her love/ generosity/fury knew no bounds.* **know one's 'on-ions;** (*Brit*) **know one's 'stuff** (*infml*) to be considered an expert at sth. **know one's own 'mind** to know very clearly what one wants or intends. **know the 'score** (*infml*) to understand the true state of affairs or the consequences of one's actions: *He knows the score: if he's late for work again he'll lose his job.* **know / tell sb a thing or two** ⇨ THING. **know one's way a'round** to be familiar with a place, subject, procedure, etc. **know what it is / what it's like (to be/do sth)** to have personal experience of being/doing sth: *Many famous people have known what it is to be poor.* **know what one's 'talking about** (*infml*) to speak from experience; to be an expert on sth: *I've lived in China, so I know what I'm talking about.* **know which side one's 'bread is buttered** (*infml*) to know where one's interests lie or what will be to one's advantage. **let it be known / make it known that ...** to tell people sth openly or indirectly: *He's let it be known that he wants no presents when he retires.* **let sb 'know** to inform sb about sth: *I don't know if I can come, but I'll let you know tomorrow.* **Lord knows** ⇨ LORD. **make oneself 'known to sb** to introduce oneself to sb: *I made myself known to the hotel manager.* **not know any 'better** to behave badly, usu because one has not been taught the correct way to behave: *Don't blame the children — they don't know any better.* **not know one's ,arse from one's 'elbow** (△ *sl derog*) to be totally ignorant, stupid or lacking in skill. **not know the first thing a'bout sb/sth / doing sth** to know nothing at all about sb/sth: *I'm afraid I don't know the first thing about gardening.* **not know sb from 'Adam** (*infml*) not to know at all who sb is. **not know the 'meaning of the word** to behave as if one does not know that such an idea exists: *'Polite — him? He doesn't know the meaning of the word.'* **not know what 'hit one** (*infml*) to be completely taken by surprise and not know how to react: *The first time I heard their music, I didn't know what had hit me.* **not know where / which way to 'look** (*infml*) to feel great embarrassment at sb's behaviour or remarks: *When he started undressing, I didn't know where to look.* **not want to know** ⇨ WANT¹. **old enough to know better** ⇨ OLD. **show sb / know / learn the ropes** ⇨ ROPE. **there's no 'knowing/'saying/'telling** it's difficult or impossible to predict: *There's absolutely no knowing how he'll react.* **(well) what do you 'know (about 'that)?** (*infml esp US*) (used to express surprise): *Well what do you know? Look who's here!* **,you 'know** (*infml*) **1** (used when reminding sb of sth): *Guess who I've just seen? Marcia! You know — Jim's wife!* **2** (used in conversation to keep the attention of the person listening or to give one time to think what to say next): *'I was feeling a bit bored, you know, and so ...'* **you 'know something/'what?** (*infml*) (used to introduce an item of news, an opinion, etc): *You 'know something? I've never really enjoyed Christmas.* **you never know** you cannot be certain: *'It's sure to rain tomorrow.' 'Oh, you never know, it could be a nice day.'* ○ *You never know when you might need those old jamjars.* **PHR V 'know about sth** to have knowledge of sth; to be aware of sth: *Not much is known about his background.* ○ *Do you know about Jack getting arrested?* **'know of sb/ sth** to have information about or experience of sth: *'Isn't tomorrow a holiday?' 'Not that I know of* (ie Not as far as I am aware).*'* ○ *Do you know of any way to stop a person snoring?* ○ *I don't know him personally, though I know 'of him.*

▶ **know** *n* **IDM in the 'know** (*infml*) belonging to a small group of people who know the truth about a particular person or situation: *Somebody in the know told me he's about to resign.*

■ **'know-all** (*US* **'know-it-all**) *n* (*infml derog*) a person who behaves as if he or she knows everything: *She's a real know-all.*

'know-how *n* [U] practical knowledge, skill or experience in sth: *financial know-how* ○ *We need somebody with the know-how to check the equipment.*

knowing /'nəʊɪŋ/ *adj* [usu attrib] showing or suggesting that one has information which is secret or known only to a few people: *a knowing smile* ○ *She gave me a knowing look* when I mentioned John's name.

▶ **knowingly** *adv* **1** intentionally; while knowing the truth or the likely consequences: *knowingly withhold crucial information* ○ *I would never knowingly lie to you.* **2** in a knowing manner: *He smiled at her knowingly.*

knowledge /'nɒlɪdʒ/ *n* **1(a)** [U, sing] the facts, information, understanding and skills that a person has acquired through experience or education: *I have only (a) limited knowledge of computer programming.* ○ *He has/shows a detailed knowledge of Renaissance art.* ○ *A baby has no knowledge of the difference between good and evil.* **(b)** [U] an organized body of information shared by people in a particular field: *specialist/scientific knowledge.* **2** the awareness of a fact or situation: *She sent it without my knowledge.* ○ *He denied all knowledge of the affair.* **IDM be common/public 'knowledge** to be known by everyone in a community or group: *Their relationship is common knowledge.* **come to sb's 'knowledge** (*fml*) to come to sb's attention; to become known by sb: *It has come to our knowledge that you have been taking time off without permission.* **to one's 'knowledge** as far as one knows personally: *To my knowledge, she has never been late before.* **to the best of one's belief/knowledge** ⇨ BEST³.

▶ **knowledgeable** /-əbl/ *adj* ~ (about sth) knowing a lot about sth: *She's extremely/immensely knowledgeable about art.* **knowledgeably** /-əbli/ *adv.*

known *pp* of KNOW: *He's a known thief* (ie It is known that he is one). ○ *This disease has no known cure.*

knuckle /'nʌkl/ *n* **1** any joint in the fingers, esp those where the fingers join the rest of the hand: *bleeding/swollen knuckles.* ⇨ picture at HAND¹. **2** (of animals) the knee or joint joining the leg to the foot, esp as a piece of meat: *pig's knuckles.* **IDM give sb / get a rap on/over the knuckles** ⇨ RAP. **near the 'knuckle** (*infml*) (of a remark, joke, etc) almost offensive.

▶ **knuckle** *v* **PHR V ,knuckle 'down to sth** (*infml*) to begin to work hard at sth: *If you want to pass that exam, you'll have to knuckle down (to some hard study).* **,knuckle 'under (to sb/sth)** (*infml*) to surrender or submit to sb/sth: *knuckle under to threats.*

knuckleduster /'nʌkldʌstə(r)/ *n* [C] (*US* **brass knuckles** [pl]) a metal cover worn over the knuckles for use as a weapon.

KO /,keɪ 'əʊ/ *abbr* (*infml*) (esp in boxing) knock out: *He was KO'd* (ie knocked out) *in the second round.*

koala /kəʊ'ɑːlə/ (also **ko'ala bear**) *n* an Australian animal with thick grey fur, large ears and no tail. Koalas live in trees and eat leaves.

kohl /kəʊl/ n [U] a black powder used esp in the East to darken the area around the eye.

kohlrabi /ˌkəʊlˈrɑːbi/ n [U] a type of cabbage with a thick round stem that is eaten as a vegetable.

kook /kuːk/ n (US derog sl) a person who acts in a strange or crazy way. ▶ **kooky** adj.

kookaburra /ˈkʊkəbʌrə/ (also **laughing jackass**) n a large Australian bird famous for the laughing sound it makes.

kopeck (also **kopek**) n a unit of money in Russia; a 100th part of a ROUBLE.

Koran (also **Qur'an**) /kəˈrɑːn; US also -ˈræn/ n the **Koran** [sing] the sacred book of the Muslims, written in Arabic, containing the word of Allah as revealed to the Prophet Muhammad. ▶ **Koranic** /kəˈrænɪk/ adj.

kosher /ˈkəʊʃə(r)/ adj **1** (of food and its preparation, sale, etc) fulfilling the requirements of Jewish law: a kosher restaurant/meal. **2** (infml) genuine; that can be trusted: There's something about him that's not quite kosher.

kowtow /ˌkaʊˈtaʊ/ v ~ (**to sb/sth**) (derog) to show sb/sth excessive respect and obedience: [V, Vpr] a refusal to kowtow (to the government's wishes).

kph /ˌkeɪ piː ˈeɪtʃ/ abbr kilometres per hour. Compare MPH.

Kraut /kraʊt/ n (sl offensive) a German.

Kremlin /ˈkremlɪn/ n the **Kremlin** (**a**) [Gp] the Russian government. (**b**) [sing] the buildings where it meets.

krill /krɪl/ n [pl v] tiny SHELLFISH found in the sea around the Antarctic. Whales (WHALE) feed on krill.

krona /ˈkrəʊnə/ n (pl **-nor** /-nɔː(r), -nə(r)/) the chief unit of money in Sweden.

krone /ˈkrəʊnə/ n (pl **-ner** /-nə(r)/) the chief unit of money in Denmark and Norway.

krypton /ˈkrɪptɒn/ n [U] (symb **Kr**) a chemical element. Krypton is a gas found in small quantities in the earth's atmosphere and is used in FLUORESCENT lamps. ⇨ App 7.

kudos /ˈkjuːdɒs; US ˈkuː-/ n [U] (infml) the praise and honour one receives for an achievement: attract/win/lose kudos ○ She did most of the work but all the kudos went to him.

Ku Klux Klan /ˌkuː klʌks ˈklæn/ n [Gp] a secret organization of white men in the southern states of the USA who are violently opposed to black people.

kumquat /ˈkʌmkwɒt/ n a fruit similar to an orange but smaller.

kung fu /ˌkʌŋ ˈfuː/ n [U] a Chinese system of fighting without weapons, similar to KARATE.

kW abbr kilowatt(s): a 2 kW electric fire.

kwashiorkor /ˌkwɒʃiˈɔːkɔː(r)/ n [U] a serious disease of children in tropical countries whose diet does not contain enough PROTEIN.

kybosh = KIBOSH.

K

Ll

L¹ (also l) /el/ n (pl **L's**, **l's** /elz/) n the 12th letter of the English alphabet: *'London' begins with (an) L/ 'L'.*

L² abbr **1** Lake: *L Windermere* (eg on a map). **2** (esp on clothing, etc) large (size). **3** /el/ (*Brit*) learner (ie sb who is learning to drive): *an L-driver.*
■ **L-plate** /'el pleɪt/ n (*Brit*) a sign showing a large red letter L, fixed to a motor vehicle that is being driven by sb learning to drive.

L³ symb the Roman NUMERAL for 50.

l abbr **1** left. Compare R. **2** (pl **ll**) line: *p* (ie page) *2, l 19 ○ verse 6, ll 8–10.* **3** litre(s).

LA /ˌel 'eɪ/ abbr Los Angeles.

la (also **lah**) /lɑː/ n (*music*) the 6th note of any major scale¹(6).

lab /læb/ n (*infml*) a LABORATORY: *a language/science lab ○ a lab assistant/technician ○ a lab coat.*

Lab /læb/ abbr (*Brit politics*) Labour (political party): *Tom Green (Lab).*

label /'leɪbl/ n **1** a piece of paper, cloth or plastic on or beside an object and describing its nature, name, owner, destination, etc: *The washing instructions are on the label. ○ Tie an address label on your luggage.* **2** a word or phrase applied to a person, group, etc, esp one that is not quite true or accurate: *hang/stick/slap a label on sb/sth ○ apply a label to sb/sth ○ A reviewer called her first novel 'super-romantic' and the label has stuck.* **3** the name of a person or company, esp one that produces records or items of fashion: *He launched his own record label. ○ You pay a lot extra for designer labels on your clothes.*
▶ **label** v (-ll-; *US* -l-) **1** to put a label or labels on sth: [Vn] *a machine for labelling wine bottles ○ Label each item carefully.* **2** (esp passive) to describe or classify sb/sth: [Vn-adj] *The envelope was labelled 'strictly private and confidential'.* [Vnn] *The press had labelled him (as) an extremist.*

labia /'leɪbɪə/ n [pl] the folds of skin at the outer opening of the female genitals.

labial /'leɪbɪəl/ adj **1** of the lips. **2** (*phonetics*) made with the lips: *labial sounds* (eg /m, p, v/).
▶ **labial** n (*phonetics*) a sound made with the lips.

labor /'leɪbə(r)/ (*US*) = LABOUR.
■ **'labor union** n = TRADE UNION.

laboratory /ləˈbɒrətri; *US* ˈlæbrətɔːri/ n a room or building used for scientific research, experiments, testing, etc: *send a specimen to the laboratory for analysis.* See also LANGUAGE LABORATORY.

laborious /ləˈbɔːrɪəs/ adj **1** (of work, etc) needing much time and effort: *a laborious job/task/process.* **2** showing signs of great effort; not flowing in a natural way: *a laborious style of writing.* See also LABOURED. ▶ **laboriously** adv.

labour¹ (*US* labor) /'leɪbə(r)/ n **1(a)** [U] work, esp hard physical work: *manual labour ○ save on labour costs.* **(b)** [C usu pl] (*fml*) a task; a piece of work: *see the results/the fruits of one's labours.* ⇨ note at WORK¹. **2** [U] workers, esp those who work with their hands, as a class or a political force: *skilled/unskilled labour ○ the free movement of labour in the European Union ○ Labour leaders met today at the Trade Union Conference. ○ labour relations* (ie between workers and employers). **3** [U, sing] the process of giving birth to a child: *go into/be in/begin labour ○ have labour pains ○ She had a difficult labour.* **4** **Labour** [Gp] (abbr **Lab**) (*Brit politics*) the Labour Party: *a Labour candidate/government/ supporter ○ Labour has said it opposes the government's housing policy.* **IDM** **a ˌlabour of 'love** a task done because one cares about sb/sth, not because it is necessary or profitable.
■ **'Labour Day** (*US* **'Labor Day**) n a public holiday in honour of working people (1 May in Britain; in the USA the first Monday in September).
'labour force n [U] everyone who can work in a country, company, etc: *a skilled labour force ○ One in ten of the labour force is now unemployed.*
ˌlabour-inˈtensive adj (of an industrial process, etc) needing to employ many people: *using traditional ˌlabour-intensive 'methods.* Compare CAPITAL-INTENSIVE.
the 'Labour Party n [Gp] (*Brit politics*) one of the major political parties in Britain, representing esp the interests of working people. See also THE CONSERVATIVE PARTY, THE LIBERAL DEMOCRATS.
'labour-saving adj [usu attrib] designed to reduce the amount of work or effort needed to do sth: *modern labour-saving devices like the washing-machine.*

labour² (*US* labor) /'leɪbə(r)/ v **1** to work or try hard: [V] *the labouring classes* [Vpr, Vp] *I've been labouring (away) at this report all morning.* [V.to inf] *They are labouring to finish the job on time.* See also LABOURING. **2** to move with difficulty and effort: [Vpr] *The van laboured up the steep mountain track.* **IDM** **labour the 'point** to continue to repeat or explain sth that has already been said and understood: *I understand what you're trying to say — there's no need to labour the point.* **PHRV** **'labour under sth** (*fml*) to be deceived or misled by a wrong belief, idea, etc: *I'm afraid he's still labouring under the delusion that he can act!*
▶ **laboured** (*US* labored) adj **1** slow and difficult: *laboured breathing.* **2** showing signs of too much effort; not natural: *his laboured attempts at humour ○ a laboured style of writing.* See also LABORIOUS 2.
labourer (*US* laborer) /'leɪbərə(r)/ n a person who does hard physical work that is not skilled: *a farm labourer.*
labouring (*US* laboring) /'leɪbərɪŋ/ n [U] doing hard physical work that is not skilled, eg digging roads: *He tried a number of labouring jobs.*

laburnum /ləˈbɜːnəm/ n [C,U] a small ornamental tree with hanging bunches of yellow flowers.

labyrinth /'læbərɪnθ/ n a complicated network of winding passages, paths, etc through which it is difficult to find one's way: *She disappeared into the labyrinth of corridors. ○ (fig) a real labyrinth of laws, rules and regulations.* Compare MAZE. ▶ **labyrinthine** /ˌlæbəˈrɪnθaɪn; *US* also -θən/ adj: *the labyrinthine complexities of party politics.*

lace

lace /leɪs/ n **1** [U] a delicate fabric with an ornamental pattern of holes and threads: *a handkerchief*

[V.to inf] = verb + *to* infinitive   [Vn.inf (no *to*)] = verb + noun + infinitive without *to*   [V.ing] = verb + *-ing* form

edged with lace ∘ *lace curtains.* See also LACY. ⇨ picture. **2** [C] a string or cord put through holes or hooks, eg in a shoe, to pull and hold two edges together: *do up/tie your shoe-laces.* ⇨ picture at SHOE.

▶ **lace** *v* **1** ~ **(sth) (up)** to fasten sth with laces: [V, Vp] *a blouse that laces (up) at the front* [Vnp] *lace one's shoes up* [also Vn]. **2** ~ **sth (with sth)** to flavour or strengthen a drink with a small amount of alcohol or a drug: [Vnpr] *a glass of milk laced with rum* [also Vn].

■ '**lace-up** *n* (usu *pl*) a shoe that is fastened with a lace: *a pair of lace-ups* ∘ *lace-up boots.*

lacerate /ˈlæsəreɪt/ *v* to injure flesh by tearing: [Vn] *His hands and knees were badly lacerated on/by the sharp stones.* ▶ **laceration** /ˌlæsəˈreɪʃn/ *n* [C, U]: *suffer multiple lacerations to the face.*

lachrymose /ˈlækrɪməʊs/ *adj* (*fml*) having a tendency to cry easily: *a lachrymose disposition.*

lack /læk/ *v* (no passive) to be without sth; to have less than enough of sth: [Vn] *lack creativity/ ambition/courage* ∘ *Her voice lacked conviction.* ∘ *They lacked the capital to develop the business.* ∘ *What he lacks in experience he makes up for in enthusiasm.* ∘ *She has the determination that her brother lacks.* **IDM** **be** '**lacking** not to be available when needed: *Money for the project is still lacking.* ∘ '*What is lacking is a master plan,*' *he said.* **be lacking in sth** not to have enough of sth: *be lacking in* '*warmth/*'*courage/*'*strength* ∘ *The book was interesting but lacking in origi*'*nality.* **have/lack the courage of one's convictions** ⇨ COURAGE.

▶ **lack** *n* [U, sing] a state of being without or not having enough of sth that is needed: *a lack of confidence/money/support* ∘ *The project was abandoned through* (ie because of) *lack of funds.*

lackadaisical /ˌlækəˈdeɪzɪkl/ *adj* lacking vigour and determination: *have a lackadaisical approach to one's studies.*

lackey /ˈlæki/ *n* **1** (formerly) a servant, usu in special uniform. **2** (*derog*) a person who acts or is treated like a servant: *The singer was surrounded by the usual crowd of lackeys and hangers-on.*

lacklustre /ˈlæklʌstə(r)/ (*US* **lackluster**) *adj* dull; without energy or life: *lacklustre eyes* ∘ *They gave a lacklustre performance.*

laconic /ləˈkɒnɪk/ *adj* using few words: *a laconic person/remark/style* ∘ *laconic humour.* ▶ **laconically** /-kli/ *adv*: '*Too bad,*' *she replied laconically.*

lacquer /ˈlækə(r)/ *n* [U] **1** a liquid substance used on metal or wood to give a hard shiny surface. **2** (*becoming dated*) a liquid sprayed on the hair to keep it in place.

▶ **lacquer** *v* to cover sth with lacquer: [Vn] *a lacquered table.*

lacrosse /ləˈkrɒs; *US* -ˈkrɔːs/ *n* [U] a game played by two teams of 10 players each who use sticks with curved nets on them to catch, carry and throw the ball.

lactation /lækˈteɪʃn/ *n* [U] (*techn*) the production of milk by women or female animals around the time when they have young.

lactic acid /ˌlæktɪk ˈæsɪd/ *n* [U] **1** an acid that forms in sour milk. **2** a substance produced in the muscles during hard exercise.

lactose /ˈlæktəʊs, -əʊz/ *n* [U] (*chemistry*) a form of sugar found in milk and used in some baby foods.

lacuna /ləˈkjuːnə/ *n* (*pl* -**nae** /-niː/ or **lacunas**) (*fml*) an empty space where sth is missing; a gap: *a lacuna in the manuscript.*

lacy /ˈleɪsi/ *adj* of or like lace: *the lacy pattern of a spider's web.*

lad /læd/ *n* **1** [C] a boy; a young man: *He's a bright lad.* ∘ *The town's changed a lot since I was a lad.* **2** **the lads** [pl] (*Brit infml*) the men in one's team,

office, pub, etc: *After work I went for a drink with the lads.* **3** [C usu *sing*] (*Brit infml*) a lively young man, esp one who has a lot of interest in women: *He has the reputation of being **a bit of a lad**.*

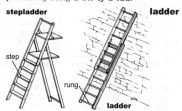

stepladder   **ladder**

step

rung

ladder

ladder /ˈlædə(r)/ *n* **1** a structure for climbing up and down sth, consisting of two upright lengths of wood, metal or rope joined to each other by short pieces of wood, etc used as steps: *climb up the rungs* (ie steps of a ladder). See also STEPLADDER. ⇨ picture. **2** a series of stages by which a person may advance in her or his career, etc: *climbing the ladder of success* ∘ *He is still on the bottom rung of the political/management ladder.* **3** (*Brit*) (*US* **run**) a fault in a woman's TIGHTS(1), etc where some threads have come undone.

▶ **ladder** *v* (**a**) [V] (of TIGHTS(1), etc) to develop a ladder(3). (**b**) [Vn] to cause TIGHTS(1), etc to develop a ladder(3).

laddie /ˈlædi/ *n* (*infml esp Scot*) (esp as a form of address) a boy; a young man. Compare LASS.

laden /ˈleɪdn/ *adj* [usu pred] ~ **(with sth)** loaded or weighed down with sth: *trees laden with apples* ∘ *a heavily laden truck* ∘ (*fig*) *a voice laden with tears.*

la-di-da /ˌlɑː di ˈdɑː/ *adj* (*infml usu derog*) behaving or speaking like the higher social classes in a way that is not natural or genuine: *I can't stand her or her* ˌla-di-da '*friends.*

ladle /ˈleɪdl/ *n* a large deep spoon with a long handle, used for serving or transferring liquids: *a* '*soup ladle.* ⇨ picture at KITCHEN.

▶ **ladle** *v* to serve food with a ladle or in large quantities: [Vnpr] *She ladled the soup into bowls.* [Vnp] *ladling out the stew.*

lady /ˈleɪdi/ *n* **1** [C] (esp in polite use) a woman: *the old lady next door* ∘ *a ladies' hockey team* ∘ *Ask that lady to help you.* ∘ *The lady at the tourist office told me it opened at 1 pm.* See also FIRST LADY. **2** [C] a woman with dignity and good manners: *She's a real lady — never loses her temper.* Compare GENTLEMAN 1, LADYLIKE. **3** [C] (esp formerly) a woman of good family and social position: *the lords and ladies of the court.* **4** (esp in Britain) a title used with the second name of a woman who is or has married a noble, or with the first name of a daughter of a noble: *Lady (Violet) Asquith* ∘ *Lady Sarah.* **5** **Ladies** [sing *v*] (*Brit*) (*US* '**ladies' room** [C]) a women's public toilet: *Is there a Ladies near here?* ⇨ note at TOILET. **IDM** ˌ**ladies and** '**gentlemen** (used by sb making a speech to address the people who are listening): *Please join me, ladies and gentlemen, in wishing the bride and groom every happiness in the future.* See panel.

■ ˌ**lady-in-**'**waiting** *n* (*pl* **ladies-in-waiting**) a woman who accompanies and looks after a queen or princess.

'**lady-killer** *n* (*infml often derog*) a man who enjoys forming relationships with women, but who does not stay in a serious relationship with any one woman.

ladybird /ˈleɪdɪbɜːd/ (*US* **ladybug** /ˈleɪdɪbʌg/) *n* a small flying insect, usu red with black spots.

ladylike /ˈleɪdilaɪk/ *adj* (*approv*) suitable for a LADY (2); polite: *ladylike behaviour* ∘ *She drank her wine with small ladylike sips.*

L

[V.speech] = verb + direct speech   [V.*that*] = verb + *that* clause   [V.*wh*] = verb + *who, how*, etc clause

1 Polite address

Ladies and gentlemen are used as the plural forms of sir and madam.

occasion	singular	plural
giving a public speech		Ladies and gentlemen, I would like to thank ...
in a shop, restaurant, etc	Yes, sir/madam, will there be anything else?	Good morning, ladies/gentlemen, can I help you?
writing formal letters	Dear Sir/Madam, Thank you for your ...	Dear Sirs, (There is no plural form of madam)

2 Referring to people

Lady and gentleman are used instead of woman and man to show politeness.

with the person present	Mr Smith, this lady/gentleman wishes to make a complaint.
	I think this lady/gentleman was in front of me.
describing behaviour	He's very gentlemanly. She's very ladylike.
referring to public toilets	the Gents (US the men's room) the Ladies (US the ladies' room) Where's the Gents, please? Where's the Ladies, please?

ladyship /ˈleɪdiʃɪp/ n (used in speaking to or about a woman who has a title): *their ladyships* ∘ *If your Ladyship will step this way, please.*

lag¹ /læg/ v (-gg-) ~ (behind sb/sth); ~ (behind) to go too slowly; to fail to go as fast as others: [Vpr] *The little boy lagged behind the rest of the walkers.* [V] *Please keep an eye on young Peter — he's inclined to lag a bit.* [Vp] *Prices are rising sharply, while incomes are lagging far behind.*
▶ **lag** (also **time-lag**) n a period of time separating two events, esp an action and its effect; a delay: *a lag of several seconds between the lightning and the thunder.* See also JET LAG, OLD LAG.

lag² /læg/ v (-gg-) [Vn, Vnpr] ~ **sth** (with sth) to cover pipes, etc with a special material to prevent the water in them from freezing or to save heat.

lager /ˈlɑːgə(r)/ n 1 [U, C] a type of light pale beer: *a pint of lager* ∘ *German lager.* 2 [C] a glass, can or bottle of this: *Two lagers, please.*
■ **lager lout** n (Brit infml) a young person, esp a young man, who drinks too much alcohol and then behaves in a noisy and unpleasant way.

laggard /ˈlægəd/ n a person, an organization, etc that is slow at doing sth: *He's no laggard when it comes to asking for more money* (ie He is very quick to do this).

lagoon /ləˈguːn/ n 1 a lake of salt water separated from the open sea by areas of sand or rocks. 2 any small area of water near a lake or river: *go swimming in the lagoon.*

lah = LA.

laid pt, pp of LAY¹.

laid-back /ˌleɪd ˈbæk/ adj (infml) (of people or their behaviour) calm and relaxed: *She always seems so laid-back.* ∘ *a ˌlaid-back apˈproach/ˈatmosphere/ˈattitude.*

lain pp of LIE².

lair /leə(r)/ n 1 a sheltered place where a wild animal regularly sleeps or rests: *the dragon's lair.* 2 a person's hiding place: *In a family argument he just retreats to his lair in the study.*

laird /leəd/ n (Scot) a LANDOWNER.

laissez-faire /ˌleɪseɪ ˈfeə(r)/ n [U] (French) the policy of allowing business companies, etc to operate and develop freely without the government interfering or controlling them: *a ˌlaissez-faire eˈconomy* ∘ *(fig) the Seventies laissez-faire approach to dressing.*

laity /ˈleɪəti/ n the laity [Gp] all the members of a Church who are not CLERGY: *involve the laity in church decision-making.* See also LAYMAN 2.

lake /leɪk/ n a large area of water surrounded by land: *go for a stroll around the lake* ∘ *take a boat out on the lake* ∘ *Lake Victoria* ∘ *the Italian Lakes* ∘ *(fig) a wine lake* (a huge supply of wine that is not being used).
■ **the ˈLake District** n [sing] (also **the Lakes** [pl]) a region of lakes and hills in NW England.

lakeside /ˈleɪksaɪd/ n [sing] the land around the edge of a lake: *lovely walks along the lakeside* ∘ *Austrian lakeside resorts.*

lamb /læm/ n 1(a) [C] a young sheep: *lambs frolicking in the fields.* ▷ picture at SHEEP. (b) [U] its flesh as food: *a leg of lamb* ∘ *lamb chops.* Compare MUTTON. 2 (infml) (used to describe or address sb with affection or pity): *You poor lamb!* **IDM** **mutton dressed as lamb** ▷ MUTTON. **one may/might as well be hanged/hung for a sheep as a lamb** ▷ HANG¹.
▶ **lambing** n [U] the time when sheep give birth to lambs or the process involved in this: *the first week of lambing* ∘ *a lambing shed.*

lambaste (also **lambast**) /læmˈbeɪst/ v to criticize sb severely: [Vn] *The opposition lambasted the government's record on the economy.*

lambswool /ˈlæmzwʊl/ n [U] the soft fine wool from lambs, used for making knitted clothes: *a lambswool jersey.*

lame /leɪm/ adj 1 unable to walk normally, eg because of an injury to one's leg: *He is lame in the left leg.* ∘ *The horse went lame.* 2 (of an excuse, argument, etc) weak and not convincing: *That was a pretty lame joke.*
■ **ˌlame ˈduck** n 1 a person or an organization that is in difficulties and unable to manage without help: *The government should not waste money supporting lame ducks.* 2 (esp US) an elected official in her or his final period of office: *a ˌlame duck ˈPresident.* ▶ **lamely** adv: *'What's next?' she asked lamely.* **lameness** n [U].

lamé /ˈlɑːmeɪ; US lɑːˈmeɪ/ n [U] a fabric in which gold or silver thread is mixed with silk, wool or cotton: *a silver lamé evening gown.*

lament /ləˈment/ v (fml) to feel or express great sorrow or regret for sb/sth: [V.speech] *'I wish we were back home,' Celia lamented.* [Vn] *He lamented the decline in standards.* [Vpr] *lament over one's dead wife* [V.that] *They lamented that so many hedges had been destroyed.*
▶ **lament** n 1 a strong expression of grief or regret: *There will be few laments for his passing.* 2 a song or poem expressing grief: *a funeral lament.*

lamentable /ˈlæməntəbl, ləˈment-/ adj that is to be regretted; very sad: *a lamentable loss of life/lack of foresight* ∘ *England's lamentable performance in the Test series.* **lamentably** /-əbli/ adv.

lamentation /ˌlæmənˈteɪʃn/ n 1 [C] an expression of grief: *lamentations about the state of the world.* 2 [U] the action of lamenting.

lamented adj (rhet or joc) (of sb/sth that has died, or been lost or removed) regretted; greatly missed: *the last movie to be shown at the much lamented Academy Cinema.*

laminated /ˈlæmɪneɪtɪd/ adj 1 (of wood, plastic, etc) made by sticking thin layers together: *a laminated table top.* 2 (of an object) covered with transparent plastic for protection: *a laminated menu/map.*
▶ **laminate** /ˈlæmɪnət/ n [U, C] laminated material.

lamp /læmp/ n **1** a device for giving light, either by the use of electricity or, esp formerly, by burning gas or oil: *a street/table/desk/bicycle lamp* ○ *read by the light of a paraffin lamp* ○ *She switched on her bedside lamp.* See also HURRICANE LAMP, STANDARD LAMP. **2** an electrical device producing RADIATION (1a), used for medical, scientific, etc purposes: *an infrared/ultraviolet lamp.*

lamplight /ˈlæmplaɪt/ n [U] light from a lamp: *Her face was pale in the lamplight.*

lamplit /ˈlæmplɪt/ adj [attrib] given light by lamps: *a lamplit room/street.*

lampoon /læmˈpuːn/ v to criticize sb/sth publicly and make them/it look ridiculous: [Vn] *His cartoons mercilessly lampooned the leading politicians of the day.*
▶ **lampoon** n a piece of writing that lampoons sb/sth.

lamppost /ˈlæmppəʊst/ n a tall post with a light at the top, beside a road or street. ⇨ picture at HOUSE¹.

lampshade /ˈlæmpʃeɪd/ n a decorative cover of glass or fabric placed over a lamp to soften its light.

LAN /læn/ abbr (*computing*) local area network (a system by which several computers in the same building can share resources and communicate with each other).

lance¹ /lɑːns; *US* læns/ n a weapon with a long wooden handle and a sharp pointed metal head.

lance² /lɑːns; *US* læns/ v to open an infected place on the body with a needle or knife: [Vn] *lance an abscess/a boil.*

lance-corporal /ˌlɑːns ˈkɔːpərəl; *US* ˌlæns-/ n (in the British army or US Marines) a NON-COMMISSIONED officer of the lowest rank. ⇨ App 6.

lancet /ˈlɑːnsɪt; *US* ˈlæn-/ n **1** a knife with a sharp point and two sharp edges, used by doctors for cutting the skin and flesh. **2** (*architecture*) a tall narrow pointed arch or window.

land¹ /lænd/ n **1** [U] the solid dry part of the earth's surface, contrasted with sea or water: *be on/reach/come to land* ○ *On land the turtle is ungainly, but in the water it is very graceful.* ⇨ note at EARTH. See also DRY LAND. **2(a)** [U] (also **lands** [pl]) an area of ground: *disputed land(s)* ○ *the land west of the mountains.* See also NO MAN'S LAND (NO), THE PROMISED LAND. **(b)** ground of the specified type: *rich/stony/forest land* ○ *arid/steppe lands* ○ *a piece of waste/derelict land.* See also WETLANDS. **(c)** ground used for a particular purpose: *100 acres of farming land* ○ *arable/grazing lands* ○ *a shortage of building land* (ie land on which to build houses). **3** the land [U] **(a)** ground or soil that is used for farming: *working the land.* **(b)** rural areas and the rural way of life, as contrasted with cities and towns: *Many farmers are leaving the land to work in industry.* **4(a)** [U] property in the form of land: *a house with 50 hectares of land adjoining it* ○ *land for sale.* See also COMMON LAND. **(b)** **lands** [pl] an area of land belonging to one person; an estate: *the duke's lands.* **5** [C] (*rhet*) a country, state or nation: *my native land* ○ *sail to distant lands* ○ *the finest orchestra in the land.* See also THE HOLY LAND, HOMELAND, COUNTRY. **IDM** **in the land of the ˈliving** (*joc*) alive. **the lie of the land** ⇨ LIE². **live off/on the fat of the land** ⇨ LIVE². **live off the land** ⇨ LIVE². **see, etc how the ˈland lies** to learn what the situation is: *Let's find out how the land lies before we tell them at home.* **spy out the land** ⇨ SPY v.
▶ **landed** adj [attrib] owning a lot of land: *the landed aristocracy/gentry.*
landless adj not owning land: *landless peasants/labourers.*
landward adj, adv /ˈlændwəd/ towards or facing the land: *on the landward side of the island.*
■ **ˈland-based** adj [usu attrib] situated on or living on the land: *land-based nuclear missiles* ○ *the dolphin's land-based ancestors.*

ˈland-agent n (*esp Brit*) a person employed to manage an estate.

ˈland-form n (*geology*) a natural feature of the earth's surface.

ˈland-locked adj almost or entirely surrounded by land: *Switzerland is completely land-locked.*

ˈland mass n a large area of land: *continental land masses.*

ˈland-mine n an explosive device laid in or on the ground, which explodes when vehicles, etc pass over it: *detonate a land-mine* ○ *His leg was blown off by a land-mine.*

land² /lænd/ v **1** ~ (sb/sth) (at...) to go or put sb/sth on land from a ship: [Vpr] *We landed at Boston.* [Vn] *sit on the harbour wall and watch the day's catch being landed* [Vnpr] *Troops have been landed at several points.* [also V]. **2(a)** to bring an aircraft down to the ground in a controlled way: [Vn] *The pilot managed to land the battered old plane safely.* **(b)** to come down through the air: [V, Vpr] *We will shortly be landing (at Kennedy airport) — please fasten your seat-belts.* [Vpr] *landing on the moon* ○ *A fly landed on his nose.* **3** to reach the ground after a jump or fall: [V] *Try to catch that leaf before it lands.* [Vpr] *He fell down the stairs, landing in a heap at the bottom.* ○ *The bag landed heavily on his foot.* **4** (of sth unpleasant or unexpected) to arrive somewhere and cause difficulties: *The complaint landed on the desk of the regional manager.* **5** (*infml*) to succeed in obtaining sth, esp when a lot of other people also wanted it: [Vn] *land a good job/a big contract.* **6** (*infml*) to strike a blow: [Vn] *Jones landed several good punches in the early rounds.* See also LANDED. **IDM** **fall/land on one's feet** ⇨ FOOT¹. **PHRV** **ˈland sb/oneself in sth** (*infml*) to get sb/oneself into difficulties: *This is a fine mess you've landed us in!* ○ *His stupid pranks are going to land him in trouble one day.* **ˌland ˈup in... / doing sth** (*infml*) to reach a final position or situation, often an undesirable one: *He landed up in hospital with several broken ribs.* ○ *We landed up spending the night in the station waiting-room.* **ˈland sb with sth/sb** (*infml*) to give sb an unpleasant task or duty to deal with: *The corporation was landed with a $1 million lawsuit.*

landfall /ˈlændfɔːl/ n [U, sing] the first sight of or approach to land after a journey by sea: *We made landfall at dusk after three weeks at sea.*

landfill /ˈlændfɪl/ n **(a)** [C, U] an area of land where waste material is buried under layers of earth: *a shallow landfill* ○ *toxic chemicals dumped at landfill sites.* **(b)** [U] the process of burying waste in this way: *a landfill operation.* **(c)** [U] waste material to be buried.

landholding /ˈlændhəʊldɪŋ/ n [C, U] possession of property in the form of land: *a map of tribal landholdings.*

landing /ˈlændɪŋ/ n **1** an act of coming or bringing sb/sth to land: *a smooth landing* ○ *Because of engine trouble the plane had to* **make an emergency landing.** ○ *a landing site* ○ (*fig*) *Hopes of a soft landing for the economy have receded.* **2** a place where people and goods can be landed from a boat or ship: *a convenient landing in a nearby cove.* **3** a level area at the top of a staircase, or between one set of stairs and another: *a first-floor landing* ○ *I left my case on the landing.* ⇨ picture at STAIRCASE.
■ **ˈlanding-craft** n (*pl* unchanged) a naval craft with a flat bottom, designed for bringing troops and equipment to the shore.
ˈlanding-gear n [U] = UNDERCARRIAGE.
ˈlanding-stage n a platform, often a floating one, on which people and goods are landed from a boat.
ˈlanding-strip n = AIRSTRIP.

landlady /ˈlændleɪdi/ n **1** a woman from whom one

rents a room, flat, house, etc for money: *I'll ask my/ the landlady if you can stay.* **2** a woman who owns or manages a pub or a guest-house (GUEST). Compare LANDLORD.

landlord /ˈlændlɔːd/ *n* **1** a person, esp a man, from whom one rents land, a house, a room, etc for money: *I was kicked out by my landlord.* **2** (*Brit*) a person, esp a man, who owns or manages a pub: *It's a nice pub, except for the landlord.* Compare LAND-LADY.

landmark /ˈlændmɑːk/ *n* **1** an object that is easily seen and recognized from a distance: *The Empire State Building is a famous/familiar landmark on the New York skyline.* **2** ~ (**in sth**) an event, a discovery, an invention, etc that marks an important point or stage in sth: *a decision which represents a landmark in the history of race relations* ∘ *a political/cultural landmark.*

landowner /ˈlændəʊnə(r)/ *n* a person who owns land, esp a large area of land: *The Duke of Westminster is one of the biggest single landowners in Britain.*

Landrover (also **Land-Rover**) /ˈlændrəʊvə(r)/ *n* (*propr*) a strong motor vehicle designed for use over rough ground.

landscape /ˈlændskeɪp/ *n* **1** (usu *sing*) all the features of an area that can be seen when looking across it: *The house is set in a magnificent landscape of rolling green hills.* ∘ *a bleak urban landscape* ∘ *Mountains dominate the Welsh landscape.* ∘ (*fig*) *the changing political landscape.* **2** a picture showing a view of the countryside: *an exhibition of oil landscapes by local artists.* **IDM** **a blot on the landscape** ⇨ BLOT.
▶ **landscape** *v* to improve the appearance of a garden, a park or an area of waste land by changing its design, planting trees and flowers, etc: [Vn] *white villas are amongst landscaped gardens.* **landscaping** *n* [U]: *a landscaping scheme.*
■ **landscape architect** (also **landscape gardener**) *n* a person whose job is to design and create attractive gardens, parks, etc.

landslide /ˈlændslaɪd/ *n* **1** (also **landslip** /ˈlændslɪp/) a mass of earth, rock, etc sliding down the side of a mountain or cliff: *be buried in a landslide.* **2** a very large majority of votes for one party in an election: *The opinion polls forecast a Democratic landslide.* ∘ *win a landslide victory.*

lane /leɪn/ *n* **1** a narrow road, esp in the country: *winding country lanes.* See also MEMORY LANE. **2** (esp in place names) a street, esp a narrow one, between buildings: *Park Lane* ∘ *the intricate maze of lanes and alleyways near the docks.* ⇨ note at ROAD. **3**(**a**) any of several sections of a wide road, eg a MO-TORWAY, marked with white broken lines and each intended for a single line of traffic: *the slow/middle/ overtaking lane of a motorway* ∘ *Don't change lanes without indicating.* ∘ *There are lane closures today on the M4.* See also BUS LANE. (**b**) any of the marked sections of track, water, etc, each intended for a competitor in a race: *The world champion is in lane four/in the outside lane.* ⇨ note at PATH. **4** a route intended for or regularly used by ships or aircraft: *one of the world's busiest shipping lanes.*

language /ˈlæŋɡwɪdʒ/ *n* **1** [U] the system of sounds and words used by humans to express their thoughts and feelings: *the origins of language* ∘ *the development of language skills in young children.* **2** [C] the particular language system used by a people or nation: *the Bantu group of languages* ∘ *one's native/first language* ∘ *He has a good command of the English language.* ∘ *How many languages do you speak?* **3** [U] a particular way or style of speaking or writing: *bad/strong/foul language* (ie words considered offensive, eg those marked △ in this dictionary) ∘ *give instructions in everyday language* (ie not specialized or technical) ∘ *poetic language.* **4**

[U] the words and phrases used by a particular group or profession: *the language of science/drug users/the courtroom* ∘ *medical language.* **5** [C, U] signs, symbols, gestures, etc used for indicating ideas or feelings: *the language of mime.* See also BODY LANGUAGE, SIGN LANGUAGE. **6** [C, U] (*computing*) a system of words, symbols and rules used in writing a PROGRAM(1): *a new programming language.* **IDM** **speak/talk the same language** to be able to understand another person because of having similar opinions or values.
■ **language laboratory** *n* a room containing special equipment to help students learn languages.

languid /ˈlæŋɡwɪd/ *adj* (*approv or derog*) moving slowly and involving very little physical effort: *languid days in the Italian sun* ∘ *a languid wave of the hand.* ▶ **languidly** *adv*: *He sprawled languidly on the sofa.*

languish /ˈlæŋɡwɪʃ/ *v* (*fml*) **1** to become weaker or fail to make progress: [V] *Tory support in the country languished steadily between general elections.* ∘ *languish in 12th place* ∘ *Share prices languished at 102p.* ∘ *The economy is languishing.* **2** ~ (**in sth**) to be forced to remain somewhere or suffer sth unpleasant for a long time: [Vpr] *languishing in a foreign jail/in bed.*

languor /ˈlæŋɡə(r)/ *n* [U, sing] the state or feeling, often pleasant, of being lazy and lacking energy: *the kind of music that induces a delightful languor* ∘ *I found it difficult to shake off my languor.* ▶ **languorous** /ˈlæŋɡərəs/ *adj*: *her soft and languorous voice/ eyes.* **languorously** *adv.*

lank /læŋk/ *adj* (*usu derog*) (of hair) straight and not attractive.

lanky /ˈlæŋki/ *adj* (**-ier**, **-iest**) (of a person) having long thin limbs, so that one's movements seem awkward: *a lanky teenager.*

lanolin /ˈlænəlɪn/ *n* [U] a fat extracted from sheep's wool and used in making skin creams, SHAMPOO(1), etc.

lantern /ˈlæntən/ *n* a metal lamp, often used outside, whose light is protected from the wind, etc by glass. It often has a handle on top so that it can be carried or hung: *I could see his face by the light of the lantern.*

lanyard /ˈlænjəd/ *n* a cord to which a knife, whistle, etc is attached. It is worn round the neck or shoulders, eg by a sailor.

lap¹ /læp/ *n* (**a**) the flat area between the stomach and knees of a person when he or she is sitting: *Come and sit on my lap.* ∘ *She had fallen asleep with the book open in her lap.* (**b**) the part of a dress, etc covering this: *She gathered the fallen apples and carried them in her lap.* **IDM** **drop/dump sth in sb's lap** (*infml*) to make sth the responsibility of sb else: *Don't try and dump the problem in my lap.* **drop/fall in/into sb's lap** (of sth pleasant) to be given to sb without their having made any effort to get it: *The job just fell into my lap. They phoned me up one day and offered it to me.* **in the lap of the gods** (of the success of a plan, etc) uncertain because of depending on luck or factors that one cannot control. **in the lap of luxury** in conditions of great comfort and wealth.
■ **lap-dog** *n* **1** a small spoilt pet dog. **2** (*derog*) a person who is completely under the influence of sb more powerful: *the government and its media lap-dogs.*

lap² /læp/ *v* **1** a single circuit of a track or RACE-COURSE: *He crashed on the tenth lap.* ∘ *hold the lap record* ∘ *do a lap of honour* (ie make a ceremonial circuit of a sports field, track, etc after winning a contest). **2** a section of a journey: *on the last lap of their round-the-world trip* ∘ *The next lap takes us into the mountains.*
▶ **lap** *v* (**-pp-**) to pass another competitor who is one

or more laps behind one: [Vn] *She's lapped three of the other runners.*

lap³ /læp/ *v* (-pp-) **1** ~ sth (up) (esp of animals) to drink sth with quick movements of the tongue: [Vn, Vnp] *a dog noisily lapping (up) water.* **2** (of water) to touch sth gently and regularly: [Vpr] *waves lapping on a beach/against the side of a boat* [V] *a gentle lapping sound* ○ *the lapping of the waves.* **PHRV** ,lap sth 'up (*infml*) to receive sth eagerly or with obvious pleasure and appreciation: *lap up sunshine/knowledge/attention* ○ *The movie got terrible reviews but the public is lapping it up.*

lapel /lə'pel/ *n* the front part of the collar of a coat or jacket that is folded back on either side of the chest: *What's that badge on your lapel?* ⇨ picture at JACKET.

lapidary /'læpɪdəri; *US* -deri/ *adj* (*fml*) (esp of written words) elegant and PRECISE(1): *lapidary style.*

lapis lazuli /ˌlæpɪs 'læzjʊli; *US* 'læzəli/ *n* [U] a bright blue stone used in making ornaments, jewellery, etc.

lapse /læps/ *n* **1** a small error, esp one caused by not concentrating: *a rare lapse of memory/concentration* ○ *A brief lapse in the final set cost her the match.* **2** ~ (from sth) (into sth) an instance or a period of bad behaviour from sb who normally behaves well: *the inevitable lapse into petty crime* ○ *It took only one lapse from virtue to finish his political career.* **3** the passing of a period of time: *after a lapse of six months* ○ *after a considerable lapse of time.*
▶ **lapse** *v* **1(a)** (of a contract, an agreement, etc) to be no longer valid, eg because of not being renewed; to EXPIRE(1): [V] *My membership of the club has lapsed.* ○ *He didn't get any compensation because his insurance policy had lapsed.* (**b**) to be no longer continued: [V] *The project had been allowed to lapse.* **2** ~ into sth to pass gradually into a usu worse state or condition: [Vpr] *The building has lapsed into decay.* [Vpr, Vp] *We spoke in French but occasionally lapsed (back) into English* ○ *lapse into silence.* **3** ~ (from sth) to stop believing in a religion or set of principles: [V] *a lapsed Catholic* [Vpr] *lapse from political commitment.*

laptop /'læptɒp/ *n* a small computer that can operate off a battery and is easily carried.

lapwing /'læpwɪŋ/ (also **peewit**) *n* a dark green and white bird with a CREST(3) on its head. Lapwings live on moors and on open ground near water.

larceny /'lɑːsəni/ *n* [C, U] (*law*) (formerly) the stealing of personal property, now called *theft.*

larch /lɑːtʃ/ *n* [C] a tree bearing cones (CONE 5) and sharp pointed leaves that fall in the winter.

lard /lɑːd/ *n* [U] a firm white substance made from the melted fat of pigs and used in cooking.
▶ **lard** *v* [Vn] to cover sth with lard, eg to stop it from becoming dry when cooked or stored. **PHRV** 'lard sth with sth (*often derog*) to include many foreign or technical terms in speech or writing, in order to appear impressive: *a lecture larded with obscure quotations.*

larder /'lɑːdə(r)/ *n* (esp formerly) a cupboard or small room used for storing food: *replenish/stock the larder.* Compare PANTRY.

large /lɑːdʒ/ *adj* (-r, -st) **1** of considerable size, extent or capacity: *a large number of people* ○ *a large amount of money* ○ *A large family needs a large house.* ○ *She inherited a large fortune.* ○ *He has a very large appetite.* ○ *large engineering companies* ○ *The club has a very large membership.* ⇨ note at FAT¹. **2** (used to describe one of a range of sizes of clothing, food and household products, etc): *Buy the large packet — it works out cheaper.* ○ *This sweater is size large.* Compare MEDIUM *adj*, SMALL. **3** wide in range,

scope or scale; broad: *take the large view* ○ *a large and complex problem.* ⇨ note at BIG. **IDM** (as) large as 'life (*joc*) (used to indicate surprise at seeing sb/sth): *I thought she'd gone to Australia but there she was, (as) large as life.* **by and 'large** in general; generally speaking: *By and large, I agree with you.* **in 'large part** to a great extent: *He was in large part to blame.* ,**larger than 'life** exaggerated in size, appearance or behaviour and likely to attract attention: *Everything about her is larger than life.* **writ large** ⇨ WRIT.
▶ **large** *n* **IDM** at 'large **1** (used after a *n*) as a whole; in general: *the opinion of students/voters/society at large.* **2** (of a criminal, a dangerous animal, etc) free; not yet captured: *The escaped prisoner is still at large.*
largely *adv* to a great extent; mostly; mainly: *a largely empty train* ○ *It was largely a matter of poor management.* ○ *The case was reopened largely because of new medical evidence.*
largeness *n* [U].
largish *adj* fairly large.
■ 'large-scale *adj* [esp attrib] **1** involving many people or things, or happening over a large area: *large scale unemployment/destruction* ○ *a large-scale police search.* **2** (of a map, model, etc) drawn or made to a scale¹(5) large enough for houses, fields, etc to be shown as well as towns and villages. Compare SMALL-SCALE.

largesse (also **largess**) /lɑː'dʒes/ *n* [U] (*fml*) a generous gift of money; GENEROSITY: *She is not noted for her largesse* (ie She is very mean).

lark¹ /lɑːk/ *n* a small brown bird with a pleasant song. **IDM** be/get up with the 'lark to get out of bed very early in the morning. See also SKYLARK.

lark² /lɑːk/ *n* (usu *sing*) (*infml*) **1** a thing done for fun or for one's amusement; an amusing adventure: *The boys didn't mean any harm — they only did it for a lark.* ○ *What a lark we had that day!* **2** (used after a *n*) an activity that one considers unpleasant or a waste of time: *this modern education lark* ○ *I don't much like this queuing lark.*
▶ **lark** *v* **PHRV** ,lark a'round/a'bout (*infml*) to enjoy oneself doing silly and amusing things: *Stop larking around and get on with your work.*

larkspur /'lɑːkspɜː(r)/ *n* [U, C] a tall garden plant with blue, pink or white flowers.

larva /'lɑːvə/ *n* (*pl* **larvae** /'lɑːviː/) an insect at the stage when it has just come out of an egg and looks like a short fat worm. ⇨ picture at BUTTERFLY.
▶ **larval** /'lɑːvl/ *adj* [attrib]: *the larval form.*

larynx /'lærɪŋks/ *n* (*pl* **larynxes** or, in technical use, **larynges** /læ'rɪndʒiːz/) (*anatomy*) (also 'voice-box) a space like a box near the top of the throat. It contains the vocal cords (VOCAL) which produce the voice. ⇨ picture at THROAT.
▶ **laryngitis** /ˌlærɪn'dʒaɪtɪs/ *n* [U] (*medical*) an infection of the larynx that makes speaking painful.

lasagne (also **lasagna**) /lə'zænjə/ *n* [U] (**a**) PASTA made in broad flat strips. (**b**) a dish made from this and containing layers of meat sauce, tomatoes and cheese.

lascivious /lə'sɪviəs/ *adj* (*derog*) feeling, expressing or causing sexual desire: *lascivious eyes/thoughts.* ▶ **lasciviously** *adv.* **lasciviousness** *n* [U].

laser /'leɪzə(r)/ *n* a device that produces a narrow, intense and highly controlled beam of light: *laser beams/radiation/physics* ○ *a laser-guided missile* ○ *Birthmarks can be removed by laser treatment.*
■ 'laser printer *n* a machine linked to a computer that produces good quality printed material by means of a laser beam.

lash¹ /læʃ/ *n* **1** = EYELASH: *long dark lashes.* **2** the flexible leather part of a whip, used for hitting people or animals: *wield the lash.* **3** a stroke from a whip or rope, given as a form of punishment: *He was given ten lashes for stealing.* ○ (*fig*) *feel the lash of sb's tongue* (ie be spoken to in a critical way).

lash² /læʃ/ *v* **1(a)** to hit a person or an animal with a whip, rope, etc: [Vn] *He was lashing the horse mercilessly.* ○ (*fig*) *The play has been lashed by the critics.* **(b)** to hit sb/sth with great force: [Vpr, Vp] *rain lashing (down) on the roof* [Vn] *waves lashing the shore.* **2** to move or move sth quickly and violently from side to side: [Vn] *a tiger lashing its tail angrily* [also Vnp, Vnpr, V]. **3** ~ **A to B/A and B together** to fasten things together securely with ropes: [Vnpr] *lash the injured climber to a stretcher* [Vnp] *a raft made of logs lashed together.* **PHR V** **ˌlash sth ˈdown** to tie sth securely in position with ropes, etc: *lash down the cargo on the deck.* **ˌlash ˈout (at sb/sth)** make a sudden violent attack with blows or words: *The horse lashed out with its back legs.* ○ *In a bitter article he lashed out at his critics.* **ˌlash ˈout (on sth)** (*Brit infml*) to spend a lot of money: *lash out on a new video recorder.*

lashing /ˈlæʃɪŋ/ *n* **1** [C] an act of whipping or beating sb/sth: *He gave the poor donkey a terrible lashing.* **2** [C] a rope, etc used to fasten things together or in position. **3 lashings** [pl] ~ **s (of sth)** (*Brit infml*) a large amount of sth, esp of food and drink: *toast with lashings of butter and home-made jam.*

lass /læs/ (also **lassie** /ˈlæsi/) *n* (esp in Scotland and N England) a girl; a young woman. Compare LAD 1, LADDIE.

lassitude /ˈlæsɪtjuːd; *US* -tuːd/ *n* [U] (*fml*) a state of feeling very tired in mind or body; lack of energy: *I felt a sudden lassitude descend on me.*

lasso /læˈsuː; *US also* ˈlæsəʊ/ *n* (*pl* **-os** or **-oes**) a long rope with a loop at one end, used for catching horses and cattle.
▶ **lasso** *v* to catch an animal using a lasso: [Vn] *lassoing wild horses.*

last¹ /lɑːst; *US* læst/ *adj* **1** coming after all others in time or order: *the last house on the left* ○ *the last time I saw her* ○ *the last question in an exam paper* ○ *December is the last month of the year.* ○ *She was last to arrive.* Compare FIRST¹. **2** [attrib] latest; most recent: *last night/week/month/summer/year* ○ *last Tuesday* ○ *in/for/during the last fortnight/few weeks* ○ *I thought her last book was one of her best.* ⇨ note at LATE¹, TIME¹. **3** [esp attrib] only remaining; final: *This is our last bottle of wine.* ○ *He knew this was his last hope of winning.* ○ *I wouldn't marry you if you were the last person on earth!* **4** (used to emphasize that sb/sth is the least likely or suitable): *It's the last thing I'd expect him to do.* ○ *She's the last person to trust with a secret.* **IDM** **at one's last ˈgasp** at the point where one can no longer continue living, fighting, etc because one is too tired or ill: *The team were at their last gasp when the whistle finally went.* **be on one's/its last ˈlegs** to be very weak or in very poor condition: *Our fridge is on its last legs — we'll have to replace it soon.* **the day, week, month, etc before ˈlast** the day, etc immediately before the most recent one; two days, etc ago: *I haven't seen him since the summer before last.* **every last ...** every person or thing in a group: *We spent every last penny we had on the house.* **first/last/next but one, etc** ⇨ FIRST¹. **first/last thing** ⇨ THING. **have the last ˈlaugh** to achieve victory over one's rivals, etc in the end. **have, etc the last word** to make the final decision in a discussion or an argument. **in the last/final analysis** ⇨ ANALYSIS. **(as) a/one's last reˈsort** the person or thing one relies on when everything else has failed: *I've tried everyone else and now you're my last resort.* **in the last reˈsort** when there are no other possible courses of action: *In the last resort we can always walk home.* **one's last/dying breath** ⇨ BREATHE. **the ˌlast ˈditch** the

last chance to avoid sth undesirable, dangerous, etc: *fight the closures to the last ditch* ○ *in a last ditch attempt to avoid war.* **the ˌlast ˈminute/ˈmoment** the latest possible time before an important event: *change one's plans at the last minute* ○ *We always leave our packing to/till the last moment.* ○ *last-minute arrangements.* **the last/final straw** ⇨ STRAW. **the ˌlast ˈword (in sth)** the most recent, fashionable, advanced, etc thing: *the last word in street fashion/military science.* **say/be one's last/final word** ⇨ WORD. **a week last Monday, etc** ⇨ WEEK.
▶ **last** *n* **the last** (*pl* unchanged) **1** the person or thing that is last or last remaining: *Sorry I'm late — am I the last?* ○ *That's the last of the butter.* ○ *These are the last of our apples.* **2** the last person or thing to be mentioned: *We invited Bill, Tom and Sue — the last being Bill's sister.* **IDM** **at (long) ˈlast** after much delay, effort, etc; in the end; finally: *At last we were home!* ○ *At long last the cheque arrived.* **breathe one's last** ⇨ BREATHE. **from first to last** ⇨ FIRST³. **hear/see the ˈlast of sb/sth** to hear/see sb/sth for the last time: *That was the last I ever saw of her.* ○ *I hope we've seen the last of the cold weather.* ○ *Unfortunately, I don't think we've heard the last of this affair.* **to/till the ˈlast** consistently, until the last possible moment, esp death: *He died protesting his innocence to the last.*

lastly *adv* finally: *Lastly, I'd like to ask you about your plans for the future.*

■ **the ˌLast ˈJudgement** *n* [sing] = JUDGEMENT DAY.
ˈlast name *n* a family name; SURNAME: *I don't know his last name.* ⇨ note at NAME¹.
the ˌlast ˈpost *n* [sing] (*Brit*) a tune played on a BUGLE at the end of the day in military camps and at military funerals: *When they sound the last post, the flag is lowered.*
the ˌlast ˈrites *n* [pl] a religious ceremony for and in the presence of a dying person: *administer the last rites to sb* ○ *receive the last rites.*

last² /lɑːst; *US* læst/ *adv* **1** after all others: *He came last in the race.* ○ *They arrived last (of all).* Compare FIRST² 1. **2** on the earlier occasion that is nearest to the present; most recently: *I saw him last/I last saw him in New York two years ago.* ○ *That was when they won the cup in 1989.* **IDM** **ˌlast but not ˈleast** last but no less important(ly) than the others: *Last but not least, I'd like to thank all the catering staff.* **ˌlast ˈin, ˌfirst ˈout** those people most recently employed, included, etc will be the first to be dismissed, excluded, etc if such action becomes necessary: *The firm will apply the principle of 'last in, first out'.*

last³ /lɑːst; *US* læst/ *v* **1** ~ **(for) sth** to continue for a period of time: [Vn] *How long do you think this fine weather will last?* [Vn, Vpr] *The war lasted (for) five years.* **2** to remain in existence; to continue to function well, etc: [V] *The pyramids were built to last forever.* [Vadv] *She won't last long in that job — it's much too demanding.* [Vnn, Vnpr] *These shoes will last you (for) the rest of your life.* **3** ~ **(out)**; ~ **(for) sth** to be adequate or enough: [V, Vp] *Will the wood last (out) till the end of the winter?* [Vn, Vnn] *We've got enough food to last (us) three days.* [also Vpr]. ⇨ note at TAKE¹. **4** ~ **sth (out)** to survive or endure sth: [Vp] *How long can they last out in these weather conditions?* [Vn, Vnp] *He's very ill and probably won't last (out) the night* (ie He will probably die before the morning).
▶ **lasting** *adj* continuing to exist or have an effect for a long time: *a lasting achievement/effect/interest/relationship/impression* ○ *a work of lasting significance* ○ *The flowers are long lasting.*

last⁴ /lɑːst; *US* læst/ *n* a block of wood or metal shaped like a foot, used in making and repairing shoes. **IDM** **stick to one's last** ⇨ STICK².

lat *abbr* latitude. Compare LONG⁵.

latch

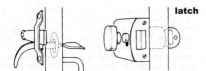

latch /lætʃ/ n **1** a small metal bar used for fastening a door or gate: *He lifted the latch and pushed open the door.* **2** a type of lock on a door that can only be opened from the outside with a key. ⇨ picture. **IDM** **on the 'latch** (esp of a door) closed but not locked: *leave the door on the latch.*

▸ **latch** v to fasten sth with a latch: [Vn] *Please latch the front gate when you leave.* **PHR V** **,latch 'on (to sth)** (*infml*) to understand an idea, sth said, etc: *If you are firm but fair, a child will soon latch on to the idea that you mean what you say.* **,latch 'on to sb/sth** (*infml*) **1** to approach sb and stay in their company (too long): *He can't have many friends because he always latches on to me at parties.* **2** to develop a strong interest in sth: *She's latched on to classical music in a big way.*

late¹ /leɪt/ adj (**-r, -st**) **1** [esp pred] after the expected or usual time: *My flight was an hour late.* ∘ *Because of the cold weather the crops are late this year.* ∘ *It's never too late to stop smoking.* ∘ *a late riser* (ie sb who gets out of bed late in the morning). Compare EARLY 1. **2** towards the end of a period of time, sb's life, etc: *What are you doing up at this late hour?* ∘ *in late summer* ∘ *She married in her late twenties* (eg when she was 28 or 29). ∘ *the late nineteenth century* ∘ *a late Victorian house* ∘ *late-night buses/movies/shopping.* Compare EARLY 2. **3** [attrib] (esp in the superlative) (most) recent: *the latest craze/fashion/trend* ∘ *her latest novel* ∘ *the latest developments/discoveries* ∘ *Have you heard the latest news?* ∘ *Here is a late news flash.* **4** [attrib] (of a person) no longer alive: *her late husband.* **IDM** **at the 'latest** no later than the time or date specified: *Applications should be in by 31 October at the latest.* ∘ *Be there by 6.30 at the latest.* **an early / a late night** ⇨ NIGHT. ▸ **lateness** /'leɪtnəs/ n [U]: *They apologized for the lateness of the train.* ∘ *He was surprised at the lateness of the hour.*

───────────────

NOTE Compare **the latest**, **the last** and **the latter**. **The latest** means 'the newest or most recent': *She always dresses in the latest fashion.* ∘ *Spielberg's latest movie opens in London next week.* **The last** refers to the final one in a sequence, after which there are no more: *What time does the last bus leave?* ∘ *the last novel she wrote before she died.* It can also refer to the item before the one being discussed: *I like this job better than my last one/than the last one I had.* ∘ *The last time we met you had a beard.* **The latter** refers to the second of two things that have been mentioned in the previous sentence, and is used mostly in quite formal writing: *Given a choice of travelling by ship or plane, most people choose the latter.* **The latter** part or half of something is the last part, or the second half: *the latter part of the story/of the 1980s.*

───────────────

late² /leɪt/ adv **1** after the expected or usual time: *get up/go to bed/arrive home late* ∘ *I sat* (ie stayed) *up late last night.* ∘ *She married late.* Compare EARLY adv 1. **2** towards the end of a period of time, sb's life, etc: *It happened late last century — in 1895, to be exact.* ∘ *As late as the 1950s, tuberculosis was still a fatal illness.* ∘ *He became an author quite late in life* (ie when he was quite old). Compare EARLY adv 2. **IDM** **late of...** (*fml*) until recently working, living, etc in the specified place: *Professor Williams, late of Oxford University.* **better late than never** ⇨ BETTER². **,late in the 'day** later than is proper or

desirable: *It's rather late in the day to say you're sorry — the harm's done now.* **of 'late** lately; recently: *I haven't seen him of late.* **sooner or later** ⇨ SOON.

▸ **later** (also **,later 'on**) adv afterwards; at a time in the future; at a later time: *I'll see you later on this afternoon.* ∘ *We met again some time later.* ∘ *Some of them were later to become her friends.*

latecomer /'leɪtkʌmə(r)/ n a person who arrives late: *Latecomers will not be admitted until the interval.*

lately /'leɪtli/ adv in recent times; recently: *Have you seen her lately?* ∘ *It's only lately that she's been well enough to go out.* ∘ *I've been doing a lot of gardening lately.* ⇨ note at RECENT.

latent /'leɪtnt/ adj [esp attrib] existing but not yet active, developed or visible: *latent abilities/talent* ∘ *latent inhibition.*

lateral /'lætərəl/ adj [esp attrib] of, at, from or towards the side or sides: *a lateral vein/artery/limb* ∘ *lateral buds/shoots/branches.* ■ **,lateral 'thinking** n [U] a way of solving problems by considering a range of ideas that may not seem logical or relevant at first: *It shows what can be done with imagination and a bit of lateral thinking.*

latex /'leɪteks/ n [U] (**a**) a thick white liquid produced by certain plants and trees, esp rubber trees. (**b**) an artificial substance resembling this, used in paints, glues, fabrics, etc: *a carpet with a latex backing.*

lath /lɑːθ; US læθ/ n (pl **laths** /lɑːðz; US læðz/) a thin narrow strip of wood used to support PLASTER(1) on the inside walls and ceilings of buildings: *a lath-and-plaster wall.*

lathe

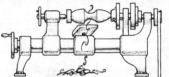

lathe /leɪð/ n a machine that shapes pieces of wood, metal, etc by holding and turning them against a fixed cutting tool. ⇨ picture.

lather /'lɑːðə(r); US 'læð-/ n [U] **1** a mass of small white bubbles produced by soap or DETERGENT when mixed with water: *shaving lather* ∘ *You get a much better lather with soft water.* **2** heavy sweat that looks like lather, esp on a horse. **3** (*infml*) a nervous or excited state: *She's in a lather about having to speak to such a large audience.* ∘ *Calm down — there's no need to get into a lather.*

▸ **lather** v **1** to form lather(1): [V] *Soap will not lather in sea water.* **2** to cover sth with lather(1): [Vn] *He lathered his face and started to shave.*

Latin /'lætɪn; US 'lætn/ n [U] the language of ancient Rome and its empire.

▸ **Latin** adj **1** of or in Latin: *Latin poetry.* **2** of the countries or peoples using languages developed from Latin, eg France, Italy, Portugal, Spain: *the Latin temperament.* Compare ROMANCE.

Latino /læ'tiːnəʊ/ adj [attrib], n (pl **-os**) (of) a person from Latin America: *Latino immigrants in the USA.* ■ **,Latin A'merica** n [U] the parts of Central and South America in which Spanish or Portuguese is the official language. **,Latin A'merican** adj ⇨ note at AMERICAN. **the ,Latin 'Church** n [sing] the Roman Catholic Church.

latitude /'lætɪtjuːd; US -tuːd/ n **1** (abbr **lat**) [U] the distance of a place north or south of the EQUATOR, measured in degrees. ⇨ picture at GLOBE. Compare

───────────────

L

───────────────

[V] = verb used alone   [Vn] = verb + noun   [Vp] = verb + particle   [Vpr] = verb + prepositional phrase

LONGITUDE. **2 latitudes** [pl] a region, esp with reference to its climate: *the northern/high latitudes* (ie regions to the north of/far from the EQUATOR). **3** [U] ~ (**in sth/to do sth**) freedom to behave, hold opinions or make decisions without restriction: *They allow their children far too much latitude.* ○ *The ruling allows states greater latitude to impose restrictions.*

latrine /ləˈtriːn/ n a toilet in a camp, etc, esp one made by digging a hole in the ground.

latter /ˈlætə(r)/ adj (*fml*) [attrib] nearer to the end of a period than to the beginning: *the latter half of the year* ○ *in the latter part of her life.*
▶ **the latter** n [sing or pl v] (also used attributively as an *adj*) the second of two things or people already mentioned: *Many support the former alternative, but personally I favour the latter (one).* ⇨ note at LATE¹. Compare FORMER.
latterly adv recently; LATELY.
■ **ˈlatter-day** adj [attrib] modern; recent: *a latter-day Robin Hood* ○ *latter-day scholars.*

lattice /ˈlætɪs/ (also **ˈlattice-work**) [U, C usu *sing*] (**a**) a framework of crossed bars with spaces between, used eg as a screen, fence or support for climbing plants. (**b**) a structure or design resembling this: *put a pastry lattice across a flan* ○ *peering through the lattice of tall reeds.*
■ **ˈlattice ˈwindow** (also **latticed window**) n a window with small pieces of glass set in a framework of metal strips.

laud /lɔːd/ v (*fml or rhet*) to praise sb/sth: [Vn] *a much-lauded production.*

laudable /ˈlɔːdəbl/ adj (*fml*) deserving praise and admiration: *a laudable aim/attempt* ○ *The campaign to save the theatre is highly laudable.* ▶ **laudably** /-əbli/ adv.

laudanum /ˈlɔːdənəm/ n [U] (formerly) a drug made from OPIUM. People used to take laudanum to calm their nerves or help them to sleep.

laudatory /ˈlɔːdətəri; US -tɔːri/ adj (*fml*) expressing or giving praise.

laugh /lɑːf; US læf/ v to make the sounds and movements of the face and body that express amusement or happiness, and sometimes also contempt or anxiety: [V] *laugh aloud/out loud* ○ *He burst out laughing.* ○ *He's so funny — he always makes me laugh.* ○ *I know they've had a bad time, but you've got to laugh, haven't you* (ie there is a funny side to it)? ○ *Don't laugh* (ie think me ridiculous), *but I've decided to teach myself Chinese.* [V.speech] *'That's stupid!' laughed Peter.* [Vpr] *Years later, we laughed about the incident.* ○ (*fig*) *a man who laughs in the face of danger.* **IDM** **laugh all the way to the ˈbank** (*infml*) to make a lot of money easily and feel very pleased about it. **laugh in sb's ˈface** to show one's contempt for sb openly. **laugh on the other side of one's ˈface** (*infml*) to be forced to change from feeling joy or satisfaction to disappointment, annoyance or regret: *He'll be laughing on the other side of his face when he reads this letter.* **laugh sb/sth out of ˈcourt** (*infml*) to dismiss sb/sth with contempt as being obviously not worth listening to: *Her story was simply laughed out of court.* **laugh till/until one ˈcries** to laugh so long or hard that there are tears in one's eyes. **laugh up one's ˈsleeve (at sb/sth)** (*infml*) to be secretly amused: *She knew the truth all along and was laughing up her sleeve at us.* **PHR V** **ˈlaugh at sb/sth 1** to show that one is amused by sb/sth: *laugh at a comedian/a joke.* **2** to mock or RIDICULE sb/sth: *We all laughed at Jane when she said she believed in ghosts.* ˌlaugh sth ˈoff (*infml*) to show that one does not care about sth or regards sth as unimportant: *He laughed off the suggestion that his job was in jeopardy.*
▶ **laugh** n **1** an act, a sound or a manner of laughing: *give/let out/break into/utter a (loud) laugh*

○ *a cynical/gentle/polite/hearty laugh* ○ *I was angry at the time, but we had a good laugh about it* (ie found it amusing) *afterwards.* ○ *I joined the drama group for a laugh* (ie for fun), *never dreaming that one day I'd be acting professionally.* ○ *His feeble attempt at humour failed to get/raise a laugh.* **2** (*infml*) an amusing incident or person: *And he didn't realize it was you? What a laugh!* ○ *He's a real laugh.* ○ (*ironic*) *Her, offer to help? That's a laugh!* **IDM** **have the last laugh** ⇨ LAST¹.

laughable /-əbl/ adj (*derog*) causing people to laugh; ridiculous: *The whole incident would be laughable if it were not so serious.* **laughably** /-əbli/ adv.

laughing /ˈlɑːfɪŋ; US ˈlæfɪŋ/ adj showing amusement, happiness, etc: *laughing faces.* **IDM** **be ˈlaughing** (*sl*) to be in a satisfactory or fortunate situation: *It's all right for you, with a good job and a nice house — you're laughing.* **be no laughing ˈmatter** to be sth serious, not to be joked about.
▶ **laughingly** adv **1** in an amused manner. **2** (*often derog*) in an amusing manner; ridiculously: *They were in what he laughingly called the boudoir.*
■ **ˈlaughing-gas** n [U] = NITROUS OXIDE.

laughing-stock n (esp *sing*) a person or thing that is mocked or treated as ridiculous: *His attempts at DIY made him the laughing-stock of the neighbourhood.*

laughter /ˈlɑːftə(r); US ˈlæf-/ n [U] the action, sound or manner of laughing: *roar with laughter* ○ *raucous/mocking/suppressed laughter* ○ *tears/peals/shrieks of laughter* ○ *a house full of laughter* (ie with a happy atmosphere).

launch¹ /lɔːntʃ/ v **1** to put sth/sb into action; to start sth: [Vn] *launch a campaign/an appeal/an inquiry* [Vnpr] *launch an attack on the government* ○ *He's launched himself on a career in the stock market.* **2** to make a new product publicly available: [Vn] *launch a share offer* ○ *The new model will be launched in July.* **3** to put a ship, esp one newly built, into the water: [Vn] *The Navy is to launch a new warship today.* ○ *The lifeboat was launched immediately to rescue the four men.* **4** to put sth into motion; to send sth on its course: [Vn] *launch a missile/rocket/torpedo* [Vnpr] *launch a satellite into orbit.* **PHR V** **ˈlaunch (oneself) into sth** to begin enthusiastically sth that is important or will take a long time: *He launched (himself) into a lengthy account of his previous job.* ˌlaunch ˈout into sth to do sth new and more exciting or profitable: *She wants to be more than just a singer and is launching out into films* (ie starting a career as a film actor).
▶ **launch** n (esp *sing*) the process of launching sth: *a book launch* ○ *The launch of the satellite was again delayed.*
launcher n (usu in compounds) (esp in military use) a device used to launch a missile, etc: *a ˌrocket/greˈnade launcher.*
■ **ˈlaunch pad** (also **ˈlaunching pad**) n a base or platform from which spacecraft, etc are launched: (*fig*) *the launch pad for a media career.*

launch² /lɔːntʃ/ n a large motor boat.

launder /ˈlɔːndə(r)/ v **1** (*fml*) to wash, dry and IRON² clothes, etc: [Vn] *Freshly laundered sheets.* **2** to transfer money obtained illegally to foreign banks, respectable businesses, etc so as to disguise its source: [Vn] *The gang laundered the drugs money through their chain of restaurants.*

launderette (also **laundrette**) /lɔːnˈdret/ n a place where the public may wash and dry their clothes in machines that operate when coins are inserted.

laundry /ˈlɔːndri/ n **1** [U] clothes, sheets, etc that have or need to be washed: *I'm going to do the laundry today.* ○ *a laundry basket.* **2** [C] a business where clothes, etc are washed: *send the sheets and towels to the laundry* ○ *a laundry van.*

Laureate /ˈlɒriət; US ˈlɔːr-/ n **1** a person who is honoured for intellectual or creative achievement: *a Nobel laureate.* **2** = POET LAUREATE.

laurel /ˈlɒrəl; US ˈlɔːr-/ n **1** an EVERGREEN bush with dark smooth shiny leaves: *a laurel hedge.* **2** (also **laurels** [pl]) honour and distinction following a great achievement: *She won laurels for her first novel.* **IDM** **look to one's ˈlaurels** to be careful not to lose one's superior position: *With so many good new actors around the older ones are having to look to their laurels.* **rest on one's laurels** ⇨ REST¹.
■ **ˈlaurel wreath** n a ring of laurel leaves worn on the head as a sign of victory or honour.

lava /ˈlɑːvə/ n [U] **(a)** hot liquid rock that comes out of a VOLCANO: *a lava flow.* ⇨ picture at VOLCANO. **(b)** a type of rock formed from this when it has cooled and hardened.

lavatory /ˈlævətri; US -tɔːri/ n (*dated or fml*) = TOILET 1. ⇨ note at TOILET.
▶ **lavatorial** adj relating to lavatories or to waste matter from the body: *lavatorial humour.*

lavender /ˈlævəndə(r)/ n [U] **1(a)** a plant with sweet-smelling pale purple flowers. **(b)** its dried flowers used to give sheets, clothes, etc a pleasant smell. **2** a pale purple colour.

lavish /ˈlævɪʃ/ adj **1** ~ (in/with sth) giving or doing sth generously or excessively: *be lavish with one's money* ○ *He was lavish in/with his praise.* **2** great in extent, rich in quality, and usu costing a lot of money: *a lavish display/meal/reception* ○ *lavish praise/illustrations/costumes/incentives.*
▶ **lavish** v **PHR V** **ˈlavish sth on/upon sb/sth** to give sth to sb/sth generously or excessively: *lavish attention/gifts on sb* ○ *lavish millions of dollars on a failed election campaign.*
lavishly adv: *lavishly decorated/illustrated.*

law /lɔː/ n **1(a)** (also **the law**) [U] all the rules established by authority or custom for regulating the behaviour of members of a community or country: *observe/obey the law* ○ *be within/outside the law* ○ *law-enforcement agencies* ○ *Stealing is against the law.* ○ *I didn't know I was breaking the law* (ie doing sth illegal). ○ *She acts as if she's above the law* (ie as if the law does not apply to her). ○ *The law is on our side* (ie We are right according to the law). See also CANON LAW, CIVIL LAW, COMMON LAW, MARTIAL LAW, STATUTE LAW. **(b)** [C] any single rule established in this way: *The new law comes into force next month.* **(c)** [U] a branch of such rules: *international/company/criminal law* ○ *the divorce/immigration/blasphemy laws.* **(d)** [U] such rules as a subject of study or the basis for the legal profession: *practise law* ○ *a law student/degree* ○ (*go to law school*) *He gave up law to become a writer.* **2** [C] a rule of action or procedure, esp in the arts or a game: *the laws of perspective/harmony* ○ *the laws of tennis.* **3** [C] a statement of fact concerning what always happens in certain circumstances; a scientific principle: *the law of gravity* ○ *the laws of chemistry.* **4 the law** [sing] (*infml*) the police: *Watch out — here comes the law!* **IDM** **be a law unto one'self/it'self** to behave in a manner that is not conventional or reliable: *She never listens to her parents — she's a law unto herself.* **go to ˈlaw (against sb)** to ask the lawcourts to decide about a problem, claim, etc. **have the ˈlaw on sb** (*infml*) to report sb to the police: *If you do that again I'll have the law on you.* **ˌlaw and ˈorder** respect for and obedience to the law throughout society: *a breakdown of law and order* ○ *establish/maintain/restore law and order.* **the ˌlaw of the ˈjungle** the survival or success of the strongest or of those with the least regard for others: *Power politics reflects the law of the jungle.* **lay down the ˈlaw** to say with real or assumed authority what should be done: *He's always laying down the law about gardening but he really*

doesn't know much about it. **the letter of the law** ⇨ LETTER. **the rule of law** ⇨ RULE. **take the law into one's own ˈhands** to act independently, often using force, to punish sb who has done sth wrong, even if one is breaking the law oneself by doing this. **there's no ˈlaw against sth** (*infml*) doing sth is allowed: *I'll stay in bed as long as I like — there's no law against it.*
▶ **lawful** /-fl/ adj **1** allowed by law; legal: *take power by lawful means.* **2** [esp attrib] recognized by law: *his lawful heir.* **lawfully** /-fəli/ adv: *a lawfully elected government.*
lawless adj **(a)** (of a country or an area) where laws do not exist or are not obeyed: *lawless regions/streets.* **(b)** (of people or actions) without respect for the law: *lawless youth.* **lawlessness** n [U].
■ **ˈlaw-abiding** adj obeying the law: *law-abiding citizens.*
ˈLaw Lord n (in Britain) a member of the House of Lords who is qualified to perform its legal work.
the ˌlaw of ˈaverages n [sing] the principle that if one extreme occurs it will be matched by the other extreme occurring, so that a normal average is maintained.

lawbreaker /ˈlɔːbreɪkə(r)/ n a person who does not obey the law; a criminal.

lawcourt /ˈlɔːkɔːt/ (also ˌcourt of ˈlaw) n a room or building in which legal cases are heard and judged. See also COURT¹ 1.

lawmaker /ˈlɔːmeɪkə(r)/ n a person who decides the laws of a country or society.

lawn¹ /lɔːn/ n [C, U] an area of short, regularly cut grass in the garden of a house or in a public park, or used for a game: *have tea on the lawn* ○ *In summer we have to mow the lawn once a week.* ○ *a ˈcroquet lawn.* ⇨ picture at HOUSE¹.
■ **ˌlawn ˈtennis** n [U] (*fml*) = TENNIS.

lawn² /lɔːn/ n [U] a type of fine material used for dresses, etc: *cotton lawn.*

lawnmower /ˈlɔːnməʊə(r)/ n a machine for cutting the grass on lawns.

lawsuit /ˈlɔːsuːt, -sjuːt/ (also **suit**) n the process of bringing a dispute, claim, etc before a lawcourt for it to be settled: *be involved in a lawsuit brought by environmental groups.*

lawyer /ˈlɔːjə(r)/ n a person trained and qualified in the law who does legal work for other people, esp a SOLICITOR: *Don't sign anything until you've consulted a lawyer.* Compare ADVOCATE n 2, ATTORNEY 1, BARRISTER.

lax /læks/ adj (*usu derog*) not strict or severe enough: *a lax attitude to health and safety regulations* ○ *lax discipline* ○ *The law is rather lax on this point.* ▶ **laxity** /ˈlæksəti/ n [U]: *moral/financial laxity.*

laxative /ˈlæksətɪv/ n, adj (a medicine, food or drink) causing or helping the bowels to empty: *take a laxative* ○ *laxative pills.*

lay¹ /leɪ/ v (*pt, pp* **laid** /leɪd/)

● **Placing something in a certain position**
1(a) to put sth/sb in a certain position: [Vnpr] *lay the book on the table* ○ *lay a blanket over the sleeping child* ○ *He laid his hand on my shoulder.* [Vnp] *lay oneself down to sleep* ○ *The horse laid back its ears.* [Vn-adj] *The storm laid the crops flat.* **(b)** to put sth in a suitable or the correct position for a particular purpose: [Vn] *lay a carpet/cable/pipe* ○ *lay the foundations of a house* ○ *lay a fire* (ie place wood, coal, etc ready for burning) ○ *lay the table* (ie put plates, knives, forks, etc on it for a meal) [Vnpr] *lay a wreath on sb's grave* ○ *lay mines/burning tyres across the road* [Vn] (*fig*) *The basis for the modern state was laid in 1945.* **2** ~ **sth (on/over sth)** to spread sth on sth; to cover sth with a layer of sth: [Vn] *lay newspaper/straw everywhere* [Vnpr] *lay*

[V.speech] = verb + direct speech   [V.*that*] = verb + *that* clause   [V.*wh*] = verb + *who, how,* etc clause

strips of meat on a grill ∘ *The grapes were laid to dry on racks.* ⇨ note at LIE².

● **Causing somebody or something to be in a certain state** **3** (*fml*) to cause sb/sth to be in a certain state or situation: [Vnpr] *lay sb under an obligation to do sth* ∘ *lay a responsibility on sb* ∘ *lay a bill before parliament.* **4** to make sth settle: [Vn] *sprinkle water to lay the dust.* **5** (*fml*) to relieve or remove sth: [Vn] *lay sb's fears.*

● **Other meanings** **6** ~ **sth (on sth)** to bet money on sth; to place a bet: [Vn] *lay a bet* [Vnpr] *lay £100 on the favourite* [Vnn, Vn.that* no passive] *I'll lay you (£5) that she won't come.* **7** (⚠ *sl*) (esp passive) (of a man) to have sex with a woman: [Vn] *hoping to get laid.* **8** (of certain creatures, esp birds and insects) to produce eggs: [Vn] *new-laid eggs* ∘ *The cuckoo lays its eggs in other birds' nests.* [Vadv] *The hens are not laying well* (ie not producing many eggs) *at the moment.* **9** (used in the combination *lay* + *n* + *prep/ infinitive*, when the phrase has the same meaning as a verb related in form to the noun): *lay the emphasis on certain points* (ie emphasize certain points) ∘ *lay stress on neatness* (ie stress it) ∘ *Who should we lay the blame on?* (ie Who should we blame?) ∘ *lay plans* (ie plan) *to do sth* ∘ *lay a trap for* (ie prepare to trap) *sb*.

IDM Most idioms containing **lay** are at the entries for the nouns or adjectives in the idioms, eg **lay claim to sth** ⇨ CLAIM²; **lay sth bare** ⇨ BARE¹. **lay it 'on ('thick / with a 'trowel)** (*infml*) to exaggerate when describing sth, praising sb, etc: *To call him a genius is laying it on a bit (too thick)!*

PHR V **lay a'bout one (with sth)** to hit wildly in all directions: *The police laid about them with clubs.*
,lay sth a'side (*fml*) **1** to abandon sth; to give sth up: *lay aside one's studies/responsibilities.* **2** (also **,lay sth 'by**) to keep sth for future use; to save sth: *lay some money aside for one's old age.*
,lay sth 'down 1 to put sth down or stop using sth: *lay down one's pen/tools* ∘ *lay down one's arms* (ie stop fighting). **2** (*fml*) to stop doing a particular job or performing a particular duty, function, etc: *lay down one's office/duties.* **3** to establish sth in or on the ground: *lay down foundations/a railway track.*
,lay sth 'down; ,lay it 'down that... to give sth as a condition, principle, etc; to establish sth: *You can't lay down hard and fast rules.* ∘ *It is laid down that all candidates must submit three copies of their dissertation.*
,lay sth 'in to provide oneself with a stock of sth: *lay in food/coal/supplies.*
,lay 'into sb/sth (*infml*) to attack sb/sth violently, with words or blows: *He really laid into her, saying she was arrogant and unfeeling.*
,lay 'off (sb) (*infml*) (esp imperative) to stop doing sth that irritates, annoys, etc sb: *Lay off! You're messing up my hair!* ∘ *Lay off him! Can't you see he's badly hurt?* **,lay 'off (sth)** (*infml*) to stop doing, using or eating sth harmful: *My doctor said I ought to lay off fatty foods for a while.* **,lay sb 'off** to dismiss a worker from a job, esp temporarily when there is no work to do: *600 employees were laid off because of the lack of new orders.*
,lay sth 'on (*Brit infml*) to provide sth; to arrange sth: *lay on a party/show/trip* ∘ *lay on food and drink* ∘ *They've laid on a bus to take guests to the airport.*
,lay sb 'out to knock sb unconscious: *He laid his opponent out in the fifth round.* **,lay sth 'out 1** to spread sth out ready for use or to be seen easily: *jewellery laid out in the shop window* ∘ *She laid out all the clothes she wanted to take with her.* **2** (often passive) to arrange sth in a planned way: *lay out a town/garden* ∘ *a well laid out magazine.* **3** to present a plan, an idea, etc for others to consider: *lay out the options* ∘ *All the terms and conditions are laid out in this document.* **4** (*infml*) to spend money: *I had to lay*

out a fortune on that car. **5** to prepare a dead body to be buried.
,lay 'over (*US*) to stop at a place on a journey: *We will lay over in Chicago.* Compare STOP OVER.
,lay sb 'up (usu passive) to cause sb to stay in bed, to be unable to work, etc: *She's laid up with a broken leg/with flu.* **,lay sth 'up 1** to save sth for the future; to store sth: *lay up supplies/fuel* ∘ *You're only laying up trouble (for yourself) by not mending that roof now.* **2** to put a ship, etc out of use, eg while it's being repaired: *lay a boat up for repairs.*

▶ **lay** *n* (⚠ *sl esp sexist*) a partner in sex(2), esp a woman: *an easy lay* (ie a person who is ready and willing to have sex).

■ **'lay-off** *n* (**a**) an instance of a worker being dismissed temporarily from a job: *There have been many lay-offs among factory workers.* (**b**) a period of time when one is not working or doing sth that one normally does regularly: *a six-week lay-off due to injury.*

lay² /leɪ/ *adj* [attrib] **1(a)** not having expert knowledge of a subject: *speaking as a lay person.* (**b**) without professional qualifications, esp in law or medicine: *a lay magistrate.* **2** not a priest; not belonging to the CLERGY: *a lay preacher.*

lay³ /leɪ/ *n* (*arch*) a poem that was written to be sung, usu telling a story.

lay⁴ *pt* of LIE².

layabout /ˈleɪəbaʊt/ *n* (*Brit infml*) a lazy person who avoids work.

lay-by /ˈleɪ baɪ/ *n* (*pl* **lay-bys**) (*Brit*) (*US* **'rest stop**) an area at the side of a road where vehicles may stop without blocking the traffic.

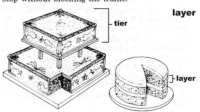

layer /ˈleɪə(r)/ *n* **1** (also /ˈleə(r)/) a thickness of material, esp one of several laid over a surface : *a layer of dust on the furniture* ∘ *remove layers of old paint* ∘ *Several thin layers of clothing will keep you warmer than one thick one.* ∘ (*fig*) *The play has several layers of meaning.* ⇨ picture. **2** (following an *adj*) a hen that lays eggs: *a poor/good layer.*
▶ **layer** *v* (esp passive) to arrange sth in layers: [Vn] *a layered skirt* ∘ *layered hair* (ie cut to several different lengths).

layette /leɪˈet/ *n* a set of clothes, nappies (NAPPY), etc for a new baby.

layman /ˈleɪmən/ *n* (*pl* **-men** /-mən/) **1** a person who does not have expert knowledge of a subject: *a book written for professionals and laymen alike* ∘ *explain sth in layman's terms.* **2** a Church member who is not a priest or a member of the CLERGY.

layout /ˈleɪaʊt/ *n* the way in which the parts of sth are arranged according to a plan: *the layout of rooms in a building* ∘ *a magazine's attractive new page layout.*

laze /leɪz/ *v* ~ (**about/around**) to rest; to relax; to be lazy: [V] *lazing by the river all day* [Vp, Vpr] *spend the afternoon lazing around (the house).* **PHR V** **laze sth away** to spend time in a lazy way: *laze away the long hot summer days.*

lazy /ˈleɪzi/ *adj* (**-ier, -iest**) **1** (*derog*) unwilling to work; doing as little work as possible: *He's not stupid, just lazy.* **2** (*derog*) showing a lack of effort or care: *a lazy piece of work* ∘ *lazy conclusions.* **3**

involving little energy or activity: *a lazy smile* ∘ *We spent a lazy day on the beach.* ► **lazily** *adv*: *a river flowing lazily beside the stream.* **laziness** *n* [U].
■ ˌlazy ˈSusan *n* (*US*) = DUMB WAITER.

lazybones /ˈleɪzɪbəʊnz/ *n* (*pl* unchanged) (*infml*) a lazy person: *Come on, lazybones, get up!*

lb *abbr* (*pl* unchanged or **lbs**) pound (weight) (Latin *libra*): *apples 20p* (ie 20 pence) *per lb* ∘ *Add 2lb sugar.* Compare OZ.

lbw /ˌel biː ˈdʌblju:/ *abbr* (in cricket) leg before wicket.

LCD /ˌel siː ˈdiː/ *abbr* (*computing*) liquid crystal display: *an LCD screen.*

LEA /ˌel iː ˈeɪ/ *abbr* (in Britain) Local Education Authority.

leach /liːtʃ/ *v* (*techn*) **1** ~ (**from sth**) (**into sth**); ~ **out/away** (of chemicals, minerals, etc) to be removed from soil, etc by water passing through it: [Vpr] *nitrates leaching from the soil into rivers* [also V, Vp]. **2** ~ **sth from sth**; ~ **sth out** (of a liquid) to make chemicals, minerals, etc drain away from the soil, etc: [Vnpr] *rain leaching pesticides from the soil* [Vn] *leached soils* [also Vnp].

lead¹ /liːd/ *v* (*pt, pp* **led** /led/) **1(a)** to show sb the way, esp by going in front: [Vnpr] *lead a guest to his room* [Vnp] *He led us out into the garden.* [also Vn]. **(b)** to guide or take sb/sth by holding, pulling, etc: [Vnpr] *lead a blind man across the road* [Vnp] *She led the horse back into the stable.* [V] *In ballroom dancing the man leads.* [Vnpr] (*fig*) *I tried to lead the discussion back to the main issue.* [also Vn]. **2(a)** to be a route or means of access: [Vpr] *A path led up the hill.* [also Vp]. **(b)** to be a connection between two or more objects: [Vpr] *a wire leading to a speaker* ∘ *the pipe leading from the water tank.* **(c)** (of a road, path, etc) to bring sb/sth to a particular position or destination: [Vnpr] *The track led us alongside a wood.* [also Vnp]. **3** ~ **sb** (**to sth**) to influence the actions or opinions of sb: [Vn] *He's too easily led.* [Vnpr] *What led you to this conclusion?* [Vnadv] *Don't let him lead you astray* (ie tempt you to do wrong). [Vn.to inf] *The evidence leads me to believe that she's lying.* ∘ *This has led scientists to speculate on the existence of other galaxies.* **4** to have a particular type of life: [Vn] *lead a miserable existence/a life of luxury/a double life.* **5** ~ (**sb/sth**) (**in sth**) to be in first place or ahead of sb/sth: [Vnpr] *lead the world in cancer research* [Vpr, Vnpr] *The champion is leading (his nearest rival) by 18 seconds.* [also Vn, V]. **6** to be the leader or head of sb/sth; to direct or control sb/sth: [Vn] *lead an army/an expedition/a strike* ∘ *lead a discussion* ∘ *lead the carol singing* ∘ *Who will lead the party in the next election?* [also V, Vnpr]. **7** (in card-games) to play first or to play sth as one's first card: [V] *It's your turn to lead.* [Vn] *lead trumps/the two of clubs.* **IDM** **the blind leading the blind** ⇨ BLIND¹. **get** (**sb**) **/ go / lead sb nowhere** to make or cause sb to make no progress; to have no successful result: *He was getting nowhere with his homework until I helped him.* ∘ *£20 goes nowhere* (ie does not buy much) *these days when you're feeding a family.* ∘ *This discussion is leading us nowhere.* **lead sb by the ˈnose** to make sb do everything one wishes; to control sb completely. **lead sb a (merry) ˈdance** to cause sb a lot of trouble, esp by making them follow from place to place. **lead sb to the ˈaltar** (*dated or joc*) to marry sb. **lead sb up the garden ˈpath** to deceive sb. **lead the ˈway (to/in sth)** to go first; to show the way: *lead the way in space research* ∘ *You lead the way and I'll follow.* **PHR V** ˌlead ˈoff (**from**) **sth** to start at a place and extend away from it: *alleyways leading off (from) the main square.* ˌlead (**sth**) ˈoff to start sth: *The first couple leads off to the right* (ie in a dance). ˌlead sb ˈon (*infml*) to persuade sb to believe or do sth by making false promises or

claims: *The salesman tried to lead me on with talk of amazing savings on heating bills.* ˈlead to sth to have sth as its result: *Eating too much fat can lead to heart disease.* ∘ *They were instantly attracted — one thing led to another and they got married.* ˌlead ˈup to sth to prepare, introduce or go before sth: *the events leading up to the strike.* ˈlead with sth **1** (*journalism*) to have sth as the main item of news: *We'll lead with the royal wedding.* **2** (in boxing) to use a particular punch to begin an attack: *lead with one's right/left.*
■ ˈlead-in *n* an introduction to a subject, etc: *He told an amusing story as a lead-in to the serious part of his speech.*

lead² /liːd/ *n* **1** [U, sing] an example set by sb's behaviour that others may copy: *He's the chief troublemaker; the others just follow his lead.* ∘ *take a/the lead in trying to end the dispute* ∘ *People expect the Church to give more of a lead on moral issues.* **2** [sing] ~ (**over sb/sth**) a distance by which one competitor, etc is in front of another: *have a lead of three metres/two lengths/half a lap (over a rival)* ∘ *The company has built up a substantial lead in laser technology.* **3** **the lead** [sing] ~ (**over sb/sth**) the first place or position, in front of sb/sth: *move/go into the lead* ∘ *take (over) the lead (from sb)/lose the lead (to sb)* ∘ *a company regaining the lead over its competitors.* **4** [C *usu sing*] a principal part in a play; a person who plays this part: *play the lead in the new Broadway hit* ∘ *the lead guitarist of the group.* **5** [C *usu sing*] (in card-games) the act or right of playing first: *Whose lead is it?* **6** [C] a piece of information or evidence that might provide the solution to a problem; a CLUE(1): *The police are investigating an important new lead.* **7** (also *esp US* **leash**) [C] a strip of leather or a cord for leading or controlling a dog: *Dogs must be kept on a lead in the park.* **8** [C] a length of wire, usu covered in plastic, that allows electrical current to pass between two pieces of equipment or from a power source to an appliance. ⇨ picture at CAR.
■ ˈlead story *n* an item of news made most prominent in a newspaper or coming first in a news broadcast.

lead³ /led/ *n* **1** [U] (*symb* **Pb**) a chemical element. Lead is a heavy soft metal, dull grey in colour, used esp formerly for water pipes or to cover roofs. It can also be added to petrol or used as a shield against dangerous RADIATION(2). ⇨ App 7. **2** [C, U] the thin black part of a pencil that marks paper.
► **leaded** /ˈledɪd/ *adj* [usu attrib] **(a)** with a cover or frame of lead: *a leaded roof/window.* **(b)** (of petrol) with lead added. Compare UNLEADED. ˌleaded ˈlight *n* (usu *pl*) a small panel of leaded glass, esp coloured, forming part of a larger window.
leaden /ˈledn/ *adj* **1** dull, heavy or slow: *a leaden heart* ∘ *moving at a leaden pace.* **2** of the colour of lead; dull grey: *leaden skies/clouds.* **3** [attrib] (*dated*) made of lead: *a leaden coffin.*
■ ˌlead-ˈfree *adj* (of petrol) without lead added.

leader /ˈliːdə(r)/ *n* **1** a person or thing that leads: *the leader of an expedition/a gang/the Opposition* ∘ *a military/political/trade union leader* ∘ *She's among the leaders* (ie of the race) *at this stage.* ∘ *This country is a world leader in health care.* See also MARKET LEADER. **2** (*US* **concert-master**) (*music*) the principal VIOLIN player of an ORCHESTRA. **3** = LEADING ARTICLE.
► **leaderless** *adj*: *Her sudden death left the party leaderless.*
leadership *n* **1** [U] being a leader: *the contest for the leadership of the Labour Party* ∘ *leadership problems.* **2** [U] the ability to be a leader: *show the qualities of leadership necessary in a team captain* ∘ *have leadership potential.* **3** [Gp] a group of leaders: *call for firm action by the union leadership.*

leading /ˈliːdɪŋ/ *adj* [attrib] **1** most important; chief: *one of the country's leading writers* ○ *play a leading role in the theatre/a political campaign, etc.* **2** in first position(s): *the leading runners.*
■ ˌleading ˈarticle (also ˈlead article, leader) (*Brit*) (*US* ˈlead story) *n* (*journalism*) a principal newspaper article by the editor, giving opinions on events, policies, etc; an EDITORIAL.
ˌleading ˈedge *n* the forward edge of an aircraft's wing.
ˌleading ˈlady, ˌleading ˈman *ns* an actor taking the chief part in a play, etc.
ˌleading ˈlight *n* (*infml approv*) a prominent member of a group: *one of the leading lights in international golf.*
ˌleading ˈquestion *n* a question that is put in such a way as to produce the desired answer.

leaf /liːf/ *n* (*pl* leaves /liːvz/) **1** [C] any of the usu green and flat parts of a plant, growing from a stem or branch or directly from the root: *lettuce/cabbage/oak leaves* ○ *sweep up the dead leaves.* See also FIG-LEAF. **2** [C] a sheet of paper, esp one forming two pages of a book: *He carefully turned the leaves of the precious volume.* **3** [U] metal, esp gold or silver, in the form of very thin sheets: *gold leaf.* **4** [C] a part of a table that can be folded or pulled into position to extend it: *a drop-leaf table.* **IDM** **come into / be in ˈleaf** to become/be covered with leaves. **take a leaf from / out of sb's ˈbook** to copy sb; to act or behave in a similar way to sb. **turn over a new leaf** ⇨ NEW.
▶ **leaf** *v* **PHRV** ˈleaf through sth to turn over the pages of a book, etc quickly; to look through sth: *leaf idly through a magazine while waiting.*
leafless *adj* having no leaves.
leafy *adj* (-ier, -iest) (**a**) covered in or having many leaves: *a leafy forest, branch, bush.* (**b**) having many trees and plants: *a leafy country lane.* (**c**) consisting of leaves: *leafy vegetables.* (**d**) made or caused by leaves: *a leafy shade.*
■ ˈleaf-mould *n* [U] soil consisting mostly of decayed leaves.

leaflet /ˈliːflət/ *n* a printed sheet of paper, usu folded and free of charge, containing information: *an explanatory leaflet* ○ *pick up a leaflet on local bus times.*
▶ **leaflet** *v* to distribute leaflets to people: [V] *a mass leafleting campaign* [also Vn].

league¹ /liːg/ *n* **1** a group of people or countries combined for a particular purpose: *the League of Nations.* **2** a group of sports clubs competing against each other: *the local darts league* ○ *the league champions* ○ *bottom of the league table.* **3** (*infml*) a class or category of excellence: *I'm not in his league* (ie He's much better than me). ○ *She's out of her league* (ie less able than all the others). **IDM** **in ˈleague (with sb)** making secret plans with sb: *He pretended not to know her but in fact they were in league (together).*

league² /liːg/ *n* (*arch*) a former measure of distance, equal to about 3 miles or 4 800 metres.

leak /liːk/ *n* **1(a)** a hole, crack, etc through which liquid or gas may wrongly get in or out: *a leak in the roof* (ie allowing rain to enter) ○ *a leak in the gas pipe* (ie allowing gas to escape). (**b**) an amount of liquid or gas that passes through this: *smell a gas leak.* **2** an act of revealing secret information, esp to the public: *a security leak.* **3** (*sl*) an act of passing URINE from the body: *have/take/go for a leak.* **IDM** **spring a leak** ⇨ SPRING³.
▶ **leak** *v* **1(a)** (of a container) to allow liquid or gas to get in or out wrongly: [V] *This boat leaks like a sieve* (ie very badly). (**b**) (of liquid or gas) to get in or out in this way: [Vp] *The rain's leaking in.* [Vpr] *Air leaked out of the balloon.* [also V]. ⇨ note at DRIP¹. **2** ~ sth (to sb) to reveal information: [Vn] *a*

leaked doucment [Vnpr] *Who leaked this to the press?* **PHRV** ˌleak ˈout (of information) to become known: *The details were supposed to be secret but they leaked out somehow.*
leakage /ˈliːkɪdʒ/ *n* **1** [U, C] the action or an instance of leaking: *the leakage of confidential information* ○ *a leakage of toxic waste.* **2** [C] a thing that has leaked: *a gas/oil leakage.*
leaky *adj* having holes or cracks that leak: *a leaky ship/kettle/roof.*

lean¹ /liːn/ *v* (*pt, pp* leant /lent/ or leaned /liːnd/) **1** to be in a sloping position; to bend: [V] *the leaning tower of Pisa* [Vpr] *lean out of the window* [Vp] *He leaned back in his chair.* **2** ~ against/on/upon sth to rest on sth in a sloping position for support: [Vpr] *a ladder leaning against the wall* ○ *lean on sb's arm/one's elbows* ○ *The old man leant upon his stick.* **3** ~ sth against/on sth to make sth rest against sth: [Vnpr] *The workmen leant their shovels against the fence and went to lunch.* **IDM** **bend/lean over backwards** ⇨ BACKWARDS. **PHRV** ˈlean on sb (*infml esp US*) to try to influence sb by threats: *If he doesn't pay soon we'll have to lean on him a little.* ˈlean on/upon sb/sth (for sth) to depend on sb/sth: *lean upon others for guidance* ○ *I need a comforting shoulder to lean on.* ˈlean to/towards sth to have a tendency towards sth: *Her political views lean towards the left.*
▶ **leaning** *n* a tendency: *have a leaning towards socialism/have socialist leanings.*
■ **lean-to** /ˈliːn tuː/ *n* (*pl* -tos /-tuːz/) a small building or shed with its roof resting against the side of a larger building, wall or fence: *They keep hens in a lean-to at the end of the garden.* ○ *a lean-to garage.*

lean² /liːn/ *adj* (-er, -est) **1** (of people or animals) without much flesh; thin and fit: *a lean athletic body.* ⇨ note at THIN. **2** (of meat) containing little or no fat: *lean beef.* **3** [esp attrib] (**a**) small in amount or quality: *a lean diet/harvest.* (**b**) (of a period of time) producing little of value: *lean years* ○ *Last season's leading goal-scorer, he's having a lean time (of it) this year.*
▶ **lean** *n* [U] the lean part of meat: *a lot of fat and not much lean.*
leanness /ˈliːnnəs/ *n* [U].

leap /liːp/ *v* (*pt, pp* leapt /lept/ or leaped /liːpt/) **1(a)** to jump high or a long way: [Vp] *The children leapt up and down with excitement.* [Vpr] *leap over a ditch/puddle* ○ *He leaped onto the train as it started to move.* ○ (*fig*) [V] *My heart leapt (for joy) at the news.* (**b**) to move quickly in the specified direction; to rush: [Vpr, Vp] *leap across the room/into one's car/upstairs* [Vpr] *They leapt into action immediately.* ○ *She leapt to her feet* (ie stood up quickly). ○ *leap to sb's defence* (ie by speaking in support of them) ○ *His name seemed to leap out at me from the page.* **2** (of prices, numbers, etc) to increase suddenly and by a large amount: [Vpr] *Shares leapt from 476p to close at 536p.* [V] *Membership has leapt in the last six months.* ⇨ note at JUMP¹. **IDM** **jump/leap to conclusions / to the conclusion that…** ⇨ CONCLUSION. ˌlook before you ˈleap (*saying*) one should consider the possible consequences before taking action. **PHRV** ˈleap at sth to accept sth eagerly, without hesitating: *She leapt at the chance to go to America.*
▶ **leap** *n* **1** a long or high jump: *He crossed the garden in three leaps.* **2** a sudden big increase or change: *a leap in prices/oil production/the number of people out of work* ○ *a leap of faith/imagination.* See also QUANTUM LEAP. **IDM** **by/in ˌleaps and ˈbounds** very rapidly: *Her health is improving in leaps and bounds.* **a leap/shot in the dark** ⇨ DARK².
leaping *adj* [attrib] moving up and down quickly and suddenly: *leaping waves/flames.*

L

■ ¹**leap-frog** n [U] a game in which each player in turn jumps with legs spread out over another who is bending down. ⇨ picture. — v (-**gg**-) to leap over sb/sth in this way: [Vn, Vpr] (fig) a company leap-frogging (over) its competitors to gain the biggest market share.

leap-frog

¹**leap year** n one year in every four years, with an extra day (29 February).

learn /lɜːn/ v (pt, pp **learnt** /lɜːnt/ or **learned** /lɜːnd/) **1** ~ (**sth**) (**from sb/sth**) to gain knowledge or skill by study, experience or being taught: learn a foreign language [V.to inf, V.wh] learn (how) to swim/to walk/to drive [Vn] learn a poem by heart (ie from memory) [Vpr] learn from one's mistakes [V] I can't drive yet — I'm still learning. [Vnpr] You can learn a lot from books. **2** ~ (**of/about**) **sth** to become aware of sth through information or observation; to realize: [V.that] learn that it's no use blaming other people [V.wh] learn what it means to be poor [Vpr] I was sorry to learn of/about your illness. [Vn] I never learned the name of this flower. **3** (sl or joc) to teach sb: [Vn] That'll learn you (eg said when punishing sb). **IDM** **learn one's** ¹**lesson** to learn what to do or not to do in future by remembering the results of one's actions: I'll never do that again — I've learned my lesson! **show sb / know / learn the ropes** ⇨ ROPE. **you/we live and learn** ⇨ LIVE².

▶ **learned** /ˈlɜːnɪd/ adj **1** having a lot of knowledge obtained by study: a learned philosopher and theologian. **2** of or for learned people: learned journals/societies ∘ the learned professions (eg law, medicine) ∘ (Brit law) (used as a term of address between lawyers in court): my learned friend.

learner n a person who is gaining knowledge or skill: a quick/slow learner ∘ I'm still only a learner, so don't expect too much. ∘ a learner driver.

learning n [U] knowledge obtained by study: a woman of great learning.

lease /liːs/ n a contract by which the owner of land or of a building allows another person to use it for a specified time, usu in return for rent: take out a lease on a commercial property ∘ The lease has four years left to run; it expires in 1999. ∘ Under the terms of the lease, you cannot keep animals in the building. **IDM** **a new lease of life** ⇨ NEW.

▶ **lease** v ~ **sth** (**to/from sb**); ~ **sth out** to permit or obtain the use of sth in exchange for rent: [Vn] lease a car/building [Vnpr] an 18-acre site leased from a local farmer [Vnp, Vnpr] He leased out some of the land (to other members of his family).

leaseback /ˈliːsbæk/ (Brit) (US **reversion**) n [U] the process of selling a property and immediately renting it back from the new owner.

leasehold /ˈliːshəʊld/ ~ (**of/on sth**) n [U] the right to use a property by means of a LEASE: have the leasehold on a house. ▶ **leasehold** adj, adv: a leasehold property ∘ own a flat leasehold. Compare FREEHOLD. ¹**leaseholder** n.

leash /liːʃ/ n (esp US) = LEAD² 7: Let the dog off the leash. **IDM** **strain at the leash** ⇨ STRAIN¹.

least /liːst/ indef det, indef pron (used as the superlative of little²) (**a**) smallest in size, amount, extent, etc: (det) He's the best teacher, even though he has the least experience. ∘ She aims to make as much money as possible with the least amount of effort. ∘ note at MUCH¹. (**b**) (pron) She gave (the) least of all towards the wedding present. ∘ That's the least of my worries (ie I have many more important things to worry about)! ∘ It's the least I can do to help (ie I feel I should do more). **IDM** **at the (very)** ¹**least** (after

amounts) and probably more than that: It'll take a year, at the very least.

▶ **least** adv to the smallest extent: just when we least expected it ∘ affecting the people who can least afford it ∘ She chose the least expensive of the hotels. ∘ one of the least performed of Shakespeare's plays. **IDM** **at** ¹**least 1** not less than: at least 3 months/£5/10 inches ∘ Cut the grass at least once a week in summer. ∘ I've known her at least as long as you have. **2** (used to be positive about sth that one has a generally negative opinion or feeling about) if nothing else is true: She may be slow but at least she's reliable. ∘ At least, he thought, they wouldn't be bored this year. **3** (used to limit or qualify sth that has been said) at any rate; ANYHOW(3): Let's at least give this approach a try. ¹**least of** ¹**all** to the smallest degree: Nobody need worry about losing their job, you least of all/least of all you. ¹**not in the** ¹**least** absolutely not; not at all: Really, I'm not in the least tired. ∘ 'Would you mind if I put the television on?' 'No, not in the least.' **not** ¹**least** especially; in particular: The documentary caused a lot of bad feeling, not least among the workers whose lives it described.

leather /ˈleðə(r)/ n **1** [U, C] a material made from animal skins treated by a special process: bikers in black leather jackets ∘ leather shoes/gloves ∘ a leather-bound book. **2 leathers** [pl] leather clothes. See also CHAMOIS LEATHER, PATENT LEATHER. **IDM** **hell for leather** ⇨ HELL.

▶ **leatherette** /ˌleðəˈret/ n [U] a material made to resemble leather.

leathery /ˈleðəri/ adj as tough as leather: leathery skin/meat/leaves.

leave¹ /liːv/ v (pt, pp **left** /left/) **1** to go away from a person or a place: [Vn] They hate leaving home. [V] Come on, it's time we left. [Vpr, Vnpr] The plane leaves (Heathrow) for Dallas at 12.35. **2(a)** to stop living at a place, belonging to a group, working for an employer, etc: [Vn] He left America in 1984 and never returned. ∘ Many children leave school at 16. [V] My secretary has threatened to leave. ∘ (Brit) go to sb's leaving party. (**b**) to leave one's wife, husband or partner permanently: [Vn] She's leaving him for another man. **3(a)** not to deal with sth: [Vn] Leave the dishes — I'll wash them up later. ∘ The lemonade was too sweet, so he left it (ie did not drink it). ∘ Why do you always leave everything until the last moment? (**b**) to cause or allow sb/sth to remain in a particular condition, place, etc: [Vn-adj] Leave the door open, please. ∘ The bomb blast left 25 people dead. [Vn.in] Don't leave her waiting outside in the rain. [Vnpr] Leave the fish in the mixture for at least an hour. **4** to cause sth to occur or remain as a result: [Vn, Vnp] a puppy leaving (behind) a trail of destruction in its wake [Vn] Red wine leaves a stain. [Vnpr] She left me with the impression that she was unhappy with her job. [Vnn] I'm afraid you leave me no choice. **5 be left** (passive) to remain for use, for sale, etc: [Vn] There are six days left before we go. ∘ Is there any coffee left? ∘ How many tickets do you have left? ∘ (fig) They are fighting for what is left of American trade unionism. [Vnpr] The only course of action left to me was to notify her employer. **6** (mathematics) to have a particular amount remaining: [Vn] Seven from ten/Ten minus seven leaves three (ie 10 − 7 = 3). **7** ~ **sth/sb** (**behind**) to fail or forget to take sth/sb with one: [Vnpr] I've left my purse on the bus. [Vn, Vnp] 'Let's drive off and leave her (behind),' he suggested callously. **8** to have family remaining alive after one's death: [Vn] He leaves a widow and two children. **9** to give a duty, position of trust, etc to another person: [Vnpr] You can leave the cooking to me. ∘ Leave an assistant in charge of the shop. ∘ **Leave it with me** — I'm sure I can sort it out. ∘ 'Where shall we eat?' 'I'll leave it entirely (up) to you (ie You can decide).' ∘ They left me with all the

washing-up. [Vn.*to* inf] *I was left to cope on my own.*
10 ~ **sth (for sb)** to deliver sth and then go away: [Vn] *How many bottles did the milkman leave today?* [Vnn, Vnpr] *Someone left you this note/left this note for you.* **11** ~ **sth to sb** to indicate that sth should be given to sb when one dies: [Vn] *How much did he leave?* [Vnpr] *leave all one's money to charity* [Vnn] *She left you £500.* **IDM** Most idioms containing **leave** are at the entries for the nouns or adjectives in the idioms, eg **leave sb in the lurch** ⇨ LURCH[1]; **leave sb cold** ⇨ COLD[1]. **leave it at 'that** (*infml*) to say or do nothing more: *We'll never agree, so let's just leave it at that, shall we?* **PHRV** ˌleave sth aˈside not to consider sth; to disregard sth: *Leaving the expense aside, do we actually need a second car?*

ˌleave sb/sth beˈhind **1** (esp passive) to make much better progress than sb else: *Britain is fast being left behind in the race for new markets.* ○ *She has left the rest of her class far behind.* **2** to leave a person, place or state permanently: *leave one's childhood behind* ○ *The train sped through the countryside leaving Edinburgh far behind.*

ˌleave 'off (doing sth) (*infml*) to stop: *Start reading from where you left off last time.* ○ *He left off playing the piano to answer the door.* ˌleave sb/sth 'off (sth) to omit sb/sth, usu from the end of sth: *You've left off a zero.* ○ *We left him off the list.*

ˌleave sb/sth 'out (of sth) not to include or mention sb/sth; to exclude or omit sb/sth: *Leave me out of this quarrel, please — I don't want to get involved.* ○ *He hadn't been asked to the party and was feeling very left out.* ○ *She left out an 'm' in 'accommodation'.* be ˌleft 'over (from sth) to remain when no longer needed: *There were lots of sandwiches left over.* ○ *We have a few coins left over from our holiday in Greece.* See also LEFTOVERS.

▶ 'leaver *n* (esp in compounds) a person who is leaving a place: *school leavers.*

leave² /liːv/ *n* [U] **1(a)** (esp in compounds). time when one has permission to be absent from work: *She's on maternity leave.* See also COMPASSIONATE LEAVE, SICK-LEAVE. **(b)** the period of time one is allowed to take as holiday from one's job: *take a month's leave* ○ *How much annual leave do you get?* ○ *She's home on leave from her regiment.* ⇨ note at HOLIDAY. **2** ~ **to do sth** (*fml*) official permission to do sth: *be given leave to appeal against the sentence* ○ *I beg leave to address the Council.* **IDM** ˌby/ˌwith your 'leave (*fml*) with your permission. **take French leave** ⇨ FRENCH. **take (one's) 'leave (of sb)** (*fml*) to say goodbye: *I took my leave of the little group.* **take ˌleave of one's 'senses** (*dated or joc*) to go mad: *Have you all taken leave of your senses?* **without as/so much as a ˌby your 'leave** (*infml*) without asking permission; rudely.

■ ˌleave of 'absence *n* [U] (*fml*) permission to be absent from one's job or from military duties: *ask for leave of absence to attend a wedding.*

'leave-taking *n* [U, sing] (*fml*) the act of saying goodbye: *a tearful leave-taking.*

-leaved /-liːvd/ (forming compound *adjs*) having leaves of the specified type or number: *a broad-leaved plant* ○ *a four-leaved clover.*

leaven /'levn/ *n* [U] a quality or influence that makes people, an atmosphere, etc less serious or more lively: *add leaven to a dry gathering.*

▶ **leaven** *v* ~ **sth (with sth)** to make sth more lively and interesting: [Vnpr] *a factual account leavened with dry humour* [also Vn]. **leavening** *n* [sing] ~ **(of sth)**

leaves *pl* of LEAF.

lechery /'letʃəri/ *n* [U] (*derog*) behaviour that shows an excessive interest in sexual pleasure.

▶ **lecher** /'letʃə(r)/ *n* (*derog*) a man who is always thinking about and looking for sexual pleasure.

lecherous /'letʃərəs/ *adj* (*derog*) having or showing an excessive interest in and desire for sexual pleasure.

lectern /'lektən/ *n* a high sloping desk for a speaker's notes or a bible in church. ⇨ picture at CHURCH.

lecture /'lektʃə(r)/ *n* **1** ~ **(to sb) (on sth)** a talk giving information about a subject to an audience or a class, often as part of a teaching programme: *give/deliver/read a lecture* ○ *attend a course/a series of lectures on Greek philosophy* ○ *go on a lecture tour.* **2** a long talk to one person or a small group of people, expressing disapproval of sth: *give sb a lecture* ○ *The policeman let me off with a lecture about speeding.*

▶ **lecture** *v* **1** ~ **(in/on sth)** to give a lecture or series of lectures: [V] *Professor Sinclair is not lecturing this term.* [Vpr] *She lectures in/on Russian literature.* ⇨ note at TEACH. **2** ~ **sb (about/on sth / doing sth)** to criticize sb about sth or for doing sth: [Vn] *Stop lecturing me!* [Vnpr] *lecture one's children about smoking.* **lecturer** /'lektʃərə(r)/ *n* **1** a person who gives lectures, esp at a college or university: *a senior lecturer in law.* **2** (*US*) a temporary or part-time (PART[1]) university teacher.

lectureship *n* the post of lecturer at a college or university (the lowest teaching grade at a British college or university).

led *pt, pp* of LEAD[1].

-led /led/ (forming compound *adjs*) influenced mainly by the specified thing: *a consumer-led campaign* ○ *a market-led economy.*

ledge /ledʒ/ *n* a narrow shelf projecting from a wall, cliff, etc: *The climbers rested on a sheltered ledge.* ○ *She put her glasses on the ledge in front of the mirror.* ○ *A bird perched on the window-ledge.*

ledger /'ledʒə(r)/ *n* a book in which a bank, business firm, etc records its financial accounts: *inspect the sales ledger.*

lee /liː/ *n* [sing] the part or side of sth providing shelter against the wind: *shelter in/under the lee of a hedge* ○ *lee slopes.*

leech /liːtʃ/ *n* **1** a small worm, usu living in water, that attaches itself to its victims and sucks their blood. It was formerly used by doctors to remove blood from sick people. **2** (*derog*) a person who aims to obtain money, fame, etc from other people's success.

leek /liːk/ *n* a vegetable related to the onion with wide flat green leaves above a long white BULB(1). ⇨ picture at ONION.

leer /lɪə(r)/ *n* (usu *sing*) an unpleasant look suggesting evil or sexual intentions: *He gave her a sly leer.*

▶ **leer** *v* ~ **(at sb/sth)** to look at sb/sth with a leer: [V] *a leering smile/face* [Vpr] *Bystanders leered at the nude painting.*

leery /'lɪəri/ *adj* [pred] ~ **(of sb/sth)** (*infml*) cautious about or suspicious of people or things; WARY: *I tend to be a bit leery of cut-price 'bargains'.*

lees /liːz/ *n* [pl] the matter left at the bottom of a bottle of wine, a barrel of beer, etc; the DREGS(1).

leeward /'liːwəd/ *or, in nautical use,* /'luːəd/ *adj, adv* on or to the side sheltered from the wind: *a harbour on the leeward side of the island.*

▶ **leeward** *n* [U] the leeward side or direction: *steer to leeward.* Compare WINDWARD.

leeway /'liːweɪ/ *n* [U] the amount of freedom to move, change, etc that is available to sb: *Most people have considerable leeway in how they spend their money.* ○ *There was little leeway for anything to go wrong.* **IDM** **make up 'leeway** (*Brit*) to recover from a bad position, esp with effort, eg because time has been lost: *She was off school for a month, so she has a lot of leeway to make up.*

left¹ *pt, pp* of LEAVE[1].

■ ˌleft-'luggage office (*Brit*) (*US* 'baggage

room) *n* a place where bags, cases, etc may be stored temporarily, eg at a bus station.

left² /left/ *adj, adv* of, on or towards the side of the body which is towards the west when a person faces north: *Fewer people write with their left hand than with their right.* ○ *Turn left here.* ○ (*sport*) *the left half/back/wing* ○ *a left-arm bowler.* Compare RIGHT⁶. **IDM** **have two left 'feet** (*infml*) to be very awkward in one's movements; to be CLUMSY. **,left, right and 'centre; ,right, left and 'centre** (*infml*) in or from all directions: *They are dishing out loans left, right and centre.* **right and left** ⇨ RIGHT⁵.

▶ **left** *n* **1** [U] (**a**) the left side or area: *She was sitting immediately to my left.* ○ *The station is on the/your left at the end of the road.* (**b**) (used after *first, second,* etc) the road, etc on the left: *Take the first left, then the second right.* **2** [C] (in boxing) a blow given with the left hand: *He knocked down his opponent with a powerful left.* **3** (also **the Left**) [Gp] (*politics*) (**a**) supporters of SOCIALISM: *a left-leaning newspaper.* (**b**) the members of a party or other group that favours a greater degree of social change, more extreme policies, etc than other members: *The Left are very upset about further privatizations.* ○ *He's on the far left of the party.* Compare RIGHT⁵ *n.*

leftist *n* (*politics*) a supporter of SOCIALISM: *prominent leftists.* — *adj*: *leftist academics.*

lefty *n* (*infml*) **1** (*derog*) a leftist: *feminists and trendy lefties.* **2** (*esp US*) a left-handed person.

■ **'left-hand** *adj* [attrib] of or on the left: *the left-hand side of the street* ○ *the top left-hand corner of the page.* Compare RIGHT-HAND. **,left-'handed** *adj* **1** (of a person) using the left hand more naturally than the right, eg for writing: *left-handed tennis players.* **2** (of a blow, catch, etc) given or taken with the left hand. **3** (of a tool) designed for use with the left hand: *,left-handed 'scissors.* — *adv* with the left hand: *Do you always write left-handed?* **,left-'hander** a left-handed person or blow. Compare RIGHT-HANDER. **,left-hand 'drive** *adj* (of a vehicle) with the steering-wheel (STEER¹) on the left of the vehicle. Compare RIGHT-HAND DRIVE.

,left-of-'centre (*US* -'center) *adj* (*politics*) supporting views more towards the left of a party: *a left-of-centre Conservative.*

the ,left 'wing *n* [Gp] (*politics*) **1** supporters of SOCIALISM: *a veteran of the left wing.* **2** the members of any group who are more in favour of change, new ideas, etc than others: *on the left wing of the Conservative party.* Compare RIGHT WING. **3** [C, U] (in football, etc) the player or position on the left side of a team on the field. Compare RIGHT WING. **,left-'wing** *adj*: **,left-wing i'deas/intel'lectuals/'policies** ○ *She's very left-wing.* **,left-'winger** *n* a supporter of the left wing.

leftovers /'leftəʊvəz/ *n* [pl] food remaining at the end of a meal: *Don't throw away the leftovers — we can have them for supper.* ▶ **leftover** *adj* [attrib]: *,leftover 'food.* ⇨ note at REST³.

leftward /'leftwəd/ *adj, adv* towards the left. ▶ **leftwards** *adv.*

leg /leg/ *n* **1** [C] each of the limbs of an animal's or a person's body used for standing and walking: *have long/short/skinny/sturdy/bandy/shapely legs* ○ *a horse's hind legs* ○ *the powerful back legs of a frog* ○ *the long thin legs of a spider* ○ *develop one's leg muscles* ○ *He's broken his leg.* See also -LEGGED, LEGGY. ⇨ picture at HUMAN. **2** [C, U] the leg of an animal used as food: *chicken legs* ○ *roast leg of lamb.* **3** [C] the part of a garment covering a leg: *a tear in the left trouser leg.* See also LEGGINGS. **4** [C] each of the parts supporting a chair, table, etc: *a chair with a broken leg.* **5** [C] (**a**) a section of a journey: *The last leg of our trip was the most tiring.* (**b**) (*sport*) each of a series of matches between the same opponents: *the second leg of their second-round match*

against Juventus. **6** [U] (in cricket) the part of the field to the left of and behind a right-handed (RIGHT⁵) BATSMAN facing the BOWLER¹(1). See also SEA LEGS. **IDM** **as fast as one's legs can carry one** ⇨ FAST¹ *adv.* **be all 'legs** (*derog*) have legs that are very long and thin. **be on one's/its last legs** ⇨ LAST¹. **cost/ pay an arm and a leg** ⇨ ARM¹. **give sb a 'leg up** (*Brit infml*) to help sb to get on a horse, climb a wall, etc or to improve their position: *Football clubs have been given a leg up by the achievements of the national side.* **have, etc one's tail between one's legs** ⇨ TAIL. **not have a ,leg to 'stand on** (*infml*) to have nothing to support one's opinion or justify one's actions. **pull sb's leg** ⇨ PULL¹. **shake a leg** ⇨ SHAKE¹. **stretch one's legs** ⇨ STRETCH. **talk the hind legs off a donkey** ⇨ TALK¹.

▶ **leg** *v* (-gg-) **IDM** **'leg it** (*infml*) to run: *leg it to the nearest telephone.*

■ **'leg-room** *n* [U] the space available for the legs of sb sitting: *There's not much leg-room in an aeroplane.*

legacy /'legəsi/ *n* **1** money or property left to a person when sb dies: *They each received a legacy of $5 000.* **2** a thing passed to sb by people who lived before them or from earlier events, etc: *the cultural legacy of the Renaissance* ○ *leave a legacy of pollution and destruction for the next generation.* Compare INHERITANCE.

legal /'liːgl/ *adj* **1** [attrib] of, based on or concerned with the law: *the company's legal adviser* ○ *the legal system/profession* ○ *seek legal advice* ○ *He may take legal action against the accountants involved.* **2** allowed or required by the law: *drink more than the legal limit of alcohol for driving* ○ *Should euthanasia be made legal?* ○ *What's the legal position on this?*

▶ **legalistic** *adj* (*usu derog*) showing very strict obedience to or respect for the law: *adopt a narrow legalistic approach to a dispute.*

legally /'liːgəli/ *adv*: *be legally responsible for sth* ○ *a legally binding document.*

■ **,legal 'aid** *n* [pl] payment from public funds for or towards the cost of legal advice or representation.

,legal pro'ceedings *n* [pl] action through the processes of the law: *take/begin/threaten legal proceedings (against sb).*

,legal 'tender *n* [U] a form of money that must be accepted if offered in payment: *The old ten-pound note is no longer legal tender.*

legality /liː'gæləti/ *n* [U] the state of being legal: *using tactics of doubtful/questionable legality* ○ *test/ determine/challenge the legality of sth in the courts.*

legalize, -ise /'liːgəlaɪz/ *v* to make sth legal: [Vn] *the 1973 ruling which legalized abortion.* ▶ **legalization, -isation** *n* [U].

legate /'legət/ *n* the official representative of the Pope in a foreign country: *a papal legate.*

legation /lɪ'geɪʃn/ *n* [CGp] a DIPLOMAT(1) below the rank of AMBASSADOR, and her or his staff, representing her or his government in a foreign country.

legato /lɪ'gɑːtəʊ/ *adj, adv* (*music*) (to be played) in a smooth even manner.

legend /'ledʒənd/ *n* **1**(**a**) [C] a story from the past that may or may not be true: *the legend of Robin Hood.* (**b**) [C] such stories gathered together: *the heroes of Greek legend* ○ *Legend has it that her career began in a circus.* ○ *The tale has passed into local legend.* **2** [C] (*infml*) an extremely famous person, esp in a particular field: *one of the great legends of early pop music* ○ *a jazz/cinema legend* ○ *He was a legend in his own lifetime/a living legend.* **3** [C] a piece of writing on sth, eg a coin. **4** [C] a key to a map.

▶ **legendary** /'ledʒəndri; *US* -deri/ *adj* **1** (*infml*) very well known; famous and inspiring admiration: *the legendary Duke Ellington* ○ *Her patience and tact*

L

were legendary. **2** of or mentioned in legend: *legendary heroes.*

-legged /-legd, -legɪd/ (forming compound *adjs*) having legs of the specified number or type: *a ˌthree-legged ˈstool* ∘ *ˌbare-ˈlegged* ∘ *ˌcross-ˈlegged.*

leggings /ˈlegɪŋz/ *n* [pl] **1** trousers for women that stretch to fit closely on the legs: *a top with matching leggings.* **2** protective outer coverings for the legs.

leggy /ˈlegi/ *adj* having long legs: *a tall leggy schoolgirl.*

legible /ˈledʒəbl/ *adj* (of written or printed words) clear enough to be read easily: *The signature was still legible.* Compare READABLE. ▶ **legibility** /ˌledʒəˈbɪləti/ *n* [U]. **legibly** /-əbli/ *adv.*

legion /ˈliːdʒən/ *n* **1(a)** a special military unit, esp of volunteers serving with the army of another country: *the French Foreign Legion.* **(b)** a battle unit of the ancient Roman army: *Caesar's legions.* **2** a large number of people who share a characteristic: *legions of admirers/photographers.*
▶ **legion** *adj* [pred] (*rhet*) very many: *The tales of his exploits are legion.*
legionary /ˈliːdʒənəri; *US* -neri/ *n, adj* a member of a LEGION(1).

legislate /ˈledʒɪsleɪt/ *v* ~ **(for/against/on sth)** to make laws: [Vpr] *legislate against discrimination in the workplace* [V.to inf] *legislate to allow prosecution of war criminals* [V] *Parliament does much more than legislate.*
▶ **legislation** /ˌledʒɪsˈleɪʃn/ *n* [U] **(a)** a law or a series of laws: *proposed new legislation on vehicle emissions.* **(b)** the process of making laws: *Legislation will be difficult and take time.*
legislative /ˈledʒɪslətɪv; *US* -leɪtɪv/ *adj* [esp attrib] involved with or concerning the making of laws: *a legislative assembly/council/body* ∘ *the legislative programme for the next session of Parliament.*
legislator /ˈledʒɪsleɪtə(r)/ *n* (*fml*) a member of a body that makes laws.
legislature /ˈledʒɪslətʃə(r)/ *n* [CGp] (*fml*) a body of people with the power to make and change laws: *the Quebec legislature.*

legit /lɪˈdʒɪt/ *adj* (*sl*) = LEGITIMATE 2: *It's all quite legit.*

legitimate /lɪˈdʒɪtɪmət/ *adj* **1** that can be defended; reasonable: *a perfectly legitimate argument/concern/expectation* ∘ *Politicians are legitimate targets for satire.* **2** in accordance with the law or rules; legal: *I'm not sure that his business is strictly legitimate.* **3** (of a child) born to parents who are legally married to each other. Compare ILLEGITIMATE.
▶ **legitimacy** /lɪˈdʒɪtɪməsi/ *n* [U] (*fml*): *claim some historical legitimacy* ∘ *question the legitimacy of sb's actions.*
legitimately *adv*: *He can now legitimately claim to be the best in the world.*
legitimize, -ise /lɪˈdʒɪtəmaɪz/ *v* (*fml*) to make sth legal or regular: [Vn] *a court ruling that legitimizes the position taken by the protestors.*

legless /ˈlegləs/ *adj* **1** without legs. **2** [pred] (*sl*) very drunk.

Lego /ˈlegəʊ/ *n* [U] (*propr*) small toy blocks of coloured plastic that can be linked together to make model houses, bridges, trains, etc: *build a space station out of Lego* ∘ *neat rows of buildings like so much Lego.*

legume /ˈlegjuːm, lɪˈgjuːm/ *n* a type of plant that has seeds in long pods (POD). Peas and beans are legumes.

legwork /ˈlegwɜːk/ *n* (*infml*) work involving much travelling about to collect information, etc: *The job involves a fair amount of legwork.*

leisure /ˈleʒə(r); *US* ˈliːʒər/ *n* [U] time free from work or other duties; spare time: *increased leisure time* ∘ *a range of leisure activities.* **IDM at ˈleisure 1** (*fml*) not occupied; free: *The rest of the day may be*

spent at leisure (ie You can do what you like). **2** without hurrying: *I'll take the report home and read it at leisure.* **at one's ˈleisure** when one has free time.
▶ **leisured** /ˈleʒəd/ *adj* [attrib] having plenty of leisure: *the leisured classes.*
leisurely *adj, adv* without hurry: *walk at a leisurely pace* ∘ *enjoy a leisurely drink.*
■ **ˈleisure centre** (*Brit*) (*US* ˈhealth club) *n* a public building with facilities for sports and other activities for people to do in their spare time.

leitmotif /ˈlaɪtməʊtiːf/ *n* (*music*) a short, constantly repeated theme in a piece of music associated with a particular person, thing or idea.

lemming /ˈlemɪŋ/ *n* a small animal similar to a mouse, living in cold northern countries. Lemmings travel in large groups and are sometimes said to follow their leaders over cliffs and into the sea where they DROWN(1): *their lemming-like readiness to rush into certain disaster.*

lemon /ˈlemən/ *n* **1** [C, U] an OVAL yellow fruit with sour juice. Slices of lemon are used to decorate food or, like the juice, as a flavouring: *lemon tea/squash* ∘ *a gin and tonic with ice and lemon* ∘ *a squeeze of lemon.* ⇨ picture at FRUIT. **2** (also ˌlemon ˈyellow) [U] a pale yellow colour. **3** [C] (*infml*) a person or thing that is found or thought to be faulty or not satisfactory. ▶ **lemony** *adj*: *a soft lemony cake.*
■ ˌlemon ˈcurd *n* [U] (*Brit*) a thick smooth jam made from lemons, sugar, eggs and butter.

lemonade /ˌleməˈneɪd/ *n* [U, C] **(a)** (*Brit*) a sweet FIZZY drink. **(b)** a drink made from LEMON juice, sugar and water.

lemur /ˈliːmə(r)/ *n* an animal similar to a monkey, found esp in Madagascar. Lemurs usu live in trees and are active at night.

lend /lend/ *v* (*pt, pp* lent /lent/) **1** ~ sth (to sb) **(a)** to give sth to sb or allow sb to use sth temporarily, on the understanding that it will be returned: *Can you lend me $5? I'll pay you back tomorrow.* [Vnpr] *I lent that video to John but he never gave it back.* [Vnn] *Lend me your pen a minute, will you?* **(b)** to provide money to sb on condition that they pay it back within a period of time and pay interest on it: [Vn] *The banks are now lending money at competitive rates of interest.* [also V]. Compare BORROW. **2(a)** ~ sth (to sth) to contribute or add sth to sth: [Vnn] *His presence lent the occasion some dignity.* [Vnpr] *A little garlic lends flavour to a sauce.* **(b)** ~ sth to sth (*fml*) to make an event, development or report more significant, more reliable, etc: [Vnpr] *lend credibility/credence/weight/significance/substance to a story* ∘ *This news lends support to earlier rumours of a ceasefire.* **IDM give/lend colour to sth** ⇨ COLOUR[1]. **lend an ˈear (to sb/sth)** to listen in a patient and sympathetic way. **lend (sb) a (helping) ˈhand (with sth)** to give sb help with sth: *I went over to see if I could lend a hand.* **lend one's name to sth** (*fml*) to allow oneself to be associated with sb: *She lent her name to many worthy causes.* **PHRV ˈlend itself to sth** to be suitable for sth: *a novel which lends itself well to dramatization for television.*
▶ **lender** *n* (*finance*) an organization or a person that lends money: *Seek help from your mortgage lender before you get too far behind with the payments.* Compare BORROWER. See also MONEYLENDER.
lending *n* [U] (*finance*) the action of lending money: *lending institutions* ∘ *Lending by banks and building societies rose by £4.9 billion last year.* **ˈlending library** *n* a library from which books may be taken away for a period of time, usu free of charge.

length /leŋθ/ *n* **1** [U] the amount sth measures or extends from one end to the other: *a river 300 miles in length* ∘ *This room is twice the length of the other, but much narrower.* ∘ *He ran the entire length of the beach.* ∘ *Her new book is about the length of (ie as*

long as) *'War and Peace'*. ⇨ App 2. ⇨ picture at
DIMENSION. ⇨ note at DIMENSION. **2** [U] the amount
of time occupied by sth: *You spend a ridiculous
length of time in the shower*. ○ *Size of pension depends
partly on length of service with the company.* **3** [C]
the size of a thing used as a unit of measurement: *I
can swim 50 lengths of the school pool.* ○ *The horse
won the race by two clear lengths* (ie by a distance
equal to twice its own length). **4** [C] a piece of sth:
timber sold in lengths of 2, 5 or 10 metres ○ *a length of
wire/string/rope.* **IDM** **at 'length 1** (*fml*) after a long
time; eventually: *'I'm still not sure,' he said at
length.* **2** taking a long time; in great detail; fully: *an
issue already examined at some/great length in these
columns* ○ *I listened at length to her story.* **full length**
⇨ FULL. **go to any, some, great, etc 'lengths (to
do sth)** to be prepared to do anything, something,
a lot, etc to achieve sth: *They went to absurd/
extraordinary lengths to keep the affair secret.* ○
*There are no lengths to which addicts will not go to
obtain their drugs.* **keep sb at arm's length** ⇨
ARM¹. **the length and 'breadth of sth** in or to all
parts of sth: *travel the length and breadth of Ireland.*
▶ **-length** (forming compound *adjs*): *a ˌknee-length
'dress* ○ *ˌfloor-length 'curtains* ○ *a ˌfeature-length
'film.***lengthen** *v* to become or make sth longer: [Vn]
lengthen a skirt [V] *the lengthening queues/shadows*
○ *The days are starting to lengthen again.* Compare
SHORTEN.
'lengthways (also **'lengthwise**) *adv* along the
length of sth: *Cut the banana in half lengthways.*
lengthy /'leŋθi/ *adj* (**-ier, -iest**) very long: *lengthy
discussions/investigations* ○ *the lengthy process of
acquiring an entry visa* ○ (*derog*) *lengthy
explanations/speeches.*
lenient /'li:niənt/ *adj* not severe, esp in punishing
people: *a lenient fine/sentence/view* ○ *I hope the judge
will be lenient with them.* ▶ **leniency** /-ənsi/ *n* [U]:
*a judge known for her leniency towards first-time
offenders.* **leniently** *adv*: *treat sb leniently.*
lens /lenz/ *n* **1** a piece of glass or other transparent
material with one or more curved surfaces. Lenses
make things appear clearer, larger or smaller when
looked through, eg in spectacles and cameras: *wipe
the lens clean* ○ *a lens cap/cover.* See also TELEPHOTO
LENS, ZOOM LENS. ⇨ picture at CAMERA, GLASS. **2** =
CONTACT LENS. **3** (*anatomy*) the transparent part of
the eye, behind the PUPIL², that focuses (FOCUS *v*)
light. ⇨ picture at EYE¹.
Lent /lent/ *n* (in the Christian religion) the period of
40 days from Ash Wednesday to the day before
Easter, during which some Christians FAST³ in memory of Christ's suffering: *give up chocolates/
smoking/meat for Lent.*
lent *pt, pp* of LEND.
lentil /'lentl/ *n* a small green, orange or brown seed,
usu dried and used as food, eg in soup or STEW.
Leo /'li:əʊ/ *n* (*pl* **-os**) (**a**) [U] the fifth sign of the
ZODIAC, the Lion. (**b**) [C] a person born under the
influence of this sign. ⇨ picture at ZODIAC. ⇨ note
at ZODIAC.
leonine /'li:ənaɪn/ *adj* (*fml*) of or like a lion: *his fine
leonine head.*
leopard /'lepəd/ *n* a large African and S Asian
animal of the cat family with a yellowish coat and
dark spots. Leopards hunt and eat other animals. ⇨
picture at CAT.
leotard /'li:ətɑːd/ *n* a garment that fits tightly over
the body from the neck down to the wrists and the
upper legs, worn by dancers, women exercising, etc.
leper /'lepə(r)/ *n* **1** a person suffering from LEPROSY.
2 a person who is rejected and avoided by others:
His unpopular views made him a social leper.
leprechaun /'leprəkɔːn/ *n* (in Irish stories) a fairy
in the shape of a little old man.
leprosy /'leprəsi/ *n* [U] an infectious disease caus-

ing painful white patches to appear on the skin and
destroying the nerves.
lesbian /'lezbiən/ *n* a HOMOSEXUAL woman. ▶ **lesbian** *adj*: *the lesbian and gay communities* ○ *a
lesbian relationship.* **lesbianism** *n* [U].
lesion /'li:ʒn/ *n* (*medical*) a wound; an injury: *painful lesions on the skin.*
less /les/ *indef det, indef pron* ~ (**sth**) (**than ... **) (used
with uncountable *ns* as the comparative of LITTLE²)
not as much (as ...); a smaller amount (of): (**a**) (*det*)
less butter/time/significance ○ *I received much/
considerably/slightly/rather/a lot less money than
the others did.* ○ *He was advised to smoke fewer
cigarettes and drink less beer.* ⇨ note at MUCH¹. (**b**)
(*pron*) *He has less to worry about now.* ○ *It is less of a
problem than I'd expected.* ○ *It'll take less than an
hour to get there.* ○ *The receptionist was less than* (ie
not at all) *helpful when we arrived.* ○ *We'll be there in
less than no time* (ie very soon).
▶ **less** *adv* ~ (**than ... **) to a smaller extent; not
so much (as): *less colourful/expensive/likely/
intelligent/successful* ○ *less often/awkwardly/
enthusiastically* ○ *I read much less now than I used to.*
○ *No less important is the work of the European
Commission.* **IDM** **any (the) 'less** (used after *not*) to
a smaller extent: *She wasn't any (the) less happy for*
(ie She was perfectly happy at) *being on her own.*
even/much/still 'less and certainly not: *No explanation was offered, still less an apology.* ○ *He's too
shy to ask a stranger the time, still less speak to a
room full of people.* **ˌless and 'less** at a continually
decreasing rate: *She found the job less and less attractive.* ○ *As time passed, she saw less and less of her
sisters.* **more or less** ⇨ MORE. **no 'less** (used to
suggest that sth is surprising or impressive, or to
show SARCASM): *She's having lunch with the Chairman of the Board, no less.* **no less than ... ** (used in
front of a number which in the circumstances one
considers high) as much as: *We won no less than 3 of
the prizes in the raffle.*
less *prep* before subtracting sth; MINUS(1) sth: *a
monthly salary of $450, less tax and insurance* ○ *send
a cheque for the catalogue price, less 10% discount.*

NOTE Less is being used more and more in spoken
and informal written English with countable (or
plural) nouns, instead of **fewer**: *There have been less
accidents on this roads since the speed limit was
reduced.* However this is still thought to be grammatically incorrect and careful speakers prefer
fewer: *fewer accidents.*

-less /-ləs/ *suff* (used widely with *ns* to form *adjs*)
without: *treeless* ○ *meaningless.* ⇨ note at INVALU-
ABLE. ▶ **-lessly** (forming *advs*): *hopelessly.*
-lessness (forming uncountable *ns*): *helplessness.*
lessee /le'siː/ *n* (*law*) a person who has use of a
building, an area of land, etc on a LEASE. ⇨ note at
LESSOR.
lessen /'lesn/ *v* to become or make sth less: *a lessening of the pain* [V] *His influence was already
lessening.* [Vn] *lessen the impact/likelihood/risk of
sth.*
lesser /'lesə(r)/ *adj* [attrib] not as great or important
as the other or others: *a lesser offence* ○ *the artist's
lesser works* ○ *one of the lesser-known Caribbean
islands* ○ *He's stubborn, and so is she, but to a lesser
degree/extent* (ie not as much). **IDM** **the ˌlesser of
two 'evils**; **the ˌlesser 'evil** the less harmful or
unpleasant of two bad choices.
lesson /'lesn/ *n* **1** a period of time given to learning
or teaching; a class(2b): *a history/English/physics
lesson* ○ *She gives piano lessons.* ○ *I'm having flying/
riding lessons.* ○ *The lesson lasted an hour.* **2** a thing
to be learnt: *The first lesson in driving is how to start
the car.* ○ (*fig*) *Other EU members can teach us a
lesson or two on industrial policy.* **3** ~ (**to sb**) an

L

experience or a model from which one can learn; an example: *a valuable/salutory lesson* ○ *Let this be a lesson to you never to play with matches!* ○ *We are still absorbing the painful/harsh lessons of this disaster.* ○ *It was a lesson not lost on* (ie learned well by) *the team manager.* **4** (*religion*) a passage from the Bible read aloud during a church service: *The first lesson is taken from St John's Gospel.* **IDM** **learn one's lesson** ⇨ LEARN. See also OBJECT LESSON.

lessor /le'sɔː(r)/ *n* (*law*) a person who gives sb use of a property on a LEASE. Compare LESSEE.

lest /lest/ *conj* (*fml*) **1** for fear that; in order that...not: *He disguised himself lest he be recognized.* ○ *Lest anyone should think my story strange, let me assure you that it is all quite true.* **2** (used after *fear, be afraid, be anxious*, etc) because of the possibility of sth happening; in case: *She was afraid lest he might drown.*

let¹ /let/ *v* (**-tt-**; *pt, pp* **let**) **1** [Vn.inf (no *to*)] (no passive) (often with the INFINITIVE omitted when the meaning is clear) (**a**) to allow sb to do sth or sth to happen without trying to stop it: *Let them splash around in the pool for a while.* ○ *Don't let your child play with matches.* (**b**) to give sb permission to do sth: *They won't let him leave the country.* ○ *She wanted to lend me some money but I wouldn't let her (do it).* ⇨ note at ALLOW. **2** to make it possible for sb/oneself/sth to go or pass in, out, etc: [Vnpr] *let sb into the house* [Vnp] *I'll give you a key so that you can let yourself in.* [Vnpr] *You've let all the air out of the tyres.* [Vnp] *Please let me past.* ○ *The dog had been let out.* ○ *The roof lets water through.* **3** [Vn.inf (no *to*)] (no passive; used in the imperative) (**a**) (with *us* as a polite way of making or responding to a suggestion or giving an instruction): *Let's go to the beach.* ○ *Let's not tell Mum for the moment.* ○ (*Brit*) *Don't let's tell Mum.* ○ *I don't think we'll succeed but let's try anyway.* ○ *'Shall we call in on Pete on the way?' 'Yes, let's.'* (**b**) (with *me* or *us* to make a polite offer of help or to introduce a remark): *Let us get those boxes down for you.* ○ *Here, let me do it.* ○ *Let us begin with a few facts.* ○ *Let me give you an example.* ○ *Let us not forget all the other people who helped.* (**c**) (used to express one's determination to oppose or resist sb/sth): *Let them attack; they won't know what's hit them!* (**d**) (used to insist that sth should happen): *Let the boy speak for himself.* ○ *Let her carry her own bag.* (**e**) (used to express an ASSUMPTION(1), eg in MATHEMATICS): *Let line AB be equal to line CD.* **4** ~ **sth (out) (to sb)** to allow sb to use a house, room, etc in return for regular payments: [Vn, Vnpr] *I let the spare room (to a lodger).* [Vnp] *They decided to let out the smaller flats at low rents.* **IDM** Most idioms containing **let** are at the entries for the nouns or adjectives in the idioms, eg **let alone** ⇨ ALONE; **let rip** ⇨ RIP. **let it 'go (at 'that)** to say or do no more about sth: *I don't entirely agree but I'll let it go at that.* ○ *I thought she was hinting at something but I let it go.* **let oneself 'go 1** to stop restraining one's feelings, desires, etc: *Come on, enjoy yourself, let yourself go!* **2** to stop being careful, tidy, etc: *He has let himself go since he lost his job.* **let sb/sth 'go, let 'go of sb/sth 1** to release one's hold of sb/sth: *let the rope go/let go of the rope* ○ *Let (me) go. You're hurting me!* **2** to allow sb to be free: *Will they let the hostages go?* **let me 'see/'think** I'm thinking or trying to remember: *Now let me see — where did he say he lived?* **let us 'say** (used when making a suggestion or giving an example): *I can let you have it for, well, let's say £100.* **to 'let** (*Brit*) available for renting: *Rooms to let* (eg on a sign outside a house).

PHRV **let sb 'down** to fail to help sb; to disappoint sb because of not being reliable: *I'm afraid she let us down badly.* ○ *This machine won't let you down.* He trudged home feeling lonely and let down. See also LET-DOWN. **let sth 'down 1** to lower sth: *We let the*

bucket down by a rope. **2** to make a garment longer, esp by lowering the HEM¹: *This skirt needs letting down.* **3** (*Brit*) to allow the air to escape from sth deliberately: *Some kids had let my tyres down.*

let sb/oneself 'in for sth (*infml*) to involve sb/oneself in sth likely to be unpleasant or cause difficulties: *I volunteered to help, and then I thought 'Oh no, what have I let myself in for!'* **let sb 'in on / into sth** (*infml*) to allow sb to share a secret: *Are you going to let them in on your plans?*

let sth 'into sth to put sth into the surface of sth so that it does not project from it: *a window let into a wall.*

let sb 'off (with sth) to punish sb lightly or not punish them at all: *They let us off lightly.* ○ *She was let off with a fine instead of being sent to prison.* **let sb 'off sth** to allow sb not to do sth or not to go somewhere: *We've been let off (school) today because our teacher is sick.* **let sth 'off** to fire a gun or make a bomb, etc: *The boys were letting off fireworks.*

let 'on (about sth / that ...) (to sb) (*infml*) to reveal a secret: *I'm getting married next week, but please don't let on (to anyone), will you?*

let sth 'out 1 to give a cry, etc: *let out a scream of terror/a gasp of delight.* **2** to make a garment looser or larger: *He's getting so fat that his trousers have to be let out around the waist.*

let 'up (*infml*) to become less strong, intense, etc; to relax one's efforts: *Will the rain ever let up?* ○ *We mustn't let up, even though we're winning.* See also LET-UP.

■ **'let-down** *n* a disappointment: *The party was a real let-down.*

'let-out *n* (*Brit*) an event, a statement, etc that allows sb to avoid a responsibility or duty: *a convenient let-out for the Minister of Education* ○ *a let-out clause in the contract.*

'let-up *n* a reduction in strength, intensity, etc: *There is no sign yet of a let-up in the recession.*

let² /let/ *n* (*Brit*) an act of renting a house, etc to or from sb; a LEASE: *Cottage available for long or short let.*

NOTE Compare **let, rent** and **hire**. In British English they all mean to allow somebody to use something for a short time in exchange for money. People **let** or **let out** accommodation, buildings or land to somebody else: *He lets (out) his house to tourists during the summer.* ○ *The biggest factory in town is to let.* You can **rent** a house, car, etc **from** somebody, or **rent** it **out** to somebody, usually for a long period of time: *We've decided to rent out our spare room.* ○ *I don't own my video. I rent it from a shop.* You can **hire** a vehicle, a building, etc, usually for a short period and for a particular purpose or a particular occasion: *Caroline and Mark hired a hall for their wedding reception.* ○ *You can easily hire a bike in Amsterdam.* A shop, etc **hires** something **out to** you: *They hire out boats by the hour.* In American English **rent** or **rent out** is used in all these ways. **Hire** can also mean 'to employ', especially in American English: *They've hired a new secretary.*

let³ /let/ *n* (in tennis) a SERVE that lands in the correct court(3) but has touched the top of the net, requiring it to be taken again. **IDM** **without let or 'hindrance** (*fml or law*) without being prevented: *A passport should enable one to travel freely, without let or hindrance.*

-let *suff* (with *ns* forming *ns*) **1** little: *booklet* ○ *piglet.* **2** unimportant; minor: *starlet.*

lethal /'liːθl/ *adj* **1** causing or able to cause death: *a lethal dose of poison* ○ *lethal weapons.* **2** harmful or causing damage: *The closure of the factory dealt a lethal blow to the town.* ○ (*joc*) *This wine's pretty lethal* (ie very strong)*!* ▶ **lethally** /'liːθəli/ *adv.*

lethargy /'leθədʒi/ *n* [U] an extreme lack of energy

or enthusiasm for doing anything; a lazy state: *She suffers from bouts of lethargy and depression.* ○ *government lethargy towards the film industry.* ► **lethargic** /ləˈθɑːdʒɪk/ *adj: The hot weather made her listless and lethargic.*

let's *short form of* LET US (LET¹).

letter /ˈletə(r)/ *n* **1** [C] a written or printed sign representing a sound used in speech: *'B' is the second letter of the alphabet.* ○ *Write your name and address in capital letters.* **2** [C] a written message addressed to a person or an organization, usu put in an envelope and sent by post: *Are there any letters for me?* ○ *We only communicate by letter.* See also COVERING LETTER, DEAD LETTER. ⟹ App 3. **IDM** **the ˌletter of the ˈlaw** the exact requirements or words of a law or rule, contrasted with its general meaning or spirit: *sticking to the letter of the law.* **to the ˈletter** paying strict attention to every detail: *keep to the letter of an agreement* ○ *I followed your instructions to the letter.*

► **lettering** /ˈletərɪŋ/ *n* [U] (**a**) the process of writing or drawing letters. (**b**) letters or words, esp with reference to their style or appearance: *gold/Roman lettering.*

■ **ˈletter-bomb** *n* an explosive device disguised as a letter and sent by post.

ˈletter-box *n* (**a**) (*esp Brit*) a narrow opening in a door through which mail is delivered. ⟹ picture at HOUSE¹. (**b**) (*US* **ˈmailbox**) a box near the main door or by the road in front of a building, to which mail is delivered. (**c**) = POSTBOX.

ˌletter of ˈcredit *n* (*finance*) a letter from a bank giving the holder authority to obtain money from another bank.

letterhead /ˈletəhed/ *n* [C] the name and address of a person, a business or an organization printed at the top of their own writing paper.

lettuce /ˈletɪs/ *n* [C,U] a plant with large thin green leaves that are usu eaten raw in a SALAD(1a): *a lettuce and tomato salad.* ⟹ picture at SALAD.

leukaemia (*US* **leukemia**) /luːˈkiːmɪə/ *n* [U] a serious disease that causes the production of too many white cells in the blood.

levee /ˈlevi/ *n* (*US*) a bank built to prevent a river from flooding: *the levees along the Mississippi.*

level¹ /ˈlevl/ *adj* **1** having a flat and even surface; not sloping: *pitch a tent on level ground* ○ *Add one level tablespoon of sugar* (ie enough to fill the spoon exactly and not in a raised heap). **2** of the same height or standard, or having the same score or position: *The two pictures aren't quite level — the one on the left is higher than the other.* ○ *France took an early lead but Wales soon drew level* (ie achieved the same score). **3** (of a voice or look) steady and not changing: *a level stare.* **IDM** **ˌlevel ˈpegging** making progress at the same rate: *The contestants were level pegging after round 3.*

■ **ˌlevel ˈcrossing** (*Brit*) (*US* **grade crossing**) *n* a place where a road and a railway cross each other at the same height. Compare CROSSING 1.

ˌlevel-ˈheaded *adj* able to judge well; sensible; calm.

level² /ˈlevl/ *n* **1** [C] a point or position on a scale of quantity, strength, value, etc: *the level of alcohol in the blood* ○ *a high level of achievement* ○ *noise/nitrate/unemployment levels* ○ *Technically, both players are on a level* (ie of the same standard). **2** [U] a relative position, stage, standard or degree of authority: *discussions at district/national level* ○ *an intermediate-level course* ○ *high-/low-level negotiations* ○ *I could use threats too, but I refuse to sink to your level* (ie behave as badly as you). See also A LEVEL. **3** [C] the height of sth, esp when measured in relation to the ground: *birds flying just above the water level* ○ *The cables are buried one metre below ground level.* ○ *The water rose to roof level.* ○ *The*

controls are at eye-level. See also SEA LEVEL. **4** [C] a floor or layer: *a multi-level parking lot* ○ *Archaeologists found pottery in the lowest level of the site.* **5** [C] = SPIRIT-LEVEL. **IDM** **on the ˈlevel** (*infml*) honest; legal: *Are you sure this deal is on the level?*

level³ /ˈlevl/ *v* (**-ll-**; *US* **-l-**) **1** to make sth equal or similar: [Vn] *level social differences* ○ *She needs to win this point to level the score.* **2** to make sth flat or smooth: [Vn] *The ground should be levelled before you plant a lawn.* **3** to destroy a building, etc completely: [Vn] *a town levelled by an earthquake.* **4** ~ **sth (at sb)** to aim a gun, etc: [Vnpr] *The hostage had a pistol levelled at his head.* [also Vn]. **PHRV** **ˈlevel sth against/at sb** to bring a charge or an accusation against sb: *level criticism at the council* ○ *accusations levelled against the directors.* **ˌlevel ˈoff/ˈout** to stop climbing or falling and become steady: *The plane levelled out at 20 000 feet.* **ˈlevel with sb** (*infml*) to tell sb the truth and not keep anything secret.

► **leveller** (*US* **leveler**) /ˈlevələ(r)/ *n* a person or thing that makes everybody equal: *Death is the great leveller.*

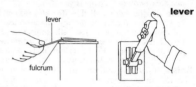

lever /ˈliːvə(r)/; *US* /ˈlevər/ *n* **1** a bar used for lifting or opening sth with one end when pressure is applied to the other end: *use a lever to prise open the window.* ⟹ picture. **2** a handle used to operate or control machinery: *the gear lever.* ⟹ picture. **3** a means of putting pressure on sb to do sth: *use the threat of sanctions as a political lever.*

► **lever** *v* to move sth with a lever: [Vnpr] *They levered the rock into position.* ○ (*fig*) *He levered himself out of bed.* [Vn-adj] *lever a crate open* [also Vn].

leverage /-ərɪdʒ; *US also* /ˈlevərɪdʒ/ *n* [U] **1** the force applied to a lever: *Use a longer handle for increased leverage.* **2** power; influence: *Her wealth gives her enormous leverage in social circles.*

■ **ˌleveraged ˈbuyout** *n* (*esp US*) a way of buying a company in which a small company borrows money on its own assets (ASSET 2) and those of the larger company it wants to buy in order to finance the deal.

leviathan /ləˈvaɪəθn/ *n* **1** (*Bible*) a large MONSTER (1a) of the sea. **2** a thing of enormous size or power: *the leviathan of government bureaucracy.*

levitate /ˈlevɪteɪt/ *v* to rise and float in the air, esp by means of magical or spiritual powers. ► **levitation** /ˌlevɪˈteɪʃn/ *n* [U]: *powers of levitation.*

levity /ˈlevəti/ *n* [U] (*fml*) the treatment of a serious matter with humour or lack of respect: *The chairman's little joke provided a rare moment of levity in an otherwise dreary meeting.*

levy /ˈlevi/ *v* (*pt, pp* **levied**) ~ **sth (on sb)** to demand and collect a payment, tax, debt, etc by authority or force; to IMPOSE(1a): [Vn] *levy interest charges* [Vnpr] *a tax levied by the government on company profits.*

► **levy** *n* (**a**) an act of levying a payment: *impose/make a levy on new cars/oil imports.* (**b**) money, etc so obtained.

lewd /ljuːd, luːd/ *adj* treating or referring to sex in a CRUDE(2) or offensive way; OBSCENE: *lewd songs/jokes* ○ *a lewd gesture.* ► **lewdness** *n* [U].

lexical /ˈleksɪkl/ *adj* (*linguistics*) of the words of a language: *lexical items* (ie words and phrases). ► **lexically** /-kli/ *adv.*

L

lexis /'leksɪs/ n [U] (linguistics) words; VOCABULARY.

lexicography /ˌleksɪ'kɒgrəfi/ n [U] the theory and practice of writing and editing dictionaries. ▶ **lexicographer** /ˌleksɪ'kɒgrəfə(r)/ n a person who writes dictionaries.

lexicon /'leksɪkən; US -kɒn/ n (pl -s) (a) (linguistics) a list of words: a lexicon of technical scientific terms. (b) a dictionary, esp of an ancient language, eg Greek or Hebrew.

ley[1] /leɪ/ n a field where grass is grown temporarily.

ley[2] /leɪ/ (also **'ley line**) n an imaginary straight line marking an ancient track that connects prominent features of the land, usu the tops of hills, churches, etc. Leys are also thought to be channels of energy.

liability /ˌlaɪə'bɪləti/ n **1** [U] ~ (**for sth**) the state of being required to do sth or accept responsibility for sth: liability for military service ○ Don't admit liability for the accident. **2** [C] (infml) a person or thing that causes one problems or puts sth at risk: Since his injury Jones has become more of a liability than an asset to the team. **3** [C usu pl] a debt; a financial obligation: a maximum liability of £500 ○ minimize one's tax liabilities. Compare ASSET.

liable /'laɪəbl/ adj [pred] **1** ~ (**for sth**) responsible by law: You will be liable for any damage caused. **2** ~ **to sth** likely to get or have sth; subject to sth: a road liable to subsidence ○ Offenders are liable to fines of up to £500. **3** ~ **to do sth** likely to do sth: We're all liable to make mistakes when we're tired.

liaise /li'eɪz/ v ~ (**with sb**) (**a**) to work closely with sb on sth of common concern: [V] liaise and exchange ideas [Vpr] It is advisable to liaise closely with the planning authorities. (**b**) to act as a link between two or more people or groups. ~ (**between A and B**): a specialist nurse liaising between hospitals, doctors and patients [also V].

liaison /li'eɪzn; US 'li:əzɒn/ n **1** [U] ~ (**between A and B**) a close working relationship involving communication between groups of people, units of an organization, etc: excellent liaison between our two departments ○ a liaison officer. **2** [C] ~ (**with sb**) (sometimes derog): vote Lib Dems' new logo. **2** [U] (law) the act of publishing such a statement: her much-publicized liaison with a Tory MP.

liar /'laɪə(r)/ n a person who tells lies, esp habitually: a good/bad liar (ie sb who can/cannot easily deceive others by telling lies).

lib /lɪb/ n (abbr) (used in the names of certain movements demanding greater freedom, fairer treatment and equal rights) liberation: gay/women's/animal lib.

libation /laɪ'beɪʃn/ n **1** (in former times) an offering of drink, usu wine, to a god. **2** (dated joc) an alcoholic drink.

Lib Dem /ˌlɪb 'dem/ abbr (Brit politics) Liberal Democrat: vote Lib Dem ○ the Lib Dems' new logo.

libel /'laɪbl/ n (**a**) [C] a false written or printed statement that damages sb's reputation: a libel printed first in 'Private Eye'. (**b**) [U] (law) the act of publishing such a statement: sue a newspaper for libel ○ a libel action brought by the actor's ex-wife ○ libel damages. Compare SLANDER. ▶ **libel** v (-ll-; US -l-) to harm sb's reputation by publishing a false statement: [Vn] She alleged that the magazine had libelled her.

libellous (US **libelous**) /'laɪbələs/ adj being or containing a libel: a libellous statement.

liberal /'lɪbərəl/ adj **1** willing to tolerate behaviour, opinions, etc different from one's own; open to new ideas: a liberal attitude to homosexuality. **2** giving or given generously: She's very liberal with promises but much less so with money. ○ a liberal helping of potatoes. **3** (of education) concerned mainly with increasing sb's general knowledge and experience, rather than with technical or professional training. **4** not strictly accurate or exact: a liberal translation

that catches the spirit of the original. **5** (politics) (**a**) favouring or based on policies that promote free trade, freedom of choice for individuals and moderate social and political change: a liberal democracy ○ liberal politicians. (**b**) **Liberal** (formerly) of the British Liberal Party. ▶ **liberal** n **1** a person who tolerates different opinions or behaviour. **2** (also **Liberal**) (politics) a member of a liberal party, esp (formerly) the British Liberal Party.

liberalism /-ɪzəm/ n [U] liberal opinions and principles, esp in politics.

liberally /-rəli/ adv: a book liberally sprinkled with illustrations ○ interpret the ruling liberally.

■ **the ˌLiberal 'Democrats** n [pl] (politics) (abbr **Lib Dems**) (in Britain) a political party favouring moderate political and social reform. Compare THE CONSERVATIVE PARTY, THE LABOUR PARTY. ˌ**Liberal 'Democrat** n (abbr **Lib Dem**) a member or supporter of the Liberal Democrats.

liberality /ˌlɪbə'ræləti/ n [U] **1** generous acts. **2** respect for political, religious or moral views that one does not agree with: a period remarkable for its liberality.

liberalize, **-ise** /'lɪbrəlaɪz/ v to free sb/sth from political, religious, legal or moral restrictions: [Vn] liberalize immigration laws. ▶ **liberalization**, **-isation** /ˌlɪbrəlaɪ'zeɪʃn; US -lə'z-/ n [U].

liberate /'lɪbəreɪt/ v ~ sb/sth (**from sth**) to free sb/sth from a situation in which they are restricted in some way: [Vn] the liberating power of theatre ○ Large areas of the country had already been liberated. [Vnpr] business liberated from state ownership. ▶ **liberated** adj showing freedom from traditional ideas in social and sexual matters: a liberated woman/lifestyle.

liberation /ˌlɪbə'reɪʃn/ n [U, sing]: the liberation of an occupied city ○ animal liberation ○ a liberation from ignorance and self-deception.

liberator n: He was hailed as the liberator of the people.

libertine /'lɪbəti:n/ n (fml derog) a man who behaves without moral principles or a sense of responsibility, esp in sexual matters.

liberty /'lɪbəti/ n **1** [U] (**a**) the state of being free from excessive restrictions placed on one's life by a governing power: restore democracy, justice and liberty ○ a society that emphasizes individual liberty. (**b**) the state of not being a prisoner or slave: fight in the courts for one's liberty. **2** [C, U] the right or power to do as one chooses: a liberty enjoyed by all citizens ○ They give their children a great deal of liberty. **3** an act or statement that may offend or annoy sb, eg because it shows lack of respect: I lent him money and now he accuses me of being mean. What a liberty! ○ The film takes considerable **liberties with** the novel on which it is based (eg by changing many details). ○ I **took the liberty of** borrowing your bike while you were away. **IDM** **at liberty** (fml) not in prison: set sb at liberty ○ The escaped convict is still at liberty. **at liberty to do sth** (fml) free from restrictions preventing one from doing sth: You're at liberty to say what you like. ○ I am not at liberty to discuss this matter further.

libidinous /lɪ'bɪdɪnəs/ adj (fml) having or showing strong sexual feelings.

libido /lɪ'bi:dəʊ, 'lɪbɪdəʊ/ n (pl -os) [U, C] (psychology) the urge or energy for sex: loss of libido.

Libra /'li:brə/ n (**a**) [U] the 7th sign of the ZODIAC, the Scales. (**b**) [C] a person born under the influence of this sign. ▶ **Libran** n, adj. ⇨ picture at ZODIAC. ⇨ note at ZODIAC.

library /'laɪbrəri, 'laɪbri; US -breri/ n **1** a building or room in which collections of books, tapes, newspapers, etc are kept for people to read, study or borrow: a public/reference/university library ○ lib-

---

[V.to inf] = verb + to infinitive   [Vn.inf (no to)] = verb + noun + infinitive without to   [V.ing] = verb + -ing form

rary opening hours ○ *a library book* ○ *a video library.*
2 (*dated or fml*) a personal collection of books,
records, films, etc: *a new edition to add to your
library.* **3** a series of books, recordings, etc issued
by the same company and similar in appearance: *a
library of classics.*
▶ **librarian** /laɪˈbreərɪən/ *n* a person in charge of or
assisting in a library. **librarianship** *n* [U]: *a diploma in librarianship.*

libretto /lɪˈbretəʊ/ *n* (*pl* **-os** or **libretti** /-tiː/) the
words that are sung and spoken in an opera or a
musical play.
▶ **librettist** /lɪˈbretɪst/ *n* the author of a libretto.

lice *pl* of LOUSE.

licence (*US* **license**) /ˈlaɪsns/ *n* **1** [C] an official
document showing that permission has been given
to do, own or use sth: *a driving licence* ○ *get an
export/television licence* ○ *lose one's licence* (ie have
permission taken away from one) ○ *goods sold under licence* (ie with permission from the
appropriate authority). See also OFF-LICENCE. **2** [U]
the use of freedom as an opportunity to behave
badly or do sth unacceptable: *They saw the manager's absence as licence to do no work.* **3** [U]
freedom to change or exaggerate words or images:
artistic/poetic licence.
■ **ˈlicence plate** (*US* **license plate**) *n* (*esp US*) =
NUMBER-PLATE. ⇨ picture at CAR.

license (also **licence**) /ˈlaɪsns/ *v* to give a licence to
sb/sth to allow them to do or use sth: [Vn.*to inf*]
shops licensed to sell tobacco [Vn] *licensed premises*
(ie where the sale of alcoholic drinks is permitted).
▶ **licensee** /ˌlaɪsənˈsiː/ *n* a person who has a licence, esp to sell alcoholic drinks.
■ **ˈlicensing laws** *n* [pl] (in Britain) laws limiting
the places and times at which alcoholic drinks may
be sold.

licentious /laɪˈsenʃəs/ *adj* (*fml*) having or showing
no moral principles in sexual matters. ▶ **licenti-
ousness** *n* [U].

lichen /ˈlaɪkən, ˈlɪtʃən/ *n* [U, C] a dry flat creeping
plant, often grey or yellow, that grows on rocks,
walls or trees. Compare MOSS.

lick /lɪk/ *v* **1(a)** to pass the tongue over the surface
of sth in order to clean it, make it wet, etc: [Vn] *lick
the back of a postage stamp* ○ *He licked his fingers.* ○
The cat was licking its fur. [Vn-adj] *He licked the
spoon clean.* **(b)** to take sth into the mouth by licking: [Vnpr] *lick honey off a spoon* [Vnp] *The cat
licked up the milk.* **2** (of waves or flames) to touch
sth lightly: [Vn] *Flames began to lick the furniture.*
3 (*sl*) to defeat sb easily: [Vn] *We thought we had
them licked.* **IDM** **get/knock/lick sth/sb into
shape** ⇨ SHAPE¹. **lick sb's ˈboots** (*infml*); (△ *sl*)
lick sb's ˈarse to show excessive respect for sb, esp
in order to gain favour from them. **lick sb/sth into
ˈshape** (*infml*) to make sb/sth efficient or ready for
use: *The new recruits will be fine once they've been
licked into shape.* **lick/smack one's lips** ⇨ LIP.
lick one's ˈwounds to try to recover one's strength
or confidence after defeat or disappointment: *Leeds
are still licking their wounds after their humiliating
defeat by Rangers.*
▶ **lick** *n* **1** [C] an act of licking sth with the tongue:
Can I have a lick of your ice-cream? **2** [sing] a small
amount of sth, esp paint: *The boat would look better
with a lick of paint.* **3** [sing] (*infml*) speed: *He started
the race at a tremendous lick.*
licking *n* [sing] (*infml*) a heavy defeat: *give sb/get a
licking.*

licorice *n* = LIQUORICE.

lid /lɪd/ *n* **1** a cover over a container, which can be
removed or opened by turning it, pulling it or raising part of it: *a dustbin lid* ○ *I can't unscrew the lid.*
⇨ picture at PAN¹. **2** = EYELID. **IDM** **flip one's lid** ⇨
FLIP. **keep a/the ˈlid on sth** to keep sth secret. **put**

the (tin) ˈlid on sth/things 1 (*Brit infml*) to be the
final act or event that causes one to become angry,
upset, etc. **2** to stop sth from happening: *put the lid
on political unrest.* **take, lift, blow, etc the ˈlid off
sth** to reveal unpleasant secrets concerning sth: *an
article that lifts the lid off the world of professional
gambling.*
▶ **lidded** *adj* [usu attrib] **1** (of containers) having a
lid: *lidded pots/tubs.* **2** (of eyes) having eyelids (EYE-
LID) of a particular type: *heavily lidded eyes.*

lido /ˈliːdəʊ/ *n* (*pl* **-os**) (*esp Brit*) a public outdoor
swimming-pool (SWIM) or part of a beach used by the
public for swimming, water sports, etc.

lie¹ /laɪ/ *v* (*pt, pp* **lied**; *pres p* **lying**) **1** ~ (**to** sb)
(**about** sth) to say sth that one knows is not true: [V]
*You could see from the expression on his face that he
was lying.* [Vpr] *Don't lie to me!* ○ *She lies about her
age.* **2** to give a false impression; to mislead: [V] *The
camera cannot lie.* **IDM** **lie through one's ˈteeth**
(*infml*) to lie greatly: *The witness was clearly lying
through his teeth.* **lie one's ˈway into / out of sth** to
get oneself into or out of a situation by lying: *He's
lied his way into the job.* ⇨ note at LIE².
▶ **lie** *n* a statement made by sb knowing that it is
not true: *His story is nothing but **a pack of lies**.* ○
That's a complete lie! See also WHITE LIE. **IDM** **give
the lie to sth** to show that sth previously stated is
not true: *These figures give the lie to reports that
business is declining.* **live a lie** ⇨ LIVE².
■ **ˈlie-detector** *n* an instrument used for showing
whether a person is telling lies: *take a lie-detector
test.*

lie² /laɪ/ *v* (*pt* **lay** /leɪ/; *pp* **lain** /leɪn/; *pres p* **lying**) **1**
to have or put one's body in a flat or resting position
on a surface: [Vpr] *lie on one's back/side/front* ○ *The
corpse lay face down in a pool of blood.* ○ *The dog was
lying fast asleep by the fire.* **2** (of a thing) to rest on a
surface: [Vpr, Vp] *Clothes were lying (about) all over
the floor.* [V-adj] *The book lay open on his desk.* ⇨
note. **3** to be, remain or be kept in a certain state:
[V-adj] *snow lying thick on the ground* ○ *These machines have lain idle since the factory closed.* [Vpr] *a
ship lying at anchor* ○ *I'd rather use my money than
leave it lying in the bank.* **4** to extend in front of one,
beneath one, etc: [Vpr] *The valley lay below us.*
[Vadv, Vpr] (*fig*) *You're still young — your whole life
lies ahead of/before you!* **5** to be situated in a specified place: [Vpr] *The town lies on the coast.* **6** ~ (**in**
sth) (of abstract things) to exist or be found: [Vadv]
It's obvious where our interests lie (ie which course
of action, etc is to our advantage). [Vpr] *The problem lies in deciding when to intervene.* **7** to be in a
particular position during a competition: [Vpr]
Thompson is lying in fourth place. [V-adj] *After five
matches Derby are lying second.* **IDM** **one has made
one's bed, so one must lie on/in it** ⇨ BED¹. **let
sleeping dogs lie** ⇨ SLEEP². **lie ˈdoggo** to remain
still and quiet. **lie heavy on sb/sth** to cause sb/sth
to feel uncomfortable or anxious: *a crime lying
heavy on one's conscience* ○ *The responsibilities of
management lay heavy on him.* ○ *The rich meal lay
heavy on my stomach.* **lie in ˈstate** (of the dead body
of an important person) to be placed on view in a
public place before burial. **lie in ˈwait (for sb)** to
hide, waiting to surprise, attack or catch sb: *He was
surrounded by reporters who had been lying in wait
for him.* **lie ˈlow** (*infml*) to try not to attract attention to oneself; to stay quiet or hidden: *The thieves
decided to lie low for a while after the robbery.* **see,
etc how the land lies** ⇨ LAND¹. **take sth lying
ˈdown** to accept an insult or offensive act without
protesting or reacting. **PHRV** **ˌlie ˈback** to do nothing except relax: *You don't have to do anything —
just lie back and enjoy the journey.*

ˌlie beˈhind sth to be the real, often hidden, reason
for sth: *What lay behind this strange outburst?*

,lie '**down** to be or get into a flat comfortable position, esp in bed, in order to sleep or rest: *Go and lie down for a while.* ○ *He lay down on the sofa and soon fell asleep.*

,lie '**in** (*Brit*); (*US*) **sleep in** (*infml*) to stay in bed after the normal time for getting up: *It's a holiday tomorrow, so you can lie in.*

'**lie with sb (to do sth)** (*fml*) to be sb's duty or responsibility: *The decision on whether to proceed lies with the Governor.* ○ *It lies with you to accept or reject the proposal.*

▶ **lie** *n* [sing] the way or position in which sth lies: *He found his ball in a difficult lie.* **IDM** **the ,lie of the 'land**; (*US*) **the ,lay of the 'land 1** the features or characteristics of an area. **2** (*infml*) the current situation or state of affairs: *I'll need to discover the lie of the land before making any decisions about the future of the business.*

■ ,**lie-'down** *n* (usu *sing*) (*Brit infml*) a short rest, esp in bed.

,**lie-'in** *n* (usu *sing*) (*infml esp Brit*) an act of staying in bed longer than usual in the morning: *look forward to a nice long lie-in on Sunday.*

NOTE Compare the verbs **lie** and **lay**. **Lie** (**lying**, **lay**, **lain**) is intransitive and has no object after it: *The children were too excited to lie down and go to sleep.* The past tense is **lay**: *I lay on the bed reading.*

Lay (**laying**, **laid**, **laid**) is transitive and is followed by an object. The past tense is **laid**: *She laid her dress on the bed.* ○ *Relatives laid some flowers at the scene of the accident.*

There is another intransitive verb **lie** (**lying**, **lied**, **lied**) which means 'to say something that is not true': *He lied about his age to get the job.*

lied /liːt/ *n* (*pl* **lieder** /'liːdə(r)/) (*music*) a German song for solo voice and piano.

liege /liːdʒ/ (also ,**liege 'lord**) *n* (formerly) a king or lord.

lien /'liːən/ *n* [C] ~ (**on/upon sth**) (*law*) the right to keep sb's property until a debt owed in connection with it, eg for repair or transport, is paid.

lieu /luː;; *Brit also* ljuː/ *n* **IDM** **in lieu (of sth)** instead: *accept a cheque in lieu of cash* ○ *work at weekends and get extra days off in lieu.*

Lieut (also **Lt**) *abbr* Lieutenant: *Lieut (James) Brown.*

lieutenant /lef'tenənt; *US* luː't-/ *n* **1** (the title of) an army or navy officer of relatively low rank. ▷ App 6. **2** (in compounds) an officer ranking next below the one specified: *lieu,tenant-'general* ○ *lieu,tenant-'colonel.* **3** a person's chief assistant.

life /laɪf/ *n* (*pl* **lives** /laɪvz/) **1** [U] the ability to grow and produce new forms that distinguishes living animals and plants from dead ones and from rocks, metals, etc: *the origins of life on earth* ○ *The body showed no signs of life.* **2** [U] living things: *animal and plant life* ○ *Is there life on Mars?* **3** [U] the state of being alive as a human being: *The riot was brought under control without loss of life* (ie without anyone being killed). ○ *Getting food to the refugees is now a matter of life and death.* **4** [U] the qualities, events and experiences of human existence: *He does not want much from life.* ○ *What do you expect? That's life* (ie These things happen and must be expected and accepted)*!* **5** [C] the existence of an individual human being: *Doctors worked through the night to save the life of the injured man.* ○ *Three lives were lost* (ie Three people died) *in the accident.* **6(a)** [C] the period between birth and death: *She lived her whole (adult) life in the country.* **(b)** [C] the period between birth and the present: *I've lived here all my life.* **7** [U] **(a)** the period between the present and death: *a friend/job/membership for life.* **(b)** (*infml*) a sentence(2) given by a lawcourt that one must spend the rest of one's life or a very long time in prison: *be given/get/do*

life. See also LIFE SENTENCE. **8** [U] **(a)** the business, pleasure and social activities of the world: *As a taxi-driver you really see* (ie experience) *life.* **(b)** activity; movement: *There are few signs of life here in the evenings.* **9** [U] liveliness; interest: *Children are always so full of life.* ○ *The show's very flat — put some more life into it.* **10** [U,C] way of living: *one's private/public/family life* ○ *city/village life* ○ *have an easy/a hard life* ○ *emigrate and start a new life in America* ○ *Her work is her life* (ie the most important thing she does). ○ *This is the life (for me)* (ie the best way to live)*!* **11** [C] a story of sb's life; a BIOGRAPHY: *write a life of Tolstoy.* **12** [U] a living model: *a portrait drawn/taken from life* ○ *a 'life class* (ie one in which art students draw, etc from living models). **13** [C] a period during which sth continues to exist or function: *throughout the life of the present government* ○ *a ,long-life 'battery.* **14** [C] (in children's games) one of a set number of chances before a player is out of the game: *You've had three lives — you've got one left.* **IDM** **at my, etc time of life** ▷ TIME[1]. **the breath of life** ▷ BREATH. **bring sb/sth to 'life** to make sb/sth more lively or interesting: *The arrival of the band brought the party to life.* ○ *Her books succeed in bringing historical characters to life.* **the change of life** ▷ CHANGE[2]. **come to 'life 1** to become more lively or interesting: *When the discussion turned to literature, she suddenly came to life.* ○ *The café only comes to life at night.* **2** to start to act or move as if alive: *In the ballet all the toys come to life.* **depart this life** ▷ DEPART. **a dog's life** ▷ DOG[1]. **end one's days/life** ▷ END[2]. **end one's life** ▷ END[2]. **a fact of life** ▷ FACT. **the facts of life** ▷ FACT. **for dear 'life/for one's 'life** as if to escape death; as hard, fast, etc as possible: *holding on for dear life* ○ *Run for your life!* **for the 'life of one** (*infml*) however hard one tries: *I cannot for the life of me remember her name.* **frighten/scare the 'life out of sb** to frighten sb very much. **full of beans/life** ▷ FULL. **have the time of one's life** ▷ TIME[1]. **in fear of one's life** ▷ FEAR[1]. **large as life** ▷ LARGE. **larger than life** ▷ LARGE. **lay down one's 'life (for sb/sth)** (*rhet*) to die in order to save sb/sth: *He laid down his life for the cause of freedom.* ,**life and 'limb** death or injury: *risk life and limb to rescue others.* **the life and 'soul of sth** (*infml*) the most lively and amusing person present at a party, etc. **a matter of life and death** ▷ MATTER[1]. **a new lease of life** ▷ NEW. **not on your 'life!** (*infml*) certainly not. **put an end to one's life/to oneself/to it all** ▷ END[1]. **a slice of life** ▷ SLICE. **take one's (own) 'life** to kill oneself. **take one's life in one's 'hands** to risk being killed: *You take your life in your hands simply crossing the road these days!* **take sb's 'life** to kill sb. **that's the story of my life** ▷ STORY[1]. **to the 'life** exactly like the original: *In the screen biography he plays Charlie Chaplin to the life.* **a walk of life** ▷ WALK[2]. a/**sb's way of life** ▷ WAY[1].

▶ **lifeless** *adj* **1** lacking liveliness; dull: *a lifeless performance.* **2** dead: *He knelt beside her lifeless body.* **3** never having had life: *lifeless stones* ○ *a lifeless planet.*

lifer /'laɪfə(r)/ *n* (*sl*) a person sentenced to spend her or his life in prison.

■ ,**life-and-'death** (also ,**life-or-'death**) *adj* [attrib] serious; extremely important; deciding between life and death: *drought victims engaged in a life-and-death struggle to survive.*

'**life cycle** *n* (*biology*) a series of forms into which a living thing changes as it develops: *the life cycle of the butterfly.*

'**life expectancy** *n* [U] **(a)** the number of years that a person is likely to live: *Women have a longer life expectancy than men.* **(b)** the length of time that sth is likely to exist or function: *the life expectancy of the average car/the present government.*

L

'life-giving adj [esp attrib] that restores or maintains life: ,life-giving 'energy/'food.

,life 'history n = LIFE STORY.

,life im'prisonment n [U] spending one's life or a very long time in prison: be sentenced to life imprisonment.

'life insurance n [U] a type of insurance that provides a specified payment on the death of the holder.

'life-jacket n a jacket without sleeves, made of light material or filled with air and used to help a person in difficulty in water to float. ⇨ picture at LIFEBELT.

,life 'peer n (Brit) a person who is given the title of a PEER¹(2) but who cannot pass the title on to a son or daughter when he or she dies.

'life preserver n (US) = LIFEBELT.

'life-saver n a thing that helps or improves sth in an important way: The radio was a life-saver during my illness — I couldn't have done without it.

'life sciences n [pl] subjects involving the study of plants, animals, etc: Biology and botany are life sciences.

'life sentence n a punishment by which sb spends their life or a very long time in prison: serve a life sentence.

,life 'size n [U] the actual size of the person or thing represented: photographs enlarged to life size. **'life-size** (also **'life-sized**) adj: a life-size(d) model of a horse.

'life-span n the length of time that sth is likely to live, continue or function: insects with a life-span of only a few hours.

'life story (also ,life 'history) n the story of a person's life: She told me her life story.

,life-sup'port adj [attrib] (of equipment) enabling sb to live in a dangerous environment, eg a spacecraft, or when natural functions of the body have failed, eg after an accident: a patient on a life-support machine/system.

,life-'threatening adj (of diseases, etc) that can cause death.

,life-'work (also ,life's-'work) n (usu sing) the main activity or most important achievement of a person's life: This hospital has been my life's-work.

lifebelt

lifebelt (US **life preserver**)   **life-jacket**

lifebelt /'laɪfbelt/ (also **'lifebuoy** /'laɪfbɔɪ/, US **life preserver**) n a ̶ ̶ ̶ng of material that floats, used for rescuing a pe....n who has fallen into water. ⇨ picture.

lifeblood /'laɪfblʌd/ n [U] **1** ~ (of sth) a thing that gives sth its essential strength and force: Good songs are the lifeblood of pop music. **2** (rhet) one's blood, seen as the thing that keeps one alive.

lifeboat /'laɪfbəʊt/ n **(a)** a small boat carried on a ship for use if the ship has to be abandoned at sea. **(b)** a boat specially built for rescuing people in danger in the sea: lifeboat crews.

lifebuoy /'laɪfbɔɪ/ n = LIFEBELT.

lifeguard /'laɪfgɑːd/ n a person employed at a beach or pool to rescue people who get into difficulty while swimming.

lifelike /'laɪflaɪk/ adj exactly like a real person or thing: a lifelike statue/drawing/toy.

lifeline /'laɪflaɪn/ n **1(a)** a line or rope thrown to rescue sb in difficulty in water. **(b)** a line attached

to sb who goes deep under the sea. **2** a thing on which sb/sth depends for their/its continued existence: Public transport is a lifeline for many rural communities.

lifelong /'laɪflɒŋ/ adj [attrib] extending throughout one's life: a lifelong friendship/commitment/ambition.

lifestyle /'laɪfstaɪl/ n the way in which an individual or a group lives: a busy/glamorous/healthy lifestyle ○ I'd like to change my lifestyle.

lifetime /'laɪftaɪm/ n the length of a person's life or a thing's existence: see many changes in one's lifetime ○ a lifetime of suffering ○ lifetime employment/ membership. **IDM the chance, etc of a 'lifetime** an exceptional opportunity, etc: have the holiday of a lifetime.

lift /lɪft/ v **1** ~ sb/sth (up) to raise sb/sth to a higher position or level: [Vnp] Lift me up, mummy — I can't see. [Vn] The government are planning to lift interest rates. [also Vnpr]. **2** to take hold of sb/sth and move them/it to a different position: [Vnpr] lift a baby out of a pram ○ lift a suitcase down from the rack. **3** to raise sb/sth or be raised to a happier state: [Vn] The sun came out and lifted our spirits. [V] Her heart lifted at the thought of him. **4** (of clouds, etc) to rise and disappear: [V] The mist began to lift. **5** to dig up vegetables; to remove plants from the ground: [Vn] lift potatoes/turnips. **6** ~ sth (from sb/sth) (infml) **(a)** to steal sth: [Vnpr] lift goods from a warehouse [also Vn]. See also SHOPLIFT. **(b)** to use sb's ideas, work, etc without asking permission or acknowledging them: [Vnpr] Many of his ideas were lifted from other authors. [also Vn]. **7** to remove or end restrictions: [Vn] lift a ban/a curfew/an embargo/a blockade. **8** to transport people or goods by air: [Vnpr] The survivors were lifted to safety by helicopter from the stricken ship. [also Vn, Vnp]. See also AIRLIFT. **IDM lift/raise a finger/hand (to do sth)** (infml) (usu negative) to make the smallest effort: He never lifts a finger to help with the housework. **lift/ raise a/one's hand against sb** ⇨ HAND¹. **PHR V lift off** (of a ROCKET(2b) or spacecraft) to rise from the launching site.

▶ **lift** n **1** (Brit) (US **elevator**) [C] a mechanical container or platform that moves up and down within a building or mine and is used for taking people or goods from one floor or level to another: a hydraulic lift ○ It's on the sixth floor — let's take the lift. See also CHAIR LIFT, SKI-LIFT. **2** [C] a free ride in a car, etc: I'll **give you a lift** to the station. ○ **hitch a lift**. **3** [U] the upward pressure of air on an aircraft in flight. Compare DRAG² 5. **4** [sing] a state of feeling better, happier, more confident, etc: Getting the job gave me a tremendous lift. **5** [sing] an act of lifting sb/sth or of being lifted. **IDM thumb a lift** ⇨ THUMB v.

■ **'lift-off** n [C, U] the act of launching a ROCKET(2b) or spacecraft: We have lift-off. See also BLAST-OFF.

ligament /'lɪgəmənt/ n a tough flexible tissue that connects bones in a person's or an animal's body: tear/strain a ligament.

ligature /'lɪgətʃə(r)/ n (techn) a thing used for joining things or tying sth very tightly, eg to stop bleeding.

light¹ /laɪt/ n **1** [U] **(a)** the natural force that makes things visible: the light of the sun/a lamp/the fire. **(b)** an amount or quality of this: the flickering light of a candle ○ The light was beginning to fail (ie It was getting dark). ○ This light is too poor to read by. ○ (fig) A soft light (ie expression) came into her eyes as she looked at him. Compare DARK². See also FIRST LIGHT. **2** [C] a source of light, esp an electric lamp: turn/switch the lights on/off ○ Far below us we could see the lights of the city. ○ A light was still burning in his study. ○ Keep going, the lights (ie traffic lights) are green. See also RED LIGHT. **3** [C] a device used to

L

produce a flame or SPARK(1a): *Have you got a light* (eg for a cigarette)? **4** [U] understanding: *I wrestled with the puzzle for ages before the light finally dawned* (ie I understood the solution). **5** [C] (*architecture*) a window or opening to let light in: *leaded lights.* **6** [U, C usu *sing*] (*art*) a part of a picture that is brighter than the areas around it: *light and shade.* See also LEADING LIGHT. **IDM** be/stand in sb's 'light to be placed between sb and a source of light: *I can't read — you're in my light.* the bright lights ⇨ BRIGHT. bring sth to 'light to reveal sth; to make sth known: *New facts have been brought to light.* cast/shed/throw 'light on sth to make sth clearer: *Recent research has shed new light on the causes of the disease.* catch the light ⇨ CATCH[1]. come to 'light to be revealed; to become known: *New evidence has recently come to light.* go out like a 'light (*infml*) to lose consciousness or fall asleep suddenly. hide one's light under a bushel ⇨ HIDE[1]. in a good, bad, favourable, etc 'light well, badly, favourably, etc: *The newspapers have presented his actions in the worst possible light.* ○ *It is hard to view his conduct in a favourable light.* in the light of sth; (*US*) in light of sth in view of sth; considering sth: *review the plans in the light of past experience.* light at the end of the 'tunnel success, happiness, etc after a long period of difficulty or hardship. see the 'light 1 to understand or accept sth after much difficulty or doubt. **2** to be converted to religious belief. see the 'light (of 'day) 1 (*rhet*) to be born. **2** (of ideas, etc) to be imagined or made public: *The notion of a Channel Tunnel first saw the light of day more than a century ago.* set 'light to sth to cause sth to start burning. sweetness and light ⇨ SWEETNESS.

▶ **light** *adj* **1** full of light; not in darkness: *a light airy room* ○ *In spring the evenings start to get lighter.* **2** pale: *light blue eyes* ○ *Light colours suit you best.* Compare DARK[1] 1,2. ‚light-'coloured *adj* (*US* -colored): *I prefer ‚light-coloured 'fabrics.*

■ 'light bulb *n* = BULB[2].

'light meter *n* a device used to measure how bright the light is before taking a photograph.

'light-pen *n* an electronic device, shaped like a pen, that can pass information to a computer screen when it touches it, or record the sale of sth when moved across a code on its label.

'light-year *n* **1** (*astronomy*) the distance that light travels in one year (about 6 million million miles). **2** light-years [pl] (*infml*) a very long time: *Racial equality still seems light-years away.*

light[2] /laɪt/ *v* (*pt, pp* lit /lɪt/ or lighted) (*Lighted* is used esp as an attributive *adj*, as in *a lighted candle*, but compare *He lit the candle* and *The candles were lit.*) **1** to begin or make sth begin burning: [Vn] *light a cigarette/candle/fire/match* [V] *This wood is so damp it won't light.* **2** to provide sth with light: [Vn] *A single bulb lit the corridor.* [Vnadv] *These streets are well/poorly lit.* [Vnpr] *Nowadays, houses are mostly lit by electricity.* **3** (*fml*) to guide sb with a light: [Vn] *His way was lit by the moon.* **PHRV** ‚light (sth) 'up (*infml*) to begin to smoke a cigarette, etc: *light up a pipe.* ‚light 'up (with sth) (of a person's face, etc) to become bright or lively: *Her eyes lit up with joy.* ‚light sth 'up 1 to make a person's face, etc bright or lively: *A rare smile lit up his stern features.* **2** to provide sth with light: *a castle lit up with floodlights* ○ *A flash of lightning lit up the sky.*

▶ 'lighting *n* [U] (**a**) equipment for providing light for a room, building, etc: *street lighting.* (**b**) the arrangement or effect of lights: *fluorescent lighting* ○ *Subtle lighting helps people relax.* ○ *help with sound and lighting* (eg in the theatre).

light[3] /laɪt/ *adj* (-er, -est) **1** easy to lift or move; not heavy: *Carry this bag — it's the lightest.* ○ *He's lost a lot of weight — he's three kilos lighter than he used to*

be. **2** (esp attrib) of less than average weight: *light summer clothes* ○ *This coat is light but very warm.* ○ *The old bridge can only be used by light vehicles.* **3** (following *ns*) less than the expected or specified weight: *This sack of potatoes is five kilos light.* **4** [esp attrib] gentle; delicate: *a light tap on the shoulder* ○ *light footsteps* ○ *apply light pressure* ○ *be light on one's feet* (ie graceful and quick). **5** [esp attrib] easy to perform; not tiring: *take a little light exercise* ○ *Since her accident she can only do light work.* **6** enjoyable and not demanding close attention: *light music/comedy/entertainment/conversation* ○ *I took some light reading* (eg a magazine) *for the train journey.* **7** easy to bear; not severe: *a light attack of indigestion* ○ *He got off with a light sentence.* **8** not intense: *light showers of rain* ○ *The wind is very light.* ○ *Trading on the Stock Exchange was light today.* **9** [esp attrib] not thick or DENSE(1,2): *light traffic* ○ *The river was visible through a light mist.* ○ *This plant will only grow in light soil.* **10(a)** (of meals) small in quantity: *a light snack/supper/ pudding.* (**b**) (of food) easy to DIGEST[2](1b) because it does not contain any rich ingredients: *a light pudding.* (**c**) (of food) containing a lot of air and rising well: *Her soufflés are always so light.* **11** [attrib] (of sleep) not deep: *My mother's a very light sleeper and wakes at the slightest noise.* **12** [esp attrib] (*US* also lite) (of drinks) low in alcohol: *a light beer/white wine.* **13** [esp attrib] cheerful; free from worry: *with a light heart* ○ *He kept his voice light.* **IDM** (as) ‚light as 'air/as a 'feather very light. make 'light of sth to treat sth as unimportant and not serious: *He made light of his injury.* make light 'work of sth to do sth quickly and with little effort: *We made light work of the tidying up.* many hands make light 'work ⇨ HAND[1].

▶ **light** *adv* with few bags or possessions : *I always travel light.*

lightly *adv* **1** gently; without force or effort: *He kissed her lightly on the cheek.* ○ *She ran lightly up the stairs.* **2** without serious consideration: *Involvement in the conflict is not to be undertaken lightly.* **3** without showing any worry or concern: *'I'll be all right,' she said lightly.* **IDM** get off 'lightly/ 'cheaply (*infml*) to escape serious punishment or trouble: *He got off lightly with a small fine.*

lightness *n* [U]: *lightness of heart* ○ *lightness of touch* (eg when playing the piano).

■ ‚light 'aircraft *n* (*pl* unchanged) a small aircraft with seats for up to about 6 passengers.

‚light-'fingered *adj* (*infml*) fond of stealing small things.

‚light-'headed *adj* feeling slightly faint or DIZZY(1a): *After four glasses of wine he began to feel lightheaded.*

‚light-'hearted *adj* (**a**) not serious; amusing or entertaining: *a light-hearted after-dinner speech.* (**b**) without cares; cheerful: *She felt light-hearted and optimistic.* ‚light-'heartedly *adv*.

‚light 'heavyweight *n* a boxer weighing between 72.5 and 79.5 kg, next above MIDDLEWEIGHT.

‚light 'industry *n* [C, U] the manufacture of small or light articles, without the use of heavy machinery.

light[4] /laɪt/ *v* (*pt, pp* lit /lɪt/ or lighted) **PHRV** 'light on/upon sb/sth (*fml*) to meet or find sb/sth by chance: *Luckily, I lit on a secondhand copy of the book.* ‚light 'out (*US sl*) (esp in the past tense) to leave quickly: *I lit out for home.*

lighten[1] /'laɪtn/ *v* **1** to become or make sth lighter in weight: [Vn] *lighten a load/pack* ○ (*fig*) *lighten the burden of taxation* [also V]. **2** to relieve sb or be relieved of care or worry: [Vn] *lighten sb's mood* [V] *My mood gradually lightened.* **3** to make sth less serious: [Vn, Vnp] *lighten (up) one's speech with a few jokes.*

lighten[2] /'laɪtn/ *v* **1** to make sth brighter: [Vn] *The* *new windows have lightened the room considerably.* **2** to become brighter: [V] *His face lightened as she told him the news.* ○ *The sky was lightening in the east.*

lighter¹ /'laɪtə(r)/ n = CIGARETTE LIGHTER.

lighter² /'laɪtə(r)/ n a boat with a flat bottom, used for transferring goods to and from ships in harbour.

lighthouse /'laɪthaʊs/ n a tower or other structure containing a strong light to warn or guide ships.

lightning¹ /'laɪtnɪŋ/ n [U] a flash of brilliant light in the sky produced by natural electricity passing between clouds or from clouds to the ground, usu followed by thunder: *be struck by lightning* ○ *forked/sheet lightning.* **IDM** **lightning never strikes (in the same place) twice** (*saying*) an unusual event is not likely to occur again in exactly the same circumstances or to the same people. **like (greased) 'lightning** very fast. **quick as lightning** ⇨ QUICK.
■ **'lightning conductor** (*Brit*) (*US* **'lightning rod**) n a metal rod or wire from the highest part of a building to the ground. Its purpose is to prevent lightning damaging the building.

lightning² /'laɪtnɪŋ/ adj [attrib] very quick or sudden: *move at/with lightning speed* ○ *Police made a lightning raid on the house.*
■ **,lightning 'strike** n a decision to stop work taken suddenly and without warning: *They called a lightning strike to protest about the dismissal of a workmate.*

lightship /'laɪtʃɪp/ n a small ship that stays at a particular place at sea where there is danger, and has a powerful light to warn and guide other ships.

lightweight /'laɪtweɪt/ adj **1** made of thinner material and weighing less than average: *lightweight shoes/trousers* ○ *a lightweight aluminium engine.* **2** containing little serious matter: *a lightweight novel/argument.* **3** (of a person) of little worth or importance.
▶ **lightweight** n **1** a person or thing of less than average weight. **2** a boxer weighing between 57 and 61 kg, next above FEATHERWEIGHT. **3** (*infml derog*) a person or thing of little influence or importance: *a political lightweight.*

lignite /'lɪgnaɪt/ n [U] a soft brown type of coal.

like¹ /laɪk/ v (not usu in the continuous tenses) **1(a)** to find sb/sth pleasant or satisfactory; to enjoy sth: [Vn] *Do you like fish?* ○ *She likes him* (ie is fond of him) *but doesn't love him.* ○ *I don't like the way he looks at me.* ○ *You've got to go to school, whether you like it or not.* [V.ing] *She's never liked swimming.* [V.n ing] *I didn't like him/his taking all the credit.* **(b)** to prefer to do sth or for sth to be made or happen in a particular way: [V.to inf] *On Sundays I like to sleep late.* [V.n to inf no passive] *He likes his guests to be punctual.* [Vn-adj] *I like my coffee strong.* **2** (in negative sentences) to be unwilling or RELUCTANT to do sth: [V.to inf] *I didn't like* (ie felt RELUCTANT) *to disturb you.* [V.ing] *He doesn't like asking for help.* **3** (used with *should/would/'d* to express a usu polite wish or preference at a particular time) [V.to inf] *Would you like something to eat?* [V.n to inf] *I'd like to think it over before deciding.* ○ *How can they afford it? That's what I'd like to know.* [V.n to inf] *We would like you to come and visit us.* ⇨ note at WANT¹. **4** (usu in questions, with *how*) to feel about sth; to respond or react to sth: [Vn] *How would you like it if such a thing happened to you?* **IDM** **if you 'like 1** (used as a polite form of agreement or suggestion): *'Shall we stop now?' 'If you like.'* ○ *If you like, we could go out this evening.* **2** (used when expressing sth in a new way or in a way that the speaker is not confident about): *This is a milestone, if you like, in the study of human genes.* **I like 'that!** (*ironic*) (used to protest that sth that has been said is not true or fair): *'She called you a cheat.' 'Well, I like*

that!' **like the 'look/'sound of sb/sth** to have received a favourable impression of sb from what one has seen of/heard about them: *I don't like the sound of that cough — shouldn't you see the doctor about it?*
▶ **likeable** (also **likable**) /'laɪkəbl/ adj easy to like; pleasant: *He's likeable enough, but a bit boring.*
likes n [pl] the things one likes: *He has so many likes and dislikes that it's impossible to please him.*

like² /laɪk/ prep **1(a)** similar to sb/sth; resembling sb/sth: *She's wearing a hat like mine.* ○ *a house built like an Arab palace* ○ *He's nothing* (ie not at all) *like his father* (ie in character or looks). ○ *That sounds like* (ie I think I can hear) *the postman.* **(b)** (used in questions to ask sb's opinion of sb/sth): *What's it like studying at a Spanish university?* ○ *This new girlfriend of his — what's she like?* **2** characteristic of sb/sth: *It's just like her to tell everyone about it.* **3** in the manner of sb/sth; to the same degree as sb/sth: *You're behaving like children.* ○ *run like the wind* (ie very fast) ○ *stories which I, like everybody else, have read in the press* ○ *Do it like this.* ○ *Don't look at me like that.* ⇨ note at AS. **4** for example: *I'm fond of modern playwrights like Pinter and Ayckbourn.* **IDM** **more 'like (it)** (*infml*) better; more satisfactory: *The roads are less crowded now — this is more like it!* **something 'like (it)** similar to what is required or desirable: *That's something like it, John.*
▶ **like** conj (*infml*) **1** in the same manner as; as well as: *No one sings the blues like she did.* ○ *It didn't turn out like I intended.* **2** (*esp US*) as if: *She acts like she owns the place.*

like³ /laɪk/ adj having similar qualities or features or in a similar situation: *They're not twins, but they're very like.* ○ *a chance to meet people of like mind* ○ *She responded in like manner.*
▶ **like** adv (used in very informal speech at any point as a meaningless addition or to qualify a word or an expression about which the speaker is not sure): *It was sort of creepy, like.* ○ *He just, like, refused to talk to me.* **IDM** **(as) like as 'not; like e'nough; most/very 'like** (*dated*) quite/very probably: *It'll rain this afternoon, as like as not.*
like n [sing] a person or thing that is similar to another: *jazz, rock and the like* (ie similar types of music) ○ *a man whose like we shall not see again* ○ *You're not comparing like with like.* **IDM** **the likes of 'sb/'sth** (*infml*) a similar person or thing: *He's a real snob — he'd never speak to the likes of 'me.*
■ **,like-'minded** adj having similar tastes or opinions: *The society offers an ideal opportunity for like-minded people to get together.*

-like suff (used widely with *n*s to form *adj*s) similar to; resembling: *childlike* ○ *ladylike* ○ *shell-like* ○ *snakelike.*

likely /'laɪkli/ adj (**-ier, -iest**) **1** ~ (**to do sth/that...**) probable or expected: *a likely cause/outcome/result* ○ *It's likely to rain.* ○ *The pain is likely to get worse.* ○ *It's likely that you'll need an operation.* **2** that seems suitable for a purpose: *a likely candidate for the job* ○ *This looks a likely place for a picnic.* **IDM** **a 'likely story** (*ironic*) (used to express disbelief about what sb has said): *He says he just forgot about it — a likely story!*
▶ **likelihood** /'laɪklihʊd/ n [U] chance; possibility: *There's no likelihood of that happening.* ○ *In all likelihood* (ie Very probably) *the meeting will be cancelled.*
likely adv **IDM** **as ,likely as 'not; most/very 'likely** (very) probably: *As likely as not she's forgotten all about it.* ○ *She's been delayed, most likely.* **not 'likely!** (*infml*) certainly not: *Me? Join the army? Not likely!*

liken /'laɪkən/ v **PHRV** **liken sth/sb to sth/sb** (*fml*) (esp passive) to compare one thing or person with another: *Life has often been likened to a journey.*

likeness /'laɪknəs/ n **1(a)** [U] being alike; resem-

L

---

bling sb/sth: *I can't see much likeness between him and his father.* (**b**) [C usu *sing*] an instance of this: *All my children share a strong family likeness.* **2** [sing] (following an *adj*) the extent to which a person, portrait, photograph, etc resembles the person portrayed: *That photo is a good likeness of David.*

likewise /ˈlaɪkwaɪz/ *adv* (*fml*) **1** the same; in the same way: *I'm going to bed and you would be well advised to* **do likewise.** **2** also: *The food was excellent, (and) likewise the wine.*

liking /ˈlaɪkɪŋ/ *n* **IDM** **for one's** ˈ**liking** to suit sb's taste, wishes, needs, etc: *The pub's too noisy for my liking.* **have a** ˈ**liking for sth** to be fond of sth: *I've always had a liking for the sea.* **take a** ˈ**liking to sb/ sth** to become fond of sb/sth: *I think she's taken a liking to me.* **to sb's** ˈ**liking** (*fml*) giving sb satisfaction; pleasing sb: *I hope the meal was to your liking.*

lilac /ˈlaɪlək/ *n* **1** [C,U] a bush with sweet-smelling purple or white flowers: *a bunch of lilac* ○ *The lilacs are in flower.* **2** [U] a pale purple colour.
▶ **lilac** *adj* of a pale purple colour.

lilliputian /ˌlɪlɪˈpjuːʃn/ *adj* (*fml*) very small: *Even America's largest banks look lilliputian in comparison with those of Japan.*

lilo /ˈlaɪləʊ/ *n* (*pl* **-os**) (*Brit propr*) a type of plastic or rubber bed that is filled with air for use eg by the sea or when camping.

lilt /lɪlt/ *n* [sing] **1** the rise and fall of the voice while speaking: *have a faint Irish lilt.* **2** a regular rising and falling pattern in music, usu accompanied by a lively rhythm. ▶ **lilting** *adj*: *a lilting song/voice.*

lily /ˈlɪli/ *n* any of various types of plant growing from a BULB(1), with large white or coloured flowers: ˈ*tiger lilies* ○ ˈ*water lilies.* **IDM** **gild the lily** ⇨ GILD.
■ **lily-livered** /ˈlɪli lɪvəd/ *adj* (*dated*) cowardly.
ˌ**lily of the** ˈ**valley** *n* [U,C] (*pl* **lilies of the valley**) a plant with small sweet-smelling white flowers shaped like bells.

limb /lɪm/ *n* **1** a leg, an arm or a wing: *aching/ trembling limbs* ○ *lose the use of your limbs.* **2** a large branch of a tree. **IDM** **life and limb** ⇨ LIFE. **out on a** ˈ**limb** (*infml*) alone; without supporters: *leave sb/ be/go out on a limb.* **tear sb limb from limb** ⇨ TEAR¹.
▶ **-limbed** /lɪmd/ (forming compound *adjs*) having limbs of the specified type: ˌ*long-*ˈ*limbed* ○ ˌ*loose-*ˈ*limbed* (ie not stiff).

limber /ˈlɪmbə(r)/ *v* to exercise in preparation for sport, etc: *do a few exercises to limber up before a race.*

limbo¹ /ˈlɪmbəʊ/ *n* **IDM** **in (a state of) limbo** in an unfinished or uncertain state: *The project must remain in limbo until the committee makes its decision.*

limbo² /ˈlɪmbəʊ/ *n* (*pl* **-os**) a West Indian dance in which the dancer bends backwards and passes under a bar that is gradually lowered.

lime¹ /laɪm/ (also ˈ**quicklime**) *n* [U] a white substance obtained by heating LIMESTONE. It is used in building materials and to help plants grow.
▶ **lime** *v* to treat soil or wood with lime: [Vn] *liming acid soils* ○ *limed oak.*

lime² /laɪm/ (also ˈ**lime-tree, linden**) *n* a tree with smooth leaves shaped like hearts, and sweet-smelling yellow flowers.

lime³ /laɪm/ *n* **1** [C] (**a**) a small round green fruit with an acid taste. (**b**) the tree on which this grows. **2** (also ˌ**lime-**ˈ**green**) [U] a pale green colour. **3** (also ˈ**lime-juice**) [U] the juice of limes used as a drink: *A lager and lime, please.*

limelight /ˈlaɪmlaɪt/ *n* [U] publicity or attention: *hog/seek/shun the limelight* ○ *be in/out of the limelight.*

limerick /ˈlɪmərɪk/ *n* a type of humorous poem with five lines, the first two rhyming (RHYME *v* 1) with the last.

limestone /ˈlaɪmstəʊn/ *n* [U] a type of white rock, containing CALCIUM, used as a building material and in making cement.

limit¹ /ˈlɪmɪt/ *n* [C] **1** a point or line beyond which sth does not extend; a boundary: *within the city limits* ○ *Fishing is forbidden within a twenty-mile limit of the coast.* ○ (*fig*) *He tried my patience to its limits.* **2** the greatest amount allowed or possible: *a* **speed limit** *of 70 mph* ○ *There's a limit to how much I'm prepared to spend.* ○ *You can't drive — you're* **over the limit** (ie you have drunk too much alcohol). **IDM** **be the limit** (*infml*) to be more than one can tolerate: *You really are the (absolute) limit!* ○ *Another rail strike — isn't that the limit!* ˌ**off** ˈ**limits** (*US*) = OUT OF BOUNDS (BOUNDS). **the sky's the limit** ⇨ SKY. **within** ˈ**limits** in a moderate way; up to a point: *I'm willing to help, within limits.*
▶ **limitless** *adj* without limit; very great: *limitless ambition/greed/wealth.*

limit² /ˈlɪmɪt/ *v* ~ **oneself/sb/sth (to sth)** to set a limit or limits to sb/sth; to restrict sb/sth: [Vnpr] *I shall limit myself to 1 500 calories per day* (ie in what I eat and drink). [Vn] *Your choice will be limited by the amount you have to spend.*
▶ **limited** *adj* restricted; few or small: *Only a limited number of places are available.* ○ *His intelligence is rather limited.* ˌ**limited e**ˈ**dition** *n* a fixed, usu small, number of copies of a book, picture, etc. ˌ**limited** ˈ**company** (also ˌ**limited lia**ˈ**bility company**) *n* (*Brit*) a business company whose members are responsible for its debts to a limited amount. See also LTD.

limiting *adj* putting limits on sth: *Lack of cash is a limiting factor.*

limitation /ˌlɪmɪˈteɪʃn/ *n* **1** [U] the action or process of limiting sb/sth or being limited: *resist any limitation of their powers.* See also DAMAGE LIMITATION. **2** [C] a condition, fact or circumstance that limits: *impose limitations on imports/expenditure.* **3** [C] a lack of ability: *I know my limitations* (ie know what I can and cannot achieve).

limo /ˈlɪməʊ/ *n* (*pl* **-os**) (*infml*) a LIMOUSINE.

limousine /ˈlɪməziːn, ˌlɪməˈziːn/ *n* a large expensive comfortable car, esp one with a glass screen separating the driver from the passengers.

limp¹ /lɪmp/ *adj* **1** not stiff or firm: *a book with limp covers* (ie flexible). **2** lacking strength or energy: *a limp handshake/gesture/response* ○ *The flowers looked limp in the heat.* ▶ **limply** *adv*.

limp² /lɪmp/ *v* **1** to walk with difficulty, esp when one foot or leg is hurt or stiff: [V] *That dog must be hurt — it's limping.* [Vp, Vpr] *The injured player limped slowly off (the field).* ⇨ note at SHUFFLE. **2** (of a ship, etc) to proceed with difficulty, esp after an accident: [Vpr] *The damaged vessel just managed to limp into harbour.*
▶ **limp** *n* [sing] a limping walk: *walk with a bad/ slight/pronounced limp.*

limpet /ˈlɪmpɪt/ *n* a small sea creature with a shell that sticks tightly to rocks: *cling/hold on (to sb/sth) like a limpet* (ie very strongly).

limpid /ˈlɪmpɪd/ *adj* (of liquids, etc) clear; transparent: *limpid eyes/water.*

linchpin /ˈlɪntʃpɪn/ *n* a person or thing that is the most important part of an organization, a plan, etc: *She was the linchpin of the team's success in the championship.*

linctus /ˈlɪŋktəs/ *n* [U] (*Brit*) a thick liquid medicine for easing sore throats and coughs.

linden /ˈlɪndən/ *n* = LIME².

line¹ /laɪn/ *n* **1** [C] (**a**) a long thin mark on the surface of sth: *a straight/wavy/dotted/diagonal line* ○ *Don't park on the double yellow lines* (ie those painted at the side of a road). ○ *Draw a line from A to B.* (**b**) a mark like a line on the skin: *a face covered in lines and wrinkles.* **2** [U] the use of lines in art:

Note the artist's delicate use of line and texture. **3 lines** [pl] a general shape; an outline: *the sleek lines of a racing car.* **4(a)** (usu **the line**) [C usu *sing*] (in sport) a mark on the ground to show the limits of a playing area, running track, etc: *be first across the (finishing) line* (ie in a race) ○ *If the ball crosses the line it's out.* **(b)** [C] a boundary: *cross the line* (ie border) *from Mexico into the USA.* See also COAST-LINE. **5** [C] a series of defensive positions where an army is fighting: *the front line* (ie that nearest to the enemy) ○ *behind enemy lines.* **6** [C] a row of people or things; a QUEUE: *a line of people waiting at the Post Office* ○ *stand/wait in line* ○ *get into line* ○ *long lines of houses.* **7** [C usu *sing*] a series of people following one another in time, esp generations of the same family: *a line of kings* ○ *in the male/female line* ○ *She comes from a long line of musicians.* **8(a)** [C] a row of words on a page of writing or in print: *page 5, line 13* ○ *Start each paragraph on a new line.* ○ *A sonnet is a poem with 14 lines.* **(b)** [C] (*infml*) a letter, esp a short one: *Write me a line if you've time.* **(c) lines** [pl] the words spoken by a particular actor: *Have you learnt your lines yet?* **(d) lines** [pl] (in some schools) a punishment in which a child is told to write out a certain sentence a number of times: *She gave me 50 lines for not doing my homework.* **9** [C] **(a)** a length of thread, rope, etc used for a particular purpose: *a 'fishing-line* ○ *Hang the clothes (out) on the line.* **(b)** (*esp nautical*) a rope: *throw sb a line.* **10** [C] a telephone or electricity wire or connection: *a bad* (eg noisy) *line* ○ *He was shouting down the line to someone.* ○ *I'm sorry, the line is engaged.* ○ *Strong winds have blown down many power lines.* See also HOT LINE, PARTY LINE, OFF-LINE, ON-LINE. **11** [C] **(a)** a single track of a railway: *The train was delayed because of ice on the line.* **(b)** a section of a railway system: *a 'branch line* ○ *the main 'line* ○ *a busy commuter line.* **12** [sing] a course of action, behaviour or thought: *the official line* ○ *a line of argument* ○ *Don't take that line with me.* ○ *The police are taking a firm/hard line on drug pushers.* **13** [sing] ~ (**of sth**) a direction or course: *be in the line of 'fire* (ie the direction in which guns, etc are fired) ○ *the line of at'tack.* See also FIRING-LINE. **14** [C] a company that provides transport for people or goods with a number of ships, aircraft, buses, etc: *a 'shipping line.* **15 the line** [sing] **(a)** (in the British army) the regular soldiers fighting on foot: *a line regiment.* **(b)** (in the US army) the regular fighting units of all kinds. **16** [sing] **(a)** an area of activity or business: *He's something in the 'banking line.* ○ *Her line is more selling than production.* ○ *That's not (much in) my line* (ie not one of my skills or interests). **(b)** a type of product: *stock a new line* (ie range of products) ○ *This shop has a nice line in winter coats.* See also ASSEMBLY LINE, PRODUCTION LINE. **IDM along the 'line** (*infml*) at some point during an activity or a process: *We obviously went wrong somewhere along the line.* ○ *He's created problems all* (ie at every stage) *along the line.* **along/on the same, etc 'lines** in the way specified: *produce another programme on the same lines* ○ *The novel develops along traditional lines.* **bring sb, come, fall, get, move, etc into 'line (with sb/sth)** to conform or make sb/sth conform: *He'll have to fall into line with the others.* **draw the line** ⇨ DRAW¹. **drop sb a line** ⇨ DROP². **the end of the line/road** ⇨ END¹. **get, have, etc one's 'lines crossed** (*infml*) to fail to communicate with or understand sb correctly. **give sb / get / have a line on sth** (*infml*) to give sb/get/ have information about sth. **hard lines** ⇨ HARD¹. **hold the 'line** keep a telephone connection open: *Hold the line while I see if she's here.* **hook, line and sinker** ⇨ HOOK¹. **in (a) 'line (with sth)** so as to form a straight line with sth: *Place your right toe in line with your left heel.* **in 'line for sth** likely to get sth: *She's in line for promotion.* **in the ˌline of 'duty**

while doing one's duty. **in 'line with sth** similar to sth; in agreement with sth: *It's in line with government policy.* **ˌlay it on the 'line** (*infml*) to state one's opinion plainly and openly: *Let me lay it on the line — I think you're cheating.* **(choose, follow, take, etc) the line of least reˈsistance** the easiest way of doing sth. **(put sth) on the 'line** (*infml*) at risk: *If this goes wrong your job's on the line.* **out of 'line (with sb/sth)** **1** not forming a straight line: *One of the soldiers is out of line.* **2** different from sth: *out of line with current thinking* ○ *Our prices are out of line with those of our competitors.* **read between the lines** ⇨ READ. **sign on the dotted line** ⇨ SIGN². **step out of line** ⇨ STEP¹. **toe the line** ⇨ TOE *v.*
■ **'line-drawing** *n* a drawing done with a pen, pencil, etc.
'line printer *n* (*computing*) a machine that prints very quickly, producing a complete line of print at a time.

line² /laɪn/ *v* **1** (esp passive) to mark sth with lines: [Vn] *lined paper* (ie with lines printed on it) [Vnpr] *a face lined with age and worry.* **2** to form a line along sth: [Vnpr] *a road lined with trees* [Vn] *Crowds of people lined the route of the procession.* **PHRV** ˌline 'up (for sth)** (*esp US*) to form a queue. **ˌline (sb) 'up** to form a line or make people form a line: *line up the suspects/get the suspects to line up.* **ˌline sth 'up** (*infml*) to arrange or organize sth: *I've got a lot lined up* (ie I'm very busy) *this week.* ○ *He's lined up a live band for the party.*
■ **'line-up** *n* **1** a line of people formed for inspection, etc: *a line-up of men in an identification parade.* **2** any set of people, items, etc arranged for a purpose: *Jones will be missing from the team line-up.* ○ *A horror movie completes this evening's TV line-up.*

line³ /laɪn/ *v* ~ **sth (with sth)** (esp passive) to cover the inside surface of sth with a layer of different material: [Vnpr] *an overcoat lined with silk* ○ *fur-lined gloves* ○ (*fig*) *The walls of the room were lined with books* [also Vn]. **IDM** **line one's (own)/sb's 'pocket(s)** to make or cause sb to make a lot of money, esp by taking advantage of a situation or by dishonest methods.

-line /-laɪn/ *comb form* (forming compound *ns*) a telephone service for the specified purpose or group of people: *helpline* ○ *Childline* ○ *Aidsline.*

lineage /'lɪniɪdʒ/ *n* [U] (*fml*) the families from which sb is descended: *have a distinguished and ancient lineage.*

lineal /'lɪniəl/ *adj* [usu attrib] (*fml*) descended directly from sb: *a lineal descendant of the company's founder.*

lineaments /'lɪniəmənts/ *n* [pl] (*fml*) the distinctive features of sth: *Her actions were marked with the lineaments of her character.*

linear /'lɪniə(r)/ *adj* **1** of or in lines: *a linear, chronological narrative.* **2** of length: *linear measurement* (eg metres, feet, inches). ⇨ App 2. ► **linearity** /ˌlɪniˈærəti/ *n* [U]. **linearly** *adv.*

linen /'lɪnɪn/ *n* [U] **1** cloth made of FLAX: *linen handkerchiefs.* **2** household things made of cloth such as sheets and tablecloths (TABLECLOTH): *a 'linen cupboard* ○ *'bed linen.* **IDM** **wash one's dirty linen in public** ⇨ WASH².

liner¹ /'laɪnə(r)/ *n* **1** a large passenger or cargo ship travelling on a regular route: *a luxury cruise liner* ○ *an ocean liner.* **2** = EYE-LINER. See also HARD-LINER, FREIGHTLINER.

liner² /'laɪnə(r)/ *n* (esp in compounds) a piece of material used to line sth: *'nappy/'bin/'drawer liners.*

linesman /'laɪnzmən/ *n* (*pl* **-men** /-mən/) an official who helps the REFEREE(1a) in certain games, eg football or tennis, esp in deciding whether or where a ball crosses one of the lines.

-ling /-lɪŋ/ *suff* **1** (with *ns* forming *ns*) little: *duckling.* **2** (with *vs* forming *ns*) (*usu derog*) a person or thing that is the object of the specified action: *hire-ling* ○ *nursling*.

linger /ˈlɪŋgə(r)/ *v* **1** to stay for a time, esp because one does not want to leave: [Vp, Vpr] *She was still lingering around (the theatre) long after the other fans had gone home.* [also V]. **2** to be slow; to spend a long time doing something: [Vpr] *linger (long) over one's meal* [V] *There's no time to linger — it'll soon be dark.* **3** to remain in existence although becoming weaker: [Vp] *Though desperately ill he could linger on* (ie not die) *for months.* [V, Vp] *The custom still lingers (on) in some parts of the country.* [V] *The smell of her perfume lingered in the empty house.*
▶ **lingering** *adj* [esp attrib] (**a**) long; slow to end: *a lingering illness* ○ *a last lingering look.* (**b**) remaining: *a few lingering doubts* ○ *a lingering sense of guilt.* **lingeringly** *adv.*

lingerie /ˈlænʒəri; US ˌlɑːndʒəˈreɪ/ *n* [U] (in shops, etc) women's clothing worn next to the skin: *lacy lingerie.*

lingo /ˈlɪŋgəʊ/ *n* (*pl* **-oes**) (*infml joc or derog*) (usu *sing*) **1** a foreign language: *He doesn't speak the lingo.* **2** expressions used by a particular group of people; JARGON: *technical lingo.*

lingua franca /ˌlɪŋgwə ˈfræŋkə/ *n* (*pl* **lingua francas**) (usu *sing*) a language used for communicating between the people of an area in which several languages are spoken: *English is becoming the lingua franca of the world.*

linguist /ˈlɪŋgwɪst/ *n* (**a**) a person who knows several foreign languages well: *She's an excellent linguist.* ○ *I'm afraid I'm no linguist* (ie I find foreign languages difficult). (**b**) a person who studies languages or linguistics.
▶ **linguistic** /lɪŋˈgwɪstɪk/ *adj* of or connected with language: *linguistic and cultural barriers* ○ *a child's innate linguistic ability.* **linguistically** *adv.*
▶ **linguistics** *n* [sing *v*] the scientific study of language or of particular languages. Compare PHILOLOGY, SEMANTICS.

liniment /ˈlɪnəmənt/ *n* [C, U] a liquid, esp one made with oil, for rubbing on the body to relieve pain.

lining /ˈlaɪnɪŋ/ *n* **1** [C, U] a layer of material used to cover the inside surface of sth: *a coat with a torn lining.* **2** [U] tissue covering the inner surface of a part of the body: *the stomach lining.* **IDM** **every cloud has a silver lining** ⇨ CLOUD[1].

link /lɪŋk/ *n* **1** ~ (**between A and B**) a person or thing that connects two or more others: *commercial/cultural/diplomatic links* ○ *a rail link* (ie service) *between the two towns* ○ *a telephone link* ○ *Police suspect there may be a link between the two murders.* See also MISSING LINK. **2** each ring or loop of a chain. ⇨ picture at CHAIN. See also CUFF-LINK.
▶ **link** *v* ~ **A to/with B; ~ A and B** (**together**); ~ **sth** (**up**) to make or suggest a connection between people or things: [Vn] *The crowd linked arms to form a barrier.* ○ *A new motorway links the two towns.* ○ *Television stations around the world are linked by satellite.* [Vnpr] *The newspapers have linked his name with hers* (ie implied that they are having an affair). ○ *Use of the spray has been linked to skin cancer.* [also Vnp]. **PHR V** **link 'up** (**with sb/sth**) to become joined or form a connection: *The two space-craft will link up (with each other) in orbit.* ○ *The school has linked up with the local history society on the project.*
■ **'link-up** *n* an act of joining two things or of being joined: *the link-up of two satellites in space.*

linkage /ˈlɪŋkɪdʒ/ *n* **1** [U, C] ~ (**between A and B**) the action of linking or being linked: *linkages between the capital and the regions.* **2** [C] a device, etc that links two or more things.

linkman /ˈlɪŋkmæn/ *n* (*pl* **-men** /-men/) a person talking on the radio or television between pro-

grammes, eg to tell people listening about future programmes.

links /lɪŋks/ *n* = GOLF-LINKS.

linnet /ˈlɪnɪt/ *n* a small brown and grey bird, common in Europe.

lino /ˈlaɪnəʊ/ *n* [U] (*Brit infml*) = LINOLEUM.

linoleum /lɪˈnəʊliəm/ (also *infml* **lino**) *n* [U] a strong cloth coated with a hard shiny substance, used as a floor covering.

linseed oil /ˌlɪnsiːd ˈɔɪl/ *n* [U] an oil made from FLAX seeds, used in paint, to protect wood, etc.

lint /lɪnt/ *n* [U] **1** a soft material used for covering wounds. **2** tiny pieces of fabric; FLUFF(1a).

lintel /ˈlɪntl/ *n* (*architecture*) a piece of wood or stone over a door or window, forming part of the frame. ⇨ picture[1].

lion /ˈlaɪən/ *n* (*fem* **lioness** /ˈlaɪənes/) **1** a large powerful animal of the cat family that eats meat and is found in parts of Africa and southern Asia. ⇨ picture at CAT. **2** (*dated*) a brave or famous person. **IDM** **beard the lion in his den** ⇨ BEARD[2]. **the 'lion's share (of sth)** (*Brit*) the largest or best part of sth when it is divided: *As usual, the lion's share of the budget is for defence.*
▶ **lionize, -ise** /-aɪz/ *v* to treat sb as a famous or important person: [Vn] *be lionized and then rejected by the press.*

lip /lɪp/ *n* **1** [C] either of the soft edges of the opening of the mouth: *the upper/lower/top/bottom lip* ○ *kiss sb on the lips* ○ *She had a cigarette between her lips.* ⇨ picture at HEAD[1]. ⇨ note at BODY. **2** [C] the edge of a hollow container or opening: *the lip of a cup/saucer/crater.* **3** [U] (*sl*) rude or IMPUDENT talk: *That's enough of your lip!* **IDM** **bite one's lip** ⇨ BITE[1]. **curl one's lip** ⇨ CURL[2]. **lick/smack one's 'lips** (*infml*) to show that one is eagerly waiting to eat or enjoy sth: *The children licked their lips as the cake was cut.* ○ *She's licking her lips at the thought of spending all that money.* **one's lips are 'sealed** one will not or must not discuss or reveal sth: *I'd like to tell you what I know but my lips are sealed.* **a stiff upper lip** ⇨ STIFF[1].
▶ **-lipped** (forming compound *adjs*) having lips of the specified kind: *ˌthin-'lipped* ○ *ˌtight-'lipped.*
■ **'lip-read** *v* (*pt, pp* **'lip-read** /-red/) [V, Vn] to understand what sb is saying by watching their lips move, not by hearing what they say. **'lip-reading** *n* [U].

'lip-service *n* **IDM** **give/pay 'lip-service to sth** to say that one approves of or supports sth while not doing so in practice: *politicians paying lip-service to environmental issues.*

lipstick /ˈlɪpstɪk/ *n* [C, U] a substance made into the shape of a small stick, used for colouring the lips: *wear lipstick.*

liquefy /ˈlɪkwɪfaɪ/ *v* (*pt, pp* **-fied**) to become or make sth liquid: [Vn] *liquefied gas* [also V].

liqueur /lɪˈkjʊə(r); US -ˈkɜːr/ *n* a strong, usu sweet, alcoholic spirit drunk in small quantities, esp after a meal: *relaxing over coffee and liqueurs.*

liquid /ˈlɪkwɪd/ *n* [C, U] a substance that flows freely, eg water, milk or oil: *She poured the dark brown liquid down the sink.* ○ *If the mixture is too dry, add more liquid.* See also WASHING-UP LIQUID.
▶ **liquid** *adj* [usu attrib] **1** in the form of a liquid; not a gas or a solid: *liquid food/fertiliser* ○ *liquid nitrogen* ○ (*joc*) *a liquid lunch* (ie beer, etc rather than food). **2** clear and clean, like water: *liquid blue eyes.* **3** (of sounds) clear, pure and flowing: *the liquid song of a blackbird.* **4** (*finance*) easily converted into cash: *liquid assets.*
■ **ˌliquid ˌcrystal dis'play** *n* (*abbr* **LCD**) a form of visual display in electronic equipment in which numbers, letters, etc become visible when an electrical current is passed through a special liquid.

liquidate /ˈlɪkwɪdeɪt/ *v* [Vn] **1** to close down a

business and use any money thus made to pay its debts. **2** to pay or settle a debt. **3** to dispose of sb/sth, esp by violent means: *He retained power by liquidating his opponents.*

▶ **liquidation** /ˌlɪkwɪˈdeɪʃn/ *n* [U] the action of liquidating sb/sth or of being liquidated: *The company has gone into liquidation.*
liquidator *n* a person responsible for liquidating a business.

liquidity /lɪˈkwɪdəti/ *n* [U] (*finance*) the state of owning things of value that can easily be changed into cash: *a lack of liquidity in smaller companies.*

liquidize, -ise /ˈlɪkwɪdaɪz/ *v* **1** [Vn] to crush vegetables, fruit, etc into a liquid. **2** to sell things in order to raise money: [Vn] *liquidize one's assets.*

▶ **liquidizer, -iser** (*Brit*) (also **blender**) *n* a device for liquidizing food.

liquor /ˈlɪkə(r)/ *n* [U] (**a**) (*esp US*) any distilled (DISTIL 1b) alcoholic drink; spirits (SPIRIT 9a): *hard liquor* ○ *a liquor store* ○ *She drinks wine and beer but no liquor.* (**b**) (*Brit*) any alcoholic drink: *intoxicating liquor.*

liquorice (also **licorice**) /ˈlɪkərɪs, -rɪʃ/ *n* [U] a black substance obtained from the root of a plant and used in medicine and sweets.

lira /ˈlɪərə/ *n* (*pl* **lire** /ˈlɪərə; *US* -reɪ/ or **liras**) (*abbr* **L**) the unit of money in Italy and Turkey.

lisp /lɪsp/ *n* (usu *sing*) a speech fault in which /s/ is pronounced as /θ/ and /z/ as /ð/: *speak with a (slight) lisp.*

▶ **lisp** *v* [V, V.speech] to speak or say sth with a lisp.

lissom (also **lissome**) /ˈlɪsəm/ *adj* thin and graceful in movement.

list¹ /lɪst/ *n* a series of written or printed names, items, figures, etc: *a shopping/wine/price list* ○ *make a list of things to do* ○ *put sb/sth on the list* ○ *take sb/sth off the list.* See also CIVIL LIST, DANGER LIST, HIT LIST, MAILING LIST, SHORT LIST, WAITING LIST.

▶ **list** *v* (**a**) to make a list of things: [Vn] *list one's priorities.* (**b**) to put things on a list: [Vnadv, Vnpr] *The books are listed alphabetically (by author).* (**c**) (*US*) to be offered for sale in a CATALOGUE(1), etc at a specified price: [Vpr] *This CD player lists at $139.*
ˌlisted ˈbuilding (*Brit*) (*US* **protected building**) *n* a building officially registered as being important because of its architecture or history and therefore protected from being altered or destroyed.
ˈlist price *n* [C usu *sing*] (*commerce*) the price at which goods are advertised for sale, eg in a CATALOGUE(1): *8% off the manufacturer's list price.* See also LISTING.

list² /lɪst/ *v* (of a ship) to lean to one side: [V, Vadv, Vpr] *The damaged vessel was listing (badly/to port).* ▶ **list** *n* [sing]: *develop a heavy list.*

listen /ˈlɪsn/ *v* **1** ~ (**to sb/sth**) to make an effort to hear sb/sth: [V] *We listened carefully but heard nothing.* ○ *Listen! What's that noise?* [Vpr] *You're not listening to me/to what I'm saying!* ⇨ note at FEEL¹. ~ (**to sb/sth**) to allow oneself to be persuaded by sb making a suggestion, giving advice, etc: [Vpr] *I never listen to* (ie believe) *what salesmen tell me.* ○ *I should never have listened to him.* ○ *Why won't you listen to reason?* [V] *I warned her not to go but she wouldn't listen.* PHRV ˈlisten (ˈout) for sth to be prepared to hear sth: *Please listen out for the phone while I'm in the garden.* ˌlisten ˈin (on/to sth) **1** to listen to a radio broadcast: *listen in to the BBC World Service.* **2** to hear sth that one is not meant to hear: *She loves listening in on other people's conversations.* ○ *The criminals did not know the police were listening in* (eg by recording their telephone calls).

▶ **listen** *n* (usu *sing*) (*infml*) an act of listening: *Have a listen and see if you like it.*
listener *n* (**a**) a person who listens: *a good listener* (ie sb who can be relied on to listen with attention

or sympathy). (**b**) a person listening to a radio programme.

listeria /lɪˈstɪəriə/ *n* [U] any of various types of bacteria that cause food poisoning (FOOD).

listing /ˈlɪstɪŋ/ *n* (**a**) a list or CATALOGUE(1): *a complete listing of all our models.* (**b**) a position on a list: *a telephone listing under Knight* ○ *a listing among the top ten billionaires* ○ (*commerce*) *a stock exchange listing* (ie for the trading of shares).

listless /ˈlɪstləs/ *adj* having no energy, liveliness or enthusiasm: *The illness left her feeling very low and listless.* ▶ **listlessly** *adv.* **listlessness** *n* [U].

lit *pt, pp* of LIGHT² 4.

litany /ˈlɪtəni/ *n* **1** a series of prayers to God for use in church services, spoken by a minister¹(3) with set responses by the people. **2** ~ (**of sth**) a long boring account of a series of events, reasons, etc: *a litany of complaints.*

lite /laɪt/ *adj US* = LIGHT³ 12.

liter (*US*) = LITRE.

literacy /ˈlɪtərəsi/ *n* [U] the ability to read and write: *basic/adult literacy.*

literal /ˈlɪtərəl/ *adj* **1** [esp attrib] (**a**) corresponding exactly to the original: *a literal transcript of a speech* ○ *a literal translation.* Compare FREE¹ 10. (**b**) concerned with the basic or usual meaning of a word or phrase: *His story is incredible in the literal sense of the word* (ie It is impossible to believe it). Compare FIGURATIVE, METAPHORICAL. **2** (*esp derog*) lacking imagination; plain and simple: *His interpretation of the music was rather too literal.*

▶ **literally** /ˈlɪtərəli/ *adv* **1** in a literal manner; exactly: *Idioms usually cannot be translated literally in another language.* ○ *When I tell someone to 'get lost' I don't expect to* ***be taken literally.*** **2** (*infml*) (used for emphasis or to intensify meaning) absolutely; completely: *I was literally bored to death!* ○ *She literally jumped out of her seat.*

literary /ˈlɪtərəri; *US* -reri/ *adj* of or concerned with literature: *literary criticism* ○ *a literary agent* (ie one acting for writers).

literate /ˈlɪtərət/ *adj* able to read and write: *Though nearly twenty he was barely literate.* Compare ILLITERATE, NUMERATE.

literati /ˌlɪtəˈrɑːti/ *n* [pl] (*fml*) educated and intelligent people who enjoy literature.

literature /ˈlɪtrətʃə(r), -tʃʊər/ *n* [U] **1** writings that are valued as works of art, esp fiction, drama and poetry (in contrast with technical books and newspapers, magazines, etc): *read/study French literature* ○ *a degree in American literature.* **2** ~ (**on sth**) writings on a particular subject: *I've read all the available literature on poultry-farming.* **3** (*infml*) printed material used eg to advertise or promote a product: *sales literature.*

-lith *comb form* (forming *n*s) of stone or rock: *monolith* ○ *megalith.* ▶ **-lithic** (forming *adj*s): *palaeolithic.*

lithe /laɪð/ *adj* moving or bending easily and gracefully (GRACEFUL): *lithe bodies.*

lithium /ˈlɪθiəm/ *n* [U] (*symb* **Li**) a chemical element. Lithium is a soft, very light, silver-white metal used in alloys (ALLOY¹) and in batteries. ⇨ App 7.

litho /ˈlaɪθəʊ/ *n* [U] (*infml*) lithography.

lithography /lɪˈθɒɡrəfi/ *n* [U] the process of printing from a smooth surface, eg a metal plate, treated so that ink sticks only to the design to be printed: *a book printed by offset lithography.*

▶ **lithograph** /ˈlɪθəɡrɑːf; *US* -ɡræf/ *n* a picture printed by lithography.
lithographic /ˌlɪθəˈɡræfɪk/ *adj.*

litigant /ˈlɪtɪɡənt/ *n* (*law*) a person involved in a claim or dispute brought before a lawcourt.

litigate /ˈlɪtɪɡeɪt/ *v* (*law*) (**a**) [V] to take a claim or dispute to a lawcourt. (**b**) [Vn] to contest a claim, etc before a lawcourt.

L

[V.speech] = verb + direct speech   [V.*that*] = verb + *that* clause   [V.*wh*] = verb + *who, how,* etc clause

▶ **litigation** /ˌlɪtɪˈgeɪʃn/ n (law) [U] the process of bringing or defending a claim, etc before a lawcourt: *run the risk of litigation* ○ *litigation costs/procedures.* **litigious** /lɪˈtɪdʒəs/ adj (*often derog*) quick to argue or to take a case to a lawcourt.

litmus /ˈlɪtməs/ n [U] a substance that turns red when in contact with an acid and blue when in contact with an ALKALI: *litmus paper* ○ (*fig*) *The outcome will be seen as a **litmus test** of government concern for conservation issues.*

litre (*US* **liter**) /ˈliːtə(r)/ n (*abbr* **l**) a unit of measurement for liquids in the metric system, equal to about 1.75 pints (PINT): *a litre bottle of wine/whisky.* ⇨ App 2.

litter /ˈlɪtə(r)/ n **1(a)** [U] small pieces of rubbish, eg paper, tins and bottles, left lying in a public place: *increased fines for dropping litter* ○ *a litter bin.* **(b)** [sing] ~ **of sth** a state of untidiness: *His room was a litter of books, clothes and dirty coffee cups.* **2** [U] **(a)** a dry substance put on a tray where pets, esp cats, can urinate (URINE), etc when indoors. **(b)** STRAW (1a), etc used for animals to lie on. **3** [CGp] all the young born to an animal at one time: *a litter of puppies.* **4** [C] (formerly) a structure consisting of a seat or bed enclosed by curtains that was carried on men's shoulders or by animals as a means of transport.

▶ **litter** v **(a)** to be scattered around a place so as to make it untidy: [Vn] *Newspapers littered the floor.* **(b)** ~ **sth (with sth)** (usu passive) to leave things around a place so as to make it untidy: [Vnpr] *His room is littered with old magazines.* [Vnp] *A number of unexploded shells were littered about.*

■ **'litter-lout** (*Brit*) (also *esp US* **'litterbug**) n (*infml derog*) a person who leaves litter in public places.

little¹ /ˈlɪtl/ adj [usu attrib] (The comparative and superlative forms, **littler** /ˈlɪtlə(r)/ and **littlest** /ˈlɪtlɪst/, are rare. It is more common to use *smaller* and *smallest*.) **1(a)** not big; small: *a little purse* ○ *a house with a little garden* ○ *a little group of tourists* ○ *She gave a little movement of impatience.* ○ *There's a little shop on the corner that sells bread.* **(b)** small when compared with others: *the little hand of the clock* ○ *'Which packet would you prefer?' 'I'll take the little one.'* ⇨ note at SMALL. **2** (used after eg *nice, pretty, sweet, nasty* to express the speaker's feelings of affection, pleasure, annoyance, etc): *a nice little room* ○ *a sweet little child* ○ *a funny little restaurant* ○ *What a nasty little man!* **3** (of distance or time) short: *It's only a little way now.* ○ *You may have to wait a little while.* **4** not important; not serious: *a little mistake/problem.* **5** young: *I had curly hair when I was little.* ○ *My little* (ie younger) *brother is 18.* **IDM** **it's no/little/small wonder** ⇨ WONDER. ▶ **littleness** n: *the littleness of man in the universe.*

■ **ˌlittle 'finger** (*US* also **pinkie**) n the smallest finger of the human hand. ⇨ picture at HAND¹. **IDM** **twist sb round one's little finger** ⇨ TWIST¹.

the **ˌlittle people** n [pl] small imaginary people with magic powers; fairies.

little² /ˈlɪtl/ indef det (used with uncountable ns) a small amount of sth; not enough: *There was little doubt in my mind.* ○ *I have very little time for reading.* ○ *We had little rain all summer.* ○ *There's little point in telling her now.* ⇨ note at MUCH¹.

▶ **little** indef pron (used as a n when preceded by *the*) a small amount: *I understood little of what he said.* ○ *We read a lot of poetry at school — I remember very little now.* ○ *The little that I have seen of his work is excellent.*

little adv not much; only slightly: *He is little known as an artist.* ○ *She left little more than an hour ago.* ○ *I slept very little last night.* ○ *Little does he know* (ie He does not know) *what trouble he's in.* **IDM** **ˌlittle by 'little** slowly; gradually: *Little by little the snow disappeared.* ○ *His English is improving little by*

little. **ˌlittle or 'nothing** hardly anything: *She said little or nothing about her experience.* **make little of sth 1** = MAKE LIGHT OF STH (LIGHT³). **2** to understand hardly anything of sth one is reading or hearing: *It's in Russian — I can make little ºof it.* Compare LESS.

little³ /ˈlɪtl/ **a little** indef det (used with uncountable ns) a small amount of sth; some but not much: *a little milk/sugar/tea* ○ *Could you give a little more attention to spelling?* ○ *I need a little help to move these books.* ○ *It caused **not a little*** (ie a great deal of) *confusion.*

▶ **a little** indef pron **1** a small amount of sth; some but not much **(a)** (referring back): *If you've got any spare milk, could you give me a little?* **(b)** (referring forward): *I've only read a little of the book so far.* **2** a short distance or time: *After a little he got up and left.* ○ *We left the car and walked for a little.*

a little (also **a little bit**) adv to some extent: *She seemed a little afraid of going inside.* ○ *These shoes are a little (bit) too big for me.* ○ *She was **not a little*** (ie very) *worried about the expense.*

littoral /ˈlɪtərəl/ n, adj (*fml*) (the part of a country that is) near the coast.

liturgy /ˈlɪtədʒi/ n a fixed form of public worship used in churches. ▶ **liturgical** /lɪˈtɜːdʒɪkl/ adj. **liturgically** /-ˈkli/ adv.

livable = LIVEABLE.

live¹ /laɪv/ adj [usu attrib] **1** having life; living: *live fish.* Compare DEAD. **2** (used esp to emphasize a surprising or unusual experience): *We saw **a real live** rattlesnake!* **3** glowing or burning: *live coals.* **4** still able to explode or light; ready for use: *several rounds of live ammunition* ○ *a live match.* **5** (of a wire, etc) connected to a source of electrical power: *That terminal is live.* **6** (of YOGHURT) still containing the bacteria needed to turn milk into YOGHURT. **7** of interest or importance at the present time: *Pollution is still very much a live issue.* **8(a)** (of a broadcast) transmitted while actually happening, not recorded previously: *live coverage of the World Cup.* **(b)** (of a musical performance or recording) given or made during a concert, not in a STUDIO(3): *a live recording made at Central Park in 1994.* **IDM** **a live 'wire** a person who is lively and full of energy.

▶ **live** adv broadcast, played or recorded at an actual performance: *This show is going out live.*

live² /lɪv/ v **1** to remain alive: [Vpr] *live to a great age* ○ *The doctors don't think he will live through the night.* [Vadv] *How long do elephants live?* [V.to inf] *She lived to see many changes.* **2** (*fml*) (less common than *be alive* in this sense) to have life; to be alive: [V] *When did Handel live?* **3** to make one's home: [Vadv] *Where do you live?* [Vpr] *live at home/in London/in an apartment.* **4** to spend one's life in a specified way: [V-n] *live and die a bachelor* [Vn] *live a peaceful life* [Vadv] *live honestly/happily/alone* ○ *He lives very well* (ie has money to enjoy the luxuries (LUXURY 2) of life). **5** (of abstract things) to remain in existence; to survive: [V, Vpr] *The memory will live (in my heart) for ever* (ie I will never forget it). **6** to enjoy life fully: [V] *I don't call that living.* ○ *I don't want to be stuck in an office all my life — I want to live!* **IDM** **be/live in each other's pockets** ⇨ POCKET. **how the other half lives** ⇨ HALF¹. **live and 'let live** (*saying*) to tolerate the opinions and behaviour of others so that they will also tolerate one's own. **live beyond/within one's 'means** to spend more/less than one earns or can afford. **live by one's 'wits** to earn money by clever and sometimes dishonest means. **live from ˌhand to 'mouth** to satisfy only one's present basic needs, esp for food: *a hand-to-mouth existence.* **live in hope (of sth / that ...)** to remain hopeful: *We live in hope that things will improve eventually.* **live in the 'past** to behave as though circumstances, values, etc have not changed from what they were previously: *She's*

---

just an old woman living in the past. **live in** ˈ**sin** (*dated or joc*) to live together as if married. **live it** ˈ**up** (*infml*) to live in a wild exciting way, usu spending a lot of money: *Now you've got more money you can afford to live it up a bit.* **live a** ˈ**lie** to suggest by one's way of living that one is different from how one really is. **live off sb's** ˈ**back** to exploit sb by using their resources, money, etc instead of one's own. **live off/on the fat of the** ˈ**land** to enjoy the best food, drink, accommodation, etc. **live off the** ˈ**land 1** to eat whatever suitable fruit, animals, etc one can find or kill: *an army forced to live off the land.* **2** to eat what one grows or produces oneself. **live** ˈ**rough** (*Brit*) to live without the usual facilities, esp out of doors: *He's a tramp and used to living rough.* **you/we live and** ˈ**learn** (used to express surprise at some new or unexpected information). **PHRV** ˈ**live by sth** to follow a particular belief, set of principles, etc: *That's a philosophy I could live by.* ˈ**live by doing sth** to earn one's living by doing sth. ˌ**live sth** ˈ**down** to live in such a way that a past embarrassment, failure, crime, etc is forgotten: *Beaten by the worst team in the league? They'll never live it down!* ˈ**live for sb/sth** to regard sb/sth as the aim or purpose of one's life: *She lives for her work.* ○ *After she died he had nothing to live for.* ˌ**live** ˈ**in/**ˈ**out** (of an employee) to live at or away from the place where one works: *They have a nanny living in.* ˈ**live off sb/sth** to receive what one needs to live from sb/sth because one has no money oneself: *live off one's parents/social security.* ˈ**live off sth** to eat only a particular type of food: *live off roots/junk food.* ˌ**live** ˈ**on** to continue to live or exist: *She lived on for many years after her husband died.* ○ *Mozart is dead but his music lives on.* ˈ**live on sth 1** to have sth as one's food: *live on (a diet of) fruit and vegetables* ○ *You can't live on 200 calories a day.* **2** to depend on sth for financial support: *live on one's salary/on £10 000 a year/on charity.* ˌ**live** ˈ**out sth 1** to do in reality what one thinks about, believes, etc: *live out one's dreams/fantasies.* **2** to spend the rest of one's life: *He lived out his days alone.* ˌ**live** ˈ**through sth** to experience sth and survive it: *He lived through both world wars.* ˈ**live together 1** to live in the same house. **2** to share a home and have a sexual relationship. ˌ**live** ˈ**up to sth** to behave as well as or be as good as expected: *He failed to live up to his principles/his reputation/his parents' expectations.* ˈ**live with sb** = LIVE TOGETHER. ˈ**live with sth** to accept or tolerate sth: *You'll have to learn to live with it, I'm afraid.*

liveable (also **livable**) /ˈlɪvəbl/ *adj* **1** (of life) worth living: *It's not the best kind of life, but it's liveable.* **2** (when predicative often followed by *in*) (of a house, etc) fit to live in: *safer and more liveable residential areas* ○ *The place looks liveable in.* **3** [pred] ~ **with** that can be dealt with: *The problem is paying the mortgage — everything else is liveable with.*

livelihood /ˈlaɪvlihʊd/ *n* (usu *sing*) a means of living; an income: *earn one's livelihood by teaching* ○ *deprive sb of his livelihood.*

livelong /ˈlɪvlɒŋ; *US* ˈlɪvlɔːŋ/ *adj* **IDM** **the livelong** ˈ**day** (*dated or rhet*) the whole length of the day.

lively /ˈlaɪvli/ *adj* (**-ier, -iest**) **1** (of a person) full of life and energy; active and enthusiastic: *She's a lively, fun-loving child.* ○ *I'm afraid I don't feel very lively today.* **2** (of a place, an event, etc) cheerful and full of interest or excitement: *a lively bar/party/ atmosphere.* **3** moving quickly from one subject to another: *a lively wit/mind/imagination* ○ *a lively*

debate/discussion. **4** (*Brit*) moving quickly or vigorously: *lively trading.* **5** strong and definite: *a lively shade of pink* ○ *show a lively interest in politics.* ▶ **liveliness** *n* [U].

liven /ˈlaɪvn/ *v* **PHRV** ˌ**liven (sb/sth)** ˈ**up** to become or make sb/sth become more lively: *Put on some music to liven things up.* ○ *The play began slowly but livened up after the interval.*

liver /ˈlɪvə(r)/ *n* **1** [C] a large organ in the body that produces BILE(1) and cleans the blood. ⇨ picture at DIGESTIVE SYSTEM. **2** [U, C] the liver of certain animals, used as food: *pig's liver* ○ *chicken livers.* ■ ˈ**liver sausage** (also *esp US* **liverwurst** /ˈlɪvəwɜːst/) *n* a SAUSAGE containing cooked and finely chopped liver, usu spread cold on bread.

livery /ˈlɪvəri/ *n* [U, C] **1** the colours, design, etc associated with a particular company or fleet of aircraft, cars, etc: *a bus painted in London Transport livery.* **2** a special uniform worn by servants: *coachmen wearing their distinctive livery.* ▶ **liveried** /ˈlɪvərid/ *adj* wearing livery: *a liveried chauffeur.* ■ ˈ**livery company** *n* any of the ancient London trade guilds (GUILD) with their own special uniforms. ˈ**livery stable** (also ˈ**livery yard**) *n* a place where horses are kept for their owners in return for payment, or where horses may be hired.

lives *pl* of LIFE.

livestock /ˈlaɪvstɒk/ *n* [U] the animals kept on a farm for use or profit, eg cattle or sheep.

livid /ˈlɪvɪd/ *adj* **1** [usu pred] (*infml*) extremely angry: *livid with rage* ○ *He'd be livid if he knew you were here.* **2** [usu attrib] of the colour of lead; bluish-grey: *a livid bruise.*

living[1] /ˈlɪvɪŋ/ *adj* **1** alive, esp now: *all living things* ○ *the finest living pianist* ○ *No man living could have done better.* **2** [attrib] used or practised; active: *living languages* (ie those still spoken) ○ *a living hope/faith/reality.* **IDM** **be living** ˈ**proof of sth / that ...** to show sth by the fact that one is alive or that sth exists: *He is living proof that engineers are not boring.* ○ *These figures are living proof of their incompetence.* **the very/living/spitting image** ⇨ IMAGE. **within/in** ˌ**living** ˈ**memory** at a time, or during the time, remembered by people still alive: *the coldest winter in living memory.* ▶ **the living** *n* [pl *v*] people who are now alive: *the living and the dead.* **IDM** **in the land of the living** ⇨ LAND[1]. ■ ˌ**living** ˈ**death** *n* [sing] an existence that is worse than being dead.

living[2] /ˈlɪvɪŋ/ *n* **1** [C usu *sing*] **(a)** a way of earning money to buy the things one needs in life: *earn one's living as a journalist/from writing* ○ **scrape a living** from part-time tutoring ○ *make a good/an adequate/a meagre living* ○ *What do you do for a living?* **2** [U] a manner or style of life: *plain/healthy living* ○ *Their standard of living is very low.* ○ *The cost of living seems to go up every day.* **3** [C] (*Brit*) a position in charge of a particular area that provides a church minister[1](3) with his income. ■ ˈ**living-room** (also *esp Brit* ˈ**sitting-room**) *n* a room in a private house for general use during the day. Compare DRAWING-ROOM. ˌ**living** ˈ**wage** *n* [sing] the lowest wage on which sb can afford a basic standard of living.

lizard

lizard /ˈlɪzəd/ *n* a reptile with a rough skin, four short legs and a long tail. ⇨ picture.

---

ll *pl* of L 2.

llama /'lɑːmə/ *n* a S American animal kept for its soft wool or for carrying loads.

lo /ləʊ/ *interj* (*arch or joc*) (used for calling attention to a surprising or amazing thing) look; see: *An extra skittle was added and, lo, tenpin bowling was born.* **IDM** **,lo and be'hold** (*esp joc or ironic*) (used to indicate surprise or annoyance): *As soon as we went out, lo and behold, it began to rain.*

load¹ /ləʊd/ *n* **1** [C] anything that is being carried or waiting to be carried, esp sth heavy: *a load of sand* ○ *porters carrying loads up the mountain.* **2** [C] (esp in compounds) the total number or amount that can be carried or put in sth, eg a vehicle: *a full load of washing* ○ *car-loads/bus-loads of tourists.* **3** [C] the amount of work to be done by a person, group or machine: *I've got a heavy workload/teaching load.* See also CASE-LOAD. **4** [C usu *sing*] a weight of responsibility, worry or grief: *a heavy load of guilt* ○ *The phone call* **took a load off my mind.** **5** the weight that is supported by a structure: *a load-bearing wall.* **6** an amount of electric current supplied by a DYNAMO(1), GENERATOR, etc. **7 loads** [pl] **~s (of sth)** (*infml*) plenty (of sth): *loads of friends/money/time* ○ *'Do you have any change?' 'Loads!'* **8 ~ of sth** [sing] a lot of sth, esp sth unpleasant or undesirable: *a load of rubbish!* ○ *He brought round a load of old junk.* **IDM** **get a load of sb/sth** (*infml esp US*) to look at sb/sth: *Get a load of that guy with the funny hat!*

load² /ləʊd/ *v* **1(a) ~ (up); ~ (up with sth); ~ sth/sb (up) (with sth); ~ sth (into/onto sth/sb)** to put a load in or on sth/sb: [Vn] *load the dishwasher* [Vnpr, Vnp] *load a lorry (up) with bricks/load bricks onto a lorry* [V, Vp] *We're still loading (up).* [also Vpr]. **(b)** to receive a load: [V] *The boat is still loading.* **2** (esp passive) to add weight to sth, eg using lead: [Vn] *a loaded dice* (ie one with weight added so that it will fall in a certain way, eg with the six on top). **3 ~ B (into A)** to put sth into a device so that it will operate: [Vn] *Be careful, that gun's loaded.* [Vnpr] *She loaded the camera with film/loaded a film into the camera.* [also V]. **4** (*computing*) to transfer data or a PROGRAM(1) into the memory of a computer: [Vn, Vnpr] *load software (from a disk)* [V] *Wait for the game to load.* **IDM** **load the 'dice (against sb)** (usu passive) to put sb at a disadvantage: *Having lost both his parents when he was a child he always felt that the dice were loaded against him.* **PHRV** **,load sb/sth 'down (with sth)** (esp passive) to make sb/sth carry a lot of heavy things: *She was loaded down with books.*

▶ **loaded** *adj* **1** full, and usu heavy: *loaded baskets.* **2** [pred] (*sl*) very rich. **3** [pred] **~ with sth** (*infml usu derog*) (of food) containing a lot of sth: *cakes loaded with calories.* **4** supporting the interests of sb: *The law is heavily loaded in favour of the consumer.* **5** having a hidden meaning or intention: *a loaded question* (ie one that is designed to make the person answering reveal more than he or she intended).

loaf¹ /ləʊf/ *n* (*pl* **loaves** /ləʊvz/) **1** [C] a mass of bread shaped and baked in one piece: *Two brown loaves and one large white, please.* ⇨ picture at BREAD. **2** [C,U] (esp in compounds) a quantity of other food formed in a solid piece: *a slice of meat loaf.* **IDM** **use one's loaf** ⇨ USE¹.

loaf² /ləʊf/ *v* (*infml*) to spend one's time not working, or not doing what one should be doing: [Vp, Vpr] *loaf around (the house all day)* [also V]. ▶ **loafer** *n* **1** a person who wastes her or his time. **2 Loafer** (*propr*) a flat leather shoe for casual wear.

loam /ləʊm/ *n* [U] a rich soil containing clay, sand and decayed vegetable matter. ▶ **loamy** *adj*.

loan /ləʊn/ *n* **1** [C] a thing that is lent, esp a sum of money: *I'm only asking for a loan — I'll pay you back.* ○ *a bank loan* (ie money lent by a bank). **2** [U] the action of lending sth or the state of being lent: (*fml*) *It's not my book — I've got it* **on loan** *from the library.* ○ *May I* **have the loan of** (ie borrow) *your bicycle?*

▶ **loan** *v* **~ sth (to sb)** (*esp US*) (*Brit fml*) to lend sth: [Vn] *a painting graciously loaned by Her Majesty the Queen* [Vnn] *I'll loan you my car for the weekend.* [also Vnpr].

loath (also **loth**) /ləʊθ/ *adj* [pred] **~ to do sth** (*fml*) unwilling; RELUCTANT: *I'm planning to sell the car soon so I'm loath to spend a lot of money on it.*

loathe /ləʊð/ *v* to feel great dislike or disgust for sb/ sth: [Vn] *loathe the smell of fried fish* [V.ing] *I loathe having to go to these conferences.*

▶ **loathing** *n* [U] **~ (for sb/sth)** great dislike or disgust: *eyes filled with loathing* ○ *feel intense loathing for sth/sth.*

loathsome /-səm/ *adj* causing great dislike or disgust: *a loathsome disease* ○ *What a loathsome creature he is!*

loaves *pl* of LOAF¹.

lob /lɒb/ *v* (**-bb-**) to hit or throw a ball or missile in a high curve through the air: [Vn] *lob a grenade* [Vnpr] *She lobbed the ball over her opponent's head.* [also V, Vnpl]. ▶ **lob** *n* a lobbed ball: *play a lob.*

lobby /'lɒbi/ *n* **1** [C] a usu large area inside the main entrance of a public building leading to other rooms: *the lobby of a hotel/theatre.* **2** [C] (in the British Parliament) a large hall open to the public and used for interviews with Members of Parliament. **3** [CGp] a group of people who try to influence politicians on a particular issue: *The anti-nuclear lobby is becoming stronger.*

▶ **lobby** *v* (*pt, pp* **lobbied**) **~ (sb) (for sth)** to try to persuade a politician to support or oppose changes to the law: [Vnpr] *lobby MPs/Congress for higher farm subsidies* [Vpr] *fishermen lobbying for higher quotas* [also V, Vn]. **lobbyist** /-ɪst/ *n* a person who lobbies.

lobe /ləʊb/ *n* **1** the soft lower part of the outer ear. ⇨ picture at HEAD¹. **2** a fairly round flat part of a body organ, esp the lungs or brain.

lobelia /ləʊ'biːliə/ *n* [C,U] a garden plant with small blue, red or white flowers.

lobotomy /ləʊ'bɒtəmi/ *n* [C,U] (*medical*) an operation involving the removal of part of the brain, esp as a way of treating severe mental disorders.

lobster /'lɒbstə(r)/ *n* **(a)** [C] a large SHELLFISH with eight legs and two long claws (CLAW 2). Its shell is black but turns bright red when it is boiled. ⇨ picture at SHELLFISH. **(b)** [U] its flesh as food. ■ **'lobster-pot** *n* a device for trapping lobsters, esp one like a basket.

local /'ləʊkl/ *adj* [esp attrib] **1** belonging or relating to a particular place or district: *a local farmer/doctor/shopkeeper* ○ *local knowledge* (ie detailed knowledge of an area that one gets esp by living there) ○ *She's a local girl* (ie from this area). ○ *have one's picture in the local paper* ○ *Following the national news we have the local news and weather.* **2** (esp medical) affecting a particular place; not general: *a local anaesthetic* (ie not one that puts you to sleep).

▶ **local** *n* **1** (usu *pl*) a person who lives in a particular place or district: *The locals tend to be suspicious of strangers.* **2** (*Brit infml*) a pub, esp near one's home: *pop into the local for a drink* ○ *Which is your local?* **locally** /-kəli/ *adv*: *She lives locally* (ie near).

■ **,local au'thority** *n* (*Brit*) a group of people responsible for the administration of a district, county, etc.

'local call *n* a telephone call to a nearby place, charged at a low rate.

'local 'colour *n* [U] typical features of the place and time in which a novel is set, used to make a story seem more real.

'local 'government *n* [U] the system of administration of a district, county, etc by elected representatives of the people who live there.

'local time *n* [U] the time in a given part of the world: *We reach Delhi at 1400 hours local time.*

locale /ləʊˈkɑːl; *US* -ˈkæl/ *n* a place where sth happens or which has particular people or events associated with it: *music conveying the atmosphere of its locale.*

locality /ləʊˈkæləti/ *n* **1** the position of sth: *trying to pinpoint the ship's exact locality.* **2** a district or area, esp one near or surrounding sth particular: *improve employment prospects for people living in the locality.*

localize, -ise /ˈləʊkəlaɪz/ *v* to restrict sth to a particular area or part; to make sth local: [Vn] *localized outbreaks of violence* ∘ *a localized infection in one part of the body.* ► **localization, -isation** /ˌləʊkəlaɪˈzeɪʃn; *US* -ləˈz-/ *n* [U].

locate /ləʊˈkeɪt; *US* ˈləʊkeɪt/ *v* (*fml*) **1** to discover the exact position or place of sb/sth: [Vn] *locate an electrical fault* ∘ *locate a town on a map* ∘ *I'm trying to locate Mr Smith. Do you know where he is?* **2** (usu passive) to establish sth in a place; to situate sth: [Vnpr] *The tourist office is located in the city centre.* [Vnadv] *The house is conveniently located, about a mile from the shopping centre.* **3** (*US*) to settle in a place; to establish oneself: [Vpr] *The company has located on the West Coast.* [also Vadv].

location /ləʊˈkeɪʃn/ *n* **1** [C] a place or position: *a suitable location for new houses* ∘ *a storage location in a computer.* **2** [C,U] an actual place or natural setting in which a film or part of a film is made: *The film was made entirely **on location** in Ireland* (ie not in a film STUDIO(2a)). **3** [U] the action of finding where sth/sb is: *responsible for the location of the missing yacht.*

loch /lɒk, lɒx/ *n* (*Scot*) (often in names) **1** a lake: *Loch Ness.* **2** a long narrow strip of sea almost surrounded by land. Compare LOUGH.

loci *pl* of LOCUS.

lock¹ /lɒk/ *n* **1** [C] a device for fastening a door, lid, etc, which requires a key to work it: *turn the key in the lock* ∘ *fit new locks on all outside doors.* See also COMBINATION LOCK. **2** [C] a section of a canal or river where the water level changes, enclosed by gates. Water can be let in or out slowly through the gates, thus raising or lowering boats in the lock from one level to the other: *take the boat through the lock.* **3** [U,sing] (*Brit*) the extent to which a vehicle's front wheels can be turned by use of the steering-wheel (STEER¹): **on full lock** (ie with the steering-wheel turned as far as it will go one way or the other) ∘ *My car has a good lock* (ie can turn within a short distance). **4** [U] the condition in which parts are fixed together so that movement is impossible: *The parts of the machine are in a state of lock.* **5** [C] (in wrestling (WRESTLE 1)) a way of holding an opponent's arm, leg, etc so that it cannot move: *have sb's arm in a lock.* IDM **lock, stock and 'barrel** including everything; completely: *They've moved abroad, lock, stock and barrel.* **(keep sth / put sth / be) under ,lock and 'key** locked up: *The criminals are now safely under lock and key.* ■ **'lock-keeper** *n* a person in charge of a canal or river lock¹(2).

lock² /lɒk/ *v* **1(a)** to fasten sth or make sth secure with a lock¹(1): [Vn] *lock a door/case/bicycle/house.* **(b)** to be able to be fastened or secured with a lock¹(1): [V] *This suitcase doesn't lock* (ie has no lock or has a lock that is broken). ▷ note at CLOSE⁴. **2** ~

(sth/sb) (in/into sth); ~ (sb/sth) (together) to become or make sb/sth become tightly fixed and unable to move: [V] *The brakes locked, causing the car to skid.* [Vpr, Vp] *The tent poles lock into each other/lock together.* [Vnpr] (*fig*) *The two sides are locked in a bitter struggle for power.* ∘ *They lay locked in each other's arms* (ie holding each other tightly). [also Vn]. PHRV **,lock sth a'way** (also **lock sth up**) to store sth in a safe place: *jewellery locked away in a safe.* **,lock 'onto sth** (of a missile, etc) to find and follow a target automatically. **,lock sb/ oneself 'out (of sth)/in** to prevent sb/oneself from entering or leaving by locking a door, etc: *At 9 pm the prisoners are locked in for the night.* ∘ *I've lost my key and I'm locked out!* ∘ *He locked himself out of the house.* **,lock (sth) 'up** to make a house, etc secure by locking the doors and windows: *Don't forget to lock up before leaving home.* **,lock sb 'up** to put sb in prison: *People like that should be locked up!* **,lock sth 'up 1** = LOCK STH AWAY. **2** to invest money so that it cannot easily be converted into cash: *All their capital is locked up in land.* ► **'lockable** *adj* that can be locked: *a lockable steering-wheel.* ■ **'lock-up** *n* **1** a prison, esp a small one where prisoners are kept for a short time. **2** (*Brit*) a usu small shop whose owner does not live in it. — *adj* [attrib] that can be locked: *a lock-up garage.*

lock³ /lɒk/ *n* **1** [C] a piece of hair that hangs or lies together: *He kept a lock of her hair as a memento.* **2** **locks** [pl] (*esp rhet or joc*) the hair of the head: *He gazed ruefully in the mirror at his greying locks.*

locker /ˈlɒkə(r)/ *n* **(a)** a small cupboard, esp one of several, where clothes can be kept, eg at a sports club: (*Brit*) ,left-'luggage lockers (ie for depositing bags, cases, etc in, eg at a railway station). **(b)** (*nautical*) a box or cupboard for storing clothes, etc in a ship. ■ **'locker-room** *n* (*esp US*) a room at a sports club, etc for changing in, with lockers for clothes, etc.

locket /ˈlɒkɪt/ *n* a small ornamental case, usu of gold or silver, that is worn on a chain round the neck and may hold sb's picture, a piece of hair, etc.

lockjaw /ˈlɒkdʒɔː/ *n* [U] (*infml*) a form of TETANUS in which the jaws become stiff and closed.

lockout /ˈlɒkaʊt/ *n* a refusal by an employer to let workers enter a factory, etc until they agree to certain conditions.

locksmith /ˈlɒksmɪθ/ *n* a person who makes and mends locks (LOCK¹ 1).

loco¹ /ˈləʊkəʊ/ *n* (*pl* **-os**) (*infml*) a railway engine: *a diesel/steam loco.*

loco² /ˈləʊkəʊ/ *adj* [pred] (*sl esp US*) mad.

locomotion /ˌləʊkəˈməʊʃn/ *n* [U] (*fml*) moving, or the ability to move, from place to place. ► **locomotive** /ˈləʊkəməʊtɪv/ *adj* of, having or causing locomotion: *locomotive power.* — *n* a railway engine: *electric/diesel/steam locomotives.*

locum /ˈləʊkəm/ *n* (also *fml* ,locum 'tenens /ˈtenenz/) *n* (*esp Brit*) a qualified person acting for a doctor or priest while they are away, eg on holiday.

locus /ˈləʊkəs/ *n* (*pl* **loci** /ˈləʊsaɪ/) (*fml or techn*) the exact place of sth: *The locus of power in the party has shifted.*

locust /ˈləʊkəst/ *n* a type of African and Asian insect that flies in huge groups, destroying all the plants and crops of a district.

locution /ləˈkjuːʃn/ *n* (*fml*) a particular way of expressing sth in words: *her strange locutions.*

lode /ləʊd/ *n* a line of metal ORE found among rocks, esp underground.

lodestar /ˈləʊdstɑː(r)/ *n* **(a)** a star that a ship, etc is steered by, esp the pole star (POLE²). **(b)** a principle that guides one's behaviour and actions.

L

lodestone /ˈləʊdstəʊn/ n a piece of metallic rock that acts as a MAGNET(1).

lodge¹ /lɒdʒ/ n **1** [C] a small house at the gates of a park or in the grounds of a large house, often occupied by a GATEKEEPER or other employee. **2** [C] a small country house for use in certain seasons: a ˈhunting/ˈfishing/ˈskiing lodge. **3** [C] a room at the main entrance to a block of flats, college, etc for the person responsible for checking people entering and leaving: the porter's lodge. **4 (a)** [CGp] the members of a branch of a society such as the Freemasons. **(b)** [C] the building where they meet: a masonic lodge. **5** the home of a BEAVER or an OTTER. **6** a Native American's tent.

lodge² /lɒdʒ/ v **1** ~ sth (with sb) (against sb) to present a statement, etc to the proper authorities for attention: [Vnpr] lodge a complaint with the police against one's neighbours [Vn] lodge an appeal/a protest/an objection. **2** ~ (sth) in sth to become or make sth fixed in sth: [Vpr, Vnpr] The bullet (was) lodged in his brain. **3** to provide sb with a place to sleep or live in for a time: [Vnpr] The refugees are being lodged in an old army camp. [also Vn]. **4** ~ (with sb / at ...) to live in sb's house, paying money for one's accommodation: [V] Where are you lodging? [Vpr] I'm lodging at Mrs Brown's (house)/with Mrs Brown. **5** ~ sth with sb / in sth to leave money, etc with sb/in sth for safety: [Vnpr] lodge valuables in the bank.
▸ **lodger** n a person who pays to live in (part of) sb's house: take (in) lodgers.

lodging /ˈlɒdʒɪŋ/ n **1** [U,C] temporary accommodation: full board and lodging (ie a room to stay in and all meals provided) ○ find a lodging for the night. **2** **lodgings** [pl] a room or rooms (not in a hotel) rented for living in: It's cheaper to live in lodgings than in a hotel.
■ **ˈlodging-house** n (dated) a house in which lodgings can be rented.

loft¹ /lɒft; US lɔːft/ n **1** a room or space directly under the roof of a house, used for storing things: a loft conversion (ie one that has been made into a room or rooms for living in). **2** a gallery or an upper level in a church or hall: the ˈorgan-loft. **3** a space under the roof of a stable, etc used for storing HAY, etc: a hayloft. **4** (US) an upper room or floor of a large shop, factory, etc, sometimes adapted for living in or for some other special purpose.

loft² /lɒft; US lɔːft/ v (esp sport) to hit, kick or throw a ball high up: [Vnpr] loft the ball over the goalkeeper [Vn] a lofted shot (eg in cricket or golf).
▸ **lofted** adj (of a golf club) shaped to hit the ball high.

lofty /ˈlɒfti; US ˈlɔːfti/ adj (-ier, -iest) **1** (fml) (not of people) very high and impressive: lofty ceilings/rooms. **2** [usu attrib] (approv) (of thoughts, aims, etc) noble; worthy of admiration: lofty ideals/principles. **3** (derog) too proud: treat sb with lofty disdain. ▸ **loftily** /-ɪli/ adv: 'I am well aware of that,' he declared loftily. **loftiness** n [U].

log¹ /lɒg; US lɔːg/ n **1(a)** a part of the trunk of a tree or of a large branch that has fallen or been cut down: birds nesting in a hollow log. **(b)** a short piece of this, esp one used in a fire: Put another log on the fire. ○ a log fire. See also YULE-LOG. **2** an official written record of events during a ship's voyage or an aircraft's flight. See also LOGBOOK 1. **IDM** as easy as falling off a log ⇨ EASY¹. sleep like a log ⇨ SLEEP².
▸ **log** v to cut down forest trees for their wood: [Vn] The whole area had been logged. **logging** n [U]: prevent the illegal logging of tropical forests ○ a logging camp.
■ **ˌlog ˈcabin** n a hut built of logs.
ˈlog-jam n a difficult situation in which little or no progress is being made: a log-jam of cases awaiting trial.

log² /lɒg; US lɔːg/ v (-gg-) **1** to enter information in an official written record or log¹(2): [Vn] The phone-call had been logged at the police station, but not followed up. **2** to achieve a certain distance or number of hours worked in a ship or plane: [Vn] The pilot had logged over 200 hours in the air. **PHR V** ˌlog ˈin/ˈon (computing) to go through the procedures to begin use of a computer system: You need a password to log in. ˌlog ˈoff/ˈout (computing) to go through the procedures to end use of a computer system.

log³ /lɒg; US lɔːg/ n (infml mathematics) a LOGARITHM: log tables.

-log (US) = -LOGUE.

loganberry /ˈləʊgənbəri; US -beri/ n a soft fruit, dark red when ripe, similar to a RASPBERRY(1).

logarithm /ˈlɒgərɪðm; US ˈlɔːg-/ n (mathematics) any of a series of numbers set out in lists which make it possible to work out problems by adding and subtracting (SUBTRACT) numbers instead of multiplying and dividing. ▸ **logarithmic** /ˌlɒgəˈrɪðmɪk; US ˌlɔːg-/ adj: a logarithmic function.

logbook /ˈlɒgbʊk/ n **1** a detailed record of things done, experienced, etc: keep a logbook. **2** a book that records official details of a motor vehicle.

loggerheads /ˈlɒgəhedz/ n **IDM** at loggerheads (with sb) disagreeing or quarrelling: The two nations are at loggerheads (with each other) over the failure of trade talks.

loggia /ˈləʊdʒə, ˈlɒdʒiə/ n a room or gallery with one or more open sides, esp one that forms part of a house and has one side open to the garden.

logic /ˈlɒdʒɪk/ n [U] **1** the science of thinking about or explaining the reasons for sth: apply logic to a problem/situation ○ study logic as a basis of philosophy. **2(a)** a particular method or system of reasoning: Aristotelian logic ○ mathematical logic. **(b)** a way of thinking or explaining sth, whether right or wrong: flawed logic ○ I fail to see the logic of his argument. **(c)** the ability to reason correctly: a test of one's logic. **3** (computing) a system or set of principles used in preparing a computer to perform a particular task.
▸ **logician** /ləˈdʒɪʃn/ n a person who is skilled in logic.

logical /ˈlɒdʒɪkl/ adj **1** following the rules of logic: a logical argument/conclusion. **2** (of an action, event, etc) natural, reasonable or sensible: the logical outcome ○ It seemed the only logical thing to do. **3** capable of thinking clearly and sensibly: a logical mind. Compare ILLOGICAL. ▸ **logically** /-kli/ adv: argue logically.

logistics /ləˈdʒɪstɪks/ n [sing or pl v] the organization of supplies and services (SERVICE 6) for any complex operation(4,6). ▸ **logistic, logistical** /ləˈdʒɪstɪkl/ adjs: Organizing famine relief presents huge logistical problems. **logistically** /-kli/ adv.

logo /ˈləʊgəʊ/ n (pl -os) a printed symbol designed for and used by a company or society as its special sign, eg in advertising.

-logue (US -log) comb form (forming ns) talk or speech: monologue ○ travelogue.

-logy comb form (forming ns) **1** a subject of study: sociology ○ theology ○ zoology. **2** a characteristic of speech or writing: trilogy ○ phraseology.
▸ **-logic(al)** comb form (forming adjs): pathological. **-logist** comb form (forming ns) a person skilled in a subject of study: biologist ○ geologist.

loin /lɔɪn/ n **1** [C, U] a piece of meat from the back or side of an animal, near the tail: some loin of pork. **2** **loins** [pl] **(a)** (euph) the sexual organs. **(b)** (dated) the lower part of the human body on both sides below the waist and above the legs. **IDM** **gird one's loins** ⇨ GIRD.

loincloth /ˈlɔɪnklɒθ/ *n* a piece of cloth worn around the body at the hips, sometimes as the only garment worn.

loiter /ˈlɔɪtə(r)/ *v* ~ **(about/around)** to stand in a public place, usu with no particular or obvious purpose: [Vpr] *loitering at street corners* [also V, Vp].

loll /lɒl/ *v* **1** ~ **(about/around)** to lie back, sit or stand in a lazy relaxed way, often while leaning against sth: [Vpr] *loll around the house* [also V, Vp]. **2** (of the head or limbs) to hang down loosely and without control: [Vpr] *The baby's head lolled against his shoulder.* [also V, Vp]. **PHRV** **loll out** (of the tongue) to hang loosely out of the mouth: *The dogs were panting, tongues lolling out.*

lollipop /ˈlɒlipɒp/ (*US also* **sucker**) *n* a large flat or round sweet on a small stick, held in the hand and sucked.
■ **lollipop man** *n* (*fem* **lollipop woman**, **lollipop lady**) (*Brit infml*) a person who carries a circular sign marked 'Stop! Children Crossing' as a warning to traffic to stop, allowing children to cross a busy road on their way to and from school.

lollop /ˈlɒləp/ *v* (*infml esp Brit*) to move with rather long awkward paces or jumps: [Vp, Vpr] *The dog was lolloping along (the road) behind him.* [also V].

lolly /ˈlɒli/ *n* (*Brit*) **1** [C] (*infml*) a LOLLIPOP. See also ICE LOLLY. **2** [U] (*sl*) money.

lone /ləʊn/ *adj* [attrib] (*esp rhet*) without companions; SOLITARY(1a): *a lone figure trudging through the snow* ○ *a lone parent* (ie one who has no husband, wife or partner to share the care of their child or children). Compare ALONE 1, LONELY 2. **IDM** **a lone wolf** a person who prefers to be, work, etc alone.
▶ **loner** *n* (*infml*) a person who avoids the company of others: *She's been a loner all her life.*

lonely /ˈləʊnli/ *adj* **1** sad because one has no friends or companions: *I live alone but I never feel lonely.* ○ *Living in a big city can be* (ie make one feel) *very lonely.* ○ *Hers is a lonely life.* **2** [attrib] without companions; SOLITARY(1a): *lonely hours spent at his desk* ○ *a lonely traveller.* **3** [attrib] (of places) far from places where people live; not often visited; remote: *a lonely stretch of road* ○ *Antarctica is the loneliest place on earth.* ⇨ note at ALONE. ▶ **loneliness** *n* [U]: *feelings of loneliness and isolation.*
■ **lonely hearts** *n* [pl] people who are seeking a friendship, esp one that will lead to marriage: *a lonely hearts column* (ie a section of a newspaper, etc containing messages from such people).

lonesome /ˈləʊnsəm/ *adj* (*esp US*) lonely: *I get lonesome when you're not here.* ⇨ note at ALONE.

long¹ /lɒŋ; *US* lɔːŋ/ *adj* (**-er** /-ŋgə(r)/; **-est** /-ŋgɪst/) **1** measuring a great or specified amount from end to end: *How long is the River Nile?* ○ *Your hair is longer than mine.* ○ *a long dress* (ie one reaching to the ankles) ○ *long-legged/-haired/-sleeved* ○ *The sleeves are a bit too long.* ○ *Is it a long way* (ie far) *to your house?* Compare SHORT¹ 1. ⇨ note at DIMENSION. **2** lasting or taking a great or specified amount of time: *a long book/film/list* (ie taking a lot of time to read/watch/deal with) ○ *He's been ill for a long time.* ○ *How long are the holidays?* ○ *They're six weeks long.* ⇨ note at LONG³. **3** seeming to last or take much more time than is the case: *ten long years.* **4** (of memory) able to remember events distant in time. **5** (*phonetics*) (of vowel sounds) taking relatively more time to make than a short vowel sound in the same position: *The vowel sound in 'caught' is long; in 'cot' it is short.* **IDM** **as long as/so long as your arm** (*infml*) very long: *There's a list of repairs as long as your arm.* **at the longest** not longer than the specified time; at the most: *He's away for short periods — a week at the longest.* **by a long way** by a great amount; easily: *He was the best performer by a long*

way. **cut a long story short** to get to the point of what one is saying quickly. **go far/a long way** ⇨ FAR¹. **go far/a long way towards sth/doing sth** ⇨ FAR¹. **go a long way 1** (of money, food, etc) to last a long time: *She makes a little money go a long way* (ie buys many things by careful spending). ○ *A little of this paint goes a long way* (ie covers a large area). **2** to be as much as one wants or can tolerate: *A little of his company goes a long way.* **have come a long way** to have made a lot of progress: *We've come a long way since those early days of the project.* **in the long/short run** ⇨ RUN². **in the long/short term** ⇨ TERM. **it's as broad as it's long** ⇨ BROAD¹. **(put on, have, wear, etc) a long face** a sad expression(1). **long haul** a long and difficult activity: *It's going to be a long haul to the final.* See also HAUL *n* 2. **a long shot** an attempt or a guess that is unlikely to succeed or to be correct but is worth a try: *It's a long shot, but it might just work.* **long in the tooth** (*Brit joc*) rather old: *He's getting a bit long in the tooth to be playing football.* **long time no see** (*infml*) (used as a greeting) it's a long time since we last met. **not by a long chalk/shot** not at all: *It's not over yet, (not) by a long chalk.* **take a long (cool/hard) look at sth** to consider a possibility, problem, etc carefully and without hurrying. **take the long view** to consider what is likely to happen, be relevant, etc over a long period of time, rather than looking only at the immediate situation.
■ **long-distance** *adj, adv* travelling or operating between distant places: *a long-distance commuter/phone call/runner* ○ *phone long-distance.*
long division *n* [U] (*mathematics*) the process of dividing one number by another with all the stages involved written down: *Can you do long division?*
long drink *n* a cool drink that is large in quantity, filling a tall glass, eg LEMONADE or beer. Compare SHORT² 2.
long johns *n* [pl] (*infml*) UNDERPANTS with long legs, sometimes extending to the ankles: *a warm pair of long johns.*
the long jump (*Brit*) (*US* the **broad jump**) *n* [sing] an ATHLETIC(2) contest of jumping as far forward as possible after running up to a mark: *competing in the long jump.*
long-life *adj* (*Brit*) (esp of milk and batteries) specially treated or made to remain fresh or last longer than the ordinary type.
long odds *n* [pl] (in betting) the remote possibility that sb/sth will win sth, so that if one bets on them one will win a relatively large amount of money. Compare SHORT ODDS.
long-range *adj* [attrib] (**a**) of or for a period of time far in the future: *a long-range weather forecast.* (**b**) (of vehicles or missiles) that can be used over great distances: *a long-range bomber.*
long-sighted (*also esp US* **far-sighted**) *adj* [usu pred] only able to see clearly what is at a distance: *She's long-sighted and needs glasses to read.* Compare SHORT-SIGHTED, FAR-SIGHTED 1.
long-term *adj* [usu attrib] of or for a long period of time: *a long-term aim/commitment.*
long-time *adj* [attrib] having lasted or existed for a long time: *a long-time friendship/admirer/ambition.*
long vacation *n* [C usu *sing*] (*Brit*) the long holiday during the summer when universities, etc are closed.
long wave *n* (*abbr* LW) a radio wave having a length of more than 1 000 metres: *a long-wave broadcast.*
long weekend *n* a WEEKEND that is made longer as a holiday by having an extra day off work at the beginning or the end of it: *have a long weekend in Amsterdam.*
long-winded *adj* (of talking or writing) going on for too long and therefore boring: *a long-winded speaker/speech/style.*

L

long² /lɒŋ; US lɔːŋ/ n **1** [U] a long time or interval: *This won't take long.* ∘ *Will you be away for long?* ∘ *I hope to write to you before long.* ⇨ note at LONG³. **2** [C] a long sound, eg a long signal in Morse Code or a long vowel or syllable in verse. **IDM** the ˌlong and (the) ˈshort of it all that needs to be said about it; the general effect or result of it.

long³ /lɒŋ; US lɔːŋ/ adv (-er /-ŋgə(r)/; -est /-ŋgɪst/) **1** for a long time: *Were you in Rome long?* ∘ *Stay as long as you like.* ∘ *long into the next century* ∘ *I won't be long* (ie will come, go, etc soon). ∘ *Long live the king!* ∘ *long-awaited/-delayed/-established/-forgotten* ∘ *long-dead/-overdue.* **2** at a time distant from a specified point of time: *long ago/before/after/since* ∘ *He died not long* (ie soon) *after (that).* ⇨ note at RECENT. **3** (with ns indicating duration) throughout the specified time: *wait all day long.* **IDM** as/so ˈlong as (used as a conj) **1** only if; on condition that: *As long as it doesn't rain we can play.* **2** (US) since; to the extent that. **be not long for this ˈworld** (rhet) to be likely to die soon. **no/any/much ˈlonger** after a certain point in time: *I can't wait any/much longer.* ∘ *He no longer lives here.* **so ˈlong** (infml) goodbye. ■ ˌlong-drawn-ˈout (also ˈlong-drawn) adj lasting a very long time, often too long; prolonged: *long-drawn-out negotiations/howls.* ˌlong-ˈlasting adj that can or does last for a long time: *long-lasting materials* ∘ *effects that are long-lasting.* ˌlong-ˈlived /-ˈlɪvd/ adj having a long life; lasting for a long time: *My family tend to be quite long-lived.* ˈlong-lost adj [attrib] not seen or heard of for a long time: *a long-lost friend.* ˈlong-running adj [attrib] (of a television series, a play, etc) that has been broadcast, performed, etc over a long period: *the longest-running show in London.* ˈlong-serving adj [attrib] having fulfilled or performed the specified position, duties, etc for a long time: *a long-serving MP.* ˌlong-ˈstanding adj [esp attrib] that has existed or lasted for a long time: *ˌlong-standing ˈgrievances.* ˈlong-stay adj [usu attrib] remaining, or intended for sb/sth to remain in, for a long time: *ˌlong-stay ˈpatients* ∘ *a ˌlong-stay ˈcar park.* ˌlong-ˈsuffering adj bearing problems, troubles, etc, esp those caused by another person, with patience: *I pity his ˌlong-suffering ˈwife.*

NOTE Both **long** and **a long time** are used as adverbial expressions of time. **Long** is not used in positive sentences unless it is modified by another adverb, eg *too* or *enough*: *I stayed out in the sun too long.* ∘ *Susan lived in India (for) a long time.* In questions you can use both expressions: *Have you been waiting long/a long time?*

In negative sentences there can be a difference in meaning. Compare: *I haven't been here for a long time* (ie It is a long time since the last time I was here) and *I haven't been here long* (ie I arrived here only a short time ago).

---

long⁴ /lɒŋ; US lɔːŋ/ v ~ for sth/~ (for sb) to do sth to want sth very much; to have a strong desire for sth or to do sth: [Vpr] *The children are longing for the summer.* [Vpr.to inf] *She longed for him to ask her out.* [V.to inf] *I'm longing to see you again.* ► **longing** /ˈlɒŋɪŋ; US ˈlɔːŋɪŋ/ n [C, U] ~ (for sb/sth) a strong desire: *a longing for home* ∘ *a deep sense of longing.* — adj [attrib] having or showing longing: *look at sb with longing eyes.* **longingly** adv: *The children gazed longingly at the toys in the window.*

long⁵ abbr longitude. Compare LAT.

longbow /ˈlɒŋbəʊ/ n (esp formerly) a bow drawn by hand, equal in length to the height of the ARCHER

and used to shoot arrows (ARROW). Compare CROSS-BOW.

longevity /lɒnˈdʒevəti/ n [U] (fml) long life: *a family noted for its longevity.*

longhand /ˈlɒŋhænd/ n [U] ordinary writing, not typed or written in SHORTHAND(1): *an essay written in longhand.* Compare SHORTHAND 1.

longitude /ˈlɒndʒɪtjuːd; US -tuːd/ n [U] (abbr long) the distance east or west of the Greenwich MERIDIAN, measured in degrees: *lines of longitude on a map.* ⇨ picture at GLOBE. Compare LATITUDE 1. ► **longitudinal** /ˌlɒndʒɪˈtjuːdɪnl; US -ˈtuːdnl/ adj **1** of longitude. **2** going downwards, not across: *longitudinal stripes* (eg on a flag). **longitudinally** /-nəli/ adv.

longways /ˈlɒŋweɪz; US ˈlɔːŋ-/ adv = LENGTHWISE.

loo /luː/ n (pl loos) (Brit infml euph) a toilet: *She's gone to the loo.* ∘ *Can I use your loo, please?* ⇨ note at TOILET.

loofah /ˈluːfə/ n [C] a long rough bath SPONGE(2a) made from the dried fruit of a tropical plant.

look¹ /lʊk/ v **1** ~ (at sb/sth) to turn one's eyes in a particular direction in order to see sb/sth: [V] *If you look carefully you can just see the church from here.* ∘ *'Has the milkman been yet?' 'I'll just look and see.'* ∘ *I was looking the other way when the goal was scored.* [V.to inf] *Look to see whether the road is clear before you cross.* [Vpr] *She looked at me and smiled.* ⇨ note. **2** ~ (for sb/sth) to search for or try to find sb/sth: [V] *I can't find my book — I've looked everywhere.* [Vpr] *Where have you been? We've been looking for you.* ∘ *Are you still looking for a job?* ∘ *Negotiators are looking for a peaceful settlement to the dispute.* **3** ~ (at sth) (esp imperative) to pay attention to sth; to observe sth: [Vpr] *Look at the time! We're going to be late.* [V] *Look, John! There's Gavin.* [V.wh] *Can't you look where you're going? You nearly knocked me over!* **4(a)** ~ to seem to be; to appear: [V-adj] *look healthy/ill/pale/puzzled/sad/tired* ∘ *That book looks interesting.* [V-n] *That looks an interesting book.* ∘ *You made me look a complete fool!* **(b)** ~ (to sb) like sb/sth; ~ (to sb) as if... / as though...** (usu not in the continuous tenses) to have the appearance of sb/sth; to suggest by appearance that...: [Vpr] *That photograph doesn't look like her at all.* ∘ *It looks like rain.* ∘ *It looks as if it's going to rain.* ∘ *You look as though you slept badly.* ⇨ note at FEEL¹. **5** to face a particular direction: [Vadv] *The house looks east.* [Vpr] *The hotel looks towards the sea.* **IDM** Most idioms containing **look** are at the entries for the nouns or adjectives in the idioms, eg **look one's age** ⇨ AGE¹; **look sharp** ⇨ SHARP. **be looking to do sth** to try to find ways of doing sth: *The government is looking to reduce inflation by a further two per cent this year.* **look ˈbad; not look ˈgood** to be considered bad behaviour or bad manners by accepted social standards: *It looks bad not going to your own brother's wedding.* **look ˈbad (for sb)** to indicate probable failure, trouble or disaster: *He's had another heart attack; things are looking bad for him, I'm afraid* (ie he is probably going to die). **look ˈgood** to be promising; to seem to be making satisfactory progress: *This year's sales figures are looking good.* **look ˈhere** (used to express protest or to ask sb to pay attention or listen to sth): *Now look here, it wasn't my fault that we missed the train.* **(not) look one'ˈself** (not) to have one's normal healthy appearance: *You're not looking yourself today* (eg You look tired or ill). **look sb ˌup and ˈdown** to examine sb in a careful or critical way. **never/not look ˈback** (infml) to be increasingly successful: *Her first novel was published three years ago and since then she hasn't looked back.* **not much to ˈlook at** (infml) not attractive in appearance: *The house isn't much to look at but it's quite spacious inside.* **to ˈlook at sb/sth** judging by the appearance

---

[V.to inf] = verb + to infinitive   [Vn.inf (no to)] = verb + noun + infinitive without to   [V.ing] = verb + -ing form

of sb/sth: *To look at him you'd never think he was a successful businessman.* **PHRV** ˌlook ¹after oneself/ sb **1** to make sure that one/sb is safe and well; to care for oneself/sb: *Who's going to look after the ¹children while you're away?* **2** to make sure that things happen to one's own or sb's advantage: *He's good at looking after himself/his own interests.* ˌlook ¹after sth to deal with or be responsible for sth: *I'm looking after his affairs while he's in hospital.*

ˌlook a¹head (to sth) to think about what is going to happen in the future: *Have you looked ahead to what you'll be doing in five years' time?*

¹look at sth **1** to examine sth closely: *Your ankle is badly swollen — I think the doctor ought to look at it.* ○ *I haven't had time to look at* (ie read) *the papers yet.* ○ *I'm taking my car to the garage to be looked at.* **2** to think about, consider or study sth: *The committee wouldn't even look at my proposal.* ○ *The implications of the new law will need to be looked at.* **3** to view or regard sth in a particular way: *The Americans look at life differently from the British.* ○ *Looked at from that point of view, his decision is easier to understand.*

ˌlook ¹back (on sth) to think about sth in one's past: *look back on one's childhood/career.*

ˌlook ¹down on sb/sth to consider sb/sth inferior to oneself; to regard sb/sth with contempt: *She looks down on people who've never been to university.*

¹look for sth to hope for sth; to expect sth: *We shall be looking for an improvement in your work this term.*

ˌlook ¹forward to sth / doing sth to be eager for sth that one expects to be enjoyable to happen: *look forward to one's retirement/the weekend/a trip to the theatre* ○ *We're really looking forward to seeing you again.*

ˌlook ¹in (on sb / at ...) to make a short visit to sb's house/a place: *The doctor will look in again this evening.* ○ *Why don't you look in (on me) next time you're in town?*

ˌlook ¹into sth to investigate or examine sth: *A working party has been set up to look into the problem.* ○ *His disappearance is being looked into by the police.*

ˌlook ¹on to watch sth without becoming involved in it oneself: *Passers-by simply looked on as he was attacked and robbed.* ¹look on sb/sth as sb/sth to regard or consider sb/sth to be sb/sth: *She's looked on as the leading authority on the subject.* ¹look on sb/sth with sth to regard sb/sth in the specified way: *I look on him/his behaviour with contempt.*

ˌlook ¹out (esp imperative) to be careful, esp in order to avoid danger: *Look out! There's a car coming.* ˌlook ¹out for sb/sth **1** to be aware of the possibility of sb coming or sth happening and try to avoid them/it: *You should look out for pickpockets.* ○ *Do look out for spelling mistakes in your work.* **2** to keep trying to find sth or meet sb: *look out for a bargain* ○ *I'll look out for you at the conference.* ˌlook sth ¹out (for sb/sth) to search for sth from among one's possessions: *I'll look out some old clothes for you to wear.*

ˌlook ¹over sth to inspect sth in order to assess its quality, extent, etc: *We must look over the house before we decide to rent it.* ˌlook sth ¹over to check sth to see what it consists of: *Here's today's post. I've looked it over and there's nothing very urgent.*

ˌlook ¹round/a¹round **1** to turn one's head in order to see sb/sth: *She looked round when she heard the noise.* **2** to examine various possibilities: *We're going to look round a little before deciding where to buy a house.* ˌlook ¹round sth to visit a place or building, eg as a tourist: *Shall we look round the cathedral this afternoon?*

ˌlook ¹through sb to ignore sb by pretending not to see them: *She just looked straight through me.* ¹look

¹through sth to examine or read sth, esp quickly: *She looked through her notes before the examination.*

¹look to sb for sth; ¹look to sb to do sth to rely on or expect sb to provide sth or do sth: *We are looking to you for help.* ○ *Many people are looking to the new council to stamp out corruption.* ¹look to sth to make sure that sth is adequate or in good condition: *The country must look to its defences.*

ˌlook ¹up (*infml*) (of business, sb's situation, etc) to become better; to improve: *Inflation is coming down and things are definitely looking up!* ˌlook ¹up (from sth) to raise one's eyes: *She looked up (from her book) as I entered the room.* ˌlook sb ¹up (*infml*) to visit or make contact with sb, esp after not having seen them for a long time: *Do look me up the next time you're in London.* ˌlook sth ¹up to search for sth in a dictionary or reference book: *Look up the time of the next train in the timetable.* ˌlook ¹up to sb to admire or respect sb: *She has always looked up to her father.*

▶ **look** *interj* (used to interrupt sb or make them listen to sth that one is saying): *Look, don't you think you're overreacting ?*

looker *n* (*infml approv sexist*) an attractive person, usu a woman: *She's a real looker!*

-looking (forming compound *adjs*) having the specified appearance: *a ˌstrange-looking ¹place* ○ *She's not ˌbad-¹looking* (ie She is quite attractive).

■ **look-alike** *n* (often used after a person's name) a person who has a very similar appearance to sb else: *a Madonna look-alike.*

¹look-in *n* **IDM** (not) give sb / get / have a ¹look-in (*Brit infml*) (not) to give sb/have a chance to take part or succeed in sth: *She talks so much that the rest of us never get a look-in.* ○ *They were forced to cut their prices in order to get a look-in.*

¹looking-glass *n* (*dated*) a mirror.

NOTE Compare **look**, **gaze**, **stare**, **peer** and **gawp**. **Look** means to direct your eyes towards a particular object: *Just look at this beautiful present.* ○ *I looked everywhere for a clean shirt this morning.* **Gaze** means to direct your eyes towards something for a long time but not really look at it because you are not concentrating your eyes on one particular thing: *He sat gazing out of the window instead of listening to the teacher.*

Stare suggests fixing your eyes on somebody or something very deliberately. It can be impolite to stare at somebody: *She stared at him in astonishment when he told her what had happened.* ○ *I noticed that one of the other passengers was staring at me.* **Peer** means to look very closely and suggests that it is difficult to see well: *He peered at me through thick glasses.* ○ *I opened the door and peered into the dark room.* **Gawp** is often used to show disapproval and means to look at someone or something in a boring way, especially with your mouth open: *Pete sits in his room gawping at the television all day.*

look² /lʊk/ *n* **1** [C usu *sing*] an act of looking at sth: *Have/Take a look at this letter.* **2** [C] a way of looking; an expression(1): *a look of pleasure/fear/ relief* ○ *I knew something was wrong — everyone was giving me funny looks* (ie looking at me in a strange way). **3** [C] a fashion; a style: *The long lean look is in this year.* ○ *a new-look hairstyle* ○ *They've given the shop a completely new look* (ie designed or decorated it differently). ○ *The house has a Mediterranean look about it.* **4** [C usu *sing*] an act of trying to find sth; a search: *I've had a good look (for it) but I can't find it anywhere.* **5** looks [pl] a person's appearance or features: *She has her father's good looks.* **IDM** by/ from the ¹look of sb/sth judging from the appearance of sb/sth: *It's going to rain today, by the look of it.* **give sb / get a dirty look** ⊳ DIRTY¹. **like the**

look/sound of sb/sth ⇨ LIKE[1]. **take a long look at sth** ⇨ LONG[1].

lookout /'lʊkaʊt/ n **1** [C] a place for watching from, eg in order to see sb, esp an enemy approaching: *a lookout tower*. **2** [C] a person who keeps watch for danger, trouble, etc: *We posted several lookouts.* **IDM** **be 'sb's lookout** (*Brit infml*) (used to refer to an action that is not considered sensible) to be sb's concern or responsibility: *If you want to waste your money, that's 'your lookout.* **be on the 'lookout for sb/sth; keep a 'lookout for sb/sth** (*infml*) = LOOK OUT FOR SB/STH: *We're always on the lookout for new investment opportunities.* ○ *Keep a sharp lookout for traffic.*

loom[1] /luːm/ n a machine for weaving cloth.

loom[2] /luːm/ v (**a**) to appear as a VAGUE(3), usu frightening or threatening, shape: [Vpr, Vp] *an enormous figure looming (up) out of the darkness/through the mist.* (**b**) to appear important or threatening and likely to happen soon: [V-adj] *The prospect of war loomed large in everyone's mind.* [V] *the looming threat of a strike.*

loony /'luːni/ adj (sl) crazy or odd(1); mad: *He does have some pretty loony ideas.*
▶ **loony** n a person who has odd ideas or behaves in an odd way.
■ **'loony-bin** n (*sl joc offensive*) a home or hospital for people with mental illness.

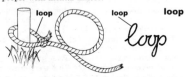

loop /luːp/ n **1(a)** a shape produced by a curve that bends right round and crosses itself: *handwriting with loops on many of the letters* ○ *The plane flew round in a wide loop.* ⇨ picture. (**b**) a length of rope, wire, etc in such a shape, usu fastened in a knot where it crosses itself: *make a loop of string to carry the package by.* ⇨ picture. **2** a complete circuit for electric current. **3** (*computing*) a set of instructions that is repeated again and again until a particular condition is satisfied. **4** an endless strip of film or tape that can be repeated continuously.
▶ **loop** v **1** to form or bend sth into a loop or loops: [Vpr, Vnpr] *strings of lanterns looping/looped between the branches of the trees* [Vn] *looped threads* [Vp] *Downstream the river loops round and flows north again.* **2** to fasten or join sth with a loop or loops: [Vnpr] *loop the rope round the post* [also Vn, Vnpl]. **IDM** **loop the 'loop** to fly or make an aircraft fly in a complete VERTICAL circle.

loophole /'luːphəʊl/ n a way of avoiding sth, esp because the words of a law, contract, etc are not clear or are badly chosen: *find/exploit a loophole in the rules* ○ *close/plug a legal loophole.*

loopy /'luːpi/ adj (sl) crazy: *It sounds a loopy idea to me.*

loose[1] /luːs/ adj (**-r, -st**) **1** detached or that can be detached from its place; not firmly fixed: *a loose tooth/thread/screw/floorboard* ○ *Be careful with that saucepan — the handle's loose.* ○ *The hook had come/worked loose (from the wall).* **2** freed from control; not tied up: *The cows had got out of the field and were (roaming) loose in the road.* ○ *Don't let that dog loose among the sheep.* ⇨ note. **3** not fastened together; not held or contained in or by sth: *loose change* (ie coins carried eg in a pocket) ○ *loose papers* ○ *nails sold loose by weight* (ie not in a packet) ○ *hair hanging loose.* **4** not organized strictly: *political parties forming a loose alliance.* **5** not exact; VAGUE(1b): *a loose translation/interpretation* ○ *loose thinking.* **6(a)** physically SLACK(1); not tense: *loose*

skin ○ *have loose bowels* (ie suffer from DIARRHOEA). (**b**) not tight or fitting closely: *loose clothing.* ⇨ note. Compare TIGHT 1,2. **7** not solid or closely packed together: *cloth with a loose weave* ○ *loose soil.* **8** [esp attrib] (*dated derog*) without moral discipline: *lead a loose and dissolute life.* **9** (of play in cricket) careless or not accurate: *some rather loose bowling.* **10** (*sport*) (of a ball) in play but not in any player's control. **IDM** **all hell broke/was let loose** ⇨ HELL. **at a loose 'end** (*US* also **at loose ends**) having nothing to do; not knowing what to do: *Come and see us if you're at a loose end.* See also LOOSE END. **break 'loose (from sb/sth)** to escape being confinement or restricted: *The dog had broken loose.* ○ *break loose from tradition.* **cut 'loose from sb/sth** to separate oneself from a group of people, their beliefs, etc: *He cut loose from his family.* **cut sth/sb/oneself 'loose (from sth)** to make sth/sb/oneself separate or free: *cut a boat loose* ○ *cut oneself loose from the past.* **have a loose 'tongue** to be in the habit of talking too freely. **have a screw loose** ⇨ SCREW n. **let sb 'loose on sth** to allow sb to do as they like with sth: *Don't let Bill loose on the garden — he'd pull up all the flowers.* **play fast and loose** ⇨ FAST[2].
▶ **loose-** (in compounds) loosely: *loose-fitting clothes.*
loosely adv in a loose manner: *hands loosely clasped* ○ *The play is loosely based on a local legend.*
looseness n [U].
■ **'loose box** n a compartment in a building or vehicle for a horse to move about freely in.
loose 'cover (*Brit*) (*US* **'slip cover**) n (usu pl) a cover for a chair, etc that can be removed.
loose 'end n (usu pl) a part of sth that has not been properly finished or explained: *tie up a few loose ends before leaving work* ○ *The play has too many loose ends.*
loose-'leaf adj [esp attrib] (of a book, etc) with pages that can be removed separately and replaced: *a loose-leaf 'file.*

NOTE The adjective **loose** has several meanings. One of these is 'not confined or tied up': *The dogs are loose in the garden.* Another meaning is 'not tight': *She wore a loose shirt and jeans.* The verb **loose** or **let loose** relates to the first sense and means 'to set free': *The guard loosed the dogs/let the dogs loose when he heard the burglar alarm.* The verb **loosen** (also **unloosen**) relates to the second sense and means 'to make something less tight': *I had to loosen my belt after that huge meal.* Note that the verb **lose** is not connected with **loose** or **loosen**. People often confuse the spelling of these words.

loose[2] /luːs/ v **1** to free sth; to allow sth to escape from control, etc: [Vn] *He loosed the brake.* [Vnpr] *anarchy loosed upon the world.* **2** to make sth loose; to UNTIE sth: [Vn] *She loosed her belt.* **3** ~ sth (**off**) (**at sb/sth**) to send off a ball, bullet, etc: [Vnpr] *He loosed off a shot at a rabbit.* [also Vn, Vnpl]. ⇨ note at LOOSE[1].

loose[3] /luːs/ n **IDM** (**be) on the 'loose** free, having escaped: *prisoners on the loose.*

loosen /'luːsn/ v to become or make sth loose or looser: [Vn] *Can you loosen the lid of this jar?* ○ *The treasury is unwilling to loosen its grip on monetary policy.* ○ *medicine to loosen a cough* (ie help to bring up the PHLEGM) [V] *This knot keeps loosening.* ⇨ note at LOOSE[1]. Compare TIGHTEN. **IDM** **loosen sb's 'tongue** to make sb talk freely: *The wine soon loosened his tongue.* **PHRV** **loosen (sth/sb) 'up** to relax or make sth/sb relax: *You should loosen up (your muscles) before playing any sport.* ○ *Don't be so nervous — loosen up a little.*

loot /luːt/ n [U] **1** goods, esp private property, taken from an enemy in war or stolen by thieves. **2** (*infml*) money; wealth.

▶ **loot** *v* to take goods from buildings, etc left without protection, eg after a violent event: [V] *soldiers killing and looting wherever they went* [Vn] *The mob looted many shops in the area.* Compare PILLAGE, PLUNDER. **looter** /ˈluːtə(r)/ *n*: *shops gutted by looters.*

lop /lɒp/ *v* (-pp-) [Vn] to cut branches, etc off a tree. **PHRV** ˌlop sth ˈoff (sth) to remove part of sth by cutting: *lop the heads off (flowers) with a stick* ○ *They managed to lop £2 million off their operating costs.*

lope /ləʊp/ *v* to run fairly fast with long relaxed steps: *The tiger loped off into the jungle.* ▶ **lope** *n* (usu *sing*): *move at a steady lope.*

lopsided /ˌlɒpˈsaɪdɪd/ *adj* with one side lower, smaller, etc than the other; not evenly balanced: *a ˌlopsided ˈgrin* ○ *have a lopsided view of things.*

loquacious /ləˈkweɪʃəs/ *adj* (*fml*) talking a lot; fond of talking. ▶ **loquacity** /ləˈkwæsəti/ *n* [U].

lord /lɔːd/ *n* **1** [C] a male ruler: *our sovereign lord the king.* **2** [sing] **(a)** **the Lord** God; Christ. **(b)** Our **Lord** Christ. **3(a)** [C] a nobleman: *She married a lord.* **(b) the Lords** [sing or pl *v*] = THE HOUSE OF LORDS: *The Lords is/are debating the issue.* Compare THE HOUSE OF COMMONS. See also LAW LORD. **4 Lord** (in Britain) **(a)** the title of certain high officials: *the Lords of the Treasury* ○ *the First Lord of the Admiralty* ○ *the Lord Mayor of London.* **(b)** used in front of the name of certain noblemen: *Lord Derby* (ie the title of the Earl of Derby). **(c) My Lord** a polite form of address to certain noblemen, judges and bishops. Compare LADY 4. **IDM** **drunk as a lord** ⇨ DRUNK. **good ˈLord; oh ˈLord** *interj* (expressing surprise, worry, etc): *Good Lord, it's you!* ○ *Oh Lord, what do we do now?* **ˈLord (ˈonly) knows** I don't know: *Lord knows what's happened to them.* **year of our Lord** ⇨ YEAR.

▶ **lord** *v* **PHRV** ˈlord it over sb (*derog*) to treat sb as inferior: *He likes to lord it over the junior staff.* ■ **the ˌLord's ˈPrayer** *n* [sing] the prayer taught by Christ to his followers, beginning 'Our Father'.

lordly /ˈlɔːdli/ *adj* (-ier, -iest) **1** (*often derog*) behaving in a proud and superior way: *dismiss people with a lordly gesture.* **2** suitable for a lord; magnificent: *a lordly mansion.*

lordship /ˈlɔːdʃɪp/ *n* (usu **Lordship**) (in Britain) a title used in speaking to or about a man with the rank or title of lord(3a,4a): *His/Your Lordship* ○ *their Lordships.*

lore /lɔː(r)/ *n* [U] the knowledge and traditions relating to sth or possessed by a particular group of people: *ˈbird lore* ○ *ˈfolklore* ○ *ˈgypsy lore* ○ *ˈCeltic lore.*

lorgnette /lɔːˈnjet/ *n* a pair of glasses held to the eyes on a long handle. Lorgnettes are rarely used now.

lorry

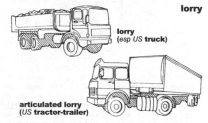

lorry (*esp US* **truck**)

articulated lorry (*US* **tractor-trailer**)

lorry /ˈlɒri; *US* ˈlɔːri/ (*esp Brit*) (also *esp US* **truck**) *n* a large strong motor vehicle for transporting goods, soldiers, etc by road: *heavy goods lorries* ○ *a lorry driver.* ⇨ picture.

lose /luːz/ *v* (*pt, pp* **lost** /lɒst; *US* lɔːst/) **1** to become unable to find sth/sb: [Vn] *I've lost my keys.* ○ *The* tickets seem to be lost/to have got lost. ○ *She lost her husband in the crowd.* **2** to have sth/sb taken away from one by accident, old age, death, etc: [Vn] *lose a leg in a car crash* ○ *lose one's hair/teeth/good looks* (ie as a result of getting old) ○ *He's lost his job.* ○ *He lost both his sons* (ie They were killed) *in the war.* ○ *She's just lost her husband* (ie He has died recently). ○ *The ship was lost at sea.* ○ *Many people lost their lives* (ie were killed). **3** to have or keep sth no longer: *lose one's confidence/composure/courage* ○ *lose one's nerve* (ie the courage to do sth) ○ *lose interest in sth/sb* (ie stop being interested in or attracted to sth/sb) ○ *lose one's balance/ equilibrium* ○ *He's lost ten pounds in weight.* ○ *I warn you, I'm rapidly losing my patience.* ○ *The train was losing speed.* **4(a)** to fail to obtain, hear or understand sth: [Vn] *His words were lost* (ie could not be heard) *in the applause.* **(b)** (*infml*) to be no longer understood by sb: [Vn] *I'm afraid you've lost me there.* **5** (*infml*) to escape from sb/sth: [Vn] *We managed to lose our pursuers in the darkness.* **6(a)** ~ **(sth) (to sb)** to be defeated; to fail to win a contest, a court case, an argument, etc: [Vn] *lose a game/a match/a race/an election* [V] *They only lost once all season.* [Vpr] *We lost to a stronger side.* [also Vnpr]. **(b)** ~ **sth (to sth/sb)** to have sth taken away by sth/ sb: [Vn, Vnpr] *Railways have lost a lot of their passenger business (to the bus companies).* **7** to have to give up sth; to fail to keep sth: [Vn] *lose one's no-claim bonus* (eg by making an insurance claim following an accident) ○ *You will lose your deposit if you cancel the holiday.* ○ *Sit down or you'll lose your seat.* **8** to waste time or an opportunity: [Vn] *We lost twenty minutes changing a tyre.* ○ *Hurry — there's no time to lose!* **9(a)** ~ **(sth) (on sth / by doing sth)** to become poorer or worse: [Vn] *The business is losing money.* [Vnpr, Vpr] *We lost (a lot) on that deal.* ○ *Poetry always loses (something) in translation.* [Vnpr] *You will lose nothing/You have nothing to lose by telling the truth.* [also V]. **(b)** to cause sb to have sth no longer: [Vnn] *His carelessness lost him the job.* **10** (of a watch or clock) to go too slowly or to become slow by a certain amount of time: [V] *A good watch neither gains nor loses.* [Vn] *This clock loses two minutes* (ie becomes two minutes behind the correct time) *a day.* **IDM** **give/lose ground** ⇨ GROUND[1]. **keep/lose one's cool** ⇨ COOL[1]. **keep/lose one's temper** ⇨ TEMPER[1]. **keep/lose track of sb/sth** ⇨ TRACK. **lose one's ˈbearings** to become lost or confused. **lose count (of sth)** to start remembering or recording a series of numbers or amounts but then forget the total before one has finished: *I lost count and had to start again.* ○ *She had lost count of the number of films they had seen together.* **lose ˈface** to suffer loss of respect and be made to feel HUMBLE(1). **lose one's ˈgrip (on sth)** to become unable to understand or control a situation, etc: *Sometimes I feel I'm losing my grip.* **lose one's ˈhead** to become unable to act in a calm or sensible way. **lose ˈheart** to stop wanting sth or wanting to do sth because of a lack of confidence. **lose one's ˈheart (to sb/sth)** to fall in love. **lose one's ˈmarbles** (*sl*) to stop behaving in a sensible way; to go crazy. **lose one's ˈmind** to become mentally ill. **lose ˈsight of sb/sth 1** to become no longer able to see sb/sth: *lose sight of land.* **2** to fail to consider sth; to forget sth: *We must not lose sight of our original aim.* **lose the ˈthread (of sth)** to be unable to follow an argument, a story, etc. **lose ˈtouch (with sb/sth)** to become no longer in contact with sb/sth: *I've lost touch with all my old friends.* ○ *Let's not lose touch with reality.* **lose one's ˈway 1** to become lost: *We lost our way in the dark.* **2** to forget the purpose or reason for sth. **a losing ˈbattle** a struggle/contest in which defeat seems certain: *It's a losing battle trying to get the work finished on time.* ○ *Researchers are fighting a losing battle against* the disease. **not lose ˈsleep / lose no ˈsleep over sth** not to worry too much about sth: *It's not worth losing sleep over.* **win or lose** ⇨ WIN. **PHR V** **ˈlose oneself in sth** to become totally absorbed in sth: *I soon lost myself in the excitement of the drama.* **ˌlose ˈout (on sth)** *(infml)* to miss an opportunity; to suffer loss: *lose out on promotion.* **ˌlose ˈout to sb/ sth** *(infml)* to be overcome or replaced by sb/sth: *small shops losing out to supermarkets.* ⇨ note at LOOSE[1].

▶ **loser** *n* a person who loses or is defeated, esp habitually: *a good/bad loser* (ie sb who accepts defeat well/badly) ∘ *a born loser* (ie sb who regularly fails in life).

loss /lɒs; *US* lɔːs/ *n* **1** [U, C usu *sing*] the action or an instance of losing or failing to keep sth/sb; the state of no longer having sth/sb: *loss of blood/sleep/ self-control/revenue* ∘ *without (any) loss of time* ∘ *experience a temporary loss of power* ∘ *The loss of this contract would be very serious.* ∘ *The famine caused widespread loss of life* (ie many deaths). ∘ *The loss* (ie death) *of his wife was a great blow to him.* **2** [C] **(a)** a person or thing lost: *announce 400 job losses* ∘ *The enemy suffered heavy losses* (ie many men killed or much equipment destroyed). **(b)** the money lost in business activity: *sell sth at a loss* (ie for less than it cost) ∘ *We made a loss on the deal.* ∘ *The company has announced heavy losses in the last year.* **3** [sing] the suffering or disadvantage caused by losing sb/ sth: *Her departure is a great loss to the orchestra.* See also DEAD LOSS. **IDM** **at a ˈloss** not knowing what to do or say: *It left him at a complete loss (for words).* ∘ *I'm at a loss what to do next.* **cut one's ˈlosses** to abandon a scheme that is not profitable before one loses too much.

■ **ˈloss-making** *adj* making a financial loss: *loss-making rural bus services.*

lost[1] *pt, pp* of LOSE.

lost[2] /lɒst; *US* lɔːst/ *adj* **1** unable to find one's way; not knowing where one is: *I realized I was completely lost.* ∘ *I got rather lost trying to find the station.* **2** [usu pred] confused or in difficulties: *We would be totally lost without your help.* ∘ *They spoke so quickly I just got lost.* **3** that cannot be found or recovered: *recalling her lost youth* ∘ *lost tribes* ∘ *The art of good conversation seems lost.* **IDM** **ˌall is not ˈlost** there is still some hope of success or recovery. **be lost for ˈwords** to be so surprised, confused, etc that one cannot think what to say. **be ˈlost in sth** to be absorbed in sth: *lost in thought/wonder/ admiration.* **be ˈlost on sb** to fail to influence or be noticed by sb: *His subtle humour was completely lost on his audience.* **be lost to sth** to be no longer aware of or influenced by sth: *When he listens to music he's lost to the world.* **get ˈlost** *(sl)* (often imperative) to go away: *Tell him to get lost.* **give sb up for ˈlost** to stop expecting that sb will be found alive. **make up for lost ˈtime** to do sth faster or more often in order to compensate for not having done it quickly or often enough before: *He didn't have a girlfriend till he was 20, but now he's making up for lost time* (ie he has had many since then). **there's little/no love lost between A and B** ⇨ LOVE[1].

■ **ˌlost ˈcause** *n* a project, ideal, etc that has failed or is certain to fail.

ˌlost ˈproperty *n* [U] *(Brit)* possessions recovered from public places and waiting to be claimed by their owners: *a ˌlost-ˈproperty office.*

lot[1] /lɒt/ *n* **the ˈlot, the whole ˈlot** [Gp] *(infml)* the whole number or amount of people or things: *That's the lot!* ∘ *Get out of my house, the (whole) lot of you!* ∘ *She expects a good salary, a company car, first-class air travel — the lot.*

lot[2] /lɒt/ **a lot, lots** *pron* *(infml)* a large number or

amount: *Have some more cake, there's lots left.* ∘ *'How many paper clips do you need?' 'A lot/Lots.'*

■ **a lot of** *det* (also *infml* **lots of**) a large number or amount of sth/sb: *What a lot of presents!* ∘ *I haven't got a lot of time.* ∘ *black coffee with lots of sugar* ∘ *A lot of people were killed in the riots.* ∘ *I saw her quite a lot of her* (ie I saw her quite often) *during the holidays.* ⇨ note at MUCH[1].

lot[3] /lɒt/ *adv* *(infml)* **1** a lot, lots (used with *adjs* and *advs*) much: *I'm feeling a lot better today.* ∘ *I eat lots less than I used to.* **2** a lot (used with *vs*) **(a)** a great amount: *I care about you a lot.* ∘ *Thanks a lot for your help.* **(b)** often: *I play tennis quite a lot in the summer.* See also A FAT LOT.

lot[4] /lɒt/ *n* **1** [CGp] *(esp Brit)* a particular group, collection or set of people or things: *The first lot of visitors has/have arrived.* ∘ *I have several lots of essays to mark this weekend.* ∘ *(infml)* *What do you lot want?* Compare BATCH 1. **2** [C] an item or a number of items sold, esp at an AUCTION sale: *Lot 46: six chairs.* **3** [C] an area of land used for a particular purpose: *a ˈparking lot* ∘ *a vacant ˈlot* (ie a building site). **4** [sing] a person's fate, luck or share of sth: *Her lot has been a hard one.* ∘ *(infml)* *That's your ˈlot* (ie That is all you are getting). **IDM** **a bad ˈlot** a person who is considered dishonest and not reliable: *His brother is a thoroughly bad lot.* **by ˈlot** using a method of selecting sb to do sth. Typically this involves everyone taking a piece of paper from a container and the one whose paper has a special mark being chosen. **cast/draw ˈlots (for sth / to do sth)** to make a selection by lot: *They drew lots for the right to go first.* **fall to sb's ˈlot to do sth** *(fml)* to become sb's task or responsibility. **throw in one's ˈlot with sb** to decide to join sb and share all their successes and problems.

loth = LOATH.

lotion /ˈləʊʃn/ *n* [C, U] a liquid medicine or beauty product for use on the skin: *soothing lotions for insect bites* ∘ *body/suntan/moisturizing lotion.*

lottery /ˈlɒtəri/ *n* **1** [C] a way of raising money by selling numbered tickets and giving prizes to the holders of numbers selected by chance: *a ˈlottery ticket.* Compare DRAW[2] 1b, RAFFLE. **2** [sing] *(often derog)* a thing whose success, outcome, etc is determined by luck: *Some people think that marriage is a lottery.*

lotto /ˈlɒtəʊ/ *n* [U] a game of chance similar to BINGO but with the numbers drawn from a container by the players instead of being called.

lotus /ˈləʊtəs/ *n* (*pl* **lotuses**) **1** a tropical plant with white or pink flowers growing on the surface of lakes, etc. **2** (in ancient Greek stories) a fruit that was said to make those who eat it feel happy, comfortable and lazy.

■ **ˈlotus position** *n* [sing] a way of sitting with one's legs crossed, used esp in YOGA(b).

loud /laʊd/ *adj* (**-er, -est**) **1** producing much noise; easily heard: *loud voices/cheers/applause* ∘ *That music's too loud — please turn it down.* ∘ *The message is coming through loud and clear.* ∘ *He has been loud in his praise of/support for the prime minister.* **2** *(derog)* (of colours, people or behaviour) forcing people to notice them/it: *That dress is a bit loud* (ie too bright), *isn't it?* ∘ *His manner is too loud.*

▶ **loud** *adv* (**-er, -est**) (used esp with *talk, sing, laugh*, etc) in a loud manner: *Speak louder — I can't hear you.* ∘ *Their baby screamed loudest of all.* **IDM** **actions speak louder than words** ⇨ ACTION. **for crying out loud** ⇨ CRY[1]. **ˌout ˈloud** aloud in a voice that can be heard: *Read the letter out loud, not to yourself.*

loudly *adv*: *a dog barking loudly* ∘ *loudly dressed.*

loudness *n* [U].

■ **ˌloud ˈhailer** *(Brit)* (*US* **bull-horn**) *n* a device like a horn held against the mouth and used to increase

loud hailer
(*US* **bull-horn**)

the sound of the voice so that it can be heard at a great distance: *The police used loud hailers to address the crowd.* ⇨ picture. Compare LOUDSPEAKER, MICROPHONE.

'**loud-mouth** *n* (*infml derog*) a person who talks too loudly or too much, esp sb who boasts. '**loud-mouthed** *adj*.

loudspeaker /ˌlaʊdˈspiːkə(r)/ (also **speaker**) *n* a part of a radio, HI-FI system, etc that changes electrical signals into sound: *a loudspeaker announcement/van.* Compare LOUD HAILER.

lough /lɒk, lɒx/ *n* (*Irish*) (esp in place names) a lake or a long strip of sea almost surrounded by land. Compare LOCH.

lounge /laʊndʒ/ *v* to sit or stand in a lazy way, esp leaning against sth: [Vp, Vpr] *lounge about/around (the house)* ○ *lounging at street corners* [also V].

▶ **lounge** *n* (**a**) a room for waiting in at an airport, etc: *the departure lounge.* (**b**) a public room in a hotel, club, etc for waiting or relaxing in. (**c**) a comfortable room in a private house for sitting and relaxing in. See also SUN LOUNGE.

lounger *n* **1** = SUN LOUNGER. **2** (*derog*) a lazy person who does no work.

■ '**lounge bar** (*Brit*) (also *esp US* '**cocktail lounge**, **sa'loon bar**) *n* a SMART[1](4), usu more expensive, bar in a pub, hotel, etc. Compare PUBLIC BAR.

'**lounge suit** *n* (*Brit*) a man's suit of matching jacket and trousers, worn esp in offices and on more formal occasions.

lour = LOWER[3].

louse /laʊs/ *n* **1** (*pl* **lice** /laɪs/) a small insect living on the bodies of people and animals, esp those living in dirty conditions. **2** (*pl* **louses**) (*sl*) a person for whom one feels contempt or disgust.

▶ **louse** *v* PHR V ,**louse sth 'up** (*sl*) to spoil or ruin sth: *You've really loused things up this time.*

lousy /ˈlaʊzi/ *adj* (**-ier, -iest**) **1** (*infml*) (**a**) very bad or ill; awful: *a lousy day/hotel* ○ *I feel lousy.* (**b**) [attrib] (used to express general contempt for sth): *She only offered me a lousy £5 for it.* **2** covered with lice (LOUSE). **3** [pred] ~ **with sth/sb** (*infml*) having too much/too many of sth/sb: *In August the place is lousy with tourists.*

lout /laʊt/ *n* a man or boy with bad manners. See also LAGER LOUT, LITTER-LOUT.

▶ **loutish** *adj* of or like a lout: *loutish behaviour.*

louvre (also **louver**) /ˈluːvə(r)/ *n* each of a set of fixed or movable strips of wood, plastic, etc designed to let air in while keeping light or rain out: *peer through the louvres of a blind.* ▶ **louvred** (also **louvered**) *adj*: *a louvred door.*

lovable /ˈlʌvəbl/ *adj* easy to love; inspiring affection: *a lovable character/rogue.*

love[1] /lʌv/ *n* **1** [U] a strong feeling of deep affection for sb/sth: *a mother's love for her children* ○ *love of one's country* ○ *He shows little love towards her.* ○ *Give my love to your sister.* Compare HATE. **2** [U] sexual affection or passion: *a love song/story* ○ *It was love at first sight* (ie They were attracted to each other the first time they met). ○ *Their love has cooled.* **3** [U, sing] great enjoyment of sth: *a love of learning/adventure/nature.* **4** [C] (**a**) a person who is loved: *Take care, my love.* ○ *She was the love of my life.* (**b**) a thing that one loves: *She's fond of all sports, but tennis is her first/greatest love.* **5** [C] (*infml esp Brit*) (a form of address used by a man to a woman or child who is not necessarily a friend, or

by a woman to a person of either sex): *Mind your head, love!* **6** [U] (in tennis) no score; NIL: *She won the first set six-love/six games to love.* IDM **be in 'love (with sb)** to feel affection and desire for sb: *I'm deeply/madly in love with her.* **be in 'love with sth** to be very fond of sth: *He's in love with the sound of his own voice* (ie talks too much). **fall in 'love (with sb/sth)** to feel a sudden strong attraction for sb/sth: *fall in love with Venice.* (**just) for 'love / for the 'love of sth** without payment or other reward: *They're all volunteers, doing it just for the love of the thing.* **for the love of 'God, etc** (*infml*) **1** (used when urging sb to do sth): *For the love of God let's get out of here!* **2** (expressing surprise, anger, etc). **a labour of love** ⇨ LABOUR[1]. **make 'love (to sb)** to have sex: *We made love (to each other).* **not for love or 'money** not by any means: *We couldn't find a hotel room for love or money.* **there's little/no 'love lost between A and B** they dislike each other: *There's never been much love lost between her and her sister.*

▶ **loveless** *adj* without love: *a loveless marriage.*

■ '**love affair** *n* a romantic or sexual relationship between two people who are in love and not married to each other.

'**love-child** *n* (*pl* **-children**) (*euph*) a child born to parents who are not married to each other.

,**love-'hate relationship** *n* an intense emotional relationship involving feelings of both love and hate.

'**love-letter** *n* a letter between two people expressing the love of one for the other.

'**love-match** *n* a marriage of two people who are in love with each other.

love[2] /lʌv/ *v* **1** to have a strong affection or deep tender feelings for sb/sth: [Vn] *love one's parents/country/wife.* **2** to like sb/sth greatly; to take pleasure in sb/sth: [Vn] *She's always loved horses.* [V.to inf, V.ing] *Children love to play/love playing.* [V.n to inf] *We'd love you to come to dinner.* [V.n ing] *I love him reading to me in bed.*

lovelorn /ˈlʌvlɔːn/ *adj* unhappy because one's love for sb is not returned by them.

lovely /ˈlʌvli/ *adj* (**-ier, -iest**) **1** beautiful; attractive: *a lovely view/house/woman* ○ *lovely hair/weather/music.* **2** (*infml*) enjoyable; pleasant: *a lovely dinner/time/story* ○ *It's lovely and warm* (ie pleasant because warm) *in here.* ○ *Isn't it a lovely day?* ⇨ note at NICE. ▶ **loveliness** *n* [U].

lovemaking /ˈlʌvmeɪkɪŋ/ *n* [U] sexual activity between two lovers, esp including having sex.

lover /ˈlʌvə(r)/ *n* **1**(**a**) [C] a partner in a sexual relationship outside marriage: *She denied that she was his lover.* Compare MISTRESS 4. (**b**) **lovers** [pl] two people who are in love or having a sexual relationship and not married to each other: *young lovers strolling in the park* ○ *It seems they had been lovers for years.* **2** [C] (often in compounds) a person who likes or enjoys sth specified: *a lover of music/horses/good wine* ○ *art-/dog-/opera-lovers.*

lovesick /ˈlʌvsɪk/ *adj* weak or ill because of being in love.

loving /ˈlʌvɪŋ/ *adj* [esp attrib] feeling or showing love: *such a loving and affectionate family* ○ *loving care/words.* ▶ **lovingly** *adv*: *old buildings lovingly restored.*

low[1] /ləʊ/ *adj* (**-er, -est**) **1** not high or tall; not extending far upwards: *a low wall/ceiling* ○ *a low range of hills* ○ *flying at a low altitude* ○ *a dress with a low neckline* ○ *The sun was low in the sky.* Compare HIGH[1]. **2**(**a**) below the usual, normal or average level, amount or intensity: *low wages/prices* ○ *low pressure* (eg of the atmosphere) ○ *the lowest temperature ever recorded* ○ *a low standard of work* ○ *a meal that is low in calories* ○ *The reservoir was very low after the long drought.* (**b**) (esp in compounds): *a*

L

low-fat yoghurt o low-alcohol beer o a low-calorie diet o low-cost housing o low-income families. **3** (of sound or a voice) not high in pitch¹(2); deep: *A man's voice is usually lower than a woman's.* **4** not loud: *a low rumble of thunder* o *Keep your voice low.* **5** lacking in energy; weak or depressed: *in a low state of health* o *feel low/in low spirits/low-spirited.* **6** ranking below others in importance or quality: *lower classes of society* o *have a low social status* o *low forms of life* (ie creatures having a relatively simple structure). **7** without culture or taste¹(6); common¹(4): *low* (ie morally unacceptable) *cunning* o *He mixes with some pretty low types.* **8** [usu attrib] (of an opinion, etc) not favourable: *have a very low opinion of sb* o *hold sb in low esteem.* **9** (of a gear) allowing a vehicle to travel at a slower speed in relation to its engine speed: *change into a lower gear when going up a hill.* **10** (of an oven, etc) warm but not hot: *cook the vegetables over a low heat* o *keep the iron on a low setting.* **11** (of light) not bright; DIM(1): *turn the lights down low.* **IDM** **at a low 'ebb** in a poor state; worse than usual: *Her spirits were at a very low ebb* (ie She was very depressed). **be/run 'low (on sth)** (of supplies) to be/become almost finished; (of people) to have used almost all one's supplies of sth: *The petrol's running low.* o *We're (running) low on petrol.* **a high/low profile** ⇨ PROFILE. **lay sb 'low** to make sb weak and ill: *The whole family was laid low by/with* (ie was ill and in bed with) *flu.*

▶ **'lowermost** *adj* lowest.

■ **lowest ˌcommon deˈnominator** *n* (*often derog*) a thing or level that appeals to or is understood by the highest number of people in a particular group: *pandering to the lowest common denominator of public taste.*

ˌlow-ˈkey *adj* not elaborate, forceful or emotional; restrained (RESTRAIN): *The wedding was a very low-key affair.* o *Officials took a very low-key approach.*

ˌlow-ˈpitched *adj* (of sounds) low in pitch¹(2); deep: *a ˌlow-pitched 'voice.* Compare HIGH-PITCHED.

'low season *n* (often **the low season**) (*Brit*) (also 'off-season) [sing] the time of year when fewest visitors go to a resort, etc. Compare HIGH SEASON.

ˌlow 'tide (also ˌlow 'water) [U,C] *n* (**a**) the tide when at its lowest level. (**b**) the time when this occurs. ⇨ HIGH TIDE. ˌlow-ˈwater mark *n* the lowest point reached by the water at low tide. Compare HIGH-WATER MARK.

low² /ləʊ/ *adv* (**-er, -est**) **1** in, at or to a low level or position: *aim/shoot low* o *bow low to the Queen.* **2** not at a high pitch¹(2): *I can't sing as low as that.* **3** quietly: *Speak lower or she'll hear you!* **IDM** **be brought 'low** to lose one's wealth or high position: *rich families brought low by the stock market collapse.* **high and low** ⇨ HIGH³. **lie low** ⇨ LIE². **stoop so low** ⇨ STOOP.

■ ˌlow-ˈlying *adj* (of land) not high, and usu fairly flat: *fog in ˌlow-lying 'areas.*

ˌlow-ˈpaid *adj* paid low wages: *They are among the ˌlowest-paid (ˌworkers) in the 'country.*

low³ /ləʊ/ *n* **1** a low level or figure: *The pound has fallen to **an all-time low** against the dollar* (ie is worth less in exchange for dollars than ever before). **2** an area of low pressure in the atmosphere: *another low moving in from the Atlantic.* Compare HIGH².

low⁴ /ləʊ/ *n* [V] to make the deep sound made by cattle; to MOO.

lowbrow /'ləʊbraʊ/ *adj* (*usu derog*) not cultured or intellectual: *a lowbrow newspaper.* Compare HIGH-BROW, MIDDLEBROW.

low-down /'ləʊdaʊn/ *adj* [attrib] (*infml*) not fair or honourable; mean²(2): *That was a pretty low-down trick to play!*

▶ **low-down** *n* [U] ~ **(on sb/sth)** (*infml*) the true facts or relevant information about sb/sth: *all the low-down on the private lives of the pop stars.*

lower¹ /'ləʊə(r)/ *adj* [attrib] situated below sth else, esp below sth of the same type or as one of a pair: *one's lower lip/jaw* o *the lower deck of a ship.* Compare UPPER, LOW¹ 6.

■ ˌlower 'case *n* [U] (in printing) small letters, eg a, b, c, not capitals: *ˌlower-case 'lettering.* Compare UPPER CASE.

ˌLower 'House (also ˌLower 'Chamber) *n* the larger, usu elected, branch of a national assembly, eg the House of Commons in Britain or the House of Representatives in the USA.

lower² /'ləʊə(r)/ *v* **1(a)** to let or bring sth/sb/oneself down: [Vnpr] *lower supplies from a helicopter to the stranded men* o *She lowered herself slowly into a chair.* [Vn] *He lowered his newspaper and looked round.* o *lower one's eyes/gaze* (ie look down) o *lower a flag/window.* (**b**) to make sth less high: *lower (the height of) the ceiling.* **2** to reduce sth or become less in amount, level, quality, etc: [Vnpr] *lower one's voice to a whisper* [Vn] *A poor diet lowers one's resistance to illness.* [V] *Stocks lowered in value.* [also Vpr]. **3** ~ **oneself (by doing sth)** (*infml*) (esp in negative sentences) to reduce one's dignity and lose respect: [Vnpr] *Don't lower yourself by asking him for help.* [also Vn]. **IDM** **raise/lower one's sights** ⇨ SIGHT¹.

lower³ (also **lour**) /'laʊə(r)/ *v* (of the sky) to be dark and threatening: [Vpr] *Huge clouds lowered over the bay.* [also V].

lowland /'ləʊlənd/ *n* (often *pl*) an area of land that is fairly flat and not very high above sea level: *farming in the fertile lowlands* o *lowland farmers* o *the Lowlands of Scotland.*

▶ **'lowlander** /-ləndə(r)/ *n* a person who lives in a lowland area.

lowly /'ləʊli/ *adj* (**-ier, -iest**) low in status or importance; HUMBLE(1): *a lowly shop assistant.*

loyal /'lɔɪəl/ *adj* ~ **(to sb/sth)** true and faithful: *security forces loyal to the President* o **remain loyal to** one's principles o *a loyal supporter of the Democratic Party.*

▶ **loyalist** *n* **1** a person who is loyal to the established ruler or government, esp during a REVOLT: *loyalist troops.* **2 Loyalist** (in Britain) a person who supports the union between Great Britain and Northern Ireland.

loyally /'lɔɪəli/ *adv.*

loyalty /'lɔɪəlti/ *n* (**a**) [U] the quality of being true and faithful in one's support of sb/sth: *swear an oath of loyalty to the monarch* o *Can I count on your loyalty?* (**b**) [C often *pl*] a strong feeling that one wants to be faithful to sb/sth: *a case of **divided loyalties** (ie of being loyal to two different and possibly conflicting causes, people, etc) o *We all have a loyalty to the company.*

lozenge /'lɒzɪndʒ/ *n* **1** a figure with four sides in the shape of a diamond. **2** a small sweet, esp one containing medicine, which is dissolved in the mouth: *throat lozenges* (ie for a sore throat).

LP /ˌel 'piː/ *abbr* long-playing (record). An LP plays for about 25 minutes on each side. Compare CD, SINGLE *n* 2.

L-plate ⇨ L².

LSD /ˌel es 'diː/ *abbr* (also *sl* **acid**) lysergic acid diethylamide (a powerful drug that affects one's mind and makes one experience things that are not real).

Lt *abbr* Lieutenant: *Lt Thomas Bailey.*

Ltd *abbr* (*Brit*) Limited (used after the name of a private limited liability company): *Pearce and Co Ltd.* Compare INC, PLC.

lubricate /'luːbrɪkeɪt/ *v* to put oil or an oily substance on or in sth so that it moves easily: [Vn]

lubricate the wheels/hinges/joints ○ (fig joc) He arrived at the meeting well lubricated with (ie having drunk a lot of) whisky.
▶ **lubricant** /'lu:brɪkənt/ n [U, C] a substance that lubricates.
lubrication /ˌlu:brɪ'keɪʃn/ n [U, C].

lubricious /lu:'brɪʃəs/ adj (fml derog) having or showing a strong interest in sexual matters.

lucerne /lu:'sɜ:n/ n [U] = ALFALFA.

lucid /'lu:sɪd/ adj **1** clearly expressed; easy to understand: a lucid explanation ○ His style is very lucid. **2** clear in one's mind; in control of one's thoughts: lucid intervals (ie during mental illness). ▶ **lucidity** /lu:'sɪdəti/ n [U]: explain a complex subject with admirable lucidity. **lucidly** adv.

luck /lʌk/ n [U] **1** success, esp when unexpected: I could hardly believe my luck when I won. ○ **With (any/a bit of) luck** we'll be home before dark. ○ I always carry one for luck. ○ They're a good team and we **wish them luck** in the final. ○ I had the luck to find him at home. ○ What a **stroke of luck** finding you here! ○ Any luck with (ie Did you manage to get) the job? ○ Our luck finally ran out (ie ended). **2** chance, esp considered as a force that causes good or bad things to happen: have good/bad/poor luck. **IDM** **as luck would 'have it** the way chance made things happen. **bad, hard, etc luck (on sb)** (used as an expression of sympathy): Bad luck, Helen, you played very well. ○ It's rotten luck on those who were beaten in the first round of the competition. **be down on one's 'luck** (infml) to have a period of bad luck. **beginner's luck** ⇨ BEGINNER. **be in / out of 'luck** to be fortunate/unfortunate: You're in luck — there's one ticket left. **the best of / good 'luck (to sb)/ (with sth)** may sb be fortunate and successful: The best of luck to both of you! ○ Good luck with your exams! **better luck next time** ⇨ BETTER¹. **just one's 'luck** (indicating that, as is often the case, sth unfortunate or annoying has happened to one): It was just my luck to go to Wimbledon the day it rained. **one's 'luck is in** one is lucky. **the luck of the 'draw** the way in which chance decides what some people become, do, get, etc and others not. **no such 'luck** one was not so fortunate: 'Did you win?' 'No such luck, I'm afraid.' **pot luck** ⇨ POT¹. **push one's luck** ⇨ PUSH¹. **tough luck** ⇨ TOUGH. **try one's luck** ⇨ TRY¹. **worse luck** ⇨ WORSE.
▶ **luckless** adj not lucky; unfortunate: the luckless owner of the stolen van.

lucky /'lʌki/ adj (-ier, -iest) having, bringing or resulting from good luck: a lucky guess/find/escape ○ a lucky break (ie a piece of good luck) ○ a lucky charm ○ Seven is my lucky number. ○ You're very lucky to be alive after that accident. ○ It's lucky she's still here. **IDM** **strike lucky** ⇨ STRIKE². **thank one's lucky stars** ⇨ THANK. **you'll be 'lucky**; **you should be so 'lucky** (ironic catchphrase) what you expect, wish for, etc is very unlikely to happen: Fifty pounds for that old radio? You'll be lucky! ▶ **luckily** /'lʌkɪli/ adv: Luckily the meeting had started late.
■ **lucky dip** (Brit) (US **lucky 'grab bag**) n (usu sing) a barrel, etc containing small prizes of various values which people select at RANDOM in return for a payment, hoping to get sth that is worth more than they have paid.

lucrative /'lu:krətɪv/ adj producing much money; profitable: a lucrative business.

lucre /'lu:kə(r)/ n [U] (derog or joc) profit or money, as a MOTIVE for doing sth: the lure of filthy lucre.

Luddite /'lʌdaɪt/ n (Brit derog) a person who is opposed to change or improvement in working methods, machines, etc in industry: the Luddite mentality.

ludicrous /'lu:dɪkrəs/ adj ridiculous; absurd: a ludicrous idea/situation. ▶ **ludicrously** adv: ludicrously tight trousers.

ludo /'lu:dəʊ/ n [U] (Brit) a simple game played with DICE and counters (COUNTER²) on a special board.

lug /lʌɡ/ v (-gg-) to carry or drag sth with great effort: [Vnpr] lug a heavy suitcase up the stairs ○ (fig infml) [Vnp] She had to lug the kids around with her all day. [also Vn]. ⇨ note at CARRY.

luggage (esp US baggage)

briefcase

handbag (US also purse)

suitcase

trunk

rucksack (US also backpack)

luggage /'lʌɡɪdʒ/ (esp Brit) (also esp US **baggage**) n [U] bags, cases, etc containing sb's belongings and taken on a journey: We can fit one more piece of luggage in the boot. ○ All luggage must be checked in at least one hour before departure. ○ Have you any hand-luggage? ⇨ picture. See also LEFT-LUGGAGE OFFICE.
■ **'luggage-rack** n (**a**) a shelf for luggage above the seats in a railway carriage, coach, etc. (**b**) = ROOF-RACK.
'luggage-van (Brit) (US **baggage car**) n a carriage for passengers' luggage on a railway train.

lugubrious /lə'ɡu:briəs/ adj sad; full of sorrow: have a lugubrious expression. ▶ **lugubriously** adv.

lugworm /'lʌɡwɜ:m/ n a large worm that lives in the sand by the sea. Lugworms are used as BAIT(1) for catching fish.

lukewarm /ˌlu:k'wɔ:m/ adj **1** (of liquids) only slightly warm: 'lukewarm 'water ○ Heat the milk until it is just lukewarm. **2** ~ (about sb/sth) not eager or enthusiastic: a ˌlukewarm re'ception/ re'sponse ○ The audience was rather lukewarm about the play.

lull /lʌl/ v **1(a)** ~ sb/sth (to sth) to make a person or an animal quiet or calm: [Vnpr] lull a baby to sleep (ie by moving it gently backwards and forwards or singing to it) [Vn] I was lulled by the boat's gentle motion. (**b**) ~ sb/sth (into sth) to calm sb, or their fears, etc, esp by deception: [Vnpr] be **lulled into a false sense of security** [also Vn]. **2** (of a storm or noise) to become quiet; to decrease: [V] By dawn the wind had lulled.
▶ **lull** n (usu sing) an interval of quiet or lack of activity: a lull before the storm/in the conversation/ during the battle.

lullaby /'lʌləbaɪ/ n a soft gentle song sung to make a child go to sleep.

lumbago /lʌm'beɪɡəʊ/ n [U] a pain in the muscles of the lower part of the back, caused by RHEUMATISM.

lumbar /'lʌmbə(r)/ adj (usu attrib) of the lower part of the back: lumbar pains ○ the lumbar region.
■ **ˌlumbar 'puncture** n (medical) the removal of fluid from the lower part of the SPINE(1) with a hollow needle.

lumber¹ /'lʌmbə(r)/ n [U] **1** (esp Brit) pieces of furniture, etc that are no longer useful and are stored away or take up space: The **lumber room** is full of old chairs we'll never use. **2** (esp US) = TIMBER 1.
▶ **lumber** v (**a**) ~ sb (with sb/sth) (usu passive) to give sb a responsibility or job that they do not want:

[Vnpr] *I got lumbered with the job of buying all the tickets.* ○ *It looks as though we're going to be lumbered with Uncle Bill for the whole weekend.* [also Vn]. (**b**) ~ **sth** (**with sth**) (esp passive) to have to find room for or carry a lot of useless things: [Vnpr] *I don't want to be lumbered with too many books.* [also Vnp].

lumber² /ˈlʌmbə(r)/ *v* to move in a slow heavy awkward way: [Vp] *A huge lorry lumbered by/past.* [Vpr] *He lumbered out of bed and into the bathroom.* [V] *the animal's slow lumbering walk.*

lumberjack /ˈlʌmbədʒæk/ (also **logger** /ˈlɒgə(r)/; *US* ˈlɔːg-/) *n* (esp in the USA and Canada) a person whose job is cutting down trees or cutting or transporting timber.

lumberyard /ˈlʌmbəjɑːd/ (*US*) *n* a yard where wood for building, etc is stored and sold.

luminary /ˈluːmɪnəri; *US* -neri/ *n* a person who inspires or influences others, esp a leading person in a particular activity: *legal/scientific/Hollywood luminaries.*

luminous /ˈluːmɪnəs/ *adj* giving out light; bright: *luminous paint* (ie paint that glows in the dark, used on watches, clocks, etc) ○ (*fig*) *the gentle, luminous quality of the music.* ▶ **luminosity** /ˌluːmɪˈnɒsəti/ *n* [U]: *the freshness and luminosity of the colours.*

lump¹ /lʌmp/ *n* **1** a hard or solid mass, usu without a regular shape: *a lump of clay* ○ *This flour is full of lumps.* ○ *Use a fork to break down the lumps of soil.* See also SUGAR-LUMP. **2** a swelling under the skin: *a nasty lump on her neck.* **3** (*infml*) a heavy, awkward or stupid person: *Do hurry up, you great lump!* IDM **have, etc a lump in one's/the throat** to feel pressure in the throat as a result of strong emotion caused by love, sadness, etc.
▶ **lump** *v* ~ **sb/sth** (**in**) **with sb/sth**; ~ **sb/sth together** (**with sb/sth**) (**as sth**) to put or consider people or things together; to treat people or things as being alike: [Vnp] *Can we lump all these items together as 'incidental expenses'?* [Vnpr, Vnp] *They are lumped (in) with the other class for certain subjects.*
lumpish /-ɪʃ/ *adj* (of a person) heavy; awkward; stupid.
lumpy *adj* full of lumps; covered in lumps: *lumpy gravy/custard* ○ *a lumpy mattress.*
■ ˌlump ˈsum *n* a single payment for a number of separate items; money paid in full rather than in several smaller amounts.

lump² /lʌmp/ *v* IDM **lump it** (*infml*) to accept sth unpleasant whether one likes it or not: *If you don't like the decision you'll just have to lump it.*

lunacy /ˈluːnəsi/ *n* [U] **1** extreme mental illness; madness. **2** very foolish behaviour: *It's sheer lunacy driving in this weather.*

lunar /ˈluːnə(r)/ *adj* (usu attrib) of the moon: *lunar rocks* ○ *a lunar eclipse.*
■ ˌlunar ˈmonth *n* the average time between one new moon and the next (about 29½ days). Compare CALENDAR MONTH.

lunatic /ˈluːnətɪk/ *n* **1** a wildly foolish person: *You're driving on the wrong side of the road, you lunatic!* **2** (*dated now offensive*) a person who is mad or severely mentally ill.
▶ **lunatic** *adj* wildly foolish: *a lunatic proposal.* IDM **the ˌlunatic ˈfringe** *n* (*derog*) those members of a political or other group whose views are regarded as wildly extreme.
■ ˌlunatic aˈsylum *n* (*dated*) a home for mentally ill people; a mental hospital.

lunch /lʌntʃ/ *n* [C, U] a meal eaten in the middle of the day: *take a **packed lunch*** (ie sandwiches, etc) *to work* ○ *a one-hour lunch break* ○ *We serve hot and cold lunches.* ○ *He's gone to/for lunch.* See also PLOUGHMAN'S LUNCH. ⇨ note at DINNER.
▶ **lunch** *v* to eat lunch: [V] *Where do you usually*

lunch? [Vpr, Vp] *We lunched (out) on cold meat and salad.*
■ ˈlunch-hour *n* a time around the middle of the day when one stops work to eat lunch: *I can meet you during my lunch-hour.*
ˈlunch-time *n* [C, U] a time around the middle of the day when lunch is normally eaten: *the lunch-time weather forecast.*

luncheon /ˈlʌntʃən/ *n* [C, U] (*fml*) lunch: *attend a charity luncheon.*
■ ˈluncheon meat *n* [U] mixed cooked meat, mainly pork, sold in a tin and usu eaten cold.
ˈluncheon voucher *n* (*abbr* **LV**) (*Brit*) (*US* ˈmeal ticket*) a ticket, given by companies to their employees, which can be exchanged for food at certain restaurants.

lung /lʌŋ/ *n* either of the two breathing organs in the chest of humans and many other animals: *lung cancer* ○ (*joc*) *a baby with a fine pair of lungs* (ie able to cry loudly). ⇨ picture at RESPIRATORY.

lunge /lʌndʒ/ *n* a sudden forward movement of the body, eg when trying to attack sb; a THRUST(1).
▶ **lunge** *v* to make a lunge: [Vpr] *He lunged wildly at his opponent.* [Vp] *She lunged out with a knife.* [also V]. ⇨ picture at FENCING.

lupin (*US* **lupine**) /ˈluːpɪn/ *n* a tall garden plant with a long pointed stem bearing many small flowers. Lupin plants may have blue, purple, pink, white or yellow flowers.

lurch¹ /lɜːtʃ/ *n* IDM **leave sb in the ˈlurch** (*infml*) to abandon sb when they are in a difficult situation.

lurch² /lɜːtʃ/ *n* [C usu *sing*] a sudden unsteady leaning or rolling movement: *The ship gave a lurch to starboard.* ○ (*fig*) *My heart gave a sickening lurch when I saw him.*
▶ **lurch** *v* to lean or roll suddenly; to STAGGER(1): [Vp, Vpr] *a drunken man lurching along (the street)* [also V].

lure /lʊə(r); *Brit also* ljʊə(r)/ *n* (**a**) a thing that attracts or is used to attract people or animals: *a high salary used as a lure to attract skilled staff.* (**b**) (usu *sing*) the attractive qualities of sth: *the lure of adventure.*
▶ **lure** *v* to attract or tempt a person or an animal: [Vnpr] *lure sb into a trap* [Vnp] *Greed lured him on.* [also Vn].

Lurex /ˈlʊəreks; *Brit also* ˈljʊə-/ *n* [U] (*propr*) a material made with a type of thread that contains a thin shiny metal strip.

lurid /ˈlʊərɪd; *Brit also* ˈljʊə-/ *adj* **1** having very bright colours or combinations of colour: *a lurid sky/sunset* ○ *dressed in a lurid orange and green blouse.* **2** violent and shocking: *The paper described the killings in lurid detail.* ▶ **luridly** *adv*.

lurk /lɜːk/ *v* **1(a)** to be or stay hidden, esp when waiting to attack or appear: [Vpr] *a suspicious-looking man lurking in the shadows* ○ *Fear lurks beneath the city's calm appearance.* [also V, Vp]. (**b**) to wait near a place trying not to attract attention: [Vpr, Vp] *He's usually lurking (about) somewhere near the bar.* [also V]. **2** to stay in the back of one's mind: [V] *a lurking doubt/suspicion.* [also Vpr]. ⇨ note at PROWL.

luscious /ˈlʌʃəs/ *adj* **1** having a rich sweet taste or smell: *luscious cakes/fruit/strawberries.* **2** (of art, clothes, etc) very rich and suggesting great pleasure to the eyes, ears, etc: *luscious silks and velvets* ○ *a picture printed in luscious shades of orange and red.* **3** sexually attractive: *a luscious young girl.*

lush /lʌʃ/ *adj* **1** growing thickly and strongly; LUXURIANT: *lush pastures/vegetation.* **2** displaying wealth and comfort: *lush decor.*

lust /lʌst/ *n* (*often derog*) [U, C] **1** ~ (**for sb**) a strong sexual desire: *curb one's lust* ○ *gratify one's lusts.* **2** ~ (**for/of sth**) an intense desire for or enjoyment of

L

sth: a lust for power/gold/adventure. See also BLOOD-LUST.

▶ **lust** *v* **PHRV** **lust after/for sb/sth** (*often derog*) to feel a strong desire for sb/sth: *lust after women* ○ *He lusted for revenge.*

lustful /-fl/ *adj* (*often derog*) filled with lust: *lustful glances.*

lustre (*US* **luster**) /ˈlʌstə(r)/ *n* [U] **1** the soft brightness of a smooth or shining surface: *the deep lustre of pearls.* **2** glory; distinction: *brave deeds adding lustre to one's name.* See also LACKLUSTRE.

▶ **lustrous** /ˈlʌstrəs/ *adj* having lustre: *lustrous hair/colours.*

lusty /ˈlʌsti/ *adj* healthy, vigorous and full of life: *lusty infants* ○ *give a lusty cheer.* ▶ **lustily** /-ɪli/ *adv: sing lustily.*

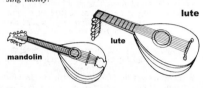

lute

lute

mandolin

lute /luːt/ *n* a musical instrument with strings, played like a guitar. Lutes were used esp in the 14th–17th centuries. ⇨ picture.

lutenist (also **lutanist**) /ˈluːtənɪst/ *n* person who plays the LUTE.

luv /lʌv/ *n* (*Brit infml*) (used esp as a form of address in writing) love: *Ta very much, luv.*

luxuriant /lʌgˈʒʊəriənt/ *adj* growing thickly and strongly: *luxuriant vegetation* ○ *luxuriant hair* ○ (*fig*) *the poem's luxuriant imagery.* Compare LUXURIOUS.

▶ **luxuriance** /-əns/ *n* [U]. **luxuriantly** *adv.*

luxuriate /lʌgˈʒʊərieɪt/ *v* ~ (**in sth**) to take great pleasure in sth; to enjoy sth as a LUXURY: [Vpr] *a cat luxuriating in the warm sunshine* ○ *luxuriate in a hot bath* [also V].

luxurious /lʌgˈʒʊəriəs/ *adj* supplied with expensive and enjoyable things; very comfortable: *live in luxurious surroundings* ○ *This car is our most luxurious model.* Compare LUXURIANT. ▶ **luxuriously** *adv.*

luxury /ˈlʌkʃəri/ *n* **1** [U] the best and most expensive food and drink, clothes, surroundings, etc; the regular use and enjoyment of these: *live in luxury* ○ *lead/live a life of luxury* ○ *luxury goods* ○ *a luxury hotel/flat/holiday.* **2** [C] a thing that is expensive

and enjoyable, but not essential: *caviar, champagne and other luxuries* ○ *We can't afford many luxuries.* **IDM** **in the lap of luxury** ⇨ LAP[1].

LW *abbr* (on radios) long wave.

-ly /-li/ *suff* **1** (used very widely with *adjs* to form *advs*) in the specified manner: *happily* ○ *stupidly.* **2** (used widely with *ns* to form *adjs*) having the qualities of: *cowardly* ○ *scholarly.* **3** (with *ns* forming *adjs* and *advs*) occurring at intervals of: *hourly* ○ *daily.*

lycée /ˈliːseɪ; *US* liːˈseɪ/ *n* (*French*) a state secondary school in France.

lychee /ˌlaɪˈtʃiː, ˈlaɪtʃiː/ *n* a small fruit, originally from China, with sweet white flesh and a single large seed in a thin reddish shell.

lying *pres p* of LIE[1,2].

lymph /lɪmf/ *n* [U] (*anatomy*) a colourless fluid from the tissues or organs of the body, containing white blood cells: *the lymph glands.*

▶ **lymphatic** /lɪmˈfætɪk/ *adj* (*anatomy*) of or carrying lymph: *the lymphatic vessels.*

lynch /lɪntʃ/ *v* (of a group of people) to kill sb believed to be guilty of a crime without a proper trial, usu by hanging: [Vn] *innocent men lynched by the angry mob* ○ (*fig*) *I can't go out and face those reporters — I'll be lynched!*

■ ˈ**lynch mob** *n* a crowd of people gathering to lynch sb.

lynx /lɪŋks/ *n* a wild animal of the cat family with spots on its fur and a short tail, noted for its excellent sight.

lyre /ˈlaɪə(r)/ *n* an ancient musical instrument with strings fixed in a frame shaped like a U. It is played with the fingers.

lyric /ˈlɪrɪk/ *adj* **1** (of poetry) expressing the writer's feelings. **2** of or composed for singing.

▶ **lyric** *n* **1** a lyric poem. **2** (esp *pl*) the words of a song: *a song with sad lyrics.*

lyrical /ˈlɪrɪkl/ *adj* expressing strong emotion or enthusiasm, esp in poetry, art, music, etc: *a lyrical description of a summer's day* ○ *She started to wax lyrical* (ie talk enthusiastically) *about her new diet.*

▶ **lyrically** /-kli/ *adv.*

lyricism /ˈlɪrɪsɪzəm/ *n* the expression of strong emotion or enthusiasm, esp in poetry, art, music, etc: *play the piano with effortless and passionate lyricism.*

lyricist /ˈlɪrɪsɪst/ *n* a person who writes the words of songs: *a pop lyricist.*

L

Mm

M¹ (also **m**) /em/ n (pl **M's**, **m's** /emz/) the 13th letter of the English alphabet: *'Moscow' starts with (an) M/ 'M'*.

M² abbr **1** (also **med**) (esp on clothing, etc) medium (size). **2** (also **m**) the Roman NUMERAL for 1 000 (Latin *mille*). **3** /em/ (*Brit*) (usu followed by a number) motorway: *heavy traffic on the M25*.

m abbr **1** (esp on forms) male (sex). **2** (esp on forms) married (status). **3(a)** metre(s): *run in the 5 000 m* (ie a race over that distance). (**b**) (*radio*) metres: *800 m long wave*. **4** million(s): *population 10 m*.

MA /ˌem ˈeɪ/ abbr (*US* **AM**) Master of Arts: *have/be an MA in Modern Languages* ○ *Marion Bell MA (London)*. Compare MSc.

ma /mɑː/ n (pl **mas**) (*infml*) (used esp as a form of address) mother: *I'm going now, Ma.* ○ *'I want my ma!' sobbed the child.*

ma'am /mæm, mɑːm/ n [sing] **1** (used esp when addressing the Queen) MADAM. **2** (*US*) (used as a polite form of address to a woman): *Can I help you, ma'am?*

Mac /mæk/ n [sing] (*US infml*) (used when addressing a man whose name one does not know): *Hey, Mac! What do you think you're doing?*

mac (also **mack**) /mæk/ n (*Brit infml*) = MACKINTOSH.

macabre /məˈkɑːbrə/ adj connected with death, and thus causing fear; GRUESOME: *a macabre ghost story*.

macadam /məˈkædəm/ n [U] a road surface made of layers of broken stones: *a macadam road*. Compare TARMAC.

macaroni /ˌmækəˈrəʊni/ n [U] a type of PASTA in the form of hollow tubes, usu cut in short pieces.
■ ˌmacaroni ˈcheese n [U] (*Brit*) a dish of macaroni with a cheese sauce.

macaroon /ˌmækəˈruːn/ n a small flat cake or biscuit made with crushed almonds (ALMOND) or COCONUT.

macaw /məˈkɔː/ n a large tropical American PARROT with brightly coloured feathers and a long tail.

mace¹ /meɪs/ n **1** an ornamental rod, carried or displayed as a sign of the authority of an official, eg a MAYOR. Compare ORB 2, SCEPTRE. **2** a large heavy club formerly used as a weapon, usu having a head with metal points.

mace² /meɪs/ n [U] a spice made from the dried outer covering of nutmegs (NUTMEG).

Mach /mɑːk, mæk/ n [U] (followed by a number) a measurement of speed, esp that of aircraft, etc. Mach one is the speed of sound: *an aircraft flying at Mach two* (ie twice the speed of sound).

machete /məˈʃeti/ n a broad heavy knife used as a cutting tool and as a weapon, esp in Latin America and the West Indies. ⇨ picture at KNIFE.

machiavellian /ˌmækiəˈveliən/ adj (*fml derog*) using clever and deceitful schemes to achieve what one wants, esp in politics: *a machiavellian person/motive/plot*.

machination /ˌmæʃɪˈneɪʃn/ n [C usu pl] a secret plot or scheme: *political machinations*.

machine /məˈʃiːn/ n **1** [C] (**a**) (often in compounds) an apparatus with several moving parts, designed to perform a particular task. Machines may be driven by electricity, steam, gas, etc or by human power: *a ˈsewing-machine/ˈwashing-machine* ○ *a life-support machine* ○ *office machines such as computers, word processors and photocopiers* ○ *I phoned her but all I got was her answering machine.* ⇨ note. (**b**) (*infml*) a particular type of machine, esp a vehicle or a household appliance: *put the clothes in the machine* (ie the washing-machine (WASHING)). **2** [CGp] a group of people that control an organization, etc or part of it: (*politics*) *the well-oiled party machine* ○ *The public relations machine covered up the firm's heavy losses.* **3** [C] (*derog*) a person who acts automatically, without having to think or show any feelings. **IDM a cog in the machine** ⇨ COG. See also FRUIT MACHINE, SLOT-MACHINE.
▶ **machine** v **1** to cut, shape, polish, etc sth with a machine: [Vn-adj] *The edge of the disc had been machined flat/smooth.* [also Vn]. **2** (*Brit*) to make clothes, etc using a sewing-machine (SEW): [Vn] *I have to machine the hem.*

machinery /məˈʃiːnəri/ n [U] **1** machines as a group or in general: *A lot of new machinery has been installed.* **2** the moving parts of a machine; a mechanism: *the machinery of a clock.* **3** ~ (**of sth / for doing sth**) the organization or structure of sth/for doing sth: *reform the machinery of government* ○ *We have no machinery for dealing with complaints.* ○ *All this will be processed by the Home Office machinery.*

machinist /məˈʃiːnɪst/ n **1** a person who operates a machine, esp a sewing-machine (SEW). **2** a person who makes, repairs or operates machines used in industry for cutting and shaping things.
■ ma'chine code (also ma'chine language) n (*computing*) a code in which instructions are written that a computer can understand and act on.

ma'chine-gun n an automatic gun giving a continuous rapid fire of bullets: *a burst/hail of machine-gun fire.* ⇨ picture at GUN. — v (**-nn-**) [Vn] to shoot sb with a machine-gun.

ma,chine-ˈmade adj made by a machine. Compare HANDMADE.

ma,chine-ˈreadable adj (*computing*) (of data) in a form that a computer can understand.

ma'chine tool n a tool for cutting or shaping materials, driven by a machine.

NOTE Compare **machine, appliance, apparatus, tool, instrument, implement, device** and **gadget**. A **machine** is designed to do a specific job and has moving parts that are powered by electricity, etc. An (**electrical**) **appliance** is a machine used in the house, such as a washing-machine or dishwasher. **Apparatus** has several pieces that must be connected and is used to perform a specific function: *the diver's breathing apparatus.*

A **tool** is an object with a simple design that you hold and use to do a particular job, eg a hammer or drill. An **instrument** is a tool designed for a technical task, especially one that requires a lot of skill. It may be small and quite delicate, eg a surgeon's knife, or have some moving parts and have a scientific use, eg a microscope. An **implement** is a tool generally used outside, especially to help with work in a garden or on a farm, eg a spade or rake.

Device is often used to show approval of a small, useful machine or instrument: *A modern kitchen has many labour-saving devices* (ie ones that save you effort and time). ○ *a clever device for locking win-*

---

dows. A **gadget** is a small modern tool that you may not need but which you can use to perform a task more easily: *The car is fitted with some clever little gadgets.*

machismo /məˈtʃɪzməʊ; *US* mɑːˈtʃiːz-/ *n* [U] (*usu derog*) aggressive pride in being male: *He combines Hollywood charisma with cowboy machismo.*

macho /ˈmætʃəʊ/ *adj* (*infml usu derog*) showing aggressive pride in being male: *He thinks it's macho to drink a lot and get into fights.*

mackerel /ˈmækrəl/ *n* (*pl* unchanged) an edible sea-fish with greenish-blue bands on its body: *a good catch of mackerel* ∘ *smoked mackerel.*

mackintosh /ˈmækɪntɒʃ/ (also *infml* **mac, mack** /mæk/) *n* (*Brit*) a coat made of material that keeps one dry in the rain.

macro- *comb form* large; on a large scale: *macro-biotic* ∘ *macroeconomics.* Compare MICRO-, MINI-.

macrobiotics /ˌmækrəʊbaɪˈɒtɪks/ *n* [sing *v*] the science of food that consists of whole grains and vegetables grown without chemical treatment. ▸ **macrobiotic** *adj* [esp attrib]: *a macrobiotic diet.*

macrocosm /ˈmækrəʊkɒzəm/ *n* **1** the **macro-cosm** [sing] the universe. **2** [C] any large complete structure containing smaller structures. Compare MICROCOSM.

macroeconomics /ˌmækrəʊˌiːkəˈnɒmɪks, -ˌekə-/ *n* [sing *v*] the study of economic factors on a large scale, eg national economies. ▸ **macroeconomic** *adj* [esp attrib]: *macroeconomic policy.*

mad /mæd/ *adj* (**-dder, -ddest**) **1(a)** mentally ill; INSANE: *He was/went completely mad.* ∘ *Please turn the radio down — the noise is driving me mad!* ∘ *the mad scene in 'King Lear'.* **(b)** (*infml esp derog*) very foolish; crazy: *She does the maddest things — like dyeing her hair purple!* ∘ *You must be mad to go swimming on a day like this.* ∘ *We decided to go mad and buy a new car, even though we couldn't afford it.* **2** (*infml*) **(a)** ~ **about/on sth/sb** very interested in or enthusiastic about sth/sb: *be mad on football/pop music* ∘ *He's mad about her* (ie likes/loves her very much). **(b)** (following *ns*) very enthusiastic about sth/sb: *a crowd of football-mad little boys* ∘ *at the age of 17 she was man-mad.* **3** ~ **(with sth)** (*infml*) very excited; wild: *make a mad dash/rush for sth* ∘ *mad with pain* ∘ *The crowd went mad with excitement.* **4** ~ **(at/with sb)** (*infml*) angry: ∘ *Don't be mad at/with me — it wasn't my fault.* **5** (of a dog) suffering from RABIES. **IDM** **hopping mad** ⇨ HOP¹. **like anything/crazy/mad** ⇨ CRAZY. **(as) mad as a ˈhatter/a March ˈhare** (*infml*) completely mad (1,2). **mad ˈkeen (on sb/sth)** (*Brit infml*) very interested in or enthusiastic about sb/sth: *She's mad keen on sailing/on that new pop group.* **stark raving/staring mad** ⇨ STARK *adv.*
▸ **madly** *adv* **1** in a wild manner as if mad: *I've been rushing around madly all day trying to find the right clothes to wear on holiday.* ∘ *The horse galloped madly off along the road.* **2** (*infml*) extremely: *madly excited/jealous* ∘ *She's madly in love with him.*
madness *n* [U] **1** the state of being mentally ill; mentally ill behaviour: *His madness cannot be cured.* **2** extremely foolish behaviour: *It is madness to go climbing in such bad weather.* **IDM** **method in one's madness** ⇨ METHOD.
■ **mad ˈcow disease** *n* [U] (*infml*) = BSE.

madam /ˈmædəm/ *n* **1** (also **Madam**) [sing] (*fml*) (a polite form of address to a woman that one does not know, whether she is married or not): *Can I help you, madam?* ∘ *Dear Madam* (ie used like *Dear Sir* in a letter) ∘ *Madam Chairman, may I be allowed to speak?* Compare MISS¹ 2. **2** [C] (*infml derog*) a girl or young woman who likes to get her own way, tell others what to do, etc: *She's a proper little madam!*

3 [C] a woman who is in charge of the prostitutes in a BROTHEL.

Madame /məˈdɑːm; *US* məˈdæm/ *n* (*abbr* **Mme**) (*pl* **Mesdames** /meɪˈdɑːm/, *abbr* **Mmes**) (a French title given to an older woman, esp one who is married or a widow or to an older woman who is not British or American): *Madame Lee from Hong Kong.*

madcap *adj* [usu attrib] typical of a person who acts in a dangerous or RECKLESS way: *madcap escapades/ideas* ∘ *a madcap character.*

madden /ˈmædn/ *v* to make sb extremely angry or annoyed: [Vn] *a wild animal maddened by pain* ∘ *It maddens me that she was chosen instead of me!* ▸ **maddening** /ˈmædnɪŋ/ *adj*: *maddening delays* ∘ *He has this maddening habit of never looking at the person he's talking to.* **maddeningly** *adv*: *Progress is maddeningly slow.*

made /meɪd/ *pt, pp* of MAKE¹. **IDM** **have (got) it made** (*infml*) to be sure of success. **(be) made for sb/each other** to be completely suited to sb/each other: *Peter and Judy seem made for one another, don't they?*
▸ **-made** (forming compound *adjs*) made or formed in a particular way, place, etc: *well-made* ∘ *strongly-made* ∘ *factory-made* ∘ *home-made* ∘ *man-made.* See also SELF-MADE.
■ ˈ**made-up** *adj* **1** with make-up (MAKE¹) on the face: *a heavily made-up face/woman.* **2** invented; not true: *made-up stories/words.*

Madeira /məˈdɪərə/ *n* [U, C] a white wine from the island of Madeira.
■ **Maˈdeira cake** *n* [U, C] a type of rich sponge cake (SPONGE).

Mademoiselle /ˌmædəmwəˈzel/ *n* (*abbr* **Mlle**) (*pl* **Mesdemoiselles** /ˌmeɪdm-/, *abbr* **Mlles**) (a French title or form of address used of or when speaking to a woman who is not married, esp a young one).

madhouse /ˈmædhaʊs/ *n* (*pl* **-houses** /-haʊzɪz/) **1** (*infml derog*) a place where there is much confusion or noise: *He has no idea how to control children — his classroom's a madhouse!* **2** (*dated*) a mental hospital.

madman /ˈmædmən/ *n* (*pl* **-men** /-mən/; *fem* **mad-woman** /-wʊmən/, *pl* **-women** /-wɪmɪn/) **(a)** a person who is mentally ill. **(b)** a foolish or crazy person.

madonna /məˈdɒnə/ *n* **1** the **Madonna** [sing] the Virgin Mary, mother of Jesus Christ. **2** [C] a statue or picture of the Virgin Mary: *There was a madonna on the altar.*

madrigal /ˈmædrɪgl/ *n* a song for several voices, usu sung without musical instruments. Madrigals are often about love and/or nature and were popular esp in the 16th century.

maelstrom /ˈmeɪlstrɒm/ *n* (usu *sing*) **1** a state of violent confusion: *be drawn/sucked into the maelstrom of war* ∘ *She experienced a maelstrom of conflicting emotions.* **2** a place in the sea where there is a very strong spinning current of water.

maestro /ˈmaɪstrəʊ/ *n* (*pl* **-os**) (often as a form of address showing respect, with a capital letter when followed by a name) a great performer, esp in the field of music: *Maestro Giulini* ∘ *The winning goal was scored by the maestro himself.*

Mafia /ˈmæfiə; *US* ˈmɑːf-/ *n* **1** the **Mafia** [Gp] a secret organization of criminals, originally in Sicily and now also in Italy and the USA: *a Mafia boss/gang/ killing/plot.* **2** **mafia** [CGp] (*derog or joc*) a group of people who have or are thought to have secret influence in society: *The town hall mafia will prevent this plan going through.*
▸ **Mafioso** /ˌmæfiˈəʊsəʊ/ *n* (*pl* **Mafiosi** /-siː/) a member of the Mafia.

magazine¹ /ˌmægəˈziːn; *US* ˈmægəziːn/ *n* **1** (also *infml* **mag** /mæg/) a type of large thin book with a paper cover, containing stories, pictures, etc and issued usu every week or every month: *women's magazines* ○ *glossy magazines* ○ *a literary magazine* ○ *a magazine article.* **2** a programme regularly broadcast on radio or television, dealing with a particular subject: *an arts/a gay magazine.*

magazine² /ˌmæɡəˈziːn; *US* ˈmæɡəziːn/ *n* **1** a store for weapons, AMMUNITION(1), explosives, etc. **2** the part of a gun that holds the bullets before they are fed into the BREECH. ⇨ picture at GUN.

magenta /məˈdʒentə/ *adj, n* [U] (of) a colour between purple and red: *flowers of deep magenta.*

maggot /ˈmæɡət/ *n* a creature like a small short worm (called a LARVA or GRUB). Maggots are the young of flies or certain other insects: *People use maggots as bait when they go fishing.*

Magi /ˈmeɪdʒaɪ/ *n* **the Magi** [pl] (*Bible*) the three wise men from the East who brought gifts to the baby Jesus.

magic /ˈmædʒɪk/ *n* [U] **1** the power of apparently using mysterious forces to change the form of things or influence events; practices based on this: *black/white magic* ○ *They believe that it was all done by magic.* ○ *This soap works **like magic** — the stains just disappear.* ○ *The paper turned green **as if by magic**.* Compare SORCERY, WITCHCRAFT. **2** tricks with mysterious results, done to entertain; the art of performing these. **3** (*approv*) (**a**) a charming or wonderful quality: *the magic of Shakespeare's poetry/of the woods in autumn.* (**b**) a thing that has such a quality: *Her playing was pure magic.* ▶ **magic** *adj* **1** used in or using magic: *a magic spell/wand/trick* ○ (*fig*) *the magic formula for success.* **2** special or important: *The appeal fund is approaching the magic figure of £500 000.* ○ *Trust is the magic ingredient in our relationship.* **3** (*infml*) wonderful; excellent: *a magic performance* ○ *It was one of those magic moments.*

magical /-kl/ *adj* **1** of, used in or like magic: *magical powers/charms/properties.* **2** (*infml*) charming; wonderful: *the magical world of Disney* ○ *a magical view over the bay* ○ *The whole experience was magical.* **magically** /-klɪ/ *adv.*

magician /məˈdʒɪʃn/ *n* a person who is skilled in magic. Compare CONJURER.

■ ˌmagic ˈcarpet *n* (in fairy stories) a carpet that is able to fly and carry people.

ˌmagic ˈeye *n* (*infml*) an electric device using a beam of light. When the beam is broken it shows that sb/sth is present, and can be used to control alarms, machinery, etc: *lifts opened and closed by a magic eye.*

ˌmagic ˈwand *n* = WAND¹ 1.

magisterial /ˌmædʒɪˈstɪəriəl/ *adj* (*fml*) **1** having or showing authority: *a magisterial manner/statement/pronouncement.* **2** [attrib] of or conducted by a magistrate: *magisterial decisions/proceedings.* ▶ **magisterially** /-iəli/ *adv*: *'Kindly remove them,' she said magisterially.*

magistrate /ˈmædʒɪstreɪt/ *n* an official who acts as a judge in the lowest courts; a Justice of the Peace: *be tried in a magistrates' court* ○ *come up before the magistrate.* ▶ **magistracy** /ˈmædʒɪstrəsi/ *n* **the magistracy** [Gp] magistrates as a group: *elected to the magistracy.*

magma /ˈmæɡmə/ *n* [U] very hot liquid rock found beneath the earth's surface. ⇨ picture at VOLCANO.

magnanimous /mæɡˈnænɪməs/ *adj* (*fml*) very generous or forgiving, esp towards a rival, an enemy, etc: *a magnanimous person/gesture/gift* ○ *He was magnanimous in victory* (ie when he won). ▶ **magnanimity** /ˌmæɡnəˈnɪməti/ *n* [U]: *show great magnanimity towards an opponent.* **magnanimously** *adv.*

magnate /ˈmæɡneɪt/ *n* a wealthy and powerful person, esp in business: *an oil magnate.*

magnesia /mæɡˈniːʃə/ *n* [U] a white powder used in liquid form as a medicine, and in industry.

magnesium /mæɡˈniːziəm/ *n* [U] (*symb* **Mg**) a chemical element. Magnesium is a metal with a silver colour that burns with a very bright flame. ⇨ App 7.

magnet /ˈmæɡnət/ *n* **1** a piece of iron or other material that can attract iron, either naturally or because of an electric current passed through it. A magnet will point roughly north and south when freely suspended. ⇨ picture. **2** ~ (**for sb/sth**) a person or thing that has a powerful attraction: *In the 1980s the area became a magnet for new investment.*

magnet

▶ **magnetism** /ˈmæɡnətɪzəm/ *n* [U] **1** (the science of) the qualities of MAGNETIC(1) substances. **2** great personal charm and attraction: *She obviously possessed enormous personal magnetism.* See also ANIMAL MAGNETISM.

magnetize, -ise /ˈmæɡnətaɪz/ *v* [Vn] **1** to make sth act like a magnet: *a magnetized screwdriver.* **2** to attract sb strongly, as if by a magnet: *He was magnetized by the charm of her personality.*

magnetic /mæɡˈnetɪk/ *adj* **1** having the properties of a MAGNET(1): *The block becomes magnetic when the current is switched on.* **2** very attractive: *a magnetic smile/personality.* **3** of or with magnetism (MAGNET 1): *magnetic properties/forces.* ▶ **magnetically** /-klɪ/ *adv.*

■ magˌnetic ˈcompass *n* = COMPASS 1.

magˌnetic ˈfield *n* an area round a MAGNET(1) where there is a magnetic force.

magˌnetic ˈnorth *n* [U] the direction roughly to the north indicated by a magnetic compass.

magˌnetic ˈtape *n* [U] a type of plastic tape used for recording sound or pictures.

magneto /mæɡˈniːtəʊ/ *n* (*pl* **-os**) a small electric GENERATOR that uses magnets (MAGNET 1) to produce electricity from the SPARK in an internal-combustion engine (INTERNAL).

Magnificat /mæɡˈnɪfɪkæt/ *n* **the Magnificat** [sing] the song of the Virgin Mary praising God, used in Church of England services.

magnificent /mæɡˈnɪfɪsnt/ *adj* splendid; remarkable; impressive: *a magnificent achievement/building/collection/display/view* ○ *She looked simply magnificent in her wedding dress.* ▶ **magnificence** /-sns/ *n* [U]: *the magnificence of the scenery.* **magnificently** *adv*: *The whole team played magnificently.*

magnifying glass
magnify

magnify /ˈmæɡnɪfaɪ/ *v* (*pt, pp* **-fied**) **1** to make sth appear larger, esp by using a LENS(1) or MICROSCOPE: [Vnpr] *bacteria magnified to 1 000 times their actual size* [also Vn]. ⇨ picture. **2** exaggerate sth: [Vn] *She tends to magnify the faults of people she dislikes.*

▶ **magnification** /ˌmæɡnɪfɪˈkeɪʃn/ *n* (**a**) [U] the action or power of magnifying sth: *viewed at high magnification.* (**b**) [C] the degree to which sth is magnified: *a magnification of between 7 and 10 times actual size.* **magnifier** /-faɪə(r)/ *n* a device that magnifies things.

■ ¹**magnifying glass** n a LENS(1) held in the hand and used for magnifying things. ⇨ picture.

magnitude /ˈmæɡnɪtjuːd; US -tuːd/ n [U] **1** (fml) the great size of sth: *The sheer magnitude of the task seemed overwhelming.* **2** the great importance of sth; the degree to which sth is important: *You don't appreciate the magnitude of her achievement.* ○ *a discovery of the first magnitude* (ie a most important discovery). **3** (astronomy) the degree of brightness of a star: *a star of the first/second magnitude.*

magnolia /mæɡˈnəʊliə/ n a tree with large sweet-smelling usu white or pink flowers.

magnum /ˈmæɡnəm/ n (pl **magnums**) a bottle containing 1.5 litres of wine or spirits: *a magnum of champagne.*

magnum opus /ˌmæɡnəm ˈəʊpəs/ n [sing] (Latin) a work of art, music or literature that is regarded as its author's greatest.

magpie /ˈmæɡpaɪ/ n **1** a noisy black and white bird that is attracted by, and often takes away, small bright objects. ⇨ picture. **2** a person who collects or keeps things, esp things of little use or value.

magpie

maharaja (also **maharajah**) /ˌmɑːhəˈrɑːdʒə/ n an Indian prince.

mahogany /məˈhɒɡəni/ n [U] **1** a hard reddish-brown wood used esp for making furniture: *a mahogany chair/desk/table/bookcase.* **2** [U] a reddish-brown colour: *with skin tanned to a deep mahogany.*

maid /meɪd/ n **1** (often in compounds) a female servant in a house or hotel: *We have a maid to do the housework.* ○ *The maid was changing the sheets when we got back to our room.* See also DAIRYMAID, HOUSEMAID, NURSEMAID. **2** (arch) a young woman who is not married; a girl: *love between a man and a maid.* See also OLD MAID.

■ ˌmaid of ˈhonour n (esp US) the principal BRIDESMAID at a wedding.

maiden /ˈmeɪdn/ n **1** (arch) a young woman who is not married; a girl. **2** (also ˌmaiden ˈover) (in cricket) an OVER³ in which no runs are scored.

▶ **maiden** adj [attrib] being the first event or act of its kind: *a maiden speech* (ie a Member of Parliament's first speech in Parliament) ○ *a maiden voyage* (ie a ship's first voyage).

■ ˌmaiden ˈaunt n an AUNT(1) who is not married.
ˈmaiden name n a woman's family name before her marriage.

maidenhair /ˈmeɪdnheə(r)/ n [U] a type of FERN with thin stems and delicate leaves.

maidenhead /ˈmeɪdnhed/ n (arch) **1** [U] the state of being a VIRGIN. **2** [C] a HYMEN.

mail¹ /meɪl/ n **1** [sing, U] the official system of collecting, transporting and delivering letters and parcels: *send a letter by airmail* ○ *The letter is in the mail.* ○ *a mail van/service/train.* **2(a)** [U] letters, parcels, etc sent by post: *Post office workers sort the mail.* ○ *There isn't much mail today.* ○ *The office mail is opened in the morning.* **(b)** [C] letters, parcels, etc delivered or collected at one time: *I want this letter to catch the afternoon mail.* ○ *Has the mail come yet?* ○ *Is there another mail in the afternoon?* Compare POST³. See also FAN MAIL, JUNK MAIL.

▶ **mail** v ~ **sth** (**to sb**) (esp US) to send sth by post: [Vn] *Don't forget to mail these letters.* [Vnn] *Mail me a new form, please.* [Vnpr] *I'll mail it to you tomorrow.* Compare POST⁴.

mailing n an act of sending large quantities of mail:

sales/weekly mailings. ¹**mailing list** n a list of names and addresses of persons to whom information, advertising material, etc is to be sent regularly: *Please add my name to your mailing list.*

■ ˌmail ˈorder n [U] a system of buying and selling goods by post: *buy sth by mail order* ○ *a mail-order business/company/firm* (ie one dealing in mail-order goods) ○ *a mail-order catalogue* (ie one that lists mail-order goods and their prices).

mail² /meɪl/ n [U] body armour made of metal rings or plates linked together, worn by soldiers in former times: *a coat of mail.*

mailbag /ˈmeɪlbæɡ/ n a strong bag in which letters, parcels, etc are carried.

mailbox /ˈmeɪlbɒks/ n (US) **1** = LETTER-BOX. **2** = POSTBOX.

mailman /ˈmeɪlmæn/ n (pl **-men** /-men/) (US) = POSTMAN.

mailshot /ˈmeɪlʃɒt/ n **(a)** a piece of advertising material sent to large numbers of people by post. **(b)** an act of sending advertising material in this way.

maim /meɪm/ v to wound or injure sb so that part of the body is permanently damaged or lost: [Vn] *killing and maiming innocent civilians* ○ *be maimed for life.*

main¹ /meɪn/ adj [attrib] (no comparative or superlative) most important; chief; principal: *the main thing to remember* ○ *the main street of a town* ○ *Be careful crossing that main road.* ○ *the main meal of the day* ○ *the main course (of a meal)* ○ *My main concern is the welfare of the children.* **IDM** **have/with an eye for/on/to the main chance** ⇨ EYE¹. **in the ¹main** in general; on the whole: *Tourists come from Europe, in the main.* ○ *The service here is in the main reliable.*

▶ **mainly** adv to the largest degree; in the majority; mostly: *You are mainly to blame.* ○ *The people in the hotel were mainly foreign tourists.*

■ ˌmain ˈclause n (grammar) a clause that can stand on its own to form a sentence.
ˌmain ˈdrag n [sing] (infml esp US) the principal street of a town or city.
ˌmain ˈline n a principal railway line between two places: *the main line from London to Coventry* ○ *a main-line station.*

main² /meɪn/ n **1** [C] **(a)** a principal pipe bringing water or gas, or a principal cable carrying electric current, from the source of supply into a building: *a burst water main* ○ *The gas main exploded and set fire to the house.* **(b)** a principal SEWER to which pipes from a building are connected. **2** the **mains** [sing or pl v] the source of water, gas or electricity supply to a building or an area: *We are/The house is not yet connected to the mains.* ○ *The electricity supply has been cut off/disconnected at the mains.* ○ *mains gas/water/electricity supply* (ie supplied from the mains) ○ *mains drainage* ○ *a mains/battery shaver* (ie one which can be operated either from a mains electricity supply or by batteries).

mainframe /ˈmeɪnfreɪm/ (also ˌmainframe comˈputer) n a large powerful computer, usu shared by many users. Compare MICROCOMPUTER, MINICOMPUTER, PERSONAL COMPUTER.

mainland /ˈmeɪnlænd/ n [sing] a large mass of land forming a country, continent, etc without its islands: *get a boat back to the mainland.* — adj [attrib]: *mainland Britain/USA.*

mainline /ˈmeɪnlaɪn/ v (sl) (of sb who is an ADDICT) to inject a drug into a large vein: [Vn] *be mainlining hard drugs* [also V].

mainsail /ˈmeɪnseɪl, ˈmeɪnsl/ n the principal sail on a ship. ⇨ picture at YACHT.

mainspring /ˈmeɪnsprɪŋ/ n (usu sing) **1** the most important part of or reason for sth: *Small companies are the mainspring of the British economy.* ○ *The love*

M

of literature was a mainspring of her life. **2** the principal spring¹(1) of a clock or watch.

mainstay /'meɪnsteɪ/ *n* the chief support; the main part of sth, enabling it to continue or be effective: *He is the mainstay of our theatre group.* ○ *Slow love songs are the mainstay of his act.*

mainstream /'meɪnstriːm/ *n* [sing] the beliefs, attitudes, etc that are shared by most people and are therefore regarded as normal or conventional; the dominant TREND in opinion, fashion, etc: *the mainstream of political thought* ○ *mainstream politics* ○ *a film director who is in the mainstream* ○ *mainstream jazz.*

maintain /meɪn'teɪn/ *v* **1** to cause sth to continue; to keep sth in existence at the same level, standard, etc: [Vn] *maintain friendly relations with sb* ○ *maintain law and order/standards* ○ *maintain prices* (ie prevent them falling or rising) ○ *The improvement in his health is being maintained.* **2** keep sth in good condition or working order by checking or repairing it regularly: [Vn] *The house is large and difficult to maintain.* ○ *Engineers maintain the turbines.* **3** to insist that sth is the case: [Vn] *maintain one's innocence* [V.that] *He has always maintained that he was not guilty of the crime.* **4** to support sb/sth financially: [Vn] *earn enough to maintain a family in comfort* ○ *This school is maintained by a charity.*

maintenance /'meɪntənəns/ *n* [U] **1** the action of maintaining sb/sth or the state of being maintained: *the maintenance of good relations between countries* ○ *price maintenance* ○ *She's taking classes in car maintenance.* ○ *money for the maintenance of one's family* ○ *a maintenance man/gang/van.* **2** (*Brit law*) money that one is legally required to pay to support sb: *He has to pay maintenance to his ex-wife.* See also ALIMONY.

maisonette (also **maisonnette**) /ˌmeɪzə'net/ *n* (*esp Brit*) a flat²(1) on two floors within a building, usu with a separate entrance.

maize /meɪz/ *n* [U] a tall CEREAL plant that produces yellow grain on large ears (EAR²). See also CORN ON THE COB, SWEET CORN.

Maj *abbr* Major: *Maj (James) Williams* ○ *Maj-Gen* (ie Major-General) (*Tom*) *Phillips.*

majestic /mə'dʒestɪk/ *adj* having or showing impressive beauty or dignity; grand; imposing (IMPOSE): *majestic views/scenery* ○ *a big house, majestic in its design.* ▶ **majestically** /-klɪ/ *adv: The cliffs rise majestically from the ocean.*

majesty /'mædʒəsti/ *n* **1** [U] impressive dignity or beauty: *the sheer majesty of the mountain scenery.* **2**(**a**) [U] royal power. (**b**) **Majesty** [C] (used with a preceding *possess det* when speaking to or about a royal person or royal people): *Thank you, Your Majesty.* ○ *at His/Her Majesty's command* ○ *Their Majesties have arrived.*

major¹ /'meɪdʒə(r)/ *adj* **1** [usu attrib] important or more important; great or greater: *a major road* ○ *play a major role in sth* ○ *the major part of sth* ○ *a major operation* (ie a medical operation that could be dangerous to a person's life) ○ *We have encountered major problems.* ○ *She has written a major novel* (ie one of high quality and great importance). Compare MINOR 1. **2** (*Brit dated or joc*) (in private schools) first or older of two brothers or boys with the same family name, esp in the same school: *Brown major.* Compare MINOR 2, SENIOR 3. **3** (*music*) (of a key¹(3a) or scale¹(6)) having two full tones (TONE¹ 6) between the first and third notes: *the major key* ○ *a major scale* ○ *the key of D major.* Compare MINOR 3.

▶ **major** *v* PHRV **'major in sth** (*US*) to specialize in a certain subject at college or university: *She majored in math and physics (at Yale).*

major *n* **1** [sing] (*music*) a major key: *shift from major to minor.* **2** [C] (*US*) (**a**) the principal subject or course of a student at college or university: *Her major is French.* (**b**) a student studying such a subject: *She's a French major.*

■ **'major 'league** *n* (*US sport*) a senior and important league, esp in BASEBALL and ice hockey (ICE¹): ˌmajor league 'baseball.

'major 'suit *n* (in card-games) spades (SPADE²) or hearts (HEART 5).

major² /'meɪdʒə(r)/ *n* (the title of) an army officer of middle rank: *Major Ronald Ferguson* ○ *He's a major in the US army.* ⇨ App 6.

■ **ˌmajor-'general** *n* (the title of) an army officer of high rank. ⇨ App 6.

majority /mə'dʒɒrəti; *US* -'dʒɔːr-/ *n* **1 the majority** [Gp] the greater number or part; most: *The majority of people prefer TV to radio.* ○ *The majority was/were in favour of the proposal.* ○ *in the vast majority of cases* ○ *majority opinion/rule* ○ *It was a **majority decision*** (ie decided by what most people wanted). ○ *Those who favour the proposed changes are in **the majority.*** Compare MINORITY. **2** [C] ~ (**over sb**) (**a**) the number by which votes for one side are more than those for the other side: *She was elected by a majority of 749.* ○ *They had a large majority over the other party at the last election.* ○ *The government does not have an **overall majority*** (ie a majority over all other parties together). (**b**) (*US*) the number by which votes for one candidate are more than those for all other candidates together. See also PLURALITY 2. **3** [U] the age when one is legally considered a full adult: *The age of majority in Britain was reduced from 21 to 18 in 1970.* IDM **the silent majority** ⇨ SILENT.

■ **ma'jority 'verdict** *n* (*law*) the VERDICT of the majority, but not all, of a JURY.

make¹ /meɪk/ *v* (*pt, pp* **made** /meɪd/)

● **Constructing or creating 1**(**a**) ~ sth (**from/out** of sth); ~ sth (**for sb**) to construct, create or prepare sth by combining materials or putting parts together: [Vn] *make a desk/a dress/a cake* ○ *make bread/cement/wine* ○ *make* (ie manufacture) *paper* ○ *God made man.* ○ *She makes her own clothes.* [Vnpr] *Wine is made from grapes.* ○ *'What is your bracelet made of?' 'It's made of gold.'* ○ *She made coffee for us all.* [Vnn] *I made myself a cup of tea.* (**b**) ~ sth **into sth** (esp passive) to put materials or parts together to produce sth: [Vnpr] *Glass is made into bottles.* (**c**) to arrange a bed so that it is ready for use: [Vn] *Please make your beds before you go out.* **2** to cause sth to appear as a result of breaking, tearing, removing material or striking: [Vnpr] *The stone made a dent in the roof of my car.* ○ *make a scratch on the surface of a table* [Vn] *The holes in the cloth were made by moths.* **3** to create or establish sth: [Vn] *These regulations were made to protect children.* ○ *Who made this ridiculous rule?* **4** to write, compose or prepare sth: [Vn] *make one's will* ○ *make a treaty with sb* ○ *She has made* (ie directed) *several movies.* ○ *I'll ask my lawyer to make a deed of transfer.*

● **Causing to become, do or appear 5** to cause sth to exist, happen or be done: [Vn] *make a noise/disturbance/mess/fuss* ○ *Sh! Don't make a sound.* ○ *It makes a change to have the house to ourselves.* ○ *She tried to make a good impression on the interviewer.* ○ *I keep making the same mistakes.* ○ *He's making good progress at school.* ○ *make an appointment.* **6** to cause sb/sth to be or become: [Vn-adj] *The news made her happy.* ○ *She made clear her objections/made it clear that she objected to the proposal.* ○ *His actions made him universally respected.* ○ *Can you make yourself understood in English?* ○ *The full story was never made public.* ○ *She couldn't make herself/her voice heard above the noise of the traffic.* **7**(**a**) to force sb to do sth: [Vn.inf (no to)] *They made me repeat the whole story.* [V.n to inf] *She must be made to comply with the rules.* [Vn] *He never cleans up his*

---

room and his mother never tries to make him. (**b**) to cause sb/sth to do sth: [Vn.inf (no *to*)] *Onions make your eyes water.* ○ *Her jokes made us all laugh.* ○ *I couldn't make my car start this morning.* ○ *What makes you say that?* ○ *I rang the doorbell several times but couldn't make anyone hear.* ○ *Nothing will make me change my mind.* ⇨ note at CAUSE. **8** to represent sb/sth as being or doing sth: [Vn-adj] *You've made my nose too big* (eg in a drawing). [Vn.inf (no *to*)] *The novelist makes his heroine commit suicide at the end of the book.* [Vn-n] *He makes Lear a truly tragic figure.* **9** to elect or appoint sb as sth: [Vn-n] *make sb king/an earl/a peer* ○ *He was made spokesman by the committee.* ○ *She made him her assistant.* **10** ~ **sth of sb/sth** to cause sb/sth to be or become sth: [Vnpr] *We'll make a tennis player of you yet* (ie turn you into a good tennis player despite the fact that you are not a good one now). ○ *This isn't very important — I don't want to make an issue of it.* ○ *Don't make a habit of it.* ○ *They've made a success of the enterprise.* ○ *You've made a terrible mess of this job.* ○ *It's important to try to make something of* (ie to achieve sth in) *your life.* [Vn-n] *She made it her business to find out who was responsible.*

• **Being or becoming something 11** to be or become sth through development; to turn out to be sth: [V-n] *If he keeps practising, he'll make an excellent musician.* ○ *He'll never make an actor.* ○ *She would have made an excellent teacher.* **12** to serve or function as sth: [V-n] *That will make a good ending to the book.* ○ *This hall would make an excellent theatre.* **13(a)** to add up to, equal or amount to sth: [V-n] *5 and 7 make 12.* ○ *A hundred cents make one dollar.* ○ *How many members make a quorum?* (**b**) to constitute, cause or lead to sth: [V-n] *His thrillers make enthralling reading.* ○ *The play makes a splendid evening's entertainment.* **14** to be a total of sth: [V-n] *That makes the tenth time he's failed his driving test!*

• **Gaining or winning 15** to earn, gain or acquire sth: [Vn] *She makes £25000 a year.* ○ *make a profit/loss* ○ *He made a fortune on the stock market.* ○ *How much do you stand to make from the deal?* **16** (in card-games, esp bridge²) (**a**) to win a trick(5) with a particular card: [Vn] *She made her ten of hearts.* (**b**) to win a trick or fulfil a contract: [Vn] *We bid game and made it.*

• **Other meanings 17** (no passive) to calculate or estimate sth to be sth: [Vn-n] *What time do you make it?/What do you make the time?* ○ *How large do you make the audience?* ○ *I make the total exactly £50.* [Vn.*that*] *I make it that we've got about 70 miles to go.* **18** (no passive) to manage to reach or go to a place or position: [Vn] *Do you think we'll make Oxford by midday?* ○ *The flight leaves in twenty minutes — we'll never make it* (ie reach the airport in time to catch it). ○ *I'm sorry I couldn't make your party last night.* ○ *Her new novel has made* (ie sold enough copies to be in) *the best-seller lists.* ○ *She'll never make* (ie win a place in) *the team.* ○ *The story made* (ie appeared on) *the front page of the national newspapers.* **19** to put sth forward for consideration; to propose sth: [Vnn] *Has she made you an offer* (ie said how much money she would pay you) *for your car?* [Vn] *make a suggestion/proposal* [Vnpr] *The employers made a new offer to the workforce.* **20** to cause or ENSURE the success of sth: [Vn] *A good wine can make a meal.* ○ *It was the beautiful weather that really made the holiday.* ○ *This news has really made my day.* **21** ~ (**as if**) **to do sth** to behave as if one is about to do sth: [V.*to* inf] *He made as if to speak.* ○ *She made to go but he held her back.* **22** (often used in a pattern with a *n*, in which *make* and the *n* have the same meaning as a *v* similar in spelling to the *n*, eg *make a decision,* ie decide; *make*

a guess (at sth), ie guess (at sth); for other expressions of this kind, see the entries for relevant *ns*).

IDM Most idioms containing **make** are at the entries for the nouns or adjectives in the idiom, eg **make love** ⇨ LOVE¹; **make merry** ⇨ MERRY. **make 'do (with sth)** to manage with sth that is not really adequate or satisfactory: *We were in a hurry so we had to make do with a quick snack.* ○ *I haven't got much money but I'll just have to make do.* **make 'good** to become rich and successful: *He made good after emigrating to America.* **make sth 'good 1** to pay for, replace or repair sth that has been lost or damaged: *She promised to make good the damage/loss.* ○ *The plaster will have to be made good before you paint it.* **2** to carry sth out; to fulfil sth: *make good a promise/threat.* **'make it** (*infml*) **1** to be successful in one's career: *He's never really made it as an actor.* **2** to succeed in reaching a place after difficulty, effort, etc: *It was a terrible journey but we finally made it.* **3** to attend sth: *I'm afraid I won't be able to make it to your party next week.* **make the 'most of sth/sb/oneself** to gain as much advantage as one can from sth/sb/oneself: *make the most of one's chances/opportunities/talents* ○ *It's my first holiday for two years so I'm going to make the most of it.* ○ *She certainly tries to make the most of herself* (eg by developing or displaying her good qualities). **make 'much of sth/sb 1** (in negative sentences and questions) to understand sth well: *I couldn't make much of what he was saying, could you?* **2** to treat sth/sb as very important; to stress or emphasize sth: *He always makes much of his humble origins.* **,make or 'break sb/sth** to be the deciding factor in making sb/sth either a success or a failure: *The council's decision will make or break the local theatre.* ○ *It's make-or-break time for the company.* **'make something of oneself** to succeed in improving one's position in life by effort.

PHR V **'make for sth 1** to move towards sth: *The ship made for the open sea.* ○ *It's getting late; we'd better make for home.* ○ *When the interval came everyone made for the bar.* **2** to help to make sth possible; to contribute or lead to sth: *The large print makes for easier reading.* ○ *Constant arguing doesn't make for a happy marriage.*
'make sb/sth into sb/sth to change or convert sb/sth into sb/sth: *We're making our attic into an extra bedroom.* ○ *The local cinema has been made into a disco.*
'make sth of sb/sth (esp with *what*) to understand the meaning or nature of sb/sth to be sth: *What do you make of it all?* ○ *What are we to make of her behaviour?* ○ *I don't know what to make of* (ie think of) *the new manager.* ○ *I can make nothing of this scribble.*
,make 'off (*infml*) to hurry or rush away, esp in order to escape: *The thieves made off in a stolen car.* **,make 'off with sth** (*infml*) to steal sth and hurry away with it: *Two boys made off with our cases while we weren't looking.*
,make 'out 1 (*infml*) (usu in questions after *how*) to manage; to survive; to FARE³: *How did he make out while his wife was away?* ○ *How are you making out with Mary?* (ie How is your relationship with her developing?). **2** (*US sl*) to engage in sexual activity. **,make sb 'out** to understand what sb's character is: *What a strange person she is! I can't make her out at all.* **,make sb/sth 'out** to manage to see sb/sth or read or hear sth: *I could just make out a figure in the darkness.* ○ *Can you make out what that sign says?* ○ *I could hear voices but I couldn't make out what they were saying.* **,make sth 'out** to write out or complete a form or document: *make out a cheque for £10* ○ *Applications must be made out in triplicate.* ○ *The doctor made out a prescription for me.* **,make sth 'out;** **,make 'out if/whether...** to understand or

M

[V] = verb used alone   [Vn] = verb + noun   [Vp] = verb + particle   [Vpr] = verb + prepositional phrase

interpret sth: *I can't make out what she wants.* ○ *How do you make that out?* (ie How did you reach that conclusion?) ○ *I can't make out if she enjoys her job or not.* ˌmake 'out that ...; ˌmake oneself/sb/sth 'out to be ... to claim; to assert; to maintain: *He made out that he had been robbed.* ○ *She's not as rich as people make out/as people make her out to be.* ○ *He makes himself out to be cleverer than he really is.*

ˌmake sth 'over (to sb/sth) to transfer the ownership of sth: *He has made over the whole property to his eldest son.*

ˌmake 'up; ˌmake oneself/sb up to put powder, LIPSTICK, etc on the face to make it more attractive or to prepare it for an appearance in the theatre, on television, etc: *She spent an hour making (herself) up before the party.* ○ *She's always very heavily made up.* ˌmake sth 'up 1 to form or constitute sth: *Animal bodies are made up of cells.* ○ *What are the qualities that make up her character?* ○ *Society is made up of people of widely differing abilities.* 2 to put sth together from several different things: *make up a bundle of old clothes for the refugees* ○ *She made up a basket of food for the picnic.* 3 to invent sth, esp in order to deceive or entertain sb: *make up an excuse* ○ *I told the children a story, making it up as I went along.* ○ *Stop making things up!* 4 to be sb/sth that completes a number or an amount required: *We still need $100 to make up the sum required.* ○ *We have ten players, so we need one more to make up a team.* 5 to replace sth lost; to compensate for sth: *Our losses will have to be made up with more loans.* ○ *Can I leave early this afternoon and make up the time tomorrow?* 6 to prepare a medicine by mixing different ingredients together: *The pharmacist made up the prescription.* 7 to create a garment out of material: *make up a dress from a pattern.* 8 to prepare a bed for use; to create a temporary bed: *We made up a bed for me on the sofa.* ○ *They made up the bed in the spare room for our guest.* ○ *The fire needs making up* (ie needs to have more coal put on it). ˌmake 'up for sth to compensate for sth: *Hard work can make up for a lack of intelligence.* ○ *Nothing can make up for the loss* (ie death) *of a child.* ○ *The beautiful autumn made up for the wet summer.* ○ *After all the delays, we were anxious to make up for lost time.* ˌmake 'up (to sb) for sth to compensate sb for the trouble or suffering one has caused them: *How can I make up for the way I've treated you?* ˌmake 'up to sb (*infml*) to be pleasant to sb in order to win their favour: *He's always making up to the boss.* ˌmake it 'up to sb (*infml*) to compensate sb for sth they have suffered or not received or for money they have spent: *I'm sorry I can't take you out today — I'll make it up to you next week.* ○ *Thanks for buying my ticket — I'll make it up to you later.* ˌmake (it) 'up (with sb) to end a quarrel or dispute with sb and become friends again: *Why don't you two kiss and make up?* ○ *Has he made it up with her yet/Have they made it up yet?*

'make it with sb (*sl*) to have sex with sb.

■ 'make-believe *n* [U] (a) the mental activity of pretending or imagining things, esp those which are better than reality: *indulge in make-believe.* (b) things imagined in this way: *live in a world of make-believe/a make-believe world.*

'make-up *n* 1 [U] cosmetics (COSMETIC) used esp by women to make themselves more attractive, or by actors: *apply/put on make-up* ○ *She never wears make-up.* 2 [sing] (a) the combination of qualities that form a person's character or personality: *Jealousy is not part of his make-up.* (b) the things, people, etc that form sth; the composition(3) of sth: *change the make-up of the committee* (ie replace some of the people who work on it). 3 [C usu *sing*] the arrangement of type, illustrations, etc on a printed page. 4 [C] (*US*) a special examination or test given to students who missed or failed an earlier one.

make² /meɪk/ *n* ~ (of sth) the name or origin of manufacture of a product; a BRAND(1): *cars of all makes* ○ *What make of radio is it?* ⇨ note at BRAND. **IDM on the 'make** (*infml derog*) trying to gain an advantage or profit for oneself.

maker /'meɪkə(r)/ *n* 1 [C] (often in compounds) a person or company that makes or produces sth: *decision/policy/programme makers* ○ *a dressmaker* ○ *a film-maker* ○ *a cabinet-maker* ○ *a watch with the maker's name on it* ○ *If it doesn't work, send it back to the makers.* See also TROUBLEMAKER. 2 **the/our Maker** [sing] the Creator; God. **IDM meet one's Maker** ⇨ MEET¹.

makeshift /'meɪkʃɪft/ *adj* used temporarily to serve a function because the real thing is not available: *use an empty crate as a makeshift table* ○ *turn the hall into a makeshift classroom.*

makeweight /'meɪkweɪt/ *n* an unimportant extra thing or person added to complete sth: *a makeweight player in the team.*

making /'meɪkɪŋ/ *n* [U] (often in compounds) the process of making or producing sth: *ingredients used in the making of bread* ○ *She finds the making of decisions difficult.* ○ *film-making* ○ *a dressmaking company* ○ *law-making.* **IDM be the 'making of sb** to cause sb to succeed or develop well: *University was the making of him.* **have the 'makings of sth** to have the qualities needed to become sth; to show the POTENTIAL to become sth: *a book with all the makings of a minor classic* ○ *She has the makings of a first-rate lawyer.* **in the 'making** in the process of developing or being made into sth: *This is the work of a great writer in the making.* ○ *This model was two years in the making.* **of one's own 'making** (of a problem, etc) caused by oneself, not sb/sth else: *His financial difficulties are entirely of his own making.*

mal- *comb form* bad or badly; not correct or correctly: *maladjusted* ○ *maladministration* ○ *malfunction.*

malachite /'mæləkaɪt/ *n* [U] a green mineral that can be polished and used for ornaments, decoration, etc.

maladjusted /ˌmælə'dʒʌstɪd/ *adj* (of a person) unable to adapt to the demands of a social environment and behave in an acceptable way: *a school for maladjusted children.* ▶ **maladjustment** /ˌmælə'dʒʌstmənt/ *n* [U, C].

maladministration /ˌmæləd,mɪnɪ'streɪʃn/ *n* [U] (*fml*) the poor or dishonest management of public affairs, business dealings, etc: *accusations of corruption and maladministration.*

maladroit /ˌmælə'drɔɪt/ *adj* (*fml*) not clever or skilful; CLUMSY: *the maladroit handling of the whole affair* ○ *maladroit management.* Compare ADROIT.

malady /'mælədi/ *n* (*fml*) a disease; an illness: (*fig*) *Violent crime is only one of the maladies afflicting modern society.*

malaise /mə'leɪz/ *n* [sing] (*fml*) (a) a general feeling of illness, without clear signs of a particular one. (b) a general lack of satisfaction or energy whose exact cause is difficult to identify: *There are signs of (a creeping) malaise in our office.* ○ *the current malaise in our society.*

malaria /mə'leəriə/ *n* [U] a disease resulting from the bite of certain types of MOSQUITO. The disease causes periods of fever and shivering (SHIVER): *a bad attack of malaria* ○ *a malaria sufferer.* ▶ **malarial** /-iəl/ *adj: malarial insects/patients/regions.*

malcontent /'mælkəntent; *US* ˌmælkən'tent/ *n* (*fml*) a person who is not satisfied with a situation and complains or causes trouble: *All the trouble is being caused by a handful of malcontents.*

male /meɪl/ *adj* 1 of the sex that does not give birth to babies: *a male horse/child/bird* ○ *a male voice.* 2 (of a plant) having flowers that produce POLLEN and

M

not seeds. **3** (*techn*) (of electrical plugs, parts of tools, etc) having a projecting part which is inserted into a SOCKET, hole, etc (the female part).
▶ **male** *n* a male person, animal, plant, etc: *a male-dominated profession*. ⇨ note at FEMALE.
maleness *n* [U].
■ ¦**male** ¦**chauvinism** *n* [U] (*derog*) the belief held by some men that men are superior to women. ¦**male** ¦**chauvinist** *n*: *She was so angry at his sexist remarks that she called him* **a male chauvinist pig**.

malefactor /ˈmælɪfæktə(r)/ *n* (*fml*) a person who does sth wrong, esp one who breaks the law: *Malefactors will be pursued and punished.*

malevolent /məˈlevələnt/ *adj* [usu attrib] having or showing a wish to do evil or cause harm to others: *a malevolent person/look/smile*. ▶ **malevolence** /-əns/ *n* [U]: *an act of sheer malevolence.* **malevolently** *adv*.

malformation /ˌmælfɔːˈmeɪʃn/ *n* **(a)** [U] the state of being badly formed or shaped: *This treatment could result in malformation of the arms.* **(b)** [C] a badly formed part, esp of the body: *a malformation of the spine.*
▶ **malformed** /ˌmælˈfɔːmd/ *adj* badly formed or shaped. Compare DEFORM.

malfunction /ˌmælˈfʌŋkʃn/ *v* (*fml*) (of an apparatus, a machine, etc) to fail to work normally or properly: [V] *The pilot died when his parachute malfunctioned.* ○ *malfunctioning body cells.* ▶ **malfunction** *n* [C, U]: *a major malfunction of the system* ○ *due to technical malfunction.*

malice /ˈmælɪs/ *n* [U] ~ (**towards sb**) the desire to harm sb; hatred for sb: *a look of pure malice* ○ *She did it out of malice.* ○ *She certainly bears you no malice.* **IDM with ¦malice a¦ˈforethought** with the deliberate intention to commit a crime.
▶ **malicious** /məˈlɪʃəs/ *adj* intended to harm sb; caused by hatred: *malicious gossip/damage* ○ *a malicious act/comment.* **maliciously** *adv*.

malign /məˈlaɪn/ *v* to say things that are unpleasant or not true about sb: [Vn] *malign an innocent person.*
▶ **malign** *adj* (*fml*) harmful: *a malign influence/intention/effect.* Compare BENIGN 1.

malignant /məˈlɪɡnənt/ *adj* **1** (of a TUMOUR or disease) that cannot be controlled and is likely to prove fatal: *malignant cells* ○ *The growth is not malignant.* Compare BENIGN 3. **2** showing a strong desire to harm people; cruel: *a malignant power/spirit.*
▶ **malignancy** /-nənsi/ *n* **1** [C] a malignant growth (4a) in the body. **2** [U] the state of being malignant.

malinger /məˈlɪŋɡə(r)/ *v* [V] (*derog*) (usu in the continuous tenses) to pretend to be ill in order to avoid work or duty. ▶ **malingerer** *n*.

mall /mæl, mɔːl/ *n* a large covered area that contains many different shops and in which traffic is not allowed: *a shopping mall.*

mallard /ˈmælɑːd; US ˈmælərd/ *n* (*pl* unchanged or **mallards**) a common type of wild duck.

malleable /ˈmæliəbl/ *adj* **1** (of metals and other substances) that can be beaten or pressed into different shapes easily. **2** (of people, ideas, etc) easily influenced or changed: *The young are more malleable than the old.* ▶ **malleability** /ˌmæliəˈbɪləti/ *n* [U].

mallet /ˈmælɪt/ *n* **1** a hammer with a large wooden head. ⇨ picture at CHISEL. **2** a hammer with a long handle and a wooden head, used for hitting the ball in CROQUET or POLO.

mallow /ˈmæləʊ/ *n* a plant with hairy stems and leaves and pink, purple or white flowers.

malnourished /ˌmælˈnʌrɪʃt; US -ˈnɜːr-/ *adj* (*fml*) suffering from MALNUTRITION. Compare UNDERNOURISHED.

malnutrition /ˌmælnjuːˈtrɪʃn; US -nuː-/ *n* (*fml*) [U] a

condition resulting from a lack of food or the right type of food: *children suffering from severe malnutrition.*

malodorous /ˌmælˈəʊdərəs/ *adj* (*fml*) having an unpleasant smell: *malodorous drains.*

malpractice /ˌmælˈpræktɪs/ *n* (*law*) **(a)** [U] careless, illegal or unacceptable behaviour by sb in a professional or official position: *medical malpractice.* **(b)** [C] an instance of this: *sent to trial for alleged malpractices.*

malt /mɔːlt, mɒlt/ *n* [U] a grain, usu BARLEY, that has been soaked in water, allowed to GERMINATE and then dried, used for making beer, WHISKY, etc: *malt whisky/vinegar.*
▶ **malt** *v* to make grain into malt: [Vn] *malted barley/wheat.*
■ ¦**malted** ¦**milk** *n* a drink made from malt and dried milk.

maltreat /ˌmælˈtriːt/ *v* (usu passive) to treat a person or an animal with violence or cruelty: [Vn] *maltreated children/cats.* ▶ **maltreatment** *n* [U]: *suffer from serious maltreatment and neglect.*

mam /mæm/ *n* (*Brit infml*) (often as a form of address) mother.

mama /məˈmɑː/ *n* (*dated Brit*) (often as a form of address) mother.

mamba /ˈmæmbə/ *n* a black or green poisonous African snake.

mamma /ˈmæmə; US ˈmɑːmə/ *n* (*infml*) (often as a form of address) mother.

mammal /ˈmæml/ *n* any of the class of animals that give birth to live babies and feed their young on milk from the breast. ▶ **mammalian** /mæˈmeɪliən/ *adj*: *mammalian species.*

mammary /ˈmæməri/ *adj* [attrib] (*biology*) of the breasts: *the mammary gland* (ie the one that produces milk).

Mammon /ˈmæmən/ *n* [U] (*usu derog*) wealth regarded as a god or an evil influence: *worship Mammon* (ie value money highly) ○ (*saying*) *You cannot serve both God and Mammon.*

mammoth /ˈmæməθ/ *n* a large hairy type of elephant, now extinct.
▶ **mammoth** *adj* [attrib] huge; IMMENSE: *a mammoth project/task.*

mammy /ˈmæmi/ *n* (*US or Brit dialect infml*) (often as a form of address) mother.

man¹ /mæn/ *n* (*pl* **men** /men/) **1** [C] an adult male human being: *clothes for men.* See also DIRTY OLD MAN. **2** [C] a human being of either sex; a person: *All men must die.* ⇨ note at FEMALE. **3** [sing] (without *the* or *a*) **(a)** the human race: *Man is mortal.* **(b)** the people of a particular period of history: *prehistoric/early/modern man* ○ *Renaissance man* ○ *the evolution of man.* ⇨ note at GENDER. **4** [C] a husband, male lover or BOYFRIEND: *Who's her new man?* ○ *be man and wife* (ie be married). **5** [C usu *pl*] a male person under the authority of sb else: *officers and men in the army/navy* ○ *The foreman gave the men* (ie the workers) *their instructions.* **6** [sing] (*dated fml*) a male servant: *My man will drive you home.* **7** [C] a present or former male member of a named university: *a Cambridge/Yale man.* **8** [sing] (*infml*) (used as a form of address, esp in a lively, angry or impatient way): *Don't just stand there, man — get a doctor!* **9** [C] a person with the qualities often associated with men such as being brave, tough, etc: *Be a man* (ie Be brave)*!* ○ *People admired him and considered him a real man.* ○ *She's more of a man than he is.* **10** [C] a piece used in games such as CHESS, draughts (DRAUGHT 3), etc: *capture all sb's men.* See also RIGHT-HAND MAN. **IDM all things to all men/people** ⇨ THING. **an angry young man** ⇨ ANGRY. **as good, well, far, much, etc as the next man** ⇨ NEXT¹. **as one ¦man** with everyone acting

M

together or in agreement: *The staff speak as one man on this issue.* **be sb's 'man** to be the person perfectly suited to a requirement: *If you need a driver, I'm your man.* ○ *If you want a good music teacher, he's your man.* **be 'man enough (to do sth)** to be brave enough: *You're not man enough to fight me!* **be one's own 'man** to act or think independently, not following others or being ordered: *He's his own man, but he doesn't ignore advice.* ○ *Working for himself meant that he could be his own man.* **be twice the man/woman** ⇨ TWICE. **ˌevery man for him'self (and the devil take the hindmost)** *(saying)* everyone must look after her or his own interests, safety, etc: *In business, it's every man for himself.* **the grand old man** ⇨ GRAND. **hit/kick a man when he's 'down** to continue to hurt or upset sb who is already defeated, depressed, etc. **the inner man** ⇨ INNER. **make a 'man (out) of sb** to turn a young man into an adult one: *The army will make a man of him.* **a ˌman about 'town** a man who frequently goes to fashionable parties, clubs, theatres, etc. **ˌman and 'boy** from youth to a later age: *He has worked for the firm for thirty years, man and boy.* **the ˌman in the 'street** the average ordinary person of either sex: *The man in the street is opposed to this idea.* **a ˌman of 'God** *(fml or rhet)* a CLERGYMAN. **a man/woman of parts** ⇨ PART[1]. **the ˌman of the 'match** *(sport)* the team member who gives the best performance in a particular game: *be voted man of the match* ○ *win the man of the match award.* **a man/woman of his/her word** ⇨ WORD. **a man/woman of the world** ⇨ WORLD. **ˌman to 'man** openly and directly, between two men: *Let's talk man to man.* ○ *a ˌman-to-man 'talk.* **a 'man's man** a man who is popular with other men, rather than with women, because of his personality. **a marked man** ⇨ MARKED. **the odd man/one out** ⇨ ODD. **the poor man's sb/sth** ⇨ POOR. **sort out the men from the boys** ⇨ SORT[2]. **time and tide wait for no man** ⇨ TIME[1]. **to a 'man** all, without exception: *To a man, they answered 'Yes'.* ○ *They were killed, to a man, in the futile attack.*

▶ **man** *interj* *(infml esp US)* (used to express surprise, admiration, etc): *Man! That's huge!*

-man (forming compound *ns*) **1(a)** (with *ns*) a person who lives in: *countryman.* **(b)** (with *adjs* and *ns*) a native of: *Irishman.* **2** (with *ns*) a man concerned with: '*businessman* ○ '*doorman* ○ '*milkman.* See also -WOMAN. ⇨ note at GENDER.

-manship (forming uncountable *ns*) the skill or quality of: *craftsmanship* ○ *sportsmanship.* See also -SHIP.

■ **'man-eater** *n* **1** a wild animal that attacks and eats human beings. **2** *(joc)* a woman who dominates men. **'man-eating** *adj*: *a man-eating lion/tiger.*

'man-hour *n* (usu *pl*) the work done by one person in one hour: *The builder reckons 15 man-hours for the job.*

ˌman of 'letters *n* a person who does literary work, eg as a writer or critic.

ˌman-'made *adj* not naturally made; artificial: ˌ*man-made 'fibres/'chemicals.*

ˌman-of-'war *n* (*pl* ˌ*men-of-'war*) *(dated)* an armed ship of a country's navy.

'man-size (also **'man-sized**) *adj* of a size suitable for a man; large: *a man-size(d) handkerchief/ breakfast.*

man² /mæn/ *v* (**-nn-**) ~ **sth (with sb)** to supply sth with men, or sometimes women, for service or to operate sth: [Vnpr] *man the boat with a replacement crew* [Vn] *the first manned space flight* ○ *Barbara will man the telephone switchboard till we get back.*

manacle /'mænəkl/ *n* (usu *pl*) either of a pair of chains or metal bands for fastening sb's hands or feet so that they cannot move freely.

▶ **manacle** *v* to fasten manacles to a person's

hands or feet: [Vn] *His hands were manacled behind his back.*

manage /'mænɪdʒ/ *v* **1** [Vn] **(a)** to be in charge of or make decisions in a business or an organization, or part of one: *manage a shop/factory/bank/hotel/ football team* ○ *manage a department/project.* **(b)** to organize or deal with sth that one has or controls, eg money, time or information: *He's good at managing his money* (ie at controlling how much he spends). ○ *a government that can manage the economy successfully* ○ *a computer program that helps you manage your data efficiently.* **(c)** to keep a person or an animal in order or under control: *manage a difficult horse* ○ *A teacher must know how to manage children.* **2(a)** ~ **(with/without sb/sth)** to continue to live or meet one's needs; to survive: [V] *The old man has had to manage on his own since his wife died.* ○ *I just can't manage on £50 a week.* [Vpr] *Can you manage with only one assistant?* [Vpr, Vp] *I can't borrow the money so I'll have to manage without (it).* [V.*to* inf] *I don't know how they managed to find us.* **(b)** to succeed in doing sth, esp with difficulty: [V, Vn] *That suitcase looks heavy. Can you manage it* (ie to lift or carry it)? ⇨ note at CAN². **(c)** (often used with *can/could*) to succeed in producing, achieving or doing sth: [Vn] *I haven't been learning French for long, so I can only manage* (ie speak) *a few words.* ○ *I'm full — I couldn't manage* (ie eat) *another thing, I'm afraid.* ○ *Despite his disappointment, he managed a smile* (ie succeeded in smiling). ○ *Can you manage lunch* (ie Are you free to have lunch with me) *on Tuesday?* ○ *I'd like to discuss it tomorrow, if you can manage the time.*

▶ **manageable** *adj* that can be managed or easily controlled: *a business/school/family of manageable size* ○ *The debt has been reduced to a manageable level.*

■ ˌ**managing di'rector** *n* the person who controls the business operations of a company.

management /'mænɪdʒmənt/ *n* **1(a)** [U] the control and making of decisions in a business or similar organization: *The failure was caused by bad management.* ○ *the government's reputation for sound economic management* ○ *a management course/ consultant.* **(b)** [CGp, U] the people who control a business or similar organization: *The management is/are considering closing the factory.* ○ *consultation between workers and management* ○ *Most managements are keen to avoid strikes.* ○ *senior/middle management* ○ *The business is under new management.* ○ *a top management job.* **2** [U] the process of dealing with or controlling people or things: *help people with the management of their problems.*

manager /'mænɪdʒə(r)/ *n* **1(a)** a person who controls a business or similar organization: *a bank/ cinema/hotel manager* ○ *the sales/marketing/personnel manager* ○ *departmental managers.* **(b)** a person who trains and organizes a sports team: *the England football manager.* **(c)** a person who deals with the business affairs of an entertainer or of a sports player or competitor. **2** (usu following an *adj*) a person who controls eg people, a household or money in the way specified: *She's not a very good manager (of money) — she always spends more than she earns.*

▶ **manageress** /ˌmænɪdʒə'res/ *n* *(Brit)* a woman who is in charge of a small business, eg a shop, restaurant or hotel.

managerial /ˌmænə'dʒɪəriəl/ *adj* of managers or management: *a managerial job/decision* ○ *managerial skills/expertise/experience/responsibility.*

mandarin /'mændərɪn/ *n* **1** [C] *(Brit)* a powerful high-ranking official, esp in the civil service (CIVIL) or a political party: *Foreign Office mandarins.* **2** [C] (formerly) a high-ranking government official in China. **3 Mandarin** [U] the official standard spoken language of China. **4** (also ˌ**mandarin** ¹**orange**) [C] a type of small orange with a loose skin. Compare SATSUMA.

mandate /ˈmændeɪt/ n **1** ~ **for sth / to do sth** (**a**) the authority to do sth, given to a government or other organization by the people who support it: *Our election victory has given us a clear mandate for our policies/to press ahead with our policies.* (**b**) (*fml*) an order given to sb to carry out a certain task or duty: *He was appointed managing director with a mandate to reverse the company's decline.* **2** (formerly) the power given to a country to govern another country or region.
▶ **mandate** /ˈmændeɪt; *Brit also* ˌmænˈdeɪt/ v (esp passive) (*fml*) to instruct sb to act or vote in a certain way: [Vn.*to* inf] *The delegates from our local branch are mandated to vote for strike action at the national conference.* [also Vn]. **mandated** adj **1** required by law or by certain rules: *mandated standards.* **2** (of a territory) placed under a mandate(2).
▶ **mandatory** /ˈmændətəri; *US* -tɔːri; *Brit also* mænˈdeɪtəri/ adj ~ (**for sb**) required by law or by certain rules; compulsory: *a mandatory life sentence for murder* ○ *Tuition is mandatory for all students.*

mandible /ˈmændɪbl/ n (*anatomy*) **1** the jaw, esp the lower jaw of a MAMMAL or a fish. ⇨ picture at SKELETON. **2** the upper or lower part of a bird's beak. **3** (in insects and similar creatures) either half of the upper pair of jaws, used for biting and seizing.

mandolin /ˈmændəlɪn, ˌmændəˈlɪn/ n a musical instrument with 6 or 8 metal strings arranged in pairs, and a curved back. ⇨ picture at LUTE.

mandrake /ˈmændreɪk/ n [U] a poisonous plant used to make drugs, esp ones which make people sleep.

mane /meɪn/ n **1** the long hair on the neck of a horse or a lion. ⇨ picture at HORSE. **2** a person's long hair: *She tossed back her thick mane of dark hair.*

maneuver (*US*) = MANOEUVRE.

manful /ˈmænfl/ adj brave or determined. ▶ **manfully** /-fəli/ adv: *stick manfully to a task* ○ *She struggled manfully to keep the little boat on course.*

manganese /ˈmæŋɡəniːz/ n [U] (*chemistry*) a chemical element. Manganese is a grey metal used in making steel and glass. ⇨ App 7.

mange /meɪndʒ/ n [U] a skin disease of hairy animals, caused by a PARASITE(1).
▶ **mangy** /ˈmeɪndʒi/ adj **1** suffering from mange: *a mangy dog.* **2** (*infml derog*) in poor condition; looking thin, weak or worn: *a mangy old blanket.*

manger /ˈmeɪndʒə(r)/ n a long open box from which horses or cattle can feed: *The baby Jesus lay in a manger.* **IDM** **a dog in the manger** ⇨ DOG¹.

mange-tout /ˌmɒːnʒ ¹tuː/ n (usu pl) a type of very small PEA in flat pods (POD), which can be cooked and eaten.

mangle¹ /ˈmæŋɡl/ v (esp passive) **1** to damage sth greatly, so that it can hardly be recognized any more: [Vn] *the mangled bodies/remains of people killed in the explosion.* **2** (of a writer, an actor, etc) to spoil a piece of work or a performance very badly: [Vn] *a mangled translation* ○ *The song was mangled beyond recognition.*

mangle

mangle² /ˈmæŋɡl/ n (esp formerly) a machine with rollers (ROLLER 1a) used for squeezing water from

clothes and making them smooth after they have been washed. ⇨ picture.

mango /ˈmæŋɡəʊ/ n [C, U] (*pl* -**oes**) a tropical fruit with sweet juicy yellow flesh: *mango-trees* ○ *mango chutney.*

mangrove /ˈmæŋɡrəʊv/ n a tropical tree that grows in wet mud at the edge of rivers and sends roots down from its branches.

mangy ⇨ MANGE.

manhandle /ˈmænhændl/ v **1** to move sth heavy with great effort: [Vnpr] *We manhandled the piano up the stairs.* **2** to treat sb roughly, eg touching, pushing or hitting them: [Vn] *I was manhandled by a gang of youths.*

manhole /ˈmænhəʊl/ n a hole in a street fitted with a lid, through which sb can enter a SEWER, etc to inspect it: *a manhole cover.*

manhood /ˈmænhʊd/ n **1** [U] the state of being an adult man: *reach manhood.* **2**(**a**) [U] the qualities of a man, eg courage, strength and sexual power: *looking for opportunities to prove their manhood.* (**b**) [sing] (*euph*) a man's PENIS. **3** [U] (*rhet*) all the men, esp of a country, considered together: *Our nation's manhood died on the battlefield.*

manhunt /ˈmænhʌnt/ n an organized search for sb, esp a criminal, usu involving many people: *Police have launched a manhunt for the bullion robbers.*

mania /ˈmeɪniə/ n **1** [U] (*psychology*) mental illness marked by extreme obsession (OBSESS), excitement or violence: *persecution mania.* **2** [C] ~ (**for sth**) (*infml*) an extreme or abnormal desire or enthusiasm: *have a mania for cleanliness/collecting things.*
▶ **maniac** /ˈmeɪniæk/ n **1** a mad person: *a homicidal maniac.* **2** (*derog or joc*) (**a**) (esp in compounds) a person who likes sth to an extreme degree: *a football maniac.* (**b**) a wild or foolish person: *He was driving like a maniac* (ie far too fast). **maniacal** /məˈnaɪəkl/ adj (*fml*) extremely violent or mad: *a maniacal attack* ○ *maniacal behaviour/laughter.*

-mania comb form (forming *ns*) mental illness or abnormal behaviour of a particular type: *klepto*¹*mania* ○ *nympho*¹*mania.*
▶ **-maniac** (forming *ns* and *adjs*) a person affected with MANIA(1) of a particular type: *dipso*¹*maniac* ○ *pyro*¹*maniac.*

manic /ˈmænɪk/ adj **1** showing wild excitement and energy: *a creative urge of almost manic intensity.* **2** (*techn*) of or affected by MANIA(1): ˌ*manic de*¹*pression.* ▶ **manically** adv.
■ ˌ**manic-de**¹**pressive** n (*psychology*) a person with a mental illness causing moods which change quickly and often between extremes of wild happiness and deep depression. **manic-depressive** adj: *a manic-depressive syndrome.*

manicure /ˈmænɪkjʊə(r)/ n [C, U] the care and treatment of the hands and nails: *do a course in manicure* ○ *have a manicure once a week.* Compare PEDICURE.
▶ **manicure** v (usu passive) to give a manicure to sb: [Vn] *beautifully manicured nails* ○ (*fig*) *a beautifully manicured lawn.*
manicurist /-kjʊərɪst/ n a person who practises manicure as a profession.

manifest¹ /ˈmænɪfest/ adj ~ (**to sb**) (**in sth**) (*fml*) clear and obvious: *a manifest truth/lie/difference.* ○ *His nervousness was manifest to all of us/in the way he spoke.*
▶ **manifest** v (*fml*) (**a**) ~ **sth** (**in sth**) to show sth clearly; to demonstrate sth: [Vn] *manifest certain characteristics/symptoms* ○ *She manifested little interest in her studies.* [Vpr] *These social tensions were manifested in the recent political crisis.* (**b**) ~ **itself** (**in sth**) to show itself; to appear: [Vn] *The symptoms manifested themselves ten days later.* ○ *Has the ghost manifested itself recently?* [also Vnpr]. **manifestly** adv: *manifestly unfair/untrue/successful.*

manifest² /ˈmænɪfest/ n a list of cargo or passengers on a ship or an aircraft: *the passenger manifest of a cruise liner.*

manifestation /ˌmænɪfeˈsteɪʃn/ n (fml) **1** [C, U] an event, an action, an object or a statement that shows sth clearly, eg illustrating or resulting from an abstract idea: *The riots are a clear manifestation of the people's discontent.* **2** [C] an appearance of a ghost or a spirit: *She claims to have seen manifestations of dead people in the haunted house.*

manifesto /ˌmænɪˈfestəʊ/ n (pl ~os) a usu printed statement of principles and policies made by a leader or a group, esp a political party, before an election: *pledges made in the Party's election manifesto ○ publish/issue a manifesto.*

manifold /ˈmænɪfəʊld/ adj (fml) of many types; many and various: *a person with manifold interests ○ The reasons for this are manifold.*
▶ **manifold** n (techn) a pipe or an enclosed space with several openings that connect with other parts, eg for taking gases into or out of cylinders (CYLINDER²) in a car engine: *the exhaust/inlet manifold.* ▷ picture at CAR.

manila /məˈnɪlə/ n [U] a type of strong brown paper: *manila envelopes.*

manipulate /məˈnɪpjuleɪt/ v **1** to control or handle sth with skill: [Vn] *manipulate the gears and levers of a machine ○ children learning how to manipulate objects while playing.* **2** (often derog) to control or influence sb/sth by clever or unfair means: [Vn] *As a shrewd politician he knows how to manipulate public opinion. ○ She uses her charm to manipulate people.*
▶ **manipulation** /məˌnɪpjuˈleɪʃn/ n [U, C] (often derog): *He made a fortune by clever manipulation of the stock market. ○ The voters are open to manipulation by the mass media.*
manipulative /məˈnɪpjələtɪv; US -leɪtɪv/ adj (often derog) (of or concerned with) manipulating sb/sth: *a manipulative politician.*
manipulator /məˈnɪpjuleɪtə(r)/ n (often derog) a person who manipulates sb/sth: *an unscrupulous manipulator.*

mankind /mænˈkaɪnd/ n [U] all human beings considered together; the human race: *the history of mankind ○ an invention of benefit to all mankind.* See also HUMANKIND. ▷ note at HUMANKIND.

manly /ˈmænli/ adj (-ier, -iest) **1** (approv) (a) (of a man) having the appearance or qualities expected of a man: *He looked so manly in his uniform.* (b) (of things) associated with such qualities; suitable for a man: *manly qualities/virtues ○ a manly pose/sport.* **2** (derog) (of a woman) having qualities or an appearance more appropriate to a man. ▶ **manliness** n [U].

manna /ˈmænə/ n [U] (in the Bible) food provided by God for the Israelites during their 40 years in the desert: (fig) *To the starving refugees the gift parcels were (like) manna from heaven* (ie an unexpected and very welcome gift or advantage).

manned pt, pp of MAN².

mannequin /ˈmænɪkɪn/ n **1** a model of a human body, used when making clothes or for displaying them in shops. **2** (dated) a person employed to display new styles of clothes by wearing them; a fashion model.

manner /ˈmænə(r)/ n **1** [sing] (fml) a way in which sth is done or happens: *the manner in which he died/of his death ○ run the business in a profitable manner ○ see that everything is done in the correct/proper manner ○ a wedding in the grand manner* (ie with great ceremony and expense). **2** [sing] a person's way of behaving towards others: *have an aggressive/a charming/a businesslike manner.* See also BEDSIDE MANNER. **3 manners** [pl] (a) polite social behaviour: *good/bad manners ○ It's bad manners to stare at*

people. ○ *He has no manners at all* (ie behaves very badly). See also TABLE MANNERS. (b) habits and customs, esp of a particular group: *18th-century aristocratic manners.* **4** [sing] (fml or rhet) the nature of a person or thing; a kind or sort of person or thing: *What manner of man is he?* **IDM** all ˈmanner of sb/sth many different types of person or thing: *The problem can be tackled in all manner of ways.* in a manner of ˈspeaking to some extent; if regarded in a certain way: *His success is, in a manner of speaking, our success too.* in the manner of sb in the style of literature or art typical of sb: *a painting in the manner of Raphael.* (as / as if) to the manner ˈborn as if one has long experience of doing sth: *She took to village life as (if) to the manner born.*
▶ **mannered** adj (derog) having a style of doing sth, esp speaking or writing, that is too elaborate and not natural: *Her prose is far too mannered and self-conscious.*
-mannered (forming compound adjs) behaving in a specified way: *ill-/well-/im peccably-ˈmannered ○ bad-/mild-mannered.*

mannerism /ˈmænərɪzəm/ n **1** [C] a particular habit of behaviour or speech: *an annoying/a characteristic/an odd mannerism.* **2** [U] the excessive use of a distinctive style in art or literature: *painting that is not free of mannerism.*
▶ **mannerist** /ˈmænərɪst/ adj of or in the style of mannerism(2).

mannish /ˈmænɪʃ/ adj (usu derog) (a) (of a woman) looking, sounding or behaving like a man. (b) (of sth belonging to a woman) more suitable for a man than for a woman: *a mannish jacket/voice/walk.*

manoeuvre (US **maneuver**) /məˈnuːvə(r)/ n **1** [C] (a) a movement performed with care and skill: *A rapid manoeuvre by the driver prevented an accident.* (b) a clever plan or movement, esp one used to deceive people: *a crafty manoeuvre to outwit his pursuers ○ a skilful political manoeuvre.* **2(a)** [C] a planned and controlled movement of armed forces: *a flanking manoeuvre* (ie round the sides of an enemy army). (b) **manoeuvres** [pl] exercises involving many troops, ships, etc: *The army is on manoeuvres in the desert.*
▶ **manoeuvre** (US **maneuver**) v (a) to move about or make sth move about by using skill and care: [V] *cyclists manoeuvring on the practice track* [Vpr] *yachts manoeuvring for position* (ie moving around to get good positions, eg in a race) [Vn] *show great skill in manoeuvring a motor bike* [Vnpr] *She manoeuvred the car slowly into the garage.* [also Vnp]. (b) to guide sb/sth somewhere using skill and often deception; to control or influence sb/sth skilfully: [Vnpr] *She manoeuvred her friends into positions of power.* [Vnp] *manoeuvre the conversation round to money* [also V, Vpr, Vn.to inf]. **manoeuvrable** (US **maneuverable**) /-vərəbl/ adj that can easily be moved into different positions: *a small, highly manoeuvrable canoe.* **manoeuvrability** (US **-neuver-**) /məˌnuːvərəˈbɪləti/ n [U]. **manoeuvring** (US **maneuvering**) /məˈnuːvərɪŋ/ n [U, C usu pl] clever and skilful behaviour, often involving deception: *He remained in office thanks to skilful political manoeuvring(s).*

manor /ˈmænə(r)/ n **1(a)** (also ˈmanor-house) a large country house surrounded by an estate. (b) this estate. **2** (Brit sl) (used esp by police officers) an area for which a particular police station is responsible.
▶ **manorial** /məˈnɔːriəl/ adj of a manor(1), esp in former times.

manpower /ˈmænpaʊə(r)/ n [U] the number of people working or available for work: *a manpower shortage ○ a need for skilled manpower.*

manqué /ˈmɒŋkeɪ; US mɑːŋˈkeɪ/ adj (following ns)

(*French*) (*fml or joc*) (of a person) who hoped to follow the specified career but did not or failed in it: *He earned his living as an architect though many felt he was an architect manqué.*

mansard /ˈmænsɑːd/ (also ˌmansard ˈroof) *n* (*techn*) a roof with a double slope, the upper part being less steep than the lower part.

manse /mæns/ *n* the house of a minister¹(3) of the church, esp in Scotland.

manservant /ˈmænsɜːvənt/ *n* (*pl* **menservants**) a male servant.

mansion /ˈmænʃn/ *n* **1** [C] a large impressive house: *the film star's Beverly Hills mansion.* **2 Mansions** [pl] (used in proper names for a block of flats): *49 Victoria Mansions, Grove Road, London.*

manslaughter /ˈmænslɔːtə(r)/ *n* [U] (*Brit law*) the crime of killing a person illegally but not intentionally: *commit manslaughter.* Compare HOMICIDE, MURDER 1.

mantelpiece /ˈmæntlpiːs/ (also *dated* **mantelshelf** /ˈmæntlʃelf/, also ˈ**chimney-piece**) *n* a shelf above a fireplace: *A clock stood on the mantelpiece.*

mantis /ˈmæntɪs/ *n* = PRAYING MANTIS.

mantle /ˈmæntl/ *n* **1** [sing] **the ~ of sb/sth** (*rhet*) the role and responsibilities of an important person or job: *assume/take on/inherit the mantle of supreme power.* **2** [C] (esp formerly) a loose garment without sleeves, worn over other clothes. **3** (*rhet*) a covering of sth: *hills with a mantle of snow.* **4** (also ˈ**gas mantle**) [C] a cover round the flame of a gas lamp that becomes very bright when heated. **5** [sing] (*geology*) the part of the Earth below the CRUST(3) and surrounding the CORE(2).

mantra /ˈmæntrə/ *n* a word, phrase or sound that is constantly repeated, esp during meditation (MEDITATE).

manual /ˈmænjuəl/ *adj* of, done with or controlled by the hands: *manual labour/workers* ○ *a manual gearbox* (ie one operated by hand with a lever, not automatically) ○ *fine embroidery requiring great manual dexterity.*
▶ **manual** *n* **1** a book containing information or practical instructions on a given subject: *a computer/car manual.* Compare HANDBOOK. **2** (*music*) a KEYBOARD(1b) of an organ, played with the hands: *a two-manual organ.*
manually /-juəli/ *adv: manually operated.*

manufacture /ˌmænjuˈfæktʃə(r)/ *v* [Vn] **1** to make goods on a large scale using machinery: *manufacture shoes/cars/cookers* ○ *exports of manufactured goods.* **2** (*usu derog*) to invent evidence, an excuse, etc: *a news story manufactured by an unscrupulous journalist.*
▶ **manufacture** *n* **1** [U] the activity of manufacturing sth: *firms engaged in the manufacture of plastics* ○ *car manufacture.* **2 manufactures** [pl] (*commerce*) manufactured goods or articles.
manufacturer *n* a person or firm that manufactures things: *send faulty goods back to the manufacturer* ○ *a clothing/a car/an electronics manufacturer.*
manufacturing *n* [U] the activity of making things by industrial processes: *the future of manufacturing in the UK* ○ *manufacturing output/processes.*

manure /məˈnjʊə(r)/ *n* [U] animal DUNG or other material, natural or artificial, spread over or mixed with soil to help plants or crops grow: *dig manure into the soil* ○ *horse/pig/chicken manure.* See also GREEN MANURE. Compare FERTILIZER.
▶ **manure** *v* to put manure on or in soil: [Vn] *well manured soil.*

manuscript /ˈmænjuskrɪpt/ *n* (*abbr* **MS**) **1** [C] a document, piece of music, etc that is written by hand, not typed or printed: *a medieval manuscript.* **2** [C] an author's work when it is written or typed,

ie is not yet a printed book: *submit a manuscript to a publisher* ○ *I read her poems in manuscript.*

Manx /mæŋks/ *adj* of the Isle of Man, its people or the language once spoken there.
■ ˌ**Manx** ˈ**cat** *n* a breed of cat with no tail.

many /ˈmeni/ *indef det, indef pron* (used with plural *ns* and *vs*) **1** a large number of people or things (**a**) (*det*): *Many people agree with privatization.* ○ *Were there many pictures by women artists?* ○ *How many children have you got?* ○ *There are too many mistakes in this essay.* ○ *He made ten mistakes in as many* (ie ten) *lines.* (**b**) (*pron*): *Many of the plants had died.* ○ *Did you know many of the people at the conference?* ○ *How many do you want?* (**c**) (used in compound *adjs*): *a many-sided/many-faceted problem* ○ *a many-headed monster.* ⇨ note at MUCH¹. **2 many a** (*fml*) (used with a singular *n* and a singular *v*) a large number of: *Many a young person has experimented with drugs.* ○ *I've been there many a time.* **IDM as many as ...** (used to indicate surprise that the number of people or things involved is so large): *There were as many as 200 people at the lecture.* **a good/ great ˈmany** very very many: *I've known him for a good many years.* **have had ˌone too ˈmany** (*infml*) to be slightly drunk. **many's the sb/sth who/that ...** there are many people/things that ...: *Many's the promise that has been broken.* (Compare: *Many a promise has been broken.*) ○ *Many's the time (that) I heard him use those words.*
▶ **the many** *n* [pl *v*] most people; the majority: *a government which improves conditions for the many.* Compare THE FEW.

Maori /ˈmaʊri/ *n* a member of the race of people who were the earliest inhabitants of New Zealand. ▶ **Maori** *adj: Maori customs/warriors.*

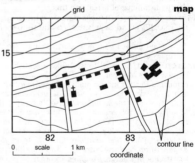

map /mæp/ *n* (**a**) a representation on paper of the earth's surface or part of it, showing countries, rivers, mountains, oceans, roads, etc: *a road-map of France* ○ *a street map of Miami* ○ *a 1:50 000 scale map of Dartmoor* ○ *find a place on the map* ○ *Can you read* (ie understand) *a map?* ○ *I'll draw you a map of how to get to my house.* ○ (*fig*) *The war redrew the map of Europe* (eg changed the national boundaries). ⇨ picture. (**b**) a similar plan showing the position of the stars, etc in the sky: *a map of the heavens.* Compare CHART 2, PLAN 2. **IDM put sb/sth on the ˈmap** to make sb/sth famous or important: *Winning the cup has put this town on the map.* **wipe sb/sth off the face of the earth / off the map** ⇨ WIPE.
▶ **map** *v* (**-pp-**) to make a map of an area: [Vn] *an unexplored region that has not yet been mapped* ○ (*fig*) *human gene mapping.* **PHRV ˈmap sth on/ onto sth** to associate a set of elements, qualities, etc with their source, cause, position on a scale, etc: *Many visual processes have yet to be mapped onto the nervous system.* ˌ**map sth ˈout** to plan or arrange sth in detail: *Her whole career is already mapped out in front of her.* ○ *She mapped out her ideas for the new project.*

M

[V.speech] = verb + direct speech   [V.*that*] = verb + *that* clause   [V.*wh*] = verb + *who, how*, etc clause

maple /'meɪpl/ n (**a**) [C] a tree with leaves that have five points. (**b**) [U] the wood of this tree: *a maple desk.*
■ ‚maple ¹syrup n [U] a sweet sticky substance obtained from a type of maple tree, often eaten with pancakes (PANCAKE 1).

mar /mɑː(r)/ v (**-rr-**) to damage or spoil sth: [Vn] *an incident that could **make or mar** his career* (ie make it a success or a failure) ○ *The big match was marred by crowd trouble.*

Mar abbr March: *3 Mar 1986.*

marathon /'mærəθən; US -θɒn/ n **1** a running race of about 42 km or 26 miles: *run a marathon* ○ *the Boston/London marathon.* **2** a task, event, etc that lasts a long time and requires a lot of effort or patience: *My job interview was a real marathon.* ○ *a marathon legal battle.*

marauding /məˈrɔːdɪŋ/ adj [attrib] (of people or animals) going about in search of things to steal, people to attack, etc: *marauding wolves* ○ *The countryside was overrun by marauding bands of armed men.* ▶ **marauder** /məˈrɔːdə(r)/ n: *nocturnal marauders.*

marble /'mɑːbl/ n **1** [U] a hard, usu white, stone, often with dark veins, which can be highly polished. It is used in building and for making statues, etc: *a slab/block of unpolished marble* ○ *marble floors* ○ *a marble sculpture/fireplace/staircase.* **2(a)** [C] a small ball of coloured glass used by children in games. (**b**) **marbles** [pl] a game played with these: *playing marbles.* **IDM** **lose one's marbles** ⇨ LOSE.
▶ **marbled** /'mɑːbld/ adj (of paper, etc) resembling the colours and patterns of marble: *a book with marbled covers* ○ *a marbled effect.*
marbling /'mɑːblɪŋ/ n [U] (**a**) a marbled pattern. (**b**) the technique of producing this.

March /mɑːtʃ/ n [U, C] (abbr **Mar**) the third month of the year. **IDM** **mad as a hatter / a March hare** ⇨ MAD.
For further guidance on how *March* is used, see the examples at *April*.

march¹ /mɑːtʃ/ v **1(a)** to walk like a soldier, with regular steps of equal length: [V] *Quick march* (ie a command to start marching)*!* [Vp] *They marched in and took over the town.* [Vn] *The army marched thirty miles over the mountains.* [also Vadv, Vpr]. (**b**) to make sb march somewhere: [Vnp] *They marched the prisoner away.* [Vnpr] *She was marched into a cell.* **2** to walk quickly, showing purpose and determination: [Vpr] *She marched into my office and demanded an apology.* [also Vp]. **3** to walk through the streets in a large group, eg in order to protest about sth; to demonstrate: [Vpr] *march for peace* [V] *The women marched and chanted.* **IDM** **get one's ¹marching orders; give sb their ¹marching orders** (infml or joc) to be told/to tell sb to go; to be dismissed/to dismiss sb: *She was totally unreliable, so she got/was given her marching orders.* **PHRV** ‚march ¹on (of abstract nouns) to proceed quickly: *Time/Progress marches on.* ¹march on ... to march to a place in order to attack it: *The army is marching on Moscow.* ○ *Angry demonstrators marched on City Hall.* ‚march ¹past (sb) (of troops) to march past a senior officer or an important guest in a PARADE(2).
▶ **marcher** n a person walking to demand sth or protest about sth: *civil-rights marchers.*
■ ¹march past n an act or a ceremony of marching past a senior officer, etc.

march² /mɑːtʃ/ n **1(a)** [C] a journey made by marching: *a long/an arduous march* ○ *a 50-mile march.* (**b**) [sing] progress when marching; advance: *the relentless march towards the enemy.* **2** [C] a procession of many people from one place to another, esp as a protest: *a peace march* ○ *The police made no attempt to break up the march.* Compare DEMONSTRATION 3. See also HUNGER MARCH. **3** [C] a

piece of music written for marching to: *a funeral march.* **4** [sing] **the ~ of sth** the steady development or forward movement of sth: *the march of progress/ mechanization.* **IDM** **on the ¹march 1** marching: *The enemy are on the march.* **2** publicly demanding sth, protesting against sth, etc: *The anti-nuclear lobby is on the march again.* **steal a march** ⇨ STEAL.

marches /'mɑːtʃɪz/ n [pl] the border area, esp between England and Scotland or England and Wales: *a little village in the Welsh marches.*

marchioness /ˌmɑːʃəˈnes/ n (**a**) the wife or widow of a MARQUIS(1). (**b**) a woman holding the same rank as a MARQUIS(1).

mare /meə(r)/ n a female horse or DONKEY. Compare FILLY, FOAL, STALLION. **IDM** **a ¹mare's nest** a discovery that seems interesting but is found to be false or worthless. **on Shanks's pony/mare** ⇨ SHANK.

margarine /ˌmɑːdʒəˈriːn; US ¹mɑːrdʒərən/ (also *Brit infml* **marge** /mɑːdʒ/) n [U] a yellow substance like butter, made from animal or vegetable fats.

margin /'mɑːdʒɪn/ n **1(a)** the blank space round the written or printed matter on a page: *leave wide/ narrow margins* ○ *notes written in the margin.* (**b**) the extreme edge or limit of sth: *the margin of a lake/pool* ○ *(fig) people living on the margins of society.* **2** (usu *sing*) (**a**) the amount of space, time, votes, etc by which sth is won: *a narrow margin between the teams in second and third place* (eg a small difference in points scored) ○ *He beat the other runners by a margin of ten seconds/by a wide margin.* ○ *She won the seat by a margin of ten votes.* (**b**) the amount of extra space, time, etc included so that one can be sure of success or safety: *a good safety margin* ○ *This is the most difficult hole on the course, with very little **margin for error**.* **3** (*commerce*) the difference between the cost of sth and the price for which it is sold: *a business operating on tight* (ie small) *margins* ○ *a substantial/comfortable profit margin.*
▶ **marginal** /-nl/ adj **1** [attrib] written in the margin of a page: *marginal notes/comments.* **2** very small; slight: *have a **marginal effect** on sth* ○ *The difference between the two estimates is marginal.* **3** having little importance; not central: *petty rivalry between marginal groups.* **4** (of land) that cannot produce enough to be profitable except when prices of farm products are high. **5** (*politics esp Brit*) won by only a small majority of votes: *a marginal seat/ constituency.* — n a seat in parliament, on a local council, etc that was won by a small majority of votes: *a Labour marginal.*
marginalize, -ise /'mɑːdʒɪnəlaɪz/ to make a person or group become or feel less important, powerful, etc: [Vn] *Western society has marginalized elderly people to a considerable extent.* **marginalization, -isation** n [U].
marginally /-nəli/ adv slightly: *marginally better/ cheaper/more risky* ○ *Local schools were only marginally affected by the strike.*
■ ¹margin of ¹error n [C usu *sing*] an amount allowed for the possibility that figures used in calculating a sum are not entirely correct: *The margin of error is 2%.*

marguerite /ˌmɑːgəˈriːt/ n a small white flower with a yellow centre.

marigold /'mærɪgəʊld/ n any of various plants with orange or yellow flowers.

marijuana (also **marihuana**) /ˌmærəˈwɑːnə/ n [U] a form of the drug CANNABIS, usu smoked for pleasure. See also CANNABIS, HASHISH.

marimba /məˈrɪmbə/ n a musical instrument like a XYLOPHONE.

marina /məˈriːnə/ n a specially designed harbour for yachts (YACHT) and small boats.

marinade /ˌmærɪˈneɪd/ n [C,U] a mixture of oil, wine, spices, etc in which fish or meat is soaked

M

before it is cooked in order to make it more tender or to give it a special taste.

▶ **marinade** (also **marinate** /ˈmærɪneɪt/) *v* ~ **sth** (**in sth**) to soak food in a marinade: [Vn] *marinated lamb* [V] *Leave the beef to marinade overnight.* [Vnpr] *marinate fish in lime-juice.*

marine¹ /məˈriːn/ *adj* **1** of, near, found in or produced by the sea: *marine mammals/organisms* ○ *a marine biologist* (ie a scientist who studies life in the sea) ○ *marine pollution.* **2** relating to ships, trade by sea, the navy, etc: *marine insurance* (ie of ships and cargo).

marine² /məˈriːn/ *n* a soldier trained to serve on land or sea, esp one in the US Marine Corps or the British Royal Marines.

mariner /ˈmærɪnə(r)/ *n* (*dated or fml*) a sailor: *a master mariner.*

marionette /ˌmæriəˈnet/ *n* a DOLL¹(1) moved by strings attached to different parts of its body. ⇨ picture at PUPPET.

marital /ˈmærɪtl/ *adj* [attrib] of marriage; between a husband and wife: *marital bliss/harmony/problems/ breakdown.*

■ ˌmarital ˈstatus *n* [U] (*fml*) (esp on official forms) the state of being single, married or divorced (DI-VORCE² 1).

maritime /ˈmærɪtaɪm/ *adj* **1** of the sea, ships or sailing: *maritime influences on climate* ○ *maritime law* ○ *great maritime powers/nations* (ie countries with powerful navies). **2** situated or found near the sea: *the maritime provinces of Canada.*

marjoram /ˈmɑːdʒərəm/ *n* [U] a plant whose sweet-smelling leaves are used in cooking.

mark¹ /mɑːk/ *n* **1(a)** a small area of dirt, a spot or a SCRATCH¹(1a) on a surface, caused eg by sth being dropped on it or by damage of some kind: *a green paint mark* ○ *scratch marks on my new car* ○ *leave dirty marks all over the kitchen floor* ○ *There's a greasy mark on this skirt.* **(b)** a noticeable spot or area on the body by which a person or animal may be recognized: *a horse with a white mark on its head* ○ *He was about six feet tall, with no **distinguishing marks**.* See also BIRTHMARK. **2(a)** a written or printed symbol; a figure, line, etc made as a sign or an indication of sth: ˌpunctuˈation marks ○ *I put a mark in the margin to indicate that I'd left something out.* ○ *White marks painted on the trees show the footpath.* See also QUESTION MARK, EXCLAMATION MARK. **(b)** a symbol, number or letter on sth to show its origin, ownership or quality: ˈlaundry marks (ie showing who a sheet, etc belongs to) ○ *cattle branded with the owner's distinctive mark.* See also TRADE MARK. **3** a visible trace; a sign or indication of a quality, feeling, etc: *bear the marks of suffering/old age* ○ *Shops remained closed as a **mark of respect** for the dead man.* **4** (*esp Brit*) a number or letter used to show the standard of sb's work or conduct: *get a good/poor mark in maths* ○ *give sb high/low marks (for sth)* ○ *get top marks.* **5** a cross made on a document instead of a signature by sb unable to write their name: *put/make one's mark (on sth).* **6** **Mark** (followed by a number) a model or type of a machine, vehicle, etc: *a Mark II estate model.* **7** (*fml*) a target: *The arrow missed its mark.* **8** a level of sth that is considered important or critical(3): *Unemployment has passed the four million mark.* **9** (in sport) the line from which a race starts or the point from which a BOWLER¹(1), etc begins his run. **IDM** **be/fall wide of the ˈmark** ⇨ WIDE. ˌhit/ˈmiss the ˈmark** to succeed/to fail in an attempt to do sth. ˌleave/make one's, its, etc ˈmark (on sth/sb)** to have an often bad effect which lasts for a long time: *War has left its mark on the countryside.* ○ *Two unhappy marriages have left their mark on her.* ˌmake one's ˈmark** to become famous and successful: *an actor who has made his mark in films.* **not**

be/feel (quite) ˌup to the ˈmark not to feel as well, lively, etc as usual: *I don't feel quite up to the mark today.* **overstep the mark** ⇨ OVERSTEP. **quick/ slow off the ˈmark** to be fast or slow in responding to a situation or understanding sth: *You have to be quick off the mark to get anything worthwhile in the sales.* **toe the mark** ⇨ TOE *v.* ˌup to the ˈmark** as good as sb/sth should be; of the required standard: *Her school work isn't quite up to the mark.*

mark² /mɑːk/ *v* **1(a)** ~ **A** (**with B**) / ~ **B on A** to make a mark on sth, eg in order to indicate ownership: [Vnpr] *mark one's name on clothes/mark clothes with one's name* ○ *The route has been marked in red.* ○ *Prices are marked on the goods.* [Vn-adj] *The teacher marked her absent.* **(b)** to become dirty or damaged: [V, Vadv] *Don't put hot dishes directly on the table, because it marks (very easily).* **2** to show the position of sth: [Vn] *This cross marks the spot where she died.* ○ *A plaque now marks his birthplace.* **3** to honour an event that one considers to be important: [Vn] *celebrations to mark the President's 75th birthday.* **4** to be a sign that sth new is about to happen: [Vn] *mark a change/a shift in* government policy ○ *mark a new phase in* international relations. **5** to give marks (MARK¹ 4) to pupils' work: [Vn] *mark examination papers* [Vadv] *Nobody likes her because she marks very hard.* [Vn-adj] *Why have you marked this sentence wrong?* **6** to give sb/sth a particular quality or character; to CHARACTERIZE sb/ sth: [Vn] *a life marked by suffering* [Vn-n] *be marked as an enemy of the poor* [also Vn-adj]. **7** (*fml*) to pay careful attention to sth; to note sth carefully: [Vn] *There'll be trouble over this, (you) mark my words.* [V.*wh*] *You mark what I say, John.* **8** (*sport*) (in a team game) to stay close to an opponent in order to prevent her or him from getting the ball: [Vnadv] *Our defence had him closely marked.* [also Vn]. **IDM** ˌmark ˈtime 1** to make marching movements without moving forward. **2** to pass one's time doing sth routine until one can do sth more interesting: *I'm just marking time in this job — I'm hoping to get into journalism.* ˌmark ˈyou** (*infml esp Brit*) but please note; but you must not forget: *She hasn't had much success yet. Mark you, she tries hard.* **PHRV** ˌmark sb ˈdown** to reduce the marks given to sb in an examination, etc: *She was marked down because of poor grammar.* ˌmark sb ˈdown (as sth)** to recognize sb to be of a particular type: *She was marked down as a brilliant student.* ˌmark sth ˈdown 1** to reduce the price of sth: *All goods have been marked down by 15%.* **2** to note sth for future use or action: *The factory is already marked down for demolition.* ˌmark sth ˈoff** to separate sth by marking a boundary: *mark the playing area off with a white line.* ˌmark sb ˈout for sth** (esp passive) to choose sb as being suitable to receive sth special: *a woman marked out for early promotion.* ˌmark sth ˈout** to draw lines to show the boundaries of sth: *mark out a tennis-court/car park.* ˌmark sth ˈup 1** to increase the price of sth: *Shares were marked up 10p to 136p.* **2** to mark or correct a text, etc, eg for printing: *mark up a manuscript.*

▶ **marked** /mɑːkt/ *adj* clear; noticeable; easily seen: *a marked difference/improvement/reluctance* ○ *Our results have been excellent, **in marked contrast** to those of our competitors.* **IDM** **a marked ˈman** a man whose actions, etc have caused him to be under suspicion, sought for punishment, etc: *He is a marked man because of his liberal views.* **markedly** /ˈmɑːkɪdli/ *adv*: *offer a markedly different approach* ○ *change/differ/improve markedly.*

marker *n* **1** a thing that indicates a position, route, etc: *boundary markers* ○ *Motorway marker posts show the distance to the nearest telephone.* **2** a type of pen that draws thick lines: *a laundry marker* ○ *a ˈmarker pen.* **3** a person who marks an examination paper. **4** words that make clear one's attitude to sth

M

or what one intends to do: *Her speech was a clear marker of current government thinking.*

marking *n* (usu *pl*) a pattern of marks or lines: *a dog with white markings on its chest.*

■ **'mark-down** *n* (usu *sing*) a reduction in price: *a mark-down of 20% on last month's price.*

'mark-up *n* (usu *sing*) **1** the difference between the cost of producing sth and the price at which it is sold: *The mark-up on food in a restaurant is at least 100%.* **2** an increase in price: *a 10% mark-up on cigarettes.*

mark³ /mɑːk/ *n* = DEUTSCHMARK: *a ten-mark note.*

market¹ /'mɑːkɪt/ *n* **1** [C] a regular gathering where people buy and sell goods: *buy vegetables at the market* ○ *a cattle/fish market* ○ *a covered/open-air market* ○ *a street market* ○ *a market stall* ○ *a market town* (ie one which has a regular market). **2** [C] the state of trade in a particular type of goods: *a dull/lively market (in coffee)* ○ *the money/financial/futures market* ○ *a rising/falling market* (ie in which eg share prices are rising/falling) ○ *The property market is very flat* (ie Few houses are being sold). **3** [sing] ~ **(for sth)** demand: *a good/poor/growing/declining market for second-hand cars* ○ *There's not much of a market for metal piping.* **4** [C] an area, a country, a section of the population, etc to which goods may be sold: *find new markets* ○ *the teenage market* ○ *foreign/domestic markets* ○ *He spotted a gap in the market and made a fortune.* See also DOWN-MARKET, UP-MARKET. **5** [sing] people buying and selling goods freely in competition with each other: *market forces/trends* ○ *a market-based/market-driven/market-led economy.* See also BLACK MARKET, STOCK MARKET. **IDM** **come on(to) the 'market** to be offered for sale: *This house only came on(to) the market yesterday.* **in the 'market for sth** interested in buying sth: *I'm not in the market for big, expensive cars.* **on the (open) 'market** available for sale to the public: *put one's car/house on the market* ○ *This type of computer is not yet on the market.* **play the 'market** (*infml*) to buy and sell stocks and shares in order to make a profit. **price oneself/sth out of the market** ⇨ PRICE *v.*

■ **'market-day** *n* [U,C] the day on which a market¹(1) is regularly held: *Thursday is market-day in Wetherford.*

ı**market 'garden** (*Brit*) (*US* ı**truck farm**) *n* a small farm where vegetables are grown for sale. ı**market 'gardener** *n.* ı**market 'gardening** *n* [U].

'market hall *n* a large covered area where a market¹(1) is held.

ı**market 'leader** *n* **(a)** the company that sells the largest quantity of a particular product: *emerge as the market leader.* **(b)** a product of which more are sold than others in competition with it: *This drug is the market leader in the treatment of thyroid deficiency.*

'market-place *n* **1** the market-place [sing] the system of buying and selling goods under competitive conditions: *Companies must be able to compete/survive in the market-place.* ○ (*fig*) *the market-place of higher education.* **2** (also ı**market 'square**) [C] an open area in a town where a market¹(1) is held.

ı**market price** *n* the price at which sth is offered for sale to the public.

ı**market re'search** (*also* ı**ri:sɜːtʃ**/ *n* [U] the study of what people buy and why, usu conducted by a company before it develops a new product, opens a new shop, etc.

ı**market 'share** *n* [U,sing] the proportion that a company has of the total volume of trading in one type of goods or services: *a loss of market share* ○ *Thomsons have a 48% market share.*

ı**market 'value** *n* [U,sing] the price at which sth would be sold if offered publicly: *buy a car at £500 below (its) current market value.*

market² /'mɑːkɪt/ *v* ~ **sth (as sth)**; ~ **sth (to sb)** to advertise and offer sth for sale: [Vnadv] *market sth imaginatively/aggressively* [Vn,Vnpr] *We need somebody to market our products (to retailers/in Germany).* [Vn-n] *It's being marketed as a low-alcohol wine.*

▶ **marketable** *adj* that can be sold; attractive to buyers, employers, etc: *a highly marketable product* ○ *marketable skills.* **marketability** /ımɑːkɪtə'bɪləti/ *n* [U].

marketeer /ımɑːkɪ'tɪə(r)/ *n* (usu in compounds) a person who favours a particular type of market¹(5): *a free marketeer* (ie one who believes that prices should be determined by competition) ○ *black marketeers.*

marketing *n* [U] **(a)** the theory and practice of presenting, advertising and selling things: *pursue effective/high-powered marketing strategies.* **(b)** the division of a company that does this: *the marketing manager/department.*

marksman /'mɑːksmən/ *n* (*pl* **-men** /-mən/) a person skilled in accurate shooting.

▶ **marksmanship** *n* [U] skill in shooting.

marl /mɑːl/ *n* [U] soil consisting of clay and LIME¹.

marlin /'mɑːlɪn/ *n* (*pl* unchanged) a large sea-fish with a long sharp nose.

marmalade /'mɑːməleɪd/ *n* [U] a type of jam made from CITRUS fruit, esp oranges, and usu eaten at breakfast.

marmoset /'mɑːməzet/ *n* a small tropical American monkey with a long thick tail.

marmot /'mɑːmət/ *n* a small European or American animal that lives in holes in the ground.

maroon¹ /mə'ruːn/ *adj, n* [U] (of) a dark brownish-red colour.

maroon² /mə'ruːn/ *v* (usu passive) to abandon sb in a place from which they cannot escape, eg an island: [Vn] *marooned sailors* [Vnpr] *sailors (left) marooned on a remote island* ○ (*fig*) *Without a car, she was marooned at home for days.*

maroon³ /mə'ruːn/ *n* a small ROCKET(1) that makes a loud noise, used to attract attention, esp at sea.

marque /mɑːk/ *n* (*fml*) a MAKE² of car, as distinct from a specific model: *the Bentley marque.*

marquee /mɑː'kiː/ *n* **1** a large tent used for public or social events: *For our wedding reception we had a big marquee in the garden.* **2** (*esp US*) a covered entrance to a theatre, cinema, hotel, etc.

marquetry /'mɑːkɪtri/ *n* [U] (the art of making) patterns or pictures on the surface of furniture with small pieces of wood, etc of different colours: *a marquetry desk.*

marquis (also **marquess**) /'mɑːkwɪs/ *n* **1** (in Britain) a nobleman of high rank, above an EARL and below a DUKE(1). **2** (in other countries) a nobleman next in rank above a COUNT³. Compare MARCHIONESS.

marram /'mærəm/ (also **marram grass**) *n* [U] a type of grass that grows esp in sand.

marriage /'mærɪdʒ/ *n* **1** [U,C] a formal, usu legally recognized, agreement between a man and a woman making them husband and wife; the state of being married: *a happy/unhappy/loveless marriage* ○ *Their marriage ended in divorce.* ○ *Her parents' experience had put her off marriage.* See also CIVIL MARRIAGE, MIXED MARRIAGE. **2** [C] a ceremony at which a couple are married; a wedding: *Her second marriage was held/took place in a registry office.* **IDM** **by 'marriage** as a result of one's marriage: *my aunt by marriage.* **give sb in 'marriage (to sb)** (*fml*) to give the care of one's daughter to her new husband.

▶ **marriageable** *adj* suitable for marriage, esp in terms of age: *daughters of marriageable age.*

■ **'marriage bureau** *n* (*pl* **bureaux**) an organization that arranges introductions between people wanting to marry.

marriage certificate *n* a legal document confirming that two people are married.

marriage guidance *n* [U] advice given by specially trained people to married couples with problems in their relationship: *a marriage guidance counsellor*.

marriage licence *n* a licence permitting a legal ceremony of marriage.

marriage of convenience *n* a marriage made in order to achieve some practical, esp financial or political, purpose, not because the two partners love each other.

married /'mærɪd/ *adj* **1(a)** ~ (**to sb**) having a husband or wife: *a married man/woman/couple* ○ *He's married to a famous writer.* ○ *Rachel and David are getting married* (ie holding their wedding) *on Saturday*. **(b)** [attrib] of or relating to marriage: *married life/bliss*. **2** [pred] ~ **to sth** so involved with sth that one has little time for other things: *married to one's work*.

marrow¹ /'mærəʊ/ *n* [U] a soft substance that fills the hollow parts of human and animal bones: *a bone marrow transplant*.

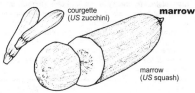

courgette
(*US* zucchini)

marrow

marrow
(*US* squash)

marrow² /'mærəʊ/ (also *Brit* **vegetable marrow**, *US* **squash**) *n* [C, U] a long, round, dark green vegetable with soft white flesh: *stuffed marrow* (ie cooked with meat, rice, etc inside). ⇨ picture. Compare COURGETTE.

marry /'mæri/ *v* (*pt, pp* **married**) **1** to take sb as a husband or wife; to get married: [Vn] *marry a doctor/a Frenchman* [V-adj, V] *They married (when they were) young*. **2** (of a priest or civil(2) official) to perform a ceremony making a couple husband and wife; to join people in marriage: [Vn] *They were married by a bishop*. **3** ~ (**sth**) (**with sth**) to combine sth or be combined successfully with sth else: [Vpr] *a lifestyle that marries well with the needs of the job* [Vn, Vnpr] *She marries wit and/with scholarship in her writing.* [also V]. **IDM** **marry money** (*infml*) to marry a rich person. **PHRV** **marry into sth** to become a part of a family or group by marrying sb from it: *He married into the aristocracy*. **marry sb off** to find a husband or wife for one's son or daughter. **marry up** (of parts or elements) to be able to be joined or combined; to match or correspond: *The two versions of the story don't quite marry up, do they?*

Mars /mɑːz/ *n* the planet fourth in order from the sun, next to the Earth.

Marsala /mɑːˈsɑːlə/ *n* [U] a dark sweet wine from Sicily.

marsh /mɑːʃ/ *n* [C, U] an area of low land which is wet because water cannot drain away from it: *cattle grazing the marshes* ○ *marsh plants*.
▶ **marshy** *adj* like or containing a marsh; wet and MUDDY: *marshy ground/fields*.
■ **marsh gas** *n* [U] = METHANE.

marshal¹ /'mɑːʃl/ *n* **1** (usu in compounds) an officer of high rank: *Field-Marshal* (ie in the Army) ○ *Air-Marshal* (ie in the Air Force). ⇨ App 6. **2** an official responsible for controlling crowds at certain public events, eg motor races or processions. **3** (*US*) **(a)** a police officer responsible for a particular area. **(b)** the head of a police or fire department in certain cities.

marshal² /'mɑːʃl/ *v* (**-ll-**; *US* **-l-**) to arrange sb/sth in proper order; to gather sb/sth together: [Vnpr] *The children were marshalled into the playground by their teachers.* [Vn] *marshal troops/forces/crowds* ○ (*fig*) *marshal one's arguments/thoughts/powers of persuasion* [also Vnp].
■ **marshalling yard** *n* a railway yard in which goods trains, etc are prepared, assembled, etc.

marshland /'mɑːʃlænd/ *n* [U, C] an area of soft wet ground: *low-lying areas which were once marshland*.

marshmallow /ˌmɑːʃˈmæləʊ; *US* ˈmɑːrʃmeləʊ/ *n* [C, U] a soft pink or white sweet.

marsupial /mɑːˈsuːpiəl/ *n, adj* (any) of a group of Australian animals, eg the KANGAROO, that carry their young in a fold of skin on the mother's stomach. See also POUCH 3a.

mart /mɑːt/ *n* a market or centre of trade: *a cattle auction mart* ○ *a used car mart*.

marten /'mɑːtɪn; *US* -tn/ *n* a small fierce animal with short legs and sharp teeth that eats smaller animals.

martial /'mɑːʃl/ *adj* (*fml*) of or associated with war: *martial music*. See also COURT MARTIAL.
■ **martial art** *n* (usu *pl*) any of the fighting sports that include JUDO and KARATE.

martial law *n* [U] military rule established in a country temporarily, eg during a time of political disturbance: *declare/proclaim/lift martial law* ○ *The country is now under martial law.*

Martian /'mɑːʃn/ *n, adj* (an imaginary inhabitant) of the planet Mars.

martin /'mɑːtɪn; *US* -tn/ *n* a bird of the SWALLOW² family.

martinet /ˌmɑːtɪˈnet; *US* -tnˈet/ *n* (usu *derog*) a person who is very strict and demands complete obedience.

martini /mɑːˈtiːni/ *n* [C, U] a drink made with GIN and French VERMOUTH: *a dry martini*.

martyr /'mɑːtə(r)/ *n* **1** a person who is killed or made to suffer greatly because of her or his religious or other beliefs: *the early Christian martyrs*. **2** (usu *derog*) a person who suffers or pretends to suffer in order to gain admiration or sympathy: *He always acts the martyr when he has to do the housework.* **3** ~ **to sth** (*infml*) a person who suffers constantly from an illness, etc: *She's a martyr to rheumatism.*
▶ **martyr** *v* (usu passive) to kill sb or make sb suffer because of their beliefs: [Vn] *He was martyred by the Romans.* **martyred** *adj* (*derog*) (of an expression or a way of speaking) showing esp pretended suffering: *She does everything with a martyred air.*

martyrdom /'mɑːtədəm/ *n* [U, C] a martyr's suffering or death: *Joan of Arc suffered martyrdom at the stake* (ie by being burnt).

marvel /'mɑːvl/ *n* **1** a person or thing that fills one with surprise and admiration: *the marvels of modern science* ○ *It's a marvel that he escaped unhurt.* ○ *She works terribly hard in spite of her illness — she's a marvel!* **2** **marvels** [pl] wonderful results or achievements: *They've performed/done marvels restoring that old cottage.*
▶ **marvel** *v* (**-ll-**; *US* **-l-**) ~ (**at sth**) to be very surprised at sth, often admiring it very much: [Vpr] *I can only marvel at such courage.* [V.that] *I never cease to marvel that she married someone like me.* [also V, V.speech].

marvellous (*US* **marvelous**) /'mɑːvələs/ *adj* (*infml*) wonderful; excellent: *a marvellous idea/writer/opportunity* ○ *marvellous weather/news* ○ *It's marvellous that we can at last buy our own house.* **marvellously** (*US* **marvelously**) *adv*.

Marxism /'mɑːksɪzəm/ *n* [U] the political and economic theory of Karl Marx (1818–83), favouring state control of production and a society without a class structure.
▶ **Marxist** /'mɑːksɪst/ *n* a supporter of Marxism.

M

───
[V.speech] = verb + direct speech   [V.that] = verb + *that* clause   [V.*wh*] = verb + *who, how*, etc clause

— *adj* relating to Marxism: *have Marxist views* ∘ *a Marxist government.*

marzipan /ˈmɑːzɪpæn, ˌmɑːzɪˈpæn/ *n* [U] a substance made from almonds (ALMOND), sugar and eggs. It is used to make sweets or to cover cakes.

mascara /mæˈskɑːrə; *US* -ˈskærə/ *n* [U] a substance for making one's eyelashes (EYELASH) look darker and thicker: *apply a coat of mascara.*

mascot /ˈmæskət, -skɒt/ *n* a person, an animal or a thing thought to bring good luck: *The club/ regimental mascot is a leopard.*

masculine /ˈmæskjəlɪn/ *adj* **1** having the qualities or appearance considered to be typical of or appropriate for men: *She looks very masculine in that suit.* ∘ *I like the solid masculine appeal of the building.* Compare EFFEMINATE, FEMININE 1. ⇨ note at FEMALE. **2** (*grammar*) (abbreviated as *masc* in this dictionary) of the male GENDER(1): *'He' and 'him' are masculine pronouns.* ∘ *'Soleil', the French word for 'sun', is masculine.* Compare FEMININE 2, NEUTER 1. ► **masculine** *n* (*grammar*) [C usu *sing*] a masculine(2) word or word form.

masculinity /ˌmæskjuˈlɪnəti/ *n* [U] the quality of being masculine.

mash /mæʃ/ *n* **1** [U] grain cooked in water until soft, used as food for animals. **2(a)** [U,C] any substance made by crushing sth into a soft mass: *a mash of wet paper and paste.* **(b)** [U] (*Brit infml*) boiled potatoes crushed into a soft mass, often with milk and butter added; mashed potatoes: ***bangers*** (ie sausages) ***and mash.*** ► **mash** *v* ~ sth (**up**) to beat or crush sth into a mash: [Vn] *mashed potato(es)/turnip(s)* [Vnpr, Vnp] *Mash the fruit (up) with a fork.* **masher** *n* an implement for mashing potatoes.

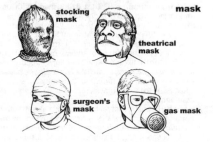

stocking mask

mask

theatrical mask

surgeon's mask

gas mask

mask¹ /mɑːsk; *US* mæsk/ *n* **1** a covering for part or all of the face, worn to disguise oneself or for protection: *bank robbers wearing stocking masks* ∘ *a gas/surgical mask* ∘ *a child wearing a Mickey Mouse mask.* ⇨ picture. ⇨ picture at FENCING. See also DEATH-MASK. **2** (usu *sing*) a manner or an expression that hides one's true character, emotions, etc: *He longed to throw off the mask of respectability.* ∘ *She conceals her worries behind a mask of cheerfulness.*

mask² /mɑːsk; *US* mæsk/ *v* **1** to cover the face with a mask: [Vn] *a masked man/gunman* [Vnpr] *The thief had masked his features with a stocking.* **2** to hide or disguise sth: *mask an unpleasant smell* ∘ *His quiet manners masked a tough determination.* ■ ˌmasked ˈball *n* a formal dance at which the guests wear masks.

ˈmasking tape *n* [U] sticky tape used when painting sth to cover an area that one does not want to get paint on: *He put masking tape round the edges of the glass while painting the window frame.*

masochism /ˈmæsəkɪzəm/ *n* [U] **(a)** (*infml*) the enjoyment of what appears to cause one trouble, anxiety, etc: *Spending your weekend correcting exam papers? That's sheer masochism!* **(b)** the practice of getting sexual pleasure from sb physically hurting

one. Compare SADISM. ► **masochist** /-kɪst/ *n*. **masochistic** /ˌmæsəˈkɪstɪk/ *adj*: *He has a masochistic streak in him.*

mason /ˈmeɪsn/ *n* **1** a person who builds in or works with stone. **2 Mason** a Freemason. ► **Masonic** /məˈsɒnɪk/ *adj* of Freemasons: *Masonic ritual.*

masonry /ˈmeɪsənri/ *n* [U] the part of a building that is made of stone and cement, etc: *brick and masonry walls* ∘ *She was injured by falling masonry.*

masque /mɑːsk; *US* mæsk/ *n* a drama in verse, often with music and dancing, popular in England in the 16th and 17th centuries.

masquerade /ˌmæskəˈreɪd; *Brit also* ˌmɑːsk-/ *n* an action, a manner, etc that appears to be genuine or sincere but is not: *Her sorrow is just a masquerade.* ► **masquerade** *v* ~ (**as sth**) to pretend to be sth that one is not: [Vpr] *a policeman masquerading as a drug-dealer* [also V].

mass¹ /mæs/ *n* **1** [C] ~ (**of sth**) **(a)** an often large quantity of sth without a definite shape, form or order: *a falling mass of rock* ∘ *There were masses of dark clouds in the sky.* ∘ *Her face was surrounded by a mass of curls.* ∘ *She began sifting through the mass of evidence.* **(b)** a large number of people or things together: *a mass of spectators* ∘ *She elbowed her way through the masses of tourists.* **2 masses** [pl] (*infml*) a large number or amount: *There were masses of people at the funeral.* ∘ *He has masses of homework to do.* ∘ *I don't need any more paper, thanks — I've got masses already.* **3 the masses** [pl] ordinary people, esp as seen by political leaders: *His simple message appealed to the masses.* **4** [sing] **the ~ of...** the majority; most: *The mass of workers do not want this strike.* **5** [U] (*physics*) the quantity of matter contained in a body (*weight* in language that is not technical). ⇨ App 8. See also LAND MASS. **IDM** **be a ˈmass of sth** to be full of or covered with: *The garden is a mass of flowers in the summer.* ∘ *His face was a mass of bruises.* ► **mass** *adj* affecting or involving a large number of people or things: *mass education/unemployment* ∘ *a mass meeting/walk-out/demonstration* ∘ *a mass murderer* ∘ *the mass destruction caused by war* ∘ *mass-circulation newspapers.* **mass** *v* to assemble or gather sb/sth together: [V, Vpr] *clouds massing (on the horizon)* [Vn] *massed armies/choirs* [Vnpr] *The general massed his troops for a final attack.* ■ **the ˌmass ˈmedia** (also ˌmass communiˈcations) *n* [pl] the means of communicating with large numbers of people, eg newspapers, television and radio.

ˌmass-proˈduce *v* to manufacture large quantities of an article using machinery: [Vn] *mass-produced cars/fridges.* **ˌmass proˈduction** *n* [U]: *the mass production of consumer goods.*

mass² (also **Mass**) /mæs/ *n* **(a)** [U,C] (esp in the Roman Catholic Church) a religious service celebrating Christ's Last Supper: *go to/hear Mass* ∘ *say a mass for their souls.* **(b)** [C] a musical arrangement for parts of this: *Beethoven's Mass in D.*

massacre /ˈmæsəkə(r)/ *n* [C,U] **1** the killing of a large number of people: *the bloody massacre of innocent civilians.* **2** (*infml*) a defeat of a team, political party, etc by a large number of points, votes, etc: *The game was a 10–0 massacre.* ► **massacre** *v* **1** [Vn] to kill large numbers of people or animals. **2** (*infml*) to defeat a team, political party, etc by a large number of points, votes, etc: [Vn] *We were massacred in the final.*

massage /ˈmæsɑːʒ; *US* məˈsɑːʒ/ *n* [U,C] the action or an instance of rubbing and pressing the body, usu with the hands, to relieve or prevent tension or pain in muscles, joints, etc: *give sb a relaxing*

M

massage ○ *The doctor recommended massage for my back pain.*
▶ **massage** *v* **1(a)** to give massage to sb, sb's muscles, etc: [Vn] *massage sb's back* ○ *(fig) The compliment served to massage my rather bruised ego.* **(b)** to rub a substance into the skin, hair, etc: [Vnpr] *massage oil into the skin.* **2** to alter figures, etc dishonestly in order to make them more acceptable: [Vn] *massage the accounts.*
masseur /mæ'sɜː(r)/ *n (fem* **masseuse** /mæ'sɜːz/) a person who practises massage as a profession.
■ **'massage parlour** (*US* **parlor**) *n (euph)* a place where men can pay for massage and/or sex with prostitutes.

massif /mæ'siːf/ *n* a group of mountains within a limited area.

massive /'mæsɪv/ *adj* **1** large, heavy and solid: *a massive building/rock.* **2** exceptionally large: *a massive increase/crowd* ○ *drink a massive amount of alcohol* ○ *suffer a massive* (ie very severe) *heart attack.* ▶ **massively** *adv*: *massively expensive/successful.* **massiveness** *n* [U].

mast /mɑːst; *US* mæst/ *n* **1** an upright post of wood or metal used to support a ship's sails. ⇨ picture at YACHT. **2** a tall pole, eg for a flag. See also HALF-MAST. **3** a tall steel structure for broadcasting radio or television signals. **IDM** **nail one's colours to the mast** ⇨ NAIL *v.*

mastectomy /mæ'stektəmi/ *n (medical)* the removal of a woman's breast by a SURGICAL operation.
master¹ /'mɑːstə(r); *US* 'mæs-/ *n* **1** *(dated)* a man who has others working for him or under him; an employer: *master and servant* ○ *The slaves feared their master.* Compare MISTRESS¹. **2** [often attrib] a worker who is skilled in a particular trade and able to teach others: *a master craftsman/builder.* **3** *(dated or joc)* the male head of a household: *the master of the house.* Compare MISTRESS². **4** the captain of a merchant ship: *a master mariner.* **5** the male owner of a dog, horse, etc: *That dog is devoted to his master.* Compare MISTRESS³. **6** *(esp Brit)* a male teacher at school; a SCHOOLMASTER: *the 'French master* (ie the man who teaches French). See also HEADMASTER, MISTRESS⁵. **7** **Master** a holder of the second university degree: *a Master of Arts/Sciences.* **8** **Master** (used esp formerly as a title for boys too young to be called Mr): *Master Charles Smith.* **9** **Master** (*Brit*) the title of the heads of certain colleges: *the Master of Balliol College, Oxford.* **10** a great artist: *a painting by an old Dutch master.* **11** *(fml)* **(a)** ~ **of sth** a person who has control of sth: *He is master of the situation.* ○ *be master of a subject* (ie know it thoroughly). **(b)** a person who is superior: *We shall see which of us is master* (eg which of us will win the fight, competition, etc). **12** an original version from which copies can be made: *the master tape/film/copy* ○ *copied from the master.* **13** [attrib] **(a)** commanding; superior; excellent: *This painting is the work of a master hand* (ie a superior and skilful artist). **(b)** main; principal: *the master bedroom.* **IDM** **(be) one's own 'master/'mistress** (to be) free and independent: *I prefer to be my own mistress, rather than work for someone else.* **serve two masters** ⇨ SERVE. See also CHOIRMASTER, GRAND MASTER, HARBOUR-MASTER, OLD MASTER, PAST MASTER.
■ **'master class** *n* a lesson, esp in music, given by a famous expert to highly skilled students.
'master-key (also **'pass key**) *n* a key made to open many different locks, each of which can also be opened by its own separate key.
ₗMaster of 'Ceremonies *n (abbr* **MC**) a person who announces guests, etc at certain formal social occasions.
'master-plan *n* a plan for success in a complex operation, etc: *It was all part of my master-plan to gain control of the company.*

'Master's degree (also **'Master's**) *n* a second higher university degree: *take a Master's degree in English.*
'master-stroke *n* a very skilful act that makes success certain: *Settling the dispute required a diplomatic master-stroke.*
master² /'mɑːstə(r); *US* 'mæs-/ *v* **1** to gain complete knowledge of or skill in sth: [Vn] *master a foreign language* ○ *She has mastered the art/technique of playing the guitar.* **2** to gain control of sth; to overcome sth: [Vn] *master one's temper/feelings.*
masterful /'mɑːstəfl; *US* 'mæs-/ *adj* **1** able to control others; dominating: *a masterful person/character/manner.* **2** skilful; excellent: *a masterful play/performance.* ▶ **masterfully** /-fəli/ *adv.*
masterly /'mɑːstəli; *US* 'mæs-/ *adj (approv)* very skilful: *their masterly handling of a difficult situation.*
mastermind /'mɑːstəmaɪnd; *US* 'mæs-/ *n* a person who is unusually intelligent, esp one who plans the work of others: *the mastermind behind the project.*
▶ **mastermind** *v* to plan and/or direct a scheme, etc: [Vn] *mastermind a campaign/robbery/project* ○ *The fraud was masterminded by an international gang.*
masterpiece /'mɑːstəpiːs; *US* 'mæs-/ (also **masterwork** /'mɑːstəwɜːk; *US* 'mæs-/) *n* a task done with great skill, esp an artist's greatest work.
mastery /'mɑːstəri; *US* 'mæst-/ *n* [U] **1** ~ (**of sth**) complete knowledge; great skill: *achieve/attain mastery of several languages* ○ *show complete mastery in one's handling of a difficult situation.* **2** ~ (**of/over sb/sth**) control: *finally gain mastery over a long illness* ○ *He struggled for mastery of his emotions.*
masthead /'mɑːsthed; *US* 'mæst-/ *n* **1** the highest part of a mast. **2** the name of a newspaper at the top of the front page.
mastic /'mæstɪk/ *n* [U] **1** a substance obtained from the bark of certain trees, used in making VARNISH. **2** a type of cement used on roofs, the frames of windows, etc to stop water getting in.
masticate /'mæstɪkeɪt/ *v* [V, Vn] *(fml)* to chew food.
▶ **mastication** /ˌmæstɪ'keɪʃn/ *n* [U].
mastiff /'mæstɪf/ *n* a breed of large strong dog, often used to guard houses.
mastitis /mæ'staɪtɪs/ *n* [U] *(medical)* a disease causing painful swelling of the breast or UDDER.
masturbate /'mæstəbeɪt/ *v* [V, Vn] to give oneself/sb sexual pleasure by stimulating the sexual organs, esp by hand. ▶ **masturbation** /ˌmæstə'beɪʃn/ *n* [U].
masturbatory /ˌmæstə'beɪtəri; *US* 'mæstərbətɔːri/ *adj* [usu attrib]: *masturbatory fantasies.*
mat¹ /mæt/ *n* **1(a)** a piece of material, made of straw, cloth, plant fibre, etc, used to cover part of a floor: *a 'doormat/'bathmat.* **(b)** a thick pad, usu of rubber or plastic, used in certain sports for competitors to land on: *a 'judo mat* ○ *The gymnast made a perfect landing on the mat.* **2** a small piece of material placed under a hot dish, or a glass, plate, etc to protect the surface underneath: *a cork 'table-mat* ○ *a 'beer mat.* **3** a thick untidy mass: *a mat of weeds/hair.*
▶ **mat** *v* **(-tt-)** (esp passive) to become or make sth a thick twisted mass: [Vn] *matted hair* [also V].
mat² = MATT.
matador /'mætədɔː(r)/ *n* a person whose task is to kill the BULL¹(1) in a BULLFIGHT.
match¹ /mætʃ/ *n* **1** [C] a game in which individuals or teams compete against each other; a contest: *a 'tennis/'wrestling/'football match* ○ *play a match against the former champions.* ⇨ note at SPORT. **2** [sing] ~ **for sb; sb's** ~ a person who is equal to sb else in skill, strength, etc: *He's no match for her* (at tennis). ○ *She's his match* (ie as good as or better than him) *when it comes to chess.* **3** [C] *(dated)* a

marriage: *She made a good match when she married him.* **4** [sing] **(a)** ~ **(for sb/sth)** a person or thing that combines well with another: *The new curtains are a perfect match for the carpet.* **(b)** ~ **(of sb/sth)** a person or thing that is similar to or very like another: *I've found a vase that's an exact match of the one we already have.* **IDM** **find/meet one's 'match (in sb)** to meet sb who has as much skill, determination, etc as oneself, and perhaps more: *He thought he could beat anyone at tennis, but he's met his match in Peter.* **the man of the match** ⇨ MAN¹. **the whole shooting match** ⇨ WHOLE.

▶ **matchless** *adj* that nothing or no one can match²(3a); supreme: *matchless beauty/skill.*

■ **,match 'point** *n* a final point needed to win a match, eg in tennis.

match² /mætʃ/ *v* **1** ~ **(with sth)** **(a)** to combine well with sth, esp in colour: [V] *a navy suit and gloves to match/matching gloves* ○ *The curtains and carpets match perfectly.* [Vn, Vpr] *These curtains won't match (with) your carpet.* **(b)** to be like or correspond to sb/sth else: [Vnadv] *a well-matched couple* [also Vn, Vpr, V]. **2** ~ **sb/sth (to/with sb/sth)** to find sb/sth that is like or corresponds to sb/sth else: [Vn] *Can you match this wallpaper?* **3(a)** to be equal to sb: [Vnpr] *No one can match her at chess.* [Vnadv] *The two players are well-matched* (ie roughly equal in ability). [also Vn]. **(b)** to find sb/sth equal to sb/ sth else: [Vn] *Can you match that story?* (ie Can you tell one that is equally good, amusing, etc?) **PHR V** **'match sth/sb against/with sth/sb** to make sth/sb compete with sth/sb else: *Match your skill against the experts in our weekly quiz.* **,match 'up** to be in agreement; to correspond: *The two statements don't match up.* **,match sth 'up (with sth)** to fit sth to sth else so as to form a complete whole: *matching up the torn pieces of the photograph.* **,match 'up to sb/sth** to be as good as or equal to sb/sth: *The film didn't match up to my expectations.*

match³ /mætʃ/ *n* a small stick or piece of cardboard used for lighting fires, etc. A match has a head made of material that bursts into flame when rubbed against a rough or specially prepared surface: *strike a match* ○ *a box of matches* ○ *put a match to sth* (ie set fire to it).

matchbox /'mætʃbɒks/ *n* a box for holding matches.

matchmaker /'mætʃmeɪkə(r)/ *n* a person who likes trying to arrange marriages or relationships between others. ▶ **matchmaking** *n* [U].

matchstick /'mætʃstɪk/ *n* the stem of a match: *with legs like matchsticks* (ie very thin) ○ *cut the carrots into matchsticks* (ie long thin shapes).

matchwood /'mætʃwʊd/ *n* [U] very small pieces of wood: *a boat reduced to matchwood* (ie completely broken up) *on the rocks.*

mate¹ /meɪt/ *n* **1(a)** (*Brit infml*) a friend or companion: *He's an old mate of mine.* ○ *I'm off for a drink with my mates.* **(b)** (*Brit sl*) used esp by men as a form of address to a man): *Sorry, mate, I can't help you.* **(c)** (in compounds) a person involved in the same specified activity, organization, etc or sharing the same accommodation: *her 'team-mates/ 'class-mates/'playmates* ○ *my 'room-mate/'flat-mate.* **2** (in job names) the assistant of a skilled worker: *a plumber's mate.* **3** an officer in the merchant navy: *the chief mate* (ie ranking just below the captain). **4(a)** either of a pair of birds or animals: *The bird seems to have lost its mate.* **(b)** (*infml*) a husband or wife. See also RUNNING MATE, SOUL MATE.

mate² /meɪt/ *v* ~ **(a)** ~ **(with sth)** (of birds or animals) to come together to have sex and produce young: [V] *the mating season* [V, Vpr] *Pandas rarely mate (with each other) in captivity.* **(b)** ~ **sth (with/to sth)** to bring birds or animals together for this purpose: [Vn, Vnpr] *We mated the grey mare (with a champion stallion).*

mate³ /meɪt/ *n* = CHECKMATE.

material¹ /mə'tɪəriəl/ *n* **1** [C, U] a substance or substances from which sth else is or can be made; a thing or things with which sth is done: *raw materials for industry* (eg oil, metals, etc) ○ *'building materials* (eg bricks, sand, glass, etc) ○ *'writing materials* (eg pens, paper, ink) ○ *We only use high-quality material for our products.* ○ (*fig*) *He is not managerial material* (ie will not become a good manager). **2** [U, C] fabric; cloth: *enough material to make a skirt and blouse* ○ *cotton/woollen material* ○ *sell 'dressmaking materials.* **3** [U] facts, information, etc to be used in writing a book, as evidence, etc: *She's collecting material for a newspaper article.*

material² /mə'tɪəriəl/ *adj* **1** [attrib] composed of or connected with physical objects rather than the mind or spirit: *the material world.* Compare IMMATERIAL 2. **2** [attrib] of physical needs or desires rather than those of the mind or spirit: *our material needs* (eg food and drink) ○ *material wealth/goods* ○ *You think too much of material comforts.* Compare SPIRITUAL 1. **3** ~ **(to sth)** (*fml or law*) important; essential; relevant: *material evidence* ○ *Is this point material to your argument?* Compare IMMATERIAL 1.

▶ **materially** /-iəli/ *adv*: *materially deprived* (ie poor) ○ *That does not materially affect my argument* (ie in a significant way).

materialism /mə'tɪəriəlɪzəm/ *n* [U] **1** (*usu derog*) a tendency to be more interested in material possessions, physical comforts, etc than in spiritual values: *the rampant materialism of modern society.* **2** (*philosophy*) the belief that only material²(2) things exist.

▶ **materialist** /mə'tɪəriəlɪst/ *n* **1** a person who believes that material possessions are all that matter in life. **2** a believer in materialism(2).

materialistic /mə,tɪəriə'lɪstɪk/ *adj*: *a materialistic person/theory/society.*

materialize, -ise /mə'tɪəriəlaɪz/ *v* **1** to become a reality; to happen: [V] *Our plans did not materialize.* ○ *The threatened strike never materialized.* **2** to take physical form; to become visible; to appear: [V] *He claimed that he could make ghosts materialize.* ○ (*infml*) *He failed to materialize* (ie did not come). ▶ **materialization, -isation** /mə,tɪəriəlaɪ'zeɪʃn; US -lə'z-/ *n* [U].

maternal /mə'tɜːnl/ *adj* **1** of or like a mother: *maternal instincts/love/mortality* ○ *She feels very maternal towards him.* **2** [attrib] related through the mother's side of the family: *She's my maternal grandfather/aunt* (ie my mother's father/sister). Compare PATERNAL. ▶ **maternally** /-nəli/ *adv.*

maternity /mə'tɜːnəti/ *n* [U] the state of being a mother: *a maternity dress* (ie one for a pregnant woman) ○ *a maternity ward/hospital* (ie for women who have just given birth).

■ **ma'ternity leave** *n* [U] a period of time during which a woman temporarily leaves her job to have a baby.

ma'ternity pay *n* [U] money paid by an employer to a woman who has temporarily left her job to have a baby. Compare PATERNITY.

matey /'meɪti/ *adj* ~ **(with sb)** (*Brit infml*) friendly: *Don't get too matey with him — he can't be trusted.*

mathematics /,mæθə'mætɪks/ *n* [sing or pl *v*] (also *Brit infml* **maths** /mæθs/ [sing or pl *v*], *US* **math** /mæθ/ [sing *v*]) the science of numbers, quantity and space. ARITHMETIC, ALGEBRA, TRIGONOMETRY and GEOMETRY are some of the branches of mathematics: *a maths teacher/lesson* ○ *His mathematics are weak* (ie He is not very good at doing sums, etc). ○ *Maths is her strongest subject.* ○ *I don't understand the mathematics* (eg the difficult sums) *here.*

▶ **mathematical** /,mæθə'mætɪkl/ *adj* of or relating

M

to mathematics: *a mathematical calculation/ formula/problem* ○ *She has a fine mathematical brain.* **mathematically** /-kli/ *adv*: *It's not mathematically enough.* ○ *She's not mathematically inclined* (ie not interested in mathematics).

mathematician /ˌmæθəməˈtɪʃn/ *n* an expert in mathematics.

matinée (also **matinee**) /ˈmætɪneɪ; *US* ˌmætnˈeɪ/ *n* an afternoon performance at a cinema or theatre.

■ **'matinée idol** *n* (*dated*) an actor who is greatly admired, esp by women.

matins (also **mattins**) /ˈmætɪnz; *US* ˈmætnz/ *n* [sing or pl *v*] the service of morning prayer, esp in the Church of England: *attend matins every Sunday.* Compare EVENSONG, VESPERS.

matri- *comb form* relating to a mother: *matricide* ○ *matriarch.* Compare PATRI-.

matriarch /ˈmeɪtriɑːk/ *n* the female head of a family or tribe. Compare PATRIARCH.

▶ **matriarchal** /ˌmeɪtriˈɑːkl/ *adj*: *a matriarchal society/system.*

matriarchy /ˈmeɪtriɑːki/ *n* a type of society in which women are the heads of families, own property and have most of the authority.

matrices *pl* of MATRIX.

matricide /ˈmætrɪsaɪd/ *n* **1** [U,C] the killing of one's own mother. **2** [C] a person who kills her or his own mother. Compare PATRICIDE.

matriculate /məˈtrɪkjuleɪt/ *v* to be admitted as a student of a college or university: *When did you matriculate?* ▶ **matriculation** /məˌtrɪkjuˈleɪʃn/ *n* [U]: *take the matriculation exam.*

matrimony /ˈmætrɪməni; *US* -məʊni/ *n* [U] (*fml*) the state of being married; marriage: *be joined in holy matrimony.*

▶ **matrimonial** /ˌmætrɪˈməʊniəl/ *adj* [usu attrib] of matrimony: *a matrimonial dispute/problem.*

matrix /ˈmeɪtrɪks/ *n* (*pl* **matrices** /ˈmeɪtrɪsiːz/ or **matrixes**) **1** the social, political, etc conditions that govern the existence and development of sth: *within the European cultural matrix.* **2** a network or GRID(2): *a matrix of paths.* **3** (*mathematics*) an arrangement of numbers, symbols, etc in a GRID(2), treated as a single quantity. ⇨ picture. **4** (*computing*) a group of circuit elements arranged to look like a GRID(2). See also DOT MATRIX PRINTER. **5** (*geology*) a mass of rock, etc in which minerals, etc are found in the ground.

matrix

$$\begin{pmatrix} 3 & 12 & 8 \\ 4 & 8 & 13 \\ 12 & 9 & 3 \end{pmatrix}$$

matron /ˈmeɪtrən/ *n* **1** a woman who manages the domestic affairs of a school, etc. **2** (formerly) a woman in charge of the nurses in a hospital (now usu called a *senior nursing officer*). **3** an older married woman, esp one with a dignified (DIGNIFY) appearance.

▶ **matronly** *adj* having the characteristics of a matron(3): *a matronly manner.*

matt (also **mat**) /mæt/ *adj* (of surfaces or colours) not shiny; dull: *a matt black enamel* ○ *Will this paint give a gloss or a matt finish?* Compare GLOSS¹ 1.

matter¹ /ˈmætə(r)/ *n* **1** [C] **(a)** an affair, a topic or a situation being considered: *get to the heart/core/ crux/root of the matter* ○ *the matter in hand/under discussion* ○ *a matter I know little about* ○ ¹*money matters* ○ *I don't discuss private matters with my colleagues.* ○ *I refuse to* **let the matter rest** (ie not take it further). ○ *We have several important matters to deal with at our next meeting.* ○ *Starting a business is* **no easy matter**. ○ *I won't let you do it — and* **that's the end of the matter** (ie I refuse to discuss it any further). ○ (*ironic*) *There's the small matter of the money you owe me.* **(b)** ~ **of sth** (**to sb**) a situation, problem or result that causes a particular

reaction in sb: *matters of growing public concern* ○ *This is a matter of considerable interest to me.* **2 the matter** [sing] ~ (**with sb/sth**) the reason for pain, problems, being unhappy, etc: *What's the matter (with you)? Why are you crying?* ○ *I asked her if* **anything was the matter**. ○ *There's* **nothing the matter with it.** **3** [U] **(a)** physical substance in general, contrasted with mind or spirit: *inert matter* ○ *study the properties of matter* ○ *The universe is composed of matter.* **(b)** substance, material or things of a specified kind: *decaying* ¹*vegetable matter* ○ ¹*waste matter* (eg from the human body) ○ ¹*reading matter* (ie books, newspapers, etc) ○ ¹*printed matter* (ie forms, documents, etc). **4** [U] (*fml*) the ideas or topic of a book, speech, etc, contrasted with its language or style: *interesting* **subject matter**. **5** [U] a substance discharged from the body: *faecal matter* ○ *an infected wound full of matter.* **IDM as a matter of 'fact** (used for emphasis) in reality; to tell the truth: *I'm going there tomorrow, as a matter of fact.* **be another / a different 'matter** to be completely different: *I can read French quite well, but speaking it fluently is a different matter.* **be no laughing matter** ⇨ LAUGHING. **for 'that matter** (used to indicate that a second category, topic, etc is as relevant as the first): *Don't talk like that to your mother, or to anyone else for that matter.* **it's all, only, etc a matter of 'time (before ...)** this consequence is inevitable though it may not happen immediately: *It's simply a matter of time before the rebels are crushed.* **make matters 'worse** to make an already difficult situation more difficult: *Her attempts to calm them down only made matters worse.* **(as) a matter of 'course** (as) a regular habit or usual procedure: *I check my in-tray every morning as a matter of course.* **a matter of 'hours, 'minutes, 'days, etc; a matter of 'pounds, 'feet, 'ounces, etc 1** not more than: *I'll be back in a matter of hours.* ○ *It's a matter of a few more miles, that's all.* **2** not less than: *It may be a matter of months before it's ready.* **a ˌmatter of ˌlife and 'death** an issue that is essential for survival, success, etc: *Of course this must have priority — it's a matter of life and death.* **a ˌmatter of o'pinion** an issue on which there is disagreement: *'She's a fine singer.' 'That's a matter of opinion.'* **a ˌmatter of 'record** a thing established as a fact by being recorded: *The minister's views on this subject are a matter of record.* **(be) a matter of sth / doing sth** a situation, a question or an issue that depends on sth else: *Dealing with such problems is all a matter of experience.* ○ *Success in business is simply a matter of knowing when to take a chance.* **mind over matter** ⇨ MIND¹. **no matter; be/make no matter (to sb) (that/whether ...)** to be of no importance to sb: *'I can't do it.' 'No matter, I'll do it myself.'* ○ *It's no matter to me whether you arrive early or late.* **no matter who, what, where, etc** whoever, whatever, wherever, etc: *Don't open the door, no matter who comes.* ○ *Don't trust him, no matter what he says.*

■ ˌmatter-of-'fact *adj* showing no emotion or imagination: *She told us the news in a very* ˌmatter-of-fact ¹*way.* ˌmatter-of-'factly *adv*.

matter² /ˈmætə(r)/ *v* ~ (**to sb**) (not in the continuous tenses or the imperative; used esp in negative sentences and questions; in sentences containing *what, who, where, if,* etc, usu with *it* as the subject) to be important: [V] *What does it matter (whether he comes or not)?* ○ *Some things matter more than others.* ○ *Does it matter if we're a bit late?* [Vpr] *It doesn't matter to me what you do.*

matting /ˈmætɪŋ/ *n* [U] rough woven material used for making mats or for packing goods: *floors covered with coconut matting.*

mattins = MATINS.

mattock /ˈmætək/ *n* a heavy tool with a long handle

and a metal head, used for breaking up soil, cutting roots, etc.

mattress /ˈmætrəs/ n a strong cloth case filled with soft or firm material and used for sleeping on. Some mattresses also contain springs.

mature¹ /məˈtʃʊə(r), -ˈtjʊə(r); US also -ˈtʊər/ adj **1(a)** fully grown or developed in mind or body: *a mature person/oak/elephant* ○ *a house with a mature garden* (ie one in which the plants, trees, etc are fully grown and well established) ○ *He's not mature enough to be given too much responsibility.* Compare IMMATURE. **(b)** (of wine or cheese) having reached a stage where its flavour has fully developed. **2** [attrib] (of thought, intentions, etc) careful and thorough: *after mature consideration/reflection.* **3** (*commerce*) (of insurance policies, etc) due for payment.
▸ **maturely** adv.
maturity /məˈtʃʊərəti, -ˈtjʊə-; US also -ˈtʊə-/ n [U] the state of being mature: *reach maturity.*
■ **ma͵ture ˈstudent** n (in Britain) a student over the age of 21 at a university or college.

mature² /məˈtʃʊə(r), -tjʊə(r); US also -ˈtʊər/ v **1** to become or make sb/sth mature: [V] *cheese/wine that matures slowly* ○ *Her character matured during these years.* ○ *My plan gradually matured.* [Vpr] *She matured into a shrewd politician.* [Vn] *Experience has matured him greatly.* **2** [V] (*commerce*) (of insurance policies, etc) to become due for payment.
▸ **maturation** /͵mætʃuˈreɪʃn/ n [U] the process of becoming or being made mature: *a slow maturation.*

matzo /ˈmætsəʊ/ n (pl **-os**) **(a)** [U] bread in the form of large thin biscuits, eaten esp by Jews at Passover. **(b)** one of these biscuits.

maudlin /ˈmɔːdlɪn/ adj foolishly sentimental or full of pity for oneself, esp when drunk.

maul /mɔːl/ v **1** ~ sb/sth (about) to handle sb/sth in a rough and unwelcome way: (*fig*) [Vn] *Her novel was badly mauled by the critics.* [also Vnp]. **2** to injure a person or an animal by tearing the flesh: [Vn] *He died after being mauled by a tiger.*

maunder /ˈmɔːndə(r)/ v ~ (on) to talk in a boring or complaining way: [V, Vp] *I mustn't keep maundering (on) about my silly problems.*

Maundy Thursday /͵mɔːndi ˈθɜːzdeɪ/ n [U] the Thursday before Easter.

mausoleum /͵mɔːsəˈliːəm/ n an ornamental building made to hold the dead body of an important person or the dead bodies of a family.

mauve /məʊv/ adj, n [U] (of) a pale purple colour.

maverick /ˈmævərɪk/ n [often attrib] a person with independent or unusual views: *Politically, she's a real maverick.* ○ *a maverick film director.*

maw /mɔː/ n (*fml*) an animal's stomach or throat: (*fig*) *a small company disappearing in the maw of a giant conglomerate.*

mawkish /ˈmɔːkɪʃ/ adj sentimental in a weak or silly way: *a mawkish film/poem.* ▸ **mawkishness** n [U].

max /mæks/ abbr maximum: *temperature 60° max.* Compare MIN 1.

maxim /ˈmæksɪm/ n a well-known saying (SAY) that expresses a general truth or rule of conduct, eg 'look before you leap'.

maximize, -ise /ˈmæksɪmaɪz/ v **1** to increase sth as much as possible: [Vn] *We must maximize profits.* **2** to make the best use of sth: [Vn] *maximize one's opportunities.* Compare MINIMIZE. ▸ **maximization, -isation** /͵mæksɪmaɪˈzeɪʃn; US -məˈz-/ n [U].

maximum /ˈmæksɪməm/ n (pl **maxima** /ˈmæksɪmə/) (usu *sing*) (abbr **max**) the greatest amount, size, intensity, etc possible or recorded: *obtain 81 marks out of a maximum of 100* ○ *develop one's skills to the maximum* ○ *The July maximum* (ie the highest temperature recorded in July) *was 30°C.* ○ *This test should take you two hours at the maximum.* ○ *This hall holds a maximum of 70 people/holds 70 people maximum.* Compare MINIMUM.
▸ **maximum** adj [attrib] as high, great, intense, etc as possible: *the maximum speed/temperature/ voltage/volume* ○ *The maximum load for this truck is one ton.*

maximal /ˈmæksɪml/ adj [usu attrib] as great as can be achieved: *try to obtain maximal benefit from the course.*

May /meɪ/ n [U, C] the fifth month of the year.
For further guidance on how *May* is used, see the examples at *April*.
■ **ˈMay Day** n [U, C] the first day of May, celebrated as a spring festival and, in some countries, as a holiday in honour of workers. Compare MAYDAY.

may¹ /meɪ/ modal v (neg **may not**; rare short form **mayn't** /ˈmeɪənt/; pt **might** /maɪt/; neg **might not**; rare short form **mightn't** /ˈmaɪtnt/) **1** (*rather fml*) (indicating permission): *You may come if you wish.* ○ *May I come in?* ○ *That was a delicious meal if I may say so.* ○ *Passengers may cross by the footbridge.* ⇨ note. **2(a)** (indicating possibility): *This coat may be Peter's.* ○ *That may or may not be true.* ○ *He may have* (ie Perhaps he has) *missed his train.* ○ *This medicine may soothe your cough.* ○ *You may disagree, but that's what I think.* ⇨ note at MIGHT¹. **(b)** (used when admitting that sth is so before introducing another point, argument, etc): *Oxford may have changed a lot in recent years, but it's still a beautiful city.* **3** (*fml*) (indicating purpose): *I'll write today so that he may know when to expect us.* **4** (used to express wishes and hopes): *May you both be very happy! ○ Long may she live to enjoy her good fortune!*

NOTE Using **may** (negative **may not**) is a polite and fairly formal way of asking for, giving or refusing permission: *May I borrow your newspaper?* ○ *You may come if you wish.* It is often used in writing: *Visitors may use the swimming-pool between 7 am and 7 pm.* ○ *Students may not use the college car park.* Children often use **may** when speaking to adults: *'Please may I leave the table?' 'No, you may not.'* Note that the short form **mayn't** is almost never used in modern English.
    Can and **cannot** (or **can't**) are used to give and refuse permission: *You can come with us if you want to.* ○ *You can't leave your bike there.*
    Could is a neutral and polite word, used mostly in requests: *'Could I use your phone?' 'Yes, of course.'* In both British and American English people use **could** when they feel uncertain: *Could I possibly arrange to see the director?*
    Must not, **mustn't** or **not be allowed to** are used to say that somebody does not have permission to do something: *We mustn't wear make-up to school.* ○ *You are not allowed to smoke anywhere in the building.*
    May is also used to talk about possibility. ⇨ note at MIGHT¹.

may² /meɪ/ n [U] the flowers of the HAWTHORN.

maybe /ˈmeɪbi/ adv perhaps; possibly: *Maybe he'll come, maybe he won't.* ○ *'Is that true?' 'Maybe, I'm not sure.'* **IDM** **that's as ˈmaybe** (used when admitting that sth may be true before introducing another point, argument, etc) that may be so.

mayday (also **Mayday**) /ˈmeɪdeɪ/ n an international radio signal used by ships and aircraft needing help: *a mayday call/signal.* See also SOS. Compare MAY DAY.

mayfly /ˈmeɪflaɪ/ n an insect that appears and lives for a short time in May.

mayhem /ˈmeɪhem/ n [U] violent disorder or confusion: *Drunken hooligans were creating mayhem on the streets.*

mayn't /ˈmeɪənt/ short form may not. ⇨ MAY¹.

mayonnaise /͵meɪəˈneɪz; US ˈmeɪəneɪz/ n [U] **(a)**

(also *US infml* **mayo**) a thick yellowish or whitish sauce made with eggs, oil and VINEGAR, used esp on cold foods. (**b**) (*Brit*) (after *ns*) a dish made with this: *Egg mayonnaise is made with mayonnaise and hard-boiled eggs.*

mayor /meə(r); *US* ˈmeɪər/ *n* (the title of) the head of the council of a city or BOROUGH, usu elected each year in Britain and every four years in the USA.
▶ **mayoral** /ˈmeərəl; *US* ˈmeɪə-/ *adj* [attrib]: *mayoral robes/duties.*
   mayoralty /ˈmeərəlti; *US* ˈmeɪər-/ *n* the office of a mayor, or the period of this.
mayoress /meəˈres; *US* ˈmeɪərəs/ *n* **1** (also ˌlady ˈmayor) a woman holding the office of mayor. **2** a mayor's wife or other woman assisting a mayor or mayoress.

maypole /ˈmeɪpəʊl/ *n* a decorated pole around which people dance on May Day.

maze

maze /meɪz/ *n* (usu *sing*) **1** a network of paths or hedges designed as a PUZZLE(2) in which one must find one's way: *We got lost in Hampton Court maze.* ○ (*fig*) *A maze of narrow alleys leads down to the sea.* ⇨ picture. **2** a complex mass of facts, etc: *finding one's way through the maze of rules and regulations.*

mazurka /məˈzɜːkə/ *n* a lively Polish dance for four or eight couples, or the music for this.

MB /ˌem ˈbiː/ *abbr* Bachelor of Medicine: *have/be an MB* ○ *Philip Watt MB, ChB.*

MBA /ˌem biː ˈeɪ/ *abbr* Master of Business Administration: *have/be an MBA* ○ *Marion Strachan MBA.*

MBE /ˌem biː ˈiː/ *abbr* Member (of the Order) of the British Empire: *be made an MBE* ○ *William Godfrey MBE.* Compare CBE.

MC /ˌem ˈsiː/ *abbr* **1** master of ceremonies. **2** (in the USA) Member of Congress: *Senator Karl B Kaufman (MC).* **3** (in the UK) Military Cross: *be awarded the/ an MC for bravery.*

MCC /ˌem siː ˈsiː/ *abbr* Marylebone Cricket Club (the governing body of English cricket).

McCoy IDM **the real thing/McCoy** ⇨ REAL.

MD /ˌem ˈdiː/ *abbr* **1** Doctor of Medicine (Latin *Medicinae Doctor*): *be an MD* ○ *David Walker MD.* **2** Managing Director: *the MD's office.*

me¹ /mi; *strong form* miː/ *pers pron* (used as the object of a *v* or of a *prep*; also used independently or after *be*) the person who is the speaker or writer: *Don't hit me.* ○ *Excuse me!* ○ *Give it to me.* ○ *Hello, it's me.* ○ *'Who's there?' 'Only me.'* Compare I².

me² = MI.

mead /miːd/ *n* [U] an alcoholic drink made from honey and water.

meadow /ˈmedəʊ/ *n* [C, U] **1** an area or field of land covered in grass used esp for HAY. **2** an area of low, often wet, land near a river: *cattle grazing in the meadows* ○ *20 acres of meadow.*

meagre (*US* **meager**) /ˈmiːgə(r)/ *adj* small in quantity and poor in quality: *a meagre diet of bread and water* ○ *supplement one's meagre income by doing odd jobs* ○ *Our appeal for help met with a meagre response.*

meal¹ /miːl/ *n* (**a**) an occasion when food is eaten:

the midday/evening meal ○ *Don't eat between meals.* (**b**) the food eaten on such an occasion: *a meal of chicken and rice* ○ *eat a big meal* ○ *a three-course meal.* IDM **make a ˈmeal of sth** (*infml*) to give sth more attention, effort, etc than it deserves or needs: *She always makes such a meal of it — I could do it in half the time!* **a square meal** ⇨ SQUARE¹.
■ ˌmeals-on-ˈwheels *n* [pl] a service in which meals are taken by car to old or sick people in their own homes.
ˈmeal-ticket *n* **1** (*infml*) a person or thing seen as a source of food or income: *There were times when he suspected he was just a meal-ticket to her.* **2** (*US*) = LUNCHEON VOUCHER.

meal² /miːl/ *n* [U] (often in compounds) grain that has been ground to a powder: ˈoatmeal. See also WHOLEMEAL.

mealtime /ˈmiːltaɪm/ *n* a time at which a meal is usu eaten.

mealy-mouthed /ˌmiːliˈmaʊðd/ *adj* (*derog*) not willing to speak in a direct or open way: *Don't be so mealy-mouthed, say what you mean!* ○ ˌmealy-mouthed poliˈticians/exˈcuses.

mean¹ /miːn/ *v* (*pt, pp* **meant** /ment/) **1** ~ sth (**to sb**) to have sth as a meaning; to SIGNIFY sth: [V] *A dictionary tells you what words mean.* [Vn] *What does this sentence mean?* [Vnpr] *These symbols mean nothing to me.* [V.that] *The flashing lights mean (that) the road is blocked.* **2** (to be likely) to result in sth; to be a sign that; to involve sth: [Vn] *Spending too much now will mean a shortage of cash next year.* ○ *Do you have any idea **what it means to** be poor?* [V.that] *The warmer weather means (that) spring is here.* [V.n ing, V.ing] *This new order will mean (us) working overtime.* **3(a)** ~ sth for sb; ~ sth (as sth); ~ sth (**to sb**) to have sth as a purpose; to intend sth: [Vnpr] *What did she mean by leaving so early?* (ie Why did she do it?) [Vn] *He means what he says* (ie is not joking, exaggerating, etc). ○ *Don't laugh! I mean it* (ie I am serious)! [V.to inf, Vn] *He means (to cause) trouble/mischief.* [Vnpr] *She meant this gift for you.* [V.that no passive] *I never meant that you should come alone.* [V.to inf] *She means to succeed.* ○ *I'm sorry I hurt you: I didn't mean to.* [Vn-n] *I wasn't serious. I meant it as a joke.* [V.n to inf] *I didn't mean you to read the letter.* ○ ***You're meant to*** (ie You are supposed to) *pay before you go in.* [Vnn] *I mean you no harm.* [Vnpr] *He means no harm to anyone.* (**b**) to intend to say sth on a particular occasion: [Vnpr] *What did he mean by that remark?* [Vn] *Do you mean Miss Anne Smith or Miss Mary Smith?* [V.that no passive] *Did he mean (that) he was dissatisfied with our service?* **4** ~ sb **for sth** (of sb's parents, fate, etc) to intend sb to be or do sth: [Vnpr esp passive] *I was never meant for the army* (ie did not have the qualities needed to become a soldier). [V.n to inf] *She was never meant to be a teacher.* ○ *His father meant him to be an engineer.* **5** ~ sth to sb (no passive) to be of value or importance to sb: [Vnpr] *Your friendship means a great deal to me.* ○ *$20 means a lot* (ie represents a lot of money) *to a poor person.* ○ *Money means nothing to him.* ○ *You know how much you mean to me* (ie how much I like you). IDM **be meant to be sth** to be generally considered to be sth: *This restaurant is meant to be excellent.* **mean ˈbusiness** (*infml*) to be serious in one's intentions: *He has the look of a man who means business.* **mean to ˈsay** (usu in questions) to admit readily: *Do you mean to say you've lost it?* ˈmean **well** (*derog*) to have good intentions, though perhaps not the will or ability to carry them out: *He's hopelessly inefficient, but I suppose he ˈmeans well.*

mean² /miːn/ *adj* (**-er, -est**) **1** not willing to give or share things, esp money; not generous: *She's too mean to make a donation.* **2** ~ (**to sb**) (of people or their behaviour) unkind: *That was a mean trick!* ○ *It* *was mean of you to eat all the food.* ○ *Don't be so mean to your little brother!* **3** (*esp US*) likely to become angry or violent; VICIOUS: *He looks like a mean character.* **4** poor in appearance, quality, etc: *mean houses in the poorest part of the city.* **5** (of a person's understanding or ability) inferior: *This should be clear even to the meanest intelligence.* **6** (*dated*) of HUMBLE(2) birth or low social rank: *The meanest labourer has the same rights as the richest landowner.* **7** (*infml approv*) very skilful, effective, etc: *a mean golfer* ○ *She certainly plays a mean game of cards.* **IDM** **no mean ¹sth** (*approv*) (usu of a person or an achievement) a very good skill: *She's no mean ¹chess player.* ○ *That was no mean ¹feat.*

▶ **meanie** /'miːni/ *n* (*infml*) an unkind or SELFISH person: *Give me some more, you meanie!*
meanly *adv.*
meanness *n* [U].

mean³ /miːn/ *n* **1** a condition, quality, course of action, etc that is in the middle between two usu undesirable extremes: *You must find a mean between frankness and rudeness.* **2** (*mathematics*) **(a)** the value found by adding together all the numbers in a group and dividing the total by the number of numbers; the average: *The mean of 13, 5 and 27 is found by adding them together and dividing by 3.* **(b)** (*esp* in relation to sth that is constantly changing) a value between two extreme values, found by adding them together and dividing the total by 2. **IDM** **the happy/golden ¹mean** a moderate course of action.

▶ **mean** *adj* [attrib] equally far from two extremes; average: *the mean sea-level* ○ *the mean temperature on a certain day.*

meander /mi'ændə(r)/ *v* **1** (of a river, etc) to follow a winding course, flowing slowly. **2(a)** (of a person) to wander without any purpose: [Vpr] *meander through the park* [Vp] *meander around/along* [also V]. **(b)** (of conversation) to proceed casually or with little purpose: [V, Vp] *The discussion meandered (on) for hours.*

▶ **meanderings** /mi'ændrɪŋz/ *n* [pl] a winding course; wandering without purpose.

meaning /'miːnɪŋ/ *n* **1** [U, C] what is referred to or indicated by eg sounds, words or signals: *sounds and patterns that convey meaning* ○ *a word with several meanings* ○ *The word is being used in its original meaning.* ○ *a poem with a deeper/hidden meaning.* **2** [U] a serious, important or useful quality; purpose: *My life seems to have lost all meaning.* ○ *With her, he learned the true meaning of love.* **IDM** **not know the meaning of the word** ⇨ KNOW.

▶ **meaning** *adj* [usu attrib] intended to communicate sth that is not directly expressed: *a meaning look/glance.*
meaningful /-fl/ *adj* **1** having some serious, important or useful quality: *a meaningful relationship/discussion.* **2(a)** intended to communicate sth that is not directly expressed: *a meaningful look/pause.* **(b)** having meaning(1): *meaningful sounds/utterances.* **meaningfully** /-fəli/ *adv.* **meaningfulness** *n* [U].
meaningless *adj* **1** without sense, purpose or reason: *meaningless chatter/violence.* **2** having no meaning(1): *a meaningless word/statement.* **meaninglessly** *adv* **meaninglessness** *n* [U].

means /miːnz/ *n* **1** [sing or pl *v*] an action, an object or a system by which a result is brought about; a method or methods: *The passport was obtained by illegal means.* ○ *Television is an effective means of communication.* ○ *There is no means of finding out what happened.* ○ *All possible means have been tried.* **2** [pl] money; wealth; what is needed to live comfortably: *be a man of means* (ie a wealthy man) ○ *She lacks the means to support a large family.* ○ *A person of your means can afford it.* **IDM** **by ¹all means** (*fml*) (used esp to invite or permit sb to do sth) of course;

certainly: *'Can I see it?' 'By all means.'* **by fair means or foul** ⇨ FAIR¹. **by means of sth** (*fml*) by using sth; with the help of sth: *lift a load by means of a crane.* **by ¹no means; not by ¹any (manner of) means** not at all: *She is by no means poor; in fact, she's quite rich.* ○ *We haven't won yet, not by any manner of means.* **the end justifies the means** ⇨ END¹. **live beyond/within one's means** ⇨ LIVE². **a ¹means to an ¹end** a thing or an action that is not interesting or important in itself but is a way of achieving sth: *I didn't enjoy my first job but saw it as a means to an end.* **ways and means** ⇨ WAY¹.

■ **¹means test** *n* an official enquiry into sb's wealth or income in order to discover if they qualify for financial help from public funds. **¹means-tested** *adj* awarded on the basis of a means test: *means-tested benefits.*

meant *pt, pp* of MEAN¹.

meantime /'miːntaɪm/ *adv* (*infml*) MEANWHILE; in the meantime. *Meantime* is less common than *meanwhile*: *Meantime, the campaign continues.*

▶ **meantime** *n* **IDM** **in the ¹meantime** MEANWHILE: *The next programme starts in five minutes: in the meantime, here's some music.*

meanwhile /'miːnwaɪl/ *adv* while sth else is happening; while waiting for sth to happen: *I went to college. Meanwhile, all my friends were getting well-paid jobs.* ○ *Leave the cake to cool. Meanwhile, make the icing.*

measles /'miːzlz/ *n* [sing *v*] an infectious disease, esp of children, with a fever and small red spots that cover the whole body. Compare GERMAN MEASLES.

measly /'miːzli/ *adj* (*infml derog*) very small in size, amount or value: *They're paid a measly £2 an hour.*

measure¹ /'meʒə(r)/ *v* **1(a)** ~ **sth (in sth);** ~ **sb/sth (up) (for sth)** to find the size, length or amount of sth by comparing it with a standard unit: [V] *measuring devices/equipment* [Vn] *measure the width of a door/the level of an electric current/the speed of a car* [V.*wh*] *an instrument that measures how much alcohol there is in the blood* [Vnpr] *Energy is measured in joules.* [Vnp] *The tailor measured me up for a suit* (eg measured my chest, arms, legs). **(b)** to judge the extent or value of sth; to assess sth: [Vn] *It's hard to measure his ability when we haven't seen his work.* **2** to be a certain size or length: [V-n] *The room measures 10 metres across/10 metres by 8 metres.* **3** to consider carefully what one says or does: [Vn] *measure one's words* ○ *She failed to measure the effect of her actions on her family.* **PHRV** **¸measure sth ¹out** to obtain an exact quantity of sth by measuring: *measure out a dose of medicine.* **¸measure ¹up (to sth/sb)** to reach the standard required or expected: *The job didn't measure up to my expectations.* ○ *The players of today simply don't measure up (to those of my youth).*

▶ **measurable** /'meʒərəbl/ *adj* **1** that can be measured: *radiation in measurable quantities* ○ *The wavelength of light is measurable with a spectrometer.* **2** noticeable; definite: *There's been a measurable improvement in his work.* **measurably** /-əbli/ *adv.*
measured *adj* **1** (of speech or writing) carefully considered; restrained: *measured words/criticism.* **2** slow and with a regular rhythm: *walk with measured steps/at a measured pace.*
measurement *n* **1** [U] the activity or process of measuring sth: *the metric system of measurement* ○ *Accurate measurement is very important in science.* **2** [C usu *pl*] the size, length or amount of sth, found by measuring: *take sb's chest/waist measurement* ○ *The measurements of the room are 20 feet by 15 feet.* ○ *This machine can give very precise measurements of pollution in the atmosphere.* ○ App 2.

■ **¹measuring-tape** *n* = TAPE-MEASURE.

measure² /'meʒə(r)/ *n* **1** an action taken to achieve a purpose: *safety measures* ○ *This is only a temporary measure.* ○ *The government is introducing new measures against/to prevent tax fraud.* **2(a)** [C] a unit used for stating the size, quantity or degree of sth: *The metre is a measure of length.* **(b)** [U, C] a system or scale of such units: *liquid/dry measure* ○ *Which measure of weight do pharmacists use?* ▷ App 2. **3** [C] a standard quantity of sth: *a measure of whisky* (ie the amount normally served in a glass, eg in a pub). **4** [C] an instrument such as a rod, tape or container marked with standard units, which is used for testing eg length or volume: *The barman uses a small silver measure for serving brandy.* See also TAPE MEASURE. **5** [sing] ~ **of sth** an indication of the extent of sth: *His resignation is a measure of how angry he is.* ○ *Words cannot always give the measure of one's feelings* (ie show how strong they are). **6** [U, sing] ~ **of sth** a certain amount of sth; some: *She achieved a/some measure of success with her first book.* **IDM** **beyond** ˈ**measure** (*fml*) very greatly: *His work has improved beyond measure.* **for good** ˈ**measure** as an extra amount of sth or as an additional item: *The pianist gave a long and varied recital, with a couple of encores for good measure.* **full/short** ˈ**measure** more or less than the correct or required amount: *I'm sure the shopkeeper gave me short measure when she weighed out the potatoes.* ○ *Lasting only 44 minutes, this CD is rather short measure.* **get/take/have the** ˈ**measure of sb** to assess/have assessed sb's character or abilities: *It took the champion a few games to get the measure of his opponent.* **have, etc one's/the full measure of sth** ▷ FULL. **in full measure** ▷ FULL. **in large, no small, some, equal, etc** ˈ**measure** (*fml*) to a great, small, some, an equal, etc extent or degree: *His failure is due in large measure to lack of confidence.* ○ *We are indebted in no small measure to our team of volunteers.* ○ *We are indebted in no small measure to our team of volunteers.* ○ *the universe can be explained entirely by mechanical processes.* ▷ **mechanically** /-klɪ/ *adv: a*

meat /miːt/ *n* **1** [U, C] the flesh of animals, esp of mammals (MAMMAL) or birds rather than fish, used as food: *a piece/slice of meat* ○ *meat-eating animals* ○ ˈ*horse meat* (ie from horses) ○ ˈ*dog meat* (ie for dogs) ○ *cooked/cold meats* ○ *a meat pie* ○ (*joc*) *a skinny boy without much meat on him.* See also RED MEAT, WHITE MEAT. **2** [U] the chief or important part of sth: *This chapter contains the meat of the writer's argument.* ▷ **meaty** *adj* (**-ier, -iest**) **1(a)** full of meat: *a meaty stew/sausage.* **(b)** like meat: *a meaty smell/taste/texture.* **2** (*approv*) having a strong, full or rich quality; SUBSTANTIAL(1): *meaty arms* ○ *a meaty book/discussion* ○ *The champion landed some meaty blows.*

meatball /ˈmiːtbɔːl/ *n* a small ball of minced (MINCE 1) meat.

Mecca /ˈmekə/ *n* **1** a city in Saudi Arabia which is the spiritual centre of Islam, being the place where Muhammad was born. **2** (also **mecca**) a place that very many people wish to visit, esp people with a shared interest: *This exhibition is a mecca for stamp collectors.*

mechanic /məˈkænɪk/ *n* a worker skilled in handling or repairing machines, eg vehicle engines: *a* ˈ*car mechanic.*

mechanical /məˈkænɪkl/ *adj* **1** of, connected with or operated by a machine or machines: *a mechanical device/toy/clock* ○ *I have little mechanical knowledge* (ie I know little about machines). ○ *The car has a few mechanical problems.* **2** (*often derog*) (of people or actions) acting or done without thought like a machine: *a mechanical movement/gesture/response* ○ *Her work had become repetitive and mechanical.* **3** relating to the physical laws of movement and cause and effect: *The universe can be explained entirely by mechanical processes.* ▷ **mechanically** /-klɪ/ *adv: a*

mechanically powered drill ○ *She recited their names mechanically, without any expression in her voice.*

mechanics /məˈkænɪks/ *n* **1** [sing *v*] **(a)** (*physics*) the science of motion and force. See also QUANTUM MECHANICS. **(b)** the practical study of machinery: *a course in car mechanics.* **2** **the mechanics** [pl] the way in which sth is done or operates: *The mechanics of staging a play are very complicated.*

mechanism /ˈmekənɪzəm/ *n* **1** a set of moving or working parts in a machine or other device: *a delicate watch mechanism* ○ *the firing mechanism of a rifle.* **2** a system of parts in a living thing which work together to perform a function: *the body's defence mechanisms against infection.* **3** a method or procedure for doing sth: *There are no mechanisms for transferring funds from one department to another.* ○ *the Exchange Rate Mechanism* (ie for controlling the values of European currencies in relation to each other).

mechanistic /ˌmekəˈnɪstɪk/ *adj* (*philosophy*) of the theory that all things in the universe are the result of physical and chemical processes: *a mechanistic explanation of the origin of life.*

mechanize, -ise /ˈmekənaɪz/ *v* (usu passive) to change eg a process or a factory so that it is run by machines instead of using people or animals: [Vn] *The country's agriculture is rapidly being/becoming mechanized.* ○ *highly mechanized factories/industrial processes* ○ *a mechanized army unit* (ie equipped with tanks rather than eg horses). ▷ **mechanization, -isation** /ˌmekənaɪˈzeɪʃn; *US* -nəˈz-/ *n* [U].

Med /med/ *n* **the Med** [sing] (*infml*) the Mediterranean Sea.

medal /ˈmedl/ *n* a flat piece of metal, usu shaped like a coin and stamped with words and a design, which is awarded to sb eg for brave actions in war, or for sporting achievement. Medals are also sometimes made to celebrate public events: *present/award medals for long service* ○ *win a silver medal in the long jump.*

▷ **medallist** (*US* **medalist**) /ˈmedəlɪst/ *n* (esp in compounds) a person who has been awarded a medal, esp for sporting achievement: *an Olympic gold/silver/bronze medallist.*

medallion /məˈdæliən/ *n* **(a)** a large MEDAL, or a piece of jewellery of similar design, that is worn around the neck and hangs down over the chest. **(b)** a thing similar in shape to this, eg an ornamental panel: *a carved stone medallion above the door.*

meddle /ˈmedl/ *v* (*derog*) **(a)** ~ **(in sth)** to interfere in sth that is not one's concern: [V] *You're always meddling.* [Vpr] *Don't meddle in my affairs.* **(b)** ~ **(with sth)** to handle sth that one ought not to, or about which one has no specialized knowledge: [Vpr] *Who's been meddling with my papers?* ○ *It's dangerous to meddle with the electrical wiring.* [also V].

▷ **meddler** *n* a person who meddles.
meddlesome /-səm/ *adj* (*fml*) fond of or in the habit of meddling.
meddling *n* [U]: *Industry should be free from political meddling.*

media /ˈmiːdiə/ *n* **the media** [sing or pl *v*] the main means of communicating with large numbers of people, esp television, radio and newspapers: *the mass media* ○ *a book that is often mentioned in the media* ○ *The media is/are to blame for starting the rumours.* ○ *a media personality* ○ *The event received excellent media coverage.* ▷ note at PLURAL. Compare MEDIUM.

mediaeval = MEDIEVAL.

median /ˈmiːdiən/ *adj* [attrib] (*mathematics*) **(a)** of or having a value in the middle of a series of such values; average: *the median value/age/price.* **(b)** situated in or passing through the middle: *a median point/line.*

▶ **median** n **1** (*mathematics*) the middle or average of a series of numbers or values. **2** (*US*) = CENTRAL RESERVATION.

mediate /'mi:dieɪt/ v **1(a)** ~ **(between sb and sb)** to try to get agreement between two or more people or groups who disagree with each other: [Vpr] *mediate in an industrial dispute* ○ *A UN mission has been sent to mediate between the warring factions.* [V] *play a mediating role.* **(b)** to achieve sth by doing this: [Vn] *mediate a peace settlement.* **2** (*fml*) to make it possible for eg an idea or a feeling to be perceived or communicated; to form a link for sth: [Vn] *institutions which mediate relations between the individual and the state* ○ *Thought is always mediated by language.*
▶ **mediation** /ˌmi:di'eɪʃn/ n [U]: *All offers of mediation were rejected.*
mediator n a person or an organization that mediates.

medic /'medɪk/ n (*infml*) a medical student or a doctor.

Medicaid /'medɪkeɪd/ n [U] a US government scheme providing medical care, esp for poor people.

medical /'medɪkl/ adj [esp attrib] **1** of the science of medicine; of curing disease: *medical treatment/knowledge/equipment* ○ *a medical examination* (ie to discover sb's state of health) ○ *the medical profession* ○ *a medical student/school* ○ *a medical certificate* (ie stating whether sb is in good health or not). **2** of the treatment of disease but not involving SURGERY(1): *The hospital has a medical ward and a surgical ward.*
▶ **medical** n (*infml*) a thorough physical and medical examination, eg before joining the army.
medically /-kli/ adv: *medically sound/unfit* ○ *medically qualified staff.*
■ **'medical officer** n (*Brit*) (*abbr* **MO**) (*US* **medical examiner**) a person, usu a doctor, employed in an organization to deal with medical and health matters.

medicament /mə'dɪkəmənt/ n (usu pl) (*fml*) a substance used in or on the body to cure illness.

Medicare /'medɪkeə(r)/ n [U] a US government scheme providing medical care, esp for old people.

medicated /'medɪkeɪtɪd/ adj containing a substance for preventing or curing infection: *medicated shampoo.*

medication /ˌmedɪ'keɪʃn/ n [U,C] (*esp US*) a drug or medicine for preventing or curing illness: *need/prescribe/administer medication.*

medicinal /mə'dɪsɪnl/ adj having healing properties; used for healing: *medicinal drugs/plants/herbs* ○ *'I only drink brandy for medicinal purposes,' he said jokingly.*

medicine /'medsn, -dɪsn/ n **1** [U] the science of preventing and curing illness and disease, eg by drugs, diet or SURGERY(1): *practise/study medicine* ○ *ethical problems in medicine* ○ *preventive/tropical/veterinary medicine.* **2** [C,U] a substance, esp a liquid, taken through the mouth, used in curing illness: *cough medicine(s)* ○ *Have you taken your medicine?* See also ALTERNATIVE MEDICINE. **IDM** **some, a little, a taste, etc of one's own 'medicine** the same bad treatment one has given to others: *Let the bully have a dose of his own medicine.* **take one's 'medicine** (*esp joc*) to submit to sth unpleasant, eg punishment, without complaining.
■ **'medicine man** n a man believed to have magical powers of healing, esp among Native Americans.

medico /'medɪkəʊ/ n (pl **-os**) (*infml*) a medical student or doctor.

medieval (also **mediaeval**) /ˌmedi'i:vl; *US also* ˌmi:d-/ adj of the Middle Ages (MIDDLE), about AD 1100–1400: *medieval history/literature/castles/Europe* ○ (*fig derog*) *Their living conditions were positively medieval* (ie very primitive).

mediocre /ˌmi:di'əʊkə(r)/ adj (*derog*) not very good; of fairly low quality: *His books are distinctly mediocre.* ○ *a mediocre actor/career/meal.*
▶ **mediocrity** /ˌmi:di'ɒkrəti/ n (*derog*) **1** [U] the quality of being mediocre: *His plays seldom rise above mediocrity.* **2** [C] a person who is mediocre in ability or personal qualities: *a government of mediocrities.*

meditate /'medɪteɪt/ v **1** ~ **(on/upon sth)** to think deeply, usu in silence, esp for religious purposes or in order to relax: [Vpr] *meditate on the sufferings of Christ* [V] *I like to meditate before an important exam.* **2** (*fml*) to plan sth in one's mind; to consider doing sth: [Vn] *meditate revenge.*
▶ **meditation** /ˌmedɪ'teɪʃn/ n **1** [U] the action or practice of meditating (MEDITATE 1): *seek peace through yoga and meditation* ○ *gaze in meditation at the holy image.* **2** [C usu pl] ~ **(on sth)** (*fml*) a written or spoken expression of serious thought: *her meditations on the causes of society's evils.*
meditative /'medɪtətɪv; *US* -teɪt-/ adj of meditation; absorbed in or involving deep thought: *a meditative mood* ○ *The tone of his later poems is more meditative.*

Mediterranean /ˌmedɪtə'reɪniən/ adj [attrib] of or similar to the Mediterranean Sea or the countries and regions which surround it: *Mediterranean countries/holiday resorts* ○ *a Mediterranean(-type) climate* (ie with hot summers and mild, fairly wet winters).

medium /'mi:diəm/ n (pl **media** /'mi:diə/ or, esp in sense 3, **mediums**) **1** [C] a means by which sth is expressed or communicated: *Commercial television is an effective medium for advertising.* ○ *Oil-paint is her favourite medium.* ○ *English is the medium of instruction* (ie All subjects are taught in English). Compare MEDIA. ⇨ note at PLURAL. **2** [C] a substance or the surroundings in which sth exists or moves or is transmitted: *bacteria growing in a sugar medium.* **3** [C] (pl **mediums**) a person who claims to be able to communicate with the spirits of dead people. **4** [sing] the middle quality, degree, etc between two extremes: *find **the happy medium*** (ie a reasonable balance) *between severity and indulgence.*
▶ **medium** adj [usu attrib] in the middle between two amounts, sizes or extremes; average: *a man of medium height/build* ○ *a medium-size(d) firm/hotel/car* ○ *a medium steak* (ie one cooked neither too lightly nor too much) ○ *In the **medium** term, profits will be reduced.*
■ **'medium wave** (*abbr* **MW**) n [U] (also **the medium wave** [sing]) a band of radio waves with a length of between 100 and 1 000 metres: *BBC World Service can be received on (the) medium wave.*

medley /'medli/ n **1** a team swimming race in which each team member uses a different stroke: *the 200 metres individual medley.* **2** a piece of music consisting of passages from other musical works: *an Irish medley.* **3** a mixture of people or things of different kinds: *a medley of flavourings.*

meek /mi:k/ adj (**-er, -est**) quiet, gentle and always ready to submit to others: *a domineering woman with a meek husband* ○ *She looks **meek and mild** but you should see her when she's angry.*
▶ **meek** n **the meek** [pl] meek people.
meekly adv: *He meekly did as he was told.*
meekness n [U].

meet¹ /mi:t/ v (pt, pp **met** /met/) **1(a)** (no passive) to come together in the same place; to CONFRONT(a) sb/sth: [V] *I hope we'll meet again soon.* [V,Vn] *We met (each other) quite by chance.* [Vn] *I met her in the street.* ○ *An amazing sight met their eyes as they entered the room.* **(b)** to come together formally for discussion: [Vadv, Vpr] *The committee meets regularly/on Fridays.* ○ *The Prime Minister met his Japanese opposite number for talks.* **(c)** to come together socially by arrangement: [V] *Let's meet* *after work and go for a drink.* **2** to go to a place and wait there for a particular person to arrive: [Vnpr] *Will you meet me at the station/off the train?* [Vn] *The hotel bus meets all incoming flights.* **3** (no passive) to see and know sb for the first time; to be introduced to sb: [Vn] *Where did you (first) meet your husband?* ○ *Meet Susan* (ie as an informal style of introduction). ○ *Pleased to meet you.* [V] *I don't think we've met (before).* **4** (no passive) to play, fight, etc together as opponents in a contest: [V, Vn] *City and United met/City met United in the final last year.* **5** to experience sth, often sth unpleasant; to ENCOUNTER sth: [Vn] *meet difficulties/disaster/one's death* ○ *Others have met similar problems.* ○ *We've met this verb form in a previous lesson.* **6** to come into contact with sth; to touch; to join: [V] *Their eyes met* (ie They looked at each other at the same time). [Vn] *His hand met hers.* [Vpr] *This belt doesn't meet round my waist any more!* **7** to do, fulfil or satisfy what is required: [Vn] *Can we meet all their requirements/conditions?* ○ *I can't possibly meet that deadline.* **8** to pay sth: [Vn] *The cost will be met by the company.* **IDM** **find/meet one's match** ⇨ MATCH¹. **make ends meet** ⇨ END¹. **meet sb's ˈeye(s)** (esp in negative sentences) to look directly at sb; to look into sb's eyes: *She was afraid to meet my eye(s).* **meet sb halfˈway** to make a compromise with sb: *If you agree to fix it all up I'll meet you halfway with the cost.* **meet one's ˈMaker** (esp joc) to die: *Poor Fred's gone to meet his Maker.* **meet one's Waterˈloo** to lose an important contest, to one's own severe disadvantage. **there is more in/to sb/sth than meets the ˈeye** sth/sth is more complex or interesting than one might at first think. **PHRV** ˌmeet ˈup (with sb) to meet sb, either by arrangement or by chance: *Let's meet up again later for a drink.* ○ *I met up with an old school friend in London.* ˈmeet with sb (esp US) to meet sb, esp for discussions: *The President met with senior White House aides.* ˈmeet with sth to be received or treated by sb in a particular way; to experience sth: *Her proposal met with much hostility/criticism.* ○ *I met with much kindness among these poor people.* ˈmeet sth with sth to react to sth in the specified way: *It's too easy to meet aggression with more aggression.*

meet² /miːt/ *n* (esp US) a sporting contest at which many competitors gather: *an athˈletics meet.* Compare MEETING 3.

meeting /ˈmiːtɪŋ/ *n* **1** an assembly of people for a particular purpose, esp for formal discussion: *have/conduct/attend a meeting* ○ *a comˈmittee/ˈstaff/ˈshareholders' meeting* ○ *What was decided at Friday's meeting?* ○ *MPs held public meetings during the election campaign.* **2** a coming together of two or more people, intentionally or by chance: *The meeting of father and son after so long was a joyful occasion.* **3** a gathering of people for a sporting contest: *a ˈrace meeting* (ie for horse-racing) ○ *an athˈletics meeting.* Compare MEET². **IDM** **a meeting of ˈminds** a close understanding between people, esp as soon as they meet for the first time.
■ ˈmeeting-house *n* a building for meetings, esp those held by Quakers.
ˈmeeting place *n* ~ (for sb) a place where people often meet: *The club is a popular meeting place for young people.*

mega /ˈmegə/ *adj* [sl] very large or great: *This song is going to be a mega hit!*

mega- /ˈmegə-/ *comb form* **1** a million; 1 000 000: *ˈmegabyte* ○ *ˈmegawatt.* **2** (esp infml) very large or great: *ˈmegastore* ○ *ˈmegastar.* ⇨ App 8.

megabyte /ˈmegəbaɪt/ *n* (abbr **MB**) a unit of computer memory equal to 1 048 576 (ie 2²⁰) bytes (BYTE): *a 40-megabyte hard disk.*

megahertz /ˈmegəhɜːts/ *n* (pl unchanged) (abbr **MHz**) one million HERTZ, a measure of radio frequency.

megalith /ˈmegəlɪθ/ *n* a large stone, esp one erected (ERECT) for ceremonial purposes in ancient times.
▶ **megalithic** /ˌmegəˈlɪθɪk/ *adj* consisting of megaliths: *a megalithic monument.*

megalomania /ˌmegələˈmeɪniə/ *n* [U] a condition in which a person has an exaggerated view of her or his own importance or power: *the President's growing megalomania.*
▶ **megalomaniac** /-niæk/ *n* a person suffering from megalomania. — *adj: megalomaniac ideas.*

megaphone /ˈmegəfəʊn/ *n* a device for speaking through that allows the voice to be heard at a distance. It is shaped like a tube that is wider at one end.

megastar /ˈmegəstɑː(r)/ *n* a very famous performer or entertainer.

megaton /ˈmegətʌn/ *n* an explosive force equal to one million tons of TNT: *10 megatons of high explosive.*

melamine /ˈmeləmiːn/ *n* [U] a type of plastic used esp as a covering for other materials: *a melamine tray/tabletop.*

melancholy /ˈmelənkəli, -kɒli/ *n* [U] (fml) deep sadness that lasts for a long time; depression.
▶ **melancholia** /ˌmelənˈkəʊliə/ *n* [U] a mental illness marked by melancholy and fear.
melancholic (also **melancholy**) /ˌmelənˈkɒlɪk/) *adj* **(a)** very sad; depressed: *a melancholy mood/person* ○ *have a melancholy nature.* **(b)** causing or expressing sadness: *melancholic songs.*

mélange /meɪˈlɑːnʒ/ *n* (French) a mixture or variety of different things: *a mélange of different cultures.*

melanin /ˈmelənɪn/ *n* [U] (techn) a dark substance in the skin and hair that causes the skin to change colour when exposed to the sun's light.

melanoma /ˌmeləˈnəʊmə/ *n* (medical) an abnormal dark spot or patch on the skin which may lead to CANCER(1): *a malignant melanoma.*

meld /meld/ *v* ~ **(sth) (into sth)** to become or make sth part of sth else; to combine; to mix: [Vpr] *dreams in which past and present meld into each other* [Vnp] *The festival melds together Christian and pagan traditions.* [also Vp, Vn].

mêlée (US **melee**) /ˈmeleɪ; US ˈmeɪleɪ-/ *n* a confused crowd of people; a confused struggle: *a mêlée of press photographers.*

mellifluous /meˈlɪfluəs/ *adj* (fml) (of music or sb's voice) sounding sweet and smooth: *speak in mellifluous tones.*

mellow /ˈmeləʊ/ *adj* (-er, -est) **1(a)** fully ripe, or smooth and pleasant in flavour or taste: *mellow fruit/wine.* **(b)** (of colour or sound) soft, rich and pleasant: *mellow autumn colours* ○ *the mellow tones of a viola* ○ *mellow stone villages.* **2** having become wise and sympathetic through age or experience. **3** (infml) relaxed and cheerful, esp as a result of being slightly drunk: *After two glasses of wine I was feeling mellow.*
▶ **mellow** *v* to become or make sth/sb mellow: [V] *Wine mellows with age.* [Vn] *Old age had now mellowed her.*

melodrama /ˈmelədrɑːmə/ *n* [U, C] **(a)** drama full of exciting events and exaggerated characters: *a gripping melodrama about mistaken identity.* **(b)** events, behaviour or language resembling drama of this kind: *all the melodrama of a major murder trial.*
▶ **melodramatic** /ˌmelədrəˈmætɪk/ *adj* (often derog) of, like or suitable for melodrama: *a melodramatic gesture/outburst/story/style of acting.*
melodramatically /-kli/ *adv.*

melody /ˈmelədi/ *n* **1** [C] a piece of music or a song with a clear or simple tune: *old Irish melodies.* **2** [C] **(a)** the main part or theme within a piece of music written for several instruments or voices. The melody is usu more clearly heard than the rest of the piece: *The melody is then taken up by the flutes.* (**b**) the musical part of a song, contrasted with the words: *Ivor Novello wrote the melody, and Noel Coward the words.* **3** [U] the arrangement of musical notes in a pleasant or ordered way.

▶ **melodic** /mə'lɒdɪk/ *adj* (**a**) [attrib] of a melody(2a): *The melodic line* (ie The main tune) *is hard to make out.* (**b**) = MELODIOUS.
melodious /mə'ləʊdiəs/ *adj* of or producing pleasant music: *melodious voices/flutes.* **melodiously** *adv.*

melon /'melən/ *n* [C,U] a large fruit of various types, with hard skin and sweet juicy flesh: *a slice of melon.* See also HONEYDEW MELON, WATER MELON. ⇨ picture at FRUIT.

melt /melt/ *v* **1** to become or make sth liquid through heating: [V] *The ice melted in the sun.* [Vn] *melted wax* ○ *The hot sun soon melted the ice.* ○ *fry mushrooms in melted butter.* **2** (of food) to become soft; to dissolve: [V] *a sweet that melts in the mouth.* ⇨ note at WATER¹. **3** to become or make sth, esp sb's feelings, gentler or softer: [Vn] *a smile that melted his heart* [V] *Her anger quickly melted* (ie disappeared). ○ *As soon as I saw her my heart melted.* **IDM** **butter would not melt in one's mouth** ⇨ BUTTER. **PHRV** **,melt (sth) a'way** to disappear or make sth disappear by melting or dissolving: *The sun has melted the snow away.* ○ (*fig*) *When the police arrived the crowd quickly melted away.* **,melt sth 'down** to melt a metal or wax object, esp so that the material can be used again: *Many of the gold ornaments were melted down to be made into coins.* **'melt into sth 1** to change gradually into sth: *One colour melted into another as the sun set.* **2** to disappear slowly into sth: *The ship melted into the darkness.*

▶ **melting** *adj* [usu attrib] causing feelings of love, affection or pity; tender: *a melting voice* ○ *his melting charm.*
■ **'melting-point** *n* [U, C] the temperature at which a solid melts: *Lead has a lower melting-point than iron.*
'melting-pot *n* (usu *sing*) a place where large numbers of people, ideas, etc are mixed together: *the vast melting-pot of American society.* **IDM** **go into/be in the 'melting-pot** to be likely to change; to be in the process of changing: *The fate of the islands is now in the melting-pot.*

meltdown /'meltdaʊn/ [U, C] *n* the accidental melting of the central part of a nuclear REACTOR, causing the release of harmful RADIATION(2): (*fig*) *a stock-market meltdown* (ie crash).

member /'membə(r)/ *n* **1** a person, or sometimes a country or an organization, belonging to a group, club or team: *Every member of her family came to the wedding.* ○ *a responsible member of society* ○ *an active/an honorary/a founding member of the society* ○ *a committee/party/band member* ○ *the members/member-states of the EU.* **2** (*fml*) (**a**) a part of the body, esp a limb: *lose a vital member.* (**b**) (*euph*) the male sexual organ; the PENIS. **3** Member (**a**) (in Britain) a Member of Parliament: *the Member for Leeds North-East.* (**b**) (in the USA) a member of the House of Representatives.

▶ **membership** *n* **1** [U] the state of being a member of a group: *apply for membership of the association* ○ *a membership card* (ie one issued to a member). **2** [CGp] the members of a club or an association: *trade unions with large membership(s)* ○ *The membership number(s) 800.*
■ **,Member of 'Parliament** *n* (*pl* **Members of Parliament**) (*abbr* **MP**) (in Britain) an elected representative in the House of Commons.
,Member of 'Congress *n* (*pl* **Members of Con-**

gress) (*abbr* **MC**) an elected member of the US Congress, esp of the House of Representatives.

membrane /'membreɪn/ *n* [C, U] **1** a piece of thin tissue that connects, covers or lines parts inside a plant or the body of an animal: *a mucous membrane* (eg inside the nose). **2** a thin layer of material, eg to protect sth against damp: *install a waterproof membrane below the concrete floor.*

memento /mə'mentəʊ/ *n* (*pl* **-oes** or **-os**) a thing that is given to or bought by sb to remind them of a person, a place or an event: *a little gift as a memento of my visit.*

memo /'meməʊ/ *n* (*pl* **-os**) (*infml*) a MEMORANDUM(1): *write/send a memo* ○ *a memo pad.*

memoir /'memwɑː(r)/ *n* **1** memoirs [pl] an account written usu by sb in public life of their own life and experiences: *politicians writing their memoirs.* **2** [C] a written record of sb's life, important events, etc, usu based on personal knowledge: *a memoir of Jane Austen.*

memorabilia /ˌmemərə'bɪliə/ *n* [pl] items that are collected or displayed, eg because they once belonged to a famous person or because they remind people of a past event: *His Beatles/theatre memorabilia fill an entire room.*

memorable /'memərəbl/ *adj* worth remembering or easily remembered, because of being very good or unusual in some way: *a memorable occasion/concert/trip.* ▶ **memorably** /-əbli/ *adv.*

memorandum /ˌmemə'rændəm/ *n* (*pl* **memoranda** /-də/) **1** ~ (**to sb**) a written note or communication, esp in business between people working for the same organization. **2** (*law*) a record of an agreement that has been reached but not yet formally prepared and signed.

memorial /mə'mɔːriəl/ *n* ~ (**to sb/sth**) an object, an institution or a custom established to remind people of a past event or a person who has died: *erect a war memorial* (ie in memory of soldiers who died in war) ○ *a memorial statue to a great statesman* ○ *hold a memorial service for victims of the disaster* ○ *winner of the Kathleen Ferrier Memorial Prize.*
■ **Me'morial Day** *n* (in the USA) a holiday, usu at the end of May, for remembering troops who died in war.

memorize, -ise /'meməraɪz/ *v* to learn sth well enough to remember it exactly: [Vn] *memorize passages from Shakespeare.*

memory /'meməri/ *n* **1(a)** [C, U] ~ (**for sth**) an individual person's power to remember things: *He has a good/poor memory for dates* (ie remembers them easily/with difficulty). ○ *lose one's memory in an accident* ○ *recite their names from memory* (ie without reading them or referring to notes) ○ *commit sth to memory* (ie learn and remember it) ○ *His name slipped my memory* (ie I forgot it). (**b**) [U] the power of the mind by which things can be remembered: *the parts of the brain responsible for memory.* **2** [C] a thought of sth that one has seen, done or experienced previously: *happy memories of childhood* ○ *I have no memory of such a request.* **3** [U] the period over which people can remember events, etc: *This hasn't happened before in recent memory.* **4** [U] what is remembered about sb after their death: *His memory will always remain with us* (ie We will always remember him). **5** [C, U] (*computing*) the part of a computer where information is stored. See also RANDOM ACCESS MEMORY. **IDM** **have a memory/mind like a sieve** ⇨ SIEVE. **if memory serves (me)** (*fml*) if I remember correctly: *She married a civil servant, if memory serves me right/correctly.* **in memory of sb/to the memory of sb** intended to remind people of sb or to honour sb who has died: *He founded the charity in memory of his late wife.* **jog sb's memory** ⇨ JOG. **refresh one's/sb's memory** ⇨ REFRESH. **within/in living memory** ⇨ LIVING¹.

■ ˌmemory ˈlane *n* [U] sentimental thoughts about one's past life and experiences: *take a trip down memory lane.*

men *pl* of MAN¹.

■ ˈmen's room *n* (*US*) a public toilet for men: *go to the men's room.* ⇨ note at TOILET.

menace /ˈmenəs/ *n* **1** [C usu *sing*] **(a)** ~ **(to sb/sth)** a thing or person that threatens to harm sb/sth: *Plastic bags are a menace to the environment.* **(b)** (*infml or joc*) a person or thing that causes trouble or danger: *That child is a menace! Take her away!* **2** [U] a threatening quality, tone or feeling: *in a speech filled with menace* ○ *a film that creates an atmosphere of menace.* **3** **menaces** [pl] (*esp law*) threatening words or actions: *demand money* **with menaces.**

▶ **menace** *v* to threaten sb/sth; to put sb/sth in danger: [Vn] *countries menaced by war.* **menacing** *adj*: *a menacing growl* ○ *Their gestures grew more menacing.* **menacingly** *adv*: *move menacingly towards sb.*

ménage /meɪˈnɑːʒ/ *n* (usu *sing*) (*fml*) the members of a household.

■ **ménage à trois** /ˌmeɪnɑːʒ ɑː ˈtrwɑ/ *n* (*pl* **ménages à trois** /ˌmeɪnɑːʒ/) (usu *sing*) (*French*) a household consisting of three people, esp a husband, wife and lover.

menagerie /məˈnædʒəri/ *n* a collection of animals kept as pets, part of a travelling show, etc.

mend /mend/ *v* **1** **(a)** (*esp Brit*) to spend time working on sth that is broken, damaged or torn so that it can be used, worn, etc again; to repair: [Vn] *mend shoes/a watch/a broken toy/a puncture* ○ *mend a hole in a sock.* **(b)** to make sth better; to improve sth: [Vn] *They tried to mend their broken marriage.* **2** to return to health; to heal: [V] *She's beginning to mend after her illness.* ○ *The broken bone is mending slowly.* **IDM** **least said soonest mended** ⇨ SAY. **mend (one's) fences (with sb)** to improve relations with sb after a disagreement or quarrel: *Both sides must mend fences to avert a crisis.* **mend one's ˈways** to improve one's habits, or way of life: *He's been to prison but there's no sign of him mending his ways.*

▶ **mend** *n* **IDM** **on the ˈmend** (*infml*) getting better after an illness or injury: *She's been very unwell, but she's on the mend now.*

mender *n* (usu in compounds) (*Brit*) a person who mends sth: *a ˈroad-mender* ○ *a ˈwatch-mender.*

mending *n* [U] the work of repairing sth, esp clothes: *do the mending.*

mendacious /menˈdeɪʃəs/ *adj* (*fml*) not telling the truth; lying: *a mendacious story/report.* ▶ **mendacity** /menˈdæsəti/ *n* [U]: *politicians accused of hypocrisy and mendacity.*

mendicant /ˈmendɪkənt/ *n, adj* (*fml*) (a person) living by begging: *mendicant friars.*

menfolk /ˈmenfəʊk/ *n* [pl] (*fml or joc*) men, esp the men of a family or community considered together: *The menfolk have all gone out fishing.* Compare WOMENFOLK.

menial /ˈmiːniəl/ *adj* (usu *derog*) (of work) not requiring much skill and often boring: *a menial task/job* ○ *menial chores like sweeping the floor.*

▶ **menial** *n* (*fml usu derog*) a person having a menial job; a servant.

meningitis /ˌmenɪnˈdʒaɪtɪs/ *n* [U] a serious disease in which the tissues enclosing the brain and spinal cord (SPINAL) become infected and swollen.

menopause /ˈmenəpɔːz/ *n* [U, C usu *sing*] (often **the menopause**) the time when a woman stops having periods (PERIOD 4), usu around the age of 50: *reach the menopause.*

▶ **menopausal** /ˌmenəˈpɔːzl/ *adj* **(a)** (of a woman) experiencing the menopause. **(b)** of the menopause: *menopausal symptoms/depression.*

menses /ˈmensiːz/ *n* (often **the menses** [pl]) (*fml or medical*) the flow of blood each month from a woman's UTERUS.

menstruate /ˈmenstrueɪt/ *v* (*fml or medical*) [V] (of a woman) to discharge blood from the UTERUS, usu once a month; to have a period(4).

▶ **menstrual** /ˈmenstruəl/ *adj* of or caused by the process of menstruating: *menstrual problems/blood* ○ *the menstrual cycle* (ie the processes that occur between the times a woman menstruates).

menstruation /ˌmenstruˈeɪʃn/ *n* [U] the process or time of menstruating.

menswear /ˈmenzweə(r)/ *n* [U] (esp in shops) clothes for men: *the menswear department of a large store.*

-ment *suff* (with *vs* forming *ns*) the action or result of: *bombardment* ○ *development* ○ *achievement.* ▶ **-mental** (forming *adjs*): *governmental* ○ *judgemental.*

mental /ˈmentl/ *adj* **1** [usu attrib] of, in or for the mind: *an enormous mental effort* ○ *a mental process/calculation/image* ○ *The experience caused him much mental suffering.* ○ **make a mental note of sth** (ie fix sth in one's mind to be remembered later). **2** [usu attrib] relating to illnesses of the mind and their treatment: *mental handicap/illness/problems/health* ○ *a mental hospital/nurse/patient.* **3** [pred] (*infml derog*) mad: *You must be mental to drive so fast!*

▶ **mentally** /ˈmentəli/ *adv* in the mind; with regard to the mind: *mentally alert/ill/retarded* ○ *I was mentally composing the letter I would write later.*

■ ˌmental ˈage *n* [C usu *sing*] the level of sb's intellectual ability, expressed in terms of the average ability for a certain age: *She is sixteen but has a ˌmental age of ˈfive.*

ˌmental aˈrithmetic *n* [U] sums done in the mind, without writing figures on paper or using eg a CALCULATOR.

mentality /menˈtæləti/ *n* [C usu *sing*] the characteristic attitude of mind or way of thinking of a person or group: *an island/siege mentality* ○ *It is very difficult to change people's mentality.*

menthol /ˈmenθɒl/ *n* [U] a solid white substance obtained from oil of PEPPERMINT(a), used to relieve pain or to give a strong cool flavour: *menthol cigarettes/toothpaste.*

mention /ˈmenʃn/ *v* ~ **sth/sb (as sth)**; ~ **sth/sb (to sb)** to write or speak about sth/sb briefly; to say the name of sth/sb: [Vn, Vnpr] *Did she mention it (to the police)?* [Vn] *Did I hear my name mentioned?* (ie Was somebody talking about me?) ○ *I'd like to thank George, Sally and others* **too numerous to mention.** [V.wh] *Did she mention when she would arrive?* [Vn-n] *He's been mentioned as a possible future prime minister.* [V.that] *It is* **worth mentioning that** *banks often close early before a holiday.* [also V, Vpr.that, V.ing]. See also ABOVE-MENTIONED. **IDM** **don't ˈmention it** (used to indicate that thanks or an apology are not necessary): *'You are so kind!' 'Don't mention it.'* **not to mention** (*infml*) (used to emphasize what follows) as well as: *He has a big house and an expensive car, not to mention a villa in France.*

▶ **mention** *n* [U, C usu *sing*] a reference to sb/sth in speech or writing: *He* **made no mention of** *her contribution.* ○ *Did the concert get a mention in the paper?* ○ *Richard* **deserves (a) special mention** *for all the help he gave us.*

mentor /ˈmentɔː(r)/ *n* a trusted adviser of sb with little experience in a particular field: *a friend and mentor to many young actors.*

menu /ˈmenjuː/ *n* **1** a list of dishes available at a restaurant or to be served at a meal: *ask for/look at the menu* ○ *What's* **on the menu** *tonight?* **2** (*computing*) a list of possible actions from which a user can choose, displayed on a computer screen.

M

────────────────────────────

[V.speech] = verb + direct speech   [V.*that*] = verb + *that* clause   [V.*wh*] = verb + *who, how,* etc clause

MEP /ˌem iː ˈpiː/ *abbr* Member of the European Parliament: *the MEP for Manchester West.*

mercantile /ˈmɜːkəntaɪl; *US also* -tiːl, -tɪl/ *adj* of trade and commerce; of merchants: *mercantile law/interests.*

mercenary /ˈmɜːsənəri; *US* -neri/ *adj* (*derog*) mainly concerned with making money or gaining some personal advantage: *Society is accused of being too mercenary.* ○ *His actions are entirely mercenary.*
▶ **mercenary** *n* a soldier hired to fight in a foreign army.

merchandise /ˈmɜːtʃəndaɪz/ *n* [U] goods bought and sold; goods for sale: *Over 200 stalls offer a wide choice of merchandise.*
▶ **merchandise** *v*.

merchandising *n* [U] (**a**) the activity of selling or promoting goods. (**b**) products associated with eg a film, a television programme or a pop star: *millions of pounds' worth of Batman merchandising.*

merchant /ˈmɜːtʃənt/ *n* **1(a)** (esp formerly) a person involved in trade or commerce: *Venice was a city of rich merchants.* (**b**) (*commerce*) a person who trades in WHOLESALE goods, often one who trades with foreign countries: *an ˌimport-ˈexport merchant* ○ *a builder's merchant* (ie one who sell supplies to the building trade). (**c**) (in compounds) a person who sells the goods specified: *a ˈcoal-merchant* ○ *a ˈwine-merchant.* ⇨ note at DEALER. **2** (*infml derog*) a person who is fond of the specified activity: *a ˈspeed merchant* (ie sb who likes to drive fast) ○ *get-rich-quick merchants.*
▶ **merchant** *adj* [attrib] relating to the transport of goods by sea: *merchant ships/shipping/seamen.*

merchantable /-əbl/ *adj* (*law*) in a fit state to be sold: *goods of merchantable quality.*

■ ˌmerchant ˈbank *n* (*Brit*) a bank that specializes in large commercial loans and financial support for industry. ˌmerchant ˈbanker *n*. ˌmerchant ˈbanking *n* [U].

ˌmerchant ˈnavy (also ˌmerchant maˈrine) *n* [CGp] a country's commercial ships and the people who work on them.

merciful ⇨ MERCY.

mercurial /mɜːˈkjʊəriəl/ *adj* **1** (of people or their moods) lively, quick to react and often changing: *a mercurial temperament/sense of humour.* **2** (*fml or medical*) of or containing MERCURY: *a mercurial ointment.*

Mercury /ˈmɜːkjəri/ *n* (*astronomy*) the planet nearest to the sun.

mercury /ˈmɜːkjəri/ (also *arch* **quicksilver**) *n* [U] (*symb* **Hg**) a chemical element. Mercury is a metal, silver in colour, often found in liquid form and used in thermometers (THERMOMETER): *mercury poisoning.* ⇨ App 7.

mercy /ˈmɜːsi/ *n* **1** [U] a kind or forgiving attitude shown towards sb one has the right or power to punish: *They showed no mercy to their captives.* ○ *God have mercy on his soul* (ie in a prayer). ○ *The prisoner begged for mercy.* ○ *a mercy dash/flight* (ie a quick journey to save sb's life). **2** [C usu *sing*] (*infml*) an event to be grateful for, eg because it stops sth unpleasant; a piece of good luck: *It's a mercy she wasn't hurt in the accident.* ○ *His death was a mercy* (eg because he was in great pain). **IDM at the mercy of sb/sth** in the power of sb/sth; under the control of sb/sth: *put oneself/be at the mercy of a mortgage lender.* **grateful/thankful for small mercies** ⇨ SMALL. **leave sb/sth to the mercy/mercies of sb/sth** to abandon sb/sth in a situation where they are likely to suffer, be treated badly, etc: *privatized companies left to the mercy of market forces.* **throw oneself on sb's mercy** (*fml*) to beg sb to treat one with mercy or in a kind or restrained way: *His lawyers advised him to throw himself on the mercy of the court and hope for a lenient sentence.*

▶ **merciful** /-fl/ *adj* ~ (**to/towards sb**) having, showing or feeling mercy: *She was merciful to the prisoners.* ○ *Death came as a merciful release.* **mercifully** /-fəli/ *adv* **1** (*infml*) (qualifying a whole sentence) to one's great relief; fortunately (FORTUNATE): *The play was very bad, but mercifully it was also short!* **2** in a merciful way: *treat sb mercifully.*

merciless *adj* ~ (**to/towards sb/sth**) showing no mercy or pity: *a merciless killer/beating* ○ *the merciless heat of the sun* ○ *The critics were merciless towards his last play.* **mercilessly** *adv*.

■ ˈmercy killing *n* [U, C] the action or an instance of killing sb out of pity, eg because they are in severe pain.

mere¹ /mɪə(r)/ *adj* (**merest**) [attrib] (no comparative form) nothing more than; no better or more important than: *The interview lasted a mere five minutes.* ○ *a mere 2% of the budget* ○ *He is no mere adviser, but the President's right-hand man.* ○ *The merest* (ie The slightest) *noise is enough to wake him.* ○ *His mere presence made her feel afraid.*
▶ **merely** *adv* only; simply: *I merely asked his name.* ○ *I meant it merely as a joke.*

mere² /mɪə(r)/ *n* (*esp Brit*) (esp in place-names) a small lake.

meretricious /ˌmerəˈtrɪʃəs/ *adj* (*fml*) apparently attractive but in fact having no value: *a meretricious style/charm.*

merge /mɜːdʒ/ *v* **1** ~ (**with/into sth**); ~ (**together**); ~ **A with B** / ~ **A and B** (**together**) (*esp commerce*) to combine or make two or more things come together and combine: [V, Vp, Vpr] *This is where the two rivers merge (together) (into one).* [Vpr] *The bank merged with its major rival.* [Vn, Vnpr] *We can merge the two businesses into a larger, more profitable one.* **2** ~ (**into sth**) to fade or change gradually into sth else: [Vpr] *Twilight merged into total darkness.* ○ *thoughts merging into dreams.*
▶ **merger** /ˈmɜːdʒə(r)/ *n* [C, U] the combining of two or more commercial companies, etc into one: *a merger between two breweries/with a rival company* ○ *The two companies/parties are considering the possibility of a merger.*

meridian /məˈrɪdiən/ *n* any imaginary circle round the earth that passes through both the North and South Poles: *the Greenwich meridian* (ie 0° LONGITUDE, which passes through the North and South Poles and Greenwich, England).

meringue /məˈræŋ/ *n* (**a**) [U] a mixture of the whites of eggs and sugar baked until crisp and used eg as a covering over sweet pies: *lemon meringue pie.* (**b**) [C] a small cake made of this.

merino /məˈriːnəʊ/ *n* (*pl* **-os**) a breed of sheep with long fine wool used in making clothes.

merit /ˈmerɪt/ *n* **1** [U] the quality of being good or worthy of, or deserving praise or reward: *a painter/painting of real merit* ○ *The plan is entirely without merit.* ○ *The team will be picked solely on merit.* ○ *She finished the season high in the order of merit.* ○ *She was awarded a certificate of merit for her piano-playing.* **2** [C often *pl*] a fact, an action or a quality that is good, or that deserves praise or reward: *The merits of the scheme are quite obvious.* ○ *This meal has the merit of simplicity/of being easy to cook.* ○ *judge each case on its (own) merits* (ie considering its particular nature or features, regardless of general circumstances or one's personal feelings).
▶ **merit** *v* (*fml*) to be worthy of sth; to deserve sth: [Vn] *merit praise/punishment/reward* ○ *Her suggestion merits consideration.*

meritocracy /ˌmerɪˈtɒkrəsi/ *n* (**a**) [C, U] a country or social system in which people of high ability or intelligence get the greatest rewards, esp political power. (**b**) [CGp] such people in a society. ▶ **meritocratic** /ˌmerɪtəˈkrætɪk/ *adj*.

M

meritorious /ˌmerɪ'tɔːrɪəs/ *adj* (*fml*) deserving praise or reward: *a prize for meritorious conduct*.

merlin /'mɜːlɪn/ *n* a small European or N American FALCON.

mermaid /'mɜːmeɪd/ *n* an imaginary creature having the body of a woman but a fish's tail instead of legs.

merry /'meri/ *adj* (**-ier, -iest**) **1** happy, cheerful and lively; full of joy: *a merry laugh/mood/throng* ○ *wish sb a merry Christmas*. **2** (*infml*) slightly drunk: *We were already merry after two glasses of wine*. **IDM** **make 'merry** (*dated*) (esp of a group of people) to enjoy oneself with singing, laughing, drinking, etc. **the ˌmore the 'merrier** the more people or things there are, the better the situation will be: *'Can I bring a friend to your party?' 'Certainly — the more the merrier!'*

▶ **merrily** /'merəli/ *adv* **1** in a happy cheerful way: *laugh/beam merrily* ○ *A fire burned merrily in the grate*. **2** without thought for the future or the consequences: *She carried on merrily, oblivious of the offence she was causing*.

merriment /'merɪmənt/ *n* [U] (*fml*) happy talk and laughter.

■ **'merry-go-round** *n* **1** (*US* also **carousel**) = ROUNDABOUT² 2. **2** a round of busy activities: *the diplomatic merry-go-round which precedes a summit conference*.

merrymaking /'merimeɪkɪŋ/ *n* [U] the process of enjoying oneself with others by singing, laughing, drinking, etc.

mesa /'meɪsə/ *n* (*pl* **mesas**) (*US*) a hill with a flat top and steep sides, common in parts of the USA.

mescaline (also **mescalin**) /'meskəlɪn/ *n* [U] a drug obtained from a type of CACTUS. Taking it makes one apparently see and experience things that are not real.

mesh /meʃ/ *n* **1(a)** [U] material made of a network of wire or thread: *a piece of wire mesh on the front of the chicken coop*. **(b)** [C usu *pl*] any of the spaces in such material: *a fish tangled in the meshes of the net*. **2** [C esp *sing*] a complex network, patterns or system: *entangled in a mesh of political intrigue* ○ *a mesh of different musical styles*.

▶ **mesh** *v* **1** ~ (**sth**) (**with sth / together**) to be in harmony or bring sth into harmony with sth else: [Vpr] *courses that will mesh with the needs of local industry* [Vnp] *The various strands of the plot are neatly meshed together*. [also V, Vadv]. **2** (of connecting parts of machines) to lock together with others; to engage: [V] *The cogs don't quite mesh*. [also Vpr, Vp]. **meshed** *adj* fitted with mesh or having meshes: *wire meshed cages*.

mesmeric /mez'merɪk/ *adj* causing people to become completely absorbed and unaware of anything happening around them: *a mesmeric rhythm*.

mesmerize, -ise /'mezməraɪz/ *v* (esp passive) to hold sb's attention completely: [Vn] *an audience mesmerized by her voice* ○ *a mesmerizing performance*.

mess¹ /mes/ *n* **1** [C usu *sing*] a dirty or untidy state: *This kitchen's a mess!* ○ *The children have* **made an awful mess** *in the bathroom*. **2** [U,C] (*infml euph*) the EXCREMENT of eg a dog or a cat: *clear up the dog mess*. **3** [C usu *sing*] a difficult or confused state or situation; a state of disorder: *My life's (in) a real mess!* ○ *She's made a terrible mess of the job* (ie done it very badly). ○ *sort out the mess* ○ (*ironic*) *A nice/fine mess you've got us into*. **4** [sing] a person/people who is/are dirty or whose clothes and hair are not tidy: *You look a mess!* ○ *You two are a mess! Get cleaned up*.

▶ **mess** *v* (*infml esp US*) to make sth untidy: [Vn] *Don't mess your hair!* **PHR V** **mess a'bout/a'round** **1** to behave in a silly annoying way, eg instead of doing sth useful: *Stop messing about and come and*

help! ○ *Don't mess about with matches!* **2** to spend time doing sth in a pleasantly casual way, without being serious or organized: *I love just messing about in the garden/in boats*. **ˌmess sb a'bout/a'round** (*Brit*) to treat sb in an unfair way, eg by not being honest with them: *Stop messing me about! Just tell me if I've got the job or not!* **ˌmess sth a'bout/a'round; ˌmess a'bout/a'round with sth** to handle sth in the wrong way, without really knowing what to do: *Don't mess the files around, I've just put them in order*. ○ *Somebody's been messing about with the radio and now it doesn't work*. **ˌmess sth 'up 1** to make sth dirty or untidy: *Who messed up my clean kitchen?* ○ *The wind has messed my hair up*. **2** to handle sth in the wrong way, so that it fails or works badly: *The government has messed up the economy*. **'mess with sb/sth** (*infml*) to interfere with sb/sth that one does not know how to handle: *Don't mess with her — she's got a violent temper*. ○ *Who's been messing with the computer?*

messy *adj* (**-ier, -iest**) **1** dirty; untidy: *a messy kitchen* ○ *He's a messy eater*. **2** making a place or people dirty: *a messy job*. **3** unpleasant and difficult or confused: *a messy situation/divorce*. **messily** *adv*: *books piled up messily in the corner* ○ *The affair ended rather messily*. **messiness** *n* [U].

mess² /mes/ *n* **(a)** (*US* also **'mess hall**) a building or room in which members of the armed forces have their meals: *the officers' mess*. **(b)** [CGp] a group of people who take their meals together in this.

message /'mesɪdʒ/ *n* ~ (**from sb**) (**to sb**) **1** a written or spoken request, piece of information, etc that is passed from one person to another indirectly: *We've had a message (to say) that your father is ill*. ○ *Jenny's not here at the moment. Can I take a message?* ○ *The ship sent a radio message asking for help*. **2** an idea or a statement from eg a writer or a religious group, which is thought to be of political, moral or social importance: *a play with a message* ○ *the prophet's message to the world* ○ *The party is not getting its message across* (ie is failing to gain public support). **IDM** **get the 'message** (*infml*) to understand an indirect remark or suggestion that sb is making: *She said it was getting late; I got the message, and left*.

messenger /'mesɪndʒə(r)/ *n* a person carrying a message, esp as a job: *send a messenger/send sth by messenger* ○ *motor-cycle messengers*.

Messiah /mə'saɪə/ *n* **1** (also **messiah**) [C] a person expected to come and save the world: *He's seen by some as the new political messiah*. **2** the Messiah [sing] (*religion*) **(a)** (for Christians) Jesus Christ. **(b)** (for Jews) a king to be sent by God. ▶ **messianic** /ˌmesi'ænɪk/ *adj*: *a messianic prophecy* ○ *a political leader speaking with messianic fervour*.

Messrs /'mesəz/ *abbr* (used as the plural of *Mr* (French *Messieurs*) before a list of names, eg *Messrs Smith, Brown and Robinson*, and before names of business firms, eg *Messrs T Brown and Co*).

messy ⇨ MESS¹.

Met /met/ *abbr* (*infml*) **1** meteorological: *the 'Met Office* ○ *the latest Met report* (ie weather forecast). **2** **the Met** the Metropolitan Opera House in New York. **3 the Met** the Metropolitan Police in London.

met *pt, pp* of MEET¹.

meta- *comb form* **1** higher; beyond: *metalanguage* ○ *metaphysics*. **2** of change: *metabolism* ○ *metamorphosis*.

metabolism /mə'tæbəlɪzəm/ *n* [U,sing] (*biology*) the chemical processes in plants or animals that change food, minerals, etc into living matter and produce energy: *An athlete has a faster metabolism than an ordinary person*.

▶ **metabolic** /ˌmetə'bɒlɪk/ *adj* [usu attrib]: *a metabolic process/disorder* ○ *have a high/low metabolic rate*.

M

metabolize, -ise /məˈtæbəlaɪz/ v (biology) to use food, minerals, etc to create new cells or energy by means of chemical processes: [Vn] We metabolize alcohol at different rates.

metal /ˈmetl/ n [C, U] a type of solid mineral substance, eg tin, iron, gold, copper, etc, which is usu hard and shiny and can usu conduct heat and electricity: a piece/lump/strip of metal ○ recycle **scrap metal** ○ a metal pipe/gate/bar ○ a metal box/chair/ sculpture. See also ALLOY¹, HEAVY METAL.

▶ **metalled** /ˈmetld/ adj (of a road) made or repaired with broken stone: a metalled road/track/ runway.

metallic /məˈtælɪk/ adj (esp attrib) of or like metal: a round metallic object ○ metallic paint (ie making sth look like metal) ○ metallic sounds/clicks (eg sounding as though metal objects are being struck together).

■ ˈmetal detector n an electronic device used for finding buried metal, eg by people searching for valuable old coins, etc.

ˈmetal fatigue n [U] weakness in metals caused by bending and stress: The aircraft wings were showing signs of metal fatigue.

metalanguage /ˈmetəlæŋgwɪdʒ/ n [C, U] (techn) the words used in talking about or describing language or a language.

metallurgy /məˈtælədʒi; US ˈmetəlɜːrdʒi/ n [U] the science of the properties of metals, their uses, methods of obtaining them, etc.

▶ **metallurgical** /ˌmetəˈlɜːdʒɪkl/ adj.

metallurgist /məˈtælədʒɪst; US ˈmetəlɜːrdʒɪst/ n an expert in metallurgy.

metalwork /ˈmetəlwɜːk/ n [U] artistic or skilled work done using metal.

metamorphose /ˌmetəˈmɔːfəʊz/ v ~ (sb/sth) (into/ to sth) (fml) to change or make sb/sth change in form or nature, esp by natural growth or development: [Vnpr] tadpoles metamorphosed into frogs [Vpr] A larva metamorphoses into a chrysalis and then into a butterfly. [also V, Vn].

▶ **metamorphosis** /ˌmetəˈmɔːfəsɪs/ n (pl metamorphoses /-əsiːz/) (fml) a change of form or nature: the metamorphosis of a larva into a butterfly ○ She had undergone an amazing metamorphosis from awkward schoolgirl to beautiful woman.

metaphor /ˈmetəfə(r)/ n [U] (a) the imaginative use of a word or phrase to describe sb/sth as another object in order to show that they have the same qualities and to make the description more forceful, eg 'She has a heart of stone': striking originality in her use of metaphor. (b) an example of this: a game of football used as a metaphor for the competitive struggle of life. Compare SIMILE.

▶ **metaphorical** /ˌmetəˈfɒrɪkl; US -ˈfɔːr-/ adj of or like a metaphor; containing metaphors: a metaphorical expression/phrase ○ use metaphorical language. Compare FIGURATIVE, LITERAL 1b.

metaphorically /-kli/ adv: I'll leave you in Robin's capable hands — **metaphorically speaking**, of course!

metaphysics /ˌmetəˈfɪzɪks/ n [sing v] the branch of philosophy dealing with the nature of existence, truth and knowledge. ▶ **metaphysical** /ˌmetəˈfɪzɪkl/ adj: metaphysical speculations/ theories.

mete /miːt/ v **PHRV** mete sth out (to sb) (fml) to cause a person, country, etc to suffer a punishment, a defeat or bad treatment: severe penalties meted out by the courts.

meteor /ˈmiːtiə(r), -iɔː(r)/ n a small piece of matter that enters the earth's atmosphere from outer space, making a bright line across the night sky as it is burnt up: a meteor shower. See also SHOOTING STAR.

▶ **meteoric** /ˌmiːtiˈɒrɪk; US -ˈɔːr-/ adj 1 (of a ca-

reer, etc) rapidly successful: a **meteoric rise** to fame. 2 of meteors.

meteorite /ˈmiːtiəraɪt/ n a piece of rock or metal from outer space that hits the earth's surface: a meteorite impact.

meteorology /ˌmiːtiəˈrɒlədʒi/ n [U] the scientific study of the earth's atmosphere and its changes, used esp for forecasting weather.

▶ **meteorological** /ˌmiːtiərəˈlɒdʒɪkl/ adj of meteorology: abnormal meteorological conditions ○ weather forecasts from the Meteorological Office.

meteorologist /ˌmiːtiəˈrɒlədʒɪst/ n an expert in meteorology.

meter¹ /ˈmiːtə(r)/ n (esp in compounds) a device that measures the amount of electricity, gas, water, etc used or records time and distance: read the ˌelecˈtricity meter ○ put 50p in the ˈgas meter ○ fares mounting up on the meter (ie of a taxi) ○ use a moisture meter to measure the amount of damp in the wall of a house. See also PARKING-METER.

▶ **meter** v to measure sth with a meter: [Vn] Domestic water supplies may be metered in future.

meter² (US) = METRE¹,².

-meter comb form (forming ns) a device for measuring sth: thermometer ○ speedometer.

methadone /ˈmeθədəʊn/ n [U] a drug used as a substitute in treating people dependent on HEROIN.

methane /ˈmiːθeɪn/ (also **marsh gas**) n [U] a gas, without colour or smell, that burns easily and is used as fuel. Natural gas consists mainly of methane: the increase in global emissions of methane.

method /ˈmeθəd/ n 1 [C] a way of doing sth: use alternative/modern/new/traditional methods of language teaching ○ scientific/educational/farming methods ○ develop a reliable method of data analysis. 2 [U] order, efficient habits, etc: The quality of his work is good but it lacks method. **IDM** (have, etc) method in one's madness behaviour that is not as strange or foolish as it seems.

▶ **methodical** /məˈθɒdɪkl/ adj (a) done in a careful logical way: a methodical approach/manner/process. (b) (of a person) doing things in a careful logical way: a methodical worker ○ He was slow, but methodical. **methodically** /-kli/ adv: She searched through the files methodically from A to Z.

methodology /ˌmeθəˈdɒlədʒi/ n [U, C] (fml or techn) a set of methods used in a particular area of activity: changes in the methodology of language teaching ○ research/scientific methodologies. **methodological** /ˌmeθədəˈlɒdʒɪkl/ adj: a methodological approach/ problem.

Methodism /ˈmeθədɪzəm/ n [U] a Christian system of beliefs that originated in the teachings of John Wesley. ▶ **Methodist** /ˈmeθədɪst/ n, adj: She was brought up (as) a Methodist. ○ a Methodist church.

meths /meθs/ n [U] (infml esp Brit) = METHYLATED SPIRITS.

methylated spirit /ˌmeθəleɪtɪd ˈspɪrɪt/ n [U] (also **methylated spirits** [pl]) a type of alcohol that is not fit for drinking, used as a fuel for lighting and heating.

meticulous /məˈtɪkjələs/ adj ~ (about sth / doing sth) giving or showing great care and attention to detail: a meticulous worker/researcher ○ do meticulous and painstaking research ○ She is meticulous about her appearance. ▶ **meticulously** adv: meticulously clean ○ a meticulously planned schedule.

métier /ˈmetieɪ/ n (French) a profession, trade or main area of activity, expert knowledge, etc: find one's (true) métier ○ He's really a poet — writing novels is not his métier.

metre¹ (US meter) /ˈmiːtə(r)/ n (abbr m) a unit of length in the metric system equal to 39.37 inches. ⇨ App 2,8.

metre² (US meter) /ˈmiːtə(r)/ n (a) [U] the rhythm of a poem, produced by the arrangement of stresses

on the syllables in each line: *the poet's use of metre.*
(**b**) [C] a particular form of this: *a metre with six beats to a line.* See also METRICAL.

-metre (*US* **-meter**) *comb form* (used in *ns* expressing a particular fraction or MULTIPLE of a metre): *a centimetre ○ a millimetre ○ a kilometre.*

metric /'metrɪk/ *adj* **1** of or based on the metric system: *metric measurements/sizes ○ British currency went metric in 1971.* **2** made, measured, etc according to the metric system: *These screws are metric.* Compare IMPERIAL 2.
■ **the ˌmetric system** *n* [sing] the decimal measuring system, using the metre, the kilogram and the litre as basic units. ⇨ App 2.
ˌmetric ˈton *n* 1 000 kilograms; one TONNE.

metrical /'metrɪkl/ (also **metric**) *adj* of or composed in verse: *poems written in a variety of metrical forms.*

Metro /'metrəʊ/ *n* (*pl* **-os**) (usu *sing*) (also **the Metro**) an underground railway system, esp the one in Paris: *travel on the Metro ○ a Metro station.* See also TUBE 4, UNDERGROUND².

metronome /'metrənəʊm/ *n* (*music*) a device that makes a regular sound like a clock, and can be set at different speeds. It helps a musician to keep the correct rhythm. ▶ **metronomic** /ˌmetrəˈnɒmɪk/ *adj: a metronomic beat.*

metropolis /mə'trɒpəlɪs/ *n* the chief city of a region or country; a capital: *a great metropolis like Tokyo ○ working in the metropolis.*
▶ **metropolitan** /ˌmetrə'pɒlɪtən/ *adj* of or in a large or capital city: *the population of metropolitan Detroit ○ living in a metropolitan district.*
■ **the ˌMetropolitan Poˈlice** *n* [Gp] (*abbr* **the Met**) the London police force.

mettle /'metl/ *n* [U] the ability to endure difficulties and to face opposition: *The next game will be a real test of his mettle. ○ She really showed/proved her mettle under pressure.* **IDM** **on one's ˈmettle** encouraged or forced to do one's best: *The team will be on their mettle for the big match.*

mew /mjuː/ *n* the soft high-pitched noise that a cat makes. See also MIAOW. ▶ **mew** *v* [V] *The kitten mewed pitifully.*

mews /mjuːz/ *n* (*pl* unchanged) (*usu Brit*) a row of stables that have been converted into houses or flats: *live in a quiet London mews ○ mews houses/ cottages.*

mezzanine /'mezəniːn, 'metsə-/ *n* **1** a raised floor between the ground floor and the first floor of a building: *a mezzanine floor/platform/walkway.* **2** (*US*) (the first few rows of) the lowest balcony in a theatre. Compare DRESS-CIRCLE.

mezzo-soprano /ˌmetsəʊ sə'prɑːnəʊ/ (also **ˈmezzo**) *n* (*music*) (**a**) a female voice between SOPRANO and CONTRALTO. (**b**) a singer with such a voice. (**c**) a musical part written for a singer with a mezzo-soprano voice.

mg *abbr* milligram(s): *1.5 mg calcium.*

Mgr *abbr* Monsignor.

MHz *abbr* megahertz.

mi¹ (also **me**) /miː/ *n* (*music*) the third note of any major scale²(6).

mi² *abbr* (*US*) = ML 1.

miaow /mi'aʊ/ *n* the crying sound made by a cat. See also MEW. ▶ **miaow** *v*: [V] *The cat was miaowing outside all night.*

miasma /mi'æzmə, mai'æ-/ *n* (esp *sing*) (*fml*) an unhealthy or unpleasant smell, atmosphere, etc: *(fig) the miasma of depression.*

mica /'maɪkə/ *n* [U] a transparent mineral easily split into thin layers: *heat-resistant mica.*

mice *pl* of MOUSE.

Michaelmas /'mɪklməs/ *n* the Christian festival of St Michael, 29 September.
■ ˌMichaelmas ˈdaisy *n* a plant with blue, white, pink or purple flowers in the autumn.

ˌMichaelmas ˈterm *n* (*Brit*) (in some universities) the autumn term.

mickey /'mɪki/ *n* **IDM** **take the ˈmickey (out of sb)** (*esp Brit*) to make sb feel foolish, esp by copying their gestures, etc or laughing at them for reasons they do not understand: *Stop taking the mickey (out of poor Susan)!*

micro /'maɪkrəʊ/ *n* (*pl* **-os**) (*infml*) a MICROCOMPUTER.

micro- *comb form* very small: *a microchip ○ a micro-organism.* ⇨ App 8. Compare MACRO-, MINI-.

microbe /'maɪkrəʊb/ *n* a tiny living thing that can only be seen under a MICROSCOPE: *a common infection caused by various microbes ○ soil microbes.* Compare VIRUS 1a.

microbiology /ˌmaɪkrəʊbaɪ'ɒlədʒi/ *n* [U] the study of very small living things, eg bacteria.
▶ **microbiologist** /-lədʒɪst/ *n* an expert in microbiology.

microchip /'maɪkrəʊtʃɪp/ (also **chip**) *n* a very small piece of SILICON or a similar material carrying a complex electronic circuit: *recent advances in microchip technology ○ a single microchip computer.*

microcomputer /'maɪkrəʊkəmpjuːtə(r)/ (also *infml* **micro**) *n* a small computer used in homes, small businesses, etc: *microcomputer software.* Compare MAINFRAME, MINICOMPUTER, PERSONAL COMPUTER.

microcosm /'maɪkrəkɒzəm/ *n* a thing, place or community regarded as representing on a small scale sth very much larger: *The school playground is a microcosm of the world at large.* Compare MACROCOSM. **IDM** **in microcosm** on a small scale: *The effects of privatization throughout industry are seen here in microcosm.*

micro-electronics /ˌmaɪkrəʊ ɪˌlek'trɒnɪks/ *n* [sing *v*] the design, manufacture and use of electronic devices with very small components. ▶ **micro-electronic** *adj.*

microfiche /'maɪkrəʊfiːʃ/ *n* [C,U] a small sheet of MICROFILM: *documents stored on microfiche.*

microfilm /'maɪkrəʊfɪlm/ *n* [U] film on which extremely small photographs are stored, esp of documents or newspapers: *scientific papers on microfilm.*

microlight /'maɪkrəʊlaɪt/ *n* a type of very small and light aircraft.

micron /'maɪkrɒn/ *n* one millionth (MILLION) of a metre.

micro-organism /ˌmaɪkrəʊ 'ɔːɡənɪzəm/ *n* (*techn*) a MICROBE: *micro-organisms in the soil.*

microphone /'maɪkrəfəʊn/ *n* an instrument that changes sound waves into electrical current. It is used esp in recording or broadcasting speech, music, etc: *speak into a microphone ○ a hand-held microphone ○ check the room for hidden microphones.*

microprocessor /'maɪkrəʊprəʊsesə(r)/ *n* (*computing*) a very small computer, or a unit of one, consisting of one or more microchips (MICROCHIP).

microscope /'maɪkrəskəʊp/ *n* an instrument for making very small objects appear larger, esp for scientific study: *examine bacteria/plants under a microscope ○ (fig) put politicians under the microscope* (ie examine their actions in great detail). ⇨ picture. See also ELECTRON MICROSCOPE.
▶ **microscopic** /ˌmaɪkrə'skɒpɪk/ *adj* **1** too small to be seen without the help of a

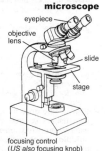

microscope

eyepiece
objective lens
slide
stage

focusing control
(*US also* focusing knob)

microscope: *a microscopic creature/particle* ○ *(fig) make a microscopic adjustment to sth.* **2** of or using a microscope: *a microscopic analysis/examination.* **microscopically** /-kli/ *adv.*

microwave /ˈmaɪkrəweɪv/ (also ˌmicrowave ˈoven) *n* a machine that cooks or heats food very quickly using ELECTROMAGNETIC waves: *microwave cookery* ○ *She reheated the soup in the microwave.*
▶ **microwave** *v* [Vn] to cook sth in a microwave.

mid /mɪd/ *adj* [attrib] the middle of: *from mid July to mid August* ○ *in the mid 1980s* ○ *She's in her mid thirties.*

mid- *comb form* in the middle of: *mid-morning coffee* ○ *a mid-air collision* ○ *a mid-season sale.*

Midas touch /ˈmaɪdəs tʌtʃ/ *n* **the Midas touch** [sing] the ability to make financial gain from whatever one does: *the pop star with the Midas touch.*

midday /ˌmɪdˈdeɪ/ *n* [U] the middle of the day; NOON: *finish work at midday* ○ *the ˌmidday ˈmeal* (ie lunch).

middle /ˈmɪdl/ *n* **1 the middle** [sing] the point, position or part which is at an equal distance from two or more points, etc; a point between the beginning and the end: *the middle of the room* ○ *be woken in the middle of the night* ○ *born in the middle of the century* ○ *a pain in the middle of his back* ○ *They were in the middle of dinner* (ie were having dinner) *when I called.* ○ *His picture was bang* (ie exactly) *in the middle of the front page.* **2** [C usu *sing*] *(infml)* a person's waist: *seize sb round the/their middle* ○ *measure fifty inches around the middle.* **IDM the middle of ˈnowhere** *(infml)* somewhere very remote or isolated: *She lives on a small farm in the middle of nowhere.* **pig/piggy/pickle in the middle** ⇨ PIG.
▶ **middle** *adj* [attrib] occupying a position in the middle: *the middle house of the three* ○ *the middle drawer* ○ *the middle-income groups in society.* **IDM (take/follow/steer) a middle ˈcourse** (to make) a compromise between two extreme courses of action.
■ ˌmiddle ˈage *n* [U] the period between youth and old age, the years from about 45 to 60: *a pleasant woman in early middle age.* ˌmiddle-ˈaged /-eɪdʒd/ *adj* of middle age: *ˌmiddle-aged ˈmen.* **middle-age(d) ˈspread** *n* [U] *(infml usu joc)* the fat around the stomach that sometimes develops in middle-aged people.
the ˌMiddle ˈAges *n* [pl] (in European history) the period from about AD 1100 to about AD 1400.
ˌ**Middle Aˈmerica** *n* [U] the middle class in the USA, esp considered as a politically conservative force.
ˌ**middle ˈclass** *n* [CGp] the social class between the lower or working class and the upper classes. It includes professional and business people: *create a new educated middle class* ○ *a ˌmiddle-class ˈbackground/ˈsuburb.*
ˌ**middle ˈdistance** *n* **1** [C] (in sport) a race distance of esp 400 or 800 metres: *a middle-distance runner.* **2 the middle distance** [sing] the part of a painting, view, etc that is neither close nor very far away: *His eyes were fixed on a small house in the middle distance.*
ˌ**middle ˈear** *n* the CAVITY inside the central part of the ear: *an infection of the middle ear.* ⇨ picture at EAR.
the ˌMiddle ˈEast *n* [sing] an area consisting of Egypt, Iran and the countries between them. Compare THE FAR EAST. **Middle Eastern** *adj*: *Middle Eastern politics.*
ˌ**middle ˈfinger** *n* the longest finger. ⇨ picture at HAND¹.
the ˈmiddle ground *n* [sing] a position in a discussion, debate, etc that avoids extremes: *occupy the political middle ground.*
ˌ**middle ˈmanagement** *n* [U with *sing* or *pl v*] *(commerce)* the people who run departments within

a business organization but who are not involved in making major policy or financial decisions. ˌ**middle ˈmanager** *n*: *a restructuring among the firm's middle managers.*
ˌ**middle ˈname** *n* a name that comes after one's first name (FIRST¹) and before one's SURNAME: *We didn't give the baby a middle name.* ⇨ note at NAME¹. **IDM be sb's middle ˈname** *(infml)* to be sb's chief characteristic: *Charm is her middle name.*
ˌ**middle-of-the-ˈroad** *adj* (of people, policies, etc) moderate; avoiding extremes: *Her political views are very middle-of-the-road.*
ˈ**middle school** *n* a school for children between 9 and 13 years old.
the ˌMiddle ˈWest *n* [sing] = MIDWEST.

middlebrow /ˈmɪdlbraʊ/ *n, adj* *(esp derog)* (a person who is) not particularly intellectual: *programmes targeted at the middlebrow audience.* Compare HIGHBROW, LOWBROW.

middleman /ˈmɪdlmæn/ *n* (*pl* **-men** /-men/) **1** a person who buys goods from the company that makes them in order to sell them to the final customer: *She wants to buy direct from the manufacturer and cut out the middleman.* **2** a person who acts as a means of communication between two or more others; an INTERMEDIARY: *He acted as a middleman in discussions between the two companies.*

middleweight /ˈmɪdlweɪt/ *n* a boxer weighing between 67 and 72.5 kg, next above WELTERWEIGHT.

middling /ˈmɪdlɪŋ/ *adj* of medium size, quality, etc: *a man of middling height.*

midfield /ˌmɪdˈfiːld/ *n* [U, sing] the central part of a sports pitch, esp in football, or the players in this position: *receive a pass in midfield* ○ *a midfield player.* ⇨ picture at FOOTBALL.

midge /mɪdʒ/ *n* a small flying insect that bites people and animals, found esp in hot damp conditions.

midget /ˈmɪdʒɪt/ *n* *(sometimes offensive)* an extremely small person.
▶ **midget** *adj* [attrib] very small: *a midget submarine.*

Midlands *n* **the Midlands** [sing or pl *v*] the middle part of a country, esp the central counties of England: *He's from the West Midlands.* ○ *a Midlands firm.* ▶ **Midland** *adj* [attrib]: *the Midland region.*

mid-life /ˈmɪd laɪf/ *adj* occurring during the middle period of one's life: *ˌmid-life ˈrestlessness.*
■ ˌ**mid-life ˈcrisis** *n* (usu *sing*) a time, esp around middle age, when a person stops feeling secure, confident, etc: *go through a mid-life crisis.*

midnight /ˈmɪdnaɪt/ *n* [U] 12 o'CLOCK at night: *at/ shortly before/just after midnight* ○ *He heard the clock strike midnight.* **IDM burn the midnight oil** ⇨ BURN.
■ **the midnight ˈsun** *n* [sing] the sun seen at midnight in summer near the North and South Poles.

mid-range /ˌmɪd ˈreɪndʒ/ *adj* [attrib] average; neither the best nor the worst that is available: *accommodation at a mid-range hotel* ○ *a mid-range saloon car.*

midriff /ˈmɪdrɪf/ *n* the middle part of the human body, between the waist and the chest: *a bare midriff.*

midshipman /ˈmɪdʃɪpmən/ *n* (*pl* **-men** /-mən/) **1** *(Brit)* a student training to be an officer in the Royal Navy. **2** *(US)* a student training to be an officer in the US Navy. ⇨ App 6.

midst /mɪdst, mɪtst/ *n* (used after a *prep*) the middle part: *in/from the midst of the crowd.* **IDM in the midst of (sth / doing sth)** while sth is happening or being done: *Stan paused in the midst of pouring his beer.* **in our/your/their midst** among or with us/you/them: *There is a traitor in our midst.*

midstream /ˌmɪdˈstriːm/ *n* [U] the middle part of a stream, river, etc: *The boat drifted out into mid-*

M

stream. **IDM** **change horses in midstream** ⇨ CHANGE¹. **in midstream** in the middle of doing sth: *The speaker stopped in midstream.*

midsummer /ˌmɪdˈsʌmə(r)/ *n* [U] the middle of summer, around 21 June: *a ˌmidsummer ˈevening.* ■ ˌMidsummer's ˈDay *n* 24 June.

mid-term /ˌmɪd ˈtɜːm/ *adj* **1** (*politics*) in the middle of the period that a government, council, etc is elected for: *a mid-term by-election victory.* **2** in the middle of the school or university term: *mid-term holidays/exams.*

midway /ˌmɪdˈweɪ/ *adj, adv* ~ (**between sth and sth / through sth**) in the middle; HALFWAY: *My house lies midway between the two villages.* ○ *reach the midway point* ○ *They scored again midway through the second half.*

midweek /ˌmɪdˈwiːk/ *n* [U] the middle of the week, ie Tuesday, Wednesday and Thursday: *a ˌmidweek ˈflight/ˈmatch* ○ *play a match* **in midweek.** ▶ **midweek** *adv* in the middle of the week: *meet/ travel/call midweek.*

Midwest /ˌmɪdˈwest/ *n* **the Midwest** (also **the Middle West**) [sing] the northern central part of the USA, from the Great Lakes to the Ohio River, Kansas and Missouri.

midwife /ˈmɪdwaɪf/ *n* (*pl* **midwives** /-waɪvz/) a person, esp a woman, trained to assist women in having their babies. ▶ **midwifery** /ˈmɪdwɪfəri; *US* -waɪf-/ *n* [U] the profession and work of a midwife: *do/take a course in midwifery.*

midwinter /ˌmɪdˈwɪntə(r)/ *n* [U] the middle of winter, around 21 December: *In midwinter the hills are covered with snow.*

mien /miːn/ *n* [sing] (*fml or rhet*) a person's appearance or manner, esp as an indication of mood: *have a sorrowful/haughty mien.*

miffed /mɪft/ *adj* (*sl*) slightly annoyed: *She was a bit miffed that he'd forgotten her name.*

might¹ /maɪt/ *modal v* (*neg* **might not**; *short form* **mightn't** /ˈmaɪtnt/) **1** (used as the past tense of *may* when reporting what sb has said): *He said he might come tomorrow.* (Compare: *'I may come tomorrow,' he said.*) **2** (indicating possibility): *He 'might get here in time, but I can't be sure.* ○ *Some of these mines might even become profitable again.* ○ *The pills might have helped him, if only he'd taken them regularly.* ○ *I know Vicky doesn't like the job, but I mightn't find it too bad.* ⇨ note. **3** (used in various polite expressions in British English) (**a**) (to make a suggestion): *You might try phoning the help desk.* ○ *I thought we might go to the zoo on Saturday.* (**b**) (to ask permission): *Might I use your phone?* ○ *If I might just add to what Mr Collins said ...* (**c**) (to make a request): *You might just (ie Please) call at the chemist on the way home.* (**d**) (*fml or joc*) (to ask for information): *How might the plans be improved upon?* ○ *And who might ˈshe be?* **4** (used to express annoyance about sth that sb could do or could have done): *I think you might at least offer to help!* ○ *Honestly, you might have told me!* **5** (used to indicate that one is not surprised that sth is true or has happened): *I might have guessed it was you that broke the window.* **6** (used to emphasize that an important point has been made): *'And where is the money coming from?' 'You* **might well** *ask!'* ○ *'He's very upset about what happened.' 'And so he might be.'*

NOTE Might and **may** are used to say that something is possible in the present or the future: *That might/may be our taxi now.* ○ *We might/may go away for the weekend if the weather's nice.* You also use **could** when you think that something is possible but not probable: *There could be a few tickets left, I suppose.*

In questions and negative sentences **might** and

may are replaced by **can** and **could**: *'Do you think they could have missed the plane?' 'Yes, they may/ might have.'*

To talk about the past **might have, may have** and **could have** (negative **might not have** or **may not have**) are used: *The plane may/might/could have been delayed.* ○ *She might/may not have had the letter yet.*

Might not or **mightn't** and **may not** (**mayn't** is extremely rare) are used to say that it is possible something will NOT happen: *She might/may not go to the party.* ○ *I mightn't be home till late this evening.*

might² /maɪt/ *n* [U] great strength or power: *America's military might* ○ *I pushed at the rock* **with all my might** *but it wouldn't move.*

mighty /ˈmaɪti/ *adj* (**-ier, -iest**) **1** (*esp rhet*) powerful; strong: *a mighty army/empire/prince* ○ *He gave a mighty blow with his hammer.* **2** great and impressive: *mighty mountain peaks* ○ *the mighty River Ganges.* **IDM** **high and mighty** ⇨ HIGH¹. ▶ **mightily** /-ɪli/ *adv* **1** (*fml*) forcefully: *They complained mightily about the way they had been treated.* **2** very: *mightily impressed/relieved.*
mighty *adv* (*infml esp US*) very: *mighty good/clever* ○ *He's mighty pleased with himself.*

migraine /ˈmiːɡreɪn, ˈmaɪɡ-; *US* ˈmaɪɡ-/ *n* [U,C] a severe type of HEADACHE(1), usu on one side of the head or face, often accompanied by NAUSEA(1) and disturbance of VISION(1a): *suffer severe migraine attacks* ○ *I'm getting a migraine.*

migrate /maɪˈɡreɪt; *US* ˈmaɪɡreɪt/ *v* ~ (**from...**) (**to...**) **1** to move from one place to go to live or work in another: [Vpr] *Men were forced to migrate to the towns to find work.* **2** (of animals, etc) to move from one place to another according to season: [V] *thousands of migrating starlings* [Vpr] *These birds migrate to North Africa in winter.*
▶ **migrant** /ˈmaɪɡrənt/ *n* a person or an animal that migrates: *migrant sea birds* ○ *He insisted he was a political refugee and not an economic migrant.*
migration /maɪˈɡreɪʃn/ *n* [U,C] an act or the process of migrating: *a period of mass migration.*
migratory /ˈmaɪɡrətri, maɪˈɡreɪtəri; *US* ˈmaɪɡrətɔːri/ *adj* having or relating to the habit of migrating: *migratory birds* ○ *the migratory instinct.*

mike /maɪk/ *n* (*infml*) a MICROPHONE.

mild /maɪld/ *adj* (**-er, -est**) **1** (of people or their behaviour) gentle and kind; not violent: *He seems very meek and mild.* ○ *He gave a mild answer, in spite of his annoyance.* ○ *She's a very* **mild-mannered** *person.* **2** not severe or harsh: *a mild punishment* ○ *a mild form of a disease* ○ *a soap that is mild on the skin.* **3** (of a flavour) not strong or bitter: *mild cheese* ○ *a mild cigar/curry.* **4** (of weather) not very cold: *the mildest winter in living memory* ○ *a pleasantly mild climate.* **5** slight: *a look of mild surprise* ○ *a mild flirtation.*
▶ **mild** *n* [U] (*Brit*) a type of beer with a mild flavour: *two pints of mild.*
mildly *adv* **1** in a gentle manner: *'Don't frown, Henry,' his mother said mildly.* **2** slightly: *mildly amusing* ○ *be mildly disappointed.* **IDM** **to put it ˈmildly** (used to indicate that one's words do not express sth as fully as they could): *Crime is a complex phenomenon, to put it mildly (ie It is extremely complex).*
mildness *n* [U].

mildew /ˈmɪldjuː; *US* -duː/ *n* [U] a tiny white FUNGUS that grows on plants, leather, food, etc in warm damp conditions: *spray roses against mildew.*
▶ **mildewed** /ˈmɪldjuːd; *US* -duːd/ *adj* affected by mildew: *mildewed walls.*

mile /maɪl/ *n* **1(a)** [C] a unit of distance equal to 1.6 km: *a 40-mile journey to work* ○ *about half a mile down the road/outside the town* ○ *an area of four*

M

square miles ○ *He drove on for mile after mile.* ○ *a mile-long procession* ○ *speeds reaching 180 miles an/ per hour* ○ *a 20-mile-an-hour speed limit.* ⇨ App 2. See also MPH, NAUTICAL MILE. **(b) miles** [pl] a large area or long distance: *cross miles of desert* ○ *miles and miles of swamp.* **2** [C usu pl] (*infml*) very much; a long way: *I feel miles* (ie very much) *better today.* ○ *The two sides in the negotiations are still miles apart.* ○ *be miles behind with one's work* ○ *You missed the target by a mile/by miles.* ○ *They live* **miles away**. **3** (esp **the mile**) [sing] a race over one mile: *He can run a four-minute mile.* **IDM** be **'miles away** (*infml*) to be thinking deeply about sth and not aware of what is happening around one. **,miles from 'anywhere/'nowhere** (*infml*) in a remote or isolated place or position. **run a 'mile (from sb/sth)** (*infml*) to show that one is very frightened of doing sth: *He'd run a mile if anyone asked him to marry them.* **see/tell sth a 'mile off** (*infml*) to see/realize sth very easily: *He's lying — you can see that a mile off.* **stand/stick out a 'mile** to be very obvious or noticeable: *Her honesty sticks out a mile.*

mileage /'maɪlɪdʒ/ *n* **1** [U, C usu *sing*] a distance travelled or to be travelled, measured in miles: *an annual mileage of around 12 000* ○ *a car with a high mileage* (ie one that has been driven many miles) ○ *Your hire car costs include unlimited mileage.* **2** [U] ~ (**in sb/sth**) (*infml*) a benefit or advantage: *He doesn't think there's any mileage in that type of advertising.* ○ *They got a lot of political mileage out of the affair.*
■ **'mileage allowance** *n* an allowance paid to cover the expenses of using one's own car on company business.

miler /'maɪlə(r)/ *n* (*infml*) a person or horse taking part in races of one mile.

milestone /'maɪlstəʊn/ *n* a very important stage or event in the development of sth: *pass/reach a milestone* ○ *His election victory was an important milestone in the country's history.*

milieu /'miːljɜː; *US* miːˈljɜː/ *n* (*pl* **milieux** or **milieus** /-jɜːz/) (usu *sing*) the social environment in which one lives or works: *come from a very different cultural/social milieu.*

militant /'mɪlɪtənt/ *adj* favouring the use of force or strong pressure to achieve one's aims: *militant elements in the trade unions* ○ *a militant speech.*
▶ **militancy** /-ənsi/ *n* [U]: *growing/increasing militancy amongst the unemployed.*
militant *n* a militant person, esp in politics: *left-wing militants.*

militarism /'mɪlɪtərɪzəm/ *n* [U] (usu *derog*) belief in increasing one's military strength to become or remain powerful, esp as government policy. ▶ **militaristic** /ˌmɪlɪtəˈrɪstɪk/ *adj*: *the militaristic tone of his speech.*

militarize, -ise /'mɪlɪtəraɪz/ *v* [Vn] **1** to send soldiers to an area: *a militarized zone.* **2** to give a military character to sb/sth. Compare DEMILITARIZE.
▶ **militarization, -isation** /ˌmɪlɪtəraɪˈzeɪʃn; *US* -rəˈz-/ *n* [U]: *the militarization of the police.*

military /'mɪlɪtri; *US* -teri/ *adj* [usu attrib] of or for soldiers or an army: *military training/discipline* ○ *a military coup/régime* ○ *military intervention* ○ *take military action.* Compare CIVILIAN.
▶ **militarily** *adj*: *militarily sensitive areas* ○ *Intervention made sense both politically and militarily.*
the military *n* [Gp] soldiers; the armed forces: *The military was/were called in to deal with the riot.*
■ **,military 'service** *n* [U] a period in which one trains or serves as a soldier: *be called up for military service* ○ *She's doing her military service.*

militate /'mɪlɪteɪt/ *v* **PHRV** **militate against sth** (*fml*) (of evidence, facts, etc) to have great force or

influence to prevent sth: *Many factors militated against the success of the venture.*

militia /məˈlɪʃə/ *n* [CGp] a trained military force whose members do not belong to a regular army but operate like one, esp to defend their country in an emergency: *local militia units.*

militiaman /-mən/ *n* (*pl* **-men** /-mən/) a member of a MILITIA.

milk¹ /mɪlk/ *n* **1** [U] the white liquid produced by female mammals (MAMMAL) as food for their young, esp that of cows or goats drunk by humans: *a pint of milk* ○ *a bottle/carton of milk* ○ *fresh goat's milk* ○ *dried/powdered milk* ○ *Do you take milk?* ○ *milk products* (eg butter, cheese, YOGHURT) ○ *a ,milk-white 'horse.* See also CONDENSED MILK, EVAPORATED MILK, SKIMMED MILK. **2** the whitish juice of certain plants and trees, eg that found inside a COCONUT: *soya milk.* **IDM** cry over spilt milk ⇨ CRY¹. ,milk and 'honey plenty of food and good things that make life easy and pleasant: *a land of/flowing with milk and honey* ○ *a time of milk and honey.* the milk of human 'kindness kindness regarded as natural to human beings: (often *ironic*) *You're so full of the milk of human kindness!*
■ **,milk 'chocolate** *n* [U] chocolate made with milk: *Do you prefer milk chocolate or plain (chocolate)?* Compare PLAIN CHOCOLATE.
'milk float *n* (*Brit*) a small, usu electric, vehicle used for delivering milk to people's houses.
'milk round *n* (esp *Brit*) the route taken by a MILK-MAN going from house to house: *do a milk round.*
,milk 'shake (also **shake**) *n* a drink of milk, and sometimes ice-cream, with an added flavour of fruit, chocolate, etc, which is mixed or shaken until it is full of bubbles: *a banana milk shake.*
'milk tooth *n* (also *esp US* **baby tooth**) (*pl* **teeth**) any of the first set of teeth in young children and animals.

milk² /mɪlk/ *v* **1** to take the milk from a cow, goat, etc: [Vn] *Cows must be milked twice a day.* [also V]. **2(a)** ~ sb/sth (**of sth**); ~ sth (**out of/from sb/sth**) to extract money, information, etc dishonestly from a person or an institution: [Vn] *milk the benefits system* [Vnpr] *His illegal deals were steadily milking the profits from the business.* **(b)** to obtain as much benefit or profit as possible from a situation: [Vn] *He milked the occasion for all it was worth, giving TV interviews and selling his story to the tabloids.* **IDM** milk/suck sb/sth dry ⇨ DRY¹.
▶ **milking** *n* [U] the process of taking milk from a cow, etc: *do the evening milking* ○ *milking machines.*

milkmaid /'mɪlkmeɪd/ *n* (esp formerly) a woman who takes the milk from cows.

milkman /'mɪlkmən/ *n* (*pl* **-men** /-mən/) a person who regularly delivers milk to people's houses.

milksop /'mɪlksɒp/ *n* (*derog*) a man or boy who is weak and easily frightened.

milky /'mɪlki/ *adj* (**-ier, -iest**) **1** mixed with or made of milk: *milky tea/coffee* ○ *a hot milky drink.* **2** of or like milk: *milky* (ie not clear) *blue eyes* ○ *milky* (ie pale or white) *skin.*
■ **the ,Milky 'Way** *n* [sing] = THE GALAXY.

mill¹ /mɪl/ *n* **1** a building fitted with machinery or apparatus for grinding grain into flour: *a 'water-mill* ○ *We walked past the old mill.* See also WINDMILL. **2** (esp in compounds) a building fitted with machinery for processing materials of a particular type: *a 'cotton-/'paper-mill.* See also SAWMILL. ⇨ note at FACTORY. **3** (esp in compounds) a device for grinding or crushing a solid substance into powder: *a 'pepper-mill.* See also RUN-OF-THE-MILL. **IDM** grist to the/one's/sb's mill ⇨ GRIST. go through/put sb through the 'mill to experience or make sb experience hard training or an unpleasant experience.
■ **'mill-wheel** *n* a large wheel turned by flowing water, used for driving a mill.

M

mill² /mɪl/ v (esp passive) to grind or crush sth in a mill: [Vn] *The grain was coarsely milled.* ○ *freshly milled pepper.* **PHRV** **mill about/around** (of people or animals) to move around in a confused mass: *Fans were milling about in the streets after the match.*

millennium /mɪˈleniəm/ n (pl **millennia** /-niə/ or **millenniums**) [C] a period of 1000 years, esp as calculated before or after the birth of Christ: *a millennium ago* ○ *the second millennium AD.*

miller /ˈmɪlə(r)/ n a person who owns or works a mill for grinding corn.

millet /ˈmɪlɪt/ n [U] a type of CEREAL plant that produces a large crop of small seeds.

milli- comb form (in the metric system) a 1000th part of: ˈmilligram ○ ˈmillimetre ○ ˈmillilitre. ⇨ App 8.

millibar /ˈmɪlibɑː(r)/ n a unit of pressure of the atmosphere.

milligram /ˈmɪligræm/ n (abbr **mg**) a 1000th of a GRAM: *a limit of 80 milligrams of alcohol per 100 millilitres of blood.*

millilitre /ˈmɪliliːtə(r)/ n (abbr **ml**) a 1000th of a litre.

millimetre (US **millimeter**) /ˈmɪlimiːtə(r)/ n (abbr **mm**) a 1000th of a metre.

milliner /ˈmɪlɪnə(r)/ n a person who makes or sells women's hats. ▶ **millinery** /-nəri; US -neri/ n [U] the business of making or selling women's hats: *the millinery department* (ie in a large store).

million /ˈmɪljən/ n, pron, det (pl unchanged or **millions**) **1** (after a, one, a number or an indication of quantity) the number 1000000: *two million dollars.* ⇨ App 2. **2 millions** [pl] an extremely large number: *an audience of millions* ○ *Millions of lives have been saved.* **3** [C often pl] (infml) a million pounds, dollars, etc: *She made her first million before she was thirty.* ○ *His idea is worth millions.* **IDM** **one, etc in a ˈmillion** a person or thing of rare or exceptional quality: *She's a wife in a million.* ○ *We haven't a chance/hope in a million* (ie We have almost no chance) *of winning.* ▶ **millionth** /ˈmɪljənθ/ n, pron, det: *a/one millionth of a second.*
For further guidance on how **million** and **millionth** are used, see the examples at *hundred* and *hundredth.*

millionaire /ˌmɪljəˈneə(r)/ n a person who has a million pounds, dollars, etc; a very rich person: *an Austrian steel millionaire* ○ *the millionaire businessman John Styles.*

millipede /ˈmɪlipiːd/ n a long thin small creature, similar to a CENTIPEDE but with two pairs of legs on each section of its body.

millisecond /ˈmɪlisekənd/ n a 1000th of a second.

millpond /ˈmɪlpɒnd/ n a pool of water used, esp formerly, for the operation of a mill: *The sea was as calm as a millpond.*

millstone /ˈmɪlstəʊn/ n either of a pair of flat circular stones used, esp formerly, for grinding grain. **IDM** **a millstone round one's/sb's ˈneck** a difficult problem or responsibility that seems impossible to solve or get rid of: *My debts were like a millstone round my neck.*

milometer /maɪˈlɒmɪtə(r)/ (also esp US **odometer**) n an instrument in a vehicle for measuring the number of miles travelled.

mime /maɪm/ n **(a)** [U] (in the theatre, etc) the technique of telling a story, etc using only expressions and gestures, and no words: *a play acted entirely in mime* ○ *a mime artist.* **(b)** [C] a performance using this technique. ▶ **mime** v to pretend to do sth using mime: [Vn] *a mimed performance* [V.ing] *She mimed hammering in a nail.* [Vpr] *They were miming to* (ie pretending to sing the words of) *their own record.* [also V].

mimetic /mɪˈmetɪk/ adj (techn or fml) copying the behaviour, etc of sb/sth else: *the mimetic skills of certain birds* ○ *mimetic dancing.*

mimic /ˈmɪmɪk/ v (-ck-) **1** to copy sb's voice, gestures, etc, esp in order to amuse people: [Vn] *mimicking sb's accent* ○ *Tom can mimic his uncle perfectly.* [also V.speech]. **2** (of creatures or things) to resemble sth closely: [Vn] *insects that mimic dead leaves to avoid being eaten by birds.* ▶ **mimic** n a person or an animal that mimics others: *She was an outstanding mimic and storyteller.*

mimicry n [U] the art of mimicking sb/sth: *her extraordinary powers of mimicry* ○ *genes concerned with mimicry in butterflies.*

mimosa /mɪˈməʊzə, -məʊsə/ n [U,C] a tree or bush with many small round sweet-smelling yellow flowers.

min abbr **1** minimum: *temperature 50° min.* Compare MAX. **2** minute(s): *fastest time 6 mins.* Compare HR.

minaret /ˌmɪnəˈret/ n a tall thin tower, usu forming part of a MOSQUE, from which Muslims are called to prayer.

minatory /ˈmɪnətəri; US -tɔːri/ adj (fml) threatening: *minatory words.*

mince /mɪns/ v **1** to cut food, esp meat, into very small pieces in a machine with revolving blades: [Vn] *minced lamb* ○ *Finely mince a kilo of lean beef.* **2** (usu derog) to walk with short delicate steps or pronounce words very carefully in order to suggest one is refined or superior in social status: [Vpr] *He came mincing towards me across the room.* [also V, Vp]. **IDM** **not mince (one's) ˈwords** to speak plainly and directly, esp when criticizing sb/sth: *My father is never one to* (ie never does) *mince words.* ▶ **mince** (Brit) (US **hamburger**) n [U] minced meat, esp BEEF: *You need a pound of mince and two onions.*

mincer (esp Brit) (US also **grinder**) n a device for mincing food, esp meat: *a mincer attachment for a food processor.*

mincing adj (usu derog) delicate, PRECISE(3) and intended to suggest one is refined: *a soft mincing voice* ○ *take short mincing steps.* ■ **ˌmince ˈpie** n a small round pie containing MINCE-MEAT, eaten esp at Christmas.

mincemeat /ˈmɪnsmiːt/ n [U] a mixture of dried fruit and PEEL, sugar, chopped apples and fat that is usu cooked in pastry, esp as mince pies (MINCE). **IDM** **make ˈmincemeat of sb/sth** (infml) to defeat sb/sth completely in a fight, a contest or an argument: *They made mincemeat of their weaker opponents.*

mind¹ /maɪnd/ n **1** [U,C] the ability to be aware of things and to think and feel; the source of one's thoughts and feelings: *have the right qualities of mind for the job* ○ *have complete peace of mind* ○ *be in a disturbed state of mind* ○ *His mind was full of dark thoughts.* ○ *All sorts of fears passed through my mind.* ○ *Wales would always be associated in my mind with that last summer with Helen.* See also FRAME OF MIND, PRESENCE OF MIND. **2** [C] **(a)** the ability to reason; one's intellectual powers: *have a brilliant/logical/mathematical mind* ○ *His mind was as sharp as ever.* **(b)** a person of outstanding intellectual ability: *one of the greatest minds of her generation.* **3** [C] a person's thoughts or attention: *Keep your minds on your work!* ○ *Her mind is completely occupied by the new baby.* **4** [C usu sing] the ability to remember; one's memory: *I can't think where I've left my umbrella — my mind's a complete blank!* **5** [U,C] a person's normal mental state: *He's 94 and his mind is going* (ie he is becoming SENILE). ○ *The tragedy affected his mind.* **IDM** **at the back of one's mind** ⇨ BACK¹. **be bored, frightened, pissed, etc out of one's ˈmind** (infml) to be

M

extremely bored, etc. **be in two ⌐minds about sth / doing sth** to feel doubtful about or hesitate over sth: *I was in two minds about leaving London: my friends were there, but the job abroad was a good one.* **be of one / the same ⌐mind (about sb/sth)** to agree or have the same opinion about sb/sth. **be/go ⌐out of one's ⌐mind** (*infml*) to be/become crazy or mad: *be out of one's mind with worry* ◦ *You must be out of your mind if you think I'm going to lend you my car!* **bear in mind** ⇨ BEAR². **bear/keep sb/sth in ⌐mind** to remember sb/sth: *We have no vacancies now, but we'll certainly bear your application in mind.* **blow one's/sb's mind** ⇨ BLOW¹. **boggle sb's/the mind** ⇨ BOGGLE. **bring/call sb's ⌐mind** to remember sb/sth: *I know her face but I can't call her name to mind.* **cast one's mind back** ⇨ CAST¹. **change one's/sb's mind** ⇨ CHANGE¹. **close one's mind to sth** ⇨ CLOSE⁴. **come/spring to ⌐mind** to present itself to one's thoughts; to occur to one: *'Have you any suggestions?' 'Nothing immediately springs to mind.'* **cross one's mind** ⇨ CROSS². **give one's ⌐mind to sth** to concentrate on or direct all one's attention to sth. **give sb a piece of one's mind** ⇨ PIECE¹. **have half a mind to do sth** (*infml*) to feel tempted to do sth but not sure about it: *He had half a mind to ask for his money back.* **have it in mind to do sth** (*fml*) to intend to do sth: *I have it in mind to ask her opinion when I see her.* **have a memory/mind like a sieve** ⇨ SIEVE. **have a mind of one's ⌐own** to form one's own opinions, make one's own decisions, etc independently of other people. **have a (good) mind to do sth** (*infml*) to have a strong desire to do sth: *I'm so angry I've a good mind to resign.* **have/keep an open mind** ⇨ OPEN¹. **have sb/sth in ⌐mind (for sth)** to be considering sb/sth as suitable for sth: *Who do you have in mind for the job?* **in one's mind's ⌐eye** in one's imagination: *In my mind's eye, I can still see the house where I was born.* **in one's right mind** ⇨ RIGHT¹. **know one's own mind** ⇨ KNOW. **lose one's mind** ⇨ LOSE. **make up one's ⌐mind** to decide: *Have you made your mind up where to go for your honeymoon?* **a meeting of minds** ⇨ MEETING. **the mind/imagination boggles** ⇨ BOGGLE. **⌐mind over ⌐matter** control of physical things by the power of the mind: *Keeping to a diet is a question of mind over matter.* **of unsound mind** ⇨ UNSOUND. **on one's ⌐mind** in one's thoughts and causing worry or concern: *My deputy has resigned, so I've got a lot on my mind just now.* ◦ *You've been on my mind all day.* **open one's/sb's mind to sth** ⇨ OPEN². **out of sight, out of mind** ⇨ SIGHT¹. **prey on sb's mind** ⇨ PREY *v*. **put sb in mind of sb/sth** to cause sb to think of or remember sb/sth: *Her way of speaking put me in mind of her mother.* **put/set sb's ⌐mind at ease/rest** to cause or enable sb to stop worrying. **put/set/turn one's ⌐mind to sth** to devote all one's attention and energy to achieving sth: *You could be a very good writer if you set your mind to it.* **speak one's mind** ⇨ SPEAK. **stick in one's mind** ⇨ STICK². **take one's/sb's mind off sth** to help one/sb not to think or worry about sth: *Hard work always takes your mind off domestic problems.* **to ⌐my mind** in my opinion: *To my mind, it's all a lot of nonsense!* **a turn of mind** ⇨ TURN².

■ **⌐mind-bending** *adj* (*infml*) influencing or altering one's state of mind: *mind-bending drugs.*

⌐mind-blowing *adj* (*infml*) astonishing because of size, intensity, etc: *the mind-blowing beauty of Africa.*

⌐mind-boggling *adj* (*infml*) extraordinary or astonishing: *Distances in space are mind-boggling.*

⌐mind-reader *n* a person who knows or claims to be able to know what another person is thinking: *How was I to know what he'd do? I'm not a mind-reader, am I?*

⌐mind-set *n* a set of attitudes or views formed by earlier events.

mind² /maɪnd/ *v* **1(a)** (used esp in questions and answers and in negative or conditional sentences; no passive) to be upset, annoyed or disturbed by sth/sb; to object to sth/sb: [Vn] *Do you mind the noise?* ◦ *I don't mind him at all; it's her I don't like.* [Vpr, V.ing] *Did she mind (about) not getting the job?* [V.wh] *I don't mind how hot it is.* [V] *They don't mind if I borrow their car occasionally.* [V.that] *She minded very much that he had not come.* **(b)** (used for asking permission or making a request in a polite way) [V] *Do you mind if I smoke?* [V.n ing] *Do you mind me/my closing the window?* [Vn] *I wouldn't mind* (ie I would very much like) *a drink.* **2** (no passive) to care or be concerned about sth: [V, V.wh] *'Would you like tea or coffee?' 'Either — I don't mind (which).'* [V.wh] *I mind (greatly) what people think about me.* **3** (*Brit*) (*US* **watch**) (no passive) to be careful about sth/sb; to pay attention to sth/sb: [Vn] *Mind* (ie Don't fall at) *that step!* ◦ *Mind your manners!* (ie Speak/Behave in a polite way.) ◦ *Mind your head!* (eg Be careful not to hit it on the low ceiling.) ◦ *Don't mind me! I won't disturb you.* [V.that] *Mind you don't cut yourself — the knife's very sharp.* ◦ *Mind you come home before 11 o'clock.* [V.wh] *Mind where you walk in those muddy boots!* **4** (*esp Brit*) to look after or attend to sb/sth: [Vn] *mind the baby* ◦ *Could you mind the phone* (ie answer it if it rings) *for five minutes?* **IDM ⌐do you ⌐mind?** (*ironic*) (used to express annoyance or disapproval): *Do you mind? I was here before you.* **I don't mind if I ⌐do** (*infml*) (used when accepting sth offered): *'Will you have a drink?' 'I don't mind if I do.'* **if you ⌐don't ⌐mind 1** (used when making a polite request or to confirm sb's agreement with what is intended) please; if it is all right: *I must ask you, if you don't mind, to read that letter more closely.* ◦ *I'll make some coffee now, if you don't mind.* **2** (used when making a polite refusal of an offer): *'Have another beer.' 'I won't, if you don't mind.'* **if you ⌐don't mind me / my ⌐saying so ...** (used to introduce a criticism or a comment that might upset or annoy sb): *If you don't mind my saying so, I don't think you should spend so much time with her.* **⌐mind one's ⌐own ⌐business 1** (esp imperative) not to interfere in other people's affairs: *'What are you reading?' 'Mind your own business!'* **2** (*infml*) to be doing sth that is not disturbing anyone: *I was just walking down the street minding my own business.* **⌐mind one's ⌐p's and ⌐q's** to be careful and polite about what one says or does. **mind/watch one's ⌐step** ⇨ STEP². **mind/watch one's tongue** ⇨ TONGUE. **⌐mind ⌐you; mind** (used to add a further comment or piece of information): *They're getting divorced, I hear — mind you, I'm not surprised.* **never ⌐mind 1** (*esp Brit*) do not worry; it does not matter: *Have you lost it? Never mind, we can buy another one.* **2** (used to emphasize that what follows is even less likely, true, etc than what has just been said): *He's not even awake, never mind dressed.* Compare LET ALONE (ALONE). **never mind (about) (doing) sth** do not think about or consider sth; do not BOTHER(2) about sth: *⌐Never mind your ⌐car, who's going to pay for the damage you've done to my fence?* ◦ *Never mind about the washing-up now.* **⌐never you ⌐mind** (*infml*) do not ask because you will not be told: *Never you mind how I found out — it's true, isn't it?* **PHRV ⌐mind ⌐out** (*Brit infml*) (esp imperative) to move and allow sb to pass: *Mind out (of the way) — you're blocking the passage.* **⌐mind ⌐out (for sb/sth)** (esp imperative) to be careful of danger, etc: *Mind out for falling rocks.*

▶ **minder** *n* (esp in compounds) a person who is employed to look after, protect, etc another person: *The boss never goes anywhere in public without one of her minders.* See also CHILD-MINDER.

minded /'maɪndɪd/ *adj* **1** [pred] ~ **(to do sth)** (*fml*) wishing strongly to do sth: *She was minded to accept* their offer. ∘ *He could do it if he were so minded.* **2** (forming compound *adjs* or following *advs*) having the type of mind specified: *a ˌstrong-minded/ ˌnarrow-minded/ˌhigh-minded ¹person* ∘ *I appeal to all ˌlike-minded ¹people to support me.* ∘ *be comˌmercially/poˌlitically/ˌtechnically ¹minded.* See also ABSENT-MINDED, BLOODY-MINDED. **3** (with *ns* forming compound *adjs*) interested in or enthusiastic about the thing specified: *She has become very ¹food-minded since her holiday in France.*

mindful /ˈmaɪndfl/ *adj* [pred] ~ **of sb/sth; ~ that...** (*fml*) conscious of sb/sth: *be mindful of one's family/ one's reputation/the risks/the need for discretion.*

mindless /ˈmaɪndləs/ *adj* **1(a)** done for no particular reason and serving no useful purpose: *mindless violence/brutality.* **(b)** acting for no particular reason or purpose: *mindless hooligans.* **2** not requiring intelligence: *a totally mindless occupation like filling supermarket shelves.* **3** [pred] ~ **of sb/sth** (*fml*) not thinking of sb/sth; not concerned with sb/sth: *mindless of personal risk.* ▶ **mindlessly** *adv*: *mindlessly destroying public property.*

mine¹ /maɪn/ *possess pron* of or belonging to me: *That book is mine.* ∘ *He's a friend of mine* (ie one of my friends). Compare MY.

mine² /maɪn/ *n* **1** a place where coal or other minerals are extracted from below the surface of the ground: *a silver mine* ∘ *go/work down a mine* ∘ *The hillside is covered in mine workings.* Compare PIT¹ 3, QUARRY². See also COALMINE. **2** a type of bomb hidden just below the surface of the ground or in the sea, for destroying vehicles, ships or people that touch or pass near it: *lay anti-personnel/anti-tank mines* ∘ *clear the coastal waters of mines.* See also LAND-MINE. **IDM a mine of inforˈmation (about/on sb/sth)** a person, book, etc that can provide a lot of information: *My grandmother is a mine of information about our family's history.*

mine³ /maɪn/ *v* **1(a)** ~ **(for sth)** to dig in the ground for coal and other minerals: [Vpr] *mining for gold/ diamonds* [also V]. **(b)** ~ **A (for sth)/~ B (from A)** to extract coal, etc from the earth by digging: [Vnpr] *mine the earth for iron ore* ∘ *Gold is mined from deep underground.* [also Vn]. **2(a)** to lay explosive mines (MINE² 2) in sth: [Vn] *mine the entrance to a harbour.* **(b)** to destroy sth by means of explosive mines: [Vn] *The cruiser was mined, and sank in five minutes.* ▶ **mining** *n* [U] the process of getting coal or other minerals from a mine: *tin-mining* ∘ *a mining village/ community* ∘ *mining equipment.*

minefield /ˈmaɪnfiːld/ *n* **1** an area of land or sea where explosive mines (MINE² 2) have been laid. **2** a situation that contains hidden dangers or difficulties: *a legal/political minefield* ∘ *Tax regulations are a minefield for the unwary.*

miner /ˈmaɪnə(r)/ *n* a person who works in a mine: *The miners went on strike.*

mineral /ˈmɪnərəl/ *n* **1** [C, U] a substance that occurs naturally in the earth and is not formed from animal or vegetable matter, eg gold or salt: *mineral deposits/resources/extraction* ∘ *the recommended daily intake of vitamins and minerals.* Compare ANIMAL, VEGETABLE 1. **2** [C usu *pl*] (*Brit fml*) (*US* **soda**) a sweet drink with bubbles of gas in it. Minerals have various flavours and do not contain alcohol: *Soft drinks and minerals sold here.* ■ **ˈmineral water** *n* [U] water from a spring in the ground that contains dissolved mineral salts or gases: *A glass of mineral water, please.*

mineralogy /ˌmɪnəˈrælədʒi/ *n* [U] the scientific study of minerals. ▶ **mineralogical** /ˌmɪnərəˈlɒdʒɪkl/ *adj*. **mineralogist** /ˌmɪnəˈrælədʒɪst/ *n* an expert in mineralogy.

minestrone /ˌmɪnəˈstrəʊni/ *n* [U] a soup made from

meat stock¹(8) and containing small pieces of vegetable and PASTA or rice.

minesweeper /ˈmaɪnswiːpə(r)/ *n* a ship used for finding and clearing away explosive mines (MINE² 2).

mineworker /ˈmaɪnwɜːkə(r)/ *n* a person who works in a mine²(1): *the National Union of Mineworkers.*

mingle /ˈmɪŋgl/ *v* **1** ~ **with sth / ~ (together); ~ A with B / ~ A and B (together)** to mix together or mix one thing with another: [V, Vp] *allow the flavours to mingle (together) for 1 hr* [Vn] *a look of mingled embarrassment and amusement* [Vnpr] *She felt intense fear mingled with excitement.* [also Vpr, Vnp]. **2** ~ **with sb/sth; ~ (together)** to move around in a place and have contact with other people: [V, Vp] *a school in which all groups mingle (together) freely and naturally* [Vpr] *Security men mingled with the crowd.*

mingy /ˈmɪndʒi/ *adj* **(-ier, -iest)** (*Brit infml*) **(a)** small; less than one expects: *What a mingy present!* **(b)** (of people) mean: *He's very mingy with his money.*

mini /ˈmɪni/ *n* (*pl* **minis**) **1** **Mini** (*propr*) a type of small car. **2** a MINISKIRT.

mini- *comb form* of small size, length, etc: ˈ*minibus* ∘ ˈ*mini-bar* ∘ ˈ*minigolf.* Compare MACRO-, MICRO-.

miniature /ˈmɪnətʃə(r); *US* ˈmɪniətʃʊər/ *n* [C] a very small detailed painting, usu of a person. **IDM in miniature** on a very small scale: *a doll's house with everything in miniature* ∘ *Through play, children act out in miniature the adult dramas of life.* ▶ **miniature** *adj* [attrib] very small; of a much smaller size than usual: *miniature dogs* (ie very small breeds) ∘ *a miniature bottle of brandy* ∘ *a miniature railway* (ie a small model one on which people may ride, eg in a park).

miniaturize, -ise *v* to make sth on a much smaller scale: [Vn] *a miniaturized skyscraper.* **miniaturization, -isation** /ˌmɪnətʃəraɪˈzeɪʃn; *US* -niətʃʊərəˈz-/ *n* [U].

mini-bar /ˈmɪni bɑː(r)/ *n* a small cupboard containing drinks, esp in a hotel room.

minibus /ˈmɪnibʌs/ *n* a small vehicle with seats for about 12 people: *hire a self-drive minibus.*

minicab /ˈmɪnikæb/ *n* (*Brit*) a taxi which is ordered in advance by telephone.

minicomputer /ˈmɪnikəmpjuːtə(r)/ *n* a computer of medium size, larger than a personal computer. Compare MAINFRAME, MICROCOMPUTER.

minim /ˈmɪnɪm/ *n* (*Brit*) (*US* **half note**) (*music*) a note that lasts half as long as a SEMIBREVE. ⇨ picture at MUSIC.

minimal /ˈmɪnɪməl/ *adj* as small as possible: *Changes can be made to the system at minimal cost.* ∘ *The risk is minimal.* ▶ **minimally** *adv*: *The room was minimally furnished.*

minimize, -ise /ˈmɪnɪmaɪz/ *v* **1** to reduce sth to the smallest amount or degree: *a production plan that will minimize manufacturing costs* [Vn] *install an alarm to minimize the risk of burglary.* **2** to reduce the true value or importance of sth: [Vn] *He minimized the value of her contribution to his research.* Compare MAXIMIZE.

minimum /ˈmɪnɪməm/ *n* (*pl* **minima** /-mə/) [C usu *sing*] **1** the least or smallest amount, degree, etc possible: *a minimum of work/effort* ∘ *keep/reduce sth to the (absolute/bare) minimum* ∘ *Repairing your car will cost a minimum of* (ie at least) *£600.* **2** (*abbr* **min**) the least or smallest amount, degree, etc allowed or recorded: *The class needs a minimum of six students to continue.* ∘ *Temperatures will fall to a minimum of 50°F.* Compare MAXIMUM. ▶ **minimum** *adj* smallest; lowest: *a minimum charge/investment/standard* ∘ *80 cents is the minimum fare on buses.* ■ ˌ**minimum ˈlending rate** *n* [sing] (*finance*) the lowest rate of interest at which a central bank lends money at any particular time.

,minimum ¹wage n [sing] the lowest wage that an employer is allowed, by law or by a union agreement, to pay: *earn the minimum wage.*

minion /'mɪnɪən/ n (esp pl) (derog or joc) an employee of low rank: *He was clearly annoyed at being treated like a minion.*

miniseries /'mɪnɪsɪəriːz/ n (esp US) a story shown on television in several parts which are broadcast within a few days of each other.

miniskirt /'mɪnɪskɜːt/ n a very short skirt.

minister¹ /'mɪnɪstə(r)/ n **1** (US **secretary**) a person at the head of a government department or a main branch of one, often a member of the CABINET(3): *the Minister of Education* ○ *the Greek Foreign Minister* ○ *a minister for science.* See also PRIME MINISTER. **2** a person, usu of lower rank than an AMBASSADOR, representing her or his government in a foreign country. **3** (in some Christian Churches) a priest: *a minister of religion.* Compare PRIEST, VICAR.
■ ,Minister of 'State n (Brit) a government minister having a rank below that of head of department.

minister² /'mɪnɪstə(r)/ v **PHRV** minister to sb/sth (fml) to care for or give active help to sb/sth: *nurses ministering to the sick and wounded.*

ministerial /,mɪnɪ'stɪərɪəl/ adj of or relating to a minister or ministers: *hold ministerial office* ○ *ministerial meetings/business* ○ *decisions taken at ministerial level.*

ministration /,mɪnɪ'streɪʃn/ n [C, U] (fml or joc) an act or the process of helping or caring for sb: *I was restored to health by the ministrations of my wife.*

ministry /'mɪnɪstri/ n **1** (US **department**) [C] a government department or the building(s) it occupies: *work in/at the ,Ministry of De'fence.* **2(a)** the ministry [Gp] ministers of religion, esp Protestant ministers, considered as a group. **(b)** [C usu sing] the duties or period of service of a minister¹(3) of religion: *enter/take up the ministry* (ie train to become a minister of religion).

mink /mɪŋk/ n **1** [C] a small fierce animal, with shiny brown fur. **2(a)** [U] its valuable fur, used for making coats, etc: *a mink coat.* **(b)** [C] a coat made from this fur: *wearing her new mink.*

minnow /'mɪnəʊ/ n a very small fish found in rivers, ponds, etc.

minor /'maɪnə(r)/ adj **1** [usu attrib] smaller, less serious or less important than others: *a minor road* ○ *minor repairs/alterations* ○ *a minor operation* ○ *suffer minor injuries* ○ *a minor part/role in a play* ○ *minor poets.* Compare MAJOR¹ 1. **2** (Brit dated or joc) (in private schools) the second or younger of two brothers or boys with the same family name: *Evans minor.* Compare MAJOR¹ 1. ⇨ JUNIOR 2. **3** (music) of or based on a scale that has a SEMITONE between its second and third notes: *a symphony in C minor* ○ *a song in a minor key* ○ *a minor third* (ie an interval of three semitones). Compare MAJOR¹ 3.
▶ **minor** n **1** (law) a person under the age of full legal responsibility, usu 18 or 21. **2** (US) a secondary field of study at a university.
minor v **PHRV** 'minor in sth (US) to study sth as a minor subject: *She minored in Italian.* Compare MAJOR¹ v.

minority /maɪ'nɒrəti; US -'nɔːr-/ n **1** [CGp] a smaller group, part, etc compared with another group: *a minority opinion/point of view* ○ *have a minority interest in a company* ○ *Only a small minority of students is/are opposed to the scheme.* ○ *A sizeable/significant minority voted against the motion.* ○ *Men are generally in the minority at parent-teacher meetings.* **2** [C] a small group in a community or nation, differing from others in race, religion, language, etc: *the rights of ethnic/racial minorities* ○ *belong to a minority group.* Compare

MAJORITY. **3** [U] (law) the state or period of being under the age of full legal responsibility. **IDM** (find oneself, be, etc) in a minority of 'one (often joc) (to be) the only person to vote for or against sth.
■ mi,nority 'government n [C, U] a government that has fewer seats in parliament than the total number held by all the other parties.

minster /'mɪnstə(r)/ n a large or important church, esp one that once belonged to a group of monks: *York Minster.*

minstrel /'mɪnstrəl/ n (in the Middle Ages) a travelling musician.

mint¹ /mɪnt/ n **1** [U] a small plant with leaves that have a pleasant fresh taste, used as a flavour in food, drinks, etc: *a sprig of mint* (eg with boiled potatoes) ○ *mint-flavoured chewing gum* ○ *mint 'sauce* (ie mint leaves chopped and mixed with VINEGAR and sugar, usu eaten with lamb). **2** [C] = PEPPERMINT: *suck a mint.* ▶ **minty** /'mɪnti/ adj: *toothpaste with a minty taste.*

mint² /mɪnt/ n **1** [C] a place where money is manufactured: *coins fresh from the mint* ○ *the Royal Mint* (ie that of the UK). **2** [sing] (infml) a very large amount of money: *make/be worth a mint.* **IDM** in mint con'dition new or as if new; perfect: *postage stamps/books in mint condition.*
▶ **mint** v to make a coin by stamping metal: [Vn] *newly-minted £1 coins.*

minuet /,mɪnju'et/ n **(a)** a slow graceful dance of the 17th and 18th centuries: *a stately minuet.* **(b)** a piece of music for this.

minus /'maɪnəs/ prep **1** (mathematics) less sth: *Seven minus three equals four (7 – 3 = 4).* **2** below zero: *a temperature of minus ten degrees centigrade (–10°C).* **3** (infml) without or lacking sth/sb: *The explosion left him minus a leg.* Compare PLUS.
▶ **minus** adj **1** (mathematics) negative: *a minus figure/quantity* (ie less than zero, eg –2x²). **2** [pred] (of marks or grades) of a standard slightly lower than the one stated: *I got B minus (B–) in the test.*
minus n **1** (also **minus sign**) the symbol –. **2** (infml) a disadvantage: *Let's consider the pluses and minuses of buying a bigger car.* Compare PLUS.

minuscule /'mɪnəskjuːl/ adj very small; tiny: *minuscule handwriting* ○ *pose only a minuscule threat to our lives.*

minute¹ /'mɪnɪt/ n **1(a)** [C] (abbr **min**) any of the 60 equal parts of an hour, equal to 60 seconds: *It's ten minutes to/past six.* ○ *I arrived a couple of minutes early/late.* ○ *My house is ten minutes' walk (away) from the shops.* ○ *We caught the bus with only minutes to spare.* ⇨ App 2. **(b)** [sing] a very short time; a moment: *It only takes a minute to make a salad.* ○ *Wait a minute — I'm nearly ready.* ○ *Will you wait for me? I won't be a minute.* **(c)** [sing] an exact point of time; an instant: *Stop it this minute* (ie immediately)! ○ *At that very minute, Tom walked in.* **2** [C] any of the 60 equal parts of a degree, used in measuring angles: *37 degrees 30 minutes (37°30').* **3** [C] an official note that records a decision or comment, or gives authority for sth to be done: *make a minute of sth.* **4** minutes [pl] a brief summary or record of what is said and decided at a formal meeting: *We read (through) the minutes of the last meeting.* ○ *Who will take* (ie make notes for) *the minutes?* **IDM** (at) any 'minute/'moment ('now) (infml) very soon: *The leading runners will enter the stadium any minute now!* in a 'minute very soon: *Our guests will be here in a minute!* just a minute/moment/second ⇨ JUST². the last minute/moment ⇨ LAST¹. ,not for a/one 'minute/'moment not at all: *I never thought for a minute that you would refuse.* the minute/moment (that)... as soon as...: *I want to see him the minute (that) he arrives.* there's one born every minute ⇨ BORN. this minute immediately; now: *Stop it this minute!* ○ *I've just this minute* woken up. **to the** ¹**minute** exactly: *The train arrived at 9.05 to the minute.* ₗ**up to the** ¹**minute** (*infml*) **1** fashionable: *Her clothes are always right up to the minute.* ○ *an* ₗup-to-the-minute ¹look/¹style. **2** having the latest information: ₗup-to-the-minute ¹news/ infor¹mation. **wait a minute/second** ⇨ WAIT¹.

▶ **minute** *v* to make a note of sth in an official document to record sth in the minutes of a meeting: [Vn] *minute an action point/a comment* ○ *There is no agenda and the proceedings are not minuted.*

■ ¹**minute-hand** *n* (usu *sing*) the hand on a watch or clock that indicates the minutes.

ₗ**minute** ¹**steak** *n* a thin piece of meat that is cooked very quickly.

minute² /maɪˈnjuːt; *US also* -ˈnuːt/ *adj* (-st; comparative rarely found) **1** very small in size or amount: *minute particles of gold-dust* ○ *water containing minute quantities of lead.* **2** containing much detail; careful and accurate: *a minute examination/ inspection* ○ *study an agreement/a contract in the minutest detail.* ▶ **minutely** *adv.*

minutiae /maɪˈnjuːʃiː; *US* mɪˈnuːʃiː/ *n* [pl] very small or unimportant details: *I won't discuss the minutiae of the contract now.*

minx /mɪŋks/ *n* (*derog or joc*) a girl who is playful or CUNNING and does not show the proper respect.

miracle /ˈmɪrəkl/ *n* **1(a)** [C] a surprising and welcome act or event which does not follow the known laws of nature and is therefore thought to be caused by God: *perform/work miracles.* (**b**) [sing] (*infml*) a remarkable or unexpected event: *an economic miracle* ○ *a miracle cure/drug* ○ *It's a miracle you weren't killed in that car crash!* **2** [C] ~ **of sth** a remarkable example or product of sth: *a miracle of modern technology.* **IDM** **do/work** ¹**miracles/**¹**wonders (for/ with sb/sth)** (*infml*) to be extremely successful in achieving positive results for/with sb/sth: *This tonic will work miracles for your depression.* ○ *He can do miracles with last night's leftovers* (eg by making them into another meal).

▶ **miraculous** /mɪˈrækjələs/ *adj* like a miracle; remarkable; contrary to what is expected: *make a miraculous recovery* ○ *a miraculous escape.* **miraculously** *adv: Miraculously, he survived the crash without injury.*

■ ¹**miracle play** (also **mystery play**) *n* a medieval drama based on events in the Bible or the lives of Christian saints.

mirage /ˈmɪrɑːʒ, məˈrɑːʒ/ *n* **1** an illusion caused by hot air conditions making one see sth that is not there, esp the appearance of a sheet of water on a hot road or in a desert. **2** any illusion or hope that cannot be fulfilled: *a mirage of equality.*

mire /ˈmaɪə(r)/ *n* [U] an area of soft deep mud: *sink into/get stuck in the mire.*

▶ **mire** *v* ~ **sb/sth in sth** (esp passive) to prevent sb/sth from making progress: [Vnpr] *The Opposition gives us the impression of a party mired in self-doubt.* [also Vn].

mirror /ˈmɪrə(r)/ *n* **1** (often in compounds) a shiny surface, usu of specially treated glass or metal, that reflects images: *a rear-view mirror* (eg in a car, to enable the driver to see what is behind) ○ *She glanced at herself in the mirror.* **2** a thing that reflects or gives a representation of sth: *Dickens's novels are a mirror of his times.*

▶ **mirror** *v* ~ **sth (in sth)** to reflect sth as in a mirror: [Vnpr] *The trees were mirrored in the still water of the lake.* [Vn] *a novel that mirrors modern society.*

■ ₗ**mirror** ¹**image** *n* a REFLECTION(1) or copy of sth that has the right side of the original object on the left and the left side on the right.

mirth /mɜːθ/ *n* [U] (*fml*) happiness and laughter: *The unexpected appearance of a dog on stage caused much mirth among the audience.* ▶ **mirthless** *adj: a*

mirthless laugh (ie showing that one is not really amused).

mis- *pref* (with *vs* and *ns*) bad; wrong; not: *misdirect* ○ *misconduct* ○ *mistrust.*

misadventure /ˌmɪsədˈventʃə(r)/ *n* **1** [C, U] (*fml*) bad luck; MISFORTUNE: *Their trip was ruined by a whole series of misadventures.* **2** [U] (*law*) a death caused by accident, not resulting from crime or lack of care and attention: *death by misadventure* ○ *return a verdict of misadventure.*

misanthrope /ˈmɪsənθrəʊp/ *n* (*fml*) a person who hates other people and avoids human society. Compare PHILANTHROPIST. ▶ **misanthropic** /ˌmɪsən-ˈθrɒpɪk/ *adj.* **misanthropy** /mɪˈsænθrəpi/ *n* [U].

misapply /ˌmɪsəˈplaɪ/ *v* (*pt, pp* **-lied**) (*fml*) (esp passive) to use sth for the wrong purpose or in the wrong way: [Vn] *misapplied rules/talents.*

▶ **misapplication** /ˌmɪsæplɪˈkeɪʃn/ *n* [U, C] a wrong use of sth: *a misapplication of the law.*

misapprehension /ˌmɪsæprɪˈhenʃn/ *n* [U, C] (*fml*) a wrong idea or mistaken belief about sth: *clear up any misapprehensions* ○ *I thought you wanted to see me but I was clearly under a misapprehension.*

misappropriate /ˌmɪsəˈprəʊprieɪt/ *v* (*fml*) to use sb else's money wrongly, esp for one's own benefit: [Vn] *The treasurer misappropriated the society's funds.* ▶ **misappropriation** /ˌmɪsəˌprəʊpriˈeɪʃn/ *n* [U].

misbegotten /ˌmɪsbɪˈɡɒtn/ *adj* [usu attrib] badly planned; not appropriate: ₗmisbegotten ¹schemes/ i¹deas.

misbehave /ˌmɪsbɪˈheɪv/ *v* ~ (**oneself**) to behave badly or in an unacceptable way: [V] *She found it difficult to handle children who misbehaved in class.* [Vn] *Harry and Tom misbehaved themselves.* ▶ **misbehaviour** (*US* **misbehavior**) /ˌmɪsbɪˈheɪvjə(r)/ *n* [U].

miscalculate /ˌmɪsˈkælkjuleɪt/ *v* (**a**) to calculate amounts, distances, measurements, etc wrongly: [Vn, V.wh] *They had miscalculated the number of chairs/how many chairs they needed.* [also V]. (**b**) to judge a situation wrongly: [Vn] *The police clearly miscalculated the crowd's response.* [also V.wh, V]. ▶ **miscalculation** /ˌmɪskælkjuˈleɪʃn/ *n* [C, U]: *The government made a serious miscalculation.*

miscarriage /ˈmɪskærɪdʒ; *Brit also* ˌmɪsˈk-/ *n* [U, C] **1** the process of giving birth to a baby before it is fully developed and able to survive: *a higher risk of miscarriage in older women* ○ *have/suffer a miscarriage.* Compare ABORTION 1. **2** (*fml*) the failure of a plan: *the miscarriage of one's hopes/schemes.*

■ ₗ**mis₊carriage of** ¹**justice** *n* [U, C] (*law*) a situation in which a lawcourt treats a person unfairly, eg by declaring them guilty of a crime when they are innocent: *Sending an innocent man to prison is a clear miscarriage of justice.*

miscarry /ˌmɪsˈkæri/ *v* (*pt, pp* **-ried**) [V] **1** (of a pregnant woman) to have a MISCARRIAGE(1). **2** (of plans, etc) to fail; to have a different result from the one intended or expected.

miscast /ˌmɪsˈkɑːst; *US* -ˈkæst/ *v* (*pt, pp* **miscast**) (usu passive) (**a**) ~ **sb (as sb/sth)** to give an actor a role for which he or she is not suitable: [Vn-n] *The young actor was badly miscast as Lear.* [also Vn]. (**b**) to give the parts in a play, etc to people who are not suitable: [Vn] *The movie was thoroughly miscast.*

miscegenation /ˌmɪsɪdʒəˈneɪʃn/ *n* [U] (*fml*) the mixing of races (RACE³ 1); the production of children by two people of different races.

miscellaneous /ˌmɪsəˈleɪniəs/ *adj* [usu attrib] of various types or from various sources: *miscellaneous items/letters/expenses* ○ *a miscellaneous collection/assortment of books.*

miscellany /mɪˈseləni; *US* ˈmɪsəleɪni/ *n* ~ (**of sth**) a

M

group or collection of different items; a mixture: *She's had a miscellany of jobs.* ○ *a miscellany of poems by different authors.*

mischance /ˌmɪsˈtʃɑːns; US -ˈtʃæns/ n [U,C] (fml) bad luck: *By pure mischance our secret was discovered.*

mischief /ˈmɪstʃɪf/ n [U] **1** behaviour, esp of children, that is annoying or does slight damage, but is not wicked: *do sth out of mischief* ○ *Those girls are fond of mischief* (eg of playing tricks). ○ *Tell the children to keep out of mischief.* ○ *He's up to* (ie planning) *(some) mischief again!* ○ *She's always getting into mischief.* **2** a desire or tendency to behave in a playful way, eg by causing trouble or mocking sb: *There was mischief in her eyes.* ○ *The kittens were full of mischief.* **3** harm or injury done to sb or to their reputation: *His malicious gossip caused much mischief until the truth became known.* **IDM** **do sb/oneself a ˈmischief** (infml or joc) to hurt sb/oneself physically: *You could do yourself a mischief on that barbed-wire fence!* **make ˈmischief** to do or say sth to upset, annoy or provoke others: *Don't let her make mischief between you — she's only jealous.*

■ **ˈmischief-making** n [U] the action of deliberately causing trouble for people, harming their reputation, etc.

mischievous /ˈmɪstʃɪvəs/ adj **1(a)** (of a person) causing, or fond of causing, trouble in a playful way: *a mischievous child.* **(b)** (of behaviour) showing a playful desire to cause trouble: *a mischievous look/ smile/trick.* **2** (fml) (of a thing) causing harm or damage: *a mischievous letter/rumour.* ▶ **mischievously** adv. *grin/whisper mischievously.*

misconceive /ˌmɪskənˈsiːv/ v (fml) (esp passive) to have a wrong idea or understanding of sth: [Vn] *The poet's intentions have been totally misconceived.* ▶ **misconceived** adj badly planned or judged; not appropriate: *a misconceived project/policy.*

misconception /ˌmɪskənˈsepʃn/ n [U,C] ~ **(about sth)**: *dispel misconceptions about the purpose of the meeting* ○ *It is a popular/common misconception* (ie Many people wrongly believe) *that in France one is guilty unless proved innocent.* Compare PRECONCEPTION.

misconduct /ˌmɪsˈkɒndʌkt/ n [U] (fml) **1** unacceptable behaviour, esp by a professional person: *allegations of gross/serious/wilful misconduct.* **2** bad management; NEGLIGENCE: *misconduct of the company's affairs.*

misconstruction /ˌmɪskənˈstrʌkʃn/ n [U,C] (fml) false or mistaken understanding of sth: *What you say is open to misconstruction* (ie could easily be understood wrongly).

misconstrue /ˌmɪskənˈstruː/ v ~ **sth (as sth)** (fml) to interpret sb's words, acts, etc wrongly: [Vn] *I don't want my remarks to be misconstrued.* [also Vn-n].

miscount /ˌmɪsˈkaʊnt/ v to count sth wrongly: [V] *We haven't enough chairs — I must have miscounted.* [also Vn].

miscreant /ˈmɪskriənt/ n (fml) a person who behaves in a way that is morally wrong or against the law.

misdeed /ˌmɪsˈdiːd/ n (usu pl) (fml) a wicked act; a crime: *be punished for one's misdeeds.*

misdemeanour (US **-demeanor**) /ˌmɪsdɪˈmiːnə(r)/ n (fml) a minor wrongdoing: *petty misdemeanours.*

misdirect /ˌmɪsdəˈrekt, -daɪˈrekt/ v **1** (esp passive) to use or apply sth wrongly or in a situation that is not the most appropriate: [Vn] *misdirected energies/ abilities/resources* ○ *misdirected* (ie not deserved) *criticism/sarcasm.* **2** ~ **sb/sth (to sth)** to send sth, or instruct sb to go to the wrong place: [Vnpr] *be misdirected to the wrong platform* ○ *The letter was misdirected to our old address.* [also Vn]. **3** [Vn] (law) (of a judge in a lawcourt) to give the JURY wrong information on a point of law. ▶ **misdirection** /ˌmɪsdəˈrekʃn, -daɪˈrek-/ n [U].

mise en scène /ˌmiːz ɒn ˈseɪn/ n [sing] (French) the arrangement of scenery, furniture, etc, eg for a play; the setting for sth.

miser /ˈmaɪzə(r)/ n (derog) a person who loves wealth and spends as little money as possible. ▶ **miserly** adj (derog) **1** like a miser; very mean: *miserly habits.* **2** hardly sufficient; very small: *a miserly amount/helping.*

miserable /ˈmɪzrəbl/ adj **1(a)** very unhappy or uncomfortable: *We were cold, wet and thoroughly miserable.* ○ *He makes her life miserable* (eg by being unkind or cruel to her). ○ *Don't look so miserable!* **(b)** making sb feel unhappy or uncomfortable; unpleasant: *miserable* (eg cold and wet) *weather* ○ *live in miserable conditions* ○ *I've had a miserable afternoon.* **2** poor in quality or quantity; too small: *How can I keep a family on such a miserable wage?* **3** [attrib] (of people) unpleasant or bad-tempered: *What a miserable old devil Scrooge was!* **4** [attrib] very disappointing: *The plan was a miserable failure.* **IDM** **miserable/ugly as sin** ⇨ SIN¹. ▶ **miserably** /-əbli/ adv: *die miserably* ○ *a miserably cold day* ○ *be miserably poor* ○ *The plan failed miserably.*

misery /ˈmɪzəri/ n **1(a)** [U] great suffering or discomfort of mind or body: *suffer the misery of toothache* ○ *lead a life of total misery.* **(b)** [C usu pl] a thing causing this; a great misfortune: *the miseries of unemployment* ○ *This dispute with the neighbours is making my life a misery.* **2** [C] (Brit infml) a person who is always miserable and complaining: *My father's a real old misery!* **IDM** **put an animal, a bird, etc out of its ˈmisery** to end the suffering of a creature by killing it. **put sb out of their ˈmisery 1** to end sb's sufferings by killing them. **2** (joc) to end sb's anxiety by telling them sth they are anxious to know: *Put me out of my misery — tell me if I've passed or not!*

misfire /ˌmɪsˈfaɪə(r)/ v **1** to fail to have the desired effect: [V] *The joke misfired completely.* **2** (of an engine, etc) to fail to start or function properly: [V, Vpr] *The engine is misfiring badly (on one cylinder).* **3** [V] (of a gun, ROCKET(2a), etc) to fail to fire correctly. Compare BACKFIRE. ▶ **misfire** n: *The first shot was a misfire.*

misfit /ˈmɪsfɪt/ n a person who is not well suited to her or his work or surroundings: *a social misfit* ○ *He always felt a bit of a misfit in the business world.*

misfortune /ˌmɪsˈfɔːtʃuːn/ n **1** [U] bad luck: *suffer great misfortune* ○ *Misfortune struck early in the voyage.* ○ *They had the misfortune to be hit by a violent storm.* **2** [C] an unfortunate condition, accident or event: *She bore her misfortunes bravely.*

misgiving /ˌmɪsˈɡɪvɪŋ/ n [U,C esp pl] ~ **(about sth / doing sth)** (fml) doubt or anxiety about the outcome or consequences of sth: *feel a sense of misgiving* ○ *I have serious misgivings about (taking) the job.*

misguided /ˌmɪsˈɡaɪdɪd/ adj wrong because of having or showing bad judgement; badly judged: *a misguided attempt to reform the company pay structure* ○ *He was certainly misguided in his decision to leave his job.* ▶ **misguidedly** adv.

mishandle /ˌmɪsˈhændl/ v **1** to manage sth wrongly or badly: [Vn] *mishandle a situation/an affair/a business deal* ○ *the mishandling of the economy.* **2** to handle or to treat sth/sb roughly: [Vn] *Wrap the parcel carefully to avoid mishandling in transit.*

mishap /ˈmɪshæp/ n [C,U] a small accident or piece of bad luck: *We had a slight mishap with the car* (eg scraped it against a wall). ○ *Our journey ended without (further) mishap.*

mishear /ˌmɪsˈhɪə(r)/ v (pt, pp **misheard** /-ˈhɜːd/) to

M

hear sb/sth wrongly so that what one thinks one hears is not what was said: [Vn] *He told me there was a towel in my room but I misheard him and thought he said 'a cow'!*

mishit /ˌmɪsˈhɪt/ v (**-tt-**; *pt, pp* **mishit**) [Vn] (in cricket, golf, etc) to hit the ball badly or in the wrong direction. ► **mishit** /ˈmɪshɪt/ n.

mishmash /ˈmɪʃmæʃ/ n [sing] ~ (**of sth**) (*infml usu derog*) a confused mixture: *not a proper plan, just a mishmash of vague ideas.*

misinform /ˌmɪsɪnˈfɔːm/ v ~ **sb** (**about sth**) (*fml*) (esp passive) to give sb wrong information; to mislead sb deliberately or without intending to do so: [Vn] *They told me the museum was open today but I was obviously misinformed.* [also Vnpr]. ► **misinformation** /ˌmɪsɪnfəˈmeɪʃn/ n [U] Compare DISINFORMATION.

misinterpret /ˌmɪsɪnˈtɜːprɪt/ v ~ **sth** (**as sth / doing sth**) to understand sth/sth wrongly; to assume sth wrongly: [Vn] *misinterpret sb's remarks* [Vn-n] *He misinterpreted her silence as (indicating) agreement.* ► **misinterpretation** /ˌmɪsɪntɜːprɪˈteɪʃn/ n [U, C]: *What you have written is open to misinterpretation* (ie could be misinterpreted).

misjudge /ˌmɪsˈdʒʌdʒ/ v **1** to form a wrong opinion of sb/sth: [Vn] *I totally misjudged his motives.* **2** to estimate sth, eg time, distance or quantity, wrongly: *They misjudged the time of their arrival and missed the plane.* ► **misjudgement** (also **misjudgment**) n [U, C]: *a serious misjudgement of popular feeling.*

mislay /ˌmɪsˈleɪ/ v (*pt, pp* **mislaid** /-ˈleɪd/) (*often euph*) to put sth where it cannot easily be found; to lose sth, usu for a short time only: [Vn] *I seem to have mislaid my passport.*

mislead /ˌmɪsˈliːd/ v (*pt, pp* **misled** /-ˈled/) ~ **sb** (**about sth**); ~ **sb** (**into doing sth**) to cause sb to have a wrong idea or impression about sb/sth: [Vn] *Don't be misled by the brochure — it's not a very nice place.* [Vnpr] *He misled me into thinking he was rich.* ► **misleading** adj giving the wrong idea or impression: *misleading instructions/advertisements/comments.* **misleadingly** adv.

mismanage /ˌmɪsˈmænɪdʒ/ v to manage sth badly or wrongly: [Vn] *mismanage one's business affairs/finances.* ► **mismanagement** n [U]: *mismanagement of natural resources/the economy.*

mismatch /ˌmɪsˈmætʃ/ v (usu passive) to match people or things wrongly or in a way that is not suitable: [Vn] *The two players were badly mismatched* (ie One was much better than the other). ► **mismatch** /ˈmɪsmætʃ/ n ~ (**between sth and sth**): *a huge mismatch between supply and demand.*

misname /ˌmɪsˈneɪm/ v to call sb/sth by a wrong name or one that is not appropriate: *I was bitten by a horse misnamed Lucky.*

misnomer /ˌmɪsˈnəʊmə(r)/ n a wrong use of a name, word or description: *'Luxury hotel' was a complete misnomer for the dilapidated building we stayed in.*

misogynist /mɪˈsɒdʒɪnɪst/ n a person, esp a man, who hates women. ► **misogynist** (also **misogynistic**) adj: *misogynist jokes.* **misogyny** n [U].

misplace /ˌmɪsˈpleɪs/ v (*fml*) (esp passive) to put sth in the wrong place: [Vn] *The book had been misplaced on the shelf.*
► **misplaced** adj **1** (of love, affection, etc) shown to the wrong person or in an unwise way: *misplaced admiration/trust/confidence.* **2** not appropriate or correct in the circumstances: *misplaced optimism* ○ *If you think deafness is funny, you have a very misplaced sense of humour.*

misprint /ˈmɪsprɪnt/ n an error in printing: *The book is full of misprints.*

mispronounce /ˌmɪsprəˈnaʊns/ v to pronounce

---

words or letters wrongly: [Vn] *She mispronounced my name.*

misquote /ˌmɪsˈkwəʊt/ v to quote sth written or spoken wrongly, deliberately or without intending to do so: [Vn] *He claimed he had been misquoted in the press.* ► **misquotation** /ˌmɪskwəʊˈteɪʃn/ n [C, U].

misread /ˌmɪsˈriːd/ v (*pt, pp* **misread** /-ˈred/) **1** ~ **sth** (**as sth**) to read sth wrongly: [Vn] *I misread the instructions on the packet.* [Vn-n] *He misread 'the last train' as 'the fast train'.* **2** to interpret sb/sth wrongly: [Vn] *misread a situation/sb's intentions.*

misrepresent /ˌmɪsˌreprɪˈzent/ v ~ **sb/sth** (**as sth**) (esp passive) to represent sb/sth wrongly; to give a false account of sb/sth: [Vn-n] *She is widely misrepresented in the press as a militant.* [also Vn, Vn-adj].
► **misrepresentation** /ˌmɪsˌreprɪzenˈteɪʃn/ n [C, U]: *a gross misrepresentation of the facts.*

misrule /ˌmɪsˈruːl/ n [U] bad government; disorder or confusion: *The country suffered years of misrule under a corrupt government.*

miss¹ /mɪs/ n **1 Miss** (**a**) (a title used with the name of a woman who is not married, or kept by a married woman, eg for professional reasons): *That's all, thank you, Miss Burton.* ○ *the Liberal candidate, Miss Janet Lipman.* ○ (*dated or fml*) *the Misses Hill.* Compare MRS, MS. (**b**) (a title given to the winner of a beauty contest in the specified country, town, etc): *Miss America* ○ *Miss Brighton* ○ *the Miss World contest.* **2 Miss** (**a**) (used as a polite form of address to a young woman, eg by the driver of a bus or by hotel staff): *I'll take your luggage to your room, Miss.* Compare MADAM. (**b**) (*esp Brit*) (used as a form of address by children to a woman teacher): *Good morning, Miss!* Compare SIR 1. **3** (*dated or joc or derog*) a young girl or woman: *She's a saucy little miss!*

miss² /mɪs/ v **1** to fail to hit, catch, reach, etc sth aimed at: [Vn] *miss the target/mark/goal* ○ *miss one's footing* (ie slip or STUMBLE, eg while climbing) ○ *The plane missed the runway by several yards.* [V.ing] *The goalkeeper just missed stopping the ball.* [V] *He shot at the bird but missed.* **2** to fail to see, hear, understand, etc sb/sth: [Vn] *The house is on the corner — you can't miss it.* ○ *I'm sorry, I missed that/missed what you said.* ○ *He completely missed the point of my joke.* **3** to fail to be present at sth; to arrive too late for sth: [Vn] *miss a meeting/a class/an appointment* ○ *He missed the train.* [Vn, V.ing] *We only missed (seeing) each other by five minutes.* **4** to fail to take advantage of sth: [Vn] *miss the chance/opportunity of doing sth* ○ *The offer of a year abroad with all expenses paid seemed too good to miss.* ○ *Don't miss our bargain offers!* [also V.ing] **5**(**a**) to notice the absence or loss of sb/sth: [Vn] *When did you first miss your purse?* ○ *He's so rich that he wouldn't miss £100.* ○ *We seem to be missing two chairs.* (**b**) to feel regret at the absence or loss of sb/sth: [Vn] *He'll be sorely missed* (eg when he retires or dies). [V.n.ing] *I miss you bringing me the paper in the mornings!* [V.ing] *Now that I've moved out of town I really miss walking to work.* **6** to avoid or to escape sth: [Vn] *If you go early you'll miss the traffic.* [V.ing] *We only just missed having a nasty accident.* **7** [V] (of an engine) to MISFIRE. **IDM hit/miss the mark** ⇨ MARK¹. **ˌmiss the ˈboat/ˈbus** (*infml*) to be too slow to take an opportunity: *If we don't apply for funding now, we'll probably miss the boat* (ie have no chance of getting any). **not ˈmiss much** (*infml*) to be aware of everything that is happening around one: *Your mother will know who's moved in — she doesn't miss much.* **not miss a ˈtrick** (*infml*) to be very alert and ready to take advantage of a situation: *She never misses a trick when it comes to cutting costs.* **PHRV ˌmiss sb/sth ˈout** to omit sb/sth: *We'll miss out* (ie not sing) *the last two verses of the song.* ○ *The printers have missed out a whole line*

M

---

here. **miss 'out (on sth)** (*infml*) to lose an opportunity to benefit from sth or to enjoy oneself: *If I don't go to the party, I'll feel I'm missing out.*

▶ **missing** *adj* **1(a)** that cannot be found or that is not in the usual place; lost: *The book had two pages missing/two missing pages.* ○ *The hammer is missing from my tool-box.* **(b)** not present: *He's always missing when there's work to be done.* **2(a)** (of a person or an animal) absent from home and impossible to find: *a police file on missing persons* ○ *They reported that their child had gone missing.* ○ *Our cat's been missing for a week.* **(b)** not present after an accident, a battle, etc but not known to have been killed: *26 passengers on the liner were reported (as) missing.*
■ **missing 'link** *n* (usu *sing*) a thing needed to complete a series. ▶ **the missing** *n* [pl *v*]: *Captain Jones is among the missing.*

miss³ /mɪs/ *n* a failure to hit, catch or reach sth that one has tried to hit, catch or reach: *score ten hits and one miss* ○ *The ball's gone right past him — that was a bad miss* (ie one he ought to have stopped, caught, etc). See also NEAR MISS. **IDM** **give sth/sb a 'miss** (*Brit infml*) **1** to omit sb/sth: *I think I'll give the fish course a miss.* **2** to decide not to do sth one normally does: *I think I'll give badminton a miss* (ie not play it) *tonight.*

missal /'mɪsl/ *n* a book containing the prayers, etc used at Mass throughout the year in the Roman Catholic Church.

misshapen /ˌmɪs'ʃeɪpən/ *adj* (esp of the body or a limb) not having the normal shape; not formed normally.

missile   missile

missile /'mɪsaɪl; *US* 'mɪsl/ *n* **1** an object or weapon that is thrown or fired at a target: *Missiles hurled at the police included stones and bottles.* ⇨ picture. **2** an explosive weapon directed at a target automatically or by means of an electronic device: *ballistic/ nuclear missiles* ○ *missile bases/sites/launching pads.* ⇨ picture. See also GUIDED MISSILE.

mission /'mɪʃn/ *n* **1** a group of people sent, esp abroad, on political or commercial business: *a British trade mission to China* ○ *go/send sb on a fact-finding mission.* **2(a)** a group of religious people sent esp to remote areas to teach others about Christianity: *a Catholic/Methodist mission in Africa.* **(b)** a building or group of buildings where the work of these people is done: *a mission station/school/ hospital.* **3** a particular task done by a person or a group: *a top-secret mission* ○ *mission control/ headquarters* ○ *The squadron flew a reconnaissance mission.* **4** a particular aim or duty that one wants to fulfil more than anything else: *Her mission in life is to help AIDS victims.*

missionary /'mɪʃənri; *US* -neri/ *n* a person sent to teach the Christian religion to people who are ignorant of it: *Catholic/Anglican missionaries* ○ *missionary work* ○ *speak with missionary zeal* (ie great enthusiasm and faith).

missis = MISSUS.

missive /'mɪsɪv/ *n* (*fml or joc*) a letter, esp a long or official one.

misspell /ˌmɪs'spel/ *v* (*pt, pp* **misspelled** or **misspelt** /-'spelt/) to spell sth wrongly: [Vn] *My name had been misspelt.* ▶ **misspelling** *n*.

misspend /ˌmɪs'spend/ *v* (*pt, pp* **misspent** /-'spent/) (esp passive) to spend or use one's money, time, etc foolishly or wrongly: [Vn] *misspent 'energy* ○ *a ˌmisspent 'youth.*

missus (also **missis**) /'mɪsɪz/ *n* **1** (*infml or joc*) (used after *the, my, your, his*) a person's wife: *How's the missus* (ie your wife)? ○ *My missus hates me smoking indoors.* **2** (*sl*) (used as a form of address to a woman): *Are these your kids, missus?* Compare MISTER 2.

mist /mɪst/ *n* **1** [U, C] a cloud of tiny drops of water hanging just above the ground. Mist is not so thick as FOG but is still difficult to see through: *hills hidden/shrouded in mist* ○ *Mist patches on the roads are making driving difficult.* ○ (*fig*) *The origins of the story are lost in the mists of time.* ○ *She looked at him through a mist of tears.* ⇨ note at FOG. **2** [sing] a fine spray of liquid, eg from an AEROSOL can: *A mist of perfume hung in the air.*
▶ **mist** *v* ~ **(sth) (up)** to cover sth or become covered with tiny drops of water: [Vn, Vnp] *Her breath misted (up) the window-pane.* [Vp] *The mirror has misted up.* [V, Vpr] *His eyes misted (with tears).* **PHRV** **ˌmist 'over** to become covered with mist: *When I drink something hot, my glasses mist over.* ○ *His eyes misted over.*

misty /'mɪsti/ *adj* (**-ier, -iest**) full of or covered with mist; not bright or clear: *a misty morning* ○ *misty weather/hills* ○ *misty rain* ○ *misty eyes/colours.* **mistily** *adv.*

mistake¹ /mɪ'steɪk/ *n* **1** an action or opinion that is foolish or wrong; an error of judgement: *This isn't my bill — there must be some mistake.* ○ *I made a mistake about Julie — she's quite nice really.* ○ *It was a big mistake to send her to boarding-school.* ○ *A week after the wedding she realized she had made a terrible mistake.* **2** a word, figure, sum, etc that is not correct: *spelling mistakes* ○ *The waiter made a mistake in adding up the bill.* **IDM** **and 'no mistake** (*infml*) without any doubt: *She's a strange woman and 'no mistake!* **by mi'stake** accidentally; in error: *I took your bag instead of mine by mistake.* **ˌmake no mi'stake (about sth)** (*infml*) do not be deceived into thinking otherwise: *Make no mistake (about it), we're facing a major financial crisis.*

NOTE Compare **mistake**, **error**, **blunder**, **fault** and **defect**. They all refer to something that has not been done correctly or properly. **Mistake** is the most general and used in most situations: *The letter had quite a few mistakes in it.* ○ *Going on a camping holiday with young children was definitely a mistake.* **Error** is used when talking about calculations, and in technical or formal contexts: *I think there are a few errors in your calculations.* A **blunder** is a stupid or careless and quite serious mistake made because of bad judgement: *A hospital blunder led to 500 cancer patients getting the wrong radiation treatment.*
Fault emphasizes a person's responsibility for a mistake: *Tom broke the window, but it was my fault for letting him play football in the house.* A **fault** can also be an imperfection in a person or thing: *There was a design fault in the train doors.* ○ *I accepted my father's faults because I loved him.* A **defect** is a serious imperfection: *The causes of many birth defects have not yet been discovered.*

mistake² /mɪ'steɪk/ *v* (*pt* **mistook** /mɪ'stʊk/; *pp* **mistaken** /mɪ'steɪkən/) **1** to be wrong or to get a wrong idea about sb/sth: [Vn] *I must have mistaken your meaning/what you meant.* ○ *You can't mistake their house — it's painted bright green.* [Vn-adj] *She mistook his smile as indicating agreement.* [Vn.to inf] *I mistook you to mean that you wanted to come.* **2** ~ **sb/sth for sb/sth** to suppose wrongly that sb/sth is sb/sth else: [Vnpr] *She is often mistaken for her twin* *sister.* **IDM** **there is/was no mistaking sb/sth** there is/was no possibility of being wrong about sb/sth: *There's no mistaking that laugh — it must be John.*

▶ **mistaken** *adj* (**a**) [usu pred] ~ (**about sb/sth**) wrong in one's opinion or judgement: *If I'm not mistaken, that's the man we saw on the bus.* ○ *You're completely mistaken about Peter.* (**b**) based on or resulting from a wrong opinion or bad judgement: *mistaken ideas/views/loyalty* ○ *a case of mistaken identity* ○ *I helped him* **in the mistaken belief that** *he needed me.* **mistakenly** *adv: He mistakenly believed that the insurance policy covered such damage.*

mister /ˈmɪstə(r)/ *n* **1** (the full form, rarely used in writing, of the abbreviation *Mr*). **2** [C] (used as a form of address to a man, esp by children): *Please, mister, can I have my ball back?* Compare MISSUS.

mistime /ˌmɪsˈtaɪm/ *v* (esp passive) to say or do sth at the wrong time: [Vn] *a mistimed* (ie not appropriate) *remark/comment* ○ *a mistimed golf shot.*

mistletoe /ˈmɪsltəʊ, ˈmɪzl-/ *n* [U] a plant with small white berries that grows esp on apple trees and is hung indoors as a Christmas decoration: *the tradition of kissing under the mistletoe.*

mistook *pt* of MISTAKE[2].

mistreat /ˌmɪsˈtriːt/ *v* (esp passive) to treat sb/sth badly or in an unkind way: [Vn] *a horse mistreated by its owner* ○ *I hate to see books being mistreated.* Compare MALTREAT. ▶ **mistreatment** *n* [U].

mistress /ˈmɪstrəs/ *n* **1** a woman in a position of authority or control: *She wants to be mistress of her own affairs* (ie to organize her own life). ○ *She is always mistress of the situation.* **2** (esp formerly) the female head of a household, esp one employing servants: *the mistress of the house* ○ *Lizzie fetched a shawl for her mistress.* Compare MASTER[1] 3. **3** a female owner of a dog or other animal: *Wooffy followed his mistress into the kitchen.* **4** a woman having a secret but regular sexual relationship, esp with a married man: *have/keep a mistress.* Compare LOVER 1. **5** (*esp Brit*) a female teacher in a school: *the* ˈFrench mistress (ie a teacher of French, not necessarily a Frenchwoman) ○ *a ballet mistress.* Compare MASTER[1] 6. **IDM** **one's own master/ mistress** ⇨ MASTER[1].

mistrial /ˌmɪsˈtraɪəl/ *n* (*law*) **1** a trial that is not considered valid because of some error in the proceedings. **2** (*US*) a trial in which the JURY cannot agree on a decision.

mistrust /ˌmɪsˈtrʌst/ *v* **1** to feel no confidence in sb/sth: [Vn] *mistrust one's own judgement.* **2** to be suspicious of sb/sth: [Vn] *mistrust sb's motives.*

▶ **mistrust** *n* [U, sing] ~ (**of sb/sth**) **1** a lack of confidence in sb/sth: *a suspicion of sb/sth: She has a deep mistrust of strangers.* **mistrustful** /-fl/ *adj* ~ (**of sb/sth**): *be mistrustful of sb's motives.* **mistrustfully** /-fəli/ *adv.*

misty ⇨ MIST.

misunderstand /ˌmɪsʌndəˈstænd/ *v* (*pt, pp* -stood /-ˈstʊd/) to interpret words, instructions, motives (MOTIVE), etc wrongly: [Vn] *Don't misunderstand me/ what I'm trying to say.*

▶ **misunderstanding** *n* **1** [U, C] a failure to understand sth correctly or in the right way: *There must be some misunderstanding — I thought I ordered the smaller model.* **2** [C] (*often euph*) a minor disagreement or quarrel: *clear up* (eg by discussion) *a misunderstanding between colleagues* ○ *We had a slight misunderstanding over the bill.*

misunderstood *adj* not appreciated for one's true character or worth: *She felt very alone and misunderstood.*

misuse /ˌmɪsˈjuːz/ *v* [Vn] **1** to use sth in the wrong way or for the wrong purpose: *misuse a word/an expression* ○ *misuse alcohol/public funds.* **2** to treat

sb/sth badly: *The company has misused and taken advantage of me.* Compare ABUSE[1].

▶ **misuse** /ˌmɪsˈjuːs/ *n* [U, C] the use of sth in the wrong way or for the wrong purpose: *the misuse of power/authority* ○ *drug misuse.*

mite[1] /maɪt/ *n* **1** [C] a small child or animal, esp as an object of sympathy: *Poor little mite!* **2** [sing] (*dated*) a very small amount: *offer sb a mite of comfort.*

▶ **a mite** *adv* (*dated infml*) a little; rather: *She seemed a mite reluctant to reply.*

mite[2] /maɪt/ *n* a tiny creature similar to a SPIDER that lives on plants, animals, carpets, etc: *house dust mites.*

mitigate /ˈmɪtɪɡeɪt/ *v* (*fml*) to make sth less severe, violent or painful: [Vn] *mitigate sb's suffering/ anger/anxiety* ○ *mitigate the severity of a punishment* ○ *mitigate the effects of global warming.* Compare MILITATE.

▶ **mitigating** *adj* [attrib] making sth less severe or serious: *mitigating circumstances/factors* (ie those that partially excuse a mistake or crime). **mitigation** /ˌmɪtɪˈɡeɪʃn/ *n* [U]: **In mitigation** (ie In order to make a crime appear less serious), *the lawyer said her client had been deeply depressed.*

mitre (*US* **miter**) /ˈmaɪtə(r)/ *n* **1** a tall pointed hat worn esp by bishops on ceremonial occasions as a symbol of their position and authority. **2** a corner joint of eg two pieces of wood with their ends cut at an angle so that together they form an angle of 90°, as in a picture frame.

▶ **mitre** (*US* **miter**) *v* (esp passive) to join two pieces of wood with a mitre(2): [Vn] *mitred corners.*

mitt /mɪt/ *n* **1** = MITTEN: *oven mitts* (ie for taking hot dishes out of an oven). **2** (in baseball) a large thick leather glove worn for catching the ball. **3** (usu *pl*) (*sl*) a hand: *I'd love to get my mitts on one of those.*

mitten /ˈmɪtn/ (also **mitt**) *n* a type of glove covering four fingers together and the thumb separately. ⇨ picture at GLOVE.

mix[1] /mɪks/ *v* **1**(**a**) ~ A **with B** / ~ A **and B** (**together**) to combine one thing with another; to BLEND things together: [Vnpr] *mix the sugar with the flour* [Vnp] *mix all the ingredients together* [Vn] *If you mix red and yellow, you get orange.* [Vn, Vnpr] (*fig*) *Don't try to* **mix business and/with pleasure.** (**b**) ~ (**with sth**) / ~ (**together**) to be able to be combined: [V] *Oil and water don't mix.* [Vpr] *Oil won't mix with water.* [also Vp]. **2** to make or prepare sth by putting several substances or ingredients together and stirring or shaking them so that they are no longer distinct: [Vn] *mix cement* [Vnn] *He mixed her a gin and tonic.* [Vnpr] *She mixed a drink for me.* **3** ~ (**with sb/sth**) (of people) to come or be together socially: [V] *He finds it hard to mix at parties.* [Vpr] *In my job, I mix with all sorts of people.* See also MIXED 4,5. **IDM** **be/get mixed** ˈup **in sth** (*infml*) to be/become involved in sth, esp sth illegal: *I don't want to get mixed up in the affair.* **be/get mixed** ˈup **with sb** (*infml*) to be/become associated with sb, esp sb dishonest: *How did she get mixed up with somebody like Roger?* **PHRV** ˌ**mix sth** ˈ**in** (esp in cooking) to combine an ingredient with others: *Mix the eggs in slowly.* ˈ**mix sth into sth 1** to add one ingredient to another and combine the two: *mix the yeast into the flour.* **2** to make sth by combining ingredients: *mix the flour and water into a smooth paste.* ˌ**mix sth** ˈ**up** to spoil the order or arrangement of a group of things: *He had mixed up all the papers on my desk.* ˌ**mix sb** ˈ**up** (**about/over sth**) to make sb become confused: *Now you've mixed me up completely!* See also MIXED-UP. ˌ**mix sb/sth** ˈ**up** (**with sb/sth**) to confuse sb/sth with sb/sth else; to be unable to distinguish between people or things: *You're always mixing me up with my sister!* ○ *I got the bags mixed up and gave you mine.*

■ **'mix-up** *n* (*infml*) a confused situation; a mistake: *There's been an awful mix-up over the dates!*

mix² /mɪks/ *n* **1** [C usu *sing*] a group of people or things of different types; a mixture: *a good social/racial mix* (eg in a group of students). **2** [C,U] a mixture of ingredients sold for the specified type of food, etc: *a packet of ᴵcake mix.*

mixed /mɪkst/ *adj* **1** composed of different qualities or elements: *The critics gave the new play a mixed reception* (ie including criticism and praise). ○ *The weather has been very mixed recently.* **2** composed of different varieties of the same thing: *a mixed salad* ○ *mixed herbs* ○ *mixed woodland* (ie of different types of tree). **3** having or showing various races or social classes: *live in a mixed society* ○ *people of mixed race.* **4** of or for members of both sexes: *a mixed school* ○ *mixed company.* **IDM** **have ˌmixed ᴵfeelings (about sb/sth)** to have some good and some bad feelings about sb/sth; to be not sure what one thinks: *She read his letter with mixed feelings.*
■ ˌmixed-aᴵbility *adj* (of a class or way of teaching) containing or for pupils of different levels of ability. ˌmixed ᴵbag *n* (*infml*) a collection of things or people, of very different types: *The competition entries were a very mixed bag.*
ˌmixed ᴵblessing *n* a thing that has advantages and also disadvantages.
ˌmixed ᴵdoubles *n* [sing *v*] a game, esp of tennis, in which a man and a woman play together as partners on each side.
ˌmixed eᴵconomy *n* an economic system in which some parts are owned by the state and others are private.
ˌmixed ᴵfarming *n* [U] the growing of crops as well as the keeping of animals.
ˌmixed ᴵgrill *n* (*Brit*) a dish of various grilled (GRILL 2a) meats and vegetables, etc: *a mixed grill of fried eggs, bacon, sausages, tomatoes and mushrooms.*
ˌmixed ᴵmarriage *n* a marriage between people of different races (RACE³) or religions.
ˌmixed ᴵmetaphor *n* a combination of two or more metaphors (METAPHOR) that do not fit together and therefore produce a ridiculous effect, eg *The hand that rocks the cradle has kicked the bucket.*
ˌmixed-ᴵup *adj* (*infml*) mentally or emotionally confused; having social problems: ˌmixed-up ᴵkids on *drugs* ○ *She felt very mixed-up after the divorce.*

mixer /ᴵmɪksə(r)/ *n* **1** a machine or device for mixing things: *a ceᴵment-mixer* ○ *a ᴵfood-mixer.* **2** (*infml*) a person who is able or unable (as specified) to mix easily with others, eg at parties: *be a good/bad mixer.* **3** a drink without alcohol that can be mixed with alcohol: *use fruit juice as a mixer.* **4** (*techn*) (**a**) (in films and broadcasting) a device that mixes signals going into it in order to produce a single combined sound or picture. (**b**) a person operating such a device: *a sound mixer.*

mixture /ᴵmɪkstʃə(r)/ *n* **1** [C,U] a substance made by mixing other substances together: *add the flour to the cake mixture* ○ *cough mixture* (ie containing several medicines). Compare COMPOUND¹ 1b. **2** [sing] a combination of two or more things or styles that are different: *The city is a mixture of old and new buildings.* ○ *We listened to the news with a mixture of surprise and horror.* ○ (*fig*) *As a nation we are an odd mixture of tolerance and prejudice.* **3** [U] the process of mixing or being mixed.

Mk *abbr* **1** mark (currency): *Mk 300.* **2** (on cars) mark (ie model or type): *Ford Granada Ghia Mk II.*

ml *abbr* (*pl* unchanged or **mls**) **1** (*US* **mi**) mile(s): *distance to village 3 mls.* **2** millilitre(s): *25 ml.*

mm¹ *abbr* (*pl* unchanged or **mms**) millimetre(s): *rainfall 6mm* ○ *a 35mm camera.*

mm² (also **mmm**) /m/ *interj* (used in writing to represent the sound made when expressing approval, agreement, hesitation, doubt, etc): *Mm, lovely cake.* ○ *Mmm? I'm sorry, I wasn't listening.*

mnemonic /nɪˈmɒnɪk/ *adj* designed to help the memory: *mnemonic verses* (eg for remembering spelling or grammar rules) ○ *a mnemonic device.*
▶ **mnemonic** *n* [C] a word, designed to help the memory: *SPIDER is a mnemonic for teachers: it stands for Solving problems, Practical work, Investigation, Discussion, Exposition, Routine skills.*

MO /ˌem ˈəʊ/ *abbr* Medical Officer, in the army, etc.

mo /məʊ/ *n* [sing] (*Brit infml*) a short period of time; a moment: *Wait a mo, I'm not quite ready.*

moan /məʊn/ *n* **1(a)** [C] a long low sad sound, usu expressing regret, pain or suffering: *the moans of the wounded.* (**b**) [sing] a similar sound as made by eg the wind: *hear the moan of the wind in the trees.* **2** [C] (*infml*) a complaint about sth: *We had a good moan about the weather.*
▶ **moan** *v* **1(a)** to produce moans or to say sth with moans: [V] *He lay on the floor moaning.* [V.speech] *'Where's the doctor?' he moaned.* (**b**) to make a moaning sound: [Vpr] *The wind was moaning through the trees.* [also V]. **2** ~ (**about sth**) (*infml*) to complain about sth: [V] *Do stop moaning and groaning all the time.* [Vpr, Vp] *He's always moaning (on) about how poor he is.*

moat /məʊt/ *n* a deep wide ditch that was dug around a castle, etc and filled with water, to protect it from enemies. ⇨ picture at CASTLE.
▶ **moated** *adj* having a moat: *a moated manor house.*

mob /mɒb/ *n* **1** [CGp] a large crowd of people, esp one that may become violent or cause trouble: *a hostile/jeering mob* ○ *An excited mob of fans rushed onto the pitch.* ○ **mob rule** (ie that is forced on others by a mob). **2** [C esp *sing*] (*infml*) a group of people engaged in a similar, esp criminal, activity; a gang.
▶ **mob** *v* (**-bb-**) (esp passive) to gather in a noisy crowd round sb either to attack or admire them: [Vn] *a pop singer mobbed by hysterical fans.*

mobile /ᴵməʊbaɪl; *US* -bl/ *adj* **1(a)** that can move or be moved easily and quickly from place to place: *a mobile phone* ○ *a mobile shop/library* (ie one inside a vehicle) ○ *a kitchen specially designed for the elderly or people who are less mobile.* (**b**) (of people) able to change class, occupation or place of residence easily: *a mobile work-force.* Compare STATIONARY. **2** (of a face, its features, etc) changing shape or expression easily and often. **3** [pred] (*infml*) having transport, esp a car: *Can you give me a lift if you're mobile?*
▶ **mobile** *n* a light ornamental hanging structure of metal, plastic, cardboard, etc, whose parts move freely in currents of air: *hang a mobile in a child's bedroom.*
mobility /məʊˈbɪləti/ *n* [U] the quality of being mobile. **moˈbility allowance** *n* (*Brit*) money from the government paid to sb with a DISABILITY to help them move around.
ˌmobile ᴵhome *n* a large CARAVAN(1a) that can be pulled behind a vehicle but is normally parked in one place and used as a home.

mobilize, -ise /ᴵməʊbəlaɪz/ *v* **1** to become or make sb/sth ready for service or action, esp in war: [V] *The troops received orders to mobilize.* [Vn] *Mobilize the troops!* **2** to organize sb/sth for a particular purpose: [Vn] *mobilize local residents to oppose the new development.* ▶ **mobilization, -isation** /ˌməʊbəlaɪˈzeɪʃn; *US* -lə'z-/ *n* [U]: *mobilization orders.*

mobster /ᴵmɒbstə(r)/ *n* a member of a gang of criminals.

moccasin /ᴵmɒkəsɪn/ *n* a flat shoe made from soft leather.

mocha /ᴵmɒkə; *US* ᴵməʊkə/ *n* [U] a type of fine coffee.

mock /mɒk/ *v* **1** ~ (**at sb/sth**) to laugh at sb/sth in

M

an unkind way; to make sb seem ridiculous, esp by
copying what they say or do: [V] *a mocking smile/
voice/laugh* [Vn] *mock sb's fears/efforts/attempts.* **2**
(*fml*) to show no respect for or fear of sb/sth; to DEFY
sb/sth: [Vn] *The heavy steel doors seemed to mock
our attempts to open them.*
▶ *adj* [attrib] (**a**) not real: *a mock battle/exam* (eg
for training or practice). (**b**) not genuine: *mock
sympathy/fear/surprise/modesty.*
mocker *n.*
mockingly *adv.*
■ **'mock-up** *n* **1** a complete model or copy of sth
made for testing, etc: *a mock-up car/submarine.* **2**
an arrangement of text, pictures, etc of sth to be
printed: *do a mock-up of a book cover.*

mockery /'mɒkəri/ *n* **1** [U] the action of mocking
sb/sth: *His smile was full of mockery.* **2** [C] ~ (**of
sth**) a worthless action or ridiculous representation
of sth: *a political system that is a mockery of democracy.* **3** [sing] a person or thing that is mocked; an
occasion when this happens. **IDM** **make a 'mockery of sth** to make sth appear foolish or worthless:
The trial made a mockery of justice.

mockingbird /'mɒkɪŋbɜːd/ *n* a black and white
American bird that can copy the songs of other
birds.

mod /mɒd/ *n* (*Brit*) a member of a group of young
people, prominent in Britain in the 1960s. Mods
liked to wear neat and fashionable clothes and to
ride motor scooters (MOTOR). Compare ROCKER.

MOD /ˌem əʊ 'diː/ *abbr* (in Britain) Ministry of
Defence.

modal /'məʊdl/ (also **modal 'verb, modal au'xiliary,
modal au'xiliary verb**) *n* (*grammar*) a verb that is
used with another verb (not a modal) to express
possibility, permission, obligation, etc. Compare
AUXILIARY *n* 3. ▶ **modal** *adj.*

NOTE The **modal verbs** are **can, could, may,
might, must, ought to, shall, should, will** and
would. Dare, need and **used to** also share some of
the features of modal verbs.
  Modal verbs have no '**s**' added to the 3rd person
singular form: *He can speak three languages.* ○ *She
will try and visit tomorrow.*
  Modal verbs are followed by the infinitive of another verb without **to**. The exceptions are **ought to**
and **used to**: *You must find a job.* ○ *You ought to stop
smoking.* ○ *I used to smoke but I gave up two years
ago.*
  Questions are formed without **do/does** in the present, or **did** in the past: *Should I invite Mary?* ○
Should I have invited Mary?
  Negative sentences are formed with **not** or the
short form **n't** and do not use **do/does** or **did**.
  At the dictionary entries for **can, dare, may,
might, must, need, shall** and **should** there are
notes which give help with how to use them.

mod cons /ˌmɒd 'kɒnz/ *n* [pl] (*Brit infml or joc*)
(used esp in advertisements) modern facilities in a
house, eg hot water, electricity, heating, telephone,
which make the house easier and more comfortable
to live in: *a house with all mod cons.*

mode /məʊd/ *n* **1** ~ (**of sth**) (**a**) (*fml*) a way or
manner in which sth happens or is done: *a mode of
action/dress/existence/operation/production/thought*
○ *Take the cheapest mode of transport.* (**b**) (*infml*) a
way of feeling or behaving: *be in holiday/work
mode.* **2** (usu *sing*) a style or a fashion in clothes,
art, drama, etc: *dress in romantic mode.* **3** (*techn*)
any of several arrangements of musical notes, eg the
major or minor scale¹(6) system in modern music. **4**
an arrangement or a setting of equipment to per-

form a certain task: *manual or automatic mode* (eg
on a camera).

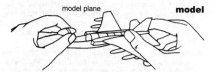
model plane   **model**

model¹ /'mɒdl/ *n* **1**(**a**) a representation of sth, usu
smaller than the original: *a model of the proposed
airport* ○ *a model train/aeroplane/car* ○ *construct a
scale model of the Eiffel Tower.* ⇨ picture. (**b**) a
design of sth that is made so that it can be copied in
another material: *a clay/wax model for a statue* (eg
to be copied in stone or metal). **2** a particular
design or type of product: *This year's new models
will be on display at the motor show.* ○ *This is the
most popular model in our whole range.* **3** a simple
description of a system, used for explaining, calculating, etc sth: *a model of a molecule* ○ *a statistical/
mathematical model* (eg used to forecast future
trends (TREND)). **4** a system used as a basis for a
copy; a pattern: *The nation's constitution provided a
model that other countries followed.* **5** ~ (**of sth**)
(*approv*) a person or thing regarded as an excellent
example to copy: *a model of tact/fairness/accuracy* ○
a model student/husband/teacher ○ *model behaviour*
○ *a model farm/prison* (ie one that has been specially
designed to be very efficient). **6**(**a**) a person employed to be painted, drawn, photographed, etc by
an artist or a photographer. (**b**) a person employed
to display clothes, hats, etc to possible buyers by
wearing them: *a 'fashion model* ○ *one of the country's
top models.* **7** a garment, hat, etc by a famous designer or a copy of this: *wear the latest Paris models.*

model² /'mɒdl/ *v* (**-ll-**; *US* **-l-**) **1** ~ **oneself/sth on
sb/sth** to take sb/sth as an example for one's action,
plans, etc: *As a young actor he modelled himself on
Olivier.* ○ *a design modelled on classical Greek architecture.* **2** to work as a model¹(6); to display clothes,
hats, etc by wearing them: [Vn] *She models swimwear in her spare time.* [also V]. **3** to make a model
of sth in clay, wax, etc; to shape clay, wax, etc to
form sth: [Vn, Vpr] *modelling (in) plasticine* [Vnpr] *a
bust modelled in clay.*
▶ **modelling** (*US* **modeling**) *n* [U] **1** the art of
making models (MODEL¹ 1a): *architectural/clay modelling* ○ *a realistic result achieved* ○ *by skilful
modelling.* **2** working as a model¹(6): *take up a
career in modelling* ○ *a modelling agency.*

modem /'məʊdem/ *n* a device linking a computer
system and eg a telephone line so that data can be
transmitted at high speeds from one computer to
another.

moderate¹ /'mɒdərət/ *adj* **1** average in amount,
intensity, quality, etc; not extreme: *moderate price
increases* ○ *travelling at a moderate speed* ○ *a
moderate-sized bathroom* ○ *a moderate breeze* (ie a
wind of medium strength). **2** not politically extreme: *a man with moderate views* ○ *moderate
policies.* **3** keeping or kept within limits that are not
excessive: *a moderate drinker* ○ *moderate wage demands.*
▶ **moderate** /'mɒdərət/ *n* a person with moderate
opinions, esp in politics.
moderately *adv* to a moderate extent; not very;
quite: *a moderately good performance* ○ *He enjoyed
the work and was moderately good at it.* ○ *She only
did moderately well in the exam.*

moderate² /'mɒdəreɪt/ *v* to become or to make sb/
sth become less intense, extreme or violent: [Vn]
exercise a moderating influence on sb ○ *He must learn
to moderate his temper.* [V] *The wind has moderated.*

M

moderation /ˌmɒdəˈreɪʃn/ n [U] the quality of being moderate; freedom from excess; restraint: *They showed a remarkable degree of moderation in not quarrelling publicly.* **IDM** **in mode'ration** (of eating, drinking alcohol, etc) in a moderate manner; not excessively: *Whisky can be good for you if taken in moderation.*

moderator /ˈmɒdəreɪtə(r)/ n **1** a person who makes sure that both sides in a dispute are represented fairly. **2** a person who makes sure that the same standards are used by different people marking an examination. **3** a Presbyterian minister[1](3) in charge of a church court.

modern /ˈmɒdn/ adj **1** [attrib] of the present or recent times; CONTEMPORARY(2): *modern European history* (eg from about 1475) ○ *Unemployment is one of the major problems of the modern world.* **2** (*usu approv*) using or having the newest methods, equipment, buildings, etc: *modern marketing techniques* ○ *one of the most modern shopping complexes in the country.* **3** [attrib] of a current or recent style of art, fashion, etc, esp one that is attempting sth new and not traditional: *modern architecture/dance.* ⇨ note at NEW.
▶ **modernity** /məˈdɜːnəti/ n [U] (*fml*) the condition of being modern: *the spread of modernity.*
■ ˌ**modern 'language** n a language that is spoken or written now, esp a European language, eg French, German, Spanish or Italian: *study modern languages at university.*

modernism /ˈmɒdənɪzəm/ n [U] modern ideas or methods in contrast to traditional ones, esp in art or religion.
▶ **modernist** /ˈmɒdənɪst/ n a believer in or supporter of modernism. — adj [attrib] of or associated with modernism: *modernist fiction.* **modernistic** /ˌmɒdəˈnɪstɪk/ adj modern in a very noticeable way: *modernistic furniture designs.*

modernize, -ise /ˈmɒdənaɪz/ v **1** to change sth so that it is suitable for modern needs or habits: [Vn] *modernize a transport system/a factory/farming methods* ○ *a fully modernized office.* **2** to adopt modern ways or ideas: [V] *If the industry doesn't modernize it will not survive.* ▶ **modernization, -isation** /ˌmɒdənaɪˈzeɪʃn; US -nə'z-/ n [U]: *the modernization of the telephone system* ○ *embark on a major modernization programme.*

modest /ˈmɒdɪst/ adj **1(a)** not large in amount, size, etc; moderate: *live on a modest income* ○ *make very modest demands* ○ *a modest improvement/success/increase.* **(b)** not particularly large, expensive or elaborate: *live in a modest little house.* **2(a)** ~ (about sth) (*approv*) not talking much or boasting about one's abilities, qualities, etc: *be modest about one's achievements* ○ *a quiet and modest man.* **(b)** rather shy: *a modest smile/suggestion.* **3** (esp of women's clothes) not emphasizing the figure or attracting attention: *a modest dress/neckline.*
▶ **modestly** adv: *be modestly dressed* ○ *'It's not as good a photo as yours,' she said modestly.*
modesty /ˈmɒdəsti/ n [U] (*usu approv*) the state of being modest: *the modesty of his political aspirations* ○ *He always detested false (ie pretended) modesty.*

modicum /ˈmɒdɪkəm/ n [sing] ~ (of sth) a small or moderate amount of sth: *His statement contains a modicum of truth.*

modify /ˈmɒdɪfaɪ/ v (*pt, pp* **-fied**) [Vn] **1** to change sth slightly, esp to improve it or make it less extreme: *The union has been forced to modify its position.* ○ *The equipment has been modified to suit local requirements.* ⇨ note at CHANGE[1]. **2** (*grammar*) (esp of an *adj* or *adv*) to limit the sense of another word: *In 'walk slowly' the adverb 'slowly' modifies the verb 'walk'.*
▶ **modification** /ˌmɒdɪfɪˈkeɪʃn/ n **(a)** [U] the action or process of modifying sth or of being modified: *The design of the spacecraft is undergoing extensive modification.* **(b)** [C] a usu small change made to sth: *The plan was approved, with some minor modifications.*

modifier /-faɪə(r)/ n (*grammar*) a word or phrase that modifies (MODIFY 2) another word or phrase.

modish /ˈməʊdɪʃ/ adj (*sometimes derog*) fashionable.

modulate /ˈmɒdjuleɪt; US -dʒə-/ v **1** to vary the strength, volume or pitch[1](2) of one's voice: [Vn] *the actor's clearly modulated tones.* **2** ~ (from sth) (to sth) (*techn*) to change from one musical key to another: [Vpr] *modulate from C major to A minor* [also V]. **3** (*fml*) to adjust or change sth: [Vn] *modulate a current/radio signal.* ▶ **modulation** /ˌmɒdjuˈleɪʃn; US -dʒə[1]-/ n [C, U].

module /ˈmɒdjuːl; US -dʒuːl/ n **1(a)** any one of a set of parts or units that are made separately and can be joined together to construct a building or piece of furniture. **(b)** a unit of a computer PROGRAM(1) that has a particular function: *a tutorial module.* **2** a unit of a spacecraft that can function independently of the main body: *the command module* (ie for the ASTRONAUT in command). **3** any one of several independent units that together form a course of study at a college or university.
▶ **modular** /ˈmɒdjələ(r); US -dʒə-/ adj **1** using a module or modules as the basis of design or construction: *modular components* ○ *modular furniture.* **2** (of a course of study) composed of separate units from which students may select a specified number.

modus operandi /ˌməʊdəs ˌɒpəˈrændiː/ n [sing] (*Latin*) a particular method of working or dealing with a task: *A chaotic hubbub of creativity was the paper's modus operandi.*

modus vivendi /ˌməʊdəs vɪˈvendiː/ n [sing] (*Latin*) a practical arrangement by which people who are quarrelling can continue to live or work together while waiting for their dispute to be settled: *We managed to achieve a kind of modus vivendi.*

moggie (also **moggy**) /ˈmɒgi/ n (*Brit infml*) a cat.

mogul /ˈməʊgl/ n a very rich, important or influential person: *Hollywood/movie/media moguls.*

mohair /ˈməʊheə(r)/ n [U] the fine soft hair of the ANGORA goat, used to make cloth or wool: *a mohair sweater.*

Mohammed = MUHAMMAD.

Mohican /məʊˈhiːkən/ n a member of a N American Indian people.
▶ **Mohican** adj **1** of or relating to the Mohicans. **2** having the hair completely off shaved except for a strip over the centre of the head from the front to the back.

moist /mɔɪst/ adj slightly wet: *moist eyes/lips* ○ *a rich moist fruit cake* ○ *Water the plant regularly to keep the soil moist.*
▶ **moisten** /ˈmɔɪsn/ v to become or make sth moist: [Vnpr] *a cloth moistened with water* [Vn, Vnpr] *She moistened her lips (with her tongue).* [also V].

moisture /ˈmɔɪstʃə(r)/ n [U] tiny drops of water on a surface, in the air, etc: *The rubber seal is designed to keep out moisture.*
▶ **moisturize, -ise** /ˈmɔɪstʃəraɪz/ v to make the skin less dry by the use of beauty creams: [Vn] *moisturizing lotion.* **moisturizer, -iser** n [C, U] a cream used for moisturizing the skin.

molar /ˈməʊlə(r)/ n any of the teeth at the back of the jaw used for crushing and chewing (CHEW) food: *upper/lower molars.* ⇨ picture at TOOTH.

molasses /məˈlæsɪz/ n [U] **1** a thick dark sweet liquid obtained from sugar while it is being refined. **2** (*US*) TREACLE.

mold (*US*) = MOULD[3]. ⇨ picture at MOULD[1].

moldering (*US*) = MOULDERING.

molding (*US*) = MOULDING.

moldy (*US*) = MOULDY.

mole[1] /məʊl/ n a small, permanent, sometimes

[V.*to* inf] = verb + *to* infinitive   [Vn.inf (no *to*)] = verb + noun + infinitive without *to*   [V.*ing*] = verb + *-ing* form

raised, dark spot on the human skin. Compare FRECKLE.

mole² /məʊl/ n **1** a small animal with dark grey fur and tiny eyes that digs tunnels under the ground to live in. **2** (*infml*) a person who works within an organization and secretly passes private and important information to another organization or country: *The authorities believe there is a mole at the Treasury.* Compare SPY.

molecule /ˈmɒlɪkjuːl/ n the smallest unit, usu consisting of a group of atoms, into which a substance can be divided without a change in its chemical nature: *A molecule of water consists of two atoms of hydrogen and one atom of oxygen.*
▸ **molecular** /məˈlekjələ(r)/ *adj* [attrib] of or relating to molecules: *molecular structure/weight* ∘ *molecular biology* .

molehill /ˈməʊlhɪl/ n a small pile of earth thrown up on the surface of the ground by a MOLE²(1) digging underground. **IDM** **make a mountain out of a molehill** ⇨ MOUNTAIN.

moleskin /ˈməʊlskɪn/ n [U] a type of strong cotton cloth with a soft surface, used for making clothes: *moleskin trousers.*

molest /məˈlest/ v (**a**) to treat sb aggressively, often causing them injury: [Vn] *an old man molested and robbed by a gang of youths.* (**b**) to attack or interfere with sb, esp a woman or child, sexually: [Vn] *He was found guilty of molesting a young girl.* ▸ **molestation** /ˌməʊleˈsteɪʃn/ n [U]. **molester** /məˈlestə(r)/ n: *a child molester.*

moll /mɒl/ n (*sl*) a female companion of a criminal.

mollify /ˈmɒlɪfaɪ/ v (*pt, pp* **-fied**) to reduce sb's anger; to make sb calmer: [Vn] *the need to mollify disgruntled customers.*

mollusc (*US* also **mollusk**) /ˈmɒləsk/ n any of the class of animals that have a soft body, no BACKBONE, and usu a hard shell: *freshwater molluscs such as snails and clams.*

mollycoddle /ˈmɒlikɒdl/ v (*derog*) to treat sb/sth with too much kindness and protection: [Vn] *He doesn't believe that children should be mollycoddled.*

Molotov cocktail /ˌmɒlətɒf ˈkɒkteɪl/ n a type of simple bomb that consists of a bottle filled with petrol.

molt (*US*) ⇨ MOULT.

molten /ˈməʊltən/ *adj* [usu attrib] melted or made liquid by heating to a very high temperature: *molten rock/metal/lava.*

mom /mɒm/ n (*US infml*) = MUM¹.

moment /ˈməʊmənt/ n **1** [C] a very brief period of time: *He thought for a moment before replying.* ∘ *It was all over in a few moments.* ∘ *She answered without a moment's hesitation.* ∘ *Could you wait a moment, please?* ∘ *One moment, please* (ie Please wait a short time). ∘ *I'll be back in a moment* (ie very soon). ∘ *We arrived not a moment too soon* (ie It was almost too late when we arrived). **2** [sing] an exact point in time: *the moment of birth* ∘ *At that (very) moment the phone rang.* ∘ *From this moment on* (ie After this) *she began to be afraid of him.* **3** [C] a time for doing sth; an occasion: *wait for the right moment* ∘ *Is this a suitable moment to discuss my salary?* **IDM** **any minute/moment** ⇨ MINUTE¹. **at the ˈmoment** at the present time; now: *Her extension is engaged at the moment. Would you like to hold or try again later?* ∘ *He's unemployed at the moment and has been for over six months.* **at short / at a moment's notice** ⇨ NOTICE. **for the ˈmoment/ˈpresent** temporarily; for now: *We're happy living in a studio for the moment but we'll want somewhere bigger one day.* **have one's/its ˈmoments** (*infml*) to have short periods that are better, more interesting, etc than usual: *The play had its moments but overall it was very disappointing.* **in the heat of the**

moment ⇨ HEAT¹. **just a minute/moment/second** ⇨ JUST². **the last minute/moment** ⇨ LAST¹. **the man, woman, boy, girl, etc of the ˈmoment** a person who is currently being talked about a lot, treated as important, etc. **the minute/moment…** ⇨ MINUTE¹. **the ˌmoment of ˈtruth** a time of crisis or testing when important decisions have to be made. **not for a/one minute/moment** ⇨ MINUTE¹. **of ˈmoment** (*fml*) very important: *These are matters of great moment.* **on the spur of the moment** ⇨ SPUR. **the psychological moment** ⇨ PSYCHOLOGICAL.

momentary /ˈməʊməntri; *US* -teri/ *adj* lasting for a very short time: *a momentary pause/interruption* ∘ *momentary regret/relief.*
▸ **momentarily** /ˈməʊməntrəli; *US* ˌməʊmənˈterəli/ *adv* **1** for a very short time: *pause momentarily.* **2** (*esp US*) very soon; immediately: *The doctor will see you momentarily.*

momentous /məˈmentəs, məʊˈm-/ *adj* very important; serious: *a momentous decision/occasion* ∘ *momentous changes.*

momentum /məˈmentəm, məʊˈm-/ n [U] **1** a force that increases the rate of development of a process: *The campaign for political change is gaining/gathering momentum.* **2** (*physics*) the quantity of motion of a moving object, measured as its mass¹(5) multiplied by its speed.

momma /ˈmɒmə/ (also **mommy** /ˈmɒmi/) n (*US infml*) = MUMMY¹.

Mon *abbr* Monday: *Mon 21 June.*

monarch /ˈmɒnək/ n a supreme ruler such as a king or queen: *the reigning monarch.*
▸ **monarchical** /məˈnɑːkɪkl/ *adj* [attrib] of a monarch or monarchy: *monarchical rule.*
monarchist /ˈmɒnəkɪst/ n a person who believes that a country should be ruled by a monarch.
monarchy /ˈmɒnəki/ n (**a**) (usu **the monarchy** [sing]) a system of government by a monarch: *plans to abolish the monarchy.* (**b**) [C] a country governed by such a system: *The United Kingdom is a constitutional monarchy.* Compare REPUBLIC.

monastery /ˈmɒnəstri; *US* -teri/ n a building in which monks live as a community. Compare CONVENT, NUNNERY.

monastic /məˈnæstɪk/ *adj* **1** of or relating to monks or monasteries (MONASTERY): *a monastic community.* **2** like life in a monastery; simple and quiet: *lead a monastic life.*
▸ **monasticism** /məˈnæstɪsɪzəm/ n [U] the way of life of monks in monasteries.

Monday /ˈmʌndeɪ, -di/ n [C, U] (*abbr* **Mon**) the second day of the week, next after Sunday: *He was born on a Monday.* ∘ *We went on the Monday and came home on the Friday* (ie on those days in a particular week). ∘ *last/next Monday* ∘ *the Monday before last* ∘ *'What's today?' 'It's Monday.'* ∘ *We'll meet on Monday.* ∘ *(Brit infml or US) We'll meet Monday* (ie on the day before next Tuesday). ∘ *'When did they meet?' '(On) Monday* (ie On the day before last Tuesday).' ∘ *I work Monday(s) to Friday(s).* ∘ *(On) Monday(s)* (ie Every Monday) *I play badminton.* ∘ *I always play badminton on a Monday.* ∘ *Monday morning/afternoon/evening* ∘ *(Brit) Monday week* (ie a week after next Monday).

monetary /ˈmʌnɪtri; *US* -teri/ *adj* [attrib] of money or currency: *the government's monetary policy* ∘ *the international monetary system* ∘ *The monetary unit of Japan is the yen.*
▸ **monetarism** /-tərɪzəm/ n [U] the policy of controlling the amount of money available as the chief method of creating or maintaining a strong economy. **monetarist** /-tərɪst/ n a person who favours monetarism. — *adj: monetarist policies.*

money /ˈmʌni/ n (*pl* in sense 4 **moneys** or **monies**) **1** [U] a means of payment, esp coins and paper notes (NOTE¹ 4), given and accepted in buying and selling:

M

have money in one's pocket ○ *earn/borrow/save/ spend/raise a lot of money* ○ *change English money into French money/francs* ○ *How much money is there in my (bank) account?* **2** [U] wealth; the total value of sb's property: *inherit money from sb* ○ *lose all one's money.* **3** [U] (*infml*) payment for work; wages: *pay/ earn good money* ○ *It's quite interesting work and the money's all right.* **4** (**moneys** or **monies**) [pl] (*arch or law*) a sum of money: *to collect all monies due.* **IDM** **be in the ˈmoney** (*infml*) to have a lot of money to spend; to be rich. **easy money** ⇨ EASY[1]. **even money** ⇨ EVEN[2]. **for ˈmy money** (*infml*) in my opinion: *For my money, he's one of the greatest comedians of all time.* **get one's ˈmoney's-worth 1** to get the full value in goods or services for the money one has spent. **2** to get the most satisfaction, enjoyment, etc out of sth. **give sb a run for their money** ⇨ RUN[2]. **good ˈmoney** a lot of money; money that is earned with hard work and not to be wasted: *I paid good money for that car and it broke down on the first day!* **have a good, etc run for one's money** ⇨ RUN[2]. **have money to ˈburn** to have so much money that one can spend it freely. **ˈmade of money** (*infml*) very wealthy: *I'm not made of money, you know!* **make ˈmoney** to make a profit; to earn a lot of money. **marry money** ⇨ MARRY. **money burns a ˈhole in sb's pocket** sb is eager to spend money or spends it quickly or extravagantly. **money for ˈjam / old ˈrope** (*Brit infml*) money or profit earned from doing sth that requires very little effort. **money ˈtalks** (*saying*) wealthy people can get special treatment and influence others. **not for love or money** ⇨ LOVE[1]. **pots of money** ⇨ POT[1]. **put ˈmoney into sth** to invest money in an enterprise, etc: *put money into a new business.* **put one's ˈmoney on sb/sth 1** to place a bet that a horse, dog, etc will win a race. **2** confidently expect sb/sth to succeed: *I'd put my money on Bill every time.* **put one's money where one's ˈmouth is** (*infml*) to show support in a practical way, not just by talking about it. **see the colour of sb's money** ⇨ COLOUR[1]. **throw one's ˈmoney about** (*infml*) to spend one's money in a careless and obvious way. See also BLOOD-MONEY, DANGER MONEY, HUSH MONEY, PIN-MONEY, POCKET-MONEY.
► **moneyed** /ˈmʌnid/ *adj* (*dated*) having a lot of money; wealthy: *the moneyed classes.*
■ **ˌmoney-back guaranˈtee** *n* a guarantee to return the money paid for sth if it is not satisfactory.
ˈmoney-box *n* (*esp Brit*) a small closed box with a narrow opening, into which coins are put as a way of saving money.
ˈmoney-maker *n* (*infml usu approv*) a product or business, etc that produces a large profit. **ˈmoney-making** *adj, n* [U]: *money-making opportunities.*
ˈmoney market *n* (esp *pl*) (*techn*) an institution, such as a bank, that deals in short-term (SHORT[1]) loans, foreign exchange, etc: *The pound had a steady day on the money markets.*
ˈmoney order *n* an official document for payment of a specified sum of money issued by a bank or post office (POST[3]).
ˈmoney-spinner *n* (*infml*) a thing that earns a lot of money: *Her last book was a real money-spinner.*
the ˈmoney supply *n* the total amount of money that exists in the economy of a country at a particular time: *control/reduce/increase the money supply.*

moneybags /ˈmʌnibægz/ *n* (*pl* unchanged) (*infml esp derog*) a rich person.

moneylender /ˈmʌnilendə(r)/ *n* a person whose business is lending money, usu at a high rate of interest[1](5).

mongol /ˈmɒŋgəl/ *n* (*offensive*) a person suffering from DOWN'S SYNDROME. ► **mongolism** /-ɪzəm/ *n* [U] (*offensive*) = DOWN'S SYNDROME.

mongoose /ˈmɒŋguːs/ *n* (*pl* **mongooses** /-sɪz/) a

mongoose

small tropical animal with fur that kills snakes, birds, rats, etc. ⇨ picture.

mongrel /ˈmʌŋgrəl/ *n* a dog of mixed breed.

monitor /ˈmɒnɪtə(r)/ *n* **1** a device used for observing, recording or testing sth: *a heart monitor* ○ *a monitor for radioactivity.* **2(a)** a VIDEO(2b) or television screen. **(b)** a computer screen. ⇨ picture at COMPUTER. **3** (*fem* **monitress** /ˈmɒnɪtrəs/) (*becoming dated*) a pupil with special duties in a school, eg helping a teacher in various ways. **4** a person who listens to and reports on foreign radio broadcasts and signals.
► **monitor** *v* **1** to watch and check sth over a period of time: [Vn] *monitor sb's performance/progress* ○ *monitor a patient's pulse.* **2** [Vn] to listen to and report on foreign radio broadcasts and signals.

monk /mʌŋk/ *n* a member of a religious community of men who live apart from the rest of society and who have made solemn promises, esp that they will not marry and will not have any possessions. Compare FRIAR, NUN.
► **monkish** *adj* of or like monks.

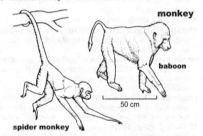
monkey
baboon
50 cm
spider monkey

monkey /ˈmʌŋki/ *n* **1** a member of the group of animals most similar to humans in appearance, esp a type with a long tail that climbs trees. ⇨ picture. **2** (*infml*) a lively, playful and sometimes annoying child: *Come here at once, you little monkey!*
► **monkey** *v* **PHRV** **ˌmonkey aˈbout/aˈround** (*infml*) to behave in a silly playful way: *Stop monkeying about!* **monkey about/around with sth** (*infml*) to play or to interfere with sth in a careless way: *monkey about with a fire extinguisher.*
■ **ˈmonkey business** *n* [U] suspicious or dishonest activities or behaviour: *There's been some monkey business going on here!*
ˈmonkey wrench *n* a tool that can be adjusted to grip or turn things of different widths. ⇨ picture at SPANNER.

mono /ˈmɒnəʊ/ *adj* of sound produced or recorded using only one sound channel: *a mono record/ recording/signal.* ► **mono** *n* [U]: *recorded in mono.* Compare STEREO.

mon(o)- *comb form* one; single: *monogamy* ○ *monomania* ○ *monorail.*

monochrome /ˈmɒnəkrəʊm/ *adj* **1** having or using images in black, white and shades of grey; black and white: *a monochrome photograph/print/ drawing* ○ *a monochrome television.* **2** having or using different shades of one colour: *a monochrome tapestry depicting a sunset.* ► **monochrome** *n* [U, C]: *painting in monochrome* ○ *illustrated with drab monochrome.*

monocle /ˈmɒnəkl/ *n* a single glass LENS for one

eye, kept in position by the muscles round the eye: *wear a monocle.*

monocotyledon /ˌmɒnəˌkɒtɪˈliːdən/ *n* (*botany*) a flowering plant that has one leaf growing from the seed at the first stage of growth.

monogamy /məˈnɒɡəmi/ *n* [U] the practice or custom of being married to only one person at a time. Compare POLYGAMY. ▸ **monogamous** /məˈnɒɡəməs/ *adj.*

monogram /ˈmɒnəɡræm/ *n* two or more letters, esp the first letters of a person's name, combined in one design and marked on items of clothing, etc. ▸ **monogrammed** *adj: a monogrammed shirt.* ⇨ picture.

monogram

monograph /ˈmɒnəɡrɑːf; *US* -ɡræf/ *n* a detailed written study of a single subject, usu appearing as a short book.

monolingual /ˌmɒnəˈlɪŋɡwəl/ *adj* speaking or using only one language: *a monolingual dictionary.* Compare BILINGUAL, MULTILINGUAL.

monolith /ˈmɒnəlɪθ/ *n* **1** a large single upright block of stone, usu shaped into a pillar or monument. **2** (*often derog*) a single huge organization, etc that never seems to change: *world banking monoliths.* ▸ **monolithic** /ˌmɒnəˈlɪθɪk/ *adj: a monolithic monument ∘ the monolithic structure of the state.*

monologue (*US* also **monolog**) /ˈmɒnəlɒɡ; *US* -lɔːɡ/ *n* **1** [C] a long speech by one person in a conversation. **2** [C,U] (**a**) a long speech in a play, film, etc spoken by one actor, esp when alone. (**b**) a dramatic story, esp in verse, told or performed by one person. Compare DIALOGUE, SOLILOQUY.

monoplane /ˈmɒnəpleɪn/ *n* an aircraft with only one set of wings. Compare BIPLANE.

monopolize, -ise /məˈnɒpəlaɪz/ *v* to have or take the greatest share of sth, so preventing others from sharing it; to dominate sth: [Vn] *monopolize a conversation ∘ try to monopolize the supply of oil* ∘ (*fig*) *Don't monopolize our guest — there are others who would like to talk to her.* ▸ **monopolization, -isation** /məˌnɒpəlaɪˈzeɪʃn; *US* -lə'z-/ *n* [U].

monopoly /məˈnɒpəli/ *n* **1** (*commerce*) (**a**) ~ (in/on sth) the sole³(2) right to supply or trade in particular goods or a particular service: *gain/hold/secure a monopoly.* (**b**) goods or a service controlled in this way: *In some countries tobacco is a government monopoly.* Compare DUOPOLY. **2** (usu *sing*) ~ in/of/on sth the sole³(2) possession or control of sth: *A good education should not be the monopoly of the rich. ∘ You can't have a complete monopoly of the car — I need to use it occasionally.* ▸ **monopolist** /-lɪst/ *n* a person or company that has a monopoly. **monopolistic** /məˌnɒpəˈlɪstɪk/ *adj* of or having a monopoly: *monopolistic practices.*

monorail /ˈmɒnəʊreɪl/ *n* [U,C] a railway system in which trains travel along a track consisting of a single rail usu placed high above the ground.

monosyllable /ˈmɒnəsɪləbl/ *n* a word with only one syllable, eg 'it' or 'no': *speak in monosyllables* (eg when not wanting to talk to sb). ▸ **monosyllabic** /ˌmɒnəsɪˈlæbɪk/ *adj* **1** having only one syllable: *a monosyllabic word.* **2** consisting of or using words of only one syllable: *monosyllabic replies* (eg saying only 'Yes' or 'No' when not wanting to give sb any information).

monotheism /ˈmɒnəʊθiːɪzəm/ *n* [U] the belief that there is only one God. Compare POLYTHEISM. ▸ **monotheist** /ˈmɒnəʊθiːɪst/ *n.* **monotheistic** /ˌmɒnəʊθiːˈɪstɪk/ *adj: monotheistic religions.*

monotone /ˈmɒnətəʊn/ *n* [sing] a dull sound or way of speaking in which the speaker's tone and volume remain the same: *talk in a monotone.*

▸ **monotone** *adj* [attrib] without varying the sound or the colour: *monotone utterances/engravings.*

monotonous /məˈnɒtənəs/ *adj* dull and never changing or varying; constant and boring: *a monotonous voice ∘ monotonous work ∘ Prices go up with monotonous regularity.* ▸ **monotonously** *adv.*

monotony /məˈnɒtəni/ *n* [U] the state of being MONOTONOUS; boring lack of variety: *relieve the monotony of everyday life.*

Monsieur /məˈsjɜː(r)/ *n* (*pl* **Messieurs** /meɪˈsjɜː(r)/) (*abbr* **M**) (in countries where French is spoken) a title used before the name of a man to refer to him, or used alone as a formal and polite form of address: *M Hercule Poirot ∘ Yes, monsieur.*

Monsignor /mɒnˈsiːnjə(r)/ *n* (*abbr* **Mgr**) the title of a priest of high rank in the Roman Catholic Church.

monsoon /ˌmɒnˈsuːn/ *n* **1** a wind in S Asia, esp in the Indian Ocean, which blows from the south-west in summer and from the north-east in winter. **2** a season of heavy rain that comes with the summer monsoon.

monster /ˈmɒnstə(r)/ *n* **1(a)** a large, ugly and frightening creature, esp an imaginary one: *monster movies ∘ a monster with three heads ∘ prehistoric monsters.* (**b**) an unusually large or ugly person, animal or thing: *Their dog is an absolute monster! ∘* (*infml*) *He's grown these monster marrows.* **2** a cruel, evil or very unpleasant person: *She talks about her boss as though he were some sex-crazed monster!*

monstrous /ˈmɒnstrəs/ *adj* **1** shocking and unacceptable; OUTRAGEOUS: *a monstrous lie/accusation ∘ monstrous crimes ∘ It's absolutely monstrous to pay men more than women for the same job.* **2** extremely large; huge: *a monstrous wave.* **3** like a MONSTER(1) in appearances; ugly and frightening.

▸ **monstrosity** /mɒnˈstrɒsəti/ *n* a thing that is very large and very ugly: *That new multi-storey car park is an utter monstrosity!*

monstrously *adv.*

montage /ˌmɒnˈtɑːʒ; *Brit* also ˈmɒnt-/ *n* (**a**) [C] a picture, film or piece of music or writing composed of many separate items put together, esp in an interesting or unusual combination. (**b**) [U] the process of making such a picture, film, etc.

month /mʌnθ/ *n* **1** (also ˌcalendar ˈmonth) any of the twelve periods of time into which the year is divided, eg May or June: *the month of August ∘ We're going on holiday next month. ∘ She earns $1 000 a month. ∘ The rent is £300 per calendar month.* **2** a period of time between a day in one month and the corresponding day in the next month, eg 3 June to 3 July: *The baby is three months old. ∘ a three-month-old baby ∘ several months later ∘ their first few months of marriage ∘ a month-long strike ∘ a six-month contract.* **IDM** **flavour of the month** ⇨ FLAVOUR. **for/in a ˌmonth of ˈSundays** (esp in negative sentences) for a very long time: *I haven't seen her for/in a month of Sundays.*

▸ **monthly** *adj* **1** done, happening, published, etc once a month or every month: *a monthly meeting/visit/magazine.* **2** paid, valid or calculated for one month: *monthly salaries ∘ a monthly season ticket ∘ a monthly income of £800.* — *adv* every month; once a month: *to be paid monthly.* — *n* a magazine published once a month: *a literary monthly.*

monument /ˈmɒnjumənt/ *n* **1** ~ (to sb/sth) a building, column, statue, etc built to remind people of a famous person or event: *a monument to soldiers killed in the war.* **2** a building, etc that is preserved because of its historical importance: *an ancient monument.* **3** ~ to sth a thing that remains as a good example of sb's qualities, deeds, achievements, etc: *This whole city is a monument to his skill as a planner and administrator.*

monumental /ˌmɒnjuˈmentl/ *adj* **1** [usu attrib] exceptionally great: *a monumental achievement/*

blunder/task ∘ *What monumental folly!* **2** [attrib] (of buildings, works of art, etc) very large, impressive and of lasting importance: *monumental paintings/ sculptures.* **3** [attrib] of or serving as a MONU-MENT(1): *a monumental inscription* (ie inscribed on a monument).

▶ **monumentally** /-təli/ *adv* extremely: *monumentally boring/successful.*

moo /muː/ *v* [V] to make the long deep sound that a cow makes. See also LOW⁴. ▶ **moo** *n*.

mooch /muːtʃ/ *v* **PHRV** **mooch about, around, etc** (*Brit infml*) to wander about slowly and with no particular purpose: *mooching around the house with nothing to do* ∘ *She mooched along, in no particular hurry.*

mood¹ /muːd/ *n* **1** the state of one's feelings or mind at a particular time: *She's in a good mood* (ie happy, tolerant, friendly, etc) *today.* ∘ *He's always in a bad mood* (ie angry, intolerant, unhappy, etc) *on Mondays.* ∘ *His mood suddenly changed and he became calm.* **2** a period of bad temper, anger, etc: *He's in a mood today — something must have upset him.* ∘ *She was in one of her moods* (ie having one of her regular periods of feeling angry, bad-tempered, etc). **3** (usu *sing*) the way a group or community feels about sth; the atmosphere in a place or among a group of people: *The mood of the meeting was distinctly pessimistic.* ∘ *I liked the way the programme captured the mood of the period.* ∘ *He is completely out of touch with* **the mood of the moment/times.** **IDM** **(be) in the mood for (doing) sth/to do sth** feeling that one would like to do sth: *I'm just not in the mood for (going to) a party tonight.* **(be) in no mood for (doing) sth/to do sth** not feeling that one would like to do sth: *He's in no mood for (telling) jokes/to tell jokes.*

▶ **moody** *adj* (**-ier, -iest**) **(a)** having moods that change quickly: *a moody and unpredictable man.* **(b)** bad-tempered or depressed and likely to show this: *I keep away from him when he's moody.* **moodily** /-ɪli/ *adv*: *staring moodily out of the window.* **moodiness** *n* [U].

■ **'mood music** *n* [U] popular music intended to create a particular, esp relaxed, atmosphere.

mood² /muːd/ *n* (*grammar*) any of three sets of verb forms that show whether what is said or written is considered certain, possible, doubtful, necessary, desirable, etc: *the indicative/imperative/subjunctive mood.*

moon¹ /muːn/ *n* **1** [sing] **(a)** (usu **the moon**) the natural body that moves round the earth once every 28 days and shines at night by light reflected from the sun: *explore the surface of the moon* ∘ *a moon landing.* **(b)** this body as it appears in the sky at a particular time: *There's no moon tonight* (ie No moon can be seen). ∘ *a crescent moon.* See also FULL MOON, NEW MOON. **2** [C] a body that moves round a planet other than the earth: *How many moons does Jupiter have?* **IDM** **many 'moons ago** a very long time ago: *All that happened many moons ago.* **once in a blue moon** ⇨ ONCE. **over the 'moon** (*infml*) extremely happy or delighted: *The whole team were over the moon at winning the competition.* **promise the earth/moon** ⇨ PROMISE².

▶ **moonless** *adj* without a visible moon: *a dark, moonless sky/night.*

moon² /muːn/ *v* ~ **(about/around)** (*infml*) to spend time doing nothing or wandering from place to place, with no purpose and without concentrating: [V] *Stop mooning and get on with some work!* [Vp] *She spent the whole summer mooning about at home.* **PHRV** **moon over sb** (*infml*) to spend one's time thinking about sb one loves, as if in a dream.

moonbeam /'muːnbiːm/ *n* a ray of light from the moon.

moonlight /'muːnlaɪt/ *n* [U] the light of the moon: *a walk by moonlight/in the moonlight.*

▶ **moonlight** *v* (*pt, pp* **-lighted**) (*infml*) to have a second job, esp at night and secretly, in addition to one's regular one during the day: [V] *a policeman who moonlights as a security guard.* **'moonlighting** *n* [U].

▶ **moonlight** *adj* [attrib] lit by the moon: *a moonlight night/picnic.*

moonlit /'muːnlɪt/ *adj* lit by the moon: *a moonlit night.*

moonshine /'muːnʃaɪn/ *n* [U] **1** foolish talk, ideas, etc; nonsense. **2** (*US*) WHISKY or other spirits made and sold illegally.

moonstruck /'muːnstrʌk/ *adj* slightly mad.

moor¹ /mɔː(r); *Brit also* mʊə(r)/ *n* (often *pl*) (*esp Brit*) a high open area of land that is not cultivated, esp one covered with HEATHER: *go for a walk on the moors* ∘ *the Yorkshire moors.*

moor² /mʊə(r); *Brit also* mɔː(r)/ *v* ~ **sth (to sth)** to attach a boat, ship, etc to a fixed object or the land with a rope or an ANCHOR, etc: [V] *We moored alongside the quay.* [Vn] *moor a yacht* [Vnpr] *The boat was moored to (a post on) the river bank.*

▶ **mooring** /'mʊərɪŋ; *Brit also* 'mɔːr-/ *n* **1 moorings** [pl] the ropes, chains, etc by which a ship, boat, etc is moored: *The boat broke its moorings and drifted out to sea.* **2** [C usu *pl*] the place where a ship, boat, etc is moored: *private moorings* ∘ *mooring ropes.*

Moor /mʊə(r)/ *n* a member of a Muslim people living in NW Africa.

▶ **Moorish** /'mʊərɪʃ/ *adj* of the Moors and their culture.

moorhen /'mʊəhen; *Brit also* 'mɔːh-/ *n* a small bird with long legs that lives near water.

moorland /'mʊələnd; *Brit also* 'mɔːl-/ *n* [U, C usu *pl*] (*esp Brit*) land that consists of moors (MOOR¹): *moorland regions.*

moose /muːs/ *n* (*pl* unchanged) a large N American deer with broad flat antlers (ANTLER). See also ELK.

moot /muːt/ *adj* **IDM** **a moot 'point/'question** a matter about which there may be disagreement or uncertainty: *It's a moot point whether men or women are better drivers.*

▶ **moot** *v* (*fml*) (usu passive) to raise a matter for discussion; to propose sth: [Vn] *The idea was first mooted some years ago.*

mop /mɒp/ *n* **1** a tool for cleaning floors. It consists of a bunch of thick strings or soft material fastened to a long handle. **2** a mass of thick, often untidy, hair: *a mop of curly red hair.*

▶ **mop** *v* (**-pp-**) **1** to clean sth with a mop: [Vn] *mop the floor.* **2(a)** to wipe the face in order to remove sweat or tears: [Vn, Vnpr] *mop one's brow (with a handkerchief).* **(b)** ~ **sth (from sth)** to wipe sth liquid from a surface using eg a cloth: [Vnpr] *mop gravy from one's chin (with a napkin)* [also Vn]. **PHRV** **,mop sth/sb 'up 1** to remove liquid by wiping it with sth that absorbs it, eg a cloth or mop: *She mopped up the pools of water on the bathroom floor.* ∘ *mop up one's gravy with a piece of bread.* **2** to complete the final parts of a task; to deal with the last remaining members of a group: *mop up the last of this year's graduates.* **3** to capture or kill the remaining small groups of people who continue to fight an army: *mop up pockets* (ie small areas) *of resistance* ∘ *continue mopping-up operations.*

mope /məʊp/ *v* (*derog*) to feel very unhappy and full of pity for oneself: [V] *Don't just sit there moping — cheer up!* **PHRV** **,mope a'bout/a'round (...)** (*derog*) to wander about a place, feeling unhappy and lacking energy and purpose: *Since he lost his job he just mopes around (the house) all day.*

moped /'məʊped/ *n* a motor cycle (MOTOR) with an

engine of low power and pedals (PEDAL 1). ⇨ picture at MOTOR CYCLE.

moquette /mɒˈket; US məʊ-/ n [U] a thick soft material used for carpets and furniture covers.

moraine /mɒˈreɪn, məˈreɪn/ n [U,C] a mass of earth, stones, etc carried along by a GLACIER and deposited when it melts.

moral¹ /ˈmɒrəl; US ˈmɔːrəl/ adj **1** [attrib] concerned with principles of right and wrong behaviour; ethical (ETHIC): *a moral question/problem/judgement/ dilemma* ○ *moral philosophy* ○ *challenge sth on moral grounds* ○ *a decline of moral standards.* **2** [attrib] based on one's sense of what is right and just, not on legal rights and obligations: *a moral responsibility/ duty/obligation* ○ *show moral courage.* **3** following right and accepted standards of behaviour; good in character: *lead a moral life* ○ *a very moral person.* Compare IMMORAL, AMORAL. **4** [attrib] able to understand the differences between right and wrong: *Human beings are moral individuals.* **5** teaching or illustrating right behaviour: *a moral drama/tale.*
▶ **morally** /-rəli/ adv **1** in relation to what is considered right behaviour: *morally wrong/ unacceptable/reprehensible* ○ *hold sb both legally and morally responsible.* **2** according to right standards of behaviour: *behave morally.*
■ **the ˌmoral maˈjority** n [Gp] the majority of people in a country, regarded as favouring strong moral standards.
ˌmoral supˈport n [U] the expression of encouragement or support for sb, rather than practical or financial help: *Would you come with me? I need some moral support.*
ˌmoral ˈvictory n a defeat that can in some ways be considered a victory, eg because the principles that one fought for were shown to be right or because one's skills or qualities were proved superior.

moral² /ˈmɒrəl; US ˈmɔːrəl/ n **1** morals [pl] standards of behaviour; principles of right and wrong: *question sb's morals* ○ *the corruption of public morals* ○ *sexual morals.* **2** [C] a practical lesson that a story, an event or an experience teaches: *The moral of this story is 'Better late than never'.*

morale /məˈrɑːl; US -ˈræl/ n [U] the amount of confidence, enthusiasm, determination, etc that a person or group has at a particular time: *affect/ raise/boost/lower/undermine sb's morale* ○ *The win was good for the team's morale.* ○ *Morale among the troops was low.*

moralist /ˈmɒrəlɪst; US ˈmɔːr-/ n (often derog) a person who has strong ideas about moral principles, esp one who tells people how they should behave.

moralistic /ˌmɒrəˈlɪstɪk; US ˌmɔːr-/ adj (usu derog) having or showing definite but narrow beliefs and judgements about what is right and wrong: *a moralistic attitude.*

morality /məˈræləti/ n **1** [U] principles concerning right and wrong or good and bad behaviour: *matters of public/private morality* ○ *standards of morality.* **2** [U] the extent to which sth is right or wrong, good or bad, etc according to moral principles: *discuss the morality of abortion/profit.* **3** [C,U] a particular system of moral principles: *Muslim/Hindu/ Christian morality.*
■ **moˈrality play** n a type of drama, popular in the 15th and 16th centuries, in which good behaviour is taught and the characters represent good and bad qualities.

moralize, -ise /ˈmɒrəlaɪz; US ˈmɔːr-/ v (usu derog) to talk or write, usu in a critical way, about right and wrong, esp in order to emphasize that one's own principles are right: [V, Vpr] *He's always moralizing (about students' behaviour).*

morass /məˈræs/ n (usu sing) **1** ~ (of sth) a situation that is confusing and complicated or prevents progress: *a morass of confusion/doubt/despair* ○ *be caught up in/bogged down in/floundering in a morass of bureaucratic procedures.* **2** a dangerous area of low soft wet land.

moratorium /ˌmɒrəˈtɔːriəm; US ˌmɔːr-/ n (pl moratoriums or moratoria /-riə/) ~ (on sth) a temporary stopping of an activity, esp by official agreement: *declare a moratorium on commercial whaling.*

morbid /ˈmɔːbɪd/ adj (of sb's mind or ideas) having or showing an interest in sad or unpleasant things, esp disease or death: *a morbid imagination/ obsession/fascination/curiosity* ○ *'He might even die.' 'Don't be so morbid.'* ▶ **morbidity** /mɔːˈbɪdəti/ n [U]. **morbidly** adv.

mordant /ˈmɔːdnt/ adj (fml) sharply critical; very sarcastic (SARCASM): *mordant criticism/wit.*

more /mɔː(r)/ indef det, indef pron ~ (sth) (than...) a greater or additional number or amount **(a)** (det): *more people/cars/money/imagination* ○ *hit the target with more luck than skill* ○ *Would you like some more coffee?* ○ *Only two more days to go!* ○ *More than 10000 people took part in the demonstration.* ○ *I know many more people who'd like to come.* **(b)** (pron): *I couldn't possibly eat any more.* ○ *I can't stand much more of this.* ○ *What more can I say* (ie in addition to what has already been said)? ○ *She earns a lot more than I do.* ○ *I'll take three more.* ○ *room for no more than three cars* ○ *I hope we'll see more of you* (ie see you more often). ⇨ note at MUCH¹. **IDM** ˌmore and ˈmore that continues to become larger in number or amount: *More and more people are buying home computers.* ○ *She spends more and more time alone in her room.*
▶ **more** adv **1** (used to form the comparative of adjs and advs with two or more syllables): *She was more intelligent/generous/frightened than her sister.* ○ *She read the letter more carefully the second time.* **2** to a greater than average degree: *programmes that appeal to the more sophisticated viewer* ○ *a course for more advanced students.* **3** to a greater extent: *I like her more than her husband.* ○ *Try to concentrate more on your work.* ○ *repeat sth once more* (ie one more time) ○ *It had more the appearance of a deliberate crime than of an accident.* **IDM** ˌmore and ˈmore increasingly: *I am becoming more and more irritated by his behaviour.* ˌmore or ˈless **1** almost: *I've more or less finished the book.* **2** approximately: *It took more or less a whole day to paint the ceiling.* ○ *I can earn $200 a night, more or less, as a waiter.* ˈmore than happy, glad, willing, etc extremely happy, etc: *I'm more than happy to take you there in my car.* ○ *It was a more than generous offer.* **no more 1** neither: *He couldn't lift the table and no more could I.* **2** not more: *You're no more capable of speaking Chinese than I am.* ○ *It's no more than a mile to the supermarket.* **no more than/nothing more than/not much more than** only; hardly different from: *Signing the forms is no more than a formality.* ○ *My new boss is not much more than a kid!* **what is ˈmore** (used for emphasis) in addition; of more importance: *He's dirty, and what's more he smells.*

moreover /mɔːrˈəʊvə(r)/ adv (used to introduce sth new that adds to or supports the previous statement) in addition; BESIDES: *They know the painting is a forgery. Moreover, they know who painted it.*

mores /ˈmɔːreɪz/ n [pl] (fml) the customs or conventions considered typical of or essential to a group or community: *social/sexual mores.*

morgue /mɔːg/ n a building in which dead bodies are kept before being buried or cremated (CREMATE); a MORTUARY.

moribund /ˈmɒrɪbʌnd; US ˈmɔːr-/ adj (fml) no longer operating effectively and about to stop or come to an end completely: *a moribund civilization/ custom/economy.*

Mormon /ˈmɔːmən/ n, adj (a member) of a religious

M

group founded in the USA in 1830, officially called 'The Church of Jesus Christ of Latter-day Saints'.

morn /mɔːn/ n (usu sing) (arch) (esp in poetry) morning.

morning /'mɔːnɪŋ/ n [C, U] (**a**) the early part of the day between dawn and NOON or before the time for lunch: *They left for Spain early this morning.* ○ *The police came round the next morning.* ○ *The discussion group meets on Friday mornings.* ○ *I'll see him tomorrow morning.* ○ *He swims every morning.* ○ *on the morning of the wedding* ○ *I've been painting the room all morning.* ○ *She works from morning till/to night.* ○ *an early morning run* ○ *read the morning papers.* (**b**) the period from midnight to noon: *He died in the early hours of Sunday morning.* **IDM** **good 'morning** (used as a polite greeting or reply to a greeting when people first see each other in the morning; sometimes also used formally when people leave each other in the morning; in informal use as a greeting often shortened to *Morning*): *Good morning, Rosalind/Miss Dixon.* ○ *Morning, Mike.* **in the 'morning 1** during the morning of the next day; tomorrow morning: *I'll ring her up in the morning.* **2** between midnight and noon, not in the afternoon or evening: *The accident must have happened at about 11 o'clock in the morning.* **morning, noon and 'night** at all times of the day and night; every day and night: *The work continues morning, noon and night.* **the other day/morning/evening/week** ⇨ OTHER.
▶ **mornings** adv in the morning; every morning: *I only work mornings.*
■ ˌmorning-'after pill n a pill that can be taken by a woman some hours after having sex to prevent her becoming pregnant.
'**morning coat** n a black jacket for men, short at the front and very long at the back, worn as part of morning dress.
'**morning dress** n [U] clothes worn by a man on very formal occasions, eg a wedding, including a morning coat and dark trousers.
'**morning sickness** n [U] a desire to VOMIT felt by a woman in the morning during the first few months after she has become pregnant.

NOTE Compare the prepositions **in** and **on** when used with time expressions. **In** is used with parts of the day like **morning**, **afternoon** and **evening**, often in combination with other time expressions: *in the morning/afternoon/evening* ○ *at 3 o'clock in the afternoon.* **In** is also used with the adjectives **early** and **late**: *in the early evening* ○ *late in the summer.*
   On is used with other adjectives, days of the week and certain other expressions: *on a beautiful spring morning* ○ *on Friday afternoon* ○ *on the previous/following day* ○ *on the morning of the 4th of September.* You do not use a preposition with **tomorrow/yesterday/this morning**, etc: *We arrived yesterday afternoon.* ○ *I'm going out this evening/tomorrow morning.* In American English **on** is often not used: *We left Friday morning and returned Sunday evening.* ○ *The course meets Wednesdays at 3.* ⇨ note at TIME¹.

morocco /mə'rɒkəʊ/ n [U] a fine soft leather made from the skins of goats or a similar material used for making shoes and covers for books.

moron /'mɔːrɒn/ n **1** (infml derog or offensive) a very stupid person: *He's an absolute moron!* **2** (techn) a person who is mentally SUBNORMAL. ▶ **moronic** /mə'rɒnɪk/ adj (infml derog): *a moronic laugh/idea.*

morose /mə'rəʊs/ adj unhappy and bad-tempered but not saying much: *a morose person/manner/expression.* ▶ **morosely** adv: *stare morosely at the sky.*

morpheme /'mɔːfiːm/ n (linguistics) the smallest

unit with meaning into which a word can be divided: *'Run-s' contains two morphemes and 'unlike-ly' contains three.*

morphine /'mɔːfiːn/ n [U] a drug made from OPIUM, used for relieving pain.

morphology /mɔː'fɒlədʒi/ n [U] **1** (biology) the scientific study of the form and structure of animals and plants. **2** (linguistics) the study of the forms of words. Compare GRAMMAR 1, SYNTAX. ▶ **morphological** /ˌmɔːfə'lɒdʒɪkl/ adj.

morris dance /'mɒrɪs dɑːns; US 'mɔːrɪs dæns/ n a traditional English dance performed by people wearing special costumes, with bells and sticks. ▶ '**morris dancer** n.

morrow /'mɒrəʊ; US 'mɔːr-/ n **the morrow** [sing] (dated) the next day after the present one or after any given day: *We must leave* **on the morrow**.

Morse Code /ˌmɔːs 'kəʊd/ n [U] a system for sending messages, using combinations of long and short sounds or flashes of light to represent letters of the alphabet and numbers: *send a message in Morse Code.*

morsel /'mɔːsl/ n ~ (**of sth**) a small amount or piece of sth, esp food: *a tasty/tiny morsel of food* ○ *She ate every morsel on her plate.*

mortal /'mɔːtl/ adj **1** that must die; that cannot live for ever: *All human beings are mortal.* ○ *Here lie the mortal remains of George Chapman* (eg as an inscription on a grave). **2** causing death; fatal: *a mortal wound/injury* ○ (fig) *Her reputation suffered a* **mortal blow** as a result of the scandal. **3** [attrib] lasting until death; showing or marked by great hatred: *mortal enemies* ○ *locked in mortal combat* (ie a fight that is only ended by the death of one of the fighters). **4** [attrib] extreme or intense: *live in mortal fear/danger.*
▶ **mortal** n a human being: (joc) *They're so grand these days that they don't talk to ordinary mortals like us any more.*
mortally /-təli/ adv **1** resulting in death: *mortally wounded.* **2** greatly; intensely: *mortally afraid.*
■ ˌmortal 'sin n [C, U] (in the Roman Catholic Church) a very serious sin that leads to the person responsible being damned (DAMN³ 1a) unless it is confessed and forgiven.

mortality /mɔː'tæləti/ n **1** [U] the state of being MORTAL(1). **2** [U] the number of deaths in a specified period of time: *the mortality rate* ○ *Infant mortality* (ie The rate at which babies die) *was 20 deaths per thousand live births in 1986.* **3** [C] a death: *traffic mortalities.*

mortar¹ /'mɔːtə(r)/ n [U] a mixture of LIME¹(1) with cement, sand and water, used in building to hold bricks, stones, etc together. ▶ **mortared** /'mɔːtəd/ adj: *Make sure all the mortared joints are firm and tight.*

mortar² /'mɔːtə(r)/ n **1** a short heavy gun for firing missiles at a high angle: *under mortar fire/attack* (ie being fired at by a mortar or mortars). **2** a strong bowl in which substances are crushed and ground with a PESTLE. ⇨ picture at PESTLE.
▶ **mortar** v [Vn] to attack sb/sth with missiles fired from mortars.

mortarboard /'mɔːtəbɔːd/ n a black cap with a stiff square top, worn by certain university teachers and students on formal occasions.

mortgage /'mɔːgɪdʒ/ n (**a**) an agreement by which money is lent by a building society (BUILDING), bank, etc for buying a house or other property, the property being the security(3): *apply for/take out a mortgage* ○ *a mortgage agreement/deed* ○ *It's difficult to get a mortgage on an old house.* (**b**) a sum of money lent in this way: *We have a mortgage of £40 000.* ○ *monthly mortgage payments* (ie money to repay the sum borrowed and the interest on it). See also HOME LOAN.

M

▶ **mortgage** v ~ sth (**to sb**) to give sb the legal right to take possession of a house or some other property as a security(3) for payment of money lent: [Vn] *He mortgaged his house in order to start a business* (ie borrowed money with his house as a security). [Vnpr] *The house is mortgaged to the bank.* **mortgagee** /ˌmɔːɡɪˈdʒiː/ n a person or an organization that lends money in mortgage agreements. **mortgagor** /ˈmɔːɡədʒɔː(r)/ n a person who borrows money in a mortgage agreement.

mortician /mɔːˈtɪʃn/ n (*US*) = UNDERTAKER.

mortify /ˈmɔːtɪfaɪ/ v (*pt, pp* -**fied**) (usu passive) to cause sb to be very ashamed or embarrassed: [Vn] *He was/felt mortified that he hadn't been invited.* ▶ **mortification** /ˌmɔːtɪfɪˈkeɪʃn/ n [U]: *She suffered the mortification of seeing her assistant promoted above her.*

mortise (also **mortice**) /ˈmɔːtɪs/ n a hole cut in a piece of wood, etc to receive the end of another piece so that the two are held together. See also TENON.
▶ **mortise** (also **mortice**) v 1 ~ A to/into B; ~ A and B together to join or fasten things with a mortise: [Vnpr] *The cross-piece is mortised into the upright post.* [also Vnp]. 2 [Vn] to cut a mortise in sth.
■ **'mortise lock** n a lock that is fitted inside a hole cut into the edge of a door, not one that is screwed onto the surface.

mortuary /ˈmɔːtʃəri; *US* ˈmɔːtʃueri/ n a room or building, eg part of a hospital, in which dead bodies are kept before being buried or cremated (CREMATE).
▶ **mortuary** adj [attrib] (*fml*) of death or burial: *mortuary rites.*

mosaic /məʊˈzeɪɪk/ n 1 [C, U] a picture or pattern made by placing together small pieces of glass, stone, etc of different colours: *ancient Roman mosaics* ○ *a design in mosaic* ○ *a mosaic floor/pavement.* 2 [C usu *sing*] ~ (**of sth**) a design or pattern composed of many different individual items: *a rich mosaic of meadows, rivers and woods.*

mosey /ˈməʊzi/ v (*US infml*) to go in a specified direction slowly and with no particular purpose: [Vp] *I'd better be moseying along* (ie leaving). ○ *Why don't you mosey over to my place after the show?* [also Vpr].

Moslem = MUSLIM.

mosque /mɒsk/ n a building in which Muslims worship.

mosquito /məsˈkiːtəʊ; *Brit also* mɒs-/ n (*pl* -**oes**) a small flying insect that sucks the blood of people and animals. One type of mosquito can spread the disease MALARIA.
■ **mos'quito-net** n a net hung over a bed, etc to keep mosquitoes away.

moss /mɒs; *US* mɔːs/ n [U, C] a very small green or yellow plant without flowers which grows in thick masses on damp surfaces or trees or stones: *moss-covered rocks/walls.* Compare LICHEN.
▶ **mossy** adj 1 covered with moss: *mossy bark.* 2 like moss: *mossy green.*

most¹ /məʊst/ *indef det, indef pron* (used as the superlative of MANY, MUCH²) 1 the greatest in number, amount or extent (**a**) (*det*): *Who do you think will get (the) most votes?* ○ *Peter made the most mistakes of all the class.* ○ *When we toured Italy we spent most time in Rome.* ○ *Most racial discrimination is based on ignorance.* (**b**) (*pron*): *We all ate a lot of cake — I probably ate (the) most* (ie more than the others ate). ○ *Harry got 6 points, Susan got 8 points, but Alison got most* (with 12). ○ *The person with the most to lose is the director.* ○ *That's the most I can do to help.* ⇨ note at MUCH¹. 2 more than half of sb/sth; the majority of sb/sth (**a**) (*det*): *Most European countries are democracies.* ○ *Most classical music sends me to sleep.* ○ *The new tax laws affect most people.* ○ *I like most vegetables.* (**b**) (*pron*): *It rained for most of the*

summer. ○ *As most of you know, I've decided to resign.* ○ *There are hundreds of verbs in English and most are regular.* ○ *He spends most of his free time in the garden.* **IDM** **at (the) 'most** as a maximum; not more than: *At (the) most I might earn £250 a night.* ○ *There were 50 people there, at the very most.* ○ *As a news item it merits a short paragraph at most.*
▶ **mostly** adv mainly; generally: *The drink was mostly lemonade.* ○ *We're mostly out on Sundays.*

most² /məʊst/ adv 1(**a**) (used to form the superlative of *adjs* and *advs* of two or more syllables): *most boring/beautiful/impressive.* ○ *The person who gave most generously to the appeal was my father.* ○ *It was the most exciting trip I've ever had.* (**b**) to the greatest extent: *What did you most enjoy?* ○ *She helped me (the) most when my parents died.* ○ *I saw her most* (ie most often) *when we were at college together.* 2(**a**) very; extremely: *We heard a most interesting talk about Japan.* ○ *I received a most unusual present from my aunt.* ○ *It was most kind of you to take me to the airport.* ○ *We shall most probably never meet again.* (**b**) absolutely: '*Can we expect to see you at church?*' '*Most certainly.*' 3 (*infml esp US*) almost: *I go to the store most every day.*
-most *suff* (with *preps* and *adjs* of position forming *adjs*): *inmost* ○ *topmost* ○ *uppermost.*

MOT /ˌem əʊ ˈtiː/ *abbr* (**a**) (in Britain) Ministry of Transport. (**b**) (also **MOT test**) (*infml*) a compulsory annual test of cars, etc over a certain age: *She took her car in for its MOT.*

mote /məʊt/ n a small piece, esp of dust.

motel /məʊˈtel/ n a hotel for motorists, with space for parking cars near the rooms.

motet /məʊˈtet/ n a short piece of church music, usu for voices only.

moth /mɒθ; *US* mɔːθ/ n an insect like a BUTTERFLY(1) but less brightly coloured. Moths fly mainly at night and are attracted to bright lights.
■ **'moth-eaten** adj 1 eaten, damaged or destroyed by moths: *moth-eaten old clothes.* 2 (*infml derog*) (**a**) looking very old and badly worn: *moth-eaten armchairs.* (**b**) old-fashioned; out of date: *moth-eaten ideas.*

mothball /ˈmɒθbɔːl; *US* ˈmɔːθ-/ n a small ball made of a strong-smelling substance, used for keeping moths (MOTH) away from stored clothes. **IDM** **in 'mothballs** stored and not used for a long time: *The scheme is to be kept in mothballs for the next few years.*
▶ **mothball** v to leave sth without using it for a long time: [Vn] *mothballed shipyards.*

mother /ˈmʌðə(r)/ n 1(**a**) (sometimes used as a form of address, usu not by young people) a woman in relation to a child or children to whom she has given birth: *My mother died when I was 6.* ○ *the relationship between mother and baby* ○ *How are you, mother?* ○ *an expectant* (ie a pregnant) *mother.* ⇨ App 4. (**b**) any female animal in relation to its young: *Look how the mother chimpanzee cares for her young.* 2 (esp as a form of address) the head of a female religious community; a Mother Superior: *Pray for me, Mother.* **IDM** **old enough to be sb's father/mother** ⇨ OLD.
▶ **mother** v 1 to care for sb/sth as a mother does; to REAR(1) sb/sth: [Vn] *piglets mothered by a sow.* 2 to treat sb with great or excessive protection or care: [Vn] *He likes to be mothered when he's ill.*
'Mothering Sunday n (*Brit*) = MOTHER'S DAY.
motherhood /-hʊd/ n [U] the state of being a mother: *She finds motherhood very rewarding.*
motherless adj having no mother.
motherly adj having or showing the kind and tender qualities of a mother: *motherly love/affection/ care* ○ *a motherly kiss.*
■ **'mother country** n (*fml*) 1 one's native country. 2 a country in relation to its colonies.
'mother-figure n an older woman that one goes to

M

---

for advice, support, help, etc. See also FATHER-FIGURE.

'mother-in-law *n* (*pl* **mothers-in-law**) the mother of one's wife or husband. ⇨ App 4.

,Mother 'Nature *n* [U] nature considered as a force that affects the world and human beings: *Leave the cure to Mother Nature. She knows best.*

,mother-of-'pearl *n* [U] the hard smooth shiny substance in various colours that forms a layer inside the shells of certain SHELLFISH and is used for making buttons, ornaments, etc: *a mother-of-pearl brooch.*

'mother's boy *n* (*infml derog*) a boy or man, esp one considered emotionally weak, whose character and behaviour are influenced too much by the protection of his mother.

'Mother's Day *n* a day on which mothers traditionally receive gifts and cards from their children. In Britain it is the fourth Sunday in Lent; in the USA it is the second Sunday in May.

,Mother Su'perior *n* the head of a female religious community.

,mother-to-'be *n* (*pl* **mothers-to-be**) a woman who is pregnant.

'mother tongue *n* the language that one first learns to speak as a child; one's native language.

motherland /'mʌðəlænd/ *n* one's native country.

motif /məʊ'tiːf/ *n* **1** a decorative design or pattern: *wallpaper with a flower motif.* **2** a theme or idea that is repeated and developed in a work of music or literature.

motion /'məʊʃn/ *n* **1** [U, sing] the act or process of moving: *the swaying motion of the ship* ○ *It is no longer in motion* (ie has stopped moving). See also PERPETUAL MOTION, SLOW MOTION. **2** [C] a particular movement; a way of moving part of the body; a gesture: *At a single motion of his hand the room fell silent.* **3** [C] a formal proposal to be discussed and voted on at a meeting: *propose/table/put forward/reject a motion of no confidence in the government* ○ *The motion was adopted/carried by a majority of six votes.* **4** [C] (*Brit fml*) (**a**) an act of emptying the bowels. (**b**) waste matter emptied from the bowels: *loose motions* (ie DIARRHOEA). **IDM** **go through the 'motions (of doing sth)** (*infml*) to pretend to do sth; to do sth but without being sincere or serious about it: *He went through the motions of welcoming her friends and then quickly left the room.* **propose a motion** ⇨ PROPOSE. **put/set sth in 'motion** to cause sth to start moving or operating: *set machinery in motion* ○ (*fig*) *put the new campaign in motion.*

▶ **motion** *v* to make a gesture to sb showing what one wants them to do, where they should go, etc: [Vpr] *He motioned to the waiter.* [Vn.*to* inf, Vpr.*to* inf] *He motioned (to) me to sit down.* [Vpr.*to* inf] *The old lady motioned for him to get out.* [Vnpr] *motion sb to a chair* [also Vnp].

motionless *adj* not moving; still: *standing perfectly motionless.*

■ **,motion 'picture** *n* a cinema film: *the motion-picture industry.*

motivate /'məʊtɪveɪt/ *v* **1** (usu passive) to be the reason for sb's action; to cause sb to act in a particular way: [Vn] *be motivated by greed/fear/love* ○ *The decision was primarily motivated by the desire to save money.* ○ *a motivating factor/force.* **2** to stimulate the interest of sb; to cause sb to want to do sth: [Vn, Vn.*to* inf] *a teacher who can motivate her pupils (to work harder).* ▶ **motivated** *adj*: *a politically motivated murder* ○ *a highly motivated individual* (ie sb who is very keen to do sth). **motivation** /,məʊtɪ'veɪʃn/ *n* [C,U]: *Most people said pay was their main motivation for working.* ○ *his powers of motivation and leadership* ○ *They lack the motivation to study.* **motivational** *adj*: *an important motiva-*

tional factor. **motivator** *n*: *Ambition is a great motivator.*

motive /'məʊtɪv/ *n ~* **(for sth)** that which causes sb to act in a particular way; a reason: *The police could not establish a motive for the murder.* ○ *question/be suspicious of sb's motives* ○ *the profit motive* (ie the desire to make a profit) ○ *She wondered if he had an **ulterior motive** in inviting her out.* ⇨ note at REASON[1].

▶ **motive** *adj* [attrib] causing movement or action: *motive power* (eg electricity, to operate machinery).

motiveless *adj*: *an apparently motiveless crime.*

motley /'mɒtli/ *adj* (*derog*) of many different types of people or things: *wearing a motley collection of old clothes* ○ *She was surrounded by a **motley crew** of musicians, singers, comedians and drunks.*

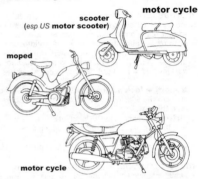

motor cycle

scooter
(*esp US* **motor scooter**)

moped

motor cycle

motor /'məʊtə(r)/ *n* **1(a)** a device that changes power into movement, used to make machines work: *an electric motor* ○ *A motor operates the zoom lens.* (**b**) a device that changes fuel, eg petrol, into energy to provide power for a vehicle, boat, etc: *He started the motor.* See also OUTBOARD MOTOR. **2** (*Brit dated or joc*) a car.

▶ **motor** *adj* [attrib] **1** having or driven by a motor: *motor vehicles* ○ *a motor mower.* **2** (*esp Brit*) of or for vehicles driven by a motor: *motor insurance* ○ *the motor trade* ○ *a motor mechanic.*

motor *v* (*Brit becoming dated*) to travel by car for pleasure: [Vpr, Vadv] *We motored (south) to the seaside.* [also Vp, V]. **motoring** /'məʊtərɪŋ/ *adj* [attrib] relating to cars or to driving: *join a motoring organization* ○ *a motoring offence.*

motorist /'məʊtərɪst/ *n* a person who drives a car: *He stopped a passing motorist.* Compare PEDESTRIAN 1.

motorized, -ised /'məʊtəraɪzd/ *adj* **1** equipped with a motor: *motorized vehicles* ○ *a motorized camera.* **2** (of troops, etc) equipped with motor vehicles: *motorized infantry.*

■ **'motor bike** *n* (**a**) (*Brit infml*) = MOTOR CYCLE: *He revved up his motor bike.* (**b**) (*US*) a small light motor cycle (MOTOR).

'motor boat *n* a small fast boat driven by an engine.

'motor car *n* (*Brit fml*) = CAR 1.

'motor cycle (also *Brit infml* **'motor bike**) *n* a road vehicle with two wheels, driven by an engine, with one seat for the driver and usu with space for a passenger behind the driver: *a motor-cycle accident.* ⇨ picture. **'motor cyclist** *n* a rider of a motor cycle: *a police motor cyclist.*

'motor scooter *n* (*esp US*) = SCOOTER 1.

motorcade /'məʊtəkeɪd/ *n* a procession of motor vehicles, often with important people travelling in them: *the presidential motorcade.*

motorway /'məʊtəweɪ/ (*Brit*) (*US* **expressway**, **freeway**, **thruway**) *n* a wide road specially built for

M

fast motor traffic, with a restricted number of places for entering and leaving. Motorways have at least two separate lanes (LANE 3) in each direction: *join/ leave the motorway at junction 19* ○ *Britain's congested motorways* ○ *a motorway service area.* ▷ note at ROAD.

mottled /'mɒtld/ *adj* marked with patches of different colours without a regular pattern: *the mottled skin of a snake* ○ *mottled purple-brown foliage.*

motto /'mɒtəʊ/ *n* (*pl* -os) a short sentence or phrase chosen and used as a guide or rule of behaviour or as an expression of the aims or ideals of a family, a country, an institution, etc: *'Live each day as it comes.' That's my motto.* ○ *Our school motto was 'Sincerity, Honour and Service'.*

mould (*US* **mold**)

mould (*US* mold)

mould¹ (*US* **mold**) /məʊld/ *n* **1** a hollow container with a particular shape, into which a soft or liquid substance is poured to set or cool into that shape: *a cake mould in the shape of a racing car.* ▷ picture. **2** (usu *sing*) a usual or expected type of sth: *She doesn't fit (into) the traditional mould of a university professor.* ○ *He is a superb striker* **in the same mould as** *Rush and Lineker.* [IDM] **break the** ˈ**mould (of sth)** to change what people expect from sth, esp in a dramatic and challenging way: *a refreshing attempt to break the mould of British politics.*

▶ **mould** *v* **1** ~ **A (into B)**; ~ **B (from / out of / in A)** to shape a soft substance into a particular form or object: [Vn, Vnpr] *mould plastic (into drainpipes)* [Vnpr] *mould a head out of/in clay* ○ *The bricks are moulded by hand.* **2** ~ **sb/sth (into sb/sth)** to guide or control the development of sb/sth; to shape or influence sb/sth: [Vn] *mould sb's character* ○ *Television moulds public opinion.* [Vnpr] *He moulded his young players into a formidable team.* **3** ~ **(sth) to/ round sth** to fit or make sth fit tightly round the shape of an object: [Vpr] *Cotton and Lycra mould beautifully to the body.* [also Vnpr].

mould² (*US* **mold**) /məʊld/ *n* [U,C] a fine soft growth(3) like fur that forms on old food or on objects left in warm wet air: *cheese covered in mould* ○ *moulds attacking the vines.*

▶ **mouldy** (*US* **moldy**) *adj* **1** covered with mould; smelling of mould: *mouldy cheese* ○ *This cucumber has gone mouldy.* **2** (*infml derog*) old and decaying: *Let's get rid of this mouldy old furniture.* **3** (*Brit infml*) unpleasant; bad: *We had a mouldy holiday — it rained every day.* **4** (*Brit infml*) unpleasant because small and mean: *They've given us a pretty mouldy pay increase this year.*

mould³ (*US* **mold**) /məʊld/ *n* [U] soft fine loose earth, esp consisting of decayed vegetable matter: *leaf-mould.*

mouldering (*US* **moldering**) /'məʊldərɪŋ/ *adj* [attrib] slowly decaying: *She dug out her mouldering albums of press cuttings.*

moulding (*US* **molding**) /'məʊldɪŋ/ *n* a line of ornamental PLASTER, carved wood, moulded plastic, etc, typically around the edge or along the top of sth: *protective mouldings round the car's doors.*

moult (*US* **molt**) /məʊlt/ *v* [V] (**a**) (of birds) to lose feathers before new feathers grow. (**b**) (of dogs, cats, etc) to lose hair: *a dog that moults all over the house.*

mound /maʊnd/ *n* **1** a mass of piled earth; a small hill: *on a grassy mound* ○ *a burial mound.* **2** a pile or

heap: *a mound of mashed potato* ○ *sitting at her desk behind a mound of reports.*

mount¹ /maʊnt/ *v* **1** to organize sth; to begin sth: [Vn] *mount an exhibition/a production/a display* ○ *mount a protest/a demonstration/an offensive/a takeover bid.* **2** ~ (**up**) (**to sth**) to increase in amount or intensity: [V] *As the numbers of refugees mount, so does the problem of finding homes for them.* ○ *Pressure is mounting for tax allowances on child care.* [Vp] *Our bills/debts/expenses are mounting up.* [Vpr] *The death toll has mounted to over 100.* **3** (*fml*) [Vn] (**a**) to go up sth: *She slowly mounted the steps.* (**b**) to go up onto sth that is raised: *The speaker mounted the rostrum.* **4** ~ **sb (on sth)** to get onto or put sb onto a horse, etc for riding: [V, Vn] *He quickly mounted (his horse) and rode away.* [Vnpr] *She mounted the boy on the horse.* ○ *The policemen were mounted on* (ie rode) *black horses.* **5** ~ **sth (on/onto/ in sth)** to put sth into place on a support; to fix sth in position for use, display or study: [Vnpr] *mount a collection of stamps in an album* ○ *mount specimens on slides* ○ *a brooch of diamonds mounted in silver* [also Vn]. [IDM] **mount** ˈ**guard (at/over sb/sth)** to act as a guard: *soldiers mounting guard at/over the palace.*

▶ **mount** *n* **1** a horse: *He patted his grey mount.* **2** a thing on which sth is mounted (MOUNT¹ 5), eg a card for a picture or a piece of glass for a SPECIMEN(2).

mounted *adj* (**a**) (of a person) on a horse: *mounted policemen.* (**b**) provided with a MOUNT(2): *a mounted photograph.*

mounting *adj* increasing: *mounting tension* ○ *mounting evidence of fraud.*

mount² /maʊnt/ *n* (*arch*, except in place names, where it is usu written *Mt*) a mountain; a hill: *Mt Etna/Everest* ○ *the Mount of Olives* ○ *St Michael's Mount.*

mountain

peak, shoulder, ridge, saddle, chimney, mountaineer, valley

mountain /'maʊntən; *US* -ntn/ *n* **1** a mass of very high rock, often going up to a point: *distant snow-capped mountains towering over the plains below* ○ *a climbing holiday in the mountains* ○ (*Mount*) *Everest is the highest mountain in the world.* ○ *a chain/range* (ie a row or series) *of mountains* ○ *a mountain chain/range* ○ *mountain peaks/paths/streams* ○ *the invigorating mountain air.* ▷ picture. **2** (often *pl*) ~ **of sth** a very large amount or number: *mountains of food/paperwork* ○ *a mountain of debts/problems.* **3** (usu *sing*) a large remaining stock that is not needed: *the European Community's butter mountain.* [IDM] **make a** ˌ**mountain out of a** ˈ**molehill** (*derog*) to make a very unimportant matter seem important.

▶ **mountaineer** /ˌmaʊntɪˈnɪə(r); *US* -ntnˈɪər/ *n* a person who is skilled at climbing mountains. ▷

M

picture. **mountaineering** n [U] the activity of climbing mountains: *a mountaineering expedition.*

mountainous /ˈmaʊntənəs/ adj **1** having many mountains: *mountainous country/terrain.* **2** huge; rising like mountains: *mountainous waves.*

■ **ˈmountain bike** n a bicycle with a strong frame, large wheels and many gears, intended esp for use on rough ground.

mountainside /ˈmaʊntənsaɪd/ n the side or slope of a mountain: *tracks leading up and down the mountainside.*

mourn /mɔːn/ v ~ **(for/over sb/sth)** to feel or show sorrow or regret for the loss of sb/sth or for sb's death: [Vn] *Few will mourn his passing.* ○ *There were many who mourned the loss of the old town hall.* [Vn, Vpr] *Today we mourn (for) all those who died in two world wars.* [also V].

▶ **mourner** n a person who mourns, esp one who attends a funeral as a friend or relative of the dead person: *Thousands of mourners accompanied the coffin through the streets.*

mournful /-fl/ adj *(sometimes derog)* (**a**) sad: *a mournful look on her face.* (**b**) depressing: *a mournful grey sky.* **mournfully** /-fəli/ adv: *'I wish I could come too,' he said mournfully.*

mourning n [U] **1** sorrow about sb's death: *declare a three-day period of national mourning* ○ *The whole country was in/went into mourning for the dead queen.* **2** special, usu dark, clothes that are worn as a sign of grief at sb's death: *His widow was dressed in mourning.*

mouse /maʊs/ n (pl **mice** /maɪs/) **1** (often in compounds) an animal like a small rat with a long thin tail. There are many different types of mouse: *a ˈhouse mouse* ○ *ˈfield mice* ○ *creeping upstairs, quiet as a mouse* ○ *The mouse scuttled back into its hole.* **2** *(computing)* a small device that is moved by hand across a surface to control the movement of the CURSOR on a computer screen. It has buttons on it for entering commands: *Use the mouse to drag the icon to a new position.* ⇨ picture at COMPUTER. **IDM** **play cat and mouse / a cat-and-mouse game with sb** ⇨ CAT. **when the cat's away, the mice will play** ⇨ CAT.

▶ **mousy** /ˈmaʊsi/ adj *(derog)* **1** (esp of hair) dull brown in colour. **2** (of people) shy and quiet; not impressive.

mousetrap /ˈmaʊstræp/ n a trap with a powerful spring for catching and killing mice.

moussaka /muːˈsɑːkə/ n [U] a Greek dish made of finely chopped meat, vegetables and cheese.

mousse /muːs/ n [C,U] **1** a cold dish made of cream, egg whites, etc mixed lightly and flavoured with sth sweet or sth SAVOURY(1): *a chocolate/ strawberry mousse* ○ *salmon/mushroom mousse.* **2** a thick liquid put on the hair to shape it or improve its condition: *styling mousse.*

moustache /məˈstɑːʃ/ (*US* **mustache** /ˈmʌstæʃ/) n **1** [C] a line of hair allowed to grow on a man's upper lip: *a bristling/drooping moustache* ○ *He had a neatly trimmed grey moustache.* ⇨ picture at HEAD[1]. **2** **moustaches** [pl] a long moustache. Compare BEARD[1].

▶ **moustached** adj [usu attrib] having a moustache.

mouth¹ /maʊθ/ n (pl **mouths** /maʊðz/) **1** the opening through which humans and animals take in food and/or the space behind this containing the teeth, tongue, etc: *He had a cigarette in his mouth.* ○ *Open your mouth wide when you sing.* ○ *Don't talk with your mouth full.* ○ *Their mouths fell open in astonishment.* ○ *A muscle twitched at the corner of her mouth.* ○ *(fig) Every time I open my mouth (ie speak) he contradicts me.* ⇨ picture at HEAD[1]. **2** a place where sth opens: *the mouth of a cave* ○ *a decorative pattern round the mouth of the bag.* **3** [C] a place where a

river enters the sea: *sailing into the mouth of the Thames.* **IDM** **born with a silver spoon in one's mouth** ⇨ BORN. **butter would not melt in one's mouth** ⇨ BUTTER. **by word of mouth** ⇨ WORD. **down in the ˈmouth** depressed. **from the horse's mouth** ⇨ HORSE. **have a big mouth** ⇨ BIG. **have one's heart in one's mouth** ⇨ HEART. **keep one's ˈmouth shut** (*infml*) to keep a secret, esp about dishonest or criminal activity: *You'd better keep your mouth shut, or else...!* **leave a bad/nasty taste in the mouth** ⇨ TASTE[1]. **live from hand to mouth** ⇨ LIVE[2]. **look a gift horse in the mouth** ⇨ GIFT. **put one's money where one's mouth is** ⇨ MONEY. **put words into sb's mouth** ⇨ WORD. **shoot one's mouth off** ⇨ SHOOT[1]. **shut your mouth/face!** ⇨ SHUT. **shut sb's mouth** ⇨ SHUT. **take the bread out of sb's mouth** ⇨ BREAD. **take the words out of sb's mouth** ⇨ WORD.

▶ **-mouthed** /-maʊðd/ (forming compound adjs) **1** having the specified type of mouth: *wide-mouthed* ○ *open-mouthed.* **2** (*usu derog*) having the specified way of speaking: *loud-mouthed* ○ *foul-mouthed.*

mouthful /-fʊl/ n (pl **-fuls**) **1** [C] as much as can easily be put into the mouth at one time: *eat a few mouthfuls of food* ○ *swallow sth in one mouthful.* **2** [sing] (*infml joc*) a word or phrase that is very long or difficult to pronounce: *His name's Timothy Thistlethwaite — quite a mouthful!*

■ **ˈmouth-organ** n = HARMONICA.

ˌmouth-to-ˌmouth reˌsusciˈtation n [U] the action of bringing sb back to consciousness by placing one's mouth over their mouth and breathing into their lungs.

ˈmouth-watering adj (*approv*) (of food or smells) making one want to eat; extremely delicious: *the mouth-watering aroma of freshly baked bread* ○ *(fig) a mouth-watering prospect.*

mouth² /maʊð/ v **1** to speak or say sth with movement of one's jaw but no sound: [Vn] *silently mouthing curses* [V.speech] *'Thank you,' she mouthed.* **2** (*derog*) to say sth in an insincere way or without understanding what is said: [Vn] *mouthing slogans* ○ *mouthing the usual platitudes about the need for more compassion.*

mouthpiece /ˈmaʊθpiːs/ n **1(a)** the part of a telephone that one speaks into: *She put her hand over the mouthpiece and shouted at the children to be quiet.* (**b**) the part of a musical instrument or pipe[1](2) that is placed between the lips. ⇨ picture at MUSICAL INSTRUMENT. **2** (*usu derog*) a person, newspaper, etc that expresses the opinions of others: *The national radio service is the mouthpiece of the government.*

mouthwash /ˈmaʊθwɒʃ/ n [U] liquid for cleaning the mouth.

movable /ˈmuːvəbl/ adj **1** that can be moved: *a machine with a movable arm for picking up objects.* **2** (*law*)(of property) that can be taken from place to place.

■ **ˌmovable ˈfeast** n a religious festival whose date may change from year to year: *(fig) It doesn't matter when we have our meeting — it's a movable feast.*

move¹ /muːv/ v **1(a)** ~ **(sb/sth)** **(about/around)** to change position or make sb/sth change position in a way that can be seen, heard or felt: [V] *It must be alive — it moved!* ○ *The bus was already moving when I jumped onto it.* ○ *Don't move — stay perfectly still.* ○ *(fig) That car was really moving (ie travelling fast)!* [Vn] *I can't move my fingers properly.* ○ *She is too ill to be moved.* ○ *Has someone moved my book?* [Vp] *He could hear someone moving about/around in the room above.* [also Vnp]. (**b**) to change position or make sb/sth change position in the specified way or in the specified direction: [Vadv] *The dancers moved very gracefully.* [Vpr] *He's moving up the school.* ○ *Philip moved towards the window.* [Vnpr] *Some men moved the target into position.* [Vnadv] *We moved our chairs a little nearer* [Vnp] *Move that bottle up to*

M

the top shelf, would you? **2** to change or change sth: [Vpr] *Russia is moving to/towards a market economy.* [Vnpr] *Let's move the meeting to Wednesday.* [Vn] *The government has not moved its position on this issue.* **3** ~ (**ahead/on**) to make progress in the specified way or direction: [V, Vp] *Time is moving on.* ○ *Share prices moved ahead today.* [Vadv, Vp] *Things are not moving (ahead) as fast as we hoped.* **4** to take action; to do sth: [V] *Unless the employers move quickly, there will be a strike.* ○ *The government has moved swiftly to dispel the rumours.* **5** ~ (**from...**) (**to...**) to change the place where one lives, has one's work, etc: [V] *We don't like it here so we've decided to move.* [Vpr] *The company's moving to Scotland.* [Vadv] *She's moved (up) north.* **6** (in CHESS and other board games) to change the position of a piece: [V] *It's your turn to move.* [Vn, Vnp] *She moved her queen (forward).* [also Vnpr]. **7** ~ **sb** (**to sth**) to cause sb to have strong feelings, esp of sympathy or sadness: [Vn] *We were deeply moved (by her plight).* [Vnpr] *Grown men were **moved to tears** at the horrific scenes.* See also MOVING 2. **8** to cause or influence sb to do sth or not to do sth: [Vn.to inf] (*fml*) *What can have moved her to behave in this way?* ○ *He works as/when the spirit moves him* (ie when he feels the desire to do so). **9** to propose sth formally for discussion and decision at a meeting: [Vn] *The Minister moved an amendment to the Bill.* [V.*that*] *Mr Chairman, I move that a vote be taken on this.* **10** to change one's attitude or make sb change their attitude: *The government won't move on this issue.* ○ *She's made up her mind and nothing will move her.* **IDM get 'moving** (*infml*) to begin, leave, etc quickly: *It's late — we'd better get moving.* **get sth 'moving** (*infml*) to cause sth to make vigorous progress: *The new director has really got things moving.* **move the 'goalposts** (*Brit infml*) to change the accepted conditions within which a particular matter is being discussed or a particular action taken. **move heaven and 'earth** to do everything one possibly can in order to achieve sth: *We moved heaven and earth to publish this book on time.* **move 'house** (*Brit*) to move one's furniture, goods, etc to another place to live in. **PHRV ,move a'long** to change to a new position, esp to avoid crowding or getting in the way of sb/sth: *Move along there, please.* ,**move 'in**; ,**move 'into sth** to start to live in one's new home: *Our new neighbours moved in yesterday.* '**move in sth** to live, be active, pass one's time, etc in a particular social group: *move in high society* ○ *She only moves in the best circles.* ,**move 'in on sb/sth** to move towards sb/sth from all directions, esp in a threatening way: *The police moved in on the terrorists.* ,**move 'off** (esp of a vehicle) to start a journey; to leave: *The signal was given, and the procession moved off.* ,**move 'on (to sth)** to move to another place, topic, etc: *I've been in this job long enough — it's time I moved on.* ○ *Can we move on to the next item on the agenda?* ,**move sb 'on** (of police) to order sb to move away from the scene of an accident, etc. ,**move 'out** to leave one's old home: *He couldn't pay his rent, so he had to move out.* ,**move 'over/'up** to change one's position in order to make room for sb: *Please move over/up so I can sit beside you.*

▶ **mover** /'mu:və(r)/ *n* a person or thing that moves in the specified way: *She's a lovely mover* (eg She dances elegantly). See also PRIME MOVER.

moving *adj* **1** [attrib] that moves: *a moving staircase* ○ *a mechanism with no moving parts* ○ *a slow-moving stream.* **2** causing one to have deep feelings, esp of sadness or sympathy: *a moving story/tribute* ○ *His speech was deeply moving.* **movingly** *adv*: *He spoke movingly of his wife's illness.*

move² /mu:v/ *n* **1** a change of place or position: *She sat watching my every move.* ○ *Keep still — don't*

make a move. **2** ~ (**towards sth / to do sth**) an action done or needing to be done to achieve a purpose: *The government's announcement is seen as the first positive move towards settling the strike.* ○ *This latest move in the dispute follows a recent increase in support for the miners.* ○ *Diplomatic moves are afoot to reduce the tension in the area.* See also FALSE MOVE. **3** ~ (**from...**) (**to/into...**) an act or the process of changing the place where one lives, works, etc: *a move from the town into the country* ○ *The office move took most of the weekend.* ○ *His new job isn't really a promotion, just a sideways move* (ie His status has remained the same). **4** an act of changing the position of a piece in CHESS or other board games when it is one's turn to play: *He beat me in ten moves.* ○ *Whose move is it?* **IDM get a 'move on** (*infml*) hurry up. **make a 'move 1** (*infml*) to start on a journey; to leave: *It's getting dark — we'd better make a move.* **2** to take action: *I decided it was time to make a move.* ○ *Let him make the first move.* **on the 'move 1** making progress: *The army is on the move.* **2** moving about from place to place: *It's hard to contact her — she's always on the move.*

movement /'mu:vmənt/ *n* **1** [U,C] the action of moving or an instance of being moved: *hand/eye movements* ○ *the gentle movement of his chest as he breathes* ○ *Loose clothing gives you greater freedom of movement.* ○ *I detected a slight movement in the undergrowth.* **2(a)** [C] an act of changing position, esp as a planned and controlled act by armed forces: *large-scale troop movements.* (**b**) **movements** [pl] actions, journeys, etc over a period of time, esp as observed and/or recorded by sb else: *The police have been keeping a close watch on the suspects' movements.* **3** [sing] ~ (**away from/towards sth**) a direction of thought or opinion; a TREND in society: *a movement towards greater freedom in fashion styles.* **4** [U,C] ~ (**in sth**) a change in amount: *not much movement in oil prices.* **5** [CGp,C] ~ (**to do sth**) a group of people with a shared set of aims or principles: *the aims/members/achievements of the Labour Movement* ○ *poets of the Romantic movement* ○ *found a mass movement to promote women's rights.* **6** [C] (*music*) one of the main divisions in a long musical work: *a symphony in four movements.* **7** [C] (*US fml*) an act of emptying the bowels.

movie /'mu:vi/ *n* (*esp US*) **1** [C] a film: *make a horror movie* ○ *Stephen Spielberg's latest movie* ○ *We went to (see) a movie.* ○ *a movie producer/star.* **2 the movies** [pl] (**a**) (also *esp US* '**movie theatre** [C]) a cinema: *Let's go to the movies tonight.* (**b**) the film industry: *She's in/She works in the movies.*

▶ '**movie-goer** *n* (*esp US*) a person who goes to the cinema, esp regularly.

mow /məʊ/ *v* (*pt* **mowed**; *pp* **mown** /məʊn/ or **mowed**) to cut grass, etc using a machine or an implement with a blade or blades: [Vn] *I mow the lawn every week in summer.* ○ *the smell of new-mown hay* [also V]. **PHRV ,mow sb 'down** to kill people, esp in large numbers: *soldiers mown down by machine-gun fire* ○ *The car went out of control and mowed down several people at the side of the road.*

▶ **mower** *n* (esp in compounds) a machine or person that mows: *a rotary/an electric mower.* See also LAWNMOWER.

MP /ˌem 'pi:/ *abbr* **1** (*esp Brit*) Member of Parliament: *Annie Hill MP* ○ *the MP for Birkenhead* ○ *Tory/Labour MPs* ○ *backbench MPs.* **2** military police.

mpg /ˌem pi: 'dʒi:/ *abbr* miles per gallon (of fuel): *This car does 40 mpg.*

mph /ˌem pi: 'eɪtʃ/ *abbr* miles per hour: *a 70 mph speed limit* ○ *driving at a steady 50 mph.* Compare KPH.

Mr /'mɪstə(r)/ *abbr* **1** (a title that comes before a

M

---

man's SURNAME or before his first name and SUR-
NAME together): *Come in, Mr Brown.* ○ *Mr John
Brown* ○ *Mr and Mrs Brown.* **2** (*fml*) (a title used to
address or refer to men in certain official positions):
Mr Chairman ○ (*esp US*) *Mr President.* Compare
MISTER.

Mrs /'mɪsɪz/ *abbr* (a title that comes before a married
woman's SURNAME or before her first name and SUR-
NAME together): *Mrs Jane Brown* ○ *Mr and Mrs
Brown.* Compare MISSUS, MISS², Ms.

MS *abbr* (*pl* **MSS**) manuscript.

Ms /mɪz, məz/ *abbr* (a title that comes before a
woman's SURNAME or before her first name and SUR-
NAME together. Some women prefer the title *Ms* to
Mrs or *Miss*, and *Ms* can be used to refer to or
address a woman when one does not know whether
she is married or not): *Ms (Mary) Green.* Compare
MISS², MRS.

MSc /ˌem es 'siː/ *abbr* Master of Science: *have/be an
MSc in Chemistry* ○ *Wendy O'Connor MSc.* Compare
MA.

Mt *abbr* Mount (esp on a map): *Mt Kenya.*

much¹ /mʌtʃ/ *indef det, indef pron* (used with
uncountable *ns*, esp after negative *vs*, in questions,
or after *as, how, so* or *too*) a large amount or quantity of sth (**a**) (*det*): *I don't have much money with me.*
○ *Did you have much difficulty finding the house?* ○
There's never very much activity here on Sundays. ○
How much water do you need? ○ *Take as much time
as you like.* ○ *There was so much traffic that we were
an hour late.* ⇨ note at VERY¹. (**b**) (*pron*): *'Is there
any mail?' 'Not (very) much.'* ○ *She never eats much
for breakfast.* ○ *Did she say much about her children?*
○ *How much is it?* (ie What is its price?) ○ *Relax as
much as you can.* ○ *I've got far too much to do.* ○ *I lay
awake for much of the night.* ○ *We didn't get to see
much else.* IDM **'not much of a...** not a good ...:
He's not much of a tennis player. ○ *I'm not much of a
correspondent* (ie I rarely write letters). **'this much**
(used to introduce sth particular or definite) what I am
about to say: *I'll say this much for him — he never
leaves a piece of work unfinished.* ○ *This much is
certain, you will never work in the police force again.*
▶ **muchness** *n* IDM **,much of a 'muchness** very
similar; almost alike: *The two candidates are much
of a muchness — it's hard to choose between them.*

Expressing quantity		
	uncountable nouns	countable nouns
positive statements	lots of money (*less fml*)	lots of coins (*less fml*)
	a lot of money	a lot of coins
	much money (*more fml*)	many coins (*more fml*)
negative statements	not much money	not many coins
	little money (*more fml*)	few coins (*more fml*)
questions	How much money?	How many coins?

1 Notice the difference between **little/few** and **a
little / a few**. If we say *'I have little money and few
interests'*, we sound disappointed and negative. If we
say *'I have a little money and a few interests'*, we
sound more positive. Compare: *He's lived here a long
time but has few friends* and *He's lived here a short
time but already has a few friends.*
2 **A lot of** can also be used in questions: *Have we got
a lot of time/cards left?* It suggests that the speaker
knows that there is/are some left and wants to know
whether the amount/number is big or small.
3 The comparative and superlative forms of **much,
many**, and **a lot of** are **more** and **(the) most**. For

little the comparative and superlative forms are
less and **(the) least** and for **few** they are **fewer** and
(the) fewest.

much² /mʌtʃ/ *adv* to a great extent or degree (used
as follows). **1** (often used with negative *vs*): *I didn't
enjoy the book (very) much.* ○ *He isn't in the office
(very) much* (ie often). ○ *Thank you very much for the
flowers.* ○ *I would very much like to see you again.* ○ *It
doesn't much matter what you wear.* ○ *Much to her
surprise he came back the next day.* **2(a)** (with past
participles used as *adjs* and also with *afraid, alive*
and *aware*, etc): *He was much angered by the report.*
○ *I'm very much aware of the lack of food supplies.* ○
the much-criticized publicity campaign ○ *a much-
needed holiday.* (**b**) (used with comparatives and
superlatives): *much slower/heavier/louder* ○ *much
more expensive* ○ *much more confidently* ○ *She's much
better today.* ○ *That was much the best meal I've had
for a long time.* ○ *I would never willingly go anywhere
by boat, much less go on a cruise.* ⇨ note at VERY.
IDM **as 'much** the same: *Please help me get this job
— you know I would do as much for you.* *'Roger
stole the money.' 'I thought/said as much* (ie That is
what I thought/said)*!'* **as much as sb can do** the
maximum that sb can do: *No ice-cream, thanks — it
was as much as I could do to finish that enormous
first course!* **'much as** although: *Much as I would
like to stay, I really must go home.* **,much the 'same**
in approximately the same condition: *The patient is
much the same this morning.* **,not much 'good at
sth** (*infml*) not very good at (doing) sth: *I'm not
much good at tennis.* **not so much sth as sth** ⇨
SO¹. **pretty much/nearly/well** ⇨ PRETTY *adv*.

muck /mʌk/ *n* **1** [U] waste matter excreted (EX-
CRETE) by farm animals; MANURE: *spread muck on the
fields* ○ *a 'muck heap.* **2** [U] (*infml esp Brit*) (**a**) dirt
or mud; FILTH(1): *Don't come in here with your boots
all covered in muck.* (**b**) anything disgusting: *I'm not
eating that muck!* ○ (*fig*) *I don't want my name
dragged through the muck* (ie my reputation harmed
by being associated with sth illegal or shocking).
IDM **make a 'muck of sth** (*Brit infml*) to do sth
badly.
▶ **muck** *v* PHRV **,muck a'bout/a'round** (*Brit
infml*) to behave in a silly way; to waste time in
useless activity: *Stop mucking about and finish your
work!* **,muck 'in** (*Brit infml*) to share tasks or accommodation equally: *You'll all have to muck in and
help.* **,muck (sth) 'out** to clean out stables, etc by
removing muck(1). **,muck sth 'up** (*infml esp Brit*) to
spoil sth: *I really mucked up my chances of getting a
good mark.*
mucky *adj* dirty: *My hands are all mucky.*

muckraking /'mʌkreɪkɪŋ/ *n* [U] (*derog*) the activity
of trying to discover things about people's background or behaviour that could damage their
reputation if made public.

mucous membrane /ˌmjuːkəs 'membreɪn/ *n* [C]
(*anatomy*) the thin wet skin that lines the nose, the
mouth and certain internal organs.

mucus /'mjuːkəs/ *n* [U] a sticky wet substance, esp
that produced by a MUCOUS MEMBRANE: *a nose
blocked with mucus* ○ *a trail of mucus left by a snail.*

mud /mʌd/ *n* [U] soft wet earth: *My shoes were
covered/plastered in/with mud.* ○ *The garden had
become a sea of mud.* ○ *a mud hut* (ie a simple house
made with mud which then dries). IDM **fling, sling,
etc 'mud (at sb)** to try to damage sb's reputation
by saying unpleasant or shocking things about
them. **one's name is mud** ⇨ NAME¹.
■ **'mud-flat** *n* (often *pl*) a stretch of mud covered by
the sea when the tide is in.
'mud-slinging *n* [U] (*derog*) trying to damage sb's
reputation by saying bad things about them.

muddle /'mʌdl/ *v* **1** ~ **sth (up)** to put sth into a state of disorder; to mix things together: [Vn] *Don't do that — you're muddling my papers!* [Vnp] *The photographs were all muddled up in a drawer.* **2 ~ sb (up)** to confuse sb mentally: [Vn, Vnp] *Don't try and explain it again or you'll muddle me (up) completely.* **3(a) ~ sb/sth (up)** to be confused about two or more things or people and therefore make mistakes in arrangements, etc: [Vn, Vnp] *I muddled (up) the dates and arrived three days late.* **(b) ~ A (up) with B** to confuse one person or thing with another: [Vnpr, Vnp] *You must be muddling me (up) with my twin brother.* **PHRV** **,muddle a'long** to live one's life with no clear purpose or plan: *We muddle along from day to day.* **,muddle 'through** to achieve one's aims even though one does not act efficiently, have the proper equipment, etc; to manage: *I expect we'll muddle through somehow!*

▶ **muddle** *n ~ (about/over sth)* (usu *sing*) **(a)** a state of disorder or confusion: *My desk's **in a real muddle.*** ◦ *There was a muddle over our hotel accommodation.* **(b)** mental confusion: *The old lady **got into a muddle** trying to set the video.*

muddled *adj* confused: *muddled thinking/motives* ◦ *his muddled version of events* ◦ *Changes to the health service have left the public feeling muddled and anxious.*

muddling *adj* causing confusion: *These tax forms are very muddling.*

■ **,muddle-'headed** *adj* not clear in thought; confused: *muddle-headed dreamers.*

muddy /'mʌdi/ *adj* (**-ier, -iest**) **1** full of or covered in mud: *muddy roads/boots.* **2** (of liquids or colours) coloured by or like mud; not clear: *a muddy stream* ◦ *muddy water* ◦ *clothes of a muddy* (ie brownish) *green.*

▶ **muddy** *v* (*pt, pp* **muddied**) to make sb/sth muddy: [Vn] *muddy one's boots.* **IDM** **muddy the 'waters** (*derog*) to make a situation confused and not clear.

mudguard /'mʌdɡɑːd/ *n* a curved cover over a wheel of a bicycle, etc. ⇨ picture at BICYCLE.

muesli /'mjuːzli/ (*Brit*) (*US* **granola**) *n* [U] a mixture of CEREAL, nuts and dried fruit, usu eaten with milk at breakfast.

muezzin /muːˈezɪn, mjuː-/ *n* a man who calls Muslims to prayer, usu from the tower of a MOSQUE.

muff¹ /mʌf/ *n* a roll of fur or other warm material into which one puts one's hands to keep them warm in cold weather. See also EARMUFF.

muff² /mʌf/ *v* (*infml derog*) to fail to achieve sth or make use of sth; to miss sth: [Vn] *He muffed a simple catch.* ◦ *She had a wonderful opportunity, but she muffed it.*

muffin /'mʌfɪn/ *n* **1** (*Brit*) (*US* **,English 'muffin**) a small flat round bun, usu eaten hot with butter. **2** (*US*) a small sweet bread roll or cake, often filled with fruit and eaten with butter.

muffle /'mʌfl/ *v* **1 ~ sb/sth (up) (in sth)** to wrap or cover sb/sth for warmth or protection: [Vnpr, Vnp] *He walked out into the snow, heavily muffled (up) in a thick coat and scarf.* **2** to make the sound of sth quieter by wrapping it, covering it in cloth, etc: [Vn] *He tried to muffle the alarm clock by putting it under his pillow.* ◦ *The fog muffled the sound of the horse's hooves.* ◦ (*fig*) *attempt to muffle the voice of opposition.*

▶ **muffled** *adj* (of sounds) not heard clearly, because an obstacle is in the way: *muffled voices/giggles from the next room.*

muffler /'mʌflə(r)/ *n* **1** a cloth worn round the neck for warmth; a SCARF. **2** (*US*) = SILENCER a.

Mufti /'mʌfti/ *n* a title given to certain Muslim legal experts or religious leaders.

mufti /'mʌfti/ *n* [U] ordinary clothes worn by people, esp soldiers, who normally wear uniform in their job: *officers in mufti.*

mug¹ /mʌɡ/ *n* **1(a)** a fairly large cup for drinking from, usu with straight sides and a handle, used without a SAUCER(1): *a coffee mug.* ⇨ picture at CUP¹. **(b)** its contents: *a mug of tea.* **2** (*sl derog or joc*) the face of a person: *What an ugly mug!* **3** (*infml*) a person who is easily deceived: *You're a mug if you believe that.* ◦ *She's no mug.* **IDM** **a 'mug's game** (*derog esp Brit*) an activity unlikely to be successful or profitable: *Trying to sell overcoats in midsummer is a real mug's game.*

■ **'mug shot** *n* (*sl*) a photograph showing sb's face, eg one of a series of such photographs of criminals, kept by the police.

mug² /mʌɡ/ *v* (**-gg-**) (*infml*) to attack and rob sb violently, esp in a public place: [Vn] *An old lady was mugged by a gang of youths in the park.* ▶ **mugger** *n.* **mugging** *n* [C, U]: *several reported muggings.*

mug³ /mʌɡ/ *v* (**-gg-**) **PHRV** **,mug sth 'up; ,mug 'up on sth** (*Brit infml*) to try to learn or REVISE(2) sth, usu in a short time for a special purpose, eg an examination: *She mugged up (on) the Highway Code before her driving test.*

muggins /'mʌɡɪnz/ *n* [sing] (*Brit infml joc*) (without *a* or *the*; often used to refer to oneself) a person who is made to look stupid, eg by being tricked into doing sth he or she does not want to do: *Muggins here locked his keys in the car!* ◦ *I suppose muggins will have to do the washing-up!*

muggy /'mʌɡi/ *adj* (of weather) warm and damp in an unpleasant way: *a muggy August day.*

Muhammad (also **Mohammed**) /məˈhæmɪd/ *n* the PROPHET(1b) who founded the religion of Islam.

mujahedin (also **mujaheddin**) /ˌmuːdʒəhəˈdiːn/ *n* [pl] (in certain Muslim countries) guerrillas (GUERRILLA) fighting esp in support of Muslim FUNDAMENTALISM.

mulatto /mjuˈlætəʊ, məˈl-/ *n* (*pl* **-os** or *esp US* **-oes**) a person who has one black parent and one white.

mulberry /'mʌlbəri; *US* -beri/ *n* **(a)** (also **'mulberry tree**) a tree with broad, dark green leaves. **(b)** its purple or white edible fruit.

mulch /mʌltʃ/ *n* a covering, eg of straw, rotting leaves or sheets of plastic, which is spread over the soil, eg to prevent it drying out, to kill weeds (WEED 1a) or to protect roots.

▶ **mulch** *v* [Vn] to cover the soil or the roots of plants with a mulch.

mule¹ /mjuːl/ *n* an animal that is the young of a DONKEY(1) or a horse, used esp for carrying loads: *She's **(as) stubborn as a mule.***

▶ **mulish** *adj* (*derog*) unwilling to change one's attitude or do what other people want one to do; STUBBORN(a).

mule² /mjuːi/ *n* a SLIPPER that is open around the heel.

mull /mʌl/ *v* **PHRV** **,mull sth 'over** to think about or consider sth long and carefully: *Thank you for your suggestion — I'd like to mull it over for a few days.*

muilah /'mʌlə/ *n* a Muslim teacher of religion and sacred law.

mulled /mʌld/ *adj* [attrib] (of wine or beer) mixed with sugar and spices and heated: *mulled claret/ale.*

mullet /'mʌlɪt/ *n* (*pl* unchanged) an edible sea-fish. The most common types are **red mullet** and **grey mullet.**

mulligatawny /ˌmʌlɪɡəˈtɔːni/ *n* [U] a soup with hot spices in it, originally from India.

mullion /'mʌliən/ *n* (*architecture*) a solid upright division between two parts of a window. ⇨ picture at CHURCH. ▶ **mullioned** /'mʌliənd/ *adj: mullioned windows.*

multi- *comb form* having many of: *multicoloured/ multifaceted* ◦ *a ,multimillio'naire* (ie a person having several million pounds, dollars, etc) ◦ *a*

₁multiracial/multi-ethnic so'ciety (ie with many different races) ○ *a ₁multi-storey 'car park/(US) ₁multi-level 'parking-lot* (ie consisting of a building with several floors) ○ *a multi-purpose tool.*

multicultural /₁mʌltɪ'kʌltʃərəl/ *adj* for or including people of several different races, religions, languages or national traditions: *a multicultural society* ○ *multicultural education.* ▶ **multiculturalism** /-ɪzəm/ *n* [U].

multifarious /₁mʌltɪ'feərɪəs/ *adj* (*fml*) of many different kinds; having great variety: *the multifarious life-forms of a coral reef* ○ *a vast multifarious organization.*

multilateral /₁mʌltɪ'lætərəl/ *adj* with two or more people or groups taking part: *a ₁multilateral a'greement* ○ *₁multilateral nuclear dis'armament* (ie involving all or most countries which have nuclear weapons). Compare BILATERAL, UNILATERAL.
▶ **multilateralism** /-ɪzəm/ *n* [U] (*politics*) the policy of seeking multilateral agreements as the best way of achieving nuclear disarmament (DISARM).

multilingual /₁mʌltɪ'lɪŋgwəl/ *adj* **1** speaking or using many languages: *multilingual children* ○ *India is a ₁multilingual 'country.* **2** written or printed in many languages: *a ₁multilingual 'phrase book.* Compare BILINGUAL, MONOLINGUAL.

multimedia /₁mʌltɪ'miːdɪə/ *adj* [attrib] involving several different methods of communication or forms of expression: *a multimedia event, including music, dance, video and a laser show.*

multinational /₁mʌltɪ'næʃnəl/ *adj* existing in or involving many countries: *a multinational company/organization* ○ *a multinational peacekeeping operation* (ie involving soldiers and observers from several countries).
▶ **multinational** *n* a company, esp a very large one, that does business in many different countries: *Some people believe that the multinationals have too much power.*

multiparty /₁mʌltɪ'pɑːti/ *adj* [attrib] involving several different political parties: *a multiparty democracy.*

multiple /'mʌltɪpl/ *adj* [attrib] having or involving many individuals, items or types: *a multiple crash on the motorway* (ie one involving many vehicles) ○ *suffer multiple injuries* ○ *houses in multiple occupation* (ie with several different people or households living in them).
▶ **multiple** *n* **1** (*mathematics*) a quantity that contains another quantity an exact number of times: *14, 21 and 28 are multiples of 7.* ○ *Traveller's cheques are available in multiples of £10, £20, £30, etc.* **2** (also *₁multiple 'store*) (*esp Brit*) a shop with many branches throughout a country.
■ *₁multiple-'choice adj* (of examination questions) showing several possible answers from which the correct one must be chosen.
₁multiple scle'rosis n [U] (*abbr MS*) a disease of the nervous system that develops over a period of time. People with the disease gradually lose control of their limbs and their speech.

multiplex /'mʌltɪpleks/ (also *₁multiplex 'cinema*) *n* a large cinema with several separate screens, eg 10 or more.

multiplication /₁mʌltɪplɪ'keɪʃn/ *n* [U] the action or process of multiplying: *children learning to do multiplication and division* ○ *an organism that grows by the multiplication of its cells* ○ *the multiplication of new restaurants in the area* ○ *the multiplication sign* (ie ×) ○ *a multiplication sum.*
■ *multipli'cation table n* a list showing the results when a number is multiplied by a set of other numbers, esp 1 to 12, in turn.

multiplicity /₁mʌltɪ'plɪsəti/ *n* [sing] ~ (*of sth*) a

large number or great variety of things: *a computer with a multiplicity of* (ie many) *uses.*

multiply /'mʌltɪplaɪ/ *v* (*pt, pp -lied*) **1** ~ A by B/ ~ A and B (*together*) to add a number to itself a particular number of times: [V] *children learning to multiply and divide* [Vnpr] *2 multiplied by 4 is/ equals/makes 8* (ie 2 × 4 = 8). [Vn, Vnpr] *Multiply 2 and 6 (together) and you get 12.* **2** to increase or make sth increase, esp greatly, in number or quantity: [V] *Our problems have multiplied since last year.* [Vn] *Buy lots of raffle tickets and multiply your chances of success.* **3** (*biology*) to produce or make sth produce out of itself large numbers of new living things: [V] *Rabbits multiply rapidly.* [Vn] *It is possible to multiply these bacteria in the laboratory.*

multitude /'mʌltɪtjuːd; *US* -tuːd/ *n* (*fml*) (**a**) [C] ~ (**of sb/sth**) (sometimes *pl* with *sing* meaning) an extremely large number of people or things: *A large multitude had assembled to hear him preach.* ○ *How will the university cope with the multitude(s) of new students?* ○ *Vast multitudes of birds visit this lake in spring.* ○ *just one of a multitude of problems/reasons.* (**b**) the multitude [Gp] (also the multitudes [pl]) (sometimes *derog*) the mass of ordinary people: *special qualities which mark her out from the multitude* ○ *demagogues who appeal to the multitude* ○ *feed the starving multitude(s).* **IDM cover/hide a multitude of sins** (*often joc*) to conceal the real, usu unpleasant, facts or situation: *The description 'produce of more than one country' can cover a multitude of sins.*
▶ **multitudinous** /₁mʌltɪ'tjuːdɪnəs; *US* -'tuːdɪnəs/ *adj* (*fml*) extremely large in number.

mum¹ /mʌm/ (*US usu* **mom** /mɒm/) *n* (*infml*) a mother: *This is my mum.* ○ *Hello, mum!* ○ *a marvellous holiday resort for mums and dads, as well as for kids.*

mum² /mʌm/ *adj* **IDM keep mum** (*infml*) to say nothing; to stay silent: *He kept mum about what he'd seen.* *₁mum's the 'word!* (*infml*) (used when asking sb to keep a secret) say nothing about this.

mumble /'mʌmbl/ *v* ~ (**about sth**); ~ sth (**to sb**) to speak or say sth in a low voice that is not clear, so that people cannot hear what is said: [V] *speak in a mumbling voice* ○ *He always mumbles when he's embarrassed.* [Vpr] *What are you mumbling about? I can't understand a word!* [Vn, Vnpr] *He mumbled something (to me) which I didn't quite catch.* [V.that] *She mumbled that she didn't want to get up yet.* [also V.speech].
▶ **mumble** *n* [sing]: *He spoke in a low mumble, as if to himself.*
mumbling *n* [U, C often *pl*] (*esp derog*) mumbled speech; speech or words whose meaning is not clear: *Nobody pays much attention to the mumblings of politicians.*

mumbo-jumbo /₁mʌmbəʊ 'dʒʌmbəʊ/ *n* [U] (*infml derog*) complicated language or ritual with no clear purpose or meaning: *I have no time for religious or scientific mumbo-jumbo.*

mummer /'mʌmə(r)/ *n* an actor in an old form of drama without words.

mummy¹ /'mʌmi/ (*US usu* **mommy** /'mɒmi/) *n* (*infml*) (used mainly by or to young children) a mother.

mummy² /'mʌmi/ *n* a body of a human being or an animal that has been mummified for burial: *an Egyptian mummy.*
▶ **mummify** /'mʌmɪfaɪ/ *v* (*pt, pp -fied*) (usu passive) to preserve a dead body by treating it with special oils and wrapping it in cloth: [Vn] *a mummified corpse.*

mumps /mʌmps/ *n* [sing *v*] a disease, esp of children, with painful swellings in the neck.

munch /mʌntʃ/ *v* ~ (**on sth**) to eat sth steadily, with much movement of the jaw: [Vn, Vpr] *munch (on) an*

---

apple [Vnpr] *He'd munched his way through a whole packet of biscuits.*

mundane /mʌn'deɪn/ *adj* (*often derog*) ordinary and with little excitement: *I lead a pretty mundane life — nothing interesting ever happens to me.* ○ *a mundane film/job* ○ *Having decided on the prizewinners, the committee moved on to more mundane matters.*

municipal /mjuː'nɪsɪpl/ *adj* [usu attrib] of a town or city with its own local government: *municipal buildings* (eg the town hall and the public library) ○ *municipal affairs/elections* (ie of the local council and its members). ▸ **municipality** /mjuːˌnɪsɪ'pælətɪ/ *n* (*fml*) a town, city or district with its own local government; the governing body of such a town, etc.

munificent /mjuː'nɪfɪsnt/ *adj* (*fml*) extremely generous; (of sth given) large in amount or splendid in quality: *a munificent benefactor/gift.* ▸ **munificence** /-sns/ *n* [U].

munitions /mjuː'nɪʃnz/ *n* [pl] military weapons, equipment and stores: *increased production of munitions in time of war.* ▸ **munition** *adj* [attrib]: *munition workers/factories.*

mural /'mjʊərəl/ *n* a painting, usu a large one, done on a wall. ▸ **mural** *adj* [attrib]: *mural art/ decoration.*

murder /'mɜːdə(r)/ *n* **1** [U, C] the illegal deliberate killing of a human being: *guilty of murder* ○ *the murder of a child* ○ *a terrorist murder* ○ *He committed six murders in one week.* ○ *This knife was probably the murder weapon.* ○ *Her latest book's a murder mystery.* See also HOMICIDE. Compare MANSLAUGHTER. **2** [U] (*infml*) (**a**) a very difficult task or an annoying unpleasant experience: *That exam was murder!* ○ *It's murder trying to find a parking place in town on a Saturday.* (**b**) ~ on sth a thing that causes great harm or discomfort to sth: *This hot weather's murder on my feet.* [IDM] **get away with 'murder** (*infml esp joc*) to succeed in ignoring rules or ordinary standards without being punished or suffering any disadvantage: *The local authorities have been getting away with murder for years.* **scream, etc blue murder** ⇨ BLUE¹.
▸ **murder** *v* **1** ~ sb (**with sth**) to kill sb illegally and deliberately: [Vn, Vnpr] *He murdered his wife (with a knife).* [V] *He condemned the terrorists as murdering beasts.* **2** (*infml*) to spoil sth by lack of skill or knowledge: [Vn] *murder a piece of music* (ie play it very badly) ○ *murder the English language* (ie speak or write it in a way that offends against correct use). **murderer** /'mɜːdərə(r)/ *n* a person who murders sb: *a double/mass murderer* (ie one who has killed two/many people). **murderess** /'mɜːdərəs/ *n* a female murderer.

murderous /'mɜːdərəs/ *adj* **1** intending or likely to murder: *a murderous villain/look/attack* ○ *a murderous-looking knife.* **2** (*infml*) very severe or unpleasant: *I couldn't stand the murderous heat.* **murderously** *adv*: *a murderously difficult piece to play.*

murk /mɜːk/ *n* [U] darkness; poor light: *peering through the murk.*
▸ **murky** *adj* (-**ier**, -**iest**) **1** dark and unpleasant; gloomy (GLOOM): *a murky night, with no moon* ○ *thick, murky fog* ○ *The light was too murky to continue playing.* **2** (of water) dirty; not clear: *the river's murky depths.* **3** (*derog or joc*) (of people's actions or character) not fully known and suspected of being not entirely moral or honest: *She had a decidedly murky past.*

murmur /'mɜːmə(r)/ *n* **1** a low continuous sound in the background: *the murmur of bees in the garden* ○ *the distant murmur of traffic.* **2** a quietly spoken word or words: *She answered in a faint murmur.* **3** a quiet expression of feeling: *a murmur of agreement/ approval/complaint* ○ *He paid the extra cost without*

a murmur (ie without complaining at all). **4** (*medical*) a faint blowing sound in the chest, usu a sign of disease or damage in the heart.
▸ **murmur** *v* **1** to make a low continuous sound: [V] *a murmuring brook* ○ *The wind murmured in the trees.* **2** to say sth in a low voice: [Vn] *murmuring words of love into her ear* [Vpr] *He was delirious, murmuring about his childhood.* [V.*that*] *He murmured that he wanted to sleep.* [also V.speech]. **3** ~ (**against/at sb/sth**) to complain about sb/sth quietly, not openly: [Vpr] *For some years the people had been murmuring against the government.* [also V, V.*that*].

muscle /'mʌsl/ *n* **1**(**a**) [C] a piece of elastic body tissue that can be tightened or relaxed to produce movement: *calf/neck/facial muscles* ○ *strain/tear/pull a muscle* ○ *exercises to develop the muscles* ○ *Don't move a muscle* (ie Stay completely still)*!* ⇨ picture. (**b**) [U] such tissue: *The heart is made of muscle.* **2** [U] physical strength: *have plenty of muscle but no brains.* **3** [U] the power to make others do as one wishes: *legal/political/ industrial muscle* ○ *a trade union with plenty of muscle.* [IDM] **flex one's muscles** ⇨ FLEX².
▸ **muscle** *v* [PHRV] **muscle 'in (on sb/sth)** (*infml derog*) to involve oneself in sth when one has no right to do so, for one's own advantage: *She resents the way her family are trying to muscle in on her success.*
■ **'muscle-bound** *adj* having large stiff muscles as the result of excessive exercise.
'muscle-man /-mæn/ *n* (*pl* -**men** /-men/) a big strong man, esp one employed to protect sb/sth.

muscular /'mʌskjələ(r)/ *adj* **1** of the muscles: *muscular contraction/tension* ○ *muscular tissue.* **2** (also **muscly** /'mʌslɪ/) having large strong muscles: *his powerful muscular arms* ○ *He was tall and muscular.*
■ **muscular 'dystrophy** *n* [U] a long illness in which the muscles become gradually weaker.

muse¹ /mjuːz/ *n* **1** **Muse** (often *pl*) (in Greek or Roman myths) each of the nine goddesses (GODDESS 1) who protected and encouraged poetry, music, dancing, history and other branches of art and literature. **2** a spirit that inspires a creative artist, esp a poet: *He felt that his muse had deserted him* (eg that he could no longer write).

muse² /mjuːz/ *v* **1** ~ (**about/on/over/upon sth**) to think in a deep or concentrated way, ignoring what is happening around one: [Vpr] *sit musing on the events of the day/on memories of the past* [also V]. **2** to say sth to oneself in a thoughtful (THOUGHT²) way: [V.speech] *'I wonder if I will ever see them again,' he mused.* [also V.*that*].

museum /mjuː'zɪəm/ *n* a building in which objects of artistic, cultural, historical or scientific interest are displayed: *a museum of natural history* ○ *a war/ maritime museum.*
■ **mu'seum piece** *n* **1** a fine example of sth suitable for a museum. **2** (*joc derog*) an old or old-fashioned thing or person: *Their old car is a real museum piece!*

mush /mʌʃ/ *n* **1** [U, sing] (*usu derog*) a soft thick mixture or mass: *overcooked vegetables turned to mush* ○ *a mush of decaying leaves.* **2** [U] (*infml derog*) writing, etc that is too sentimental: *a romantic novel full of mush.*
▸ **mushy** *adj* **1** like mush: *mushy peas.* **2** (*infml derog*) weak and sentimental: *mushy stories.*

mushroom /'mʌʃrʊm, -ruːm/ *n* a FUNGUS with a fairly round flat head and a stem. Most mushrooms can be eaten: *grilled/fried mushrooms* ○ *a button*

M

mushroom (ie a small one with a round head) ○
mushroom soup. ⇨ picture at FUNGUS. Compare
TOADSTOOL.

▶ **mushroom** *v* [V] **1** (usu **go mushrooming**) to
gather mushrooms in a field or wood. **2** (*sometimes
derog*) to spread or increase in number rapidly: *new
housing mushrooming all over the city.*

■ **'mushroom cloud** *n* a cloud that forms in the air
after a nuclear explosion.

musical notation

notes		rests
○	semibreve (*US* whole note)	▬
♩	minim (*US* half note)	▬
♩	crotchet (*US* quarter note)	↯
♪	quaver (*US* eighth note)	↯
♪	semiquaver (*US* 1/16 note)	↯
♫	demisemiquaver (*US* 1/32 note)	↯

♯ sharp   ♮ natural   ♭ flat

time signature — tie — leger line

key signature   bar

music /'mjuːzɪk/ *n* [U] **(a)** the arrangement of
sounds in a pleasing sequence or combination to be
sung or played on instruments: *compose/study music*
○ *classical/rock music* ○ *a music lesson/teacher* ○
What sort of music do you like? **(b)** compositions of
this kind: *Mozart's music* ○ *play/write a piece of
music* ○ *The poem has been set to music* (ie had
music written for it). See also CHAMBER MUSIC, COUN-
TRY MUSIC, FOLK-MUSIC. **(c)** the written or printed
signs representing such compositions: *read music* ○ *I
had to play it without the music.* See also SHEET
MUSIC. ⇨ picture. **IDM face the music** ⇨ FACE².
music to one's 'ears information that pleases one
very much: *The news of his resignation was music to
my ears.*

■ **'music box** *n* (*US*) = MUSICAL BOX.

'music-hall *n* (*Brit*) **(a)** [C] (esp in the late 19th and
early 20th centuries) a theatre presenting shows
with a variety of different types of entertainment, eg
singing, dancing and comic acts. **(b)** [U] such entertainment: *perform in music-hall* ○ *music-hall
comedians/jokes.*

'music stand *n* a light, usu folding, frame for holding sheets of printed music for sb playing.

musical /'mjuːzɪkl/ *adj* **1** [usu attrib] of or for
music: *a musical director* (eg of a film/show/
broadcast) ○ *a musical entertainment/performance* ○
musical talent/skill. **2** fond of or skilled in music:
She's very musical. **3** sounding pleasant like music:
have a musical voice.

▶ **musical** (also ˌmusical 'comedy) *n* a light amusing play or film with songs and usu dancing: *a
revival of an old Hollywood musical.*

musicality /ˌmjuːzɪˈkæləti/ *n* [U] the state of being
musical: *the admirable musicality of the performers.*

musically /-kli/ *adv* **1** in or of music: *musically*

gifted/talented/ignorant. **2** in a way that is pleasing
to listen to: *play/sing/speak musically.*

■ **'musical box** (*esp Brit*) (*US* **'music box**) *n* a box
containing a mechanical device that produces a
tune when the box is opened.

ˌmusical 'chairs *n* [pl] **1** a game with music in
which players go round a row of chairs (always one
fewer than the number of players) until the music
stops, when the one who finds no chair to sit on has
to leave the game. The person who sits on the last
chair when the music stops wins. **2** (*often derog*) a
situation in which people frequently exchange jobs
or positions: *His appointment as finance director
follows a long period of musical chairs involving top
management.*

ˌmusical 'instrument *n* = INSTRUMENT 3. ⇨ picture.

musician /mjuˈzɪʃn/ *n* **(a)** a person who plays a
musical instrument: *The band consists of ten musicians.* **(b)** a person who is skilled at writing or
playing music: *She is a fine musician.*

▶ **musicianship** *n* [U] art and skill in writing or
performing music.

musk /mʌsk/ *n* [U] a substance with a strong smell
produced by a certain type of male deer. It is used in
making PERFUME(1): *musk-roses* (ie a type of rose
that smells like musk).

▶ **musky** *adj* smelling like musk: *a musky scent.*

musket /'mʌskɪt/ *n* an early type of gun with a long
barrel used by soldiers.

▶ **musketeer** /ˌmʌskəˈtɪə(r)/ *n* (formerly) a soldier
armed with a musket.

musketry /'mʌskɪtri/ *n* [U] (*dated*) muskets generally, or their use: *the distant sound of musketry.*

muskrat /'mʌskræt/ *n* a large water animal of N
America with a strong smell and valuable fur.

Muslim /'mʊzlɪm, 'mʌz-, -ləm/ (also **Moslem**
/'mɒzləm/) *n* a person whose religion is Islam.

▶ **Muslim** (also **Moslem**) *adj* of Muslims and Islam:
a Muslim community/leader ○ *the Muslim faith.*

muslin /'mʌzlɪn/ *n* [U] a thin fine cotton cloth, used
for dresses, curtains, etc.

mussel /'mʌsl/ *n* a small edible SHELLFISH with a
black shell in two parts. ⇨ picture at SHELLFISH.

must /məst; *strong form* mʌst/ *modal v* (*neg* **must
not**; *short form* **mustn't** /'mʌsnt/) **1** (used to indicate that it is necessary that sth happens): *I must go
to the bank to get some money.* ○ *When you enter the
building you must show the guard your pass.* ○ *Cars
must not park in front of the entrance.* ○ *You mustn't
open the oven door before the cake is ready.* ○ (*Brit*)
We mustn't be late, must we? ○ '*Must you go so soon?*'
'*Yes, I must.*' ⇨ note. ⇨ note at SHOULD, MAY. **2**
(used for advising or recommending): *We must see
what the authorities have to say.* ○ *I must ask you not
to do that again.* **3** (used to indicate that one thinks
sth is likely or logical): *You must be hungry after
your long walk.* ○ *She must be having a lot of problems with the language.* ○ *You must be Mr Smith — I
was told to expect you.* ○ *They must be twins.* ○ *He
must have known* (ie Surely he knew) *what she
wanted.* ○ *We must have read the same report.* **4**
(used for insisting that sb does sth): *You 'must put
your name down for the team.* ○ *You simply 'must
read this book — it's so wonderful.* ○ *It's from my
boyfriend, if you 'must know.* ○ '*Must you make so
much noise?*'

▶ **must** *n* (*infml*) a thing that must be done, seen,
heard, etc: *His new novel is a must for all lovers of
crime fiction.*

NOTE Must and **have to** are used in the present to
say that something is necessary. **Must** is used when
the speaker expects or orders something to be done:
You must be home by 11 o'clock. ○ *You must be careful
crossing the road.* ○ *I must wash the car tomorrow.*

You use **have to** when the situation makes something necessary or when a person other than the

speaker is giving an order: *I have to collect the children from school at 3 o'clock.* ∘ *You have to pay for the tickets in advance.* ∘ *Nurses have to wear a uniform.*

There are no past or future forms of **must**. To talk about the past you use **had to** and **has had to**. **Will have to** is used to talk about the future. Questions with **have to** are formed using **do**: *I had to wait half an hour for a bus.* ∘ *We'll have to borrow the money we need.* ∘ *Do the children have to wear a uniform?*

In negative sentences both **must not** and **don't have to** (also **don't need to** and **need not**) are used. **Must not** is used when the speaker expects or orders somebody not to do something: *Passengers must not smoke until the signs have been switched off.* The short form **mustn't** is used especially in British English: *You mustn't leave the gate open.*

Don't have to, **don't need to** or **need not** are used when it is not necessary to do something: *You don't have to pay for the tickets in advance.* ∘ *She doesn't have to/doesn't need to work at weekends.* The short form **needn't** is used especially in British English.

Must not is also used to talk about permission. ⇨ note at MAY.

mustache (*US*) = MOUSTACHE.

mustang /'mʌstæŋ/ *n* a small American wild horse.

mustard /'mʌstəd/ *n* [U] **1** a hot-tasting yellow or brown PASTE¹(3) made from the crushed seeds of the mustard plant and eaten with food, esp certain meats. The mustard plant has yellow flowers and long thin seed pods (POD): *a jar of mustard* ∘ *mustard powder* ∘ *French/English/Dijon mustard.* **2** [U] a fairly dark yellow colour: *a mustard (yellow) sweater.* **IDM keen as mustard** ⇨ KEEN¹. ■ '**mustard gas** *n* [U] a poisonous gas that burns the skin.

muster /'mʌstə(r)/ *n* a gathering of people or things, esp for inspection: *muster stations* (ie places where people assemble in an emergency). **IDM pass muster** ⇨ PASS¹.
▶ **muster** *v* **1** to come or bring people together, esp for a military PARADE(2): [V] *The troops mustered (on the square).* [Vn] *muster the troops.* **2** ~ **sth (up)** (often after *can, could,* etc) to succeed in creating a particular feeling or attitude in oneself or in other people: [Vn] *muster public support for sth* ∘ *muster all one's courage* ∘ *He addressed her* **with all the** politeness **he could muster.** [Vnp] *I couldn't muster up much enthusiasm for it.*

musty /'mʌsti/ *adj* damp and smelling STALE(1) or of mould²: *a musty attic* ∘ *the musty smell of old books.*

mutable /'mju:təbl/ *adj* (*fml*) that can or is likely to change. ▶ **mutability** /ˌmju:tə'bɪləti/ *n* [U].

mutant /'mju:tənt/ *n* (**a**) (*biology*) a living thing that differs physically from its parents as a result of GENETIC change. (**b**) (*infml*) (esp in stories about space, the future, etc) a living thing with an abnormal and frightening appearance as a result of GENETIC change.
▶ **mutant** *adj* differing as a result of GENETIC change: *a mutant gene* ∘ *a mutant strain of a virus.*

mutation /mju:'teɪʃn/ *n* (*esp techn*) (**a**) [U] the action or process of changing in form or structure: (*biology*) *mutation of cells* ∘ (*linguistics*) *vowel mutation.* (**b**) [C] a change in form or structure: *mutations in plants caused by radiation.* (**c**) [C] a new living thing resulting from such a change.
▶ **mutate** /mju:'teɪt; *US* 'mju:teɪt/ *v* ~ (**into sth**) to change or make sth change in form or structure: [V] *cells that mutate* [Vn] *cells mutated by a virus* [Vpr] *organisms that mutate into new forms.*

mute /mju:t/ *adj* **1** silent; making no sound: *stare in mute astonishment/sympathy* ∘ *remain mute.* **2** (*dated*) (of people) unable to speak; DUMB(1). **3** (of a

letter in a written word) not pronounced when the word is spoken: *The 'b' in 'dumb' is mute.*
▶ **mute** *n* **1** (*music*) (**a**) a piece of metal, plastic, etc used to soften the sounds produced from an instrument with strings. (**b**) a device placed in the opening of an instrument that is blown, in order to change the quality of the sounds produced. ⇨ picture at MUSICAL INSTRUMENT. **2** (*dated*) a person without the power of speech.

mute *v* (esp passive) to make the sound of sth, esp a musical instrument, quieter or softer, esp with a mute: [Vn] *The strings are muted throughout the closing bars of the symphony.* **muted** *adj* **1** (of sounds) quiet, soft and low: *They spoke in muted voices.* **2** not openly or strongly expressed: *muted excitement/criticism.* **3** (of musical instruments) fitted with a mute: *muted violins.* **4** (of colours) not bright; subdued (SUBDUE): *muted greens and blues.*
'**mute button** *n* a device on a telephone for temporarily preventing the person making a call from hearing what is being said in the room of the person receiving it.
mutely *adv* in silence; without speaking.

mutilate /'mju:tɪleɪt/ *v* to injure or damage sb/sth very severely, eg by breaking or tearing off a necessary part: [Vn] *The prisoners' arms and legs had been cut off and their mutilated bodies thrown into the ditch.* ∘ *Intruders slashed and mutilated several paintings.* ▶ **mutilation** /ˌmju:tɪ'leɪʃn/ *n* [U, C]: *Thousands suffered death or mutilation as a result of the bomb attacks.*

mutinous /'mju:tənəs/ *adj* refusing to obey orders or instructions: *mutinous soldiers/workers* ∘ *mutinous behaviour/looks.*

mutiny /'mju:təni/ *n* [U, C] refusal to obey the proper authorities, esp by soldiers or sailors: *Having failed to seize control of the ship, the crew were tried for mutiny.* ∘ *The team manager nearly had a mutiny on his hands.*
▶ **mutineer** /ˌmju:tə'nɪə(r)/ *n* a person who is guilty of mutiny.
mutiny *v* (*pt, pp* **-nied**) [V, Vpr] ~ (**against sb/sth**) to refuse to obey orders; to be guilty of mutiny.

mutt /mʌt/ *n* (*derog or joc*) a dog, esp one of no particular breed.

mutter /'mʌtə(r)/ *v* **1** ~ (**sth**) (**to sb/oneself**) (**about sth**) to speak or say sth in a low voice that is hard to hear: [V] *Don't mutter! I can't hear you.* [Vpr, Vp] *Sarah was muttering (away) to herself as she washed the dishes.* [Vn, Vnpr] *He muttered something (to the sales assistant) about losing his wallet.* [also V.*that*, V.speech]. **2** ~ (**about/against/at sb/sth**) to complain privately or in a way that is not openly expressed: [Vpr] *For some time people had been muttering about the way she ran the shop.* [also V].
▶ **mutter** *n* (usu *sing*) a low sound or words that are not clear or distinct.
muttering /'mʌtərɪŋ/ *n* [U] (**a**) words spoken in a low voice, often to oneself. (**b**) (also **mutterings** [pl]) complaints that are expressed privately, not openly.

mutton /'mʌtn/ *n* [U] the meat from a fully grown sheep: *a leg/shoulder of mutton* ∘ *mutton stew.* Compare LAMB 1b. **IDM mutton dressed as** '**lamb** (*Brit infml derog*) an older person dressed in a style suitable for a younger person.

mutual /'mju:tʃuəl/ *adj* **1** (of a feeling or an action) felt or done by each towards the other: *mutual affection/suspicion* ∘ *mutual aid/support* ∘ *The dislike between us was mutual.* **2** (*infml*) shared by two or more people: *We met at the house of a/our mutual friend* (ie a friend of both of us)*, Peter Cox.* **3** (*fml*) (of people) having the same specified relationship to each other: *mutual well-wishers.* ▶ **mutuality** /ˌmju:tʃu'æləti/ *n* [U] (*fml*): *a mutuality of interest.*
mutually /-uəli/ *adv*: *mutually agreed working*

M

musical instruments

Playing an instrument

When speaking generally about playing musical instruments, **the** is usually used before the name of the instrument:

- *She decided to take up (= start learning to play)* **the** *flute.*
- *I've been playing* **the** *piano since I was twelve.*
- *He played* **the** *trumpet in a dance band.*

The is not used when two or more instruments are mentioned:

- *She teaches violin, cello and piano.*

The preposition **on** is used to say who is playing which instrument:

- *The recording features James Galway on the flute.*
- *She sang and he accompanied her on the piano.*

The is not usually used when you are talking about pop or jazz musicians:

- *Eric Clapton on guitar*
- *Miles Davis played trumpet.*

Describing instruments

There are four **sections** of instruments in an **orchestra**: **strings**, **woodwind**, **brass** and **percussion**.

Specific adjectives are used before the names of musical instruments to describe the type of instrument it is:

- *a tenor saxophone*
- *a bass drum*
- *a classical guitar*

Grammar point

The names of instruments are used like adjectives before other nouns:

- *a clarinet lesson*
- *Chopin's Piano Concerto No 1*
- *She's going to do her cello practice.*

strings

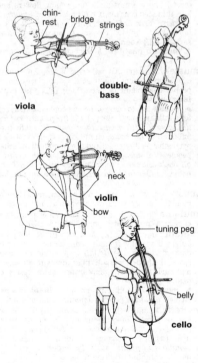

chin-rest   bridge   strings

viola

double-bass

neck

violin

bow

tuning peg

belly

cello

woodwind

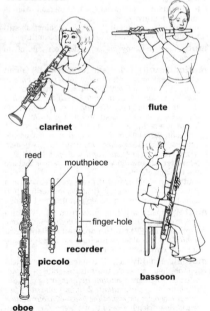

flute

clarinet

reed

mouthpiece

finger-hole

recorder

piccolo

bassoon

oboe

M

People who play instruments

At the entry in the dictionary for a particular musical instrument there might be a word, ending in **-ist** or **-er**, which means 'somebody who plays this instrument':

● *The violinist lifted his bow.*
● *the South African drummer, Louis Moholo*

If there is no special word, you use **player** after the name of the instrument:

● *the quartet's viola player*

When talking about pop music or jazz, people often use **player** even when there is a word for the person like **saxophonist** or **bassist**:

● *a brilliant young sax player*
● *We're looking for a new bass player.*

Music for instruments

Music is **composed** or **written for** an instrument. In a piece of music written for a group of instruments, each has a different **part** to play:

● *There are parts for oboe and bassoon.*

A **solo** is a part for one instrument playing alone. A **soloist** plays it:

● *a very accomplished violin soloist*
● *I love the saxophone solo on this song.*

In an orchestra playing classical music, **first**, **second** and **principal** are used with certain instruments to describe a player's position or importance:

● *She plays first horn in the National Children's Orchestra.*
● *He became principal cellist within a few years.*

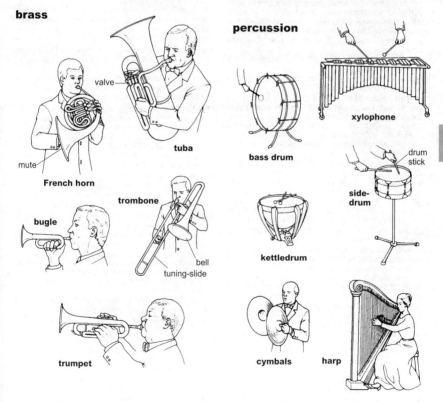

brass

valve

mute

tuba

French horn

bugle

trombone

bell
tuning-slide

trumpet

percussion

xylophone

bass drum

drum stick

side-drum

kettledrum

cymbals   harp

M

hours ∘ *The two arguments are not **mutually exclusive*** (ie It is possible to accept parts of both). ∎ **'mutual fund** *n* (*US*) = UNIT TRUST.

,mutual in'surance company *n* an insurance company in which some or all of the profits are divided among the holders of policies.

Muzak /'mjuːzæk/ *n* [U] (*propr often derog*) continuous recorded light music often played in shops, restaurants, factories, etc.

muzzle /'mʌzl/ *n* **1(a)** the nose and mouth of an animal, esp a dog or fox. (**b**) a guard placed over this part of an animal's head to prevent it biting people. ⇨ picture at HORSE. **2** the open end of a gun, out of which the bullets are fired: *a ,muzzle-loading 'gun.* Compare BREECH.
▶ **muzzle** *v* [Vn] **1** (esp passive) to put a muzzle on a dog, etc. **2** (*derog*) to prevent a person, society or newspaper from expressing their opinions freely: *accuse the government of muzzling the press.*

muzzy /'mʌzi/ *adj* (*Brit*) **1** unable to think in a clear way; confused: *Those drugs make me feel muzzy.* ∘ *Her mind was muzzy from sleep and cold.* **2** not clear; blurred (BLUR): *muzzy eyesight.*

MV /,em 'viː/ *abbr* motor vessel.

MW *abbr* **1** (*radio*) medium wave. **2** (*techn*) megawatt(s).

my /maɪ/ *possess det* **1** of or belonging to the speaker or writer: *Where's my hat?* ∘ *My feet are cold.* ∘ *He always forgets my birthday.* **2** (used before a *n* or an *adj* as a form of address, showing affection or sympathy, or sometimes lack of patience or superior status): *my dear/darling/love* ∘ *my dear fellow/girl/ Mary.* **3** (used in exclamations): *My goodness, what a surprise!* ∘ *My God, look at the time!* Compare MINE[1].

mycology /maɪ'kɒlədʒi/ *n* [U] the science or study of fungi (FUNGUS).

mynah /'maɪnə/ *n* a large dark bird of SE Asia that can copy human speech.

myopia /maɪ'əʊpiə/ *n* [U] **1** (*medical*) inability to see distant things clearly. **2** (*derog*) inability to consider or plan for the future: *the prevalent educational myopia at national level.* ▶ **myopic** /maɪ'ɒpɪk/ *adj*: *myopic eyes* ∘ (*derog*) *a myopic attitude/outlook* ∘ *myopic advisers.* See also SHORT-SIGHTED.

myriad /'mɪriəd/ *n* an extremely large number: *Each galaxy contains myriads/a myriad of stars.*
▶ **myriad** *adj* [attrib] too many to count: *demands made by the myriad charities in existence today.*

myrrh /mɜː(r)/ *n* [U] a sticky substance with a sweet smell but a bitter taste that is obtained from plants and used for making INCENSE[1] and PERFUME(1).

myrtle /'mɜːtl/ *n* [U] a bush with shiny leaves and sweet-smelling white flowers.

myself /maɪ'self/ *reflex, emph pron* (only taking the main stress in sentences when used emphatically) **1** (*reflex*) (used when the speaker or writer is also the person affected by an action): *I ,cut myself with a 'knife.* **2** (*emph*) (used to emphasize the speaker or writer): *I my'self will present the prizes.* ∘ *I said so my'self only last week.* **IDM** **(all) by my'self 1** alone: *I sat by myself in the waiting-room.* **2** without help: *I finished the crossword (all) by my'self.*

mysterious /mɪ'stɪəriəs/ *adj* **1** difficult to understand or explain: *a mysterious event/crime/letter* ∘ *He resigned in mysterious circumstances.* **2** keeping or liking to keep things secret: *He was being very mysterious, and wouldn't tell me what he was up to.* ∘ *She gave me a mysterious look* (ie suggesting secret knowledge). ▶ **mysteriously** *adv*: *The main witness had mysteriously disappeared.* ∘ *Mysteriously, there was no answer when I phoned.*

mystery /'mɪstri/ *n* **1** [C] (**a**) a thing of which the cause or origin is not known or impossible to explain: *the mystery/mysteries of life* ∘ *a crime that is an unsolved mystery* ∘ *a mystery guest/tour* (ie kept secret until the last possible moment) ∘ *It's a mystery to me why they chose him for the job.* ∘ *Their motives **remain a mystery**.* (**b**) (*infml*) a person about whom not much is known or can be learned: *He's a bit of a mystery!* **2** [U] the condition of being secret or not known: *His past is **shrouded in mystery*** (ie One cannot find out the truth about it). ∘ *Mystery surrounds her disappearance.* **3** [U] a sense that sth secret or exciting may soon be discovered or revealed: *The cave was full of mystery.* ∘ *'You'll find out after dinner,' she said with an air of mystery.* **4** [C] a religious truth or belief that is beyond human understanding: *the mystery of the Incarnation.* **5** **mysteries** [pl] secret religious ceremonies: (*fig*) *initiate new recruits into the mysteries* (ie customs and practices) *of army life.* **6** [C] a story or play about a crime or other event that seems difficult to explain: *a murder mystery* ∘ *a mystery thriller.* ∎ **'mystery play** *n* = MIRACLE PLAY.

mystic /'mɪstɪk/ (also **mystical** /'mɪstɪkl/) *adj* **1** having hidden meaning or spiritual power: *mystic rites/forces.* **2** of or based on MYSTICISM: *the world's mystic religions* ∘ *mystical writings.* **3** causing feelings of deep respect and wonder: *mystic beauty* ∘ *Watching the sun rise over the mountain was an almost mystical experience.*
▶ **mystic** *n* a person who tries to become united with God and so reach truths beyond human understanding.
mystically /-kli/ *adv*.

mysticism /'mɪstɪsɪzəm/ *n* [U] the belief that knowledge of God and of real truth may be reached by directing one's mind or through spiritual INSIGHT(1a), independently of reason and the senses: *Christian mysticism* ∘ *There is a strong element of mysticism in his poetry.*

mystify /'mɪstɪfaɪ/ *v* (*pt, pp* **-fied**) to make sb uncertain or confused through lack of information or understanding; to PUZZLE *v* sb: *(by) her mystifying disappearance* ∘ *I'm mystified — I just can't see how he did it.* ▶ **mystification** /,mɪstɪfɪ'keɪʃn/ *n* [U]: *the mystification of the reader* ∘ *There was a look of mystification on his face.*

mystique /mɪ'stiːk/ *n* [sing] an air of mystery and importance that attracts one's interest or admiration: *the mystique of space exploration* ∘ *The tiger has a mystique that has always been respected.*

myth /mɪθ/ *n* **1(a)** [C] a story that originated in ancient times, esp one concerning the early history of a people or explaining natural events, such as the seasons: *a Creation myth* (ie about how the world began) ∘ *ancient Greek myths.* (**b**) [U] such stories generally: *famous in myth and legend.* **2** [C] a thing or person that is imaginary or not true: *the myth of a classless society* ∘ *The rich uncle he boasts about is only a myth.*
▶ **mythical** /'mɪθɪkl/ (also **mythic** /'mɪθɪk/) *adj* **1** existing only in myth: *mythical heroes* ∘ *mythic creatures.* **2** imaginary; invented: *that mythical 'rich uncle' he boasts about.*

mythology /mɪ'θɒlədʒi/ *n* [U, C] myths in general, or a particular group of myths: *study Greek mythology/ancient mythologies.*
▶ **mythological** /,mɪθə'lɒdʒɪkl/ *adj* of or in myths or mythology: *mythological explanations* ∘ *Pluto, the mythological king of the underworld.*

myxomatosis /,mɪksəmə'təʊsɪs/ *n* [U] an infectious and usu fatal disease of rabbits.

M

Nn

N¹ (also **n**) /en/ n (pl **N's, n's** /enz/) **1** the 14th letter of the English alphabet: *'Nicholas' begins with (an) N/'N'*. **2** (*mathematics*) (used to represent a number whose value is not specified). See also NTH.

N² abbr **1** (*US* also **No**) north; northern: *N California* ○ *London N14 6BS* (ie as a postal code). **2** (esp on electric plugs) neutral (connection).

n abbr noun.

NAAFI (also **Naafi**) /'næfi/ abbr (*Brit*) Navy, Army and Air Force Institutes (an organization providing shops and places to eat for British soldiers, etc in England and abroad): *a NAAFI canteen*.

nab /næb/ v (**-bb-**) (*infml*) (**a**) to catch sb doing sth wrong; to arrest sb: [Vnpr, Vn] *He was nabbed (by the police) for speeding*. (**b**) to take or catch sb/sth: [Vn] *I tried to nab him as he was leaving the meeting.* ○ *Who's nabbed my pen?*

nadir /'neɪdɪə(r)/ n [sing] **1** the lowest point; a time of greatest depression, despair, etc: *Company losses reached their nadir in 1992*. **2** the part of the sky directly below an observer. Compare ZENITH 1.

naff /næf/ adj (*Brit sl*) (used as a general term of disapproval) lacking taste or style; worthless; not fashionable: *That's a pretty naff idea!*

nag¹ /næg/ v (**-gg-**) **1** ~ (**at sb**) to complain or criticize sb continuously: [Vn, Vpr] *He nagged (at) her all day long*. [V] *Stop nagging, I'll do it as soon as I can*. [Vn.to inf] *She's been nagging me to mend that lamp for weeks*. **2** to worry or hurt sb continuously: [Vn] *a nagging pain/doubt/suspicion/worry* [Vn, Vpr] *The problem had been nagging (at) me for weeks*.

nag² /næg/ n (*infml often derog*) a horse, esp one that is old or ill.

nail /neɪl/ n **1** a thin hard layer covering the outer tip of the human finger or toe: *clean/cut/bite one's nails*. See also FINGERNAIL, TOENAIL. ⇨ picture at HAND¹. **2** a small thin piece of metal with a sharp point at one end and a usu flat head at the other. Nails are used esp for fixing things together or for hanging things on a wall, etc: *hammer in a nail*. ⇨ picture at HAMMER. Compare SCREW n 1. **IDM** **fight, etc tooth and nail** ⇨ TOOTH. **hard as nails** ⇨ HARD¹. **hit the nail on the head** ⇨ HIT¹. **a nail in sb's/sth's 'coffin** a thing that makes sb's death, or the end, failure, etc of sb/sth certain to happen soon: *The strike was the last nail in the company's coffin*. **on the 'nail** (*infml*) (of payment) without delay: *I want cash on the nail*.
▶ **nail** v **1** (*infml*) to catch or arrest sb: [Vn] *Have the police nailed the man who did it?* **2** [Vn] (*infml*) to show sth to be false. **IDM** **nail one's colours to the 'mast** (*esp Brit*) to declare openly and firmly what one believes, who one supports, etc. **PHRV** **,nail sth 'down 1** to make a carpet, lid, etc secure with nails. **2** to define sth exactly: *The reasons why some children do badly at school are difficult to nail down*. **,nail sb 'down (to sth)** to force sb to give a firm promise or to say exactly what they intend to do: *She says they come, but I can't nail her down to a specific time*. **,nail sth 'on; ,nail sth on/onto/to sth** to fasten sth to sth with nails: *nail the l 1 on (the crate)* ○ *nail a sign to the wall*. **,nail sth 'up 1** to fasten sth with nails so that it hangs from a wall, post, etc. **2** to make a door, window, etc secure with nails so that it cannot easily be opened.

■ **'nail-biting** adj causing great tension or anxiety: *a nail-biting end to the match*.
'nail-brush n a small stiff brush for cleaning the nails of the fingers. ⇨ picture at BRUSH¹.
'nail-file n a small flat file³ for shaping the nails of the fingers.
'nail-scissors n [pl] small, usu curved, SCISSORS for cutting the nails of the fingers and toes: *a pair of nail-scissors*.
'nail varnish (also **varnish**) (*Brit*) (*US* **'nail polish**) n [U] a liquid that is applied to the nails of the fingers and toes to give them a hard shiny surface or colour when dry.

naive (also **naïve**) /naɪ'iːv/ adj **1** (*esp derog*) (**a**) showing lack of experience, wisdom or judgement: *a naive person/remark/question* ○ *be politically naive*. (**b**) foolishly ready to believe what one is told: *You weren't so naive as to believe him, were you?* **2** natural and innocent in speech and behaviour: *Their approach to life is refreshingly naive*.
▶ **naively** (also **naïvely**) adv.
naivety (also **naïvety** /naɪ'iːvəti/, **naïveté** /naɪ'iː-vəteɪ/) n [U] the quality of being naive: *His work is a curious blend of sophistication and naivety*.

naked /'neɪkɪd/ adj **1**(**a**) without clothes on: *a naked body* ○ *as naked as the day he was born* ○ *She stood there completely naked*. (**b**) [usu attrib] without the usual covering: (*Brit*) *a naked light* (eg an electric BULB(2) without a shade) ○ *a naked sword* (ie one without its SHEATH(1a)) ○ *naked trees* (ie without leaves). **2** not disguised: *the naked truth* ○ *naked aggression/emotion/fear*. **IDM** **the naked 'eye** the normal power of the eyes to see, without the use of a TELESCOPE, a MICROSCOPE, etc: *Microbes are too small to be seen by the naked eye*. **stark naked** ⇨ STARK. ▶ **nakedly** adv: *nakedly aggressive/commercial*.
nakedness n [U].

namby-pamby /,næmbi 'pæmbi/ adj (*derog*) weak; foolishly sentimental.

name¹ /neɪm/ n **1** [C] a word or words by which a person, an animal, a place or a thing is known and spoken to or about: *My name is Peter*. ○ *Write your name and address here, please*. ○ *Do you know the name of this flower?* See also CODE-NAME, HOUSEHOLD NAME, MAIDEN NAME, PET NAME. **2**(**a**) [sing] a reputation, esp a good one: *The company has always had a name for reliability*. ○ *This kind of behaviour gives students a bad name*. ○ *She made a name for herself/made her name as a writer of children's fiction*. (**b**) [attrib] (*esp US*) (in compounds) having a name that is generally known: *a big-name company*. **3** [C] a famous person: *Some of the biggest names in the art world were at the party*. **IDM** **answer to the name of sth** ⇨ ANSWER². **be sb's middle name** ⇨ MIDDLE. **a big noise/shot/name** ⇨ BIG. **by 'name** using the name or names of sb/sth: *The headteacher knows all the pupils by name*. ○ *I only know her by name* (ie from hearing others speak about her, not personally). **by/of the name of** named: *a young actor by the name of William Devlin*. **call sb names** ⇨ CALL¹. **drop names** ⇨ DROP². **enter one's 'name / put one's 'name down (for sth)** to apply to enter a school, college, course, competition, etc. **give a dog a bad name** ⇨ DOG¹. **give one's 'name to sth** to invent or originate sth which then becomes known by one's own name: *Charles Mac-*

N

intosh gave his name to a type of raincoat. **in the name of** 'sb/'sth **1** by the authority of sth: *I arrest you in the name of the law.* **2** calling sb/sth to witness: *In God's name, what are you doing?* **3** for the sake of sth: *They did it all in the name of friendship.* **in** '**name only** not in reality: *The park exists in name only; houses have been built on the site now.* **lend one's name to sth** ⇨ LEND. **one's name is** '**mud** one is not liked or avoided because of sth one has done: *They won't invite me. My name is mud at the moment.* **name names** ⇨ NAME². **the name of the** '**game** the main purpose or most important aspect of an activity: *Hard work is the name of the game if you want to succeed in business.* **put a** '**name to sb/sth** to know or remember what sb/sth is called: *I've heard that tune before but I can't put a name to it.* **take sb's name in** '**vain** to use a name, esp God's, without proper respect. **(have sth) to one's** '**name** (to possess sth) as one's own: *an Olympic athlete with five gold medals to his name* ○ *She hasn't a penny to her name* (ie is very poor). **under the name (of)** 'sth using sth as a name instead of one's real name: *He writes under the name (of) Nimrod.*
■ '**name-dropping** *n* [U] the practice of casually mentioning the names of famous people one knows or pretends to know in order to impress others: *Name-dropping won't get you accepted any quicker.* '**name-drop** *v* (**-pp-**) [V].
'**name-plate** *n* a sign on or beside a door showing the name of a company or of the person living or working there: *a doctor's name-plate.*

NOTE Your **first name** in English-speaking countries is the name your parents give you when you are born and is the name friends and people in your family use when they speak to you. In Christian countries, **Christian name** is sometimes used for **first name**. **Forename** is a formal word for **first name** and is often found on application forms, etc.
The name that is common to your family is your **surname**, **family name** or **last name**. It is often used with the titles Mr, Ms, Mrs or Miss. These titles are *not* used with first names alone.
Your **full name** is all the names you have, including your **middle names** (ie other names your parents gave you) which you do not say very often.

---

name² /neɪm/ *v* **1** ~ sb/sth (**after sb**); (*US*) ~ sb/sth (**for sb**) to give a name to sb/sth: [Vnpr] *He was named after his father* (ie given his father's first name). [Vn-n] *They named their son John.* [also Vn]. **2** to give the name(s) of sb/sth; to identify sb/sth: [Vn] *Can you name all these plants?* ○ *Police have named a man they would like to question.* ○ *Everyone was there: John, Karen, Philip,* **to name but a few** (ie giving only these as examples). **3** to state sth exactly; to specify sth: [Vn] *Name your price* (ie Say what price you want to charge). ○ *They're engaged, but they haven't yet* **named the day** (ie chosen and announced the day on which they will get married). [Vn] *Chairs, tables, cupboards —* **you name it** (ie anything you can imagine), *she makes it.* **4** ~ sb (**as sth**) to choose or appoint sb for a position: [Vn-n] *She has been named as the new head of department.* [also Vn]. **IDM** **name** '**names** to give the name of a person or people involved in sth, esp sth wrong or illegal: *He said someone had lied but wouldn't name names.*

nameless /'neɪmləs/ *adj* **1(a)** [esp attrib] having no name or no known name: *a nameless grave* ○ *the nameless thousands who built the pyramids.* (**b**) not mentioned by name: *a nameless source in the government* ○ *a well-known public figure* **who shall be/ remain nameless** (ie whose name I will not mention). **2** [esp attrib] (**a**) (esp of emotions) not easy to describe: *a nameless longing/fear.* (**b**) too

terrible to describe: *the nameless horrors of the prison camp.*

namely /'neɪmli/ *adv* that is to say; to be specific: *Only one boy was absent, namely Scott.* ○ *Shareholders drew their own conclusions, namely that it was time to sell out.*

namesake /'neɪmseɪk/ *n* a person or thing having the same name as another: *She's my namesake but we're not related.*

nanny /'næni/ *n* (*Brit*) **1** a child's nurse. **2** (also **nan** /næn/) (*infml*) (esp as a form of address) a grandmother.

nanny-goat /'næni gəʊt/ *n* a female goat. ⇨ picture at GOAT. Compare BILLY-GOAT.

nap¹ /næp/ *n* a short sleep, esp during the day: *have/ take a quick nap after lunch.* See also CATNAP.
▶ **nap** *v* (**-pp-**) [V] to have a short sleep. **IDM** **catch sb napping** ⇨ CATCH¹.

nap² /næp/ *n* [U] the short fine threads or hairs on the surface of certain fabrics, eg VELVET, usu lying or brushed in one direction. Compare PILE⁴.

napalm /'neɪpɑːm/ *n* [U] a jelly made from petrol that burns and is used in making bombs.

nape /neɪp/ *n* (usu *sing*) the back part of the neck: *Her hair was caught at the nape in a gold bow.* ⇨ picture at HEAD¹.

napkin /'næpkɪn/ *n* **1** (also '**table napkin**) a piece of cloth or paper used at meals for protecting one's clothes and wiping one's lips and fingers. **2** (*Brit dated or fml*) = NAPPY.

nappy /'næpi/ (also *fml* **napkin**) (*Brit*) (*US* **diaper**) *n* a piece of soft cloth or other thick covering folded round a baby's bottom and between its legs to absorb or hold its body waste: *change the baby's nappy* ○ *a disposable nappy* (ie one that is made to be used once only).

narcissism /'nɑːsɪsɪzəm/ *n* [U] (*psychology*) an abnormal and excessive love or admiration for oneself.
▶ **narcissistic** /ˌnɑːsɪ'sɪstɪk/ *adj*.

narcissus /nɑː'sɪsəs/ *n* (*pl* **narcissuses** /nɑː'sɪsəsɪz/ or **narcissi** /nɑː'sɪsaɪ/) a plant, growing from a BULB¹, that produces long leaves and white or yellow flowers in spring: *The daffodil is a type of narcissus.*

narcotic /nɑː'kɒtɪk/ *n* **1** a substance causing one to sleep or become very relaxed and feel no pain: *The juice of this fruit is a mild narcotic.* **2** (*often pl*) a drug that affects the mind: *trafficking in narcotics* ○ *a narcotics agent* (ie one investigating the illegal trade in narcotics).
▶ **narcotic** *adj* of or having the effect of a narcotic: *a narcotic effect/substance.*

nark /nɑːk/ *n* (*Brit sl*) a person who informs the police about people involved in crimes.

narked /nɑːkt/ *adj* (*Brit sl*) annoyed: *extremely narked at being ignored.*

narrate /nə'reɪt; *US* 'næreɪt/ *v* to tell a story; to give a written or spoken account of sth: [Vn] *narrate one's adventures in central Asia* ○ *The story is narrated by Sarah Holt.*
▶ **narration** /nə'reɪʃn, næ'r-/ *n* (**a**) [U] the telling of a story. (**b**) [C] a story; an account of events.
narrator *n* a person who narrates sth.

narrative /'nærətɪv/ *n* **1** [C] a spoken or written account of events; a story: *a gripping narrative of/ about their journey up the Amazon.* **2** [U] the telling of a story: *a master of narrative* ○ *The novel contains more narrative than dialogue.*
▶ **narrative** *adj* telling a story: *narrative literature* ○ *narrative poems* ○ *the narrative structure.*

narrow /'nærəʊ/ *adj* (**-er, -est**) **1** small in width in relation to length: *a narrow bed/bridge/channel/ path* ○ *The lane was too narrow for cars to overtake.* Compare BROAD¹ 1, THIN 1, WIDE 1a. **2** [usu attrib] with only a small margin; only just achieved: *have a*

---

narrow escape from death ○ be elected by a narrow
majority (eg when voting is 67 to 64) ○ have a narrow
lead over (ie be not far ahead of) the rest. **3** limited
in range or scope; having little interest in general
issues or sympathy for the opinions of others: a
narrow mind ○ She takes a rather narrow view of the
subject. **4** limited in numbers or variety; small or
restricted: a narrow circle of friends ○ within the
narrow confines of political life. **5** strict; exact: What
does the word mean in its narrowest sense? **IDM** **the
straight and narrow** ▷ STRAIGHT¹.
▶ **narrow** v to become or make sth narrower: [V]
The road narrows here. ○ The gap between the two
parties has narrowed considerably. ○ Her eyes narrowed (ie She partly closed them) menacingly. [Vn]
He narrowed his eyes and frowned. **PHRV** **narrow**
sth 'down to reduce the number of possibilities or
choices: We've narrowed down the list to three possible candidates.
narrowly adv **1** only just; by only a small margin:
be narrowly defeated ○ He narrowly avoided a
collision/escaped death. **2** closely; carefully: observe
someone narrowly.
narrowness n [U]: the narrowness of the road ○
narrowness of mind.
narrows n [pl] a narrow channel connecting two
larger areas of water.
■ **,narrow-'minded** /'maɪndɪd/ adj not ready to
listen to or tolerate the views of others: a narrow-
minded bigot. **,narrow-'mindedness** n [U].
narwhal /'nɑːwəl/ n a white WHALE from the Arctic
region. The male narwhal has a long TUSK.
NASA /'næsə/ abbr (in the USA) National Aeronautics and Space Administration.
nasal /'neɪzl/ adj of, for or relating to the nose: nasal
sounds (eg /m, n, ŋ/) ○ the nasal passages ○ a nasal
voice (ie produced through both the nose and the
mouth).
nascent /'næsnt/ adj (fml) beginning to exist; not
yet fully developed: a nascent industry/talent ○ nascent democracies.
nasturtium /nə'stɜːʃəm; US næ-/ n a garden plant
with edible red, orange or yellow flowers and round
flat leaves.
nasty /'nɑːsti; US 'næsti/ adj (-ier, -iest) **1** not nice;
unpleasant: a nasty smell/taste ○ There's so much
cheap and nasty stuff in the shops nowadays. Compare NICE. **2(a)** unkind; full of spite: What a nasty
man! ○ Don't be nasty to your little brother. ○ She has
a nasty temper. **(b)** morally bad: nasty stories ○ She's
got a thoroughly nasty mind. See also VIDEO NASTY.
3(a) dangerous; threatening: a nasty corner (ie dangerous for cars going fast) ○ The weather is too nasty
for sailing. ○ He had a nasty look in his eye. ○ He
turned nasty (ie became aggressive) when I refused
to go with him. **(b)** painful; severe: a nasty cut/
wound ○ She had a nasty skiing accident. ○ The news
gave me a nasty shock. **4** unfortunate; not welcome:
I've got **a nasty feeling** it's going to rain. ○ His
predictions have **a nasty habit** of turning out to be
true. **IDM** **leave a bad/nasty taste in the mouth**
▷ TASTE¹. **a nasty piece of 'work** (infml) an unpleasant person or one who cannot be trusted. ▶
nastily adv. **nastiness** n [U].
nation /'neɪʃn/ n a large community of people, usu
sharing a common history, culture and language,
and living in a particular territory under one government: industrialized nations ○ Her plight touched
the nation. ▷ note at COUNTRY.
■ **,nation-'state** n a nation of people forming an
independent state: advocate the establishment of a
separate nation-state.
national /'næʃnəl/ adj [usu attrib] **1** of a nation;
common to or characteristic of a whole nation: a
national treasure/institution/campaign ○ national
and local news ○ national and international issues ○

our national character ○ The decision was made **in
the national interest** (ie for the benefit of the
nation). **2** owned, controlled or financially supported by the State: a national theatre/library.
▶ **national** n a citizen of a particular nation: He's a
French national working in Italy. ▷ note at CITIZEN.
nationally /'næʃnəli/ adv: attract criticism both locally and nationally.
■ **,national 'anthem** n a song or hymn adopted by
a nation, used to express loyalty to and love of one's
country and sung esp on ceremonial occasions.
,national con'vention n (US) an assembly of a
major political party, esp to nominate a candidate
for election as President.
,national cur'riculum n (pl curricula) (usu sing)
(in Britain) a programme of study in all major
subjects followed by all pupils in state schools: attainment targets in the national curriculum.
,national 'debt n (usu sing) the total amount of
money owed by a country to those who have lent it
money.
the ,National 'Front n [Gp] (in Britain) a political
party with extreme views, esp on RACIAL issues.
,national 'grid n [sing] (Brit) a network of electric
power lines linking the major power stations.
the ,National 'Guard n [sing] (esp US) a trained
military force partly maintained by individual
States but available for national service in an emergency.
the ,National 'Health Service n [sing] (abbr NHS)
(in Britain) a public service providing medical care,
paid for by taxes: I got my hearing-aid on the National Health (Service).
,National In'surance n [U] (abbr NI) (in Britain) a
system of compulsory payments made by employees
and employers to enable the State to provide assistance to people who are ill, unemployed or retired:
National Insurance contributions.
,national 'park n an area of country whose natural
beauty is protected and maintained by the State for
the public to enjoy: The area was designated a national park.
,national 'service n [U] a period of compulsory
service in the armed forces of one's country: do
one's national service.
the ,National 'Trust n [sing] (in Britain) a society
founded in 1895 to preserve places of natural beauty
or historic interest.
nationalism /'næʃnəlɪzəm/ n [U] **1** a strong feeling
of love and pride in one's own country: (sometimes
derog) a surge of cultural nationalism. Compare PAT-
RIOTISM. **2** a desire for political independence by a
nation that is controlled by another or is part of
another; a policy based on this: Welsh nationalism.
▶ **nationalist** /'næʃnəlɪst/ n, adj [attrib] (a person)
supporting nationalism(2): Scottish nationalists (ie
those who want Scotland to have its own parliament) ○ nationalist demands/movements/sympathies.
nationalistic /,næʃnə'lɪstɪk/ adj strongly favouring
nationalism: nationalistic fervour during the World
Cup.
nationality /,næʃə'næləti/ n **1** [U,C] membership
of a particular nation: Fill in your name, address
and nationality on the form. ○ apply for/have/hold
French nationality ○ The conference brought together
scientists of all nationalities. **2** [C] a national group
forming part of a nation: concern for the
rights of minority nationalities in the country.
nationalize, -ise /'næʃnəlaɪz/ v to transfer sth
from private ownership to ownership by the State:
[Vn] nationalize the railways/the coal-mines/the steel
industry ○ the nationalized sector of the economy.
Compare DENATIONALIZE, PRIVATIZE. ▶ **nationalization, -isation** /,næʃnəlaɪ'zeɪʃn; US -lə'z-/ n [U]: the
nationalization of the railways.
nationwide /,neɪʃn'waɪd/ adj, adv over the whole

N

of a nation: *a ˌnationwide ˈsurvey/camˈpaign* ○ *The company has over 300 stores nationwide.*

native /'neɪtɪv/ *n* **1(a)** a person born in a place, country, etc, and associated with it by birth: *a native of Miami/Italy/the north-east/these parts.* **(b)** a local inhabitant: *She speaks the language like a native.* **2** (*dated usu offensive*) a person born in a place, esp one who is not white and considered by visitors and those who have settled there to be inferior: *The early colonists and settlers enslaved the natives.* **3** an animal or a plant that lives or grows naturally in a certain area: *The kangaroo is a native of Australia.* ▶ **native** *adj* **1** associated with the place and circumstances of one's birth: *native speakers of English* (ie those whose first language is English) ○ *leave one's native land/city* ○ *Her native language/tongue is German.* **2** (*sometimes derog or offensive*) of natives (NATIVE 2): *native customs/rituals.* **3** (of qualities) belonging to a person's basic personality or character, not acquired by education, training, etc: *have a great deal of native charm/intelligence/wit.* **4** ~ **to ...** (of plants, animals, etc) originating in a place: *plants native to America* (eg tobacco, potatoes) ○ *The tiger is native to India.* **IDM** **go ˈnative** (*often joc*) (of a person abroad) to adopt the customs of the local people and abandon those of one's own: *He's emigrated to the USA and gone completely native.*
■ ˌNative Aˈmerican (also *dated* **Amerindian**) *n* a member of any of the peoples that were the original inhabitants of North America. See also RED INDIAN.

nativity /nə'tɪvəti/ *n* **1 the Nativity** [sing] the birth of Christ, celebrated by Christians at Christmas. **2 Nativity** [C] a picture of the birth of Christ.
■ na'tivity play *n* a play about the birth of Christ.

NATO (also **Nato**) /'neɪtəʊ/ *abbr* North Atlantic Treaty Organization (an arrangement made between several European countries, USA, Canada and Iceland to give each other military help if necessary): *the NATO alliance/allies.*

natter /'nætə(r)/ *v* ~ **(away/on) (about sth)** (*Brit infml*) to talk casually for a long time, esp about unimportant things: [Vpr, Vp] *nattering (on) about his family* [V] *I can't sit here nattering — I've got work to do.*
▶ **natter** *n* [sing] (*Brit infml*) an informal conversation: *have a good natter.*

natty /'næti/ *adj* (*dated infml*) **1** neat and fashionable: *a natty dresser* ○ *buy a natty new suit.* **2** well designed: *a natty briefcase.*

natural /'nætʃrəl/ *adj* **1** [attrib] of, existing in or caused by nature(1); not made or caused by human beings: *natural phenomena/forces/disasters* ○ *the natural world* (ie of trees, rivers, animals and birds) ○ *animals living in their natural state* (ie wild) ○ *a country's natural resources* (ie its coal, oil, forests, etc) ○ *a flower's natural beauty.* **2** of or in agreement with the character or personality of a living thing: *the natural agility of a cat.* **3** [attrib] **(a)** (of people) born with a certain skill, ability, etc: *He's a natural leader.* ○ *She's a natural linguist* (ie learns languages easily). **(b)** (of qualities, etc) with which one is born; INHERENT: *He has a natural talent for music.* **4** as is to be expected; normal: *die a natural death/die of natural causes* (ie not by violence, etc, but normally, of old age) ○ *It's only natural to worry about your children.* ○ *She was the natural choice for the job.* **5** relaxed and not pretending to be sb/sth different: *her natural friendliness* ○ *It's difficult to look natural when you're feeling nervous.* **6** (*music*) (used after the name of a note) neither sharp(11b) nor flat²(5): *B natural.* ⇨ picture at MUSIC. **7** [attrib] (of a son or daughter) related by blood: *He's not our natural son — we adopted him when he was three.* **8** based on human reason alone: *natural law/virtue.*
▶ **natural** *n* **1** (*music*) **(a)** a normal musical note,

not its sharp(11b) or flat²(5) form. **(b)** the sign (♮) indicating such a note in printed music. **2** ~ **(for sth)** a person considered to be perfectly suited for a job, an activity, etc: *He's a natural for the role of Puck.* ○ *She didn't have to learn how to run: she's a natural.*

naturalness *n* [U] the state or quality of being natural: *a novel admired for the naturalness of the dialogue.*
■ ˌnatural ˈchildbirth *n* [U] a method of giving birth to children in which the mother is not given drugs and does special breathing and relaxing exercises.
ˌnatural ˈgas *n* [U] a gas found in the earth, not manufactured: *power stations running on natural gas.*
ˌnatural ˈhistory *n* [U] the study of plants and animals: *a natural history programme on TV.*
ˌnatural ˈscience *n* [pl] the sciences used in the study of the physical world, eg CHEMISTRY, PHYSICS, BIOLOGY, BOTANY, GEOLOGY. Compare LIFE SCIENCES.
ˌnatural seˈlection *n* [U] the theory that living things develop, survive and die out according to their ability to adapt themselves to their environment.

naturalism /'nætʃrəlɪzəm/ *n* [U] **1** the style of art and literature in which things are presented in a real and detailed way. **2** (*philosophy*) the theory that rejects explanations not based on natural causes and laws.
▶ **naturalistic** /ˌnætʃrə'lɪstɪk/ *adj* copying nature closely: *a naturalistic style/writer/painter.*

naturalist /'nætʃrəlɪst/ *n* a person who studies animals, plants, birds and other living things.

naturalize, -ise /'nætʃrəlaɪz/ *v* (usu passive) **1** to make sb from another country a citizen of the specified country: [Vn] *a naturalized American who was born in Poland.* **2** to introduce a plant or an animal into a country where it is not native: [Vn] *The grey squirrel is now naturalized in Britain.* ▶ **naturalization, -isation** /ˌnætʃrəlaɪ'zeɪʃn; US -lə'z-/ *n* [U]: *naturalization papers* (ie documents proving a person has been made a citizen of a country).

naturally /'nætʃrəli/ *adv* **1** by nature(4a): *a naturally gifted actor* ○ *She's naturally musical.* **2** of course; as might be expected: *'Did you answer her letter?' 'Naturally!'* ○ *Naturally, as a beginner, I'm not a very good driver yet.* **3** without artificial help, special treatment, etc: *plants that grow naturally in chalky soils* ○ *Her hair curls naturally.* **4** without exaggerating; in a normal way: *Try to act naturally, even if you're feeling tense.* **5** easily; almost without trying: *Most sports come naturally to him.*

nature /'neɪtʃə(r)/ *n* **1** [U] the whole universe and every created, not artificial, thing: *the wonders of nature* ○ *manufactured substances not found in nature.* **2** (often **Nature**) [U] the forces that control the events of the physical world: *contrary to the laws of Nature* ○ *It's best to let nature take its course.* ○ *man's constant attempts to control nature.* See also MOTHER NATURE. **3(a)** [C, U] the typical qualities and characteristics of a person or an animal: *appeal to sb's better nature* (ie the generous part of their character) ○ *It's against his nature* (ie not his natural reaction) *to be unkind.* ○ *There is no cruelty in her nature.* ○ *Cats and dogs have quite different natures — dogs like company, cats are independent.* ○ *She is proud by nature.* See also HUMAN NATURE, SECOND NATURE. **(b)** [sing] the basic qualities or character of a thing: *Chemists study the nature of gases.* ○ *He knows nothing of the nature of my work.* **4** [sing] a kind, sort or class: *Things of that nature do not interest me.* **IDM** **against ˈnature** not natural; not moral: *a crime against nature.* **(go, etc) back to ˈnature** returning to the simple type of life that existed before complex political and industrial societies developed: *man's yearning to get back to nature.* **in the nature of** '**sth** similar to sth; a type of sth: *His speech was in the nature of an a¹pology.*

▶ **-natured** (forming compound *adjs*) having qualities or characteristics of the specified kind: ¦*good-*¹*natured.*

■ '**nature reserve** *n* an area of land protected for the benefit of its animals, plants, physical features, etc.

'**nature study** *n* [U] the study of plants, animals, insects, etc, esp in school.

'**nature trail** *n* a path through woods or countryside, along which interesting plants, animals, etc can be seen.

naturism /'neɪtʃərɪzəm/ *n* [U] (*Brit*) = NUDISM. ▶ **naturist** /'neɪtʃərɪst/ *n* (*Brit*) = NUDIST.

naught = NOUGHT 2.

naughty /'nɔːti/ *adj* (**-ier, -iest**) **1** (used esp when talking to or about children) behaving badly: *one of the naughtiest children in the class* ○ *It was very naughty of you not to tell me where you were going.* **2** (*infml*) connected with sex in a rude or funny way: *a naughty joke/word.* ▶ **naughtily** *adv.* **naughtiness** *n* [U].

nausea /'nɔːzɪə, 'nɔːsɪə/ *n* [U] **1** a feeling of wanting to be sick: *overcome by nausea after eating too much.* **2** a feeling of extreme dislike or disgust: *filled with nausea at the sight of cruelty to animals.*

▶ **nauseate** /'nɔːzɪeɪt, 'nɔːsɪeɪt/ *v* to make sb feel nausea: *The idea of eating raw meat nauseates me.* **nauseating** *adj*: *nauseating food* ○ *a nauseating person* ○ *The smell was quite nauseating.* **nauseatingly** *adv.*

nauseous /'nɔːzɪəs, 'nɔːsɪəs; *US* 'nɔːʃəs/ *adj* **1** feeling nausea or disgust: *She felt nauseous and weak.* **2** causing nausea; disgusting: *a nauseous account of the murder.*

nautical /'nɔːtɪkl/ *adj* of ships, sailors or sailing: *nautical terms.*

■ ¦**nautical** '**mile** (also **sea mile**) *n* a measure of distance at sea, about 1852 metres.

naval /'neɪvl/ *adj* of a navy; of ships of war: *a naval officer/uniform/battle* ○ *naval forces* ○ *a naval power* (ie a country with a strong navy).

nave /neɪv/ *n* the long central part of a church, where people attending a service mostly sit. ⇨ picture at CHURCH.

navel /'neɪvl/ *n* a small hollow in the middle of the stomach where the cord attaching a baby to its mother was cut at birth. ⇨ picture at HUMAN.

navigable /'nævɪgəbl/ *adj* (of seas, rivers, etc) suitable for ships, boats, etc to sail on: *The Rhine is navigable from Strasbourg to the sea.*

navigate /'nævɪgeɪt/ *v* **1** to find the position and direct the course of a ship, an aircraft, a car, etc, using maps, instruments, etc: [V] *navigate by the stars* ○ *I'll drive: you navigate* (ie tell me which way to go). [Vnpr] *navigate a ship through coastal waters* [Vn] *We navigated our way south.* **2** to sail along, over or through a sea, river, etc: [Vn] *The upper reaches of the river are too dangerous to navigate.*

▶ **navigation** /ˌnævɪ'geɪʃn/ *n* [U] **1** the action, process or art of navigating: *navigation by satellite* ○ *a navigation chart* ○ *an expert in navigation* ○ *in-car navigation systems to beat urban traffic problems.* **2** movement of ships over water or aircraft through the air: *an increase in navigation through the canal.* **navigational** *adj*: *navigational aids.*

navigator *n* a person who navigates, esp in a ship or an aircraft.

navvy /'nævi/ *n* (*Brit*) a person employed to do hard physical work, eg on a building site.

navy /'neɪvi/ *n* **1**(**a**) [C] a country's military force of ships and their crews: *exercises involving the navies of the USA, Britain and France.* (**b**) **the navy, the**

Navy [Gp] a country's fighting ships and their crews, considered as an institution: *join the navy* ○ *an officer/sailor in the Royal/US Navy.* See also MERCHANT NAVY. ⇨ App 6. **2** [U] = NAVY BLUE.

■ ¦**navy** '**blue** (also **navy**) *adj, n* [U] dark blue: *a navy (blue) dress/suit.*

nay /neɪ/ *adv* (*dated or rhet*) **1** and more than that; and indeed: *Such a policy is difficult, nay, impossible to justify.* **2** (*arch*) no. Compare YEA.

Nazi /'nɑːtsi/ *n, adj* **1** (a member) of the German National Socialist Party founded by Hitler. **2** (*derog*) (a person) holding extreme views on people of other races and prepared to use violence to express them. ▶ **Nazism** /'nɑːtsɪzəm/ *n* [U].

NB (also **nb**) /ˌen 'biː/ *abbr* (used before a written note) take special notice that; note well (Latin *nota bene*).

NBC /ˌen biː 'siː/ *abbr* (in the USA) National Broadcasting Company: *heard it on NBC.*

NCO /ˌen si: 'əʊ/ *abbr* a non-commissioned officer: *promoted to NCO rank.*

NE *abbr* north-east; north-eastern: *the NE corner of the island.*

Neanderthal /ni'ændətɑːl/ *adj* of an extinct type of human being living in Europe during the Stone Age: *Neanderthal artefacts* ○ (*fig derog*) *Neanderthal* (ie very old-fashioned) *opinions.*

neap tide /'niːp taɪd/ (also '**neap**) *n* a tide when there is least difference between high and low water. Compare SPRING TIDE.

near¹ /nɪə(r)/ *adj* (**-er** /'nɪərə(r)/, **-est** /'nɪərɪst/) (**near** and **nearer** [usu pred]; **nearest** [pred] or [attrib]) **1** within a short distance of space or time; close: *His house is very near.* ○ *Where's the nearest bank?* ○ *The nearest house to ours is 2 miles away.* ○ *Some of the nearer branches caught fire.* ○ *We hope to move to Bath in the near future* (ie very soon). ⇨ note at NEXT². **2** coming next after sb/sth: *a 12-point lead over her nearest rival.* **3** (esp superlative) similar in size, quality, etc: *This is the nearest colour we have in stock.* ○ *the nearest equivalent to the model you want* ○ *He was the nearest thing to* (ie the person most like) *a father she had ever had.* ○ *Five hundred would be a nearer estimate.* See also ONO. **4** having a close family connection: *the near relations of the deceased.* **5** (no comparative or superlative) having almost all the qualities or features of sth: *a near riot/tragedy* ○ *reach near starvation* ○ *a near impossibility/certainty.* **IDM** **a close/near thing** ⇨ THING. **one's** ¦**nearest and** '**dearest** (*joc*) one's close family: *spend Christmas with one's nearest and dearest.* **to the nearest ...** (followed by a number when counting or measuring approximately): *budgeting to the nearest £100 for the cost of repairs* ○ *The time is measured to the nearest 100th of a second.* ▶ **nearness** *n* [U]: *the moon's nearness to the earth* ○ *the nearness of death.*

■ **the** ¦**Near** '**East** *n* [sing] the countries on the eastern shores of the Mediterranean Sea.

¦**near** '**miss** *n* **1** a situation in which a serious accident or disaster is only just avoided: *a near miss by two aircraft over southern England.* **2** a bomb or shot that lands near its target but not on it.

¦**near-**'**sighted** *adj* (*esp US*) = SHORT-SIGHTED.

near² /nɪə(r)/ *adv* **1** at a short distance away in time or space: *Lee found some shops quite near.* ○ *Don't come any nearer or I'll shoot.* ○ *Our final exams are drawing near.* ○ *The threat of a rail strike moved a step nearer today.* **2** (esp in compounds) almost: *a near-perfect performance* ○ *a near-impregnable position* ○ *near-certain success.* **IDM** **as near as** as accurately as: *There were about 3 000 people there, as near as I could judge.* **as** ¦**near as** '**damn it** / '**dammit**; **as** ¦**near as makes no** '**difference** (*infml esp Brit*) an amount that is not much more or less, so that the difference does not matter: *It will*

[V.speech] = verb + direct speech   [V.*that*] = verb + *that* clause   [V.*wh*] = verb + *who, how*, etc clause

N

cost £350, or as near as dammit. **far and near/wide** ⇨ FAR[1]. **not anywhere near / nowhere near** far from; not at all: *I've nowhere near enough money for the fare.* ○ *There wasn't anywhere near enough food for all of us.* **sail close/near to the wind** ⇨ SAIL[2]. **so ˌnear and ˌyet so 'far** (used to comment on an attempt that was almost successful but in fact failed).

near³ /nɪə(r)/ (also **near to**) *prep* (*near to* not usu used before the name of a place, person, festival, etc) **1(a)** not far from sb/sth; close to sb/sth: *The supermarket is very near (to) the library.* ○ *near the Italian border* ○ *She was sitting near (to) the window.* ○ *Bradford is near Leeds.* **(b)** a short period of time from sth: *My birthday is very near Christmas.* ○ *a nuclear power station near (to) the end of its working life.* **2** (used esp before a number) approaching sth; a small amount above or below sth: *report profits near to £10m* ○ *Share prices are near their record high of last year.* **3** similar in quality, size, etc to sth: *a state near to death* ○ *No one else comes near her in intellect.* **4** friendly with or emotionally close to sb: *It's very difficult to get near him.* **5** ~ **sth / doing sth** approaching a particular state; almost or on the point of doing sth: *children near starvation* ○ *She was near to tears (ie almost crying).* ○ *We were near to being killed.* **IDM** **close/dear/near to sb's heart** ⇨ HEART. **close/near to home** ⇨ HOME[1]. ▶ **'nearer (to)** *prep*: *He's nearer 70 than 60.* ○ *Go and sit nearer the fire.* ○ *I'll think about it nearer the time.* ○ *The company has cut its profit forecasts from around $11m to nearer $8m.* **'nearest (to)** *prep*: *This colour is nearest to the original.* ○ *John is nearest me in age.*

near⁴ /nɪə(r)/ *v* to approach or come close to sth in space or time: [Vn] *We were at last **nearing the end of** our journey.* ○ *The project is **nearing completion**.* ○ *She's nearing 40.*

nearby /ˌnɪə'baɪ/ *adj* [usu attrib] near in position; not far away: *a ˌnearby 'church/'river/'town* ○ *The shop nearby sells milk.* ○ *The beach is quite nearby.* ▶ **nearby** *adv* at a short distance from sb/sth: *They live nearby.*

nearly /'nɪəli/ *adv* not completely; almost; very close to: *nearly empty/full/finished* ○ *It's nearly one o'clock.* ○ *It's nearly time to leave.* ○ *They gave us nearly everything we needed.* ○ *We're nearly there now.* ○ *There's nearly £100 here.* ○ *She very nearly died.* **IDM** **not 'nearly** far from; much less than; not at all: *There isn't nearly enough time to learn all these new words.* ○ *We aren't nearly ready for the inspection.* **pretty much/nearly/well** ⇨ PRETTY *adv*. ⇨ note at ALMOST.

nearside /'nɪəsaɪd/ **the nearside** *n* [sing] (*Brit*) (for a driver, etc) the left side of a road or of a vehicle or an animal on a road: *The driver lost control, veered to the nearside and crashed into a van.* ○ *keep to the nearside lane.* Compare OFFSIDE[2].

neat /niːt/ *adj* **1(a)** (of things) arranged in a tidy way; done carefully: *a neat cupboard/room* ○ *neat work/writing* ○ *arranged in neat rows/piles* ○ *We managed to get the garden looking **neat and tidy**.* **(b)** (of people) liking to keep things in order and do things carefully; tidy: *a neat worker/dresser.* **2(a)** (of clothes) simple and elegant: *a neat uniform/dress.* **(b)** having a pleasing shape or appearance: *her small neat face.* **3** not wasting time and effort; skilful; efficient: *a neat way of doing the job* ○ *a neat solution to the problem* ○ *He gave a neat summary of the financial situation.* **4** (*infml esp US*) (as a general term of approval) good; excellent: *a really neat movie/idea/car.* **5** (*US* usu **straight**) (esp of spirits or wines) not mixed with water: *a neat whisky/vodka* ○ *drink one's whisky neat* ○ *weed-killer applied neat to the lawn.* ▶ **neatly** *adv*: *neatly trimmed hair* ○ *summarize the situation very neatly* ○ *The box fitted neatly into the drawer.* **neatness** *n* [U].

nebula /'nebjələ/ *n* (*pl* **nebulae** /-liː/ or **nebulas**) a mass of dust or gas seen in the night sky, sometimes glowing very bright, at other times dark and visible only when next to brighter objects.

nebulous /'nebjələs/ *adj* not clear; VAGUE(1): *nebulous ideas/plans/concepts.*

necessarily /ˌnesə'serəli/ *Brit also* 'nesəsərəli/ *adv* as an inevitable result; in all cases: *Just because they're rich it doesn't necessarily mean they're happy.*

necessary /'nesəsəri; *US* -seri/ *adj* **1** essential for a purpose; needed: *It didn't seem necessary for us to meet/necessary that we meet.* ○ *Changes can easily be made where necessary.* ○ *Is it absolutely/really necessary to send him to hospital?* ○ *If necessary, I'm prepared to come again tomorrow.* ○ *I haven't got the necessary tools.* ○ *I'll make the necessary arrangements.* **2** that must be; inevitable; logical: *accept the necessary consequences of one's actions.* **IDM** **a ˌnecessary 'evil** a thing that is undesirable and possibly harmful but must be accepted for practical reasons: *The loss of jobs is regarded by some as a necessary evil in the fight against inflation.* ▶ **necessaries** *n* [pl] the things needed for sth: *the necessaries of life.*

necessitate /nə'sesɪteɪt/ *v* (*fml*) to make sth necessary: [Vn] *policy changes which will necessitate a fundamental reorganization* [V.ing] *Increased traffic necessitated widening the road.* [V.n ing] *The demands of the job may necessitate you working unsocial hours.*

necessity /nə'sesəti/ *n* **1** [U] ~ **(of/for sth)**; ~ **(to do sth)** circumstances that force one to do sth; the state of being necessary; the need for sth: *recognize the necessity for improved child-care facilities* ○ *I don't think there's any necessity to draw up a written agreement at this stage.* ○ *The final decision will of necessity (ie necessarily) rest with her parents.* ○ *The government was spared the necessity of instituting an official enquiry.* ○ *There's absolutely no necessity for you to be involved.* **2** [C] a necessary thing: *the basic necessities of life* ○ *Air-conditioning was an absolute necessity.* **IDM** **make a virtue of necessity** ⇨ VIRTUE.

neck

crew neck

polo-neck
(*US* turtle-neck)

V-neck

turtle-neck
(*US* mock
turtle-neck)

neck /nek/ *n* **1** [C] **(a)** the part of the body that connects the head to the shoulders: *wrap a scarf round one's neck* ○ *She fell out of the window and broke her neck.* ○ *Giraffes have very long necks.* ○ *He craned (ie stretched) his neck to see over the heads of the crowd.* ⇨ picture at HEAD[1]. **(b)** the part of a garment that goes around this: *My shirt is a little tight in the neck.* ⇨ picture. See also CREW NECK, POLO-NECK, TURTLE-NECK, V-NECK. **2** [U] the flesh of an animal's neck eaten as food: *buy some neck of lamb.* **3** [C] a narrow part of sth, like a neck in shape or position: *the neck of a bottle/violin* ○ *a neck of land.* ⇨ picture at MUSICAL INSTRUMENT. **IDM** **breathe down sb's neck** ⇨ BREATHE. **by the scruff of the/one's neck** ⇨ SCRUFF. **ˌget it in the 'neck** (*infml*) to be severely criticized or punished for sth: *You'll get it in the neck if you're caught* *stealing.* **a millstone round one's/sb's neck** ⇨ MILLSTONE. ₁**neck and** ¹**neck (with sb/sth)** (in horse-racing or in a contest, struggle, etc) with neither competitor having an advantage or a lead; level: *The leading runners are neck and neck.* ₁**neck of the** ¹**woods** (*infml*) a particular place, esp one where one is not expected to be: *What are you doing in this neck of the woods?* **a pain in the neck** ⇨ PAIN. **risk/save one's** ¹**neck** to risk/save one's life; to risk/avoid great danger: *He won't help you — he's only interested in saving his own neck.* **stick one's neck out** ⇨ STICK². **up to one's/the ears/eyes/ eyebrows/neck in sth** ⇨ EAR. **wring sb's neck** ⇨ WRING.

▶ **neck** *v* (*infml*) (usu in the continuous tenses) (of couples) to kiss each other in a sexual way: [V] *The two of them were necking on a park bench.*

necklace /ˈnekləs/ *n* an ornament of jewels or beads (BEAD 1a), worn around the neck: *a diamond necklace.*

neckline /ˈneklaɪn/ *n* the edge or shape of a garment, esp that of a woman, at or below the neck: *a dress with a high/low/plunging neckline.*

necktie /ˈnektaɪ/ *n* (*dated or US*) = TIE¹ 1.

necromancy /ˈnekrəʊmænsi/ *n* [U] the art or practice of communicating by magic with the dead in order to learn about the future.

▶ **necromancer** /-sə(r)/ *n* a person who practises necromancy.

necropolis /nəˈkrɒpəlɪs/ *n* (*pl* **necropolises** /-lɪsɪz/) a CEMETERY, esp a large ancient one.

nectar /ˈnektə(r)/ *n* [U] a sweet liquid produced by flowers and collected by bees for making honey: (*fig*) *After their long walk the beer tasted like nectar.*

nectarine /ˈnektəriːn/ *n* a type of PEACH(1a) with a smooth skin.

née /neɪ/ *adj* (used after the name of a married woman and before her father's family name) born with the name: (*Mrs*) *Jane Smith, née Brown.*

need¹ /niːd/ *modal v* (*neg form* **need not**; *short form* **needn't** /ˈniːdnt/) (used only in negative sentences and questions, after *if* and *whether* or with *hardly, scarcely, no one,* etc; not in the continuous tenses) **1** (indicating obligation): *You needn't finish that work today.* ◦ *He asked whether he need send a deposit.* ◦ *If she wants anything, she need only ask.* ◦ *I need hardly tell you* (ie You must already know) *that the work is dangerous.* ◦ *Nobody need be afraid of catching the disease.* ⇨ note at MUST. **2** (used with *have* + a past participle to indicate that actions in the past were or may have been unnecessary): *You needn't have hurried.* ◦ *She needn't have come in person — a letter would have been enough.* ◦ *Need you have paid so much?* ⇨ note at NEED².

need² /niːd/ *v* **1** to require sth/sb because they are important or useful, and not simply because one would like to have them: [Vn] *That dog needs a bath.* ◦ *Do you need any help?* ◦ *He needed six points for a win.* ◦ *What we need is some proof.* ◦ *Don't go — I may need you.* ◦ *Food aid is badly/urgently needed.* [V.to inf] *I need to get some sleep.* [V.ing] *The garden doesn't need watering — it rained last night.* **2** (indicating obligation) [V.to inf] *I didn't need to go to the bank — I borrowed some money from Mary.* ◦ *All you need to do is (to) fill in this form.* ◦ *A dog needs to be taken out for a walk every day.* ◦ *Will we need to show our passports?* ⇨ note at MUST.

NOTE When you are asking questions about whether something is necessary, you can use either **need¹** (modal verb) or **need²**: *Need we really leave so early?* ◦ *Do we really need to leave so early?* The use of the modal verb is more formal.

To say that it is not necessary to do something, you can use **need not** (also **needn't**) or **do/does not need to** (also **don't/doesn't need to**): *You needn't go home yet.* ◦ *You don't need to go home yet.*

When you say that it is not necessary to have something, only **do/does not need** is possible: *We don't need a car in the city* (NOT *We need not a car in the city*).

To talk about the past you use **didn't need, didn't need to** or **needn't have**: *We didn't need very much money on holiday as we stayed with friends.* ◦ *I didn't need to wait very long for the bus* (ie the bus came quickly). **Needn't have** is only used to talk about something somebody did in the past that was not necessary: *You needn't have waited for me* (ie you waited for me but it was not necessary).

need³ /niːd/ *n* **1** [sing, U] ~ (**for sth**); ~ (**for sb**) to **do sth** circumstances in which sth is lacking or necessary, or which require sth to be done; a necessity: *create/identify a need for sth* ◦ *He stressed the need for a cautious approach.* ◦ *The house is in need of a thorough clean.* ◦ *She felt a need to talk to someone about it.* ◦ *There's no need for you to go yet.* **2 needs** [pl] basic necessities or requirements: *supply a baby's needs* ◦ *satisfy/meet sb's needs* ◦ *pupils with special educational needs* ◦ *Will £20 be enough for your immediate needs?* **3** [U] the state of being without food, money, etc: *charities feeding people in need* ◦ *He helped me in my hour of need.* See also NEEDY. **IDM a friend in need** ⇨ FRIEND. **if need** ¹**be** if necessary: *There's always food in the freezer if need be.* ◦ *If need be, I can do extra work at the weekend.*

▶ **needful** /-fl/ *adj* (*dated*) necessary: (*rhet or joc*) *Will you do the needful* (ie do what is required)*?*

needless *adj* not necessary: *needless work/trouble/ worry.* **IDM** ₁**needless to** ¹**say** as you already know or would expect: *Needless to say, he kept his promise.*

needlessly *adv*: *Patients are dying needlessly.*

needle /ˈniːdl/ *n* **1** [C] a small thin piece of polished steel with a point at one end and a hole for thread at the other, used in sewing: *the eye of a needle* ◦ *She threaded the needle expertly.* See also PINS AND NEEDLES. **2** [C] a long thin piece of plastic, metal, polished wood, etc without a hole but with a pointed end or a hook: ¹*knitting needles* ◦ *a* ¹*crochet needle.* **3** [C] a thin, usu metal piece, POINTER(1) in an instrument for measuring, etc: *the speedometer needle* ◦ *The compass needle swung round.* **4** [C] a pointed hollow end of a SYRINGE: *disposable needles for injecting drugs.* ⇨ picture at INJECTION. **5** [C] a thing like a needle(1) in shape, appearance or use, eg the thin pointed leaf of a PINE¹ tree or a pointed rock: *dead pine needles.* ⇨ picture at PINE¹. **6** [C] a STYLUS used in playing records. **7** [U] (*infml*) anger or hostility, esp in situations where people are rivals: *A certain amount of needle has crept into* (ie gradually appeared in) *this game.* ◦ *a needle game/match* (ie one in which the competitors are very fierce rivals). **IDM a needle in a** ¹**haystack** a thing that is almost impossible to find because it is hidden among many other things: *Searching for one man in this big city is like looking for a needle in a haystack.* **sharp as a needle** ⇨ SHARP.

▶ **needle** *v* (*infml*) to provoke or annoy sb, esp with words: [Vn] *I could see that my questions were needling him.*

needlewoman /ˈniːdlwʊmən/ *n* (*pl* **-women** /-wɪmɪn/) a woman who sews, usu skilfully; a SEAMSTRESS: *an expert needlewoman.*

needlework /ˈniːdlwɜːk/ *n* [U] sewing or embroidery (EMBROIDER 1).

needn't /ˈniːdnt/ *short form* need not ⇨ NEED¹.

needy /ˈniːdi/ *adj* (**-ier, -iest**) without the things that are needed for life, ie food, clothes, etc; very poor: *a needy family* ◦ *help the poor and needy.*

ne'er-do-well /ˈneə duː wel/ *n* a useless or lazy person: *How is that ne'er-do-well brother of yours?*

nefarious /nɪˈfeəriəs/ *adj* (*fml*) wicked: *nefarious deeds/activities.*

neg *abbr* negative.

negate /nɪˈgeɪt/ *v* (*fml*) **1** to cancel the effect of sth; to NULLIFY sth: [Vn] *Attempts to standardize human performance can negate the purpose of study.* **2** [Vn] to deny the existence of sb/sth.
▶ **negation** /nɪˈgeɪʃn/ *n* (usu *sing*) (*fml*) the absence or opposite of sth: *This theory is a negation of all traditional beliefs.*

negative /ˈnegətɪv/ *adj* **1** (abbreviated as *neg* in this dictionary) (of words, sentences, etc) expressing refusal or DENIAL; indicating 'no' or 'not': *a negative sentence/question/adverb* ○ *give sb a negative answer.* Compare AFFIRMATIVE. **2(a)** lacking in helpful qualities or characteristics; not having or showing an interested attitude, aiming to improve sth, etc: *He has a very negative approach to his work.* ○ *She was still critical of the proposals, but not as negative about them as before.* **(b)** (of an effect) harmful: *eliminate the negative side-effects of a drug.* **3** (of the results of a test or an experiment) indicating that a substance or condition is not present: *Her pregnancy test was negative.* **4** (*mathematics*) (of a number or quantity) less than zero. **5** containing or producing the type of electric charge carried by an ELECTRON: *the negative terminal of a battery.* Compare POSITIVE.
▶ **negative** *n* **1** a word or statement that expresses or means refusal or DENIAL: *'No', 'not' and 'neither' are negatives.* ○ (*fml*) *She answered in the negative* (ie said 'no'). **2** a developed photographic film, etc on which the light and dark areas of the actual objects or scene are reversed and from which positive pictures can be made: *Don't throw the negatives away.*
negatively *adv*: *react negatively* ○ *negatively charged electrons.*
negativity *n* [U] a negative(2) attitude.

neglect /nɪˈglekt/ *v* **1** to give no or not enough care or attention to sb/sth: [Vn] *accuse sb of neglecting their studies/children/health* ○ *research into neglected and unexamined areas.* **2** (*fml*) to fail or forget to do sth, esp carelessly; not to do what one ought to do: [V.to inf] *He neglected to write and say 'Thank you'.* See also NEGLIGENCE.
▶ **neglect** *n* [U] the act of neglecting sb/sth or state of being neglected: *The buildings are crumbling because of years of neglect.* ○ *She was severely criticized for neglect of duty.* ○ *The garden was in a state of total neglect.*
neglected *adj* showing or suffering from a lack of care or attention: *abused and neglected children* ○ *The house looked sadly neglected.*
neglectful /-fl/ *adj* ~ (**of sth/sb**) (*fml*) in the habit of neglecting persons or people: *neglectful of one's appearance/responsibilities/family.*

negligée /ˈneglɪʒeɪ; *US* ˌneglɪˈʒeɪ/ *n* a woman's light dressing-gown (DRESSING): *She looked stunning in her silk negligée.*

negligence /ˈneglɪdʒəns/ *n* [U] lack of proper care and attention; careless behaviour: *The accident was the result of negligence.* ○ *They sued the doctor for medical negligence.* ○ (*law*) *be accused of criminal negligence* (ie that can be punished by law).

negligent /ˈneglɪdʒənt/ *adj* not giving proper care and attention to sth; careless: *be negligent of one's duties/responsibilities* ○ *The council was negligent in the way that it looked after the girl.* ▶ **negligently** *adv*.

negligible /ˈneglɪdʒəbl/ *adj* of little importance or size; not worth considering: *a negligible amount/error/effect* ○ *Losses in trade this year were negligible.*

negotiable /nɪˈgəʊʃiəbl/ *adj* **1** that can be settled by discussion: *The salary is negotiable.* **2** (of a cheque, BOND(2), etc) that can be exchanged for cash or passed to another person instead of cash: *negotiable securities.* **3** (of rivers, roads, etc) that can be

crossed, passed along or over, etc: *It is an excellent route for walkers, but not negotiable by vehicles.*

negotiate /nɪˈgəʊʃieɪt/ *v* **1(a)** ~ (**with sb**) (**for/about sth**) to try to reach agreement by discussion: [Vpr] *negotiate for a bank loan* ○ *We've decided to negotiate with the employers about our wage claim.* [V] *They refuse to negotiate.* ○ *be in a strong negotiating position* ○ *negotiating machinery/skills.* **(b)** ~ **sth** (**with sb**) to arrange or settle sth in this way: *negotiate a deal/sale/treaty* ○ *moves towards a negotiated settlement of the hostage crisis* [also Vnpr]. **2** to get over or past an obstacle, etc successfully: [Vn] *The climbers had to negotiate a steep rock face.*
■ **the neˈgotiating table** *n* [sing] a formal meeting to discuss how to settle an issue or a dispute: *Both sides still refuse to come to the negotiating table.*
▶ **negotiator** *n* a person who takes part in negotiations, esp because it is her or his job: *a skilled negotiator* ○ *the union's chief negotiator.*

negotiation /nɪˌgəʊʃiˈeɪʃn/ *n* [C often *pl*, U] discussion aimed at reaching an agreement: *the latest round of pay negotiations* ○ *enter into/open/conduct/ resume/break off negotiations with sb* ○ *A settlement was reached after lengthy negotiations.* ○ *be in negotiation with sb* ○ *A treaty is currently under **negotiation** in Vienna.* ○ *The price is a matter of/for negotiation.*

Negress /ˈniːgres/ *n* (*sometimes offensive*) a Negro woman or girl.

Negro /ˈniːgrəʊ/ *n* (*pl* **-oes** /-əʊz/) (*sometimes offensive*) a member of the race of MANKIND that has a black skin and originated in Africa.

Negroid /ˈniːgrɔɪd/ *adj* having the physical characteristics that are typical of Negroes.

neigh /neɪ/ *v* [V] to make the long high cry of a horse.
▶ **neigh** *n* a neighing cry.

neighbour (*US* **neighbor**) /ˈneɪbə(r)/ *n* **1(a)** a person living next to or near another: *Turn your radio down, or you'll wake the neighbours.* ○ *They are close/near neighbours of ours* (ie live not far from us). ○ *She's had a disagreement with her **next-door** neighbour* (ie the person who lives in the house beside hers). **(b)** a country or thing that is next to or near another: *Cambodia's northern neighbours* ○ *Britain's nearest neighbour is France.* **2** (*dated or rhet*) any other human being: *Love your neighbour.*
▶ **neighbouring** (*US* **-boring**) /ˈneɪbərɪŋ/ *adj* [attrib] situated or living next to or near to sb/sth: *the neighbouring country/town/village/farm* ○ *In neighbouring Andhra Pradesh 120 people have died.*

neighbourhood (*US* **-borhood**) /ˈneɪbəhʊd/ *n* (a) [C] a district; an area near a particular place: *a Catholic/poor/middle-class neighbourhood* ○ *We live in a rather rich/affluent neighbourhood.* ○ *drink in a neighbourhood bar.* **(b)** [CGp] the people living there: *She is liked by the whole neighbourhood.* **IDM** **in the neighbourhood of** approximately: *a sum in the neighbourhood of £500.*
■ ˌneighbourhood ˈwatch *n* [U] a scheme in which a group of people living in an area watch each other's houses regularly to discourage anyone from trying to enter them illegally.

neighbourly (*US* **-borly**) /ˈneɪbəli/ *adj* kind and friendly. ▶ **neighbourliness** (*US* **-borliness**) *n* [U]: *in a spirit of good neighbourliness.*

neither /ˈnaɪðə(r), ˈniːðə(r)/ *indef det, indef pron* not one nor the other of two things or people **(a)** (*det*) *Neither team liked the arrangement.* ○ *Neither answer is correct.* ○ *Neither Martha nor Jane could comfort me.* ○ *Neither one of us could understand German.* ○ (*fml*) *In neither case was a decision reached.* **(b)** (*pron*) *I chose neither of them.* ○ *They produced two reports, neither of which contained any concrete suggestions.* ○ *'Which is your car?' 'Neither, mine's being repaired.'*

N

▶ **neither** adv **1** (used before a modal v or an aux v placed in front of its subject) not either: He doesn't like Beethoven and neither do I. ○ I haven't been to New York before and neither has my sister. ○ 'Did you see it?' 'No.' 'Neither did I.' **2** neither...nor... not...and not: I neither know nor care what happened to him. ○ The hotel is neither spacious nor comfortable.

NOTE Note that you use a singular noun and verb after **neither** and **either**: Neither candidate was suitable for the job. ○ Either candidate will be suitable for the job. **Neither of, either of, none of** or **any of** can be followed by a plural noun and a singular or a plural verb. A plural verb is especially common in speaking: Neither of my parents has/have a car. ○ Does/Do either of you like strawberries? ○ None of the staff speaks/speak a foreign language. ○ Does/Do any of the children play a musical instrument? You can also use a singular or a plural verb after **neither...nor**: Neither the television nor the video works/work properly.

nemesis /'neməsɪs/ n [U, sing] (fml) punishment or ruin that is deserved and cannot be avoided: He **met his nemesis**.

neo- comb form new; modern; in a later form: neo-lithic ○ neo-Georgian ○ neo-fascist.

neoclassical /ˌniːəʊ'klæsɪkl/ adj of or in a style of art, literature or music that is based on or influenced by the classical style, esp of ancient Greece and Rome: neoclassical architecture.

neocolonialism /ˌniːəʊkə'ləʊniəlɪzəm/ n [U] the use of economic or political pressure by powerful countries to obtain or keep influence over other countries, esp former colonies.

neolithic /ˌniːə'lɪθɪk/ adj of the later part of the Stone Age: neolithic man.

neologism /ni'ɒlədʒɪzəm/ n a new word or expression: There are many neologisms in computing terminology.

neon /'niːɒn/ n [U] a chemical element. Neon is a colourless gas that glows with a bright light when an electric current is passed through it: neon lights/signs. ⇨ App 7.

neonatal /ˌniːə'neɪtəl/ adj of or relating to a child that has just been born: a neonatal intensive care unit.

nephew /'nefjuː, 'nevjuː/ n the son of one's brother or sister, or the son of one's husband's or wife's brother or sister. ⇨ App 4. Compare NIECE.

nepotism /'nepətɪzəm/ n [U] the practice among people with power or influence of favouring their own relatives, esp by giving them jobs: achieve promotion through nepotism.

Neptune /'neptjuːn; US -tuːn/ n (astronomy) a distant planet, eighth in order from the sun.

nerve /nɜːv/ n **1** [C] a long strand or mass of strands carrying impulses of sensation or of movement between the brain and all parts of the body: pain caused by a trapped nerve ○ nerve endings ○ nerve fibres/tissues. ⇨ picture at TOOTH. **2 nerves** [pl] (infml) a condition in which one is very nervous and worried; the feelings that produce this: suffer from (an attack of) nerves ○ actors showing signs of first-night nerves ○ Everyone's nerves are on edge after the accident. ○ frayed nerves. **3(a)** [U] the courage to do sth risky or dangerous: I don't ride any more; I had a bad fall and **lost my nerve**. ○ It takes a lot of nerve to be a racing driver. ○ I wouldn't **have the nerve** to try anything like parachuting. **(b)** [sing] (infml) a rude attitude that upsets others: **What a nerve!** She borrowed my bike without asking! ○ He's **got a nerve**, trying to tell me what to do. ○ I didn't think you'd **have the nerve** to show your face here again. See also WAR OF NERVES. **IDM a bag/bundle of** 'nerves in a very nervous condition: I

was a bundle of nerves at the interview. **get on sb's** 'nerves (infml) to irritate or annoy sb: Stop whistling! It's/You're getting on my nerves! **have nerves of steel**: to be not easily upset or frightened. **hit/touch a (raw/sensitive)** 'nerve to refer to a subject that causes sb pain, anger, etc: You hit a raw nerve when you mentioned his first wife. **strain every nerve** ⇨ STRAIN[1].

▶ **nerve** v ~ **oneself for sth / to do sth** to give oneself the courage, strength or determination to do sth: [Vn.to inf] I nerved myself to go to the dentist. [Vnpr] She's nerving herself for a final confrontation.
nerveless adj **1** lacking strength: The knife fell from her nerveless fingers. **2** very brave: a nerveless racing driver.
■ 'nerve-cell n a cell that carries impulses in nerve tissue.
'nerve-centre (US -center) n a place from which a large factory, organization, project, etc is controlled and instructions sent out: the nerve-centre of an election campaign.
'nerve gas n a poisonous gas that affects the nervous system, used in war.
'nerve-racking adj causing great mental strain: a nerve-racking wait for exam results.

nervous /'nɜːvəs/ adj **1** ~ (of sth / doing sth) not confident; afraid: Interviews always make me nervous. ○ I'm nervous of being alone at night. ○ Do you feel nervous about getting married? **2** tense; excited: full of nervous energy ○ a nervous race-horse ○ She gave a nervous laugh. ○ (fig) nervous trading on the stock market. **3** of the body's nerves: a nervous disorder/condition/disease ○ suffering from nervous exhaustion. ▶ **nervously** adv: She glanced nervously behind her. **nervousness** n [U]: He tried to hide his nervousness.
■ ˌnervous 'breakdown n a period of mental illness that causes one to feel depressed, tired and physically weak: have/recover from a nervous breakdown.
'nervous system n the system of nerves throughout the body of a person or an animal. See also CENTRAL NERVOUS SYSTEM.

nervy /'nɜːvi/ adj (infml) **1** (Brit) anxious; UNEASY: I didn't think she was the nervy type. **2** (US) lacking respect, esp in a bold or cheerful way: a nervy kid.

-ness /nəs/ suff (with adjs forming uncountable ns) the quality, state or character of being: dryness ○ blindness ○ silliness.

nest /nest/ n **1(a)** a place or structure chosen or made by a bird for laying its eggs and sheltering its young: sparrows building a nest of twigs and dry grass. **(b)** a place where certain other creatures live, or produce and keep their young: an ants' nest ○ a wasps' nest. **2** a secret or protected place: a nest of thieves ○ a love nest. **3** a group or set of similar things of different sizes made to fit inside each other: a nest of boxes/tables/bowls. **IDM feather one's nest** ⇨ FEATHER[2]. **a hornet's nest** ⇨ HORNET. **a mare's nest** ⇨ MARE.
▶ **nest** v to make and use a nest: [V] nesting robins ○ Swallows are nesting in the garage. ○ the nesting season.
■ 'nest egg n a sum of money saved for future use: a tidy little nest egg of £5 000.

nestle /'nesl/ v **1** to settle comfortably in a warm soft place: [Vpr, Vp] nestle (down) among the cushions [Vpr] They nestled in front of the fire. **2** to put or hold sb/sth or to lie in a partly hidden or sheltered position: [Vpr] She nestled the baby in her arms. ○ a bird nestling in the reeds ○ The village nestled snugly at the foot of the hill. **3** ~ **sth against, on, etc sth** to push one's head, shoulder, etc against, etc sth in a gentle and LOVING way: [Vnpr] She nestled her head on his shoulder.

N

nestling /'nestlɪŋ/ *n* a bird that is too young to leave the nest.

net¹ /net/ *n* (**a**) [U] loose open material made of string, thread, wire, etc woven or tied together: *a piece of nylon net* ○ *net curtains.* See also NETTING. (**b**) [C] (esp in compounds) a piece of this used for a particular purpose, eg catching fish, holding hair in place, etc: *a 'tennis net* ○ *a 'hair-net* ○ *a mos'quito net* ○ *'fishing-nets* ○ *kick/hit the ball into the back of the net* (eg in football or hockey). ⇨ picture at TENNIS. See also SAFETY NET. **IDM** **cast one's net wide** ⇨ CAST¹. **slip through the net** ⇨ SLIP¹. **spread one's net** ⇨ SPREAD.

▶ **net** *v* (**-tt-**) **1** to catch or obtain sth/sb with or as if with a net: [Vn] *They netted a good haul of fish.* ○ *A swoop by customs officers has netted 15 people so far.* **2** cover plants, etc with a net or nets: [Vn] *netted raspberry canes.* **3** (*sport*) to kick, hit, etc a ball into the goal: [Vn] *Gascoigne netted the only goal.*

net² (*Brit* also **nett**) /net/ *adj* **1** [attrib] (**a**) (of money) remaining when nothing more is to be taken away: *a net profit of £500* ○ *a salary of $30 000 net* ○ *What do you earn, net of tax* (ie after tax has been paid)? (**b**) (of a price) to be paid in full; fixed: *a net price of £7.50* ○ *Are these prices net?* (**c**) (of weight) of the contents only, excluding the container or the wrapping paper: *calculate the net weight of the goods.* Compare GROSS² 4. **2** [attrib] (of an effect, etc) final, after all the major factors have been considered: *The net result is that small shopkeepers are being forced out of business.* ○ *The UK is a net importer of food* (ie It imports more than it exports).

▶ **net** *v* (**-tt-**) to gain sth as a net profit: [Vn] *She netted £500 from the sale.*

netball /'netbɔːl/ *n* [U] a team game in which players score by throwing a ball so that it falls through a high ring with a net hanging from it.

nether /'neðə(r)/ *adj* [attrib] (*arch*) lower: *the nether regions/world* (ie the world of the dead, hell).

netting /'netɪŋ/ *n* [U] string, wire, etc woven or tied into a net: *wire netting.*

nettle /'netl/ *n* a common wild plant with hairs on its leaves that STING²(1) if touched. **IDM** **grasp the nettle** ⇨ GRASP.

▶ **nettle** *v* to make sb slightly angry; to irritate sb: [Vn] *My remarks clearly nettled her.*

network /'netwɜːk/ *n* **1** a complex system of roads, etc crossing each other: *a rail/road/canal network* ○ *a network of underground cables/pipes.* **2** a closely linked group of people, companies, etc: *a communications/transportation/distribution network* ○ *set up a network of financial advice centres.* **3** a group of broadcasting stations that link up to broadcast the same programmes at the same time: *the three big US television networks.* **4** a system of computers linked together: *a local area network.* **IDM** **the old boy network** ⇨ OLD.

▶ **networked** *adj* [usu attrib] (**a**) connected to a network: *networked computer systems.* (**b**) broadcast on a network: *nationally networked TV.*

networking *n* [U] **1** a system in which people in different rooms, buildings, etc are linked by means of a computer network: *networking software.* **2** a system of selling in which one person organizes others and receives a COMMISSION(2) on their sales: *increase sales through networking.* **3** a system of developing and maintaining professional contact with people in the same business or field.

neural /'njʊərəl/ *adj* (*techn*) of or relating to a nerve or the nervous system: *neural processes.*

neuralgia /njʊəˈrældʒə; *US* nʊ-/ *n* [U] (*medical*) a sharp pain felt along a nerve, usu in the head or face. ▶ **neuralgic** /njʊəˈrældʒɪk/ *adj*.

neuritis /njʊəˈraɪtɪs; *US* nʊ-/ *n* [U] (*medical*) INFLAMMATION of a nerve or nerves.

neur(o)- *comb form* of a nerve or nerves: *a neurosis* ○ *a neurosurgeon.*

neurology /njʊəˈrɒlədʒi; *US* nʊ-/ *n* [U] the scientific study of nerves and their diseases.

▶ **neurological** /ˌnjʊərəˈlɒdʒɪkl; *US* ˌnʊ-/ *adj*: *neurological research.*

neurologist /njʊəˈrɒlədʒɪst; *US* nʊ-/ *n* an expert in neurology.

neurosis /njʊəˈrəʊsɪs; *US* nʊ-/ *n* (*pl* **neuroses** /-əʊsiːz/) **1** (*medical*) a mental illness that causes depression or abnormal behaviour, often with physical symptoms but with no sign of disease. **2** any strong worry or fear: *her neurosis about her excess weight.*

neurotic /njʊəˈrɒtɪk; *US* nʊ-/ *adj* having or showing an abnormal anxiety or obsession about sth; caused by or suffering from NEUROSIS: *neurotic fears/ outbursts* ○ *a neurotic person* ○ (*infml*) *She's neurotic about turning lights off to save electricity.*

▶ **neurotic** *n* a neurotic person.

neurotically /-kli/ *adv*.

neuter /'njuːtə(r); *US* 'nuː-/ *adj* **1** (*grammar*) (of a word) neither MASCULINE(2) nor FEMININE(2): *a neuter noun.* **2** (of plants and animals) having no or only partly developed sex organs.

▶ **neuter** *v* to remove part of the sex organs of an animal: [Vn] *We had our tom-cat neutered.*

neutral /'njuːtrəl; *US* 'nuː-/ *adj* **1**(**a**) not supporting or helping either side in a dispute, contest, war, etc: *a neutral country/observer/position* ○ *be/remain politically neutral.* (**b**) belonging to a country that does not support either side in a war: *neutral territory/ ships* ○ (*fig*) *meet on neutral ground* (ie in a place that does not belong to, or have a particular connection with, any of the people who are meeting). **2**(**a**) having no distinct or positive qualities: *provide a neutral background for a display* ○ *'So you told her?' he said in a neutral tone of voice.* (**b**) (of colours) not strong or vivid, eg grey or light brown: *neutral clothes/wallpaper* ○ *a neutral colour scheme.* **3** (*chemistry*) neither acid nor alkaline (ALKALI).

▶ **neutral** *n* **1** [C] a person, country, colour, etc that is neutral. **2** [U] the position of the gears of a vehicle in which the engine is not connected with the parts operated by it: *slip (the gears) into neutral* ○ *leave the car in neutral.*

neutrality /njuːˈtræləti; *US* nuː-/ *n* [U] the condition of being neutral(1a), esp in war: *political neutrality* ○ *adopt a position of neutrality.*

neutralize, -ise *v* to take away the effect or special quality of sth by using sth with the opposite effect or quality: [Vn] *neutralize a poison/an acid/a threat.* **neutralization, -isation** /ˌnjuːtrəlaɪˈzeɪʃn; *US* -ləˈz-/ *n* [U].

neutrally /-rəli/ *adv*.

neutron /'njuːtrɒn; *US* 'nuː-/ *n* (*physics*) a tiny piece of atomic matter that carries no electric charge and that forms part of the NUCLEUS(1b) of an atom. Compare ELECTRON, PROTON.

never /'nevə(r)/ *adv* **1** at no time in the past or the future; on no occasion; not ever: *She never comes to visit us.* ○ *He has never been abroad.* ○ *I will never agree to their demands.* ○ *'Would you do that?' 'Never.'* ○ *Never in all my life have I heard such nonsense!* ○ *I'll never (ever) stay at that hotel again.* **2** (used for emphasis, in certain expressions) not: *I waited for ages but he never turned up.* ○ *That's never a Picasso!* ○ *That will never do* (ie is completely unacceptable). ○ *He never so much as smiled* (ie did not smile even once). ○ *'I told my boss exactly what I thought of him.' 'You never did!'* (ie 'Surely you didn't!') ○ (*infml*) *'You took my bike.' 'No, I never (did).'* ○ (*dated or joc*) *Never fear* (ie Do not worry), *everything will be all right.* **IDM** **on the never-never** (*Brit infml*) by hire purchase (HIRE): *buy a new car on the never-never.* (**well,**) **I never (did)!** (used to express surprise or disapproval): *Well, I never! Fancy getting married and not telling us!*

▶ **never** *interj* (*infml*) surely not; I do not believe it: *'I got the job.' 'Never!'*

■ ˌnever-ˈending *adj* seeming to last for ever: *a never-ending supply of jokes* ○ *I'm tired of your never-ending complaints.*

ˌnever-ˈnever land *n* [sing] an imaginary place where everything is wonderful: *a never-never land of low prices and widespread subsidies.*

nevermore /ˌnevəˈmɔː(r)/ *adv* (*arch*) never again; at no future time.

nevertheless /ˌnevəðəˈles/ *adv* in spite of this; however; still: *This defeat was widely predicted but it is disappointing nevertheless.* ○ *The old system had its flaws, but nevertheless it was preferable to the new one.*

new /njuː; *US* nuː/ *adj* (-er, -est) **1** not existing before; introduced, made, invented, etc recently or for the first time: *a new film/novel/car/idea* ○ *new clothes/furniture.* See also BRAND-NEW. **2(a)** ~ (to sb) already existing but not seen, experienced, etc before; not familiar: *learn new words in a foreign language* ○ *a new* (ie recently discovered) *star* ○ *Everything in the department still seems very new to her.* **(b)** ~ (to sth) (of a person) not yet familiar with sth because one has only just started, arrived, etc: *I am new to this town.* ○ *They are still new to the work.* ○ *You're new here, aren't you?* **3** changed from the previous one(s); different: *a new job/teacher/home* ○ *make new friends.* **4** freshly produced: *new potatoes/carrots* (ie ones dug from the soil early in the season) ○ *new* (ie freshly baked) *bread.* ➪ note. **5** (usu with *the*) modern; of the latest type: *the new morality* ○ *the newest fashions/colours* ○ *a new breed/type of explorer.* **6** [usu attrib] **(a)** just beginning: *a new day* ○ *a new era in the history of our country.* **(b)** beginning again; fresh: *start a new life* ○ *This government offers new hope to the people.* **(c)** having fresh energy, courage, health, etc: *She looks a new woman since she changed jobs.* **ᴵᴰᴹ** **brave new world** ➪ BRAVE. **break fresh/new ground** ➪ GROUND¹. **new/fresh blood** ➪ BLOOD¹. **(as) ˌgood as ˈnew** in very good condition, as when new: *I'll just sew up the lining and the coat will be as good as new.* **a ˌnew lease of ˈlife**; (*US*) **a ˌnew lease on ˈlife** the chance to live or last longer or with a higher quality of life: *Since recovering from her operation, she's had a new lease of life.* ○ *A bit of oil and some paint could give that old bike a new lease of life.* **teach an old dog new tricks** ➪ TEACH. **turn over a new ˈleaf** to change one's way of life to become a better, more responsible person: *Becoming a father made him turn over a new leaf.*

▶ **new-** (forming compound *adjs*): *new-laid eggs* ○ *enjoying their new-found freedom* ○ *new-style trains/contracts.*

newly *adv* (usu before a past participle) recently: *signs of newly acquired wealth* ○ *a newly married couple.* ˈnewly-wed *n* (usu *pl*) a person who has recently married.

newness *n* [U].

■ ˌNew ˈAge *adj* of or belonging to a cultural movement that rejects modern western values and promotes greater spiritual awareness and a more integrated (INTEGRATE) approach to life: *New Age travellers/music.*

ˌnew ˈbroom *n* a new person in a senior post who is likely to make a lot of changes.

ˌnew ˈdeal *n* new arrangements or social conditions, esp when these are seen as better than earlier ones: *The government has promised a new deal for farmers.*

ˌnew ˈmoon *n* **(a)** the moon when it is seen as a thin CRESCENT(1). **(b)** the time when the moon is in this shape: *after the next new moon.* Compare FULL MOON.

the ˌNew ˈTestament *n* [sing] the second part of

the Bible, concerned with the teachings of Christ and his earliest followers.

ˈnew town *n* (*Brit*) a complete town planned and built at one time.

ˌnew ˈwave (also **New Wave**) *n* [U, sing] **(a)** a movement introducing new styles or fashions in art, etc: *New-Wave films/designs.* **(b)** a style of rock³ music popular in the 1970s: *early teen encounters with punk and new wave.*

the ˌNew ˈWorld *n* [sing] North and South America. Compare THE OLD WORLD.

ˌnew ˈyear *n* [U, sing] the beginning of the year: *Happy New Year!* ○ *I'll see you in the new year.* ˌNew Year's ˈDay (*US* ˈNew Year's) *n* [U] 1 January. ˌNew Year's ˈEve *n* [U] 31 December.

ᴺᴼᵀᴱ Compare **new**, **contemporary** and **modern**. **New** usually refers to something that has not been done before, or that has been produced, found, etc a very short time ago: *What's Lucy's new baby called?* ○ *I've bought a new computer.* ○ *Is your car new or second-hand?* **Modern** and **contemporary** are used to talk about things which exist in the present time, especially things created in a new style that has not been tried before: *Do you like modern architecture?* ○ *the Institute of Contemporary Arts.* **Modern** can refer to a longer period up to the present: *modern English* (ie since 1500). **Contemporary** does not always refer to the present but can also refer to what was happening at a particular time in the past: *Shakespeare's plays tell us a lot about contemporary life* (ie the life of the 16th century).

newborn /ˈnjuːbɔːn/ *adj* [attrib] recently born: *newborn babies.*

newcomer /ˈnjuːkʌmə(r)/ *n* a person who has recently arrived in a place or started an activity: *a newcomer to the village/to opera.*

newel /ˈnjuːəl; *US* ˈnuːəl/ (also ˈnewel post) *n* post at the top or bottom of a staircase.

newfangled /ˌnjuːˈfæŋgld/ *adj* [usu attrib] (*usu derog*) (of ideas or things) modern or fashionable in a way that many people dislike or refuse to accept: *I don't like all these ˌnewfangled ˈgadgets/ˈmethods.*

news /njuːz; *US* nuːz/ *n* **1(a)** [U] new or fresh information; report(s) of recent events: *What's the latest news?* ○ *Have you heard the news? Mary's engaged!* ○ *I want to hear all your news.* ○ *It's **news to me*** (ie I haven't heard about it before). ○ *Have you any news of Pete?* (ie Have you heard anything about/from him?) ○ *the home/foreign news pages in a newspaper* ○ *a news item/report/broadcast/bulletin* ○ *She is always **in the news*** (ie Her activities are regularly reported in the press, on television, etc). **(b)** **the news** [sing *v*] a regular broadcast of the latest news on the radio or television: *listen to the news* ○ *What time's the news on BBC2?* ○ *We heard it on the news.* **2** [U] a person, a thing or an event that is considered interesting enough to be reported as news: *Pop stars are always news.* **ᴵᴰᴹ** **break the ˈnews (to sb)** to be the first to tell sb about sth, esp sth that will make them unhappy. ˌno news is ˈgood news (*saying*) if there were bad news we would hear it, so since we have heard nothing we can assume that all is well.

▶ **newsy** *adj* (*infml*) full of interesting and entertaining news: *a newsy letter.*

■ ˈnews agency *n* an organization that gathers news and sells it to newspapers and television and radio companies.

ˈnews room *n* the room at a newspaper office or a radio or television station where news is received and prepared for printing or broadcasting.

ˈnews-sheet *n* a small newspaper with few pages.

ˈnews-stand *n* = BOOKSTALL.

newsagent /ˈnjuːzeɪdʒənt; *US* ˈnuːz-/ (*Brit*) (*US*

N

newsdealer) *n* a shopkeeper who sells newspapers and magazines, and often sweets and cigarettes.

newscast /ˈnjuːzkɑːst; *US* -kæst/ *n* a news report on radio or television.

▶ **'newscaster** (*Brit* also **newsreader**) *n* a person who reads the news on television or radio.

newsdealer /ˈnjuːzdiːlə(r); *US* ˈnuːz-/ *n* (*US*) = NEWSAGENT.

newsflash /ˈnjuːzflæʃ; *US* ˈnuːz-/ (also **flash**) *n* a short item of important news broadcast on radio or television, sometimes interrupting a programme.

newsletter /ˈnjuːzletə(r); *US* ˈnuːz-/ *n* an informal printed report giving information about the activities of a club or society and sent regularly to its members.

newspaper /ˈnjuːspeɪpə(r); *US* ˈnuːzp-/ *n* (**a**) [C] a printed publication appearing daily or weekly and containing news, advertisements and articles on various subjects: *reading a newspaper* ○ *newspaper cuttings.* (**b**) [U] paper taken from a newspaper: *a parcel wrapped in newspaper.*

newspaperman /ˈnjuːspeɪpəmæn; *US* ˈnuːzp-/ *n* (*pl* **-men** /-men/) a journalist.

newsprint /ˈnjuːzprɪnt; *US* ˈnuːz-/ *n* [U] the paper on which newspapers are printed.

newsreader /ˈnjuːzriːdə(r); *US* ˈnuːz-/ *n* (*Brit*) = NEWSCASTER.

newsreel /ˈnjuːzriːl; *US* ˈnuːz-/ *n* a short cinema film of recent events.

newsworthy /ˈnjuːzwɜːði; *US* ˈnuːz-/ *adj* interesting or important enough to be reported as news: *Nothing very newsworthy happened last week.*

newt /njuːt; *US* nuːt/ *n* a small animal with short legs and a long tail that can live in water or on land. **IDM** **pissed as a newt** ⇨ PISSED.

next¹ /nekst/ *adj* [attrib] ~ (**to sb/sth**) **1** (usu with *the*) coming immediately after sb/sth in order, space or time: *the next name on the list* ○ *Who's next, please* (eg at a shop)? ○ *How far is it to the next petrol station?* ○ *the next house to ours* (Compare: *the house next to ours*) ○ *The next train to Baltimore is at 10.00.* ○ *The next time I saw her she was working in London.* ○ *The next six months will be the hardest.* ○ *I fainted and the next thing I knew I was in hospital.* **2** (used without *the* before eg *Monday, week, summer, year*) the one immediately following: *Next Thursday is 12 April.* ○ *I'm going skiing next winter.* ⇨ note at TIME¹. **IDM** **better luck next time** ⇨ BETTER¹. **first/last/next but one, etc** ⇨ FIRST¹. **as good, well, far, much, etc as the 'next man** as good, well, etc as the average person: *I can enjoy a joke as well as the next man, but this is going too far.* **from one day to the next** ⇨ DAY. **the next world** the place where one goes after death, according to some religious beliefs.

▶ **the next** *n* [sing] a person or thing that is next: *She finished one novel and immediately started the next.*

■ **ₙnext 'door** *adv* in, into or being the next room, house, building, etc: *The cat is from the house next door.* ○ *The manager's office is just next door.* ○ *We live next door to a pub.* **'next-door** *adj* [attrib]: *our ₙnext-door 'neighbours* ○ *the ₙnext-door 'house/'office.*

ₙnext of 'kin *n* [C, U] (*pl* unchanged) (*fml*) one's closest living relation or relations: *Her next of kin has/have been informed.* ○ *The form must be signed by next of kin.*

next² /nekst/ *adv* **1** after sth else; then; afterwards: *What did you do next?* ○ *Next we visited Tokyo.* ○ *What comes next* (ie follows)? **2** (with superlatives) following in the specified order: *The next oldest building is the church.* **3** (used after question words to express surprise): *You're learning to be a parachutist? Whatever next!*

■ **ₙnext-'best** *adj* to be preferred to any others if one's first choice is not available: *The next-best thing is to abandon the project altogether.*

next to *prep* **1** in or into a position immediately to one side of sb/sth; beside sb/sth: *Peter sat next to me on the sofa.* ○ *I've put the bed next to the window.* **2** following in order after sb/sth: *Next to skiing her favourite sport was skating.* **3** almost: *Painting the ceiling proved next to impossible without a ladder.* ○ *I got it for* **next to nothing** *in a sale.* ○ *My horse came next to last in the race.*

NOTE Compare **next** and **nearest**. (**The**) **next** means 'the one that follows' in a series of events, places or people: *When is your next appointment?* ○ *Turn left at the next traffic-lights.* ○ *Who's next?* (**The**) **nearest** means 'the closest' in time or distance: *My party will be on the Saturday nearest to my birthday.* ○ *Where's the nearest supermarket?* Notice the difference between the prepositions **nearest** (**to**) and **next to**: *Janet's sitting nearest the window* (ie of all the children). ○ *Sarah's sitting next to the window* (ie beside it).

nexus /ˈneksəs/ *n* [sing] a complex series of connections: *the nexus between industry and political power.*

NFL /ˌen ef ˈel/ *abbr* (in the USA) National Football League.

NHS /ˌen eɪtʃ ˈes/ *abbr* (in Britain) National Health Service: *The NHS is under-funded.* ○ *an NHS hospital.*

NI *abbr* **1** (in Britain) National Insurance: *NI contributions.* **2** Northern Ireland.

nib /nɪb/ *n* a metal point of a pen.

nibble /ˈnɪbl/ *v* **1(a)** ~ (**at sth**) to take small bites of sth: [Vn] *fish nibbling the bait* ○ *She nibbled his ears playfully.* [Vpr] *Mice have been nibbling at the cheese.* (**b**) to eat small amounts of food, esp between meals: [V] *I put on weight because I was constantly nibbling.* **2** ~ (**at sth**) to show cautious interest in an offer, etc: [V] *'Is he interested in the deal?' 'He's nibbling.'* [Vpr] *He nibbled at the idea, but would not make a definite decision.*

▶ **nibble** *n* **1** [C] an act of nibbling: *I felt a nibble on the end of my line.* **2 nibbles** [pl] small biscuits, etc eaten with a drink before a meal.

nibs /nɪbz/ *n* **IDM** **his nibs** (*Brit infml joc*) (used to refer to a person who is, or thinks he or she is, more important than other people).

nice /naɪs/ *adj* (-**r**, -**st**) **1(a)** pleasant; agreeable: *a nice day/smile/remark* ○ *nice weather/children* ○ *That tastes nice!* ○ *One of the nicest things about her is her sense of humour.* ○ *We had a nice time at the beach.* ○ *Nice to meet you!* ○ *I asked him in the nicest possible way* not to park in front of my garage. (**b**) ~ (**to sb**) kind; friendly: *It's very nice of you to let me stay.* ○ *He's not very nice to her when he's had a few drinks.* Compare NASTY. **2** (*ironic*) bad; unpleasant: *This is a nice mess you've got us into!* ○ *That's a nice thing to say!* **3** fine; SUBTLE(1): *a nice distinction* ○ *a nice point of law* (ie one that may be difficult to decide). **4** (usu in negative expressions) honest: *She's not too nice in her business methods.* **5** (*approv*) (used before *adjs* to emphasize how pleasant or comfortable sth is): *a nice comfy bed* ○ *a nice cold drink* ○ *You need a nice hot bath.* **IDM** **nice and** (used before *adjs* or *advs*) (*infml approv*) pleasantly; in a way that is welcome: *It was nice and cool in the woods.* ○ *Everybody arrived nice and early.* **nice work if you can 'get it** (used to express envy of sb's good luck): *'He was paid £200 for a 10-minute speech.' 'Nice work if you can get it!'*

▶ **nicely** *adv* **1** in a pleasant or neat manner: *nicely dressed* ○ *It was a difficult thing to say, but he put it very nicely.* **2** (*infml*) very well; perfectly: *That will suit me nicely.* ○ *My tomato plants are coming along very nicely.* ○ *The programme is nicely timed to coincide with the opening of the exhibition.* **IDM** **do 'nicely** (esp in the continuous tenses) to make good

progress: *Her new business is doing very nicely.* ○ *The patient is doing nicely.*
niceness *n* [U].

> **NOTE** **Nice** is a general word which is often used in speaking where another adjective would describe something in a more precise way. **Enjoyable** and **pleasant** describe an experience that you like (a holiday, a party, an evening, etc). **Good** describes the standard or quality of something (the weather, a restaurant, etc). **Pretty** describes the pleasing appearance of something (a dress, a garden, etc). **Friendly**, **kind** and **pleasant** can all be used to describe people. **Lovely**, **delightful**, **charming** and **sweet** are all used to mean **very nice**: *It was a lovely meal!* ○ *a delightful old house* ○ *Your new boyfriend is charming.* ○ *What a sweet baby!*

nicety /ˈnaɪsəti/ *n* **1** [C usu *pl*] a fine distinction or detail: *I won't go into all the legal niceties of the case.* ○ *observe diplomatic/social niceties* (ie of polite behaviour). **2** [U] (*fml*) accuracy; precision: *the nicety of his judgement.* **IDM** **to a** ˈ**nicety** exactly right: *You judged the distance to a nicety.*

niche /nɪtʃ/ *Brit also* ni:ʃ/ *n* **1** a hollow place, esp in a wall, used eg to display a work of art: *Two small candles and some flowers were placed in a niche.* ⇨ picture. **2** a suitable and satisfying role, job or way of life: *carve/create/find a niche for oneself in* the music business. **3** an opportunity in business, etc: *find a niche in the market.* **4** (*biology*) the conditions in which a species can live successfully: *birds exploiting a previously unoccupied niche.*

niche   niche

nick[1] /nɪk/ *n* a very small cut: *Make a nick in the cloth with the scissors.* **IDM** **in good, bad, etc** ˈ**nick** (*Brit infml*) in good, etc condition or health: *She's in pretty good nick for a 70-year-old.* ○ *The car's in poor nick.* **in the** ˌ**nick of** ˈ**time** only just in time; at the last moment: *We arrived in the nick of time.*
▶ **nick** *v* to make a nick in sth: [Vn] *nick one's chin while shaving.*

nick[2] /nɪk/ *n* **the nick** [sing] (*Brit sl*) a prison or a police station: *She spent a year in the nick.* ○ *The burglar was taken to the local nick.*
▶ **nick** *v* (*Brit infml*) **1** ~ **sb** (**for sth**) to arrest sb: [Vnpr] *He was nicked for stealing.* [also Vn]. **2** ~ **sth** (**from sb/sth**) to steal sth: [Vn] *Who's nicked my pen?* [also Vnpr].

nickel /ˈnɪkl/ *n* **1** [U] (*symb* Ni) a chemical element. Nickel is a metal used in making special types of steel and other alloys (ALLOY[1]), etc: *nickel-plated steel wire.* ⇨ App 7. **2** [C] a coin of the USA or Canada, worth 5 cents. ⇨ note at CENT[1].

nick-nack = KNICK-KNACK.

nickname /ˈnɪkneɪm/ *n* an informal, often humorous name based on a person's real name or connected with her or his appearance or habits: *Her nickname was 'Rabbit' because of her big front teeth.*
▶ **nickname** *v* (esp passive) to give a nickname to sb: [Vn-n] *She was nicknamed 'Madonna'.*

nicotine /ˈnɪkətiːn/ *n* [U] an oily substance in tobacco that is dangerous to one's health: *teeth/fingers stained with nicotine.*

niece /niːs/ *n* a daughter of one's brother or sister or of one's husband's or wife's brother or sister. ⇨ App 4. Compare NEPHEW.

nifty /ˈnɪfti/ *adj* (**-ier, -iest**) (*infml*) **1(a)** skilful and accurate: *a footballer's nifty footwork* ○ *He's a nifty performer on the guitar.* **(b)** simple and effective; useful: *a nifty little gadget for peeling potatoes.* **2** fashionable; attractive: *wearing a nifty new outfit.*

niggardly /ˈnɪɡədli/ *adj* mean; not generous: *a niggardly attitude* ○ *They pay a niggardly 3% on loans.*
nigger /ˈnɪɡə(r)/ *n* (⚠ *derog offensive*) a black person.

niggle /ˈnɪɡl/ *v* **1** ~ (**at sb**) (**about/over sth**) to criticize sb/sth or spend too much time on unimportant details: [Vpr] *Stop niggling about every penny we spend.* [V, Vpr] *You never say anything nice — all you do is niggle (at me).* **2** to irritate or worry sb slightly: [Vn] *His untidiness constantly niggled her.* [also V].
▶ **niggle** *n* **1** a minor criticism: *My only niggle about the meal was the cost of the wine.* **2** a minor pain: *He gets the occasional niggle in his right shoulder.* **3** a small worry, doubt, etc: *have a few niggles about his fitness for the match on Saturday.*
niggling /ˈnɪɡlɪŋ/ (*also* **niggly** /-li/) *adj* **1** too unimportant to give time or attention to: *Don't waste time on niggling details.* **2** causing continual slight worry or annoyance: *a niggling pain* ○ *niggling doubt* ○ *She had a niggling feeling that something was wrong at home.*

nigh /naɪ/ *adv, prep* **1** (*arch or rhet*) near (to): *The end of the world is nigh!* **2** ~ **on** (*dated or rhet*) almost: *spend nigh on £500 a month on food* ○ *It's nigh on impossible to find a good gardener.* See also WELLNIGH.

night /naɪt/ *n* [C, U] **1(a)** the time of darkness in each 24 hours: *He phoned me up at 11 o'clock at night.* ○ *The fire started on Saturday night.* ○ *These animals only come out at night.* ○ *She was ill in the night.* ○ *We sat up all night (long) talking.* ○ *We spent the night with friends in London.* ○ *The same noise was heard night after night* (ie every night). ○ *Night fell* (ie It became dark). **(b)** the evening: *We watched television last night.* ○ *What shall we do on Friday night?* **2** an evening on which a specified activity takes place: *the first/last night of a play.* **IDM** **all right on the night** ⇨ RIGHT[1]. **an early/a late** ˈ**night** a night when one goes to bed earlier/later than usual: *You've been having too many late nights recently.* **by day/night** ⇨ DAY. **have a good/bad** ˈ**night** to sleep well/badly during the night. **in the/at dead of night** ⇨ DEAD. **make a** ˈ**night of it** to spend much of the night in celebrating, eg at a party. **morning, noon and night** ⇨ MORNING. ˌ**night and** ˈ**day/** ˌ**day and** ˈ**night** continuously; all the time: *machines kept running night and day.* **night** ˈ**night** (used by or to children) good night: *'Night night, sleep tight!'* **a night** ˈ**out** an evening spent enjoying oneself away from home: *I enjoy an occasional night out at the theatre.* **spend the night with sb/together** ⇨ SPEND. **things that go bump in the night** ⇨ THING.
▶ **nightie** *n* (*infml*) = NIGHTDRESS.

nightly *adj, adv* happening, done, etc at night or every night: *the nightly bombardment* ○ *The film is on twice nightly.*

nights *adv* (*esp US*) regularly each night: *I can't sleep nights.* ○ *He works nights.*

■ ˈ**night-life** *n* [U] entertainments available at night in a particular town or area: *There's not much night-life here.*

ˈ**night-light** *n* a weak light that is kept on in a bedroom at night.

ˈ**night-long** *adj, adv* lasting all night: *engage in night-long discussions.*

ˈ**night safe** *n* a container in the outside wall of a bank where money, etc can be deposited when the bank is closed.

ˈ**night school** *n* [U, C] lessons given in the evening for adults in a wide range of subjects, eg languages, sport or cooking: *learn Japanese at night school* ○ *go to night school on Tuesdays.*

ˈ**night-time** *n* the time of darkness: *It's pretty noisy at night-time.* ○ ˌ*night-time* ˈ*fears.*

ˌ**night-**ˈ**watchman** /-mən/ *n* (*pl* **-men** /-mən/) a man employed to guard a building, eg a factory, at night.

NOTE Compare **at night, by night, in the night, during the night** and **on a...night. At night** is used when something habitually happens during the night: *Nocturnal animals such as bats and owls only come out at night.* ○ *I don't like driving at night.* **By night** has the same meanings as **at night.** It is used especially in contrast with the day, or to describe how something looks, feels, etc when it is dark: *The guide takes you on a tour of Paris by night.* ○ *The desert is a place of scorching heat by day and bitter cold by night.*

In the night usually refers to the night that has just finished: *I'm exhausted. The baby woke up three times in the night.* **During the night** can also be used in this way, meaning 'while it was night': *It rained hard during the night.* **On** is used when you describe a particular night: *on a night in May* ○ *on a cold winter's night.* For further information on prepositions of time ⇨ note at TIME[1].

nightcap /'naɪtkæp/ n **1** a usu alcoholic drink taken before going to bed: *What about a nightcap?* **2** (formerly) a soft cap worn in bed.

nightclothes /'naɪtkləʊðz/ n [pl] clothes worn in bed.

nightclub /'naɪtklʌb/ n a club open until late at night for drinking, dancing and entertainment.

nightdress /'naɪtdres/ (also **nightgown**, *infml* **nightie** /'naɪti/) n a long loose garment worn by a woman or girl in bed.

nightfall /'naɪtfɔ:l/ n [U] the time each day when it becomes dark: *We hope to be back by nightfall.*

nightgown /'naɪtgaʊn/ n a NIGHTDRESS.

nightingale /'naɪtɪŋgeɪl; US -tng-/ n a small brown bird, the male of which has a beautiful song.

nightjar /'naɪtdʒɑ:(r)/ n a brown bird, active at night, with a long tail and a harsh cry.

nightmare /'naɪtmeə(r)/ n **1** a very frightening dream: *I have recurring nightmares about falling off a cliff.* **2** (*infml*) a very frightening or unpleasant experience: *getting to the airport was an absolute nightmare.* ○ *It's time to put the nightmare of the last ten years behind us.* ▶ **nightmarish** /'naɪtmeərɪʃ/ *adj*: *nightmarish problems.*

nightshirt /'naɪtʃɜ:t/ n a boy's or man's long shirt worn in bed.

nihilism /'naɪɪlɪzəm/ n [U] **1** the total rejection of all religious and moral principles as a basis for behaviour. **2** the belief that nothing really exists. ▶ **nihilist** /-ɪst/ n a believer in nihilism. **nihilistic** /ˌnaɪɪˈlɪstɪk/ *adj*.

nil /nɪl/ n [U] nothing, esp as the score in certain games; zero: *Bayern Munich won the match three nil/three goals to nil.* ○ *The chances of it happening are absolutely nil.* ⇨ note at NOUGHT.

nimble /'nɪmbl/ *adj* (**-r** /'nɪmblə(r)/, **-st** /'nɪmblɪst/) **1** quick and accurate in movement: *sewing with nimble fingers* ○ *She's very nimble on her feet.* **2** (of the mind) able to think and understand quickly: *a nimble tactical brain.* ▶ **nimbly** /'nɪmbli/ *adv*: *leaping nimbly over the fence.*

nimbus /'nɪmbəs/ n (*pl* **nimbuses** /-bəsɪz/ or **nimbi** /-baɪ/) a large grey rain cloud.

nimby /'nɪmbi/ n (*joc derog*) (formed from the first letters of *not in my back yard*) a person who claims to be in favour of sth, but objects if it is not convenient for herself or himself personally: *adopt a nimby attitude to the proposal for a new motorway.*

nincompoop /'nɪŋkəmpu:p/ n (*dated infml*) a foolish person.

nine /naɪn/ n, pron, det the number 9. **IDM** ˌ**nine to** ˈ**five** the normal working hours in an office: *I work nine to five.* ○ *a nine-to-five job.*

▶ **nine-** (in compounds) having nine of the thing specified: *a nine-hole golf-course.*

ninth /naɪnθ/ pron, det 9th. — n each of nine equal parts of sth.
For further guidance on how *nine* and *ninth* are used, see the examples at *five* and *fifth.*

ninepin /'naɪnpɪn/ n **IDM** ˌ**go down like** ˈ**ninepins** to become ill in great numbers: *There's a lot of flu about — people are going down* (ie catching the disease) *like ninepins.*

nineteen /ˌnaɪnˈti:n/ n, pron, det the number 19. **IDM** ˌ**talk, etc nineteen to the dozen** ⇨ DOZEN. ▶ **nineteenth** /ˌnaɪnˈti:nθ/ n, pron, det.
For further guidance on how *nineteen* and *nineteenth* are used, see the examples at *five* and *fifth.*

ninety /'naɪnti/ n, pron, det **1** the number 90. **2 the nineties** n [pl] the numbers, years or temperature from 90 to 99. **IDM** ˌ**in one's nineties** between the ages of 90 and 100. ˌ**ninety-nine** ˌ**times out of a** ˈ**hundred** almost always. ▶ **ninetieth** /'naɪntiəθ/ n, pron, det.
For further guidance on how *ninety* and *ninetieth* are used, see the examples at *five* and *fifth.*

ninny /'nɪni/ n (*infml*) a foolish person: *Don't be such a ninny!*

nip /nɪp/ v (**-pp-**) **1(a)** to squeeze sb/sth hard, eg between the finger and thumb, causing pain; to pinch sb/sth: [Vn] *A crab nipped my toe while I was paddling.* [Vnpr] *She nipped me on the arm.* **(b)** to take small bites with the front teeth: [Vn] *That dog nipped my ankle!* **2** (of frost, cold wind, etc) to damage or harm sth, esp plants: [Vn] *The icy breeze nipped the young blooms.* ○ *The cold nipped his cheeks and made him gasp.* **3** (*Brit infml*) to go somewhere quickly: [Vp] *The car nipped in* (ie got in quickly) *ahead of me.* [Vp, Vpr] *She has just nipped out* (to the bank). [Vpr] *a motor bike nipping in and out of the traffic.* ⇨ note at WHIZZ. **IDM** **nip sth in the** ˈ**bud** to stop or destroy sth at an early stage in its development: *She wanted to be an actress, but her parents nipped that idea in the bud.* **PHRV** ˌ**nip sth** ˈ**off (sth)** to remove a part of sth with one's fingers. ▶ **nip** n **1** a sharp pinch or bite: *The dog gave me a nasty nip on the leg.* **2** a feeling of cold: *There's a distinct nip in the air.* **3** (*infml*) a small drink, esp of spirits: *a nip of brandy.* See also NIPPY.

nipper /'nɪpə(r)/ n (*Brit infml*) a small child: *a cheeky young nipper.*

nipple /'nɪpl/ n **1(a)** a small dark part of the breast that sticks out. Babies can suck milk through a woman's nipples. ⇨ picture at HUMAN. **(b)** (*esp US*) = TEAT 2. **2** a thing shaped like a nipple, used eg to direct oil, etc into a machine.

nippy /'nɪpi/ *adj* (**-ier, -iest**) (*infml*) **1** quick: *a nippy little car.* **2** cold: *It's a bit nippy today, isn't it?*

nirvana /nɪəˈvɑːnə/ n [U] (in Buddhism and Hinduism) a state of perfect happiness and freedom in which the individual becomes absorbed into the supreme spirit.

nit /nɪt/ n **1** the egg or young form of a LOUSE(1) or other insect, esp the type that lives in human and animal hair: *Shampoo thoroughly to get rid of nits.* **2** (*infml esp Brit*) a stupid person. ■ ˈ**nit-picking** *adj, n* (*infml derog*) looking for small errors or faults when it is not necessary: *nit-picking criticism* ○ *There's been far too much nit-picking.*

nitrate /'naɪtreɪt/ n [U,C] any of several chemical compounds containing NITROGEN, used esp to make soil more FERTILE(1): *We need to cut nitrate levels in water.*

nitric acid /ˌnaɪtrɪk ˈæsɪd/ n [U] a powerful colourless acid that can destroy most substances.

nitrogen /'naɪtrədʒən/ n [U] (*symb* **N**) a chemical element. Nitrogen is a gas without colour, taste or smell that occurs in large quantities in the earth's atmosphere. ⇨ App 7. ▶ **nitrogenous** /naɪ-ˈtrɒdʒənəs/ *adj*.

nitroglycerine (also *esp US* **nitroglycerin**) /ˌnaɪtrəʊˈglɪsəriːn, -rɪn/ *n* [U] a powerful liquid explosive.

nitrous oxide /ˌnaɪtrəs ˈɒksaɪd/ (also **laughing-gas**) *n* [U] a gas used esp formerly by dentists to prevent one feeling pain: *nitrous oxide emissions from heavy goods vehicles.*

nitty-gritty /ˌnɪti ˈgrɪti/ *n* **the nitty-gritty** [sing] (*infml*) the most important aspects or details of a situation, an activity, etc: *We only got down to the real nitty-gritty at the end of the meeting.*

nitwit /ˈnɪtwɪt/ (also **nit**) *n* (*infml*) a stupid or foolish person: *He's a complete nitwit.*

No (also **no**) (*pl* **Nos**, **nos**) (*US symb* **#**) number: *room no 145* (eg in a hotel) ∘ *No 10 (Downing Street)* (ie the official residence of the British Prime Minister). **2** (*US*) North; Northern.

no /nəʊ/ *neg det* **1** (used with countable *ns* in the singular or plural, or with uncountable nouns) not any; not one; not a: *No words can express my grief.* ∘ *No student is to leave the room.* ∘ *There was no bread left in the supermarket.* ∘ *No two people think exactly alike.* **2** (used to indicate that sth is not allowed): *No smoking.* ∘ *No dogs in the restaurant.* **3** (used before an *adj* to express the exact opposite of what is said): *It was no easy matter* (ie It was very difficult). ∘ *She's no fool* (ie She is intelligent).

▶ **no** *interj* (used to give a negative reply): '*Would you like a drink?*' '*No, thank you.*' ∘ '*Is it raining?*' '*No, it isn't.*' ∘ '*Haven't you finished?*' '*No, not yet.*'
IDM **yes and no** ⇨ YES.

no *neg adv* (used before comparative *adjs* and *advs*) not: *This book is no more exciting than his others.* ∘ *If you're no better by tomorrow I'll call the doctor.*

noes /nəʊz/ *n* [pl] the total number of people voting 'no' in a formal debate, eg in Parliament: *The noes have it* (ie Those voting 'no' are in the majority).

■ **no-ball** *n* (in cricket) a ball bowled in a way that is not permitted by the rules and for which the opponents are given a run²(9).

no-claims bonus *n* (*Brit*) a reduction in the annual cost of one's insurance if one has not made a claim to the insurance company in the previous year: *lose one's no-claims bonus.*

no-fault *adj* [attrib] (*US*) of a type of car insurance that pays for damage after an accident before it has been established whose fault it was.

no-go area *n* an area of a city, etc which the police or army do not enter, usu because this would be dangerous or would cause trouble. Compare NO GO.

no-hoper *n* (*infml derog*) a person who is considered useless: *a bunch of no-hopers running the country.*

no man's land *n* [U] an area of land between the borders of two countries or between two armies and so under the control of neither.

no-nonsense *adj* [attrib] without fuss; simple and direct: *a no-nonsense approach/attitude/manner.*

no one *neg pron* = NOBODY.

no-show *n* (*infml*) a person who is expected at an event, has a ticket for a journey, etc but does not appear for it.

nob /nɒb/ *n* (*sl derog esp Brit*) a member of the upper class or a wealthy person: *He acts as if he's one of the nobs.*

nobble /ˈnɒbl/ *v* (*Brit infml*) **1** [Vn] to prevent a horse from winning a race by eg giving it drugs. **2** to influence sb to help one, esp illegally, eg by offering them money: [Vn] *There's no point in trying to nobble the jury.*

nobility /nəʊˈbɪləti/ *n* **1** [U] the quality of being noble, esp in mind or character: *his integrity and nobility of purpose.* **2** **the nobility** [Gp] people of

high social rank who have titles, eg a DUKE or an EARL: *marry into the nobility.* Compare ARISTOCRACY.

noble /ˈnəʊbl/ *adj* (**-r** /ˈnəʊblə(r)/, **-st** /ˈnəʊblɪst/) **1** having a high social rank, esp from birth: *a family of noble descent.* **2** having or showing very fine personal qualities, eg honour and honesty: *a noble leader/mind/gesture* ∘ *noble sentiments* ∘ *He died for a noble cause.* **3** impressive in size or appearance; splendid: *a noble building/horse.*

▶ **noble** *n* a person of noble birth or rank.
nobly /ˈnəʊbli/ *adv*: *nobly born* ∘ *thoughts nobly expressed.*

nobleman /ˈnəʊblmən/ *n* (*pl* **-men** /-mən/; *fem* **noblewoman** /-wʊmən/, *pl* **-women** /-wɪmɪn/) a person of noble birth or rank. Compare ARISTOCRAT, COMMONER.

noblesse oblige /nəʊˌbles əˈbliːʒ/ (*French saying*) people of high rank must accept the responsibilities of their position, eg helping people in need.

nobody /ˈnəʊbədi/ (also **no one** /ˈnəʊ wʌn/) *neg pron* not anyone; no person: *Nobody was at home.* ∘ *When I arrived there was nobody there.* ∘ *He found that nobody could speak English.* ⇨ note at GENDER.

▶ **nobody** *n* a person of no importance: *a bunch of nobodies.* See also ANYBODY 3.

nocturnal /nɒkˈtɜːnl/ *adj* done, happening or active in the night: *a nocturnal visit/trip* ∘ *nocturnal animals.* Compare DIURNAL 1.

nocturne /ˈnɒktɜːn/ *n* a short piece of music in a romantic style, esp for the piano.

nod /nɒd/ *v* (**-dd-**) **1(a)** to move one's head down and then up again quickly, in order to give the answer 'yes' or to show that one agrees or understands: [V, Vn] *She nodded (her head) in agreement.* [V] *I asked her if she wanted to come and she nodded.* [Vn] *She nodded her approval.* (**b**) ~ **sth** (**at/to sb**) to make this movement in order to greet sb or give them a signal: [Vn] *nod a greeting* [Vpr] *He nodded to me in welcome.* [Vpr.to inf] *He nodded to me to leave the room.* (**c**) ~ **(to/towards sb/sth)** to move one's head in order to indicate the direction of sb/sth: [Vpr] *I asked where his wife was and he nodded towards the garden.* **2** to move one's head up and down several times: [V] *He sat nodding in time to the music.* **3** to let one's head fall forward when one is falling asleep: [V] *He sat nodding by the fire.* **4** (of flowers, etc) to move up and down in the wind: [V] *nodding pansies.* **IDM** **have a nodding acquaintance with sb/sth** to know sb/sth slightly: *I have no more than a nodding acquaintance with her work.* **PHRV** **nod off** (*infml*) to fall asleep for a short time while sitting in a chair: *He nodded off by the fire.*

▶ **nod** *n* an act of nodding: *give a nod of recognition/agreement.* **IDM** **give sb/get the nod** (*infml*) to give sb/obtain permission to do or continue doing sth: *Plans for a new bypass were finally given the nod.* **a nod is as good as a wink (to a blind horse/man)** (*saying*) a suggestion, HINT(1), etc can be understood without anything further being said. **on the nod** (*Brit infml*) by general agreement and without discussion: *The proposal went through* (ie was approved) *on the nod.*

node /nəʊd/ *n* **1** (*botany*) (**a**) a small swelling on a root or branch. (**b**) a place on the stem of a plant from which a branch or a leaf grows. **2** (*anatomy*) a small hard mass of tissue, eg on a joint in the human body: *lymph nodes.* **3** (*techn*) a point at which two lines or systems meet or cross. ▶ **nodal** /ˈnəʊdl/ *adj*.

nodule /ˈnɒdjuːl; *US* ˈnɒdʒuːl/ *n* a small round lump or swelling, esp on a plant.

Noel /nəʊˈel/ *n* (esp in songs or on cards) Christmas.

noggin /ˈnɒgɪn/ *n* (*dated or rhet*) a small alcoholic drink.

noise /nɔɪz/ *n* **1** [C, U] a sound, esp when it is loud or unpleasant or disturbs or worries one: *the noise*

N

of jet aircraft ○ a rattling noise ○ What's that noise? ○ Don't make so much noise. ○ noise pollution. **2** [U] (radio) (**a**) electrical disturbance that spoils reception of a radio broadcast: When atmospheric pressure is high, there's always a lot of noise. (**b**) (computing) a signal that interrupts a PROGRAM(1), often causing an error. **3 noises** [pl] (following adjs) remarks expressing the specified feeling, which may or may not be genuine: make encouraging/sympathetic/ polite noises ○ He made all the right noises (ie said what people wanted or expected him to say). **IDM a big noise/shot/name** ⇨ BIG. **make a 'noise (about sth)** to complain loudly: She made a lot of noise about the poor food. **make 'noises (about sth)** (infml) to speak indirectly about one's attitude or intentions, esp so that other people should know: Staff are making noises about some of the recent committee decisions.
▶ **noiseless** adj making little or no noise: with noiseless footsteps. **noiselessly** adv.

noisome /ˈnɔɪsəm/ adj (fml) extremely unpleasant; offensive: a noisome sight/smell.

noisy /ˈnɔɪzi/ adj (-ier, -iest) (**a**) making or causing a lot of noise: noisy children/games ○ a noisy welcome ○ Stop being so noisy! (**b**) full of noise: a noisy classroom/café ○ I can't work in here — it's far too noisy. ▶ **noisily** /-ɪli/ adv: chattering noisily.

nomad /ˈnəʊmæd/ n **1** a member of a tribe or people that moves with its animals from place to place and has no permanent home. **2** a person who does not stay long in one place. ▶ **nomadic** /nəʊˈmædɪk/ adj: nomadic herdsmen ○ live/lead a nomadic life/existence.

nom de plume /ˌnɒm də ˈpluːm/ n (pl noms de plume /ˌnɒm də ˈpluːm/) (French) a pen-name (PEN[1]).

nomenclature /nəˈmenklətʃə(r); US ˈnəʊmən- kleɪtʃər/ n (fml) (**a**) [C,U] a system of naming things, esp in a particular branch of science: botanical nomenclature. (**b**) [U] the names used in such a system: learn the nomenclature.

nominal /ˈnɒmɪnl/ adj **1** existing, etc in name only; not real or actual: the nominal ruler of the country ○ the nominal value of the shares. **2** (of a sum of money) very small and far below the real cost or value: pay a nominal rent ○ She charged only a nominal fee for her work. ▶ **nominally** /-nəli/ adv: be nominally in command.

nominate /ˈnɒmɪneɪt/ v **1(a)** ~ sb (for/as sth) to propose formally that sb should be chosen for a position, an honour, an office or a task: [Vnpr] She has been nominated for the Presidency. [Vn.n] He was nominated as best actor. [also Vn.to inf]. (**b**) ~ sb (to/as sth) to appoint sb to an office: [Vnpr] be nominated to a committee [Vn] nominate a spokesperson [Vn.to inf] He was nominated to speak on our behalf. [Vn-n] The board nominated her as the new director. **2** ~ sth (as sth) to decide formally on a date or place for an event: [Vn-n] 1 December has been nominated as the day of the election. [also Vn].

nomination /ˌnɒmɪˈneɪʃn/ n (**a**) [U] the action of nominating (NOMINATE 1) sb or the state of being nominated: membership of the Society is by nomination only. (**b**) [C] an instance of this: How many nominations have there been (ie How many people have been nominated) so far?

nominative /ˈnɒmɪnətɪv/ n (grammar) (in certain languages) the special form of a noun, a pronoun or an adjective when it is (part of) the subject of a verb. ▶ **nominative** adj: 'I', 'we', 'she' and 'they' are all nominative pronouns.

nominee /ˌnɒmɪˈniː/ n **1** a person who is nominated (NOMINATE 1) for an office, a position, etc. **2** (commerce) a person in whose name money is invested in a company, etc.

non- pref (used widely with ns, adjs and advs) not:

nonsense ○ non-fiction ○ non-alcoholic ○ non-profit- making ○ non-committally. ⇨ note at UN-.

nonagenarian /ˌnɒnədʒəˈneəriən, ˌnəʊn-/ n, adj (a person who is) of any age from 90 to 99.

non-aggression /ˌnɒn əˈgreʃn/ n [U, esp attrib] (of an agreement between two countries) committed not to attack each other: a non-aggression pact/treaty ○ a policy of non-aggression.

non-alcoholic /ˌnɒn ælkəˈhɒlɪk/ adj (of a drink) containing no alcohol: non-alcoholic lager.

non-aligned /ˌnɒn əˈlaɪnd/ adj (of a state) not supported by or supporting any major world power, eg the USA, China: the non-aligned countries/nations. ▶ **non-alignment** /ˌnɒn əˈlaɪnmənt/ n [U] the principle or practice of being non-aligned: follow a policy of non-alignment.

non-appearance /ˌnɒn əˈpɪərəns/ n [U] (fml) the failure to appear or be present: the non-appearance in court of the defendant.

non-attendance /ˌnɒn əˈtendəns/ n [U] the failure to be present in a place where one is expected: The chairman received three apologies for non-attendance at the meeting.

nonce-word /ˈnɒns wɜːd/ n a word invented for one particular occasion.

nonchalant /ˈnɒnʃələnt/ adj appearing or feeling calm and relaxed, not showing anxiety, interest or enthusiasm: try to appear/look/sound nonchalant. ▶ **nonchalance** /-ləns/ n [U]: He received the trophy with surprising nonchalance. **nonchalantly** adv: nonchalantly lighting a cigarette ○ He strolled nonchalantly past as if he had all the time in the world.

non-combatant /ˌnɒn ˈkɒmbətənt/ n a person who does not fight in a war, even though he or she may be in the armed forces, eg an army doctor or CHAPLAIN.

non-commissioned /ˌnɒn kəˈmɪʃnd/ adj not having a commission(5) in the army, etc: non-commissioned officers such as sergeants or corporals.

noncommittal /ˌnɒnkəˈmɪtl/ adj not showing what one thinks, which side one supports, etc; not committing oneself: a noncommittal attitude/reply/letter ○ She was very noncommittal about my suggestion. Compare COMMIT 4. ▶ **noncommittally** adv.

non-compliance /ˌnɒn kəmˈplaɪəns/ n [U] a refusal or failure to obey an order, a rule, etc: impose a fine for non-compliance with the safety regulations.

non compos mentis /ˌnɒn ˌkɒmpəs ˈmentɪs/ adj [pred] (Latin) not able to think clearly; not in one's right mind: I'd had a few beers and was completely non compos mentis. Compare COMPOS MENTIS.

nonconformist /ˌnɒnkənˈfɔːmɪst/ n, adj **1** (a person) who does not conform to normal social conventions: rather nonconformist ideas about child-rearing ○ He was a real nonconformist at school; he got into trouble the whole time. **2 Nonconformist** (a member) of a PROTESTANT Church that does not conform to the beliefs and practices of the Church of England. Compare DISSENTER.
▶ **nonconformity** (also **nonconformism**) n [U] **1** failure to conform to normal social conventions. **2** the beliefs and practices of Nonconformist Churches.

non-contributory /ˌnɒn kənˈtrɪbjətri; US -tɔːri/ adj (of an insurance or PENSION[1] scheme) in which regular payments are paid by the employer, not the employee: non-contributory benefits.

non-cooperation /ˌnɒn kəʊˌɒpəˈreɪʃn/ n [U] the failure to cooperate, esp as a form of protest: An all-out strike is unlikely but some forms of non-cooperation are being considered.

nondescript /ˈnɒndɪskrɪpt/ adj (derog) (of a person or thing) with no remarkable or interesting features, characteristics, etc; dull: *a nondescript landscape/face/voice* ○ *wear nondescript clothes.*

none /nʌn/ *indef pron* **1** ~ **(of sb/sth)** (used to refer to a plural *n* or *pron*) not one; not any: *I planted hundreds of seeds but none (of them) has/have come up.* ○ *None of these pens works/work.* ○ *None of them has/have replied yet.* **2** ~ **(of sth)** (used to refer to an uncountable *n* or a *pron*) not any: *I wanted some string but there was none in the house.* ○ *'Is there any bread left?' 'No, none at all.'* ○ *None of this money is mine.* **3** (*rhet*) (with comparatives and *than*) no one: *Everybody loved him, but none more so than I.* **IDM** **¹none but** only: *None but the freshest eggs are used in our cakes.* **none ¹other than** (used for emphasis) no one else but: *The new arrival was none other than the President himself.* **will have none of sth; want none of sth** to want nothing to do with sth; to refuse to accept sth, esp sb's bad behaviour: *I'll have none of your impudence, thank you.*

▶ **none** *adv* **1** (used with *the* and a comparative) not at all: *After hearing her talk on computers, I'm afraid I'm none the wiser.* ○ *He's none the worse for falling into the river.* **2** (used with *too* and *adjs* or *advs*) not very: *He was looking none too pleased.* ○ *She's none too well this morning.*

■ **¹none the ¹less** (also **nonetheless**) *adv* nevertheless: *It's not cheap but I think we should buy it none the less.*

nonentity /nɒˈnentəti/ *n* **1** (*derog*) a person without any special qualities or achievements; an unimportant person: *How could such a nonentity become chairman of the company?* **2** a thing that does not exist or exists only in the imagination.

non-event /ˌnɒn ɪˈvent/ *n* (*infml*) an event that is expected to be important or interesting, but is in fact a disappointment: *The party was a non-event; hardly anyone came.*

non-existent /ˌnɒn ɪgˈzɪstənt/ *adj* not existing; not real: *a non-existent danger/problem/threat* ○ *In those days health care was virtually non-existent.* ○ *My German is non-existent, I'm afraid* (ie I speak no German).

non-fiction /ˌnɒn ˈfɪkʃn/ *n* [U] a book or piece of writing that deals with facts, not imaginary stories: *the non-fiction shelves in the library.* Compare FIC-TION 1.

non-flammable /ˌnɒn ˈflæməbl/ *adj* (of clothes, materials, etc) not catching fire easily: *non-flammable pyjamas for children* ○ *non-flammable adhesive.* ⇨ note at INVALUABLE.

non-intervention /ˌnɒn ɪntəˈvenʃn/ (also **non-interference** /ˌnɒn ɪntəˈfɪərəns/) *n* [U] the principle or practice of not becoming involved in the disputes of others, esp in international affairs: *adopt a policy of non-intervention.*

no-no /ˈnəʊ nəʊ/ *n* [sing] (*infml*) a thing that is not permitted or accepted: *Smoking in this house is a no-no now.*

non-observance /ˌnɒn əbˈzɜːvəns/ *n* [U] (*fml*) the failure to keep or observe a rule, custom, etc: *accused of non-observance of the terms of the agreement.*

nonpareil /ˌnɒnpəˈreɪl; *US* -ˈrel/ *n* [sing], *adj* [attrib] (*fml*) (a person or thing) without a rival, esp in good qualities: *a nonpareil of the film world.*

non-payment /ˌnɒn ˈpeɪmənt/ *n* [U] (*fml*) failure to pay a debt, fine, etc: *He was taken to court for non-payment of rent.*

nonplus /ˌnɒnˈplʌs/ *v* (**-ss-**; *US* **-s-**) (esp passive) to surprise and confuse sb so much that they do not know what to do, think, etc: [Vn] *I was completely nonplussed by his reply.*

non-prescription /ˌnɒn prɪˈskrɪpʃn/ *adj* [attrib] (esp of drugs) that can be bought directly by a customer without a special form from a doctor, etc.

non-profit-making /ˌnɒn ˈprɒfɪt meɪkɪŋ/ *adj* (of

an enterprise) that does not aim to make a profit: *a non-profit-making organization* ○ *a children's charity that is non-profit-making.*

non-proliferation /ˌnɒn prəˌlɪfəˈreɪʃn/ *n* [U] a limiting of the increase in number and spread of sth: *a non-proliferation treaty aimed at stopping the spread of nuclear weapons.*

non-refundable /ˌnɒn rɪˈfʌndəbl/ *adj* (of a sum of money) that cannot be returned: *Please note that your deposit is non-refundable.*

non-renewable /ˌnɒn rɪˈnjuːəbl/ *adj* (esp of natural resources like gas and oil) that cannot be replaced after use: *Most of our energy comes from non-renewable resources.*

non-resident /ˌnɒn ˈrezɪdənt/ *adj* (*fml*) **1** (of a person, company, etc) not based permanently in a particular country: *Tax exemption only applies to those with non-resident status.* **2(a)** not living in a place of work: *This apartment block has a non-resident caretaker.* **(b)** (also **non-residential** /ˌnɒn rezɪˈdenʃl/) (of a job) that does not require one to live in one's place of work: *a non-resident(ial) post.*

▶ **non-resident** *n* **1** a person not living permanently in a particular country: *Student fees are higher for non-residents.* **2** a person not staying at a hotel, etc: *The bar is open to non-residents.*

nonsense /ˈnɒnsns; *US* -sens/ *n* **1** [U] spoken or written words that have no meaning or make no sense: *The computer's producing absolute nonsense.* ○ *This so-called translation is pure nonsense.* **2(a)** [U] foolish talk, ideas, etc: *You're talking nonsense!* ○ *'I won't go.' 'Nonsense! You must go!'* **(b)** [U] foolish or unacceptable behaviour: *Stop that nonsense, children, and get into bed!* ○ *He won't stand for any nonsense from the staff.* **IDM** **make a ¹nonsense of sth** to reduce the value of sth greatly: *This discovery makes a nonsense of all previous theories.* ○ *If people can bribe judges and policemen, it makes a complete nonsense of the legal system.* **stuff and nonsense** ⇨ STUFF¹.

▶ **nonsensical** /nɒnˈsensɪkl/ *adj* stupid; absurd: *a nonsensical argument/remark/suggestion.* **nonsensically** /-kli/ *adv.*

non sequitur /ˌnɒn ˈsekwɪtə(r)/ *n* (*Latin*) a statement that does not follow in a logical way from the previous one; a piece of false reasoning.

non-slip /ˌnɒn ˈslɪp/ *adj* that does not slip or helps to prevent sb/sth slipping: *non-slip mats.*

non-smoker /ˌnɒn ˈsməʊkə(r)/ *n* **1** a person who does not smoke tobacco. **2** a section of a train, etc in which smoking is forbidden. ▶ **non-¹smoking** *adj*: *a non-smoking area in a restaurant.*

non-standard /ˌnɒn ˈstændəd/ *adj* not standard: *non-standard ¹dialects/¹forms/varieties* ○ *non-standard ¹English.*

non-starter /ˌnɒn ˈstaːtə(r)/ *n* (*infml*) a thing or person that has no chance of success: *As a business proposition it's a non-starter.*

non-stick /ˌnɒn ˈstɪk/ *adj* (of a pan, surface, etc) covered with a substance that prevents food sticking to it during cooking: *a ˌnon-stick ¹frying-pan.*

non-stop /ˌnɒn ˈstɒp/ *adj, adv* **1** (of a train, journey, etc) without any stops: *a non-stop flight to Tokyo* ○ *fly non-stop from New York to Paris.* **2** (done) without stopping: *ˌnon-stop ¹talk/¹work* ○ *He chattered non-stop all the way.*

non-U /ˌnɒn ˈjuː/ *adj* (*dated Brit infml*) (of language, behaviour or dress) not characteristic of the upper social classes; not socially acceptable to certain people: *a ˌnon-U ¹accent.* Compare U².

non-union /ˌnɒn ˈjuːnɪən/ *adj* [usu attrib] **1** not belonging to a trade union: *non-union labour/members/workers.* **2** (of a business, company, etc) not having trade union members: *a ˌnon-union ¹factory/¹industry.*

N

non-violence /ˌnɒn ˈvaɪələns/ *n* [U] the policy of using peaceful methods, not force, to bring about political or social change: *Gandhi's policy of non-violence.* ► **non-violent** /-lənt/ *adj*: *a non-violent protest/demonstration.*

non-White /ˌnɒn ˈwaɪt/ *n, adj* (a person) not belonging to any of the races with pale skins.

noodle /ˈnuːdl/ *n* (usu *pl*) a long thin strip of PASTA used in soups, etc: *chicken noodle soup* ○ *Chinese food is often served with rice or noodles.*

nook /nʊk/ *n* a sheltered quiet place or corner: *a shady nook in the garden* ○ *sit in a cosy nook by the fire.* **IDM** **every** ˌnook and ˈcranny (*infml*) every part of a place; everywhere: *The wind blew into every nook and cranny.*

noon /nuːn/ *n* [sing] (used without *a* or *the*) 12 o'clock in the middle of the day: *The library closes at noon on Saturdays.* ○ *The conference opens at twelve noon.* ○ *the noon deadline for the end of hostilities.* **IDM** **morning, noon and night** ⇨ MORNING.

noonday /ˈnuːndeɪ/ (also **noontide** /-taɪd/) *n* [sing] (*dated or rhet*) NOON: *sitting in the noonday sun.*

noose /nuːs/ *n* a loop in one end of a rope, with a knot that allows the loop to get smaller as the other end of the rope is pulled: *tighten the noose round sb's neck* ○ *a hangman's noose.* ⇨ picture.

noose

nope /nəʊp/ *interj* (*infml*) no: *'Have you seen my pen?' 'Nope.'*

nor /nɔː(r)/ *conj, adv* **1** (used after *neither* to indicate a second or further alternative) and not: *I have neither the time nor the patience to listen to his complaints.* **2** (used after a negative statement to introduce another, with the subject following the *v*): *This isn't the main reason, nor is it the most important.* ○ *My parents don't like him, and nor do I.* Compare NEITHER.

nor'- ⇨ NORTH.

Nordic /ˈnɔːdɪk/ *adj* **1** of the countries of Scandinavia. **2** of or relating to the Germanic people of N Europe, who are typically tall, with blue eyes and blond hair: *Nordic features.*

norm /nɔːm/ *n* **1** (often with *the* when *sing*) a standard or pattern, esp of social behaviour, that is typical of a group: *cultural/social norms* ○ *Criminal behaviour seems to be the norm in this neighbourhood.* **2** [C] a required standard, amount, level, etc of sth: *Few companies are prepared to break the 7% pay norm.*

normal /ˈnɔːml/ *adj* **1** typical, usual or expected: *Her temperature is normal.* ○ *accept some unhappiness as a normal part of life* ○ *start work at the normal time* ○ **lead/live a normal life** ○ *We are open during normal office/business hours.* ○ *In/ under normal circumstances, I would say 'yes'.* ○ *In the normal course of events I would have told him at once.* **2** not suffering from any mental disorder: *People who commit such crimes aren't normal.* Compare ABNORMAL. ► **normal** *n* [U] the usual state, level, standard, etc: *Her temperature is above/below normal.* ○ *Things have returned to normal.*

normality /nɔːˈmælɪti/ (also *esp US* **normalcy** /ˈnɔːmlsi/) *n* [U] the state of being normal: *seek a return to normality.*

normalize, -ise /ˈnɔːməlaɪz/ *v* **1** to have or bring back a normal friendly relationship, esp after a dispute or war: [Vn,Vnpr] *normalize trading relations (with the West)* [also V]. **2** to make sth fit the normal pattern; to make sth standard: [Vn] *normalize an author's odd spelling.* **normalization, -isation** /ˌnɔːməlaɪˈzeɪʃn; *US* -ləˈz-/ *n* [U]: *the normalization of relations.*

normally /ˈnɔːməli/ *adv*: *It's normally much warmer than this in July.* ○ *Train services are running normally.*

Norman /ˈnɔːmən/ *adj* **1** (*architecture*) of the style introduced into England in the 11th century by the **Normans** from northern France, who defeated the English in 1066; ROMANESQUE: *a Norman arch/ cathedral.* **2** of the Normans: *the Norman Conquest.*

normative /ˈnɔːmətɪv/ *adj* (*fml*) describing or setting standards or rules of language or behaviour which should be followed: *a normative argument/ grammar.*

north /nɔːθ/ *n* [U, sing] (*abbr* N) **1** (usu **the north**) the direction to one's left when one is facing the rising sun: *cold winds from the north* ○ *He lives to the north of* (ie further north than) *here.* ○ *Do you know which way is north?* Compare EAST, SOUTH, WEST. See also MAGNETIC NORTH, TRUE NORTH. **2** **the north**, **the North** the part of any country, etc that lies further north than other parts: *the North of Japan* ○ *The north is less expensive to live in than the south.* ► **north** *adj* [attrib] (**a**) of, in or towards the north: *North London* ○ *a north wall* (ie one facing north). (**b**) coming from the north: *a north wind* (ie blowing from the north). **north** *adv* to or towards the north: *sail/drive (due) north.* **IDM** **up** ˈnorth (*infml*) to or in the north: *He's gone to live up north.*

northward /ˈnɔːθwəd/ going towards the north: *a northward course.*

northwards /ˈnɔːθwədz/ (also **northward**) *adv* towards the north. ⇨ note at FORWARD[2].

■ **the** ˈ**North Country** *n* [sing] the northern part of England.

ˌ**north-**ˈ**east** *n* [sing], *adj, adv* (*abbr* NE) (the direction or region) HALFWAY between north and east. ˌ**north-**ˈ**easterly** *adj* (**a**) towards the north-east. (**b**) (of winds) blowing from the north-east. — *n* a wind from the north-east. ˌ**north-**ˈ**eastern** /-ˈiːstən/ *adj* of, from or situated in the north-east. ˌ**north-**ˈ**eastwards** /-ˈiːstwədz/ (also ˌ**north-**ˈ**eastward**) *adv* towards the north-east.

the ˌ**North** ˈ**Pole** *n* [sing] the point on the Earth that is furthest north. ⇨ picture at GLOBE.

ˌ**north-**ˈ**west** *n* [sing], *adj, adv* (*abbr* NW) (the direction or region) HALFWAY between north and west. ˌ**north-**ˈ**westerly** *adj* (**a**) towards the north-west. (**b**) (of winds) blowing from the north-west. — *n* a wind from the north-west. ˌ**north-**ˈ**western** /-ˈwestən/ *adj* of, from or situated in the north-west. ˌ**north-**ˈ**westwards** /-ˈwestwədz/ (also ˌ**north-**ˈ**westward**) *adv* towards the north-west.

northbound /ˈnɔːθbaʊnd/ *adj* travelling or leading towards the north: *northbound traffic* ○ *the northbound lane of the interstate highway.*

northerly /ˈnɔːðəli/ *adj* **1** to, towards or in the north: *travel in a northerly direction.* **2** (of winds) from the north. ► **northerly** *n* a wind from the north: *cold northerlies bringing rain.*

northern /ˈnɔːðən/ *adj* [usu attrib] of, from or situated in the north: *the northern region/frontier/ climate* ○ *the northern hemisphere.* ⇨ picture at GLOBE. ► **northerner** /ˈnɔːðənə(r)/ *n* a person born or living in the northern part of a country. **northernmost** /-məʊst/ *adj* [usu attrib] furthest to the north.

■ **the** ˌ**northern** ˈ**lights** *n* [pl] = AURORA BOREALIS.

Nos ⇨ No.

nose[1] /nəʊz/ *n* [pl] **1** [C] the part of the face above the mouth, used for breathing and for smelling things: *She wrinkled her nose in disgust* (eg because of an unpleasant smell). ○ *Stop picking your nose* (ie taking out pieces of dirt with the finger)! ⇨ picture at HEAD[1]. ⇨ note at BODY. **2** [C] the front part of eg an aircraft: *He brought the plane's nose up and made a*

perfect landing. ➭ picture at AIRCRAFT. **3** [sing] (**a**) ~ **for sth** (*infml*) an ability to find or detect sth: *a reporter with a nose for scandal.* (**b**) a sense of smell: *a dog with a good nose.* **4** (of wine) a pleasing distinctive smell. **IDM be no skin off one's nose** ➭ SKIN. **blow one's nose** ➭ BLOW¹. **cut off one's nose to spite one's ¹face** (*infml*) to harm oneself while taking revenge on sb else. **follow one's nose** ➭ FOLLOW. **get up sb's ¹nose** (*sl esp Brit*) to annoy sb: *Her remarks really got up my nose!* **have one's nose in ¹sth** (*infml*) to be reading sth with great attention and interest: *Peter's always got his nose in a book.* **keep one's ¹nose clean** (*infml*) to avoid doing anything wrong, illegal, etc: *If you keep your nose clean, you'll do well in this firm.* **keep one's/ sb's nose to the ¹grindstone** (*infml*) to keep oneself/sb working hard. **lead sb by the nose** ➭ LEAD¹. **look down one's ¹nose at sb/sth** (*infml*) to treat sb/sth with contempt: *They look down their noses at people less successful than themselves.* ₁**nose to ¹tail** (*Brit*) (of traffic) with each vehicle very close to the one in front: *cars crawling nose to tail for miles.* **on the ¹nose** (*sl*) exactly: *You've hit it* (ie described or understood it) *on the nose!* **pay through the nose** ➭ PAY². **plain as the nose on one's face** ➭ PLAIN¹. **poke/stick one's nose into ¹sth** (*infml*) to interfere in sth that is not one's concern: *Don't go poking your nose into other people's business!* **powder one's nose** ➭ POWDER *v*. **put sb's ¹nose out of joint** (*infml*) to upset or annoy sb, eg by not paying attention to them or hurting their pride. **rub sb's nose in it** ➭ RUB¹. **thumb one's nose at sb/sth** ➭ THUMB *v*. **turn one's ¹nose up at sth** (*infml*) to treat sth with contempt: *She turned her nose up at my small donation.* (**right**) **under sb's** (**very**) ¹**nose** (*infml*) **1** directly in front of sb: *I put the bill right under his nose so that he couldn't miss it.* **2** openly, but usu without being noticed: *They were having an affair under my very nose, and I didn't even realize!* **with one's nose in the air** (*infml*) indicating that one thinks one is superior to other people: *She walked straight past us with her nose in the air.*
▶ **-nosed** /-nəʊzd/ (forming compound *adjs*) having a nose of the specified colour, shape, etc: *red-nosed* ○ *long-nosed.*

nose² /nəʊz/ *v* **1** to move forward slowly and carefully: [Vpr, Vp] *The plane nosed (down) cautiously through the dense cloud.* [Vnpr] *The taxi nosed its way into the middle lane.* [Vadv] (*fig*) *The Democrats are nosing ahead in the opinion polls.* **2** (of animals) to search or smell sth with the nose: [Vpr] *a dog nosing into an old rucksack* [Vnp] *Timmy nosed out a rat.* [also Vn]. **PHRV ₁nose a¹bout/a¹round/¹round** (*infml derog*) to look around a place or ask people questions in order to discover sth interesting: *a reporter nosing around for news* ○ *I caught him nosing round my garden.* ₁**nose sth ¹out** (*infml*) to discover sth by searching carefully: *reporters nosing out all the details of the affair.*

nosebag /¹nəʊzbæg/ (*US* ¹**feedbag**) *n* a bag containing food for a horse, hung from its head.

nosebleed /¹nəʊzbliːd/ *n* a flow of blood coming from the nose: *have a nosebleed.*

nosedive /¹nəʊzdaɪv/ *n* **1** an aircraft's sudden sharp fall towards the ground with the nose¹(2) first: *go into a sudden nosedive.* **2** (*commerce*) a sudden steep fall or drop: *Prices/shares/profits have taken a nosedive.*
▶ **nosedive** *v* **1** [V] (of an aircraft, etc) to descend sharply with the nose¹(2) pointing towards the ground. **2** to fall sharply: [V] *Demand for oil has nosedived.*

nosegay /¹nəʊzgeɪ/ *n* a small bunch of sweet-smelling flowers worn on a dress or carried in the hand.

nosering /¹nəʊzrɪŋ/ *n* a ring in the nose of an animal for leading it, or of a person as an ornament.

nosey (also **nosy**) /¹nəʊzi/ *adj* (**-ier, -iest**) (*infml usu derog*) showing great interest and curiosity in other people's affairs: *nosey neighbours* ○ *Don't be so nosey — it's none of your business.* ▶ **nosiness** *n* [U].
■ ₁**Nosey ¹Parker** (also ₁**Nosy ¹Parker**) *n* (*Brit infml derog*) a person who is nosey: *I caught that Nosey Parker reading my diary.*

nosh /nɒʃ/ *n* (*sl esp Brit or Austral*) [U] food: *cheap nosh.*
■ ¹**nosh-up** *n* (*sl esp Brit*) a meal, esp a large one: *Let's go for a nosh-up at Sally's place.*

nostalgia /nɒ¹stældʒə/ *n* [U] the feeling of sadness mixed with pleasure when one thinks of a happy period, event, etc earlier in one's life: *middle-aged couples wallowing in nostalgia.*
▶ **nostalgic** /nɒ¹stældʒɪk/ *adj* of, feeling or causing nostalgia: *be nostalgic for the lost peace of the countryside.* **nostalgically** /-kli/ *adv*: *looking back nostalgically to my childhood in Africa.*

nostril /¹nɒstrəl/ *n* either of the two openings at the bottom of the nose through which a person or an animal breathes: *flared nostrils.* ➭ picture at HEAD¹.

nostrum /¹nɒstrəm/ *n* (*fml derog*) a medicine made by sb who is not a proper doctor or chemist: (*fig*) *a nostrum put forward as a cure for unemployment.*

not /nɒt/ *adv* **1**(**a**) (used with auxiliary and modal *vs* to form the negative; often contracted to *-n't* /nt/ in speech and informal writing): *She did not see him.* ○ *You may not get the job.* ○ *They aren't here.* ○ *I mustn't forget.* ○ *It's cold today, isn't it?* ○ *Wouldn't you like to go home?* (**b**) (used with non-finite *vs* to form the negative): *He warned me not to be late.* ○ *I was sorry not to have seen him.* ○ *She accused me of not telling the truth.* **2**(**a**) (used in short answers after* believe, expect, hope, trust*, etc instead of a clause beginning with *that* and containing a negative *v*): *'Will it rain?' 'I hope not'* (ie I hope that it will not rain).' ○ *'Did she pass?' 'I'm afraid not.'* ○ (*fml*) *'Does he know?' 'I believe not.'* (**b**) (used to indicate the negative alternative after questions with *Are you, Can he, Shall we*, etc): *Is she ready or not?* ○ *I don't know if/whether he's telling the truth or not.* **3** (used to reply in the negative to part or all of a question: *'Are you hungry?' 'Not hungry, just very tired.'* ○ *'Would you like some more?' 'Not for me, thank you.'* **4**(**a**) (used before *ns* or *prons* to exclude a person or group): *She likes most kinds of music but not jazz.* ○ *'Who wants to come for a walk?' 'Not me!'* (**b**) (used before *all* or *every* to exclude some members of the group): *Not everybody agrees with you.* ○ *Not all children enjoy television.* **5** (used to show that the opposite of the following word or phrase is intended): *Somebody not a million miles from here* (ie very close) *is responsible for this mess.* ○ *We plan to meet again in the not too distant future* (ie quite soon). **IDM ₁not at ¹all 1** (used for accepting sb's thanks): *'Thank you for all your help.' 'Not at all.'* **2** (used for saying 'yes' to a request): *'Do you mind if I open the window?' 'Not at all.'* **3** definitely not: *'Did you enjoy it?' 'Not at all.'* **not only ... (but) also** (used to emphasize an additional factor or feature): *He not only acts but also writes his own plays.* ¹**not that** though one is not suggesting that: *She hasn't written to me — not that she said she would.*

notable /¹nəʊtəbl/ *adj* ~ (**for sth**) worthy of attention or notice: *a notable success/discovery* ○ *make a notable contribution to scientific research* ○ *The town is notable for its ancient harbour.* ○ *With a few notable exceptions, everybody gave something.*
▶ **notable** *n* a famous or important person: *The usual local notables were there.*
notably /¹nəʊtəbli/ *adv* **1** (used for giving a good example of sth): *This is true of many English towns,*

N

notably Bath and Oxford. **2** particularly: *a notably talented young violinist.*

notary /'nəʊtəri/ (also ‚notary 'public) *n* a person with official authority to be a witness when sb signs a legal document.

notation /nəʊ'teɪʃn/ *n* [U, C] a system of signs or symbols used to represent numbers, amounts, musical notes, etc: *musical/scientific notation.*

notch /nɒtʃ/ *n* **1** ~ (in/on sth) a cut shaped like a V in an edge or a surface: *For each day he spent on the island, he cut/made a notch on a stick.* ⇨ picture at GROOVE. **2** a level or grade: *turn the sound up another notch* ○ *He needs to lift his game a notch if he wants to win.* See also TOP-NOTCH. **3** (*US*) a narrow mountain pass.
▶ **notch** *v* [Vn] to make a notch in sth. **PHR V** ‚notch sth 'up (*infml*) to score sth; to achieve sth: *notch up heavy gains/losses* ○ *They notched up their ninth win in a row.*

note[1] /nəʊt/ *n* **1** [C] a short written record to help one remember sth: *make a note of the dates* ○ *She lectured without notes.* ○ *He sat taking notes of everything that was said.* **2** [C] (**a**) a short informal letter: *a note of thanks* ○ *leave a note for the milkman* ○ *a suicide note.* (**b**) an official letter sent from the representative of one government to another: *An exchange of notes quickly followed the incident.* **3** [C] a short comment on or explanation of a word or passage in a book: *a new edition of 'Hamlet', with copious notes* ○ *see note 3, page 259.* See also FOOT-NOTE. **4** (also 'banknote, *US* usu bill) [C] a piece of paper money issued by a bank: *a £5 note* ○ *We only exchange notes and traveller's cheques.* See also CREDIT NOTE. **5** [C] (**a**) a single sound of a certain pitch[1](2) and length, made by the voice or a musical instrument: *sing/play the first few notes of a tune.* (**b**) a sign used to represent such a sound in written or printed music. ⇨ picture at MUSIC. (**c**) any one of the keys of a piano, etc: *the black notes and the white notes.* **6** [sing] ~ (of sth) a matter, a state or an indication of sth: *The book ended on an optimistic note.* ○ *On a more serious note* (ie Speaking more seriously), *I'd like to consider...* ○ *On a slightly different note* (ie Changing the subject slightly), *let's think about what we'll do this weekend.* ○ *There was a note of self-satisfaction in his speech.* **7** [U] notice; attention: *a performance worthy of note* ○ *Take note of what he says* (ie pay attention to it). **IDM** compare notes ⇨ COMPARE. of 'note of importance or great interest: *a singer/writer of some note* ○ *Nothing of particular note happened.* hit/strike the right/wrong 'note to do, say or write sth that is suitable/not suitable for a particular occasion. strike/sound a 'note (of 'sth) to express feelings, views, etc of the stated kind: *She sounded a note of caution in her speech.* ○ *The article struck a deeply pessimistic note.* strike/sound a false note ⇨ FALSE.
▶ **notelet** /'nəʊtlət/ *n* a small folded sheet of paper or card with a picture on the front, for writing a short letter on.

note[2] /nəʊt/ *v* (*esp fml*) to pay attention to sth; to observe sth: [Vn] *Please note my words.* [V.that] *She noted (that) his hands were dirty.* ○ *It is worth noting* (ie It is an interesting fact) *that the most successful companies had the lowest prices.* [V.wh] *Note how I do it, then copy me.* **PHR V** note sth down to record sth in writing; to write sth down: *The police officer noted down every word she said.*
▶ **noted** *adj* ~ (for/as sth) well-known; famous: *a noted pianist* ○ *a town noted for its fine buildings/as a health resort.*
■ 'noteworthy *adj* deserving to be noted because of being unusual, interesting or impressive: *It is note-worthy that only 5% of senior managers are women.* ○ *a noteworthy performance by a young soloist.*

notebook /'nəʊtbʊk/ *n* a small book for writing notes (NOTE[1] 1) in.
■ ‚notebook com'puter *n* a very small computer that is easy to carry around.

notepad /'nəʊtpæd/ *n* a block of sheets of paper for writing on.

notepaper /'nəʊtpeɪpə(r)/ *n* [U] paper for writing letters on.

nothing /'nʌθɪŋ/ *neg pron* not anything; no single thing: *a box with nothing in it* ○ *Nothing (else) matters to him apart from his job.* ○ *I've had nothing to eat since lunchtime.* ○ *There's nothing you can do to help.* ○ *The doctor said there was nothing (serious) wrong with me.* ○ *There is nothing as refreshing as lemon tea.* ○ *Their chances of winning had faded to nothing.* ○ *'What's that in your pocket?' 'Oh, nothing* (ie nothing important, nothing that concerns you).' ○ *It used to cost nothing to visit a museum.* ○ (*infml*) *He's five foot nothing* (ie exactly five feet tall). **IDM** be 'nothing to sb to be a person for whom sb has no feelings: *I used to love her but she's nothing to me any more.* for 'nothing **1** without payment; free: *We could have got in for nothing — nobody was collecting tickets.* **2** with no reward or result; to no purpose: *All that preparation was for nothing because the visit was cancelled.* have nothing on sb (*infml*) **1** to have much less of a certain quality or ability than sth/sb: *Today's pop music has got 'nothing on the old Broadway musicals.* **2** (of the police, etc) to have no information that could show sb to be guilty of sth: *They can't arrest him because they've got nothing 'on him.* not for 'nothing for a very good reason: *Not for nothing was he called the king of rock and roll.* 'nothing but only; no more/less than: *His speech was nothing but hot air.* ○ *Nothing but a miracle can save her now.* ○ *I want nothing but the best for my children.* 'nothing if not (*infml*) extremely; very: *The trip was nothing if not varied.* 'nothing less than (used to emphasize how great or extreme sth is): *His negligence was nothing less than criminal.* ○ *It was nothing less than a disaster.* nothing 'like (*infml*) **1** not at all like: *It looks nothing like a horse.* **2** absolutely not: *Her cooking is nothing like as good as yours.* ○ *I had nothing like enough time to answer all the questions.* ‚nothing 'much not a great amount of sth; nothing of great value or importance: *There's nothing much in the fridge.* ○ *I got up late and did nothing much all day.* ‚nothing 'to it very simple: *I did the crossword in half an hour — there was nothing to it.* sweet nothings ⇨ SWEET[1]. there is/was nothing (else) 'for it (but to do sth) there is no other action to take except the one specified: *There was nothing else for it but to resign.*
▶ **nothingness** *n* [U] the state of not being; the state of being nothing: *the desert's endless expanse of nothingness* ○ *Our spirits dissolve into nothingness.*

notice /'nəʊtɪs/ *n* **1** [U] attention; observation: *Take no notice/Don't take any notice of what you read in the papers.* ○ *It was Susan who brought the problem to my notice* (ie told me about it). ○ *It has come to my notice* (ie I have heard or been told) *that you have been stealing.* ○ *It will not have escaped (your) notice that there have been some major changes in the company.* **2** [C] (**a**) a sheet of paper giving written or printed news or information, usu displayed publicly: *pin a notice on the board.* (**b**) a board or a sign displaying information: *a notice saying 'Keep Off The Grass'.* (**c**) a small advertisement or announcement in a newspaper or magazine: *notices of births, deaths and marriages.* **3** [U, C] (**a**) information or a warning of what will happen: *You must give proper notice* (ie tell people in advance) *of changes in the arrangements.* ○ *Prices may be altered without notice.* ○ *The bar is closed until further notice.* (**b**) a formal letter or state-

---

ment saying that one will leave a job or house at a specified time: *He has handed in his notice* (ie announced that he is going to leave his job). ○ *My contract says that I must give a month's notice if I intend to leave the company.* ○ *500 workers have been issued with redundancy notices.* **4** [C] a short review of a book, play, etc in a newspaper or magazine: *The play received good notices.* **IDM** **at short / at a moment's 'notice** not long in advance; without warning or time for preparation: *The meeting was cancelled at short notice.* ○ *You must be ready to leave at a moment's notice.* **not take a blind bit of notice** ⇨ BLIND¹.

▶ **notice** *v* **1** to become aware of sth/sb; to see or observe sth/sb: [V] *Didn't you notice? He's dyed his hair.* [Vn] *He got into the building without being noticed.* [V.that] *I noticed (that) he left early.* [Vn.*in*, Vn.inf (no *to*)] *Did you notice him coming in/ come in?* [also V.*wh*]. **2** to pay attention to sb: [Vn] *a young actor trying desperately to be noticed by the critics* ○ *She just wants to be noticed, that's why she dresses so strangely.* ○ *My husband hardly seems to notice me any more.*

noticeable /-əbl/ *adj* ~ **(in sth)** easily seen or noticed; clear or definite: *The effects of the drug were noticeable in his behaviour.* ○ *There's been a noticeable improvement in her handwriting.* ○ *It was noticeable that she was in a bad mood.* **noticeably** /-əbli/ *adv*.

■ **'notice-board** (*Brit*) (*US* **'bulletin board**) *n* a board for notices (NOTICE 2a) to be displayed on.

notify /'nəʊtɪfaɪ/ *v* (*pt, pp* **-fied**) ~ **sb (of sth)**; ~ **sth to sb** to inform sb of sth or report sth to sb, esp formally or officially: [Vn, Vnpr] *Have the authorities been notified (of this)?* ○ *notify us of your intentions/notify your intentions to us in writing* [Vn.*that*] *He notified us that he was going to leave.*

▶ **notifiable** /'nəʊtɪfaɪəbl/ *adj* [esp attrib] (*fml*) (of diseases) that must by law be reported to the public health authorities because they are so dangerous: *Typhoid is a notifiable disease.*

notification /ˌnəʊtɪfɪ'keɪʃn/ *n* [U, C] (*fml*) the action of informing sb about sth: *receive notification of sth* ○ *No visits may be made to the prison without prior notification.*

notion /'nəʊʃn/ *n* **1** [C] ~ **(that…)** an idea or a belief: *a political system based on the notions of equality and liberty* ○ *the notion that all human beings are born equal* ○ *I had a vague notion that she originally came from Poland.* ○ *His head is full of silly notions.* **2** ~ **(of sth)** an awareness or understanding of the nature or extent of sth: *Do you have the slightest notion (of) what this means?* ○ *She has no notion of the difficulty of this problem.*

notional /'nəʊʃənl/ *adj* assumed to be actual or real for a particular purpose; based on guesses, estimates or abstract ideas: *My calculation is based on notional figures, since the actual figures are not yet available.* ○ *a notional exchange rate for agricultural transactions.* ▶ **notionally** /'nəʊʃənəli/ *adv*: *The notes B♯ and C are notionally distinct, although they sound the same.*

notorious /nəʊ'tɔːriəs/ *adj* ~ **(for/as sth)** (*derog*) well-known for some bad quality or deed: *a notorious criminal/area of the city* ○ *She's notorious for getting drunk at parties.* ○ *The bar is notorious as a meeting-place for drug pushers.* ▶ **notoriety** /ˌnəʊtə'raɪəti/ *n* [U] fame for being bad in some way: *He achieved (a certain) notoriety as a reckless gambler.* **notoriously** *adv*: *It is notoriously difficult to find cheap accommodation in London.*

notwithstanding /ˌnɒtwɪθ'stændɪŋ, -wɪð-/ *prep* ~ **(that …)** (*fml*) (can also follow the *n* to which it refers) without being affected by sth; in spite of sth: *Notwithstanding a steady decline in numbers, the*

school has had a very successful year. ○ *Language difficulties notwithstanding, he soon grew to love the country and its people.* ○ *The contract is invalid, notwithstanding that the goods have been delivered.* ▶ **notwithstanding** *adv* (*fml*) in spite of this; however; nevertheless.

nougat /'nuːgɑː; *US* 'nuːgət/ *n* [U] a hard sweet made with nuts, sugar or honey, and the whites of eggs.

nought /nɔːt/ *n* **1** the figure 0: *The first player scored nought.* ○ *write three noughts on the blackboard* ○ *nought point one* (ie 0.1). ⇨ App 2. **2** (also **naught**) (*arch*) (in certain phrases) nothing: *His efforts came to nought* (ie were unsuccessful).

■ **ˌnoughts and 'crosses** (*Brit*) (*US* ˌtick-tack-'toe*) *n* [U] a game in which two players take turns to write 0s or Xs in a set of nine squares, with each trying to complete a row of three 0s or three Xs.

NOTE The figure **0** has several different names in English. Compare **zero**, **nought**, **O** and **nil**. **Zero** is used especially in scientific, medical and economic contexts, and to talk about temperature: *The temperature here rarely falls below zero.* ○ *The government wants to achieve zero inflation.*

Nought is often used in British English to talk about the figure 0, as part of a number: *A million is 1 followed by six noughts (1 000 000).* ○ *We sell clothes for children aged nought to six (0–6).* When saying or reading a telephone or bank account number, etc in British and American English we say the figure 0 as a letter 'O': *My account number is 0204381 (O-two-o-four-three-eight-one).* ○ *The code is 47005 (four seven double-o five).*

Nil is used when talking about the score in a team game, for example in football: *The final score was 3–0 (three nil).* It is also sometimes used to mean 'nothing at all': *The prospects of getting work were nil.* In American English **zero** is commonly used in all these cases.

noun /naʊn/ *n* (*grammar*) (abbreviated as *n* in this dictionary) a word used to name or identify any of a class of things, people, places or ideas, or a particular one of these. See also COMMON NOUN, COUNT NOUN, PROPER NOUN.

■ **'noun phrase** *n* (*grammar*) a phrase whose function in a sentence is equivalent to that of a noun, eg the phrase *Living alone* in the sentence *Living alone has its advantages.*

nourish /'nʌrɪʃ/ *v* **1** to keep a person, an animal or a plant alive and well with food: [Vn] *badly nourished children* ○ *Most plants are nourished by water drawn up through their roots.* ○ (*fig*) *Our literary tradition is continually nourished by new writers.* **2** (*fml*) to allow a feeling to continue and develop: *For some time I had nourished a wish to write my memoirs.*

▶ **nourishing** *adj*: *nourishing food.*

nourishment *n* [U] food that keeps sb/sth alive and well: *obtain nourishment from the soil* ○ (*fig*) *books that provide intellectual nourishment.*

nous /naʊs/ *n* [U] (*Brit infml*) common sense (COMMON¹); practical intelligence: *None of them had the nous to shut the door when the fire started.*

nouveau riche /ˌnuːvəʊ 'riːʃ/ *n* (*pl* **nouveaux riches** /ˌnuːvəʊ 'riːʃ/) (*French derog*) a person who has recently become rich, esp one who displays her or his wealth in a very obvious manner. ▶ **nouveau riche** *adj*.

nouvelle cuisine /ˌnuːvel kwɪ'ziːn/ *n* [U] (*French*) a modern style of cooking that avoids heavy foods and emphasizes the way dishes are presented.

Nov *abbr* November: *21 Nov 1983.*

nova /'nəʊvə/ *n* (*pl* **novas** or **novae** /-viː/) (*astronomy*) a star that suddenly becomes much brighter for a short period. Compare SUPERNOVA.

novel¹ /'nɒvl/ *n* an invented story in PROSE, long enough to fill a complete book: *read/write a novel* ○ *the novels of Jane Austen* ○ *historical/science-fiction/romantic novels.*

novel² /'nɒvl/ *adj* (*esp approv*) new and strange; of a type not known before: *a novel idea/design/experience.*

novelette /ˌnɒvə'let/ *n* a short novel, esp one of poor literary quality.

novelist /'nɒvəlɪst/ *n* a writer of novels.
▸ **novelistic** /-'lɪstɪk/ *adj* (*fml*) characteristic of or used in novels: *a novelistic device/convention/style.*

novella /nə'velə/ *n* (*pl* **novellas**) a short novel.

novelty /'nɒvlti/ *n* **1** [U] the quality of being new, different or strange: *At first he played with the computer all the time, but the novelty soon **wore off*** (ie he grew bored with it). ○ *There's a certain novelty (value) in this approach.* **2** [C] a previously unknown thing, situation or experience; a new or strange thing or person: *A car that can run on electricity is still something of a novelty.* **3** [C] a small toy, ornament, etc of low value: *a chocolate egg with a plastic novelty inside.*
▸ **novelty** *adj* [attrib] intended to be amusing or striking, because of being different or unusual: *one of those novelty hats with a hand holding a hammer stuck on it.*

November /nəʊ'vembə(r)/ *n* [U, C] (*abbr* **Nov**) the 11th month of the year, next after October.
For further guidance on how *November* is used, see the examples at *April.*

novice /'nɒvɪs/ *n* **1** a person who is new and has little experience in a job or situation: *She's a complete novice as a reporter.* ○ *an excellent computer for novices and experts alike* ○ *a novice writer/salesman/cook.* **2** (in horse-racing) a horse that has not yet won a major race. **3** a person who has just joined a religious community but is not yet a monk or a nun. Compare POSTULANT.

now /naʊ/ *adv* **1(a)** at the present time: *Where are you living now?* ○ *People used to go to the cinema, but now they watch television more.* ○ *It's now ten years since we got married.* **(b)** at or from this moment, but not before: *Now* (eg After all these interruptions) *I can get on with my work.* ○ *Start writing now.* ○ *I am now ready to answer your questions.* **(c)** (used after a *prep* or as the subject of a *v*) the present time: *I never realized I loved you until now.* ○ *He should have arrived by now.* ○ *Now is the best time to visit the gardens.* Compare THEN 1. **2** (used to express annoyance at the latest in a series of annoying actions or events): *Now the government wants to tax food!* ○ *What do you want now?* **3(a)** (used without reference to time, to emphasize or draw attention to what is about to be said, eg in a story): *Now the country was ruled by a handsome prince.* ○ *The phone's ringing. Now who can that be?* **(b)** (used to express a mild warning or order): *Now be quiet for a few moments and listen to this.* ○ *No cheating, now.* **IDM (every) now and a'gain/'then** from time to time; occasionally: *I like to go to the opera now and then.* ○ *Every now and again she checked to see if he was still asleep.* **ˌnow, 'now; ˌnow 'then** (used when expressing mild disapproval or warning sb): *Now, now,/Now then, that's enough noise.* **now ... now** at one time ... at another time: *Her moods kept changing — now happy, now sad.* **(it's) ˌnow or 'never** this is the only opportunity sb will have to do sth: *If you want to ask her to marry you, it's now or never. She's leaving the country tomorrow.* '**now then 1** ⇨ NOW, NOW. **2** (used to introduce a statement that makes a suggestion or invites a response): *Now then, who wants to come for a walk?* **now for 'sb/'sth** (used when turning to a fresh activity or subject): *Now for a quick swim before lunch.* ○ *And now for some travel news.*

▸ **now** *conj* ~ (**that**) ... because the specified thing is happening or has just happened: *Now (that) you mention it, I do remember the incident.* ○ *Now you've passed your test you can drive on your own.*

nowadays /'naʊədeɪz/ *adv* at the present time, in contrast with the past: *Nowadays, many children prefer watching TV to reading.*

nowhere /'nəʊweə(r)/ *indef adv* not at or to any place; no place: *This animal is found in Australia, and nowhere else.* ○ *There was nowhere for me to sit* (eg because all the seats were occupied). ○ *'Where are you going this weekend?' 'Nowhere special.'* ○ *Nowhere is the effect of government policy more apparent than in agriculture.* ○ (*infml*) *One of the horses I backed came second; the rest were/came nowhere* (ie were not among the first three to finish the race). **IDM nowhere to be 'found/'seen; nowhere in 'sight** impossible for anyone to find or see: *The children were nowhere to be seen.* ○ *The money was nowhere to be found.* ○ *A peace settlement is nowhere in sight* (ie is not likely in the near future).

nowt /naʊt/ *neg pron* (*Brit dialect infml*) nothing: *There's nowt wrong with you.*

noxious /'nɒkʃəs/ *adj* (*fml*) harmful, poisonous or very unpleasant: *noxious substances/fumes* ○ (*fig*) *The racists are spreading noxious propaganda.*

nozzle /'nɒzl/ *n* a piece at the end of a pipe or tube, with a narrow opening in it, through which a stream of air or liquid is directed.

nr *abbr* near (eg in the address of a small village): *Oakley, Nr Basingstoke, Hants.*

NRA /ˌen ɑːr 'eɪ/ *abbr* **1** (in the USA) National Rifle Association. **2** (in Britain) National Rivers Authority.

NSPCC /ˌen es ˌpiː siː 'siː/ *abbr* (in Britain) National Society for the Prevention of Cruelty to Children.

nth /enθ/ *adj* (*infml*) [attrib] the latest or last in a long series: *You're the nth person to ask me that* (ie Many others have asked me the same thing). ○ *For the nth time, you can't go!*

nuance /'njuːɑːns; *US* 'nuː-/ *n* [C, U] (*usu approv*) a slight difference, often difficult to detect, in eg meaning, colour or sb's feelings: *appreciate delicate nuances of language* ○ *a performance with little nuance or expression.*
▸ **nuanced** /-ɑːnst/ *adj* containing nuances.

nub /nʌb/ *n* [sing] **the ~ (of sth)** the central or essential point of a problem or situation: *The nub of the problem is our poor export performance.*

nubile /'njuːbaɪl; *US* 'nuːbl/ *adj* (of girls or young women) **1** sexually attractive: *a photograph of a nubile young woman.* **2** (*fml*) old enough and suitable for marriage.

nuclear /'njuːklɪə(r); *US* 'nuː-/ *adj* [usu attrib] **1(a)** using, producing or resulting from nuclear energy: *a nuclear power-station/reactor* ○ *nuclear fuel/waste* ○ *the nuclear industry* ○ *nuclear-powered submarines.* **(b)** of or relating to weapons that use this type of energy: *a nuclear weapon/bomb/missile* ○ *a nuclear explosion/attack/war* ○ *nuclear disarmament.* Compare CONVENTIONAL 2. **2** (*physics*) of the NUCLEUS(1b) of an atom: *nuclear particles/physics.*
■ **ˌnuclear 'energy** (also **ˌnuclear 'power**) *n* [U] an extremely powerful form of energy produced by the splitting of the nuclei (NUCLEUS 1b) of atoms. Nuclear energy can be used to produce electricity: *the government's nuclear-power programme.*
ˌnuclear 'family *n* (*sociology*) the family considered as mother, father and children only, and not including any less close relations.
ˌnuclear-'free *adj* [esp attrib] (of eg a country or region) not having or allowing any nuclear weapons or materials: *campaign for a nuclear-free world.*
ˌnuclear 'winter *n* a period without light, heat or

growth which it is believed would follow a nuclear war.

nucleic acid /njuːˌkliːɪk ˈæsɪd, -ˌkleɪɪk; *US* nuː-/ either of two acids, DNA and RNA, that occur in all living cells.

nucleus /ˈnjuːkliəs; *US* ˈnuː-/ *n* (*pl* **nuclei** /-kliaɪ/) **1(a)** (*biology*) the central part of a living cell. **(b)** (*physics*) the positively charged central part of an atom, containing most of its mass. See also PROTON, NEUTRON. **2** the central part of sth around which other parts are situated, collected or gathered: *The fortress was the nucleus of the ancient city.* ◦ *These paintings will form the nucleus of a new collection.*

nude /njuːd; *US* nuːd/ *adj* (eg of a human figure in art) wearing no clothes; naked: *a nude woman/model* ◦ *He posed nude for an artist/a photographer.* ◦ *nude sunbathing.*

▶ **nude** *n* **(a)** a naked human figure, esp in art or photography: *a reclining nude.* **(b)** a work of art showing such a figure: *Michelangelo's nudes.* **IDM** **in the ˈnude** wearing no clothes; naked: *swimming in the nude.*

nudism /-ɪzəm/ (also **naturism**) *n* [U] the practice of not wearing clothes, esp outdoors, for health reasons.

nudist /-ɪst/ (also **naturist**) *n* a person who practises nudism: *a private beach for nudists* ◦ *a nudist beach/camp/magazine.*

nudity /ˈnjuːdəti; *US* ˈnuː-/ *n* [U] the state of being naked: *too much nudity on TV.*

nudge /nʌdʒ/ *v* **1** to touch or push sb, esp with one's elbow, to draw their attention to sth: [Vn, Vnpr] *I nudged her (on the arm) and pointed to the man across the street.* **2** to push sth/sb gently or gradually: [Vn] *The horse nudged my pocket with its nose.* ◦ *The front of the car just nudged the gatepost.* [Vnpr] *He nudged the ball past the goalkeeper.* **3** ~ **sb into/towards (doing) sth** to try to make sb do sth, using gentle force or encouragement: [Vnpr] *He's trying to nudge his colleagues into accepting the deal.* **4** to move or make sth move close to a particular value, level or state: [Vn] *Inflation is nudging 20%.* [Vnpr] *This afternoon's sunshine could nudge the temperature above freezing.*

▶ **nudge** *n* a slight push, esp with the elbow: *She gave me a nudge in the ribs.* ◦ (*fig*) *He's capable of hard work, but he needs a nudge now and again.*

NOTE Compare **nudge, prod, jab, poke** and **stab**. These verbs all describe pushing something such as a finger or stick into part of a person's body or into an object. **Nudge** means to push or touch somebody gently to get their attention: *Polly nudged her husband. 'Are you awake?' she asked.*

Prod means to push something with your fingers or something pointed in order to examine it: *The cook prodded the potatoes to see if they were cooked.* ◦ *She prodded the ground with her stick.* If a person **jabs** something into somebody or something, or **jabs** somebody with something, they hit them quickly with a sharp object: *The nurse jabbed a needle into my arm.* ◦ *She jabbed me with her knitting-needle.*

Poke is used in the same patterns and means 'to push sharply': *He poked a stick into the fire/poked the fire with a stick.* **Poke** and **prod** are often used together in a disapproving way to mean 'to examine the body': *When the doctor had finished poking and prodding me I was allowed to get dressed.* **Stab** means to hit or push with an object such as a knife, in order to cause injury: *His killer stabbed him with a knife.*

nugatory /ˈnjuːɡətəri; *US* ˈnuːɡətɔːri/ *adj* (*fml*) worthless; having no purpose; not valid: *a nugatory offer/idea/argument.*

nugget /ˈnʌɡɪt/ *n* **1** a lump of a valuable metal or mineral, eg gold, found in the earth. **2** a small thing, eg an idea or a fact, that is regarded as valuable: *a book full of nuggets of useful information.*

nuisance /ˈnjuːsns; *US* ˈnuː-/ *n* (esp *sing*) ~ (**to sb**) a thing, a person or behaviour that is annoying or causes trouble: *The noise from his stereo was a nuisance to the neighbours.* ◦ *It's a nuisance having to buy a separate ticket for each journey.* ◦ *Stop* **making** *a* **nuisance of yourself** *and do something useful instead.*

null /nʌl/ *adj* **IDM** ˌnull and ˈvoid (*law*) having no legal force; not valid: *The contract has been declared null and void.*

▶ **nullify** /ˈnʌlɪfaɪ/ *v* (*pt, pp* **-fied**) **1** to make eg an agreement or an order lose its legal force: [Vn] *a court decision nullifying a marriage/a government decree.* **2** (*fml*) to make sth lose its effect; to act against sth: [Vn] *An unhealthy diet will nullify the effects of training.*

nullity /ˈnʌləti/ *n* [U] (*fml or law*) the lack of legal force or the state of not being valid, esp of a marriage: *a decree of nullity* (ie a legal statement declaring a marriage null and void).

NUM /ˌen juː ˈem/ *abbr* (in Britain) National Union of Mineworkers.

numb /nʌm/ *adj* (of a part of the body) having lost all physical feeling or the power to feel, eg because of cold or pain: *My fingers were/went numb with cold.* ◦ (*fig*) *The shock left me numb.* ◦ *She was numb with terror.*

▶ **numb** *v* **1** to make sth/sb numb: [Vn] *her numbed fingers/feet* ◦ *The injection will numb your gums for a while.* **2** to give sb such an emotional shock that they are no longer capable of thinking or acting: [Vn] *She was completely numbed by her father's death.* **numbing** *adj* emotionally shocking or depressing: *the numbing monotony of the factory routine.* ▶ **numbly** *adv: 'I can't believe he's dead,'* *she said numbly.* **numbness** *n* [U].

number /ˈnʌmbə(r)/ *n* **1** [C] an idea, a symbol or a word indicating a quantity of units: *Think of a number. Multiply it by 2.* ◦ *Can you read the numbers on the doors/tickets?* ◦ *My telephone number is 622998.* ◦ *What's the registration number of your car?* See also CARDINAL NUMBER, ORDINAL NUMBER, SERIAL NUMBER. **2** [C] (*abbrs* **No**, **no**, *US symb* **#**) (used before a figure to indicate the place of sth in a series): *the passenger in seat number 32* ◦ *Her record reached number 6 in the charts.* ◦ *No 10 Downing Street is the official residence of the British Prime Minister.* **3** (*sing or pl* in form; always taking a plural verb when preceded by *a/an*) a quantity or an amount of people or things: *A large number of people have applied.* ◦ *The number of people applying has increased this year.* ◦ *Considerable numbers of* (ie Very many) *animals have died.* ◦ *People are emigrating in increasing numbers.* ◦ *The university will have to expand owing to pressure of numbers* (ie of students). ◦ *A number of* (ie some) *problems have arisen.* ◦ *Count the number of books on the shelf.* ◦ *We were fifteen in number* (ie there were fifteen of us). **4** [sing] (*fml*) a group or quantity of people: *one of our number* (ie one of us) ◦ *among their number* (ie among them) ◦ *Their philosophy is the greatest happiness for the greatest number.* **5** [C] an issue of a newspaper or magazine: *the current number of 'Vogue'* . See also BACK NUMBER. **6** [C] a song or dance, esp one of several in a performance: *sing a slow, romantic number.* **7** [sing] (preceded by an *adj* or *adjs*) (*sl*) an item, eg a dress or car, that is admired: *She was wearing a black leather number.* ◦ *That new Fiat is a fast little number.* **8** [U] (*grammar*) a property of certain parts of speech, eg nouns and verbs, showing whether one or more than one thing or person is being spoken of. Number is often shown by variation in the form of the word: *'Men'* *is plural in number.* ◦ *The subject of*

N

a sentence and its verb must agree in number. See also ONE'S OPPOSITE NUMBER. **IDM** **any 'number of sth/sb** many things or people: *There are any number of good restaurants to choose from.* **by 'numbers** following a sequence of instructions identified by numbers: *painting by numbers.* **a cushy number** ⇨ CUSHY. **have (got) sb's 'number** (*infml*) to know what sb is really like and what their intentions really are: *He thinks he can fool me but I've got his number.* **in round figures/numbers** ⇨ ROUND[1]. **one's 'number is up** (*infml*) the time has come when sb will die or be ruined: *When the wheel came off the car I thought my number was up!* **,number 'one** (*infml*) **1** the most important or best person or thing: *This company is number one in the oil business.* ○ *the number one problem/priority* ○ *the world's number one tennis player.* **2** oneself: *Looking after number one is all he thinks about.* **there's safety in numbers** ⇨ SAFETY. **times without number** ⇨ TIME[1]. **weight of numbers** ⇨ WEIGHT[1].

▶ **number** *v* **1** to give a number to sth: [Vn] *The seats aren't numbered.* [Vn-n] *The doors were numbered 2, 4, 6 and 8.* [Vnpr] *We'll number them from one to ten.* [V] *I couldn't work out the numbering system for the hotel rooms.* **2** to amount or add up to a certain number: [Vn] *We numbered 20* (ie There were 20 of us) *in all.* **IDM** **sb's/sth's days are numbered** ⇨ DAY. **PHRV** **'number (sb/sth) among sth** to include sb/sth or to be included in a particular group or category: *I number her among my closest friends.* ○ *The string quartets number among his finest works.*

numberless *adj* too many to be counted. ⇨ note at INVALUABLE.

■ **'number crunching** *n* [U] (*computing infml*) the rapid processing of very large quantities of numbers, using a computer.

'number-plate (*esp Brit*) (also *esp US* **'licence plate, 'license plate**) *n* a metal or plastic plate on a vehicle that shows its registration number (REGISTRATION). ⇨ picture at CAR.

numeral /'nju:mərəl; *US* 'nu:-/ *n* a symbol representing a number. Compare ARABIC NUMERAL, ROMAN NUMERAL.

numerate /'nju:mərət; *US* 'nu:-/ *adj* having a good basic knowledge of ARITHMETIC; able to understand and work with numbers: *teach children to be numerate.* Compare LITERATE. ▶ **numeracy** /'nju:mərəsi; *US* 'nu:-/ *n* [U].

numerator /'nju:məreɪtə(r); *US* 'nu:-/ *n* the number above the line in a fraction, eg 3 in ¾. Compare DENOMINATOR.

numerical /nju:'merɪkl; *US* nu:-/ (also **numeric** /-ɪk/) *adj* of or relating to numbers: *in numerical order* ○ *numeric values.*
▶ **numerically** /-kli/ *adv* in terms of numbers: *The enemy were numerically superior* (ie There were more of them).

numerous /'nju:mərəs; *US* 'nu:-/ *adj* (*fml*) a large number of people or things; many: *her numerous friends* ○ *on numerous occasions.*

numinous /'nju:mɪnəs; *US* 'nu:-/ *adj* (*fml*) indicating or suggesting the presence of a god; having a strong religious or spiritual quality: *The poem has a certain numinous mystery.*

numismatics /,nju:mɪz'mætɪks; *US* ,nu:-/ *n* [sing *v*] the study of coins and medals (MEDAL).
▶ **numismatist** /nju:'mɪzmətɪst; *US* nu:-/ *n* a person who collects coins or medals.

nun /nʌn/ *n* a woman living in a female religious community who has promised to serve God all her life: *She became a Catholic nun.* Compare MONK.
▶ **nunnery** /'nʌnəri/ *n* (*dated*) a house where a group of nuns live: a CONVENT. Compare MONASTERY.

nuncio /'nʌnsɪəʊ/ *n* (*pl* **-os**) a representative of the Pope in a foreign country.

nuptial /'nʌpʃl/ *adj* [attrib] (*fml*) of marriage or of a wedding: *the nuptial ceremony* ○ *nuptial bliss.*
▶ **nuptials** *n* [pl] (*fml or rhet*) a wedding: *the day of his nuptials.*

nurse[1] /nɜ:s/ *n* **1** a person trained to help a doctor to look after sick or injured people: *a qualified/registered nurse* ○ *a dental nurse* ○ *a psychiatric nurse* (ie one who works in a hospital for people with mental illnesses) ○ *Nurse Jones will be looking after you.* ○ *Come quickly, Nurse.* See also DISTRICT NURSE. **2** (also **'nursemaid**) a woman or girl employed to look after babies or small children in their own homes. Compare NANNY 1, NURSERY NURSE.

nurse[2] /nɜ:s/ *v* **1** to care for sick or injured people; to look after sb: [Vnp] *be nursed back to good health* [Vn] *She nursed her mother until she died.* **2** to hold sb/sth carefully, esp in a loving way: [Vn] *nurse a child/puppy* ○ *Still nursing our wounds, we made our way home.* [Vnpr] *nurse a fragile vase in one's arms.* **3** to give special care to sth; to help sth to develop: [Vn] *nurse young plants* [Vnpr] *new recruits nursed through the training period* [Vn] *nurse a cold* (ie keep warm, stay in bed, etc in order to cure it quickly). **4** to hold a strong feeling in one's mind for a long time: [Vn] *nurse feelings of revenge* ○ *nurse a grievance.* **5(a)** [V] (of a baby) to suck milk from a woman's breast. **(b)** (of a woman) to feed a baby with milk from her breast: [Vn] *nursing mothers.*
▶ **nursing** *n* [U] the art or practice of looking after sick or injured people: *train for a career in nursing* ○ *the nursing profession* ○ *nursing care/staff.*
■ **'nursing home** *n* a small, usu privately owned, hospital, esp one where old people live and are looked after: *Eventually she had to give up her flat and go into a nursing home.*

nursemaid *n* = NURSE[1] 2.

nursery /'nɜ:səri/ *n* **1** (also **day nursery**) a place where young children are cared for, usu while their parents are at work, etc: *Charlie goes to a day nursery.* Compare CRÈCHE, NURSERY SCHOOL. **2** a room in a house for the special use of young children: *We've turned the smallest bedroom into a nursery for our new baby.* **3** a place where young plants and trees are grown for sale or for planting elsewhere.
■ **'nursery nurse** *n* a person trained to look after small children.
'nursery rhyme *n* a simple traditional poem or song for children.
'nursery school *n* a school for children from 2 or 3 to 5 years old. Compare PLAYGROUP.
'nursery slopes (*Brit*) (*US* **'bunny slopes**) *n* [pl] gentle slopes suitable for people in the early stages of learning to SKI.

nurseryman /'nɜ:sərimən/ *n* (*pl* **-men**) a person who owns or works in a NURSERY(3).

nurture /'nɜ:tʃə(r)/ *v* (*fml*) **(a)** to care for and encourage the growth of sb/sth: [Vn] *nurture delicate plants* ○ *children nurtured by loving parents.* **(b)** to help the development of sth: [Vn] *nurture a friendship/a talent/a new project.* **(c)** to feel and develop sth for a long time: *nurture an ambition/a hope.*
▶ **nurture** *n* [U] care; encouragement; support.

nut /nʌt/ *n* **1** (often in compounds) a fruit of certain trees, consisting of a hard shell with a softer part inside that can be eaten. ⇨ picture: *chopped nuts* ○ *nuts and raisins* ○ *a Brazil nut* ○ *a hazelnut.* ⇨ picture. **2** a small piece of metal with a hole through the centre, used for screwing onto a BOLT[1](2) to secure it. Nuts and bolts are used to hold pieces of wood, machinery, etc together: *tighten a nut* ○ *a wheel nut.* ⇨ picture at BOLT[1]. **3** (*sl*) a person's head: *He cracked his nut on the ceiling.* **4** (*sl derog*) **(a)** (*Brit* also **nutter**) a foolish or mad person: *He's a bit of a nut, if you ask me.* ○ *The guy's a complete nutter.* **(b)** (after a *n*) a person

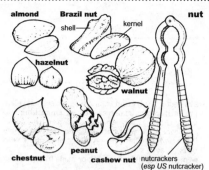

almond   Brazil nut   nut
shell   kernel
hazelnut
walnut
chestnut   peanut
cashew nut   nutcrackers
(esp US nutcracker)

who is very interested in the thing specified: *a motor-bike/football/health nut*. **IDM** **do one's 'nut** (*Brit sl*) to be very angry: *She'll do her nut when she sees the broken window*. **a hard/tough 'nut (to 'crack)** (*infml*) **1** a difficult problem or situation to deal with. **2** a person who is difficult to persuade, influence, etc. **the ,nuts and 'bolts (of sth)** (*infml*) the basic practical details: *master the nuts and bolts of the newspaper business*. **,off one's 'nut** (*sl*) mad: *You must be off your nut!*
▶ **nutty** *adj* (**-ier, -iest**) **1** tasting of or containing nuts: *a nutty flavour*. **2** (*sl*) slightly crazy: *She's got some nutty friends*. **IDM** **(as) ,nutty as a 'fruit cake** (*sl*) completely crazy.
■ **,nut-'brown** *adj* having a dark rich brown colour: *,nut-brown 'eyes*.
'nut-house *n* (*sl offensive*) mental hospital.

nutcase /'nʌtkeɪs/ *n* (*sl*) a mad or foolish person: *He's a complete nutcase!*

nutcrackers /'nʌtkrækəz/ *n* [pl] (also *esp US* **nut-cracker** [sing]) an implement for cracking open the shells of nuts. ⇨ picture at NUT.

nutmeg /'nʌtmeg/ *n* [U] a spice made from the hard seed of an E Indian tree: *Add a pinch of grated nutmeg*.

nutrient /'njuːtrɪənt; *US* 'nuː-/ *n* (*fml*) a substance that helps a living thing to grow: *lack of essential nutrients* ○ *Plants draw minerals and other nutrients from the soil*.

nutrition /njuˈtrɪʃn; *US* nuː-/ *n* [U] the process of providing and receiving food necessary for health

and growth; nourishment (NOURISH): *give advice on cleanliness and nutrition* ○ *children not receiving adequate nutrition* ○ *an expert in animal nutrition*. See also MALNUTRITION.
▶ **nutritional** /-ʃənl/ *adj*: *the nutritional value of a food* ○ *Read the nutritional information on the packet*. **nutritionally** /-ʃənəli/ *adv*.
nutritionist /-ʃənɪst/ *n* an expert in nutrition.
nutritious /njuˈtrɪʃəs; *US* nuː-/ *adj* (*fml*) (of food) healthy; helping the body to grow: *a nutritious meal*.
nutritive /'njuːtrətɪv; *US* 'nuː-/ *adj* (*fml*) = NUTRITIONAL: *Plant material is poor in nutritive value*.

nuts /nʌts/ *adj* [pred] (*sl*) **1** crazy; mad: *Stop that, will you? It's driving me nuts*. **2** ~ **about sb/sth; ~ on sth** very much in love with sb or very enthusiastic about sth: *I'm absolutely nuts about her*. ○ *He's nuts on cars*.

nutshell /'nʌtʃel/ *n* the hard covering around the softer inside part of a nut. **IDM** **(put sth) in a nutshell** (to say sth) in very few words: *To put it in a nutshell, we're bankrupt*.

nutter /'nʌtə(r)/ *n* (*Brit sl*) = NUT 4a.

nuzzle /'nʌzl/ *v* to press or rub sb/sth gently with the mouth or nose: [Vn] *The cow licked and nuzzled its calf*. [Vpr, Vp] *The dog nuzzled (up) against me on the sofa*.

NW *abbr* north-west; north-western: *NW Australia* ○ *6 miles NW of Ilkley*.

NY *abbr* New York.

NYC *abbr* New York City.

nylon /'naɪlɒn/ *n* **1** [U] a very artificial fibre used for making clothing, rope, brushes, etc: *This material is 45% nylon*. ○ *a nylon strap/tent*. **2** **nylons** [pl] (*dated*) women's stockings (STOCKING) or TIGHTS(1) made of nylon.

nymph /nɪmf/ *n* **1** (in Greek and Roman myths) a spirit of nature in the form of a young woman. Nymphs lived esp in rivers and woods. **2** (*biology*) a young insect that has a similar form to the adult: *a dragonfly nymph*.

nymphet /'nɪmfət/ *n* (*infml*) a young girl regarded as sexually desirable.

nympho /'nɪmfəʊ/ *n* (*pl* **-os**) (*infml*) a NYMPHOMANIAC.

nymphomaniac /,nɪmfəˈmeɪnɪæk/ *n* (*often derog*) a woman who has an excessive desire for sex.

NZ *abbr* New Zealand.

Oo

O¹ (also **o**) /əʊ/ *n* (*pl* **O's, o's** /əʊz/) **1** the 15th letter of the English alphabet: *There are two O's in Oxford.* **2** (in saying telephone, etc numbers aloud) zero: *My number is six o double three* (ie 6033). ○ *He's in room one o two* (ie 102). ⇨ note at NOUGHT.

O² /əʊ/ *interj* = OH: *O God, not another bill!* ○ *O the shame of it!*

o' /ə/ *prep* (used in written English to represent an informal pronunciation of *of*): *Would you like a cup o' coffee?* See also O'CLOCK, WILL-O'-THE WISP, CAT-O'-NINE-TAILS.

oaf /əʊf/ *n* (*pl* **oafs**) a stupid or awkward person, esp a man: *Mind where you're treading, you clumsy oaf!* ▶ **oafish** *adj*: *oafish behaviour.*

acorn

oak

oak /əʊk/ *n* (**a**) [C] a tree with tough hard wood, common in many parts of the world: *a forest of oaks* ○ *an oak tree/leaf.* ⇨ picture. (**b**) [U] the wood of this tree: *The table is (of) solid oak.* ○ *oak panelling* ○ *a carved oak door.*
▶ **oaken** /ˈəʊkən/ *adj* [attrib] (*fml*) made of oak.

OAP /ˌəʊ eɪ ˈpiː/ *abbr* (*Brit*) old-age pensioner: *a queue of OAPs in the post office.*

oar /ɔː(r)/ *n* a long pole with a flat blade, pulled by hand in order to drive a boat through the water: *She lowered/dipped the oars into the water.* ⇨ picture at ROWING-BOAT. **IDM** **put/stick one's 'oar in** (*Brit infml*) to give an opinion, some advice, etc without being asked; to interfere: *I was getting along very nicely until Patrick stuck his oar in.*
■ **'oarlock** *n* (*US*) = ROWLOCK.

oarsman /ˈɔːzmən/ *n* (*pl* **-men** /-mən/) a person who rows a boat, esp as a member of a team.

OAS /ˌəʊ eɪ ˈes/ *abbr* Organization of American States.

oasis /əʊˈeɪsɪs/ *n* (*pl* **oases** /-siːz/) **1** an area with water and trees, etc in a desert. **2** a pleasant place or period of time in the middle of sth unpleasant, dull, etc: *The study was an oasis of calm in a noisy household.*

oat ⇨ OATS.

oath /əʊθ/ *n* (*pl* **oaths** /əʊðz/) **1** a solemn promise to do sth or a solemn declaration that sth is true: *take/swear an oath* of loyalty to the Queen ○ *Before giving evidence the witness had to take the oath.* ○ *Government employees swear an oath not to reveal official secrets.* **2** an offensive word or phrase used to express anger, surprise, etc; a swear-word (SWEAR): *He hit his finger with the hammer and uttered a string of oaths.* **IDM** **on/under 'oath** (*law*) having sworn to tell the truth in a court of law: *They testified under oath that she had been with them.* ○ *The judge reminded the witness that she was still under oath.*

oatmeal /ˈəʊtmiːl/ *n* [U] **1** flour made from crushed OATS, used in PORRIDGE, etc. **2** a light brown colour.

oats /əʊts/ *n* [pl] grain from a type of CEREAL(1) plant grown in cool climates as food, eg for making POR-RIDGE: *Give the horse some oats.* ○ *fields of ripe barley and oats* ○ *porridge oats.* **IDM** **be getting one's 'oats** (*infml*) to have sex regularly. **sow one's wild oats** ⇨ SOW¹.
▶ **oat** *adj* [attrib] containing or made from oats: *oat cakes* ○ *oat bran.*

OAU /ˌəʊ eɪ ˈjuː/ *abbr* Organization of African Unity.

obdurate /ˈɒbdjʊərət; *US* -dər-/ *adj* (*fml usu derog*) (of a person or an attitude) refusing to change in any way; STUBBORN(1): *an obdurate refusal* ○ *He remained obdurate: he would press ahead regardless.* ▶ **obduracy** /ˈɒbdjʊərəsi; *US* -dər-/ *n* [U]. **obdurately** *adv.*

OBE /ˌəʊ biː ˈiː/ *abbr* (in Britain) Officer (of the Order) of the British Empire: *be (made) an OBE* ○ *Matthew Silkin OBE.*

obedient /əˈbiːdiənt/ *adj* ~ (**to sb/sth**) doing what one is told to do; willing to obey: *obedient children* ○ *His dog is very obedient.* ○ *The party is naturally obedient to the will of its leader.* Compare DISOBEDI-ENT. ▶ **obedience** /-əns/ *n* [U] ~ (**to sb/sth**): *The tribes were forced to accept obedience to the Jewish law.* ○ *He expected unquestioning/blind obedience from his men.* **obediently** *adv*: *She whistled, and the dog came obediently.*

obeisance /əʊˈbeɪsns/ *n* (*fml*) **1** [U] obedience to or respect for sb/sth: *make obeisance to* the great leaders of the past. **2** [C] a deep bow of respect or obedience.

obelisk /ˈɒbəlɪsk/ *n* a tall pointed stone pillar with four sides, set up in memory of a person, an event, etc.

obese /əʊˈbiːs/ *adj* (*fml or medical*) (of people) very fat: *She is grossly obese.* ○ *Obese patients are advised to change their diet.* ⇨ note at FAT¹. ▶ **obesity** /əʊˈbiːsəti/ *n* [U]: *Obesity can increase the risk of heart disease.*

obey /əˈbeɪ/ *v* to do what one is told or required to do by sb: [V] *Soldiers are trained to obey without question.* [Vn] *obey the law/the rules* ○ *It's not my fault — I was only obeying orders.* ○ *They refused to obey me.* Compare DISOBEY.

obfuscate /ˈɒbfʌskeɪt/ *v* (*fml derog*) to make sth confused or difficult to understand, esp deliberately: *He accused the government of obfuscating the issue.* ▶ **obfuscation** *n* [U].

obituary /əˈbɪtʃʊəri; *US* -tʃueri/ *n* a printed notice of a person's death, often with a short account of her or his life and achievements: *He writes obituaries for the local newspaper.*

object¹ /ˈɒbdʒɪkt/ *n* **1** a solid thing that can be seen and touched: *a distant object* ○ *surrounded by famil-iar household objects* ○ *inanimate objects* ○ *Weird glass and plastic objects lined the shelves.* **2** ~ **of sth** a person or thing to which sth is done or towards which a particular feeling or thought is directed: *an object of desire/pity/admiration* ○ *The church is my main object of interest.* See also SEX OBJECT. **3** a thing aimed at; a purpose; an intention: *She left college* **with the object of** *going into business.* ○ *His one/sole object in life is to earn as much money as possible.* ○ *You can't do that — it would defeat the whole* **object of the exercise** (ie completely spoil your plan). **4** (*grammar*) a noun, or a phrase or

---

clause behaving like a noun, which refers to a person, thing, etc affected by the action of a verb, or which depends on a PREPOSITION. For example, in *He took the money* and *He took what he wanted*, *'the money'* and *'what he wanted'* are direct objects (DIRECT[1]), and in *I gave him the money*, *'him'* is an indirect object (INDIRECT). Compare SUBJECT[1] 6. **IDM** **expense, money, etc is no 'object** expense, etc is not important, not a limiting factor, etc: *He always travels first class — expense is no object to him.*

■ **'object-lesson** *n* (usu *sing*) a practical example of what should or should not be done in a particular situation, etc: *Her calm handling of the emergency was an object-lesson to us all.*

object² /əb'dʒekt/ *v* **1** ~ (**to sb/sth**); ~ (**to doing sth**) to say that one is not in favour of sb/sth; to protest: [V] *She wanted to cut down the hedge, but her neighbour objected.* [Vpr] *I strongly object to being charged a fee for using my credit card.* ○ *They objected to the plan on the grounds that it was too expensive.* **2** to give sth as a reason for opposing sb/sth: [V.that] *I objected that he was too young for the job.* [V.speech] *'But he's too young,' I objected.*

▶ **objector** *n* a person who objects: *objectors to the plans for a new factory.* See also CONSCIENTIOUS OBJECTOR.

objection /əb'dʒekʃn/ *n* (**a**) ~ (**to sth / doing sth**) a statement or feeling of dislike, disapproval or opposition: *lodge a formal objection to sth* ○ *The government dismissed/countered objections that the trial was not fair.* ○ *I'd like to come too, if you've no objection.* (**b**) ~ (**to/against sb/sth**) a reason for objecting: *raise/put forward/voice a number of objections to the proposals* ○ *My main objection to the plan is that it would be too expensive.*

▶ **objectionable** /-ʃənəbl/ *adj* causing objection or disapproval; unpleasant: *an objectionable smell* ○ *highly objectionable remarks* ○ *I myself didn't find anything objectionable in his behaviour.*

objective /əb'dʒektɪv/ *adj* **1** not influenced by personal feelings or opinions; fair: *an objective report/account/assessment* ○ *objective criteria* ○ *He finds it difficult to remain objective where his son is concerned.* **2** (*philosophy*) having existence outside the mind; that can be observed and proved; real: *objective knowledge.* Compare SUBJECTIVE.

▶ **objective** *n* a thing aimed at or wished for; a purpose: *achieve one's main/primary/key/ultimate objective* ○ *the company's long-term financial objectives* ○ *set realistic aims and objectives for oneself* ○ *Our objective is a world without poverty.*

objectively *adv: see/view/judge things objectively* ○ *objectively true.*

objectivity /ˌɒbdʒek'tɪvəti/ *n* [U] the state of being objective: *scientific objectivity.*

objet d'art /ˌɒbʒeɪ 'dɑː/ *n* (*pl* **objets d'art** /ˌɒbʒeɪ 'dɑː/) (*French*) a small decorative or artistic object: *a house full of antique furniture and objets d'art.*

obligated /'ɒblɪgeɪtɪd/ *adj* ~(**to do sth**) (*fml*) legally or morally forced to do sth: *He felt obligated to do sth.*

obligation /ˌɒblɪ'geɪʃn/ *n* (**a**) [C] a law, a promise, an influence, etc that forces one to do sth; a duty: *fulfil one's professional/social obligations* ○ *the obligations imposed by parenthood/citizenship* ○ *release sb from their obligations* ○ *You are **under no obligation** to pay for goods which you did not order.* (**b**) [U,C usu *sing*] the condition of being forced to do sth, esp by one's conscience: *They attended the party more out of a sense of obligation than anything else.* ○ *We must recognize our obligation to future generations and protect our environment.* ○ *You may examine the books in your own home for ten days without cost or obligation* (ie to buy them).

obligatory /ə'blɪgətri; *US* -tɔːri/ *adj* (*fml*) required by rule, law or custom; compulsory: *He gave her the*

usual obligatory kiss on the cheek. ○ *It is obligatory to remove your shoes before entering the mosque.*

oblige /ə'blaɪdʒ/ *v* **1** (usu passive) to force or require sb by law, agreement or moral pressure to do sth: [Vn.*to* inf] *The law obliges parents to send their children to school.* ○ *They were obliged to sell their house in order to pay their debts.* ○ *You are not obliged to answer these questions, but it would help us if you did.* ○ *Don't feel obliged to stay if you're busy.* **2** ~ **sb** (**with sth / by doing sth**) (*fml*) to do what sb wants as a favour: [V] *We'd be happy to oblige.* [Vn, Vnpr] *The Princess refused to oblige the photographers (by posing with her sons).*

▶ **obliged** *adj* [pred] ~ (**to sb**) (**for sth / doing sth**) (*dated*) (used esp when expressing thanks or making a polite request) grateful to sb for performing a particular service: *I'm **much obliged** to you for helping us.* ○ *I'd be obliged if you'd check what I've written.*

obliging *adj* willing to help: *an obliging porter* ○ *He is always very obliging.* **obligingly** *adv: They had obligingly reserved a room for me.*

oblique /ə'bliːk/ *adj* **1** not expressed directly: *an oblique comment/hint/reference.* **2** (of a line) sloping at an angle.

▶ **oblique** (also **slash**) *n* a mark (/) used to separate numbers, words, etc as in *4/5 people, male/female, lunch and/or dinner, 25/7/1949.* ⇨ App 3.

obliquely *adv* indirectly: *refer to her problems only obliquely.*

obliterate /ə'blɪtəreɪt/ *v* **1** to remove all signs of sth; to destroy sth completely: [Vn] *The entire village was obliterated by the tornado.* ○ *She tried to obliterate the memory of her childhood.* **2** to cover the sight, sound, etc of sth: [Vn] *The view was totally obliterated by the fog.* ▶ **obliteration** /əˌblɪtə'reɪʃn/ *n* [U].

oblivion /ə'blɪviən/ *n* [U] **1** a state in which one is no longer aware or conscious of what is happening: *drink oneself into oblivion* ○ *slide/sink/slip into oblivion.* **2** the state of being forgotten, esp by the public: *rescue sb from political oblivion* ○ *His work fell/sank into oblivion after his death.*

oblivious /ə'blɪviəs/ *adj* [usu pred] ~ (**of/to sth**) not aware of or not noticing sth: *oblivious of one's surroundings* ○ *oblivious to what was happening* ○ *oblivious to danger.* ▶ **obliviousness** *n* [U].

oblong /'ɒblɒŋ; *US* -lɔːŋ/ *n* a flat shape with four straight sides and four angles of 90°, longer than it is wide: *The only light came from a tiny oblong of glass in the roof.* See also RECTANGLE. ▶ **oblong** *adj: an oblong mirror.*

obloquy /'ɒbləkwi/ *n* [U] (*fml*) **1** strong public criticism of sb/sth: *In the face of public obloquy, he was forced to resign.* **2** loss of public respect: *hold sb up to obloquy.*

obnoxious /əb'nɒkʃəs/ *adj* very unpleasant; offensive: *obnoxious behaviour* ○ *He is the most obnoxious man I know.* ▶ **obnoxiously** *adv*.

oboe /'əʊbəʊ/ *n* (*music*) a wind instrument shaped like a tube and played by blowing through a double REED(2). ⇨ picture at MUSICAL INSTRUMENT.

▶ **oboist** /-ɪst/ *n* a person who plays the oboe.

obscene /əb'siːn/ *adj* (of words, pictures, behaviour, etc) offensive or disgusting by accepted moral standards, esp in sexual matters: *obscene phone calls/gestures/language* ○ *obscene books/films/literature* ○ *It's obscene to spend so much on food when millions are starving.*

▶ **obscenely** *adv: behave obscenely* ○ *be obscenely rich.*

obscenity /əb'senəti/ *n* (**a**) [U] obscene behaviour or language: *laws against obscenity.* (**b**) [C] an obscene word or act: *scribble obscenities on the wall* ○ *He screamed obscenities at her.*

obscurantism /ˌɒbskjuː'ræntɪzəm; *US* ɒb'skjʊərənt-*

ɪzəm/ n [U] (fml) the practice of deliberately preventing sb from understanding or discovering sth: *the struggle of science against religious obscurantism.* ▶ **obscurantist** n, adj: *obscurantist religions/ myths.*

obscure /əbˈskjʊə(r)/ adj **1** not easily or clearly seen or understood: *I found the lecture very obscure.* ○ *The origins of the disease are still rather obscure.* **2** not well-known: *an obscure German poet* ○ *an obscure corner of the world.*
▶ **obscure** v to prevent sth from being seen, heard, understood, etc: [Vn] *Her face was partially obscured by the shadows.* ○ *Mist obscured the view.* ○ *The facts of the case may have been deliberately falsified or obscured.*
obscurely adv.
obscurity /əbˈskjʊərəti/ n **1** [U] the state of not being well-known: *content to live in obscurity* ○ *After years of working in obscurity, he at last found recognition.* **2** [C] a thing that is not clear and is therefore difficult to understand: *a philosophical essay full of obscurities.* **3** [U] darkness; poor light.

obsequies /ˈɒbsəkwiz/ n [pl] (fml) funeral ceremonies: *royal/state obsequies.*

obsequious /əbˈsiːkwiəs/ adj ~ (to sb) (derog) too willing to obey or serve sb; showing excessive respect for sb: *give an obsequious smile.* ▶ **obsequiously** adv. **obsequiousness** n [U].

observable /əbˈzɜːvəbl/ adj [usu attrib] that can be seen or noticed: *an observable lack of enthusiasm* ○ *no observable signs of life.*

observance /əbˈzɜːvəns/ n **1** [U] ~ (of sth) the practice of obeying a law or keeping a custom, festival, holiday, etc: *the observance of school rules* ○ *the observance of Christmas* ○ *strict observance of basic human rights.* **2** [C] (fml) an act performed as part of a religious or traditional ceremony: *religious observances.*

observant /əbˈzɜːvənt/ adj **1** quick at noticing things: *The thief was spotted by an observant shop assistant.* ○ *Journalists are trained to be observant.* **2** (fml) careful to obey laws or to keep customs, traditions, etc: *She's a Catholic, but not particularly observant.*

observation /ˌɒbzəˈveɪʃn/ n **1** [U] the action of watching sb/sth carefully so as to notice things: *his astonishing powers of observation* ○ *close and careful observation of an animal's behaviour* ○ *We escaped observation* (ie were not seen). ○ *The patient was kept under observation all night.* ○ *The police have been keeping him under observation for weeks.* ○ *an observation platform/post/tower from which scenery, wild animals, enemy forces, etc can be watched.* **2** [C] a spoken or written remark or comment based on sth one has seen, heard, etc: *make some witty observations about human behaviour* ○ *record scientific observations.*

observatory /əbˈzɜːvətri; US -tɔːri/ n a special building from which the stars, the weather, etc can be observed by scientists.

observe /əbˈzɜːv/ v **1** to see and notice sb/sth; to watch sb/sth carefully: [V] *He observes keenly, but says little.* [Vn] *observe the behaviour of birds* [V.that] *She observed that he'd left but made no comment.* [V.wh] *They observed how the tiny wings were fitted to the body.* [V.n to inf only passive] *The woman was observed to follow him closely.* [Vn.ing, Vn.inf (no to)] *The police observed the man entering/enter the bank.* **2(a)** to obey rules, laws, etc: [Vn] *observe the speed limit* ○ *observe a cease-fire.* **(b)** to celebrate festivals, birthdays, etc: *Do they observe Christmas?* **3** (fml) to make a remark: [V.that] *He observed that it would probably rain.* [V.speech] *'It may rain,' he observed.*
▶ **observer** n **1** a person who observes: *a detached/ an independent observer* ○ *This is clear even to a* casual observer. ○ *Most art forms require a contribution from the observer.* **2** a person who attends a conference, lesson, etc to listen and watch but not to take part: *an observer at a summit conference* ○ *send sb along as an observer.* **3** a person trained to notice and record enemy aircraft, positions, etc: *the Royal Observer Corps.*

obsess /əbˈses/ v (usu passive) to fill the mind of sb continually so that they can think of nothing else: [Vn] *be obsessed by/with the fear of death* ○ *He's completely obsessed with her.* ○ *She became obsessed with the idea that she was being watched.*
▶ **obsession** /əbˈseʃn/ n ~ (with/about sth/sb) **1** [U] the state of being obsessed: *His obsession with computers began six months ago.* ○ *Her fear is bordering on obsession.* **2** [C] a thing or person that obsesses sb; a fixed idea that fills the mind: *suffer from an obsession with cleanliness* ○ *Dieting has become an obsession with him.* **obsessional** /əbˈseʃənl/ adj of, having or causing obsession: *have an obsessional fear of men* ○ *a tale of obsessional love.*
obsessive /əbˈsesɪv/ adj of or having an obsession: *obsessive behaviour* ○ *an obsessive concern for neatness* ○ *She's obsessive about punctuality.* — n (medical) a person who has an obsession: *sporting obsessives* ○ *The psychiatrist has done a lot of work with obsessives.* **obsessively** adv: *obsessively concerned with one's appearance* ○ *He worries obsessively about money.*

obsolescent /ˌɒbsəˈlesnt/ adj becoming out of date; going out of use: *obsolescent technology* ○ *Electronic equipment quickly becomes obsolescent.* ▶ **obsolescence** /-ˈlesns/ n [U]: *a product with built-in/planned obsolescence* (ie deliberately designed by the manufacturer not to last long).

obsolete /ˈɒbsəliːt, ˌɒbsəˈliːt/ adj no longer used; out of date: *obsolete words found in old texts* ○ *skills which are now becoming obsolete.*

obstacle /ˈɒbstəkl/ n a thing that blocks one's way or makes movement, progress, etc difficult: *fall over an unseen obstacle in the path* ○ *remove obstacles to world peace* ○ *place obstacles in the way of sth* ○ *A lack of qualifications can be a major obstacle to career progress.*
■ **'obstacle race** n a race in which the competitors have to climb over, under, through, etc various natural or artificial obstacles.

obstetrics /əbˈstetrɪks/ n [sing v] (medical) the branch of medicine concerned with the birth of children. Compare GYNAECOLOGY.
▶ **obstetric** /əbˈstetrɪk/ adj: *obstetric medicine/ practice.*
obstetrician /ˌɒbstəˈtrɪʃn/ n a doctor who specializes in obstetrics.

obstinacy /ˈɒbstɪnəsi/ n [U] the fact of being OB-STINATE(1): *Sheer obstinacy prevented her from apologizing.*

obstinate /ˈɒbstɪnət/ adj **1** (often derog) refusing to change one's opinion or decisions, despite attempts to persuade one: *The obstinate old man refused to go to hospital.* ○ *He has an obstinate streak* (ie Some of his behaviour is very obstinate). **2** difficult to overcome, remove, etc: *obstinate resistance* ○ *an obstinate rash on his face* ○ *an obstinate stain on the carpet.* ▶ **obstinately** adv: *ideas to which he obstinately clung* ○ *He obstinately refused to help.*

obstreperous /əbˈstrepərəs/ adj (fml) (of people or their behaviour) very noisy and difficult to control: *obstreperous behaviour/children* ○ *He becomes obstreperous when he's had a few drinks.* ▶ **obstreperously** adv.

obstruct /əbˈstrʌkt/ v **1** to be or get in the way of sb/sth; to block sth: [Vn] *Parked cars obstructed his view of the road.* ○ *He was charged with obstructing the highway.* **2** to prevent sb/sth deliberately from making progress; to put difficulties in the way of sb/ sth: [Vn] *be charged with obstructing the police in the* course of their duty ○ *obstruct a player on the football field* ○ *obstruct the passage of a bill through Congress* (ie try to prevent a law being passed).

obstruction /əb'strʌkʃn/ *n* **1** [U] the action of obstructing (OBSTRUCT) sb/sth: *obstruction of the factory gates* ○ *be arrested for obstruction.* **2** [C] a thing that obstructs (OBSTRUCT) sb/sth: *an operation to remove an obstruction in the throat* ○ *obstructions on the road* (eg fallen trees) ○ *Your car is causing an obstruction* (ie getting in the way of others). **3** [U] (*sport*) the offence of unfairly preventing the movement of a player in the other team: *be penalized for obstruction.*
▶ **obstructionism** /-ʃənɪzəm/ *n* [U] deliberate obstruction of plans, laws, etc.
obstructionist /-ɪst/ *n, adj.*

obstructive /əb'strʌktɪv/ *adj* causing or intended to cause an OBSTRUCTION: *an obstructive lung disease* ○ *an agricultural policy obstructive to small farmers* ○ *Her attitude was unhelpful and obstructive.* ▶ **obstructively** *adv.*

obtain /əb'teɪn/ *v* **1** (*rather fml*) to get or acquire sth by making an effort: [Vn] *obtain permission/information/advice/approval* ○ *I managed to obtain the book I wanted.* [Vnpr] *Vitamins and fibre are best obtained from/through natural food.* **2** (*fml*) (of rules, customs, etc) to be in use; to exist: [V] *The situation changes when these conditions no longer obtain.*
▶ **obtainable** *adj* that can be obtained: *Full details are obtainable from any post office.* ○ *Are his records still obtainable?*

obtrude /əb'truːd/ *v* (*fml*) **1** ~ (**sth/oneself**) (**on/upon sb**) to become or make sth/oneself noticeable, esp in a way that is not welcome: [Vnpr] *obtrude one's opinions on others* [Vpr] *He didn't realize how much he was obtruding on her grief.* [also V]. **2** to stick out: [V, Vpr] *On the lower slopes rocks and bushes were already obtruding (through the snow).*
▶ **obtrusive** /əb'truːsɪv/ *adj* noticeable in an unpleasant way; disturbing: *I find the music in the bar very obtrusive.* ○ *Try to wear less obtrusive colours.*
obtrusively *adv: obtrusively bright/loud.*

obtuse /əb'tjuːs; *US* -'tuːs/ *adj* (*fml derog*) slow to understand; stupid: *He's being deliberately obtuse.* ○ *She cannot possibly be so obtuse.* ▶ **obtusely** *adv.*
obtuseness *n* [U].
■ **ob₁tuse ₁angle** *n* (*geometry*) an angle between 90° and 180°. ⇨ picture at ANGLE.

obverse /'ɒbvɜːs/ *n* **1** (*techn*) the side of a coin or MEDAL that has the head or main design on it: *The head of the Queen appears on the obverse of British coins.* Compare REVERSE² 4. **2** (*fml*) the logical opposite of sth: *The obverse of love is hate.*

obviate /'ɒbvieɪt/ *v* (*fml*) to remove sth; to make sth unnecessary: [Vn] *obviate dangers/problems* ○ *The new road obviates the need to drive through the town.*

obvious /'ɒbviəs/ *adj* easily seen or understood; clear: *It was obvious to everyone that the child had been badly treated.* ○ *Spending less money is the obvious answer to his financial problems.* ○ *Ann's teaching experience made her the obvious choice for the job.* ○ *I may be **stating the obvious**, but without more money the project cannot survive.*
▶ **obviously** *adv* as can easily be seen or understood; clearly: *He was obviously drunk.* ○ *Obviously we don't want to spend too much money.* ⇨ note at HOPEFUL.
obviousness *n* [U].

occasion /ə'keɪʒn/ *n* **1** [C] a particular time when sth happens: *on this/that occasion* ○ *on rare occasions* ○ *on the occasion of her daughter's wedding* ○ *I've met him on several occasions.* ○ *On one occasion* (ie Once) *he rang me in the middle of the night.* ○ *I bought this dress specially for the occasion.* **2** [sing] ~ (**for sth**) a suitable or right time for sth: *A funeral is hardly an*

occasion for practical jokes. ○ *I'll wear it if the occasion arises* (ie if I get the opportunity). **3** [C] a special event, ceremony or celebration: *a great/historic/social occasion* ○ *The wedding was a memorable occasion.* **4** [U] (*fml*) a reason or cause: *I've had no occasion to visit him recently.* ○ *She never has much occasion to speak French in her new job.* **IDM** **on oc₁casion(s)** occasionally; from time to time. **rise to the occasion** ⇨ RISE². **a sense of occasion** ⇨ SENSE.
▶ **occasion** *v* (*fml*) to be the cause of sth: [Vn] *The incident occasioned a great deal of comment.* ○ *The delay was occasioned by the need to consult senior management.* [Vnn] *The decision occasioned us much anxiety.* [also Vnpr].

NOTE Occasion, **opportunity** and **chance** all mean a time when it is possible to do something. **Chance** and **possibility** are also used to suggest that something might happen.
   Occasion suggests a time that is socially suitable for the activity: *A wedding is an occasion for celebration.* **Opportunity** and **chance** suggest it is possible for you to do something because the circumstances are good or lucky at that time: *I had the opportunity to spend a year in Paris while I was a student.* ○ *The meeting will provide a good opportunity for us to make a decision.* ○ *I hope you get the chance to relax while you're away.* ○ *Listeners will have the chance to air their views on the phone-in tonight.*
   Chance can also refer to how probable something is: *What are your chances of being promoted?* You cannot say 'somebody has the possibility to do something', but you can say that there is a **possibility of** something, or a **possibility that** something could happen: *Is there any possibility of a cure?* ○ *There is the possibility that interest rates may be cut.* **Occasion** may refer to the particular time when something happens: *The most memorable occasions are often the ones you didn't plan.*

occasional /ə'keɪʒənl/ *adj* [usu attrib] **1** happening or done from time to time; not regular: *He pays me occasional visits.* ○ *There will be occasional showers during the day.* ○ *I don't drink much alcohol, just the occasional glass of wine.* **2** (*fml*) written or meant for a special event: *occasional verses* (eg written to celebrate an anniversary).
▶ **occasionally** /-nəli/ *adv* now and then; at times: *He visits me occasionally.*
■ **oc₁casional table** *n* a small table used for different things at different times.

Occident /'ɒksɪdənt/ *n* **the Occident** [sing] (*fml*) the countries of the West, ie Europe and America. Compare ORIENT¹.
▶ **occidental** *adj* (*fml*) of or from the Occident.

occult /'ɒkʌlt; *US* ə'kʌlt/ *adj* involving magical or SUPERNATURAL powers: *occult powers/rituals.*
▶ **the occult** *n* [sing] occult practices, ceremonies, powers, etc: *He's interested in the occult.*

occupant /'ɒkjəpənt/ *n* (**a**) a person who lives in or uses a house, room, etc: *The previous occupants of the house had left it in a terrible mess.* (**b**) a person who is in a car, seat, etc: *The car was badly damaged but its occupants were unhurt.*
▶ **occupancy** /-pənsi/ *n* (*fml*) [U] the action or period of occupying a house, land, etc: *a change of occupancy* ○ *Prices are based on full occupancy of an apartment.*

occupation /ˌɒkjuˈpeɪʃn/ *n* **1** [C] (*fml*) a job or profession: *Please state your name, age and occupation on the form.* ⇨ note at JOB. **2** [C] a way of spending time: *His favourite occupation is fishing.* **3** [U] (**a**) the action by a group of people or an army from one country of moving into and taking control of another country, a town, etc: *the German occupation of France during the Second World War.* (**b**) the period of time during which a country, town, etc is controlled in this way. **4** [U] the action of living in or using a house, room, piece of land, etc: *The new house is now ready for occupation.*

▶ **occupational** /-ʃənl/ *adj* [attrib] of, caused by or connected with a person's job: *occupational health/diseases* ○ *The average salary varies from one occupational group to another.* ,**occu,pational 'hazard** *n* a risk or danger connected with a particular job: *Explosions, though infrequent, are an occupational hazard for coal-miners.* ,**occu,pational 'therapy** *n* [U] a way of helping people to recover from illness or injury by giving them special work to do. ,**occu,pational 'therapist** *n*.

occupier /'ɒkjupaɪə(r)/ *n* a person who lives in or uses a house, room, piece of land, etc; an OCCUPANT: *The letter was addressed to the occupier of the house.* See also OWNER-OCCUPIER.

occupy /'ɒkjupaɪ/ *v* (*pt, pp* **-pied**) **1** to live in or use a house, room, piece of land, etc: [Vn] *The house next door has not been occupied for over a year.* ○ *A firm of solicitors occupies the fourth floor.* **2** to move into and take control of a country, town, etc, esp by military force: [Vn] *The army occupied the enemy's capital.* ○ *the occupied territories.* **3** to fill space, time or a position: [Vn] *The bed occupied most of the room.* ○ *Looking after a large family occupies most of her time.* ○ *He occupies a senior position in the company.* **4** ~ **sb/oneself (in doing sth / with sth)** to fill sb's/one's time or keep sb/oneself busy (doing sth/with sth): [Vn] *How does he occupy himself now that he's retired?* ○ *She needs something to occupy her mind.* [Vnpr] *The child occupied himself in playing video games.* **5** to move into a building and stay there as a protest against sth: [Vn] *The rebel forces have occupied the television station.*

▶ **occupied** *adj* [pred] **1** in use; filled: *The toilet was occupied.* ⇨ note at EMPTY¹. **2** ~ **(in doing sth / with sth)** busy: *He's fully occupied in looking after/with three small children.* ○ *She kept herself occupied knitting clothes for refugees.*

occur /ə'kɜ:(r)/ *v* (**-rr-**) **(a)** to take place; to happen: [V] *When did the accident occur?* ○ *The explosion occurred just after midnight.* **(b)** to exist; to be found: [Vpr] *natural sugars occurring in fruit* ○ *Child abuse occurs in all classes of society.* ○ *The disease occurs most frequently in rural areas.* [also V]. ⇨ note at HAPPEN. **2** ~ **to sb** (of an idea or a thought) to come into sb's mind: [Vpr] *An idea has occurred to me.* [Vpr.that] *The thought occurred to me that I might have made a mistake.* ○ *Didn't it ever occur to you that I would be worried?* [Vpr.to inf] *It never occurred to her to ask for help.*

occurrence /ə'kʌrəns/ *n* **1** [C] an event; an incident; a happening: *a rare occurrence* ○ *Robbery is now an everyday occurrence.* **2** [U] (*fml*) the fact or frequency of sth happening: *In adults the occurrence of cancer increases with age.*

NOTE Compare **occurrence, event, incident** and **happening. Occurrence** is quite a formal word meaning something that happens: *Divorce has become a common occurrence.* An **event** often refers to something important happening: *The tourist guide lists the major events happening in the town throughout the year.* ○ *The events of 1989 ended the Cold War.*

An **incident** is often not very important but is something you remember: *The movie is based on a real-life incident.* An **incident** can also refer to a crime or an accident: *The incident took place in the early hours of Sunday morning.*

A **happening** is usually something unusual that has occurred: *There have been a few strange happenings in this town recently.* Note that you can also use the verb **happen** to talk about something that has occurred: *I want you to describe what happened in as much detail as possible.*

---

ocean /'əʊʃn/ *n* **(a)** (usu **the ocean**) [sing] the mass of salt water that covers most of the earth's surface: *the ocean floor* ○ *an ocean voyage.* **(b)** (usu **Ocean**) [C] each of the large seas into which this is divided: *the Atlantic/Pacific/Indian/Arctic/Antarctic Ocean.* **IDM** **a drop in the bucket/ocean** ⇨ DROP¹. **oceans of sth** (*Brit infml*) lots of sth: *oceans of food and drink.*

▶ **oceanic** /,əʊʃi'ænɪk/ *adj* [usu attrib] (*fml*) of, like or found in the ocean: *an oceanic climate* ○ *oceanic plant life.*

oceanography /,əʊʃə'nɒgrəfi/ *n* [U] the scientific study of the ocean. **oceanographer** *n* a specialist in oceanography.

■ **'ocean-going** *adj* [attrib] (of ships) made for crossing the sea, not for journeys along the coast or up rivers.

ocelot /'ɒsəlɒt/ *n* a large wild cat with a yellow and black coat found in Central and South America.

och /ɒk, ɒx/ (*Scot or Irish*) *interj* (used to express surprise, regret, agreement, disagreement, etc): *Och, aye* (ie Oh, yes)*!*

ochre (*US* also **ocher**) *n* [U] /'əʊkə(r)/ **(a)** a type of red or yellow earth used as a colouring in paints and dyes. **(b)** the colour of ochre. ▶ **ochre** *adj*: *red roofs and ochre walls.*

o'clock /ə'klɒk/ *adv* (used with the numbers 1 to 12 when telling the time, to specify an exact hour): *He left eleven five and six o'clock.* ○ *go to bed at/after/before eleven o'clock.*

Oct *abbr* October: *6 Oct 1931.*

octagon /'ɒktəgən/; *US* -gɒn/ *n* (*geometry*) a flat shape with eight straight sides and eight angles.

▶ **octagonal** /ɒk'tægənl/ *adj* shaped like an octagon: *an octagonal coin/table/tower.*

octane /'ɒkteɪn/ *n* a chemical substance in petrol, used as a measure of its quality: *high-octane fuel.*

octave /'ɒktɪv/ *n* (*music*) **(a)** the difference or space between the first and the last in a series of eight notes on a musical scale¹(6): *play an octave higher* ○ *Her voice has a range of three octaves.* **(b)** the 8th note in such a series.

octet /ɒk'tet/ *n* **(a)** a group of eight singers or musicians: *a jazz octet.* **(b)** a piece of music for an octet.

oct(o)- *comb form* having eight of sth: *octagon* ○ *octogenarian* ○ *octopus.*

October /ɒk'təʊbə(r)/ *n* [U,C] (*abbr* **Oct**) the 10th month of the year, next after September.
For further guidance on how *October* is used, see the examples at *April.*

octogenarian /,ɒktədʒə'neəriən/ *n* a person between 80 and 89 years of age.

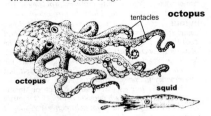

tentacles **octopus**

octopus

squid

octopus /'ɒktəpəs/ *n* (*pl* **-es**) a sea animal with a soft round body and eight long tentacles (TENTACLE 1). ⇨ picture. Compare SQUID.

ocular /'ɒkjələ(r)/ *adj* [esp attrib] (*fml*) **1** of or connected with the eyes or sight: *ocular muscles/defects.* **2** that can be seen; visual: *ocular proof.*

oculist /'ɒkjəlɪst/ *n* a specialist in treating eye disorders.

OD /ˌəʊ ˈdiː/ v (*3rd pers sing pres t* **OD's**, *pres p* **OD'ing**, *pt* **OD'd**) ~ (**on sth**) (*infml*) = OVERDOSE v.

odd /ɒd/ adj (**-er**, **-est**) **1(a)** strange; unusual; PECULIAR(1): *an odd tale* ○ *All this is very odd.* ○ *You find his books in the oddest places.* ○ *The oddest thing about it was its colour.* (**b**) (*often derog*) behaving in a strange way: *She lives with some very odd characters.* ○ *What an odd man!* **2** (no comparative or superlative) (of numbers) leaving one remaining when divided by two: *1,3,5 and 7 are odd numbers.* Compare EVEN² 4. **3** [usu attrib] (no comparative or superlative) (**a**) remaining when the other of a pair or the others of a set is/are missing: *an odd shoe/ glove* ○ *two odd volumes of an encyclopedia* ○ *You're wearing odd socks* (ie two that do not form a pair). (**b**) remaining after the rest has been used: *She made a cushion out of odd bits of material.* **4** (no comparative or superlative; usu placed directly after a number) a little more than: *five hundred odd* (ie slightly more than 500) ○ *thirty-odd* (ie between 30 and 40) *years later.* **5** [attrib] (no comparative or superlative) happening or occurring occasionally and not at regular or fixed intervals: *weed the garden at odd times/moments* ○ *The landscape was bare except for the odd cactus.* ○ *I read very little — only the odd magazine.* **6** [attrib] (often **the odd**) spare; that one can give to sb: *When you've got an odd five minutes, I'd like to speak to you.* ○ *Can you spare the odd 50p for a cup of tea, sir?* **IDM** **the/an odd man/ one ˈout 1** a person or thing that remains when all the others have been put into pairs or groups: *There's always an odd man out when the children are divided into teams.* **2** a person or thing that is different from the others: *Banana, grape, apple, rose — which of these is the odd one out?* **3** (*infml*) a person who cannot fit easily into the group or society of which he or she is a member: *At school she always felt the odd one out.*

▶ **odd** (forming compound *adjs*): *an odd-looking house* ○ *an odd-sounding name.*

oddly *adv* in a strange manner: *behave oddly* ○ *be oddly dressed* ○ *She looked at him very oddly.* ○ **Oddly enough**, *we were just talking about the same thing.*

oddness *n* [U]: *the oddness of her appearance* ○ *His oddness frightened her.*

■ **ˌodd ˈjobs** *n* [pl] small jobs of various types, usu done for other people: *do odd jobs around the house.* ˌodd ˈjob man /mæn/ *n* (*pl* men /-men/) a person paid to do odd jobs.

oddball /ˈɒdbɔːl/ *n* (*infml*) a person who appears strange or ECCENTRIC(1): *My boss is a real oddball.* ▶ ˈoddball *adj* [attrib]: *oddball designs/projects.*

oddity /ˈɒdəti/ *n* **1** [U] the quality of being odd(1): *I was puzzled by the oddity of her remark.* **2** [C] an unusual act, event, person or thing: *a grammatical oddity* ○ *He's treated as something of an oddity in the neighbourhood.*

oddment /ˈɒdmənt/ *n* (usu *pl*) a piece or an item remaining from a larger piece or set: *a chair sold as an oddment at the end of the sale* ○ *a patchwork quilt made out of oddments.* Compare ODDS AND ENDS.

odds /ɒdz/ *n* [pl] **1** the chances that sth will or will not happen: *The odds are in your favour* (ie You are likely to succeed). ○ *The odds are (heavily) against him* (ie He is unlikely to succeed). ○ *The odds are that* (ie It is probable that) *she'll win.* **2** strong opposition or great disadvantages: *a victory in the face of hopeless/overwhelming odds* ○ **Against all the odds** *she achieved her dream of becoming a ballerina.* **3** (in betting) the difference in amount or RATIO between the money bet on a horse, etc and the money that will be paid if it wins: *The horse was running at odds of ten to one.* ○ *The odds are five to one on the defending champion.* ○ *I'll lay odds of* (ie bet) *three to one that he'll get the job.* **IDM** **be at ˈodds (with sb) (over/on sth)** to be disagreeing or quarrelling with sb about sth: *He's always at odds with his father over politics.* **have the cards/odds stacked against one** ⇨ STACK v. **it makes no ˈodds** (*esp Brit*) it makes no difference; it is of no importance: *It makes no odds to me whether you go or stay.* **over the ˈodds** (*Brit infml*) more than is expected or necessary: *The firm pays over the odds in order to keep its staff.*

■ ˌodds and ˈends *n* (*infml*) small articles; items of various sorts, usu without much value: *He's moved most of his stuff — there are just a few odds and ends left.* Compare ODDMENT.

ˌodds-ˈon *adj* very likely to happen, win, etc: *the ˌodds-on ˈfavourite* ○ *It's odds-on that he'll be late.*

ode /əʊd/ *n* a poem addressed to a person or thing, or celebrating some special event: *Keats's 'Ode to Autumn'.*

odious /ˈəʊdiəs/ *adj* (*fml*) very unpleasant; disgusting: *What an odious man!* ○ *I find his flattery odious.*

odium /ˈəʊdiəm/ *n* [U] (*fml*) general or widespread hatred or disgust felt towards sb, esp because of sth they have done: *behaviour that exposed him to odium and ridicule.*

odometer /əʊˈdɒmɪtə(r)/ *n* (*esp US*) = MILOMETER.

odorous /ˈəʊdərəs/ *adj* (*dated fml*) having a usu pleasant smell.

odour (*US* **odor**) /ˈəʊdə(r)/ *n* (*fml*) [C] a distinctive, usu unpleasant, smell: *a characteristic fishy odour* ○ *a lingering odour of cigarette smoke* ○ *emit/give off a pungent odour* ○ (*fig*) *The scandal has left rather a nasty odour.* See also BODY ODOUR. **IDM** **be in good/ bad ˈodour (with sb)** to be in/out of favour with sb: *I'm in rather bad odour with my parents.*

▶ **odourless** *adj* without a smell: *an odourless liquid.*

odyssey /ˈɒdəsi/ *n* a long journey full of experiences.

OECD /ˌəʊ iː siː ˈdiː/ *abbr* Organization for Economic Cooperation and Development.

Oedipus complex /ˈiːdɪpəs kɒmpleks; *US* ˈed-/ (*psychology*) the unconscious sexual desire of a child for the parent of the opposite sex, esp of a boy for his mother, and the resulting jealous feelings towards the other parent.

o'er /ɔː(r)/ *adv*, *prep* (*arch*) over.

oesophagus (also *esp US* **esophagus**) /iˈsɒfəgəs/ *n* (*pl* **-phaguses** or **-phagi** /-gaɪ/) (*medical*) the tube through which food passes from the mouth to the stomach: *cancer of the oesophagus.* ⇨ picture at DIGESTIVE SYSTEM, THROAT. Compare GULLET.

oestrogen /ˈiːstrədʒən/ (also *esp US* **estrogen** /ˈes-/) *n* [U, C] any of a group of hormones (HORMONE) produced by the ovaries (OVARY 1), which develop the characteristic sexual features of the female body and prepare the body to reproduce. Oestrogen is also produced artificially, eg for use in CONTRACEPTION: *have an oestrogen deficiency.* Compare PROGESTERONE.

oeuvre /ˈɜːvrə/ *n* [sing] (*French*) all the works of a writer, artist, etc: *Picasso's oeuvre.*

of /əv/ *adv*; *strong form* ɒv/ *prep* **1(a)** (followed by a possess *pron* or by a *n*, usu with 's) belonging to sb; owned by or associated with sb: *a friend of mine* ○ *an acquaintance of my wife's* ○ *that house of theirs in the country.* (**b**) (followed by a *n*) belonging to sth; part of sth: *the handle of the umbrella* ○ *the lid of the box.* **2** relating to sb's role, status or position: *the role of the teacher* ○ *the rights of man* ○ *the privileges of the élite* ○ *the responsibilities of a nurse.* **3** originating from a specific background or living in a place: *a woman of Italian descent* ○ *a man of humble origin* ○ *the miners of Wales* ○ *the inhabitants of the area.* **4** (esp referring to sb's works as a whole) created by sb: *the works of Milton* (Compare: *a poem by Milton*) ○ *the paintings of Monet* ○ *the songs of*

John Lennon. **5(a)** concerning or showing sb/sth: *stories of crime and adventure* ○ *a photograph of my dog* ○ *a picture of the Pope* ○ *a map of India.* **(b)** about sb/sth: *I've never heard of such places.* ○ *He told us of his travels.* **6** (indicating the material used to make sth): *a dress of blue silk* ○ *shirts made of cotton* ○ *a house (built) of stone.* Compare FROM 8. **7(a)** (indicating what is measured, counted or contained): *a pint of milk* ○ *2 kilos of potatoes* ○ *3 sheets of paper* ○ *a box of matches* ○ *a bottle of lemonade.* **(b)** (indicating the size, level or extent of sth): *an increase of 2.5%* ○ *a diameter of 5 cms.* **(c)** (showing the relationship between part and the whole of sth): *a member of the football team* ○ *for six months of the year.* **(d)** (used after *some, many, a few,* etc and between a numeral or superlative *adj* and a *pron* or *det*): *some of his friends* ○ *a few of my CDs* ○ *not much of the food* ○ *six of them* ○ *five of the team* ○ *the last of the girls* ○ *the brightest of all the students.* **8(a)** (used in expressions showing distance in space or time): *a town 5 miles north of Derby* ○ *within 100 yards of the station* ○ *at the time of the revolution* ○ *Within a year of their divorce he had remarried.* ○ *(US) a quarter of eleven* (ie 10.45 am or pm). **(b)** (used when saying a date): *the twenty-second of July* ○ *the first of May.* **(c)** *(dated)* frequently happening at a specified time: *They used to visit me of a Sunday* (ie on Sundays). **9** (used after *ns* formed from *vs*) **(a)** (introducing the object of the action expressed by the preceding *n*): *a lover of* (ie sb who loves) *classical music* ○ *fear of the dark* ○ *the forging of a banknote* ○ *There was no hope of his being elected.* **(b)** (introducing the subject of the action expressed by the preceding *n*): *have the support of the voters* ○ *the feelings of a rape victim towards her attacker* ○ *the love of a mother for her child* ○ *an outbreak of cholera.* **10** so that sb no longer has or suffers from sth: *rob sb of sth* ○ *deprived of his mother's protection* ○ *relieved of responsibility* ○ *cure sb of drug addiction.* **11** (indicating a cause): *die of pneumonia* ○ *ashamed of one's behaviour* ○ *proud of being captain.* **12** in relation to sth; concerning sth: *the result of the debate* ○ *the time of departure* ○ *the topic of conversation* ○ *a dictionary of English* ○ *the Professor of Mathematics* ○ *a director of the company* ○ *his chance of winning* ○ *sure of one's facts.* **13** (used before a *n* or a phrase that specifies what the preceding *n* refers to): *the city of Dublin* ○ *the issue of housing* ○ *on the subject of education* ○ *at the age of 16.* **14** (introducing a phrase that describes a preceding *n*): *a coat of many colours* ○ *a girl of ten* (ie who is ten years old) ○ *a woman of genius* ○ *a matter of great importance* ○ *an item of value.* **15** (used between two *ns,* the first of which describes the second): *He's got the devil of a temper.* ○ *Where's that fool of a receptionist?* **16** (used to show whose behaviour is being described by *It is/was + adj*): *It was kind of you to offer.* ○ *It's wrong of your friend to suggest it.* **IDM** **of ¹all** (used before a *n* to indicate the least likely or appropriate example): *I'm surprised that you'd ¹all people think that.* ○ *A flat tyre, today of all days!* **of ₁all the ¹sth** (used to express anger at sb's behaviour): *Of ₁all the ¹cheek/¹nerve!*

off¹ /ɒf; *US* ɔːf/ *adj* **1** [pred] **(a)** ~ **(with sb)** *(infml esp Brit)* (esp after *rather, very, slightly,* etc) not polite or friendly: *She sounded rather off on the phone.* ○ *He was a bit off with me this morning.* **(b)** not acceptable: *They want to cut our expenses — that's a bit off, isn't it?* **(c)** not well: *You look a bit off this morning, Mary.* **2** [pred] (of food) no longer fresh enough to eat or drink: *This fish has gone off.* ○ *The milk smells/tastes decidedly off.* **3** [attrib] = OFFSIDE².
■ **¹off chance** *n* [sing] a slight possibility: *There is still an off chance that the weather will improve.* ○ *He came* **on the off chance of** *finding me at home.*

off² /ɒf; *US* ɔːf/ *adv part* For the special uses of **off** in

phrasal verbs, look at the verb entries. For example, the meaning of **come off** is given in the phrasal verb section of the entry for **come**. **1(a)** at or to a point distant in space; away from a place: *The town is still five miles off.* ○ *He ran off with the money.* ○ *Sarah's off in India somewhere.* ○ *Be off/Off with you!* (ie Go away!) **(b)** at a point distant in time; away: *Summer is not so far off.* **2** (indicating removal or separation, esp from the human body): *He's had his beard shaved off.* ○ *take one's coat/tie off* ○ *Don't leave the toothpaste with the top off.* Compare ON² 3. **3** starting a journey or race: *She's off to Hong Kong tomorrow.* ○ *I must be off soon.* ○ *They're off* (ie The race has begun). **4** *(infml)* (of sth arranged or planned) not going to happen; cancelled: *The wedding/engagement is off.* ○ *The miners' strike is off.* Compare ON² 6. **5(a)** not connected or functioning: *The water/gas/electricity is off.* **(b)** (of appliances) not being used: *The TV/radio/light is off.* ○ *Make sure the central heating is off.* Compare ON² 4. **6** *(esp Brit)* (of an item on a MENU(1)) no longer available or being served: *The fish with almonds is off today.* **7** away from work or duty: *I think I'll take the afternoon off* (ie not work this afternoon). ○ *She's off today.* ○ *I've got three days off next week.* **8** taken from the price: *shoes with £5 off* ○ *All shirts have 10% off.* **9** (in the theatre) behind or at the sides of the stage; not on the stage: *noises/voices off.* **IDM** **be ₁off for ¹sth** *(infml)* to have supplies of sth: *How are we ₁off for ¹coffee?* (ie How much have we got?) Compare WELL OFF FOR STH, BADLY OFF FOR STH. **₁off and ¹on / ₁on and ¹off** from time to time; now and again: *It rained on and off all day.*
▶ **off** *n* [sing] **1 the off** the start of a race: *They're ready for the off.* **2 the off** (in cricket) the half of the field towards which a batsman is facing when waiting to receive a ball: *play the ball to the off* ○ *the off stump.* Compare LEG 6.
■ **¹off of** *prep (sl esp US)* = OFF³.

off³ /ɒf; *US* ɔːf/ *prep* For the special uses of **off** in phrasal verbs, look at the verb entries. For example, the meaning of **take sth off sth** is given in the phrasal verb section of the entry for **take¹**. **1** down or away from a position on sth: *fall off a ladder/ tree/horse/wall* ○ *The rain ran off the roof.* ○ *The ball rolled off the table.* ○ *Keep off the grass.* ○ *Cut another slice off the loaf.* ○ *Take a packet off the shelf.* ○ *They were only 100 metres off the summit when the accident happened.* ○ *(fig) We're getting right off the subject.* ○ *Scientists are still a long way off (finding) a cure.* **2** (esp of a road or street) leading away from sth: *a narrow lane off the main road* ○ *a bathroom off the main bedroom.* **3** at some distance from sth: *a big house off the main street* ○ *an island off the coast of Cornwall* ○ *The ship sank off Cape Horn.* **4** *(infml)* not wishing or needing to take sth: *I'm off* (ie not drinking) *alcohol for a week.* ○ *He's finally off drugs* (ie He no longer takes them).

off- /ɒf; *US* ɔːf/ *pref* (used widely to form *ns, adjs, vs* and *advs*) not on; away or at a distance from: *off-stage* ○ *off-peak* ○ *offshore* ○ *offload.*

offal /¹ɒfl; *US* ¹ɔːfl/ *n* [U] the internal parts of an animal, eg the heart, brain, LIVER, etc, used as food for humans or animals: *beef/sheep offal.*

offbeat /₁ɒf¹biːt; *US* ₁ɔːf-/ *adj (infml)* unusual; not conventional: *₁offbeat ¹humour* ○ *an offbeat TV comedy* ○ *Her style of dress is distinctly offbeat.*

offcut /¹ɒfkʌt; *US* ¹ɔːf-/ *n* a piece of wood, paper, etc remaining after the main piece has been cut: *buy some timber offcuts to build kitchen shelves.*

off-day /¹ɒf deɪ; *US* ¹ɔːf/ *n (infml)* a day when one does things badly, is not lucky, etc: *Even the best players sometimes have off-days.*

offence (*US* **offense**) /ə¹fens/ *n* **1** [C] ~ **(against sth)** an instance of breaking a rule or law; an illegal act; a crime: *commit an offence* ○ *an offence against* society/humanity/the state ○ a **capital offence** (ie one that may be punished by death) ○ *sexual offences* ○ *be charged with a serious offence* ○ *Because it was his **first offence*** (ie the first crime of which he was found guilty), *the punishment was not too severe.* **2** [U] ~ (**to sb/sth**) the action of upsetting or insulting; behaviour that upsets or insults sb: *I'm sorry — I **meant no offence** when I said that.* ○ *I'm sure he didn't mean to **cause offence** (to you).* ○ *She **took offence at** (ie was offended by) something I said.* ○ *There's no need to **take offence.*** **3** [C] ~ (**to sb/sth**) (*fml*) a thing that makes sb feel upset, annoyed or insulted: *The new shopping centre is an offence to the eye* (ie is unpleasant to look at). **IDM no of'fence** (used to explain that one does not intend to upset or insult sb): *No offence, madam, but you'll have to move your car.*

offend /ə'fend/ v **1(a)** (esp passive) to make sb feel upset or insulted; to hurt sb's feelings: [Vnpr, Vn] *She was offended at/by his sexist remarks.* [Vn] *She may be offended if you don't reply to her invitation.* [V] *TV programmers have to be careful not to offend.* **(b)** to be annoying or unpleasant to sb/sth: [Vn] *an ugly building that offends the eye* ○ *The colour scheme offends me.* **2** ~ (**against sth/sb**) to do wrong to sb/sth; to commit an offence(1) against sth/sth: [V] *criminals who persistently offend* [Vpr] (*fml*) *His conduct offended against the rules of decent behaviour.*
▶ **offender** n a person who offends, esp by breaking a law: *a persistent offender* ○ *sex offenders.* See also FIRST OFFENDER.
offending adj [attrib] causing annoyance or difficulty: *There were complaints, so the offending products were recalled to the factory and destroyed.* ○ *The offending paragraph was deleted.*

offense /ə'fens/ n [Gp, U] (*US sport*) an attacking team or section; a method of attack: *Their team had a poor offense.* ○ *Their offense was badly planned.* Compare DEFENCE 3.

offensive /ə'fensɪv/ adj **1(a)** causing sb to feel upset, insulted or annoyed: *offensive remarks/language/behaviour* ○ *I find your attitude most offensive.* Compare INOFFENSIVE. **(b)** very unpleasant; disgusting: *an offensive smell* ○ *She finds tobacco smoke offensive.* **2** (*fml*) used for or connected with attack; aggressive: *offensive weapons/operations.* Compare DEFENSIVE.
▶ **offensive** n an aggressive action, campaign or attitude; an attack: *launch a major offensive* ○ *an air offensive.* **IDM be on the of'fensive** to be making an attack; to act aggressively: *Liverpool were on the offensive for most of the first half.* **go on (to)/take the of'fensive** to begin to attack: *In meetings she always takes the offensive before she can be criticized.*
offensively adv: *offensively loud music* ○ *play offensively.*
offensiveness n [U].

offer /'ɒfə(r); US 'ɔːf-/ v **1** ~ **sth** (**to sb**) (**for sth**) to put forward sth to be considered, so it can then be either accepted or refused; to present sth: [Vnpr] *She is offering a reward for the return of her lost bracelet.* ○ *He offered £150 000 for the house.* [Vn] *I've been offered a job in Japan.* [Vnn] *He offered her a cigarette.* ○ *We offered him the house for $200 000.* **2** ~ **sth** (**to sb**) to show or express willingness or the intention to do, give, etc sth: [V] *I don't think they need help, but I think I should offer anyway.* [Vn] *They offered no resistance.* [V.to inf] *We offered to leave.* [Vnn] *We offered him a lift, but he didn't accept.* [Vnpr] *The company offered the job to someone else.* **3** (*rather fml*) to give opportunity for sth; to provide sth: [Vn] *The job offers prospects of promotion.* ○ *The trees offered welcome shade from the sun.* **4** ~ **sth/sb** (**up**) (**to sb**) (**for sth**) (*fml*) to present or give sth to God: [Vnp, Vnpr] *She offered (up) a*

prayer *(to God) for her husband's safe return.* [also Vn, Vnn]. **IDM have sth to offer** to have sth available to be enjoyed, used, etc: *the luxuries that a first-class hotel has to offer* ○ *a young man with a great deal to offer* (ie who is clever, talented, etc). **offer** (**sb**) **one's 'hand** (*fml*) to extend one's hand for sb to hold or shake, eg as a sign of friendship: *She smiled and offered her hand.*
▶ **offer** n **1** [C] ~ (**to sb/to do sth**) a statement offering to do or give sth to sb: *an offer of help from the neighbours* ○ *your kind offer to help* ○ *an offer of marriage* (ie a proposal(2)). **2** [C] ~ (**for sth**) an amount offered: *a firm offer* (ie one that is genuine and not likely to be withdrawn) ○ *I've had an offer of £2 200 for the car.* ○ *They made (me) an offer which I couldn't refuse.* ○ *The original price was £3 000, but I'm **open to offers*** (ie prepared to consider offers of less than that). See also ONO. **IDM on 'offer 1** available: *vocational courses currently on offer.* **2** (*esp Brit*) for sale at a reduced price: *Baked beans are on offer this week at the local supermarket.* **under 'offer** (*Brit*) (of a building for sale) having sb who has made an offer to buy: *The property is currently under offer.*
offering /'ɒfərɪŋ; US 'ɔːf-/ n a thing offered, esp as a gift or contribution: *a church offering* ○ *He gave her a box of chocolates as a **peace offering*** (ie in the hope of ending a quarrel, etc). ○ *I don't think much of the offerings on TV these days.* See also BURNT OFFERING.

offertory /'ɒfətri; US 'ɔːfətɔːri/ n [sing] (*fml*) money collected during a religious service or left in a special box in a church: *Money should be put in the offertory box.*

offhand /,ɒf'hænd; US ,ɔːf-/ adj (*derog*) (of behaviour, speech, etc) too casual; ABRUPT(2): *He was rather offhand with me.* ○ *I don't like his offhand manner.*
▶ **offhand** adv without previous thought: *I don't know offhand how much money I earn.* ○ *Offhand, I can't think of anyone who could help you.*

office /'ɒfɪs; US 'ɔːf-/ n **1** [C] **(a)** a room, set of rooms or building used as a place of business, esp for administrative work: *She works in our Paris office.* ○ *Our office is in the centre of the town.* ○ *We ought to inform **head office.*** ○ *an 'office job* ○ *office equipment such as word processors and photocopiers* ○ *'office workers.* **(b)** a usu small room in which a particular person works: *a lawyer's office* ○ *Some secretaries have to share an office.* **2** [C] (*US*) a place where a doctor sees her or his patients: *the pediatrician's office.* **3** [C] (often in compounds) a room or building used for a particular purpose, esp to provide a service: *the lost 'property office* ○ *a 'ticket office at a station* ○ *the local 'tax office* ○ *the 'Post Office.* See also BOX-OFFICE, REGISTRY OFFICE. **4 Office** [C] (esp in compounds) a government department, including the staff, their work and their duties: *work at/in the 'Foreign Office.* **5** [C, U] a public position of trust and authority, esp in government; the work and duties connected with this: *seek/accept/leave/resign office as a cabinet minister* ○ *hold the office of mayor* ○ *The party has been **out of office*** (ie has not formed a government) *for many years.* ○ *The present administration took office in 1989.* ○ *Which political party is **in office** in your country?* **IDM through sb's good 'offices** (*fml*) with sb's kind help: *through the good offices of our embassies overseas.*
■ **'office block** n a usu large building containing offices, usu belonging to more than one company: *tall concrete office blocks* ○ *The bank and the building society are in the same office block.*
'office boy n (*fem* **'office girl**) (*dated*) a young person employed to do less important duties in an office.
'office-holder (also **'office-bearer**) n a person who holds an office(5): *All the office-bearers have to be elected.*

O

'**office hours** n [pl] the hours during which business is regularly conducted: *Office hours vary from company to company.*

officer /ˈɒfɪsə(r); US ˈɔːf-/ n **1** a person appointed to command others in the armed forces: *naval/army/ air force officers* ○ *commissioned and non-commissioned officers* ○ *the officers and men of the regiment* ○ *the officers' mess.* **2** (often in compounds) a person with a position of authority or trust, eg in the government or a society: *executive and clerical officers* ○ *a customs officer* ○ *a probation officer* ○ *officers of state* (ie ministers in the government) ○ *the Chief Medical Officer* ○ *We had to vote to appoint all three officers: President, Secretary and Treasurer.* See also PETTY OFFICER, RETURNING OFFICER, WARRANT-OFFICER. **3** (often as a form of address) a police officer: *Officer Bailey* ○ *Yes, officer, I saw it happen.*

official /əˈfɪʃl/ adj **1** of or relating to a position of authority or trust: *official responsibilities/powers/ records* ○ *in his official capacity as mayor.* **2** said, done, etc with authority; recognized by authority: *an official announcement/statement/decision* ○ *the official biography of the President* ○ *The news is almost certainly true although it's not yet official.* **3** for, suitable for or characteristic of people holding office (5); formal: *an official reception/dinner* ○ *written in an official style.* Compare UNOFFICIAL.
▶ **official** n a person who holds a public office(5), eg in national or local government: *government officials* ○ *the officials of a political party.*
officialdom /-dəm/ n [U] (fml often derog) (a) officials as a group: *persuade officialdom to take environmental protection seriously.* (b) the methods by which public officials perform their duties, exercise power, etc: *The play is an attack on petty officialdom.*
officialese /əˌfɪʃəˈliːz/ n [U] (derog) the formal language of official documents, regarded as difficult to understand: *The report is refreshingly free of the usual officialese.*
officially /əˈfɪʃəli/ adv **1** in an official manner; formally: *I've been officially invited to the wedding.* ○ *We already know who's got the job, even though we haven't yet been told officially.* **2** as announced publicly, esp by officials, though not necessarily true in fact: *Officially, the director is in a meeting — actually, he's playing golf.*
■ **oˌfficial reˈceiver** n = RECEIVER 4.

officiate /əˈfɪʃɪeɪt/ v ~ (**at sth**) to perform the duties of a public office(5): [Vpr] *The bishop will officiate at the wedding* (ie perform the marriage ceremony). [also V].

officious /əˈfɪʃəs/ adj (derog) too ready or willing to give orders, offer advice or help, or use one's authority: *I'm tired of being pushed around by officious civil servants.* ▶ **officiously** adv. **officiousness** n [U].

offing /ˈɒfɪŋ; US ˈɔːf-/ n **IDM** **in the offing** (infml) likely to appear or happen soon; not far away: *I've heard there are more staff changes in the offing.*

off-key /ˌɒf ˈkiː; US ˌɔːf-/ adj, adv **1** out of tune: *sing off-key.* **2** not fitting or appropriate: *Some of his remarks were rather off-key.*

off-licence /ˈɒf laɪsns/ n (Brit) a shop or part of a pub where alcoholic drinks are sold to be taken away.

off-line /ˌɒf ˈlaɪn; US ˌɔːf-/ adj (computing) (using equipment) that is not controlled by a central processing unit: *off-line storage.* Compare ON-LINE.

offload /ˌɒfˈləʊd; US ˌɔːf-/ v ~ **sb/sth** (**on/onto sb**) to get rid of sth/sb that is not wanted, esp by passing it/them on to sb else: [Vn] *nervous dealers trying to offload stocks in a hurry* [Vnpr] *We'll be able to come if we can offload the children onto my sister.*

off-peak /ˌɒf ˈpiːk; US ˌɔːf-/ adj [attrib] in or used at a time that is less popular or less busy, and there-

fore usu cheaper: *off-peak elecˈtricity* ○ *ˌoff-peak ˈholiday prices.* Compare PEAK[1] 1.

off-putting /ˈɒf pʊtɪŋ; US ˈɔːf-/ adj (infml esp Brit) unpleasant; disturbing: *I found his aggressive manner rather off-putting.*

off-season /ˈɒf siːzn; US ˈɔːf-/ n [sing] (in business and holiday travel) the least active time of the year; the period when there are few orders or visitors: *Many hotels close completely in the off-season.*

offset /ˈɒfset; US ˈɔːf-/ v (**-tt-**; pt, pp **offset**) ~ **sth** (**against sth**) to compensate for sth; to balance sth: [Vn] *We had to put up prices to offset the increased cost of materials.* [Vnpr] *There are certain expenses that you can offset against tax.*

offshoot /ˈɒfʃuːt; US ˈɔːf-/ n a thing or part that grows or develops from sth: *an offshoot of the parent company* ○ *remove and transplant offshoots from a plant.*

offshore /ˌɒfˈʃɔː(r); US ˌɔːf-/ adj [usu attrib] **1** at sea not far from the land: *an offshore ˈoil rig/ˈisland/ ˈanchorage* ○ *ˌoffshore ˈfishing.* **2** (of winds) blowing from the land towards the sea: *ˌoffshore ˈbreezes.* **3** (commerce) (of goods, funds, etc) made or registered abroad: *offshore banking.* Compare ONSHORE, INSHORE.

offside[1] /ˌɒfˈsaɪd; US ˌɔːf-/ adj, adv (sport) (**a**) (of a player in football, hockey, etc) in a position where the ball may not be legally played, between the ball and the opponents' goal: *The forwards are all offside.* (**b**) of or relating to such a position: *be in an ˌoffside poˈsition* ○ *the ˌoffˈside rule.* Compare ONSIDE.

offside[2] /ˌɒfˈsaɪd; US ˌɔːf-/ (also **off**) adj [attrib] (Brit) on the side of a vehicle or an animal on the road furthest from the edge of the road: *the rear ˌoffside ˈtyre* ○ *the off front wheel of a car.* Compare NEARSIDE.

offspring /ˈɒfsprɪŋ; US ˈɔːf-/ n (pl unchanged) (fml or joc) (**a**) a child or children of a particular person or couple: *She's the offspring of a scientist and a musician.* ○ *Their offspring are all very clever.* (**b**) the young of an animal: *How many offspring does a cat usually have?*

off-stage /ˌɒf ˈsteɪdʒ; US ˌɔːf-/ adj, adv not on the stage; not visible to the audience: *an ˌoff-stage ˈscream* ○ *At this point in the play, most of the actors are off-stage.* Compare ON-STAGE.

off-street /ˈɒf striːt; US ˈɔːf-/ adj [attrib] not on the public road: *off-street parking only.*

off-white /ˌɒf ˈwaɪt; US ˌɔːf-/ n, adj not pure white, but white with a little grey or yellow in it: *paint a room off-white* ○ *ˌoff-white ˈpaint.*

oft /ɒft; US ɔːft/ adv (arch) (esp in compounds) often: *an oft-repeated warning.*

often /ˈɒfn, ˈɒftən; US ˈɔːfn/ adv (**-er**, **-est**) **1** many times; at short intervals; frequently: *We often go there.* ○ *We have often been there.* ○ *We've been there quite often.* ○ *It very often rains here in April.* ○ *I hope to visit you oftener in future.* ○ *How often* (ie At what intervals) *do the buses run?* **2** in many instances; commonly: *Old houses are often damp.* **IDM** **as ˌoften as ˈnot**; **more ˌoften than ˈnot** very frequently: *Even when it's fine the buses are late more often than not.* **ˌevery so ˈoften** occasionally; from time to time. **once too often** ⇨ ONCE.

ogle /ˈəʊgl/ v ~ (**at sb**) (derog) to look or stare at sb, esp a woman, in a way that suggests sexual interest: [Vn, Vpr] *She dislikes being ogled (at).* [also V].

ogre /ˈəʊgə(r)/ n (fem **ogress** /ˈəʊgres/) **1** (in stories) a cruel and frightening giant who eats people. **2** a very frightening person: *My boss is a real ogre.*

oh (also **O**) /əʊ/ interj **1** (used for emphasis or when reacting to sth that has been said): *Oh yes I will.* ○ *Oh dear!* ○ *Oh well, never mind.* **2** (expressing surprise, fear, joy, etc): *Oh look!* ○ *Oh, how horrible!*

---

3 (used to attract sb's attention): *Oh Pam, can you come over here for a minute?* Compare AH.

ohm /əʊm/ *n* the unit of electrical resistance(5).

OHMS /ˌaʊ eɪtʃ em ˈes/ *abbr* (*Brit*) (esp on official forms, envelopes, etc) On Her/His Majesty's Service.

oi /ɔɪ/ *interj* (*Brit*) (used to call attention, esp in an angry way): *Oi, you! Get out of my garden!*

-oid *suff* (with *adjs* and *ns*) resembling; similar to: *humanoid* ○ *rhomboid.*

oil rig

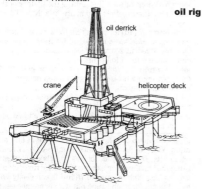

oil derrick

crane   helicopter deck

oil /ɔɪl/ *n* **1** [U] any of various thick liquids that do not mix with water and usu burn easily, obtained from animals, plants or minerals: ˈcoconut/ ˈsunflower/ˈvegetable oil ○ ˌolive ˈoil ○ ˈcooking oil ○ ˌcod-liver ˈoil ○ ˈsalad oil. **2** [U] (**a**) PETROLEUM found in rock underground: *drilling for oil in the desert* ○ *crude oil.* (**b**) (often in compounds) a form of this used esp as fuel or to make machinery move easily: *an* ˈoil-heater/-lamp/-stove ○ ˈengine oil ○ *Put some oil in the car.* **3** [U] any of various thick liquids used on the hair, skin, etc as a COSMETIC: ˈsun-tan oil ○ ˈbath oil. **4**(**a**) **oils** [pl] paints made by mixing colouring matter in oil: *paint in oils.* (**b**) [C] (*infml*) a picture painted with these. **IDM** **burn the midnight oil** ⇨ BURN. **pour oil on troubled water** ⇨ POUR. **strike gold/oil** ⇨ STRIKE².
▸ **oil** *v* to put oil on or into sth, eg to make part of a machine run smoothly: [Vn] *oil a lock/one's bicycle/ a stiff hinge.* **IDM** **oil the ˈwheels** to make sth happen smoothly and without problems: *Having friends on the council helped to oil the wheels (of the campaign).*
■ ˌoil-ˈfired *adj* (of a heating system, etc) burning oil as fuel: ˌoil-fired central ˈheating.
ˈoil-paint (also ˈoil-colour, *US* **-color**) *n* [C, U] = OILS (OIL 4a).
ˈoil-painting *n* **1** [U] the art of painting using oils (OIL 4a): *She enjoys oil-painting.* **2** [C] a picture painted in oils (OIL 4a). **IDM** **be no ˈoil-painting** (*Brit infml joc*) to be a plain¹(5) or ugly person.
ˈoil rig *n* a structure with which to extract oil from under the ground or under the sea. ⇨ picture.
ˈoil-slick *n* = SLICK *n*.
ˈoil-tanker *n* a large ship with tanks for carrying oil, esp PETROLEUM.
ˈoil well *n* a hole made in the ground to obtain PETROLEUM.

oilcan /ˈɔɪlkæn/ *n* a can containing oil, esp one with a long thin part at the top for applying oil to machinery. ⇨ picture at CAN¹.

oilcloth /ˈɔɪlklɒθ, *US* -klɔːθ/ *n* [U] cotton material treated with oil to make it resist water. It is used as a covering for shelves, tables, etc.

oilfield /ˈɔɪlfiːld/ *n* an area where oil is found in the ground or under the sea: *North Sea oilfields.*

oilman /ˈɔɪlmæn/ *n* (*pl* **-men** /-men/) a man who works in the oil industry.

oilskin /ˈɔɪlskɪn/ *n* (**a**) [U] cloth treated with oil to make it resist water. (**b**) [C] a coat, etc made of this material. (**c**) **oilskins** [pl] a set of clothes made of this material: *Sailors wear oilskins in stormy weather.*

oily /ˈɔɪli/ *adj* (**-ier, -iest**) **1** of or like oil: *an oily liquid.* **2** covered or soaked with oil; containing much oil: *oily hair* ○ *an oily skin* ○ *an oily rag* ○ *oily food.* **3** (*derog*) trying too hard to win favour by insincere praise, being very polite, etc: *He smiled at me in an oily manner.* ▸ **oiliness** *n*.

oink /ɔɪŋk/ *interj, n* (used to represent the sound a pig makes).

ointment /ˈɔɪntmənt/ *n* [C, U] a smooth oily substance rubbed on the skin to heal injuries, etc or as a COSMETIC. **IDM** **a/the fly in the ointment** ⇨ FLY².

okay (also **OK**) /ˌəʊˈkeɪ/ *adj, adv* (*infml*) all right; satisfactory or in a satisfactory way: *I hope the children are okay.* ○ *I think I did OK in the exam.* ○ *We'll go to the cinema tomorrow, OK?* (ie is that agreed?) ○ *Whatever you want to wear is OK by/with me.*
▸ **okay** (also **OK**) *interj* (*infml*) all right; yes: *'Will you help me?' 'OK.'* ○ *Okay, children, let's clear up the room now.*
okay (also **OK**) *v* (*infml*) to agree to sth; to approve of sth: [Vn] *He okayed/OK'd my idea.*
okay (also **OK**) *n* [sing] (*infml*) agreement; permission: *Have they given you their okay?* ○ *We've got the OK from the director at last.* Compare A-OK.

okra /ˈəʊkrə, ˈɒkrə/ *n* [U] the long green seed cases of an African plant, used as a vegetable.

old /əʊld/ *adj* (**-er, -est**) ⇨ note at ELDER¹. **1** (with a period of time or with *how*) of a particular age: *He's forty years old.* ○ *At fifteen years old he left school.* ○ *How old is this building?* ○ *A seven-year-old* (ie A child who is seven years of age) *should be able to read.* ⇨ note at AGE¹. **2** having lived a long time; advanced in age; no longer young: *Old people are not as active as young people.* ○ *He's too old for you to marry.* ○ *What will she do when she is/gets/grows old?* **3**(**a**) having been in existence or use for a long time: *old customs/beliefs/habits* ○ *old clothes/cars/ houses* ○ *the same old excuses* ○ *This carpet's getting pretty old now.* (**b**) [attrib] belonging to past times; not recent or modern: *old religious practices* ○ *Things were different in the ˈold days.* **4** [attrib] known for a long time; familiar(1): *an old friend of mine* (ie one I have known for a long time, but not necessarily old in years) ○ *We're old rivals* (ie We have been rivals for a long time). **5** former; previous, but not necessarily old in years: *in my old job* ○ *at my old school* ○ *I prefer the chair in its old place.* ○ *We had a larger garden at our old house.* ⇨ note. **6** [attrib] (*infml or joc*) (used as a term of affection or to refer casually to sth): *Dear old John!* ○ *Good old Angela!* ○ *You're a funny old thing!* ○ *The old legs aren't as strong as they used to be.* **7** [attrib] (*infml*) (used for emphasis): *Any old thing* (ie Anything whatever) *will do.* **IDM** ˈany old how (*infml*) in a careless or untidy way: *The books were scattered round the room any old how.* **a chip off the old block** ⇨ CHIP¹. **for ˈold times' sake** because of tender or sentimental memories of one's past. **the ˈgood/ˈbad old days** an earlier period of time in one's life or in history that is seen as better/worse than the present: *We often meet to talk about the good old days at school.* **a/the grand old man** ⇨ GRAND. **have/give sb a high old time** ⇨ HIGH¹. **money for jam/old rope** ⇨ MONEY. **no fool like an old fool** ⇨ FOOL¹. **of ˈold** of, in or since former times: *in days of old* ○ *We know him of old* (ie have known him for a long time and so know him well). (**as) old as the ˈhills** very old; ancient: *This dress is as old as the hills.* **old ˈboy, ˈchap, ˈman, etc** (*dated infml*) (used esp by older men of the middle and upper classes as a familiar form of address when talking to another man): *Excuse me, old man, can I borrow your newspaper?* **(be) old enough to be sb's 'father/'mother** very much older than sb: *You can't marry him — he's old enough to be your father!* **(be) old enough to know 'better** old enough to act in a more sensible way than one did: *Have you been drawing on the walls? I thought you were old enough to know better.* **,old 'hat** (*infml derog*) not new or original; old-fashioned: *His ideas are all terribly old hat.* **(have) an old head on young 'shoulders** (to be) a more mature person than is expected for one's age. **an old 'wives' tale** an old and usu foolish idea or belief. **one of the 'old school** an old-fashioned or conservative person. **settle an old score** ⇨ SETTLE¹. **the same old story** ⇨ SAME¹. **teach an old dog new tricks** ⇨ TEACH. **tough as old boots** ⇨ TOUGH. **young and old** ⇨ YOUNG.

▶ **the old** *n* [pl v] old people: *The old feel the cold weather more than the young.*

oldie /ˈəʊldi/ *n* (*infml*) an old person or thing: *This record is a real oldie.*

oldish *adj* rather old.

■ **,old 'age** *n* [U] the later part of life; the state of being old: *He's getting very bad-tempered in his old age.* ○ *Old age can bring many problems.* **,old-age 'pension** *n* (*Brit*) a regular income paid by the state to people above a certain age. **,old-age 'pensioner** *n* (*abbr* **OAP**) (also **pensioner, senior citizen**) a person who receives an old-age pension.

'old boy *n* (*fem* **'old girl**) **1** a former pupil of a particular school: *an old boys' reunion.* **2 ,old 'boy/ 'girl** (*infml*) an old person: *the old girl who lives next door.* **IDM the ,old 'boy network** (*Brit infml*) the tendency among old boys, esp of private schools, to help each other in later life.

the 'old country *n* [sing] the country where one was born, esp when one has left it to live elsewhere.

,Old 'English *n* [U] = ANGLO-SAXON 3.

,old-e'stablished *adj* [attrib] having been in existence a long time: *,old-e,stablished 'customs/be'liefs/ 'companies.*

,old-'fashioned *adj* (*often derog*) **1** out of date; not modern: *,old-fashioned 'clothes/'styles.* **2** believing in old ways, ideas, customs, etc: *My aunt is very old-fashioned.* ○ *She gave me an ,old-fashioned 'look* (ie one expressing disapproval).

,old 'flame *n* a former lover: *She met one of her old flames at the party.*

old girl *n* ⇨ OLD BOY.

the ,old 'guard *n* [Gp] the original or conservative members of a group.

,old 'hand *n* ~ **(at sth / doing sth)** a person with a lot of experience and skill in a particular activity: *She's an old hand at dealing with the press.*

,old 'lag *n* (*Brit infml*) a person who has been in prison many times.

,old 'maid *n* (*derog*) a single(2) woman who is thought to be too old for marriage. **,old-'maidish** *adj* (*derog*) having characteristics thought to be typical of an old maid, eg disliking anything rude or rough, etc; PRIM(1).

,old 'man *n* (*infml*) one's father or husband or employer, etc: *How's your old man* (eg your husband) *these days?*

,old 'master *n* (**a**) an important painter of the past, esp of the 13th–17th centuries in Europe. (**b**) a picture painted by such a person.

,Old 'Nick *n* (*dated infml joc*) the devil.

,old 'people's home (also **,old 'folks' home**) *n* (*infml*) a place where old people live and are cared for: *His mother is in an old folks' home.*

,old school 'tie *n* (*esp Brit*) **1** a tie worn by former pupils of a particular school. **2** the principle of excessive or sentimental loyalty to one's former

school and fellow pupils or traditional values, ideas, etc.

,old 'stager *n* (*infml*) a person with long experience in a particular activity.

'old-style *adj* [attrib] typical of former times; old-fashioned: *an old-style Conservative politician.*

,old 'sweat *n* (*Brit infml*) a person, esp a soldier, with many years' experience.

the ,Old 'Testament *n* [sing] the first of the two main divisions of the Bible, telling the history of the Jews and their beliefs. Compare THE NEW TESTAMENT.

'old-time *adj* [attrib] belonging to or typical of former times: *,old-time 'dancing.* **,old-'timer** *n* a person who has lived in a place or been associated with a club, job, etc for a long time.

,old 'woman *n* (*infml*) **1** one's wife or mother. **2** (*derog*) a man who is easily frightened or who worries too much about unimportant things.

'old-world *adj* [attrib] belonging to past times; not modern: *a cottage with old-world charm.*

the ,Old 'World *n* [sing] Europe, Asia and Africa. Compare THE NEW WORLD.

NOTE Compare **old, aged, elderly, ancient** and **antique**. You can use **old** to talk about people, animals or objects. It usually describes somebody or something that has lived or existed for a long time: *an old woman/dog/church.* An **old friend** is somebody you have known for a long time but who is not necessarily old in age: *Kate's an old friend of mine — we were at school together.* **Old** can also mean 'former' or 'previous': *He was much happier at his old school.* ○ *my sister's old boyfriend.*

Aged is more formal than **old** and is used to describe very old people who have possibly become physically weak. **Elderly** is a polite word to describe old people and is often used in official language: *There are increasing numbers of elderly people in western societies.* People may also say **older person/ people** as a polite way of saying somebody is not young: *Many older people in Britain live alone on low incomes.*

Ancient and **antique** are usually only applied to things. Something **ancient** existed thousands of years ago: *the ancient Greek civilization* ○ *She's studying ancient history.* **Antique** describes an object which has survived from the past and so is valuable now: *He collects antique furniture.*

olde /əʊld, ˈəʊldi/ *adj* [attrib] (*arch or joc*) (esp in names of places) old; of a past age: *a pub that tries to recreate the flavour of Olde England.*

olden /ˈəʊldən/ *adj* [attrib] (*arch*) of a past age: *in olden times/days.*

oleander /ˌəʊliˈændə(r)/ *n* [C,U] a Mediterranean bush with red, white or pink flowers and tough leaves.

O level /ˈəʊ levl/ = ORDINARY LEVEL. Compare A LEVEL, GCSE.

olfactory /ɒlˈfæktəri/ *adj* (*fml*) of or relating to the sense of smell: *the olfactory nerves/organs.*

oligarchy /ˈɒlɪgɑːki/ *n* **1(a)** [U] a form of government in which a small group of people hold all the power. (**b**) [CGp] these people as a group. **2** [C] a country governed by an oligarchy.

olive /ˈɒlɪv/ *n* **1(a)** [C] a small bitter green or black fruit. Olives are used for food and for their oil: *stuffed olives* ○ *put olives in a salad.* (**b**) [C] the tree on which this fruit grows: *olive trees* ○ *a grove of olives.* **2** (also **,olive-'green**) [U] the yellowish green colour of an olive.

▶ **olive** *adj* **1** yellowish green: *olive paint.* **2** (of the skin) yellowish brown: *an olive complexion.*

■ **'olive branch** *n* a symbol of peace; a thing said or done to show that one wishes to make peace with sb:

807

on

He *held out an olive branch* to the workers by agreeing to discuss their grievances.
‚olive 'oil n [U] oil extracted from olives.

Olympiad /ə'lɪmpiæd/ n an instance of the holding of the modern Olympic Games: *The 21st Olympiad took place in Montreal.*

Olympian /ə'lɪmpiən/ adj (fml) (of manners, etc) very impressive or superior: *maintain an air of Olympian detachment.*

Olympic /ə'lɪmpɪk/ adj [attrib] of or connected with the Olympic Games: *an Olympic athlete* ○ *break the Olympic 5000 metres record.*
■ **the O‚lympic 'Games** (also **the Olympics**) n [pl] an international sports festival held every four years in a different country: *the 1992 Barcelona Olympics.*

OM /‚əʊ 'em/ abbr (in Britain) Order of Merit: *be awarded the OM* ○ *Henry Moore OM.*

ombudsman /'ɒmbʊdzmən, -mæn/ n (pl **-men** /-mən/) an official appointed by a government to investigate and report on complaints made by citizens against public authorities.

omega /'əʊmɪgə; US əʊ'megə/ n the last letter of the Greek alphabet (Ω, ω).

omelette (also **omelet**) /'ɒmlət/ n a dish of eggs beaten together and fried, often with cheese, meat, vegetables, etc or with a sweet filling: *a ham and mushroom omelette.*

omen /'əʊmen, -mən/ n ~ (of sth) an event regarded as a sign that sth good or bad will happen in the future: *a good/bad omen* ○ *an omen of victory* ○ *words of ill omen.*

ominous /'ɒmɪnəs/ adj suggesting that sth bad is going to happen; threatening: *an ominous silence* ○ *Those black clouds are/look a bit ominous.* ▶ **ominously** adv.

omission /ə'mɪʃn/ n **1** [U] the action of omitting or leaving out sb/sth: *The play was shortened by the omission of two scenes.* ○ *His omission from the team is rather surprising.* ○ (fml) *sins of omission* (ie not doing things that should be done). **2** [C] a thing that is omitted: *There are some notable omissions in/from the list.*

omit /ə'mɪt/ v (-tt-) **1** to fail to do sth: [V.to inf] *She omitted to mention that the gun was loaded.* **2** to EXCLUDE(3) sth; to leave sth out: [Vn] *This chapter may be omitted.*

omni- comb form all; everywhere: *omnipotence* ○ *omniscience* ○ *omnivorous.*

omnibus /'ɒmnɪbəs/ n (pl **-buses**) **1** a large book containing a number of books or stories, eg by the same author: *an omnibus volume/edition.* **2** a radio or television programme combining several recent broadcasts in a series: *the omnibus edition of East-enders.* **3** (dated) a bus.

omnipotent /ɒm'nɪpətənt/ adj (fml) having very great power or power without limit: *an omnipotent deity.* ▶ **omnipotence** /-təns/ n [U].

omnipresent /‚ɒmnɪ'preznt/ adj (fml) present everywhere: *the omnipresent squalor/dread.*

omniscient /ɒm'nɪsiənt/ adj (fml) knowing everything: *Christians believe that God is omniscient.* ▶ **omniscience** /-siəns/ n [U].

omnivorous /ɒm'nɪvərəs/ adj (fml) **1** eating all types of food, esp both plants and meat: *an omnivorous diet.* **2** making use of everything available: *an omnivorous reader.*

on[1] /ɒn/ prep For the special uses of **on** in phrasal verbs, look at the verb entries. For example, the meaning of **turn on sb** is given in the phrasal verb section of the entry for **turn[1]**. **1** (also fml **upon**) **(a)** in or into a position covering, touching or forming part of a surface: *a picture on the wall* ○ *a drawing on the blackboard* ○ *dirty marks on the ceiling* ○ *Leave*

the glasses on the table. ○ *sit on the grass* ○ *leaves floating on the water* ○ *travel on the continent* (Compare: *in Europe*) ○ *the diagram on page 5* (Compare: *in the next chapter/paragraph*) ○ *stick a stamp on an envelope* ○ *a carpet on the floor* ○ *hit sb on the head.* **(b)** supported by or attached to sb/sth: *a roof on a house* ○ *stand on one foot* ○ *lie on one's back* ○ *a blister on one's foot* ○ *a ring on one's finger* ○ *lean on me/on my arm* ○ *a flag on a pole* ○ *a coat on a hook* ○ *hanging on a string* ○ *riding on a bicycle/on horse-back* ○ *a hat on one's head* ○ *sit on a chair* ○ (fig) *have sth on one's mind.* **2** in or into a large public vehicle: *on the plane from London to New York* ○ *travel on the bus/the tube/the coach* (Compare: *travel by bus, etc; sitting in the bus, etc*) ○ *have lunch on the train.* **3** (used esp with *pers prons*) being carried by sb; in the possession of sb: *Have you got any money on you?* ○ *The burglar was caught with the stolen goods still on him.* ⇨ note at WEAR[1]. **4(a)** (indicating a time when sth happens; in US English often with *on* omitted): *on Sunday(s)* ○ (US) *They're arriving Sunday.* ○ *on May the first/the first of May* ○ *on the evening of May the first* (Compare: *in the evening*) ○ *on this occasion* ○ *on a sunny day in August* ○ *on your birthday/Christmas day.* Compare IN[2] 3, AT 3. ⇨ note at MORNING[1], TIME. **(b)** (also **upon**) at or immediately after the time or occasion of sth: *On my arrival home/On arriving home I discovered the burglary.* ○ *On (my) asking for information I was told I must wait.* ○ *He flew home on the death of his parents.* **5** about sth/sb: *speak/write/lecture on Shakespeare* ○ *an essay on political economy* ○ *a programme on 20th-century music* ○ *while we're on the subject* (ie talking about it). ⇨ note at ABOUT[3]. **6** (indicating membership of a group or an organization): *be on the committee/staff/jury/panel* ○ *Which/Whose side are you on* (ie Which of two or more different views do you support)? **7** eating, drinking, etc, esp regularly: *live on bread and water* ○ *gorge oneself on sweets* ○ *be on* (ie unable to stop taking) *heroin* ○ *Most cars run on petrol.* ○ *The doctor put me on these tablets.* **8** (indicating direction) towards sb/sth: *march on the capital* ○ *turn one's back on sb* ○ *pull/draw a knife on sb* (ie to attack them) ○ *creep up on sb* ○ *On the left you can see the palace.* **9** (sometimes fml **upon**) at or near a place or time: *a town on the coast* ○ *a house on the main road* ○ *a house on a council estate* ○ *a village on the border* ○ *drive on the M25* ○ *boats moored on both sides of the river* ○ *hedges on either side of the road* ○ *I moved to Leeds just on* (ie almost exactly) *a year ago.* **10** (also fml **upon**) (indicating a basis or reason for sth) as a result of sth; because of sth: *a story based on fact* ○ *have sth on good authority* ○ *arrested on a charge of theft* ○ *On your advice I applied for the job.* ○ *You have it on my word* (ie I promise you it will happen, etc). **11** supported financially by sb/sth: *live on a pension/one's savings/a student grant* ○ *be on a low wage* ○ *feed a family on £50 a week* ○ *an operation on the National Health Service* ○ (infml) *Drinks are on me* (ie I will pay for them). **12** by means of sth; using sth: *play a tune on the flute* ○ *information available on computer/disc/tape* ○ *broadcast on the TV/radio* ○ *speak on the telephone.* **13** (also fml **upon**) (indicating an increase, esp of cost): *a tax on tobacco* ○ *charge interest on the loan* ○ *a strain on our resources.* **14** with regard to sb/sth; so as to affect sb/sth: *a ban on imports* ○ *He's rather hard on his kids.* ○ (infml) *Don't go too heavy on the* (ie give me too much) *sugar.* **15** compared with sth/sb: *This month's unemployment figures are 20000 up on last month.* **16** (indicating an activity, a purpose or a state): *on business/holiday* ○ *go on an errand* ○ *on loan for a week* ○ *on special offer.* **17** (indicating a telephone number by which a person may be contacted): *You can phone me on 0181-530 3906.* **18** (also fml **upon**) (fml) (of repeated things) in addition to

[V.speech] = verb + direct speech   [V.that] = verb + that clause   [V.wh] = verb + who, how, etc clause

sth; following sth: *suffer disaster on disaster* ○ *Wave (up)on wave of violence spread through the city.*

on² /ɒn/ *adv part* For the special uses of **on** in phrasal verbs, look at the verb entries. For example, the meaning of **get on** is given in the phrasal verb section of the entry for **get**. **1** (indicating continued activity, progress or state): *He worked on without a break.* ○ *If you like a good story, read on.* ○ *They wanted the band to play on.* ○ *The war still went on* (ie continued). ○ *He slept on through all the noise.* **2** (indicating movement forward or progress in space or time): *run/walk/hurry on to the end of the lane* ○ *Please send my letter on to my new address.* ○ *from that day on* (ie from then until now) ○ *On with the show* (ie Let it begin/continue)! **3(a)** (of clothes) in position on sb's body; being worn: *Put your coat on.* ○ *Why doesn't she have her glasses on?* ○ *Your hat's not on straight.* **(b)** in the correct position above or forming part of sth: *Make sure the lid is on.* ○ *Leave it with the cover on.* ○ *The skirt is finished — I'm now going to sew a pocket on.* Compare OFF² 2. **4(a)** (esp of an electrical apparatus, etc or a power supply) in action or use; being operated: *The lights were all on.* ○ *The TV is always on in their house.* ○ *Someone has left the tap on* (ie The water is running). ○ *I can smell gas — is the oven on?* ○ *Make sure you put the handbrake on.* **(b)** available or connected: *We were without electricity for three hours but it's on again now.* ○ *Is the water on?* Compare OFF² 5. **5** (of a performance, play, etc) in progress: *The show was already on when we arrived.* ○ *The strike has been on now for six weeks.* ○ *There's a war on, you know.* **6** planned to take place in the future: *Is the match on at 2 pm or 3 pm? The postal strike is still on* (ie has not been cancelled). Compare OFF² 4. **7** (of programmes, films, entertainments, etc) that can be seen; being performed: *Look in the TV guide to see what's on.* ○ *There's a good play on at the local theatre.* ○ *What time is the news on?* **8** arranged to take place; happening: *Have we got anything on* (ie any plans, appointments, etc) *for this evening?* **9(a)** (of a performer) on the stage; performing: *I'm on in five minutes.* ○ *What time is the group on?* Compare OFF² 9. **(b)** (of a worker) on duty; working: *The night nurse is/goes on at 7 pm.* Compare OFF² 7. **10** in or into a vehicle; inside: *The bus driver waited until everybody was on.* ○ *Four people got on.* **11** with the specified part in front or at the point of contact: *enter the harbour broadside on* ○ *The cars crashed head on.* **IDM** **be 'on** (*infml esp Brit*) to be practical, right or acceptable: *That just isn't on.* ○ *You're on* (ie I accept the bet, suggestion, etc)! **be 'on (for sth)** (*infml*) to be ready to take part in sth: *Are you on for tomorrow's game?* **be/go/keep 'on about sth** (*infml derog*) to talk in a boring or complaining way about sth: *What's he on about now?* **be/go/keep 'on at sb (to do sth)** (*infml derog*) to annoy or tire sb with frequent requests, criticisms, etc: *He was on at me again to lend him money.* ○ *They kept on at him until he confessed.* Compare BE ONTO SB (ONTO). **off and on / on and off** ⇨ OFF². **,on and 'on** without stopping; continuously: *He kept moaning on and on.* ■ **on to** *prep* = ONTO.

once /wʌns/ *adv* **1** on one occasion only; one time: *I've only been there once.* ○ *He cleans his car once a week.* ○ *She only sees her parents once every six months.* **2(a)** at some time in the past: *I once met your mother.* ○ *He once lived in Zambia.* **(b)** formerly: *This book was famous once, but nobody reads it today.* **3** (in negative sentences or questions) ever; at all: *He never once offered/He didn't once offer to help.* **IDM** **,all at 'once 1** suddenly: *All at once the door opened.* ○ *All at once she lost her temper.* **2** all together; all at one time: *I can't do everything all at once — you'll have to be patient.* ○ *The bills came all at once.* **at 'once 1** immediately; without delay:

Come here at once! ○ *She fell asleep almost at once.* **2** at the same time: *Don't all speak at once!* ○ *I can't do two things at once.* ○ *The film is at once humorous and moving.* **(just) for 'once; just this 'once** on this occasion only, as an exception: *Just for once he arrived on time.* ○ *Can't you be nice to each other just this once?* **once a'gain; once 'more** one more time; another time: *I'll tell you how to do it once again.* ○ *Let's play it once more.* **once and for 'all** now and for the last time; finally: *I'm warning you once and for all.* ○ *He's travelled a lot but now he's back home once and for all.* **,once 'bitten, ,twice 'shy** (*saying*) after an unpleasant experience one is careful to avoid sth similar. **once in a blue 'moon** (*infml*) very rarely or never: *I only see her once in a blue moon.* **(every) ,once in a 'while** occasionally: *Once in a while we go to a restaurant, but usually we eat at home.* **,once or 'twice** a few times: *I don't know the place well, I've only been there once or twice.* **,once too 'often** one time more than is sensible or safe: *You've tried that trick once too often.* **,once upon a 'time** (used as the beginning of esp children's stories) a long time ago in the past: *Once upon a time there was a beautiful princess.* ▶ **once** *conj* as soon as; when: *Once you learn the basic rules, it's easy to play.* ○ *How would we cope once the money had gone?* **the once** *n* [sing] (*infml*) the one time; on one occasion: *She's only done it the once so don't be too angry.* ■ **'once-over** *n* [sing] (*infml*) a rapid inspection or piece of work: *Before buying the car I gave it the once-over.* ○ *The carpet needs a quick once-over with the hoover.*

oncoming /'ɒnkʌmɪŋ/ *adj* [attrib] advancing towards or approaching one: *face the oncoming traffic.*

one¹ /wʌn/ *n, pron, det* **1** the number 1. **2** (used rather than *a* before *hundred*, *thousand*, *dozen*, etc or before a unit of weight or measurement when one wishes to be formal or exact or to emphasize a number or amount): *The fee will be one hundred and fifty pounds.* ○ *The distance between them was over one thousand metres.* **3** (used for emphasis) a single; just one: *There's only one piece of cake left.* ○ *I found eight people living in one room.* **4(a)** an individual in a group or set: *One of my friends lives in Brighton.* ○ *She's the only one who tried to help me.* ○ *One place I'd really like to visit is Bali.* **(b)** (used for emphasis and always stressed) a specific person or thing; the only one: *He's the 'one person I can always trust.* ○ *The 'one way to succeed is to work hard.* **(c)** (indicating a particular but not specified period of time): *one morning/afternoon last week* ○ *One day* (ie At an indefinite time in the future) *you'll be grateful for my advice.* **5** (*usu fml*) (used with a person's name to show that the speaker does not know the person) a certain(5); a¹(9): *The author of the article turned out to be one Stanley Carter.* **6** (used with *the other*, *another* or *other(s)*) to show a contrast: *The two girls are so alike that strangers find it difficult to tell (the) one from the other.* ○ *I see you add the egg before the milk — that's 'one way of doing it* (ie there are other, possibly better, ways). **7** the same: *They all went off in one direction.* ○ *The workers were all of one mind* (ie all had the same opinion). **8** (*infml esp US*) (used instead of *a* or *an* to emphasize the *n* or phrase that follows it): *It was one hell of a match* (ie a very good and exciting match). ○ *That's one handsome guy!* **IDM** **be all one to sb** ⇨ ALL³. **be at 'one (with sb/sth)** to be in agreement with sb/sth: *I'm at one with you.* ○ *We are at one on this subject.* **get one 'over sb/sth** (*infml*) to gain an advantage over sb/sth: *They got one over us in the end by deciding to speak in German.* **get sth in 'one** (*infml*) to understand a point, an explanation, etc immediately: *'We have to attract younger customers.' 'Exactly, you've got it in one!'* **I, you, etc / sb for 'one** certainly I, you, etc/

sb, if no one else: *I for one have no doubt that he's lying.* ○ *Lots of people would like to come — your mother for one.* **in a minority of one** ➪ MINORITY. **(₁all) in ¹one** combined: *He's the club President, Treasurer and Secretary (all) in one.* ○ *an ₁all-in-one* sham¹poo *and* con¹ditioner. **number one** ➪ NUMBER. **₁one after a¹nother / the ¹other** first one person or thing, and then another, and then another, up to any number or amount: *The bills keep coming, one after another.* **₁one and ¹all** (dated infml) everyone: *A Happy New Year to one and all!* **₁one and ¹only** (used for emphasis) only; SOLE³(1): *Here he is — the one and only Michael Jackson!* **₁one and the ¹same** (used for emphasis) the same: *I've only just discovered that my two favourite authors are one and the same (person).* **₁one by ¹one** separately and in order: *go through the items on a list one by one.* **₁one or ¹two** a few: *One or two people didn't come.* **₁one ¹up (on/over sb)** in a position of advantage over sb; one step ahead of sb: *Your teaching experience puts you one up on the other candidates.*
For further guidance on how *one* is used, see the examples at *five*.

▶ **one-** (in compounds) having one of the thing specified: *a one-act play* ○ *a one-piece swimsuit.*

¹oneness *n* [U] a feeling of harmony or identity with sb/sth: *a sense of oneness with nature.*

■ **₁one-armed ¹bandit** *n* (*Brit*) = FRUIT MACHINE.

₁one-horse ¹race *n* [sing] a race or contest in which one person, team, etc is far ahead of the rest and certain to win.

₁one-¹liner *n* (*infml*) a short joke or funny remark in a play, comedy programme, etc: *deliver some good one-liners.*

₁one-¹man *adj* [attrib] involving or run by one person alone: *the introduction of one-man buses* ○ *union resistance to one-man operation of machines.* **₁one-man ¹band** *n* a musician, usu in the street, playing several instruments at the same time: (*fig*) *I run the business as a one-man band.* **₁one-man ¹show** *n* a public performance by one person of dramatic or musical items normally requiring several performers.

₁one-night ¹stand *n* (*infml*) a sexual relationship that lasts for a single night: *I was hoping for a lasting affair, not just a one-night stand.*

₁one-¹off *adj* [attrib] made or happening only once: *a ₁one-off ¹payment.* **₁one-¹off** *n* [sing] a thing that is made or happens only once: *Her novel was just a one-off.*

₁one-parent ¹family (also **₁single-parent ¹family**, **₁lone parent ¹family**) *n* a family in which children live with only one of their parents, eg after a DIVORCE¹.

₁one-¹sided *adj* **1** (esp of opinions, etc) unfair; showing prejudice: *a ₁one-sided ¹argument* ○ *The press was accused of being very one-sided.* **2** involving people who do not have the same ability, intensity of feeling, etc as each other: *It was a very one-sided game — we won easily.* ○ *Their relationship is very one-sided.*

¹one-time *adj* [attrib] former: *his ₁one-time ¹business partner.*

₁one-to-¹one *adj* with one member of one group corresponding to one of another: *a ₁one-to-one* re¹lationship ○ *teaching on a one-to-one basis* (ie with one teacher for each student).

₁one-track ¹mind *n* a mind that can think only of a single subject or has only one interest: *He's got a one-track mind — all he ever thinks about is sex!*

one-¹upmanship *n* [U] (*infml*) the art of getting and keeping an advantage over other people.

₁one-¹way *adj* [attrib] **1** moving or allowing movement in one direction only: *₁one-way ¹traffic* ○ *a ₁one-way ¹street/¹system.* **2** permitting one to travel to a place but not back from it: *a ₁one-way ¹ticket.* Compare SINGLE *n* 1. **3** (of a mirror) acting as a mirror to the person in front of it but used by people in the

next room as a window to see what that person is doing.

one² /wʌn/ *indef pron* **1** (used as the object of a *v* or *prep* to avoid the repetition of *a* or *an + n*): *I forgot to bring a pen. Can you lend me one?* (Compare: *I can't find my pen. Have you seen it?*) ○ *There have been a lot of burglaries in this area. I read about one this morning.* See also PROP-WORD. **2 ~ of** (used with a plural *n* preceded by a *det*, eg *the, my, your, these*, etc to indicate a member of a class or group): *She's knitting a sweater for one of her grandchildren.* ○ *We think of you as one* (ie a member) *of the family.*

▶ **one** *n* **1** (never taking main stress) (used after *this, that, which* or after an *adj* which cannot stand alone): *I prefer ¹that one.* ○ *Which ones have you ¹read?* ○ *Your plan is a ¹good one.* ○ *Her new car goes faster than the ¹old one.* **2 the one(s)** (used with a group of words that identify the person(s) or thing(s) being considered): *Our hotel is the one nearest the beach.* ○ *Students who do well in examinations are often the ones who ask questions in class.* **IDM a ¹one** (*infml esp Brit*) (used to show surprise and amusement at sb's behaviour): *He is a one, your son. Never out of trouble!* **the one about sb/sth** the joke about sb/sth: *Do you know/Have you heard the one about the bald policeman?*

NOTE In formal speech or writing the use of the nouns **one/ones** is avoided in the following cases:
1 After a possessive (eg *your, Mary's*) unless it is followed by an adjective: *This is my car and that's my husband's.* ○ *My cheap camera takes better pictures than his expensive one.*
2 When showing a contrast with two adjectives: *The students compared British and/with American universities.* It is less formal to say: *The students compared British universities with American ones.*
3 After *these* and *those*: *Do you prefer these designs or those* (more formal than *those ones*)? **One/Ones** may be used after *which*, even in formal speech, to show singular and plural: *Here are the designs. Which one/ones do you prefer?* (ie You can choose one or several of them.)

one³ /wʌn/ *n* (used, esp *pl*, after an *adj*, to refer to a person or people not previously specified): *It's time the little ones were in bed.* ○ *pray to the Holy One* (ie God) *for forgiveness.*

▶ **one** *pron* (*fml*) a person with a particular characteristic: *She was never one to gossip* (ie the sort of person who does). ○ *He's not one who is easily frightened.* **IDM (be) one for (doing) sth** (to be) a person who is good at or spends a lot of time doing sth: *She's a great one for (solving) puzzles.*

■ **₁one a¹nother** *pron* each for or with the other or others; each other: *listening to one another's records* ○ *We help one another when we can.*

one⁴ /wʌn/ *pers pron* (*fml*) (used as the subject or object of a *v*, or after a *prep* to refer to people generally, including the speaker or writer): *In these circumstances one prefers to be alone.* ○ *One must be sure of one's facts before making a public accusation.*

onerous /¹əʊnərəs/ *adj* (*fml*) demanding much effort or causing much difficulty: *onerous duties/tasks.*

oneself /wʌn¹self/ *reflex, emph pron* (only taking the main stress in sentences when used emphatically) **1** (*reflex*) (used when people in general cause and are also affected by an action): *one's ability to wash and ¹dress oneself.* **2** (*emph*) (used to emphasize *one*): *One could easily arrange it all one¹self.* **IDM (all) by one¹self 1** alone. **2** without help.

ongoing /¹ɒngəʊɪŋ/ *adj* [usu attrib] continuing to exist or go forward: *an ongoing debate* ○ *ongoing research.*

onion /¹ʌnjən/ *n* [C, U] a round white vegetable with many layers inside each other. Onions have a strong smell and flavour and are used in cooking:

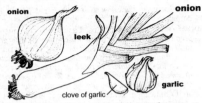

onion   onion   leek   garlic   clove of garlic

plant a row of onions ○ *spring onions* ○ *onion soup.* ⇨ picture. **IDM** **know one's onions** ⇨ KNOW.

on-line /ˌɒn ˈlaɪn/ *adj* (*computing*) (of equipment or a process) connected to and controlled by a central computer: *an ˌon-line ˈticket booking system* ○ *The data entry terminal is connected to an on-line database while editing is taking place.* Compare OFF-LINE.

onlooker /ˈɒnlʊkə(r)/ *n* a person who watches sth happening without getting involved: *By the time the ambulance had arrived, a crowd of onlookers had gathered.*

only¹ /ˈəʊnli/ *adj* [attrib] **1** with no other or others of the same group, style, etc existing or present; SOLE³(1): *She was the only person who could do it.* ○ *His only answer was a grunt.* ○ *This is the only painting in this style that we have.* ○ *She's their only daughter.* ○ *We were the only people there.* **2** most worth considering; best: *She's the only woman for the job.* ○ *It's the only place to eat.* **IDM** **one and only** ⇨ ONE¹.
 ■ ˌonly ˈchild *n* (*pl* ˈchildren) a child with no brothers or sisters: *My mother was an only child.* ○ *Only children are sometimes lonely.*

only² /ˈəʊnli/ *adv* **1** (used to MODIFY(2) a word or phrase and placed close to it in written or formal spoken style; in informal speech, stress may show which word, etc is modified, so that *only* may have various positions) and no one or nothing else; solely (SOLE³): *I only saw ˈMary* (ie I saw Mary and no one else). ○ *I only ˈsaw Mary; I didn't speak to her.* ○ *Only ˈmembers may use the bar.* ○ *Only ˈfive people were hurt in the accident; the rest escaped uninjured.* ○ *He only lives a ˈmile away.* ○ *We only waited a few ˈminutes but it seemed like hours.* ○ *Children may enter but only if accompanied by an adult* (eg on a sign). ○ *If you do that, it will only make matters worse.* ○ *We can only guess* (ie We cannot be certain about) *what happened.* **2** no longer ago than: *I saw him only yesterday.* **3** not until: *They arrive only on Thursday.* **IDM** **if only** ⇨ IF. **not only ... but (also)** both ... and: *He not only read the book, but (also) remembered what he had read.* **only ˈjust 1** not long ago/before: *We've only just arrived.* ○ *I've only just moved to Boston.* **2** almost not; SCARCELY(1): *He only just caught the train.* ○ *I've got enough money to buy her a present, but only just.* **only to do sth** (used to indicate sth that happens immediately afterwards, esp sth that causes surprise, disappointment, sadness, etc): *I arrived at the shop only to find I'd left all my money at home.* **only too** very: *I shall be only too pleased to help if I can.* ○ *Children can be difficult, as we know only too well.* **you're only young ˈonce** (*saying*) let young people have what enjoyment and freedom they can get, because they will have to work and worry later in their lives: *Enjoy the disco — you're only young once.*

only³ /ˈəʊnli/ *conj* (*infml*) except that; but: *I'd love to come, only I have to work.* ○ *This book's well written, only it's rather depressing.* ○ *He's always making promises, only he never keeps them.* ○ *He would probably do well in the examination only he gets very nervous.*

ono /ˌəʊ en ˈəʊ/ *abbr* (esp in small private advertisements) or near offer: *Lady's bike £35 ono* (ie the person selling it might accept £30).

onomatopoeia /ˌɒnəˌmætəˈpiːə/ *n* [U] a combina-
tion of sounds in a word that resembles or suggests what the word refers to, eg *hiss, cuckoo, thud.* ▶ **onomatopoeic** /-ˈpiːɪk/ *adj*: *'Sizzle' and 'hush' are onomatopoeic words.*

onrush /ˈɒnrʌʃ/ *n* [sing] (*fml*) a strong forward rush or flow: *an onrush of water* ○ *the onrush of powerful feelings.*

onset /ˈɒnset/ *n* [sing] a beginning, esp of sth unpleasant: *the onset of winter/disease/old age.*

onshore /ˈɒnʃɔː(r)/ *adj* [usu attrib], *adv* **1** (of wind) blowing from the sea towards the land: *an onshore breeze.* **2** on or near the shore: *an onshore development.* Compare OFFSHORE.

onside /ˌɒnˈsaɪd/ *adj* [usu pred], *adv* (*sport*) (of a player in football, hockey, etc) in a position where the ball may legally be played, ie behind the ball or with the necessary number of opponents between the player and the goal: *He was definitely onside when he scored that goal.* Compare OFFSIDE¹.

onslaught /ˈɒnslɔːt/ *n* ~ (**against/on sb/sth**) a fierce attack: *survive an onslaught by enemy forces* ○ *an onslaught against/on government housing policies.*

on-stage /ˌɒnˈsteɪdʒ/ *adj, adv* on the stage, visible to the audience: *She walked slowly on-stage.* Compare OFF-STAGE.

onto (also **on to**) /ˈɒntə; *before vowels, and finally,* ˈɒntu/ *prep* moving to a position on a surface: *move the books onto the second shelf* ○ *step out of the train onto the platform* ○ *Water was dripping onto the floor.* ○ *The crowd ran onto the field.* ○ *The child climbed up onto his father's shoulders.* Compare OFF³ 1. **PHR V** **be ˈonto sb 1** (*infml*) to pursue sb in order to find out about their illegal activities: *The police are onto him about the stolen car.* **2** to be talking to sb in order to inform them of sth or persuade them to do sth: *Have you been onto the solicitor yet?* ○ *My mother's been onto me for ages about the mess in my room.* Compare GET ONTO SB (GET). **be ˈonto sth** to have some information or evidence that could lead to an important discovery: *When did you realize you were onto something really big?*

ontology /ɒnˈtɒlədʒi/ *n* [U] (*philosophy*) a branch of thought concerned with the nature of existence. ▶ **ontological** /ˌɒntəˈlɒdʒɪkl/ *adj*.

onus /ˈəʊnəs/ *n* (usu **the onus**) [sing] (*fml*) a duty or responsibility for doing sth: *The report puts the onus of caring for children firmly on the parents.*

onward /ˈɒnwəd/ *adj* [attrib] (*esp fml*) directed or moving forward: *an onward journey/movement* ○ *the onward march of time.* ▶ **onward** (also **onwards** /ˈɒnwədz/) *adv: from the 1980s onwards* ○ *The library is open from 10 am onwards.* ⇨ note at FORWARD².

onyx /ˈɒnɪks/ *n* [U] a stone that has layers of different colours in it, used for ornaments, etc: *an onyx paperweight.*

oodles /ˈuːdlz/ *n* [pl] **~s** (**of sth**) (*infml*) great amounts of sth; lots: *have oodles of money/hot water.*

oomph /ʊmf/ *n* [U] (*infml*) energy; enthusiasm; liveliness: *You're singing the right notes but the song needs more oomph.*

ooze /uːz/ *v* (**a**) ~ **from/out of sth**; ~ **out/away** (of thick liquids) to come or flow out slowly: [Vp] *Some of the toothpaste had oozed out.* ○ (*fig*) *Their courage was oozing away.* [Vpr] *Black oil was oozing out of the engine.* ○ *Blood was still oozing from the wound.* (**b**) ~ (**with**) **sth** to let sth out in this way: [Vpr] *toast oozing with butter* [Vn] *The wound was oozing pus.* ○ (*fig*) *They oozed confidence* (ie were clearly very confident). [Vn,Vpr] *She was simply oozing (with) charm.* [also V]. ⇨ note at DRIP¹.
 ▶ **ooze** /uːz/ *n* **1** [U] a soft liquid mud, esp at the bottom of a river, lake, etc. **2** [sing] a slow flow: *a steady ooze of blood from a wound.*

op¹ /ɒp/ *n* (*infml*) = OPERATION 1.

---

op² (also **Op**) *abbr* opus: *Beethoven's Piano Sonata in E major, Op 109*.

opacity /əʊˈpæsəti/ *n* [U] the quality of being OPAQUE: *the opacity of frosted glass* ○ *the opacity of her argument.*

opal /ˈəʊpl/ *n* [C, U] a usu white or colourless precious stone, used in jewellery, in which changes of colour are seen: *a bracelet made of opals* ○ *an opal ring.*

▶ **opalescent** /ˌəʊpəˈlesnt/ *adj* (*fml*) changing colour like an opal: *an opalescent sky.*

opaque /əʊˈpeɪk/ *adj* **1** not allowing light to pass through; not transparent: *opaque glass* ○ *opaque tights.* **2** (of a statement, piece of writing, etc) not clear; difficult to understand: *use opaque language* ○ *The report was full of technical jargon that is opaque to me.*

op art /ˈɒp ɑːt/ *n* [U] a style of modern art that gives the illusion of movement by the particular use of patterns and colours.

OPEC /ˈəʊpek/ *abbr* Organization of Petroleum Exporting Countries.

open¹ /ˈəʊpən/ *adj* **1** allowing things or people to go or be taken in, out or through; not closed: *leave the door open* ○ *sleep in a room with the windows open* ○ *with both eyes open* ○ *The dog escaped through the open gate.* ○ *The door burst open and the children rushed in.* **2** [usu attrib] not enclosed, confined or blocked: *open country* (ie without forests, buildings, etc) ○ *the open road* ○ *open fields* (ie without hedges or fences) ○ *crack open a nut* ○ *break open a safe* ○ *He prefers open fires to stoves or radiators.* **3** [usu pred] ready for business; admitting customers or visitors: *The banks aren't open yet.* ○ *The shop isn't open on Sundays.* ○ *Doors* (eg of a theatre) *open at 7.00 pm.* ○ *Is the new school open yet?* ○ *She declared the festival open.* ○ *He kept two bank accounts open.* **4(a)** spread out; no longer folded: *The flowers are all open now.* ○ *The book lay open on the table.* **(b)** not fastened: *a blouse open at the neck* ○ *His coat was open.* **5** [attrib] not covered; bare; exposed: *an open wound* (ie one in which the skin is broken or damaged) ○ *an open drain/sewer.* **6** ~ (**to sb/sth**) that anyone can enter, visit, etc; public: *an open debate/competition/championship/scholarship* ○ *The gardens are open to the public.* ○ *She was tried in open court* (ie with the public being freely admitted to hear the trial). **7(a)** not kept hidden or secret; known to all: *an open quarrel/scandal* ○ *their open display of affection.* **(b)** willing to talk; honest; frank: *an open character* ○ *He was quite open about his reasons for leaving.* **8** not finally decided or settled: *Let's leave the matter open.* ○ *Is the job/vacancy/position still open* (ie available, not filled)*?* **9** [usu attrib] (of cloth, etc) with wide spaces between the threads: *an open texture/weave.* **IDM** **be an ˌopen ˈsecret** to be known to many people, though not officially acknowledged: *Their love affair is an open secret.* **be / lay oneself (wide) open to sth** to behave so that one is likely to receive criticism, etc: *You're laying yourself wide open to accusations of dishonesty.* **have/keep an ˌopen ˈmind (about/on sth)** to be willing to listen to or accept new ideas, consider other people's suggestions, etc: *I'm not convinced your idea will work, but I'll keep an open mind for the moment.* **in the ˌopen ˈair** not inside a house or building; outside: *picnics in the open air* ○ *sleeping in the open air.* **keep one's ˈears/ˈeyes open** to be alert and quick to hear or notice things. **keep an eye open/out** ⇨ EYE¹. **keep/leave one's options open** ⇨ OPTION. **leave the door open** ⇨ DOOR. **an ˌopen ˈbook** a person who is easily understood and has no secrets: *He/His mind/His life is an open book.* **ˈopen to sb** possible for or available to sb: *There are only two options open to her.* **ˈopen to sth** willing to receive sth: *open to persuasion/suggestion(s).* **ˌthrow sth**

ˈopen (to sb) to make sth available to everybody: *throw the debate open to the audience* ○ *throw one's house open to the public.* **wide open** ⇨ WIDE. **with one's eyes open** ⇨ EYE¹. **with ˌopen ˈarms** with great affection or enthusiasm: *He welcomed us with open arms.*

▶ **the ˈopen** *n* [sing] open space or country; the open air: *The children love being out in the open.* Compare IN THE OPEN AIR. **IDM** **bring sth / be / come (out) in(to) the ˈopen** to make esp secret plans, ideas, etc known to the public; to be/become known to the public: *Now the scandal is out in the open, the President has a lot of questions to answer.*

openly *adv* not secretly; honestly; in public: *discuss a subject openly* ○ *go somewhere openly* (ie where one might be expected to go secretly).

openness *n* [U] honesty; frankness (FRANK¹): *We were surprised by her openness when talking about her private life.*

■ **ˌopen-ˈair** *adj* [attrib] being or happening in the open air; outside: *an ˌopen-air ˈswimming-pool/ˈconcert.*

ˌopen-and-ˈshut *adj* easily decided or proved; obvious: *He's clearly guilty — it's an ˌopen-and-shut ˈcase.*

ˈopen day *n* a day when the public may visit a place normally closed to them: *an open day at the local primary school.*

ˌopen-ˈdoor *adj* [attrib] (of a policy, system, etc) not restricted; allowing people free access to information, etc.

ˌopen-ˈended *adj* without any limits, restrictions or aims set in advance: *an ˌopen-ended diˈscussion* ○ *ask ˌopen-ended ˈquestions.*

ˌopen-ˈhanded *adj* giving freely; generous.

ˌopen-ˈhearted *adj* sincere; kind.

ˌopen-heart ˈsurgery *n* [U] (*medical*) an operation on the heart during which the blood is kept flowing by a machine.

ˌopen ˈhouse *n* [U] a place or situation in which all visitors are welcome: *We keep open house at all times here.* ○ *It's open house — anyone can come.*

ˌopen ˈletter *n* a letter, usu of protest or comment, addressed to a person or group, but intended to be made public, esp by being printed in a newspaper: *The students wrote an open letter to the Minister of Education.*

ˌopen ˈmarket *n* [sing] the process of buying and selling goods, services, etc in public and without restrictions: *available on the open market.*

ˌopen-ˈminded *adj* willing to consider new ideas; without prejudice: *She wished her parents were more open-minded about her friends.* **ˌopen-ˈmindedness** *n* [U].

ˌopen-ˈmouthed /-maʊðd/ *adj* with the mouth open, esp showing great surprise: *The child stared open-mouthed at the huge cake.*

ˌopen-ˈnecked *adj* [attrib] worn without a tie: *an open-necked shirt.*

ˌopen-ˈplan *adj* (of a building) having large rooms and few internal walls: *an ˌopen-plan ˈoffice.*

ˌopen ˈprison *n* a prison with fewer restrictions than usual on prisoners' movements, etc.

ˌopen ˈquestion *n* a matter on which different views are possible; a question that is not yet decided or answered: *How many people will lose their jobs remains an open question.*

the ˌopen ˈsea *n* [U] an area of sea away from land: *We left port and headed for the open sea.*

ˌopen ˈsesame *n* [sing] ~ (**to sth**) an easier way of gaining sth that is usu difficult to obtain: *Having a degree is not an open sesame to immediate employment these days.*

ˌopen ˈverdict *n* an official decision stating that the exact cause of sb's death is not known: *After the inquest on the drowned man, an open verdict was recorded.*

open² /'əʊpən/ v **1(a)** to become open; to be opened: [V] *The door opened and in walked Alan.* [also Vadv]. **(b)** to make sth be open, eg to allow access or to reveal contents: [Vn, Vnadv] *open a box/a parcel/ an envelope/one's mouth (wide)* [Vnn] *open the window a crack/fraction/bit/little* (ie open it slightly) [Vnpr] *She opened the door for the cat to come in.* **2** to cut or make a passage through sth or an opening in sth: [Vn] *open a mine/well/tunnel* [Vnpr] *open a new road through a forest.* **3** ~ **(sth) (out)** to spread or spread sth flat; to UNFOLD(1a): [Vn, Vnp] *open a map (out) on the table* [Vn] *open a book/a newspaper* ○ *Open your hand — I know you're hiding something.* [V] *The flowers are opening.* **4(a)** to start sth: [Vn] *open an account* (eg at a bank) ○ *open a meeting/a debate.* **(b)** to be ready or make sth ready for use or business: [Vn] *open a business* ○ *The new supermarket opened last week.* ○ *Banks don't open on Sundays.* **(c)** to declare officially and with ceremony that a new building or event is open: [Vn] *open a garden fête* ○ *The Queen opens Parliament.* **IDM the heavens opened** ⇨ HEAVEN. **open one's/sb's eyes (to sth)** to make one/sb realize the truth about sth: *Foreign travel opened his eyes to poverty for the first time.* **open the ¦floodgates (of sth)** to release a great force of emotion, destruction, protest, etc previously held under control. **open / pour out one's heart to sb** ⇨ HEART. **open one's/sb's mind to sth** to make one/sb aware of and interested in sth: *The experience opened his mind to religion.* **PHRV ¦open into/onto sth** to give access to sth; to lead to sth: *This door opens onto the garden.* ○ *The two rooms open into each other.* **¦open ¦out** to become bigger and wider: *The street opened out into a small square.* **¦open ¦out (to sb)** to communicate more freely. **¦open ¦up 1** (*infml*) to talk freely and openly: *After a few drinks he began to open up a bit.* **2** to begin shooting: *Anti-aircraft guns opened up.* **3** (esp imperative) to open a door: *Open up or we'll break the door down!* **¦open (sth) ¦up 1** to become or make sth available: *New opportunities/ markets are opening up for us.* ○ *open up undeveloped land* ○ *His stories opened up new worlds of the imagination.* **2** to begin or make sth ready for business: *There's a new Thai restaurant opening up nearby.* ○ *He never opens up shop on a Sunday.* **3** (*infml*) to create a gap or lead; (of a gap or lead) to develop: *open up a 10-second/3-point lead* ○ *A clear gap had opened between them.* **4** to open or make sth open: *Too much exercise might open up your wound.* **¦open sth ¦up** to make sth visible or accessible; to UNWRAP, UNDO(1), UNLOCK(1), etc sth: *open up a package* ○ *open up the boot of a car.* **¦open (sth) with sth** to begin by showing, using or talking about sth: *The story opens with a murder.* ○ *The company opens the season with a performance of Carmen.*
▶ **opener** /'əʊpnə(r)/ n **1** (usu in compounds) a thing that opens sth: *a ¦can-opener* ○ *a ¦bottle-opener.* See also EYE-OPENER. **2** (in cricket) either of the two batsmen who open play. **IDM for ¦openers** (*infml*) for a start; as a beginning: *For openers we'll get rid of this old furniture.*

opencast /'əʊpənkɑːst; US -kæst/ adj [usu attrib] (of mines, etc) in which coal, etc is extracted at or from a level near the earth's surface: *¦opencast ¦coal-mining.*

opening /'əʊpnɪŋ/ n **1** [C] a way in, out or through sth; a gap: *an opening in a hedge/fence* ○ *an opening in the clouds.* **2** [C esp *sing*] a beginning: *the opening of a book/speech/film.* **3** [sing] the process of becoming open or making sth open: *watch the opening of a flower* ○ *the long-awaited opening of the new library.* **4** [C] a ceremony to celebrate a new public building, etc being ready for use: *Many attended the opening of the new sports centre.* **5** [C] **(a)** an available position or opportunity in a business or firm: *There*

are few openings in publishing for new graduates. **(b)** a good opportunity to do or talk about sth; favourable conditions: *excellent openings for trade* ○ *The last speaker gave me the opening I was waiting for.*
▶ **opening** adj [attrib] first: *his opening remarks* ○ *the opening chapter of a book.*
■ **¦opening hours** n [pl] the times during which a shop, bank, library or pub is open for business: *Opening hours are 11 am to 7 pm today.*
¦opening ¦night n (usu *sing*) a night on which a new play or film is performed or shown to the public for the first time: *The president attended the opening night of the opera.*
¦opening-time n [U] (*Brit*) the time at which pubs may legally open and begin to serve drinks.

opera /'ɒprə/ n **(a)** [C] a dramatic work in which all or most of the words are sung to music: *hear operas by Verdi and Puccini.* **(b)** [U] dramatic works of this type as an art form or entertainment: *go to the opera* ○ *an opera singer* ○ *the opera season* ○ *We're very fond of opera.* See also SOAP OPERA. **(c)** [C] a company performing opera: *the Vienna State Opera.*
▶ **operatic** /ˌɒpə'rætɪk/ adj of or for an opera: *operatic arias.*
■ **¦opera-house** n a theatre for the performance of operas.

operate /'ɒpəreɪt/ v **1(a)** (*fml*) to work; to function: [Vadv] *How does the machine operate?* [V] *The alarm was not operating.* **(b)** to make a machine, etc work; to control sth: [Vn] *operate machinery* ○ *He operates the lift.* ○ *The radio is operated by batteries.* **2** to have or produce an effect; to be in action: [V] *A new timetable is now operating.* [Vpr] *The new law operates to our advantage.* **3** to do business; to manage or direct sth: [Vpr] *The company operates from offices in London.* [Vn] *flights operated by Air France* ○ *They operate three factories and a huge warehouse.* [V] *operating costs/expenses.* **4** (of soldiers, the police, etc) to conduct an action, usu as part of a larger campaign: [Vpr] *bombers operating from bases in the North.* [V] *Police speed traps are operating on this motorway.* **5** ~ **(on sb) (for sth)** to treat sb by cutting part of their body open and eg removing or repairing a diseased or injured organ: [V, Vpr] *The doctors decided to operate (on her) immediately.*
▶ **operable** /'ɒpərəbl/ adj **(a)** that can be treated by means of a medical operation: *The tumour is operable.* **(b)** that can be used: *The mill machinery is still operable.*
■ **¦operating system** n a set of programs (PROGRAM 1) that control the way a computer works and how other programs use its resources.
¦operating table n a special table on which medical operations are performed: *The patient died on the operating table.*
¦operating theatre (also **¦theatre**, *esp US* **¦operating room**) n a room in a hospital used for operations.

operation /ˌɒpə'reɪʃn/ n **1** (also *infml* **op**) [C] ~ **(on sb/sth) (for sth)**; ~ **(to do sth)** (*medical*) the cutting open of part of a person's body, in order to remove or repair a diseased or injured part: *have/undergo an operation for appendicitis* ○ *perform an operation to amputate his leg* ○ *a liver transplant operation.* **2** [C] a business company: *a huge multinational electronics operation.* **3** [C usu *pl*] an activity in a particular area of industry, business, etc: *a company involved in building/banking operations* ○ *operations research* (ie the study of business operations in order to improve their efficiency). **4** [C] an activity, often involving several people and/or spread over a period of time: *mount a rescue/security operation* ○ *a massive police operation covering the entire country.* **5(a)** [C] an act performed by a machine: *The computer performs the whole operation in less than 3*

seconds. (**b**) [U] the way in which sth works: *super-vise the machine's operation.* **6** [C often *pl*] a movement of ships, troops, etc in war or during training: *the operations room* (ie from which they are controlled) ○ *the officer in charge of operations* ○ *take part in Operation Bumble-bee.* **IDM** **be in ope'ration; bring sth / come into ope'ration** to be/become or make sth be/become effective: *When does the plan come into operation?* ○ *Is this rule in operation yet?*
▶ **operational** /-ʃənl/ *adj* (*fml*) **1** of, for or used in operations: *early operational problems* ○ *operational costs.* **2** [usu pred] ready for use; ready to act: *The inter-city line to Leeds is now fully operational again.* **operationally** *adv.*

operative /ˈɒpərətɪv; *US* -reɪt-/ *adj* (*fml*) [usu pred] operating; effective; in use: *This law becomes operat-ive on 12 May.* ○ *The station will be operative again in January.* **IDM** **the operative word** the most signi-ficant word in a phrase, etc: *The boss is hopping mad about it — 'mad' being the operative word.*
▶ **operative** *n* (*fml*) a worker, esp a skilled MANUAL worker: *factory operatives.*

operator /ˈɒpəreɪtə(r)/ *n* **1** a person who operates equipment or a machine: *a fork-lift truck operator* ○ *a computer operator.* **2** a person who operates a telephone SWITCHBOARD, esp at the telephone ex-change (TELEPHONE): *Dial 100 for the operator.* **3** a person who runs or owns a business or an industry: *Our holiday was cancelled when the tour operator went bankrupt.* **4** (*infml esp derog*) a person acting in the specified way, usu dishonestly: *He's a smooth/slick/shrewd/clever operator.*

operetta /ˌɒpəˈretə/ *n* a short light musical comedy.

ophthalmic /ɒfˈθælmɪk/ *adj* (*medical*) of or for the eye: *ophthalmic surgery.*
■ **oph,thalmic op'tician** *n* = OPTICIAN 2.

ophthalmology /ˌɒfθælˈmɒlədʒi/ *n* [U] (*medical*) the scientific study of the eye and its diseases.
▶ **ophthalmologist** /-lədʒɪst/ *n* a person specializ-ing in ophthalmology.

opiate /ˈəʊpiət/ *n* (*fml*) a drug containing OPIUM, used for relieving pain or to help sb sleep.

opinion /əˈpɪniən/ *n* **1** [C] ~ (**of/about sb/sth**) a belief or judgement about sb/sth, not necessarily based on fact or knowledge: *What's your opinion of the new President?* ○ *In* '*my opinion, it's a very sound investment.* ○ *We should* **ask** *Bill's* **opinion about** *the layout of the equipment.* ○ *The chairman's opinion should be sought.* ○ *What are his political opinions?* ○ *It is my opinion that he should resign.* **2** [U] the beliefs or views of a group; what people in general think: *Opinion is shifting in favour of the new scheme.* ○ *The project seems excellent, but local/popular opinion is against it.* **3** [C] a professional estimate or piece of advice: *get a lawyer's opinion on the question* ○ *If you don't mind, I'd like a second* (ie somebody else's) *opinion before I make the decision.* **IDM** **be of the opinion that ...** (*fml*) to believe or think that...: *I'm of the opinion that we should take a risk.* **one's considered opinion** ⇨ CONSIDER. **have a good, bad, high, low, etc opinion of sb/sth** to think well, badly, etc of sb/sth: *The boss has a very high opinion of her.* ○ *She has a poor opinion of your written work.* **a matter of opinion** ⇨ MATTER¹.
▶ **opinionated** /-eɪtɪd/ (also ,**self-o'pinionated**) *adj* (*derog*) holding very strong views which one is not willing to change : *He is very opinionated and likes to have the last word in an argument.*
■ **o'pinion poll** *n* = POLL¹ 2.

opium /ˈəʊpiəm/ *n* [U] a drug obtained from POPPY seeds, used esp formerly to relieve pain or to help people sleep. Opium is also taken for its effects on the mind and is illegal in many countries: *opium*

smuggling ○ *Karl Marx said that religion was the opium of the people* (ie sth that gives false satisfac-tion or compensation for the harsh conditions of their lives).

opossum /əˈpɒsəm/ (*US* also **possum** /ˈpɒsəm/) *n* a type of small American or Australian animal that lives in trees and carries its young in a POUCH(3a).

opponent /əˈpəʊnənt/ *n* (**a**) ~ (**at/in sth**) a person who is against another person in a game, a fight, a struggle or an argument: *a political opponent* ○ *They easily defeated their opponents in Saturday's game.* (**b**) ~ (**of sth**) a person who is against sth and tries to change or destroy it: *opponents of abortion.*

opportune /ˈɒpətjuːn; *US* -tuːn/ *adj* (*fml*) **1** (of time) suitable or favourable for a purpose: *arrive at an opportune moment.* **2** (of an action or event) done or coming at the right time: *an opportune remark/statement/intervention* ○ *Your arrival was most op-portune.* Compare INOPPORTUNE. ▶ **opportunely** *adv.*

opportunism /ˌɒpəˈtjuːnɪzəm; *US* -ˈtuːn-/ *n* [U] (*esp derog*) the practice of looking for and using oppor-tunities to gain an advantage for oneself, without considering if this is fair or right: *political opportun-ism.* ▶ **opportunist** /-ɪst/ *n, adj* (*esp derog*): *He was a charmer and an opportunist.* ○ *opportunist burg-lars.* **opportunistic** /ˌɒpətjuːˈnɪstɪk; *US* -tuːn-/ *adj* (*esp derog*): *opportunistic behaviour.*

opportunity /ˌɒpəˈtjuːnəti; *US* -ˈtuːn-/ *n* [C,U] ~ (**for/of doing sth**); ~ (**to do sth**) a favourable time, occasion or set of circumstances for doing sth: *have/get/find/create an opportunity* ○ *a company promot-ing* **equal opportunities** *for women* ○ *an area with few job opportunities* ○ *have no/little/not much op-portunity for hearing good music* ○ *a great/golden/marvellous opportunity to travel* ○ *a wasted opportunity* ○ *I had no opportunity to discuss it with her.* ○ *Don't miss this opportunity — it may never come again.* ○ *I'd like to* **take this opportunity** *to thank my colleagues.* ○ *He is rude to me* **at every opportunity.** ⇨ note at OCCASION.

oppose /əˈpəʊz/ *v* to express strong disapproval of or disagreement with sth/sb, esp with the aim of preventing or changing a course of action: [Vn] *oppose the building of a new tower block* ○ *oppose the motion in a debate* ○ *oppose government policy on privatization* [also V.ing, Vn.ing].
▶ **opposed** *adj* ~ (**to sth**) **1** strongly against sth: *She seems violently opposed to your going abroad.* **2** very different from sth: *Our views are diametric-ally opposed on this issue.* **IDM** **as opposed to** in contrast to: *I am here on business as opposed to pleasure.*
opposing *adj* [attrib] opposite; on the opposite side: *opposing views/factions* ○ *an opposing player.*

opposite /ˈɒpəzɪt, ˈɒpəsɪt/ *adj* **1** [usu attrib] ~ (**to sb/sth**) having a position on the other side of sb/sth; facing: *on the opposite page* ○ *We sat at opposite ends of the table (to each other).* **2** (used after the *n*) facing the speaker or a specified person or thing: *I could see smoke coming out of the windows of the house directly opposite.* **3** [attrib] entirely different; contrary: *travelling in opposite directions* ○ *contact with* **the opposite sex** (ie of men with women or women with men) ○ *Their opinions are entirely op-posite.*
▶ **opposite** *adv*: *There's a newly married couple living opposite.* ○ *The woman sitting opposite is a detective.*
opposite *prep* ~ (**to sb/sth**) **1** on the other side of a specific area from sb/sth; facing sb/sth: *I sat oppos-ite to him during the meal.* ○ *The bank is opposite the supermarket.* ○ *Put the chair in the corner opposite the door.* **2** (of actors) taking a part in a play, film, etc as the partner of sb: *She had always dreamed of appearing opposite Robert Redford.*

opposite *n* ~ **(of sth)** a word or thing that is as different as possible from sth: *Hot and cold are opposites.* ∘ *What is the opposite of heavy?* ∘ *I thought she would be small and blonde but she's completely the opposite.*
■ **one's ‚opposite 'number** *n* (usu *sing*) a person with a similar job or position to one's own in another group or organization: *having talks with his opposite number in the White House.*

opposition /‚ɒpə'zɪʃn/ *n* **1** [U] ~ **(to sb/sth)** the state or action of opposing sb/sth; resistance: *Delegates expressed strong opposition to the scheme.* ∘ *The army came up against/met (with) fierce opposition in every town.* **2 the opposition** [Gp] competitors; rivals: *The opposition is/are mounting a strong challenge to our business.* **3 the Opposition** [Gp] (*politics esp Brit*) Members of Parliament of the political party or parties opposing the government: *the leader of the Opposition* ∘ *Opposition MPs* ∘ *We need an effective Opposition.* **4** [U, C] (*fml*) the state of being opposite: *the opposition between the sacred and the profane.* **IDM in oppo'sition (to sb/sth) 1** opposing: *We found ourselves in opposition to several colleagues on this issue.* **2** forming the Opposition: *The Conservative Party was in opposition for the first time in years.* ▶ **oppositional** /-ʃənl/ *adj* (*fml*): *oppositional tactics.*

oppress /ə'pres/ *v* **1** to rule or treat sb in a continually cruel or harsh way: [Vn] *The people are oppressed by a ruthless military dictator.* **2** to make sb feel anxious, uncomfortable or unhappy: [Vn] *oppressed by worry/poverty/work* ∘ *The heat oppressed him and made him ill.*
▶ **oppressed** *adj* treated in a cruel or harsh way: *an oppressed people/group/class.* **the oppressed** *n* [pl *v*] oppressed people: *the oppressed of the world.*
oppression /ə'preʃn/ *n* [U]: *a tyrant's oppression of his people* ∘ *victims of oppression.*
oppressive /ə'presɪv/ *adj* **1** cruel or unfair: *oppressive laws/rules/measures.* **2** hard to bear; causing distress: *oppressive weather* ∘ *He found the silent house oppressive.* **oppressively** *adv*: *oppressively hot.*
oppressor *n* a person or group that oppresses sb; a cruel or harsh ruler: *suffer at the hands of an oppressor.*

opprobrious /ə'prəʊbriəs/ *adj* (*fml*) (of words, etc) showing contempt; rude(1): *opprobrious remarks.*
▶ **opprobrium** /-briəm/ *n* [U] (*fml*) **(a)** harsh criticism; contempt: *incur the opprobrium of one's colleagues.* **(b)** public shame and DISGRACE¹(1): *suffer opprobrium.*

ops /ɒps/ *n* [pl] (*infml*) = OPERATIONS.

opt /ɒpt/ *v* to decide to do sth; to choose to do sth: [V.to inf] *He opted to go to Stanford rather than Yale.* **PHR V 'opt for sth** to decide on sth; to choose sth: *Very few students are opting for science courses.* ⇨ note at CHOOSE. **‚opt 'out (of sth)** to choose not to be involved in sth: *I think I'll opt out of this game.* ∘ *an opted-out school/hospital* (ie one no longer under local authority control but funded from central government).
■ **'opt-out** *n* an instance of choosing not to take part in sth: *an opt-out from the treaty* ∘ *an opt-out clause in the agreement.*

optic /'ɒptɪk/ *adj* [esp attrib] of or concerned with the eye or the sense of sight: *the optic nerve* (ie from the eye to the brain). ⇨ picture at EYE¹.
▶ **optics** *n* [sing *v*] the scientific study of sight and of light in relation to it. See also FIBRE OPTICS.

optical /'ɒptɪkl/ *adj* [esp attrib] **1** of the sense of sight: *optical effects.* **2** concerned with or used for improving the way one sees sth: *optical instruments such as microscopes and telescopes.* ▶ **optically** /-kli/ *adv*.

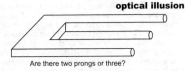
optical illusion

Are there two prongs or three?

■ **‚optical 'fibre** *n* [C, U] a thin glass thread through which light can be transmitted.
‚optical il'lusion *n* a thing that deceives one's eyes: *A mirage is an optical illusion.* ∘ *I thought I saw a ghost but it was just an optical illusion.* ⇨ picture.

optician /ɒp'tɪʃn/ *n* **1** a person who makes and sells spectacles and contact lenses (CONTACT). **2** (also **oph‚thalmic op'tician**) a person qualified to examine the eyes and recommend and issue spectacles: *go to the optician's* ∘ *The optician said I needed new glasses.*

optimism /'ɒptɪmɪzəm/ *n* [U] the tendency to expect the best in all things; confidence in the success of a course of action: *be full of optimism for the future* ∘ *There is a new feeling of optimism in the country.* Compare PESSIMISM.
▶ **optimist** /-mɪst/ *n* a person who is always hopeful and expects the best in all things.
optimistic /‚ɒptɪ'mɪstɪk/ *adj* ~ **(about sth)** expecting the best; confident: *an optimistic view of events* ∘ *She's not optimistic about the outcome.* **optimistically** /-kli/ *adv*.

optimize, -ise /'ɒptɪmaɪz/ *v* (*fml*) to make sth as good or as favourable as possible: [Vn] *seeking to optimize standards of health and safety at work.*

optimum /'ɒptɪməm/ (also **optimal** /'ɒptɪməl/) *adj* [attrib] (*fml*) best or most favourable: *the optimum temperature for the growth of plants* ∘ *enjoy optimum economic conditions.*
▶ **optimum** *n* (*pl* **optimums** or **optima** /-mə/) (usu *sing*) (*fml*) the best or most favourable result, set of conditions, etc: *For efficient fuel consumption a speed of 60 mph is about the optimum.*

option /'ɒpʃn/ *n* **1** [U] the power or freedom of choosing; choice: *I have little/no option but to go* (ie I have to go). ∘ *He did it because he had no other option.* ∘ *have the option of taking early retirement* ∘ *He was given one month's imprisonment without the option of a fine.* **2** [C] a thing that is or may be chosen; a choice: *You have only one option.* ∘ *There are various options open to you.* **3** [C] ~ **(on sth)** (*commerce*) the right to buy or sell sth at a certain price within a certain time: *We have a 12-day option on the house.* See also SOFT OPTION. **IDM keep/leave one's 'options open** to avoid making a decision now, so that one still has a choice later: *Don't commit yourself now — keep your options open until you leave university.*
▶ **optional** /-ʃənl/ *adj* that may be chosen or not, as one wishes; not compulsory: *optional subjects at school* ∘ *The CD player is an optional extra in this car* (ie It will cost extra if one chooses to have it).

opulent /'ɒpjələnt/ *adj* (*fml*) **1** made or decorated in an expensive style; LUXURIOUS: *opulent furnishings/villas/surroundings.* **2** abundant: *opulent vegetation.* ▶ **opulence** /-ləns/ *n* [U]. **opulently** *adv*.

opus /'əʊpəs/ *n* (*pl* **opera** /'ɒpərə/) (usu *sing*) (*abbr* **op**) **1** each of the musical compositions of a COMPOSER, usu numbered in order of publication: *Beethoven's opus 112.* **2** (*fml*) a work of art, esp on a large scale. See also MAGNUM OPUS.

or /ɔː(r)/ *conj* **1** (introducing an alternative): *Is it green or blue?* ∘ *Are you coming or not?* ∘ *Is the baby a boy or a girl?* Compare EITHER...OR... **2** (introducing esp the last of a series of alternatives): *I'd like it to be black, (or) white or grey.* **3** if not; otherwise: *Turn the heat down or the cake will burn.* Compare

OR ELSE (ELSE). **4** (after a negative) and neither: *He can't read or write.* ○ *They never dance or sing.* Compare NEITHER... NOR... **5** (used between two numbers to show approximately how many): *He drank six or seven pints of beer.* ○ *It was the third or fourth time I'd tried it.* **6(a)** (introducing a word or phrase that explains or means the same as another): *geology, or the science of the earth's crust* ○ *It weighs a kilo, or just over two pounds.* **(b)** (introducing a contrasting idea): *He was obviously lying — or was he?* **IDM** **or somebody/something/somewhere**; **somebody/something/somewhere or other** (*infml*) (used to express uncertainty about a person, thing or place): *He's a factory supervisor or something.* ○ *'Who told you?' 'Oh, somebody or other, I've forgotten who.'* ○ *It's somewhere or other in the kitchen.*

-or *suff* (with *vs* forming *ns*) a person or thing that does: *actor* ○ *governor* ○ *resistor*. Compare -EE, -ER.

oracle /ˈɒrəkl; *US* ˈɔːr-/ *n* **1** [C] **(a)** (in ancient Greece) a holy place where the gods could be asked about the future: *the oracle at Delphi.* **(b)** the answer given, which often had hidden meaning. **(c)** the priest or priestess (PRIEST 2) giving the answers: *consult the oracle.* **2** [C usu *sing*] a person considered able to give reliable advice: *My sister's the oracle on investment matters.* **3 Oracle** [U] (*Brit propr*) a news and information service transmitted from a computer source to specially made televisions.
▶ **oracular** /əˈrækjələ(r)/ *adj* (*fml or joc*) of or like an oracle; with hidden meaning: *oracular utterances.*

oral /ˈɔːrəl/ *adj* **1** spoken; not written: *an oral examination* ○ *stories passed on by oral tradition* (ie from one generation to the next without being written) ○ *oral history.* **2** of, by or for the mouth: *oral hygiene* ○ *oral contraceptives* ○ *oral sex* (ie in which one partner's sex organs are stimulated by the mouth of the other).
▶ **oral** *n* a spoken examination(1): *He failed the oral.*
orally /ˈɔːrəli/ *adv* **1** through the spoken word: *tribal legends that have been passed down orally.* **2** of, by or for the mouth: *not to be taken orally* (eg, of medicines, not to be swallowed).

orange /ˈɒrɪndʒ; *US* ˈɔːr-/ *n* **1** [C] **(a)** a round juicy edible fruit with a thick skin that is reddish-yellow when ripe: *oranges, lemons and other citrus fruits* ○ ˈorange peel ○ ˈorange juice. ⇨ picture at FRUIT. See also BLOOD ORANGE. **(b)** (also ˈorange tree) the tree on which this fruit grows: *an orange grove.* **2** [U] the reddish-yellow colour of an orange: *a pale shade of orange.* ⇨ picture at SPECTRUM. **3** [U, C] a drink made from or tasting of oranges: *Would you like some orange?* ○ *a gin and orange.*
▶ **orange** *adj* of the colour orange: *an orange hat.*
orangeade /ˌɒrɪndʒˈeɪd; *US* ˌɔːr-/ *n* [U, C] a FIZZY drink with an orange flavour.
■ ˈ**orange blossom** *n* [U, C] the white sweet-smelling flowers of the orange tree: *Orange blossom is traditionally associated with weddings.*
ˌ**orange** ˈ**squash** *n* [U, C] (*Brit*) a drink made by adding water to orange juice or orange SYRUP(2).

orangery /ˈɒrɪndʒəri; *US* ˈɔːr-/ *n* a place, esp a glass building, where orange trees are grown.

orang-utan /ɔːˌræŋuːˈtæn; *US* əˈræŋətæn/ (also **orang-outang** /-æŋ/) *n* a large APE with long arms and reddish hair, found in Borneo and Sumatra. ⇨ picture at APE.

oration /ɔːˈreɪʃn/ *n* (*fml*) a formal speech made on a public occasion, esp as part of a ceremony: *a funeral oration.*

orator /ˈɒrətə(r); *US* ˈɔːr-/ *n* (*fml*) a person who makes formal speeches in public or who is good at public speaking: *a fine political orator.*
▶ **oratorical** /ˌɒrəˈtɒrɪkl; *US* ˌɔːrəˈtɔːr-/ *adj* (*fml*

sometimes derog) of orators or the art of public speaking: *oratorical skills/gestures.*

oratorio /ˌɒrəˈtɔːriəʊ; *US* ˌɔːr-/ *n* (*pl* **-os**) a musical composition for singers and an ORCHESTRA, usu with a theme from the Bible: *Handel's oratorios.* Compare CANTATA.

oratory¹ /ˈɒrətri; *US* ˈɔːrətɔːri/ *n* a room for private prayer or worship.

oratory² /ˈɒrətri; *US* ˈɔːrətɔːri/ *n* [U] public speaking, esp when used skilfully to influence an audience: *The crowd were entranced by her oratory.*

orb /ɔːb/ *n* **1** (*arch or fml*) an object shaped like a ball, esp the sun, the moon or one of the planets: *an orb of golden light.* **2** an ornamental ball with a cross on top, carried by a king or queen as part of their ceremonial dress. Compare SCEPTRE, MACE¹ 1.

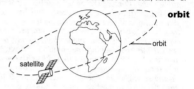

orbit /ˈɔːbɪt/ *n* **1 (a)** a path followed by a planet or moon round another body: *the earth's orbit round the sun.* **(b)** a path followed by an object, eg a spacecraft, round a planet, star, etc: *a space station in orbit round the moon* ○ *a satellite put into orbit round the earth.* ⇨ picture. **2** (usu *sing*) an area of power or influence; the scope(2) of sth: *Marketing does not come/fall **within the orbit** of his department.*
▶ **orbit** *v* to move in orbit round sth: [V] *a laboratory orbiting in space* [Vn] *the first man to orbit the earth.*
orbital /ˈɔːbɪtl/ *adj* of an orbit round sth: *a spacecraft's orbital distance from the earth* ○ *an orbital motorway* (ie round the outside of a city). — *n* (*Brit*) (*US* **beltway**) a road passing round the outside of a city: *take the London orbital.*

orchard /ˈɔːtʃəd/ *n* a piece of land, usu enclosed, in which fruit trees are grown: *apple orchards.*

orchestra /ˈɔːkɪstrə/ *n* [CGp] a usu large group of people playing various musical instruments together: *a dance/string/symphony orchestra* ○ *She plays the flute in the school orchestra.* ○ *He conducts the London Symphony Orchestra.* Compare BAND² 1.
▶ **orchestral** /ɔːˈkestrəl/ *adj* [usu attrib] of, for or by an orchestra: *orchestral instruments/music* ○ *an orchestral concert.*
■ ˈ**orchestra pit** *n* the place in a theatre just in front of the stage where the orchestra sits and plays for an opera, a ballet, etc.

orchestrate /ˈɔːkɪstreɪt/ *v* **1** to arrange a piece of music for an ORCHESTRA to play: [Vn] *piano pieces orchestrated by the composer.* **2** (*sometimes derog*) to arrange sth carefully in order to produce a desired result: [Vn] *The demonstration was carefully orchestrated so as to attract the maximum publicity.* ▶ **orchestration** /ˌɔːkɪˈstreɪʃn/ *n* [C, U].

orchid /ˈɔːkɪd/ *n* a plant, usu with flowers of unusual shapes and brilliant colours, having one PETAL larger than the other two. There are many different types of orchid: *Many wild orchids are becoming rare.* ○ *She wore a single orchid on her evening dress.*

ordain /ɔːˈdeɪn/ *v* **1** to make sb a priest or minister(3): [Vn-n] *He was ordained (as a) priest last year.* [also Vn]. See also ORDINATION. **2** (*fml*) (of God, the law, fate, etc) to order or command sth; to decide sth in advance: [V.that] *Fate had ordained that they would never meet again.* [also Vn].

ordeal /ɔːˈdiːl, ˈɔːdiːl/ *n* a difficult or painful experience, esp one that tests a person's character or ability to endure sth: *the ordeal of divorce* ○ *The hostages went through a terrible ordeal.*

order¹ /'ɔːdə(r)/ *n* **1** [U] the way in which people or things are placed or arranged in relation to each other: *names written in alphabetical order* ○ *a list of events in chronological order* (ie according to times, dates, etc) ○ *arranged in order of size/merit/ importance.* **2** [U] the state of being carefully and neatly arranged: *put/leave/set one's affairs/ papers/accounts* **in order** ○ *Get your ideas into some kind of order before beginning to write.* Compare DISORDER 1. **3** [U] the state that exists when people obey laws, rules or authority: *Some teachers find it difficult to keep order in their classes/to keep their classes in order.* ○ *The police are trying to restore public order.* Compare DISORDER 2. **4** [C] ~ **(for sb to do sth);** ~ **(that…)** a command or an instruction given by sb in authority: *Soldiers must obey orders.* ○ *He gave orders for the work to be started/that the work should be started immediately.* ○ *My orders prevent me from leaving the camp* (ie I have been instructed not to leave it). ○ *He takes (his) orders only from the president.* ○ *I'm under orders not to let any strangers in.* See also TALL ORDER. **5** [C] ~ **(for sth) (a)** a request to make or supply goods: *fill an order* (ie supply the goods asked for) ○ *place/ receive an order for 65 aircraft* ○ *He gave his order to the waiter.* **(b)** the goods supplied: *The stationery order has arrived.* See also MAIL ORDER, SIDE ORDER. **6** [C] a formal written instruction that allows the holder to be paid money or to do sth: *You can cash the order at any post office.* ○ *an eviction order* ○ *obtain a court order to allow a divorced man to visit his children.* See also BANKER'S ORDER, MONEY ORDER, POSTAL ORDER, STANDING ORDER. **7** [U] the system of rules or procedures at public or committee meetings, or in Parliament, the lawcourts, etc: *bring/call a meeting to order* (ie make people observe the rules) ○ *The delegates refused to come to order.* See also POINT OF ORDER. **8** [C *esp sing*] (*fml*) the way that a society, the world, etc is constituted or arranged: *the natural order of things* ○ *The old order in Europe saw rapid change in the late 1980s.* **9** [C *esp pl*] (*derog or joc*) a social class: *the lower orders.* **10** [CGp] (*biology*) a group of related animals or plants below a class(7) and above a family(4): *the order of primates.* **11(a)** [CGp] a group of people appointed to a special class as an honour or a reward: *The Order of the Garter is an ancient order of chivalry.* **(b)** [C] a sign, BADGE(a), etc worn by members of such a group: *wear all one's orders and medals.* **12** [CGp] a group of people, esp monks or nuns, living under religious rules: *the monastic orders* ○ *the Order of Dominican Friars.* **13** [C] a style of ancient Greek or Roman architecture using a characteristic type of column: *the five classical orders of architecture* ○ *the Doric order.* **14** [sing] (*fml*) a type; a sort: *skills of the highest order.* **IDM** **be in/take (holy) 'orders** to be/become a priest. **by 'order (of sb/sth)** according to directions given by a person in authority: *by order of the Governor* ○ *No Parking. By Order* (eg on a notice). **get one's marching orders; give sb their marching orders** ⇨ MARCH¹. **in apple-pie order** ⇨ APPLE. **in 'order 1** able to be used; valid: *Is your work permit in order?* **2** as it should be: (*fml*) *Is everything in order, Sir?* **in 'order (to do sth)** (*fml*) allowed according to the rules of a meeting, etc: *Is it in order to speak now?* **in order that** (*fml*) with the intention that; so that: *He left early in order that his children would not be alone in the house.* **in order to do sth** with the purpose or intention of doing sth: *She arrived early in order to get a good seat.* **in running/working 'order** (esp of machines) working well or smoothly: *The engine has been tuned and is now in perfect working order.* **in short order** ⇨ SHORT¹. **law and order** ⇨ LAW. **of/in the order of**

sth (*fml*) about sth; approximately sth: *Her salary is in the order of £350 a week.* **on 'order** requested but not yet received: *I've got two books on order at the bookshop.* **the ,order of the 'day 1** the state of things at a particular time: *Pessimism seems to be the order of the day.* **2** a major action or procedure that has been decided upon: *Free trade is the order of the day.* **Order! Order!** (used to call attention to the fact that the usual rules or procedures at a debate, meeting, etc are not being observed). **,out of 'order 1** (of a machine, etc) not working properly: *The phone is out of order.* **2** not arranged properly or neatly: *I checked the files and some of the papers were out of order.* **3** (*fml*) not allowed by the rules of a formal meeting, etc: *His objection was ruled to be out of order.* **4** (*Brit infml*) behaving in a way that is not acceptable or right: *Taking my car without asking was totally out of order.* **a/the pecking order** ⇨ PECK. **put/set one's house in order** ⇨ HOUSE¹. **(made) to order** (made) according to a customer's special requirements: *The shop will tailor a suit to order.* **under starter's orders** ⇨ STARTER.

■ **'order book** *n* a record kept by a business of orders for products, equipment, etc from customers: *have a full order book* (ie many orders).

'order-form *n* a printed form to be completed by a customer ordering goods: *fill in an order-form.*

'order-paper *n* (*Brit*) a written or printed programme of business for a committee, Parliament, etc on a particular day.

order² /'ɔːdə(r)/ *v* **1** to give an order¹(4) to sb; to command sb to do sth: [Vn] *The chairman ordered silence.* [Vnpr] *The boy was ordered out of the room.* [V.that] *The judge ordered that the prisoner should be released.* [Vn.to inf] *We ordered him to leave immediately.* [V.speech] *'Sit down!' she ordered.* **2** ~ **sth (for sb/oneself)** to request sb to supply or make goods, etc: [Vn, Vnpr] *I've ordered a new carpet (from the store).* [Vnpr] *We don't have the book in stock but we can order it for you.* [Vnn] *He ordered himself a new suit.* **3** ~ **sth (for sb/oneself)** to request sb to bring food, drink, etc in a hotel, restaurant, etc: [V] *We haven't ordered yet.* [Vn] *I've ordered a steak.* [Vnn] *He ordered himself a double whisky.* [Vnn, Vnpr] *I've ordered you a pizza/ordered a pizza for you.* **4** (*fml*) to put sth in order; to arrange or direct sth: [Vn] *I need time to order my thoughts.* **PHR V** **,order sb a'bout/a'round** to keep telling sb to do things: *Even as a boy he was always ordering his friends about.* **,order sb 'out (of…)** to order sb to leave a place: *They were ordered out of the city.*

▶ **ordered** /'ɔːdəd/ *adj* carefully or well arranged: *an ordered life/existence.* Compare DISORDERED.

NOTE Compare **order, tell, instruct, direct** and **command.** In everyday situations you use **tell** when you want somebody to do something: *He told me to phone back tomorrow.* ○ *I was told to get my hair cut.* ○ *We told the builder to finish the job as quickly as possible.* **Order** is stronger and is used when people in authority expect you to obey: *A policeman ordered me to stop the car.* **Instruct** and **direct** suggest giving an exact description of what you must do and are used in business or legal situations: *I have been instructed by the company to refund the cost of the tickets.* ○ *The judge directed the defendant to answer the question.* **Command** is used mainly in military situations: *The officer commanded his men to stop shooting.*

orderly¹ /'ɔːdəli/ *adj* **1** arranged in a neat and careful way; in good order: *files in orderly sequence* ○ (*fig*) *have an orderly mind.* **2** behaving well; peaceful: *an orderly football crowd.* Compare DISORDERLY.

▶ **orderliness** /'ɔːdəlinəs/ *n* [U].

orderly² /'ɔːdəli/ *n* **1** (also **medical orderly**) a worker in a hospital, usu doing jobs that do not require special training. **2** an army officer's assistant.

ordinal /'ɔːdɪnl; *US* -dənl/ (also ˌordinal ˈnumber) *n* a number defining a thing's position in a series: *'First', 'second', and 'third' are ordinals.* Compare CARDINAL².

ordinance /'ɔːdɪnəns/ *n* [C, U] (*fml*) an order, a rule or a law made by a government or an authority: *the ordinances of the City Council* ○ *by ordinance of the mayor.*

ordinand /'ɔːdɪnænd/ *n* a person who is preparing to become a priest.

ordinary /'ɔːdnri; *US* 'ɔːrdəneri/ *adj* normal; usual: *an ordinary sort of day* ○ *in the ordinary course of events* ○ *ordinary people like you and me* ○ *We were dressed up for the party but she was still in her ordinary clothes.* ○ (*derog*) *a very ordinary meal* (ie not interesting). Compare EXTRAORDINARY 1. **IDM in the ordinary way** (*esp Brit*) if the circumstances are usual: *In the ordinary way, she's not a nervous person.* **out of the ˈordinary** unusual; exceptional: *His behaviour was nothing out of the ordinary* (ie not unusual).

▶ **ordinarily** /'ɔːdnrəli; *US* ˌɔːrdn'erəli/ *adv* **1** in an ordinary manner: *behave quite ordinarily.* **2** as a general rule; usually: *an ordinarily obedient child* ○ *Ordinarily, I find this job easy, but today I'm having problems.*

■ ˈOrdinary level (also O level) *n* (formerly in British education) an examination at the lowest level in the General Certificate of Education.

ˌordinary ˈseaman *n* a sailor of the lowest rank on a ship. ⇨ App 6.

ordination /ˌɔːdɪ'neɪʃn; *US* -dn'eɪʃn/ *n* [U, C] the action or ceremony of making sb a priest or minister¹(3). See also ORDAIN.

ordnance /'ɔːdnəns/ *n* [U] military supplies and materials: *an ordnance depot.*

■ the ˌOrdnance ˈSurvey *n* [sing] (*Brit*) (the government department that prepares) accurate and detailed maps of Great Britain: *an Ordnance Survey map.*

ordure /'ɔːdjʊə(r); *US* -dʒər/ *n* [U] (*fml*) solid waste from the body of a person or an animal; EXCREMENT.

ore /ɔː(r)/ *n* [U, C] rock, earth, etc from which metal can be obtained: *iron ore* ○ *imported metal ores.*

oregano /ˌɒrɪ'ɡɑːnəʊ; *US* ə'reɡənəʊ/ *n* [U] a plant used to give flavour in cooking. It is a type of MARJORAM.

organ¹ /'ɔːɡən/ *n* **1** a part of an animal or a plant that has a particular purpose: *the organs of speech* (ie the tongue, teeth, lips, etc) ○ *the reproductive organs* ○ *The eye is the organ of sight.* ○ *internal organs* ○ *an organ transplant.* **2** (*esp joc*) a PENIS: *the male organ.* **3** (*fml*) an official organization that has a special purpose; a means of getting work done: *Parliament is the chief organ of government.* **4** (*fml*) a means of communicating the views of a particular group or party: *organs of public opinion* (ie newspapers, television, radio) ○ *The People's Daily is the official organ of the Chinese Communist Party.*

organ² /'ɔːɡən/ *n* **1** (*US* also ˈpipe-organ) a musical instrument like a large piano from which sounds are produced by air forced through pipes: *play the organ in church* ○ *organ music.* **2** any similar type of instrument without pipes: *an eˌlectric ˈorgan* ○ *a ˈmouth-organ* ○ *a ˈbarrel-organ.* Compare HARMONIUM.

▶ **organist** *n* a person who plays an organ: *a church organist.*

■ ˈorgan-grinder *n* a person who plays a barrel-organ (BARREL): (*joc*) *He's only the organ-grinder's monkey* (ie an unimportant person who does what he is told to do).

ˈorgan-loft *n* a place above the ground floor of a church, etc where an organ stands.

organdie (*US* also **organdy**) /'ɔːɡəndi/ *n* [U] a type of fine, slightly stiff, cotton material: *a white organdie blouse.*

organic /ɔː'ɡænɪk/ *adj* **1** (*fml*) of or affecting an organ or organs of the body: *organic diseases/ disorders* ○ *organic injury.* **2** [esp attrib] of, found in or formed by living things: *organic substances/ compounds/matter* ○ *rich organic soil* ○ (*fig*) *the organic growth of this sector of industry* (ie natural and slow, as if of a living thing). Compare INORGANIC. **3** [esp attrib] (of food, farming methods, etc) produced or practised without artificial chemicals: *organic vegetables* ○ *organic horticulture.* **4** (*fml*) made of related parts; arranged as a system: *an organic society.* ▶ **organically** /-klɪ/ *adv*: *organically grown tomatoes* ○ *The doctor said there was nothing organically wrong with me.*

■ orˌganic ˈchemistry *n* [U] the chemistry of CARBON(1) compounds. Compare INORGANIC CHEMISTRY.

organism /'ɔːɡənɪzəm/ *n* (*fml*) **1(a)** a living being, esp a very small one, with parts that work together: *study the effects of pollution on organisms in water* ○ *Every new organism begins as a single cell.* **(b)** an individual plant or animal: *a living organism.* **2** a system composed of parts which are dependent on each other.

organization, -isation /ˌɔːɡənaɪ'zeɪʃn; *US* -nə'z-/ *n* **1** [U] **(a)** the activity of organizing sth: *the organization of a conference* ○ *the organization of detailed information.* **(b)** the condition or state of being organized, esp in a tidy or efficient way: *She is brilliant but her work lacks organization.* **2** [C] an organized group of people; a system: *the World Health Organization* ○ *work for a business/charity organization.* ▶ **organizational, -isational** /-ʃənl/ *adj* [esp attrib]: *excellent organizational skills.*

organize, -ise /'ɔːɡənaɪz/ *v* **1** ~ sb/sth (into sth) to put sb/sth into working order; to arrange parts, people, etc into an efficient system: [Vn] *organize a political party/a government/a club* ○ *She loves to organize people.* [Vnpr] *She organized the class into four groups.* **2** to make arrangements or preparations for sth: [Vn] *organize a picnic/a protest meeting/an expedition* ○ *Who's organizing the sandwiches?* ⇨ note at ARRANGE. **3** ~ sb (into sth) to form workers into a trade union (TRADE¹), etc: [Vn] *organize the work force* ○ *organized labour* [Vnpr] *organize peasant farmers into a co-operative* [V] *To protect your rights you need to organize.*

▶ **organized, -ised** *adj* **1** showing good order; efficient: *a highly organized person* ○ *a well-organized office.* Compare DISORGANIZED. **2** arranged and controlled, esp on a large scale: *a badly organized event* ○ *fight organized crime.*

organizer, -iser *n*: *the organizers of a festival/ petition/strike.*

orgasm /'ɔːɡæzəm/ *n* [U, C] the most intense moment of sexual excitement, or an instance of this: *reach orgasm* ○ *have an orgasm.*

▶ **orgasmic** /ɔː'ɡæzmɪk/ *adj* of or like an orgasm: *the orgasmic pleasure of winning.*

orgiastic /ˌɔːdʒɪ'æstɪk/ *adj* (*fml*) of or like an ORGY; wild: *orgiastic revels.*

orgy /'ɔːdʒi/ *n* **1** (*often derog*) a wild party, usu with a lot of drinking and/or sexual activity: *a drunken orgy.* **2** ~ (of sth) (*infml*) an excessive amount of a particular activity: *an orgy of killing and destruction* ○ *an orgy of spending before Christmas.*

orient¹ /'ɔːrɪənt/ *n* the Orient [sing] (*fml or rhet*) the countries of the East, esp eastern Asia: *perfumes and spices from the Orient.* Compare OCCIDENT.

orient² /'ɔːrɪənt/ *v* [Vn, Vnpr] (*esp US*) = ORIENTATE.

oriental /ˌɔːrɪ'entl/ *adj* of or from the countries of the East, esp eastern Asia: *oriental art* ○ *a department of oriental studies.* Compare OCCIDENTAL.

[V] = verb used alone [Vn] = verb + noun [Vp] = verb + particle [Vpr] = verb + prepositional phrase

▶ **Oriental** n (*sometimes offensive*) a person from the East, esp from Japan or China.

orientalist /-təlɪst/ n a person who studies the language, arts, etc of oriental countries.

orientate /'ɔ:riənteɪt/ (also *esp US* **orient**) v **1** ~ sb/sth (to/towards sb/sth) (usu passive) (**a**) to direct the interest of sb to sth: [Vnpr] *Our students are orientated towards the science subjects.* [also Vn]. (**b**) to direct or aim sth at sb/sth; to design sth specially for sb/sth: [Vnpr] *policies orientated to the needs of the people.* [Vn] *We run a commercially orientated operation.* **2** ~ **oneself** (**a**) to establish one's position in relation to one's surroundings, the points of the COMPASS(1), etc: [Vn] *The mountaineers found it difficult to orientate themselves in the fog.* (**b**) to make oneself familiar with a new situation: [Vn] *It took him some time to orientate himself in his new school.* Compare DISORIENTATE.

▶ **orientation** /ˌɔ:riən'teɪʃn/ n [U] the action of orientating oneself or the state of being orientated: *the orientation of new employees* ○ *the orientation of birds during flight* ○ *one's sexual orientation* (ie whether one is attracted to people of the opposite sex, the same sex or both sexes).

-orientated (also **-oriented**) (forming compound adjs) directed towards: *a ¹sports-orientated course* ○ *become more profit orientated.*

orienteering /ˌɔ:riən'tɪərɪŋ/ n [U] the sport of finding one's way across country on foot using a map and a COMPASS(1): *go/take up orienteering.*

orifice /'ɒrɪfɪs/ n (*fml*) an outer opening in the body, etc: *the nasal/anal orifice.*

origin /'ɒrɪdʒɪn/ n **1** [C,U] the point where sth starts; a source: *the origins of life on earth* ○ *be foreign in origin* ○ *words of Latin origin* ○ *The origins of the custom are unknown.* **2** [C *esp pl*] a person's social background, family, etc: *ethnic/rural/middle-class origins.*

original /ə'rɪdʒənl/ adj **1** [attrib] existing from the beginning; first or earliest: *Most of the original inhabitants have left for the mainland.* ○ *I prefer your original plan to this one.* **2** (*usu approv*) (**a**) newly created or formed; fresh: *an original idea* ○ *His designs are highly original.* (**b**) able to produce new ideas; creative: *an original thinker/writer/painter* ○ *have an original mind.* **3** painted, written, etc by the artist; not copied: *an original Constable* ○ *The original manuscript has been lost; this is a copy.*

▶ **original** n **1 the original** [C] the earliest form of sth, from which copies can be made: *This painting is a copy; the original is in Madrid.* ○ *Send out the photocopies and keep the original.* **2 the original** [sing] the language in which sth was first written: *read Homer in the original* (ie in ancient Greek). **3** [C *esp sing*] (*infml esp joc*) a person who thinks, behaves, dresses, etc unusually.

originality /əˌrɪdʒə'næləti/ n [U] the state or quality of being original(2): *have/lack/show originality.*

originally /-nəli/ adv **1** from or in the beginning: *The school was originally quite small.* ○ *Originally, we were going to Italy, but then we booked a holiday in Greece.* **2** in an original(2) way: *speak/think/write originally.*

■ **o,riginal 'sin** n [U] (*religion*) (in Christianity) a condition of wickedness thought to be present in everybody from birth.

originate /ə'rɪdʒɪneɪt/ v (*fml*) **1** ~ **in** sth; ~ **from/with** sb to start from or to occur first in sth; to have sth/sb as a cause or beginning: [Vpr] *The disease is thought to have originated in the tropics.* ○ *The style of architecture originated with the ancient Greeks.* [Vadv] *How did these ideas originate?* **2** to create sth new: [Vn] *originate a new style of dancing.* ▶ **originator** n.

ormolu /'ɔ:məlu:/ n [U] a mixed metal with a gold colour used to decorate furniture, make ornaments, etc: *an ormolu clock.*

ornament /'ɔ:nəmənt/ n **1** [C] a thing designed to add beauty to sth, but usu without practical use: *The mantelpiece was crowded with china ornaments.* **2** [U] (*fml*) decoration; adornment (ADORN): *architectural ornament* ○ *The clock is simply for ornament; it doesn't work any more.*

▶ **ornament** /'ɔ:nəment/ v ~ sth (with sth) (esp passive) to add decoration to sth: [Vnpr] *a dress elaborately ornamented with lace* [also Vn].

ornamental /ˌɔ:nə'mentl/ adj of or for ornament: *Ornamental copper pans hung on the wall.*

ornamentation /ˌɔ:nəmen'teɪʃn/ n [U] things that add decoration to sth: *a plain facade without ornamentation.*

ornate /ɔ:'neɪt/ adj (**a**) decorated in a rich way: *ornate carvings in a church* ○ *That style of architecture is too ornate for my taste.* (**b**) (*often derog*) (of written or spoken words) using elaborate language to achieve an impressive effect; not simple in style or vocabulary: *use ornate descriptions* ○ *written in an ornate style.* ▶ **ornately** adv.

ornery /'ɔ:nəri/ adj (*US infml*) bad-tempered.

ornithology /ˌɔ:nɪ'θɒlədʒi/ n [U] the scientific study of birds. ▶ **ornithological** /ˌɔ:nɪθə'lɒdʒɪkl/ adj: *an ornithological journal/society.* **ornithologist** /ˌɔ:nɪ'θɒlədʒɪst/ n.

orotund /'ɒrəʊtʌnd/ adj (*fml sometimes joc*) (of the voice) grand; impressive; full of dignity.

orphan /'ɔ:fn/ n a child whose parents are dead: *He has been an orphan since he was five.* ○ *orphan girls/boys.*

▶ **orphan** v (usu passive) to make a child an orphan: [Vn] *She was orphaned in the war.*

orphanage /'ɔ:fənɪdʒ/ n a home for children who are orphans.

orth(o)- comb form correct; standard: *orthography* ○ *orthopaedic.*

orthodontics /ˌɔ:θə'dɒntɪks/ n [sing v] (*medical*) the treatment of problems concerning the position of the teeth and jaws.

▶ **orthodontic** adj: *orthodontic treatment.*
orthodontist /-'dɒntɪst/ n a specialist in orthodontics.

orthodox /'ɔ:θədɒks/ adj **1** (esp of beliefs or behaviour) generally accepted or approved; of a normal or usual type: *orthodox medicine* ○ *Her ideas are very orthodox.* Compare HETERODOX, UNORTHODOX. **2** (*religion*) following strictly the older, more traditional practices: *orthodox Jews.* **3 Orthodox** of or belonging to the Orthodox Church: *an Orthodox bishop/community/monastery.*

▶ **orthodoxy** /'ɔ:θədɒksi/ n **1(a)** [U] the state of being orthodox or holding orthodox beliefs: *a radical economist battling against financial orthodoxy.* (**b**) [C *esp pl*] (*fml*) an orthodox belief, practice or policy: *challenge traditional/entrenched orthodoxies.* **2 Orthodoxy** [U] (*religion*) the Orthodox Church, its beliefs and teachings.

■ **the ,Orthodox 'Church** (also **the ,Eastern ,Orthodox 'Church**) n [sing] a branch of the Christian Church, found esp in eastern Europe, Russia and Greece, which recognizes the Patriarch of Constantinople (ie Istanbul) as its supreme bishop: *the Greek/Russian Orthodox Church.*

orthography /ɔ:'θɒɡrəfi/ n [U] (*fml*) the system of spelling in a language: *The two languages are essentially the same, but their orthography is different.* ▶ **orthographic** /ˌɔ:θə'ɡræfɪk/ adj.

orthopaedics (also *esp US* **orthopedics**) /ˌɔ:θə'pi:dɪks/ n [sing v] (*medical*) the branch of medicine that deals with injuries and diseases of bones or muscles.

▶ **orthopaedic** (also *esp US* **orthopedic**) /ˌɔ:θə'pi:dɪk/ adj of or concerning orthopaedics: *an* *orthopaedic hospital/surgeon* ○ *orthopaedic surgery on his spine.*

-ory *suff* (with *vs* and *ns* forming *adjs*): *inhibitory* ○ *congratulatory.*

oryx /'ɒrɪks; *US* 'ɔːr-/ *n* a large African ANTELOPE with long straight horns.

OS /ˌəʊ 'es/ *abbr* (in Britain) Ordnance Survey: *an OS map.*

Oscar /'ɒskə(r)/ *n* an annual award in the form of a small statue presented in the USA for excellence in the cinema, eg in directing, acting or composing: *This movie was nominated for/won four Oscars.* See also ACADEMY AWARD.

oscillate /'ɒsɪleɪt/ *v* **1** ~ (between sth and sth) (*fml*) to keep moving between extremes of feeling, behaviour or opinion: [Vpr] *Manic depressives oscillate between depression and elation.* [V] *Her moods have been oscillating wildly since she came off the drug.* Compare VACILLATE. **2** to move repeatedly and regularly from one position to another and back again: [V, Vp] *Watch how the needle oscillates (back and forth) as the current continually changes.* ○ *an oscillating pendulum.* **3** [V] (*physics*) (of electric current, radio waves, etc) to change in strength or direction at regular intervals. ▸ **oscillation** /ˌɒsɪ'leɪʃn/ *n* (*fml*) **1** [U] the action of oscillating: *the oscillation of the compass needle/of radio waves* ○ *the economy's continual oscillation between growth and recession.* **2** [C] a single swing or movement of a thing or person that is oscillating: *oscillations of government policy.*

oscillator /-tə(r)/ *n* (*physics*) an instrument for producing electrical oscillations.

oscilloscope /ə'sɪləskəʊp/ *n* (*physics*) an instrument that shows variations in electrical current as waves in a line on the screen of a cathode-ray tube (CATHODE).

osier /'əʊzɪə(r); *US* 'əʊʒər/ *n* a type of WILLOW(a) tree. Its flexible shoots are used for making baskets.

osmosis /ɒz'məʊsɪs/ *n* [U] **1** (*biology or chemistry*) the gradual spread of a liquid through a solid part of sth: *The moisture spreads through the walls by osmosis.* **2** the gradual process of learning or being influenced by sth, as a result of being in close contact with it: *People can sometimes learn languages by osmosis.* ▸ **osmotic** /ɒz'mɒtɪk/ *adj.*

osprey /'ɒspreɪ/ *n* a large brown and white bird that feeds on fish.

ossify /'ɒsɪfaɪ/ *v* (*pt, pp* **-fied**) (esp passive) **1** (*fml derog*) to become or make sth rigid and unable to change: [Vn] *an ossified political system* [also V]. **2** [V, Vn] to become or make sth hard like bone; to change into bone. ▸ **ossification** /ˌɒsɪfɪ'keɪʃn/ *n* [U] (*fml*) the process or action of ossifying: *the ossification of traditional practices.*

ostensible /ɒ'stensəbl/ *adj* [attrib] stated or appearing to be true, but not necessarily so: *The ostensible reason for his absence was illness.* ▸ **ostensibly** /-əbli/ *adv*: *Troops were sent in, ostensibly to protect the civilian population.*

ostentation /ˌɒsten'teɪʃn/ *n* [U] (*derog*) the exaggerated display of eg wealth, knowledge or skill, intended to impress people or fill them with envy: *The Governor lives modestly, without pretension or ostentation.*

ostentatious /ˌɒsten'teɪʃəs/ *adj* (*derog*) (**a**) showing or liking ostentation: *dress in a very ostentatious manner.* (**b**) (of an action) done in a very public or exaggerated way so that people will notice, but not usu sincere: *her ostentatious concern for the poor.* ▸ **ostentatiously** *adv*: *flirting ostentatiously.*

osteo- *comb form* of or concerning bone or the bones: *osteopath* ○ *osteoarthritis.*

osteoarthritis /ˌɒstiəʊɑː'raɪtɪs/ *n* [U] (*medical*) a

painful disease of the joints of the body that causes them to swell and become stiff.

osteopathy /ˌɒsti'ɒpəθi/ *n* [U] (*medical*) the treatment of certain diseases based on the manipulation (MANIPULATE) of the bones and muscles. ▸ **osteopath** /'ɒstiəpæθ/ *n* a person who practises osteopathy. Compare CHIROPRACTOR. **osteopathic** /ˌɒstiə'pæθik/ *adj.*

osteoporosis /ˌɒstiəʊpə'rəʊsɪs/ *n* [U] (*medical*) a condition in which the bones become weak and easily broken, eg because of a lack of CALCIUM.

ostler /'ɒslə(r)/ *n* (formerly) a man who looked after horses at an INN.

ostracize, -ise /'ɒstrəsaɪz/ *v* to exclude sb from a group, eg a club or a social gathering; to refuse to meet or talk to sb: [Vn] *He was ostracized by his colleagues for refusing to support the strike.* ▸ **ostracism** /-sɪzəm/ *n* [U] (*fml*) the action of ostracizing sb; the state of being ostracized: *social ostracism.*

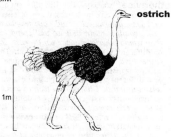

ostrich

1m

ostrich /'ɒstrɪtʃ/ *n* **1** a very large African bird with a long neck and long legs. Ostriches cannot fly, but they can run very fast. ▷ picture. **2** (*infml*) a person who refuses to face unpleasant facts: *the ostriches who still believe that there won't be a war.*

other /'ʌðə(r)/ *indef det* **1** additional or different to people or things mentioned or implied: *Mr Harris and Mrs Bate and three other teachers were there.* ○ *Other members may disagree but I feel that the subscription should not be increased.* ○ *Are there any other questions?* ○ *I can't see you now — some other time, perhaps.* ○ *I took the job because there wasn't any other/there was no other work available.* ○ *She has no close friends other than me.* Compare ANOTHER. **2** (used after *the, my, your, his,* etc with a singular *n*) the second of two people or things, the first of which has already been mentioned or implied: *Hold the bottle and pull the cork out with the other hand.* ○ *My other sister is a doctor.* ○ *You may continue on the other side of the paper.* **3** (used after *the* or a possessive with a plural *n*) those remaining in a group: *The other books belong to John.* ○ *I haven't read 'Cymbeline' but I've read all Shakespeare's other plays.* **IDM** **the ˌother ˈday/ˈmorning/ˈevening/ˈweek** recently: *I saw him in town the other day.* ▸ **other** *pron* **1** [sing] (**a**) (used after *the* or a possess *det*) the second person or thing of two or the one remaining of a group: *He raised one arm and then the other.* ○ *Ten members of the team are English and the other is Welsh.* (**b**) (used esp after *one* or *any*) a person or thing that is additional to or different from those mentioned or implied: *Answer one question from Section A, one from Section B, plus one other.* ○ *This option is preferable to any other.* **2** **others** [pl] (**a**) (used after *the* or a *possess det*) the remaining persons or things in a group: *I went swimming while the others played tennis.* ○ *I can't do questions 4 and 5 but I've done all the others.* ○ *These shoes are dirty — I'll have to wear my others.* (**b**) people or things that are additional to or different from those mentioned or implied: *Some people came by car, others came on foot.* ○ *Two buildings were destroyed by the bomb and many/several/ten others were damaged.* ○ *a parliament consisting of 100 Socialists, 90 Conservatives and 10 others* (ie from various parties) ○ *We must help others less fortunate than ourselves.*

other *adv* **IDM** **other than** (esp after a negative) **1** except: *He never speaks to me other than to ask for something.* **2** different or differently from; not: *I have never known him to behave other than selfishly.* ○ *She seldom appears other than happy.*

otherness *n* [U] (*fml*) the quality of being different or strange: *Westerners have always been fascinated by the otherness of Oriental civilization.*

■ ˌother ˈwoman *n* (usu *sing*) a woman with whom a married man is having a romantic or sexual relationship outside marriage.

other-worldly /ˌʌðə ˈwɜːldli/ *adj* concerned with or thinking about spiritual or intellectual, rather than practical, matters.

otherwise /ˈʌðəwaɪz/ *adv* **1** in different or opposite conditions or circumstances; if not; or else: *I had no problems, otherwise I would have telephoned you.* ○ *These changes mean that we will spend less money than would otherwise have been the case.* **2** in other or different respects; apart from that: *The rent is rather high, but otherwise the house is fine.* ○ *He was slightly bruised, but otherwise unhurt.* **3** in another or a different way; differently: *mulled wine, otherwise known as Glühwein* ○ *I wanted to see him, but he was otherwise engaged* (ie doing something else). ○ *The project was a failure, and it's no use pretending otherwise.* **IDM** **or otherwise** (indicating an alternative or a contrast to what has just been stated): *the desirability or otherwise of these changes* ○ *We insure against all damage, accidental or otherwise.* **know different/otherwise** ⇨ KNOW.

otiose /ˈəʊtiəʊs; *US* ˈəʊʃiəʊs/ *adj* (*fml*) (of language, ideas, etc) serving no useful purpose; unnecessary: *long, otiose descriptions.*

OTT /ˌəʊ tiː ˈtiː/ *abbr* (*infml esp Brit*) over the top (ie excessive): *His behaviour was definitely OTT.*

otter /ˈɒtə(r)/ *n* a small animal that has four webbed (WEB) feet, a flat tail and thick brown fur. Otters live in rivers and eat fish. ⇨ picture.

otter

ottoman /ˈɒtəmən/ *n* a long soft hollow seat, but without a back or arms, often used as a box for storing things.

OU /ˌəʊ ˈjuː/ *abbr* (in Britain) Open University: *an OU degree in maths.*

ouch /aʊtʃ/ *interj* (expressing sudden pain): *Ouch! That hurt!* See also OW.

ought to /ˈɔːt tə; *before vowels and finally* ˈɔːt tu/ *modal v* (*neg* **ought not to**, *short form esp Brit* **oughtn't to** /ˈɔːtnt/) **1** (used to indicate what is considered morally right or socially correct, and often, esp in the negative, to criticize sb's actions): *Children ought to respect their parents.* ○ *'Ought I to write to say thank you?' 'Yes, I think you ought (to).'* ○ *You ought to apologize.* ○ *You ought to have apologized* (ie but you didn't). ○ *Such things ought not to be allowed.* ○ *They oughtn't to let their dog run on the road.* ○ *She ought to have been more tactful.* **2** (used to indicate a desirable or expected state, esp when one is criticizing the current situation): *Children ought to be able to read by the age of 7.* ○ *There ought to be more buses during the rush hour.* **3** (used to give advice or recommend a course of action): *You ought to improve your French before going to work in Paris.* ○ *We ought to be leaving now.* ○ *This cake's*

delicious. You ought to try some. ⇨ note at SHOULD. **4** (used to draw a probable or logical conclusion): *If he started out at nine, he ought to be here by now.* ○ *That ought to be enough food for all of us.* ○ *Oughtn't the water to have boiled by now?*

Ouija board /ˈwiːdʒə bɔːd/ *n* (*propr*) a board marked with letters of the alphabet and other signs, used in seances (SEANCE) to receive messages said to come from the dead.

ounce /aʊns/ *n* **1** [C] (*abbr* **oz**) a unit of weight, $\frac{1}{16}$ of a pound, equal to 28.35 grams (GRAM). ⇨ App 2. **2** [sing] ~ **of sth** (*infml*) (used esp with negative *vs*) a very small quantity of sth; any: *There's not an ounce of truth in his story.* ○ *If you had an ounce of integrity, you'd apologize to her at once.*

our /ɑː(r), ˈaʊə(r)/ *possess det* **1** of or belonging to us: *our daughter/dog/house* ○ *our two children* ○ *We showed them some of our photos.* ○ *Our suspicions were aroused by his strange behaviour.* ○ *Our main export is rice.* ○ *We need to safeguard the future of our planet.* **2** belonging to or working for the same organization as oneself: *And now, over to our Rome correspondent…* ○ *Our managing director has just resigned.* **3 Our** (used to refer to or address God or a holy person): *Our Father* (ie God) ○ *Our Lady* (ie the Virgin Mary).

▶ **ours** /ɑːz, ˈaʊəz/ *possess pron* of or belonging to us: *Their house is similar to ours, but ours has had a loft conversion.* ○ *Ours was an unhappy marriage.* ○ (*infml*) *That dog of ours has been causing trouble again!*

ourselves /ɑːˈselvz, aʊəˈselvz/ *reflex, emph pron* (only taking the main stress in sentences when used emphatically) **(a)** (*reflex*) (used when oneself and another person or other people together cause and are affected by an action): *We shouldn't blame ourselves for what happened.* ○ *Let's just relax and enjoy ourselves.* ○ *We'd like to see it for ourselves.* ○ *Psychology provides us with knowledge about ourselves.* **(b)** (*emph*) (used to emphasize *we* or *us*; sometimes used instead of these words): *We've often thought of going there ourselves.* ○ *The only people there were ourselves.* **IDM** **by ourselves 1** alone. **2** without help.

-ous *suff* (with *ns* forming *adjs*) having the qualities or character of: *poisonous* ○ *mountainous* ○ *glorious.*
▶ **-ously** *suff* (forming *advs*): *grievously.* **-ousness** *suff* (forming uncountable *ns*): *spaciousness.*

oust /aʊst/ *v* ~ **sb** (**from sth / as sth**) to remove sb from a job or position of power, sometimes in order to take their place oneself: [Vn, Vnpr] *oust a rival (from office)* [Vn-n, Vnpr] *He was ousted (from his position) as chairman.*

out /aʊt/ *adv part* For the special uses of **out** in phrasal verbs, look at the verb entries. For example, the meaning of **burst out** is given in the phrasal verb section of the entry for **burst[1]**. **1** away from the inside of a place: *open the door and run out into the garden/corridor* ○ *Can you show me the way out?* ○ *She shook the bag and some coins fell out.* ○ *It's cold out.* ○ *Out you go!* (ie Go out!) Compare IN[1] 1. **2(a)** away from or not at one's home or place of work: *I phoned Lynn but she was out.* ○ *The manager is out at the moment.* ○ *We went out for a walk.* ○ *Let's go out this evening/have an evening out* (eg go to the cinema or a restaurant). Compare IN[1] 2. **3** (indicating a long distance away from a place, eg from land, from one's country or from a town): *The boats are all out at sea.* ○ *She's working out in Australia.* ○ *He lives right out in the country.* **4** away from the edge of a place: *The boy dashed out into the road.* ○ *Don't lean out, you might fall.* **5** (of a book, etc) not in the library; borrowed by sb else: *The book you wanted is out (on loan).* **6** (of the tide) away from the shore; low: *I like walking on the wet sand when the tide is out.* Compare IN[1] 5. **7** (esp of the sun) visible from the earth and not hidden by clouds: *It was a clear* night and the stars were out. **8** (of flowers) fully open: *The daffodils are out.* **9(a)** published or issued: *Her new book is out.* ○ *There's a warrant out for his arrest.* (**b**) revealed or known; no longer hidden: *The secret is out.* ○ *Out with it* (ie Say what you know)*!* **10** clearly and loudly so that people can hear: *call/cry/shout out* ○ *say sth out loud* ○ *the need to speak out about injustice.* **11** (*infml*) (used with superlative *adjs*) in existence; among known examples: *If you believe that, you're the biggest fool out.* **12** (*infml*) having declared to other people that one is HOMOSEXUAL: *I've always known I was gay, but I've only been out for two years.* **13** (*infml*) on strike: *bring the miners out* ○ *The dockers are out.* **14** not in power or in office: *Most people want this government out.* Compare IN¹ 8. **15** (*infml*) not fashionable: *Miniskirts are out this year.* Compare IN¹ 7. **16** (*infml*) not possible or not allowed: *Swimming in the sea is out until the weather gets warmer.* ○ *I'm trying to lose weight, so cakes and sweets are out!* **17** (*sport*) (**a**) (in eg cricket or baseball) no longer batting (BAT¹ *v* 1), having been dismissed: *The captain/The whole side was out for 106* (ie after having made 106 runs in cricket). ○ (*US*) *Johnson struck out in the second inning.* (**b**) (of a ball, eg in tennis) having landed outside the playing area: *He lost the point because the ball was out.* Compare IN¹ 9b. **18** ~ (**in sth**) not correct or exact; wrong: *I was slightly out in my calculations.* ○ *We're ten pounds out in our accounts* (ie We have £10 more or less than we should have). ○ *Your guess was a long way out* (ie completely wrong). **19** (of fire, lights or burning materials) not or no longer burning or lit: *All the lights were out in the streets.* ○ *The candle has gone out.* ○ *The bonfire has burnt (itself) out.* ○ *He stubbed his cigarette out.* **20** unconscious: *He was out for more than an hour before the nurses could bring him round.* (**a**) to the end; completely: *hear sb out* ○ *work out a plan* ○ *fight it out* (ie settle a dispute by fighting). See also ALL OUT (ALL³), TIRE SB/ONESELF OUT. (**b**) (*infml*) (of periods of time) finished; at an end: *He'll have spent all that money before the week/month/year is out.* **IDM** **be out for sth/to do sth** to be trying to get or do sth; to be determined to obtain sth: *I'm not out for revenge.* ○ *In our society, people are out for what they can get* (ie seeking their own advantage). ○ *The company is out to capture the Canadian market.* ₁**out and** ¹**about 1** fit enough to go outdoors again after an illness: *It's good to see old Mr Jenkins out and about again.* **2** travelling around a place: *We've been out and about talking to people all over the country.* ▶ **out** *n* **IDM** **the ins and outs** ⇨ IN³. ■ **out of** /¹aʊt əv/ *prep* **1(a)** moving away from the inside of a place: *jump out of bed* ○ *go out of the house* ○*fly out of the cage.* Compare INTO. (**b**) situated away from or outside a place that is enclosed or considered as a unit; not in a place: *Mr Green is out of town this week.* ○ *Fish can survive for only a short time out of water.* Compare IN² 1. **2** at a specified distance from a place: *The ship sank 10 miles out of Stockholm.* **3** because of sth; having sth as one's reason: *do sth out of mischief/spite/malice* ○ *help sb out of pity* ○ *ask out of curiosity.* **4** by using sth; from sth: *She made a skirt out of the material I gave her.* Compare FROM 8, OF 6. **5** from among a number or set: *Choose one out of the six.* ○ *This is only one example out of several I could give you.* **6** having sth as its origin or source; from sth: *drink beer out of the can* ○ *pay for a new car out of one's savings* ○ *a scene out of a play by Miller.* **7** lacking sth; without sth: *be out of* (ie have no) *flour/sugar/tea* ○ *He's been out of work for six months.* **8** not in the condition specified by the following *n*: *He's still in intensive care but out of danger.* ○ *She'll never get out of debt.* **9** so as to take or discover sth from sb, esp as a result of acting dishonestly: *cheat sb out of their money* ○ *Don't worry, I'll get the truth out of him.* **10** not concerned

with sth; not involved in sth: *It's a dishonest scheme and I'm glad to be out of it.* ○ *We're out of the championships.* **IDM** **'out of it** (*infml*) sad because of not being included in sth: *We've only just moved here so we still feel a little out of it.* ○ *She looks rather out of it — perhaps she doesn't speak English.*

out- *pref* **1** (with *vs* and *ns* forming transitive *vs*) to a greater extent than; greater or better than: *outlive* ○ *outgrow* ○ *outnumber* ○ *outwit.* **2** (with *ns*) separate; isolated: *outhouse* ○ *outpost.* **3** (with *vs* forming *ns*, *adjs* and *advs*) outward; away from; publicly: *outburst* ○ *outgoing* ○ *outspokenly.*

outage /¹aʊtɪdʒ/ *n* (*US*) a period of time when the supply of electricity, etc is not operating: *We were stuck in the elevator during the outage.*

out-and-out /₁aʊt ən ¹aʊt/ *adj* [attrib] in every respect; complete: *an* ₁*out-and-out* ¹*crook/re*¹*bellion.*

outback /¹aʊtbæk/ *n* (usu **the outback**) [sing] (esp in Australia) a remote area, far from the coast, where few people live: *be lost in the outback.*

outbid /₁aʊt¹bɪd/ *v* (**-dd-**; *pt*, *pp* **outbid**) ~ **sb** (**for sth**) to offer more money than another person in order to buy sth, eg at an AUCTION: [Vn,Vnpr] *She outbid me (for the vase).*

outboard /¹aʊtbɔːd/ *adj* (*techn*) on, towards or near the outside of a ship or an aircraft: *outboard wing panels.*
▶ ¹**outboard** *n* = OUTBOARD MOTOR.
■ ₁**outboard** ¹**motor** (also ₁**outboard** ¹**engine,** ¹**outboard**) *n* an engine that is attached to, but can be removed from, the outside of the back of a boat. ⇨ picture at DINGHY.

outbound /¹aʊtbaʊnd/ *adj* (*fml*) travelling to a destination from one's base, rather than returning home: *outbound flights/passengers.*

outbreak /¹aʊtbreɪk/ *n* a sudden appearance or start of sth, eg of disease or violence: *a fresh outbreak of typhoid/hostilities/rioting* ○ *Outbreaks of rain are expected in the afternoon.*

outbuilding /¹aʊtbɪldɪŋ/ *n* a building, eg a shed or stable, that is separate from the main building: *a large farmhouse with several outbuildings.* Compare OUTHOUSE.

outburst /¹aʊtbɜːst/ *n* a sudden violent expression, esp of strong emotion: *an outburst of laughter/anger* ○ *sporadic outbursts of violence* ○ *He later regretted his outburst.*

outcast /¹aʊtkɑːst; *US* -kæst/ *n* a person who is driven away from home, friends or society, or who has no place in society: *an outcast from society* ○ *People with the disease are treated as social outcasts.*
▶ **outcast** *adj.*

outclass /₁aʊt¹klɑːs; *US* -¹klæs/ *v* (esp passive) to be much better than sb/sth: [Vn] *In design and quality of manufacture the cars were totally outclassed by their Italian competitors.*

outcome /¹aʊtkʌm/ *n* the effect or result of an action or event: *What was the outcome of your meeting?* ○ *Further hardship will be the inevitable outcome of these spending cuts.*

outcrop /¹aʊtkrɒp/ *n* a large mass of rock that stands above the surface of the ground: *perched on a rocky outcrop.*

outcry /¹aʊtkraɪ/ *n* ~ (**over/against sth**) a strong public protest: *There has been an outcry from environmental groups over/against the proposal to build the new airport.*

outdated /₁aʊt¹deɪtɪd/ *adj* no longer current; old-fashioned: ₁*outdated e*¹*quipment/*¹*working methods/* tra¹*ditions* ○ *Her ideas on education are pretty outdated.* Compare OUT-OF-DATE.

outdistance /₁aʊt¹dɪstəns/ *v* to move faster than and leave behind a competitor in a race, etc: [Vn] *She easily outdistanced the other runners.*

outdo /₁aʊt¹duː/ *v* (*3rd pers sing pres t* **-does** /-¹dʌz/; *pt* **-did** /-¹dɪd/; *pp* **-done** /-¹dʌn/) to do more or better than sb: *a contest in which each tries to outdo the others in strength* ○ **Not to be outdone** (ie Not wanting to let sb else do better) *she tried again.*

outdoor /ˈaʊtdɔː(r)/ *adj* [attrib] **1** used, done or existing in the open air, rather than in a building or house: *outdoor clothing/activities* ○ *an outdoor swimming-pool.* Compare INDOOR. **2** fond of activities done in the open air: *He's not really an outdoor type.*

outdoors /ˌaʊtˈdɔːz/ *adv* in or into the open air; outside; not inside a house or building: *Farm workers spend most of their time outdoors.* ○ *I don't like to go outdoors after dark.* Compare INDOORS.
▶ **the outdoors** *n* [sing] the open air and the countryside, esp far away from towns and cities: *Come to Canada and enjoy* **the great outdoors**.

outer /ˈaʊtə(r)/ *adj* [attrib] **(a)** further from the inside or centre: *the outer rim of the wheel* ○ *the outer suburbs of the city* ○ (*fig*) *explore the outer* (ie most extreme) *fringes/limits of human experience.* **(b)** on the outside of sth: *the outer layers of the skin* ○ *outer garments* ○ *the outer walls of a house.* **(c)** (esp in names of places) most remote: *Outer Mongolia* ○ *the Outer Hebrides.* Compare INNER.
▶ **outermost** /ˈaʊtəməʊst/ *adj* furthest from the inside or centre; most remote: *the outermost planet* ○ *the outermost layers of the earth's crust.* Compare INNERMOST.
■ ˌouter ˈspace *n* [U] = SPACE¹ 5: *strange creatures from outer space.*

outface /ˌaʊtˈfeɪs/ *v* to defeat an opponent by remaining firm and confident: [Vn] *She outfaced her rivals by refusing to resign.*

outfall /ˈaʊtfɔːl/ *n* (*techn*) the place where a river, drain, etc flows out into the sea: *a sewage outfall.*

outfield /ˈaʊtfiːld/ *n* **the outfield** (*sport*) **(a)** [U] (in cricket and baseball) the part of the field furthest from the batsmen or the batter (BAT¹): *a difficult catch in the outfield.* **(b)** [Gp] the players in this part of the field.
▶ **outfielder** *n* a player in the outfield.

outfight /ˌaʊtˈfaɪt/ *v* (*pt, pp* **outfought** /-ˈfɔːt/) [Vn] to fight better than an opponent in battle or in sport.

outfit /ˈaʊtfɪt/ *n* **1** [C] clothes worn together as a set, esp for a particular occasion or purpose: *a skiing outfit* ○ *She bought a new outfit for her daughter's wedding.* **2** [C] all the equipment or articles needed for a particular purpose: *a bicycle repair outfit.* **3** [CGp] (*infml*) a group of people working together; an organization: *a small publishing outfit.*
▶ **outfitter** *n* (often *pl* with *sing v*) (*dated or fml*) a shop or business supplying clothes, esp for men or children: *visit a gentlemen's outfitters* ○ *They are the official school outfitters.*

outflank /ˌaʊtˈflæŋk/ *v* [Vn] **(a)** to move round the side of an opponent, esp in order to attack from behind: *Instead of confronting the enemy directly, Napoleon simply outflanked them.* **(b)** to gain an advantage over sb, esp by taking an unexpected action: *They found themselves outflanked by the rival takeover bid.*

outflow /ˈaʊtfləʊ/ *n* ~ (**from sth**) an outward flow, esp of liquid or money: *a steady outflow of oil from the tank* ○ *illegal outflows of currency.*

outfox /ˌaʊtˈfɒks/ *v* to gain an advantage over sb by being more clever and CUNNING(1): [Vn] *He easily outfoxed reporters waiting outside his house.*

outgoing /ˈaʊtɡəʊɪŋ/ *adj* **1** friendly and cheerful with other people: *an outgoing personality* ○ *She's very outgoing.* **2** [attrib] **(a)** leaving a particular office, post or position: *the outgoing government/president.* **(b)** moving or going away from a certain place: *an outgoing tide* ○ *outgoing flights/passengers* ○ *This telephone should be used for outgoing calls.* Compare INCOMING.

outgoings /ˈaʊtɡəʊɪŋz/ *n* [pl] the amount of money

a business or a person spends, esp regularly: *monthly outgoings on rent and food.*

outgrow /ˌaʊtˈɡrəʊ/ *v* (*pt* **outgrew** /-ˈɡruː/; *pp* **outgrown** /-ˈɡrəʊn/) [Vn] **1** to grow too big to be able to wear or fit into sth: *He's already outgrown his school uniform.* ○ *The company has outgrown its offices.* **2** to grow faster, taller or larger than another person: *He's already outgrown his older brother.* **3** to stop doing sth or lose interest in sth as one grows older: *outgrow bad habits/childish interests* ○ *He has outgrown his passion for pop music.* Compare GROW OUT OF STH (GROW).

outgrowth /ˈaʊtɡrəʊθ/ *n* (*fml*) **1** a natural development or result of sth: *One outgrowth of this research has been the renewed public interest in the subject.* **2** a thing that grows out of another thing: *an outgrowth from the brain.*

outgun /ˌaʊtˈɡʌn/ *v* (**-nn-**) to have greater military strength than sb: [Vn] (*fig*) *The England team was completely outgunned and outwitted.*

outhouse /ˈaʊthaʊs/ *n* (*pl* **-houses** /-haʊzɪz/) *n* **1** a small building, eg a shed, outside the main building: *She did her painting in one of the outhouses.* Compare OUTBUILDING. **2** (*US*) a toilet that is enclosed but separate from the main building.

outing /ˈaʊtɪŋ/ *n* **1** ~ (**to ...**) a trip, usu a fairly short one, taken for pleasure or entertainment: *go on an outing to the seaside* ○ *a family outing.* **2** (*infml*) an appearance in an outdoor sports contest: *In/On his only outing last season, the horse finished fifth.*

outlandish /aʊtˈlændɪʃ/ *adj* (*usu derog*) looking or sounding strange: *outlandish clothes/behaviour.* ▶ **outlandishly** *adv.*

outlast /ˌaʊtˈlɑːst; *US* -ˈlæst/ *v* to exist or operate for a longer time than sb/sth: [Vn] *This clock has outlasted several owners.* ○ *I believe that jazz will outlast rock music in popular taste.* Compare OUTLIVE.

outlaw /ˈaʊtlɔː/ *n* (esp formerly) a person who has broken the law and is hiding to avoid being caught: *a band of outlaws.*
▶ **outlaw** *v* **1** to declare sth to be illegal: [Vn] *plans to outlaw computer hacking* ○ *the outlawed nationalist party.* **2** [Vn] (formerly) to make or declare sb an outlaw.

outlay /ˈaʊtleɪ/ *n* [C esp *sing*, U] ~ (**on sth**) (*commerce*) money spent at the beginning of a project or on an item of equipment, eg to help the future development of a business: *an outlay of £100 000 on new machinery* ○ *Apart from the initial outlay, there are other costs to be considered when buying a car.* ○ *Starting this kind of business requires little financial outlay.*

outlet /ˈaʊtlet/ *n* ~ (**for sth**) **1** (*commerce*) a place that sells goods made by a particular company or of a particular type; a shop: *The business has 34 retail outlets in this state alone.* **2** a means of releasing energy, strong feelings or talents of a person: *Children need an outlet for their energy.* ○ *Trained musicians can find few professional outlets.* **3** a pipe or hole through which eg water or steam can come out of sth: *a sewage outlet* ○ *the outlet valve on the engine.* Compare INLET 2. **4** (*US*) = SOCKET 2.

outline /ˈaʊtlaɪn/ *n* **1** a statement of the main facts or points: *an outline for an essay/a lecture* ○ *an outline of Roman history* ○ *describe a plan in (broad) outline* ○ *an outline agreement/proposal* (ie one yet to be fully worked out). **2** a line or lines indicating the shape or outer edge of sth: *an outline map of Italy* ○ *She could see only the outline(s) of the roof in the dim light.*
▶ **outline** *v* **1** ~ **sth (to sb)** to give a short general description of sth: [Vn, V.*wh*] *We outlined our proposals and how we intended to proceed.* [also Vnpr]. **2** to draw or mark the outer edge of sth: [Vnpr] *The important paragraph is outlined in red ink.* [also Vn].

outlive /ˌaʊtˈlɪv/ v to live longer than sb: [Vnpr] *He outlived his wife by three years.* [Vn] *(fig) The machines had **outlived their usefulness** (ie were no longer useful and could be disposed of).* Compare OUTLAST.

outlook /ˈaʊtlʊk/ n **1** ~ (on sth) a person's attitude to life and the world in general: *a tolerant/confident/pessimistic outlook* ○ *people of widely differing outlooks* ○ *Meeting her has changed his whole outlook on life.* **2** ~ (for sth) (usu *sing*) (**a**) what seems likely to happen; the probable future for sb/sth: *a bright outlook for trade* ○ *a bleak outlook for the unemployed.* (**b**) the weather as forecast for the next few days: *The outlook for the weekend is dry and sunny.* **3** a view on which one looks out: *The house has a pleasant outlook over the valley.*

outlying /ˈaʊtlaɪɪŋ/ adj [attrib] far from a centre or a city; remote: *outlying areas/districts/villages.*

outmanoeuvre (*US* **-maneuver**) /ˌaʊtməˈnuːvə(r)/ v to do better than an opponent, etc by acting more skilfully and cleverly: [Vn] *The government has been successfully outmanoeuvred by the Opposition.*

outmoded /ˌaʊtˈməʊdɪd/ adj (*often derog*) no longer fashionable or in use: *outmoded ideas/beliefs/views* ○ *outmoded forms of transport.*

outnumber /ˌaʊtˈnʌmbə(r)/ v to be greater in number than sb/sth: [Vn] *The demonstrators were heavily/vastly outnumbered by the police.* ○ *In this profession, men outnumber women by two to one* (ie there are twice as many men as women).

out-of-date /ˌaʊt əv ˈdeɪt/ adj [attrib] **1** old-fashioned and no longer useful: *an out-of-date dictionary/institution.* **2** no longer valid: *an out-of-date driving-licence.* See also OUT OF DATE (DATE¹). See also UP-TO-DATE.

outpace /ˌaʊtˈpeɪs/ v to go faster than sb/sth; to be more than sth: [Vn] *He easily outpaced the other runners.* ○ *Demand is outpacing production.*

out-patient /ˈaʊtpeɪʃnt/ n a person who goes to a hospital for treatment but continues to live at home: *the out-patient department.* Compare IN-PATIENT.

outperform /ˌaʊtpəˈfɔːm/ v to perform better than sb/sth: *The strong economy has helped some smaller banks to outperform their larger rivals.* ▶ **outperformance** n [U].

outplay /ˌaʊtˈpleɪ/ v to play much better than and so defeat sb: [Vn] *We were totally outplayed by the visiting team.*

outpoint /ˌaʊtˈpɔɪnt/ v (in boxing, etc) to defeat sb by scoring more points: [Vn] *He was easily outpointed by the champion.*

outpost /ˈaʊtpəʊst/ n **1** a small military camp at some distance from the main army, used for observing an enemy's movements, etc. **2** a small town or group of buildings established in a distant part of a country.

outpouring /ˈaʊtpɔːrɪŋ/ n **1** a large amount of sth produced in a short time: *a remarkable outpouring of new ideas.* **2** (usu *pl*) an expression of very strong feelings: *outpourings of public grief.*

output /ˈaʊtpʊt/ n [U, sing] **1** the amount of sth that a person, a machine or an organization produces: *The average output of the factory is 20 cars a day.* ○ *Manufacturing output has increased by 8% in two years.* **2** (*techn*) the information produced by a computer: *data ouput* ○ *an output device.* Compare INPUT. **3** the power, energy, etc produced by an apparatus: *an output of 100 watts.* ▶ **output** v (-**tt**-; *pt, pp* **output**) (*computing*) to supply information, results, etc: [Vn] *The computer can output the data in seconds.* Compare INPUT v.

outrage /ˈaʊtreɪdʒ/ n **1** [U] a strong feeling of anger and shock: *There has been public outrage over the recent terrorist attacks.* ○ *She was filled with a sense*

of *outrage.* **2** [C] an act or event that is violent, cruel or very wrong and that shocks people or makes them very angry: *commit/perpetrate outrages against the civilian population.* ▶ **outrage** /ˈaʊtreɪdʒ/ v to make sb very shocked, angry or upset: [Vn] (esp passive): *Many people have been outraged by the latest tax increases.* ○ *A page of outraged letters followed the article.*

outrageous /aʊtˈreɪdʒəs/ adj **1** very shocking and unacceptable: *outrageous behaviour* ○ *I refuse to pay such outrageous prices!* **2** very unusual and quite shocking: *wear outrageous clothes* ○ *She says the most outrageous things sometimes.* ▶ **outrageously** adv: *outrageously expensive clothes* ○ *She behaved outrageously.*

outrank /ˌaʊtˈræŋk/ v to be of higher rank than sb; to be much better than sb/sth: [Vn] *Colonel Jones outranks everyone here.* ○ *In sheer skill he outranks the other contenders for the title.*

outré /ˈuːtreɪ; *US* uːˈtreɪ/ adj (*French derog*) (esp of behaviour, ideas, etc) very unusual and quite shocking: *outré modern fashions.*

outreach /ˈaʊtriːtʃ/ n [U] the activity of an organization in contacting and providing a service or advice to people in the community, esp outside its usual centres: *outreach youth workers in remote rural areas.*

outrider /ˈaʊtraɪdə(r)/ n a person riding a motor cycle (MOTOR) or a horse in front of or beside the vehicle of an important person in order to guard her or him: *The President's car was escorted by motor cycle outriders.*

outrigger /ˈaʊtrɪgə(r)/ n a wooden structure projecting from the side of a boat or ship in order to keep it steady in the water.

outright /aʊtˈraɪt/ adv **1** openly and honestly, without hiding anything: *I told him outright what I thought of his behaviour.* **2** not gradually; immediately: *Most of the crash victims were killed outright.* ○ *We had saved enough money to buy the house outright.* **3** clearly and completely: *He won outright.* ○ *She denied outright having been there.* ▶ **outright** adj [attrib] complete and clear, without any doubt: *an outright ban/rejection/victory* ○ *She was the outright winner.*

outrun /ˌaʊtˈrʌn/ v (*pt* **outran** /-ˈræn/; *pp* **outrun**) **1** to run faster or further than sb/sth: [Vn] *Can a man outrun a horse?* **2** to develop faster than sth: [Vn] *Demand for the new model is outrunning supply.*

outsell /ˌaʊtˈsel/ v (*pt, pp* **outsold** /-ˈsəʊld/) to sell more or be sold in greater quantities than sb/sth: [Vn] *We're now outselling our main rivals.* ○ *This model outsells all the others in our range.*

outset /ˈaʊtset/ n **IDM** **at/from the (very) outset (of sth)** at/from the beginning of sth: *At the outset of her career she was full of ambition.* ○ *His innocence was clear from the very outset.*

outshine /ˌaʊtˈʃaɪn/ v (*pt, pp* **outshone** /-ˈʃɒn/) to be much better than sb/sth: [Vn] *He far outshines the rest of the class.*

outside¹ /ˌaʊtˈsaɪd/ n (**a**) (usu **the outside**) [C usu *sing*] the outer side or surface of sth: *The outside of the house needs painting.* ○ *You can't open the door from the outside.* ○ *There is a list of the ingredients on the outside of the packet.* ○ *She seems calm on the outside but I know how worried she really is.* (**b**) [sing] the area that is near or around a building, etc: *walk around the outside of the building* ○ *I didn't go into the church — I only saw it from the outside.* (**c**) [sing] the lane or part of a road nearest to the middle: *overtake sb on the outside.* (**d**) [sing] the side of a pavement or path that is nearest to the road. (**e**) [sing] the part of a curving road or track furthest from the inner or shorter side of the curve. (**f**) [sing] the world outside a particular group, organization, institution, etc: *get help from outside* ○

life **on the outside** (eg not in prison). Compare
INSIDE[1]. **IDM** **at the outside** at the most; as a maximum: *room for 75 people at the outside* ∘ *With tips I
can earn £150 a week, at the very outside.*

▶ **outside** /ˈaʊtsaɪd/ *adj* [attrib] **1** of, on or facing
the outer side: *a house with only two outside walls* ∘
the outside appearance. **2(a)** not in the main building; not internal: *an outside toilet.* **(b)** not included
in or connected with a group, an organization, etc:
We plan to use an outside firm of consultants. ∘ *She
has a lot of* **outside interests** (ie not connected with
her work). ∘ *The* **outside world** (ie the people,
places, activities, etc that are not part of one's normal life and experience) *seemed hostile and
frightening to them.* **3** (of a choice, possibility, etc)
very small: *have an* **outside chance** *of winning.* **4**
(of a number) the maximum being considered: *My
outside price is $100 000.* ∘ *150 is an outside estimate.*
5 (of a telephone call or line) connected to a place
that is outside the building or organization: *You
have to pay to make an outside call.*
■ ‚outside ˈbroadcast *n* (*esp Brit*) a programme
filmed or recorded in a place other than the main
STUDIO(1).
‚outside ˈlane *n* (usu *sing*) the section of a road or
MOTORWAY that is nearest to the centre, ie nearest to
the right in countries where vehicles drive on the
left.

outside² /ˌaʊtˈsaɪd/ (also *esp US* **outside of**) *prep* **1**
on or to a place on the outside of sth: *You can park
your car outside our house.* ∘ *Leave your muddy boots
outside the door.* ∘ *Don't go outside the school playground.* Compare INSIDE² 1. **2** away from or not in a
particular place: *It's the biggest theme park outside
the USA.* **3** near to a particular place: *a small
village just outside Leeds.* **4** not within sth: *The
matter is outside my area of responsibility.* ∘ *You may
do as you wish outside working hours.* ∘ *The decision
has been criticized by people outside the organization.*
▶ **outside** *adv* **1** on or to the outside: *Please wait
outside.* ∘ *The house is painted green outside.* **2** in or
to a place that is not in a building: *It's warm enough
to eat outside.* ∘ *Go outside and see if it's raining.*

outsider /ˌaʊtˈsaɪdə(r)/ *n* **1** a person who is not, or
is not accepted as, a member of a society, group, etc:
*We can't do this by ourselves — we'll need the help of
an outsider.* ∘ *Although she's lived there for ten years,
the neighbours still treat her as an outsider.* ∘ *To an
outsider it may appear to be a glamorous job.* **2** a
person or an animal taking part in a race or competition but not expected to win: *It was won by a
complete outsider.* ∘ *Amazingly, the job went to* **a
rank outsider**.

outsize /ˈaʊtsaɪz/ (also **outsized** /ˈaʊtsaɪzd/) *adj*
[usu attrib] (*euph*) (esp of clothes) larger than the
standard sizes: *outsize dresses for larger ladies.*

outskirts /ˈaʊtskɜːts/ *n* [pl] the parts of a town or
city that are furthest from the centre: *They live on
the outskirts of Paris.*

outsmart /ˌaʊtˈsmɑːt/ *v* to gain an advantage by
being cleverer than sb: [Vn] *She always managed to
outsmart her political rivals.*

outspoken /aʊtˈspəʊkən/ *adj* ~ **(in sth)** saying
openly exactly what one thinks: *an outspoken critic
of the government* ∘ *be outspoken in one's remarks.* ▶
outspokenly *adv*: *outspokenly critical.* **outspokenness** *n* [U]: *Her outspokenness has made her a lot of
enemies.*

outspread /ˌaʊtˈspred/ *adj* spread or stretched out
as far as possible: *with arms/wings outspread.*

outstanding /aʊtˈstændɪŋ/ *adj* **1** exceptionally
good; excellent: *an outstanding player/piece of work/
performance* ∘ *an area of outstanding natural
beauty.* **2** [usu attrib] very obvious or easily noticed: *the outstanding features of the landscape* ∘ *an
issue of outstanding importance.* **3** (of payment,

work, problems, etc) not yet paid, done, solved, etc:
have outstanding debts of over £5 000 ∘ *A good deal of
work is still outstanding.*
▶ **outstandingly** *adv* exceptionally: *outstandingly
successful* ∘ *play outstandingly well.*

outstay /ˌaʊtˈsteɪ/ *v* to stay longer than sb: [Vn]
outstay all the other guests. **IDM** **outstay/overstay
one's welcome** ⇨ WELCOME.

outstretched /ˌaʊtˈstretʃt/ *adj* (with limbs, wings,
etc) stretched or spread out as far as possible: *He
ran towards her with ‚arms outˈstretched/with ‚outstretched ˈarms.*

outstrip /ˌaʊtˈstrɪp/ *v* (**-pp-**) **1** to become larger,
more important, etc than sb/sth: [Vn] *Demand is
currently outstripping production.* **2** to run faster
than sb in a race so that one passes them: [Vn] *She
soon outstripped the slower runners.*

out-take /ˈaʊt teɪk/ *n* a piece of a film that is
removed before the film is shown because it contains a mistake.

out-tray /ˈaʊt treɪ/ *n* a tray for holding letters or
documents that have been dealt with and are ready
to be posted or handed to sb else. Compare IN-TRAY.

outvote /ˌaʊtˈvəʊt/ *v* (esp passive) to defeat sb by
gaining a larger number of votes: [Vn] *They were
outvoted by the other committee members.*

outward /ˈaʊtwəd/ *adj* [attrib] **1** (of a journey)
going out or away from a place that one is going to
return to: *Our luggage got lost on the outward journey.* **2** of or on the outside: *There were no outward
signs that the house was being lived in.* ∘ **To (all)
outward appearances** (ie As far as one can see
from the outside) *the child seems very happy at
school.* **3** in one's expressions or actions, in contrast
to one's true feelings: *She shows no outward sign of
the sadness she must feel.* ∘ *An outward show of
confidence concealed his nervousness.* Compare IN-
WARD.
▶ **outwardly** *adv* on the surface; apparently:
*Though badly frightened, she remained outwardly
calm.*
outwards /-wədz/ (*Brit*) (also *esp US* **outward**) *adv*
towards the outside; away from the centre or from a
particular point: *The two ends of the wire must be
bent outward(s).* ∘ *The door opens outwards.* ∘ *The
city is spreading outwards.* ∘ *Lie on your stomach
with your elbows pointing outwards.* ⇨ note at FOR-
WARD². ‚outward ˈbound *adj* going away from
home, etc: *The ship is outward bound.* ‚**Outward
ˈBound** *n* (in Britain) a scheme that provides adventure training and other outdoor activities for young
people: *an Outward Bound course.*

outweigh /ˌaʊtˈweɪ/ *v* to be greater or more important than sth: [Vn] *The advantages* **far outweigh** *the
disadvantages.* ∘ *The risks are vastly outweighed by
the potential benefits.*

outwit /ˌaʊtˈwɪt/ *v* (**-tt-**) to overcome or defeat sb/sth
by doing sth clever or CUNNING(1): [Vn] *The escaped
man has so far succeeded in outwitting the police.* ∘
He spends his life trying to outwit the system.

outworn /ˈaʊtwɔːn/ *adj* [usu attrib] no longer useful; old-fashioned: *outworn practices in industry.*
Compare WORN-OUT.

ouzo /ˈuːzəʊ/ *n* [U] a strong Greek alcoholic drink
made from ANISEED and usu drunk with water: *a
glass of ouzo.*

ova *pl* of ovum.

oval /ˈəʊvl/ *adj* shaped like an egg: *an oval brooch/
mirror* ∘ *an oval-shaped face.* ▶ **oval** *n*: *The
swimming-pool is a large oval.*

ovary /ˈəʊvəri/ *n* **1** either of the two organs in
women and female animals, birds and fish that produce eggs. ⇨ picture at REPRODUCTION. See also
OVUM. **2** (*botany*) the part of a plant that produces
seeds.

▶ **ovarian** /əʊˈveəriən/ adj [attrib] of an ovary or the ovaries: *an ovarian cyst.*

ovation /əʊˈveɪʃn/ n a long and enthusiastic show of appreciation from an audience: *The team received/were given a rapturous/tumultuous/enthusiastic ovation.* See also STANDING OVATION.

oven /ˈʌvn/ n an enclosed space shaped like a box and usu part of a COOKER(1), in which things are cooked or heated: *take the bread out of the oven* ◦ *a gas/electric oven* ◦ *Bake in a pre-heated oven for 35 minutes.* ◦ *Open a window, it's like an oven* (ie very hot) *in here!* Compare MICROWAVE, STOVE¹. **IDM** **have a bun in the oven** ⇨ BUN.

■ ˌoven-ˈready adj bought already prepared and ready for cooking: *ˌoven-ready ˈchickens.*

ovenproof /ˈʌvnpruːf/ adj suitable for use in a hot oven: *an ovenproof dish.*

ovenware /ˈʌvnweə(r)/ n [U] dishes that can be used for cooking food in an oven.

over¹ /ˈəʊvə(r)/ adv part For the special uses of **over** in phrasal verbs, look at the verb entries. For example, the meaning of **take sth over** is given in the phrasal verb section of the entry for **take¹**. **1(a)** downwards and outwards from an upright position: *Don't knock that vase over.* ◦ *The wind must have blown it over.* ◦ *He bent over to pick up the book.* ◦ *She leaned over and whispered in his ear.* **(b)** from one side to another side: *Turn the patient over onto his front.* ◦ *Turn over the page.* ◦ *The car skidded off the road and rolled over and over down the slope.* **(c)** across a street, an open space, etc: *Take these letters over to the post office.* ◦ *He rowed us over to the other side of the lake.* ◦ *He has gone over to/is over in France.* ◦ *Let's ask some friends over* (ie to our home). ◦ *Put the tray over there* (eg on the other side of the room). **2** so as to cover sb/sth entirely: *The lake is completely frozen over.* ◦ *Cover her over with a blanket.* **3** remaining; not used or needed: *If there's any food (left) over, put it in the fridge.* ◦ *I'll have just $10 over when I've paid my debts.* ◦ *7 into 30 goes 4 with 2 over.* **4** above; more: *children of fourteen and over* ◦ *It's two metres long or a bit over.* See also ABOVE¹ 2. Compare UNDER 4. ⇨ note at AGE¹. **5** (*esp US*) again: *He repeated it several times over until he could remember it.* ◦ *We did the house over* (ie decorated it) *and bought new furniture.* **6** ended: *Their relationship is over.* ◦ *By the time we arrived the meeting was over.* ◦ *Thank goodness that's over.* **7** (indicating a change of position or loyalty): *He's gone over to the enemy* (ie joined them). ◦ *Please change the wheels over* (eg put the front wheels at the back). **8** (used when communicating by radio): *Message received. Over* (ie It is your turn to speak). **IDM** **(all) over aˈgain** a second time from the beginning: *He did the work so badly that I had to do it all over again myself.* **over against sth** in contrast with sth: *the benefits of private education over against state education.* ˌover and ˈover (aˈgain) many times; repeatedly: *I've told you ˌover and ˌover aˈgain not to do that.* ◦ *Say the words over and over to yourself.*

over² /ˈəʊvə(r)/ prep For the special uses of **over** in phrasal verbs, look at the verb entries. For example, the meaning of **get over sth** is given in the phrasal verb section of the entry for **get**. **1** (not able to be replaced by *above* in this sense) resting on the surface of sb/sth and partly or completely covering them/it: *Spread a cloth over the table.* ◦ *She put a rug over the sleeping child.* ◦ *He wore an overcoat over his suit.* ◦ *He put his hand over her mouth to stop her screaming.* ⇨ note at ABOVE². **2** in or to a position higher than and not touching sb/sth; above sb/sth: *They held a large umbrella over her.* ◦ *The balcony juts out over the river.* ◦ *There was a lamp (hanging) over the table.* Compare ABOVE² 1, UNDER 1. ⇨ note at ABOVE². **3(a)** from one side of sth to the other; across sth: *a bridge over the river* ◦ *run over the grass* ◦ *escape over the border* ◦ *look over the hedge.* **(b)** on the far or opposite side of sth: *He lives over the road/way.* ◦ *Over the river is private land.* **(c)** so as to cross sth and be on the other side: *climb over a wall* ◦ *jump over the stream* ◦ *go over the mountains.* **4** (esp with *all*) in or on all or most parts of sth/a place: *Snow is falling (all) over the country.* ◦ *He's famous all over the world.* ◦ *He sprinkled sugar over his cereal.* **5** more than a specified time, amount, cost, etc: *over 3 million copies sold* ◦ *She stayed in Lagos (for) over a month.* ◦ *He's over two metres tall.* ◦ *She's well over fifty.* Compare UNDER 4. ⇨ note at ABOVE². **6** (indicating control, command or authority): *He ruled over a great empire.* ◦ *She has only the director over her.* ◦ *He has little control over his emotions.* Compare UNDER 5, BELOW. **7(a)** (indicating the passing of time) while doing, having, eating, etc sth; during sth: *discuss it over lunch* ◦ *Over the next few days they got to know the town well.* **(b)** throughout a period; during sth: *We shall be away over* (ie until after) *Christmas and the New Year.* **(c)** past a particular, usu difficult, stage or period: *We're over the worst of the recession.* ◦ *It took her ages to get over her illness.* **8** because of or concerning sth; about sth: *an argument over money* ◦ *a disagreement over the best way to proceed.* **9** transmitted by sth; on sth: *We heard it over the radio.* ◦ *She wouldn't tell me over* (ie when speaking on) *the phone.* **10** louder than sth: *I couldn't hear what he said over the noise of the traffic.* **IDM** ˌover and aˈbove besides sth; in addition to sth: *The waiters get good tips over and above their wages.* ◦ *There are other factors over and above those we have discussed.*

over³ /ˈəʊvə(r)/ n (in cricket) a series of six balls bowled from one end of the WICKET(1b) by the same person: *dismiss two batsmen in the same over.*

over- pref **1** (with *ns* forming *ns, vs, adjs* and *advs*) from above; outside; across: *overcoat* ◦ *overarching* ◦ *overhang* ◦ *overall* ◦ *overhead.* Compare SUPER-. **2** (used widely with *vs, ns, advs* and esp *adjs*) to excess; too much; more than usual: *overgeneralize* ◦ *overwork* ◦ *overemphasis* ◦ *overtime* ◦ *overambitious* ◦ *over-anxious* ◦ *overconfident* ◦ *over-sensitive* ◦ *overindulgence* ◦ *over-aggressively.* Compare HYPER-.

overact /ˌəʊvərˈækt/ v [V, Vn] (*derog*) to act a part in a play, etc in an exaggerated way.

overall¹ /ˌəʊvərˈɔːl/ adj [attrib] **(a)** including everything; total: *an overall increase of £1.3 million* ◦ *the overall cost of the carpet including sales tax and fitting.* **(b)** taking everything into account; general: *an overall improvement* ◦ *The overall effect/impression is very good.* ◦ *This information will help us to build up an overall picture of the situation.*

▶ **overall** adv **1** including everything; in total: *how much will it cost overall?* **2** on the whole; generally: *Overall it's been a good match.*

overall² /ˈəʊvərɔːl/ n **1** [C] (*Brit*) (*US* **smock**) a loose coat worn over other clothes to protect them from dirt, etc: *The lab assistant was wearing a white overall.* ⇨ picture at APRON. **2 overalls** [pl] **(a)** (*US* **coverall** [C]) a loose garment made of heavy material and covering the body, arms and legs, usu worn over other clothing by workers to protect them from dirt, etc: *The mechanic was wearing a pair of blue overalls.* See also BOILER SUIT. **(b)** = DUNGAREES.

overarching /ˌəʊvərˈɑːtʃɪŋ/ adj covering a wide range of topics, interests, activities, etc: *the overarching themes of race, violence and disorder.*

overarm /ˈəʊvərɑːm/ adj, adv (of throwing a ball) with the arm swung over the shoulder: *bowl/throw overarm.* Compare UNDERARM.

overawe /ˌəʊvərˈɔː/ v (usu passive) to impress sb so much that they remain silent and feel respect or fear: [Vn] *He was overawed by the rather grand surroundings.*

overbalance /ˌəʊvəˈbæləns/ v **(a)** to lose one's bal-

O

ance and fall: [V] *He overbalanced and fell into the water.* (**b**) to make sb/sth fall or turn over: [Vn] *If you stand up you'll overbalance the canoe.*

overbearing /ˌəʊvəˈbeərɪŋ/ *adj* (*derog*) trying to dominate other people in an unpleasant way: *an overbearing father/manner.*

overblown /ˌəʊvəˈbləʊn/ *adj* **1** (*fml*) too elaborate; trying too hard to be impressive: *the usual overblown hype on the book cover.* **2** (of flowers) past their best: *ˌoverblown ˈroses.*

overboard /ˈəʊvəbɔːd/ *adv* over the side of a ship or boat into the water: *fall/jump/be washed overboard.* **IDM** **go ˈoverboard** (*infml often derog*) to be extremely enthusiastic about sth/sb: *The critics have gone overboard about her new play.* **throw sth/ sb ˈoverboard** to abandon sb/sth; to stop supporting sb/sth: *Principles were thrown overboard in the scramble to get elected.*

overbook /ˌəʊvəˈbʊk/ *v* to reserve seats, rooms, etc for too many passengers or visitors on an aircraft, in a hotel, etc: [Vn] *The flight was heavily overbooked.* [also V]. Compare DOUBLE-BOOK.

overburden /ˌəʊvəˈbɜːdn/ *v* ~ **sb** (**with sth**) (usu passive) to give sb/sth more work, worry, etc than they/it can deal with: [Vn] *gravely overburdened hospital services* [Vnpr] *be overburdened with guilt/ debt/committee meetings.*

overcapacity /ˌəʊvəkəˈpæsəti/ *n* [U, sing] (*commerce*) the resources to produce more goods, handle more business, etc than is needed at a particular time: *problems of overcapacity in the car industry.*

overcast /ˌəʊvəˈkɑːst; *US* -ˈkæst/ *adj* (of the sky) covered with cloud; dull: *a dark, ˌovercast ˈday* ∘ *It's a bit overcast — it might rain.*

overcharge /ˌəʊvəˈtʃɑːdʒ/ *v* **1** ~ (**sb**) (**for sth**) to charge sb too much money for sth, usu deliberately: [V, Vn] *Always check your bill; he has a habit of overcharging (people).* [Vnpr, Vnn] *We were overcharged (£5) for the wine.* [also Vpr]. Compare UNDERCHARGE. **2** to fill or load sth too full or too heavily: [Vn] *overcharge an electric circuit/a battery* [Vnpr] (*fig*) *a poem overcharged with emotion.*

overcoat /ˈəʊvəkəʊt/ *n* a long warm coat worn over other clothes in cold weather.

overcome /ˌəʊvəˈkʌm/ *v* (*pt* **overcame** /-ˈkeɪm/; *pp* **overcome**) **1** to succeed in dealing with or controlling sth: [Vn] *overcome an obstacle/a difficulty* ∘ *overcome one's fear of flying* ∘ *He overcame a strong temptation to run away.* **2** (*fml*) to defeat sb: [Vn] *Rangers finally overcame Celtic in a close match.* **IDM** **be overcome by/with sth** to be strongly affected by sth: *She was overcome by embarrassment/grief/ curiosity.* ∘ *The dead woman had been overcome by smoke and fumes.*

overcompensate /ˌəʊvəˈkɒmpenseɪt/ *v* ~ (**for sth**) (**by doing sth**) to try to correct an error or a weakness by taking measures that are too strong and cause a different problem: [Vpr] *He had overcompensated for the strength of the wind, and taken the aircraft off course.* [also V].

overcook /ˌəʊvəˈkʊk/ *v* to cook food for longer than is necessary: [Vn] *overcooked vegetables.*

overcrowded /ˌəʊvəˈkraʊdɪd/ *adj* (of a place) with too many people or things in; too crowded: *ˌovercrowded ˈbuses/ˈtrains/ˈschools/ˈprisons* ∘ *a room overcrowded with ornaments* ∘ *Shopping centres get very overcrowded just before Christmas.*

▶ **overcrowding** /ˌəʊvəˈkraʊdɪŋ/ *n* [U] the state of having too many people in one place: *action to reduce the serious overcrowding in prisons.*

overdo /ˌəʊvəˈduː/ *v* (*pt* **overdid** /-ˈdɪd/; *pp* **overdone** /-ˈdʌn/) **1** to do, perform or express sth too fully or for too long; to exaggerate sth: [Vn] *She really overdid the sympathy* (ie did not seem sincere). ∘ *He was trying to be helpful but he rather*

overdid it. **2** to use too much of sth: [Vn] *Don't overdo the salt in the food.* ∘ *The garden statues are rather overdone.* **3** (usu passive) to cook sth for too long: [Vn] *The fish was overdone and very dry.* **IDM** **over ˈdo it/things** to work, study or exercise too hard or for too long: *He's been overdoing things recently.* ∘ *You must stop overdoing it — you'll make yourself ill.*

overdose /ˈəʊvədəʊs/ *n* too much of a drug, esp more than is safe for one: *take a massive overdose of sleeping tablets* ∘ (*fig*) *We've had an overdose of party politics this week* (ie heard too much about it).

▶ **overdose** *v* /ˌəʊvəˈdəʊs/ (*infml* OD) ~ (**on sth**) to take an excessive and dangerous amount of a drug: [V, Vpr] *He overdosed (on heroin) and went into a coma.*

overdraft /ˈəʊvədrɑːft; *US* -dræft/ *n* a sum of money lent to sb by a bank, allowing them to spend more money than is in their account: *run up a large overdraft* ∘ *He has a huge overdraft to pay off.* ∘ *I took out an overdraft to pay for my new car.*

overdraw /ˌəʊvəˈdrɔː/ *v* (*pt* **overdrew** /-ˈdruː/; *pp* **overdrawn** /-ˈdrɔːn/) to take out more money from a bank account than it contains: [Vn] *Don't overdraw (your account) without telling us in advance.*

▶ **overdrawn** /ˌəʊvəˈdrɔːn/ *adj* (**a**) [pred] (of a person) having taken more money from one's account than one has in it: *I'm overdrawn by £500.* (**b**) (of an account) with more money taken out than was paid or left in: *a heavily overdrawn account.*

overdressed /ˌəʊvəˈdrest/ *adj* (*usu derog*) wearing clothes that are too formal or too elegant for the occasion: *I feel rather overdressed in this suit — everyone else is wearing jeans!*

overdrive /ˈəʊvədraɪv/ *n* [U] **1** a mechanism providing an extra gear above the normal top gear in a vehicle: *be in overdrive.* **2** a state of great or excessive activity: *As the wedding day approached the whole family went into overdrive.*

overdue /ˌəʊvəˈdjuː; *US* -ˈduː/ *adj* [usu pred] not having arrived, or not done, paid, etc by the required or appropriate time: *The second instalment for the washing machine is overdue.* ∘ *Her baby is two weeks overdue.* ∘ *These forms were long overdue.*

over-easy /ˌəʊvər ˈiːzi/ *adj* (*US*) (of fried eggs) turned over when almost cooked and fried briefly on the other side.

overeat /ˌəʊvərˈiːt/ *v* (*pt* **overate** /-ˈet/; *pp* **overeaten** /-ˈiːtn/) to eat more than one needs or more than is healthy: [V] *There is a tendency to overeat at Christmas.*

overemphasis /ˌəʊvərˈemfəsɪs/ *n* [U, sing] ~ (**on sth**) too much emphasis or importance: *an overemphasis on arts subjects.* ▶ **overemphasize, -ise** *v*: *The importance of adequate preparation cannot be overemphasized.*

overestimate /ˌəʊvərˈestɪmeɪt/ *v* to estimate sth to be larger, better, more important, etc than it really is: [Vn] *I overestimated the amount of milk we'd need for the weekend.* ∘ *The importance of these findings cannot be overestimated* (ie is very great). ▶ **overestimate** /-mət/ *n* (usu *sing*): *I'm expecting about 100 people but that may be an overestimate.* Compare UNDERESTIMATE.

overexpose /ˌəʊvərɪkˈspəʊz/ *v* [Vn] (*esp passive*) **1** to expose a film, etc for too long or in too bright a light. Compare UNDEREXPOSE. **2** to allow sb/sth to be seen or heard about too often by the public. ▶ **overexposure** *n* [U].

overfishing /ˌəʊvəˈfɪʃɪŋ/ *n* [U] the process of taking so many fish from a river, the sea, etc that the number of fish in it becomes very low.

overflow /ˌəʊvəˈfləʊ/ *v* **1** to be so full that the contents go over the sides or beyond the limits: [V] *Your bath is overflowing.* ∘ *overflowing ashtrays* ∘ *The hospitals are filled/full to overflowing (with* *patients*). [Vn] *The river overflowed its banks.* ⊏⟩ picture at OVERLAP. **2** ~ **(into)** sth to spread beyond the limits of a full room, etc: [Vpr] *The meeting overflowed into the streets.* [also Vn]. **3** ~ **with sth** to be very full of sth, esp a feeling: [Vpr] *overflowing with happiness/kindness/gratitude* ○ *His heart overflowed with love.*

▶ **overflow** /ˈəʊvəfləʊ/ n **1** [U] **(a)** the action of a liquid flowing over the edge of sth: *stop the overflow from the cistern.* **(b)** liquid that overflows: *Put a bowl underneath to catch the overflow.* **2** (also ˈoverflow pipe) [C] a pipe that allows excess liquid to escape: *The overflow from the bath is blocked.* **3** [U, sing] a number of people or things that do not fit into the space available: *a large overflow of population from the cities* ○ *an overflow car park.*

overfly /ˌəʊvəˈflaɪ/ v (*pt* **overflew** /-ˈfluː/; *pp* **overflown** /-ˈfləʊn/) (of an aircraft) to fly over a place: [Vn] *overfly a war zone* [V] *the noise from overflying planes.*

overground /ˈəʊvəɡraʊnd/ adj, adv (*Brit*) on the surface of the ground: *a new overground route through Kent.* Compare UNDERGROUND[2] 1.

overgrown /ˌəʊvəˈɡrəʊn/ adj **1** [pred] ~ **(with sth)** covered with plants that have been allowed to grow wild: *walls overgrown with ivy* ○ *The garden's completely overgrown (with weeds).* **2** [usu attrib] (*often derog*) having grown too large too ᶠast: *an overgrown village* ○ (*fig joc*) *He behaves like an ˌover grown ˈschoolboy.*

overgrowth /ˈəʊvəɡrəʊθ/ n [U] excessive growth: *the overgrowth of fibrous tissue.*

overhang /ˌəʊvəˈhæŋ/ v (*pt, pp* **overhung** /-ˈhʌŋ/) to hang or extend outwards over sth: [Vn] *Dramatic cliffs overhang the beach.* [V] *The road is dark with overhanging trees.*

▶ **overhang** /ˈəʊvəhæŋ/ n **(a)** the part of sth that overhangs: *shelter under the overhang of the cliff.* **(b)** the amount by which sth overhangs.

overhaul /ˌəʊvəˈhɔːl/ v **1** to examine sth carefully and thoroughly and make any necessary changes or repairs: [Vn] *have an engine overhauled* ○ *The language syllabus needs to be completely overhauled.* **2** to come from behind sb/sth and pass them/it: [Vn] *He overhauled the leader in the final lap.*

▶ **overhaul** /ˈəʊvəhɔːl/ n a thorough examination of sth followed by any necessary changes or repairs: *a thorough/major/massive/complete overhaul of the coal industry* ○ *The heating system is due for an overhaul.*

overhead /ˈəʊvəhed/ adj **1** raised above the ground and above one's head: *overhead lighting/cables/power lines* ○ *an overhead railway.* **2** [attrib] of or relating to the general expenses involved in running a company or an organization: *increasing overhead costs.*

▶ **overhead** /ˌəʊvəˈhed/ adv above one's head; in the sky: *birds flying overhead* ○ *Lightning flashed overhead.*

overhead n [U] (*US*) = OVERHEADS.

■ ˌoverhead proˈjector n (*abbr* **OHP**) a device that projects images onto a wall or screen above and behind the person operating it: *I need an overhead projector for my talk.*

overheads /ˈəʊvəhedz/ n [pl] (*Brit*) (*US* **overhead** [U]) regular expenses involved in running a business or an organization, eg on rent, lighting, insurance, heating and wages: *cut back on/reduce our overheads.*

overhear /ˌəʊvəˈhɪə(r)/ v (*pt, pp* **overheard** /-ˈhɜːd/) to hear sb talking when one is not involved in the conversation or without their knowledge: [Vn] *overhear snatches/bits of conversation from the next table* [Vn.ing] *I overheard them quarrelling.* [Vn.inf (no to)] *I overheard him say he was going to France.* Compare EAVESDROP.

overjoyed /ˌəʊvəˈdʒɔɪd/ adj [usu pred] ~ **(at sth / to do sth)** extremely happy: *He'll be overjoyed at your news.* ○ *She was overjoyed to see us.*

overkill /ˈəʊvəkɪl/ n [U] (*derog*) excessive use or REPETITION(1) of sth, so that its impact or effect is reduced: *Media overkill is threatening to ruin the event.*

overland /ˈəʊvəlænd/ adj, adv across the land; by land, not by sea or air: *an overland route/journey* ○ *travel overland to Pakistan.*

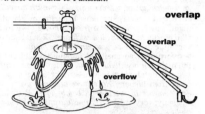

overlap

overlap

overflow

overlap /ˌəʊvəˈlæp/ v (**-pp-**) **1** to extend over sth, esp another similar object, so as to cover it partly: [V, Vn] *The wooden planks overlap (one another).* **2** to happen at the same time: [V, Vpr] *The two conferences overlap (by one day).* **3** to cover part of the same area of interest, responsibility, etc: [V] *Our jobs overlap slightly, which sometimes causes difficulties.*

▶ **overlap** /ˈəʊvəlæp/ n **1** [C] the part or amount of an object which covers sth: *an overlap of 5 cms on each roof tile.* ⊏⟩ picture. **2** [sing] a period of time in which two events, activities, etc happen together: *We need an overlap of at least a week so that John can teach Ann the job.* **3** [U] ~ **(between sth and sth)** a common area of interest, knowledge, etc: *There's a huge overlap between maths and physics.*

overlay /ˌəʊvəˈleɪ/ v (*pt, pp* **overlaid** /-ˈleɪd/) ~ **sth (with sth)** (usu passive) **1** to put one thing on top of another, esp a thin layer of sth over the surface of sth else: [Vnpr] *wood overlaid with gold* [also Vn]. **2** to add sth to sth else so that it seems to cover it: [Vnpr] *The place was overlaid with memories of his childhood.* ▶ **overlay** /ˈəʊvəleɪ/ n: *gold overlay* ○ *a complex overlay of social conventions.*

overleaf /ˌəʊvəˈliːf/ adv on the other side of the page of a book, etc: *See picture overleaf.* ○ *Conditions of sale are listed overleaf.*

overload /ˌəʊvəˈləʊd/ v (esp passive) **1** to put too great a load on or into sth: [Vn] *an overloaded ferry/lorry* [also Vnpr]. **2** ~ **sb (with sth)** to give sb/sth too much of sth: [Vnpr] *He's overloaded with work/responsibilities.* [also Vn]. **3** to put too great a demand on a computer, an electrical system, etc, causing it to fail: [Vn] *The lights fused because the system was overloaded.*

▶ **overload** /ˈəʊvələʊd/ n [U, sing] an excessive amount of sth: *an overload of demands on hospital services* ○ *We're all suffering from information overload.*

overlook /ˌəʊvəˈlʊk/ v **1(a)** to fail to see or notice sth; to miss sth: [Vn] *a fact that is all too easily overlooked.* **(b)** to see a mistake, wrongdoing, etc but decide officially to ignore it: [Vn] *We can't afford to overlook such serious offences.* **(c)** to consider sb/sth not good or important enough and so ignore them/it: [Vn] *Despite her qualifications she has been repeatedly overlooked for the job.* **2** to have or give a view of a place from above it: [Vn] *a flat overlooking Central Park* ○ *Our garden is overlooked by our neighbours' windows.*

overlord /ˈəʊvələːd/ n (esp formerly) a person with supreme power over many people.

overly /ˈəʊvəli/ adv (before an *adj*) too; excessively;

[V.speech] = verb + direct speech   [V.*that*] = verb + *that* clause   [V.*wh*] = verb + *who, how*, etc clause

particularly: *The pay offer isn't overly generous, is it?* ○ *I am not overly impressed by his work.* Compare OVER-.

overmanned /ˌəʊvəˈmænd/ *adj* (of a company, etc) having more workers than are necessary: *Management decided the office was overmanned.* Compare OVERSTAFFED, UNDERMANNED. ▶ **overmanning** /ˌəʊvəˈmænɪŋ/ *n* [U].

over-much /ˌəʊvəˈmʌtʃ/ *adj, adv* (esp with a negative *v*) too much; very much: *His book did not display ˌover-much ˈtalent.* ○ *Don't worry over-much about it.*

overnight /ˌəʊvəˈnaɪt/ *adv* **1** during or for the night: *stay overnight at a friend's house* ○ *We travelled overnight because it was cheaper.* **2** suddenly or very quickly: *She became famous overnight.*

▶ **overnight** /ˈəʊvənaɪt/ *adj* [attrib] **1** during or for the night: *an overnight stop in Rome* ○ *an overnight bag* (ie containing things needed for a night spent away from home) ○ *Have there been any overnight developments in the London bomb story?* **2** (*infml*) suddenly; very quickly: *The restaurant was an overnight success.*

overpass /ˈəʊvəpɑːs; *US* -pæs/ *n* (*esp US*) = FLYOVER 1.

overpay /ˌəʊvəˈpeɪ/ *v* (*pt, pp* **overpaid** /-ˈpeɪd/) ~ **sb** (**for sth / doing sth**) to pay too much; to pay sb too highly: [Vnpr] *I think he's grossly overpaid for doing what he does.* [Vn, Vnpr] *They overpaid me (by £10) this week.* Compare UNDERPAY. ▶ **overpayment** /-ˈpeɪmənt/ *n*.

overplay /ˌəʊvəˈpleɪ/ *v* to attach too much importance to sth: [Vn] *He tends to overplay his role in the negotiations.* Compare UNDERPLAY. **IDM** **overplay one's ˈhand** to spoil one's chance of success by judging that one is in a stronger position than one really is: *The union is in danger of overplaying its hand in the current dispute.*

overpower /ˌəʊvəˈpaʊə(r)/ *v* **1** to defeat or gain control of sb/sth completely because of one's superior strength: [Vn] *The police quickly overpowered the few demonstrators.* **2** to be so strong or intense as to affect or disturb sb seriously: [Vn] *He was overpowered by the cigarette smoke.*

▶ **overpowering** /ˌəʊvəˈpaʊərɪŋ/ *adj* very strong or powerful: *an overpowering feeling of sadness* ○ *The smell from the sewers was almost overpowering.*

overrate /ˌəʊvəˈreɪt/ *v* (esp passive) to have too high an opinion of sb/sth; to put too high a value on sb/sth: [Vn] *In my opinion, he/his work has been greatly overrated.* Compare UNDERRATE.

overreach /ˌəʊvəˈriːtʃ/ *v* ~ **oneself** (*esp derog*) (no passive) to fail by trying to achieve more than is possible: [Vn] *In making these promises, the government clearly overreached itself.*

overreact /ˌəʊvəriˈækt/ *v* ~ (**to sth**) to react too strongly or too intensely to difficulty, danger, bad news, etc: [Vpr] *financial markets overreacting to political changes* [V] *She tends to overreact when things go wrong.* ▶ **overreaction** /-ˈækʃn/ *n* [U, sing] ~ (**to sth**): *an overreaction by the stock market* ○ *The council is accused of overreaction to shopkeepers' complaints.*

override /ˌəʊvəˈraɪd/ *v* (*pt* **overrode** /-ˈrəʊd/; *pp* **overridden** /-ˈrɪdn/) [Vn] **1** to use one's superior authority to reject sth that has already been decided and to ignore the objections or claims of others: [Vn] *override sb's views/decisions/wishes.* **2** to be more important than sth: [Vn] *Considerations of safety override all other concerns.* **3** to interrupt an automatic device and control it oneself: [Vn] *Use this key if you need to override any of the programmed instructions.*

▶ **overriding** /ˌəʊvəˈraɪdɪŋ/ *adj* [attrib] more important than any other considerations: *a question of* **overriding** *importance/interest* ○ *Unemployment seemed the overriding problem.*

overrule /ˌəʊvəˈruːl/ *v* to use one's superior authority to change a decision, reject a proposal, etc: *overrule a claim/an objection* ○ *The Court of Appeal overruled the earlier decision.*

overrun /ˌəʊvəˈrʌn/ *v* (*pt* **overran** /-ˈræn/; *pp* **overrun**) **1** (esp passive) (of sth undesirable) to spread over and occupy a place in great numbers: [Vn] *a warehouse overrun by rats* ○ *They overran the enemy positions in less than a week.* **2** to continue beyond or exceed the time allowed or the expected cost: [Vpr] *The lecturer overran by ten minutes.* [Vn] *The news programme overran its allotted time.* ▶ **overrun** /ˈəʊvərʌn/ *n*: *a cost overrun* ○ *a six-month construction overrun.*

overseas /ˌəʊvəˈsiːz/ *adj* (in Britain used to refer to countries outside Europe) at, to, with, from, etc places or countries across the sea; foreign: ˌoverseas ˈtrade/comˈpetitors/ˈmarkets/ˈearnings ○ ˌoverseas ˈstudents.

▶ **overseas** *adv* abroad: *go/live/travel overseas.*

oversee /ˌəʊvəˈsiː/ *v* (*pt* **oversaw** /-ˈsɔː/; *pp* **overseen** /-ˈsiːn/) [Vn] to supervise sb/sth and make sure that everything is done properly: [Vn] *oversee sb's work* ○ *He is responsible for overseeing day-to-day operations.*

▶ **overseer** /ˈəʊvəsɪə(r)/ *n* (*dated*) a person whose job is to oversee sb/sth.

oversexed /ˌəʊvəˈsekst/ *adj* having stronger sexual desire than is usual.

overshadow /ˌəʊvəˈʃædəʊ/ *v* [Vn] **1** to make sb/sth seem less important or noticeable; to dominate sb/sth: [Vn] *Despite his professional success, he was always overshadowed by his wife.* ○ *Reports of the earthquake overshadowed all other news.* **2** to throw a shadow over sth: [Vn] *The garden is overshadowed by large trees.* **3** to make an occasion less happy than it should be: [Vn] *The victory was overshadowed by the terrible loss of life.*

overshoot /ˌəʊvəˈʃuːt/ *v* (*pt, pp* **overshot** /-ˈʃɒt/) to go further or beyond a target, destination, etc: [Vn] *The aircraft overshot the runway.* [Vpr, Vnpr] *The missile overshot (its target) by a couple of miles.*

oversight /ˈəʊvəsaɪt/ *n* **1** [U, C] a failure to notice or do sth: *The error wasn't deliberate but due to oversight.* ○ *Through an unfortunate oversight your letter was left unanswered.* **2** [U] the responsibility of supervising sb/sth: *give sb/have oversight of broadcasting standards.*

oversimplify /ˌəʊvəˈsɪmplɪfaɪ/ *v* (*pt, pp* **-fied** /-faɪd/) to distort the accuracy of sth by expressing it in terms that are too simple: [Vn] *His analysis consistently oversimplifies the situation/problem/matter.* ▶ **over-simplification** /ˌəʊvəˌsɪmplɪfɪˈkeɪʃn/ *n* [C usu pl, U]: *This is a gross oversimplification of the facts.*

oversized /ˈəʊvəsaɪzd/ (also **oversize** /-saɪz/) *adj* of more than the usual size: *an oversized helmet/class.*

oversleep /ˌəʊvəˈsliːp/ *v* (*pt, pp* **overslept** /-ˈslept/) to sleep longer or later than one intended: [V] *I overslept and was late for work.*

overspend /ˌəʊvəˈspend/ *v* (*pt, pp* **overspent** /-ˈspent/) ~ (**on sth**) to spend too much money or more than the planned amount: [Vpr] *The company overspent on labour.* [Vn] *The council has overspent its budget again.* [also V]. ▶ **overspend** /ˈəʊvəspend/ *n* [sing]: *a £200 000 overspend.*

overspill /ˈəʊvəspɪl/ *n* [U] (*esp Brit*) people who are moved out of a crowded place, esp part of a city, to an area where there is more space: *build new houses for London's overspill* ○ *an overspill housing development.*

overstaffed /ˌəʊvəˈstɑːft; *US* -stæft/ *adj* (of an office, etc) having more members of staff than are necessary. Compare OVERMANNED, UNDERSTAFFED.

overstate /ˌəʊvəˈsteɪt/ *v* to express or state sth too strongly; to exaggerate sth: [Vn] *We must be careful* *not to overstate the case.* ○ *The importance of a good education cannot be overstated.* Compare UN-DERSTATE. ▶ **overstatement** /ˌəʊvəˈsteɪtmənt/ *n* [C, U]: *a gross overstatement of the economic benefits* ○ *his fondness for overstatement.*

overstay /ˌəʊvəˈsteɪ/ *v* to stay longer than the arranged or expected period of time: [Vn] *overstay one's visit to sb.* **IDM** **outstay/overstay one's welcome** ⇨ WELCOME.

overstep /ˌəʊvəˈstep/ *v* (**-pp-**) to go beyond what is normal or permitted: [Vn] *overstep the boundaries of one's authority* ○ *overstep the bounds of modesty.* **IDM** **overstep the ˈmark** to do or say more than one should or more than is wise or acceptable; to go too far: *I've tolerated your rudeness in the past, but this time you've overstepped the mark.*

overstock /ˌəʊvəˈstɒk/ *v* ~ **sth** (**with sth**) (**a**) to have too large a supply or stock of sth: [Vnpr] *a store overstocked with furniture.* [also Vn]. (**b**) to put more animals in an area than there is food or space for: [Vn] *an overstocked field.* [also Vnpr].

overstretch /ˌəʊvəˈstretʃ/ *v* ~ **oneself/sb/sth** to make excessive demands on available resources: [Vn] *an overstretched prison service* ○ *They had overstretched themselves to buy a £300 000 dream house.*

oversubscribed /ˌəʊvəsəbˈskraɪbd/ *adj* (*esp finance*) (of sth for sale) applied for in greater quantities than are available: *The share offer was hugely oversubscribed.*

overt /əʊˈvɜːt, ˈəʊvɜːt/ *adj* [usu attrib] done or shown openly or publicly; not secret or hidden: *an overt display of jealousy/hostility.* Compare COVERT[1]. ▶ **overtly** *adv*: *overtly political activities.*

overtake /ˌəʊvəˈteɪk/ *v* (*pt* **overtook** /-ˈtʊk/; *pp* **overtaken** /-ˈteɪkən/) **1** (*esp Brit*) to come from behind and pass a moving person or vehicle: [Vn] *overtake a tractor* [V] *It's dangerous to overtake on a bend.* **2** to increase in number or amount so as to be more than sth else: [Vn] *These figures could be overtaken by the end of the year.* ○ *Italy's economy has overtaken that of its nearest competitors.* **3** (*esp passive*) (of unpleasant events) to happen to sb/sth suddenly and without warning: [Vn] *be overtaken by fear/surprise/bad weather* ○ *The diplomatic mission was overtaken by events* (ie by circumstances changing rapidly). ○ *The same fate overtook France several years later.*

overtax /ˌəʊvəˈtæks/ *v* to make too great demands on sb/sth: [Vn] *overtax sb's strength/patience.*

overthrow /ˌəʊvəˈθrəʊ/ *v* (*pt* **overthrew** /-ˈθruː/; *pp* **overthrown** /-ˈθrəʊn/) to remove sb/sth from a position of power using force: [Vn] *The rebels tried to overthrow the government.* ▶ **overthrow** /ˈəʊvəθrəʊ/ *n* (usu *sing*) an act of overthrowing sb/sth: *the peaceful overthrow of communism.*

overtime /ˈəʊvətaɪm/ *n* [U] **1** time worked in addition to one's normal working hours: *do 2 hours overtime* ○ *unions imposing a ban on overtime* ○ *overtime pay/earnings.* **2** (*US sport*) = EXTRA TIME. ▶ **overtime** *adv*: *work overtime* ○ (*fig*) *My brain was working overtime* (ie very hard) *trying to think where I'd seen him before.*

overtone /ˈəʊvətəʊn/ *n* (usu *pl*) an attitude, emotion, etc that is suggested or implied in addition to what is actually stated: *a speech containing moral/racial/sexual/political overtones* ○ *overtones of despair.* Compare UNDERTONE 2.

overture /ˈəʊvətʃʊə(r), -tjʊə(r)/ *n* **1** [C] a piece of music written as an introduction to an opera, a ballet, a musical play, etc: *Prokofiev's overture to Romeo and Juliet.* **2** [C usu *pl*] ~ (**to sb**) a friendly approach or proposal made to sb with the aim of starting discussions, establishing a relationship, etc: *He began making overtures to a number of*

merchant banks. ○ *All overtures of peace were rejected.*

overturn /ˌəʊvəˈtɜːn/ *v* **1** to turn over or be turned over: [V] *The car overturned and burst into flames.* [Vn] *He overturned the boat.* ○ *The boys ran down the street overturning boxes of fruit and vegetables.* **2** to reverse a legal decision, result, etc: [Vn] *The court overturned the ruling.* ○ *The Labour candidate overturned the previous Conservative majority of 4000.*

overuse /ˌəʊvəˈjuːz/ *v* to use sth too much or too often: [Vn] *one of the most overused words in politics.* ▶ **overuse** /ˌəʊvəˈjuːs/ *n* [U, sing]: *prevent the overuse of fertilizer.*

overview /ˈəʊvəvjuː/ *n* a short general description or account of sth, without much detail: *Let me give you an overview of the company's plans for the next five years.*

overweening /ˌəʊvəˈwiːnɪŋ/ *adj* [attrib] (*fml derog*) showing excessive confidence, pride, etc: *overweening arrogance/power.*

overweight /ˌəʊvəˈweɪt/ *adj* **1** (of people) too heavy; fat: *an overweight ˈchild* ○ *According to my doctor I'm 8 kilos overweight.* Compare UNDER-WEIGHT. ⇨ note at FAT[1]. **2** heavier than is usual or allowed: *If your luggage is very overweight, you'll have to pay an excess charge.*

overwhelm /ˌəʊvəˈwelm/ *v* **1** to defeat sb completely because of superior numbers, strength, skill, etc: [Vn] *be overwhelmed by the enemy forces* ○ *They overwhelmed our defences within hours.* **2** (of water, etc) to cover sb/sth quickly and completely: [Vn] *The skiers were overwhelmed by an avalanche.* [Vnpr] (*fig*) *We don't want to overwhelm you with requests for information.* **3** (often passive) to have a very strong emotional effect on sb: [Vn] *I was overwhelmed by feelings of despair.* ○ *I felt completely overwhelmed by the kindness I had received.* Compare OVERCOME 3.

▶ **overwhelming** *adj* **1** very great; very strong: *overwhelming support for our policies* ○ *have an overwhelming urge to be sick* ○ *The evidence against him was overwhelming.* **2** complete; total: *an overwhelming victory.* **overwhelmingly** *adv*: *overwhelmingly successful/generous.*

overwork /ˌəʊvəˈwɜːk/ *v* **1** to work or make a person or an animal work too hard or too long: [V] *You'll be ill if you go on overworking like this.* [Vn] *We're overworked and underpaid.* **2** (*esp passive*) to use a word, an idea, etc too much and so make it weaker in meaning or effect: [Vn] *an overworked metaphor/expression.* ▶ **overwork** /ˌəʊvəˈwɜːk/ *n* [U] the practice of working too hard or too long: *stress caused by overwork.*

overwrite /ˌəʊvəˈraɪt/ *v* (*pt* **overwrote** /-ˈrəʊt/; *pp* **overwritten** /-ˈrɪtn/) [Vn] (*computing*) to destroy data on a file by entering and saving new data over it.

overwrought /ˌəʊvəˈrɔːt/ *adj* in a state of nervous excitement, anxiety, etc: *be in a very overwrought state* ○ *I'm sorry about yesterday — I was rather overwrought.*

ovoid /ˈəʊvɔɪd/ *adj* (*fml*) shaped like an egg.

ovulate /ˈɒvjuleɪt/ *v* [V] (*medical*) (of a woman or a female animal) to produce ova (OVUM) from an OVARY(1). ▶ **ovulation** /ˌɒvjuˈleɪʃn/ *n* [U]: *methods of predicting ovulation.*

ovum /ˈəʊvəm/ *n* (*pl* **ova** /ˈəʊvə/) (*biology*) a female cell capable of developing into a baby when fertilized (FERTILIZE 1) by male SPERM(1).

ow /aʊ/ *interj* (expressing sudden pain). Compare OUCH.

owe /əʊ/ *v* **1** ~ (**sb**) **for sth**; ~ **sth** (**to sb**) to have an obligation to pay for sth already received or to pay back a loan: [Vn] *She owes $10 000.* [Vnn] *They owe me £150.* [Vnpr] *He owes rent to Sam.* ○ *I owe you for* *last night's meal.* **2** ~ **sth to sb/sth** to recognize sb/ sth as the cause or source of sth: [Vnpr] *He owes his success more to his contacts than to his ability.* ○ *Her style owes much to Hemingway.* **3** ~ **sth to sb** to be under a moral obligation to behave towards sb in a particular way: [Vnn] *owe one's parents respect* [Vnpr] *owe loyalty to a political party* ○ *We owe it to our customers to give them the best possible service.* **4** to feel gratitude to sb because they have helped one: [Vnn] *I owe my teachers a great deal.* [Vnpr] *I owe a lot to my wife and children.* **IDM owe sb one** (*infml*) to owe sb a favour: *Thanks, David. I 'owe you one.*

owing /ˈəʊɪŋ/ *adj* [pred] (of money that has been earned or lent) not yet paid: *£5 is still owing.*
■ **owing to** *prep* because of or on account of sth: *Owing to torrential rain, the game was cancelled.* ⇨ note at DUE[1].

owl /aʊl/ *n* a bird with large round eyes that hunts small animals at night. Owls are traditionally regarded as wise: *hear the hoot of an owl.* ⇨ picture.
▶ **owlish** *adj* looking serious or wise, esp because of the shape of one's face and eyes: *Her owlish glasses make her look too studious.* **owlishly** *adv.*

owl
barn-owl

own[1] /əʊn/ *det, pron* **1** (used after possessives to emphasize personal possession or responsibility, or the individual character of sth) belonging to oneself, itself, ourselves, etc: *I saw it with my own eyes* (ie I didn't hear about it from someone else). ○ *It was her own idea.* ○ *This is my own house/This house is my own* (ie not rented, etc). ○ *Our children are grown up and have children of their own.* ○ *I have my very own room at last.* ○ *Your day off is your own* (ie You can spend it as you wish). ○ *For reasons of his own* (ie particular reasons that perhaps only he knew about), *he refused to join the club.* ○ *The accident happened through no fault of her own.* ○ *He wants to come into the business on his own terms.* **2** done or produced by and for oneself: *She makes all her own clothes.* ○ *He has to cook his own meals.* **IDM come into one's/its 'own** to have the opportunity to show one's/its qualities or abilities: *This car really comes into its own on rough ground.* ○ *She really came into her own when the children were ill.* **get one's 'own back (on sb)** (*infml*) to do sth to sb in return for harm, injury, etc they have done to oneself: *I'll get my own back on him one day, I swear!* **hold one's 'own (against sb/sth) (in sth)** to maintain one's position against attack, competition, etc and not become weaker: *Business isn't good but we're managing to hold our own.* ○ *She can hold her own against anybody in an argument.* ○ *The patient is holding her own although she is still very ill.* **(all) on one's 'own 1** alone: *I'm all on my own today.* ○ *She lives on her own.* **2** without being helped or supervised; alone: *He can be left to work on his own.* ⇨ note at ALONE.
■ **'own 'brand** (also *Brit* **,own 'label,** *US* **'store brand**) *n* [often attrib] goods in a shop marked with the name of the shop or store instead of that of the manufacturer: *He designs for both Chanel and his own brand.* ○ **,own label 'products.**
,own 'goal *n* (*Brit*) **(a)** a goal scored accidentally by a member of a team against her or his own side. **(b)** a silly mistake made against one's own interests, which embarrasses one but amuses other people: *The proposals threatened their own jobs and were seen as a spectacular own goal.*

own[2] /əʊn/ *v* **1** to have sth as one's property; to possess sth: [Vn] *This house is mine; I own it.* ○ *They*

owned just a few goats and some chickens. ○ *a privately/publicly/jointly owned company* ○ *An investment trust owns 12% of the shares.* **2** (*fml*) **(a)** to admit or acknowledge that sth is true: [V.that] *I own (that) it was entirely my fault.* [Vn-n] *He owned the boy as his son.* [Vn] *She was finally forced to own the truth.* **(b)** ~ **(to sth/doing sth)** to confess that one has or is doing sth: [Vpr] *She owned to a feeling of profound jealousy.* **PHRV ,own 'up (to sth/doing sth)** to admit or confess that one is to blame for sth: *Nobody owned up to breaking the window.* ○ *Eventually she owned up.*

owner /ˈəʊnə(r)/ *n* a person who owns sth: *the owner of a black Mercedes* ○ *boat owners* ○ *the dog's owner.* See also LANDOWNER.
▶ **ownership** *n* [U] the state or right of being an owner: *a growth in house ownership* ○ *be in private/ joint/public ownership* ○ *The ownership of the land is disputed.* ○ *The restaurant is under new ownership.*
■ **,owner-'occupied** *adj* (of a house, etc) lived in by the owner, not rented to sb else: *Most of the houses in this street are owner-occupied.* **,owner-'occupier** *n* a person who owns the house he or she lives in.

ox /ɒks/ *n* (*pl* **oxen** /ˈɒksn/) **1** a BULLOCK used, esp formerly, for pulling carts, agricultural equipment, etc. Compare BULL[1] 1, STEER[2]. **2** (esp *pl*) (*dated*) any domestic cow or BULL[1](1). See also CATTLE.

Oxbridge /ˈɒksbrɪdʒ/ *n* (*Brit*) the universities of Oxford and Cambridge considered together, esp in contrast to newer British universities: *Oxbridge graduates.* Compare REDBRICK 1.

Oxfam /ˈɒksfæm/ *abbr* Oxford Committee for Famine Relief (a charity that raises money in Britain and distributes aid to the developing world): *a concert in aid of Oxfam* ○ *an Oxfam shop.*

oxide /ˈɒksaɪd/ *n* [C, U] (*chemistry*) a compound of oxygen with another substance: *iron oxide* ○ *an oxide of tin.*

oxidize, -ise /ˈɒksɪdaɪz/ *v* **(a)** to combine or cause sth to combine with oxygen. **(b)** to form or become covered with RUST(1). ▶ **oxidization, -isation** /ˌɒksɪdaɪˈzeɪʃn; *US* -dəˈz-/ (also **oxidation** /ˌɒksɪˈdeɪʃn/) *n* [U].

Oxon /ˈɒksɒn/ *abbr* **1** (esp in addresses) Oxfordshire (Latin *Oxonia*). **2** (esp in degree titles) of Oxford University (Latin *Oxoniensis*): *Alice Tolley MA (Oxon).* Compare CANTAB.

oxtail /ˈɒksteɪl/ *n* the tail of an ox, used esp for making soup.

oxyacetylene /ˌɒksiəˈsetəliːn/ *n* a mixture of oxygen and ACETYLENE gas which produces a very hot flame, used esp for cutting or joining metal: *oxyacetylene torches.*

oxygen /ˈɒksɪdʒən/ *n* [U] (*symb* **O**) a chemical element. Oxygen is a gas without colour, taste or smell, which is present in the air and necessary for all forms of life on earth: *suffer from lack of oxygen* ○ *Oxygen was in short supply on the higher slopes.* ⇨ App 7.
▶ **oxygenate** /-eɪt/ *v* [Vn] to supply, treat or mix sth with oxygen.
■ **'oxygen mask** *n* a mask placed over the nose and mouth through which a person can breathe oxygen, eg in an aircraft or a hospital: *Oxygen masks will drop from the overhead lockers in an emergency.*
'oxygen tent *n* a small tent placed over a sick person who needs an extra supply of oxygen.

oyster /ˈɔɪstə(r)/ *n* a large flat SHELLFISH. Some types of oyster can be eaten and others produce pearls (PEARL 1a): *boys diving for pearls in the oyster beds.* ⇨ picture at SHELLFISH. **IDM the world is one's oyster** ⇨ WORLD.
■ **'oyster-catcher** *n* a type of black and white sea bird that eats SHELLFISH.

[V.*to* inf] = verb + *to* infinitive   [Vn.inf (no *to*)] = verb + noun + infinitive without *to*   [V.*ing*] = verb + -*ing* form

oz *abbr* (*pl* unchanged or **ozs**) ounce (Italian *onza*): *Add 4 oz sugar.* ⇨ App 2.

ozone /ˈəʊzəʊn/ *n* [U] (**a**) (*chemistry*) a colourless gas with a strong smell: *ozone depletion* (ie in the ozone layer). (**b**) (*Brit infml*) air that smells fresh and pure as at the seaside: *Just breathe in that ozone!*

■ ˌozone-ˈfriendly *adj* not containing substances that will damage the ozone layer: *ozone-friendly aerosols/fridges.* ⇨ note at USER-FRIENDLY.

ˈozone hole *n* an area in the ozone layer where the amount of ozone has been greatly reduced, so that harmful rays from the sun can pass through it: *an ozone hole over the Arctic.*

ˈozone layer *n* [sing] a layer of ozone high above the earth's surface that helps to protect the earth from the sun's harmful rays.

O

Pp

P¹ (also **p**) /piː/ n (pl **P's**, **p's** /piːz/) the 16th letter of the English alphabet: *'Philip' begins with (a) P/'P'*. **IDM mind one's p's and q's** ⇨ MIND².

P² *abbr* (on road signs) parking.

p *abbr* **1** (pl **pp**) page: *see p 34 and pp 63-72*. **2** /piː/ (Brit infml) penny; pence: *a 49p stamp* ○ *The minimum charge for a call is 20p.* ⇨ note at PENNY. Compare D 2. **3** (music) quietly; softly (SOFT) (Italian *piano*). Compare F 3.

PA /ˌpiː ˈeɪ/ *abbr* **1** personal assistant: *She works as PA to the managing director.* **2** Press Association. **3** public address (system): *The announcement was made on/over the PA (system).*

pa¹ /pɑː/ n (infml esp US) father.

pa² *abbr* per year (Latin *per annum*): *salary £29 000 pa* ○ *an increase of 3.2% pa.*

pace¹ /peɪs/ n **1** [C] **(a)** a single step in walking or running: *She took two paces forward.* ○ *To be a really good runner he needs to lengthen his pace a little.* **(b)** the length of a large step, used as a measurement: *Competitors must stand at a distance of 20 paces from each other.* **2** [U, sing] the rate or speed of movement, esp of walking or running: *at a good/fast/slow/walking pace* ○ *quicken one's pace* ○ *She slackened her pace so I could keep up with her.* ○ *The ball **gathered pace** as it rolled down the hill.* **3** [U, sing] **(a)** the speed or rate at which sth progresses, develops, changes, etc: *increasing the pace of reform* ○ *I like the slow pace of life in the country.* See also PACY. **(b)** the fast speed or rate of sth: *He gave up his job in advertising because he couldn't take/stand the pace.* ○ *This novel lacks pace* (ie Its plot develops too slowly). **IDM at a snail's pace** ⇨ SNAIL. **force the pace** ⇨ FORCE². **go through / show one's ˈpaces** to show others what one is capable of: *We watched the horses going through their paces.* **keep ˈpace (with sb/sth)** to develop or increase at the same rate as sb/sth: *The company must keep pace with changes in the market.* ○ *Are wages keeping pace with inflation?* **put sb/sth through their/its ˈpaces** to give sb/sth tasks to perform in order to test their/its ability or quality: *put a new car through its paces* ○ *Youngsters will be put through their paces by qualified instructors.* **set the ˈpace 1** to be quicker than others to introduce new products, ideas, changes, etc and so force others to make the same changes in order to remain in business: *This company is setting the pace in the home computer market.* **2** to run ahead of other competitors in a race at a speed which they try to copy: *Willis set the pace in the first mile.*

pace² /peɪs/ v **1** to walk with slow or regular steps, eg when one is anxious or annoyed: [Vp, Vpr] *He paced up and down (the platform), waiting for the train.* [Vp] *She seemed agitated, restlessly pacing about.* [Vn] *He paced the streets all night long.* **2** to set the rate or speed at which sth happens or develops: [Vnadv] *The play was badly paced.* **3** ~ **oneself** to find the right speed and rhythm of work, life, etc for oneself: *You need to pace yourself in a job like this.* **PHRV pace sth off/out** to measure sth by taking regular steps across it: *She paced out the length of the room.*

pace³ /ˈpɑːkeɪ, ˈpɑːtʃeɪ, ˈpeɪsɪ/ prep (Latin fml) (used to express polite disagreement with sb's opinion) with respect to sb: *Pace Professor Maxwell, the evidence suggests…*

pacemaker /ˈpeɪsmeɪkə(r)/ n **1** (also **ˈpace-setter**) a runner in a race who deliberately starts at a faster speed than he or she will be able to continue at, sometimes in order to help another runner to win: *Early pacemakers tend to fade before the finish.* ○ (fig) *an inner city project regarded as a pace-setter for the rest of Britain.* **2** an electronic device placed under the skin near the heart to make the heart beat in a more regular way: *be fitted with a pacemaker.*

pachyderm /ˈpækidɜːm/ n (techn) a type of animal with very thick skin, eg an elephant.

pacific /pəˈsɪfɪk/ adj (fml) making or loving peace; peaceful: *Their intentions are purely pacific.*

pacifism /ˈpæsɪfɪzəm/ n [U] the belief that war and violence are wrong and that all disputes can be settled by discussion.
▶ **pacifist** /-ɪst/ n a person who believes in pacifism and would refuse to fight in a war: *a lifelong/convinced/confirmed pacifist* ○ *pacifist principles.*

pacify /ˈpæsɪfaɪ/ v (pt, pp **-fied**) **1** to make sb calm and quiet: [Vn] *He was furious at first, but I managed to pacify him.* **2** [Vn] to establish peace in an area or a country where there is war.
▶ **pacification** /ˌpæsɪfɪˈkeɪʃn/ n [U]: *the pacification of the rebel states.*
pacifier n (US) = DUMMY 3.

pack¹ /pæk/ n **1** [C] a small paper or cardboard container in which several of the same item are packed together; a packet: *a pack of cigarettes/beefburgers/Christmas cards* ○ *a six-pack of beer* (ie six cans of beer wrapped and sold together) ○ *They are £5.80 for a pack of four.* **2** a set of different items packed together for a particular purpose: *a membership/an information/a home buyers' pack* ○ *I gave her one of those Chinese cookery starter packs with all the different sauces and spices.* **3** [C] **(a)** a number of things wrapped or tied together for carrying, esp on the back: *donkeys carrying packs of wool.* **(b)** a large bag with straps that fit over the shoulders and an opening at the top: *long-distance walkers carrying huge packs.* See also BACKPACK, HAVERSACK, RUCKSACK. **4** [CGp] ~ **(of sb/sth)** (often derog) a number of people or things: *a pack of reporters* ○ *He told me a pack of lies.* ○ *They **lead the pack** of European car manufacturers.* **5** [CGp] **(a)** a group of animals that hunt together: *packs of dogs roaming the streets* ○ *Wolves hunt in packs.* **(b)** a group of dogs kept for hunting: *a pack of hounds.* **6** [CGp] an organized group of Cub Scouts or Brownies. **7** [C] (US **deck**) a complete set of 52 playing-cards (PLAYING-CARD). **IDM the joker in the pack** ⇨ JOKER. See also FACE-PACK, ICE-PACK.
■ **ˈpack-animal** n an animal used for carrying loads, eg a horse.
ˈpack ice n [U] a large mass of ice floating in the sea, formed from smaller pieces which have frozen together.

pack² /pæk/ v **1(a)** ~ **(sth) (in/into sth)** to put one's possessions into a container for transport or storage: [V, Vn] *Haven't you packed (your suitcase) yet?* [Vn, Vnpr] *All these books need to be packed (into boxes).* **(b)** ~ **into sth** to fit into a container for transport or storage: [Vnpr] *My clothes won't all pack into this case.* **2** ~ **sth (in sth) (a)** to protect sth that breaks easily by surrounding it with soft material: [Vnpr] *pack china in newspaper* ○ *glass packed in*

[Vnn] = verb + noun + noun [V-adj] = verb + adjective For more help with verbs, see Study pages **B4–8**.

straw [also Vn]. (**b**) to store fruit, meat, fish, etc in a substance in order to preserve it: [Vnpr] *fresh shell-fish packed in ice* ○ *sardines packed in oil/brine.* **3** to put food, manufactured goods, etc into a container for storage or sale: [Vnpr] *meat packed in Cellophane* [Vn] *She packs eggs.* **4** ~ **sth** (**with sth/sb**) (esp passive) to fill or crowd sth with people or things: [Vn, Vnpr] *Chanting fans packed the stadium/The stadium was packed with chanting fans.* ○ *The show played to packed houses* (ie large audiences). [Vnpr] *This book is packed with useful information.* [Vn] *The restaurant was packed* (ie crowded). [Vnp] *Everyone was packed together on the station platform.* See also ACTION-PACKED. **5** to form or make sth form a hard thick mass: [Vnpr] *The wind had packed the snow against the door.* [also Vpr]. **6** (*US infml*) to carry sth regularly: [Vn] *He packs a gun.* **7** ~ **sth with sb** (*derog*) to choose the members of a committee, etc so that they are likely to support one: [Vnpr] *He packed the board with like-minded colleagues.* **IDM** **pack one's 'bags** (*infml*) to leave one's home or family permanently, esp after a disagreement: *The next time he hit her she packed her bags and left.* **pack a (hard, etc) 'punch** (*infml*) **1** (of a boxer) to be capable of hitting sb very hard. **2** to have a very powerful effect: *Her cocktails pack quite a punch!* **send sb packing** ⇨ SEND. **PHRV** ,**pack sth a'way** to put sth into a box, cupboard, etc because it is not needed: *As soon as he finished university, he packed away all his notes.*

,**pack (sb/sth)** '**in**; ,**pack (sb/sth)** '**into sth** to fill a limited space completely: *All six of us were packed into the tiny car.* ○ *The show has been packing them in for months* (ie attracting large audiences). ,**pack it** '**in** (*Brit infml*) (esp imperative) to stop doing or saying sth that angers or annoys sb else: *I'm sick of your complaining — just pack it in, will you?* ,**pack sth** '**in** (*infml*) to leave or abandon sth: *She's packed in her job.* ○ *Smoking's bad for you — you ought to pack it in.* ,**pack sth** '**in**; ,**pack sth** '**in/'into sth** to do a lot of things in a limited time: *She managed to pack a lot of sightseeing into three days.*

,**pack sb** '**off (to …)** to send sb away, esp because one does not want them with one: *She packed the children off to bed.* ○ *In the summer we were packed off to stay with our grandparents.*

,**pack sth** '**out** (esp passive) to fill a theatre, cinema, etc completely: *Opera houses are packed out wherever she sings.*

,**pack** '**up** (*infml esp Brit*) (of a machine, an engine, etc) to stop working or operating; to break down (BREAK¹): *My car has packed up.* ,**pack (sth)** '**up 1** to put one's possessions into cases, etc before leaving a place: *He packed up his things and left.* **2** (*infml*) to stop doing sth: *Business is terrible — I might as well pack up and go home.* ○ *When did you pack up that job you had in Japan?*

▶ **packer** *n* a person, company or machine that packs goods, esp food.
■ ,**packed** '**lunch** *n* sandwiches, fruit, etc prepared at home and taken to work, school, etc to eat for lunch: *He takes a packed lunch to work every day.*

package /'pækɪdʒ/ *n* **1(a)** an object or objects wrapped in paper or packed in a box; a parcel: *The postman delivered a large package.* (**b**) a box, etc in which things are packed. **2** (*US*) = PACKET 1. **3** (also '**package deal**) a set of proposals offered or accepted as a whole: *a benefits/an aid/an economic package* ○ *agree on a **package of measures** to reduce the trade deficit.* **4** (*computing*) a closely related set of programs (PROGRAM 1) for a particular application, sold and used as a single unit: *a new word-processing package.*

▶ **package** *v* **1** to make sth into or put sth in a bag, box, etc, eg to sell it: [Vn] *packaged foods* [Vnpr] *They are packaged in 2 kg and 5 kg bags.* [Vnadv]

Their products are always attractively packaged. **2** to represent sb/sth in a particular way: [Vn-n] *She did not want to be packaged as a feminist writer.*
packaging *n* [U] materials used to wrap or protect goods: *Attractive packaging helps to sell products.*
■ '**package holiday** (also '**package tour**) *n* a holiday organized by a travel agent, for which one pays a fixed price that includes the cost of transport, accommodation and often some meals.

packet /'pækɪt/ *n* **1** [C] (**a**) (*US* usu **package** or **pack**) a small paper or cardboard container in which goods are packed for selling: *a packet of biscuits/cigarettes/crisps* ○ *an empty cereal packet* ○ *packet soup.* (**b**) a small parcel: *She took out a small packet from her bag.* **2** [sing] (*infml*) a large amount of money: *Buying your children's school uniform can cost (you) a packet.*

packing /'pækɪŋ/ *n* [U] **1** the process of packing one's possessions, goods, etc: *Have you finished your packing* (eg to go on holiday)? **2** material used for packing delicate objects: *Put plenty of packing round it.* ○ *add £2.50 for postage and packing.*
■ '**packing-case** *n* a usu wooden box or case for storing or transporting goods.

pact /pækt/ *n* an agreement between two or more people, groups or countries: *a suicide pact* ○ *sign a non-aggression pact* ○ *They made a pact not to tell anyone.*

pacy /'peɪsi/ *adj* moving or progressing quickly: *a pacy thriller.*

pad¹ /pæd/ *n* **1** a thick piece of soft material used eg to protect sth from rubbing against sth else, or to improve the shape or increase the size of sth: *put a pad of cotton wool and gauze over a wound* ○ *a jacket with 'shoulder-pads.* **2** (usu *pl*) a piece of thick flexible material worn in certain sports, eg football and cricket, to protect the legs and ankles. ⇨ picture at CRICKET¹, HOCKEY. See also SHIN-PAD. **3** a number of sheets of paper for writing or drawing on, fastened together at one edge: *a 'writing pad.* **4** the soft part under the foot of certain animals, eg dogs and foxes. **5** a flat surface from which a spacecraft is launched or on which it lands. See also LAUNCHING PAD. **6** (usu *sing*) (*dated infml*) the place where sb lives: *Come back to my pad.*

pad² /pæd/ *v* (**-dd-**) (esp passive) to add soft material to a container, garment, etc, eg to help protect sth/sb or to change the shape or increase the size of sth: [Vn] *a padded envelope* (ie for sending delicate objects through the post) ○ *a padded bra/jacket* ○ *padded earphones.* **PHRV** ,**pad sth** '**out 1** to put soft material into a garment in order to give it a particular shape: *pad out the shoulders of a dress.* **2** to make a book, an essay, a speech, etc longer by adding unnecessary material: *I padded out my essay with lots of quotations.*

▶ **padding** *n* [U] **1** soft material used for padding things. **2** unnecessary material in an essay, etc: *His speech was virtually all padding.*
■ ,**padded** '**cell** *n* a room in a hospital for mentally ill people, with soft walls to prevent violent patients from injuring themselves.

pad³ /pæd/ *v* (**-dd-**) to walk with steady steps making a soft dull sound: [Vp, Vpr] *pad about (the house) in one's slippers.*

paddle¹ /'pædl/ *n* **1** [C] a short pole with a broad blade at one or both ends, used to move a small boat, esp a CANOE, through the water. ⇨ picture at CANOE. Compare OAR. **2** [sing] an act or a period of using the paddle in a boat. **3** [C] an instrument or a part of a machine shaped like a paddle, esp one used for beating or mixing food.

▶ **paddle** *v* to move a small boat through the water using a paddle: [Vpr] *paddle across the river* [Vadv, Vnadv] *We paddled (the canoe) slowly upstream.* [also Vp, Vn, Vnpl]. **IDM** **paddle one's own**

paddle-steamer

ca'noe (*infml*) to depend on oneself and no one else; to be independent.

■ 'paddle-steamer *n* a boat powered by steam and moved by a wheel with a number of boards attached which push against the water as the wheel turns. ⇨ picture.

paddle² /'pædl/ *v* (a) to walk with bare feet in shallow water: [Vpr, Vp] *paddling (about) at the water's edge* [also V]. Compare WADE 1. (b) to move one's feet or hands gently in water, eg while sitting: [Vnpr] *paddle one's toes in the water*.
▶ paddle *n* [sing] an act or a period of paddling: *Let's go for a paddle*.
■ 'paddling pool (*US* 'wading pool) *n* a shallow pool in which children may paddle.

paddock /'pædək/ *n* 1 a small field where horses are kept or exercised. 2 an enclosure at a course or track where horses or cars assemble and are shown before a race.

paddy¹ /'pædi/ (also 'paddy-field) *n* a field where rice is grown.

paddy² /'pædi/ *n* (usu *sing*) (*Brit infml*) a fit of anger or temper: *be in a paddy*.

Paddy /'pædi/ *n* (*infml offensive*) an Irish person.

padlock /'pædlɒk/ *n* a type of lock¹(1) with a loop at one side that is opened with a key. It is used for fastening things, eg two ends of a chain, together. ⇨ picture at CHAIN.
▶ padlock *v* to fasten sth with a padlock: [Vn] *The gate was securely padlocked*. [Vnpr] *She padlocked her bike to the railings*.

padre /'pɑːdreɪ/ *n* (*infml*) (often as a form of address) a religious minister¹(3) in the armed forces: *Good morning, padre!* Compare CHAPLAIN.

paean /'piːən/ *n* (*fml*) a song of praise or victory: *a paean of praise*.

paediatrics (*US* pediatrics) /ˌpiːdɪˈætrɪks/ *n* [sing *v*] the branch of medicine concerned with children and their illnesses.
▶ paediatric (*US* pedi-) *adj*: *a paediatric ward* (ie for sick children).
paediatrician (*US* pedi-) /ˌpiːdɪəˈtrɪʃn/ *n* a doctor who specializes in paediatrics.

paedophilia (*US* pedo-) /ˌpiːdəˈfɪliə/ *n* [U] the condition of being sexually attracted to children.
▶ paedophile (*US* pedo-) /'piːdəʊfaɪl/ *n* a person who is sexually attracted to children.

paella /paɪˈelə/ *n* [U] a Spanish dish of rice, chicken, fish and vegetables, cooked and served in a large shallow pan.

pagan /'peɪgən/ *n* (*sometimes derog*) 1 a person who is not a believer in any of the world's chief religions, esp as viewed by those who are believers. 2 (formerly) a person who did not believe in Christianity. Compare ATHEIST, HEATHEN 1. ▶ pagan *adj*: *pagan worship of the sun*. paganism /-ɪzəm/ *n* [U].

page¹ /peɪdʒ/ *n* 1(a) (*abbr* p) one side of a sheet of paper in a book, magazine, etc: *read a few pages of a book* ○ *the sports page* (ie in a newspaper) ○ *You'll find the quotation on page 35*. See also FRONT-PAGE, FULL-PAGE. (b) this sheet of paper itself: *Several pages have been torn out of the book*. See also YELLOW PAGES. 2 (*rhet*) an episode or a period of history: *a glorious page of Arab history*.

page² *v* [Vn] 1 to call the name of sb over a public-

address system (PUBLIC), eg at an airport, in order to give them a message. 2 to contact sb by sending radio signals to a device that they carry. The device makes a noise when receiving the signals: *Can you page Dr Berry, please?* ○ *Europe-wide radio paging services*.
▶ pager *n* a device operated by radio signals, used for receiving messages.

page³ /peɪdʒ/ (also 'page-boy) *n* (a) (*Brit*) (*US* 'bell-boy) a boy or young man, usu in uniform, employed in a hotel or club to carry cases, open doors for people, etc. (b) a small boy attending a woman when she gets married.

pageant /'pædʒənt/ *n* 1 a public entertainment consisting of a procession of people in costume, or an outdoor performance of scenes from history: (*fig*) *the pageant of history* (ie history as a succession of colourful events). 2 a brilliant display or spectacle.
▶ pageantry /'pædʒəntri/ *n* [U] elaborate display and ceremony: *all the pageantry of a coronation*.

pagoda /pəˈgəʊdə/ *n* a religious building in India and E Asia. It is usu a tall tower with several levels, each of which has its own roof extending over the floor below. ⇨ picture.

paid *pt, pp* of PAY².
▶ paid *adj* [usu attrib] (of work, etc) for which people receive money: *take paid leave*. IDM put paid to sth ⇨ PAY².
■ 'paid-up *adj* [attrib] having paid all the money owed to a club, political party, etc: *She's a (fully) ˌpaid-up 'member*.

pagoda

pail /peɪl/ *n* a bucket: *a pail of water*.

pain /peɪn/ *n* 1(a) [U] the physical suffering or discomfort caused by injury or illness: *be in (great) pain* ○ *feel no/not much/a lot of pain* ○ *a cry of pain* ○ *suffer from acute back pain* ○ *Her back causes/gives her a lot of pain*. (b) [C] a feeling of suffering or discomfort in a particular part of the body: *have a pain in one's back/chest/shoulder* ○ *stomach pains* ○ *muscular **aches and pains*** ○ *This should ease the pain*. (c) [U] mental suffering or distress: *the pain of separation* ○ *He caused his family much pain*. 2 [C] (*infml*) an annoying or boring person or thing: *She can be a real pain when she's in a bad mood*. ○ *We've missed the last bus — what a pain!* IDM a pain in the 'arse/'neck (*infml*) an annoying or boring person or thing. on/under pain/penalty of sth (*fml*) with the threat of the specified punishment if one does not obey: *Prisoners were forbidden to approach the fence under pain of death*.
▶ pain *v* (no passive) to cause sb pain or distress: [Vn] *My foot is still paining me*. ○ *It pains me to have to tell you this*. pained *adj* annoyed or offended: *give sb a pained look*.

painful /-fl/ *adj* 1 causing or making one feel pain: *a painful blow on the shoulder* ○ *Her shoulder is still painful*. 2 causing distress or embarrassment: *a painful experience/memory/conversation* ○ *His embarrassment was painful to watch*. 3 causing trouble or difficulty: *the painful process of stripping the paint off the wall*. painfully /-fəli/ *adv*: *Her thumb is painfully swollen*. ○ *He was **painfully aware** of his lack of experience*. ○ *Progress has been painfully slow*.

painless *adj* not causing pain or distress: *The treatment is quite painless*. painlessly *adv*.

painkiller /'peɪnkɪlə(r)/ *n* a drug that reduces pain: *She's on* (ie taking) *painkillers*. ▶ painkilling *adj*: *a painkilling drug/injection*.

pains /peɪnz/ *n* [pl] IDM be at pains to do sth to take great care or make a particular effort to do sth:

She was at great pains to stress the advantages of the new system. **for one's pains** in return for one's efforts or trouble: *She looked after her sick mother for 10 years and got no thanks at all for her pains.* **take (great) pains (with / over / to do sth)** to take great care or make a careful effort to do sth: *She always takes great pains with her work.* ○ *Great pains have been taken to ensure the safety of passengers.*

painstaking /ˈpeɪnzteɪkɪŋ/ *adj* done with, requiring or taking great care or trouble: *a painstaking task/investigation* ○ *with painstaking attention to detail* ○ *a painstaking student/worker.* ▶ **painstakingly** *adv.*

paint¹ /peɪnt/ *n* **1(a)** [U] a substance applied to a surface in liquid form to give it colour: *white/black/yellow paint* ○ *give the door a fresh coat of paint* ○ *The paint is still wet* (ie It has not dried yet). **(b)** [U] a layer of dried paint on a surface: *The paint is starting to peel off.* **2 paints** [pl] tubes or blocks of paint, often in a set: *a box/set of oil-paints* ○ *The artist brought his paints with him.*

paint² /peɪnt/ *v* **1** to put paint onto sth: [Vn] *paint a door/wall/house* [Vn-adj] *paint the ceiling white* [also V]. **2** to make a picture using paints; to portray or represent sb/sth in paint: [Vpr] *paint in oils/water-colours* [Vn] *paint a picture/a portrait/a landscape* [Vnpr] *Someone had painted a beard on the poster of the prime minister.* ○ *(fig) In her latest novel she paints a gloomy picture of life in the next century.* [V] *My paint paints well* (ie is a good artist). **3** *(dated or joc)* to put colouring substances onto the face, etc: [Vn] *She spends hours painting her face.* **IDM** **not as black as it/one is painted** ⇨ BLACK¹. **paint the town ˈred** *(infml)* to go out and enjoy a lively noisy time in bars, clubs, etc, esp in order to celebrate sth. **PHRV** **ˌpaint sth ˈout** to cover a part of a painting by putting more paint on top: *Some of the original figures seem to have been painted out.* **ˌpaint ˈover sth** to cover sth with paint: *paint over the dirty marks on the wall.*

paintbox /ˈpeɪntbɒks/ *n* a box containing a set of paints.

paintbrush /ˈpeɪntbrʌʃ/ *n* a brush used for applying paint. ⇨ picture at BRUSH¹.

painter¹ /ˈpeɪntə(r)/ *n* **1** a person whose job is painting buildings, walls, windows, etc: *work as a painter and decorator.* **2** an artist who paints pictures: *a famous painter* ○ *a portrait/landscape painter.*

painter² /ˈpeɪntə(r)/ *n* a rope fastened to the front of a boat, used for tying it to a post, ship, etc.

painting /ˈpeɪntɪŋ/ *n* **1** [U] the process or art of using paint: *wash and rub down the walls in preparation for painting* ○ *Her hobbies include music and painting.* **2** [C] a picture that has been painted: *a famous painting by Rembrandt.*

paintwork /ˈpeɪntwɜːk/ *n* [U] a painted surface or surfaces: *The paintwork is in good condition.* ○ *A stone hit the car and damaged the paintwork.*

pair /peə(r)/ *n* **1** [C] two things of the same kind, usu used, worn, etc together: *a pair of gloves/shoes/socks/earrings* ○ *a huge pair of eyes.* **2** [C] an object consisting of two parts joined together: *a pair of binoculars/tights/scissors/underpants* ○ *I've broken my glasses — I'll have to buy a new pair.* **3** [pl v] two people closely connected or doing sth together: *the happy pair* (ie the newly married couple) ○ *(infml) You've behaved very badly, the pair of you!* **4** [CGp] one male and one female animal of the same species that are breeding together: *a pair of swans nesting by the river.* **5** [C] two horses linked together to pull a carriage, etc: *a coach and pair.* See also AU PAIR. **IDM** **in ˈpairs** two at a time; in twos: *These earrings are only sold in pairs.* **show a clean pair of heels** ⇨ SHOW².

▶ **pair** *v* **1** ~ A with B; ~ A and B **(together)** (esp passive) to arrange people or things in a pair or pairs: [Vnpr] *be paired with sb in a doubles match* [also Vnp, Vn]. **2** [V] (of animals) to come together in order to breed. **PHRV** **ˌpair (sb/sth) ˈoff (with sb)** to form or make sb/sth form a pair or pairs: *The students had all paired off by the end of term.* ○ *She's always trying to pair her friends off with each other.* **ˌpair ˈup (with sb)** to form a pair or pairs in order to work, play a game, etc together.

Paisley /ˈpeɪzli/ *n* [often attrib] a detailed pattern of curved figures that look like feathers: *a Paisley tie/dressing-gown.*

pajamas *(esp US)* = PYJAMAS.

pal /pæl/ *n* *(dated infml)* **1** a friend: *We've been pals for years.* **2** *(infml)* (used as an aggressive form of address to a man): *Now look here, pal, you're asking for trouble!*

▶ **pal** *v* **(-ll-)** **PHRV** **ˌpal ˈup (with sb)** *(Brit)*; *(US)* **ˌpal aˈround (with sb)** *(infml)* to become friendly with sb.

pally /ˈpæli/ *adj* ~ **(with sb)** *(infml)* friendly: *She's become very pally with the boss.* ○ *They've become very pally (with each other).*

palace /ˈpæləs/ *n* **1** the official home of a ruler, an ARCHBISHOP or a bishop: *Buckingham Palace* ○ *a presidential palace.* **2(a)** any large splendid house: *Compared to ours their house is a palace.* **(b)** (used in the names of large public buildings, eg hotels and cinemas): *Crystal Palace* ○ *Strand Palace Hotel.*

palae(o)- (also *esp US* **pale(o)-**) *comb form* of ancient times; very old: *palaeolithic* ○ *palaeontology.*

palaeolithic (also *esp US* **paleo-**) /ˌpæliəʊˈlɪθɪk, ˌpeɪl-/ *adj* of or relating to the early part of the Stone Age.

palaeontology (also *esp US* **paleon-**) /ˌpæliɒnˈtɒlədʒi, ˌpeɪl-/ *n* [U] the study of fossils (FOSSIL 1) as a guide to the history of life on earth. ▶ **palaeontologist** (also *esp US* **paleon-**) /-ədʒɪst/ *n* an expert in palaeontology.

palatable /ˈpælətəbl/ *adj* **(a)** pleasant to taste: *add a few herbs to make the stew more palatable.* **(b)** pleasant or acceptable to the mind: *The truth is not always very palatable.*

palatal /ˈpælətl/ *adj* *(phonetics)* (of a speech sound) made by placing the tongue against or near the PALATE(1) (usu the hard palate).

palate /ˈpælət/ *n* **1** the roof of the mouth: *the hard/soft palate* (ie its front/back part). See also CLEFT PALATE. ⇨ picture at THROAT. **2** (usu *sing*) a sense of taste; an ability to distinguish one taste from another: *a wine that will delight even the most jaded palate.*

palatial /pəˈleɪʃl/ *adj* **(a)** like a palace. **(b)** extremely large or splendid: *a palatial dining room/hotel/residence.*

palaver /pəˈlɑːvə(r); *US* -ˈlæv-/ *n* [U, sing] *(infml derog)* fuss or trouble, often with a lot of talk or argument: *What a palaver we had to go through to get a new visa!* ○ *Cut the palaver — let's get to the point.*

pale¹ /peɪl/ *adj* **(-r, -est)** **1** (of a person, the face, etc) having little colour; or less colour than usual: *have a pale complexion* ○ *be/go pale with anger/fear/shock* ○ *Are you feeling all right? You look rather pale.* ○ *He went/turned **deathly pale** at the news.* **2(a)** (of colours) not bright or vivid; not dark: *pale blue eyes* ○ *a pale sky.* **(b)** (of light) not strong; faint: *the pale light of dawn.* **IDM** **green/pale about the gills** ⇨ GILL¹.

▶ **pale** *v* ~ **(at sth)** to become pale: [V, Vpr] *He/His face paled visibly (at the news).* **PHRV** **ˈpale beside / in comparison with sth** to seem less important, great, etc in comparison with sth: *Investment in British Rail pales in comparison with the*

P

amount invested in continental railways. ○ *Their other problems **paled** into insignificance beside this latest catastrophe.*
palely /ˈpeɪlɪ/ *adv.*
paleness *n* [U].

pale² /peɪl/ *n* **IDM** **be₎yond the ˈpale** considered unacceptable or unreasonable by people in general: *His remarks were clearly beyond the pale.*

pale(o)- ⇨ PALAE(O)-.

palette /ˈpælət/ *n* a thin board on which an artist mixes colours when painting, with a hole for the thumb to hold it by.
■ ˈ**palette-knife** *n* (**a**) a thin flexible knife used by artists for mixing and applying paints. (**b**) a knife with a broad thin flexible blade for spreading substances in cooking: *spread icing on a cake with a palette-knife.*

palimpsest /ˈpælɪmpsest/ *n* **1** a piece of usu ancient writing material from which the original writing has been removed to create space for new writing. **2** a novel, play, set of ideas, etc that appears to consist of several layers, with each new layer changing or hiding the previous ones.

palindrome /ˈpælɪndrəʊm/ *n* a word or phrase that reads the same backwards as forwards, eg *madam* or *nurses run.*

paling /ˈpeɪlɪŋ/ *n* [U,C usu *pl*] a fence made of pointed metal or wooden posts: *erect new paling* ○ *a row of white palings.*

palisade /ˌpælɪˈseɪd/ *n* [C] a strong fence made of pointed wooden stakes or iron poles, esp one used to defend a building: *a timber palisade* ○ *a palisade fence.*

palish /ˈpeɪlɪʃ/ *adj* rather pale: *a dark shape against a palish background.*

pall¹ /pɔːl/ *v* to become boring or less interesting because of having been experienced too often: [V] *Lying on a beach doing nothing begins to pall after a while.*

pall² /pɔːl/ *n* **1** a cloth spread over a COFFIN. **2** a dark or heavy covering: *A **pall of smoke** hung over the town.*

pallbearer /ˈpɔːlbeərə(r)/ *n* a person who walks beside or helps to carry the COFFIN at a funeral.

pallet¹ /ˈpælət/ *n* a wooden or metal tray or platform for carrying or storing goods: *The pallets of books are stacked on top of each other by a fork-lift truck.*

pallet² /ˈpælət/ *n* **1** a MATTRESS filled with straw. **2** a hard narrow bed.

palliasse /ˈpæliæs; US pælˈjæs/ *n* a MATTRESS filled with straw.

palliate /ˈpælieɪt/ *v* (*fml*) to make disease less severe or unpleasant, without removing its cause: [Vn] *Many modern drugs palliate but do not cure illness.*

palliative /ˈpæliətɪv/ *n, adj* **1** (a medicine) that reduces pain without removing its cause: *Aspirin is a palliative (drug).* **2** (*usu derog*) (a thing) that reduces the harmful effects of sth without removing its cause: *short-term palliative measures to satisfy public opinion.*

pallid /ˈpælɪd/ *adj* **1** (of a person, the face, etc) pale, esp because of illness: *have a pallid complexion/ skin.* **2** weak or dull: *a pallid sun* ○ *pallid lyrics.*

pallor /ˈpælə(r)/ *n* [U] a pale colouring of the face, caused eg by illness or fear: *Her cheeks had a sickly pallor.*

pally ⇨ PAL.

palm¹ /pɑːm/ *n* the inner surface of the hand between the wrist and the fingers: *sweaty palms* ○ *read sb's palm* (ie say what will happen to sb by looking at the lines on their palm) ○ *He held the bird in the palm of his hand.* ⇨ picture at HAND¹. **IDM** **cross sb's palm with silver** ⇨ CROSS². **grease sb's**

palm ⇨ GREASE *v*. **have sb in the ₎palm of one's ˈhand** have complete power or control over sb.
▶ **palm** *v* [Vn] to hide a coin, card, etc in the hand when performing a trick. **PHRV** ₎**palm sb ˈoff (with sth)** (*infml*) to persuade sb to accept sth by lying to them: *He tried to palm me off with some excuse about the bus being late.* ₎**palm sb/sth ˈoff (on/onto sb)** (*infml*) to get rid of sb/sth that one does not want by persuading sb else to accept them/it: *I managed to palm the night shift off on(to) Harry.* ₎**palm sth ˈoff as sth** (*infml*) to pretend that sth is what it is not, esp in order to sell it: *He was trying to palm cheap copies off as original works of art.*

palm² /pɑːm/ (also ˈ**palm tree**) *n* a tree that grows in warm or tropical climates, with no branches and a mass of large wide leaves at the top. There are several types of palm tree: *a ˈdate palm* ○ *a ˈcoconut palm* ○ *palm fronds/groves.* ⇨ picture.

palm tree

■ ˈ**palm oil** *n* [U] oil obtained from the fruit of certain types of palm, widely used in cooking and in making soap, candles, etc.
₎**Palm ˈSunday** *n* the Sunday before Easter.

palmist /ˈpɑːmɪst/ *n* a person who claims to be able to interpret a person's character or tell her or his future by looking at the lines on the palm of that person's hand.
▶ **palmistry** /ˈpɑːmɪstri/ *n* [U] the art or practice of a palmist.

palpable /ˈpælpəbl/ *adj* **1** that can be felt or touched: *a palpable sense of loss/relief.* **2** clear to the mind; obvious: *His statement is palpable nonsense.* ▶ **palpably** /-əbli/ *adv.*

palpitate /ˈpælpɪteɪt/ *v* **1** [V] (of the heart) to beat rapidly. **2** ~ (**with sth**) (of a person or a part of the body) to shake or TREMBLE(1a) because of fear, excitement, etc: [Vpr] *palpitating with terror* [also V].
▶ **palpitation** /ˌpælpɪˈteɪʃn/ *n* **1** [U] the action of palpitating. **2 palpitations** [pl] rapid beating of the heart: *I get palpitations if I drink too much coffee.* ○ (*fig*) *The thought of flying gives me palpitations* (ie makes me very nervous).

palsy /ˈpɔːlzi/ *n* [U] an illness causing one to be unable to move and making the limbs TREMBLE(1a). See also CEREBRAL PALSY.
▶ **palsied** /ˈpɔːlzid/ *adj* affected with palsy.

paltry /ˈpɔːltri/ *adj* (*usu derog*) (**a**) very small; unimportant: *a paltry amount/sum.* (**b**) worthless; not worth accepting or considering: *a paltry excuse.*

pampas /ˈpæmpəs; US -əz/ **the pampas** *n* [sing or pl *v*] a large area of land in S America that is covered in grass and without trees. Compare PRAIRIE, SAVANNAH, STEPPE, VELD.
■ ˈ**pampas-grass** *n* [U] a type of tall ornamental grass with silver-white flowers like feathers.

pamper /ˈpæmpə(r)/ *v* (*often derog*) to treat a person or an animal with too much kindness, attention or comfort: [Vn] *a pampered child of rich parents* ○ *pamper oneself with a luxuriously deep bath.*

pamphlet /ˈpæmflət/ *n* a small book with a paper cover, usu containing information on a specific subject or expressing political or religious opinions: *produce/publish a political pamphlet.*
▶ **pamphleteer** /ˌpæmfləˈtɪə(r)/ *n* a person who writes pamphlets.

pan¹ /pæn/ *n* (often in compounds) **1(a)** a usu metal container with a handle or handles, used for cooking food in: *pots and pans* ○ *Cook the pasta in a large pan of boiling water.* ⇨ picture. See also FRYING-PAN, SAUCEPAN. (**b**) the amount contained in this: *a pan of hot fat.* **2** (*Brit*) the bowl of a lavatory. **3** either of the dishes on a pair of scales (SCALE³ 1). ⇨ picture at

pan

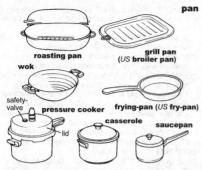

roasting pan

grill pan
(*US* broiler pan)

wok

safety-valve

pressure cooker

frying-pan (*US* fry-pan)

casserole

saucepan

lid

SCALE³. **4** a metal dish in which small stones are washed to separate them from gold or other valuable minerals. See also BEDPAN, DUSTPAN. **IDM** **a flash in the pan** ⇨ FLASH¹.
▶ **pan** *v* (**-nn-**) **1** ~ (**for sth**) to wash small stones in a pan in order to find gold or other valuable minerals: [Vpr] *prospectors panning for gold* [also V]. **2** (*infml*) to criticize sth severely: [Vn] *The film was panned by the critics.* **PHRV** **pan 'out** (*infml*) (of events or circumstances) to develop in a particular way: *It depends how things pan out.*

pan² /pæn/ *v* (**-nn-**) (*cinema or broadcasting*) (**a**) to move a camera, etc to the right or left so as to follow a moving object or to show a wide view: [Vnpr] *He panned the camera across the faces of the crowd.* [also Vn]. (**b**) (of a camera, etc) to move in this way: [Vpr] *The shot panned slowly across the room.* [also V].

pan- *comb form* of or relating to all or the whole of: *pan-African* ○ *pan-global* ○ *pandemic*.

panacea /ˌpænə'siːə/ *n* ~ (**for sth**) an answer or cure for all diseases or troubles: *There's no single panacea for the country's economic ills.*

panache /pə'næʃ, pæ-/ *n* [U] a manner that has style and confidence: *She dresses with great panache.*

panama /'pænəmɑː/ (also ˌpanama 'hat) *n* a hat made of a fine woven material like straw.

panatella /ˌpænə'telə/ *n* a long thin CIGAR.

pancake /'pænkeɪk/ *n* **1** [C] a flat round cake made with flour, eggs and milk, fried on both sides. Pancakes are usu eaten hot, and sometimes rolled up with a sweet or SAVOURY(1) filling: *toss a pancake* (ie to fry the other side). **2** [U] make-up (MAKE¹) for the face consisting of powder pressed into a flat solid cake. **IDM** **flat as a pancake** ⇨ FLAT¹.
■ **'Pancake Day** *n* (*infml*) (in Britain) Shrove Tuesday, when pancakes are traditionally eaten.

pancreas /'pæŋkrɪəs/ *n* a GLAND near the stomach. It produces substances which help to break down food in the body. ⇨ picture at DIGESTIVE SYSTEM.
▶ **pancreatic** /ˌpæŋkri'ætɪk/ *adj* of or relating to the pancreas: ˌpancreatic 'juice/'cancer.

panda /'pændə/ *n* **1** (also ˌgiant 'panda) a large rare black and white animal similar to a bear. Pandas are found in China and Tibet. **2** (also ˌred 'panda) an Indian animal like a RACCOON, with brown fur and a long thick tail.
■ **'panda car** *n* (*Brit*) a small police car.

pandemic /pæn'demɪk/ *adj* (of a disease) occurring over a whole country or the whole world.
▶ **pandemic** *n* a pandemic disease. Compare ENDEMIC, EPIDEMIC 1.

pandemonium /ˌpændə'məʊnɪəm/ *n* [U] wild and noisy disorder or confusion: *Pandemonium broke out when the news was announced.* ○ *Pandemonium reigned in the classroom until the teacher arrived.*

pander /'pændə(r)/ *v* **PHRV** **'pander to sth/sb** (*derog*) to try to satisfy a worthless, weak or im-

moral desire, or to please sb who has this: *newspapers pandering to the public love of scandal.*

p and p (also **p & p**) /ˌpiː ən 'piː/ *abbr* (*Brit*) (the price of) postage and packing: *price £28.95 including p and p.*

pane /peɪn/ *n* a single sheet of glass in a window: *a pane of glass* ○ *a 'window-pane.* ⇨ picture at HOUSE¹.

panegyric /ˌpænə'dʒɪrɪk/ *n* (*fml*) a speech or piece of writing praising sb/sth.

panel

panel /'pænl/ *n* **1** [C] a strip of wood, glass or metal forming part of the surface of a door, wall, ceiling, etc. Panels are usu raised above or sunk below the area around them: *a ceiling with carved wooden panels* ○ *One of the glass panels in the front door was smashed.* ⇨ picture. **2** [C] a piece of metal forming a section of the outer frame of a vehicle: *a 'panel-beater* (ie sb whose job is to knock out depressions in panels with a hammer). **3** [C] a strip of material inserted into a garment: *The sleeves had lace panels.* **4** [C] a flat board on which the controls and instruments of an aircraft, a car, etc are fixed: *an 'instrument panel* ○ *a con'trol panel.* **5** [CGp] a team of people chosen to take part in a game, discussion, etc on radio or television, usu with an audience: *a panel of experts* ○ *a 'panel game.* See also PANELLIST.

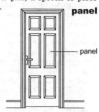

panel

▶ **panel** *v* (**-ll-**; *US* **-l-**) (esp passive) to cover or decorate sth with panels: [Vn] *a panelled room/ceiling/wall.* **panelling** (*US* **paneling**) *n* [U] **1** a series of panels, eg on a wall: *a room with fine oak panelling.* **2** wood used for making panels.

panellist (*US* **panelist**) /'pænəlɪst/ *n* a member of a panel(5).

pang /pæŋ/ *n* ~ (**of sth**) **1** (usu *pl*) a sudden sharp feeling of pain: *pangs of hunger.* **2** a feeling of painful emotion: *feel a pang of jealousy/remorse/guilt/conscience.*

panhandle¹ /'pænhændl/ *n* (*US*) a narrow piece of land extending from one State into another: *the Texas panhandle.*

panhandle² /'pænhændl/ *v* [V] (*US infml*) to beg for money in the street.

panic /'pænɪk/ *n* [C, U] (**a**) a sudden feeling of great fear that cannot be controlled: *be in a (state of) blind panic (about sth)* ○ *I got into a panic when I found the door was locked.* ○ *The thought of flying fills me with panic.* ○ *a panic decision* (ie one made in a state of panic). (**b**) a fear that spreads quickly through a group of people: *There was (an) immediate panic when the alarm sounded.* ○ *The bank's collapse caused (a) panic on the Stock Exchange* (ie The value of shares fell quickly). ○ (*infml*) *There's no panic* (ie no need for panic) *we've got plenty of time.* **IDM** **'panic stations** (*dated infml*) a state of alarm or emergency: *It was panic stations when the police arrived to search the building.*
▶ **panic** *v* (**-ck-**) to feel or make a person or an animal feel panic: [V] *Don't panic!* [Vn] *The gunfire panicked the horses.* **PHRV** **'panic sb into doing sth** (often passive) to make sb do sth unwise or act too quickly because of panic: *The banks were panicked into selling sterling.*
panicky /'pænɪki/ *adj* (*infml*) affected or caused by panic: *a panicky voice/feeling* ○ *Don't get panicky!*
■ **'panic-stricken** *adj* in a state of panic; extremely frightened: *She sounded panic-stricken on the phone.*

pannier /'pænɪə(r)/ *n* **1** each of a pair of bags or boxes on either side of the back wheel of a bicycle or motor cycle (MOTOR). **2** each of a pair of baskets

---

[V] = verb used alone   [Vn] = verb + noun   [Vp] = verb + particle   [Vpr] = verb + prepositional phrase

carried on either side of its back by a horse or DONKEY.

panoply /ˈpænəpli/ n (fml) a complete or splendid collection of things: *a panoply of weapons* ○ *The government has promised a whole panoply of social and economic improvements.*

panorama /ˌpænəˈrɑːmə; US -ˈræmə/ n **1** a view of a wide area: *From the summit there is a superb panorama of the Alps.* **2** a view of a constantly changing scene or series of events: *The book presents a panorama of social history since the Middle Ages.* ▶ **panoramic** /ˌpænəˈræmɪk/ adj: *a panoramic view from the top of the tower.*

pan-pipes /ˈpæn paɪps/ n [pl] a musical instrument made of a series of pipes of different length fixed together and played by blowing across the open ends. ⇨ picture.

pan-pipes

pansy /ˈpænzi/ n **1** a garden plant with a short stem and broad flat flowers of various bright colours. ⇨ picture at FLOWER. **2** (infml derog) a man whose behaviour or manners are like a woman's; a male HOMOSEXUAL.

pant /pænt/ v to breathe with short quick breaths, usu with the mouth open, after doing sth tiring or because it is very hot: [Vadv] *He was panting heavily as he ran.* [V.speech] *'How much farther is it?' she panted.* [also V]. **IDM** **puff and pant** ⇨ PUFF². **PHR V** **pant along, down, etc** to walk or run in the specified direction while panting: *The dog panted along the road beside me.* **pant for sth** (only in the continuous tenses) to show by one's rapid breathing that one needs to drink, get one's breath, etc: *panting for breath/a cool drink.* **pant sth out** to say sth with difficulty, while panting: *He panted out the message.*

▶ **pant** n (usu pl) a short quick breath: *breathe in short pants.*

pantaloons /ˌpæntəˈluːnz/ n [pl] (esp formerly) trousers of various types.

pantechnicon /pænˈteknɪkən/ (Brit) (US **moving van**) n a large van used for moving furniture from one house to another.

pantheism /ˈpænθiːɪzəm/ n [U] **1** the belief that God can be identified with all the forces of nature and with all natural things. **2** a willingness to accept the worship of all gods. ▶ **pantheist** /-θiːɪst/ n. **pantheistic** /ˌpænθiˈɪstɪk/ adj.

pantheon /ˈpænθiːən; US -θiɒn/ n **1** a building in which famous dead people of a nation are buried or honoured. **2** all the gods of a nation or people: *the ancient Egyptian pantheon.* **3** (esp in ancient Greece and Rome) a temple dedicated (DEDICATE 3) to all the gods. **4** a group of famous or important people: *a pantheon of brilliant performers from all over the world.*

panther /ˈpænθə(r)/ n **1** a LEOPARD, esp a black one. **2** (US) a PUMA.

panties /ˈpæntiz/ n [pl] (infml) short UNDERPANTS worn by women; KNICKERS.

pantihose (also **pantyhose**) /ˈpæntihəʊz/ n [pl v] (US) = TIGHTS 1.

pantile /ˈpæntaɪl/ n a curved TILE(1) used for roofs.

panto /ˈpæntəʊ/ n (pl **pantos** /ˈpæntəʊz/) (Brit infml) = PANTOMIME 1.

pantomime /ˈpæntəmaɪm/ n **1** (Brit) [C,U] a type of play with music, dancing and jokes, based on a fairy story and usu performed at Christmas: *go to a pantomime* ○ *act/appear in pantomime.* **2** [U] the use of movement and expression of the face and body to

indicate meaning or tell a story. **3** [C usu sing] a ridiculous event or situation, esp with a lot of confusion.

■ **pantomime dame** n a comic female character in a pantomime, usu acted by a man.

pantry /ˈpæntri/ n a small room or large cupboard close to a kitchen, for keeping food, etc in.

pants /pænts/ n [pl] **(a)** (Brit) UNDERPANTS or KNICKERS: *a pair of pants* ○ *Where are my pants?* **(b)** (esp US) trousers: *ski pants* ○ *I've known him since he was in short pants* (ie still a child). **IDM** **bore, scare, etc the pants off sb** (infml) to make sb extremely bored, scared, etc. **by the seat of one's pants** ⇨ SEAT¹. **catch sb with their pants/trousers down** ⇨ CATCH¹. **wear the pants/trousers** ⇨ WEAR¹.

pantsuit n = TROUSER SUIT.

pap /pæp/ n [U] **1** soft or almost liquid food such as that suitable for babies or people who are ill. **2** (derog) books, magazines, entertainment, etc that have no worth or value: *How can you bear to read such pap!*

papa /pəˈpɑː; US ˈpɑːpə/ n (dated infml) (used esp by children as a form of address) a father. Compare POP³, POPPA.

papacy /ˈpeɪpəsi/ n **(a)** **the papacy** [sing] the position or authority of the Pope. **(b)** [C usu sing] the period of time when a POPE is in office: *during the papacy of John Paul II.*

▶ **papal** /ˈpeɪpl/ adj of the Pope or the papacy: *papal authority.*

paparazzo /ˌpæpəˈrætsəʊ/ n (pl **paparazzi** /-tsi/) [usu pl] a journalist or photographer who follows famous people around in order to get interesting stories or photographs.

papaw = PAWPAW.

papaya = PAWPAW.

paper /ˈpeɪpə(r)/ n **1** (often in compounds) [U] a material made in thin sheets and used for writing, printing or drawing on, or for wrapping and packing things: *a piece/sheet of paper* ○ *writing-paper* ○ *tissue-paper* ○ *recycled paper* ○ *a paper bag/handkerchief/towel.* See also BLOTTING-PAPER, CREPE PAPER, GREASEPROOF PAPER, NOTEPAPER, TOILET PAPER, WRAPPING PAPER. **2** [C] a newspaper: *Where's today's paper?* ○ *a daily/Sunday paper* ○ *a national/local paper.* See also EVENING PAPER. **3** [C] **(a)** (usu pl) a piece of paper which has been written on: *His desk is always covered with papers.* **(b)** **papers** [pl] official documents, esp showing sb's identity, purpose, etc: *Immigration officials will ask to see your papers.* **4** [C] **(a)** a set of examination questions on a particular subject: *The geography paper was difficult.* **(b)** the written answers to examination questions: *She spent the evening marking exam papers.* **5** an article (2) or essay, esp one read to or written for specialists: *He's giving/reading a paper at the conference on the results of his research.* See also GREEN PAPER, WHITE PAPER. **6** [C,U] WALLPAPER: *a pretty striped paper for the bedroom.* **IDM** **on paper 1** in writing: *Could you put a few ideas down on paper?* **2** when judged from written or printed evidence; in theory(4): *It's a fine plan on paper, but will it work in practice?* ○ *She looks good on paper* (ie has good qualifications). **not worth the paper it's written on** ⇨ WORTH. **put pen to paper** ⇨ PEN¹.

▶ **paper** v to decorate the walls of a room by covering them with WALLPAPER: [Vn] *We're papering the bathroom.* **IDM** **paper over the cracks (in sth)** to try to hide a problem or fault, esp in a way that is not likely to be successful: *Critics of government policy argue that the new measures introduced to fight crime are simply papering over the cracks.* **PHR V** **paper sth over 1** to cover sth with WALLPAPER: *We papered over the stains on the wall.* **2** to try to hide a problem or fault, esp in a way that is not likely to be successful.

papery /'peɪpəri/ *adj* like paper in texture; thin and dry: *wrinkled, papery skin*.

■ **'paper-boy** *n* (*fem* **'paper-girl**) a boy or girl who delivers newspapers to people's houses.

'paper-chase *n* a run across country in which the leader drops a trail of pieces of paper for the other runners to follow.

'paper-clip *n* a piece of bent wire or plastic used for holding sheets of paper together. ⇨ picture at CLIP¹.

'paper-knife *n* a knife used for opening envelopes, etc.

ˌpaper 'money *n* [U] money in the form of notes (NOTE¹ 4), not coins.

'paper-pusher *n* (*US*) = PEN-PUSHER.

'paper round *n* a job of regularly delivering newspapers to houses; the route taken when doing this: *Some children do a paper round before school.*

ˌpaper 'tiger *n* a person or thing that seems or claims to be powerful or threatening but is not really so.

ˌpaper-'thin *adj* (of objects) very thin and delicate: *beautiful paper-thin material* ○ (*fig*) *a paper-thin line between success and failure.*

paperback /'peɪpəbæk/ *n* [C,U] a book with a flexible paper cover: *a cheap paperback* ○ *a paperback book/edition* ○ *When is it coming out in paperback?* Compare HARDBACK.

paperweight /'peɪpəweɪt/ *n* a small heavy object put on top of loose papers to keep them in place.

paperwork /'peɪpəwɜːk/ *n* [U] the written work that is part of a job, such as filling in forms, writing letters and reports, etc: *There's a lot of paperwork involved.*

papier mâché /ˌpæpieɪ 'mæʃeɪ; *US* ˌpeɪpər mə'ʃeɪ/ *n* [U] (*French*) paper mixed with glue, or flour and water, etc and used for moulding into boxes, trays, ornaments, etc.

papist /'peɪpɪst/ *n, adj* (*derog*) (used esp by Protestants) (a) Roman Catholic.

paprika /'pæprɪkə; *US* pə'priːkə/ *n* [U] a red powder made from a type of sweet pepper(2) and used as a spice.

papyrus /pə'paɪrəs/ *n* (**a**) [U] a tall water plant with thick stems used in ancient times in Egypt to make paper. (**b**) [U] this paper. (**c**) [C] (*pl* **papyri** /pə'paɪriː/) a document written on this paper.

par¹ /pɑː(r)/ *n* [U] (in golf) the number of strokes considered necessary for a good player to complete a hole(4) or course: *a 5-par hole* ○ *Par for the course is 72.* ○ *She went round the course in three under* (ie three strokes less than) *par.* Compare BIRDIE 2, BOGEY¹ 1, EAGLE 2. **IDM** **below/under 'par** (*infml*) less well, good, etc than is usual or expected: *I'm feeling a bit below par today.* ○ *Teaching in some subjects has been under par.* **be ˌpar for the 'course** (*infml*) to be what one would expect to happen or expect sb to do: *She was an hour late, but I'm told that's about par for the course for her.* **on a par with sb/sth** equal in importance, quality, etc to sb/sth: *As a writer she was on a par with the great novelists.* **up to 'par** (*infml*) as good/well as usual : *I didn't think her performance was up to par.*

par² (also **para** /'pærə/) *abbr* paragraph: *see par 19* ○ *paras 39–42* (eg in a contract).

para /'pærə/ *n* (*infml*) a paratrooper (PARATROOPS).

para- *pref* (forming *ns*) **1** beside; near: *parameter* ○ *paramilitary.* **2** beyond: *parapsychology* ○ *paranormal.*

parable /'pærəbl/ *n* (esp in the Bible) a story told to illustrate a moral or spiritual truth: *Jesus taught in parables.* ○ *the parable of the prodigal son.*

parabola /pə'ræbələ/ *n* (*geometry*) a curve like the path of an object thrown into the air and falling back to earth. ⇨ picture.

parabola

▶ **parabolic** *adj* parabolic curves.

parachute /'pærəʃuːt/ *n* a device attached to people or objects to make them fall slowly and safely when dropped from an aircraft. It consists of a large folded piece of cloth, attached by strings to the person or object, which opens out in the air to form an umbrella shape above them/it: *land by parachute* ○ *a parachute jump/drop.*

▶ **parachute** *v* to drop or cause sb/sth to drop by parachute from an aircraft: [V] *She enjoys parachuting.* [Vpr] *We parachuted into enemy territory.* [Vnpr] *Supplies were parachuted into the earthquake zone.* [also Vn].

parachutist /-ɪst/ *n* a person who drops from an aircraft using a parachute.

parade /pə'reɪd/ *n* [C] **1** a public procession, esp to celebrate a special day or event: *a May Day/an Easter/a Victory Parade* ○ *a parade of players before a football match* ○ *a fashion parade* (ie one in which models display new clothes to an audience). **2** a formal gathering of troops for inspection, etc: *a military parade.* **3** (*often derog*) an obvious display of sth in order to impress people: *He's always **making a parade** of his wealth.* **4** (esp in names) a street of shops or a public place for walking: *walk along North Parade* ○ *a shopping parade.* **IDM** **on parade** taking part in a procession or parade: *The regiment is on parade.* ○ (*fig*) *Many smart new hats were on parade at the wedding.*

▶ **parade** *v* **1** to walk or make a person or an animal walk in a procession or in order to display sth: [Vpr] *The demonstrators paraded through the city.* [Vp] *She paraded up and down in her new hat.* [Vnpr] *The horses are being paraded round the enclosure.* [also V, Vn, Vnpr]. **2** to display sth in order to attract attention or impress people: [Vn] *She never paraded her learning or experience.* [Vnpr] *The hostages were paraded in front of the cameras.* **3** to gather together for inspection, etc: [Vn] *The colonel paraded his troops.* ○ (*fig*) *Many arguments were paraded in favour of this policy.* [also V]. **4** ~ (**sb/ sth**) **as sth** to try to appear or make sb/sth appear good or important in a particular way, esp when they are not: [Vpr] *Several versions of the story were parading as the truth.* [Vn-n usu passive]: *This man had been paraded as a hero of the people.*

■ **pa'rade-ground** *n* a place where soldiers gather for inspection, etc.

paradigm /'pærədaɪm/ *n* **1** (*fml*) a type of sth; a pattern; a model: *a paradigm for others to copy* ○ *shifting paradigms of morality.* **2** (*grammar*) a set of all the different forms of a word: *verb paradigms.* ▶ **paradigmatic** /ˌpærədɪɡ'mætɪk/ *adj.*

paradise /'pærədaɪs/ *n* **1** [sing without *a* or *the*] heaven: *the idea of hell as an alternative to paradise.* **2**(**a**) [C] an ideal or perfect place: *This island is a paradise for bird-watchers.* See also FOOL'S PARADISE. (**b**) [U] a state of perfect happiness: *Being alone is his idea of paradise.* **3** **Paradise** [sing without *a* or *the*] (in the Bible) the garden of Eden, where Adam and Eve lived.

paradox /'pærədɒks/ *n* **1** [C] a person, thing or situation that has two contrary features and is therefore rather strange: *It is a paradox that professional comedians often have unhappy lives.* **2**(**a**) [C] a statement containing opposite ideas that make it seem absurd or unlikely although it is or may be true: *'More haste, less speed' is a well-known paradox.* (**b**) [U] the use of this in writing, etc: *a work* *full of paradox and ambiguity.* ► **paradoxical** /ˌpærəˈdɒksɪkl/ *adj.* **paradoxically** /-kli/ *adv.*

paraffin /ˈpærəfɪn/ (also **'paraffin oil**) (*Brit*) (*US* **kerosene**) *n* [U] an oil obtained from PETROLEUM, coal, etc and used as a fuel for heat and light: *a paraffin heater/lamp/stove.*
■ **'paraffin wax** *n* [U] a white substance like wax, obtained from PETROLEUM and used esp for making candles.

paragon /ˈpærəgən; *US* -gɒn/ *n* (**a**) ~ **of sth** a person who is a perfect example of a particular quality: *be seen as a paragon of virtue.* (**b**) a completely perfect person: *I make no claim to be a paragon.*

paragraph /ˈpærəɡrɑːf; *US* -ɡræf/ *n* **1** a distinct section of a piece of writing, usu consisting of several sentences dealing with a single theme. The first sentence of a paragraph starts on a new line: *begin a new paragraph* ∘ *See paragraph 15 of the handbook.* **2** a short report in a newspaper: *There's a paragraph on the accident in the local paper.*

parakeet /ˈpærəkiːt/ *n* a type of small PARROT(1), usu with a long tail. Compare BUDGERIGAR.

parallel /ˈpærəlel/ *adj* **1(a)** (of two or more lines) running side by side, with the same distance between them at every point: *parallel lines.* ⇨ picture at CONVERGE. (**b**) [pred] ~ **to/with sth** (of a line) having this relationship with another one: *The road runs parallel with the canal.* ∘ *The road and the canal are parallel to each other.* **2** very similar in type or taking place at the same time: *a parallel case/career/development.*
► **parallel** *n* **1** [U, C] a person, a situation, an event, etc that is the same as or similar to another: *an achievement without parallel in modern times* ∘ *There are interesting parallels* (ie similar features) *in the two situations.* **2** [C] a comparison: *It is possible to draw a parallel between their experience and ours.* **3** (also ˌparallel of ˈlatitude) [C] an imaginary line on the earth's surface, or a corresponding line on a map, parallel to and passing through all points the same distance north or south of the EQUATOR: *the 49th parallel.* **IDM** **in ˈparallel (with/to sth/sb)** happening or doing sth at the same time, and often related: *The two projects will move forward in parallel (with each other).*
parallel *v* (-ll-) (esp passive) **1** to be equal or similar to sth; to match sth: [Vn] *His performance has never been paralleled.* ∘ *Her experiences parallel mine in many ways.* **2** to happen at the same time as sth, esp because of being connected with it: [Vn] *The rise in interest rates was paralleled by a fall in house prices.*
parallelism /-ɪzəm/ *n* [U] the state of being parallel: *Don't exaggerate the parallelism between the two cases.*
■ ˌparallel ˈbars *n* [pl] a pair of bars on posts, used for GYMNASTICS.

parallelogram /ˌpærəˈleləɡræm/ *n* (*geometry*) a flat shape with four straight sides, the opposite sides being parallel and equal to each other. ⇨ picture at QUADRILATERAL.

paralyse (*US* **paralyze**) /ˈpærəlaɪz/ *v* **1** to cause a person or an animal to have no feeling in or control of all or part of the body: [Vn] *The accident left her paralysed from the chest/neck/waist down.* ∘ *She is paralysed in both legs.* **2** ~ **sb/sth** (**with sth**) (esp passive) to prevent sb/sth from moving or acting normally: [Vnpr] *be paralysed with fear/horror/shock* [Vn] *a country paralysed by industrial disputes* ∘ *paralysing shyness/heat.*

paralysis /pəˈræləsɪs/ *n* (*pl* **paralyses** /-siːz/) **1** [C, U] a loss of feeling in or control of all or part of the body, caused by a disease of an injury to the nerves: *suffer from paralysis of the right leg* ∘ *The paralysis affects his right leg and he can only walk with difficulty.* **2** [U] a total inability to move, act,

operate, etc: *the growing paralysis of Europe's air traffic control system.*

paralytic /ˌpærəˈlɪtɪk/ *adj* **1** suffering from PARALYSIS(1). **2** (*Brit infml*) very drunk: *She was/got completely paralytic last night.*

paramedic /ˌpærəˈmedɪk/ *n* a person whose job is helping doctors, etc with medical work: *ambulancemen and other paramedics.* ► **paramedical** /-ɪkl/ *adj*: *paramedical skills/services/staff.*

parameter /pəˈræmɪtə(r)/ *n* (usu *pl*) any of the factors that limit the way in which sth can be done: *We have to work within established parameters of time and money.*

paramilitary /ˌpærəˈmɪlətri; *US* -teri/ *adj* [attrib] **1** of or relating to a military force that is organized like but not part of the official army of a country: *an illegal paramilitary organization* ∘ *paramilitary activity.* **2** relating to and helping the official army of a country: *paramilitary police.*
► **paramilitary** *n* a member of a paramilitary group or organization.

paramount /ˈpærəmaʊnt/ *adj* (*fml*) **1** more important than anything else; supreme: *This matter is of paramount importance.* ∘ *Paramount in my mind is a concern for public safety.* **2** having supreme power and authority: *a paramount chief/leader.*

paranoia /ˌpærəˈnɔɪə/ *n* [U] **1** a mental illness in which sb wrongly believes that they are hated or being badly treated by others or that they are somebody very important. **2** (*infml*) an abnormal tendency to be suspicious of and lack trust in other people. ► **paranoiac** /ˌpærəˈnɔɪɪk, -ˈnɔɪæk/ *n, adj* = PARANOID.

paranoid /ˈpærənɔɪd/ (also **paranoiac**) *adj* of, like, suffering from or showing PARANOIA: *paranoid fears* ∘ *paranoid schizophrenia* ∘ *She's paranoid about what other people think of her.*
► **paranoid** (also **paranoiac**) *n* a paranoid person.

paranormal /ˌpærəˈnɔːml/ *adj* that cannot be explained by science or reason: *paranormal pheˈnomena.*
► **the paranormal** *n* [sing] paranormal events or subjects: *an interest in the paranormal.*

parapet /ˈpærəpɪt, -pet/ *n* **1** a low protective wall along the edge of a bridge, roof, BALCONY, etc. **2** (in war) a protective wall of earth, stones, etc along the front edge of a TRENCH.

paraphernalia /ˌpærəfəˈneɪliə/ *n* [U] a large number of small articles or personal possessions, esp the equipment needed for a particular activity: *skiing paraphernalia* ∘ *surrounded by all the paraphernalia of family life.* ⇨ note at PLURAL.

paraphrase /ˈpærəfreɪz/ *n* an account or expression of the meaning of sth written or said, using different words, esp in order to make it easier to understand.
► **paraphrase** *v* to express the meaning of sth written or said, using different words, esp in order to make it easier to understand: [Vn] *paraphrase a speech in colloquial English.*

paraplegia /ˌpærəˈpliːdʒə/ *n* [U] PARALYSIS of the lower part of the body, including the legs.
► **paraplegic** /ˌpærəˈpliːdʒɪk/ *n, adj* (a person) suffering from paraplegia: *She's (a) paraplegic.* ∘ *paraplegic ˈsports* (ie of or for paraplegics).

parapsychology /ˌpærəsaɪˈkɒlədʒi/ *n* [U] the study of mental powers that apparently exist but that cannot be explained by current scientific knowledge.

paraquat /ˈpærəkwɒt/ *n* [U] (*propr*) an extremely poisonous liquid for killing weeds (WEED 1a).

parasite /ˈpærəsaɪt/ *n* **1** an animal or plant that lives on or in another and gets its food from it: *fleas, lice and other parasites.* **2** (*derog*) a person who

always relies on or makes use of others and gives nothing in return: *live as a parasite on society.*
▶ **parasitic** /ˌpærəˈsɪtɪk/ (also **parasitical** /ˌpærəˈsɪtɪkl/) *adjs* (**a**) living as a parasite; like a parasite: *a parasitic plant/worm* ○ (*fig*) *He lives a parasitic existence, constantly borrowing money from his friends.* (**b**) caused by a parasite: *a parasitic disease.* **parasitically** /-klɪ/ *adv.*

parasol /ˈpærəsɒl; *US* -sɔːl/ *n* a light UMBRELLA(1) used to give shade from the sun. Compare SUNSHADE.
⇨ picture at HOUSE¹.

paratroops /ˈpærətruːps/ *n* [pl] soldiers trained to drop from aircraft by PARACHUTE.
▶ **paratroop** *adj* [attrib] of or consisting of para-troops: *a paratroop regiment.*
paratrooper /ˈpærətruːpə(r)/ *n* a member of a group of paratroops.

parboil /ˈpɑːbɔɪl/ *v* to boil food until it is partly cooked: [Vn] *Potatoes can be parboiled before roast-ing.*

parcel /ˈpɑːsl/ *n* **1** (*US* also **package**) a thing or things wrapped up for carrying or sending by post: *There's a parcel for you.* ○ *She was carrying a parcel of books under her arm.* **2** a piece of land, esp on an estate: *They own a cottage and a small parcel of land.* **IDM** **part and parcel of sth** ⇨ PART¹.
▶ **parcel** *v* (**-ll-**; *US* **-l-**) **PHRV** ˌparcel sth ˈout to divide sth into parts or portions: *He parcelled out the land into small plots.* ˌparcel sth ˈup to make sth into a parcel; to wrap sth up: *She parcelled up the books.*
■ ˈparcel bomb *n* a bomb wrapped up to look like a normal parcel and sent by post.

parched /pɑːtʃt/ *adj* **1** hot and dry; dried out with heat: *earth parched by the sun* ○ *the parched deserts of Africa* ○ *parched lips* (eg of a person with a fever). **2** very thirsty: *Give me a drink — I'm parched.*

parchment /ˈpɑːtʃmənt/ *n* **1**(**a**) [U] material made from the skin of sheep or goats and used, esp for-merly, for writing on. (**b**) [C] a piece of this material which has been written on. **2** [U] a type of paper made to resemble parchment.

pardon¹ /ˈpɑːdn/ *n* (*rather fml*) **1** [U] ~ (**for sth**) the action of forgiving sb for sth: *ask/seek sb's pardon for sth.* **2** [C] an official decision not to punish sb for a crime: *be granted a royal pardon* (ie by the king or queen). **IDM** **beg sb's pardon** ⇨ BEG. **I beg your pardon** ⇨ BEG.

pardon² /ˈpɑːdn/ *v* ~ **sb** (**for sth/doing sth**) (*usu fml*) to forgive or excuse sb for sth: [Vn] *pardon an offence/a fault* ○ *The place was, if you'll pardon the expression, a dump.* [Vnpr] *He begged her to pardon him for his rudeness.* [V.n *ing,*Vnpr] *Pardon me* (*for*) *asking/Pardon my asking, but isn't that my hat you're wearing?* Compare EXCUSE² 1. **IDM** **par-don me** = I BEG YOUR PARDON (BEG).
▶ **pardon** (*US* also ˌpardon ˈme) *interj* (used to ask sb to repeat sth because one did not hear it).
pardonable /ˈpɑːdnəbl/ *adj* that can be forgiven or excused: *a pardonable error.*

pare /peə(r)/ *v* **1** to trim sth by cutting away the edges: [Vn] *pare one's fingernails* [Vnpr] (*fig*) *The original plot had been pared to the bone* (ie re-duced to the minimum). **2** ~ **sth** (**off**) to cut away the skin or outer covering from sth: [Vn] *pare an apple* [Vnp] *She pared off the thick peel with a knife.* **PHRV** **pare sth down** to reduce sth greatly: *We have pared down our expenses to a minimum.*
▶ **parings** /ˈpeərɪŋz/ *n* [pl] pieces that have been cut off.

parent /ˈpeərənt/ *n* **1** (usu *pl*) a father or mother: *May I introduce you to my parents* (ie my father and mother)? ○ *Denise and Martin have recently become parents.* See also SINGLE PARENT. ⇨ App 4. **2** an animal or plant from which others are produced: *the parent bird/tree.*
▶ **parentage** /-ɪdʒ/ *n* [U] the fact of who one's parents are; one's origin(2): *a person of unknown parentage* (ie having parents whose identity is not known) ○ *of humble parentage.*
parental /pəˈrentl/ *adj* [usu attrib] of or relating to a parent or parents: *parental affection/love/support* ○ *children lacking parental care.*
parenthood /ˈpeərənthʊd/ *n* [U] the state of being a parent: *the responsibilities of parenthood.*
parenting /ˈpeərəntɪŋ/ *n* [U] the care and bringing up of children by their parents: *good/bad parenting.*
■ ˌparent ˈcompany *n* a commercial company that owns or controls one or more other companies.
ˌparent-ˈteacher association *n* (*abbr* PTA) an organization of the teachers and parents of the chil-dren at a school, formed to improve relations and understanding between them.

parenthesis /pəˈrenθəsɪs/ *n* (*pl* **parentheses** /-əsiːz/) **1** [C] a word, phrase or sentence inserted as an extra explanation or idea into a passage which would be complete without it. In writing it is usu separated from the rest by brackets (BRACKET 2), dashes (DASH¹ 4) or commas (COMMA). **2** [C usu *pl*] either of a pair of round brackets (BRACKET 2), ie (), used to enclose an additional word, phrase, etc. ⇨ App 3.
▶ **parenthetic** /ˌpærənˈθetɪk/ (also **parenthetical** /-ɪkl/) *adj*, of relating to or added as a parenthesis (1): *parenthetical remarks.* **parenthetically** /-klɪ/ *adv.*

par excellence /ˌpɑːr ˈeksəlɑːns; *US* ˌeksəˈlɑːns/ *adv* (*French approv*) (used after a *n*) better than all others of its kind: *He is the elder statesman par excellence.*

pariah /pəˈraɪə/ *n* a person who is not acceptable to society; an OUTCAST: *be treated as a pariah.*

parish /ˈpærɪʃ/ *n* **1** [C] an area that has its own church and clergyman (CLERGY): *He is vicar of a large rural parish.* ○ *a parish church* ○ *a parish priest* ○ *parish boundaries.* **2** [C] (in England) a small country area, esp a village, that has its own local government: *the parish council.* Compare BOROUGH 1. **3** [CGp] the people living in a parish, esp those who attend church regularly.
▶ **parishioner** /pəˈrɪʃənə(r)/ *n* an inhabitant of a parish, esp one who attends church regularly.
■ ˌparish ˈclerk *n* an official with various duties in connection with a parish church.
ˌparish-ˈpump *adj* [attrib] of or relating to local affairs: ˌparish-pump ˈpolitics.
ˌparish ˈregister *n* a book recording the christen-ings (CHRISTEN 1), marriages and burials that have taken place at a particular parish church.

Parisian /pəˈrɪziən; *US* -ʒn/ *adj* of or relating to Paris.
▶ **Parisian** *n* a native or inhabitant of Paris.

parity /ˈpærəti/ *n* [U] (*fml*) **1** the state of being equal, esp as regards status or pay: *parity of treatment/incomes* ○ *Primary school teachers are de-manding parity with* (ie the same pay as) *those in secondary schools.* **2** (*finance*) the state of one cur-rency being equivalent in value with another.

park¹ /pɑːk/ *n* **1** [C] a public garden or area of land in a town where people go to walk, play, relax, etc: *strolling in the park* ○ *a park bench* ○ *Hyde Park.* **2** [C] an enclosed area of land, usu with fields and trees, attached to a large country house. **3** [C] (in compounds) an area of land used for a particular purpose: *an industrial park.* See also AMUSEMENT PARK, BALLPARK, CAR PARK, NATIONAL PARK, SAFARI PARK, THEME PARK. **4**(**a**) [C] (*US*) a piece of land for playing sports, esp baseball. (**b**) **the park** [sing] (*Brit*) a football pitch.
■ ˌpark-and-ˈride *n* a system designed to reduce traffic in towns, etc by providing regular public

P

transport between large car parks on the edge of a town and the town centre: *use the park-and-ride* ○ *park-and-ride service.*

park² /pɑːk/ *v* **1** to stop driving and leave a vehicle for a time, eg at the side of a road or in a car park (CAR 1): [V, Vn] *There's nowhere to park (the car).* [Vn] *a line of parked cars* [Vpr, Vnpr] *You can't park (your car) in this street.* [Vnadv] *You are/Your car is very badly parked.* **2** (*infml*) **(a)** to leave sb/sth in a place for a time: [Vnadv] *Park your luggage here while you buy a ticket.* [also Vnpr]. **(b)** ~ **oneself** to sit down: [Vnpr] *Park yourself in that chair while I make you a cup of tea.* [also Vnadv].

parka /ˈpɑːkə/ *n* a very warm jacket or coat with a HOOD¹(1) lined with fur.

parkin /ˈpɑːkɪn/ *n* [U] (*Brit*) a type of cake made with GINGER(1), oatmeal and TREACLE.

parking /ˈpɑːkɪŋ/ *n* [U] **(a)** the action of stopping a vehicle at a place and leaving it there for a time: *There is no parking between 9 am and 6 pm.* ○ *Look out for a* ˈ*parking space.* ○ *a* ˈ*parking fine* (ie for parking illegally). **(b)** a space or an area for leaving vehicles: *Is there any parking near the theatre?*
■ ˈ**parking-lot** *n* (*US*) = CAR PARK.
ˈ**parking-meter** *n* a device into which one puts coins as payment for parking a car beside it for a period of time.
ˈ**parking-ticket** *n* an official notice, usu put on a car, ordering one to pay a fine for parking illegally: *I got a parking-ticket today.*

Parkinson's disease /ˈpɑːkɪnsnz dɪziːz/ (also **Parkinsonism** /ˈpɑːkɪnsənɪzəm/) *n* [U] a severe disease that causes the muscles to become weak and the limbs to shake.

Parkinson's law /ˈpɑːkɪnsnz lɔː/ *n* [U] (*joc*) the idea that work will always take as long as the time available for it.

parkland /ˈpɑːklænd/ *n* [U] open land with fields and groups of trees: *The house stands in 500 acres of rolling parkland.*

parkway /ˈpɑːkweɪ/ *n* (*US*) a wide road with trees, grass, etc along the sides and/or the central strip.

parlance /ˈpɑːləns/ *n* [U] (*fml*) a particular way of speaking or of using words: *in common/legal/modern/official parlance.*

parley /ˈpɑːli/ *n* (*pl* **-eys**) (*dated*) a meeting between enemies or opponents to discuss terms for peace, etc: *arrange a parley with sb.*
▶ **parley** *v* [V, Vpr] ~ (**with sb**) (*dated*) to have a parley.

parliament /ˈpɑːləmənt/ *n* **1 Parliament** [Gp] (in Britain) the group of people responsible for making and changing laws in the United Kingdom. Parliament consists of the House of Commons, the House of Lords and the King or Queen: *the* ˌ*Houses of* ˈ*Parliament* ○ *a* ˌ*Member of* ˈ*Parliament* ○ *The issue was debated in Parliament.* ○ *get into* (ie be elected a Member of) *Parliament* ○ *the State Opening of Parliament* (ie the ceremony in which the King or Queen opens a new SESSION(1) of Parliament). **2** [CGp] Parliament as it exists during the period of time between one general election (GENERAL¹) and the next: *adjourn/dissolve (a) Parliament* ○ *The government is unlikely to get the bill through within (the lifetime of) this Parliament.* **3** [CGp] a group of people that makes the laws of a country: *the French/German parliament.* **4** [C] the building where a parliament meets.
▶ **parliamentarian** /ˌpɑːləmənˈteəriən/ *n* a member of a parliament, esp an experienced and skilful one: *one of our most eminent parliamentarians.*
parliamentary /ˌpɑːləˈmentri/ *adj* [usu attrib] of or relating to a parliament: *parliamentary debates/procedures/committees* ○ *a parliamentary recess.* Compare UNPARLIAMENTARY.

parlour (*US* **parlor**) /ˈpɑːlə(r)/ *n* **1** (*dated*) a room in

a private house for sitting in, entertaining visitors, etc. **2** (in compounds) (*esp US*) a shop providing certain goods or services: *a* ˈ*beauty/an ice-*ˈ*cream/a* ˈ*funeral parlour.* See also MASSAGE PARLOUR.
■ ˈ**parlour game** *n* a game played in the home, esp a game with words.

parlous /ˈpɑːləs/ *adj* (*fml or rhet*) full of danger or uncertainty; very bad: *the parlous state* of international relations ○ *English tennis is in a parlous condition.*

Parmesan /ˌpɑːmɪˈzæn; *US* ˈpɑːrməzɑːn/ *n* [U] a hard cheese made in Italy, usu grated (GRATE² 1) and served on PASTA.

parochial /pəˈrəʊkiəl/ *adj* **1** [usu attrib] (*fml*) of or relating to a church PARISH(1): *parochial matters.* **2** (*derog*) showing interest in a local or limited area only; narrow(3): *a parochial attitude/event* ○ *He is rather too parochial in his outlook.* ▶ **parochialism** /-ɪzəm/ *n* [U].

parody /ˈpærədi/ *n* ~ (**of sth**) **1** [C, U] speech, writing or music that deliberately copies and exaggerates the style of a writer, musician, etc in order to be amusing: *a parody of a Shakespearian sonnet/an operatic aria/a well-known politician* ○ *She has a gift for parody.* **2** [C] a thing that is done so badly that it seems deliberately to mock what is intended: *The trial was a parody of justice.*
▶ **parodist** /-ɪst/ *n* a person who writes parodies.
parody *v* (*pt, pp* **-died**) to make a parody(1) of sb/sth; to copy sb/sth in an exaggerated amusing way: [Vn] *parody an author/a style/a poem.*

parole /pəˈrəʊl/ *n* [U] the release of a prisoner before the end of a sentence(2) if he or she promises to behave well, or temporarily for a special purpose: *let sb out/release sb* **on parole** ○ *be on parole* ○ *He's hoping to get/win parole.* ○ *the parole system.*

paroxysm /ˈpærəksɪzəm/ *n* a sudden attack or violent expression of eg laughter, anger, etc: *paroxysms of coughing/giggling* ○ *He went into a paroxysm of rage* (ie became very angry).

parquet /ˈpɑːkeɪ; *US* pɑːrˈkeɪ/ *n* [U] a floor covering made of wooden blocks arranged in a pattern: *a parquet floor.*

parricide /ˈpærɪsaɪd/ *n* **1** [C, U] the killing of one's father or mother or a close relation. **2** [C] a person guilty of this. Compare PATRICIDE.

parrot /ˈpærət/ *n* **1** any of various types of usu tropical bird with curved beaks and bright colourful feathers. Some parrots are kept as pets and can be trained to copy human speech. ⇨ picture. **2** (*esp derog*) a person who repeats sb else's words or copies their actions without thinking. **IDM** **sick as a parrot** ⇨ SICK.

parrot

▶ **parrot** *v* [Vn] (*derog*) to repeat sb's words or copy their actions without thinking.
■ ˈ**parrot-fashion** *adv* (*derog*) without thinking about or understanding the meaning of sth: *learn/repeat sth parrot-fashion.*

parry /ˈpæri/ *v* (*pt, pp* **parried**) **1** to turn aside a blow⁽¹⁾(1), a shot¹(6) or an attack by using one's own weapon or one's hand to block it: [Vn] *His shot was parried by the goalkeeper.* ⇨ picture at FENCING. **2** to avoid having to answer a question: [V.speech] *parry an awkward question* [V] *'I'm not sure about that,' he parried.*
▶ **parry** *n* an act of parrying a blow etc, esp in boxing or fencing (FENCE² 1).

parse /pɑːz; *US* pɑːrs/ *v* [Vn] (*grammar*) **(a)** to describe the part of speech (PART¹), GRAMMATICAL form and function of a word in a particular sentence, etc.

(**b**) to divide a sentence into parts and describe their grammatical form, function, etc.

Parsee /ˌpɑːˈsiː/ *n* a member of a religious group in India whose ancestors originally came from Persia.

parsimony /ˈpɑːsɪmənɪ; *US* -məʊnɪ/ *n* [U] (*fml usu derog*) extreme unwillingness (UNWILLING) to spend money or use resources; meanness (MEAN² 1).

▶ **parsimonious** /ˌpɑːsɪˈməʊnɪəs/ *adj* (*fml usu derog*) very unwilling to spend money or use resources; mean²(1). **parsimoniously** *adv*.

parsley /ˈpɑːslɪ/ *n* [U] a small plant with curling green leaves that are used for flavouring and decorating food: *parsley sauce*.

parsnip /ˈpɑːsnɪp/ *n* (**a**) [C,U] a long, pale yellow vegetable, usu eaten cooked: *roast parsnips*. (**b**) [C] the plant that produces this vegetable as its root. ⇨ picture at TURNIP.

parson /ˈpɑːsn/ *n* **1** (in the Church of England) a VICAR or RECTOR(1a) of a PARISH(1). **2** (*infml*) any Protestant CLERGYMAN.

▶ **parsonage** /-ɪdʒ/ *n* a parson's house.

■ **parson's ˈnose** (*US* **pope's ˈnose**) *n* (*infml*) the piece of flesh at the tail end of a cooked bird, esp a chicken.

part¹ /pɑːt/ *n* (often without *a* when singular) **1** [C] ~ (**of sth**) some but not all of a thing: *We spent (a) part of our vacation in Maine.* ○ *The early part of her life was spent in Paris.* ○ *She had a miserable trip — she was ill for part of the time.* ○ *The film is good in parts.* ○ *Parts of the book are interesting.* ○ *We've done the difficult part of the job.* ○ *Part of the building was destroyed in the fire.* ○ *The worst part was having to wait three hours in the rain.* **2** [C] ~ (**of sth**) (**a**) a distinct portion of a human or an animal body or of a plant: *the parts of the body* ○ *Which part of your leg hurts?* See also PRIVATE PARTS. (**b**) a usu essential piece of a machine or structure: *lose one of the parts of the lawnmower* ○ *the working parts of a machine* ○ *spare parts.* **3** a member of sth: *work as part of a team* ○ *We think of you as part of the family.* **4(a)** an area or a region of a country, town, etc: *Which parts of Australia have you visited?* ○ *Which part of London do you come from?* ○ *Do come and visit us if you're ever in our part of the world.* (**b**) **parts** [pl] (*infml*) a region or an area: *She's not from these parts.* ○ *He's just arrived back from foreign parts.* **5** [C] a section of a book, television programme, etc, esp as much as is published or broadcast at one time: *an encyclopedia published in 25 weekly parts* ○ *Henry IV, Part II* ○ *The final part will be shown next Sunday evening.* **6** [C] (**a**) a role played by an actor in a play, film, etc: *He took/played the part of Hamlet.* ○ *She was very good in the part.* ○ (*fig*) *He's always acting/playing a part* (ie pretending to be what he is not). (**b**) the words spoken by an actor playing a particular role: *Have you learnt your part yet?* **7** [C usu *sing*] ~ (**in sth**) a person's share in an activity: *He had no part in the decision.* ○ *I want no part of this sordid business.* ○ *She plays an active part in local politics.* ○ *We all have a part to play in the fight against crime.* **8** (*music*) music for a particular voice or instrument in a group singing or playing together: *a song in four parts* ○ *play the piano part.* **9** [C] each of several equal portions of a whole: *a sixtieth part of a minute* ○ *Add three parts wine to one part water.* **10** [C] (*US*) = PARTING 2. **IDM** **the best/better part of sth** most of sth, esp a period of time; more than half of sth: *I spent the best part of an hour trying to find my car keys.* ○ *We've lived here for the better part of a year.* ○ *You must have drunk the best part of a bottle of wine last night.* **discretion is the better part of valour** ⇨ DISCRETION. **for the ˈmost part** mostly; usually: *The contributors, for the most part, are professional scientists.* **for ˈmy, ˈhis, ˈtheir, etc part** speaking for myself, etc; personally: *For my part, I don't mind where we eat.* **in large part** ⇨

LARGE. **in ˈpart** to a certain extent; partly: *His success was due in part to luck.* **look the ˈpart** to have an appearance or wear clothes suitable for a particular job, role or position: *I think he must be a sea captain — he certainly looks the part.* **a man/woman of (many) ˈparts** a person with many skills or talents. **on the part of sb / on sb's ˈpart** made or done by sb: *It was an error on my part.* **part and parcel of sth** an essential part of sth: *Keeping the accounts is part and parcel of my job.* **take sth in good ˈpart** to accept sth slightly unpleasant without becoming offended: *He took the teasing in good part.* **take ˈpart (in sth)** to be involved in sth; to PARTICIPATE in sth: *take part in a discussion/demonstration/game/fight/celebration* ○ *How many countries took part in the last Olympic Games?* **take sb's ˈpart** to support sb, eg in an argument: *His mother always takes his part.*

▶ **part** *adv* partly: *She is part French, part English.* ○ *Her feelings were part anger, part relief.*

partly *adv* to some extent; not completely: *She was only partly responsible for the accident.* ○ *It was partly her fault.*

■ **ˌpart-exˈchange** *n* [U] a method of buying sth in which an article, eg a car, is given as part of the payment for a more expensive one: *offer/take sth in part-exchange.*

ˌpart of ˈspeech *n* (*grammar*) each of the classes into which the words of a language are divided according to grammar, eg noun, adjective, verb.

ˌpart-ˈtime *adj, adv* for only a part of the day or week in which people work: *ˌpart-time emˈployment* ○ *She's looking for a ˌpart-time ˈjob.* ○ *ˌpart-time ˈworkers* ○ *work part-ˈtime.* Compare FULL-TIME. **ˌpart-ˈtimer** *n* a part-time worker.

part² /pɑːt/ *v* **1** (*fml*) (**a**) ~ (**from sb**) to go away or separate from sb: [V-n] *We parted the best of friends* (ie went away from each other with no feeling of anger, eg after a quarrel). [V] *They exchanged a final kiss before parting.* [Vpr, V] *She has parted from her husband/She and her husband have parted* (ie started to live apart). (**b**) ~ **sb (from sb)** to separate sb from sb else: [Vnpr] *The children were parted from their father.* [also Vn]. **2** to divide or make sth divide; to form separate parts: [V] *Her lips parted in a smile.* ○ *The crowd parted to let them through.* ○ *The clouds parted and the sun shone through.* [Vn] *The police parted the crowd.* **3** to separate the hair of the head along a line and comb the hair away from it: [Vnpr] *He parts his hair in the middle.* [also Vn]. **IDM** **part ˈcompany (with sb/sth) 1** to go different ways or separate after being together: *We parted company at the bus-stop.* ○ *He and his agent have parted company/He has parted company with his agent.* ○ *It is on political questions that their views part company* (ie are different). **2** to disagree with sb: *I'm afraid I have to part company with you there.* **PHRV** **ˈpart with sth** to give or sell sth to sb else: *He hates parting with* (ie spending) *his money.* ○ *Despite her poverty, she refused to part with her grandmother's ring.*

partake /pɑːˈteɪk/ *v* (*pt* **partook** /-ˈtʊk/; *pp* **partaken** /-ˈteɪkən/) (*dated or fml*) **1** ~ (**of sth**) to eat or drink a part or an amount of sth: [Vpr] *They invited us to partake of their simple meal.* [also V]. ~ (**in sth**) to take part in an activity: [Vpr] *partake in the social life of the village* [also V]. **PHRV** **parˈtake of sth** to have some of a quality: *His letters partake of the artistic spirit of his surroundings.*

partial /ˈpɑːʃl/ *adj* **1** of or forming a part; not complete: *a partial recovery* (eg after an illness) ○ *a partial eclipse of the sun* ○ *Our trip was only a partial success.* **2** [pred] ~ **to sb/sth** liking sb/sth very much: *He's (rather) partial to a glass of brandy after dinner.* **3** [usu pred] ~ **(towards sb/sth)** (*usu derog*) showing too much favour to one person or side, eg in a contest or a dispute: *The referee was accused of being partial (towards the home team).* Compare IM-PARTIAL.

▶ **partiality** /ˌpɑːʃiˈæləti/ *n* **1** [U] (*derog*) being partial(3): *He judged the case without partiality.* Compare IMPARTIALITY. **2** [C] ~ **for sb/sth** (*fml*) a special fondness (FOND 2) for sb/sth: *She has a partiality for French cheese.*

partially /ˈpɑːʃəli/ *adv* **1** not completely; partly: *The road was partially blocked by a fallen tree.* ○ *a society for the blind and partially sighted.* **2** (*derog*) in a partial(3) manner.

participant /pɑːˈtɪsɪpənt/ *n* ~ (**in sth**) a person who takes part in sth: *All the participants in the debate had an opportunity to speak.*

participate /pɑːˈtɪsɪpeɪt/ *v* ~ (**in sth**) to take part or become involved in an activity: [Vpr] *participate in a competition/discussion/meeting* ○ *She participates actively in local politics.* [V, Vpr] *How many countries will be participating (in the Olympic Games)?*

▶ **participation** /pɑːˌtɪsɪˈpeɪʃn/ *n* [U] ~ (**in sth**) the action of taking part in sth: *Union leaders have called for the active participation of all members in the day of protest.*

participle /ˈpɑːtɪsɪpl/ *n* (*grammar*) a word formed from a verb, ending in *-ing* (*present participle*) or *-ed*, *-en*, etc (*past participle*). Participles are used in verb phrases (eg *She is going* or *She has gone*) or as adjectives (eg *a fascinating story*): 'Hurrying' and 'hurried' are the present and past participles of 'hurry'.

▶ **participial** /ˌpɑːtɪˈsɪpiəl/ *adj* consisting of or being a participle: 'Loving' in 'a loving mother' and 'polished' in 'polished wood' are participial adjectives.

particle /ˈpɑːtɪkl/ *n* **1** a very small bit or piece of sth: *particles of dust/dust particles* ○ *He choked on a particle of food.* ○ (*fig*) *There's not a particle of truth in her story.* **2** (*physics*) any of various types of small pieces of matter of which atoms are composed: *particle physics.* See also ALPHA PARTICLE, ELEMENTARY PARTICLE. **3** (*grammar*) a minor part of speech, esp a short word that does not change its form. See also ADVERBIAL PARTICLE.

particular /pəˈtɪkjələ(r)/ *adj* **1** [attrib] relating to one person or thing rather than others; individual: *his particular problems* ○ *I usually agree with her, but in this particular case I think she's wrong.* ○ *Is there any particular colour you would prefer?* **2** [attrib] more than usual; special; exceptional: *a matter of particular importance* ○ *for no particular reason* ○ *She took particular care not to damage the parcel.* **3** ~ (**about/over sth**) giving close attention to detail; difficult to please; FUSSY(2): *She's very particular about what she wears.* ○ *She's a very particular person.* **IDM in parˈticular** especially; particularly: *The whole meal was good but the fish in particular was excellent.* ○ *'Is there anything in particular you'd like for dinner?'*

▶ **particular** *n* (often *pl*) (*fml*) a piece of information; a detail; a fact: *Her account is correct in every particular.* ○ *The police officer took down all the particulars about the missing child.*

particularity /pəˌtɪkjuˈlærəti/ *n* [U] (*fml*) **1** the quality of being individual or particular(1). **2** attention to detail; being exact.

particularize, -ise /pəˈtɪkjələraɪz/ *v* [V, Vn] (*fml*) to name or state sth specially or one by one; to specify items.

particularly *adv* especially: *I like all her novels, but her latest is particularly good.* ○ *The meal was delicious, particularly the dessert.* ○ *I don't particularly want to see him today.*

parting /ˈpɑːtɪŋ/ *n* **1(a)** [U] the action of leaving or being separated from sb: *the sadness of parting* ○ *a parting kiss.* **(b)** [C] an instance of this: *their final*

parting. **2** [U, C] the action or an instance of dividing into parts: *the parting of the clouds.* **3** (*US* **part**) [C] a line on a person's head where the hair is divided and combed in different directions: *a side/centre parting.* ⇨ picture at HAIR. **IDM a/the ˌparting of the ˈways** a point at which two people must separate.

■ **ˌparting ˈshot** *n* a final remark, esp an unkind one, made by sb as they leave.

partisan /ˌpɑːtɪˈzæn, ˈpɑːtɪzæn; *US* ˈpɑːrtəzn/ *n* **1** an enthusiastic supporter of a person, group or cause. **2** a member of an armed group formed to fight secretly against enemy soldiers who are occupying its country.

▶ **partisan** *adj* (*often derog*) showing too much support for one person, group or cause(3); biased (BIAS *v*): *partisan views/feelings* ○ *You must listen to both points of view and try not to be partisan.*

partisanship /-ʃɪp/ *n* [U].

partition /pɑːˈtɪʃn/ *n* **1** [U] the division of one country into two or more countries: *the partition of Germany after the war.* **2** [C] a structure that divides a room or space into two parts, esp a thin wall in a house.

▶ **partition** *v* (esp passive) to divide sth into parts: [Vn] *India was partitioned in 1947.* **PHRV partition sth off** to separate one area, part of a room, etc from another with a partition(2): *We've partitioned off one end of the kitchen to make a breakfast room.*

partitive /ˈpɑːtətɪv/ *adj* (*grammar*) (of a word or phrase) indicating a part or quantity of sth.

▶ **partitive** *n* (*grammar*) a partitive word or phrase: *'Some' and 'any' are partitives.*

partner /ˈpɑːtnə(r)/ *n* **1** a person who takes part in an activity with another or others, esp one of the owners of a business: *a senior/junior partner in a law firm* ○ *business partners* ○ *They were partners in crime.* **2** either of two people dancing together or playing tennis, cards, etc on the same side, against others: *dancing partners* ○ *be sb's partner at bridge/badminton.* **3** either of two people who are married to one another or having a sexual relationship with one another. ⇨ note. **4** a country or an organization that has an agreement with another or others: *Britain's EU partners.* See also SLEEPING PARTNER, SPARRING PARTNER.

▶ **partner** *v* to be the partner(2) of sb: [Vn] *partner sb at whist/tennis.*

partnership /-ʃɪp/ *n* **(a)** [U] ~ (**with sb**) the state of being a partner or partners, esp in business: *She worked in partnership with her sister/They worked in partnership.* ○ *He went/entered into partnership with her brother.* ○ *He and his brother went/entered into partnership.* **(b)** [C] ~ (**with sb**) a group of two or more people working, playing, etc together as partners: *a successful partnership.* **(c)** [C] a business with two or more owners.

NOTE Many men and women in Western countries live together as husband and wife without being legally married. They usually refer to the other person as their **partner** rather than **boyfriend** or **girlfriend**: *Helen lives with her partner in Los Angeles.* You can use **partner** if you do not know whether somebody is married: *Where does your partner work?*

partook *pt* of PARTAKE.

part-owner *n* a person who owns sth together with one or more others: *Tim is part-owner of the flat.* **ˌpart-ˈownership** *n* [U].

partridge /ˈpɑːtrɪdʒ/ *n* (*pl* **partridges** or *pl* unchanged) a wild bird hunted for food or sport. Partridges have brown feathers, round bodies and short tails.

party /ˈpɑːti/ *n* **1** [C] (esp in compounds) a social event, often in a person's home, to which people are invited in order to enjoy themselves, eg by eating, drinking, dancing, etc: *a 'birthday party* ○ *a 'dinner party* ○ *a 'garden party* ○ *a 'party dress* ○ *I'm giving/having/holding a party next Saturday night.* See also HEN-PARTY, HOUSE PARTY, STAG-PARTY. **2** [CGp] (used esp in compounds or before *ns*) a political organization whose members all have the same aims and beliefs, usu one that is trying to win elections to parliament: *The main political parties in the United States are the Democrats and the Republicans.* ○ *She's a member of the 'Labour Party.* ○ *a left-wing/right-wing/centre party* ○ *the party 'leader/'policy/mani'festo* ○ *party 'interests/'funds/'members* ○ *the 'party system* (ie government based on political parties). **3** [CGp] a group of people working or travelling together: *a party of schoolchildren/tourists.* See also SEARCH-PARTY, WORKING PARTY. **4** [C] (*fml*) a person or people forming one side in a legal agreement or dispute, or taking part in some other activity: *the guilty party* (ie the person who is to blame for sth) ○ *Is this solution acceptable to all parties concerned?* ○ *Local shopkeepers and other interested parties* (ie people involved in or affected by the situation) *were invited to the meeting.* See also THIRD PARTY. **IDM** **be (a) party to sth** to be involved in, know about or support an action, a plan, etc: *be party to an agreement/a dispute/a decision* ○ *They refused to be party to any violence.*

▶ **party** *v* (*pt, pp* **partied**) (*infml*) to enjoy oneself at a party(1): [V] *partying all night long.*

■ **'party-goer** *n* a person attending a party.

'party line *n* a telephone line shared by two or more customers who each have their own number.

ˌparty 'line *n* (usu *sing*) the official policies of a political party: *Some MPs refused to **follow/toe the party line** on defence.*

'party piece *n* (*Brit esp joc*) an act that sb often does at parties, etc to entertain others, eg performing a trick or singing a song.

ˌparty 'politics *n* [sing or pl *v*] political activity carried out through, by or for parties. **ˌparty po'litical** *adj* of or relating to a political party or parties: *a party political broadcast by the Republican Party.*

ˌparty 'spirit *n* [U] enthusiasm for parties (PARTY 1).

ˌparty-'wall *n* a wall that divides two buildings or rooms and that belongs to the owners of both properties.

parvenu /'pɑːvənjuː; *US* -nuː/ *n* (*pl* **-us**) (*derog*) a person who has suddenly risen from a low social or economic position to one of wealth or power: *parvenu bureaucrats.*

pass¹ /pɑːs; *US* pæs/ *v* **1(a)** to move forward or to the other side of sb/sth: [Vn] *pass a barrier/sentry/checkpoint* [V] *The street was so crowded that cars were unable to pass.* [Vn] (*fig*) *Not a word passed her lips* (ie She said nothing). **(b)** to leave sb/sth on one side or behind as one goes forward; to go past sb/sth: [Vn] *Turn right after passing the Post Office.* ○ *She passed me in the street without even saying hello.* ○ *I pass the church on my way to work.* ○ *A car passed me at 90 mph.* ○ *Unemployment has now passed the three million mark.* [V] *I hailed a passing taxi.* **2(a)** to go or move in the specified direction: [Vpr] *The procession passed slowly along the street.* ○ *We passed through Pennsylvania on our way to Ohio.* ○ *We passed from the corridor into a large hall.* [Vp] *He glanced at her and then passed on* (ie continued to walk forward). [Vadv] *A plane passed low overhead.* **(b)** to make sth move in the specified direction or to be in a certain position: [Vnpr] *pass a thread through the eye of a needle* ○ *pass a rope round a post* ○ *She passed her hand across her forehead.* **3 ~ sth (to sb)** to give sth to sb by handing it to them: [Vnn, Vn] *Pass (me) the salt, please.* [Vnp] *They passed the photograph around* (ie from one person to the next). [Vnp, Vnn] *Pass that book over/Pass me (over) that book.* [Vnpr] *She passed the letter to Mary.*

[Vn] *He was sent to prison for passing bad cheques* (ie issuing worthless cheques). **4 ~ (sth) (to sb)** (in football, hockey, Rugby, etc) to kick, hit or throw the ball to a player of one's own side: [Vnpr, Vpr] *He passed (the ball) to the winger.* [also V, Vn]. **5 ~ to sb** to be transferred from one person to another, esp by being inherited: [Vpr] *On his death, the title passed to his eldest son.* **6 ~ from sth to/into sth** to change from one state or condition to another: [Vpr] *pass from boyhood to manhood* ○ *Water passes from a liquid to a solid state when it freezes.* **7(a)** (of time) to go by; to be spent: [V] *Six months passed, and we still had no news of them.* ○ *The holidays passed far too quickly.* ○ *We grew more anxious **with each/every passing day.*** **(b)** to occupy or spend time: [Vn] *We sang songs to **pass the time*** (ie to make the passage of time less boring). ○ *How did you pass the evening?* **8** to come to an end; to be over: [V] *They waited for the storm to pass.* ○ *The dizziness will soon pass.* **9(a)** to achieve the required standard in an examination, a test, etc: [V, Vn] *You'll have to work hard if you want to pass (your finals).* [Vn] *She hasn't passed her driving test yet.* **(b)** to examine sb/sth and declare them/it to be satisfactory or acceptable: [Vn] *The examiners passed all the candidates* (ie decided that their work was of the required standard). **10(a)** to approve a law, proposal, etc by voting: [Vn] *Congress passed the bill.* ○ *The motion was passed by 12 votes to 10.* **(b)** (esp of a law, proposal, etc) to be approved or accepted by a parliament, an assembly, etc: [Vn] *This film will never pass the censors* (eg because it is too violent). [also V] **11** to be allowed or tolerated: [V] *I don't like it, but I'll **let it pass*** (ie will make no objections). ○ *Her provocative remarks passed without comment* (ie People ignored them). **12 ~ (on sth)** to say that one does not know the answer to a question, esp during a QUIZ(1): [Vpr] *'What's the capital of Peru?' 'I'll have to pass on that one.'* [V] *All right, I pass. What's the answer?* ○ *'Who wrote "Ulysses"?' 'Pass* (ie I do not know)!' **13 ~ sth (on sb/sth)** to pronounce or declare sth: [Vn, Vnp] *pass sentence (on sb found guilty of a crime)* ○ *pass judgement (on sb/sth)* [Vn] *pass a remark.* **14 ~ (between A and B)** to happen; to be said or done: [Vpr] *after all that has passed between them* [V-adj] *His departure from the party passed unnoticed.* **15** to go beyond the limits of sth: [Vn] *pass belief* (ie be impossible to believe) ○ *pass one's comprehension* (ie be impossible for one to understand). **16** [V] (in card-games) to refuse to play a card or make a bid when it is one's turn. **17** to send sth out from the body as or with URINE or FAECES: [Vn] *If you're passing blood you ought to see a doctor.* **IDM** **make/pass water** ⇨ WATER¹. **ˌpass the 'buck (to sb)** (*infml*) to transfer the responsibility or blame for sth to sb else. **pass the 'hat round/around** (*infml*) to collect money, eg to help sb who is ill, to buy food and drink for a party, etc. **pass 'muster** to be accepted as adequate or satisfactory. **pass the time of 'day (with sb)** to greet sb and have a short conversation with them. **PHRV** **'pass as sb/sth** = PASS FOR SB/STH.

ˌpass a'way 1 (also **pass 'on**) (*euph*) to die: *His mother passed away last year.* **2** to stop existing: *civilizations that have passed away.*

ˌpass 'by (sb/sth) to go past: *I saw the procession pass by.* ○ *The procession passed right by my front door.* **ˌpass sb/sth 'by** to occur without affecting sb/sth: *The whole business passed him by* (ie He was hardly aware that it was happening). ○ *She feels that life is passing her by* (ie that she is not gaining from or enjoying the opportunities and pleasures of life).

ˌpass sth 'down (esp passive) to pass sth from one generation to the next: *knowledge which has been passed down over the centuries.*

'pass for/as sb/sth to be accepted as sb/sth: *He speaks French well enough to pass for a Frenchman.*

'pass 'into sth to become a part of sth: *Many foreign words have passed into the English language.* ○ *His deeds have passed into legend* (ie because they were so brave, important, etc).

ıpass 'off 1 (of an event) to take place and be completed: *The demonstration passed off without incident.* **2** (of pain, the effects of a drug, etc) to come to an end gradually; to disappear: *The numbness in your foot will soon pass off.* **ıpass sb/oneself/sth 'off as sb/sth** to represent sb/sth falsely as sb/sth: *She passed him off as* (ie pretended that he was) *her husband.* ○ *He escaped by passing himself off as a guard.*

ıpass 'on = PASS AWAY. **ıpass 'on (to sth)** to move from one activity, stage, etc to another: *Let's pass on to the next item on the agenda.* **ıpass sth 'on (to sb)** to hand or give sth to sb else, esp after receiving or using it oneself: *Pass the book on to me when you've finished with it.* ○ *I passed your message on to my mother.* ○ *She caught my cold and passed it on to* (ie infected) *her husband.*

ıpass 'out to lose consciousness; to FAINT². **ıpass 'out (of sth)** (*Brit*) to leave a military college after completing a course of training: *a passing-'out ceremony/parade.*

ıpass sb 'over to fail to consider sb for promotion in a job, esp when they deserve it or think they deserve it: *He was passed over in favour of a younger man.* **ıpass 'over sth** to ignore or avoid sth: *They chose to pass over her rude remarks.* ○ *Sex is a subject he prefers to pass over* (eg because it embarrasses him).

ıpass 'through to go through a town, etc, stopping there for a short time but not staying: *We were passing through, so we thought we'd come and say hello.*

ıpass sth 'up (*infml*) to choose not to make use of a chance, an opportunity, etc: *Imagine passing up an offer like that!*

pass² /pɑːs; *US* pæs/ *n* **1** ~ **(to sb)** (in football, hockey, Rugby, etc) an act of kicking, hitting or throwing the ball to a player in one's own team: *a long pass to the half-back.* **2(a)** a paper or card giving sb permission, eg to enter, leave or be absent from a place: *All visitors must show their passes before entering the building.* ○ *There is no admittance without a security pass.* **(b)** any of various types of bus ticket or train ticket. A pass may allow sb to travel regularly along a particular route over a specified period of time or to travel at a reduced fare or free of charge: *a monthly bus pass* (ie one that is valid for a month). **3** a successful result in an examination: *She got a pass in French.* ○ *2 passes and 3 fails.* **4** a road or way over or through mountains: *The pass was blocked by snow.* **5** an act of going or moving past or over sth: *The helicopter made several passes over the village before landing.* **IDM** **come to such a 'pass / to a pretty 'pass** (*dated or joc*) to reach a sad or difficult state: *Things have come to a pretty pass when the children have to prepare their own meals.* **make a pass at sb** (*infml*) to try to attract sb sexually.

passable /'pɑːsəbl; *US* 'pæs-/ *adj* **1** [usu pred] **(a)** (of roads) clear of obstacles, esp snow, and therefore in a fit state to be driven on: *The mountain roads are not passable until late spring.* **(b)** (of a river) that can be crossed. Compare IMPASSABLE. **2** fairly good but not excellent; adequate: *have a passable knowledge of German.*
▶ **passably** /-əbli/ *adv* in an adequate or acceptable way.

passage /'pæsɪdʒ/ *n* **1** [U] **(a)** the process of passing: *the passage of time.* **(b)** the action of going past, through or across sth: *guarantee sb safe passage through the country.* **(c)** the freedom or right to go through or across sth: *They were denied passage*

through the occupied territory. **2** [C usu *sing*] a way through sth: *force a passage through the crowd.* **3** [*sing*] a journey from one place to another by ship or plane; the cost of a ticket for this: *book one's passage to New York* ○ *He worked his passage to Australia* (eg paid for the journey by doing jobs on the ship he was travelling on). **4** (also **'passageway**) [C] a narrow way through sth, esp with walls on both sides; a CORRIDOR(1). **5** [C] a structure like a tube in the human body, through which air, waste matter, etc passes: *the nasal passages* ○ (*infml*) *the back passage* (ie the ANUS). **6** [C] a short section from a book, speech, piece of music, etc quoted or considered on its own: *a passage from the Bible.* **7** [U] the passing of a BILL¹(4) by a parliament so that it becomes law.

passbook /'pɑːsbʊk; *US* 'pæs-/ *n* = BANK-BOOK.

passé /'pæseɪ, 'pɑːs-; *US* pæ'seɪ/ *adj* [usu pred] (*French*) out of date; old-fashioned; past the best: *Her ideas on food are distinctly passé* ○ *He was a fine actor but he's a bit passé now.*

passenger /'pæsɪndʒə(r)/ *n* **1** a person travelling in a car, bus, train, plane, ship, etc, other than the driver, the pilot or a member of the crew: *The driver was killed in the crash but both passengers escaped unhurt.* ○ *the passenger seat* (ie the seat next to the driver's seat in a motor vehicle) ○ *a passenger train* (ie one carrying passengers rather than goods). **2** (*infml derog esp Brit*) a member of a team, crew, etc who does not do as much work as the others: *This firm can't afford (to carry) passengers.*

passer-by /ˌpɑːsə 'baɪ; *US* ˌpæsər/ *n* (*pl* **passers-by** /ˌpɑːsəz 'baɪ/) a person who is going past sb/sth, esp by chance: *Police asked passers-by if they had seen the accident happen.*

passim /'pæsɪm/ *adv* (*Latin*) (of names or subjects referred to in notes, etc) occurring throughout or at several points in a book, an article, etc.

passing /'pɑːsɪŋ; *US* 'pæs-/ *adj* [attrib] **(a)** lasting for a short time; brief: *a passing thought/fancy/glance.* **(b)** casual; CURSORY: *a passing reference/remark* ○ *He bears more than a passing resemblance to* (ie looks quite like) *your brother.*
▶ **passing** *n* **1** [U] the process of going by: *the passing of time/the years.* **2** (*fml*) **(a)** the end: *the passing of the old year* (ie on New Year's Eve). **(b)** (*euph*) death: *The country mourns his passing.* **IDM** **in passing** as a matter of secondary importance; casually; by the way: *mention sth in passing.*

passion /'pæʃn/ *n* **1(a)** [U,C] a strong feeling, eg of hate, love or anger: *a man of violent passions* ○ *a crime of passion* ○ *She argued with great passion.* ○ *Passions were running high at the meeting* (ie People were in an angry or emotional state). **(b)** [*sing*] an angry state: *fly into a passion* (ie become very angry). **2** [U] ~ **(for sb)** intense, esp sexual, love: *His passion for her made him blind to everything else.* **3** [*sing*] **(a)** ~ **for sth** a great enthusiasm for or enjoyment of sth: *have a passion for chocolate/detective stories/tennis.* **(b)** a thing for which sb has great enthusiasm: *Horse-racing is her passion.* ○ *Music is a passion with him.* **4 the Passion** [*sing*] (*religion*) the suffering and death of Christ.
▶ **passionless** *adj* without emotion or enthusiasm: *a passionless performance.*
■ **'passion-flower** *n* a climbing plant with brightly coloured flowers .
'passion-fruit *n* [C,U] the edible fruit of certain types of passion-flower: *passion-fruit ice-cream.*
'passion-play *n* a play about the Passion of Christ.

passionate /'pæʃənət/ *adj* **1(a)** caused by or showing intense sexual love: *a passionate kiss/lover/relationship.* **(b)** caused by or showing strong feelings: *a passionate plea for mercy* ○ *her passionate support for our cause* ○ *a passionate defender of civil liberties.* **2** dominated or easily affected by strong feelings: *a passionate nature/temperament/woman.*

[V.*to* inf] = verb + *to* infinitive   [Vn.inf (no *to*)] = verb + noun + infinitive without *to*   [V.*ing*] = verb + *-ing* form

▶ **passionately** adv: He loved her passionately. ◦ He believes passionately in freedom of speech. ◦ passionately fond of tennis.

passive /ˈpæsɪv/ adj **1** accepting what happens or is done to one without responding actively or as-serting oneself; not active: play a passive role in a marriage ◦ a passive observer of events ◦ passive obedience/acceptance ◦ His passive face concealed a deep anger. **2** (grammar) of the form of a verb used when the subject is affected by the action of the verb, as in Her leg was broken and He was bitten by a dog: a passive sentence. Compare ACTIVE.
▶ **passive** (also ˌpassive ˈvoice) n [sing] (grammar) the passive form of a verb, verb phrase or sentence: In the sentence 'He was seen there', 'was seen' is in the passive. Compare ACTIVE n.
passively adv.
passiveness (also **passivity** /pæˈsɪvəti/) n [U] the state or quality of being passive.
■ ˌpassive reˈsistance n [U] the activity of oppos-ing a government or an enemy who has occupied one's country, by refusing to obey orders or laws, not by violent means.
ˌpassive ˈsmoking n [U] the breathing in of smoke from other people's cigarettes, etc.

passkey /ˈpɑːskiː/ n **(a)** a key to a door or gate given to people who have a right to enter. **(b)** = MASTER-KEY.

Passover /ˈpɑːsəʊvə(r); US ˈpæs-/ n the Jewish reli-gious festival in memory of the freeing of the Jews from being slaves in Egypt.

passport /ˈpɑːspɔːt; US ˈpæs-/ n **1** an official docu-ment issued by the government of a particular country, identifying the holder as a citizen of that country and allowing her or him to travel abroad: hold a Canadian passport ◦ go through passport control. **2** ~ **to sth** a thing that enables one to achieve sth: The only passport to success is hard work.

password /ˈpɑːswɜːd/ n **(a)** a secret word or phrase that one needs to know in order to be allowed into a place: give the password. **(b)** a secret word that one must type in order to use a computer system.

past¹ /pɑːst; US pæst/ adj **1** gone by in time: in past years/centuries/ages ◦ in times past ◦ The time for discussion is past. **2** [attrib] gone by recently; just finished or ended: The past month has been a diffi-cult one for him. ◦ I've seen little of her in the past few weeks. **3** [attrib] belonging to an earlier time: past happiness ◦ past and present students of the college ◦ past achievements/failures/generations/presidents ◦ Let's forget about who owes what — it's all past history. **4** [attrib] (grammar) (of a verb form) indic-ating a state or an action in the past: The past tense of 'take' is 'took'.
▶ **past** n **1** the past [sing] **(a)** the time that has gone by: I've been there many times in the past. **(b)** things that happened in an earlier time; past events: memories of the past ◦ look back on/remember/regret the past. **2** [C] a person's past life or career, esp when he or she has a bad reputation: We know nothing of his past. ◦ She's a woman with a 'past'. **3** (also **past tense**) [sing] (grammar) (abbreviated as pt in this dictionary) the form of a verb used to describe actions in the past: The past of the verb 'take' is 'took'. **IDM** **live in the past** ⇨ LIVE². **a thing of the past** ⇨ THING.
■ ˌpast ˈmaster n ~ (in/of sth); ~ (at sth/doing sth) a person who has a lot of skill or experience in a particular activity; an expert: She's a past master at (the art of) getting what she wants.
ˌpast ˈparticiple n (grammar) (abbreviated as pp in this dictionary) (in English) a PARTICIPLE used in the present perfect, past perfect and PASSIVE(2) forms of verbs (eg beaten, sung, pretended), and sometimes as an adjective.

ˌpast ˈperfect adj, n = PLUPERFECT.

past² /pɑːst; US pæst/ prep **1** (US also time) later than sth; after sth: half past t[...] (minutes) past six ◦ There's a bus at twenty min[...] past the hour (ie at 1.20, 2.20, 3.20, etc). ◦ We arrive[...] at two o'clock and at ten past (ie ten minutes past two). ◦ It was past midnight when we got home. **2** on the far side of sth; from one side to the other of sth/sb: We live in the house just past the church. ◦ If you look past the town hall you'll see the police station. ◦ She walked past the shop. ◦ He hurried past me without stopping. **3(a)** beyond or above a certain point: Unemployment is now past the 3 million mark. ◦ I didn't get past the first question in the exam. ◦ The flowers are past their best. **(b)** beyond the limits of sth/doing sth: I'm past caring (ie I no longer care) what happens to me. **(c)** beyond the age of sth: He's past his prime. ◦ She's long past retirement age. **IDM** ˈpast it (infml) too old to do what one was once capable of; too old to be used for its normal function: In some sports you're past it by the age of 25 these days. ◦ That overcoat is looking decidedly past it.
▶ **past** adv part from one side to the other of sth: walk/march/go/rush past.

pasta /ˈpæstə; US ˈpɑːstə/ n [U] a food made from flour, eggs and water, hard when dry and soft when cooked. There are many types and shapes of pasta, each with a different name: a pasta sauce (ie to eat with pasta) ◦ Macaroni, spaghetti and ravioli are all types of pasta. Compare NOODLE.

paste¹ /peɪst/ n **1** [sing] a soft wet mixture, esp of a powder and a liquid: a smooth/thin/thick paste ◦ She mixed the flour and water to a paste. **2** [U] a mixture of flour and water used to stick things together, esp to stick paper to a wall. **3** [U] (esp Brit) (esp in compounds) a mixture of ground meat, fish, etc for spreading on bread: anchovy paste. **4** [U] a sub-stance like glass used to make artificial jewellery.

paste² /peɪst/ v **(a)** to stick sth to sth else or in the specified place, using PASTE¹(2): [Vnpr] paste posters onto the wall ◦ paste pictures into a scrapbook [Vnp] paste pieces of paper together ◦ paste up an advertise-ment ◦ paste the edges down. **(b)** to make sth by sticking pieces of paper together: [Vn] children cut-ting and pasting paper crowns for themselves.

pasteboard /ˈpeɪstbɔːd/ n [U] a type of thin board made by fastening thin sheets of paper together.

pastel /ˈpæstl; US pæˈstel/ n **1(a)** [C,U] a stick of soft coloured chalk used for drawing: a box of pas-tels ◦ a landscape in pastel. **(b)** a picture drawn with pastels. **2** a pale delicate colour: pastel shades/colours.

pastern /ˈpæstən/ n the part of a horse's foot be-tween the FETLOCK and the HOOF. ⇨ picture at HORSE.

pasteurize, -ise /ˈpɑːstʃəraɪz; US ˈpæs-/ v [Vn] to heat a liquid, esp milk, to a certain temperature and then cool it, in order to kill harmful bacteria. ▶ **pasteurization, -isation** /ˌpɑːstʃəraɪˈzeɪʃn; US ˌpæstʃərəˈzeɪʃn/ n [U].

pastiche /pæˈstiːʃ/ n **1** [C] a literary, musical or artistic work in the style of another author, artist, etc. **2** [C] a literary, musical or artistic work con-sisting of elements from various sources. **3** [U] the art of composing pastiches: He has a gift for pas-tiche.

pastille /ˈpæstəl; US pæˈstiːl/ n a small sweet for sucking, esp one containing medicine for a sore throat: fruit pastilles ◦ throat pastilles.

pastime /ˈpɑːstaɪm; US ˈpæs-/ n a thing done regu-larly for enjoyment rather than work: Photography is her favourite pastime.

pasting /ˈpeɪstɪŋ/ n [sing] **1** a severe beating. **2** a heavy defeat: The team took a real pasting.

pastor /ˈpɑːstə(r); US ˈpæs-/ n a minister¹(3), esp of a Nonconformist church.

pastoral /ˈpɑːstərəl; US ˈpæs-/ adj **1(a)** portraying

P

side, esp in a sentimental ...ral *scene/poem/painting* ○ ...ᵼ relating to country life or ...ᵼ of animals: *a tribe of pas-* ...ᵼ work of a priest or teacher ...ᵼ advice, esp in addition to her ...uties: *pastoral care/duties/*

...:mi/ *n* [U] smoked BEEF(1) with a stron...

pastry /ˈpeɪ...ᵼ *n* **1** [U] a mixture of flour, fat and water which is baked and used as a base or covering for pies, etc: *pastry tarts.* **2** [C] an item of food made entirely or partly of pastry: *Danish pastries.* See also PUFF PASTRY.

pasture /ˈpɑːstʃə(r); *US* ˈpæs-/ *n* **1(a)** [U] land covered with grass and similar plants, suitable for feeding animals: *acres of rich pasture* ○ *put a flock out to pasture.* **(b)** [C] a piece of this. **2 pastures** [pl] the circumstances of one's life, work, etc: *find greener/richer/better/lusher pastures* (ie a better way of life, etc) ○ (*rhet*) *She decided it was time to move on to pastures new* (ie a new job, place to live, etc).
▶ **pasture** *v* **1** to put animals in a pasture to feed on grass: [Vn] *pasture one's sheep on the village common.* **2** [V] (of animals) to feed on grass.

pastureland /ˈpɑːstʃəlænd; *US* ˈpæs-/ (*also* **pasturage**) /ˈpɑːstʃərɪdʒ; *US* ˈpæs-/ *n* [U] land where animals can feed on grass.

pasty¹ /ˈpæsti/ *n* (*esp Brit*) a piece of pastry folded round a filling of meat, fruit, jam, etc. See also CORNISH PASTY.

pasty² /ˈpeɪsti/ *adj* **1** of or like PASTE¹(1): *a pasty substance* ○ *mix to a pasty consistency.* **2** pale and looking ill: *a pasty face/complexion* ○ *a pasty-faced youth.*

pat¹ /pæt/ *v* (-tt-) **1** to tap sb/sth gently with the open hand or with a flat object: [Vn] *pat a dog* ○ *pat sb's hand* ○ (*Brit*) *pat a ball* (ie so that it bounces up and down) [Vnpr] *pat a child on the head* (ie as a sign of affection). **2** to put sth in a specified position or state by patting: [Vnpr] *She patted her hair into place/shape* [Vnp] *She patted down a few wisps of hair.* [Vn-adj] *He patted his face dry (with a towel).* **IDM** **pat sb/oneself on the ˈback** to praise or CONGRATULATE sb/oneself.
▶ **pat** *n* **1** a gentle tap with the open hand or with a flat object: *She gave the child a pat on the head.* ○ *He gave her knee an affectionate pat/gave her an affectionate pat on the knee.* **2** ~ (**of sth**) a small mass of sth, esp butter, that has been shaped by patting. See also COW-PAT. **IDM** **a ˌpat on the ˈback (for sth/doing sth)** praise or approval: *give sb/get a pat on the back* ○ *She deserves a pat on the back for all the hard work she's done.*

pat² /pæt/ *adv* **IDM** **have/know sth off ˈpat** to know sth perfectly so that one can repeat it at any time: *He had all the answers off pat.* ○ *She knows the rules off pat.* **stand ˈpat** (*esp US*) to refuse to change a decision one has made, an opinion one holds, etc.
▶ **pat** *adj* **1** exactly right; appropriate. **2** (*derog*) too quick; GLIB: *Her answer was too pat to be convincing.*

patch¹ /pætʃ/ *n* **1** a piece of material placed over a hole or a damaged or worn place to cover or strengthen it: *a jacket with leather patches on the elbows* ○ *a patch on the inner tube of a tyre* ○ *She sewed a patch onto the knee of her jeans.* **2** a pad worn over an injured eye to protect it: *He wears a black patch over his right eye.* **3** a part of a surface that is different in colour, texture, etc from the area around it: *a black dog with a white patch on its neck* ○ *damp patches on a wall* ○ *He's developing a bald patch.* **4** ~ (**of sth**) a small area of sth: *patches of fog/ice/sunlight* ○ *patches of blue in a cloudy sky* ○ *The ground is wet in*

patches. **5** a small piece of land, esp one used for growing vegetables: *a ˈcabbage/ˈvegetable patch.* **6** (*Brit infml*) an area in which sb, eg a police officer, works or which they know well: *He knows every house in his patch.* **7** (*infml*) a period of time of the specified type, esp a difficult or unhappy one: *Their marriage has been going through a bad/sticky patch.* **IDM** **not be a ˈpatch on sb/sth** (*infml*) to be much less successful, interesting, etc than sb/sth: *This book isn't a patch on her others.*

patch² /pætʃ/ *v* **(a)** to cover a hole or a worn place with a patch: [Vn] *patch a hole in a pair of jeans.* **(b)** ~ **sth (up)** to mend a garment by covering a hole or worn place with a patch: [Vnp] *patch up an old pair of jeans* [Vn] *The elbows of your jersey are worn — I'll need to patch them.* **PHRV** **ˌpatch sth/sb ˈup 1** to repair sth or treat sb's injuries, esp quickly or temporarily: *He managed to patch up his bike after the accident.* ○ *The doctor will soon patch you up.* **2** to settle or resolve a quarrel, dispute, etc: *They patched up their differences.*

patchouli /ˈpætʃuli, pəˈtʃuːli/ *n* **(a)** [C] a sweet-smelling plant grown in E Asia. **(b)** [U] the PERFUME(1) made from this plant.

patchwork /ˈpætʃwɜːk/ *n* **1** [U] a type of NEEDLEWORK in which small pieces of cloth with different designs are sewn together: *a patchwork bedcover/cushion/quilt.* **2** [sing] a thing consisting of various small pieces or parts: *a patchwork of fields seen from the plane* ○ *a patchwork of small communities.*

patchy /ˈpætʃi/ *adj* **1** existing in or having patches: *patchy fog/mist/cloud.* **2** not of the same quality throughout; not even²(2): *a patchy essay/novel/performance* ○ *His work is rather patchy.* ○ *My knowledge of German is patchy* (ie not complete). ▶ **patchily** *adv.* **patchiness** *n* [U].

pate /peɪt/ *n* (*arch or joc infml*) the top part of the head: *a shiny bald pate.*

pâté /ˈpæteɪ; *US* pɑːˈteɪ/ *n* [U] a type of rich PASTE¹(3) made of finely ground meat or fish: *liver/duck/mackerel pâté.*
■ **pâté de foie gras** /ˌpæteɪ də fwɑː ˈɡrɑː; *US* pɑːˌteɪ/ *n* [U] (*French*) pâté made from the LIVER(2) of a goose.

patella /pəˈtelə/ *n* (*pl* **patellae** /-liː/) (*anatomy*) the KNEECAP. ⇨ picture at SKELETON.

patent¹ /ˈpeɪtnt, ˈpætnt; *US* ˈpætnt/ *adj* [usu attrib] obvious; clear: *a patent lie* ○ *his patent dislike of the plan* ○ *a patent disregard for the truth.* ▶ **patently** *adv*: *It was patently obvious that he was lying.*

patent² /ˈpætnt, ˈpeɪtnt; *US* ˈpætnt/ *n* **1(a)** an official document giving the holder the sole right to make, use or sell an invention and preventing others from copying it: *take out* (ie obtain) *a patent to protect an invention* ○ *patent applied for* (eg marked on goods not yet protected by a patent). **(b)** the right given by this. **2** an invention or process that is protected by a patent: *It's my patent.*
▶ **patent** *adj* [attrib] **1** (of an invention, a product, etc) protected by or having a patent. **2** made and sold by a particular firm: *patent medicines* (ie ones that can be bought without a doctor's PRESCRIPTION(1a)) ○ (*joc*) *his patent* (ie personal) *remedy for hangovers.*
patent *v* [Vn] to obtain a patent for an invention or a process.

patentee /ˌpeɪtnˈtiː; *US* ˌpætn-/ *n* a person who obtains or holds a patent.
■ **ˌpatent ˈleather** *n* [U] leather with a hard shiny surface, used for shoes and bags.
ˈpatent office *n* an office or a government department that issues patents.

paterfamilias /ˌpeɪtəfəˈmɪliæs; *US* ˌpætə-/ *n* [sing] (*fml or joc*) the male head of a family or household.

paternal /pəˈtɜːnl/ *adj* **1** of or like a father: *paternal affection/authority* ○ *have a paternal concern for sb's* *welfare* (ie like that of a father for his child). **2** related through one's father: *her paternal grandmother* (ie her father's mother). Compare MATERNAL. ▶ **paternally** /-nəli/ *adv*.

paternalism /pəˈtɜːnəlɪzəm/ *n* [U] (*sometimes derog*) the policy of governments or employers of controlling people by providing them with what they need, but giving them no responsibility or freedom of choice. ▶ **paternalistic** /pəˌtɜːnəˈlɪstɪk/ *adj*: *paternalistic attitudes/employers*.

paternity /pəˈtɜːnəti/ *n* [U] the state or fact of being the father of a child: *He denied paternity of the boy*. ■ **paˈternity leave** *n* [U] time taken off work by the father of a new baby.

paˈternity suit *n* a court case intended to establish formally the identity of a child's father, esp so that he may be required to support it. Compare MATERNITY.

path /pɑːθ; *US* pæθ/ *n* (*pl* **paths** /pɑːðz; *US* pæðz/) **1** (also **ˈpathway**, **ˈfootpath**) a way or track made for or by people walking: *Keep to the path or you'll lose your way*. ○ *The path follows the river and then goes up through the woods*. ○ *We took the path across the fields*. ⇨ picture at HOUSE[1]. **2** a line along which sb/sth moves: *the path of a tornado* ○ *Three men blocked her path*. ○ *She threw herself **in the path of** (ie in front of) an oncoming vehicle*. ○ (*fig*) *She has had a difficult path through life*. See also FLIGHT PATH. **3** a course of action: *I strongly advised him not to take that path*. **4** (usu *sing*) ~ **to sth** a way to reach or achieve sth: *the path to victory/ruin/economic recovery*. **IDM** **cross sb's path** ⇨ CROSS[2]. **lead sb up the garden path** ⇨ LEAD[1]. **the primrose path** ⇨ PRIMROSE. **smooth sb's/the path/way** ⇨ SMOOTH[2]. ▶ **pathless** *adj*: *pathless forests*.

NOTE Compare **path**, **track** and **lane**. A **path** or **footpath** is a narrow way marked out for people to walk along, between houses in a town, or across fields, besides rivers, etc in the country: *Just follow the path and you won't get lost*. A **track** is a rough path in the country that has been formed by people, animals or vehicles constantly using it: *We walked along a track through the forest*. A **lane** is a narrow road in the country. It can also refer to one of the sections of a wide road that is marked for a single line of traffic to use: *a six-lane motorway* ○ *You're in the wrong lane if you want to turn left*. A train travels along a **track**: *The railway track runs along the shore of Lake Superior*. Runners in an athletics stadium run in individual **lanes**. The specially prepared area used for running is called the **track**.

-path ⇨ -PATHY.

pathetic /pəˈθetɪk/ *adj* **1** causing one to feel pity or sadness: *pathetic cries for help* ○ *the pathetic sight of starving children*. **2** (*infml*) extremely inadequate; useless; worthless: *a pathetic attempt/performance/ excuse — You're pathetic — you can't even boil an egg!* ▶ **pathetically** /-kli/ *adv*: *a pathetically thin child* ○ *The dog was whimpering pathetically*.

pathfinder /ˈpɑːθfaɪndə(r); *US* pæθ-/ *n* a person or thing that goes before others and shows the way.

patho- *comb form* disease: *pathology*.

pathogen /ˈpæθədʒən/ *n* an agent(2b) that causes disease: *the spread of pathogens into the water system*. ▶ **pathogenic** /-ˈdʒenɪk/ *adj*.

pathological /ˌpæθəˈlɒdʒɪkl/ *adj* **1** (*infml*) not reasonable or sensible: *a pathological fear/hatred* ○ *a pathological liar* (ie a person who cannot stop himself telling lies). **2** of or caused by a physical or mental illness: *pathological depression*. **3** of or relating to PATHOLOGY. ▶ **pathologically** /-kli/ *adv*: *pathologically disturbed*.

pathology /pəˈθɒlədʒi/ *n* [U] the scientific study of diseases. ▶ **pathologist** /pəˈθɒlədʒɪst/ *n* an expert in pathology, esp one who examines the body of dead people to discover the cause of death: *The police pathologist's report indicated that she died from a blow to the head*.

pathos /ˈpeɪθɒs/ *n* [U] a quality, esp in literature or drama, that causes a feeling of pity or sadness: *a performance full of pathos and anger*.

-pathy *comb form* (forming *ns*) **1** a method of treating disease: *homeopathy* ○ *osteopathy*. **2** a feeling: *telepathy*.
▶ **-path** *comb form* (forming *ns*) **1** a doctor using a particular method of treating disease: *homeopath* ○ *osteopath*. **2** a person suffering from a disease: *psychopath*.
-pathic *comb form* (forming *adjs*): *homeopathic* ○ *telepathic*.

patience /ˈpeɪʃns/ *n* [U] **1** ~ (**with sb/sth**) the ability to accept delay, annoyance or suffering without complaining: *People have **lost patience with** (ie have become annoyed about) the slow pace of reform*. ○ *After three hours of waiting for the train, our patience was exhausted*. ○ *She has little patience with* (ie can hardly tolerate) *anyone who doesn't share her views*. ○ *It's enough to try* (ie test) *the patience of a saint!* **2** ~ (**for sth / to do sth**) the ability to keep doing sth that requires a lot of effort: *Learning to walk again after his accident required great patience*. ○ *I haven't the patience to do embroidery*. **3** (*Brit*) (*US* **solitaire**) a card-game for one player.

patient[1] /ˈpeɪʃnt/ *adj* ~ (**with sb/sth**) having or showing PATIENCE(1,2): *patient research/questioning/ determination* ○ *You'll have to be patient with my mother — she's rather deaf*. ▶ **patiently** *adv*: *wait/ sit/listen patiently*.

patient[2] /ˈpeɪʃnt/ *n* (**a**) a person who is receiving medical treatment, esp in a hospital. (**b**) a person who is registered with a doctor, dentist, etc and is treated by her or him when necessary: *I have been a patient of Dr Davis for many years*.

patina /ˈpætɪnə; *US* pəˈtiːnə/ *n* [sing] **1(a)** a usu green or black layer that forms on the surface of metals, esp old BRONZE or copper. (**b**) a similar layer that forms on other surfaces: *roof-tiles with a patina of moss and lichen* ○ (*fig*) *strip off the thin patina of respectability*. **2** a shiny surface on old wood.
▶ **patiˈnation** *n* [U,C] a layer covering the surface of sth: *The original patination had been black*.

patio /ˈpætɪəʊ/ *n* (*pl* **-os** /-əʊz/) an outdoor area with a hard surface next to a house, where people can sit: *Let's have lunch out **on the patio***. Compare VERANDA.

patisserie /pəˈtiːsəri/ *n* **1** [C] a shop selling pastries and cakes. **2** [U] pastries and cakes generally.

patois /ˈpætwɑː/ *n* (*pl* unchanged /-twɑːz/) a form of language spoken by the ordinary people of a region and different from the standard language of the country: *He speaks the local patois*.

patri- *comb form* of a father: *patricide* ○ *patriarch*. Compare MATRI-.

patriarch /ˈpeɪtriɑːk/ *n* **1** the male head of a family or tribe. Compare MATRIARCH. **2** Patriarch (in the Eastern Orthodox and Roman Catholic Churches) a bishop of high rank. **3** an old man who is greatly respected.
▶ **patriarchal** /ˌpeɪtriˈɑːkl/ *adj* **1** of or like a patriarch. **2** ruled or controlled by men: *a patriarchal society*.
patriarchate /-eɪt/ *n* a position or period of office of a Patriarch of the Church.
patriarchy /-ki/ *n* (**a**) [U] control or government by men. (**b**) [C] a society, country, etc controlled or governed by men.

patrician /pəˈtrɪʃn/ *n* (*fml*) a member of the highest social class; an ARISTOCRAT. Compare PLEBEIAN *n*.
▶ **patrician** *adj* of or like a patrician: *patrician airs/authority*.

patricide /'pætrɪsaɪd/ n (fml) (**a**) [C,U] the act of killing one's own father. (**b**) [C] a person who does this. Compare MATRICIDE, PARRICIDE.

patrimony /'pætrɪməni; US -məʊni/ n [U] (fml) property inherited from one's father or ancestors.

patriot /'pætrɪət, 'peɪt-; US 'peɪt-/ n a person who loves her or his country, esp one who is ready to defend it against an enemy: a true patriot.
▶ **patriotic** /ˌpætri'ɒtɪk, ˌpeɪt-; US ˌpeɪt-/ adj having or showing love of one's country: patriotic men and women ∘ patriotic songs/fervour.
patriotism /-ɪzəm/ n [U] love of one's country and willingness to defend it: an upsurge of patriotism.

patrol /pə'trəʊl/ v (-ll-) to go round an area to check that it is secure or safe and that there is no trouble: [Vn, Vpr] Troops regularly patrol (along) the border. [also V].
▶ **patrol** n **1** an act of patrolling an area: Security guards make hourly patrols of the site. **2** one or more people or vehicles that patrol an area: a naval/army/police patrol ∘ a police pa'trol car. **3** a group of 6–8 members of a Scout troop or a Guide company.
IDM **on patrol** patrolling a particular area: Terrorists attacked two soldiers on foot patrol.
■ **pa'trol wagon** n (US) = BLACK MARIA.

patron /'peɪtrən/ n (fem **patroness** /ˌpeɪtrən'es; US 'peɪtrənəs/) **1** a person who gives money or support to a person, an organization, a cause(3) or an activity: a wealthy patron of the arts. Compare SPONSOR 1. **2** (fml) a customer of a shop, restaurant, theatre, etc: Patrons are requested to leave their bags in the cloakroom.
■ ˌpatron 'saint n a saint regarded as protecting a particular person or place: St Christopher is the patron saint of travellers.

patronage /'pætrənɪdʒ/ n [U] **1** the support and encouragement given by a PATRON(1): patronage of the arts ∘ Without the patronage of several large firms, the festival could not take place. ∘ He's under the Prime Minister's patronage. Compare SPONSORSHIP. **2** the right or power to appoint sb to or recommend sb for an important position: dependent on patronage to advance their careers.

patronize, **-ise** /'pætrənaɪz; US 'peɪt-/ v **1** (derog) to treat sb in a way that appears friendly, but clearly displays that one feels superior to them: [Vn] He resented the way she patronized him. [also V]. **2** (fml) to be a regular customer of a shop, etc: [Vn] The restaurant is patronized by many politicians and journalists.
▶ **patronizing**, **-ising** adj (derog) showing that one feels superior: a patronizing manner/attitude/smile/tone of voice ∘ I wish he wouldn't be so patronizing! **patronizingly**, **-isingly** adv.

patsy /'pætsi/ n (US infml derog) a person who is stupid or easily cheated.

patter /'pætə(r)/ n **1** [sing] the sound of quick light steps or taps: the patter of rain on a roof ∘ the patter of footsteps. **2** [U, sing] the rapid continuous talk of a person telling jokes, performing tricks, selling sth, etc, intended to entertain, distract one's attention, persuade one to buy sth, etc.
▶ **patter** v to make quick light tapping sounds: [Vpr] rain pattering on the windowpanes [also Vp].
PHR V to walk with quick light steps in the specified direction: [Vp, Vpr] She pattered along (the corridor) in her bare feet.

pattern /'pætn/ n **1** a way in which sth happens, moves, develops or is arranged: patterns of behaviour/behaviour patterns ∘ the pattern of worldwide economic decline ∘ These sentences all have the same grammatical pattern. ∘ The murders all seem to follow a set/similar pattern (ie occur in a similar way). **2** an excellent example; a model: This company's profit-sharing scheme sets the pattern for others to follow. **3** an arrangement of lines, shapes,

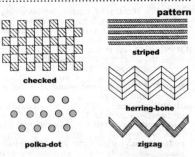

pattern

striped

checked

herring-bone

polka-dot

zigzag

colours, etc, esp as a decorative design on clothes, carpets or wallpaper: a checked/flowery/Paisley/geometric pattern ∘ a dress with a pattern of tiny roses. ➪ picture. **4** a design or set of instructions from which sth is to be made: follow a knitting pattern. **5** a sample of cloth or other material: a book of carpet/wallpaper patterns.
▶ **pattern** v **1** to create a pattern on sth: [Vn] a landscape patterned by vineyards. **2** ~ sth on sth to use sth as a model for sth; to copy sth: [Vnpr] a new approach patterned on Japanese ideas. **patterned** /'pætənd/ adj ~ (with sth) decorated with a pattern: patterned china/wallpaper ∘ a blue shawl patterned with silver moons.

patterning /'pætənɪŋ/ n [U] **1** the design, arrangement or distribution of shapes, events, elements, etc in a pattern: a bird with black and white patterning on its wings. **2** (fml) the forming of fixed ways of behaviour by copying or repeating sth: the patterning of child-parent relationships.

paucity /'pɔːsəti/ n [sing] (fml) ~ (of sth) a small amount; not enough of sth: a paucity of evidence.

paunch /pɔːntʃ/ n a fat stomach, esp a man's: a middle-aged paunch ∘ You're getting quite a paunch.
▶ **paunchy** adj having a paunch.

pauper /'pɔːpə(r)/ n a very poor person: a pauper's grave ∘ He died a pauper.

pause /pɔːz/ n **1** ~ (in sth) a temporary stop in action or speech: There was a long pause before she answered. ∘ He slipped out during a pause in the conversation. ∘ After a short pause, they continued climbing. ∘ The rain fell without pause. ➪ note at BREAK². **2** (music) a sign (⌢) over a note¹(5b) or rest²(3) to indicate that it should be longer than usual. **IDM** **give 'pause to sb**; **give (sb) pause for 'thought** to make sb think seriously about sth or hesitate before doing sth: The institution's social value should give pause to those who seek to destroy it. ∘ The interpretation of the play gave pause for thought. **a pregnant pause/silence** ➪ PREGNANT.
▶ **pause** v ~ (for sth) to make a pause: [V] He paused for a moment before continuing. [Vpr] speak without pausing for breath (ie very quickly).

pave /peɪv/ v ~ sth (with sth) (esp passive) to cover a surface with flat stones or bricks: [Vn] a paved area outside the back door [Vnpr] The path is paved with concrete slabs. **IDM** **pave the 'way (for sb/sth)** to create a situation in which sb will be able to do sth or sth can happen: economic policies that will pave the way for industrial expansion.
▶ **paving** n [U] (**a**) a surface of flat stones: weeds growing through cracks in the paving. (**b**) the stones, etc used for this: lay concrete paving.
■ 'paving stone n a flat piece of stone used for paving paths, etc.

pavement /'peɪvmənt/ n **1** [C] (Brit) (US sidewalk) a raised path with a surface of flat stones or Tarmac at the side of a road for people to walk on: Don't ride your bicycle on the pavement. **2** [C,U] an area or surface of flat stones: a broad stretch of pavement ∘ a *pavement café* **3** [U] (*US*) the hard surface of a road or street.

■ **'pavement artist** *n* a person who draws on the pavement with coloured chalks, esp in order to earn money from people passing.

pavilion /pə'vɪlɪən/ *n* **1** (*Brit*) a building next to a sports ground, used by players and spectators: *a cricket pavilion.* **2** a building used as a shelter, eg in a park. **3** a large ornamental building used for concerts, dances, etc: *the Royal Pavilion in Brighton.* **4** a temporary building, esp a large tent used to display items at an exhibition.

paw /pɔː/ *n* **1** a foot of an animal with claws (CLAW 1a) or nails: *a cat's/dog's paw.* **2** (*infml joc or derog*) a person's hand: *Take your dirty little paws off me!*
▶ **paw** *v* ~ (**at**) **sth 1(a)** (of an animal) to feel or scratch sth with the paws: [Vpr] *The dog pawed at his sleeve.* [also Vn]. **(b)** (esp of a horse or BULL¹(1)) to scrape the ground, etc with the foot: [Vn, Vpr] *The mare was snorting and pawing (at) the ground.* **2** to touch sb/sth with the hands in a rough or awkward way or in a sexually unacceptable manner: [Vn] *He can't be near a woman without pawing her.* [also Vpr].

pawn¹ /pɔːn/ *n* **1** any of the eight CHESS pieces of the smallest size and least value. ⇨ picture at CHESS. **2** a person or group whose actions are controlled by others: *They are being used as political pawns in the struggle for power.*

pawn² /pɔːn/ *v* to leave an object with a PAWN-BROKER in exchange for money. The object is returned to the owner if he or she pays back the money within a specified time. If not, it may be sold: [Vn] *He pawned his gold watch to pay the rent.*
▶ **pawn** *n* **IDM** **in pawn** pawned: *My ring is in pawn.*

pawnbroker /'pɔːnbrəʊkə(r)/ *n* a person who lends money in exchange for articles left with her or him.

pawnshop /'pɔːnʃɒp/ *n* a place where a PAWN-BROKER works.

pawpaw (also **papaw** /'pɔːpɔː/, **papaya** /pə'paɪə/) *n* a tropical fruit with green skin, edible orange flesh and small black seeds.

pay¹ /peɪ/ *n* [U] the money paid to sb for regular work: *a pay rise/award/increase* ∘ *a 6.5% pay offer* ∘ *holiday/redundancy pay* ∘ *pay negotiations/ bargaining* ∘ *He doesn't like the job, but the pay is good.* ∘ note at INCOME. See also SICK-PAY. **IDM** **in the pay of sb/sth** (*usu derog*) secretly employed by a person or group: *a spy in the pay of the enemy.*
■ **'pay-claim** *n* (*Brit*) a demand for an increase in pay, esp one made by a union for its members.
'pay-day *n* a day of the week or month on which wages or salaries are paid.
'pay-packet (*Brit*) (also **'wage-packet**) *n* an envelope containing an employee's wages.
'pay phone *n* a telephone operated by coins, usu in a public place.

pay² /peɪ/ *v* (*pt, pp* **paid** /peɪd/) **1(a)** ~ (**sb**) (**for sth**); ~ **sth** (**to sb**) (**for sth**) to give sb money for work, goods, services, etc: [V, Vpr] *They tried to leave the restaurant without paying (for their meal).* [Vpr] *Are you paying in cash or by cheque?* ∘ *Her parents paid for her to go* (ie paid the cost of her travel) *to America.* [Vn] *Have you paid the milkman this week?* [Vnpr] *How much did you pay for your car?* ∘ *pay sb by the hour/by the job* ∘ *Have you paid that money to the bank yet?* [Vnn] *You haven't paid me the money you owe me.* [Vadv] *My firm pays well* (ie pays high wages). [Vn.to inf] *You're not paid to sit around doing nothing!* **(b)** ~ **sth** (**to sb**) to give what is owed; to settle a demand or an amount due: [Vn] *pay rent* ∘ *pay a bill/debt/fine* [Vnn] *He paid the kidnappers a ransom of £50 000 for his son.* [Vnpr] *Membership fees should be paid to the club secretary.*

2(a) (of a business, etc) to be profitable: [V] *It's difficult to make farming pay.* **(b)** (often with *it* as subject) to result in some advantage or profit for sb: [V] *Crime doesn't pay.* [V.to inf] *It pays to be honest with the taxman.* [Vn.to inf] *It would pay (you) to use an accountant.* **3** ~ (**for sth**) to suffer or be punished for one's beliefs or actions: [V, Vpr] *I'll make him pay (for those remarks).* [Vpr] *Many paid with their lives.* **4** (with certain *ns*) to give or make the specified thing: [Vn, Vnpr] *Some of you weren't **paying attention** (to what I said).* [Vnpr] *She **paid no heed** to* (ie took no notice of) *our warning.* [Vnn] *He **paid me the compliment** of saying he admired my work.* ∘ *I promised to **pay them a visit.*** **IDM** **cost/pay an arm and a leg** ⇨ ARM¹. **give/pay lip-service to sth** ⇨ LIP-SERVICE. **he who pays the piper calls the 'tune** (*saying*) the person who provides the money for sth should control how it is spent. **pay 'court to sb** to treat sb with great respect in order to gain favour: *leaders paying court to the new president.* **pay 'dividends** to produce benefits or advantages: *A cautious approach will pay dividends.* **pay the 'penalty (for sth/doing sth)** to suffer because of bad luck, an error or wrongdoing: *The England team are paying the penalty for lack of match practice.* **pay a/the 'price (for sth)** to suffer a disadvantage or loss in return for sth one has gained: *Our troops recaptured the city, but they paid a heavy price* (ie many were killed). **pay one's re'spects (to sb)** (*fml*) to visit sb as a sign of respect for them: *I intend to call on your mother and pay my respects.* ∘ *Thousands came to **pay their last respects** to the murdered policeman* (eg by attending his funeral). **pay through the 'nose (for sth)** (*infml*) to pay far too much money for sth: *You'll pay through the nose for a house in that area.* **pay one's/ its 'way** (of a person or business, etc) to earn enough to support oneself/itself: *The freight business must pay its own way without subsidies.* **put 'paid to sth** (*infml*) to stop or destroy sth: *The argument she had with her manager has probably put paid to any hopes of promotion.* **there will be/was the 'devil/'hell to pay** (*infml*) there will be/was a lot of trouble: *There was hell to pay when we got home that night.* **PHRV** **,pay sb 'back (sth)**; **,pay sth 'back** to return money to sb that one has borrowed from them: *Have you paid back the money you owe yet?* ∘ *I'll pay you back next week.* **,pay sb 'back (for sth)** to punish sb or get one's revenge(1a) for sth sb has done: *I'll pay him back for the trick he played on me.*
,pay sth 'in; **,pay sth into sth** to put money into a bank account: *pay a cheque into one's account.*
,pay 'off (*infml*) (of a risky policy, course of action, etc) to bring good results; to be successful: *The gamble paid off.* **,pay sb 'off 1** to pay the wages of sb and dismiss them from a job: *pay off the crew of a ship.* **2** (*infml*) to give money to sb to prevent them from doing sth; to BRIBE sb. **,pay sth 'off** to finish paying money owed for sth: *pay off one's debts/a loan/a mortgage.*
,pay sth 'out 1 to pay a large sum of money for sth: *I had to pay out £400 to get my car repaired!* ∘ *We're paying out $800 a month on our mortgage.* See also PAYOUT. **2** to release or pass a length or rope through one's hands.
,pay 'up to pay all the money that is owed for sth: *I'll take you to court unless you pay up immediately.*
▶ **payable** /'peɪəbl/ *adj* [pred] **(a)** that must be paid: *No import duty is payable.* **(b)** that may be paid: *The price is payable in instalments.*
payee /,peɪ'iː/ *n* a person to whom sth is paid.
payer *n* a person who pays or who has to pay for sth.
■ **,pay-as-you-'earn** *n* [U] (*Brit*) (*abbr* **PAYE**) a method of collecting tax due on a person's income by deducting it from her or his wages or salary.

'pay-bed *n* (*Brit*) a bed in a public hospital for which the user has paid as a private patient.

ˌpaying 'guest *n* a person who lives in sb's house and pays for her or his food and accommodation.

'pay-off *n* (*infml*) **1** an act or occasion of paying money, esp a BRIBE, to sb: *a secret pay-off*. **2** a deserved benefit, reward or punishment: *We have invested in new equipment and are now seeing the pay-off in school science classes.*

PAYE /ˌpiː eɪ waɪ 'iː/ *abbr* (*Brit*) (of income tax) pay-as-you-earn.

payload /'peɪləʊd/ *n* **1** the part of the load of a ship, an aircraft, etc for which payment is received, eg passengers and cargo, but not fuel. **2** the explosive power of a bomb or missile. **3** the equipment carried by a spacecraft or SATELLITE(1).

paymaster /'peɪmɑːstə(r)/ *n* **1** an official who pays troops, workers, etc. **2** (usu *pl*) (*derog*) a person who pays sb else to do sth, esp sth illegal, for her or him and who therefore controls their actions: *The paymasters of these petty crooks are the big crime syndicates.*

■ **ˌPaymaster 'General** *n* (*Brit*) the minister in charge of the department of the Treasury through which payments are made.

payment /'peɪmənt/ *n* ~ (**for sth**) **1** [U] the action of paying sb/sth or of being paid: *We would be grateful for prompt payment of your account.* ○ *Payment of subscriptions should be made to the club secretary.* **2** [C] a sum of money paid: *make ten monthly payments of £50* ○ *Would you accept $50 as payment for the work?* **3** [U, sing] a reward or gesture of gratitude for sth: *We'd like you to accept this gift in payment for your kindness.* ○ (*ironic*) *Personal abuse was the only payment he got for his efforts.*

payout /'peɪaʊt/ *n* a usu large payment of money: *an insurance payout.*

payroll /'peɪrəʊl/ *n* (**a**) a list of people employed by a company and the amount of money to be paid to each of them: *a firm with 500 employees on the payroll* (ie one that employs 500 people). (**b**) the total amount of wages and salaries paid to the employees of a company.

payslip /'peɪslɪp/ *n* (*Brit*) a piece of paper given to an employee showing how much he or she has been paid and how much tax, insurance, etc has been deducted (DEDUCT).

PC /ˌpiː 'siː/ *abbr* **1** personal computer. **2** (*pl* **PCs**) (in Britain) police constable: *PC (Tom) Marsh.* Compare WPC.

pc *abbr* (*US* **pct**) (*symb* **%**) per cent: *20 pc.*

PE /ˌpiː 'iː/ *abbr* physical education: *do PE at school* ○ *a PE lesson.* Compare PT.

pea /piː/ *n* (**a**) a round green seed that grows with others in a POD and is eaten cooked as a vegetable: *pea soup.* (**b**) the climbing plant that produces these.

■ **ˌpea-'green** *adj, n* (having) a bright green colour like that of peas.

peace /piːs/ *n* **1**(**a**) [U] freedom from war or violence: *a peace formula/plan/movement/treaty* ○ *peace studies/negotiations/talks* ○ *make peace between the warring factions* ○ *a UN force sent to keep the peace* (ie to prevent people from quarrelling or fighting) ○ *The two communities live together in peace (with one another).* ○ *After years of fighting the people longed for peace.* (**b**) [sing] a period of this: *the search for a lasting peace.* **2** [U] a state of calm or quiet: *disturb the peace* ○ *enjoy the peace of a summer evening/the countryside* ○ *I would work better if I had a bit of peace and quiet.* ○ *He just wants to be left in peace* (ie not to be disturbed). ○ *peace of mind* (ie freedom from worry) ○ *She never felt at peace (with herself).* ○ *May he rest in peace* (eg carved on the stone at sb's grave). **3** [U] a state of harmony and friendship: *be at peace with the world* ○ *There's never any peace between her brothers.* See also BREACH OF THE

PEACE, JUSTICE OF THE PEACE. **IDM** **ˌhold one's 'peace/'tongue** (*dated*) to remain silent although one would like to say sth. **make one's peace with sb** to end a quarrel with sb, esp by saying that one is sorry. **rest in peace** ⇨ REST¹.

■ **the 'Peace Corps** *n* [Gp] (*US*) an organization that sends young people to work as volunteers (VOLUNTEER 3) in developing countries.

'peace dividend *n* (usu *sing*) money not needed to be spent on the defence of a country, eg as a result of disarmament (DISARM 2): *a peace dividend of at least $12 billion.*

'peace-keeping *adj* [attrib] intended to help maintain peace and prevent war: *peace-keeping operations/duties* ○ *a peace-keeping force/mission.*

'peace-loving *adj* preferring to live in peace and avoid quarrelling: *peace-loving citizens.*

'peace-offering *n* a present offered to show that one is willing to make peace or that one is sorry for sth: *I bought her some flowers as a peace-offering.*

peaceable /'piːsəbl/ *adj* **1** not liking to quarrel; wishing to live in peace with others: *a peaceable temperament/person.* **2** not involving argument or fighting; peaceful: *a peaceable settlement/discussion.* ▶ **peaceably** /-əbli/ *adv*: *live peaceably with one's neighbours.*

peaceful /'piːsfl/ *adj* **1** not involving war or violence: *a peaceful demonstration/reign/revolution/solution* ○ *people of different religions living in peaceful coexistence* ○ *peaceful uses of nuclear power.* **2** promoting or living in peace: *peaceful aims* ○ *a peaceful society.* **3** quiet; calm: *a peaceful evening/scene/death* ○ *It's so peaceful out here in the country.* ▶ **peacefully** /-fəli/ *adv*: *die/sleep peacefully.* **peacefulness** *n* [U].

peacemaker /'piːsmeɪkə(r)/ *n* a person who persuades people or countries to make peace.

peacetime /'piːstaɪm/ *n* [U] a period when a country is not at war. Compare WARTIME.

peach /piːtʃ/ *n* **1**(**a**) [C] a round juicy fruit with yellow flesh, soft yellow and red skin and a rough stone: *peaches and cream.* ⇨ picture at FRUIT. (**b**) (also **'peach tree**) [C] the tree on which this grows. Compare NECTARINE. **2** [sing] ~ (**of a sth**) (*infml approv*) an exceptionally good or attractive person or thing: *That was a peach of a shot!* **3** [U] a pinkish-orange colour.

▶ **peachy** *adj* like a peach in colour or texture.

■ **ˌpeach 'Melba** *n* [U] a sweet dish made with ice-cream, peaches and RASPBERRY(1) sauce.

peacock

peacock /'piːkɒk/ *n* a large male bird with long blue and green tail feathers which it can spread out like a fan: *She looked as elegant/proud as a peacock.* ⇨ picture.

■ **ˌpeacock 'blue** *adj, n* [U] (having) a bright greenish-blue colour.

peahen /'piːhen/ *n* a large brown bird, the female to a PEACOCK.

peak¹ /piːk/ *n* **1** (usu *sing*) the point of highest intensity, value or achievement: *Traffic reaches a peak between 8 and 9 in the morning.* ○ *She's at the peak of her career.* ○ *peak periods/production* ○ *em-*

ploy additional staff during the peak summer season ○ *peak hours* (ie when demand for sth, eg electricity, is highest) ○ *peak viewing time* (ie when the greatest number of people are watching television) ○ *peak rate calls* (ie made during the busiest period and charged at the highest rate). Compare OFF-PEAK. **2(a)** a pointed top, esp of a mountain: *The plane flew over snow-covered peaks.* ▷ picture at MOUNTAIN. **(b)** a mountain with a pointed top: *The climbers made camp halfway up the peak.* **3** the pointed front part of a cap. ▷ picture at HAT. **4** any shape, edge or part of sth that becomes narrow and pointed at the end: *the peak of a roof* ○ *hair combed into a peak.*

▶ **peaked** *adj* having a peak: *a peaked cap/roof.*

peak² /piːk/ *v* to reach the highest point or value: [V] *Toy sales peak just before Christmas.* ○ *Demand for electricity peaks in the early evening.* [Vpr] *The rate of increase peaked at 34%.*

▶ **peaky** *adj* (*infml*) ill or pale: *look a bit peaky.*

peal /piːl/ *n* **1** ~ (of sth) a loud burst of sound: *a peal of thunder* ○ *break into peals of laughter.* **2(a)** a loud ringing of a bell or a set of bells: *A peal of bells rang out.* **(b)** a musical pattern that can be rung on a set of bells. **(c)** a set of bells with different notes in harmony with each other.

▶ **peal** *v* ~ (out) to sound in a peal: [Vpr, Vp] *The bells pealed (out) across the countryside.* [Vpr] *Ellen pealed with laughter.* [also V].

peanut /ˈpiːnʌt/ *n* **1** (also **groundnut**) [C] an edible nut that grows in a thin crisp shell underground: *a packet of salted peanuts* ○ *peanut oil.* ▷ picture at NUT. **2 peanuts** [pl] (*infml*) a very small amount of money: *work for peanuts* ○ *He gets paid peanuts for doing that job.*

■ ˌpeanut ˈbutter *n* [U] a thick soft PASTE¹(3) made from peanuts that have been roasted and ground, usu eaten spread on bread.

pear /peə(r)/ *n* **(a)** a sweet juicy yellow or green fruit with a round shape that becomes narrower towards the stem. ▷ picture at FRUIT. **(b)** (also ˈpear tree) the tree on which this grows.

pearl /pɜːl/ *n* **1(a)** a small, hard, shiny white or bluish-grey ball that forms inside the shells of certain oysters (OYSTER) and is of great value as a jewel: *a string of pearls* ○ *a pearl necklace.* **(b)** a copy of this made artificially. See also MOTHER-OF-PEARL, SEED-PEARL. **2** a thing resembling a pearl in shape or colour: *pearls of dew on the grass.* **3** a very precious or highly valued thing: *pearls of wisdom.* IDM **pearls before ˈswine** valuable things given or offered to people who do not appreciate them.

▶ **pearly** *adj* of or like a pearl: *pearly white teeth.*

the ˌPearly ˈGates *n* [pl] (*joc*) the gates of heaven.

■ ˌpearl ˈbarley *n* [U] BARLEY ground into small round grains, used esp in soups.

peasant /ˈpeznt/ *n* **1** (esp formerly or in poorer countries) a poor farmer owning or renting a small piece of land which he or she cultivates: *peasant farmers/farming.* **2** (*infml derog*) a rough, rude or ignorant person.

▶ **peasantry** /ˈpezntri/ *n* [Gp] all the peasants of a region or country: *the local peasantry.*

pease-pudding /ˌpiːz ˈpʊdɪŋ/ *n* [U] (*esp Brit*) a dish of dried peas (PEA) soaked and boiled until they are soft.

peashooter /ˈpiːʃuːtə(r)/ *n* a toy weapon consisting of a small tube from which dried peas are shot by blowing through the tube.

peat /piːt/ *n* [U] a soft black or brown substance formed from decaying plants. It occurs instead of soil near the surface of the ground, esp in cool wet areas, and is used for burning as a fuel or to improve garden soil: *peat bogs* ○ *a peat fire* (ie one in which cut pieces of peat are burned).

▶ **peaty** *adj* of or containing peat: *peaty soil.*

pebble /ˈpebl/ *n* a small stone made smooth and round by the action of water, eg in a stream or by the sea. IDM **not the only pebble on the ˈbeach** not the only person who matters or who has to be considered.

▶ **pebbly** *adj* covered with pebbles: *a pebbly beach.*

■ ˈpebble-dash *n* [U] cement mixed with small pebbles, used for covering the outside walls of houses.

pecan /ˈpiːkən, prˈkæn; US prˈkɑːn/ *n* an edible nut with a smooth pinkish-brown shell. It grows on trees in the southern USA.

peccadillo /ˌpekəˈdɪləʊ/ *n* (*pl* **-oes** or **-os** /-ləʊz/) a small unimportant offence or sin: *minor sexual peccadilloes.*

peccary /ˈpekəri/ *n* a type of wild hairy animal like a pig, found in Central and S America.

peck /pek/ *v* **1** ~ (at sth) **(a)** (of birds) to hit sth with the beak: [V] *hens pecking in the yard* [Vpr] *birds pecking at the berries* [Vn] *The lamb had been pecked by crows.* **(b)** to make sth by hitting with the beak: [Vnpr] *The birds had pecked a hole in the sack.* **2** ~ sb (on sth) (*infml*) to kiss sb lightly and quickly: [Vnpr] *peck sb on the cheek* [also Vn]. IDM **a/the ˈpecking order** (*infml*) the order of importance amongst the members of a group in relation to each other: *Newcomers have to accept their position at the bottom of the pecking order.* PHRV **ˈpeck at sth** (of people) to eat very small amounts of food, esp because one is not hungry: *She sat nervously pecking at her meal.* **ˌpeck sth ˈout** to remove sth by pecking: *Vultures had pecked out the dead goat's eyes.*

▶ **peck** *n* (usu *sing*) **1** an act of pecking sb/sth: *The parrot gave me a sharp peck on the finger.* **2** (*infml*) a quick kiss: *She gave her aunt a peck on the cheek.*

pecker /ˈpekə(r)/ *n* (*US sl*) a PENIS. IDM **keep one's ˈpecker up** (*Brit infml*) to remain cheerful in spite of difficulties.

peckish /ˈpekɪʃ/ *adj* (*Brit infml*) slightly hungry: *feel a bit peckish.*

pectin /ˈpektɪn/ *n* [U] (*chemistry*) a substance similar to sugar that forms in ripe fruit and causes jam to set.

pectoral /ˈpektərəl/ *adj* **1** of the chest or breast: *pectoral muscles* ○ *a pectoral fin.* **2** worn on the chest or breast: *a pectoral cross* (ie one worn by a bishop).

▶ **pectorals** (also *infml* **pecs**) *n* [pl] (*often joc*) chest muscles.

peculiar /prˈkjuːliə(r)/ *adj* **1** odd or strange, esp in a rather unpleasant way: *a peculiar taste/smell/noise* ○ *I had a peculiar feeling that I had been there before.* ○ *My keys have disappeared — it's most peculiar!* ○ *She was behaving in a very peculiar way.* **2** (*infml*) ill: *I'm feeling rather peculiar — I think I'll lie down for a while.* **3** [pred] ~ **to sb/sth (a)** belonging only to sb/sth: *an accent peculiar to this region* ○ *a flavour peculiar to food cooked on an open fire* ○ *a species of bird peculiar to Asia.* **(b)** used or practised only by sb/sth: *techniques peculiar to accident investigation.* **4** [attrib] (*dated or fml*) special or particular: *his own peculiar way of doing things.*

▶ **peculiarity** /prˌkjuːliˈærəti/ *n* **1** [U] the quality of being peculiar. **2** [C] an odd or unusual feature, quality, habit, etc: *a general peculiarity* ○ *peculiarities of dress/behaviour/diet.* **3** [C] a distinctive feature; a characteristic: *a peculiarity of this disease.*

peculiarly *adv* **1** in a peculiar(1) manner: *behave most peculiarly.* **2** more than usually; especially: *a peculiarly difficult time.*

pecuniary /prˈkjuːniəri; US -ieri/ *adj* (*fml*) of or involving money: *a pecuniary advantage/gain/loss.*

pedagogue (*US* **-gog**) /ˈpedəgɒg/ *n* (*arch or fml*) a teacher.

▶ **pedagogy** /ˈpedəgɒdʒi/ *n* [U] (*fml*) the study of methods and styles of teaching. **pedagogic** /ˌpedəˈgɒdʒɪk/ (also **pedagogical** /-ɪkl/) *adj* of or concerning teaching methods: *pedagogic skills/ theory.* **pedagogically** /-kli/ *adv.*

pedal /'pedl/ *n* **1** a flat bar that drives or controls a machine, eg a bicycle or a car, when pressed down by the foot or feet: *One of the pedals on my bike has broken.* ○ *the brake/clutch pedal* (eg of a car) ○ *a pedal boat* (ie one driven by pedals).* ▷ picture at BICYCLE. **2** a bar on a musical instrument, eg a piano, an organ or a HARP, that is operated by the foot in order to produce or affect sound: *the loud/ soft pedal* (ie on a piano).* ▷ picture at PIANO¹.
▶ **pedal** *v* (**-ll-**; *US* also **-l-**) **1(a)** to press a pedal or pedals: [V] *pedal hard to make the machine run smoothly.* **(b)** to move by pedalling: [Vadv] *pedal fast* [Vpr] *pedal down the hill* [Vp] *pedal along* [also V]. **2** to move or operate a machine by pedalling: [Vnpr] *pedal a bicycle across the field* [also Vn].
■ **'pedal bin** *n* (*Brit*) a bin for rubbish, usu in a kitchen, with a lid that opens when a pedal is pressed.

pedalo /'pedələʊ/ (*pl* **-os**) a small pleasure boat operated by pedals (PEDAL 1).

pedant /'pednt/ *n* (*derog*) a person who is too concerned about small details or rules, esp when learning or teaching.
▶ **pedantic** /pɪ'dæntɪk/ *adj* (*derog*) of or like a pedant: *a pedantic insistence on the rules.* **pedantically** /-kli/ *adv.*
pedantry /'pedntri/ *n* [U] too much emphasis on formal rules or small details: *an unnecessary display of pedantry.*

peddle /'pedl/ *v* ~ **sth** (**to sb**) **1** to try to sell goods by going from house to house or from place to place: [Vn] *peddle one's wares* [Vn, Vnpr] *be arrested for peddling illegal drugs* (*to addicts*).* ▷ note at SELL. **2** to spread or promote sth, eg an idea or a rumour, in an attempt to get it accepted: [Vn] *peddle malicious gossip* [Vnpr] *peddling his crazy theories to anyone who will listen.*
▶ **peddler** /'pedlə(r)/ *n* **1** a person who sells illegal drugs. **2** (*US*) = PEDLAR.

pedestal /'pedɪstl/ *n* the base of a column or statue, etc.* ▷ picture.
IDM **knock sb off their pedestal/perch** ▷ KNOCK². **to put/place sb on a 'pedestal** to admire sb greatly, esp without noticing their faults.
■ **ˌpedestal 'basin** *n* a BASIN(1) supported by a central column.

pedestal

pedestrian /pə'destrɪən/ *n* a person walking in the street, not sb in a vehicle: *Two pedestrians were injured when the car skidded.*
▶ **pedestrian** *adj* **1** lacking imagination or excitement; dull: *a pedestrian description of events* ○ *Life in the suburbs can be pretty pedestrian.* **2** [attrib] of or for pedestrians: *a pedestrian walkway.*
pedestrianize, -ise *v* to make a street or part of a town into an area for pedestrians only: [Vn] *a pedestrianized shopping zone.*
■ **peˌdestrian 'crossing** (*Brit*) (*US* **crosswalk**) *n* a part of a road specially marked with lines, etc where vehicles must stop to allow pedestrians to cross. See also PELICAN CROSSING, ZEBRA CROSSING, BELISHA BEACON.
peˌdestrian 'precinct *n* (*Brit*) a part of a town, esp a shopping area, where vehicles may not enter.
pedi- *comb form* of the feet: *pedicure.*
pedicure /'pedɪkjʊə(r)/ *n* [C, U] care and treatment of the feet for medical reasons or to improve their appearance. Compare MANICURE.
pedigree /'pedɪgriː/ *n* **1** [C] **(a)** the official record

of the animals from which an animal has been bred: *very knowledgeable about livestock and pedigrees* ○ *looking for animals with pedigrees.* **(b)** an animal descended from a known line of usu specially chosen animals of the same breed: *The best pedigrees fetch very high prices.* **2** [C, U] a line of ancestors, esp when these belonged to the upper classes of society: *proud of his long pedigree* ○ *people without pedigree.* **3** [C, U] the background, history, etc of a person or thing, esp when this is impressive: *a director with a distinguished business pedigree* ○ *products with a long pedigree going back to the early days of the industry.*
▶ **pedigree** *adj* [attrib] (of an animal) descended from a known line of usu specially chosen animals of the same breed: [attrib]: *pedigree cattle/dogs.*

pediment /'pedɪmənt/ *n* (*architecture*) the front part, usu in the shape of a TRIANGLE(1), above the entrance of a building in the ancient Greek style.* ▷ picture at COLUMN.

pedlar (*US* **peddler**) /'pedlə(r)/ *n* (esp formerly) a person who travels from place to place or from house to house trying to sell small articles.

pee /piː/ *v* (*pt pp* **peed**) (*infml*) to urinate (URINE): [Vpr] *a dog peeing against a fence* [also V].
▶ **pee** *n* (*infml*) **(a)** [U] URINE. **(b)** [sing] an act of urinating: *go for/have a quick pee.*

peek /piːk/ *v* ~ (**at sth**) to look at sth quickly and often secretly when one should not: [V] *No peeking!* [Vpr] *peek over the fence* ○ *She peeked at the present inside the paper.* Compare PEEP¹ 1, PEER². ▶ **peek** *n* [sing] ~ (**at sb/sth**): *take a quick peek* (*at what is*) *behind the curtain.*

peekaboo /ˌpiːkə'buː/ (*Brit* also **peepbo** /'piːpbəʊ, 'piːpəʊ/) *n* [U] a simple game played to amuse young children, in which one hides one's face and then reveals it, saying 'Peekaboo!' or 'Peepbo!'.

peel /piːl/ *v* **1(a)** ~ **sth** (**for sb**) to take the skin off fruit, vegetables, etc: [Vn] *peel a banana/an apple/a potato* [Vnn] *Would you peel me an orange?* [Vnpr] *Could you peel these prawns for me?* **(b)** ~ **(sth) away/off** to be removed or cause sth to be removed from the surface of sth: [Vnp] *peel away the outer layer* [Vp] *The label will peel off if you soak it in water.* **(c)** to have a skin or outer layer which comes off: [Vadv] *oranges that peel easily.* **2(a)** ~ (**off**) (of a covering) to come off in strips or small pieces: [V] *The wallpaper is peeling.* ○ *After sunbathing, my skin began to peel.* [Vp] *The bark of plane trees peels off regularly.* **(b)** (of a surface) to lose strips or small pieces of its covering: [V] *Put on some cream to stop your face from peeling.* ○ *The walls have begun to peel.* **IDM** **keep one's eyes peeled/skinned** ▷ EYE¹. **PHRV** **ˌpeel 'off** (of cars, aircraft, etc) to leave a group and turn to one side: *The leading vehicles in the motorcade peeled off to the right.* **ˌpeel (sth) 'off** (*infml*) to remove some or all of one's clothes, esp when one is hot or before exercise: *peel off one's sweater* ○ *You look hot — why don't you peel off?*
▶ **peel** *n* [U] the outer covering or skin of fruit, vegetables, etc: *lemon/orange peel.* ▷ picture at FRUIT. Compare RIND, SKIN 3, ZEST 3.
peeler *n* (esp in compounds) a device for peeling fruit, vegetables, etc: *a potato peeler.* ▷ picture at POTATO.
peelings /'piːlɪŋz/ *n* [pl] the parts of fruit or vegetables that have been removed by peeling.

peep¹ /piːp/ *v* **1** ~ (**at sth**) to look quickly and secretly at sth, esp through a small opening: [Vpr] *peep at a secret document* ○ *be caught peeping through the keyhole* [Vp] *She moved the curtain a little and peeped out.* [also V]. Compare PEEK, PEER². **2** (of light) to appear through a small opening: [Vpr] *daylight peeping through the curtains* [also Vp]. **3** to appear slowly or partly: [Vp] *The moon peeped out*

Geographical names

This list shows the English spelling and pronunciation of geographical names except for those relating to the British Isles which are shown on page **C6**.

If a country has a different word for the adjective and the person from the country, both are given, (eg **Denmark**; **Danish**, **Dane**). To make the plural of a word for a person from a particular country, add **-s**, except for **Swiss** and words ending in **-ese** (eg *Japanese*), which stay the same, and for words that end in **-man** or **-woman**, which change to **-men** or **-women** (eg *three Frenchmen*).

Afghanistan /æfˈgænɪstɑːn; US -stæn/; Afghan /ˈæfgæn/, Afghani /æfˈgɑːni/, Afghanistani /æfˌgænɪˈstɑːni; US -ˈstæni/

Africa /ˈæfrɪkə/; African /ˈæfrɪkən/

Albania /ælˈbeɪniə/; Albanian /ælˈbeɪniən/

Algeria /ælˈdʒɪəriə/; Algerian /ælˈdʒɪəriən/

America ⇨ (the) United States (of America)

America /əˈmerɪkə/; American /əˈmerɪkən/

Andorra /ænˈdɔːrə/; Andorran /ænˈdɔːrən/

Angola /æŋˈgəʊlə/; Angolan /æŋˈgəʊlən/

Antarctica /ænˈtɑːktɪkə/; Antarctic /ænˈtɑːktɪk/

Antigua and Barbuda /ænˌtiːgə ən bɑːˈbjuːdə/; Antiguan /ænˈtiːgən/, Barbudan /bɑːˈbjuːdən/

(the) Arctic Ocean /ˌɑːktɪk ˈəʊʃn/; Arctic

Argentina /ˌɑːdʒənˈtiːnə/, the Argentine /ˈɑːdʒəntaɪn/; Argentinian /ˌɑːdʒənˈtɪniən/, Argentine

Armenia /ɑːˈmiːniə/; Armenian /ɑːˈmiːniən/

Asia /ˈeɪʃə, ˈeɪʒə/; Asian /ˈeɪʃn, ˈeɪʒn/

Australia /ɒˈstreɪliə, ɔːˈs-/; Australian /ɒˈstreɪliən, ɔːˈs-/

Austria /ˈɒstriə, ˈɔːs-/; Austrian /ˈɒstriən, ˈɔːs-/

Azerbaijan /ˌæzəbaɪˈdʒɑːn/; Azerbaijani /ˌæzəbaɪˈdʒɑːni/, Azeri /əˈzeəri/

(the) Bahamas /bəˈhɑːməz/; Bahamian /bəˈheɪmiən/

Bahrain, Bahrein /bɑːˈreɪn/; Bahraini, Bahreini /bɑːˈreɪni/

Bangladesh /ˌbæŋgləˈdeʃ/; Bangladeshi /ˌbæŋgləˈdeʃi/

Barbados /bɑːˈbeɪdɒs/; Barbadian /bɑːˈbeɪdiən/

Belarus /bɪˌeləˈruːs/; Belorussian /bɪˌeləˈrʌʃn/

Belgium /ˈbeldʒəm/; Belgian /ˈbeldʒən/

Belize /bəˈliːz/; Belizean /bəˈliːziən/

Benin /beˈniːn/; Beninese /ˌbenɪˈniːz/

Bhutan /buːˈtɑːn/; Bhutani /buːˈtɑːni/, Bhutanese /ˌbuːtəˈniːz/

Bolivia /bəˈlɪviə/; Bolivian /bəˈlɪviən/

Bosnia-Herzegovina /ˌbɒzniə ˌhɜːtsəgəˈviːnə/; Bosnian /ˈbɒzniən/

Botswana /bɒtˈswɑːnə/; Botswanan /bɒtˈswɑːnən/, (person: Motswana /mɒtˈswɑːnə/, people: Batswana /bætˈswɑːnə/)

Brazil /brəˈzɪl/; Brazilian /brəˈzɪliən/

Brunei Darussalam /ˌbruːnaɪ dæˈruːsælæm/; Brunei, Bruneian /bruːˈnaɪən/

Bulgaria /bʌlˈgeəriə/; Bulgarian /bʌlˈgeəriən/

Burkina /bɜːˈkiːnə/; Burkinese /bɜːkɪˈniːz/

Burundi /bʊˈrʊndi/; Burundian /bʊˈrʊndiən/

Cambodia /kæmˈbəʊdiə/; Cambodian /kæmˈbəʊdiən/

Cameroon /ˌkæməˈruːn/; Cameroonian /ˌkæməˈruːniən/

Canada /ˈkænədə/; Canadian /kəˈneɪdiən/

(the) Cape Verde Islands /ˌkeɪp ˈvɜːd aɪləndz/; Cape Verdean /ˌkeɪp ˈvɜːdiən/

(the) Caribbean Sea /ˌkærəˈbiːən ˈsiː/; Caribbean

Central African Republic /ˌsentrəl ˌæfrɪkən rɪˈpʌblɪk/

Chad /tʃæd/; Chadian /ˈtʃædiən/

Chile /ˈtʃɪli/; Chilean /ˈtʃɪliən/

China /ˈtʃaɪnə/; Chinese /ˌtʃaɪˈniːz/

Colombia /kəˈlɒmbiə/; Colombian /kəˈlɒmbiən/

Comoros /ˈkɒmərəʊz/; Comoran /kəˈmɔːrən/

Congo /ˈkɒŋgəʊ/; Congolese /ˌkɒŋgəˈliːz/

Costa Rica /ˌkɒstə ˈriːkə/; Costa Rican /ˌkɒstə ˈriːkən/

Côte d'Ivoire /ˌkəʊt diːˈvwɑː/

Croatia /krəʊˈeɪʃə/; Croatian /krəʊˈeɪʃən/

Cuba /ˈkjuːbə/; Cuban /ˈkjuːbən/

Cyprus /ˈsaɪprəs/; Cypriot /ˈsɪpriət/

(the) Czech Republic /ˌtʃek rɪˈpʌblɪk/; Czech /tʃek/

Denmark /ˈdenmɑːk/; Danish /ˈdeɪnɪʃ/, Dane /deɪn/

Djibouti /dʒɪˈbuːti/; Djiboutian /dʒɪˈbuːtiən/

Dominica /ˌdɒmɪˈniːkə/; Dominican /ˌdɒmɪˈniːkən/

(the) Dominican Republic /dəˌmɪnɪkən rɪˈpʌblɪk/; Dominican /dəˈmɪnɪkən/

Ecuador /ˈekwədɔː(r)/; Ecuadorian /ˌekwəˈdɔːriən/

Egypt /ˈiːdʒɪpt/; Egyptian /iˈdʒɪpʃn/

El Salvador /el ˈsælvədɔː(r)/; Salvadorean /ˌsælvəˈdɔːriən/

Equatorial Guinea /ˌekwəˌtɔːriəl ˈgɪni/; Equatorial Guinean /ˌekwəˌtɔːriəl ˈgɪniən/

Eritrea /ˌerɪˈtreɪə/; Eritrean /ˌerɪˈtreɪən; US -ˈtriːən/

Estonia /eˈstəʊniə/; Estonian /eˈstəʊniən/

Ethiopia /ˌiːθiˈəʊpiə/; Ethiopian /ˌiːθiˈəʊpiən/

Europe /ˈjʊərəp/; European /ˌjʊərəˈpiːən/

Fiji /ˈfiːdʒiː; US ˈfiːdʒiː/; Fijian /ˌfiːˈdʒiːən; US ˈfiːdʒiən/

Finland /ˈfɪnlənd/; Finnish /ˈfɪnɪʃ/, Finn /fɪn/

France /frɑːns; US fræns/; French /frentʃ/; Frenchman /ˈfrentʃmən/, Frenchwoman /ˈfrentʃwʊmən/

Gabon /gæˈbɒn; US -ˈbəʊn/; Gabonese /ˌgæbəˈniːz/

(the) Gambia /ˈgæmbiə/; Gambian /ˈgæmbiən/

Georgia /ˈdʒɔːdʒə/; Georgian /ˈdʒɔːdʒən/

Germany /ˈdʒɜːməni/; German /ˈdʒɜːmən/

Ghana /ˈgɑːnə/; Ghanaian /gɑːˈneɪən/

Gibraltar /dʒɪˈbrɔːltə(r)/; Gibraltarian /ˌdʒɪbrɔːlˈteəriən/

Greece /griːs/; Greek /griːk/

Grenada /grəˈneɪdə/; Grenadian /grəˈneɪdiən/

Guatemala /ˌgwɑːtəˈmɑːlə/; Guatemalan /ˌgwɑːtəˈmɑːlən/

Guinea /ˈgɪni/; Guinean /ˈgɪniən/

Guinea-Bissau /ˌgɪni bɪˈsaʊ/

Guyana /gaɪˈænə/; Guyanese /ˌgaɪəˈniːz/

Haiti /ˈheɪti/; Haitian /ˈheɪʃn/

Holland /ˈhɒlənd/ ⇨ (the) Netherlands

Honduras /hɒnˈdjʊərəs; US -ˈdʊə-/; Honduran /hɒnˈdjʊərən; US -ˈdʊə-/

Hong Kong /ˌhɒŋ ˈkɒŋ/

Hungary /ˈhʌŋgəri/; Hungarian /hʌŋˈgeəriən/

Iceland /ˈaɪslənd/; Icelandic /aɪsˈlændɪk/

India /ˈɪndiə/; Indian /ˈɪndiən/

Indonesia /ˌɪndəˈniːziə; US -ˈniːʒə-/; Indonesian /ˌɪndəˈniːziən; US -ʒn/

Iran /ɪˈrɑːn/; Iranian /ɪˈreɪniən/

Iraq /ɪˈrɑːk/; Iraqi /ɪˈrɑːki/

Israel /ˈɪzreɪl/; Israeli /ɪzˈreɪli/

Italy /ˈɪtəli/; Italian /ɪˈtæliən/

Jamaica /dʒəˈmeɪkə/; Jamaican /dʒəˈmeɪkən/

Japan /dʒəˈpæn/; Japanese /ˌdʒæpəˈniːz/

Jordan /ˈdʒɔːdn/; Jordanian /dʒɔːˈdeɪniən/

Kazakhstan /ˌkæzækˈstɑːn/; Kazakh /kəˈzæk/

Kenya /ˈkenjə/; Kenyan /ˈkenjən/

Kirgyzstan /ˌkɪəgɪzˈstɑːn/; Kirgyz /ˈkɪəgɪz; US kɪərˈgiːz/

Kiribati /ˈkɪrəbæs/

Korea /kəˈrɪə; US kəˈriːə/; North Korea, North Korean /ˌnɔːθ kəˈrɪən; US kəˈriːən/; South Korea, South Korean /ˌsaʊθ kəˈrɪən; US kəˈriːən/

Kuwait /kuˈweɪt/; Kuwaiti /kuˈweɪti/

Laos /laʊs/; Laotian /ˈlaʊʃn; US leɪˈəʊʃn/

Latvia /ˈlætviə/; Latvian /ˈlætviən/

Lebanon /ˈlebənən; US -nɒn/; Lebanese /ˌlebəˈniːz/

Lesotho /ləˈsuːtuː/; Sotho /ˈsuːtuː/, (person: Mosotho /məˈsuːtuː/, people: Basotho /bəˈsuːtuː/)

Liberia /laɪˈbɪəriə/; Liberian /laɪˈbɪəriən/

Libya /ˈlɪbiə/; Libyan /ˈlɪbiən/

Liechtenstein /ˈlɪktənstaɪn, ˈlɪxt-/; Liechtenstein, Liechtensteiner /ˈlɪktənstaɪnə(r), ˈlɪxt-/

Lithuania /ˌlɪθjuˈeɪniə/; Lithuanian /ˌlɪθjuˈeɪniən/

Luxembourg /ˈlʌksəmbɜːg/; Luxembourg, Luxembourger /ˈlʌksəmbɜːgə(r)/

Madagascar /ˌmædəˈgæskə(r)/; Madagascan /ˌmædəˈgæskən/, Malagasy /ˌmæləˈgæsi/

Malawi /məˈlɑːwi/; Malawian /məˈlɑːwiən/

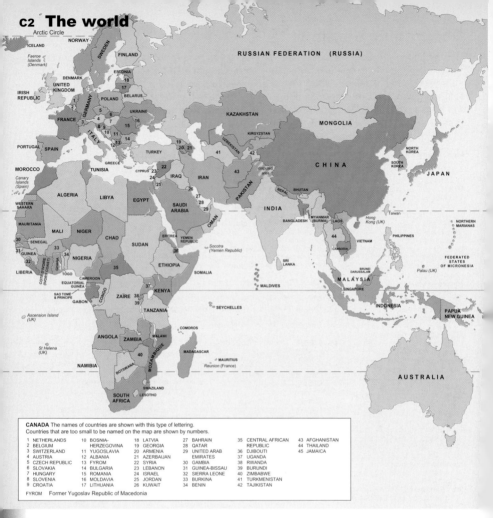

CANADA The names of countries are shown with this type of lettering.
Countries that are too small to be named on the map are shown by numbers.

1	NETHERLANDS	10	BOSNIA-	18	LATVIA	27	BAHRAIN
2	BELGIUM		HERZEGOVINA	19	GEORGIA	28	QATAR
3	SWITZERLAND	11	YUGOSLAVIA	20	ARMENIA	29	UNITED ARAB
4	AUSTRIA	12	ALBANIA	21	AZERBAIJAN		EMIRATES
5	CZECH REPUBLIC	13	FYROM	22	SYRIA	30	GAMBIA
6	SLOVAKIA	14	BULGARIA	23	LEBANON	31	GUINEA-BISSAU
7	HUNGARY	15	ROMANIA	24	ISRAEL	32	SIERRA LEONE
8	SLOVENIA	16	MOLDOVA	25	JORDAN	33	BURKINA
9	CROATIA	17	LITHUANIA	26	KUWAIT	34	BENIN

35	CENTRAL AFRICAN
	REPUBLIC
36	DJIBOUTI
37	UGANDA
38	RWANDA
39	BURUNDI
40	ZIMBABWE
41	TURKMENISTAN
42	TAJIKISTAN

43	AFGHANISTAN
44	THAILAND
45	JAMAICA

FYROM   Former Yugoslav Republic of Macedonia

Malaysia /mə'leɪzɪə; US -'leɪʒə/;
   Malaysian /mə'leɪzɪən; US -'leɪʒn/
(the) Maldives /'mɔːldiːvz/;
   Maldivian /mɔːl'dɪvɪən/
Mali /'mɑːli/; Malian /'mɑːlɪən/
Malta /'mɔːltə/; Maltese /ˌmɔːl'tiːz/
Mauritania /ˌmɒrɪ'teɪnɪə; US
   ˌmɔːr-/; Mauritanian
   /ˌmɒrɪ'teɪnɪən; US ˌmɔːr-/
Mauritius /mə'rɪʃəs; US mɔː-/;
   Mauritian /mə'rɪʃn; US mɔː-/
Mexico /'meksɪkəʊ/; Mexican
   /'meksɪkən/
Moldova /mɒl'dəʊvə/; Moldovan
   /mɒl'dəʊvən/
Monaco /'mɒnəkəʊ/; Monacan
   /'mɒnəkən/, Monégasque
   /ˌmɒni'gæsk/
Mongolia /mɒŋ'gəʊlɪə/; Mongolian
   /mɒŋ'gəʊlɪən/, Mongol /'mɒŋgl/
Montserrat /ˌmɒntsə'ræt/;
   Montserratian /ˌmɒntsə'reɪʃn/
Morocco /mə'rɒkəʊ/; Moroccan
   /mə'rɒkən/
Mozambique /ˌməʊzæm'biːk/;
   Mozambiquean /ˌməʊzæm'biːkən/
Myanmar /mi,æn'mɑː(r)/
Namibia /nə'mɪbɪə/; Namibian
   /nə'mɪbɪən/
Nauru /'naʊru/; Nauruan
   /naʊ'ruːən/

Nepal /nɪ'pɔːl/; Nepalese /ˌnepə'liːz/
(the) Netherlands /'neðələndz/;
   Dutch /dʌtʃ/, Dutchman
   /'dʌtʃmən/, Dutchwoman
   /'dʌtʃwomən/
New Zealand /ˌnjuː 'ziːlənd; US
   ˌnuː/; New Zealand, New Zealander
   /ˌnjuː 'ziːləndə(r); US ˌnuː/
Nicaragua /ˌnɪkə'rægjuə; US
   -'rɑːgwə/; Nicaraguan
   /ˌnɪkə'rægjuən; US -'rɑːgwən/
Niger /niː'ʒeə(r); US 'naɪdʒər/;
   Nigerien /niː'ʒeərɪən/
Nigeria /naɪ'dʒɪərɪə/ Nigerian
   /naɪ'dʒɪərɪən/
Norway /'nɔːweɪ/; Norwegian
   /nɔː'wiːdʒən/
Oman /əʊ'mɑːn/; Omani /əʊ'mɑːni/
Pakistan /ˌpɑːkɪ'stɑːn; US 'pæk-
   ɪstæn/; Pakistani /ˌpɑːkɪ'stɑːni; US
   ˌpækɪ'stæni/
Panama /'pænəmɑː/; Panamanian
   /ˌpænə'meɪnɪən/
Papua New Guinea /ˌpæpuə ˌnjuː
   'gɪni; US ˌnuː/; Papuan /'pæpuən/
Paraguay /'pærəgwaɪ; US -gweɪ/;
   Paraguayan /ˌpærə'gwaɪən; US
   -'gweɪən/
Peru /pə'ruː/; Peruvian /pə'ruːvɪən/
(the) Philippines /'fɪlɪpiːnz/;

Philippine /'fɪlɪpiːn/, Filipino
   /ˌfɪlɪ'piːnəʊ/
Poland /'pəʊlənd/; Polish /'pəʊlɪʃ/,
   Pole /pəʊl/
Portugal /'pɔːtʃʊgl/; Portuguese
   /ˌpɔːtʃu'giːz/
Qatar /'kʌtɑː(r)/; Qatari /kʌ'tɑːri/
Romania /ru'meɪnɪə/; Romanian
   /ru'meɪnɪən/
Russia /'rʌʃə/; Russian /'rʌʃn/
Rwanda /ru'ændə/; Rwandan
   /ru'ændən/
San Marino /ˌsæn mə'riːnəʊ/; San
   Marinese /ˌsæn ˌmærɪ'niːz/
Sao Tomé and Principe /ˌsaʊ
   tə,meɪ ən 'prɪnsɪpeɪ/
Saudi Arabia /ˌsaʊdi ə'reɪbɪə/;
   Saudi /'saʊdi/, Saudi Arabian
   /ˌsaʊdi ə'reɪbɪən/
Senegal /ˌsenɪ'gɔːl/; Senegalese
   /ˌsenɪgə'liːz/
(the) Seychelles /seɪ'ʃelz/;
   Seychellois /ˌseɪʃel'wɑː/
Sierra Leone /siˌerə li'əʊn/;
   Sierra Leonean /siˌerə li'əʊnɪən/
Singapore /ˌsɪŋə'pɔː(r), ˌsɪŋgə-; US
   'sɪŋgəpɔːr/; Singaporean
   /ˌsɪŋə'pɔːrɪən, ˌsɪŋgə-/
Slovakia /sləʊ'vɑːkɪə, -'væk-/;
   Slovak /'sləʊvæk/

GREENLAND
(Denmark)

Alaska
(USA)

CANADA

UNITED STATES OF AMERICA

Azores
(Portugal)

Hawaiian
Islands
(USA)

Bermuda (UK)

Johnston
Atoll (USA)

Tropic of Cancer

MEXICO

BAHAMAS

CUBA

DOMINICAN
REPUBLIC

BELIZE
HONDURAS

45

HAITI

PUERTO
RICO

West
Indies

Cape
Verde
Islands

GUATEMALA
EL SALVADOR
NICARAGUA

COSTA RICA

PANAMA

TRINIDAD AND TOBAGO

VENEZUELA

GUYANA

SURINAM

FRENCH GUIANA

MARSHALL
ISLANDS

Palmyra
Atoll (USA)

Kiritimati
(Kiribati)

COLOMBIA

NAURU

KIRIBATI

Equator

Galapagos
Islands
(Ecuador)

ECUADOR

SOLOMON
ISLANDS

TUVALU

Tokelau
(New Zealand)

PERU

BRAZIL

VANUATU

WESTERN
SAMOA

FIJI

TONGA

French
Polynesia
(France)

Cook
Islands
(New Zealand)

BOLIVIA

PARAGUAY

New
Caledonia
(France)

Tropic of Capricorn

Pitcairn
Islands (UK)

Easter
Island
(Chile)

San Felix
Islands
(Chile)

CHILE

ARGENTINA

URUGUAY

Kermadec
Island
(New Zealand)

Juan
Fernandez
Islands (Chile)

NEW
ZEALAND

Chatham
Islands
(New Zealand)

Auckland Island
(New Zealand)

Scale at the equator

0   3000   6000 km

Falkland
Islands (UK)

South
Georgia
(UK)

Slovenia /sləʊˈviːniə/; Slovene /ˈsləʊviːn/, Slovenian /sləʊˈviːniən/
(the) Solomon Islands /ˈsɒləmən ˈaɪləndz/
Somalia /səˈmɑːliə/; Somali /səˈmɑːli/
(the Republic of) South Africa /ˌsaʊθ ˈæfrɪkə/; South African /ˌsaʊθ ˈæfrɪkən/
Spain /speɪn/; Spanish /ˈspænɪʃ/, Spaniard /ˈspænɪəd/
Sri Lanka /sri ˈlæŋkə; US -ˈlɑːŋ-/; Sri Lankan /sri ˈlæŋkən; US ˈlɑːŋ-/
St Kitts and Nevis /snt ˌkɪts ən ˈniːvɪs; US semt/
St Lucia /snt ˈluːʃə; US semt/
St Vincent and the Grenadines /snt ˈvɪnsnt ən ðə ˈgrenədiːnz; US semt/
Sudan /suˈdɑːn; US -ˈdæn/; Sudanese /ˌsuːdəˈniːz/
Surinam /ˌsʊərɪˈnæm/; Surinamese /ˌsʊərɪnæˈmiːz/
Swaziland /ˈswɑːzilænd/; Swazi /ˈswɑːzi/
Sweden /ˈswiːdn/; Swedish /ˈswiːdɪʃ/, Swede /swiːd/
Switzerland /ˈswɪtsələnd/; Swiss /swɪs/
Syria /ˈsɪriə/; Syrian /ˈsɪriən/

Taiwan /taɪˈwɑːn/; Taiwanese /ˌtaɪwɑːˈniːz/
Tajikistan /tæˌdʒiːkɪˈstɑːn/; Tajik /tæˈdʒiːk/
Tanzania /ˌtænzəˈniːə/; Tanzanian /ˌtænzəˈniːən/
Thailand /ˈtaɪlænd/; Thai /taɪ/
Tibet /tɪˈbet/; Tibetan /tɪˈbetn/
Togo /ˈtəʊgəʊ/; Togolese /ˌtəʊgəˈliːz/
Tonga /ˈtɒŋə, ˈtɒŋgə/; Tongan /ˈtɒŋən, ˈtɒŋgən/
Trinidad and Tobago /ˌtrɪnɪdæd ən təˈbeɪgəʊ/; Trinidadian /ˌtrɪnɪˈdædiən/, Tobagan /təˈbeɪgən/, Tobagonian /ˌtəʊbəˈgəʊniən/
Tunisia /tjuˈnɪziə; US tuˈniːʒə/; Tunisian /tjuˈnɪziən; US tuˈniːʒn/
Turkey /ˈtɜːki/; Turkish /ˈtɜːkɪʃ/, Turk /tɜːk/
Turkmenistan /tɜːkˌmenɪˈstɑːn/; Turkmen /ˈtɜːkmen/
Tuvalu /tuːˈvɑːluː/; Tuvaluan /ˌtuːvɑːˈluːən/
Uganda /juːˈgændə/; Ugandan /juːˈgændən/
Ukraine /juːˈkreɪn/; Ukrainian /juːˈkreɪniən/
(the) United Arab Emirates /juːˌnaɪtɪd ˌærəb ˈemɪrəts/

(the) United States of America /juːˌnaɪtɪd ˌsteɪts əv əˈmerɪkə/; American /əˈmerɪkən/
Uruguay /ˈjʊərəgwaɪ/; Uruguayan /ˌjʊərəˈgwaɪən/
Uzbekistan /ʊzˌbekɪˈstɑːn/; Uzbek /ˈʊzbek/
Vanuatu /ˌvænuˈɑːtuː/
(the) Vatican City /ˌvætɪkən ˈsɪti/
Venezuela /ˌvenəˈzweɪlə/; Venezuelan /ˌvenəˈzweɪlən/
Vietnam /ˌviːetˈnæm; US -ˈnɑːm/; Vietnamese /ˌviːetnəˈmiːz/
(the) West Indies /ˌwest ˈɪndiz/; West Indian /ˌwest ˈɪndiən/
Western Samoa /ˌwestən səˈməʊə/; Samoan /səˈməʊən/
Yemen Republic /ˌjemən rɪˈpʌblɪk/; Yemeni /ˈjeməni/
Yugoslavia /ˌjuːgəʊˈslɑːviə/; Yugoslavian /ˌjuːgəʊˈslɑːviən/, Yugoslav /ˈjuːgəʊslɑːv/
Zaïre /zɑːˈɪə(r)/; Zairean /zɑːˈɪəriən/
Zambia /ˈzæmbiə/; Zambian /ˈzæmbiən/
Zimbabwe /zɪmˈbɑːbwi/; Zimbabwean /zɪmˈbɑːbwiən/

Canada and the United States of America

C4

Legend

- —— international boundary
-) national boundary
- ■ capital city
- • city
-) river
- ◎ lake
- ▲ peaks or highest points
- ▒ land over 1500 metres

Scale: 0 — 500 — 1000 km

Canada

Northwest Territories

Arctic Ocean

Beaufort Sea

Ellesmere Island

Queen Elizabeth Islands

Devon Island

Baffin Bay

Baffin Island

Somerset Island

Prince of Wales Island

Parry Islands

Melville Island

Banks Island

Victoria Island

Southampton Island

Labrador Basin

Newfoundland

St John's

Hudson Bay

Great Bear Lake

Great Slave Lake

Yellowknife

Mackenzie

Lake Athabasca

Yukon

Yukon

Mackenzie Mountains

Yukon Mountains

Brooks Range

Alberta

Edmonton

Calgary

Mt Robson 3954

Peace

British Columbia

Rocky Mountains

Mt Waddington 4042

Mt Columbia 3747

Vancouver

Victoria

Fraser

Saskatchewan

Saskatoon

Regina

Saskatchewan

Manitoba

Winnipeg

Lake Winnipeg

Ontario

Thunder Bay

Lake Superior

Great Lakes

Québec

Québec

Montréal

Ottawa

Chicoutimi-Jonquière

St Lawrence

New Brunswick

Moncton

St John

Nova Scotia

Sydney

Halifax

Prince Edward Island

United States of America

Alaska

Mt McKinley 6194

Anchorage

Alaska Range

Yukon

Washington

Seattle

Mt Rainier 4392

Oregon

Portland

Eugene

Columbia

Montana

Great Falls

Billings

Rocky Mountains

Missouri

North Dakota

Bismarck

Grand Forks

Minnesota

Maine

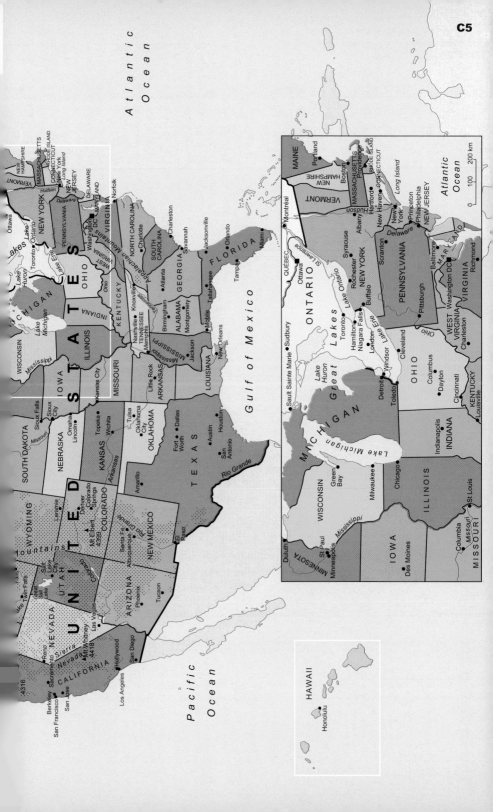

The British Isles

Britain or **Great Britain** /ɡreɪt ˈbrɪtn/ (GB) is a geographical area consisting of **England** /ˈɪŋɡlənd/, **Scotland** /ˈskɒtlənd/ and **Wales** /weɪlz/ (but not **Ireland** /ˈaɪələnd/).

The name **Britain** is often also incorrectly used to refer to the political state, officially called the **United Kingdom of Great Britain and Northern Ireland**. This is abbreviated to the **United Kingdom** or the **UK**.

The **British Isles** is a group of islands that includes Britain, Ireland and a number of smaller islands. The **Irish Republic** (also the **Republic of Ireland**; formerly **Eire** /ˈeərə/) is an independent state occupying the southern part of the island of Ireland.

To refer to the nationality of the people of Britain or the United Kingdom, you use the adjective **British**. **English** describes people from **England** and should not be used to describe people from **Ireland**, **Scotland** and **Wales** who are **Irish**, **Scottish** and **Welsh** respectively. There is further information in the notes at the entries for **British** and **Scottish**.

There are special adjectives and nouns to describe people from some cities, eg a person from London is a **Londoner** /ˈlʌndənə(r)/, from Dublin a **Dubliner** /ˈdʌblɪnə(r)/, from Glasgow a **Glaswegian** /ɡlɑːzˈwiːdʒən; *US* ɡlæs-/, from Manchester a **Mancunian** /mænˈkjuːniən/, and from Liverpool a **Liverpudlian** /ˌlɪvəˈpʌdliən/. A Londoner who speaks with the local accent is also called a **Cockney** /ˈkɒkni/. **Brummie** /ˈbrʌmi/ is an informal name for a person from Birmingham.

Atlantic Ocean

SCOTLAND

Shetland Islands

Orkney Islands

The Minch

Outer Hebrides
WESTERN ISLES

Inner Hebrides

Skye
Mull
Coll
Tiree
Islay
Jura

NORTH WEST HIGHLANDS
Moray Firth
Inverness
Loch Ness
HIGHLAND
GRAMPIAN MOUNTAINS
Aberdeen
Dee
Spey
Tay
TAYSIDE
Dundee
1344m Ben Nevis
CENTRAL
Loch Lomond
Forth
Firth of Tay
FIFE
Firth of Forth
Edinburgh
LOTHIAN
STRATHCLYDE
Firth of Clyde
Glasgow
Clyde
Tweed
SOUTHERN UPLANDS
BORDERS

NORTHERN IRELAND

UNITED KINGDOM
Scotland
Northern Ireland
England
Wales
IRISH REPUBLIC

Legend

- - - - international boundary

——— national boundary

⌒ boundaries of districts in Northern Ireland, counties in the Irish Republic, England and Wales, and regions and island areas in Scotland

■ capital city

● city or town

river

lake

▲ peaks or highest points

land 200–500 metres above sea level

land over 500 metres above sea level

0   50   100 km

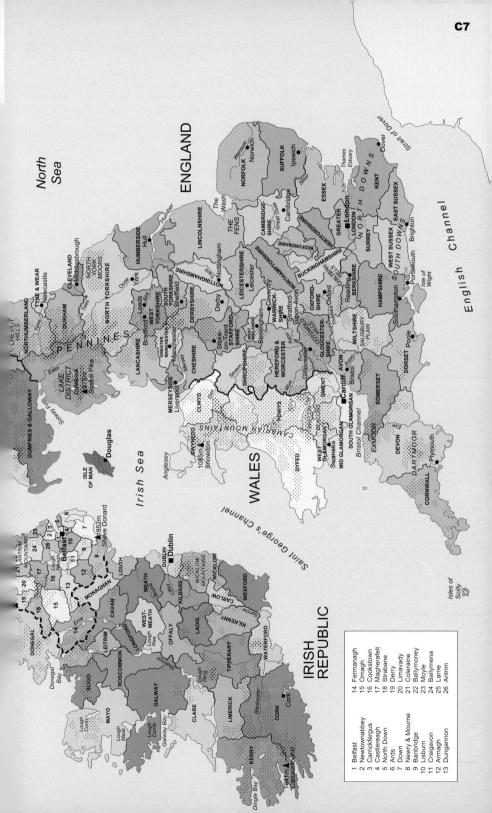

North Sea

ENGLAND

CHEVIOT HILLS

NORTHUMBERLAND

TYNE & WEAR
Newcastle

DUMFRIES & GALLOWAY

Solway Firth

CLEVELAND
Middlesbrough

DURHAM

NORTH YORK MOORS

LAKE DISTRICT
CUMBRIA
Scafell Pike 978m

P E N N I N E S

NORTH YORKSHIRE
York
Ouse
Tees
Eden

HUMBERSIDE
Hull
Humber

LINCOLNSHIRE

NOTTINGHAMSHIRE
Nottingham

THE FENS
The Wash

NORFOLK
Norwich
Wensum

SUFFOLK
Ipswich
Stour

LANCASHIRE
Aire
LEEDS
Bradford
WEST YORKSHIRE
SOUTH YORKSHIRE
Sheffield

DERBYSHIRE
Derby

LEICESTERSHIRE
Leicester

NORTHAMPTONSHIRE

CAMBRIDGE-SHIRE
Cambridge
Great Ouse

BEDFORDSHIRE

HERTFORDSHIRE

ESSEX

GREATER LONDON
London
Thames Estuary

KENT
NORTH DOWNS
Dover
Strait of Dover

MERSEYSIDE
Liverpool
Mersey
GREATER MANCHESTER
Manchester

CHESHIRE

STAFFORD-SHIRE
Stoke-on-Trent

Birmingham
WEST MIDLANDS

WARWICK-SHIRE
Coventry
Stratford-Avon

OXFORD-SHIRE
Oxford
Thames

BUCKINGHAMSHIRE

BERKSHIRE
Reading

SURREY

WEST SUSSEX
SOUTH DOWNS
Brighton
EAST SUSSEX

Chilterns

SHROPSHIRE

HEREFORD & WORCESTER
Severn
Wye

GLOUCESTER-SHIRE
Gloucester

AVON
Bristol
Avon

WILTSHIRE
SALISBURY PLAIN

HAMPSHIRE
Southampton
Portsmouth
Isle of Wight

English Channel

CLWYD
Dee

GWYNEDD
Snowdon 1085m
Anglesey

C A M B R I A N   M O U N T A I N S

POWYS

WALES

DYFED

BRECON BEACONS

GWENT

MID GLAMORGAN
WEST GLAMORGAN
Swansea
SOUTH GLAMORGAN
Cardiff

Bristol Channel

SOMERSET

EXMOOR
Exe

DEVON

DARTMOOR

DORSET
Poole

CORNWALL
Plymouth

Irish Sea

Douglas
ISLE OF MAN

Saint George's Channel

Isles of Scilly

IRISH REPUBLIC

DONEGAL
Donegal Bay

LEITRIM

SLIGO
Lough Mask
Lough Corrib

MAYO

ROSCOMMON
Shannon

GALWAY
Galway Bay

CLARE

KERRY
Carrauntoohill 1041m
Dingle Bay

LIMERICK

CORK
Cork
Blackwater

TIPPERARY
Lough Derg

WATERFORD

KILKENNY

CARLOW
Barrow

WEXFORD

LAOIS

OFFALY

KILDARE

DUBLIN
Dublin

WICKLOW
WICKLOW MOUNTAINS

MEATH
Boyne

WEST-MEATH
Lough Ree

LONGFORD

CAVAN

MONAGHAN

LOUTH

Lough Neagh
Lough Erne
Erne

ANTRIM MOUNTAINS
Belfast
Slieve Donard 852m

North Channel

1	Belfast	14 Fermanagh
2	Newtownabbey	15 Omagh
3	Carrickfergus	16 Cookstown
4	Castlereagh	17 Magherafelt
5	North Down	18 Strabane
6	Ards	19 Derry
7	Down	20 Limavady
8	Newry & Mourne	21 Coleraine
9	Banbridge	22 Ballymoney
10	Lisburn	23 Moyle
11	Craigavon	24 Ballymena
12	Armagh	25 Larne
13	Dungannon	26 Antrim

Central Europe

C8

Legend:
- international boundary
- ■ capital city
- • city
- ~ river/canal
- lake
- land over 1000 metres
- land over 2000 metres
- ▲ peaks or highest points
- FYROM Former Yugoslav Republic of Macedonia

from behind the clouds. [Vpr] *green shoots peeping through the soil.*

▶ **peep** *n* (esp *sing*) a quick secret look, esp through a small opening: *have a peep through the window* ○ *take a peep at the baby asleep in her cot.*

■ **'peep-hole** *n* a small opening in a wall, door, curtain, etc through which one may look.

,Peeping 'Tom *n* (*derog*) a person who likes to watch people when they do not know they are being watched, esp when they are taking off their clothes; a VOYEUR.

'peep-show *n* an exhibition of small pictures in a box, viewed through a small opening.

peep² /piːp/ *n* **1** [C] a short weak high sound such as that made by young birds, mice, etc. **2** (also **'peep**) [C] the sound of a car's horn(3). **3** [sing] (*infml*) a sound made by sb, esp sth said: *I haven't **heard a peep out of** the children for over an hour.*

▶ **peep** *v* [V] to make a peep.

peer¹ /pɪə(r)/ *n* **1** (usu *pl*) (**a**) a person who is equal to another in rank, status or ability: *be judged by one's peers* ○ *gain the respect of one's peers* ○ *As a goal-scorer he has few peers.* (**b**) a person who is the same age as another: *He doesn't spend enough time with his peers.* ○ *be heavily influenced by one's peers at school.* **2** (*fem* **peeress** /'pɪeres/) (in Britain) a member of the NOBILITY(2): *peers of the realm* (ie those who may sit in the House of Lords). See also LIFE PEER.

▶ **peerage** /'pɪərɪdʒ/ *n* **1** [Gp] all the peers (PEER 2), as a group: *elevate/raise sb to the peerage* (ie to make them a peer or peeress). **2** [C] the rank of a peer¹(2) or peeress: *inherit a peerage.*

peerless *adj* superior to all others; without equal: *a peerless performance.*

■ **'peer group** *n* a group of people of approximately the same age or status: *mix with one's peer group* ○ *peer-group pressure.*

peer² /pɪə(r)/ *v* ~ (**at sth/sb**) to look closely or carefully at sth, esp when unable to see it well: [Vadv] *peer shortsightedly* [Vpr] *peer at sb over one's glasses* ○ *peer into the mist/out of the window/over the wall/through a gap* [Vp] *He went to the window and peered out.* ▷ note at LOOK¹. Compare PEEK, PEEP¹ 1.

peeve /piːv/ *v* (*infml*) (esp passive or with *it* as subject) to annoy sb; to make sb bad-tempered: [Vn.*that*] *It peeves me that they're so unreliable.*

▶ **peeved** *adj* ~ (**about sth**) (*infml*) annoyed: *He sounded rather peeved on the phone.*

peevish /'piːvɪʃ/ *adj* easily annoyed, esp by unimportant things; bad-tempered: *a peevish child/voice* ○ *He was looking slightly peevish.* **peevishly** *adv.*

peewit (also **pewit**) /'piːwɪt/ *n* = LAPWING.

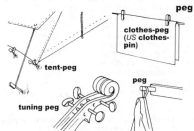

peg

clothes-peg
(US clothespin)

tent-peg

peg

tuning peg

peg¹ /peg/ *n* **1** a short piece of wood, metal or plastic, usu narrower at one end than the other, used for holding things together, hanging things on, marking a position, etc. **2(a)** such a device fastened to a wall or door, on which clothes, etc may be hung: *Hang your hat/coat on the peg by the door.* ▷ pic-

ture. (**b**) (also **'tent-peg**) such a device hammered into the ground to hold one of the ropes of a tent in place. ▷ picture. (**c**) = CLOTHES-PEG. (**d**) (also **'tuning peg**) each of several wooden screws for making the strings of a musical instrument tighter or looser. ▷ picture. ▷ picture at MUSICAL INSTRUMENT. **IDM a peg to 'hang sth on** a reason, an excuse or an opportunity for doing sth: *He uses this issue as a peg to hang his ideas on.* ,**off the 'peg** (*Brit*); (*US*) ,**off the rack** (of clothes) not made specially according to a person's particular measurements: *buy a suit off the peg* ○ *an ,off-the-peg 'suit.* **a square peg** ▷ SQUARE¹. ,**take sb 'down a peg (or two)** to make sb realize that they are not as important, good, etc as they think they are: *He's too arrogant — he needs to be taken down a peg or two.*

■ **'peg-leg** *n* (*dated*) an artificial leg, esp a wooden one.

peg² /peg/ *v* (**-gg-**) **1** (esp passive) to fasten sth with pegs (PEG¹ 1): [Vnpr, Vnp] *peg a tent (down) to the ground* ○ *peg the clothes (out) on the line* [also Vn]. **2** ~ **sth (at sth)** (esp passive) to fix or keep wages or prices at a certain level: [Vnpr] *Pay increases were pegged at five per cent.* [Vn] *Keep public transport fares pegged.* **3** ~ **sb (as sth)** (*US infml*) to classify sb: [Vn-n] *She pegged him as a big spender.* **IDM level pegging** ▷ LEVEL¹. **PHRV peg away (at sth)** (*infml*) to continue working hard at or trying to achieve sth difficult: *He kept pegging away at his thesis all summer.* **peg out** (*Brit infml*) to die. **peg sth out** to mark an area of land with pegs (PEG¹ 1): *peg out a claim* (ie mark out the land of which one claims ownership).

pejorative /pɪ'dʒɒrətɪv; *US* -'dʒɔːr-/ *adj* (*fml*) expressing contempt and criticism or disapproval: *pejorative remarks/comments/words.* ▶ **pejoratively** *adv.*

Pekinese (also **Pekingese**) /,piːkɪ'niːz/ *n* (*pl* unchanged or **Pekineses**) a small dog with short legs, long hair and a short flat nose, originally from China. ▷ picture at DOG¹.

pelagic /pə'lædʒɪk/ *adj* (*techn*) (**a**) (of fishing, etc) done on the open sea. (**b**) (of fish, etc) living near the surface of the open sea.

pelican /'pelɪkən/ *n* a large water bird with a bag of skin under its long beak for storing food.

■ ,**pelican 'crossing** *n* (*Brit*) a pedestrian crossing (PEDESTRIAN) with traffic lights that are operated by pedestrians. See also PEDESTRIAN CROSSING, ZEBRA CROSSING.

pellagra /pə'lægrə/ *n* [U] (*medical*) a disease that results from inadequate diet. It causes the skin to crack and often leads to insanity (INSANE).

pellet /'pelɪt/ *n* **1** a small ball of usu soft material such as bread or wet paper, made eg by rolling it between the fingers: *paper pellets.* **2** a small metal ball that is fired from a gun: *lead pellets.*

pell-mell /,pel'mel/ *adv* in a hurry and in great disorder; HEADLONG(2): *The children rushed pell-mell down the stairs.*

pellucid /pə'luːsɪd/ *adj* (*fml*) very clear: *pellucid skin/prose/water.*

pelmet /'pelmɪt/ *n* (also *esp US* **valance**) *n* a strip of wood, cloth, etc placed above a window to hide a curtain rail. Compare VALANCE.

pelt¹ /pelt/ *v* **1** ~ **sb (with sth)** to throw sth at sb repeatedly as an attack: [Vn] *pelt sb with snowballs/stones/rotten tomatoes.* **2** ~ (**down**) (often with *it* as subject) (of rain, etc) to fall very heavily: [V] *shelter from the pelting rain* [Vpr] *It was pelting with rain.* [Vp] *The snow was pelting down.* **3** to run very fast in the specified direction: [Vpr] *pelting down the hill.* [also Vp].

pelt² /pelt/ *n* the skin of an animal, esp with the fur or hair still on it: *beaver pelts.*

pelvis /ˈpelvɪs/ n (anatomy) the wide curved framework of bones at the lower end of the SPINE(1). ⇨ picture at SKELETON.
▶ **pelvic** /ˈpelvɪk/ adj of or relating to the pelvis: *pelvic bones/movements.*

pen¹ /pen/ n **1** [C] (often in compounds) an instrument for writing with ink, consisting of a pointed piece of split metal, a metal ball, etc, fixed into a metal or plastic holder: *a fountain pen ○ a ball-point pen ○ a felt-tip pen ○ (rhet) a new book from the pen of* (ie written by) *Kingsley Amis.* See also BIRO, LIGHT-PEN. **2** [sing] (rhet) the occupation of writing: *He lives by his pen.* **IDM** **put pen to ˈpaper** (fml) to write or start to write sth, eg a letter. **a slip of the pen/tongue** ⇨ SLIP².
▶ **pen** v (-nn-) (fml) to write sth: [Vn] *She penned a few words of thanks.*
■ ˌpen-and-ˈink adj [esp attrib] drawn with a pen: *pen-and-ink drawings/sketches.*
ˈpen-friend (also ˈpen-pal) n a person with whom one becomes friendly by exchanging letters, esp sb in a foreign country whom one has never met.
ˈpen-name n a name used by a writer instead of her or his real name; a NOM DE PLUME.
ˈpen-pusher (esp Brit) (US also **paper-pusher**) n (infml derog) a person with a boring job, esp in an office, which involves a lot of writing.

pen² /pen/ n a small piece of land surrounded by a fence in which farm animals are kept: *a ˈsheep pen.* See also PLAY-PEN.
▶ **pen** v (-nn-) **PHRV** ˌpen sb/sth ˈin/ˈup to shut a person or an animal in, or as if in, a pen: *pen up the chickens for the night ○ She feels penned in by her life as a housewife.*

pen³ /pen/ n (US infml) a prison.

penal /ˈpiːnl/ adj [esp attrib] **1** of, relating to or used for punishment, esp by law: *penal laws/reforms ○ the penal system ○ a penal colony/settlement* (ie a place where criminals are sent as a punishment) *○ Criminals could at one time be sentenced to* **penal servitude** (ie prison with hard physical work). **2** punishing sb very severely: *penal taxation* (ie so heavy that it seems like a punishment). **3** that can be punished by law: *a penal offence.*
■ ˈpenal code n a system of laws relating to crime and its punishment.

penalize, -ise /ˈpiːnəlaɪz/ v **1** ~ sb (for sth) (**a**) to punish sb for breaking a rule or law by making them suffer a penalty or disadvantage: [Vn] *People who drive when they are drunk should be heavily penalized.* [Vnpr] *Will we be penalized for incorrect spelling in the exam?* (**b**) (in sports and games) to punish sb for breaking a rule by giving an advantage to their opponent: [Vn] *Persistent foul play will be severely penalized. ○ He was penalized for a foul* (eg A free kick was awarded to the other team). **2** to put sb into an unfavourable position or at a disadvantage, esp unfairly: [Vn] *The new law penalizes the poorest members of society.*

penalty /ˈpenlti/ n **1** ~ (for sth) (**a**) a punishment for breaking a law, rule or contract: *a penalty clause in a contract.* (**b**) a particular form or level of punishment: *the ˈdeath penalty ○ It is an offence to travel without a valid ticket — penalty £100. ○ The maximum penalty for this crime is 10 years' imprisonment.* **2** a disadvantage suffered as a result of an action or a circumstance: *One of the penalties of fame is loss of privacy.* **3**(**a**) (in sports and games) a disadvantage imposed (IMPOSE 1a) on a player or team as a punishment for breaking a rule: *The referee awarded a penalty (kick) to the home team.* (**b**) (in football) a goal scored with a penalty kick: *The only goal was a penalty in the second half.* **IDM** **on/under pain/penalty of sth** ⇨ PAIN. **pay the penalty** ⇨ PAY².
■ ˈpenalty area (also ˈpenalty box) n (in football)

the area in front of the goal within which a breaking of the rules by the defenders is punished by the award of a penalty(3a) to the attacking team. ⇨ picture at FOOTBALL.
ˌpenalty ˈshoot-out n (in football) a way of deciding the winner when both teams have the same score at the end of a game. Each team takes a certain number of penalty kicks and the team that scores more wins.

penance /ˈpenəns/ n **1** [C, U] ~ (for sth) a punishment that one gives oneself to show that one is sorry for having done wrong: *an act of penance ○ do penance* (ie perform an act that shows one is sorry) *for one's sins ○ (joc) She made him cook the dinner as (a) penance for forgetting her birthday.* **2** [U] (in the Roman Catholic and Orthodox Churches) a ritual act to gain forgiveness (FORGIVE) of one's sins by confessing them to a priest and doing sth that he tells one to do as a punishment.

pence pl of PENNY. ⇨ note at PENNY.

penchant /ˈpɒ̃ʃɒ̃/; US ˈpentʃənt/ n ~ for sth a special enjoyment of or tendency towards sth: *She has a penchant for Mexican food.*

pencil /ˈpensl/ n (**a**) [C] an instrument for drawing or writing with, consisting of a thin stick of GRAPHITE or coloured chalk enclosed in a long thin piece of wood or fixed in a metal or plastic case: *a pencil drawing.* (**b**) [U] writing done with a pencil: *Should I sign my name in pencil or ink? ○ Pencil rubs out easily.* See also BLUE PENCIL.
▶ **pencil** v (-ll-; US -l-) to write, draw or mark sth with a pencil: [Vn] *She pencilled the rough outline of a house.* **PHRV** **pencil sth in** to write an arrangement that might be changed later, eg in a diary: *Let's pencil in 3 May for the meeting.*
■ ˈpencil-case (US also ˈpencil pouch) n a small bag, box, etc for holding pencils and pens.
ˈpencil-sharpener n a device for making pencils sharp.

pendant /ˈpendənt/ n **1** an ornament that hangs from a chain worn round the neck. **2** a piece of decorated glass hanging from a CHANDELIER.

pending /ˈpendɪŋ/ adj [pred] (fml) (**a**) waiting to be decided or settled: *There is a legal case pending.* (**b**) going to happen soon: *A decision on this matter is pending.*
▶ **pending** prep (fml) while waiting for sth to take place or happen; until sth: *She was held in custody pending trial.*

pendulous /ˈpendjələs; US -dʒələs/ adj (fml) hanging down loosely and swinging from side to side: *pendulous breasts.*

pendulum /ˈpendjələm; US -dʒələm/ n **1** a weight hung from a fixed point so that it can swing freely, esp a rod with a weight at the bottom that regulates the mechanism of a clock. ⇨ picture. **2** a change from one state of affairs to the opposite one, esp when this happens regularly: *The pendulum of public opinion has swung dramatically.*

pendulum

pendulum

penetrable /ˈpenɪtrəbl/ adj (fml) that can be penetrated. Compare IMPENETRABLE.

penetrate /ˈpenɪtreɪt/ v **1** ~ (into/through) sth to make a way into or through sth: [Vn] *The bullet penetrated his lung. ○ The party has been penetrated by extremists. ○ A shrill cry penetrated the silence.* [Vpr] *Our troops have penetrated deep into enemy territory. ○ The heavy rain had penetrated right through her coat.* **2** to see or show a way into or

through sth: [Vn] *Our eyes could not penetrate the darkness.* ○ *The headlamps penetrated the fog.* ○ *We soon penetrated his disguise* (ie saw who he really was). **3** to understand or discover sth that is difficult to understand or hidden: [Vn] *It was impossible to penetrate the mystery.* ○ *He seemed to be able to penetrate my thoughts.* **4** to be understood or realized by sb: [V] *I explained the problem to him several times but it didn't seem to penetrate.* [Vn] *Nothing we say penetrates his thick skull!* **5** [Vn] *(fml)* (of a man) to put the PENIS into the VAGINA of a woman.
▶ **penetrating** *adj* **1** having or showing the ability to think and understand deeply: *a penetrating mind/question/thinker* ○ *a penetrating look/glance/stare.* **2** (of a voice or sound) loud and harsh: *a penetrating cry/shriek/yell.*

penetration /ˌpenɪˈtreɪʃn/ *n* [U] **1** the action or process of penetrating sth: *our penetration of the enemy's defences.* **2** *(fml)* the ability to think and understand sth deeply: *her powers of penetration.* **3** *(fml)* an action of putting the PENIS into a female's VAGINA.

penetrative /ˈpenɪtrətɪv; US -treɪtɪv/ *adj* **1** involving PENETRATION: *penetrative sex.* **2** (of sb's mind, thoughts, etc) having or showing deep understanding; sharp: *a penetrative analysis.*

penguin /ˈpeŋgwɪn/ *n* a black and white sea bird living in the Antarctic. Penguins cannot fly but use their wings for swimming. ⇨ picture.

penguin

1m

penicillin /ˌpenɪˈsɪlɪn/ *n* [U] a substance obtained from mould² used as a drug to prevent or treat infections caused by bacteria.

peninsula /pəˈnɪnsjələ; US -nsələ/ *n* an area of land almost surrounded by water or projecting far into the sea: *the Iberian peninsula* (ie Spain and Portugal).
▶ **peninsular** /-lə(r)/ *adj* of or like a peninsula.

penis /ˈpiːnɪs/ *n* the organ with which a male person or animal has sex and urinates (URINE). ⇨ picture at REPRODUCTION.

penitence /ˈpenɪtəns/ *n* [U] ~ (**for sth**) sorrow or regret for having done sth wrong: *show penitence for one's sins.*

penitent /ˈpenɪtənt/ *adj* feeling or showing sorrow or regret for having done sth wrong: *a penitent sinner.*
▶ **penitent** *n* a penitent person, esp one who is doing religious PENANCE(2).

penitential /ˌpenɪˈtenʃl/ *adj (fml)* of or concerning PENITENCE or PENANCE: *a penitential life.*

penitentiary /ˌpenɪˈtenʃəri/ *n (US)* a prison.

penknife /ˈpennaɪf/ (also *esp US* **pocket knife**) *n (pl* **-knives** /-naɪvz/) small knife with one or more blades that fold down into the handle, usu carried in the pocket. ⇨ picture at KNIFE.

pennant /ˈpenənt/ (also **pennon** /ˈpenən/) *n* (**a**) a long narrow pointed flag, esp one used on a ship for signalling or to show the ship's identity. ⇨ picture at FLAG¹.

penniless /ˈpenɪləs/ *adj* having no money; very poor: *a penniless beggar.*

penny /ˈpeni/ *n (pl* **pennies** /ˈpeniz/ or *Brit* **pence** /pens/) **1** *(abbr* **p**) a small British BRONZE(1) coin and unit of money. There are 100 pence in one pound (£1): *He had a few pennies in his pocket.* ○ *Potatoes are 20 pence a pound.* ○ *These pencils cost 40p each.* ⇨ note. **2** *(abbr* **d**) a former British BRONZE(1) coin in use until 1971. There were twelve pennies in one SHILLING. **3** *(US)* a cent. ⇨ note at CENT. **IDM** be ˌtwo/ten a ˈpenny **1** to be very

cheap: *Lobsters are two a penny where I come from.* **2** to exist in large quantities and be easy to obtain: *Good jobs aren't exactly ten a penny these days.* ˌin for a ˈpenny, ˌin for a ˈpound *(Brit saying)* having started to do sth, it is worth spending as much time or money as is necessary to complete it. **the ˈpenny drops** *(infml esp Brit)* sb finally understands or realizes sth that they had not understood or realized before: *I had to explain the riddle to her several times before the penny dropped.* **a ˌpenny for your ˈthoughts** *(catchphrase)* (used for asking sb what they are thinking about). **a pretty penny** ⇨ PRETTY. **spend a penny** ⇨ SPEND. **turn up like a bad ˈpenny** *(infml)* (of a person) to appear when one is not welcome or not wanted, esp habitually. **worth every penny** ⇨ WORTH.
■ ˌpenny arˈcade *n (US)* = AMUSEMENT ARCADE.
ˌpenny ˈfarthing *n (Brit)* an early type of bicycle with a large front wheel and a small back wheel.
ˈpenny-pincher *n (infml derog)* a mean person; a person who dislikes spending money. **ˈpenny-pinching** *adj, n* [U].
ˌpenny ˈwhistle *n* = TIN WHISTLE.

NOTE A **penny** is one of a hundred **pence** that make up a British pound. In American English a **penny** is a one cent coin. **Pennies** refers to a number of coins of one penny or one cent. **Pennies** is also used to mean small amounts of money: *She saved her pennies all year to buy the children presents at Christmas.* In Britain **pence** or **p** is used to talk or write about a sum of money: *20 pence or 20p.* ○ *It costs 40p on the bus.* ○ *The apples were 75 pence a kilo.* Note that people often say only the numbers when talking about pounds and pence. *This T-shirt was only 1.99* (ie one ninety nine) *in the market.* When talking about an individual coin you can say **a** 5/10, etc **p**, or **a** 5/10 **p piece**: *The drinks machine doesn't take 50ps.* ○ *Have you got a twenty pence piece for the phone?*
In negative sentences **not a penny** means 'no money at all': *It didn't cost a penny* (ie It cost nothing). ○ *His parents refused to give him a penny* (ie would not give him any money). If you **count the pennies**, you are careful about how much you spend: *We didn't count the pennies in those days and spent what we liked.* ○ *He's a bit mean with money and counts every penny.*

pension¹ /ˈpenʃn/ *n* [C, U] a sum of money paid regularly by a government to people above a certain age and to widowed (WIDOW) or disabled (DISABLE) people, or by former employers or financial institutions to retired people: *an old-age pension* ○ *a retirement pension* ○ *an army pension* ○ *draw one's pension* (eg obtain it regularly from a Post Office in Britain) ○ *live on a pension* ○ *a pension fund* ○ *a pension plan/scheme* (ie a system in which people receive a pension according to how much they have contributed to the pension fund).
▶ **pension** *v* **PHRV** ˌpension sb ˈoff *(esp Brit)* (usu passive) to allow or force sb to retire, and to pay them a pension: *He was pensioned off and his job given to a younger man.* ○ *(fig infml) That old car of yours should have been pensioned off years ago.*
pensionable /ˈpenʃənəbl/ *adj* giving sb the right to receive a pension: *a pensionable job/salary* ○ *She is of pensionable age.*
pensioner /ˈpenʃənə(r)/ *n* a person who is receiving a pension, esp from the government: *an old-age pensioner.* See also OAP, SENIOR CITIZEN.

pension² /ˈpɒsjɔ̃; US paːnsˈjəʊn/ *n (French)* a small private hotel in certain European countries, esp France.

pensive /ˈpensɪv/ *adj* thinking deeply about sth, esp

in a sad or serious way: *a pensive expression/look/ mood* ○ *She looked pensive when she heard the news.* ▶ **pensively** adv.

penta- *comb form* having or consisting of five of sth: *pentagon* ○ *pentathlon.*

pentagon /ˈpentəgən; *US* -gɒn/ *n* **1** [C] (*geometry*) a flat shape with five straight sides and five angles. **2 the Pentagon** [sing] (**a**) the large building near Washington that is the headquarters of the US Department of Defense and the US armed forces. (**b**) the leaders of the US armed forces: *a spokesman for the Pentagon.* ▶ **pentagonal** /penˈtægənl/ *adj* having five sides.

pentameter /penˈtæmɪtə(r)/ *n* a line of verse containing five stressed syllables.

pentathlon /penˈtæθlən, -lɒn/ *n* a sports event in which each competitor takes part in five different sports, ie running, riding, swimming, shooting and fencing (FENCE² 1). See also DECATHLON.

Pentecost /ˈpentɪkɒst; *US* -kɔːst/ *n* [sing] **1** a Jewish festival that takes place 50 days after the second day of the Passover. **2** (*Brit* also **Whit Sunday**) (in the Christian Church) the 7th Sunday after Easter, when the coming of the Holy Ghost to the Apostles (APOSTLE 1) is celebrated. ▶ **Pentecostal** /ˌpentɪˈkɒstl; *US* -ˈkɔːstl/ *adj* of a religious group that emphasizes gifts from God, esp the power to heal the sick, and celebrates them in very enthusiastic services.

penthouse /ˈpenthaʊs/ *n* a house or flat at the top of a tall building, often thought to be a desirable place to live: *a luxury penthouse flat/apartment/ suite.*

pent up /ˌpent ˈʌp/ *adj* (of feelings, impulses, etc) that cannot be expressed or released: *emotions that have been pent up for too long* ○ *ˌpent-up ˈanger/ ˈenergy/fruˈstration.*

penultimate /penˈʌltɪmət/ *adj* [attrib] before the last one; last but one: *the penultimate day of the month.*

penurious /pəˈnjʊəriəs; *US* -ˈnʊr-/ *adj* (*fml*) very poor.

penury /ˈpenjəri/ *n* [U] (*fml*) extreme poverty: *living in penury* ○ *reduced to penury.*

peony /ˈpiːəni/ *n* a garden plant with large round pink, red or white flowers.

people /ˈpiːpl/ *n* **1** [pl v] persons: *Were there many people at the party?* ○ *streets crowded with people* ○ *He meets a lot of famous people in his job.* ○ *Many old people live alone.* **2** [pl v] persons in general: *Some people are very inquisitive.* ○ *Most people wouldn't agree with you.* ○ *People drive very badly in this country.* ○ *This kind of social problem worries people.* ⇨ note at GENDER¹. **3**(**a**) [C] a nation, race, tribe or community; all the persons belonging to this: *the English-speaking peoples* ○ *The Spartans were a war-like people.* (**b**) [pl v] those persons who live in a particular place or have a particular nationality: *the people* (ie inhabitants) *of London* ○ *the British/ French/Russian people.* ⇨ note. **4 the people** [pl v] the citizens of a country, esp in contrast with those who govern them: *The President no longer has the support of the people.* **5 the people** [pl v] ordinary persons who do not have a special rank or position in society: *the common people* ○ **a man of the people** (eg a politician who is popular with ordinary people). **6** [pl v] an important person's supporters or employees: *His people worked hard to get him elected.* **7** [pl v] (*infml*) others who work for the same company or organization as oneself: *I'll have to talk to my people and get back to you about the contract.* **8** [pl v] (*infml*) a person's relatives: *She's spending Christmas with her people.* **9** [pl v] those who work in a particular field or are involved in a particular area of activity: *Arts people get a fair amount of government support.* See also BOAT

PEOPLE. **IDM** **all things to all men/people** ⇨ THING. **people (who live) in glass houses shouldn't throw ˈstones** (*saying*) one should not criticize others when one has faults oneself.
▶ **people** *v* ~ **sth** (**with sth**) (usu passive) to fill a place, an area, etc with people; to live in a place, an area, etc: [Vn] *a village peopled by hardy seafolk* [Vnpr] *He believes the world is peopled with idiots.*

NOTE Compare **person, persons** and **people**. **People** is the usual plural form of **person**. *How many people went to the party?* The plural form **persons** is mostly used in legal language and other formal or written contexts: *holiday apartments accommodating 1–6 persons.* ○ *Persons under the age of 18 are not admitted.* The countable noun **a people** (plural **peoples**) means a nation, tribe or race: *Ancient Egyptians were a fascinating people.* ○ *The French-speaking peoples of the world.*

PEP /pep/ (*pl* **PEPs**) *abbr* (*Brit*) Personal Equity Plan (a government scheme to encourage ordinary people to invest money in industry, etc).

pep /pep/ *n* [U] (*infml*) liveliness; energy and enthusiasm: *The captain was trying to put some pep into the team.*
▶ **pep** *v* (*pp, pt* **-pp-**) **PHR V** **pep sb/sth up** (*infml*) to make sb/sth more lively or energetic: *A walk in the fresh air will pep you up.*
■ **ˈpep pill** *n* (*infml*) a pill containing a drug that stimulates the nervous system.
ˈpep talk *n* (*infml*) a talk intended to encourage sb to work harder, try to win, have more confidence, etc: *She gave us all a pep talk before the game.*

pepper /ˈpepə(r)/ *n* **1** [U] a hot-tasting powder made from the dried berries of certain plants, used to add flavour to food: *a dash of pepper.* **2** [C] a hollow, roughly round vegetable, usu red, green or yellow and eaten raw or cooked: *peppers stuffed with meat and rice.*
▶ **pepper** *v* **1** [Vn] to put pepper on food. **2** ~ **sb/ sth with sth** to hit sb/sth repeatedly with small objects, esp shots: [Vnpr] *The wall had been peppered with bullets.* ○ (*fig*) *pepper sb with questions.* **3** ~ **sth with sth** to include large numbers of sth in sth: [Vnpr] *speech peppered with swear-words* ○ *an essay peppered with spelling mistakes.*

peppery /ˈpepəri/ *adj* **1** tasting strongly of pepper: *a peppery sauce.* **2** easily made angry: *a peppery old colonel.*
■ **ˈpepper-mill** *n* a container in which dried pepper berries are ground to powder by hand for putting on food.
ˈpepper-pot (*US* also **ˈpepperbox**) *n* a small container with holes in the top, used for putting pepper on food. Compare SALT-CELLAR.

peppercorn /ˈpepəkɔːn/ *n* a dried berry that is ground to make pepper. **ˌpeppercorn ˈrent** *n* (*Brit*) a very low rent.

peppermint /ˈpepəmɪnt/ *n* (**a**) [U] a type of MINT¹(1) that produces an oil with a strong flavour. This oil is used in making sweets and in medicine. (**b**) (also **mint**) [C] a sweet flavoured with oil of peppermint: *suck a peppermint* ○ *peppermint creams.*

peptic ulcer /ˌpeptɪk ˈʌlsə(r)/ *n* an ULCER in the DIGESTIVE system.

per /pə(r); *strong form* pɜː(r)/ *prep* (used to express rates, prices, etc) for each unit of time, length, etc: *£60 per day* ○ *£2 per person* ○ *calculated per square yard* ○ *45 revolutions per minute* ○ *100 miles per hour.* **IDM** **ˈas per sth** (*infml*) according to sth: *work done as per instructions.*

perambulation /pəˌræmbjuˈleɪʃn/ *n* [C,U] (*fml or joc*) a walk through or round a place, esp for pleasure and without hurrying.

perambulator /pəˈræmbjuleɪtə(r)/ *n* (*Brit fml*) a PRAM.

per annum /pər ˈænəm/ *adv* for each year: *earning $30 000 per annum.*

per capita /pə ˈkæpɪtə/ *adv, adj* for each person: *Per capita income rose sharply last year.* ○ *average earnings per capita.*

perceive /pəˈsiːv/ *v* **1** (*fml*) to become aware of sb/ sth; to notice or observe sb/sth: [Vn] *I perceived a change in his behaviour.* [V.that] *She perceived that he was unhappy.* [Vn] *We had already perceived how the temperature fluctuated.* [V.n *to* inf only passive] *The patient was perceived to have difficulty in breathing.* [Vn.*in*] *I perceived someone standing behind me.* **2** ~ sth (**as sth**) to interpret or understand sth in a certain way: [Vn] *education that meets the perceived needs of children* ○ *That is not the way I perceive the situation.* [Vn-n] *I perceived his comment as a challenge.* [also Vn-adj]. See also PERCEPTIBLE, PERCEPTION.

per cent (*US* **percent**) /pəˈsent/ *adj, adv* in or for every hundred: *a fifty per cent (ie 50%) increase in price* ○ *working twenty per cent harder.*
▶ **per cent** (*US* also **percent**) *n* [C usu *sing*, but with *sing* or *pl v*] one part in every hundred; PERCENTAGE: *half a per cent (ie 0.5%)* ○ *Over sixty per cent of all families own/owns a television.* ○ *What per cent of the population read/reads books?* ⟹ App 2.

percentage /pəˈsentɪdʒ/ *n* **1** [C] the rate, number or amount in each hundred: *The figure is expressed as a percentage.* ○ *The salesmen get a percentage (ie a commission) on everything they sell.* ○ *a percentage increase in ticket prices.* **2** [sing or pl *v*] proportion: *What percentage of his income is taxable?* ○ *An increasing percentage of the population own their own homes.* ⟹ App 2.

perceptible /pəˈseptəbl/ *adj* ~ (**to sb**) (*fml*) **1** that can be felt or noticed with the senses: *perceptible movements/sounds* ○ *a perceptible smell.* **2** great enough to be noticed: *a perceptible change/ deterioration/improvement/increase/loss of colour* ○ *effects that are barely perceptible.* ▶ **perceptibly** /-əbli/ *adv*: *The patient has improved perceptibly.*

perception /pəˈsepʃn/ *n* (*fml*) **1** [U] the ability to see, hear or understand things; awareness: *improve one's powers of perception.* **2** [U] a deeper natural understanding and awareness than is usual; INSIGHT(1a): *His analysis of the problem showed great perception.* **3** [C] a way of seeing, understanding or interpreting sth: *Our perceptions of the world around us are constantly changing.*

perceptive /pəˈseptɪv/ *adj* (*approv*) **1** having or showing understanding or INSIGHT(1a): *a perceptive analysis/comment/judgement.* **2** quick to notice and understand things: *It's very perceptive of you to notice that!* ▶ **perceptively** *adv*. **perceptiveness** *n* [U]: *show rare perceptiveness.*

perch¹ /pɜːtʃ/ *n* **1** a place where a bird rests, esp a branch or a bar or rod for this purpose, eg in a bird's cage: *The parrot shuffled along its perch.* **2** (*infml*) a high seat or position: *He watched the game from his precarious perch on top of the wall.* **IDM** **knock sb off their pedestal/perch** ⟹ KNOCK².
▶ **perch** *v* (**on sth**) **1** ~ (of a bird) to land and stay on a branch, etc: [Vpr] *The birds perched on the television aerial.* [also V]. **2** ~ (**on sth**) (esp of a person) to sit, esp on sth high or narrow: [Vpr] *perch dangerously on a narrow ledge* ○ *We had to perch on high stools at the bar.* [also V].

perched /pɜːtʃt/ *adj* [pred] **1** (esp of a bird) resting or sitting on sth: *sit perched on a branch.* **2** placed in a high or dangerous position: *a castle perched high above the river.*

perch² /pɜːtʃ/ *n* (*pl* unchanged) a common edible fish that lives in rivers and lakes.

perchance /pəˈtʃɑːns; *US* -ˈtʃæns/ *adv* (*arch*) perhaps.

percipient /pəˈsɪpiənt/ *adj* (*fml*) quick to notice or understand things; PERCEPTIVE(2): *a percipient on-looker.*

percolate /ˈpɜːkəleɪt/ *v* ~ (**through sth**)/ ~ (**through**) (of a liquid, gas, etc) to move gradually through a surface containing tiny holes or spaces: [Vpr] *Water had percolated through the rocks.* [Vp] *Nitrates may take 20 years to percolate through to the underground streams.* ○ (*fig*) *The news took some time to percolate through.* [also V].
▶ **percolator** *n* a pot for making and serving coffee, in which boiling water is repeatedly forced up a central tube and passes down again through ground coffee.

percussion /pəˈkʌʃn/ *n* **1** [U] musical instruments that are played by striking, beating or tapping with a stick, etc, eg drums: *percussion instruments* ○ *The track features Joey Langton on percussion.* **2** **the percussion** (also **perˈcussion section**) [Gp] the players of percussion instruments in an ORCHESTRA. ⟹ picture at MUSICAL INSTRUMENT.
▶ **percussionist** /-ʃənɪst/ *n* a person who plays percussion instruments.

perdition /pɜːˈdɪʃn/ *n* [U] (*fml religion*) punishment lasting for ever after death: *be damned to perdition.*

peregrination /ˌperəɡrɪˈneɪʃn/ *n* (*fml or joc*) a journey, esp a long slow one: *his peregrinations in southern Europe.*

peregrine /ˈperɪɡrɪn/ (also ˌperegrine ˈfalcon) *n* a large grey and white bird that can be trained to hunt and catch small birds and animals.

peremptory /pəˈremptəri/ *adj* (*fml esp derog*) (esp of sb's manner or behaviour) insisting on immediate attention or obedience: *a peremptory summons/ reply/tone of voice* ○ *She finally lost patience with his incessant peremptory demands.*
▶ **peremptorily** /-trəli/ *adv* in a way that allows for no discussion or refusal; in a harsh or ABRUPT(2) way: *'Is this yours?' she demanded peremptorily.*

perennial /pəˈreniəl/ *adj* **1(a)** constantly occurring: *a perennial problem/complaint/favourite.* (**b**) lasting for a long time: *a perennial source of hope.* **2** (of plants) living for more than two years.
▶ **perennial** *n* a perennial plant.
perennially /-niəli/ *adv*.

perestroika /ˌperəˈstrɔɪkə/ *n* [U] (esp in the former Soviet Union) the reform of the economic and political system: *the main architects/opponents of perestroika.*

perfect¹ /ˈpɜːfɪkt/ *adj* **1(a)** having everything that is necessary; complete and not damaged: *in perfect condition* ○ *an absolutely perfect set of teeth.* (**b**) exact; PRECISE(2): *a perfect copy/match/fit* ○ *perfect accuracy/timing.* (**c**) the best of its kind; ideal: *a perfect score* (ie one in which no marks or points have been lost) ○ *a perfect example of Picasso's early style* ○ *the perfect crime* (ie one in which the criminal is never discovered) ○ (*ironic*) *The weather was less than perfect* (ie not very good at all). (**d**) excellent; very good: *She spoke perfect English.* ○ *That was a perfect evening.* (**e**) ~ (**for sb/sth**) highly suitable for sb/sth; exactly right: *It was a perfect day for a picnic.* ○ *She is the perfect choice for the job.* ○ *'Will 2 o'clock be OK for you?' 'Perfect, thanks.'* **2** (*grammar*) (of a verb TENSE²) composed of part of the verb *have* with the past PARTICIPLE of the main verb: *'I have eaten' is the present perfect tense of the verb 'eat', and 'I had eaten' is the past perfect.* **3** [attrib] (*infml*) total; absolute: *perfect nonsense* ○ *a perfect fool/pest/ stranger.* **IDM** **practice makes perfect** ⟹ PRACTICE.
▶ **perfect** *n* **the perfect** [sing] (*grammar*) the perfect tense: *The verb is in the perfect.* ○ *the present/ past perfect.*

perfectly *adv* **1** in a perfect way: *perfectly formed* ○ *The trousers fit perfectly.* **2** completely; quite: *be perfectly happy/normal/safe/right/clear* ○ *I wish you'd stop fussing. I'm perfectly all right.* ○ *'What do*

[V.speech] = verb + direct speech   [V.*that*] = verb + *that* clause   [V.*wh*] = verb + *who, how*, etc clause

*you mean?' 'You **know perfectly well** what I mean.'*
3 (*dated infml*) extremely; absolutely: *What perfectly awful weather!*

perfect² /pə'fekt/ v to make sth perfect or complete: [Vn] *perfect an art/a system/a method of doing sth* ○ *a violinist who spent years perfecting her technique.*

perfection /pə'fekʃn/ n **1** [U] (**a**) the state of being perfect; the absence of faults: *aim/strive/search for perfection* ○ *His performance was little short of perfection.* (**b**) the highest state or quality possible: *Her singing was perfection itself.* **2** [U] the process of improving sth so that it becomes perfect: *They are working on the perfection of their new paint formula.* **IDM** **to per'fection** to exactly the right degree; perfectly: *a dish cooked to perfection* ○ *He timed his run to perfection.*

▶ **perfectionist** /-ʃənɪst/ n (*sometimes derog*) a person who tries to get every detail correct and is not satisfied with anything less than perfection: *As a cook she's such a perfectionist that she insists on using only the finest ingredients.* **perfectionism** /pə'fekʃənɪzəm/ n [U].

perfidy /'pɜːfədɪ/ n [U] (*fml or rhet*) actions which betray a person or a principle; treachery (TREACHEROUS 1): *In Act 2 he learns of Giovanni's perfidy and swears revenge.*

▶ **perfidious** /pə'fɪdɪəs/ adj ~ (**to/towards sb**) (*fml*) deceitful or TREACHEROUS: *their perfidious influence.*

perforate /'pɜːfəreɪt/ v to make a hole or holes through sth: [Vn] *perforated bricks/plastic bags* ○ *a perforated ulcer* ○ *A metal spike had perforated the fuel tank.*

▶ **perforation** /ˌpɜːfə'reɪʃn/ n a small hole or series of small holes, esp in paper: *tear the sheet of stamps along the perforations.*

perforce /pə'fɔːs/ adv (*arch or fml*) because it is necessary or inevitable: *They had perforce to abandon the attempt on the summit.*

perform /pə'fɔːm/ v **1** to do sth, eg a piece of work, or sth one has been ordered or has agreed to do: [Vn] *perform a miracle/an experiment/a remarkable feat* ○ *perform an operation to save sb's life* ○ *perform a vital service for the community.* **2** to act in an official way at sth; to conduct sth: [Vn] *perform a ceremony/rite.* **3** to act a play, do tricks, play a piece of music, etc to entertain an audience: [Vn] *The play/concerto was first performed in 1987.* ○ *perform somersaults* [V] *watch sb perform* [Vpr] *perform (skilfully) on the flute* [Vnadv] *I'd like to see it performed live.* **4** to work or function: [Vadv] *The new drug has performed well in tests.* ○ *How is the new car performing?*

▶ **performer** n **1** a person who performs for an audience: *a talented cabaret performer.* **2** a person or thing that behaves or functions in the specified way: *a skilled performer in goal* ○ *Today's star performer was ICI, up 26p to 525p.*

■ **the per,forming 'arts** n [pl] arts such as drama, music and dance which are performed for an audience.

performance /pə'fɔːməns/ n **1** [C] (**a**) an act of performing a play, a concert or some other entertainment: *attend the evening/matinée performance of Swan Lake.* (**b**) the way a person performs in a play, concert, etc: *Brando's finest/greatest performance* ○ *a rare live performance by the band.* **2**(**a**) [C] an action or achievement, considered in relation to how successful it is: *an impressive/a spectacular/a strong/an inspired performance by the national team* ○ *performance-related pay* ○ *performance targets* ○ *He criticized the recent poor performance of the company.* (**b**) [U] the ability to operate efficiently, react quickly, etc: *high performance cables* ○ *I am impressed by the machine's overall/all-round performance.* **3** [sing] the process of performing sth: *the performance of one's duties.* **4** [sing] (*infml*) an

act involving a lot of unnecessary fuss or trouble: *You should have seen the trouble I had getting the children to go to school — what a performance!* ○ *He goes through the whole performance of checking the oil and water every time he takes the car out.*

perfume /'pɜːfjuːm/ n [C, U] **1** a sweet-smelling liquid, often made from plants, used esp on the body: *He caught a faint whiff of some expensive French perfume.* **2** a pleasant smell: *the fragrant perfume of the flowers.*

▶ **perfume** /'pɜːfjuːm; US pər'fjuːm/ v (*esp passive*) **1** to put perfume in or on sth: [Vn] *perfumed deodorants/candles* [Vnpr] *a hand lotion perfumed with rosemary.* **2** (of flowers, etc) to give a pleasant smell to sth: [Vn] *Roses perfumed the air.* **perfumed** adj having or producing a strong perfume: *heavily perfumed hyacinths.*

perfumery /pə'fjuːmərɪ/ n a place where perfumes are made or sold: *the perfumery counters of department stores.*

perfunctory /pə'fʌŋktərɪ/ adj (*fml*) (of an action) done as a duty or routine, without care or interest: *a perfunctory examination/greeting/nod* ○ *She gave him no more than a perfunctory 'So glad you could come.'* ▶ **perfunctorily** /-trəlɪ/ adv.

pergola /'pɜːɡələ/ n a framework made of wooden posts and bars around which plants can be trained to grow, eg forming a covered walk in a garden.

perhaps /pə'hæps, præps/ adv **1** possibly; MAYBE: *'Why isn't she here?' 'Perhaps she's ill.'* ○ *Perhaps the weather will change tomorrow.* **2** (used when one does not want to give a firm opinion): *It is, perhaps, the best known of his works.* **3** (used when making a rough estimate): *He was alone for perhaps half an hour.* **4** (used when one agrees or accepts sth reluctantly): *'Don't you think we should ask your father first?' 'Well, perhaps so.'* **5** (used when making a polite request, offer or suggestion): *Perhaps you'd like some tea.* ○ *I wondered if, perhaps, you'd glance over this letter for me.* ○ *Perhaps you would be kind enough to* (ie Please) *open the door for me.*

peri- *pref* around: *periscope* ○ *perimeter.*

peril /'perəl/ n (*rhet or fml*) **1** [U] serious danger: *be in great/grave/dire peril* ○ *We **ignore** these warnings **at our peril**.* **2** [C usu *pl*] a dangerous situation or circumstance: *a book warning of the perils of drug abuse* ○ *These birds are able to survive the perils of the Arctic winter.*

▶ **perilous** /'perələs/ adj (*fml or rhet*) full of risk; dangerous: *a perilous journey across the mountains* ○ *leaning at a perilous angle* ○ *the perilous state of the region.* **perilously** adv: *perilously fast/steep* ○ *They were **perilously close** to the edge of the precipice.*

perimeter /pə'rɪmɪtə(r)/ n a boundary around an area: *Guards patrol the perimeter of the airfield.* ○ *a perimeter fence.*

period /'pɪərɪəd/ n **1** a length or portion of time: *a prolonged period of peace/recovery/uncertainty* ○ *aiming to reduce traffic at peak periods* ○ *a £200m investment programme over a 4-year period* ○ *This compares with a 4% increase for the same period in 1993.* ○ *This offer is available for a limited period only.* ○ *There will be showers and sunny periods tomorrow.* See also COOLING-OFF PERIOD. **2**(**a**) a portion of time in the life of a person, nation or CIVILIZATION: *a painting from Picasso's blue period* ○ *during the period of the French Revolution* ○ *The house is 18th century and contains much furniture of the period* (ie of the same century). ○ *period costumes/furniture.* (**b**) (*geology*) a portion of time in the development of the Earth's surface: *the Jurassic period.* **3** a lesson in school, etc: *a free period* ○ *We have three periods of geography a week.* **4** a flow of blood that occurs for a few days each month from the body of a woman when she is not pregnant: *have a period* ○ *period pains.* **5** (*esp US*) (**a**) = FULL STOP

⇨ App 3. (**b**) (*infml*) (added to the end of a statement to stress that no further discussion is possible): *We can't pay higher wages, period.*

■ **'period piece** *n* an object, a play, a piece of music, etc dating from a particular period of history: *It is being staged as a period piece, a spirited evocation of life in the Thirties.*

periodic /ˌpɪəriˈɒdɪk/ (also **periodical** /-kl/) *adj* occurring or appearing at intervals: *experiencing periodic attacks of dizziness* ○ *a periodical review of expenditure.*

▶ **periodical** *n* a magazine, etc that is published at regular intervals, eg every week or every month. **periodically** /-kli/ *adv* at intervals: *update sth periodically.*

■ **the ˌperiodic 'table** *n* [sing] (*chemistry*) a list of all the chemical elements arranged according to their atomic weights. ⇨ App 7.

peripatetic /ˌperipəˈtetɪk/ *adj* (*fml*) going from place to place, eg in order to work: *peripatetic music teachers.*

periphery /pəˈrɪfəri/ *n* (*fml*) (usu *sing*) **1** the edge or boundary of an area: *industrial development on the northern periphery of the town* ○ *objects at the periphery of her vision.* **2** a position on the outside of a social, political, etc group; the FRINGE(3): *minor poets on the periphery of the movement.*

▶ **peripheral** /-ərəl/ *adj* **1** ~ (**to sth**) of secondary or minor importance: *Fund-raising is peripheral to their main activities.* **2** of or on a periphery: *peripheral vision* ○ *peripheral zones.* **3** (*computing*) (of a device) that can be attached to and used with a computer but is not an essential part of it. — *n* (*computing*) a peripheral device: *display units, printers and other peripherals.* **peripherally** /-ərəli/ *adv.*

periscope /ˈperiskəʊp/ *n* an apparatus with mirrors and lenses (LENS 1) arranged in a tube so that the user has a view of the area above, eg the surface of the sea from a SUBMARINE(1) when it is under water. ⇨ picture.

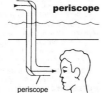

periscope

perish /ˈperɪʃ/ *v* **1** (*fml or rhet*) to be destroyed; to die: [V] *Thousands of people perished in the earthquake.* ○ *They vowed to succeed or perish in the attempt.* **2** (of rubber) to rot; to lose its elastic quality: [V] *The seal on the bottle has perished.* **IDM** ˌperish the 'thought (*infml*) (used to show that one finds a suggestion either absurd or not welcome) may it never happen: *I'm not suggesting that pubs should never close — perish the thought!*

▶ **perishable** *adj* (esp of food) likely to decay or go bad quickly: *perishable goods/commodities.* **perishables** *n* [pl] things, esp food, that go bad or decay quickly.

perishing *adj* (*esp Brit*) **1** extremely cold: *It's perishing outside.* **2** (*dated sl*) (used to express annoyance) DAMN[2]: *I can't get in — I've lost the perishing key!*

peritonitis /ˌperitəˈnaɪtɪs/ *n* [U] (*medical*) a painful and serious condition in which the inside wall of the abdomen becomes inflamed (INFLAME).

periwinkle /ˈperiwɪŋkl/ *n* **1** a plant that grows along the ground and has blue or white flowers. **2** = WINKLE.

perjure /ˈpɜːdʒə(r)/ *v* ~ **oneself** (*law*) to tell a lie, esp in a lawcourt, after one has sworn to tell the truth: [Vn] *Several witnesses perjured themselves in order to protect the accused.*

▶ **perjury** /ˈpɜːdʒəri/ *n* [U] (*law*) the action of perjuring oneself, esp in a lawcourt: *be found guilty of (committing) perjury.*

perk¹ /pɜːk/ *n* (*infml*) (usu *pl*) (**a**) money or goods received as a right from one's employer: *Perks offered by the firm include a car and free health insurance.* (**b**) an advantage or a benefit considered by an employee as part of a particular job or position: *She regards free stationery as one of the perks of the job.*

perk² /pɜːk/ *v* **PHRV** ˌperk 'up (*infml*) to become more cheerful or lively, esp after a period of illness or sadness: *He felt depressed but soon perked up when his friends arrived.* ○ (*fig*) *Share prices perked up a little towards the end of the day's trading.* ˌperk **sb/sth 'up** (*infml*) **1** to make sb feel more cheerful or lively: *A cup of coffee will perk you up.* **2** to make one's clothes, a room, a garden, etc look better or more exciting: *You need a bright red scarf to perk up that grey suit.*

▶ **perky** *adj* (**-ier, -iest**) (*infml*) **1** lively and cheerful: *He's still in bed, but he seems quite perky.* **2** too full of confidence; cheeky (CHEEK): *a perky grin.* **perkiness** *n* [U].

perm /pɜːm/ (also *fml* ˌpermanent 'wave, *US* permanent) *n* a method of changing the style of one's hair, in which it is treated with chemicals and set in waves or curls that last for several months: *have a perm.*

▶ **perm** *v* to give sb's hair a perm: [Vn] *Her hair has been permed.*

permafrost /ˈpɜːməfrɒst; *US* -frɔːst/ *n* [U] soil that is permanently frozen deep beneath the earth's surface, esp in POLAR regions.

permanence /ˈpɜːmənəns/ (also **permanency** /-nənsi/) *n* [U] the state or condition of continuing or remaining for a long time: *a longing for some sense of permanence and continuity in a fast-changing world* ○ *questioning the permanence of their commitment to peace.*

permanent /ˈpɜːmənənt/ *adj* lasting or expected to last for a long time or for ever: *a permanent tan/feature/exhibition* ○ *the permanent members of the UN Security Council* ○ *The burnt-out buildings are a permanent reminder of the disaster.* ○ *The company is now taking on workers on a permanent basis.* Compare IMPERMANENT, TEMPORARY.

▶ **permanent** *n* (*US*) = PERM.
permanently *adv*: *be permanently disabled* ○ *She is now based permanently in the USA.*

■ ˌpermanent 'secretary *n* (*Brit*) a senior official in the British civil service (CIVIL): *the Permanent Secretary to the Treasury.*
ˌpermanent 'wave *n* (*fml*) = PERM.

permeate /ˈpɜːmieɪt/ *v* (*fml*) to spread to every part of sth: [Vn] *a distrust of strangers permeating the whole community* [Vn, Vpr] *The smell of cooking permeated (through) the house.*

▶ **permeable** /ˈpɜːmiəbl/ *adj* (*techn*) that can be permeated by liquids or gases; POROUS: *permeable materials/soils.* Compare IMPERMEABLE **permeability** /ˌpɜːmiəˈbɪləti/ *n* [U].

permeation /ˌpɜːmiˈeɪʃn/ *n* [U] (*fml*): *the permeation of information technology in schools.*

permissible /pəˈmɪsəbl/ *adj* (*fml*) that is or can be allowed: *permissible levels of nitrates in water.*

permission /pəˈmɪʃn/ *n* [U, C] ~ (**to do sth**) the action of allowing sb to do sth; CONSENT *n*: *request/seek sb's permission* ○ *She asked (for) permission to leave early.* ○ *She refused to give/grant her permission.* ○ *They were refused permission to leave the country.* ○ *They entered the area without permission.* ○ *poems reprinted by kind permission of the author* ○ *The soldiers had special permission to attend the ceremony.* ○ *obtain the necessary permissions to reproduce illustrations.* ⇨ note at ALLOWANCE. See also PLANNING PERMISSION.

permissive /pəˈmɪsɪv/ *adj* [usu attrib] (*often derog*) (**a**) allowing great freedom of behaviour, esp to children or in sexual matters: *permissive parents.*

[V] = verb used alone   [Vn] = verb + noun   [Vp] = verb + particle   [Vpr] = verb + prepositional phrase

(**b**) showing this freedom: *permissive attitudes/ behaviour* ○ *grow up in a permissive society.*

▶ **permissiveness** *n* [U] the state of being permissive in attitude or behaviour: *encouraging permissiveness.*

permit /pə'mɪt/ *v* (**-tt-**) (*fml*) **1** to give permission for sth; to allow sth: [Vn] *Dogs are not permitted in the hotel.* ○ *He is below the permitted age to hold a driving licence.* [V.*ing*] *We do not permit smoking in the office.* [Vn-n] *The prisoners were permitted two hours' exercise a day.* ○ *Wallis permitted himself a wry smile.* [Vn.*to* inf] *The council will not permit you to build here.* **2** to make sth possible: [V] *Parliament should be recalled as soon as circumstances permit.* ○ *I'll come tomorrow, weather permitting* (ie if the weather doesn't prevent me). [Vn] *The new one-way system permits the free flow of traffic at all times.* [Vn.*to* inf] *These vents permit hot air to enter.* ⇨ note at ALLOW. **PHRV** per'mit of sth (*fml*) (esp in negative sentences; no passive) to admit sth as possible; to tolerate sth: *The situation does not permit of any delay.*

▶ **permit** /'pɜːmɪt/ *n* an official document that gives sb the right to do sth, esp to go somewhere: *apply for a work/travel/fishing permit* ○ *You cannot enter a military base without a permit.* ⇨ note at ALLOWANCE.

permutation /ˌpɜːmjuː'teɪʃn/ *n* (*fml*) a variation in the order of a set of things: *The coloured pieces can be arranged in endless permutations and combinations.* ○ *The permutations of x, y and z are xyz, xzy, yxz, yzx, zxy and zyx.*

pernicious /pə'nɪʃəs/ *adj* (*fml*) having a very harmful effect on sb/sth, esp in a gradual or SUBTLE(1) way: *pernicious lies/myths/doctrines* ○ *a pernicious influence on society.*

pernickety /pə'nɪkəti/ *adj* (*infml or derog*) worrying too much about unimportant details; FUSSY(2): *It seems almost pernickety to object to the last few sentences of such an excellent report.*

peroration /ˌperə'reɪʃn/ *n* (*fml*) the last part of a speech that gives a forceful summary of what has been said before.

peroxide /pə'rɒksaɪd/ (also ˌhydrogen pe'roxide) *n* [U] a colourless liquid used to kill bacteria and to BLEACH hair: *a woman with peroxide blonde hair.*

perpendicular /ˌpɜːpən'dɪkjələ(r)/ *adj* (**a**) ~ (**to sth**) at an angle of 90° to another line or surface: *a line drawn perpendicular to the direction of travel.* (**b**) at an angle of 90° to the ground: *perpendicular cliffs.*

▶ **perpendicular** *n* **1** [C] perpendicular line. **2** (also **the perpendicular**) [U] perpendicular position or direction: *The wall is a little out of (the) perpendicular.*

perpetrate /'pɜːpətreɪt/ *v* (*fml*) to commit a crime, make an error, etc: [Vn] *perpetrate a dreadful outrage* ○ *violence perpetrated against innocent victims* ○ *Many computer frauds are perpetrated by authorized users.*

▶ **perpetration** /ˌpɜːpə'treɪʃn/ *n* [U].

perpetrator *n* a person who commits a crime or does sth considered wrong: *the perpetrator of a hoax.*

perpetual /pə'petʃuəl/ *adj* [usu attrib] **1** without interruption; continuous: *the perpetual noise of traffic* ○ *live in a state of perpetual fear.* **2** (*infml*) frequently repeated: *How can I work with these perpetual interruptions?* **3** permanent during life: *He was elected perpetual president.* ▶ **perpetually** /-tʃuəli/ *adv.*

■ per,petual 'motion *n* [U] movement, eg of an imagined machine, that would continue for ever without needing power from an outside source.

perpetuate /pə'petʃueɪt/ *v* (*fml*) to make sth continue: [Vn] *perpetuate a problem/belief/tradition* ○ *These measures will only perpetuate the hostility be-*

tween the two groups. ▶ **perpetuation** /pəˌpetʃu'eɪʃn/ *n* [U].

perpetuity /ˌpɜːpə'tjuːəti; *US* -'tuː-/ *n* **IDM** in perpetuity (*fml*) for ever; permanently: *an annual income granted in perpetuity* ○ *preserve places of natural beauty in perpetuity.*

perplex /pə'pleks/ *v* to make sb feel confused; to worry sb: [Vn] *I was perplexed by his strange behaviour.*

▶ **perplexed** *adj* confused or worried: *a perplexed expression/look* ○ *The audience looked perplexed.* ○ *She tried to explain her behaviour to her perplexed parents.* **perplexedly** /-ɪdli/ *adv.*

perplexing *adj*: *The whole affair is very perplexing.* **perplexity** /-əti/ *n* **1** [U] the state of being perplexed; confusion(1): *She looked at us in perplexity.* **2** [C] a complicated or difficult situation or thing: *try to cope with the perplexities of life.*

perquisite /'pɜːkwɪzɪt/ *n* (*fml*) **1** (also *infml* **perk**) (esp *pl*) money or goods given or regarded as a right in addition to one's pay: *Perquisites include the use of the company car.* **2** a special advantage or right enjoyed as a result of one's position: *Politics in Britain used to be the perquisite of the property-owning classes.*

perry /'peri/ *n* [U] an alcoholic drink made from PEAR juice. Compare CIDER.

pers *abbr* person.

per se /ˌpɜː 'seɪ/ (*Latin*) by or of itself: *The drug is not harmful per se, but is dangerous when taken with alcohol.*

persecute /'pɜːsɪkjuːt/ *v* **1** ~ **sb** (**for sth**) (esp passive) to treat sb in a cruel way, esp because of their race[3](1), their political or religious beliefs, etc: [Vn, Vnpr] *Throughout history religious minorities have been persecuted (for their beliefs).* **2** to pursue and annoy sb continually: [Vn] *He accused the media of persecuting him and his family.*

▶ **persecution** /ˌpɜːsɪ'kjuːʃn/ *n* [U, C]: *face/suffer persecution for one's beliefs* ○ *He came to realize that this persecution complex* (ie feeling that people were persecuting him) *was only in his mind.* ○ *be the victims of frequent persecutions.*

persecutor *n* a person who persecutes others: *He tried to escape from the hands of his persecutors.*

persevere /ˌpɜːsɪ'vɪə(r)/ *v* ~ (**at/in/with sth**); ~ (**with sb**) (*usu approv*) to continue trying to do sth, esp in spite of difficulty: [V] *If you persevere I'm sure you'll succeed.* [Vpr] *She persevered in her efforts to win the championship.* ○ *He was hopeless at French, but his teacher persevered with him.*

▶ **perseverance** /ˌpɜːsɪ'vɪərəns/ *n* [U] continued steady effort to achieve an aim; steadfastness: *show great perseverance in the face of extreme hardship* ○ *After months of disappointment, his perseverance was finally rewarded.*

persevering /ˌpɜːsɪ'vɪərɪŋ/ *adj* showing continued steady effort: *A few persevering climbers finally reached the top.*

Persian /'pɜːʃn, 'pɜːʒn; *US* 'pɜːrʒn/ *adj* of Persia (now called Iran), its people or its language.

▶ **Persian** *n* **1** [C] an inhabitant of Persia. **2** [U] the language of Persia (now usu called *Iranian* or *Farsi*).

■ ˌPersian 'carpet (also ˌPersian 'rug) *n* a carpet of traditional design from the Near East, made by hand from silk or wool.

ˌPersian 'cat (also **Persian**) *n* a breed of cat with long hair.

persimmon /pə'sɪmən/ *n* a sweet orange tropical fruit like a large TOMATO, which grows on trees.

persist /pə'sɪst/ *v* **1** ~ (**in sth/in doing sth/with sth**) to continue to do sth, esp with determination and in spite of difficulty, opposition, argument or failure: [V] *If you persist, you will annoy them even more.* [Vpr] *He will persist in wearing that dreadful tie.* ○ *She persists in the belief/in believing that she is* *being persecuted.* ○ *They persisted with the agricultural reforms, despite opposition from the farmers.* [also V.speech]. **2** to continue to exist: [V] *Fog will persist throughout the night.* ○ *You should seek medical advice if the pain persists.*

▶ **persistence** /-əns/ *n* [U] **1** continuing to do sth in spite of difficulties: *His persistence was rewarded when they finally agreed to resume discussions.* **2** the continuing existence of sth: *The doctor couldn't explain the persistence of the high temperature.*

persistent /-ənt/ *adj* **1** refusing to give up: *She eventually married the most persistent of her admirers.* **2(a)** continuing without interruption: *persistent noise/rain/pain* ○ *persistent questioning.* **(b)** occurring frequently: *persistent attacks of coughing* ○ *Despite persistent denials, the rumour continued to spread.* **persistently** *adv.*

person /ˈpɜːsn/ *n* (*pl* **people** /ˈpiːpl/ or, esp in formal use, **persons**) ⇨ note at PEOPLE. **1(a)** a human being as an individual: *He's just the person we need for the job.* ○ *Here she is — the very person we were talking about!* ○ *I had a letter from the people who used to live next door.* **(b)** (used after *ns*): *I'm not really a chess/competition/theatre person* (ie I don't like chess/competitions/the theatre very much). **2** (*fml or derog*) a human being, esp not identified: *A certain person* (ie somebody that I do not wish to name) *told me about it.* ○ *Any person found leaving litter will be prosecuted.* ○ *The fare is £10 per person.* ○ (*law*) *She was accused of conspiring with* **(a) person or persons unknown** (eg said when charging sb in court). **3** (*grammar*) (abbreviated as *pers* in this dictionary) any of the three classes of personal pronouns. The first person '*I/we*' refers to the person(s) speaking, the second person '*you*' refers to the person(s) spoken to, and the third person '*he, she, it, they*' refers to the person(s) or thing(s) spoken about. **4** (*religion*) (in Christianity) each of the three forms of God (*Father, Son* and *Holy Spirit*). The three persons of God are the *Trinity.* **IDM** **about/on one's** ˈ**person** carried about with one, eg in one's pocket: *Relatives of the dead man were traced through an address found on his person.* **be no/not be any respecter of persons** ⇨ RESPECTER. **in** ˈ**person** physically present: *The winner will be there in person to collect the prize.* ○ *You may apply for tickets in person or by letter.* **in the person of sb** (*fml*) in the form or shape of sb: *Help arrived in the person of his father.* ○ *The firm has an important asset in the person of the sales director.*

▶ **-person** (forming compound *ns*) a person concerned with: *salesperson* ○ *spokesperson.* ⇨ note at GENDER.

■ ˌ**person-to-**ˈ**person** *adj* **1** between individuals: *person-to-person meetings.* **2** (*esp US*) (of a telephone call) made through the OPERATOR(2) to a particular person and paid for from the time that person answers the phone.

persona /pəˈsəʊnə/ *n* (*pl* **personae** /-niː, -naɪ/) the character of a person as presented to others or as others perceive it: *His public persona was of a great joker but his friends knew him as a serious, often moody man.* See also DRAMATIS PERSONAE.

■ **perˌsona non** ˈ**grata** /nɒn ˈɡrɑːtə, nəʊn/ *n* [sing] (*Latin*) a person who is not welcome or acceptable to others, esp to a foreign government: *He was declared persona non grata and forced to leave the country.*

personable /ˈpɜːsənəbl/ *adj* having a pleasant appearance or manner: *The salesman was a very personable young man.*

personage /ˈpɜːsənɪdʒ/ *n* (*fml or joc*) a person, esp a famous or important one: *Political and royal personages from many countries attended the funeral.*

personal /ˈpɜːsənl/ *adj* **1** [attrib] of or belonging to a particular person rather than a group or an organization: *personal affairs/feelings* ○ *a car for*

your personal use only ○ *give sth the* **personal touch** (ie make it individual or original) ○ *a novel written from* **personal experience.** **2** not of one's public or professional life; private: *a letter marked 'Personal'* ○ *We'll join you later — we have something personal to discuss first.* ○ *His* **personal life** *is a mystery to his colleagues.* **3** [attrib] done or made by a particular person: *The President made a* **personal appearance** *at the event.* ○ *I shall give the matter my personal attention.* **4** [attrib] done or made for a particular person: *a personal account* (ie a bank account, etc in a person's name) ○ *We offer a personal service to our customers.* ○ *Will you do it for me as a personal favour?* **5** referring to a person's private life or concerns, esp in a way that suggests disapproval or criticism: *The argument was becoming too personal.* ○ *Try to avoid making personal comments.* **6** [attrib] of the body: *personal cleanliness/hygiene* ○ *personal danger/injury.*

▶ **personally** /-ənəli/ *adv* **1** not represented by another; in person: *All letters will be answered personally.* ○ *All meals are personally supervised by the restaurant owner.* **2** as a person: *I don't know him personally, but I've read his books.* **3** (often at the beginning of a statement) as far as I am concerned; for myself: *Personally, I don't like him at all.* ○ *Personally speaking/Speaking for myself, I'm in favour of the scheme.* ⇨ note at HOPEFUL. **IDM** **take sth** ˈ**personally** to be offended by sth: *I'm afraid he took your remarks personally.*

■ ˌ**personal as**ˈ**sistant** *n* (*abbr* **PA**) a secretary who assists an official or a manager.

ˈ**personal column** *n* a column in a newspaper or other publication for private messages or short advertisements.

ˌ**personal com**ˈ**puter** *n* (*abbr* **PC**) a small computer designed for use at home or in an office. ⇨ picture at COMPUTER.

ˌ**personal** ˈ**pronoun** *n* (*grammar*) (abbreviated as *pers pron* in this dictionary) any of the pronouns *I, me, she, her, he, him, we, us, you, they, them, it, one.*

ˌ**personal** ˈ**stereo** *n* = WALKMAN.

personality /ˌpɜːsəˈnæləti/ *n* **1** [C] the characteristics and qualities of a person seen as a whole: *have an artistic/an assertive/a likeable/a strong personality* ○ *personality traits* ○ *People usually wear clothes that express their personality.* **2** [U,C] qualities that make sb different and interesting: *We need someone with lots of personality to organize the party.* ○ *She was very beautiful, but seemed to lack personality.* See also SPLIT PERSONALITY. **3** [C] a famous person, esp in the world of entertainment or sport: *personalities from the theatre world* ○ *a television/sports personality.*

■ **perso**ˈ**nality cult** *n* (*often derog*) the excessive admiration of a famous person, esp a political leader.

personalize, -ise /ˈpɜːsənəlaɪz/ *v* **1** (esp passive) to mark sth to show that it belongs to a particular person: [Vnpr] *handkerchiefs personalized with her initials* [Vn] *a personalized number-plate* (ie one on a car, with letters chosen by the owner). **2** to cause sth to become concerned with personal matters or feelings rather than with general issues: [Vn] *We don't want to personalize the argument.*

personify /pəˈsɒnɪfaɪ/ *v* (*pt, pp* **-fied**) **1(a)** to treat sth as if it were a human being: [Vn] *The sun and the moon are often personified in poetry.* **(b)** to represent an idea, a quality, etc in human form: [Vn-n] *Justice is often personified as a blindfolded woman holding a pair of scales.* [also Vn] **2** to be an example in human form of a quality or characteristic, esp one possessed to an extreme degree: [Vn] *He personifies the selfishness of modern society.* ○ *He is kindness personified.*

▶ **personification** /pəˌsɒnɪfɪˈkeɪʃn/ *n* **1** [U] the

action of treating sth as a human being or of representing it in human form: *the personification of autumn in Keats's poem.* **2** [C usu *sing*] ~ **of sth** a person who possesses a quality or characteristic to an extreme degree: *He looked the personification of misery.* ○ *She was the personification of elegance.*

personnel /ˌpɜːsəˈnel/ *n* **1** [pl *v*] the people employed in an organization; staff(1a): *skilled/trained personnel* ○ *sales/technical/security personnel* ○ *Army personnel are not allowed to leave the base.* **2** [U, Gp] a department in a firm which deals with employees, esp with their appointment and welfare: *work in personnel/in the personnel department* ○ *Personnel is/are organizing the training of new members of staff.*

■ ˌper·son'nel **carrier** *n* a military vehicle for transporting troops, etc.

perspective

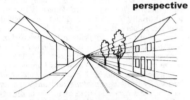

perspective /pəˈspektɪv/ *n* **1** [U] the art of drawing solid objects on a flat surface so as to give the right impression of their height, width, depth and position in relation to each other: *a perspective drawing* ○ *The artist shows a fine command of perspective.* ⇨ picture. **2** [C] a view(2), esp one stretching into the distance: *get a perspective of the whole valley.* **3** [C] a particular attitude towards sth; a point of view (POINT¹): *see things from a global/feminist/Christian perspective* ○ *gain a different perspective on the problem* ○ *keep a sense of perspective* (ie see things in a balanced way). **IDM in / into / out of perspective 1** showing the right/wrong relationship between visible objects: *draw the buildings in perspective* ○ *That tree on the left of the picture is out of perspective.* **2** in a way that does not exaggerate any aspect/that exaggerates some aspects: *keep a problem in perspective* (ie not think it is worse than it is) ○ *put the events into an international perspective* ○ *get things badly out of perspective.*

Perspex /ˈpɜːspeks/ *n* [U] (*propr*) a strong transparent plastic material that is often used instead of glass.

perspicacious /ˌpɜːspɪˈkeɪʃəs/ *adj* (*fml*) having or showing great judgement or INSIGHT(1a); PERCEPTIVE: *a perspicacious remark* ○ *He was perspicacious enough to realize that things were soon going to change.* ▶ **perspicaciously** *adv.* **perspicacity** /ˌpɜːspɪˈkæsəti/ *n* [U].

perspire /pəˈspaɪə(r)/ *v* (*fml*) to give out sweat through the skin: [V] *perspiring profusely after a game of squash.*
▶ **perspiration** /ˌpɜːspəˈreɪʃn/ *n* [U] **(a)** sweat: *Beads of perspiration stood out on his forehead.* **(b)** the process of giving out sweat: *Perspiration cools the skin in hot weather.*

persuade /pəˈsweɪd/ *v* **1** ~ **sb** (**into sth / doing sth**) to lead sb to do sth through reasoning or argument: [Vn, Vn.to inf] *Please try and persuade her (to come with us).* [Vn] *She is easily persuaded.* [Vnpr] *He can persuade himself into believing anything he wants to believe.* **2** ~ **sb** (**of sth**) (*rather fml*) (esp passive) to make sb believe sth; to convince sb: [Vn] *I am not fully persuaded by the evidence.* [Vn.that] *She finally persuaded us that she was telling the truth.* [Vnpr] *He was eventually persuaded of the value of regular exercise.*

persuasion /pəˈsweɪʒn/ *n* **1** [U] the action of per-

suading sb or of being persuaded: *She has great powers of persuasion.* ○ *After a lot of persuasion, he agreed to come.* ○ *Gentle persuasion is more effective than force.* ○ *I wasn't planning to go, but I'm open to persuasion.* **2** [C] a set of esp religious or political beliefs: *people of all persuasions.*

persuasive /pəˈsweɪsɪv/ *adj* able to persuade; convincing: *have a persuasive manner* ○ *persuasive arguments/reasons/excuses.* ▶ **persuasively** *adv.* **persuasiveness** *n* [U]: *the persuasiveness of his argument.*

pert /pɜːt/ *adj* (esp of a girl or young woman) showing or suggesting a cheerful lack of respect; cheeky (CHEEK): *a pert reply* ○ *her pretty, pert face.* ▶ **pertly** *adv.* **pertness** *n* [U].

pertain /pəˈteɪn/ *v* ~ **(to sth)** (*fml*) **1** to be connected with or relevant to sth: [Vpr] *evidence pertaining to the case* [V] *The same rules no longer pertain.* **2** (esp *law*) to belong to sth as a part of it: [Vpr] *the manor and the land pertaining to it.*

pertinacious /ˌpɜːtɪˈneɪʃəs; US -tnˈeɪʃəs/ *adj* (*fml*) holding firmly to an opinion or a course of action; STUBBORN(1). ▶ **pertinaciously** *adv.* **pertinacity** /ˌpɜːtɪˈnæsəti; US -tnˈæ-/ *n* [U].

pertinent /ˈpɜːtɪnənt; US -tənənt/ *adj* ~ **(to sth)** (*fml*) relevant to sth: *pertinent comments/points/questions* ○ *remarks not pertinent to the matter we are discussing.* ▶ **pertinently** *adv: pertinently observed detail.* **pertinence** /-əns/ *n* [U].

perturb /pəˈtɜːb/ *v* (*fml*) (esp passive) to make sb very worried; to disturb(3) sb: [Vn] *I was surprised but not perturbed by his sudden outburst.*
▶ **perturbation** /ˌpɜːtəˈbeɪʃn/ *n* [U, C] (*fml*) the state or an instance of being perturbed.
perturbed /-ˈtɜːbd/ *adj: a rather perturbed young man* ○ *feel increasingly perturbed about her behaviour.*

peruse /pəˈruːz/ *v* (*fml or joc*) to read sth, esp carefully or thoroughly: [Vn] *peruse a document* ○ *Would you care to peruse the wine list?* ▶ **perusal** /pəˈruːzl/ *n* [U, sing]: *knowledge gained by regular perusal of newspapers* ○ *a brief perusal of the agenda.*

pervade /pəˈveɪd/ *v* to spread to and be perceived in every part of sth: [V] *a pervading atmosphere of warmth* [Vn] *The smell of flowers pervaded the house.* ○ *Her work is pervaded by nostalgia for a past age.*

pervasive /pəˈveɪsɪv/ *adj* present and seen or felt everywhere: *a pervasive smell of damp* ○ *Her influence is all pervasive.* ▶ **pervasively** *adv.* **pervasiveness** *n* [U].

perverse /pəˈvɜːs/ *adj* (of people or their actions, intentions, etc) showing a deliberate and STUBBORN(1) desire to behave in a way that is wrong, unreasonable or unacceptable: *a perverse child* ○ *a perverse decision/judgement* (ie one that ignores the facts or evidence) ○ *a perverse desire to shock* ○ *his perverse refusal to see a doctor* ○ *It would be perverse to take a different view.* ○ *She takes a perverse pleasure in upsetting her parents.* ▶ **perversely** *adv: She continued, perversely, to wear shoes that hurt her feet.* **perversity** *n* [U].

perversion /pəˈvɜːʃn; US -ʒn/ *n* **1(a)** [U] (esp sexual) behaviour or desires that are considered abnormal or unacceptable: *sexual perversion.* **(b)** [C] an instance of this: *His craving for publicity has become almost a perversion.* **2** [U, C] the changing of sth from right to wrong, or an instance of this: *the perversion of innocence/justice* ○ *Her account was a perversion of the truth.*

pervert /pəˈvɜːt/ *v* **1** to turn sth away from its proper nature or use: [Vn] *pervert the truth/the course of justice.* **2** to make sb, their mind, etc turn away from what is considered right or natural: [Vn] *pervert (the mind of) a child* ○ *a potentially great man perverted and destroyed by power* ○ *Do pornographic books pervert those who read them?*

[Vnn] = verb + noun + noun   [V-adj] = verb + adjective   For more help with verbs, see Study pages **B4–8**.

▶ **pervert** /'pɜːvɜːt/ n (derog) a person whose (esp sexual) behaviour is considered abnormal or unacceptable.

perverted adj showing PERVERSION(1): a perverted desire to make others suffer ∘ sexually perverted acts.

peseta /pə'seɪtə/ n the unit of money in Spain.

pesky /'peski/ adj (infml esp US) causing trouble; annoying: pesky mosquitoes.

peso /'peɪsəʊ/ n (pl -os) the unit of money in many Latin American countries and the Philippines.

pessary /'pesəri/ n (medical) 1 a small piece of solid medicine placed in a woman's VAGINA and left to dissolve to cure an infection. 2 a device placed in a woman's VAGINA to prevent her becoming pregnant or to support the WOMB.

pessimism /'pesɪmɪzəm/ n [U] the tendency to be sad and anxious and to believe that the worst will happen: There is general pessimism in the company about future job prospects. Compare OPTIMISM.

▶ **pessimist** /-ɪst/ n a person who expects the worst to happen: It's easy to sell insurance to a pessimist. Compare OPTIMIST.

pessimistic /,pesɪ'mɪstɪk/ adj ~ (about sth): have a pessimistic view of life ∘ be pessimistic about the future ∘ I think the original sales figures were too pessimistic. **pessimistically** /-kli/ adv.

pest /pest/ n 1 an insect or animal that destroys plants, food, etc: Stores of grain are frequently attacked by pests, especially rats. ∘ garden pests such as slugs or greenfly ∘ pest control. Compare VERMIN 1. 2 (infml) an annoying person or thing: That child is an absolute pest — he keeps ringing the doorbell and then running away!

pester /'pestə(r)/ v ~ sb (for sth); ~ sb (with sth) to annoy or disturb sb, esp with frequent requests: [Vn] He told the photographers to stop pestering him. ∘ The horses were continually pestered by flies. [Vnpr] Beggars pestered him for money. ∘ He pestered her with requests for help. [Vn.to inf] They keep pestering me to read to them.

pesticide /'pestɪsaɪd/ n [C, U] a chemical substance used to kill pests (PEST 1), esp insects: crops sprayed with pesticide ∘ vegetables grown without the use of pesticides. See also INSECTICIDE.

pestilence /'pestɪləns/ n [U] (arch) any fatal infectious disease that spreads quickly through large numbers of people.

▶ **pestilential** /,pestɪ'lenʃl/ adj 1 [attrib] (infml) very annoying. 2 (arch) of or like a pestilence.

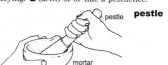

pestle ▸ **pestle**

mortar

pestle /'pesl/ n a heavy tool with a round end used for crushing and grinding foods, drugs, etc to powder, esp in a special bowl called a mortar. ⇨ picture.

pet /pet/ n 1 an animal or a bird kept as a companion and treated with care and affection: They have many pets, including three cats. ∘ a pet mouse/hamster ∘ pet food ∘ a pet shop (ie where animals are sold as pets). 2 (often derog) a person treated with special favour, esp in a way that seems unfair to others: She's **teacher's pet**. 3 [attrib] a thing that is given special attention by sb: Filling in forms is my **pet hate**. ∘ Once he starts talking about censorship you can't stop him — it's his **pet subject**. 4 (infml) (used as a term of affection, esp for a child or young woman): Be a pet and post this letter for me. ∘ That's kind of you, pet.

▶ **pet** v (-tt-) 1 [Vn] to treat an animal, etc with

affection, esp by stroking it. 2 (infml) (of two people) to kiss and touch each other sexually: [V] heavy (ie passionate) petting.

■ **'pet name** n a name used to show affection. A pet name may be different from, or a short form of, a person's real name. ⇨ App 5.

petal /'petl/ n any of the delicate coloured divisions of the head of a flower: a flower with five petals ∘ 'rose petals. ⇨ picture at FLOWER.

▶ **-petalled** (US **-petaled**) /'petld/ (forming compound adjs) having the specified number or type of petals: a four-petalled flower.

petard /pe'tɑːd/ n **IDM** **hoist/hoisted by/with one's own petard** ⇨ HOIST.

peter /'piːtə(r)/ v **PHR V** **peter out** to decrease or fade gradually before coming to an end: The path petered out at the edge of the wood. ∘ The protest campaign soon petered out for lack of support.

petit bourgeois /,peti 'bʊəʒwɑː/ n [sing], adj (a member) of the lower middle class in society.

petite /pə'tiːt/ adj (approv) (of a girl or woman) having a small and attractive figure.

petition /pə'tɪʃn/ n ~ (to sb) 1 a formal written request, esp one signed by many people appealing to sb in authority: organize/present/sign a petition ∘ a petition against closing the Steel Works ∘ a petition for tighter safety standards ∘ **get up** (ie start) a petition about sth. 2 (law) a formal application made to a court of law.

▶ **petition** v ~ for/against sth; ~ sb (for sth) to make a formal request to sb for sth: [Vnpr] petition the government for equal opportunities at work [Vn, Vn.to inf] petition Parliament (to allow shops to open on Sunday). **PHR V** **petition for sth** (law) to make a formal request for sth in a court of law: petition for divorce. **petitioner** /-ʃənə(r)/ n a person who petitions, esp in a court of law.

petrel /'petrəl/ n a black and white sea bird that can fly far from land.

petrify /'petrɪfaɪ/ v (pt, pp -fied) 1 to make sb very frightened, esp so they are unable to think or act: [Vn] The idea of making a speech in public petrified him. 2 to change or make sth change into stone: [Vn] petrified trees [V] (fig) Without new ideas institutions tend to petrify. ▶ **petrified** adj: an expression of fear ∘ She was absolutely petrified (with fright).

petro- comb form 1 of petrol: petrochemical. 2 of rocks: petrology.

petrochemical /,petrəʊ'kemɪkl/ n [C] any of various substances obtained from oil or natural gas: the petrochemical industry.

petrol /'petrəl/ (US **gasoline**, **gas**) n [U] a liquid obtained by refining PETROLEUM, used as fuel in car engines, etc: fill a car up with petrol ∘ the petrol tank of a car ∘ an increase in petrol prices ∘ leaded/unleaded petrol ∘ petrol-driven vehicles. ⇨ picture at CAR. Compare DIESEL 2.

■ **'petrol bomb** n a simple bomb made of a bottle filled with petrol that explodes when it is thrown and hits something.

'petrol station (Brit) (also **'filling station**, **'service station**, US **'gas station**) n a place beside a road where petrol and other goods are sold to motorists. Compare GARAGE 2.

petroleum /pə'trəʊliəm/ n [U] mineral oil that forms under the ground or the sea and is extracted through holes bored (BORE¹) beneath it. Petroleum is refined to produce petrol, PARAFFIN, DIESEL oil, etc.

■ **pe,troleum 'jelly** (US also **petrolatum** /,petrə'leɪtəm/) n a substance obtained from petroleum, used eg on the skin as an OINTMENT or to LUBRICATE machinery.

petrology /pə'trɒlədʒi/ n [U] the scientific study of rocks.

petticoat /'petɪkəʊt/ n a light loose garment hanging from the shoulders or the waist, worn by a girl or woman under a dress: *white lacy petticoats*.

pettifogging /'petɪfɒgɪŋ/ adj (*dated or derog*) (**a**) (of a person) paying too much attention to unimportant detail. (**b**) unimportant; TRIVIAL: *pettifogging objections*.

pettish /'petɪʃ/ adj (*derog*) (**a**) (of a person) bad-tempered, like a child that is not allowed to do what it wants to do. (**b**) (of a remark or an act) said or done in a bad-tempered or unreasonable way: *a pettish jerk of the hand*. ▶ **pettishly** adv.

petty /'peti/ adj (-**ier**, -**iest**) (*derog*) **1**(**a**) small or TRIVIAL; unimportant: *petty details/squabbles/restrictions* ○ *petty crime/theft* (ie the theft of articles of small value) ○ *petty criminals/thieves/offenders*. (**b**) concerned with small and unimportant matters: *petty observance of the regulations*. **2** unkind or mean²(2): *petty spite/jealousy* ○ *a petty desire for revenge*. ▶ **pettiness** n [U].
■ ˌpetty ˈcash n [U] a usu small amount of money kept in an office for small payments.
ˌpetty ˈofficer n (*abbr* PO) an officer in the navy. ⇨ App 6.

petulant /'petjʊlənt/ US -tʃə-/ adj bad-tempered or unreasonable, esp because one cannot do or have what one wants: *a petulant and jealous wife* ○ *petulant children*. ▶ **petulantly** adv. **petulance** /-əns/ n [U]: *He tore up the letter in a fit of petulance*.

petunia /pə'tjuːniə; US -'tuː-/ n a garden plant with white, pink, purple or red flowers.

pew /pjuː/ n **1** any of the long seats with a back that are placed in rows in a church for people to sit on. ⇨ picture at CHURCH. **2** (*Brit infml joc*) a seat: *Take a pew* (ie Sit down)!

pewit = PEEWIT.

pewter /'pjuːtə(r)/ n [U] (**a**) a grey metal made by mixing tin with lead, used esp formerly for making cups, dishes, etc: *a pewter tankard*. (**b**) objects made of this: *a fine collection of old pewter*.

PG /ˌpiː 'dʒiː/ abbr (of films) parental guidance, ie containing scenes not suitable for young children.

PGCE /ˌpiː dʒiː siː 'iː/ abbr (in Britain) Postgraduate Certificate of Education.

pH /ˌpiː 'eɪtʃ/ n [sing] (*chemistry*) a measurement of the acid¹(1) or ALKALI level of a solution or a substance. A reading of below 7 indicates that the solution is acidic (ACID¹), and above 7 that it is alkaline (ALKALI): *a pH of 7.5* ○ *test the pH level of the soil*.

phalanx /'fælæŋks/ n a number of people standing close together for a particular purpose: *a solid phalanx of riot police*.

phallus /'fæləs/ n (*pl* **phalluses** or rarely **phalli** /-laɪ/) (**a**) (*fml*) a PENIS, esp when hard and swollen. (**b**) an image of this, used esp in certain religions. ▶ **phallic** /'fælɪk/ adj of or like a phallus: *phallic imagery/symbols*.

phantasm /'fæntæzəm/ n (*fml*) a thing seen in the imagination; an illusion.
▶ **phantasmagoria** /ˌfæntæzmə'gʊriə; US -'gɔːriə/ n (*fml*) a changing scene of real or imagined figures, eg as seen in a dream or created as an effect in a film. **phantasmagorical** /-'gɒrɪkl; US -'gɔːrɪkl/ adj.

phantom /'fæntəm/ n **1** a ghost: *the phantom of his dead father* ○ *the legend of the phantom ship*. **2** [often attrib] (**a**) any imagined thing; an illusion: *phantom visions created by a tormented mind* ○ *a phantom pregnancy* (ie a condition in which a woman wrongly believes she is pregnant and in which some of the symptoms of being pregnant may appear). (**b**) anything that has been thought or said to exist but does not: *phantom assets/contracts* ○ *The much publicized world market turned out to be a phantom*.

Pharaoh /'feərəʊ/ n (the title of) the ruler of ancient Egypt.

Pharisee /'færɪsiː/ n **1** a member of an ancient Jewish religious group, known for their strict obedience to the traditional and written law. **2** (*derog*) a person who pretends to have high moral and religious standards but is not good or religious in a genuine way; a hypocrite (HYPOCRISY).

pharmaceutical /ˌfɑːmə'suːtɪkl; Brit also -'sjuː-/ (esp *pl*) a drug or medicine: *the development of new pharmaceuticals* ○ *a pharmaceuticals company*. ▶ **pharmaceutical** adj of or connected with the making and distribution of pharmaceuticals: *the pharmaceutical industry* ○ *Japan's top ten pharmaceutical companies*.

pharmacist /'fɑːməsɪst/ n a person who has been trained to prepare medicines and sell them to the public: *waiting for the pharmacist to make up her prescription* ○ *buy cough medicine at the pharmacist's* (ie pharmacist's shop). Compare CHEMIST.

pharmacology /ˌfɑːmə'kɒlədʒi/ n [U] the scientific study of drugs and their use in medicine.
▶ **pharmacological** /ˌfɑːmələ'lɒdʒɪkl/ adj: *pharmacological research*.
pharmacologist /-'kɒlədʒɪst/ n a person who specializes in pharmacology.

pharmacopoeia (US also **pharmacopeia**) /ˌfɑːmələ'piːə/ n a book containing a list of medicines and drugs and directions for their use, esp one published officially for use in a particular country.

pharmacy /'fɑːməsi/ n **1** [C] (**a**) (US also **drugstore**) a shop or part of a shop where medicines and drugs are sold. (**b**) a place, eg in a hospital, where medicines are prepared. **2** [U] the study of the preparation of medicines and drugs: *be trained in pharmacy*. See also DISPENSARY.

pharynx /'færɪŋks/ n (*pl* **pharynges** /fə'rɪndʒiːz/) (*anatomy*) the place at the back of the mouth and nose where the passages to the nose and to the mouth connect with the throat. ⇨ picture at THROAT.
▶ **pharyngitis** /ˌfærɪn'dʒaɪtɪs/ n [U] (*medical*) a disease causing painful swelling of the pharynx.

phase /feɪz/ n **1** a stage in a process of change or development: *a phase of history* ○ *the second phase of a project* ○ *buildings constructed during Phase 1* ○ *the most exciting phase of one's career* ○ *My son is going through a difficult phase.* ○ *In young children being fussy about food is usually only a **passing phase**.* **2** each of the shapes of the bright parts of the moon that are visible at given times, esp the new moon (NEW), the first quarter, the last quarter and the full moon (FULL). **IDM in/out of phase** being/not being in the same state at the same time: *The two sets of traffic lights were out of phase* (ie Their changes did not correspond with each other) *and several accidents occurred*.
▶ **phase** v (esp passive) to plan or do sth in stages: [Vn] *a phased withdrawal of troops* ○ *Cutbacks were phased over a 5-year period*. **PHRV** ˌphase sth ˈin to introduce sth gradually or in stages: *The new regulations will be phased in from August*. ˌphase sth ˈout to withdraw or stop using sth gradually or in stages: *The old filing system will have been phased out by 1998*.

PhD /ˌpiː eɪtʃ 'diː/ abbr Doctor of Philosophy: *have/be a PhD in History* ○ *Bill Crofts PhD*.

pheasant /'feznt/ n (**a**) [C] (*pl* unchanged or **pheasants**) a large bird

pheasant

with a long tail, the male of which is brightly coloured. Pheasants are sometimes shot for sport and food. ⇨ picture. (**b**) [U] its flesh prepared as food: *roast pheasant.*

phenol /ˈfiːnɒl/ *n* [U] = CARBOLIC.

phenomenal /fəˈnɒmɪnl/ *adj* very remarkable; extraordinary: *the phenomenal success of her books* ○ *The rocket travels at a phenomenal speed.* ○ *The response to the appeal fund has been phenomenal.*
▶ **phenomenally** /-nəli/ *adv* to an extraordinary degree: *Interest in the subject has increased phenomenally.*

phenomenology /fɪˌnɒmɪˈnɒlədʒi/ *n* [U] (*techn*) the branch of philosophy that concentrates on what is perceived by the senses in contrast to what is independently real or true about the world.

phenomenon /fəˈnɒmɪnən; *US* -nɒn/ *n* (*pl* **phenomena** /-ɪnə/) **1** a fact or an event, esp in nature or society: *natural/social/historical phenomena* ○ *A total eclipse of the sun is a rare phenomenon.* ○ *Bankruptcy is a common phenomenon in an economic recession.* **2** a remarkable person, thing or event: *the phenomenon of their rapid rise to power.*

pheromone /ˈferəməʊn/ *n* a substance produced by an animal as a chemical signal, to attract another animal of the same species.

phew /fjuː/ *interj* (a short soft sound made by blowing out or sucking in one's breath, used to express relief or surprise): *Phew! That was a close thing — I thought he was going to hit us.*

phial /ˈfaɪəl/ (also **vial** /ˈvaɪəl/) *n* a small glass container, eg for liquid medicine or PERFUME(1).

philander /fɪˈlændə(r)/ *v* (*usu derog*) (of a man) to have a lot of casual sexual relationships with women: [V] *He spent his time drinking and philandering.* ○ *She complained to everyone of Henry's philandering.*
▶ **philanderer** /-dərə(r)/ *n* (*derog*) a man who philanders: *Roger's a terrible philanderer.*

philanthropy /fɪˈlænθrəpi/ *n* [U] kindness and good deeds inspired by concern for people's welfare.
▶ **philanthropic** /ˌfɪlənˈθrɒpɪk/ *adj*: *philanthropic organizations* (eg to help poor people) ○ *philanthropic motives.*
philanthropist /fɪˈlænθrəpɪst/ *n* a person who is concerned for the welfare or benefit of others and who supports good causes, esp by giving money: *The university was founded by a millionaire philanthropist.* Compare MISANTHROPE.

philately /fɪˈlætəli/ *n* [U] the collection and study of postage stamps (STAMP² 1).
▶ **philatelic** /ˌfɪləˈtelɪk/ *adj*.
philatelist /fɪˈlætəlɪst/ *n* a person who collects or knows a lot about postage stamps (STAMP² 1).

-phile *comb form* (forming *ns* and *adjs*) (a person who is) fond of: *Anglophile* ○ *bibliophile.* Compare -PHOBE.

philharmonic /ˌfɪlɑːˈmɒnɪk/ *adj* (used in the names of orchestras, music societies, etc) devoted to music: *the Boston Philharmonic Orchestra.*

-philia *comb form* (forming *ns*) (esp abnormal) love of: *paedophilia.* ⇨ -PHOBIA.

philistine /ˈfɪlɪstaɪn; *US* -stiːn/ *n* (*derog*) a person who has no interest in or understanding of the arts, or is HOSTILE(1) to them: *He dismissed critics of his work as philistines.* ▶ **philistine** *adj* (*derog*) [usu attrib]: *a philistine attitude.* **philistinism** /-tɪnɪzəm/ *n* [U] (*derog*): *the philistinism of the popular press.*

phil(o)- *comb form* liking or being fond of: *philanthropy* ○ *philology.*

philology /fɪˈlɒlədʒi/ *n* [U] the science or study of the development of language or of a particular language. Compare LINGUISTICS.
▶ **philological** /ˌfɪləˈlɒdʒɪkl/ *adj* of or concerning philology.

philologist /fɪˈlɒlədʒɪst/ *n* an expert in philology.

philosopher /fəˈlɒsəfə(r)/ *n* **1(a)** a person who has developed a particular set of theories and beliefs: *the Greek philosopher Aristotle.* (**b**) a person who studies or teaches philosophy: *political philosophers.* **2** (*infml*) a person who thinks deeply about things: *He seems to be a bit of a philosopher.*

philosophy /fəˈlɒsəfi/ *n* **1(a)** [U] the search for knowledge and understanding of the nature and meaning of the universe and of human life: *moral philosophy* ○ *the philosophy of history* ○ *a philosophy lecturer.* (**b**) [C] a particular set or system of beliefs resulting from this search for knowledge: *the philosophy of Jung* ○ *conflicting philosophies.* **2** [C] a set of beliefs or an attitude to life that is a guiding principle for behaviour: *one's philosophy of life* ○ *free-market philosophies* ○ *Take every opportunity that presents itself — that's my philosophy!*
▶ **philosophical** /ˌfɪləˈsɒfɪkl/ (also **philosophic** /-ˈsɒfɪk/) *adj* **1(a)** of philosophy: *philosophical principles/speculations.* (**b**) devoted to philosophy: *philosophical writings/discussions.* **2** (of people) thinking deeply about things: *a philosophical character.* **3** ~ (**about sth**) having or showing courage and a calm attitude towards sth: *She was/seemed remarkably philosophical about her loss.* ○ *He took the news with a philosophical smile.* **philosophically** /-kli/ *adv*: *She accepted the court's decision philosophically.* **philosophize, -ise** /fəˈlɒsəfaɪz/ *v* ~ (**about/on sth**) (*often derog*) to talk about serious matters, esp in a boring or POMPOUS way: [Vpr] *philosophizing about the nature and existence of a god* [also V].

phlegm /flem/ *n* [U] a thick substance which forms in the nose and throat, esp when one has a cold, and which can be removed by coughing, etc.
▶ **phlegmatic** /fleɡˈmætɪk/ *adj* not easily made angry or upset; calm: *a phlegmatic temperament.*

phobia /ˈfəʊbiə/ *n* an extreme or abnormal dislike or fear of sth: *learn to control/conquer one's phobia about flying.*

-phobia *comb form* (forming *ns*) an extreme or abnormal fear of: *claustrophobia* ○ *xenophobia.* Compare -PHILIA.
▶ **-phobe** *comb form* (forming *ns*) a person who dislikes sth: *Anglophobe* ○ *xenophobe.* Compare -PHILE.
-phobic *comb form* (forming *adjs*) having or showing extreme or abnormal fear of: *claustrophobic* ○ *xenophobic.*

phoenix /ˈfiːnɪks/ *n* (in stories) a bird of the Arabian desert, said to live for several hundred years before burning itself and then being born again from its ashes.

phone /fəʊn/ *n* (**a**) a telephone: *The phone is ringing — answer it, will you?* ○ *I must just* **make a quick phone call.** ○ *the phone bill* ○ *order sth over the phone* ○ *a portable phone* ○ *He gave them his phone number.* See also CAR PHONE, ENTRYPHONE, PAY PHONE. (**b**) the part of the telephone that one speaks into; the RECEIVER(1): *My little girl picked up the phone.* ○ *He banged the phone down.* ○ *I took the phone off the hook.* See also ANSWERPHONE. **IDM** **be on the ˈphone 1** to be talking to sb using the phone: *He's been on the phone to Rachel for an hour.* **2** (*Brit*) (of a person, business, etc) to have a telephone: *I'm afraid I'm not on the phone.*
▶ **phone** *v* ~ (**sb**)(**up**) to make a telephone call to sb: [V] *Did anybody phone?* [Vp, Vnp] *Phone (them) up and find out what time the play starts, will you?* [Vpr] *I asked them to phone for a taxi.* [Vn] *Don't forget to phone New York.* ○ *For further information phone 0181 690 9368.* **PHR V** **phone in** to make a telephone call to one's place of work or to a radio or television station: *Hundreds of listeners phoned in to complain.*

■ **'phone book** n = TELEPHONE DIRECTORY.

'phone box (also **'phone booth**, **'telephone box**, **'telephone kiosk**, *Brit* **'call-box**) n a small structure of various designs containing a public telephone, eg in the street or at a station.

'phone-in (*Brit*) (*US* **'call-in**) n a radio or television programme in which questions, comments, etc made by ordinary people on the telephone are broadcast: *a live phone-in show.*

'phone tapping n = TELEPHONE TAPPING.

-phone *comb form* **1** (forming ns) an instrument using or making sound: *a telephone* ○ *a dictaphone* ○ *a xylophone.* **2** (forming adjs) speaking a particular language: *anglophone* ○ *francophone.*

▶ **-phonic** *comb form* (forming adjs) of an instrument using or making sound: *telephonic.*

phoneme /'fəʊniːm/ n (*linguistics*) any one of the set of smallest distinctive speech sounds in a language that distinguish one word from another: *In English, the 's' in 'sip' and the 'z' in 'zip' represent two different phonemes.*

▶ **phonemic** /fə'niːmɪk/ adj of or concerning phonemes.

phonetic /fə'netɪk/ adj (*linguistics*) **1** (of a method of writing speech sounds) using a symbol for each distinct sound or sound unit: *a phonetic symbol/alphabet/transcription.* **2** (of spelling) corresponding closely to the sounds represented: *Spanish spelling is phonetic.* **3** of or concerning the sounds of human speech.

▶ **phonetically** /-klɪ/ adv.

phonetics n [sing v] the study of speech sounds and their production.

phoney (also **phony**) /'fəʊni/ adj (-ier, -iest) (*infml derog*) (**a**) (of a person) pretending or claiming to be what one is not: *There's something very phoney about him.* (**b**) (of a thing) false: *a phoney American accent* ○ *phoney insurance claims* ○ *The story sounds phoney to me.*

▶ **phoney** (also **phony**) n (pl **-neys** or **-nies**) a phoney person or thing: *The man's a complete phoney.*

■ **,phoney 'war** n a period of time during which opponents are at war but do not fight: (*fig*) *His speech marked the end of the phoney war and the start of an intense campaign for votes.*

phon(o)- *comb form* of sound or sounds: *phonetic.*

phonology /fə'nɒlədʒi/ n [U] (*linguistics*) the study of speech sounds, esp in a particular language. ▶ **phonological** /ˌfəʊnə'lɒdʒɪkl/ adj.

phony = PHONEY.

phooey /'fuːi/ interj (*infml*) (used to indicate that one does not believe or has contempt for sth that has just been said).

phosphate /'fɒsfeɪt/ n [C, U] any salt or compound containing PHOSPHORUS, esp one used for helping plants to grow: *phosphate-free washing powder* ○ *the use of nitrates and phosphates to fertilize the soil.*

phosphorescent /ˌfɒsfə'resnt/ adj (**a**) producing light without heat or with so little heat that it cannot be felt. (**b**) producing a faint GLOW(1) in the dark: *phosphorescent toadstools.* Compare FLUORESCENT. ▶ **phosphorescence** /-sns/ n.

phosphorus /'fɒsfərəs/ n [U] (*symb* P) (*chemistry*) a chemical element. Phosphorus is a pale yellow poisonous substance resembling wax that glows in the dark and catches fire easily. ⇨ App 7.

photo /'fəʊtəʊ/ n (pl **-os** /-təʊz/) (*infml*) = PHOTOGRAPH: *She took a photo of us.* ○ *a colour photo* ○ *a photo frame/album.*

■ **'photo booth** n a small enclosed structure where one can put money in a machine and get a photograph of oneself in a few minutes, eg in a post office or at a railway station.

'photo-call n a time arranged in advance when

photographers or television cameras are officially invited to take pictures of a famous person.

,photo 'finish n (esp in horse-racing) a finish of a race where the leaders are so close together that only a photograph of them passing the winning-post (WIN) can show which is the winner.

'photo opportunity n an occasion when a famous person can deliberately take advantage of a dramatic situation or setting to be photographed by press photographers or television cameras.

photo- *comb form* **1** of or using light: *photosynthesis.* **2** of or using photography: *photocopy* ○ *photogenic.*

photocopy /'fəʊtəʊkɒpi/ n a photographic copy of sth written, printed or drawn.

▶ **photocopy** v (pt, pp **-pied**) (**a**) to make a photographic copy of sth written, printed or drawn: [Vn] *photocopy a form/a letter* ○ *Can you get these photocopied for me by 3 o'clock?* [V] *He's doing some photocopying.* (**b**) to be able to be photocopied: [V] *These old maps probably won't photocopy very well.* **photocopier** /-piə(r)/ n a machine used for making photocopies.

photofit /'fəʊtəʊfɪt/ n a picture of a person, esp one wanted by the police, made by putting together photographs of different features of the face.

photogenic /ˌfəʊtəʊ'dʒenɪk/ adj looking attractive in photographs: *I'm not very photogenic.* ○ *a photogenic village.*

photograph /'fəʊtəɡrɑːf; *US* -ɡræf/ (also *infml* **photo**) n a picture formed by means of the chemical action of light on film, and then transferred to specially prepared paper: *get a photograph enlarged* ○ *The book is illustrated with colour photographs and drawings.* ○ *His photograph appeared in the local paper.* ○ *Please enclose a recent passport-sized photograph of yourself.* ○ *This photograph of the ship was taken in July 1992.*

▶ **photograph** v **1** to take a photograph of sb/sth: [Vn] *photograph the bride/a military base/a rare plant.* **2** to appear in a particular way in photographs: [Vadv] *He photographs well/badly.* Compare FILM² 1. **photographer** /fə'tɒɡrəfə(r)/ n a person who takes photographs, esp as a job: *pose for photographers* ○ *one of the top wildlife/fashion/portrait photographers in the world* ○ *a competition open to both amateur and professional photographers.* Compare CAMERAMAN.

photographic /ˌfəʊtə'ɡræfɪk/ adj [usu attrib] of, used in or produced by photography: *photographic equipment/images/techniques* ○ *a photographic record of the event.* **,photographic 'memory** n (usu sing) the ability to remember things in great detail after seeing them. **photographically** /-klɪ/ adv.

photography /fə'tɒɡrəfi/ n [U] the art or process of taking photographs: *colour/flash/aerial photography* ○ *Her hobby is photography.* ○ *Did you see that film about Antarctica — the photography was superb!*

photon /'fəʊtɒn/ n (*physics*) a unit of ELECTROMAGNETIC energy.

Photostat (also **photostat**) /'fəʊtəstæt/ n (*propr*) a PHOTOCOPY: *a Photostat copy.*

photosynthesis /ˌfəʊtəʊ'sɪnθəsɪs/ n [U] the process by which green plants convert carbon dioxide (CARBON) and water into food using energy from sunlight.

phrase /freɪz/ n **1**(**a**) (*grammar*) a group of words without a verb, esp one that forms part of a sentence: *'The green car' and 'at half past four' are phrases.* See also NOUN PHRASE. (**b**) a group of words forming a short expression, esp an IDIOM(3) or a clever, striking way of saying sth: *a memorable/well-chosen/significant phrase* ○ *learn a few phrases of Hindi* ○ *She was, in her own evocative phrase, a*

[Vnn] = verb + noun + noun   [V-adj] = verb + adjective   For more help with verbs, see Study pages **B4–8**.

woman without a past. See also CATCHPHRASE. **2** (*music*) a short distinct passage forming part of a longer passage. **IDM** **to coin a phrase** ⇨ COIN *v.* **a turn of phrase** ⇨ TURN².

▶ **phrasal** /ˈfreɪzl/ *adj* of or concerning a phrase.

■ **phrasal verb** *n* (abbreviated as *phr v* in this dictionary) a simple verb combined with an adverb or a PREPOSITION, or sometimes both, to make a new verb with a meaning that is different from that of the simple verb, eg *go in for, win over, blow up.*

▶ **phrase** *v* **1** to express sth in words in the specified way: [Vnadv] *phrase one's criticism very carefully* [Vnpr] *regulations phrased in terms of national security.* **2** to divide music into phrases, esp in performance: [Vnadv] *an elegantly phrased aria* [also Vn]. **phrasing** *n* [U] **1** (*music*) the manner of dividing a passage into phrases, in composing or performing: *The singer was criticized for her poor phrasing.* **2** = PHRASEOLOGY.

phraseology /ˌfreɪziˈɒlədʒi/ *n* [U] the choice or arrangement of words; the wording (WORD): *The phraseology was typical of a school report, with expressions like 'tries hard' and 'could do better'.*

■ **phrase book** *n* a book listing common expressions translated into another language, esp for use by travellers in a foreign country: *buy a Spanish phrase book for one's holiday.*

phut /fʌt/ *adv* **IDM** **go phut** (*infml*) (esp of electrical or mechanical things) to stop functioning; to fail or break down (BREAK¹): *The washing-machine has gone phut.*

phylum /ˈfaɪləm/ *n* (*pl* **phyla** /-lə/) (*biology*) a major group to which animals or plants belong.

physical /ˈfɪzɪkl/ *adj* **1(a)** of or for the body: *physical fitness/strength* ○ *physical exercise/education/training* ○ *physical contact* ○ *physical and mental changes of old age.* **(b)** actual; in person: *She was intimidated by his physical presence.* **2** of or concerning things that can be experienced through the five senses, eg touch or sight, rather than perceived through the mind or spirit: *the physical world/universe.* **3** of or according to the laws of nature: *It is a physical impossibility to be in two places at once.* **4** [attrib] of the natural features of the world: *physical geography* ○ *a physical map* (ie one showing mountains, rivers, etc). **5** [attrib] of or concerning natural forces and things that are not alive: *the physical sciences* ○ *physical chemistry.* **6** (*infml euph*) using violence: *Are you going to co-operate or do we have to get physical?*

▶ **physical** *n* (*infml*) a medical examination to see if one is fit.

physicality /ˌfɪzɪˈkæləti/ *n* [U] the condition or quality of being physical: *the sheer physicality of his piano playing.*

physically /-kli/ *adv* **1** in a way that relates to the body: *be physically exhausted/fit/handicapped/abused* ○ *I don't find him physically attractive.* ○ *He did not provide her with the support she needed, either emotionally or physically.* **2** according to the laws of nature: *That's physically impossible!*

■ **physical jerks** *n* [pl] (*infml*) exercises done to keep fit.

physician /fɪˈzɪʃn/ *n* (*dated or fml*) a doctor, esp one specializing in areas of treatment other than SURGERY(1). Compare SURGEON.

physicist /ˈfɪzɪsɪst/ *n* an expert in PHYSICS: *a nuclear physicist.*

physics /ˈfɪzɪks/ *n* [sing v] the scientific study of the properties of matter and energy, eg heat, light, sound, GRAVITY(1), and the relationships between them: *nuclear physics* ○ *the laws of physics* ○ *a physics textbook* ○ *study the physics of the electron.*

physio /ˈfɪziəʊ/ *n* (*pl* **-os**) (*infml*) **1** [U] PHYSIOTHERAPY. **2** a physiotherapist (PHYSIOTHERAPY).

physio- *comb form* **1** of or relating to nature or

natural forces or functions: *physiology.* **2** physical: *physiotherapy.*

physiognomy /ˌfɪziˈɒnəmi; *US* -ˈɒɡnəmi/ *n* (*fml*) the shape and features of a person's face.

physiology /ˌfɪziˈɒlədʒi/ *n* [U] **(a)** the scientific study of the normal functions of living things: *reproductive physiology* ○ *the anatomy and physiology of the brain.* **(b)** the way in which a particular living thing functions: *plant physiology* ○ *the physiology of the snake.*

▶ **physiological** /ˌfɪziəˈlɒdʒɪkl/ *adj* **(a)** of or concerning the functions of living things: *the physiological effects of space travel* ○ *physiological adaptations/changes.* **(b)** of or concerning physiology: *physiological research.* **physiologically** *adv.*
▶ **physiologist** /ˌfɪziˈɒlədʒɪst/ *n* an expert in physiology.

physiotherapy /ˌfɪziəʊˈθerəpi/ (also *infml* **physio**) *n* [U] the treatment of disease, injury or weakness in the joints or muscles by exercises, MASSAGE and the use of light and heat: *have two hours of physiotherapy daily.*

▶ **physiotherapist** /-pɪst/ (also *infml* **physio**) *n* a person trained to give physiotherapy.

physique /fɪˈziːk/ *n* the general appearance and size of a person's body, esp of the muscles: *a fine/muscular/well-developed physique* ○ *He doesn't have the physique for such heavy work.*

pi /paɪ/ *n* (*geometry*) the symbol (π) representing the RATIO of the CIRCUMFERENCE of a circle to its DIAMETER, ie 3.14159.

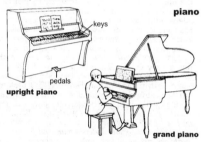

piano

keys

pedals

upright piano

grand piano

piano¹ /piˈænəʊ/ *n* (*pl* **-os** /-nəʊz/) (also *fml* **pianoforte** /piˌænəʊˈfɔːti; *US* -tei/) a large musical instrument played by pressing the black or white keys of a KEYBOARD(1b), thus causing small hammers to strike metal strings to produce different notes: *play a tune on the piano* ○ *a piano teacher/lesson* ○ *piano music* ○ *Ravel's piano concerto in G* ○ *He composed several short pieces for (the) piano.* ⇨ picture. See also GRAND PIANO, UPRIGHT PIANO.

▶ **pianist** /ˈpɪənɪst/ *n* a person who plays the piano: *a famous concert/jazz pianist* ○ *a good/an accomplished pianist.*

piano² /ˈpjɑːnəʊ/ *adv, adj* (*music*) (*abbr* **p**) soft(ly). Compare FORTE².

piazza /piˈætsə; *US* piˈɑːzə/ *n* a public square, esp in an Italian town.

pic /pɪk/ *n* (*infml*) a picture.

picaresque /ˌpɪkəˈresk/ *adj* (*fml*) (of a style or type of literature) describing the adventures of a person who is rather rough and dishonest but easy to like.

piccolo /ˈpɪkələʊ/ *n* (*pl* **-os** /-ləʊz/) a small musical instrument similar to a FLUTE but producing higher notes. ⇨ picture at MUSICAL INSTRUMENT.

pick¹ /pɪk/ *v* **1** to choose or select sb/sth from a group of people or things, esp after careful thought: [Vn] *She picked the largest cake on the plate.* ○ *He's been picked to play for the first team.* ○ *He picked his words carefully* (eg tried to express himself so as not to annoy sb). ⇨ note at CHOOSE. **2** to gather and remove flowers, vegetables, etc from the place where they grow: [Vn] *flowers freshly picked from the garden* ○ *pick plums/strawberries/broad beans* ○ *go blackberry picking* [Vnn] *Please can you pick me a lettuce?* [also Vnpr]. **3(a)** ~ **sth (from/off sth)** to remove sth from a surface, esp with one's fingers: [Vnpr] *pick a hair from one's collar* ○ *pick the nuts off the top of the cake.* (**b**) to remove small pieces of matter from sth, esp in order to clean it: [Vn-adj] *The dogs picked the bones clean* (ie removed all the meat from the bones). [Vn] *pick one's teeth* (ie use a small pointed piece of wood, etc to remove tiny pieces of food from one's teeth) ○ *Stop picking* (ie removing dried MUCUS from the inside of) *your nose!* **4** to open a lock without a key, esp by using a piece of bent wire or a pointed tool: [Vn] *The burglars had picked the lock on the back door.* **IDM** **have a bone to pick with sb** ⇨ BONE. **pick and 'choose** to make a selection from a number of things, esp in a slow, careful or FUSSY(2) way: *You have to take any job you can get — you can't pick and choose.* **pick sb's 'brains** (*infml*) to question sb who knows a lot about sth in order to obtain information that one can use oneself: *Can I pick your brains about the best hi-fi system to buy?* **pick a 'fight/'quarrel (with sb)** to cause a fight/quarrel with sb deliberately, eg by behaving aggressively. **pick 'holes in sth** to find faults in sth: *It was easy to pick holes in his argument.* **pick sb's 'pocket** to steal money, etc from sb's pocket. **pick/pull/tear sth to pieces** ⇨ PIECE¹. **pick/pull/tear sth to pieces** ⇨ PIECE¹. **pick up the bill/tab** (*infml*) to pay for sth, esp sth expensive: *Taxpayers will have to pick up the bill.* **pick up the 'pieces/'threads** to restore one's life or a situation to a more normal state, esp after a shock or disaster: *Their lives were shattered by the tragedy and they are still trying to pick up the pieces.* **pick up 'speed** to go faster: *The train began to pick up speed.* **pick one's 'way** to walk carefully, choosing the driest, safest, etc places to put one's feet: *She picked her way delicately along the muddy path.* **PHRV** **'pick at sth** **1** to eat food in very small amounts or without having an appetite for it: *Sparrows picked at the crumbs.* ○ *He never seems hungry and just picks at his food.* **2** to pull sth with repeated small movements: *He picked at the knots uselessly with cold fingers.*

pick sb 'off to aim carefully at a person, an animal, etc, esp one of a group, and shoot her, him or it: *A sniper hidden on a roof picked off three of the soldiers on patrol.*

'pick on sb **1** to blame, punish or criticize sb repeatedly and often unfairly: *She felt that her teachers were picking on her.* **2** to choose sb, esp for an unpleasant task: *I know they need someone to go to the meeting, but why did they have to pick on me!*

pick sb/sth 'out **1** to choose sb/sth from a number of people/things: *She was picked out from thousands of applicants for the job.* ○ *He picked out the ripest peach.* **2** to distinguish sb/sth from people or things around them: *pick out sb/sb's face in a crowd* ○ *The window frames are picked out in blue against the white walls.* **pick sth 'out** **1** to play a tune, eg on the piano, esp in a HESITANT way and without having written music to follow. **2** to discover or recognize sth after careful study: *pick out recurring themes in an author's work.*

pick sth 'over to examine fruit, clothing, etc carefully, esp in order to select the best or throw away what is bad: *Pick over the lentils in case there are any stones amongst them.*

pick 'up **1** to become better; to improve: *Trade always picks up in the spring.* ○ *We're waiting until the weather picks up a bit.* See also PICK-UP 4. **2** (*infml*) to start again; to continue: *Let's pick up where we left off* (ie finished) *yesterday.* **pick oneself 'up** to stand up again after falling: *He picked himself up and brushed himself down.* **pick**

sb 'up **1** to go somewhere to collect sb in one's car, esp having previously arranged to do so: *I'll pick you up at 7 o'clock.* **2** to stop and allow sb to get into one's car and travel with one: *He picked up a hitchhiker.* **3** to rescue sb from the sea, from an isolated place, etc: *The lifeboat picked up all the survivors.* **4** (*infml often derog*) to begin talking to sb whom one has never met before with the intention of having a casual sexual relationship with them: *He picked up the girl at a college disco.* ○ *She's living with some man she picked up on the beach.* See also PICK-UP 2. **5** (*infml*) (of the police) to arrest sb: *The police picked him up as he was trying to leave the country.* **6** to criticize sb for sth they have just said: *Stop picking me up all the time!* **pick sb/sth 'up** **1** to take hold of and lift sb/sth: *He bent down and picked up the book from the floor.* ○ *She picked up the telephone and dialled his number.* ○ *He picked the child up in his arms and held him tight.* **2** to see or hear sb/sth, esp by means of electronic apparatus: *They picked up the yacht on their radar screen.* ○ *I'm surprised you can pick up Capital Radio this far out of London.* **pick sth 'up** **1** to learn a foreign language, a technique, etc by hearing or seeing it often, rather than by making a deliberate effort: *pick up bad habits* ○ *She soon picked up French when she went to live in Paris.* **2** to hear or learn news, gossip, etc, esp by chance: *See if you can pick up anything about their future plans.* ○ *Where on earth did you pick up that idea?* **3** to identify sth: *Scientists can now pick up early signs of the disease.* **4** to collect sth: *I've got to pick up my coat from the cleaners.* See also PICK-UP 3. **5** to buy sth, esp cheaply or by luck: *pick up a bargain* ○ *She picked up a valuable first edition at a book sale.* **6** to obtain or acquire sth: *I'll pick something up* (ie buy sth) *for dinner on my way home.* ○ *We picked up a little money doing odd jobs.* ○ *I've picked up a terrible cold from somewhere.* **7** to find and follow a route, etc: *pick up a trail/a scent* ○ *We'll pick up the motorway near Coventry.* **8** to discuss further sth that has already been mentioned: *Can I just pick up the point you made earlier?*

► **picker** *n* (esp in compounds) a person or thing that picks flowers, vegetables, etc: *apple pickers.*

■ **pick-me-up** /'pɪkmiʌp/ *n* (*infml*) a drink, esp medicine or an alcoholic drink taken as a TONIC(1) when one feels weak, tired or ill.

'pick-up *n* **1** (also **'pick-up truck**) a small van or truck with low sides and no roof at the back, used eg by farmers. ⇨ picture at JEEP. **2** (*infml derog*) a person with whom one has a sexual relationship after meeting them by chance: *casual pick-ups.* **3** an occasion when sb/sth is collected: *the security van's daily pick-up from the bank.* **4** ~ (**in sth**) (*infml*) an improvement: *the seasonal pick-up in house prices.*

pick-your-'own *adj* [usu attrib] (*abbr* **PYO**) (of fruit or vegetables) picked by the customer on the farm where they are grown: *pick-your-own strawberries* ○ *a pick-your-own farm.*

pick² /pɪk/ *n* [sing] **1** a choice; a right of selecting: *Which one would you like? Take your pick* (ie choose whichever you like). ○ *The winner has first pick of the prizes.* **2** the ~ **of sth** the best example or examples of sth: *We're reviewing the pick of this month's new books.* ○ (*infml*) *I think we got the pick of the bunch* (ie the best of a number of things or people).

pick³ /pɪk/ (also **pickaxe**, US **pickax**) *n* a large heavy tool consisting of a curved iron bar with sharp ends fixed at the centre to a wooden handle. It is used for breaking rocks, hard ground, etc: *wield a pickaxe.* ⇨ picture at AXE. See also ICE-PICK, TOOTH-PICK.

pickaxe (US also **pickax**) /'pɪkæks/ *n* = PICK³. ⇨ picture at AXE.

picket /'pɪkɪt/ n **1(a)** a worker or group of workers who stand outside the entrance to a factory, etc during a strike to try to persuade others not to enter: *Five pickets were injured in the scuffle with police.* ○ *men on picket duty.* See also FLYING PICKET. **(b)** a person or a group of people who stand outside a particular place to protest about sth. **2** an occasion on which people act as pickets: *a mass picket* ○ *organize/mount/hold a peaceful picket of the embassy.* **3** a pointed piece of wood set into the ground: *a picket fence.*

▶ **picket** v **(a)** to place pickets outside a place of work to prevent people from entering: [Vn] *The union is picketing all the company's offices.* ○ *The conference centre will be picketed.* **(b)** to act as a picket at a place of work: [V] *Some of the members did not want to picket.* [also Vn].

picketing n [U] the action of holding a picket or being a picket: *Picketing and other intimidation will be made illegal.*

■ **'picket line** n a line or group of pickets outside a place: *Fire crews refused to cross the picket line.*

pickings /'pɪkɪŋz/ n [pl] profits or gains that are easily or dishonestly earned or obtained: *He promised us* **rich pickings** *if we bought the shares immediately.* ○ *There were only slim pickings to be had on the stock market.*

pickle /'pɪkl/ n **(a)** [U] vegetables or fruit preserved in VINEGAR or salt water: *dill pickle* ○ *a cheese and pickle sandwich.* **(b)** [C usu pl] a particular vegetable or fruit preserved in this way: *a lime pickle* ○ *The dish was accompanied by a variety of pickles.* Compare CHUTNEY, RELISH 2. **IDM** **in a (sorry, pretty, etc) 'pickle** in a difficult or unpleasant situation. **pickle in the middle** (*US*) = PIG/PIGGY IN THE MIDDLE (PIG).

▶ **pickle** v to preserve vegetables, etc in VINEGAR, etc: [Vn] *pickled cucumber/onions/walnuts* ○ *herrings pickled in brine.* **pickled** adj (*infml*) drunk.

pickpocket /'pɪkpɒkɪt/ n a person who steals money, etc from other people's pockets, esp in crowded places.

picky /'pɪki/ adj (*infml derog*) difficult to please; FUSSY(2); CHOOSY: *a picky eater* ○ *She's very picky about which television programmes they watch.*

picnic /'pɪknɪk/ n **(a)** a meal packed in a box, etc and eaten later as part of a short trip taken for pleasure: *We'll go to the river and take a picnic with us.* ○ *We had a picnic by the lake.* ○ *a picnic area/basket/lunch.* **(b)** a short trip that includes a picnic: *It's a nice day — let's go for/on a picnic.* **IDM** **be no 'picnic** (*infml*) to be difficult and cause a lot of problems: *Bringing up a family when you are unemployed is no picnic.*

▶ **picnic** v (**-ck-**) to have a picnic: [Vpr] *They were picnicking in the woods.* [also V]. **picnicker** n a person who is having a picnic: *Picnickers are requested not to leave litter* (eg on a notice).

pictorial /pɪk'tɔːriəl/ adj **1(a)** in or using pictures: *a pictorial account/record of the expedition.* **(b)** having pictures; illustrated: *a pictorial encyclopedia.* **2** of or relating to pictures: *the pictorial composition of a photograph.* ▶ **pictorially** adv /-əli/

picture /'pɪktʃə(r)/ n **1** [C] **(a)** a painting, drawing, sketch, etc, esp as a work of art: *hang a picture on the wall* ○ *His picture of lions won a prize.* ○ *The little girl drew a picture of her house and coloured it in.* **(b)** a photograph: *They showed us their wedding pictures.* ○ *She's taking a picture of the children.* **(c)** a drawing or photograph of a person; a portrait: *Will you paint my picture?* ○ *He's got his picture (ie a picture showing him) in the paper.* **2** [C] an image on a television screen: *dramatic satellite pictures of the war* ○ *The picture is much clearer with the new aerial.* **3(a)** [C] a cinema film: *a low-budget picture* ○ *Have you seen her latest picture?* See also MOTION

PICTURE. **(b) the pictures** [pl] (*dated Brit infml*) the cinema: *We don't often go to the pictures.* **4** [C usu sing] **(a)** an account or description of sth that enables one to form a mental picture or impression of it: *Her book gives a good/colourful picture of everyday life in ancient Rome.* ○ *The picture presented by the report was misleading.* **(b)** a mental picture; an idea about sth: *Her description helped the police to build up an accurate picture of what had happened.* ○ *In his mind he* **formed a picture of** *where they would live.* ○ *If you study the figures closely, a gloomy/disturbing/grim picture emerges.* **5 the picture** [sing] the general situation with regard to sb/sth: *The overall picture is unchanged.* **6** (usu **a picture**) [sing] (*infml*) a beautiful person, object or scene: *The girls* **were/looked a picture** *in their pretty dresses.* **IDM** **in the 'picture** (*infml*) fully informed about sth: *Our plans are now well advanced so I need to put you in the picture.* **be/look the picture of 'health, 'happiness, etc** (*infml*) to look very healthy, happy, etc. **get the 'picture** (*infml*) to understand or appreciate a situation, esp one that is being described: *There we all were — each of us hoping that someone else would speak first. You get the picture?*

▶ **picture** v **1(a)** to form a mental image of sb/sth; to imagine sb/sth: [V.wh] *He tried to picture what it would be like to spend months entirely alone.* [Vn.ing] *She pictured him lying dead on the roadside.* [Vn] *I can still picture the house I grew up in.* **(b)** ~ **sb/sth as sth** (esp passive) to present sb/sth in a particular way: [Vn-n] *He is often pictured as an outsider.* **2** (esp passive) to show sth/sb in a picture: [Vnpr] *They were pictured against a background of flowers.* [Vnadv] *The winner was Mark Davis, pictured above with the competition judges.*

■ **'picture-book** n a book with many pictures, esp one for children.

'picture-gallery n a room or building in which paintings are displayed.

,picture 'postcard n a POSTCARD with a picture on one side.

'picture rail n a narrow strip of wood attached to the walls of a room below the ceiling and used for hanging pictures from.

'picture window n a very large window consisting of a single piece of glass. ⊳ picture at HOUSE¹.

picturesque /,pɪktʃə'resk/ adj **1** forming a pretty scene; charming: *a picturesque cottage/fishing village/stone bridge/setting.* **2** (of language) strong and vivid; striking. ▶ **picturesquely** adv. **picturesqueness** n [U].

piddle /'pɪdl/ v [V] (*infml*) to urinate (URINE).

piddling /'pɪdlɪŋ/ adj [esp attrib] (*infml derog*) small; unimportant: *piddling sums of money.*

pidgin /'pɪdʒɪn/ n [C,U] any of several languages resulting from contact between Europeans and local peoples, eg in W Africa and SE Asia, containing elements of the local language and esp English, French or Dutch: *speak in pidgin* ○ *pidgin English.* Compare CREOLE.

pie /paɪ/ n [C,U] **(a)** meat or fruit cooked in a dish lined with pastry and with a covering of pastry: *a slice of apple pie* ○ *a helping of steak and kidney pie* ○ *a pie dish* ○ *Have some more pie.* **(b)** (*US*) this without a top covering of pastry: *pecan pie.* Compare FLAN, TART¹. See also COTTAGE PIE, CUSTARD PIE, MINCE PIE, PORK PIE, SHEPHERD'S PIE. **IDM** **as easy as pie** ⊳ EASY¹. **eat humble pie** ⊳ EAT. **have a finger in every pie** ⊳ FINGER¹. **,pie in the 'sky** (*infml*) an event that is planned or hoped for but very unlikely to happen: *Their ideas about reforming the prison system are just pie in the sky.*

■ **'pie chart** n a diagram consisting of a circle divided into sections that each represent a specific proportion of the whole, eg in order to show spending in various areas in relation to total expenditure: *draw a pie chart.* ⇨ picture at CHART.

,pie-'eyed *adj* (*infml*) drunk.

piebald /ˈpaɪbɔːld/ *adj* (esp of a horse) having patches on it of two colours, usu black and white. Compare SKEWBALD.

piece¹ /piːs/ *n* **1** (usu *pl*) (**a**) any of the parts of which sth is made: *He lost one of the pieces of his model engine.* ○ *He took the clock to pieces.* ○ *The furniture is delivered in pieces and you have to assemble it yourself.* ○ *The bridge was dismantled piece by piece.* (**b**) any of the bits or parts into which sth breaks: *The vase broke/shattered into a thousand pieces.* ○ *The cup lay in pieces on the floor.* ○ *hack/pull/rip sth to pieces* ○ *The boat was smashed to pieces on the rocks.* **2** ~ (**of sth**) (esp with *of* and an uncountable *n*) (**a**) an amount or a unit of sth: *a piece of chalk* ○ *a piece of paper* ○ *buy a piece of glass to fit the window frame* ○ *put another piece of wood on the fire* ○ *get a piece of grit in one's eye.* (**b**) a slice, lump, etc of a food: *He cut her a large piece of bread/cake/meat/cheese.* ⇨ note. **3**(**a**) a single article; an item of a particular type: *a piece of furniture/jewellery/luggage.* (**b**) (esp after a number in compounds) any of the parts of a set: *a jigsaw with 1 000 pieces* ○ *a 28-piece dinner service* ○ *a 50-piece orchestra* (ie with 50 players). (**c**) any of a set of small objects or figures used in board games: *One of the white chess pieces is missing.* **4** ~ **of sth** a single instance or example of sth: *a piece of advice/information/luck/news/research* ○ *a fine/brilliant/inspired piece of work.* **5** ~ (**of sth**) (**a**) (in art, music, etc) a single work or composition: *a piece of music/poetry/sculpture* ○ *In some ways this piece is more a*

There is usually a specific word to describe a piece of something, depending on its shape, size or how it was made. The table shows some examples.

Food

cut into	
a thin, flat piece	a *slice* of bread, cheese, tomato, etc
pieces from a circle, usually of equal size	a *slice* of cake, pizza, melon, etc
a triangular shape	a *wedge* of lemon
a square piece	a *chunk/cube* of meat, fruit, etc.

broken into	
very small pieces	bread**crumbs**, biscuit **crumbs**, etc
small flat pieces	**flakes** of fish, corn**flakes**, etc

A substance

made or cut into a	
large square shape	a *block* of wood, ice
small square shape	a *cube* of sugar, an ice-**cube**
large rectangular shape	a *slab* of concrete, stone **slabs**
small rectangular shape	a *bar* of soap, chocolate
very thin, flat piece	a *sheet* of paper, plastic

torn or broken into a small piece that is	
not valuable	a *scrap* of paper, material, cloth
thin and sharp	a *splinter* of wood, glass
old and delicate or valuable	a *fragment* of glass, stone, a photograph

---

more a musical comedy than a ballet. See also MU-SEUM PIECE, PARTY PIECE. (**b**) an essay or a newspaper article: *Did you read Mary Kenny's piece in today's paper?* See also SET PIECE. **6** a coin: *a 50p piece* ○ *a five-cent piece.* **IDM** **bits and pieces** ⇨ BIT¹.

give sb a piece of one's 'mind (*infml*) to tell sb exactly what one thinks, esp when one disapproves of their behaviour. **go to 'pieces** (*infml*) (of a person) to be extremely afraid or upset and lose control of oneself: *He went completely to pieces when they told him she was dead.* **in one 'piece** (*infml*) (of a person) safe and not harmed, esp after a dangerous experience: *They were lucky to get back in one piece.* **a nasty piece of work** ⇨ NASTY. (**all**) **of a 'piece with sth** (*fml*) consistent with sth: *The new measures are all of a piece with the government's policy.* **pick/pull/tear sb to 'pieces** (*infml*) to criticize sb severely, esp when they are not present. **pick/pull/tear sth to 'pieces** (*infml*) to argue against sth; to find fault with sth. **pick up the pieces/threads** ⇨ PICK¹. **a piece/slice of the action** ⇨ ACTION. **a ,piece of 'cake** (*infml*) a thing that is very easy: *The exam was a piece of cake.* **say one's piece** ⇨ SAY. **the villain of the piece** ⇨ VILLAIN.

■ **'piece-work** *n* [U] work paid for by the amount done and not by the hours worked.

piece² /piːs/ *v* **PHRV** ,piece sth to'gether **1** to discover a story, facts, etc from separate pieces of evidence: *This account of their journey has been pieced together from personal letters and diaries.* **2** to make or assemble sth from individual pieces: *piece together torn scraps of paper in order to read what was written.*

pièce de résistance /ˌpiːˌes də reˈzɪstɒs; US ˌreziːˈstɑːns/ *n* (*pl* **pièces de résistance** /ˌpiːˌes də/) (*French*) (esp of creative work) the most important or impressive item: *The architect's pièce de résistance was the city's opera house.*

piecemeal /ˈpiːsmiːl/ *adv* one part at a time; piece by piece: *companies broken up and sold off piecemeal.*

▶ **piecemeal** *adj* arriving, done, etc piecemeal: *a piecemeal approach* ○ *piecemeal changes/reforms.*

pied /paɪd/ *adj* (esp of birds) of two or more different colours, esp black and white.

pied-à-terre /ˌpjeɪd ɑː ˈteə(r)/ *n* (*pl* **pieds-à-terre** /ˌpjeɪd ɑː/) (*French*) a small flat, usu in a town, that one does not live in as one's main home but keeps for use when necessary: *They live in Scotland but have a pied-à-terre in London.*

pier

pier /pɪə(r)/ *n* **1** a large structure built from the land out above the sea at a resort. Piers are used by people to walk along and often have restaurants and places of entertainment on them: *the fair at the end of the pier.* ⇨ picture. **2** a low structure of wood or iron built from the land out into the sea or a lake, where boats can stop and load or UNLOAD(1b) passengers or goods: *take the river bus from the pier.* Compare JETTY. **3** (*techn*) a pillar.

pierce /pɪəs/ *v* **1**(**a**) (of sharp pointed instruments) to go into or through sth: [Vn] *The arrow pierced his shoulder.* ○ (*fig rhet*) *A stab of resentment pierced her heart.* (**b**) to make a hole in or through sth, esp with

---

[Vnn] = verb + noun + noun   [V-adj] = verb + adjective   For more help with verbs, see Study pages **B4–8**.

sth sharp: [Vnpr] *pierce holes in the bottom of a tin* [Vn] *earrings for pierced ears.* **2(a)** (of light, sound, etc) to penetrate sth quickly and suddenly: [Vn] *Her shrieks pierced the air.* [Vpr] *The beam of the searchlight pierced through the darkness.* **(b)** to force a way through sth: [Vn, Vpr] *They failed to pierce (through) the stout Liverpool defence.*

▶ **piercing** *adj* **1** (of voices, sounds, etc) very high and loud; SHRILL(1): *A piercing shriek rent the air.* **2(a)** (of eyes) very bright and seeming to see through the person they are looking at: *her piercing blue eyes.* **(b)** (of a look) very direct; searching: *the cold piercing gaze of the lawyer.* **3** (of a feeling, comment, etc) very strong, and direct: *his piercing analysis/intelligence.* **4** (of wind, cold, etc) bitter; penetrating: *a piercing breeze/chill.* **piercingly** *adv*: *a piercingly cold wind.*

pierrot /ˈpɪərəʊ/ *n* a CLOWN(1) whose face is painted white and who is dressed in loose white clothes.

piety /ˈpaɪəti/ *n* [U] strong belief in a religion, shown in one's worship and general behaviour; the state of being PIOUS(1): *She is renowned for her piety.* ○ *put on a show of piety.*

piffle /ˈpɪfl/ *n* [U] (*infml derog*) nonsense; rubbish: *That's absolute piffle!*

piffling /ˈpɪflɪŋ/ *adj* (*derog*) very small and unimportant or ridiculous: *piffling complaints.*

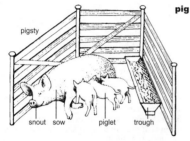

pig

pigsty

snout   sow   piglet   trough

pig /pɪɡ/ *n* **1** a domestic or wild animal with pink or black skin, short legs, a broad nose and a short tail that curls: *The pigs were grunting and squealing in their sty.* ⇨ picture. See also BOAR, GUINEA-PIG, HOG 1, SOW², SWINE 2. **2** (*infml derog*) **(a)** a person who is selfish and greedy and shows bad manners: *Don't be such a pig!* ○ *The greedy pig's eaten all the biscuits!* ○ *He made a pig of himself with the ice-cream* (ie ate too much). **(b)** a difficult or unpleasant thing, task, etc: *a pig of a job/day/exam.* **3** (*sl derog offensive*) a police officer. **IDM** **buy a pig in a poke** ⇨ BUY. **make a ¹pig's ear (out) of sth** (*infml*) to do sth badly; to make a mess of sth. **pig/piggy in the ¹middle** (*Brit*); (*US*) **pickle in the middle 1** a children's game in which two people throw a ball, etc to each other over the head of another person who has to try to catch it. **2** a person who is caught between two people who are fighting or arguing, and suffers because of it. **pigs might ¹fly** (*ironic saying esp Brit*) (used to show that one does not believe sth is true or will ever happen): *Tom give up smoking? Yes, and pigs might fly!*

▶ **pig** *v* (**-gg-**) **PHRV** ¹pig ¹out (on sth) (*sl esp US*) to eat a lot of sth: *We pigged out on pizza and chicken wings.*

piggery /ˈpɪɡəri/ *n* a place where pigs are kept or bred.

piggy /ˈpɪɡi/ *n* (*infml*) (used by or when talking to young children) a little pig. — *adj* (*infml derog*) (of features, etc) like those of a pig: *He has nasty piggy eyes.* **¹piggy bank** *n* a container with a SLOT(1) in the top for putting coins etc in. Piggy banks are used esp by children for saving money in and are often in the shape of a pig. Compare MONEY-BOX.

■ **¹pig-iron** *n* [U] a form of iron that is not pure.

pigeon /ˈpɪdʒɪn/ *n* a fairly large bird, usu grey and white in colour, sometimes shot for food. Some pigeons live on buildings in towns: *pigeon droppings* ○ *The pigeons cooed softly.* ○ *a ¹homing pigeon* (ie one trained for a sport to fly home after being released some distance away). ⇨ picture. See also CARRIER PIGEON, CLAY PIGEON, STOOL-PIGEON, WOODPIGEON. **IDM** **one's pigeon** (*Brit infml*) one's responsibility or business: *I don't care where the money comes from — that's not ¹my pigeon.* **put/set the cat among the pigeons** ⇨ CAT.

pigeon

■ **¹pigeon-hole** *n* any of a set of small boxes open at the front, esp in a desk for keeping papers in, or fixed on a wall for messages, letters, etc: *The hotel clerk put the note in her pigeon-hole.* — *v* **1** to classify sb/sth, esp in a rigid manner; to give sb/sth a label(2): [Vn] *a writer that the critics could not pigeon-hole* [also Vn-n]. **2** to put sth aside to be dealt with later and then ignore or forget it: [Vn] *The scheme was pigeon-holed after a brief discussion.*

piggyback /ˈpɪɡibæk/ *n* a ride on a person's back while he or she is walking: *Give me a piggyback, Daddy!* ▶ **piggyback** *adv*: *carry sb piggyback.*

pigheaded /ˌpɪɡˈhedɪd/ *adj* refusing to change one's opinion; STUBBORN(1): *He's obstinate and pigheaded.* ▶ **¹pig¹headedness** *n* [U].

piglet /ˈpɪɡlət/ *n* a young pig. ⇨ picture at PIG.

pigment /ˈpɪɡmənt/ *n* [U, C] **(a)** colouring matter that occurs naturally in the skin, hair, etc of living creatures. **(b)** [U, C] a substance that gives colour to dyes, paint, etc: *Only natural pigments are used to dye the wool.*

▶ **pigmentation** /ˌpɪɡmenˈteɪʃn/ *n* [U] the colouring of the skin, hair, etc by pigment: *patches of brown pigmentation on the face.*

pigmy = PYGMY.

pigskin /ˈpɪɡskɪn/ *n* [U] leather made from a pig's skin: *¹pigskin ¹gloves.*

pigsty /ˈpɪɡstaɪ/ (also **sty**) *n* **1** (*US* also **¹pigpen** /ˈpɪɡpen/) a building in which pigs are kept. ⇨ picture at PIG. **2** (*infml derog*) a very dirty or untidy place: *Honestly, this room's a pigsty!*

pigtail /ˈpɪɡteɪl/ *n* **1** (*US* **braid**) a short length of hair twisted into a PLAIT, usu worn one either side of the head by young girls: *a fat child with pigtails.* ⇨ picture at PLAIT. **2** a short length of hair, held in a loose bunch by eg an elastic band, that hangs from the back of a pig: *They grabbed hold of his pigtail and jerked his head back.* ⇨ picture at PLAIT.

pike¹ /paɪk/ *n* (*pl unchanged*) a large fish that lives in rivers, lakes, etc and has very sharp teeth.

pike² /paɪk/ *n* a type of spear with a long wooden handle, formerly used as a weapon by soldiers on foot.

pike³ /paɪk/ *n* (*dialect*) (in N England) a pointed top of a hill: *the Langdale Pikes.*

pikestaff /ˈpaɪkstɑːf/ *n* **IDM** **plain as a pikestaff** ⇨ PLAIN¹.

pilaf /ˈpiːlæf; *US* pɪˈlɑːf/ (also **pilau** /ˈpiːlaʊ/) *n* [U, C] an eastern dish of rice, vegetables and spices, often with meat or fish.

pilaster /pɪˈlæstə(r)/ *n* a flat ornamental column that projects from the wall of a building.

pilchard /ˈpɪltʃəd/ *n* a small sea-fish similar to a HERRING, eaten as food.

pile¹ /paɪl/ *n* **1** a number of things lying one on top of another: *a pile of books/clothes/wood* ○ *a huge pile of dirty washing* ○ *He arranged the notes in neat piles.* ○ *She looked in horror at the mounting pile of correspondence.* **2** (often *pl*) ~ **of sth** (*infml*) a lot of sth: *companies sitting on a pile of cash* ○ *I've got piles/a*

---

pile of work to do. **3** (*fml or joc*) a large impressive building or group of buildings: *tourists tramping round his ancestral pile.* See also PILES. **IDM** **(the) bottom/top of the 'pile** of least/greatest importance or status: *people at the bottom of the social pile* ○ *Top of the pile is the recording with Domingo.* **make a 'pile** (*infml*) to earn a lot of money: *I bet they made an absolute pile out of the deal.*

pile² /paɪl/ *v* **(a)** ~ **sth (up)** to put things one on top of the other; to form a pile of things: [Vnpr] *She piled furniture into the spare room.* ○ *Goods of every kind were piled around me.* [Vnp] *Pile the logs up outside the door.* [also Vn]. **(b)** ~ **A in(to)/on(to) B;** ~ **B with A** to load sth with sth: [Vnpr] *Pile plenty of coal on the fire.* ○ *She piled everything into a suitcase and left.* [Vnadv] *The sink was piled high with dishes.* [Vnpr] (*fig*) *The situation grew more serious as blunder was piled on blunder.* **IDM** **pile it 'on** (*infml*) to exaggerate: *It's probably not as bad as she says — she does tend to pile it on.* **pile on the 'agony** (*infml*) to make an unpleasant situation worse: *The latest tax increase is just piling on the agony.* **PHR V** **pile into sth / out of sth; pile in/out (of a number of people)** to enter/leave sth in a rush, without order or control: *The children piled noisily out of the bus.* ○ *The taxi arrived and we all piled in.* **,pile 'up** to increase in quantity; to accumulate: *Evidence was piling up against them.* ○ *Her debts are piling up.*
■ **'pile-up** *n* a crash involving several vehicles: *Thick fog has caused several pile-ups on the motorway.*

pile³ /paɪl/ *n* a heavy column of wood, metal or concrete placed upright in the ground, a river, etc, eg as a foundation for a building or support for a bridge: *pile moorings.*
■ **'pile-driver** *n* **1** a machine for forcing piles into the ground. **2** a very heavy blow, kick, etc.

pile⁴ /paɪl/ *n* [U] the soft surface of carpets or of fabrics such as VELVET, formed by many small threads: *the thick pile of a bath towel* ○ *a deep pile carpet.* Compare NAP².

piles /paɪlz/ *n* [pl] = HAEMORRHOIDS.

pilfer /'pɪlfə(r)/ *v* ~ **(sth) (from sb/sth)** to steal things of little value or in small quantities: [V] *He was caught pilfering.* [Vpr, Vnpr] *She had been pilfering (small amounts) from the petty cash for months.* ▶ **pilferage** /'pɪlfərɪdʒ/ *n* [U]: *losses due to damage or pilferage.*

pilgrim /'pɪlgrɪm/ *n* a person who travels to a holy place for religious reasons, eg to show respect for a particular saint: *Muslim pilgrims on their way to Mecca* ○ *devout pilgrims visiting the shrine.* ▶ **pilgrimage** /-ɪdʒ/ *n* [C,U] a journey made by a pilgrim: *go on/make an annual pilgrimage to Benares* ○ *a place of pilgrimage* (ie one visited by pilgrims). **2** [C] a journey to a place associated with sb/sth that one respects: *a pilgrimage to Shakespeare's birthplace.*

pill /pɪl/ *n* **1** [C] a small flat round piece of medicine made to be swallowed whole: *a vitamin pill* ○ *Take three pills daily after meals.* Compare CAPSULE. See also PEP PILL, SLEEPING-PILL. **2 the pill** [sing] (*infml*) a pill taken regularly by women to prevent them becoming pregnant: *She's on the pill* (ie taking contraceptive (CONTRACEPTION) pills). ○ *My doctor says I should go on the pill.* **IDM** **a bitter pill** ⇨ BITTER. **sugar/sweeten the pill** to make sth unpleasant seem less unpleasant.

pillage /'pɪlɪdʒ/ *n* [U] (*fml*) the action of stealing or damaging property, esp by soldiers in war: *horrific accounts of widespread rape and pillage.*
▶ **pillage** *v* to rob sb/sth of goods, crops, etc with violence, as in war: [Vn] *The town was pillaged by the invading army.* [Vnpr] (*fig*) *money pillaged from*

pension funds [V] *They went looting and pillaging.* See also LOOT, PLUNDER.

pillar /'pɪlə(r)/ *n* **1(a)** a tall upright piece of stone, wood or metal used eg as support for a building, or as an ornament or a MONUMENT. ⇨ picture at CHURCH. **(b)** a thing in the shape of this: *a pillar of fire/smoke.* **2** ~ **of sth (a)** a strong supporter of sth; an important member of sth: *a pillar of the Church/the establishment* ○ *a scandal involving several pillars of society* (ie highly respected people). **(b)** a fundamental part or feature of a system, an organization, etc: *dismantling the pillars of apartheid* ○ *eroding one of the great pillars of domestic policy, the benefits system.* **IDM** **(go, be driven, etc) from ,pillar to 'post** (to go, etc) from one person or thing to another without achieving anything.
■ **'pillar-box** *n* (*dated Brit*) a box in the street for posting letters in. It is about five feet high and painted bright red: *pillar-box red.* Compare LETTER-BOX, POSTBOX.

pillbox /'pɪlbɒks/ *n* a small concrete shelter for soldiers, often partly underground, from which a gun can be fired.

pillion /'pɪliən/ *n* a seat for a passenger behind the driver of a motor cycle (MOTOR): *a pillion passenger/seat.* ▶ **pillion** *adv*: *ride pillion.*

pillory /'pɪləri/ *v* (*pt, pp* **-ried** /-lərid/) (esp passive) to attack or mock sb/sth publicly: [Vn] *She was pilloried in the press for her extravagant parties.*
▶ **pillory** *n* (usu *sing*) a wooden frame, with holes for the head and hands, into which people were locked in former times as a punishment. ⇨ picture.

pillory

pillory

pillow /'pɪləʊ/ *n* a cushion used to support the head, esp in bed: *plump up the pillows* ○ *She lay back/fell back onto her pillow.*
▶ **pillow** *v* to rest or support sth on or as if on a pillow: [Vn] *He lay with his head pillowed in her lap.*

pillowcase /'pɪləʊkeɪs/ (also **'pillowslip** /'pɪləʊslɪp/) *n* a cloth cover for a PILLOW, which can be removed.

pilot /'paɪlət/ *n* **1** a person who operates the controls of an aircraft: *a fighter pilot* ○ *The accident was caused by pilot error.* ⇨ picture at HANG-GLIDING. **2** a person with special knowledge of a canal, the entrance to a harbour, etc, whose job is to guide ships through them. See also AUTOMATIC PILOT, COPILOT.
▶ **pilot** *adj* [attrib] done as an experiment, esp on a small scale, to test sth before it is introduced on a large scale: *a 'pilot project/study/survey* ○ *a pilot edition of a new language course.*
pilot *v* **1** ~ **sb/sth (through sth)** to act as a pilot of sth: [Vn] *pilot a plane* [Vnpr] *pilot a ship through the Panama Canal* ○ (*fig*) *pilot a bill* (ie help its progress) *through parliament.* **2** to test sth by means of a pilot scheme: [Vn] *Schools in this area are piloting the new biology course.*
■ **'pilot-light** *n* a small flame that burns continuously, eg on a gas COOKER or BOILER(2), and lights a larger flame when the gas is turned on.
'Pilot Officer *n* (*Brit*) an officer in the Royal Air Force. ⇨ App 6.

pimento /pɪ'mentəʊ/ *n* (*pl* **-os**) a small red pepper(2) with a mild taste.

pimp /pɪmp/ *n* a man who controls prostitutes and lives on the money they earn.
▶ **pimp** *v* [V, Vpr] ~ **(for sb)** to find customers for a prostitute or BROTHEL; to act as a pimp.

pimple /'pɪmpl/ *n* a small raised spot on the skin: *a pimple on one's chin* ○ *teenage pimples.* See also GOOSE-PIMPLES.

▶ **pimply** /ˈpɪmpli/ *adj* having pimples: *pimply skin* ○ *a pimply youth.*

pin¹ /pɪn/ *n* **1** [C] **(a)** a short thin piece of stiff wire with a sharp point at one end and a round head at the other, used for fastening together pieces of cloth, paper, etc. **(b)** (esp in compounds) a similar piece of wire with a sharp point and a decorated head, used for a special purpose: *a diamond pin* ○ *a lapel pin.* See also TIE-PIN. **2** [C] (esp in compounds) a short piece of wood or metal for various special purposes: *a 2-pin electric plug* ○ *Stainless steel pins were inserted into his spine to strengthen it.* ➪ picture at SOCKET. See also DRAWING-PIN, HAIRPIN, NINEPIN, ROLLING-PIN, SAFETY PIN. **3** [C] a piece of metal on a hand grenade (HAND¹) that stops it from exploding. **4 pins** [pl] (*infml*) legs: *He's not as quick on his pins as he was.* **5** (in golf) a stick with a flag on top of it, placed in a hole to mark its position: *The ball stopped 5 feet short of the pin.* **IDM** **for two ˈpins** (*Brit*) (used to indicate that one could easily be persuaded to do sth, even though one realizes it would not be sensible): *For two pins I'd tell my boss what I think of him.* **hear a pin drop** ➪ HEAR.

■ **ˈpin-money** *n* [U] a small amount of money for extra expenses: *She earns a bit of pin-money doing ironing for other people.*

ˌpins and ˈneedles *n* [U] a tingling (TINGLE 1) sensation in a part of the body, esp a limb, caused by the blood flowing again after being stopped by pressure: *He woke with pins and needles in his foot.*

pin² /pɪn/ *v* **(-nn-)** ~ **sth (to/on sth/sb)**; ~ **sth (together)** to attach sth with a pin or pins: [Vnp] *Pin the bills together so you don't lose them.* [Vnpr] *a note pinned to the document* ○ *The medal was pinned to/on his chest.* ○ (*fig*) *We're* ***pinning all our hopes on you*** (ie relying on you completely). [also Vn]. **PHR V** **ˈpin sb/sth against/to/under sth** to make it impossible for sb/sth to move: *They pinned him against the wall.* ○ *His arms were pinned to his sides.* ○ *She was pinned under the wreckage of the car.* **ˌpin sth ˈback/ˈdown/ˈup** to fasten sth with pins in the position specified: *He was pinning the notice back up on the board.* ○ *She pinned up her long hair to keep cool.* **ˌpin sb ˈdown 1** to make sb unable to move, esp by holding them firmly: *He was pinned down by his attackers.* **2** to make sb be specific or declare their intentions clearly: *She's a difficult person to pin down.* **ˌpin sb ˈdown (to sth / doing sth)** to make sb agree to sth: *You'll find it difficult to pin him down to (naming) a price.* **ˌpin sth ˈdown** to define sth exactly: *There's something wrong with the colour scheme but I can't quite pin it down.* **ˌpin sth on sb** to make sb seem responsible or take the blame for sth: *The bank manager was really to blame, though he tried to pin the whole fiasco on a clerk.*

■ **ˈpin-up** *n* (*infml*) **(a)** a picture of an attractive person, eg a film star or a model, for fixing on a wall. **(b)** a person shown in such a picture.

PIN /pɪn/ *abbr* (also **PIN number** *n*) a personal identification number (issued by a bank, etc to a customer for use with a CASHCARD).

pinafore /ˈpɪnəfɔː(r)/ *n* (*esp Brit*) a loose garment without sleeves, worn over clothes to keep them clean. ➪ picture at APRON.

pinball /ˈpɪnbɔːl/ *n* [U] a game in which small metal balls are guided down a sloping board and score points by bouncing off numbered pins and other obstacles: *a pinball machine.*

pince-nez /ˌpæ̃s ˈneɪ/ *n* (*pl* unchanged) [sing or pl *v*] a pair of spectacles with a spring that fits on the nose, instead of parts at the sides which fit over the ears.

pincer /ˈpɪnsə(r)/ *n* **1 pincers** [pl] a tool made of two crossed pieces of metal and used for gripping and pulling things, eg for pulling nails out of wood:

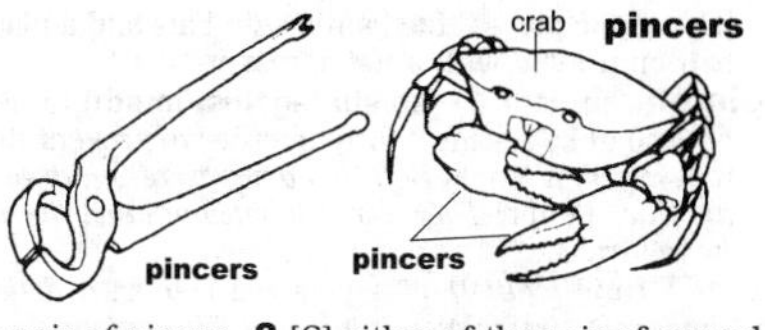

a pair of pincers. **2** [C] either of the pair of curved claws (CLAW 2) of certain types of SHELLFISH: *the crab's pincers.* ➪ picture. ➪ picture at SHELLFISH.

■ **ˈpincer movement** *n* a military attack by forces advancing on an enemy position from two sides.

pinch /pɪntʃ/ *v* **1(a)** to take or hold sth in a tight grip between the thumb and finger: [Vn] *He pinched the child's cheek playfully.* [Vnp] *To stop a bleeding nose, tilt the head back and pinch the nostrils together.* **(b)** to hurt sb by holding their flesh in this way: [Vn] *The little girl was crying because somebody had pinched her.* ○ *I was so amazed I had to pinch myself in case it was all a dream.* **(c)** to have sth in a tight grip between two hard things that are pressed together: [Vn] *The door pinched my finger as it shut.* **2** (esp of shoes) to hurt sb because of being too tight: [V, Vn] *These new shoes pinch (me).* **3** ~ **sth (from sb/sth)** (*Brit infml*) to take sth without the owner's permission; to steal sth: [Vnpr] *He's been pinching money from the cashbox.* [Vn] *Who's pinched my dictionary?* **PHR V** **ˌpinch sth ˈoff/ˈout** to remove sth by pinching: *pinch off the dead flowers.*

▶ **pinch** *n* **1** an act of pinching sb/sth between the finger and thumb: *She gave him a pinch (on the arm) to wake him up.* **2** as much as can be held between the tips of the thumb and first finger: *Add a pinch of salt.* **IDM** **at a ˈpinch** (*infml*) just possibly, if it is absolutely necessary: *We can get six people round this table, at a pinch.* **feel the pinch** ➪ FEEL¹. **take sth with a pinch of ˈsalt** to think that sth is not likely to be true; to believe sth only partly.

pinched *adj* (of a person's face, etc) pale and tense, eg because of cold, hunger or worry: *her thin, pinched features.*

pincushion /ˈpɪnkʊʃn/ *n* a small pad used for sticking pins in when they are not being used.

pine¹ /paɪn/ *n* **(a)** (also **ˈpine tree**) [C] a tree that produces cones (CONE 5) and has thin sharp leaves throughout the year. Pines grow in cool northern regions: *a pine forest* ○ *pine needles* ○ *pine-scented soap* (ie smelling of pines). ➪ picture. **(b)** [U] its pale soft wood, used in making furniture, floors, etc: *a solid pine dresser.*

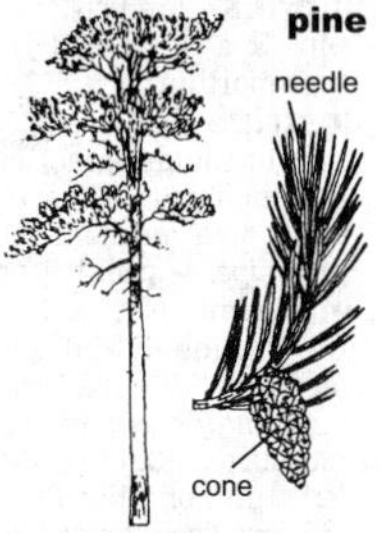

pine² /paɪn/ *v* **1** [V] to be very unhappy, esp because sb has died or gone away. **2** ~ **(for sb/sth)** to want or miss sb/sth very much: [Vpr] *a dog pining for its master.* **PHR V** **pine away** to become ill or grow thin and weak because of grief until one dies: *She lost all interest in living and just pined away.*

pineapple /ˈpaɪnæpl/ *n* [C, U] a large juicy tropical fruit with sweet yellow flesh and a prickly skin: *fresh/tinned pineapple* ○ *a can of pineapple chunks/rings* ○ *a glass of ˈpineapple juice.* ➪ picture at FRUIT.

ping /pɪŋ/ *n* the short sharp ringing sound, eg of a hard object hitting a hard surface: *the ping of a spoon hitting a glass* ○ *There was a loud ping as the guitar string broke.*

▶ **ping** *v* to make a ping: [V] *a sudden pinging sound.*

ping-pong /ˈpɪŋpɒŋ/ (*infml*) (also **ˈtable tennis**) *n*

[U] a game played like tennis with bats and a plastic ball on a table with a net across it.

pinion /'pɪnɪən/ v ~ **sb/sth (against/to sth)** to tie or hold sb or sb's arms tightly in order to prevent them moving: [Vn, Vnpr] *Both his arms were pinioned (to his side).* [Vnpr] *They were pinioned against the wall by the truck.*

pink¹ /pɪŋk/ adj **1** of a pale red colour: *a delicate shade of rose/salmon pink* ○ *a pink glow in the evening sky* ○ *go/turn pink with embarrassment.* See also SHOCKING PINK. **2** (*infml*) having or showing slightly left-wing (LEFT²) political views. Compare RED¹ 4. **IDM** **be tickled pink** ⇨ TICKLE.
▶ **pink** n **1** [U, C] a pink colour: *pale pinks and blues* ○ *Pink is her favourite colour.* **2** [U] pink clothes: *dressed in pink.* **3** [C] a garden plant with sweet-smelling pink, red or white flowers. **IDM** **in the 'pink** (*infml joc*) in very good health; very well.
pinkish adj slightly pink: *a pinkish glow/tint.*
■ **,pink 'gin** n [U, C] a drink of gin mixed with a special liquid that gives it a bitter flavour.

pink² /pɪŋk/ (*US* **ping** /pɪŋ/) v [V] (of a car engine) to make small explosive sounds when not running properly; to knock²(5).

pinkie (also **pinky**) /'pɪŋki/ n (*Scot or US*) the smallest finger of the human hand; the little finger (LITTLE¹). ⇨ picture at HAND¹.

pinking shears /'pɪŋkɪŋ ʃɪəz/ n [pl] special SCISSORS used for cutting fabric in a way that prevents it from fraying (FRAY² 1) at the edges. ⇨ picture at SCISSORS.

pinnacle /'pɪnəkl/ n **1** the highest point; the PEAK¹(1): *reach the pinnacle of one's career/fame.* **2** a high pointed piece of rock. **3** a small pointed ornament built on to a roof. ⇨ picture at CHURCH.

pinny /'pɪni/ n (*Brit infml*) a PINAFORE.

pinpoint /'pɪnpɔɪnt/ n a very small area, esp of light.
▶ **pinpoint** adj [attrib] absolutely exact: *navigate a plane with pinpoint accuracy.*
pinpoint v (**a**) to find the exact position of sth: [Vn] *pinpoint the spot on a map.* (**b**) to define sth exactly: [Vn] *pinpoint the areas in most urgent need of help* ○ *It's difficult to pinpoint precisely what went wrong.*

pinprick /'pɪnprɪk/ n **1** a PRICK²(3b) caused by a pin. **2** a thing that is annoying although small and unimportant.

pinstripe /'pɪnstraɪp/ n (**a**) [C] a very narrow white line in the design of cloth, esp of the type used for making formal suits: *a pinstripe suit.* (**b**) [U, C] such cloth or a garment made of it: *dressed in (a) grey pinstripe.* ▶ **pinstriped** adj.

pint /paɪnt/ n **1** (*abbr* **pt**) (**a**) (*Brit*) a unit of measure for liquids and some dry goods, 1/8 of a GALLON (equal to 0.568 of a litre): *a pint of beer/milk/shrimps* ○ *Add half a pint of double cream.* (**b**) (*US*) a similar measure (equal to 0.473 of a litre). ⇨ App 2. **2** (*Brit*) (**a**) a pint of milk: *Two pints today, please.* (**b**) a pint of beer: *They stopped at the pub for a pint.* **IDM** **put a quart into a pint pot** ⇨ QUART.
■ **'pint-sized** adj (*infml*) very small.

pioneer /,paɪə'nɪə(r)/ n **1** a person who is the first to study and develop a new area of knowledge, culture, etc: *architectural pioneers* ○ *pioneer work* ○ *They were pioneers in the field of microsurgery.* **2** a person who is among the first to go into an area or a country to settle or work there: *land cleared by the early pioneers* ○ *pioneer wagons* ○ *the pioneer spirit.*
▶ **pioneer** v to be the first person to develop new methods; to help the early development of sth: [Vn] *She pioneered the use of the drug.* ○ *The design was pioneered in the 1970s.*
pioneering adj [usu attrib] introducing new ideas and methods: *the pioneering early days of radio* ○ *pioneering research.*

pious /'paɪəs/ adj **1** having or showing a deep re-

spect for God and religion: *a pious Muslim.* **2** (*derog*) only pretending to be moral and good to impress other people; insincere: *She's always ready with her pious phrases.* ○ *He dismissed his critics as pious do-gooders.* **3** sincere but unlikely to be fulfilled: *Such reforms seem likely to remain merely pious hopes.* ▶ **piously** adv.

pip¹ /pɪp/ (*esp Brit*) (*US also* **seed**) n a small hard seed in a fruit: *apple/grape/orange pips.* ⇨ picture at FRUIT.

pip² /pɪp/ n (usu *pl*) a short high sound used esp as a time signal on the radio or telephone: *The news will follow the pips at 6 o'clock.* ○ *The pips tell a caller from a pay phone that his time has run out.*

pip³ /pɪp/ v (**-pp-**) (*Brit infml*) (*esp passive*) to defeat sb by a small margin or just before they win: [Vn] *She led after 70 holes, only to be pipped by Laura Davis.* [Vnpr] *Both times Richards pipped him for the match award.* ○ *We didn't win the contract: we were pipped at the post* (ie just beaten) *by another firm.*

pipe¹ /paɪp/ n **1** [C] (esp in compounds) a tube through which liquids or gases can flow: *plastic/lead/copper pipes* ○ *a burst 'water-pipe* ○ *a leaking 'gas-pipe* ○ *a cracked/blocked 'drainpipe.* See also EXHAUST-PIPE, WINDPIPE. **2** [C] a narrow tube with a bowl at one end, used for smoking tobacco: *smoke a pipe* ○ *He puffed on/at his pipe.* ○ *a packet of 'pipe tobacco.* **3** (*music*) (**a**) [C] a musical instrument consisting of a single tube, played by blowing. (**b**) **pipes** [pl] a set of these joined together. See also PAN-PIPES. (**c**) [C] each of the tubes from which sound is produced in an organ²(2). (**d**) **pipes** [pl] = BAGPIPES. **IDM** **put 'that in your pipe and smoke it** (*infml*) you have to accept what I have said, whether you like it or not.
■ **'pipe-cleaner** n a flexible piece of wire covered with soft material, used for cleaning inside a tobacco pipe.

pipe² /paɪp/ v **1** to transport water, gas, etc in pipes: [Vnpr] *pipe water into a house/to a farm* ○ *pipe oil across the desert* [also Vn]. **2** [Vn, Vnpr] (esp passive) to transmit music, a radio programme, etc by wire or cable. **3(a)** [Vn] (of a bird) to whistle or sing sth. (**b**) [V.speech, Vn] (of a person, esp a child) to say sth in a high voice. **4** to welcome or indicate the arrival of sb by the sound of a pipe: [Vnadv, Vnpr] *pipe the captain aboard/on board* [Vnp] *pipe the guests in.* **5** to put a decoration on a cake with a thin line of ICING: [Vn] *pipe 'Happy Birthday' on a cake.* **PHRV** **,pipe 'down** (*infml*) (esp imperative) to be less noisy; to stop talking: *Kids, pipe down, will you? I'm on the phone.* **pipe up** (*infml*) to begin to sing or speak, esp suddenly and in a high voice.
■ **,piped 'music** n [U] recorded music played continuously, eg in large shops, in order to make the customers, etc feel comfortable.

pipedream /'paɪpdriːm/ n a hope or plan that is impossible to achieve or not practical.

pipeline /'paɪplaɪn/ n a series of connected pipes, usu underground, for transporting oil, gas, etc to a distant place: *lay a pipeline.* **IDM** **in the 'pipeline** (of changes, laws, proposals, etc) being prepared or discussed; about to happen: *Important new laws are already in the pipeline.*

piper /'paɪpə(r)/ n a person who plays music on a pipe, esp the BAGPIPES. **IDM** **he who pays the piper calls the tune** ⇨ PAY².

pipette /pɪ'pet/ n (esp in chemistry) a narrow tube used in a laboratory for transferring or measuring small quantities of liquids.

pipework /'paɪpwɜːk/ n [U] a network of pipes in a house, under the ground, etc.

piping /'paɪpɪŋ/ n [U] **1** a pipe or pipes of the specified type or length: *ten metres of lead piping.* **2(a)** a folded strip of fabric, often enclosing a cord, used to decorate a garment, cushion, etc: *the piping on his uniform.* (**b**) lines of ICING or cream used to decorate a cake, etc: *a piping bag.* **3** the action or sound of playing a pipe¹(3) or pipes: *We heard their piping in the distance.*

▶ **piping** *adj* (esp of a person's voice) high-pitched. [IDM] **piping 'hot** (*approv*) (of liquids or food) very hot: *Serve the soup piping hot.*

pipit /'pɪpɪt/ *n* (esp in compounds) a small brown bird with a pleasant song: *meadow/rock pipits.*

pippin /'pɪpɪn/ *n* a type of apple that can be eaten raw.

pipsqueak /'pɪpskwiːk/ *n* (*infml* or *derog*) a usu young person that one regards as unimportant or not worthy of respect.

piquant /'piːkənt/ *adj* **1** having a pleasantly sharp taste: *The peppers give the sauce a piquant flavour.* **2** pleasantly exciting and stimulating to the mind: *a piquant bit of gossip.*

▶ **piquancy** /-ənsi/ *n* [U] the quality or state of being piquant: *the delicate piquancy of the soup* ◦ *The situation is given an added piquancy since the two men are also rivals in love.*

pique /piːk/ *n* [U] a feeling of annoyance or resentment (RESENT), usu because one's pride has been hurt: *When he realized nobody was listening to him, he left the room in a fit of pique.* ◦ *Out of pique they refused to accept the compromise offered.*

▶ **piqued** *adj* [pred] having a feeling of pique: *She seemed rather piqued by my remarks.* ◦ *He was piqued to discover that he hadn't been invited.*

piracy /'paɪrəsi/ *n* [U] **1** the practice of robbing ships at sea. **2** [U] illegal copying or broadcasting: *attempts to eliminate product piracy.*

piranha /pɪ'rɑːnə/ *n* a small tropical American river fish that attacks and eats live animals.

pirate /'paɪrət/ *n* **1** (esp formerly) a person on a ship who attacks and robs other ships at sea: *the notorious pirate Captain Kidd* ◦ *a pirate crew/ship/flag.* **2** a person who copies illegally sth protected by COPYRIGHT, esp in order to sell it: *a pirate edition/video/tape.* **3** a person or a company that broadcasts without a licence: *pirate radio stations* ◦ *interference with radio reception caused by pirates.* See also PIRACY.

▶ **pirate** *v* to use or copy illegally printed or recorded material which is protected by COPYRIGHT, esp for profit: [Vn] *circulate a pirated edition of a computer game.* ⇨ note at SMUGGLE.

piratical /ˌpaɪ'rætɪkl/ *adj* like a pirate(1): *His beard and black eye-patch gave him an almost piratical look.*

pirouette /ˌpɪru'et/ *n* a rapid turn or spin made esp by a dancer while balanced on the point of the toe or the ball of the foot: *She pranced in little pirouettes around the kitchen.* ▶ **pirouette** *v* [Vpr] *pirouetting round the stage* [also V].

Pisces /'paɪsiːz/ *n* (**a**) [pl] the 12th sign of the ZODIAC, the Fishes. (**b**) [C] a person born under the influence of this sign. ▶ **Piscean** *n, adj* ⇨ picture at ZODIAC. ⇨ note at ZODIAC.

piss /pɪs/ *v* (△ *sl*) [V] to urinate (URINE). [IDM] **'piss oneself (laughing)** to laugh very hard, esp at sb else's mistake, behaviour, etc. [PHRV] **ˌpiss (sb) a'bout/a'round** (*Brit*) to behave in a foolish way, or in a way that is deliberately not helpful to sb or wastes time: *Stop pissing about and get on with your work.* ◦ *The job centre pissed me around for hours before they finally gave me the right form.* **'piss down** (*Brit*) to rain heavily. **ˌpiss 'off** (*esp Brit*) (esp imperative) to go away: *Why don't you just piss off and leave me alone?* **ˌpiss sb 'off** to make sb annoyed or bored: *I'm pissed off with the way the company has treated me.*

▶ **piss** *n* (△ *sl*) (**a**) [U] URINE. (**b**) [sing] an act of urinating (URINE): *go for/have a piss.* [IDM] **take the 'piss (out of sb/sth)** to mock sb/sth.

pissed *adj* (△ *Brit sl*) drunk. [IDM] **(as) pissed as a 'newt** very drunk.

■ **'piss-up** *n* (△ *Brit sl*) an occasion when a large amount of alcohol is drunk.

pistachio /pɪ'stæʃiəʊ, -'tɑːʃiəʊ/ *n* (*pl* **-os**) (also pi'stachio nut) a small nut with a green edible KERNEL: *pistachio ice-cream.*

piste /piːst/ *n* a track of firm snow for skiing (SKI) on: *skiing off piste* (ie where the snow is deep and soft).

pistol /'pɪstl/ *n* a type of small gun, held and fired with one hand: *an automatic pistol* ◦ *a pistol shot.* ⇨ picture at GUN. See also WATER-PISTOL. [IDM] **hold a pistol to sb's 'head** to try to force sb to do sth they do not want to do by using threats.

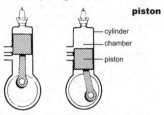

piston

— cylinder
— chamber
— piston

piston /'pɪstən/ *n* a round plate or short CYLINDER(1b), usu of metal, that fits closely inside a tube and moves up and down or backwards and forwards inside it. It is used eg in engines to cause other parts to move by means of a rod connecting it to them. ⇨ picture. See also CONNECTING-ROD.

pit¹ /pɪt/ *n* **1** [C] a large and usu deep hole or opening in the ground: *dig/excavate a pit* ◦ (*fig*) *You seem to think my bank account is a bottomless pit!* **2** [C] (esp in compounds) a hole in the ground, usu with steep sides, from which esp minerals are dug out: *a 'chalk-pit* ◦ *a 'gravel-pit.* See also SANDPIT. **3** [C] a COALMINE: *go down the pit* (ie work as a miner) ◦ *pit closures.* **4** **the pits** [pl] (in motor racing) a place near the track where cars can stop for fuel, new tyres, etc during a race. See also ARMPIT, ORCHESTRA PIT, PIT STOP. [IDM] **the pit of the/one's 'stomach** the bottom of the stomach, thought to be the place where strong feelings, esp of fear, are felt: *He had a sudden sinking feeling in the pit of his stomach.* **be the 'pits** (*infml esp US*) to be very bad or the worst example of sth: *The food in this restaurant is the pits!*

▶ **pit** *v* (-tt-) ~ **sth (with sth)** (esp passive) to make small hollow places on a surface: [Vn] *Acid had pitted the surface of the silver.* [Vnpr] *a face pitted with smallpox* ◦ *The surface of the moon is pitted with craters.* [PHRV] **'pit sb/sth against sb/sth** to test sb/sth in a struggle or competition with sb/sth: *pit oneself against the reigning champion* ◦ *He decided to pit his wits against the bureaucracy of the tax office.*

■ **'pit-head** *n* the entrance of a COALMINE and the offices, machinery, etc in the area around it: *a ˌpit-head 'ballot* (ie a vote, esp about union matters, taken at the pit-head).

'pit-prop *n* a large piece of wood used to support the roof of a part of a COALMINE from which coal has been removed.

'pit stop *n* **1** (in motor racing) an occasion when a car stops in the pits (PIT¹ 4) during a race. **2** (*US*) a brief stop during a journey for a rest, a meal, etc.

pit² /pɪt/ *n* (*esp US*) = STONE 5.

▶ **pit** *v* (-tt-) (usu passive) to remove stones from fruit: [Vn] *pitted olives.*

pit-a-pat /ˌpɪtə'pæt/ (also **pitter-patter** /'pɪtə pætə(r)/) *adv* with quick light steps or taps: *Her heart went pit-a-pat.* See also PATTER 1. ▶ **pit-a-**

[V] = verb used alone   [Vn] = verb + noun   [Vp] = verb + particle   [Vpr] = verb + prepositional phrase

pat (also **pitter-patter**) *n*: *the soft pit-a-pat of rain on the roof.*

pitch¹ /pɪtʃ/ *n* **1** [C] (*Brit*) an area of ground prepared and marked for a game; a sports ground or field: *a 'football/'cricket/'hockey pitch* ○ *a pitch invasion by the team's supporters.* ⇨ picture at CRICKET¹, FOOTBALL. **2** [sing, U] the quality of a musical note, a voice, etc, esp how high or low it is: *A train whistle seems to have a higher pitch as the train approaches.* **3(a)** [U, sing] the degree or intensity of sth: *a frenetic pitch of activity* ○ *Speculation has reached such a pitch that a decision will have to be made immediately.* See also FEVER PITCH. **(b)** [sing] ~ **of sth** the highest point of sth: *This dancer's talents have reached a/the pitch of perfection.* **4** (also **'sales pitch**) [C usu *sing*] talk or arguments used by a person trying to sell things: *a clever sales pitch* ○ *The representatives of each company were given ten minutes to make their pitch.* **5** [C] the act or manner of throwing sth, eg the ball in baseball. **6** [C] (*esp Brit*) a place in a street or a market where a person has a stall to sell things, or where a street entertainer usu performs. **7** [U] (*techn*) the movement of a ship up and down on the water, or of an aircraft in the air. Compare ROLL¹ 3a. **8** [C] (*techn*) the degree of slope, esp of a roof. **IDM queer sb's pitch** ⇨ QUEER *v*.

pitch² /pɪtʃ/ *v* **1(a)** to express or set sth at a particular level: [Vnpr] *an explanation pitched at a level suitable for a young child* [Vnadv] *pitch one's hopes high* ○ *Their prices are pitched lower than those of their competitors.* **(b)** (*music*) to set a piece of music or one's voice at a certain pitch¹(2): [Vnadv] *a high-/low-pitched voice* ○ *The song is pitched too low for me.* [Vnpr] *Should we pitch it in a higher key?* **2** to throw sb/sth in the specified direction, esp in a rough manner: [Vnpr] *pitch a stone into the river* ○ *People just pitch their rubbish over the wall.* ○ (*fig*) *The new President has been pitched straight into a crisis.* [Vnp] *The carriage overturned and the passengers were pitched out.* **3** (*sport*) **(a)** (of a ball bowled in cricket or hit in golf) to strike the ground: [V] *He hit it before it pitched.* [Vadv] *The ball pitched short.* [also Vpr]. **(b)** [Vnadv, Vnpr, Vnp] (in cricket or golf) to make a ball bowled or hit strike the ground at the specified place. **(c)** [V, Vn] (in baseball) to throw the ball to the batter (BAT¹). **4** to fall heavily, esp forwards or outwards: [Vadv] *He suddenly pitched forward out of his seat.* [also Vp]. **5** (of a ship or an aircraft) to move up and down in the air: [V] *The ship pitched and rolled and many passengers were sick.* Compare ROLL² 7a. **6** to set up a tent or camp, esp for a short time: [Vn] *They **pitched camp** near the river.* **PHRV 'pitch for sth** (*infml*) to make a bid for sth; to try to obtain sth: *Several firms are pitching for the contract.* **pitch 'in**; **pitch 'into sth** (*infml*) to become involved in sth: *Two players started fighting, and then the rest of the team pitched in.* ○ *For once, I pitched into the housework with a light heart.* **pitch 'in (with sth)** to offer help or support: *They pitched in with contributions of money.* ○ *The neighbours pitched in and we soon finished the job.*

► **pitched** *adj* (of a roof) sloping from a ridge; not flat. **pitched 'battle** *n* **(a)** a violent fight or argument: *Rioters fought a pitched battle with the police.* **(b)** a military battle fought with troops arranged in prepared positions.

pitch³ /pɪtʃ/ *n* [U] a black substance made from tar or coal. Pitch is sticky and almost liquid when hot, and hard when cold, and is used to fill cracks or spaces, eg between the wooden boards of a ship or to prevent water coming through roofs.
■ **pitch-'black** *adj* completely black or dark: *a pitch-black night.*
pitch-'dark *adj* completely dark; with no light at all: *It's pitch-dark outside — you won't be able to see a thing.*

pitcher¹ /pɪtʃə(r)/ *n* **1** (esp formerly) a large container for liquids, with one or two handles and a lip for pouring. **2** (*esp US*) **(a)** a jug. **(b)** the amount of liquid contained in this: *a pitcher of water/wine.*

pitcher² /pɪtʃə(r)/ *n* (in baseball) the player who throws the ball to the batter (BAT¹).

pitchfork /pɪtʃfɔːk/ *n* a fork with a long handle and two sharp metal points, used esp on a farm for lifting and moving cut grass, etc.
► **pitchfork** *v* **PHRV 'pitchfork sb into sth** to force sb into a situation or a job, esp suddenly: *He was pitchforked into politics in 1980.*

piteous /pɪtɪəs/ *adj* (*fml*) deserving or causing pity: *a piteous cry/sight* ○ *The horse was in a piteous condition.* Compare PITIABLE, PITIFUL. ► **piteously** *adv.*

pitfall /pɪtfɔːl/ *n* ~ **(for sb)** a danger or difficulty, esp one that is hidden or not immediately obvious: *This text presents many pitfalls for the translator.*

pith /pɪθ/ *n* **1** [U, sing] a soft dry white substance inside the skin of oranges and certain other fruits. **2** [sing] the essential or most important part of sth: *the need for pith and precision in one's writing* ○ *the pith of her argument.* Compare CORE 3.
► **pithy** *adj* (*approv*) brief but full of meaning: *a pithy comment/observation/saying.* **pithily** /-ɪli/ *adv.*

pitiable /pɪtɪəbl/ *adj* **1** deserving or causing one to feel pity: *The refugees were in a pitiable state/condition.* **2** (*derog*) deserving contempt: *a pitiable lack of talent.* Compare PITEOUS, PITIFUL. ► **pitiably** /-əbli/ *adv.*

pitiful /pɪtɪfl/ *adj* **1** causing one to feel pity: *The horse was **a pitiful creature/sight** (eg because it was very thin or sick).* ○ *Their suffering was pitiful to see.* **2** (*derog*) deserving contempt: *pitiful efforts/excuses/lies.* Compare PITEOUS, PITIABLE. ► **pitifully** /-fəli/ *adv*: *The dog was whining pitifully.* ○ *Their standard of living remains pitifully low.* ○ (*derog*) *The fee is pitifully low/inadequate.*

pitiless /pɪtɪləs/ *adj* **1** showing no pity; cruel: *a pitiless killer/tyrant.* **2** very harsh or severe, and never ending: *a scorching, pitiless sun.* ► **pitilessly** *adv.*

piton /pi:tɒn/ *n* (*sport*) a short pointed metal bar with a ring at one end through which a rope can be passed. Pitons are hammered into rocks or cracks between rocks to support people climbing mountains, etc.

pitta /pi:tə; *Brit also* pɪtə/ (also **'pitta bread**) *n* [U, C] a type of flat bread that can be split open and filled with meat, SALAD(1a), etc, eaten esp in Greece and the Middle East. ⇨ picture at BREAD.

pittance /pɪtns/ *n* (usu *sing*) (*derog*) a very small or inadequate amount of money paid to sb as wages or an allowance: *work all day for a pittance* ○ *She could barely survive on the pittance she received as a widow's pension.*

pitter-patter = PIT-A-PAT.

pituitary /pɪtjuːɪtəri; *US* -tuːəteri/ (also **pi'tuitary gland**) *n* a small GLAND at the base of the brain. It produces hormones (HORMONE) that influence the body's growth and development.

pity /pɪti/ *n* **1** [U] ~ **(for sb/sth)** a feeling of sorrow caused by the suffering and troubles of others: *be full of pity for the starving animals* ○ *be moved to pity by sb's suffering* ○ *I have/feel very little pity for convicted murderers.* ○ **Have pity on** (ie Have some sympathy for) *the people who have to go out in this dreadful weather!* ○ *I **took pity on** the beggar and gave him some money.* **2** [sing] ~ **(that...)** a cause for mild regret or annoyance: *It's a (great) pity the weather isn't better for our outing today.* ○ *What a* *pity (that) you can't come with us tonight.* ○ *It seems a pity to waste this food.* ○ (*infml*) *This dress is really nice. Pity it's so expensive.* **IDM for pity's 'sake** (used to express anger or an urgent need for sth to be done): *For pity's sake, please help us!* **more's the 'pity** (*infml*) (used to express regret) unfortunately (UNFORTUNATE): *'Was the bicycle insured?' 'No, more's the pity!'* See also PITEOUS, PITIABLE, PITIFUL, PITILESS.

▶ **pity** *v* (*pt, pp* **pitied**) to feel pity for sb: [Vn] *Pity the poor sailors at sea in this storm!* ○ *His widow is much to be pitied.* **pitying** *adj* showing pity and sometimes also contempt: *He received only pitying looks/smiles from his audience.* **pityingly** *adv*.

pivot /ˈpɪvət/ *n* **1** the central point, pin or column on which sth turns or is balanced: *The machine-gun swings round on its pivot.* ⇨ picture at SCALE³. **2** the central or most important person or thing: *His sculpture provides the pivot of the whole exhibition.* ○ *This assertion is the pivot of her whole argument.*

▶ **pivot** *v* (**a**) ~ (**on sth**) to turn on or as if on a pivot: [Vpr] *She pivoted on her heels and marched out of the room.* [also V]. (**b**) (usu passive) to provide sth with a pivot; to fix sth on a pivot: [Vnpr] *The wipers are pivoted at the bottom of the windscreen.* [also Vn]. **PHRV 'pivot on sth** (no passive) (of an argument, etc) to depend entirely on sth: [Vpr] *The whole novel pivots on this single incident.*

pivotal /-tl/ *adj* of great importance because other things depend on it; central: *a pivotal decision/ character* ○ *a pivotal role/position in European affairs.*

pixel /ˈpɪksl/ *n* (*computing*) any of the individual dots on a computer screen, which together form the whole display.

pixie /ˈpɪksi/ *n* (esp in children's stories) a small fairy, often portrayed with pointed ears and a pointed hat.

pizza /ˈpiːtsə/ *n* [C, U] a baked Italian dish consisting of a flat, usu round, piece of DOUGH(1) covered with tomatoes, cheese and often pieces of vegetables, meat or fish.

▶ **pizzeria** /ˌpiːtsəˈriːə/ *n* a restaurant that specializes in pizzas.

pizzicato /ˌpɪtsɪˈkɑːtəʊ/ *adj, adv* (*music*) using the fingers instead of the bow to play the string of a VIOLIN or a similar instrument.

pkt *abbr* (eg in a RECIPE(1)) packet: *1 pkt chopped walnuts.*

Pl *abbr* (esp in an address) Place: *Grosvenor Pl.*

pl *abbr* plural.

placard /ˈplækɑːd/ *n* a written or printed notice designed to be publicly displayed, eg by being fixed to a wall or carried on a stick: *They carried placards saying: 'Stop racist murders!'* ⇨ picture at FLAG¹.

placate /pləˈkeɪt; *US* ˈpleɪkeɪt/ *v* to make sb less angry; to calm or satisfy sb: [Vn] *These concessions are unlikely to placate extremists.*

▶ **placatory** /pləˈkeɪtəri; *US* ˈpleɪkətɔːri/ *adj* placating or designed to placate sb: *a placatory remark/ smile.*

place¹ /pleɪs/ *n* **1** [C] a particular area or position: *Is this the place where it happened?* ○ *This would be a good place for a picnic.* ○ *I can't be in two places at once.* **2** [C] a city, town or village: *the place where I was born* ○ *We saw so many places on the tour I can't remember them all.* ○ *Paris is a big place.* **3** [C] a particular building, room or outdoor site: *This office is a great place to work.* ○ *We were looking for a place to eat* (eg a restaurant). ○ *'I hate these places,' he said as he entered the hospital.* ○ *He loves to be seen in all the right places* (ie at all the important social events). ○ (*infml*) *Let's get out of this place!* **4** [C] (esp in compounds or fixed phrases) a building or area of land used for a particular purpose: *a ˈmeeting-place/ ˈhiding-place* ○ (*fml*) *places of entertainment* (eg theatres or cinemas) ○ *a place of worship* (eg a

church) ○ *a place of learning* (eg a university) ○ *He can usually be contacted at his place of work.* See also RESTING-PLACE. **5** [C] a particular spot or area on a surface, eg on the body: *I have a tattoo in an embarrassing place.* ○ *The paint was peeling off the wall in several places.* ○ *You can still see the place where the picture used to hang.* **6** [C] a particular passage or point in eg a book, play or piece of music: *Use a bookmark to mark your place.* ○ *The audience laughed in all the right places* (eg when watching a play). ○ *The singer had obviously lost her place* (ie could not remember what came next). **7** [C] a seat or position, esp one reserved for or occupied by a person or vehicle: *Come and sit here — I've kept you a place.* ○ *Return to your places and get on with your work.* ○ *Four places were laid/set* (ie prepared so that four people could eat) *at the table.* ○ *Let's change/ swap* (ie exchange) *places so you can see better.* ○ *I went to buy a newspaper and lost my place in the queue.* ○ *the place of honour at the head of the procession* ○ *There's only one place left in the car park.* ⇨ note at SPACE. **8** [sing] (**a**) ~ (**in sth**) the role, position or function of sth/sb in relation to others: *a debate about the place of computers in modern society* ○ *have an assured place in history* ○ *There will always be a place for you here if you decide to return.* (**b**) a person's rank or role in society: *know/forget one's place* (ie behave/not behave according to one's social position) ○ *It's not your place* (ie your proper role) *to give advice.* **9** [C] (**a**) an opportunity to study, eg at a school or university: *She was awarded a place at the National School of Music.* ○ *The ballet school offers free places to children who are exceptionally talented.* ○ *There are very few places left on the course.* (**b**) membership of a sports team: *She worked hard for her place in the Olympic team.* ○ *He lost his place in the first team.* **10** [C] (**a**) ~ (**for sth**) a natural or proper position for sth: *Put everything away in its right place.* ○ *There's a place for your luggage above the seat.* (**b**) (usu with a negative) a suitable, proper or safe area for sb to be: *A railway station is no place for a child to be left alone at night.* ○ *This town isn't the kind of place I'd like to live in.* **11** [sing] a house or flat; a person's home: *They have a flat in town as well as a place in the country.* ○ *I'm fed up with living with my parents, so I'm looking for a place of my own.* ○ (*infml*) *We're having the party at ˈmy place.* ○ *She likes her husband to help around the place.* **12** [C usu *sing*] (**a**) (in a competition) a position among the winning competitors: *He finished in third place.* (**b**) (in horse-racing) a position among the first three, esp second or third: *Did you back the horse for a place or to win?* **13** [C] (*mathematics*) the position of a figure after a decimal point: *calculated/correct to 5 decimal places* (eg 6.57132). **14** Place [sing] (*abbr* Pl) (as part of a name for a short street or square): *ˌLangham ˈPlace.* **IDM all 'over the place/shop** (*infml*) **1** everywhere: *Firms are going bankrupt all over the place.* **2** in a mess; in a state of disorder: *Her hair was all over the place.* ○ *Your calculations are all over the place* (ie completely wrong). **change/swap 'places (with sb)** (usu negative) to be in sb else's situation or circumstances: *I'm perfectly happy — I wouldn't change places with anyone.* **fall/slot into 'place** (of a set of facts or series of events) to begin to make sense in relation to each other: *It all began to fall into place when detectives found her will.* **give 'place to sb/sth** (*fml*) to be replaced by sb/sth: *Houses and factories gave place to open fields as the train gathered speed.* **'go places** (*infml*) (esp in the continuous tenses) to be increasingly successful, eg in one's career: *two young people who are really going places.* **have one's heart in the right place** ⇨ HEART. **if I was/were in your shoes/place** ⇨ SHOE. **in the 'first place** (used at the end of a sentence or clause) **1** (used after stating the original purpose or most important reason for sth): *We need to make a decision; that's why we're all here in the first place.* **2** at an earlier, more appropriate time: *Why didn't you tell us that in the first place?* **in the ¹first, ¹second, etc place** (used at the beginning of a sentence or clause, eg when making points in an argument): *Well, in the first place he's got all the right qualifications, and secondly...* **in ¹my, ¹your, etc place** in my, your, etc situation or circumstances: *If I were in her place I'd sell the lot.* **in ¹place** in the right, proper or usual position, eg ready for sth: *All the actors were in place so the play could begin.* ○ *Leave everything in place, just as it was when we arrived.* **in place of sb/sth; in sb's/sth's ¹place** instead of sb/sth; replacing sb/sth: *The chairman was ill so his deputy spoke in his place.* ○ *Williams was selected in place of the injured Roberts.* **out of ¹place 1** not in the right, proper or usual place: *The librarian noticed that some of the books were out of place.* **2** not suitable or acceptable; not belonging in a particular situation: *Her criticisms were quite out of place.* ○ *Victorian furniture is out of place in a modern house.* ○ *I felt out of place at my husband's school reunion.* **a place in the ¹sun** equal or shared privileges: *Nations that had been oppressed for centuries were now fighting for a place in the sun.* **pride of place** ⇨ PRIDE. **put oneself in sb else's / sb's ¹place** to imagine oneself in sb else's situation or circumstances. **put sb in their (proper) ¹place** to make sb feel ashamed or embarrassed by making them aware that they have been too bold or done sth unacceptable: *He tried to kiss her but she quickly put him in his place.* **take ¹place** (of a meeting, a social event, etc) to be held; to occur; to happen: *When does the ceremony take place?* ○ *We may never discover what took place (between them) that night.* ⇨ note at HAPPEN. **take sb's/sth's place; take the place of sb/sth** to replace sb/sth: *She couldn't attend the meeting so her assistant took her place.* ○ *Nothing could take the place of the family/paintings he had lost.*

■ **¹place-mat** *n* a mat on a table on which a person's plate is put.

¹place-name *n* a name of a city, town, hill or other place¹(2): *an expert on the origin of place-names.*

¹place-setting *n* a set of knives, forks, spoons, etc or plates or dishes for one person.

place² /pleɪs/ *v* **1** to put sth/sb in a particular place, esp carefully and deliberately: [Vnadv] *a cleverly placed bugging device* [Vnpr] *He placed the money on the counter/his hand on my shoulder.* ○ *A bomb had been placed under the seat.* **2** (more formal than *put*) to put sb in the situation or circumstances specified: [Vnpr] *place sb in command* ○ *place sb under arrest* ○ *place sb in a difficult position/in an embarrassing situation* ○ *place one's faith/trust in sb/sth* ○ *Responsibility for concluding an agreement was placed in his hands* (ie He was made responsible for it). **3 ~ sth on sth** to take a certain attitude or point of view towards sth; to consider sth in a certain way: [Vnpr] *place a high value on honesty* ○ *The team manager places great emphasis on attacking play.* **4** to make a judgement about sb/sth in comparison with others; to classify sb/sth: [Vnpr] *I would place her among the world's greatest sopranos.* **5** (esp in negative sentences) to identify sb/sth from memory or past experience: [Vn] *I've seen his face before but I can't place him.* ○ *She has a foreign accent that I can't quite place.* **6** to issue an instruction or request, esp to order goods or make a bet: [Vnpr] *They have placed an order with us for three new aircraft.* ○ *I'd like to place an advertisement in your newspaper.* [Vn] *Place your bets now!* **7 ~ sb (in sth); ~ sb (with sb/sth)** to find a home, job or course for sb: [Vn] *The agency places about 2000 secretaries a year.* [Vn] *They placed the children with foster-parents.* **8** (esp sport) (usu passive) to award sb/sth a particular position

in a competition or race: [Vn-adj] *The horse was placed third.* [Vnadv] *United are well placed just one point behind the League leaders.* **IDM be well placed for sth / to do sth 1** to be in a good position or have a good opportunity to do sth, esp with an advantage over others: *The firm is well placed to take advantage of the new trade agreement.* **2** to be situated in a good position: *The hotel is well placed for a variety of restaurants.* **put/place a premium on sb/sth** ⇨ PREMIUM. **to put/place sb on a pedestal** ⇨ PEDESTAL.

▸ **placed** *adj* [pred] (esp of horses) **(a)** (*Brit*) finishing first, second or third in a race. **(b)** (*US*) finishing second in a race.

placement /ˈpleɪsmənt/ *n* [U, C] the action of placing sb/sth: *the placement of the ball* ○ *The students spend the third year of the course on (a) placement with an industrial firm.*

placing *n* the position of sb/sth in an order or a list: *The young athlete was satisfied with his final placing.* ○ *Chart placings are determined by the number of records sold.*

placebo /pləˈsiːbəʊ/ *n* (*pl* **-os**) **1** (*medical*) a substance that has no physical effect, used when testing new drugs or given to a patient whose illness is imaginary: *the placebo effect* (ie the effect of taking a placebo and feeling better). **2** (*esp derog*) an action designed only to please or calm sb: *These measures are simply a placebo and do not deal with the real causes of dissent.*

placenta /pləˈsentə/ *n* (*pl* **placentae** /-tiː/ or **placentas**) (*anatomy*) an organ lining the WOMB of a pregnant woman which provides food for the developing baby through the UMBILICAL CORD, and which comes out of the womb after birth.

placid /ˈplæsɪd/ *adj* **(a)** (of a person or an animal) not easily excited or irritated: *a placid temperament/smile.* **(b)** calm and peaceful, with very little movement: *the placid waters of the lake.* ▸ **placidly** *adv: cows placidly munching grass.* **placidity** /pləˈsɪdəti/ *n* [U].

plagiarize, -ise /ˈpleɪdʒəraɪz/ *v* ~ **sth (from sb/sth)** to take sb's ideas or words and use them as if they were one's own: [Vn, Vnpr] *Whole passages of the book are plagiarized (from earlier studies of the period).* [also V].

▸ **plagiarism** /-rɪzəm/ *n* [U, C] the action or an instance of plagiarizing: *be accused of plagiarism and breach of copyright.*

plagiarist /-rɪst/ *n* a person who plagiarizes.

plague /pleɪg/ *n* **1(a)** (also **the plague**) [U, sing] = BUBONIC PLAGUE: *an outbreak of plague.* **(b)** [C] any infectious disease that kills many people: *the new plague of Aids.* **2** [C] ~ **of sth** large numbers of an animal or insect that come into an area and cause great trouble or damage: *a plague of flies/locusts/rats.* **IDM avoid sb/sth like the plague** ⇨ AVOID. ▸ **plague** *v* ~ **sb (with sth) 1** to cause trouble or difficulty to sb/sth, esp continually or repeatedly: [Vn] *the strikes which plagued British industry in the 1970s* [Vnpr] *a team plagued with injury.* **2** (esp passive) to cause suffering or discomfort to sb: [Vn] *be plagued by doubts/jealousy* [Vnpr] *She was plagued with arthritis.* **3** to annoy sb, esp by repeatedly asking them questions or demanding their attention: [Vnpr] *plague sb with questions/requests for money* [Vn] *a pop star plagued by autograph hunters.*

plaice /pleɪs/ *n* [C, U] (*pl* unchanged) a type of flat sea-fish eaten as food. See also FLOUNDER².

plaid /plæd/ *n* **1** [C] a long piece of woollen cloth, worn over the shoulders as part of Scottish ceremonial dress. **2** [U] cloth with a TARTAN pattern, used for making clothes, esp kilts (KILT): *a plaid jacket/skirt.*

plain¹ /pleɪn/ *adj* (**-er, -est**) **1** easy to see, hear or understand; clear: *The markings along the route are quite plain.* ○ *He* **made it plain** *(to us) that we should leave.* ○ *She made her annoyance plain.* ○ *There is no more money — do I make myself plain?* **2** (of words) not trying to deceive; frank and direct: *The plain truth/fact is I don't want to go.* ○ *a politician with a reputation for plain speaking.* **3(a)** not decorated or elaborate; ordinary and simple: *a plain but very elegant dress* ○ *plain food/cooking* ○ *plain cake* (eg without fruit). **(b)** without a pattern or marking on it: *plain fabric/wallpaper/tiles* ○ *write on plain paper* (ie without lines). **4** [attrib] (used for emphasis) ordinary; basic: *You don't need any special skills for this job, just plain common sense.* ○ *I don't use a word processor, just a plain, old-fashioned typewriter.* **5** (*derog*) (esp of a woman) not beautiful or attractive. **IDM** **in plain ˈEnglish** simply and clearly expressed: *a document written in plain English.* **(as) plain as a ˈpikestaff;** (*Brit*) **as plain as the nose on one's ˈface** very obvious. **plain ˈsailing** simple and free from trouble: *Once the design problems were solved, it was all/everything was plain sailing.*

▶ **plain** *adv* (*infml*) absolutely; simply: *That is just plain stupid.*

plainly *adv* (**a**) obviously; clearly: *He plainly intended to ignore my advice.* ○ *There is plainly a need for more consultation.* ○ *That is plainly absurd.* ○ *Plainly, my presence was unwelcome.* (**b**) easily: *The mountain tops are plainly visible from the village.*
plainness *n* [U].

■ ˌplain ˈchocolate *n* [U] dark chocolate with a slightly bitter taste, made without extra milk being added. Compare MILK CHOCOLATE.
ˌplain ˈclothes *n* ordinary clothes, not uniform, esp as worn by police officers on duty: *The policemen were* **in plain clothes.** **ˈplain-clothes** *adj* [attrib]: *a ˌplain-clothes deˈtective.*
ˌplain ˈflour *n* [U] flour that does not contain baking-powder (BAKE). Compare SELF-RAISING FLOUR.

plain² /pleɪn/ *n* a large area of flat land: *ride across the vast, grassy plain* ○ *the Great Plains of the American Midwest.*

plainsong /ˈpleɪnsɒŋ/ (also **plainchant** /-tʃɑːnt; US -tʃænt/) *n* [U] medieval church music for a number of voices singing together.

plaintiff /ˈpleɪntɪf/ (also **complainant**) *n* (*law*) a person who brings a legal action against sb in a lawcourt: *The jury found for the plaintiff.* Compare DEFENDANT.

plaintive /ˈpleɪntɪv/ *adj* sounding sad or full of sorrow, esp in a weak complaining way: *a plaintive cry/voice.* ▶ **plaintively** *adv.*

plait

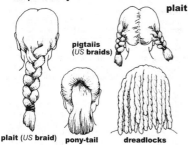

pigtails
(US braids)

plait (US braid)   pony-tail   dreadlocks

plait /plæt/ (*US* **braid**) *n* hair divided into three parts which are woven together and tied at the end: *wear one's hair in plaits/in a plait.* ⇨ picture.
▶ **plait** *v* (**a**) to weave strands of hair, rope, etc together to make a plait: [Vn] *plait one's hair* ○ *plaited pastry.* (**b**) to make sth by doing this: [Vn] *a plaited belt.*

plan /plæn/ *n* **1** ~ (**for sth/doing sth**); ~ (**to do sth**) an idea or a method that has been thought about in detail in advance; an intention: *a plan to produce/ for producing energy from waste material* ○ *a development plan* (eg for an industry or an area) ○ *a carefully worked-out plan* ○ *What are your plans for the holidays?* ○ *He's already* **making plans** *for his retirement.* ○ *There has been* **a change of plan** (ie it was decided not to do what was planned). ○ *The Chancellor said he* **had no plans to** *increase taxes.* ○ *The best plan* (ie The best thing to do) *would be to ignore it completely.* ○ *If everything* **goes according to plan** (ie happens as I expect) *I shall be back before dark.* ○ *Let's consider our* **plan of attack/ campaign** (ie the way to approach the problem). See also MASTER-PLAN. **2(a)** a detailed diagram or map of part of a town, a group of buildings, etc: *a plan of the royal palace and its surroundings* ○ *a plan of the town centre/the London Underground.* (**b**) (esp *pl*) ~ (**for sth**) an outline drawing of a building or structure, showing the position and size of the various parts in relation to each other: *draw up plans for an extension to the house* ○ *The architect submitted the plans for approval.* (**c**) a diagram of the parts of a machine: *plans of early flying machines.* Compare CHART, GROUND-PLAN, MAP. **3** a way of arranging sth, esp when shown on a drawing: *a seating plan* (eg showing where people are to sit at a table). **4** (esp in compounds) a financial arrangement, enabling a person to earn interest on money, receive an income when he or she retires, etc: *a pension/a savings/an investment plan.*

▶ **plan** *v* (**-nn-**) **1** to make a plan for sth; to decide sth in advance: [Vn] *plan a garden* ○ *a well-planned city/essay/campaign.* **2** (**a**) ~ (**for/on sth**) to make preparations for sth that is expected to happen: [Vpr] *plan for the future/one's retirement* ○ *I had planned for 20 guests, but only 10 arrived.* ○ *We hadn't planned on (having) twins!* [also V]. ⇨ note at ARRANGE. (**b**) ~ (**on doing sth**) to make plans to do sth; to intend to do sth: [V.to inf] *When do you plan to take your holiday?* [Vn] *We're planning a holiday in France next summer.* [Vpr] *I'd planned on having a quiet evening at home, until you turned up!* **PHRV** ˌplan sth ˈout to consider sth in detail in advance: *plan out one's annual expenditure* ○ *plan out a new traffic system for the town.* **planner** *n* (**a**) (also ˌtown ˈplanner) a person who works in or studies town planning. (**b**) a person who makes plans: *military planners.* **ˈplanning** *n* [U] (**a**) the action or process of making plans for sth: *The thing I enjoy most about holidays is the planning!* See also FAMILY PLANNING. (**b**) = TOWN PLANNING. **ˈplanning permission** *n* [U] a licence to build a new building or change an existing one, issued by a local authority: *You have to get planning permission from City Hall.*

plane¹ /pleɪn/ *n* **1** an aircraft or AEROPLANE: *travel by plane* ○ *board a plane in Rome* ○ *a plane crash* ○ *The plane landed at Geneva.* **2(a)** (*esp geometry*) any flat or level surface: *the horizontal/vertical plane.* (**b**) an imaginary flat surface through or joining material objects: *The knee is a joint that can only move in one plane.* **3** a level of thought, existence or development: *reach a higher plane of achievement* ○ *They seem to exist on a different spiritual plane.*

▶ **plane** *adj* [attrib] **1** completely flat; level: *a plane surface.* **2** (of angles, figures, etc) lying in a PLANE¹(2): *Plane geometry is concerned with two-dimensional figures, such as triangles.*

plane² /pleɪn/ *n* a tool, consisting of a blade set in a flat surface, which makes the surface of wood smooth by shaving very thin layers from it. ⇨ picture.

▶ **plane** *v* to use a plane on sth: [Vn] *plane the edge of a plank* [Vnp] *plane the surface down* [Vn-adj] *plane the wood smooth.* **PHRV** ˌplane sth aˈway/ˈoff

plane

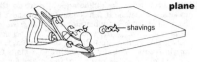

shavings

to remove sth with a plane: *plane away the bumps on a surface.*

plane³ /pleɪn/ (also **¹plane-tree**) *n* any of several types of tree with spreading branches, broad leaves and thin bark that comes off easily.

planet /'plænɪt/ *n* any of the bodies in space that move around a star (such as the sun) and receive light from it: *the planets of our solar system* ○ *the planet Venus.*

▶ **planetarium** /ˌplænɪ'teəriəm/ *n* (*pl* **planetariums** or **planetaria** /-ɪə/) a building in which a curved ceiling respresents the sky, and moving images of the stars and planets are projected onto it, to show their changing positions. Planetariums are built to entertain and educate people.

planetary /'plænətri; *US* -teri/ *adj* [attrib] of or like a planet or planets: *planetary activity* ○ *a planetary system.*

plangent /'plændʒənt/ *adj* (*fml*) **1** (of sounds) beating loudly: *plangent electronic keyboards.* **2** (of sounds or images) expressing sadness.

plank /plæŋk/ *n* **1** a long narrow flat piece of cut wood used for making floors, etc. **2** any of the main points in the policy of an organized group, esp a political party: *Increased spending on roads is the main plank of the government's transport policy.* **IDM** **thick as two short planks** ⇨ THICK. **walk the plank** ⇨ WALK¹.

▶ **planking** *n* [U] planks used to make a floor, etc: *a table made of rough planking.*

plankton /'plæŋktən/ *n* [U] the tiny forms of plant and animal life that live in the water of seas, rivers, lakes, etc.

plant¹ /plɑːnt; *US* plænt/ *n* **1** [C] (**a**) a living thing that grows in the earth and usu has a stem, leaves and roots: *¹plant life* ○ *Plants need light and water.* (**b**) any of the smaller kinds of these as distinct from bushes or trees: *garden/flowering/indoor plants* ○ *grow tomato plants.* See also HOUSE-PLANT, POT PLANT. **2(a)** [U] the machinery, equipment, etc used in an industrial or manufacturing process: *¹plant hire* (ie renting of machines or equipment) ○ *The firm has made a huge investment in new plant.* (**b**) [C] a piece of machinery or equipment: *The farm has its own ¹power plant.* **3** [C] a place where an industrial or manufacturing process takes place; a factory: *a ¸car as'sembly plant* ○ *a ¹chemical plant* ○ *a nuclear re'processing plant.* ⇨ note at FACTORY. **4** [C] (*infml*) (**a**) a thing placed deliberately so that its discovery will make an innocent person appear guilty; a piece of false or misleading evidence: *He claimed that the drugs found in his house were a plant.* (**b**) a person who joins a group of criminals, enemies, etc to report to others on their activities: *They discovered that he was a police plant.* (**c**) a person who joins an audience, a group, etc to encourage others to respond in a certain way: *There were several plants in the studio audience to start people laughing or clapping.*

plant² /plɑːnt; *US* plænt/ *v* **1(a)** to put plants, seeds, etc in the ground to grow: [Vn] *plant flowers around the pool* ○ *We planted beans and peas in the vegetable garden.* ○ *Plant them in rows one metre apart.* (**b**) ~ **sth (with sth)** to put bushes, trees, flowers, etc in a garden, pot, etc: [Vn] *plant a garden* [Vnpr] *plant the border with spring flowers* ○ *mountain slopes planted with conifers.* Compare SOW¹. **2(a)** to place sth in the specified position firmly or forcefully: [Vnpr] *He planted his feet firmly on the ground.* [Vnadv] *She*

stood with her feet planted wide apart. (**b**) (*infml*) to put or fix sth/oneself in a particular place: [Vnpr] *plant a bomb on an aeroplane* ○ *He planted himself in front of the fire.* **3** (*infml*) (**a**) ~ **sth (on sb)** to hide sth where it will be found in order to deceive sb or make an innocent person seem guilty: [Vnpr] *plant stolen goods on sb* [Vn, Vnpr] *She claimed that the drugs had been planted (on her).* (**b**) ~ **sb (in sth)** to send sb to join a group, esp to report secretly on its members: [Vnpr] *The police had planted a spy in the gang.* ○ *The speaker's supporters had been planted in the audience and they applauded loudly.* [also Vn]. **4** ~ **sth (in sth)** to fix or establish an idea, etc in sb's mind: [Vn] *plant doubts/suspicions/rumours* [Vnpr] *Who planted that notion in your head?* **5** to give sb a kiss, etc in a particular place: [Vnpr] *He planted a kiss on her cheek.* **PHRV** **¸plant sth 'out** to place plants in the ground so that they have enough room to grow: *plant out tomato seedlings.*

▶ **planter** *n* (often in compounds) **1** a person who is responsible for growing crops, esp in tropical countries: *a ¹sugar-planter/¹rubber-planter/¹tea-planter.* **2** a machine for planting seeds, etc. **3** a container in which plants are grown: *a strawberry planter.*

plantain¹ /'plæntɪn/ *n* (**a**) [C,U] a tropical fruit, similar to a BANANA but less sweet and usu cooked before being eaten. (**b**) [C] the large plant on which this grows.

plantain² /'plæntɪn/ *n* a common wild plant with small green flowers and broad flat leaves that spread out close to the ground.

plantation /plɑːn'teɪʃn; *US* plæn-/ *n* **1** a large piece of land, esp in a tropical country, where tea, cotton, sugar, tobacco, etc are grown: *a plantation owner.* **2** an area of land planted with trees: *plantations of fir and pine* ○ *forestry plantations.*

plaque¹ /plæk; *Brit also* plɑːk/ *n* a flat piece of stone, metal, etc, usu with a name and dates on, fixed on a wall in memory of a person or an event: *a bronze plaque on the house where the poet was born.*

plaque² /plɑːk; *US* plæk/ *n* [U] (*medical*) a substance that forms on teeth and encourages the growth of harmful bacteria: *remove plaque by brushing your teeth regularly.* Compare TARTAR¹.

plasma /'plæzmə/ (also **plasm** /'plæzəm/) *n* [U] **1** (*anatomy*) the colourless liquid part of blood, in which the blood cells float. Blood plasma is sometimes given to people who need it, eg during a medical operation. **2** (*physics*) a gas that contains approximately equal numbers of positive and negative charges and is present in the sun and most stars.

plaster /'plɑːstə(r); *US* 'plæs-/ *n* **1** [U] a smooth mixture of LIME¹(1), sand, water, etc that becomes hard when dry and is used for making a smooth surface on walls and ceilings: *The plaster will have to dry out before you can paint the room.* **2** (also ¸plaster of 'Paris) [U] a white powder mixed with water that becomes very hard when dry, used for making moulds, holding broken bones in place, etc: *She broke her leg two weeks ago and it's still in plaster.* **3** [C,U] = STICKING-PLASTER.

▶ **plaster** *v* (**a**) [Vn] to cover a wall, etc with plaster(1). (**b**) ~ **A with B / ~ B on(to) A** to cover sth with a lot of sth, as one puts plaster on a wall: [Vnpr] *hair plastered with oil* ○ *an artist who plasters the paint on the canvas* ○ *plaster the room with posters.* **PHRV** **¸plaster sth 'down** to make sth lie flat by having a wet or sticky substance on it: *Her hair was plastered down with sweat.* **plastered** *adj* (*sl*) drunk: *be/get plastered.* **plasterer** /'plɑːstərə(r)/ *n* a person whose job is to put plaster(1) on walls and ceilings.

■ **¹plaster cast** (**a**) a mould made with thin material and plaster of Paris to hold a broken bone in

---

[V.*to* inf] = verb + *to* infinitive   [Vn.inf (no *to*)] = verb + noun + infinitive without *to*   [V.*ing*] = verb + *-ing* form

place. (**b**) a mould, eg for a small statue, made of plaster of Paris.

plasterboard /ˈplɑːstəbɔːd/ n [U] a building material made of sheets of cardboard with PLASTER(1) between them, used for inside walls and ceilings.

plasterwork /ˈplɑːstəwɜːk/ n [U] the dry PLASTER(1) on ceilings, often formed into decorative shapes and patterns: *ornamental/rococo plasterwork*.

plastic /ˈplæstɪk/ n **1** [U, C usu pl] any of several chemically produced substances that can be formed into shapes when heated or made into thin threads and used to make various artificial fabrics: *the use of plastics in industry* ∘ *Many items are/use are made out of plastic.* ∘ *Plastic is often used instead of leather.* **2** **plastics** [sing v] the science of making plastics. **3** [U] (*infml*) credit cards (CREDIT): *Do you think they take plastic?*

▶ **plastic** adj **1** (of goods) made of plastic: *a plastic bag/bucket/spoon.* **2** (of materials or substances) easily shaped or moulded: *Clay is a plastic substance.* **plasticity** /plæˈstɪsəti/ n [U] the state or quality of being able to be moulded or shaped.

■ ˌplastic ˈarts n [pl] art forms that involve moulding or making models, eg in clay or wax, or representing things so that they appear solid: *The plastic arts include sculpture, pottery and painting.*

ˌplastic exˈplosive n [U, C] an explosive material that can easily be formed into different shapes or moulded around the object it is used to destroy.

ˌplastic ˈsurgeon n a person who is qualified to perform plastic surgery.

ˌplastic ˈsurgery n [U] the repairing or replacing of injured or damaged tissue on the surface of the body, eg after a person has been badly burned.

Plasticine /ˈplæstəsiːn/ n [U] (*propr*) a substance similar to clay but which does not harden like clay, used for making things, esp by children: *plasticine animals.*

plate

plate

dish

bowl

plate¹ /pleɪt/ n **1** [C] (**a**) (often in compounds) a flat round dish made usu of clay, china or plastic, from which food is served or eaten: *a ˈdinner/ˈdessert/ ˈsoup plate* ∘ *paper ˈplates.* ⇨ picture. (**b**) the contents of this: *a plate of stew/sandwiches.* (**c**) a similar plate, usu made of metal or wood, used to collect money from people at a church service: *pass round the plate* ∘ *put £5 in the plate.* See also HOT-PLATE. **2** [U] (**a**) spoons, forks, dishes, bowls, etc made of gold or silver, esp for use at meals: *display the family plate.* (**b**) dishes, bowls, cups, etc made of gold or silver for use in a church: *The plate is kept in a locked cupboard.* **3** [U] (often in compounds) metal other than silver or gold that has been covered with a thin layer of silver or gold: *a silver plate teapot* ∘ *The cutlery is plate, not solid silver.* **4** [C] (**a**) a thin flat sheet of metal, glass, etc: *The ship's hull is made of welded steel plates.* (**b**) (*biology*) a thin flat piece of horn, bone, etc: *The armadillo has a protective shell of bony plates.* **5** [C] (*geology*) any of the large rigid sheets of rock that compose the earth's surface: *the oceanic plate* ∘ *mountains that formed when two plates collided.* **6** [C] a small piece of metal with eg a name or number on it: *a name plate* ∘ *a brass ˈplate* (eg at the entrance to the place where a doctor, dentist or lawyer works). See also NUMBER-PLATE. **7** [C] (**a**) a photograph used as an illustration in a book: *a ˈcolour plate* ∘ *See plate 4.* (**b**) a sheet of metal, plastic, rubber, etc treated so that words or

pictures can be printed from it: *a printing plate.* (**c**) (in photography) a sheet, esp of glass, coated with chemicals, which reacts to light and on which an image is formed. **8** (also **denture**) [C] a thin piece of plastic which fits inside the mouth and holds artificial teeth. **IDM** **on a ˈplate** (*infml*) with little or no effort from the person concerned: *You can't expect promotion to be handed to you on a plate.* **on one's ˈplate** occupying one's time or energy: *have enough/ a lot/too much on one's plate.*

▶ ˈplateful /-fʊl/ n (pl **-fuls**) the amount that a plate¹(1a) holds: *She ate three platefuls of spaghetti!*

■ ˌplate ˈglass n [U] very clear glass of fine quality made in thick sheets, used eg for doors and shop windows.

ˈplate-rack n a wooden or plastic frame in which food plates are stored or left to dry after being washed. ⇨ picture at RACK¹.

ˌplate tecˈtonics /tekˈtɒnɪks/ n [sing v] (*geology*) the study of the structure and formation of the earth's surface through the movement of its plates (PLATE¹ 5).

plate² /pleɪt/ v **1** ~ sth (**with sth**) (esp passive) to cover another metal with a thin layer of esp gold or silver: [Vnpr] *a copper tray plated with silver* [Vn] *gold-plated dishes.* See also ELECTROPLATE. **2** to cover a vehicle with metal plates: [Vn] *armour-plated trucks.*

▶ **plating** n [U] **1** a thin covering, of metal, esp silver or gold, on another metal: *The plating is beginning to wear off.* **2** a layer or covering, esp of metal plates: *protected with steel plating.*

plateau /ˈplætəʊ; US plæˈtəʊ/ n (pl **plateaux** or **plateaus** /-təʊz/) **1** a large area of fairly level land high above the area around it. **2** a state of little or no change following a time of growth or progress: *Prices have now reached a plateau after a period of rapid inflation.*

platelayer /ˈpleɪtleɪə(r)/ n (*Brit*) a person whose job is to lay and repair railway tracks.

platelet /ˈpleɪtlət/ n any of the tiny cells shaped like discs in the blood that help it to become hard when bleeding occurs.

platform /ˈplætfɔːm/ n **1** a flat surface raised above the level of the ground or floor, used by public speakers or performers, so that they can be seen by their audience: *Coming onto the platform now is tonight's conductor, Jane Glover.* ∘ *appear on the same platform/share a platform with sb* (ie make speeches, etc at the same public meeting) ∘ *Your questions will be answered from the platform.* **2** a flat surface built next to and at a higher level than a railway track, where passengers get on and off trains: *Which platform does the Brighton train arrive/depart from?* ∘ *Your train is waiting at platform 5.* **3** (usu *sing*) (*Brit*) the open area at the entrance to a bus where passengers get on and off: *No standing on the platform.* **4** (usu *sing*) (*politics*) the main policies and aims of a political party, esp as stated before an election: *fight the election/come to power on a platform of economic reform.* **5** a raised level surface, eg one on which equipment stands or from which it is operated: *a mobile launch platform* (eg for rockets) ∘ *an oil platform.* **6** a thick sole of a shoe: *platform soles/shoes.*

platinum /ˈplætɪnəm/ n [U] (*symb* Pt) a chemical element. Platinum is a greyish-white metal, often used in making expensive jewellery and, esp with other metals, in industry: *a sapphire in a platinum setting.* ⇨ App 7.

■ ˌplatinum ˈblonde n, adj (*infml*) (a person, usu a woman, whose hair is) very fair or silver in colour, often as a result of being dyed (DYE¹).

platitude /ˈplætɪtjuːd; US -tuːd/ n (*fml derog*) a remark or statement that has been used too often in similar situations to be interesting: *We'll have to* listen to more platitudes about the dangers of over-spending. ► **platitudinous** /ˌplætɪˈtjuːdɪnəs; US -ˈtuːdənəs/ adj (fml): The speeches were mechanical and platitudinous.

platonic /pləˈtɒnɪk/ adj (of love or a friendship between two people) close and deep but not sexual: a platonic relationship ∘ He said that his feelings for her were entirely platonic.

platoon /pləˈtuːn/ n a small group of soldiers under the command of a LIEUTENANT(1).

platter /ˈplætə(r)/ n a large shallow dish for serving food, esp meat or fish: a silver platter.

platypus /ˈplætɪpəs/ (also ˌduck-billed ˈplatypus) n (pl **platypuses**) a small Australian animal covered in fur and with a beak like a duck, webbed (WEB) feet and a flat tail. Platypuses lay eggs but give milk to their young.

plaudit /ˈplɔːdɪt/ n (usu pl) (fml) applause, praise or any other sign of approval: a man anxious to win plaudits from the critics.

plausible /ˈplɔːzəbl/ adj **1** (of a statement, an excuse, etc) seeming to be right or reasonable; that can be believed: She could find no plausible explanation for its disappearance. ∘ His story was/sounded perfectly plausible. **2** (derog) (of a person) skilled in producing convincing arguments, esp in order to deceive people: a plausible liar. Compare IMPLAUSIBLE. ► **plausibility** /ˌplɔːzəˈbɪləti/ n [U]: the plausibility of her alibi. **plausibly** /-əbli/ adv: He argued very plausibly for the proposal's acceptance.

play¹ /pleɪ/ v

● **Doing things for amusement 1(a)** ~ (**with sb/sth**) to do things for pleasure, as children do; to enjoy oneself, rather than work: [Vpr] play with a ball/toy/dog [V] children playing in the park ∘ You'll have to play inside today. ∘ There's a time to work and a time to play. (**b**) ~ (**at**) sth (no passive) (esp of children) to pretend to be sth or do sth for amusement: [Vn, Vpr] Let's play (at) pirates. **2** ~ sth (**on sb**) to trick sb for amusement: [Vn, Vnpr] play a joke/trick (on sb).

● **Taking part in a game 3** ~ (**sth**) (**with/against sb**); ~ sb (**at sth**) to be involved in a game; to compete against sb in a game: [Vn] play football/chess/cards [Vn, Vnpr] Have you played her (at squash) yet? [Vpr, Vnpr] play (darts) with one's friends ∘ He plays (hockey) for Cleveland. [Vpr] On Saturday France play(s) against Wales. [V] Do footballers hear the crowd when they're playing? **4** to gamble at or on sth: [Vpr] play at the roulette table [Vn] play the stock market (ie buy and sell shares, etc to make money) [also V]. **5(a)** to take a particular position in a team: [Vpr] Who's playing in goal? [Vn-n] I've never played centre-forward before. (**b**) ~ sb (**as sth**) to include sb in a team: [Vn] play Collins as centre-forward [Vn, Vnpr] I think we should play Bill (on the wing) in the next match. **6** (in sport) to make or try to make contact with the ball, etc in the specified manner: [V, Vpr] She played (at the ball) and missed. [Vnpr] In soccer, only the goal-keeper may play the ball with his hands. [Vn] play a fast backhand volley. **7** (of a sports field, etc) to be in a certain condition for play: [Vadv] a pitch that plays well/poorly (ie allows the ball to move easily, slowly, etc). **8(a)** to move a piece in CHESS, etc: [Vn] She played her bishop. (**b**) to put a card face upwards with its value displayed on the table in a game of cards: play one's ace/a trump [V] She played out of turn!

● **Producing music or sound 9(a)** ~ (**sth**) (**on sth**); ~ sth (**to sb**) to perform on a musical instrument; to perform music: [Vn] play the piano/violin/flute (well) [Vpr] play to an audience [Vnpr] play a tune on the guitar [Vnn] play sb a piece by Chopin/a Beethoven sonata [V] In the distance a band was playing. (**b**) (of music) to be performed: [V] I could hear music playing on the radio. **10(a)** ~ sth (**for sb**) to make a CD, CASSETTE, etc produce sound: [Vn, Vnn] Can you play (me) her latest recording? [Vnpr] Play that jazz tape for me, please. (**b**) (of a CD, etc) to produce sound: [V] There was an old blues record playing in the next room.

● **Acting 11(a)** to act in a drama, etc; to act the role of sb: [Vn] play (the part of) Ophelia ∘ Lilia was played by Helen Mirren. (**b**) ~ (**to sb**) (of a drama) to be performed: [Vpr] a production of 'Carmen' playing to packed houses [also V]. **12** (no passive) to behave in a specified way; to act as if one were a particular type of person: [V-adj] play dead (ie pretend to be dead in order to trick sb) [V-n] play the politician/the diplomat/the wronged wife ∘ Stop playing the fool (ie acting foolishly).

● **Other meanings 13(a)** to move quickly and lightly, esp often changing direction: [Vpr] sunlight playing on/over the surface of the lake ∘ A smile played on/about her lips. (**b**) to direct esp light or water to a specified place: [Vnpr] play the torch beam over the walls ∘ The firemen played their hoses on the burning building. (**c**) (of fountains) to produce a steady stream of water: [V] Fountains were playing in the park. **14** [Vn] to make a fish become tired and weak by pulling against the line.

▪ **IDM** Most idioms containing **play** are at the entries for the nouns or adjectives in the idioms, eg **play the game** ⇨ GAME¹. **have money, time, etc to ˈplay with** (infml) to have plenty of money, time, etc for doing sth. **what sb is ˈplaying at** (usu expressing anger or annoyance) what sb is doing: I don't know ˈwhat he thinks he's playing at.

▪ **PHRV** ˌplay aˈbout/aˈround (**with sb/sth**) **1** to behave or handle sth in a casual careless way: Stop playing about and get on with the job. ∘ Don't play around with my expensive tools! **2** to have an affair or FLIRT(1) with sb: Her husband is always playing around. ∘ She's playing around with her sister's boyfriend.

ˌplay aˈlong (**with sb/sth**) to pretend to be in agreement with sb/sth: (infml) I decided to play along with her idea.

ˈplay at sth / being sth to do sth without much effort or enthusiasm: He's only playing at his job in the city: he's much more interested in being a racing driver.

ˌplay sth ˈback (**to sb**) to allow the material recorded on a tape, VIDEO(2c), etc to be heard or seen: I rewound the cassette and played her voice back to her. See also PLAY-BACK.

ˌplay sth ˈdown to try to make sth appear less important than it is: The government is trying to play down its involvement in the affair. See also DOWNPLAY.

ˌplay sb ˈin, ˈout, etc to play music as sb enters, leaves, etc a place: The band played the performers onto the stage. ˌplay oneself ˈin to play slowly and carefully at the beginning of a game.

play A off against B (Brit); (US) **play A off B** to put two people or groups in competition with each other, esp for one's own advantage: She played her two rivals off against each other and got the job herself.

ˌplay ˈon (sport) to continue to play; to start playing again: Some of the players claimed a penalty but the referee told them to play on. ˈplay on/upon sth to take advantage of sb's feelings, etc: Her speech played heavily on the angry mood of her audience.

ˌplay sth ˈout to be involved with or concentrate on sth, often while important events are happening around one: a power struggle being played out by the rival factions ∘ Their love affair was played out against the backdrop of war. ˌplay oneself/itself

---

[Vnn] = verb + noun + noun   [V-adj] = verb + adjective   For more help with verbs, see Study pages **B4–8**.

'**out** to become weak and no longer useful or relevant: *The revolution's fervour had played itself out.*

ǀ**play (sb)** ǀ**up** (*infml*) to cause sb problems, pain or difficulties: *My shoulder is playing (me) up today.* ○ *The children have been playing up all day* (eg by being noisy). ǀ**play sth** ǀ**up** to try to make sth appear more important than it is: *She played up her past achievements just to impress us.*

'**play with oneself** (*euph*) to MASTURBATE. '**play with sth** to consider an idea, etc but not seriously: *She's playing with the idea of starting her own business.*

■ '**play-back** *n* (**a**) [U] the action or process of playing music, showing a video, etc that has been recorded previously. (**b**) [C] a repeat of a particular passage of music, piece of film, etc: *a television play-back of the finish of the race.*

ǀ**played** '**out** *adj* [pred] (*infml*) exhausted; finished; no longer useful: *Is this theory played out* (ie no longer worth considering)?

'**play-off** *n* a match between two players or teams that are level, to decide which will be the winner: *a European cup play-off.*

play² /pleɪ/ *n* **1** [U] activity done for amusement and enjoyment, esp by children: *the happy sounds of children* **at play** ○ *the advantages of learning through play* ○ *a play area.* **2** (*sport*) (**a**) [U] the playing of a game: *Rain prevented any further play in the match.* ○ *Tennis players need total concentration during play.* (**b**) [U] the manner of playing a game: *There was some excellent play in yesterday's match.* ○ *They were penalized for too much rough play.* See also FAIR PLAY, FOUL PLAY. (**c**) [C] (*esp US*) an action or a move in a game: *a fine defensive/passing play.* (**d**) [U] the position of a ball in relation to the lines of a court, field, etc and the rules of the game being played: *The ball went out of play.* ○ *He just managed to keep the ball* **in play.** **3** [C] a work written to be performed by actors; a drama: *a radio play* ○ *act/take part in a play* ○ *She has just written a new play.* ○ *We went to see her new play at the Playhouse last night.* See also MIRACLE PLAY, MYSTERY PLAY, PASSION-PLAY. **4** [U] scope for free and easy movement: *We need more play on the rope.* ○ *There shouldn't be so much play in the steering-wheel.* **5** [U] the activity or operation of sth; the influence of sth on sth else: *the free play of market forces* ○ *The financial crisis has* **brought** *new factors* **into play.** ○ *Personal feelings should not* **come into play** *when one makes business decisions.* **6** [U] a light, quick, constantly changing movement: *the play of sunlight on water.* **IDM call sth into play** ⇨ CALL¹. **child's play** ⇨ CHILD. **make a** '**play for sb/sth** (*esp US*) to perform actions that are designed to achieve a desired result: *She was making a play for the leadership of the party.* **a play on** '**words** a clever and amusing use of language; a PUN: *The advertising slogan was a play on words.* **the state of play** ⇨ STATE¹.

▶ **playlet** /'pleɪlət/ *n* a short play²(3).

■ '**play-acting** *n* [U] the action of pretending to have feelings, attitudes, etc.

'**play-pen** *n* a small movable enclosure with wooden bars or NETTING in which a baby or small child can play safely.

'**play-room** *n* a room in a house for children to play in.

playboy /'pleɪbɔɪ/ *n* a rich man who spends his time enjoying himself.

player /'pleɪə(r)/ *n* **1** a person who plays a game: *a game for four players* ○ *She's an excellent* '*tennis player.* ⇨ picture at DART¹, HOCKEY, SNOOKER. **2** a person who plays a musical instrument: *a* '*trumpet player.* **3** (*dated or fml*) an actor: *amateur players.* See also RECORD-PLAYER.

playful /'pleɪfl/ *adj* **1** fond of playing; full of fun: *a playful kitten* ○ *be in a playful mood.* **2** done in fun;

not serious: *a playful punch on the arm* ○ *playful remarks.* ▶ **playfully** /-fəli/ *adv.* **playfulness** *n* [U].

playground /'pleɪgraʊnd/ *n* **1** an area of land, often with swings and slides, etc where children play, eg as part of a school: *children talking* **in the playground.** See also ADVENTURE PLAYGROUND. **2** an area where particular people like to enjoy themselves: *The island has become a playground for rich businessmen.*

playgroup /'pleɪgruːp/ (*also* '**playschool**) *n* [C, U] a group of children below school age who meet regularly and play together while supervised by adults: *Jenny goes to playgroup twice a week.* Compare NURSERY SCHOOL.

playhouse /'pleɪhaʊs/ (*pl* **-houses** /-haʊzɪz/) *n* **1** a theatre. **2** (*Brit*) a model of a house large enough for a child to play in.

playing-card

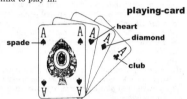

heart
diamond
spade
club

playing-card /'pleɪɪŋ kɑːd/ (*also* **card**) *n* any of a set of 52 cards with numbers and symbols printed on one side, used for playing various games: *a pack of playing-cards.* ⇨ picture.

playing-field /'pleɪɪŋ fiːld/ *n* (*sport*) a field with special markings, used for outdoor team games: *a game of football on the school playing-field.*

playmate /'pleɪmeɪt/ *n* a friend with whom a child plays.

playschool /'pleɪskuːl/ *n* = PLAYGROUP.

plaything /'pleɪθɪŋ/ *n* **1** a toy. **2** a person treated as an unimportant object of amusement by sb else: *the mere plaything of fate* ○ *She seemed content with her life as a rich man's plaything.*

playtime /'pleɪtaɪm/ *n* [U, C] the time used for having fun and relaxing, esp outdoors at school: *The children are outside during playtime.* ○ *They have three playtimes during the day.*

playwright /'pleɪraɪt/ *n* a person who writes plays.

plaza /'plɑːzə; *US* 'plæzə/ *n* **1** an outdoor square, esp in a Spanish town. Compare PIAZZA. **2** (*esp US*) a small shopping centre.

PLC (*also* **plc**) /ˌpiː el 'siː/ *abbr* (*Brit*) Public Limited Company: *Lloyd's Bank PLC.* Compare INC, LTD.

plea /pliː/ *n* **1** (*fml*) ~ (**for sth**) an urgent emotional request; an appeal: *a plea for forgiveness/money/more time* ○ *He was deaf to* (ie refused to listen to) *her pleas.* **2** (*law*) a statement made by or for a person charged with an offence in court: *enter a plea of guilty/not guilty.*

■ '**plea bargaining** *n* [U] an arrangement by which a DEFENDANT in a court of law admits to being guilty of a lesser crime in the hope of receiving a lighter punishment.

plead /pliːd/ *v* (*pt, pp* **pleaded**; *US* **pled** /pled/) **1** ~ (**with sb**) (**for sth**) to make repeated urgent requests to sb for sth: [Vpr] *plead for mercy* ○ *She pleaded with him not to leave her.* [V.to inf] *The boy pleaded to be allowed to ride on the tractor.* [also V]. **2** to offer sth as an explanation or excuse, esp for failing to do sth or for doing sth wrong: [Vn] *He apologized for not coming to the party, pleading pressure of work.* **3** (*law*) (**a**) to present a case to a court of law: [Vn] *They employed a top lawyer to plead their case.* (**b**) [Vpr] ~ **for/against sb** (of a lawyer) to speak for sb accused of an offence in a court of law. **4** (*law*)

(of sb on trial in a court of law) to state that one is guilty, not guilty, or not responsible for one's actions as a basis on which the trial proceeds: [V-adj] *plead guilty/not guilty* [Vadv] *How do you plead?* (ie Said by the judge at the start of the trial). [Vn] *Counsel for the accused said that he intended to plead insanity* (ie that his client was mad and therefore not responsible for his actions). **5 ~ (for)** sth to argue in support of sth: [Vn] *plead the cause of political prisoners* [Vpr] *plead for a halt in the trading of wild birds.*
▶ **pleadingly** *adv* in an emotional and begging manner: *look/speak pleadingly.*

pleasant /'pleznt/ *adj* (-er, -est) (a) ~ (to sth) giving pleasure to the mind, feelings or senses; enjoyable: *a pleasant meal/evening/view/walk* ○ *a pleasant atmosphere/experience/surprise* ○ *live in pleasant surroundings* ○ *music that is pleasant to the ear.* ⇨ note at NICE. **(b)** ~ (to sb) polite and friendly: *a pleasant smile/voice/manner* ○ *Please try to be pleasant to the guests.* ○ *What a pleasant young man!*
▶ **pleasantly** *adv*: *smile pleasantly* ○ *We were pleasantly surprised* at the profit we made.
pleasantness *n* [U].

pleasantry /'plezntri/ *n* (usu *pl*) (*fml*) a friendly casual remark, usu made in order to appear polite: *They exchanged pleasantries for a few minutes before saying goodbye.*

please /pli:z/ *v* **1** to make sb happy: [Vn] *It's difficult to please everybody.* ○ *Our main aim is to please the customers.* ○ *He's a very hard/difficult man to please.* ○ *There's no pleasing some people* (ie some people are impossible to please). **2** (in subordinate clauses often beginning with *as* or *what*) (*fml*) **(a)** to think desirable or appropriate; to choose: [V] *You may stay as long as you please.* **(b)** to want; to like: [V] *You can't always do exactly as you please.* ○ *That child behaves just as he pleases.* ○ *She has so much money she can buy anything she pleases.* **IDM** **if you** '**please 1** (*fml or dated*) (used when making a polite request): *Come this way, if you please.* **2** (*dated esp Brit*) (used to express annoyance when reporting sth, esp sth unexpected): *And now, if you please, I've got to rewrite the whole report!* ○ *He says the food isn't hot enough, if you please.* ,**please** '**God** may God let it happen; if it is pleasing to God: *Please God, things will start to improve soon.* ,**please your**'**self** (*ironic*) do as you like; I don't care what you do: '*I don't want to come for a walk.' 'Please yourself.'*
▶ **please** *interj* **1(a)** (used as a polite way of making a request or giving an order): *Please come in.* ○ *Come in, please.* ○ *Two cups of coffee, please.* ○ *Tickets, please.* ○ *Quiet, please!* **(b)** (used to add force to a request or statement): *Please don't leave me here alone!* ○ *Please, please, don't be late!* ○ *Please, I don't understand what I have to do!* ○ *Children, please! I'm trying to work.* **2** (*infml*) (used when accepting an offer emphatically) yes: '*Do you want some help?' 'Please!'* **IDM** ,**yes,** '**please** (used as a polite way of accepting the offer of sth) I accept and am grateful: '*Would you like some coffee/a lift?' 'Yes, please.'*
pleased *adj* **1** ~ (with sb/sth) feeling or showing satisfaction or pleasure: *Your mother will be very pleased (with you).* ○ *Are you pleased with your new house?* ○ (*sometimes derog*) *He looks rather pleased with himself* (ie pleased with what he has done). **2** ~ to do sth happy to do sth: *I was very pleased to be able to help.* ○ *We were pleased to hear the news.* ○ (*fml*) *Pleased/I'm pleased to meet you* (ie said when being introduced to sb). ○ (*fml*) *Thank you for your invitation, which I am very pleased to accept.* **IDM** **(as)** ,**pleased as** '**Punch** very pleased.
pleasing *adj* ~ (to sb/sth) giving pleasure; pleasant: *a pleasing colour scheme/shape* ○ *music that is pleasing to the ear* ○ *The results are pleasing to both of us.* **pleasingly** *adv*: *a pleasingly relaxed atmosphere.*

pleasure /'pleʒə(r)/ *n* **1(a)** [U] a state or feeling of being happy or satisfied: *a work of art that has given pleasure to millions of people* ○ *a life spent in pursuit of pleasure* ○ *It gives me great pleasure to welcome our speaker.* ○ *She takes (no/great) pleasure in her work.* ○ *Has she gone to Paris on business or for pleasure* (ie for work or for fun)*?* **(b)** [C] a thing that gives happiness or satisfaction: *the pleasures of living in the country* ○ *She has few pleasures left in life.* ○ *It's been a pleasure meeting you.* ○ '*Thank you for doing that.' 'It's a pleasure.'* **2** [U] (*dated fml*) what a person wants; a desire: *You are free to come and go at your pleasure* (ie as you wish). **IDM** **have the** '**pleasure of sth/doing sth** (used to make polite requests, issue invitations, etc): *May I have the pleasure of this dance?* ○ (*fml or joc*) *Are we to have the pleasure of seeing you again?* **with** '**pleasure** (*fml*) one is pleased to accept, agree, etc: '*Will you join us?' 'Thank you, with pleasure.'* ○ '*May I borrow your car?' 'Yes, with pleasure.'* Compare DISPLEASURE.
▶ **pleasurable** /'pleʒərəbl/ *adj* giving pleasure; enjoyable: *a highly pleasurable experience/activity.*
pleasurably /-əbli/ *adv*.
■ '**pleasure boat** *n* (*dated*) a boat used for short tourist trips: *pleasure boat trips round the harbour.* '**pleasure-craft** *n* (*pl* unchanged) a pleasure boat.

pleat /pli:t/ *n* a permanent fold in a piece of cloth, made by sewing the top or side of the fold: *a shirt with narrow pleats at the front.*
▶ **pleated** /'pli:tɪd/ *adj* having pleats: *a pleated skirt.*

plebeian /plə'bi:ən/ *adj* **1** (*fml*) of the lower social classes: *of plebeian origins.* **2** (*derog*) lacking in culture or education; VULGAR(1): *plebeian tastes.*
▶ **plebeian** *n* (*usu derog*) a person belonging to the lower social classes, esp in ancient Rome. Compare PATRICIAN.

plebiscite /'plebɪsɪt, -saɪt/ *n* (*politics*) a direct vote by the people of a country on a matter of national importance: *hold a plebiscite* ○ *The question of which state the area should belong to was decided by (a) plebiscite.* Compare REFERENDUM.

plebs /plebz/ *n* (usu **the plebs**) [pl] (*infml derog*) ordinary unimportant people, esp of the lower social classes.

plectrum /'plektrəm/ *n* (*pl* **plectrums** or **plectra** /-trə/) (*music*) a small piece of metal, wood, plastic or bone used for plucking the strings of a guitar or similar instrument.

pled *pt, pp* of PLEAD.

pledge /pledʒ/ *n* **1** ~ (**to do** sth) a solemn promise: *give a pledge never to reveal the secret* ○ *a pledge of support* ○ *The government has failed to honour its election pledge.* **2** a thing given to sb as a sign of friendship, love, etc or as a guarantee of good faith: *gifts exchanged as a pledge of friendship.* **3** an article left with a PAWNBROKER in exchange for money. **IDM** **sign/take the** '**pledge** (*esp joc*) to make a solemn promise never to drink alcohol.
▶ **pledge** *v* **1(a)** ~ sth (**to sb/sth**) (*fml*) to promise solemnly to give sth, eg one's support: [Vn] *pledge a donation* [Vnpr] *pledge loyalty to the king/the flag* ○ *be pledged to secrecy* [also Vnn]. **(b)** ~ **sb/oneself** (**to sth/to do sth**); ~ **sth/that...** to promise solemnly that sb/one will do sth or support a cause, etc: [Vn.to inf, Vnpr] *The government has pledged itself to reduce bureaucracy/to increased expenditure on AIDS research.* [V.to inf, V.that] *The union have pledged never to strike/pledged that they will never strike.* **2** to leave sth with sb as a pledge(2): [Vn] *He's pledged his mother's wedding ring.*

plenary /'pli:nəri/ *adj* (of meetings, etc) to be attended by all who have the right to attend: *a plenary session of the assembly/conference.*

plenipotentiary /ˌplenɪpə'tenʃəri/ *n* a person, eg

[V.*to* inf] = verb + *to* infinitive   [Vn.inf (no *to*)] = verb + noun + infinitive without *to*   [V.*ing*] = verb + -*ing* form

an AMBASSADOR, with full powers to act on behalf of her or his government, esp in a foreign country. ▶ **plenipotentiary** adj.

plenteous /'plentiəs/ adj (fml) PLENTIFUL.

plentiful /'plentɪfl/ adj existing or available in large quantities or numbers: a plentiful supply of fresh vegetables ∘ Strawberries are plentifᵤl at the moment. Compare SCARCE. ▶ **plentifully** /-fəli/ adv .

plenty /'plenti/ pron a number or an amount that is sufficient for sb or more than they need: plenty of eggs/money/time ∘ 'Do you need more milk?' 'No thanks, there's plenty in the fridge.' ∘ They always gave us plenty to eat.
▶ **plenty** n [U] a situation in which there is a large supply of food, money, etc: Everyone is happier **in** times of plenty. ∘ We had food and drink **in plenty**.
plenty adv **1** (used with more) a lot: We have plenty more of them in the warehouse. ∘ There's plenty more paper if you need it. **2** (infml) (used with big, long, tall, etc followed by enough) easily: The rope was plenty long enough to reach the ground.

plethora /'pleθərə/ n [sing] (fml) a quantity greater than what is needed or can be used; an excess: The report contained a plethora of detail.

pleurisy /'plʊərəsi/ n [U] (medical) a serious illness affecting the delicate lining of the THORAX(1) and the lungs, causing severe pain in the chest or sides.

plexus ⇨ SOLAR PLEXUS.

pliable /'plaɪəbl/ adj **1** easily bent, shaped or twisted; flexible: Cane is pliable when wet. **2** (of a person) easily influenced: the pliable minds of children.

pliant /'plaɪənt/ adj **1** easily bent without breaking: the pliant twigs of young trees. **2** (sometimes derog) adapting or changing easily; easily influenced: a pliant husband. ▶ **pliancy** /'plaɪənsi/ n [U]. **pliantly** adv.

pliers /'plaɪəz/ n [pl] a tool with long flat metal jaws in which sth, eg wire, can be held firm when the jaws are closed so that it can be bent or twisted: a pair of pliers.

plight¹ /plaɪt/ n [sing] a serious and difficult situation or condition: the plight of the homeless ∘ They were in a desperate plight, having lost all their possessions in the fire.

plight² /plaɪt/ v **IDM** **plight one's 'troth** (arch) to make a promise, esp to marry sb.

plimsoll /'plɪmsəl/ (also **pump**) (Brit) (US **sneaker**) n a light canvas sports shoe with rubber soles: a pair of white plimsolls.

plinth /plɪnθ/ n a block of stone on which a column or statue stands. ⇨ picture at COLUMN.

plod /plɒd/ v (-dd-) ~ (along/on) to walk slowly with heavy steps or with difficulty: [Vadv] Labourers plodded home through the muddy fields. [Vpr, Vp] We plodded (on) through the rain for several hours. [also V]. ⇨ note at STAMP¹ **PHRV** **plod a'long/'on** to proceed or progress slowly: 'How's the book?' 'Oh, I'm plodding along.'
▶ **plodder** n (usu derog) a person who works slowly and with determination, but who lacks imagination.
plodding adj (derog): a plodding speech/account.

plonk¹ /plɒŋk/ n (usu sing) (infml) a low sound, eg of sth fairly heavy dropping: to hear a plonk.
▶ **plonk** v **PHRV** **'plonk oneself/sth (down) in/on sth** (infml) to drop or put oneself/sth down heavily or in a hurried way: He plonked the groceries on the kitchen floor and ran upstairs. ∘ We plonked ourselves (down) by the fire.

plonk² /plɒŋk/ n [U] (infml esp Brit) cheap wine of poor quality.

plop /plɒp/ n (usu sing) a short sound, eg of a small object dropping into water.
▶ **plop** v (-pp-) to fall with a plop: [Vp] The fish

plopped back into the river. [Vpr] (fig) A memo plopped onto my desk.

plosive /'pləʊsɪv, 'pləʊzɪv/ n, adj (phonetics) a consonant sound made by closing the air passage and then releasing the air in a way that can be heard, eg /t/ and /p/ in top.

plot¹ /plɒt/ n a small marked piece of land used or intended for a special purpose: a building plot ∘ a vegetable plot ∘ a small plot of land.
▶ **plot** v (-tt-) ~ sth (on sth) (**a**) to mark sth on a map, chart or diagram: [Vn] plot a ship's course [Vnpr] earthquake centres plotted on a world map. (**b**) to draw a line or curve by connecting points on a GRAPH: [Vn, Vnpr] plot a temperature curve (on a graph).

plot² /plɒt/ n **1** a plan or an outline of the events in a play or novel: The plot was too complicated for me to follow. **2** ~ (to do sth) a secret plan made by several people to do sth, usu sth wrong or illegal: hatch/devise a plot to overthrow the government ∘ The police have uncovered a plot to kidnap the President's daughter. **IDM** **the plot 'thickens** (catchphrase) the situation is becoming more complicated or mysterious.
▶ **plot** v (-tt-) ~ (with sb) (against sb); ~ (to do sth) to make a secret plan to do sth; to take part in a plot: [Vpr] plot with others against the state [Vn] She is plotting her revenge. [V.to inf] They were plotting to overthrow the government. [also V]. **plotter** n.

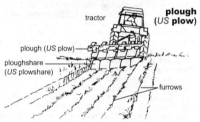

plough
(US plow)
tractor
plough (US plow)
ploughshare
(US plowshare)
furrows

plough (US **plow**) /plaʊ/ n **1** [C] a farming implement with a curved blade, pulled by animals or by a tractor. It is used for digging and turning over the soil, esp before seeds are planted. ⇨ picture. See also SNOWPLOUGH. **2 the Plough** (Brit) (US also **the ,Big 'Dipper**) [sing] (astronomy) the seven brightest stars in the group of the Great Bear, visible only from the northern half of the world. **IDM** **under the 'plough** (of land) used for growing crops and not for keeping animals on.
▶ **plough** (US **plow**) v ~ sth (up) to dig and turn over the surface of land with a plough: [Vn] ploughed fields [Vnp] The meadow has been ploughed up. **PHRV** **plough sth back (in)**; **plough sth back (into sth)** **1** to turn over growing crops, grass, etc with a plough and mix them into the soil in order to improve its quality. **2** to invest profits back in the business that produced them. **plough into sth/sb** to crash violently into sth/sb: The car went out of control and ploughed into the side of a bus. **plough on (with sth)** to continue slowly and with difficulty: He ploughed on with his lengthy explanation even though few people were listening. **plough (one's way) through sth 1** to force a way through sth: plough one's way through the mud ∘ The ship ploughed through the waves. **2** to make progress slowly or with difficulty: plough through legal textbooks/a pile of documents/mountains of work.

ploughman (US **plow-**) /'plaʊmən/ n (**-men** /-mən/) a man who guides a PLOUGH(1), esp one pulled by animals.
■ **,ploughman's 'lunch** n (Brit) a meal of bread and cheese with PICKLE(1a) and SALAD(1a), usu eaten in a pub.

ploughshare (US **plowshare**, **share**) /'plaʊʃeə(r)/

[V.speech] = verb + direct speech   [V.that] = verb + that clause   [V.wh] = verb + who, how, etc clause

n the broad blade of a PLOUGH. ⇨ picture at PLOUGH 1. **IDM** **turn swords into ploughshares** ⇨ SWORD.

plover /ˈplʌvə(r)/ *n* a bird with long legs and a short tail that lives on wet ground, esp near the sea. ⇨ picture.

plover

ploy /plɔɪ/ *n* words or actions that are carefully planned to win an advantage over sb else: *a marketing ploy* ○ *It was all a ploy to distract attention from his real aims.*

pluck¹ /plʌk/ *v* **1** ~ sth (off/out) to remove sth from where it is growing by pulling it; to pick sth: [Vnpr] *pluck a rose from the garden* [Vn] *pluck one's eyebrows* (ie remove hairs from them to make them neater) [Vnp] *pluck out a grey hair.* **2** [Vn] to pull the feathers off a dead bird, eg a chicken, in order to prepare it for cooking. **3** ~ sth (from sth); ~ (at sth) to hold sth with the fingers and pull it: [Vn, Vpr] *The child was plucking (at) her mother's skirt.* [Vnpr] *He plucked a handkerchief from his pocket.* **4** ~ sb from sth to rescue sb from a difficult or unpleasant situation: [Vnpr] *a sailor plucked from a sinking ship by a helicopter* ○ *She was plucked from obscurity to take part in the new TV series.* **5** (*US* also **pick**) to sound the strings of a musical instrument by pulling and releasing them: [Vn] *pluck the strings of a guitar.* **PHRV** **pluck sth 'up** to raise or increase one's courage or spirits: *I finally plucked up the/enough courage to tell her.*

pluck² /plʌk/ *n* [U] (*infml*) courage: *She showed a lot of pluck in dealing with the burglars.*
▶ **plucky** *adj* having or showing pluck; brave.

plug /plʌɡ/ *n* **1(a)** a plastic or rubber device with metal pins that fit into holes in a SOCKET(2) to make an electrical connection: *a three-/two-pin plug* ○ *Put the plug in the socket.* ○ *I'll have to change the plug on the hair-drier.* ⇨ picture at SOCKET. **(b)** (*infml*) an electric SOCKET(2). **2(a)** a piece of metal, rubber or plastic that fits tightly into a hole, eg in a bath or barrel: *Pull (out) the plug and let the water drain away.* See also EARPLUG. **(b)** (*US*) = STOPPER. **3** = SPARK-PLUG. **4** (*infml*) a piece of favourable publicity in the media for a commercial product, eg a book or recording: *The programme gave his new show a nice plug.* **IDM** **pull the plug on sb/sth** ⇨ PULL¹.
▶ **plug** *v* (**-gg-**) **1** to fill a hole or block sth with a plug: [Vn] *plug a leak in the roof* ○ (*fig*) *The government will have to raise taxes to plug the gap between revenue and spending.* **2** (*infml*) to mention sth favourably in the media, esp repeatedly: [Vn] *They've been plugging his new show on the radio.* **3** (*infml esp US*) to shoot or hit sb: [Vn-adj] *He'd been plugged full of holes.* [also Vn, Vnpr]. **PHRV** **plug a'way (at sth)** to work hard and steadily at sth: *She's been plugging away at her French for months.* **plug sth 'in** to connect sth to the electricity supply with a plug(1a): *plug in the vacuum cleaner* ○ *The tape recorder wasn't plugged in.* Compare UNPLUG.

plughole /ˈplʌɡhəʊl/ (*Brit*) (*US* **drain**) *n* a hole into which a plug(2a) fits, esp in a sink, bath, etc: *wash/pour sth down the plughole.*

plum /plʌm/ *n* **1(a)** [C] a soft round fruit with a smooth red or purple skin, sweet flesh and a fairly flat pointed stone. ⇨ picture at FRUIT. **(b)** [C] (also **plum tree**) a tree on which this grows. **2** [U] a dark reddish-purple colour. **3** (*infml*) (often attrib) a thing considered good or worth having, esp a job with good pay: *She's got a plum job in the BBC.*
■ **plum 'pudding** *n* [C, U] = CHRISTMAS PUDDING.

plumage /ˈpluːmɪdʒ/ *n* [U] the feathers covering a bird's body: *be in summer/winter plumage.*

plumb¹ /plʌm/ *v* **1** [Vn] to test sth by using a PLUMB-LINE. **2** (*fml or rhet*) to try to understand sth thoroughly: [Vn] *plumb the mysteries of the universe.*

IDM **plumb the depths of sth** to reach the lowest point of sth: *plumb the depths of despair* ○ *The film plumbs new depths of bad taste.* **PHRV** **plumb sth 'in** to connect an appliance, eg a washing-machine (WASHING) to pipes that can supply it with water: *I've plumbed in the new dishwasher.*

plumb² /plʌm/ *adv* **1** exactly: *plumb in the middle.* **2** (*US infml*) quite; absolutely: *He's plumb stupid.*

plumber /ˈplʌmə(r)/ *n* a person whose job is to fit and repair pipes, tanks, etc that supply and store water for use in a building.

plumbing /ˈplʌmɪŋ/ *n* [U] **1** the system of pipes, tanks, etc that supply and store water for use in a building: *There is something wrong with the plumbing.* **2** the work of a PLUMBER: *We employed a local man to do the plumbing.*

plumb-line /ˈplʌm laɪn/ *n* a cord with a weight attached to one end, used to find the depth of water or to test whether a wall, etc is straight.

plume /pluːm/ *n* **(a)** a feather, esp a large one used as a decoration. **(b)** an ornament of feathers or similar material, worn in the hair or on a hat or HELMET: *a plume of ostrich feathers.* **(c)** a thing that rises and curves in the air in the shape of a feather: *a plume of smoke.* **plumed** *adj* having or decorated with a plume or plumes: *a plumed hat.*

plummet /ˈplʌmɪt/ *n* a weight attached to a line, eg to keep the FLOAT²(1a) upright when fishing.
▶ **plummet** *v* to fall steeply or rapidly: [V] *House prices have plummeted in this area.* [Vp, Vpr] *A single slip could send them plummeting down (the mountainside).*

plummy /ˈplʌmi/ *adj* **1** like a PLUM(1a) in colour, taste or texture: *plummy lips* ○ *a wine with a plummy taste.* **2** (*Brit usu derog*) (of a voice) rich and deep in tone, in a way that is thought typical of the English upper class: *a plummy accent.*

plump /plʌmp/ *adj* **(a)** (*usu approv*) (esp of an animal, a person, or a part of the body) having a pleasantly full round shape; having plenty of flesh: *a plump chicken/face* ○ *a baby with plump cheeks.* **(b)** (*euph*) fat: *She's rather short and plump.* ⇨ note at FAT¹.
▶ **plump** *v* ~ sth (up/out) to make sth full and round: [Vn, Vnp] *plump (up) the cushions/pillows.* **PHRV** **plump (oneself/sb/sth) 'down** to fall or drop sth suddenly and heavily: *plump down the heavy bags* ○ *plump (oneself) down in a chair.* **plump for sb/sth 1** (*Brit*) to make a considered decision in favour of sb/sth: *The committee plumped for the most experienced candidate.* ○ *We finally plumped for a holiday by the sea.* **2** (*US*) to support sb/sth enthusiastically: *plump for one's local team.*
plumpness *n* [U].

plunder /ˈplʌndə(r)/ *v* to steal goods from a place, esp during a time of war or civil disorder: [V] *The invaders advanced, killing and plundering as they went.* [Vnpr] *plunder a palace of its treasures* [Vn] *Robbers had plundered the graves thousands of years before.*
▶ **plunder** *n* [U] **1** the action of plundering: *the profits of plunder.* **2** goods that have been plundered: *They loaded the carts with plunder.* Compare LOOT, PILLAGE.

plunge /plʌndʒ/ *v* **1(a)** ~ sth in(to sth) to put sth into sth else quickly and with force: [Vnpr] *plunge a rod into a blocked drain* ○ *He plunged his hand deep into his pocket.* [also Vnp]. **(b)** ~ in(to sth) to jump or fall into sth quickly and with force: [Vpr] *plunge into the icy water* [also Vp]. **2** to move or make sb/sth move suddenly and violently forwards and downwards: [Vpr] *The car plunged over the cliff.* [Vnadv] *The sudden jolt plunged her forward.* [V] *Share prices plunged as a result of the gloomy economic forecast.* [also Vnpr]. **3** to enter or make sb/sth enter a specified state or condition: [Vnpr] *The*

[Vnn] = verb + noun + noun   [V-adj] = verb + adjective   For more help with verbs, see Study pages **B4–8**.

news plunged us into despair. [Vpr,Vnpr] *The country (was) plunged into civil war after the death of its President.*

▶ **plunge** *n* (**a**) [C esp *sing*] a sudden violent movement or fall: *a plunge into debt/chaos.* (**b**) [C] an act of jumping or diving (DIVE¹ 1) into water: *a refreshing plunge in the lake.* **IDM** **take the ˈplunge** to take a bold and important step, esp after thinking about it for some time: *They have finally decided to take the plunge and get married.*

plunger *n* **1** a part of a device that can be pushed down, eg in a SYRINGE when sb is giving an injection (INJECT 1) or in a coffee pot when the coffee has brewed (BREW 2a). **2** a rubber cup fixed onto a handle, used for clearing a blocked pipe by means of SUCTION.

pluperfect /ˌpluːˈpɜːfɪkt/ (also **past perfect**) *adj, n* (*grammar*) (of) a TENSE² of a verb formed in English with *had* and a past participle that expresses an action completed before a particular point in the past, eg 'Since he *had* not *received* my letter, he did not come'.

plural /ˈplʊərəl/ *n* (*grammar*) (abbreviated as *pl* in this dictionary) a form of a noun or verb which refers to more than one person or thing: *The plural of 'child' is 'children'.* ○ *The verb should be in the plural* (eg 'have' not 'has' in 'they have'). Compare SINGULAR.

▶ **plural** *adj* **1** (*grammar*) of or having the plural form: *Most plural nouns in English end in 's'.* **2** of more than one: *a plural society* (ie one with more than one ethnic group).

NOTE There are a lot of nouns in English of Latin or Greek origin. They often end in **-us, -a, -um, -on**, etc. The plural forms of these nouns can cause difficulty. **1** Some, especially scientific terms, have kept their original singular and plural forms: *bacillus, bacilli* ○ *larva, larvae* ○ *criterion, criteria*. **2** Many, especially those in general use, now only have a regular English plural form: *arena, arenas* ○ *circus, circuses* ○ *electron, electrons*. **3** Some have alternative plural forms, which are both acceptable. The Latin form is more formal: *focus, focuses/foci* ○ *formula, formulas/formulae* ○ *spectrum, spectrums/ spectra*. **4** There is uncertainty with some nouns as to whether they are singular or plural: *This data is correct* and *These data are correct* are both acceptable. **Paraphernalia** (a Greek plural) is used as a singular noun: *All my fishing paraphernalia is in the car.* **Media** (*sing* **medium**) is sometimes incorrectly used as a singular noun: *The media are* (NOT *is*) *often accused of being biased.*

pluralism /ˈplʊərəlɪzəm/ *n* [U] **1(a)** the existence in one society of a number of groups that belong to different races or have different political or religious beliefs. (**b**) the principle that these different groups can live together in peace in one society. **2** (*usu derog*) the holding of more than one office at one time, esp in the Church.

▶ **pluralist** /ˈplʊərəlɪst/ *n* a supporter of pluralism.
pluralist (also **pluralistic**) /ˌplʊərəˈlɪstɪk/ *adj*: *a pluralist society.*

plurality /plʊəˈræləti/ *n* **1** [C] (*fml*) a large number: *a plurality of influences/peoples.* **2** [C] (*US politics*) a majority of less than 50%; a majority that is not absolute. Compare MAJORITY 1. **3** [U] (*grammar*) the state of being PLURAL(1).

plus /plʌs/ *prep* (**a**) with the addition of sth/sb: *Two plus five is seven.* ○ *The cost is £22, plus £1 for postage.* (**b**) (*infml*) as well as sth/sb: *We've got to fit five people plus all their luggage in the car.* Compare MINUS 3.

▶ **plus** *adj* **1** (following a number) more than the amount or number indicated: *The work will cost*

$10 000 plus. **2** above zero: *The temperature is plus four degrees.*

plus *n* (*pl* **pluses** /ˈplʌsɪz/) **1** the sign +: *He seems to have put a plus instead of a minus.* **2** (*infml*) a positive quality; an advantage: *Knowledge of French is a plus in her job.* Compare MINUS *n* 2.

■ **ˌplus-ˈfours** *n* [pl] wide loose trousers ending just below the knees, where they fit closely: *a pair of plus-fours.*

ˈplus point *n* an aspect of sth that may be seen as a good thing; an advantage: *One of the hotel's plus points is that it is very central.*

plush /plʌʃ/ *n* [U] a type of silk or cotton cloth with a thick soft surface like VELVET.

▶ **plush** (also **plushy**) *adj* (*infml*) extremely comfortable and expensive; SMART¹(4): *a plush hotel/ restaurant.*

Pluto /ˈpluːtəʊ/ *n* the planet that is furthest from the sun.

plutocracy /pluːˈtɒkrəsi/ *n* (**a**) [U] government by the richest people of a country. (**b**) [C] a country governed in this way.

▶ **plutocrat** /ˈpluːtəkræt/ *n* (*often derog*) a person who is powerful because of his wealth.

plutonium /pluːˈtəʊniəm/ *n* [U] (*symb* **Pu**) (*chemistry*) a chemical element. Plutonium is RADIOACTIVE and used esp in nuclear weapons and as a fuel in nuclear power stations. ⇨ App 7.

ply¹ /plaɪ/ *n* [U] (esp in compounds) **1** a layer of wood or thickness of cloth: *three-ply wood.* **2** a strand of rope or wool: *three-/four-ply knitting wool.*

ply² /plaɪ/ *v* (*pt, pp* **plied** /plaɪd/) **1** (of ships, buses, etc) to go regularly from one point to another and back again: [Vnpr] *ply the routes between the islands* [Vpr] *ferries that ply between England and France* [Vn] *ships that ply the South China Sea.* **2** (*fml*) to use a tool or weapon: [Vn] *ply the oars* (ie row a boat). **IDM** **ply one's ˈtrade** to work at a skilled job. **ply for ˈhire** (of taxi drivers, people hiring boats, etc) to wait in a place looking for passengers: *taxis plying for hire at the airport.* **PHRV** **ˈply sb with sth 1** to give or offer sb food and drink repeatedly: *She plied us with cakes.* **2** to keep asking sb questions.

plywood /ˈplaɪwʊd/ *n* [U] board made by sticking thin layers of wood on top of each other: *sheets of plywood* ○ *plywood furniture.*

PM /ˌpiːˈem/ *abbr* (*infml esp Brit*) Prime Minister: *an interview with the PM.*

pm (*US* **PM**) /ˌpiːˈem/ *abbr* after noon (Latin *post meridiem*): *at 3 pm* (ie 3 o'CLOCK in the afternoon). Compare AM².

PMT /ˌpiː em ˈtiː/ *abbr* premenstrual tension.

pneumatic /njuːˈmætɪk; *US* nuː-/ *adj* **1** filled with air: *a pneumatic tyre.* **2** worked by air under pressure: *a pneumatic drill.*

pneumonia /njuːˈməʊniə; *US* nuː-/ *n* [U] a serious illness affecting one or both lungs, causing difficulty in breathing.

PO /ˌpiːˈəʊ/ *abbr* **1** (also **po**) postal order. **2** Post Office: *PO Box 7427* (eg in an address).

poach¹ /pəʊtʃ/ *v* (**a**) to cook fish, fruit, etc by heating it gently in a small amount of liquid: [Vnpr] *apricots poached in white wine* [also Vn]. (**b**) to cook an egg by removing it from its shell and putting it in water that is nearly boiling.

poach² /pəʊtʃ/ *v* **1** to catch birds, animals or fish on sb else's property without permission: [V, Vn] *He was caught poaching (hares).* **2(a)** ~ (**on sth**) to be active in an area that properly belongs to sb else: [Vpr] *Rival salesmen were poaching on his territory.* [also V]. (**b**) to take ideas, staff, etc from sb/sth, esp in a deceitful or unfair way: [Vn] *A rival firm poached our best computer programmers.*

▶ **poacher** *n* a person who poaches.

pocked /pɒkt/ *adj* ~ **(with sth)** having holes or depressions in the surface: *The moon's surface is pocked with small craters.*

pocket /'pɒkɪt/ *n* **1(a)** a small piece of material sewn into or onto a garment and forming a small bag for carrying things in: *a coat/jacket/trouser pocket* ○ *He picked up his keys and put them in his pocket.* ○ *a pocket dictionary/calculator/guide* (ie one small enough to fit in a pocket). **(b)** a container resembling this, eg on the inside of a car door or in a SUITCASE: *You will find information about safety procedures in the pocket in front of you* (eg on an aircraft). **2** (usu *sing*) money that one has available for spending; financial means: *prices to suit every pocket* ○ *The expedition was a drain on her pocket.* **3** a small isolated group or area: *pockets of unemployment* ○ *a few isolated pockets of opposition/resistance to the new regime.* **4** = AIR POCKET. **5** (*sport*) any of the holes or string bags beneath them situated round the edges of a table for pool²(3), SNOOKER or BILLIARDS. ➪ picture at SNOOKER. **IDM** **be in sb's 'pocket** to be controlled or strongly influenced by sb. **be/live in each other's 'pockets** to be (too) close to or spend (too) much time with each other. **dig into one's pocket(s)** ➪ DIG. **have sb in one's 'pocket** to have influence or power over sb. **,in/,out of 'pocket** having gained/lost money as a result of sth: *Even after paying all our expenses, we were still over £100 in pocket.* ○ *His mistake left us all out of pocket.* ○ *,out-of-pocket ex'penses* (ie money that one has spent and which will be returned, eg by one's employer). **line one's/sb's pocket** ➪ LINE³. **money burns a hole in sb's pocket** ➪ MONEY. **pick sb's pocket** ➪ PICK¹. **put one's hand in one's pocket** ➪ HAND¹.
▶ **pocket** *v* **1** to put sth into one's pocket: [Vn] *She quickly slipped the note without reading it.* **2** to keep or take sth for oneself, esp dishonestly: [Vn] *She pays $2 for them, sells them for $4 and pockets the difference.* ○ *He was given £20 for expenses, but pocketed most of it.* **3** [Vn] (eg in BILLIARDS) to hit a ball into a pocket(5).

pocketful /-fʊl/ *n* (*pl* **-fuls**) the amount a pocket holds: *a pocketful of coins.*
■ **'pocket knife** *n* (*esp US*) = PENKNIFE. ➪ picture at KNIFE.
'pocket money *n* [U] **(a)** (*Brit*) a small amount of money given to a child by its parents, esp on a regular basis. **(b)** money for small expenses.

pocketbook /'pɒkɪtbʊk/ *n* **1** a small book for writing in. **2(a)** = WALLET. **(b)** (*US*) a PURSE¹(1) or small bag for a woman.

pock-mark /'pɒk mɑːk/ *n* a hollow mark left on the skin after a spot¹(2) has healed.
■ **'pock-marked** *adj* having pock-marks or marks resembling them: *a pock-marked face* ○ *walls pock-marked with bullets.*

pod /pɒd/ *n* a usu long thin case containing seeds that develops from the flowers of various plants, esp peas (PEA) and beans.

podgy /'pɒdʒi/ *adj* (*infml usu derog*) (of people or parts of the body) short and fat: *podgy fingers.* ➪ note at FAT¹.

podiatry /pə'daɪətri/ *n* [U] (*US*) = CHIROPODY. ▶ **podiatrist** /-trɪst/ *n* (*US*) = CHIROPODIST.

podium /'pəʊdiəm/ *n* a small platform for a person to stand on while conducting a group of musicians, giving a speech, etc.

poem /'pəʊɪm/ *n* a piece of creative writing in verse, esp one expressing deep feelings: *write/compose poems.*

poet /'pəʊɪt/ *n* (*fem* **poetess** /,pəʊɪ'tes/) a writer of poems.
■ **,Poet 'Laureate** (also **Laureate**) *n* **(a)** (in Britain) a poet officially appointed to write poems for state occasions. **(b)** (*esp US*) a poet regarded as the most famous or typical of her or his country or region.

poetic /pəʊ'etɪk/ *adj* **1** (*approv*) of or suggesting poetry, esp in being imaginative, graceful and showing deep feeling: *a poetic rendering of a piano sonata.* **2** [attrib] = POETICAL 1: *his entire poetic output.*
▶ **poetical** /-kl/ *adj* **1** [attrib] of or being poetry: *the poetical works of Keats.* **2** [attrib] = POETIC 1.
poetically /-kli/ *adv.*
■ **po,etic 'justice** *n* [U] a suitable or deserved punishment or reward.
po,etic 'licence *n* [U] the freedom to change the normal rules of language when writing verse, eg by reversing word order or changing meaning: *allow oneself/indulge in a bit of poetic licence.*

poetry /'pəʊətri/ *n* [U] **1** a collection of poems or poems in general: *epic/lyric/dramatic/pastoral/symbolist poetry* ○ *Dryden's poetry* ○ *a poetry book* ○ *a poetry reading.* Compare PROSE, VERSE 1. **2** (*approv*) a beautiful and graceful quality: *a ballet dancer with poetry in every movement.*

po-faced /'pəʊ feɪst/ *adj* (*Brit infml derog*) with a solemn expression, esp of disapproval.

pogo stick /'pəʊgəʊ stɪk/ *n* a pole, with bars for standing on and a spring at the bottom end, used as a toy for jumping about on.

pogrom /'pɒgrəm; *US* 'pəʊgrəm/ *n* an organized persecution (PERSECUTE) or killing of a particular group or class of people, esp because of their race or religion.

poignant /'pɔɪnjənt/ *adj* affecting one's feelings deeply; making one sad or full of pity: *a poignant scene/phrase/moment.* ▶ **poignancy** /-jənsi/ *n* [U]: *songs of great poignancy and beauty.* **poignantly** /-jəntli/ *adv.*

poinsettia /pɔɪn'setiə/ *n* a tropical plant with large red leaves that grow to look like flowers. It is sometimes grown indoors in pots.

point¹ /pɔɪnt/ *n* **1** [C] a narrow, usu sharp, end of sth; a tip: *the point of a pin/knife/pencil* ○ *the point of the jaw* (eg as the target for a punch in boxing) ○ *The stake had been sharpened to a vicious-looking point.* See also GUNPOINT, KNIFE-POINT. **2** [C] (often **Point** as part of a name) a narrow piece of land projecting from the coast into the sea: *The ship rounded the point.* ○ *Pagoda Point.* **3** [C] **(a)** any dot used in writing or printing, eg as a full stop (FULL) or before a decimal: *a decimal point* ○ *Two point six (2.6) means the same as* $2\frac{6}{10}$. ➪ App 2. **(b)** a tiny dot or mark of light or colour: *stars seen as points of light in a dark sky.* See also FOCAL POINT. **4** [C] (*esp geometry*) a position on a drawing, map, etc: *Lines AB and CD intersect at the point P.* See also VANISHING-POINT. **5** [C] a particular place or area: *an assembly/a rallying/a meeting point* ○ *Guards had been posted at several points around the perimeter.* See also VANTAGE POINT. **6** [C] a particular time or instant: *He was at the point of death* (ie about to die). ○ *At one point I though she was going to refuse.* ○ *The argument started to get very violent, at which point I left.* See also TURNING-POINT. **7** [C] a particular stage in a process of change or development: *boiling-/freezing-/melting-point* ○ *reach danger/crisis point* ○ *We had reached the point where some of our assets had to be sold off.* ○ *There comes a point when some action is necessary.* **8** [C] any of the 32 marks round a COMPASS(1): *the cardinal points* (ie the four main points: N, E, S and W) ○ *People came from all points of the compass* (ie every direction). **9** [C] **(a)** a unit of measurement or value: *a point on a scale* ○ *The pound fell several points on the international markets today.* **(b)** an individual mark or score, added to others to make a total score: *We need one more point to win the game.* **10** [C] a specific item or detail: *the main points of a* story/a discussion/an argument ○ points of differ-ence/similarity/agreement/disagreement ○ explain a theory point by point (ie explain each individual idea in it, in order) ○ One point in favour of her plan is its cheapness. **11** [C] **(a)** a thing said as part of a discussion: Dr Rose made a number of interesting points in his speech. **(b)** an effective argument: 'But she might not agree.' 'You've got a point there/ That's a point (ie I had not thought of that).' See also TALKING-POINT. **12** (usu the point) [sing] the matter under discussion; the essential part or aspect of sth: The point (at issue) is this... ○ Let's stop discussing trivial details and come/get to the point. ○ The speaker kept wandering off/away from the point. **13** [U, sing] the essential meaning, fea-ture, purpose or value of sth: get/see/miss the point of sth ○ I'm afraid you've missed my point. ○ There's no/not much point in complaining; they never take any notice. **14** [U] (fml) power and ur-gency (URGENT 2); effectiveness (EFFECTIVE): words/ remarks that have/lack point. **15** [C] a distinctive feature or characteristic: sb's good/strong/bad/ weak points ○ I'm afraid honesty is not his strong point (ie he is not honest). See also SELLING-POINT. **16** [C] (Brit) (often in compounds) an electrical SOCKET(2), into which a plug is put: a power/cooker/ shaver point. **17** points [pl] (in ballet) the tips of the toes: dancing on points. **18** points [pl] (Brit) (US switch [C]) a set of movable rails at a place where a railway line divides into two tracks, which can be altered to allow a train to use either track: change the points. **19** [U] (after a number) a unit of meas-urement for the size of letters in printing, word-processing (WORD), etc: Choose a smaller font size, eg 9 point. **IDM** beside the ꞌpoint not relevant. a case in point ⇨ CASE¹. the finer points ⇨ FINE¹. have one's ꞌpoints to have certain good aspects or qual-ities but not be entirely satisfactory: Taking a holiday in November has its points. if/when it comes to the ꞌpoint if or when the moment for a difficult action or decision arrives: If it came to the point, would you sacrifice your job for your prin-ciples? in point of ꞌfact in reality; actually: He said he would pay, but in point of fact he has no money. labour the point ⇨ LABOUR². make one's ꞌpoint to make one's feelings or opinions known: All right, you've made your point — now keep quiet and let the others say what they think. make a ꞌpoint of doing sth to be particularly careful to do sth because one considers it important or necessary: I make a point of checking that all the windows are shut whenever I go out. a moot point/question ⇨ MOOT. not to put too fine a point on it ⇨ FINE¹. on the ꞌpoint of sth/doing sth just about to do sth: I was on the point of going to bed when you rang. ○ The company is on the point of collapse. on ꞌpoints (in a competi-tion) by the number of points scored: Arsenal are level on points, but have played fewer games. a ꞌpoint of deꞌparture **1** a place or time at which a journey begins. **2** a starting point for a discussion or an enterprise: Let's take 'Das Kapital' as a point of departure for our survey of Marxism. a ꞌpoint of ꞌhonour a matter of great importance to one's hon-our or reputation: I always pay my debts punctually — it's a point of honour with me. the ꞌpoint of ꞌno reꞌturn the point at which one has to do sth that one has decided to do and cannot withdraw from it. ꞌpoint ꞌtaken (used to indicate acceptance of a criti-cism that has been made). score a point/points ⇨ SCORE². a sore point ⇨ SORE. stretch a point ⇨ STRETCH. take sb's ꞌpoint to understand and accept sb's argument. to the ꞌpoint relevant and appropriate: remarks that were very much to the point ○ His speech was short and to the point. to the point of sth to a degree that can be described as sth: His manner was abrupt to the point of rudeness. up to a (certain) ꞌpoint to some extent; in some

degree: I agree with you up to a (certain) point.
■ ꞌpoint-duty n [U] (Brit) the controlling of traffic by a police officer standing in the middle of the road, eg where roads cross.
ꞌpoint of ꞌorder n (pl points of order) (in formal discussions, eg debates) a matter of correct proced-ure according to the rules: On a point of order, Mr Chairman, can associate members vote on this mat-ter?
ꞌpoint of ꞌview n (pl points of view) an attitude; an opinion: This is unacceptable from my point of view. ○ What's your point of view on nuclear power?
ꞌpoint-to-ꞌpoint n (Brit) a race on horses over a marked course across fields, etc with jumps.

point² /pɔɪnt/ v **1** ~ (at/to sb/sth) to direct people's attention towards sb/sth by extending one's finger towards them/it: [V] It's rude to point. [Vpr] 'That's the man who did it,' she said, pointing at me. ○ He pointed to a tower on the distant horizon. **2** to indic-ate position, direction, time, level, etc on a device: [Vadv] A compass needle points north. [Vpr] The clock hands pointed to twelve (ie It was NOON or midnight). **3** ~ sth (at/towards sb/sth) to aim or direct sth: [Vn, Vnpr] point one's finger (at sb/sth) [Vnpr] point a gun at sb ○ point a telescope at/ towards the moon. **4** to face or be turned in a particular direction: [Vadv] A hedgehog's spines point backwards. [also Vpr]. **5** to give force to sth; to make sth noticeable: [Vn] a story that points a moral. **6** to fill the spaces between bricks with cement or MORTAR¹: [Vn] point a wall/chimney. **IDM** point a/the ꞌfinger (at sb) (infml) to accuse sb openly. point the ꞌway (to/towards sth) to show the possibility of future development: tax reforms which point the way to a more prosperous future. **PHRV** ꞌpoint sth ꞌout (to sb) to direct attention to sth: point out a mistake ○ point out to sb the stupidity of their behaviour ○ I must point out that further delay would be unwise. ꞌpoint to sth to suggest that sth is likely; to indicate sth: All the evidence points to his guilt. ꞌpoint sth ꞌup to give special emphasis to a particular aspect of sth; to show sth very clearly: The recent disagreement points up the differences between the two sides.
▶ **pointed** adj **1** having a sharp tip, end, etc: a pointed instrument/tool ○ a pointed hat. **2** directed clearly against a particular person or her or his behaviour: a pointed comment/remark/rebuke ○ She made some pointed references to his careless work.
pointedly adv in a way that indicates criticism of a particular person or suggests one's intentions clearly: She stared pointedly at me. ○ He looked point-edly at the door (eg indicating that I should open it, close it, leave, etc).
pointing n [U] the cement or MORTAR¹ put in the spaces between the bricks of a wall, etc: Check the pointing is in good condition.

point-blank /ˌpɔɪnt ꞌblæŋk/ adj [attrib] **1** (of a shot) aimed or fired at very close range: He shot her at ˌpoint-blank ꞌrange. **2** (of sth said) direct and immediate, and often rather rude: a ˌpoint-blank reꞌfusal.
▶ **point-blank** adv in a point-blank manner; dir-ectly: fire point-blank at sb ○ refuse point-blank to do sth ○ I asked him point-blank what he was doing there.

pointer /ꞌpɔɪntə(r)/ n **1** a long thin piece of metal, plastic, etc which moves to indicate figures, posi-tions, etc on a scale, DIAL(2), etc. **2** a rod or stick used to point to things on a map, chart, etc. **3** (infml) a piece of advice: Could you give me a few pointers on how to tackle the job? **4** ~ (to sth) a thing that shows likely future developments: Eco-nomic pointers suggest a slowing down in the rate of growth. **5** a large hunting dog trained to stand still with its nose pointing in the direction of hunted birds, etc which it smells.

pointillism /ˈpɔɪntɪlɪzəm, ˈpwænt-/ n [U] a technique of painting developed in France in the late 19th century, in which the picture is built up from tiny dots of different colours. ▶ **pointillist** /-lɪst/ n, adj: pointillist art/artists.

pointless /ˈpɔɪntləs/ adj with little or no sense, aim or purpose: a pointless remark ○ It is pointless owning a car if you can't drive it! ▶ **pointlessly** adv. **pointlessness** n [U]: the pointlessness of his existence.

poise /pɔɪz/ v to be or keep sth balanced or suspended: [Vpr] The hawk poised in mid-air ready to swoop. [Vnpr] He poised the javelin in his hand before throwing it.
▶ **poise** n [U] **1** the graceful and balanced position or movement of the body; the control of this: move with the assured poise of a ballet dancer. **2** quiet confidence, dignity and SELF-CONTROL: a woman of great poise ○ She seemed embarrassed for a moment but quickly recovered her poise.

poised adj **1** [pred] ~ (in, on, above, etc sth) in a state of balance: poised on tiptoe/in mid-air ○ a cup poised on the edge of a table (ie likely to fall off if lightly touched) ○ (fig) poised between the old way of life and the new. **2** [pred] ~ (in/on/above/for sth); ~ (to do sth) (of people, animals, etc) in a state of physical tension, ready for action: poised on the edge of the swimming-pool (ie ready to jump in) ○ (fig) The party is poised (ie ready) for a return to power. ○ The company is poised to expand its overseas operation. **3** showing calm SELF-CONTROL; full of poise(2): a poised young lady ○ a poised manner.

poison /ˈpɔɪzn/ n [C, U] **1** a substance causing death or harm if taken into the body or absorbed: rat poison ○ poison for killing weeds ○ commit suicide by taking poison ○ a poison pill ○ poison gas (ie esp as used to kill people in war). **2** an extremely harmful or unpleasant thing or person: the poison of racial hatred ○ He can be absolute poison!
▶ **poison** v ~ sb/sth (with sth) **1(a)** to give poison to a living thing; to kill or harm sb/sth with poison: [Vnpr] His wife poisoned him with arsenic. [Vn] Are our children being poisoned by lead in the atmosphere? (**b**) to infect sth with poison; to put poison in or on sth: [Vn] a poisoned foot ○ a poisoned arrow/ dart [Vn, Vnpr] These companies are poisoning our rivers (with chemical waste). **2(a)** to harm sth morally; to CORRUPT²(1) sth: [Vnpr] poison sb's mind with propaganda [also Vn]. (**b**) to fill sth with suffering, hatred, etc; to spoil or ruin sth: [Vn] a quarrel which poisoned our friendship [also Vnpr]. **IDM** **a poisoned ˈchalice** a thing given to sb that appears attractive but later proves harmful or unpleasant: As the war became more unpopular the job of Foreign Secretary began to seem more like a poisoned chalice.
poisoner /ˈpɔɪzənə(r)/ n a person who murders sb by means of poison. **poisoning** /ˈpɔɪzənɪŋ/ n [U, C] an action or instance of giving or taking poison; the result of this: lead poisoning (ie poisoning by lead³(1)). See also BLOOD-POISONING, FOOD POISONING.
poisonous /ˈpɔɪzənəs/ adj **1(a)** using poison as a means of attacking enemies or PREY(1a): poisonous snakes/insects ○ a lizard with a poisonous bite. (**b**) causing death or illness if taken into the body: poisonous plants/chemicals. **2** (derog) (**a**) morally harmful: the poisonous doctrine of racial superiority. (**b**) full of spite; malicious (MALICE): sb with a poisonous tongue (ie who spreads bad or false rumours about people).

■ ˌpoison-ˈpen letter n an offensive letter sent deliberately to upset the person who receives it.

poke¹ /pəʊk/ v **1(a)** ~ sb/sth (with sth) to push sb/ sth sharply with a stick, one's finger, etc: [Vn, Vnpr] poke the fire (with a poker) (ie to make it burn more

strongly) [Vnpr] poke sb in the ribs (ie push them with one's finger, etc in a friendly way). (**b**) ~ sth in sth to make a hole in sth by pushing one's finger, a sharp instrument, etc through it: Poke two holes in the sack so you can see through it. (**c**) ~ at sth to make repeated small pushing movements at sth: [Vpr] She poked at her lunch unenthusiastically. **2** to put or move sth in a specified direction, with a sharp push: [Vnpr] poke food through the bars of a cage ○ He poked his head round the door to see if she was in the room. [Vnp] Don't poke her eye out with that stick! ▷ note at NUDGE. **IDM** **poke ˈfun at sb/ sth** to mock sb/sth: He enjoys poking fun at others. **poke/stick one's nose into sth** ▷ NOSE¹. **PHR V** ˌpoke aˈbout/aˈround (infml) to search for sth in a casual way: What were you doing poking about in my room? **poke out of/through sth**; **poke out/ through/up** to be visible coming through a hole, gap, etc; to PROTRUDE: a pen poking out (of sb's pocket) ○ I can see a finger poking through (a hole in your glove). ○ A few daffodils were already poking up (ie starting to grow).
▶ **poke** n an act of poking sb/sth: give the fire a poke ○ give sb a poke in the ribs.

poke² /pəʊk/ n **IDM** **buy a pig in a poke** ▷ BUY.

poker¹ /ˈpəʊkə(r)/ n a strong metal rod or bar for moving or breaking up coal in a fire.

poker² /ˈpəʊkə(r)/ n [U] a card-game for two or more people in which the players bet on the values of the cards they hold.

■ ˈpoker-face n (infml) a face that shows no sign of what the person is thinking or feeling. ˈpoker-faced adj: a poker-faced expression.

poky /ˈpəʊki/ adj (infml derog) (of a place) small; limited in space: a poky little room.

polar /ˈpəʊlə(r)/ adj [attrib] **1** of or near the North or South Pole: polar ice ○ polar explorers. **2** of (one of) the poles of a MAGNET(1): polar attraction. **3** (fml or techn) directly opposite in character or tendency: Is it sensible to think of men and women as **polar opposites**?
■ ˈpolar bear n a white bear living near the North Pole. ▷ picture at BEAR¹.

polarity /pəˈlærəti/ n **1** [U] ~ (between A and B) the state of having two opposite tendencies, opinions, etc: the growing polarity between the left and right wings of the party. **2** [U, C] (techn) the condition of having two poles with contrary qualities: the polarity of a magnet ○ reversed polarity/ polarities.

polarize, -ise /ˈpəʊləraɪz/ v **1(a)** ~ (into sth) (of people, views, etc) to separate into two groups which are completely opposite to each other: [V] Public opinion has polarized on this issue. [also Vpr]. (**b**) ~ sb/sth (into sth) to make people, views, etc separate in this way: [Vn] The issue has polarized public opinion. [also Vnpr]. **2** [Vn] (physics) to make waves of light, etc VIBRATE(1) in a single direction. **3** (techn) to give POLARITY(2) to sth: [Vn] polarize a magnet. ▶ **polarization, -isation** /ˌpəʊləraɪˈzeɪʃn; US -rəˈz-/ n [C, U]: the polarization of attitudes.

Polaroid /ˈpəʊlərɔɪd/ n (propr) **1(a)** [U] a thin transparent film put on sun-glasses (SUN), car windows, etc to reduce the brightness of sunlight. (**b**) **Polaroids** [pl] sun-glasses (SUN) treated with Polaroid. **2** [C] (also **Polaroid ˈcamera**) a camera that can produce photographs within seconds after the picture has been taken. (**b**) a photograph taken with such a camera.

pole¹ /pəʊl/ n a long thin piece of wood or metal, used esp as a support for sth or for pushing boats, etc along: a tent/flag/telegraph pole ○ a punt/barge/ ski pole. ▷ picture at SKIING, VAULT². See also TOTEM-POLE. **IDM** **up the ˈpole** (infml esp Brit) crazy; wildly wrong.

▶ **pole** v to push a boat, etc along by using a pole: [Vnpr] *pole a punt up the river* [also Vnp].

■ **'pole position** n [U, C] the leading position at the start of a motor race.

'**pole-vault** n (*sport*) a jump over a high bar, using a long pole which is held in the hands. — v [V] to perform such a jump. '**pole-vaulter** n. '**pole-vaulting** n [U]. ⇨ picture at VAULT².

pole² /pəʊl/ n **1** either of the two points at the opposite ends of the line on which the earth or any other planet turns: *the North/South Pole.* ⇨ picture at GLOBE. **2** (*physics*) either of the two ends of a MAGNET(1), or the positive or negative point of an electric battery. **3** either of two opposite or contrasting extremes: *Our points of view are at opposite poles.* **IDM** **be 'poles apart** to be widely separated; to have nothing in common: *The two sides in the dispute are still poles apart* (ie are far from reaching an agreement or a compromise).

■ '**pole star** n the North Star, the star that is near the North Pole in the sky.

pole-axe (*US* also **pole-ax**) /'pəʊl æks/ v **1** to hit sb/sth down with a very heavy blow: [Vn] *He was pole-axed by a left hook to the jaw.* **2** (usu passive) to affect sb very greatly with surprise and distress: [Vn] *We were all pole-axed by the news.*

polecat /'pəʊlkæt/ n **1** a small European animal of the WEASEL family which has dark brown fur and an unpleasant smell. **2** (*US*) = SKUNK 1.

polemic /pə'lemɪk/ n (*fml*) **1(a)** [C] a speech, piece of writing, etc containing very forceful arguments for or against sth/sb: *He launched into a fierce polemic against the government's policies.* **(b)** [U] such speeches, writing, etc: *engage in polemic.* **2 polemics** [pl] the art or practice of arguing a case formally and usu forcefully.

▶ **polemical** /-ɪkl/ (also **polemic**) adj (*fml*) **1** [attrib] of polemics: *polemic(al) skills.* **2** arguing a case very forcefully, often when many people disagree with it: *a polemic(al) article/speech.*

polemicist /pə'lemɪsɪst/ n a person who is skilled in polemics.

police /pə'liːs/ n (usu **the police**) [pl v] (the members of) an official organization whose job is to keep public order, prevent and solve crime, etc: *the local/ state/national police* ○ *a police car/enquiry/raid/ report* ○ *call out the riot police* ○ *There were over 100 police on duty at the demonstration.* ○ *The police have not made any arrests.* See also THE METROPOLITAN POLICE, SECRET POLICE.

▶ **police** v to keep order in a place with or as if with police; to control sth: [Vn] *The teachers on duty are policing the school buildings during the lunch hour.* ○ (*fig*) *a committee to police the new regulations* (ie make sure they are obeyed) ○ *community policing* ○ *policing strategy/measures.*

■ **po,lice 'constable** n (*abbr* **PC**) (also **constable**) (in Britain and some other countries) a police officer of the lowest rank.

po'lice dog n a dog trained to find or attack suspected criminals.

po'lice force n the police officers of a country, district or town.

po'lice officer n a member of the police force.

po'lice state n (*derog*) a country controlled by political police, usu a TOTALITARIAN state.

po'lice station n the office of a local police force: *The suspect was taken to the nearest police station for questioning.*

policeman /pə'liːsmən/ n (*pl* **-men** /-mən/) a male member of the police force.

policewoman /pə'liːswʊmən/ n (*pl* **-women** /-wɪmɪn/) (*abbr* **PW**) a female member of the police force.

policy /'pɒləsi/ n **1** [U, C] ~ (**on sth**) a plan of action, statement of ideals, etc proposed or adopted

by a government, political party, business, etc: *according to our present policy* ○ *adopt fresh policies* ○ *US foreign/domestic policy* ○ *a policy-making body* ○ *What is the Labour Party's policy on immigration?* ○ (*saying*) *Honesty is the best policy* (ie the best principle for people to live by). **2** [C] the terms of a contract of insurance, or a written statement of this: *a 'fire-insurance policy* ○ *a 'policy document.*

policyholder /'pɒləsihəʊldə(r)/ n a person or group holding an insurance policy.

polio /'pəʊliəʊ/ (also *fml* **poliomyelitis** /ˌpəʊliəʊˌmaɪə'laɪtɪs/) n [U] an infectious disease affecting the nerves in the SPINE(1) and often resulting in an inability to move or control parts of the body: *polio vaccine.*

polish /'pɒlɪʃ/ v **1** ~ sth (**up**) (**with sth**) to make sth smooth and shiny by rubbing, esp after first putting on a special substance to produce this result: [Vnpr] *polish shoes with a brush and a cloth* [Vn] *polish the floor* [Vnp] *polish up some old brass candlesticks.* **2** ~ sth (**up**) to improve sth by correcting it, making small changes or adding new material: [Vn, Vnp] *polish (up) a speech/an article.* **PHRV** ,**polish sth 'off** (*infml*) to finish sth quickly: *polish off a big plateful of stew* (ie eat it all) ○ *polish off a bit of work.* ,**polish sth 'up** to improve a skill, one's reputation, etc by working at it: *The country needs to polish up its image abroad.*

▶ **polish** n **1** [U, C] a substance used for polishing: *wax polish* ○ *'furniture/'floor/'shoe polish* ○ *a tin of metal polish* ○ *apply polish to sth.* See also FRENCH POLISH, NAIL VARNISH. **2** [sing] a shiny surface, etc obtained by polishing: *a table-top with a good polish.* **3** [sing] an act of polishing sth: *give the floor a thorough polish.* **4** [U] (*approv*) a fine or elegant quality or style; REFINEMENT(3): *He's still young and lacks polish and sophistication.* ○ *The choir sang with clarity, precision and polish.* **IDM** **spit and polish** ⇨ SPIT¹.

polished adj **1** shiny from polishing: *polished wood.* **2** elegant; refined: *polished manners* ○ *a polished style/performance.*

polisher n a machine for polishing: *a floor polisher.*

politburo /'pɒlɪtbjʊərəʊ/ n (*pl* **-os**) the chief committee of a Communist party responsible for making policy, esp in the former USSR.

polite /pə'laɪt/ adj (~**er**, ~**est**) **1** having or showing that one has good manners and consideration for other people: *a polite child* ○ *make polite conversation* ○ *It wasn't very polite of you to serve yourself without asking.* Compare IMPOLITE. **2** [attrib] (*fml*) typical of people in society who regard themselves as superior to and more refined than others: *a rude word not used in polite society/company.* ▶ **politely** adv. **politeness** n [U].

politic /'pɒlɪtɪk/ adj (*fml*) (of actions) well judged; PRUDENT: *When the fight began, he thought it politic to leave.* See also THE BODY POLITIC.

political /pə'lɪtɪkl/ adj **1** of the state; of government; of public affairs in general: *political rights/ liberties* ○ *a political system.* **2** of the conflict or competition between two or more parties: *a political party/debate/crisis* ○ *political skill/know-how/ opinions* ○ *a party political broadcast* (eg to explain a party's policies). **3** (of actions) considered to be harmful to the state or government: *a political offence/crime* ○ *imprisoned on political grounds* ○ *a political prisoner.* **4** (of people) interested in or active in politics: *She is very political (in outlook).* ○ *I'm not a political animal* (ie person). **5** (*euph derog*) concerned with power, status, etc within an organization rather than with matters of principle: *I suspect that he was dismissed for political reasons.* ○ *It must have been a political decision.*

▶ **politically** /-kli/ adv with regard to politics: *a politically active person* ○ *a politically sensitive issue* ○

It makes sense politically as well as economically.
po,litically cor'rect *adj* (*abbr* **PC**) showing political correctness.
po,litical a'sylum *n* [U] (*fml*) = ASYLUM 1.
po,litical cor'rectness *n* [U] (*sometimes derog*) the principle of avoiding language or behaviour that may offend particular groups of people; an excessive display of or belief in this.
po,litical ge'ography *n* [U] GEOGRAPHY(1) dealing with boundaries, communications, etc between countries.
po,litical 'science (also **politics**) *n* [U] the academic study of government and political institutions.
politician /ˌpɒləˈtɪʃn/ *n* a person whose job is concerned with political affairs, esp as an elected member of parliament, etc.
politicize, -ise /pəˈlɪtɪsaɪz/ *v* to make sb/sth more interested in or aware of politics; to give a political character to sth: [Vn] *Trade unions are becoming increasingly politicized.* ▶ **politicization, -isation** /pəˌlɪtɪsaɪˈzeɪʃn/ *n* [U].
politicking /ˈpɒlətɪkɪŋ/ *n* [U] (*often derog*) political activity, esp to win votes or support: *A lot of politicking preceded the choice of the new director.*
politics /ˈpɒlətɪks/ *n* **1(a)** [sing or pl *v*] political affairs or life: *party politics* ○ *local politics* ○ *He's thinking of going into politics* (eg trying to become a Member of Parliament, Congress, etc). **(b)** [pl] political views or beliefs: *What are your politics?* **(c)** [sing *v*] (*derog*) competition between political parties: *They're not concerned with welfare: it's all politics!* **2** [U] = POLITICAL SCIENCE: *She's reading politics at university.* **3** [sing *v*] (*derog*) matters concerned with acquiring or exercising power within a group or an organization: *get involved in office politics* ○ *sexual politics* (ie concerning relationships of power in sexual matters or between the sexes).
polity /ˈpɒləti/ *n* (*fml*) **1** [U] the form or process of government. **2** [C] a society as an organized state.
polka /ˈpɒlkə; *US* ˈpəʊlkə/ *n* a lively dance of eastern European origin, or a piece of music for this.
■ **'polka dot** *n* (usu *pl*) a large round dot, one of many forming a regular pattern on cloth: *a polka-dot scarf.* ⊳ picture at PATTERN.
poll¹ /pəʊl/ *n* **1(a)** [C] (also **the polls** [pl]) the process of voting at an election; the counting of votes: *be successful at the polls* ○ *The result of the poll has now been declared.* ○ *The country is going to the polls* (ie voting in a political election) *today.* **(b)** [sing] the number of votes cast: *head the poll* (ie have the largest number of votes). **2** [C] a survey of public opinion conducted by putting questions to a representative selection of people: *a public opinion poll* ○ *We're conducting a poll among students.* See also DEED POLL, GALLUP POLL, EXIT POLL, STRAW POLL.
■ **'poll tax** *n* a tax to be paid at the same rate by every person or every adult in the community.
poll² /pəʊl/ *v* **1** (of a candidate at an election) to receive a certain number of votes: [Vn] *Mr Hill polled over 3 000 votes.* **2** to ask sb for their opinion as part of a public opinion poll: [Vn] *Of those polled, seven out of ten said they preferred brown bread.*
▶ **polling** *n* [U] **(a)** voting: *heavy polling* (ie in large numbers). **(b)** the conducting of public opinion polls. **'polling-booth** *n* a small, partly enclosed stand in a polling-station where people vote by marking a card, etc. **'polling-station** *n* a building where people go to vote in an election. **'polling-day** *n* [U, C] a day on which people vote in an election: *a week before polling-day.*
pollard /ˈpɒləd, -lɑːd/ *v* (esp passive) to cut off the top of a tree so that many new thin branches will grow, forming a thick head of leaves: [Vn] *The willows need to be pollarded.*
▶ **pollard** *n* a pollarded tree.

pollen /ˈpɒlən/ *n* [U] fine, usu yellow, powder formed in flowers, which can FERTILIZE(1) other flowers when carried to them by the wind, insects, etc.
■ **'pollen count** *n* a number indicating the amount of pollen in the air, used as a guide for people who are affected by it: *I get hay fever when there's a high pollen count.*
pollinate /ˈpɒləneɪt/ *v* [Vn] to FERTILIZE(1) a plant with POLLEN. ▶ **pollination** /ˌpɒləˈneɪʃn/ *n* [U].
pollster /ˈpəʊlstə(r)/ *n* (*infml*) a person who conducts a POLL¹(2) of public opinion.
pollute /pəˈluːt/ *v* ~ **sth (with sth)** to make sth dirty or no longer pure, esp by adding harmful or unpleasant substances to it: [Vn] *polluted air* [Vnpr] *rivers polluted with chemical waste from factories* ○ (*fig*) *pollute the minds of the young with foul propaganda.*
▶ **pollutant** /-ənt/ *n* a substance that pollutes, eg smoke or waste products from factories: *release pollutants into the atmosphere.*
polluter *n* a person or group of people that pollutes.
pollution /pəˈluːʃn/ *n* [U] **(a)** the process of polluting sth or the state of being polluted: *the pollution of our beaches with oil.* **(b)** substances that pollute: *beaches covered with pollution.*
polo /ˈpəʊləʊ/ *n* [U] a game in which players riding on horses try to hit a ball into a goal using long wooden hammers. See also WATER POLO.
■ **'polo-neck** (*Brit*) (*US* **turtle-neck**) *n* a high round collar made of a thick piece of material turned over: *a polo-neck 'sweater.* ⊳ picture at NECK.
polonaise /ˌpɒləˈneɪz/ *n* a slow dance of Polish origin or a piece of music for this.
poltergeist /ˈpəʊltəɡaɪst; *Brit also* ˈpɒlt-/ *n* a type of ghost that makes loud noises, throws objects about, etc.
poly /ˈpɒli/ *n* (*pl* **polys**) (*infml*) = POLYTECHNIC.
poly- *comb form* many: *polygamy* ○ *polyphonic.*
polyandry /ˌpɒliˈændri/ *n* [U] the custom of having more than one husband at the same time. ▶ **polyandrous** /ˌpɒliˈændrəs/ *adj.*
polyanthus /ˌpɒliˈænθəs/ *n* (*pl* **polyanthuses**) [U, C] a garden plant of the PRIMROSE(1) family, with several flowers, often of different colours, on one stem.
polyester /ˌpɒliˈestə(r); *US* ˈpɒliestər/ *n* [U, C] an artificial fabric used for making clothes, etc: *a polyester shirt.*
polyethylene /ˌpɒliˈeθəliːn/ *n* [U] (*US*) = POLYTHENE.
polygamy /pəˈlɪɡəmi/ *n* [U] the custom of having more than one wife at the same time. Compare MONOGAMY. ▶ **polygamous** /pəˈlɪɡəməs/ *adj: a polygamous marriage/society.*
polyglot /ˈpɒliɡlɒt/ *adj* (*fml*) knowing, using or written in many languages: *a polyglot nation* ○ *a polyglot edition.*
▶ **polyglot** *n* a person who speaks many languages.
polygon /ˈpɒliɡən; *US* -ɡɒn/ *n* (*geometry*) a flat shape with many (usu five or more) straight sides and angles. ▶ **polygonal** /pəˈlɪɡənl/ *adj.*
polymath /ˈpɒlimæθ/ *n* (*fml approv*) a person who knows a lot about many different subjects.
polymer /ˈpɒlimə(r)/ *n* (*chemistry*) a natural or artificial compound composed of large molecules (MOLECULE) which are themselves made from combinations of small simple molecules.
polymorphous /ˌpɒliˈmɔːfəs/ (also **polymorphic** /-fɪk/) *adj* (*fml*) having or passing through many stages of development, growth, etc.
polyp /ˈpɒlɪp/ *n* **1** (*biology*) a small and very simple type of sea creature with a body shaped like a tube: *Coral is formed by certain types of polyp.* **2** (*medical*) any of several types of abnormal growth, eg in the nose.

polyphony /pəˈlɪfəni/ n [U] the combination of several different patterns of musical notes to form a single piece of music; COUNTERPOINT. ▶ **polyphonic** /ˌpɒliˈfɒnɪk/ adj.

polypropylene /ˌpɒliˈprəʊpəliːn/ n [U] a type of strong plastic widely used in making moulded objects, eg toys and chairs.

polystyrene /ˌpɒliˈstaɪriːn/ (also esp US **Styrofoam**) n [U] a type of very light plastic which has been expanded with a special gas. Polystyrene is usu white in colour and is used for making containers, preventing heat loss, etc: a polystyrene cup.

polysyllable /ˈpɒlisɪləbl/ n a word of several (usu more than three) syllables. ▶ **polysyllabic** /ˌpɒlisɪˈlæbɪk/ adj.

polytechnic /ˌpɒliˈteknɪk/ (also infml **poly**) n (esp formerly in Britain) a college for higher education, esp in scientific and technical subjects. Most polytechnics in Britain are now called, and have the same status as, universities.

polytheism /ˈpɒliθiːɪzəm/ n [U] the belief in or worship of more than one god. Compare MONOTHEISM. ▶ **polytheistic** /ˌpɒliθiːˈɪstɪk/ adj.

polythene /ˈpɒliθiːn/ (US **polyethylene**) n [U] (Brit) a type of plastic in the form of thin flexible sheets, used for making bags, as a wrapping material, etc: polythene sheeting.

polyunsaturated /ˌpɒliʌnˈsætʃəreɪtɪd/ adj (of many vegetable and some animal fats) having a chemical structure which does not encourage the harmful formation of CHOLESTEROL in the blood: Polyunsaturated margarine is very popular. Compare SATURATED 3, UNSATURATED.

polyurethane /ˌpɒliˈjʊərəθeɪn/ n [U] a type of plastic used in making paints: polyurethane gloss (ie a paint that dries with a hard shiny surface).

pom /pɒm/ n (Austral or NZ sl often derog) = POMMY.

pomander /pəˈmændə(r)/ n a ball or container of mixed sweet-smelling substances, eg flowers, leaves, spices, etc, used to give a pleasant smell to cupboards, rooms, etc.

pomegranate /ˈpɒmɪgrænɪt/ n a round fruit with a thick skin. When ripe it has a reddish centre full of large juicy seeds. Pomegranate trees grow chiefly in N Africa and W Asia: pomegranate juice/seeds.

pommel /ˈpɒml/ n 1 the round part of a SADDLE(1) that sticks up at the front. 2 the round part on the end of the handle of a sword.

pommy /ˈpɒmi/ (also **pom**) n (Austral or NZ sl often derog) a British person.

pomp /pɒmp/ n [U] splendid or magnificent display, esp at a public event: all the **pomp and ceremony** of a royal wedding. **IDM** ˌpomp and ˈcircumstance magnificent and/or ceremonial display and procedure.

pom-pom /ˈpɒmpɒm/ n a small woollen ball used for decoration, esp on a hat.

pompous /ˈpɒmpəs/ adj (derog) feeling, or showing that one feels, that one is much more important than other people: a pompous official ∘ pompous language (ie too grand or formal). ▶ **pomposity** /pɒmˈpɒsəti/ n [U]: deflate/puncture/prick sb's pomposity ∘ He is entirely without pomposity. **pompously** adv.

ponce /pɒns/ n (Brit) 1 a man who lives with a prostitute and lives on the money she earns. 2 (infml offensive) a man who acts in an EFFEMINATE way or is thought to be HOMOSEXUAL.
▶ **ponce** v **PHR V** ˌponce aˈbout/aˈround (Brit infml derog) 1 (of a man) to act in an EFFEMINATE way. 2 to fail to do sth quickly or effectively; to waste time: Stop poncing about and get that job finished!

poncho /ˈpɒntʃəʊ/ n (pl -os) a type of CLOAK(1)

made from a large piece of cloth with a hole in the middle for the head.

pond /pɒnd/ n a small area of still water, esp one used or made as a place for cattle to drink or as an ornamental garden pool: a fish pond ∘ a duck pond ∘ pond life (ie animals living in a pond).

ponder /ˈpɒndə(r)/ v ~ (on/over sth) to think about sth carefully and for a long time, esp in trying to reach a decision; to consider: [V] You have pondered long enough — it is time to decide. [Vn,Vpr] We need time to ponder (on) the significance of these events. [V.wh] I am pondering how to respond.

ponderous /ˈpɒndərəs/ adj 1 slow and awkward because of great weight: a fat man's ponderous movements. 2 (derog) (of speech, written style, etc) without vigour; too solemn; dull: ponderous attempts at wit. ▶ **ponderously** adv. **ponderousness** n [U].

pong /pɒŋ/ n (Brit infml often joc) a strong, usu unpleasant, smell: What a horrible pong! ▶ **pong** v (Brit infml often joc): [V] Your feet pong!

pontiff /ˈpɒntɪf/ n (fml) a POPE: the Supreme Pontiff in Rome.

pontifical /pɒnˈtɪfɪkl/ adj (fml) of, or characteristic of, a POPE or bishop.

pontificate¹ /pɒnˈtɪfɪkeɪt/ v ~ (about/on sth) (derog) to speak as if one were the only person who knew the facts or had the right opinions about sth: [Vpr] He sat there pontificating about the legal system although it was clear that he knew very little about it. [also V].

pontificate² /pɒnˈtɪfɪkət/ n the position or period in office of a POPE.

pontoon¹ /pɒnˈtuːn/ n (a) (also **vingt-et-un**, **blackjack**) [U] a card-game in which players try to acquire cards with a value totalling 21. (b) [C] (in this game) a score of 21 from two cards.

pontoon² /pɒnˈtuːn/ n any of several boats or hollow metal structures joined together to support a temporary road over a river, etc: a pontoon bridge.

pony /ˈpəʊni/ n a type of small horse: a Shetland pony. **IDM** on Shanks's pony/mare ⇨ SHANK.
■ ˈpony-tail n a bunch of hair drawn back and tied at the back of the head so that it hangs like a horse's tail. ⇨ picture at PLAIT.
ˈpony-trekking n [U] the activity of riding across country on ponies for pleasure.

pooch /puːtʃ/ n (sl esp US) a dog.

poodle /ˈpuːdl/ n a breed of dog with thick curling hair which is often cut into an elaborate pattern. ⇨ picture at DOG¹.

poof /pʊf/ (also **poofter** /ˈpʊftə(r)/) n (Brit sl derog or offensive) a male HOMOSEXUAL.

pooh /puː/ interj (used to express disgust at a bad smell): Pooh! This egg is bad.

pooh-pooh /ˌpuː ˈpuː/ v (infml) to treat an idea, a suggestion, etc with contempt; to dismiss sth as worthless: [Vn] They pooh-poohed our scheme for raising money.

pool¹ /puːl/ n 1 a small area of still water, esp one that has formed naturally: an undisturbed forest pool. 2 a shallow patch of water or other liquid lying on a surface: After the rainstorm, there were pools on the roads. ∘ The body was lying in a pool of blood. ∘ (fig) pools of light/shade. 3 = SWIMMING-POOL.

pool² /puːl/ n 1 [C] a common fund of money, esp collected from all the players in a gambling game. 2 [C] (a) a common supply of money, goods or services which are available to a group of people to be used when needed: a pool of cars used by the firm's salesmen ∘ a pool car. (b) a group of people available for work when required: a pool of doctors available for emergency work ∘ a ˈtyping pool. 3 [U] a game played with usu 16 coloured balls on a table, similar to SNOOKER. 4 the pools [pl] (Brit) = FOOTBALL

poolside

POOLS: *do the pools every week* ○ *have a win on the pools.*

▶ **pool** *v* to put money, resources, etc into a common fund: [Vn] *They pooled their savings for a holiday abroad.* ○ (*fig*) *If we pool our ideas, we may find a solution.*

poolside /ˈpuːlsaɪd/ *n* [sing often attrib] the area around a swimming-pool (SWIM): *sunbathe at the poolside* ○ *a poolside bar.*

poop /puːp/ *n* (**a**) the back end of a ship; the STERN². (**b**) (also **poop deck**) the raised deck at the back end of a ship.

pooped /puːpt/ (also ˌpooped ˈout) *adj* [pred] (*infml esp US*) very tired.

poor /pʊə(r); *Brit also* pɔː(r)/ *adj* (**-er, -est**) **1** having very little money with which to buy one's basic needs: *She was too poor to buy clothes for her children.* ○ *He came from a poor family.* ○ *the poorer countries of the world.* **2** [pred] ~ **in sth** having sth only in very small quantities; lacking in sth: *a country poor in minerals* ○ *soil poor in nutrients.* **3**(**a**) not good or adequate, esp in contrast with what is usual or expected: *the party's poor performance in the election* ○ *We had a poor crop of raspberries this year.* ○ *Attendance at the concert was very poor.* (**b**) of low quality: *poor food/light/soil* ○ *a poor diet* ○ *be in poor health* ○ *having a poor opinion of sb* (ie not respecting them) ○ *Her remarks were in very poor taste.* (**c**) inferior: *his poor attempts to be witty* ○ *Watching the event on television was a poor substitute for actually being there.* ○ *She came a poor second* (ie a long way behind the winner). (**d**) (of a person) not good or skilled at sth: *a poor judge of character* ○ *a poor loser* (ie one who shows anger at losing in games or sports) ○ *a poor sailor* (ie sb who easily gets sick at sea). **4** (*esp infml*) deserving pity or sympathy; unfortunate: *The poor little puppy had been abandoned.* ○ *Poor fellow, his wife has just died.* ○ *'I've been feeling ill all week.' 'Poor you!'* **IDM** **the ˌpoor man's ˈsb/ˈsth** a person or thing that is an inferior or cheaper alternative to a well-known person, institution, food, etc: *Sparkling white wine is the poor man's champagne.*

▶ **the poor** *n* [pl *v*] people with little money or few possessions: *raising money for the poor and needy.*

■ ˌpoor reˈlation *n* a person or thing with less power, status or respect than others of the same type: *Some people may regard radio as the poor relation of broadcasting.*

ˌpoor ˈWhite *n* (*usu derog or offensive*) a member of a class of poor white people, esp in the southern USA.

poorly /ˈpʊəli; *Brit also* ˈpɔːli/ *adv* in a poor(3) manner; badly: *poorly dressed* ○ *The street is poorly lit.* ○ *She was poorly prepared for the interview.* **IDM** **poorly ˈoff** (*infml*) having very little money: *He left her very poorly off.*

▶ **poorly** *adj* [esp pred] (*infml esp Brit*) not well; ill: *The child has been poorly all week.* ○ *You look rather poorly to me.* ⇨ note at SICK.

pop¹ /pɒp/ *n* **1** [C] a short sharp explosive sound: *The cork came out of the bottle with a loud pop.* **2** [U] (*infml*) a FIZZY drink containing no alcohol: *a bottle of pop.*

▶ **pop** *adv* with a pop¹ (1): *It came out pop.* ○ *The balloon went pop* (ie burst).

pop² /pɒp/ *n* [UC usu *pl*] (*infml*) a modern popular style, esp in music: *pop music/culture* ○ *a pop singer/song/concert/group/star* ○ *top of the pops* (ie the most popular current recordings) ○ *a pop video* (ie made to accompany a pop song). Compare CLASSICAL 2.

■ ˈpop art *n* [U] a style of art developed in the 1960s. It was based on popular culture and used material such as advertisements, film images, etc.

ˈpop festival *n* a large, usu outdoor, gathering of

people to hear performances by pop musicians, sometimes lasting several days.

pop³ /pɒp/ *n* (*infml esp US*) (used esp as a form of address) **1** a father. Compare PAPA, POPPA. **2** any older man.

pop⁴ /pɒp/ *v* (**-pp-**) **1**(**a**) to make a short sharp explosive sound, as when a CORK(2) comes out of a bottle: [V] *Champagne corks were popping throughout the celebrations.* (**b**) to make sth burst with such a sound: [Vn] *The children were popping balloons.* **2** (*infml*) to take a drug, esp habitually: [Vn] *popping pills.* **IDM** **pop the ˈquestion** (*infml*) to make a proposal of marriage. **PHRV** **ˌpop across, down, out etc** (*esp Brit*) to come or go quickly or suddenly in the direction specified: *He's just popped down the road to the shops.* ○ *She's popped over to see her mother.* ○ *He's only popped out for a few minutes.* ○ *Where's Tom popped off to?* ○ *Her eyes nearly popped out of her head* (ie with surprise and delight) *when she saw what she had won.* **ˈpop sth across, in, into, etc sth** to put or take sth somewhere quickly or suddenly: *pop a letter in the post* ○ *She popped the tart into the oven.* ○ *He popped his head round the door to say goodbye.* **ˌpop ˈin** to make a brief visit: *She often pops in for coffee.* **ˌpop sth ˈin** (*esp Brit*) to deliver sth as one is passing: *I'll pop the books in on my way home.* **ˌpop ˈoff** (*infml*) to die: *She said she had no intention of popping off for some time yet.* **ˌpop ˈup** (*infml*) to appear or occur, esp when not expected: *He seems to pop up in the most unlikely places.*

■ ˈpop-eyed *adj* (**a**) having eyes that are naturally wide open. (**b**) having eyes wide open with surprise, fear, strain, etc: *She was pop-eyed with amazement.*

ˈpop-up *adj* [attrib] **1** (of a children's book, etc) containing pictures on stiff paper that rise up to form a scene, etc as the pages are turned: *a pop-up story-book.* **2** (of an automatic toaster (TOAST¹)) that operates by pushing the TOAST¹ quickly upwards when it is ready.

pop⁵ *abbr* population: *pop 12 m* (ie 12 million).

popadam = POPPADAM.

popcorn /ˈpɒpkɔːn/ *n* [U] seeds of MAIZE that have been heated so that they burst and form light whitish balls. Popcorn can be eaten with salt or sugar added.

pope /pəʊp/ *n* the head of the Roman Catholic Church who is also the Bishop of Rome: *the election of a new pope* ○ *Pope John Paul.*

▶ **popery** /ˈpəʊpəri/ *n* [U] (*derog*) Roman Catholicism.

popish /ˈpəʊpɪʃ/ *adj* (*derog*) of or relating to Roman Catholicism: *popish forms of worship.*

■ ˌpope's ˈnose *n* (*US infml*) = PARSON'S NOSE.

popgun /ˈpɒpɡʌn/ *n* a child's toy gun that shoots eg a CORK(2) with a popping sound.

poplar /ˈpɒplə(r)/ *n* [C] a type of tall straight tree with soft wood.

poplin /ˈpɒplɪn/ *n* [U] a type of shiny, usu cotton, cloth used for making clothes.

poppa /ˈpɒpə/ *n* (*US infml*) (used esp as a form of address) father. Compare PAPA, POP³.

poppadam (also **poppadom, popadam**) /ˈpɒpədəm/ *n* a thin crisp Indian bread eaten with CURRY¹, etc.

popper /ˈpɒpə(r)/ *n* (*Brit infml*) = PRESS-STUD.

poppet /ˈpɒpɪt/ *n* (*Brit infml*) (used esp as a term of affection for a child): *How's my little poppet today?* ○ *Don't cry, poppet.*

poppy /ˈpɒpi/ *n* a wild or cultivated plant with large, often bright red, flowers, whitish juice and small black seeds. OPIUM is obtained from one type of poppy: *poppy fields.* ⇨ picture at FLOWER.

poppycock /ˈpɒpikɒk/ *n* [U] (*infml*) nonsense: *You're talking complete poppycock!*

Popsicle /ˈpɒpsɪkl/ *n* (*US propr*) = ICE LOLLY.

populace /'pɒpjələs/ (usu **the populace**) n [Gp] (*fml*) the general public; ordinary people: *He had the support of large sections of the local populace.* ∘ *The populace at large is/are opposed to sudden change.*

popular /'pɒpjələ(r)/ adj **1(a)** liked, admired or enjoyed by many people: *a hugely/immensely/universally popular politician* ∘ *This design has always been popular.* ∘ *Jogging is the most popular form of exercise among the under-40s.* (**b**) ~ **with sb** liked, admired or enjoyed by a particular person or group: *measures popular with the electorate* ∘ *I'm not very popular with the boss* (ie He is annoyed with me) *at the moment.* **2** [attrib] (a) (*sometimes derog*) suited to the taste or the educational level of the general public: *popular music* ∘ *the popular press* ∘ *novels without popular appeal* ∘ *popular* (ie simplified) *science.* (**b**) (of beliefs, etc) held by a large number of people: *a popular misconception* ∘ **Contrary to popular opinion**, *women are not worse drivers than men.* **3** [attrib] of or by the people: *a popular uprising* ∘ *a leader with widespread popular support* ∘ *in response to popular demand.*
▶ **popularly** adv by many or most people: *a popularly held belief* ∘ *It is popularly believed that...* ∘ *The mountain is* **popularly known as** *Arthur's Seat.*
■ **popular front** n a political party representing left-wing (LEFT²) groups.

popularity /ˌpɒpjuˈlærəti/ n [U] the quality or state of being liked or admired by many people: *win/gain/enjoy/widespread popularity with the voters* ∘ *the continuing popularity of road transport* ∘ *Her books have grown in popularity recently.*

popularize, -ise /'pɒpjələraɪz/ v **1** to make sth generally liked: [Vn] *Her books have done much to popularize the sport.* **2** to make sth known or available to the general public, esp by presenting it in a form that can be easily understood: [Vn] *popularize new theories in medicine* ∘ *a popularizing author.* ▶ **popularization, -isation** /ˌpɒpjələraɪˈzeɪʃn; *US* -rə'z-/ n [U].

populate /'pɒpjuleɪt/ v (usu passive) (**a**) to live in an area and form its population: [Vn] *deserts populated only by nomadic tribesmen* ∘ *densely/heavily/sparsely/thinly populated regions.* (**b**) to move to an area and fill it with people: [Vn] *The islands were gradually populated by settlers from Europe.*

population /ˌpɒpjuˈleɪʃn/ n **1** [CGp] (**a**) the people who live in an area, a city, a country, etc: *control population growth* ∘ *the ageing populations of Western European countries* ∘ *Muslims make up 55% of the population.* (**b**) a particular group or type of people or animals living in an area, etc: *the entire working population* ∘ *the immigrant population* ∘ *Iraq's civilian population.* (**c**) the total number of people living somewhere: *What is the population of Ireland?* ∘ *a city with a population of over 10 million.* **2** [U] the degree to which an area has been populated: *areas of dense/sparse population.*
■ **population centre** (*US* **center**) n an area where there are a lot of people: *The problem affects the main population centres, not the smaller towns.*
population explosion n a sudden large increase in population.

populism /'pɒpjəlɪzəm/ n [U] a type of politics that claims to represent the interests of ordinary people: *For all her professed populism, she was a remote figure.* ▶ **populist** /-ɪst/ n, adj: *presenting himself as a populist* ∘ *a right-wing populist leader* ∘ *populist theories.*

populous /'pɒpjələs/ adj (*fml*) having a large population; heavily populated: *the populous areas near the coast* ∘ *The world's most populous country.*

porcelain /'pɔːsəlɪn/ n [U] (**a**) a hard white shiny material made by baking clay and used for making cups, plates, ornaments, etc: *a fine porcelain vase.* (**b**) objects made of this: *a valuable collection of antique porcelain.*

porch /pɔːtʃ/ n **1** a covered entrance to a building, esp a church or house. ➪ picture at CHURCH, HOUSE¹. **2** (*US*) = VERANDA. ➪ picture at VERANDA.

porcupine /'pɔːkjupaɪn/ n an animal covered with long sharp quills (QUILL 2) which protect it when it is attacked.

pore¹ /pɔː(r)/ n any of the tiny openings in the surface of the skin or of a leaf, through which MOISTURE can pass: *blocked pores* ∘ *The fine leaf pores close at night.* ∘ (*fig*) *He was oozing wickedness from every pore.* See also POROUS.

pore² /pɔː(r)/ v **PHRV** **pore over sth** to study sth by looking at it very carefully: *She was poring over an old map of the area.* ∘ *He spent hours poring over the rows of figures.*

pork /pɔːk/ n [U] the flesh of a pig eaten as food: *roast pork* ∘ *a leg of pork* ∘ *pork sausages* ∘ *Muslims do not eat pork.* See also BACON, GAMMON, HAM 1b.
■ **pork-barrel** n (*US sl*) government money spent on local projects in order to win votes: *pork-barrel politics.*
pork pie n a pie made of pastry filled with pork, often eaten cold.

porn /pɔːn/ n [U] (*infml*) = PORNOGRAPHY. See also HARD PORN, SOFT PORN.

porno /'pɔːnəʊ/ adj (*infml*) = PORNOGRAPHIC: *a porno movie/magazine.*

pornography /pɔːˈnɒɡrəfi/ n [U] (**a**) the describing or showing of naked people or sexual acts in order to cause sexual excitement: *laws on pornography.* (**b**) books, films, etc that do this: *the trade in pornography.*
▶ **pornographer** /pɔːˈnɒɡrəfə(r)/ n a person who produces or sells pornography.
pornographic /ˌpɔːnəˈɡræfɪk/ adj of or relating to pornography: *pornographic magazines/material/movies.*

porous /'pɔːrəs/ adj allowing liquid or air to pass through, esp slowly: *a porous material* ∘ *porous rocks like sandstone and limestone* ∘ *He added sand to the soil to make it more porous.*
▶ **porosity** /pɔːˈrɒsəti/ n [U] the quality or state of being porous.

porphyry /'pɔːfəri/ n [U] a type of hard red rock which contains red and white crystals, and may be polished and made into ornaments.

porpoise /'pɔːpəs/ n a sea MAMMAL similar to a DOLPHIN.

porridge /'pɒrɪdʒ; *US* 'pɔːr-/ (*US* also **oatmeal**) n [U] a soft food made by boiling a CEREAL(1b) in water or milk. Porridge is eaten hot, esp at breakfast: *porridge oats* ∘ *a bowl of porridge with milk and sugar.*

port¹ /pɔːt/ n **1** [C] a town or city with a harbour, esp one where ships load and UNLOAD(1b) cargo: *fishing ports* ∘ *continental ports* ∘ *Rotterdam is a major port.* ∘ *the port authorities.* **2** [C,U] a place where ships load and UNLOAD(1b) cargo or shelter from storms; a harbour: *a naval port* ∘ *The ship spent four days in port.* ∘ *They reached port at last.* **IDM** **any port in a storm** (*saying*) in times of trouble or difficulty one takes whatever help is available.
■ **port of call 1** a place where a ship stops during a voyage. **2** (*infml*) a place where a person goes or stops, esp during a journey: *My first port of call was the chemist's.*

port² /pɔːt/ n [U] the side of a ship or an aircraft that is on the left when one is facing forward: *The ship was leaning over to port.* ∘ *the port side/engine* ∘ *on the port bow.* Compare STARBOARD.

port³ /pɔːt/ n (**a**) [U] a strong sweet, usu dark red, wine made in Portugal. Port is drunk esp at the end of a meal. (**b**) [C] a glass of this: *I'll have a port and lemon, please.*

portable /'pɔːtəbl/ *adj* that can be easily carried; not fixed permanently in place: *a portable heater/phone/computer.*

▶ **portability** /ˌpɔːtə'bɪləti/ *n* [U]: *I bought it for its portability, not its appearance.*

portable *n* a portable version of sth: *The document had been typed on a small portable* (ie a portable TYPEWRITER).

Portakabin /'pɔːtəkæbɪn/ *n* (*Brit propr*) a room or set of rooms designed to be moved and put together quickly, eg as a temporary office.

portal /'pɔːtl/ *n* (often *pl*) (*fml or rhet*) a DOORWAY or gate, esp a grand and impressive one: *enter the hallowed portals of Broadcasting House.*

portcullis /pɔːt'kʌlɪs/ *n* a strong heavy iron GRAT-ING raised or lowered at the entrance to a castle. ⇨ picture at CASTLE.

portend /pɔː'tend/ *v* (*fml*) to be a sign or warning of sth in the future: [Vn] *This could portend a change of government policy.*

portent /'pɔːtent/ *n* ~ (**of sth**) (*fml*) a sign or warning of a future event, often an unpleasant one; an OMEN: *The event proved to be a portent of the disaster that was to come.* ○ *We shall try to reach an agreement, but the portents are not good.*

▶ **portentous** /pɔː'tentəs/ **1** of or like a portent: *portentous events/signs.* **2** (*derog*) solemn in a way that is intended to impress people: *adopt a portentous tone.* **portentously** *adv*: '*No good will come of this,' she announced portentously.* **portentousness** *n* [U].

porter /'pɔːtə(r)/ *n* **1** a person whose job is carrying people's LUGGAGE and other loads, eg in railway stations, airports, hotels, markets, etc: *a hospital porter* ○ *I tipped the porter $10.* **2** (*Brit*) (*US* **doorman**) a person whose job is to be on duty at the entrance to a hotel, large building, etc: *the night porter* ○ *The hotel porter will call a taxi for you.* **3** (*US*) a person whose job is helping passengers on a train, esp in a sleeping-car (SLEEP²).

portfolio /pɔːt'fəʊliəʊ/ *n* (*pl* **-os**) **1(a)** a thin flat case for carrying loose papers, documents, drawings, etc. (**b**) a set of pieces of work collected by sb as an example of their skills, eg to show to sb who may give them a job: *prepare a portfolio of one's best photos.* **2** a set of investments owned by a person, bank, etc: *My stockbroker manages my portfolio for me.* **3** (*fml*) the position and special duties of a government minister: *She resigned her portfolio.* ○ *a Minister without portfolio* (ie one without responsibility for a particular department).

porthole /'pɔːthəʊl/ *n* a usu round window in the side of a ship or an aircraft.

portico /'pɔːtɪkəʊ/ *n* (*pl* **-oes** or **-os**) (*architecture*) a roof supported by columns, esp one forming an entrance to a large building: *an elegant classical portico.*

portion /'pɔːʃn/ *n* **1** a part or share into which sth is divided: *be supported by a substantial/sizeable portion of the population* ○ *devote a small portion of one's budget to sth* ○ *The centre portion of the bridge collapsed.* ○ *You give this portion of the ticket to the inspector and keep the other.* **2** an amount of food suitable for or served to one person: *a generous portion of roast duck* ○ *She cut the pie into six portions.* ○ *Do you serve children's* (ie smaller) *portions?*

▶ **portion** *v* **PHRV** **portion sth 'out (among/between sb)** to divide sth into shares to give to several people: *She portioned out the money equally between both children.* ○ *The work was portioned out fairly.* See also APPORTION.

Portland stone /ˌpɔːtlənd 'stəʊn/ *n* [U] a type of yellowish-white limestone used for building.

portly /'pɔːtli/ *adj* (esp of an older man) having a rather fat body: *his portly figure* ○ *portly members of the city council.*

portmanteau word /pɔː'mæntəʊ wɜːd/ *n* an invented word that combines parts of two words and their meaning, eg *motel* from *motor* and *hotel*, or *brunch* from *breakfast* and *lunch*.

portrait /'pɔːtreɪt, -trət/ *n* **1** a painting, drawing or photograph of a person, esp of the face alone: *She had her portrait painted.* ○ *a portrait painter.* ⇨ picture at CARICATURE. Compare LANDSCAPE 2. See also SELF-PORTRAIT. **2** a description or impression of sth: *The book contains/paints a fascinating portrait of life at the court of Henry VIII.*

▶ **portraitist** /-ɪst/ *n* a person who makes portraits: *a skilled portraitist.*

portraiture /-tʃə(r); *US* -tʃʊər/ *n* [U] the art of making portraits.

portray /pɔː'treɪ/ *v* ~ **sb/sth (as sb/sth) 1** to show sb/sth in a picture, by acting, etc: [Vn-n] *a picture of the general portraying him as a Greek hero* [Vn] *Non-professional actors were used to portray the local people.* **2** to describe or give an impression of sb/sth, esp when one is not giving a complete and fair picture: [Vn-n] *He has often been portrayed as a cold, calculating character.* [also Vn-adj, Vnadv].

▶ **portrayal** /pɔː'treɪəl/ *n* **1** [C] a description, an impression or a representation: *He is best known for his portrayal of Falstaff.* **2** [U] the action of portraying sth: *the portrayal of sex and violence on television.*

pose /pəʊz/ *v* **1** to create or present a difficulty, a threat, a question, etc: [Vn] *pose a risk/dilemma/danger* ○ *The heat is posing problems for the whole team.* ○ *In this issue, we pose the question: 'Is there life after parenthood?'* ○ *Pollution poses a serious threat to the environment.* **2** ~ (**for sb/sth**) to sit or stand in a particular position in order to be painted, drawn or photographed: [V] *He had to pose in the nude.* [Vpr] *The artist asked her to pose for him.* ○ *The press wanted the band to pose for a photo.* **3** ~ **as sb/sth** to claim or pretend to be sb/sth: [Vpr] *He posed as a successful businessman.* ○ *The detective posed as a mourner at the victim's funeral.*

▶ **pose** *n* **1** a position in which a person poses: *a relaxed pose for the camera* ○ *She adopted a stiff, formal pose.* **2** (*derog*) a way of behaving that is not natural, sincere, etc, but only intended to impress people: *His concern for the poor is only a pose.* **IDM** **strike an attitude/a pose** ⇨ STRIKE².

poser *n* **1** (*infml*) an awkward or difficult question or problem. **2** = POSEUR.

poseur /pəʊ'zɜː(r)/ (also **poser** /'pəʊzə(r)/) *n* (*derog*) a person who behaves in a way that is not natural, sincere, etc but intended merely to impress people: *Some people admired him greatly while others considered him a poseur.*

posh /pɒʃ/ *adj* (**-er, -est**) (*infml*) (**a**) elegant or expensive; SMART¹(4): *a posh car/hotel* ○ *a posh wedding* ○ *You look very posh in your new suit.* (**b**) (*Brit sometimes derog*) typical of or belonging to the upper class of society: *a posh accent* ○ *They live in the posh part of town.*

posit /'pɒzɪt/ *v* (*fml*) to suggest or assume sth as a fact: [Vn] *posit the existence of some form of divine being.*

position /pə'zɪʃn/ *n* **1** [C] (**a**) a place where sb/sth is: *He moved the furniture back to its usual position.* ○ *From his position on the cliff top, he had a good view of the harbour.* ○ *Plant your rose-bush in a sunny position.* (**b**) (esp *pl*) (*techn*) a place where a fighting force has placed men and guns: *attack the enemy positions.* **2** [U] (**a**) the place where sb/sth should be; the right place: *Her husband took his position at her side.* ○ *The runners got into position on the starting-line.* ○ *The chairs were all out of position.* (**b**) the state of being placed where one has an advantage over one's rivals in a contest, war, etc: *Candidates had been manoeuvring/jostling for position even before the leadership became vacant.* **3** [C, U] a way in which sb/sth is placed or arranged; a POSTURE(1a): *sit/lie in a comfortable position* ○ *be in an upright/a horizontal position* ○ *The soldiers have to stand for hours without changing position.* ○ *The vase was in a precarious position on the window-sill.* **4** [C] ~ (**on sth**) a view or an opinion held by sb: *He set out/stated the government's official position on the issue.* ○ *She has made her position very clear.* **5** [C esp *sing*] a situation or circumstances, esp when they affect one's power to act: *in a position of power/strength/authority* ○ *You realize that this puts me in a very awkward position?* ○ *The company's financial position is very sound.* ○ *He was in the unenviable position of having to choose between imprisonment and exile.* ○ *What would you do in my position?* ○ (*fml*) *I'm afraid I am* **not in a position to** (ie I cannot) *help you.* **6(a)** [C] a place or rank in relation to others: *discuss the position of women in society* ○ *the company's market position* ○ *'What is his position in class?' 'He's third from the top.'* (**b**) [U] high rank or status: *people of position* ○ *Wealth and position were not important to her.* **7** [C] (*fml*) a job: *a senior position in/with a big company* ○ *I should like to apply for the position of assistant manager.* ○ *She had worked for the firm for twenty years and was in a position of trust.* **8** [C] (*sport*) (in team games) a set of functions considered as the responsibility of a particular player: *'What position does he play/is he?' 'Centre-forward.'*

▶ **position** *v* to place or arrange sth/sb/oneself in a particular way or position: [Vn] *position the aerial correctly* ○ *Note the positioning of the goalkeeper's feet.* [Vnpr] *She positioned herself near the door.* ○ *Alarms are positioned at strategic points around the prison.*

positional /-ʃənəl/ *adj* of or relating to position: *a player with poor positional skills.*

positive /'pɒzətɪv/ *adj* **1(a)** having a helpful and CONSTRUCTIVE intention or attitude towards sth: *make positive proposals/suggestions* ○ *have a positive approach* ○ *Try to be more positive in dealing with the problem.* (**b**) showing confidence and OPTIMISM: *a positive attitude/feeling/response* ○ *project a positive image* ○ *We welcome this move, and feel very positive about it.* ○ *positive thinking* (ie a determined mental attitude that helps one achieve success). (**c**) showing a pleasing increase or improvement: *positive aspects/factors/elements* ○ *a positive growth rate* ○ *There have been (some) positive developments in the crisis.* **2** with no possibility of doubt; clear and definite: *positive instructions/orders* ○ *make a positive commitment to sth* ○ *We have no positive evidence of her involvement.* **3** ~ (**about sth/that...**) (of a person) confidently holding an opinion; convinced: *Are you absolutely positive that it was after midnight?* ○ *She was quite positive about the amount of money involved.* **4** (of the results of a test or an experiment) indicating that a substance is present: *get a positive reaction* ○ *be HIV-positive* ○ *The tests proved positive.* ○ *The athlete* **tested positive for** *steroids.* **5** (*infml*) absolute; complete: *Her behaviour was a positive outrage.* ○ *It was a positive miracle that we arrived on time.* **6** (used to emphasize that sth is true): *On stage, short sight is a positive advantage.* **7** (*mathematics*) (of a quantity) greater than zero. **8** (*techn*) containing or producing the type of electrical charge produced by rubbing glass with silk: *a positive charge* ○ *the positive terminal of a battery.* See also PROTON. Compare NEGATIVE.

▶ **positive** *n* **1** a positive quality or aspect. **2** a number greater than zero. **3** a photograph printed from a NEGATIVE(2).

positively *adv* **1** in a positive(1,2) way; with complete certainty; firmly: *think positively* ○ *Her attacker has now been positively identified by the police.* ○ *'I*

won't hear of it,' she said positively. ○ *He has said that this will be positively his last appearance.* **2** (used to emphasize sth that sounds surprising, or to make a dramatic contrast to the previous statement): *She was positively glowing with excitement.* ○ *Some diets may be positively dangerous.*

■ **positive dis,crimin'ation** *n* [U] (*Brit*) the practice or policy of deliberately favouring people who are often treated in an unfair way, eg because of their race.

positive 'vetting *n* [U] (*Brit*) the process of thoroughly checking the background and character of a candidate for a job in the civil service (CIVIL) that involves access to secret material.

positivism /'pɒzətɪvɪzəm/ *n* [U] a system of philosophy based on things that can be seen or proved rather than on ideas. ▶ **positivist** /-vɪst/ *n.*

posse /'pɒsi/ *n* [C] (**a**) (*esp US*) a group of people brought together by an officer of the law to find a criminal, maintain order, etc: *The sheriff rounded up a posse.* (**b**) any small group of people who share an aim or a characteristic: *He was followed everywhere by a posse of journalists.*

possess /pə'zes/ *v* [not in the continuous tenses] **1** (*fml*) (**a**) to have or own sth: [Vn] *He decided to give away everything he possessed and become a monk.* ○ *Iran possesses 10% of the world's known oil reserves.* ○ *She admitted possessing illegal drugs.* ○ *We possess Marx's notes on some of these works.* (**b**) to have sth as a quality or characteristic: [Vn] *There are few actors who don't possess some musical skills.* ○ *The new prime minister possesses a strong will.* **2** (esp passive) to control or dominate a person's mind: [Vn] *She seemed to be possessed (by the devil).* ○ *She was suddenly possessed by an overwhelming jealousy.* ○ *He is possessed by the idea that he is being followed.* [Vn.to *inf*] *Whatever possessed you to do that?* **IDM** **be possessed of sth** (*fml*) to have a quality: *She is possessed of a wonderfully calm temperament.* **like one pos'sessed** violently or with great energy, as if taken over by madness or an evil spirit: *He fought like a man possessed.*

▶ **possessor** *n* (*fml or joc*) a person who possesses sth: *He is now the* **proud possessor** *of a driving-licence.*

possession /pə'zeʃn/ *n* **1** [U] (**a**) the state of having, owning or controlling sth: *caught* **in possession of** *stolen goods* ○ *one of the many treasures in their possession* ○ *fight for/win/get possession of the ball* ○ *The possession of a passport is essential for foreign travel.* ○ *On her father's death, she came into possession of a vast fortune.* ○ *You cannot legally* **take possession** *of the property until three weeks after the contract is signed.* (**b**) (*infml*) the state of possessing an illegal drug or drugs: *charged with possession.* See also VACANT POSSESSION. **2** [C esp *pl*] a thing that is possessed; a piece of property: *her most prized/treasured possessions* ○ *He lost all his possessions in the fire.* **3** [C] a country controlled or governed by another: *The former colonial possessions are now independent states.*

possessive /pə'zesɪv/ *adj* **1** ~ (**about sth/sb**) (**a**) treating sb as if one owns them; demanding total attention or love: *possessive parents* ○ *He's terribly possessive about his girlfriends.* (**b**) showing a desire to own things and not willing to share what one owns: *Jimmy's very possessive about his toys.* **2** (*grammar*) (abbreviated as *possess* in this dictionary) of or showing possession: *the possessive case* ○ *'Anne's', 'the boy's' and 'the boys'' are possessive forms.* ○ *'Yours', 'his', etc are possessive pronouns.*

▶ **possessive** *n* (*grammar*) **1** [C] a possessive word or form: *'Ours' is a possessive.* **2 the possessive** [sing] the possessive case[1](8). Compare GENITIVE.

possessively *adv.*

possessiveness *n* [U].

possibility /ˌpɒsəˈbɪləti/ n **1** [U] ~ (of sth / doing sth); ~ (that...) the state or fact of being possible; likelihood (LIKELY): *within/beyond the bounds of possibility* ○ *There is now no possibility of new funds being made available.* ○ *We must face the possibility that he may never return.* ○ *He refused to rule out the possibility of a tax increase.* ⇨ note at OCCASION. **2** [C] a thing that is possible; a thing that may exist or happen: *discuss/consider/explore/investigate a wide range of possibilities* ○ *Bankruptcy is a real/strong/distinct possibility if sales don't improve.* **3(a)** [C] an opportunity: *new export possibilities* ○ *the possibilities now open to writers.* **(b) possibilities** [pl] the condition of being capable of being used or improved; POTENTIAL (n): *The house is very dilapidated but it has possibilities.* ○ *She saw the possibilities of the scheme from the beginning.*

possible /ˈpɒsəbl/ adj **1(a)** that can be done: *It should be possible to develop a form of tape that cannot be copied.* ○ *Try to give as much detail as possible* (ie as much as you can) *in your answer.* ○ *We will get your order to you as soon as possible.* ○ *Shelter the plants from sun and wind, if (at all) possible* (ie if you can). ○ *Avoid caffeine and other stimulants whenever/wherever possible* (ie when you can). ○ *It is quite/perfectly possible for someone to know a huge amount of history without being able to draw any lessons from it.* ○ (fml) *The doctor will come at the earliest possible opportunity.* ○ *We did all that was humanly possible* (ie that humans could do) *to save his life.* **(b)** that can exist or happen, though not certain to: *a possible future leader* ○ *the possible side-effects of the drug* ○ *Frost is possible, although unlikely, at this time of year.* ○ *It seems possible that the rule will now be relaxed.* ○ *It is just possible that we may be late.* **2** reasonable or acceptable: *a possible solution to the dispute* ○ *There are several possible explanations.* Compare IMPOSSIBLE. **IDM** **the best of both worlds / all possible worlds** ⇨ BEST³.
▶ **possible** n (infml) a person who is suitable for selection, eg for a job or a sports team: *They interviewed 30 people of whom five were possibles.*

possibly /-əbli/ adv **1** perhaps: *a serious, possibly fatal, disease* ○ *'Will you be leaving next week?' 'Possibly.'* ○ *This conference is possibly the most important event of his presidency.* ○ *Could you possibly* (ie Please will you) *open that window for me?* **2(a)** with a reasonable amount of effort, GOOD-WILL(1), etc: *I will come as soon as I possibly can.* ○ *I can't possibly lend you so much money.* ○ *You can't possibly carry all that luggage.* **(b)** (used to emphasize that one feels strongly that sth is difficult, strange, unreasonable, etc): *You can't possibly think that I had anything to do with it!*

possum /ˈpɒsəm/ n (US) = OPOSSUM. **IDM** **play ˈpossum** (infml) to pretend to be asleep or unaware of sth in order to deceive sb.

post¹ /pəʊst/ n **1** [C] (esp in compounds) a piece of metal or wood set upright in the ground to support sth, mark a position, etc: *a rusty old post* ○ *Tie the tennis net to the posts.* ○ *ˈboundary posts* (ie marking a boundary). See also GATEPOST, GOALPOST, LAMP-POST, SIGNPOST. **2** [sing] the place where a race starts or finishes: *the ˈstarting/ˈfinishing/ˈwinning post.* **3** [C usu sing] (infml) = GOALPOST: *The ball hit/grazed the post.* **IDM** **deaf as a post** ⇨ DEAF. **first past the ˈpost** winning in an election because one has received the most votes though not necessarily an absolute majority: *a first-past-the-post system.* **from pillar to post** ⇨ PILLAR.
▶ **post** v ~ **sth (up)** to display a notice, etc in a public place: [Vn] *Have the exam results been posted yet?* [Vnp] *Pictures of the three suspects have been posted up all over the shopping centre.* See also POSTER a.

post² /pəʊst/ n **1** a job; a position of paid employ-

ment: *fill a post* ○ *several vacant teaching posts* ○ *She was appointed to the post of general manager.* ○ *He will take up his post in July.* ○ *She was offered a Cabinet post in the new government.* **2** a place where a person is on duty, esp a soldier or an official: *a Customs post* ○ *He was rushed to the first aid post.* ○ *The guards were ordered not to leave their posts.* See also LAST POST, STAGING POST, TRADING POST.
▶ **post** v **1** ~ **sb (to sth)** to appoint sb to a job or a responsibility: [Vnadv] *post sb abroad* [Vnpr] *After several years in London, he was posted to the embassy in Moscow.* **2** ~ **sb (at/on sth)** to place a soldier, etc at her or his post²(2): [Vn, Vnpr] *We posted sentries (at the gates).* **posting** /-ɪŋ/ n (esp Brit) an appointment to a post²(1), esp an official one: *offer sb a three-month posting in Cyprus* ○ *He expects that his next posting will be (to) Paris.*

post³ /pəʊst/ (also esp US **mail**) n **(a)** [U] letters, parcels, etc: *There was a lot of post this morning.* ○ *He's dealing with his post at the moment.* **(b)** [U] the official transport and delivery of these: *send sth by post* ○ *I'll put/get it in the post to you first thing in the morning.* ○ *It should get there next day if you send it by first class post.* **(c)** [C] any of the regular collections from a POSTBOX or deliveries to a house, etc, of letters and parcels: *catch/miss* (ie be in time/too late for) *the last post* ○ *Has the post arrived yet?* ○ *The parcel came in this morning's post.* ○ *a post van.*
■ **ˌpost-ˈfree** adv, adj without any charge made for posting, or with the charge already paid: *The book will be delivered post-free.*
ˈpost office n **1** [C] a building or room where one can buy stamps, send parcels, collect government payments one is entitled to, etc: *queuing up for her pension at a post office counter.* **2** **the ˈPost Office** [sing] the public organization responsible for the transport and delivery of letters, etc. **ˈpost-office box** (also **PˈO box**) n a small numbered cupboard at a post office where letters are kept until the person or company they are for collects them.
ˌpost-ˈpaid adj, adv with the charge for delivery already paid.

post⁴ /pəʊst/ (also esp US **mail**) v **(a)** to put a letter, etc into a POSTBOX or take it to a post office (POST³): [Vn] *Could you post this letter for me?* ○ *obtain a certificate of posting.* **(b)** ~ **sth (to sb)** to send a letter, etc to sb: [Vnn, Vnpr] *They will post me the tickets/post the tickets to me as soon as they get my cheque.* **IDM** **keep sb ˈposted** to keep sb informed of the latest developments or news: *They promised to keep him posted about the sales of his book.*

post- pref (with ns, vs and adjs) after: *a postgraduate* ○ *postdate* ○ *a post-Impressionist* ○ *the post-1945 period.* Compare ANTE-, PRE-.

postage /ˈpəʊstɪdʒ/ n [U] the amount charged or paid for sending letters, etc by post: *What was the postage on that parcel?* ○ *The tapes are $10.00 each, including postage and packing.*
■ **ˈpostage stamp** n (fml) = STAMP² 1.

postal /ˈpəʊstl/ adj **(a)** relating to or concerned with the post³(1b): *postal charges/workers/offices/services* ○ *delays in the postal system.* **(b)** sent by post³(1b): *Postal applications/bookings must be received by 12 December.* ○ *If you will be out of the country on election day, you may apply for a postal vote.*
■ **ˈpostal code** n = POSTCODE.
ˈpostal order (Brit) (US **ˈmoney order**) n an official piece of paper bought from a post office (POST³), representing a particular sum of money. It can be posted to a specified person who can exchange it for that sum.

postbag /ˈpəʊstbæg/ n **1** (US **mailbag**) a bag used by a POSTMAN for carrying letters, etc. **2** (infml esp Brit) letters received, esp by sb important or by a newspaper, television station, etc, at a particular time: *We had a huge postbag on the subject from our readers.*

postbox /ˈpəʊstbɒks/ (also **mailbox**) *n* a metal box in which letters to be sent through the post are placed. See also PILLAR-BOX.

postcard /ˈpəʊstkɑːd/ *n* a card for sending messages by post without an envelope. Postcards often have a picture or photograph on one side: *She sent him a (picture) postcard of Venice.* ○ *Answers on a postcard, please, to this address.* See also PICTURE POSTCARD.

postcode /ˈpəʊstkəʊd/ (also **postal code**, *US* **Zip code**) *n* a group of numbers, or letters and numbers, that is used as part of an address so that letters can by separated into groups by machine: *Her postcode is CB11 3AD.*

postdate /ˌpəʊstˈdeɪt/ *v* to put a date on a document, etc that is later than the actual date: [Vn] *a ˌpostdated ˈcheque* (ie one which cannot be exchanged for cash until the date written on it). Compare ANTEDATE, BACKDATE.

poster /ˈpəʊstə(r)/ *n* (**a**) a large notice, often with a picture on it, that is displayed in a public place: *put up election posters* ○ *display a poster advertising the circus* ○ *a poster campaign.* (**b**) a large printed picture: *Her bedroom walls are covered with posters of her favourite pop stars.*

poste restante /ˌpəʊst ˈrestɑːnt; *US* reˈstɑːnt/ (*US* also **general delivery**) *n* [U] a department in a post office (POST³) to which letters for a person may be sent and where they are kept until he or she collects them.

posterior /pɒˈstɪəriə(r)/ *adj* (*techn*) situated behind or at the back: *the posterior deltoid muscle.* Compare ANTERIOR.
▶ **posterior** *n* (*infml joc*) a person's bottom(3): *She has a rather large posterior.*

posteriori ⇨ A POSTERIORI.

posterity /pɒˈsterəti/ *n* [U] all future generations of people: *plant trees for the benefit of posterity* ○ *have sth recorded/preserved for posterity* ○ *Posterity will remember him as a truly great man.*

postgraduate /ˌpəʊstˈɡrædʒuət/ (*US* **graduate**) *adj* (of studies, etc) done after taking a first degree: *a postgraduate course/diploma* ○ *do postgraduate work/research.*
▶ **postgraduate** *n* a person doing postgraduate studies. Compare GRADUATE¹, UNDERGRADUATE.

posthumous /ˈpɒstjʊməs; *US* ˈpɒstʃəməs/ *adj* (**a**) happening or given after death: *posthumous fame/earnings* ○ *the posthumous award of a medal for bravery.* (**b**) (of a literary work) published after its author's death: *a number of posthumous essays.* ▶ **posthumously** *adv: The prize was awarded posthumously.*

postindustrial /ˌpəʊstɪnˈdʌstriəl/ *adj* (of a place or community) no longer relying on heavy industry (HEAVY): *a postindustrial city/economy developing its potential for tourism.*

postman /ˈpəʊstmən/ (*US* **mailman**) (*pl* **-men** /-mən/) *n* a person employed to collect and deliver letters, etc: *our local postman.*

postmark /ˈpəʊstmɑːk/ *n* an official mark stamped on letters, parcels, etc showing the place and date of posting and making the stamps unable to be used again: *an envelope with a Bristol postmark.*
▶ **postmarked** *adj* (followed by a *n*) having a postmark with the specified place, time, etc on it: *The letter was postmarked Tokyo 9 March.*

postmaster /ˈpəʊstmɑːstə(r); *US* -mæst-/ *n* (*fem* **postmistress** /-mɪstrəs/) a person in charge of a post office (POST³).
■ **ˌPostmaster ˈGeneral** *n* (*pl* **Postmasters General**) (usu *sing*) the person in charge of the POSTAL system of a country.

post-modern /ˌpəʊst ˈmɒdn/ *adj* (*techn*) relating to a style of art, architecture, etc that reacts against modern tendencies: *post-modern designs/buildings.*
▶ **post-modernism** *n* [U]. **post-modernist** *adj.*

post-mortem /ˌpəʊst ˈmɔːtəm/ *n* ~ (**on sb/sth**) **1** a medical examination of a person's body made after death in order to find the cause of death: *carry out a post-mortem* ○ *The post-mortem examination revealed that the victim had been poisoned.* **2** a discussion or review of an event after it has happened: *hold a post-mortem on the party's election defeat.*

postnatal /ˌpəʊstˈneɪtl/ *adj* (**a**) occurring in the period after the birth of a child: *At least one in ten women suffer from ˌpostnatal deˈpression.* (**b**) of or for a baby that has just been born: *postnatal care* ○ *a postnatal nurse/unit.* Compare ANTENATAL, PRENATAL.

postoperative /ˌpəʊstˈɒpərətɪv/ *adj* (*fml or techn*) occurring in or relating to the period after an operation(1): *suffer severe postoperative bleeding.*

postpone /pəˈspəʊn/ *v* ~ **sth** (**to/until sth**) (often passive) to cause or arrange for an event, etc to happen at a later time: [Vnpr] *The match was postponed to the following Saturday because of bad weather.* [Vn] *a postponed fourth-round match* [Vnpr, Vnadv] *The exhibition has had to be postponed for two months/indefinitely.* [V.ing] *Let's postpone making a decision until we have more information.* Compare CANCEL 1. ▶ **postponement** *n* [U, C]: *Rain caused the postponement of several race-meetings.* ○ *His lawyer is seeking a postponement of the hearing.*

postprandial /ˌpəʊstˈprændiəl/ *adj* [usu attrib] (*fml or joc*) happening immediately after a meal: *enjoy a postprandial nap.*

postscript /ˈpəʊstskrɪpt/ *n* ~ (**to sth**) **1** (*abbr* PS) an extra message added at the end of a letter after the signature: *She scribbled a quick postscript about her visit to David.* **2** facts or information added to sth after it is completed: *Their son's death a month later forms a tragic postscript to the story.*

postulant /ˈpɒstjʊlənt; *US* -tʃəl-/ *n* a person who lives among monks and nuns in preparation for entering a religious order. Compare NOVICE 3.

postulate /ˈpɒstjʊleɪt; *US* -tʃəl-/ *v* (*fml*) to suggest or accept that sth is true, esp as a basis for reasoning or discussion: [Vn] *The report postulated a grain harvest of over 80 million tons.* [V.that] *She postulates that a cure will be found by the year 2000.*
▶ **postulate** /ˈpɒstjʊlət; *US* -tʃəl-/ *n* (*fml*) a statement that is assumed to be true.

posture /ˈpɒstʃə(r)/ *n* **1(a)** [C usu *sing*] a position of the body: *an awkward/slumped posture* ○ *his composed/dignified posture.* (**b**) [U] the way in which a person holds herself or himself when standing, walking or sitting: *correcting sb's posture* ○ *She has very good posture.* **2** [C] a way of considering sth; an attitude: *The newly-elected government has adopted an uncompromising/a defensive posture on the issue of immigration.* Compare STANCE.
▶ **posture** *v* to pretend to be sth that one is not: [Vn] *He postured as a political activist.* [also V]. **posturing** /ˈpɒstʃərɪŋ/ *n* [U, C esp *pl*] (*derog*) behaviour that is not natural or sincere but is intended to attract attention or to have a particular effect: *the political posturings of recent weeks* ○ *The unions need to stop all this posturing and get down to serious talking.*

postwar /ˌpəʊstˈwɔː(r)/ *adj* [usu attrib] existing or happening in the period after a war, esp World War II or a recent major war: *the postwar era/years* ○ *postwar reconstruction* ○ *in postwar Iran.*

---

posy /ˈpəʊzi/ n a small bunch of flowers: *A little girl presented a posy to the Princess.*

pot

coffee pot

teapot

flowerpot

pot of paint
(*esp US* **can of paint**)

pot¹ /pɒt/ n **1** [C] (**a**) a round container made of glass, plastic, metal, etc for storing or cooking things in: *women making pots from local clay* ○ *an empty yoghurt pot* ○ *a chicken ready for the pot* ○ *She got out all her pots and pans.* ⇨ picture. (**b**) (esp in compounds) any of various types of container made for a particular purpose: *a ˈcoffee pot* ○ *a ˈpepper-pot.* ⇨ picture. See also CHAMBER-POT, CHIMNEY-POT, FLOWERPOT, LOBSTER-POT, MELTING-POT, POTTED, POTTERY. (**c**) the amount contained in a pot: *stir a pot of paint* ○ *Please bring me another pot of coffee.* See also HOTPOT. **2** [C] a FLOWERPOT: *a pot of geraniums on the window-sill.* **3** [C] a TEAPOT: *Is there any tea left in the pot?* **4 the pot** [sing] (*esp US*) (**a**) the total amount of the bets made in a card-game. (**b**) all the money given by a group of people for a common purpose, esp for buying food. **5** [U] (*sl*) = MARIJUANA. **6** [C] = POT-SHOT: *take/have a pot at goal.* **IDM** **go to ˈpot** (*infml*) to be spoilt or ruined: *The firm is going to pot under the new management.* **keep the ˈpot boiling** to keep interest in sth alive. **the pot calling the kettle ˈblack** (*saying*) the person who accuses sb of having a fault has the same fault herself or himself: *She accused us of being extravagant — talk about the pot calling the kettle black!* **ˌpot ˈluck** the chance that whatever is available is good, acceptable, pleasant, etc: *It's pot luck whether you get good advice or not.* ○ *You are welcome to eat with us, but you'll have to take pot luck.* ○ *We don't usually book hotels — we just take pot luck.* **a pot of ˈgold** a large prize or reward that sb hopes for but is unlikely to get: *the prospect of a pot of gold when the statue was sold.* **ˈpots of money** (*infml*) a very large amount of money: *Her father has got pots of money.* **put a quart into a pint pot** ⇨ QUART.
■ **ˌpot-ˈbelly** n a large stomach that sticks out. **ˌpot-ˈbellied** adj (of a person) having a pot-belly.
ˈpot-boiler n (*derog*) a book or work of art produced only to earn money: *She produced/turned out regular pot-boilers while also working on her masterpiece.*
ˈpot plant n (*Brit*) a plant grown in a FLOWERPOT, usu indoors.
ˈpot-shot (also **pot**) n ~ (**at sb/sth**) (*infml*) a shot made without taking careful aim: *Somebody took a pot-shot at him as he was walking the dog.*

pot² /pɒt/ v (**-tt-**) **1** ~ sth (**up**) to plant sth in a pot¹(2): [Vn] *compost for potting young plants* [Vn, Vnp] *He's busy potting (up) chrysanthemum cuttings.* **2** (in BILLIARDS, etc to succeed in hitting a ball into a pocket(5): [Vn] *pot the black (ball).* **3** to kill sth by shooting it: [Vn] *They potted dozens of rabbits.*
▶ **potted** /ˈpɒtɪd/ adj [attrib] **1** planted in a pot¹(2): *a house full of potted plants.* **2** preserved in a pot¹(1a). **3** (*Brit often derog*) (of a book, story etc) in a short simple form: *a potted history of England* ○ *She gave her parents a potted account/version of the night's events.* **4** (*US infml*) drunk.
■ **ˈpotting shed** n (*Brit*) a shed where seeds and young plants are grown in pots (POT¹ 2) before being planted outside.

potable /ˈpəʊtəbl/ adj (*fml or joc*) fit for drinking.

potash /ˈpɒtæʃ/ n [U] a compound of POTASSIUM used to improve soil for farming and in making soap.

potassium /pəˈtæsiəm/ n [U] (*symb* **K**) a chemical element. Potassium is a soft shiny metal, silver in colour, that occurs in rocks and in the form of mineral salts and is essential for all living things. ⇨ App 7.

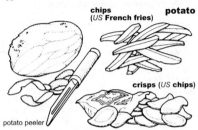

chips
(*US* **French fries**)

potato

crisps (*US* **chips**)

potato peeler

potato /pəˈteɪtəʊ/ n (pl **-oes**) (**a**) [C] a round white vegetable with a brown or red skin. Potatoes grow as the underground roots of a plant: *The potatoes are ready to be dug up.* ⇨ picture. (**b**) [U, C] this vegetable cooked and served as food: *a plate of mince with mashed potato* ○ *boiled/roast/fried/jacket potatoes* ○ *Would you like another potato?* See also COUCH POTATO.
■ **poˌtato ˈcrisp** (*Brit*) (*US* **poˈtato chip**) n = CRISP n 1.

potent /ˈpəʊtnt/ adj **1**(**a**) having great power: *a potent and dynamic force.* (**b**) having a strong effect: *a potent drug/drink.* (**c**) likely to persuade people; convincing: *potent arguments/reasoning.* **2** (of males) capable of having sex. See also IMPOTENT 2. ▶ **potency** /-nsi/ n [U]: *religious/political potency* ○ *boil alcohol to reduce its potency* ○ *sexual potency.* **potently** adv.

potentate /ˈpəʊtnteɪt/ n (esp formerly) a ruler with direct power over his people: *the splendid court of an Eastern potentate.*

potential /pəˈtenʃl/ adj [attrib] (**a**) that can or may in future develop into sth: *a potential source of conflict* ○ *a potential leader/champion* ○ *The book is a potential best seller.* (**b**) existing and capable of being developed or used: *potential energy/power/resources* ○ *a device with many potential applications.* ▶ **potential** n [U] (**a**) ~ (**for sth**) the possibility of sth happening or being developed: *the potential for foreign investment* ○ *She recognized the potential for error in the method being used.* (**b**) qualities that exist and can be developed: *seek to fulfil one's potential* ○ *She has artistic potential/has potential as an artist.*
potentiality /pəˌtenʃiˈæləti/ n (*fml*) a power or quality that exists but has not been developed: *The potentialities of the average person are not fully used.*
potentially /-ʃəli/ adv: *a potentially disastrous situation* ○ *It could potentially appeal to a wide audience.*

pothole /ˈpɒthəʊl/ n **1** a deep hole or cave formed in rock, esp by the action of water. **2** a rough hole in the surface of a road made by traffic and bad weather.
▶ **ˈpotholer** n a person who explores potholes (POTHOLE 1) in rock.
ˈpotholing n [U]: *go potholing.*

potion /ˈpəʊʃn/ n (*dated or rhet*) a drink of medicine or poison, or a liquid used in magic: *a magic/love potion.*

pot-pourri /ˌpəʊ pʊˈriː; *Brit also* ˌpəʊ ˈpʊri/ n **1** [C, U] a mixture of dried flowers and spices used for making a room, cupboard, etc smell pleasant. **2** [C] a mixture of various things that were not originally intended to form a group: *a pot-pourri of tunes.*

[V.*to* inf] = verb + *to* infinitive   [Vn.inf (no *to*)] = verb + noun + infinitive without *to*   [V.*ing*] = verb + *-ing* form

potter¹ /ˈpɒtə(r)/ (*Brit*) (*US* **putter** /ˈpʌtər/) *v* ~ (**about/around** (**sth**)) to work or move without hurry or effort, doing a number of small tasks or not concentrating on anything in particular: [V] *He loves pottering in the garden.* [Vp] *potter about at the exhibition* [Vpr] *We spent the afternoon pottering around the old part of the town.*

potter² /ˈpɒtə(r)/ *n* a person who makes clay pots by hand.
▶ **pottery** /ˈpɒtəri/ *n* **1** [U] pots, dishes, etc made esp by hand with clay that is baked in an oven: *a valuable collection of Japanese pottery.* **2** [U] the skill of making pots, etc, esp by hand: *a pottery class* ○ *She is learning pottery.* **3** [C] a place where pottery is made.
■ ˌpotter's ˈwheel *n* a flat revolving disc on which wet clay is shaped to make pots.

potty¹ /ˈpɒti/ *adj* (*Brit infml*) (**a**) foolish or mad: *I think you're potty to sell that house.* ○ *That noise is driving me potty!* (**b**) ~ **about sb/sth** extremely enthusiastic about sb/sth: *She's potty about jazz/Mike.*

potty² /ˈpɒti/ *n* (*infml*) a bowl used by small children as a toilet.
■ ˈpotty-training *n* the process of teaching a young child to use a potty so that it no longer needs to wear a NAPPY.

pouch /paʊtʃ/ *n* **1** (often in compounds) a bag made esp of leather and carried in a pocket or attached to a belt: *a ˈkey/toˈbacco pouch* ○ *She kept her money and passport in a pouch hanging round her neck.* **2** an area of loose hanging skin, eg under the eyes of a sick person. **3**(**a**) a pocket of skin on the stomach in which a female MARSUPIAL, eg a KANGAROO, carries her young. (**b**) a pocket of skin in the cheeks of certain animals, in which they carry and store food: *a hamster's pouch.*

pouffe (also **pouf**) /puːf/ (*Brit*) (*US* **hassock**) *n* a large thick cushion used as a seat or for resting the feet on.

poultice /ˈpəʊltɪs/ *n* a soft substance spread on a cloth, sometimes heated and put on a sore place on the body to ease pain, reduce swelling, etc: *apply a poultice.*

poultry /ˈpəʊltri/ *n* (**a**) [pl *v*] chickens, ducks, geese (GOOSE 1), kept for eating or for their eggs: *keep poultry* ○ *poultry farming.* (**b**) [U] the meat of these birds eaten as food: *eat plenty of fish and poultry.*

pounce /paʊns/ *v* ~ (**on/upon sb/sth**) (**a**) to make a sudden attack, moving forwards or down in order to catch sb/sth: [V] *We saw the tiger about to pounce.* [Vpr] *The hawk pounced on its prey and carried it off.* ○ *We hid behind the bushes, ready to pounce on the intruder.* (**b**) to notice and take advantage of a mistake, remark, etc quickly and eagerly: [Vpr] *He pounced on me and accused me of lying.* ○ *They pounced on the only word they could understand.* [also V].

pound¹ /paʊnd/ *n* **1** [C] (*symb* £) (**a**) (also ˌpound ˈsterling) the chief unit of British money; 100 pence: *a ten-pound note* ○ *a pound coin* ○ *I've spent £25 on food today.* ○ *Total losses were estimated at over three million pounds.* See also STERLING. (**b**) the unit of money of several other countries, eg Cyprus, Egypt, Ireland, Israel and Malta. (**c**) **the pound** [sing] the value of the British pound on international money markets: *the strength/value of the pound (against other currencies)* ○ *The pound closed slightly higher at $1.634.* See also GREEN POUND. **2** [C] (*abbr* **lb**) a standard measure of weight, equal to 0.454 of a kilogram: *Apples are sold by the pound.* ○ *I've put on two pounds this week* (ie I weigh two pounds more). ○ App 2. **IDM in for a penny, in for a pound** ⇨ PENNY. (**have, want, demand, etc**) **one's pound of** ˈflesh (to insist on) receiving the full amount that is legally due to one even when it is morally

offensive to do so: *Their distress had no effect on him — he was determined to have his pound of flesh.*

pound² /paʊnd/ *n* (**a**) a place where motor vehicles that have been parked illegally are kept until their owners pay to have them released. (**b**) a place where cats and dogs that have been found wandering in the street are kept until their owners claim them. See also IMPOUND.

pound³ /paʊnd/ *v* **1**(**a**) to hit sth with repeated heavy blows: [Vpr] *the sound of feet pounding on the stairs* ○ *Someone was pounding at/on the door.* [Vp] *The heavy guns pounded away all day.* [Vn] *pound enemy positions* ○ *He was pounding the keyboard until midnight.* (**b**) ~ **sth** (**to sth**) to crush or beat sth with repeated heavy blows: [Vn, Vnpr] *pounding garlic (to a paste)* [Vnpr] *The ship was pounded to pieces against the rocks.* **2** ~ (**with sth**) (esp of the heart) to beat heavily: [V, Vpr] *My heart was pounding (with fear).* [V] (*fig*) *a pounding bass line.* **PHR V** ˈpound along, down, up, etc to move in the direction specified with heavy rapid steps: *The horses came pounding along the track.* ˌpound sth ˈout to produce sth with heavy blows: *pounding out a tune on the piano.*

poundage /ˈpaʊndɪdʒ/ *n* [U] a charge of a certain sum per pound in value or weight of sth.

pounder /ˈpaʊndə(r)/ *n* (in compounds) (**a**) a thing that weighs a specified number of pounds: *a three-pounder* (eg a fish weighing 3 lb) ○ *a quarter-pounder* (ie a BURGER containing a quarter of a pound of meat). (**b**) a gun that fires a shell weighing the specified number of pounds: *an eighteen-pounder.*

pounding /ˈpaʊndɪŋ/ *n* **1** a sound or feeling of sth beating heavily: *There was a pounding in his head.* **2** an instance of sb/sth being severely damaged or heavily defeated: *The team took a terrible pounding.*

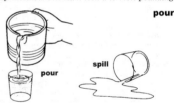
pour

pour /pɔː(r)/ *v* **1** (esp of a liquid) to flow, esp downwards, in a continuous stream: [Vpr] *Blood was pouring from the wound.* ○ *Tears were pouring down his face.* ○ *The ceiling collapsed and rubble poured into the room.* [Vp] *I knocked over the bucket and the water poured out all over the floor.* **2** to make a liquid flow from a container in a continuous stream: [Vnpr] *pour milk into a jug* [Vnp] *She poured out all the water remaining.* [Vn] *Although I poured it carefully, I still managed to spill some.* ⇨ picture. **3** to serve a drink, soup, sauce, etc by holding the container at an angle and letting the liquid flow out into a cup or dish in a controlled way: [V, Vn] *Shall I pour (the tea)?* [Vn, Vnp] *I've poured (out) two cups of coffee.* [Vnpr] *I've poured coffee into your cup by mistake.* [Vnn] *Shall I pour you some water?* [Vnpr] *I've poured a glass of wine for you.* [Vadv] *This teapot doesn't pour well.* **4** (of rain) to fall heavily: [V] *It's pouring outside.* [Vp] *The rain was pouring down.* **5** to come or go somewhere continuously in large numbers: [Vpr] *Commuters were pouring into the station.* [Vp] *The fans poured out after the game, cheering wildly.* [Vp, Vpr] *Letters of complaint have poured in(to the office).* **IDM it never rains but it pours** ⇨ RAIN². **open / pour out one's heart to sb** ⇨ HEART. **pour oil on troubled ˈwater(s)** to try to settle a disagreement or dispute. **pour ˈscorn on sb/sth** to speak with contempt about sb/sth: *She poured scorn on my suggestion.* **pour/throw cold**

water on sth ⇨ COLD¹. **PHRV** ‚pour ¹out (of an account, one's feelings, etc) to be told or expressed freely and fully: *When he realized we knew the truth, the whole story came pouring out.* ‚pour sth ¹out to express one's feelings, give an account of sth, etc freely and fully: *She poured out her troubles to me over a cup of coffee.*

pout /paʊt/ *v* to push the lips, or the bottom lip, forward in order to express annoyance or to look sexually attractive: [V] *a child that always pouts when teased* ○ *a model with smouldering eyes and pouting lips* [Vn] *pout one's lips provocatively.*
▶ **pout** *n* (esp *sing*) a pouting expression of the face.

poverty /¹pɒvəti/ *n* **1** [U] the state of being poor: *live in poverty* ○ *conditions of abject/grinding poverty.* **2** [U, sing] the state of existing in amounts that are too small; lack: *His work displays (a) poverty of imagination.* **3** [U] the state of being inferior; poor quality: *the poverty of the soil* ○ *They were recognizable by the poverty of their dress.*
■ **the ¹poverty line** [sing] the minimum level of income needed to buy the basic necessities of life: *live below the poverty line.*
¹poverty-stricken *adj* extremely poor: *poverty-stricken families/areas.*
¹poverty trap *n* (usu *sing*) a situation in which sb stays poor even when they get a job because state benefits are reduced or taxes increased as their income rises.

POW /‚piː əʊ ¹dʌblju:/ *abbr* prisoner of war: *a POW camp.*

powder /¹paʊdə(r)/ *n* **1** [C, U] **(a)** a mass of very small fine dry pieces or grains: *lumps of chalk crushed to (a) powder* ○ *The snow was like powder.* **(b)** (esp in compounds) a substance in this form that has a particular use: *¹chilli/¹curry powder* ○ *¹face powder* ○ *a range of ¹washing powders.* See also SOAP POWDER, TALCUM POWDER. **2** [U] = GUNPOWDER. **IDM** **keep one's ¹powder dry** to remain cautious and ready for a possible emergency: *The problem may not arise, but there's no harm in keeping our powder dry.*
▶ **powder** *v* to put powder on sth: [Vn] *powder one's face/nose.* **IDM** **powder one's ¹nose** (*euph*) (of a woman) to go to the toilet. **powdered** *adj* (of a substance that is naturally liquid) dried and made into powder: *powdered milk/eggs* ○ *The detergent is sold in powdered form.* ‚powdered ¹sugar *n* [U] (*US*) = CASTER SUGAR.
powdery /¹paʊdəri/ *adj* like powder: *a light fall of powdery snow.*
■ **powder ¹blue** *adj, n* (of) a pale blue colour.
¹powder-keg *n* **1** a small barrel for holding GUNPOWDER. **2** a dangerous situation that may suddenly become very violent: *The country is a powder-keg waiting to explode.*
¹powder-puff *n* a soft round pad used for applying powder to the face.
¹powder-room *n* (*euph*) a women's toilet in a department store, hotel, theatre, etc.

power /¹paʊə(r)/ *n* **1** [U] (in people) the ability or opportunity to do sth or to act: *It is not in/within my power* (ie I am unable or not in a position) *to help you.* ○ *I will do everything in my power to help you.* **2(a)** [U] (also **powers** [pl]) a particular ability of the body or mind: *He has lost the power of speech.* ○ *The drug affects sms powers of concentration.* ○ *He had to use all his powers of persuasion.* **(b)** **powers** [pl] all the abilities of a person's body or mind: *a woman of impressive intellectual powers* ○ *be at the height of one's powers* (ie when one is strongest in mind and body). **3** [U] the strength or energy contained in sth: *The ship was helpless against the power of the storm.* ○ *The power of her performance affected the whole audience.* ○ *They were impressed by the power of her arguments.* ⇨ note at

STRENGTH. See also FIRE-POWER. **4** [U] **(a)** control over others: *the power of the law* ○ *have sb in one's power* (ie be able to do what one wishes with sb) ○ *have power over sb/sb's future* ○ *fall into sb's power* ○ *He made the mistake of underestimating the power of the press.* **(b)** political control; rule: *take/seize/lose power* ○ *The government came to/into power at the last election.* ○ *The present regime has been in power for two years.* **5** [C esp *pl*] a right possessed by or given to a person or group; authority: *military/ legal/economic power(s)* ○ *The powers of the police must be clearly defined.* ○ *The President has exceeded his powers* (ie has done more than he or she is allowed or has the right to do). **6** [C] a person, group or state with great authority or influence: *world powers* (ie countries with the most influence in international affairs) ○ *an allied/enemy power.* **7** [U] **(a)** energy that can be gathered and used for operating sth: *wind/nuclear/hydroelectric power.* **(b)** the public supply of electricity: *They've switched off the power.* **(c)** [attrib] operated by mechanical or electrical energy: *power ¹brakes/¹steering* ○ *¹power tools.* **(d)** (of an engine, etc) capacity or performance: *a car's power of acceleration* ○ *boost/increase/ reduce engine power.* **8** [C esp *sing*] (*mathematics*) the result obtained by multiplying a number by itself a certain number of times: *4 to the power of 3 is 4³* (ie 4 × 4 × 4 = 64). **9** [U] the capacity of a LENS(1) for making objects appear larger: *the power of a microscope/telescope.* **10** [C] a good or evil spirit that controls the lives of others: *the powers of darkness* (ie the forces of evil or of the Devil) ○ *She believed in the existence of a benevolent power.* **IDM** **the corridors of power** ⇨ CORRIDOR. **do sb a ¹power of good** (*infml*) to be very good for sb's physical or mental health: *A holiday would do us all a power of good.* **more power to sb's ¹elbow** (*Brit infml*) (used to express support for or encouragement to sb doing sth): *She is campaigning for an improved bus service — more power to her elbow!* **the (real) power behind the ¹throne** the person who really controls an organization, a country, etc, in contrast to the person who is legally in charge: *The President's wife was suspected of being the real power behind the throne.* **the ‚powers that ¹be** (*often ironic*) the people who control an organization, a country, etc: *The powers that be are still trying to decide what should be done.*
▶ **power** *v* **1** (esp passive) to supply sth with the energy that enables it to operate: [Vn] *aircraft powered by jet engines* ○ *toys powered by batteries.* **2** to move very quickly and with great power: [Vpr, Vnpr] *He powered (his way) into the lead.* [also Vp, Vnp].
powered *adj* (usu in compounds) equipped with or operated by the specified type of energy: *solar-powered heating.* See also HIGH-POWERED.
■ **¹power-base** *n* the main support for a politician or political party: *His power-base is in the south of the country.*
¹power-broker *n* a person who influences how much political power others have.
¹power cut *n* an interruption in the supply of electricity: *The violent storms caused several power cuts.*
¹power line *n* a cable supplying electric power.
‚power of at¹torney *n* [U, C] (*law*) the right to act on sb's behalf in business or financial matters.
¹power point *n* (*Brit*) a SOCKET(2) on a wall, etc where electrical appliances can be attached to the electrical supply by a plug.
¹power-sharing *n* [U] a system or policy in which two or more parties or groups agree to share responsibility for making decisions, taking political action, etc.
¹power station (*US* **¹power plant**) *n* a building where electricity is produced: *a coal-fired power-station* ○ *a nuclear power-station.*

powerboat /ˈpaʊəbəʊt/ n a boat with an engine, esp a very powerful one, for racing, etc.

powerful /ˈpaʊəfl/ adj (**a**) having great power: *a powerful explosion* ○ *a powerful engine/motor bike/ computer* ○ *a powerful voice*. (**b**) having a strong effect: *a powerful image/drug/speech* ○ *a powerful feeling of regret/sympathy/anger*. (**c**) physically strong: *powerful muscles*. (**d**) having great control or influence: *a powerful enemy/nation/organization/ ruler*. ▶ **powerfully** /-fəli/ adv: *He is powerfully built* (ie has a large strong body).

powerhouse /ˈpaʊəhaʊs/ n (pl -**houses** /-haʊzɪz/) a person, a group, an organization, etc that is very strong and full of energy: *The department is seen as a powerhouse of new ideas*.

powerless /ˈpaʊələs/ adj **1** without power or strength: *render sb powerless* ○ *be in a powerless position*. **2** [pred] ~ **to do sth** completely unable to do sth: *I feel powerless to help*. ○ *They were powerless to resist*. ▶ **powerlessness** n [U]: *I feel a terrible sense of powerlessness*.

pox /pɒks/ n **the pox** [sing] (*dated*) = SYPHILIS. See also CHICKENPOX, SMALLPOX.

pp abbr **1** pages. **2** /ˌpiː ˈpiː/ (before a signature) on behalf of (Latin *per procurationem*): *pp J E Symonds* (eg signed by his secretary in his absence). **3** (*music*) very quietly (Italian *pianissimo*). Compare FF 3.

PPS /ˌpiː piː ˈes/ abbr (*Brit*) Parliamentary Private Secretary: *She is PPS to the Chancellor*.

PR /ˌpiː ˈɑː(r)/ abbr **1** proportional representation. **2** public relations: *a PR assistant/job/department*.

pr abbr **1** (pl **prs**) pair. **2** price.

practicable /ˈpræktɪkəbl/ adj that can be put into practice or carried out; that is likely to work: *a practicable scheme/solution/suggestion* ○ *He did not consider that such an arrangement was practicable*. Compare IMPRACTICABLE. ▶ **practicability** /ˌpræktɪkəˈbɪləti/ n [U]. **practicably** /-əbli/ adv: *as soon as is practicably possible*.

practical /ˈpræktɪkl/ adj **1** concerned with reality and action rather than theory and ideas: *practical experience/skills* ○ *He's better at practical tasks than those that require intellectual thought*. ○ *Where can I get some really practical advice?* Compare THEORETICAL 1. **2** suitable for the purpose for which it was intended; useful: *a practical, modern kitchen* ○ *Cool, loose-fitting clothes would be more practical for this kind of holiday*. Compare IMPRACTICAL. **3** that can be done or is likely to work in real circumstances: *find a practical way out of the problem* ○ *It wouldn't be practical to take the car because there won't be anywhere to park*. **4(a)** (of a person) able to make things function or to deal with what circumstances require: *She's very practical when it comes to mending things*. (**b**) (of a person) sensible and realistic: *We must be practical and work out the cost first*. **5** that is so in effect; VIRTUAL: *a practical certainty* ○ *The owner's brother has in practical control of the firm for years*. **IDM** **for (all) ˈpractical purposes** as far as really matters; in reality: *The game has another ten minutes to go, but for all practical purposes it's already over*.
▶ **practical** n (*infml*) a practical(1) examination or lesson, eg in a scientific subject: *a physics practical*. **practicality** /ˌpræktɪˈkæləti/ n **1** [U] the quality or state of being sensible and realistic: *He questioned the practicality of the proposal*. **2 practicalities** [pl] practical(1) matters rather than theories or ideas: *We need to discuss practicalities like time and cost*.
practically /-kli/ adv **1** almost; nearly: *practically impossible/invisible/unchanged* ○ *His work is practically unknown here*. **2** in a practical(4) manner: *She's very practically minded*.
■ **ˌpractical ˈjoke** n a trick played on sb which

makes them look foolish and is intended to amuse others: *The children put salt in the sugar bowl as a practical joke*. **ˌpractical ˈjoker** n.
ˌpractical ˈnurse n (*US*) a nurse with less training than a registered nurse (REGISTER²).

practice /ˈpræktɪs/ n **1** [U] the actual doing of sth; action as contrasted with ideas: *put a plan into practice* ○ *The idea would never work in practice*. **2(a)** [U] regularly repeated exercise or training done in order to improve one's skill at sth: *an hour's practice every day* ○ *a practice game* ○ *Playing the piano well requires a lot of practice*. ○ *With practice you could get quite good at this*. (**b**) [C] a period of time spent doing this: *The players will meet for a practice in the morning*. **3(a)** [U] a way of doing sth that is common, habitual or expected: *It is stand- ard practice to ask hotel guests for their passports when they check in*. ○ *Paying bills promptly is good financial practice*. ○ *Are such methods common practice in this country?* See also CODE OF PRACTICE, SHARP PRACTICE. (**b**) [C] a thing done regularly; a habit or custom: *the practice of closing shops on Sundays* ○ *I had a short sleep after lunch, as is my usual practice*. **4** [U, C] the work or business of a doctor, lawyer, etc: *a doctor working in general prac- tice* (ie as a family doctor) ○ *a medical/dental/legal practice* ○ *a group practice* (ie several doctors work- ing together as a group from the same building) ○ *buy a country practice* ○ *My solicitor is no longer in practice*. See also GENERAL PRACTICE, PRIVATE PRAC- TICE. **IDM** **ˌin / ˌout of ˈpractice** having/not having spent time recently doing sth that requires skill: *It's important to keep in practice*. ○ *If you don't play regularly, you soon get out of practice*. **ˌpractice makes ˈperfect** (*saying*) practising sth repeatedly makes it possible to become very good at it.

practise (*US* **practice**) /ˈpræktɪs/ v **1** to do sth repeatedly or regularly in order to improve one's skill: [V] *I haven't been practising enough*. [Vn] *She's practising a new piece on the piano*. ○ *I need to practise my Italian before my trip to Rome*. [V.ing] *Practise reversing the car into the garage*. **2** to do sth regularly as part of one's normal behaviour: [Vn] *practise self-restraint* ○ *practise ancient customs*. **3** ~ (**as sth**) to work as a doctor, lawyer, etc: [V] *Does he still practise?* [V-n] *She practised as a solicitor for many years*. [Vn] *practise law/medicine/dentistry*. **IDM** **ˌpractise what one ˈpreaches** to do habitu- ally oneself what one tells others to do. **PHRV** **ˈpractise sth on/upon sb** to do sth to sb, esp in order to take advantage of them: *practise deception on people*.
▶ **practised** (*US* **-ticed**) /-tɪst/ adj ~ (**in sth**) expert, esp as a result of much practice or experience: *practised in the art of deception* ○ *The men worked with practised skill*.
practising (*US* **-ticing**) adj [attrib] currently active or engaged in a profession, religion, etc: *a practising lawyer/Christian*.

practitioner /prækˈtɪʃənə(r)/ n **1** a person who works in a profession, esp medicine: *a medical prac- titioner*. See also GENERAL PRACTITIONER. **2** a person who regularly does a particular activity, esp one requiring skill: *an outstanding practitioner of the art of management*.

praesidium = PRESIDIUM.

pragmatic /prægˈmætɪk/ adj treating things in a sensible and realistic way to produce results; con- cerned with actual circumstances rather than general theories: *a politician with a pragmatic ap- proach* ○ *a pragmatic solution to the problem*. ▶ **pragmatically** /-kli/ adv: *respond pragmatically to a crisis*.

pragmatics /prægˈmætɪks/ n [sing v] (*linguistics*) the study of the way in which language is used to express or interpret real intentions in particular situations, esp when the actual words used may appear to mean sth different.

pragmatism /ˈprægmətɪzəm/ n [U] (fml) thinking about or treating things in a practical way rather than according to general theories: *a foreign policy built on economic pragmatism.* ▸ **pragmatist** /-tɪst/ n: *A pragmatist is always flexible in dealing with problems.*

prairie /ˈpreəri/ n a flat wide area of land covered with grass, esp in N America; a plain. Compare PAMPAS, SAVANNAH, STEPPE, VELD.

praise¹ /preɪz/ v **1** ~ sb/sth (for sth); ~ sb/sth as sth to express approval or admiration for sb/sth: [Vn] *She praised his cooking.* [Vnpr] *He praised her for all her hard work.* [Vn-adj] *Critics praised the work as highly original.* **2** to express respect, honour or gratitude to God: [Vn] *praise the Lord.*

praise² /preɪz/ n [U] **1** the expression of approval or admiration for sb/sth: *an achievement worthy of great praise* ○ *It's important to give praise where it is due* (ie praise people when they deserve it). ○ *His teachers are full of praise for his work.* ○ *He received high praise for his scientific research.* ○ *He spoke in praise of all the members of the rescue team.* **2** the worship of God: *a hymn of praise* ○ *Praise be (to God)* (ie expressing relief or joy)! **IDM** **damn sb/sth with faint praise** ⇨ DAMN³. **sing sb's/sth's praises** ⇨ SING.

▸ **ˈpraiseworthy** /-wɜːði/ adj deserving praise: *a very praiseworthy achievement/effort/performance.* **praiseworthiness** n [U].

pram /præm/ (Brit) (also fml **perambulator**, US **buggy**, **baby carriage**) n a carriage with four wheels for a baby to go out in, pushed by a person on foot.

prance /prɑːns; US præns/ v **1** to move in the specified direction in an excited or proud manner, with exaggerated steps: [Vpr] *She was prancing along in her new outfit.* ○ *He pranced out of the room in a fury.* [Vp] *They were prancing about* (ie jumping or dancing happily) *to the music.* **2** [V] (of a horse) to move with high steps. [also Vp,Vpr].

prank /præŋk/ n a playful or foolish trick: *a childish prank* ○ *play a prank on sb.*

▸ **prankster** /ˈpræŋkstə(r)/ n a person who plays pranks.

prat /præt/ n (Brit sl) a very foolish or stupid person: *Don't be such a prat!*

prate /preɪt/ v [V, Vpr, Vp] ~ (on) (about sth) (dated derog) to talk foolishly or too much.

prattle /ˈprætl/ v ~ (on/away) (about sb/sth) (usu derog) to talk a lot, esp about unimportant things: [Vp] *She was prattling on about her latest boyfriend.* [also Vpr, V].

▸ **prattle** n [U] (usu derog) talk about unimportant things: *full of childish/idle prattle.*

prawn /prɔːn/ n a type of edible sea creature like a large SHRIMP(1): *a prawn cocktail* (ie a dish of prawns served with MAYONNAISE).

praxis /ˈpræksɪs/ n [U] (fml) an accepted way of doing sth: *the contemporary praxis of the church.*

pray /preɪ/ v **1** ~ (to sb) (for sb/sth) to offer thanks, make requests, etc to God: [V] *They knelt down and prayed.* [Vpr] *The priest prayed for the dying man.* ○ *They prayed (to God) for an end to their sufferings/ for their sufferings to end.* [V.that] *They prayed that she would recover.* [V.to inf] *She prayed to be forgiven.* [also V.speech]. **2** ~ (for sth) to hope very much: [Vpr] *Our holiday starts tomorrow and we're praying for good weather.* [V.that] *I was praying that nobody would notice my mistake.* **3** (dated or fml) (imperative only; used when adding emphasis to a question or request, sometimes ironically) please: *And what, pray, would be the point of doing that?*

■ **ˌpraying ˈmantis** n a large insect. It holds its front legs in a position that suggests sb praying, while waiting to catch another insect, etc.

prayer /preə(r)/ n **1(a)** [C] ~ (for sth) a solemn request or expression of thanks to God or to an object of worship: *say one's prayers* ○ *a prayer for forgiveness/rain/success* ○ *He arrived, as if in answer to her prayers.* **(b)** [C] a fixed form of words used for this: *prayers he had learnt as a child.* See also THE LORD'S PRAYER. **(c)** [U] the action of praying: *They knelt in prayer.* ○ *She believed in the power of prayer.* **2** prayers [pl] a regular, sometimes informal, meeting in which prayers are said: *have family/ morning/evening/daily prayers.* **4** [C usu sing] a thing for which one hopes very much: *My one prayer is that he will walk again.* **IDM** **not to have a ˈprayer (of doing sth)** (infml) to have no chance of doing sth: *They haven't got a prayer of winning.*

■ **ˈprayer-book** n **(a)** a book containing prayers, for use in church, etc. **(b)** the **ˈPrayer Book** (also the ˌBook of ˌCommon ˈPrayer) [sing] the prayer-book used in Anglican services.

ˈprayer-mat n a small carpet on which Muslims kneel when praying.

pre- pref (used fairly widely with vs, ns and adjs) before: *pre-heat* ○ *pre-war* ○ *prehistoric.* Compare ANTE-, POST-.

preach /priːtʃ/ v **1(a)** ~ (to sb) (about/against/on sth) to make a religious speech, esp in church; to give a SERMON(1a): [Vn] *preach a sermon every Sunday* [Vpr] *The vicar preached to the congregation for half an hour.* ○ *He preached against violence.* [also V]. **(b)** to make a religion or belief known by talking about it publicly; to teach sth: [Vn] *preach the Gospel/the word of God* ○ *They preached the new doctrines throughout Europe.* **2** to try to persuade people to accept, follow or support a belief, a method, etc: [Vn] *He was always preaching the virtues of capitalism.* **3** ~ (at/to sb) (often derog) to give sb strong advice on morals, behaviour, etc, esp in an annoying way: [V, Vpr] *I am tired of listening to you preach (at me).* [Vpr] *You are in no position to preach to me about honesty.* **IDM** **practise what one preaches** ⇨ PRACTISE. **preach to the conˈverted** to speak to people in support of views that they already hold: *Rousing speeches to faithful party members is simply preaching to the converted.*

▸ **preacher** n a person who preaches in church, esp a CLERGYMAN: *a good preacher* ○ *a preacher famous for his inspiring sermons.*

preamble /priˈæmbl, ˈpriːæmbl/ n [C,U] ~ (to sth) a statement or introduction that comes before sth spoken or written: *'Why are you here?' she demanded, without preamble.* ○ *The phrase is explained in the preamble to the report.*

prearranged /ˌpriːəˈreɪndʒd/ adj arranged in advance: *a prearranged meeting/signal.*

precarious /prɪˈkeəriəs/ adj **1** not safe; dangerous: *He was unable to get down from his precarious position on the rocks.* **2** depending on chance; uncertain: *She makes a rather precarious living as a novelist.* ▸ **precariously** adv: *perch/balance precariously on top of sth* ○ *live on a precariously small income.* **precariousness** n [U].

pre-cast /ˌpriː ˈkɑːst; US ˈkæst/ adj (of concrete) made into blocks ready for use in building.

precaution /prɪˈkɔːʃn/ n ~ (against sth) an action taken in advance to avoid danger, prevent problems, etc: *take an umbrella just as a precaution* ○ *fire precautions/precautions against fire* ○ *I took the precaution of locking everything in the safe.* ▸ **precautionary** /prɪˈkɔːʃənəri; US -neri/ adj: *take precautionary measures/steps.*

precede /prɪˈsiːd/ v to come or go before sb/sth in time, order, position, etc; to happen before sth: [Vn] *the events that preceded this* ○ *The President entered, preceded by members of the security staff.* ○ *She preceded me in the job.* [V] *This point has been dealt with in the preceding paragraph.* **PHRV** **precede**

[V.to inf] = verb + to infinitive   [Vn.inf (no to)] = verb + noun + infinitive without to   [V.ing] = verb + -ing form

sth with sth to do or say sth to introduce sth else: *She preceded her speech with a vote of thanks to the committee.*

precedence /ˈpresɪdəns/ *n* [U] ~ (**over sb/sth**) the right or requirement to come before sb/sth else in time, order, etc; PRIORITY(2): *a list of the guests in order of precedence* (ie in order of social rank) ○ *People who arrive first should have precedence.* ○ *The needs of the community must* **take precedence** *over individual requirements.*

precedent /ˈpresɪdənt/ *n* [C, U] **1** an earlier decision, case, etc that is regarded as an example or a rule to be followed in similar circumstances later: *a ruling that* **set a precedent** *for future cases* ○ *a case that established a precedent* ○ *a decision without precedent.* **2** [C] a similar event or action that happened earlier: *historical precedents* ○ *There is no precedent for such a measure.* See also UNPRECEDENTED.

precept /ˈpriːsept/ *n* [C, U] (*fml*) a rule or guide, esp for behaviour: *moral/ideological/religious precepts* ○ *Children learn far more by example than by precept.*

precinct /ˈpriːsɪŋkt/ *n* **1** [C] (*Brit*) an area in a town for specific or restricted use, esp a shopping area where vehicles may not enter: *a shopping precinct* ○ *a pedestrian precinct.* **2** [C] an area enclosed by definite boundaries, esp the walls of a cathedral, church or college. **3** [C] (*US*) an administrative area within a city or county served by its own police force, etc or electing its own representatives: *an election precinct* ○ *a police precinct.* **4(a)** **precincts** [pl] boundaries; limits: *No parking is allowed within the hospital precincts.* (**b**) [C] the area around a place: *within the city precincts* ○ *the station precinct.*

precious /ˈpreʃəs/ *adj* **1** of great value, esp because of being very beautiful, rare or expensive: *Gold and silver are* **precious metals**. ○ *The crown is set with* **precious stones,** *including diamonds and rubies.* **2** ~ (**to sb**) very important to sb; greatly loved by sb: *a few precious moments together* ○ *a precious memento of happier times* ○ *Each life is precious.* ○ *She is very precious to him.* ○ *I lead a busy life so my free time is precious to me.* ○ (*infml ironic*) *She talks about nothing except her precious car!* **3** (*derog*) too concerned with elegant language and manners: *a rather precious young man.* **4** (*infml often ironic*) great: *A precious lot of* (ie very little) *good that will do!*

▶ **precious** *adv* (used before *little, few*) (*infml*) very: *Precious few people can afford prices like that.* ○ *She has precious little to be cheerful about.*

preciousness *n* [U]: *the preciousness of an old friendship* ○ *a style of writing that is prone to preciousness.*

precipice /ˈpresəpɪs/ *n* a very steep side of a cliff, mountain or rock: *a house perched above an 80 ft precipice* ○ (*fig*) *The country's economy was* **on the edge of a/the precipice** (ie in danger of collapsing).

precipitate /prɪˈsɪpɪteɪt/ *v* (*fml*) **1** to cause sth, esp sth bad, to happen suddenly or sooner: [Vn] *events that precipitated his fall from power.* **2** ~ **sb/sth into sth** to throw sb/sth suddenly into a particular state or condition: [Vnpr] *The assassination of the president precipitated the country into war.*

▶ **precipitate** /prɪˈsɪpɪtət/ *adj* (of an action) done or happening suddenly or without care or thought; RASH²: *a precipitate decline in government fortunes* ○ *To go ahead without further consultation would have been precipitate — even foolhardy.* **precipitately** *adv.*

precipitation /prɪˌsɪpɪˈteɪʃn/ *n* [U] (*techn or fml*) the amount of rain, snow, etc that falls in an area: *a heavy precipitation* ○ *a more oceanic climate with increased precipitation and strong winds.*

precipitous /prɪˈsɪpɪtəs/ *adj* (*fml*) **1** extremely high

or steep: *a precipitous hillside/slope.* **2** sudden and dramatic: *a precipitous fall/drop in grain prices.* ▶ **precipitously** *adv*: *perched precipitously on the edge of a cliff.*

précis /ˈpreɪsiː; *US* preɪˈsiː/ *n* [U, C] (*pl* unchanged /-iːz/) a much shorter version of an article, a speech, etc giving the main points or ideas from it; a summary.

▶ **précis** *v* (*pp* **précised** /-siːd/*pres p* **précising** /-siːɪŋ/) to make a précis of sth: [Vn] *précising a scientific report.*

precise /prɪˈsaɪs/ *adj* **1** stated clearly and accurately: *give precise details/instructions/measurements* ○ *a clear and precise description of the incident.* **2** [attrib] exact; particular: *at that* **precise moment** ○ *What were her precise words?* ○ *It cost about $1000, I think — I'm not sure of the precise amount.* **3** taking care to be exact and accurate, esp about minor details: *a precise worker/manner* ○ *The answer is 100, or 99.8* **to be precise.** ○ (*often derog*) *a person with a very prim and precise manner.*

▶ **precisely** *adv* **1(a)** exactly; just: *at 2 o'clock precisely* ○ *do precisely the opposite of what was asked* ○ *I can't remember precisely what happened.* ○ *That is precisely what I mean.* ○ *It is precisely because I care about them that I won't let them go to nightclubs with their friends.* (**b**) in a PRECISE(2) manner; carefully: *time/judge/define sth precisely* ○ *He enunciated the words very precisely.* **2** (used to express agreement with a statement, often suggesting that it states sth that is obvious or has already been said by oneself): *'He was drunk again?' 'Precisely.'*

precision /prɪˈsɪʒn/ *n* [U] accuracy: *carve the chicken with surgical precision* ○ *He approached the task with military precision.* ○ *Look at the precision and craftsmanship of her drawings.* ○ *precision bombing/engineering* ○ *precision instruments/tools* (ie those designed for very accurate work, measurements, etc).

preclude /prɪˈkluːd/ *v* ~ **sth;** ~ **sb from doing sth** (*fml*) to prevent sth from happening or sb doing sth; to make sth impossible: [Vn] *Financial constraints preclude excavation of more than part of the site.* [Vnpr] *His appearance for the England B team does not preclude him from playing for Ireland at full international level.*

precocious /prɪˈkəʊʃəs/ *adj* (**a**) (*sometimes derog*) (of a child) having developed particular abilities at an earlier age than usual: *Their precocious daughter can already play the piano at the age of three.* (**b**) (of behaviour, ability, etc) showing this development: *display a precocious talent for computing.* ▶ **precociously** *adv.* **precociousness,** **precocity** /prɪˈkɒsəti/ *ns* [U].

preconceived /ˌpriːkənˈsiːvd/ *adj* [attrib] (of an idea, opinion, etc) formed in advance and not based on sufficient information or experience: *He had no* **preconceived ideas** *about what careers his children should follow.*

preconception /ˌpriːkənˈsepʃn/ *n* (often *pl*) ~ (**about sb/sth**) an opinion or idea formed in advance and not based on sufficient information or experience: *common preconceptions about life in China.* See also MISCONCEPTION.

precondition /ˌpriːkənˈdɪʃn/ *n* a condition that is required to exist or be done for sth else to happen or exist: *negotiate without any preconditions* ○ *A cessation of violence is a necessary precondition for any talks.*

precursor /priːˈkɜːsə(r)/ *n* ~ (**of/to sth**) (*fml*) a person or thing that comes before sb/sth more important, larger or more highly developed: *researching a book on Freud's precursors* ○ *small disturbances that were precursors of the revolution to come.*

predate /ˌpriːˈdeɪt/ *v* to happen or exist at an earlier

[V.speech] = verb + direct speech   [V.*that*] = verb + *that* clause   [V.*wh*] = verb + *who, how,* etc clause

date than sth/sb: [Vn] *Few of the town's fine buildings predate the earthquake of 1755.* Compare POSTDATE.

predator /ˈpredətə(r)/ *n* **1** an animal that kills and eats other animals: *deter/ward off/fend off potential predators* ○ *Young rabbits provide food for a variety of predators.* **2** (*derog*) a person who exploits others, esp financially or sexually: *The public want to protect their domestic industry from foreign predators.*

predatory /ˈpredətri; US -tɔːri/ *adj* **1** (of animals) living by killing other animals for food: *predatory birds/instincts.* **2** (*derog*) (of people or their behaviour) seeking to exploit others for financial or sexual reasons: *his predatory advances/interests* ○ *predatory companies.*

predecease /ˌpriːdɪˈsiːs/ *v* (*law*) to die before sb: [Vn] *Most men predecease their wives.*

predecessor /ˈpriːdɪsesə(r); US ˈpredəs-/ *n* **1** a person who held a position, job, etc before sb else: *The decision was made by my predecessor as manager.* **2** a thing that has been followed or replaced by sth else: *The latest car phones are much more efficient than their predecessors.* Compare SUCCESSOR.

predestination /ˌpriːdestɪˈneɪʃn/ *n* [U] the theory or belief that everything that happens has been decided in advance by God and that humans cannot change it.

predestined /ˌpriːˈdestɪnd/ *adj* ~ (**to do sth**) (*fml*) already decided or determined by fate: *It seemed that his failure was predestined.* ○ *They were predestined to spend their lives together.*

predetermine /ˌpriːdɪˈtɜːmɪn/ *v* (*fml*) to decide or fix sth in advance: *the ability to predetermine the sex of embryos* ○ *predetermined strategies/responses* ○ *A person's health is often genetically predetermined.*

predeterminer /ˌpriːdɪˈtɜːmɪnə(r)/ *n* (*grammar*) a word that can precede a DETERMINER in a sentence, eg *all* in 'all the students', *twice* in 'twice the price', *such* in 'such a lot of rain'.

predicament /prɪˈdɪkəmənt/ *n* (*fml*) a difficult or unpleasant situation, esp one in which it is difficult to know what to do: *a financial predicament* ○ *I'm afraid we're in a bit of a predicament.*

predicate¹ /ˈpredɪkət/ *n* (*grammar*) a part of a statement that says sth about the subject, eg 'is short' in 'Life is short'. Compare SUBJECT¹ 6.

predicate² /ˈpredɪkeɪt/ *v* (*fml*) **1** ~ sth on/upon sth (esp passive) to base sth on sth; to do or decide sth as a consequence of sth: [Vnpr] *The project was predicated on the assumption that the economy was expanding.* **2** to declare or assert that sth is the case: [V.that] *predicate that the market collapse was caused by weakness of the dollar* [also Vn].

predicative /prɪˈdɪkətɪv; US ˈpredɪkeɪtɪv/ *adj* (*grammar*) (abbreviated as *pred* in this dictionary) (of an adjective) coming after a verb such as *be, become, get, seem, look.* Many adjectives, eg *old,* can be either predicative, as in 'The man is very old', or attributive, as in 'an old man'. Some, like *asleep,* can only be predicative. Compare ATTRIBUTIVE. ▶ **predicatively** *adv.*

predict /prɪˈdɪkt/ *v* to say in advance that sth will happen; to forecast sth: [Vn] *accurately predict the outcome/result/possible consequences of sth* ○ *City analysts confidently predict a turnover of $300 million.* [V.that] *She predicted that the election result would be close.* [V.wh] *It is too early to predict who will win.* [V.n to inf] *Pre-tax profits are predicted to fall sharply.*

▶ **predictable** /-əbl/ *adj* (**a**) that can be predicted: *predictable behaviour/results/weather* ○ *a weak and predictable plot.* (**b**) (*often derog*) (of a person) behaving in a way that can be predicted: *I knew you'd say that — you're so predictable!* ○ *Opposition to the proposal came from predictable quarters.* **predictability** /prɪˌdɪktəˈbɪləti/ *n* [U]. **predictably** *adv:*

Predictably enough, the medical profession have condemned the proposals.

prediction /prɪˈdɪkʃn/ *n* **1** [C] a statement that sth will happen; a FORECAST: *the UN's predictions of famine* ○ *widespread predictions that interest rates will rise* ○ *Her predictions came true.* **2** [U] the action of predicting sth: *set up a new centre for the prediction of climate change.*

predictor *n* a person, an instrument, etc that predicts sth: *Cholesterol level is the strongest predictor of heart disease.*

predictive *adj* [usu attrib] (*fml*) concerned with predicting the future: *predictive dreams/studies.*

predilection /ˌpriːdɪˈlekʃn; US ˌpredl'ek-/ *n* (usu *sing*) ~ (**for sth**) (*fml*) a preference; a special enjoyment of sth: *have a predilection for Japanese food.*

predispose /ˌpriːdɪˈspəʊz/ *v* ~ **sb to sth / to do sth** (*fml*) to influence sb to have the specified attitude, condition, etc or to a particular action: [Vnpr] *a stressful career that predisposed him to heart attacks* [V.n to inf] *Her natural tolerance predisposed her to forgive him.*

▶ **predisposition** /ˌpriːdɪspəˈzɪʃn/ *n* (usu *sing*) [U, C] ~ (**to/towards sth**) (**of sth**) **1** the state of mind or body that makes sb likely to act in a particular way, suffer from a particular condition, etc: *a predisposition to depression/premature hair loss.*

predominant /prɪˈdɒmɪnənt/ *adj* **1** having more power or influence than others: *the predominant opinion in the party* ○ *The Socialists were predominant in the last Parliament.* **2** most noticeable or important: *the predominant feature/factor in sth* ○ *Her predominant characteristic is honesty.*

▶ **predominance** /-əns/ *n* [U, sing] ~ (**of sth**) **1** the state of being greater in number: *a predominance of liberals in the party.* **2** the state of being stronger or more influential than sb/sth: *American predominance in space research.*

predominantly *adv* mainly; for the most part: *a predominantly English-speaking population.*

predominate /prɪˈdɒmɪneɪt/ *v* **1** ~ (**over sb/sth**) to have control, power or influence over sb/sth: [V] *Fear of chaos and revolution still predominated among the middle classes.* [Vpr] *No single group predominates over another.* **2** to be greater in number, amount, etc: [V] *a colour scheme in which red predominates* ○ *Oak trees predominate in this forest.*

pre-eminent /priˈemɪnənt/ *adj* superior to all others; outstanding: *a scientist pre-eminent in her field* ○ *He enjoyed a pre-eminent position among the writers of his day.*

▶ **pre-eminence** /-əns/ *n* [U] ~ (**in sth**): *awards for those who achieve pre-eminence in public life.*

pre-eminently *adv* to a very great extent; above all: *an activity in which she has been pre-eminently successful.*

pre-empt /priˈempt/ *v* **1** to prevent sth happening by taking action to stop it: [Vn] *Her departure pre-empted any further questions.* **2** to do sth before sb else: [Vn] *I was preparing to speak when she pre-empted me.* **3** (*US*) (esp in television) to replace the planned programme: [Vn] *'Roseanne' will be pre-empted by a special news bulletin.*

▶ **pre-emption** /priˈempʃn/ *n* [U] (*commerce*) the opportunity of one person or group to buy goods, shares, etc: *Existing shareholders will have pre-emption rights.*

pre-emptive /-tɪv/ *adj* intended to prevent sb taking action, esp against oneself: *launch a pre-emptive attack/strike.*

preen /priːn/ *v* ~ **oneself/itself** **1** (*often derog*) (**a**) (of a person) to spend a lot of time making oneself look attractive and then admiring one's appearance: [Vn] *girls preening themselves in front of the mirror* [also V]. (**b**) to show that one is very pleased with oneself: [Vnpr] *He sat preening himself on his witty* *remark.* [also Vn]. **2** [V, Vn] (of a bird) to clean itself or make its feathers smooth with its beak.

pre-exist /ˌpriːɪgˈzɪst/ *v* (**a**) to exist from an earlier time: [V] *a pre-existing relationship/medical condition.*
▶ **pre-existence** /-əns/ *n* [U] an earlier form of existence, esp of the soul.
pre-existent /-ənt/ *adj.*

prefab /ˈpriːfæb/ *n* (*infml*) a PREFABRICATED building.

prefabricated /ˌpriːˈfæbrɪkeɪtɪd/ *adj* (of a building) manufactured in sections that can be assembled later: *a prefabricated house/shed.* ▶ **prefabrication** /ˌpriːfæbrɪˈkeɪʃn/ *n* [U].

preface /ˈprefəs/ *n* a statement at the beginning of a book, esp one that explains the author's aims. Compare FOREWORD, INTRODUCTION 3a.
▶ **preface** *v* **1** ~ **sth with sth** (esp passive) to provide a book, etc with a preface: [Vn] *Each chapter is prefaced by an apposite quotation.* [Vnpr] *He prefaced the diaries with a short account of how they were discovered.* **2** ~ **sth by sth / with sth / by doing sth** to begin or introduce a speech, etc: [Vnpr] *She prefaced her talk with an apology.*

prefatory /ˈprefətri; *US* -tɔːri/ *adj* [usu attrib] (*fml*) acting as a PREFACE or an introduction to sth: *a prefatory note.*

prefect /ˈpriːfekt/ *n* **1** (in some British schools) an older pupil who is given authority over younger pupils and certain other responsibilities. **2** (also **Prefect**) the chief administrative officer of an area in certain countries, eg France and Japan.
▶ **prefecture** /ˈpriːfektʃə(r)/ *n* (in certain countries) an area of administration: *citizens of Nagasaki Prefecture.*

prefer /prɪˈfɜː(r)/ *v* (**-rr-**) ~ **sth** (**to sth**) (not in the continuous tenses) to choose sth rather than sth else; to like sth better: [Vn] *plants that prefer full sunlight* ○ *'Coffee or tea?' 'I'd prefer tea, thanks.'* ○ *the preferred candidate* [Vnpr] *I prefer sorbet to ice-cream.* [Vn, Vnpr] *A local firm is to be preferred (to one from outside the area).* [Vn-adj] *I prefer my coffee black.* [V.to inf] *She actually prefers to do things by herself.* ○ *He decided he'd prefer not to say anything.* [V.n to inf] *Their father prefers them to be home early.* [V.ing] *I prefer walking to cycling.* ○ (*Brit fml*) [V.that] *I would prefer that you did not/prefer it if you did not print this story.* **IDM** **prefer/press charges** ⇨ CHARGE[1].
▶ **preferable** /ˈprefrəbl/ *adj* (not used with *more*) ~ (**to sth / doing sth**) more desirable or suitable; to be preferred to sth: *Written authority is preferable.* ○ *Anything was preferable to the strained atmosphere at home.* ○ *He finds country life infinitely preferable to living in the city.* **preferably** /ˈprefrəbli/ *adv* more than anything, etc else; as a first choice; if possible: *She wanted a cake, preferably one with chocolate icing.* ○ *They want to buy a new house, near the university preferably.*

preference /ˈprefrəns/ *n* **1(a)** [U, sing] ~ (**for sth**) a greater interest in or desire for sb/sth than sb/sth else: *It's entirely a matter of personal/individual preference.* ○ *Many people have expressed a clear/definite/marked/strong preference for smaller schools.* ○ *The most popular pets, in order of preference, are: dogs, horses, cats…* (**b**) [C] a thing that is liked better or best: *a study of consumer preferences.* **2** [U] favour shown to one person or group rather than another: *Employees who have worked here for many years will be given preference in the allocation of parking spaces.* **IDM** **in preference to sb/sth** rather than sb/sth: *She was chosen in preference to her sister.*
■ **'preference shares** (*US* **pre,ferred 'shares**) *n* [pl] (*finance*) shares on which a firm must pay inter-

est to the holders before distributing profits to holders of ordinary shares.

preferential /ˌprefəˈrenʃl/ *adj* giving, receiving or showing preference(2): *preferential import duties/tariffs/interest rates* ○ *Why should single mothers get/receive preferential treatment when it comes to housing?* ▶ **preferentially** /-ʃəli/ *adv.*

preferment /prɪˈfɜːmənt/ *n* [U] (*fml*) promotion to a higher position or rank: *academic/ecclesiastical preferment.*

prefigure /ˌpriːˈfɪgə(r); *US* -gjər/ *v* (*fml*) to have particular qualities or features that suggest or indicate in advance sth that will happen in the future: [Vn] *worrying events that may prefigure a head-on clash.*

prefix /ˈpriːfɪks/ *n* **1** (abbreviated as *pref* in this dictionary) a letter or group of letters added to the front of a word to change its meaning, eg *un-* in *unhappy, co-* in *cooperate.* Compare AFFIX[2], SUFFIX. **2** (*dated*) a word, eg *Dr, Ms*, placed before a person's name as a title.
▶ **prefix** /ˈpriːfɪks/ *v* ~ **A to B / ~ B with A** to add sth at the beginning or as an introduction: [Vnpr] *In Britain telephone calls prefixed with 0800 are free of charge.*

pregnant /ˈpregnənt/ *adj* (of a woman or female animal) having a baby or young animal developing in the WOMB: *My wife is pregnant.* ○ *Sue became/got pregnant almost at once.* ○ *My daughter was pregnant with her third child at the time.* ○ *She was six months pregnant (ie had been pregnant for six months).* ○ *Tom got his girlfriend pregnant, so they're getting married.* **IDM** **a pregnant 'pause/'silence** (*fml*) a pause/silence full of meaning that is not openly expressed: *There was a pregnant pause before she answered my question.*
▶ **pregnancy** /-nənsi/ *n* (**a**) [U] the state or period of being pregnant: *the later stages of pregnancy* ○ *These drugs should not be taken during pregnancy.* ○ *The pregnancy test was positive.* (**b**) [C] a situation of being pregnant: *unplanned/unwanted pregnancies* ○ *the increase in teenage pregnancies* ○ *She's had three pregnancies in four years.*

preheat /ˌpriːˈhiːt/ *v* ~ **sth** (**to sth**) to heat an oven to a certain temperature before putting food in it to cook: [Vn, Vnpr] *₁Preheat the 'oven (to 220°C).*

prehensile /prɪˈhensaɪl; *US* -sl/ *adj* (of a part of an animal's body) able to hold and grip things: *the monkey's prehensile tail.*

prehistoric /ˌpriːhɪˈstɒrɪk; *US* -ˈstɔːrɪk/ *adj* of or concerning the time before history was first recorded: *in prehistoric times* ○ *prehistoric man/graves/cave paintings.* Compare HISTORIC.

prehistory /ˌpriːˈhɪstri/ *n* **1** [U] the period before history was first recorded: *study Mexican prehistory.* **2** [sing] the earliest stages of the development of sth: *the prehistory of the Earth.*

prejudge /ˌpriːˈdʒʌdʒ/ *v* to make a judgement about sb/sth in advance and without having adequate information: [Vn] *We mustn't prejudge the issue.*

prejudice /ˈpredʒudɪs/ *n* ~ (**about/against sb/sth**) (**a**) [U] dislike or DISTRUST of a person, group, custom, etc that is based on fear or false information rather than on reason or experience, and that influences one's attitude and behaviour towards them: *He was a tireless opponent of racial prejudice.* ○ *combat public ignorance and prejudice.* (**b**) [C] an instance of this: *She came up against all the old prejudices about mixing a career with motherhood.* ○ *The incident reinforced/confirmed her prejudices.* **IDM** **without 'prejudice (to sth)** (*esp law*) without having an effect on an existing right or claim: *The firm agreed to pay compensation without prejudice (ie without affecting LIABILITY(1)).*
▶ **prejudice** *v* **1** to cause sb to have a prejudice; to influence sb: [Vn] *The jury were told that they must*

not allow their feelings to prejudice them. **2** to cause harm to a case, claim, etc: [Vn] *The judge said the chances of a fair trial had been prejudiced by the press coverage.*

prejudiced *adj* ~ **(against / in favour of sb/sth)** (*usu derog*) having or showing prejudice: *a wildly prejudiced view* ○ *He went to the head teacher alleging that I was prejudiced against his daughter.* ○ *The committee seemed to be prejudiced in favour of farmers' interests.*

prejudicial /ˌpredʒuˈdɪʃl/ *adj* ~ **(to sth)** (*fml*) causing or likely to cause harm to a person's rights, interests, etc: *developments prejudicial to the company's future.*

prelate /ˈprelət/ *n* (*fml*) a CLERGYMAN of high rank, eg a bishop.

preliminary /prɪˈlɪmɪnəri; *US* -neri/ *adj* coming before a more important action or event: *After a few preliminary remarks she came to the main point of the meeting.* ○ *preliminary inquiries/talks* ○ *announce the **preliminary results** of the survey/tests* ○ (*sport*) *a preliminary contest/heat/round* (ie held before a main contest in order to exclude weaker players or teams).

▶ **preliminary** *n* (usu *pl*) ~ **(to sth)** a preliminary action, event or measure done in preparation for sth: *the necessary preliminaries to a peace conference* (eg discussions about procedures) ○ *We skipped the usual preliminaries.*

prelude /ˈpreljuːd/ *n* **1** ~ **(to sth)** an action or event that happens before another more important one and forms an introduction to it: *Could the growing number of bankruptcies be the prelude to general economic collapse?* **2** (*music*) a short piece of music, esp an introduction to a longer piece: *Rachmaninov's G major prelude* ○ *the prelude to Act II.*

premarital /ˌpriːˈmærɪtl/ *adj* happening before marriage: *premarital sex.*

premature /ˈpremətʃə(r); *US* ˌpriːməˈtʊər/ *adj* **1(a)** happening before the proper or expected time: *premature baldness/ageing/death* ○ *the premature closing of the exhibition.* (**b**) (of a baby or its birth) born or occurring at least three weeks before the expected time: *The baby was five weeks premature.* **2** ~ **(in doing sth)** (*derog*) happening, done, made, etc too soon: *a premature conclusion/decision/judgement* ○ *His comments may prove to be a little premature.* ○ *I think it's premature for us to talk about sending troops in.* ▶ **prematurely** *adv*: *born/die prematurely* ○ *prematurely bald/grey.*

premeditated /ˌpriːˈmedɪteɪtɪd/ *adj* planned in advance: *a premeditated decision/murder* ○ *The attack was clearly premeditated.* Compare UNPREMEDITATED.

▶ **premeditation** /priːˌmedɪˈteɪʃn/ *n* [U].

premenstrual /ˌpriːˈmenstruəl/ *adj* (*techn*) occurring or experienced before menstruation (MENSTRUATE): *Many women suffer from premenstrual tension/syndrome, which causes them to have headaches and feel irritated or depressed.* See also PMT.

premier /ˈpremiə(r); *US* prɪˈmɪər, ˈpriːmɪər/ *adj* [attrib] first in importance or position: *one of France's premier chefs* ○ *Britain's premier exporter of drilling equipment* ○ (*sport*) *the premier league/division.*

▶ **premier** *n* (esp in news reports) a head of a government; a prime minister (PRIME¹): *her first act as premier* ○ *The French premier.* **premiership** [U] the position or period of office of a premier: *a candidate for the premiership* ○ *gain/resign the premiership.*

première /ˈpremɪeə(r); *US* prɪˈmɪər/ *n* the first public performance of a new play or showing of a film: *attend the **world première** of her new play* ○ *a gala première* ○ *The movie had its première in Chicago last year.*

▶ **première** *v* (usu passive) to perform a play or show a film to the public for the first time: *The film was premièred at the Cannes festival.*

premise (also **premiss**) /ˈpremɪs/ *n* (*fml*) a statement or an idea on which reasoning is based: *a false premise* ○ *Let's start from the basic premise that we all have certain rights.* ○ *I'm working on the premise that we shall have very little support.*

premises /ˈpremɪsɪz/ *n* [pl] a house or an office together with any buildings or land near to it that are owned by the same person or company: *rent shop/business/commercial premises* ○ *The firm is looking for larger premises.* ○ *No toxic substances are allowed **on the premises**.* ○ *He was asked to leave the premises immediately.* ○ *He was escorted **off the premises**.*

premium /ˈpriːmiəm/ *n* **1** an amount of money to be paid regularly for an insurance policy: *pay a monthly premium of £20* ○ *The annual premium is now due.* **2** an additional payment, eg one added to interest¹(5) payments: *A premium of 2% is paid on long-term investments.* ○ *You have to pay a high premium for express delivery.* **IDM** **at a ˈpremium 1** rare or difficult to obtain, and therefore more expensive or more highly valued than usual: *Space is at a premium in this building.* **2** (*finance*) above the normal or usual value: *Shares are selling at a premium.* **put/place a premium on sb/sth** to consider sb/sth particularly valuable or important: *The company places a high premium on interpersonal skills.*

▶ **premium** *adj* [attrib] (**a**) (of a price, etc) very high: *premium rents.* (**b**) (of a product) of the best quality: *premium sherry.*

■ **ˈPremium Bond** *n* (*Brit*) a government BOND(2) that offers the chance of winning money as a prize each month, instead of paying any interest¹(5).

premonition /ˌpriːməˈnɪʃn, ˌprem-/ *n* ~ **(of sth / that…)** a feeling that sth is going to happen, esp sth unpleasant: *a premonition of disaster* ○ *I had a premonition that my life was about to change.*

▶ **premonitory** /prɪˈmɒnɪtəri; *US* -tɔːri/ *adj* (*fml*) giving a warning of sth about to happen: *premonitory signs/feelings/dreams.*

prenatal /ˌpriːˈneɪtl/ *adj* (*esp US*) = ANTENATAL.

preoccupation /priːˌɒkjuˈpeɪʃn/ *n* **1(a)** [C] an idea or a subject that a person thinks about very often or all the time: *His main preoccupation at that time was getting enough to eat.* ○ *The nature of truth is one of the preoccupations of modern philosophy.* (**b**) [U, C] ~ **with sth** a state of constantly thinking or worrying about sth: *She found his preoccupation with money irritating.* **2** [U] a mood or state of mind in which one pays little attention to anything but one's own thoughts: *He was sitting at his desk with an air of preoccupation.*

preoccupy /priːˈɒkjupaɪ/ *v* (*pt, pp* **-pied**) to engage sb's mind or thoughts so that they cannot think of other things: [Vn] *Health worries preoccupied him constantly.* ○ *The students' thoughts are naturally preoccupied by their forthcoming exams.*

▶ **preoccupied** *adj* (**a**) ~ **(with sth)** busy with sth, so that one is unable to think about or deal with anything else: *I've been too preoccupied with my work to even think about taking a holiday.* (**b**) not paying attention to sb/sth because one is thinking or worrying about sth else: *She seemed preoccupied all the time I was talking to her.*

preordain /ˌpriːɔːˈdeɪn/ *v* (usu passive) to decide or determine sth before it actually happens: [Vn] *Our lives are/have been preordained by supernatural forces.* [V.n *to* inf] *They seemed preordained to meet.* [also V.*that*].

prep /prep/ *n* (*infml*) [U] (*Brit*) school work to be done after lessons, at the end of the day; HOMEWORK(1).

[V.*to* inf] = verb + *to* infinitive   [Vn.inf (no *to*)] = verb + noun + infinitive without *to*   [V.*ing*] = verb + *-ing* form

■ **'prep school** *n* = PREPARATORY SCHOOL.

prepack /ˌpriː'pæk/ (also **pre-package** /-'pækɪdʒ/) *v* to put goods into packs ready for sale before distribution to shops: [Vn] *prepacked fruit/cheese/ meat.*

prepaid /ˌpriː'peɪd/ *adj* paid or paid for in advance: *a prepaid envelope* (ie one on which the POSTAGE has already been paid) ○ *The delivery charge was prepaid.*

preparation /ˌprepə'reɪʃn/ *n* **1** ~ **(for sth) (a)** [U] the action or process of preparing: *the preparation of meals* ○ *You can't pass an exam without preparation.* ○ *These injuries have interrupted the team's preparation for next week's match.* ○ *The advertising campaign is still in preparation.* ○ *The team has trained hard in preparation for the match.* **(b)** [C usu *pl*] ~ **(for sth)** an activity or a thing that is done to prepare for sth: *The country is making preparations for war/to go to war.* ○ *Was your university course a good preparation for your career?* **2** [C] a substance that has been specially prepared for use as eg a medicine or drug: *a pharmaceutical preparation* ○ *a preparation for concealing skin blemishes.*

preparatory /prɪ'pærətrɪ; US -tɔːrɪ/ *adj* preparing for sth; done in advance of sth: *preparatory investigations/measures/meetings* ○ *a preparatory course for students entering the university next year* ○ *a series of preparatory sketches.* **IDM** **pre'paratory to sth** (*fml*) (used like a preposition) in preparation for sth; in advance of sth: *Security checks had been carried out preparatory to the President's arrival.*

■ **pre'paratory school** (also **'prep school**) *n* **1** (*Brit*) a private(6) school for pupils between 7 and 13 years old whose parents pay for their education. Compare PUBLIC SCHOOL. **2** (*US*) a school, usu a private one, that prepares students for college.

prepare /prɪ'peə(r)/ *v* **1** ~ **(sth/sb/oneself) (for sb/ sth)** to get ready or make sth/sb ready: [V] *I had no time to prepare.* [Vn] *have everything prepared beforehand* [Vpr, Vn] *The police are preparing (themselves) for trouble at next week's demonstration.* [Vnpr] *A hotel room is being prepared for them/their arrival.* [V.to inf, Vn.to inf] *The troops prepared (t'.emselves) to go into battle.* **2** to make food ready to be eaten or cooked: [Vn] *He was in the kitchen preparing lunch.* ○ *Prepare the fish by wiping it with a damp paper towel.* **3** ~ **sth (from sth)** (*chemistry*) to make a chemical substance, eg from other substances: [Vn] *prepare penicillin in the laboratory* [also Vnpr]. **IDM** **prepare the 'ground (for sth)** to make it possible or easier to develop sth: *The committee will prepare the ground for next month's summit.* ○ *Early experiments with rockets prepared the ground for space travel.*

▶ **prepared** *adj* [pred] **1** ~ **(for sth)** able to deal with sth: *I knew there were problems, but I was not prepared for this! We'll be better prepared next time.* **2** ~ **to do sth** willing to do sth: *I am prepared to lend you the money if you promise to pay it back next week.* ○ *They seem prepared to compromise.* **3** done, made, written, etc in advance: *The spokesman read out a prepared statement.* ○ *I often buy prepared meals at the supermarket.* **preparedness** /prɪ'peərɪdnəs/ *n* [U] the state of being prepared, ready or willing: *his preparedness to break the law* ○ *The troops are in a state of preparedness.*

prepayment /ˌpriː'peɪmənt/ *n* [C, U] payment in advance: *a funeral prepayment plan.*

preponderant /prɪ'pɒndərənt/ *adj* (*fml*) greater than others in amount, influence or importance: *Melancholy is the preponderant mood of the poem.* ▶ **preponderance** /-əns/ *n* [sing]: *a preponderance of blue-eyed people in the population.* **preponderantly** *adv.*

preposition /ˌprepə'zɪʃn/ *n* (*grammar*) (abbreviated as *prep* in this dictionary) a word or group of words (eg *in, from, to, out of, on behalf of*) used before a noun or pronoun to show eg place, position, time or method. ▶ **prepositional** /-ʃənl/ *adj*: *a prepositional phrase* (ie a preposition and the noun following it, eg *at night, after breakfast*).

prepossessing /ˌpriːpə'zesɪŋ/ *adj* (*fml*) (esp after a negative) making a good or strong impression; attractive: *He/His appearance is not very prepossessing.* Compare UNPREPOSSESSING.

preposterous /prɪ'pɒstərəs/ *adj* (*fml*) completely unreasonable; absurd or shocking: *The accusation/ suggestion is preposterous.* ▶ **preposterously** *adv.*

preppy (also **preppie**) /'prepɪ/ *n* (*US infml*) a person attending an expensive private school, or sb who looks like such a person.

Pre-Raphaelite /ˌpriː 'ræfəlaɪt/ *n* (*art*) a member of a group of British 19th-century artists who painted in a style similar to that of Italian painting before the time of Raphael. ▶ **Pre-Raphaelite** *adj*: *a Pre-Raphaelite portrait.*

pre-record /ˌpriː rɪ'kɔːd/ *v* (esp passive) to record music, a television programme, etc in advance, to be broadcast later: [Vn] *a pre-recorded interview* ○ *watch pre-recorded highlights of a football match.* Compare LIVE[1] 8.

▶ **pre-recorded** *adj* (of a CASSETTE or VIDEO(2c)) with sound or pictures already recorded on it.

prerequisite /ˌpriː'rekwəzɪt/ *n* ~ **(for/of/to sth)** (*fml*) a thing required as a condition for sth to happen or exist: *A degree is a prerequisite for employment at this level.*

prerogative /prɪ'rɒgətɪv/ *n* a right or privilege, esp one belonging to a particular person or group: *It is the prime minister's prerogative to decide when to call an election.* ○ *the ˌroyal pre'rogative* (ie the special powers and rights of a king or queen, eg to dissolve parliament) ○ *A President has the prerogative of pardoning criminals.*

Pres *abbr* President: *Pres Clinton.*

presage /'presɪdʒ, prɪ'seɪdʒ/ *v* (*fml*) to be a sign that sth will happen, usu sth unpleasant: *Dark clouds usually presage rain.* [Vn] *a military defeat which presaged the end of the Roman Empire.* ▶ **presage** /'presɪdʒ/ *n* (*fml*) a sign that sth will happen, usu sth unpleasant: *a presage of doom.*

Presbyterian /ˌprezbɪ'tɪəriən/ *adj* (of a Church, esp the national Church of Scotland) governed by elders (ELDER[1] *n* 3) who are all equal in rank. Compare EPISCOPAL. ▶ **Presbyterian** *n* a person who is a member of the Presbyterian Church. **Presbyterianism** /-ɪzəm/ *n* [U] the beliefs of Presbyterians, or their system of church government.

presbytery /'prezbɪtrɪ; US -terɪ/ *n* **1** an administrative court of the PRESBYTERIAN Church. **2** a house where a Roman Catholic priest lives. **3** (in a church) the eastern part of the CHANCEL, beyond the CHOIR(2).

preschool /ˌpriː'skuːl/ *adj* [attrib] of the time or age before a child is old enough to go to school: *a ˌpreschool 'child/a child of preschool age* ○ *ˌpreschool edu'cation.*

prescient /'presiənt/ *adj* (*fml*) knowing or appearing to know about things before they happen: *prescient remarks/warnings.* ▶ **prescience** /-əns/ *n* [U]: *She showed great prescience in selling her shares just before the market crashed.*

prescribe /prɪ'skraɪb/ *v* ~ **sth (for sb/sth) 1** (of a doctor) to advise or order the use of a medicine or medical treatment: [Vn] *The doctor prescribed some pills to help me to sleep.* ○ *The optician prescribed tinted lenses.* ○ *Do not exceed the prescribed dose.* [Vnpr] *Ask her to prescribe something for that cough.* [Vn-n] *The doctor prescribed rest as the best cure.* **2** to declare with authority that sth should be done or that a rule should be followed: [Vn] *a prescribed form of words* ○ *a prescribed text* (ie one that has to be studied, eg for an examination) [V.*that*] *Police regulations prescribe that an officer's number must be clearly visible.* [Vnpr] *You can't prescribe fixed standards for art.* [also V.*wh*].

prescription /prɪˈskrɪpʃn/ *n* **1(a)** [C, U] ~ (**for sth**) a written instruction, issued by a doctor, that enables one to buy and use a medicine or get other forms of treatment: *The doctor gave me a prescription for antibiotics.* ○ *This drug is available only on prescription.* (**b**) [C] a medicine prepared as a result of such an instruction: *The chemist made a mistake when making up the prescription.* ○ *prescription charges.* **2** [C] ~ (**for sth**) a recommended course of action: *a prescription for sustainable development.* **3** [U] the action of prescribing (PRESCRIBE 1) sth: *The prescription of drugs is a doctor's responsibility.*

prescriptive /prɪˈskrɪptɪv/ *adj* (*fml*) **1(a)** stating what should be done; making rules or giving instructions: *a prescriptive approach/judgement/role.* (**b**) (*linguistics*) telling people how they ought to use a language: *a prescriptive grammar of English.* Compare DESCRIPTIVE 2. **2** (of rights and institutions) made legal or acceptable by continued existence over a long period: *prescriptive rights* ○ *a prescriptive monarchy.*

presence /ˈprezns/ *n* **1** [U] the state of being present in a place: *dogs trained to detect the presence of explosives* ○ *Your presence is requested at a meeting of shareholders.* ○ *Her presence during the crisis had a calming effect.* Compare ABSENCE. **2** [C] a number of people, esp soldiers or police officers, in a place for a particular purpose: *a massive police presence at the football match* ○ *The United Nations maintains a military presence in the area.* **3** [C usu *sing*] a person or thing that is or seems to be present in a place: *a ghostly presence* ○ *The President's adviser has been a constant presence at those meetings.* **4** [U, sing] (*approv*) the impression a person makes on others by her or his behaviour or personality: *a man of great presence* ○ *The power of Olivier's stage presence can never be forgotten.* **IDM** **be admitted to, shown into, etc sb's** ˈ**presence** (*fml*) to be brought to a room or place in order to meet sb very important: *The ambassador was ushered into the King's presence.* **in the** ˈ**presence of sb / in sb's** ˈ**presence** in the place where sb is; with sb there: *He made the accusation in the presence of witnesses.* ○ *She asked them not to discuss the matter in her presence.* **make one's presence** ˈ**felt** to make others aware of one's presence or existence, eg by the strength of one's personality or by one's superior authority: *The new chairman is certainly making his presence felt!* ■ ˌ**presence of** ˈ**mind** *n* [U] the ability to remain calm and take quick sensible action in a crisis: *The boy had the presence of mind to turn off the electricity supply.*

present¹ /ˈpreznt/ *adj* **1** [pred] ~ (**at sth**) (**a**) (of a person) in a particular place at a particular time: *Were you present when the news was announced?* ○ *The mistake was obvious to all (those) present.* ○ *Everybody present welcomed the decision.* ○ *There were 200 people present at the meeting.* (**b**) ~ (**in sth**) (of things) existing in a place at a particular time: *a machine which measures how much radioactivity is present (in the atmosphere)* ○ *Analysis showed that traces of arsenic were present in the body.* ○ *The threat of war is still present.* Compare ABSENT¹ 1. **2** [attrib] existing or happening now: *the present situation/difficulties/arrangements* ○ *the present owner/occupant of the house* ○ *a list of all the club members, past and present* ○ *You can't use it in its present condition.* ○ *If prices continue to increase at the present rate...* **IDM** **present company**

exˈcepted (used when making a critical remark to exclude people present from the criticism) what I am saying does not apply to you: *People tend to drink too much at parties, present company excepted, of course.*
▶ **present** *n* (usu **the present**) [sing] (**a**) the time now passing; the present time: *artists of the past, present and future* ○ *an escape from the harsh realities of the present.* (**b**) (*grammar*) = PRESENT TENSE. **IDM** **at** ˈ**present** at this time; now: *I'm afraid I can't help you just at present.* **for the moment/present** ⇨ MOMENT. **no time like the present** ⇨ TIME¹. ■ **the** ˌ**present** ˈ**day** *n* [sing] modern times; the situation that exists in the world now: *This custom has survived to the present day.* ○ ˌ*present-day exˈperiences/*ˈ*fashions/*ˈ*life.* ˌ**present** ˈ**participle** *n* (*grammar*) (abbreviated as *pres p* in this dictionary) the form of the verb that in English ends in *-ing*, eg *going, having, swimming.* It can sometimes be used as an adjective. Compare VERBAL NOUN. **the** ˌ**present** ˈ**perfect** *n* [sing] (*grammar*) the verb TENSE² in English that is formed with the present tense of *have* and the past PARTICIPLE of the verb, as in *she has eaten.* **the** ˌ**present** ˈ**tense** *n* [sing] (*grammar*) (abbreviated as *pres t* in this dictionary) the verb TENSE² that expresses an action or a state happening or existing at the time of speaking: *The verb is in the present tense.* Compare PAST¹ *n* 3.

NOTE Compare **present, current** and **actual. Present** means 'existing or happening now': *How long have you been in your present job?* **Current** suggests a situation that exists now, but which may be temporary: *The factory cannot continue its current level of production.* ○ *the current crisis in the government.* Note that **actual** cannot be used to mean **current**. It means 'real or exact': *I need the actual figures, not just an estimate.* ○ *His actual age was 45, not 40 as stated on the form.*

present² /ˈpreznt/ *n* a thing given to sb as a gift: *birthday/Christmas/wedding presents* ○ *This book was a present from my brother.* ○ *He liked my old typewriter so much, I made him a present of it* (ie gave it to him).

present³ /prɪˈzent/ *v* **1** ~ **sb with sth**; ~ **sth (to sb)** to give sth to sb, esp formally at a ceremony: [Vn] *A local celebrity presented the prizes.* [Vnpr] *Colleagues presented the retiring chairman with a gold watch/ presented a gold watch to the retiring chairman.* **2(a)** ~ **sth (for sth)**; ~ **sth (to sb)** to show or offer sth for other people to look at or consider: [Vn] *present one's passport at the border* ○ *Several interesting papers were presented at the conference.* [Vnadv] *a well-presented analysis* [Vnpr] *present one's designs for approval/consideration* ○ *They presented a petition to the governor.* (**b**) ~ **sth/sb/oneself as sth** to show sth/sb/oneself from a certain point of view; to show a certain aspect of sth/sb/oneself: [Vn-n] *He likes to present himself as the saviour of his people.* [Vnpr] *The country presents a modern, go-ahead face to the world.* **3(a)** ~ **sb with sth**; ~ **sth (to sb)** to cause sth to occur or be experienced: [Vn, Vnpr] *Your request presents (us with) certain problems.* [Vnpr] *Army life presents many difficulties/ challenges/opportunities to the new recruit.* ○ *The President has suddenly been presented with a crisis.* (**b**) ~ **itself (to sb)** (of an opportunity, a solution, etc) to occur or become available: *A new problem suddenly presented itself.* **4(a)** to appear in and introduce a programme on radio or television: [Vn] *He used to present a gardening programme on BBC 2.* (**b**) to produce a show, play, broadcast, etc for the public: *The National Theatre is presenting a new production of 'Hamlet'.* ○ *Starlight Productions presented the Chinese Children's Choir in concert.* (**c**) to introduce and advertise a new product to the public: *Acme Fashions present their new range of children's clothing.* **5** ~ **sb** (**to sb**) (*fml*) to introduce sb formally, esp to sb of higher rank or status: [Vn, Vnpr] *May I present my fiancé (to you)?* **6** ~ **oneself at, for, in, etc sth** (*fml*) to attend or appear somewhere for a formal event: [Vnpr] *You will be asked to present yourself for interview.* ○ *I have to present myself in court on 20 May.* **7** ~ **sth** (**to sb**) (*fml*) to offer or express sth in speech or writing: [Vn, Vnpr] *present one's apologies/compliments/greetings (to sb).* **8** to give sb a bill or cheque that they should pay: [Vn] *Has the builder presented his bill yet?* ○ *The cheque was presented* (ie at a bank) *on 21 March.* **IDM** pre,sent ˈarms (of soldiers) to hold a RIFLE¹ upright in front of the body as a mark of respect.

▶ **presenter** *n* a person who presents a radio or television programme.

presentable /prɪˈzentəbl/ *adj* fit to appear or be shown in public; clean, tidy or attractive: *I've got several suits but not one of them is presentable.* ○ *I must go and make myself presentable before the guests arrive.* ▶ **presentably** /-əbli/ *adv.*

presentation /ˌprezn'teɪʃn; *US also* ˌpriːzen-/ *n* **1** [U] (**a**) the way in which sth is presented: *I admire the clear, logical presentation of her arguments.* ○ *The government needs to improve the presentation of its policies.* (**b**) the action of presenting sth: *The trial was adjourned following the presentation of new evidence to the court.* **2** [C] (**a**) the act of giving sb a gift or prize, esp at a formal ceremony: *We want to make her a presentation to celebrate her 40 years with the firm.* ○ *The President will* **make the presentation** (ie will hand over the gift) *himself.* ○ *a presentation copy* (ie a free book presented by the publisher (PUBLISH) or the author). (**b**) the ceremony itself: *the school's annual presentation of prizes.* **3** [C] (*esp commerce*) a meeting or talk at which eg a new product or business idea is presented: *I gave a presentation to local teachers on our new range of textbooks.* **4** [C] a production of a play, etc in a theatre: *We went to the première of their new presentation.* **5** [C, U] (*medical*) the position of a baby in the mother's body just before birth.

▶ **presentational** /-ʃənl/ *adj* of or relating to the presentation of sth, eg of new products or policies: *the advertising manager's presentational skills.*

presentiment /prɪˈzentɪmənt/ *n* (*fml*) a feeling that sth, esp sth unpleasant, will happen: *a presentiment of trouble ahead.*

presently /ˈprezntli/ *adv* **1** after a short time; soon: *I'll be with you presently.* ○ *Presently, the two men re-emerged from the house.* **2** (*esp US*) at the present time; now: *The book is presently unavailable.*

NOTE When **presently** means 'soon' it usually comes at the end of the sentence: *She'll be here presently.* When it means 'after a short time' it often comes at the beginning: *Presently, I heard her leave the house.* **Presently**, can also mean 'now' or 'currently' and comes next to the verb: *The train service presently carries 20000 passengers daily.* ○ *Your proposal is presently being considered.*

preservation /ˌprezə'veɪʃn/ *n* [U] **1** the action of preserving sth: *the preservation and conservation of wildlife* ○ *the preservation of works of art/academic standards* ○ *a preserˈvation order* (ie one that makes it illegal to destroy sth, esp a building, because of its historical value). **2** the degree to which sth has not been affected by eg age or weather: *The paintings were in an excellent state of preservation.* Compare CONSERVATION.

preservative /prɪˈzɜːvətɪv/ *n* [C, U] a substance used for preserving sth or preventing decay: *food free from preservatives* ○ *treat the fence with (a) wood preservative.* ▶ **preservative** *adj* [esp attrib]: *timber treated with a preservative solution.*

preserve¹ /prɪˈzɜːv/ *v* **1**(**a**) to keep sth in its original state or in good condition: [Vn] *preserving old aircraft/the English countryside* ○ *preserve the value of an investment* ○ *Efforts to preserve the peace have failed.* [Vn-adj] *This vase has been preserved intact.* [also Vn-n]. (**b**) to prevent sth, esp food, from decaying by treating it in a particular way: [Vnpr] *apricots preserved in syrup* [Vn] *preserve a dead body by embalming it* ○ *Wax polish preserves wood and leather.* **2** ~ **sb/sth** (**from sth**) to keep sb/sth alive, or safe from harm or danger: [Vn, Vnpr] *preserve endangered species (from extinction).* **3** to keep or continue to have a particular quality or feature: [Vn] *She managed to preserve her sense of humour in a difficult situation.* Compare CONSERVE¹.

▶ **preserver** *n* [C, U] a person or thing that preserves sth: *treat the garden fence with (a) wood preserver.*

preserve² /prɪˈzɜːv/ *n* **1** [C] an activity, an interest, etc regarded as exclusive to a particular person or group: *She regards negotiating prices with customers as her special preserve.* ○ *Fishing is a traditionally male preserve.* **2** [U, C] (*fml*) fruit preserved in the form of jam: *strawberry preserve.* Compare CONSERVE².

pre-set /ˌpriːˈset/ *v* (**-tt-**; *pt, pp* **pre-set**) to adjust a device or piece of equipment before one needs to use it: [Vn.to inf] *She may pre-set to record the match.* [Vn] *The video was pre-set to record the match.* [Vn] *The driver can pre-set the maximum speed of the car.*

preside /prɪˈzaɪd/ *v* ~ (**at/over sth**) to lead or be in charge of a conference, meeting, etc: [V] *the presiding officer/judge* ○ *Whoever presides will need patience and tact.* [Vpr] *The Prime Minister presides at/over meetings of the Cabinet.* **PHRV** pre'side over sth to be responsible for a situation or be in charge when it happens: *The President's wife will personally preside over the health reforms.* ○ *The present director has presided over a rapid decline in the firm's profitability.*

presidency /ˈprezɪdənsi/ *n* the office(5), or term of office, of a president: *be elected to the presidency (of the United States/of the International Olympic Committee)* ○ *talks begun during Reagan's presidency* ○ *Belgium currently holds the presidency of the European Union.*

president /ˈprezɪdənt/ *n* **1 President** the head of state (HEAD¹) in the USA and many modern republics: *the President of the United States* ○ *President Clinton/De Gaulle* ○ *Yes, Mr President.* **2** (also **President**) the head of certain organizations, colleges, etc: *He was made president of the cricket club/students' union.* ○ *The Prince of Wales is Honorary President of the charity.* **3** (*esp US*) the head of a bank or business firm. ▶ **presidential** /ˌprezɪˈdenʃl/ *adj*: *a presidential candidate/election/decision* ○ *compare parliamentary and presidential systems of government* ○ (*US*) *a presidential year* (ie one in which an election for president is held).

presidium (also **praesidium**) /prɪˈsɪdiəm/ *n* a permanent powerful committee of government, esp in Communist countries: *the presidium of the ruling socialist party.*

press¹ /pres/ *n* **1**(**a**) (often **the Press**) [Gp] newspapers, magazines, the news sections of radio and television, and the journalists who work for them: *The Press was/were not allowed to attend the trial.* ○ *The incident was widely reported* **in the press**. ○ *the local/national/foreign press* ○ *a press photographer* ○ *issue a press statement* (ie one to the press) ○ *the music press* (ie newspapers and magazines about music, esp pop music) ○ *the freedom of the press/press freedom* (ie the right of journalists to report events and express opinions freely). Compare MEDIA. See also GUTTER PRESS. (**b**) [U, sing] treatment given to or opinions expressed about sb/sth in the press: *get/be given a good/bad press* ○ *The company received a lot of bad press during the year.* **2(a)** (also **'printing-press**) [C] a machine for printing books, etc: *The news is hot off the press* (ie has just been printed in the newspapers). **(b)** [U] the process of printing: *prepare a book for press* ○ *Prices are correct at the time of going to press* (ie being printed). See also STOP PRESS. **3** [C] a business for printing and publishing books: *Oxford University Press.* **4** [C] (esp in compounds) a device or machine used for pressing things, eg to make them flat or to extract juice from them: *a 'trouser-press* ○ *a 'wine-/ 'cider-press* ○ *an 'olive-press.* **5** [C usu *sing*] the act of applying pressure with the hand or with sth held in the hand: *Those shirts need a press* (ie with a hot iron). **6** [sing] a crowd of people packed tightly together: *He thrust his way through the press of people.* **7** [C] (*dated*) a large cupboard, usu with shelves, eg for clothes: *a linen press.*

■ **'press agency** *n* = NEWS AGENCY.

'press agent *n* a person employed by eg a theatre to organize advertising and publicity in the press.

'press-box *n* a place reserved for journalists at a public event, eg a sports contest.

'press conference *n* a meeting at which a prominent person talks to journalists, eg in order to announce a decision or an achievement or to answer questions: *The Minister called a press conference as soon as the figures were known.*

'press cutting (also *esp US* **'press clipping**) *n* = CUTTING¹ 1.

'press gallery *n* a place reserved for journalists observing the proceedings in a parliament or law-court.

'press office *n* a department, eg of a business firm or political party, which provides information about it to the press and answers journalists' questions.

'press officer *n* a person in charge of or working for a press office.

'press release *n* an official announcement or account of sth given to the press, eg by a government department, political party or business firm: *The company issued a press release to end speculation about its future.*

press² /pres/ *v* **1(a)** ~ **(sth/sb/oneself) against sth; ~ sth to sth; ~ sth together** to push sth or to be pushed closely and firmly against sth: [Vnpr] *The child pressed her face against the window.* ○ *He pressed a handkerchief to his nose.* [Vnp] *She pressed her lips together.* [Vpr] *My boot is pressing against a blister on my toe.* [also Vp]. **(b)** to push or squeeze part of a device, etc in order to make it operate: [Vn] *press a button/switch/key* ○ *He pressed the buzzer on his intercom.* [V.to inf, Vadv] *Press (here) to open.* [Vpr, Vp] *The driver pressed (down) hard on the accelerator.* [Vn-adj] *She pressed the door/lid firmly shut.* [also Vnp]. **(c)** ~ **sth into/onto sth** to put sth in a place by pushing it firmly: [Vnpr] *press money into sb's hand.* **(d)** to squeeze a person's arm or hand, esp as a sign of affection: [Vn] *He gently pressed his wife's arm to comfort her.* **2** ~ **sb (for sth)** to make strong efforts to persuade or force sb to do sth: [Vn] *When/If pressed, he will admit that he knew about the affair.* [Vnpr] *The bank is pressing us for repayment of the loan.* [Vn.to inf] *They are pressing us to make a quick decision.* **3** to make one's case forcefully or repeatedly: [Vn] *I don't wish to press the point, but you do owe me £200.* ○ *She is still pressing her claim for compensation.* ○ *They were determined to press their case at the highest level.* **4** (of people packed together in a crowd) to move in the specified direction by pushing: [Vpr] *The photographers pressed round the royal visitors.* [Vpr, Vadv] *The crowds were pressing (forward) against the barriers.* [Vp] (*fig*) *all the unwelcome thoughts that were pressing in on him.* **5(a)** to make

sth flat or smooth by using force or putting sth heavy on top: [Vn] *press flowers* (eg between pages of a book) [Vn-adj] *press the soil flat with the back of a spade.* **(b)** to make clothes smooth by applying pressure with a hot iron: [Vn] *My suit needs pressing.* See also IRON² 1. **6** to apply force or weight to fruit or vegetables, esp in order to squeeze juice from them: [Vn] *press grapes to make wine* [Vnpr] *press the juice out of/from an orange.* **7** to make sth by applying force or weight to a material: [Vn] *a machine for pressing gramophone records* [Vnpr] *press car bodies out of sheets of metal* [Vnp] *press out shapes from a piece of card.* **IDM** **prefer/press charges** ⇨ CHARGE¹. **,press sth 'home** to obtain as much advantage as possible from a situation by being determined in one's attacking or argument: *press home one's advantage* ○ *press home an argument/an attack/a point.* **,press sb/sth into 'service** to use sb/sth for a purpose that they were not trained or intended for because there is no one or nothing else available: *Every type of boat was pressed into service to rescue passengers from the sinking ferry.* **PHRV** **,press a'head/'on (with sth)** to continue doing sth in a determined way; to hurry forward: *'Shall we stay here for the night?' 'No, let's press on.'* ○ *The company is pressing ahead with its plans for a new warehouse.* **'press for sth** to make repeated and urgent requests for sth: *The unions are pressing for improved working conditions.* **'press sth on sb** to insist that sb accepts sth, esp against their will: *She kept pressing cakes and biscuits on us.* ○ *The firm is trying to press new contracts on its employees.*

▶ **pressed** *adj* (usu *pred*) **1** ~ **(for sth)** having hardly enough of sth, esp time or money: *We're a bit pressed — can I call you back later?* ○ *I'm very pressed for cash at the moment — can I pay you next week?* **2** ~ **(to do sth)** having difficulty in doing or achieving sth: *You would be hard pressed to find a better secretary.* ○ *The government was pressed to retain its majority.*

pressing *adj* that needs to be dealt with quickly or immediately; urgent: *deal with the most pressing matters/problems/questions first* ○ *a pressing need for more nurses* ○ *He left the meeting early, saying he had a pressing engagement.*

pressing *n* **(a)** a thing made by pressing (PRESS² 7) a material: *The factory assembles car bodies from pressings made in Japan.* **(b)** a number of such things made at one time: *The second pressing was of much higher quality than the first.*

■ **press-stud** /'pres stʌd/ (also **popper**, *US* **'snap fastener**) *n* a small metal or plastic fastening device for clothes, made of two parts that can be pressed together.

'press-up (*US* **'push-up**) *n* (usu *pl*) an exercise in which a person lies facing the floor and, keeping the back straight, raises the upper part of the body by pressing down on the hands.

press-gang /'pres gæn/ *n* [CGp] **(a)** (formerly) a group of people employed to force men to join the army or navy. **(b)** any group that forces others to do sth.

▶ **press-gang** *v* ~ **sb (into sth / doing sth)** (*infml*) to make sb do sth, esp unwillingly: [Vnpr] *We were press-ganged into helping with the housework.* [also Vn].

pressman /'presmæn/ *n* (*pl* **-men** /-men/) (*Brit*) a journalist.

pressure /'preʃə(r)/ *n* **1** [U] **(a)** the force or weight of sth pressing continuously on or against sth that it touches: *the pressure of the crowd against the barriers* ○ *The pressure of the water caused the dam to burst.* **(b)** an amount of this: *exert/maintain/relieve pressure on sth* ○ *pump up/reduce the tyre pressure* ○ *apply gentle pressure to stop the flow of blood* ○ *water*

[V.*to* inf] = verb + *to* infinitive　　[Vn.inf (no *to*)] = verb + noun + infinitive without *to*　　[V.*ing*] = verb + *-ing* form

passing through the pipes at high pressure ○ *a pres-sure chamber* ○ *a pressure gauge* (ie an instrument for measuring the pressure of liquid, gas, air, etc). See also BLOOD PRESSURE. **2** [U] the weight of the air in the atmosphere: *A band of high/low pressure is moving across the country.* See also ATMOSPHERIC PRESSURE. **3** [U, C] ~ (**of sth**); ~ (**to do sth**) a strong need to achieve sth or to behave in a certain way, causing anxiety or difficulty: *She has very little free time because of pressure of work.* ○ *The pressures of city life forced him to move to the country.* **IDM** **bring 'pressure to bear on sb (to do sth)** to use force or strong influence to make sb do sth: *The council brought pressure to bear on the landlord to improve his property.* **put 'pressure on sb (to do sth)** to force or try to force sb to do sth, esp quickly: *put pressure on sb to make a decision* ○ *The birth of twins put pressure on them to find a bigger house.* **under 'pressure 1** (of a liquid or gas) forced into a container: *The gas is stored under pressure in the tank.* ○ *The beer comes out of the barrel under pressure.* **2** influenced by an urgent need or forced necessity: *work under pressure* ○ *put sb/come under pressure (to do sth).* **3** suffering stress: *She is constantly under pressure and it is affecting her health.* ▶ **pressure** *v* [Vn, Vnpr, Vn.to inf] = PRESSURIZE 1.
■ **'pressure-cooker** *n* a strong metal pot with a tight lid in which food can be cooked quickly by steam under high pressure. ⇨ picture at PAN¹.
'pressure group *n* [CGp] a group that tries to influence governments or other organizations, esp by holding public meetings and talking and writing to (important) people about their cause: *an environmental pressure group trying to stop the building of a new motorway.*

pressurize, -ise /'preʃəraɪz/ *v* **1** (also **pressure**) ~ **sb** (**into sth/doing sth**) to force, influence or persuade sb to do sth: [Vn] *I need time — don't pressurize me!* [Vnpr] *She was pressurized into accepting the job.* [Vn.to inf] *He felt that he was being pressurized to resign.* **2** (esp passive) to keep the air pressure in a SUBMARINE(1), an aircraft, etc constant and similar to that on the surface of the earth: [Vn] *a pressurized cabin* ○ *The compartments are all fully pressurized.* ▶ **pressurization**, **-isation** /ˌpreʃəraɪˈzeɪʃn; US -rəˈz-/ *n* [U].

prestige /preˈstiːʒ/ *n* [U] **1** respect based on good reputation, past achievements, etc: *lose/regain/win prestige* ○ *social/academic prestige* ○ *He suffered a loss of prestige when the book didn't sell.* **2** the power to impress others, esp as a result of wealth, position, appearance, etc: *a job that carries great prestige* ○ *the prestige value of owning a Rolls Royce* ○ *Congress agreed to fund the project because of its prestige.*
▶ **prestigious** /preˈstɪdʒəs/ *adj* having or bringing prestige: *one of the world's most prestigious orchestras.*

presto /'prestəʊ/ **IDM** **hey presto** ⇨ HEY.

presumably /prɪˈzjuːməbli; US -ˈzuː-/ *adv* it may be supposed: *Presumably the plane was late because of the fog.* ○ *You came by car, presumably?*

presume /prɪˈzjuːm; US -ˈzuːm/ *v* **1** to suppose sth to be true; to take sth for granted (GRANT): [V.that] *I presume (that) you still want to come.* [Vadv] *'Are the neighbours away on vacation?' 'I presume so.'* [Vn-adj, V.n to inf] *In English law, an accused person is presumed (to be) innocent until proved guilty.* [Vn-adj] *Twelve passengers are missing, presumed dead.* **2** (*fml*) to dare to do sth; to be so bold as to do sth: [V.to inf] *I wouldn't presume to argue with you.*

presumption /prɪˈzʌmpʃn/ *n* **1(a)** [U] ~ (**of sth**) the action of supposing sth to be true: *the presumption of guilt/innocence.* **(b)** [C] a thing that is considered to be true or very probable: *The article is based on too many false presumptions.* **2** [U] (*fml*)

behaviour that is too bold or proud: *She was infuriated by his presumption in not consulting her first.*

presumptive /prɪˈzʌmptɪv/ *adj* (*fml esp law*) based on reasonable belief: *presumptive evidence.* See also HEIR PRESUMPTIVE.

presumptuous /prɪˈzʌmptʃuəs/ *adj* (of people or their behaviour) too bold or confident: *Would it be presumptuous of me to ask you to contribute?*

presuppose /ˌpriːsəˈpəʊz/ *v* **1** to assume sth to be true before it is proved: [Vn] *Teachers sometimes presuppose background knowledge that their students do not possess.* **2** to require sth as a condition; to imply sth: [Vn] *Solutions presuppose problems, as answers presuppose questions.* [V.that] *Approval of the plan presupposes that the money will be made available.*
▶ **presupposition** /ˌpriːsʌpəˈzɪʃn/ *n* (*fml*) a thing that is presupposed: *make an unjustified presupposition.*

pre-tax /ˌpriːˈtæks/ *adj* before tax has been taken away: *pre-tax 'income/'profits/'surplus.*

pretence (US **pretense**) /prɪˈtens/ *n* **1(a)** [U] the action of pretending; deception: *Their friendliness was only pretence.* ○ *Their way of life was all pretence.* **(b)** [sing] ~ **of sth** a false show of sth: *make a pretence of loyalty/grief* ○ *She kept up the pretence that she still loved him.* **2** [C] ~ **to sth/doing sth** a claim to a desirable quality: *I make little/no pretence to being an expert on the subject.* **IDM** **under false pretences** ⇨ FALSE.

pretend /prɪˈtend/ *v* **1** to make oneself appear to be sth or to be doing sth in order to deceive others or in play: [V] *The time has come to stop pretending!* [V.that] *She pretended (that) she was not at home when we rang the bell.* [V.to inf] *The children pretended to drive the car.* ○ *I don't pretend (ie claim) to know as much about it as he does.* **2** to claim sth falsely, esp as an excuse: [Vn] *She pretended illness as an excuse.* ○ *His pretended concern did not fool me.* **PHRV** **pre'tend to sth** (*fml*) to make a claim to sth: *I don't pretend to any great understanding of music.*
▶ **pretender** *n* ~ (**to sth**) a person whose claim to sth is disputed.

pretension /prɪˈtenʃn/ *n* **1** [C usu *pl*] ~ (**to sth/doing sth**) a claim or the making of one: *have social/literary/artistic pretensions* ○ *He has/makes no pretensions to being an expert on the subject.* **2** [U] PRETENTIOUS behaviour: *live modestly, without pretension.*

pretentious /prɪˈtenʃəs/ *adj* (*derog*) claiming importance, value or style, esp without good cause: *expressed in pretentious language* ○ *a pretentious person/film/name.* ▶ **pretentiousness** *n* [U].

preternatural /ˌpriːtəˈnætʃrəl/ *adj* (*fml*) beyond what is natural or normal; unusual: *preternatural power/force/ability* ○ *a preternatural gift for knowing what others are thinking.* ▶ **preternaturally** *adv.*

pretext /'priːtekst/ *n* ~ (**for sth/doing sth**) a reason given for doing sth that is not the real reason; an excuse: *He came to see me on/under the pretext of wanting to borrow a book.* ○ *We'll have to find a pretext for not going to the party.*

prettify /'prɪtɪfaɪ/ *v* (*pt, pp* **-fied**) (*usu derog*) to make sth pretty in a SUPERFICIAL(3a) way: [Vn] *The old farm cottages are being prettified as holiday homes.* Compare BEAUTIFY.

pretty /'prɪti/ *adj* (**-ier, -iest**) pleasing and attractive, without being very beautiful or magnificent: *a pretty girl/face/village* ○ *a pretty boy* (ie one who looks too much like a girl) ○ *What a pretty dress!* ○ *She looks as pretty as a picture* (ie very pretty). ○ *The bodies of the victims were not a pretty sight* (ie were shocking or unpleasant to look at). ⇨ note at BEAUTIFUL, NICE. **IDM** **come to such a pass/a pretty**

pass ⇨ PASS². **not just a pretty 'face** sb who is not only attractive but also has other more important or useful qualities: *Don't underestimate her — she's not just a pretty face, you know.* **a pretty 'penny** a lot of money: *Renovating the house will cost a pretty penny.*

▶ **pretty** *adv* fairly; quite: *The situation seems pretty hopeless.* ○ *She seemed pretty satisfied with the result.* ⇨ note at FAIRLY. **IDM** **pretty much/nearly/well** almost: *The two designs are pretty much the same.* ○ *I'm pretty nearly as tall as he is.* ○ *My patience is pretty well exhausted.* **be sitting pretty** ⇨ SIT.

prettily /'prɪtɪli/ *adv* in a pretty or charming way: *She decorated the room very prettily.* ○ *She smiled prettily as she accepted the flowers.*

prettiness *n* [U]: *People commented on the prettiness of the cottage.*

pretzel /'pretsl/ *n* a crisp salty biscuit made in the shape of a knot or stick.

prevail /prɪ'veɪl/ *v* **1** ~ **(in sth)** to exist or happen generally; to be widespread: [V] *the living conditions that then prevailed* [Vpr] *The use of animals for ploughing still prevails in many countries.* **2** ~ **(against/over sb/sth)** *(fml)* to fight successfully against sb/sth; to defeat sb/sth: [V, Vpr] *Virtue will prevail (against evil).* [Vpr] *The invaders prevailed over the native population.* **PHRV** **pre'vail on/upon sb to do sth** *(fml)* to persuade sb to do sth: *May I prevail on you to make a speech after dinner?*

▶ **prevailing** *adj* [attrib] **(a)** most usual or widespread: *the prevailing customs/fashions/conditions.* **(b)** (of a wind) that blows in an area most frequently: *The prevailing wind here is from the southwest.*

prevalent /'prevələnt/ *adj* ~ **(among/in sth/sb)** *(fml)* existing or happening generally; widespread: *diseases prevalent in the Third World* ○ *an attitude prevalent among university students.* ▶ **prevalence** /-əns/ *n* [U]: *a decline in the prevalence of cigarette smoking.*

prevaricate /prɪ'værɪkeɪt/ *v* *(fml)* ~ **(on/over sth)** to speak or act in a way that misleads others or avoids revealing the truth about a situation; to equivocate (EQUIVOCAL): [V.speech] *'Who?' she prevaricated, knowing perfectly well who he meant.* [Vpr] *The government has deliberately prevaricated over the EU directive.* [also V]. ▶ **prevarication** /prɪ,værɪ'keɪʃn/ *n* [U, C]: *The report was full of lies and prevarications.*

prevent /prɪ'vent/ *v* ~ **sb/sth (from doing sth)** to stop sb doing sth or to stop sth happening: [Vn] *Your prompt action prevented a serious accident.* [Vn, Vnpr] *prevent the spread of a disease/a disease from spreading* [V.n ing] *Nobody can prevent us/our getting married.* ▶ **preventable** *adj*: *preventable accidents/deaths.*

prevention /prɪ'venʃn/ *n* [U] the action of preventing sth: *accident/crime prevention* ○ *the prevention of cruelty to animals.* **IDM** **prevention is better than 'cure** *(saying)* it is easier to prevent sth happening than to undo the damage later.

preventive /prɪ'ventɪv/ (also **preventative** /prɪ'ventətɪv/) *adj* preventing or intended to prevent sth undesirable, eg disease or trouble: *preventive measures/powers* ○ *preventative medicine.*

preview /'priːvjuː/ *n* **(a)** a showing of a film, an exhibition, a play, etc before it is shown to the general public: *a press preview* (ie one for journalists only) ○ *We attended a **sneak preview** of the winter fashion collection.* **(b)** a report or description of a film, a performance of a play, etc before it is shown to the general public: *a preview of next week's programme.*

▶ **preview** *v* to have or give a preview of sth: [Vn] *paintings previewed at the Cologne Art Fair.*

previous /'priːviəs/ *adj* [attrib] coming before in time or order; former: *We had met on two previous occasions.* ○ *He was there the previous day.* ○ *Who was the previous owner?* ○ *I am unable to attend because of a previous engagement.* ○ *The criminal had had four previous convictions.* ○ *She had no previous experience of publishing.* ▶ **previously** *adv*: *She had previously worked in television.*

pre-war /,priː'wɔː(r)/ *adj* [esp attrib] occurring or existing before a war, esp the Second World War: *in the pre-war period* ○ *,pre-war 'cars/'housing/ ma'chinery* ○ *Industrial production has only just reached pre-war levels.*

prey /preɪ/ *n* **(a)** an animal, bird, etc hunted and killed by another for food: *The lion stalked its prey through the long grass.* ○ *Mice and other small creatures are the owl's prey.* **(b)** a person who is taken advantage of or harmed by another: *She was **easy prey** for dishonest salesmen.* **IDM** **be/fall 'prey to sth** *(rather fml)* **1** to become a VICTIM(1) of sb/sth: *young people falling prey to drugs* ○ *The zebra fell prey to the lion.* **2** (of a person) to be greatly troubled or disturbed by sth: *She was prey to irrational fears.* ▶ **prey** *v* **IDM** **prey on sb's 'mind** to trouble sb greatly: *The thought that he was responsible for her death preyed on his mind.* **PHRV** **'prey on/upon sb/ sth 1** to hunt or catch an animal, etc for food: *hawks preying on small birds.* **2** to make sb one's VICTIM(1); to take advantage of or attack sb: *bogus social workers preying on old people.*

price /praɪs/ *n* **1** an amount of money for which sth may be bought or sold: *a woollen sweater, price $29.95* ○ *Prices are rising/falling/going up/going down/shooting up/plummeting.* ○ *I can't afford it at that price.* ○ *charge high prices* ○ *He sold the house at/ for a good price.* ○ *Ask the builder to give you a price* (ie say how much he will charge) *for the work.* ○ *The price of cigarettes is set to rise again.* See also CUT-PRICE, COST PRICE, LIST PRICE, MARKET PRICE. ⇨ note. **2** what must be done, given or experienced in order to get or keep sth: *Loss of independence was a high price to pay for peace.* ○ *Being recognized wherever you go is the price you pay for being famous.* ○ *No price is too high for winning their respect.* **3** the ODDS(3) in betting: *Six to one is a good price for that horse.* See also STARTING-PRICE. **IDM** **at a 'price** at a high price: *Fresh strawberries are now available — at a price!* **at 'any price** whatever the cost may be: *The people want peace at any price.* **beyond 'price** *(esp rhet)* extremely valuable; so valuable that it cannot be bought. **cheap at/for the price** ⇨ CHEAP. **everyone has their 'price** *(saying)* everyone can be bribed (BRIBE *v*) in some way. **not at 'any price** in no circumstances, however favourable: *I wouldn't have my sister's children to stay again — not at any price!* **pay a/the price** ⇨ PAY². **a 'price on sb's head** a reward offered for capturing or killing sb: *He knew it was dangerous to be seen — there was a price on his head.* **put a 'price on sth** to value sth in terms of money: *You can't put a price on that sort of loyalty.* **'what price ...?** *(Brit infml)* (used when sth promised or expected seems unlikely to happen) see how worthless it was: *What price peaceful protest now?* ○ *What price all your promises now?*

▶ **price** *v* **1** ~ **sth (at sth)** to fix the price of sth at a particular level: [Vnpr] *The agent priced the house at the right level for the market.* ○ *Even the cheapest was priced at £5.* [Vnadv] *These goods are priced too high.* [also Vn]. **2** to know nearly or exactly the price or value of sth: [Vn] *I don't know enough about porcelain to be able to price these plates.* **3** to mark goods with a price: [Vn] *The assistant priced the garments before putting them on display.* **IDM** **price oneself/ sth out of the 'market** to charge such a high price for one's goods, services, etc that no one buys them.

priceless *adj* **1** too valuable to be priced: *priceless jewels/paintings/treasures* ○ *(fig) Her one priceless asset is her common sense.* ⇨ note at INVALUABLE. **2**

(*dated infml*) very amusing or absurd: *You look absolutely priceless in that hat!*

pricey /'praɪsi/ *adj* (**-ier, -iest**) [usu pred] (*infml*) expensive: *This restaurant is a bit pricey for me.*

■ **'price-fixing** *n* [U] (*usu derog*) the practice of setting prices by agreement among companies in competition with each other, esp so as to keep them artificially high.

'price-list *n* a list of current prices for goods on sale.

'price tag *n* (**a**) a label showing the price of sth. (**b**) ~ (**on sth**) the cost of sth: *The government regard the price-tag on the new fighter plane as too high.*

'price war *n* a situation in which companies, etc selling goods repeatedly reduce their prices in order to attract buyers.

NOTE Price and cost both mean the amount of money you need to buy something. Price is generally used of objects which you can buy and sell: *the price of vegetables/houses/cars.* Cost usually relates to services or processes: *the cost of growing vegetables/decorating the house ○ production costs ○ the cost of living.* Charge is the amount of money you are asked to pay for a service: *electricity and gas charges ○ There is a small charge for parking.* Price, cost and charge are also verbs: *The tickets were priced at £25. ○ Our holiday didn't cost very much. ○ How much do they charge for advertising?*

prick¹ /prɪk/ *v* **1(a)** ~ **sth** (**with sth**) to make a tiny hole in sth with a sharp point: [Vnpr] *prick holes in paper with a pin* [Vn] *He pricked the balloon and it burst.* (**b**) ~ **sth** (**on/with sth**) to make a hole in the skin so that it hurts or bleeds: [Vnpr] *She pricked her finger on/with a needle.* [Vn] *Be careful — the thorns will prick you.* **2** make sb feel a slight pain as if being pricked: [V] *She felt a slight pricking sensation in her throat.* [Vn] *He could feel tears pricking his eyes.* **3** to cause mental discomfort to sb: [Vn] *His conscience is pricking him now that he realizes what he has done.* **IDM** **prick up one's 'ears 1** (of an animal, esp a horse or dog) to raise the ears as if listening. **2** (of a person) to begin suddenly to pay attention to what is being said: *The children pricked up their ears when they heard the word 'ice-cream'.* **PHRV** **,prick sth 'out** to plant young plants in small holes made in the soil.

prick² /prɪk/ *n* **1** (⚠ *sl*) a PENIS. **2** (*sl derog*) a stupid or unpleasant man: *Don't be such a prick!* **3(a)** an act of pricking (PRICK¹ 1) sth: *I gave my finger a prick with a needle.* (**b**) a pain caused by being pricked (PRICK¹ 1): *I can still feel the prick.* ○ (*fig*) *the pricks of conscience.* **IDM** **kick against the pricks** ⇨ KICK¹.

prickle /'prɪkl/ *n* **1(a)** a small pointed growth(3) on the stem or leaf of a plant; a small THORN(1). (**b**) a small pointed growth(3) on the skin of certain animals: *a hedgehog's prickles.* **2** a pricking (PRICK¹ 2) sensation on the skin: *She felt a prickle of fear/excitement.*

▶ **prickle** *v* to have or make sb/sth have a feeling of being pricked (PRICK¹ 2): [V,Vn] *The woollen cloth prickled (my skin).* [V] *My scalp began to prickle as I realized the horrible truth.*

prickly /'prɪkli/ *adj* **1(a)** covered with prickles (PRICKLE 1): *prickly rose-bushes.* (**b**) having or causing a sensation of prickling (PRICKLE *v*): *a prickly feeling/sensation ○ My skin feels prickly.* **2** (*infml*) (of a person) easily becoming angry or offended: *He can be rather prickly to deal with.* **,prickly 'heat** *n* [U] a skin condition common in hot climates, with small red spots that ITCH(1). **,prickly 'pear** *n* (**a**) a type of CACTUS covered with prickles (PRICKLE 1a). (**b**) its edible fruit, shaped like a PEAR.

pride /praɪd/ *n* **1(a)** [U] ~ (**in sb/sth**) a feeling of pleasure or satisfaction that one gets from doing sth well, or from owning or being responsible for sth

excellent or widely admired: *You should **take** more **pride in** your appearance. ○ She looked with pride at the result of her work. ○ He felt a glow of pride as people stopped to look at his garden.* (**b**) [sing] **the ~ of sth** a person or thing that is an object or source of such a feeling: *The new sports centre was the pride of the town.* **2** [U] (*derog*) a too high opinion of oneself or one's achievements: *He was puffed up with pride.* **3** [U] knowledge of one's own worth or character; a sense of dignity and respect for oneself: *Her pride was hurt. ○ Having to accept the money was a blow to her pride.* **4** [CGp] a group of lions. **IDM** **pride comes/goes before a 'fall** (*saying*) if you are too proud(2) of yourself, sth will happen to make you look foolish. **pride of 'place** the most prominent or important position, because of being the best or most preferred: *Your picture has pride of place on my mantelpiece.* **sb's pride and 'joy** a person or thing that sb is very proud of: *The baby is their pride and joy.*

▶ **pride** *v* **PHRV** **'pride oneself on sth / doing sth** to be proud of sth: *He prides himself on always remaining calm in an emergency.*

priest /priːst/ *n* **1** a person appointed to perform religious duties and ceremonies in the Roman Catholic, Orthodox or Anglican Church: *a parish priest ○ the ordination of women priests.* Compare CHAPLAIN, CLERGYMAN, MINISTER¹ 3, VICAR. **2** (*fem* **priestess** /'priːstes/) a person who performs religious ceremonies in a religion which is not Christian.

▶ **the priesthood** /-hʊd/ *n* (**a**) [sing] the position of a priest: *enter the priesthood.* (**b**) [Gp] priests in general, esp in a particular Church or country: *the Catholic/Spanish priesthood.*

priestly *adj* [usu attrib] of, like or relating to a priest: *priestly duties.*

prig /prɪg/ *n* (*derog*) a person who behaves as if he or she is morally superior to everyone else, and disapproves of what others do.

▶ **priggish** *adj* of or like a prig. **priggishness** *n* [U].

prim /prɪm/ *adj* (*usu derog*) **1** (of a person) always behaving correctly and easily shocked by anything that is rude: *You can't tell that joke to her — she's much too **prim and proper**.* **2** rather formal in appearance, behaviour or manner: *a prim little dress with a white collar.* ▶ **primly** *adv: He didn't reply, but just smiled primly.*

prima ballerina /ˌpriːmə ˌbæləˈriːnə/ *n* a leading woman ballet dancer.

primacy /'praɪməsi/ *n* **1** [U] (*fml*) the leading position or position of greatest importance: *the primacy of language/religion/personal experience ○ Can the party maintain its primacy for another year?* **2** [C] the position of an archbishop.

prima donna /ˌpriːmə ˈdɒnə/ *n* **1** a leading woman opera singer. **2** (*derog*) a person who thinks he or she is very important and behaves badly when things go wrong or others do not do as he or she wants.

primaeval = PRIMEVAL.

prima facie /ˌpraɪmə ˈfeɪʃi/ *adj* [attrib], *adv* (*esp law*) based on what seems at first to be true or real, without further or deeper investigation: *prima facie evidence* (ie sufficient to establish sth legally, unless it is found to be false later) ○ *Prima facie, there is a strong case against him.*

primal /'praɪml/ *adj* [attrib] (*fml*) first or original; PRIMEVAL: *the loss of their primal innocence ○ primal desires/fears/instincts.*

primary /'praɪməri; *US* -meri/ *adj* **1** [usu attrib] earliest in time or order of development: *primary causes ○ in the primary stage of development ○ The disease is still in its primary stage.* **2** [usu attrib] most important; fundamental: *The primary aim of this course is to improve your spoken English. ○ We* *need to establish the primary cause of the problem.* ○ *Health care is of primary importance.* ○ *Our primary concern must be the children.* ○ *primary stress/accent* (ie the strongest stress given, when speaking, to a syllable in a word or compound, shown in this dictionary by the mark* '). **3** [attrib] of or for primary education: *primary teachers* ○ *teaching at primary level.* Compare SECONDARY, TERTIARY.

▶ **primarily** /praɪ'merəli; *Brit also* 'praɪmərəli/ *adv* mainly: *The problem is not primarily a financial one.* ○ *The purpose of the programme is primarily educational.*

primary (*also* ˌprimary e'lection) *n* (in the USA) an election in which people in certain states vote to select party candidates for a future major election: *the presidential primaries.*

■ ˌprimary 'colour (*US* 'color) *n* any of the three colours, red, yellow and blue, from which all other colours can be obtained by mixing.

ˌprimary edu'cation *n* [U] education in the first years of school, for children between 5 and 11 years old.

ˌprimary 'health care *n* [U] the treatment of health problems by a general practitioner (GENERAL¹), not by doctors in a hospital.

'primary school *n* **1** (*Brit*) a school for children between 5 and 11 years old. **2** (*US* also ele'mentary school, 'grade school, 'grammar school) a school for children between 6 and 8 years old.

primate¹ /'praɪmeɪt/ *n* an ARCHBISHOP: *the Primate of all England* (ie the Archbishop of Canterbury) ○ *the Primate of England* (ie the Archbishop of York).

primate² /'praɪmeɪt/ *n* a member of the most highly developed order of mammals (MAMMAL) that includes human beings, apes (APE) and monkeys.

prime¹ /praɪm/ *adj* [attrib] **1** most important; chief; fundamental: *Her prime motive was personal ambition.* ○ *My prime concern is to protect my property.* ○ *It is a matter of prime importance.* ○ *The prime cause of the trouble was bad management.* ○ *He's a **prime suspect** in the case.* **2** of the best quality; excellent: *prime (cuts of) beef* ○ *a prime site for development.* **3** having all the expected or typical qualities: *That's a **prime example** of what I was talking about.*

■ ˌprime 'minister *n* the chief minister in a government.

ˌprime 'mover *n* a person or thing that is the first or major influence in the development of sth: *He believes that economic factors are the prime movers of change.*

ˌprime 'number *n* (*mathematics*) a number that can be divided exactly only by itself and 1, eg 7, 17, 41.

'prime time *n* [U] (in broadcasting) the time when the highest number of people are watching or listening: *prime-time* 'advertising/'shows/'television.

prime² /praɪm/ *n* [sing] a state or time of greatest strength, beauty, vigour, etc; a state of highest perfection: *be in the prime of life/youth* ○ *When is a man in his prime?* ○ *She is past her prime.*

prime³ /praɪm/ *v* **1** to make sth ready for use or action; to prepare sth: [Vn] *prime a fuse* ○ *The bomb was primed, ready to explode.* **2** [Vn] to prepare wood, metal, etc for painting by covering it with a substance that helps the paint to stay on the surface. **3** ~ **sb** (**with sth**) to supply sb with information before a particular event, sometimes dishonestly, so that they know how to act: [Vn] *The witness had been primed by a lawyer.* [Vnpr] *The new manager was clearly well primed with information before he arrived.* **IDM** prime the 'pump to encourage the growth of a new or weak business or industry by investing money in it. See also PUMP PRIMING.

primer¹ /'praɪmə(r); *US* 'prɪmər/ *n* (*dated*) a book that contains the basic facts of a school subject for people beginning to learn it: *a Latin primer.*

primer² /'praɪmə(r)/ *n* [U,C] a substance used to PRIME³ (2) a surface for painting.

primeval (*also* **primaeval**) /praɪ'miːvl/ *adj* [usu attrib] (**a**) of the earliest period of the history of the world: *primeval rocks.* (**b**) very ancient: *primeval forests/wilderness.* (**c**) based on instinct rather than reason, as if from the earliest period of human life: *primeval desires/urges.*

primitive /'prɪmətɪv/ *adj* **1** [usu attrib] of or at an early stage of social development: *primitive culture/rituals/societies* ○ *primitive man.* **2** (*often derog*) simple and fundamental, as if from an earlier period of history; not comfortable or convenient: *Living conditions in the camp were pretty primitive.* ○ *The cave provided a primitive shelter from the storm.*

▶ **primitive** *n* (**a**) a painter or SCULPTOR of the period before the Renaissance. (**b**) an artist who paints in a simple style without or as if without any formal artistic training. (**c**) an example of the work of a primitive.

primogeniture /ˌpraɪməʊ'dʒenɪtʃə(r)/ *n* [U] (*law*) the fact of being the first child born in a family: *He inherited the property by **right of primogeniture*** (ie because he was the eldest son).

primordial /praɪ'mɔːdiəl/ *adj* [usu attrib] (*fml*) existing at or from the beginning, esp of the world or the universe: *primordial gases* ○ *a primordial swamp.* ▶ **primordially** /-diəli/ *adv.*

primrose /'prɪmrəʊz/ *n* **1** [C] a wild plant that has pale yellow flowers in spring; one of these flowers. **2** [U] a pale yellow colour. **IDM** the primrose 'path (*rhet*) an easy life, esp one that leads to disaster: *follow the primrose path to ruin.*

▶ **primrose** *adj* of a pale yellow colour.

primula /'prɪmjələ/ *n* a plant or flower of the PRIMROSE(1) family. Primulas are of various colours and sizes and commonly grown in gardens.

Primus /'praɪməs/ (*pl* -**es**) (*also* 'Primus stove) *n* (*propr*) a small movable cooker that burns oil and is used esp by people camping.

prince /prɪns/ *n* **1** a male member of a royal family who is not the king, esp (in Britain) a son or GRANDSON of the king or queen: *the Prince of Wales* (ie the heir to the British throne). **2** a male royal ruler, esp of a small state: *Prince Rainier of Monaco.* **3** (in some countries) a nobleman. **4** ~ **of/among sth** an excellent or outstanding man in a particular field: *Bocuse, a prince among chefs.*

▶ **princely** *adj* (**a**) [usu attrib] of, like or ruled by a prince: *princely states.* (**b**) splendid or generous: *a princely gift/sum.*

■ ˌPrince 'Consort *n* (a title often given to) the husband of a ruling queen.

princess /ˌprɪn'ses/ *n* (**a**) a female member of a royal family who is not the queen, esp (in Britain) the daughter or GRANDDAUGHTER of the king or queen: ˌPrincess 'Margaret. (**b**) the wife of a prince.

■ ˌPrincess 'Royal *n* (esp in Britain) (a title often given to) the eldest daughter of the king or queen.

principal /'prɪnsəpl/ *adj* [attrib] first in rank or importance; chief; main: *build new roads to link the country's principal cities* ○ *The Danube is one of the principal rivers of Europe.* ○ *The principal aim of the scheme is to bring employment to the area.*

▶ **principal** *n* **1** (the title of) the person with the highest authority in an organization, esp in certain schools and colleges: *the Principal of Edinburgh University.* **2** a person who takes a leading part in a play, an opera, etc: *a principal actor/role.* **3** (usu sing) (*finance*) an amount of money lent or invested on which interest¹(5) is paid: *repay principal and interest.* **4** a person for whom another acts as her or his agent, eg in business or law.

principally /-pli/ *adv* for the most part; mainly: *The book is principally aimed at beginners.* ○ *The scheme failed principally because of a lack of finance.*

■ ˌprincipal ˈparts *n* [pl] (*grammar*) the forms of a verb from which all other forms can be made. In English these are the INFINITIVE, the past TENSE² and the past PARTICIPLE.

principality /ˌprɪnsɪˈpæləti/ *n* **1** [C] a country ruled by a prince: *the principality of Monaco*. **2 the Principality** [sing] (*Brit*) Wales.

principle /ˈprɪnsəpl/ *n* **1** [C] a basic general truth that is the foundation of sth, eg a subject or a system of moral behaviour: *the basic principles of geometry* ○ *the principle of equality of opportunity for all* ○ *Discussing all these details will get us nowhere: we must get back to first principles*. **2(a)** [C usu *pl*] a guiding rule for personal behaviour: *live according to one's principles* ○ *She seems to have no principles at all when it is a question of making money.* ○ *It would be against my principles to lie to you.* **(b)** [U] these rules: *a woman of (high) principle* ○ *He is completely without principle* (ie does not behave morally) ○ *It is a matter of principle with her to answer her children's questions honestly.* **3** [sing] a general or scientific law shown in the way a thing works, or used as the basis for constructing a machine, etc: *These devices both work on the same principle.* ○ *The system works on the principle that heat rises.* **IDM in principle 1** as far as basic principles are concerned: *There's no reason in principle why people couldn't travel to Mars* (ie It is possible, though it has not yet been done). **2** in general but not in detail: *They have agreed to the proposal in principle but we still have to negotiate the terms.* **on principle** because of one's principles or beliefs: *Many people are opposed to abortion on principle.*

▶ **principled** *adj* based on or having (esp good) principles of behaviour: *a (high-)principled man* ○ *a principled stand against federalism.*

print¹ /prɪnt/ *n* **1** [U] letters, words, numbers, etc appearing in printed form: *Headlines are written in large print.* ○ *The print is too small for me to read without glasses.* See also THE SMALL PRINT. **2** [C] a mark left on a surface where sth, eg a foot, has been pressed on it: *The lion left its prints in the sand.* See also FINGERPRINT, FOOTPRINT. **3** [C] **(a)** a picture or design made by printing from a surface covered in ink: *an old Japanese print* ○ *a series of prints of 19th-century life.* **(b)** a photograph printed from a negative(2): *colour prints.* **4** [C,U] cotton fabric with a pattern on it: *She bought a flowery print to make a summer dress.* ○ *a print dress.* **IDM in print 1** (of a book) still available from the publisher: *Is that volume still in print?* **2** (of a person's work) printed in a book, newspaper, etc: *It was the first time he had seen himself/his work in print.* ˌout of ˈprint (of a book) no longer available from the publisher: *Her first novel is out of print now but you may find a second-hand copy.*

print² /prɪnt/ *v* **1(a)** ~ sth (in/on sth) to make letters, pictures, etc on sth by pressing a surface covered in ink against it: [Vn] *The first 64 pages of the book have been printed.* ○ *They bought a new machine to print the posters.* [Vnpr] *The poems were printed on a small hand-operated press.* ○ (*fig*) *The events had printed themselves on her memory* (ie could not be forgotten). **(b)** to make books, pictures, etc in this way: [Vn] *The publisher has printed 30 000 copies of the book.* ○ *The firm specializes in printing calendars.* **2** to publish in printed form: [Vnpr] *The story was printed in all the national newspapers.* [also Vn]. **3** to write without joining the letters together: [V] *Children learn to print when they first go to school.* [Vn] *He printed his name in capitals at the bottom of the picture.* **4** ~ sth (in/on sth) to press a mark or design on a surface: [Vnpr] *print letters in the sand* [also Vn]. **5** to make a design on a piece of paper or fabric by pressing a surface against it which has been coloured with ink or dye: [Vnpr] *print a design*

on a T-shirt* [Vn] *printed cotton/wallpaper.* **6** ~ sth (off) to make a photograph from a negative *n*(2): [Vn, Vnp] *How many copies shall I print (off) for you?* **IDM the ˌprinted ˈword** what is published in books, newspapers, etc: *the power of the printed word to influence people's attitudes.* **PHRV** ˌprint (sth) ˈout (*computing*) (of a machine) to produce information from a computer in printed form. See also PRINTOUT.

▶ **printable** /-əbl/ *adj* fit to be published or printed: *His comment when he heard the news was not printable* (ie was very rude)*!*

printer *n* **1** a machine for printing text onto paper, esp one linked to a computer. **2(a)** a person whose job is printing. **(b)** an owner of a printing firm.

printing *n* **1** [U] the action or art of printing: *The invention of printing caused important changes in society.* ○ *a printing error.* **2** [C] a number of copies of a book printed at one time; an impression(6): *a first printing of 5 000 copies.* **3** letters written separately rather than joined together. ˈprinting-press *n* a machine for printing books, newspapers, etc.

■ ˌprinted ˈcircuit *n* an electric circuit using thin strips of material instead of wires to carry the current.

ˈprinted matter *n* [U] (also ˌprinted ˈpapers [pl]) printed material, eg newspapers and magazines, which may be sent by post at a reduced rate.

printout /ˈprɪntaʊt/ *n* [U,C] material produced in printed form from a computer: *Get me a printout of last month's sales figures, please.*

prior¹ /ˈpraɪə(r)/ *adj* [attrib] existing or coming before in time, order or importance: *I'll have to refuse your invitation because of a prior engagement.* ○ *They have a prior claim to the property* (ie one based on an earlier legal agreement).

■ ˈprior to *prep* (*fml*) before sth: *We received no notification prior to the event.*

prior² /ˈpraɪə(r)/ *n* (*fem* **prioress** /ˈpraɪərəs; *Brit also* ˌpraɪəˈres/) **(a)** a person who is head of a religious group or of a house of monks or nuns. **(b)** (in an ABBEY) a person next in rank below an ABBOT or ABBESS.

▶ **priory** /ˈpraɪəri/ *n* a building where monks or nuns live governed by a prior or a prioress.

priority /praɪˈɒrəti; *US* -ˈɔːr-/ *n* **1(a)** [C] a thing that is regarded as more important than others: *You must decide what your priorities are.* ○ *You've got your priorities all wrong/back to front.* ○ *Housework is low on her list of priorities.* ○ *Improved housing is a (top) priority.* **(b)** [U] ~ (over sth) a high or top place among various things to be done: *The government gave (top) priority to reforming the legal system.* ○ *The search for a new vaccine took priority over all other medical research.* ○ *Priority cases, such as homeless families, get dealt with first.* **2** [U] ~ (over sb/sth) **(a)** the right to have or do sth before others: *I have/take priority over you because I've worked here longer.* **(b)** the right to proceed before other traffic: *Vehicles coming from the right have priority.*

▶ **prioritize, -ise** /praɪˈɒrətaɪz/ *v* to give sth priority: [Vn] *Prioritizing your work can help reduce stress.*

prise /praɪz/ (also *esp US* **prize** /praɪz/, *US* **pry** /praɪ/) *v* to use force to separate sb/sth from sth else: [Vnp] *She used a screwdriver to prise off/up the lid.* ○ *The referee needed all his strength to prise the two boxers apart.* [Vn-adj] *The box had been prised open.* [also Vnpr]. **PHRV** ˌprise sth ˈout of sb to force sb to reveal sth they know: *She refused to tell us, and nothing we could do could prise the information out of her.*

prism /ˈprɪzəm/ *n* **(a)** (*geometry*) a solid figure with ends that are parallel and of the same size and shape, and with sides whose opposite edges are equal and parallel. **(b)** a transparent object of this shape, with usu TRIANGULAR(1) ends and made of glass, which separates ordinary light into the colours of the rainbow. ⇨ picture at SPECTRUM.

prismatic /prɪz'mætɪk/ *adj* (*techn*) of, like or using a PRISM: *the prismatic spectrum* ○ *a prismatic compass.*

prison /'prɪzn/ *n* **1** [C] (**a**) a place where people are kept as a punishment for crimes they have committed or while waiting for tr\'al: *the prison population* (ie the total number of prisoners in a country) ○ *The prisons are overcrowded.* (**b**) (*derog*) a place from which sb cannot escape: *Now that he was disabled, his house had become a prison to him.* **2** [U] the condition of being kept in a prison: *He was sent to prison for five years.* ○ *She's gone to/is in prison.* ○ *escape from/be released from/come out of prison.* ⇨ note at SCHOOL¹.

▶ **prisoner** *n* **1** a person kept in prison, as a punishment or while waiting for trial: *a prison built to hold 500 prisoners* ○ *Prisoner at the bar* (ie being tried), *do you plead guilty or not guilty?* **2** a person, an animal, etc that has been captured and is being kept confined: *They are holding her daughter prisoner and demanding a ransom of £50 000.* ○ *He was taken prisoner* (ie captured) *by rebel soldiers.* ○ (*fig*) *She has been burgled so often that she has become a virtual prisoner in her own home* (ie because she is afraid to go out). **,prisoner of 'conscience** *n* (*pl* prisoners of conscience) a person kept in prison because he or she has committed an act of social or political protest. **,prisoner of 'war** *n* (*pl* prisoners of war) (*abbr* POW) a person, usu a member of the armed forces, captured during a war by the enemy and kept in a prison camp until the end of the war.

■ **'prison camp** *n* a guarded camp where prisoners, esp prisoners of war or political prisoners, are kept.

prissy /'prɪsi/ *adj* (*infml derog*) (of a person) too careful and correct, and appearing to be easily shocked by rude behaviour, etc.

pristine /'prɪstiːn/ *adj* (**a**) in the original condition: *a pristine copy of the book's first edition.* (**b**) (*approv*) fresh and clean, as if new: *a pristine layer of snow* ○ *The car was in pristine condition.*

privacy /'prɪvəsi; *US* 'praɪv-/ *n* [U] **1** the state of being alone and not watched or disturbed: *A high wall round the estate protected their privacy.* ○ *He preferred to read in the privacy of his study.* **2** the state of freedom from interference (INTERFERE) or public attention: *Newspapers often fail to respect the individual's right to privacy.* ○ *She complained that the questions were an invasion of (her) privacy.*

private /'praɪvət/ *adj* **1** (*esp attrib*) of, belonging to or for the use of one particular person or group only; personal: *private property* ○ *a private income/ private means* (ie money not earned as a salary, etc but coming from personal property, investments, etc) ○ *father's own private chair, which no one else is allowed to use* ○ *a private letter* (ie about personal matters) ○ *'Is this a hotel?' 'No, it's a private house.'* **2**(**a**) not (to be) revealed to others; secret: *I'm not going to tell you about it; it's private.* ○ *That's my private opinion.* (**b**) (of a person) not liking to share thoughts and feelings with others: *He's a rather private person.* **3** (of a conversation, meeting, etc) involving only a small number of people, usu two, and kept secret from others: *I'd like a private chat with you.* **4**(**a**) (of a place) quiet and free from people who may interrupt: *Let's find a private spot where we can sit and talk.* (**b**) [usu pred] (of people) not disturbed by others; alone together: *Let's go upstairs where we can be a bit more private.* **5**(**a**) [attrib] having no official role or position: *a private citizen* ○ *She is acting as a private individual in this matter.* (**b**) not connected with one's work or official position: *The Queen is making a private visit to Canada.* ○ *Some people are fascinated by the private lives of public figures.* **6** of, belonging to or managed by an individual or an independent company rather than the state: *private industry* ○ *private education/ medicine* ○ *a private pension plan.* Compare PUBLIC.

▶ **private** *n* **1** [C] a soldier of the lowest rank: *Private (Alan) Smith* ○ *He enlisted as a private.* ⇨ App 6. **2 privates** [pl] (*infml*) = PRIVATE PARTS. **IDM** **in private** with no one else present: *She asked to see him in private.*

privately *adv*: *a privately-owned firm* ○ *The matter was arranged privately.* ○ *He supported the official policy in public, but privately he was convinced it would fail.*

■ **,private 'company** *n* a business firm that does not issue shares to the general public. Compare PUBLIC COMPANY.

,private de'tective (also **,private in'vestigator**, *infml* **,private 'eye**) *n* a DETECTIVE not employed by a police force.

,private 'enterprise *n* [U] business or industry managed by independent companies or private individuals, not controlled by the state.

,private 'member *n* (in Britain) a member of the House of Commons who is not a minister. **,private 'member's bill** *n* (in Britain) a bill¹(4) presented to Parliament by a private member.

,private 'parts *n* [pl] (*euph*) the sexual organs.

,private 'patient *n* (*Brit*) a person treated by a doctor other than under the National Health Service.

,private 'practice *n* **1** [U] the practice of one's profession as an independent person and not an employee: *architects/solicitors in private practice.* **2** (*Brit*) (**a**) [U] the providing of medical care by independent doctors, dentists, etc outside the National Health Service: *I'm going into private practice when I qualify.* (**b**) [C] a place providing this care: *My NHS dentist has left to form a private practice.*

,private 'school *n* **1** (*Brit*) a school supported financially entirely by money paid by the parents of students attending it, not by the government. **2** (*US*) a school not receiving its main financial support from the government. Compare PUBLIC SCHOOL.

,private 'secretary *n* a SECRETARY(1) dealing with sb's more important personal and secret affairs.

the ,private 'sector *n* [sing] the part of the economy not under direct state control: *the rapid growth of the private sector* ○ *private sector pay rises.* Compare PUBLIC SECTOR.

privateer /ˌpraɪvə'tɪə(r)/ *n* (esp formerly) a ship used for attacking and robbing other ships.

privation /praɪ'veɪʃn/ *n* (*fml*) **1** [U, C usu *pl*] a lack of basic comforts and things necessary for life: *a life of privation and misery* ○ *The survivors suffered many privations before they were rescued.* **2** [C usu *sing*] a state of not having sth, not necessarily sth essential: *She didn't find the lack of a car a great privation.*

privatize, -ise /'praɪvətaɪz/ *v* to transfer sth from state control or ownership to private ownership: [Vn] *privatize the railways* ○ *British Telecom was privatized in 1984.* Compare DENATIONALIZE, NATIONALIZE. ▶ **privatization, -isation** /ˌpraɪvətaɪ-'zeɪʃn; *US* -tə'z-/ *n* [U]: *the privatization of the steel industry.*

privet /'prɪvɪt/ *n* [U] a bush with small leaves that stay green throughout the year, and small white flowers. It is often used for garden hedges: *a privet hedge.*

privilege /'prɪvəlɪdʒ/ *n* **1** [C] a special right or advantage available only to a particular person or group of people: *Older children have/enjoy special privileges.* ○ *People who abuse their parking privileges will have them removed.* ○ *Education should be seen as a universal right, not as a special privilege.* **2** [U] (*derog*) the rights and advantages possessed by the rich and powerful people in a society: *She had* led *a life of luxury and privilege.* **3** [sing] a thing that gives one great enjoyment and that most people do not have the opportunity to do: *It was a great privilege hearing her sing/to hear her sing.* **4** [C, U] a special legal right to do or say things without risking punishment: *an Act which granted the trade unions certain legal privileges* ○ *parliamentary privilege* (ie a special right given to members of a parliament to say particular things without risking legal action).

▶ **privileged** *adj* **1(a)** (*sometimes derog*) having privilege or privileges: *be in a privileged position* ○ *She came from a privileged background.* ○ *The government uses its power solely in the interests of the privileged few.* (**b**) [pred] honoured: *We are very privileged to have Senator Dobbs with us this evening.* **2** legally protected from being made public: *privileged information.*

privy¹ /'prɪvi/ *adj* [pred] ~ **to sth** (*fml*) sharing in the secret of sth: *I wasn't privy to the negotiations.*

privy² /'prɪvi/ *n* (*dated*) a toilet, esp an outdoor one.
■ **the ,Privy 'Council** *n* [Gp] (*Brit*) a group of respected and experienced politicians appointed by the king or queen, formerly as advisers on affairs of state, but now usu as a personal honour for its members.
the ,privy 'purse *n* [sing] (*Brit*) an amount of money given by the British government for the private expenses of the king or queen.

prize¹ /praɪz/ *n* **1** an award given to the winner of a competition, race, etc: *be awarded the Nobel prize for physics* ○ *She won/took first prize.* ○ *a prizewinning book/architect/design* ○ *She won £5 000 in prize money.* ○ *Her book gained several literary prizes.* ○ *There are no prizes for guessing who Dan's taking out tonight* (ie It is obvious). See also CONSOLATION PRIZE. **2** a thing of value that is worth struggling to achieve: *The greatest prize of all — world peace — is now within our grasp.*
▶ **prize** *adj* [attrib] (**a**) winning or likely to win a prize: *prize cattle* ○ *a prize bloom.* (**b**) excellent of its kind: *That's a prize example of what I mean.* (**c**) (*dated infml*) complete: *I made a prize idiot of myself.*
prize *v* to value sth highly: [Vn] *The portrait of her mother was her most prized possession.* ○ *I prize my independence too much to get married just yet.*
■ **'prize-giving** *n* a usu annual school ceremony at which prizes are given to students who have done especially well.
'prize-fight *n* a boxing match fought for money.
'prize-fighter *n*.

prize² (*esp US*) = PRISE.

pro¹ /prəʊ/ *n* **IDM the ,pros and 'cons** the advantages and disadvantages of sth: *Let's examine the pros and cons.*

pro² /prəʊ/ *n* (*pl* **pros**) (*infml*) a professional, esp in sport: *a golf pro* ○ *a pro athlete* ○ *a young boxer who's just turned pro* ○ (*approv*) *He's a real pro.*
■ **'pro-am** *n, adj* (a competition) involving professional and AMATEUR(1) players: *a ,pro-am 'golf tournament.*

pro- *pref* (with *ns* and *adjs*) in favour of; supporting: *,pro-a'bortion/,pro-'life* ○ *,pro-government 'forces.* Compare ANTI- 1.

proactive /prəʊ'æktɪv/ *adj* (of a person, policy, etc) creating or controlling a situation by causing things to happen rather than reacting to events, etc.

probability /,prɒbə'bɪləti/ *n* **1** [U] the state of being probable: *There's very little probability that anyone will try to escape.* ○ *What is the probability of its success?* **2** [C] a thing that is probable; a probable event or result: *A fall in interest rates is a strong probability in the present economic climate.* ○ *In planning for the future, we need to consider a whole range of probabilities and possibilities.* ○ *The magistrate*

will make a decision on **the balance of probabilities. 3** [C] (*mathematics*) a RATIO expressing the chances that a certain event will occur: *The species has a 50% probability of extinction within 5 years.*
IDM in ,**all proba'bility** it is very likely that: *In all probability he's already left.*

probable /'prɒbəbl/ *adj* likely to happen, exist or be true: *the most probable explanation/outcome/cause* ○ *It seems probable that the police are right about this.*
▶ **probable** *n* ~ (**for sth**) a person or thing most likely to be chosen, eg for a sports team or as the winner: *All four players are probables for the national team, to be announced tomorrow.* Compare POSSIBLE, IMPROBABLE.
probably /-əbli/ *adv* almost certainly: *He's probably stuck in a traffic jam.* ○ *You're probably right.* ○ *'Will you be coming?' 'Probably (not)'.*

probate /'prəʊbeɪt/ *n* (*law*) [U] the official process of proving that a will⁴(5) is correct: *grant probate* ○ *a probate court/application.*
▶ **probate** *v* [Vn] (*US law*) to prove that a will⁴(5) is genuine.

probation /prə'beɪʃn; *US* prəʊ-/ *n* [U] **1** (*law*) the system by which a person found guilty of a crime is not sent to prison, but is legally required to report regularly to an official for a fixed period of time: *He was sentenced to three years' probation.* ○ *She was convicted of reckless driving and put on probation for three years.* ○ *be under a probation order.* **2** the testing of a person's abilities or behaviour to find out if he or she is suitable, esp for a job: *a three-month period of probation/probation period for new members of staff.*
▶ **probationary** /prə'beɪʃnri; *US* prəʊ'beɪʃəneri/ *adj* of, for or doing probation: *a probationary period* ○ *a young probationary teacher.*
■ **pro'bation officer** *n* an official whose job is to supervise people on probation.

probe /prəʊb/ *n* **1** a tool for examining a place which cannot be reached otherwise, esp a thin instrument with a BLUNT(1) end used by a doctor in medical examinations and operations. **2** (also **'space probe**) a spacecraft without people on board which obtains information about space and transmits it back to earth. **3** ~ (**into sth**) (used esp in newspapers) a thorough and careful investigation of sth: *set up a probe into the disappearance of government funds.*
▶ **probe** *v* **1** to explore, examine or enter sth with or as if with a probe(1): [Vn] *He probed the swelling gently with his finger.* ○ *Searchlights probed the night sky.* **2** ~ (**into sth**) to investigate or examine sth closely: [Vpr] *I became more puzzled the more deeply I probed into his past life.* [Vn] *a weekly TV programme that probed government scandals in the 1980s.* **3** to ask sb questions intended to make them tell one things that are personal or secret: [V.speech] *'You said he got very angry?' Maggie probed.* [Vn] *She never probed Lucy, aware that she would never get the truth.* **probing** *adj* intended to discover the truth: *probing questions.*

probity /'prəʊbəti/ *n* [U] (*fml*) the quality of being honest and worthy of trust: *raise doubts as to sb's probity.*

problem /'prɒbləm/ *n* **1** a thing that is difficult to deal with or understand: *a knotty problem* ○ *serious/pressing economic problems* ○ *We've got a minor problem with the car — it won't start!* ○ *We've run into a few technical/practical problems.* ○ *You'll have to mend that leak or it will cause/create problems later.* ○ *The government must tackle/confront/address the housing problem in the inner cities.* ○ *Travel is/poses/presents a problem for him now that he's in a wheelchair.* ○ *The problem first arose in 1993.* ○ (*infml*) *'Will you be able to get me tickets for the game?' 'Of course,*

no problem (ie It will be easy).' ○ *Stop worrying about their marriage — it's not your problem.* ○ *a newspaper's problem page* (ie for readers' letters about their problems, and suggested solutions). **2** a question to be answered or solved, esp by reasoning or calculating: *a mathematical problem* ○ *She found the answer to the problem.* ○ *develop problem-solving strategies.*
▶ **problematic** /ˌprɒbləˈmætɪk/ (also **problematical**) *adj* difficult to deal with or understand; awkward and complex: *The marketing of such a product may prove problematic.*
■ **'problem child** *n* a child who continually behaves badly, does not learn well, etc.

procedure /prəˈsiːdʒə(r)/ *n* **1** [C,U] a formal or official order or way of doing things, esp in business, law politics, etc: *follow the agreed/correct/established/normal/usual/proper/standard procedure(s)* ○ *parliamentary procedure* ○ *The police are reviewing their crowd control procedures.* **2** [C] ~ **(for sth)** a series of actions that need to be completed in order to achieve sth: *the standard procedure for making a complaint* ○ *Registering a birth or death is a straightforward procedure.* ▶ **procedural** /prəˈsiːdʒərəl/ *adj*: *procedural changes/difficulties/irregularities.*

proceed /prəˈsiːd, prəʊ-/ *v* **(a)** *(rather formal)* to go on to a further or to the next stage: [V] *arguments about whether the trial should proceed* ○ *Work is proceeding slowly.* [Vpr] *The project never proceeded past the planning stage.* [V.to inf] *He proceeded to explain the scheme in more detail.* ○ *(ironic) Having said he wasn't hungry he then proceeded to eat half a packet of biscuits!* **(b)** ~ **(with sth)** *(fml)* to begin or continue sth: [Vpr] *Please proceed with your report.* [V] *All right, nurse, you may proceed.* **(c)** *(fml)* to move or travel in a particular direction: [Vpr] *From the city centre proceed along Maple Street until you reach the station.* ○ *Proceed with extreme caution.*
PHRV **pro'ceed against sb** *(law)* to take legal action against sb. **pro'ceed from sth** *(fml)* to be caused by or originate from sth: *the evils that proceed from human greed.*

proceedings /prəˈsiːdɪŋz/ *n* [pl] **1** ~ **(against sb / for sth)** the process of using a lawcourt or other official body to settle a dispute or disagreement: *institute divorce/bankruptcy/extradition proceedings* ○ *The firm has started legal proceedings to protect its name.* ○ *She threatened to bring proceedings against him.* **2** an ordered series of actions, esp at a meeting, ceremony, etc: *The proceedings will begin with a speech to welcome the guests.* ○ *The proceedings were interrupted by the fire alarm.* **3** ~ **(of sth)** a published report or record of a discussion, meeting, conference, etc: *His paper was published in the proceedings of the Kent Archaeological Society.*

proceeds /ˈprəʊsiːdz/ *n* [pl] ~ **(of/from sth)** the money gained by selling sth, giving a performance, etc; profits: *Here's your share of the proceeds from the sale of the car.* ○ *They gave a concert and donated the proceeds to charity.*

process¹ /ˈprəʊses; US ˈprɒses/ *n* **1** a series of actions or tasks performed in order to do, make or achieve sth: *begin the difficult/gradual process of reforming the education system* ○ *Unloading the cargo was a slow process.* ○ *Teaching him to walk again was a long and painful process* (ie a slow and difficult one). ○ *We're still in the process of selling our house.* ○ *I was moving some furniture and twisted my ankle in the process* (ie while doing it). ○ *an opportunity to advance the peace process* ○ *the decision-making process* ○ *the selection process.* **2** a series of changes, esp ones that happen naturally: *the digestive processes* ○ *a normal part of the ageing process* ○ *He began the slow process of recovery.* **3** a method of doing or making sth, esp one used in industry: *the processes used in cement production* ○

technical changes in the process of movie-making ○ *They have developed a new process for rustproofing car bodies.*
▶ **process** *v* **1** to put a raw material, food, etc, through an industrial or a manufacturing process in order to change it, preserve it, etc; to treat sth: [Vn] *Most of the food we buy is processed in some way.* ○ *processed cheese* ○ *I sent three rolls of photos away to be processed.* ○ *a sewage processing plant.* **2** to deal officially with a document, request, etc: [Vn] *It may take a few weeks for your application to be processed.* **3** [Vn] to perform a series of operations on sth in a computer. See also DATA PROCESSING, WORD PROCESSING. **processor** *n* a machine that processes things. See also FOOD PROCESSOR, MICROPROCESSOR, WORD PROCESSOR.

process² /prəˈses/ *v* to walk or move in or as if in procession: [Vpr] *The bishops, priests and deacons processed slowly through the cathedral.* [also Vp].

procession /prəˈseʃn/ *n* **1** [C] **(a)** a number of people, vehicles, etc moving along in a controlled way, esp as part of a ceremony: *a 'funeral procession* ○ *The procession made its way slowly down the hill.* **(b)** [U] the action of moving forward in this way: *The choir entered the church in procession.* **2** [C] a large number of people who come one after the other: *An endless procession of visitors came to the house.*
▶ **processional** /-ʃənl/ *adj* of, for or used in a procession, esp a religious one: *a processional hymn.*

proclaim /prəˈkleɪm/ *v* **1** to make sth, esp sth important or dramatic, known officially or publicly; to announce sth: [Vn] *proclaim a public holiday* [Vnadv] *They dare not proclaim their intentions too loudly.* [V.that] *Banners proclaim that change must come soon.* [V.speech] *'Our very existence is threatened,' he proclaimed.* [Vn-n] *After its independence India was proclaimed a republic.* [also V.wh]. **2** *(fml)* to show sth clearly; reveal: [Vn-n, V.that] *His accent proclaimed him a Scot/that he was a Scot.*
▶ **proclamation** /ˌprɒkləˈmeɪʃn/ *n* **(a)** [C] a public statement: *issue/make an official proclamation* ○ *sign the proclamation of independence.* **(b)** [U] the action of proclaiming sth: *by public proclamation.*

proclivity /prəˈklɪvəti/ *n* ~ **(for/to sth / doing sth)** *(fml)* a natural tendency to do sth, esp sth considered strange or bad: *have a proclivity to sudden violent rages* ○ *his unusual sexual proclivities.*

procrastinate /prəʊˈkræstɪneɪt/ *v* *(fml derog)* to delay or postpone action: [V] *He procrastinated until it was too late to do anything at all.* ▶ **procrastination** /prəʊˌkræstɪˈneɪʃn/ *n* [U,C] *(fml derog)*: *She condemned the government's procrastination.*

procreate /ˈprəʊkrieɪt/ *v* *(fml)* to reproduce sexually: [V] *the urge to procreate.* ▶ **procreation** /ˌprəʊkriˈeɪʃn/ *n* [U]: *They regard sex as only for procreation.*

proctor /ˈprɒktə(r)/ *n* *(US)* a person responsible for supervising students in an examination. Compare INVIGILATOR.

procurator fiscal /ˌprɒkjʊreɪtə ˈfɪskl/ *n* (in Scotland) a public official whose job is to decide whether people suspected of crime should be brought to trial.

procure /prəˈkjʊə(r)/ *v* *(fml)* **1** ~ **sth (for sb)** to obtain sth, esp with care or effort; to acquire sth: [Vnpr, Vnn] *Can you procure a copy of the report for me/procure me a copy?* [Vn] *He was responsible for procuring spare parts.* ○ *procure the services of a lawyer* ○ *The party failed to procure sufficient votes.* **2** to find prostitutes for clients: [Vnpr] *He was accused of procuring an under-age girl for unlawful sex.* [also V, Vn].
▶ **procurement** *n* [U] *(fml)* the process of obtaining sth: *the procurement of goods/raw materials/supplies* ○ *be in charge of weapons procurement.*

procurer /-'kjʊərə(r)/ n (*fem* **procuress** /-'kjʊəres/) a person who finds prostitutes for clients.

prod /prɒd/ v (**-dd-**) **1** ~ (**at sb/sth**) to push sb/sth with a finger or a pointed object; to POKE(1) sb/sth: [Vnpr] *He prodded me in the ribs with his rifle.* [Vpr] *They prodded at the animal through the bars of its cage.* [also Vn,V]. ⇨ note at NUDGE. **2** ~ **sb** (**into sth / doing sth**) (*infml*) to make or try to make a slow or unwilling person do sth; to encourage sb: [Vn.*to* inf] *He needs to be prodded to do anything like that.* [Vnpr] *The museum had prodded him into leaving his art collection to them.*
▶ **prod** n **1** an act of prodding sb/sth; a POKE: *She gave the man a sharp prod with her umbrella.* **2** (*infml*) an act of reminding sb to take action: *If you don't receive an answer by next week,* **give** *them a gentle* **prod.**
prodding n [U] the action of prodding sb/sth: *He needed no prodding.* ○ *A little judicious prodding may be necessary at this stage.*

prodigal /'prɒdɪgl/ adj (*fml derog*) spending money or resources too freely; EXTRAVAGANT(1a): *a prodigal administration.* **IDM** **the prodigal** (**'daughter/'son**) a person who leaves her or his home and wastes money on eg a life of pleasure, but who later regrets this and returns: *So, the prodigal (son) has returned!*
▶ **prodigality** /ˌprɒdɪ'gæləti/ n [U].

prodigious /prə'dɪdʒəs/ adj (*fml*) very great in size, amount or degree, esp so as to cause admiration or surprise: *their prodigious achievement/output/energy/talent* ○ *The government sank prodigious amounts of public money into the scheme.* ▶ **prodigiously** adv: *a prodigiously gifted/talented artist.*

prodigy /'prɒdədʒi/ n a person, esp a young person, with unusual or remarkable qualities or abilities: *a 14-year-old tennis prodigy* ○ *a child/an infant prodigy* (ie a child who is unusually talented for her or his age, esp in music or MATHEMATICS).

produce /prə'djuːs; US -'duːs/ v **1**(**a**) to make or manufacture sth, esp in large quantities: [Vn] *a fashion house producing well-styled casual clothes* ○ *America has produced more cars than ever this year.* ○ *locally produced wines* ○ *The organization has produced a booklet to help small investors.* See also MASS-PRODUCE. (**b**) to grow or supply sth, esp in large quantities: [Vn] *The region has produced over half the country's wheat crop.* ○ *This soil produces good tomatoes.* **2** to create sth using skill: [Vn] *produce a poem/work of art* ○ *She produced a hot meal for us within 20 minutes.* **3** to create sth as part of a natural process; to bear or grow sth: [Vn] *The plant is producing new leaves.* ○ *His cow has produced a calf.* ○ *The cows are producing a lot of milk.* ○ *The boiler blew up, producing clouds of smoke.* **4** to cause a particular result or situation: [Vn] *His announcement produced a violent reaction among the crowd.* ○ *The war produced a surge of patriotic feeling.* ○ *A phone call to the manager soon* **produced results** (ie achieved the desired effect). **5** ~ **sth** (**from / out of sth**) to show or provide sth so that it can be examined or used: [Vn] *produce a ticket for inspection* ○ *He can produce evidence to support his allegations.* [Vnpr] *The man suddenly produced a gun from his pocket.* **6** to arrange the performance of a play, an opera, etc or the making of a film or television programme: [Vn] *produce a documentary* ○ *She is producing 'Romeo and Juliet' at the local theatre.* Compare DIRECT² 1b, PRODUCT, PRODUCTION, PRODUCTIVE.
▶ **produce** /'prɒdjuːs; US -duːs/ n [U] things that have been produced (PRODUCE 1b), esp by farming: *fresh produce* ○ *organic/dairy produce* ○ *It says on the bottle 'Produce of France'.*

producer /prə'djuːsə(r); US -'duː-/ n **1** a person, company, country, etc that produces goods or materials: *small-scale egg producers* ○ *the world's major*

gold producer. Compare CONSUMER. **2**(**a**) a person in charge of a film, play etc, who obtains the money to pay for it, and arranges rehearsals (REHEARSE), filming, publicity, etc. Compare DIRECTOR 2. (**b**) a person or company that arranges for a television or radio programme, a record, etc to be made: *an independent producer.*

product /'prɒdʌkt/ n **1** a thing that is grown or produced, usu for sale: *cereal/dairy/meat/pharmaceutical products* ○ *marketing a range of beauty products* ○ *launch a new product.* See also END-PRODUCT, GROSS NATIONAL PRODUCT. **2** [C] a thing or substance produced during a natural, chemical or manufacturing process: *dispose of the waste products of the manufacturing process* ○ *the products of combustion.* See also BY-PRODUCT. **3** [C] ~ **of sth** (**a**) a thing or state that is the result of sth: *a product of evolution* ○ *the products of genius* (eg great works of art). (**b**) a person who has been greatly influenced by sth: *She is the product of an intellectual middle-class background.* **4** [C] (*mathematics*) a quantity obtained by multiplying one number by another: *The product of 4 and 10 is 40.*

production /prə'dʌkʃn/ n **1** [U] the action of manufacturing, growing, extracting, etc things, esp in large quantities: *oil/car/egg/energy production* ○ *the amount of land available for food production* ○ *a fall in industrial production* ○ *Production of the new aircraft will start next year.* ○ *The new weapons system will be* **in production** *by the end of the year.* ○ *More tests are needed before it* **goes into production.** ○ *That model* **went out of production** *five years ago.* ○ *production costs/managers/processes/difficulties.* See also MASS PRODUCTION. **2** [U] the quantity produced: *a fall/increase in production* ○ *production levels.* **3**(**a**) [C] a thing that has been produced, esp a play or film: *This is Spielberg's most ambitious production to date.* ○ *a new production of 'King Lear'.* (**b**) [U] the process of producing a film, play, etc: *her involvement in film production.* **IDM** **on production of sth** (*fml*) by/when showing sth: *On production of your membership card, you will receive a discount on all your purchases.*
■ **pro'duction line** n a sequence of groups of machines and workers, in which each group performs part of the production process: *Cars are checked as they come off the production line.*

productive /prə'dʌktɪv/ adj **1** producing or able to produce goods or crops, esp in large quantities: *highly productive farming land/manufacturing methods* ○ *Africa's long-term* **productive capacity.** **2** achieving a lot; useful: *It wasn't a very productive meeting.* ○ *I spent a very productive hour in the library.* **3** [pred] ~ **of sth** (*fml*) resulting in sth; causing sth: *The changes were not productive of better labour relations.* See also COUNTER-PRODUCTIVE. ▶ **productively** adv: *spend one's time productively.*

productivity /ˌprɒdʌk'tɪvəti/ n [U] efficiency, esp in industry, measured by comparing the amount produced with the time taken or the resources used to produce it: *high/improved/increased/enhanced productivity* ○ *Our productivity is only about 40% of Japanese levels.* ○ *a productivity agreement/deal* (ie an agreement between management and unions that the cost of higher wages will be paid for by an increase in productivity).

Prof *abbr* (as a title) Professor: *Prof Mike Harrison.*

prof /prɒf/ n (*infml*) PROFESSOR: *go and see the prof.*

profane /prə'feɪn/ adj (*fml*) **1** having or showing contempt for God or holy things; blasphemous (BLASPHEME): *profane acts/language.* **2** [attrib] not sacred; SECULAR(1): *songs of sacred and profane love.*
▶ **profane** v (*fml*) [Vn] to treat a sacred thing with contempt or lack of respect.
profanity /prə'fænəti; US prəʊ-/ n (*fml*) (**a**) [U] profane behaviour, esp the use of profane language.

(**b**) [C esp *pl*] a profane word or phrase: *He uttered a stream of profanities.*

profess /prə'fes/ *v* (*fml*) **1** to claim sth, often falsely: [Vn, V.*to* inf] *I don't profess expert knowledge of/profess to be an expert in this subject.* [Vn] *She professed her innocence.* **2** to state openly that one has a belief, feeling, etc: [Vn-adj] *He professed himself satisfied with the progress made.* [Vn] *They all profess a belief in competition.* **3** to have or belong to a religion: [Vn] *profess Islam.*
▸ **professed** *adj* [attrib] **1** claimed, sometimes falsely: *her professed love of children.* **2** openly declared: *a professed Christian/anarchist* ○ *The government stuck to its professed intentions.*

profession /prə'feʃn/ *n* **1(a)** [C] a paid occupation, esp one that requires advanced education and training, eg architecture, law or medicine: *advising college leavers on their choice of profession* ○ *the acting/teaching/dental profession* ○ *enter/go into/join the medical profession* ○ *She is a lawyer by profession.* ○ *He was a man of 45, at the very top of his profession.* (**b**) **the profession** [CGp] all the people working in a particular profession: *The Health Service reforms are opposed by leading members of the profession* (ie the medical profession). ○ *The legal profession* (ie lawyers) *has/have always resisted change.* ⇨ note at JOB. **2** [C] ~ **of sth** a public statement or claim of sth: *a profession of belief/faith/loyalty* ○ *His professions of concern did not seem sincere.*

professional /prə'feʃənl/ *adj* **1(a)** [attrib] of, relating to or belonging to a profession: *professional associations/bodies* ○ *professional ethics/codes of practice* ○ *a distinguished professional career* ○ *You will need to* **seek/take professional advice** *about your claim for compensation.* ○ *The doctor was accused of* **professional misconduct**. (**b**) (*approv*) having or showing the skill or qualities of a professional person: *a very professional piece of work* ○ *She is extremely professional in her approach to her job.* ○ *Many of the performers were of professional standard.* Compare UNPROFESSIONAL. **2(a)** doing as a job sth which others do only as an interest or a HOBBY: *a professional boxer/tennis player* ○ *a professional cook/photographer/musician* ○ *After he won the amateur championship he* **turned professional** (ie began to earn money from his sport). (**b**) (of sport, etc) done as a job: *the world of professional football/golf.* Compare AMATEUR 1.
▸ **professional** *n* **1** a person qualified or employed in one of the professions: *nurses and other committed health professionals* ○ *You need a professional to sort out your finances.* **2** (also *infml* **pro**) a sportsman(2) player or performer: *a top golf professional.* **3** (also *infml* **pro**) (*approv*) a highly skilled and experienced person: *This survey is the work of a real professional.*
professionalism /-ʃənəlɪzəm/ *n* [U] **1** (*approv*) (**a**) the skill or qualities required or expected of members of a profession: *These soldiers are performing their duties with courage and professionalism.* (**b**) great skill and ability: *impressed by the professionalism of her performance.* **2** the practice of using professional players in sport: *Increased professionalism has changed the game radically.*
professionally /-ʃənəli/ *adv* (**a**) in a professional way: *The product has been marketed very professionally.* (**b**) by a professional person: *The burglar alarm should be professionally installed.* (**c**) in the knowledge and skill of a profession: *professionally qualified people.* (**d**) as a paid occupation: *He plays golf professionally.*
■ **pro,fessional 'foul** *n* (*euph*) (in sport, esp football) a deliberate FOUL¹, esp one committed in order to stop the game when a member of the opposing team seems certain to score.

professor /prə'fesə(r)/ *n* (*abbr* **Prof**) **1** (often as a title) a university teacher of the highest grade: *Professor (James) Brown* ○ *She was made (a) professor at the age of 40.* ○ *be appointed Professor of Chemistry* ○ *a university professor* ○ *a professor in engineering.* **2** (*US*) a teacher at a university or college.
▸ **professorial** /ˌprɒfə'sɔːriəl/ *adj* of or like a professor: *a professorial post* ○ *professorial duties.*
professorship *n* the position of a professor at a university: *accept/hold a professorship in History* ○ *She was appointed to a professorship at Columbia University.*

proffer /'prɒfə(r)/ *v* ~ **sth** (**to sb**) (*fml*) to offer sth to sb: [Vnpr] *proffer advice/help/thanks to sb* [Vn] *A variety of reasons were proffered for the long delay.* ○ *She proffered her resignation.* [Vnn] *He proffered me his hand in a gesture of friendship.*

proficient /prə'fɪʃnt/ *adj* ~ (**in/at sth / doing sth**) doing or able to do sth in a skilled or an expert way because of training and practice: *a proficient driver* ○ *be proficient in English/at operating a computer* ○ *She has become reasonably proficient at her job.* ▸ **proficiency** /-nsi/ *n* [U] ~ (**in sth / doing sth**): *develop/show/increase proficiency* ○ *a test of proficiency (in English)* ○ *reach a high level of proficiency.*

profile /'prəʊfaɪl/ *n* **1** a view from the side, esp of the human face: *his handsome profile* ○ *The Queen's head appears* **in profile** *on British stamps.* **2** the edge or outline of sth seen against a background: *the profile of the tower against the sky.* **3** a report or description of sb/sth in a newspaper article, broadcast programme, etc: *The magazine publishes a profile of a leading sports personality each month.* ○ *The programme will present a profile of the British nuclear industry.* **4** a public image of oneself, one's business, one's clients, etc: *increase/raise one's profile* ○ *The deal will improve our corporate profile.* **IDM** **a ,high/,low 'profile** a noticeable or INCONSPICUOUS way of behaving, so as to attract/avoid public attention: *adopt/keep/maintain a low profile* ○ *high-profile politicians* ○ *Texas Instruments has the highest market profile at the moment.*
▸ **profile** *v* to write or make a profile(3) of sb/sth: [Vn] *His private life was endlessly profiled in leading magazines.*

profit¹ /'prɒfɪt/ *n* **1** [C, U] money gained in business, esp the difference between the amount earned and the amount spent: *sell sth at a profit* ○ *operate at a profit* ○ *show a clear/healthy/fat profit* ○ *The sale generated record profits.* ○ *They* **make a profit** *of ten pence on every copy they sell.* ○ *Profits for the last six months rose/fell by 7%.* ○ *Should public transport be run for profit?* ○ *There's very little profit in publishing poetry these days.* ○ *They're only interested in a quick profit.* **2** [U] (*fml*) advantage or benefit gained from sth: *It is a book that any aspiring musician could read with profit.*
▸ **profitless** *adj* without profit; worthless: *profitless talk.*
■ **,profit and 'loss account** *n* a list that shows the amount of money spent compared with the amount earned by a business in a particular period: *enter an item in the profit and loss account.*
'profit margin *n* the difference between the cost of buying or producing sth and the price for which it is sold: *increase the profit margin to 20%.*
'profit-sharing *n* [U] the system of dividing a portion of a company's profits among its employees: *a profit-sharing scheme.*
'profit-taking *n* [U] (*commerce*) the sale of shares (SHARE¹ 3) at a time when profit will be gained.

profit² /'prɒfɪt/ *v* **PHRV** **'profit by/from sth** to obtain an advantage or benefit from sth: *profit by one's experiences/mistakes.* ○ *small companies profiting from changes in the employment laws* ○ *Farmers have profited from the improved weather conditions.*

profitable /'prɒfɪtəbl/ *adj* bringing profit or advantage: *make a profitable investment* ○ *one of the most profitable airlines in the world* ○ *She spent a very profitable afternoon in the library.* ▶ **profitability** /ˌprɒfɪtə'bɪləti/ *n* [U]: *increase profitability.* **profitably** /-əbli/ *adv*: *run a business profitably* ○ *She spent the weekend profitably.*

profiteering /ˌprɒfɪ'tɪərɪŋ/ *n* [U] (*derog*) the activity of deliberately making too large a profit, esp by exploiting people in difficult times, eg in a war or during FAMINE. ▶ **profiteer** *n*.

profiterole /prə'fɪtərəʊl/ *n* a small hollow bun of light pastry, usu filled with cream and covered with chocolate.

profligate /'prɒflɪgət/ *adj* (*fml derog*) using money, resources, etc in a way that wastes them; EXTRAVAGANT(1a): *profligate spending* ○ *a profligate lifestyle.* ▶ **profligacy** /'prɒflɪgəsi/ *n* [U] (*fml derog*) profligate behaviour, acts, etc: *financial profligacy.*

pro forma /ˌprəʊ 'fɔːmə/ *n* (*pl* **pro formas**) an (INVOICE) that gives details of goods being sent and is sent to the customer in advance of the goods themselves.

profound /prə'faʊnd/ *adj* **1** (*fml*) (of a state or quality) deep; intense; very great: *a profound silence/shock* ○ *have a profound distrust/dislike of sth* ○ *have a profound influence/effect on sth/sb* ○ *Since she'd left, changes to the company had been profound.* **2**(**a**) having or showing great knowledge or understanding of a subject: *a profound awareness of the problem* ○ *Her book is literate, thoughtful, at times profound.* (**b**) needing much study or thought: *the profound mystery of life.* ▶ **profoundly** *adv* deeply; extremely; to a very great extent: *a profoundly disturbing book* ○ *She was profoundly shaken by the news.* ○ *Our lives are **profoundly affected** by what happened to us in childhood.*

profundity /prə'fʌndəti/ *n* (*fml*) **1** [U] depth of knowledge, thought, etc: *a work that lacks profundity and analytical precision.* **2** [C esp *pl*] a statement, idea, etc that has deep meaning: *philosophical profundities.*

profuse /prə'fjuːs/ *adj* in large amounts; ABUNDANT: *profuse apologies/thanks* ○ *profuse bleeding.* ▶ **profusely** *adv*: *apologize/sweat profusely.* **profusion** /prə'fjuːʒn/ *n* [sing, U] ~ **of sth** (*fml*) a large quantity of sth: *a profusion of colours/flowers* ○ *Roses grew **in profusion** against the old wall.*

progenitor /prəʊ'dʒenɪtə(r)/ *n* (*fml*) **1** a person or a thing that comes before sth; an ancestor. **2** a person who originates an artistic, intellectual or political movement, etc: *the progenitors of modern art.*

progeny /'prɒdʒəni/ *n* [pl *v*] (*fml or joc*) the young of humans or animals: *He appeared, surrounded by his numerous progeny.* ○ (*fig*) *He claimed that modern science was not the progeny of* (ie a direct product of) *traditional science but a different subject altogether.*

progesterone /prə'dʒestərəʊn/ *n* [U] a sex HORMONE that prepares and maintains the WOMB for carrying a baby and is used in CONTRACEPTION because it prevents ovulation (OVULATE). Compare OESTROGEN.

prognosis /prɒg'nəʊsɪs/ *n* (*pl* **prognoses** /-siːz/) (**a**) a forecast of the probable development of sth: *The long-term prognosis for the company's future is very encouraging.* (**b**) (*medical*) a forecast of the likely course of a disease or an illness: *make a prognosis* ○ *The prognosis is not good.* Compare DIAGNOSIS.

prognostication /prɒgˌnɒstɪ'keɪʃn/ *n* (*fml*) a thing that is predicted: *His gloomy prognostications proved to be false.*

program /'prəʊgræm/ *n* **1** (*computing*) a series of instructions in code that control the operations of a computer: *a program written for financial analysts* ○ *a spreadsheet program* ○ *run a test program.* **2** (*US*) = PROGRAMME.

▶ **program** *v* (**-mm-**; *US* also **-m-**) **1** (*computing*) to instruct a computer, etc to do sth by putting a program into it: [V.n *to* inf] *The computer is programmed to warn users before information is deleted.* [also Vn]. **2** (*US*) = PROGRAMME *v*.

programmable /'prəʊgræməbl, prəʊ'græm-/ *adj* that can be controlled by a computer program: *a programmable remote control for the video.*

programme (*US* **program**) /'prəʊgræm/ *n* **1** a film, play, etc that is broadcast on television or radio: *an arts/discussion programme* ○ *Which programme do you want to watch?* ○ *Did you see the programme about/on Indian wildlife last night?* **2** a plan of future events, activities, etc: *draw up a training programme for new staff* ○ *launch a major investment programme* ○ *follow a fitness programme* ○ *What's the programme* (ie What are we going to do) *tomorrow?* **3**(**a**) a series of items in a concert, on a course of study, etc: *plan a programme of lectures for first-year students* ○ *The programme includes two Mozart sonatas.* (**b**) a printed piece of paper or thin book that gives information about an event, the names of the actors in a play, etc: *buy a theatre programme* ○ *look in the programme to see what time the fireworks start.*

▶ **programme** (*US* **program**) *v* (**-mm-**; *US* also **-m-**) (usu passive) **1** ~ **sth** (**for sth**) to make a programme or of for sth; to put sth on a programme; to plan or arrange sth: [Vnpr] *The final section of the motorway is programmed for completion next month.* [also Vn]. **2**(**a**) to cause sb/sth to do sth or behave in a particular way, esp automatically: [Vn.*to* inf] *A woman's body is programmed to produce as much milk as her baby needs.* (**b**) to give a machine instructions to do sth: [Vn.*to* inf] *The video is programmed to switch itself on at ten o'clock.* [also Vn].

■ **'programme music** *n* [U] music intended to suggest a story, picture, etc.

'programme note *n* a short description or explanation in a programme(3b) of a musical work, a play, an actor's career, etc.

programmer /'prəʊgræmə(r)/ *n* a person whose job is writing programs (PROGRAM 1) for computers.

programming /'prəʊgræmɪŋ/ *n* [U] **1** the activity of writing computer programs (PROGRAM 1): *a programming language* ○ *end-user programming.* **2** the selection of television or radio programmes by broadcasting companies: *politically balanced programming.*

progress /'prəʊgres; *US* 'prɒg-/ *n* [U] **1** forward movement: *The walkers were making slow progress up the rocky path.* ○ *The yacht made good progress with a following wind.* **2** advance or development, esp towards a better state: *evolutionary/scientific/technological progress* ○ *the progress of civilization* ○ *My son is making good progress at school.* ○ *The patient is making slow progress after her operation.* ○ *Strike leaders have reported some progress in the talks to settle the dispute.* ○ *ask for a 'progress report on the situation.* **IDM** **in progress** (*fml*) being done or made: *The discussion/trial/inquiry is now in progress.* ○ *Please be quiet — examination in progress.*

▶ **progress** /prə'gres/ *v* **1** to make progress; to advance or develop towards a better or finished state: [V] *She progressed very slowly after the accident.* ○ *I asked how the sale of the house was progressing.* ○ *In some ways, civilization does not seem to have progressed much in the last century.* **2** to move forward in time: [V] *The weather became colder as the day progressed.*

progression /prə'greʃn/ *n* (*fml*) **1** [U] ~ (**from sth**)

(to sth) the process of moving forward or developing, esp in stages or gradually: *career progression* ∘ *follow a natural/logical progression from childhood to adolescence.* **2** [C] a sequence or series: *a long progression of sunny days.*

progressive /prə'gresɪv/ *adj* **1(a)** (*approv*) advancing in social conditions or efficiency: *a progressive firm/nation.* **(b)** favouring or showing rapid progress or reform: *progressive ideas* ∘ *progressive schools/education* ∘ *progressive reforms* ∘ *a progressive political party.* **2** happening or developing steadily: *a progressive disease* ∘ *a progressive reduction in the number of staff.*
▶ **progressive** *n* [usu pl] a person who supports a progressive(1b) policy or adopts progressive methods: *political battles between progressives and conservatives.*
progressively *adv* (often with a comparative) increasingly; by degrees: *get progressively harder/slower/weaker* ∘ *His eyesight is becoming progressively worse.*
progressivism *n* [U]: *political/social progressivism.*
■ **pro'gressive tense** *n* = CONTINUOUS TENSE.

prohibit /prə'hɪbɪt; *US* prəʊ-/ *v* (*fml*) **1** ~ **sth**; ~ **sb (from doing sth)** (esp passive) to forbid sth or sb from doing sth, esp by laws, rules or regulations: [Vn] *Parking without a permit is prohibited.* [Vnpr] *He was prohibited from taking part in the vote.* **2** to make sth impossible; to prevent sth: [Vn] *The high cost prohibits the widespread use of the drug.*

prohibition /ˌprəʊɪ'bɪʃn; *US* ˌprəʊə'bɪʃn/ *n* **1** [U] the action of forbidding sth or the state of being forbidden: *the prohibition of alcohol/drugs* ∘ *They voted in favour of the prohibition of smoking in public areas.* **2** [C] ~ **(against sth)** a law or regulation that forbids sth: *a prohibition against shops opening on Sunday.* **3 Prohibition** [U] a period of time (1920–1933) when the making and selling of alcoholic drinks was forbidden by law in the USA.
▶ **prohibitionist** /-ʃənɪst/ *n* a person who supports the prohibition of sth by law, esp the sale of alcoholic drinks.

prohibitive /prə'hɪbətɪv; *US* prəʊ-/ *adj* **1(a)** preventing or intending to prevent people using or buying sth: *a prohibitive tax on imported cars.* **(b)** (of prices, etc) so high that one cannot afford to buy: *prohibitive costs* ∘ *The cost of property in the city is prohibitive.* **2** that prohibits: *prohibitive legislation/regulations.* ▶ **prohibitively** *adv*: *Private medical care is becoming prohibitively expensive.*

project¹ /'prɒdʒekt/ *n* **1(a)** a piece of work, etc that is organized carefully and designed to achieve a particular aim; a plan: *a research project* ∘ *set up an inner city housing project* ∘ *run a conservation project to protect wildlife.* **(b)** any planned activity: *a knitting/writing project.* **2** a piece of school or college work in which students do their own research and present the results: *a history project* ∘ *My class is doing a project on the First World War.*

project² /prə'dʒekt/ *v* **1** (esp passive) **(a)** to plan a scheme, an activity, etc: [Vn] *a projected collaboration between two major research institutions* ∘ *a projected road improvement scheme.* **(b)** to estimate sth, esp a change in the size, amount or cost of sth: [Vn] *projected growth/profits/results* ∘ *a projected deficit of £8 million* ∘ *the increased fuel consumption projected by British Gas* [Vn.to inf] *The unemployment rate is projected to fall by 7%.* **2** ~ **sth (into sth)** to send or throw sth outwards or forward: [Vnpr] *an apparatus to project missiles into space* [Vn] *Actors must learn to project their voices.* [also Vnadv]. **3** ~ **sth (on/onto sth)** to cause light, shadow, a photographic image, etc to fall on a surface: [Vnpr] *project spotlights onto the stage* ∘ *Images are projected onto the retina of the eye.* [also Vn]. **4** to extend outwards beyond a surface: [V] *a projecting*

beam [Vpr] *a balcony that projects over the street.* **5** to present sth/sb/oneself to others in a way that creates a strong or favourable impression: [Vn] *try to project an image of reliability and strength.* **PHRV** **pro'ject sth onto sb** (*psychology*) to think, esp in an unconscious way, that sb shares one's own feelings, usu unpleasant ones: *You mustn't project your guilt onto me* (ie assume that I feel as guilty as you do).

projectile /prə'dʒektaɪl; *US* -tl/ *n* (*fml or techn*) **(a)** an object that is or is designed to be shot forward, esp from a gun: *fire a projectile.* **(b)** any object thrown as a weapon.

projection /prə'dʒekʃn/ *n* **1** [C] an estimate of future situations or trends (TREND), etc based on a study of present ones: *sales projections for the next financial year* ∘ *Our original projection has now been revised downwards.* **2(a)** [U] the action of projecting sth: *the projection of images onto a screen* ∘ *the projection of one's feelings onto others.* **(b)** [C] a thing that is projected, esp a mental image viewed as reality. **3** [C] a thing that extends outwards from a surface: *a projection of rock from the cliff-face.*
▶ **projectionist** /-ʃənɪst/ *n* a person whose job is to project films onto a screen, esp in a cinema.

projector /prə'dʒektə(r)/ *n* an apparatus for projecting photographs or films onto a screen: *a 'slide projector* ∘ *The projector broke down.*

prolapse /'prəʊlæps/ *n* (*medical*) a condition in which an organ of the body has slipped forward or down so as to be out of place: *a uterine prolapse.* ▶ **prolapsed** /prəʊ'læpst/ *adj*: *a prolapsed womb.*

proletarian /ˌprəʊlə'teəriən/ *adj* (often *derog*) of or concerning the PROLETARIAT: *a proletarian novel* ∘ *a proletarian revolution.*

proletariat /ˌprəʊlə'teəriət/ *n* **the proletariat** [Gp] (*dated or derog*) the class of workers who do not own the means of production and who earn their living by working for wages, esp in industry: *the growth of the urban proletariat* ∘ *Communism aimed to establish the dictatorship of the proletariat.* Compare BOURGEOISIE.

proliferate /prə'lɪfəreɪt/ *v* **1** (of plants, animals and cells) to reproduce rapidly; to multiply: [V] *cancer cells proliferating* ∘ *a pond in which minute organisms proliferate.* **2** to increase rapidly in numbers: [V] *At Christmastime biographies of the famous proliferate in the bookshops.*
▶ **proliferation** /prəˌlɪfə'reɪʃn/ *n* [U,sing] **(a)** a rapid growth or increase in numbers: *the proliferation of cancer cells* ∘ *the danger of nuclear proliferation* (ie the spread of nuclear weapons to countries that do not already possess them). **(b)** a large number of a particular thing: *Buyers are confused by the sheer proliferation of models available.*

prolific /prə'lɪfɪk/ *adj* **1** (of plants, animals, etc) producing a lot of fruit, flowers, young, etc: *prolific vegetation* ∘ *a prolific harvest* ∘ *prolific milk yields.* **2** (of a writer, an artist, etc) producing many works: *a prolific author* ∘ *a prolific period in the composer's life* ∘ *In later years, she became even more prolific.* ▶ **prolifically** /-kli/ *adv*: *a prolifically flowering plant.*

prolix /'prəʊlɪks; *US* prəʊ'lɪks/ *adj* (*fml*) (of a speech, writer, etc) using too many words and therefore boring to listen to or read: *writing that is prolix and unfocussed* ∘ *a prolix speaker.* ▶ **prolixity** /prəʊ'lɪksəti/ *n* [U].

prologue (*US* also **prolog**) /'prəʊlɒg; *US* -lɔːg/ *n* ~ **(to sth)** **1** a separate part of a poem or play that introduces it: *a short prologue* ∘ *the 'Prologue' to the 'Canterbury Tales'.* Compare EPILOGUE. **2** an act or event that is an introduction to sth or leads up to sth; the first in a series of events: *The signing of the agreement was a prologue to better relations between the two countries.*

prolong /prə'lɒŋ; *US* -'lɔːŋ/ *v* to make sth last longer; to extend sth: [Vn] *drugs that help to prolong*

life ○ *They prolonged their visit by a few days.* ○ *Don't prolong the agony — just tell us who's won!*
► **prolongation** /ˌprəʊlɒŋˈɡeɪʃn; US -lɔːŋ-/ n [U] (*fml*) the action of prolonging sth: *the artificial prolongation of human life* ○ *further atrocities that led to the prolongation of the war.*

prolonged *adj* [usu attrib] continuing for a long time: *prolonged negotiations* ○ *a prolonged absence* ○ *skin damage resulting from prolonged exposure to the sun* ○ *endure a **prolonged period** of economic uncertainty.*

prom /prɒm/ n (*infml*) **1** (*Brit*) = PROMENADE CONCERT: *go to the last night of the proms.* **2** (*Brit*) = PROMENADE 1. **3** (*US*) a formal dance, esp one held by a class in high school (HIGH¹) or college at the end of a term.

promenade /ˌprɒməˈnɑːd; US -ˈneɪd/ n **1** (*Brit infml* prom) a public place for walking, esp one beside the sea at a resort: *stroll along the promenade at Brighton.* **2** (*dated or fml*) a walk or ride taken in public for exercise or pleasure.
► **promenade** v (*dated or fml*) to take a relaxed walk or ride in public, esp in order to meet or be seen by others.
■ ˌpromenade ˈconcert (also *infml* prom) n (*Brit*) a concert at which part of the audience stands or sits on the floor.

prominent /ˈprɒmɪnənt/ *adj* **1** distinguished or important: *play a prominent part/role in sth* ○ *a prominent politician/activist/dissident* ○ *She was prominent in the fashion industry.* **2** easily seen: *the most prominent feature in the landscape* ○ *The house is in a prominent position in the town square.* **3** projecting from sth: *prominent cheek-bones/teeth.*
► **prominence** /-əns/ n [U, sing] the state of being prominent: *a young actor who has recently come/risen/shot to prominence* ○ *The newspapers are giving undue prominence to the story.*
prominently *adv*: *issues that are expected to figure/feature prominently in the debate* ○ *The notice was prominently displayed.*

promiscuous /prəˈmɪskjuəs/ *adj* (*derog*) **1** having many sexual partners: *promiscuous behaviour* ○ *a promiscuous society* ○ *She did not regard herself as promiscuous.* **2** (*fml*) not carefully chosen: *the promiscuous use of words like 'nice' or 'good'* (ie when sth should be described more exactly). ► **promiscuity** /ˌprɒmɪˈskjuːəti/ n [U]: *sexual promiscuity.*

promise¹ /ˈprɒmɪs/ n **1** [C] ~ (**of sth**) a written or spoken declaration that one will definitely give or do or not do sth: *keep/make/break/go back on a promise* ○ *extract a promise from sb* ○ *The government failed to keep its election promise of more arts funding.* ○ (*ironic*) *'I'll never come and see you again.' 'Is that a promise?'* **2** [U] an indication of future success or good results: *Her work/She **shows** great promise.* ○ *He failed to fulfil his early promise.* **3** [U, sing] ~ **of sth** an indication that sth may be expected to come or occur; a possibility or hope of sth: *a promise of future happiness* ○ *The day dawned bright and clear with the promise of warmth and sunshine.*

promise² /ˈprɒmɪs/ v **1** ~ **sth** (**to sb**) to make a promise to sb; to tell sb that one will definitely give or do or not do sth: [V] *I can't promise, but I'll do my best.* [Vn] *The president has promised a thorough investigation into the affair.* ○ *The promised aid was not forthcoming.* [V.to inf] *He promised to help me.* ○ *You've got to promise not to tell anyone.* [Vnn] *I have promised myself a quiet weekend.* ○ *She promised her grandson an ice-cream if he stopped crying.* [Vnpr] *I can't lend you my bike — I've promised it to Sally.* [Vn.that] *She promised me (that) she would be there.* [V.that] *'Promise you won't forget!' 'I promise.'* [also V.speech]. **2** (*fml*) to make sth seem likely: [Vn] *The clouds promised rain.* [V.to inf] *It promises to be*

warm this afternoon. **IDM** **I (can) ¹promise you** (*infml*) (used as a form of encouragement or as a threat) you can be sure: *You'll really enjoy it, I promise you.* ○ *If you don't stop messing around, you'll regret it, I promise you!* **promise (sb) the ¹earth/¹moon** (*infml*) to make promises that one is unlikely to be able to keep: *Politicians promise the earth before an election, but things are different once they are in power.*
■ **the ˌpromised ¹land** n [sing] any place or situation in which one expects to find happiness and security: *reach the promised land of equal equality.*
► **promising** *adj* (**a**) likely to do well; full of promise¹ (2): *a promising newcomer* ○ *He was voted the most promising young player of 1993.* (**b**) indicating future success or good results; hopeful: *The weather doesn't look too promising.* ○ *'I've been called for a second interview.' 'That sounds promising.'* ○ *His cough is better now, so that's a promising sign.*
promisingly *adv*: *The day started promisingly enough, but by lunchtime it began to rain.*

promissory note /ˈprɒmɪsəri nəʊt/ n a signed document containing a promise to pay a stated sum of money on demand or on a specified date.

promo /ˈprəʊməʊ/ *adj* [attrib], n (*infml*) (of or relating to) publicity for a performer or a commercial product: *make a short promo video.*

promontory /ˈprɒməntəri; US -tɔːri/ n an area of high land that extends out into the sea or a lake. ⇨ picture at COAST.

promote /prəˈməʊt/ v **1** to help the progress of sth; to encourage or support sth: [Vn] *an organization that aims to promote enjoyment of the countryside* ○ *a training course that promotes better communication between employers and their staff* ○ *a harmless drug that helps to promote sleep.* **2** to give publicity to sth in order to sell it: [Vn] *promote a record/film/product* ○ *a publicity campaign to promote her new book* ○ *We're promoting it worldwide.* **3** ~ **sb** (**from sth**) (**to sth**) (esp passive) to raise sb to a higher position or rank: [Vn] *She worked hard and was soon promoted.* [Vnpr] *He was promoted to sergeant/sales manager.* ○ *be promoted from the ranks* ○ *He's celebrating — his football team has been promoted to the First Division.* Compare DEMOTE.
► **promoter** n (**a**) a person or company that organizes sth or provides the money for sth, esp an artistic performance or a sporting event: *a boxing promoter* ○ *the show's UK promoters.* (**b**) ~ **of sth** a supporter of sth: *an enthusiastic promoter of many good causes.*

promotion /prəˈməʊʃn/ n **1(a)** [U] the process of raising sb or of being raised to a higher position or more important job: *a job with excellent promotion prospects* ○ *the team's promotion from Division 2 to Division 1* ○ *apply for/gain/win promotion.* (**b**) [C] an instance of this: *a well-deserved promotion* ○ *The new job is a promotion for her.* **2(a)** [U] advertising or some other activity intended to increase the sales of a product or service: *She is responsible for sales promotion.* ○ *ban tabacco promotion.* (**b**) [C] an advertising or publicity campaign for a particular product: *book/record promotions* ○ *We are doing a special promotion of our paperback list.* **3** [U] ~ **of sth** activity that helps or encourages the progress or success of an aim, a principle or a movement: *They worked for the promotion of world peace.*
► **promotional** /-ʃənl/ *adj* of or relating to promotion(2): *promotional activities/material/work* ○ *a promotional tour by the author.* See also PROMO.

prompt¹ /prɒmpt/ *adj* **1** done without delay; immediate: *a prompt reply* ○ *Prompt payment of the invoice would be greatly appreciated.* **2** ~ (**in doing sth**) (of a person) acting without delay: *We are always prompt in paying our bills.*

[V.speech] = verb + direct speech   [V.*that*] = verb + *that* clause   [V.*wh*] = verb + *who, how,* etc clause

P

▶ **prompt** *adv* (in relation to a specified time) exactly: *at 6 o'clock prompt.*

promptly *adv* **1** without delay: *act promptly in an emergency.* **2** exactly at the time specified: *They left promptly at 5 o'clock.* **3** (used when sth is done in an amusing, sudden or unexpected way): *He shouted 'Mind the wire', leapt the fence and promptly fell over.*

promptness *n* [U]: *act with great promptness and efficiency.*

prompt² /prɒmpt/ *v* **1** to inspire or cause a feeling or an action: [Vn] *The ban on smoking was prompted by complaints from members of staff.* ○ *What prompted that remark, I wonder?* **2** to cause sb to do sth: [Vn.to inf] *What prompted him to be so generous?* ○ *The accident prompted her to renew her insurance.* [also Vn]. **3(a)** to help a speaker by suggesting the words that could or should follow: [Vn] *The speaker was rather hesitant and had to be prompted occasionally by the chairman.* [V.speech] *'And then what happened?' he prompted.* **(b)** to follow the text of a play and help an actor if he or she forgets the words, by saying the next line quietly: [V] *Will you prompt for us at the next performance?* [Vn] *The leading actor had to be prompted several times.*

▶ **prompt** *n* an act of prompting or words spoken to prompt an actor, a speaker, etc: *She needed an occasional prompt.*

prompter *n* a person who prompts in a play.

prompting *n* [C,U] an act of urging or persuading sb to do sth: *Despite several promptings from his parents the boy refused to apologize.* ○ *He did it without any prompting from me.*

promulgate /ˈprɒmlgeɪt/ *v* (*fml*) **(a)** to make sth widely known: [Vn] *promulgate a belief/an idea/a theory.* **(b)** to announce a new law, etc officially; to PROCLAIM(1) sth: [Vn] *The American Declaration of Independence was promulgated in January 1776.* ▶ **promulgation** /ˌprɒmlˈgeɪʃn/ *n* [U]: *the promulgation of a treaty.*

prone /prəʊn/ *adj* **1** [pred] ~ **to sth / to do sth** likely to suffer from, do or get sth: *be prone to illness/infection/injury* ○ *land prone to flooding* ○ *Such marriages are particularly/notoriously prone to fail.* See also ACCIDENT-PRONE. Compare LIABLE 2,3. **2** lying flat, esp with one's face downwards: *lying prone* ○ *in a prone position.* Compare PROSTRATE 1, SUPINE 1. ▶ **proneness** /ˈprəʊnnəs/ *n* [U]: *proneness to injury.*

prong /prɒŋ; *US* prɔːŋ/ *n* each of the two or more long pointed parts of a fork: *One of the prongs of the garden fork went through his foot.* ⇨ picture at FORK.

▶ **-pronged** (forming compound *adjs*) having the number or type of prongs specified: *a ˌfour-pronged ˈfork* ○ (*fig*) *a ˌthree-pronged atˈtack* (ie one made by three separate forces, usu advancing from different directions).

pronominal /prəʊˈnɒmɪnl/ *adj* (*grammar*) of or like a pronoun: *a pronominal reference to an object* (ie the use of the word 'it' to replace the name of the object).

pronoun /ˈprəʊnaʊn/ *n* (*grammar*) (abbreviated as *pron* in this dictionary) a word used in place of a noun or noun phrase, eg *he, it, hers, me, them,* etc: *demonstrative/interrogative/possessive/relative pronouns.* See also PERSONAL PRONOUN.

pronounce /prəˈnaʊns/ *v* **1** to make the sound of a word or letter in a particular way: [Vn] *People pronounce words like 'castle' and 'bath' differently in different parts of the country.* ○ *Very few people can pronounce my name properly.* ○ *The 'b' in 'debt' is not pronounced.* See also PRONUNCIATION, UNPRONOUNCEABLE. **2** to declare or announce sth, esp formally, solemnly or officially: [Vn] *pronounce an opinion/a judgement* [Vn-adj] *She was pronounced dead on arrival at the hospital.* [Vn-n] *The play was pronounced*

a success. [V.that] *The doctor pronounced that he was fit enough to return to work.* [V.speech] *'It's definitely an antique,' he pronounced.* **PHRV** **proˈnounce (sth) for/against sb/sth** (*law*) to pass judgement in court in favour of/against sb/sth: *pronounce (sentence) against the accused.* **proˈnounce on/upon sth** to express one's opinion on sth, esp formally: *Only an unwise critic would pronounce on the artist's meaning.*

▶ **pronounceable** /-əbl/ *adj* (of sounds or words) that can be pronounced: *I find some of the place-names barely pronounceable.*

pronounced *adj* **1** very noticeable: *He walked with a pronounced limp.* **2** (of opinions, etc) strongly felt; definite: *She has very pronounced views about art.*

pronouncement *n* ~ **(on sth)** a formal statement or declaration: *make an official pronouncement on changes in transport policy.*

pronto /ˈprɒntəʊ/ *adv* (*infml*) at once; quickly: *It's got to be done pronto!*

pronunciation /prəˌnʌnsiˈeɪʃn/ *n* **1(a)** [U] the way in which a language is spoken: *a student's guide to English pronunciation.* **(b)** [C] the way in which a word is pronounced: *What is the correct pronunciation of this word?* **2** the way a person speaks the words of a language: *His pronunciation of English is still not good, but it is improving.*

proof¹ /pruːf/ *n* **1** [U] evidence that shows, or helps to show, that sth is true or is a fact: *ask sb for proof of identity/ownership* ○ *provide written/scientific/legal proof* ○ *We need more proof before we can accuse him of stealing.* ○ *The size of the audience was proof of his popularity.* **2** [C esp *pl*] a test copy of printed material produced so that mistakes can be corrected: *check/correct/read the proofs of a book* ○ *colour proofs* (ie of a book, etc with colour photographs or illustrations). **3** [U] a measure of the strength of alcoholic drinks in which the strongest measure is 100%: *This whisky is 70% proof.* **4** [U] the testing of whether sth is true or a fact: *Is the claim capable of proof?* **IDM** **be living proof of sth/that…** ⇨ LIVING¹. **the proof of the ˈpudding (is in the ˈeating)** (*saying*) the real value of sth/sth can be judged only from practical experience and not from appearance or theory.

proof² /pruːf/ *adj* **1** [pred] ~ **against sth** (*fml*) **(a)** providing protection against sth: *Their clothing was not proof against the bitter weather.* **(b)** that can resist sth: *proof against temptation.* **2** (in compounds) that can resist sth or protect against sth specified: *dishwasher-proof plates* ○ *rainproof/windproof clothing* ○ *medicine bottles with childproof caps.* See also DAMP-PROOF COURSE, BULLETPROOF, FIREPROOF, SOUNDPROOF, WATERPROOF.

▶ **proof** *v* [Vn] (*fml*) to treat sth in order to make it proof against sth, esp fabric in order to make it WATERPROOF.

proofread /ˈpruːfriːd/ *v* (*pt, pp* **-read** /-red/) to read and correct a piece of written or printed work: [Vn] *proofread four pages an hour* ○ *be/get paid £8.50 an hour for proofreading.* **ˈproofreader** *n*: *work as a proofreader for a publishing company.*

prop¹ /prɒp/ *n* **1** a piece of wood, metal, etc used to support sth or keep sth in position: *Props were used to prevent the roof collapsing.* ⇨ picture. See also PIT-PROP. **2** a person or thing that gives help or support to sb/sth: *He doesn't think of her as a person, just as an emotional prop.* **3** (*sport*) (in Rugby) a player at either side of the front row of a SCRUM(1).

▶ **prop** *v* (**-pp-**) **(a)** to support sth or keep sth in position: *Her patient lay propped on the pillows.* [Vn-adj] *He used a box to prop the door open/ajar.* [also Vn]. **(b)** ~ **sb/sth (up) against sth** to lean sb/sth against sth: [Vnpr] *a bicycle propped against the wall* ○ *He propped his guitar against a speaker.* [also Vnpl]. ⇨ picture. **PHRV** **ˌprop sth ˈup 1** to

prop

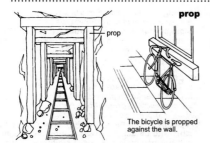

prop

The bicycle is propped against the wall.

raise sth and support it by putting sth under it or against it: *The roof will have to be propped up while repairs are carried out.* ○ *A five-month-old baby cannot sit unaided — she has to be propped up with pillows.* ○ *He propped himself up on one elbow.* **2** (*often derog*) to support sth that would otherwise fail: *The industry is propped up by the government.*
■ **'prop-word** *n* (*grammar*) the word *one* (or *ones*) when used to stand for a noun, esp a noun that has been mentioned previously, as in *'Which piece would you like?' 'I'd like the bigger one.'*

prop² /prɒp/ (also *fml* **property**) *n* (usu *pl*) a movable object used on a theatre stage, in a film, etc: *stage props* ○ *personal props.*

propaganda /ˌprɒpəˈgændə/ *n* [U] (*usu derog*) ideas or statements that are intended as publicity for a particular cause, esp a political one, and are often exaggerated or false: *a propaganda campaign/ exercise/message* ○ *be subjected to enemy propaganda* ○ *The play is sheer political propaganda.*
▶ **propagandist** /-dɪst/ *n* (*often derog*) a person who creates or spreads propaganda: *propagandists for the government* ○ *a political propagandist* ○ *propagandist films* ○ *a propagandist organization.*
propagandize, -ise /-daɪz/ *v* [V] (*fml usu derog*) to spread or organize propaganda.

propagate /ˈprɒpəgeɪt/ *v* **1** (*fml*) to spread an idea, a belief, knowledge, etc more widely: [Vn] *religious leaders who travelled overseas to propagate their faith.* **2(a)** to grow and increase the number of plants: [Vn] *propagate plants from seeds and cuttings.* **(b)** (of plants) to reproduce: [V] *Plants won't propagate in these conditions.* [Vn] *Trees propagate themselves by seeds.*
▶ **propagation** /ˌprɒpəˈgeɪʃn/ *n* [U]: *the propagation of plants from cuttings.*
propagator *n* a thing that propagates: *tomato plants growing in a heated propagator* (ie a glass or plastic box that keeps them warm).

propane /ˈprəʊpeɪn/ *n* [U] a colourless gas found in natural gas and PETROLEUM and used as a fuel.

propel /prəˈpel/ *v* (-ll-) **1** to move, drive or push sth/ sb forward: [Vn] *mechanically propelled vehicles* ○ *a boat propelled by eight oars.* **2** to move sb forcefully in a particular direction or into a particular situation: [Vnpr] *A hand on her shoulder propelled her along the corridor at amazing speed.* ○ *His addiction to drugs propelled him towards a life of crime.* [also Vnp, Vnadv].
▶ **propellant** (also **propellent**) /-ənt/ *n* [C, U] **(a)** a thing or substance that propels sth, eg the fuel that fires a ROCKET(2a). **(b)** a gas that forces out the contents of an AEROSOL container.
propeller *n* a device with two or more blades, fixed to a revolving rod for propelling a ship or an aircraft: *start the propellers.*
■ **pro,pelling 'pencil** *n* a pencil with a lead³(2) that can be moved down for writing by turning or pushing the top of the pencil.

propensity /prəˈpensəti/ *n* ~ (**for/to sth**); ~ (**for doing / to do sth**) (*fml*) a tendency to do sth, esp sth

undesirable: *show a propensity for/to violence* ○ *She has a propensity to exaggerate.* ○ *He shows a marked propensity for getting into debt.*

proper /ˈprɒpə(r)/ *adj* **1(a)** [attrib] genuine; being in fact what it is called: *ensure that sb receives proper training/care* ○ *She hadn't had a proper holiday for years.* ○ *Make sure you have a proper breakfast, not just a cup of coffee!* **(b)** (following *ns*) in its true form; itself: *Students do a year's foundation course before they start the degree course proper.* **2(a)** that fits, belongs or is suitable; appropriate: *use the proper tool for the job* ○ *This isn't the proper lid for this pan but it will do for now.* **(b)** [attrib] according to the rules; right or correct: *the proper way to hold the bat* ○ *maintain the proper standards of professional conduct* ○ *Please put the books back in their proper places.* ○ *I can't help with your application; you will have to go through the proper channels.* Compare RIGHT¹ 1. **3** according to or respecting social conventions; respectable: *I'm not sure that's a proper subject for a school debate.* ○ *He always behaves in a rather formal and proper way.* Compare IMPROPER. See also PROPRIETY. **4** [attrib] (*infml*) thorough; complete: *We're in a proper mess now.* ○ *Please give this room a proper clean.*
▶ **properly** *adv* in a correct or suitable way: *behave properly* ○ *not properly equipped/trained* ○ *The photocopier isn't working properly.*
■ **,proper 'noun** (also **,proper 'name**) *n* (*grammar*) a name of a person, place, institution, etc, written with a CAPITAL¹(3) letter at the start, eg *Jane, Mr Smith, Paris, Europe, the Rhine, the Houses of Parliament.*

property /ˈprɒpəti/ *n* **1** [U] a thing or things owned; a possession or possessions: *government property* ○ *Be careful not to damage other people's property.* ○ *He was charged with being in possession of stolen property.* **2(a)** [U] land and buildings: *property owners* ○ *buy/sell property* ○ *invest money in property* ○ *the property market* ○ *a property developer* ○ *Private Property — Keep Out.* **(b)** [C] (*fml*) a piece of land and its buildings: *industrial/residential properties* ○ *own a property in the West Country* ○ *A fence divides the two properties.* **3** [C esp *pl*] (*fml*) a special quality or characteristic that sth has: *compare the physical properties of two substances* ○ *Certain plants have medicinal* (ie healing) *properties.* **4** [C usu *pl*] (*fml*) = PROP². See also INTELLECTUAL PROPERTY, PUBLIC PROPERTY.
▶ **propertied** /ˈprɒpətid/ *adj* (*fml*) owning property, esp land: *The tax will affect only the propertied classes.*

prophecy /ˈprɒfəsi/ *n* **(a)** [C] a statement that tells what will happen in the future: *a self-fulfilling prophecy* ○ *religious prophecies.* **(b)** [U] the power of saying what will happen in the future: *He seemed to have the gift of prophecy.*

prophesy /ˈprɒfəsaɪ/ *v* (*pt, pp* **-sied**) to say what will happen in the future: [Vn] *prophesy disaster* [V.that] *As a young man, he prophesied that he would be the England captain by the age of 25.* [also V.speech].

prophet /ˈprɒfɪt/ *n* **1(a)** [C] (esp in the Christian, Jewish and Muslim religions) a person who teaches religion and is, or claims to be, inspired by God: *an Old Testament prophet* ○ *Hebrew prophets.* **(b)** the **Prophet** [sing] Muhammad, who founded the Muslim religion. **2** [C] a person who says, or claims to be able to say, what will happen in the future: *If we had listened to all you prophets of doom* (ie people who express negative opinions), *we would never have started the project.* **3** [C] ~ (**of sth**) a person who speaks for or tries to spread a new belief, cause, theory, etc: *William Morris was one of the early prophets of socialism.*

prophetess /ˈprɒfɪtes, ˌprɒfɪˈtes/ *n* a woman who is a PROPHET.

P

prophetic /prəˈfetɪk/ adj (fml) **1** describing or showing what will happen in the future: curiously prophetic remarks ∘ a prophetic warning. **2** of or relating to a PROPHET or prophets: the prophetic books of the Old Testament ∘ prophetic zeal. ▶ **prophetically** /-kli/ adv: 'He will know before long,' she added prophetically.

prophylactic /ˌprɒfɪˈlæktɪk/ adj (medical) tending to prevent a disease: prophylactic treatment. ▶ **prophylactic** n (fml or techn) **1** a prophylactic medicine, device or course of action. **2** (esp US) = CONDOM.

propinquity /prəˈpɪŋkwəti/ n [U] (fml) (a) the state of being near in space or time: live in close propinquity to each other. (b) close family relationship.

propitiate /prəˈpɪʃieɪt/ v (fml) to win the favour of sb, esp sb who is IMPATIENT(1) or angry, by a pleasing act: [Vn] They offered sacrifices to propitiate the gods. ▶ **propitiation** /prəˌpɪʃiˈeɪʃn/ n [U] ~ (for sth): in propitiation for their sins. **propitiatory** /prəˈpɪʃiətri; US -tɔːri/ adj (fml) intended to propitiate sb.

propitious /prəˈpɪʃəs/ adj ~ (for sth/sb) (to do sth) (fml) giving or indicating a good chance of success; favourable: It was not a propitious time to start a new business. ∘ Circumstances could hardly be less propitious for a strike. ▶ **propitiously** adv: The holiday began propitiously but then everything started to go wrong.

proponent /prəˈpəʊnənt/ n ~ (of sth) (fml) a person who supports a cause, theory, etc: one of the leading proponents of aromatherapy.

proportion /prəˈpɔːʃn/ n **1** [CGp] a part or share of a whole; a fraction(1): Water covers a large proportion of the earth's surface. ∘ The proportion of regular smokers increases sharply with age. ∘ A higher proportion of Americans go on to higher education than is the case in Britain. **2** [U] ~ (of sth to sth) the relationship of one thing to another in quantity, size, etc; RATIO: The proportion of men to women in the college has changed dramatically over the years. ∘ The basic ingredients are limestone and clay in the proportion 2:1. **3** [U, C usu pl] a correct or ideal relationship in size, degree, etc between one thing and another, or between the parts of a whole: It is rare for the iron and silica to be present in just the right proportions. ∘ A garden design should reflect nature in shape, proportion and size. **4** proportions [pl] measurements or dimensions; size: a food shortage that could soon reach alarming proportions ∘ a room of modest proportions. **5** [U] (mathematics) the equal relationship between two pairs of numbers: '4 is to 8 as 6 is to 12' is a statement of proportion. **IDM** **in proˈportion** in the correct relation to other things: You haven't drawn the figures in the foreground in proportion. ∘ The problem of hooliganism should be kept in proportion — only a small number of young people act in this way. ∘ Her figure is perfectly in proportion. **in proˈportion to sth** relative to sth: The garden is very long in proportion to its width. **out of (all) proˈportion (to sth)** larger, more serious, etc in relation to sth than is necessary or appropriate: They earn salaries out of all proportion to their ability. ∘ The media have blown the incident up out of all proportion. **out of proˈportion (to sth)** in the wrong relation to other things: I've drawn the head out of proportion to (the size of) the body. ∘ a severe punishment that was out of proportion to the crime. ▶ **proportioned** adj (esp in compounds) having the proportions (PROPORTION 4) as specified: a well proportioned room ∘ his perfectly proportioned body.

proportional /prəˈpɔːʃənl/ adj ~ (to sth) (fml) corresponding in size, amount or degree to sth; in the correct proportion: For a joint of meat, the length of cooking time is proportional to its weight. ▶ **propor-**

tionally /-ʃənəli/ adv: Farmers pay proportionally less for water than urban ratepayers.
■ **proˌportional ˌrepresenˈtation** n [U] (abbr PR) a system that gives each party in an election a number of seats in relation to the number of votes its candidates receive. Compare FIRST PAST THE POST (POST¹).

proportionate /prəˈpɔːʃənət/ adj ~ (to sth) (fml) in proportion to sth; PROPORTIONAL: Increasing production costs resulted in proportionate price increases for the consumer. ▶ **proportionately** adv: Costs have risen, and prices will rise proportionately.

proposal /prəˈpəʊzl/ n **1(a)** [C] ~ (for sth / doing sth); ~ (to do sth) a suggestion; a plan or scheme: put forward a proposal for better health care ∘ submit a proposal to build more office accommodation ∘ Various proposals were examined and rejected. (b) [U] the action of suggesting sth or putting sth forward: the proposal of new terms for a peace treaty. **2** [C] an offer of marriage, esp from a man to a woman: She had had/received many proposals (of marriage) but preferred to remain single.

propose /prəˈpəʊz/ v **1** to offer or put forward sth for consideration; to suggest sth: [Vn] a proposed visit ∘ proposed cuts in public spending ∘ a ban on tobacco advertising proposed by the European Commission ∘ The government is proposing changes to the current legislation. [V.that] It was proposed that membership fees should be increased. [V.ing] She proposed setting up a new committee. Compare SECOND⁴, OPPOSE. **2** to have sth as one's plan or intention; to intend: [V.to inf] I propose to make an early start tomorrow. [V.ing] How do you propose getting home? [also Vn]. **3** ~ (sth) (to sb) to suggest or offer marriage to sb, esp formally: [V, Vpr] He was trying to decide whether he should propose (to her). [Vn] He had proposed marriage, unsuccessfully, twice already. [also Vnpr]. **4** ~ sb for sth; ~ sb as sth to put forward sb as a member of a society, for a position, etc; to NOMINATE(1a) sb: [Vnpr, Vn-n] I propose Mary Kelly for membership/as chairman of the committee. [also Vn]. **IDM** **propose sb's ˈhealth** to ask people to drink to sb's health and happiness: I would like to propose the health of the bride and bridegroom. **propose a ˈmotion** to be the main speaker in favour of a formal proposal in a debate. ▶ **proposer** n a person who proposes sth/sb, esp a motion(3) or a candidate for a position, etc. Compare SECONDER.

proposition /ˌprɒpəˈzɪʃn/ n **1** a thing that is proposed, esp in business; a suggestion: a viable business/commercial proposition ∘ The fact that we won't have to pay transport costs makes it an **attractive proposition** for us. **2** (infml) a matter to be dealt with; a problem or task: Writing a biography of a living person is a tricky proposition. **3** ~ (that...) a statement that expresses a judgement or an opinion: The proposition that the individual is more important than society is common in Western philosophy. ▶ **proposition** v to propose having sex to sb, esp in a direct or offensive way: She was propositioned several times in the course of the evening.

propound /prəˈpaʊnd/ v (fml) to put sth forward for consideration or solution: [Vn] propound an idea/a policy/a scheme ∘ the theory of natural selection, first propounded by Charles Darwin.

proprietary /prəˈpraɪətri; US -teri/ adj (usu attrib) **1(a)** (of goods) manufactured and sold by a particular firm: proprietary medicines ∘ proprietary brands of food. (b) (abbreviated as propr in this dictionary) (of a name) owned and used only by a particular firm: 'Hoover' is a proprietary name and may not be used by other makers of vacuum cleaners. Compare BRAND NAME. **2** of or relating to an owner or ownership: proprietary rights/attitudes ∘ She cast a proprietary eye over her newly painted shop.

proprietor /prəˈpraɪətə(r)/ n (fem **proprietress** /prəˈpraɪətrəs/) the owner of a business, hotel, etc: a newspaper proprietor ○ Please address all complaints to the proprietor.

▶ **proprietorial** /prəˌpraɪəˈtɔːrɪəl/ adj (often derog) of, like or relating to a proprietor: have a proprietorial air ○ journalists protesting against proprietorial influence on editorial policy.

propriety /prəˈpraɪəti/ n (fml) **1(a)** [U] the state of being correct in one's social or moral behaviour: have no sense of propriety ○ behave with perfect propriety ○ The way tourists dress sometimes offends local standards of propriety. **(b) the proprieties** [pl] the details or rules of correct behaviour: She was careful to observe the proprieties. ○ The company had acted in accordance with all legal proprieties. **2** [U] ~ (of sth) the condition of being right or suitable: A social worker questioned the propriety of separating children from their parents.

propulsion /prəˈpʌlʃn/ n [U] the action or process of driving sth forward: jet propulsion (ie propulsion by means of jet engines) ○ The fish uses its tail fins for propulsion through the water.

▶ **propulsive** /prəˈpʌlsɪv/ adj (fml) that drives sth forward: propulsive power/forces.

pro rata /ˌprəʊ ˈrɑːtə/ adj, adv (fml) in proportion to sth: If production costs go up, there will be a pro rata increase in prices/prices will increase pro rata.

prosaic /prəˈzeɪɪk/ adj (usu derog) **(a)** ordinary and not showing any imagination: a prosaic style/writer ○ a prosaic description of the scene. **(b)** dull; not romantic: a prosaic job ○ the prosaic side of life. ▶ **prosaically** /-kli/ adv.

proscenium /prəˈsiːnɪəm/ n (in a theatre) the part of the stage in front of the curtain: He prefers working in a traditional theatre with a **proscenium arch** (ie an arch that forms a frame for the stage where the curtain is opened).

proscribe /prəˈskraɪb; US prəʊ-/ v (fml) to state officially that sth is dangerous or forbidden: [Vn] proscribed books/drugs/practices. ▶ **proscription** /prəˈskrɪpʃn; US prəʊ-/ n [U, C]: the law's proscription of deviant sexual practices.

prose /prəʊz/ n [U] written or spoken language that is not in verse: write in prose ○ a prose writer. Compare POETRY 1, VERSE 1.

prosecute /ˈprɒsɪkjuːt/ v **1(a)** ~ sb (for sth / doing sth) to bring a criminal charge against sb in a court of law: [Vnpr] He was prosecuted for exceeding the speed limit. [Vn] **Trespassers will be prosecuted** (eg on a notice). [V] The police decided not to prosecute. **(b)** (of a lawyer) to represent a person or an organization that prosecutes sb: [V] the prosecuting lawyer/counsel. **2** (fml) to continue with sth: [Vn] prosecute a war/an attack.

▶ **prosecutor** /ˈprɒsɪkjuːtə(r)/ n a person who prosecutes in a court of law, esp on behalf of the public: the public/state prosecutor's office.

prosecution /ˌprɒsɪˈkjuːʃn/ n **1(a)** [U] the action of prosecuting sb or the process of being prosecuted for a criminal offence: be liable to/face prosecution for tax evasion. **(b)** [C] an instance of this: The police brought a prosecution against the company's directors for fraud. **2 the prosecution** [Gp] a person or an organization that prosecutes in a court of law, together with their lawyers, etc: Mr Hughes acted as counsel for the prosecution. ○ The prosecution lack(s) sufficient evidence. Compare DEFENCE 2b. **3** [U] the ~ of sth (fml) the action of carrying out or the process of being occupied with sth: be in favour of the vigorous prosecution of the war.

proselytize, -ise /ˈprɒsələtaɪz/ v (fml) to try to persuade others to accept one's own beliefs, religion, etc: [V] proselytizing aims/activities/zeal.

prosody /ˈprɒsədi/ n [U] (the study of) the patterns of sounds and rhythms in poetry and speech.

prospect¹ /ˈprɒspekt/ n **1** [U] ~ (of sth / doing sth) the chance or hope that sth will happen: There is no immediate prospect of a peace settlement. ○ Many young families have little or no prospect of buying their own homes. ○ A fascinating contest seems in **prospect**. **2** [sing] an idea of what may or will happen: a daunting/an exciting/a terrifying prospect ○ She viewed the prospect of a week alone in the house with alarm. **3 prospects** [pl] the chances of being successful: Further training would improve your job prospects. ○ Long-term employment prospects for young people still look gloomy. **4** [C] a candidate or competitor who is likely to be successful: She's a good prospect for the American team. **5** [C] (dated) a wide view of an area of land, etc: a magnificent prospect of the lake with the mountains in the background.

prospect² /prəˈspekt; US ˈprɒspekt/ v ~ (for sth) to search for gold, minerals, oil, etc: [V, Vpr] The company is prospecting (for gold) in that area.

▶ **prospector** n a person who explores a region looking for gold, minerals, etc.

prospective /prəˈspektɪv/ adj [attrib] expected to be or to occur; future or possible: be worried about prospective changes in the law ○ the prospective Labour candidate at the next election ○ show the house to a prospective buyer.

prospectus /prəˈspektəs/ n a printed document, thin book, etc giving details of and advertising a college, a new business, etc: look at prospectuses from several universities ○ The company will publish/launch its new prospectus tomorrow.

prosper /ˈprɒspə(r)/ v to be successful, esp financially: [V] The business is prospering.

prosperity /prɒˈsperəti/ n [U] the state of being successful, esp financially: economic/industrial/material prosperity ○ Tourism has brought (an increase in) prosperity to the islands.

prosperous /ˈprɒspərəs/ adj rich and successful: a prosperous country/economy/industry ○ The north of the region is still more prosperous than the south.

prostate /ˈprɒsteɪt/ n (also **prostate gland**) n (anatomy) an organ in the body of male human beings and animals that releases a fluid in which sperms (SPERM 1) float. ⇨ picture at REPRODUCTION.

prosthesis /prɒsˈθiːsɪs/ n (pl **prostheses** /-ˈθiːsiːz/) (medical) an artificial part of the body, eg a limb, an eye or a tooth: A prosthesis was fitted after the amputation. ▶ **prosthetic** /prɒsˈθetɪk/ adj: a prosthetic limb/appliance.

prostitute /ˈprɒstɪtjuːt; US -tuːt/ n a person who offers herself or himself for sex(2) with sb in return for money.

▶ **prostitute** v [Vn] ~ oneself (derog) **1** to use one's abilities, etc wrongly or in a way that is not worthy of them, esp in order to earn money: [Vn] a musician who prostitutes her talent/herself by writing advertising jingles. **2** [Vn] to act as a prostitute.

prostitution /ˌprɒstɪˈtjuːʃn; US -ˈtuːʃn/ n **1** [U] the practice of working as a prostitute: earn money by/from prostitution. **2** [C, U] ~ of sth the use of one's abilities, etc in a way that is not worthy of them.

prostrate /ˈprɒstreɪt/ adj **1** lying stretched out on the ground with one's face downwards: fall prostrate in worship ○ They found her prostrate on the floor. Compare PRONE 2, SUPINE 1. **2** ~ (with sth) overcome by sth; defeated or helpless: She was prostrate with grief after his death.

▶ **prostrate** /prɒˈstreɪt; US ˈprɒstreɪt/ v **1** ~ oneself to throw oneself on the floor and lie with one's face downwards: [Vn] They prostrated themselves as a sign of worship. ○ The pilgrims prostrated themselves before the altar. **2** (esp passive) (of illness, weather, etc) to make sb helpless: [Vn] The shock nearly prostrated her. **prostration** /prɒˈstreɪʃn/ n [U] **1** the action of lying with one's face downwards,

P

esp in worship. **2** extreme physical weakness: *a state of prostration brought on by the heat.*

prosy /ˈprəʊzi/ *adj* (of a writer, speaker, book, speech, style, etc) dull; lacking in imagination.

protagonist /prəˈtægənɪst/ *n* **1(a)** (*fml*) a major character in a drama: *the leading/chief/main protagonist* ○ *the play's doomed protagonist.* **(b)** the main person in a story or a real event: *leave the protagonists to fight it out between themselves.* **2** ~ **(of sth)** a leader of a movement in a course of action, etc: *a leading protagonist of the conservation movement.*

protean /ˈprəʊtiən, prəʊˈtiːən/ *adj* (*fml*) that can change quickly and easily: *a protean character.*

protect /prəˈtekt/ *v* **1** ~ **sb/sth (against/from sth)** to keep sb/sth safe from harm, injury, etc; to defend sb/sth: [Vn] *protect the environment* [Vnpr] *protect young children from harm* ○ *Make sure the young plants are protected from frost.* ○ *The interests of part-time workers should be protected.* **2** to guard one or more industries of a country against competition by taxing foreign goods: [Vn] *a heavily protected industry.* **3** ~ **sb/sth (against sth)** (*techn*) (esp passive) (of an insurance policy, etc) to promise to pay the necessary costs in case of injury, fire, etc: [Vnpr] *be protected against loss of income.*
■ **pro₁tected ˈbuilding** *n* (*US*) = LISTED BUILDING.

protection /prəˈtekʃn/ *n* **1** ~ **(for sb) (against sth)** **(a)** [U] the action of protecting sb/sth or the condition of being protected: *Use a suncream that gives adequate protection against harmful ultraviolet rays.* ○ *The union is campaigning for greater protection (for staff) against unfair dismissal.* **(b)** [C] a thing that protects: *legal protections for unions* ○ *consumer protections.* **2** [U] the system of protecting an industry by taxing foreign goods: *provide protection for the car industry by imposing import duties on foreign goods.* **3** [U] the system of paying money to criminals so that one's business will not be attacked by them: *paying protection money* ○ *The gang were running protection rackets in all the big cities.*
▶ **protectionism** /-ʃənɪzəm/ *n* [U] the principle or practice of protecting a country's own industries: *increase agricultural/industrial protectionism.* **protectionist** /-ʃənɪst/ *adj*: *protectionist measures/policies* ○ *a protectionist government.*

protective /prəˈtektɪv/ *adj* **1** [esp attrib] that protects or is intended to protect sth/sb: *a protective layer of varnish* ○ *the earth's protective ozone layer* ○ *Workers who handle asbestos need to wear protective clothing.* ○ *protective legislation/tariffs.* **2** ~ **(of sth / towards sb)** having or showing a wish to protect sth/sb: *feel fiercely protective towards one's children* ○ *He put his arm round her in a protective gesture.* ○ *She was extremely protective of her public image.* ▶ **protectively** *adv*: *act protectively towards one's children.* **protectiveness** *n* [U].
■ **pro₁tective ˈcustody** *n* [U] the state of being kept in prison for one's own safety.

protector /prəˈtektə(r)/ *n* **1** a person or an organization that protects sb/sth: *the company's image as a protector of the environment.* **2** a thing made or designed to give protection: *wear ear protectors against machine noise.*

protectorate /prəˈtektərət/ *n* a country that is controlled and protected by a more powerful country. Compare COLONY 1a.

protégé (*fem* **protégée**) /ˈprɒtəʒeɪ; *US* ˈprəʊt-/ *n* a person whose welfare and career are looked after by an influential person, esp over a long period: *a young protégé of the violinist Yehudi Menuhin.*

protein /ˈprəʊtiːn/ *n* [C,U] a substance found in meat, eggs, fish, certain vegetables, etc that is an important part of the diet of humans and animals: *essential proteins and vitamins* ○ *protein deficiency* ○ *Peas, beans and lentils are a good source of vegetable protein.*

pro tem /ˌprəʊ ˈtem/ *adv* (*infml*) for now; temporarily: *This arrangement will have to do pro tem.*

protest¹ /ˈprəʊtest/ *n* **(a)** [C] a statement or an action that shows one's strong disapproval or disagreement: *The union organized/staged a protest against the redundancies.* ○ *Parking restrictions were introduced following protests from local residents.* **(b)** [U] the showing of strong disapproval or disagreement in a statement or an action: *The minister resigned in protest against the decision.* ○ *a protest demonstration/march* ○ *a protest vote* (ie one against the party in power rather than for an opposing party). **IDM** **under ˈprotest** unwillingly and after making protests: *She paid the fine under protest.*

protest² /prəˈtest/ *v* **1** ~ **(about/against/at sth)** to express strong disagreement or disapproval about sth: [Vpr] *They protested strongly at the cuts in public spending.* ○ *Demonstrators protested against the new legislation.* [V] *I really must protest — you have no right to make such an accusation.* [Vn] (*US*) *A demonstration was planned to protest the mistreatment of prisoners.* **2** to declare sth solemnly or firmly, esp in reply to an accusation: [Vn] *He protested his innocence.* [V.that] *She protested that she had never seen him before.* [V.speech] *'But I did tell you!' she protested.*
▶ **protester** *n* a person who protests: *A group of protesters gathered outside the embassy.*

Protestant /ˈprɒtɪstənt/ *n*, *adj* (a member) of any part of the Christian Church that separated from the Church of Rome in the 16th century, or of their branches which formed later: *a Protestant church/minister/service.* Compare ROMAN CATHOLIC.
▶ **Protestantism** /-ɪzəm/ *n* [U] the system of beliefs, teachings, etc of the Protestants.

protestation /ˌprɒtəˈsteɪʃn/ *n* (*fml*) a strong declaration: *protestations of love/innocence/loyalty* ○ *Despite their protestations, they were glad to accept our help.*

prot(o)- *comb form* (forming *n*s and *adj*s) first or original; having others develop from it or follow it: *prototype* ○ *protoplasm* ○ *protozoan.*

protocol /ˈprəʊtəkɒl; *US* -kɔːl/ *n* **1** [U] a system of rules governing formal occasions, eg meetings between governments, officials, etc: *the protocol of diplomatic visits* ○ *a breach of protocol* ○ *Protocol demands that formal dress be worn on such occasions.* **2** [C] (*fml*) the first or original version of an agreement, in writing.

proton /ˈprəʊtɒn/ *n* a very small piece of matter with a positive electric charge, which is present inside all atoms. Compare ELECTRON, NEUTRON.

protoplasm /ˈprəʊtəplæzəm/ (also **plasma**) *n* [U] (*biology*) a colourless substance like jelly from which all plants and animals are formed.

prototype /ˈprəʊtətaɪp/ *n* the first model or design of sth from which other forms are copied or developed: *the prototype for future school buildings* ○ *a prototype supersonic aircraft.* ▶ **prototypical** /ˌprəʊtəˈtɪpɪkl/ *adj.*

protozoan /ˌprəʊtəˈzəʊən/ (also **protozoon** /-ˈzəʊɒn/) *n* (*pl* **protozoans** or **protozoa** /-ˈzəʊə/) a very small living thing, usu having only one cell, which can only be seen under a MICROSCOPE.
▶ **protozoan** /ˌprəʊtəˈzəʊən/ *adj* of or like a protozoan.

protracted /prəˈtræktɪd; *US* prəʊ-/ *adj* (*often derog*) lasting longer than expected or longer than usual: *a protracted lunch break* ○ *protracted delays/disputes/negotiations.*

protractor /prəˈtræktə(r); *US* prəʊ-/ *n* an instrument, usu in the form of a SEMICIRCLE with degrees (0° to 180°) marked on it, used for measuring and drawing angles.

protrude /prəˈtruːd; *US* prəʊ-/ *v* ~ **(from sth)** to extend from a place or from a surface; to stick out:

[V] *protruding eyes/lips/teeth* ○ *a protruding chin*
[Vpr] *He managed to hang on to a piece of rock protruding from the cliff face.* ○ *Several pens protruded from his top pocket.*

▶ **protrusion** /prə'truːʒn; *US* prəʊ-/ *n* (**a**) [C] a thing that protrudes: *rocky protrusions on the surface of the cliff.* (**b**) [U] the action of protruding.

protuberant /prə'tjuːbərənt; *US* prəʊ'tuː-/ *adj* (*fml*) curving or swelling outwards from a surface; prominent: *protuberant ears.*

▶ **protuberance** /-əns/ *n* (*fml*) a protuberant thing; a swelling: *The diseased trees are marked by protuberances on their bark.*

proud /praʊd/ *adj* (**-er, -est**) **1** (*approv*) (**a**) ~ (**of sb/sth**); ~ (**to do sth / that...**) feeling or showing pride (1a): *a proud father* ○ *She's very proud of her new car.* ○ *They were rather proud of their success/of being so successful.* ○ *They were proud to be chosen/that they had been chosen for the team.* ○ *Your achievements are something to be proud of.* ○ (*ironic*) *I hope you feel proud of yourself — you've ruined the game!* (**b**) causing pride(1a): *It was a proud day for us when we won the trophy.* ○ *The portrait was his proudest possession.* (**c**) having or showing dignity, independence or respect for oneself: *She had been too proud to ask for help.* ○ *They are a proud and independent people.* **2** (*derog*) feeling that one is better or more important than others; ARROGANT: *She was too proud to admit she was wrong.* ○ *He is too proud now to be seen with his former friends.* **3** (*fml*) splendid; imposing (IMPOSE): *The statue stands tall and proud in the main square.* **4** ~ (**of sth**) (*Brit techn*) standing out from or extending above sth: *The cement should be/stand proud of the surface and then be smoothed down later.* See also HOUSE-PROUD.

▶ **proud** *adv* **IDM** **do sb 'proud 1** (*infml*) to treat sb very well, by giving them plenty of good food and entertainment: *The college did us proud at the centenary dinner.* **2** (*US*) to be a source of pride to sb: *Her calmness during the crisis did her proud.*
proudly *adv* in a proud(1,3) manner: *She proudly displayed her prize.*

prove /pruːv/ *v* (*pp* **proved**; *US* **proven** /'pruːvn/) ⇨ note. **1** ~ **sth** (**to sb**) to show that sth is true or certain by means of facts or evidence: [Vn, V.*that*] *prove sb's guilt/(that) sb is guilty* [Vn] *Nobody will believe you unless you have evidence to prove your case.* ○ *She claimed that money had been wasted and our financial difficulties seemed to prove her point.* [Vnpr] *Can you prove it to me?* [Vpr.*that*] *I shall prove to you that the witness is lying.* [Vn-adj] *They said I wouldn't succeed, but I proved them wrong.* Compare DISPROVE. See also PROOF[1] 1,4. **2** ~ (**oneself**) **sth** to be seen or found to be sth; to turn out to be sth: [V-adj] *The old methods proved best after all.* [V.*to* inf] *The task proved to be more difficult than we'd expected.* [V-n, Vn-n] *He proved (himself) a better driver than the world champion.* [also Vn-adj]. **IDM** **the exception proves the rule** ⇨ EXCEPTION.

▶ **provable** /-əbl/ *adj* that can be proved: *a provable case of negligence.*

NOTE Prove and shave have alternative past participle forms: **proved/proven** and **shaved/shaven**. The irregular form **proven** is more common in American English than in British English. **Shaven** and **proven** are mostly used adjectively: *a well-proven method* ○ *a shaven head.*

proven /'pruːvn, 'prəʊvn/ *adj* (*approv*) that has been tested or demonstrated: *a man of proven ability.* **IDM** **not 'proven** (in Scottish law) a VERDICT(1) in a criminal trial that there is not enough evidence to prove sb is innocent or guilty, and that they must therefore be set free.

provenance /'prɒvənəns/ *n* [U] (*fml*) the place that sth originally came from: *the provenance of a word* ○

antique furniture of doubtful provenance (eg that may not be genuine).

provender /'prɒvɪndə(r)/ *n* [U] (*dated or joc*) food.

proverb /'prɒvɜːb/ *n* a short well-known sentence or phrase that states a general truth about life or gives advice, eg 'Better safe than sorry' or 'Don't put all your eggs in one basket'.

▶ **proverbial** /prə'vɜːbiəl/ *adj* **1** of or expressed in a proverb: *proverbial wisdom* ○ *He is the proverbial square peg in a round hole.* **2** well-known and talked about by a lot of people: *His obstinacy is proverbial.*
proverbially /-biəli/ *adv.*

provide /prə'vaɪd/ *v* **1** ~ **sb** (**with sth**); ~ **sth** (**for sb**) (**a**) to make sth available for sb to use by giving or lending it: [Vn] *The management will provide food and drink.* ○ *Please return this form in the envelope provided.* [Vnpr] *This book will provide you with all the information you need.* ○ *Can you provide accommodation for thirty people?* (**b**) to offer or present an answer, example, opportunity, etc: [Vn] *Let us hope his research will provide the evidence we need.* [Vnpr] *The painting provides us with one of the earliest examples of the use of perspective.* **2** (*fml*) to state as a requirement: [V.*that*] *A clause in the agreement provides that the tenant shall pay for repairs to the building.* See also PROVISION **PHR V** **pro'vide against sth** (*fml*) to make preparations in case sth happens: *Health insurance can provide against possible loss of income.* **pro'vide for sb** to give sb money and the things that they need to live, eg food and clothing: *They worked hard to provide for their large family.* ○ *He didn't provide for his wife and children in his will* (ie didn't leave them money to live on). **pro'vide for sth 1** to make the necessary plans to deal with something that may happen in the future: *The planners had not provided for a failure of the power system.* **2** (*fml*) (of a law, etc) to make it possible for sth to be done later: *The right of individuals to appeal to a higher court is provided for in the constitution.*

▶ **provider** *n* a person or group that provides, esp a person who supports a family: *The eldest son is the family's only provider.* ○ *providers of employment/loans/services.*

provided /prə'vaɪdɪd/ (also **provided that, providing** /prə'vaɪdɪŋ/, **providing that**) *conj* on the condition that; only if: *I will agree to go provided/providing (that) my expenses are paid.* ○ *Provided you have the money in your account, you may withdraw up to £100 a day.*

providence /'prɒvɪdəns/ *n* [U] the way in which God or nature cares for and protects all creatures: *trust in divine providence.* **IDM** **tempt fate/providence** ⇨ TEMPT.

provident /'prɒvɪdənt/ *adj* (*fml*) careful in planning for future needs: *Some farmers had been provident in the good years but others were ruined by the bad harvests.* Compare IMPROVIDENT.
■ **'Provident Society** (also **'Provident Association**) *n* = FRIENDLY SOCIETY.

providential /ˌprɒvɪ'denʃl/ *adj* (*fml*) lucky because it occurs just at the right time: *their providential departure just before the floods.* ▶ **providentially** /-ʃəli/ *adv.*

providing ⇨ PROVIDED.

province /'prɒvɪns/ *n* **1** [C] any of the parts into which a country is divided for the purposes of government: *Canada has ten provinces.* Compare COUNTY, STATE[1] 3. **2** **the provinces** [pl] all the parts of a country except the capital city: *The show will tour the provinces after it closes in London.* ○ (*derog*) *He found life in the provinces boring.* **3** [sing] (*fml*) a person's particular area of knowledge, interest or responsibility: *The matter is outside my province* (ie I cannot or need not deal with it). ○ *Adventure*

P

---

stories were traditionally the province of male writers.

provincial /prə'vɪnʃl/ *adj* **1** [attrib] (**a**) of a province(1): *the provincial government* ○ *provincial taxes.* (**b**) of the provinces (PROVINCE 2): *provincial newspapers/theatres/towns.* **2** (*derog*) typical of the provinces (PROVINCE 2); having or showing a narrow or limited view of life and current affairs: *provincial attitudes.*
▶ **provincial** *n* (*usu derog*) a person who lives in or comes from the provinces (PROVINCE 2): *Whenever I go to New York I feel like a provincial.*
provincialism /-ɪzəm/ *n* (*derog*) [U] a provincial(2) attitude, esp one that shows a concern only for one's own small area: *He wanted to escape from the provincialism of the small town where he had been brought up.*
provincially /-ʃəli/ *adv.*

provision /prə'vɪʒn/ *n* **1** ~ **of sth** (**a**) [U] the giving or lending of sth to sb: *housing/education provision* ○ *The government is responsible for the provision of health care.* (**b**) [C usu *sing*] an amount of sth that is provided: *The provision of specialist teachers is being increased.* **2** [U] ~ **for sth/sb**; ~ **against sth** preparation that is made to meet future needs or in case sth happens: *make provision for one's old age* ○ *provision for his wife and children* ○ *provision against possible disaster* ○ *The present law makes no provision for this.* **3 provisions** [pl] supplies of food and drink, esp for a journey: *The expedition set out with enough provisions for two weeks.* **4** [C] a condition or requirement in a legal document: *under the provisions of the agreement* ○ *She accepted the contract **with the provision that** it would be revised after a year.*
▶ **provision** *v* ~ **sb/sth** (**with sth**) (*fml*) (esp passive) to supply sb/sth with provisions of food or other things that are needed: [Vnpr] *provisioned for a long voyage* [also Vn].

provisional /prə'vɪʒənl/ *adj* arranged or provided for the present time only, but possibly to be changed later; temporary: *a provisional government* ○ *The booking is only provisional.* ○ *a provisional driving-licence* (ie one that has to be obtained before one can start to learn to drive). ▶ **provisionally** /-nəli/ *adv*: *The meeting has been provisionally arranged for 3.00 pm next Friday.*

proviso /prə'vaɪzəʊ/ *n* (*pl* **-os**; *US* also **-oes**) a thing that is required as part of an agreement; a condition: *I agreed to go, with the proviso that my family should come with me.*

provocation /ˌprɒvə'keɪʃn/ *n* (**a**) [U] the action of making sb angry by deliberately doing sth annoying or offensive; the action of provoking sb/sth or of being provoked: *He reacted with violence only **under provocation*** (ie when provoked). ○ *She loses her temper **at/on the slightest provocation**.* (**b**) [C] a thing that provokes: *The police remained calm in the face of repeated provocations.*

provocative /prə'vɒkətɪv/ *adj* **1** intended to make people become angry, annoyed, etc: *a provocative comment/remark/speech* ○ *Ignore him — he's just being provocative.* **2** intended to make sb sexually excited or interested: *make a provocative gesture* ○ *She was dressed to look provocative.* ▶ **provocatively** *adv.*

provoke /prə'vəʊk/ *v* **1(a)** to make a person or an animal angry or annoyed: [Vn] *I am not easily provoked, but this behaviour is intolerable!* ○ *If you provoke the dog, it will attack you.* (**b**) ~ **sb into doing sth/to do sth** to make sb do sth by continually annoying them or treating them in a certain way: [Vnpr] *His selfish behaviour finally provoked her into leaving him.* [Vn.*to* inf] *He was provoked by their repeated questioning to say more than he had intended.* **2** to cause a particular reaction in sb: [Vn]

provoke laughter/riots/smiles/violence ○ *His speech provoked an angry reaction/response from the crowd.*
▶ **provoking** *adj* (*dated or fml*) annoying: *It is very provoking of her to be so late.* See also THOUGHT-PROVOKING.

provost /'prɒvəst; *US* 'prəʊvəʊst/ *n* **1(a)** (*Brit*) (the title of) the head of certain university colleges. (**b**) (*US*) a senior administrative officer in certain universities. **2** (*Scot*) the head of a town or BOROUGH(1) council.

prow /praʊ/ *n* (*fml*) the pointed front part of a ship or boat; the bow³(1).

prowess /'praʊəs/ *n* [U] (*fml*) outstanding skill or ability: *academic/sporting prowess* ○ *We admire his prowess as an oarsman.*

prowl /praʊl/ *v* **1(a)** to move quietly and carefully, esp when hunting for sth: [Vp] *dogs prowling about at night* [Vpr] *burglars prowling in the grounds of the house* [also V]. (**b**) to move about, through or in a place in this way: [Vn] *thieves prowling the streets at night.* **2** to walk or wander, eg because one is anxious or unable to relax: [Vpr] *prowl round the house* [Vp] *I could hear him prowling about in his bedroom all night.* [also V].
▶ **prowl** *n* **IDM (be/go) on the 'prowl** (to be/go) prowling: *There was a fox on the prowl near the chicken coop.*
prowler *n* a person or an animal that prowls.

NOTE Compare **prowl**, **skulk**, **lurk**, **slink**, **sneak**, **sidle**, **steal**, **creep** and **tiptoe**. These verbs describe people or animals moving slowly and quietly because they do not want to be noticed. **Prowl** (**about, around**, etc) suggests an animal looking for food, or a criminal looking for something to steal: *Wolves prowled the forest in search of prey.* ○ *I thought I saw someone prowling around outside the house.* **Skulk** (**about, around**, etc) refers to someone moving around where they cannot be seen, possibly angrily, or waiting to do something bad: *He skulked about the hall, waiting for the police to leave.*
Lurk also describes waiting secretly: *I felt sure there was a man lurking in the bushes.* A person or an animal **slinks** (**off, away**, etc) when they feel ashamed or frightened, or are going to do something bad: *A fox came slinking through the trees towards the hen-house.* People **sneak** (**in, out**, etc) when they are doing something they feel guilty about: *She tried sneaking into the cinema without paying.*
Sidle describes the way somebody moves when they are trying not to be noticed or are nervous about what they intend to do: *The boy sidled past the teacher and then ran out of the door.* People **steal** (**in, out**, etc) in great secrecy: *She stole out of the house in the middle of the night.*
Creep also suggests secrecy and moving very quietly: *I didn't hear her creeping up behind me.*
Tiptoe means to walk very quietly on your toes so that nobody can hear you: *They tiptoed upstairs so as not to wake the baby.*

proximate /'prɒksɪmət/ *adj* (*fml*) next before or after in time, order, etc; nearest: *the proximate cause of injury.*

proximity /prɒk'sɪməti/ *n* [U] ~ (**to sth**) (*fml*) the state or fact of being near sth/sb in space or time: *in the proximity of* (ie near) *the building* ○ *houses built **in close proximity** to each other* ○ *The restaurant benefits from its proximity to several cinemas.*

proxy /'prɒksi/ *n* **1** [C] a person who is given the authority to act on behalf of another: *act as sb's proxy* ○ *He made his wife his proxy.* **2** [U] the authority to represent sb else, esp in voting at an election: *vote by proxy* ○ *a proxy vote.*

prude /pruːd/ *n* (*derog*) a person who is or claims to

be easily shocked by anything rude or INDECENT(1), esp things connected with sex.
▶ **prudery** /'pruːdəri/ n [U] (derog) the behaviour or attitude of a prude.
prudish /'pruːdɪʃ/ adj (derog) of or like a prude: have a prudish dislike of rude jokes.

prudent /'pruːdnt/ adj acting with or showing care and thought for the future; showing good judgement: make a prudent investment ○ Instead of moving house it might be more prudent to stay where we are. Compare IMPRUDENT. ▶ **prudence** /-dns/ n [U] (fml): exercise prudence in balancing expenditure against income. **prudently** adv: act prudently in a crisis.

prune¹ /pruːn/ n a dried PLUM(1a): stewed prunes.

prune² /pruːn/ v **1** ~ sth (from/off sth); ~ sth (away/back/off) to trim the shape of a tree, bush, etc by cutting away some of the branches, etc, esp to encourage new shoots to grow: [Vn] Prune back the longer branches. [also Vnpr]. ⇨ note at CLIP². **2** ~ sth (of sth); ~ sth (down) to reduce the extent of sth by cutting unnecessary parts: [Vn] prune expenditure [Vnpr] Try to prune your essay of irrelevant detail. [Vnp] I'm pruning down my Christmas card list this year. ▶ **pruning** n [U]: the pruning of overseas forces ○ Careful pruning at the right time is the secret of success with roses. ○ My article could do with a bit of pruning.

prurient /'prʊəriənt/ adj (fml derog) having or showing excessive interest in sexual matters: show a prurient interest in the details of a rape case. ▶ **prurience** /-əns/ n [U].

prussic acid /ˌprʌsɪk 'æsɪd/ n [U] a very poisonous acid.

pry¹ /praɪ/ v (pt, pp **pried** /praɪd/) ~ (into sth) to inquire with too much curiosity into other people's private affairs: [V] safe from prying eyes [Vpr] I don't want them prying into my affairs.

pry² /praɪ/ v (pt, pp **pried** /praɪd/) (US) = PRISE: [Vnp, Vnpr] pry the lid off (a can) [Vn-adj] pry the can open [Vnpr] pry information out of sb.

PS /ˌpiː 'es/ abbr (esp at the end of a letter) postscript (Latin postscriptum): Love from Tessa. PS I'll bring the car.

psalm /saːm/ n a sacred song or poem, esp one of those in the Book of Psalms in the Old Testament: The choir sang the 23rd Psalm.
▶ **psalmist** /-ɪst/ a writer of psalms.

psalter /'sɔːltə(r)/ n a book containing a collection of sacred songs with their music, for use in public worship.

psephology /si'fɒlədʒi/ n [U] the study of how people vote in elections.
▶ **psephological** /ˌsiːfə'lɒdʒɪkl/ adj: psephological analysis.
psephologist /si'fɒlədʒɪst/ n an expert in psephology.

pseud /sjuːd, suːd/ n (infml derog) a person who pretends to know a lot about sth, be very artistic, etc in order to impress others: She's just a pseud — she knows nothing about the theatre really. ▶ **pseud** adj: a pseud remark ○ I think he's rather pseud.

pseudo /'sjuːdəʊ, 'suː-; US 'suː-/ adj (infml) not genuine; pretended or insincere: pseudo poetry ○ I like real folk music, not the pseudo variety.

pseud(o)- comb form not genuine; false or pretended: pseudonym ○ pseudo-intellectual ○ pseudo-science.

pseudonym /'sjuːdənɪm, 'suː-; US 'suː-/ n a person's name that is not her or his real name, esp one used by an author: Mark Twain was the pseudonym of Samuel Langhorne Clemens. ○ She writes **under a pseudonym**. Compare PEN-NAME.

▶ **pseudonymous** /sjuː'dɒnɪməs, suː-; US suː-/ adj (fml) writing or written under a pseudonym: a pseudonymous author.

psi abbr pounds (pressure) per square inch (eg on tyres).

psoriasis /sə'raɪəsɪs/ n [U] a skin disease that causes rough red patches.

psst /pst/ interj (used to attract sb's attention secretly): Psst! Let's get out now before they see us!

psych /saɪk/ v ~ sb (out / out of sth) (infml) to make an opponent feel less confident by appearing very confident or aggressive oneself: [Vn, Vnp] Her arrogant behaviour on court psyched her opponent (out) completely. [Vnpr] He was psyched out of the match/race. **PHRV** ˌpsych sb/oneself 'up (esp passive) to prepare sb/oneself mentally for sth: She had really psyched herself up for the exams.

psyche /'saɪki/ n the human soul or mind: painful memories buried deep in his psyche ○ Her book is an exploration of the American psyche.

psychedelia /ˌsaɪkə'diːliə/ n [U] music, art, culture, etc based on the experiences produced by PSYCHEDELIC(1) drugs.

psychedelic /ˌsaɪkə'delɪk/ adj **1** (of drugs) that make the user HALLUCINATE: Mescalin and LSD are psychedelic drugs. **2** having intensely vivid colours, sounds, etc like those experienced while hallucinating (HALLUCINATE): psychedelic clothes/music.

psychiatry /saɪ'kaɪətri, sə-/ n [U] the study and treatment of mental illness. ⇨ note at PSYCHOLOGY.
▶ **psychiatric** /ˌsaɪki'ætrɪk/ adj: a psychiatric clinic ○ psychiatric treatment.
psychiatrist /-ɪst/ n a specialist in psychiatry: receive treatment for depression from a psychiatrist ○ the psychiatrist's couch (ie for patients to lie on during treatment).

psychic /'saɪkɪk/ adj **1** (also **psychical** /'saɪkɪkl/) concerned with events or processes that seem to be outside physical or natural laws: psychic energy/ forces. **2** able or seeming to be able to exercise powers outside physical or natural laws: psychic healing ○ She claims to be psychic and to be able to foretell the future. **3** (also **psychical**) of the soul or mind: sb's psychic development ○ psychical disorders.
▶ **psychic** n a person who claims or appears to be able to exercise powers outside physical or natural laws.
psychically /-kli/ adv: be psychically healthy/ disturbed.

psycho /'saɪkəʊ/ n (pl **-os**) (infml derog) a person who behaves in a very abnormal, esp violent, way: Don't let him drive — he's a complete psycho behind the wheel. ▶ **psycho** adj.

psych(o)- comb form of the mind: psychiatry ○ psychology ○ psychotherapy.

psychoanalysis /ˌsaɪkəʊə'næləsɪs/ n [U] a method of treating sb's mental problems or disorders by making them aware of experiences in their early life and tracing the connection between these and their present behaviour or feelings.
▶ **psychoanalyse** /ˌsaɪkəʊ'ænəlaɪz/ (also **analyse**, US **-lyze**) v [Vn] to treat or investigate sb by means of psychoanalysis.
psychoanalyst /ˌsaɪkəʊ'ænəlɪst/ (also **analyst**) n a person who practises psychoanalysis. ⇨ note at PSYCHOLOGY.
psychoanalytic /ˌsaɪkəʊˌænə'lɪtɪk/ (also **psychoanalytical** /-ɪkl/) adj. **psychoanalytically** /-ɪkli/ adv.

psychology /saɪ'kɒlədʒi/ n **1** [U] the science or study of the mind and how it functions: child psychology ○ educational psychology. Compare PSYCHIATRY. **2** [sing] (infml) the mental characteristics of a person or group: the psychology of the teenager.
▶ **psychological** /ˌsaɪkə'lɒdʒɪkl/ adj **1** of or affecting the mind: the psychological development of a

child ○ *psychological needs/problems* ○ *the psychological complexity of the novel* ○ *try to gain a* **psychological advantage** *over your opponent.* **2** of or relating to psychology: *psychological methods/ research.* **IDM** **the ˌpsychological ˈmoment** the most appropriate time to do sth, in order to achieve success: *We're going to have to ask for more money — it's just a question of finding the (right) psychological moment.* **psychologically** /-kli/ *adv.* **ˌpsychoˈlogical ˈwarfare** *n* [U] the attempt to destroy an enemy's will to fight a war by convincing them that they cannot win, changing their beliefs, etc.

psychologist /-dʒɪst/ *n* an expert in psychology: *an educational/research/child psychologist.*

NOTE Psychology is the study of the mind and human and animal behaviour. A **psychologist** is a person who studies the mind and behaviour to find out more about it. He or she may also work with people to help solve problems, etc. **Psychiatry** is the area of medicine that treats mental illness. A **psychiatrist** is a doctor who works in this area. **Psychoanalysis** is a form of treatment used in **psychiatry** which examines a person's life and experiences. This is also often called **analysis** and is practised by a **psychoanalyst**. **Psychotherapy** is the general name for all forms of treatment in this area. A person who practises it is called a **psychotherapist**. The words **therapy** and **therapist** are used in connection with various forms of treatment for problems and illnesses of the mind.

---

psychopath /ˈsaɪkəʊpæθ/ *n* a person suffering from a severe mental or emotional disorder, esp one who behaves in a violently aggressive way. ► **psychopathic** /ˌsaɪkəʊˈpæθɪk/ *adj: a psychopathic disorder/killer.*

psychosis /saɪˈkəʊsɪs/ *n* (*pl* **psychoses** /-siːz/) [C, U] a severe mental illness that affects the whole personality. See also PSYCHOTIC.

psychosomatic /ˌsaɪkəʊsəˈmætɪk/ *adj* **1** (of disease) caused or made worse by mental stress: *The symptoms may have been psychosomatic in origin.* **2** dealing with the relationship between the mind and the body.

psychotherapy /ˌsaɪkəʊˈθerəpi/ *n* [U] the treatment of mental disorders by discussing problems, etc, rather than giving drugs or other medical treatment.

► **psychotherapist** /-pɪst/ *n* a person who treats people by using psychotherapy. ⊏> note at PSYCHOLOGY.

psychotic /saɪˈkɒtɪk/ *adj* (*medical*) of or suffering from severe mental illness: *a psychotic disorder.*

► **psychotic** *n* (*medical*) a person suffering from severe mental illness. See also PSYCHOSIS.

PT /ˌpiː ˈtiː/ *abbr* physical training: *do PT* ○ *a PT lesson.* Compare PE.

pt *abbr* **1** part: *Shakespeare's Henry IV Pt 2.* **2** (*pl* **pts**) pint: *½ pt milk.* **3** (*pl* **pts**) point: *The winner scored 10 pts.* **4** (esp on a map) port: *Pt Moresby.*

PTA /ˌpiː tiː ˈeɪ/ *abbr* parent-teacher association (in schools).

PT boat /ˌpiː tiː ˈbəʊt/ *n* (*US*) a small fast boat used for attacking enemy ships with torpedoes (TORPEDO).

Pte (*Brit*) (*US* **Pvt**) *abbr* Private (soldier): *Pte (Jim) Hill.*

pterodactyl /ˌterəˈdæktɪl/ *n* a flying reptile that lived millions of years ago.

PTO /ˌpiː tiː ˈəʊ/ *abbr* (eg at the bottom of a page) please turn over .

pub /pʌb/ (also *fml* **public house**) *n* (*Brit*) a building where people go to drink and to meet their friends. Pubs serve alcoholic and other drinks, and often also food: *a pub lunch* ○ *They've gone down/round to the pub for a drink.* Compare INN, TAVERN. ⊏> note at INN.

■ **ˈpub crawl** *n* (*Brit infml*) a visit to several pubs

one after another, drinking at each of them: *go on a pub crawl.*

puberty /ˈpjuːbəti/ *n* [U] the stage when a person's sexual organs are developing and he or she becomes capable of having children: *reach the age of puberty.*

pubescent /pjuːˈbesnt/ *adj* of or at the stage when a person's sexual organs are developing and he or she becomes capable of having children: *pubescent boys/girls.*

pubic /ˈpjuːbɪk/ *adj* [attrib] of or on the part of the body near the sexual organs: *pubic hair* ○ *the pubic bone.* ⊏> picture at REPRODUCTION.

public /ˈpʌblɪk/ *adj* **1** (esp attrib) (**a**) of or concerning people in general: *a danger to public health* ○ *The campaign was designed to increase public awareness of the problem.* ○ **Public opinion** *was opposed to the war.* ○ *26 December is a public holiday in Britain.* ○ *It's* **public knowledge** (ie It is generally known that) *she's expecting a baby.* (**b**) provided, esp by government, for the use of people in general; not private: *public spending* ○ *public services/education/ libraries* ○ *a/the public highway* ○ *a public telephone* ○ *I came by public transport* (ie train, bus, etc). (**c**) known about by many people through newspapers, television, etc: *He is one of the most admired public figures.* **2** open or known to people in general: *a public apology* ○ *a public place* ○ *Details of the government report have not been made public.* Compare PRIVATE. **IDM** **go ˈpublic** (of a company) to become a public company by selling shares to the public. **in the ˈpublic ˈeye** well known to or often seen by many people in newspapers, on television, etc.

► **public** *n* [Gp] (**a**) **the ˈpublic** people in general: *complaints from members of the public* ○ *Is Buckingham Palace open to the public?* ○ *The public has/have a right to know what is in this report.* (**b**) a group of people who share a particular interest or who have sth in common: *the theatre-going public* ○ *She knows how to keep her public* (eg the readers of her books) *satisfied.* **IDM** **common/public knowledge** ⊏> KNOWLEDGE. **in ˈpublic** when other people, esp strangers, are present: *She was appearing in public* (ie in front of people in general) *for the first time since her illness.* Compare IN PRIVATE. **wash one's dirty linen in public** ⊏> WASH².

publicly /-kli/ *adv: He announced publicly that he was resigning.* ○ *This information is not publicly available.*

■ **ˌpublic-adˈdress system** *n* (*abbr* ˌPˈA system) an electronic system designed to AMPLIFY(1) sound, used at public meetings, sports events, etc.

ˌpublic ˈbar *n* (*Brit*) a bar¹(1) in a pub with simpler or less comfortable furniture than other bars. Compare LOUNGE BAR.

ˌpublic ˈcompany (also ˌpublic ˌlimited ˈcompany) *n* (*abbrs* **plc, PLC**) (*Brit*) a company that sells shares in itself to the public: *The pension fund owns shares in several major public companies.*

ˌpublic conˈvenience *n* (*Brit*) a toilet provided for the public to use. ⊏> note at TOILET.

ˌpublic ˈhouse *n* (*Brit fml*) = PUB.

ˌpublic ˈnuisance *n* **1** (*law*) an illegal act that harms people in general: *be charged with committing a public nuisance.* **2** (*infml*) a person or people who behave in a way that annoys people in general: *People who park on the pavement are a public nuisance.*

ˌpublic ˈproperty *n* [U] a thing that is known to everybody or anyone: *Her photograph appeared in every national newspaper and her private life became public property.*

ˌpublic ˈprosecutor *n* a lawyer acting for the state who tries to prove people guilty in a court of law.

the ˌPublic ˈRecord Office *n* [sing] (*Brit*) the place where official records, esp of people's births, deaths

---

and marriages, are kept and made available to the public.

‚public re'lations n [sing or pl v] (abbr ‚P¹R) **1** the work of presenting a good image of an organization to the public, esp by providing information: *She works in public relations.* **2** the state of the relationship between an organization and the public: *Our company supports local artistic events; it's good for public relations.*

‚public 'school n **1** (in Britain, esp England) a private school for pupils between 13 and 18 years old whose parents, etc pay for their education. Public schools usu provide food and accommodation for pupils. Compare PREPARATORY SCHOOL. **2** (esp in the US, Australia and Scotland) a local school, paid for by the state, which provides free education.

the ‚public 'sector n [sing] the part of an economy, industry, etc that is controlled by the state: *public-sector housing.* Compare THE PRIVATE SECTOR.

‚public 'spirit n [U] willingness to do things that help the public in general. **‚public-'spirited** adj: *a public-spirited woman.*

‚public u'tility n (fml) an organization that supplies water, electricity, gas, etc to the public.

‚public 'works n [pl] building work, eg of roads, hospitals, schools, etc, which is paid for by the government: *a public works programme.*

publican /'pʌblɪkən/ n a person who owns or manages a pub.

publication /ˌpʌblɪ'keɪʃn/ n **1(a)** [U] the action of printing a book, magazine, etc and making it available to the public: *the date of publication* ∘ *It was clear, even before publication, that the book would be a success.* **(b)** [C] a book, magazine, etc that has been published: *specialist publications.* **2** [U] the action of making sth known to the public: *publication of the exam results* ∘ *The government have delayed publication of the trade figures.*

publicist /'pʌblɪsɪst/ n **1** a person whose job is to make sth known to the public. **2** a writer or specialist in current affairs, eg a political journalist.

publicity /pʌb'lɪsəti/ n [U] **1** notice or attention from the newspapers, television, etc: *avoid/shun/seek publicity* ∘ *Their wedding took place amid a blaze of* (ie very intensive) *publicity.* **2** the giving of information about sth in order to attract the attention of the public; advertising: *There has been a lot of publicity for her new film.* ∘ *a* **publicity campaign** (ie a series of activities designed to attract the attention of the public) ∘ *The band dressed up as spacemen as a* **publicity stunt**.

publicize, -ise /'pʌblɪsaɪz/ v to give the public information about sth: [Vn] *an advertising campaign to publicize the new film* ∘ *a well-publicized attempt to break the world speed record.*

publish /'pʌblɪʃ/ v **1(a)** to prepare and print a book, magazine, etc and make it available to the public: [Vn] *This book was published by Oxford University Press.* ∘ *The journal is published monthly.* **(b)** (of a newspaper or magazine) to print sth for the public to read: [Vn] *Her letter was published in The Guardian.* **(c)** (of an author) to have one's work printed and made available to the public: [Vn] *He has published several articles on the subject.* ∘ *She has just published her first novel.* **2** to make sth known to the public: [Vn] *The firm publishes its accounts in August.*
▶ **publisher** n (often pl with sing meaning) a person or company that publishes books, newspapers, etc: *Several publishers are competing in the same market.* ∘ *My publishers offered me a generous advance.*
publishing n [U] the profession or business of publishing books: *She was offered a job in publishing.* See also DESKTOP PUBLISHING. **'publishing house** n a company that publishes books.

puce /pjuːs/ adj, n [U] (of) a brownish purple colour: *The man's face was puce with rage.*

puck /pʌk/ n a hard rubber disc used instead of a ball in ice hockey (ICE¹). ⊏> picture at HOCKEY.

pucker /'pʌkə(r)/ v ~ (sth) (up) to form or make sth form small folds: [V, Vp] *The child's face puckered (up) and he began to cry.* [Vn] *pucker one's lips* (ie tighten them, eg as if for a kiss) ∘ *puckered seams* [also Vnp].

puckish /'pʌkɪʃ/ adj playful and MISCHIEVOUS(1): *a puckish grin.*

pud /pʊd/ n (Brit infml) = PUDDING 1,2a.

pudding /'pʊdɪŋ/ n **1** [C,U] (Brit) a sweet food eaten at the end of a meal: *There isn't a pudding today.* ∘ *What's for pudding?* See also AFTERS, DESSERT. **2(a)** [C,U] a cooked sweet or SAVOURY(1) dish made from flour, rice or bread with fat, eggs, etc. Puddings are usu eaten hot: *some bread and butter pudding* ∘ *a rice pudding* ∘ *steak and kidney pudding* ∘ *Christmas/plum pudding.* **(b)** [C] a thing that is like this in texture or appearance: (*derog or joc*) *a pudding face.* See also BLACK PUDDING, YORKSHIRE PUDDING. **IDM the proof of the pudding** ⊏> PROOF¹.
■ **'pudding basin** n (Brit) a deep round bowl used for mixing or for cooking puddings.

puddle /'pʌdl/ n [C] a small pool of water, or other liquid, esp rain that has gathered on the ground.

pudenda /pjuː'dendə/ n [pl] (fml) the external sexual organs, esp of a woman.

pudgy /'pʌdʒi/ adj (-ier, -iest) (infml) short and fat; PODGY: *pudgy fingers* ∘ *a pudgy child.*

puerile /'pjʊəraɪl; US -rəl/ adj (derog) silly and CHILDISH(b): *puerile behaviour* ∘ *Some people think he's amusing, but in my opinion his jokes are puerile.*

puff¹ /pʌf/ n **1** [C] **(a)** a short light blowing of air, wind, etc: *a puff of wind.* **(b)** an amount of smoke, steam, etc that is blown out: *a puff of smoke* ∘ (*fig*) *puffs of white cloud in the sky* ∘ (*joc*) *vanish in a puff of smoke* (ie disappear quickly). **(c)** an act of breathing in smoke from a cigarette or pipe and blowing it out again: *She lit the cigarette and took a few puffs.* **2** [C] (esp in compounds) a hollow piece of pastry filled with cream, jam, etc: *a cream puff.* **3** [U] (*infml esp Brit*) = BREATH 1: *be out of puff* (ie breathing very quickly, esp after exercise). See also POWDER-PUFF.
▶ **puffy** adj soft and swollen in appearance: *puffy clouds* ∘ *Your eyes look rather puffy. Have you been crying?* **puffiness** n [U].
■ **'puff-ball** n a type of FUNGUS(1) with a round head. It bursts when ripe to release its spores (SPORE).
‚puff 'pastry n [U] a type of light pastry used for pies, cakes, etc.
‚puff 'sleeve (also **‚puffed 'sleeve**) n a sleeve on a dress or other piece of clothing that is gathered (GATHER 7) at the shoulder and narrower at the lower edge, so that it forms a round shape.

puff² /pʌf/ v **1(a)** (of air, wind, smoke, etc) to blow or come out in puffs (PUFF¹ 1b); to make air, wind, smoke, etc do this: [Vpr] *Smoke was puffing out of the chimney.* [Vnpr] *Don't puff smoke into people's faces.* [also Vn, Vp]. **(b)** ~ (at/on) sth to smoke a cigarette or pipe in puffs (PUFF¹ 1c): [Vpr, Vp] *puff (away) at/on a cigarette* [Vn] *He sat puffing his pipe.* **2** (*infml*) to breathe loudly or quickly, eg after running: [V] *He was puffing hard when he reached the station.* **IDM huff and puff** ⊏> HUFF¹. **‚puff and 'blow** (*infml*) **1** (also **‚puff and 'pant**) to breathe quickly and loudly after physical effort: *arrive puffing and panting at the top of the hill.* **2** = HUFF AND PUFF. **(be) puffed up with 'pride, etc** (*usu derog*) (to be) too full of pride, etc. **PHRV puff along, in, out, up, etc** to move in the specified direction, sending out small clouds of smoke or steam, or breathing quickly and loudly: *The train puffed into the station.* ∘ *She puffed up the hill.* **‚puff sth 'out** to make sth larger, esp by filling it with air: *puff out*

P

one's cheeks ○ *The bird puffed out its feathers.* ,puff (sth) 'up to swell or make sth swell: *Her face puffs up if she eats bananas — she's allergic to them.*
▶ **puffed** (also ,puffed 'out) *adj* [usu pred] (*infml esp Brit*) (of a person) breathing with difficulty; out of breath: *I'm quite puffed out after climbing all those stairs.*

puffin /'pʌfɪn/ *n* a black and white sea bird with a large, brightly coloured beak, common in the N Atlantic. ⇨ picture.

puffin

pug /pʌg/ *n* a small dog with short hair and a broad flat face that has deep folds of skin.

pugilist /'pju:dʒɪlɪst/ *n* (*fml*) (**a**) a boxer, esp a professional one. (**b**) a person who enjoys fighting, arguing, etc: *a parliamentary pugilist.* ▶ **pugilism** /-lɪzəm/ *n* [U]. **pugilistic** /,pju:dʒɪ'lɪstɪk/ *adj*.

pugnacious /pʌg'neɪʃəs/ *adj* (*fml*) (of people or their behaviour) always eager to quarrel or fight; aggressive. ▶ **pugnaciously** *adv*. **pugnacity** /pʌg'næsəti/ *n* [U]: *He defended his position with great pugnacity.*

puke /pju:k/ *v* ~ (**sth**) (**up**) (*sl*) to be sick; to VOMIT: [V, Vp] *The baby puked (up) all over me.* [Vnp] *I puked up my dinner.* ▶ **puke** *n* [U]: *covered in puke.*

pukka /'pʌkə/ *adj* (*Brit*) **1** genuine: *pukka walking boots.* **2** of good quality; excellent: *Thanks — you've done a pukka job!*

pull

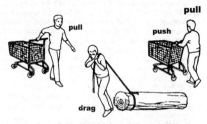

pull · push · drag

pull¹ /pʊl/ *v* **1** to hold sth firmly and use force in order to move it or try to move it towards oneself: [V] *You push and I'll pull.* ○ *Don't pull so hard or the handle will come off.* [Vn] *Stop pulling her hair!* [Vpr] *I pulled at/on the rope to see if it was secure.* [Vnpr] *She pulled him gently towards her.* [Vnadj, Vnp] *Pull the door shut/to.* ⇨ picture. **2** to remove sth from a place by pulling: [Vn] *pull* (ie extract) *a tooth* [Vnp] *Pull the plug out.* ○ *She reached in her pocket and pulled out a notebook.* ○ *He pulled off his boots.* ○ *She spent the afternoon pulling up weeds.* [Vnpr] *They managed to pull the child out of the river just in time.* ○ *He pulled a gun on me* (ie produced it, eg from a pocket, and aimed it at me). **3** to move sb/sth in the specified direction by pulling: [Vnpr] *Pull your chair nearer the table.* [Vnp] *He pulled his trousers up/pulled up his trousers.* ○ *She pulled her sweater on/pulled on her sweater.* ○ *Her hair was pulled back into a tight bun.* **4** to hold or be attached to sth and move it along behind one while moving: [Vn, Vnpr] *The horse was pulling a heavy cart (along the road).* [Vn] *The child pulled the toy train along behind her.* **5** to move one's body or a part of one's body in the specified direction, esp using force: [Vnp] *The dog snapped at her so she quickly pulled back her hand.* [Vp] *He tried to kiss her but she pulled away.* [V-adj, Vn-adj] *John pulled (himself) free and ran off.* **6** to open or close curtains, etc: [Vn, Vnpr] *pull the blinds (back).* **7** to damage a muscle, etc by using too much force: [Vn]

pull a ligament/muscle/tendon. **8** to move a switch, etc towards oneself or down in order to operate a machine or piece of equipment: [Vn] *Pull the lever to start the motor.* ○ *Don't pull the trigger yet.* **9** to move or make a vehicle move sideways: [Vpr] *The wheel is pulling to the left.* [Vpr, Vnpr] *She pulled (the van) to the right to avoid the dog.* **10** ~ **sb/sth** (**in**) to attract the interest or support of sb/sth: [Vn] *a campaign to pull in the voters.* **11** (*dated sl*) to attract sb sexually: [Vn] *He can still pull the girls.* **12** (of an engine, etc) to work hard and use a lot of effort in order to operate: [V] *The old car pulled hard as we drove slowly up the hill.* **13** (*infml*) to succeed in playing a trick on sb, committing a crime, etc: [Vn] *They pulled a bank job* (ie robbed a bank). ○ *He's pulling some sort of trick.* **14** to hold oars (OAR) and draw them through the water in order to move a boat along: [Vpr, Vnpr] *They pulled (the boat) towards the shore.* [also V]. **15** to move a handle on a large container causing beer to flow out: [Vn] *She works in the local pub pulling pints.* **IDM pick/pull/tear sb to pieces** ⇨ PIECE¹. **pick/pull/tear sth to pieces** ⇨ PIECE¹. **pull/make faces / a face** ⇨ FACE¹. **pull a 'fast one (on sb)** (*infml*) to trick sb. **pull sb's 'leg** (*infml*) to play a joke on sb, esp by making sb believe sth that is not true: *Don't worry — I was only pulling your leg.* **pull the 'other one (— it's got 'bells on)** (*Brit infml*) (used to indicate that one does not believe what sb has just said). **pull out all the 'stops** (*infml*) to make the greatest effort possible in order to achieve sth: *The airline pulled out all the stops to get him there in time.* **pull the 'plug on sb/sth** (*infml*) to put an end to sb's project, a plan, etc: *The BBC pulled the plug on the series after only five episodes.* **pull one's 'punches** (*infml*) (usu negative) to criticize sb less strongly than one is able to: *He certainly didn't pull any punches when it came to telling me what he thought of my work.* **pull 'rank (on sb)** to make use of one's place or status in society or at work to gain unfair advantages over sb. **pull the rug (out) from under sb's 'feet** (*infml*) to take help or support away from sb suddenly. **pull one's 'socks up** (*Brit infml*) to try to improve one's performance, work, behaviour, etc: *You'll be dropped from the team if you don't pull your socks up.* **pull 'strings (for sb)**; (*US*) **pull 'wires (for sb)** (*infml*) to use one's influence in order to obtain an advantage for sb: *Her father pulled a few strings to get her into university.* **pull the 'strings** to control events or the actions of other people: *Most people think that our politicians run the country, but who is really pulling the strings?* **pull oneself up by one's (own) 'bootstraps** (*infml*) to try to improve one's position in society by one's own efforts. **pull one's 'weight** to work as hard as everybody else in a job, an activity, etc: *We can only win if everyone in the team pulls their weight.* **pull the 'wool over sb's eyes** (*infml*) to hide one's real actions or intentions from sb; to deceive sb: *It's no use trying to pull the wool over my eyes — I know exactly what's going on.* **PHRV ,pull a'head (of sb/sth)** to move in front of sb/sth: *The car behind pulled ahead (of me) as soon as the road was clear.*
'pull at/on sth to breathe in the smoke from a cigarette, etc by taking long deep breaths: *He lit his pipe and pulled on it thoughtfully.*
,pull a'way (from sth) (of a vehicle) to start moving away: *We waved as the bus pulled away.*
,pull (sb) 'back 1 (of an army) to withdraw; to make an army withdraw: *The troops were forced to pull back after the battle.* 2 to decide not to proceed with sth one was intending to do because of possible problems: *Their sponsors pulled back at the last minute.*
,pull sth 'down to destroy a building or other structure completely: *The old cinema has been pulled down.*

ₗ**pull sb** ˈ**in** (*infml*) to bring sb to a police station in order to ask them questions about a crime; to arrest sb. ₗ**pull** ˈ**in sth** (*infml*) to earn the specified large amount of money: *He's pulling in at least £50 000 a year.* ₗ**pull** ˈ**in (to sth)**; ₗ**pull** ˈ**into sth 1** (of a train) to enter a station and stop: *The train pulled in (to the station) and the passengers got off.* **2** (*Brit*) (of a vehicle or its driver) to move to the side of the road or to a specified place and stop: *The police car signalled to us to pull in.* ○ *She pulled into a garage to check the tyres.*

ₗ**pull** ˈ**off (sth)** (of a vehicle or its driver) to leave the road in order to stop for a short time: *pull off the motorway to fill up with petrol.* ₗ**pull sth** ˈ**off** (*infml*) to succeed in doing sth very difficult: *pull off a deal/ coup* ○ *I never thought you'd pull it off.*

ₗ**pull** ˈ**out** (of a vehicle or its driver) to move away from the side of the road, etc: *A car suddenly pulled out in front of me.* ₗ**pull** ˈ**out (of sth)** (of a train) to leave a station: *I arrived just as the last train was pulling out.* ₗ**pull (sb/sth)** ˈ**out (of sth)** to withdraw or make sb/sth withdraw from sth: *They are pulling their troops out of the war zone.* ○ *The project became so expensive that we had to pull out.*

ₗ**pull (sth)** ˈ**over** (of a vehicle) to move or (of a driver) to move a vehicle to the side of the road in order to stop or to let sth pass: *She saw the ambulance coming up behind her and pulled (her car) over.*

ₗ**pull** ˈ**round** (*Brit infml*) to get better again, after an illness: *He seems to be pulling round.*

ₗ**pull (sb)** ˈ**through (sth) 1** to recover or help sb recover from a serious illness, operation, etc: *She's very ill but the doctor thinks she will pull through.* ○ *The love and support of his family helped to pull him through (his illness).* **2** to succeed or to help sb to succeed in doing sth very difficult: *I relied on my instincts to pull me through.*

ₗ**pull to**ˈ**gether** to act, work, etc together with other people in an organized way and without fighting: *If it is to stand any chance of winning the next election, the party must pull together.* ₗ**pull oneself to**ˈ**gether** to take control of one's feelings and behave in a calm way: *Stop crying and pull yourself together!*

ₗ**pull** ˈ**up** (of a vehicle or its driver) to stop: *The driver/car pulled up at the traffic-lights.* ₗ**pull sb** ˈ**up** (*Brit infml*) to criticize sb for sth they have done wrong: *He was pulled up by the chairman for inaccuracies in the report.*

■ ˈ**pull-in** *n* (*Brit infml*) a café by the side of a road, where motorists can stop for a meal or a drink.

ˈ**pull-out** *n* (**a**) a part of a magazine, etc that can be pulled out and kept separately: *Free with this month's issue: a special 32-page pull-out guide to health and fitness.* (**b**) the act of withdrawing an army, etc from a place.

ˈ**pull-up** *n* (usu *pl*) an exercise in which one grips a high bar and pulls the body up by bending the arms.

NOTE Compare **pull**, **drag**, **haul**, **tow**, **trail** and **draw**. All these verbs mean to use strength or force to move something towards you. **Pull** has the widest meaning. A vehicle, an animal or a person can pull an object that is behind it: *We pulled the boat out into the water.* ○ *A tractor was pulling a trailer across the yard.* **Drag** suggests that the object is heavy or difficult to move without a lot of effort, so you need to pull it along the ground: *She dragged the heavy suitcases into the house.* ○ *He had been dragged from the car in the dark.*

Haul often means pulling or raising a heavy object, especially with a rope: *The fishermen hauled in their nets and headed for home.* ○ *Elephants are sometimes used for hauling timber.* **Tow** suggests a vehicle pulling another, usu damaged, vehicle which is attached to it by a rope or chain: *My car broke down and it had to be towed to a garage.*

People **trail** objects behind them carelessly or for no particular reason: *The little boy went upstairs trailing his teddy bear behind him.* People may also **trail** their arms or hands in the water when travelling in a boat. **Draw** is more formal than **pull** and is used especially in writing: *Rosie drew her chair close and whispered confidentially.* **Draw** is also often used to describe animals pulling vehicles: *Cinderella's coach was drawn by six white horses.* ○ *a horse-drawn carriage.*

pull² /pʊl/ *n* **1** [C] ~ **(at/on sth)** an act of pulling sth: *A pull on the rope will make the bell ring.* ○ *I felt a pull at my sleeve and turned round.* **2** [sing] the ~ **(of sth)** (**a**) a strong physical force making sth move in a particular direction: *The tides depend on the pull of the moon.* ○ *The pull of the current carried us downstream.* (**b**) a strong force influencing a person's emotions, behaviour, etc: *He felt the pull of the sea again.* **3** [U] (*infml*) power and influence over other people: *She has a lot of pull with the board of directors.* **4** [C] ~ **(at sth)** (**a**) an act of breathing in smoke from a cigarette, pipe, etc: *She took a long pull at her cigarette.* (**b**) an act of drinking sth deeply: *He took another pull at his beer.* **5** [sing] a long walk up a hill or mountain that requires a lot of effort: *It was a long pull (up) to the top of the crag.* **6** [C] (esp in compounds) a handle for pulling sth: *a* ˈ*bell-pull.* See also RING-PULL.

pullet /ˈpʊlɪt/ *n* a young domestic hen, esp at the age when it begins to lay eggs.

pulley /ˈpʊli/ *n* an apparatus consisting of a wheel over which a rope or chain is stretched. It is used for lifting or lowering heavy things. ⇨ picture.

pulley

Pullman /ˈpʊlmən/ *n* (*pl* **Pullmans**) (also ˈ**Pullman car**, *US* ˈ**parlor car**) (esp formerly) a type of specially comfortable railway carriage.

pullover /ˈpʊləʊvə(r)/ *n* = JERSEY 1.

pulmonary /ˈpʌlmənəri; *US* -neri/ *adj* [attrib] (*medical*) of or affecting the lungs: *the pulmonary arteries* ○ *pulmonary diseases.*

pulp /pʌlp/ *n* **1**(**a**) [U] the soft inner part of fruit; the flesh: *Scoop out the pulp and serve it with sugar.* ○ *tomato pulp.* (**b**) [U, sing] a soft wet substance made esp by crushing or beating sth: *If you cook the vegetables for too long, you'll reduce them to an unattractive pulp.* ○ *Mash the beans (in)to a pulp.* ○ (*fig*) *His face had been **beaten to a pulp** (ie very badly beaten).* (**c**) [U] a soft substance, made from crushed wood, cloth or other material, which is used for making paper: ˈ*wood pulp.* **2** [U] (*derog*) books, magazines, etc that are of poor quality, eg because they are badly written or written simply to shock people reading them: *pulp fiction.*

▶ **pulp** *v* to make sth into a pulp: [Vn] *Unsold copies of the book were pulped.*

pulpy *adj* **1** like or containing a lot of pulp(1): *a pulpy consistency.* **2** (*infml derog*) (of a book or magazine) of poor quality, eg because it is badly written or written simply to shock people: *a pulpy romance.*

pulpit /ˈpʊlpɪt/ *n* a small raised and usu enclosed platform in a church where a priest, etc stands to speak to the people there. Pulpits are usu made of wood or stone: (*fig*) *The policy has been widely condemned from the pulpit* (ie by members of the CLERGY). ⇨ picture at CHURCH.

pulsar /ˈpʌlsɑː(r)/ *n* (*astronomy*) a star, not usu visible, that sends out regular rapid radio signals. Compare QUASAR.

pulsate /pʌlˈseɪt; US ˈpʌlseɪt/ v **1** (also **pulse**) to expand and contract with strong regular movements: [V] *A vein was pulsating on his forehead.* **2** to shake with strong regular movements or sounds; to VIBRATE(1): [V] *pulsating rhythms* ○ *dancing all night in some pulsating disco.* **3** ~ (**with sth**) to be full of excitement, energy, etc: [Vpr] *The streets were pulsating with life.* [V] *a pulsating game.* ▶ **pulsation** /pʌlˈseɪʃn/ n [C,U]: *the pulsation(s) of the blood in the body.*

pulse¹ /pʌls/ n **1** (usu *sing*) the regular beating of blood through the body, esp as felt on the inside of the wrist: *have a rapid/strong/weak pulse* ○ *one's 'pulse rate* (ie the number of times that one's heart beats in one minute) ○ *The doctor took/felt my pulse* (ie counted how many times it beat in one minute). ○ *Fear set her pulse racing.* **2** a strong regular beat in music: *the throbbing pulse of the drums.* **3(a)** a single VIBRATION of sound, light, electric current, etc: *The machine emits sound pulses.* **(b)** (usu *sing*) a series of these: *The machine is operated by an electronic pulse.* **IDM** **have/keep one's finger on the pulse** ⇨ FINGER¹.
▶ **pulse** v **1** ~ (**through sth**) to move with strong regular movements; to beat: [Vpr] *blood pulsing through his veins* ○ (*fig*) *excitement pulsing through the city.* [also V]. **2** [V,Vpr]. = PULSATE 1. **3** ~ (**with sth**) to be full of excitement, energy, etc: [Vpr] *a painting pulsing with colour* [also V].

pulse² /pʌls/ n (usu *pl*) the usu dried seeds of certain plants, eg peas or beans, used as food: *Pulses are a good source of protein.*

pulverize, -ise /ˈpʌlvəraɪz, ˈpʊl-/ v **1** (*fml*) to crush sth into a fine powder: [Vn] *a machine that pulverizes nuts.* **2** (*infml*) to destroy or defeat sb/sth completely: [Vn] *We absolutely pulverized the opposition.*

puma /ˈpjuːmə; US ˈpuːmə/ (also **cougar, panther**) n a large American animal of the cat family with greyish-black fur.

pumice /ˈpʌmɪs/ (also **'pumice-stone**) n [U] a grey rock that is very light in weight. It is used in powder form for cleaning and polishing, and in pieces for rubbing on the skin to soften it.

pummel /ˈpʌml/ v (-ll-; US also -l-) to hit sb/sth repeatedly, esp with the fists (FIST); to beat sb/sth: [Vn] *She pummelled his chest with her free hand.*

pump¹ /pʌmp/ n **1** (esp in compounds) a machine for forcing liquid, gas or air into, out of or through sth, eg water from a WELL⁴(1a), petrol from a tank, air into a tyre or oil through a pipe: *a petrol/foot/bicycle pump* ○ *A pump in the boiler sends hot water round the central heating system.* See also STOMACH-PUMP. ⇨ picture at BICYCLE. **2** an act of pumping: *After several pumps, the water began to flow.* **IDM** **prime the pump** ⇨ PRIME³.
▶ **pump** v **1(a)** to make air, water, etc move in a specified direction by using a pump or sth that operates like a pump: [Vnpr] *Pump air into a tyre* ○ *pump water from a well* ○ *The heart pumps blood round the body.* [Vn-adj] *The lake had been pumped dry.* [V] *You will need to pump hard for several minutes to fill the tank.* [also Vn]. **(b)** (of a liquid) to move in a specified direction as if forced by a pump: [Vpr] *Blood was pumping out of the wound in his leg.* [also Vp]. **2(a)** to move vigorously in and out or up and down: [V] *His heart was pumping with excitement.* [also Vadv]. **(b)** (*infml*) to move sth vigorously up and down: [Vn] *I pumped the brakes but nothing happened.* [Vn,Vnp] *He pumped my hand (up and down) vigorously.* **3** to fill sb/sth with sth: [Vn-adj] *He was pumped full of drugs.* **4** ~ sb (**for sth**) (*infml*) to try to obtain information from sb by asking a lot of questions: [Vnpr] *We tried to pump him for more details.* [also Vn]. **IDM** **pump 'iron** (*infml*) to exercise the body using weights in order to strengthen the muscles. **PHRV** **pump sth 'in/**

'into sth to put a lot of money, effort, etc into sth: *The government has pumped a great deal of money into the project.* **pump sth 'out** (*infml*) to produce sth in large quantities: *loudspeakers pumping out rock music* ○ *Our cars pump out thousands of tonnes of poisonous fumes every year.* **pump sth 'up** fill a tyre, etc with air using a pump.

■ **'pump priming** n [U] (*esp US*) investment, esp by a government, in order to encourage growth in a business or an industry.

'pump-room n (*Brit*) (esp formerly) the room at a SPA where people go to drink the special water.

pump² /pʌmp/ n a light soft shoe worn for dancing, sport, etc.

pumpernickel /ˈpʌmpənɪkl/ n [U] a type of heavy, dark brown RYE bread eaten esp in Germany.

pumpkin /ˈpʌmpkɪn/ n [C,U] a very large round fruit with a thick skin and many seeds. Its orange flesh is used as a vegetable and, esp in the USA, as a filling for pies: *Children often make lanterns out of pumpkins at Hallowe'en.* ○ *pumpkin pie/soup.*

pun /pʌn/ n ~ (**on sth**) the humorous use of a word that has two meanings, or of different words that sound the same; a play on words: *The newspapers were full of puns on the Prime Minister's name, with headlines like 'a Major success.'*
▶ **pun** v (-nn-) [V] to make a pun or puns.

Punch /pʌntʃ/ n **IDM** **pleased as Punch** ⇨ PLEASED.

punch¹ /pʌntʃ/ v **1** ~ (**sb**) (**in/on sth**) to hit sb/sth hard with the FIST: [Vnpr] *punch sb in the face/stomach* [Vn] *He was repeatedly kicked and punched.* ○ (*fig*) *He was punching the air* (ie moving his fist quickly through the air) *in triumph.* **2** to press buttons or keys on a computer, telephone, etc in order to operate it: [Vn] *He began punching the keyboard.* ○ *She punched the wrong number.* **PHRV** **punch sth 'in/'into sth** to give information to a computer by pressing the keys: *punch in all his details* ○ *She punched my name into the computer.*
▶ **punch** n **1** [C] a blow given with the FIST: *give sb a punch on the nose/(US) in the nose* ○ *The fight became serious when people started throwing punches.* **2** [U] the power to interest, excite, etc sb: *a speech with plenty of punch* ○ *The article lacks real punch.* **IDM** **pack a punch** ⇨ PACK². **pull one's punches** ⇨ PULL¹.

puncher n: *He's a heavy/strong/powerful puncher.*
punchy adj (-ier, -iest) (*infml*) having PUNCH¹ n(2): *a punchy argument/debate.*

■ **'punch-drunk** adj **(a)** (of a boxer) unsteady or confused because of damage to the brain as a result of being repeatedly punched on the head. **(b)** in a confused state, eg after working very hard: *Parents and teachers have been left punch-drunk by repeated government efforts to reform the education system.*

'punch-line n the last few words of a joke or story which give it humour.

'punch-up n (*Brit infml*) a physical fight: *The argument ended in a punch-up.*

punch² /pʌntʃ/ n a tool or machine for cutting holes in leather, metal, paper, etc.
▶ **punch** v ~ sth (**in sth**) to make a hole in sth with a punch: [Vn] *punch a train ticket* [Vnpr] *punch holes in a sheet of metal.* **PHRV** **punch (sb) 'in/'out** (*US*) = CLOCK (SB) IN/OUT. **'punch card** (also **'punched 'card**) n a card on which information is recorded by punching holes in it, used formerly for giving instructions or data to a computer.

punch³ /pʌntʃ/ n [U] a drink made from wine or spirits mixed with water, fruit juice, sugar, spices, etc and drunk hot or cold: *rum punch.* Compare CUP¹.

■ **'punch-bowl** n a bowl in which punch is mixed and served: *a glass punch-bowl.*

Punch and Judy show /ˌpʌntʃ ən ˈdʒuːdi ʃəʊ/ n (in Britain) a traditional comic PUPPET(1) show for children in which the character Punch fights with his wife Judy.

punchbag /'pʌntʃbæg/ (*Brit*) (*US* **'punching bag**) *n* a heavy stuffed bag, hung on a rope, which is punched for exercise or training, esp by boxers.

punchball /'pʌntʃbɔːl/ *n* a heavy leather ball, fixed on a spring, which is punched (PUNCH¹) for exercise or training, esp by boxers.

punctilious /pʌŋk'tɪliəs/ *adj* (*fml esp approv*) very careful to carry out one's duties correctly; showing great attention to details of behaviour: *a punctilious butler* ○ *a punctilious observance of the formalities.* ▶ **punctiliously** *adv*: *observe the rules punctiliously.* **punctiliousness** *n* [U].

punctual /'pʌŋktʃuəl/ *adj* happening or doing sth at the agreed or proper time: *a punctual start to the meeting* ○ *be punctual for an appointment* ○ *The tenants are always punctual in paying the rent.* ▶ **punctuality** /ˌpʌŋktʃu'æləti/ *n* [U]. **punctually** /'pʌŋktʃuəli/ *adv*: *arrive/depart punctually.*

punctuate /'pʌŋktʃueɪt/ *v* **1** ~ **sth** (**with sth**) to interrupt sth at intervals: [Vn] *Her speech was punctuated by bursts of applause from the crowd.* ○ *He constantly punctuates his sentences with hand gestures.* **2** to divide writing into sentences, phrases, etc by using special marks, eg full stops, question marks, etc: [Vn] *The transcription of his speech needs to be punctuated.* [also V].
▶ **punctuation** /ˌpʌŋktʃu'eɪʃn/ *n* [U] the action or system of punctuating: *mistakes in spelling and punctuation.*
■ **ˌpunctu'ation mark** *n* any of the marks used to punctuate writing: *Punctuation marks include commas, colons, full stops, question marks, etc.* ⇨ App 3.

puncture /'pʌŋktʃə(r)/ *n* (**a**) a small hole in a tyre made by a sharp point: *The car had a puncture.* ○ *I got a puncture on the way and arrived late.* ○ *mend a puncture.* (**b**) any similar small hole in sth: *She had two small puncture marks in her skin where the snake had bitten her.*
▶ **puncture** *v* **1**(**a**) to make a small hole in sth: [Vn] *puncture a tyre/balloon* ○ *She was taken to the hospital with broken ribs and a punctured lung.* (**b**) (of a tyre, etc) to get a puncture: [V] *Both his tyres punctured on the stony road.* **2** to reduce sb's pride, confidence, etc: [Vn] *puncture sb's illusions/complacency.*

pundit /'pʌndɪt/ *n* (*often joc*) a person who knows a lot about a particular subject; an expert: *a panel of well-known television pundits* ○ *The pundits disagree on the best way of dealing with the problem.*

pungent /'pʌndʒənt/ *adj* **1** having a strong sharp taste or smell: *the pungent smell of garlic.* **2** strong, direct and often critical: *pungent remarks/criticism/satire* ○ *a pungent style of writing.* ▶ **pungency** /-nsi/ *n* [U]. **pungently** *adv*.

punish /'pʌnɪʃ/ *v* (**a**) ~ **sb** (**for sth / doing sth**) (**by/with sth**) to make sb suffer, eg by sending them to prison or by making them pay money, because they have broken the law or done sth wrong: [Vn] *Those responsible for this crime will be severely punished.* [Vnpr] *How should society punish a man for the murder of his wife/for murdering his wife?* ○ *She was punished with ten years in prison.* ○ *They used to punish the children by sending them to bed early.* (**b**) ~ **sth** (**by/with sth**) to cause sb to suffer for a particular crime or wrongdoing: [Vn] *Aggressive behaviour should always be punished.* [Vnpr] *punish dangerous driving with heavy fines.*
▶ **punishable** *adj* ~ (**by sth**) (of a crime, etc) that can be punished, esp by law: *This crime is punishable by death in some countries.* ○ *Giving false information to the police is a punishable offence.*
punishing *adj* [usu attrib] that makes one very tired or weak: *a punishing routine/schedule* ○ *a punishing defeat.*

punishment *n* **1**(**a**) [U] the action of punishing sb or of being punished: *to escape punishment* ○ *capital punishment* (ie punishment by death). See also COR-PORAL PUNISHMENT. (**b**) [C] a way in which a person is punished: *The punishments inflicted on the children were too severe.* ○ *The punishment should fit the crime.* **2** [U] rough treatment: *He works as a miner, and his body has taken a lot of punishment over the years.*

punitive /'pjuːnətɪv/ *adj* (*fml*) (**a**) intended as punishment: *take punitive action against sb* ○ *carry out a punitive raid on a rebel village.* (**b**) very severe; harsh: *punitive taxation.* ▶ **punitively** *adv*.

punk /pʌŋk/ *n* **1**(**a**) (also ˌpunk **'rock**) [U] a type of loud violent rock³ music popular amongst young people esp in the late 1970s and early 1980s. Punk often expresses a protest against conventional attitudes and behaviour: *a punk band/record.* (**b**) (also ˌpunk **'rocker**) [C] a person who likes punk music and dresses like punk musicians, eg by wearing metal chains, clothes with holes in and brightly coloured hair: *a punk hairstyle.* **2** [C] (*infml derog esp US*) a young man or boy who is regarded with contempt because he behaves in a rude or violent way or because he is considered unimportant.

punnet /'pʌnɪt/ *n* (*esp Brit*) a small light square basket in which soft fruits are often sold: *The strawberries are 90p a punnet.*

punster /'pʌnstə(r)/ *n* a person who often makes puns (PUN).

punt¹ /pʌnt/ *n* a long shallow boat with a flat bottom and square ends which is moved by pushing the end of a long pole against the bottom of a river.
▶ **punt** *v* to travel in a punt, esp for pleasure: [V] *She soon learned to punt.* ○ *They often go punting on the river.* [also Vpr, Vp].

punt² /pʌnt/ *v* [Vn] to kick a football after it has dropped from the hands and before it reaches the ground.
▶ **punt** *n* a kick made by punting the ball.

punt³ /pʌnt/ *v* (*infml*) [V] to risk money by investing, playing games of chance, etc; to gamble. ▶ **punt** *n* (*infml*): *Investors did not feel it was a good punt.*

punt⁴ /pʊnt/ *n* the unit of the money in the Republic of Ireland.

punter /'pʌntə(r)/ *n* (**a**) a person who gambles. (**b**) (*infml derog*) a person who buys or uses a particular product or service; a customer or client: *It's important to keep the punters happy.* ○ *The average punter will not notice the difference.*

puny /'pjuːni/ *adj* (**-ier**, **-iest**) (*usu derog*) (**a**) small and weak: *puny limbs/muscles* ○ *The newborn lamb was a puny little creature.* (**b**) very poor in ability, quality, amount or size: *They laughed at my puny efforts at rock-climbing.* ○ *We're only getting a puny 1% pay rise this year.*

pup /pʌp/ *n* **1**(**a**) = PUPPY 1. (**b**) a young animal of various species: *a mother seal and her pup.* **2** = PUPPY 2. **IDM** **sell sb / buy a pup** (*Brit infml*) to sell sb/be sold sth that is worthless, or worth much less than the price paid for it.

pupa /'pjuːpə/ *n* (*pl* **pupae** /'pjuːpiː/) an insect in the stage of development between a LARVA and an adult insect. ⇨ picture at BUTTERFLY. Compare CHRYSALIS.
▶ **pupate** /pjuː'peɪt; *US* 'pjuːpeɪt/ *v* [V] (*techn*) (of an insect LARVA) to develop into a pupa.

pupil¹ /'pjuːpl/ *n* (**a**) (*esp Brit*) a person, esp a child, who is taught in school or privately: *There are 30 pupils in the class.* ○ *a former pupil of the school* ○ *She takes private pupils as well as teaching in a school.* (**b**) a person who is taught and influenced by an expert, eg in the arts: *The painting is the work of one of Rembrandt's pupils.*

pupil² /'pjuːpl/ *n* the dark circular opening in the

centre of the eye that becomes smaller in bright light and larger in the dark. ⇨ picture at EYE[1].

puppet

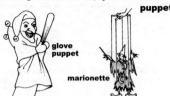

glove puppet

marionette

puppet /'pʌpɪt/ n **1** a small figure of a person or an animal that can be made to move, eg by pulling strings attached to its limbs, or by putting one's hand inside it. Puppets are used for telling a story or as a form of entertainment: *a Batman puppet* ○ *a puppet theatre/show.* ⇨ picture. See also GLOVE PUPPET, MARIONETTE. **2** (*usu derog*) a person or group whose actions are controlled by another: *a puppet government/state* (ie one controlled by another power) ○ *The union representative was accused of being a puppet of the management.*
▶ **puppeteer** /ˌpʌpɪ'tɪə(r)/ n a person who performs with a puppet(1) or puppets.
puppetry /'pʌpɪtri/ n [U] the art of making and controlling puppets (PUPPET 1).

puppy /'pʌpi/ (also **pup** /pʌp/) n **1** a young dog: *a spaniel puppy.* **2** (*dated infml derog*) a proud or rude young man: *You insolent young puppy!*
■ **'puppy-fat** (*Brit*) (*US* **baby fat**) n [U] (*infml*) fat on the body of a child which disappears as the child grows older. ⇨ note at FAT[1].
'puppy love (also **calf-love**) n [U] (*infml*) a strong, usu temporary, feeling of love, esp between older children or young adults. Compare CRUSH[2] 2.

purchase[1] /'pɜːtʃəs/ n (*fml*) **1(a)** [U,C] the action or process of buying sth: *the date of purchase* ○ *loans for the purchase of equipment* ○ *The receipt is your proof of purchase.* ○ *House purchases are on the increase.* ○ *a compulsory purchase order* (ie one issued by a public authority on sb's property, usu in order to destroy it and build a road, new houses, etc). See also HIRE PURCHASE. **(b)** a thing bought: *He laid his purchases out on the table.* ○ *He was seen **making a purchase** at the station bookstall.* **2** [sing, U] a firm hold or grip on sth, eg on a flat surface: *The climbers had difficulty getting a/any purchase on the rock face.*
■ **'purchase price** n the price paid or to be paid for sth: *The purchase price is less if you pay by cash.*
purchase[2] /'pɜːtʃəs/ v ~ **sth** (**from sb/with sth**) (*fml*) to buy sth: [Vnpr] *purchase a house with a loan from a building society* [Vn] *Employees are encouraged to purchase shares in the firm.* ○ (*fig*) *The firm's financial stability was purchased at the cost of its independence.*
▶ **purchaser** n (*fml*) a person who buys sth: *houses at prices attractive to potential/prospective purchasers.* Compare VENDOR 2.
purchasing n [U] (*commerce*) the activity of buying things, eg in a business firm: *the company's purchasing manager.* **'purchasing power** [U] **(a)** money available to buy goods with: *Inflation reduces the purchasing power of people living on fixed incomes.* **(b)** the value of a unit of money measured in terms of what it can buy: *a decline in the purchasing power of the dollar.*

purdah /'pɜːdə/ n [U] the system in certain Muslim and Hindu societies of keeping women from public view, eg by giving them a separate room in the house or special clothing to wear when they go outside: *keep sb/be/live **in purdah**.*

pure /pjʊə(r)/ adj (-r /'pjʊərə(r)/; -st /'pjʊərɪst/) **1(a)** not mixed with any other substance, colour,

emotion, etc: *pure gold/silk/wool* ○ *made from 100% pure cotton* ○ *water of the purest blue* ○ *pure bliss/joy/pleasure.* **(b)** clean and not mixed with any harmful substances: *pure water* ○ *The air is so pure in these mountains.* **(c)** not of mixed race, breed or origin: *The cat is a pure Siamese.* **2** [attrib] (used for emphasis; not in the comparative) nothing but; complete; SHEER[1](1): *They met by pure accident/chance/coincidence.* ○ *pure folly/extravagance/nonsense* ○ *do sth out of pure kindness/malice/mischief* ○ *Reports that he may resign are pure speculation* (ie probably not true). **3** without evil or sin, esp sexual sin; innocent or morally good: *pure thoughts* ○ *His motives were pure.* ○ (*rhet*) *pure in body and mind/pure in heart.* **4** (of sound) clear and steady: *a pure note/voice.* **5** (*usu approv*) having no complicated or unnecessary elements; simple: *the clean, pure lines of classical architecture.* **6** [attrib] dealing with theory only; studied for its own sake without immediate practical application: *pure mathematics/science/research.* Compare APPLIED. See also PURIFY, PURITY. **IDM** **,pure and 'simple** (used after the n referred to) and nothing else; only this: *It's laziness, pure and simple.* ○ *The reason for the change is lack of money, pure and simple.*
▶ **purely** adv only; entirely: *Their meeting was purely accidental/coincidental.* ○ *He bought the house purely as an investment.*
■ **'pure-bred** adj (of an animal) of one single breed; not of mixed stock: *a pure-bred Alsatian dog.* See also THOROUGHBRED.

purée /'pjʊəreɪ; *US* pjʊə'reɪ/ n [U,C] (often in compounds) food in the form of a thick liquid made eg by crushing fruit or cooked vegetables in a small amount of water: *make apple/tomato/chestnut purée* ○ *a raspberry purée.*
▶ **purée** v (*pt, pp* **puréed**) to make food into a purée: [Vn] *puréed carrots.*

purgative /'pɜːɡətɪv/ n, adj (a substance, esp a medicine) that causes the bowels to empty: *This oil acts as a purgative/has a purgative effect.*

purgatory /'pɜːɡətri; *US* -tɔːri/ n [U] **1** (also **Purgatory**) (in Roman Catholic teaching) a place or condition in which the souls of dead people are made pure by suffering in preparation for Heaven: *a prayer for the souls in purgatory.* **2** (*esp infml or joc*) any place or condition of suffering: *Getting up at four in the morning is sheer purgatory!*

purge /pɜːdʒ/ v **1** ~ **oneself/sb/sth** (**of sth**); ~ **sth from sth** to make oneself/sb/sth pure by removing sth bad or undesirable: [Vnpr] *She wanted to purge these unhappy memories from her mind/purge her mind of these unhappy memories.* [also Vn]. **2** ~ **sth** (**of sb**); ~ **sb** (**from sth**) to rid an organization, esp a political party, of people considered to be undesirable: [Vnpr] *purge the party of extremists/purge extremists from the party* ○ *Officers who were not loyal to the king were purged.*
▶ **purge** n an act of ridding an organization of people who are considered undesirable: *a purge of disloyal members* ○ *political purges that followed the change of government.*

purify /'pjʊərɪfaɪ/ v (*pt, pp* **-fied**) **(a)** ~ **sth** (**of sth**) to make sth pure by removing dirty, harmful or undesirable substances: [Vn] *the water is purified as it passes through the rock.* ○ *Water-purifying tablets* ○ *purified air* [Vnpr] *The soil has to be purified of all bacteria.* **(b)** to make sb pure by removing their sins, esp in a religious ceremony: [Vn] *Hindus purify themselves by bathing in the river Ganges.* ▶
purification /ˌpjʊərɪfɪ'keɪʃn/ n [U]: *a water-purification plant* ○ *the purification of souls.*

purist /'pjʊərɪst/ n a person who considers it very important that things should be correct or genuine, eg in the use of language or in the arts: *Purists may*

be shocked by the changes made to the text of the play.
▶ **purism** /'pjʊərɪzəm/ n [U] (*fml*).

puritan /'pjʊərɪtən/ n **1** (*usu derog*) a person who has extremely strict moral attitudes and who tends to regard pleasure as a sin: *the puritans who want to clean up television* (eg by not allowing bad language, sex and violence). **2 Puritan** a member of the group of English Protestants in the 16th and 17th centuries who wanted simpler forms of worship.
▶ **puritan** adj **1 Puritan** of or relating to the Puritans: *Puritan Ministers/doctrines.* **2** = PURITANICAL.
puritanical /ˌpjʊərɪ'tænɪkl/ adj (*usu derog*) having or involving very strict moral attitudes: *a puritanical view/upbringing/society* ○ *My grandparents were very puritanical.*
puritanism /'pjʊərɪtənɪzəm/ n [U] **1 Puritanism** the practices and beliefs of the Puritans. **2** very strict moral attitudes.

purity /'pjʊərəti/ n [U] the state or quality of being pure: *purity of colour/form/sound* ○ *test the purity of the water* ○ *question the purity of sb's motives.*

purl /pɜːl/ (also 'purl stitch) n [C,U] a stitch in knitting that produces ridges on the upper side: *a purl row.*
▶ **purl** v to knit sth in purl stitch: [Vn] *Knit one* (ie make one plain stitch), *purl one.* [also V].

purlieus /'pɜːljuːz/ n [pl] (*fml or rhet*) the area near or surrounding a place: *a fashionable residence in the purlieus of the capital.*

purloin /pɜː'lɔɪn, 'pɜːlɔɪn/ v ~ **sth** (**from sb/sth**) (*fml or joc*) to steal sth or use sth without permission: [Vnpr] *use techniques purloined from the media* [also Vn].

purple /'pɜːpl/ adj **1** having the colour of red and blue mixed together: *a purple flower/dress/bruise* ○ *He/His face was/went purple with rage.* **2** [attrib] (*fml*) (of writing or speech) elaborate or exaggerated in style, esp when expressing strong emotion: *purple passages/patches/prose.*
▶ **purple** n [U,C]: *dressed all in purple* ○ *the deep purples of plums and blackberries.*
purplish /'pɜːplɪʃ/ adj rather purple in colour: *a purplish light/sky.*
■ ˌPurple 'Heart n (*US*) a MEDAL awarded to a soldier who has been wounded in battle.

purport /pə'pɔːt/ v (*fml*) to claim or pretend to be sth; to be intended to appear as sth: [V.*to* inf] *The document purports to be an official statement.*
▶ **purported** adj [attrib] (*fml*) claimed, reported or assumed to be the case: *a purported disagreement between members of the government* ○ *the purported ringleader of the plot.* **purportedly** adv: *a letter purportedly written by Shakespeare.*
purport /'pɜːpɔːt/ n [sing] ~ **of sth** (*fml*) the general meaning or intention of sth: *I do not understand the purport of your question.*

purpose /'pɜːpəs/ n **1** [C] (**a**) an intention, an aim or a function of sth; a reason for doing sth: *What is the purpose of the meeting?* ○ *Getting rich seems to be her only purpose in life.* ○ *The building is no longer used for its original purpose.* ○ *a dual-purpose tool* (ie with two different functions) ○ *He went to her house with the sole purpose of threatening her.* ○ *We have found an office that will serve our purpose.* (**b**) **purposes** [pl] the requirements of a particular situation: *These gifts count as income for tax purposes.* ○ *for administrative/medical/insurance purposes* ○ *For the purposes of our argument, let us assume that sales rise by 5%.* **2** [U] (**a**) meaning; satisfaction: *Her work for charity gives a sense of purpose to her life.* (**b**) (*fml*) the ability to plan sth and work effectively to achieve it; determination: *Her approach to the job lacks purpose.* **IDM** **at cross purposes** ⇨ CROSS³. **for practical purposes** ⇨ PRACTICAL. **on 'purpose** not by accident; intentionally: *'Was it broken accidentally?' 'No, he did it on purpose.'* ○ *She*

does these things on purpose to annoy me. **to all intents and purposes** ⇨ INTENT². **to little/no/some 'purpose** (*fml*) with little/no useful result or effect: *Money has been invested in the scheme to very little/to no useful purpose.*
▶ **purposeful** /-fl/ adj (**a**) showing determination to achieve sth: *They set about dealing with the problem in a purposeful way.* (**b**) (*fml*) having a useful purpose: *Young people's energies should be directed towards more purposeful activities.* **purposefully** /-fəli/ adv: *He strode purposefully into the meeting.*
purposeless adj without a purpose: *a purposeless existence.*
purposely adv on purpose; intentionally: *He was being purposely slow.*
purposive /'pɜːpəsɪv/ adj (*fml*) having a clear and definite purpose: *acting in a purposive manner.*
■ ˌpurpose-'built adj (*esp Brit*) made for a particular purpose: *a ˌpurpose-built 'factory/'stadium.*

purr /pɜː(r)/ v (**a**) (of a cat) to make a low continuous sound in the throat, esp when pleased or comfortable: [V] *purring contentedly on my lap.* (**b**) (of machinery) to make a similar smooth regular sound; to move making such a sound: [Vp] *The car purred along smoothly in top gear.* [also V, Vpr]. (**c**) to speak in a low voice, eg when expressing happiness or satisfaction: [V.speech] *'I'm having such a lovely time,' she purred.* [Vpr] *purr with anticipation/delight* [also V].
▶ **purr** n (esp sing) a purring sound: *the purr of a contented cat/a car engine.*

purse¹ /pɜːs/ n **1** [C] a small bag made of leather, plastic, etc for carrying money, esp coins, in: *She took a coin from her purse and gave it to the child.* Compare WALLET. **2** [sing] money available for spending: *excursions to suit every purse* ○ *Should spending on the arts be met out of the public purse?* See also PRIVY PURSE. **3** [C] (*sport*) a sum of money given as a prize: *fighting for a purse of $500000.* **4** [C] (*US*) = HANDBAG. ⇨ picture at LUGGAGE.
■ 'purse-strings n [pl] the way in which money is spent: *get a tighter grip on the purse-strings* ○ *The government controls/holds the purse-strings.*

purse² /pɜːs/ v to form one's mouth into a small tight round shape: [Vn] *Her lips were pursed in concentration/disapproval.*

purser /'pɜːsə(r)/ n an officer responsible for the welfare of passengers on a ship or an aircraft.

pursuance /pə'sjuːəns; *US* -'suː-/ n **IDM** **in (the) pursuance of sth** (*fml*) while performing sth; in the course of sth: *costs incurred in pursuance of a claim against a travel agent.*

pursuant /pə'sjuːənt; *US* -'suː-/ adj ~ **to sth** (*fml*) (usu following ns) conforming to sth: *be given power pursuant to Section 95 of the Companies Act 1985.*

pursue /pə'sjuː; *US* -'suː/ v **1** to follow or chase sb/sth, esp in order to catch them/it: [Vn] *bank robbers closely/hotly pursued by the police* ○ *She was pursued by photographers everywhere she went.* ○ (*fig*) *His eyes pursued her throughout the evening.* **2** (*fml*) to do, have or take part in sth: [Vn] *pursue a policy of non-intervention* ○ *pursue a goal/an aim/an ideal* ○ *All students have to pursue a two-year course in mathematics.* **3** (*fml*) to continue to be interested or involved in sth; to proceed further with sth: [Vn] *She decided to pursue her studies after obtaining her first degree.* ○ *pursue legal action* ○ *The suggestion is not worth pursuing.*
▶ **pursuer** n a person who pursues (PURSUE 1) sb: *He managed to avoid/outwit his pursuers.*

pursuit /pə'sjuːt; *US* -'suːt/ n **1** ~ **of sth** the action of looking for or trying to find sth: *people travelling round the country in pursuit of work* ○ *the relentless pursuit of wealth/power* ○ *his single-minded pursuit of perfection.* **2** [U] the action of following or chasing sb/sth in order to catch them/

it: *a red Ferrari with two police cars* **in pursuit** ○ *The police* **gave pursuit** (ie started chasing them) *immediately.* **3** [C usu *pl*] a thing to which one gives one's time and energy; an occupation or an activity: *outdoor/leisure/artistic/scientific pursuits.* **IDM** **in hot pursuit** ⇨ HOT.

purulent /ˈpjʊərələnt/ *adj* (*medical*) of, containing or discharging PUS: *a purulent discharge from the ear.*

purvey /pəˈveɪ/ *v* ~ **sth** (**to sb**) (*fml*) to supply or make available food, services or information, esp as one's business: [Vn] *a newspaper purveying subversive ideas* [also Vnpr].
▶ **purveyor** *n* (*fml*) a person or company that supplies or makes sth available: *Brown and Son, purveyors of fine wines.*

purview /ˈpɜːvjuː/ *n* (*fml*) [U] the scope of sb's activities or influence: *questions that lie outside/that do not come within the purview of the present inquiry.*

pus /pʌs/ *n* [U] a thick yellowish liquid formed in and coming out from an infected wound: *The bandage was soaked in blood and pus.*

push¹ /pʊʃ/ *v* **1** to stand behind sth/sb and use esp one's hands to move it/them away from oneself or to a different position: [V] *Don't push until I tell you to.* [Vn] *He was pushing a pram.* [Vnpr] *Let's push the table nearer the wall.* ○ *He pushed a plate of biscuits towards me.* ○ *She pushed the car onto the verge.* [Vnadj] *The dog pushed the door open.* [Vnadv] *He pushed her to and fro on the swing.* [Vpr] *He pushed (hard) against the door with his shoulder.* ⇨ picture at PULL¹. **2** to move forward by forcing one's way through a group of people or things: [Vp, Vpr] *The crowd pushed past (us).* [Vnp, Vnpr] *We had to push our way through (the crowd).* [V] *There's no need to push, Roy, we've got plenty of time.* ○ *There was a lot of pushing and shoving to get a good view of the finish.* **3** to put one's body or part of one's body in a particular position: [Vnpr] *She pushed her head further under the blanket.* [Vnp] *He pushed himself up from the sofa.* **4** to press a switch, button, etc in order to make sth operate: [Vn] *Push the doorbell.* ○ *You can get sugar (in your coffee) by pushing the red button.* **5** to advance quickly through an area: [Vpr, Vp] *The army pushed (on) towards the Nile.* **6** ~ **sb** (**into sth / doing sth**); ~ **sb** (**for sth / to do sth**) (*infml*) to urge sb to do sth that they may not want to do; to put pressure on sb: [Vn] *You'll have to push him or he'll do no work at all.* ○ *She pushes her children too hard.* [Vnpr] *She was pushed into going to university by her parents.* ○ *push sb for an explanation/for payment* [Vn.*to inf*] *We pushed him to take up science.* **7** (*infml*) to work hard in order to persuade people to buy goods, accept an idea, etc; to promote sth: [Vn] *We must be pushing the new model hard.* ○ *Unless you push your claim, you will not get satisfaction.* **8** (*infml*) to sell illegal drugs: [Vn] *She was arrested for pushing heroin.* ⇨ note at SELL. **IDM** **be pushing sth** (*infml*) to be nearly the specified age: *He must be pushing* ˈ*60 by now.* **push the** ˈ**boat out** (*Brit infml*) to spend more money than usual to celebrate sth: *This is the last time we'll see her, so let's really push the boat out.* **push one's** ˈ**luck** (*infml*) to take a risk with sth because one is too confident of success: *You didn't get caught last time, but don't push your luck!* **push up (the)** ˈ**daisies** (*infml joc*) to be dead and in one's grave: *I'll be pushing up the daisies by the time this project is finished!* **PHRV** **push sb a'bout/a'round** (*infml*) to give sb orders in an unpleasant way: *She left because she didn't like being pushed round by her manager.* **push a'head/'on** to continue as fast as possible on one's way: *Let's push on — it'll be dark soon.* **push a'head/'forward/'on (with sth)** to continue doing sth in a determined way: *push ahead with one's*

ˈ*plans* ○ *We ignored all the interruptions and pushed* ˌ*on with the* ˈ*meeting.*
push a'long (*infml*) to leave a place: *It's late — I'd better be pushing along now.*
ˈ**push for sth** to make repeated and urgent requests for sth: *push for electoral reform.*
ˌ**push** ˈ**forward** to force others to consider or notice sth: *He repeatedly pushed forward his own claim.* ˌ**push oneself** ˈ**forward** (*often derog*) to try to attract attention to oneself for one's own advantage.
ˌ**push** ˈ**in** to go in front of other people who are already waiting for sth: *I was standing in the queue and this man pushed in (in front of me).*
ˌ**push** ˈ**off 1** (*infml*) (often imperative) to go away: *Push off! We don't want you here.* ○ *They obviously didn't want us to stay, so we pushed off.* **2** to make a boat move away from the shore, etc by pushing against it with an oar.
ˌ**push** ˈ**out** (*infml*) to produce sth in large quantities: *factories pushing out cheap cotton goods.*
ˌ**push sb/sth** ˈ**over** to make sb/sth fall by pushing.
ˌ**push sth** ˈ**through (sth)** to get sth officially accepted or completed quickly: *push reforms through* ○ *push a plan through the committee stage.*
ˌ**push sth** ˈ**up** to make the price, value, etc of sth increase: *A shortage of building land will push property values up.*
▶ **pushed** *adj* [pred] (*infml*) **1** ~ **for sth** not having enough of sth: *be very pushed for money/space/time.* **2(a)** ~ (**to do sth**) having difficulty doing sth: *We'll be pushed to get there in time.* (**b**) busy: *I'm a bit pushed at the moment — can I ring you back?*
pusher 1 (*infml*) a person who sells illegal drugs. **2** a person or thing that pushes sb/sth: *a wheelchair pusher.* See also PEN-PUSHER.
■ ˈ**push-bike** *n* (*Brit infml*) a bicycle: *an old push-bike.*
ˈ**push-button** *adj* [attrib] operated by pressing a button or buttons: *a radio with push-button tuning* ○ *a push-button phone.*
ˈ**push-up** *n* (*esp US*) = PRESS-UP.

push² /pʊʃ/ *n* **1** [C] an act of pushing sth/sb: *The car won't start — I need a push.* ○ *He gave me a violent push in the back.* ○ *The whole system can be activated* **at the push of a button.** **2** [C] a large and determined military attack: *It was decided to postpone the big push until the spring.* **3** [U] (*infml*) determination to succeed: *He hasn't enough push to be a successful salesman.* **IDM** **at a** ˈ**push** (*infml esp Brit*) only with difficulty: *We can provide accommodation for six people at a push.* **give sb / get the** ˈ**push** (*infml esp Brit*) **1** to dismiss sb/to be dismissed from one's job: *He got the push when the new manager came.* **2** to end one's relationship with sb: *He gave his girlfriend the push.* **when** ˌ**push comes to** ˈ**shove** when there is no other choice; when everything else has failed.
■ ˈ**push-start** *v* [Vn] to start a vehicle by pushing it along to make the engine turn. ˈ**push-start** *n.*

pushcart /ˈpʊʃkɑːt/ *n* a small cart pushed by hand.

pushchair /ˈpʊʃtʃeə(r)/ (*Brit*) (also *esp US* **stroller**) *n* a small folding chair on wheels in which a baby or small child is pushed from place to place.

pushover /ˈpʊʃəʊvə(r)/ *n* (*infml*) (**a**) a thing that is very easily done or won: *The match was certainly no pushover.* (**b**) a person who is easily persuaded or influenced: *Borrowing money from her is easy — she's a pushover.*

pushy /ˈpʊʃi/ *adj* (*infml derog*) trying constantly to draw attention to oneself; openly ambitious: *a pushy wife* ○ *He made himself unpopular by being so pushy.*
▶ **pushiness** *n* [U].

pusillanimous /ˌpjuːsɪˈlænɪməs, ˌpjuːzɪ-/ *adj* (*fml*) frightened of taking risks; cowardly: *a pusillanim-*

ous minister. ▶ **pusillanimity** /ˌpjuːsɪləˈnɪməti, ˌpjuːzɪ-/ *n* [U]. **pusillanimously** *adv*.

puss /pʊs/ *n* **1** (*esp Brit*) (used for calling or talking to a cat: *Puss, puss, where are you?* **2** [sing] (*sl esp US*) the face: *a smack in the puss.*

▶ **pussy** /ˈpʊsi/ *n* **1** (also **ˈpussy-cat**) (used by and when talking to small children) a cat. **2** (⚠ *sl*) the female sexual organs, esp the VULVA.

■ **ˈpussy willow** *n* a small tree that has soft furry (FUR) grey flowers in spring.

pussyfoot *v* ~ (**about/around**) (*infml usu derog*) to be cautious or careful in expressing one's opinions in order to avoid annoying or upsetting sb: [Vp] *Stop pussyfooting around and say what you mean.* [also V].

pustule /ˈpʌstjuːl; *US* -tʃuːl/ *n* (*medical*) a small spot on the skin, esp one containing PUS.

put /pʊt/ *v* (**-tt-**; *pt, pp* **put**) **1** to move sth into a particular place or position; to place sth somewhere: [Vnpr] *She put the book on the table.* ○ *Did you put sugar in my coffee?* ○ *She put her arm round his shoulders.* ○ *It's time to put the baby to bed.* [Vnadv] *Where did you put the scissors?* ○ *He put the newspaper aside and turned to speak to me.* [Vnp] *Put your hand up if you want more paper.* **2** to fit or fix sth to sth else: [Vnpr] *Will you please put a patch on these trousers?* ○ *We must put a new lock on the front door.* **3** to move sth into a particular place or position using force: [Vnpr] *She put a knife between his ribs.* ○ *He put his fist through a plate-glass door.* **4** to cause sb/sth to go to a particular place: [Vnpr] *Her family put her in an old people's home.* ○ *put a satellite into orbit* ○ *It was the year the Americans put a man on the moon.* **5** to write sth or make a mark on sth: [Vnpr] *put one's signature to a document* [Vnadv] *Put your name here.* [Vn] *I couldn't read what he had put.* **6** to bring sb/sth into the specified state or condition: [Vnpr] *I was put in charge of the office.* ○ *The incident put her in a bad mood.* ○ *She immediately put me at (my) ease.* ○ *Your decision puts me in an awkward position.* ○ *I will try to put the matter into perspective.* ○ *His refusal to cooperate puts our plans at risk.* ○ *Let's put your suggestion into practice.* ○ *The injury to her back will put her out of action for several weeks.* **7** ~ **sth on/onto/to sth** to make sb/sth feel sth or be affected by sth; to IMPOSE(1b) sth on sb/sth: [Vnpr] *He new job has **put a great strain on** him.* ○ *They **put pressure on** him to resign.* ○ *It put the onus on her to make the final decision.* ○ *They put all the blame on/onto me.* ○ *It's time you **put a stop to** this childish behaviour.* **8** ~ **sth on sth** to give or attach a particular level of importance, trust, value, etc to sth: [Vnpr] *Our company puts the emphasis on quality.* ○ *He put a limit on the amount we could spend on the project.* **9** to rank or classify sb/sth at the specified level: [Vnpr] *I put her in the top rank of modern novelists.* ○ *As a writer I'd put him on a par/level with Joyce.* **10** to express or state sth in a particular way or form: [Vnadv] *She put it very tactfully.* ○ *The meat was — how shall I put it? — a little overdone.* ○ *As T S Eliot puts it …* ○ *To put it simply/Put simply, we accept their offer or go bankrupt.* ○ *'The election result was a disaster for the country.' 'I wouldn't put it quite like that.'* [Vnpr] *Can you help me put this letter into good English, please?* **11** (*sport*) [Vn] to throw the SHOT. Compare SHOT-PUT. **IDM** Most idioms containing **put** are at the entries for the nouns or adjectives in the idioms, eg **put one's foot in it** ⇨ FOOT¹; **put/set sb/sth right** ⇨ RIGHT¹. **not put it ˈpast sb (to do sth)** (*infml*) (used with *would*) to consider sb capable of doing sth wrong, illegal, etc: *I wouldn't put it past him to steal money from his own family!* **put it to sb that …** to challenge sb to dare to disagree with what one is going to say: *I put it to you that you*

are the only person who had a motive for the crime. **put sb ˈthrough it** (*infml*) to force sb to experiencesth difficult or unpleasant: *They really put me through it (ie asked me difficult questions, etc) at the interview.* **put toˈgether** (used after a *n* or *ns* referring to a group of people or things) combined; in total: *Your department spent more last year than all the other departments put together.* **PHR V** **put (sth) aˈbout** (*nautical*) (of a ship) to change direction; to make a ship change direction. **put sth aˈbout** to spread or circulate false news, rumours, etc: *Someone has been putting it about that you're planning to resign.*

put sth above sth ⇨ PUT STH BEFORE/ABOVE STH.

put oneself/sth aˈcross/ˈover (to sb) to communicate one's ideas, feelings, etc successfully to sb: *She's not very good at putting her views across in meetings.*

put sth aˈside to ignore or forget sth; to DISREGARD sth: *They decided to put aside their differences.* **put sth aˈside/ˈby 1** to save sth, esp a sum of money, for use later: *She's put aside a tidy sum for her retirement.* **2** to reserve an item for a customer to collect later: *We'll put the suit aside for you, sir.*

ˈput sth at sth to calculate or estimate sb/sth to be the specified age, weight, amount, etc: *I would put him/his age at about 55.* ○ *The damage to the building is put at over £1 million.*

put sb aˈway (*infml*) (often passive) to send sb to prison, to a mental hospital, etc: *He was put away for ten years for armed robbery.* **put sth aˈway 1** to put sth in a box, drawer, etc because one has finished using it: *It's time to put your toys away now.* ○ *I'm just going to put the car away (ie in the garage).* **2** to save money to spend later: *She's got a few thousand pounds put away for her retirement.* **3** (*infml*) to eat or drink a large quantity of food or drink: *He must have put away half a bottle of whisky last night.* ○ *I don't know how he manages to put it all away!* **4** (*US*) = PUT STH DOWN 5.

put sth ˈback 1 to return sth to its proper place; to replace sth: *Please put the dictionary back on the shelf when you've finished with it.* **2** to move the hands of a clock back to correct the time shown or because of an official change of time: *Tonight we have to remember to put the clocks back one hour.* **3** to move sth to a later time or date; to POSTPONE sth: *This afternoon's meeting has been put back to next week.* **4** to cause sth to be delayed: *Poor trading figures put back our plans for expansion.* ○ *The drivers' strike has put back our deliveries by over a month.*

ˈput sth before/above sth to treat or regard sth as more important than sth else: *He puts his children's welfare before all other considerations.*

put sth by ⇨ PUT STH ASIDE/BY.

put (sth) ˈdown (of an aircraft or its pilot) to land; to land an aircraft: *He put (the glider) down in a field.* **put sb ˈdown** (*infml*) to make sb appear stupid or silly in front of other people: *He's always putting his wife ˈdown in public.* See also PUT-DOWN.

put sth ˈdown 1 to place sth on a table, shelf, etc: *Put that knife down before you hurt somebody!* ○ *I can't put this book down (ie I do not want to stop reading it because I am enjoying it so much).* **2** to write sth; to make a note of sth: *I'm having a party next Saturday — put it down in your diary so you don't forget.* **3** to stop or suppress sth by force: *put down a rebellion/a revolt/an uprising ○ The military government is determined to put down all political opposition.* **4** (*esp Brit*) (often passive) to kill an animal, usu by giving it a drug, because it is old or sick: *The horse broke a leg in the fall and had to be put down.* ○ *We had our old cat put down.* **5** (*esp Brit*) to store wine, etc for future use: *put down six cases of claret last year.* **put sb ˈdown as sb** to consider or judge sb to be sth: *From the way he spoke, I put* *him down as a retired naval officer.* ˌ**put sb ˈdown for sth** to put sb's name on a list, etc for sth: *Put me down for three tickets for Saturday's performance.* ○ *They've put their son down for the local school.* ˈ**put sth down to sth 1** to consider that sth is caused by or is the result of sth: *What do you put her success down to?* ○ *I put it all down to her hard work and initiative.* **2** to charge an amount or item to a particular person's account: *Would you put these shoes down to my account, please?*

put sth forth (*fml*) ⇨ PUT STH OUT/FORTH.

ˌ**put oneself/sb ˈforward** to propose or recommend oneself/sb as a candidate for a job or position: *He has put himself forward for a place on the national executive.* ○ *Can I put you/your name forward for club secretary?* ˌ**put sth ˈforward 1** to move the hands of a clock forward to correct the time shown or because of an official change of time: *Put your watch forward — you're five minutes slow.* **2** to move sth to an earlier time or date: *We've put forward (the date of) our wedding by one week.* **3** to propose or suggest sth for discussion: *put forward an argument/a plan/a suggestion* ○ *She is putting forward radical proposals for electoral reform.*

ˌ**put sb ˈin 1** to employ sb to do a particular job: *put in a caretaker/a security man.* **2** to elect a political party to govern a country: *The electorate put the Conservatives in in 1983.* ˌ**put (sth) ˈin** to interrupt another speaker in order to say sth: *'But what about us?' he put in.* ○ *Could I put in a ˈword at this point?* ˌ**put sth ˈin 1** to fit or INSTALL(1) sth: *We put the central heating in when we moved here.* ○ *We're having a new shower put in.* **2** to include sth in a letter, story, etc: *If you're writing to your mother, don't forget to put in something about her coming to stay at Easter.* **3** to present sth formally; to submit sth: *put in a claim for damages/higher wages.* ˌ**put sth ˈin; ˈput sth into sth / doing sth 1** to devote time, effort, etc to sth: *She often puts in twelve hours' work a day.* ○ *We've put a great deal of time and effort into this project.* ○ *She's putting a lot of work into improving her French.* **2** to invest or give money: *He's put all his savings into that house.* ○ *She put £5 in for Sandra's leaving present.* ˌ**put ˈin (at...) / ˈput into...** (of a ship, its crew, etc) to enter a port or harbour: *The boat put in at Lagos/put into Lagos for repairs.* ˌ**put ˈin for sth** to apply formally for sth: *put in for a pay rise* ○ *Are you going to put in for that job?* ˌ**put oneself/sb/sth ˈin for sth** to enter oneself/sb/sth for a competition: *She's put herself in for the 100 metres and the long jump.*

ˌ**put sb ˈoff 1** (*esp Brit*) (of a vehicle or its driver) to stop in order to allow sb to leave: *I asked the bus driver to put me off near the town centre.* **2** to cancel a meeting or an appointment with sb: *We've invited friends to supper and it's too late to put them off now.* ○ *She put him off with the excuse that she had too much work to do.* **3** to make sb feel dislike, lack of trust, etc: *He's very clever, but his manner does tend to put people off.* ○ *Don't be put off by his gruff exterior; he's really very kind underneath.* See also OFF-PUTTING. ˌ**put sb ˈoff (sth)** to disturb sb who is busy with sth; to distract sb: *Don't put me off when I'm trying to concentrate.* ○ *The sudden noise put her off her game.* ˌ**put sb ˈoff sth / doing sth** to make sb lose their interest in or enthusiasm for sth: *The accident put her off ˈdriving for life.* ○ *She was put off ˈscience by bad teaching at school.* ˌ**put sth ˈoff** to switch sth off (SWITCH): *Could you put the lights off before you leave?* ˌ**put sth ˈoff; put off doing sth** to put sth to a later time or date; to delay (doing) sth: *We've had to put our wedding off until September.* ○ *This afternoon's meeting will have to be put off.* ○ *She keeps putting off going to the dentist.*

ˌ**put sth ˈon 1** to dress oneself in sth: *put on one's ˈcoat/ˈgloves/ˈhat* ○ *Which dress shall I put on for the party?* **2** to apply sth to one's skin: *put on lipstick/*

hand cream ○ *She's just putting on her make-up.* **3** to switch sth on (SWITCH); to operate sth: *put on the light/oven/radio/television* ○ *Let's put the kettle on and have a cup of tea.* ○ *She put on the brakes suddenly.* **4** to make sth begin to play[1](10): *put on a record/tape/CD* ○ *Do you mind if I put some music on?* **5** to grow fatter, heavier or taller, esp by the specified amount: *put on five kilos in weight* ○ *She always puts on weight during the winter.* ○ *He must have put on three inches this year already.* **6** to provide sth specially: *The city is putting on extra buses during the holiday period.* **7** to produce or present a play, an exhibition, etc: *The local drama club are putting on 'Macbeth' at the Playhouse.* **8** to move the hands of a clock forward to show a later time. **9** to pretend to have a particular feeling, quality or characteristic; to assume a particular expression, etc: *put on a Boston accent/a wounded expression* ○ *Don't put on that innocent look — we know you ate all the biscuits.* ○ *He seems very sincere, but it's all put on.* ˌ**put sth ˈon sth 1** to add an amount of money to the price or cost of sth: *The government has put ten pence on the price of a gallon of petrol.* **2** to place a tax, etc on sth: *put a duty on wine.* **3** to bet money on sth: *I've put £10 on Black Widow in the next race.* ○ *I've never put money on a horse.* ˌ**put sb ˈonto sb 1** to help sb to find, meet or see sb; to tell sb about a person who may be useful to them: *put sb onto a dentist/plumber* ○ *Could you put me onto a good accountant?* **2** to inform the police, etc where sb is, so they can be caught: *An anonymous telephone call put detectives onto the gang's whereabouts.* ˌ**put sb ˈonto sth** to inform sb of the existence of sth interesting, pleasant, etc; to tell sb about sth: *Who put you onto this restaurant? It's superb!'*

ˌ**put oneself ˈout** (*infml*) to make a special effort to do sth for sb: *Please don't put yourself out on my account.* ○ *She's always ready to put herself out to help others.* ˌ**put sb ˈout 1** to cause sb trouble, extra work, etc: *I hope our arriving late didn't put them out.* **2** to upset or offend sb: *She was most put out by his rudeness.* ○ *He looked really put out.* **3** to make sb unconscious: *These sleeping tablets will put him out for a few hours.* ˌ**put sth ˈout 1** to take sth out of one's house and leave it, eg for sb to collect: *put out the dustbins/the empty milk bottles* ○ *Have you put the cat out yet?* **2** to place sth where it will be noticed and used: *put out ashtrays and bowls of peanuts before the party* ○ *put out clean towels for the guests.* **3** to produce sth, esp for sale: *The plant puts out 500 new cars a week.* See also OUTPUT. **4** to issue, publish or broadcast sth: *put out a call for a doctor* ○ *Police have put out a description of the man they wish to question.* **5** to stop sth burning; to EXTINGUISH(a) sth: *put out a candle/cigarette/pipe* ○ *Firemen soon put the fire out.* **6** to switch sth off (SWITCH): *put out the lamp/light/gas fire.* **7** to push a bone out of its normal position; to DISLOCATE(1) sth: *She fell off her horse and put her shoulder out.* **8** to make a figure, result, calculation, etc wrong: *The devaluation of the pound has put our estimates out by several thousands.* ˌ**put sth ˈout/ˈforth** to develop or produce new shoots, leaves, etc. ˌ**put sth ˈout (to sb)** to give a job or task to a worker who is not one's employee or to a firm that is not part of one's own group or organization, so that the work will be done in another place: *A lot of editing is put out to freelancers.* ○ *All repairs are done on the premises and not put out.* ˌ**put ˈout (to... /from...)** (of a boat or its crew) to leave a harbour, port, etc and go towards the open sea: *put out to sea* ○ *We put out from Liverpool.*

put oneself/sth over (to sb) ⇨ PUT ONESELF/STH ACROSS/OVER (TO SB). ˌ**put sth ˈover on sb** (*infml*) to persuade sb to accept a claim, story, etc that is not true: *Don't try to put one over on me!*

ˌ**put sth ˈthrough** to proceed with and complete

successfully a plan, programme, etc: *put through a business deal* ○ *The government is putting through some radical new legislation.* ¦**put sb ¦through sth 1** to make sb experience sth very difficult or unpleasant: *You have put your family through a lot recently.* ○ *Trainee commandos are put through an exhausting assault course.* **2** to arrange or pay for sb to attend a school, college, etc: *He put all his children through university.* ¦**put sb/sth ¦through (to sb/...)** to connect sb by telephone: *put a call through to the regional office* ○ *Could you put me through to the manager, please?*

¦**put sb to sth** to cause sb trouble, difficulty, etc: *I do hope we're not putting you to too much trouble.*

¦**put sth to sb 1** to express, communicate or submit sth to sb: *Your proposal will be put to the board of directors.* **2** to ask sb a question: *The audience are now invited to put questions to the speaker.* ○ *The call for a strike must be put to the union as a whole.*

¦**put sth to¦gether** to make or repair sth by fitting parts together; to assemble sth: *put together a model aeroplane* ○ *put together an essay/a meal/a case for the defence.* See also PUT TOGETHER in the idioms section.

¦**put sth towards sth** to give money as a contribution to sth: *Here's £50 to put towards your skiing trip.*

¦**put ¦up sth** to offer or show a particular level of skill, determination, etc in a fight or contest: *They surrendered without putting up much of a fight.* ○ *The team put up a splendid performance* (ie played very well). ¦**put sb ¦up 1** to provide food and accommodation for sb in one's own house: *We can put you up for the night.* **2** to present sb as a candidate in an election: *The Green Party hopes to put up more candidates in the next election.* ¦**put sth ¦up 1** to raise sth or put it in a higher position: *put up a flag* ○ *She's put her hair up* (ie She is wearing it in a COIL(2) on top of her head). **2** to build or construct sth: *put up a building/fence/memorial/tent.* **3** to fix or fasten sth in a place where it will be seen; to display sth: *put up Christmas decorations/a notice/a poster* ○ *The team will be put up on the notice-board.* **4** to raise or increase sth: *My landlord's threatening to put the rent up by £20 a week.* **5** to provide or lend money: *A local businessman has put up the £500 000 needed to save the club.* **6** to present an idea, etc for discussion or consideration: *put up an argument/a case/a proposal.* ¦**put ¦up (at...)** to obtain food and lodging at a place; to stay somewhere for the night: *They put up at a motel.* ¦**put (oneself) ¦up for sth** to offer oneself as a candidate for sth: *She is putting (herself) up for election to the committee.* ¦**put sb ¦up (for sth)** to propose sb for an official position: *We want to put you up for club treasurer.* ¦**put sb ¦up to sth / doing sth** (*infml*) to urge or encourage sb to do sth wrong or foolish: *Some of the older boys must have put him 'up to it.* ¦**put ¦up with sb/sth** to tolerate or bear sb/sth: *I don't know how she puts up with him/his drinking.*

■ ¦**put-down** *n* (usu *sing*) a remark made by sb in order to make another person look stupid or silly: *She was unable to think of an effective put-down.*

¦**put-up ¦job** *n* (usu *sing*) (*Brit infml*) a question, scheme, etc intended to trick or deceive sb.

¦**put-upon** *adj* (of a person) badly treated by sb who exploits one's willingness, kindness, etc for their own advantage: *his much put-upon wife* ○ *I'm beginning to feel just a little put-upon.*

putative /ˈpjuːtətɪv/ *adj* [attrib] (*fml*) generally supposed to be the thing specified: *He's referred to in the document as the putative father.*

putrefy /ˈpjuːtrɪfaɪ/ *v* (*pt, pp* **-fied**) to rot and produce a very bad smell; to become PUTRID(1): [V] *putrefying corpses.*
▶ **putrefaction** /ˌpjuːtrɪˈfækʃn/ *n* [U] the process of putrefying: *the stink of putrefaction.*

putrescent /pjuːˈtresnt/ *adj* (*fml*) in the process of rotting and beginning to smell very bad: *a putrescent corpse.* ▶ **putrescence** /-sns/ *n* [U].

putrid /ˈpjuːtrɪd/ *adj* **1** (esp of animal or vegetable matter) that has rotted and so smells very bad: *a pile of rotten, putrid fish* ○ *the putrid smell of rotting fish.* **2** (*infml*) very unpleasant; very bad: *Why did you paint the room that putrid colour?*

putsch /pʊtʃ/ *n* a sudden attempt to remove a government by force.

putt /pʌt/ *v* (in golf) to hit the ball gently so that it rolls across the ground into or nearer to the hole, usu from a position on the GREEN²(4): [V] *You need a lot more practice at putting.* [also Vn].
▶ **putt** *n*: *hole/sink a putt* ○ *She took three putts* (ie to get the ball into the hole) *from the edge of the green.*
putter *n* **1** a golf club used for putting. **2** a person who putts.

■ ¦**putting-green** *n* an area of smooth short grass for putting on, esp one with several holes like a very short golf course where people can practise putting.

putter /ˈpʌtə(r)/ *v* **1** (of a boat or vehicle) to produce from its engine a series of sounds with a slow regular rhythm, as it moves: [Vp, Vpr] *barges puttering along (the river).* **2** (*US*) = POTTER¹.

putty /ˈpʌti/ *n* [U] a soft oily substance that hardens after a few hours. It is used esp for fixing glass in window frames. **IDM** **(be) putty in sb's 'hands** (to be) easily influenced or controlled by sb: *He adores her — he's putty in her hands.*

puzzle /ˈpʌzl/ *n* **1** (usu *sing*) a thing that is difficult to understand or answer; a mystery: *The reason for his actions remains a puzzle to historians.* **2** (often in compounds) a question or toy that is designed to test a person's knowledge, skill, intelligence, etc: *do a crossword puzzle* ○ *find the answer to/solve a puzzle* ○ *set a puzzle for sb/set sb a puzzle.* **3** (*esp US*) = JIGSAW 1. ⇨ picture at JIGSAW.
▶ **puzzle** *v* to make sb confused because they do not understand or explain sth: [Vn] *Her reply puzzled me deeply.* ○ *He puzzled his brains* (ie thought hard) *to find the answer.* **PHRV** ¦**puzzle over sth** to think hard about sth in order to understand or explain it: *She's been puzzling over this problem for weeks.* ¦**puzzle sth ¦out** to find the answer to sth by thinking hard: *puzzle out a riddle* ○ *I'm trying to puzzle out what this letter says — it's written in German.* **puzzled** *adj* unable to understand or explain sth; confused: *She listened with a puzzled expression on her face.* ○ *I am puzzled that he hasn't replied to my letter.* ○ *We are puzzled (about) what to do next.* **puzzler** /ˈpʌzlə(r)/ *n* (*infml*) a person or thing that puzzles one: *That question is a real puzzler!* **puzzlement** /ˈpʌzlmənt/ *n* [U] the state of being puzzled: *He stared at me with a look of puzzlement on his face.* **puzzling** /ˈpʌzlɪŋ/ *adj*: *a puzzling statement/decision/attitude.*

PVA /ˌpiː viː ˈeɪ/ *abbr* polyvinyl acetate (a chemical substance used in certain types of paint and glue).

PVC /ˌpiː viː ˈsiː/ *abbr* polyvinyl chloride (a strong plastic material used for clothing, floor coverings, pipes, etc).

pw *abbr* per week: *£300 pw.*

pygmy (also **pigmy**) /ˈpɪɡmi/ *n* **1** **Pygmy** a member of a tribe of very short people living in Africa or SE Asia. **2** a very small person or species of animal or plant: *a pygmy shrew.*

pyjamas (*US* **pajamas**) /pəˈdʒɑːməz; *US* -ˈdʒæm-/ *n* [pl] **1** a loose jacket and trousers worn for sleeping in, esp by men and children: *a pair of pyjamas* ○ *He was wearing striped pyjamas.* **2** loose trousers tied round the waist, worn by Muslims of both sexes in certain Asian countries. **IDM** **be the cat's whiskers/pyjamas** ⇨ CAT. ▶ **pyjama** (*US* **pajama**) *adj* [attrib]: *one's pyjama bottom(s)/top/trousers/jacket.*

pylon /ˈpaɪlən; *US* ˈpaɪlɒn/ *n* a tall metal structure used for carrying electricity cables high above the ground.

PYO /ˌpiː waɪ ˈəʊ/ *abbr* pick-your-own.

pyramid /ˈpɪrəmɪd/ *n* **1(a)** a large stone structure with a flat square or triangular base and sloping sides that meet in a point at the top. The ancient Egyptians built pyramids as burial places for their kings and queens. **(b)** (*geometry*) a solid figure of this shape with a base of three or more sides. ⇨ picture at SOLID. **(c)** a thing or pile of things that has the shape of a pyramid: *a pyramid of tins in a shop window.* **2** an organization or a system seen as a structure in which the higher the level, the fewer the people or things that occupy that level: *the social pyramid.*
▶ **pyramidal** /pɪˈræmɪdl/ *adj* having the shape of a pyramid.
■ **pyramid 'selling** *n* [U] (*commerce*) a method of selling goods in which sb pays for the right to sell a company's goods and then sells part of that right to other people.

pyre /ˈpaɪə(r)/ *n* a large pile of wood for burning a dead body as part of a funeral ceremony: *a funeral pyre.*

Pyrex /ˈpaɪreks/ *n* [U] (*propr*) a type of hard glass that does not break at high temperatures. It is used esp in making bowls, dishes, etc for cooking food in: *a Pyrex dish.*

pyrites /paɪˈraɪtiːz; *US* pəˈraɪtiz/ *n* [U] a shiny yellow mineral that is a natural compound of SULPHUR and another metal, eg iron: *iron/copper pyrites.*

pyromania /ˌpaɪrəʊˈmeɪniə/ *n* [U] a mental illness that causes a strong desire to set fire to things: *suffer from pyromania.*
▶ **pyromaniac** /-niæk/ *n* a person who suffers from pyromania.

pyrotechnics /ˌpaɪrəˈtekniks/ *n* **1** [sing *v*] the making of fireworks (FIREWORK). **2** [pl] (*fml*) a public display of fireworks (FIREWORK) as an entertainment. **3** [pl] (*sometimes derog*) a brilliant display of skill, eg by a speaker, a musician, etc. ▶ **pyrotechnic** *adj* [usu attrib].

Pyrrhic victory /ˌpɪrɪk ˈvɪktəri/ *n* a victory that was not worth winning because the winner has lost so much in winning it.

python /ˈpaɪθn; *US* ˈpaɪθɒn/ *n* a large tropical snake that kills animals for food by winding its long body around them and crushing them.

Qq

Q¹ (also **q**) /kjuː/ *n* (*pl* **Q's, q's** /kjuːz/) the 17th letter of the English alphabet: *'Queen' starts with (a) Q/'Q'.* **IDM** **mind one's p's and q's** ⇨ MIND².

Q² *abbr* question. Compare A³.

QB /ˌkjuː ˈbiː/ *abbr* (*Brit law*) Queen's Bench.

QC /ˌkjuː ˈsiː/ *abbr* (*Brit law*) Queen's Counsel: *Anthony Scrivener QC.* Compare KC.

QED /ˌkjuː iː ˈdiː/ *abbr* that is what I intended to prove and I have proved it (Latin *quod erat demonstrandum*).

QE2 /ˌkjuː iː ˈtuː/ *abbr* Queen Elizabeth the Second (a ship): *a luxury cruise on the QE2.*

qr *abbr* quarter(s).

qt *abbr* quart(s).

qua /kweɪ, kwɑː/ *prep* (*fml*) in the capacity or character of sth; as sth: *The church has always supported the legitimacy of the state qua state.*

quack¹ /kwæk/ *v* [V] to make the sound made by a duck.
▶ **quack** *n* the sound a duck makes.

quack² /kwæk/ *n* (*infml derog*) (**a**) a person who dishonestly claims to have special knowledge and skill, esp in medicine: *quack doctors/cures.* (**b**) (*Brit sl*) a doctor.
▶ **ˈquackery** /-əri/ *n* [U] (*derog*) the methods or behaviour of a quack².

quad /kwɒd/ *n* (*infml*) **1** = QUADRANGLE. **2** = QUADRUPLET.

quadrangle /ˈkwɒdræŋgl/ *n* an open square area with buildings all round it, esp in a school or college.

quadrant /ˈkwɒdrənt/ *n* **1** a quarter of a circle or of its CIRCUMFERENCE. ⇨ picture at CIRCLE. **2** an instrument for measuring angles, esp in order to check one's position at sea or to look at the stars.

quadraphonic (also **quadrophonic**) /ˌkwɒdrəˈfɒnɪk/ *adj* (of recorded or broadcast sound) transmitted through four channels. Compare MONO, STEREO.

quadr(i)- *comb form* (forming *ns* and *adjs*) **1** having four parts: *quadrilateral* ○ *quadruped.* **2** being one of four parts: *quadrant* ○ *quadruplet.*

quadrilateral

square	rectangle
rhombus	parallelogram
trapezium (US trapezoid)	trapezoid (US trapezium)

quadrilateral /ˌkwɒdrɪˈlætərəl/ *n, adj* (*geometry*) (a) flat shape) with four straight sides. ⇨ picture.

quadrille /kwəˈdrɪl/ *n* (esp formerly) a dance for four or more couples, in which they form a square.

quadrophonic ⇨ QUADRAPHONIC.

quadruped /ˈkwɒdruped/ *n* (*tech*) a creature with four feet. Compare BIPED.

quadruple /ˈkwɒdrupl; *US* kwɒˈdruːpl/ *adj* [usu attrib] having or made of four parts, people or groups: *a quadruple alliance.*
▶ **quadruple** *n, adv, det* four times as much or as many as sth: *We need quadruple the number of players we've got for a full orchestra.*
quadruple /kwɒˈdruːpl/ *v* to multiply sth or be multiplied by four: [V] *Their profits have quadrupled since 1989.* [Vn] *They've quadrupled their output in the last five years.*

quadruplet /ˈkwɒdruplət; *US* kwɒˈdruːp-/ (also *infml* **quad**) *n* (usu *pl*) each of four children born to the same mother at one birth.

quaff /kwɒf; *US* kwæf/ *v* (*dated or rhet*) to drink sth, esp an alcoholic drink, quickly: [Vn] *They spent the evening quaffing champagne.*

quagmire /ˈkwæɡmaɪə(r), ˈkwɒɡ-/ *n* **1** an area of soft wet ground: *The heavy rain had turned the field into a quagmire.* **2** a difficult and dangerous situation from which it is hard to escape: *He got bogged down in the political quagmire.*

quail¹ /kweɪl/ *n* (*pl* unchanged or **quails**) [C] a small brown bird whose flesh and eggs are eaten as food.

quail² /kweɪl/ *v* ~ (**at/before sb/sth**) to feel or show fear: [Vpr] *She quailed at the prospect of addressing such a large audience.* [also V].

quaint /kweɪnt/ *adj* attractive because of being unusual or old-fashioned: *quaint old customs.* ▶ **quaintly** *adv*. **quaintness** *n* [U].

quake /kweɪk/ *v* **1** (of the earth) to shake: [V] *They felt the ground quake as the bomb exploded.* **2** ~ (**with sth**) (**at sth**) (of people) to shake because of fear, cold, etc; to TREMBLE(1a): [Vpr] *quaking with fear/cold* ○ *She was quaking in her boots at the thought of a meeting with her boss.* [also V].
▶ **quake** *n* (*infml*) = EARTHQUAKE.

Quaker /ˈkweɪkə(r)/ *n* a member of the Society of Friends, a Christian religious group that meets without any formal ceremony and is strongly opposed to violence and war.

qualification /ˌkwɒlɪfɪˈkeɪʃn/ *n* **1** [C] (**a**) a quality or skill that makes sb suitable for a particular job or activity: *Previous teaching experience is a necessary qualification for the post.* (**b**) an official proof, eg a degree or DIPLOMA, that one has successfully completed a course, passed an exam, etc: *a teaching/nursing/postgraduate qualification* ○ *He left school with no formal qualifications.* **2** [C, U] a statement that makes the meaning of a previous statement less strong or less general: *She gave her approval to the scheme but not without several qualifications.* ○ *I can recommend him without qualification.* **3** [U] the action of qualifying.

qualify /ˈkwɒlɪfaɪ/ *v* (*pt, pp* **-fied**) **1**(**a**) ~ (**as sth**) to reach the standard of ability, knowledge, etc required in order to enter a particular profession, eg by successfully completing a course or by passing an exam: [V, V-n] *She won't qualify (as a doctor) until next year.* [V] *How many years does it take to qualify?* (**b**) ~ **sb** (**for sth**) to give sb the skills,

---

[V] = verb used alone [Vn] = verb + noun [Vp] = verb + particle [Vpr] = verb + prepositional phrase

knowledge, etc to do sth: [Vnpr] *The training course will qualify you for a better job.* [Vn.*to* inf] *The test qualifies you to drive heavy vehicles.* **2** ~ **(sb) (for sth)** to have or give sb the right to do sth: [Vnpr] *Residence in the area automatically qualifies you for membership.* [Vpr] *After six months you'll qualify for a pay review.* [V.*to* inf] *Eighteen-year-olds qualify to vote.* [V] *To qualify, you must have lived in this country for three years or more.* [also Vn.*to* inf]. **3** ~ **(for sth)** to be of a high enough standard to enter a contest; to defeat another person or team in order to enter or to continue in a contest: [V] *England failed to qualify.* [Vpr] *They qualified for the World Cup in Italy.* **4** ~ **(sth) as sth** to have or consider that sth has a particular quality: [V-n] *It's an old building, but it doesn't quite qualify as an ancient monument!* [also Vn-n]. **5** to make the meaning of a previous statement less strong or less general: [Vn] *I feel I must qualify my earlier remarks in case they are misinterpreted.* **6** (*grammar*) (of a word) to describe another word in a particular way: [Vn] *In 'the open door', 'open' is an adjective qualifying 'door'.*
▶ **qualified** *adj* **1(a)** ~ **(for sth)** having completed the necessary training or passed an examination in order to enter a particular profession: *a qualified doctor* ○ *She's extremely well qualified for the job.* ○ *It takes three years to become qualified.* **(b)** [pred] having the knowledge or skills to do sth: *I'm not really qualified to comment on this matter.* **2** limited: *give the scheme only qualified approval.*
qualifier /-faɪə(r)/ *n* **1** (*grammar*) a word, esp an adjective or adverb, that qualifies (QUALIFY 6) another word. **2(a)** a person, team, etc that qualifies (QUALIFY 3) for sth, esp one that has won the first part of a competition, etc and is now entitled to take part in the next round: *The final brings together two qualifiers from each heat.* **(b)** a match, etc in which the winning team qualifies (QUALIFY 3) for the next round of the competition: *a World Cup qualifier.*

qualitative /ˈkwɒlɪtətɪv; *US* -teɪt-/ *adj* [usu attrib] of or concerned with quality: *qualitative analysis* ○ *There has been little qualitative improvement in their work.* Compare QUANTITATIVE. ▶ **qualitatively** *adv.*

quality /ˈkwɒləti/ *n* **1(a)** [U, C] the standard of sth when compared to other things like it; how good or bad sth is: *goods of the highest quality/high-quality goods* ○ *the **quality of life** in rural areas* ○ *This paper is very poor quality.* ○ *There are many different qualities of gold and silver.* **(b)** [U] a high standard or level: *contemporary writers **of quality*** ○ *We aim to provide quality at reasonable prices.* ○ *We specialize in quality furniture.* **2** [C] **(a)** a usu good characteristic: *personal qualities such as honesty and generosity* ○ *possess/lack leadership qualities* ○ *She has all the qualities of a good teacher.* **(b)** a special or distinguishing feature: *a particular quality of light in her paintings* ○ *His voice has a rich melodic quality.*
■ **'quality control** *n* [U] the practice of checking the quality of a product by testing samples: *Quality control is an important part of the manufacturing process.*
ˌquality 'newspaper (also **quality**) *n* (usu *pl*) a newspaper considered as being for people with a high educational standard. Quality newspapers are usu printed on a large size of paper and contain mainly serious news and reports: *a leading quality paper like 'The Times'.* Compare TABLOID *n.*

qualm /kwɑːm, kwɔːm/ *n* (usu *pl*) ~ **(about sth)** a feeling of doubt or worry about whether what one is doing is right: *He had no qualms about cheating his employer.*

quandary /ˈkwɒndəri/ *n* a state of not being able to decide what to do in a difficult situation: *leave sb/be **in a quandary**.*

quango /ˈkwæŋɡəʊ/ *n* (*pl* **-os**) (*often derog*) an organization that operates independently but with support from the government.

quantify /ˈkwɒntɪfaɪ/ *v* (*pt, pp* **-fied**) to express or measure the quantity of sth: [Vn] *The extent of the risk to health is difficult to quantify.* ▶ **quantifiable** *adj*: *It has no quantifiable value.* **quantification** /ˌkwɒntɪfɪˈkeɪʃn/ *n* [U].

quantitative /ˈkwɒntɪtətɪv; *US* -teɪt-/ *adj* [usu attrib] of or concerned with quantity: *quantitative analysis.* Compare QUALITATIVE.

quantity /ˈkwɒntəti/ *n* **1** [U] the measurement of sth by stating how much of it there is: *His reputation as a writer is based more on quantity than on quality* (ie He writes a lot but he does not write very well). **2(a)** [C, U] an amount or number of sth: *a huge quantity of food* ○ *Add a small quantity of raisins.* ○ *Alcohol can be bad for you if consumed in large quantities.* **(b)** a large amount or number of sth: *It's cheaper to buy goods **in quantity**.* **IDM** **an unknown quantity** ⇨ UNKNOWN.
■ **'quantity surveyor** *n* a person who calculates the quantity of materials needed for constructing buildings, etc and how much they will cost.

quantum /ˈkwɒntəm/ *n* (*pl* **quanta** /-tə/) **1** (*physics*) a very small quantity of ELECTROMAGNETIC energy. **2** (*fml*) a quantity of sth, esp a very small one.
■ **ˌquantum 'leap** (also **ˌquantum 'jump**) *n* a sudden, great and important change, improvement or development: *This discovery marks a quantum leap forward in the fight against cancer.*
ˈquantum theory (also **ˌquantum meˈchanics**) *n* [U] (*physics*) a theory or system based on the idea that energy exists in units that cannot be divided.

quarantine /ˈkwɒrəntiːn; *US* ˈkwɔːr-/ *n* [C usu *sing*, U] a period of time when an animal or a person that has or may have a disease is kept away from others in order to prevent the disease from spreading: *The dog was kept in quarantine for six months.* ○ *quarantine regulations/restrictions.*
▶ **quarantine** *v* [Vn] to put an animal or a person into quarantine.

quark /kwɑːk/ *n* (*physics*) any of several very small parts of matter from which it is assumed that atoms are formed.

quarrel /ˈkwɒrəl; *US* ˈkwɔːrəl/ *n* **1** ~ **(with sb) (about/over sth)** an angry argument or disagreement: *a family quarrel* ○ *quarrels between husbands and wives about who should do the housework.* ⇨ note at ARGUMENT. **2** ~ **with sth** (often in negative sentences) a reason for complaining about or for disagreeing with sb/sth: *I have no quarrel with his methods.* **IDM** **pick a fight/quarrel** ⇨ PICK[1].
▶ **quarrel** *v* (**-ll-**; *US* **-l-**) ~ **(with sb) (about/over sth)** to have an angry argument or disagreement: [V] *Stop quarrelling, children!* [Vpr] *She quarrelled with her brother about the terms of their father's will.* ○ *There's no sense in quarrelling over the past.* **PHR V** **ˈquarrel with sth** (often in negative sentences) to disagree with or complain about sth: *I can't quarrel with your conclusions.* ○ *Few people will quarrel with this basic principle.*
quarrelsome /-səm/ *adj* fond of starting quarrels.

quarry¹ /ˈkwɒri; *US* ˈkwɔːri/ *n* a person or an animal that is being hunted or chased: *The hunters lost sight of their quarry in the forest.* ○ *journalists relentlessly pursuing their quarry.*

quarry² /ˈkwɒri; *US* ˈkwɔːri/ *n* a place where stone, etc is dug out of the ground: *a chalk/slate/limestone quarry.* Compare MINE² 1.
▶ **quarry** *v* (*pt, pp* **quarried**) ~ **A for B/B from A;** ~ **sth out (of sth)** to extract stone, etc from a quarry: [Vnpr] *quarrying the hillside for granite* ○ *clay quarried from open pits* [also Vn, Vnpr, Vpr].

quart /kwɔːt/ *n* (*abbr* **qt**) a unit for measuring liquids, equal to 2 pints or approximately 1.14 litres in the UK, and equal to 0.94 of a litre in the USA. ⇨

App 2. **IDM put a quart into a pint ¹pot** (to try to) do sth that is impossible, esp to put sth into a space that is too small for it.

quarter /'kwɔ:tə(r)/ n **1** [C] each of four equal parts of sth: *a quarter of a mile* ○ *The programme lasted (for) an hour and a quarter* (ie 75 minutes). ○ *Cut the apples into quarters.* ○ *About three quarters of the theatre was full.* ⇨ App 2. ⇨ note at HALF¹. **2** [C] fifteen minutes before or after every hour: *It's (a) quarter to/(US) of four now — I'll meet you at quarter past/(US) after.* ⇨ App 2. **3** [C] three months, esp as a period for which rent or other payment is made, or a firm's earnings are calculated: *The rent is due at the end of each quarter.* ○ *Our gas bill for the last quarter was unusually high.* ○ *Sales are ▶p 10% on the same quarter last year.* **4** [C] (**a**) a direction or region: *Her travels had taken her to all quarters of the globe.* (**b**) a district or part of a town: *a residential quarter* ○ *the historic quarter of the city.* **5** [C] a person or group of people, esp as a possible source of help, information, etc: *As her mother has always been against the idea, she could expect no help from that quarter.* ○ *Support for the scheme has come from some unexpected quarters.* **6** [C] (US) (a coin worth) 25 cents: *It'll cost you a quarter.* ⇨ note at CENT¹. **7** [C] the period twice a month when the moon is a quarter visible: *The moon is in its first/last quarter.* **8** [C usu *sing*] the back part of a ship's side: *on the port/starboard quarter.* **9** [C] a unit of weight, 28 pounds in the UK or 25 pounds in the USA; a quarter of a HUNDREDWEIGHT. **10 quarters** [pl] accommodation, esp for soldiers: *live in married quarters* ○ *move to more comfortable living quarters.* **11** [U] (*dated or fml*) pity or MERCY(1) shown towards an enemy or an opponent who is in one's power: *His business rivals knew they could expect no quarter from such a ruthless adversary.* **IDM at/from close quarters** ⇨ CLOSE¹.
▶ **quarter** v **1** to divide sb/sth into four parts: [Vn] *peel and quarter an apple.* **2** to provide sb with lodgings: [Vnpr] *troops quartered in a nearby village.* [also Vnadv].
■ **¹quarter day** n (*Brit*) the first day of a quarter(3), when payments become due.
¡**quarter-'final** n (in sport, etc) any of four contests or matches to decide the players or teams for the semifinals (SEMIFINAL).
¹**quarter-note** n (US) = CROTCHET.
¹**quarter sessions** n [pl] a court of law with limited powers to try criminal cases, held every three months in certain US states and formerly in Britain.

quarterdeck /'kwɔ:tədek/ n the part of the upper deck of a ship near the back, usu reserved for officers.

quarterly /'kwɔ:təli/ adj, adv produced or occurring once every three months: *receive quarterly bank statements* ○ *pay the rent quarterly.*
▶ **quarterly** n a magazine, etc published four times a year.

quartermaster /'kwɔ:təmɑ:stə(r); US -mæs-/ n an army officer in charge of stores and accommodation.

quartet /kwɔ:'tet/ n **1**(**a**) a group of four people playing music or singing together: *the Amadeus Quartet.* (**b**) a piece of music for such a group: *a Beethoven string quartet.* **2** a set of four people or things: *the last in a quartet of novels.*

quarto /'kwɔ:təʊ/ n (pl -os) (*techn*) (**a**) a size of page made by folding a standard sheet of paper twice to form eight pages. (**b**) a book with pages of this size: *a quarto volume.*

quartz /kwɔ:ts/ n [U] any of various types of hard mineral substance: *a vein of quartz in hard rock* ○ *Quartz crystals are used to make very accurate clocks and watches.*

quasar /'kweɪzɑ:(r)/ n (*astronomy*) a very distant object like a star. Quasars appear to shine very brightly for a limited period. Compare PULSAR.

quash /kwɒʃ/ v **1** to reject sth and declare it no longer valid: [Vn] *quash a verdict/decision/conviction* ○ *The sentence was quashed by the appeal court judge.* **2** to take action to stop sth: [Vn] *quash rumours* ○ *The rebellion was quickly quashed.*

quasi- /'kweɪzaɪ-, 'kweɪsaɪ-/ *pref* (forming *adjs* and *ns*) **1** partly; almost: *a quasi-official body* ○ *a quasi-religious experience.* **2** that appears to be sth but is not really so: *a quasi-scientific explanation.*

quatercentenary /ˌkwætəsen'ti:nəri; US -'tenəri/ n a 400th anniversary: *celebrate the quatercentenary of Shakespeare's birth.*

quatrain /'kwɒtreɪn/ n a poem, or verse of a poem, consisting of four lines.

quaver /'kweɪvə(r)/ v **1** (of a voice or a musical sound) to shake or move slightly off a note, eg because one is nervous: [V] *in a quavering voice* ○ *His voice quavered with emotion.* ○ *Her top notes quavered a little.* **2** to say sth in a voice that is not calm or steady: [V.speech] *'Have I passed my test?' he quavered.*
▶ **quaver** n **1** (usu *sing*) a sound that does not remain steady: *You could hear the quaver in her voice.* **2** (US **eighth note**) a note in music that lasts half as long as a CROTCHET. ⇨ picture at MUSIC.
quavery /'kweɪvəri/ adj: *speak with a quavery voice.*

quay /ki:/ n a stone or metal platform in a harbour where boats come in to load, etc: *We tied up on the quay.*

quayside /'ki:saɪd/ n [sing] a QUAY and the area near it: *crowds waiting at/on the quayside to welcome them.*

queasy /'kwi:zi/ adj (-ier, -iest) **1** feeling sick or tending to feel sick: *Travelling by coach makes me queasy.* ○ *His stomach still felt queasy.* **2** slightly nervous or worried about sth. ▶ **queasily** adv. **queasiness** n [U]: *These tablets may cause queasiness.*

queen /kwi:n/ n **1**(**a**) (the title of) the female ruler of an independent state, usu inheriting the position by right of birth: *Queen Elizabeth II* ○ *the Queen of the Netherlands* ○ *be made/crowned queen.* Compare KING 1. (**b**) the wife of a king. **2**(**a**) a woman, place or thing regarded as best or most important in some way: *Ruth Rendell, the queen of detective-story writers* ○ *an American movie queen* ○ *Venice, the queen of the Adriatic.* (**b**) a woman or girl chosen to hold the most important position in a festival or celebration: *Queen of the May* (ie a girl chosen to lead a procession, dance, etc to celebrate spring) ○ *a carnival/beauty queen.* **3** a female insect that produces eggs for the whole group: *A hive cannot exist without a queen bee.* **4**(**a**) the most powerful piece in CHESS. ⇨ picture at CHESS. (**b**) (in a pack of cards) any of the four cards with the picture of a queen on: *the queen of hearts.* **5** (*sl derog*) a male homosexual who behaves in a feminine way. **IDM the King's/Queen's bee** ⇨ ENGLISH. **turn King's/Queen's evidence** ⇨ EVIDENCE. **the uncrowned king/queen** ⇨ UNCROWNED.
▶ **queen** v **IDM ¹queen it (over sb)** (*derog*) (of a woman) to behave in an unpleasant and superior way towards other people: *Since her promotion, she queens it over everyone else in the office.*
queenly adj of, like or suitable for a queen: *sit in queenly dignity* ○ *give a queenly wave.*
■ ¡**queen 'bee 1** the female bee that produces eggs in a HIVE(1). **2** a woman who behaves as if she is the most important person in a particular place or group.
¡**queen 'consort** n the wife of a king.
¡**queen 'mother** n the widow of a king and mother of a reigning king or queen.
¡**Queen's 'Bench (Division)** n ⇨ KING'S BENCH.
¡**Queen's 'Counsel** n ⇨ KING'S COUNSEL.

queer /kwɪə(r)/ *adj* **1** strange; odd: *The meat had a queer smell.* ○ *a queer mood/feeling.* **2** (*sl derog offensive*) (esp of men) HOMOSEXUAL. **3** (*dated infml*) slightly ill: *I woke up feeling rather queer.*
▶ **queer** *n* (*sl derog offensive*) a homosexual man.
queer *v* IDM **queer sb's 'pitch** (*Brit infml*) to spoil sb's plans or chances of getting sth.
queerly *adv*: *He looked at me queerly.*
queerness *n* [U].

quell /kwel/ *v* (**a**) to end sth, esp by force: [Vn] *quell the rebellion/opposition/unrest.* (**b**) to suppress feelings, etc: [Vn] *quell sb's fears/anxieties/doubts.*

quench /kwentʃ/ *v* **1** to satisfy one's thirst by drinking: [Vn] *a thirst-quenching drink of cold water* ○ *I need something to quench my thirst.* **2** to stop sth burning: [Vn] *quench the flames* ○ (*fig*) *quench sb's ardour/desire/passion.*

querulous /ˈkwerələs, -rjə-/ *adj* complaining; showing that one is irritated: *in a querulous tone of voice* ○ *a querulous child.* ▶ **querulously** *adv.* **querulousness** *n* [U].

query /ˈkwɪəri/ *n* **1** a question, esp one that expresses a doubt about sth: *have/raise a query about sth* ○ *We will be pleased to deal with/handle any queries you may have.* **2** a question mark (?): *Put a query against that.*
▶ **query** *v* (*pt, pp* queried) **1** to express doubt about sth: [Vn] *query a statement/suggestion/conclusion* ○ *query the amount charged* [V.wh] *He queried whether it was really necessary.* **2** to ask sb a question: [V.speech] *'What's that?' she queried.* [Vnpr] *The minister was queried about his plans for the industry.*

quest /kwest/ *n* (*fml or rhet*) **1** ~ (**for sth**) the act of seeking sth; a long search for sth: *the quest for truth/knowledge/happiness* ○ *He set off **in quest of** adventure.*
▶ **quest** *v* (*fml or rhet*) to try to find sth; to search: [V] *have a questing attitude to life.*

question¹ /ˈkwestʃən/ *n* **1** [C] a sentence, etc that asks for information: *ask a lot of questions* ○ *Question 3 is quite difficult.* ○ *I will be happy to answer questions at the end.* ○ *I'd like to put a question to the speaker.* **2** [C] ~ (**of sth**) a matter or an issue which is or needs to be settled: *What about the question of security?* ○ *I've got the job. Now it's a question of finding somewhere to live.* ○ *This raises the question of how we finance the project.* ○ *I'm afraid he's dying — it's merely a question of time.* **3** [U] doubt or uncertainty: *There is no/some question about his honesty.* ○ *Her sincerity is **beyond question**.* ○ *His suitability for the post is **open to question**.* IDM **beg the question** ⇨ BEG. **bring sth / come into 'question** to raise or become an issue for further consideration, discussion, etc: *It does bring into question the whole purpose of the Nato alliance.* ○ *Sunday trading laws came into question again recently.* **call sth into question** ⇨ CALL¹. **in 'question 1** being considered or discussed: *The woman in question is sitting over there.* ○ *The job in question is available for three months only.* **2** in doubt: *The future of public transport is now in question.* **a moot point/question** ⇨ MOOT. **out of the 'question** not worth discussing because it is impossible: *A new bicycle is out of the question — we can't afford it.* **pop the question** ⇨ POP⁴. **there is, was, etc some/no question of** there is a/no possibility of: *There was some question of selling the business.* ○ *There is no question of anyone being made redundant.*
■ **'question mark** *n* (**a**) the symbol (?) used in writing after a question. ⇨ App 3. (**b**) a doubt: *There's a question mark against his name — I'm not convinced he's the right man for the job.*
'question-master (also *esp US* **'quiz-master**) *n* a person who asks the questions in a QUIZ(1), esp on television or radio.

'question time *n* [U] (in a parliament) the period of time when ministers answer questions from members of parliament.

question² /ˈkwestʃən/ *v* **1** ~ **sb** (**about/on sth**) to ask sb a question or questions: [Vn] *They questioned her closely about her previous job.* ○ *He was questioned by the police for six hours.* ○ *Of those questioned, over 50% said they knew they should take more exercise.* **2** to express or feel doubt about sth: [Vn] *Her loyalty has never been questioned.* ○ *I just accepted what he said — I never thought to question it.* [V.wh] *He also questioned whether it was solely the lorry driver's fault.*
▶ **questionable** *adj* **1** that can be doubted: *a questionable assumption/decision/result* ○ *It is questionable how necessary the changes are.* **2** dishonest; that causes suspicion: *questionable earnings* ○ *a questionable lifestyle.* **questionably** /-əbli/ *adv.*
questioner *n* a person who asks questions, esp in a broadcast programme or a public debate.
questioning *n* [U] an occasion or period of asking sb questions about sth: *be subjected to hostile/persistent questioning* ○ *The police brought him in for questioning.*
questioningly *adv* using a gesture or tone of voice in a way that asks a question: *look at sb questioningly* ○ *raise an eyebrow questioningly.*

questionnaire /ˌkwestʃəˈneə(r)/ *n* a written or printed list of questions to be answered by a number of people, esp as part of a survey: *Please fill in/complete and return the enclosed questionnaire.*

queue /kjuː/ *n* (*esp Brit*) a line of people, vehicles, etc waiting for sth or to do sth: *the cinema/lunch/ticket queue* ○ *By 7 o'clock a long queue had formed outside the cinema.* ○ *People had to stand in a queue for hours to buy a ticket.* ○ *Is this the queue for the bus?* ○ *join a queue of cars at the traffic-lights.* IDM **jump the queue** ⇨ JUMP¹.
▶ **queue** *v* ~ (**up**) (**for sth**) to wait in a queue: [V] *We queued for an hour but didn't get in.* [Vpr] *Queue here for taxis.* [Vp] *They're queuing up to see a film.*

quibble /ˈkwɪbl/ *n* an objection or criticism, esp an unimportant one: *quibbles over the exact amount* ○ *I only have a few minor quibbles about your essay — basically it's very good.*
▶ **quibble** *v* ~ (**over/about/with sth**) to argue about small differences or disagreements: [V] *The company should pay up now, and stop quibbling.* [Vpr] *50p isn't worth quibbling about.* ○ *She's very efficient — no one would quibble with that.*

quiche /kiːʃ/ *n* [C, U] an open pie filled with a mixture of eggs and milk with bacon, cheese, etc: *a slice of mushroom quiche.*

quick /kwɪk/ *adj* (**-er, -est**) **1(a)** moving fast or doing sth in a short time: *a quick worker/reader* ○ *She was quick to point out all the mistakes I'd made.* ○ *quick to respond/react/learn* ○ *It's quicker by train.* (**b**) done in a short time: *have a quick bath/drink* ○ *I'll just have a quick look in that shop.* ○ *make a quick recovery* (ie from an illness) ○ *'Have you finished already? That was quick!'* ○ *Are you sure this is the quickest way?* ○ *He fired three shots **in quick succession**.* See also DOUBLE-QUICK. **2(a)** [attrib] lively; active; alert: *quick wits* ○ *Her quick reactions/thinking saved the boy's life.* (**b**) easily provoked; sensitive: *He's got a quick temper* (ie He becomes angry very readily). ○ *She's always very quick to take offence* (ie is easily offended). (**c**) ~ (**at sth**) intelligent; competent: *He's not as quick as his sister.* ○ *His spelling's poor but he's very quick at figures.* IDM **make a fast/quick buck** ⇨ BUCK³. **(as) quick as a 'flash; (as) quick as 'lightning** very quickly: *He got the answer as quick as a flash.* **quick/slow off the mark** ⇨ MARK¹. **quick/slow on the draw** ⇨ DRAW². **quick/slow on the uptake** ⇨ UPTAKE.
▶ **quick** *adv* (**-er, -est**) quickly: *Come as quick as*

you can. ○ *He's just trying to get rich quick.* ○ *Let's see who responds/reacts quickest.*

quick *n* [sing] soft tender flesh, esp below the fingernails: *She has bitten her nails (down) to the quick.* **IDM** **cut sb to the ¹quick** to upset sb deeply by saying or doing sth unkind: *Their insults cut her to the quick.*

quickly *adv*: *speak/write/run/learn very quickly* ○ *do/finish sth as quickly as possible.*

quickness *n* [U] **1** speed: (*saying*) *The quickness of the hand deceives the eye.* **2** intelligence: *She amazes me with her quickness and eagerness to learn.*

■ **,quick-'fire** *adj* rapid: *a series of ,quick-fire ¹deals.*

¹quick one *n* (*infml*) a drink, usu an alcoholic one, taken quickly: *Have you got time for a quick one before you go?*

,quick-'tempered *adj* likely to become angry very quickly: *a ,quick-tempered ¹woman.*

,quick-'witted *adj* able to think quickly; intelligent: *a ,quick-witted ¹student/re¹sponse.*

quicken /ˈkwɪkən/ *v* **1** to become or make sth quicker (QUICK 1): [V] *a quickening heart/pulse rate* ○ *The quickening pace of events.* [Vnpr] *We quickened our steps to a run.* [also Vn]. **2** (*fml*) to become or make sth more active: [Vn] *a play that quickened her interest in contemporary drama* [also V].

quickie /ˈkwɪki/ *n* (*infml*) a thing that is made or done very quickly: *go to a pub for a quickie* (ie a quick drink).

quicklime /ˈkwɪklaɪm/ *n* [U] = LIME¹.

quicksand /ˈkwɪksænd/ *n* [C often *pl*, U] wet deep sand into which people or things will sink.

quicksilver /ˈkwɪksɪlvə(r)/ *n* [U] = MERCURY: *like quicksilver* (ie very quick or quickly).

▶ **quicksilver** *adj* [attrib] (of mood, actions or behaviour) moving or changing very quickly: *the quicksilver delicacy of her playing.*

quickstep /ˈkwɪkstep/ *n* a dance with quick steps, or a piece of music for this: *play/dance a quickstep.*

quid /kwɪd/ *n* (*pl* unchanged) (*Brit infml*) one pound in money: *Can you lend me five quid?* ○ *It only costs a couple of quid to get in.* **IDM** **quids ¹in** in a position where one has profited or can profit from sth: *If you sell your house now, you'll be quids in.*

quid pro quo /ˌkwɪd prəʊ ¹kwəʊ/ *n* (*pl* **quid pro quos**) a thing given in return for sth else: *What do they want as a quid pro quo for releasing the hostages?*

quiescent /kwiˈesnt/ *adj* (*fml*) quiet; not active: *a quiescent volcano* ○ *It is unlikely that the terrorists will remain quiescent for long.* ▶ **quiescence** /-sns/ *n* [U].

quiet /ˈkwaɪət/ *adj* (**-er, -est**) **1** with very little or no noise: *her quiet voice/footsteps* ○ **Be quiet!** ○ *I'll be* (**as**) **quiet as a mouse.** ○ *Please can you keep the children quiet while I'm on the phone?* ○ *The room suddenly went very quiet.* **2(a)** without many people or much activity: *The roads are usually quieter in the afternoon.* ○ *lead a quiet life* ○ *Business is quiet at this time of the year.* ○ *Their wedding was very quiet.* (**b**) without disturbance or interruption: *have a quiet smoke* ○ *have a quiet evening at home.* **3** (of a person) gentle; not forceful: *She was a quiet person but friendly.* **4** not expressed loudly; restrained: *have a quiet confidence* ○ *She takes a quiet satisfaction in her work.* ⇨ note. **IDM** **keep quiet about sth; keep sth quiet** to say nothing about sth: *I've decided to resign but I'd rather you kept quiet about it for now.*

▶ **quiet** *n* [U] the state of being quiet; calm: *the quiet of the countryside* ○ *Can we have a bit of peace and quiet in here, please!* **IDM** **on the ¹quiet** secretly: *have a drink on the quiet.*

quiet *v* ~ (**sb/sth**) (**down**) (*esp US*) to become quiet or make sb/sth quiet: [Vn] *quiet a frightened horse*

[V] *After a while her sobs quieted.* [Vp] *Quiet down, kids!* [also Vnp].

quieten /ˈkwaɪətn/ *v* ~ (**sb/sth**) (**down**) (*esp Brit*) to become or make sb/sth less disturbed, noisy, etc: [V] *By 2 am the party had quietened.* [Vp] *Quieten down and get on with your work.* [Vn] *quieten a frightened child* ○ *quieten sb's anxiety/suspicions.*

quietly *adv*: *speak/move/sob quietly* ○ *This engine runs very quietly.* ○ *She slipped quietly out of the room.* ○ *He is quietly confident of victory.* ○ *He was a quietly-spoken man.*

quietness *n* [U]: *the quietness of the countryside* ○ *His quietness worried her.*

NOTE Quiet, silent and calm can all be used to describe both people and things and generally describe a lack of sound or movement. A **silent** film has no speech and a **silent** machine makes no noise. **Quiet** can mean **silent**: *Please be quiet, I'm trying to work.* A **quiet** street, suburb, etc is not noisy or busy. **Quiet** can also mean without disturbance or excitement: *Politicians must sometimes wish for a quieter life.* **Still** means 'not moving': *Stand still!* ○ *the still surface of the lake.* It may suggest a lack of sound or movement: *Everyone had gone to bed and the house was completely still.* A **calm** person is not nervous or excited in difficult situations: *Stay calm and call an ambulance immediately.* If the weather or the sea is **calm** there is not very much wind: *It was a calm day and the water seemed peaceful and inviting.*

quietism /ˈkwaɪətɪzəm/ *n* [U] an attitude to life based on a calm acceptance of things as they are without trying to resist or change them. ▶ **quietist** /-ɪst/ *n, adj.*

quietude /ˈkwaɪətjuːd; *US* -tuːd/ *n* [U] (*fml*) the state of being still; calm: *the quietude of a cathedral.*

quiff /kwɪf/ *n* (*Brit*) a piece of hair, esp of a man, brushed up above the forehead: *a quiff of blond hair that kept falling into his eyes.*

quill /kwɪl/ *n* **1(a)** (also **¹quill-feather**) a large feather from the wing or tail of a bird. ⇨ picture at FEATHER. (**b**) (also **,quill ¹pen**) a pen made from the hollow stem of such a feather. **2** (usu *pl*) a long sharp stiff SPINE(2) of a PORCUPINE.

quilt /kwɪlt/ *n* a thick covering for a bed, made of layers of cloth filled with soft material: *a patchwork quilt.* Compare DUVET, EIDERDOWN.

quilted /ˈkwɪltɪd/ *adj* (of a jacket, cushion, etc) made of pieces of cloth filled with soft material that is held in place by lines of stitches: *a quilted jacket/dressing-gown.*

quin /kwɪn/ (*US* **quint** /kwɪnt/) *n* (*infml*) = QUINTUPLET.

quince /kwɪns/ *n* (**a**) a hard bitter fruit shaped like a pear, used for making jam, etc: *quince jelly.* (**b**) a tree on which it grows: *a flowering quince.*

quincentenary /ˌkwɪnsenˈtiːnəri; *US* -senˈtenəri/ *n* a 500th anniversary.

quinine /kwɪˈniːn, ˈkwɪniːn; *US* ˈkwaɪnaɪn/ *n* [U] a drug used to treat fever, esp MALARIA.

quint (*US*) = QUIN.

quintessence /kwɪnˈtesns/ *n* [sing] **the ~ of sth** (*fml*) **1** the essential part of a theory, speech, condition, etc: *a painting that captures the quintessence of Viennese elegance.* **2** the perfect example of a quality: *She was the quintessence of hospitality.* ▶ **quintessential** /ˌkwɪntɪˈsenʃl/ *adj*: *quintessential beauty.* **quintessentially** /-ʃəli/ *adv*: *a sense of humour that is quintessentially British.*

quintet /kwɪnˈtet/ *n* (**a**) a group of five people playing music or singing together. (**b**) a piece of music for such a group: *Schubert's 'Trout' Quintet.*

quintuplet /ˈkwɪntjuːplət; *US* kwɪnˈtʌplət/ (also

infml **quin**, *US* **quint** *n* (usu *pl*) any of five children born to the same mother at one birth.

quip /kwɪp/ *n* a quick and clever remark: *He always manages to end with a quip.* ▶ **quip** *v* (-pp-) [V.speech] to make a quip or quips.

quirk /kwɜːk/ *n* **1** a strange habit or type of behaviour: *Everyone has their own little quirks and eccentricities.* **2** a strange thing that happens, esp accidentally: *By **a quirk of fate** they had booked into the same hotel.* ▶ **quirky** *adj*: *a quirky character/event/coincidence.*

quisling /ˈkwɪzlɪŋ/ *n* (*derog*) a person who helps an enemy occupying her or his country; a TRAITOR.

quit /kwɪt/ *v* (-tt-; *pt*, *pp* **quit** or, in British use, **quitted**) **1** to leave a place, job, etc: [V] *If I don't get a pay rise I'll quit.* ○ *Tenants who refuse to accept leases are given **notice to quit** (ie ordered to leave the accommodation).* [Vn] *He quit school at 16.* **2** (*infml*) to stop doing sth: [V.ing] *I've quit smoking.* [also V]. **IDM** **be ˈquit of sb/sth** be rid of sb/sth; be freed from sb/sth: *I'm glad to be quit of the responsibility.* ○ *You're well quit of him (ie fortunate because he has left).* **double or quits** ⇨ DOUBLE⁴. ▶ **quitter** *n* (*often derog*) a person who gives up easily and does not finish a task he or she has started: *I knew you weren't a quitter.*

quite /kwaɪt/ *adv* **1** (used esp with *adjs* or *advs* that refer to a gradable quality; not used with a negative) to some extent; not very; fairly: *quite big/small/good/cold/warm/interesting* ○ *They had to wait quite a long time.* ○ *He plays quite well.* ○ *I quite like opera.* ○ *I found the test quite hard.* ⇨ note at FAIRLY. **2** (used esp with *adjs* or *advs* that refer to a gradable quality; not used with a negative) perfectly; completely; very: *He's quite happy at his new school* ○ *You'll be quite comfortable here.* ○ *I can see it quite clearly.* **3** (used with *adjs* or *advs* to emphasize sth; not used with a negative): *quite delicious/spectacular/amazing/incredible* ○ *a quite extraordinary experience* ○ *The view was quite breathtaking.* ○ *That was quite the nicest meal I've ever had.* ○ *She performed quite brilliantly.* ⇨ note. **4** (used esp with words that refer to an absolute quality) completely; entirely: *quite empty/perfect/enough* ○ *Are you quite sure/certain?* ○ *He has quite recovered from his illness.* ○ *I don't think that's quite right.* ○ *I quite agree/understand.* ○ *'Do you mind waiting?' 'No, that's quite all right.'* **5** (also *fml* **quite so**) (used to express agreement or understanding): *'It's not something we want to have talked about.' 'Quite (so).'* ○ *'He's bound to feel shaken after his accident.' 'Quite.'* **IDM** **not quite 1** almost; slightly less (than): *The theatre was not quite full.* ○ *'There must be 1000 people here.' 'Not quite that many.'* ○ *It's almost like being in the Alps, but not quite.* **2** (expressing uncertainty) not entirely: *It wasn't quite as simple as I thought it would be.* ○ *I don't quite know what to do next.* ○ *Those shoes don't quite go with that dress.* **quite a few** ⇨ FEW². **quite a ˈlot (of)** a considerable number or amount: *We drank quite a lot of wine.* **ˈquite a**; **ˈquite some** /-sʌm/ (*approv esp US*) (used to indicate that a person or thing is unusual): *It must be quite some car.* ○ *We had quite a party.* **quite ˈsomething** (used to show approval of sb/sth unusual or special): *You decorated the whole house yourself? That's quite something!* ▶ **quite** *det* (used before *a/the* + noun phrase as an intensifier): *She's quite a beauty/swimmer.* ○ *We found it quite a change when we moved to London.* ○ *He's quite the little gentleman, isn't he?*

NOTE In American English, **quite** can be used to mean 'very' or 'absolutely': *The service in that restaurant was quite bad.* The expression **quite nice** can therefore mean 'very nice' in American English: *Thank you for the flowers, that was quite nice of you.*

In British English this sentence would not be very polite because **quite nice** usually means 'fairly nice'.

In both British and American English people say **really** when they want to show approval or pay a compliment: *Thank you for the flowers, it was really nice of you.* ○ *The film was really good.*

Quite comes before **a** or **an** when it is used with an adjective before a noun: *The house is quite small.* ○ *It's quite a small house* (NOT *It's a quite small house*).
⇨ note at FAIRLY.

quits /kwɪts/ *adj* **IDM** **be quits (with sb)** *infml* (of two people) not to owe each other anything after money, etc has been paid back: *I'll give you £5 and then we're quits.* **call it quits** ⇨ CALL¹. **double or quits** ⇨ DOUBLE⁴.

quiver¹ /ˈkwɪvə(r)/ *v* to shake or TREMBLE(1a) slightly: [V] *quivering leaves* ○ *His voice quivered with emotion.* ○ *'I'm sorry,' she said, her lip quivering.* ▶ **quiver** *n* a quivering sound or movement: *A quiver of excitement ran through the audience.* ○ *the quiver of an eyelid.*

quiver² /ˈkwɪvə(r)/ *n* a case for carrying arrows ARROW(1). ⇨ picture at ARCHERY.

quixotic /kwɪkˈsɒtɪk/ *adj* having fine romantic ideals and good intentions that are not at all practical or realistic.

quiz /kwɪz/ *n* (*pl* **quizzes**) **1** a contest, esp on television or radio, in which people try to answer questions to test their knowledge: *take part in a quiz* ○ *a sports/music/general knowledge quiz* ○ *a quiz game/programme/show.* **2** (*US*) an informal written test or examination given to students. ▶ **quiz** *v* (-zz-) **(a)** ~ **sb (about sb/sth)** to ask sb questions: [Vnpr] *She was quizzed by detectives about the theft.* [Vn] *70% of the people quizzed said they agreed with the President.* **(b)** [Vn] (*US*) to give students a quiz(2). ■ **ˈquiz-master** *n* = QUESTION-MASTER.

quizzical /ˈkwɪzɪkl/ *adj* (of a smile, look, etc) expressing slight, esp amused, confusion: *a quizzical glance* ○ *His expression was quizzical.* ▶ **quizzically** /-kli/ *adv*: *She looked at me quizzically.*

quoit /kɔɪt, kwɔɪt/ *n* **(a)** [C] a ring in a game that is thrown onto an upright PEG¹(1). **(b)** **quoits** [sing *v*] the game in which this is done: *play deck quoits* (ie on a ship).

quorum /ˈkwɔːrəm/ *n* [sing] the minimum number of people who must be present at a meeting of a committee, etc before it can proceed and its decisions can be considered valid: *have/achieve a quorum.*

quota /ˈkwəʊtə/ *n* **1** a limited number or amount of people or things that is officially allowed: *introduce a strict import quota on grain.* **2** a fixed amount of sth that must be done, given or received: *get one's full quota of sleep* ○ *I'm going home now — I've done my quota of work for the day.*

quotation /kwəʊˈteɪʃn/ *n* **1** (also *infml* **quote**) [C] a group of words taken from a book, play, speech, etc and repeated, usu by sb who is not the original author: *a dictionary of quotations* ○ *a quotation from Shakespeare.* See also MISQUOTATION. **2** [U] the action of quoting: *Support your argument by quotation.* **3** (also *infml* **quote**) [C] the price that sb says they would charge for a piece of work: *a written quotation* ○ *You should get a number of quotations from different builders.* Compare ESTIMATE¹ 3. **4** [C] (*finance*) a statement of the current price of stocks or commodities: *the latest quotations from the Stock Exchange.* ■ **quoˈtation marks** (also *infml* **quotes**, *Brit* **inverted commas**) *n* [pl] a pair of marks (' ' or " ") used at the beginning and end of words that are being quoted. ⇨ App 3.

quote /kwəʊt/ *v* **1** ~ **(sth)** **(from sb/sth)** to repeat words that were previously said or written by another person in speech or writing: [Vn] *to quote Keats/the Bible* ○ *Please quote your account number in all correspondence.* ○ *The book provides, to quote the author, 'food for the imagination'.* ○ *I think he's going to resign, but please **don't quote me on that** (ie because I am not sure if it is true).* [Vpr] *She quoted from a government document.* [Vnpr] *He's always **quoted as saying** she disagrees with the decision.* [V] *She said, and I quote, 'Life is meaningless without love.'* See also MISQUOTE. **2** to mention sb/ sth in support of a statement: [Vn, Vnn] *Can you quote me an example of what you mean?* **3** to say how much one will charge for a piece of work: [Vnn] *They quoted us £200 for installing a new shower unit.* [also Vn, Vnpr]. Compare ESTIMATE². **4** ~ **sth (at sth)** *(finance)* to give a price for shares, etc: [Vn, Vnpr] *ordinary shares quoted on the stock exchange (at 55p a share).*

▶ **quote** *n* *(infml)* **1** [C] = QUOTATION 1,3. **2 quotes** [pl] = QUOTATION MARKS: *His words are in quotes.*
IDM **'quote (... 'unquote)** (used when speaking to show the beginning (and end) of a statement or piece of writing that is being quoted, esp when the speaker disagrees with it): *This quote startlingly original novel unquote is both boring and badly written.*

quotable *adj* that can be or that deserves to be quoted: *(infml) a speech full of quotable quotes.*

quoth /kwəʊθ/ *v* (used only in the 1st and 3rd person singular past tense) *(arch)* said: [V.speech] *'Alas,' quoth I/he/she.*

quotient /ˈkwəʊʃnt/ *n* **1** a degree or an amount of a specified quality or characteristic: *As food supplies slowly disappeared, their misery quotient increased.* **2** *(mathematics)* a number obtained when one number is divided by another.

qv /ˌkjuː ˈviː/ *abbr* *(fml)* which may be referred to (Latin *quod vide*) (used eg to direct a reader to another part of a book, etc for further information).

Q

Rr

R¹ (also **r**) /ɑː(r)/ n (pl **R's** , **r's** /ɑːz/) the 18th letter of the English alphabet: *'Rabbit' begins with (an) R/ 'R'*. **IDM** **the three ¹Rs** reading, writing and ARITH-METIC, regarded as the basis of an education.

R² abbr **1** Queen; King (Latin *Regina*; *Rex*): *Elizabeth R*. **2** (also symb ®) (*commerce*) registered as a trade mark (TRADE¹): *Kodak®* **3** (*US politics*) Republican. See also D². **4** River: *R Thames/Mississippi R* (eg on a map).

r abbr right. Compare L 1.

rabbi /ˈræbaɪ/ n (pl **rabbis**) a Jewish religious leader or teacher of Jewish law: *the Chief Rabbi* (eg of Jewish communities in Britain) ○ *Rabbi Lionel Blue*.
▶ **rabbinical** /rəˈbɪnɪkl/ (also **rabbinic**) adj of rabbis; of Jewish teaching or law.

rabbit /ˈræbɪt/ n (**a**) [C] a small animal with greyish brown fur, long ears and a short tail. Rabbits live in holes in the ground. Compare HARE. See also HUTCH. (**b**) [U] its flesh eaten as food: *rabbit pie*.
▶ **rabbit** (*Brit*) v [V] (usu **go rabbiting**) to hunt rabbits. **PHRV** **,rabbit ¹on (about sb/sth)** (*infml derog*) to talk continuously, usu about things that are not important or interesting: *What are you rabbiting on about?*
■ **¹rabbit warren** n **1** an area of land full of holes and tunnels made by wild rabbits. **2** (*derog*) a building or part of a city with many narrow passages or streets: *The council offices were a real rabbit warren.*

rabble /ˈræbl/ n [Gp] (**1**) a large disorderly (DISORDER) group of people; a MOB(1): *He was met by a rabble of noisy, angry youths*. **2** **the rabble** (*derog*) the lower social classes: *speeches appealing to the rabble*.
■ **¹rabble-rouser** n a person who makes speeches to crowds of people intending to make them very angry or excited, esp for political aims. **¹rabble-rousing** adj, n [U]: *a rabble-rousing speaker/speech*.

Rabelaisian /ˌræbəˈleɪziən/ adj full of rude jokes about sex and the body, in the style of the French writer Rabelais: *Rabelaisian prose*.

rabid /ˈræbɪd, ˈreɪb-/ adj **1** suffering from RABIES: *a rabid dog*. **2** (usu attrib) (of feelings or opinions) violent or extreme: *rabid hate/greed* ○ *rabid socialism*.

rabies /ˈreɪbiːz/ n [U] a disease that causes madness and often death in dogs and other animals. Humans can also catch rabies, usu by being bitten by an animal that has the disease.

RAC /ˌɑːr eɪ ˈsiː/ abbr (in Britain) Royal Automobile Club.

raccoon (also **racoon**) /rəˈkuːn; *US* ræ-/ (also *US infml* **coon**) n (**a**) [C] a small greyish-brown N American animal with black markings on its face and its thick furry tail. (**b**) [U] its fur: *a raccoon cap*.

race¹ /reɪs/ n **1** ~ (**against/with sb/sth**); ~ (**between A and B**) (**a**) [C] a contest between runners, horses, vehicles, etc to see which is the fastest: *to win/lose/run a race* ○ *to come first/second/last in a race* ○ *a ¹horse-race* ○ *a ¹boat race* ○ *a five-kilometre race* ○ *Let's have a race to the end of the beach.* ○ (*fig*) *The process of getting food to the starving villagers is now **a race against time** (ie an attempt to do or finish sth before a particular time).* (**b**) **the races** [pl] a race meeting: *a day at the races*. ⇨ note at

SPORT. **2** [sing] a situation in which a number of people, groups, organizations, etc are competing for sth: *join the race for the presidency* ○ *The race is now on* (ie has begun) *to find a cure for this disease.* See also ARMS RACE, RAT RACE.
■ **¹race meeting** n (*Brit*) a series of races, esp for horses, held at one course over one day or several days.

race² /reɪs/ v **1** ~ (**against**) **sb/sth** to take part in a race against sb/sth: [Vpr] *The drivers were racing against each other.* ○ *The cars raced round the track.* [Vnpr] *Come on, I'll race you to school* (ie try to get there before you do). [V.to inf] *Manufacturers everywhere are racing to find substitutes for CFCs.* [also Vn, Vn.to inf]. **2**(**a**) to move very fast: [Vpr] *He raced along the road.* ○ *Thick white clouds raced across the sky.* [Vadv] *The days seemed to race past.* ○ *He raced off to catch the train.* [also V.to inf]. ⇨ note at RUN¹. (**b**) to move sb/sth very fast: [Vnpr] *The patient had to be raced to hospital.* **3**(**a**) to compete in races: [V] *She races at all the big meetings.* (**b**) to make an animal or a vehicle compete in races: [Vn] *race pigeons/dogs* ○ *race cars/bikes in rallies.* **4** (esp of the heart) to beat very fast: [V] *Her heart was racing with excitement.* **5** to operate at high speed: [V] *The driver waited for the green light, his engine racing.* ○ *Her mind raced, running over the possibilities.* [also Vp, Vpr].
▶ **racer** n (**a**) a horse, boat, car, etc used for racing. (**b**) a person who competes in races: *ski racers*.
racing n [U] (**a**) the sport of racing horses: *a ¹racing stable* (ie for horses trained to race). See also FLAT-RACING. (**b**) (usu in compounds) any sport that involves competing in races: *Grand Prix motor racing* ○ *a ¹racing driver* ○ *¹greyhound racing* ○ *a ¹racing car/ yacht* (ie designed for racing).

race³ /reɪs/ n **1** [C, U] any of the groups into which humans can be divided according to their physical characteristics, eg colour of skin, colour and type of hair, shape of eyes and nose: *the Caucasian/ Mongolian race* ○ *people of mixed race* ○ *There should be no discrimination on the grounds of sex, race or religion.* **2** [C] a group of people who have the same culture, history, language, etc: *the Spanish/ Germanic/Nordic races.* **3** [C] any of the main species, breeds or types of animals or plants: *breed a race of cattle that can survive drought.* See also THE HUMAN RACE. **4** [U] (*fml*) family origins; ancestry (ANCESTOR): *people of ancient and noble race.*
■ **,race re¹lations** n [pl] the relationships between people of different races who live in the same community: *attempts to improve race relations in our inner cities* ○ *race relations legislation.*
¹race riot n a violent disturbance between groups of people of different races in the same community.

racecourse /ˈreɪskɔːs/ (*Brit*) (*US* **racetrack**) n a track where horses race.

racegoer /ˈreɪsɡəʊə(r)/ n a person who regularly goes to horse-races (HORSE).

racehorse /ˈreɪshɔːs/ n a horse that is bred and trained to run in races.

racetrack /ˈreɪstræk/ n **1** a track for races between vehicles or runners. **2** (*US*) = RACECOURSE.

racial /ˈreɪʃl/ adj connected with or resulting from race³(1); happening or existing between people of

---

different races: *racial pride/purity* ○ *racial discrimination/prejudice/violence/segregation* ○ *the fight for racial equality.* ▶ **racialism** /-ʃəlɪzəm/ *n* [U] = RACISM. **racialist** /-ʃəlɪst/ *n, adj* = RACIST. **racially** /-ʃəli/ *adv: a racially diverse community* ○ *racially motivated violence.*

racism /ˈreɪsɪzəm/ (also **racialism**) *n* [U] (*derog*) (**a**) the belief that some races (RACE³ 1) are superior to others. (**b**) unfair treatment or dislike of sb because they are of a different race: *take measures to combat racism* ○ *victims of racism.* ▶ **racist** /ˈreɪsɪst/ (also **racialist**) *n, adj: She's a racist.* ○ *racist groups/thugs* ○ *racist abuse/attacks/remarks.*

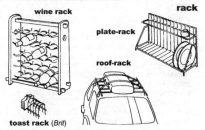

wine rack

rack

plate-rack

roof-rack

toast rack (*Brit*)

rack¹ /ræk/ *n* **1** (often in compounds) a framework, usu with bars or pegs (PEG¹ 1), for holding things or for hanging things on: *a 'vegetable rack* ○ *a 'wine rack* (ie for holding wine bottles) ○ *racks of clothes displayed in a shop* ○ *He hung the towels neatly on the rack.* ○ *Cool the cakes on a wire rack.* ⊏> picture. See also ROOF-RACK, TOAST RACK. **2** a shelf or container for light cases, coats, etc above the seats of a bus, train, plane, etc: *a 'luggage rack* ○ *He reached up and put his briefcase in the rack.* **3** a part of a machine consisting of a bar with teeth into which those of a wheel or gear fit. **4** (usu **the rack**) (formerly) an instrument of TORTURE(1) consisting of a frame on which a person's arms and legs were tied and then pulled in opposite directions, stretching the body: *put sb on the rack.* **IDM off the rack** (*US*) = OFF THE PEG (PEG¹). **on the 'rack** suffering severe physical or mental pain.

rack² (also **wrack**) /ræk/ *v* (often passive) to cause sb great physical or mental pain: [Vnpr] *racked with pain/fever* [Vn] *racked by (feelings of) guilt/remorse/doubt* ○ *Violent sobs racked her whole body* ○ *a racking cough* ○ (*fig*) *a country racked by civil war.* **IDM rack one's 'brain(s)** to try very hard to think of sth or remember sth: *We racked our brains for an answer.* ○ *I've been racking my brains trying to remember his name.*

rack³ /ræk/ *n* **IDM go to ˌrack and 'ruin** to be in or get into a bad state because of lack of care and attention: *They let the house go to rack and ruin.* ○ *This country is going to rack and ruin; we need a change of government.*

racket¹ (also **racquet**) /ˈrækɪt/ *n* **1** [C] a piece of sports equipment used for hitting the ball, etc in tennis, SQUASH¹(3) or BADMINTON. It has an OVAL frame, with strings stretched across and down it. ⊏> picture at SQUASH¹, TENNIS. **2 rackets** (also **racquets**) [sing *v*] a game for two or four people played with rackets and a small hard ball in a court with four walls. Compare SQUASH¹ 3.

racket² /ˈrækɪt/ *n* (*infml derog*) **1** [sing] a loud unpleasant noise: *Stop making that terrible racket!* **2** [C] a dishonest or illegal way of getting money: *protection/extortion/drugs rackets* ○ *be involved in the smuggling racket.*
▶ **racketeer** /ˌrækəˈtɪə(r)/ *n* (*derog*) a person who makes money through dishonest or illegal activities. **racketeering** *n* [U]: *be charged with fraud and racketeering.*

raconteur /ˌrækɒnˈtɜː(r)/ *n* a person who is good at telling stories in an interesting and amusing way: *She's a brilliant raconteur.*

racoon = RACCOON.

racy /ˈreɪsi/ *adj* (**-ier, -iest**) (of speech, writing, etc) lively, and perhaps slightly shocking, often in the way it deals with sex: *a racy description of New York life* ○ *racy stories.*

radar /ˈreɪdɑː(r)/ *n* [U] a system for finding out the position and movement of solid objects, esp aircraft and ships, when they cannot be seen, by sending out short radio waves which they reflect: *locate an aircraft by radar* ○ *enemy radar* ○ *a radar operator/scanner/installation* ○ *The plane disappeared off the radar screen.* Compare SONAR. ■ **'radar trap** (also **'speed trap**) *n* a section of road where the police use a radar device to detect vehicles travelling faster than they should.

raddled /ˈrædld/ *adj* (*Brit*) (of a person, face, etc) looking very tired; WORN²(2).

radial /ˈreɪdiəl/ *adj* of or arranged like rays; having bars, lines, etc that go outwards from a central point: *radial spokes* (eg in a bicycle wheel). ▶ **radial** (also **ˌradial 'tyre**) *n* a tyre with the cords inside arranged so that they are at right angles (RIGHT¹) to the outside part. This strengthens the tyre so that the vehicle is easier to control on wet surfaces. Compare CROSS-PLY. **radially** /-ɪəli/ *adv.*

radiant /ˈreɪdiənt/ *adj* **1** [attrib] sending out light or heat; shining or glowing brightly: *the radiant sun* ○ *radiant heaters.* **2** ~ (**with sth**) showing great happiness, love or beauty: *his radiant face/smile* ○ *her radiant beauty* ○ *She was radiant with joy/health.* **3** [attrib] (*techn*) sent out by RADIATION(1a): *radiant heat/energy.*
▶ **radiance** /-əns/ *n* [U] the quality of being radiant (1,2): *the sun's radiance* ○ *Her face shone with joy and radiance.*
radiantly *adv: smile radiantly.*

radiate /ˈreɪdieɪt/ *v* **1**(**a**) (of a person) to send out a clear and strong feeling of sth: [Vn] *radiate charm/confidence/enthusiasm/health.* (**b**) ~ **from sb/sth** (of a feeling) to be sent out by sb/sb's eyes, etc: [Vpr] *Love and kindness seemed to radiate from her.* **2**(**a**) to send out rays of light or heat: [Vn] *a stove that radiates warmth.* (**b**) ~ **from sth** (of light or heat) to be sent out from sth by RADIATION(1a): [Vpr] *warmth radiating from the stove.* Compare IRRADIATE 1. **3** ~ (**from / out from sth**) (of lines, etc) to spread out like rays from a central point: [Vpr] *Five roads radiate from the new roundabout.* [also V].

radiation /ˌreɪdiˈeɪʃn/ *n* **1** [U] (**a**) the sending out of heat, energy, etc in the form of rays. (**b**) the heat, energy, etc sent out like this: *ultraviolet radiation.* **2** [U,C] powerful and dangerous rays sent out from RADIOACTIVE substances: *be exposed to radiation* ○ *a low/high level of radiation* ○ *a radiation leak from a nuclear power station* ○ *the radiations emitted by radium.* **3** (also **radiation therapy**) [U] the treatment of CANCER(1) and other diseases using radiation. Compare CHEMOTHERAPY, RADIOTHERAPY. ■ **ˌradi'ation sickness** *n* [U] the illness caused when the body is exposed to high radiation.

radiator /ˈreɪdieɪtə(r)/ *n* **1** a hollow metal device for heating rooms. Radiators are usu connected by pipes through which hot water is pumped: *install a central heating system with a radiator in each room.* **2** a device for cooling the engine of a vehicle or an aircraft: *a radiator grille.* ⊏> picture at CAR.

radical /ˈrædɪkl/ *adj* [usu attrib] **1** of or from the root or base; fundamental: *a radical flaw/error/fault in the system.* **2**(**a**) thorough or complete: *radical reforms/changes.* (**b**) new and different: *radical designs/ideas.* **3** favouring thorough or complete political or social reform; holding extreme views: *a radical politician/thinker/writer* ○ *radical politics.*

▶ **radical** *n* a person with radical(3) opinions: *political/religious radicals.*

radicalism /-kəlɪzəm/ *n* [U] belief in radical(3) ideas and principles: *political/social radicalism.*

radicalize, -ise *v* to make sb/sth more radical(3): [Vn] *an emerging radicalized clergy.*

radically /-klɪ/ *adv*: *radically altered/modified* ○ *have radically different views.*

radii *pl* of RADIUS.

radio /ˈreɪdɪəʊ/ *n* (*pl* **-os**) **1** [U] the process of sending and receiving messages through the air by ELECTROMAGNETIC waves: *contact a ship at sea by radio* ○ *ˈradio waves/signals.* **2** (often **the radio**) [U, sing] the activity or industry of broadcasting programmes for people to listen to: *I heard it* **on the radio.** ○ *a play specially written for radio* ○ *a radio programme/announcer/station.* **3** [C] (**a**) an apparatus for receiving programmes broadcast to the public by means of radio signals: *turn the radio on/off* ○ *a portable radio* ○ *a car radio* ○ *a radio-cassette player.* See also CLOCK RADIO. (**b**) an apparatus, eg on ships or planes, for sending and receiving radio messages: *a radio receiver/transmitter* ○ *hear a gale warning on/over the ship's radio.*

▶ **radio** *v* (*pt, pp* **radioed**) to send a message by radio: [Vpr] *radio (to sb) for help* [Vn, Vnn] *radio (sb) one's position* [V.that, Vn.that] *We radioed (the coast-guards) that we were in trouble.*

■ **ˈradio car** *n* a car equipped with a radio for communication.

ˌradio-conˈtrolled *adj* controlled from a distance by radio signals: *a ˌradio-controlled model ˈaeroplane.*

ˌradio ˈtelescope *n* an apparatus for finding stars, following the course of spacecraft, etc by means of radio waves from outer space.

radio- *comb form* of RADIATION or radioactivity (RADIOACTIVE): *radioactive* ○ *radiologist* ○ *radiotherapy.*

radioactive /ˌreɪdɪəʊˈæktɪv/ *adj* sending out powerful and dangerous rays that are produced when atoms are broken up: *radioactive chemicals/materials/particles* ○ *radioactive contamination of farmland* ○ *radioactive fallout/waste* ○ *Radium and uranium are radioactive elements.* ▶ **radioactivity** /ˌreɪdɪəʊækˈtɪvəti/ *n* [U]: *a rise in the level of radioactivity.*

radiocarbon /ˌreɪdɪəʊˈkɑːbən/ *n* [U] a RADIOACTIVE form of carbon present in the materials of which living things are formed, used in carbon dating (CARBON): *radiocarbon analysis.*

radiography /ˌreɪdɪˈɒɡrəfi/ *n* [U] the process of taking X-RAY photographs.

▶ **radiographer** /-ɡrəfə(r)/ *n* **1** a person who takes X-RAY photographs in a hospital. **2** a person trained to use X-rays in the treatment of CANCER(1), etc.

radiology /ˌreɪdɪˈɒlədʒi/ *n* [U] the study and use of different types of RADIATION(3) in medicine, eg to treat diseases. ▶ **radiologist** /-ɪst/ *n.*

radiotherapy /ˌreɪdɪəʊˈθerəpi/ *n* [U] the treatment of disease by RADIATION(3): *a course of radiotherapy.* Compare CHEMOTHERAPY. ▶ **radiotherapist** *n.*

radish /ˈrædɪʃ/ *n* a small hot-tasting red or white root vegetable, eaten raw in salads (SALAD 1): *a bunch of radishes.*

radium /ˈreɪdɪəm/ *n* [U] a chemical element. Radium is a RADIOACTIVE metal used in the treatment of certain diseases, eg CANCER(1): *radium therapy.* ⇨ App 7.

radius /ˈreɪdɪəs/ *n* (*pl* **-dii** /-dɪaɪ/) **1(a)** a straight line from the centre of a circle or SPHERE(1a) to any point on its outer edge or surface. (**b**) the length of this line as a measurement: *calculate the radius of a circle.* ⇨ picture at CIRCLE. Compare DIAMETER.

2 a circular area measured by its radius: *Police searched all the woods within a six-mile radius/within a radius of six miles.* **3** (*anatomy*) (**a**) the shorter bone in the part of the human arm between the hand and the elbow. ⇨ picture at SKELETON. (**b**) a similar bone in the lower part of an animal's leg or a bird's wing.

radon /ˈreɪdɒn/ *n* [U] a chemical element. Radon is a RADIOACTIVE gas. ⇨ App 7.

RAF /ˌɑːr eɪ ˈef *or, in infml use,* ræf/ *abbr* (in Britain) Royal Air Force: *an RAF pilot.*

raffia /ˈræfɪə/ *n* [U] long thin material from the leaves of a type of palm², used for weaving mats, etc.

raffish /ˈræfɪʃ/ *adj* wild and not respectable in appearance, but quite attractive: *He had the raffish air of a showman.*

raffle /ˈræfl/ *n* a way of making money for a good cause by selling tickets with numbers on them. Later some numbers are chosen and prizes given to the people whose tickets match them: *sell raffle tickets* ○ *win a box of chocolates in a raffle.* Compare DRAW² 1b, LOTTERY 1.

▶ **raffle** *v* [Vn, Vnp] ~ **sth (off)** to offer sth as a prize in a raffle.

raft¹ /rɑːft; *US* ræft/ *n* (**a**) a flat structure of logs, barrels, etc tied together and used as a boat or a floating platform: *build a makeshift raft* ○ *a raft race.* (**b**) a small boat of rubber, plastic, etc that is filled with air: *an inflatable raft.*

▶ **rafting** *n* (*sport*) [U] the activity of travelling on a raft: *go white water rafting on the Colorado River.*

raft² /rɑːft; *US* ræft/ *n* (usu *sing*) ~ **(of sth)** (*infml*) a large number or amount: *a raft of rules and regulations.*

rafter /ˈrɑːftə(r)/; *US* ˈræf-/ *n* any of the parallel sloping beams that support a roof: *a room with exposed rafters.*

rag¹ /ræɡ/ *n* **1** [C, U] a piece of old, often torn, cloth used esp for cleaning things: *an oily rag* ○ *Wipe off the excess dirt with an old rag.* See also GLAD RAGS. **2** [C] (*dated infml usu derog*) a newspaper: *I read it in the local rag.* **IDM** **chew the fat/rag** ⇨ CHEW. **in ˈrags** wearing clothes that are very old and torn: *be dressed in rags.* (**from**) **ˌrags to ˈriches** from extreme poverty to wealth: *a classic tale of rags to riches* ○ *Hers was a true rags-to-riches story.* **a red rag to a bull** ⇨ RED¹.

■ **ˈrag-bag** *n* [sing] an odd mixture of things: *a rag-bag of ideas.*

ˌrag ˈdoll *n* a soft DOLL¹(1) made from pieces of cloth: *She lay unconscious in the road like a rag doll.*

the ˈrag trade *n* [sing] (*dated infml*) the business of designing, making and selling clothes, esp for women: *go into the rag trade.*

ˈrag week *n* [usu *sing*] (*Brit*) an annual event when students collect money for charity by organizing a series of entertainments.

rag² /ræɡ/ *v* (**-gg-**) [Vn, Vnpr] ~ **sb (about/for sth)** (*dated Brit infml*) to mock or TEASE(1) sb.

rag³ /ræɡ/ *n* a piece of RAGTIME music.

ragamuffin /ˈræɡəmʌfɪn/ *n* (*dated*) a person, esp a child, in dirty torn clothes.

rage /reɪdʒ/ *n* [U, C] violent anger or an instance of this: *be crimson with rage* ○ *fly into an uncontrollable rage* ○ *She was filled with rage at the thought of cruelty to animals.* ○ *She was at the mercy of his frequent drunken rages.* ○ (*fig*) *The storm's rage finally abated.* **IDM** **be all the fashion/rage** ⇨ FASHION.

▶ **rage** *v* **1** ~ **(at/against sb/sth)** to feel or express violent anger: [Vpr] *He raged against the injustice of it all.* ○ *I raged inwardly for hours at the decision.* [V.speech] *'You idiots!' he raged.* [also V]. **2(a)** (of storms, battles, etc) to continue violently: [V] *Outside, a storm raged.* ○ *The battle raged overhead.* ○ *The argument raged for days.* (**b**) (esp of illnesses) to spread rapidly: [Vpr] *A flu epidemic raged through the school for weeks.* [also V]. **raging** *adj* [attrib] (**a**) very strong or painful: *a raging hunger/thirst/passion* ○ *have a raging headache/toothache.* (**b**) (of natural forces) very powerful: *a raging inferno* ○ *raging blizzards.*

ragged /ˈrægɪd/ *adj* **1**(**a**) (of clothes) old and torn: *a ragged coat/suit* ○ *His sleeves were ragged at the cuffs.* (**b**) (of people) wearing old or torn clothes: *a ragged and barefoot old man.* **2** having an outline, edge or surface that is not straight or even: *a ragged edge to the lawn* ○ *a ragged line of soldiers.* **3** not smooth or regular: *The choir gave a rather ragged performance.* ▶ **raggedly** *adv.* **raggedness** *n* [U].

raglan /ˈræɡlən/ *adj* [attrib] (**a**) (of a sleeve) that is sewn to the front and back of a garment in a sloping line from the neck to under the arm. (**b**) (of a garment) having sleeves of this kind: *a raglan jumper.*

ragout /ræˈɡuː, ˈræɡuː/ *n* [C,U] pieces of meat and vegetables boiled together; a STEW.

ragtime /ˈræɡtaɪm/ *n* [U] music, played esp on the piano, that originated in the USA in the 1890s and developed into JAZZ: *a ˌragtime ˈband.*

raid /reɪd/ *n* ~ (**on sth**) **1** a surprise attack on an enemy by troops, ships or aircraft: *make/launch a bombing raid on enemy bases.* See also AIR RAID. **2** a surprise attack on a building, etc in order to commit a crime: *an armed bank raid.* **3** a surprise visit by the police, etc, eg to arrest people or to seize stolen goods: *Police seized drugs in a **dawn raid** on the house.*
▶ **raid** *v* to make a raid on a place: [Vn] *Customs men raided the house.* ○ (*fig*) *The children have been raiding the fridge again* (ie for food to eat). **raider** *n* a person, a ship, an aircraft, etc that makes a raid: *bank raiders.* **ˈraiding party** *n* a group of people who go out to make a raid, esp a group of soldiers.

rail¹ /reɪl/ *n* **1** [C] (**a**) a bar or a connected series of bars made of wood or metal for people to hold for support or to form a barrier of some kind: *hold onto the rail at the edge of the ice-rink* ○ *a wooden rail in front of an altar.* See also GUARD-RAIL, HANDRAIL, RAILING. (**b**) a bar fixed to a wall for hanging things on: *a ˈpicture rail* ○ *a ˈcurtain rail.* (**c**) (esp *pl*) each of the two metal bars forming the track that trains run on. ⇨ picture at FLANGE. **2** [U often attrib] railways as a means of transport: *travel/send sth by rail* ○ *the country's rail network* ○ *What's the **rail fare** to Glasgow?* ○ *the cost of **rail travel**.* **IDM** **go off the ˈrails** (*Brit infml*) **1** to start behaving in a strange or abnormal way: *When his wife died he went completely off the rails.* **2** to lose control; to stop functioning properly: *The company has gone badly off the rails.* **jump the rails/track** ⇨ JUMP¹.
▶ **rail** *v* **PHRV** **ˌrail sth ˈin/ˈoff** to surround or separate sth with rails: *The statues were railed off to prevent people touching them.*

rail² /reɪl/ *v* **PHRV** **ˈrail at/against sb/sth** (*fml*) to complain about sb/sth strongly and angrily: *He railed against fate.* ○ *She railed at him and accused him of being lazy.*

railcard /ˈreɪlkɑːd/ *n* (*Brit*) a card that allows sb to travel by train at a reduced cost: *buy a student railcard.*

railhead /ˈreɪlhed/ *n* the point at which a railway ends.

railing /ˈreɪlɪŋ/ *n* (often *pl*) a fence made of metal bars: *park railings* ○ *I chained my bike to the iron railings.*

raillery /ˈreɪləri/ *n* [U] (*fml*) friendly fun or joking.

railroad /ˈreɪlrəʊd/ *n* (*US*) a railway.
▶ **railroad** *v* **PHRV** **ˈrailroad sb into (doing) sth** (*infml*) to force sb to do sth: *I won't be railroaded into buying a car I don't want!* **ˌrailroad sth ˈthrough (sth)** (*infml*) to get sth passed, accepted,

etc quickly by applying pressure: *railroad a bill through Congress.*

railway /ˈreɪlweɪ/ (*US* **railroad**) *n* **1** (*Brit* also **ˈrail-way line**) a track with rails on which trains run: *The railway is still under construction.* **2** (often *pl*) a system of railway tracks, together with the trains that run on them, and the organization and people needed to operate them: *work on/for the railways* ○ *a railway station/carriage/worker* ○ *an electric railway* ○ *a model railway.*

railwayman /ˈreɪlweɪmən/ (also **railman** /ˈreɪlmən/) *n* (*pl* **-men** /-mən/) (*Brit*) (*US* **railroader**) a person who works for a railway company.

raiment /ˈreɪmənt/ *n* [U] (*arch*) clothing.

rain¹ /reɪn/ *n* **1** [U,sing] water that falls from the clouds in separate drops; all of these drops: *heavy/torrential/driving rain* ○ *We've had a lot of rain this month.* ○ *Don't go out in the rain.* ○ *It's **pouring with rain** (ie It is raining very hard).* ○ *It looks like rain* (ie as if it is going to rain). ○ *A light rain began to fall.* See also ACID RAIN, RAINY. **2 the rains** [pl] the season of heavy continuous rain in tropical countries: *The rains come in September.* **3** [sing] ~ **of sth** a great number of things falling like rain: *a rain of arrows/bullets.* **IDM** **come ˌrain, come ˈshine; (come) ˌrain or ˈshine** whether there is rain or sun; whatever happens: *Every morning, rain or shine, he goes out jogging.* **right as rain** ⇨ RIGHT¹.
■ **ˈrain check** *n* (*esp US*) a ticket given for later use when a match, show, etc is cancelled because of rain. **IDM** **take a rain check (on sth)** (*infml*) to refuse an invitation or offer but say that one might accept it later: *Thanks for the invitation, but I'll have to take a rain check on it.*
ˈrain forest *n* a thick forest in tropical parts of the world that have a lot of rain: *the Amazon rain forest.*

rain² /reɪn/ *v* **1** (used with *it*) (of rain) to fall: [V] *It's still raining* (ie Rain is still falling). ○ *It rained hard all day.* ○ *Has it stopped raining?* **2**(**a**) ~ **on sb/sth** to fall like rain on sb/sth: [Vpr] *Fragments of glass rained on them from above.* (**b**) ~ **sth on sb/sth** to make sth fall like rain on sb/sth: [Vnpr] *The volcano erupted, raining hot ashes on the villages below.* **3** to bring sth down repeatedly and with force: [Vnpr] *He attacked the man, raining blows to his head and shoulders.* **IDM** **it never rains but it ˈpours** (*saying*) (said when one piece of bad luck is or is likely to be followed by another): *First my car broke down, then I lost my key — it never rains but it pours!* **rain cats and ˈdogs** (used esp in the continuous tenses) (*infml*) to rain very heavily. **PHRV** **ˌrain ˈdown (sth)** to flow or come down in large quantities: *Tears rained down her cheeks.* ○ *Loose rocks rained down (the hillside).* **ˌrain ˈdown (on sb/sth)** to come down on sb/sth in large quantities: *Fire-bombs rained down on the military convoy.* ○ *Abuse rained down on the noisy students from the open windows.* **be ˌrained ˈoff**; (*US*) **be ˌrained ˈout** (of an event) to be prevented from taking place or continuing because of rain: *The match was rained off twice.*

rainbow /ˈreɪnbəʊ/ *n* an arch of different colours that is formed in the sky when the sun shines through rain: *silks dyed in all the colours of the rainbow* ○ (*fig*) *When the flowers bloom, the fields are a rainbow of bright colours.*

raincoat /ˈreɪnkəʊt/ *n* a light coat that keeps the person wearing it dry in the rain.

raindrop /ˈreɪndrɒp/ *n* a single drop of rain.

rainfall /ˈreɪnfɔːl/ *n* [U] the total amount of rain that falls in a particular area in a certain amount of time: *an average annual rainfall of 10 cm.*

rainproof /ˈreɪnpruːf/ *adj* that can keep rain out: *a rainproof jacket.*

rainstorm /ˈreɪnstɔːm/ *n* a storm with very heavy rain.

---

rainwater /ˈreɪnwɔːtə(r)/ n [U] water that has fallen as rain: *collect rainwater from gutters in a barrel.*

rainy /ˈreɪni/ adj (-ier, -iest) having or bringing a lot of rain: *a rainy afternoon/day* ∘ *the ˈrainy season in Kenya* ∘ *rainy weather.* **IDM** **save, keep, etc sth for a ˌrainy ˈday** to save sth, esp money, for a time when one may need it.

raise /reɪz/ v **1(a)** to lift or move sth to a higher level: [Vn] *raise one's hand* ∘ *She raised the gun and fired.* [Vnpr] *He raised his eyes from his work.* [Vnpr, Vnp] *raise a sunken ship (up) to the surface.* **(b)** to move sth/sb/oneself to an upright position: [Vn] *We raised the fence and fixed it in position.* [Vnpr, Vnp] *He raised himself (up) on one elbow.* Compare LOWER² 1. **2 ~ sth (to sth)** to increase the amount or level of sth: [Vn] *raise salaries/prices/taxes* ∘ *raise standards of service* ∘ *Don't tell her about the job until you know for sure — we don't want to **raise her hopes** (ie give her too much hope).* ∘ *raise public awareness of an issue* [Vnpr] *He raised his offer to £500.* ∘ *raise the temperature to 80°.* Compare LOWER² 2. **3** to bring or collect sth together; to manage to obtain sth: [Vn] *raise money/a loan* ∘ *raise funds for charity.* See also FUND-RAISING. **4(a)** to make sth be heard: [Vn] *A passer-by* **raised the alarm** *when he saw smoke pouring from the building.* **(b)** to mention sth for discussion or attention: [Vn] *The book raises many important issues/questions.* ∘ *I'm glad you raised the subject of money.* **5** to make sth occur or appear: [Vn] *raise doubts/fears/suspicions in people's minds* ∘ *The plans for a new motorway have raised angry protests from local residents.* ∘ *He told them all his best jokes, but he couldn't even raise a smile.* ∘ *The horses' hooves raised a cloud of dust.* **6(a)** (*esp US*) to care for a child, etc until it is able to look after itself: [Vn] *My parents died when I was very young, so I was raised by my aunt.* **(b)** [Vn] to breed particular farm animals; to grow particular crops. **7** to end a restriction on sb/sth: [Vn] *raise a blockade/a ban/an embargo.* **8** (*Brit infml*) to get in contact with sb: [Vn] *I can't raise her on the phone.* **IDM** **lift/raise a finger/hand** ⇨ LIFT. **lift/raise a/one's hand against sb** ⇨ HAND¹. **raise one's ˈeyebrows (at sth)** (esp passive) to show that one disapproves of or is surprised by sth: *Eyebrows were raised/There were a lot of raised eyebrows when he arrived at the party without his wife.* **raise one's ˈglass (to sb)** to hold up one's glass and wish sb happiness, good luck, etc before one drinks. **raise sb's hackles** ⇨ HACKLES. **raise ˈhell** (*infml*) to protest angrily; to cause a disturbance. **raise the ˈroof** to produce or make sb produce a lot of noise inside a building, eg by cheering or shouting: *a singer capable of raising the roof every time he performs.* **raise/lower one's sights** ⇨ SIGHT¹. **raise sb's ˈspirits** to make sb feel more cheerful: *The sunny weather raised my spirits a little.* **raise the ˈtemperature** to increase tension, hostility, etc: *Her sudden outburst raised the temperature of the discussion.* **raise one's ˈvoice** to speak more loudly, esp because one is angry. **PHRV** **ˈraise sth to sb/sth** to build or ERECT²(1) a statue, etc in honour or memory of sb/sth: *raise a memorial to those killed in the war.*
► **raise** n (*US*) = RISE¹ 2: *get a raise of $200.*

raised /reɪzd/ adj higher than the area around: *a raised platform.*

-raiser (forming compound *ns*) a person or thing that raises sth: *a ˈfund-raiser.* See also CURTAIN-RAISER.

NOTE Compare **raise** (transitive) and **rise** (intransitive). When somebody **raises** something, they lift it to a higher position: *He raised his head from the pillow and switched off the alarm clock.* When a person **rises**, he or she stands up or gets up from a lower position: *She rose from her chair.* When some-thing **rises**, it moves to a higher position: *The helicopter rose into the air.*

The nouns **rise** in British English and **raise** in American English mean an increase in pay: *Should I ask my boss for a rise/raise?* ∘ *a three per cent pay rise/raise.*

raisin /ˈreɪzn/ n a dried sweet GRAPE, used in cakes, etc.

raison d'être /ˌreɪzõ ˈdetrə/; *US* -zõn-/ n [sing] (*French*) the most important reason for sb's/sth's existence: *Work seems to be her sole raison d'être.*

raj /rɑːdʒ/ n (also **the Raj**) [U] (the period of) British rule in India before 1947: *life under the Raj.*

rajah /ˈrɑːdʒə/ n (formerly) an Indian king or prince.

rake

rake¹ /reɪk/ n a tool with a long handle and a row of metal points at the end for gathering fallen leaves, making soil smooth, etc. ⇨ picture.
► **rake** v **1(a)** to move sth using a rake: [Vnpr] *rake leaves into a pile* [Vnp] *She raked up the grass cuttings.* [also Vn]. **(b)** to make sth level using a rake: [Vn, Vn-adj] *rake the soil (smooth)* (eg before planting seeds). **(a)** to fire a gun at or point a camera, light, etc at sth while moving it from one side to the other: [Vnpr] *They raked the enemy ranks with machine-gun fire.* ∘ *The bird-watcher raked the trees with his binoculars.* [also Vn]. **(b)** [Vn] (esp of a light) to move slowly across sth. **PHRV** **ˌrake aˈround (for sth)** to search carefully: *We raked around in the files, but couldn't find the letter.* **ˌrake sth/it ˈin** (*infml*) to earn a lot of money: *raking in the profits* ∘ *Her last two novels were best sellers, so she's really raking it in!* **ˌrake sb/sth ˈup** (*infml*) to bring people or things together, esp when this is difficult to do: *We need to rake up two more players to form a team.* **ˌrake sth ˈup** (*infml*) to remind people of sth that it would be better to forget: *rake up old quarrels/grievances* ∘ *Don't rake up the past.*
■ **ˈrake-off** n (*infml*) a share of profits, esp from dishonest or illegal activity: *She got a 5% rake-off from the deal.*

rake² /reɪk/ n (*dated*) a man, esp a rich and fashionable one, considered as having low moral standards, eg because he drinks or gambles a lot or has sex with many women.
► **rakish** /ˈreɪkɪʃ/ adj **1** of or like a rake²: *a rakish appearance/smile.* **2** showing cheerful casual confidence: *a hat worn* **at a rakish angle** (eg on the back of the head). **rakishly** adv.

rake³ /reɪk/ n [sing] the amount by which sth, esp the stage in a theatre, slopes.
► **raked** /reɪkt/ adj placed at or having a sloping angle: *a raked stage/running track* ∘ *The seat back is raked for extra comfort.*

rally /ˈræli/ v (*pt, pp* **rallied**) **1(a) ~ (round/behind/to sb/sth); ~ (round)** (of people) to come together in order to support sb/sth when there is danger, need, etc: [Vp, Vpr] *When their mother was ill, the children all rallied round (her).* [Vpr] *Her colleagues rallied to her defence when she was accused of stealing.* [also V]. **(b) ~ sb/sth (round sb)** to bring people, support, etc together in this way: [Vn, Vnpr] *The Prime Minister has managed to rally public opinion (to his side).* ∘ *The leader rallied his men (round him).*

[V] *The **rallying cry** of* (ie call for support by) *the party leaders.* **2** to recover health, strength, etc after an illness or time of weakness: [Vpr] *The pound rallied today against the German mark.* [V] *The team rallied after a poor first half.* **3** (*finance*) [V] (of share prices, etc) to increase after a fall. ▶ **rally** *n* **1** [C] a large, usu political, public meeting: *attend/address a party rally* ○ *organize/hold/ stage a* ¦*peace rally.* **2** [sing] a recovery of health, strength, etc, eg after an illness or a time of weakness: *an unexpected/late rally of shares on the Stock Market.* **3** [C] (in tennis, etc) a series of strokes before a point is scored: *That was a great rally!* **4** [C] a race for motor vehicles over public roads: *rally driving.*

ram¹ /ræm/ *n* **1** an adult male sheep. ⇨ picture at SHEEP. Compare EWE. **2** = BATTERING RAM. **3** a device in a machine for striking with great force.

ram² *v* (**-mm-**) **1(a)** ~ **into** sth to crash against sth; to strike or push sth with great force: [Vpr] *The car rammed into the bus.* ○ *The ice skater rammed into the barrier.* (**b**) (of a vehicle) to strike or run into another vehicle deliberately in an attempt to stop it or destroy it: [Vn] *The police van was rammed by a stolen car.* **2** ~ sth **in, down, into, on,** etc to push sth firmly into place by ramming: [Vnpr] *ram clothes into a suitcase* [Vnp] *He rammed his foot down on the accelerator.* **IDM** ¦**ram sth** ¦**home** to emphasize a point, an argument, etc very strongly: *The accident has rammed home the message that careless driving costs lives.*

RAM /ræm/ *abbr* (*computing*) random access memory: *data stored in RAM chips.* Compare ROM.

Ramadan /ˌræmə¦dæn, -¦dɑːn/ *n* the 9th month of the Muslim year, when Muslims do not eat or drink anything between SUNRISE and SUNSET(1).

ramble /¦ræmbl/ *v* **1** to walk for pleasure, esp in the countryside: [Vpr] *ramble along country lanes* [also V, Vp]. **2** ~ (**on**) (**about sb/sth**) to talk or write a lot in a disorganized (DISORGANIZE) way: [Vpr, Vp] *The old man rambled (on) happily about the past.* [also V]. **3** (of plants) to grow or climb over other plants, hedges, etc with long shoots: [Vpr] *roses rambling over an old stone wall* [also V]. ▶ **ramble** *n* a walk for pleasure: *go for/on a gentle ramble in the country* ○ *an organized nature ramble.* **rambler** /¦ræmblə(r)/ *n* **1** a person who walks in the countryside, esp as part of an organized group: *She's a keen rambler.* **2** a plant, esp a rose, that rambles (RAMBLE 3).
rambling *adj* **1** (esp of buildings or streets) spreading in various directions with no regular pattern: *a rambling old house* ○ *a maze of narrow, rambling streets.* **2** (*derog*) (of talk, writing, etc) often changing subjects; not properly connected: *a long, rambling letter/speech.* **3** (of a plant) growing or climbing with long shoots: *rambling roses.* — *n* **1** [U] the activity of walking for pleasure in the countryside: *a rambling club* ○ *go rambling on Sundays.* **2** [C usu *pl*] things that are said or written in a long, badly organized way: *incoherent ramblings.*

rambunctious /ræm¦bʌŋkʃəs/ *adj* (*infml esp US*) = RUMBUSTIOUS.

ramekin /¦ræməkɪn/ *n* a small dish for baking and serving an individual portion of food.

ramification /ˌræmɪfɪ¦keɪʃn/ *n* (usu *pl*) any of a large number of complex or unexpected results that follow an action or a decision: *These changes in the law are bound to have widespread social and economic ramifications.*

ramp /ræmp/ *n* **1** a slope that joins two parts of a road, path, building, etc when one is higher than the other: *push a wheelchair up/down a ramp.* **2** (*Brit*) a small ridge built across a road to make vehicles go more slowly.

rampage /ræm¦peɪdʒ, ¦ræmpeɪdʒ/ *v* to rush around wildly or violently: [Vpr, Vp] *mobs rampaging (about) through the streets* [also V]. ▶ **rampage** *n* **IDM be/go on the** ¦**rampage** to go about behaving violently or causing destruction: *After the match, some football fans went on the rampage in the city centre.*

rampant /¦ræmpənt/ *adj* **1** (of disease, crime, etc) existing or spreading everywhere in a way that cannot be controlled: *rampant inflation/corruption* ○ *Food was scarce and disease (was) rampant.* **2** (of plants) growing very thickly or fast: *rampant tropical vegetation.* ▶ **rampantly** *adv*.

rampart /¦ræmpɑːt/ *n* (esp *pl*) a high wide wall of stone or earth with a path on top, built around a castle, fort, etc to defend it: *Visitors can walk along the castle ramparts.*

ramrod /¦ræmrɒd/ *n* an iron rod formerly used for pushing the explosive material into a gun. **IDM (as) stiff/straight as a** ¦**ramrod** very straight: *He stood as stiff as a ramrod.* ○ *Her back was straight as a ramrod.*

ramshackle /¦ræmʃækl/ *adj* (**a**) (of houses, vehicles, etc) almost collapsing: *a ramshackle old cottage.* (**b**) (of an organization or a system) badly organized or designed: *ramshackle government policies.*

ran *pt* of RUN¹.

ranch /rɑːntʃ; *US* ræntʃ/ *n* a large farm, esp in N America or Australia, where cattle, sheep, etc are bred: *run a cattle ranch in Texas* ○ *a ranch house* ○ *ranch hands* ○ *a sheep ranch in Australia.* ▶ **rancher** *n* a person who owns, manages or works on a ranch.
ranching *n* [U] the activity of running a ranch: *cattle/sheep ranching.*

rancid /¦rænsɪd/ *adj* (**a**) (of foods containing a lot of fat) tasting or smelling bad because they are old: *rancid oil* ○ *The butter has gone/turned rancid.* (**b**) (of smells or tastes) unpleasant, like old fat: *There was a rancid smell in the kitchen.*

rancour (*US* **-cor**) /¦ræŋkə(r)/ *n* [U] bitter or angry feelings; spite: *There was rancour in his voice/eyes.* ○ *She accepted the decision **without rancour**.* ▶ **rancorous** /¦ræŋkərəs/ *adj*: *rancorous debate.*

rand /rænd; *in South Africa, commonly* rɑːnt/ *n* the unit of money in the Republic of South Africa; 100 cents.

R and D /ˌɑːr ən ¦diː/ *abbr* (*commerce*) research and development: *extra funds for R and D* ○ *an R and D programme.*

random /¦rændəm/ *adj* (usu attrib) done, chosen, etc without method or conscious choice; HAPHAZARD: *take a random sample/selection for testing* ○ *books in random order* ○ *The noises seemed to occur at random intervals.* ▶ **random** *n* **IDM at** ¦**random** without method or conscious choice: *open a book at random* (ie not at any particular page) ○ *The terrorists fired into the crowd at random.* ○ *People in the supermarket were chosen at random to try out the new products.* **randomly** *adv*: *people randomly chosen to take part in a survey.* ■ ¦**random** ¦**access** *n* [U] (*computing*) a process that allows information in a computer to be stored or recovered quickly without reading through items stored previously. Compare DIRECT ACCESS, READ ONLY. ¦**random** ¦**access** ¦**memory** *n* [U] (*abbr* **RAM**) computer memory used temporarily to store data that can be changed or removed. Compare READ-ONLY MEMORY.

randy /¦rændi/ *adj* (**-ier, -iest**) (*infml esp Brit*) sexually excited: *feel randy.*

rang *pt* of RING².

range¹ /reɪndʒ/ *n* **1** [C] a number of different things of the same general type: *stock a whole range of*

R

goods ○ *The new model comes in an exciting range of colours.* ○ *Guests can participate in a **wide range** of leisure activities.* **2** [C] the limits between which sth varies: *people with a broad/limited/narrow range of experience* ○ *Most of the students are in the age range 17–20.* ○ *The annual range of temperature is from –10°C to 40°C.* ○ *There's a wide range of ability in the class.* ○ *It's difficult to find a house we like within our price range.* **3(a)** [U] the distance within which one can see or hear; the distance over which sounds will travel: *It is outside my range of vision.* ○ *They live within range of the transmitter.* See also LONG-RANGE, SHORT-RANGE. **(b)** [U, sing] the distance to which a gun will shoot, or over which a missile, etc will travel: *in/within/out of (firing) range* ○ *shoot at point-blank range* (ie at sth very close) ○ *The gun has a range of five miles.* **(c)** [C] the distance that a vehicle, etc will travel before it needs more fuel. **4** [C] **(a)** an area of ground with targets for soldiers, etc to practise shooting: *an army range* ○ *a 'rifle-range.* **(b)** an area within which rockets (ROCKET 1) and missiles are fired. **5** [C] a line or row of mountains, hills, etc: *the Andes mountain range.* **6 the range** [sing] (*US*) a large open area for keeping cattle. **7** [C] an old type of cooking STOVE[1]: *a kitchen range.* See also FREE-RANGE.

range[2] /reɪndʒ/ *v* **1** ~ **between A and B /** ~ **from A to B** to vary or extend between specified limits: [Vpr] *The students' ages range from 16 to 21.* ○ *Prices range between $7 and $10.* ○ *subjects ranging from accounting to zoology* ○ *The fields range in size from half an acre to six acres.* **2(a)** (esp passive) to arrange oneself/sb/sth in a line or lines, or in a specified way: [Vnpr] *flowerpots ranged in rows on the window-sill* ○ *The spectators had ranged themselves/were ranged along the whole route of the procession.* **(b)** ~ **sb/oneself with/against sb/sth** to place sb/oneself in a particular group: *On this issue, she has ranged herself with the Opposition.* **3(a)** to wander freely over or through an area: [Vadv] *At this stage, the young animals do not range far from the family.* [also Vadv]. **(b)** (used about sth that is written or spoken) to cover a number of different subjects: [Vpr] *a discussion ranging over many different topics* [also Vadv]. See also WIDE-RANGING.

rangefinder /'reɪndʒfaɪndə(r)/ *n* a device for finding the distance of sb/sth to be shot at or photographed.

ranger /'reɪndʒə(r)/ *n* a person whose job is to look after a park, a forest or an area of countryside.

rangy /'reɪndʒi/ *adj* (**-ier, -iest**) tall and thin, with long limbs: *his slim, rangy figure.*

rank[1] /ræŋk/ *n* **1** [C, U] a position in a scale of responsibility, quality, social status, etc: *a painter of the first/top rank* (ie one of the very best) ○ *people of (high) rank* ○ *Britain is no longer **in the front rank** of European powers.* See also RANKING. **2** [C, U] a position or grade in the armed forces, police, etc: *be promoted to the rank of colonel* ○ *officers of high rank* ○ *military ranks* ○ *The unit consisted of 5 officers and 40 **other ranks*** (ie soldiers who were not officers). **3(a)** [C] a line or row of soldiers, police officers, etc standing next to each other: *ranks of marching infantry* ○ *keep/break ranks* (ie remain/fail to remain in line). **(b) the ranks** [pl] ordinary soldiers, ie not officers: *join/serve in the ranks* ○ *rise from the ranks* (ie be made an officer after serving as an ordinary soldier) ○ (*fig*) *join the ranks of the unemployed* (ie become unemployed). **4** [C] a line or row of things or people: *fir trees in **serried ranks*** ○ *Take the taxi at the head of the rank* (ie the first in the line). See also TAXI RANK. **IDM break 'ranks** to leave a group, esp to show that one no longer supports it: *Large numbers of MPs felt compelled to break ranks over the issue.* **close ranks** ⇨ CLOSE[4]. **pull rank** ⇨ PULL[1].

▶ **rank** *v* (not used in the continuous tenses) **1** to place sb/sth in a particular position or regard sb/sth in a particular way according to quality, achievement, etc: [Vnadv] *I rank her achievement very highly.* [Vnpr] *I rank her among/alongside the country's best writers.* ○ *Only four players are ranked above him.* **2** to have a rank or place: [Vpr] *Her work ranks with the best of the decade.* [V-adj] *He currently ranks second in the world.* [V] (*esp US*) *You just don't rank!* [also Vadv]. See also HIGH-RANKING. **,ranking 'officer** *n* [sing] (*US*) the officer having the highest rank of those present.

■ **the ,rank and 'file** *n* [Gp] **1** the ordinary soldiers who are not officers. **2** the ordinary members of an organization: *the rank and file of the workforce* ○ *rank-and-file workers/members/supporters.*

rank[2] /ræŋk/ *adj* **1** having a strong unpleasant smell: *the rank smell of rotting vegetation.* **2** [attrib] (*esp derog*) complete and UTTER[1]: *a rank beginner* ○ *rank insolence/stupidity/nonsense* ○ *The winning horse was a **rank outsider**.* **3** (of plants, etc) growing too thickly: *rank grass.*

ranking /'ræŋkɪŋ/ *n* a position in a scale, esp of skill at a sport: *He has improved his ranking this season from 67th to 30th.* ○ *Graf retained her No 1 world ranking.*

rankle /'ræŋkl/ *v* ~ **(with sb)** to cause bitter or angry feelings: [Vpr] *The insult still rankled with him.* [V] *This happened twenty years ago, but it still rankles.*

ransack /'rænsæk/ *v* **1** ~ **sth (for sth)** to search a place thoroughly: [Vnpr] *I've ransacked the house for those papers, but I can't find them.* [also Vn]. **2** to go through a place stealing and destroying things: [Vn] *The apartment had been ransacked and all her valuables stolen.*

ransom /'rænsəm/ *n* [U, C] money paid for the release of a person held as a prisoner: *The kidnappers demanded a ransom of £50 000 from his family.* ○ *They paid over $2 million in ransom (money).* **IDM hold sb to 'ransom 1** to keep sb as a prisoner and demand a ransom for her or him. **2** (*derog*) to take strong action to force sb to do what one wants: *By threatening strike action the unions are holding the country to ransom.* **a king's ransom** ⇨ KING.

▶ **ransom** *v* [Vn] to obtain the release of sb by paying a ransom.

rant /rænt/ *v* (*derog*) to speak loudly or angrily, esp for a long time: [Vp] *He kept ranting on (at us) about how unfair it was.* [also Vpr, V, V.speech]. **IDM ,rant and 'rave** to show one's anger by shouting and complaining about sth loudly: *You can rant and rave all you like, but you'll still have to pay the fine.*

rap /ræp/ *n* **1** [C] a quick sharp blow or knock: *a sharp rap on the elbow* ○ *There was a rap at/on the door.* **2** [U] a type of rock[3] music with a fast strong rhythm and words which are spoken rapidly rather than sung: *a rap song/artist* ○ *listen to some rap.* **IDM beat the rap** ⇨ BEAT[1]. **give sb / get a rap on/over the 'knuckles** (*infml*) to give sb/receive criticism; to blame sb/be blamed for sth: *get a rap over the knuckles for being late.* **take the 'rap (for sth)** (*infml esp US*) to accept punishment, esp for sth one has not done, in order to protect sb.

▶ **rap** *v* (**-pp-**) **1(a)** to hit sb quickly and sharply: [Vn] *She rapped my knuckles.* **(b)** to knock or tap lightly and quickly: [Vpr] *rap at/on the door* ○ *She rapped on the table to get their attention.* **2** [V] (*US sl*) to talk rapidly and continuously. **PHRV ,rap sth 'out 1** to say sth suddenly and sharply: *rapping out orders.* **2** to express sth by tapping sounds: *The prisoner rapped out a message on the cell wall.*

rapacious /rə'peɪʃəs/ *adj* (*fml*) greedy, esp for money: *rapacious capitalists.*

▶ **rapacity** /rə'pæsəti/ *n* [U] GREED(2), esp for money.

rape[1] /reɪp/ v to force sb to have sex when they do not want to: [Vn] *She claimed she had been raped.*
▶ **rape** n **1(a)** [U] the crime of raping sb: *to commit rape* ∘ *Rape is on the increase.* ∘ *rape victims.* **(b)** [C] an instance of this: *a rise in the number of rapes.* **2** [U] (*fml*) the act of destroying or spoiling sth: *the rape of our countryside* (eg by building on it).
rapist /'reɪpɪst/ n a person who commits rape: *a convicted rapist.*

rape[2] /reɪp/ n [U] a plant with bright yellow flowers. It is grown for its leaves, which are used as food for farm animals, and for its seed, from which oil is made: *a field of rape* ∘ ˌrape-seed 'oil ∘ ˌoilseed 'rape.

rapid /'ræpɪd/ adj **(a)** happening in a short time: *rapid growth/change/expansion* ∘ *a rapid rise/decline in sales* ∘ *The patient made a rapid recovery.* **(b)** moving or acting quickly; fast: *a rapid pulse/heartbeat* ∘ *ask several questions in rapid succession.*
▶ **rapidity** /rə'pɪdəti/ n [U]: *The disease is spreading with alarming rapidity.*
rapidly adv: *a rapidly growing economy* ∘ *The work is progressing rapidly.*
rapids n [pl] a part of a river where the water flows very fast, usu over rocks: *shoot the rapids* (ie travel quickly along them in a boat).
■ 'rapid-fire adj [attrib] (of questions, etc) spoken or produced very quickly, one after the other.
ˌrapid 'transit n [U] (*US*) the system of fast public transport in cities, eg by underground railway.

rapier /'reɪpiə(r)/ n (esp formerly) a light thin sword with two sharp edges: (*fig*) *rapier wit.* ⇨ picture at SWORD.

rapport /ræ'pɔ:(r)/ n [U, sing] ~ (**with sb / between A and B**) a close relationship in which people understand each other very well: *strike up/establish a (close) rapport with sb* ∘ *He has a very good rapport with his pupils.* ∘ *There was little rapport between the two women.*

rapprochement /ræ'prɒʃmɒ̃, ræ'prəʊʃmɒ̃; *US* ˌræprəʊʃ'mɑ:/ n [sing] ~ (**with sb / between A and B**) (*fml*) a renewing of friendly relations, esp between countries or groups which were former enemies: *bring about a rapprochement between warring states/factions.*

rapt /ræpt/ adj so interested in what one is seeing or hearing that one is not aware of anything else: *a rapt audience* ∘ *She listened to the speaker with rapt attention.* ∘ *He watched her with a rapt expression.*

rapture /'ræptʃə(r)/ n [U] a feeling of intense delight: *gazing in/with rapture at the beautiful image.* **IDM** be in, go into, etc 'raptures (about/over sb/ sth) to feel or express great delight or enthusiasm: *The critics went into raptures about her last film.*
▶ **rapturous** /'ræptʃərəs/ adj [usu attrib] expressing great delight or enthusiasm: *rapturous applause* ∘ *give sb a rapturous welcome/reception.* **rapturously** adv.

rare[1] /reə(r)/ adj (**-r, -st**) **1(a)** being one of only a few that exist: *a rare book/bird/butterfly.* **(b)** not often happening or seen; unusual: *a rare disease/ occurrence/sight* ∘ *I only saw her on the rare occasions I went into her family's shop.* ∘ *It is extremely rare for the weather in April to be this hot.* See also RARITY.
▶ **rarely** adv not often; SELDOM: *an odd little man who rarely spoke* ∘ *She is rarely seen in public nowadays.* ∘ *a rarely-performed play* ∘ (*fml*) *Rarely has the President looked so ill at ease.*

NOTE A thing or an event is **rare** when it is found or happens infrequently: *She gave a rare interview on television.* It may once have been common: *The tiger is now a rare animal.* Rare can also mean having a special value or quality: *music of rare quality and emotional depth.* Something, usually a thing you use every day, is **scarce** when it is hard to get because there is not very much of it available: *Water is scarce in the desert.*

rare[2] /reə(r)/ adj (usu of meat) cooked so that the inside is still red: *He likes his steak (medium-)rare.*

rarebit /'reəbɪt/ n = WELSH RAREBIT.

rarefied /'reərɪfaɪd/ adj [usu attrib] **1** (of air) containing less oxygen than usual; thin: *the rarefied air of the Andes.* **2** (*often derog*) concerned with high, esp academic, standards and so having no connection with the lives of ordinary people: *university professors living in a rarefied academic atmosphere.*

raring /'reərɪŋ/ adj [pred] ~ **to do sth** (*infml*) very eager to do sth: *She has recovered from her operation and is raring to get back to work.* **IDM** ˌraring to 'go extremely eager to start: *When can we begin? We're all raring to go!*

rarity /'reərəti/ n **1** [U] the quality of being rare. **2** [C] a thing that is unusual; a thing that has great value because it is rare: *Rain is a rarity in this country.* ∘ *ancient scrolls and other rarities.*

rascal /'rɑ:skl; *US* 'ræskl/ n **1** (*joc*) a playful or cheeky (CHEEK) person, esp a child, who likes playing tricks: *Give me my keys back, you little rascal!* **2** (*dated*) a dishonest and bad person.

rash[1] /ræʃ/ n **1** [C us *sing*] a patch of tiny red spots on the skin: *a 'nettle-rash* ∘ *I break out/come out in a rash* (ie A rash appears on my skin) *if I eat chocolate.* ∘ *The heat brought her out in* (ie caused) *a red itchy rash.* **2** [*sing*] ~ **of sth** a series of esp unpleasant things occurring or appearing one after the other within a short period of time: *the recent rash of strikes in the steel industry* ∘ *There has been a rash of burglaries in the area over the last month.*

rash[2] /ræʃ/ adj (of people or their actions) acting or done without careful consideration of the possible results: *Don't do anything rash — you don't need to make a decision until tomorrow.* ∘ *You shouldn't make rash promises.* ∘ *It would be rash of them to make up their minds before they've heard all the evidence.* ▶ **rashly** adv: *She had rashly promised to lend him the money.* **rashness** n [U]: *In a moment of rashness, I agreed to help.*

rasher /'ræʃə(r)/ n a thin slice of bacon: *a fried egg and two rashers of bacon for breakfast.*

rasp /rɑːsp; *US* ræsp/ n **1** [sing] an unpleasant harsh sound: *the rasp of a saw on wood.* **2** [C] a metal tool with a long blade covered with rows of sharp points, used for making rough surfaces smooth.
▶ **rasp** v **1(a)** ~ **sth (out)** to say sth in an unpleasant harsh voice: [Vn, Vnp] *rasp (out) orders* [V.speech] *'Keep quiet!' he rasped.* **(b)** to make an unpleasant harsh sound: [V] *a rasping voice/cough* ∘ *She lay in bed, her breath rasping painfully in her throat.* **2** to rub sth with, or as if with, a rasp: [Vn, Vn-adj] *rasp the surface (smooth).*

raspberry /'rɑːzbəri; *US* 'ræzberi/ n **1** a small edible soft fruit, red when ripe, or the bush on which it grows: *raspberries and cream* ∘ *raspberry jam.* **2** (*Brit*) (*US* ˌBronx 'cheer) (*infml*) a sound made with the tongue and lips to show dislike, contempt, etc: *give/blow sb a raspberry* ∘ *The teacher got a raspberry as she turned her back.*

Rastafarian /ˌræstə'feəriən/ (also *infml* **Rasta**) n, adj (a member) of a Jamaican religion whose followers worship the former Ethiopian EMPEROR Haile Selassie as God. ▶ **Rastafarianism** n [U].

rat /ræt/ n **1** a small animal with a long tail that looks like a large mouse. **2** (*infml derog*) **(a)** a person who is not loyal or who deceives sb: *You rat! How can you lie to your own wife?* **(b)** an unpleasant person. **IDM** smell a rat ⇨ SMELL[1].
▶ **rat** v (**-tt-**) (*infml*) **(a)** ~ **(on sth)** to break an agreement or a promise: [Vpr] *They accused the government of ratting on their commitment to provide*

more housing. [also V]. (**b**) ~ (**on sb**) to reveal a secret; to betray sb: [Vpr] *He threatened to rat on his own brother!* [also V].

rats *interj* (*dated infml*) (used to express annoyance): *Oh rats! I've forgotten my keys.*

ratter *n* a dog or cat that catches rats: *Terriers are good ratters.*

■ **the ˈrat race** *n* [sing] (*infml derog*) a way of life in which everybody competes fiercely to be more successful than everybody else: *get caught up in/get out of the rat race.*

ratatat, rat-a-tat-tat = RAT-TAT.

ratatouille /ˌrætəˈtwiː, -ˈtuːi/ *n* [U] a dish made of stewed (STEW) vegetables.

ratbag /ˈrætbæg/ *n* (*sl derog*) an unpleasant or disgusting person.

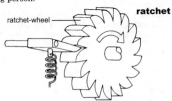

ratchet

ratchet-wheel

ratchet /ˈrætʃɪt/ *n* a device consisting of a wheel or bar with a piece of metal that fits between the teeth allowing movement in one direction only. ⇨ picture.

rate¹ /reɪt/ *n* **1** a measurement of how fast or how many times sth happens in relation to sth else: *walk at a/the rate of 5 kilometres an hour* ○ *produce cars at a rate of 50 a/per week* ○ *the rising rate of unemployment* ○ *the annual ˈbirth/diˈvorce rate* ○ *a high ˈpass/ ˈfailure rate* (eg in an examination) ○ *the exˈchange rate/the rate of exˈchange* (ie the number of units of one currency given in exchange for one unit of another). **2** a fixed charge, payment or value: *postal/advertising/insurance rates* ○ *a low/high hourly rate of pay* ○ *the basic rate of tax* ○ *special reduced rate for children/students* ○ *Surveys offered at reasonable rates.* ○ *Interest rates have fallen from 8% to 5%.* See also BASE RATE. **3** a speed of movement, change, etc: *The incidence of such crimes is increasing at a steady/terrifying rate.* ○ *His pulse rate dropped suddenly.* ○ *At the rate you work, you'll never finish!* **4** (usu *pl*) (*Brit*) a tax on land and buildings paid to the local authority by a business and formerly also by all property owners: *set a rate of 66 pence in the pound* (ie 66 pence for every pound of a property's value). Compare COUNCIL TAX, FIRST-RATE, SECOND-RATE, THIRD-RATE. **IDM** **at ˈany rate 1** whatever happens or may have happened: *Well, that's one good piece of news at any rate.* **2** (used when correcting or stating more exactly sth that one has previously said): *He said he'll be coming tomorrow. At any rate, I think that's what he said.* **3** (used to indicate that what one has just said is not as important as what one is about to say): *There were 60 people there, or maybe 70. I don't know. At any rate, the room was packed.* **at a rate of ˈknots** (*infml*) very rapidly. **at ˈthis/ˈthat rate** (*infml*) if this/that continues; doing things this/that way; if this/that is typical: *At this rate, we'll soon be bankrupt.* **the going rate** ⇨ GOING.

■ **ˈrate-capping** *n* [U] (*Brit*) the placing by the government of an upper limit on the rates (RATE¹ 4) that a local authority can charge.

rate² /reɪt/ *v* **1** ~ sth at sth; ~ sb/sth as sth to estimate the worth or value of sb/sth: [Vnpr] *What do you rate his income at?* [Vnadv] *She is **highly rated** as a novelist.* [Vn-n] *He is widely rated as one of the best players in the world.* [Vn] (*infml*) *I don't rate this play* (ie think it is good) *at all.* **2** to regard

sb/sth as sth: [Vnpr] *Do you rate Tom among your friends?* **3** to rank or be regarded in a specified way: [V-adj] *That task rates low on my priority list.* [V-n] *This must rate as one of the worst meals I have ever eaten!* **4** (*infml*) to deserve sth: [Vn] *The incident didn't even rate a mention in the local paper.*

ratepayer /ˈreɪtpeɪə(r)/ *n* (*Brit*) (formerly) a person who pays taxes to the local authority on the land and buildings he or she owns.

rather /ˈrɑːðə(r); US ˈræðər/ *adv* **1** (often indicating slight criticism, disappointment or surprise) to a certain extent; fairly (**a**) (used before *adjs* and *advs*): *It's rather cold outside.* ○ *The instructions were rather complicated.* ○ *She fell and hurt her leg rather badly.* ○ *I didn't fail the exam; in fact I did rather well!* (**b**) (used before comparatives): *This hotel is rather more expensive than the others.* ○ *The patient has responded to the treatment rather better than expected.* (**c**) (used before *too*): *I tried the trousers on, but they were rather too big for me.* ○ *He spoke rather too quickly for me to understand.* **2** to a moderate extent; quite (**a**) (used before *a, the* and *like*): *It seems rather a good idea.* ○ *It's rather a shame that Anne missed the concert.* ○ *Alan looks rather like his mother.* (**b**) (used before a *v*): *I rather suspect we're making a big mistake.* ○ *We were rather hoping you'd be free on Friday.* ○ *He rather resented having to do Jane's work as well as his own.* ⇨ note at FAIRLY. **3**(**a**) (used to correct sth one has said previously, or to give more accurate information): *She worked as a secretary, or rather, a personal assistant.* ○ *In the end he had to walk — or rather run — to the office.* (**b**) (used to introduce an idea that is different or opposite to the idea that one has stated previously): *The walls were not white, but rather a sort of dirty grey.* **IDM** **rather you, him, etc than ˈme** (*infml*) (used for saying that one would not like to do sth that another person is going to do): *'I'm going climbing tomorrow.' 'Rather you than me!'* **would rather... (than)** (usu shortened to *'d rather*) would prefer to: *She'd rather die than lose the children.* ○ *Would you rather walk or take the bus?* ○ *'Do you mind if I smoke?' 'Well, I'd rather you didn't.'*

▶ **rather** /*also* ˌrɑːˈðɜː(r)/ *interj* (*dated Brit*) (used when replying to a suggestion, etc and always stressed) certainly: *'How about a trip to the coast?' 'Rather!'*

■ **rather than** *prep* in preference to sb/sth; instead of sb/sth: *I think I'll have a cold drink rather than coffee.* ○ *It's management that's at fault rather than the workforce.* ○ *Why didn't you ask for help, rather than trying to do it on your own?*

ratify /ˈrætɪfaɪ/ *v* (*pt, pp* **-fied**) (*fml*) to make an agreement, a contract, etc officially valid, usu by signing it: [Vn] *Heads of twelve European governments will meet to ratify the treaty.* ▶ **ratification** /ˌrætɪfɪˈkeɪʃn/ *n* [U].

rating /ˈreɪtɪŋ/ *n* **1**(**a**) the classifying or ranking of sb/sth according to quality, etc: *a high/low popularity/credibility rating* ○ *give medical research a high-priority rating* ○ *poor ratings in the opinion polls.* See also CREDIT RATING. (**b**) (often *pl*) the popularity of a television or radio programme as measured by the number of people viewing or listening: *The show has gone up in the ratings.* **2** (*esp Brit*) (in the navy) a sailor who is not an officer.

ratio /ˈreɪʃiəʊ/ *n* (*pl* **-os**) a relation between two amounts, which shows how many times one contains the other: *a student/teacher ratio of 20:1* ○ *The ratios of 1 to 5 and 20 to 100 are the same.* ○ *The ratio of women to men in the factory is three to one.* Compare PROPORTION 2.

ratiocination /ˌrætɪɒsɪˈneɪʃn; US ˌræʃi-/ *n* [U] (*fml*) the process of logical and methodical reasoning.

ration /ˈræʃn/ *n* **1** [C] a fixed quantity, esp an amount of food, fuel, etc that one is officially allowed to have when there is not enough for everybody to have as much as they want: *the weekly butter/meat/petrol ration* (eg during a war) ○ *a ration card/book* (ie entitling the holder to a ration). **2 rations** [pl] a fixed amount of food supplied regularly to a soldier, etc: *We're on short rations* (ie allowed less than usual) *until fresh supplies arrive.*

▶ **ration** *v* ~ **sb/sth (to sth)** (esp passive) to limit the amount of sth that sb is allowed to have: [Vnpr] *People were rationed to one egg a week.* ○ *Bread was rationed to one loaf per family.* [also Vn]. **PHRV** ,**ration sth ¹out** to distribute fixed amounts of sth to a group of people: *ration the remaining water out among the survivors.* **rationing** *n* [U] the system of limiting the amount of food, clothing, etc that people are allowed to have when there is not enough for everybody to have as much as they want: *The government may have to introduce petrol rationing.*

rational /'ræʃnəl/ *adj* **1** (of a person) able to think and make decisions based on reason: *Man is a rational being.* **2** (of ideas or actions) based on reason; sensible; reasonable: *rational behaviour* ○ *a rational argument/explanation/decision.* **3** able to think clearly and normally: *No rational person would behave like that.* Compare IRRATIONAL.

▶ **rationality** /ˌræʃə'næləti/ *n* [U] the quality of being rational.
rationally /-ʃnəli/ *adv*: *think/behave/argue rationally.*

rationale /ˌræʃə'nɑːl; *US* -'næl/ *n* ~ **(behind/for/of sth)** the principles or reasons on which sth is based: *What is the rationale behind this decision?*

rationalism /'ræʃnəlɪzəm/ *n* [U] the theory that all behaviour, opinions, etc should be based on reason, not on feelings or religious belief.

▶ **rationalist** /-lɪst/ *n* a person who believes in rationalism. **rationalist** (also **rationalistic** /ˌræʃnəlɪstɪk/) *adj*: *rationalist theories.*

rationalize, -ise /'ræʃnəlaɪz/ *v* **1** (to try) to explain or understand one's actions, feelings, etc by giving logical reasons for them, esp when these are not true or appropriate: [V] *He's constantly rationalizing.* [Vn] *She rationalized her decision to buy a car by saying that it would save her money on bus fares.* **2** to make changes in a business, system, etc in order to increase efficiency and reduce waste: [Vn] *rationalize the factory's production/distribution.* ▶ **rationalization, -isation** /ˌræʃnəlaɪ'zeɪʃn; *US* -lə'z-/ *n* [C,U]: *Rationalization of the company resulted in several job losses.*

rattan /ræ'tæn/ *n* [C,U] a climbing plant found esp in Malaysia. It has long thin stems that are used for making furniture, etc.

rat-tat /ˌræt 'tæt/ (also **rat-a-tat** /ˌræt ə 'tæt/, **rat-a-tat-tat** /ˌræt ə tæt 'tæt/) *n* [sing] the sound of knocking, esp on a door: *a sharp rat-tat at/on the front door.*

rattle /'rætl/ *v* **1(a)** to make short sharp sounds quickly, one after the other; to shake while making such sounds: [V] *The windows were rattling in the wind.* ○ *Hailstones rattled on the tin roof.* **(b)** to make sth do this: [Vn] *The wind rattled the windows.* ○ *She rattled the money in the tin.* **2** (*infml*) (esp passive) to make sb nervous, worried or frightened: [Vn] *She was clearly rattled by the question.* **PHRV** **rattle a¹long, ¹off, ¹past, etc** move with a rattling sound: *The old bus rattled along the stony road.* ○ *A cart rattled past (us).* ,**rattle a¹way/¹on** to talk quickly and for a long time, esp about sth that is not important or interesting: *He rattled on for hours about his job.* ,**rattle sth ¹off** to say or repeat sth quickly and without much effort: *The child rattled off the poem he had learnt.* ,**rattle ¹through sth** to do sth quickly: *We rattled through lunch in 20 minutes.*

▶ **rattle** *n* **1** a rattling sound: *the rattle of bottles/chains* ○ *the harsh rattle of machine-gun fire.* **2(a)** a

baby's toy that makes a rattling sound when it is shaken. **(b)** an instrument that makes a rattling sound, used by spectators at a football match.
rattling /'rætlɪŋ/ *adv* (*dated*) very: *The book is a rattling good read.*

rattlesnake /'rætlsneɪk/ (also *US infml* **rattler** /'rætlə(r)/) *n* a poisonous American snake that makes a rattling noise with its tail when it is angry or afraid. ▷ picture at SNAKE.

ratty /'ræti/ *adj* **1** (*Brit infml*) easily made angry; bad-tempered: *He gets ratty with me when I'm late.* **2** (*US infml*) untidy and in bad condition: *long ratty hair.*

raucous /'rɔːkəs/ *adj* (of a sound) loud and rough: *We could hear the sound of raucous laughter coming from the pub across the street.* ▶ **raucously** *adv.* **raucousness** *n* [U].

raunchy /'rɔːntʃi/ *adj* (*infml*) **(a)** (*Brit*) showing or suggesting strong sexual desire; sexy (SEX): *a raunchy joke/story* ○ *Their stage act was fairly raunchy.* **(b)** (*US*) = OBSCENE.

ravage /'rævɪdʒ/ *v* to damage sth badly; to destroy sth: [Vn] *forests ravaged by fire* ○ *Rebel forces are ravaging the countryside.* ○ (*fig*) *a face ravaged by disease.*

▶ **the ravages** *n* [pl] ~ **of sth** the damaging effect of sth; the destruction done by sth: *the ravages of war* ○ (*fig*) *The ravages of time had spoilt her looks.*

rave /reɪv/ *v* **1** ~ **(at/against/about sb/sth)** to talk wildly or angrily as if in a fever or mad: [Vpr] *The patient began to rave incoherently at the nurses.* [also V]. **2** ~ **(about sb/sth)** (*infml*) to speak or write about sb/sth with great enthusiasm or admiration: [Vpr] *Everyone's raving about her latest film.* [V.speech] *'The best comedian this century,' raved the 'Daily Telegraph'.* [also V]. **IDM** **rant and rave** ▷ RANT.

▶ **rave** *n* (*Brit infml*) a large party for young people, with dancing to fast electronic music, popular esp in the late 1980s and early 1990s: *all-night raves* ○ *the rave scene.*
rave *adj* [attrib] (*infml*) very enthusiastic: *The play got rave reviews in the papers.*
raver *n* (*Brit infml*) **1** (*dated or ironic*) a person who leads a wild and exciting social life: *be a real/right little raver.* **2** a person who goes to raves.
raving *adj* [attrib] **1** talking or behaving wildly: *He was carrying on like a raving lunatic.* **2** absolute; complete: *Their daughters were all raving beauties.* — *adv* **IDM** **stark raving/staring mad** ▷ STARK *adv.*
ravings *n* [pl] wild or mad talk: *the ravings of a demented old man.*
■ ¹**rave-up** *n* (*dated Brit infml*) a lively party with dancing and drinking.

ravel /'rævl/ *v* (**-ll-**; *US* also **-l-**) (esp passive) (of woven or knitted fabric) to separate into threads: [V] *an old cardigan with ravelled cuffs.* See also UNRAVEL 1. Compare FRAY¹.

raven /'reɪvn/ *n* a large bird like a CROW¹ with shiny black feathers and a harsh cry.

▶ **raven** *adj* [attrib] (of hair) black and shiny: *silky raven hair.*

ravening /'rævənɪŋ/ *adj* [attrib] (*rhet*) (esp of animals) fierce and wild because of hunger: *ravening wolves.*

ravenous /'rævənəs/ *adj* **(a)** very hungry: *When's supper? I'm ravenous!* **(b)** (of hunger, etc) very great: *a ravenous appetite.* ▶ **ravenously** *adv*: *eat ravenously* ○ *She's always ravenously hungry.*

ravine /rə'viːn/ *n* a deep narrow valley with steep sides.

ravioli /ˌrævi'əʊli/ *n* [U] an Italian dish of small squares of PASTA filled with meat, cheese, etc and usu served with a sauce.

ravish /'rævɪʃ/ *v* **1** (*fml or rhet*) (esp passive) to fill sb with great delight: [Vn] *He was ravished by the*

beauty of the music. **2** [Vn] (*arch*) to RAPE¹ a woman or girl.
▶ **ravishing** *adj* very beautiful; delightful: *a ravishing smile* ∘ *You look ravishing in that dress!* **ravishingly** *adv*: *ravishingly beautiful.*

raw /rɔː/ *adj* **1** not cooked: *raw meat/vegetables* ∘ *eat oysters raw.* **2** [usu attrib] (**a**) in the natural state, ie before being processed or made into sth else: *raw silk/sewage* ∘ *raw sugar* (ie not refined). (**b**) not yet organized or analysed: *feed raw data into a computer.* **3** naturally strong; not controlled or refined: *songs full of raw emotion* ∘ *raw energy.* **4**(**a**) (of a part of the body) sore because the skin has come off: *There's a nasty raw patch on my arm where I burned it on the cooker.* (**b**) (of a wound) not healed. **5** [usu attrib] (of a person) new to an activity or a job and therefore lacking experience or skills: *raw recruits* (eg in the army). **6** (of the weather) cold and wet: *raw north-east winds* ∘ *a raw February morning.* **7** honest and truthful, esp about unpleasant things: *a raw portrayal of working-class life.* **IDM** **a raw/ rough deal** ⇨ DEAL².
▶ **raw** *n* **IDM** **in the ˈraw 1** not made to seem better, pleasanter, etc than it is: *The documentary shows life in the raw.* **2** (*infml*) without clothes; naked.
rawness *n* [U].
■ **ˌraw-ˈboned** *adj* (*usu derog*) very thin, so that the bones show under the skin: *a ˌraw-boned ˈface.*
ˌraw maˈterial *n* (often *pl*) a natural substance which is used to make sth else: *Coal, oil and minerals are the raw materials of industry.* ∘ (*fig*) *Her family's exploits provide the raw material for her novels.*

rawhide /ˈrɔːhaɪd/ *n* [U] leather that has not been treated: *a rawhide whip.*

ray¹ /reɪ/ *n* **1**(**a**) a narrow beam of light, heat or other energy: *the rays of the sun* ∘ *ultraviolet rays.* See also X-RAY, COSMIC RAYS. (**b**) ~ **of** sth a small amount of sth good or of sth that one is hoping for: *a few rays of hope* ∘ *It's a ray of comfort (for us) in these troubled times.* **2** any one of a number of lines, bands, etc coming out from a centre. **IDM** **a ˌray of ˈsunshine** (*infml*) a person or thing that makes life brighter or more cheerful.

ray² /reɪ/ *n* an edible sea-fish with a large broad flat body and a long tail.

ray³ /reɪ/ *n* (*music*) the second note of any major scale¹(6).

rayon /ˈreɪɒn/ *n* [U] a smooth silky fabric made from CELLULOSE(1): *rayon shirts.*

raze /reɪz/ *v* (esp passive) to destroy a building, town, etc completely, so that no part is left standing: [Vnpr] *During the war, whole villages were razed to the ground.* [also Vn].

razor /ˈreɪzə(r)/ *n* an instrument with a sharp blade, used for removing hair from the skin: *a disposable razor* ∘ *an electric razor.* See also SHAVER.
■ **ˈrazor-blade** *n* a thin sharp piece of metal that is used in a razor, esp one that can be thrown away when it is no longer sharp.
ˌrazor-ˈsharp *adj* extremely sharp: *ˌrazor-sharp ˈteeth* ∘ *He is known for his razor-sharp wit.*

razz /ræz/ *v* (*US infml*) to mock or TEASE(1) sb: [Vn] *kids razzing the teacher.*

razzle /ˈræzl/ *n* **IDM** **be/go (out) on the razzle** (*infml*) to be/go out to celebrate and enjoy oneself, eg in clubs or bars.

razzmatazz /ˌræzməˈtæz/ (also **razzamatazz** /ˌræzəməˈtæz/) *n* [U] (*infml*) noisy exciting activity that is intended to attract and impress people: *all the razzamatazz of showbiz.*

RC /ˌɑː ˈsiː/ *abbr* Roman Catholic: *St Mary's RC Church.*

Rd *abbr* (in street names) road: *12 Ashton Rd.*

RE /ˌɑː ˈiː/ *abbr* religious education: *an RE teacher.*

re¹ = RAY³.

re² /riː/ *prep* (used in formal written English) with reference to sth/sb; on the subject of sth/sb: *Re your letter of 1 September…*

re- *pref* (used widely with *vs* and related *ns, adjs* and *advs*) again: *reapply* ∘ *redecoration* ∘ *re-entered* ∘ *reassuringly.*

NOTE In many verbs beginning with **re-** the prefix is pronounced /rɪ-/, /ri-/ or /re-/ and it may have lost its original meaning of 'again' or 'back': /rɪ-/ *recall, repair*; /ri-/ *react*; /re-/ *represent.* Other verbs have had **re-** added to them with the meaning of 'again' and it is pronounced /ˌriː-/: *remarry, recreate.* There are a few verbs which fit into both groups and a hyphen is sometimes used to show the distinction: *recount* /rɪˈkaʊnt/ = 'tell a story', *re-count* /ˌriː ˈkaʊnt/ = 'count again'; *recover* /rɪˈkʌvə(r)/ = 'get back' or 'become well again', *re-cover* /ˌriː ˈkʌvə(r)/ = 'supply with a new cover'.

reach /riːtʃ/ *v* **1**(**a**) to go as far as sb/sth/a place; to get to or arrive somewhere: [Vn] *reach York by one o'clock* ∘ *reach the end of the book* ∘ *reach a speed of 500 mph* ∘ *The rescuers reached him just in time.* (**b**) to achieve sth; to obtain sth: [Vn] *reach a conclusion/decision/verdict* ∘ *reach maturity* ∘ *You'll understand these things when you reach my age.* ∘ *The appeal fund has reached its target of £10 000.* See also FAR-REACHING. **2** ~ **for** sth; ~ **out (to sb/sth)** to stretch out one's hand in order to touch or take sth: [Vpr] *He reached for a pencil.* ∘ *She reached across the table for the jam.* [Vp] (*fig*) *We must reach out to those in need.* **3** ~ sth (**down**) **for sb** (*infml*) to stretch one's hand out or up and take sth; to get and give sth to sb: [Vnpr, Vnp, Vnn] *Could you reach (me) that box (down) from the top of the wardrobe?* **4** ~ (**to**) sth to extend to sth; to be able to stretch up, out, etc and touch sth: [V] *Can you get me that book from the top shelf? I can't reach.* [Vn] *My feet can hardly reach the pedals.* [Vpr] *She wore a dress that reached (down) to her ankles.* **5** to communicate with sb: [Vn] *You can reach her at home on 01355-694162.* [Vnpr] *I can't reach him by phone/on the phone.* ∘ *We could reach more people by advertising.* **IDM** **reach comes to / reaches sb's ears** ⇨ EAR¹. **hit/make/ reach the headlines** ⇨ HEADLINE. **reach for the ˈstars** to be very ambitious.
▶ **reach** *n* **1** [sing] the extent to which a hand, etc can be stretched out: *a boxer with a long reach.* **2** [C usu *pl*] a continuous stretch of a river between two bends: *the upper/lower reaches of the Thames.* **IDM** **beyond / out of / within (one's/sb's) ˈreach 1** outside or inside the distance that a hand, etc can be stretched out: *have/keep a dictionary within (arm's) reach* ∘ *The top shelf is well out of/beyond my reach.* ∘ *Keep those medicines out of reach of the children/out of the children's reach.* **2** beyond or within sb's/sth's authority, influence, ability, etc: *concepts beyond the reach of present scientific knowledge* ∘ *Such highly-paid jobs are out of reach for someone with no qualifications.* ∘ *House prices are beyond the reach of many young couples.* **within (easy) ˈreach (of sb/sth)** inside a distance that can be travelled (easily): *The hotel is within easy reach of the beach.*
reachable *adj* that can be reached: *reachable by road/within an hour.*

react /riˈækt/ *v* **1**(**a**) ~ (**to sb/sth**) to change or behave in a particular way as a result of or in response to sth: [V] *I nudged her but she didn't react.* [Vadv] *You never know how she's going to react.* [Vpr] *React positively/negatively to a suggestion* ∘ *People can react badly to certain food additives.* ∘ *She reacted to her father's death by becoming angry and bitter.* (**b**) ~ (**against sb/sth**) to respond to sb/sth with hostility, resistance, etc: [Vpr] *react strongly against tax increases* ∘ *People often react against the* *way their parents brought them up.* [also V]. **2** ~ **with sth;** ~ **(together)** *(chemistry)* (of substances) to change by coming into contact with sth: [Vpr] *Iron reacts with water and air to produce rust.* [V,Vp] *Sodium and water react (together).*

reaction /ri'ækʃn/ *n* **1** [U,C] ~ **(to sb/sth)** a response to a situation, an act, an influence, etc: *What was his reaction to the news?* ○ *My immediate reaction was one of disbelief.* ○ *the shocked reaction of schools to the education cuts* ○ *The new play got rather a mixed reaction from the audience.* **2** [sing] a physical response, usu a bad one, to a drug, chemical substance, etc: *have an **allergic reaction** to dairy products* ○ *I had a bad reaction after my typhoid injection.* **3** [sing,U] ~ **(against sth)** a change from one attitude, feeling or condition to the opposite: *This permissiveness was a reaction against Victorian puritanism.* **4** [U] opposition to esp political progress or reform: *The forces of reaction made change difficult.* **5** [U,C] chemical change produced by two or more substances acting upon each other; an instance of this: *nuclear reaction.* See also CHAIN REACTION.

▶ **reactionary** /ri'ækʃənri; *US* -neri/ *n, adj* (of) a person or group opposing progress or reform, esp in politics: *a reactionary government* ○ *reactionary forces.*

reactivate /ri'æktɪveɪt/ *v* to bring sth back into operation; to make sth active again: [Vn] *reactivate public interest in the plight of the homeless.*

reactive /ri'æktɪv/ *adj* **1** showing a reaction or response: *be positively/negatively reactive to other people's suggestions* ○ *The police continue to favour a reactive rather than a preventive strategy.* **2** *(chemistry)* tending to react(2): *highly reactive substances.*

reactor /ri'æktə(r)/ (also **nuclear reactor**) *n* an apparatus for the controlled production of nuclear energy: *plans to build a new reactor near the coast.* See also FAST BREEDER REACTOR.

read /riːd/ *v* (*pt, pp* **read** /red/) **1** (used in the simple tenses or with *can/be able*) to look at and understand the meaning of written or printed words or symbols: [V] *teach children (how) to read and write* ○ *learn (how) to read* [Vn] *read shorthand/ Chinese (characters)/Braille/music* ○ *I can't read your writing.* ○ *I can't read that road sign without my glasses.* **2** ~ **sth (to sb/oneself)** to go through written or printed words, etc silently or aloud to others: [V] *I never have enough time to read/for reading.* [Vn] *read a book/a magazine/the newspaper* ○ *a novel that is not read much these days* (ie few people read it) [Vpr] *The children were told to read quietly to themselves for half an hour.* ○ *She read (to us) from her book.* [Vnadv] *He read the poem aloud.* [Vnp] *He read the article through twice.* ○ *Read this over for mistakes.* [V.wh] *Read what the instructions say.* [Vnpr,Vnn] *She read a story to us/read us a story.* See also PROOFREAD. **3** to discover or find out about sb/sth by reading: [Vn] *read the news/the share prices* [Vpr] *I read about her death in today's paper.* [V.that] *I read that he had resigned.* **4** ~ **(for) sth** *(Brit)* to study a subject, esp at a university: [Vn] *read English/law at Oxford* [Vpr] *read for a physics degree* ○ *read for the Bar* (ie study law to become a BARRISTER). **5** to discover the contents or meaning of sth; to interpret sth in a particular way: [Vn] *read sb's mind/thoughts* ○ *read sb's lips* (ie look at the movements of sb's lips to learn what they are saying) ○ *read (sb's fortune in) the cards* ○ *Doctors must be able to read symptoms correctly.* ○ *How do you read the present situation?* [Vn-n] *Silence must not always be read as consent.* See also LIP-READ. **6** to show sth; to have sth written on it: [V.speech] *The sign reads 'Keep Left.'* ○ *I've changed the last paragraph. It now reads as follows...* **7(a)** (of measuring instruments) to indicate a certain weight, pressure, etc: [Vn]

What does the thermometer read? **(b)** to receive information from instruments: [Vn] *read the gas/ electricity meter* [V.wh] *I can't read what the thermometer says.* **8** to give a certain impression when read: [Vadv] *The story reads well/badly.* [Vpr] *The poem reads like* (ie sounds as if it is) *a translation.* **9** to hear and understand sb speaking on a radio set: [Vn, Vn-adj] *'Are you reading me?' 'I'm reading you loud and clear.'* **10** ~ **A for B;** ~ **B as A** to replace one word, etc with another when correcting a text: [Vnpr] *For 'neat' in line 3 read 'nest'.* [also Vn-n]. **IDM** ,**read between the** '**lines** to look for or discover a meaning in sth that is not openly stated. ,**read sb like a** '**book** *(infml)* to understand sb's thoughts, motives (MOTIVE), etc clearly: *I can read you like a book: you're not sorry at all.* ,**read (sb) the** '**Riot Act** *(Brit)* to declare forcefully to sb that sth must stop: *When he arrived late again, the teacher read him the Riot Act.* ,**take it/sth as** '**read** to assume sth without a need for discussion: *We can take it as read that you want the job.* **PHRV** ,**read** '**on** to continue reading: *That's the story so far. Now read on.*

,**read sth** '**back** to read a message, etc aloud so that its accuracy can be checked: *I'll dictate the letter and then you can read it back to me.*

,**read sth** '**into sth** to assume that sth means more than it does: *You have read too much into what she said. I'm sure she didn't mean it!*

,**read sth** '**out** to read sth aloud, esp to others: *She read out the letter to the whole family.*

,**read sb/sth** '**up;** ,**read** '**up on sb/sth** to read a lot about or make a special study of a subject: *I've got to read Nelson up/read up on Nelson for the history exam.*

▶ **read** /riːd/ *n* [sing] *(infml esp Brit)* **1** a period or act of reading: *have a long/quiet/little read* ○ *Can I have a read of your magazine?* **2** (with an *adj*) a book, etc considered as sth worth reading: *The novel is/makes an excellent read.*

read /red/ *adj* (preceded by an *adv*) having knowledge gained from reading: *a well-read person* ○ *be widely read in the classics.*

readable /'riːdəbl/ *adj* **1** that is easy or enjoyable to read: *a highly readable style/essay/article.* **2** (of written words, etc) that can be read. Compare LEGIBLE. **readability** /,riːdə'bɪləti/ *n* [U].

■ ,**read-only** '**memory** *n* (*abbr* ROM) *(computing)* a computer memory storing data that cannot be altered or removed: *The most important programs are in the read-only memory.* Compare RANDOM-ACCESS.

'**read-out** *n* *(computing)* information obtained from a computer on a screen or in printed form.

readdress /,riːə'dres/ (also **redirect**) *v* ~ **sth (to sb/ sth)** to change the address on a letter, etc: [Vn,Vnpr] *She asked me to readdress any mail for her (to her new home).*

reader /'riːdə(r)/ *n* **1** a person who reads, esp one who is fond of reading: *an avid/a slow reader* ○ *a book that will appeal to the general reader* ○ *Happy Christmas to all our readers* (eg as a notice in a newspaper, magazine, library, etc). ○ *He's a great reader of science fiction.* **2** a book intended to give students practice in reading: *graded English readers* (eg for foreign learners). **3 Reader** ~ **(in sth)** *(Brit)* a senior university teacher of a rank immediately below a PROFESSOR(1): *Reader in English Literature.* **4** (also **publisher's** '**reader**) a person employed to read books, articles, etc and say whether or not they are suitable for publication. **5** (also '**proof-reader**) a person employed to read and correct early copies of books, etc before they are printed. **6** (also **lay reader**) a person appointed to read aloud parts of a service in church. **7** *(techn)* an electronic device with a special LENS(1) that can read printed text and automatically store it on a computer.

▶ **readership** n **1** [sing] the number or type of readers of a newspaper, magazine, etc or of a particular writer: *The Daily Echo has a readership of over ten million.* ○ *a newspaper with a conservative readership* ○ *an author who has/commands a large readership.* **2** [C] ~ (**in sth**) (*Brit*) the position of a Reader(3): *hold/have a readership in Maths.*

readily, readiness ⇨ READY.

reading /'riːdɪŋ/ n **1** [U] (**a**) the action of a person who reads: *be fond of reading* ○ *reading matter* (ie books, newspapers, etc) ○ *a reading-lamp/-light* (ie one placed to help sb reading) ○ *have a good reading knowledge of French* (ie understand written French well). (**b**) books, etc intended to be read: *heavy/light reading* (eg for study/entertainment) ○ *Her articles make interesting reading.* **2** [C] an amount indicated or registered by a measuring instrument: *take a thermometer reading.* **3** [C] a way in which sth is interpreted or understood: *a feminist/Marxist reading of a text* ○ *What is your reading of the situation?* **4** [C] (**a**) an entertainment at which sth is read to an audience; a passage read in this way: *a poetry-/play-reading* ○ *readings from Dickens.* (**b**) a formal announcement of sth to an audience: *the reading of a will/of marriage banns.* (**c**) a formal reading aloud of a passage from the Bible: *a reading from St John's gospel.* **5** [C] (in a parliament) each of the stages of debate through which a Bill must pass before it can become law.
■ **'reading age** n one's ability to read, measured by comparing it with the average ability of children of the specified age: *adults with a reading age of eight.*
'reading-room n a room in a library, club, etc where people can read or study.

readjust /ˌriːə'dʒʌst/ v **1** ~ (**oneself**) (**to sth**) (no passive) to adapt oneself again to a situation one has been in previously: [Vnpr, Vpr] *It's hard to readjust (oneself) to life back home after working abroad.* [V, Vpr] *You need time to readjust* (to living alone). [also Vn]. **2** to set or adjust sth again: [Vn] *readjust the engine tuning/television set.* ▶ **readjustment** n [U,C]: *go through a period of readjustment* ○ *make minor readjustments to the wiring.*

readmit /ˌriːəd'mɪt/ v ~ **sb** (**to sth**) (esp passive) **1** to allow sb to become a member of a group or an organization again: [Vnpr] *be readmitted to the United Nations.* **2** to enter a hospital again as a patient: [Vn, Vnpr] *She was readmitted* (to hospital) *three days later.* ▶ **readmission** /ˌriːəd'mɪʃn/ (also **readmittance**) /ˌriːəd'mɪtns/ n [U] ~ (**to sth**): *seek readmission to the Commonwealth.*

ready /'redi/ adj (**-ier**, **-iest**) **1** ~ (**for sth / to do sth**) (**a**) (of a person) fully prepared for sth or to do sth: *get ready for a journey* ○ *Are you ready to start work?* ○ *'Shall we go?' 'I'm ready when you are!'* ○ *Volunteers were ready and waiting to pack the food in boxes.* (**b**) completed and available for use: *Come on, dinner's ready!* ○ *The contract will be ready to sign in two weeks.* **2** [pred] ~ **to do sth** on the point of doing sth; about to do sth: *She looked ready to collapse at any minute.* **3** ~ (**for sth / to do sth**) (of a person) willing and eager: *He's always ready to help his friends.* ○ *Don't be so ready to find fault.* ○ *I was very angry and ready for a fight.* **4**(**a**) [attrib] quick and intelligent: *have a ready wit.* (**b**) [pred] ~ **with sth** (of a person) quick to give sth: *be always ready with advice/affection.* **5** easily available or obtained: *Keep your dictionary ready to hand.* ○ *This account provides you with a ready source of income.* ○ *There's a ready market for antiques* (ie Buyers are easily found for them). See also ROUGH-AND-READY. **IDM make 'ready (for sth)** to prepare: *make ready for the President's visit.*
▶ **readily** /-ɪli/ adv **1** without hesitating; willingly: *His suggestion was readily accepted.* ○ *She readily*

agreed *to help.* **2** without difficulty; easily: *Spare parts are readily available.*
readiness /'redinəs/ n [U] **1** ~ (**for sth**) the state of being ready or prepared: *the troops' readiness for battle* ○ *have everything in readiness for an early start.* **2** ~ (**to do sth**) willingness or eagerness: *her readiness to help.* **3** quickness and ease: *readiness of wit.*

ready n **the ready** [sing] (also **readies** [pl]) (*infml*) available money; cash: *not have enough of the ready.* **IDM at the 'ready** ready for immediate action or use: *He had his camera/gun at the ready.*

ready adv (used before a past participle, esp in compounds) already: *ready cooked/mixed* ○ *ready-printed forms.*

ready v (*pt, pp* **-died**) ~ **oneself/sb/sth** (**for sth**) to make oneself/sb/sth ready; to prepare oneself/sb/sth: [Vnpr] *party workers readying themselves for the next election* ○ *ships readied for battle* [also Vn].
■ **ˌready-'made** adj **1** (esp of clothes) made in standard sizes, not to the measurements of a particular customer: *a ˌready-made 'suit* ○ *ready-made curtains.* **2** (esp of food) prepared in advance: *ready-made pastry/frozen meals.* **3** very appropriate; ideal: *We have no ready-made answers.*
ˌready 'money (also **ˌready 'cash**) n [U] (*infml*) coins and notes; money that is immediately available: *payment by ready money.*

reaffirm /ˌriːə'fɜːm/ v to state sth again positively and definitely: [Vn] *reaffirm one's loyalty* [V.that] *She reaffirmed that she was prepared to help.* ▶ **reaffirmation** /ˌriːˌæfə'meɪʃn/ n [U].

reagent /ri'eɪdʒənt/ n (*chemistry*) a substance used to cause a chemical reaction, esp in order to detect the presence of another substance.

real /'riːəl; *Brit* also rɪəl/ adj **1**(**a**) existing as a thing or occurring as a fact; not imagined, supposed or pretended: *real and imagined fears/illnesses* ○ *Was it a real person you saw or a ghost?* ○ *Real life is sometimes stranger than fiction.* ○ *The growth of violent crime is a very real problem.* ○ *There's no real possibility of them changing their minds.* ○ *She has no real chance of passing the exam.* (**b**) [attrib] actual or true, not just appearing so: *Who is the 'real manager of the firm* (ie the person who does the work of managing it)? ○ *Tell me the 'real reason.* ○ *A lot of politicians seem to be out of touch with the real 'world.* ○ *See the 'real Africa on one of our walking safaris.* (**c**) likely to happen; possible: *The ending of the story is all too real.* ○ *This is a very real situation.* **2** genuine; not artificial: *real silk/gold/pearls* ○ *Is that real hair or a wig?* **3** [attrib] (used for emphasis) complete; thorough; serious: *The camping trip was a real disaster.* ○ *They present a real barrier to progress.* **4** [attrib] (of money, incomes, etc) assessed by their power to buy things: *Real incomes have gone up by 10% in the past year.* ○ *This represents a reduction of 5% in real terms* (ie when price rises, etc have been allowed for). **IDM for 'real** (*infml*) **1** seriously: *This isn't just a practice game — this time it's for real.* **2** genuine: *I don't think her tears were for real.* **the ˌreal 'thing/Mc'Coy** /məˈkɔɪ/ (*infml*) the genuine article or thing: *It's a US air-force flying jacket, the real McCoy.* ○ *Are you sure it's the real thing* (ie love), *not just infatuation?*
▶ **real** adv (*US or Scot infml*) very; really: *have a real fine time/a real good laugh* ○ *I'm real sorry.*
■ **ˌreal 'ale** n [U,C] (*Brit*) beer that is made and stored in the traditional way.
'real estate n [U] **1** (*US*) (**a**) houses or land: *investors buying New York real estate.* (**b**) the business of selling houses or land for building. **2** (also **realty**, **real property**) (*law*) property consisting of land or buildings. **'real estate agent** n [U] = ESTATE AGENT.
ˌreal-'life adj [attrib] as actually occurred, existed,

etc; not fictional (FICTION): *a film based on ˌreal-life eˈvents.*

ˌreal ˈtime *n* [U] (*computing*) the very short time it takes a computer system to react to data and respond in an appropriate manner: *To make the training realistic the simulation operates in real time.* ○ *real-time missile guidance systems.*

realign /ˌriːəˈlaɪn/ *v* **1** to make sth face or go in a different direction: [Vn] *proposals to realign the runway.* **2** ~ (oneself) (with sth) (*esp politics or finance*) to form sb/sth or be formed into new groups: [Vpr, Vnpr] *The party may realign (itself) with Labour in a new coalition.* [Vnadv] *If sterling is realigned downwards, the debt could increase.* [also Vn]. ▶ **realignment** *n* [U, C]: *the realignment of car wheels* ○ *political realignments.*

realism /ˈriːəlɪzəm; *Brit also* ˈrɪəl-/ *n* [U] **1** an attitude of mind in which one accepts a situation as it is and is prepared to deal with it, without pretending it is different: *a new air/mood of realism.* **2** the quality of being very like the person, thing or situation that is described: *the gritty realism of television programmes like 'Grange Hill'.* **3** (in art and literature) the representation of familiar things as they really are. Compare CLASSICISM 1, ROMANTICISM. ▶ **realist** *n* **1** a person who is prepared to deal with a situation as it is without pretending it is different: *I'm a realist — I know you can't change people overnight.* **2** a writer, painter, etc whose work shows realism(3): *a realist novel/style.*

realistic /ˌriːəˈlɪstɪk; *Brit also* ˌrɪəl-/ *adj* **1** having or showing a sensible and practical idea of what can be done, achieved, etc: *a realistic approach/ assessment/view* ○ *A 2% pay rise is more realistic.* ○ *Be realistic and don't try to change too much too soon.* ○ *Is this a realistic* (ie an appropriate) *salary for such a responsible job?* **2** (in art and literature) showing realism(3). **realistically** /-klɪ/ *adv*: *Realistically, this is unlikely to happen quickly.*

reality /rɪˈælətɪ/ *n* **1** [U] the quality of being real or of resembling sth that is real: *the lifelike reality of his paintings.* **2** [U] one's true personal situation and the problems that exist in one's life; the real world, as contrasted with one's ideals and illusions: *escape from the reality of everyday existence* ○ *face (up to)* (ie accept) *reality* ○ *bring sb back to reality* (ie make them think about the situation as it is, not as they would like it to be). **3** [C often *pl*] a thing that is actually experienced or seen; a thing that is real: *the harsh realities of poverty/unemployment* ○ *He cannot grasp the realities of the situation.* ○ *The dream/idea will soon become a reality* (ie exist in fact, not just in sb's mind). **IDM in reˈality** in actual fact; really: *The house looks very old, but in reality it was built only 40 years ago.* See also VIRTUAL REALITY.

realize, -ise /ˈriːəlaɪz; *Brit also* ˈrɪəl-/ *v* **1** (not used in the continuous tenses) to become aware of or accept sth as a fact; to begin to understand sth: [Vn] *realize one's mistake* ○ *realize the extent of the damage* [V.*that*] *She realized that he had been lying.* [V.*wh* no passive]: *I fully realize why you did it.* **2** (esp passive) to make one's dreams, ideas, plans, etc happen: [Vn] *realize one's hopes/ambitions* ○ *realize designs for the stage* ○ *her worst fears were realized* (ie The things she was most afraid would happen did happen). **3** (*fml*) **(a)** to convert property, shares, etc into money by selling them: [Vn] *realize one's assets.* **(b)** (of goods, etc) to be sold for a price: [Vn] *The furniture realized £900 at the sale.* **(c)** to get money from selling sth: [Vn, Vnpr] *How much did you realize (on those paintings)?* ▶ **realizable, -isable** /-əbl/ *adj* that can be realized (REALIZE 2,3): *realizable objectives/assets.*

realization, -isation /ˌriːəlaɪˈzeɪʃn; *Brit also* ˌrɪəl-; *US* -ləˈz-/ *n* [U, sing]: *the realization of his greatest*

ambition ○ *the realization of the company's assets* ○ *I was struck by the sudden realization that I would probably never see her again.*

really /ˈriːəlɪ; *Brit also* ˈrɪəl-/ *adv* **1** in actual fact; truly: *What do you really think about it?* ○ *Don't worry — it's not really that important.* ○ *Your name is on the car's documents, but who really owns it?* ○ *You're not really supposed to go in there.* ⇨ note at HOPEFUL. **2** thoroughly; very: *a really charming person* ○ *a really cold/fast/long journey.* ⇨ note at QUITE. **3** (used to express interest, surprise, mild protest or doubt): *'We're going to Japan next month.' 'Oh, really?'* ○ *'She's resigned.' 'Really? Are you sure?'* ○ *You really shouldn't smoke.* ○ *'Shut up!' 'Well, really!'*

realm /relm/ *n* **1** (*fml or rhet*) a country ruled by a king or queen: *the defence of the realm* ○ *coins/peers/ laws of the realm.* **2** a field of activity or interest: *in the realm of literature/science* ○ *Here, I think, he's moving into the realms of fantasy.*

realpolitik /reɪˈɑːlpɒlɪtiːk/ *n* [U] (*German*) an approach to politics based on the actual circumstances and needs of one's own people, not on morals or ideals.

realtor /ˈriːəltə(r)/ *n* (*US*) = ESTATE AGENT.

realty /ˈriːəltɪ/ *n* [U] = REAL ESTATE.

ream /riːm/ *n* **1** [C] (*techn*) 500 sheets of paper. **2** **reams** [pl] (*infml*) a large quantity of paper or writing: *write reams (and reams) of bad verse.*

reap /riːp/ *v* **1** to cut and gather a crop, esp grain: [Vn] *reap (a field of) barley* [also V]. **2** to receive or obtain some advantage as a result of one's own or others' actions: [Vn] *reap the rewards/benefits of years of study* ○ *reap the fruits of one's labours.* **IDM** (ˌsow the ˈwind and) ˌreap the ˈwhirlwind (*saying*) (to start sth that seems harmless and) to have to suffer unexpected and serious consequences. ▶ **reaper** *n* a person who reaps: (*fig*) *Death, the grim reaper.*

reappear /ˌriːəˈpɪə(r)/ *v* to appear again after being absent or not visible: [V] *After a few minutes John reappeared with a tray.* [Vpr] *The moon reappeared from behind a cloud.* ▶ **reappearance** /-rəns/ *n* [U, C]: *the reappearance of the symptoms* ○ *making a welcome reappearance at the National Theatre.*

reapply /ˌriːəˈplaɪ/ *v* (*pt, pp* reapplied) **1** ~ (for sth) to make another formal request for sth or to do sth: [Vpr] *reapply for a loan/visa* [V] *Previous applicants for the post need not reapply.* **2** to use sth or make a rule, etc operate again: [Vn] *The formula was reapplied when privatizing the railways.* **3** to put or spread a substance on a surface: [Vn] *reapplying her lipstick/sunscreen.*

reappoint /ˌriːəˈpɔɪnt/ *v* to give sb a position they formerly held; to appoint sb again to a particular position: [Vn-n] *She was reappointed as national coach for a further two years.* [also Vn]. ▶ **reappointment** *n* [U].

reappraisal /ˌriːəˈpreɪzl/ *n* [U, C usu *sing*] the action of examining sth again to see whether it or one's attitude to it should be changed: *a reappraisal of the situation/problem* ○ *a radical reappraisal of the role of broadcasting.*

reappraise /ˌriːəˈpreɪz/ *v* to assess again the quality or value of sth: [Vn] *reappraise a role/strategy.*

rear¹ /rɪə(r)/ *n* **1** (usu **the rear**) [sing] the back part: *a kitchen in/at/to the rear of the house* ○ *a view of the house taken from the rear* ○ *attack the enemy's rear* ○ *a car's rear doors/lights/wheels/window.* Compare FRONT 1. **2** (also **rear end**) [C usu *sing*] (*infml euph*) the part of the body one sits on; the buttocks (BUTTOCK): *a kick in/on the rear.* **IDM** **bring up the ˈrear** to be or come last, eg in a procession or race. ▶ **rearmost** /ˈrɪəməʊst/ *adj* furthest back: *the rearmost section of the aircraft.*

rearward /ˈrɪəwəd/ *adj, n* [U] (towards) the back of sth: *rearward seats.*

---

rearwards /ˈrɪəwədz/ (also **rearward**) adv towards the back.

■ ˌrear ˈadmiral /ˌrɪər ˈædmərəl/ n (the title of) a senior officer in a navy: ˌRear Admiral (Brian) ˈKing. ⇨ App 6.

ˌrear-view ˈmirror n a mirror in which a driver can see the traffic, etc behind. ⇨ picture at CAR.

rear² /rɪə(r)/ v **1(a)** to care for young children or animals, etc until they are fully grown: [Vn] rear a family ○ The male bird helps the female to rear the young. **(b)** [Vn] to breed animals or birds: rear cattle/poultry. Compare RAISE 6. **2** ~ (**up**) (of a horse, etc) to raise itself on its back legs: [V, Vp] The horse reared (up) in fright. **3** to raise one's head: [Vn] The snake reared its head. ○ (fig) terrorism *rearing its ugly head* again.

rearguard /ˈrɪəɡɑːd/ n (usu **the rearguard**) [Gp] a group of soldiers guarding the back of an army, esp when it is withdrawing after a defeat. Compare VANGUARD.

■ ˌrearguard ˈaction n (sing) a struggle continued even when it is unlikely to succeed: *fighting a rearguard action* to save the party from an overwhelming election defeat.

rearm /riˈɑːm/ v to supply an army, etc with weapons again, or with better weapons: [V, Vn] fear of the rebels rearming/being rearmed. ▶ **rearmament** /riˈɑːməmənt/ n [U]: a major programme of rearmament.

rearrange /ˌriːəˈreɪndʒ/ v **1** to place sth in a different position or order: [Vn] rearrange the furniture/one's books ○ Do you like the way I've rearranged the room? **2** to change plans, etc that have already been made: [Vn, Vnpr] Can we rearrange the meeting (for next week)? ▶ **rearrangement** n [U, C]: make some rearrangements.

reason¹ /ˈriːzn/ n **1** [U, C] ~ (for sth/doing sth); ~ (to do sth); ~ (why.../that...) the cause of sth or of sb doing sth; a fact, situation, etc that explains or justifies sth: What are your reasons for leaving/the reasons for your leaving the job? ○ Actually, I did it for entirely the opposite reason. ○ The reason why I'm late is that/because I missed the bus. ○ We aren't going, *for the simple reason that* we can't afford it. ○ We *have (good/no) reason to believe* that he is lying. ○ *For some/some reason or another* I never actually went to see him. ○ *All the more reason* for avoiding/to avoid him ○ That is not an adequate/a sufficient reason for sacking him. ○ (fml) He was excused *by reason of* (ie because of) his age. ○ She complained, *with reason* (ie rightly), that she had been underpaid. ⇨ note. **2** [U] the power of the mind to think, understand, form opinions, etc: the conflict between faith and reason. **3** one's reason [sing] one's health of mind: *lose one's reason* (ie go mad). **4** [U] what is right, practical or possible; common sense (COMMON¹): see/listen to/hear/be open to (ie be prepared to accept) reason ○ There's a good deal of reason in what you say. ○ I'll do anything *within reason* to earn a living. ○ I tried to persuade her but she was *beyond (all) reason*. **IDM for reasons / some reason best known to one**ˈ**self** (esp joc) for reasons that are hard for others to discover or understand: For reasons best known to himself, he drinks tea from a beer glass. **rhyme or reason** ⇨ RHYME. **it/that ˌstands to ˈreason** it/that is obvious to everyone: It stands to reason that nobody will work without pay.

NOTE Compare **reason, cause, justification, ground** and **motive**. The **cause** of something is what makes it happen: Police are investigating the cause of the explosion. ○ No cause for her ill health could be found. ○ the causes of the First World War. **Reason** has the widest use. A **reason** is the explanation that people give for why something has happened or why they have done something: She

didn't give a reason for her decision. ○ Police cannot name the man for legal reasons.

Reason and **justification** can both mean that an explanation is acceptable to people: The police had no reason to suspect him/no justification for suspecting him. When there is a valid reason for believing something, there is a valid reason for it: There should be no cause for jealousy between us. **Ground** is the legal justification for an action, and is usually used in the plural: I left my job on medical grounds. ○ She had good grounds for divorce. A **motive** is the feeling or desire inside somebody that makes them act: The murderer did not seem to have a motive.

reason² /ˈriːzn/ v **(a)** to use one's power to think, understand, form opinions, etc: [V] man's ability to reason. **(b)** (no passive) to come to a conclusion through this process: [V.that] He reasoned that if we started at 6 am we would be there by midday. [V] Wouldn't that extra £500, he reasoned, solve all his problems? **PHRV** ˌreason sth ˈout to find an answer to a problem by considering various possible solutions: The police are still trying to reason out how the thief got in. ˈreason with sb to argue in order to convince or persuade sb: I reasoned with him for hours about the danger, but he wouldn't change his mind. ○ There's no reasoning with that woman (ie She won't listen to arguments).

▶ **reasoned** adj [attrib] (of an argument, etc) presented in a logical way: a reasoned approach to the problem ○ She put a (well-)reasoned case for increasing the fees.

reasoning n [U] **(a)** the action or process of using one's ability to think, form opinions, etc: powers of reasoning. **(b)** arguments produced when doing this: Your reasoning on this point is faulty.

reasonable /ˈriːznəbl/ adj **1(a)** (of people) having good judgement; fair and sensible: No reasonable person could refuse. ○ She's perfectly reasonable in her demands. **(b)** (of opinions, etc) practical or fair; based on good sense: a reasonable attitude/conclusion ○ a reasonable suspicion/fear/belief ○ It's not reasonable to expect a child to understand sarcasm. ○ Is the accused guilty *beyond reasonable doubt*? **2** as much as is appropriate or due; moderate: a reasonable fee/offer/claim ○ He demands to be given reasonable access to his son. **3** (of prices, etc) not too expensive; acceptable: Ten pounds for a good dictionary seems reasonable enough. Compare UN-REASONABLE. **4** [esp attrib] fairly good; average: reasonable weather/health/food ○ There's a reasonable chance that he'll come.

▶ **reasonableness** n [U].

reasonably /-əbli/ adv **1** in a logical and sensible way: discuss the matter calmly and reasonably. **2** to a moderate or acceptable degree; fairly or quite: reasonably good/cheap/intelligent/accurate ○ a reasonably-priced book ○ He seems reasonably satisfied with it.

reassemble /ˌriːəˈsembl/ v **1** to meet together again as a group: [V] Parliament reassembles next week after the summer recess. **2** to fit the parts of sth together again after it has been taken apart: [Vn] reassemble a clock/an engine.

reassert /ˌriːəˈsɜːt/ v **1** to make sth clear or obvious after a period when it was not so; to assert oneself/sth again: [Vn] reassert one's authority/control ○ The time had come for her to reassert herself. **2** to state sth again: [V.that] He reasserted that all parties should be involved in the negotiations. [also Vn]. ▶ **reassertion** n [U, sing].

reassess /ˌriːəˈses/ v [Vn] to judge again the quality or value of sth, or one's ideas about sth. ▶ **reassessment** n [U, C].

reassure /ˌriːəˈʃʊə(r)/, Brit also -ˈʃɔː(r)/ v ~ sb (**about sth**) to remove sb's fears or doubts; to make sb confident again: [Vnpr] *The police reassured her about her child's safety.* [Vn.*that*] *He was reassured that her illness was not dangerous.* [Vn] *He looked as though he needed reassuring.*

▶ **reassurance** /-rəns/ *n* **1** [U] the action of reassuring sb or of being reassured: *want/need/demand reassurance.* **2** [C] a thing that reassures: *Despite reassurances I remained worried.*

reassuring *adj* removing one's doubts or fears: *a reassuring glance/word/pat on the back* ○ *She was kind and reassuring.* **reassuringly** *adv*: *speak reassuringly.*

reawaken /ˌriːəˈweɪkən/ *v* to make sth exist or become active again: [Vn] *reawaken interest/ memories/old fears.*

rebate /ˈriːbeɪt/ *n* an amount by which a debt, tax, etc can be reduced: *qualify for a rent/tax rebate.* Compare DISCOUNT¹.

rebel /ˈrebl/ *n* (**a**) a person who fights against, or refuses to serve, the established government: *rebel forces.* (**b**) a person who resists authority or control: *She has always been something of a rebel.*

▶ **rebel** /rɪˈbel/ *v* (**-ll-**) ~ (**against sb/sth**) **1** [V, Vpr] to fight against or resist the established government. **2** to resist authority or control; to protest strongly against sth: [Vpr] *He finally rebelled against his strict upbringing.* [also V].

rebellion /rɪˈbeljən/ *n* [U, C] ~ (**against sb/sth**) **1** esp violent resistance to the established government: *rise (up) in open rebellion* ○ *stage a rebellion against the military rulers.* **2** the action of resisting authority or control: *a rebellion against the proposed tax increases.*

rebellious /rɪˈbeljəs/ *adj* showing a desire to rebel; not easily controlled: *rebellious tribes* ○ *a child with a rebellious temperament.* **rebelliously** *adv*. **rebelliousness** *n* [U].

rebirth /ˌriːˈbɜːθ/ *n* [U, sing] **1** the process of coming or bringing sth back into existence or use: *the seasonal cycle of death and rebirth* ○ *the rebirth of European fascist parties.* **2** a complete spiritual change in which a person finds a stronger religious faith, is converted to a new religion, etc.

reborn /ˌriːˈbɔːn/ *adj* [pred] **1** having experienced a complete spiritual change. Compare BORN-AGAIN. **2** existing or active again; brought back to life: *Hope was reborn.*

rebound /rɪˈbaʊnd/ *v* **1** ~ (**from/off sth**) to bounce back after hitting sth: [Vpr] *The ball rebounded from/off the wall into the road.* [also V]. **2** ~ (**on sb**) to have an adverse effect on the person doing sth: [V, Vpr] *The scheme rebounded (on her) in a way she had not expected.*

▶ **rebound** /ˈriːbaʊnd/ *n* (*esp commerce*) a positive reaction occurring after sth negative: *a rebound in oil exports.* **IDM** **on the 'rebound** **1** while bouncing back: *hit a ball on the rebound.* **2** while still affected by a failed relationship with sb: *She quarrelled with Paul and then married Peter on the rebound.*

rebuff /rɪˈbʌf/ *n* an unkind refusal or rejection of an offer, a request or a friendly gesture: *Her kindness to him was met with a cruel rebuff.*

▶ **rebuff** *v* [Vn] to give a rebuff to sb.

rebuild /ˌriːˈbɪld/ *v* (*pt, pp* **rebuilt** /ˌriːˈbɪlt/) **1** to build or put sth together again: [Vn] *rebuild the city after the earthquake* ○ *We rebuilt the engine* (ie took it to pieces and put it together again) *using some new parts.* **2** to form sth again; to restore sth: [Vn] *rebuild sb's confidence/hopes/health* ○ *After the divorce, he had to rebuild his life completely.*

rebuke /rɪˈbjuːk/ *v* ~ **sb** (**for sth/doing sth**) (*fml*) to express sharp or strong disapproval to sb, esp officially: [Vnpr] *He was publicly rebuked by the committee for ignoring club rules.* [also Vn]. ▶ **rebuke** *n*: *administer a stern rebuke (to sb).*

rebut /rɪˈbʌt/ *v* (**-tt-**) [Vn] (*fml*) to say or prove that a

charge, a piece of evidence, etc is false. ▶ **rebuttal** /-tl/ *n* [C, U] (*fml*): *deliver a firm rebuttal of the accusations* ○ *The allegations met with immediate rebuttal.*

recalcitrant /rɪˈkælsɪtrənt/ *adj* (*fml*) resisting authority or discipline: *a recalcitrant child/attitude.* ▶ **recalcitrance** /-əns/ *n* [U].

recall /rɪˈkɔːl/ *v* **1** to bring sth/sb back into the mind; to remember sth: [Vn] *I can't recall his name.* [V.speech] *'This road used to be much narrower,' she recalled.* [V] *If I recall correctly, I left the keys on the shelf.* [V.*that*] *She recalled that he had left early that day.* [V.*wh*] *Try to recall exactly what happened.* [V.*ing*] *I recall seeing him there.* [V.n *ing*] *I recall her giving me the key.* **2(a)** ~ **sb** (**from...**) (**to...**) to order sb to return from a place: [Vn, Vnpr] *recall an ambassador (from his post)* [Vn] *recall (Members of) Parliament* (eg for a special debate). (**b**) to order sth to be returned: [Vn] *recall library books.*

▶ **recall** /rɪˈkɔːl, ˈriːkɔːl/ *n* **1** [sing] an order to sb/ sth to return: *his surprise recall to the Welsh team* ○ *the temporary recall of embassy staff.* **2** [U] the ability to remember: *a person gifted with total recall* (ie able to remember every detail) ○ *My powers of recall are not what they were.* **IDM** **beyond/past re'call** that cannot be brought back to the original state or cancelled: *Once the missiles are launched they are beyond recall.* ○ *Some pictures are damaged beyond recall.*

recant /rɪˈkænt/ *v* (*fml*) to withdraw or reject as false sth that one has previously said or believed: [Vn] *recant one's former opinions in public* [also V]. ▶ **recantation** /ˌriːkænˈteɪʃn/ *n* [U, C].

recap /ˈriːkæp/ *v* (**-pp-**) ~ (**on**) **sth** (*infml*) = RECAPITULATE [V, Vn] *Let me recap (the points we have agreed so far).* [also V.*wh*, Vpr]. ▶ **recap** *n* (*infml*) = RECAPITULATION.

recapitulate /ˌriːkəˈpɪtʃuleɪt/ (also *infml* **recap**) *v* to state again or give a summary of the main points of a discussion: [V.*wh*, Vpr] *Let me just recapitulate (on) what we've agreed so far.* [also V, Vn]. ▶ **recapitulation** /ˌriːkəpɪtʃuˈleɪʃn/ (also *infml* **recap**) *n* [C, U].

recapture /ˌriːˈkæptʃə(r)/ *v* **1** to capture again a person or an animal that has escaped, or sth previously taken by an enemy: [Vn] *recapture escaped prisoners* [Vnpr] *The town was recaptured from the enemy.* **2** to experience again or reproduce past emotions, etc: [Vn] *She tried to recapture the happiness of her youth.* ○ *recapture a period atmosphere* (eg in a play or film). ▶ **recapture** *n* [U]: *the recapture of towns occupied by the rebels.*

recast /ˌriːˈkɑːst; US -ˈkæst/ *v* (*pt, pp* **recast**) **1** ~ **sth** (**as sth**) to put sth, esp sth written or spoken, into a new form: [Vn] *recast a paragraph/chapter* ○ *the recasting of economic policy* [Vn-n] *She recast her lecture as a radio talk.* **2** to change the actors in a play, etc or the role of a particular actor: [Vn-n] *I've been recast as Brutus.* [also Vn].

recce /ˈreki/ *n* [C, U] (*Brit infml*) = RECONNAISSANCE: *make/do a quick recce of the area.*

recd *abbr* received: *recd $9.50.*

recede /rɪˈsiːd/ *v* **1** ~ (**from sth**) to move backwards from a previous position or away from an observer, or to appear to do this: [V, Vpr] *As the tide receded (from the shore) we were able to look for shells.* [Vpr] *We headed for the open sea and the coast receded into the distance.* [V] (*fig*) *The prospect of bankruptcy has now receded* (ie is less likely). **2** to slope backwards: *a receding chin* ○ *He has a receding hairline/He is receding* (ie His hair has stopped growing at the front of his head).

receipt /rɪˈsiːt/ *n* **1** [U] ~ (**of sth**) (*fml*) the action of receiving sth or of being received: *acknowledge receipt of a letter/an order* ○ *Your membership card* *will be despatched* **on receipt of** *the completed application form.* ○ *(fml) We are* **in receipt of** *your letter of the 15th.* **2** [C] ~ **(for sth)** a written or printed statement that goods have been paid for: *get a receipt for your expenses* ○ *sign a receipt.* **3 receipts** [pl] the money received by a business: *net/ gross receipts.*

receivable /rɪˈsiːvəbl/ *adj* (usu following *ns*) (*commerce*) (of bills, accounts, etc) for which money has not yet been received: *bills receivable.*
▸ **receivables** *n* [pl] (*commerce*) money that is owed to a business.

receive /rɪˈsiːv/ *v* **1(a)** ~ **sth (from sb/sth)** to get or accept sth that has been sent or given to one: [Vn] *receive a letter/present/phone call/grant* ○ *receive insults/thanks/congratulations.* **(b)** (*esp Brit*) to buy or accept stolen goods, knowing that they are stolen: [V] *get 4 years in prison for receiving* [also Vn]. **2** to experience sth: [Vn] *receive a good education* ○ *receive severe injuries/blows* [Vnpr] *We received a warm welcome from our hosts.* **3** ~ **sb (with sth)** (**as sth**) (*fml*) (*esp passive*) to welcome or entertain a guest, esp formally: [Vn] *The ambassador was received by the head of state.* [Vnpr] *She was received with warm applause.* [Vn-n] *He was received as a hero.* **4** ~ **sb (into sth)** to allow sb to enter, eg as a guest, member, etc; to admit sb: [Vnpr] *He has been received into the Church.* [also Vn]. **5** ~ **sb/sth (with sth)** (*esp passive*) to react to sb/sth in a specified way: [Vnpr] *My suggestion was received with disdain.* [Vnadv] *How was the play received?* ○ *The reforms have been well received by the public.* **6** to be given sb's careful thought; to have sb's attention: *He said the idea would receive serious consideration.* **7(a)** to convert broadcast signals into sounds or pictures: [Vnpr] *receive a programme via satellite* [also Vn]. **(b)** to be able to hear a radio message being sent by sb: [Vn] *Are you receiving me?* [Vn-adj] *I am receiving you loud and clear.* **IDM** **be at/on the re'ceiving end (of sth)** (*infml*) to be the one who suffers sth unpleasant: *The party in power soon learns what it's like to be on the receiving end of political satire.*
▸ **received** *adj* [attrib] widely accepted as correct, though not necessarily so: *received opinion/ pronunciation* ○ *change received ideas about education* ○ *The received wisdom is that it is impossible to produce good wine from this soil.*

receiver /rɪˈsiːvə(r)/ *n* **1** the part of a telephone that receives the sound of sb's voice and is held to the ear: *pick up/lift/put down/replace the receiver.* **2** a piece of radio or television equipment that converts broadcast signals into sound or pictures: *a satellite receiver.* **3(a)** a person who receives sth. **(b)** a person who buys or accepts stolen goods, knowing that they have been stolen. **4** (also **of,ficial re'ceiver**) (*law*) an official appointed by a court to handle the financial affairs of a company that is BANKRUPT(1): *call in the receiver* ○ *put the business in the hands of a receiver.*
▸ **receivership** /-ʃɪp/ *n* [U, C] (*law*) the state of being under the control of a receiver(4): **go into/be in receivership.**

recent /ˈriːsnt/ *adj* [usu attrib] that existed, happened, began, was done, etc not long ago or not long before: *a recent event/development/occurrence* ○ *his most recent visit to Poland* ○ *There have been many changes* **in recent years.** ○ *She was keen to forget her recent failure.*
▸ **recently** *adv* not long ago or not long before; in recent times: *He has recently been made a director.* ○ *She hasn't been feeling well recently.* ○ *Until recently they were living in Edinburgh.* ○ *More recently, his name was linked with that of a local councillor.*

NOTE Recently, **not long ago** and **lately** show that an action happened in the recent past. **Recently** has the widest use, in postitive and negative statements and questions, with the past and perfect tenses: *Did she have a party recently?* ○ *They've recently bought a car.* **Not long ago** is only used in positive statements with the past tenses: *They moved house not long ago.* ○ *Not long ago, we went to Amsterdam for the weekend.* **Lately** is used with the perfect tense, especially for questions and negative statements: *Have you been to the movies lately?* ○ *I haven't seen Jane lately.* ○ *He's only lately/recently started working here.* ○ *There have been so many natural disasters lately/recently.*

receptacle /rɪˈseptəkl/ *n* ~ **(for sth)** (*fml*) a container in which sth is placed or stored: (*fig*) *The seas have been used as a receptacle for a range of industrial toxins.*

reception /rɪˈsepʃn/ *n* **1** [U] the action of receiving sb/sth or of being received: *her reception into the religious order* ○ *a reception area/camp/centre* (ie where refugees (REFUGEE), etc are received and given temporary accommodation). **2** [sing] the way in which a person or group of people reacts to sth: *The play was given an enthusiastic reception by the critics.* **3** [U] the area in a hotel or an office building where guests, visitors or clients are welcomed, registered, etc: *the reception desk* ○ *Wait for me* **at/in reception.** **4** [C] a formal social occasion to welcome sb or celebrate sth: *official receptions for the foreign visitors* ○ *hold a wedding reception.* **5** [U] the quality and efficiency of receiving broadcast signals: *Reception of the BBC World Service is poor here.*
▸ **receptionist** /-ʃənɪst/ *n* a person employed to make appointments and receive clients or visitors in a hotel, an office building, a doctor's SURGERY(2a), etc.
■ **re'ception room** *n* (used esp when advertising houses for sale) a living-room (LIVING²).

receptive /rɪˈseptɪv/ *adj* ~ **(to sth)** able or willing to consider or accept new ideas, suggestions, etc: *a receptive person/mind/attitude/audience* ○ *be very receptive to new developments.* ▸ **receptiveness**, **receptivity** /ˌriːsepˈtɪvəti/ *ns* [U].

recess /rɪˈses, ˈriːses/ *n* **1** [C, U] **(a)** a period of time when the work of a parliament, a committee, the lawcourts, etc is stopped: *break for the summer recess* ○ *Parliament/Congress is* **in recess.** **(b)** (*US*) a break between classes at school. ⇨ note at BREAK². **2** [C] a space in a room where part of a wall is set back from the main part; an ALCOVE: *put a bookcase in the recess.* **3** [C] a hollow space inside sth: *a drawer with a secret recess.* **4** [C usu *pl*] (*esp rhet*) a remote or secret place: *the dark recesses of a cave* ○ (*fig*) *in the innermost recesses of one's mind.*
▸ **recess** *v* (*US*) to take or order sth to take a recess(1a): [V] *The Commission recessed.* [Vn] *The hearing was recessed.* **recessed** *adj* placed in a recess(2); set back: *recessed shelves/lighting.*

recession /rɪˈseʃn/ *n* **1** [C, U] a period of economic DECLINE² in a country, with reduced trade and industrial activity and many people unemployed: *The recession has had an enormous impact on tourism.* ○ *The whole country is* **in recession.** See also DEPRESSION 2. **2** [U] a movement back from a previous position: *the gradual recession of the flood water.*
▸ **recessionary** *adj* [attrib] **(a)** of economic DECLINE²: *in the present recessionary period/conditions/ times.* **(b)** likely to result in a period of economic DECLINE²: *recessionary policies.*

recessive /rɪˈsesɪv/ *adj* (*biology*) (of characteristics inherited from a parent, such as the colour of the eyes or of the hair) not appearing in a child but remaining hidden because of the presence of stronger, more dominant characteristics.

recharge /ˌriːˈtʃɑːdʒ/ *v* to fill sth again, esp a battery with electrical power: [Vn] (*rhet*) *Please recharge your glasses and drink to the bride and* *groom!* **IDM** **recharge one's 'batteries** (*infml*) to regain one's strength and energy by resting and relaxing for a time. ▸ **rechargeable** *adj*: *rechargeable batteries.*

recherché /rə'ʃeəʃeɪ/ *adj* (*fml usu derog*) too unusual or OBSCURE(1) to be easily understood.

recidivist /rɪ'sɪdɪvɪst/ *n* (*fml*) a person who commits crimes repeatedly and is unable to stop even after being punished. ▸ **recidivism** /-ɪzəm/ *n* [U].

recipe /'resəpi/ *n* **1** ~ (**for sth**) a set of instructions for preparing a food dish, including a list of ingredients required: *recipe books/cards* ○ *Please can I have the recipe for this — it's delicious.* **2** ~ **for sth** a method of achieving sth: *What is his recipe for success?* ○ *His plans are **a recipe for** (ie are likely to lead to) **disaster**.*

recipient /rɪ'sɪpiənt/ *n* ~ (**of sth**) (*fml*) a person who receives sth: *recipients of awards.*

reciprocal /rɪ'sɪprəkl/ *adj* given and received in return; mutual: *reciprocal trade deals* ○ *a reciprocal relationship between teachers and students.* ▸ **reciprocally** /-kli/ *adv.*

reciprocate /rɪ'sɪprəkeɪt/ *v* **1** (*fml*) (**a**) to give and receive sth in return; to make a mutual exchange of sth: [Vn] *reciprocate greetings/compliments/gifts.* (**b**) to return a feeling, gesture, greeting, etc: [V] *He reciprocated by wishing her good luck.* [Vn] *His smile was not reciprocated.* **2** (*techn*) (of parts of a machine) to move backwards and forwards in a straight line: [V] *reciprocating pistons.* ▸ **reciprocation** /rɪˌsɪprə'keɪʃn/ *n* [U].

reciprocity /ˌresɪ'prɒsəti/ *n* [U] (*fml*) the principle or practice of mutual exchange, esp of giving advantages or privileges in return for advantages or privileges received: *reciprocity of rights and obligations* ○ *reciprocity in trade (between countries).*

recital /rɪ'saɪtl/ *n* **1** [C] a public performance of music or poetry by a single performer or a small group: *give a piano recital* ○ *a Chopin recital.* Compare CONCERT. **2** [C] a detailed account of a series of events, problems, etc: *I had to listen to a long recital of all his misfortunes.*

recitation /ˌresɪ'teɪʃn/ *n* **1** [C, U] the speaking in public of a piece of literature that one has learnt: *give recitations from Dickens* ○ *his dream-like recitation of the ballad.* **2** [C] an act of saying a series of things aloud: *She continued her rapid recitation of the week's events.*

recitative /ˌresɪtə'tiːv/ *n* [C, U] (*music*) a part of an opera or ORATORIO sung in the rhythm of ordinary speech with many words on the same note.

recite /rɪ'saɪt/ *v* **1** ~ (**sth**) (**to sb**) to say a piece of literature aloud from memory, esp to an audience: [Vnpr] *recite a speech from 'Hamlet' to the class* [also V, Vpr, Vn]. **2** ~ **sth** (**to sb**) to state names, facts, etc one by one; to give a list of sth: [Vn] *recite the names of all the European capitals* [Vnpr] *They recited all their grievances to me.*

reckless /'rekləs/ *adj* ~ (**of sth**) (of people or their actions) without thinking or caring about the consequences or the danger involved: *cause death by reckless driving* ○ *make a reckless decision* ○ *He showed **a reckless disregard** for his own safety.* ▸ **recklessly** *adv.* **recklessness** *n* [U].

reckon /'rekən/ *v* **1** (not used in the continuous tenses; esp passive) to consider that sb/sth is as specified: [Vnpr] *She is reckoned among our best reporters.* [V.that] (*infml*) *I reckon (that) he's too old for the job.* [Vn-n, Vn.to inf] *She is reckoned (to be) the cleverest pupil in the class.* **2(a)** (*infml*) (no passive) to think or assume; to consider: [V.that] *I reckon (that) it'll be ready by Friday.* ○ *The news won't worry her, I reckon.* ○ *What do you reckon our chances are of arriving on time?* (**b**) to expect: [V.to inf] *We reckon to finish by midday.* **3** to calculate sth: [Vn] *reckon the total volume of imports* ○ *Hire charges are reckoned from the date of delivery.*

[V.that] *I reckon it will cost about £100.* **PHRV** **'reckon on (doing) sth** to rely on sth or on sth happening: *We're reckoning on moving house in May.* ○ *You can't always reckon on (having) good weather.* **ˌreckon sth 'up** to find the sum or total of sth: *reckon up bills/accounts/costs.* **'reckon with sb/sth** **1** to take sb/sth into account; to consider the possibility of sth: *I didn't reckon with getting caught up in so much traffic.* **2** to face sb/sth; to have to deal with sb/sth: *They had many difficulties to reckon with.* **3** (esp passive) to consider sb/sth important; to take sb/sth seriously: *Her next opponent is **a force to be reckoned with**.* ○ *He's a person to reckon with.* **'reckon without sb/sth** to fail to take sb/sth into account; to fail to consider the possibility of sth: *We wanted a quiet holiday, but we had reckoned without (the noise from) the other guests.*

reckoning /'rekənɪŋ/ *n* [U] the action of calculating or estimating sth: *the reckoning of debts/accounts* ○ *By my reckoning, you still owe me £5.* **IDM** **a day of reckoning** ⇨ DAY. **in / into / out of the 'reckoning** (*esp Brit*) (esp in sport) among/not among the possible winners; among/not among those likely to be successful: *They played badly all season and were never in the reckoning for the championship.*

reclaim /rɪ'kleɪm/ *v* **1** ~ **sth** (**from sb/sth**) to seek to get sth back after having given it to sb, lost it, etc: [Vn] *reclaim tax/lost property* ○ *efforts to reclaim territory lost in the war.* [also Vnpr]. **2** ~ **sth** (**from sth**) to make land fit to cultivate, eg by draining it or bringing water to it: [Vn] *reclaimed marshland/ desert* [Vnpr] *reclaim an area from the sea.* **3** ~ **sth** (**from sth**) to recover raw material from waste products so that it can be used again: [Vn, Vnpr] *reclaim glass (from old bottles).* See also RECYCLE. ▸ **reclaim** *n* (usu *sing*) a place where one collects one's cases, etc after travelling on an aircraft: *waiting at the baggage reclaim.* **reclamation** /ˌreklə'meɪʃn/ *n* [U]: *land reclamation* ○ *the reclamation of scrap material.*

recline /rɪ'klaɪn/ *v* **1** to lean or lie back in a flat or nearly flat position: [Vpr] *recline on a sofa/a grassy bank* [V] *a reclining figure* (eg in a painting) ○ *a reclining chair/seat* (ie one with a back that can be moved from an upright into a sloping position). **2** [Vn] to move the back of a seat into a sloping position.

recluse /rɪ'kluːs/ *n* a person who lives alone and likes to avoid other people: *live/lead the life of a (virtual) recluse.*

recognition /ˌrekəg'nɪʃn/ *n* [U] the action of recognizing sb/sth or of being recognized: *He stared at her without recognition.* ○ (*fml*) *The USA has announced its recognition of the new regime.* ○ *an award **in recognition of** one's services/achievements* ○ *He has won wide/international recognition in the field of tropical medicine.* **IDM** **beyond / out of (all) recog'nition** so much that recognition is very difficult: *The town has changed beyond all recognition since I was last here.*

recognize, -ise /'rekəgnaɪz/ *v* (not used in the continuous tenses) **1** ~ **sb/sth** (**by/from sth**) to be able to identify again sb/sth that one has seen, heard, etc before; to know sb/sth again: [Vn] *recognize a tune/an old friend* [Vnpr] *I recognized her by her red hair/from the photograph you showed me.* **2** to admit or be aware that sth exists or is true; to acknowledge sth: [Vn, V.that] *They failed to recognize the problem/that there was a problem.* [Vnn, Vn.to inf] *Smoking is generally recognized as/ recognized to be one of the major causes of heart disease.* **3** ~ **sb/sth** (**as sth**) to accept sth as officially valid or genuine; to approve of sth officially: [Vn] *recognized schools/qualifications* ○ *recognize sb's claim to ownership* ○ (*fml*) *Britain has refused to recognize the new regime.* [Vn.to inf, Vn-n]

He was recognized to be the lawful heir/recognized as the lawful heir. **4** to show official appreciation for sb's ability or achievements, eg by giving them an award: [Vn] *The Queen recognized his services to the state by awarding him a knighthood.*

▶ **recognizable**, **-isable** /ˈrekəgnaɪzəbl, ˌrekəgˈnaɪzəbl/ *adj* that can be recognized (RECOGNIZE 1): *She was barely recognizable as the girl I had known at school.* **recognizably**, **-isably** /-əbli/ *adv*: *a recognizably similar style.*

recoil /rɪˈkɔɪl/ *v* **1** ~ (from sb/sth); ~ (at sth) **(a)** to move one's body quickly away from sb/sth with a feeling of fear, disgust, etc: [Vpr] *He recoiled in horror at the sight of the corpse.* ○ *She recoiled from his embrace.* [also V]. **(b)** to react to sth with a feeling of fear, disgust, etc: [Vpr] *He recoiled from the idea of killing another man.* [also V]. **2** [V] (of guns) to move suddenly backwards when fired. **PHR V** **recoil on sb** (*fml*) (of a harmful action) to have a bad effect on the person who did it.

▶ **recoil** /ˈriːkɔɪl/ *n* [U, sing] a sudden backward movement, esp of a gun when fired.

recollect /ˌrekəˈlekt/ *v* (not used in the continuous tenses; usu not passive) (*rather fml*) to be able to remember sth from the past: [V] *As far as I recollect, you came late.* [Vn] *recollect one's childhood/sb's name* [V.that] *I recollect that you denied it.* [V.wh] *Can you recollect how it was done?* [V.ing] *She can recollect meeting the king.* [V.n ing] *No one can recollect her leaving.* [also V.speech].

recollection /ˌrekəˈlekʃn/ *n* (*rather fml*) **(a)** [U] the ability to RECOLLECT or the action of recollecting sth; memory: *I have no recollection of meeting her before.* ○ **To the best of my recollection** (ie If I remember correctly), *I was not present at that meeting.* ○ *My recollection of events differs from hers.* **(b)** [C often *pl*] a thing, event, etc that is remembered: *vivid/clear/vague recollections of her youth* ○ *One of my earliest recollections is a visit to London Zoo when I was three or four.*

recommence /ˌriːkəˈmens/ *v* (*fml*) to start again or start doing sth again: [V] *The meeting will recommence at 2.* [Vn] *recommence work.*

recommend /ˌrekəˈmend/ *v* **1** ~ sb/sth (to sb) (for sth / as sth) to praise sb/sth and say that they are suitable for a purpose; to speak favourably of sb/sth: [Vn, Vnpr] *recommend a good restaurant/book/ plumber (to sb)* [Vnpr] *The hotel is highly recommended for its excellent facilities.* ○ *What would you recommend for removing ink stains?* ○ *She was strongly recommended for the post by a colleague.* [Vn-n] *I can recommend him as an extremely good hairdresser.* **2** to suggest a course of action; to advise sth: [Vn] *My doctor has recommended a long period of rest.* [V.that] *I'd recommend (that) you see a solicitor.* [V.ing, V.n ing] *I recommended (your) meeting him first.* [V.n to inf] *We recommend you to book early to avoid disappointment.* [also V.wh]. **3** ~ sb/ sth (to sb) (of a quality, etc) to make sb/sth attractive: [Vn] *a plan with nothing/little/much to recommend it* [also Vnpr].

▶ **recommendation** /ˌrekəmenˈdeɪʃn/ *n* **1** [U] the action of recommending sb/sth: *I stayed there on your recommendation* (ie because you recommended it) *and I loved it!* **2** [C] **(a)** a statement, letter, etc that recommends sb/sth, esp a person for a job: *write/give sb a (letter of) recommendation* ○ *My previous employer's personal recommendation got me my new job.* **(b)** a course of action, etc that is recommended: *The judge made certain recommendations to the court.* ○ *There has been a recommendation from union leaders that the offer of 5% be rejected.* **3** [C usu *sing*] a quality, etc that makes sb/sth attractive: *The food here isn't particularly good but its one recommendation is that it's cheap.*

recompense /ˈrekəmpens/ *v* ~ sb (for sth) (*fml*) to give sb a reward for sth they have done or compensate sb for loss, harm, etc, usu with money: [Vnpr] *recompense employees for working overtime* ○ *recompense her for the loss of her job* [also Vn].

▶ **recompense** *n* [sing, U] ~ (for sth) (*fml*) a thing, usu money, that is given as a reward for sth or compensates sb: *receive adequate recompense for one's services/efforts* ○ *The victim was awarded $10 000 as recompense for loss of income after the accident.*

reconcile /ˈrekənsaɪl/ *v* **1** ~ sth (with sth) to find a way to make two or more ideas, situations, etc agree with each other when actually they seem to be in opposition: [Vn] *reconcile different political views* [Vnpr] *reconcile the evidence with the facts* ○ *She finds it difficult to reconcile her career ambitions with the need to bring up her children.* **2(a)** (esp passive) ~ sb (with sb) to make people become friends again, eg after quarrelling: [Vn] *We were reconciled when he apologized.* [Vnpr] *After years of not speaking to each other, she was finally reconciled with her father.* **(b)** to reach agreement on sth that causes disagreement; to settle sth: [Vn] *They are unable to reconcile their differences.* **3** ~ sb/oneself to sth to accept or make sb accept an unpleasant situation because there is nothing one can do to change it: [Vnpr] *It took a long time to reconcile them to the fact that their father would not come back.* ○ *He cannot reconcile himself to a lifetime of unemployment.*

▶ **reconcilable** /-əbl, ˌrekənˈsaɪləbl/ *adj*.

reconciliation /ˌrekənsɪliˈeɪʃn/ *n* **1** [U] ~ (between A and B); ~ (with sth) the process of making two or more ideas, situations, etc agree with each other when actually they seem to be in opposition: *the reconciliation of attitudes/opinions.* **2** [sing] ~ (between A and B); ~ (with sth) an end to a disagreement: *bring about a reconciliation between the two sides.*

recondite /ˈrekəndaɪt/ *adj* (*fml*) (of subjects, ideas, etc) not known about or understood by many people.

recondition /ˌriːkənˈdɪʃn/ *v* (esp passive) to repair sth so that it is in good condition again: [Vn] *a reconditioned engine/cooker* ○ *It's not a new typewriter — it's been reconditioned.*

reconnaissance /rɪˈkɒnɪsns; US ˈkɒnəzəns/ (also *Brit infml* **recce**) *n* [C, U] a survey of an area, esp for military purposes: *make an aerial reconnaissance of the island* ○ *troops engaged in reconnaissance* ○ *a reconnaissance flight/satellite/mission.*

reconnoitre (US **-ter**) /ˌrekəˈnɔɪtə(r)/ *v* to make a survey of an area, esp for military purposes: [Vn] *The platoon was sent to reconnoitre the village before the attack.* [also V].

reconsider /ˌriːkənˈsɪdə(r)/ *v* to think about sth again, esp because there is doubt about a previous opinion, decision, etc: [Vn] *reconsider one's decision/ position* ○ *The company was forced to reconsider its plans to expand the business.* [V] *I strongly urge you to reconsider.* [also V.wh]. ▶ **reconsideration** /ˌriːkənsɪdəˈreɪʃn/ *n* [U].

reconstitute /ˌriːˈkɒnstɪtjuːt; US -tuːt/ *v* (esp passive) **1** (*fml*) to change the form or organization of an official group: [Vn] *a reconstituted board/panel/ committee.* **2** to change dried food back to its original state by adding water: [Vn] *reconstitute dried milk/powdered soup.* ▶ **reconstitution** /ˌriːˌkɒnstɪˈtjuːʃn; US -ˈtuːʃn/ *n* [U].

reconstruct /ˌriːkənˈstrʌkt/ *v* **1** to construct or build again sth that has been damaged or destroyed: [Vn] *The cathedral was reconstructed after the fire.* **2** ~ sth (from sth) to create a full description of sth that has existed or happened by using the facts that are known: [Vn, Vnpr] *Police are trying to reconstruct the victim's last movements (from eyewitness reports).* ○ *The film is an attempt to reconstruct everyday life during the war.*

▶ **reconstruction** /ˌ-'strʌkʃn/ n **1(a)** [U] the action or process of reconstructing sth or of being reconstructed: *the postwar reconstruction of Germany* ○ *plans for the reconstruction of the city centre.* **(b)** [C] a copy of sth that no longer exists: *The chapel is a reconstruction of one that originally stood on this site.* **2** [C] an attempt to create a full description of sth that has happened by using the facts that are known: *a reconstruction by detectives of the events leading up to a murder* (eg by using actors at the place where it was committed).

record¹ /'rekɔːd; *US* 'rekərd/ n **1** [C] ~ **(of sth)** a permanent account, esp in a document or on computer, of facts, events, etc: *records of births, marriages and deaths* ○ *public/medical records* ○ *keep a record of one's expenses.* **2** [sing] ~ **(for sth)** the facts, events, etc known, but not always written down, about the past of sb/sth: *He had a distinguished war record* (eg He won medals (MEDAL), etc for his conduct). ○ *She has a criminal record* (ie has previously been found guilty of committing a crime or crimes). ○ *The airline has an impressive safety record.* ○ *The school has a poor record for exam passes.* See also TRACK RECORD. **3** [C] (also **disc**, dated '**gramophone record**) a thin circular piece of plastic on which sound, esp music, has been recorded: *a pop/jazz/hit record* ○ *a record collection/sleeve* ○ *put on/play a record* ○ *a record company* (ie one which produces and sells records). **4** [C] the best performance or the highest or lowest level ever reached, esp in sport: *beat/break* (ie do better than) *a record* ○ *an Olympic/world/all-time record* ○ *She holds the world record for the 100 metres.* ○ *a record score/time* ○ *record profits/sales* ○ *Unemployment last month reached a record high* (ie its highest ever level). **IDM** **(just) for the 'record** (used for showing that one wants a statement to be officially noted and remembered, esp in order to correct sth previously stated): *Just for the record, I would like to clarify something my colleague said earlier.* **a matter of record** ⇨ MATTER¹. **,off the 'record** (of statements) not for publication; not to be treated as official: *The vice-president admitted, (strictly) off the record, that the talks had failed.* **on 'record** (of facts, events, etc) noted or recorded, esp officially: *Last summer was the wettest on record.* **on (the) 'record** (of statements) publicly known and noted, published or broadcast: *be/go on (the) record as saying that the law should be changed* ○ *put one's views/objections on (the) record.* **put/set the 'record straight** to give a correct version of facts, events, etc that have previously been wrongly stated or described: *To put the record straight, I do not support that idea and never have done.*

■ '**record-breaker** n a person or thing that breaks a record¹(4). '**record-breaking** adj [attrib]: *a record-breaking jump/time/victory.*

'**record-holder** n a person holding a sports record¹(4).

'**record-player** n (*becoming dated*) (also *dated* **gramophone**) a machine for reproducing sound from records (RECORD¹ 3).

record² /rɪ'kɔːd/ v **1** to write down or put into a computer or onto film facts or events so that they can be remembered or referred to in the future: [Vn] *Their childhood is recorded in diaries and photographs of those years.* ○ *record the minutes/proceedings of a meeting* [V.*wh*] *Historians record how Rome fell.* [also V.*that*]. **2** to say or do sth publicly that is noted, written down or remembered: [Vn] *record one's opinions in a meeting* ○ *At the inquest, the coroner recorded a verdict of accidental death.* ○ *Manchester United have recorded their sixth win of the season.* **3(a)** ~ **(sth)** **(from sth)** **(on sth)** to preserve sound or pictures on tape or film so that they can be listened to or watched again later: [V]

To record, press both buttons. [Vpr, Vnpr] *record (a programme) from the radio/television* [Vnpr] *record an interview on video* [Vn] *a recorded programme/concert* [Vn.*ing*] *record sb playing the piano.* **(b)** to perform music so that it can be preserved on tape and reproduced later: [Vn] *The band is currently in the studio recording their new album.* [also V]. **4** (of measuring instruments) to show sth; to register sth: [Vn] *The thermometer recorded a temperature of 40°C.*

■ **re,corded de'livery** n [U] (*Brit*) a method of sending post in which the person who receives the letter or parcel must sign a form to confirm that it has been delivered: *send a letter (by) recorded delivery.*

recorder /rɪ'kɔːdə(r)/ n **1** a machine for recording (RECORD² 3) sound or pictures, or both: *a tape/cassette recorder* ○ *a 'video recorder.* See also FLIGHT-RECORDER. **2** a wooden or plastic musical instrument consisting of a single tube into which one blows while covering a series of holes with one's fingers. Recorders are often played by children. ⇨ picture at MUSICAL INSTRUMENT. **3** (*Brit*) a judge in certain lawcourts.

recording /rɪ'kɔːdɪŋ/ n **(a)** [C] sound or pictures that have been preserved on tape, film or record¹(3): *make a video recording of a wedding* ○ *a live/studio recording* ○ *a good recording of the opera on tape/video.* **(b)** [U] the process of preserving sound or pictures on tape, etc: *during the recording of the show* ○ *recording equipment* ○ *a recording studio/session/artist.*

recount /rɪ'kaʊnt/ v ~ sth **(to sb)** to give a detailed account of sth; to tell sb about sth: [Vn, Vnpr] *recount one's story/adventures/experiences (to a friend)* [V.*wh*, Vpr.*wh*] *He recounted (to her) in vivid detail how he had caught the thief.* [also V.speech].

re-count /ˌriː 'kaʊnt/ v [Vn] to count sth, esp votes, again. ▶ **re-count** /'riː kaʊnt/ n: *The unsuccessful candidate demanded a re-count of the votes.*

recoup /rɪ'kuːp/ v to get back money that one has spent or lost: [Vn] *We hope to recoup our initial investment in the first year.* ○ *The dollar recouped early losses on Wall Street today.*

recourse /rɪ'kɔːs/ n [U] (*fml*) a source of help in a difficult situation, or the use of this: *Your only recourse is legal action.* ○ *They managed to solve the dispute without recourse to a court of law.* **IDM** **have recourse to sb/sth** (*fml*) to use sb/sth as a source of help in a difficult situation: *I hope the doctors won't have recourse to surgery.*

recover /rɪ'kʌvə(r)/ v **1** ~ **(from sb/sth)** to return to a normal state of health, mind, strength, etc: [Vpr] *He's now fully recovered from his illness.* ○ *recover from the shock/surprise of seeing sb* [V] *After a period of decline, the economy is beginning to recover.* **2(a)** to get back one's health, the use of one's senses, etc: [Vn] *recover one's sight/hearing* ○ *recover consciousness* ○ *I'm slowly recovering my strength after the operation.* **(b)** to get back control of oneself, one's actions or one's emotions: [Vn] *The skater quickly recovered his balance.* ○ *She recovered herself/her composure and smiled.* **3** ~ sth **(from sb/sth)** to regain possession of sth or get back sth stolen or lost: [Vn] *recover stolen goods/lost property* [Vnpr] *Six bodies were recovered from the wreckage.* **4** ~ sth **(from sb/sth)** to regain money, time, etc that one has spent or lost: [Vnpr] *recover damages/costs/expenses from sb* [Vn] *The team recovered its lead in the second half.*

▶ **recoverable** /ˌ-rəbl/ adj **1** that can be regained after having been spent or lost: *recoverable deposits/losses/assets.* **2** that can be obtained from the ground: *recoverable oil reserves.*

re-cover /ˌriː 'kʌvə(r)/ v ~ sth **(in/with sth)** to put a

[V.speech] = verb + direct speech   [V.*that*] = verb + *that* clause   [V.*wh*] = verb + *who*, *how*, etc clause

recovery /rɪˈkʌvəri/ n **1** [U,C usu *sing*] ~ **(from/in sth)** a return to a normal state of health, mind, strength, etc: *make a quick/speedy/good/slow recovery (from illness)* ○ *She is on the road to* (ie making progress towards) *recovery.* ○ *a recovery in consumer spending* ○ *The team staged a dramatic recovery in the second half.* **2** [U] ~ **(of sth/sb)** the action or process of regaining possession or use of sth: *the recovery of the missing diamonds* ○ *a reˈcovery vehicle* (ie one for taking a vehicle that cannot be driven to a place for repair) ○ *It is hoped that the operation will bring about the recovery of his sight.* **3** [U] (also reˈcovery room [C]) the room in a hospital where patients are kept immediately after an operation: *The patient is in recovery.*

re-create /ˌriː kriˈeɪt/ v to create the atmosphere, style, etc of sth that existed in the past: [Vn] *The film successfully re-creates the glamour of 1940s Hollywood.* ▶ **re-creation** /-ˈeɪʃn/ n [U, C].

recreation /ˌrekriˈeɪʃn/ n [C, U] an activity done for enjoyment when one is not working: *walk and climb mountains for recreation* ○ *funds for leisure and recreation* ○ *Among her recreations are chess and gardening.*
▶ **recreational** /-ʃənl/ adj of or for recreation: *recreational activities/facilities.*
■ **recreˈation ground** n an area of land used by the public for sports or games.
recreˈation room n **1** a room in a school, a hospital, an office block, etc in which people can relax, play games, etc: *the nurses' recreation room.* **2** (US) a room in a private house used for games, entertainment, etc.

recrimination /rɪˌkrɪmɪˈneɪʃn/ n [C usu *pl*, U] an accusation in response to an accusation from sb else: *bitter/angry/furious recriminations* ○ *Let's not indulge in mutual recrimination.* ▶ **recriminatory** /rɪˈkrɪmɪnətri; US -tɔːri/ adj: *recriminatory remarks.*

recrudescence /ˌriːkruːˈdesns/ n [U] (*fml*) the appearance again of sth unpleasant or undesirable: *prevent the recrudescence of civil disorder.*

recruit /rɪˈkruːt/ n **1** a person who has recently joined the armed forces or police and is not yet trained: *new/recent/raw* (ie not experienced) *recruits* ○ *drilling recruits on the parade ground.* **2** ~ **(to sth)** a person who has recently joined or may join an organization, a company, a club, etc: *advertise for recruits to voluntary work from among the young unemployed.*
▶ **recruit** v **1** ~ **(sb) (to sth);** ~ **sb (as sth)** to find new people to join a company, an organization, etc: [V, Vn] *recruit (staff) on a regular basis* ○ *a recruiting officer/poster/drive* [Vn, Vnpr] *recruit new members (to the club)* [Vn-n] *recruit sb as a spy.* **2** to persuade sb to do or assist in doing sth: [Vn.*to* inf] *We recruited some friends to help us move house.* **3** to form an army, a party, etc by gaining supporters: [Vn] *recruit a task force.* **recruiter** n. **recruitment** n [U]: *the recruitment of workers/teachers/new party members* ○ *a company's recruitment drive/policy/problems* ○ *a recruitment agency.*

rectal /ˈrektəl/ adj (anatomy) of the RECTUM: *a rectal thermometer.*

rectangle /ˈrektæŋgl/ n (geometry) a flat shape with four straight sides and four angles of 90°. ⇨ picture at QUADRILATERAL.
▶ **rectangular** /rekˈtæŋgjələ(r)/ adj having the shape of a rectangle.

rectify /ˈrektɪfaɪ/ v (pt, pp **-fied**) to put sth right; to correct sth: [Vn] *rectify an error/omission* ○ *Steps should be taken to rectify the situation.* ▶ **rectification** /ˌrektɪfɪˈkeɪʃn/ n [U].

rectilinear /ˌrektɪˈlɪniə(r)/ adj **1** in a straight line:

rectilinear motion. **2** having straight lines: *a rectilinear figure.*

rectitude /ˈrektɪtjuːd; US -tuːd/ n [U] (*fml*) morally correct behaviour and attitudes; honesty: *a person of exemplary moral rectitude.*

recto /ˈrektəʊ/ n (pl **-os**) the page on the right side of an open book: *on the recto page.* Compare VERSO.

rector /ˈrektə(r)/ n **1(a)** (in the Church of England) a priest in charge of a PARISH(1) from which he or she receives income directly. Compare VICAR. **(b)** (in the Roman Catholic Church) a priest in charge of a church or a religious community. **2** (in Britain) the head of certain universities, colleges, schools or religious institutions.
▶ **rectory** /ˈrektəri/ n a rector's house.

rectum /ˈrektəm/ n (pl **rectums** or **recta**) (anatomy) the lower end of the large INTESTINE, through which solid waste passes out of the body at the ANUS. ⇨ picture at DIGESTIVE SYSTEM.

recumbent /rɪˈkʌmbənt/ adj [usu attrib] (*fml*) (esp of a person) lying down: *a recumbent figure* (eg in a painting or sculpture).

recuperate /rɪˈkjuːpəreɪt; -ˈkuː-/ v **1** ~ **(from sth)** (*fml*) to recover after being ill, tired, weak, etc; to regain health, energy or strength: [Vpr] *He is still recuperating from his operation.* [Vn] *recuperate one's strength after a hard climb* [also V]. **2** to get back money spent or lost: [Vn] *He hoped to recuperate at least part of his investment.*
▶ **recuperation** /rɪˌkjuːpəˈreɪʃn, -ˌkuː-/ n [U]: *have great powers of recuperation* ○ *recuperation of costs/expenses.*
recuperative /rɪˈkjuːpərətɪv, -ˈkuː-/ adj (*fml*) helping one to recuperate: *the recuperative effects of sea air.*

recur /rɪˈkɜː(r)/ v (**-rr-**) to happen again; to happen repeatedly: [V] *The symptoms tend to recur.* ○ *a recurring problem/error/illness* ○ *This theme recurs regularly throughout the opera.*
▶ **recurrence** /rɪˈkʌrəns/ n [U,C usu *sing*] the fact or process of sth happening again: *the recurrence of an illness/error/problem/theme* ○ *the need to prevent a recurrence of the situation.*
recurrent /-ənt/ adj [usu attrib] happening often or regularly: *recurrent attacks/fits/headaches* ○ *a recurrent problem/theme/nightmare.*
■ **reˌcurring ˈdecimal** n a decimal fraction in which the same figures are repeated without end, eg 3.999, 4.014014: *The recurring decimal 3.999… is also described as 3.9 recurring.*

recycle /ˌriːˈsaɪkl/ v **(a)** to treat things that have already been used so that they can be used again: [Vn] *recycle newspaper/packaging/tin cans* ○ *the recycling of plastics* ○ *a recycling plant/scheme.* **(b)** (esp passive) to obtain the material for new products from things that have been used, by treating them: [Vn] *ˌrecycled ˈglass* (eg from old bottles) ○ *envelopes made from recycled paper.* See also RECLAIM 3. ▶ **recyclable** /ˌriːˈsaɪkləbl/ adj: *recyclable materials/bags/plastic.*

NOTE When you **recycle** glass, paper, etc, you use it again, or it is collected so that it can be made into new glass, paper, etc: *The government wants everyone to recycle 25% of their household waste.* Glass or paper that is **recycled** is made from material that has been used before. If something is **recyclable**, it can be used again or collected so that it can be made into new material: *A lot of plastics are now recyclable.*

red¹ /red/ adj (**-dder, -ddest**) **1** of the colour of fresh blood or a similar colour: *a red dress/car* ○ *red lips* ○ *a red sky* ○ *Maple leaves turn red in the autumn.* ○ *red-painted doors* ○ *red-tiled roofs.* ⇨ picture at SPECTRUM. **2(a)** (of the eyes) surrounded by red skin: *Her eyes were red with weeping.* ○ *be red-eyed with* fatigue. (**b**) (of the face) bright red, eg because of anger or effort: *go/be red (in the face) with embarrassment* ○ *be red-faced and sweating.* See also BLOOD-RED. **3** (of hair or an animal's fur) of a reddish-brown colour: *a red-haired woman* ○ *red deer/squirrels.* **4** (*infml often derog*) having very left-wing (LEFT²) political opinions. Compare PINK¹ 2. **IDM** **paint the town red** ⇨ PAINT². **(as) red as a 'beet-root**, (*US*) **(as) red as a 'beet** having a very red face, esp because one is embarrassed: *He went as red as a beetroot when I asked about his new girlfriend.* **(like) a red rag to a 'bull** a thing that makes sb become very angry. ▶ **redness** *n* [U, sing]: *redness of the skin.*

■ **red a'lert** *n* [U, C] a situation in which emergency services are expecting and ready for an emergency to occur: *put the police/hospitals on red alert.*

red-'blooded *adj* [usu attrib] (*infml*) full of energy and strength; VIRILE: *red-blooded young males.*

red 'cabbage *n* [U, C] a type of CABBAGE(1) with red leaves.

red 'card *n* (in football, etc) a card shown by the REFEREE(1a) to a player who is being sent off the field. Compare YELLOW CARD.

red 'carpet (usu **the red carpet**) *n* (usu *sing*) a strip of red carpet laid on the ground for an important visitor to walk on when he or she arrives: *roll out the red carpet* ○ (*usu fig*) *give sb the red-carpet treatment.*

red 'cent *n* [sing] (*US*) (esp after a negative) a very small amount of money: *I didn't get a red cent for it.*

red 'corpuscle (also **red cell**) *n* a blood cell that carries oxygen to the body tissues and carbon dioxide (CARBON) away from them. Compare WHITE CORPUSCLE.

the Red 'Crescent *n* [sing] an organization in Muslim countries that works to relieve suffering caused by natural disasters, help victims of war, etc.

the Red 'Cross *n* [sing] an international organization that works to relieve suffering caused by natural disasters, help victims of war, etc: *Red Cross officials/doctors.*

red 'flag *n* **1** a flag used for warning of danger, eg on roads or railways. **2** a symbol of revolution or COMMUNISM(2).

red 'giant *n* a large star towards the end of its life that gives out a reddish light.

red-'handed *adj* **IDM** **catch sb red-handed** ⇨ CATCH¹.

red-'headed *adj* ⇨ REDHEAD.

red 'herring *n* a fact, an argument, an event, etc that leads people's attention away from the main point: *The plot is full of red herrings to distract the reader.*

red-'hot *adj* **1** (of metal or burning coal, etc) so hot that it glows red: *a red-hot poker.* **2** showing or causing great enthusiasm or strong feeling: *red-hot protest.* **3** (*infml*) (of news) completely new and exciting or shocking: *a red-hot story.*

Red 'Indian (also **redskin**) *n* (△ *dated offensive*) a Native American; an American Indian.

red-'letter day *n* an important day or a day that stays in the memory because of sth good that happened then.

red 'light *n* a signal telling the driver of a vehicle to stop: *go through a red light* (ie not stop at one).

red-'light district *n* a part of a town where there are many prostitutes.

red 'meat *n* [U] meat that has a dark colour when cooked, eg BEEF(1) or lamb. Compare WHITE MEAT.

red 'pepper *n* **1** [C] the ripe red fruit of the CAPSICUM plant. **2** [U] = CAYENNE.

red 'setter *n* = IRISH SETTER.

red 'tape *n* [U] (*derog*) complicated official rules and regulations, esp when these are considered unnecessary; excessive BUREAUCRACY(2): *It takes weeks* *to go through all the red tape involved in getting planning permission.*

red 'wine *n* [U, C] wine made from dark grapes (GRAPE). Compare ROSÉ, WHITE WINE.

red² /red/ *n* **1** [U, C] a red colour: *light/clear/deep/dark red* ○ *the reds and browns of the woods in autumn* (ie of the leaves, etc) ○ *There's too much red in the painting.* ○ *The traffic lights were on red.* **2** [U] red clothes: *be dressed in red.* **3** [U] red wine: *Would you prefer red or white?* **4** [C] (*infml often derog*) a person with very left-wing (LEFT²) political opinions: *a union infiltrated by reds.* **IDM** **the red** [U] (*infml*) a situation of owing money to a bank because one has spent more money than is in one's account: *be in/out of the red* ○ *go into/get out of the red* ○ *My bank account is £50 in the red.* **see red** (*infml*) to become very angry suddenly: *Her remarks really made me see red.*

redbreast /'redbrest/ *n* (*rhet*) a ROBIN.

redbrick /'redbrɪk/ *adj* **1** (of universities in Britain) founded relatively recently, in contrast with much older universities. Compare OXBRIDGE. **2** (of a building) made from bricks of a red-brown colour: *an ugly redbrick chapel/house.*

redcoat /'redkəʊt/ *n* (formerly) a British soldier.

redcurrant /,red'kʌrənt/ *n* a small round red edible berry: *redcurrant 'jelly.*

redden /'redn/ *v* **1** to become or make sth become red: [V] *The smoke made her eyes redden.* [Vn] *redden one's lips with lipstick.* **2** (of a person or the face) to become pinker than usual because of embarrassment, anger, effort, etc; to BLUSH(1): [V] *She stared at him and he reddened.* [Vpr] *He reddened at the mention of her name.*

reddish /'redɪʃ/ *adj* fairly red: *reddish fur/hair.*

redecorate /,riː'dekəreɪt/ *v* to decorate a room, etc again, esp to put new paint or WALLPAPER on walls: [V] *We'll have to redecorate when we move in.* [Vn] *redecorate a house/the living-room/an office.* ▶ **redecoration** *n* [U].

redeem /rɪ'diːm/ *v* **1(a)** to do sth or have a quality that compensates for the faults or bad aspects of sth: [Vn] *The acting was not good enough to redeem the awfulness of the play.* ○ *He redeemed his earlier poor performance by scoring two excellent goals.* ○ *The sole redeeming feature of this job is the good salary.* (**b**) ~ **oneself** to do sth that compensates for sth bad one has done or puts one back into favour with others: [Vn] *He has a chance to redeem himself in tonight's match.* **2(a)** ~ **sth** (**from sb/sth**) to get sth back from sb by paying them back the money they lent one in exchange: [Vn, Vnpr] *I redeemed my watch (from the pawn shop).* (**b**) to pay the full sum of money owed to sb; to clear a debt: [Vn] *redeem a mortgage/loan.* (**c**) to convert sth, eg shares or vouchers (VOUCHER 1) into cash or goods: [Vn] *This coupon can be redeemed at any of our branches.* **3** [Vn, Vnpr] ~ **sb** (**from sth**) (in Christianity) to free or save sb from sin.

▶ **redeemable** /-əbl/ *adj* ~ (**against sth**): *gift tokens redeemable at any garden centre* ○ *These vouchers are redeemable against any holiday listed in the brochure.*

the Redeemer *n* [sing] Jesus Christ.

redemption /rɪ'dempʃn/ *n* [U] (*fml*) the action of redeeming sth/sb or the process of being redeemed: *the redemption of a loan* ○ *the redemption of the world from sin.* **IDM** **beyond/past re'demption** too bad to be improved or saved: *When they scored their third goal we knew the match was beyond redemption.*

▶ **redemptive** *adj* /rɪ'demptɪv/ *adj* (*fml*) of redemption; redeeming: *the redemptive power of love.*

redeploy /,riːdɪ'plɔɪ/ *v* to give new positions or tasks to sb: [Vn] *redeploy troops elsewhere* ○ *The company hopes that some workers can be redeployed* at other sites. ► **redeployment** n [U]: *the redeployment of staff/resources.*

redevelop /ˌriːdɪˈveləp/ v to change an area by removing (some of the) existing buildings and building new ones: *redevelop a city centre/housing estate/derelict site.* ► **redevelopment** n [U]: *inner-city redevelopment* ○ *The site was sold for redevelopment.*

redhead /ˈredhed/ n a person with reddish-brown hair.
■ **ˌred-ˈheaded** adj (of a person) having reddish-brown hair.

redirect /ˌriːdəˈrekt/ v 1 [Vn] = READDRESS. 2 to send, etc sth in a different direction: [Vn] *redirect the ball.* 3 to use resources, etc in a different, more desirable, way: [Vnpr] *redirect funds to more immediate needs* ○ *redirect your energies into more worthwhile activities* [also Vn]. ► **redirection** n [U, sing]: *the redirection of mail* ○ *a sudden redirection of economic policy.*

redistribute /ˌriːdɪˈstrɪbjuːt/ v to share sth out in a different way: [Vn] *redistribute jobs/power/land.* ► **redistribution** /ˌriːdɪstrɪˈbjuːʃn/ n [U, sing]: *the redistribution of wealth/labour/resources.*

redo /ˌriːˈduː/ v (pt **redid** /-ˈdɪd/; pp **redone** /-ˈdʌn/) to do sth again or differently: [Vn] *You'll have to redo this letter, I'm afraid.* ○ *We're redoing the work we did last term.* ○ *I'll just redo my hair.* ○ *We've just redone the kitchen* (ie decorated it again).

redolent /ˈredələnt/ adj [pred] ~ **of/with sth** (fml) 1 smelling strongly of sth: *The cottage was redolent of lavender and furniture polish.* ○ *The air was redolent with the smell of exotic spices.* 2 making one think of sth: *a place redolent of history and tradition.* ► **redolence** /-əns/ n [U]: *an all-pervading redolence of incense.*

redouble /ˌriːˈdʌbl/ v to make sth greater, stronger, more intense, etc: [Vn] *We must redouble our efforts if we want to succeed.* ○ *redoubled enthusiasm/strength/vigour.*

redoubt /rɪˈdaʊt/ n a small fort or defensive position.

redoubtable /rɪˈdaʊtəbl/ adj (fml) deserving to be feared and respected: *a redoubtable opponent/fighter.*

redound /rɪˈdaʊnd/ v PHRV **reˈdound to sth** (fml) to contribute greatly to one's/sb's reputation, etc; promote sth: *Her hard work redounds to her credit/to the honour of the school.*

redress /rɪˈdres/ v (fml) to put right a wrong; to compensate for sth: [Vn] *redress an injustice/a grievance* ○ *redress the damage done.* IDM **redress the ˈbalance** to make things equal again: *The team has more men than women so we must redress the balance* (ie include more women in it).
► **redress** /rɪˈdres, ˈriːdres/ n [U] ~ **(for/against sth)** (fml) (the right to claim) compensation for a wrongdoing one has suffered: *seek legal redress for unfair dismissal* ○ *In such circumstances, you have no redress.*

redskin /ˈredskɪn/ n (△ dated offensive) = RED INDIAN.

reduce /rɪˈdjuːs; US -ˈduːs/ v 1 ~ **sth (from sth) (to/by sb)** to make sth smaller in size, quantity, number, degree, price, etc: [Vn] *reduce pressure/speed/visibility reduced by fog* ○ *increase profits by reducing costs* ○ *Giving up smoking reduces the risk of heart disease.* ○ *This shirt was greatly/much reduced in the sale.* [Vnpr] *reduce prices by 10%* ○ *The number of staff was reduced from 40 to 25.* 2 [V] (infml esp US) to lose weight by being on a special diet. PHRV **reˈduce sb (from sth) to sth** to make sb lower in rank or status: *reduce a sergeant to the ranks* (ie make him an ordinary soldier). **reˈduce sb/sth (from sth) to sth / doing sth** (usu passive) to bring or force sb/sth into a specified, usu worse, state or condition: *reduce sb to tears* ○ *a beautiful building reduced to ashes/rubble/ruins* ○ *They were reduced to*

begging in the streets. ○ *Overwork has reduced him to a physical wreck.* **reˈduce sth to sth** to change sth to a more general or basic form: *reduce a problem to two main issues.*
► **reducible** /-əbl/ adj ~ **(to sth)** (fml) that can be reduced: *A culture is not reducible to the desires of the individuals comprising it.* Compare IRREDUCIBLE.
■ **reˌduced ˈcircumstances** n [pl] (euph) the state of being poor after being relatively wealthy: *be living in reduced circumstances.*

reduction /rɪˈdʌkʃn/ n 1(a) [U] the action of reducing sth or the state of being reduced: *ˈnoise/ˈweight reduction* ○ *aim for a reduction of fat in one's diet.* (b) [C] an instance of reducing sth: *a marked reduction in size/weight* ○ *a reduction in the number of law graduates* ○ *price reductions.* (c) [C] the amount by which sth is reduced, esp in price: *sell sth at a huge reduction* ○ *special ticket reductions for children under 12.* 2 [C] a copy of a map, picture, etc made by reducing the size of the original one. Compare ENLARGEMENT.

redundant /rɪˈdʌndənt/ adj 1 (esp Brit) no longer in employment because there is no more work available: *redundant car workers* ○ *The company plans to make a further 50 staff redundant.* 2 no longer needed: *redundant factories/farm buildings.* 3 unnecessary: *The picture has too much redundant detail.*
► **redundancy** /-ənsi/ n 1 [U] (a) (esp Brit) the state of being redundant(1): *a high level of redundancy among unskilled workers* ○ *compulsory/voluntary redundancy* ○ *take/accept redundancy* ○ *redundancy payments.* (b) material that is redundant(3): *Natural language is characterized by redundancy* (ie words that perform no particular function). 2 [C] (esp Brit) a worker made redundant(1): *The factory closure will result in 200 redundancies.*
redundantly adv.

redwood /ˈredwʊd/ n [C,U] a very tall tree with reddish wood that grows esp in California.

re-echo /ˌriː ˈekəʊ/ v (of sounds, thoughts, etc) to be repeated again and again: [Vpr] *Their shouts re-echoed through the valley.* [V] *His unkind words kept re-echoing in my mind.*

reed /riːd/ n 1 [C] a type of tall grass with a hollow stem growing near water: *reed beds* (ie where they grow) ○ *The edge of the lake was fringed with reeds.* 2 [C] a thin strip of metal or wood in certain musical instruments that produces sound when air is blown over it: *reed instruments like the oboe and the clarinet.* ⇨ picture at MUSICAL INSTRUMENT. IDM **a broken reed** ⇨ BROKEN².
► **reedy** adj 1 full of reeds (REED 1): *reedy river banks.* 2 (derog) (of voices or sounds) high, thin and harsh.

re-educate /ˌriː ˈedʒukeɪt/ v to educate sb to think or behave in a new or different way: [Vn, Vn.to inf] *We must re-educate people (to eat more healthily).* ► **re-education** /ˌriː edʒuˈkeɪʃn/ n [U].

reef¹ /riːf/ n a ridge of rock, sand, etc at or near the surface of the sea: *a coral reef* ○ *the Great Barrier Reef.*

reef² /riːf/ n a part of a sail that can be tied or rolled up to make the sail smaller in a strong wind.
► **reef** v [Vn] to reduce the size of a sail by tying or rolling up one or more reefs.
■ **ˈreef-knot** (US **square-knot**) n a type of double knot that will not slip or undo easily.

reefer /ˈriːfə(r)/ n 1 (also **reefer jacket**) a short thick woollen jacket, usu dark blue, with two rows of buttons. 2 (sl) a cigarette containing MARIJUANA.

reek /riːk/ n [sing] a strong unpleasant smell: *the reek of stale tobacco smoke.*
► **reek** v ~ **(of sth) (a)** to smell very strongly of sth: [Vpr] *His breath reeked of tobacco.* ○ *The room reeked of cheap perfume.* [also V]. **(b)** to suggest sth

---

[V.to inf] = verb + to infinitive   [Vn.inf (no to)] = verb + noun + infinitive without to   [V.ing] = verb + -ing form

strongly, esp sth unpleasant or suspicious: [Vpr] *Their actions reek of corruption.*

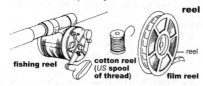

reel

fishing reel   **cotton reel**   reel
         (US spool
         of thread)   **film reel**

reel¹ /riːl/ (also *esp US* **spool**) *n* (**a**) a long or round object on which thread, wire, camera film, etc is wound: *a 'cotton reel ○ a reel on a fishing-rod.* ⇨ picture. (**b**) the film, wire, thread, etc wound round this: *a reel of cotton ○ a new reel of film.* ⇨ picture.
▶ **reel** *v* PHRV ˌreel **sth ¹in/¹out** to wind sth on or off a reel: *Reel in the line slowly or you'll lose the fish.*
ˌreel **sth ¹off** to say or repeat sth quickly without having to stop and think about it: *reel off a poem/a list of names/a set of instructions.*

reel² /riːl/ *v* **1** to move in a very unsteady way, eg because one is drunk or has been hit: [V] *By the end of the fight, he was reeling.* [Vpr] *They reeled out of the pub, both completely drunk.* [Vp] *She reeled back from the force of the blow.* **2** to seem to be spinning round and round, usu as a result of a shock or great emotion: [Vpr] *be reeling from/with/under the shock* ○ *His mind reeled at the news.* [V] *The very idea of winning £10 million sets my head reeling.*

reel³ /riːl/ *n* a lively Scottish or Irish dance, usu for two or four couples, or the music of this: *dance a highland reel.*

re-elect /ˌriː ɪˈlekt/ *v* ~ **sb (to sth); ~ sb (as sth)** to elect sb again: [Vn] *He will almost certainly be re-elected.* [Vnpr] *She was re-elected to the board of governors.* [Vn-n] *The committee voted to re-elect him (as) president.* ▶ **re-election** /-ˈlekʃn/ *n* [U]: *stand for re-election.*

re-enter /ri ˈentə(r)/ *v* to enter sth or a place again: [V, Vn] *re-enter (the room) by another door.*
▶ **re-entry** /ri ˈentri/ *n* [U] **1** the action of entering a place, etc again: *a re-entry course/programme for nurses* (ie for nurses returning to work after a long time doing other things) ○ *to be refused re-entry without a visa.* **2** the return of a spacecraft into the earth's atmosphere: *The capsule gets very hot **on re-entry**.*

re-examine /ˌriː ɪgˈzæmɪn/ *v* to examine or think about sth again: [Vn] *re-examine a witness/a court case* ○ *It's worthwhile to re-examine one's beliefs and values from time to time.* ▶ **re-examination** /ˌriː ɪgˌzæmɪˈneɪʃn/ *n* [U, sing]: *call for a complete re-examination of a court case.*

ref¹ /ref/ *n* (*infml*) a sports REFEREE(1).

ref² /ref/ *abbr* (*commerce*) reference: *our ref 14A; your ref 392* (eg at the top of a business letter).

refectory /rɪˈfektri/ *n* a large room for meals in a religious or educational institution: *a refectory table.*

refer /rɪˈfɜː(r)/ *v* (**-rr-**) PHRV reˈfer **to sb/sth 1** to mention or speak of sth: *The victims were not referred to by name.* ○ *This incident in his childhood is never referred to again.* **2** to relate to or describe sb/sth: *This paragraph refers to the events of last year.* ○ *When I said some people are stupid, I wasn't referring to you.* **3** to look at sth or ask a person for information: *refer to a dictionary/an expert* ○ *The speaker referred to his notes repeatedly.* reˈfer **to sb/ sth as sth** to describe sb/sth as sth: *He always refers to his wife as 'my other half'.* reˈfer **sb/sth to sb/sth** to send sb/sth to sb/sth for help, advice, action, a decision, etc: *The doctor referred me to a psychiatrist.* ○ *The case was referred to the Court of Appeal.* ○ *I was referred to the manager/the enquiry office.* ○ *The reader is referred to page 13 for a fuller*

account of this affair. ○ *May I refer you to my letter of 14 May?*
▶ **referral** /rɪˈfɜːrəl/ *n* (**a**) [U] the action of sending sb/sth or being sent to sb/sth for help, action, advice, a decision, etc: *the referral of such cases to a doctor.* (**b**) [C] a person or thing sent to sb/sth in this way: *several referrals from the clinic.*

referee /ˌrefəˈriː/ *n* **1(a)** (also *infml* **ref**) (*sport*) an official who controls a sports game and makes sure that players do not break the rules: *He was sent off for arguing with the referee.* ⇨ picture at BOXING, FOOTBALL, HOCKEY. Compare UMPIRE. (**b**) a person who is asked to settle a dispute, an argument, etc: *Each time my neighbours had a fight, I had to act as referee.* **2** (*Brit*) a person who supplies a usu written statement about the character or ability of sb applying for a job, a place at a university, etc: *The principal often acts as (a) referee for his students.*
▶ **referee** *v* to act as a referee in a game: [V] *In my 22 years of refereeing I had never seen such violence.* [Vn] *Who refereed the match?*

reference /ˈrefərəns/ *n* **1** ~ (**to sb/sth**) (**a**) [U] the action of mentioning sb/sth: *I'd hoped she would talk about her books, but she only made **passing reference** to them.* ○ *Try to avoid making any reference to his illness.* (**b**) [C] a statement, etc that mentions sb/sth: *His jokes include many topical references.* ○ *The book is full of references to places I know.* **2** ~ (**to sb/sth**) the action of asking sb for help, advice, approval, etc: *She should not have done it without reference to me first.* **3** [U] the action of looking at sth for information: *Keep this list of numbers near the phone **for easy reference**.* ○ *The guidebook may be useful **for future reference**.* **4** [C] ~ (**to sb/sth**) a note in a book, etc that indicates the source of information used by the author: *There is a list of references at the end of each chapter.* See also CROSS-REFERENCE. **5** [C] a piece of information that indicates where sth/sb is, can be found, etc: *a 'map reference* ○ *Each book in the library carries a reference mark on the cover.* **6** [U] (*fml*) a connection or relationship between things: *These facts **bear/ have no reference to** (ie are not relevant to) the matter under discussion.* ○ *I am writing **with/in reference to** (ie about) your job application.* See also FRAME OF REFERENCE, TERMS OF REFERENCE. **7** [C] (*abbr* **ref**) (*commerce*) a way of identifying who has sent a letter; the number of a file, etc: *Please quote our reference when replying.* **8** [C] (a person willing to make) a usu written statement about sb's character or abilities, esp when they are applying for a new job: *give/quote sb/sb's name as a reference* ○ *You can use your present employer as a reference.* ○ *provide/supply sb with a reference* ○ *She came to us with excellent references.* Compare TESTIMONIAL 1.
■ ˈreference **book** *n* a book, eg an encyclopedia or a dictionary, in which one can look up facts, information, etc, but which one does not normally read right through.
ˈreference **library** *n* a library of books that can be read or referred to but not borrowed.

referendum /ˌrefəˈrendəm/ *n* (*pl* **referendums** or **referenda**) [C, U] a vote taken on an important issue by all the people of a country, etc: ***hold a referendum** on ending military service* ○ *settle a national issue by referendum.* Compare PLEBISCITE.

refill /ˌriːˈfɪl/ *v* [Vn] to fill sth again: *refill one's glass/ tank/cigarette lighter.*
▶ **refill** /ˈriːfɪl/ *n* (**a**) (a container holding) a quantity of a substance used to refill sth: *a packet of refills for a cartridge pen.* (**b**) (*infml*) another drink of the same type: *Would you like a refill?*

refine /rɪˈfaɪn/ *v* **1** to make a substance pure: [Vn] *the process of refining sugar/oil.* **2** to improve sth by making small changes to it: [Vn] *refine earlier sys-*

tems/designs/techniques/theories ○ *We need to refine our process of selection.*

▶ **refined** *adj* (*sometimes derog*) having high standards of politeness and manners, or showing an ability to judge good quality, good style, etc: *a man of refined tastes in music and wine* ○ *refined ladies drinking tea in the afternoon.*

refiner *n* a person, company or machine that refines (REFINE 1) substances: *sugar refiners.*

refinery /-nəri/ *n* a factory, etc where sth is refined (REFINE): *a 'sugar/oil refinery.*

refinement /rɪˈfaɪnmənt/ *n* **1** [C] a small change or addition to sth that improves it: *architectural refinements* ○ *all the refinements of modern computer technology.* **2** [U] the action of refining sth or the process of sth being refined: *the refinement of oil/sugar.* **3** [U] the quality of being refined (REFINE): *The house has an atmosphere of elegant refinement.*

refit /ˌriːˈfɪt/ *v* (**-tt-**) ~ **sth** (**with sth**) to repair or fit new parts, equipment, etc to sth: [Vn] *refit a ship/car/kitchen/factory* [also Vnpr]. ▶ **refit** /ˈriːfɪt/ *n*: *The hotel has undergone a complete refit.*

reflate /riːˈfleɪt/ *v* to increase the amount of money in use in a country, usu in order to increase demand for goods and so stimulate the economy: [V, Vn] *We need to reflate (the economy) as a matter of urgency.* Compare DEFLATE 3, INFLATE 3. ▶ **reflation** /riːˈfleɪʃn/ *n* [U]. **reflationary** /riːˈfleɪʃnri; *US* -neri/ *adj*: *reflationary policies/measures.*

reflect /rɪˈflekt/ *v* **1** ~ **sb/sth** (**in sth**) (esp passive) to show the image of sb/sth on the surface of sth such as a mirror, water or glass: [Vn] *See how beautifully the river reflects the trees.* [Vnpr] *She could see herself reflected in his eyes.* ○ *He looked at his face reflected in the mirror.* **2** [Vn] to throw back heat, light, sound, etc from a surface: *The white houses reflect the glare of the sun.* ○ *We need a building material which absorbs sound, and doesn't reflect it.* **3** to be a feature or an aspect of sth that indicates sth. about its true nature or qualities: [Vn] *The financial markets today were simply reflecting the strength of the German economy.* ○ *Certain laws need changing to reflect changing attitudes in society.* ○ *Her interest in gardening is reflected in her novels.* **4** ~ (**on/upon sth**) to consider or think deeply about sth: [Vpr] *reflect on a problem* [V] *Before I decide, I need time just to sit and reflect.* [V.that] *He reflected sadly that he had probably made the wrong decision about the job.* [also V.speech, V.wh]. **IDM** **reflect well, badly, etc on sb/sth** to make sb/sth appear to be good, bad, etc: *This scandal is bound to reflect badly on the police as a whole.*

■ **re**,**flected** ˈ**glory** *n* [U] (*derog*) admiration, praise, etc given to sb, not because of what they have achieved themselves, but because of what sb they are connected with has done: *basking in the reflected glory of his wife's success.*

reflection (*Brit* also **reflexion**) /rɪˈflekʃn/ *n* **1** an image reflected by a mirror, a shiny surface, water, etc: *admiring his reflection in the mirror.* **2** [U] the action or process of reflecting (REFLECT 2) heat, sound, light, etc. **3** [C] an indication of sth: *Your clothes are often a reflection of your personality* ○ *These events are a sad reflection on the state of our inner cities.* **4(a)** [U] long and careful consideration: *She decided, on further reflection, to accept his offer after all.* ○ *A moment's reflection would have shown you that you were wrong.* **(b)** [C often *pl*] a written or spoken expression of sth that has been carefully considered: *a book of his reflections on childhood.* **5** [C] an account or description of sth: *The article is an accurate reflection of events that day, in my opinion.*

reflective /rɪˈflektɪv/ *adj* **1** tending to think deeply about things; thoughtful (THOUGHT²): *a quiet and reflective man* ○ *in a reflective mood.* **2** capable of

reflecting sth, esp light: *reflective car number plates* ○ *On dark nights children should wear reflective clothing.* ▶ **reflectively** *adv*: *He sat puffing reflectively on his pipe.*

reflector /rɪˈflektə(r)/ *n* a thing that reflects heat, light or sound: *a reflector fitted to the back of a bicycle.* ⇨ picture at BICYCLE.

reflex /ˈriːfleks/ *n* a movement or an action that one cannot control, made in response to sth: *have quick/slow/normal reflexes* ○ *test sb's reflexes* ○ *a reflex movement/response* ○ *Almost as a* **reflex action**, *I grab my diary when the phone rings.* See also CONDITIONED REFLEX.

■ ,**reflex** ˈ**angle** *n* an angle of more than 180°.

reflexion (*Brit*) = REFLECTION.

reflexive /rɪˈfleksɪv/ *adj* (*grammar*) (abbreviated as *reflex* in this dictionary) (of a word or the form of a word) showing that the action of the verb is performed on its subject: *In 'He cut himself', 'cut' is a reflexive verb and 'himself' is a reflexive pronoun.*

refloat /ˌriːˈfləʊt/ *v* [Vn] to make a boat, ship, etc float again, eg after it has become stuck on the bottom in shallow water.

reform /rɪˈfɔːm/ *v* to become or make sb/sth better by correcting or making improvements: *reform one's ways/habits* ○ *reform the electoral system* ○ *He's given up drink and is now a reformed character.*

▶ **reform** *n* **(a)** [U] (esp in social or political matters) the action of reforming sth or the process of being reformed: *a government committed to reform* ○ *demands for electoral/constitutional reform* ○ *reform laws/bills/measures.* **(b)** [C] an official change in the way sth is done or organized: *carry out reforms in education* ○ *economic reforms.*

reformer *n* a person who works for political or social change: *a social/political/religious reformer.*

reˈ**formist** *adj* in favour of esp gradual change in political or social matters: *a strongly reformist administration* ○ *He is reformist rather than revolutionary.*

re-form /ˌriː ˈfɔːm/ *v* to form again, esp into a different group or pattern: [V] *political groups that are constantly breaking up and re-forming* ○ *It took the soldiers about a minute to re-form.*

reformation /ˌrefəˈmeɪʃn/ *n* **1(a)** [U] the action of reforming sth/sb or the process of being reformed: *the reformation of criminals.* **(b)** [C] a great change for the better in social, religious or political affairs. **2 the Reformation** [sing] the 16th-century movement in Europe for reform of the Roman Catholic Church, which resulted in the establishment of Protestant Churches.

reformatory /rɪˈfɔːmətri; *US* -tɔːri/ (also **re**ˈ**form school**) *n* (*dated or US*) an institution to which young criminals are sent instead of going to prison. See also APPROVED SCHOOL, BORSTAL.

refract /rɪˈfrækt/ *v* (of water, air, glass, etc) to make a ray of light change direction when it enters at an angle: [Vn] *Light is refracted when passed through a prism.* ▶ **refraction** /rɪˈfrækʃn/ *n* [U]: *A stick held in the water will appear to bend, showing refraction (of light).* ⇨ picture at SPECTRUM.

refractory /rɪˈfræktəri/ *adj* (*fml*) difficult to control; very badly behaved: *a boy trying to control his refractory pony.*

refrain¹ /rɪˈfreɪn/ *n* **1** the lines of a song or poem which are repeated, esp at the end of each verse: *I'll sing the verses and you all join in for the refrain.* **2** a comment or complaint that is often repeated: *Complaints about poor food in schools have become a familiar refrain.* ○ *The protest began with a small group, but then others took up the refrain.*

refrain² /rɪˈfreɪn/ *v* ~ (**from sth/doing sth**) (*rather fml*) to stop oneself doing sth, esp sth that one would like to do: [Vpr] *refrain from comment/criticism* ○ *Customers are kindly requested to refrain from smoking.*

[Vnn] = verb + noun + noun   [V-adj] = verb + adjective   For more help with verbs, see Study pages **B4–8**.

o *She has wisely refrained from criticizing the government in public.* [also V].

refresh /rɪ'freʃ/ v to make sb/sth look or feel stronger, less tired, fresher, etc: [Vn] *The long sleep refreshed her.* o *Carrie went upstairs to refresh her make-up.* **IDM** **refresh one's/sb's memory (about sb/sth)** to remind oneself/sb of sth, esp with the help of sth that can be seen or heard: *Perhaps this photo will refresh your memory.*
▸ **refreshing** adj **1** making one feel stronger, less tired or more alert: *a nice refreshing shower/sleep/drink* o *The breeze was cool and refreshing.* **2** pleasantly new or different: *It's refreshing to see some new faces in the company.* o *I find his directness very refreshing.* **refreshingly** adv: *refreshingly honest/original/different* o *a speech refreshingly free from hypocrisy.*
■ re'**fresher course** n a short course of instruction in which one learns about new ideas, methods and developments in one's profession: *go on/attend a refresher course.*

refreshment /rɪ'freʃmənt/ n **1(a)** [U] (*fml or joc*) food and drink: *Would you like some refreshment?* o *liquid refreshment* (ie drink) o *a refreshment room* (eg at a railway station where food and drink are sold). **(b) refreshments** [pl] small quantities of food and drink, esp provided for or sold to people in a public place or at a public event: *Light refreshments will be served during the break.* o *Tickets include the price of refreshments.* **2** [U] the process of becoming refreshed (REFRESH).

refrigerate /rɪ'frɪdʒəreɪt/ v make food, etc cold in order to keep it fresh or preserve it: [Vn] *keep meat/milk refrigerated* o *refrigerate container trucks.*
▸ **refrigeration** /rɪˌfrɪdʒə'reɪʃn/ n [U]: *Keep all meat products under refrigeration.*
refrigerator /rɪ'frɪdʒəreɪtə(r)/ n (*rather fml*) (also *infml* **fridge** /frɪdʒ/) a small cupboard or room specially designed to keep food, etc cold. Compare FREEZER.

refuel /ˌriː'fjuːəl/ v (**-ll-**; *US* **-l-**) to fill sth or be filled again with fuel: [Vn] *refuel a car/plane* [V] *We landed at Bahrain to refuel.* o *a refuelling stop.*

refuge /'refjuːdʒ/ n **1(a)** [U] ~ (**from sb/sth**) shelter or protection from danger, trouble, etc: *a place of refuge* o *seek refuge from the storm/fighting* o *take refuge in the US Embassy* o *give sb refuge.* **(b)** [C] a place, person or thing that provides this: *establish a refuge for rare birds* o *For her, poetry is a refuge from the problems of the world.* **2** [C] (*Brit*) = TRAFFIC ISLAND.

refugee /ˌrefjʊ'dʒiː/ n a person who has been forced to leave his or her country, home, etc for political or religious reasons, or because there is a war, shortage of food, etc: *a steady flow of refugees from the war zone* o *set up* ˌrefu'gee *camps* o *economic/political refugees.*

refulgent /rɪ'fʌldʒənt/ adj (*fml*) (of a light) very bright.

refund /rɪ'fʌnd/ v ~**sth (to sb)** to pay back money received or spent: [Vn] *refund a deposit* [Vnpr] *Your travelling expenses will be refunded to you.* [Vnn] *We guarantee to refund you your money in full if you are not satisfied with your purchase.*
▸ **refund** /'riːfʌnd/ n [C, U] a sum of money paid back: *claim/obtain/pay a tax refund* o *ask for a refund on unused theatre tickets* o *If you are not satisfied, return the goods within 14 days for replacement or refund!*
refundable adj: *a refundable deposit* o *Tickets are not refundable.*

refurbish /ˌriː'fɜːbɪʃ/ v [Vn] to restore and decorate a building, etc; to develop and improve sth: *a recently refurbished hotel* o *The flat will be completely refurbished for the new tenants.* ▸ **refurbishment** n

[U, C]: *The hotel is closed for refurbishments.* o *carry out tasteful refurbishments to Victorian buildings.*

refusal /rɪ'fjuːzl/ n **(a)** [U] the action of refusing or being refused: *the refusal of a request/an invitation/an offer.* **(b)** [C] an act of refusing: *a blunt/flat/curt refusal* o *His refusal to discuss the issue is most annoying.* See also FIRST REFUSAL.

refuse¹ /'refjuːs/ n [U] rubbish: *kitchen/garden/household refuse* o *a refuse bag/dump/bin* o *refuse disposal.*
■ '**refuse collector** n (*fml*) = DUSTMAN.

refuse² /rɪ'fjuːz/ v to say or show that one is unwilling to give, accept or do sth: [Vn] *refuse one's consent/help/permission* o *refuse a gift/an offer/an invitation* o *Our application for visas was refused.* [V] *He was asked to join but he refused.* [V.to inf] *The car absolutely refused to start.* [Vnn] *I was refused access to my medical notes.*

refute /rɪ'fjuːt/ v **1** to prove sth to be wrong: [Vn] *refute a claim/a theory/an argument.* **2** to say that sth is wrong or not true; to deny sth: [Vn] *He refuted all suggestions that he was planning to resign.* ▸ **refutable** /-əbl/ adj. **refutation** /ˌrefjuː'teɪʃn/ n [C, U]: *His article is a wholesale refutation of modernization.*

regain /rɪ'ɡeɪn/ v **1** to get sth back again after losing it; to recover sth: [Vn] *regain consciousness* o *regain one's freedom/health/sight/composure* o *The former president's attempt to regain power.* **2** to reach a place or position again: [Vn] *regain one's footing/balance* (eg after slipping).

regal /'riːɡl/ adj of, like or fit for a king or queen; royal: *regal splendour/power* o *have a regal appearance/bearing* o *She dismissed him with a regal gesture.* ▸ **regally** /-ɡəli/ adv.

regale /rɪ'ɡeɪl/ v **PHRV** **regale sb with sth** to amuse or entertain sb with stories, jokes, etc: *She regaled us with tales of her life in the theatre.*

regalia /rɪ'ɡeɪliə/ n [U] the special clothes worn and objects carried at official ceremonies: *a portrait of the queen in full regalia.*

regard¹ /rɪ'ɡɑːd/ v **1** (*fml*) to look steadily at sb/sth in the specified way: [Vnadv] *She regarded him closely/intently/curiously, etc.* **2** ~ **sb/sth (with sth)**; ~ **sb/sth as sth** to consider or think about sb/sth in the specified way: [Vnadv] *Her work/She is very highly regarded.* [Vnpr] *regard sb/sth with affection/approval/distaste/suspicion* [Vn-adj] *regard sth as essential* [Vn-n] *regard sth as a success/a failure/a disaster* o *He's widely regarded as one of our best young writers.* o *She regards me as a rival (for her job).* **IDM** **as regards sb/sth** (*fml*) concerning or in connection with sb/sth: *I have little information as regards his past.* o *As regards the second point in your letter...*
▸ **regarding** prep with reference to sb/sth; concerning sb/sth: *She said nothing regarding your request.*

regard² /rɪ'ɡɑːd/ n (*fml*) **1** [U] ~ **to/for sb/sth** attention to or concern for sb/sth: *drive without regard for/to speed limits* o *have/pay/show little regard for the feelings of others.* **2** [U] ~ (**for sb/sth**) respect: *hold sb in high/low regard* (ie have a good/bad opinion of sb) o *have a great/the utmost regard for sb's judgement/intelligence/achievements* o *Children no longer have proper regard for their parents and teachers.* **3 regards** [pl] (used esp at the end of a letter) kind wishes; greetings: *With kind/warm regards, Yours ...* o *Please give/send my regards to your brother.* **IDM** **in/with regard to sb/sth** (*fml*) in connection with sb/sth: *a country's laws in regard to human rights* o *Do you have anything else to say with regard to your job application?* **in this/that re'gard** (*fml*) in connection with the point previously mentioned: *I have nothing further to say in this regard.*

▶ **regardless** *adv* paying no attention; despite the circumstances: *The weather was terrible but we pressed on regardless.* ○ *I protested, but she carried on regardless.* **regardless of** *prep* paying no attention to sth/sb; despite sth/sb: *regardless of the consequences/danger/expense* ○ *The club welcomes all new members, regardless of age.* ○ *He carries on working, regardless of whether he's tired or not.*

regatta /rɪˈɡætə/ *n* a sporting event at which races between boats are held: *hold a sailing regatta.*

regd *abbr* (*commerce*) registered.

regency /ˈriːdʒənsi/ *n* [C] the period of government by a REGENT.
▶ **Regency** *adj* [usu attrib] of the period 1810–20, when George, Prince of Wales, acted as REGENT in Britain: *Regency architecture/furniture.*

regenerate /rɪˈdʒenəreɪt/ *v* **1** to make sb/sth strong and vigorous again: [Vn] *regenerate industry/ the economy/derelict land* ○ *After his vacation he felt regenerated.* **2** (*biology*) to grow or make sth grow again: [V] *Once destroyed, brain cells do not regenerate.* [Vn] *If the woodland is left alone, it will regenerate itself in a few years.* ▶ **regeneration** /rɪˌdʒenəˈreɪʃn/ *n* [U]: *the regeneration of cells in the body* ○ *economic/environmental regeneration.* **regenerative** /rɪˈdʒenərətɪv/ *adj*: *the regenerative powers of nature.*

regent /ˈriːdʒənt/ (*often* **Regent**) *n* a person appointed to rule a country while the King or Queen is too young, old, ill, etc, or is absent: *act as regent.*
▶ **regent** (*often* **Regent**) *adj* (following *ns*) performing the duties of a Regent: *the Prince Regent.*

reggae /ˈreɡeɪ/ *n* [U] a type of West Indian popular music and dance with strong rhythms.

regicide /ˈredʒɪsaɪd/ *n* (**a**) [U] the crime of killing a king or a queen. (**b**) [C] a person who commits this crime.

regime /reɪˈʒiːm/ *n* (**a**) a method or system of government: *a socialist/fascist/totalitarian/military regime.* (**b**) a method or system of organizing or doing sth: *a dietary regime* ○ *Many employees are critical of the present regime.*

regimen /ˈredʒɪmən/ *n* (*medical or fml*) a set of instructions about diet, exercise, behaviour, etc aimed at improving sb's health or changing their way of life: *follow a strict regimen* ○ *a daily regimen of 15 minutes of body exercises.*

regiment /ˈredʒɪmənt/ *n* [CGp] **1** a large military group, usu under the command of a COLONEL(a): *an infantry/a cavalry/an armoured/a tank regiment* ○ *enlist in the 1st Battalion of the Lancashire Regiment.* **2** ~ **of sth/sb** a large number of things or people: *A whole regiment of volunteers turned up to help.*
▶ **regiment** /ˈredʒɪment/ *v* (*esp derog*) (usu passive) to force strict discipline on sb/sth; to organize people or things into rigid groups, patterns, etc: [Vn] *a highly regimented society/lifestyle* ○ *trees planted in regimented lines.* **regimentation** /ˌredʒɪmenˈteɪʃn/ *n* [U]: *She rebelled against the regimentation of school life.*

regimental /ˌredʒɪˈmentl/ *adj* [attrib]: *a regimental mascot/band/parade* ○ *regimental headquarters/ colours.*

region /ˈriːdʒən/ *n* **1** [C] an area, usu without fixed limits: *the Arctic/desert/tropical regions* ○ *one of the most densely populated regions in North America* ○ *pains in the abdominal region.* **2** [C] an administrative division of a country. **3 the regions** [pl] all of a country except the capital: *develop new rail services to the regions.* **IDM in the region of sth** (of a number, weight, price, etc) about sth: *earn (somewhere) in the region of £20 000 a year.*
▶ **regional** /-nl/ *adj* [usu attrib] of a region: *re-*

gional variations in pronunciation ○ *the conflict between regional and national interests* ○ *regional councils/elections/newspapers.* **regionally** /-nəli/ *adv*: *regionally based television companies.*

register[1] /ˈredʒɪstə(r)/ *n* **1** an official list or record of names, items, etc; a book containing such a list: *a parish register (ie of births, marriages and deaths)* ○ *be on the electoral register/the register of voters* ○ *make entries in a register* ○ *Could you sign the hotel register please, sir?* ○ *The class teacher called the (names on the) register.* ○ *He was struck off the register by the General Medical Council for negligence.* See also CASH REGISTER. **2** (a part of) the range of a human voice or a musical instrument: *notes in the upper/middle register* ○ *the lower register of a clarinet/tenor.* **3** (*linguistics*) the range of vocabulary, grammar, etc used by speakers in particular social circumstances or professional contexts: *The essay suddenly switches from a formal to an informal register.*
■ **ˈregister office** *n* = REGISTRY OFFICE.

register[2] /ˈredʒɪstə(r)/ *v* **1** ~ **(at/for/with sth);** ~ **sth (in sth);** ~ **(sb) as sth** to record a name, an event, a sale, etc in a list for official purposes: [Vn] *register a birth/marriage/death* ○ *register a company/a trade mark* ○ *a registered child-minder* [Vpr] *register at a hotel* ○ *register for a course/an exam/a degree* ○ *register with a doctor/dentist* ○ *register one's car/the birth of a child/a patent* [Vnpr] *register a house in one's own name.* [Vn-n] *She is registered (as) disabled/ unemployed.* [also V]. **2** to make sth known officially or publicly, esp so that it is recorded: [Vn] *Thousands have registered their hostility to the new legislation by signing a petition.* **3**(**a**) (of a figure, etc) to indicate or record sth: [V] *The meter just didn't register; it must have been faulty.* [Vn] *an earth tremor registering 1.5 on the Richter Scale* ○ *The thermometer registered 32°C.* ○ *The stock exchange has registered huge losses this week.* (**b**) to show or indicate an emotion by one's expression, actions, etc: [Vn] *register one's disgust/disapproval/ amusement* ○ *Her face registered dismay.* **4** (*infml*) (esp in negative sentences) to be recognized or noted mentally: [V] *I told him when and where to meet us, but it can't have registered.* ○ *Her name doesn't register at all.* **5** to send sth by post, paying extra to protect it against loss or damage: [Vn] *send a registered letter* ○ *send a parcel by registered post.*
■ **ˌregistered ˈnurse** *n* (*US*) a trained nurse licensed by a state authority.
ˌregistered ˈtrade mark *n* (*abbr* **R**, *symb* ®) a sign or name, etc of a manufacturer, etc which is officially recorded and protected from use by others.

registrar /ˌredʒɪˈstrɑː(r), ˈredʒɪstrɑː(r)/ *n* **1** a person whose job is to keep official records, esp of births, marriages and deaths. **2** the chief administrative officer in a university: *Applications should be addressed to the registrar.* **3** (*Brit*) a qualified hospital doctor who is being trained as a specialist: *a surgical registrar* ○ *a junior orthopaedic registrar.*

registration /ˌredʒɪˈstreɪʃn/ *n* **1** [U] the action of registering sth/sb or of being registered: *the registration of letters/parcels* ○ *the registration of students for a course/examination* ○ *Please queue here for registration.* ○ *registration fees.* **2** [C] an instance of this: *vehicle/birth/death registrations.*
■ **regiˈstration number** *n* a series of letters and numbers displayed at the front and back of a vehicle to identify it. ▷ picture at CAR.

registry /ˈredʒɪstri/ *n* a place, eg in a church or university, where registers are kept.
■ **ˈregistry office** (also **ˈregister office**) *n* a place where civil(2) marriages are performed and where records of births, marriages and deaths are made: *Are they getting married in a church or a registry office?*

Regius professor /ˌriːdʒiəs prəˈfesə(r)/ n (Brit) a PROFESSOR(1), esp at Oxford or Cambridge, who holds a university position established or approved by a king or queen.

regress /rɪˈgres/ v ~ (**to sth**) to return to an earlier or less advanced form or state: [Vpr] She regressed to her old habits. [also V].

▶ **regression** /rɪˈgreʃn/ n [U,C] the process of regressing: regression to an earlier stage of emotional development.

regressive adj (usu derog) becoming or making sth less advanced: The Opposition condemned the policy as a regressive measure. Compare PROGRESSIVE 1.

regret¹ /rɪˈgret/ v (-tt-) (**a**) to feel sad, sorry or disappointed about sth, eg a loss or a missed opportunity: [Vn] His death was regretted by all. ○ If you go now, you'll regret it (ie You will wish you had stayed). ○ You ought to buy a microwave; you won't regret it. ○ I don't regret what I said. [V.ing, V.n ing] I regret (his) ever having raised the matter. [V.that] (fml) **It is to be regretted that** so many young people leave school without qualifications. (**b**) (used to express such feelings in a formal and polite way, eg when giving bad or unpleasant news) [Vn] We regret any inconvenience caused. ○ The terrorists issued a statement regretting the boy's death. [V.that] I regret that I cannot help. [V.to inf] We regret to inform you that your application has been unsuccessful. ○ The experiment was a failure, I regret to say.

▶ **regrettable** /-əbl/ adj that is or should be regretted: a regrettable failure/lapse/mistake ○ Her rudeness was most regrettable. ○ **It is regrettable that** the police were not informed sooner. **regrettably** /-əbli/ adv: regrettably slow progress ○ Regrettably, the experiment ended in failure.

regret² /rɪˈgret/ n [U,C] a feeling of sadness or disappointment, esp at the loss of sb/sth: feel regret about a missed opportunity ○ express regret at sb's death ○ It is with profound/deep/great regret that I have to announce the closure of the factory. ○ Much to my regret, I am unable to accept your invitation. ○ I have no regrets about leaving. ○ My only regret is that I didn't leave sooner.

▶ **regretful** /-fl/ adj feeling or expressing regret: 'I'll have to go now.' She sounded regretful. **regretfully** /-fəli/ adv with regret; sadly (SAD): He shook his head regretfully. ○ Regretfully, I must decline.

regroup /ˌriːˈgruːp/ v ~ (**sth**) (**for sth**) to form or form sb/sth into fresh groups; to organize sb/oneself/sth in a different way: [Vpr, Vnpr] The enemy regrouped (their forces) for a new attack. [V] (fig) After its election defeat, the party needs to regroup. [also Vn].

regular /ˈregjələ(r)/ adj **1** following a constant or definite pattern, esp with the same time or space between individual instances: lampposts placed **at regular intervals** ○ regular breathing ○ a regular pulse/heartbeat ○ have regular habits/follow a regular routine (ie do the same things at the same times every day) ○ regular meetings/visits/payments ○ The equipment is checked **on a regular basis**. ○ She writes a regular column for a national newspaper. **2** arranged evenly or in an organized pattern: her regular teeth/features ○ jets flying in a regular formation. **3** [attrib] (**a**) (of people) doing the same thing or going to the same place often: our regular customers/readers/listeners ○ a regular offender (ie against the law) ○ He was a regular visitor to her house. (**b**) (of people) visited when necessary; usual: my regular doctor/dentist. **4**(**a**) done or happening often; frequent: taking regular exercise ○ Strikes were a regular occurrence during the 1970s. ○ She suffered regular abuse from her uncle. (**b**) lasting or happening over a long period: a regular job/income ○ She could find no regular employment. **5** normal; proper; correct: Those without regular visas were refused

entry. ○ He applied for the job through the regular channels (ie in the accepted way). **6** [attrib] (esp US) ordinary; not special: a regular deck of cards ○ He's just a regular guy. **7** (esp US) of an average size: Tubs of popcorn come in three sizes: small, regular and large. **8** [attrib] belonging to the permanent professional armed forces or police force of a country: a regular soldier/army ○ regular troops. **9** (grammar) (esp of verbs or nouns) having normal inflected (INFLECT 2) forms: The past participle of regular verbs ends in '-ed'. **10** (infml often ironic) (used for emphasis) thorough; complete: It turned into a regular brawl. ○ You're a regular little charmer, aren't you?

▶ **regular** n **1** a regular(8) member of the armed forces. **2** (infml) a regular customer or user, eg at a shop or restaurant: He's one of our regulars.

regularity /ˌregjuˈlærəti/ n [U] the state of being regular: the striking regularity of her features ○ the regularity of her daily routine/her attendance at church ○ Economic crises recur with monotonous regularity.

regularly adv **1**(**a**) at regular intervals or times: The cleaning lady arrives regularly at eight every morning. (**b**) frequently: He regularly appears on television. **2** in a balanced or regular manner: The garden is laid out regularly.

regularize, -ise /ˈregjələraɪz/ v to make sth lawful or correct: [Vn] Illegal immigrants are being given the opportunity to regularize their position.

regulate /ˈregjuleɪt/ v **1** to control sth by means of rules and restrictions: [Vn] regulate one's conduct/expenditure ○ measures to regulate the traffic (eg restrictions on speed) ○ The activities of credit companies are regulated by law. ○ Privatized industries are overseen by a regulating body. **2** to adjust an apparatus or a mechanism so that it functions as desired; to control speed, pressure, etc in this way: regulate a clock/radiator ○ This valve regulates the flow of water.

▶ **regulator** n **1** a person or an organization that officially regulates (REGULATE 1) an area of business or industry: the gas industry regulator. **2** a device that regulates (REGULATE 2) sth: a pressure/temperature regulator.

regulatory /ˈregjələtəri; Brit also ˌregjuˈleɪtəri; US ˈregjələtɔːri/ adj [esp attrib] having the power to regulate(1): regulatory bodies/authorities/agencies.

regulation /ˌregjuˈleɪʃn/ n **1** [C usu pl] a rule or restriction made by an authority: too many **rules and regulations** ○ fire/safety/building regulations ○ regulations concerning/governing the sale of weapons ○ That is contrary to/against (the) regulations. **2** [U] the action or process of regulating sth; control: international regulation of banking and tax laws.

▶ **regulation** adj [attrib] required by the regulations; correct: in regulation uniform ○ The player was suspended for the regulation eight matches.

regurgitate /rɪˈgɜːdʒɪteɪt/ v **1** (fml) to bring food that has been swallowed back up into the mouth again: [Vn] The bird regurgitates half-digested food to feed its young. **2** (derog) to repeat sth one has heard or learnt without really thinking about it: [Vn] The students are simply regurgitating my lectures. ▶ **regurgitation** /rɪˌgɜːdʒɪˈteɪʃn/ n [U].

rehabilitate /ˌriːəˈbɪlɪteɪt/ v [Vn] **1** to help sb to have a normal life again after they have been in prison or hospital for a long time: rehabilitate prisoners/the disabled in the community. **2** to restore sb/sth to their/its former higher status or position: rehabilitate a disgraced former leader. **3** to restore sth, esp a building, to good condition after it has been left to decay: The warehouses have been rehabilitated and converted into artists' studios. ○ (fig) measures to rehabilitate the country's ailing economy. ▶ **rehabilitation** /ˌriːəˌbɪlɪˈteɪʃn/ n [U]: the

R

rehabilitation of drug addicts ○ *a rehabilitation centre for psychiatric patients.*

rehash /ˌriːˈhæʃ/ v (derog) to put ideas or material into a new form with no great change or improvement: [Vn] *The group is rehashing its old hits.* ○ *His essay was just a rehashed version of my lecture notes.*
▶ **rehash** /ˈriːhæʃ/ n [sing] rehashed material: *a rehash of last summer's programme.*

rehear /ˌriːˈhɪə(r)/ v (pt, pp **reheard** /ˌriːˈhɜːd/) [Vn] (law) to hear or consider again a case in a lawcourt.
▶ **rehearing** n an opportunity for a case to be heard again: *apply for a rehearing.*

rehearse /rɪˈhɜːs/ v **1(a)** ~ (**for sth**) to practise a play, piece of music, etc for public performance: [V] *They are rehearsing for a new TV show.* ○ *rehearse with a full cast/orchestra* [Vn] *rehearse an opera.* **(b)** ~ **sb** (**for sth**) to supervise or train sb who is practising in this way: [Vnpr] *rehearse the actors for the fight scene* [Vnadv] *The musicians were well rehearsed.* [also Vn]. **2** to prepare in one's mind or practise privately what one is going to say to sb: [Vnpr] *He rehearsed the interview in his mind beforehand.* **3** (usu derog fml) to give a list of things, esp things that have been mentioned many times before: [Vn] *rehearse one's grievances* ○ *a well-rehearsed argument.*
▶ **rehearsal** /-sl/ n [C, U] a practice performance of sth, eg a play or piece of music: *have/hold/stage a rehearsal* ○ *perform a piece without rehearsal* ○ *a new production of 'Oklahoma' currently* **in rehearsal** ○ *a rehearsal room* ○ (fig) *This incursion is seen as a rehearsal for a full-scale invasion.* See also DRESS REHEARSAL.

reheat /ˌriːˈhiːt/ v to heat cooked food again after it has been left to go cold: [Vn] *Leave the soup to stand for two hours and then reheat it.*

rehouse /ˌriːˈhaʊz/ v to give sb a new house or home: [Vn] *tenants rehoused by the local authority during building repairs.*

Reich /raɪk, raɪx/ n (usu sing) (esp formerly) the German state or empire: *the Third Reich* (ie Germany under Hitler's rule (1933–1945)).

reign /reɪn/ v **1** ~ (**over sb/sth**) to rule as king or queen: [V] *the reigning monarch* ○ *George VI reigned from 1936 to 1952.* ○ (fig) *the reigning champion/Miss World* [also Vpr]. **2** (of an idea, a feeling or an atmosphere) to be dominant: [V] *Silence reigned* (ie There was complete silence). [V-adj] *Chaos reigns* **supreme** *in our house.*
▶ **reign** n the period of rule of a king, queen, EMPEROR, etc: **in/during the reign of** *King Alfred* ○ (fig) *his reign as director of the National Theatre.*
ˌ**reign of** ˈ**terror** n (pl **reigns of terror**) a period during which there is a lot of violence and many people are killed by the ruler or people in power: *fleeing from a reign of terror.*

reimburse /ˌriːɪmˈbɜːs/ v ~ **sth** (**to sb**); ~ **sb** (**for sth**) (usu fml) to pay back money to sb which they have spent or lost: [Vn] *My expenses were fully reimbursed.* [Vnpr] *We will reimburse the customer for any loss or damage.* [also Vnn]. ▶ **reimbursement** n [U, C]: *seek/receive reimbursement of medical expenses.*

rein /reɪn/ n **1(a)** [C often pl] a long, narrow, usu leather, band fastened around the neck of a horse. The rider holds and pulls the reins in order to guide and control the horse: *Don't let go of the reins!* ○ *ride* **on a short/long rein** (ie use more/less control). **(b) reins** [pl] a similar device for restraining a small child. **2 reins** [pl] **the ~s** (**of sth**) (esp rhet) the state of being in control or being the leader of sth: *hold/take up the reins of government* (ie govern/begin to govern). **IDM** **give, etc free/full** ˈ**rein to sb/sth** to give complete freedom of action or expression to sb/sth: *give free rein to town planners* ○ *allow*

one's imagination free rein. **keep a tight rein on sb/sth** ⇨ TIGHT.
▶ **rein** v **PHRV** ˌ**rein sth** ˈ**in**; ˌ**rein sb/sth** ˈ**back 1** to restrain or control sb/sth: *rein in public expenditure* ○ *The leader needs to rein back the extremists in his party.* **2** to slow down or stop a horse by pulling back the reins.

reincarnate /ˌriːɪnˈkɑːneɪt/ v ~ **sb/sth** (**in/as sb/sth**) (usu passive) to put the soul of a dead person in another body: [Vnpr] *be reincarnated in animal form* [also Vn-n, Vn].
▶ **reincarnation** /ˌriːɪnkɑːˈneɪʃn/ n **(a)** [U] the belief that after sb's death their soul transfers to a new body. **(b)** [C usu sing] a person or an animal in whom a soul is reincarnated: *He believes he is a/the reincarnation of Napoleon.*

reindeer /ˈreɪndɪə(r)/ n (pl unchanged) a large deer with long antlers (ANTLER) like branches. Reindeer live in cold northern regions: *a herd of reindeer* ○ *reindeer meat/skins.* Compare CARIBOU.

reinforce /ˌriːɪnˈfɔːs/ v **1(a)** to strengthen or emphasize a feeling, an idea, a habit, etc: [Vn] *reinforce sb's opinion/argument/conviction* ○ *Such jokes tend to reinforce racial stereotypes.* **(b)** to cause a process to continue or increase in intensity: [Vn] *Political instability has reinforced the country's economic decline.* **2** to improve sb's status or position; to increase sb's power: [Vn] *The Prime Minister's position has been reinforced following his successful visit to the USA.* **3** to make a structure or a material stronger, eg by adding another material to it: [Vnpr] *Concrete panels reinforced with steel.* [Vn] *reinforce a wall/bridge* ○ *Buildings have been reinforced to withstand earthquakes.* ○ *reinforced plastic/steel.* **4** to send more troops or military equipment to a place: [Vn] *The United Nations is reinforcing its military presence in the country.* [Vnpr] *The garrison must be reinforced against attack.*
▶ **reinforcement** n **1 reinforcements** [pl] extra soldiers, police officers or military equipment sent to a place: *an urgent request for reinforcements.* **2** [U, sing] the action or process of reinforcing sth: *the reinforcement of existing prejudices by the media.*
■ ˌ**reinforced** ˈ**concrete** n [U] concrete with metal bars or wires inside it to make it stronger.

reinstate /ˌriːɪnˈsteɪt/ v ~ **sb/sth** (**in/as sth**) **(a)** to restore sb to a previous position, esp an important one: [Vn-n] *reinstate sb as manager* [Vnpr] (fig) *Sue is now reinstated in his affections* (eg after a quarrel). [also Vn]. **(b)** to restore sth to its previous position; to bring sth back into force: [Vn] *reinstate the death penalty* [Vn-n] *Tennis has been reinstated as an Olympic sport.* ▶ **reinstatement** n [U].

reinsurance /ˌriːɪnˈʃʊərəns; Brit also -ˈʃɔːr-/ n [U] (finance) the practice of insurance companies buying their own insurance against losses resulting from claims made against them.

reinterpret /ˌriːɪnˈtɜːprɪt/ v to interpret sth in a new or different way: [Vn] *Historians are continually reinterpreting the events of the past.* ▶ **reinterpretation** /-ˈteɪʃn/ n [U, C]: *a radical reinterpretation of Shakespeare's 'Hamlet'.*

reintroduce /ˌriːɪntrəˈdjuːs; US -ˈduːs/ v **1** to bring into force again a former rule, system, etc: [Vn] *reintroduce the death penalty/foreign exchange controls.* **2** to put a species of plant, bird or animal back in a region where it used to live. ▶ **reintroduction** n [U, C].

reinvent /ˌriːɪnˈvent/ v to change sth so much that it appears to be sth completely new: [Vn] *Rembrandt virtually reinvented the art of painting.* **IDM** **reinvent the wheel** (usu derog) to spend a lot of effort creating sth which in fact already exists or is known: *We already have a fair and efficient tax system. Why reinvent the wheel?*

reinvest /ˌriːɪnˈvest/ v ~ (**sth**) (**in sth**) (finance) to

---

[Vnn] = verb + noun + noun   [V-adj] = verb + adjective   For more help with verbs, see Study pages **B4–8**.

invest money made from one investment in other investments, etc: [Vnpr] *The company's profits are reinvested in new equipment.* [also Vpr, Vn, V]. ▶ **reinvestment** *n* [U, C].

reissue /ˌriːˈɪʃuː/ *v* ~ **sth (as sth)** to issue sth again, esp sth that has not been available for some time: [Vn] *reissue a book/stamp/coin* [Vnpr] *old jazz recordings reissued on compact disc* [Vn-n] *The novel was reissued as a paperback.*
▶ **reissue** *n* a thing reissued, esp an old book or recording newly available: *a reissue of a 1953 recording of 'Don Giovanni'.*

reiterate /riˈɪtəreɪt/ *v* (*fml*) to repeat sth that has already been said, esp for emphasis: [Vn] *reiterate an argument/a demand/an offer* [V.that] *Let me reiterate that we are fully committed to this policy.* ▶ **reiteration** /riˌɪtəˈreɪʃn/ *n* [U,C usu *sing*]: *a reiteration of her previous statement.*

reject /rɪˈdʒekt/ *v* **1** to refuse to accept or consider sth given or offered: [Vn] *reject a gift/an argument/ a decision/a possibility/a suggestion* ○ *a rejected candidate/applicant* ○ *The proposal was firmly/flatly rejected.* ○ *After the transplant his body rejected* (ie failed to adapt to) *the new heart.* **2** to put aside or not use sb/sth that is not of an adequate quality or standard: [Vn] *Imperfect articles are rejected by our quality control.* ○ *Previously rejected players have been brought back into the team.* [Vn-adj] *The army doctors rejected several recruits as unfit.* **3** to fail to give a person or an animal due attention, care or affection: [Vn] *The child was rejected by its parents.* ○ *The lioness rejected the smallest cub.*
▶ **reject** /ˈriːdʒekt/ *n* a rejected thing or person: *The rejects* (ie damaged or spoiled goods) *are sold off cheaply.* ○ *reject china/furniture/clothing.*
rejection /rɪˈdʒekʃn/ *n* [U, C]: *Her proposal met with unanimous rejection/continual rejections.* ○ *a rejection letter/slip* (ie a formal letter or note saying that one is not being offered a job, one's book has not been accepted for publication, etc).

rejig /ˌriːˈdʒɪg/ *v* (**-gg-**) (*Brit infml*) to make changes in sth; to arrange sth differently: [Vn] *rejig the kitchen to fit in the new cooker* ○ *The whole plan will have to be rejigged.*

rejoice /rɪˈdʒɔɪs/ *v* ~ **(at/in/over sth)** (*dated or fml*) to feel or show great joy: [Vpr] *rejoice over a victory* ○ *rejoice at/in sb's success/the misfortunes of a rival* [V] *There is no reason to rejoice.* [V.to inf] *We rejoiced to see our son well again.* [V.that] *We rejoiced that the war was over.* **PHRV** re**ˈjoice in sth** (*joc*) to have or enjoy having a particular name or title which may seem amusing or unusual to others: *She rejoiced in the name of Cassandra Postlethwaite.*
▶ **rejoicing** *n* (**a**) [U] happiness; joy; celebration: *a hymn of rejoicing* ○ *There was much/loud rejoicing after the victory.* (**b**) **rejoicings** [pl] expressions of joy; celebrations: *great rejoicings.*

rejoin¹ /ˌriːˈdʒɔɪn/ *v* to join sb/sth again after leaving them/it: [Vn] *rejoin a club/the army* ○ *She made a detour and rejoined us on the other side of the wood.* ○ *He rejoined his regiment after a few days' leave.* ○ *This lane rejoins the main road further on.* [also V].

rejoin² /rɪˈdʒɔɪn/ *v* (*fml*) (no passive) to say sth as a sharp or amusing reply: [V.speech] *'You're wrong!' she rejoined.*

rejoinder /rɪˈdʒɔɪndə(r)/ *n* (*fml*) a reply, esp a sharp or amusing one: *'No!' was his curt rejoinder.*

rejuvenate /rɪˈdʒuːvəneɪt/ *v* to make sb/sth look or feel younger or more lively: [Vn] *feel rejuvenated after a long holiday* ○ *This cream will rejuvenate your skin/complexion.* ○ (*fig*) *rejuvenate antique furniture/ derelict areas.* ▶ **rejuvenation** /rɪˌdʒuːvəˈneɪʃn/ *n* [U, sing]: *the rejuvenation of a flagging career.*

rekindle /ˌriːˈkɪndl/ *v* to make sth become active again; to revive sth: [Vn] *rekindle interest/*

enthusiasm/hope* ○ *These pay increases may rekindle inflation.*

re-laid *pt, pp* of RE-LAY.

relapse /rɪˈlæps/ *v* ~ **(into sth/doing sth)** to fall back into a previous condition or into a worse state after making an improvement: [Vpr] *relapse into bad habits* ○ *relapse into unconsciousness/silence/ crime* [V] *She managed to give up smoking for two months but then relapsed.*
▶ **relapse** /rɪˈlæps, ˈriːlæps/ *n* an instance of relapsing, esp after partial recovery from an illness: *have/suffer a relapse.*

relate /rɪˈleɪt/ *v* **1** ~ **sth (to/with sth)** to establish a connection between eg ideas, events or situations; to link or associate sth with sth else: [Vn] *I found it difficult to relate the two concepts in my mind.* [Vnpr] *In future, pay increases will be related to improved productivity.* **2** ~ **sth (to sb)** (*fml*) to give a spoken or written account of sth; to tell a story: [Vn] *relate one's experiences/the events of the last week* [V.wh, Vpr.wh] *She related (to them) how it happened.* [also Vnpr, V.that, Vpr.that]. **PHRV** re**ˈlate to sth/sb 1** to be connected with sth/sb; to refer to sth/ sb: *statements/documents/statistics relating to economic policy* ○ *Does the new law relate only to theft/ motorists?* **2** (*infml*) to be able to understand and have sympathy with sb/sth: [Vpr] *Some adults can't relate to children.* ○ *Our product needs an image that people can relate to.*
▶ **related** *adj* ~ **(to sth/sb) 1** connected or associated with sth/sb: *crime related to drug abuse* ○ *pollution, conservation and other related topics.* **2** in the same family, group, etc: *related species/ languages* ○ *We're distantly related.* ○ *He is related to her by marriage.* Compare UNRELATED. **relatedness** *n* [U].

relation /rɪˈleɪʃn/ *n* **1 relations** [pl] ~ **s (between sb/sth and sb/sth)**; ~ **s (with sb/sth)** links, contacts or dealings between people, groups or countries: *diplomatic/international/trade relations* ○ *the friendly relations (existing) between our two countries* ○ *US-Chinese relations* ○ *sexual relations* ○ *community relations* (eg between different races in the same country) ○ *Relations between us are rather strained* (ie difficult or awkward) *at present.* ○ *break off (all) relations with one's family.* See also INDUSTRIAL RELATIONS, PUBLIC RELATIONS, RACE RELATIONS. **2** [U] ~ **(between sth and sth)**; ~ **(to sth)** a close connection between two or more things: *the relation of cause and effect* ○ *the relation between rainfall and crop yields* ○ *Your conclusion bears no relation to the rest of your essay.* **3(a)** [C] a person in the same family as another; a person who is related to another: *a close/near/distant relation of mine* ○ *a relation by marriage.* (**b**) [U] ~ **(to sb)** a family connection: *Is he any relation (to you)?* ○ *His surname is also Brady but we're no relation.* See also BLOOD RELATION, POOR RELATION. **IDM** **in relation to sth/sb 1** concerning sth/sb; with reference to sth/sb: *his comments in relation to this affair.* **2** with reference to the amount, level or size of sth; in proportion to sth: *Temperature varies in relation to pressure.* ○ *You've drawn the people too large in relation to the buildings.*
▶ **relational** /-ʃənl/ *adj* (*fml or techn*) existing or considered in relation to sth else: *Science tells us about the structural and relational properties of objects.* ○ (*computing*) *a relational database* (ie one that can recognize the connection between stored items of information).

NOTE Compare **relation**, **relations** and **relationship**. A **relation** is somebody in your family: *A relation of mine is coming to stay.* The way people are connected in a family is their **relationship**: *'What's your relationship to John?' 'He's my brother-in-law.'* A **relationship** is a friendship and strong

R

emotional connection between two people: *Their relationship broke up after three years.* It can also refer to the way people or things are connected and affect each other: *Do you have a good relationship with your parents?* ○ *Britain has a special relationship with the USA.* **Relations** are the official connections or friendships between countries, organizations, etc: *Relations between the two countries have improved.* **Relation** and **relationship** can mean a similarity or connection between things: *Is there a relation/relationship between violence on television and violent crime?*

relationship *n* **1** ~ (between A and B); ~ (with sb) **(a)** links, contacts or dealings between people, groups or countries: *They have a very close relationship.* ○ *Ours is a purely business/professional relationship.* ○ *the special relationship between Britain and the USA* ○ *I have a good working relationship with my boss.* See also LOVE-HATE RELATIONSHIP. **(b)** a loving or sexual association between two people: *have a relationship with sb* ○ *Their affair did not develop into a lasting relationship.* **2** ~ (between A and B); ~ (of A to B) the way in which certain things, ideas, events, etc are connected; the state of being connected: *the relationship between thought and language* ○ *examine the relationship of his artistic style to that of his contemporaries* ○ *The level of tax bears no relationship to people's ability to pay.* **3** ~ (between A and B); ~ (of A to B) the state of being related by birth or marriage: *a father-son relationship* ○ *I'm not sure of their exact relationship — I think they're cousins.* ⇨ note at RELATION.

relative /'relətɪv/ *adj* **1(a)** ~ (to sth) considered in relation to or in proportion to sth/sb else: *the relative merits of the two plans/candidates/cars* ○ *the position of the sun relative to the earth.* **(b)** [attrib] to a moderate or fairly high degree, esp compared to other people or things or to previous circumstances: *They are living in relative comfort.* ○ *Given the team's run of defeats, this draw was a relative success.* Compare ABSOLUTE 4. **2** ~ to sth (*fml*) (following *ns*) having a connection with sth; referring to sth: *the facts/papers relative to the case.* **3** [attrib] (*grammar*) (abbreviated as *rel* in this dictionary) referring to an earlier noun, clause or sentence: *In the phrase 'the man who came', 'who' is a relative pronoun and 'who came' is a relative clause.*
▶ **relative** *n* a person who is related to another; a person in the same family as another: *friends and relatives* ○ *close/distant relatives.*
relatively *adv* **(a)** in relation, proportion or comparison to sth/sb else: *Considering the smallness of the car, it is relatively roomy inside.* ○ *People spend relatively less on food than they did ten years ago* (ie as a proportion of their total spending). ○ *Relatively speaking, this matter is unimportant.* **(b)** to a moderate degree; quite: *In spite of her illness, she is relatively cheerful.*

relativism /'relətɪvɪzəm/ *n* [U] (*fml*) the belief that truth is not always and generally valid, but can be judged only in relation to other things, eg one's personal circumstances.

relativity /,relə'tɪvəti/ *n* [U] **1** (*physics*) Einstein's theory of the universe, which states that all motion is relative and treats time as a fourth dimension related to space. **2** the state of being relative(1a): *a philosopher who emphasizes the relativity of all perception/progress.*

relaunch /,ri:'lɔ:ntʃ/ *v* to start or present sth again, esp in a completely new or different way: [Vn] *relaunch a product/magazine/political party.* ▶ **relaunch** /'ri:lɔ:ntʃ/ *n*: *a party to mark the relaunch of the appeal.*

relax /rɪ'læks/ *v* **1(a)** to rest after work or effort, eg by doing sth enjoyable: [V] *Just relax and enjoy the movie.* ○ *I like to relax with a good book/glass of wine*

when I get home from work. **(b)** to become or make sb become less anxious, worried or formal in manner: [V] *I'll only relax when I know you're safe.* ○ *Relax! Everything will be all right.* [Vn] *A drink after work relaxed him.* **2** to become or make sth become less tight, stiff or tense: [V] *Let your muscles relax slowly.* [Vpr] *His face relaxed into a smile.* [Vn] *a massage to relax the muscles* ○ *relax one's grip (on sth)* ○ (*fig*) *The dictator refuses to relax his grip on power.* **3** to let rules, regulations, etc become less strict or rigid: [Vn] *We could relax the entry requirements slightly in your case.* **4** to allow one's effort or attention to become less intense: [Vn] *You cannot afford to relax your vigilance/concentration for a moment.*
▶ **relaxation** /,ri:læk'seɪʃn/ *n* **1(a)** [U] rest and enjoyment: *The President doesn't have much time for relaxation.* **(b)** [C] an activity done for this purpose: *Fishing is his favourite relaxation.* **2** [U] the action of relaxing sth: *some relaxation of the rules.*
relaxed *adj* **1** not feeling or showing anxiety or tension; calm or rested: *a relaxed atmosphere in the classroom* ○ *She looked very relaxed after her weekend trip.* **2** not having or applying strict rules, an organized plan, etc: *a relaxed teaching style* ○ *Her father is fairly relaxed about/takes a fairly relaxed attitude towards discipline.*
relaxing *adj* helping people to become less tense or anxious: *a relaxing bath/drink/holiday.*

relay /'ri:leɪ/ *n* **1** (also **'relay race**) a race between teams in which each member runs or swims part of the total distance, the next member starting when the previous one finishes: *the 4 × 100 m relay* (ie with each of four people in a team running or swimming 100 metres) ○ *a relay team/runner.* **2** a fresh set of people or animals taking the place of others that have finished a period of work or some other activity: *Rescuers worked in relays to save the trapped miners.* Compare SHIFT² 2. **3(a)** (*radio*) an electronic device for receiving signals and transmitting them again with greater strength, thus increasing the distance over which they are carried: *a relay station/satellite.* **(b)** a programme or message broadcast in this way: *a relay from Radio Hamburg.*
▶ **relay** /'ri:leɪ, rɪ'leɪ/ *v* (*pt, pp* **relayed**) ~ sth (from…) (to…) **1** to receive sth, eg a message, and pass it on: [Vnpr] *relay the colonel's orders to the troops* ○ *Bribes were relayed to officials via secret bank accounts.* [also Vn]. **2** to broadcast a programme by passing signals through a transmitting station: [Vnpr] *a concert relayed (live) from the Royal Albert Hall* [also Vn].

re-lay /,ri:'leɪ/ *v* (*pt, pp* **re-laid** /-'leɪd/) [Vn] to lay eg pipes, a carpet, etc again.

release /rɪ'li:s/ *v* **1** ~ oneself/sb/sth (from sth) to allow a person or an animal to come out of a place; to set sb/sth free: [Vn, Vnpr] *release a prisoner/hostage (from captivity)* [Vnpr] *release the horses into the field* ○ *She gently released herself from his arms/embrace.* ○ (*fig*) *Death released him from his sufferings.* **2** ~ sth (from sth) to allow sth to fly, fall, etc freely: [Vn] *release an arrow* [Vn] *release toxic gases into the atmosphere* ○ *The bullet is released from the gun at very high speed.* **3** to free sb from an obligation: [Vnpr] *release sb from a contract/a promise/an undertaking* ○ *release a monk from his vows* [Vn] (*often euph*) *The club is releasing some of its older players.* **4(a)** ~ sth (to sb/sth) to allow news, facts or information to be made known: [Vnpr] *The results of the opinion poll have just been released to the media.* [Vn] *Police have released no further details about the accident.* **(b)** to make sth available to the public: [Vn] *release a movie/book/record* [Vnpr] *new products released onto the market.* **5** to make sth/sb available that was previously restricted in some way: [Vn] *The new bypass will go* *ahead as soon as the government releases the funds.* [Vnpr, Vn.*to* inf] *The new appointments will release existing staff for other projects/to work on other projects.* **6** to make sth less tight or firm; to let go: [Vn] *release one's grip (on sth)* ○ *Release the tension on the wire by loosening this screw.* ○ *The policeman refused to release my arm.* **7** to remove sth from a fixed position, causing sth to move, work or function: [Vn] *release the clutch/handbrake* ○ *release a switch* ○ *release the trigger of a gun/the shutter of a camera.*

▶ **release** *n* **1** [U, C] ~ **(from sth)** the action of releasing sb/sth or the state of being released: *an order for sb's release from prison* ○ *Death is often a welcome release from pain.* ○ *a release of tension* ○ *the release of toxic gases into the atmosphere* ○ *delay the release of a film/record/book* ○ *The movie is on general release* (ie is being shown widely at cinemas). ○ *the release mechanism of a lock.* **2** [C] a thing that is released (RELEASE 4b), esp a new record or film: *the latest new releases.* See also PRESS RELEASE.

relegate /'relɪgeɪt/ *v* **1** ~ **sb/sth (to sth)** to give sb/ sth a lower or less important rank, task or state: [Vnpr] *I have been relegated to the role of a mere assistant.* ○ *relegate old files to the storeroom* ○ *The issue has been relegated to the margins of politics.* [also Vn]. **2** ~ **sb (from sth) (to sth)** (*esp Brit*) (esp passive) to transfer a sports team to a lower division: [Vn, Vnpr] *Will Spurs be relegated (from the Premier Division/to the First Division)?* ▶ **relegation** /ˌrelɪ'geɪʃn/ *n* [U]: *teams threatened with relegation.*

relent /rɪ'lent/ *v* **1** ~ **(in sth)** to decide to be less strict, harsh or determined: [V] *She finally relented and let the children stay up late to watch TV.* [Vpr] *The police will not relent in their fight against crime.* **2** to become less intense: [V] *The pressure of this job never relents.* **3** (of bad weather) to improve: [V] *The rain relented just long enough for me to go shopping.*

▶ **relentless** *adj* **1** never ending; constant: *her relentless pursuit of perfection* ○ *relentless questioning/criticism* ○ *the relentless heat of the sun.* **2** not relenting (RELENT 1); strict or harsh: *be relentless in punishing offenders* ○ *a relentless enemy.* **relentlessly** *adv.*

relevant /'reləvənt/ *adj* ~ **(to sth/sb)** closely connected with sth; appropriate in the circumstances: *a highly relevant argument/point/suggestion* ○ *have all the relevant documents ready* ○ *gather information relevant to a public enquiry.* ▶ **relevance** /-əns/ *n* [U]: *have/bear some/no relevance to the matter in hand* ○ *historical events of contemporary relevance.* **relevantly** *adv: The applicant has experience in teaching, and, more relevantly, in industry.*

reliable /rɪ'laɪəbl/ *adj* consistently good in quality or performance, and able to be trusted: *a reliable assistant/witness/goalkeeper* ○ *a reliable watch/car* ○ *a reliable service/supply/source of information* ○ *My memory's not very reliable these days.*

▶ **reliability** /rɪˌlaɪə'bɪləti/ *n* [U] the quality of being reliable: *the reliability of public transport* ○ *What do you look for in buying a car — speed or reliability?* **reliably** /-əbli/ *adv: I am **reliably informed** (ie told by a reliable source) that he's about to resign.*

reliance /rɪ'laɪəns/ *n* [U] ~ **(on/upon sth/sb)** confidence or trust in sth/sb; the state of being dependent on sth/sb: *his total/increasing reliance on his wife* ○ *the country's reliance on imported oil* ○ *Don't **place too much reliance** on his advice.*

▶ **reliant** /-ənt/ *adj* ~ **on/upon sth/sb** [pred] having reliance on sth/sb; depending on sth/sb: *He's heavily reliant on bank loans.* See also SELF-RELIANT.

relic /'relɪk/ *n* **1** ~ **(of/from sth)** an object, a ruined building, a tradition, etc surviving from a past age: *relics of ancient civilizations* ○ *an interesting linguistic relic* ○ *a relic from the 1960s* ○ (*rhet*) *the books and records that were the relics of her youth.* **2** (esp *pl*) a part of the body or clothes or possessions of a

holy person kept after her or his death as sth to be deeply respected. ⇨ note at REST³.

relief¹ /rɪ'liːf/ *n* **1** [U, sing] **(a)** ~ **(from sth)** the easing or removing of pain, distress or anxiety: *doctors working for the relief of suffering* ○ *The drug brings/gives some relief from pain.* ○ *The weekend came as a welcome relief.* **(b)** the feeling that results from this: *a sense of relief* ○ *cries/tears of relief* ○ *I **breathed/heaved a sigh of relief** when I heard he was safe.* ○ *To my great relief/Much to my relief, I wasn't late.* ○ *It's **a great relief to** find you here.* ○ *'What a relief! They're safe!'* **2** [U] food, money, medical supplies, etc given to people in need, eg in a disaster area: *send relief to/provide relief for those made homeless by the earthquake* ○ *committees for famine relief* ○ *re'lief funds/supplies/organizations/ workers.* **3** [U, C] money given by the government to people in special need or difficulty: *qualify for tax relief* ○ *temporary financial relief for those adversely affected by the new law.* **4** [U] ~ **(from sth)** a pleasant break or change from sth that was difficult or boring: *The interruptions provided some **comic/ light relief** in an otherwise dull speech.* **5** [CGp] a group of police officers or soldiers replacing another group on duty: *'B' Relief come(s) on duty at 9 o'clock.* Compare SHIFT² 2b. **6** [sing] ~ **(of sth)** the action of freeing a town from a SIEGE(1a): *the relief of Mafeking.*

▶ **relief** *adj* [attrib] **(a)** (of a bus, train, etc) additional to a regular service: *A relief coach service was provided to carry the extra passengers.* **(b)** replacing sb and doing their job after they have finished work for the day, gone on holiday, etc: *a re'lief driver/ crew.*

■ **re'lief road** *n* a road that vehicles can use to avoid an area of heavy traffic, esp a road built for this purpose. Compare BYPASS 1.

relief² /rɪ'liːf/ *n* **1** (*art*) **(a)** [U] a method of carving or moulding in which a design projects from a flat surface: *in high/low relief* (ie with the design projecting a lot/a little from its background). **(b)** [C] a design or carving made in this way: *murals and reliefs of scenes from mythology.* **2** [U] the use of colours, dark areas contrasted with light, etc to make sth more prominent or noticeable: *The hills **stood out in sharp relief** against the dawn sky.* ○ (*fig*) *Performance-related pay has been **thrown into sharp/stark relief** by the current controversy.* **3** [U] the differences of height between mountains, hills and valleys on the earth's surface: *the stunning relief of the Grand Canyon.*

■ **re'lief map** *n* a map that uses various colours, etc to indicate the different heights of hills, valleys, etc.

relieve /rɪ'liːv/ *v* **1** to reduce or remove pain, distress, anxiety, etc: [Vn] *drugs to relieve the pain/ discomfort* ○ *relieve suffering/hardship among refugees.* **2** to make sth less difficult or serious; to reduce the level or intensity of sth: [Vn] *efforts to relieve famine in Africa* ○ *relieve the pressure on working mothers* ○ *The bypass relieves traffic jams in the city centre.* **3** to introduce variety into sth: [Vn] *relieve the tedium/boredom/monotony of waiting* ○ *Not a single tree relieved the flatness of the plain.* **4** to release sb from a duty or task by taking their place or finding sb else to do so: [Vn] *relieve a sentry/workmate/driver* ○ *You'll be relieved at six o'clock.* **5** [Vn] to end the SIEGE(1a) of a town, fort, etc by an enemy army. **6** [Vn] ~ **oneself** (*euph*) to empty one's BLADDER(1) or bowels. **PHR V** **re'lieve sb of sth 1** (*often joc*) to help sb by taking from them sth they are carrying, holding, etc: *Let me relieve you of your coat and hat.* ○ (*ironic*) *The thief relieved him of* (ie stole) *his wallet.* **2** (*fml*) to carry out a task or duty for sb else or instead of them: *The new secretary will relieve us of some of the paperwork.* **3** to dismiss sb from a job, position, etc: *relieve*

Mr Brett of his post as manager ○ *The general was relieved of his command/duties.*

▶ **relieved** *adj* feeling or showing relief[1](1b): *a relieved smile/look/expression* ○ *We were very relieved to hear you were safe.*

religion /rɪˈlɪdʒən/ *n* **1** [U] belief in the existence of a god or gods, esp the belief that they created the universe and gave human beings a spiritual nature which continues to exist after the death of the body. **2** [C] a particular system of faith and worship based on religious belief: *the Christian/Jewish/Hindu religion* ○ *practise one's religion.* **3** [sing] a controlling influence on one's life; a thing that one feels very strongly about: *Football is like a religion for Bill.* ○ *I approve of being punctual but she* **makes a religion of it.**

religious /rɪˈlɪdʒəs/ *adj* **1** [attrib] of or connected with religion or a particular religion: *religious worship/belief/faith* ○ *a religious service.* **2** (of a person) believing in and practising a religion; DE-VOUT(1): *She's very religious.* **3** [attrib] of a group of people committed to a religion, eg monks: *a religious house* (ie a MONASTERY or CONVENT). **4** very careful or exact: *pay religious attention to detail* ○ *be religious in one's observance of protocol.*

▶ **religiously** *adv* **1** in a religious(1) way. **2** very carefully or exactly: *I followed the instructions religiously.* ○ *She phones him religiously every day.*
religiousness *n* [U].

relinquish /rɪˈlɪŋkwɪʃ/ *v* ~ **sth (to sb)** *(fml)* to stop having, doing or claiming sth; to give sth up (GIVE[1]): [Vn] *relinquish control of a company* ○ *relinquish one's position as Governor* ○ *He had relinquished all hope that she was alive.* ○ *relinquish the struggle for freedom* [Vn, Vnpr] *relinquish one's grip/hold (on power)* [Vnpr] *She relinquished possession of the house to her sister.*

reliquary /ˈrelɪkwəri; *US* -kweri/ *n* a container for relics (RELIC 2) of a holy person.

relish /ˈrelɪʃ/ *n* **1** [U] ~ **(for sth)** great enjoyment, pleasure or satisfaction: *eat with great/considerable/obvious relish* ○ *have a relish for party politics* ○ *She savoured the joke* **with relish. 2** [C,U] vegetables mixed or cooked with spices, etc and served with plainer food to add flavour: *cucumber/sweetcorn relish.* Compare PICKLE 1, SAUCE 1.

▶ **relish** *v* to enjoy or get pleasure from sth: [Vn] *relish a meal/drink/joke* [V.ing] **relish the idea/thought/prospect of sth/doing sth** ○ *I don't relish having to get up so early.* [also V.n ing].

relive /ˌriːˈlɪv/ *v* to live through an experience, etc again, esp in one's imagination: [Vn] *relive the horrors of war* ○ *I relived that fateful day over and over in my mind.*

reload /ˌriːˈləʊd/ *v* [V, Vn] to load sth, esp a gun or a camera, again.

relocate /ˌriːləʊˈkeɪt; *US* ˌriːˈləʊkeɪt/ *v* ~ **(sb/sth) (from...) (to...)** (esp of a company) to move or move one's factory, offices, etc to a new place: [V] *take the decision to relocate* [Vadv, Vpr] *We're relocating (to) just south of Newcastle.* [Vn, Vnpr] *The company is to relocate its headquarters and most of its staff (to the Midlands).* ▶ **relocation** /ˌriːləʊˈkeɪʃn/ *n* [U]: *the relocation of industry* ○ *the cost of relocation* ○ *relocation allowances/expenses* (eg for those starting a new job in a different area).

reluctant /rɪˈlʌktənt/ *adj* unwilling and therefore slow to act, agree, etc: *a reluctant helper/supporter/admirer* ○ *She was very reluctant to admit her mistake.* ▶ **reluctance** /-əns/ *n* [U, sing]: *She made a great show of reluctance, but finally accepted our offer.* ○ *He only came* **with great/with a marked reluctance. reluctantly** *adv*: *They reluctantly agreed.*

rely /rɪˈlaɪ/ *v* *(pt, pp relied)* **PHRV** **reˈly on/upon sb/sth (to do sth) 1** to need or be dependent on sb/sth:

Nowadays we rely increasingly on computers to regulate the flow of traffic in the town. ○ *He relied on you(r) supporting him.* **2** to trust or have confidence in sb/sth: [Vpr] *You can rely on me to keep your secret.* ○ *She cannot be relied on to tell the truth.*

remain /rɪˈmeɪn/ *v* (usu not in the continuous tenses) **1** to be still present after other parts have been removed, used or dealt with: [V] *Very little of the house remained after the fire.* ○ *Only about half of the original workforce remains.* ○ *I feel sorry for her, but* **the fact remains that** *she lied to us.* ○ *leave the remaining points for our next meeting* ○ *There were only ten minutes remaining.* **2** to continue to be sth; to stay in the same condition: [V-adj] *remain standing/seated* ○ *He remained silent.* [Vadv] *Let things remain as they are.* [V-n] *In spite of their quarrel, they remained the best of friends.* **3** *(fml)* to be still needing to be done, said, etc: [V.to inf] *It* **remains to be seen** (ie It will only be known later) *whether you are right.* ○ *Much remains to be done.* ○ *Nothing remains except for me to say goodbye.* **4** *(esp fml)* to stay in the same place; to stay and not leave with others: [Vpr] *I remained in Mexico City until May.* ○ *The aircraft remained on the ground.* [V, Vp] *She left, but I remained (behind).*

remainder /rɪˈmeɪndə(r)/ *n* **1** (usu **the remainder**) [Gp] the remaining people, things or time; the rest[3]: *She kept a few of his books but gave away the remainder.* ○ *We spent the remainder of the day sightseeing.* **2** [C usu sing] *(mathematics)* the number left after one number has been divided into another, or one number has been subtracted (SUBTRACT) from another: *Divide 2 into 7, and the answer is 3,* (with) *remainder 1.* ⇨ note at REST[3]. **3** [C] the copies of a book still not sold when there is no longer a great demand for it. Remainders are usu sold at a reduced price.

▶ **remainder** *v* [Vn] (esp passive) to sell copies of a book at a reduced price.

remains /rɪˈmeɪnz/ *n* [pl] **1** what is left after other parts have been removed, used or dealt with: *the remains of a meal/chicken* ○ *the remains of a defeated army* ○ *I rescued the remains of my slipper from the dog.* **2** ancient buildings, etc that have partly survived when others were destroyed; ruins: *the remains of an abbey/of ancient Rome.* **3** *(fml)* a dead body: *His* **mortal remains** *are buried in the churchyard.* ○ *Investigators found a trench containing human remains.* ⇨ note at REST[3].

remake /ˌriːˈmeɪk/ *v* *(pt, pp remade /-ˈmeɪd/)* [Vn] to make eg a film or recording again or differently.

▶ **remake** /ˈriːmeɪk/ *n* a thing remade: *The movie is a remake of the 1932 original.*

remand /rɪˈmɑːnd; *US* -ˈmænd/ *v* (esp passive) to send an accused person away after a brief appearance at a lawcourt to wait for trial at a later date, esp while further evidence is being gathered: [Vnpr] *The accused was* **remanded in custody** (ie sent to prison until the date of the trial) *for a week.* ○ *He was* **remanded on bail** (ie allowed to wait at home for the trial). [also Vn].

▶ **remand** *n* [U] the state of having been remanded: *a remand prisoner* ○ *prisoners* **on remand** (ie waiting for their trial).

■ **reˈmand centre** *n* *(Brit)* a place where young people accused of crimes are sent temporarily to wait for trial.

remark /rɪˈmɑːk/ *v* ~ **on/upon sth/sb** to say or write sth as a comment; to observe sth: [Vpr] *I couldn't help remarking on her youth.* ○ *The similarity between them has often been remarked on.* [V.speech] *'I thought it was odd,' he remarked.* [V.that] *Critics remarked that the play was not original.*

▶ **remark** *n* **1** [C] a thing said or written as a comment: *make pointed/cutting/rude remarks* ○ *The* best way to treat a remark like that is to ignore it. **2** [U] (dated or fml) notice: There was nothing worthy of remark.

remarkable /-əbl/ adj ~ **(for sth)** unusual or exceptional; worth noticing: a remarkable person/ achievement/event/book ○ a boy who is remarkable for his maturity. **remarkably** /-əbli/ adv: Remarkably, his only injury was a bruised elbow. ○ She's remarkably tall for her age.

remarry /ˌriːˈmæri/ v (pt, pp **-ried**) **(a)** to marry a person after one's wife or husband has died or after a DIVORCE¹(1): [V] The widower did not remarry. **(b)** to marry the same person a second time: [Vn] She remarried her former husband ten years after their divorce. ▸ **remarriage** /ˌriːˈmærɪdʒ/ n [U, C].

rematch /ˈriːmætʃ/ n (usu sing) a match¹(1) or game¹(3) played again between the same people or teams.

remedy /ˈremədi/ n ~ **(for sth) 1** (fml) a treatment, medicine, etc that cures a disease or relieves pain: a popular remedy for flu/toothache/cramp ○ herbal remedies. **2** a way of dealing with or removing sth undesirable: seek a remedy for injustice ○ He found a remedy for his grief in constant hard work.
▸ **remedial** /rɪˈmiːdiəl/ adj [attrib] **1** providing, or intended to provide, a remedy or cure: undergo remedial treatment/therapy for a bad back ○ take **remedial action** against unemployment ○ undertake **remedial work** on a bridge. **2** for or consisting of pupils who are slower at learning or have fallen behind the others: remedial classes/lessons/groups.
remediable /rɪˈmiːdiəbl/ adj for which there is a remedy.
remedy v (pt, pp **-died**) to correct, change or improve sth undesirable: [Vn] remedy injustices/ mistakes/losses/deficiencies ○ The situation could not be remedied.

remember /rɪˈmembə(r)/ v (not usu in the continuous tenses) **1(a)** to have or keep in the memory sth that was said, done or agreed previously; to recall(1) sth to one's memory: [Vadv] If I remember rightly the party starts at 8 pm. [V] 'Have you met my brother?' 'Not as far as I remember.' [Vn] I can't/ don't remember his name. ○ Robert's contribution should also be remembered. [V.that] Remember (that) we're going out tonight. [V.wh] Do you remember where you put the key? [V.ing] I remember posting the letters. [V.n ing] I remember him objecting to the scheme. [Vn-n] He remembered her as a slim young girl. **(b)** to do what one intends or is expected to do at the appropriate time; not to forget to do sth: [V.to inf] Don't forget to ring your father. **2** to give money, etc to sb/sth: [Vn] Please remember (ie do not forget to give a tip to) the waiter. ○ remember sb in one's will ○ Auntie Jill always remembers my birthday (eg by sending a card or present). **3** to mention or think with respect about sb, esp in one's prayers: [Vn] remember the sick, the old and the needy ○ a church service to remember the war dead. **PHRV** re**'member sb to sb** to pass greetings from one person to another: Please remember me to Jenny when you see her.

remembrance /rɪˈmembrəns/ n (fml) **1** [U] the process of remembering sb/sth; memory: a service in remembrance of those killed in the war ○ a chapel of remembrance (ie in a church). **2** [C] a thing given or kept in memory of sb/sth: He sent us a small remembrance of his visit.

■ Re,membrance 'Sunday (also Re'membrance Day) n (in Britain) the Sunday nearest to 11 November, on which those killed in war, esp the wars of 1914–18 and 1939–45, are remembered in church services, prayers, etc.

remind /rɪˈmaɪnd/ v ~ **sb (of/about sth)** to tell sb again about sth or to do sth; to help sb to remember sth that they may have forgotten: [Vn] Do I have to

remind you yet again? ○ **That** (eg What you have just said, done, etc) **reminds me**, I must feed the cat. [Vnpr] 'Don't forget the camera.' 'Remind me of/ about it nearer the time.' [Vn.that] Travellers to the region are reminded that malaria tablets are advisable. [Vn.to inf] Remind me to answer that letter. [also Vn.wh]. **PHRV** re**'mind sb of sb/sth** to cause sb to remember or think about sb/sth because of certain similar features or mental associations: He reminds me of his brother. ○ This song reminds me of France.
▸ **reminder** n **1** a thing that reminds sb, or a way of reminding sb, about sth or to do sth: be a constant/permanent/salutary/timely reminder of the futility of war ○ The sudden cold weather served as **a reminder** that winter was not yet over. **2** a letter or note sent to inform sb that it is time for them to do sth: I've received another reminder from the electricity board (ie to pay a bill).

reminisce /ˌremɪˈnɪs/ v ~ **(about sth/sb)** to think, talk or write about past events and experiences, usu with enjoyment: [Vpr] She often reminisced about her youth. [also V].

reminiscence /ˌremɪˈnɪsns/ n **1** [U] the recalling (RECALL 1) of past events and experiences: reminiscence of childhood. **2 reminiscences** [pl] **(a)** a spoken or written account of one's remembered experiences: the writer's reminiscences of his life abroad. **(b)** thoughts, words, feelings, etc that remind sb of sth else: Her work is full of reminiscences of earlier poetry.

reminiscent /ˌremɪˈnɪsnt/ adj **1** [pred] ~ **of sb/sth** reminding one of or suggesting sb/sth: His style is faintly reminiscent of Picasso's. **2** concerned with thinking about past events and experiences: in a reminiscent mood.

remiss /rɪˈmɪs/ adj [pred] ~ **(in sth)** (fml) careless about doing sth one should do: I have been very remiss in my duty. ○ It was remiss of her to forget to pay the bill.

remission /rɪˈmɪʃn/ n **1** [U, C] **(a)** the reduction of a prison sentence because of good behaviour: get (a) remission of six months/get six months' remission. **(b)** the cancelling, or reduction of a debt, payment, penalty, etc: full/partial remission of exam fees ○ various tax remissions. **2** [U, C] a reduction in force or degree, esp of pain or disease: The drug produced dramatic remissions in some patients. **3** [U] the forgiving of sins by God.

remit¹ /rɪˈmɪt/ v (**-tt-**) (fml) **1** ~ **sth (to sb)** to send money, etc to a person or place, esp by post: [Vn] remit a fee/cheque [Vnpr] Payment will be remitted to you in full. **2** to cancel or free sb from a punishment, debt, payment, etc: [Vn] remit a prison sentence ○ remit a tax/a fine/fees. **PHRV** re**'mit sth to sb** (law) (esp passive) to send a matter to be decided to an authority: The case has been remitted for rehearing before another judge.

remit² /ˈriːmɪt, rɪˈmɪt/ n [sing] the area of control or influence that an official person or group has: extend/widen/alter a remit ○ be given a remit to protect the landscape ○ Staff recruitment is outside our remit.

remittance /rɪˈmɪtns/ n **(a)** [C] a sum of money sent in payment for sth: Please return the completed form with your remittance. **(b)** [U] the sending of money in payment for sth: Remittance may be made by credit card or by cheque.

remix /ˌriːˈmɪks/ v [Vn] to record music again, esp by mixing it with sounds, voices, etc recorded before. ▸ **remix** /ˈriːmɪks/ n: a dance/disco remix ○ The band released a remix of their first single.

remnant /ˈremnənt/ n **1** (often pl) **(a)** an amount or part of sth that remains: the remnants of a meal ○ a few remnants of furniture and household goods. **(b)** a trace of sth that survives: the last remnants of a *traditional way of life.* ➪ note at REST³. **2** a small piece of material or carpet left over from a roll and sold at a reduced price: *a remnant sale* ○ *cushions made from remnants.*

remodel /ˌriːˈmɒdl/ *v* (**-ll-**; *US* **-l-**) to change the structure or shape of sth: [Vn] *plans to remodel the education system* ○ *The inside of the old house was completely remodelled.*

remonstrance /rɪˈmɒnstrəns/ *n* [C, U] (*fml*) a protest: *Our remonstrances produced no effect.* ○ *There was no word of remonstrance.*

remonstrate /ˈremənstreɪt; *US* rɪˈmɒnstreɪt/ *v* ~ (**with sb**) (**about sth**) (*fml*) to make a protest or complaint about sb/sth: [Vpr] *We remonstrated with the neighbours about the noise.* [also V, V.speech].

remorse /rɪˈmɔːs/ *n* [U] ~ (**for sth/doing sth**) deep regret for having done sth wrong: *He was filled/overcome with remorse for not having visited his dying father.* ○ *The prisoner showed no remorse for his crimes.*

▶ **remorseful** /-fl/ *adj*: *He looked genuinely remorseful.* **remorsefully** /-fəli/ *adv*.

remorseless *adj* **1** without pity or regret: *remorseless cruelty.* **2** that cannot be stopped; strong and continuous: *a remorseless struggle* ○ *the remorseless rise of inflation.* **remorselessly** *adv*: *events leading remorselessly to war.*

remote /rɪˈməʊt/ *adj* (**-r, -st**) **1(a)** ~ (**from sth**) far away from where other people live; isolated: *a remote area/village/farmhouse* ○ *in the remotest* (ie most distant) *parts of Asia* ○ *live in a house remote from any town or village.* (**b**) [attrib] far away in time: *in the remote past/future.* (**c**) [attrib] distant in relationship: *a remote ancestor/cousin.* (**d**) ~ (**from sth**) separate in feeling, interest, etc; not connected with sth: *an abstract theory that seems rather remote from everyday life.* **2** (of people or behaviour) not very friendly or interested: *a remote expression* ○ *He seems rather remote.* **3** small; slight: *a remote possibility/chance* ○ *I haven't* **the remotest idea** *who did it.* ○ *The prospect of her recovery is increasingly remote.*

▶ **remotely** *adv* (usu in negative sentences) to a very small or slight degree: *not remotely amusing/interesting/possible.*

remoteness *n* [U]: *the remoteness of the mountains* ○ *remoteness from everyday life.*

■ **re·mote con'trol** *n* [U, C] control of a machine or device from a distance, usu by radio or electrical signals: *a remote control handset* (eg for switching channels on a television set) ○ *click/press the remote control* ○ *The car doors can be locked by remote control.* **re·mote-con'trolled** *adj*: *reˌmote-controlled 'cameras.*

remould ➪ RETREAD.

remount /ˌriːˈmaʊnt/ *v* **1** [V, Vn] to get on a horse, bicycle, etc again. **2** [Vn] to go up a ladder, hill, etc again. **3** [Vn] to put a picture, photograph, etc on a new mount¹(2).

▶ **remount** /ˈriːmaʊnt/ *n* a fresh horse for a rider.

remove¹ /rɪˈmuːv/ *v* **1(a)** ~ **sth/sb** (**from sth**) to take sth/sb away from a place or to another place: [Vn, Vnpr] *remove the dishes* (*from the table*) [Vnpr] *remove one's hand from sb's shoulder* ○ *The paintings were removed to a museum.* ○ *They were removed from the English class* (eg to have special lessons). (**b**) to take off clothing, etc from the body: [Vn] *remove one's hat/coat/gloves/glasses* [Vnpr] *remove the bandages/plaster from sb's arm.* **2** ~ **sth** (**from sth**) (**a**) to make sth disappear; to get rid of sth: [Vnpr] *remove doubts/fears from sb's mind* [Vn] *an operation to remove a tumour* ○ *remove problems/difficulties/objections* ○ *The threat of redundancy was suddenly removed.* (**b**) to get rid of sth by cleaning: [Vnpr] *remove graffiti from the subway walls* ○ *remove stains from clothing* [Vn] *She removed her*

make-up with a tissue. **3** ~ **sb** (**from sth**) to dismiss sb from a post, etc: [Vnpr] *He was removed from his position as chairman.* [also Vn]. **IDM** **once, twice, etc re'moved** (of a COUSIN(1)) belonging to a different generation: *He's my cousin's son so he's my first cousin once removed.*

▶ **removable** /-əbl/ *adj* that can be removed or detached: *removable cushion covers* ○ *a removable luggage rack.*

removal /-vl/ *n* **1** [U] the process of removing sth/sb or of being removed: *his removal from office* ○ *stain removal.* **2** [C] the transfer of furniture, etc to a different home: *house removals* ○ *a reˈmoval van/firm/service.*

removed *adj* [pred] ~ (**from sth**) very different: *a way of life that is* **far removed** *from our own.*

remover *n* **1** (in compounds) a thing that removes sth: *a stain/paint/nail varnish remover.* **2** (esp *pl*) a person or business that moves sb's furniture, etc to a new house: *a firm of furniture removers.*

remove² /rɪˈmuːv/ *n* ~ (**from sth**) a stage or degree of difference or distance from sth: *The book enables children to experience* **at one remove** (*from reality*) *a wide range of emotions.*

remunerate /rɪˈmjuːnəreɪt/ *v* [Vn, Vnpr] ~ **sb** (**for sth**) (*fml*) (usu passive) to pay sb for work or services.

▶ **remuneration** /rɪˌmjuːnəˈreɪʃn/ *n* [U] (*fml* or *rhet*) payment.

remunerative /rɪˈmjuːnərətɪv/ *adj* (*fml*) for which one is well paid: *a highly remunerative job/post/position.*

renaissance /rɪˈneɪsns; *US* ˈrenəsɑːns/ *n* **1 the Renaissance** [sing] the period in the 14th, 15th and 16th centuries during which there was a renewed interest in art and literature, inspired by a fresh study of ancient Greek art, ideas, etc: *Renaissance art/literature.* **2** [C] any similar renewed interest among people in general: *Folk music is currently enjoying a renaissance.*

renal /ˈriːnl/ *adj* [usu attrib] (*medical*) of or concerning the kidneys (KIDNEY 1): *renal tissue/failure.*

rename /ˌriːˈneɪm/ *v* to give a new name to sb/sth; to name sb/sth again: [Vn] *rename a street/country/company* [Vn-n] *The polytechnic was renamed 'City University'.*

renascent /rɪˈnæsnt/ *adj* (*fml*) becoming active again; reviving: *renascent nationalism.*

rend /rend/ *v* (*pt, pp* **rent** /rent/) (*arch* or *fml*) to tear sth apart with force or violence; to split sth: [Vnpr] *a country rent in two by civil war* [Vnp] *The tent was rent apart.* [Vn] (*fig*) *Loud screams rent the air.* See also HEART-RENDING.

render /ˈrendə(r)/ *v* (*fml*) **1** to cause sb/sth to be in a specified condition: [Vn-adj] *render sth harmless/useless/obsolete/invalid* ○ *Hundreds of people were rendered homeless by the earthquake.* **2** ~ **sth** (**for sth**); ~ **sth** (**to sb**) to give sth in return for sth or because it is expected: [Vn] *render homage/obedience/allegiance* ○ *a reward for services rendered* [Vnn, Vnpr] *render sb a service/render a service to sb* [Vnpr] *render help to the disaster victims* ○ *render thanks to God.* **3** to present or send in an account for payment: [Vn] *account rendered £50.* **4** to give a performance of music, a play, a character, etc; to portray sb/sth in painting, etc: [Vnadv] *The piano solo was well/poorly rendered.* ○ *The artist had rendered her gentle smile perfectly.* [also Vnpr]. **5** ~ **sth** (**into sth**) to express sth in another language; to translate sth: [Vnpr] *a concept that is difficult to render into English* [also Vn]. **6** to cover stone or brick with a first layer of PLASTER(1): [Vn] *a rendered building/façade/exterior.* **PHRV** ˌ**render sth 'down** to make fat, etc liquid by heating it; to melt sth.

▶ **rendering** /ˈrendərɪŋ/ *n* **1** a performance of or way of interpreting a piece of music or a dramatic

R

role: *a moving rendering of a Schubert song* ○ *his rendering of Hamlet.* **2** a version or translation (TRANSLATE) of sth written: *a rendering in Spanish of the original Arabic.* **3** a first layer of PLASTER(1) on stone or brick.

rendezvous /ˈrɒndɪvuː/ *n* (*pl* unchanged /-vuːz/) **1** ~ (**with sb**) a meeting at an agreed time or the place chosen for it: *arrange/make a rendezvous with Bill at the café at two o'clock* ○ *a secret rendezvous.* **2** a place where a particular group of people often meet: *The café is a popular lunchtime rendezvous.*

▶ **rendezvous** *v* (*pt* **rendezvoused** /-vuːd/) ~ (**with sb**) to meet sb at a rendezvous: [V, Vpr] *We arranged to rendezvous (with them) at the hotel at 6 o'clock.*

rendition /renˈdɪʃn/ *n* (*fml*) the way in which a dramatic role or a piece of music, etc is performed: *give a spirited rendition of a Bach chorale.*

renegade /ˈrenɪgeɪd/ *n* (*fml derog*) **1** a person who deserts a cause(3), political party, religious group, etc: *a renegade priest/spy/soldier.* **2** any person living outside or in opposition to society: *bands of renegades in the mountains.*

renege /rɪˈniːg, rɪˈneɪg/ *v* ~ (**on sth**) (*fml*) to fail to keep a promise, an agreement, etc: [Vpr] *renege on a contract/deal/debt* [V].

renew /rɪˈnjuː; *US* -ˈnuː/ *v* **1(a)** to begin sth again, eg after a pause or an interruption: [Vn] *renew peace talks* ○ *renewed outbreaks of terrorist violence* ○ *renew one's efforts/attempts to break a record.* (**b**) to make or form sth again after a period of time: [Vn] *renew a friendship/a relationship/an acquaintance* ○ *The pilot managed to renew contact with the control tower.* (**c**) to say or state sth again: [Vn] *renew a request/complaint/criticism/protest* ○ *I renewed my offer of help.* **2** to make sth valid for a further period of time: [Vn] *renew a passport/permit/lease/contract* ○ *renew one's subscription to a journal/membership of a club* ○ *renew one's library books* (ie extend the period for borrowing them) *for another week.* **3** to replace sth with new of the same kind: [Vn] *renew worn tyres/a roof* ○ *The light bulb needs renewing.* **4** (esp passive) to give new strength or energy to sth: [Vn] *work with renewed enthusiasm/interest* ○ *After praying, I felt spiritually renewed.* ○ *He came to regard her with renewed affection.*

▶ **renewable** /-əbl/ *adj* that can be renewed (RENEW 2): *Is the permit renewable?*

renewal /-ˈnjuːəl; *US* -ˈnuːəl/ *n* [U,C] the renewing of sth or an instance of this: *urban renewal* (eg removing old buildings to build better houses) ○ *permit renewals* ○ *the renewal date* (eg of a library book) ○ *Any renewal of negotiations will be welcomed.*

rennet /ˈrenɪt/ *n* [U] a substance that makes milk become thick and sour and is used in making cheese.

renounce /rɪˈnaʊns/ *v* (*fml*) **1** [Vn] (**a**) to agree to give up ownership or possession of sth, esp formally: *renounce a claim/title/legal right/privilege.* (**b**) to give up a habit; to abandon sth: *renounce strong drink/cigarettes* ○ *They've renounced their old criminal way of life.* **2** ~ **sb/sth** (**for sth**) to reject or stop following sb/sth: [Vn] *renounce terrorism/violence/war* ○ *renounce a treaty/an agreement* ○ *renounce one's earlier ideals/principles/convictions* [Vnpr] *a painter who renounced classicism for/in favour of a more romantic style.* **3** to refuse to associate with or acknowledge sth/sb: [Vn] *He renounced his former business partners.* ▶ **renouncement** *n* [U] = RENUNCIATION.

renovate /ˈrenəveɪt/ *v* to get old buildings back into good condition: [Vn] *The house has been completely renovated and modernized.* ▶ **renovation** /ˌrenəˈveɪʃn/ *n* [U,C usu *pl*]: *buildings in need of renovation* ○ *renovation work/plans/grants* ○ *The college is closed for renovation.* ○ *carry out extensive renovations to a hospital.*

renown /rɪˈnaʊn/ *n* [U] (*fml*) the state of being famous; fame: *win renown (as a singer)* ○ *an artist of (great/international) renown.*

▶ **renowned** *adj* ~ (**as/for sth**) famous: *renowned as an actress/for her acting.*

rent¹ /rent/ *n* [U,C] a regular payment made for the use of land, buildings, a telephone, machinery, etc: *owe three weeks' rent/be three weeks behind with the rent* ○ *pay the rent monthly* ○ *pay a high/low rent for farmland* ○ *a rent book/agreement/collector* ○ *rent control* ○ *Rents are going up again.* **IDM** **for rent** (esp on printed signs) available to be rented. Compare TO LET (LET¹).

▶ **rent** *v* **1** ~ **sth** (**from sb**) to pay rent for the use of sth: [Vnpr] *rent a holiday cottage from an agency* [Vn] *Did you buy your video or is it rented?* **2** ~ **sth** (**out**) (**to sb**) to allow sb to use sth in return for rent: [Vnpr, Vnp] *Mr Hill rents this land (out) to us at £500 a year.* [Vn, Vnn] *She finally agreed to rent (me) the room.* ⇨ note at LET².

rentable *adj* available or suitable for renting.

rental /ˈrentl/ *n* **1** [C] the amount of rent paid or received: *pay a telephone rental of £20 a quarter.* **2** [U] the renting of sth: *a car rental company* ○ *rental charges.*

■ **ˌrent-ˈfree** *adj, adv* for which rent is not paid: *a ˌrent-free ˈhouse* ○ *occupy rooms rent-free.*

rent² /rent/ *n* a torn place in material, etc; a tear¹.

rent³ *pt, pp* of REND.

renunciation /rɪˌnʌnsiˈeɪʃn/ (also **renouncement** /rɪˈnaʊnsmənt/) *n* [U,sing] the formal act or declaration of giving sth/sb up: *a/the renunciation of nuclear weapons/a sinful life.*

reopen /ˌriːˈəʊpən/ *v* to open sth or be opened again after a period of time: [Vn] *reopen a shop under a new name* ○ *reopen a discussion/debate/dialogue* ○ *The murder inquiry/case/trial was reopened.* ○ (*fig*) *reopen old wounds* (ie remind sb or be reminded of painful experiences, disagreements, etc in the past) [V] *School/Parliament reopens next week.* ▶ **reopening** /ˌriːˈəʊpənɪŋ/ *n* [U,C]: *the reopening of an old theatre.*

reorder /ˌriːˈɔːdə(r)/ *v* **1** to order sth again; to order fresh supplies of sth: [Vn] *Have you reordered the stationery?* [also V]. **2** to put sth in a new order: [Vn] *reorder the books on the shelf.*

▶ **reorder** *n* a demand for more or fresh supplies: *put in a reorder for Oxford dictionaries.*

reorganize, **-ise** /riːˈɔːgənaɪz/ *v* to organize sth again or in a different way: [Vn] *reorganize the accounts department* [also V]. ▶ **reorganization**, **-isation** /riːˌɔːgənaɪˈzeɪʃn; *US* -nəˈz-/ *n* [U,C].

Rep *abbr* (*US*) **1** Representative (in Congress). **2** Republican (party). Compare DEM.

repaid *pt, pp* of REPAY.

repair¹ /rɪˈpeə(r)/ *v* [Vn] **1** to mend sth that is broken or damaged: *repair a road/puncture/watch/shirt.* **2** to put sth right or compensate for sth: *repair an error/omission* ○ *repair a broken marriage* ○ *Can the damage to international relations be repaired?* Compare FIX¹ 7, MEND 1.

▶ **repair** *n* **1** [C usu *pl*] ~ (**to sth**) an act or result of repairing sth: *The shop is closed for repairs* (ie while repair work is being done). ○ *Heel repairs while you wait* (eg in a shoe shop). **2** [U] repairing or being repaired: *a road under repair* ○ *The vase was (damaged) beyond repair* (ie could not be repaired). ○ *a bike repair shop.* **IDM** **in good, bad, etc reˈpair** in good, bad, etc condition: *keep a car in good repair.*

repairable /-əbl/ *adj*: *The road is repairable at public expense.* Compare IRREPARABLE.

repairer *n* a person who repairs things: *a watch repairer.*

repair² /rɪˈpeə(r)/ *v* **PHRV** **reˈpair to ...** (*fml or joc*) to visit a place, esp frequently or in large numbers: *We all repaired to the nearest pub.*

reparation /ˌrepəˈreɪʃn/ n (fml) **1** [U] ~ (for sth) the action of compensating for wrong or damage done: *make reparation (to God) for one's sins.* **2 reparations** [pl] compensation for war damage, paid by a defeated enemy: *exact heavy reparations.*

repartee /ˌrepɑːˈtiː/ n [U] conversation that consists of quick clever comments and replies: *indulge in brilliant/witty repartee* ○ *be good at (the art of) repartee.*

repast /rɪˈpɑːst; US -ˈpæst/ n (fml or rhet) a meal: *enjoy a light/simple repast.*

repatriate /ˌriːˈpætrieɪt; US -ˈpeɪt-/ v ~ **sb (to sth)** to send or bring sb back to their own country: *repatriate refugees/prisoners of war/immigrants* [also Vnpr]. ▶ **repatriation** /ˌriːˌpætriˈeɪʃn; US -ˌpeɪt-/ n [U, C]: *voluntary/forced repatriation.*

repay /rɪˈpeɪ/ v (pt, pp **repaid** /rɪˈpeɪd/) **1** ~ **sth (to sb)** to pay back money owed to sb: [Vn] *repay a debt/mortgage/loan* [Vn, Vnpr] *If you lend me $20, I'll repay it (to you) tomorrow.* [Vn, Vnn] *Has she repaid you (the money she borrowed)?* **2** ~ **sb (for sth)**; ~ **sth (with sth)** to give sb sth in return for help, kindness, etc: [Vn, Vnpr] *How can I ever repay (you for) your kindness?* [Vnpr] *The firm repaid her hard work with a bonus.* **3** to be worth giving the thing specified: [Vn] *The report would repay closer scrutiny.*

▶ **repayable** /-əbl/ adj that can or must be repaid: *The loan is repayable in monthly instalments.*

repayment n (**a**) [U] the process of paying sth back: *the repayment of debts.* (**b**) [C] a sum of money paid back: *mortgage/loan repayments* ○ *Repayments can be spread over two years.*

rep¹ /rep/ n (infml) a representative(2,3): *a sales rep* ○ *elect a union rep.*

rep² /rep/ n [U] (infml) = REPERTORY 1: *act/appear in rep.*

repeal /rɪˈpiːl/ v [Vn] to withdraw a law, etc officially. ▶ **repeal** n [U].

repeat /rɪˈpiːt/ v **1(a)** to say or write sth more than once: [Vn] *repeat a comment/promise/demand* ○ *Am I repeating myself?* (ie Did I say this before?) ○ *She repeated what she had said.* [V.that] *I repeat: the runway is not clear for take-off.* [also V.speech]. (**b**) to do or make sth more than once: [Vn] *repeat an action/attempt/attack* ○ *Such bargain offers can't be repeated.* ○ *Repeat the exercise several times before going on to the next one.* ○ *The programme is repeated on Wednesday at 9 pm.* (**c**) ~ **(itself)** to happen more than once: [V] *a repeating pattern/beat* [Vn] *Does history/the past repeat itself?* (ie Do similar events or situations happen again later?) **2(a)** to say aloud sth that one has heard or learnt: [Vn] *Repeat each sentence after me.* ○ *He repeated what she had said word for word.* [also V.speech]. (**b**) ~ **sth (to sb)** to tell sb else sth that one has heard or been told: [Vn] *The story is too well-known to bear repeating.* [Vn, Vnpr] *Don't repeat what I said (to anyone) — it's confidential.* **3** ~ **(on one)** (of food) to continue to be tasted from time to time after being eaten: [V, Vpr] *Do you find that onions repeat (on you)?* **4** (used esp with *not* to emphasize that one has just said) [Vn] *I will not, repeat not, allow you to make remarks like that.*

▶ **repeat** n **1** an act of repeating sth; a thing repeated: *a repeat performance/showing* ○ (*commerce*) *a repeat order* (ie for a further supply of the same goods). **2** a radio or television programme that has been broadcast before: *'Is it a new series?'* *'No, only repeats.'* **3** (*music*) a mark indicating a passage that is to be repeated.

repeatable adj [usu pred] that can be repeated: *His comments are not repeatable* (eg because they were very rude).

repeated adj [attrib] done, said or happening again and again: *repeated blows/warnings/accidents.* **re-**

peatedly adv again and again: *He begged her repeatedly to stop.*

▶ **repeater** n (techn) a gun that can be fired several times without being loaded again.

repel /rɪˈpel/ v (**-ll-**) [Vn] **1** to drive or push sb/sth back or away: *repel an attacker/attack/invasion* ○ *The surface repels moisture* (ie does not allow it to penetrate). **2** to cause a feeling of horror or disgust in sb: *Gratuitous violence repels most people.* ○ *She was repelled by his filthy appearance.* **3** to push sth away from itself by an INVISIBLE(1) force: *North magnetic poles repel each other.*

▶ **repellent** /-ənt/ adj **1** ~ **(to sb)** causing strong dislike or disgust: *a repellent smell* ○ *repellent attitudes/images/behaviour* ○ *I find his selfishness repellent.* ○ *The idea is repellent to me.* **2** (in compounds) that cannot be penetrated by the specified substance: *a water-repellent fabric.* — n [U] **1** a chemical that repels insects: *mosquito repellent.* **2** a substance used to treat fabric, stone, etc so that water does not penetrate it.

repent /rɪˈpent/ v ~ **(of sth)** (fml) to feel regret or sorrow about sth that one has done or failed to do: [V, Vpr] *Repent (of your sins) and ask God's forgiveness.* [Vn] *He soon repented his actions.*

▶ **repentance** /-əns/ n [U] ~ **(for sth)** regret or sorrow for sth bad that one has done: *show no sign of repentance.*

repentant /-ənt/ adj feeling or showing that one repents: *She wasn't in the least repentant.* ○ *He looked suitably repentant.*

repercussion /ˌriːpəˈkʌʃn/ n (usu pl) an indirect and usu unpleasant effect or result of sth; a consequence: *the social/political repercussions of the case* ○ *His resignation will have serious repercussions on/for the firm.*

repertoire /ˈrepətwɑː(r)/ (also fml **repertory**) n (**a**) all the plays, songs, pieces of music, etc that a performer or group of performers knows and is able to perform: *add to/extend one's repertoire* (ie learn sth new) ○ *have a wide repertoire of classical pieces* ○ *That tune is not in my repertoire.* (**b**) all the skills, etc that a person has and is able to use: *the developing verbal repertoire of young children.*

repertory /ˈrepətri; US -tɔːri/ n **1** (also infml **rep**) [U] the performing of several plays for short periods by the same group of actors in the same theatre: *act/work in repertory* ○ *play repertory for two years* ○ *a repertory actor/theatre/company.* **2** [C] (fml) = REPERTOIRE.

repetition /ˌrepəˈtɪʃn/ n **1** [U, C] the repeating of sth or a thing repeated: *learn by repetition* ○ *His speech was full of repetition(s) and pauses.* ○ *I want no repetition of this behaviour* (ie Do not do it again). **2** [C] a thing that has been done or said before; a copy: *He gave a repetition of yesterday's talk.*

▶ **repetitious** /ˌrepəˈtɪʃəs/, **repetitive** /rɪˈpetətɪv/ adjs (usu derog) containing too much repetition, and therefore boring: *a repetitive job/tune* ○ *repetitive questions* ○ *repetitious work.* **repetitiously**, **repetitively** advs. **repetitiousness**, **repetitiveness** ns [U].

rephrase /ˌriːˈfreɪz/ v to say sth again in different words, esp to make the meaning clearer: [Vn] *rephrase a remark/question/point.*

replace /rɪˈpleɪs/ v **1** to take the place of sb/sth: [Vn] *Machines have replaced people in many areas of industry.* ○ *Can anything replace a mother's love?* [Vn-n] *His deputy replaced him as leader.* **2** ~ **sb/sth (with sb/sth)** to exchange sb/sth for sb/sth that is better or newer: [Vn, Vnpr] *The battery needs replacing (with a new one).* [Vn] *He is inefficient and must be replaced.* **3** to put sth back in its place: [Vnpr] *replace the book on the shelf* [Vn] *replace the receiver* (ie after using the telephone).

▶ **replaceable** /-əbl/ *adj* that can be replaced. Compare IRREPLACEABLE.

replacement *n* **1** [U] the action of replacing sth or of being replaced: *the replacement of worn parts.* **2** [C] ~ (**for sb/sth**) a person or thing that takes the place of another: *hip replacements* ○ *find a replacement for Sue* (ie sb to do her work) *while she is ill* ○ *replacement staff.*

replay /ˌriːˈpleɪ/ *v* [Vn] **1** to play again a sports event, eg a football match that neither team won. **2** to play again sth recorded on tape or VIDEO(2c).

▶ **replay** /ˈriːpleɪ/ *n* **1** a replayed match. **2** the playing again of a short section of a recording, eg to look more carefully at sth: *a slow-motion replay of a goal being scored.*

replenish /rɪˈplenɪʃ/ *v* (*fml*) **1** ~ sth (**with sth**) to fill sth again: [Vn] *Let me replenish your glass* (eg with more wine). [also Vnpr]. **2** to get a further supply of sth: [Vn] *replenish one's stocks of pet food/ notepaper/light bulbs.* ▶ **replenishment** *n* [U].

replete /rɪˈpliːt/ *adj* [pred] ~ (**with sth**) (*fml*) **1** well provided or supplied with sth; filled with sth: *a game replete with drama and high tension.* **2** very full of food: *replete with turkey and plum pudding after Christmas lunch.*

replica /ˈreplɪkə/ *n* **1(a)** a close or exact copy of sth, eg a painting. (**b**) a model of sth made on a smaller scale[1](1): *make a replica of the Eiffel Tower.* **2** a person or thing that closely resembles sb/sth: *She was a cheerful replica of her mother.*

▶ **replicate** /ˈreplɪkeɪt/ *v* (*fml*) to be or make an exact copy of sth; to reproduce sth: [Vn] *The results of the experiment could not be replicated by other researchers.* ○ *The virus replicates itself a number of times in the computer.* **replication** /ˌreplɪˈkeɪʃn/ *n* [U, C].

reply /rɪˈplaɪ/ *v* (*pt, pp* **replied**) ~ (**to sb/sth**) (**with sth**) (**a**) to say or make an answer, in speech or writing; to respond: [Vpr] *fail to reply to a question/ letter/accusation* ○ *I replied with a short note.* [V.speech] *'Certainly not,' she replied.* [V.that] *He replied that he was busy.* [V] *Why doesn't he reply?* (**b**) to give an answer in the form of an action: [Vpr] *He replied with a nod.* ○ *The enemy replied to our fire* (ie fired back at us). [also V].

▶ **reply** *n* **1** [U] an action of replying to sb/sth: *She made no reply.* ○ *What did he do in reply to your challenge?* **2** [C] an answer in speech or writing; a response: *get/have/receive several replies to an advertisement* ○ *a reply-paid envelope* (ie one sent so that the person replying does not have to pay to send the reply). Compare ANSWER[1].

report[1] /rɪˈpɔːt/ *v* **1** ~ (**on sb/sth**) (**to sb/sth**); ~ sth (**to sb**) to give a spoken or written account of sth heard, seen, done, studied, etc; to describe sth: [Vpr] *report on recent developments* [Vn, Vpr] *report on progress made* [Vn] *report a debate/strike/ kidnapping* [Vnpr] *They reported their findings to the professor.* [V.wh] *I reported how he had reacted.* [V.ing, V.n ing] *She reported (his) having seen the gunman.* [Vn-adj] *The doctor reported the patient fit and well.* [also V.speech]. **2(a)** to make sth known, esp by publishing or broadcasting; to announce sth: [Vn, V.that] *A special news bulletin reported his death/reported that he had died.* [Vn] *The company reports pre-tax profits of over £50 million.* [V.n to inf] *She is reported to be making a good recovery in hospital.* [V.ing] *Journalists reported being fired on.* [also V.n ing, Vn-adj]. (**b**) ~ (**on**) sth to write about or send news as a journalist or reporter: [Vn] *There is still nothing definite to report.* [Vp] *This is Mark Tully reporting on the Indian elections for the BBC.* [also V.that,Vpr.that, V]. **3** ~ sb (**for sth**); ~ sb/sth (**to sb**) to make a formal complaint or accusation about an offence or the person who committed it: [Vnpr] *report an official for insolence* [Vn, Vnpr] *re-*

port a burglary/an accident (to the police) [Vn] *an increase in the number of reported rapes.* **4(a)** ~ (**to sb/sth**) **for sth** to tell sb that one has arrived, eg for work or for an appointment: [Vpr] *report for duty at 7 am* ○ *Please report to reception/the receptionist on arrival.* (**b**) to say formally that one/sb is in a particular state or condition: [V-adj] *He reported sick.* [Vn-adj] *The child was reported missing on Friday.* **5** ~ **to sb/sth** to be responsible to a person or department that supervises one's work: [Vpr] *All representatives report (directly) to the sales manager.* **PHR V** **re·port** **ˈback (from sth)** to return: *The officer reported back from leave on Sunday night.* **re·port** **ˈback (to sb/sth)** to give a spoken or written account of sth one has been asked to do or investigate: *He was requested to report back to the committee about/on his findings.*

▶ **reportage** /rɪˈpɔːtɪdʒ, ˌrepɔˈtɑːʒ/ *n* [U] the reporting of news or the typical style in which journalists do this: *a piece of dramatic reportage.*

reportedly *adv* according to what some people say: *The star is reportedly very ill.*

reporter *n* a person who reports news for newspapers, radio or television: *a reporter from The Guardian* ○ *our City/financial reporter* ○ *an on-the-spot reporter* (ie one who is at the scene of an event). Compare JOURNALIST.

■ **re·ported** **ˈquestion** *n* = INDIRECT QUESTION.

re·ported **ˈspeech** *n* [U] = INDIRECT SPEECH.

report[2] /rɪˈpɔːt/ *n* **1** [C] ~ (**on sth**) a spoken or written account of sth heard, seen, done, studied, etc, esp one that is published or broadcast: *reliable/ conflicting/detailed reports* ○ *produce/submit/draw up regular progress reports* ○ *a government report on crime* ○ *the school governors' report to parents* ○ *a firm's annual/monthly reports* (ie on its financial position) ○ *law reports* (ie written records of trials, etc in the lawcourts) ○ *radio/TV/press reports on the crash.* **2(a)** [C] a story or piece of information that may or may not be true: *reports of UFO sightings* ○ *I have only her report to go on.* (**b**) (*fml*) gossip or rumour: *Report has it* (ie People are saying) *that...* **3** [U] (*fml*) the way in which sb/sth is spoken of; reputation: *be of good/bad report.* **4** [C] (*Brit*) a written statement about a pupil's or an employee's work and behaviour: *a ˈschool report* ○ *get a good/ bad report.* **5** [C] an explosive sound, like that of a gun being fired: *the sharp report of a pistol/firework* ○ *The cork came out of the bottle with a loud report.*

■ **reˈport card** *n* (*US*) a school report[2](4).

repose /rɪˈpəʊz/ *v* (*fml*) **1(a)** to rest; to lie: [Vpr] *a picture of a nude reposing on a couch.* (**b**) ~ sth **on sb/sth** to lay an arm, etc on sb/sth for support: [Vnpr] *repose one's head on a cushion.* **2** to be kept in a place: [Vpr] *The vase now reposes in the British Museum.* **PHR V** **repose sth in sth/sb** (*fml*) to place one's trust, etc in sb/sth: *He reposed too much confidence in her/in her promises.*

▶ **repose** *n* [U] (*fml or rhet*) **1** rest; sleep: *disturb sb's repose* ○ *Her face is sad in repose.* **2** a peaceful state or time: *odd moments of repose.*

repository /rɪˈpɒzətri; *US* -tɔːri/ *n* **1** a place where things are kept or stored, esp a WAREHOUSE or museum: *a furniture repository* ○ *a repository for old legal documents.* **2** a person or book that has a lot of information, secrets, etc: *My father is a repository of local knowledge/folklore.*

repossess /ˌriːpəˈzes/ *v* to take back from sb property or goods for which payment is owed: [Vn] *repossess furniture* ○ *repossessed homes.* ▶ **repossession** /ˌriːpəˈzeʃn/ *n* [U, C]: *seek a repossession order* ○ *a huge rise in repossessions.*

reprehensible /ˌreprɪˈhensəbl/ *adj* (*fml*) deserving blame or criticism: *Your conduct/attitude is most reprehensible.*

represent¹ /ˌreprɪˈzent/ v **1** (esp passive) to be a member of a particular group and be present to speak or act on its behalf: [Vn] *Women were not represented in the government at that time.* ○ *Our school was well represented at the meeting* (ie A lot of people from our school were there). **2** to act or speak officially for sb: [Vn] *Members of Parliament representing Welsh constituencies* ○ *Our firm is represented at the conference by Mr James Hall.* ○ *Who is representing you* (ie acting as your lawyer) *in the case?* **3** (esp passive) to take the place of sb; to act as a substitute for sb: [Vn, Vnpr] *The President was represented (at the funeral) by the Vice-president.* **4(a)** to be; to constitute: [Vn] *These changes represent a threat to international security.* ○ *Indirectly, his words represented an accusation.* ○ *A pay rise of 5% represents an annual increase of £400 for the lowest-paid workers.* **(b)** to be the result of sth: [Vn] *This new car represents years of research.* **(c)** to be an example or expression of sth; to be typical of sth: [Vn] *Those comments do not represent all our views.* ○ *His new piece represents a major new trend in modern music.* **5** to be a symbol or EQUIVALENT of sb/sth: [Vn] *Phonetic symbols represent sounds.* ○ *What does x represent in this equation?* **6** to show an image of sb/sth; to DEPICT sb/sth: [Vn] *The picture represents a hunting scene.* [Vn-n] *The king is represented as a villain in the play.* **7** ~ **sth (to sb)** (*fml*) to try to make sth clear to sb: [Vn] *represent the rashness of a plan* [Vnpr] *They represented their grievances to the Governor.* [Vpr.that] *The lawyer represented to the court that the defendant was mentally unstable.* [also V.that]. **8** (*fml*) to describe sb/sth, often falsely, as having a certain character or qualities: [Vnpr] *Why do you represent the matter in this way?* [Vn-adj] *The risks were represented as negligible.* [Vn-n] *I am not what you represent me to be.* [also Vnadv].
▶ **representation** /ˌreprɪzenˈteɪʃn/ n **1** [U] the action of representing sb/sth or the state of being represented: *effective representation* (ie in Parliament) *of voters' interests* ○ *The firm needs more representation in China.* **2 representations** [pl] ~**s (to sb)** (*fml*) formal statements made to sb in authority, eg to make known one's opinion or to make a protest: **make representations to** *the council about the state of the roads* ○ *Union representations failed to influence the management's position.* **3** [C] (*fml*) a thing, esp a picture or model, that shows an image of sb/sth: *plastic representations of dinosaurs.* See also PROPORTIONAL REPRESENTATION. **representational** *adj* (esp of art) trying to portray things as they really are: *representational paintings.*

represent² /ˌriːprɪˈzent/ v [Vn] to give or send a cheque, bill, etc again for payment.

representative /ˌreprɪˈzentətɪv/ *adj* **1** ~ **(of sb/ sth)** **(a)** showing most of the ideas or opinions found amongst a particular group of people: *Is a questionnaire answered by 500 people truly representative of national opinion?* **(b)** containing examples of a number of types: *a representative sample/selection/survey* ○ *a representative collection of European insects.* **(c)** typical of a class or group: *The building is very representative of 1980s architecture.* **2** consisting of a group of people chosen by the rest to speak and act on their behalf: *representative institutions/ governments.*
▶ **representative** n ~ **(of sb/sth) 1** a typical example of a class or group: *representatives of the younger generation.* **2** (also *infml* **rep**) (*commerce*) an agent of a firm, esp a person who travels about selling its products: *act as sole representatives of the company in Turkey* ○ *their representative for the Middle East.* **3(a)** a person chosen or appointed to take the place of another or others: *the Queen's representative at the ceremony.* **(b)** a person chosen or elected to speak and act on behalf of others, eg in

a law-making body(4); a DELEGATE¹: *our representative* (ie MP) *in the House of Commons* ○ *send a representative to the negotiations* ○ *a representative of the Fire Brigade Union.* See also HOUSE OF REPRESENTATIVES.

repress /rɪˈpres/ v **1(a)** to restrain or stop an impulse: [Vn] *repress an urge to scream* ○ *repress a sneeze/smile/cough.* **(b)** (usu passive) to make sb restrain or hide their emotions, thoughts, etc: [Vn] *His childhood was repressed and solitary.* **2** to prevent discussion, protest, etc by force in order to stop others becoming influential or powerful: [Vn] *All opposition is brutally repressed by the regime.*
▶ **repressed** *adj* not happy or fulfilled because one has hidden or not acknowledged one's emotions and desires: *her emotionally repressed mother* ○ *repressed anger/desire/fear.*
repression /rɪˈpreʃn/ n **1** [U] the action of repressing sb/sth or the state of being repressed: *victims of government repression* ○ *the repression of free speech.* **2** (*psychology*) [U] the action of forcing desires and urges, esp those in conflict with accepted standards of behaviour, out of one's conscious mind, often resulting in unusual behaviour: *sexual repression.*
repressive /rɪˈpresɪv/ *adj* tending to repress(2); harsh or severe: *a repressive regime/law/measure.* **repressively** *adv.* **repressiveness** n [U].

reprieve /rɪˈpriːv/ v **1** to cancel or delay a punishment for sb, esp sb condemned to death: [Vn] *reprieve a condemned prisoner.* **2** to give sb/sth temporary relief from danger, trouble, etc: [Vn] *Three of the pits due for closure have been reprieved.*
▶ **reprieve** n (usu *sing*) **1** an official order cancelling or delaying a punishment, esp a death sentence(2): *grant (sb) a reprieve* ○ *The prisoner won/ was given a last-minute reprieve.* **2** temporary relief from danger, trouble, etc: *The gallery has won a temporary reprieve and will re-open in May.*

reprimand /ˈreprɪmɑːnd; *US* -mænd/ v ~ **sb (for sth)** to express severe disapproval of sb or their actions, esp officially: [Vnpr] *The company was reprimanded and fined £500 for failing to submit accounts.* [Vn] *The headmaster was severely reprimanded.*
▶ **reprimand** n [C, U] a spoken or written statement officially expressing severe disapproval of sb or their actions: *receive a stiff/severe/sharp/public reprimand* ○ *a letter of reprimand.*

reprint /ˌriːˈprɪnt/ v **(a)** [Vn] to print copies of a book, etc again, with few or no changes. **(b)** (of a book, etc) to be printed again: [V] *The dictionary is reprinting with minor corrections.*
▶ **reprint** /ˈriːprɪnt/ n **(a)** a new impression(6) of a book with few or no changes: *The work is into its fifth reprint.* **(b)** such a reprinted book. Compare EDITION 3.

reprisal /rɪˈpraɪzl/ n [C, U] an act of showing aggression or violence, esp political or military, towards those who have shown aggression, etc to oneself; retaliation (RETALIATE): *fears of reprisals against his family* ○ *After one of their aircraft was shot down they **took** reprisals.* ○ *They shot 10 hostages **in** reprisal.*

reproach /rɪˈprəʊtʃ/ v (*fml*) **(a)** ~ **sb/oneself (for sth / doing sth)** to blame or criticize sb/oneself, esp in a sad or disappointed way, for failing to do sth: [Vnpr] *She reproached him gently for forgetting their anniversary.* ○ *You have nothing to reproach yourself for* (ie that you need regret). [also Vn]. **(b)** ~ **sb/ oneself with sth** to criticize sb/oneself for a fault: [Vnpr] *She reproached him with aloofness.*
▶ **reproach** n **1(a)** [U] blame; criticism: *a word/ look/sigh of reproach* ○ *Her manners are **above/ beyond reproach*** (ie perfect). **(b)** [C] a word, remark, etc that criticizes sb: *heap reproaches on sb.*

2(a) [U] (*fml*) a state of shame or loss of honour: *bring reproach upon oneself.* (**b**) [sing] ~ (**to sb/sth**) a person or thing that brings shame upon sb/sth: *Poverty is/The poor are a constant reproach to our society.*
reproachful /-fl/ *adj* expressing blame or criticism: *a reproachful look/tone.* **reproachfully** /-fəli/ *adv.*
reprobate /ˈreprəbeɪt/ *n* (*fml or joc*) a person who spends a lot of time doing things which society in general considers IMMORAL(1), eg drinking alcohol or gambling: *You old reprobate!* ▶ **reprobate** *adj* [attrib]: *reprobate behaviour.*
reproduce /ˌriːprəˈdjuːs; *US* -ˈduːs/ *v* **1** ~ **sth** (**as sth**) to cause sth to be seen or heard again, or to occur again: [Vn] *The charm of the novel has been faithfully (ie accurately) reproduced in the film.* ○ *Can this effect be reproduced in a laboratory?* [Vn-n] *The computer reproduced the data as a set of diagrams.* **2** to make a copy of a picture, etc: [Vn] *This copier can reproduce colour photographs.* ○ *All paintings in this book are reproduced courtesy of the National Gallery.* **3** to have a specified quality when copied: [Vadv] *Some colours reproduce better than others.* **4** (of people, animals, plants, etc) to produce young: [V, Vn] *Reptiles reproduce (themselves) by laying eggs.* ▶ **reproducible** /-əbl/ *adj.*
reproduction /ˌriːprəˈdʌkʃn/ *n* **1** [U] the action or process of reproducing sth or of being reproduced: *Compact disc recordings give excellent sound reproduction.* **2** [U] the process of producing young: *sexual reproduction* ○ *study reproduction in shellfish.* **3** [C] a thing that has been reproduced, esp a copy of a work of art: *Is that painting an original or a reproduction?* ○ *reproduction furniture* (ie made as a copy of an earlier style).
▶ **reproductive** /ˌriːprəˈdʌktɪv/ *adj* [usu attrib] of or for the reproduction of young: *reproductive organs/systems.* ⇨ picture.
reproof /rɪˈpruːf/ *n* (*fml*) (**a**) [U] blame or disapproval: *She ignored her father's look of reproof.* (**b**) [C] a remark, etc expressing this: *receive a mild reproof from the teacher.*
reprove /rɪˈpruːv/ *v* ~ **sb** (**for sth/doing sth**) (*fml*) to criticize sb severely; to show that one disapproves of sb: [Vnpr] *The priest reproved people for not attending church more often.* [also Vn]. ▶ **reproving** *adj* [usu attrib]: *a reproving glance.* **reprovingly** *adv.*
reptile /ˈreptaɪl; *US* -tl/ *n* any of the class of cold-blooded (COLD[1]) animals that have skin covered with scales and that lay eggs: *Snakes, lizards, tortoises and crocodiles are all reptiles.*
▶ **reptilian** /repˈtɪliən/ *adj* of or like a reptile: *our reptilian ancestors* ○ (*fig derog*) *He licked his lips in an unpleasantly reptilian way.*

republic /rɪˈpʌblɪk/ *n* (**a**) a system of government in which there is an elected president, but no king or queen. The people of the country elect the government. (**b**) a country having such a system: *a constitutional republic* (eg the USA) ○ *the Republic of Ireland.* Compare MONARCHY.
republican /rɪˈpʌblɪkən/ *adj* of or like a republic; supporting the principles of a republic: *a republican movement/party/government* ○ *republican sympathies* ○ *the Irish Republican Army.*
▶ **republican** *n* **1** a person who supports republican government. **2** Republican (**a**) one of the two main political parties in the USA. Compare DEMOCRAT 2. (**b**) a person in Northern Ireland who believes that that country should be part of the Republic of Ireland and not be ruled by Great Britain.
republicanism /-ɪzəm/ *n* [U] support for republican principles.
■ **the Reˈpublican Party** *n* [sing] one of the two main political parties in the USA. Compare THE DEMOCRATIC PARTY.
repudiate /rɪˈpjuːdieɪt/ *v* (*fml*) **1(a)** to refuse to accept sth; to reject sth: [Vn] *repudiate a charge/view/claim/suggestion.* (**b**) to refuse to do sth that is required by an authority or an agreement: [Vn] *repudiate a treaty/contract/vow* ○ *repudiate* (ie refuse to pay) *one's debts.* **2** to refuse to deal with or be connected with sb any longer; to DISOWN sb: [Vn] *repudiate one's son/lover/former friend.* ▶ **repudiation** /rɪˌpjuːdiˈeɪʃn/ *n* [U].
repugnant /rɪˈpʌgnənt/ *adj* ~ (**to sb**) (*fml*) causing a feeling of strong dislike or disgust: *I find his racist views deeply repugnant.* ○ *The idea of eating meat is repugnant to me.* ○ *All food was repugnant to me during my illness.*
▶ **repugnance** /-nəns/ *n* [U] ~ (**at/for/towards sth/sb**) (*fml*) strong dislike or disgust: *the moral repugnance felt by many at this brutal massacre* ○ *She could not overcome her physical repugnance for him.*
repulse /rɪˈpʌls/ *v* (*fml*) **1** [Vn] to force an attacker or an attack to RETREAT(1a) by fighting. **2** to refuse to accept sb's offer, help, etc, often in a rude way; to reject sb/sth: [Vn] *repulse sb's kindness/sympathy/assistance* ○ *She repulsed his advances.* **3** (esp passive) to make sb feel strong dislike or disgust: [Vn] *repulsed by the horrible smell.* Compare REPEL 1,2.
repulsion /rɪˈpʌlʃn/ *n* [U] **1** a feeling of strong dislike or disgust: *be filled with repulsion.* **2** (*physics*) the force by which bodies tend to push each other away: *There are forces of attraction and repulsion between atoms.* Compare ATTRACTION.
repulsive /rɪˈpʌlsɪv/ *adj* **1** causing a feeling of strong dislike or disgust: *a repulsive sight/smell/person* ○ *Picking your nose is a repulsive habit.* **2**

male   **reproductive systems**

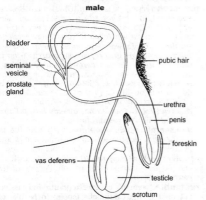

bladder
seminal vesicle
prostate gland
pubic hair
urethra
penis
foreskin
vas deferens
testicle
scrotum

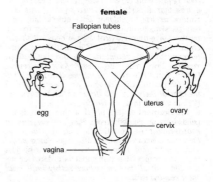

female

Fallopian tubes
uterus
ovary
egg
cervix
vagina

(*physics*) causing REPULSION(2): *repulsive forces.* ▶ **repulsively** *adv*: *repulsively ugly.* **repulsiveness** *n* [U].

reputable /'repjətəbl/ *adj* having a good reputation; respected or known to be of good quality: *a highly reputable firm/shop/accountant.* Compare DISREPUTABLE.

reputation /ˌrepjuˈteɪʃn/ *n* [U,C] ~ (**for sth/doing sth**) the opinion that people in general have about what sb/sth is like: *a school with an excellent/enviable/unrivalled reputation* ○ *a good/bad reputation as a doctor* ○ *have a reputation for laziness/for being lazy* ○ *compromise/ruin sb's reputation* ○ *establish/build up/make a reputation (for oneself)* ○ *live up to one's reputation* (ie behave, perform, etc as one is expected to).

repute /rɪˈpjuːt/ *n* [U] (*fml*) reputation: *a player of international repute* ○ *know sb only by repute* ○ *a house of ill repute* (ie a BROTHEL). **IDM** **of reˈpute** (*fml*) having a good reputation: *wines of repute* ○ *a doctor of (some) repute.*

▶ **reputed** /-tɪd/ *adj* [usu pred] ~ (**to be sth/to have done sth**) generally thought to be sth or to have done sth, although this is not certain: *He is reputed to be the best surgeon in Paris.* ○ *the house reputed to have been the poet's birthplace* ○ *She has sold her share of the company for a reputed £7 million.* **reputedly** *adv*.

request /rɪˈkwest/ *n* ~ (**for sth/that…**) (**a**) an act of politely asking for sth: *make an official request for more money* ○ *your request that I should destroy the letter* ○ *Catalogues are available on request* (ie if one asks for them). ○ *I came at my mother's request/at the request of my mother* (ie because she asked me to). ○ *The writer's name and address were withheld by request* (ie because he or she requested it). (**b**) a thing asked for in this way: *Her request was granted.* ○ *a radio request programme* (ie in which music, etc is played that has been requested by people listening).

▶ **request** *v* ~ **sth (from/of sb)** (*fml*) to ask politely for sth: [Vn] *He requested a loan from the bank.* [V.n to inf] *She received a letter requesting her to attend the award ceremony.* ○ *You are (kindly) requested not to smoke.* [V.that, Vpr.that] *They requested (of the terrorists) that they free the hostages.* [also Vnpr]. ⇨ note at ASK.

■ **reˈquest stop** *n* (*Brit*) a place where a bus will stop only if a passenger signals it to do so.

requiem /'rekwiəm, -iem/ *n* (**a**) (also ˌ**requiem ˈmass**) a special Christian ceremony for a person who has recently died, at which people pray for her or his soul. (**b**) a piece of music for this.

require /rɪˈkwaɪə(r)/ *v* (usu not in the continuous tenses) **1** (*rather fml*) to need or depend on sb/sth: [Vn] *Do you require any assistance?* ○ *Deciphering the code requires an expert.* [V.that] *The situation requires that I (should) be there.* [V.ing] *All cars require servicing regularly.* **2** ~ **sth (of sb)** (*fml*) (esp passive) to order or demand sth, esp from a position of authority: [Vn] *I have done all that is required by law.* ○ *an old building that does not meet the required safety standards* ○ '*Hamlet' is required reading* (ie must be read) *for the course.* [V.that, Vnpr] *It is required (of me) that I give evidence.* [V.n to inf] *Civil servants are required to sign the Official Secrets Act.* **3** (*fml*) to wish to have sth: [Vn] *Is that all that you require, sir?*

▶ **requirement** *n* (esp *pl*) **1** a thing that is depended on or needed: *goods that are surplus to requirements* (ie more than is needed) ○ *Our immediate requirement is extra staff.* ○ *Our latest model should meet your requirements exactly* (ie be just what you want). **2** a thing that is ordered or demanded: *Not all foreign visitors satisfy/fulfil legal entry requirements.*

requisite /'rekwɪzɪt/ *adj* [attrib] (*fml*) required or necessary: *have/lack the requisite experience for the job* ○ *The firm employs the requisite number of women.*

▶ **requisite** *n* ~ (**for/of sth**) (*fml*) a thing that is needed for a purpose: *toilet requisites* (eg soap, PERFUME(1), etc) ○ *A university degree has become a requisite for a career in this field.*

requisition /ˌrekwɪˈzɪʃn/ *n* [C, U] ~ (**on sb**) (**for sth**) an official, usu written, demand for the use of property or materials, esp by an army during a war or by certain people in an emergency: *a supply requisition* ○ *a requisition form/order.*

▶ **requisition** *v* ~ **sth (from sb)**; ~ **sth as sth** to demand the use of sth by a requisition: [Vn, Vnpr] *requisition ships (from the merchant navy)* [Vn-n] *The town hall was requisitioned as army headquarters.*

requite /rɪˈkwaɪt/ *v* (*fml*) to give sth in return for sth else; to REPAY(2) sth: [Vn] *the joys of requited love.* Compare UNREQUITED. ▶ **requital** /-tl/ *n* [U] (*fml*): *be killed in requital for one's crimes.*

re-route /ˌriː ˈruːt/ *v* to send sb/sth by a different route: [Vn] *re-route traffic/shipping/freight/luggage* [Vnpr] *My flight was re-routed via Athens.*

rerun /ˌriːˈrʌn/ *v* (**-nn-**; *pt* **reran**; *pp* **rerun**) [Vn] **1** to show a film or television programme or play a tape again. **2** to run a race again.

▶ **rerun** /'riːrʌn/ *n* a film or television programme that is shown again: *a rerun of a popular play/series* ○ (*fig*) *We don't want a rerun of Monday's fiasco.*

resale /'riːseɪl, ˌriːˈseɪl/ *n* [U] the sale to another person of sth that one has bought: *a house up for resale.*

reschedule /ˌriːˈʃedjuːl; *US* ˌriːˈskedʒuːl/ *v* [Vn] **1** to change a plan, esp so that sth happens later than originally intended. **2** (*finance*) to arrange for a loan, etc to be paid back later than originally planned.

rescind /rɪˈsɪnd/ *v* (*law*) to withdraw a law, contract, etc and declare that it is no longer valid: *rescind an agreement/order/act.* See also ANNUL.

rescue /'reskjuː/ *v* ~ **sb/sth (from sth/sb)** to save or bring away sb/sth from a dangerous or harmful situation: [Vnpr] *rescue sb from drowning/a fire/bankruptcy* ○ *You rescued me from an embarrassing situation.* ○ *The house was rescued from demolition.* [Vn] *Police rescued the hostages.*

▶ **rescue** *n* (**a**) [U] the action of rescuing sb/sth or of being rescued: *a rescue party/attempt/operation* ○ *A wealthy sponsor came to their rescue with a generous donation.* (**b**) [C] an instance of this: *Ten fishermen were saved in a daring sea rescue off the Welsh coast.*
rescuer *n*.

research /rɪˈsɜːtʃ, 'riːsɜːtʃ/ *n* [U] (also *esp Brit* **researches** [pl]) ~ (**into/on sth**); ~ (**on sb**) careful study or investigation, esp in order to discover new facts or information: *scientific/clinical/historical research* ○ *a startling piece of research on cancer/into the causes of cancer* ○ *be engaged in/carry out/do research* ○ *What do their researches show?* ○ *a research worker/grant/degree.* See also MARKET RESEARCH.

▶ **research** /rɪˈsɜːtʃ/ *v* ~ (**into/on sth**); ~ (**on sb**) to do research on sth/sb: [Vn] *a well-researched book* [Vpr] *researching into the causes of cancer among children* [Vn] *The subject has already been fully researched.* [also V]. **researcher** *n*.

■ **reˌsearch and deˈvelopment** *n* [U] (*abbr* **R & D**) (in industry, etc) the scientific search for new and improved products and manufacturing processes.

resell /ˌriːˈsel/ *v* (*pt, pp* **resold** /ˌriːˈsəʊld/) to sell sth one has bought to another person: [Vn] *resell the goods at a profit.*

resemble /rɪˈzembl/ *v* ~ **sb/sth (in sth)** (no passive; not used in the continuous tenses) to be like or similar to another person or thing: [Vn] *She resembles her mother.* [Vnpr] *an object resembling a turnip in shape.*

▶ **resemblance** /rɪˈzembləns/ *n* [U,C] ~ **(to sb/ sth)**; ~ **(between A and B)** the fact or an instance of being like or similar to another person or thing: *a striking/strong/close/passing resemblance* ○ *a family resemblance* ○ *There is a degree of resemblance between the two boys.* ○ *The film bears/has/shows little or no resemblance to the novel.*

resent /rɪˈzent/ *v* to feel bitter or angry about sth insulting, offensive, etc: [Vn] *I bitterly resent your criticism.* [V.n ing] *Does she resent me/my being here?* [also V.ing].

▶ **resentful** /-fl/ *adj* feeling or showing that one resents sth: *a resentful silence/look/voice* ○ *She felt angry and resentful at what had happened.* ○ *He was deeply resentful of her interference.* **resentfully** /-fəli/ *adv.*

resentment *n* [U,sing] the action or an instance of resenting sb/sth: *bear/feel/show no resentment against/towards anyone* ○ *She felt a deep-seated resentment at/of/over the way she had been treated.*

reservation /ˌrezəˈveɪʃn/ *n* **1** [C] a reserved seat, room, etc; a record of this: *a flight/hotel reservation* ○ *make/hold reservations (in the name of Baker).* Compare BOOKING. **2** [U,C esp *pl*] a reason or reasons for not agreeing to a plan, accepting an idea, etc: *express initial/major/minor/serious reservations about the offer* ○ *I support this measure without reservation* (ie completely). ○ *I have my reservations* (ie doubts) *about his ability to do the job.* **3** [C] (*Brit*) a strip of land along the centre of a road, dividing the traffic on either side: *the central reservation.* **4** [C] an area of land in the USA reserved for Native Americans to live in.

reserve¹ /rɪˈzɜːv/ *v* ~ **sth (for sb/sth)** **1** to keep sth for a special reason or to use at a later time: [Vnpr] *He told us to reserve our strength for the next day's climb.* ○ *These seats are reserved for special guests.* [Vn] *I decided to reserve (my) judgement until I knew all the facts.* **2** to have or keep a specified power: [Vn] *The management reserves the right to refuse admission.* ○ (*law*) *All rights reserved* (eg for a publishing company). **3** to order a seat, table, etc for use by a particular person at a future time: [Vn] *reserve two theatre tickets* [Vnpr] *reserve a table/ room for two in the name of Hill.*

reserve² /rɪˈzɜːv/ *n* **1** [C usu *pl*, U] a thing kept for later use; an extra amount available when needed: *dwindling oil reserves* ○ *have great reserves of capital/energy/stock* ○ *the ˈgold reserve* (ie to support the issue of paper money) ○ *a reserve (petrol) tank* ○ *funds kept/held in reserve.* **2** [C] an extra player chosen in case a substitute is needed in a team. **3** [C] a piece of land reserved esp as a protected area for animals and plants: *a ˈbird/ˈgame/ˈwildlife reserve.* **4**(**a**) **the reserve** [sing] forces outside the regular armed services and available to be called out in an emergency. (**b**) **reserves** [pl] military forces kept back, for use when needed. **5** [U] reasons that prevent one agreeing to a plan, accepting an idea, etc: *We accept your statement without reserve* (ie fully). ○ *He spoke without reserve* (ie freely) *of his time in prison.* **6** (also **reˈserve price**) [C] (*Brit*) the lowest price that will be accepted, esp for an item at an AUCTION: *The painting failed to reach its reserve and was withdrawn.* **7** [U] the tendency to avoid showing one's feelings or expressing one's opinions to other people: *For once, she lost/dropped her customary reserve and became quite lively.*

▶ **reservist** /rɪˈzɜːvɪst/ *n* a member of a country's reserve forces: *reservist soldiers.*

reserved /rɪˈzɜːvd/ *adj* (of people or their character) slow to show feelings or express opinions: *a reserved manner.* Compare UNRESERVED.

reservoir /ˈrezəvwɑː(r)/ *n* **1** a natural or artificial lake used as a source or store of water for a town, etc. **2** ~ **of sth** a large supply or collection of sth: *a reservoir of information/facts/knowledge* ○ *a reservoir of skilled labour.*

reset /ˌriːˈset/ *v* (**-tt-**; *pt, pp* **reset**) **1**(**a**) to place sth in position again: [Vn] *reset a diamond in a ring* ○ *reset a broken bone.* (**b**) to set a measuring instrument to give a new reading: [Vn] *reset a dial/gauge/ control* [Vnpr] *reset your watch to local time.* **2** [Vn] to prepare a new set of questions for an exam, a test, etc.

resettle /ˌriːˈsetl/ *v* to settle or help people to settle again in a new country or area: [Vn] *resettle refugees/farmers* [also V]. ▶ **resettlement** *n* [U]: *a resettlement agency/programme/scheme/site.*

reshape /ˌriːˈʃeɪp/ *v* to shape or form sth again or in a different way: [Vn] *reshape the economy* ○ *reshape one's body/life.*

reshuffle /ˌriːˈʃʌfl/ *v* [Vn] to change round the jobs done by a group of people, esp in a government. ▶ **ˈreshuffle** *n*: *plan a Cabinet reshuffle.*

reside /rɪˈzaɪd/ *v* ~ **in/at…** (*fml*) (**a**) to have one's home in a certain place; to live: [Vadv] *reside abroad* [Vpr] *reside at 10 Elm Terrace* ○ *reside in college.* (**b**) to exist or be kept in a certain place: [Vpr] *exhibits currently residing at the museum* [also Vadv]. **PHR V** **reˈside in/with sb/sth** (*fml*) (of power or a quality) to be present in or belong to sb/sth: *Supreme authority resides with the President.* ○ *The film's interest resides mainly in the beautiful photography.*

residence /ˈrezɪdəns/ *n* (*fml*) **1** (also **residency**) [C] a house, esp a large or impressive one: *10 Downing Street is the British Prime Minister's official residence.* ○ *a desirable country/family/Georgian residence for sale* (eg in an advertisement). **2** (also **residency**) [U] (**a**) the fact of living in a particular place: *a hall of residence/residence hall* (eg for university students) ○ *take up residence* (ie go and live) *in college.* (**b**) the period of this: *be granted temporary/permanent residence in a country.* **IDM** **in ˈresidence** living in a particular place because of one's work or duties: *The royal standard flies when the Queen is in residence.* ○ *Students must remain in residence during the academic year.* ○ *a writer/an artist/a musician in residence* (eg at a college or in a community which pays her or him to work there for a period of time).

residency /ˈrezɪdənsi/ *n* [U,C] (*fml*) **1** = RESIDENCE 2: *be granted permanent residency in Britain.* **2** the employment of an artist, musician, etc to work at a particular place for a period of time.

resident /ˈrezɪdənt/ *n* **1** a person who lives or has a home in a place, not a visitor: *a (local) residents' association.* **2** a person staying in a hotel: *The restaurant is open to non-residents.*

▶ **resident** *adj* having a home in a place: *the town's resident population* (ie not tourists or visitors) ○ *be resident abroad/in the USA.*

residential /ˌrezɪˈdenʃl/ *adj* [esp attrib] **1** containing or suitable for private houses: *a residential area/suburb/district* (ie one in which there are no offices, factories, etc). **2** connected with or based on residence(2): *a residential home for the elderly* ○ *a residential language course.*

residue /ˈrezɪdjuː; *US* -duː/ *n* ~ (**of sth**) **1** a small amount of sth that remains after the main part is taken or used: *pesticide residues in food.* **2** (*law*) a part of a dead person's estate remaining after all debts, charges, gifts, etc have been settled: *The residue was left to Cancer Research.* ⇨ note at REST³.

▶ **residual** /rɪˈzɪdjuəl; *US* -dʒuː/ *adj* [usu attrib] left over as a residue(1); remaining: *residual chalk deposits* (ie left after rocks have been worn away) ○ *a few residual faults in the computer program.*

---

residuary /rɪˈzɪdjuəri; US -dʒueri/ adj **1** (techn) of a residue(1). **2** (law) of the residue(2) of an estate: a residuary legatee/gift/bequest.

resign /rɪˈzaɪn/ v ~ **(from sth)** to give up one's job, position, etc: [V, Vpr] The mayor resigned (from office). [Vn] She resigned her directorship and left the firm. [V-n, Vn-n] I resigned (my post) as chairman. Compare RETIRE 1 **PHR V** re'sign oneself to sth / doing sth to accept and be ready to endure sth as inevitable: They had clearly resigned themselves to defeat/to being defeated.
▶ **resigned** adj ~ **(to sth / doing sth)** having or showing patient acceptance of sth unpleasant: a resigned look/smile/gesture ○ She seems resigned to not having a holiday this year. **resignedly** /-nɪdli/ adv: 'I suppose I must,' she said resignedly.

resignation /ˌrezɪgˈneɪʃn/ n **1** ~ **(from sth)** **(a)** [U, C] the action or an instance of resigning: He is considering resignation (from the board). ○ Further resignations are expected. **(b)** [C] a letter, etc to one's employers stating that one wishes to resign: offer/tender/send in/give in/hand in one's resignation ○ We haven't yet received his resignation. **2** [U] patient willingness to accept or endure sth: accept failure with resignation.

resilient /rɪˈzɪliənt/ adj **1(a)** (approv) (of a person) quickly recovering from shock, injury, depression, etc: physically/mentally resilient ○ She is very resilient to change. **(b)** (of animals, plants, etc) quickly recovering from injury, damage, etc: Temperate forests are more resilient than tropical ones. **2** (of an object or a substance) springing back to its original form after being bent, stretched, crushed, etc: made of a tough, resilient fabric.
▶ **resilience** /-əns/ (also **resiliency** /-nsi/) n [U] **1(a)** the ability of people to recover quickly from shock, injury, etc: Her natural resilience helped her to overcome the crisis. **(b)** the ability of animals, plants, etc to recover quickly from injury, damage, etc. **2** the ability of objects to spring back after being bent, stretched, etc: an alloy combining strength and resilience.
resiliently adv.

resin /ˈrezɪn; US ˈrezn/ n [C, U] **1** a sticky substance that is produced by certain trees and is used in making VARNISH(1a), medicine, etc. **2** a similar substance made artificially, used in making plastics. ▶ **resinous** /ˈrezɪnəs; US ˈrezənəs/ adj: the resinous scent of pine trees.

resist /rɪˈzɪst/ v **1** to use force in order to prevent sth happening or being successful: [Vn] resist an enemy/attack ○ He was charged with resisting arrest. [V] He didn't try to resist. **2** to oppose a plan, an idea, etc: [Vn] resist the call for reform [also V]. **3** to endure sth without being damaged or harmed by it: [Vn] resist corrosion/damp/frost/disease. **4** to succeed in not yielding to sth/sb: [Vn] resist temptation/chocolate [V.ing] Jill couldn't resist making jokes about his baldness.
.> **resister** n a person who resists: passive resisters.
resistible adj that can be resisted. Compare IRRESISTIBLE.

resistance /rɪˈzɪstəns/ n **1** [U, sing] ~ **(to sth/sb)** the action of using force to oppose sth/sb: armed resistance ○ put up (a) passive resistance ○ The demonstrators offered little or no resistance to the police. **2** [U, sing] ~ **(to sth)** dislike of or opposition to a plan, an idea, etc: The idea met with some resistance. ○ The firm must overcome its resistance to new technology. ○ There is a resistance to any reallocation of resources. **3** [U, sing] ~ **(to sth)** the power to endure sth without damage or harm: the body's natural resistance to disease ○ build up (a) resistance to infection. **4** [U, sing] ~ **(to sth)** a force that stops the progress of sth: a low wind resistance (eg in the design of planes or cars). **5** [U, C] (physics) the property of not con-

ducting heat or electricity; a measurement of this. **6** (often **the Resistance**) [Gp] a secret organization resisting the authorities, esp in a country occupied by an enemy: a resistance fighter. **IDM** **the line of least resistance** ⇨ LINE¹.

resistant /rɪˈzɪstənt/ adj ~ **(to sth)** offering resistance: a resistant strain of virus ○ bacteria that have become resistant to antibiotics ○ be resistant to change.
▶ **-resistant** (forming compound adjs): ˈwater-/ˈheat-/ˈstain-resistant.

resistor /rɪˈzɪstə(r)/ n a device providing resistance (5) to electric current in a circuit.

resit /ˌriːˈsɪt/ v (-tt-; pt, pp resat) [Vn] (Brit) to take an examination or test again, usu after failing.
▶ **resit** /ˈriːsɪt/ n a second or further attempt at an examination or test: candidates for the September resit.

resolute /ˈrezəluːt, -liːuːt/ adj ~ **(in sth)** having or showing great determination: a resolute action/refusal/approach/measure ○ be resolute in one's demands for peace. Compare IRRESOLUTE. ▶ **resolutely** adv: remain resolutely independent.

resolution /ˌrezəˈluːʃn, -ljuːʃn/ n **1** [U] the quality of being RESOLUTE or firm; determination: show great resolution ○ a man lacking in resolution ○ His speech ended on a note of resolution. **2** [C] a firm decision to do or not to do sth: make/keep good resolutions ○ her resolution never to marry ○ a **New Year resolution** (eg not to smoke in the new year ahead). **3** [C] a formal statement of opinion agreed on by a committee or assembly, esp by means of a vote: pass/carry/adopt/reject a resolution ○ a resolution in favour of/demanding better conditions ○ a resolution that conditions should be improved. **4** [U] (fml) the action of solving or settling problems, doubts, etc: the resolution of a dispute/a difficulty/a doubt/an issue. **5** [U, sing] the process of separating sth or being separated into parts: a computer screen/printer with a high resolution (ie one that produces a good-quality image made up of many small dots, close together).

resolve /rɪˈzɒlv/ v (fml) **1** ~ **on/upon/against sth / doing sth** to decide firmly; to determine(3): [V.to inf] resolve never to give up [Vpr] He resolved on/against (making) an early start. [V.that] She resolved that she would never see him again. **2** (of a committee or an assembly) to make a decision by a formal vote: [V.that] The council resolved that the compulsory purchase order (should) be revoked. [V.to inf] The union resolved to strike by 36 votes to 15. **3** to solve or settle problems, doubts, etc: [Vn] resolve an argument/a difficulty/a crisis ○ Her arrival did little to resolve the situation. **4** ~ **sth (into sth)** to separate sth into its parts: [Vnpr] resolve a complex argument into its basic elements [Vn] (techn) the **resolving power** of a lens (ie its ability to MAGNIFY (1) things clearly).
▶ **resolve** n (fml) **1** [C] a thing one has firmly decided to do: make a resolve not to smoke ○ show/keep/break one's resolve. **2** [U] the quality of being firm or determined: be strong/weak in one's resolve ○ His opposition served only to strengthen our resolve.
resolved adj [pred] (of a person) determined or RESOLUTE: I was fully/firmly resolved not to see him.

resonant /ˈrezənənt/ adj (fml) **1** (of sound) deep, clear and continuing to ECHO²(1): rich resonant notes/voices. **2** ~ **with sth** (of a place) filled with the sound of sth: alpine valleys resonant with the sound of church bells. **3** (of a room, musical instrument, etc) causing sounds to ECHO²(1) inside it or around it. **4** having the power to bring images, feelings, memories, etc into sb's mind: a poem filled with resonant images ○ The house was still resonant with memories of his childhood.
▶ **resonance** /-əns/ n (fml) **1** [U] the quality of being resonant. **2** [C, U] the sound produced in an

object by sound waves from another object. **3** [C,U] (in a piece of writing, music, etc) the power to bring images, feelings, memories, etc into the mind of the reader, listener, etc; the images, feelings, memories, etc produced in this way: *profound resonances of Greek mythology.*
resonantly *adv.*
resonate /'rezəneɪt/ *v* [V, Vpr] ~ **(with sth)** *(fml)* to produce or be filled with resonance. **resonator** /-tə(r)/ *n* an apparatus for increasing the resonance of sound, esp in a musical instrument.

resort /rɪ'zɔːt/ *v* **PHRV** **resort to sth** to make use of sth, esp sth bad or unpleasant, as a means of achieving sth, often because no other course of action is possible: *resort to violence/terrorism* ○ *If negotiations fail we will have to resort to strike action.*
▶ **resort** *n* **1** [C] a place where a lot of people go on holiday: *seaside/ski/mountain resorts* ○ *Brighton is a popular English coastal resort.* **2** [sing] a person or thing that provides help in a difficult situation: *The judge has announced his decision, and our only resort is an appeal to a higher court.* **3** [U] ~ **to sth** the action of resorting to sth: *talk calmly, without resort to threats.* **IDM** **a/one's last resort** ⇨ LAST¹. **in the last resort** ⇨ LAST¹.

resound /rɪ'zaʊnd/ *v* **1(a)** ~ **(through sth)** (of a sound, voice, etc) to fill a place with sound; to ECHO²(1): [V, Vpr] *Church bells resounded (through the valley).* **(b)** ~ **(with/to sth)** (of a place) to be filled with sound: [Vpr] *The hall resounded with applause.* ○ *The stadium resounded to the chants of the football fans.* [also V]. **2** ~ **through**, **around**, etc **sth** *(fml)* (of fame, an event, etc) to be talked about or repeated by many people: [Vpr] *Her name resounded throughout Europe.* Compare REVERBERATE.
▶ **resounding** *adj* [attrib] **1** filling a place with sound: *resounding applause* ○ *His head hit the floor with a resounding thud.* **2** (of an event, etc) very great; remarkable: *win a resounding victory* ○ *The party was a resounding success.* **resoundingly** *adv.*

resource /rɪ'sɔːs, -'zɔːs; US 'riːsɔːrs/ *n* **1** [C usu *pl*] a supply of sth that a country, an organization or an individual has and can use, esp to increase wealth: *a country rich in natural resources such as oil, coal and gas* ○ *mineral/agricultural resources* ○ *resource allocation* ○ *The company lacks the financial resources to invest in new technology.* ○ *The organization's success is largely due to the way it manages its human resources* (ie its staff). ○ *We agreed to pool our resources* (ie so that everybody contributes sth). **2** [C usu *pl*] a thing that gives help, support or comfort when needed: *He has no inner resources and hates being alone.* ○ *She had no brothers or sisters and so was often left to her own resources* (ie left to amuse herself as a child). ○ *a resource file/room* (eg containing materials for teachers). **3** [U] *(fml)* the ability to find quick, clever and efficient ways of doing things.
▶ **resource** *v* to provide sth with resources: [Vn] *inadequate resourcing of schools* ○ *The scheme must be properly resourced.*
resourceful /-fl/ *adj* clever at finding ways of doing things. **resourcefully** /-fəli/ *adv.* **resourcefulness** *n* [U].

respect¹ /rɪ'spekt/ *n* **1** [U] ~ **(for sb/sth)** the feeling of admiration for sb/sth because of their good qualities or achievements; polite behaviour resulting from this: *a mark/token of respect* ○ *have a deep/ sincere respect for sb* ○ *win/lose the respect of sb* ○ *Children should show respect for their teachers.* ○ *I have the greatest respect for you/hold you in the greatest respect.* ○ *With respect, sir, I disagree.* Compare DISRESPECT. See also SELF-RESPECT. **2** [U] ~ **(for sb/sth)** consideration or care: *have some/little/no respect for sb's feelings* ○ *Many young people show very little respect for traditional values.* **3** [C] a

particular aspect or detail: *in this respect* ○ *in some/ all/many/several/most respects* ○ *In what respect do you think the film is biased?* **in respect of sth** *(fml or commerce)* **1** as regards sth; with special reference to sth: *price rises in respect of gas and water costs.* **2** in payment for sth: *money received in respect of overtime worked.* **with due respect** ⇨ DUE¹. **with respect to sth** *(fml or commerce)* concerning sth: *This is true with respect to English but not to French.* ○ *I am writing with respect to your recent enquiry.*
▶ **respects** *n* [pl] *(fml)* polite greetings: *Give my respects to your parents.* **IDM** **pay one's respects** ⇨ PAY².

respect² /rɪ'spekt/ *v* **1** ~ **sb/sth (for sth)** to admire or have a high opinion of sb/sth because of sth: [Vn, Vnpr] *I respect (you for) your honesty.* [Vn] *a respected scientist.* **2(a)** to show consideration or care for sth/sb: [Vn] *respect sb's wishes/opinions/ feelings* ○ *respect the environment* (eg by protecting it) ○ *Please respect my (desire for) privacy.* [Vn·n] *Children should be respected as human beings.* **(b)** to avoid interfering with or harming sth; to agree to recognize sth: [Vn] *respect sb's rights/privileges* ○ *respect cultural differences.*
▶ **respecter** *n* **IDM** **be no / not be any respecter of ¹persons** to treat everyone in the same way, without being influenced by their importance, wealth, etc: *Death is no respecter of persons.*
respecting *prep* *(fml)* relating to sth; concerning sth: *laws respecting property* ○ *information respecting the child's whereabouts.*

respectable /rɪ'spektəbl/ *adj* **1** considered by society to be good, proper or correct; decent in appearance or behaviour: *a respectable married couple* ○ *a respectable middle-class background/ upbringing* ○ *dress in a respectable way.* **2** quite good or large; not causing shame or embarrassment: *There was quite a respectable crowd at the match on Saturday.* ○ *She earns a respectable salary.*
▶ **respectability** /rɪ,spektə'bɪləti/ *n* [U].
respectably /-əbli/ *adv* in a respectable manner: *respectably dressed* ○ *a respectably married woman* ○ *a respectably large audience.*

respectful /rɪ'spektfl/ *adj* ~ **(to/towards sb)**; ~ **(of sth)** feeling or showing respect: *respectful of other people's opinions* ○ *The crowd listened in respectful silence.* ○ *We stood at a respectful distance as the funeral procession went by.* Compare DISRESPECTFUL.
▶ **respectfully** /-fəli/ *adv.*

respective /rɪ'spektɪv/ *adj* [attrib] belonging or relating separately to each of the people or things already mentioned: *They are each well-known in their respective fields.* ○ *After the party we all went off to our respective rooms.*
▶ **respectively** *adv* in the same order as the people or things already mentioned: *Julie Wilson and Mark Thomas, aged 17 and 19 respectively.*

respiration /,respə'reɪʃn/ *n* [U] *(fml)* the action of breathing: *respiration rate.* See also ARTIFICIAL RESPIRATION.

respirator /'respəreɪtə(r)/ *n* [C] **1** a device worn over the nose and mouth to allow sb to breathe although they are surrounded by smoke, gas, etc: *fire-fighters wearing respirators.* **2** an apparatus that enables sb to breathe over a long period when they are unable to do so naturally: *put the patient on a respirator.*

respire /rɪ'spaɪə(r)/ *v* *(fml)* to breathe: [V] *Some reptiles respire through their skin.*
▶ **respiratory** /rə'spɪrətri, 'respərətri; US 'respərətɔːri/ *adj* [esp attrib] *(medical)* of or for breathing air: *respiratory diseases such as bronchitis and asthma* ○ *the respiratory tract/system.* ⇨ picture.

respite /'respaɪt; US 'respɪt/ *n* **1** [U,sing] ~ **(from sth)** a short period of rest or relief from sth difficult

R

the respiratory system

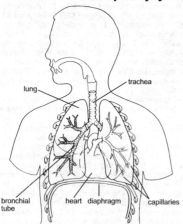

lung

trachea

bronchial tube   heart   diaphragm   capillaries

or unpleasant: *enjoy a moment's respite* ○ *a brief/ temporary/welcome respite from pain/worry/stress* ○ *There has been no respite from the fighting.* **2** [C] a short delay allowed before sth difficult or unpleasant must be done: *We are prepared to grant him temporary respite, after which the debt must be repaid in full.*

resplendent /rɪ'splendənt/ *adj* [usu pred] ~ **(in sth)** (*fml*) bright and colourful in an impressive way; splendid: *resplendent in his red and gold uniform* ○ *the resplendent tail feathers of the male peacock.* ▶ **resplendently** *adv.*

respond /rɪ'spɒnd/ *v* **1** ~ **(to sb/sth) (with sth)** (*rather fml*) to give a spoken or written answer: [V] *I asked where he'd been, but he didn't respond.* [Vpr] *She responded to my letter with a phone call.* [V.speech] *'I don't know,' she finally responded.* [V.that] *When asked for his reaction he responded that he was not surprised.* **2** ~ **(to sth) (with sth / by doing sth)** to do sth as a reaction to sth: [Vpr] *She responded (to my question) with a smile/with indignation.* ○ *He kicked the dog, which responded by growling.* ○ *How did they respond to the news?* **3** ~ **(to sth)** to react quickly or favourably (to sb/sth): [Vpr] *The car responds well to the controls.* ○ *The patient is not responding to treatment.* ○ *Animals respond to kindness.* [also V].

respondent /rɪ'spɒndənt/ *n* **1** a person who answers questions, esp in a survey or QUESTIONNAIRE: *60% of the respondents said they were opposed to the new law.* **2** (*law*) a person accused of sth, esp in a DIVORCE¹(1) case.

response /rɪ'spɒns/ *n* ~ **(to sb/sth) 1** [C, U] a spoken or written answer: *She made no response.* ○ *In response to your inquiry...* ○ *I received an encouraging response to my letter of application.* **2** [C, U] an action or feeling produced in answer to sth; a reaction: *an emotional/enthusiastic/positive response to the news* ○ *I knocked on the door, but there was no response.* ○ *The tax cuts produced a favourable public response.* ○ *My initial response was one of surprise.* ○ *We sent out over a thousand letters, but the response rate was very low* (ie few people replied). **3** [C usu pl] (*religion*) a part of a church service that is said or sung by the CONGREGATION(1) or CHOIR(1) in answer to the priest.

responsibility /rɪˌspɒnsə'bɪləti/ *n* **1** [U] ~ **(for sb/ sth)** the state or fact of being responsible: *Her new job means taking on more responsibility.* ○ *take/ assume/accept/bear full responsibility for the con-*

sequences ○ *The IRA has claimed/admitted responsibility for the attack.* ○ *a Minister with special responsibility for women's affairs* ○ *The manufacturers **disclaim all responsibility** for damage caused by misuse.* ○ *She feels a strong sense of responsibility towards her employees.* **2** [C] ~ **(to sb)** a duty for which a person is responsible: *the various responsibilities of the post* ○ *Our business is a joint/ shared responsibility.* ○ *It's my responsibility to lock the doors.*

responsible /rɪ'spɒnsəbl/ *adj* **1** [pred] ~ **(for sb/ sth)**; ~ **(for doing sth)** having the job or duty of doing sth or caring for sb/sth, so that one may be blamed if sth goes wrong: *the Minister responsible for environmental issues* ○ *The driver is responsible for the safety of his passengers.* ○ *Parents should be responsible for teaching their children the difference between right and wrong.* **2** [pred] ~ **(for sth)** being the cause of sth and so able to be blamed for it: *Who's responsible for this mess?* ○ *Smoking is responsible for many cases of lung cancer.* ○ *She is mentally ill and cannot **be held responsible** for her actions.* **3** [pred] ~ **to sb/sth** having to report to sb/ sth with authority or in a higher position and explain to them what one has done: *be directly responsible to the President.* **4(a)** (of people or their actions or behaviour) capable of being trusted; reliable and sensible: *behave like responsible citizens/ adults* ○ *show a responsible attitude.* Compare IRRESPONSIBLE. **(b)** [esp attrib] (of jobs, etc) needing sb who can be relied on; involving important duties: *a highly responsible position/role.*
▶ **responsibly** /-əbli/ *adv* in a reliable or sensible way: *act/behave responsibly.*

responsive /rɪ'spɒnsɪv/ *adj* ~ **(to sb/sth) 1** responding with interest or enthusiasm; sympathetic: *a responsive class/audience* ○ *be responsive to suggestions/ideas/criticisms.* **2** [usu pred] reacting quickly and favourably: *a flu virus that is not responsive to treatment* ○ *a horse responsive to the wishes of its rider* ○ *Managers should be more responsive to the needs of their staff.* ▶ **responsively** *adv.* **responsiveness** *n* [U].

rest¹ /rest/ *v* **1(a)** to relax, sleep or do nothing after a period of activity or because of illness: [V] *lie down and rest for an hour after lunch* ○ *The nurse said we couldn't visit him because he was resting.* ○ (*fig*) *He will never rest* (ie never have peace of mind) *until he knows the truth.* **(b)** to cause or allow sth/sb to do this: [Vn] *Sit down and rest your legs.* ○ *Are you rested enough to go on?* See also RIP. **2** ~ **(sth) on/ against sth** to lie or be placed on/against sth for support: [Vpr, Vnpr] *Her elbows rested/She rested her elbows on the table.* [Vnpr] *Rest the ladder against the wall.* **3** (*fml*) (of a subject being talked about) to be left without further discussion: [V] *let the matter/topic/affair rest* ○ *The matter cannot rest there — I demand an apology.* **4** (*esp law*) to bring one's argument to an end; to have no more to say about sth, esp because one believes that one's point has been proved: [Vn] *I rest my case.* **IDM** **rest as͟sured (that...)** (*fml*) to be certain that...: *You may rest assured that everything possible is being done.* **rest on one's 'laurels** (*esp derog*) to feel so satisfied with what one has already done or achieved that one does not try to do any more. **PHRV** **'rest on sb/sth** (no passive) **1** to depend on or rely on sb/sth: *The team's hopes of a medal now rest on Gunnell.* **2** (of a look, etc) to be directed for a time at sb/sth: *Her eyes travelled slowly around the room and finally rested on me.* **'rest on sth** (no passive!) to be based on sth: *an argument/a claim resting on a false assumption* ○ *The whole theory rests on a very simple idea.* ○ *The success of the play rests largely on the performances of the main actors.* **'rest with sb (to do sth)** (*fml*) to be sb's responsibility to do sth:

The decision rests entirely with you. ○ *It rests with management to justify their actions.*

■ '**resting-place** *n* (*euph*) a grave: *his final resting-place in the local churchyard.*

rest² /rest/ *n* **1** [C, U] ~ (**from sth**) a period or the action of relaxing, sleeping or doing nothing after a period of activity, etc: *have a good night's rest* ○ *stop for a well-earned rest* ○ *have/take a rest from all your hard work* ○ *Sunday is a day of rest.* ○ *Try to get some rest now — you've got a busy day tomorrow.* ▷ note at BREAK². **2** [C] (often in compounds) an object that is used to support sth: *a rest for a billiard cue* ○ *an armrest* (eg on a seat or chair). See also FOOTREST, HEADREST. **3** [C] (*music*) an interval of silence between notes, or a sign that indicates this: *The trumpets have six bars' rest.* ▷ picture at MUSIC. **IDM** **at** '**rest 1** not moving. **2** free from trouble or anxiety: (*euph*) *be/lie at rest* (ie be buried) *in one's grave.* **come to** '**rest** (of a moving object) to stop moving: *The car crashed through the barrier and came to rest in a field.* **give sth/it a** '**rest** (*infml*) to stop doing sth for a while: *If you've hurt your ankle you should give sport a rest for a few weeks.* ○ *Oh, give it a rest, will you? You've been complaining all day!* **lay sb to** '**rest** (*euph*) to bury sb: *She was laid to rest beside her late husband.* **lay/put sth to** '**rest** to prove that sth is not true: *An official announcement finally laid speculation to rest.* **put/set sb's mind at ease/rest** ▷ MIND¹.
  ▶ **restful** /-fl/ *adj* ~ (**to sb/sth**) giving a relaxed peaceful feeling: *restful sleep* ○ *a restful Sunday afternoon.* ○ *Pastel colours are restful to the eye.*

■ '**rest area**, '**rest stop** *ns* (*US*) = LAY-BY.

'**rest-cure** *n* a long period of rest, usu in bed, as medical treatment for stress, anxiety, etc: (*fig ironic*) *This job's certainly no rest-cure!*

'**rest-day** *n* a day spent resting, esp during a sports competition.

'**rest-home** *n* a place where old or sick people are cared for.

'**rest room** *n* (*US euph*) a public toilet, eg in a theatre, restaurant, etc. ▷ note at TOILET.

rest³ /rest/ *n* **the** ~ (**of sth**) **1** [sing] the remaining part of sth: *the rest of the world/my life/her money* ○ *watch the rest of a film* ○ *Take what you want and throw the rest away.* **2** [pl v] the remaining people or things; the others: *Paul and I are playing tennis this afternoon. What are the rest of you going to do?* ○ *The first question was difficult, but the rest were quite easy.* **IDM** **and** (**all**) **the** '**rest** (**of it**) (*infml*) and everything else that could be mentioned or that one expects: *He wants a huge house and an expensive car and all the rest of it.* ○ *She believes in God and heaven and hell and the rest.* **for the** '**rest** (*fml*) as far as other matters are concerned; apart from that: *The book contains some interesting passages about the author's childhood. For the rest, it is rather dull.*

NOTE When speaking about who or what remains from an original total, you say **the rest** or, in a more formal context, **the remainder**: *Some children stay on after school for activities; the rest/the remainder (of them) go home.* ○ *We spent a few days sightseeing and the rest of the time at the beach.* If something has been partly used or destroyed, what is left are **the remains** or **the remnants**: *You should not keep the remains of medicines.* ○ *The remnants of the man's clothes were found by the river.* **Remains** is also used of old buildings or dead bodies: *the remains of an old castle* ○ *human remains.* A **relic** is a historical object and reminder of the past: *The museum is full of Egyptian and Roman relics.* **Leftovers** are pieces of food that have not been eaten: *Put the leftovers in the fridge; we can have them for lunch tomorrow.* A **residue** is what is left after a process, especially a chemical one, has taken place: *There is a green*

residue in the bottom of the test-tube. In a mathematical calculation **the remainder** (in arithmetic), or **the balance** (in a business context), is the amount left after subtracting or dividing numbers.

---

restate /ˌriːˈsteɪt/ *v* to say sth again or in a different way: [Vn] *restate one's position/case/commitment.* ▶ **restatement** *n* [C, U].

restaurant /ˈrestrɒnt; *US* -tərənt/ *n* a place where meals are prepared, served and eaten. Compare CAFÉ.
  ▶ **restaurateur** /ˌrestərəˈtɜː(r)/ *n* (*fml*) a person who owns and runs a restaurant.

■ '**restaurant car** *n* (*Brit*) = DINING-CAR.

restitution /ˌrestɪˈtjuːʃn; *US* -ˈtuː-/ *n* [U] ~ (**of sth**) (**to sb/sth**) **1** (*fml*) the action of giving sth that was lost or stolen back to its proper owner: *the restitution of property to the owner.* **2** (*law*) compensation, esp in the form of money, for injury, etc: *make restitution for the damage done* ○ *restitution claims.*

restive /ˈrestɪv/ *adj* unable to be still or quiet; difficult to control, esp because one is not satisfied with sth: *Another hour passed and the crowd grew/became increasingly restive.* ▶ **restiveness** *n* [U].

restless /ˈrestləs/ *adj* **1** unable to be still or quiet because one is bored, anxious, IMPATIENT(1), etc: *The audience was becoming restless.* ○ *The children always get restless on long journeys.* ○ *After five years in the job, he was beginning to feel restless.* **2** without rest or sleep: *a restless night.* ▶ **restlessly** *adv*: *The lion paced restlessly up and down in its cage.* **restlessness** *n* [U].

restock /ˌriːˈstɒk/ *v* ~ **sth** (**with sth**) to fill sth with new or different things to replace those used, sold, etc: [Vn] *restock the freezer for Christmas* [Vnpr] *restock the library shelves with new books* ○ *restock a lake/river with fish.*

restoration /ˌrestəˈreɪʃn/ *n* **1** [U, C] the work of restoring a ruined building, an old painting, etc to its original condition; an example of this: *undergo a lengthy process of restoration* ○ *The palace is closed during restoration/closed for restoration work.* ○ *The statue is in need of restoration.* ○ *the museum restoration fund.* **2** [U] ~ (**to sb/sth**) the action of returning sth to a former owner, place or condition: *the restoration of stolen property* ○ *the restoration of the Elgin marbles to Greece* ○ *the restoration of her eyesight* ○ *the restoration of order after the riots.* **3** [U, C] ~ (**to sb/sth**) the action of introducing sth again, eg after it has been withdrawn; an instance of this: *the restoration of old customs* ○ *We demand an immediate restoration of our right to vote.* **4** **the Restoration** [sing] the return of the monarchy (MONARCH) in Britain in 1660, when Charles II became king; the period following this: *Restoration comedy/ poetry.*

restorative /rɪˈstɔːrətɪv/ *adj* making sb feel strong, healthy, etc again: *the restorative powers of sea air* ○ *a restorative cup of tea.*
  ▶ **restorative** *n* [C] (*dated or joc*) a drink, esp an alcoholic one, intended to make sb feel better, stronger, etc: *The brandy acted as a restorative.*

restore /rɪˈstɔː(r)/ *v* **1(a)** ~ **sb** (**to sth**); ~ **sth** (**to sb**) to bring sb/sth back to a former condition: [Vn] *restore sb's beauty/sight/confidence* ○ *Law and order were quickly restored after the riots.* [Vnpr] *restore sb to good health* [Vn, Vnpr] *The deposed king was restored (to power/to his throne).* (**b**) ~ **sb/sth to sth** to bring sb/sth back to a former place or position: [Vnpr] *restore laid-off workers to their old jobs.* **2** ~ **sth** (**to sb**) to bring sth back into use, eg after it has been withdrawn: [Vn] *restore ancient traditions/ ceremonies* ○ *restore old laws/taxes/charges* ○ *restore*

[V] = verb used alone   [Vn] = verb + noun   [Vp] = verb + particle   [Vpr] = verb + prepositional phrase

diplomatic relations with Britain [also Vnpr]. **3 ~ sth (to sth)** to repair a ruined building, work of art, etc so that it is like the original: [Vn] *restore a Roman fort/a vintage car/an oil painting/a china vase* [Vnpr] *The hall has been lovingly restored to its original splendour.* Compare RENOVATE. **4 ~ sth (to sb/sth)** (*fml*) to give sth that was lost or stolen back to sb: [Vn, Vnpr] *restore the stolen paintings (to their former owner)* [Vn] *restore the water supply.*

▶ **restorer** *n* [C] a person whose job is to restore(3) things, eg old buildings and works of art: 'picture/ 'furniture restorers.*

restrain /rɪˈstreɪn/ *v* **~ oneself/sb/sth (from sth / doing sth)** to keep onself/sb/sth under control; to prevent onself/sb/sth from doing sth: [Vn] *restrain one's anger/laughter/tears* ○ *restrain the urge to hit sb* ○ *Can't you restrain your dog?* [Vnpr] *I had to restrain myself from saying something rude.*

▶ **restrained** *adj* **1** calm; not showing emotion: *a restrained rebuke/protest/discussion* ○ *He was furious, but his manner was very restrained.* See also UNRESTRAINED. **2** not colourful or highly decorated: *The room was furnished in an elegant, restrained style.*

restraint /rɪˈstreɪnt/ *n* **1** [C usu *pl*] **~ (on sb/sth)** a thing that limits or controls sb/sth; a restriction: *restraints on government spending* ○ *break free from the restraints of convention* ○ *impose wage restraints.* **2** [U] the quality of behaving in a calm or moderate way: *talk/weep without restraint* ○ *The police appealed to the crowd for restraint.* ○ *He showed/ exercised considerable restraint in ignoring these insults.* **3** [U] the action of restraining sb/sth or of being restrained: *He could only be prevented from hitting the guard by physical restraint.*

restrict /rɪˈstrɪkt/ *v* **~ oneself/sb/sth (to sth / doing sth)** to put a limit on oneself/sb/sth: [Vn] *Having small children tends to restrict one's freedom.* ○ *Fog severely restricted visibility.* ○ *restrict the number of students in a class* [Vnpr] *families restricted to (having) one child* ○ *restrict oneself to one glass of wine a day* ○ *Speed is restricted to 30 mph in towns.* ○ *Entry to the club is restricted to members only.*

▶ **restricted** *adj* **1** controlled or limited in some way: *restricted access/movement/development* ○ *The shop sells a very restricted range of books.* ○ *In modern houses, space is often quite restricted.* ○ (*Brit*) *a restricted area* (ie where speed or parking is strictly controlled). **2** [esp attrib] **(a)** (*Brit*) (of land) open only to certain people, esp because things happen there which the authorities want to keep secret: *enter a restricted zone.* **(b)** (*esp US*) declared officially secret and available only to certain people: *a restricted document.*

restriction /rɪˈstrɪkʃn/ *n* **(a)** [U] the action of restricting sb/sth or of being restricted: *Tourists are now able to visit most East European countries without restriction.* **(b)** [C esp *pl*] **~ (on sth)** a law, etc that restricts sb/sth: *speed/price/import restrictions* ○ *place/impose/enforce a restriction* ○ *The government has agreed to lift restrictions on trade with Britain.* ○ *There is no restriction on the amount you can withdraw as long as your account stays in credit.* ○ *The sale of firearms is subject to many legal restrictions.*

restrictive /rɪˈstrɪktɪv/ *adj* preventing people from doing what they want; limiting: *She finds living with her aunt rather restrictive.*

■ re,strictive 'practices *n* [pl] (*Brit often derog*) (esp in industry) agreements or ways of working which make an organization less efficient than it could be in order to prevent competition or protect people's jobs, esp by limiting the price at which goods may be sold or the amount of goods that may be produced.

restructure /ˌriːˈstrʌktʃə(r)/ *v* to organize sth in a new way; to give a new or different structure to sth: [Vn] *restructure an organization/a proposal/the economy.* ▶ **restructuring** *n* [U,C usu *sing*]: *The company is undergoing (a) complete restructuring.*

result /rɪˈzʌlt/ *n* **1(a)** [C, U] **~ (of sth)** the effect or outcome of sth: *She died as a result of her injuries.* ○ *The failure of the company was a direct result of poor management.* ○ *I was late, with the result that* (ie so that) *I missed my train.* ○ *They ignored my advice, with disastrous results.* ○ *She is looking for a new job, so far without result.* ○ *The net result of the government's policies has been inflation on a massive scale.* **(b)** results [pl] a successful and pleasing outcome: *begin to show/produce/achieve results* ○ *a football manager who knows how to get results from his players.* **2** [C] **(a)** (esp *pl*) **~ (of sth)** a statement of the score, marks or name of the winner in a sporting event, a competition, an examination, etc: *the 'football/'racing results* ○ *get good/bad exam results* ○ *announce the election results* ○ *The result of the match was a draw.* **(b)** **~ (of sth)** a statement of the outcome of a scientific or medical test: *When will you get the result of your X-ray?* **(c)** (esp *sing*) (*Brit infml*) (esp in football) a victory: *We badly need a result from this match.* **3** [C] the answer to a mathematical (MATHEMATICS) problem.

▶ **result** /rɪˈzʌlt/ *v* **~ (from sth)** to occur as a result(1a): [Vpr] *injuries resulting from a fall* [V] *It was a large explosion and the resulting damage was extensive.* **PHR V** re'sult in sth to cause sth; to have sth as a result: *Our efforts resulted in success/failure.* ○ *There has been an accident on the motorway, resulting in long delays.* ○ *The incident resulted in his being dismissed from his job.*

resultant /-ənt/ *adj* [attrib] (*fml*) happening as a result or consequence: *the growing economic crisis and resultant unemployment.*

resume /rɪˈzuːm; *Brit also* -ˈzjuː-/ *v* (*fml*) **1** to begin sth again or continue sth after stopping for a time: [Vn] *resume production* ○ *resume one's studies/duties* ○ *After several months she left hospital and tried to resume a normal life.* [V] *Talks will resume in Washington in a few weeks' time.* [V.ing] *The two sides have resumed fighting.* **2** to take or occupy sth again: [Vn] *resume one's seat* (ie sit down again) ○ *resume possession of a title.*

résumé /ˈrezjumeɪ; *US* ˈrezəmeɪ/ *n* **1** a summary: *give a résumé of the evidence/plot/meeting.* **2** (*US*) = CURRICULUM VITAE.

resumption /rɪˈzʌmpʃn/ *n* [U, sing] (*fml*) the action of beginning sth again after an interruption: *no immediate resumption of building work* ○ *a resumption of hostilities/negotiations/diplomatic relations.*

resurface /ˌriːˈsɜːfɪs/ *v* **1** to put a new surface on a road, etc: [Vn] *The main street is closed for resurfacing.* **2** to come to the surface again: [V] *The submarine resurfaced.* ○ (*fig*) *Old prejudices began to resurface.*

resurgent /rɪˈsɜːdʒənt/ *adj* [usu attrib] (*fml*) reviving after a period of little activity, poor performance, lack of popularity, etc: *a resurgent economy* ○ *resurgent hope/nationalism.* ▶ **resurgence** /-əns/ *n* [U, sing]: *a sudden resurgence of interest in West African art* ○ *a resurgence in fighting to the south of the city.*

resurrect /ˌrezəˈrekt/ *v* **1** to revive a practice, an idea, an argument, etc; to bring sth back into use: [Vn] *resurrect old customs/traditions* ○ *His speech threatens to resurrect the debate about education in Britain.* **2** to bring sb back to life again: [Vn] (*joc*) *That noise is enough to resurrect the dead!*

▶ **resurrection** /ˌrezəˈrekʃn/ *n* **1** the Resurrection [sing] (in Christian belief) **(a)** the event or time when Jesus became alive again three days after his death. **(b)** the time of the Last Judgement when all dead people will become alive again. **2** [U, sing] (*fml*) a new beginning: *the resurrection of the troubles in Northern Ireland.*

resuscitate /rɪˈsʌsɪteɪt/ v (*fml*) to bring sb/sth back to consciousness: [Vn] *resuscitate a boy pulled from the river* ○ (*fig*) *He tried to resuscitate the idea a couple of years later.* ▶ **resuscitation** /rɪˌsʌsɪˈteɪʃn/ n [U]: *their frantic efforts/attempts at resuscitation.* See also MOUTH-TO-MOUTH RESUSCITATION.

retail /ˈriːteɪl/ n [U] the practice of selling goods in small quantities to the general public: *outlets* (ie shops) *for the retail of leather goods* ○ *retail businesses/traders* ○ *The manufacturer's recommended retail price is £9.99.* Compare WHOLESALE.
▶ **retail** v **1** (a) to sell sth: [Vn] *The firm manufactures and retails its own range of exclusive clothing.* (b) ~ **at/for sth** to be sold at a specified price: [Vpr] *Both cars will retail at roughly $40 000.* **2** [Vn, Vnpr] ~ **sth** (**to sb**) (*fml*) to give details, esp of gossip, etc, to others. **retailing** n [U] the business of selling goods to the general public: *buy shares in a textiles and retailing group.*
retailer n a person who sells goods to the general public: *one of the country's largest food retailers.*
■ **retail price index** n [sing] a list of the prices of certain common retail goods, showing how these change from month to month.

retain /rɪˈteɪn/ v (*esp fml*) **1** to continue to have sth; to keep sth: [Vn] *retain one's freedom/independence* ○ *try to retain a flexible approach* ○ *a player struggling to retain his place in the team* ○ *The ceremony retains an aura of mystery.* ○ *We retained the original fireplace when we decorated the room.* ○ *The police retained control of the situation.* [Vn-n] *Military intervention was retained as a possible future course of action.* **2** to hold or contain sth: [Vn] *Clay soil retains water.* ○ *This information is no longer retained within the computer's main memory.* **3** (*techn*) to secure the services of sb, esp a lawyer, by paying for them in advance or by making regular payments: [Vn] *retain a barrister/consultant* ○ *a retaining fee.* See also RETENTION.
▶ **retainer** n **1** (*techn*) a sum of money paid to sb in advance for services that they agree to provide when they are required: *She was paid $30 an hour plus a $500 a month retainer.* **2** (*arch or joc*) a servant, esp one who has been with a family or person for a long time: *the king's retainers.*
retaining adj [attrib] designed or intended to keep sth in the correct position: *a retaining screw/strap* ○ *a retaining wall* (ie one that supports a mass of earth or confines water in a RESERVOIR(1)).

retake /ˌriːˈteɪk/ v (*pt* **retook** /-ˈtʊk/; *pp* **retaken** /-ˈteɪkən/) **1** (esp of an army) to capture sth again: [Vn] *retake a position/town* ○ (*fig*) *He fought back to retake the lead two laps later.* **2** to take an examination, etc again: [Vn] *retake the physics paper.*
▶ **retake** /ˈriːteɪk/ n (*infml*) **1** a second or further attempt at filming a scene: *do several retakes.* **2** a second or further attempt to pass an examination.

retaliate /rɪˈtælieɪt/ v ~ (**against sb/sth**) (**by doing sth / with sth**) to harm, injure, etc sb because they have upset one or caused one harm or injury: [Vpr] *The boy slapped his sister, who retaliated by kicking him.* ○ *They threatened to retaliate against similar cross-border raids.* [V] *They are likely to retaliate.* ▶ **retaliation** /rɪˌtæliˈeɪʃn/ n [U] ~ (**against sb/sth**); ~ (**for sth**) *the danger of retaliation against UN aid workers* ○ *The shooting may have been in retaliation for the recent sectarian murders.* **retaliatory** /rɪˈtæliətri; US -tɔːri/ adj: *take retaliatory measures* ○ *The raid was purely retaliatory.*

retard /rɪˈtɑːd/ v (*fml*) to slow the progress or development of sb/sth; to HINDER sb/sth: [Vn] *Lack of sun retards plant growth.* ○ *retarding efforts to agree on a common foreign policy.*

▶ **retardation** /ˌriːtɑːˈdeɪʃn/ n [U]: *mental retardation.*
retarded adj mentally less developed than is normal for one's age: *a home for severely retarded young people.*

retch /retʃ/ v to make sounds and movements as if one is about to VOMIT, but without doing so: [Vpr] *She retched at the smell and hurried to open a window.* [also V].

retell /ˌriːˈtel/ v (*pt, pp* **retold** /-ˈtəʊld/) to tell a story, etc again in a different way or in a different language: [Vn] *Greek myths retold for children.*

retention /rɪˈtenʃn/ n [U, sing] (*fml*) **1(a)** the continued possession or use of sth: *retention of one's rights/privileges* ○ *the full retention of one's (mental) faculties.* **(b)** the continued existence of sth: *The government wanted to close the research establishment, but an official report argued for its retention.* **2** the ability to remember things: *show an amazing retention of facts/details.* **3** the action of holding sth in position or stopping it from coming out: *the retention of flood waters* ○ *suffer from retention of urine* (ie failure to pass it out from the BLADDER(1)).

retentive /rɪˈtentɪv/ adj (of the memory) having the ability to remember facts, impressions, etc easily; not forgetting things.

rethink /ˌriːˈθɪŋk/ v (*pt, pp* **rethought** /-ˈθɔːt/) to think again about a policy, course of action, etc, esp in order to change it: [Vn] *rethink an attitude/a strategy/an approach* [V] *The public outcry has prompted some hasty rethinking at the Department of Education.* ▶ **rethink** /ˈriːθɪŋk/ n [sing]: *a major/ radical rethink of company policy.*

reticent /ˈretɪsnt/ adj ~ (**about sth**) not revealing one's thoughts or feelings readily: *be reticent about one's plans* ○ *He seemed strangely reticent about his past.* ▶ **reticence** /-sns/ n [U] (*fml*): *She overcame her natural reticence and talked freely about her marriage.*

reticule /ˈretɪkjuːl/ n (*arch or joc*) a woman's small bag, usu made of cloth and with a string that can be pulled tight to close it.

retina /ˈretɪnə; US ˈretənə/ n (*pl* **retinas** or **retinae** /-niː/) (esp *sing*) a layer of MEMBRANE(1) at the back of the eye that is sensitive to light and sends an image of what is seen to the brain. ⇨ picture at EYE¹.

retinue /ˈretɪnjuː; US ˈretənuː/ n [CGp] a group of people accompanying an important person: *The Queen was flanked by a full retinue of bodyguards and attendants.* ○ (*joc*) *the conference organizer and her retinue of helpers.*

retire /rɪˈtaɪə(r)/ v **1(a)** ~ (**from sth**) to stop doing one's regular work, esp because one has reached a particular age: [V] *Judges should retire at 65.* ○ *The company's official retiring age is 60.* [Vadv] *She has decided to retire early* (ie before reaching the usual age). [Vpr] *He will retire from the army next year.* [V-n] *He retired as manager of the team in 1993.* **(b)** (esp passive) to cause an employee to do this: [Vn] *I was retired on medical grounds.* Compare RESIGN 1. **2** ~ (**from...**) (**to...**) (*fml*) (of an army, etc) to move back without being forced to, esp in order to organize troops, resources, etc in a new way: [Vpr] *The battalion retired to prepared positions.* [also V]. Compare RETREAT 1a. **3(a)** ~ (**from...**) (**to...**) (*fml*) to go away, esp to somewhere quiet or private: [V, Vpr] *The jury retired (from the courtroom) to consider their verdict.* [Vpr] *After lunch he retired to his study.* **(b)** (*fml or rhet*) to go to bed: [V] *I decided to retire early with a book.* **4** ~ (**from sth**) (in sport) to stop playing in the middle of a game, match, etc, esp because of injury: [Vpr] *The boxer retired from the contest with eye injuries.* [V-adj] *The batsman retired hurt.* [also V].

R

▶ **retired** adj having retired from work: a retired Civil Servant.

retiring /rɪˈtaɪərɪŋ/ adj preferring not to be with other people; shy: a quiet, retiring girl.

retirement /rɪˈtaɪəmənt/ n (**a**) [U,C] the event of retiring or state of having retired from work: be above/below retirement age/the age of retirement ∘ urge staff to **take early retirement** (ie retire before the usual age) ∘ She was now approaching retirement. ∘ a retirement pension ∘ There have been several retirements in the company this year. ∘ He has announced his retirement from international football. ∘ He **came out of retirement** to win a medal at the Commonwealth Games. ∘ He lives **in retirement** in Scotland. (**b**) [U, sing] the period of one's life after one has retired: enjoy retirement ∘ We all wish you a long and happy retirement.

retort /rɪˈtɔːt/ v to make a quick, esp angry, reply to an accusation or a challenge: [V.speech] 'Nonsense!' she retorted. [V.that] He retorted that it was my fault as much as his. ▶ **retort** n: She bit back (ie stopped herself from making) a sharp retort and changed the subject.

retouch /ˌriːˈtʌtʃ/ v [Vn] to improve or alter a photograph, painting, etc by making minor changes.

retrace /rɪˈtreɪs/ v **1** to go back along exactly the same path or route that one has just come along: [Vn] We **retraced our steps** to the car and continued our journey. **2** to discover and follow the route taken by sb else: retrace the explorer's original route ∘ Police are retracing the last known movements of the missing child.

retract /rɪˈtrækt/ v (fml) **1** to withdraw a statement, charge, etc: [Vn] He made a false confession which he later retracted. [also V]. **2** to refuse to honour or keep an agreement: [Vn] retract a promise/an offer. **3** to move or pull sth back or in: [Vn] retract the landing gear (ie of an aircraft) [V] The undercarriage failed to retract. ▶ **retractable** /-əbl/ adj that can be moved or pulled in: a knife with a retractable blade.

retraction /rɪˈtrækʃn/ n (**a**) [C] a statement saying that one no longer believes or wishes to be associated with sth one has said or written previously: publish a full retraction of the story. (**b**) [U] the action of retracting sth or of being retracted.

retrain /ˌriːˈtreɪn/ v to train or train sb for a new type of work or to use new equipment: [V] nurses retraining for work in the community [V-n] She retrained as a primary school teacher. [Vn.to inf] retrain staff to use new technology [also Vn]. ▶ **retraining** n [U]: the retraining of out-of-work miners ∘ go on a retraining course.

retread /ˈriːtred/ n a type made by putting a new rubber surface onto an old worn tyre.

retreat /rɪˈtriːt/ v **1**(**a**) to move back or withdraw when faced with danger or difficulty: [V] the sound of his retreating footsteps [V, Vpr] force the enemy to retreat (behind their lines) [Vpr] crowds retreating before police fire hoses [Vn] We retreated half a mile in order to get across the river. Compare ADVANCE² 1, RETIRE 2. (**b**) to change one's decisions or attitude because of criticism, threats, etc from other people: [V] The President retreated in the face of hostile public opinion. [Vpr] retreat from a demand. **2** to go away to a place where one will not be disturbed: [Vpr] After the scandal, she retreated from the public eye. ∘ Embarrassed, she retreated to her bedroom. ∘ (fig) retreat into a world of fantasy. **3** to become smaller in size or extent: [V] The flood water/glacier slowly retreated. **4** (esp finance) to become lower in value: [Vn, Vnpr] Share prices retreated 45p (to 523p).

▶ **retreat** n **1** [U,C usu sing] the action or an instance of retreating: an orderly retreat from the camp ∘ The rebels are **in retreat**. ∘ The minister made an undignified/embarrassing retreat from his earlier position. **2** the retreat [sing] a signal for an army to retreat: sound the retreat (eg on a drum or BUGLE). **3** [C] a quiet or private place: spend the weekends at a country retreat. **4** [U,C] a period when one stops one's usual activities and goes to a quiet place for prayer and thought: go into/be in retreat ∘ make an annual retreat. **IDM** **beat a retreat** ⇨ BEAT¹.

retrench /rɪˈtrentʃ/ v (fml) to reduce one's expenses: [V] Inflation has forced the company to retrench. ▶ **retrenchment** n [U,C]: a period of sharp retrenchment and redundancies.

retrial /ˌriːˈtraɪəl/ n (usu sing) a new trial of sb who has already been tried (TRY¹ 3a): The judge **ordered a retrial** because new evidence had come to light.

retribution /ˌretrɪˈbjuːʃn/ n [U] ~ (**for sth**) (fml) punishment that is considered to be morally right and fully deserved: his fears of divine retribution ∘ seek revenge and retribution for the latest terrorist outrages.

▶ **retributive** /rɪˈtrɪbjətɪv/ adj [attrib] (fml) happening or inflicted as retribution.

retrieve /rɪˈtriːv/ v **1** ~ sth (**from sb/sth**) (esp fml) to get sth back, esp from a place where it should not be: [Vnpr] retrieve yesterday's newspapers from the dustbin ∘ She bent to retrieve her comb from under the seat. [Vn] The police have managed to retrieve some of the money. **2** (esp computing) to find or extract stored information: [Vn, Vnpr] retrieve data (from a disk) [Vnpr] retrieve an address from the files. **3** (fml) to make a situation, etc better or right again; to restore sth: [Vn] retrieve one's losses/ honour ∘ You can only retrieve the situation by apologizing to him publicly.

▶ **retrievable** /-əbl/ adj.

retrieval /-vl/ n [U] (fml) the process of retrieving sth or of being retrieved: a match lost beyond all hope of retrieval ∘ (computing) information/data retrieval.

retriever n a breed of large dog. Retrievers can be trained to bring back birds, etc that have been shot.

retro- pref (with adjs and ns) back or backwards: retroactive ∘ retrograde.

retroactive /ˌretrəʊˈæktɪv/ adj (fml) taking effect from a past date: retroactive legislation ∘ The new law was made retroactive to 1 January. ▶ **retroactively** adv.

retrograde /ˈretrəɡreɪd/ adj (fml) getting worse; returning to a less good condition: Closing small village schools is **a retrograde step**.

retrogressive /ˌretrəˈɡresɪv/ adj returning to old-fashioned ideas or methods: a retrogressive change.

retrospect /ˈretrəspekt/ n **IDM** **in retrospect** looking back on a past event or situation: Her success seems, in retrospect, little short of miraculous. ∘ In retrospect, it's easy to see where we went wrong.

▶ **retrospection** /ˌretrəˈspekʃn/ n [U] (fml) the action of looking back on past events or experiences.

retrospective /ˌretrəˈspektɪv/ adj **1** looking back on the past: retrospective views/guilt ∘ a retrospective exhibition of the painter's work. **2** (of laws, payments, etc) applying to the past as well as the future: a retrospective pay award ∘ The legislation was made retrospective. — n an exhibition tracing the development of a painter, SCULPTOR, etc: a major retrospective of the photographer Dorothy Wilding. **retrospectively** adv: Mortgage interest relief can be claimed retrospectively.

retsina /retˈsiːnə/ n [U,C] Greek white wine that is given a special flavour with RESIN(1).

return¹ /rɪˈtɜːn/ v **1** ~ (**to ...**) (**from ...**) to come or go back to a place: [Vpr, Vadv] return (home) from a trip [Vpr] They recently returned to Paris from London. ∘ His eyes returned to the headline. [V] She returned to collect her umbrella. **2** ~ sth (**to sth/sb**) to bring, give, put or send sth back to a place: [Vnpr]

Please return this book to the library for me. [Vn] *She returned his pen.* [Vn-adj] *I returned the letter unopened.* [Vnn] *He never returned me my £5.* **3** (of a feeling, etc) to come back again: [V] *doubts/suspicions/symptoms that constantly return* ○ *Tell me if the pain returns.* **4** ~ **to sth** to go back to a particular subject, habit or state: [Vpr] *I shall return to this point* (ie discuss it again) *later.* ○ *They returned to the pre-1985 voting system.* ○ *The bus service has returned to normal.* **5** to feel, say or do the same in response: [Vn] *return an invitation* (ie send an invitation to sb who has previously sent an invitation to oneself) ○ *return a greeting/stare/compliment/favour* ○ *He could not return her love/affection.* ○ *The enemy returned (our) fire.* **6** (in certain sports) to hit the ball, etc back to one's opponent during play: [Vn] *return a shot/service/volley.* **7** *(fml)* (esp of a JURY(1)) to give a verdict: [Vn] *The inquest returned a verdict of accidental death.* **8** ~ **sb (to sth)**; ~ **sb (as sth)** (esp passive) to elect sb to a parliament: [Vnpr] *She was returned to Parliament with a decreased majority.* [Vn-adj] *He was returned unopposed as MP for Bath.* **9** to give sth as profit; to yield sth: [Vn] *Our investment accounts return a high rate of interest.*

▸ **returnable** /-əbl/ *adj* that can or must be returned: *returnable bottles/crates* ○ *The deposit is not returnable.*

returnee /rɪ͵tɜː'niː/ *n* (*US*) a person who returns or is taken home from abroad, esp unwillingly: *Returnees were not punished for leaving the country.*

■ **re'turning officer** *n* (*esp Brit*) an official who is responsible for arranging an election in a CON-STITUENCY and announcing the result.

return² /rɪ'tɜːn/ *n* **1** [sing] ~ (**to...**) (**from...**) an act of coming or going back to a place: *I was told the news on my return home* (ie when I got back) *(from Italy).* ○ *on the return trip/voyage/flight* ○ *I saw the play on its return to the Haymarket Theatre.* **2** (*Brit*) (*US* **round-trip ticket**) [C] a ticket for a journey to a place and back again: *a weekend/period return* ○ *a ͵day re'turn to London* (ie valid only for the day of issue). Compare SINGLE 4. **3** [U,C] ~ (**to sth/sb**) the action of bringing, giving, putting or sending sth back: *We would appreciate the prompt return of all library books.* ○ *The deposit is refunded on return of the vehicle.* ○ *Her return of service* (eg at tennis) *was very accurate.* **4** [sing] ~ (**to sth**) an act of coming or going back to an earlier state or condition: *a return of my doubts/suspicions/symptoms* ○ *his return to consciousness* ○ *the return of spring* ○ *a return to normal working hours/old habits.* **5** [C] an official report or statement, esp one made in reply to a formal demand: *complete one's ¹income-tax return* ○ *the e'lection returns* (ie the numbers of votes for each candidate at an election). **6** [C esp *pl*] ~ (**on sth**) a profit from a business deal, etc: *disappointing returns on capital/investment* ○ *investors looking for quick returns* ○ *You should get a good return on these shares.* **7** [C] a theatre ticket bought by sb and then sold back to the theatre: *queuing at the box office for returns.* **IDM** **by re'turn (of ¹post)** (*Brit*) by the next post³(1c): *Please reply by return of post.* ○ *Write now and we will send you a free sample by return.* **in return (for sth)** as payment or reward for sth: *I bought him a drink in return for his help.* **many happy returns** ⇨ HAPPY. **the point of no return** ⇨ POINT¹. **sale or return** ⇨ SALE.

■ **re͵turn 'fare** *n* (*Brit*) the cost of a journey to a place and back again: *the return fare to Sydney.*

re͵turn 'game (also **re͵turn 'match**) *n* a second game or match between the same opponents: *They played a return match the following week.*

re͵turn 'ticket (*Brit*) (*US* ͵**round-trip 'ticket**) *n* = RETURN² 2.

reunify /͵riː'juːnɪfaɪ/ *v* to join two or more territ-

ories into a single political unit again: [Vn] *a reunified Germany.* ▸ **reunification** *n* [U].

reunion /riː'juːnɪən/ *n* **1** [C] a meeting, esp after a long period of separation: *an emotional reunion between the two sisters.* **2** [C] a social gathering of people who were formerly friends, who once worked together, etc: *a family reunion at Christmas* ○ *have/hold an annual reunion of war veterans* ○ *a reunion dinner/celebration.* **3** the action of becoming a single group or organization again: *the reunion of the Democrats with the Liberals.*

reunite /͵riːju'naɪt/ *v* **1** ~ **sb/sth (with sb/sth)** (esp passive) to cause two or more people to come together again; (of two or more people) to come together again: [Vnpr] *Parents were reunited with their lost children.* [also Vn,Vpr,Vp]. **2** to join together again separate areas or separate groups within an organization, etc: [Vn] *He said that the island must be reunited before joining the European Community.* ○ *This issue at last reunited the Tory Party.*

reuse /͵riː'juːz/ *v* to use sth again: [Vn] *reuse an old envelope.*

▸ **reuse** /͵riː'juːs/ *n* [U]: *attempts to stop the reuse of needles by addicts.*

reusable /͵riː'juːzəbl/ *adj* that can be used again: *reusable batteries/envelopes.*

rev /rev/ *n* (usu *pl*) (*infml*) a revolution of an engine: *doing a steady 4000 revs (per minute).*

▸ **rev** *v* (**-vv-**) ~ (**sth**) (**up**) to make an engine run quickly, eg when starting a car: [V,Vn] *Don't rev (the engine) so hard.* [Vp] *I could hear him/his car revving up outside.* [also Vnp].

Rev (also **Revd**) *abbr* (used before a name) Reverend: *the Rev George Hill.* Compare RT REV.

revalue /͵riː'væljuː/ *v* **1** to assess the value of sth again: [Vn,Vnpr] *have your house revalued (at today's prices).* **2** (*finance*) to increase the exchange value of a currency: [Vn] *The franc is to be revalued.* Compare DEVALUE 1. ▸ **revaluation** /͵riːvæljuˈeɪʃn/ *n* [U,C usu *sing*]: *property revaluation* ○ *the need for a further revaluation of the yen.*

revamp /͵riː'væmp/ *v* (*infml often derog*) to give sth a new form or structure, often in a way that is not very thorough; to improve the appearance of sth: [Vnpr] *revamp an old comedy routine with some new jokes* [Vn] *a revamped kitchen* ○ *the revamped Communist Party, now called the Socialist Party.* ▸ **revamp** *n* [sing]: *a revamp of the programme's traditional format.*

reveal /rɪ'viːl/ *v* **1** ~ **sth (to sb)** to make facts, etc known: [Vn] *reveal secrets/details* ○ *reveal one's methods/feelings/sources* [V.that] *I can now reveal that the Princess is to marry in August.* [V.wh] *I can't reveal who told me.* [V.n.to inf] *Her evidence revealed the young men to be innocent.* [Vnpr] *The doctor did not reveal the truth to him.* [Vpr.that] *A member of the union committee revealed to the press that the teachers were going on strike.* [also Vpr.wh]. **2** to cause or allow sth to be seen: [Vn] *Her smile revealed two rows of white even teeth.* ○ *A closer examination/inspection revealed a crack in the vase.* [Vn-adj] *Industrial tribunals have been revealed as powerless and inadequate.* See also REVELATION, REVELATORY.

▸ **revealing** *adj* **1** making facts, attitudes, etc known: *a revealing slip of the tongue* ○ *This document is extremely revealing.* **2** (of a woman's dress, etc) allowing more of the body to be seen than is usual or acceptable: *She was wearing a rather revealing silk blouse.* **revealingly** *adv*.

reveille /rɪ'væli; *US* 'revəli/ *n* [U] a signal played on a drum, BUGLE, etc to wake soldiers in the morning: *Reveille was at 0600 hours.*

revel¹ /'revl/ *v* (**-ll-**; *US* **-l-**) **PHRV** **'revel in sth / doing sth** to get great delight from sth: *She was* *clearly revelling in her new-found freedom.* ∘ *Some people seem to revel in annoying others.*

revel² *n* (usu *pl*) (*dated*) noisy celebrations: *midnight revels.*
▶ **reveller** (*US* **reveler**) /ˈrevələ(r)/ *n* (*dated or joc*) a person who is enjoying herself or himself in a noisy way, esp after drinking alcohol: *late-night revellers leaving the pubs.*

revelation /ˌrevəˈleɪʃn/ *n* **1** [C, U] the making known of sth that was secret or hidden: *divine revelation of truth* ∘ *She was stunned by the revelation that he was already married.* **2** [C] a thing which is revealed, esp sth surprising: *revelations about her private life in the press.* **IDM** **be a revelation (to sb)** to cause a lot of surprise, usu because of being better than or different from what was expected: *His Hamlet was a revelation to the critics.*

revelatory /ˌrevəˈleɪtəri; *US* ˈrevələtɔːri/ *adj* revealing sth that was not known or suspected; giving an INSIGHT(2) into sth: *His performance of the piece was competent but scarcely revelatory.*

revelry /ˈrevlri/ *n* [U, C usu *pl*] noisy celebrations: *sounds of drunken revelry.*

revenge /rɪˈvendʒ/ *n* **1** [U] (**a**) deliberate punishment or injury inflicted in return for what one has suffered: *an act of revenge* ∘ *He swore to* **take his revenge on/against** *their families.* ∘ *The policemen were apparently killed* **in revenge for** *the attack on demonstrators last week.* (**b**) the desire to inflict this: *done in the spirit of revenge.* **2** [U] (*sport*) the defeat of a person or team that beat one in a previous game: *England beat Belgium 2–1, exacting revenge for their 6–5 defeat last season.* ∘ *His opponent was intent on/thirsting for revenge.*
▶ **revenge** *v* **PHRV** **reˈvenge oneself on sb; be reˈvenged on sb** to get satisfaction by deliberately inflicting injury on sb in return for injury inflicted by them on oneself.
revengeful /-fl/ *adj* feeling or showing a desire for revenge.

revenue /ˈrevənjuː; *US* -nuː/ *n* [U] (also **revenues** [pl]) income, esp the total annual income of a state or an organization: *extra sources of government revenue* ∘ *sales and advertising revenue* ∘ *a slump in oil revenues* ∘ *increased revenues from sales of personal computers* ∘ *revenue raised/generated by the new tax* ∘ *This one drug accounts for 50% of the company's revenues.* See also THE INLAND REVENUE.

reverberate /rɪˈvɜːbəreɪt/ *v* **1(a)** (of a sound) to be repeated several times as an ECHO¹(1b): [Vpr] *The piercing sound of a hunting horn reverberated through the forest.* (**b**) ~ (**with sth**) (of an atmosphere or a place) to seem to shake and be disturbed because of a loud noise: [Vpr] *The room reverberated with the noise of the shot.* [also V]. **2** to have a severe and upsetting effect: [V, Vpr] *Repercussions of the case continue to reverberate (in/through the financial world).*
▶ **reverberation** /rɪˌvɜːbəˈreɪʃn/ *n* [U, C usu *pl*] **1** a loud noise repeated as an ECHO¹(1b): *the reverberation of thunder.* **2** undesirable effects of sth that spread amongst a large number of people: *the continuing reverberations of the scandal.*

revere /rɪˈvɪə(r)/ *v* (*fml*) to feel deep respect or admiration for sb/sth: [Vn] *a teacher revered by generations of students* [Vn-n] *Many of the hit songs of the sixties are now revered as classics.*

reverence /ˈrevərəns/ *n* [U] ~ (**for sb/sth**) a feeling of deep respect or admiration for sb/sth: *The crowd knelt in reverence and worship.* ∘ *He has a deep reverence for the traditions of the Church.*

reverend /ˈrevərənd/ *adj* **the Reverend** (*abbrs* **Rev, Revd**) (used as the title of a member of the CLERGY): *the Reverend Charles Dodgson.* See also RIGHT REVEREND.

■ **ˌReverend ˈMother** *n* (usu *sing*) (the title of) the nun in charge of a CONVENT; the Mother Superior.

reverent /ˈrevərənt/ *adj* feeling or showing great respect and admiration: *a reverent voice/atmosphere/pause.* ▶ **reverently** *adv*: *speak reverently of sb* ∘ *She reverently turned the brooch over in her hand.*

reverential /ˌrevəˈrenʃl/ *adj* (*fml*) caused by or showing REVERENCE: *a reverential hush/tone/whisper.* ▶ **reverentially** /-ʃəli/ *adv*: *He dropped his voice reverentially.*

reverie /ˈrevəri/ *n* [U, C] (*fml*) a state in which one ignores what is happening around one and has pleasant thoughts: *be deep/sunk/lost in reverie* ∘ *She fell/drifted into a reverie.*

revers /rɪˈvɪə(r)/ *n* (*pl* unchanged /-ˈvɪəz/) (usu *pl*) the edge of a coat, jacket, etc, turned back to show the reverse¹ side, esp at the LAPEL.

reversal /rɪˈvɜːsl/ *n* [C, U] **1** a change of sth to the opposite of what it was: *a dramatic reversal of their earlier decision/policy* ∘ *a reversal of the usual procedures/trends.* **2** a change from being successful to having problems or suffering defeat: *the team's recent reversal* ∘ *His luck suffered a cruel/sharp reversal.* **3** an exchange of positions, functions, etc between two people: *role reversal/reversal of roles* (eg between a husband and his wife when the husband looks after the house and children while the wife works).

reverse¹ /rɪˈvɜːs/ *adj* [attrib] ~ (**of/to sth**) contrary or opposite to what has been mentioned: *have the reverse effect* ∘ *go in the reverse direction* ∘ *Statistics showed a reverse trend to that recorded in other countries.* ∘ *The three winners were announced in reverse order* (ie the person in third place being announced first, etc).
■ **reˌverse ˈgear** *n* [C, U] = REVERSE² 3.

reverse² /rɪˈvɜːs/ *n* **1** **the reverse (of sth)** [sing] the thing that is the contrary or opposite to what has just been mentioned: *In hot weather, the reverse happens/applies.* ∘ *Children's shoes aren't cheap — quite the reverse.* ∘ *You might think that young people would now be abandoning smoking, but exactly the reverse of this is true.* **2** [C] (*fml*) a change from making successful progress to having problems or suffering defeat: *the government's recent reverses* ∘ *a reverse at the polls* (ie a poor election result) ∘ *We suffered some serious financial reverses.* **3** (also **reverse gear**) [U] the mechanism used to make a vehicle travel backwards: *Put the car into reverse.* ∘ (*fig*) *The arms race has gone into reverse.* **4** [sing] the back of a coin, medal, piece of cloth, etc: *the reverse of a painting* ∘ *a maker's mark on the reverse of a plate.* **5** [C] a device that turns sth over or back: *an automatic ribbon reverse* (eg on a printer (PRINT²)). **IDM** **in reˈverse** from the end towards the start; backwards: *Ambulances have 'AMBULANCE' printed in reverse on their bonnets.*

reverse³ /rɪˈvɜːs/ *v* **1(a)** to make a vehicle travel backwards: [Vpr] *She reversed round the corner.* [Vp] *The garage was open, so I reversed in.* [Vnpr] *He reversed the car into a tree.* [also V, Vn, Vnp]. (**b**) (of a vehicle) to travel backwards: [V] *Watch out! That van is reversing.* **2(a)** to make sth the opposite of what it was; to change sth completely: [Vn] *reverse a procedure/process/trend* ∘ *The brothers are trying to reverse the decline of their father's company.* (**b**) to exchange two positions, functions, etc: [Vn] *Husband and wife have reversed roles.* ∘ *She used to work for me, but our situations are now reversed.* **3** to replace a previous decision, law, etc with a new one: [Vn] *reverse the decision of a lower court* ∘ *reverse a decree/judgement* ∘ *Local clergy are campaigning to have the decision reversed.* **4** to turn sth the opposite way round, turn the bottom of sth to face the top, or turn the inside of sth to the outside: [Vn] *Writing is*

reversed in a mirror. **IDM** **reverse the ˈcharges** (*US* also ˌcall colˈlect) to make a telephone call that will be paid for by the person receiving it, not the person making it: *You can reverse the charges when you ring me.* ○ *make a reverse charge call to New York.*

▶ **reversible** /-əbl/ *adj* that can be reversed: *a reversible coat/pillowcase* (ie one that can be used with either side turned to the outside) ○ *Is this trend reversible?* **reversibility** /rɪˌvɜːsəˈbɪləti/ *n* [U].

■ **reˈversing light** (*Brit*) (*US* **backup light**) *n* a white light at the back of a vehicle which comes on when the vehicle is reversing.

reversion /rɪˈvɜːʃn; *US* -ˈvɜːrʒn/ *n* **1** [U, sing] an act or a process of reverting to sth; a return: *a reversion to swamp/old methods/former habits* ○ *the reversion of Hong Kong to Chinese rule.* **2** (*US law*) = LEASE-BACK.

revert /rɪˈvɜːt/ *v* **PHR V** reˈvert to sth (**a**) to return to a former state or condition: *fields that have reverted (back) to moorland.* (**b**) to return to a former practice or habit: *revert to smoking when under stress* ○ *After her divorce she reverted to (using) her maiden name.* ○ *Once a socialist, she has now reverted to type* and votes Tory like her parents. (**c**) (*fml*) to return to an earlier topic: *To revert/ Reverting to your earlier question, ...* ○ *The conversation kept reverting to the subject of money.* **PHR V** reˈvert to sb/sth (*law*) (of property, rights, etc) to return or pass to the original owner, the state, etc: *If he dies without an heir, his property reverts to the state.* See also REVERSION.

revetment /rɪˈvetmənt/ *n* (*techn*) stones or other material used to strengthen a wall, hold back a bank of earth, etc.

review /rɪˈvjuː/ *n* **1** [U, C] a new examination of sth, with the possibility or intention of changing it if this is considered desirable or necessary: *The terms of the contract are **subject to review** periodically/ every six months.* ○ *carry out/conduct a radical review of manufacturing methods* ○ *a ˈrent review* ○ *Our selection procedures are currently **under review**.* ○ *Your case is **coming up for review** in May.* ○ *a policy review body.* **2** [C] a survey or report of a subject or of past events: *publish an annual/ monthly review of progress* ○ *present a review of the year's sport* ○ *a wide-ranging review of recent developments in wildlife conservation.* **3** [C] a report by sb in a newspaper or magazine giving her or his opinion of a book, film, etc: *The play got excellent/ mixed/unfavourable reviews in the American press.* ○ *His production of 'Macbeth' opened to **rave reviews**.* **4** [C] (*fml*) a ceremonial display and inspection of troops, etc: *hold a review of the fleet.*

▶ **review** *v* **1(a)** to examine or consider sth again, with the possibility of changing it if this is thought desirable or necessary: [Vn] *The council met to review the budget.* ○ *The government is reviewing the situation.* (**b**) to think about past events, eg to try to understand why they happened; to SURVEY(2) sth: [Vn] *review one's successes and failures* ○ *review one's progress.* **2** to write a review of a book, film, etc for publication: [Vn] *The play was (well/favourably) reviewed in the Daily Mail.* **3** [Vn] to inspect troops, a fleet, etc in a ceremonial way. **reviewer** *n* a person who writes reviews of books, etc: *The Washington Post's book reviewer* ○ *a play which reviewers have praised highly.*

revile /rɪˈvaɪl/ *v* ~ sb (**for sth / doing sth**) (*fml*) (esp passive) to criticize sb/sth in angry and insulting language: [Vnpr] *The government is regularly reviled for running down the welfare state.* [also Vn].

revise /rɪˈvaɪz/ *v* **1** to change sth in order to correct or improve it: [Vn] *present revised proposals/ estimates to the committee* ○ *revise a manuscript before publication* ○ *revise one's opinion of sb* [Vnadv]

The sales forecast for July has been revised upwards. **2** ~ (**sth**) (**for sth**) (*Brit*) to look again at work that one has done, in preparation for an examination: [Vn] *revise English literature* [V, Vpr] *I'm staying in tonight to revise (for my physics exam).*

▶ **revision** /rɪˈvɪʒn/ *n* (**a**) [U, C] the action of revising sth: *Their policies are currently undergoing radical/drastic revision.* ○ *carry out a final revision of the manuscript* ○ (*Brit*) *do some revision for the exams* ○ *make some revision notes.* (**b**) [C] a change or set of changes to sth: *They made some hasty revisions to the schedule.*

■ **the Reˌvised ˌStandard ˈVersion** *n* [sing] the version of the Bible made in 1946–57.

the Reˌvised ˈVersion *n* [sing] the version of the Bible made in 1870–84, based on the Authorized Version.

revisionism /rɪˈvɪʒənɪzəm/ *n* [U] (*often derog*) changes to, or doubts about, standard political ideas or practices, esp Marxism. ▶ **revisionist** /-ʒənɪst/ *n, adj*: *the activities of revisionists* ○ *revisionist tendencies.*

revisit /ˌriːˈvɪzɪt/ *v* to visit a place again, esp after a long period of time: [Vn] *revisit one's old haunts.*

revitalize, -ise /riːˈvaɪtəlaɪz/ *v* to put new life into sth; to make sth stronger or more lively: [Vn] *revitalize an industry/the economy/education* ○ *new ways to revitalize your hair* ○ *Her appointment as leader revitalized the party.* ▶ **revitalization, -isation** /ˌriːˌvaɪtəlaɪˈzeɪʃn; *US* -lə'z-/ *n* [U]: *the promised revitalization of the public transport system.*

revival /rɪˈvaɪvl/ *n* **1** [U, C] an improvement in the condition or strength of sth; a recovery: *the revival of hope/interest* ○ *a brief revival in the political fortunes of the Democratic Party* ○ *Our economy is undergoing a revival.* **2** [U, C] the process of bringing sth back into existence, use, fashion, etc: *the revival of old customs/values/skills* ○ *the revival of nationalism* ○ *a religious/commercial/political revival* ○ *Folk music is currently enjoying a revival.* **3** [C] a new production of a play, etc that has not been performed for some time: *put on a revival of John Osborne's 'Look Back in Anger'.*

▶ **revivalism** /-vəlɪzəm/ *n* [U] the process of creating or increasing interest in sth, esp religion: *jazz/ Christian revivalism.*

revivalist /-vəlɪst/ *n* a person who tries to promote sth, esp religion, and make it more popular. — *adj* [attrib]: *revivalist crusades/styles.*

revive /rɪˈvaɪv/ *v* **1** to come back or bring sb/sth back to health, strength or consciousness: [V] *The flowers will revive in water.* ○ *Our failing spirits revived.* [Vn] *She fainted but the brandy soon revived her.* ○ *an attempt to revive the flagging tourist trade.* **2** to bring sth back into existence, use, fashion, etc: [Vn] *revive old practices/customs* ○ *revive a plan/ policy/debate* ○ *stories which revive memories* ○ *efforts to revive the miniskirt* ○ *The poor trade figures have revived fears of higher interest rates.* **3** to produce again a play, etc that has not been performed for some time: [Vn] *revive a 1930s musical.* See also REVIVAL.

revivify /ˌriːˈvɪvɪfaɪ/ *v* (*pt pp* **-fied**) [Vn] (*fml*) give new life or liveliness to sth.

revocation /ˌrevəˈkeɪʃn/ *n* [U] (*fml*) the cancelling of a law, licence, etc: *the revocation of the contract.*

revoke /rɪˈvəʊk/ *v* (*fml*) to withdraw or cancel a law, licence, etc: [Vn] *revoke planning permission* ○ *He had his sentence revoked.*

revolt /rɪˈvəʊlt/ *v* **1** ~ (**against sb/sth**) (**a**) to show violent resistance to authority: [Vpr] *revolting against a military dictatorship* [V] *The people threatened to revolt.* (**b**) to express protest about sth: [Vpr] *revolt against parental discipline* ○ *Public opinion may revolt against such heavy casualties.* [also V]. **2**

to make sb feel horror or disgust: [Vn] *The violent scenes in the film revolted me.* ○ *I was revolted by the smell of whisky on his breath.*
▶ **revolt** *n* (**a**) [U] the action or state of protesting against or resisting authority: *a period of open/armed/political revolt* ○ *stir/incite militant party members to revolt* ○ *The people rose in revolt.* (**b**) [C] a protest or violent act of resistance against authority: *a Communist-led revolt* ○ *The army easily put down/crushed the revolt.* ○ *face a revolt amongst one's supporters.* Compare REVOLUTION 1.

revolting /rɪ'vəʊltɪŋ/ *adj* causing disgust or horror; extremely unpleasant: *a revolting mixture of pasta and curry* ○ *His feet smelt absolutely revolting.* ▶ **revoltingly** *adv.*

revolution /ˌrevə'luːʃn/ *n* **1** [C,U] an attempt to change the system of government, esp by force: *the French Revolution of 1789* ○ *a peaceful/bloodless revolution* ○ *stir up revolution.* **2** [C] ~ (**in sth**) a complete or dramatic change of method, conditions, etc: *a revolution in printing techniques/sexual attitudes* ○ *a technological/cultural revolution.* **3** [C,U] ~ (**on/round sth**) a movement in a circle round a point, esp of one planet round another: *the revolution of the earth on its axis round the sun* ○ *make/describe a full revolution.* See also COUNTER-REVOLUTION, INDUSTRIAL REVOLUTION.
▶ **revolutionary** /-ʃənəri; *US* -neri/ *adj* **1** [usu attrib] of political revolution: *revolutionary movements/leaders/posters.* **2** involving a complete or dramatic change: *a revolutionary idea* ○ *The consequences of genetic engineering are revolutionary.* — *n* (esp *pl*) a person who begins or supports a political revolution: *a regime overthrown by revolutionaries.*
revolutionize, -ise /-ʃənaɪz/ *v* to make sth change completely or in a dramatic way: [Vn] *This chip could revolutionize the design of computers.*

revolve /rɪ'vɒlv/ *v* **1** ~ (**around/round sth**) (of a planet, etc) to move around sth in a circle: [Vpr] *The earth revolves round the sun.* [also V]. **2** to go round in a circle; to ROTATE(1): [V] *The machine cuts the grass as its blades revolve.* **PHRV** **re'volve around sb/sth** to have sb/sth as its chief concern; to centre on sb/sth: *My life revolves around my job.* ○ *He thinks that everything revolves around him.*
▶ **revolving** *adj* [usu attrib] that can turn in a circle: *The theatre has a revolving stage.* **revolving 'door** *n* an entrance to a hotel, etc consisting of usu four glass sections that turn together round a central post.

revolver /rɪ'vɒlvə(r)/ *n* a small gun with a container for bullets that turns so that several shots can be fired quickly. ▷ picture at GUN.

revue /rɪ'vjuː/ *n* [C,U] a type of show performed on stage, consisting of a mixture of jokes, songs and dances about current or recent events: *a satirical revue* ○ *act/perform in revue.*

revulsion /rɪ'vʌlʃn/ *n* [U,sing] ~ (**against/at/over/from sth**) a feeling of disgust or horror: *feel a sense of revulsion at the bloodshed* ○ *She experienced a revulsion from the sights and smells around her.* ○ *The government expressed its shock and revulsion over the murder.*

reward /rɪ'wɔːd/ *n* **1** [C,U] a thing that is given or received in return for doing sth good, working hard, etc: *the emotional rewards of motherhood* ○ *get one's just reward for one's efforts* ○ *The money was a reward for forty years of loyal service.* ○ *He reaped/received considerable financial reward for his work.* **2** [C] a sum of money offered for helping the police to find a criminal or for finding and returning lost property: *a £10 000 reward has been offered for the return of the stolen painting.*
▶ **reward** *v* ~ **sb** (**for sth / doing sth**) (**with sth**) (esp passive) to give a reward to sb: [Vnpr] *She was*
rewarded for her efforts/for working hard with a pay rise. ○ *The audience rewarded his remark with loud applause.* [Vn] *Our long climb was finally rewarded by magnificent views from the summit.* ○ *After hours spent searching their patience was finally rewarded when they found the missing document.* **rewarding** *adj* (of an activity, etc) worth doing; satisfying: *a rewarding trip/pastime* ○ *Teaching is not very rewarding financially* (ie not very well paid).

rewind /ˌriː'waɪnd/ *v* (*pt, pp* **rewound** /-'waʊnd/) to make a tape in a CASSETTE player or a video recorder (VIDEO) go backwards: [V, Vn] *Rewind (the tape) and play it again.*

rewire /ˌriː'waɪə(r)/ *v* to put new electrical wires into a building, etc: [Vn] *The house has been completely rewired.*

rework /ˌriː'wɜːk/ *v* to make changes to sth in order to improve it or make it more accurate, suitable, etc: [Vn] *rework the original story so that it appeals to modern readers* ○ *I think you should rework your sums.* ▶ **reworking** *n*: *a reworking of Shakespeare's 'Hamlet'.*

rewrite /ˌriː'raɪt/ *v* (*pt* **rewrote** /-'rəʊt/; *pp* **rewritten** /-'rɪtn/) ~ **sth** (**for sth**); ~ **sth** (**as sth**) to write sth again in a different or better way: [Vnpr, Vn-n] *rewrite the script for radio/as a radio play* [Vn] *an attempt to rewrite history* ○ *This essay will have to be completely rewritten.*
▶ **rewrite** /'riːraɪt/ *n* a thing that is rewritten: *do a total rewrite of the original speech.*

rhapsody /'ræpsədi/ *n* **1** (*music*) (often in titles) a romantic piece of music that is not regular in form, usu in one movement: *Liszt's Hungarian Rhapsodies.* **2** [usu *pl*] the expression of great enthusiasm or delight in speech or writing: *rhapsodies of praise.*
▶ **rhapsodic** /ræp'sɒdɪk/ *adj.*
rhapsodize, -ise /'ræpsədaɪz/ *v* [V, Vpr] ~ (**about/over sb/sth**) (*fml*) to talk or write with great enthusiasm about sb/sth.

rhesus /'riːsəs/ (also **'rhesus monkey**) *n* a small monkey common in N India, often used in scientific experiments.

rhetoric /'retərɪk/ *n* [U] **1** the art of using language in an impressive way, esp to influence people in public speaking. **2** (*often derog*) speech or writing that sounds important and impressive but is often insincere or exaggerated: *the empty rhetoric of politicians* ○ *a powerful piece of rhetoric.*

rhetorical /rɪ'tɒrɪkl; *US* -'tɔːr-/ *adj* **1** (abbreviated as *rhet* in this dictionary) of the art of rhetoric(1): *the rhetorical devices of classical literature.* **2** (*often derog*) in or using rhetoric(2): *rhetorical speeches.* **3** (of a question) asked only to produce an effect or make a statement rather than to get an answer, eg *Who cares?* (ie No one cares): *'What can I do?' he asked. It was a rhetorical question.* ▶ **rhetorically** /-kli/ *adv*: *'Why me?' she asked rhetorically.*

rheumatic /ru'mætɪk/ *adj* of, causing or affected by RHEUMATISM: *rheumatic complaints/pains/joints* ○ *a rheumatic old man.*
■ **rheu,matic 'fever** *n* [U] an infectious disease that causes fever, with swelling and pain in the joints.

rheumatism /'ruːmətɪzəm/ *n* [U] a disease that makes the muscles and joints painful, stiff and swollen: *suffer from rheumatism.* Compare ARTHRITIS.

rheumatoid arthritis /ˌruːmətɔɪd ɑː'θraɪtɪs/ *n* [U] a disease that causes the joints, esp of the hands, wrists, knees and feet, to become swollen and painful.

rhinestone /'raɪnstəʊn/ *n* a colourless jewel intended to look like a diamond, used in cheap jewellery: *rhinestone buttons.*

rhino /'raɪnəʊ/ *n* (*pl* unchanged or **-os** /-nəʊz/)

(*infml*) a RHINOCEROS: *a black/white rhino* ○ *rhino horn.* ⇨ picture.

rhinoceros /raɪˈnɒsərəs/ *n* (*pl* unchanged or **rhinoceroses**) a great heavy animal of Africa and S Asia which has very thick skin and either one or two horns on its nose.

rhizome /ˈraɪzəʊm/ *n* (*botany*) the thick stem of certain plants. It grows along or under the ground and has roots and shoots growing from it. ⇨ picture at FLOWER.

rhododendron /ˌrəʊdəˈdendrən/ *n* a bush with large red, purple, pink or white flowers and leaves which it keeps throughout the year.

rhomboid /ˈrɒmbɔɪd/ *n* (*geometry*) a flat shape with four straight sides, the opposite sides being parallel and equal to each other. ⇨ picture at QUADRILATERAL.

rhombus /ˈrɒmbəs/ *n* (*pl* **rhombuses**) (*geometry*) a flat shape with four straight equal sides and four angles which are not right angles (RIGHT¹). ⇨ picture at QUADRILATERAL.

rhubarb /ˈruːbɑːb/ *n* [U] **1** a garden plant with thick red stems that are cooked and eaten like fruit: *rhubarb pie.* **2** (a word that a group of actors repeat on stage to give the impression of a lot of people speaking at the same time).

rhyme /raɪm/ *n* **1** [U] the quality shared by words or syllables that have or end with the same sound as each other, esp when such words, etc are used at the ends of lines of poetry, eg *day, away; visit, is it; puff, rough*: *a poem/story in rhyme.* **2** [C] ~ (**for sth**) a word that has the same sound as another: *Can you think of a rhyme for 'yellow'?* **3** [C] a short poem in which the word or syllable at the end of each line has the same sound as the word at the end of another line: *She made up a little rhyme to amuse the children.* See also NURSERY RHYME. **IDM** **ˌrhyme or ˈreason** (usu in negative sentences) logic or sense: *a decision without rhyme or reason* ○ *There seems to be no rhyme or reason to English spelling.*

▶ **rhyme** *v* **1** ~ (**with sth**) (of words, syllables or lines of a poem) to have or end with the same sound: [Vpr] *'Gift' rhymes with 'lift'.* [V] *'Though' and 'through' don't rhyme.* **2** ~ **sth** (**with sth**) to put together words that sound the same, eg when writing poetry: [Vn, Vnpr] *You can rhyme 'girl' and/with 'curl'.* [Vn] *rhymed verse.* **rhyming** *adj*: *rhyming couplets.*

■ **ˈrhyming slang** *n* [U] a way of speaking in which words are replaced with rhyming words or phrases. For example, in COCKNEY rhyming slang 'apples and pears' means 'stairs'.

rhythm /ˈrɪðəm/ *n* **1** [C, U] a strong regular repeated pattern of sounds or movements: *dance to the rhythm of the drums* ○ *play the same tune in/with a different rhythm* ○ *Latin-American rhythms* ○ *the rhythm of her breathing* ○ *She's a great dancer — she has a natural sense of rhythm* (ie the ability to move in time to a fixed beat). **2** [U, C] a constantly repeated sequence of events or processes: *the rhythm of the tides/seasons* ○ *biological rhythms* (eg of the human body).

▶ **rhythmic** /ˈrɪðmɪk/ (also **rhythmical** /ˈrɪðmɪkl/) *adj* having rhythm: *the rhythmic quality of African music* ○ *the rhythmic tread of marching feet* ○ *His breathing became slow and rhythmic.* **rhythmically** /-kli/ *adv.*

■ **ˌrhythm and ˈblues** (*abbr* **R and B**) *n* [U] a type of popular music based on the blues (BLUE² 3a).

ˈrhythm section *n* the part of a dance band that supplies the rhythm, usu consisting of drums, BASS¹(1) and sometimes piano.

rib /rɪb/ *n* **1** [C] any of the curved bones extending from the BACKBONE(1) round the chest. Humans and animals have twelve pairs of ribs: *broken/cracked/bruised ribs* ○ *a rib injury* ○ *nudge/dig/poke sb in the ribs.* ⇨ picture at SKELETON. **2** [C] a piece of

meat from the ribs of an animal, with one or more bones attached. See also SPARE-RIB. **3** [C] a curved piece of wood or metal that forms part of the structure of sth, eg a boat or building, and helps to strengthen it. **4** [U, C] a stitch in knitting that produces a raised pattern of lines: *cuffs knitted in rib.*

▶ **rib** *v* (**-bb-**) ~ **sb** (**about/for/over sth**) (*infml*) to mock sb in a friendly way; to TEASE(1) sb: [Vn, Vnpr] *She was ribbed mercilessly (about her accent).*

ribbed *adj* (esp of fabrics) having raised lines: *ribbed tights* ○ *a ribbed sweater.* **ribbing** *n* [U] **1** a pattern of raised lines in knitting. **2** ~ (**about/for/over sth**) (*infml*) friendly teasing (TEASE 1): *He got a lot of ribbing at school for his mistake.*

ribald /ˈrɪbld, ˈraɪbɔːld/ *adj* (*fml or rhet*) referring to sexual matters in a rude but humorous way: *ribald humour/remarks/laughter.*

▶ **ribaldry** /ˈrɪbldri, ˈraɪb-/ *n* [U] (*fml or rhet*) ribald language or behaviour.

ribbon /ˈrɪbən/ *n* **1**(**a**) [U] silk, nylon or other material in a narrow strip, used for tying sth or for decoration: *a parcel wrapped in tissue paper and tied with satin ribbon* ○ *a length of velvet ribbon.* (**b**) [C] a piece of this: *Her hair was tied back with a black ribbon.* ○ (*fig*) *Ribbons of black smoke rose from the chimneys.* **2** [C] a ribbon of a special colour and pattern, awarded to sb esp in the armed forces because of their achievements and worn on a jacket, etc. **3** [C] a long narrow strip of material that contains ink and is used in a TYPEWRITER and some computer printers. **IDM** **cut, tear, etc sth to ˈribbons** to cut, tear, etc sth very badly: *The wind tore the sails to ribbons.* ○ *Don't walk on the broken glass — you'll cut your feet to ribbons!*

ribcage /ˈrɪbkeɪdʒ/ *n* the structure of ribs (RIB 1) round the chest.

rice /raɪs/ *n* [U] (**a**) a type of grass grown on wet land in hot countries, esp in E Asia, producing seeds that are cooked and used as food: *rice fields/paddies.* (**b**) these seeds: *grains of rice* ○ *a bowl of boiled/fried rice* ○ *long-/short-grain rice* ○ *brown rice* (ie without its outer covering removed).

■ **ˈrice-paper** *n* [U] a type of thin edible paper made from the straw of rice plants and used as a base for small cakes, etc.

ˌrice ˈpudding *n* [C, U] a sweet dish made by cooking rice in milk and sugar.

rich /rɪtʃ/ *adj* (**-er, -est**) (in meanings 1, 2 and 3 the opposite of *poor*) **1** having a lot of money or property; wealthy: *the rich countries of the world* ○ *grow/become/get richer and richer* ○ *The business deal made him a very rich man.* **2**(**a**) [pred] ~ **in sth** producing or having a large supply of sth: *Oranges are rich in vitamin C.* ○ *a play rich in humour* ○ *a fertilizer rich in nitrogen.* (**b**) (of soil) containing a lot of minerals, etc and so good for growing plants in: *rich, well-drained soil.* **3**(**a**) producing or produced in large quantities: *a rich harvest* ○ (*fig*) *The book is a rich source of ideas.* (**b**) complex and interesting: *She leads a rich and varied life.* ○ *Rome has an immensely rich history.* **4** (of food) containing a large amount of fat, butter, eggs, spices, etc: *a rich fruit cake* ○ *a rich creamy sauce.* **5**(**a**) (of colours or sounds) pleasantly deep and strong: *the rich colours of autumn leaves* ○ *a rich soothing voice.* (**b**) (of smells or tastes) pleasantly smooth and strong: *the rich aroma of freshly ground coffee.* **6** valuable and beautiful: *rich fabrics/furnishings.* **7** (*infml*) (of a criticism, etc) not reasonable, esp because the person criticizing has the same fault: *'He said you were lazy.' 'That's (a bit) rich* coming from someone who never gets up before midday!' **IDM** **strike it rich** ⇨ STRIKE².

▶ **the rich** *n* [pl v] people who have a lot of money or property: *take from the rich and give to the poor.*

richly *adv* **1** in a generous manner: *She was richly* rewarded *for her trouble.* **2** in an elaborate and splendid manner: *a richly-decorated robe.* **3** fully: *a richly deserved success* ○ *Her success was richly earned.*

richness *n* [U] the quality or state of being rich: *the richness and diversity of Japanese culture* ○ *the richness of the furnishings* ○ *The painting has an amazing richness of colour.*

riches /'rɪtʃɪz/ *n* [pl] wealth; money and valuable possessions: *amass great riches* ○ *He claims to despise riches.* ○ *(fig) the riches of Oriental art* ○ *the natural riches of the soil.* **IDM** **rags to riches** ⇨ RAG¹.

Richter scale /'rɪktə skeɪl/ *n* **the Richter scale** [sing] *(geology)* scale¹(2) from 0 to 8 for measuring the intensity of an EARTHQUAKE: *measuring 7.3 on the Richter scale.*

rick¹ /rɪk/ *v* to strain a joint, etc: [Vn] *rick one's ankle/back.*

rick² /rɪk/ *n* a large pile of HAY or straw built in a regular shape and often covered to protect it from rain.

rickets /'rɪkɪts/ *n* [sing or pl *v*] a children's disease that is caused by poor diet and results in the bones becoming soft and badly formed.

rickety /'rɪkəti/ *adj (infml)* not strong or firm; likely to collapse: *rickety wooden stairs* ○ *a rickety bridge/gate/shed.*

rickshaw /'rɪkʃɔ:/ *n* **(a)** a small light vehicle with two wheels pulled by one or more people, used in some Asian countries to carry passengers: *ride in a rickshaw.* **(b)** a similar vehicle like a bicycle with three wheels, having a seat for passengers behind the driver.

ricochet /'rɪkəʃeɪ/ *v (pt, pp* **ricocheted** /-ʃeɪd/; **ricochetted** /-ʃetɪd/) ~ **(off sth)** (of a bullet, etc) to strike a surface and bounce back off it at an angle: [Vpr] *The stone ricocheted off the wall and hit a passer-by.* [also V].
▶ **ricochet** *n* **(a)** [U] the action of striking a surface and bouncing back off it: *the constant ricochet of bricks and bottles off police riot shields.* **(b)** [C] a bullet, etc that does this: *be hit by a ricochet.*

rid /rɪd/ *v* (**-dd-**; *pt, pp* **rid**) **IDM** **be/get 'rid of sb/sth** to be/become free of sb/sth that causes one annoyance or trouble: *He's a boring nuisance! I'm glad to be rid of him.* ○ *get rid of dry skin/fascism* ○ *The shop ordered 20 copies of the book and now it can't get rid of* (ie sell) *them.* **PHRV** **'rid oneself/sb/sth of sb/sth** to make oneself/sb/sth free from sb/sth that causes annoyance or trouble: *rid the house of mice* ○ *rid oneself of guilt.*

riddance /'rɪdns/ *n* **IDM** **good 'riddance (to sb/sth)** (said to express relief, etc at being free of sb/sth that caused one annoyance or trouble): *He's gone at last, and good riddance (to him)!*

ridden /'rɪdn/ **1** *pp* of RIDE². **2** *adj* (usu in compounds) full of or dominated by sth specified: *ˌflea-ridden 'lodgings* ○ *be 'guilt-ridden* ○ *(fml) She was ridden by/with guilt.*

riddle¹ /'rɪdl/ *n* **1** a question, statement or description, not easily understood at first, that has a clever answer: *ask/tell sb a riddle* ○ *know the answer to/solve a riddle* ○ *speak/talk in riddles.* **2** a person, event, etc that is not easy to understand: *the riddle of how the universe originated* ○ *She's a complete riddle, even to her parents.*

riddle² /'rɪdl/ *v* ~ **sb/sth (with sth)** (esp passive) to make many holes in sb/sth: [Vn] *Sniper fire riddled the building.* [Vnpr] *The car was riddled with bullet holes.* **PHRV** **be 'riddled with sth** to be full of sth, esp sth bad or undesirable: *They are riddled with disease.* ○ *The administration is riddled with corruption.* ○ *His essay is riddled with mistakes.*

ride¹ /raɪd/ *n* **1** a journey or part of a journey in or on a vehicle: *a ride on the back of a motor bike* ○ *He*

gave *me a ride in his Landrover.* ○ *Can I hitch a ride with you?* ○ *The ride from the airport passes through quiet countryside.* ○ *It's only a five-minute 'bus-ride into town.* See also JOYRIDE. **2** a journey on a horse, etc, often for pleasure: *an early-morning ride* ○ *go for a 'donkey-ride* ○ *It's a three-day ride to the coast.* ○ *(fig) Give me a ride on your shoulders, Daddy.* **3** the way riding in a car, etc feels: *The luxury model gives a smoother ride.* ○ *(fig) The company looks to be in for a bumpy ride* (ie a difficult time) *this year.* ○ *(fig) The bill* **had an easy/a rough ride** (ie passed easily/with difficulty) *through the Commons.* **4 (a)** an amusement at a FAIR³(1), which people pay to sit or stand on for a short time while it moves round fast, swings from side to side, etc: *The rides on the promenade were still open.* **(b)** a period of time spent on such an amusement: *have a ride on the Big Dipper.* **IDM** **have/give sb a rough ride** ⇨ ROUGH¹. **take sb for a 'ride** *(infml)* to deceive or cheat sb.

ride² /raɪd/ *v (pt* **rode** /rəʊd/; *pp* **ridden** /'rɪdn/) **1(a)** to travel on a horse, etc: [Vpr] *They rode along narrow country lanes.* ○ *children riding on donkeys* [Vp] *She turned and rode back to the village.* **(b)** to go out regularly on a horse for pleasure: [V] *Do you ride much?* ○ *She hasn't been out riding since the accident.* **2** to sit on and control an animal or a bicycle: [Vn] *ride a horse/camel/bicycle* [Vnpr] *He rode his new bike over the rough mountain tracks.* ○ *a jockey who has ridden six winners this season* [Vnadv] *He rode the horse too hard.* **3** to go through or over sth on a horse, bicycle, etc: [Vn] *ride the prairies/moors.* **4** ~ **(in/on sth)** to travel in a vehicle as a passenger: [Vpr] *ride in a bus/on a train* ○ *You can ride in the back (of the car) with your brother.* [Vp] *They rode off in his car.* [Vn] *(US) ride the bus to work.* ⇨ note at TRAVEL. **5** to float or be supported on water, etc: [Vn] *riding the waves on a surfboard* [Vn, Vpr] *gulls riding (on) the wind* [Vpr] *ships riding at anchor.* **6** [Vn] to yield to a punch, etc so as to reduce the effect. **IDM** **let sth 'ride** *(infml)* to take no immediate or further action on sth: *I'll let things ride for a week and see what happens.* **ride for a 'fall** (used esp in the continuous tenses) to act in a risky way which makes disaster likely. **ride 'high** (used esp in the continuous tenses) to be successful: *The company is riding high this year.* **ride 'roughshod over sb/sth** to treat sb/sth harshly, without concern or with contempt: *He rode roughshod over the wishes of the people.* **PHRV** **'ride on sth** to depend on sth: *My whole future is riding on this interview.* **ˌride sth 'out** to continue as normal during a difficult time until it passes: *Do you think we can ride out the recession?* **ˌride 'up** (of clothing) to move gradually upwards, out of position: *Your skirt's riding up.*

▶ **rider** *n* **1(a)** a person who can ride a horse: *a poor/an experienced/a talented rider* ○ *She's no rider* (ie cannot ride well). **(b)** a person riding on a horse: *Three riders were approaching.* **2** a person riding a bicycle, etc: *a motor-cycle rider.* **3** ~ **(to sth)** an additional remark following a statement, etc: *We should like to add a rider to the previous remarks.*

ridge /rɪdʒ/ *n* **1** a line along the top where two sloping surfaces meet: *the ridge of a roof* ○ *ridge tiles* ○ *a series of ridges in a ploughed field* ○ *There are ridges on the soles to help the boots grip the surface.* Compare FURROW 1. **2** a narrow area of high land along the top of a line of hills; a long mountain range. ⇨ picture at MOUNTAIN, PLATEAU 1. **3** *(techn)* a long narrow region of high pressure in the atmosphere. Compare TROUGH 3.
▶ **ridge** *v* (usu passive) to cover sth with or make sth into ridges: [Vn] *a slightly ridged surface.*

ridicule /'rɪdɪkjuːl/ *n* [U] language or behaviour intended to make sb/sth appear foolish or absurd:

incur/excite ridicule ∘ *be held up/exposed to ridicule* ∘ *He's become an object of ridicule.*

▶ **ridicule** *v* to make sb/sth look foolish; to mock sb/sth: [Vn] *The opposition ridiculed the government's attempt to explain the mistake.*

ridiculous /rɪ'dɪkjələs/ *adj* deserving to be laughed at; absurd: *You look ridiculous in those tight trousers.* ∘ *What a ridiculous idea!* ∘ *Don't be ridiculous!* **IDM** **from the sublime to the ridiculous** ⇨ SUBLIME. ▶ **ridiculously** *adv*: *be ridiculously cheap/expensive.* **ridiculousness** *n* [U].

riding /'raɪdɪŋ/ *n* [U] the sport or activity of going about on a horse: *enjoy/take up riding* ∘ '*riding lessons/holidays* ∘ *a* '*riding-school* (ie for people learning to ride a horse) ∘ '*riding boots.*
■ '**riding-crop** *n* = CROP 5.

rife /raɪf/ *adj* [pred] (*fml*) (**a**) (esp of bad things) widespread; common: *an area where crime is rife* ∘ *Speculation is rife in the City.* (**b**) ~ **with sth** full of sth bad: *The country was rife with rumours of war.*

riff /rɪf/ *n* a short repeated pattern of notes in popular music, esp JAZZ: *a guitar riff.*

riffle /'rɪfl/ *v* ~ (**through**) **sth** (*Brit*) to turn over sth, eg the pages of a book, quickly and casually: [Vn, Vpr] *Weary commuters riffled (through) their evening papers.*
▶ **riffle** *n* (*US*) an area of rough shallow water in a stream.

riff-raff /'rɪf ræf/ *n* [U] (*derog*) the least respectable section of society: *mix with the riff-raff.*

rifle¹ /'raɪfl/ *n* a gun with a long barrel(2), usu fired from the shoulder. ⇨ picture at GUN.
■ '**rifle-range** *n* 1 [C] a place for practising shooting with rifles. 2 (also '**rifle-shot**) [U] the distance that a rifle bullet will travel: *be out of/within rifle-range.*

rifle² /'raɪfl/ *v* ~ (**through**) **sth** to search through sth, looking for sth to steal: [Vn] *The safe had been rifled and many documents taken.* [Vpr] *Someone had rifled through all her drawers.*

rifleman /'raɪflmən/ *n* (*pl* **-men** /-mən/) a soldier armed with a rifle.

rift /rɪft/ *n* 1 a split, crack or break in sth: *a rift in the clouds.* 2 a serious disagreement between friends, members of a group, etc: *a growing rift between the two factions.*
■ '**rift-valley** *n* a valley with steep sides formed when two parallel cracks develop in the earth's surface and the land between them sinks.

rig¹ /rɪg/ *v* (**-gg-**) [Vn, Vnpr] ~ **sth** (**with sth**) to fit a ship or boat with equipment, eg ropes and sails. **PHRV** ,**rig oneself/sb 'out (in/with sth)** (esp passive) to provide sb with equipment or clothes: *rigged out with everything we needed for a week's camping* ∘ *a cavalry regiment rigged out in green and gold.* ,**rig sth 'up** to build a structure, etc quickly or with whatever materials are available: *rig up a shelter for the night.*
▶ **rig** *n* 1 (esp in compounds) the equipment needed for a special purpose: *an* '*oil/*'*gas/*'*drilling rig.* 2 the way that a ship's masts (MAST 1), sails, etc are arranged.
rigging *n* [U] the arrangement of ropes, etc that support a ship's masts (MAST 1) and sails: *The sailors climbed up into the rigging.* ⇨ picture at YACHT.

rig² /rɪg/ *v* (**-gg-**) (*often derog*) to manage or control sth so that it produces a result or situation to one's own advantage: [Vn] *rig the market* (ie cause an artificial rise or fall in share prices, etc in order to make illegal profits) ∘ *He claimed that the election had been rigged.* ▶ **rigging** *n* [U]: *allegations of* '*vote/e*'*lection rigging.*

right¹ /raɪt/ *adj* 1 [usu pred] (of behaviour, actions, etc) morally good or justified; required by law or duty: *Is it ever right to kill?* ∘ *You were quite right to*

refuse/in refusing his offer. ∘ *It seems only right to warn you of the risk.* 2 true or correct as a fact: *Actually, that's not quite right.* ∘ *Did you get the answer right?* ∘ *Have you got the right money* (ie exact amount) *for the bus fare?* ∘ *What's the right time?* ∘ '*Mr Stewart, isn't it?' 'Yes, that's right.'* 3 correct in one's opinion or judgement: *They were right about her being lazy.* ∘ *You're right to be cautious.* ∘ *Am I right in thinking we've met before?* 4 ~ (**for sth/sb**) the best of a number of possible choices; most suitable: *He's the right man for the job.* ∘ *That coat's just right for you.* ∘ *Is this the right way to the zoo?* ∘ *She has all the right contacts* (ie knows the people in a position to help her career, etc). 5 (also ,**all 'right**) normal; in good health or condition: *'Do you feel all right?' 'No, I don't feel (quite) right today.'* ∘ *Things aren't right between her parents.* 6 (of a side of a piece of fabric) intended to be the outer side of a garment, etc and to be seen: *Place the pattern pieces on the right side of the material.* 7 [attrib] (*Brit infml*) (esp in derogatory phrases) real; complete: *You made a right mess of that!* ∘ *She's in a right (old) temper!* Compare WRONG. **IDM** **get on the right/wrong side of sb** ⇨ SIDE¹. **get sth 'right/ 'straight** (sometimes used as a threat) to understand sth clearly: *Let's get this right once and for all.* ∘ *Let's get one thing straight — I give the orders round here, OK?* **have one's heart in the right place** ⇨ HEART. **hit/strike the right/wrong note** ⇨ NOTE¹. **(not) in one's right 'mind** (not) mentally normal. **not (quite) right in the 'head** (*infml*) foolish; slightly mad; ECCENTRIC(1). **on the right/wrong side of sb/sth** ⇨ SIDE¹. **on the right/wrong track** ⇨ TRACK. **put/set sb/sth right** to correct sb/sth: *put one's* '*watch right* (ie to the correct time) ∘ *I want to set/put you* '*right on one or two matters.* **right (you are)!** (*Brit also* ,**right-'oh!**) (*infml*) (used to indicate one's agreement with a suggestion or to acknowledge an order or, esp *US*, a request). (**as**) **right as 'rain** (*infml*) in excellent health or working order. **start off on the right/wrong foot** ⇨ START².
▶ **rightly** *adv* 1 in a just manner; properly: *act rightly.* 2 with good reason; with justification (JUSTIFY): *She's been sacked, and rightly so.* ∘ *Quite rightly, the press has given extensive coverage to the debate.* ∘ *He was rightly furious at the decision.* 3 correctly: *If I remember rightly…* ∘ *As you rightly point out, we can't afford a new car.*
rightness *n* [U]: *the rightness* (ie justice) *of their cause* ∘ *the rightness of his decision.*
■ '**right angle** *n* an angle of 90°: *Place the table at right angles/at a right angle to the wall.* ⇨ picture at ANGLE, TRIANGLE. '**right-angled** *adj* having or consisting of a right angle: *a right-angled triangle/corner.*
,**right-'minded** *adj* having sound and honest opinions; honourable and just: *All ,right-minded* '*people will surely be shocked by this outrage.*

right² /raɪt/ *adv* 1 exactly; directly: *sitting right beside you* ∘ *The wind was right in our faces.* 2 all the way; completely: *a fence right around the garden* ∘ *Go right to the end of the road.* ∘ *I fell right to the bottom of the stairs.* ∘ *The pear was rotten right through.* ∘ *The handle came right off in my hand.* 3 correctly: *Have I guessed right or wrong?* 4 in a satisfactory manner: *Nothing seems to be going right for me today.* 5 immediately: *I must answer that phone, but I'll be right back.* **IDM** **right/straight a'way/'off** without delay; immediately: *I want it typed right away, please.* ∘ *I told her right/straight off what I thought of her.* **right 'now** immediately; at this moment. **see sb 'right** (*US* also **do sb 'right**) to make sure that sb has all they need or want: *You needn't worry about running out of money — I'll see you right.* **serve sb right** ⇨ SERVE. **too 'right!** (*infml*) (used to indicate enthusiastic agreement).
■ ,**Right 'Honourable** *adj* [attrib] (*Brit*) (used to

R

address or refer to certain people of high rank, eg earls and government ministers): *my Right Honourable friend, the Secretary of State for the Environment.* Compare HONOURABLE 2.

,**Right** '**Reverend** *adj* [attrib] (used to address or refer to a bishop): *the Right Reverend Richard Harries, Bishop of Oxford.*

right³ /raɪt/ *n* **1** [U] what is good, just, honourable, etc: *know the difference between right and wrong* ○ *You did right to tell me the truth.* **2** [U, C] ~ **(to sth / to do sth)** a just, proper or legal claim; a thing that one is entitled to do or have by law: *What right have you/What gives you the right to do that?* ○ *You have no right to stop me from going in there.* ○ *exercise one's legal rights* ○ *have no rights as a US citizen* ○ *animal rights campaigners* ○ *the right to remain silent* ○ *Everyone has a right to a fair trial.* ○ *Do the police have the right of arrest in this situation?* ○ *He's quite within his rights to demand an enquiry.* ○ *I know my rights.* See also CIVIL RIGHTS, HUMAN RIGHTS. **3** rights [pl] a legal authority or claim to sth: *buy/own the movie/translation/foreign rights (of a book)* (ie the authority to make a film of it, translate it, sell it abroad, etc) ○ *all rights reserved* (ie protected or kept for the owners of the book, film, etc). See also COPYRIGHT. **IDM be in the 'right** to have justice and truth on one's side. **by right of sth** (*fml*) because of sth: *The Normans ruled England by right of conquest.* **by 'rights** if justice were done: *By rights, half the reward should be mine.* **do 'right by sb** to treat sb fairly. **in one's own 'right** because of one's personal claims, qualifications, efforts, etc, not because of one's association with sb else: *Her husband's a poet, and she's also an author in her own right.* **(as) of 'right / by 'right** (*fml*) because of having the legal or moral claim; as is just: *The property belongs to her as of right.* **put/set sb/sth to 'rights** to correct sb/sth; to put things in order: *It took me ages to put things to rights after the workmen had finished.* **the rights and 'wrongs of sth** the true facts. **two wrongs don't make a right** ⇨ WRONG *n.*
■ ,**right of a**'**bode** *n* [U] a claim recognized by law that entitles one to live in a certain place.

,**right of 'way** *n* (*pl* ,**rights of 'way**) **1** [C] **(a)** the legal authority to pass over another person's land without needing to ask for permission: *No public right of way.* **(b)** a path subject to such authority: *Is there a right of way across these fields?* **2** [U] (on a road) the authority to proceed while another vehicle must wait: *I have the right of way/It's my right of way at this junction.*

'**rights issue** *n* (*commerce*) an offer of new shares in a company at a reduced price to people who already have shares in it.

right⁴ /raɪt/ *v* [Vn] **1** to return oneself/itself/sth to a proper, correct or upright position: *I righted some chairs and we sat down amongst the debris.* ○ *The horse stumbled, then miraculously righted itself.* **2** to correct oneself/itself/sth: *right a wrong* ○ *The fault will probably right itself if you give it time.*

right⁵ /raɪt/ *adj* of, on or towards the side of the body which is towards the east when a person faces north: *my right eye* ○ *In Britain we drive on the left side of the road, not the right side.* Compare LEFT². **IDM** ,**give one's right 'arm for sth/to do sth** (*infml*) (used for expressing a strong wish to make a great personal sacrifice in order to have or do sth): *I'd have given my right arm to be there with them.*
▶ **right** *adv* to the right side: *He looked neither right nor left.* ○ *Turn right at the end of the street.* **IDM** **left, right and centre; right, left and centre** ⇨ LEFT². ,**right and 'left** everywhere: *She owes money right and left.*

right *n* **1(a)** [U] the right⁵ side or direction: *the first turning to/on the right.* **(b)** [sing] (used with *first,*

second, etc) a road, etc on the right⁵ side: *take the first right and then second left.* **2 the Right** [Gp] (*politics*) the political party or members of a party who support more traditional social values, private enterprise and control of industry by private companies rather than by the state: *The Right in British politics is represented by the Conservative Party.* Compare LEFT² *n.*

rightist *n, adj* (a member) of a political party or group whose members support traditional social values, private enterprise, etc.

■ ,**right 'bank** *n* [sing] the bank of a river on its right side as it flows from the source.

'**right-hand** *adj* [attrib] **1** of or for the right hand: *a right-hand glove.* **2** on or towards the right side: *make a right-hand turn* ○ *the top right-hand corner.* Compare LEFT-HAND. ,**right-'handed** *adj* **(a)** (of a person) using the right hand more, or with more ease, than the left hand. **(b)** (of a tool) designed for use with the right hand. — *adv* with the right hand: *play tennis right-handed.* ,**right-'hander** *n* **(a)** a right-handed person. **(b)** a blow or stroke made with the right hand. Compare LEFT-HANDER. ,**right-hand 'drive** *adj* (of a vehicle) with the steering-wheel (STEER¹) on the right of the vehicle. Compare LEFT-HAND DRIVE. ,**right-hand 'man** *n* [sing] a chief assistant; a most reliable person helping one: *He was the governor's right-hand man.*

,**right-of-'centre** *adj* having political opinions that tend more towards traditional values than to social reform: *a right-of-centre party/candidate.*

,**right 'turn** *n* a turn to the right so that one is in a position at right angles (RIGHT¹) to the original one.

,**right 'wing** *n* **1** [Gp] (*politics*) those who support more traditional or conservative policies than others in the same group or party: *She's on the right wing of the Labour Party.* **2** [C, U] (in football, etc) the player or position on the right side of a team on the field: *playing (on the) right wing.* Compare LEFT WING. ,**right-'wing** *adj*: ,*right-wing o*'*pinions* ○ *This newspaper's views are very right-wing.* ,**right-'winger** *n* **1** a person on the right wing of a political party: *He was barracked by Tory right-wingers.* **2** a person playing on the right wing of eg a football team. Compare WING 6, WINGER.

righteous /'raɪtʃəs/ *adj* **1** that can be morally justified: *righteous anger/indignation.* **2** (*fml*) doing, thinking, etc what is morally right: *righteous people/thoughts.* ▶ **righteously** *adv.* **righteousness** *n* [U].

rightful /'raɪtfl/ *adj* [attrib] just, proper or legal: *a rightful claim* ○ *his rightful place/position* ○ *the rightful owner/king.* ▶ **rightfully** /-fəli/ *adv*: *They must have what is rightfully theirs.*

right-on /,raɪt 'ɒn/ *adj* (*infml*) aware of and sympathetic to current social and political issues, esp involving groups who are not well represented: *a ,right-on 'feminist.*

rightward /'raɪtwəd/ *adj, adv* on or to the right: *a rightward movement* ○ *moving rightward.* ▶ **rightwards** *adv.*

rigid /'rɪdʒɪd/ *adj* **1** stiff; not bending or changing shape: *a rigid support for the tent* ○ *She sat in her chair, rigid and staring.* ○ *Her face was rigid with terror.* **2** strict; firm; that cannot be changed or adapted: *a man of rigid principles* ○ *rigid categories* ○ *impose rigid controls* ○ *The schedule is far too rigid.* ▶ **rigidity** /rɪ'dʒɪdəti/ *n* [U, C]: *The rigidity of the metal caused it to crack.* ○ *the rigidities of the social structure.* **rigidly** *adv*: *rules/procedures that are rigidly applied* ○ *be rigidly opposed to any change.*

rigmarole /'rɪgmərəʊl/ *n* [C usu *sing*] (*derog*) **1** a complicated procedure which is often not necessary: *go through the whole rigmarole of filling out forms.*

2 a long complicated story or statement: *I've never heard such a rigmarole.*

rigor mortis /ˌrɪgə ˈmɔːtɪs/ *n* [U] the process by which the body becomes stiff after death: *Rigor mortis had already set in.*

rigour (*US* **rigor**) /ˈrɪgə(r)/ *n* (*fml*) **1** [U] the quality of being severe or strict: *be treated with the utmost rigour of the law* ○ *apply scientific/intellectual rigour to an investigation.* **2** **rigours** [pl] harsh and difficult conditions: *face/survive the rigours of an Arctic winter/of prison life.*
▶ **rigorous** /ˈrɪgərəs/ *adj* (*fml*) **1** severe; strict: *rigorous discipline.* **2** strictly accurate or detailed: *rigorous attention to detail* ○ *a rigorous search/examination/analysis.* **3** (of weather, etc) harsh: *a rigorous climate.* **rigorously** *adv*: *The regulations are rigorously enforced.*

rile /raɪl/ *v* (*infml*) to annoy sb; to irritate sb: [Vn] *Don't get riled.* [Vn.that] *It riles me that he won't agree.*

rim /rɪm/ *n* **1** an edge or a border of sth that is circular or approximately circular: *the rim of a cup/bowl/lake/volcano* ○ *a pair of glasses with gold rims.* **2** the edge of a wheel on which a tyre is fitted. ▷ picture at BICYCLE.
▶ **rim** *v* (**-mm-**) to form or be a rim for sth: [Vn] *a huge lake rimmed by glaciers.*
rimless *adj* (of spectacles) having lenses (LENS 1) held in place only at the sides and with no frames round them.
-rimmed (forming compound *adjs*) having a rim or rims of the type specified: *steel-rimmed glasses* ○ *red-rimmed eyes* (eg from crying).

rime /raɪm/ *n* [U] (*esp rhet*) frost.

rind /raɪnd/ *n* [C, U] the hard outer skin or covering of certain fruits, esp oranges and lemons (LEMON 1), and of some types of cheese and bacon: *grated lemon rind* ○ *cut off the* ˈ*bacon rind.* Compare PEEL *n*, SKIN 3, ZEST 3.

ring¹ /rɪŋ/ *n* **1** a small circular band of precious metal, often with a valuable stone or stones set in it, worn esp on a finger: *a gold* ˈ*ring* ○ *a diamond* ˈ*ring.* See also ENGAGEMENT RING, WEDDING RING. **2** (esp in compounds) a circular band of any material: *a* ˈ*napkin-ring* ○ *a* ˈ*key-ring* ○ *a child's inflatable ring* (ie worn round the waist when learning to swim) ○ *the rings of Saturn.* **3** a circle: *blow* ˈ*smoke-rings* (ie circles of tobacco smoke from the mouth) ○ *children standing in a ring* ○ *There were dark rings round her eyes from lack of sleep.* **4** a group of people working together, esp secretly: *a* ˈ*spy ring* ○ *a ring of dealers controlling prices at an auction.* **5** an enclosed space in which animals and/or people perform or compete, with seats all around for spectators: *a circus ring* ○ *knock sb out of the ring* (ie in boxing) ○ *The next competitor rode into the ring.* See also BULLRING. **6** a small flat plate which can be heated by gas or electricity and is used for cooking on: *put the kettle on the ring* ○ *turn off the* ˈ*gas ring.* **IDM** **run** ˈ**rings round sb** (*infml*) to do things much better than sb.
▶ **ring** *v* (*pt, pp* **-ed**) **1** ~ **sb/sth (with sth)** (esp passive) to surround sb/sth: [Vn, Vnpr] *The area was ringed by/with police.* [Vn] *A high fence ringed the prison camp.* **2** to make a circular mark round sth: [Vn, Vnpr] *Ring the correct answer (with your pencil).* **3** [Vn] to put a metal ring on the leg of a bird so as to be able to identify it in future.
■ ˈ**ring-binder** *n* (*Brit*) a file for holding papers, in which metal rings go through holes in the edges of the pages, holding them in place.
ˈ**ring finger** *n* the third finger, usu of the left hand, on which a wedding ring is traditionally worn. ▷ picture at HAND¹.
ˈ**ring-pull** *n* a small piece of metal with a ring attached which is pulled to open cans of drink, etc.

ˈ**ring road** (*Brit*) (*US* **beltway**) *n* a road built around a town to reduce traffic in the centre.

ring² /rɪŋ/ *v* (*pt* **rang** /ræŋ/; *pp* **rung** /rʌŋ/) **1** (also *esp US* **call**) ~ **sb/sth (up)** to TELEPHONE sb/sth: [Vn] *I'll ring you tonight.* [V] *David rang while you were out.* [Vnpr] *Ring up the station and find out when the train is due.* [Vnpr] *He rang the studio from the car phone.* [V.to inf] *She rang to say she'd be late.* [Vpr, Vp] *I'm ringing (up) about your advert in today's paper.* [Vpr] *I'll ring for a taxi.* **2** to make a long clear sound: [V] *Will you answer the telephone for me if it rings?* ○ *The doorbell rang loudly.* [Vnpr] *The bells rang for evensong.* [Vpr] *She left the stage with the applause **ringing in her ears**.* **3** to make a bell, etc sound: [Vn] *ring the fire-alarm* [Vpr] *ring the bell for school assembly.* **4** ~ **(for sb/sth)** to call for attention by making a bell, etc sound: [V] '*Did you ring, sir?' asked the stewardess.* [Vpr] *ring for the maid/for service* ○ *Someone is ringing at the door* (ie ringing the DOORBELL). **5** (of a clock or bell) to mark the time by striking: [Vn] *This clock only rings the hours* (ie rings on the hour but not at quarter or half past or quarter to the hour). **6** ~ **(with sth)** to be filled with sounds: [Vpr] *The playground rang with children's shouts.* [also V]. **7** to produce a certain effect when heard: [Vn-adj] *Her words rang hollow* (ie sounded insincere). ○ *His story may seem incredible, but it rings* (ie seems likely to be) *true to me.* **8** (of the ears) to be filled with a ringing or humming (HUM 2) sound: [V] *The music was so loud it made my ears ring.* **IDM** **ring a** ˈ**bell** (*infml*) to remind one of sth in a VAGUE(1) way; to sound familiar: *His name rings a bell; perhaps we've met at a conference.* **ring the** ˈ**changes (on sth)** to vary one's routine, style, choices, etc: *ring the changes on the businessman's traditional dark suit and tie.* **PHRV** ˌ**ring (sb)** ˈ**back** (*Brit*) **1** to TELEPHONE sb again later after finding them not available: *Tell her I'll ring (her) back later.* **2** to TELEPHONE sb who called while one was not available: *Ask her to ring me back today, please.* ˌ**ring** ˈ**off** (*Brit*) to end a telephone conversation: *He rang off before I could explain.* ˌ**ring** ˈ**out** to sound loudly and clearly: *A pistol shot rang out.* ˌ**ring sth** ˈ**up** to record an amount on a cash register (CASH): *She rang up all the items and they came to £26.45.*
▶ **ring** *n* **1** (*Brit infml*) (*US* **call**) [C] a telephone call: *I'll **give you a ring** tomorrow.* **2** [C] an act of ringing a bell; the sound of a bell: *give two rings on the bell* ○ *There was a ring at the door.* **3** [sing] a loud clear sound: *the ring of hooves on the cobblestones.* **4** [sing] ~ **(of sth)** a particular quality shown by sth one hears: *His explanation has a/the* **ring of truth** *about it.* ○ *That tune has a familiar ring.*

ringer *n* **1** (also **bell-ringer**) a person who rings bells, eg in a church. **2** (*US*) a horse or an ATHLETE (1) illegally entered in a race under a false name. **IDM** **be a dead ringer for sb** ▷ DEAD.

ringleader /ˈrɪŋliːdə(r)/ *n* (*usu derog*) a person who leads others in crime or in opposing authority.

ringlet /ˈrɪŋlət/ *n* [C esp *pl*] a long curl of hair hanging down from sb's head.

ringmaster /ˈrɪŋmɑːstə(r)/ *n* a person in charge of a CIRCUS(1) performance.

ringside /ˈrɪŋsaɪd/ *n* [U] the area immediately beside a boxing ring, CIRCUS(1) ring, etc: *at the ringside* ○ *a* ˌ*ringside* ˈ*seat.*

ringworm /ˈrɪŋwɜːm/ *n* [U] a skin disease, esp of animals or children, producing round red patches.

rink ▷ ICE-RINK, SKATING-RINK.

rinse /rɪns/ *v* **1** to wash sth with clean water: [Vn] *Rinse the pasta with boiling water.* **2** to wash sth quickly, often without soap: [Vn] *rinse one's hands before eating.* **3** to remove soap from sth with clean water after washing it: [Vn] *Rinse your hair thoroughly after shampooing it.* **PHRV** ˌ**rinse sth** ˈ**off** to

R

remove dirt, soap, etc from sth: *Rinse off the salt after swimming.* ,**rinse sth 'out** to remove dirt, etc from sth with water: *He rinsed the bucket out under the hose.* **rinse sth out of / from sth** to remove dirt, soap, etc from sth with water: *I rinsed the shampoo out of my hair.*
▶ **rinse** *n* **1** [C] an act of rinsing sth: *Give your hair a good rinse after shampooing it.* ○ *The washing-machine has just started its rinse cycle.* **2** [C,U] a liquid for putting temporary colour into the hair: *a blue rinse.*

riot /'raɪət/ *n* **1** [C] a wild or violent protest by a crowd of people: *Riots broke out in several areas.* ○ *The police succeeded in quelling the riot.* ○ *(fig) There'll be a riot* (ie People will be very angry) *if the government doesn't invest more in this service.* **2** [sing] ~ **of sth** a large or splendid display of sth: *The flower-beds were a riot of colour.* **3 a riot** [sing] *(infml)* a very amusing thing or person: *She's an absolute riot!* **IDM read the Riot Act** ⇨ READ. **run 'riot** to behave in a wild and violent way: *Protesters ran riot through the town.* ○ *(fig) weeds running riot in the garden* ○ *Inflation is running riot and prices are out of control.*
▶ **riot** *v* to take part in a riot: [Vpr] *After the match, the fans rioted.* [V] *They are rioting against food prices.* **rioter** *n*. **rioting** *n* [U]: *renewed outbreaks of rioting.*
riotous /-əs/ *adj* **1** *(fml or law)* protesting in a wild and violent way: *a riotous assembly* (ie of people) ○ *charged with riotous behaviour.* **2** [attrib] wild; out of control: *a riotous party* ○ *riotous laughter* ○ *Riotous* (ie expensive) *living had drained his fortune.* **riotously** *adv* extremely: *riotously funny.*
■ **'riot gear** *n* [U] the equipment used by the police when dealing with riots: *The police were in full riot gear, with shields and helmets.*
'riot police *n* [pl *v*] police trained to deal with people rioting.

rip /rɪp/ *v* (-pp-) **(a)** to tear sth by pulling it sharply in different directions: [Vnpr] *rip a piece of cloth in two* [Vn] *I've ripped my jeans.* [also Vnadv]. **(b)** ~ **sth open** to open sth by pulling in this way: [Vn-adj] *rip open a letter* ○ *My cat had its ear ripped open by a dog.* **(c)** (of material) to tear or become torn: [Vadv] *Be careful with that dress; it rips easily.* **IDM let 'rip (about/against/at sb/sth) 1** to speak violently or with great passion: *let rip about the government's incompetence.* **2** to act or proceed without restraint: *an opportunity for actors and audience alike to let rip* ○ *At 50 yards from the finishing line the jockey really let rip.* **let sth 'rip** *(infml)* **1** to allow a car, machine, etc to go at its top speed: *Let her/it rip!* **2** to allow sth to develop naturally, without attempting to control it: *Inflation was just let rip.* **PHRV ,rip sb 'off** *(infml)* to cheat sb, esp financially: *Tourists complain of being ripped off by local taxi-drivers.* ,**rip sth 'off** *(sl)* to steal sth: *Somebody's ripped off my wallet.* **rip sth 'off (sth) / out** to remove sth roughly and quickly: *rip the cover off (a book)* ○ *rip a kitchen out* ○ *He ripped off his clothes and dived in.* ,**rip sth 'up** to tear sth violently into small pieces: *He ripped up the report and threw it in the bin.*
▶ **rip** *n* a long tear: *There's a big rip in my sleeve.*
■ **'rip-off** *n* (usu *sing*) *(infml)* an act of deceiving sb, stealing sth, charging sb too much, etc: *£2.50 for a cup of coffee? What a rip-off!*
'rip-roaring *adj* [attrib] *(infml)* **(a)** wild and noisy: *a rip-roaring speech/performance.* **(b)** very great, good, etc: *The play was a rip-roaring success.*

RIP /,ɑːr aɪ 'piː/ *abbr* (on graves, etc) may he/she/they rest in peace (Latin *requiescat/requiescant in pace*): *James Dent RIP.*

ripe /raɪp/ *adj* **1** (of fruit, grain, etc) ready to be gathered and used, esp for eating: *Are the apples ripe*

enough to eat yet? ○ *The corn will be ripe soon.* Compare UNRIPE. **2** (of cheese) fully mature or developed: *ripe Brie or Camembert.* **3** (of a person's age) advanced: *live to a ripe old age.* **4** [pred] ~ **(for sth)** ready; fit; prepared: *land that is ripe for development* ○ *a nation ripe for revolution.* **IDM the time is ripe for sth/sb to do sth** ⇨ TIME¹.
▶ **ripen** /'raɪpən/ *v* to become or make sth ripe: [V] *ripening corn* [Vn] *peaches ripened by the sun* ○ *To ripen green tomatoes, leave them on a sunny window-sill.*
ripeness *n* [U].

riposte /rɪ'pɒst/ *n* *(fml)* a quick clever reply or response, esp to criticism: *a witty riposte* ○ *deliver an effective riposte to the threatened take-over.*
▶ **riposte** /rɪ'pɒst/ *v* [V, V.speech, V.*that*] *(fml)* to deliver a riposte.

ripple /'rɪpl/ *n* **1** [C] **(a)** a small wave or series of waves: *She threw a stone into the pond and watched the ripples spread.* **(b)** a thing like this in appearance or movement: *slight ripples on the surface of the metal.* **2** [C usu *sing*] a gentle rising and falling sound: *a ripple of laughter/excitement/interest/unease.* **3** [U] ice-cream with added flavour in lines like ripples running through it: *some raspberry/chocolate ripple.*
▶ **ripple** *v* to move or make sth move in ripples: [V] *corn rippling in the breeze* ○ *rippling muscles* [Vn] *wind rippling the lake* [Vpr] *Shock waves rippled through the hall.*

rise¹ /raɪz/ *n* **1(a)** an upward movement or progress: *the rise and fall of the British Empire* ○ *His rise to power was very rapid.* **(b)** ~ **(in sth)** an increase in amount, number or intensity: *a rise in the price of meat/the value of the dollar/the average temperature.* **2** *(Brit)* (*US* **raise**) an increase in wages or salary: *demand a rise from next October.* **3** an upward slope; a small hill: *a church situated on a small rise* ○ *At the top of the rise they paused for a rest.* **IDM get a rise out of sb** to cause sb to show annoyance or make an angry response by saying sth to provoke them. **give 'rise to sth** *(fml)* to cause sth: *Her disappearance gave rise to the wildest rumours.*

rise² /raɪz/ *v* (*pt* **rose** /rəʊz/, *pp* **risen** /'rɪzn/) **1** to come or go upwards; to reach a high or higher level or position: [Vpr] *smoke rising from the chimney* [V] *rising flood water* [Vn, Vpr] *The river has risen (by) several metres.* [V] *(fig) new tower blocks rising* (ie being built) *nearby.* ⇨ note at RAISE. **2** *(fml)* to get up from a lying, sitting or kneeling position: [V] *He was accustomed to rising* (ie getting out of bed) *early.* [Vpr] *We rose from the table.* [V.*to* inf] *He rose to welcome me.* **3** *(fml)* (of a group of people) to end a meeting; to ADJOURN(1): [V] *The House* (ie Members of the House of Commons) *rose at 10 pm.* **4** to increase in number or amount: [V] *rising fuel bills/ divorce rates* ○ *The cost of living continues to rise.* [Vpr] *Unemployment rose by 3% last year.* ○ *Air pollution has risen above an acceptable level.* **5** (of a sound) to become louder and usu higher in pitch¹(2): [V, Vpr] *Her voice rose (in anger).* **6** (of the wind) to begin to blow more strongly: [V] *The wind is rising — I think there's a storm coming.* **7** (of a feeling) to begin and increase in intensity: [V, Vp] *He felt anger rising (up) within him.* **8** to become more cheerful and confident: [V, Vpr] *Her spirits rose (at the news).* **9** (of the colour of one's skin) to become pink or red with embarrassment or shame: [V] *The boy's colour rose and he lowered his eyes.* **10** (of hair) to become upright instead of lying flat: [V] *The hair on the back of my neck rose when I heard the scream.* **11** to reach a higher rank, status or position in society, popularity, one's career, etc: [V] *a rising young politician* [Vpr] *He rose from the ranks to become an officer.* **12** ~ **(up) (against sb/sth)** *(fml)* to begin to fight

against one's ruler or government or against a foreign army; to REBEL: [Vpr, Vp] *rise (up) in revolt* ○ *rise (up) against the invaders* [also V]. **13(a)** (of the sun, moon, etc) to appear above the horizon: [V] *The sun rises in the east.* Compare SET¹ 18. **(b)** to be or become visible above the surroundings: [Vpr] *a cathedral rising above the rooftops.* **14** (of land) to slope upwards: [V] *The ground rose steeply all around.* **15** (of a river) to begin to flow; to have its source: [V] *The Thames rises in the Cotswold Hills.* **16** (of cakes, bread, etc) to swell because of the action of YEAST or baking-powder (BAKE): [V] *My cake is a disaster — it hasn't risen.* **17** ~ **(from sth)** to come to life again: [Vpr] *rise from the ashes/the dead* [also V]. **draw oneself up / rise to one's full height** ⇨ FULL. **make sb's gorge rise** ⇨ GORGE¹. **make sb's hackles rise** ⇨ HACKLES. **rise and shine** (*catchphrase*) (usu imperative) to get out of bed and be active. **rise to the bait** to react when one is being provoked or tempted: *As soon as I mentioned money he rose to the bait, and became really interested.* **rise to the oc'casion** to prove oneself able to deal with an unexpected problem, situation, etc. **PHRV rise a'bove sth** to show oneself able to deal with problems and not let them prevent one's progress: *She had the courage and determination to rise above her physical disability.* **rise to sth** to show oneself able to deal with an unexpected situation, problem, etc: *Luckily, my mother rose to the occasion/challenge/task.*
▶ **riser** *n* **1** an upright piece of wood, stone, etc between each of the steps of a STAIRCASE. **2** a person who habitually gets out of bed at the specified time in the morning: *an early/a late 'riser.*
rising *n* [C] an armed protest against authority; a REVOLT: *Troops were brought in to suppress the rising.*
■ **rising 'damp** *n* [U] damp coming up from the ground into the walls of a building.

risible /ˈrɪzəbl/ *adj* (*fml usu derog*) fit to be laughed at; ridiculous: *risible attempts to fabricate evidence.*

risk /rɪsk/ *n* **1(a)** [C,U] ~ **(of sth / that...)** the possibility of meeting danger or of suffering harm or loss: *Is there any risk of the bomb exploding?* ○ *I'm prepared to take* (ie accept) *that risk.* ○ *a calculated risk* (ie one taken with full knowledge of the dangers) ○ *There's a risk of her developing pneumonia/ that she'll develop pneumonia.* ○ *an investment involving a high degree of risk* ○ *an all-risks insurance policy.* **2** [C] a person or thing that is a source of risk: *He's a good/poor insurance risk.* ○ *Many people see it as a major health/security risk.* **IDM at one's own risk** taking responsibility for one's own safety, possessions, etc: *Persons swimming beyond this point do so at their own risk.* ○ *Cars are left at their owners' risk* (eg on a notice). **at 'risk** threatened by the possibility of loss, failure, etc; in danger: *put one's life at risk* ○ *be at risk from drought* ○ *children at risk of contracting AIDS* ○ *My job is at risk.* **at the 'risk of (doing sth)** although there is the possibility of doing sth: *At the risk of sounding ungrateful, I must refuse your offer.* **at risk to oneself/sb/sth** with the possibility of losing or injuring oneself/sb/sth: *He saved the child at considerable risk to himself/to his own life.* **run the 'risk (of doing sth); run 'risks** to do sth that exposes one to a danger or the possibility of sth bad happening: *We can't run the risk (of losing all that money).* ○ *He runs more risk of being injured.* ○ *She runs the same risks as everyone else.*
▶ **risk** *v* **1** to expose sb/sth to danger: [Vn] *risk one's health/life.* **2** to accept the possibility of sth bad occurring: [Vn] *risk failure/arrest* [V.ing] *risk getting caught in a storm.* **3** to do sth knowing that it is dangerous, may not succeed, etc: [Vn, V.ing] *You should not risk marriage/marrying unless you*

are absolutely sure about it. **IDM risk/save one's neck** ⇨ NECK.

risky *adj* (**-ier, -iest**) full of danger; full of the possibility of failure, loss, etc: *a risky undertaking* ○ *The investment was too risky.* **riskily** /-ɪli/ *adv*.

risotto /rɪˈzɒtəʊ/ *n* (*pl* **-os**) [C,U] an Italian dish of rice cooked with vegetables, meat, fish, etc.

risqué /ˈrɪskeɪ; *US* rɪˈskeɪ/ *adj* (of a story, etc) rather rude and likely to shock or offend some people.

rissole /ˈrɪsəʊl/ *n* a small flat mass of chopped meat and spices that is cooked by frying.

rite /raɪt/ *n* [C] a religious or other solemn ceremony: *marriage/funeral rites* ○ *initiation rites* (eg those performed when a new member joins a secret society). See also THE LAST RITES.
■ **rite of 'passage** *n* (often *pl*) a ceremony or event, eg marriage, marking an important stage in a person's life.

ritual /ˈrɪtʃuəl/ *n* **1(a)** [U] actions that are always done at a fixed time and in the same way, esp as part of a religious or other ceremony: *an interest in pagan ritual.* **(b)** [C] a particular set of such actions: *the ritual of the Catholic Church/the Japanese tea ceremony.* **2** [C] (*esp joc*) a procedure regularly followed in exactly the same way every time: *He went through the ritual of filling and lighting his pipe.*
▶ **ritual** *adj* [attrib] of or done as a ritual: *a ritual dance* ○ *ritual phrases of greeting.*
ritualize, -ise /ˈrɪtʃuəlaɪz/ *v* to make sth into, or perform sth as, a ritual: [Vn] *ritualized displays of aggression in the animal world.*
ritually /ˈrɪtʃuəli/ *adv*.
ritualism /-ɪzəm/ *n* [U] (*esp derog*) the regular or excessive practice of ritual. **ritualistic** /ˌrɪtʃuəˈlɪstɪk/ *adj*.

ritzy /ˈrɪtsi/ *adj* (*infml*) expensive and elegant; SMART¹(4): *a ritzy nightclub.*

rival /ˈraɪvl/ *n* ~ **(to sb/sth) (for/in sth)** a person or thing competing with another: *business rivals* ○ *rivals in love* ○ *a new rival for the Democratic nomination* ○ *the only possible rival to the president* ○ *a rival bid/firm/offer.*
▶ **rival** *v* (**-ll-**; *US* also **-l-**) ~ **sb/sth (for/in sth)** to seem or be as good as sb/sth; to be COMPARABLE to sb/sth: [Vn] *a view rivalling anything the Alps can offer* [Vnpr] *Golf cannot rival football for/in excitement.*
rivalry /ˈraɪvlri/ *n* [U,C] ~ **(with sb/sth)**; ~ **(between A and B)** the state of being rivals; competition between people wanting the same thing: *a country paralysed by political rivalries* ○ *He pursued a friendly/bitter rivalry with his brother.* ○ *An intense rivalry has grown up between the two teams.*

riven /ˈrɪvn/ *adj* [pred] ~ **(by/with sth)** (*fml or rhet*) split; violently divided: *a family riven by ancient feuds.*

river /ˈrɪvə(r)/ *n* [C] **1** a large natural stream of water flowing in a channel: *the River Thames* ○ *the Mississippi River* ○ *the mouth of the river* (ie where it enters the sea) ○ *river traffic.* Compare CANAL 1. **2** a large flow of any substance: *a river of lava* ○ (*fig rhet*) *rivers of blood.* **IDM sell sb down the river** ⇨ SELL.
■ **river-bank** *n* the ground along the side of a river: *walk along the river-bank.*
river-bed *n* the ground over which a river usu flows: *It's so long since it rained that the river-bed is dry.*

riverside /ˈrɪvəsaɪd/ *n* [sing] the ground along either side of a river: *a riverside restaurant.*

rivet /ˈrɪvɪt/ *n* a metal pin or bolt for fastening two pieces of leather, metal, etc together, one end being hammered or pressed flat to prevent slipping.
▶ **rivet** *v* (usu passive) **1** to fasten sth with a rivet or rivets: [Vn] *riveted steel plates* [Vnpr] *be riveted in place* [Vnp] *The knife handles are made of two pieces*

R

riveted together. **2** to fix sb/sth in one place so that they/it cannot move: [Vn, Vnpr] *We stood riveted (to the spot).* [Vnpr] *All eyes were riveted on the speaker.* **3** to attract and hold sb's complete attention: [Vn] *I was absolutely riveted by her story.* **riveting** adj (*approv*) holding the attention completely; extremely interesting: *an absolutely riveting performance.*

riviera /ˌrɪviˈeərə/ n (often **Riviera**) a region by the sea famous for its climate and beauty and containing many holiday resorts: *the French/Italian/ Cornish Riviera.*

rivulet /ˈrɪvjələt/ n a small stream: (*fig*) *Rivulets of sweat ran down his face.*

RM /ˌɑːr ˈem/ abbr (in Britain) Royal Marines: *Capt Tom Pullen RM.*

RN /ˌɑːr ˈen/ abbr **1** (in the USA) registered nurse. Compare SRN. **2** (in Britain) Royal Navy: *Capt L J Grant RN.*

RNA /ˌɑːr en ˈeɪ/ abbr (*chemistry*) ribonucleic acid (a substance present in living cells): *RNA molecules.*

RNIB /ˌɑːr en aɪ ˈbiː/ abbr (in Britain) Royal National Institute for the Blind.

RNLI /ˌɑːr en el ˈaɪ/ abbr (in Britain) Royal National Lifeboat Institution.

roach¹ /rəʊtʃ/ n (*pl* unchanged) a small European fish found in rivers, lakes, etc.

roach² /rəʊtʃ/ n (*US infml*) = COCKROACH.

road /rəʊd/ n **1(a)** a way between places, esp one with a prepared surface which vehicles can use: *the road to Bristol/the Bristol road* ○ *main/major/minor roads* ○ *a city/suburban/country/mountain road* ○ ˌroad ˈsafety ○ ˈroad junctions ○ ˈroad signs. See also ACCESS ROAD, RING ROAD, SERVICE ROAD, SLIP-ROAD. **(b)** (in compounds) of or concerning such a way or ways: *a ˈroad-map of Scotland* ○ *be considerate to other ˈroad-users.* **2** Road (*abbr* Rd) (in names of roads, esp in towns): *35 York Road, Boston, MA.* ⇨ note. **3** the way to achieving sth: *go down/take the road of privatization* ○ *be on the road to success/ recovery.* See also MIDDLE-OF-THE-ROAD. **IDM by ˈroad** in or on a road vehicle: *It's about 50 miles by road.* ○ *It's cheaper to transport goods by road than by rail.* **the end of the line/road** ⇨ END¹. **hit the road** ⇨ HIT¹. **one for the ˈroad** (*infml*) a final drink before leaving for home. **on the ˈroad 1** travelling, esp as a firm's sales representative or a performer: *The band has been on the road for almost a month.* **2** (of a car) in use; able to be driven: *get the car back on the road.* **3** moving from place to place, without having a permanent home: *It's not difficult to survive on the road.*
▶ ˈroadie n (*infml*) a person who works with a pop group, etc when they are on tour, esp one who helps to move their equipment.
■ ˈroad-hog n (*infml*) a person who drives without care and consideration for others.
ˈroad-house n (*dated*) a pub, restaurant, etc on a main road in the country.
ˈroad sense n [U] the ability to behave in a sensible way while walking, driving, etc on roads.
ˈroad show n **1** a performance given by a group of travelling entertainers, esp a pop group. **2** a radio or television programme broadcast away from the studio.
ˈroad tax n (esp in Britain) a tax paid by the owner of a vehicle that allows her or him to drive it on public roads.
ˈroad test n a test of a vehicle, esp a new model, on public roads: *The new sports model achieved 170 miles an hour in road tests.* ˈroad-test v [Vn] to test a vehicle in this way.

NOTE In a town or city, **street** is the most general word for a road lined with buildings: *a street map of London.* In British English **street** is not used for roads outside towns but streets in towns are also often called **Road**: *Oxford Street* ○ *Edgware Road.* An **avenue** is usually a wide street lined with trees. In older American cities **streets** often run across **avenues**: *the old theatre at* (ie at the corner of) *53rd St and 5th Ave.* An **alley** or a **lane** is a narrow street between buildings.

Roads, or **highways** in American English, connect towns and villages: *a road map of Ireland.* **Motorways** in British English (**freeways**, **expressways** or **highways** in American English) are built for long-distance traffic to avoid towns. A **lane** is also a narrow road in the country. **Highway** is not used very often in British English except in certain official phrases: *the Highway Code.* **Road**, **Street** and **Avenue** are the most common words used in street names and are often written as **Rd**, **St** and **Ave**.

roadblock /ˈrəʊdblɒk/ n a barrier put across a road by the police or army so that they can stop and search vehicles.

roadside /ˈrəʊdsaɪd/ n an edge of a road: *cars parked by/at the roadside* ○ *a ˌroadside ˈcafé*

roadway /ˈrəʊdweɪ/ n [C, U] a road, or the part of a road used by vehicles, contrasted with the part used by eg people walking: *major roadways* ○ *a section of roadway.*

roadworks /ˈrəʊdwɜːks/ n [pl] (*Brit*) work that involves building or repairing roads: *delays caused by major roadworks.*

roadworthy /ˈrəʊdwɜːði/ adj (of a vehicle) fit to be driven on a public road. ▶ ˈroadworthiness n [U].

roam /rəʊm/ v to walk or travel without any definite aim or destination: [Vpr] *roaming over the plains* [Vp] *just roaming about/around* [Vadv] *Horses roamed freely.* [Vn] *He used to roam the streets for hours on end.*

roan /rəʊn/ n, adj [attrib] an animal, esp a horse, having brown hair mixed with white or grey.

roar /rɔː(r)/ n a long loud deep sound, esp like that made by a lion: *the roar of the crowd/flames/sea/ traffic* ○ *a roar of applause/disapproval* ○ *roars of laughter.*
▶ **roar** v **1(a)** to make a roar: [V] *tigers roaring in their cages* ○ *The crowd roared.* ○ *He just roared* (ie laughed loudly) *when I told him.* [Vpr] *roar with laughter/pain* ○ *roar for attention* ○ *The engine roared into life.* **(b)** ~ sth **(out)** to express sth with a roar: [Vnp] *roar out an order* [Vn] *The crowd roared its approval.* [V.speech] *'How dare you say that!' he roared.* **2** to move quickly in the specified direction making a loud, deep sound: [Vp] *roaring about on a motorbike* [Vpr] *Cars roared past us.* ○ *He roared up the hill.*
roaring /ˈrɔːrɪŋ/ adj [attrib] **(a)** extremely noisy: *roaring thunder/guns.* **(b)** (of a fire) large, bright and noisy: *a roaring bonfire.* **IDM do a ˈroaring trade (in sth)** to sell sth very quickly; to do excellent business in sth. **a ˌroaring sucˈcess** a very great success. — adv extremely and noisily: *be roaring drunk.* **the ˌroaring ˈforties** n [pl] a part of the Atlantic Ocean between LATITUDE(1) 40° and 50° S, where there are many storms.

roast /rəʊst/ v **1(a)** to cook meat, etc in an oven, or over a fire: [Vn] *roast a joint of meat/a chicken/some potatoes.* **(b)** to be cooked in this way: [V] *the smell of roasting meat.* ⇨ note at COOK. **2** to dry sth and turn it brown using intense heat: [Vn] *roast coffee beans/peanuts/chestnuts.* **3** (*infml*) to expose oneself/sb to the heat of a fire, the sun, etc: [Vn] *roast one's toes in front of the fire* [V] *We're going to lie in the sun and roast for two weeks.* **4** (*infml* or *joc*) to criticize sb/sth harshly: [Vn] *The critics really roasted her new play.*

▶ **roast** adj [attrib] cooked in an oven, etc: *roast beef/chestnuts.*

roast n **1** [C] a joint of meat that has been roasted or is meant for roasting: *order a roast from the butcher.* **2** [C] (*esp US*) an outdoor party at which food is roasted.

roasting adj (*infml*) very hot: *I'm roasting in this sweater.* — n [sing] harsh and angry criticism: *My dad gave me a real roasting for coming home late.*

■ '**roasting tin** (also *Brit* '**roasting tray**, *US* '**roasting pan**) n a large, usu metal, tray with raised sides for roasting meat, etc. ⇨ picture at PAN¹.

rob /rɒb/ v (-bb-) ~ sb/sth (of sth) **1** to take property from a person or place illegally: [Vn] *be accused of robbing a bank* (*infml*) *I was robbed (of my cash and cheque-book).* ⇨ note. **2** to prevent sb/sth having sth, esp sth needed or deserved: [Vnpr] *be robbed of sleep by noisy neighbours* ○ *A last-minute goal robbed them of almost certain victory.* [also Vn].

▶ **robber** n a person who robs people; a thief.

robbery /'rɒbəri/ n [U,C] the action or an instance of stealing; THEFT: *be convicted of armed robbery* ○ *three robberies in one week.* **IDM** **daylight robbery** ⇨ DAYLIGHT.

NOTE Compare **rob**, **steal** and **burgle**. A robber or thief **robs** a place such as a bank, **robs** a person, or **robs** a person **of** things, especially money: *He was robbed of all his money and clothes.* A thief **steals** things, or **steals** things **from** a place or a person: *My bike's been stolen.* A burglar **burgles** a house by forcing a way into it and stealing things from it: *We arrived home from our holiday to find the house had been burgled.* People can also say they have been **burgled**: *We were burgled three times in a month.*

robe /rəʊb/ n **1** (esp in compounds) a long loose outer garment: *a beach-robe* ○ *Many Arabs wear long flowing robes.* **2** (esp pl) such a garment worn as a sign of rank or office, or for a ceremony: *coro¹nation robes* ○ *cardinals in scarlet robes.* **3** (*US* also **bathrobe**) a dressing-gown (DRESSING).

▶ **robe** v ~ sb/oneself (in sth) (*fml*) (esp passive) to dress sb/oneself in a robe: [Vn] *black-robed judges* [Vnpr] *professors robed in their ceremonial gowns.*

robin /'rɒbɪn/ n (**a**) (also ,robin 'redbreast) (**b**) a small brown European bird with a red breast. (**b**) (*US*) a larger N American bird resembling this. See also ROUND ROBIN.

robot /'rəʊbɒt/ n **1** (also **automaton**) a machine that can perform the actions of a person and which operates automatically or is controlled by a computer: *Many tasks on the production line in car factories are now performed by robots.* **2** (esp derog) a person who seems to behave without thinking. Compare AUTOMATON 2.

▶ **robotic** /rəʊ'bɒtɪk/ adj like a robot; stiff and mechanical: *robotic movements.* **robotics** n [sing v] the science of designing and operating robots.

robust /rəʊ'bʌst/ adj **1** vigorous; healthy and strong: *a robust young man/plant* ○ *a robust appetite.* **2** strong and able to survive rough treatment: *a robust chair/computer.* **3** firm and full of energy and determination: *a robust speech/response* ○ *take a more robust view.* **4** (*derog*) not delicate or refined: *a rather robust sense of humour.* **5** (of wine) full of flavour and colour.

▶ **robustly** adv in an energetic or vigorous way; strongly: *robustly defending the government's record* ○ *robustly made furniture.*

robustness n [U].

rock¹ /rɒk/ n **1(a)** [U,C] the hard solid material forming part of the surface of the earth or similar planets: *They drilled through several layers of rock to reach the oil.* ○ *igneous/lunar rocks.* (**b**) [C] a mass of this standing above the earth's surface or out of the sea: *the Rock of Gibraltar* ○ *The ship hit some rocks*

and sank. **2** [C] (**a**) a large detached piece of rock; a BOULDER: *clambering over the rocks at the foot of the cliff* ○ *The sign said 'Danger: falling rocks'.* (**b**) (*US*) a small stone: *That boy threw a rock at me.* **3** (*Brit*) (*US* ,rock 'candy) [U] a type of hard sweet, usu made in long sticks and sold esp at holiday resorts by the sea: *a stick of Brighton rock.* **IDM** **on the 'rocks** **1** (of a ship) having hit some rocks and breaking apart. **2** (*infml*) (of a marriage, business, etc) in danger of failing; at a severe crisis. **3** (*infml*) (of drinks) served with pieces of ice but no water: *Scotch on the rocks.* (**as**) **solid/steady as a 'rock** strong and firm; extremely reliable: *an invaluable player, steady as a rock.*

■ ,rock-'bottom n [U] (used without the) the lowest point or level: *Prices have hit/reached rock-bottom.* ○ ,rock-bottom (ie bargain) 'prices.

'**rock-cake** n a small cake with a hard rough surface, usu containing dried fruit.

'**rock-climbing** n [U] the sport or activity of climbing rock surfaces.

'**rock-garden** n = ROCKERY. ⇨ picture at HOUSE¹.

,rock-'hard adj extremely hard, strong or tough: *a rock-hard body/bed* ○ *The chicken was still rock-hard from the freezer.* ○ *He may look soft, but underneath he's rock-hard.*

'**rock-salt** n [U] common salt as a solid mineral.

,rock-'solid (also ,rock-'steady) adj unlikely to collapse, be changed, etc: *a rock-solid de¹fence/ex¹cuse* ○ *rock-solid Tory voters* ○ ,rock-steady 'nerves.

rock² /rɒk/ v **1** to move or make sb/sth move gently backwards and forwards, or from side to side: [Vnpr] *rock a baby to sleep* [V,Vn] *He sat rocking (himself) in his chair.* [Vn,Vnpr] *Our boat was rocked (from side to side) by the waves.* [Vp] *He rocked back on his heels* [also Vnp]. **2** to shake or make sth shake violently: [V] *The whole house rocked as the bomb exploded.* [Vn] *The town was rocked by an earthquake.* **3** to disturb or shock sb/sth greatly: [Vn] *The scandal rocked the government.* **IDM** **rock the 'boat** (*infml*) to do sth that upsets a delicate situation and causes difficulties: *Things are progressing well — please don't (do anything to) rock the boat.*

▶ **rocker** n **1** either of the two curved pieces of wood on which a rocking-chair rests. **2** = ROCKING-CHAIR. **3** (also 'rocker switch) a switch that changes from the 'on' to the 'off' position by means of a rocking action. **IDM** ,off one's 'rocker (*sl*) mad; crazy: *You must be off your rocker!*

rocky /'rɒki/ adj (-ier, -iest) unsteady; tending to rock or shake: *This chair is a bit rocky.* ○ (*fig*) *a rocky marriage* ○ *The programme got off to a rocky start.*

■ '**rocking-chair** (also **rocker**) n a chair mounted on rockers (ROCK²) so that it can be rocked backwards and forwards by the person sitting on it.

'**rocking-horse** n a wooden horse mounted on rockers (ROCK²) or springs so that it can be rocked backwards and forwards by a child sitting on it.

rock³ /rɒk/ (also '**rock music**) n [U] a type of loud modern popular music with a strong beat, played on electric guitars (GUITAR), etc: *hard/punk rock* ○ *a 'rock band/star.*

▶ **rock** v to dance to rock music: [Vnp] *rocking the night away* [Vpr] *rock to the beat* [also V]. **rocker** n **1** (also **Rocker**) (*Brit*) a member of a group of young people in Britain, esp in the 1960s, who liked to wear leather jackets, ride motor cycles (MOTOR) and listen to rock music. Compare MOD. **2** a person who performs, dances to, or enjoys rock music: *a funk/heavy/punk rocker* ○ *an ageing rocker.*

■ ,rock and 'roll (also ,rock 'n' 'roll) n [U] an early simple form of rock music: *a rock 'n' roll singer.*

rockabilly /'rɒkəbɪli/ n [U] (esp in the USA) a type of popular music combining rock and roll (ROCK³) and HILL-BILLY music.

rocker ⇨ ROCK², ROCK³.

rockery /ˈrɒkəri/ (also **rock-garden**) n a bank of large stones with plants growing between them. ⇨ picture at HOUSE¹.

rocket

rocket /ˈrɒkɪt/ n **1** a device containing an explosive powder that shoots into the air when lit and then explodes: a diˈstress rocket (ie used to signal for help). ⇨ picture. **2(a)** a device in the shape of a tube that is driven through the air by gases released when fuel is burned inside it. Rockets are used eg to shoot missiles or launch spacecraft. **(b)** a missile or spacecraft moved by rocket power: a space rocket ∘ A rocket smashed into the side of the building. ∘ a ˈrocket attack. ⇨ picture. **IDM give sb/get a ˈrocket** (Brit infml) to criticize/be criticized angrily for sth one has done.
▸ **rocket** v **1** to increase very rapidly: [Vpr] Pre-tax profits rocketed to £8.7m. [V] House prices are rocketing. **2** to move extremely quickly: [Vp] rocket along/off/past [Vpr] He rocketed to stardom (ie became famous) overnight. **3** to attack sth with rockets (ROCKET 1): [Vn] Fighters rocketed the presidential palace.

rocky /ˈrɒki/ adj (-ier, -iest) **1** consisting of rock: a rocky outcrop/promontory/coastline. **2** full of rocks: a rocky hillside/channel ∘ rocky soil. See also ROCKY.

rococo /rəˈkəʊkəʊ/ adj, n [U] (of) a style in furniture, architecture, music, etc with much elaborate decoration, common in Europe in the 18th century: a rococo fountain ∘ She had a passion for Italian rococo.

rod /rɒd/ n **1** (often in compounds) a thin straight piece of wood or metal: a glass/steel rod ∘ a ˈmeasuring-rod ∘ ˈpiston-rods. See also LIGHTNING ROD. **2** a stick used for hitting people as a punishment. **3** = FISHING-ROD. **4** (US sl) a small gun. **IDM a rod/stick to beat sb with** ⇨ BEAT¹. **make a rod for one's own ˈback** to do sth likely to cause trouble for oneself later. **rule with a rod of iron** ⇨ RULE v. **spare the rod and spoil the child** ⇨ SPARE².

rode pt of RIDE².

rodent /ˈrəʊdnt/ n any of a group of small animals with strong sharp front teeth: Rats, squirrels and beavers are all rodents.

rodeo /ˈrəʊdɪəʊ, rəʊˈdeɪəʊ/ n (pl -os) (esp in the USA) an exhibition or contest in which cowboys (COWBOY 1) show their skill at catching animals with ropes, riding cattle and wild horses, etc.

roe¹ /rəʊ/ n [U, C] the mass of eggs inside a female fish (**hard roe**) or the SPERM(1) of a male fish (**soft roe**), eaten as food.

roe² /rəʊ/ n (pl unchanged or **roes**) (also ˈ**roe-deer**) a type of small deer.

roger¹ /ˈrɒdʒə(r)/ interj (in radio communications) your message has been received and understood.

roger² /ˈrɒdʒə(r)/ v [Vn] (⚠ Brit sl) (of a male) to have sex with sb.

rogue /rəʊg/ n **1** (dated) a dishonest man or one without principles. **2** (joc esp approv) a person who behaves badly, esp in a playful or harmless way: He's a charming rogue. **3(a)** a wild animal driven away or living apart from the main group, and possibly dangerous: a ˌrogue ˈelephant. **(b)** a person or thing behaving differently from the accepted standard and usu in a way to cause trouble: rogue (ie unexpected) storms ∘ a rogue missile flying out of control.
▸ **roguish** /ˈrəʊgɪʃ/ adj (usu approv) playful; MISCHIEVOUS(1): He gave her a roguish look. **roguishly** adv.
■ ˌ**rogues' ˈgallery** n a collection of photographs of criminals kept by the police and used for identifying people suspected of committing crimes, etc.

roistering /ˈrɔɪstərɪŋ/ adj [attrib] (dated) having fun in a noisy cheerful way: roistering men waving bottles of wine. ▸ **roistering** n [U].

role (also **rôle**) /rəʊl/ n **1** an actor's part in a play, film, etc: play a variety of roles ∘ the title role. **2** a function that a person or thing typically has or is expected to have: play a key/central/major/vital/ significant role ∘ take a more active role in sth ∘ the role of the teacher in the learning process.
■ ˈ**role model** n a person who may be taken as an example to be copied: None of my teachers were particularly good role models.
ˈ**role-play** (also ˈ**role-playing**) n [U] an activity in which people act a situation. It is used esp in training people to develop communication skills or in treating mentally ill people.

roll

toilet roll (US **toilet paper roll**)   **roll of film**   **roll of cloth**

roll¹ /rəʊl/ n **1** [C] **(a)** a tube made by turning a sheet of flexible material over and over on itself without pressing it flat: a roll of carpet/film/cloth ∘ Wallpaper is sold in rolls. See also TOILET ROLL. ⇨ picture. **(b)** a thing with this shape: a man with rolls of fat around his stomach. **2** [C] **(a)** an individual portion of bread, long or round in shape, often eaten with butter and a filling: Six brown rolls, please. ⇨ picture at BREAD. Compare BUN 1. **(b)** (Brit) (following a n or ns) one of these containing the specified filling: a cheese roll ∘ a bacon and tomato roll. See also SAUSAGE ROLL, SPRING ROLL, SWISS ROLL. **3(a)** [C, sing] a rolling movement from side to side or over and over: a horse enjoying a roll in the grass ∘ two rolls of the dice ∘ The slow, steady roll of the ship made us feel sick. Compare PITCH¹ 7. **(b)** [C] an exercise in which one puts one's head and knees close together and turns one's body over, forwards or backwards, on the ground: do a forward roll. **4** [C usu sing] an official list or register, esp of names: the electoral roll (ie the list of people who may vote in an election) ∘ be included in the roll of benefactors. See also PAYROLL. **5** [C] a steady continuous sound: the distant roll of thunder ∘ A drum roll/A roll on the drums preceded the most dangerous part of the performance. See also ROCK AND ROLL. **IDM on a ˈroll** (infml) experiencing a prolonged period of success, good luck, progress, etc.
■ ˈ**roll bar** n a metal bar used to strengthen the roof of a car and to protect the people inside if the car turns over.
ˈ**roll-call** n [U, C] the reading aloud of a list of names to check whether everyone is present: Roll-call will be at 7 am. ∘ (fig) a distinguished roll-call (ie list) of former champions.
ˌ**roll of ˈhonour** (Brit) (US ˈ**honor roll**) n (usu sing) a list of people whose achievements are honoured, esp those who have died in battle.
ˌ**roll-top ˈdesk** n a desk with a flexible cover that rolls up into the top part of the desk.

roll² /rəʊl/ v **1** to turn over and over, or make sth round turn over and over, and move in a particular direction: [Vpr] *The ball rolled down the hill.* ○ *waves rolling onto the beach* [Vp] *The coin fell and rolled away.* [Vnpr] *delivery men rolling barrels across a yard* [also Vnp]. **2** to turn or make sth turn over and over or round and round while remaining in the same place: [Vpr] *a porpoise rolling in the water* [Vnpr] *rolling a pencil between his fingers* [V, Vn] *His eyes rolled/He rolled his eyes strangely.* **3** ~ **over;** ~ **sb/sth over** to turn or make sb/sth turn over to face a different direction: [Vnpr, Vnp] *roll a baby (over) onto its stomach* [Vp] *She rolled over to let the sun brown her back.* [Vpr] *He rolled onto his back.* **4(a)** to make sth or be made into the shape of a ball or tube: [Vnpr, Vnp] *roll string/wool (up) into a ball* [Vnp] *roll up a carpet/a map/a blind* [Vnn] *He rolled himself a cigarette.* [Vn] *I always roll my own (cigarettes).* ○ *a rolled umbrella* [Vpr, Vp] *The hedgehog rolled (up) into a spiky ball.* Compare UNROLL 1. **(b)** to fold the edge of a piece of clothing, etc over and over onto itself to make it shorter: [Vnp] *roll up one's sleeves* ○ *roll back the carpet* [Vnpr] *She rolled her trousers to her knees.* **5** to wrap or cover oneself/sb/sth in sth: [Vnpr] *roll the meat in breadcrumbs* [Vnpr, Vnp] *He rolled himself (up) in his blanket.* **6** to make sth flat with a heavy implement: [Vnp] *roll out the pastry* [Vn] *roll a lawn* [Vn-adj] *roll the ground flat* [also Vnpr]. **7(a)** to move or make sb/sth move or rock from side to side: [V] *walk with a rolling gait* [V, Vp] *The ship was rolling heavily (to and fro).* [Vnpr] *The huge waves rolled the ship from side to side.* [also Vpr]. Compare PITCH² 5. **(b)** to move forwards and backwards or from side to side without control: [Vpr, Vp] *We were rolling (about) with laughter.* **8** to move smoothly and steadily in space or time: [Vpr] *cars rolling off the assembly line* [Vadv] *The traffic rolled slowly forwards.* [Vp] *Clouds rolled away from the summit.* ○ *The years roll by/on.* **9** to make a long deep continuous sound: [V] *rolling drums* ○ *The thunder rolled.* [Vn] *roll one's r's* (ie by letting one's tongue VIBRATE(1) with each 'r' sound). **10(a)** (of machines, etc) to operate or begin operating: [V] *keep the presses/cameras rolling.* **(b)** [Vn] to make machines, etc begin operating. **IDM** **be 'rolling (in money, etc)** (*sl*) to have a lot of money: *What do you mean, he can't afford it? He's absolutely rolling (in money)!* **heads will roll** ⊳ HEAD¹. **rolled into 'one** combined in one person or thing: *He's an artist, a scientist and a businessman (all) rolled into one.* **rolling in the 'aisles** much amused; helpless with laughter: *He soon had us rolling in the aisles.* **roll/slip/trip off the tongue** ⊳ TONGUE. **roll 'up!** **roll 'up!** (used to invite people passing to join an audience). **roll up one's 'sleeves** to prepare to work or fight. **set/start/keep the ball rolling** ⊳ BALL¹. **PHRV** **roll sth 'back 1** to turn or force sb/sth back or further away: *roll back Communism* ○ *roll back the frontiers of space.* **2** (*esp US*) to reduce prices, etc: *roll back inflation.* **roll sth 'down 1** to open sth, eg by turning a handle: *roll down a car window.* **2** to make a rolled piece of clothing, etc hang or lie flat; to UNROLL(1) sth: *roll down a blind/one's sleeves.* **roll 'in** (*infml*) **1** to arrive in great numbers or quantity: *Offers of help are still rolling in.* **2** to arrive casually: *She rolled in for work two hours late.* **roll (sth) 'on 1** to apply, spread, etc sth onto a surface with a ROLLER(1a), or be applied, etc in this way: *The paint is easy to roll on/rolls on easily.* **2** (*Brit*) (used in the imperative) come soon: *Roll on spring/the holidays!* **roll 'up** (*infml*) (of a person or vehicle) to arrive: *Bill finally rolled up two hours late.*

▶ **rolling** *adj* [attrib] **1** rising and falling; undulating (UNDULATE): *rolling hills/countryside.* **2** done, etc in regular stages or at regular intervals over a

period of time: *a rolling programme/schedule of motorway repairs.*
■ **,rolled 'oats** *n* [pl] OATS that have had their dry outer layer removed and have then been crushed.
,rolling 'drunk *adj* [pred] so drunk that one cannot control one's movements.
'rolling-pin *n* a tube made of wood or glass used for rolling DOUGH(1) or pastry flat, etc. ⊳ picture at KITCHEN.
'rolling-stock *n* [U] engines, carriages or other vehicles used on a railway.
,rolling 'stone *n* a person who does not settle happily to live and work in one place.
'roll-on *n* a liquid for the body applied by means of a ball that moves round in the neck of its container: *roll-on deodorants.*
,roll-,on ,roll-'off *adj* [usu attrib] (*abbr* **ro-ro**) (of a ship) designed to allow vehicles to be driven onto and off it: *a ,roll-on ,roll-off 'ferry.*
'roll-up *n* (*infml*) a cigarette made by hand by rolling tobacco in a piece of special paper: *He always smokes roll-ups.*

roller /'rəʊlə(r)/ *n* **1(a)** a tube used for making sth flat or spreading it over a surface: *a garden roller* (ie for use on a lawn) ○ *a 'road-roller* ○ *Apply paint with a roller for even coverage.* See also STEAMROLLER. **(b)** a tube on which sth is placed to enable it to be moved: *The huge machine was moved to its new position on rollers.* **(c)** a tube on which sth is wound: *a 'roller blind* (ie a type of window BLIND³(1) wound on a roller) ○ *a roller towel.* **(d)** (also **curler**) a small tube of plastic around which hair is wound to make it curl: *put her hair in rollers.* **2** a long swelling wave: *rollers crashing on the beach.*
■ **'roller-coaster** (*Brit* also **switchback**) *n* a type of railway with open cars, tight turns and very steep slopes ridden for fun, eg at a FAIR³(1).
'roller skate (also **skate**) *n* a type of shoe with small wheels fitted to the bottom: *a pair of roller skates.* ⊳ picture at SKATE¹. **'roller-skate** *v* to move smoothly over hard surfaces wearing a pair of roller skates: [V] *go roller-skating.* **'roller-skating** *n* [U].

rollicking /'rɒlɪkɪŋ/ *adj* [attrib] very lively and amusing: *a rollicking good family film.*

rollmop /'rəʊlmɒp/ *n* a raw piece of HERRING which is rolled up and preserved in VINEGAR.

roly-poly /,rəʊli 'pəʊli/ (also **,roly-poly 'pudding**) *n* [C, U] a sweet dish made of pastry with jam spread on it which is rolled up and baked or boiled.
▶ **roly-poly** *adj* [attrib] (*infml*) (of people) short and rather fat: *his roly-poly body.*

ROM /rɒm/ *abbr* (*computing*) read-only memory: *ROM chips.* Compare RAM. See also CD-ROM.

romaine /rəʊ'meɪn/ *n* (*US*) = COS¹.

Roman /'rəʊmən/ *adj* **1(a)** of Rome: *Roman women* ○ *the Roman dialect.* **(b)** of the ancient Roman republic or empire: *Roman remains* ○ *a Roman temple/villa/road.* **2** of the Christian Church of Rome; Roman Catholic: *the Roman rite.* **3 roman** (of printing type) in ordinary upright form: *Definitions in this dictionary are printed in roman type.* Compare ITALIC.
▶ **Roman** *n* **1** [C] a member of the ancient Roman republic or empire: *after the Romans invaded Britain.* **2** [C] a native or inhabitant of the city of Rome. **3 roman** [U] roman(3) type. **IDM** **when in 'Rome (do as the 'Romans do)** (*saying*) one should change one's habits to suit the customs of the place one is living in or of the people one is living with.
■ **the ,Roman 'alphabet** *n* [sing] the letters A to Z, used esp in West European languages.
,Roman 'candle *n* a long FIREWORK that shoots out bright coloured stars.
,Roman 'Catholic (also **Catholic**) *n, adj* (a member) of the Christian Church that acknowledges the Pope as its head: *He's (a) Roman Catholic.* Compare

PROTESTANT. ¸**Roman Ca'tholicism** n [U] the faith of the Roman Catholic Church: *convert to Roman Catholicism.*

¸**Roman 'nose** n a nose with a high bridge¹(3a).

¸**roman 'numeral** n any of the Roman letters or groups of letters still used to represent numbers, eg I = 1, V = 5, X = 10, C = 100: *Henry VIII* ○ *Copyright BBC MCMXCIII (1993).* Compare ARABIC NUMERAL.

Romance /rəʊˈmæns/ adj [attrib] of those languages which are descended from Latin: *French, Italian and Spanish are Romance languages.*

romance /rəʊˈmæns/ n **1(a)** [C] an exciting and pleasant love affair, often not taken very seriously: *a holiday/teenage/secret romance.* **(b)** [U] a feeling of intensity and pleasure, usu associated with a love affair: *Spring is here and there's romance in the air.* ○ *Here's how to put some romance back into your marriage.* **2** [U] a feeling of excitement and adventure: *the romance of travel* ○ *There was an air of romance about the old castle.* **3** [C] a story of love, excitement and adventure, often set in the past: *a medieval romance* ○ *She prefers romances to detective stories.*
 ▶ **romance** v [V] to tell people interesting and exciting stories about oneself which are not true.

Romanesque /ˌrəʊməˈnesk/ adj, n [U] (of) the style of architecture current in western Europe between about 900 and 1200 AD, with round arches, thick walls and tall pillars: *a beautiful Romanesque doorway.* Compare NORMAN 1.

Romano- comb form Roman; of Rome: *Romano-British settlements.*

romantic /rəʊˈmæntɪk/ adj **1** [esp attrib] connected or concerned with love or a love affair: *a romantic candlelit dinner* ○ *a romantic attachment/feeling* ○ *a romantic story/scene.* **2** appealing to the imagination and affecting the emotions intensely: *romantic music* ○ *romantic mountain scenery* ○ *The view is very romantic.* **3** (of people, their characters, etc) highly imaginative and emotional; concerned with ideals rather than reality: *a romantic view of life* ○ *She has a dreamy romantic nature.* **4** (also **Romantic**) [esp attrib] (of music, literature, etc, esp in the 19th century) noted for depth of feeling rather than form or intellectual ideas; preferring wild nature, passion, etc to order and restraint: *the Romantic movement* ○ *Keats is one of the greatest Romantic poets.*
 ▶ **romantic** n **1** a person who is highly imaginative and emotional and concerned with ideals rather than reality. **2** (also **Romantic**) a romantic(4) artist.
 romantically /-kli/ adv: *be romantically involved with sb* ○ *Their names have been linked romantically.*
 romanticism /rəʊˈmæntɪsɪzəm/ n [U] **1** romantic(1) feelings, attitudes or behaviour. **2** (also **Romanticism**) a romantic(4) tendency in literature, art and music, esp in the 19th century. Compare CLASSICISM 1, REALISM 3. **romanticist** /-tɪsɪst/ n.
 romanticize, -ise /-tɪsaɪz/ v (often derog) to make sth seem more exciting, more interesting or better than it really is: [V] *Don't romanticize — stick to the facts.* [Vn] *a novel that refuses to romanticize the grim realities of war.*

Romany /ˈrɒməni, ˈrəʊm-/ n **1** [C] a GYPSY. **2** [U] the language of the gypsies (GYPSY).
 ▶ **Romany** adj [usu attrib] of gypsies (GYPSY) or their language.

romp /rɒmp/ v (esp of children or animals) to play together in a lively way with much running, jumping, etc: [Vp] *puppies romping about/around in the garden* [also V]. **IDM** **romp home / to victory** to win, succeed, etc easily: *The favourite romped home.* ○ *The Liberal Democrats have romped to victory in the latest by-election.* **PHRV** ¸**romp a'way/a'head** to rise, make progress, etc very rapidly: *The Hang Seng index continued to romp ahead.* ○ *They*

romped away at the beginning of the season and now look set to win the championship. ○ *He romped away with first prize.* **'romp in** to win, succeed, etc easily: *They romped in with profits of $12m.* ¸**romp 'through (sth)** (infml) to do sth with little difficulty or effort: *She romped through her exams.*
 ▶ **romp** n **1** [sing] an act of romping: *children having a romp in the garden.* **2** [C] an amusing but not serious film, book, play, etc: *His latest film is an enjoyable romp.* **3** [C] an amusing but not serious piece of sexual activity: *politicians involved in sex romps with call-girls.*

rompers /ˈrɒmpəz/ n [pl] (also **'romper-suit** [C]) a garment worn by a baby, covering the upper body and the legs.

rondo /ˈrɒndəʊ/ n (pl -os) a piece of music in which the main theme returns a number of times.

rood /ruːd/ n a large cross in a church, esp one on or above the screen that divides the priests and choir from the public.

roof /ruːf/ n (pl **roofs**) a structure covering or forming the top of a building, vehicle, etc: *a flat/sloping/ pitched roof* ○ *a thatched/tiled/slate roof* ○ *The roof is leaking again.* ○ *fly above the roofs of the city* ○ *the roof of one's mouth* ○ *The roof of the tunnel caved in, killing twelve miners.* See also SUN-ROOF. ⇨ picture at CAR, HOUSE¹. **IDM** **go through the 'roof** (infml) **1** to become very angry: *She went through the roof when I told her I'd crashed her car.* **2** (of prices, etc) to rise very rapidly: *Property prices have gone through the roof.* **have a 'roof over one's head** to have somewhere to live: *The house is very small but at least we've got a roof over our heads.* **hit the ceiling/roof** ⇨ HIT⁴. **raise the roof** ⇨ RAISE. **under one / the same 'roof** in the same house or building: *Although divorced, they continued to live under the same roof.* **under one's 'roof** in one's home: *I won't have that man under my roof again.*
 ▶ **roof** v ~ sth (over/in); ~ sth (with sth) to cover sth with a roof; to be a roof for sth: [Vnpr] *a garage roofed with tiles* [Vnp] *a plan to roof in the stadium* [also Vn].
 -roofed (forming compound adjs) having a roof of the specified type or colour: *red-roofed cottages.*
 roofing n [U, usu attrib] **1** material used for roofs: *'roofing tiles/slates/felt.* **2** the process of building roofs: *a roofing contractor.*
 ■ **'roof-garden** n a garden on the flat roof of a building.
 'roof-rack n a metal frame for carrying LUGGAGE, etc attached to the roof of a vehicle. ⇨ picture at CAR, RACK¹.

rooftop /ˈruːftɒp/ n the outer surface of a roof: *flying over the rooftops of Paris* ○ *Prisoners staged a rooftop protest about living conditions.* **IDM** ¸**shout, etc sth from the 'rooftops** to talk about sth in a very public way that may embarrass or annoy sb: *I told you about it in confidence — you don't have to go and shout it from the rooftops.*

rook¹ /rʊk/ n a large black bird. Rooks build their nests in groups: *the loud cawing of rooks.*
 ▶ **rookery** /-əri/ n a group of rooks' nests.

rook² /rʊk/ n = CASTLE 2. ⇨ picture at CHESS.

rook³ /rʊk/ v (infml) to cheat sb, eg by charging too high a price for sth: [Vn] *The waiter rooked us — we paid far too much for the wine.*

rookie /ˈrʊki/ n (infml) a person who has just started a job, an activity, etc and who has little experience: *a rookie police officer* ○ *They give all the unpleasant tasks to the rookies.*

room /ruːm, rʊm/ n **1(a)** [C] a part of a building that has its own walls, floor and ceiling and is usu entered from inside the building: *a dining/living room* ○ *a simply furnished room* ○ *He's in the next room.* ○ *teachers sitting in the staff room.* See also BALLROOM, BATHROOM, BEDROOM. **(b)** a bedroom in a

hotel, etc or in a house where one is staying as a guest: *I want to book a double/single room for two nights.* ○ *I'll show you to your room.* ○ *She lets out rooms to students.* See also GUEST-ROOM. **2 rooms** [pl] a set of rooms, usu rented, for living in; lodgings: *He's staying in rooms in Kensington.* **3** [U] ~ **(for sb/sth);** ~ **(to do sth)** space that can be used for a purpose, eg where sth can be put: *Is there enough room for me in the car?* ○ *This table **takes up too much room**.* ○ *Can you **make room** on that shelf for more books?* ○ ***standing room only*** (ie no room to sit down, eg in a bus or theatre). See also LEG-ROOM. ⇨ note at SPACE. **4** [U] ~ **(for sth)** the possibility of sth existing or happening: *There's (plenty of) **room for improvement** in your work* (ie It is not as good as it could be). ○ *There's **no room for doubt*** (ie The situation is quite clear). ○ *The government has little **room for manoeuvre*** (ie will find it difficult to change its position, policy, etc). **5** all the people in a room: *The whole room broke into applause.* **IDM be cramped for room/space** ⇨ CRAMP². **no room to swing a ¦cat** (*infml saying*) not enough space to live or work in.
▶ **room** *v* (*US*) to have lodgings; to share a room or set of rooms with sb: [Vpr] *He's rooming with my friend Alan.* [Vp] *We roomed together.*
-roomed (forming compound *adjs*) having rooms of the specified number or type: *a ten-roomed house.*
roomful /-fʊl/ *n* (*pl* **-fuls**) the amount or number of people or things a room will hold: *a whole roomful of antiques* ○ *I was shown into a roomful of strangers.*
roomy *adj* (**-ier, -iest**) (*approv*) having plenty of space to contain things or people: *a surprisingly roomy car/bungalow.* **roominess** *n* [U].
■ **¦rooming-house** *n* (*US*) a building where rooms with furniture in can be rented.
¦room-mate *n* a person living in the same room or set of rooms as another, eg in a college or lodgings. Compare FLATMATE.
¦room service *n* [U] a service provided in a hotel, by which guests can order food and drink to be brought to their rooms: *Call room service and ask for some sandwiches.*
roost /ruːst/ *n* a usu high place above the ground where birds settle to sleep. **IDM come home to roost** ⇨ HOME³. **rule the roost** ⇨ RULE *v*.
▶ **roost** *v* (of birds) to settle for sleep: [V] *a roosting place for pigeons* [also Vpr].
rooster /ˈruːstə(r)/ *n* (*esp US*) = COCK¹ 1.

root¹ /ruːt/ *n* **1** [C] the part of a plant that grows under the ground, absorbing water and minerals: *pull a plant up by* (ie including) *the roots* ○ *Vines have very long roots.* ○ *root crops/vegetables, eg carrots or potatoes.* See also GRASS ROOTS. **2** [C] the part of a hair, tooth, nail or tongue that attaches it to the rest of the body: *pull hair out by the roots.* **3** [C esp sing] the origin or basis of sth: ***The root of the problem*** *is his relationship with his father.* ○ *What lies **at the root of** this matter?* ○ *Money is often said to be **at the root of all evil**.* ○ *We need to tackle the root (cause) of the trouble.* **4 roots** [pl] family origins or connections; feelings attaching one to a particular place in which one or one's family lives or has lived: ***put down*** (ie establish) ***roots*** *in a place* ○ *pull up one's roots* (ie move away from a place where one has been for a long time) ○ *Many Americans have roots in Europe.* **5** [C] (*linguistics*) the part of a word on which its other forms are based; a word from which other words are formed: *'Walk' is the root of 'walks', 'walked', 'walking' and 'walker'.* ○ *'Feminine' comes from the Latin root 'femina' meaning 'woman'.* **6** [C] (*mathematics*) a quantity which, when multiplied by itself a certain number of times, produces another quantity: *4 is the square root of 16 (4 × 4=16) and the cube root of 64 (4 × 4 × 4=64).* **IDM ¦root and ¦branch** thoroughly; completely: *destroy an*

organization *root and branch* ○ *root-and-branch reforms.* **take ¦root 1** (of a plant) to develop a root or roots: *The cuttings I took from your roses haven't taken root.* **2** to become established: *a country where democracy has never really taken root.*
▶ **rootless** *adj* having no roots (ROOT 4): *a rootless wandering life.* **rootlessness** *n* [U].
■ **¦root beer** *n* [U,C] (*US*) a sweet drink, not alcoholic, that is flavoured with the roots of various plants.

root² /ruːt/ *v* (of a plant) to develop roots and begin to grow: [Vadv] *This type of plant roots easily.* ○ *deep-rooted grasses* [also V, Vpr]. **PHRV ¦root (a¦bout/ a¦round) for sth** (of people) to search for sth by moving things or turning things over: *What are you doing rooting around in my desk?* ○ *She was rooting (about) in her bag for her keys.* ○ *pigs rooting (around) for acorns.* **¦root for sb/sth** (no passive) (*infml*) to support sb/sth enthusiastically; to cheer for sb/sth: *We're rooting for the college baseball team.* ○ *Good luck in your exams — we're all rooting for you!* **¦root sth/sb ¦out 1** to find and destroy or remove sth completely: *their determination to root out corruption* ○ *a fresh attempt to root out troublemakers.* **2** to find sth/sb after searching for a long time: *I've managed to root out a copy of the original document.* **¦root sb to ¦sth** to cause sb to remain still in a place and unable to move: *Fear rooted him to the spot.* **¦root sth ¦up** to dig or pull up a plant with the roots.
▶ **rooted** *adj* **1** [pred] fixed in one place and unable to move: *We were/stood rooted to the ground/ spot in terror.* **2** deeply and firmly established: *The idea is firmly rooted in his mind.* ○ *have a rooted objection to sth* ○ *deeply-rooted differences.* **3** originating in or from sth: *beliefs rooted in the past.*

rope /rəʊp/ *n* **1** [C,U] thick cord or wire made by twisting finer cords or wires together: *We tied his feet together with (a) rope.* ○ *coils of rope on the quayside* ○ *They tied a (piece of) rope to the branch and used it as a swing.* See also SKIPPING-ROPE, TOW-ROPE. ⇨ picture at BOXING. **2** [C] a number of similar things held together by a string or thread passed through the middle of each: *a rope of onions/ pearls.* **3 the rope** [sing] (*infml or rhet*) death by hanging: *bring back the rope* (ie the death penalty). **IDM at the end of one's rope** ⇨ END¹. **give sb enough ¦rope** to give sb the freedom to do what they like, esp in the hope that what they do will make them look foolish, destroy their reputation, etc: *He's a fool — give him enough rope and he's sure to hang himself.* **give sb plenty of / some ¦rope** to allow sb much/some freedom to act in the way they think best. **money for jam / old rope** ⇨ MONEY. **on the ¦ropes** (*infml*) (in boxing) forced to the edge of the ring¹(5) and near defeat: (*fig*) *After a string of by-election defeats the government is clearly on the ropes.* **show sb / know / learn the ¦ropes** to explain to sb/know/learn the procedures or rules for doing sth: *She's just joined the department — it'll take her a week or two to learn the ropes.*
▶ **rope** *v* to tie a person or thing to another person or thing, or to tie people or things together, with a rope: [Vnp] *climbers roped together for safety* [Vnpr] *They roped her to a chair.* **PHRV ¦rope sb ¦in (to do sth)** (*infml*) (esp passive) to persuade sb to take part in an activity: *All her friends have been roped in to help with the show.* **¦rope sth ¦off** to separate one area from another using a rope, tape, etc: *rope off the scene of the accident.*
■ **¦rope-¦ladder** *n* a ladder made of two long ropes connected by a series of short pieces of wood, etc at regular intervals.

ropy (also **ropey**) /ˈrəʊpi/ *adj* (*Brit infml*) poor in quality, health, etc; not secure: *ropy old furniture* ○ *a ropy marriage* ○ *I'm feeling pretty ropey today.*

R

ro-ro /ˈrəʊrəʊ/ *abbr* roll-on roll-off (ROLL²).

rosary /ˈrəʊzəri/ *n* (**a**) (esp in the Roman Catholic Church) a string of beads (BEAD 1a) used for counting prayers as they are said: *wooden rosary beads*. (**b**) [sing] these prayers: *say/recite the rosary*.

rose¹ *pt* of RISE².

rose² /rəʊz/ *n* **1** [C] a sweet-smelling flower that grows on a bush and usu has thorns (THORN 1) on its stems. There are many different types of rose: *a ˈrose bush ○ a climbing rose ○ I prune the roses. ○ a bunch of red roses ○ a wild/cultivated rose.* ⇨ picture at FLOWER. **2** [C] a pink colour: *a rose-pink blouse.* **3** [C] a piece of metal or plastic with small holes in it that can be attached to a pipe or a watering-can (WATER) for watering plants. **IDM** **a bed of roses** ⇨ BED¹. **come up ˈroses** (*infml*) (of a situation) to develop in a very favourable way: *New job, new boyfriend — everything's coming up roses at last.* **not all ˈroses** (*infml*) not all pleasant: *Being a film star is not all roses by any means.* **look at/see sth through rose-coloured/rose-tinted ˈspectacles, etc** to see things as more positive or favourable than they really are.

■ **ˈrose-hip** *n* = HIP².

ˈrose-water *n* [U] a sweet-smelling liquid made from roses, sometimes used in cooking.

ˌrose-ˈwindow *n* an ornamental circular window, usu in a church.

rosé /ˈrəʊzeɪ; US rəʊˈzeɪ/ *n* [U, sing] any light pink wine: *an excellent (bottle of) rosé ○ rosé wines.* Compare RED WINE, WHITE WINE.

roseate /ˈrəʊziət/ *adj* [usu attrib] (*rhet*) deep pink: *the roseate hues of dawn.*

rosebud /ˈrəʊzbʌd/ *n* the flower of a rose before it is open: *a rosebud mouth* (ie one that is small and round).

rosemary /ˈrəʊzməri; US -meri/ *n* [U] a bush with narrow sweet-smelling leaves which are used to give flavour to food: *lamb with rosemary and garlic ○ Rosemary is the symbol of remembrance.*

rosette /rəʊˈzet/ *n* **1** a round decoration made of RIBBON(1a) worn by supporters of a sports club or a political party, or to show that sb has won a prize: *The fans are all wearing Manchester United rosettes. ○ the Democratic candidate with his big blue rosette.* **2** a thing that grows or is made in the shape of a rose: *a rosette of leaves ○ a rosette carved on each corner of the table.*

rosewood /ˈrəʊzwʊd/ *n* [U] a hard dark wood with a pleasant smell, used for making furniture: *a rosewood table.*

rosin /ˈrɒzɪn; US ˈrɒzn/ *n* [U] a type of RESIN(1) used on the strings and bows of musical instruments.

▶ **rosin** *v* [Vn] to rub sth with rosin.

roster /ˈrɒstə(r)/ *n* a list of people's names and the duties they have to perform at a particular time: *The monthly roster involves a week of night duty.* Compare ROTA.

▶ **roster** *v* (*Brit*) to place sb on a roster: [Vn] *introduce more flexible rostering.*

rostrum /ˈrɒstrəm/ *n* (*pl* **rostrums** or **rostra** /-trə/) a raised platform on which a person stands to make a speech, conduct music, receive a prize, etc: *climb onto/mount the rostrum.*

rosy /ˈrəʊzi/ *adj* (**-ier, -iest**) **1** (esp of skin) pink and healthy in appearance: *rosy cheeks.* **2** likely to be satisfactory; promising: *The prospects for rapid growth couldn't be rosier. ○ She painted a rosy picture of the firm's future.*

rot /rɒt/ *v* (**-tt-**) (**a**) to decay naturally and gradually: [V] *a heap of rotting leaves ○ rotting vegetation* [Vp] *The wood has rotted away completely.* [V] (*fig*) *He was thrown into prison and left to rot.* (**b**) to make sth decay: [Vn] *Oil and grease will rot the rubber of your tyres.* [Vnp] *Eating too much sugar can rot your teeth away.*

▶ **rot** *n* [U] **1** the process or state of rotting: *The roof timbers are full of rot* (ie rotted wood). See also DRY ROT. **2** (*dated Brit infml*) nonsense: *Don't talk such utter rot!* **IDM** **the rot sets ˈin** things begin to get steadily worse: *The rot really set in when three senior managers resigned within a week.* **stop the rot** ⇨ STOP¹.

rota /ˈrəʊtə/ *n* (*pl* **rotas**) (*esp Brit*) a list showing duties to be done or the names of people to do them in turn: *work on a rota system ○ the weekly cleaning rota.* Compare ROSTER.

rotary /ˈrəʊtəri/ *adj* [usu attrib] (**a**) (*fml*) (of motion) moving round a central point; circular. (**b**) (of a machine, an engine, etc) using this type of motion: *a rotary drill/lawnmower.*

▶ **rotary** *n* (*US*) = ROUNDABOUT² 1.

rotate /rəʊˈteɪt; US ˈrəʊteɪt/ *v* **1** to move or make sth move in circles round a central point: [V] *the rotating blades of a helicopter* [Vn] *Try to rotate your wrist.* [Vpr] *rotate through 360 degrees.* **2** to happen or make sth happen in turns or in a particular order: [Vn] *the technique of rotating crops* [Vnpr] *The post of chairman rotates among members of the committee.*

▶ **rotation** /rəʊˈteɪʃn/ *n* **1**(**a**) [U] the action of rotating: *the rotation of the Earth on its axis.* (**b**) [C] one complete movement of this type. **2** [C, U] a regular organized sequence of things or events: *the rotation of crops/crop rotation* (ie changing the crops grown each year on the same land). **IDM** **in roˈtation** one after the other in order: *crops planted in rotation ○ The two men worked in rotation, taking turns to do the digging.* **rotational** /-ʃənl/ *adj.*

rote /rəʊt/ *n* [U] the process of learning sth by repeated study rather than by understanding the meaning: *learn sth by rote ○ rote learning.*

rotisserie /rəʊˈtɪsəri/ *n* a piece of equipment for roasting meat, etc on a revolving metal rod.

rotor /ˈrəʊtə(r)/ *n* a part of a machine that revolves round a central point: *rotor blades on a helicopter.* ⇨ picture at HELICOPTER.

rotten /ˈrɒtn/ *adj* **1** (of food and other substances) decayed; having gone bad or soft: *rotten eggs/fruit/wood ○ The window frames are completely rotten.* **2** (*infml*) very bad; very unpleasant: *a rotten job/holiday ○ She's got a rotten cold. ○ We had rotten weather all week. ○ That was a rotten thing to do! ○ The police force is rotten to the core* (ie completely CORRUPT(1)). **3** (*infml*) not well; ill: *feel/look rotten.* ▶ **rottenly** *adv* (*infml*) very badly: *play rottenly.* **rottenness** *n* [U].

rotter /ˈrɒtə(r)/ *n* (*dated Brit infml*) a person who behaves towards sb in a way that is considered morally wrong, cruel or mean²(2,3): *He's a complete rotter!*

Rottweiler /ˈrɒtwaɪlə(r), -vaɪlə(r)/ *n* a breed of large dog that can be very fierce.

rotund /rəʊˈtʌnd/ *adj* (*fml or joc*) (of a person) round and fat: *I'd recognize that rotund figure anywhere!* ▶ **rotundity** *n*: *He demonstrates that rotundity is no obstacle to agility.*

rotunda /rəʊˈtʌndə/ *n* a round building or hall, esp one with a curved roof.

rouble (also **ruble**) /ˈruːbl/ *n* the chief unit of money in Russia. See also KOPECK.

roué /ˈruːeɪ/ *n* (*dated derog*) a man, esp an older one, who lives in an IMMORAL(2) way, esp by having sexual relationships with many women.

rouge /ruːʒ/ *n* [U] (*dated*) a red powder used for giving colour to the cheeks.

▶ **rouge** *v* [Vn] to colour the cheeks with rouge.

rough¹ /rʌf/ *adj* (**-er, -est**) **1**(**a**) (of a surface) not smooth or level: *rough ground ○ rough hands ○ rough material.* Compare SMOOTH¹. (**b**) (of the sea, etc) not calm: *When the sea is very rough, the ferry* *doesn't sail.* ○ *We had a rough crossing from Dover.* **2** using excessive force; rather violent; not gentle: *rough behaviour* ○ *The children are very rough with their toys.* ○ *Rugby is a rough sport.* ○ *That area of the city is quite rough* (ie dangerous) *after dark.* ○ *The parcel had received some rough handling in the post.* **3** (of sth in its early stages) done, etc quickly and without detail; not exact: *a rough sketch/outline/ calculation/translation* ○ *a rough draft of his speech* ○ *Give me a rough idea of your plans.* ○ *I'll give you a rough estimate of the costs.* **4** difficult; unpleasant; not peaceful: *You look as though you've had a rough night.* ○ *Why should I do all the rough work?* **5** harsh in taste, sound, etc: *a rough wine/voice* ○ *Your engine sounds a bit rough — you'd better have it checked.* **6** (*infml*) not well; not looking happy: *I feel pretty rough — I'm going to bed.* ○ *You look rough, John. Is anything the matter?* **IDM** be **'rough (on sb) 1** (*infml*) be unpleasant or UNLUCKY for sb: *Losing his job was rough on him.* **2** to be too severe or angry with sb: *I'm sorry I was so rough on you.* **have / give sb a rough 'ride** to experience/make sb experience a lot of criticism and opposition: *The new chairman was given a rough ride by certain members of the committee.* **a raw/rough deal** ⇨ DEAL².

▶ **roughly** *adv* **1** in a rough(2,3) manner: *treat sb/ speak roughly* ○ *Add the roughly chopped celery.* **2** approximately: *It should cost roughly £10.* ○ *It's about forty miles,* **roughly speaking.** ○ *I know roughly what to expect at the interview.*

roughness *n* [U] the quality or state of being rough: *the roughness of his chin.*

■ **,rough-and-'ready** *adj* simple and not carefully prepared, but effective or adequate: *have a rough-and-ready approach to home decorating* ○ *The accommodation is rather rough-and-ready, I'm afraid.*

,rough-and-'tumble *n* [U] rough but often enjoyable activity, fighting, etc: *the rough-and-tumble of political life* ○ *She found it hard to get used to the rough-and-tumble of the other children.* — *adj* [attrib]: *rough-and-tumble games.*

,rough 'diamond (*Brit*) (*US* **,diamond in the 'rough**) *n* a person who lacks good manners, education, etc but who is considered to have great ability, charm, etc.

,rough 'edges *n* [pl] the aspects of a person's character or of a thing that are not properly finished or not ready or suitable: *It'll take a few months to knock the rough edges off the new trainees.*

,rough 'justice *n* [U] punishment that is unfair, or fair but not official or expected.

'rough stuff *n* [U] violent behaviour: *We don't want any rough stuff in this pub.*

rough² /rʌf/ *adv* in a rough manner: *a team that is notorious for playing rough.* **IDM** **live rough** ⇨ LIVE². **sleep rough** ⇨ SLEEP².

■ **,rough-'hewn** *adj* shaped or carved roughly: *a cabin made of ,rough-hewn 'logs* ○ *his handsome ,rough-hewn 'face.*

rough³ /rʌf/ *n* **1** (also **the rough**) [U] the part of a golf course where the grass is long and the ground less even, and where it is more difficult to play the ball: *be in/get out of the rough.* ⇨ picture at GOLF. Compare FAIRWAY. **2** [C] a rough¹(3) drawing or design: *Have you seen the (artwork) roughs for the new book?* **3** [C] (*infml*) a violent criminal: *beaten up by a gang of roughs.* **IDM** **in 'rough** without great accuracy; approximately: *I've drawn it in rough, to give you an idea of what it will look like.* **take the ,rough with the 'smooth** to accept what is unpleasant or difficult as well as what is pleasant or easy: *In marriage you have to learn to take the rough with the smooth.*

rough⁴ /rʌf/ *v* **IDM** **'rough it** (*infml*) to live without the usual comforts of life: *roughing it in a student flat* ○ *You may have to rough it a bit if you come to*

stay. **PHR V** **,rough sth 'out** to draw, describe or prepare sth without details: *He roughed out some ideas for the new buildings.* **,rough sb 'up** (*infml*) to attack sb physically.

roughage /'rʌfɪdʒ/ *n* [U] the substances in certain foods that help the body to DIGEST²(1a) what one eats: *For roughage, eat plenty of fresh fruit and wholesome bread.*

roughcast /'rʌfkɑːst; *US* -kæst/ *n* [U] a substance containing small stones, used for covering the outside walls of buildings.

roughen /'rʌfn/ *v* to become or make sth rough: [Vn] *a face roughened by the sun and wind* ○ *Roughen the surface before applying the paint.*

roughneck /'rʌfnek/ *n* a rough violent person.

roughshod /'rʌfʃɒd/ *adv* **IDM** **ride roughshod over sb/sth** ⇨ RIDE².

roulette /ruːˈlet/ *n* [U] a game in which a ball is dropped onto a moving wheel that has holes with numbers on it. The players bet on where the ball will be when the wheel stops: *play roulette* ○ *a roulette wheel.* See also RUSSIAN ROULETTE.

round¹ /raʊnd/ *adj* **1** shaped like a circle or a ball: *a round mirror/window/table* ○ *a small round stone* ○ *People used to think the world was flat instead of round.* **2** (esp of a part of the body) full and curved: *round cheeks* ○ *small, round hands.* **3** [attrib] full; complete: *a round dozen* (ie not less than twelve) ○ *a round* (ie considerable) *sum of money.* **IDM** **in round 'figures/'numbers** given to the nearest 10, 100, 1000, etc; not given in exact figures or numbers: *In round figures, there are about 3000 students taking the course.*

▶ **roundish** *adj* approximately round in shape.

roundly *adv* in a forceful and thorough way: *be roundly condemned/criticized/defeated* ○ *'It wouldn't hurt you to work a bit harder,' she said roundly.*

roundness *n* [U].

■ **,round-'eyed** *adj* with the eyes wide open in surprise, fear, etc: *stare round-eyed with terror/ wonder.*

,round 'robin *n* **1** a letter, etc expressing the opinions or wishes of a number of people, each of whom sign it in turn. **2** (*sport esp US*) a competition in which each player plays every other player in turn: *a round-robin match/tournament.*

,round-'shouldered *adj* (*derog*) with the shoulders bent forward or sloping downwards: *Sit up straight — you're getting round-shouldered!*

'round-table *adj* [attrib] (of a meeting, etc) in which those present have equal status and rights: *,round-table dis'cussions/'talks* ○ *a ,round-table a'greement between management and union.*

,round 'trip *n* **(a)** (*Brit*) a journey to one or more places and back again, often by a different route. **(b)** (*US*) = RETURN² 2: *a ,round-trip 'ticket.*

round² /raʊnd/ *adv part* (*esp Brit*) (also *esp US* **around**) For the special uses of **round** in phrasal verbs, look at the verb entries. For example, the meaning of **come round to sth** is given in the phrasal verb section of the entry for **come.** ⇨ note. **1** moving in a circle; rotating (ROTATE 1): *Everybody joins hands and dances round.* ○ *How do you make the wheels go round?* ○ *children spinning round and round* ○ (*fig*) *The thought kept going round and round in her head.* **2** completing a full cycle(1): *How long does it take the minute hand of the clock to go round once?* ○ *Spring will soon come round again.* **3** measuring or marking the edge or outside of sth: *a young tree measuring only 18 inches round* ○ *They've built a high fence* **all round** *to keep intruders out.* **4(a)** on all sides of sb/sth; close to sb/sth: *A large crowd had gathered round to watch.* **(b)** at various places in an area: *People stood round waiting for something to happen.* **5** so as to face a different, usu the opposite, direction: *turn the car round and drive* *back again* ∘ *She looked/turned/swung round at the sound of his voice.* **6** to the other side of sth: *We walked round to the back of the house.* **7** by a route that is longer than the most direct one: *It's quickest to walk across the field — going round by road takes much longer.* ∘ *The road's blocked — you'll have to drive round.* **8** to various different places or positions: *move all the furniture round* ∘ *go round interviewing people about local traditions.* **9** (*infml*) to or at a specified place, esp where sb lives: *go round to the local shop* ∘ *I'll be round in an hour.* ∘ *We've invited the Frasers round this evening.* **10** to or for all members of a group in turn: *Pass the biscuits round.* ∘ *The news was quickly passed round.* ∘ *Have we* **enough cups to go round?** IDM **round a'bout 1** near; in the surrounding (SURROUND) area: *the countryside/villages round about.* **2** approximately: *We're leaving round about midday.* ∘ *A new roof will cost round about £3 000.*

NOTE **Round** and **around** can be prepositions or adverbs and are used in many phrasal verbs. **Around** is used in British and American English, and **round** is used especially in British English: *The earth goes round/around the sun.* ∘ *They live round/around the corner.* ∘ *We travelled round/around India.*

round³ /raʊnd/ *n* **1(a)** a regular sequence of activities, visits, etc: *the daily round of school life* ∘ *Her life is* **one long round** *of meetings/parties.* ∘ *We did/went the rounds of* (ie visited in turn) *our relations at Christmas.* (**b**) a regular route taken, esp by sb delivering or collecting sth or visiting sb: *a postman's/milkman's round* ∘ *doctors* **on their rounds** (ie visiting their patients) ∘ *The health and safety officer is making his rounds/his usual round* (ie of inspection). See also MILK ROUND. **2** a series of meetings or discussions: *the next round of the peace talks* ∘ *a new round of pay bargaining.* **3** (*sport*) (**a**) a stage in a contest, competition, etc: *a qualifying round* ∘ *The fight only lasted five rounds.* ∘ *Norwich were knocked out in the third round of the Cup.* (**b**) a complete circuit of a course: *play a round* (ie 18 holes) *of golf* ∘ *She jumped a clear round* (ie in SHOWJUMPING). **4** a number of drinks bought by one person for all the others in a group: *buy a round* ∘ *It's my round* (ie my turn to pay for the next set of drinks). **5(a)** a complete slice of bread: *a round of toast.* (**b**) a sandwich made with two slices of bread: *two rounds of cheese and tomato and one of beef.* **6** a circular object or piece of sth: *Cut the pastry into small rounds, one for each pie.* **7(a)** a single shot or series of shots from one or more guns: *They fired several rounds at us.* (**b**) a bullet, etc available to be fired: *We've only three rounds of ammunition left.* **8** a short period of applause: *She got a big* **round of applause** *for her performance.* **9** a musical composition for two or more voices in which each sings the same tune but starts at a different time. IDM **do/go the 'round(s) (of sth)** (of news, etc) to circulate: *The rumour quickly went the rounds (of the village).* **in the 'round 1** (of a theatre, play, etc) with the audience almost all around the stage. **2** (of SCULPTURE(2), etc) made so that it can be viewed from all sides: *His work should be seen in the round.*

round⁴ /raʊnd/ (*esp Brit*) (also *esp US* **around**) *prep.* ⇨ note at ROUND¹. **1** having sth as the central point of a circular movement: *sail round the world* ∘ *The earth moves round the sun.* **2** to or at a point on the other side of sth: *walk round the car* ∘ *There's a petrol station round the next bend.* **3** placed at or covering all sides of sth: *a scarf round his neck* ∘ *sitting round the table.* **4** to or at various points in sth: *look round the room* ∘ *There were soldiers positioned all round the town.*

round⁵ /raʊnd/ *v* **1** to make sth into the shape of a circle or a ball: *round the lips* (eg when making the

sound /uː/) ∘ *stones rounded by the action of water.* **2** to go round sth: *We rounded the corner/bend at high speed.* PHRV **round sth 'off 1** to end or complete sth well or in a satisfactory way: *round off a meal with a good brandy* ∘ *He rounded off his political career by becoming Minister of Trade and Industry.* **2** to take the sharp edges off sth: *She rounded off the corners of the table with sandpaper.* **'round on sb** to speak suddenly and angrily to sb: *She was amazed when he rounded on her and called her a liar.* ,round **sb/sth 'up** to gather people, animals or things together in one place: *cowboys rounding up cattle* ∘ *The guide rounded us up and led us back to the coach.* ,round **sth 'up/'down** to increase/decrease a figure, price, etc to the nearest whole number: *It came to £3.97, rounded up to £4.*

▶ **rounded** *adj* **1** having a round shape: *rounded hills* ∘ *a knife with a rounded end* ∘ *a well rounded figure.* **2** (*approv*) possessing a pleasing depth or wide range of characteristics, abilities, etc: *wine with a smooth rounded flavour* ∘ *The book provides a rounded picture of his early life.*

■ **'round-up** *n* (usu *sing*) **1** the act of gathering together people, animals or things into one place: *a round-up of suspects/stray cattle.* **2** a summary: *a news round-up.*

roundabout¹ /'raʊndəbaʊt/ *adj* [usu attrib] not using the shortest or most direct route, form of words, etc: *take a roundabout route* ∘ *a roundabout way of saying sth* ∘ *I heard the news in a roundabout way.*

roundabout² /'raʊndəbaʊt/ *n* **1** (*Brit*) (*US* **traffic circle**) a road JUNCTION in the form of a circle round which all traffic has to go in the same direction: *approach/go round a roundabout.* Compare CIRCUS 3. **2** (also **merry-go-round**, *US* **carousel**, **whirligig**) a revolving platform with model horses, cars, etc for children to ride on at a fair. IDM **swings and roundabouts** ⇨ SWING².

roundel /'raʊndl/ *n* **1** a small circle carved into wood, stone, etc as a decoration. **2** a mark on esp military aircraft indicating which country they belong to.

rounders /'raʊndəz/ *n* [sing *v*] a game for two teams, played with a bat and ball. The players of one team hit the ball and run round a circuit, stopping at any of four bases, while the other team chase the ball and try to get them out. Compare BASEBALL.

Roundhead /'raʊndhed/ *n* a supporter of Parliament in the English Civil War. Compare CAVALIER.

roundsman /'raʊndzmən/ *n* (*pl* **-men** /-mən/) (*dated*) a person who delivers goods, esp food, to people's houses.

rouse /raʊz/ *v* **1** ~ **sb** (**from sth**) to wake sb: [Vn, Vnpr] *I was roused (from my sleep) by the door-bell ringing.* **2** to make sb/oneself want to do sth; to stimulate sb/oneself: [Vnpr] *rouse sb/oneself to action* ∘ *Their visit roused her from her apathy/depression.* [Vn] *You need to rouse yourself and take more interest in other people.* [also Vn.to inf]. **3** to cause a particular feeling or attitude to exist: [Vn] *rouse sb's anger/jealousy/indignation* ∘ *What first roused your suspicions?* ∘ *The new law is bound to rouse a lot of opposition.* **4** to make sb annoyed or angry: [Vn] *When he's roused, he can be quite frightening!* See also AROUSE.

▶ **rousing** *adj* [usu attrib] exciting and encouraging; vigorous: *a rousing speech/performance* ∘ *The team was given a rousing reception by the fans.*

roustabout /'raʊstəbaʊt/ *n* (*US*) a man with no special skills who works eg on an oil rig (OIL) or in a CIRCUS(1).

rout /raʊt/ *n* [C, U] a total defeat: *After our fifth goal the match became a rout.* IDM **put sb to 'rout** (*fml*) defeat sb completely: *They put the rebel army to rout.*

▶ **rout** *v* to defeat sb completely: [Vn] *He resigned after his party was routed in the election.*

route /ruːt; *US also* raʊt/ *n* **1(a)** a way to go or send

sth from one place to another: *We drove home by the quickest route.* ○ *an escape route* ○ *a much used holiday route* ○ *Which route did you take/follow?* ○ *They've cut off our supply routes.* ○ *(fig) the route to success.* (**b**) a fixed path or course: *a bus route* ○ *the main shipping routes across the Atlantic.* **2** (*esp US*) (used before the number of a major road): *Take Route 69.* See also EN ROUTE.
▶ **route** *v* (*pres p* **routing** or, rarely, **routeing**; *pp* **routed**) to send sth by a specified route: [Vnpr] *This flight is routed to Chicago via New York.* ○ *routing data via satellite.*
■ **'route march** *n* a long march, esp one made by soldiers in training.

routine /ruːˈtiːn/ *n* **1** [C, U] a fixed and regular way of doing things: *Keep to/follow a* **set routine.** ○ *do sth* **as a matter of routine** ○ *establish a new routine* ○ *Now he's left, it'll be back to the old routine.* **2** [C] a set sequence of movements, esp in a dance: *go through a skating routine.*
▶ **routine** *adj* **1** usual; regular: *routine tasks/chores/duties* ○ *the routine procedure* ○ *routine maintenance.* **2** (*derog*) normal or usual and, as a result, boring or without special interest: *a rather routine existence/production of 'Romeo and Juliet'.* **routinely** *adv*: *We routinely check safety levels of radiation.* ○ *They are routinely abused and beaten.*

roux /ruː/ *n* (*pl* unchanged) (in cooking) a mixture of melted fat and flour used as a base for sauces.

rove /rəʊv/ *v* (*esp rhet*) to wander from place to place; to move around in a place: [V] *a roving reporter/correspondent* ○ *a roving* (ie not faithful) *husband* [Vn] *bands of hooligans roving the streets* [Vpr] *(fig) His eyes continually roved around the room.* **IDM** **have a roving 'eye** to be always looking for a chance to start a new sexual relationship.
▶ **rover** *n* a person who likes to travel or move around rather than be settled in one place: *She's always been something of a rover.*

row¹ /rəʊ/ *n* a number of people or things arranged in a tidy line: *a row of books/houses/desks/seats* ○ *standing in a row/in rows* ○ *plant a row of cabbages* ○ *sit in the front/back row at the cinema.* See also DEATH ROW. **IDM** **in a 'row** without a break; in succession: *This is the third day in a row that it's rained.* ○ *If a team wins the championship three times in a row, they keep the cup.*
■ **'row house** *n* (*US*) a terraced (TERRACE) house.

rowing-boat
(*esp US* **row-boat**)

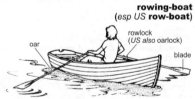

oar
rowlock
(*US also* oarlock)
blade

row² /rəʊ/ *v* (**a**) to move a boat through the water by using oars (OAR): [Vpr, Vnpr] *row (the boat) across the lake* [Vadv, Vp] *row ashore/out to sea* [also V, Vn]. (**b**) to transport sb/sth in this way: [Vnp, Vnpr] *He rowed us across the river.* [also Vn].
▶ **row** *n* (usu *sing*) a trip or period of time spent rowing a boat: *go for a row* ○ *a long and tiring row.*
rower *n* a person who rows a boat. See also OARSMAN.
■ **'rowing-boat** (also *esp US* **'row-boat**) *n* a small boat that one rows. ⇨ picture.
'rowing-machine *n* an exercise machine on which one makes rowing movements.

row³ /raʊ/ *n* (*infml*) **1** [C] a noisy or violent argument; a quarrel: *a family row* ○ *I think they've had a row.* ○ *the continuing row over the government's defence policy.* ⇨ note at ARGUMENT. **2** [sing] a loud

unpleasant noise: *How can I read with this row going on?* ○ *What a row they're making!*
▶ **row** *v* ~ **(with sb)** to quarrel noisily: [V] *They're always rowing.* [Vpr] *He's rowing (with his employers) over money.*

rowan /ˈrəʊən, ˈraʊən/ (also **'rowan tree**) *n* a type of tree that has red berries in autumn.

rowdy /ˈraʊdi/ *adj* (**-ier, -iest**) (*derog*) creating a lot of noise and disorder: *a group of rowdy teenagers* ○ *address a rowdy meeting* ○ *The party got a bit rowdy.*
▶ **rowdily** *adv*.
rowdiness *n* [U].
rowdy *n* (*dated derog*) a rowdy person.

rowlock /ˈrɒlək, ˈrəʊlɒk/ (*US also* **oarlock**) *n* a device fixed on the side of a boat for keeping an OAR in position. ⇨ picture at ROWING-BOAT.

royal /ˈrɔɪəl/ *adj* [usu attrib] **1** of a king or queen: *the royal family* ○ *limitations on royal power* ○ *the royal visit to Canada.* **2** belonging to the family of a king or queen: *the royal princesses/palaces.* **3** in the service of or supported by a king or queen or their family: *the Royal Air Force* ○ *the Royal Society of Arts* ○ *the Royal Opera House.* **4** suitable for a king, etc; splendid: *a royal welcome.* **IDM** **the royal 'we'** the use of 'we' by a king or queen to refer to himself or herself.
▶ **royal** *n* (usu *pl*) (*infml*) a member of the royal family: *the young royals.*
royalist /ˈrɔɪəlɪst/ *n* a person who supports the system of having a king or queen: *a convinced royalist* ○ *royalist troops.* Compare REPUBLICAN *n.*
royally /ˈrɔɪəli/ *adv* in a splendid manner: *We were royally entertained.*
■ **ˌroyal 'blue** *adj, n* [U] (of) a deep bright blue colour.
ˌRoyal Com'mission *n* (*Brit*) a group of people officially appointed by the king or queen, at the government's request to investigate and report on a particular matter: *set up a Royal Commission on/to review the security services.*
ˌRoyal 'Highness *n* (used as the title of a royal person, esp a prince or princess): *His Royal Highness, Prince Edward* ○ *Their Royal Highnesses, the Duke and Duchess of York.*
ˌroyal 'jelly *n* [U] a substance produced by worker bees which is fed to the young queen bee: *health food products containing royal jelly.*

royalty /ˈrɔɪəlti/ *n* **1** [U] a royal person or royal people: *in the presence of royalty* ○ *a shop patronized by royalty.* **2** [C] (**a**) a payment made to a writer, composer, etc each time a book is sold, a work performed, etc: *royalties on CD sales* ○ *a royalty cheque* ○ *an advance against future royalties.* (**b**) a payment made by a mining or oil company to the owner of the land being mined.

rpm /ˌɑː piː ˈem/ *abbr* revolutions per minute (used as a measurement of engine speed): *2 500 rpm.*

RSA /ˌɑːr es ˈeɪ/ *abbr* (in Britain) Royal Society of Arts.

RSC /ˌɑːr es ˈsiː/ *abbr* (in Britain) Royal Shakespeare Company: *an RSC production.*

RSM /ˌɑːr es ˈem/ *abbr* Regimental Sergeant-Major.

RSPB /ˌɑːr es piː ˈbiː/ *abbr* (in Britain) Royal Society for the Protection of Birds.

RSPCA /ˌɑːr es ˌpiː siː ˈeɪ/ *abbr* (in Britain) Royal Society for the Prevention of Cruelty to Animals.

RSVP /ˌɑːr es viː ˈpiː/ *abbr* (esp on invitations) please reply (French *répondez s'il vous plaît*).

Rt Hon *abbr* (*Brit*) Right Honourable: *(the) Rt Hon Richard Scott.* Compare HON 2.

Rt Rev (also **Rt Revd**) *abbr* Right Reverend: *(the) Rt Rev George Hill.* Compare REV.

RU *abbr* Rugby Union.

rub¹ /rʌb/ *v* (**-bb-**) **1(a)** ~ **(sth) (with sth)** to move one's hand, an object, etc backwards and forwards

R

repeatedly on a surface while pressing: [V] *If you keep rubbing, the paint will come off.* [Vn] *He rubbed his eyes.* ○ *She rubbed her chin thoughtfully.* [Vnpr] *Rub the surface with a damp cloth. She rubbed her hand across her face.* [Vpr, Vnpr] *The cat was rubbing (itself) against my legs.* (**b**) ~ **sth (together)** to move two surfaces against each other in this way: [Vn, Vnpr] *She rubbed her hands (together) in delight.* (**c**) ~ **(on/against sb/sth)** (of a surface) to move backwards and forwards repeatedly on another surface while pressing against it, esp causing pain or damage: [V] *The heel of my shoe is rubbing* (ie against my foot). [Vpr] *The wheel is rubbing on the mudguard.* **2** to cause sth to reach the specified state by rubbing: [Vn-adj] *rub the surface smooth* ○ *rub one's hair dry (with a towel).* **3** ~ **sth (in/into/on/over sth)** to press a soft or liquid substance into sth by rubbing: [Vnpr] *Rub the lotion in/into your skin.* [Vnpr] *He rubbed the cream on her back.* **IDM** **rub sb's 'nose in it** (*infml*) to remind sb repeatedly of their mistakes in a cruel way. **rub 'salt into the wound / sb's wounds** to make a painful experience even more painful for sb. **rub 'shoulders with sb** to meet sb famous socially or as part of one's job: *He's rubbing shoulders with film stars all the time.* **rub sb up the wrong 'way** (*infml*) to make sb angry or annoyed, often without intending to, by doing or saying sth that offends them: *She tends to rub people up the wrong way.* **PHR V** **rub a'long (with sb/together)** (*Brit infml*) (of two or more people) to live or work together in a reasonably friendly way. **rub (sb/oneself/sth) 'down** to rub sb, oneself, a horse, etc hard with eg a towel to make the skin dry and clean: *The players paused to rub (themselves) down between games.* **rub sth 'down** to make sth smooth by rubbing: *Rub the wood down well with fine sandpaper before painting.* **rub it 'in** to remind sb repeatedly of sth they would like to forget, eg a past mistake: *I know it was a silly thing to do, but there's no need to rub it in!* **rub (sth) 'off (sth)** to remove sth or be removed by rubbing: *Rub the mud off your trousers.* ○ *Who's rubbed my figures off the blackboard?* ○ *These stains won't rub off.* **rub 'off (on/onto sb)** (*infml*) (of personal qualities, behaviour, etc) to be transferred to sb as a result of spending time with a person who has those qualities, etc: *Let's hope some of his good luck rubs off on me!* **rub sb 'out** (*US sl*) to murder sb. **rub sth 'out** to remove the marks made by a pencil, etc, by using a RUBBER¹(2): *rub out a mistake/word/drawing.* **rub sth 'up** to polish sth by rubbing.
► **rubbing** *n* a copy of an inscription (INSCRIBE) or picture carved in metal or stone, made by placing paper over it and rubbing with a pencil, piece of coloured wax, etc: *take a brass rubbing* (eg of a decoration on a TOMBSTONE).

rub² /rʌb/ *n* **1** [C usu *sing*] an act or instance of rubbing: *Give your shoes a rub before you go out.* **2** **the rub** [sing] (*dated or rhet*) a problem or difficulty: *One needs employment in order to secure a place to live. There's/There lies the rub.*

rubber¹ /'rʌbə(r)/ *n* **1** [U] a strong elastic substance which keeps out water. It is made from the juice of a tropical plant or produced artificially, and is used to make tyres, etc: *rubber plantations in Malaysia* ○ *rubber gloves/boots/bullets* ○ *foam rubber.* **2** [C] (*Brit*) (also *esp US* **eraser**) a small piece of rubber or some other substance used for removing pencil marks, etc from paper. **3** [C] (*infml esp US*) a CONDOM.
► **rubberized, -ised** /'rʌbəraɪzd/ *adj* treated or covered with rubber: *rubberized waterproof cloth.*
rubbery /'rʌbəri/ *adj* like rubber in appearance or texture: *rubbery lips/features* ○ *Don't cook the meat for too long or it will become rubbery.*
■ **,rubber 'band** (also **elastic band**, *US* **elastic**) *n* a

thin circular piece of rubber used for holding things together: *a pile of papers with a rubber band round them.*
'rubber plant *n* a plant with thick shiny green leaves, often grown indoors.
,rubber 'stamp 1 a small device held in the hand and used for printing the date, the name of an organization, etc on a document. **2** (*derog*) a person or group that automatically gives approval to the actions or decisions of others. **,rubber-'stamp** *v* [Vn] (*often derog*) to approve sth automatically and without considering it properly.
rubber² /'rʌbə(r)/ *n* a competition in certain sports and card-games, consisting of three or five games played between the same players or teams: *Let's play another rubber.*

rubbish /'rʌbɪʃ/ *n* [U] **1** (*esp Brit*) (*US* also **garbage**, **trash**) (**a**) things that one does not want any more; waste material: *household rubbish* ○ *The dustmen haven't collected the rubbish yet.* ○ *a 'rubbish dump/heap/tip* ○ *a 'rubbish bin.* (**b**) worthless or poor quality material: *The film is (a load of) rubbish.* **2** (*infml*) foolish talk, ideas, etc; nonsense: *Rubbish! You're not fat!* ○ *Don't talk rubbish!* ○ *You don't believe all that rubbish, do you?*
► **rubbish** *v* (*infml*) to criticize sb/sth severely or treat them as worthless: [Vn] *The film was rubbished by the critics.* ○ *He rubbished all my ideas, saying they were impractical.*
rubbishy *adj* (*infml*) of very poor quality: *rubbishy TV serials.*

rubble /'rʌbl/ *n* [U] bits of broken stone, rock or bricks, esp from a building that has been damaged or destroyed: *a road built on a foundation of rubble* ○ *dig people out of the rubble* ○ *The building was reduced to (a pile of) rubble by the explosion.*

rubella /ruː'belə/ *n* [U] (*medical*) = GERMAN MEASLES.

Rubicon /'ruːbɪkən; *US* -kɒn/ *n* **IDM** **cross the Rubicon** ⇨ CROSS².

rubicund /'ruːbɪkənd/ *adj* (*fml*) (of a person's face) having a healthy red colour: *rubicund complexion* ○ *a cheerful, rubicund policeman.*

ruble = ROUBLE.

rubric /'ruːbrɪk/ *n* [C] (*fml*) a title, an instruction or a rule printed in a document or book, usu in a different style from the rest of the text.

ruby /'ruːbi/ *n* **1** [C] a dark red precious stone: *a ruby ring.* **2** [U] the colour of rubies; dark red: *ruby velvet* ○ *ruby red lips.*
■ **,ruby 'wedding** *n* the 40th anniversary of a wedding.

RUC /,ɑː juː 'siː/ *abbr* Royal Ulster Constabulary.

ruched /ruːʃt/ *adj* decorated with material, eg lace, which is drawn together in small folds: *a dress with ruched sleeves* ○ *ruched curtains/blinds.*

ruck¹ /rʌk/ *n* **1** [C] (*sport*) (in Rugby football) a loose SCRUM(1). **2** **the ruck** [sing] ordinary people or things: *He was eager to get out of the ruck and distinguish himself in some way.*

ruck² /rʌk/ *v* **PHR V** **ruck 'up** (of cloth) to form untidy folds: *Your dress has rucked up at the back.*

rucksack /'rʌksæk/ (*US* also **backpack**) *n* a bag carried on the back and attached by bands that go over the shoulders, used for carrying one's belongings while walking, climbing, etc. ⇨ picture at LUGGAGE. Compare HAVERSACK.

ruckus /'rʌkəs/ *n* (*pl* **ruckuses** /'rʌkəsɪz/) (usu *sing*) *infml esp US*) a noisy disturbance: *cause a ruckus.*

ructions /'rʌkʃnz/ *n* [pl] (*infml*) angry protests or arguments; trouble: *The affair has caused serious ructions within the Tory party.*

rudder /'rʌdə(r)/ *n* (**a**) VERTICAL piece of wood or metal at the back of a boat, used for steering. ⇨ picture at YACHT. (**b**) VERTICAL piece of metal at the

back of an aircraft, used for controlling its HORI-ZONTAL movement. ⇨ picture at AIRCRAFT.
▶ **rudderless** *adj* with no one in control and therefore not moving in a particular direction: *Without a firm leader, the government is rudderless.*

ruddy¹ /'rʌdi/ *adj* **1** (*approv*) (of a person's face) having a healthy red colour: *ruddy cheeks* ○ *a ruddy complexion.* **2** (*fml*) reddish: *a ruddy glow in the sky.*
▶ **ruddiness** *n* [U].

ruddy² /'rʌdi/ *adj* [attrib], *adv* (*dated Brit infml*) = BLOODY²: *He's a ruddy idiot.* ○ *She left a ruddy great* (ie very big) *pile of work for me to do.*

rude /ru:d/ *adj* (**-r, -st**) **1** (of people or their behaviour) showing no respect or consideration; not polite: *a rude remark* ○ *It's rude to interrupt when somebody is speaking.* ○ *She was rude to me (about my cooking).* ○ *It was rude of them not to phone and say they would be late.* **2** concerned with sex in a way that may embarrass or offend people: *a rather rude joke* ○ *rude words.* **3** [attrib] sudden, unpleasant and unexpected: *The news that he was to lose his job came as a rude shock.* ○ *If you think it's going to be easy finding a flat, you're in for* **a rude awakening.** **4** [attrib] (*dated or fml*) simple and roughly made; primitive: *a rude shelter of branches and leaves.* **IDM** **in rude 'health** (*dated*) in very good health.
▶ **rudely** *adv* **1** in a way that is not polite: *She rudely ignored me.* **2** in a sudden unpleasant way: *The tranquillity was rudely interrupted by a loud ring on the doorbell.* **3** in a primitive way: *a rudely-constructed wooden hut.*
rudeness *n* [U]: *She was offended by his rudeness.*

rudiments /'ru:dɪmənts/ *n* [pl] **the ~s** (**of sth**) the most basic and essential facts or principles of a subject: *learn/grasp the rudiments of economics.*
▶ **rudimentary** /ˌru:dɪ'mentri/ *adj* **1** dealing with simple or basic matters, ideas, etc: *He received only a rudimentary education.* ○ *I have only a rudimentary understanding/knowledge of Latin.* **2** basic and not properly developed: *a village with rudimentary sanitation* ○ *Some dinosaurs had only rudimentary teeth.*

rue /ru:/ *v* (*pres p* **rueing** or **ruing**; *pt, pp* **rued**) (*dated or fml*) to regret sth because it has bad results: [Vn] *He rued the day he had joined the army.*
▶ **rueful** /'ru:fl/ *adj* showing sadness or regret: *give a rueful smile/grin.* **ruefully** /'ru:fəli/ *adv*: *John ruefully admitted his mistake.* ○ *She quitted ruefully.*

ruff /rʌf/ *n* **1** a ring of differently coloured or marked feathers or fur round the neck of a bird or an animal. **2** a wide stiff FRILL worn as a collar, esp in the 16th century.

ruffian /'rʌfiən/ *n* (*dated*) a violent man, esp one involved in crime: *a gang of ruffians.*

ruffle /'rʌfl/ *v* **1 ~ sth (up)** to disturb the smooth surface of sth: [Vn] *a breeze ruffling the calm surface of the lake* ○ *ruffled sheets* ○ *Don't ruffle my hair, I've just combed it.* [Vnp] *The bird ruffled up its feathers.* **2** (esp passive) to make sb annoyed, worried or confused: [Vn] *She was obviously ruffled by the question.* ○ *He never gets ruffled, even under pressure.* **IDM** **ruffle sb's 'feathers** (*infml*) to upset or annoy sb. **smooth sb's ruffled feathers** ⇨ SMOOTH².
▶ **ruffle** *n* a strip of material gathered in a number of small folds and used to decorate the edge of a garment, esp at the wrist or neck.

rug /rʌg/ *n* **1** a piece of thick, usu woollen, material that covers part of a floor: *a rug in front of the fire* ○ *a hearth rug.* **2** (*Brit*) a piece of thick warm material used as covering for the legs, etc: *a 'travelling-rug.* **IDM** **pull the rug from under sb's feet** ⇨ PULL¹. **snug as a bug in a rug** ⇨ SNUG.

Rugby /'rʌgbi/ (also **Rugby 'football**) *n* [U] a form of football played with an OVAL ball which may be kicked or carried: *a Rugby ball/club/match/player.* ⇨ picture.

goalposts — **Rugby**
try line
Rugby ball

■ **Rugby 'League** *n* [U] a professional form of Rugby, with 13 players in a team.
Rugby 'Union (also *infml esp Brit* **rugger**) *n* [U] an AMATEUR(1) form of Rugby, with 15 players in a team.

rugged /'rʌgɪd/ *adj* **1** rough and UNEVEN(1), with many rocks: *a rugged coastline* ○ *rugged country/scenery/mountains.* **2** (*esp approv*) (of a man) having strong features: *a rugged face* ○ *his rugged good looks.* **3** strong and not easily broken; designed to be used in severe conditions, bad weather, etc: *a rugged vehicle.* **4** (of a person) tough and determined but perhaps not showing good manners: *a rugged individualist.* ▶ **ruggedly** *adv*: *ruggedly handsome.* **ruggedness** *n* [U].

rugger /'rʌgə(r)/ *n* [U] (*infml esp Brit*) Rugby Union football.

ruin /'ru:ɪn/ *v* **1** to severely damage or spoil sth: [Vn] *The crops were ruined by the late frost.* ○ *The island has been ruined by tourism.* ○ *It poured with rain and my shoes got/were ruined.* ○ *The mistake ruined his chances of ever becoming President.* **2** to make sb lose all their money, their position, etc: [Vn] *If she loses the court case it will ruin her.* ○ *a ruined man.*
▶ **ruin** *n* **1** [U] the state or process of being severely damaged or destroyed: *a city reduced to a state of ruin by war* ○ *The house has fallen into ruin through years of neglect.* **2** [U] (**a**) the complete loss of all one's money, one's position, etc: *face financial ruin* ○ *The government's failure to act on this matter led ultimately to its ruin.* (**b**) the cause of this: *Gambling was his ruin.* **3** [C often *pl*] the parts of a building or town that remain after it has fallen down or been destroyed: *the ruins of the castle* ○ *the ancient ruins of Pompeii* ○ *The abbey is now a ruin.* **IDM** **go to rack and ruin** ⇨ RACK³. **in 'ruins** severely damaged or destroyed: *An earthquake left the whole town in ruins.* ○ *His career/reputation is/lies in ruins.* ○ *Their economic policy is in ruins.*
ruination /ˌru:ɪ'neɪʃn/ *n* [U] the action or process of ruining sth or of being ruined: *the ruination of the countryside.*
ruined *adj* (of a building, town, etc) with only some parts remaining because it has been partially destroyed, allowed to fall down, etc: *a ruined church/city.*
ruinous /'ru:ɪnəs/ *adj* **1** costing far more money than one can afford to spend: *ruinous expenditure.* **2** leading to ruin: *the ruinous effects of the strike.* **3** (*fml*) in ruins: *ruinous castles.* **ruinously** *adv*: *ruinously expensive court case.*

rule /ru:l/ *n* **1** [C] a statement of what can, should or must be done in particular circumstances or when playing a game: *the rules of football* ○ *observe/obey/follow the rules* ○ *draw up a set of* **rules and regulations** ○ *It is a school rule that someone must be on duty at all times.* ○ *He has* **broken the rules** *and will have to be disqualified.* ○ *Don't get annoyed with me — I don't make the rules!* See also GROUND RULE. **2** [C usu *sing*] a usual practice or habit; the normal state of things: *He makes it a rule never to borrow money.* ○

R

Cold winters here are the exception rather than the rule (ie are rare). ○ *As a (general) rule I'm home by six.* **3** [U] authority; government: *democratic/majority rule* ○ *a long spell of Republican rule* ○ *a country formerly under French rule* ○ *mob rule* (ie the state that exists when a violent crowd takes control). See also HOME RULE. **4** [C] a straight measuring device used by carpenters, etc. See also SLIDE-RULE. **5** [C] a straight line drawn by hand or printed. **IDM** bend/stretch the 'rules to change or interpret the rules, laws, etc in a way that suits a particular situation. **the exception proves the rule** ⇨ EXCEPTION. **the rule of 'law** the condition in which every member of society, including its rulers, accepts the authority of the law: *The hallmark of his tyranny was a complete disregard for the rule of law.* **a rule of 'thumb** a rough practical method of assessing or measuring sth, usu based on past experience rather than on exact measurement, etc and therefore not completely reliable in every case or in every detail: *As a rule of thumb, you should cook a chicken for 20 minutes for each pound that it weighs.* **work to 'rule** to follow the rules of one's occupation in an excessively strict way in order to cause delay, as a form of industrial protest. See also WORK-TO-RULE.

▸ **rule** *v* **1** ~ **(over sb/sth)** to govern sb/sth; have authority over sb/sth: [Vpr] *She once ruled over a vast empire.* [V, Vn] *Charles I ruled (England) for eleven years.* **2** (usu passive) to have power or influence over sb, sb's feelings, etc: [Vn] *Don't allow yourself to be ruled by your emotions.* ○ *She let her heart rule her head* (ie acted according to her emotions, rather than logical thoughts). **3** to give an official decision: [Vpr] *The judge ruled in favour of/against the plaintiff.* [V.that, Vn-adj] *The chairman ruled that the question was out of order/ruled the speaker out of order.* [V.n to inf] *The court ruled the action to be illegal.* **4** to draw a line using a ruler(2), etc: [Vn] *Do you want ruled paper* (ie with parallel lines printed on it) *or plain?* **IDM** **rule the 'roost** to be the dominant person in a group. **rule (sb/sth) with a rod of 'iron** to govern a group of people, a country, etc very harshly. **PHRV** ,rule sth 'off to separate sth from the next section of writing by drawing a line below it. ,rule sb/sth 'out (as sth) to exclude sb/sth: *That possibility can't be ruled out altogether* (ie It must continue to be considered). ○ *His age effectively ruled him out as a possible candidate.*

rulebook /'ruːlbʊk/ *n* the written set of rules governing a game or particular circumstances: *There's nothing in the rulebook to say you can't play in jeans if you want to.*

ruler /'ruːlə(r)/ *n* **1** a person who rules or governs: *the country's military rulers.* **2** a straight strip of wood, plastic, metal, etc used for measuring or for drawing straight lines.

ruling /'ruːlɪŋ/ *adj* [attrib] that rules; dominant: *the ruling class/party/body.*
▸ **ruling** *n* an official decision: *appeal against/dispute the court's ruling* ○ *When will the committee give/make its ruling?*

rum[1] /rʌm/ *n* [U, C] a strong alcoholic drink made from the juice of sugar-cane (SUGAR).

rum[2] /rʌm/ *adj* (*dated Brit infml*) odd; PECULIAR(1): *He's a rum character.*

rumba /'rʌmbə/ *n* a lively dance that originated in Cuba: *dance/do the rumba.*

rumble[1] /'rʌmbl/ *v* (**a**) to make a deep low continuous sound: [V] *thunder rumbling in the distance* ○ *I'm so hungry that my stomach's rumbling.* (**b**) to move in the specified direction making such a sound: [Vpr] *tanks rumbling through the streets* [Vp] (*fig*) *Discussions rumble on over the siting of the new airport.* [also Vadv].

▸ **rumble** *n* **1** [U, C usu *sing*] a rumbling sound: *the low rumble of surf/gunfire* ○ *There was a rumble of approval from the government benches.* **2** [C] (*US sl*) a street fight between gangs.

rumbling *n* **1** a deep low continuous sound: *the rumbling of the volcano.* **2** (esp *pl*) (**a**) signs that people are not satisfied with sth: *rumblings of discontent/unease in the coal industry.* (**b**) a rumour: *takeover rumblings.*
■ **'rumble strip** *n* (*infml*) any of a series of rough strips across a road, eg before a ROUNDABOUT[2](1). The noise made when a vehicle drives over them is intended to make the driver go more slowly.

rumble[2] /'rʌmbl/ *v* (*Brit sl*) to realize the true character of sb/sth: [Vn, V.wh] *He looks suspicious — do you think he's rumbled us/what we're up to?*

rumbustious /rʌm'bʌstʃəs/ (also *esp US* **rambunctious**) *adj* (*infml*) cheerful in a lively noisy way; BOISTEROUS(1).

ruminant /'ruːmɪnənt/ *n, adj* (an animal) of the type that brings back food from its stomach and chews it again: *Cows and sheep are ruminants.*

ruminate /'ruːmɪneɪt/ *v* ~ **(about/on/over sth)** to think deeply: [Vpr] *sit ruminating on recent events* [also V].
▸ **rumination** /ˌruːmɪ'neɪʃn/ *n* [U].
ruminative /'ruːmɪnətɪv; *US* -neɪtɪv/ *adj* tending to ruminate; thoughtful: *in a ruminative mood.* **ruminatively** *adv.*

rummage /'rʌmɪdʒ/ *v* ~ **(among/in/through sth) (for sth);** ~ **(about/around)** to turn things over and esp make them untidy while searching for sth: [Vp] *rummage around in the attic* [Vpr] *The doctor rummaged in his bag for a stethoscope.*
▸ **rummage** *n* [*sing*] an act of rummaging: *have a good rummage around.*
■ **'rummage sale** *n* [*sing*] (*US*) = JUMBLE SALE.

rummy /'rʌmi/ *n* [U] a simple card-game in which players try to form sets or sequences of cards.

rumour (*US* **rumor**) /'ruːmə(r)/ *n* (**a**) [C] a story that is spread by being talked about but may not be true: *The rumour began with an anonymous telephone call to a newspaper.* ○ *There's a nasty rumour going round/circulating/spreading about your father.* ○ *Oh yes, I did hear a vague rumour that he was leaving.* ○ *There are strong/persistent rumours of an impending merger.* (**b**) [U] information spread like this: *Many of the stories were based on rumour and gossip.* ○ *Rumour has it* (ie People say) *that he was murdered.*

▸ **rumoured** (*US* **rumored**) *adj* reported as a rumour: *They bought the house at a rumoured price of £600 000.* ○ *It's widely rumoured that she's going to resign.* ○ *She is rumoured to be on the point of resigning.*

rump /rʌmp/ *n* **1** [C] (**a**) an animal's buttocks (BUTTOCK): *He slapped the horse on the rump.* (**b**) (*joc*) a person's bottom. **2** (also ,rump 'steak) [C, U] a piece of BEEF(1) cut from near the rump. **3** [C] (*derog*) a small or unimportant part left from a larger group: *The election reduced the party to a rump.*

rumple /'rʌmpl/ *v* to make sth untidy or creased (CREASE *v* 1): [Vn] *The bed was rumpled where he had slept.* ○ *She rumpled his hair playfully.* Compare CRUMPLE 1.

rumpus /'rʌmpəs/ *n* (usu *sing*) a disturbance; noise; UPROAR(1): *kick up/make/cause/create a rumpus.*
■ **'rumpus room** *n* (*US dated*) a room in a private house used esp for games, parties, etc.

run[1] /rʌn/ *v* (**-nn-**; *pt* **ran** /ræn/; *pp* **run**) **1** to move at a speed faster than a walk, never having both or all the feet on the ground at the same time: [V] *He cannot run because he has a weak heart.* ○ *They turned and ran when they saw us coming.* ○ *Can you run as fast as Mike?* [V.to inf] *She ran/came running to meet us.* ○ *I had to run to catch the bus.* [Vp] *She* *ran out to see what was happening.* ○ *The dogs ran off as soon as we appeared.* [Vadv] *He ran home in tears to his mother.* ⇨ note. **2(a)** to cover the specified distance by running: [Vn] *Who was the first man to run a mile in under four minutes?* See also RUN A MILE (MILE). **(b)** to practise running as a sport: [V] *You're very unfit; you ought to take up running.* ○ *She used to run when she was at college.* **(c)** ~ (**in sth**) to take part or compete in a running race: [V, Vpr] *Christie will be running (in the 100 metres) tonight.* [Vn] *run the marathon* ○ *Lewis ran a fine race to take the gold medal.* **(d)** (esp passive) to cause a race to take place: [Vn] *The Derby will be run in spite of the bad weather.* See also RUNNER 1. **3** to go quickly or hurry from one place to another within an area: [Vp, Vpr] *I've been running around (town) all morning buying Christmas presents.* **4(a)** (of buses, trains, etc) to travel backwards and forwards on a particular route: [V] *Buses to Oxford run every half hour.* ○ *The ferries don't run on Christmas Day.* [Vpr] *Trains run between London and Brighton throughout the day.* **(b)** to put buses, trains, etc in service: [Vn] *London Transport run extra trains during the rush hour.* **5** to drive sb to a place in a car: [Vnpr] *Can I run you to the station?* [also Vnp, Vnadv]. **6** to move forward smoothly or easily, esp on wheels: [Vpr] *Trains run on rails.* ○ *Sledges run well over frozen snow.* **7(a)** to move, esp quickly, in the specified direction: [Vpr] *The van ran down the hill out of control.* ○ *The car ran off the road into a ditch.* ○ *A shiver ran down my spine.* **(b)** to cause sth to move in the specified direction: [Vnpr] *She ran her fingers nervously through her hair.* ○ *I ran my eyes over the page.* **8** (of a ship or its crew) to sail or steer to the specified place: [Vadv] *We/The ship ran aground.* [also Vpr]. **9(a)** to extend in the specified direction: [Vpr] *A fence runs round the whole field.* ○ *He has a scar running across his left cheek.* [V-adj] *The road runs parallel to the railway.* **(b)** to make sth extend in the specified direction: [Vnpr] *We ran a cable from the lights to the stage.* **10(a)** ~ (**for sth**) to continue for the specified period of time without stopping: [Vpr] *Her last musical ran (ie was performed regularly) for six months on Broadway.* ○ *Election campaigns in Britain run for three weeks.* [V] *The critics predict this play will run and run!* **(b)** to operate or be valid for the specified period of time: [Vn] *The lease on my house has only a year to run.* [also Vpr]. **11** to bring or take sth into a country illegally and secretly: [Vnpr] *He used to run guns across the border.* See also RUNNER 2. ⇨ note at SMUGGLE. **12** (of a story, an argument, etc) to have the specified words, contents, etc: [V] *She poisoned her husband, or so the story runs.* [V.speech] *'Ten shot dead by gunmen,' ran the newspaper headline.* **13(a)** (of a liquid) to flow: [Vpr] *The River Rhine runs into the North Sea.* ○ *The tears ran down her cheeks.* ○ *Water was running all over the bathroom floor.* [Vn] ~ **sth** (**for sb**) to cause a liquid to flow: [Vnpr] *She ran hot water into the bowl.* [Vn] *run the hot tap* [Vnn, Vnpr] *Could you run me a hot bath/run a hot bath for me?* **(c)** (of a tap, etc) to send out a liquid: [V] *Who left the tap running?* ○ *Your nose is running* (ie MUCUS is flowing from it). ○ *The smoke makes my eyes run.* ⇨ note at DRIP¹. **(d)** (*techn* or *fml*) (of the sea, the tide, a river, etc) to rise higher or flow more quickly: [V-adj] *The tide was running strong.* [also V]. **(e)** ~ **with sth** (usu in the continuous tenses) to be covered with a flowing liquid: *His face was running with sweat.* ○ *The bathroom floor is running with water.* **14(a)** (of dye or colour in a piece of clothing) to dissolve and spread: [V] *I'm afraid the colour ran when I washed your new skirt.* **(b)** (of a solid substance) to melt: [V] *It was so hot that the butter ran.* ○ *The wax began to run.* [Vpr] (*fig*) *The tears blurred his eyes and the words of her letter*

began to run into one another. See also RUNNY 2. **15(a)** to pass into or reach the specified state; to become: [V-adj] *The river ran dry* (ie stopped flowing) *during the drought.* ○ *Supplies are running short/low.* ○ *We've run short of milk.* ○ *You've got your rivals running scared.* **(b)** ~ **at sth** (used esp in the continuous tenses) to be at or near the specified level: [Vpr] *Inflation was now running at 26 per cent.* ○ *Sales are running at barely half their 1992 level.* **16(a)** to be in charge of sth; to manage sth: [Vn] *run a hotel/a shop/a language school* ○ *He has no idea how to run a successful business.* ○ *Stop trying to run my life for me!* ○ *The shareholders want to have more say in how the company is run.* ○ *a badly-run company.* See also RUNNING 2. **(b)** to own and use a vehicle or a machine: [Vn] *I can't afford to run a car on my salary.* **17** to make a service, course of study, etc available to people; to organize sth: [Vn] *The college runs summer courses for foreign learners of English.* **18(a)** to operate or function: [V] *Stan had the chain-saw running.* [Vpr] *Our van runs on* (ie uses) *diesel.* [Vadv] (*fig*) *Her life has run smoothly up to now.* **(b)** (esp in the continuous tenses) (of an event, a train, etc) to happen, arrive, etc at the specified time: [V-adj] *The trains are running late.* [V-n, Vpr] *I'm afraid programmes are running (a few minutes) behind schedule this evening.* [Vadv] *The murderer was given three life sentences, to run concurrently.* **(c)** to carry out a test over a period of time: [Vn] *The consultant decided to run some more tests on the blood samples.* **19** to make sth operate or function: [Vn] *Could you run the engine for a moment?* ○ *Can you run this program on the computer for me?* [Vnpr] *I can run my electric razor off* (ie with power from) *the mains.* **20** ~ (**for sb/sth**); ~ (**in sth**) to be a candidate in an election for a political position; to stand¹(14): [V] *Reagan ran a second time in 1980.* [Vpr] *How many candidates are running for the Presidency/in the Presidential election?* **21** (of a newspaper or magazine) to print and publish sth as an item or a story: [Vn] *The Guardian is running a series of articles on the Russian economy.* **22** (*esp US*) (of a woven or knitted piece of clothing) to LADDER(a): [V] *Nylon tights sometimes run.* **IDM** Most idioms containing **run** are at the entries for the nouns or adjectives in the idioms, eg **run riot** ⇨ RIOT. **come ˈrunning** to be eager to do what sb wants: *She knew she only had to telephone and he would come running.* **ˈrun for it** (esp imperative) to run in order to escape from sb/sth: *Here come the police — run for it!* **PHRV ˈrun across sb/sth** to meet sb or find sth by chance: *I ran across my old friend Jean in Paris last week.*

ˌrun **ˈafter sb** (no passive) **1** to run to try to catch sb; to chase sb: *The dog was running after a rabbit.* **2** (*infml*) to seek sb's company in order to have a romantic or sexual relationship with them: *She runs after every good-looking man she meets.*

ˌrun **aˈlong** (*infml*) (used in the imperative to tell sb, esp a child, to go away): *Run along now, children, I'm busy.*

ˈrun **at sb** (no passive) to run towards sb to attack or as if to attack them: *He ran at me with a knife.*

ˌrun **aˈway (from sb/...)** to leave sb/a place suddenly; to escape from sb/a place: *Louise had a sudden urge to throw her homework at the teacher and run away.* ○ *He ran away from home at the age of thirteen.* See also RUNAWAY. ˌrun **aˈway from sth** to try to avoid sth because one is shy, lacking in confidence, etc: *run away from a difficult situation* ○ *Her suicide bid was an attempt to run away from reality.* ˌrun **aˈway with one** (of a feeling) to gain complete control of one; to dominate one: *Her imagination tends to run away with her.* ˌrun **aˈway with sb; run aˈway (together)** (also *infml* ˌrun **ˈoff with sb,** ˌrun **ˈoff (together)**) to leave home, one's husband etc with sb, in order to have a relationship

---

R

with or marry them: *She ran away with her boss/ She and her boss ran away (together).* ,**run a**'**way with sth** to win sth clearly or easily: *The champion ran away with the match.*

,**run sth** '**back** to wind a tape, VIDEO(2c), etc back to an earlier point in order to see or hear it again.

,**run sth** '**by/**'**past sb** (*infml esp US*) to show sb sth or tell sb about an idea, a proposal, etc in order to get their reaction to it. ,**run back** '**over sth** to discuss or consider sth again; to REVIEW(1) sth: *I'll run back over the procedure once again.*

,**run (sth)** '**down 1** to lose power or stop functioning; to make sth do this: *My car battery has run down; it needs recharging.* ○ *If you leave your headlights on you'll soon run down the battery.* **2** (often in the continuous tenses) to stop functioning gradually or become smaller in size or number; to make sth do this: *British manufacturing industry has been running down for years.* ○ *The local steelworks is being run down and is likely to close within three years.* ○ *The company is running down its sales force.* See also RUN-DOWN. ,**run sb/sth** '**down 1** (esp of a vehicle or its driver) to hit sb/sth and knock them/it to the ground: *The cyclist was run down by a car/motorist.* **2** to criticize sb/sth in an unkind way: *He's always running down his wife's cooking in public.* **3** (*esp Brit*) to find sth/sb after looking for it/them for a long time: *I finally ran the book down in the university library.*

,**run sb** '**in** (*infml*) to arrest sb and take them to a police station: *He was run in for drunk and disorderly behaviour.* ,**run sth** '**in** (*Brit*) to prepare the engine of a new car for normal use by driving slowly and carefully: *Don't drive your new car too fast until you've run it in.*

,**run** '**into sb** to meet sb by chance: *Guess who I ran into today?* ○ *I ran into an old schoolfriend at the supermarket this morning.* '**run into sth 1** to meet or enter an area of bad weather while travelling: *We ran into a patch of thick fog just outside Naples.* **2** to experience difficulties, problems, etc: *The project is running into financial difficulties.* ○ *run into debt/ danger/trouble.* **3** (no passive) to reach the specified level or amount of sth: *Her income runs into six figures* (ie is more than £100 000 or $100 000). ○ *The publishers are hoping the book will run into a second edition.* '**run (sth) into sb/sth** to crash into sb/sth or make a vehicle do this: *The bus went out of control and ran into a shop front.* ○ *She ran* (ie drove) *her car into a tree while reversing.*

,**run (sth)** '**off 1** (*Brit*) (of a liquid) to drain or flow out of a container. **2** to make a liquid do this. ,**run sth** '**off 1** to copy or reproduce sth on a machine: *Could you run (me) off twenty copies of the agenda?* **2** to cause a race to be run: *The heats of the 200 metres will be run off tomorrow.* See also RUN-OFF. ,**run** '**off with sth (together)** (*infml*) = RUN AWAY WITH SB. ,**run** '**off with sth** to steal sth and take it away: *The treasurer has run off with the club's funds.*

,**run** '**on** to continue without stopping; to go on longer than is necessary or expected: *The meeting will finish promptly — I don't want it to run on.* '**run on sth** (no passive) (of thoughts, a discussion, etc) to have sth as a subject; to be concerned with sth: *His thoughts kept running on what her remarks could have meant.*

,**run** '**out** (of an agreement, a document, etc) to become no longer valid: *The lease on our apartment runs out in a few months.* ○ *My visa has run out.* ,**run** '**out (of sth)** (of a supply of sth) to be used up or finished; (of a person) to use up or finish a supply of sth: *Our fuel ran out/We ran out of fuel.* ○ *Time is running out for the trapped miners.* ○ *Could I have a cigarette? I seem to have run out.* ,**run** '**out on sb** (*infml*) to abandon sb, esp when they particularly need one's help: *He ran out on her when she became*

pregnant. ,**run sb** '**out** (often passive) (in cricket) to dismiss a batsman who is trying to make a run²(9) by hitting the WICKET(1a) with the ball before the batsman has reached the CREASE(3).

,**run** '**over** (of a container or its contents) to OVERFLOW(1): *The bath (water) is running over.* ,**run** '**over sb**; ,**run sb** '**over** (of a vehicle or its driver) to knock a person or an animal down and pass over their body or a part of it: *I ran over a cat last night.* ○ *Two children were run over by a speeding driver/a speeding vehicle and killed.* ,**run** '**over sth** to read through or practise sth quickly: *She ran over her notes before giving the lecture.* ○ *I always run over my lines before going on stage.*

,**run** '**through sth 1** (no passive) to pass quickly through sth: *An angry murmur ran through the crowd.* ○ *Thoughts of revenge kept running through his mind.* **2** (no passive) to be present in every part of sth: *A deep melancholy runs through her poetry.* ○ *There is a deep-seated conservatism running through our society.* **3** to discuss, examine or read sth quickly: *He ran through the names on the list.* **4** to repeat sth quickly or briefly: *And now we'll run through the main points of the news again.* ○ *Could we run through your proposals once again?* **5** to perform, act or REHEARSE(1) sth: *Could we run through Scene 3 again, please?* See also RUN-THROUGH. **6** to use up or spend money carelessly: *She ran through the entire estate within two years.*

'**run to sth** (no passive) **1** to extend to or reach the specified amount or size: *The book runs to nearly 800 pages.* **2** (of a person) to have enough money for sth; (of money) to be enough for sth: *We can't run to a new car.* ○ *Our funds won't run to a trip abroad this year.*

,**run** '**up** (of a person bowling in cricket, an ATHLETE (1), etc) to gather speed by running before releasing the ball, jumping, etc. See also RUN-UP. ,**run sth** '**up 1** to allow a bill, debt, etc to accumulate: *You'll run up a big gas bill if you leave the heater on all the time.* **2** to make a piece of clothing quickly, esp by sewing: *run up a blouse/dress/skirt.* **3** to raise sth, esp a flag: *run up the Union Jack.* ,**run** '**up against sth** to meet or experience a difficulty, problem, etc: *The government is running up against considerable opposition to its privatization plans.*

■ '**run-around** *n* (*infml*) **IDM** give sb the '**run-around** to treat sb badly by not giving them the help or information they need or by deceiving them: *My lawyer's never available when I ring — I think he's giving me the run-around.*

'**run-down** *n* (usu *sing*) **1** an act of reducing the size of an industry, a company, etc: *the government's gradual run-down of the coal industry.* **2** ~ (**of/on sth**) (*infml*) a detailed analysis or description (of sth): *give sb/get a run-down on sth* ○ *I want a complete run-down on the situation.*

,**run-**'**down** *adj* **1** in bad condition; neglected (NEGLECT); DILAPIDATED: *a ,run-down* '*area/*'*town/* '*industry* ○ *The whole city is in a very run-down state.* **2** tired and slightly ill, esp from working hard: *be/ feel/get run-down* ○ *You look pretty run-down. Why don't you take a few days off?*

'**run-in** *n* **1** ~ (**to sth**) a period of time leading to an event or the preparation for it: *during the run-in to the Christmas.* **2** ~ (**with sb**) a quarrel, disagreement or fight: *have a run-in with the police.*

'**run-off** *n* an extra vote or race held to decide the winner when an election or a race has ended in a tie¹(6): *a run-off ballot/election.*

'**run-through** *n* a practice or rehearsal (REHEARSE): *There will be a run-through of the whole play tonight.*

'**run-up** *n* **1** ~ (**to sth**) a period of time leading to an event: *during the run-up to Christmas.* **2** an act or a distance of running in order to gain speed before bowling, jumping, etc: *a fast/short run-up.*

***

R

NOTE Compare **run**, **trot**, **gallop**, **race** and **sprint**. When describing movement that is faster than walking, **run** is the most usual word. You **run** as a sport or when you are in a hurry: *I was late so I had to run for the train.* People **jog** when they run steadily and not very fast as a form of physical exercise: *She jogs every morning to keep fit.* **Trot** and **gallop** are mainly used to describe how horses run. **Trot** means to walk quite quickly with short steps: *The pony started to trot more steadily.* **Gallop** means to run fast: *A solitary horse galloped around the field.* **Race** suggests that you need to run fast, not always in a competition: *She raced to the window to stop the child from climbing out.* **Sprint** means to run as fast as possible over a short distance: *I sprinted across the square to the station.*

run² /rʌn/ *n* **1** [C] an act or a period of running on foot: *I go for a run every morning.* ○ *Catching sight of her, he* **broke into a run.** ○ *It started to rain heavily and we had to* **make a run for it.** **2** [C] an instance or a period of travelling by car, train, etc: *take the car out for a run in the country.* **3** [C] a route taken by vehicles, ships, etc: *This ferry operates on the Dover-Calais run.* **4** [C] a series of performances: *The play had a good run/a run of six months/a limited run.* ○ *It's just finished its run on Broadway.* ○ *France maintained their unbeaten run in the World Cup by beating Norway 1–0 last night.* See also DRY RUN, DUMMY RUN, TRIAL RUN. **5** [C] a period or succession; a spell³(1): *a run of bad luck* ○ *We've enjoyed an exceptional run of fine weather recently.* **6** [C usu *sing*] ~ **on sth** a sudden demand for sth by a lot of people: *a run on sterling following its rise in value against the dollar* ○ *When the new currency measures were announced, there was a* **run on the bank** (ie a sudden withdrawing of money by many customers). **7** [C] (often in compounds) an enclosed area in which domestic animals, birds, etc are kept: *a* 'chicken-run. **8** [C] a usu sloping track for a particular purpose, esp sport: *a* 'ski-run ○ *a to*'boggan run. **9** [C] a point scored in cricket or baseball: *He was in for 20 minutes before scoring his first run.* ○ *Our team won by 87 runs.* See also HOME RUN. **10** [sing] **the ~ of sth** the tendency or TREND of sth: *After 40 minutes Spurs scored, against the run of play* (ie although they had looked less likely to score than their opponents). ○ *The run of the cards favoured me* (ie I was dealt good cards). **11** [C] (*music*) a series of notes sung or played quickly up or down the scale. **12** [C] = LADDER 3: *get a run in one's tights.* **13 the runs** [pl] (*sl*) DIARRHOEA. **IDM at a** 'run running: *He started off at a run but soon tired and slowed to a walk.* **the common, general, ordinary, etc run (of sth)** the average type or class: *He was completely different from the normal run of people I knew.* **give sb a (good, etc) run for their** 'money to give sb challenging competition or opposition: *They may win the game, but we'll give them a good run for their money.* **give sb / get / have the** 'run of sth to give sb/get/have permission to make full use of sth: *He gave me the run of his library.* ○ *Her dogs have the run of the house.* **have a good, excellent, etc run for one's** 'money to get reward, interest, enjoyment, etc, esp in return for effort: *I don't mind retiring at 45; I've had an excellent run for my money* (ie a very satisfying career). **in the** 'long/'short run with regard to the far/near future: *Her present unpopularity is not going to help in the short run, of course, but in the longer run she may still be the best election hope for the Democrats.* **on the** 'run **1** trying to avoid being captured: *have/keep the enemy on the run* ○ *He's on the run from the police.* **2** (*infml*) continuously active and moving about: *I've been on the run all day and I'm exhausted.*
■ '**run-of-the-**'**mill** *adj* (*often derog*) not special; ordinary: *a* ˌrun-of-the-mill de'tective story.

runabout /ˈrʌnəbaʊt/ *n* (*infml*) a small light car, esp one for making short journeys in towns.

runaway /ˈrʌnəweɪ/ *adj* [attrib] **1** (of a person) having run away: *a hostel for runaway children.* **2** (of an animal or a vehicle) no longer under the control of its rider or driver: *a runaway horse/truck/train.* **3** happening very rapidly or easily: *the country's runaway inflation rate* ○ *a runaway victory/win* ○ *the* **runaway success** *of her last play.*
▶ **runaway** *n* a person who has run away: *her work with young runaways.*

rune /ruːn/ *n* **1** any of the letters in an ancient Germanic alphabet that was carved on wood or in stone. **2** a similar mark with a mysterious or magic meaning. ▶ **runic** *adj*: *runic signs.*

rung¹ *pp* of RING².

rung² /rʌŋ/ *n* **1** a piece of wood, etc forming a step in a ladder. ⇨ picture at LADDER. **2** a level or rank in society, one's career, an organization, etc: *start on the lowest/bottom rung of the salary scale* ○ *the first rung of the career/property ladder.*

runnel /ˈrʌnl/ *n* (*fml*) a small stream or channel: *The tears made runnels down her make-up.*

runner /ˈrʌnə(r)/ *n* **1** a person or an animal that runs, esp one taking part in a race: *a long-distance/cross-country/marathon runner* ○ *a list of runners and riders.* See also FRONT RUNNER. **2** (esp in compounds) a person who takes the specified goods illegally into or out of an area: 'gun-runners. **3** a strip of metal or wood on which sth slides or moves along: *sledge runners.* **4** a creeping plant stem that can put roots down: *strawberry runners.* **IDM do a** 'runner **(on sb)** (*Brit sl*) to leave or run away from sb in a hurry.
■ ˌrunner 'bean *n* (*Brit*) (also *esp US* ˌstring 'bean) (**a**) a type of climbing bean plant. (**b**) each of the long green pods (POD) growing from this, eaten as a vegetable.

runner-up /ˌrʌnər ˈʌp/ *n* (*pl* **runners-up** /ˌrʌnəz ˈʌp/) ~ **(to sb)** a person or team finishing second in a race or competition: *50 runners-up will each receive a £20 gift voucher.* ○ *They finished runners-up behind Sweden.*

running /ˈrʌnɪŋ/ *n* [U] **1** the action or sport of running: *take up running* ○ *running shoes.* **2** the activity of managing or operating sth: *the day-to-day running of a shop/business/country* ○ *the* **running costs** *of a car* (eg of fuel, repairs, insurance). **IDM in/out of the** 'running **(for sth)** (*infml*) having some/no chance of succeeding or achieving sth: *be in the running for a management post/a company car.* **make the** 'running (*Brit infml*) to set the speed at which sth is done; to take the lead in doing sth: *Mike is rather shy, so Sue had to make all the running in their relationship.*
▶ **running** *adj* **1** [pred] (following a number and a *n*) in succession; one after the other: *She has now won the championship three times running.* ○ *For the second day running, my car wouldn't start.* **2** [attrib] continuous; not interrupted: *The police were involved in a* **running battle** *with demonstrators.* **3** [attrib] (of water) (**a**) flowing: *I can hear running water.* (**b**) supplied through taps: *All the hotel's rooms have hot and cold running water.* **4** [attrib] (of sore areas on the body, etc) having liquid or PUS coming out: *an animal covered in* **running sores.** **IDM in running/working order** ⇨ ORDER¹. **(go and) take a running** 'jump (*dated sl*) (often imperative) go away: *He wanted to borrow money again, so I told him to go and take a running jump.*
■ ˌrunning 'commentary *n* a spoken description of events as they occur, esp by a person broadcasting on radio or television: *keep up/give a running commentary on the game.*
'**running mate** *n* (*politics esp US*) a candidate for a

supporting position in an election: *Bill Clinton's running mate, Al Gore.*

‚running re'pairs *n* [pl] minor repairs or replacement of parts.

‚running 'total *n* a total, eg of costs or expenses, which includes each new item as it occurs.

runny /'rʌni/ *adj* (*infml*) **1** (of the nose or eyes) producing a lot of liquid MUCUS, eg when one has a cold: *I've got a sore throat and a runny nose.* **2** (*sometimes derog*) more liquid than is usual or expected: *runny jam/sauce/cake-mixture* ○ *Omelettes should be runny* (ie not fully cooked) *in the middle.*

runt /rʌnt/ *n* **1** a small weak animal, esp the smallest and weakest of the young born from the same mother at the same time: *nine healthy piglets and one runt.* **2** (*derog*) a weak or unimportant person.

runway /'rʌnweɪ/ *n* a hard surface along which aircraft take off and land: *The plane taxied down the runway.*

rupee /ruː'piː/ *n* a unit of money in India, Pakistan and certain other countries.

rupture /'rʌptʃə(r)/ *n* **1** [C, U] (*fml*) (a) an ending of friendly relations: *deep ruptures within the party.* (b) a breaking away from sth: *a rupture with traditional ideas.* **2** [C] (*medical*) (a) an injury in which a part of the body breaks apart or bursts: *the rupture of a blood-vessel.* (b) a HERNIA in the stomach: (*infml*) *I nearly gave myself a rupture lifting that bookcase.*
▶ **rupture** *v* **1(a)** to burst or break an organ or a tissue, etc in the body; (of an organ, a tissue, etc) to burst or break: [Vn] *a ruptured appendix/spleen* [also V]. (b) ~ **oneself** to cause oneself to have a rupture(2b): [Vn] *He ruptured himself trying to lift a wardrobe.* **2** (*fml*) to cause a connection, union, etc to end: [Vn] *the risk of rupturing East-West relations.* **3** (of a container) to crack or break open; to cause a container to crack or break open: [Vn] *a ruptured fuel tank* [also V].

rural /'rʊərəl/ *adj* (usu attrib) of, in or suggesting the countryside or agriculture: *remote/isolated/rural areas* ○ *rural communities/bus services/MPs* ○ *life in rural Britain* ○ *a rural economy.* Compare RUSTIC 1, URBAN.

Ruritanian /ˌrʊərɪ'teɪnɪən/ *adj* like or full of romantic adventures.

ruse /ruːz/ *n* a deceitful way of doing sth or getting sth; a trick: *think up a ruse for getting into the cinema without paying.*

rush¹ /rʌʃ/ *v* **1(a)** to go or come with great speed: [V] *Don't rush: take your time.* [Vpr] *Water went rushing through the lock gates.* ○ *The children rushed out of school.* [Vp] *Don't rush away/off — I haven't finished.* [V.to inf] *People rushed to buy the shares.* (b) to transport or send sb/sth with great speed: [Vnpr] *Ambulances rushed the injured to hospital.* [Vnp] *Relief supplies were rushed in.* [Vnn] *Please rush me your current catalogue.* **2** ~ **(sb) (into sth / doing sth)** to act or make sb act without proper thought or consideration: [Vpr] *I'm afraid she rushed into marriage.* [Vnpr] *Don't let them rush you into signing the contract.* [Vn] *Don't rush me — I need time to think about it.* **3** to try to attack or capture sb/sth suddenly: [Vn] *rush the enemy's positions/defences* ○ *Fans rushed the stage after the concert.* **IDM** **rush/run sb off their feet** ⇨ FOOT¹. **PHRV** **‚rush sth 'out** to produce sth very quickly: *The editors rushed out a piece on the crash for the late news.* **‚rush sth 'through (sth)** to make sth become official policy, etc very quickly: *rush a bill through Parliament.*

rush² /rʌʃ/ *n* **1** [sing] a sudden rapid movement forward: *She made a rush for the door.* ○ *People were trampled in the headlong rush.* ○ *The tide comes in with a sudden rush here.* **2** [sing] a sudden increase of sth; a SURGE(2): *a rush of blood to the cheeks* ○ *a rush of adrenalin* ○ *work in a rush of enthusiasm* ○ *a*

rush of cold air. **3** [sing, U] (*infml*) a period of great activity or hurry: *I'm in a dreadful/mad rush so I can't stop.* ○ *I do my shopping in September to avoid the Christmas rush.* ○ *'I'll be with you in a minute.' 'Don't worry, there's no rush.'* ○ *a rush job* (ie one done as quickly or as soon as possible). **4** [C] ~ **on/ for sth** a sudden great demand for goods, etc: *The unexpected wet weather caused a rush on umbrellas.* **5 rushes** [pl] (*techn*) the first print of a cinema film before it is edited (EDIT 1b).
■ **'rush hour** *n* the time each day when roads are most full of traffic and trains and buses are most crowded because people are going to or coming from work: *the morning/evening rush hour* ○ *I got caught in the rush hour traffic.* ○ *I try to avoid the rush hour if I can.*

rush³ /rʌʃ/ *n* a plant that grows near water and has a long thin stem. These stems can be dried and used for making baskets, the seats of chairs, etc: *rush matting.*
▶ **rushy** *adj* full of rushes.

rusk /rʌsk/ *n* a hard crisp biscuit, esp one used for feeding babies.

russet /'rʌsɪt/ *adj* reddish-brown in colour: *the russet autumn leaves.*
▶ **russet** *n* **1** [C, U] a reddish-brown colour. **2** [C] a reddish-brown apple.

Russian /'rʌʃn/ *adj* of Russia, its culture, its language or its people: *Russian folklore/dancing.*
▶ **Russian** *n* **1** [C] a person from Russia or, loosely, the former USSR. **2** [U] the language of Russia and the official language of the former USSR.
◘ **‚Russian rou'lette** *n* [U] a dangerous game in which one shoots at one's own head a gun containing a bullet in only one of its chambers (CHAMBER 6), without knowing if it will fire or not: *play (at) Russian roulette.*

rust /rʌst/ *n* [U] **1** a reddish-brown substance that forms on iron or steel by the action of water and air: *patches of rust* ○ *The axle was badly corroded by/ with rust.* **2** a reddish-brown colour: *rust colour.*
▶ **rust** *v* to be affected with rust: [V] *old rusting farm implements* ○ *Brass doesn't rust.* [Vp] *The hinges had rusted away* (ie been destroyed by rust).
rusted *adj*: *The underneath of the car was badly rusted.*
rusty *adj* (**-ier, -iest**) **1** affected with rust: *rusty nails.* **2** (usu pred) (*infml*) of a poor quality or standard through lack of practice: *My German/ tennis/singing is pretty rusty.*

rustic /'rʌstɪk/ *adj* (usu attrib) **1** (*approv*) typical of the country or country people; simple and not refined: *rustic simplicity* ○ *the rustic charm of the village.* Compare RURAL. **2** made of rough wood; not neatly finished, polished, etc: *a rustic bench/bridge/ fence.*
▶ **rustic** *n* (*often derog*) a person from the countryside.

rustle /'rʌsl/ *v* **1** to make or cause sth to make a dry light sound like paper, leaves, etc moving or rubbing together: [V] *Her silk dress rustled as she moved.* ○ *the sound of the trees rustling in the breeze* [Vn] *I wish people wouldn't rustle their bags of popcorn during the movie.* **2** [Vn] (*US*) to steal cattle or horses. **PHRV** **‚rustle sth/sb 'up** (*infml*) to prepare or provide sth/sb, esp without much warning: *I can rustle up some eggs and bacon for you.* ○ *We managed to rustle up a few helpers to hand out leaflets.*
▶ **rustle** *n* [sing] a rustling sound: *hear a rustle in the bushes* ○ *the rustle of paper/leaves/silk.*

rustler /'rʌslə(r)/ *n* (*US*) a person who steals cattle or horses.

rustling /'rʌslɪŋ/ *n* **1** [C, U] a sound made by sth that rustles: *a rustling noise* ○ *mysterious rustlings at night* ○ *the rustling of sweet-papers/dry leaves.* **2** [U] the stealing of cattle or horses.

---

rustproof /ˈrʌstpruːf/ *adj* (of metal) treated to prevent rusting (RUST *v*).

rut¹ /rʌt/ *n* [C] **1** a deep track made by a wheel or wheels in soft ground: *The tractor ruts led to a farm gate.* **2** a fixed and boring way of life: *I feel as though I'm **stuck in a rut** — I need a new job.* ○ *It's easy to **get into a rut** unless you keep trying new things.*
▶ **rutted** *adj* marked with ruts: *a deeply rutted track.*

rut² /rʌt/ *n* (also **the rut**) [U] the time of the year when male animals, esp deer, are sexually excited and active: *Stags fight during the rut.* ▶ **rutting** *adj*: *rutting stags* ○ *the rutting season.*

rutabaga /ˌruːtəˈbeɪgə/ *n* [C, U] (*esp US*) = SWEDE. ⇨ picture at TURNIP.

ruthless /ˈruːθləs/ *adj* (of people or their behaviour) having or showing no pity or feeling for others; hard and cruel: *a ruthless dictator* ○ *be utterly ruthless in one's determination to succeed* ○ *The campaign was conducted with ruthless efficiency.* ▶ **ruthlessly** *adv*: *be ruthlessly efficient.* **ruthlessness** *n* [U].

-ry ⇨ -ERY.

rye /raɪ/ *n* [U] a plant grown for its grain, which is used for making flour or WHISKY, or as food for cattle: *rye bread* ○ *rye whisky* ○ *rye grass.* ⇨ picture at CEREAL.

R

Ss

S¹ (also **s**) /es/ *n* (*pl* **S's, s's** /'esɪz/) the 19th letter of the English alphabet: *'Say' begins with (an) 'S'.*
■ **'S-bend** *n* a bend in a road or pipe shaped like an S.

S² *abbr* **1** (*pl* **SS**) Saint: *SS Philip and James.* Compare ST. **2** (indicating size, esp on clothing) small. **3** (*US* also **So**) south; southern: *S Yorkshire.*

s *abbr* (in former British currency) shilling(s).

SA *abbr* South Africa.

-s' /s, z, ɪz/ *suff* **1** (forming the end of a plural *n* to indicate that sth belongs to the people, animals or things mentioned): *the cats' tails* ○ *their wives' jobs.* **2** (sometimes forming the end of a singular *n* ending in *s*, to indicate possession): *Charles' room.* ⟹ App 3.

-'s¹ /s, z, ɪz/ *suff* **1(a)** (added to the end of a singular *n* to indicate that sth belongs to the person, animal, or thing mentioned): *the woman's hat* ○ *Peter's desk* ○ *the dog's paw* ○ *the book's cover.* **(b)** (used to refer to a particular shop or to sb's home): *I'll call at the chemist's* (ie the chemist's shop) *on the way home.* ○ *Shall we go round to David's* (ie David's house) *tonight?* ○ *I bought it at Lewis's.* **2** (added to the end of a plural *n* that does not end in *s* to indicate that sth belongs to the people, etc mentioned): *children's clothes* ○ *the women's quarters.* **3** (sometimes added to letters or numbers to form the plural): *in the 1990's* ○ *'Accommodation' has two c's and two m's.* ⟹ App 3.

-'s² /s, z/ *short form* (*infml*) **1** (used after *he, she* or *it* and *when, where, what, who* or *how*) is: *She's still in the bath.* ○ *What's he doing now?* ○ *It's time to go now.* **2** (used after *he, she* or *it* and *where, what, who* or *how*) has: *Who's taken my pen?* ○ *Where's he gone?* ○ *It's gone wrong again.* **3** (used after *let* when making a suggestion that includes oneself and others) us: *Let's go to the pub for lunch.* ⟹ App 3.

sabbath /'sæbəθ/ *n* (usu **the sabbath**) [sing] (*religion* or *fml*) the day of the week intended for rest and worship of God, Saturday for Jews and Sunday for Christians: *keep/break the Sabbath* (ie not work/ play on the Sabbath) ○ *the sabbath day.*

sabbatical /sə'bætɪkl/ *n* a period of time given at intervals for esp university teachers, for study, travel, etc: *take a year's sabbatical in Rome* ○ *be on sabbatical* ○ *a sabbatical term/year.*

sable /'seɪbl/ *n* [U] the fur of a small Arctic animal, used for making coats or artists' brushes: *a sable coat.*

sabotage /'sæbətɑːʒ/ *n* [U] damage done deliberately and secretly to transport, machinery, equipment, etc in order to prevent an enemy or a rival from succeeding or as a form of protest: *Investigators examining the wreckage of the aircraft have not ruled out sabotage.* ○ *economic/industrial sabotage.*
▶ **sabotage** *v* to damage, destroy or spoil sth deliberately and secretly: [Vn] *sabotage a missile/a telephone exchange* ○ *sabotage sb's plans/business* ○ *sabotage the chances of a diplomatic solution.*
saboteur /ˌsæbə'tɜː(r)/ *n* a person who commits sabotage.

sabre (*US* **saber**) /'seɪbə(r)/ *n* **1** a heavy sword with a curved blade. ⟹ picture at SWORD. **2** a light sword with a thin blade, used in fencing (FENCE² 1). Compare FOIL³.

■ **'sabre-rattling** *n* [U] attempts to frighten sb by threatening to attack or punish them: *The situation calls for calm discussion, not sabre-rattling.*
ˌ**sabre-toothed** *adj* having very long curved teeth.

sac /sæk/ *n* a part of an animal or plant shaped like a bag: *These toads have an inflatable sac on their throats.*

saccharin /'sækərɪn/ *n* [U] a very sweet substance sometimes used instead of sugar.
▶ **saccharine** /-riːn/ *adj* (*derog*) too sweet or sentimental: *saccharine music* ○ *a saccharine smile.*

sacerdotal /ˌsæsə'dəʊtl/ *adj* (*fml*) of a priest or priests.

sachet /'sæʃeɪ; *US* sæ'ʃeɪ/ *n* **1** a sealed plastic or paper packet containing a small amount of a product: *a sachet of sugar/sauce/shampoo.* **2** a small bag containing a sweet-smelling substance, placed among clothes, etc to give them a pleasant smell.

sack¹ /sæk/ *n* **1** [C] **(a)** a large bag made of strong material used for storing and carrying eg cement, coal or flour: *plastic rubbish sacks* ○ *The sack split and the rice poured out.* **(b)** this and its contents: *We get through a sack of potatoes every month.* **2** [C] (*US*) **(a)** any bag. **(b)** a bag and its contents: *a sack of candy* ○ *two sacks of groceries.* **3 the sack** [sing] (*infml esp US*) bed: *He caught them in the sack together.* **IDM** **hit the hay/sack** ⟹ HIT¹.
▶ **sackful** /-fʊl/ *n* (*pl* **-fuls**) the quantity held by a sack: *two sackfuls of flour.*
sacking *n* [U] rough cloth used for making sacks.
■ **'sack race** *n* a race in which competitors put both legs in a sack and move forward by jumping.

sack² /sæk/ *v* (*infml esp Brit*) to dismiss sb from a job; to fire²(3) sb: [Vn] *be sacked for incompetence.*
▶ **the sack** *n* [sing] an order to leave a job: *give sb/get the sack.*
sacking *n* an act of sacking sb or of being sacked: *Further sackings are expected.*

sack³ /sæk/ *v* [Vn] (esp formerly) to steal or destroy property in a captured town.
▶ **sack** *n* (usu **the sack**) [sing] the act or process of sacking a town: *the sack of Troy.*

sackcloth /'sækklɒθ/ *n* [U] rough cloth used for making sacks. **IDM** ˌ**sackcloth and 'ashes** signs that one is very sorry for sth: *Just because I was wrong she expects to see me in sackcloth and ashes.*

sacrament /'sækrəmənt/ *n* **1** [C] any of several rituals in the Roman Catholic, Anglican and other Christian Churches through which Christians believe they are specially blessed by God: *the sacrament of baptism.* **2 the 'sacrament** (also **the** ˌ**Holy 'Sacrament**) [sing] (in Christianity) the bread and wine of the Eucharist: *receive the sacrament.*
▶ **sacramental** /ˌsækrə'mentl/ *adj* [esp attrib] of or connected with the sacraments: *sacramental wine.*

sacred /'seɪkrɪd/ *adj* **1** connected with God or a god, or considered to be holy: *a sacred rite/place/ image* ○ *sacred buildings such as churches, mosques, temples and synagogues* ○ *sacred music* (ie for use in religious services) ○ *sacred writings* (eg the Koran or the Bible). **2** ~ (**to sb**) regarded with great respect: *Her marriage is sacred to her.* ○ *Sacred to the memory of...* (eg on a grave) ○ (*joc*) *They've changed the time of the news* — *nothing is sacred these days.* **3** (*fml*) (of an obligation, etc) regarded as important; solemn: *hold a promise sacred* ○ *regard sth*

---

as a sacred duty. ▶ **sacredness** *n* [U]. See also
SANCTITY.

■ ¡**sacred** ¡**cow** *n* (usu *sing*) (*derog*) an established
idea, institution, etc that many people treat with
more than reasonable respect by thinking that it
should not be changed or criticized: *This pricing
policy owes little to that sacred cow, the free market.*

sacrifice /ˈsækrɪfaɪs/ *n* **1(a)** [U] the action of giving up (GIVE¹) sth that one values for the sake of sth
more important or valuable: *The minister insisted
there had been no sacrifice of principles.* ∘ *He became
a top sportsman not without some sacrifice to himself*
(ie only by training very hard, giving up many
social activities, etc). **(b)** [C] a thing that one gives
up in this way: *financial sacrifices* ∘ *Her parents
made many **sacrifices** so that she could get a university education.* **2** ~ (**to sb**) **(a)** [U] the offering of
sth valuable to a god, often an animal killed in a
special ritual: *the sacrifice of an ox to Jupiter* ∘
human sacrifice. **(b)** [C] a thing offered in this way:
kill a sheep as a sacrifice.
▶ **sacrifice** *v* **1** ~ **sth** (**to/for sth**) to lose or give up
sth for the sake of sth more important or valuable:
[Vn] *soldiers who sacrificed their lives during the
fight for independence* [Vnpr] *The car's designers
have sacrificed comfort for greater economy* (ie have
made the car less comfortable in order to be able to sell
it at a lower price). ∘ *In her writing clarity is sometimes
sacrificed to brevity.* **2** ~ **to sb**; ~ **sth** (**to sb**) to make a
sacrifice(2) of sth to sb: [Vpr] *sacrificing to idols*
[Vn, Vnpr] *They sacrificed a lamb (to the gods).*
sacrificial /ˌsækrɪˈfɪʃl/ *adj* [usu attrib] of or like a
sacrifice: *sacrificial blood/offerings/victims* ∘ *the sacrificial cost of an undertaking.*

sacrilege /ˈsækrəlɪdʒ/ *n* [U,C usu *sing*] the action
of treating a sacred thing or place without respect:
(*fig*) *She regarded the damage done to the painting as
sacrilege.* ∘ *Blaring radios are a sacrilege in such a
secluded part of the countryside.* ▶ **sacrilegious**
/ˌsækrəˈlɪdʒəs/ *adj*: *Harming these animals is considered sacrilegious.*

sacristan /ˈsækrɪstən/ *n* a person who is responsible for the contents of a church and prepares the
ALTAR for services.

sacristy /ˈsækrɪsti/ *n* a room in a church where a
priest prepares for a service and where various
objects used in worship are kept.

sacrosanct /ˈsækrəʊsæŋkt/ *adj* (*often ironic*) too
important to be changed, disturbed or argued about:
*She'll work till late in the evening, but her weekends
are sacrosanct.*

sad /sæd/ *adj* (**-dder, -ddest**) **1** showing or causing
sorrow or regret; unhappy: *a sad look/event/story* ∘
John is sad because his dog has died. ∘ *I'm sad you're
leaving.* ∘ *It was a sad day for us all when the village
school closed down.* ∘ *Why is she looking so sad?* ∘ *It
is sad that he did not live to see his book published.*
∘ *The divorce left him **sadder but wiser**.* **2** [attrib]
deserving blame or criticism; bad: *a sad state of
affairs* ∘ *a sad case of cruelty* ∘ *It's a sad fact that
many of those who die in road accidents are under 25.*
3 worse than is deserved, so making one feel
pity or regret: *a sad fate* ∘ *This once beautiful ship is
in a sad condition now.* **IDM** **sad to ˈsay** (used esp at
the beginning of a sentence) unfortunately (UNFOR-
TUNATE): *Sad to say, the house has now been
demolished.*
▶ **sadden** /ˈsædn/ *v* (esp passive) to make sb feel
sad: [Vn.*to* inf] *It saddens me to see all their efforts
wasted.* [Vn] *We were all saddened by her death.*
sadly *adv* **1** unfortunately (UNFORTUNATE): *Sadly,
we have no more money.* ⇨ note at HOPEFUL. **2**
much; badly: *a sadly neglected garden* ∘ *They had
hoped to win and were sadly disappointed.* **3** in a sad
manner: *She looked at him sadly.*
sadness *n* **1** [U] the state of being sad: *The occa-*

sion was tinged with sadness. **2** [C usu *pl*] a thing
that makes one sad: *It was a great sadness to him
that he never had children.*

saddle /ˈsædl/ *n* **1** a seat, often made of leather, for
a rider on a horse, etc: *spend hours **in the saddle***
(ie riding a horse). ⇨ picture at BICYCLE. See also
SIDE-SADDLE. **2** a seat on a bicycle or motor cycle
(MOTOR): *sit on the saddle and lean forwards.* **3** a
joint of meat from the back of an animal: *a saddle of
lamb/venison.* **IDM** **in the ˈsaddle** in a position of
authority and control: *The director hopes to remain
in the saddle for a few more years yet.*
▶ **saddle** *v* ~ **up**; ~ **sth** (**up**) to put a saddle on a
horse: [Vp] *saddle up and ride off* [Vn, Vnp] *saddle
one's pony (up).* **PHRV** **ˈsaddle sb with sth** (esp
passive) to give sb an unpleasant responsibility,
task, etc: *be saddled with a large mortgage* ∘ *I've been
saddled with the job of organizing the conference.*
saddler /ˈsædlə(r)/ *n* a person who makes saddles
and leather goods for horses. **saddlery** /ˈsædləri/ *n*
[U] **(a)** goods made or sold by a saddler. **(b)** the art
of making these.
■ **ˈsaddle-bag** *n* **1** either of a pair of bags put over
the back of a horse, etc. **2** a bag attached to the back
of a bicycle saddle.
ˈsaddle-sore *adj* (of a rider) sore and stiff after
riding.

sadism /ˈseɪdɪzəm/ *n* [U] **(a)** enjoyment from watching or inflicting physical or mental suffering:
accusations of sadism in the treatment of prisoners.
(b) sexual pleasure obtained from this. Compare
MASOCHISM.
▶ **sadist** /ˈseɪdɪst/ a person who practises sadism.
sadistic /səˈdɪstɪk/ *adj*: *sadistic laughter* ∘ *take sadistic pleasure/delight in sth.*

sado-masochism /ˌseɪdəʊ ˈmæsəkɪzəm/ *n* [U] the
enjoyment of both inflicting and experiencing pain,
esp during sexual activity. ▶ **sado-masochist**
/ˌseɪdəʊ ˈmæsəkɪst/ *n.* **sado-masochistic** /ˌseɪdəʊ
ˌmæsəˈkɪstɪk/ *adj.*

sae /ˌes eɪ ˈiː/ *abbr* **1** self-addressed envelope. **2**
stamped addressed envelope: *enclose sae for reply.*

safari /səˈfɑːri/ *n* (*pl* **safaris**) [U,C] a trip to see or
hunt wild animals, esp in E Africa: *go/be on safari* ∘
return from (a) safari.
■ **saˈfari park** *n* a park in which wild animals move
around freely and are watched by visitors from
their cars.

safe¹ /seɪf/ *adj* (**-r, -st**) **1** [pred] ~ (**from sth/sb**)
protected from danger and harm; secure: *be safe
from attack/attackers* ∘ *You'll be safe here.* ∘ *Will the
car be safe outside?* ∘ *Your secret is safe with me.* ∘
*They enjoyed their vacation, **safe in the knowledge
that** friends were looking after the house.* **2** [pred]
not damaged, hurt, lost, etc: *The missing child was
found **safe and well/safe and sound**.* ∘ *She got
back safe from her adventure.* ∘ *The plane crashed
but the crew are safe.* **3** not likely to cause or lead to
damage, injury, loss, etc: *a safe car/speed/road* ∘
safer methods of testing drugs ∘ *Is that ladder safe?* ∘
It's not safe to go out alone at night. ∘ *Are the toys
safe for small children?* ∘ *a safe investment* (ie one
that will not lose money). **4** (of a place) providing
security or protection: *a safe haven for threatened
species* ∘ *Put the key in a safe place* (ie where it will
not be lost or stolen). **5(a)** [usu attrib] (of a person)
unlikely to do dangerous things; cautious: *a safe
driver/worker.* **(b)** (*often derog*) showing a cautious
attitude: *a safe choice* ∘ *They appointed a safe person
as the new manager* (eg one unlikely to make
changes, offend people, etc). ∘ *It would be safer to
allow an extra £20.* **6** based on good reasons or
evidence; reliable: *It's safe to assume that there
will always be a demand for new software.* ∘ *a safe
verdict.* **IDM** **better safe than sorry** ⇨ BETTER². **for**

safe 'keeping to be kept safely and protected from harm: *Before the game I gave my watch to my wife for safe keeping.* **in safe 'hands** protected by sb from harm: *I believed he was in safe hands — I wouldn't have left him otherwise.* **in (sb's) safe 'keeping** being kept safely and protected from harm by sb: *Can I leave the children in your safe keeping?* **on the 'safe side** taking no risks: *Although the sun was shining, I took an umbrella (just) to be on the safe side.* **play (it) 'safe** to avoid risks: *The roads might be busy, so we'd better play safe and catch the earlier bus.* **(as) 'safe as 'houses** very safe: *Don't worry, their jobs are safe as houses.* **a 'safe 'bet** a thing that is certain to happen or be suitable: *A black dress is always a safe bet.* ○ *It's a safe bet that the problem will get worse.*

▶ **safely** *adv* **1(a)** without being damaged, hurt or lost: *They arrived home safely.* **(b)** so as not to cause harm: *Drive safely!* ○ *Broken bottles should be safely disposed of.* **(c)** so as to be protected from harm: *The original disks are locked away safely.* **2** without any possibility of being wrong: *We can safely say/assume that he will accept the job.* **3** without any harm or problems being caused as a result: *These recommendations can safely be ignored.* **4** with no possibility of change or of sth going wrong: *He's now safely dead and buried.* ○ *The exams are safely over.*

■ **'safe 'conduct** *n* **(a)** [U] freedom from the danger of attack, arrest, etc when passing through an area: *The robbers wanted safe conduct to the airport for themselves and their hostages.* **(b)** [C] a document guaranteeing this.

'safe deposit *n* a building containing heavily protected rooms and safes which people may rent for storing valuable things in. **'safe-deposit box** *n* a small safe in such a building.

'safe house *n* a house used by criminals, people hiding from the authorities, etc, where they can stay without being discovered or disturbed.

the 'safe period *n* [sing] the time just before and during a woman's period(4), when she is unlikely to become pregnant.

'safe 'seat *n* (*Brit*) a CONSTITUENCY(1) in which the candidate of a particular party has a lot of support and is unlikely to be defeated in an election.

'safe 'sex *n* [U] sexual activity in which people take measures to protect themselves from AIDS and other sexual diseases, eg by using a CONDOM.

safe² /seɪf/ *n* a strong box or cupboard with a complicated lock, used for storing valuable things in.

safeguard /'seɪfɡɑːd/ *n* ~ (**against sb/sth**) a thing that serves as a protection from harm, risk or danger: *We make copies of our computer disks as a safeguard against accidents.* ○ *insist on/provide adequate safeguards for people involved in the project.*

▶ **safeguard** *v* to protect sb/sth: [Vn] *safeguard sb's rights/interests/privacy* ○ *safeguard the environment.*

safety /'seɪfti/ *n* [U] **(a)** the state of being safe: *I'm worried about the safety of the children (ie I am afraid something may happen to them).* ○ *We're keeping you here for your own safety.* ○ *road safety (ie being safe when using the roads).* **(b)** the state of not being dangerous: *I'm worried about the safety of the treatment.* **(c)** the ability to keep or make sb/sth safe: *We reached the safety of the river bank (ie a place where we would be safe).* ○ *safety precautions* ○ *a safety harness/bolt.* **IDM** **'safety 'first** (*saying*) safety is the most important thing. **there's 'safety in 'numbers** (*saying*) being in a group makes one feel more confident.

■ **'safety-belt** *n* = SEAT-BELT.

'safety-catch *n* a device that prevents a gun being fired or a machine operating accidentally: *Is the safety-catch on?*

'safety curtain *n* a curtain that can be lowered between the stage and the main part of a theatre to prevent the spread of fire.

'safety glass *n* [U] tough glass that does not break into sharp pieces, used eg for car windows.

'safety island (also **'safety zone**) *n* (*US*) = TRAFFIC ISLAND.

'safety match *n* a match³ that will only catch fire when rubbed against a special surface, eg the side of the box containing it.

'safety net *n* **1** a net placed underneath acrobats (ACROBAT), etc to catch them if they should fall. **2** an arrangement that helps to prevent disaster if sth goes wrong: *a financial safety net* ○ *If I lose my job, I've got no safety net.*

'safety pin *n* a pin with the point bent back towards the head and covered by a guard when closed: *He fixed the card to his lapel with a safety pin.*

'safety razor *n* a RAZOR with a guard to prevent the blade cutting the skin.

'safety-valve *n* **1** a device that releases steam or pressure in a machine when it becomes too great. ⇨ picture at PAN¹. **2** a harmless way of releasing feelings of anger, annoyance, etc: *Sport is a good safety-valve for the tension that builds up at work.*

saffron /'sæfrən/ *n* [U] bright orange strands obtained from certain CROCUS flowers, used in cooking to give colour and flavour to food.

▶ **saffron** *adj* bright orange-yellow: *saffron robes.*

sag /sæɡ/ *v* (**-gg-**) **1** to hang or curve down under weight or pressure: [V] *a sagging roof* ○ *The tent began to sag as the canvas became wet.* ○ *Your skin starts to sag as you get older.* **2** to become weaker or fewer: [V] *Interest/hopes/morale began to sag.* ○ *Exports sagged in the first quarter of the year.*

▶ **saggy** /'sæɡi/ *adj* tending to sag: *a saggy mattress.*

saga /'sɑːɡə/ *n* **1** a long story of brave deeds, esp of Icelandic or Norwegian origin. **2** a story of a long series of events or adventures: *The Forsyte Saga* ○ *the ongoing saga of boardroom intrigue* ○ *Do you want to hear the latest episode in our house-hunting saga?*

sagacious /sə'ɡeɪʃəs/ *adj* (*fml*) showing wisdom and good judgement: *a sagacious person/decision.*

▶ **sagacity** /sə'ɡæsəti/ *n* [U] (*fml*) the quality of being sagacious; wisdom and good judgement: *political sagacity.*

sage¹ /seɪdʒ/ *n* [U] a small plant with sweet-smelling greyish-green leaves that are used in cooking: *dried sage* ○ *sage and onion stuffing* (eg used to stuff a chicken).

sage² /seɪdʒ/ *n* (*fml*) a very wise man: *consult the sages.*

▶ **sage** *adj* [usu attrib] (*fml*) wise or appearing to be wise: *a sage judge/priest/ruler* ○ *a sage comment/rejoinder.*

sagely *adv*: *She nodded sagely.*

sagebrush /'seɪdʒbrʌʃ/ *n* [U] a plant smelling like SAGE¹ that grows in the USA.

Sagittarius /ˌsædʒɪ'teəriəs/ *n* **(a)** [U] the 9th sign of the ZODIAC, the Archer. **(b)** [C] a person born under the influence of this sign. ▶ **Sagittarian** /-'teəriən/ *n, adj.* ⇨ picture at ZODIAC. ⇨ note at ZODIAC.

sago /'seɪɡəʊ/ *n* [U] hard white grains made from the soft inside of a type of PALM², usu cooked with milk as a PUDDING(1).

sahib /sɑːb, 'sɑːɪb/ *n* (used, esp formerly, in India as a form of address) a European man, usu with some social or official status.

said /sed/ **1** *pt, pp* of SAY. **2** *adj* [attrib] (*fml*) = AFOREMENTIONED: *the said company.*

sail¹ /seɪl/ *n* **1(a)** [C] a sheet of canvas or other material against which the wind blows and drives a ship or boat through the water: *hoist/lower/change the sails.* **(b)** [U] sails: *put on more sail* ○ *There was too little wind for the yacht to be under sail* (ie using sails to drive it along). ○ *the age of sail* (ie when ships all used sails). **2** [sing] (**a**) a voyage or trip on water for pleasure: *go for a sail*. (**b**) a voyage of a specified length: *a three-day sail to our destination*. **3** [C] a set of boards attached to the arm of a WINDMILL. The wind blows against these, turning the arms and creating power to drive machinery. ▷ picture at WINDMILL. **IDM** **in/under full sail** ▷ FULL. **set ˈsail (from/to/for ...)** to begin a voyage: *a liner setting sail from Southampton* ○ *We set sail (for France) at high tide*. **take the wind out of sb's sails** ▷ WIND[1].

sail[2] /seɪl/ *v* **1(a)** to travel on water in a ship or boat using sails or engine power: [Vpr] *sail up/along the coast* ○ *sail into harbour* [Vp] *a dinghy sailing by*. (**b**) (usu **go sailing**) to travel on water in a boat with sails, esp as a sport: [V] *We spent the weekend sailing off the south coast*. ▷ note at TRAVEL. **2 ~ (from ...) (for/to ...)** (of a ship or the crew and passengers) to begin a voyage; to leave a harbour: [V] *When does the ferry sail?* [Vpr] *He sailed for the West Indies (from Portsmouth) on HMS Minerva*. **3** to travel by ship across or on a sea or an ocean: [Vn] *sail the Aegean in a cruiser*. **4** to have the skill to control a boat: [V] *Do you sail?* [Vn] *She sails her own yacht.* [Vnpr] *He sailed the boat between the islands.* **5** to move in a smooth or very confident way in the direction specified: [Vpr] *clouds sailing across the sky* ○ *The manager sailed into the room.* [Vp] *She sailed past, ignoring me completely.* **IDM** **sail close/ near to the ˈwind** to behave in a way that is risky or nearly illegal: *He'd been sailing close to the wind for years and this time he took one risk too many.* **PHRV** **ˌsail ˈthrough (sth)** to pass an examination or a test without difficulty: *She sailed through her finals.*

▶ **sailing** *n* **1** [U] travelling in a boat with sails, esp as a sport: *I love sailing.* ○ *a ˈsailing club/dinghy.* **2** [C] a voyage made regularly; the departure of a ship on a voyage: *six sailings a day from Dover to Ostend.* **IDM** **plain sailing** ▷ PLAIN[1]. **ˈsailing-boat** (also **ˈsailing-ship**) *n* a boat or ship that uses sails.

sailboard /ˈseɪlbɔːd/ *n* = WINDSURFER 1a.

sailboat /ˈseɪlbəʊt/ *n* (*US*) a boat driven by sails.

sailcloth /ˈseɪlklɒθ; *US* -klɔːθ/ *n* [U] canvas, esp for sails.

sailor /ˈseɪlə(r)/ *n* a member of a ship's crew, esp one below the rank of officer. **IDM** **a good/bad ˈsailor** a person who rarely/often becomes sick at sea in rough weather.
■ **ˈsailor suit** *n* a suit for a child made in the style of a sailor's uniform.

saint /seɪnt *or, in British use before names,* snt/ *n* **1** (*abbrs* **St**) a person declared to be holy by the Christian Church because of her or his qualities or good works: *the gospel of St John* ○ *St Andrew's Road.* See also PATRON SAINT. **2** a very good, kind or patient person: *She's a saint to go on living with that man.* ○ *His behaviour would try the patience of a saint.*

▶ **sainted** *adj* [usu attrib] (*dated or joc*) declared to be or regarded as a saint: *And how is my sainted sister?*

sainthood *n* [U].

saintly *adj* of or like a saint; very holy or good: *a saintly way of life* ○ *a saintly expression on her face.* **saintliness** *n* [U].
■ **ˈsaint's day** *n* a day of the year when a particular saint is celebrated, and on which, in some countries, people who are named after that saint also have celebrations.

sake[1] /seɪk/ *n* **IDM** **for God's, goodness', Heaven's, etc ˈsake** (used as an *interj*) by itself or before or after a command or request to express annoyance): *For God's sake, stop that awful noise!* ○ *Oh, for Heavens sake!* ○ *For goodness' sake! How can you be so stupid?* **for old times' sake** ▷ OLD. **for**

sth's **ˈown sake** because of the interest or value sth has, not for any benefit it may bring: *I'm studying history for its own sake, not because it will help me get a job.* ○ *believers in art for its own/for art's sake.* **for pity's sake** ▷ PITY. **for the sake of sb/ sth**; **for sb's/sth's sake** in order to help sb/sth or because one likes sb/sth: *They stayed together for the sake of the children.* ○ *I'll help you for your sister's sake* (eg because I like her and want to save her trouble). ○ *Can't you compromise just this once, for all our sakes?* **for the sake of sth / doing sth** in order to get or keep sth: *We made concessions for the sake of peace.* ○ *She argues for the sake of arguing/for the sake of it* (ie because she likes arguing).

sake[2] (also **saki**) /ˈsɑːki/ *n* [U] a Japanese alcoholic drink made from rice.

salacious /səˈleɪʃəs/ *adj* (*fml derog*) (of speech, books, pictures, etc) treating sexual matters in a frank and OBSCENE way: *salacious gossip.* ▶ **salaciousness** *n* [U].

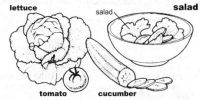
lettuce salad salad tomato cucumber

salad /ˈsæləd/ *n* **1** [C, U] (**a**) (a dish of) chopped, usu raw, vegetables, eg LETTUCE, TOMATO and CUCUMBER, mixed or served together, often with oil and VINEGAR or MAYONNAISE: *prepare/mix a salad* ○ *have cold meat and salad for lunch* ○ *three-bean salad* ○ *potato salad* (ie containing chopped cooked potatoes and MAYONNAISE) ○ *a salad bowl* ○ *a ˈside salad* (ie a small bowl of salad eaten with a meal). ▷ picture. (**b**) (*Brit*) a dish of a specified food served with salad: *make a/ some chicken/ham salad.* See also FRUIT-SALAD. **2** [U] a green vegetable, eg LETTUCE, suitable for eating raw. See also GREEN SALAD. **IDM** **one's ˈsalad days** (*dated or rhet*) a time when one is young and without much experience.
■ **ˈsalad cream** *n* [U] (*Brit*) a type of MAYONNAISE. **ˈsalad-dressing** *n* [U] a mixture, usu of oil, VINEGAR, salt and pepper, for putting on salad.

salamander /ˈsæləmændə(r)/ *n* an animal like a LIZARD that lives both on land and in water.

salami /səˈlɑːmi/ *n* (*pl* **salamis**) [U, C] a type of SAUSAGE, originally from Italy, with a strong flavour and usu eaten cold.

salary /ˈsæləri/ *n* a fixed regular payment, usu made every month to employees doing esp professional or office work: *be on/have a salary of £18 000* ○ *Has your salary been paid into your bank account yet?* ○ *Should doctors' salaries be higher?* ○ *He finds it difficult to manage on his salary.* ○ *a salary agreement/scale.* Compare WAGE[1]. ▷ note at INCOME.

▶ **salaried** *adj* (**a**) (of a person) receiving a salary: *salaried staff.* (**b**) (of a job) for which a salary is paid.

sale /seɪl/ *n* **1** [U] the action or process of selling sth or of being sold: *the sale of cars/clothes/machinery* ○ *The money was raised by the sale of raffle tickets.* ○ *They are currently negotiating the sale of one of their subsidiary companies.* **2(a)** [C] an act of selling sth: *I haven't **made a sale** all week.* ○ *She gets $10 commission on each sale.* (**b**) **sales** [pl] the amount of sth sold: *increased sales of ice-cream in the hot weather* ○ *Sales are up* (ie More goods have been sold) *this month.* **3** [C] (in a shop, etc) an occasion when goods are sold at lower prices than usual: *hold an end-of-season sale* ○ *the January sales* (ie when many shops reduce their prices) ○ *buy goods at/in the sales* ○ *sale prices/goods.* **4** [C] an AUCTION. **IDM** **for ¹sale** intended to be sold, usu by or on behalf of the owner: *I'm sorry — this painting's not for sale.* ○ *They've put their house up for sale.* **on ¹sale 1** available to be bought, esp in a shop: *The new model is not yet on sale in Britain.* ○ *Tickets go on sale on 15 February.* **2** (*US*) being offered at a reduced price: *All video equipment is on sale today and tomorrow.* **(on) ¹sale or re¹turn** (of goods) supplied to a shop-keeper with an agreement that he or she can send back any items that are not sold without having to pay for them. See also CAR-BOOT SALE, GARAGE SALE, JUMBLE SALE.

■ **¹sales clerk** *n* (*US*) = SHOP ASSISTANT.

¹sales department *n* (usu *sing*) the department of a company concerned with selling its products, as distinct from eg manufacturing them.

¹sales pitch *n* = PITCH¹ 4.

¹sales representative (also *infml* **¹sales rep**) *n* an employee of a company who travels around an area selling its goods.

¹sales slip *n* (*US*) a RECEIPT.

¹sales talk *n* [U] talk aimed at persuading sb to buy sth.

¹sales tax *n* [U,C] (in certain countries) a tax on the money received when sth is sold, added to the price by the person selling.

saleable /¹seɪləbl/ *adj* fit for sale; that sb will want to buy: *not in a saleable condition* ○ *The houses are highly saleable.*

saleroom /¹seɪlruːm, -rʊm/ (*US* **¹salesroom** /¹seɪlz-/) *n* a room where goods are sold at an AUCTION.

salesman /¹seɪlzmən/ *n* (*pl* **-men** /-mən/) a man whose job is to sell goods, eg in a shop.
▶ **¹salesmanship** *n* [U] skill in selling goods.

salesperson /¹seɪlzpɜːsn/ *n* (*pl* **-people** /-piːpl/) a person whose job is to sell goods, eg in a shop.

saleswoman /¹seɪlzwʊmən/ *n* (*pl* **-women** /-wɪmɪn/) a woman whose job is to sell goods, eg in a shop.

salient¹ /¹seɪlɪənt/ *adj* [attrib] most noticeable or important; main: *the salient points of a speech* ○ *She pointed out all the salient features of the new design.*

salient² /¹seɪlɪənt/ *n* an outward curve in a military line of attack or defence, or the corner of a fort.

saline /¹seɪlaɪn; *US* -liːn/ *adj* [attrib] (*fml*) containing salt: *a saline lake* ○ *Use a saline solution for cleaning contact lenses.* ▶ **salinity** /sə¹lɪnəti/ *n* [U]: *the high salinity of the soil.*

saliva /sə¹laɪvə/ *n* [U] liquid produced in the mouth that helps one swallow and DIGEST²(1a) food.
▶ **salivary** /¹sælɪvəri, sə¹laɪvəri; *US* ¹sæləveri/ *adj* [attrib] of or producing saliva: *the salivary glands.*
salivate /¹sælɪveɪt/ *v* (*fml*) to produce saliva, esp excessively: *The smell of that cooking made him salivate.* **salivation** /¹sælɪ¹veɪʃn/ *n* [U].

sallow¹ /¹sæləʊ/ *adj* (of a person's skin or face) pale and yellowish and not healthy: *She looked sallow and drawn.* ▶ **sallowness** *n* [U].

sallow² /¹sæləʊ/ *n* a type of WILLOW tree that does not grow very tall.

sally /¹sæli/ *n* **1(a)** a sudden attack, esp by troops surrounded by the enemy: *make a successful sally.* **(b)** (*infml*) a quick journey: *a brief sally to the shops.* **2** a lively or humorous remark: *sallies of sarcasm.*
▶ **sally** *v* (*pt, pp* **sallied**) **PHRV** ¹**sally ¹out/¹forth** (*dated or joc*) to go out from somewhere to do sth: *After lunch we sallied forth for a short walk.*

salmon /¹sæmən/ *n* (*pl* unchanged) **(a)** [C] a large fish with pink flesh. People sometimes fish for salmon with a rod and line as a sport: *a salmon farm.* **(b)** [U] its flesh used as food: *smoked salmon* ○ *a salmon salad/mousse.*

■ **¹salmon-¹pink** *n, adj* the colour of a salmon's flesh; orange-pink.

salmonella /¹sælmə¹nelə/ *n* [U] a germ that causes food poisoning (FOOD): *eggs infected with salmonella* ○ *cases of salmonella poisoning.*

salon /¹sælɒn; *US* sə¹lɒn/ *n* **1** a place where customers go for hair or beauty treatment: *a ¹beauty salon* ○ *a ¹hairdressing salon.* **2(a)** (formerly) a regular gathering of guests at the house of a woman of high society: *a literary salon* (ie with writers, etc as guests). **(b)** a room used for this.

saloon /sə¹luːn/ *n* **1** (also **sa¹loon car**) (*Brit*) (*US* **sedan**) a car in which the part where the driver and passengers sit is separated from the storage area at the back: *a Rover 800 saloon.* ⇨ picture at HATCH-BACK. **2** a public room or building for a specified purpose: *the ship's ¹dining-saloon* ○ *a ¹billiard-saloon.* **3** (also **sa¹loon bar**) = LOUNGE BAR. **4** (*US*) a place where alcoholic drinks may be bought and drunk; a bar¹(1a).

salsa /¹sælsə; *US* ¹sɑːlsə/ *n* [U] **1** a type of Latin American dance music. **2** a sauce eaten with Mexican food.

salsify /¹sælsəfi/ *n* [U] (*US* also **oyster-plant** [C]) a plant with a long root cooked as a vegetable.

salt /sɔːlt, sɒlt/ *n* **1** (also **common salt**) [U] a white substance used to give a better flavour to food or to preserve it. Salt is obtained from mines and is also found in sea water: *put too much salt in the soup* ○ *foods with a high salt content* ○ *salt and vinegar flavour crisps* ○ *¹table salt* (ie in powder form so that it can be shaken onto food) ○ *Would you pass the salt, please.* ○ *¹sea salt* ○ *a ¹salt-mine* ○ *winds carrying salt spray* (ie from the sea). See also ROCK-SALT. **2** [C] a chemical compound of a metal and an acid: *mineral salts.* **3** **salts** [pl] a substance like salt in taste or form: *¹bath salts* (ie used to give a pleasant smell to bath water). See also SMELLING-SALTS. **4** [C] (*dated infml*) an experienced sailor: *an old salt.* **IDM** **like a dose of salts** ⇨ DOSE. **rub salt into the wound / sb's wounds** ⇨ RUB¹. **the salt of the ¹earth** a very good, honest, kind person or group of people: *You can trust her — she's the salt of the earth.* **take sth with a pinch of salt** ⇨ PINCH *n*. **worth one's salt** ⇨ WORTH.

▶ **salt** *v* **1** (esp passive) to put salt on or in food: [Vn] *salted peanuts* ○ *a pan of boiling salted water.* **2** to preserve food with salt: [Vn] *salted beef/pork.* **3** [Vn] to put salt on roads, etc to melt ice or snow. **PHRV** ¹**salt sth a¹way** to save money, etc secretly and usu dishonestly: *She salted away most of the profits from the business.*
salt *adj* [attrib] containing, tasting of or preserved with salt: *salt water* ○ *salt marshes* ○ *the salt flats of Utah* ○ *salt beef/pork.*
salty *adj* (**-ier, -iest**) **1** containing or tasting of salt. **2** (of speech, humour, etc) vigorous and vivid: *her salty language.* **saltiness** *n* [U].

■ **¹salt-cellar** (*US* **¹salt-shaker**) *n* a small container for salt used at the table, usu with one hole at the top through which it is poured. Compare PEPPER-POT.

¹salt-water *adj* [attrib] of the sea: *a salt-water lagoon/fish.* Compare FRESHWATER.

SALT (also **Salt**) /sɔːlt/ *abbr* Strategic Arms Limitation Talks: *the Salt treaties.*

saltpetre (*US* **-peter**) /¹sɔːlt¹piːtə(r), ¹sɒlt-/ *n* [U] a white powder used for preserving food or for making matches and GUNPOWDER.

salubrious /sə¹luːbrɪəs/ *adj* (*fml*) (of surroundings, etc) pleasant and healthy; not dirty: *the less salubrious parts of town.*

salutary /¹sæljətri; *US* -teri/ *adj* having a good effect: *a salutary lesson/experience* ○ *The accident is a salutary reminder of the dangers of climbing.*

salutation /ˌsæljuˈteɪʃn/ n (fml) **1(a)** [U] greeting or respect: *raise one's hand in salutation.* **(b)** [C] a sign or expression of this, eg a word or a kiss: *the shouts and salutations of the bystanders.* **2** [C] the words used in a letter to address the person being written to, eg *Dear Sir.*

salute /səˈluːt/ n **1(a)** an action, esp the action of firing a gun, performed to show honour or respect or to welcome sb: *fire a ten-gun salute.* **(b)** a gesture of respect to a senior officer, etc made by raising the fingers of the right hand to the side of the forehead: *give a salute* ∘ *The officer returned the sergeant's salute* (ie saluted in reply to such a gesture). **2** a gesture of greeting, respect or loyalty: *He raised his hat as a friendly salute.* ∘ *a salute to democracy/the new year* ∘ *They raised their glasses in salute.* **IDM** **take the saˈlute** (of a person of high rank) to acknowledge with a salute the salutes of soldiers marching past.

▶ **salute** v **1** to make a salute to sb/sth: [Vn] *saluting the flag* [V, Vn] *The guard stepped back and saluted (the general).* **2** (fml or rhet) to show admiration and respect for a person, an achievement, etc: [Vn] *salute sb's courage and self-sacrifice* ∘ *Today we salute all those who died for their country.*

salvage /ˈsælvɪdʒ/ n [U] **(a)** the removal of a damaged ship and its cargo from the sea, or the removal of property likely to be damaged by fire, floods, etc for future use, repair, etc: *Salvage of the wreck was delayed by bad weather.* ∘ *a salvage company* (ie one that recovers damaged ships, etc from the sea) ∘ *The painting was thoroughly burnt and beyond salvage.* **(b)** property rescued in this way.

▶ **salvage** v ~ **sth (from sth) 1** to save a ship or property from loss, fire, destruction, etc: [Vn, Vnpr] *Iron bars were salvaged (from the sunken freighter).* **2** to save sth from harm, disaster, difficult circumstances, etc: [Vn] *She took them to court in an attempt to salvage her reputation.* [also Vnpr].

salvation /sælˈveɪʃn/ n [U] **1** (religion) the saving of a person's soul from sin and its consequences; the state of being saved in this way: *pray for the salvation of the world.* **2** a way of avoiding loss, disaster, etc: *Music is my salvation* (ie helps me forget my problems).

■ **the Salˌvation ˈArmy** n [sing] a Christian organization whose members wear military uniforms and work esp to help the poor.

salve /sælv, sɑːv; US sæv/ n [C, U] (esp in compounds) any oily substance used on wounds, burns, etc to help them heal: *ˈlip-salve.*

▶ **salve** v to help to reduce feelings of guilt or anxiety: [Vn] *The gift was his way of salving his conscience.*

salver /ˈsælvə(r)/ n a tray, usu of metal, on which letters, drinks, etc are placed before they are handed to people: *a silver salver.*

salvo /ˈsælvəʊ/ n (pl **-os** or **-oes**) **1** an act of firing several guns at the same time: *Another salvo exploded near our position.* Compare VOLLEY 1. **2** a sudden, vigorous or aggressive act or series of acts: *the opening salvo in the election contest.*

sal volatile /ˌsæl vəˈlætəli/ n [U] a type of smelling-salts (SMELL¹).

Samaritan /səˈmærɪtən/ n **the Samaritans** [pl] an organization devoted to giving help and friendship to people in despair, esp over the telephone. **IDM** **a ˌgood Saˈmaritan** a person who gives sympathy and help to people in trouble.

samba /ˈsæmbə/ n (usu sing) a dance originating in Brazil or a piece of music for this: *dance the samba.*

same¹ /seɪm/ adj **1** the ~ sb/sth (as sb/ sth / that...) (also sometimes preceded by this/that/ these/those) exactly the one or ones referred to or mentioned; not different; IDENTICAL(1): *We have lived*

in the same house for twenty years. ∘ *He took it off the top shelf and put it back in the same place.* ∘ *He is the same age as his wife.* ∘ *She's aged a lot but she is still the same fun-loving person I knew at university.* ∘ *They both said the same thing.* ∘ *She did it for the same reason.* ∘ *I saw the mistake at the (very) same moment that she did.* ∘ *I resigned last Friday and left that same day.* **2** the ~ sb/sth (as sb/sth / that...) one that is exactly like the one referred to or mentioned; exactly matching: *I saw the same shoes last week for £5 less.* ∘ *I bought the same car as yours/that you did* (ie another car of that type). **IDM** **amount to / come to / be the same ˈthing** to have the same result, meaning, etc: *You can pay by cash or cheque: it comes to the same thing.* **at the same ˈtime 1** at once; together: *Don't all speak at the same time.* ∘ *She was laughing and crying at the same time.* **2** (introducing a fact, etc that must be considered) nevertheless; yet: *You've got to be firm, but at the same time you must be sympathetic.* **be all ˈone / all the ˈsame to sb** to be unimportant to sb what will happen: *It's all the same to me whether we eat now or later.* **be in the same ˈboat** to be in the same difficult or unfortunate circumstances: *She and I are in the same boat — we both failed the exam.* **be of one / the same ˈmind** ⇨ MIND¹. **by the same ˈtoken** (fml) in a corresponding way; following from the same argument: *She must be more reasonable, but by the same token you must try to understand her point of view.* **in the same ˈbreath** immediately after saying sth that suggests the opposite intention or meaning: *He praised my work and in the same breath told me I would have to leave.* **on a different / the same wavelength** ⇨ WAVELENGTH. **the ˌsame old ˈstory** what usually happens: *It's the same old story: everybody wants to go on holiday, but nobody is prepared to make the arrangements.* **speak/talk the same language** ⇨ SPEAK. **tarred with the same brush** ⇨ TAR v.

▶ **the same** adv in the same way; similarly: *I still feel the same about it.* ∘ *Babies all look the same to me.* ∘ *The two words are spelled differently, but pronounced the same.*

sameness n [U] the quality of being the same; lack of variety: *the tedious sameness of winter days indoors.*

samey /ˈseɪmi/ adj (Brit infml derog) not changing enough: *The music is all a bit samey.*

same² /seɪm/ pron **1** the ~ (as sb/sth/...) **(a)** the same thing or things: *He and I said the same.* ∘ *I think the same (as you do) about this.* ∘ *I would do the same again.* ∘ (infml) *'I'll have a coffee.' 'Same for me, please* (ie I will have one, too).*' **(b)** the same number, colour, shape, size, quality, etc: *Their ages are the same.* ∘ *Have you got another pair the same?* ∘ *He'd like one the same as yours.* **2** the ~ (Brit fml or joc) the same person or thing mentioned: *'Was it George who telephoned?' 'The same* (ie Yes, it was George).*' **3** (fml or joc) (used in bills, etc) the previously mentioned thing: *To dry-cleaning suit, £8; to repairing same, £4.50.* **IDM** **ˌall/ˌjust the ˈsame** in spite of this; nevertheless: *All the same, there's some truth in what she says.* ∘ *He's not very reliable, but I like him just the same.* ∘ *I didn't need your screwdriver, but thanks all the same* (ie for lending it). **be all one to sb; be all the same to sb** ⇨ ALL³. **ˌone and the ˈsame** the same person or thing: *It turns out that her aunt and my cousin are one and the same.* **(the) ˌsame aˈgain** (said as a request to sb to serve the same drink as before): *Same again, please!* **ˌsame ˈhere** (infml) the same thing applies to me; I am, think, etc the same: *'I hate this book.' 'Same here.'* ∘ *'I'm not very good at history.' 'Same here.'* **(the) ˌsame to ˈyou** (used as an answer to a greeting, an insult, etc): *'Happy Christmas!' 'And the same to you!'* ∘ *'Get lost!' 'Same to you!'*

samosa /səˈməʊsə/ n a crisp fried pastry made in

the shape of a TRIANGLE and filled with meat or vegetables cooked with spices.

samovar /ˈsæməʊvɑː(r)/ n a container for heating water, used esp in Russia for making tea.

sampan /ˈsæmpæn/ n a small boat with a flat bottom, used along the coasts and rivers of China.

sample /ˈsɑːmpl; US ˈsæmpl/ n **1(a)** one of a number of things, or one part of a whole, that can be examined in order to see what the rest is like; a SPECIMEN(1): a sample of his handwriting o a ˈblood/ˈurine sample o samples of curtain material. **(b)** a number of people chosen randomly (RANDOM) from a larger group: The survey covers a representative sample of the population. **2** a small amount of a product given free of charge: give away free samples of a new perfume o a sample pack/sachet.
▶ **sample** v to try or examine sth by experiencing it or by tasting it: [Vn] sample the delights of Chinese cooking o We sampled opinion among the workers (ie asked some of them) about changes in working methods.

sampler /ˈsɑːmplə(r); US ˈsæm-/ n **1** a piece of cloth decorated with different stitches to show sb's skill in NEEDLEWORK and often displayed on a wall. **2** a small amount of a product given or sold to people for them to try and see whether they like it: a sampler pack.

samurai /ˈsæmʊraɪ/ n (pl unchanged) **(a) the samurai** [pl] (formerly) the military class in Japan. **(b)** [C] a member of this class.

sanatorium /ˌsænəˈtɔːriəm/ n (pl sanatoriums or sanatoria /-riə/) (US also sanitarium /ˌsænəˈteəriəm/, sanitorium /ˌsænəˈtɔːriəm/; pl -ria) a place like a hospital where patients who have a lasting illness or who are recovering from an illness are treated.

sanctify /ˈsæŋktɪfaɪ/ v (pt, pp -fied) **1** to make sb/sth holy: [Vn] a life sanctified by prayer. **2** (esp passive) to make sth seem right, legal, etc; to justify sth: [Vn] a practice sanctified by time/tradition. ▶ **sanctification** /ˌsæŋktɪfɪˈkeɪʃn/ n [U].

sanctimonious /ˌsæŋktɪˈməʊniəs/ adj (derog) showing that one feels morally superior to other people: a sanctimonious smile/voice/newspaper editorial. ▶ **sanctimoniously** adv. **sanctimoniousness** n [U].

sanction /ˈsæŋkʃn/ n **1** [U] (fml) permission or approval for an action, a change, etc: The book was translated without the sanction of the author. o The conference gave its official sanction to the change of policy. **2** [C] ~ (against sth) a threatened penalty that makes people obey laws, rules, etc: the need for effective sanctions against computer hacking. **3** [C usu pl] ~ (against sb) a measure taken to force a country to obey international law, respect human rights, etc: apply/tighten/lift economic sanctions.
▶ **sanction** v to give one's permission for sth; to approve sth: [Vn] They won't sanction a further cut in interest rates.

sanctity /ˈsæŋktəti/ n [U] the state of being holy or sacred: believe in the sanctity of life/marriage o She radiates sanctity.

sanctuary /ˈsæŋktʃuəri; US -ueri/ n **1** [C] a sacred place, eg a church, temple or MOSQUE. **2(a)** [C usu sing] a place where sb is protected from people wishing to arrest or attack them: The fleeing rebels found a sanctuary in the cathedral. o a sanctuary for political refugees. **(b)** [U] such protection: claim/seek/take/be offered sanctuary in the embassy. **3** [C] an area where birds and wild animals are protected and encouraged to breed: a ˈbird sanctuary.

sanctum /ˈsæŋktəm/ n **1** a private room, office, etc where sb can go and not be disturbed: I was allowed once into his inner sanctum. **2** a holy place.

sand /sænd/ n **1** [U] very small fine grains of rock. Sand is found on beaches, in rivers, deserts, etc: mix sand and cement to make concrete. **2** [U, C usu pl] an

area of sand, eg on a beach: children playing on the sand(s)/in the sand. **3** sands [pl] (used in names) a mass of sand in a river or the sea: the Goodwin Sands. **IDM** bury/hide one's head in the sand ▷ HEAD¹. the sands are running ˈout there is not much time left: The sands are running out: we must have the money by tomorrow. shifting sands ▷ SHIFT¹.
▶ **sand** v **1** ~ sth (down) to make esp wood smooth with SANDPAPER: [Vnp] The bare wood must be sanded down. [Vn-adj] The floor has been sanded smooth. [also Vn]. **2** [Vn] to put sand on a surface.
sander (also ˈsanding machine) n a machine for sanding surfaces, eg by means of a revolving pad or drum¹(2) with SANDPAPER on it.
sandy adj (-ier, -iest) **1** like, covered with or containing sand: a sandy beach o sandy soil. **2** (of hair) yellowish-red.
■ ˈ**sandbar** n a mass of sand at the point where a river or harbour joins the sea.
ˈ**sand-dune** n = DUNE. ▷ picture at COAST¹.

sandal   flip-flop (US thong)   **sandal**

sandal /ˈsændl/ n a type of light shoe worn esp in warm weather. Its upper part is either partly open or consists of bands or cords that attach the sole to the foot. ▷ picture. Compare BOOT¹ 1, SHOE 1.
▶ **sandalled** adj wearing sandals.

sandalwood /ˈsændlwʊd/ n [U] **(a)** a hard wood with a sweet smell, sometimes used for making fans, etc. **(b)** the PERFUME(1) obtained from this wood: sandalwood soap.

sandbag /ˈsændbæg/ n a bag filled with sand, used as a defence against rising floods.
▶ **sandbag** v (-gg-) to put sandbags in or around sth: [Vn] sandbag the doorway to keep the water out.

sandbank /ˈsændbæŋk/ n a bank or mass of sand in a river or the sea: a boat struck on a sandbank.

sandblast /ˈsændblɑːst; US -blæst/ v [Vn] to clean or decorate a stone wall, etc by aiming a jet of sand at it from a special machine.

sandbox /ˈsændbɒks/ n (US) = SANDPIT.

sandcastle /ˈsændkɑːsl; US -kæsl/ n a pile of sand shaped to look like a castle, usu made by a child on a beach.

sandfly /ˈsændflaɪ/ n a flying insect common on beaches.

sandman /ˈsændmæn/ n the sandman [sing] an imaginary person who makes children fall asleep.

sandpaper /ˈsændpeɪpə(r)/ n [U] strong paper covered with sand or a similar substance, used for rubbing surfaces smooth.
▶ **sandpaper** v to smooth sth with sandpaper: [Vn, Vnp] sandpapering (down) an old pine table.

sandpiper /ˈsændpaɪpə(r)/ n a small bird living near the banks of lakes and rivers.

sandpit /ˈsændpɪt/ (Brit) (US sandbox) n a hollow place partly filled with sand for children to play in.

sandstone /ˈsændstəʊn/ n [U] a type of rock formed of grains of sand tightly pressed together.

sandstorm /ˈsændstɔːm/ n a storm in a desert area in which sand is blown through the air by the wind.

sandwich /ˈsænwɪdʒ, -wɪtʃ; US -wɪtʃ/ n **1** two or more slices of bread with a layer of food, eg meat, cheese or SALAD, between them: ham/chicken/cucumber sandwiches o a sandwich bar/box/filling. See also CLUB SANDWICH. **2** (esp Brit) a type of cake consisting of two sections with cream or jam between them: a jam sandwich.

▶ **sandwich** v PHRV **'sandwich sb/sth between sb/sth** (esp passive) to press sb/sth into a small space between other people or things: *I was sandwiched between two fat men on the bus.* ○ *Their property is sandwiched between the golf course and the river.*

■ **'sandwich-board** n either of two connected boards advertising sth. The boards are hung over the shoulders of a person who walks about in the streets to display them.

'sandwich course n (*Brit*) an educational course in which there are periods of study between periods of working in a company, in industry, etc.

sane /seɪn/ *adj* (**-r, -st**) **1** having a normal healthy mind; not mad: *It's hard to stay sane under such awful pressure.* **2** having or showing good judgement; sensible; reasonable: *a sane person/decision/policy.* See also SANITY.

sang *pt of* SING.

sang-froid /ˌsɒŋ 'frwɑː/ n [U] the quality of remaining calm in a dangerous situation or in an emergency: *He reacted to the crisis with characteristic sang-froid.*

sangría /'sæŋgrɪə, sæŋ'griːə/ n [U] (*Spanish*) a drink of red wine mixed with fruit and lemonade.

sanguinary /'sæŋgwɪnəri; *US* -neri/ *adj* (*fml*) **1** involving many people being injured or killed; BLOODY[1](2): *a sanguinary battle.* **2** fond of killing people; BLOODTHIRSTY(1): *a sanguinary ruler.*

sanguine /'sæŋgwɪn/ *adj* ~ (**about sth**) (*fml*) hopeful; optimistic (OPTIMISM): *She remained sanguine about our chances of success.* ○ *He* **takes a less sanguine view** *of the future than most analysts.*

sanitarium, sanitorium (*US*) = SANATORIUM.

sanitary /'sænətri; *US* -teri/ *adj* **1** [attrib] of or concerned with the removal of human waste and keeping places free from dirt, etc: *sanitary ware* (ie toilets, etc) ○ *inadequate sanitary facilities in prisons* ○ *sanitary regulations* ○ *a sanitary inspector.* Compare INSANITARY. **2** free from dirt or substances that may cause disease; clean; hygienic (HYGIENE): *Conditions in the refugee camps were far from sanitary.*

■ **'sanitary towel** (*US* **'sanitary napkin**) n a soft cotton pad used by a woman for absorbing the blood during a period(4). Compare TAMPON.

sanitation /ˌsænɪ'teɪʃn/ n [U] systems that protect people's health, esp those that dispose efficiently of human waste: *a place with no proper sanitation.*

sanitize, -ise /'sænɪtaɪz/ v (esp passive) **1** to make sth free from anything that may damage health: [Vn] *sanitized dustbins.* **2** (*derog*) to make sth, eg an account of an event, less disturbing, shocking, etc: [Vn] *a sanitized version of a story.*

sanity /'sænəti/ n [U] **1** the state of having a normal healthy mind: *doubt/question sb's sanity* ○ *He* **kept his sanity** *by writing poetry.* **2** the state of being sensible or reasonable; good sound judgement: *try to restore some sanity to a ridiculous situation.*

sank *pt of* SINK[1].

sanserif /ˌsæn'serɪf/ n [U] (in printing) a form of type[2] without serifs (SERIF). ⇨ picture at SERIF.

Santa Claus /'sæntə klɔːz/ (also *infml* **santa**) (*esp Brit*) = FATHER CHRISTMAS.

sap[1] /sæp/ n [U] the liquid in a plant that carries food to all parts of it: *Maple syrup is made from the sap of the sugar maple tree.*

▶ **sappy** *adj* full of sap.

sap[2] /sæp/ v (**-pp-**) ~ **sb/sth (of sth)** to make sb/sth weak or destroy sth gradually over a period of time: [Vn] *The long trek sapped our energy/strength.* ○ *Years of failure have sapped his confidence.*

sap[3] /sæp/ n (*infml*) a stupid person who is easily tricked or treated unfairly: *The poor sap never knew his wife was cheating him.*

sapient /'seɪpɪənt/ *adj* (*fml*) wise. ▶ **sapience** /-əns/ n [U] **sapiently** *adv.*

sapling /'sæplɪŋ/ n a young tree.

sapper /'sæpə(r)/ n a soldier whose job is to build or repair roads, bridges, etc.

sapphire /'sæfaɪə(r)/ n (**a**) [C] a clear, bright blue jewel. (**b**) [U] its colour. ▶ **sapphire** *adj* bright blue.

sapwood /'sæpwʊd/ n [U] the soft outer layers of the wood of a tree, inside the bark.

Saracen /'særəsn/ n an Arab or a Muslim at the time of the Crusades.

sarcasm /'sɑːkæzəm/ n [U] remarks that imply the opposite of what they appear to mean and are intended to upset or mock sb: *heavy/bitter sarcasm* ○ *'And is that free and fair trade?' she asked, with more than a hint of sarcasm in her voice.* Compare IRONY.

▶ **sarcastic** /sɑː'kæstɪk/ (also *Brit infml* **sarky**) *adj* using or expressing sarcasm: *sarcastic comments/wit* ○ *People who didn't like him said he was very sarcastic.* Compare IRONIC. **sarcastically** /-klɪ/ *adv*: *'Don't mind me, I only live here,' she said sarcastically.*

sarcophagus /sɑː'kɒfəgəs/ n (*pl* **sarcophagi** /sɑː'kɒfəgaɪ/) a stone COFFIN, esp one with carved decoration, used in ancient times.

sardine /ˌsɑː'diːn/ n a young PILCHARD or a similar fish, cooked and eaten fresh or preserved in tins in oil or tomato sauce. IDM **(packed, squashed, etc) like sar'dines** (*infml*) pressed tightly together in a way that is uncomfortable or unpleasant: *The ten of us were squashed together like sardines in this tiny room.*

sardonic /sɑː'dɒnɪk/ *adj* showing that one thinks one is superior or that one is not taking sb/sth seriously; mocking: *a sardonic smile/grin.* ▶ **sardonically** /-klɪ/ *adv*: *'You could always pray for a miracle,' he added sardonically.*

sarge /sɑːdʒ/ n (*infml*) (used esp as a form of address) = SERGEANT.

sari /'sɑːri/ n a long piece of cotton or silk cloth that is wrapped round the body and worn as the main garment esp by Indian women.

sarky /'sɑːki/ *adj* (*Brit infml*) = SARCASTIC: *Don't get sarky with me!*

sarong /sə'rɒŋ; *US* -'rɔːŋ/ n a long piece of cloth wrapped round the body from the waist or the armpits (ARMPIT) downwards by Malaysian and Indonesian men and women.

sartorial /sɑː'tɔːrɪəl/ *adj* [attrib] (*fml*) of clothes or a person's style of dress: *sartorial elegance/details.* ▶ **sartorially** /-rɪəli/ *adv.*

SAS /ˌes eɪ 'es/ *abbr* (in Britain) Special Air Service (a group of highly trained soldiers who are used on very secret or difficult operations).

sash[1] /sæʃ/ n a long strip of cloth worn around the waist or over one shoulder, eg as part of a uniform or as decoration.

sash[2] /sæʃ/ n either of a pair of windows, one above the other, which are opened and closed by sliding them up and down inside the frame.

■ **'sash-cord** n a cord with a weight at one end running over a PULLEY and attached to a window, allowing it to be kept open in any position.

ˌsash-'window n a window consisting of two sashes. ⇨ picture at HOUSE[1].

sashay /sɑː'ʃeɪ; *US* sæ'ʃeɪ/ v (*US infml*) to walk or move in a casual way, intending to attract attention: [Vpr] *sashay into the room* [also Vp].

sass /sæs/ n [U] (*US infml*) rude talk; impudence (IMPUDENT): *Don't give me any of your sass!* ▶ **sass** v (*US infml*) to be rude to sb: [Vn] *Don't you dare sass me!*

sassy *adj* (**-ier, -iest**) (*infml esp US*) **1** rude; showing lack of respect. **2** (*dated*) lively and fashionable: *a real sassy dresser.*

Sassenach /ˈsæsənæk, -næx/ *n* (*Scot derog or joc*) an English person.

Sat *abbr* Saturday: *Sat 3 May.*

sat *pt, pp* of SIT.

Satan /ˈseɪtn/ *n* the Devil.
▶ **satanic** /səˈtænɪk/ *adj* **1** (often **Satanic**) connected with or characteristic of Satan: *satanic rites* (eg involving the worship of Satan). **2** (*esp rhet*) wicked; evil.
Satanism /ˈseɪtənɪzəm/ *n* [U] the worship of Satan.
▶ **Satanist** /ˈseɪtənɪst/ *n*.

satchel /ˈsætʃəl/ *n* a small leather or canvas bag, usu hung from a strap over the shoulder and used for carrying school books, etc.

sated /ˈseɪtɪd/ *adj* [usu pred] ~ (**with sth**) (*fml*) having had so much of sth that one does not want any more: *sated with pleasure.*

satellite /ˈsætəlaɪt/ *n* **1** an electronic device that is sent into space and moves round a planet: *a weather satellite* (ie one that helps to record and forecast the weather) ○ *a com,muni'cations satellite* (ie one that transmits to a place or places on Earth telephone messages or radio and television signals received from another part of the Earth) ○ *satellite TV* (ie television channels broadcast by use of a satellite) ○ *a satellite link/picture/broadcast/station.* ⇨ picture at ORBIT. **2** a natural body in space that moves round a larger body, esp a planet: *The moon is the Earth's satellite.* **3** a country or an organization dependent on and controlled by another more powerful country or organization: *a satellite state.*
■ **'satellite dish** *n* a device in the shape of a dish that receives signals transmitted by a satellite(1).

satiate /ˈseɪʃieɪt/ *v* (*fml*) (usu passive) to provide sb with so much of sth that they do not want any more: [Vn] *feel satiated after Christmas dinner* [Vnpr] *be satiated with pleasure.* ▶ **satiation** /ˌseɪʃiˈeɪʃn/ *n* [U].

satiety /səˈtaɪəti/ *n* [U] (*fml*) the state or feeling of being satiated (SATIATE).

satin /ˈsætɪn; *US* ˈsætn/ *n* [U] silk material that is shiny and smooth on one side: *a white satin dress/ribbon.*
▶ **satin** *adj* [usu attrib] smooth like satin: *The paint has a satin finish.*
satiny *adj* having the appearance or texture of satin: *her satiny skin.*

satire /ˈsætaɪə(r)/ *n* (**a**) [U] the art or practice of mocking people, institutions, etc and making them appear ridiculous in order to show how foolish, wicked or INCOMPETENT they are: *a work full of coarse/cruel/savage satire* ○ *political satire.* (**b**) [C] ~ (**on sb/sth**) a piece of writing, a play, a film, etc that uses this art: *The book is a stinging/biting satire on American politics.*
▶ **satirical** /səˈtɪrɪkl/ (also **satiric** /səˈtɪrɪk/) *adj* containing or using satire: *a satirical play/cartoon/ magazine* ○ *His poems are witty and satirical.* **satirically** /-kli/ *adv.*
satirist /ˈsætərɪst/ *n* a person who writes, performs or uses satire.
satirize, -ise /ˈsætəraɪz/ *v* to attack sb/sth using satire: [Vn] *famous personalities satirized in comedy shows.*

satisfaction /ˌsætɪsˈfækʃn/ *n* **1** [U] ~ (**at/with sth**) a feeling of pleasure because one has sth or has achieved sth: *She can look back on her career with great satisfaction.* ○ *get/obtain/derive satisfaction from sth* ○ *a look of smug satisfaction* ○ *do the work to the satisfaction of the client* ○ *He never had the satisfaction of seeing his paintings recognized and admired.* See also JOB SATISFACTION. **2** [U] ~ **of sth** the action of fulfilling a need, desire, demand, etc:

the satisfaction of one's goals. **3** [U] the state of being certain or convinced about sth: *He couldn't prove to my satisfaction that his offer was genuine.* **4** [C] a thing that gives pleasure and happiness: *the satisfactions of being a parent.* **5** [U] (*fml*) (**a**) an acceptable response to a complaint, eg compensation or an apology: *When I didn't get any satisfaction from the local branch I wrote to the head office.* (**b**) (*dated*) revenge for an insult to one's honour or reputation. Compare DISSATISFACTION.

satisfactory /ˌsætɪsˈfæktəri/ *adj* of an acceptable nature or standard; good enough for a purpose: *a satisfactory attempt/explanation/meal/piece of work* ○ *The result of the experiment was satisfactory.* ○ *Her school report says her French is satisfactory but not outstanding.* Compare UNSATISFACTORY. ▶ **satisfactorily** /-təRəli/ *adv*: *This incident has never been satisfactorily explained.* ○ *The patient is progressing satisfactorily.*

satisfy /ˈsætɪsfaɪ/ *v* (*pt, pp* **-fied**) **1** to do sth or give sb sth that is acceptable or adequate, so that they feel pleased or CONTENT[1]: [Vn] *Nothing satisfies him: he's always complaining.* ○ *She wasn't satisfied by my explanation.* **2** to fulfil a need, desire, demand, etc; to meet a requirement: [Vn] *satisfy sb's hunger/ curiosity* ○ *satisfy demand for a product* ○ (*fml*) *She has satisfied the conditions for entry into the college.* **3** to convince sb by giving them proof or by persuading them: [Vn] *My assurances don't satisfy him: he's still sceptical.* [Vnpr] *satisfy the police as to/of one's innocence* [Vn.that] *Once I had satisfied myself that it was the right decision, I went ahead.* See also SATISFACTION.
▶ **satisfied** *adj* ~ (**with sb/sth**) feeling or showing satisfaction; CONTENT[1]: *thousands of satisfied customers* ○ *a satisfied smile* ○ *I felt quite satisfied with my day's work.* ○ (*ironic*) *It's your fault I missed my train — I hope you're satisfied!* Compare DISSATISFIED.
satisfying *adj* giving satisfaction: *a satisfying meal/result.* **satisfyingly** *adv.*

satsuma /sætˈsuːmə/ *n* (*Brit*) a type of small orange with a loose skin. Compare MANDARIN 4.

saturate /ˈsætʃəreɪt/ *v* **1** to make sth completely wet; to soak sth: [Vn] *continuous heavy rain had saturated the fields.* **2** ~ **sth/sb** (**with/in sth**) (esp passive) to fill sth/sb completely with sth so that no further addition is possible or desirable: [Vn, Vnpr] *The market is saturated (with good used cars)* (ie There are too many of them for sale). [Vnpr] *be saturated in Indian history and culture.*
▶ **saturated** *adj* **1** [usu pred] completely wet; soaked: *I went out in the rain and got saturated.* **2** [usu attrib] (*chemistry*) (of a solution(3)) containing the greatest possible amount of the substance that has been dissolved in it. **3** [usu attrib] (of fats) containing chemicals combined in such a way that they cannot be easily processed by the body when eaten: *dairy products high in saturated fats.* Compare POLYUNSATURATED, UNSATURATED.
saturation /ˌsætʃəˈreɪʃn/ *n* [U] the process of saturating sth or the state of being saturated. — *adj* [attrib] (**a**) covering or affecting an extremely large area: *saturation bombing of the city.* (**b**) happening to the greatest extent possible: *saturation coverage of a news story.* **,satu'ration point** *n* [U, sing] **1** the stage at which no more can be absorbed, accepted, added, etc: *So many refugees have arrived that the camps have reached saturation point.* **2** (*chemistry*) the stage at which no more of a substance can be absorbed into a solution.

Saturday /ˈsætədeɪ, -di/ *n* [C, U] (*abbr* **Sat**) the 7th and last day of the week, next after Friday.
For further guidance on how *Saturday* is used, see the examples at *Monday.*

Saturn /ˈsætɜːn, -tən/ *n* (*astronomy*) the large planet,

6th in order of distance from the sun, with rings composed of tiny pieces of ice around it.

saturnine /ˈsætənaɪn/ adj (fml) (of people or their appearance) solemn; gloomy (GLOOM): a saturnine mood/temperament.

satyr /ˈsætə(r)/ n (in Greek and Roman myths) a god of the woods who is half man and half goat.

sauce /sɔːs/ n **1** [C, U] a liquid consisting of various ingredients that is served and eaten with food to add flavour to it: tomato/soy/chilli sauce ○ slices of veal in a white wine and cream sauce ○ make a chocolate/raspberry sauce for the ice-cream ○ What sauces go best with fish? ○ a sauce bottle. Compare GRAVY 1, TARTAR SAUCE, WHITE SAUCE. **2** [U, sing] (infml) rude behaviour that shows lack of respect for sb: That's enough of your sauce, young man! ○ He's got a sauce, criticizing me for something he does himself! **3 the sauce** [sing] (US sl) alcoholic drinks: Keep off the sauce! **IDM** **what is ˌsauce for the ˈgoose is ˌsauce for the ˈgander** (saying) what one person is allowed to do, another person must be allowed to do in similar circumstances: Isn't this a case of sauce for the goose?

▶ **saucy** adj (-ier, -iest) rude or INDECENT(1) in an amusing or harmless way: a saucy comedian/answer/postcard. **saucily** /-ɪli/ adv.

■ **ˈsauce-boat** (also **gravy boat**) n a type of long JUG(a) or dish in which sauce or GRAVY(1) is served.

saucepan /ˈsɔːspən; US -pæn/ n a metal pot, usu round and with a lid and a long handle, used for cooking things over heat. ⇨ picture at PAN¹.

saucer /ˈsɔːsə(r)/ n **1** a small shallow curved dish on which a cup stands: washing the cups and saucers. ⇨ picture at CUP¹. **2** anything shaped like a saucer, eg the dish¹(3) of a radio telescope (RADIO).

sauerkraut /ˈsaʊəkraut/ n [U] CABBAGE(1) that has been cut into small pieces and pickled (PICKLE).

sauna /ˈsɔːnə, ˈsaʊnə/ n **(a)** a period of sitting or lying in a special room heated to a very high temperature by steam from burning wood or coal: have a sauna. **(b)** a room for this: sit in the sauna. Compare TURKISH BATH.

saunter /ˈsɔːntə(r)/ v to walk slowly and without hurrying: [Vpr] saunter down the road [Vp] He sauntered by with his hands in his pockets. [also Vadv].

▶ **saunter** n [sing] a slow casual walk: go for/have a saunter around the shops.

sausage

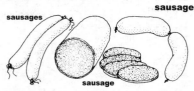

sausages

sausage

sausage /ˈsɒsɪdʒ; US ˈsɔːs-/ n [C, U] a mixture of minced (MINCE 1) meat, and other ingredients in a long thin edible skin. Sausages are cooked and eaten whole or served cold cut in slices: pork/beef sausages ○ grill some sausages ○ 200 grams of garlic sausage. ⇨ picture. See also LIVER SAUSAGE. **IDM** **not a ˈsausage** (infml) nothing at all: 'Did you buy anything?' 'Not a sausage.'

■ **ˈsausage-dog** n (infml) a DACHSHUND.

ˈsausage meat n [U] minced (MINCE 1) meat mixed with other ingredients, used for making sausages.

ˌsausage ˈroll n (Brit) a small tube of pastry containing cooked sausage meat.

sauté /ˈsəʊteɪ; US səʊˈteɪ/ adj [attrib] (of food) quickly fried in a little hot fat: sauté potatoes.

▶ **sauté** v (pt, pp **sautéed** or **sautéd**; pres p **sautéing**) to fry food in a little hot fat: [Vn] Sauté the onions for 5 minutes. ⇨ note at COOK.

savage /ˈsævɪdʒ/ adj **1(a)** wild and fierce: a savage lion/wolf ○ a savage attack by a big dog. **(b)** cruel or very violent; VICIOUS: savage criticism/fighting ○ The article was a savage attack on the government's record. ○ He has a savage temper. **2** extremely severe: savage cuts in public spending ○ The decision was a savage blow for the local residents. **3** (dated offensive) primitive; not civilized (CIVILIZE): savage tribes.

▶ **savage** n (dated offensive) a member of a primitive tribe: an island inhabited by savages ○ (derog) He described the terrorist attack as the work of savages.

savage v **1** to attack sb violently, causing serious injury: [Vn] She was savaged by a large dog. **2** to criticize sb/sth severely: [Vn] a novel savaged by the reviewers.

savagely adv: be savagely attacked/criticized ○ 'You would say that!' retorted Lynn savagely.

savagery /ˈsævɪdʒri/ n [U] cruel and violent behaviour; cruelty: The police have been appalled by the savagery of the attacks.

savannah (also **savanna**) /səˈvænə/ n [C, U] a plain in hot countries that is covered in grass but has few trees. Compare PAMPAS, PRAIRIE, STEPPE, VELD.

savant /ˈsævənt; US sæˈvɑːnt/ n (fml) a person of great learning.

save¹ /seɪv/ v **1** ~ sb/sth (from sth / doing sth) to make or keep sb/sth safe from harm, loss, etc; to rescue sb/sth: [Vn] save sb's life ○ It was too late for the doctors to save her and she died that night. [Vnpr] save sb from drowning ○ save a person from himself (eg from the results of his own foolish actions) ○ Can the firm be saved from closure? [Vn] He's trying to save their marriage. ○ She saved the set (ie at tennis) by winning the next game. **2** ~ (sth) (up) (for sth) to keep money for future use; to accumulate money instead of spending it, esp in order to buy sth: [V] you spend too much — you should start saving. [Vpr, Vp] I'm saving (up) for a new bike. [Vp] We've been saving up to go to Australia. [Vn] save some money every month [Vnp] She's managed to save up a few hundred pounds. [Vnpr] save money for a house. **3** ~ sth (for sth) to keep sth for future use; not to use all of sth: [Vn] Don't eat all that chocolate now — save some of it. [Vnpr] Save your strength for the hard work you'll have to do later. [Vnn, Vnpr] Save me some of those sweets/save some for me! **4** ~ (on) sth; ~ sth (on sth) to avoid wasting sth or using more than is necessary: [Vpr] save on time and money by shopping at the supermarket [Vnpr] save money on decorating by doing it yourself [Vn] Book early and save £50! **5** to avoid or help sb to avoid sth that is unpleasant or difficult: [Vnn] Order the goods by phone and save yourself a journey. ○ This will save us a lot of trouble. [Vn] explain sth clearly to save confusion [Vnpr] Her parents' gift saved her from having to borrow from the bank. [V.ing, V.n.ing] Walking to the office saves (me) spending money on bus fares. See also LABOUR-SAVING. **6** ~ sb (from sth) to set sb free from sin: [Vn, Vnpr] He came into the world to save us (from our sins). **7** (sport) to prevent an opponent's shot from going into the goal: [Vn] The goalkeeper saved several close-range shots. **IDM** **risk/save one's neck** ⇨ NECK. **save one's/sb's ˈbacon** (infml) to avoid or help sb avoid failure, loss, etc that seemed likely: I was nearly bankrupt, but your loan saved my bacon. **save one's ˈbreath** to avoid wasting time and effort talking because it is useless to do so: Save your breath — you'll never persuade her. **save the ˈday/situˈation** to prevent failure, disaster, etc when this seems certain to happen: Disagreements threatened to wreck the peace talks, but the President's intervention saved the situation. **save (sb's) ˈface** to preserve one's/sb's pride or reputation; to avoid or help sb to avoid embarrassment, loss of dignity, etc: She'd actually been sacked, but she saved face by telling everyone she'd resigned. **save one's**

S

(own) '**skin** (*infml usu derog*) to act without concern for others in order to escape punishment, loss, injury, etc oneself: *When the rest of the gang were arrested, he saved his own skin by giving evidence against them.*

▶ **save** *n* (in football, etc) an act of preventing a goal from being scored: *He made some amazing saves.*

saver *n* **1** a person who saves money regularly, esp in a bank or building society (BUILDING): *The rise in interest rates is good news for savers.* **2** (*Brit*) a travel ticket that costs less than the usual price: *an off-peak saver* ∘ *a saver ticket.* See also LIFE-SAVER.

-saving (forming compound *adjs*) that makes sth unnecessary or prevents waste of sth: *labour-saving devices* ∘ *energy-saving modifications.*

■ ¸**saving** '**grace** *n* (*usu sing*) a good quality that compensates for the otherwise poor qualities of sb/sth: *He may be mean and unreliable, but his one saving grace is his sense of humour.*

save² /seɪv/ (also **save for**) *prep* (*dated or fml*) except sth/sb: *We know nothing about her save (for) her name.*

▶ **save** *conj* (*dated or fml*) except: *He told us nothing about himself save that he came from Germany.*

saving /'seɪvɪŋ/ *n* **1** [C] an amount of sth not used or wasted: *a great saving of time and money* ∘ *achieve big savings on fuel through greater efficiency.* **2** **savings** [pl] money saved, esp in a bank or building society (BUILDING) account: *keep one's savings in the bank.*

■ '**savings account** *n* **1** (*Brit*) any type of bank account that earns a higher level of interest¹(5) than a current account (CURRENT¹) or deposit account (DE-POSIT²). **2** (*US*) any type of account that earns interest¹(5).

¸**savings and** '**loan association** *n* (*US*) = BUILDING SOCIETY.

'**savings bank** *n* a bank that pays interest¹(5) on money deposited but does not provide other services for its customers.

saviour (*US* **savior**) /'seɪvɪə(r)/ *n* **1** a person who rescues or saves sb/sth from danger, failure, loss, etc: *The new manager has been hailed as the saviour of the club.* **2** **the Saviour, Our Saviour** Jesus Christ.

savoir-faire /¸sævwɑː 'feə(r)/ *n* [U] (*French approv*) the ability to behave in the appropriate way in social situations: *possess/display/lack savoir-faire.*

savory (*US*) = SAVOURY.

savour (*US* **savor**) /'seɪvə(r)/ *n* (*usu sing*) a taste or flavour that sth has, esp a pleasant one: *soup with a slight savour of garlic* ∘ (*fig*) *Life seems to have lost some of its savour* (ie its enjoyable quality).

▶ **savour** *v* **1** to enjoy the taste or flavour of sth, esp by eating or drinking it slowly: [Vn] *savour the finest French cuisine.* **2** to enjoy an experience or feeling thoroughly; to RELISH sth: [Vn] *a chance to savour the rewards of success* ∘ *It was a day to savour.* ∘ *I wanted to savour every moment.* PHRV '**savour of sth** (no passive) to contain a suggestion or trace of sth, esp sth bad: *Her attitude savours of hypocrisy.*

savoury (*US* **savory**) /'seɪvəri/ *adj* **1** (of food) having a salty or sharp flavour, not a sweet one: *a savoury sauce/spread/snack/dish.* **2** having an appealing and attractive taste or smell. **3** (usu in negative sentences) morally acceptable or respectable: *not a very savoury topic for discussion* ∘ *I gather his past life was not altogether savoury.* Compare UNSAVOURY.

▶ **savoury** (*US* **savory**) *n* **1** (usu *pl*) a food with a salty or sharp flavour: *Peanuts, olives and other savouries were served with the drinks.* **2** a savoury(1) dish, usu served at the end of a meal.

savoy /sə'vɔɪ/ *n* a type of CABBAGE(1) with wrinkled (WRINKLE) leaves.

savvy /'sævi/ *n* [U] (*sl*) understanding of the realities of life; common sense (COMMON¹): *He has a lot of savvy.*

▶ **savvy** *adj* (*sl*) having common sense (COMMON¹); SHREWD: *Why can't you be a bit more savvy?*

savvy *v* [V, Vn] (*sl*) (esp in the imperative or present tense) to understand.

saw¹ *pt* of SEE¹.

saw² /sɔː/ *n* (often in compounds) a tool that has a long blade with sharp teeth on one of its edges. A saw is moved backwards and forwards by hand or driven by electrical, etc power and is used for cutting wood, metal, etc: *use a saw to cut the wood for shelves* ∘ *cutting logs with a* '*power saw.* See also CHAIN-SAW, CIRCULAR SAW, HACKSAW.

▶ **saw** *v* (*pt* **sawed**; *pp* **sawn** /sɔːn/, *US* **sawed**) **1** to use a saw; to cut sth with a saw: [V] *spend half an hour sawing* [Vpr] *saw into the branch* [Vn] *saw wood* [Vnpr] *saw a branch into logs/in two* [Vnpr] *saw the plank right through.* ⇨ note at CUT¹. **2** ~ (**away**) (**at sth**) to move sth backwards and forwards as if using a saw: [Vpr, Vp] *sawing (away) at her violin* [Vn, Vpr] *He was sawing (at) the bread with a blunt knife.* PHRV ¸**saw sth** '**down** to cut sth and bring it to the ground using a saw: *saw a tree down.* ¸**saw sth** '**off (sth)** to cut sth off with a saw: *saw a branch off (a tree)* ∘ *a sawn-off shotgun* (ie one with most of the barrel cut off, used esp by criminals because it is easier to carry and conceal). ¸**saw sth** '**up** to cut sth into pieces with a saw: *All the trees have been sawn up into logs.*

saw³ /sɔː/ *n* (*dated*) a wise saying (SAY) or PROVERB: *You know the old saw: 'More haste, less speed.'*

sawdust /'sɔːdʌst/ *n* [U] tiny pieces of wood that fall as powder from wood as it is cut with a SAW².

sawmill /'sɔːmɪl/ *n* a factory in which wood is cut into boards, etc by machinery.

sax /sæks/ *n* (*infml*) = SAXOPHONE.

saxifrage /'sæksɪfreɪdʒ/ *n* [U, C] a small plant with white, yellow or red flowers that grows among rocks in the hills or is cultivated in gardens.

Saxon /'sæksn/ *n* a member of a people once living in NW Germany, some of whom settled in Britain in the 5th and 6th centuries.

▶ **Saxon** *adj* of the Saxon people or their language: *Saxon kings/times/churches.* See also ANGLO-SAXON.

saxophone
/'sæksəfəʊn/ (also *infml* **sax**) *n* a metal musical instrument that one plays by blowing through it and pressing keys with the fingers. It is used mainly in JAZZ and dance music: *tenor/ alto/soprano saxophones* ∘ *a saxophone solo.* ⇨ picture.

saxophone

key

saxophone

▶ **saxophonist** /sæk'sɒfənɪst; *US* 'sæksəfəʊnɪst/ *n* a musician who plays the saxophone.

say /seɪ/ *v* (*3rd pers sing pres t* **says** /sez/; *pt, pp* **said** /sed/) **1** ~ **sth (to sb)** to speak or tell sb sth, using words: [V.speech] *'Hello!' she said.* [Vn] *Did you say £2.60 or £2.16?* ∘ *Be quiet, I've got something to say.* ∘ *Having said that* (ie Despite what I have just said), *I agree with your other point.* [Vnpr] *She said nothing to me about it.* ∘ *If you damage the car, your father will have plenty to say about it* (ie he will be angry). [V.that] *He said (that) his friend's name was Sam.* ∘ *They say/It's said* (ie People claim) *that he's a genius.* [Vpr.that] *He said to me that he was going to resign.* [V.wh] *He finds it hard to say what he feels.*

[Vpr] *I said to myself* (ie thought) *'That can't be right!'* [Vadv] *So you say* (ie I think it may be wrong). [V.*to* inf] *She said to meet her here.* ⇨ note. **2** to repeat words, phrases, etc that one has learned: [Vn] *say a short prayer/poem* ○ *Try to say that line with more conviction.* **3** to express an opinion on sth: [Vn] *My wife thinks I'm lazy — what do you say?* [Vn] *Say what you like* (ie Although you disagree) *about her, she's still a fine singer.* [Vnpr] *I'll say this (for them), they're a very efficient company.* [V.*that*] *I can't say I blame her for resigning* (ie I think she was justified). ○ *I would say he's right.* ○ *I say* (ie suggest) *we go without them.* ○ *I wouldn't say they were rich* (ie In my opinion they are not rich). [V.*wh*] *It's hard to say what caused the accident.* [V] *'When will the picture be finished?' 'I couldn't/can't say* (ie I don't know).*'* **4** (no passive) to suggest or give sth as an example or a possibility: [Vn] *You could learn to play chess in, (let's) say, three months.* ○ *Let's take any writer, say* (ie for example) *Dickens…* [V.*that*] *Say (that) you lose your job: what would you do then?* **5** ~ *sth (to sb)* to make thoughts, feelings, etc clear to sb by using words, gestures, etc: [Vnpr] *This poem doesn't say much to me.* [Vn] *Just what is the artist trying to say in her work?* ○ *Her angry glance said it all.* **6** (no passive) (of sth written or visible) to give certain information or instructions: [Vn] *a notice saying 'Keep Out'* ○ *The clock says three o'clock.* [V.*that*] *The instructions say (that) one should leave it to set for four hours.* [V.*wh*] *The book doesn't say where he was born.* [V.*to* inf] *The guidebook says to turn left.* **IDM** **easier said than done** ⇨ EASY². **enough said** ⇨ ENOUGH². **go without saying** to be very obvious or easy to predict: *It goes without saying that I'll help you.* **have a good word to say for sb/sth** ⇨ WORD. **have something, nothing, etc to say for oneself** to be ready, unwilling, etc to talk, eg to give one's views or justify sth one has done: *She hasn't got much to say for herself* (ie doesn't take part in conversation). ○ *He's got too much to say for himself* (ie He talks too much about himself in a way that is annoying). ○ *You're late for work again — what have you got to say for yourself?* **I dare say** ⇨ DARE. **if you don't mind me/my saying so…** ⇨ MIND². **I'll say!** (*infml*) (used for emphasis) yes; certainly: *'Does she see him often?' 'I'll say! Nearly every day.'* **I must say** (used when emphasizing an opinion): *Well, I must say, that's the funniest thing I've heard all week.* **I say** (*Brit dated*) **1** (used to express surprise, shock, etc): *I 'say! What a huge cake!* **2** (used to attract sb's attention or to introduce a subject of conversation): *I say, can you lend me five pounds?* **it says a 'lot, very 'little, etc for sb/sth** it indicates a good/bad quality that sb/sth has: *It says a lot for her* (ie shows how patient she is) *that she never lost her temper.* ○ *It doesn't say much for our efficiency* (ie It shows that we are not very efficient) *that the order arrived a week late.* **I wouldn't say 'no (to sth)** (*infml*) (used to indicate that one would like sth or to accept sth offered): *'Fancy some coffee?' 'I wouldn't say no.'* ○ *I wouldn't say no to a pizza.* **least 'said ,soonest 'mended** (*saying*) a bad situation will be resolved most quickly if nothing more is said about it. **the less said the 'better**; (*infml*) **the least said…** the best thing to do is to say as little as possible about sth: *'How did you get on in your driving test?' 'The least said the better* (ie I failed and I don't want to discuss it).*'* **let us 'say** let us suppose or imagine: *Let's say you don't get a place at university — what will you do instead?* **mean to say** ⇨ MEAN¹. **needless to say** ⇨ NEEDLESS. **never say 'die** (*saying*) don't give up hope: *Never say die: we might still get there.* **no sooner said than done** ⇨ SOON. **not be 'saying much** not to be a remarkable fact or statement: *She's a better player than me, but as I'm no good at all, that's not*

saying much. **not say boo to a 'goose**; (*US*) **not say boo to 'anyone** to be very or too shy or gentle: *He's such a nervous chap he wouldn't/couldn't say boo to a goose.* **'not to say** (used for suggesting that a stronger way of describing sb/sth is justified): *a difficult, not to say impossible, task.* **one can't say 'fairer (than 'that)** (*Brit infml*) one is being reasonable or generous, esp when making an offer: *Look, I'll give you £100 for it. I can't say fairer than that.* **put in / say a word for sb** ⇨ WORD. **sad to say** ⇨ SAD. **say/be one's last/final word** ⇨ WORD. **say 'no (to sth)** to refuse an offer, a suggestion, etc: *If you don't invest in these shares, you're saying no to a potential fortune.* **,say no 'more** (*infml*) I understand exactly what you mean, so it is unnecessary to say anything further: *'He came home with lipstick on his face.' 'Say no more!'* **,say one's 'piece** to say in full exactly what one feels or thinks: *Once I'd said my piece I wasn't quite so annoyed with her.* See also HAVE ONE'S SAY. **say 'what?** (*US sl*) (used to express surprise at what sb has just said) what did you say?: *'He's getting married.' 'Say what?'* **say 'when** (used to ask sb to indicate when one should stop pouring a drink or serving food for them because they have enough). **say the 'word** to give an order; to make a request: *Just say the word, and I'll go.* **strange to say** ⇨ STRANGE. **suffice to say** ⇨ SUFFICE. **'that is to say** in other words: *three days from now, that's to say on Friday.* **there's no knowing/saying/telling** ⇨ KNOW. **to say the 'least** without exaggerating at all; to use the mildest expression: *I was surprised at what he said, to say the least.* **to say 'nothing of sth** (used when introducing a further fact or thing, usu implying that it is either of lesser or of greater importance than the one already mentioned): *Her knowledge and experience were invaluable, to say nothing of her kindness and courtesy.* See also NOT TO MENTION (MENTION). **well 'said!** I agree completely: *'I believe we must stand up for ourselves.' 'Well said, John.'* **,what do/would you 'say (to sth / doing sth)?** would you like sth/to do sth?: *Let's go to Mexico together. What do you say?* ○ *What do you say to going to the theatre tonight?* ○ *What would you say to a whisky?* **what/whatever sb says 'goes** (*infml*) the specified person has total authority and must be obeyed: *My wife wants the kitchen painted white, and what she says goes.* **when ,all is said and 'done** when everything is taken into account: *I know you're upset, but when all's said and done it isn't exactly a disaster.* **you can say 'that again** I agree with you completely; you are absolutely right: *'He's in a bad mood today.' 'You can say that again!'* **you don't 'say!** (*infml*) (used to express surprise): *'We're going to get married.' 'You don't say!'* **you 'said it!** (*infml*) that is very true: *'The food was awful!' 'You said it!'* ○ *'I looked a right fool wearing that Donald Duck outfit.' 'You said it!'*

▶ **say** *n* [sing, U] ~ (**in sth**) the right or power to contribute one's opinion or be involved in sth: *have no/not much/some/any say (in a matter)* ○ *I want a say in the management of the business.* **IDM** **have one's 'say** to express one's view fully: *Don't interrupt her — let her have her say.* See also SAY ONE'S PIECE.

say *interj* (*US infml*) (**a**) (used for expressing surprise or pleasure): *'I've just been given a pay rise.' 'Say, that's wonderful!'* (**b**) (used for attracting sb's attention or introducing a topic of conversation): *Say! How about a Chinese meal tonight?*

saying /ˈseɪɪŋ/ *n* a well-known phrase, expression or PROVERB: *'More haste, less speed,' as the saying goes.*

■ **'say-so** *n* [sing] (*infml*) **1** a statement made by sb for which they offer no proof: *Don't take it just on my say-so — see for yourself.* **2** permission to do sth: *He can't do it without the say-so of all twelve of the directors.*

NOTE Compare **say** and **tell**. **Say** never has a person as the object. **Tell** can have two objects.

You **say** something, or **say** something **to** somebody.
You **tell** somebody something. You **tell** a story, or a joke.
You **tell** somebody **to do** something.

Anne said	*'I'm tired.'*	
	that she was tired.	
Anne told		*that she was tired.*
	me	*a story.*
	the children	*to go to bed.*

S-bend ⇨ S¹.

scab /skæb/ *n* **1** [C] a hard dry covering that forms over a wound as it heals. **2** [U] a disease of skin or plants causing a rough surface: *sheep scab.* **3** [C] (*infml derog*) a worker who refuses to join a strike, or who takes the place of sb on strike; a BLACKLEG: *scab labour.*
▶ **scabby** *adj* covered with scabs or scab: *scabby hands/apples.*

scabbard /'skæbəd/ *n* a holder for the blade of a sword, etc, esp one hanging from a belt; a SHEATH(1). ⇨ picture at SWORD.

scabies /'skeɪbiːz/ *n* [U] a skin disease that makes one ITCH(1) a lot.

scabious /'skeɪbiəs/ *n* [U] a wild or cultivated plant with blue, pink or white flowers.

scabrous /'skeɪbrəs; *US* 'skæb-/ *adj* (*fml*) **1** (of animals, plants, etc) having a rough surface. **2** INDECENT(1); sexually offensive: *scabrous novels.*

scads /skædz/ *n* [pl] ~ (**of sth**) (*infml esp US*) large numbers or amounts of sth: *scads of money/people.*

tubular scaffolding

scaffold

scaffold /'skæfəʊld/ *n* **1** a platform on which people are executed: *die on the scaffold* ∘ *go to the scaffold* (ie be executed). **2** a structure of scaffolding: *a scaffold bridge* ∘ *scaffold poles.* ⇨ picture.
▶ **scaffolding** /'skæfəldɪŋ/ *n* [U] metal poles and wooden boards joined together and put next to a building for builders (BUILD), painters, etc to stand on when working high up, or to support a platform for a speaker, etc: *put up/work on/climb scaffolding* ∘ *The statue is surrounded by scaffolding.* ⇨ picture.

scalar /'skeɪlə(r)/ *n, adj* (*mathematics*) (a quantity) having size but no direction. Compare VECTOR 1.

scalawag (*US*) = SCALLYWAG.

scald /skɔːld/ *v* **1** to burn oneself or part of one's body with boiling liquid or steam: [Vn, Vnpr] *scald one's hand (with hot fat)* [Vn] *She was badly scalded when the boiler exploded.* **2** [Vn] to heat esp milk until it is almost boiling.
▶ **scald** *n* an injury to the skin from boiling liquid or steam: *For minor burns and scalds, cool the affected area under running water.*
scalding *adj* hot enough to scald: *scalding water/tea* ∘ (*fig*) *scalding tears.* — *adv*: *scalding* (ie very) *hot.*

scale¹ /skeɪl/ *n* **1** [C usu *sing*, U] the relative size, extent, etc of sth: *entertain on a large scale* (eg hold expensive parties with many guests) ∘ *On a global scale, 77% of energy is created from fossil fuels.* ∘ *Here was corruption on a grand scale.* ∘ *achieve*

economies of scale in production (ie producing many items to reduce the price of each one) ∘ *The scale of commercial activity has declined.* ∘ *It was impossible to comprehend the full scale of the disaster.* See also FULL-SCALE, LARGE-SCALE, SMALL-SCALE. **2** [C] (**a**) a range of values forming a system for measuring or grading sth: *a scale of fees/charges/taxation* ∘ *a five-point pay scale* ∘ *evaluate performance on a scale from 1 to 10* ∘ *The salary scale goes from £12 500 to £20 000.* See also SLIDING SCALE. (**b**) a particular system of units: *the decimal scale.* See also RICHTER SCALE. **3** [C] (**a**) a series of marks at regular intervals on eg a ruler or a THERMOMETER for the purpose of measuring sth: *This ruler has one scale in centimetres and another in inches.* (**b**) an instrument marked in this way: *How much does it read on the scale?* **4** [C usu *sing*] all the different levels of sth considered as an ordered whole: *rise up the social scale* ∘ *At the other end of the scale we find gross poverty.* **5** [C] a relation between the actual size of sth and a map, diagram, etc which represents it: *a scale of ten kilometres to the centimetre* ∘ *a scale of 1:25 000* ∘ *Plans are being drawn at/to a much larger scale* (ie to show a relatively small area in detail). ∘ *a scale model/drawing.* ⇨ picture at MAP. **6** [C] (*music*) a series of notes arranged at fixed intervals in an upward or downward order, esp a series of eight starting on a KEYNOTE: *the scale of F* (ie with F as the keynote) ∘ *practise scales on the piano.* Compare OCTAVE. **IDM** **to scale** with the parts of a map, model, etc in the same proportion to each other as they are in the thing represented: *draw a map of an area to scale.*
▶ **scale** *v* **PHR V** **scale sth 'down/'up** to reduce/increase the size or number of sth: *scale up production to meet demand* ∘ *We are scaling down the number of trees to be felled.* ∘ *the scaling down of military forces.*

scale² /skeɪl/ *n* **1**(**a**) [C] any of the thin plates of hard material covering the skin of many fish and reptiles: *scrape the scales from a herring.* ⇨ picture at FISH¹. (**b**) [C] a thing resembling this: *buds with a covering of sticky scales.* **2** (also **fur**) [U] the hard greyish-white material sometimes deposited inside kettles (KETTLE), pipes, etc by water when it is heated: *lime scale.* **3** [U] a hard layer of material that forms on teeth, esp when they are not cleaned regularly; PLAQUE².
▶ **scale** *v* [Vn] to remove the scales (SCALE² 1a) from fish. Compare DESCALE.
scaly *adj* covered with scale or scales: *scaly skin/ferns/monsters* ∘ *a kettle that is scaly inside.*

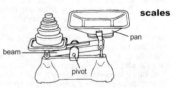

scales

pan
beam
pivot

scale³ /skeɪl/ *n* **1** **scales** [pl *v*] (*US* also **scale** [C]) an instrument for weighing people or things: *a pair of scales* ∘ *bathroom/kitchen/weighing scales.* ⇨ picture. **2** [C] either of the two pans on a balance¹(5): (*fig*) *the scales of justice.* **IDM** **tip the balance/scale** ⇨ TIP².

scale⁴ /skeɪl/ *v* to climb up sth steep, eg a wall or a cliff: [Vn] *a surgeon who has scaled the heights of his profession.*

scallion /'skæliən/ *n* (*esp US*) = SPRING ONION.

scallop *n* /'skɒləp; *US* 'skæl-/ **1**(**a**) a type of edible SHELLFISH with two shells shaped like fans. (**b**) (also **'scallop shell**) either shell of this, sometimes used for cooking or serving food in. **2** any one of a series of small curves cut on the edge of fabric, pastry, etc for decoration.

▶ **scallop** v to decorate sth with scallops (SCALLOP 2): [Vn] *a scalloped hem.*

scallywag /'skæliwæg/ (*US* **scalawag** /'skælə-wæg/) n (*infml joc*) a person, esp a child, who behaves badly but in a harmless way: *You naughty little scallywag!*

scalp /skælp/ n **1** the skin of the head excluding the face: *Regular treatment of the scalp will control dandruff.* **2** part of the scalp and the hair rooted in it, formerly cut off a dead enemy by some N American Indians as a sign of victory: (*fig*) *In his fight to expose official corruption he has claimed some notable scalps.*

▶ **scalp** v to take the scalp(2) from an enemy: [Vn] (*fig infml*) *He'll scalp me* (ie punish me severely) *if he finds me here!*

scalpel /'skælpəl/ n a small sharp light knife used by doctors performing operations.

scam /skæm/ n (*infml*) a dishonest scheme: *a betting/currency scam.*

scamp /skæmp/ n a child who enjoys playing tricks and causing trouble: *That little scamp Jimmy has hidden my slippers again!*

scamper /'skæmpə(r)/ v to run with quick bouncing steps, esp because of fear or excitement: [Vnpr] *The children scampered up the steps laughing.* [V] *the sound of scampering feet* [Vp] *The rabbit scampered away/off in fright.* ⇨ note at SCURRY.

scampi /'skæmpi/ n [U] a dish of large prawns (PRAWN), usu fried: *I'll just have some scampi.*

scan /skæn/ v (**-nn-**) **1** to look at every part of sth carefully; to examine sth with great attention: [Vnpr] *He scanned the horizon for any sign of land.* [Vn] *She scanned his face anxiously.* **2** to look quickly but not very thoroughly at a document, letter, etc: [Vn] *She scanned the newspaper over breakfast.* **3** (of a light, RADAR, etc) to pass across an area: [Vn] *Concealed video cameras scan every part of the town centre.* **4** (*computing*) to pass an electronic beam over sth in order to put it in the memory of a computer: [Vnpr] *Documents and diagrams can be scanned into the computer.* [also Vn]. **5** (*medical*) to obtain an image of a person's body or part of it on a computer after taking an X-RAY(2a) or using ULTRA-SOUND techniques. **6(a)** [Vn] to analyse the rhythm of a line of verse, as in 'Mary/'had a/'little/'lamb. **(b)** (of verse) to have a regular rhythm according to fixed rules: [V] *a line that does not scan.*

▶ **scan** n an act of scanning sb/sth: *have a quick scan through the job adverts* ○ *do/have a 'brain scan.*

scanner n (*techn*) **1** a device used by doctors to produce a picture of the inside of a person's body on a computer screen after eg taking a series of X-rays (X-RAY 2a) or using ULTRASOUND techniques. **2** a device that can be passed across a document, etc in order to store its contents in a computer. **3** a device for receiving and sending esp RADAR signals.

scansion /'skænʃn/ n [U] **(a)** the action of scanning (SCAN 6a) verse. **(b)** the way in which verse scans (SCAN 6b).

scandal /'skændl/ n **1(a)** [U, C] behaviour considered to be morally or legally wrong, causing or likely to cause public shock or anger: *The scandal broke* (ie became known to the public) *in 1994.* ○ *attempts to hush up the scandal* ○ *A series of corruption scandals led to the fall of the government.* **(b)** [U, sing] public feelings of shock and anger at behaviour considered morally or legally wrong: *Her arrest for theft caused* (a) *scandal in the village.* **2** [U] talk about things people have done or are thought to have done which are considered morally wrong and shocking: *spread scandal* ○ *Further scandal concerning the bishop appeared in yesterday's tabloids.* **3** [sing] an action, attitude, etc that is considered wrong and shocking: *It is a scandal that*

the defendant was declared innocent. ○ *The council's failure to act is a scandal.*

▶ **scandalize, -ise** /'skændəlaɪz/ v to shock sb by doing sth they consider is not proper or is morally wrong: [Vn] *scandalize the neighbours by sunbathing naked on the lawn.*

scandalous /'skændələs/ adj **1** causing public anger or disgust; shocking: *scandalous behaviour/talk/pictures* ○ *It is scandalous that you were treated so badly.* **2** [attrib] (of reports or rumours) containing scandal(2). **scandalously** adv: *scandalously low pay.*

scandalmonger /'skændlmʌŋgə(r)/ n (*derog*) a person who spreads scandal(2).

scansion ⇨ SCAN.

scant /skænt/ adj [attrib] (*fml*) hardly enough; not very much: *pay scant attention to sb's advice* ○ *behave with scant regard/respect for my feelings* ○ *Information on their migration routes is scant.*

▶ **scanty** adj small in size or amount; hardly large enough: *a scanty bikini* ○ *scanty evidence.* **scantily** adv: *scantily clad/dressed.*

-scape suff (with ns forming ns) a view of sth: *landscape* ○ *seascape* ○ *moonscape.*

scapegoat /'skeɪpgəʊt/ (also esp US **fall guy**) n a person who is blamed or punished for the wrongdoing or faults of sb else: *He has been made the scapegoat for the government's incompetence.*

scapula /'skæpjʊlə/ n (pl **scapulae** or **scapulas**) (*anatomy*) a shoulder-blade (SHOULDER). ⇨ picture at SKELETON.

scar /skɑː(r)/ n **1** a mark left on the skin by a wound, burn, etc after it has healed: 'scar tissue ○ *Will the cut leave a scar?* ○ (*fig*) *bullet scars on walls.* **2** a feeling of great sadness, guilt, etc after an unpleasant experience: *the scars of war* ○ *emotional scars* ○ *Her years in prison left a scar.* **3** an area of a hill or cliff where there is bare rock and no grass, etc.

▶ **scar** v (**-rr-**) to leave a scar or scars on sb/sth: [Vn] *a face scarred by acne* ○ (*fig*) *a scarred landscape* ○ *battle-scarred soldiers* ○ *The experience scarred her for life.*

scarce /skeəs/ adj (**-er, -est**) not easily obtained and usu found only in small quantities: *scarce resources* ○ *Money/Labour was scarce.* ○ *Food soon became scarcer and more expensive.* Compare PLENTIFUL. ⇨ note at RARE. **IDM** ,**make oneself 'scarce** (*infml*) to go away and not attract attention: *I could tell they wanted to be left alone so I made myself scarce.*

▶ **scarcity** /'skeəsəti/ n [C, U] the lack of sth or difficulty of obtaining it; SHORTAGE: *frequent scarcities of raw materials* ○ *The scarcity of food forced prices up.*

scarcely /'skeəsli/ adv **1** only just; almost not: *There were scarcely a hundred people present.* ○ *I scarcely know him.* ○ *We can scarcely afford the rent.* **2** only a short time before: *Scarcely had she entered the room when the phone rang.* **3** (used to suggest that sth is very unlikely) surely not: *You can scarcely expect me to believe that!* ⇨ note at ALMOST. Compare BARELY, HARDLY 1.

scare /'skeə(r)/ v **(a)** to frighten sb: [Vn] *That noise scared me.* [Vnadv] *The thought of my exams next week scares me stiff* (ie makes me feel extremely frightened). **(b)** to become frightened: [Vadv] *He scares easily.* **IDM** **frighten/scare the daylights out of sb** ⇨ DAYLIGHTS. **frighten/scare the life out of sb** ⇨ LIFE. **frighten/scare sb to death** ⇨ DEATH. **scare the 'shit out of sb** to frighten sb vey much. **PHRV** ,**scare sb a'way/'off** to make sb leave, stay away, etc by frightening or alarming them: *light a fire to scare off the wolves* ○ *He scares people away by being so brash.* **scare sb into doing sth** to frighten sb in order to make them do sth: *They scared him into handing over the keys.*

▶ **scare** *n* (usu *sing*) (**a**) a sudden feeling of fear: *You did give me a scare, creeping up on me like that!* (**b**) anxiety or alarm about sth: *The explosion at the chemical factory caused a major pollution scare.* ○ *a* '*scare story* (eg a newspaper report that spreads alarm).

scared *adj* ~ (**of sb/sth**); ~ (**of doing sth / to do sth**) frightened: *scared of being attacked/to go out alone* ○ *a scared look/face* ○ *I'm scared of snakes.* ○ *Didn't you feel scared?* ⇨ note at AFRAID.

scary /'skeəri/ *adj* (**-ier, -iest**) (*infml*) causing fear or alarm: *a scary ghost story* ○ *The last part of the climb was quite scary.*

scarecrow /'skeəkrəʊ/ *n* a figure made to resemble a person that is dressed in old clothes and put in a field to frighten birds away.

scaremonger /'skeəmʌŋgə(r)/ *n* (*derog*) a person who frightens people by spreading alarming news, rumours, etc. ▶ **scaremongering** *n* [U]: *journalists accused of scaremongering.*

scarf /skɑːf/ *n* (*pl* **scarfs** /skɑːfs/ or *esp Brit* **scarves** /skɑːvz/) a piece of material worn for ornament or warmth round the neck or, by women, over the shoulders or hair.

scarlet /'skɑːlət/ *adj, n* [U] (of) a bright red colour: *scarlet flowers* ○ *dressed all in scarlet* ○ *She blushed scarlet when I swore.*

■ ,**scarlet** '**fever** *n* [U] an infectious disease causing red marks on the skin.

,**scarlet** '**woman** *n* (*dated derog or joc*) a prostitute; a woman who has sexual relations with many partners.

scarp /skɑːp/ *n* a very steep slope.

scarper /'skɑːpə(r)/ *v* (*Brit sl*) to run away; to leave quickly: [V] *The baby's father scarpered as soon as I told him I was pregnant.*

scary ⇨ SCARE.

scathing /'skeɪðɪŋ/ *adj* ~ (**about sb/sth**) (of criticism, etc) severe; harsh; showing contempt or SCORN: *a scathing remark/rebuke/review* ○ *a scathing attack on the government* ○ *The report was scathing about the lack of safety precautions.* ▶ **scathingly** *adv*: *She wrote scathingly of his work.*

scatter /'skætə(r)/ *v* **1** to move or make people or animals move, usu quickly, in different directions: [V] *The crowd scattered.* [Vn] *The police scattered the crowd.* **2(a)** to throw sth in different directions; to put sth here and there: [Vn, Vnpr] *scatter seed (over the ground)* [Vnpr] *scatter grit on the road* [Vnp] *A few cushions were scattered about.* (**b**) ~ **sth with sth** to cover a surface, etc with sth thrown over it in small quantities: [Vnpr] *scatter the lawn with grass seed.*

▶ **scatter** (also **scattering** /'skætərɪŋ/) *n* [*sing*] a small amount or number of things scattered or spread apart: *a scatter of hailstones* ○ *a scattering of applause/houses.*

scattered *adj* lying far apart; not close together: *a few scattered settlements* ○ *a thinly scattered population* ○ *sunshine with scattered showers.*

NOTE When you **scatter** things you throw them in different directions in order to spread them across an area. You can also scatter an area such as the ground or a field *with* things: *We scattered seeds on the ground/scattered the ground with seeds for the birds.* **Scatter over/around** suggests the result is untidy or unplanned: *Clothes were scattered around the room.* **Sprinkle** means to throw water, sand, salt, etc intentionally over a small area: *Sprinkle the herbs over the rice before serving.* ○ *She sprinkled some oil on her hands.* **Strew** is usually used in the past participle form **strewn** and suggests that things have been thrown either intentionally or carelessly: *The streets were strewn with flowers.* ○ *There was litter strewn all over the garden.*

scatterbrain /'skætəbreɪn/ *n* (*infml*) a person who forgets things or who cannot concentrate on one thing for very long. ▶ '**scatterbrained** *adj.*

scatty /'skæti/ *adj* (*Brit infml*) **1** slightly mad; crazy: *The noise would drive anyone scatty.* **2** tending to forget things: *Your scatty son has forgotten his key again.*

scavenge /'skævɪndʒ/ *v* **1** ~ (**for sth**) (of an animal or a bird) to search for decaying flesh as food: [Vpr] *a crow scavenging for carrion* ○ *Badgers will scavenge from sheep and lamb carcasses.* [also V]. **2** ~ (**for**) **sth** (of a person) to search through waste for items that one can use: [Vpr] *tramps scavenging through dustbins* [Vn, Vnpr] *They scavenge junk (from the rubbish site) and sell it.*

▶ **scavenger** *n* an animal, a bird or a person that scavenges.

scenario /sə'nɑːriəʊ; *US* -'nær-/ *n* (*pl* **-os**) **1** ~ (**for sb/sth**) an imagined sequence of future events: *a likely/a possible/an alternative scenario for the company's future* ○ *The worst scenario is/would be closure of the factory.* **2** a written outline of a film, play, etc giving details of the scenes and plot.

scene /siːn/ *n* **1** [C usu *sing*] a real or imagined place where sth happens: *the scene of the accident/crime/battle* ○ *Police **reached the scene** too late to prevent a riot.* ○ *Reporters **arrived/were on the scene** (ie at the place) soon after the bomb exploded.* **2** [C] a situation or an incident in real life: *the horrific scene(s) after the earthquake* ○ *There were scenes of violence in the capital today.* **3** [C usu *sing*] a display of emotion or anger: *make a scene* ○ *There was quite a scene when she refused to pay.* **4** [C] a view of everything in sight: *a delightful rural scene* ○ *gazing in amazement at the scene before them* ○ *They went abroad for a **change of scene** (ie to see and experience new surroundings).* **5** [C] a picture of an area showing the activities of people or animals in it: *scenes of Venice* ○ *He paints woodland scenes.* **6** [C] (**a**) (usu *sing*) a place represented on the stage of a theatre: *The **scene is set** in Normandy.* (**b**) the painted background, etc representing such a place; the scenery(2): *The scenes are changed during the interval.* **7** [C] (**a**) a sequence of continuous action in a play, film, etc: *a nude/sex/love scene* ○ *The scene in the hospital was very moving.* (**b**) a part of an act in a play or an opera; a section within such a part: *Act 1, Scene 2 of 'Macbeth'* ○ *the duel scene in 'Hamlet'.* **8 the scene** [*sing*] (esp after a *n*) (*infml*) the current situation in a particular area of activity or way of life: *the* '*music/*'*folk scene* ○ *a newcomer on the* '*fashion scene* ○ *the po*'*litical scene* ○ *After years at the top, she simply vanished from the scene.* IDM **behind the** '**scenes 1** out of sight of the audience; behind the stage. **2** in secret; without being known to the public: *political deals done behind the scenes.* **not one's** '**scene** (*infml*) not sth one is interested in: *I'm not going to the disco — it's just not my scene.* **set the** '**scene (for sth) 1** to describe a place or a situation in which sth is about to happen: *The opening chapter does little more than set the scene.* **2** to help to cause sth: *His arrival set the scene for another argument.*

scenery /'siːnəri/ *n* [U] **1** the natural features of an area, eg mountains, valleys, rivers and forests: *mountain scenery* ○ *stop to admire the scenery.* **2** the painted background used to represent natural features or buildings, etc on a theatre stage.

scenic /'siːnɪk/ *adj* [usu attrib] having or showing beautiful natural scenery: *an area of scenic beauty* ○ *the scenic splendours of the Rocky Mountains* ○ *take the scenic route home.* ▶ **scenically** /-kli/ *adv.*

scent /sent/ *n* **1(a)** [U] the characteristic smell of sth, esp a pleasant one: *the scent of pines/new-mown hay* ○ *These flowers have no scent.* (**b**) [C] a particular type of smell: *a delicate scent of lavender* ○ *a musky* *scent.* **2** [U] (*esp Brit*) a usu liquid substance with a pleasant smell obtained from animals, flowers, plants, etc and worn esp by women on the skin; PERFUME(1): *a bottle of scent* ○ *put some scent on before going out* ○ *a ¹scent bottle.* **3(a)** [U, C usu *sing*] a smell left behind by people and animals that enables dogs, etc to follow their track: *follow/lose/pick up/recover the scent* ○ *Hounds hunt by scent.* **(b)** [sing] a trail of evidence or signs that helps sb to find sb/sth: *Scientists are on the scent of a cure.* ○ *He grew a beard to put/throw reporters off the scent* (ie to stop them following him). **4** [sing] ~ **of sth** a feeling of the presence of sth: *a scent of danger/fear/trouble/victory.*

▶ **scent** *v* **1(a)** to discover sth by the sense of smell: [Vn] *The dog scented a rat.* **(b)** to begin to suspect the presence or existence of sth: [Vn] *scent a crime* ○ *scent victory* ○ *scent blood* (ie the possibility of defeating sb and gaining REVENGE(1a)) ○ *The press have already scented a story.* **2** ~ **sth (with sth)** (esp passive) to give sth a certain scent: [Vn] *scented candles/notepaper/soap* ○ *roses that scent the air* [Vnpr] *a handkerchief scented with lavender.*

scepter (*US*) = SCEPTRE.

sceptic (*US* **skeptic**) /ˈskeptɪk/ *n* **1** a person who doubts that a claim, statement, etc is true: *The government must still convince the sceptics that its policy will work.* **2** a person who does not think religious teachings are true.

▶ **sceptical** (*US* **skep-**) /-kl/ *adj* ~ **(of/about sth)** unwilling to believe sth; doubtful that claims, statements, etc are true or that sth will happen: *I'm rather sceptical about his chances of winning, despite what the papers say.* **sceptically** (*US* **skep-**) /-kli/ *adv.*

scepticism (*US* **skep-**) /ˈskeptɪsɪzəm/ *n* [U, sing] a sceptical attitude: *treat a report with scepticism* ○ *have a healthy scepticism about public relations.*

sceptre (*US* **scepter**) /ˈseptə(r)/ *n* an ornamental rod carried by a king or queen as a sign of royal power, eg at a state ceremony. Compare MACE¹ 1, ORB 2.

schedule /ˈʃedjuːl; *US* ˈskedʒuːl/ *n* **1(a)** a programme of work to be done or of planned events: *a factory production schedule* ○ *have a full/tight/busy schedule* (ie have many things to do) ○ *a project that is ahead of/on/behind schedule* ○ *Everything is running to schedule.* **(b)** = TIMETABLE: *The fog disrupted airline schedules.* **2** a list of items or points of agreement: *a spare parts schedule* ○ *Schedule 4 of the Companies Act.*

▶ **schedule** *v* ~ **sth (for sth)** (esp passive) to include sth in a schedule; to arrange sth for a certain time: [Vn] *a scheduled flight/service* (ie one that happens regularly) ○ *One of the scheduled events is a talk on alternative medicine.* [Vnpr] *The sale is scheduled for tomorrow.* [V.n to inf] *She is scheduled to give a speech in Brussels tonight.*

schema /ˈskiːmə/ *n* (*pl* **schemata** /-mətə, skiːˈmɑːtə/) (*fml*) an outline or representation of a plan, a theory, an arrangement, etc.

schematic /skiːˈmætɪk/ *adj* in the form of a plan or chart: *a schematic diagram of the structure of the organization.* ▶ **schematically** /-kli/ *adv.*

scheme /skiːm/ *n* **1** ~ **(for sth/for doing sth/to do sth)** a plan or an arrangement for doing or organizing sth: *an imaginative scheme to raise/for raising money* ○ *training/pension/insurance schemes* ○ *another one of his hare-brained/grandiose schemes.* **2** an ordered system; an arrangement: *a coordinated ¹lighting scheme.* See also COLOUR SCHEME. **IDM** **the ¹scheme of things** the way things are or are planned: *This department has little influence in the overall scheme of things.*

▶ **scheme** *v* **(a)** to plan, esp secretly, to do sth for one's own benefit: [Vpr] *rebels scheming against*

their leader [V.to inf] *They are scheming to discredit her.* [also V]. **(b)** to plan secretly sth to one's own advantage: [Vn] *Her enemies are scheming her downfall.* **schemer** *n* a person who schemes. **scheming** *adj* often making secret and dishonest schemes: *her scheming nephew.*

scherzo /ˈskeətsəʊ/ *n* (*pl* **-os**) a lively vigorous piece of music, usually playful or comic; such a section in a larger work.

schism /ˈsɪzəm/ *n* [U, C] strong disagreement within an organization, esp a religious one, causing its members to divide into separate groups HOSTILE(1a) to each other: *a schism within the Anglican Church* ○ *the threat of schism within the government.* ▶ **schismatic** /sɪzˈmætɪk/ *adj*: *schismatic religious movements.*

schizoid /ˈskɪtsɔɪd/ *adj* resembling or suffering from SCHIZOPHRENIA: *schizoid tendencies.*

schizophrenia /ˌskɪtsəˈfriːniə/ *n* [U] (*medical*) a mental illness in which a person is unable to link her or his thoughts and feelings to real life, suffers from delusions (DELUSION 2) and withdraws increasingly from social relationships into a life of the imagination.

▶ **schizophrenic** /ˌskɪtsəˈfrenɪk/ *adj* of or suffering from schizophrenia: *a schizophrenic personality* ○ *We didn't realize he was schizophrenic.* — *n* a person suffering from schizophrenia: *She was diagnosed a schizophrenic while at university.*

schlepp (also **schlep**) /ʃlep/ *v* (**-pp-**) (*US sl*) **1** to carry sth that is heavy or awkward a long way: [Vnpr] *We had to schlepp those boxes across town.* [also Vn]. **2** to spend a lot of energy or effort doing sth: [Vpr] *I really don't fancy schlepping all the way down there.* [also Vp, Vadv].

schlock /ʃlɒk/ *n* [U] (*US sl*) things that are cheap and of inferior quality; TRASH(1): *stores full of schlock.*

schmaltz /ʃmɔːlts/ *n* [U] (*infml*) the quality of being excessively sentimental, esp in the arts. ▶ **schmaltzy** *adj*: *a schmaltzy script.*

schmo /ʃməʊ/ (also **schmuck** /ʃmʌk/) *n* (*US sl derog*) a foolish person: *I wouldn't be caught dead dancing with that schmo!*

schnapps /ʃnæps/ *n* [U] a strong alcoholic drink made from grain.

scholar /ˈskɒlə(r)/ *n* **1** a student who has been awarded money, esp after a competitive examination, to help pay for her or his education: *a British Council scholar.* **2** a person who has a deep knowledge of an academic subject: *a Greek/history scholar.*

▶ **scholarly** *adj* **1** involving or connected with academic study: *a scholarly journal* ○ *scholarly pursuits.* **2** showing the learning, care and attention typical of a scholar: *be more scholarly in one's approach to a problem* ○ *a scholarly young woman.*

scholarship /ˈskɒləʃɪp/ *n* **1** [C] an award of money to sb to help pay for their education: *win a scholarship to the university* ○ *a music scholarship.* **2** [U] the learning, methods or standards of a good SCHOLAR(2): *a distinguished work of scholarship.*

scholastic /skəˈlæstɪk/ *adj* **1** [usu attrib] (*fml*) of schools and education: *one's scholastic achievements.* **2** of scholasticism.

▶ **scholasticism** /skəˈlæstɪsɪzəm/ *n* [U] a system of philosophy taught in universities in the Middle Ages, based on religious principles.

school¹ /skuːl/ *n* **1** [C] **(a)** an institution for educating children: *attend a good/the local school* ○ *the use of computers in schools* ○ *school holidays/rules* ○ *a school bus/building/report* ○ *Which school do you go to?* **(b)** the buildings used by such an institution: *build a new school.* See also BOARDING-SCHOOL, COMPREHENSIVE SCHOOL, FINISHING-SCHOOL, FIRST SCHOOL,

GRAMMAR SCHOOL, HIGH SCHOOL, JUNIOR SCHOOL, MIDDLE SCHOOL, NIGHT SCHOOL, NURSERY SCHOOL, PLAYSCHOOL, PREPARATORY SCHOOL, PRIVATE SCHOOL, PUBLIC SCHOOL, SECONDARY SCHOOL, SUNDAY SCHOOL. **(c)** an institution for teaching a particular subject: *go to 'art/'drama/'ballet school.* **2** [U] (used without *the*) **(a)** the process of being educated in a school¹(1a): *old enough for/to go to school* ○ *two more years of school* ○ *(Brit) the school-'leaving age* (ie the age until which children must attend school) ○ *I hate school!* ○ *He left school when he was sixteen.* **(b)** the time when teaching is done in a school; lessons: *meet friends before school* ○ *after-school activities* ○ *School begins at 9 am.* ○ *There will be no school* (ie no lessons) *tomorrow.* ⇨ note. **3 the school** [sing] all the pupils or all the pupils and teachers in a school: *Soon, the whole school knew about it.* **4** [C] *(US infml)* a college or university: *famous schools like Yale and Harvard.* **5** [C] a department of a university concerned with a particular area of study: *the ¹law/¹medical/¹history school* ○ *the School of ¹Dentistry.* **6** [C] a course, usu for adults, on a particular subject: *a summer school for music lovers/on modern art.* **7** [C usu sing] *(infml)* an experience or activity that provides discipline or instruction: *the hard school of life.* **8** [C] a group of writers, artists, etc sharing the same principles, views, methods or style: *the Dutch/Venetian school of painting* ○ *the Hegelian school* (ie of writers on philosophy who were influenced by Hegel). **IDM** **one of the old school** ⇨ OLD. **a school of 'thought** a group of people with similar views: *I don't belong to the school of thought that favours radical change.* **teach school** ⇨ TEACH.

▶ **school** *v* ~ **sb/oneself/sth (in sth)** to train sb/oneself/an animal: [Vn] *school a horse* [Vnpr, Vn.to inf] *school oneself in patience/to be patient* [Vnpr] *be well schooled in the basic techniques of drawing.*

schooling *n* [U] the education one receives at school: *He had very little schooling.* ○ *Who's paying for her schooling?*

■ **'school age** *n* [U] the age or period when a child normally attends school: *a child of school age.*

'school-days *n* [pl] the period of one's life when one attends school: *look back fondly on one's school-days.*

'school friend (also **schoolfellow, schoolmate**) *n* a friend who attends or attended the same school as oneself: *I met an old* (ie former) *school friend yesterday.*

,school-'leaver *n* (Brit) a person who has recently left school: *jobs for school-leavers.*

NOTE In British and American English when a **school, church, prison,** etc is being referred to as an institution, you do not need to use **the** after a preposition: *She went to university in York.* ○ *He was sent to prison for a year.* ○ *I can't believe your daughter is in college already.*

If you are going to a **hospital** as a patient you say: *I'm going to hospital.* If you are going as a visitor you say: *I'm going to the hospital to visit my friend.* In American English you always talk about going to **the hospital.**

When you are talking about the specific building, **the** is used: *We went to the school to discuss our daughter's progress.* ○ *I saw her leaving the hospital/ leaving the church* (ie going out of the building).

---

school² /sku:l/ *n* a large number of fish or whales (WHALE), etc swimming together; a SHOAL¹.

schoolboy /'sku:lbɔɪ/ *n* a boy at school: *schoolboy humour.*

schoolchild /'sku:ltʃaɪld/ *n* (*pl* **schoolchildren** /-tʃɪldrən/) (usu *pl*) a child attending school.

schoolfellow /'sku:lfeləʊ/ *n* = SCHOOL FRIEND.

schoolgirl /'sku:lgɜ:l/ *n* a girl at school: *a 13-year-old schoolgirl.*

schoolhouse /'sku:lhaʊs/ *n* (esp formerly) a building used as a school, esp a small one in a village.

schoolmaster /'sku:lmɑ:stə(r)/ *n* (*fem* **schoolmistress** /'sku:lmɪstrəs/) a teacher in a school, esp a private school.

schoolmate /'sku:lmeɪt/ *n* = SCHOOL FRIEND.

schoolteacher /'sku:lti:tʃə(r)/ *n* a teacher in a school.

schooner /'sku:nə(r)/ *n* **1** a type of ship with two or more masts (MAST 1) and sets of sails. **2 (a)** *(Brit)* a tall glass for SHERRY. **(b)** *(US)* a tall glass for beer.

schwa /ʃwɑː/ *n* (*phonetics*) **(a)** a vowel sound that occurs in parts of words that are not stressed, eg the 'a' in 'about' or the 'e' in 'moment'. **(b)** the PHONETIC symbol for this, /ə/.

sciatic /saɪˈætɪk/ *adj* [usu attrib] *(anatomy)* of the hip or of the **sciatic nerve**, which goes from the PELVIS to the THIGH.

▶ **sciatica** /saɪˈætɪkə/ *n* [U] pain affecting or near the sciatic nerve.

science /ˈsaɪəns/ *n* **(a)** [U] the study of the structure and behaviour of the physical and natural world and society, esp through observation and experiment: *demand more funding for science in the universities* ○ *professionals in science and industry* ○ *a science teacher/writer/museum/course.* **(b)** [U,C] a particular area of this: *medical science* ○ *computer science* ○ *the science of engineering* ○ *study one of the sciences.* Compare ART¹ 3. See also DOMESTIC SCIENCE, NATURAL SCIENCE, POLITICAL SCIENCE, SOCIAL SCIENCE.

IDM **blind sb with science** ⇨ BLIND².

▶ **scientist** /ˈsaɪəntɪst/ *n* a person who studies one or more of the natural or physical sciences: *a research scientist* ○ *forensic/nuclear scientists.*

■ **,science 'fiction** (also *infml* **sci-fi**) *n* [U] a type of writing based on imagined scientific discoveries of the future, and often dealing with space travel, life on other planets, etc.

'science park *n* a group of buildings with facilities for scientific research or the development of industries based on science.

scientific /ˌsaɪənˈtɪfɪk/ *adj* **(a)** [attrib] of, used in or involved in science: *a scientific discovery/ instrument/study/adviser* ○ *scientific research.* **(b)** using methods based on those of science: *scientific farming* ○ *They are very scientific in their approach.*

▶ **scientifically** /-klɪ/ *adv.*

sci-fi /ˌsaɪ ˈfaɪ/ *n* [U] *(infml)* = SCIENCE FICTION.

scimitar /ˈsɪmɪtə(r)/ *n* a short curved sword with one sharp edge. ⇨ picture at SWORD.

scintilla /sɪnˈtɪlə/ *n* [sing] ~ **of sth** *(fml)* (usu in negative sentences) a tiny amount of sth: *There was not a scintilla of truth in the claim.*

scintillating /ˈsɪntɪleɪtɪŋ/ *adj* brilliant; amusing in a clever way: *a scintillating performance/display* ○ *(ironic) That was a very scintillating conversation!*

scion /ˈsaɪən/ *n* **1** *(fml or rhet)* a young member of a family, esp a noble one. **2** a piece of a plant, esp one cut to make a new plant.

scissors

nail clippers

scissors

pinking shears

gardening shears

hairdresser's clippers

secateurs

[V.*to* inf] = verb + *to* infinitive   [Vn.inf (no *to*)] = verb + noun + infinitive without *to*   [V.*ing*] = verb + -*ing* form

scissors /ˈsɪzəz/ n [pl] an instrument consisting of two blades joined in the middle with a ring at the end of each through which one puts one's thumb and a finger in order to open and close them. Scissors are used for cutting eg paper or cloth: *a pair of scissors.* ⇨ picture.

sclerosis /skləˈrəʊsɪs/ n [U] (*medical*) a condition in which soft tissue in the body becomes abnormally hard. See also MULTIPLE SCLEROSIS.
▶ **sclerotic** /skləˈrɒtɪk/ *adj* of or having sclerosis.

scoff¹ /skɒf; *US* skɔːf/ v ~ (**at sb/sth**) to speak with contempt about sb/sth; to JEER at or mock sb/sth: [Vpr] *scoff at other people's beliefs* [V] *Don't scoff — he's quite right.* ▶ **scoffer** n.

scoff² /skɒf/ v (*Brit infml*) to eat a lot of sth quickly: [Vn] *Who scoffed all the biscuits?*

scold /skəʊld/ v ~ **sb** (**for sth / doing sth**) to speak angrily to sb, esp a child, because they have done sth wrong: [Vnpr] *He scolded me because I left the window open.* [Vnpr] *She scolded herself for her silliness/for being so silly.* [also V]. ▶ **scolding** n (usu *sing*): *give sb/get a (good) scolding for being late.*

scone /skɒn, skəʊn/ n (*esp Brit*) a small baked cake made of flour, fat and milk. Scones are often eaten with butter or cream and jam.

scoop /skuːp/ n **1**(**a**) a tool with a handle and an open curved surface, used for picking up and moving grain, flour, sugar, etc. ⇨ picture.

scoop

(**b**) a similar small tool with a round bowl at one end, used esp for serving ice-cream. (**c**) an amount picked up by a scoop: *two scoops of mashed potato.* **2**(**a**) a piece of important or exciting news made public by a newspaper, radio station, etc before its rivals: *a royal scoop.* (**b**) a large profit or amount of money: *Pensioner in £500 000 Pools Scoop* (eg as a HEADLINE).
▶ **scoop** v **1**(**a**) to move or lift sth with, or as if with, a scoop(1): [Vnpr] *scoop rice out of a sack* ∘ *She scooped ice-cream into their bowls.* [Vnp] *The children were scooping up fistfuls of sand.* [also Vn]. ~ **sth** (**out**) to make a hole or hollow part in sth with, or as if with, a scoop: [Vnpr] *scoop a hole in the sand* [Vnp] *scoop out the inside of a melon.* **2** ~ **sb/ sth** (**up**) to move or lift sb/sth with a quick flowing movement: [Vnp] *She scooped him up into her arms.* [Vnpr] *He scooped his anorak off the peg as he passed.* **3** [Vn] (**a**) to act before a rival, etc to make news public: *She scooped all the national newspapers to get the story.* (**b**) to get sth, esp a large profit or amount of money: *He scooped £50 000 in the lottery.* ∘ *She scooped all three awards.*

scoot /skuːt/ v (*infml*) to go somewhere in a hurry: [V] *I'd better scoot or I'll be late.* [Vp] *She's gone scooting off to Edinburgh for the weekend.* [also Vpr].

scooter /ˈskuːtə(r)/ n **1** (also *esp US* **ˈmotor scooter**) a light motor cycle (MOTOR), usu with small wheels, a low seat and a curved metal shield protecting the driver's legs. ⇨ picture at MOTOR CYCLE. **2** a child's vehicle with a front and back wheel connected by a narrow board and with handles connected to the front wheel by an upright bar. The rider holds the handles, puts one foot on the board and pushes against the ground with the other foot.

scope /skəʊp/ n [U] **1** ~ (**for sth / to do sth**) the opportunity to do or achieve sth: *a job with plenty of scope for original ideas* ∘ *There is certainly scope for improvement in the economy.* **2** the range or extent of matters being dealt with, studied, etc: *Their powers are rather limited in scope.* ∘ *Does feminist literature come within the scope of your programme?* ∘ *Police are broadening the scope of their enquiries.*

-scope *comb form* (forming *ns*) an instrument for looking through or observing with: *microscope* ∘ *oscilloscope* ∘ *telescope.*
▶ **-scopic(al)** *comb form* (forming *adjs*): *microscopic(al)* ∘ *telescopic.*
-scopy *comb form* (forming *ns*) (**a**) the action or process of observing: *spectroscopy.* (**b**) the use of an instrument like a MICROSCOPE, TELESCOPE, etc: *microscopy.*

scorch /skɔːtʃ/ v **1** to burn and damage a surface by making it too hot: [Vn] *scorch one's fingers* ∘ *I scorched my shirt when I was ironing it.* ∘ *The fire had scorched my desk.* **2** to become or make sth become dry and brown, esp from the heat of the sun: [V] *The leaves will scorch if you water them in the sun.* [Vn] *a scorched landscape.* **3** (*infml*) to go in the direction specified at a very high speed: [Vpr, Vp] *motor cyclists scorching (off) down the road* [Vpr] *scorch to a 6–1 victory.*
▶ **scorcher** n (*infml*) **1** a very hot day: *It's a real scorcher today!* **2** a remarkable stroke, shot, etc: *His first goal was a scorcher.*
scorching *adj* very hot: *a scorching day* ∘ *It's scorching outside.* ∘ (*fig*) *a scorching condemnation of government inactivity.* — *adv*: *a **scorching** hot day.*
■ **scorched ˈearth policy** n (usu *sing*) a policy of destroying anything that may be useful to an advancing enemy.
ˈscorch mark n a mark made on a surface by scorching: *scorch marks on a shirt/lawn.*

score¹ /skɔː(r)/ n **1**(**a**) [C] a number of points, goals, etc made by a player or team in a game or gained in a competition, etc: *a high/low score* ∘ *75 was an excellent score in these conditions.* See also SCOREBOARD. (**b**) [sing] the points, goals, etc made by both players or teams: *keep (the) score* (ie keep a record of the score as each point, goal, etc is made) ∘ *What's the score now?* ∘ *The final score was 4–3.* **2** [C] a number of marks gained in a test, an examination, etc: *a score of 120 in the IQ test.* **3** [C] (**a**) a written or printed version of a piece of music showing what each instrument is to play or what each voice is to sing: *an orchestral score* ∘ *the score for/of Verdi's 'Requiem'.* (**b**) the music written for a film, play, etc: *a stirring score by William Walton.* **4**(**a**) [C] (*pl* unchanged) a set or group of 20: *a score of people* ∘ *mosquitoes by the score* (*arch or rhet*) *He lived four score* (ie 80) *years.* (**b**) **scores** [pl] very many: *Scores of people were fainting in the heat.* **5** [C] a cut or SCRATCH²(1) on a surface: *deep scores on the rock* ∘ *scores made by a knife on the bark of a tree.*
IDM **know the score** ⇨ KNOW. **on ˈthat/ˈthis score** with regard to that/this; as far as that/this is concerned: *You don't have to worry on that score.*
settle a score; settle an old score ⇨ SETTLE¹.
▶ **scoreless** *adj* without either team making a score: *a scoreless draw* (eg in football).
■ **ˈscore draw** n the result of a football match in which both teams get an equal number of goals.
ˈscore-sheet (also **ˈscore-card**) n a piece of paper on which a score is recorded.

score² /skɔː(r)/ v **1**(**a**) to gain points, goals, etc in a game or competition: [V] *The home team has yet to score.* [Vn] *Hughes scored two goals before half-time.* ∘ *He scored a century* (ie 100 runs in cricket). (**b**) to keep a record of the points, etc gained in a game or competition: [V] *Who's going to score?* **2** to gain marks in a test or an examination: [Vn] *She scored 120 in the history test.* **3** to succeed; to achieve an advantage: [Vn, Vnpr] *The movie scored an instant success (with the public).* [V] *She's scored again with her latest hit single.* [Vpr] *In heavy traffic a bicycle can really score over other forms of transport.* **4** ~ **sth** (**for sth**) (esp passive) to arrange music for one or more musical instruments: [Vnpr] *a piece scored for violin, viola and cello* [also Vn]. **5** to make a cut or SCRATCH²(1) on a surface: [Vn] *rocks scored by a* glacier ∘ *score trees that are due to be felled* [Vnpr] *Score the card with a knife or scissors before folding it.* **6** ~ **(with sb)** (*sl*) to have sex with a new partner: [V, Vpr] *Did you score (with her) last night?* **IDM** ₁**score a ¹point/¹points (against/off/over sb)** = SCORE OFF SB. **PHRV** ¹**score off sb** to make sb appear foolish, eg by making a clever amusing remark: *When he appears on TV chat shows he's only interested in trying to score off the other guests.* ₁**score sth ¹out/¹through** to draw a line or lines through sth: *Her name had been scored out on the list.*

▶ **scorer** *n* **1** a person who keeps a record of points, goals, etc scored in a game. **2** a player who scores goals, runs, etc: *a prolific goal-scorer.*

scoreboard /'skɔ:bɔ:d/ *n* a board on which a score, eg at cricket, is shown.

scoreline /'skɔ:laɪn/ *n* the final score in a game, competition, etc: *Following a 3–1 scoreline, United stay top of the league.*

scorn /skɔ:n/ *n* [U] ~ **(for sth/sb)** a strong feeling that sth/sb is worthless and deserves only contempt, often shown by tone of voice or expression: *dismiss a suggestion with scorn* ∘ *She did nothing to conceal her scorn for the others.* **IDM** **pour scorn on sb/sth** ⇨ POUR.

▶ **scorn** *v* **1** to feel or show scorn for sb/sth: [Vn] *She scorns the efforts of amateur singers.* ∘ *He was privately scorned by his fellow officers.* **2(a)** to refuse sth because one is too proud(2) to accept it: [Vn] *scorn sb's invitation/advice/offer.* **(b)** (*fml*) to refuse to do sth because one is too proud: [V.to inf] *scorn to ask for help.*

scornful /-fl/ *adj* showing or feeling scorn: *a scornful laugh/glance/rejection/dismissal* ∘ *be scornful of other people's efforts.* **scornfully** /-fəli/ *adv*: *Jake looked at her scornfully.*

Scorpio /'skɔ:piəʊ/ *n* **(a)** [U] the 8th sign of the ZODIAC, the Scorpion. **(b)** [C] (*pl* **-os**) a person born under the influence of this sign. ▶ **Scorpian** *n, adj.* ⇨ picture at ZODIAC. ⇨ note at ZODIAC.

scorpion /'skɔ:piən/ *n* a small creature with eight legs, two of which form claws (CLAW 2), and a long tail which can bend up over its body to give a poisonous sting. ⇨ picture.

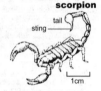

scorpion

tail

sting

1cm

Scot /skɒt/ *n* a native of Scotland.

Scotch /skɒtʃ/ *adj* **1** (also **Scottish**, except in certain fixed expressions) of Scotland: *Scotch beef/ whisky.* ⇨ note at SCOTTISH. **2** = SCOTS.

▶ **Scotch** *n* **(a)** [U] WHISKY made in Scotland. **(b)** [C] a glass of this: *Have a Scotch!*

■ ₁**Scotch ¹broth** *n* [C, U] a thick soup containing cooked grain and vegetables.

₁**Scotch ¹egg** *n* (*Brit*) a boiled egg enclosed in sausage meat (SAUSAGE) and fried.

¹**Scotch tape** *n* [U] (*US propr*) a transparent sticky tape sold in rolls, used esp for sticking paper, card, etc to other things. See also SELLOTAPE.

scotch /skɒtʃ/ *v* to stop sth; to put an end to sth completely: [Vn] *His appearance in public scotched rumours that he had fled the country.* ∘ *Plans for a merger have been scotched.*

scot-free /₁skɒt 'fri:/ *adv* without punishment or harm: *They got off/escaped scot-free because of lack of evidence.*

Scotland Yard /₁skɒtlənd 'jɑ:d/ *n* [Gp] the main office of the London police, esp the Criminal Investigation Department, now officially called *New Scotland Yard: Scotland Yard's anti-terrorist squad* ∘ *They called in Scotland Yard* (ie asked for the help of

this department). ∘ *Scotland Yard has/have been brought in.*

Scots /skɒts/ *adj* of Scotland, its people or its DIALECT of English: *a Scots family/industrialist* ∘ *Scots law.* ⇨ note at SCOTTISH.

▶ **Scots** *n* a DIALECT of English spoken in Scotland: *speak Scots.*

Scotsman /'skɒtsmən/ *n* (*pl* **-men** /-mən/) a man born in Scotland.

Scotswoman /'skɒtswʊmən/ *n* (*pl* **-women** /-wɪmɪn/) a woman born in Scotland.

Scottish /'skɒtɪʃ/ *adj* (abbreviated as *Scot* in this dictionary) of Scotland, its people or its DIALECT of English: *Scottish dancing* ∘ *the Scottish Highlands* ∘ *speak with a Scottish accent.*

NOTE The adjective **Scottish** is used to describe the people and things of Scotland and **Scots** is only used to describe its people, its law and its language: *the Scottish islands* ∘ *top Scottish/Scots rock bands.* **Scotch** is only used to describe products of Scotland, such as whisky, beef or wool, and is considered derogatory or old-fashioned if it is used in any other way. The noun **Scotch** means whisky, and the noun **Scots** is the Scottish dialect of English. A person who comes from Scotland is a **Scot**: *The Scots won their match against England.*

scoundrel /'skaʊndrəl/ *n* (*becoming dated*) a person who shows no moral principles or conscience.

scour¹ /'skaʊə(r)/ *v* **1** ~ **sth (out)** to make the dirty surface of sth clean or bright by rubbing it with sth rough: [Vn] *scour the pots and pans* ∘ *a scouring pad* [Vnp] *scour out a saucepan.* **2** (of water, a river, etc) to make a deep channel by flowing over sth and removing soil, rock, etc: [Vn] *crags deeply scoured by wind and rain* [Vnpr, Vnp] *The torrent scoured (out) a gully in the hillside.*

▶ **scourer** /'skaʊərə(r)/ *n* a pad of stiff nylon or wire used for scouring kitchen pans, etc.

scour² /'skaʊə(r)/ *v* ~ **sth (for sb/sth)** to search a place or thing thoroughly for sb/sth: [Vnpr, Vn] *Police scoured the woods (looking) for the body.* [Vnpr] *He spent hours scouring magazines for information.*

scourge /skɜ:dʒ/ *n* **1** a whip used esp formerly for punishing people. **2** (usu *sing*) a person or thing that causes trouble or suffering: *the scourge of war/ disease/inflation* ∘ *These pirates were the scourge of the South China Sea.* ∘ *Rabbits are a scourge in some rural areas.*

▶ **scourge** *v* to hit sb with a scourge: [Vn] (*fig*) *policies designed to scourge and oppress workers.*

Scouse /skaʊs/ *n* [U] **1** the DIALECT of Liverpool. **2** (also **Scouser** /'skaʊsə(r)/) [C] a native of Liverpool.

▶ **Scouse** *adj* of or relating to Liverpool: *Scouse comedians.*

scout /'skaʊt/ *n* **1** a person, an aircraft, etc sent ahead to get information about the enemy's position, strength, etc. See also TALENT-SCOUT. **2** Scout (also *esp dated* ₁**boy ¹scout**) a member of a branch of the Scout Association, an organization which aims to develop boys' characters through discipline, outdoor activities and public service: *join the Scouts* ∘ *a scout troop/hut.* Compare GIRL GUIDE.

▶ **scout** *v* (*infml*) **PHRV** ₁**scout a¹round/a¹bout (for sb/sth)** to look in various places to find sb/sth: *scouting around auction rooms for antique furniture* ∘ *We'd better start scouting about for a new secretary.*

Scoutmaster /'skaʊtmɑ:stə(r); *US* -mæst-/ *n* a person who leads a troop of Scouts.

scowl /skaʊl/ *n* an angry look or expression.

▶ **scowl** *v* ~ **(at sb/sth)** to look at sb/sth with a scowl: [V] *Stop scowling.* [Vpr] *The receptionist scowled at me.* ⇨ note at SMIRK.

Scrabble /'skræbl/ *n* [U] (*propr*) a game in which the players make a pattern of words on a board from letters printed on small, usu plastic, blocks: *playing Scrabble.*

scrabble /ˈskræbl/ *v* **1** ~ (about) (for sth) to feel about roughly with the fingers, trying to find sth one cannot see: [Vp] *scrabbling about under the table for a 50p piece* [Vpr] *She scrabbled in her bag for her spectacles.* [also V]. **2** to scratch sth noisily: [V] *mice scrabbling behind the skirting-board* [Vpr] *Tommy was scrabbling at the door to be let in.* **3** to scratch and scrape the ground trying to keep one's balance and not fall: [Vpr] *The children were scrabbling up the slope.* ∘ *feet scrabbling for a foothold.*

scraggy /ˈskrægi/ *adj* (*derog*) thin and showing a lot of bone: *a scraggy neck* ∘ *scraggy sheep.*

scram /skræm/ *v* (-mm-) (*sl*) (esp imperative) to go away quickly: [V] *Scram! I don't want you here!*

scramble /ˈskræmbl/ *v* **1** to move quickly using one's hands to help one: [Vpr] *The girl scrambled over the wall.* ∘ *scramble to one's feet* [Vadv] *scramble ashore* [Vp] *They forced an opening and scrambled through.* **2** ~ (for sth) to struggle or compete with others, esp in order to get sth or a share of sth: [Vpr] *players scrambling for possession of the ball* [V.to inf] *They were all scrambling to get the best bargains.* **3** to change the way a telephone conversation or a broadcast sounds so that only sb with a special device is able to understand it: [Vn] *scrambled satellite signals.* **4** to mix things together so that they have no order; to JUMBLE things: [Vn] *scrambled thoughts.* **5** (esp passive) to mix the white and yellow parts of eggs together and cook them with milk and butter in a pan: [Vn] *scrambled eggs on toast* ∘ *eat scrambled egg for breakfast.* **6** to order that planes should take off immediately in an emergency: [Vn] *Two squadrons were scrambled to intercept the enemy aircraft.*
▶ **scramble** *n* **1** [sing] an act of walking or climbing with difficulty or over rough ground: *a scramble over the rocks at the seashore.* **2** [sing] ~ (for sth) a rough struggle to get sth: *There was a mad/frantic scramble for the best seats.* ∘ (*fig*) *a scramble for university places.* **3** [C] a race for motor cycles (MOTOR) over rough ground.
scrambler /ˈskræmblə(r)/ *n* a device for scrambling telephone conversations, etc.

scrap¹ /skræp/ *n* **1(a)** [C] a small piece of sth, usu not wanted: *scraps of paper/cloth/wood.* ∘ (*fig*) *scraps of news/information.* ⊳ note at PIECE¹. **(b)** **scraps** [pl] food left after a meal: *Give the scraps to the dog.* **2** [sing] (usu with a negative) a small amount of sth: *There's not a scrap of truth in the claim.* ∘ *'Does he have evidence to support this?' 'Not a scrap!'* **3** [U] articles that are not wanted but are of some value for the material they are made of: *A man comes round regularly collecting scrap.* ∘ *sell an old car for scrap* (ie so that any good parts can be used again) ∘ *scrap iron* ∘ *a scrap (metal) merchant.*
▶ **scrap** *v* (-pp-) (often passive) to dispose of sth that is useless or no longer wanted: [Vn] *scrap a car/ship* ∘ (*fig*) *Plans to extend the airport may have to be scrapped.* ∘ *The scrapping of veterinary health checks.*

scrappy *adj* (-ier, -iest) **1** consisting of individual sections, events, etc that are not linked together or organized into a whole: *a scrappy essay/supper/game of football.* **2** not tidy or neat: *frayed, scrappy edges.* **scrappily** /-ɪli/ *adv.*
■ **'scrap heap** *n* a pile or heap of scrap¹(3). **IDM** **on the 'scrap heap** no longer wanted; useless: *Unemployed people often feel they are on the scrap heap.*
'scrap paper *n* [U] (*esp Brit*) loose bits of paper, often partly used, for writing notes on.

scrap² /skræp/ *n* ~ (with sb) (*infml*) a fight or rough quarrel: *get into a scrap* ∘ *He had a scrap with his sister.*

▶ **scrap** *v* (-pp-) ~ (with sb) to fight; to quarrel: [V] *He was always scrapping at school.* [also Vpr].

scrapbook /ˈskræpbʊk/ *n* a book with blank pages for sticking pictures, newspaper cuttings, etc in.

scrape¹ /skreɪp/ *v* **1(a)** to move a sharp or hard implement across a surface, eg in order to clean it or remove sth from it: [Vn] *scraping new potatoes* [Vnp] *scrape out a dirty saucepan* [Vn-adj] *scrape the path clear of snow.* **(b)** ~ **sth from/off sth** to use a sharp tool to remove sth, eg mud or paint, from sth: [Vnp] *scrape away the top layer* [Vnp, Vnpr] *scrape the rust off (sth)* [Vnpr] *scrape paint from a door.* **2(a)** ~ **sth (against/on/along sth)** to rub or cause sth to rub accidentally against sth rough, sharp, etc, resulting in damage or injury: [Vn] *I fell and scraped my knee.* [Vnpr] *I scraped the side of my car against a wall.* **(b)** ~ **sth from/off sth**; ~ **sth away/off** to remove sth, eg skin or paint, accidentally in this way: [Vnpr] *She's scraped the skin off her elbow.* [also Vnp]. **3** ~ **(sth) against/along/on sth** to rub or make sth rub against sth, making a harsh noise: [Vpr] *Bushes scraped against the car windows.* ∘ *The ship's hull scraped along the side of the dock.* [Vnpr] *Don't scrape your chair on the floor.* [Vp] (*derog*) *We could hear her scraping away on her violin.* **4** ~ **sth (out)** to make a hollow place with a sharp tool, a CLAW(1), etc: [Vnpr] *scrape a hole in the ground* [also Vnp]. **5** to achieve sth with difficulty: [Vn] *scrape a narrow victory* ∘ *They barely scraped 51% of the vote.* ∘ *scrape a living* [Vadv] *He scraped home* (ie just won) *by 15 votes.* **IDM** **bow and scrape** ⊳ BOW². **scrape (the bottom of) the 'barrel** to use the worst items or people because they are the only ones available: *It's really scraping the barrel when you have to bring players out of retirement to make up a team.* **PHRV** **,scrape a'long/'by (on sth)** to manage to live with difficulty: *I can just scrape by on what my parents give me.* **,scrape sth 'back/'up** to pull one's hair tightly back from one's face: *She wore her hair scraped back.* **,scrape 'in; ,scrape into sth** to get a job in a company, a place in a school, etc with difficulty: *She just scraped into university with the minimum qualifications.* **,scrape sth 'out** to remove sth from inside sth else, using a sharp or hard tool: *scrape out the flesh of a melon.* **,scrape 'through (sth)** to succeed with difficulty in doing sth, esp in passing an examination: *She only just scraped through the test.* **,scrape sth to'gether/'up** to gather or collect sth with some difficulty: *We scraped together an audience of fifty for the play.* ∘ *Can you scrape up enough money to buy a car?*
▶ **scraper** *n* a tool used for scraping, eg for scraping mud from shoes or ice from a car.
scraping *n* (usu *pl*) a small bit produced by scraping: *scrapings from the bottom of the pan.*

scrape² /skreɪp/ *n* **1** (esp *sing*) an act or a sound of scraping: *the scrape of a pen on paper/of sb's fingernail on a blackboard.* **2** an injury or a mark made by scraping: *a nasty scrape on the elbow* ∘ *a scrape on the car door.* **3** (*infml*) an awkward situation caused by foolish behaviour or by not thinking about the consequences of one's actions: *She's always getting into scrapes.*

scrappy ⊳ SCRAP¹.
scrapyard /ˈskræpjɑːd/ *n* a place where scrap¹(3) is collected.

scratch¹ /skrætʃ/ *v* **1(a)** to make marks on or in a surface with sth sharp; to make a shallow wound in the skin in this way: [V, Vn] *That cat won't scratch (you).* [Vpr] *The dog is scratching at the door.* [Vn] *You've scratched the table with your knife.* **(b)** to make sth by scratching: [Vn] *scratch a line on a surface* [Vn, Vnp] *scratch (out) a hole in the soil* [Vnpr] *He'd scratched his name in the bark of the tree.* **(c)** to remove sth by scratching: [Vnpr] *scratch the rust off the lock* [Vnp] *Mind he doesn't scratch* *your eyes out.* [Vnpr] (*fig*) *Her name had been scratched off the list.* **2** to rub the skin, esp with the nails, to stop it itching (ITCH 1): [V, Vn] *Stop scratching (yourself).* [Vn] *Scratching the rash will only make it worse.* **3** ~ **sb/oneself/sth (on sth)** to get oneself or a part of the body scratched by accident: [Vn] *She scratched herself while pruning the roses.* [Vnpr] *He's scratched his hand on a nail.* **4** to make a harsh unpleasant sound: [V] *My pen scratches.* **5** ~ **(sb/sth) (from sth)** to withdraw or make sb/sth withdraw from competing in a race, competition, etc: [V, Vpr] *I had to scratch (from the marathon) because of illness.* [Vn, Vnpr] *The horse had to be scratched (from its first race).* **IDM scratch one's 'head** to think hard in order to find an answer to sth: *We've been scratching our heads over this problem.* **scratch the 'surface (of sth)** to deal with only a small part of a subject or a problem: *This article is short and only scratches the surface of the topic.* ○ *The famine is so bad, aid can only scratch the surface.* ¡**you scratch 'my back and ¡I'll scratch 'yours** (*saying*) if you help me I will help you, esp in a way that is unfair to others. **PHRV ¡scratch a'bout/a'round (for sth) 1** to scratch the ground, etc in search of sth: *chickens scratching about in the farmyard.* **2** to look for sth in various places: *scratching around in the rubble looking for bits of junk* ○ (*fig*) *She was scratching around for something to say.*

■ **'scratch pad** *n* (*esp US*) a pad of scrap paper.

scratch² /skrætʃ/ *n* **1** [C] a mark, a cut or an injury made by scratching: *Her hands were covered with scratches from the thorns.* ○ *It's only a scratch* (ie a very slight injury). ○ *He escaped without a scratch* (ie was not hurt at all). **2** [sing] an act or a period of scratching sth/oneself: *I like a good scratch!* **IDM start (sth) from 'scratch** ⇨ START². **(be/come) up to 'scratch; (bring sb/sth) up to 'scratch** as good as sth should be; satisfactory: *Is her schoolwork up to scratch?* ○ *We'll have to bring the house up to scratch before we sell it.*

▶ **scratch** *adj* **1** (*esp Brit*) using whatever people or materials are available: *a scratch meal/team/orchestra.* **2** with no HANDICAP(3b) given: *a scratch golfer/player/race.*

scratchy *adj* **1** making the skin ITCH: *scratchy clothes/wool.* **2** (of a record, etc) making odd noises when played because of scratches on its surface. **3** (of a pen) making a scratching sound when writing. **4** (of writing or drawings) rough or carelessly done.

scrawl /skrɔːl/ *v* to write or draw sth in a rough, careless or hurried way: [Vpr] *Who's scrawled all over the wall?* [Vnpr] *She scrawled a few words on a postcard.* [also Vn, V].

▶ **scrawl** *n* (**a**) [sing] a rough, careless or hurried way of writing: *I could hardly read his childish scrawl.* (**b**) [C] a note, etc written in this way: *Her signature was an illegible scrawl.*

scrawny /'skrɔːni/ *adj* (*derog*) not having much flesh on the bones: *the scrawny neck of a turkey.* ⇨ note at THIN.

scream /skriːm/ *v* **1(a)** to give a long high-pitched cry of fear, pain or excitement: [Vpr] *The fans screamed with delight when they saw him.* ○ *We all screamed with laughter* (ie laughed noisily). [V, Vpr, Vp] *She screamed (out) (in terror).* [Vn-adj] *The baby was screaming itself hoarse.* ○ note at SHOUT. (**b**) to cry sth in this way: [Vn, Vnpr] *demonstrators screaming obscenities (at the police)* [V.speech] *'Help!' she screamed.* [V.that, Vp] *He screamed (out) that there was a fire.* [Vpr.to inf] *He screamed at me to stop.* [also Vnpl]. **2(a)** (of the wind, a machine, etc) to make a loud high-pitched sound: [V] *Lights flashed and sirens screamed.* ○ *I pressed the accelerator till the engine screamed.* (**b**) to move quickly in the specified direction or way making such a sound: [Vpr] *The wind screamed through the trees.* [Vp] *Racing cars screamed past.* [also Vadv].

▶ **scream** *n* **1** [C] a loud high-pitched cry or noise: *the screams of the wounded* ○ *screams of laughter/ excitement.* **2** [sing] (*dated infml*) a person or thing that causes laughter: *He's an absolute scream.*

screamingly *adv* extremely: *screamingly funny/ obvious.*

scree /skriː/ *n* [U, C] an area of small loose stones, esp on a mountain, which slide when walked on: *a scree slope* ○ *ferns poking through the scree.*

screech /skriːtʃ/ *v* **1(a)** to give a harsh high-pitched cry: [Vpr, Vp] *screech (out) in pain* [V] *monkeys screeching in the trees.* (**b**) to say sth in this way: [Vn, Vnp] *screech (out) a warning* [Vnpr] *The child screeched insults at us.* [also V.speech]. **2(a)** to make a harsh high-pitched sound: [V] *The brakes screeched as the car stopped.* (**b**) to move in the specified direction or way making such a sound: [Vpr] *screech to a halt* [Vp] *jets screeching past* [also Vadv].

▶ **screech** *n* [sing] a screeching cry or sound: *the screech of tyres/gulls.*

screed /skriːd/ *n* **1** [C] a long and usu not very interesting speech or piece of writing. **2** [C, U] a layer of material, eg cement, spread over a floor to make it smooth: *a concrete screed.*

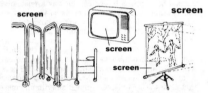

screen /skriːn/ *n* **1** [C] a fixed or movable upright structure used for dividing a room, concealing sth, protecting sb, etc. Screens can consist of solid panels or of cloth, etc over wooden or metal frames: *get undressed behind a screen* ○ *screens round a hospital bed* ○ *a fire screen.* ⇨ picture. **2** [C] a thing that conceals sb/sth or gives protection, eg from the weather: *a screen of trees* ○ (*fig*) *He was using his business activities as a screen for crime.* See also SUNSCREEN. **3** [C] a wood or stone structure that partly separates the main area of a church from the ALTAR or the CHOIR. ⇨ picture at CHURCH. **4** [C] (**a**) a blank surface onto which pictures or films are projected. ⇨ picture. (**b**) a blank surface, esp on a television or part of a computer, on which pictures or data are shown. ⇨ picture. ⇨ picture at COMPUTER. **5** often **the screen** [sing] the film industry or cinema films: *write for the screen* ○ *a star of stage and screen* (ie appearing in plays and films) ○ *the small screen* (ie television) ○ *a screen actor/performance* ○ *It's only a year since she made her screen debut.* **6** [C] a frame with a fine wire net stretched across it to keep out flies, etc: *a 'door-screen* ○ *a 'window-screen.* See also THE SILVER SCREEN, WINDSCREEN.

▶ **screen** *v* **1** ~ **sth/sb (off) (from sth/sb); ~ sth/ sb (against sth)** to conceal, protect or shelter sth/sb with or by forming a screen: [Vn] *The bushes will screen us while we change.* [Vnpr] *The trees screen the house from view.* ○ *The wall screens us against the wind.* [Vnp] *A bookcase screens off part of the room.* **2** to protect sb from blame, punishment, etc: [Vn] *She tried to screen him by lying to the police about his whereabouts.* **3** ~ **sb/sth (for sth)** to examine or test sb/sth to find out if there is any disease, fault, etc present: [Vnpr] *screen women for breast cancer* [Vn] *Government employees are regularly screened by the security services* (ie checked to make sure they are suitable and able to be trusted). **4** to show a film, etc in a cinema or on television: [Vn] *The documentary will be screened tonight on Channel 4.* **screening** *n* **1** [C] a showing of a film, television programme, etc:

the film's first screening in this country. **2** [U, C] the testing or examining of sb/sth for disease, faults, etc: *cancer screening* ○ *A fifth of all applicants fail during the initial screening.*

■ '**screen test** *n* a test to see if sb is suitable to appear in a cinema film.

screenplay /'skriːnpleɪ/ *n* the words for a film.

screenwriter /'skriːnraɪtə(r)/ *n* a person who writes the words for films. Compare PLAYWRIGHT, SCRIPTWRITER.

screw /skruː/ *n* **1** [C] a metal pin like a nail with a SPIRAL ridge (or thread) along it and a line or cross cut into its head. Screws are turned

screw

screw — thread

and pressed into wood, metal, etc with a SCREW-DRIVER so as to fasten things together: *a wood screw* (ie for use in wood). ⇨ picture. Compare NAIL. See also CORKSCREW. **2** [C] an act of turning a screw; a turn: *The nut isn't tight enough yet: give it another screw.* **3** [C] a propeller (PROPEL), esp of a ship or motor boat: *a twin-screw cruiser.* **4** [C] (*Brit sl*) a prison officer. **5** [sing] (⚠ *sl*) (**a**) an act of sex: *have a screw with sb* ○ *All he wants is a screw.* (**b**) a partner in sex(2): *be a good screw.* **IDM** **have a** '**screw loose** to be slightly odd in one's behaviour. **put the** '**screws on** (**sb**) to force sb to do sth by frightening and threatening them: *The landlord's putting the screws on to get her to leave.* **a turn of the screw** ⇨ TURN².

▶ **screw** *v* **1** to fasten sth or make it tight with a screw or screws: [Vnpr] *screw a bracket to the wall* ○ *screw a lock on the door* [Vnp] *screw all the parts together* [also Vn].

screw on → **screw**

screw off

2(**a**) to twist sth round; to make sth tighter by twisting: [Vnp, Vnpr] *screw the lid on (the jar)* [Vnp] *screw a bulb in* ○ *screw one's head round* (ie in order to look over one's shoulder) [Vn-adj] *screw the nut tight.* (**b**) to be attached by screwing: [Vpr] *This type of bulb screws into the socket.* [Vp] *Does this lid screw on, or do you just press it down?* ⇨ picture. **3** ~ **sb** (**for sth**) (*sl*) to cheat sb, esp by making them pay too much for sth: [Vn] *We've been screwed.* [Vnpr] *How much did they screw you for* (ie How much did you have to pay)? **4** (⚠ *sl*) (**a**) (of two people) to have sex: [V] *a couple screwing in the back of a car.* (**b**) (esp of a man) to have sex with sb: [Vn] *He accused me of screwing his wife.* **IDM** **have one's head screwed on** ⇨ HEAD¹. **screw** '**him,** '**you,** '**that, etc** (⚠ *sl*) (used in the imperative to express one's annoyance about sb/sth). **screw up one's** '**courage** to force oneself to be brave: *I finally screwed up my courage and went to the dentist.* **PHRV** ,**screw sth** '**from /** '**out of sb** to force sb to give sth: *They screwed the money out of her by threats.* ,**screw** '**up** (*sl esp US*) to handle a situation very badly: *I was trying to help, but I screwed up again.* ,**screw sth** '**up 1** to fasten sth with screws: *screw up a crate.* **2** to fasten sth by turning it: *I screwed up the jar and put it back in the cupboard.* Compare UNSCREW. **3** to make paper, etc into a tight ball: *I screwed up the letter and threw it on the fire.* **4** to tense¹ *v* the muscles of the face or the eyes when the light is too strong, when one feels pain, etc: *The bitter drink made her screw up her face.* **5** (*sl*) to handle a situation very badly; to make a mess of sth: *Don't ask them to organize the trip, they'll only screw everything up.* ,**screw sb** '**over** (*US*) to cheat sb.

screwy *adj* (*infml*) strange, ECCENTRIC or crazy: *She's really screwy!* ○ *What a screwy idea!*

■ '**screwball** *n* (*US infml*) an ECCENTRIC or crazy person: *a screwball comedy.*

,**screwed-**'**up** *adj* (**a**) upset and not completely able to deal with problems in life: ,*screwed-up* '*kids* ○ *I'm still screwed-up about the accident.* (**b**) twisted into a ball: *a screwed-up tissue/paper bag.* (**c**) (of the face or eyes) tense with worry, effort, etc.

'**screw-topped** (also '**screw-top**) *adj* (of a container) having a top or lid that screws (SCREW *v*2) onto it.

screwdriver

Phillips screwdriver

handle

screwdriver

screwdriver /'skruːdraɪvə(r)/ *n* a tool with a blade that fits into the head of a screw to turn it when driving it into place or removing it. ⇨ picture.

scribble /'skrɪbl/ *v* **1** to write sth very fast or carelessly: [Vnpr] *scribbling figures on the back of an envelope* [Vn] *some scribbled notes* [Vnp] *She scribbled down his comments.* [Vp] *He was still at his desk, scribbling away feverishly.* **2** to draw or make marks that have no meaning: [Vpr] *a child scribbling all over a book.*

▶ **scribble** *n* **1** [U, sing] very fast or careless writing: *I can't read this scribble.* **2** [C esp *pl*] marks that have no meaning: *a book with scribbles all over it.*

scribbler /'skrɪblə(r)/ *n* (*derog*) an author, a journalist, etc: *Fleet Street scribblers.*

scribe /skraɪb/ *n* a person who made copies of writings before printing was invented.

scrimmage /'skrɪmɪdʒ/ *n* **1** a confused struggle or fight: *a scrimmage round the bargain counter.* **2** (in American football) a sequence of play that begins with the placing of the ball on the ground.

scrimp /skrɪmp/ *v* to manage to live on very little money, esp so as to be able to pay for sth: [V] *We had to scrimp and save to pay the bills.*

scrip /skrɪp/ *n* (*techn*) an extra share in a business company issued instead of a DIVIDEND: *a scrip issue.*

script /skrɪpt/ *n* **1** [C] a written text of a play, film, broadcast, talk, etc: *That line isn't in the original script.* **2** [U] writing done by hand: *his neat script.* See also MANUSCRIPT. **3** [C, U] a system of writing: *a document in Cyrillic script.* **4** [C] (*Brit*) a candidate's written answer or answers in an examination: *The examiner had to mark 150 scripts.*

▶ **script** *v* (esp passive) to write a script for a film or a television or radio play, etc: [Vn] *Everything on the radio at that time was scripted down to the last comma.* **scripted** *adj* read from a script: *a scripted talk.*

scripture /'skrɪptʃə(r)/ *n* **1** Scripture [U] (also **the Scriptures** [pl]) the Bible: *a* '*Scripture lesson* ○ *quote from the Scriptures.* **2** **scriptures** [pl] the holy writings of a religion other than Christianity: *Vedic scriptures.*

▶ **scriptural** /'skrɪptʃərəl/ *adj* of or based on the Bible: *scriptural references* ○ *her wide scriptural knowledge.*

scriptwriter /'skrɪptraɪtə(r)/ *n* a person who writes scripts (SCRIPT 1) for films, television and radio plays, etc. Compare SCREENWRITER.

scroll /skrəʊl/ *n* **1**(**a**) a roll of paper or PARCHMENT for writing, etc to on: *Chinese scroll paintings.* (**b**) an ancient book written on such a roll: *the Dead Sea Scrolls.* **2** anything curved as though it has been rolled like a scroll, esp an ornamental design cut in stone or wood.

▶ **scroll** *v* (**a**) to move text on a computer screen gradually up or down in order to display different parts of it: [Vp] *Scroll down as far as section 3.* [also V, Vpr, Vn, Vnpr, Vnp]. (**b**) [V, Vpr, Vp] (of text displayed on a computer) to be moved up or down in this way.

Scrooge /skruːdʒ/ n (usu *sing*) (*derog*) a person who is mean with money.

scrotum /ˈskrəʊtəm/ n (pl **scrotums** or **scrota**) (usu *sing*) the bag of skin enclosing the testicles (TESTICLE) in most male animals. ⇨ picture at RE-PRODUCTION.

scrounge /skraʊndʒ/ v ~ (**sth**) (**from/off sb**) (*infml often derog*) to persuade sb to give one sth, or to take sth without asking permission: [Vpr, Vnpr] *She's always scrounging (money) off her brother.* [Vn] *We managed to scrounge a few bottles of wine.*
▶ **scrounge** n [IDM] **on the ˈscrounge** (*infml*) trying to borrow or obtain sth by scrounging: *If you're on the scrounge again, I've no money.*
scrounger n: *He thinks people on government benefits are all lazy scroungers.*

scrub¹ /skrʌb/ v (-bb-) **1(a)** ~ **sth** (**down/out**) to clean sth thoroughly by rubbing it hard, esp with a brush and soap and water: [Vn] *scrub the floor* ∘ *little boys with freshly scrubbed necks* [V, Vp] *He was down on his knees, scrubbing (away).* [Vnp] *Scrub the doors down before painting them.* ∘ *scrub out a saucepan* [Vn-adj] *The walls were now scrubbed clean of graffiti.* **(b)** ~ **sth off** (**sth**) to remove sth in this way: [Vnp, Vnpr] *It took ages to scrub the paint off (the children's hands).* **2** (*infml*) to cancel a plan, etc: [Vn] *We were going for a picnic, but we had to scrub it because of the rain.* [PHR V] **ˌscrub ˈup** (*medical*) (of a SURGEON) to wash one's hands and arms thoroughly before operating on sb.
▶ **scrub** n [sing] an act of scrubbing sth: *give the floor a good scrub.*
■ **ˈscrubbing-brush** (*US* also **ˈscrub-brush**) n a stiff brush for scrubbing floors, etc. ⇨ picture at BRUSH¹.

scrub² /skrʌb/ n [U] **(a)** bushes and small trees: *The bird disappeared into the scrub.* **(b)** (also **scrubland** /ˈskrʌblənd/) an area of land covered with these.
▶ **scrubby** /ˈskrʌbi/ adj **(a)** covered with scrub: *a scrubby hillside.* **(b)** (of trees, etc) small; not fully developed.

scruff /skrʌf/ n [IDM] **by the scruff of the/one's ˈneck** holding the back of an animal's or a person's neck: *She grabbed him by the scruff of his neck and threw him out.*

scruffy /ˈskrʌfi/ adj (-ier, -iest) (*infml*) dirty or untidy: *a scruffy little town* ∘ *You can't go to a job interview looking so scruffy!*
▶ **scruff** n (*Brit infml*) a scruffy person: *He's a bit of a scruff.*
scruffily adv.
scruffiness n [U].

scrum /skrʌm/ n (*Brit*) **1(a)** (also *fml* **scrummage**) a part of a Rugby game when certain players of both sides link themselves together with their heads down to push against the other side. The ball is then thrown between them and each side tries to get possession of it: *taking the ball from a scrum.* **(b)** the group of players arranged in this way. **2** a struggling mass of people: *a scrum of photographers.*

scrummage /ˈskrʌmɪdʒ/ n (*fml*) = SCRUM 1.

scrumptious /ˈskrʌmpʃəs/ adj (*infml*) (esp of food) extremely enjoyable; DELICIOUS: *scrumptious desserts.*

scrunch /skrʌntʃ/ v **1** to make a harsh crushing noise: [V] *the sound of footsteps scrunching on the gravel path.* **2** ~ **sth** (**up**) to crush sth, esp with one's hands: [Vnp] *She took out the remaining chocolate and scrunched up the box.* [Vnpr] *Jill scrunched his letter into a ball.* **3** ~ **sth** (**up**) to make sth smaller: *scrunch up one's face/shoulders.* ▶ **scrunch**

n [sing]: *the scrunch of her shoes on the gravel.* Compare CRUNCH.

scruple /ˈskruːpl/ n [U, C often *pl*] a feeling that prevents one from doing or allowing sth that one thinks may be wrong: *moral/religious scruples* ∘ *He **had no scruples about** buying stolen goods.* ∘ *She is totally **without scruple**.*
▶ **scruple** v (*fml*) (usu in negative sentences) to hesitate to do sth because of one's scruples: [V.to inf] *She wouldn't scruple to tell a lie if she thought it would be to her advantage.*

scrupulous /ˈskruːpjələs/ adj **1** extremely careful and thorough; paying great attention to details: *a scrupulous inspection of the firm's accounts* ∘ *be scrupulous about hygiene.* **2** ~ (**in sth/doing sth**) careful not to do wrong; absolutely honest: *scrupulous in all her business dealings* ∘ *behave with scrupulous honesty/fairness.* ▶ **scrupulously** adv: *scrupulously fair/honest/clean* ∘ *She **scrupulously avoided** any mention of his ex-wife.*

scrutineer /ˌskruːtəˈnɪə(r)/; *US* -tnˈɪər/ n (*Brit*) a person who checks that an election or other vote is conducted correctly and fairly.

scrutinize, -ise /ˈskruːtənaɪz/ v to look at or examine sth carefully or thoroughly: [Vn] *He scrutinized minutely all the documents relating to the trial.*

scrutiny /ˈskruːtəni/ n [U] (*fml*) careful and thorough examination: *Their findings will repay careful scrutiny.* ∘ *Though attractive, the idea does not **stand up to/bear** (too much) **scrutiny**.* ∘ *In 1994 the problem again came under the **close/intense/rigorous scrutiny** of the Department of Education.*

scuba-diving /ˈskuːbə daɪvɪŋ/ n [U] the activity of going under water using special breathing apparatus. This consists of a CYLINDER(1b) of compressed (COMPRESS¹) air and a tube through which one breathes the air: *go scuba-diving* ∘ *a scuba-diving school.*

scud /skʌd/ v (-dd-) (esp of clouds) to move fast and smoothly in a straight line: [Vpr] *clouds scudding across the sky* [also Vp, Vadv].

scuff /skʌf/ v **(a)** to mark or scrape sth, esp a shoe: [Vn] *a scuffed leather case* [Vnpr] *I scuffed the toe of my boot on the step.* **(b)** to mark or scrape a surface with one's shoes: [Vn] *The lino on the floor was scuffed and torn.*
▶ **scuff** (also **ˈscuff-mark**) n a mark made by scuffing.

scuffle /ˈskʌfl/ n ~ (**with sb**) a confused struggle between people who are close together: *be involved in a scuffle with other passengers* ∘ *Scuffles broke out between police and demonstrators.*
▶ **scuffle** v ~ (**with sb**) to be involved in a scuffle: [Vpr] *scuffle with reporters.* **scuffling** n [U] a low noise of movement that is not distinct: *He could hear whispering and scuffling on the other side of the door.*

scull /skʌl/ n **(a)** [C usu *pl*] either of a pair of small oars (OAR) used by a single person rowing, one in each hand. **(b)** **sculls** [pl] a race between light boats with pairs of sculls: *single/double sculls* (ie with one/two people in each boat).
▶ **sculling** n [U] the sport of racing with sculls: *a sculling coach.*
sculler n a person who rows with sculls.

scullery /ˈskʌləri/ n a small room next to the kitchen, esp in a large house, where dishes, etc are washed.

sculpt /skʌlpt/ v = SCULPTURE v: [Vn] *a beautifully sculpted head* [also Vnpr].

sculptor /ˈskʌlptə(r)/ n (fem **sculptress** /ˈskʌlptrəs/) a person who does SCULPTURE.

sculpture /ˈskʌlptʃə(r)/ n **1** [U] the art of making figures, objects, etc by carving wood or stone, shaping clay, pouring metal into moulds, etc: *the techniques of sculpture in stone.* **2** [C, U] a work or

---

works made in this way: *a bronze sculpture of Venus* ○ *a display of Degas sculptures* ○ *a collector of modern sculpture.*

▶ **sculptural** /ˈskʌlptʃərəl/ *adj* [esp attrib] of, like or connected with sculpture: *sculptural decoration.*

sculpture (also **sculpt**) *v* (esp passive) (**a**) to represent sb/sth in sculpture; to make a sculpture: [Vnpr] *figures sculptured in marble* ○ *sculpture a statue out of hard wood.* (**b**) to make sth into a sculpture: [Vn] *a sculptured archway* [Vnpr] *sculpture the clay into a bust.*

scum /skʌm/ *n* **1** [U, sing] a layer of dirt or bubbles on the surface of a liquid: *stinking water covered by a thick green scum.* **2** [pl *v*] a person or people for whom one feels contempt: *Don't waste your sympathy on scum like that.* ○ *She regards drug dealers as **the scum of the earth*** (ie as the worst people there are).

▶ **scummy** *adj* of or containing scum(1): *cold, scummy tea.*

scupper /ˈskʌpə(r)/ *v* (*Brit infml*) to cause sth/sb to fail; to ruin sth/sb: [Vn] *scupper sb's chances/hopes* ○ *We're scuppered!* ○ *The project was scuppered by opposition from the trade unions.*

scurrilous /ˈskʌrələs/ *adj* very rude and insulting, and often intended to damage sb's reputation: *scurrilous rumours/attacks/gossip* ○ *He wrote a scurrilous piece about me in the local press.* ▶ **scurrilously** *adv.*

scurry /ˈskʌri/ *v* (*pt, pp* **scurried**) to run with short quick steps: [Vpr] *people scurrying about the house carrying armfuls of holly* ○ *mice scurrying across the floor* ○ *The rain **sent** everyone **scurrying for** shelter.* [Vp] *Crowds scurried past.*

▶ **scurry** *n* [sing] an act or a sound of scurrying: *hear a scurry of feet.*

NOTE Scurry, **scuttle** and **scamper** all describe the way people or animals run with short, quick steps. **Scurry** or **scuttle** (**about**, **away**, **off**, etc) means to run in a hurry in order to escape from danger, etc: *The rain sent us scurrying for cover in a shop doorway.* ○ *A beetle scuttled away when I lifted the stone.* **Scurry** can also show busy or hurried activity: *Everyone scurried about looking for an empty seat.* **Scamper** (**around**, **away**, **off**, etc) is usually used of small animals or children. It suggests them playing happily or running away when surprised: *A family of rabbits scampered away as we approached.*

scurvy /ˈskɜːvi/ *n* [U] a disease of the blood caused by a lack of VITAMIN C from not eating enough fruit and vegetables.

scuttle¹ /ˈskʌtl/ *v* to run with short quick steps: [Vp] *the sound of mice scuttling about* [Vpr] *The rain sent people scuttling for shelter.* ⇨ note at SCURRY.

scuttle² *v* [Vn] **1** to sink a ship deliberately by letting water into it or making holes in its side or bottom. **2** to cause sth to fail deliberately: *scuttle a peace plan.*

scuttle³ /ˈskʌtl/ *n* = COAL-SCUTTLE.

scythe /saɪð/ *n* a tool with a slightly curved blade attached to a long handle, used for cutting long grass, corn, etc. Compare SICKLE.

▶ **scythe** *v* to cut grass, etc with a scythe: [V] *workers scything in the meadow* [Vn] *scythe the grass* [Vpr, Vnpr] (*fig*) *She managed to scythe (her way) through all the red tape.*

SDLP /ˌes diː el ˈpiː/ *abbr* (*Brit politics*) (in N Ireland) Social and Democratic Labour Party.

SE *abbr* South-East; South-Eastern: *SE Asia* ○ *London SE9 2BX* (ie as a POSTCODE).

sea /siː/ *n* **1** [U] (often **the sea**, also *esp rhet* **seas** [pl]) the salt water that covers most of the earth's surface and surrounds its continents and islands: *fly over land and sea* ○ *travel by sea* ○ *people going on holiday in search of sun, sand and sea* ○ *The waste*

was dumped in the sea. ○ *The river flows into the sea near Portsmouth.* ○ *the cold sea(s) of the Antarctic* ○ *freedom of the seas* ○ *roam the seas* ○ *a sea voyage* ○ *a hotel room with a sea view.* See also THE HIGH SEAS, THE OPEN SEA. **2** [C] (often **Sea**, esp as part of a name) (**a**) a particular area of the sea, smaller than an ocean: *the Mediterranean Sea* ○ *the South China Sea.* (**b**) a large lake with fresh water or salt water: *the Caspian Sea* ○ *the Sea of Galilee.* **3** [C] (also **seas** [pl]) the state or movement of the waves of the sea: *The tanker was foundering in **heavy/rough/ mountainous seas.*** **4** [sing] ~ **of** sth a large amount of sth covering a large area: *I stood amid a sea of corn.* ○ *He looked down at the sea of faces beneath him.* **IDM at** **ˈsea 1** on a ship, etc on the sea: *spend three months at sea.* **2** not knowing what to do; confused: *She tried to follow the instructions, but was soon completely at sea.* **between the devil and the deep blue sea** ⇨ DEVIL¹. **go to ˈsea** to become a sailor. **out to ˈsea** away from land to where the sea is deepest: *We gazed out to sea.* ○ *She fell overboard and was swept out to sea.* **put (out) to ˈsea** to leave a port or harbour by ship or boat. **there are other fish in the sea; there are more fish in the sea** ⇨ FISH¹.

■ ˌsea ˈair *n* [U] air at the SEASIDE, thought to be good for the health: *a breath of sea air.*

ˈsea anemone *n* a small simple sea creature in the shape of a tube with a ring of tentacles (TENTACLE) around the mouth. There are many different types of sea anemone.

the ˈsea bed *n* [sing] the floor of the sea.

ˈsea bird *n* any bird which lives close to the sea, eg on cliffs, islands, etc, and takes food from it.

ˈsea breeze *n* a wind blowing from the sea towards the land, esp during the day.

ˈsea change *n* (usu *sing*) a strong and noticeable change: *one of those momentous events which cause a sea change in public attitudes.*

ˈsea dog *n* an old or experienced sailor.

ˈsea-fish *n* (*pl* unchanged) any fish that lives in the sea, rather than in lakes, rivers, etc.

ˈsea front (often **the sea front**) *n* [sing] the part of a town facing the sea: *a hotel **on the sea front*** ○ *a seafront restaurant.*

ˌsea-ˈgreen *adj, n* (of) a bluish-green colour.

ˈsea horse *n* a small fish that swims upright and has a body that looks like the head of a horse.

ˈsea legs *n* [pl] the ability to walk easily on the DECK¹(1a) of a moving ship and not to feel sick at sea: *I feel a bit odd — I haven't got my sea legs yet.*

ˈsea level *n* [U] the level of the sea measured at a point between high tide and low tide, used as the basis for measuring the height of all places on land: *50 metres above/below sea level.*

ˈsea lion *n* a large seal¹ of the Pacific Ocean.

ˈSea Lord *n* (in Britain) any of the four naval members of the Board of Admiralty.

ˈsea power *n* **1** [U] the ability to control the seas with a strong navy. **2** [C] a country with a strong navy.

ˈsea shell *n* the shell of a small creature living in the sea, often found empty when the creature has died: *a large collection of sea shells.*

ˈsea urchin *n* a small sea animal with a round prickly shell.

ˌsea ˈwall *n* a wall built to stop the sea flowing onto the land.

ˈsea water *n* [U] salt water from the sea.

seaboard /ˈsiːbɔːd/ *n* the part of a country that is along its coast: *Australia's eastern seaboard.*

seaborne /ˈsiːbɔːn/ *adj* carried in ships: *seaborne trade* ○ *a seaborne invasion.*

seafarer /ˈsiːfeərə(r)/ *n* (*dated or fml*) a sailor.

seafaring /ˈsiːfeərɪŋ/ *adj* [attrib], *n* [U] (of) work or travel on the sea: *a seafaring nation.*

seafood /ˈsiːfuːd/ *n* [U] edible fish or SHELLFISH from the sea: *Seafood is our speciality.* ○ *a* ˈseafood *restaurant* ○ *a* ˌseafood ˈcocktail.

seagoing /ˈsiːgəʊɪŋ/ *adj* [attrib] (of ships) built for crossing the sea: *a seagoing vessel.*

seagull /ˈsiːgʌl/ *n* = GULL¹: *the cry of seagulls overhead.*

seal

seal

seal¹ /siːl/ *n* an animal that lives near and in the sea and eats fish. Some seals are hunted for their thick fur. ⇨ picture.

▶ **sealing** *n* [U] the activity of hunting seals.

seal

seal

sealing an envelope   making a seal

seal² /siːl/ *n* **1** [C] **(a)** a piece of wax, lead or other soft material, usu stamped with a design and fixed to a document to show that it is genuine, or to a letter, packet, etc to prevent it being opened before it reaches its destination: *The letter bears the seal of the king.* ○ *(fig) The project has been given the government's* ***seal of approval*** (ie has been officially approved). **(b)** a piece of metal, a ring, etc with a design used for stamping a seal. ⇨ picture. **2** [C] a thing used instead of a seal, eg a piece of paper stuck across the opening of a letter, etc. **3(a)** [C] a substance, strip of material, etc used to fill a gap or crack so that air, liquid, etc cannot enter or escape: *a rubber seal in the lid of a jar* ○ *I've bought a seal to put around the edge of the bath.* **(b)** [sing] protection given by this: *The putty gives a good seal round the window.* **IDM** **set the ˈseal on sth** (*fml*) to confirm or complete sth: *His election to the premiership set the seal on a remarkable political career.*

▶ **seal** *v* **1(a)** [Vn] to stick the FLAP(1) to the main part of an envelope in order to close it. ⇨ picture. **(b)** ~ **sth** (**up**) to fasten or close eg a letter or parcel securely: [Vn] *a sealed bid at an auction* ○ *sealed ballot boxes* [Vn, Vnp] *a parcel sealed (up) with adhesive tape.* **(c)** ~ **sth** (**up**) to close sth tightly or put a substance or strip of material on sth to stop air, liquid, etc entering or escaping: [Vn] *hermetically sealed containers* ○ *The jar must be well/tightly/properly sealed.* [Vn, Vnp] *Seal (up) the window to prevent draughts.* [also Vnpr]. **2** (*law*) to put a seal²(1,2) on sth, eg a legal document to indicate that it is genuine: [Vn] *an agreement signed, sealed and delivered in the presence of witnesses.* **3** to prevent anyone passing through a place: [Vn] *The army immediately sealed the country's borders.* **4** (*fml*) to settle sth in a way that cannot be changed; to decide sth: [Vn] *seal victory with a goal in the final minute* ○ *in the weeks before the GATT deal was sealed* ○ *Her* ***fate was*** *effectively* ***sealed*** (ie No one could stop what was going to happen to her). **IDM** **one's lips are sealed** ⇨ LIP. **PHRV** ˌseal sth ˈin to keep sth in by sealing: *Our foil packets seal the flavour in.* ˌseal sth ˈoff to prevent anyone or anything entering or leaving an area: *Police sealed off all the exits.* ○ *The district remained sealed off yesterday as army engineers inspected the buildings.*

sealant /ˈsiːlənt/ *n* [U, C] a substance used to stop

air, liquid, etc entering or escaping from sth: *mend the hole and paint some sealant on.*

■ ˈsealing-wax *n* [U] a type of wax that melts quickly when heated and hardens quickly when cooled, used, esp formerly, for sealing letters, etc.

seam /siːm/ *n* **1(a)** a line along which two edges, esp of cloth, are joined or sewn together: *the seams down the side of his trousers.* ⇨ picture at SEW. **(b)** a line where two edges meet, eg of wooden boards. **2** a layer of sth between layers of other material, eg a layer of coal between rock: *strike a* ***rich seam*** *of iron ore.* **IDM** **be bursting/bulging at the ˈseams** (*infml*) to be very full: *Their house is bursting at the seams already, without their taking in a lodger.* **be coming/falling apart at the ˈseams** (*infml*) to be in a very bad condition and likely to collapse: *This government's transport policy is coming apart at the seams.*

▶ **seamed** *adj* ~ (**with sth**) having a seam or seams: *seamed stockings/tights* ○ (*fig*) *an old man with a brown seamed face.*

seamless *adj* without a seam(1a): *seamless stockings* ○ (*fig*) *the seamless urban sprawl.* **seamlessly** *adv*: *splice/weave things together seamlessly.*

seaman /ˈsiːmən/ *n* (*pl* -**men** /-mən/) a sailor, esp one in a navy below the rank of an officer. ⇨ App 6. See also ABLE SEAMAN.

▶ ˈseamanship /-mənʃɪp/ *n* [U] skill in handling and managing a boat or ship.

seamstress /ˈsiːmstrəs, ˈsem-/ *n* a woman who sews, esp as a paid job.

seamy /ˈsiːmi/ *adj* (-**ier**, -**iest**) unpleasant; SORDID: *a seamy vice scandal* ○ *the seamier side of human nature.*

seance (also **séance**) /ˈseɪɒs/ *n* a meeting at which people try to talk with the spirits of the dead: *hold/attend a seance.*

seaplane /ˈsiːpleɪn/ *n* an aircraft designed so that it can take off from and land on water.

seaport /ˈsiːpɔːt/ *n* a town with a harbour used by large ships: *the Baltic seaports.*

sear /sɪə(r)/ *v* to burn a surface: [Vn] *The body was seared and blackened.*

▶ **searing** *adj* [usu attrib] extremely strong: *a searing pain* ○ *the searing heat of the tropical summer* ○ (*fig*) *The novel is a searing indictment of poverty.*

search /sɜːtʃ/ *v* **1(a)** ~ (**sth**) (**for sth/sb**); ~ **through/among sth** (**for sth/sb**) to look carefully in order to find sth/sb: [V] *We searched for hours but couldn't find the book.* [Vpr] *searching in the dark for the light switch* (ie feeling for it with one's hands) ○ *She searched through her drawers/among her belongings for the missing photo.* [Vn] *The homes of suspected terrorists are regularly searched by the police.* ○ (*computing*) *search a database.* **(b)** ~ **sb** (**for sth**) to look at everything in a person's pockets and examine her or his body and clothes to see if anything is concealed there: [Vnpr] *The police searched her for drugs.* [also Vn]. **2** ~ **for sth;** ~ **sth** (**for sth**) to think hard and carefully, eg in order to find the answer to a problem: [Vpr] *philosophers searching for the truth* ○ *search for the right words to express one's feelings* [Vn] *I searched my memory, but couldn't remember her name.* ○ *Search your conscience and ask if you're not equally to blame.* [also Vnpr]. See also SOUL-SEARCHING. **IDM** ˌsearch ˈme (*infml*) I don't know: *'Where's the newspaper?' 'Search me, I haven't seen it.'* **PHRV** ˌsearch ˈout sth to look for or find sth by searching: *search out new opportunities* ○ *We've searched out some of your favourite recipes.*

▶ **search** *n* an act of searching: *a search for a missing aircraft* ○ *carry out/make repeated searches for explosives* ○ *the search for knowledge/a compromise* ○ *do a search of a database* ○ ***The search is on*** (ie has begun) *to find Britain's best young cook.* **IDM** **in**

search of sb/sth looking for sb/sth: *go in search of a cheap hotel* ∘ *soldiers/athletes in search of glory* (ie trying hard to achieve victory or success).
searcher *n* a person who is searching for sth: *a searcher after knowledge.*
searching *adj* seeking the truth; keen and penetrating (PENETRATE): *a searching question/interview/ examination* ∘ *She gave me a searching look.* **searchingly** *adv.*
■ **'search-party** *n* [CGp] a group of people who join together to search for a person or thing: *send out a search-party.*
'search warrant *n* an official document that allows the police to search a building or other place eg to look for stolen property.

searchlight /'sɜːtʃlaɪt/ *n* a powerful lamp whose beam can be turned in any direction, used eg to look for enemy aircraft at night.

seascape /'siːskeɪp/ *n* a picture of a scene at sea: *paint seascapes.*

seashore /'siːʃɔː(r)/ *n* (usu **the seashore**) [U] the land along the edge of the sea, esp when it consists of sand or rocks: *a body washed up on the sea-shore.*

seasick /'siːsɪk/ *adj* [esp pred] feeling sick or wanting to VOMIT as the result of the motion of a ship: *be/ get seasick.* ▶ **seasickness** *n* [U].

seaside /'siːsaɪd/ *n* (often **the seaside**) [U] a place by the sea, esp a holiday resort: *spend two weeks at/ by the seaside* ∘ *a seaside town/hotel.* ⇨ note at COAST[1].

season[1] /'siːzn/ *n* **1** a part of the year distinguished by its particular type of weather, esp one of the four traditional periods into which the year is divided, ie spring, summer, autumn and winter: *the 'dry/'rainy season* ∘ *the cycle of the seasons.* **2(a)** the time of the year when sth is easily available or common, or when a certain activity takes place: *the 'football/'baseball/'flat-racing season* ∘ *They've won the League for the last three seasons.* ∘ *the 'growing/ 'breeding season* ∘ *the 'holiday/'tourist season* ∘ *The hotels are usually full during the (summer) season.* ∘ *the season of goodwill/the festive season* (ie Christmas) ∘ *Strawberries are now in season* (ie available in large quantities). ∘ *Fruit is more expensive/Hotels are cheaper out of season.* See also CLOSE SEASON, HIGH SEASON, OFF-SEASON, THE SILLY SEASON. **(b)** a series of concerts, plays or films, esp with a particular theme: *a short season of silent film classics* ∘ *the summer season at the Royal Opera House.* **IDM** **in 'season** (of a female animal) ready to MATE[2]. **the season's 'greetings** (used as a greeting at Christmas).
■ **'season ticket** *n* a ticket that allows sb eg to make as many journeys, go to as many sports matches as they wish within a specified period: *a monthly season ticket for the Paris metro* ∘ *Manchester United season ticket holders.*

season[2] /'siːzn/ *v* **1** ~ *sth* (**with sth**) to add flavour to food, eg with salt, pepper or other spices: [Vnadv] *highly seasoned sauces* [Vnpr] *Season the lamb with garlic and rosemary.* [also Vn]. **2** (usu passive) to make wood fit for use by exposing it to the weather: [Vn] *furniture made of oak that has been well seasoned.*
▶ **seasoned** *adj* [usu attrib] (of a person) having much experience of a particular activity or situation: *a seasoned professional/traveller/political campaigner.*
seasoning *n* [U, C] a substance used to season food: *Stir in the lemon rind and seasoning.* ∘ *Salt and pepper are the two most common seasonings in cooking.*

seasonable /'siːznəbl/ *adj* usual or appropriate for the time of year: *seasonable snow showers* ∘ *seasonable clothes.*

seasonal /'siːzənl/ *adj* **1** happening during a particular season; varying with the seasons: *seasonal work* (eg picking fruit) ∘ *seasonal variations in unemployment/prices.* **2** typical of or suitable for the time of year, esp Christmas: *Everybody was full of seasonal goodwill/the seasonal spirit.* ▶ **seasonally** /-nəli/ *adv*: *the seasonally adjusted unemployment figures* (ie excluding the variations that occur in the different seasons).

seat[1] /siːt/ *n* **1(a)** a thing made or used for sitting on, eg a chair, BENCH(1a) or box: *She leaned back in her seat.* ∘ *He put his shopping on the seat beside him.* ∘ *take a seat* (ie sit down) ∘ *a stone seat in the garden* ∘ *a window/corner seat* (ie one near a window/in a corner) ∘ *a child seat* (ie for a child, eg in a car). See also BACK SEAT. ⇨ picture at CAR. **(b)** the part of this on which one actually sits: *a chair with a leather seat and a wooden back.* **2** a place where one pays to sit in a public vehicle or in a theatre, cinema, etc: *There are no seats left on the flight.* ∘ *He put his shopping on the seat beside him.* ∘ *book/reserve two seats for the concert* ∘ *seat prices.* ⇨ note at SPACE. **3(a)** a place as a member of a law-making assembly, a council or a committee: *a seat on the city council/in Parliament* ∘ *take one's seat* (ie begin one's duties, esp in Parliament) ∘ *win/ lose a seat* (ie in an election) ∘ *The Democrats have a majority of 21 seats in the Senate.* **(b)** an area of the country that elects a Member of Parliament: *a seat in Devon.* See also SAFE SEAT. **4** (*fml*) a place where sth is based, or where an activity is carried on: *Washington is the seat of government of the USA.* ∘ *a university town renowned as a seat of learning.* See also COUNTY SEAT. **5** (also **'country 'seat**) a large house in the country, usu the centre of a large estate belonging to a member of the upper class: *the family seat in Norfolk.* **6(a)** (*fml*) the part of the body on which a person sits: the buttocks (BUTTOCK). **(b)** the part of a garment, esp trousers, covering this: *a hole in the seat of his trousers.* See also THE HOT SEAT. **IDM** **bums on seats** ⇨ BUM[1]. **by the seat of one's pants** relying on instinct rather than careful thought or skill. **in the driving seat** ⇨ DRIVING. **on the edge of one's seat** ⇨ EDGE[1]. **take a back seat** ⇨ BACK SEAT.
▶ **-seater** (forming compound *ns* and *adjs*) (of a vehicle or place) with the specified number of seats: *a ,ten-seater 'minibus* ∘ *a ,thousand-seater 'stadium* ∘ *a fast little ,two-'seater* (ie car) ∘ *an ,all-seater 'stadium* (ie where everyone has a seat).
■ **'seat-belt** (also **'safety-belt**) *n* a belt attached to a seat in an aircraft, a car, etc worn by a passenger to avoid being thrown forward if an accident happens: *Fasten your seat-belts!* ∘ *The seat-belt sign is on.* ⇨ picture at CAR.

seat[2] /siːt/ *v* **1** (*fml*) (esp passive) to cause sb/ oneself to sit: [Vn] *Please be/remain seated, ladies and gentlemen.* [Vnpr] *a statue of a woman seated on a horse* ∘ *She seated herself on the sofa/at the piano.* ∘ *Seat the boy next to his brother.* **2** (of a place) to have seats for a specified number of people: *a hall that seats 500 (people).* See also DEEP-SEATED.
▶ **seating** *n* [U] places to sit; seats: *rearrange the seating* ∘ *a hall with a seating capacity of 500.*

seaward /'siːwəd/ *adj, adv* towards the sea; in the direction of the sea: *looking seaward.* ▶ **'seawards** /-wədz/ *adv.*

seaway /'siːweɪ/ *n* a deep channel cut through the land along which large ships can pass.

seaweed /'siːwiːd/ *n* [U, C] a plant growing in the sea or on rocks at the edge of the sea.

seaworthy /'siːwɜːði/ *adj* (of a ship) in a suitable condition for a sea voyage: *make a damaged ship seaworthy again.* ▶ **'seaworthiness** *n* [U].

sebaceous /sɪ'beɪʃəs/ *adj* [attrib] (*techn*) producing an oily substance in the body: *the sebaceous glands in the skin.*

[V.speech] = verb + direct speech　　　[V.*that*] = verb + *that* clause　　　[V.*wh*] = verb + *who, how,* etc clause

sec¹ /sek/ n (*infml*) a second³(2): *I'll be with you in a sec.*

sec² (also **Sec**) *abbr* secretary: *first sec, HM Embassy, Moscow.*

secateurs /ˌsekəˈtɜːz/ n [pl] (*esp Brit*) a gardening tool like a pair of strong scissors for cutting plants, small branches, etc: *a pair of secateurs.* ⇨ picture at SCISSORS.

secede /sɪˈsiːd/ v ~ (**from sth**) (*fml*) to withdraw from membership of a state or an organization of states; to become independent: [Vpr] *Latvia seceded from the Soviet Union in 1991.* [also V].

▶ **secession** /sɪˈseʃn/ n [U,C] ~ (**from sth**) (*fml*) the action of seceding. **secessionist** /-ˈseʃənɪst/ n, adj (a person) favouring the secession of one part of a country from the rest.

seclude /sɪˈkluːd/ v ~ **oneself/sb** (**from sb/sth**) (*fml*) to keep oneself/sb apart from others: [Vn] *seclude patients for long periods* [Vnpr] *seclude oneself from the world.*

▶ **secluded** adj (**a**) (of a place) not visited or seen by many people: *a secluded garden/beach/spot.* (**b**) away from the company of others: *lead a secluded life* ∘ *The monks live secluded from the outside world.*
seclusion /sɪˈkluːʒn/ n [U] the state of being away from others or in a private place: *in the seclusion of one's own home.*

second¹ /ˈsekənd/ pron, det **1**(**a**) ~ (**to sb/sth**) 2nd; next in time, order or importance: *the second of June* ∘ *He was (the) second to arrive.* ∘ *She published her first novel last year and now she's written a second.* ∘ *You're the second (person) to ask me that.* ∘ *She was/came/finished second to the Ethiopian champion in the marathon.* ∘ *the second month of the year* ∘ *This is the second time it's happened.* ∘ *Daniel is her second son.* ∘ *Osaka is the second largest city in Japan/Japan's second city.* ∘ *She's in the second team.* ∘ (*fml*) *He is second only to my own son in my affections.* See also TWO. (**b**) [attrib] another; additional; extra: *a second helping of soup* ∘ *Italy scored a second goal just after half-time.* ∘ *My wife and I decided not to have a second child.* **2** [attrib] of the same quality or standard as a previous one: *The press are calling him a second Olivier* (ie saying that he has as much talent as Olivier). **IDM** ˌsecond to ˈnone as good as the best: *As a dancer, he is second to none.*

▶ **second** adv second in order or importance: *I agreed to speak second.* ∘ *He puts his family first and his job second.*

secondly adv in the second place; in addition; also: *Firstly, it's too expensive; and secondly, it's very ugly.* ⇨ note at FIRST².

■ ˌsecond ˈballot n a part of an election, esp of a leader, in which people choose from among the candidates who got most votes in the previous round of voting: *force/avoid a second ballot.*

ˌsecond-ˈbest adj **1** next after the best: *my ˌsecond-best ˈsuit* ∘ *the second-best solution.* **2**(**a**) not as good as one would really like; not ideal: *I like live music; for me records are definitely second-best.* (**b**) failing to win or to do as well as sth/sb else, eg in a competition: *The two teams are quite evenly matched but this time Arsenal came off second-best.* — n [U]: *I'm used to high quality and won't accept second-best.*

ˌsecond ˈchamber (also **upper chamber**) n the upper house in a law-making body.

ˌsecond ˈclass n [U] (**a**) a standard of accommodation in a hotel, on a train, etc that is of lower quality than first class: *travel in second class* ∘ *second-class ˈcarriages/comˈpartments/ˈpassengers.* (**b**) a category of mail that takes longer than first-class mail to reach its destination: *Second class is cheaper.* ∘ *ˌsecond-class ˈletters/ˈstamps.* Compare FIRST-CLASS.

ˌsecond-ˈclass adj **1** of the second-best or second most important group or category: *a ˌsecond-class deˌgree in ˈhistory* ∘ *ˌsecond-class hoˈtels/ˈroads.* **2**

(*derog*) much less good than the best; second-rate (SECOND¹): *a ˌsecond-class ˈschool* ∘ *The old are treated as ˌsecond-class ˈcitizens* (ie not treated as well as other members of society). — adv: *go/travel second-class* ∘ *It takes longer if you send it second-class.*

the ˌsecond ˈcoming n [sing] (*religion*) the return of Jesus Christ at the Last Judgement.

ˌsecond ˈcousin n a child of a COUSIN(1) of one of one's parents. See also ONCE, TWICE, ETC REMOVED (REMOVE¹).

ˌsecond-ˈguess v **1** to guess in advance what is going to happen or what sb is going to do: [Vn] *Don't try to second-guess the outcome.* ∘ *Good chess players can second-guess their opponents' thoughts.* **2** to comment on or criticize sb/sth afterwards, after an event has happened or a decision has been taken: [Vn] *The prime minister showed a remarkable willingness to second-guess her most senior ministers.*

ˌsecond-ˈhand adj, adv **1** previously owned by sb else: *a ˌsecond-hand ˈcar/ˈsuit/ˈcamera* ∘ *a ˌsecond-hand ˈbookshop* (ie a shop selling second-hand books) ∘ *I rarely buy anything second-hand.* **2** (*often derog*) (of news, information, etc) obtained from others, not from one's own knowledge or experience: *ˌsecond-hand ˈgossip* ∘ *get news second-hand.*

ˌsecond ˈhome n **1** a house or flat owned by sb in addition to their main residence, which they use only part of the time, esp for holidays: *second homes lying empty in the Welsh countryside.* **2** [sing] a place, eg a city or a country, that sb knows well and has strong connections with, but which is not their home: *I was born in New York, but France is my second home.*

ˌsecond ˈlanguage n (usu *sing*) a language learned by sb in addition to the language they learned to speak first.

ˌsecond lieuˈtenant n an army officer below LIEUTENANT(1) in rank. ⇨ App 6.

ˈsecond name n (usu *sing*) (**a**) a SURNAME: *I don't know his second name.* (**b**) another personal name: *Do you have a second name?*

ˌsecond ˈnature n [U] ~ (**to sb**) (**to do sth**) the tendency always to behave in a similar way so that one does it by instinct: *Secrecy and deception had become second nature to her.* ∘ *It was second nature to me to use such language.*

the ˌsecond ˈperson n [sing] (*grammar*) the form of a word used when addressing sb. In the phrase *you are*, the verb *are* is in the second person and the word *you* is a second-person pronoun: *the second ˌperson ˈsingular/ˈplural.*

ˌsecond-ˈrate adj of poor quality; not very good: *a ˌsecond-rate ˈactor/perˈformance/ˈrestaurant* ∘ *His novels are very second-rate.*

ˌsecond ˈsight n [U] the ability to see into the future, or to see events happening far away as if one were present.

ˌsecond-ˈstring adj [attrib] (of a sports player) being a substitute, rather than a regular player: *a second-string team/side.*

ˌsecond ˈwind n [U] new strength or energy to continue with sth that made one tired: *She's got/found her second wind.*

second² /ˈsekənd/ n **1** [C] (*Brit*) a university degree of the second class: *get a (good) second in economics at Oxford.* **2** (also ˌsecond ˈgear) [U] the second lowest forward gear in a car, etc: *Are you in first or second?* ∘ *Change down from third to second.* **3** [C usu *pl*] a manufactured article that has a fault and is therefore sold cheaper: *These plates are seconds.* **4 seconds** [pl] (*infml*) a second portion of food: *Are there any seconds?* **5** [C] a person who assists a boxer or sb fighting a DUEL(1).

■ ˌsecond in comˈmand n [sing] a person who is next below sb in rank and who takes charge when they are absent: *the sales director and her second in command* ∘ *He is second in command of the regiment.*

[Vnn] = verb + noun + noun   [V-adj] = verb + adjective   For more help with verbs, see Study pages **B4–8.**

second³ /'sekənd/ n **1** (symb ") (**a**) any of the 60 equal parts of a minute, used in measuring time: *The winning time was 1 minute 5 seconds.* ⇨ App 2. (**b**) any of the 60 equal parts of a minute, used in measuring angles: *1 ° 6' 10"* (ie one degree, six minutes, and ten seconds). **2** (also *infml* **sec**) a short time; a moment: *I'll be ready in a second.* ○ *The food was on the table in seconds.* **IDM** **just a minute/ moment/second** ⇨ JUST². **wait a minute/second** ⇨ WAIT¹.
■ **'second hand** n (usu *sing*) the hand on some watches and clocks that records seconds. Compare SECOND-HAND.

second⁴ /'sekənd/ v **1** to support sb's idea or proposal at a meeting so that it can be discussed or voted on: [Vn] *Mrs Smith proposed the motion and Mr Jones seconded (it).* ○ (joc) *'Let's go to the cinema.' 'I'll second that.'* Compare PROPOSE 1. **2** to support or assist sb: [Vn] *I was ably seconded in this research by my son.*
▶ **seconder** n a person who seconds a proposal, etc. Compare PROPOSER.

second⁵ /sɪ'kɒnd/ v ~ sb (**from sth**) (**to sth**) (*esp Brit*) to transfer sb temporarily from their usual job to other duties or another position: [Vnpr] *a manager seconded from a regional branch to head office* [also Vn]. ▶ **secondment** n [C,U]: *a two-month secondment* ○ *an officer on secondment overseas.*

secondary /'sekəndri; US -deri/ adj **1** ~ (**to sth**) coming after sth that is first or primary; of less importance, value, etc than what is primary: *a secondary issue/role* ○ *secondary stress* (eg on the first syllable of '₁uni'versity') ○ *secondary picketing* (eg of a firm that is thought to be helping the employers of the workers on strike) ○ *Such considerations are secondary to our main aim of improving efficiency.* ○ *Her age is only of secondary importance.* **2** caused by, coming from, etc sth that is original or primary: *a secondary effect/factor* ○ *green is a secondary colour* (ie one produced by mixing two primary colours, yellow and blue) ○ *a secondary infection* (ie one which occurs as a result of another illness). **3** [attrib] of or for secondary education: *secondary teachers.* Compare PRIMARY, TERTIARY. ▶ **secondarily** /-drəli; US ₁sekən'derəli/ adv.
■ **₁secondary edu'cation** n [U] education for young people of (usu) 11–18 years.
'secondary school n a school for young people of (usu) 11–18 years.

secrecy /'si:krəsi/ n [U] the state of being secret or keeping sth secret: *The meeting was held in great secrecy.* ○ *Everyone involved was sworn to secrecy* (ie had to promise not to tell anyone). ○ *The whole affair is still shrouded in secrecy.*

secret /'si:krət/ adj **1** ~ (**from sb**) that is not known or seen, or must not be known or seen, by others: *a secret marriage/document/meeting* ○ *keep sth secret from one's family* ○ *Secret talks were held between the government and the rebel leaders.* **2** [attrib] not declared or admitted to others: *a secret drinker* ○ *I'm a secret fan of soap operas on TV.* **3** [esp pred] (*fml*) fond of having or keeping secrets; SECRETIVE. **4** [attrib] (of a place) hidden or quiet: *my secret hideaway in the country.*
▶ **secret** n **1** a thing that is not or must not be known by other people: *keep a secret* (ie not tell it to anyone else) ○ *The wedding date's a big secret.* ○ *Shall we let him in on* (ie tell him) *the secret?* ○ *He made no secret of his dislike for me* (ie made it very clear). **2** the best or only way of doing or achieving sth that not many people know: *What's the secret of your success?* ○ *The secret of good design is simplicity.* **3** anything not properly understood or difficult to understand; a mystery: *the secrets of creation/nature.* **IDM** **be an open secret** ⇨ OPEN¹.

in 'secret without others knowing: *meet in secret* ○ *leave the country in secret.*
secretly adv: *He posted the letter secretly.*
■ **₁secret 'agent** (also **agent**) n a person working secretly for a government and trying to find out secret information, esp the military secrets of another government; a SPY.
₁secret 'ballot n a way of voting or an occasion when people vote secretly: *elected by secret ballot.*
₁secret po'lice n [pl v] a police force that works in secret to make sure that citizens behave as their government wants.
₁secret 'service n (usu *sing*) a government department responsible for protecting its government's military and political secrets and discovering those of other governments.

secretariat /₁sekrə'teəriət, -iæt/ n **1** the administrative department of a large organization. **2** the staff or office of a Secretary-General or of a government secretary(4a): *the UN secretariat in New York.*

secretary /'sekrətri; US -teri/ n **1** a person employed in an office, usu working for another person, dealing with letters, typing, keeping records, etc and making appointments and arrangements: *a legal/ medical secretary* ○ *Please contact my secretary to make an appointment.* **2** an official of a club, society, etc who deals with writing letters, keeping records, and making business arrangements: *the membership secretary.* **3** (in Britain) the principal assistant of a government minister, an AMBASSADOR, etc. **4 Secretary** (**a**) = SECRETARY OF STATE. (**b**) (*US*) the head of a government department: *Secretary of the Treasury.* See also HOME SECRETARY, PERMANENT SECRETARY.
▶ **secretarial** /₁sekrə'teəriəl/ adj of or for secretaries or their work: *secretarial staff/duties/training/ colleges.*
■ **₁Secretary-'General** n (*pl* **Secretaries-General**) the chief official in charge of a large organization: *the UN Secretary-General.*
₁Secretary of 'State n **1** (also **Secretary**) (in Britain) the head of a major government department: *the Secretary of State for Education/Employment* ○ *the Education/Employment Secretary.* **2** (in the USA) the head of the government department that deals with foreign affairs.

secrete /sɪ'kri:t/ v (*fml*) **1** (of part of a plant, an animal or a person) to produce a liquid substance: [Vn] *Saliva is secreted by glands in the mouth.* ○ *Some animals secrete poisonous substances as a means of defence.* **2** to hide sth in a secret place: [Vnpr] *money secreted in a drawer* [also Vn].
▶ **secretion** /sɪ'kri:ʃn/ n (*fml*) (**a**) [U] the process by which liquid substances are produced by parts of the body or of plants: *the secretion of bile by the liver.* (**b**) [C] such a substance: *normal bodily secretions.*

secretive /'si:krətɪv/ adj liking to keep things secret or to hide one's thoughts, feelings, etc: *have a secretive nature* ○ *be shy and secretive.* ▶ **secretively** adv: *act secretively.* **secretiveness** n [U].

sect /sekt/ n (*sometimes derog*) a group of people who share esp religious beliefs or opinions different from those of a larger group from which they have separated: *a minor Christian sect.*

sectarian /sek'teəriən/ adj **1** of a SECT or sects: *sectarian violence* (ie between members of different religious sects). **2** (*derog*) showing a lack of concern for those outside one's own SECT, class, etc: *sectarian prejudices/views.* ▶ **sectarianism** /-ɪzəm/ n [U] (*often derog*): *sectarianism and discrimination in religion.*

section /'sekʃn/ n **1** [C] any of the parts into which sth may be or has been divided: *This section of the road is closed.* ○ *The library has a large biology section.* **2** [C] any of a number of parts that can be fitted together to make a structure: *the three sections*

of a fishing-rod ○ *The shed comes in sections that you assemble yourself.* **3** [C] a separate group within a larger body of people: *the brass section of the orchestra* ○ *Farm workers make up only a small section of the population.* See also RHYTHM SECTION. **4** [C] a department of an organization, institution, etc: *head of the finance section* ○ *the section dealing with customer complaints.* **5** [C] a separate part of a document, book, etc: *section 4, subsection 2 of the treaty* ○ *the financial section of the newspaper* ○ *The report has a section on accidents at work.* **6** [C] a view or representation of sth seen as if cut straight through from top to bottom: *This illustration shows a section through a leaf.* See also CROSS-SECTION. **7** (*medical*) (**a**) [C, U] the process of cutting or separating sth in an operation(1): *the section of a diseased organ.* See also CAESAREAN. (**b**) [C] a piece cut or separated in this way: *examine a section of tissue under the microscope.*
▶ **section** *v* **1** to separate sth into sections: [Vnpr] *a library sectioned into subject areas* [Vnp] *Part of the town had been sectioned off.* [also Vn]. **2** [Vn] (*medical*) to cut or separate tissue, etc.
sectional /-ʃənl/ *adj* **1** [usu attrib] of a group or groups within a community, etc: *support sectional interests* ○ *sectional jealousies/rivalry.* **2** made or supplied in sections: *sectional buildings.* **sectionalism** /-ʃənəlɪzəm/ *n* [U] (*usu derog*) too much concern for the good of one's own section of the community, rather than that of everybody.

sector /'sektə(r)/ *n* **1** a part or branch of a particular area of activity, esp of a country's economy: *the manuˈfacturing sector* (ie all the manufacturing industries of a country) ○ *the ˈservice sector* (eg hotels, restaurants, etc). See also THE PRIVATE SECTOR, THE PUBLIC SECTOR. **2** a part of a circle lying between two straight lines drawn from the centre to the edge. ⇨ picture at CIRCLE. **3** any of the parts of a battle area, or of an area under military control: *an enemy attack in the southern sector.*

secular /'sekjələ(r)/ *adj* **1** not concerned with spiritual or religious affairs; of this world: *secular education/art/music* ○ *the secular powers of the State.* **2** (of priests) not belonging to a community of monks: *the secular clergy* (eg PARISH(1) priests).
▶ **secularism** /-lərɪzəm/ *n* [U] the belief that laws, education, etc should be based on facts, science, etc rather than religion. **secularist** /-lərɪst/ *adj*: *secularist beliefs/philosophies.*
secularize, -ise /-lərɑɪz/ *v* (*fml*) to make sth secular; to remove sth from control of the church: [Vn] *We live in a more secularized society.*

secure /sɪ'kjʊə(r)/ *adj* **1** ~ (**about sth**) not feeling worry, doubt, etc: *feel secure about one's future* ○ *Children need to feel secure.* ○ *She was happy, **secure in the knowledge** that her family loved and respected her.* **2** not likely to be lost or to fail; certain; guaranteed: *make a secure investment* ○ *have a secure job* ○ *Her place in the history books is secure.* **3** ~ (**against/from sth**) safe; protected: *The strongroom is as secure as we can make it.* ○ *Are we secure from attack here?* ○ *When you're insured, you're secure against loss.* **4** firmly fixed; not likely to fall, be broken, etc: *a secure base/foundation/foothold* ○ *Is that ladder secure?*
▶ **secure** *v* **1** ~ **sth** (**for sb/sth**) (*fml*) to obtain sth, sometimes with difficulty: [Vn] *secure a bank loan* [Vnpr] *They've secured government backing for the project.* [Vnn] *The film secured him recognition as an actor.* [also Vn]. **2** to fix sth firmly; to fasten sth: [Vn] *Secure all the doors and windows before leaving.* **3** ~ **sth** (**against/from sth**) to make sth safe; to protect sth: [Vn, Vnpr] *secure a building (from collapse)* [Vnpr] *Can the town be secured against attack?* [Vn] (*fig*) *The new law secures the rights of the mentally ill.*
securely *adv*: *securely bolted/fastened/fixed.*

security /sɪ'kjʊərəti/ *n* **1** [U] freedom or protection from danger or worry: *children who lack the security of a good home* ○ *have the security of a guaranteed pension.* See also SOCIAL SECURITY. **2** [U] measures taken to guarantee the safety of a country, person, thing of value, etc: *a security guard/officer* ○ *national security* (ie the defence of a country) ○ *security forces* (eg police or troops) ○ *a security van* (eg for transporting money) ○ *a high security prison* (ie for dangerous criminals) ○ *There was **tight security** for the Pope's visit* (eg Many police officers guarded him). **3** [C, U] a thing of value, eg one's house, that can be used to make sure that one will pay back borrowed money or keep a promise: *lend money **on security*** (ie in return for sth given as security) ○ *give sth as (a) security.* Compare GUARANTEE¹ 1. **4** [C often *pl*] a document or certificate showing who owns shares (SHARE¹ 3), etc: *government securities* (ie for money lent to a government).
■ **the Seˈcurity Council** *n* [sing] the part of the United Nations concerned with keeping the peace.
seˈcurity risk *n* a person who may be a danger to a country, an organization, etc because of her or his political beliefs, personal habits, etc, or who may reveal secrets to an enemy: *She's a poor/good security risk.*

sedan /sɪ'dæn/ *n* **1** (*US*) = SALOON 1. ⇨ picture at HATCHBACK. **2** (also **se,dan-ˈchair**) a box containing a seat for one person, carried on poles by two people, esp in the 17th and 18th centuries.

sedate¹ /sɪ'deɪt/ *adj* calm and steady; full of dignity: *walk at a sedate pace* ○ *a sedate old lady.* ▶ **sedately** *adv*: *walk sedately.* **sedateness** *n* [U].

sedate² /sɪ'deɪt/ *v* to give sb a drug that calms the nerves or makes them sleep: [Vn] *She is heavily sedated.*
▶ **sedation** /sɪ'deɪʃn/ *n* [U] a state of rest or sleep as a result of being sedated: *The patient is **under (heavy) sedation.***
sedative /'sedətɪv/ *n* a drug or medicine that sedates: *give sb a sedative.* Compare TRANQUILLIZER. — *adj* [usu attrib]: *a sedative drug/injection.*

sedentary /'sedntri; *US* -teri/ *adj* (*rather fml*) (**a**) (of work) done sitting down: *a sedentary job/occupation.* (**b**) (of people) spending a lot of time sitting down: *a sedentary worker.*

sedge /sedʒ/ *n* [U] a plant like grass that grows in wet ground or near water.

sediment /'sedɪmənt/ *n* [U] **1** the solid material that settles to the bottom of a liquid: *the sediment at the bottom of a wine bottle.* **2** sand, stones, mud, etc carried by water or wind and left somewhere, eg at the bottom of a lake, a river, the sea, etc.
▶ **sedimentary** /ˌsedɪ'mentri/ *adj* of or like sediment(2); formed from sediment: *sedimentary rocks/layers.*
sedimentation /ˌsedɪmen'teɪʃn/ *n* [U] (*geology*) the process of depositing sediment(2).

sedition /sɪ'dɪʃn/ *n* [U] words or actions intended to make people oppose the authority of the state: *be charged with sedition.*
▶ **seditious** /sɪ'dɪʃəs/ *adj* of, causing or spreading sedition: *seditious activities/speeches/writings.*

seduce /sɪ'djuːs; *US* -'duːs/ *v* **1** ~ **sb** (**from sth**); ~ **sb** (**into sth/doing sth**) (*fml*) to persuade sb to do sth they would not usu agree to do; to tempt sb: [Vnpr] *Higher salaries are seducing many teachers into industry.* ○ *I let myself be seduced into buying a new car.* [also Vn]. **2** to persuade sb, esp sb younger or less experienced than oneself, to have sex: [Vn] *She claimed that he had seduced her.*
▶ **seducer** *n* a person who seduces sb, esp into having sex.

seduction /sɪ'dʌkʃn/ *n* **1** [U, C] the action of seducing (SEDUCE 2) sb or an instance of being seduced: *the art of seduction* ○ *her seduction by an older man.*

2 [C usu*pl*] (*fml*) a tempting or attractive feature: *the seductions of country life.*

seductive /sɪˈdʌktɪv/ *adj* tending to SEDUCE or tempt sb; attractive: *a seductive woman/smile/look* ○ *This offer of a high salary and a company car is very seductive.* ▶ **seductively** *adv*. **seductiveness** *n* [U].

sedulous /ˈsedjʊləs; *US* ˈsedʒələs/ *adj* (*fml*) showing much hard work, steady effort or care: *a sedulous researcher/journalist* ○ *pay sedulous attention to details.* ▶ **sedulously** *adv*: *He sedulously avoided any mention of the subject.*

see¹ /siː/ *v* (*pt* **saw** /sɔː/; *pp* **seen** /siːn/)

● **Using the eyes 1** (not in the continuous tenses) to become aware of sb/sth by using the eyes; to perceive sb/sth: [Vn] *He looked for her but couldn't see her in the crowd.* ○ *I looked out of the window but saw nothing.* [V.*that*] *He could see (that) she had been crying.* [V.*wh*] *If you watch carefully you will see how I do it/how it is done.* ○ *Did you see what happened?* [Vn-adj] *I hate to see you unhappy.* [Vn.*in*] *She was seen running away from the scene of the crime.* [Vn.inf (no *to*)] *I saw you put the key in your pocket.* [V.n *to* inf only passive] *She was seen to enter the building about the time the crime was committed.* **2** (not usu in the continuous tenses; often used with *can* and *could*) to have or use the power of sight: [V] *If you shut your eyes you can't see.* ○ *She will never (be able to) see again* (ie she has become blind). [Vpr] *On a clear day you can see for miles from the top of the tower.* ○ *Move out of the way, please — I can't see through you!* [V.*to* inf] *It was getting dark and I couldn't see to read.* ⇨ note at FEEL¹.

● **Looking at sth 3** (not usu in the continuous tenses) to look at or watch sth: [Vn] *In the evening we went to see a movie.* ○ *Have you seen the new production of 'Hamlet' at the Playhouse?* ○ *Fifty thousand people saw the match.* **4** (only in the imperative) to look at sth in order to find information: [Vn] *See page 158.*

● **Meeting people 5** (not usu in the continuous tenses) to be near and recognize sb; to meet sb by chance: [Vn] *I saw your mother in town today.* ○ *Guess who I saw at the party yesterday?* **6(a)** to visit sb: [Vn] *Come and see us again soon.* **(b)** ~ sb (about sth) to have a meeting with sb: [Vn] *I'm seeing my solicitor tomorrow.* ○ *You ought to see* (ie discuss your illness, etc with) *a doctor.* [Vnpr] *What is it you want to see* (ie talk with) *me about?* **7** to receive a call or visit from sb: [Vn] *The manager can only see you for five minutes.* ○ *She's too ill to see anyone at present.* **8** (used esp in the continuous tenses) to spend time in the company of sb: [Vn] *She doesn't want to see him any more.* ○ *She's seeing* (ie having a relationship with) *a married man.*

● **Grasping with the mind or imagination 9** (not usu in continuous tenses) to perceive sth with the mind; to understand sth: [V] *'The box opens like this.' 'Oh, I see.'* [Vn] *He didn't see the joke.* ○ *I don't think she saw the point of the story.* ○ *I can see* (ie recognize) *the advantages of the scheme.* [V.*that*] *Can't you see (that) he's deceiving you?* [V.*wh*] *Do you see what I mean?* **10** (not usu in the continuous tenses) to have an opinion of sth: [Vnadv] *I see things differently now.* ○ *Lack of money is the main problem, as I see it* (ie in my opinion). [Vnpr] *Try to see the matter from her point of view.* **11** (not in the continuous tenses) to view sth as a future possibility; to imagine sb/sth as sth: [Vn.*in*] *I can't see her changing her mind.* [Vn-n] *Her colleagues see her as a future director.*

● **Discovering or checking sth 12** (not usu in the continuous tenses) **(a)** to find out or discover sth by looking or searching or asking: [V] *'Has the milkman been yet?' 'I'll just go and see.'* ○ *'Is he going*

to recover?' 'I don't know, we'll just have to **wait and see.'** [V.*wh*] *Could you go and see what the children are doing?* [V.*that*] *I see (that)* (ie I have read in the newspapers that) *interest rates are going up again.* **(b)** to find out or discover sth by thinking or considering: [V.*that*] *'Do you think you'll be able to help us?' 'I don't know, I'll have to see.'* [V.*wh*] *I'll see what I can do to help.* **13** (not usu in the continuous tenses) to make sure; to check: [V.*that*] *See that all the doors are locked before you leave.* ○ *Could you see (that) the children are in bed by 8 o'clock?* ○ *I'll see that it's done.*

● **Experiencing or witnessing 14** (not in the continuous tenses) to experience or suffer sth: [Vn] *He has seen a great deal in his long life.* ○ *These shoes have seen a lot of wear* (ie have been worn a lot). **15** (not in the continuous tenses) **(a)** to be the time when an event happens: [Vn] *This year sees the tercentenary of Handel's birth.* **(b)** to be the scene or setting of sth: [Vn] *This stadium has seen many thrilling football games.* **(c)** to be alive or present to witness sth: *I hope I never (live to)* **see the day** *that computers replace books.*

● **Other meanings 16** to go with sb to help or protect them: [Vnpr] *I saw the old lady across* (ie helped her to cross) *the road.* [Vnadv] *May I see you home* (ie go with you as far as your house)? [Vnp] *My secretary will see you out* (ie of the building). **17** (in gambling games) to bet the same amount as another player.

IDM Most idioms containing **see** are at the entries for the nouns or adjectives in the idioms, eg **see the light** ⇨ LIGHT¹; **see red** ⇨ RED². **for all (the world) to ˈsee** clearly visible. **ˌsee for oneˈself** to find out or observe sth in order to be convinced or satisfied: *If you don't believe me, go and see for yourself!* **seeing that …**; (*infml*) **seeing as (how) …** in view of the fact that …; since …; because …: *Seeing that he's been ill all week he's unlikely to come.* **see a lot, nothing, etc of sb** to be often, never, etc in the company of sb: *They've seen a lot/nothing/little/more/less of each other recently.* **ˈsee you; (Iˈll) be ˈseeing you** (*infml*) goodbye: *I'd better be going now. See you!* **see you aˈround** (*infml*) = SEE YOU.

PHRV **ˈsee about sth / doing sth** to deal with sth; to attend to sth: *I must see about* (ie prepare) *lunch soon.* ○ *I'll have to see about getting the roof repaired.* ○ *He says he won't help us, does he? Well, we'll soon see about that* (ie I will insist that he does help).
ˈsee sth in sb/sth to find sb/sth attractive or interesting: *I can't think what she sees in him.*
ˌsee sb ˈoff 1 to go to a railway station, airport, etc to say goodbye to sb who is about to start a journey: *We all went to the airport to see her off.* **2** to force sb to leave a place, eg by chasing them: *Some boys were trespassing in our garden but I saw them off pretty quickly.*
ˌsee sth ˈout (not in the continuous tenses) to last until the end of sth: *We have enough logs to see the winter out.*
ˌsee ˈover sth to visit and examine or inspect a place carefully: *We need to see over the house before we can make you an offer.*
ˌsee ˈthrough sb/sth (not in the continuous tenses) to realize the truth about sb/sth so that one is not deceived: *We saw through him from the start.* ○ *I can see through your little game* (ie am aware of the trick you are trying to play on me). **ˌsee sth ˈthrough** (not usu in the continuous tenses) not to abandon a task, project, etc until it is finished: *She's determined to see the job through.* **ˌsee sb ˈthrough (sth)** (not in the continuous tenses) to satisfy the needs of sb or give help or support to sb for a particular, esp difficult, period of time: *Her courage and good humour saw her through the bad times.* ○ *That overcoat*

S

should see me through the winter. ∘ *I've only got $50 to see me through until pay-day.*
¹**see to sth** to attend to or deal with sth: *The photocopier isn't working; I'll have to get somebody to see to it.* ∘ *Will you see to the arrangements for the next committee meeting?* ¹**see to it that...** to make sure that...: *See to it that you're ready on time!*
■ ¹**see-through** *adj* (of material) very thin so that one can see through it: *a ₗsee-through ¹blouse.*

see² /si:/ *n* (*fml*) the district for which a bishop or an ARCHBISHOP is responsible; the office or authority of a bishop or an archbishop. See also THE HOLY SEE.

seed /si:d/ *n* **1(a)** [C] the part of a plant from which a new plant of the same kind can grow: *a tiny poppy seed* ∘ *sow a row of lettuce seeds.* ⇨ picture at FRUIT. **(b)** [U] a quantity of these for planting, feeding birds, etc: *a handful of grass seed* ∘ *Did you grow these vegetables from seed* (ie rather than from small plants)? **(c)** [attrib] (to be) used for planting: *seed corn/potatoes.* **2** [C] (*US*) = PIP¹. **3** [C usu *pl*] ~ (of sth) a cause or beginning of sth: *Are the seeds of criminal behaviour sown early in life?* ∘ *This planted the seeds of doubt in my mind.* **4** [C] (esp in tennis) any of the players thought to be the best in a particular competition. Competitions are arranged so that seeds do not play against each other until the later rounds: *The final is between the first and second seeds.* **5** [U] (*dated fml*) SEMEN. **IDM** **go/run to ¹seed 1** (of a plant) to produce flowers and seeds instead of just leaves. **2** to begin to look untidy or become less able, efficient, etc: *He started to drink too much and gradually ran to seed.*
▶ **seed** *v* **1(a)** (of a plant) to produce seed. **(b)** [Vn] ~ **itself** (of a plant) to reproduce itself with its own seed. **2** ~ **sth** (**with sth**) to plant seed in sth: [Vn] *a newly-seeded lawn* [Vnpr] *seed a field with wheat.*
seeded *adj* **1** (esp in tennis) selected as a seed(4): *seeded players.* **2** (of fruit) with the seeds removed: *seeded raisins.*
seedless *adj* having no seeds: *seedless grapes/oranges.*
■ ¹**seed-bed** *n* **1** an area of fine soil for planting seeds in. **2** a place or situation in which sth develops: *The university was a seed-bed of protest among intellectuals.*
¹**seed-cake** *n* [C, U] a cake containing esp CARAWAY seeds.
¹**seed-pearl** *n* a small PEARL(1).

seedling /¹si:dlɪŋ/ *n* a young plant newly grown from a seed: *tomato seedlings.*

seedsman /¹si:dzmən/ *n* (*pl* **-men** /-mən/) a person who grows and sells seeds.

seedy /¹si:di/ *adj* (**-ier, -iest**) **1** untidy, dirty or not respectable in appearance: *a seedy old tramp* ∘ *a cheap hotel in a seedy part of town.* **2** [usu pred] (*infml*) not very well; rather ill: *feeling seedy.* ▶ **seediness** *n* [U]: *the seediness of his lodgings.*

seek /si:k/ *v* (*pt, pp* **sought** /sɔ:t/) (*fml*) **1** ~ (**after/for**) **sth** to look for sth; to try to find or get sth: [Vn] *seek happiness/comfort/wealth* ∘ *seek shelter from the rain* [Vn, Vpr] *seeking (for) solutions to current problems* ∘ *young graduates seeking (after) success in life.* **2** ~ **sth** (**from sb**) to ask sb for sth: [Vn] *seek help/advice/information* [Vnpr] *You must seek permission from the manager.* **3** to attempt to do sth; to try: [V.*to* inf] *seek to bring the conflict to an end* ∘ *They sought to mislead us.* **IDM** **seek one's ¹fortune** to try to find a way to become rich and successful. **PHRV** ₗ**seek sb/sth ¹out** to look for and find sb/sth: *seek out new experiences* ∘ *It sometimes helps to seek out people with similar problems to your own.* See also HIDE-AND-SEEK, SELF-SEEKING.
▶ **seeker** *n* (often in compounds) a person who seeks the specified thing: *asylum/gold/fun seekers* ∘ *seekers after truth.*

seem /si:m/ *v* ~ (**to sb**) (**to be**) **sth**; ~ **like sth** (not used in continuous tenses) to give the impression of being or doing sth; to appear: [V-adj] *She seems happy (to me).* ∘ *Do whatever seems best.* [V-n, Vpr, V.*to* inf] *It seems (to me) (to be) the best solution.* ∘ *It seemed like a disaster at the time.* [V.*that*, Vpr.*that*] *It seems (to me) that she's right.* [V.*that*] *It would seem that...* (ie a cautious way of saying '*It seems that...*') [Vadv] '*She's leaving.*' '*So it seems* (ie People say so).*' [V.*to* inf] *They seem to know what they're doing.* ∘ *I can't seem to* (ie It seems that I can't) *stop coughing.* **IDM** **it seems/seemed as if.../as though...** the impression is/was given that...: *It always seemed as if/though they would marry in the end.*
▶ **seeming** *adj* [attrib] (*fml*) appearing to be sth, but perhaps not actually being this in reality; APPARENT(2): *seeming intelligence/interest/anger* ∘ *Despite his seeming deafness, he could hear every word.*
seemingly *adv* in appearance; apparently: *They were seemingly unaware of the decision.*

seemly /¹si:mli/ *adj* (*dated* or *fml*) acceptable and suitable in polite society: *Try and behave in a more seemly manner.* ∘ *It would be more seemly to tell her after the funeral.* ▶ **seemliness** *n* [U].

seen *pp* of SEE¹.

seep /si:p/ *v* ~ **through (sth)/into sth/out (of sth)/away** (of liquids) to flow slowly and in small quantities through sth: [Vpr] *water seeping through the roof of the tunnel* [Vp] *Oil is seeping out through a crack in the tank.* ∘ (*fig*) *Their power is seeping away.* ⇨ note at DRIP¹.
▶ **seepage** /¹si:pɪdʒ/ *n* [U] the process of seeping through sth: *prevent water seepage into a building.*

seer /sɪə(r)/ *n* (*dated* or *rhet*) a person who claims to see into the future and tells people what will happen.

seersucker /¹sɪəsʌkə(r)/ *n* [U] a thin, usu cotton, fabric raised up in rows across its surface: *a seersucker tablecloth.*

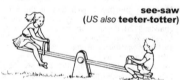

see-saw
(*US also* **teeter-totter**)

see-saw /¹si:sɔ:/ *n* **1** (*US also* **teeter-totter**) [C] a long board balanced on a central support for esp children to play on. A person sits at each end and makes the see-saw move up and down: *have a go on the see-saw.* ⇨ picture. **2** a series of rises and falls: *a see-saw in prices/trading.*
▶ **see-saw** *v* [V] **1** to play on a see-saw. **2** to rise and fall or move from one position, opinion, etc to another repeatedly: [V] *Prices see-saw according to demand.* [Vadv] *The game see-sawed back and forth.*

seethe /si:ð/ *v* **1** (of liquids) to move about making bubbles or waves as if boiling: [V] *They fell into the seething waters of the rapids.* **2** ~ (**with sth**) **(a)** (esp in the continuous tenses) to be very angry, upset, etc: [V, Vpr] *She was seething (with rage) at his remarks.* **(b)** to be crowded: [Vpr] *streets seething with excited crowds* [V] *a seething mass of humanity.*

segment /¹segmənt/ *n* **1** a part of sth which is separated from the other parts or which can be considered separately: *She cleaned a small segment of the painting.* ∘ *Lines divided the area into segments.* **2** any one of the several sections of an orange, a LEMON, etc: *grapefruit segments.* **3** (*geometry*) a part of a circle separated from the rest by a single line. ⇨ picture at CIRCLE.
▶ **segment** /seg¹ment/ *v* to separate sth into

segments: [Vn] *a segmented body/market.*
segmentation /ˌsegmen'teɪʃn/ *n* [U, C] the division of sth into segments: *market segmentation.*

segregate /'segrɪgeɪt/ *v* ~ **sb/sth (from sb/sth)** **1** to put sb/sth in a place away from others; to isolate sb/sth: [Vn] *segregate cholera patients* [Vnpr] *He served most of his sentence segregated from the other prisoners.* **2** to separate a group of people from the rest of the community, esp because of their race³(1) or religion, and treat them differently: [Vnpr] *Protestants segregated from Catholics* [Vn] *segregated schools/residential areas* (ie for the use of one particular group of people). Compare INTEGRATE.
▶ **segregation** /ˌsegrɪ'geɪʃn/ *n* [U] the action of segregating people or things or the state of being segregated: *a policy of racial segregation.*

seismic /'saɪzmɪk/ *adj* [usu attrib] of or caused by earthquakes (EARTHQUAKE): *seismic activity/tremors/ data.*

seismograph /'saɪzməgrɑːf; *US* -græf/ *n* an instrument for detecting earthquakes (EARTHQUAKE) and for recording how strong they are and how long they last.

seismology /saɪz'mɒlədʒi/ *n* [U] the science or study of earthquakes (EARTHQUAKE). ▶ **seismologist** /-dʒɪst/ *n.*

seize /siːz/ *v* **1** to take hold of sth/sb suddenly or violently; to GRAB sth/sb: [Vnpr] *She seized me by the wrist.* [Vn] *He seized my bag and ran off with it.* **2(a)** to take possession of sth or capture sb/sth, using force: [Vn] *seize the airport in a surprise attack* ○ *The army has seized power.* ○ *The men were seized* (ie arrested) *as they left the building.* **(b)** (of the police, etc) to use one's authority to take property, esp stolen goods, illegal drugs, etc, away from sb by force: [Vn] *20 kilos of heroin were seized yesterday at Heathrow.* ○ *All the company's assets were seized.* **3** to see an opportunity, etc and use it eagerly: [Vn] *seize the chance to make some money* ○ *seize a three-stroke lead* ○ *Seize any opening you can.* **4** (esp passive) (of a strong feeling, desire, etc) to affect sb suddenly and deeply: [Vn] *Panic seized us.* ○ *We were seized by a sudden impulse to run.* **PHRV** '**seize on/ upon sth** to recognize sth and use it eagerly: *She seized on my suggestion and began work immediately.* ○ *The critics seized on my mistake.* ˌ**seize** '**up** (of moving machinery) to stop working because sth is wrong: *Your engine will seize up if you don't put some more oil in.* ○ *(fig) My joints seem to seize up in the cold weather.*
▶ **seizure** /'siːʒə(r)/ *n* **1** [U,C] the action or an instance of seizing sth by force or legal authority: *the seizure of power by the army* ○ *the seizure of contraband by Customs officers* ○ *Police reports claim that substantial seizures of cocaine have been made.* **2** [C] a sudden violent attack of illness, esp in the brain; a stroke¹(8): *have a seizure* ○ *epileptic seizures.*

seldom /'seldəm/ *adv* not often; rarely: *She very seldom leaves the house.* ○ *The island is seldom, if ever, visited.* ○ *Seldom have I seen such brutality.*

select /sɪ'lekt/ *v* ~ **sb/sth (as sth)** to choose sb/sth carefully, esp as being the best or most suitable: [Vn] *select a gift/candidate/wine* ○ *selected poems of T S Eliot* [Vnpr] *select a card from the rack* [Vn-n] *be selected as the team leader* [Vn.to inf] *Who has been selected to chair the meeting?* ⇨ note at CHOOSE.
▶ **select** *adj* **1** [usu attrib] carefully chosen, esp as the best out of a larger group: *a select bibliography.* **2** (of a society, club, gathering, etc) admitting only certain people; exclusive: *a select group of top scientists* ○ *a documentary shown to a select audience* ○ *This area is very select* (ie Only the most wealthy, respectable, etc people live here).
selector *n* **1** a person who selects people, eg the members of a national sports team: *the England*

selectors. **2** a device that selects sth, eg the correct gear in a vehicle.
■ **se,lect com'mittee** *n* a small committee of a parliament, congress, etc appointed to investigate a particular matter or area of activity: *the Defence Select Committee* ○ *the Commons Select Committee on trade and industry.*

selection /sɪ'lekʃn/ *n* **1** [U] the process of selecting sb/sth or the state of being selected: *the selection of a football team* ○ *the selection process* ○ *I'm delighted about my selection as leader.* **2** [C] (**a**) a number of selected items or people: *read selections from 18th century English poetry* ○ *a selection of milk and plain chocolates.* (**b**) a collection of a particular thing from which some can be selected: *a shop with a huge selection of paperbacks.* See also NATURAL SELECTION.
■ **se'lection committee** *n* a committee appointed to select people, eg the members of a sports team.

selective /sɪ'lektɪv/ *adj* **1** of or for certain specific people or things: *the selective training of recruits* ○ *a selective pesticide* (ie one that kills certain insects only). **2** ~ (**about sb/sth**) tending to choose carefully: *I'm very selective about the books I read.* ○ *This school is academically selective.* ▶ **selectively** *adv*: *The document had been selectively leaked to the press.* **selectivity** /sə,lek'tɪvəti/ *n* [U]: *A feature of such reports is their selectivity in what they mention and what they omit.*

self /self/ *n* (*pl* **selves** /selvz/) **1(a)** [U] (also **the self** [sing]) (*fml*) a person's inner being¹(1b), including the mind and spirit; the EGO: *the conscious self* ○ *a sense of self* ○ *the search for self/one's inner self.* (**b**) [C usu *sing*] a person's nature or personality; the qualities that make one individual: *He was not his usual cheerful self today.* ○ *one's better self* (ie one's good qualities) ○ *By doing that he showed his true self* (ie what he is really like). ○ *She's her old self again* (ie has returned to her normal behaviour, health, etc). **2** [U] one's own interest, advantage or pleasure: *You always put self first.* ○ *She has no thought of self* (ie is always more concerned for other people). **3** [C] (*commerce or rhet*) myself, yourself, himself, etc: *a cheque payable to self* (ie to the person whose signature is on it) ○ *We look forward to seeing your wife and your good self* (ie you). **IDM a shadow of one's/its former self** ⇨ SHADOW.

self- *comb form* of, to or by oneself or itself: ˌ*self-con'trol* ○ ˌ*self-ad'dressed* ○ ˌ*self-¹taught.*

self-absorbed /ˌself əb'sɔːbd/ *adj* only concerned about or interested in oneself: *He's too self-absorbed to care about us.* ▶ **self-absorption** /-əb'sɔːpʃn/ *n* [U].

self-access /ˌself 'ækses/ *n* [U] a method of learning which enables a student to choose and use appropriate learning materials for private study: *The books are colour-coded for self-access.* ○ *self-access materials/centres.*

self-addressed /ˌself ə'drest/ *adj* [usu attrib] (of an envelope that will be used for a reply) addressed to oneself.

self-adhesive /ˌself əd'hiːsɪv/ *adj* covered on one side with a sticky substance, and so able to stick to surfaces without glue, etc being applied: *self-adhesive floor tiles.*

self-advertisement /ˌself əd'vɜːtɪsmənt/ *n* [U] the promotion of one's own talents and abilities.

self-appointed /ˌself ə'pɔɪntɪd/ *adj* [usu attrib] having decided to be sth, usu without the agreement of others: *a self-appointed judge/expert/critic.*

self-assembly /ˌself ə'sembli/ *adj* [attrib] (esp of furniture) bought in separate parts that have to be fitted together by the buyer.

self-assertive /ˌself ə'sɜːtɪv/ *adj* expressing one's views, demands, etc confidently; ASSERTIVE. ▶ **self-assertion** /-ə'sɜːʃn/, **self-assertiveness** *ns* [U].

S

self-assured /ˌself əˈʃʊəd; *Brit also* -ˈʃɔːd/ *adj* having or showing confidence in one's ability, position, etc: *a very self-assured young woman.* ▶ **self-assurance** /-əˈʃʊərəns; *Brit also* -ˈʃɔːr-/ *n* [U].

self-awareness /ˌself əˈweənəs/ *n* [U] the state of knowing one's own character, feelings, etc.

self-catering /ˌself ˈkeɪtərɪŋ/ *adj* [usu attrib] (of a holiday, accommodation, etc) providing facilities for people to cook their own meals: *self-catering chalets.*

self-centred (*US* **-centered**) /ˌself ˈsentəd/ *adj* (*derog*) thinking too much about oneself and too little about others: *her self-centred attitude.* ▶ **self-centredness** (*US* **-centered-**) *n* [U].

self-confessed /ˌself kənˈfest/ *adj* [attrib] openly admitting that one is sth usu considered bad: *a ˌself-confessed alcoˈholic/ˈthief.*

self-confident /ˌself ˈkɒnfɪdənt/ *adj* having confidence in oneself, one's abilities, etc: *a self-confident person/manner/reply* ○ *learn to be more self-confident.* ▶ **self-confidence** /-dəns/ *n* [U].

self-congratulation /ˌself kənˌgrætʃəˈleɪʃn/ *n* [U] satisfaction with and praise for one's own achievements: *speeches of self-congratulation.* ▶ **self-congratulatory** /ˌself kənˈgrætʃələtəri/ *adj.*

self-conscious /ˌself ˈkɒnʃəs/ *adj* **1** nervous or awkward because one is shy or worried about what other people think of one: *a ˌself-conscious ˈsmile* ○ *be self-conscious about one's appearance.* **2** strongly aware of who or what one is or what one is doing. ▶ **self-consciously** *adv.* **self-consciousness** *n* [U].

self-contained /ˌself kənˈteɪnd/ *adj* **1(a)** (of a person) quiet and not depending on the company of others. **(b)** complete in itself; independent: *The story consists of several self-contained plots which are woven together.* **2** [usu attrib] (*esp Brit*) (of accommodation) having no shared facilities, and usu having its own private entrance: *a ˌself-contained ˈflat/maisoˈnette.*

self-contradictory /ˌself ˌkɒntrəˈdɪktəri/ *adj* containing or expressing two or more ideas or statements that are not consistent with each other.

self-control /ˌself kənˈtrəʊl/ *n* [U] the ability to control one's behaviour or not to show one's feelings: *show/exercise great self-control in not becoming angry* ○ *lose one's self-control.* ▶ **self-controlled** *adj.*

self-defeating /ˌself dɪˈfiːtɪŋ/ *adj* (of a course of action, etc) likely to achieve the opposite of what is intended: *Punishing the demonstrators is self-defeating and will only encourage further demonstrations.*

self-defence (*US*) (also **-defense**) /ˌself dɪˈfens/ *n* [U] the defence of one's body, actions, rights, etc: *kill sb in self-defence* (ie while defending oneself against attack) ○ *He had nothing to say in self-defence* (ie to explain or justify his behaviour).

self-denial /ˌself dɪˈnaɪəl/ *n* [U] refusing to do or have the things one would like, either from necessity or for moral reasons.

self-determination /ˌself dɪˌtɜːmɪˈneɪʃn/ *n* [U] **1** the right of a nation, country, etc to decide what form of government it will have or whether it will be independent of another country or not. **2** the right or opportunity of individuals to control their own fates.

self-discipline /ˌself ˈdɪsəplɪn/ *n* [U] the ability to apply oneself steadily to a particular task without being distracted or influenced by one's desires, feelings, etc: *an athlete's self-discipline* ○ *Dieting demands self-discipline.*

self-drive /ˌself ˈdraɪv/ *adj* [attrib] (*Brit*) **1** (of a vehicle) that one can hire and drive oneself: *a ˌself-drive ˈcar/ˈvan* ○ *a ˌself-drive ˈhire firm.* **2** (of a holiday) on which one takes and drives one's own car.

self-educated /ˌself ˈedʒukeɪtɪd/ *adj* educated

more by one's own efforts than by schools, teachers, etc.

self-effacing /ˌself ɪˈfeɪsɪŋ/ *adj* not trying to impress people; very modest: *He is charming but self-effacing.*

self-employed /ˌself ɪmˈplɔɪd/ *adj* working independently for customers or clients and not for an employer: *become self-employed.* ▶ **the self-employed** *n* [pl *v*] self-employed people: *pensions for the self-employed.* **self-employment** /-ɪmˈplɔɪmənt/ *n* [U]: *a person in self-employment.*

self-esteem /ˌself ɪˈstiːm/ *n* [U] a good opinion of one's own character and abilities: *a man with **high/ low** self-esteem* ○ *undermine/raise sb's self-esteem.*

self-evident /ˌself ˈevɪdənt/ *adj* clear without any need for proof, explanation or further evidence; obvious: *Her sincerity/The conclusion is self-evident.*

self-examination /ˌself ɪɡˌzæmɪˈneɪʃn/ *n* [U] the study of one's own behaviour and the reasons for it, esp in order to judge whether it is acceptable.

self-explanatory /ˌself ɪkˈsplænətri; *US* -tɔːri/ *adj* not needing further explanation; easy to understand: *The diagram is self-explanatory.*

self-expression /ˌself ɪkˈspreʃn/ *n* [U] the expression of one's feelings, thoughts, etc, eg in writing, painting, dancing, etc.

self-fulfilling /ˌself fʊlˈfɪlɪŋ/ *adj* (esp of a PROPHECY) certain to happen because of events caused by its being made.

self-government /ˌself ˈɡʌvənmənt/ *n* [U] the government or control of a country, an organization, etc by its own people or members, not by others. ▶ ˌself-ˈgoverning *adj.*

self-help /ˌself ˈhelp/ *n* [U] the use of one's own efforts, resources, etc to achieve things, without depending on others: *a self-help group* ○ *encourage self-help and mutual support for single parents.*

self-important /ˌself ɪmˈpɔːtənt/ *adj* (*derog*) thinking that one is much more important than one really is; POMPOUS. ▶ **self-importance** /-təns/ *n* [U].

self-imposed /ˌself ɪmˈpəʊzd/ *adj* (of a duty, task, etc) that sb forces upon themselves: *a ˌself-imposed ˈlimit/ˈexile.*

self-indulgent /ˌself ɪnˈdʌldʒənt/ *adj* (*derog*) allowing oneself to do or have what one enjoys without control: *self-indulgent feelings/habits* ○ *The novel is too long and self-indulgent.* ▶ **self-indulgence** /-dʒəns/ *n* [U]: *a life of gross self-indulgence.*

self-inflicted /ˌself ɪnˈflɪktɪd/ *adj* (of an injury, a wound, etc) that one inflicts deliberately on oneself.

self-interest /ˌself ˈɪntrəst/ *n* [U] concern for one's own interests or personal advantage: *act purely from/out of self-interest.* ▶ **self-interested** *adj.*

selfish /ˈselfɪʃ/ *adj* (*derog*) thinking first of one's own interests, needs, etc without concern for others; not sharing what one has with others; (of an action) done for selfish reasons: *selfish behaviour* ○ *When you have children, you have to become less selfish.* ▶ **selfishly** *adv.* *act/behave selfishly.* **selfishness** *n* [U]: *act out of pure selfishness.*

selfless /ˈselfləs/ *adj* (*fml approv*) thinking more of the needs and welfare of others than of one's own; UNSELFISH: *selfless devotion to one's children.* ▶ **selflessly** *adv:* *Each member of the group worked selflessly to achieve a common aim.* **selflessness** *n* [U].

self-locking /ˌself ˈlɒkɪŋ/ *adj* (eg of a door) locking automatically when closed.

self-made /ˌself ˈmeɪd/ *adj* [usu attrib] having become successful, rich, etc by one's own efforts: *a ˌself-made ˈman/ˈwoman.*

self-opinionated /ˌself əˈpɪnjəneɪtɪd/ *adj* (*derog*)

[V.*to* inf] = verb + *to* infinitive   [Vn.inf (no *to*)] = verb + noun + infinitive without *to*   [V.*ing*] = verb + -*ing* form

always wanting to express one's own strong views without considering that they could be wrong.

self-pity /ˌself ˈpɪti/ n [U] (*often derog*) pity for oneself: *a letter full of complaints and self-pity.*

self-portrait /ˌself ˈpɔːtreɪt/ n a portrait of oneself: *a self-portrait by Van Gogh.*

self-possessed /ˌself pəˈzest/ adj calm and confident, esp at times of stress or difficulty: *She seemed very self-possessed in front of the TV cameras.*
▶ **self-possession** /-pəˈzeʃn/ n [U] the control of one's emotions and behaviour; confidence: *keep/lose/regain one's self-possession.*

self-preservation /ˌself prezəˈveɪʃn/ n [U] the protection of oneself from harm or destruction; the natural urge to survive: *the instinct for self-preservation.*

self-raising flour /ˌself ˈreɪzɪŋ flaʊə(r)/ n (*US* **self-rising flour** /-ˈraɪzɪŋ-/) n [U] flour containing a substance which makes cakes, etc rise during baking. Compare PLAIN FLOUR.

self-reliant /ˌself rɪˈlaɪənt/ adj relying on one's own abilities and efforts; independent: *She lives alone and is totally self-reliant.* ▶ **self-reliance** /-ˈlaɪəns/ n [U].

self-respect /ˌself rɪˈspekt/ n [U] a feeling of pride in oneself: *lose all self-respect.*
▶ **self-respecting** adj [attrib] (esp in negative sentences) having self-respect: *No self-respecting doctor would refuse to treat a sick person.*

self-righteous /ˌself ˈraɪtʃəs/ adj (*derog*) feeling or acting as if one believes one is always right: *a self-righteous person/attitude/remark* ○ *self-righteous anger/condemnation.* ▶ **self-righteously** adv. **self-righteousness** n [U].

self-rule /ˌself ˈruːl/ n [U] the governing of a country or part of a country by its own people.

self-sacrifice /ˌself ˈsækrɪfaɪs/ n [U] (*approv*) the giving up of things that one wants for oneself to help others or for a good purpose: *Her work with refugees involved considerable self-sacrifice.* ▶ **self-sacrificing** adj [usu attrib].

selfsame /ˈselfseɪm/ adj [attrib] (used after *the, this, that,* etc) very same: *She said the selfsame thing to me.* ○ *They were both born on that selfsame day.*

self-satisfied /ˌself ˈsætɪsfaɪd/ adj (*derog*) too pleased with oneself and one's own achievements: *a self-satisfied person/attitude/grin.*

self-seeking /ˌself ˈsiːkɪŋ/ adj (*derog*) having or showing concern for one's own interests before those of others. ▶ **self-seeking** n [U].

self-service /ˌself ˈsɜːvɪs/ n [U] a system of service in a restaurant, shop, etc in which customers take what they want and then pay for it. ▶ **self-service** adj: *a self-service petrol-station.*

self-styled /ˌself ˈstaɪld/ adj [attrib] (*sometimes derog*) using a name, title, etc which one has given oneself, esp without having any right to do so: *self-styled leaders/experts/poets.*

self-sufficient /ˌself səˈfɪʃnt/ adj ~ (**in sth**) able to fulfil one's own needs, without help from others: *a country self-sufficient in grain* (ie producing all the grain it needs) ○ *Even when she was ill she still managed to be self-sufficient.* ▶ **self-sufficiency** /-ˈfənsi/ n [U].

self-supporting /ˌself səˈpɔːtɪŋ/ adj (of a person, a business, a country, etc) having or earning enough to support oneself or itself, without help from others: *A rain forest is a self-supporting ecosystem.*

self-willed /ˌself ˈwɪld/ adj (*derog*) determined to do what one wants: *a troublesome self-willed child.*

sell /sel/ v (*pt, pp* **sold** /səʊld/) **1** ~ (**sth**) (**to sb**) (**at/for sth**) to give goods, etc to sb in exchange for money: [Vpr,Vnpr] *sell (sth) at a high price/a loss/a discount* [V, Vn] *Is she likely to sell (the car)?* ○ *sell furniture by auction* [Vnpr] *I sold my car (to a friend)*

for £750. [Vnn] *Will you sell me your camera?* **2**(**a**) to offer or have a stock of sth for sale: [Vn] *a shop selling fruit/clothes/electrical goods* ○ *Do you sell stamps?* (**b**) (of a person selling goods, etc) to persuade people to buy sth: [Vn] *I sell insurance.* **3** ~ (**at/for sth**) to be sold; to find buyers: [V] *It's a marvellous book, but will it sell?* [Vadv] *The new model car is selling well.* [Vpr] *The badges sell at 50p each.* [Vn] *Their last record sold millions.* **4** to make people want to buy sth: [Vn] *It is not price but quality that sells our shoes.* ○ *Her name will help to sell the product.* ⇨ note. **5** (*infml*) ~ **sth/sb/oneself** (**to sb**) to make sb believe that sth/sb/one is good, useful, worth having, etc: [Vnn] *the best way to sell people a new proposal* [Vnpr] *You'll never sell ideas like that to the voters.* [Vn] *You have to sell yourself* (ie persuade people that you are the most suitable person) *at a job interview.* **6** ~ **oneself** (**to sb**) to accept money, a reward, etc from sb for doing sth bad: [Vn] *Are artists who work in advertising selling themselves?* [also Vnpr]. **IDM** **be 'sold on sth/sb** (*infml*) to be enthusiastic about sth/sb: *I like the house but I'm not sold on the area.* **be sold 'out (of sth)** to have sold all the stock, tickets, etc: *The match was completely sold out.* ○ *We're sold out of bread, I'm afraid.* **go/sell like hot cakes** ⇨ HOT. **sell one's 'body** (*rhet*) to work as a prostitute. **sell sb down the 'river** (*infml*) to betray sb, usu for one's own advantage. **sell sb / buy a pup** ⇨ PUP. **sell sth/sb/oneself 'short** **1** not to recognize the true value of sth/sb/oneself: *Don't sell yourself short: your work is very good.* **2** to cheat sb in value or quantity. **3** (*commerce*) to sell shares (SHARE[1] 3), etc that one does not yet own at an agreed price, in hope of being able to buy them soon at a lower price and so make a profit. **sell one's 'soul (to the devil)** to do anything, even sth dishonest, in return for money, fame, etc: *She'd sell her soul to get that job.* **PHR V** **ˌsell sth 'off** to sell things at reduced prices in order to get rid of them, eg because they have not sold well: *sell off old stock.* **ˌsell 'out** to be all sold: *The show has sold out* (ie There are no tickets left). **ˌsell 'out (of sth)** to sell one's whole supply of sth: *We've sold out (of milk) but we'll be getting some more in later.* **ˌsell 'out (to sb)** to give up or change one's beliefs: *She's sold out and left the party.* **ˌsell (sth) 'out (to sb)** to sell all or part of one's share in a business: *She has decided to sell out (her share of the company) and retire.* **ˌsell sb 'out** to betray sb: *They sold us out by agreeing to work during the strike.* **ˌsell (sth) 'up** to sell all one's property, one's home, etc, eg when leaving the country or retiring: *They sold up and moved to the south of France.*
▶ **sell** n [sing] (*infml*) a deception; a disappointment: *It's a real sell — the menu seems cheap but they charge extra for vegetables.* See also HARD SELL.
■ **'sell-by date** n a date, esp one marked on food products, by which sth must be sold in shops: *This yoghurt is past its sell-by date.*
'sell-off n a sale of government shares (SHARE[1] 3) or services to individuals or private companies: *the electricity/water sell-off.*
'selling-point n a feature of sth that makes it attractive, esp to buyers: *The hotel's private golf course is one of its strongest selling-points.*
'selling price n the price at which sth is sold. Compare COST PRICE.
'sell-out n **1** an event for which all the tickets have been sold: *Every concert they gave was a sell-out.* ○ *a sell-out crowd/tour.* **2** (*infml*) an instance of betraying or being betrayed: *Radicals in the party attacked his policies as a sell-out to capitalism.*

NOTE Compare **sell, peddle, push** and **flog**. Sell is the most general word and means to give something in exchange for money: *They are selling their house and moving to the country.* ○ *Do you sell magazines* *here?* **Peddle** is often used in a disapproving way to describe selling things that are of low quality, and is also used to talk about things such as ideas, religion or dreams: *Gangs who peddle fake perfume to bargain-hunters.* ○ *He was accused of peddling garbage in his newspaper.* **Peddle** is also used in connection with illegal drugs. **Push** is informal and means to sell and promote illegal drugs: *He began pushing heroin while he was still at school.* **Flog** is an informal word suggesting that what somebody is selling is not worth very much, and is therefore difficult to sell: *He tried to flog me a broken television.*

seller /ˈselə(r)/ n **1** (often in compounds) a person who sells sth: *a ¹bookseller* ○ *a ¹newspaper seller* ○ *The seller is required to carry out repairs before completion of the sale.* **2** (esp following an *adj*) a thing that is sold, esp in the manner specified: *The book has been a steady seller for years.* See also BEST SELLER.
  ■ ¸seller's ¹market n a situation in which goods are either popular or needed, so that the people selling have an advantage: *It's a seller's market for vintage cars* (ie Many people will pay high prices for them).

Sellotape /ˈseləteɪp/ n [U] (*Brit propr*) a usu transparent sticky tape(3): *mend a torn map with Sellotape* ○ *a role of Sellotape.* See also SCOTCH TAPE.
  ▶ **sellotape** v to stick Sellotape on sth; to mend or fix sth with Sellotape: [Vn, Vnp] *sellotape the parcel (up)* ○ *sellotape torn pieces of paper (together)* [Vnpr] *sellotape a notice to the wall.*

selvage (also **selvedge**) /ˈselvɪdʒ/ n an edge of material woven so that threads cannot come loose: *fold the fabric with the selvages together.*

selves pl of SELF.

semantic /sɪˈmæntɪk/ adj [usu attrib] of the meaning of words and sentences: *semantic analysis.*
  ▶ **semantics** n [sing v] the branch of linguistics (LINGUIST) dealing with the meanings of words and sentences.

semaphore /ˈseməfɔː(r)/ n **1** [U] a system of sending signals by holding the arms or two flags in certain positions to represent letters of the alphabet: *send a message by semaphore.* **2** [C] a device with red and green or yellow and white lights on movable arms, used for signalling on railways: *semaphore signals.*
  ▶ **semaphore** v to send messages by semaphore: [V.that, Vpr.that] *semaphore (to sb) that help is needed/to send help* [also V, Vn, Vpr.*wh*].

semblance /ˈsembləns/ n [sing, U] ~ **of sth** an outward appearance of being sth; a state of resembling sth: *put on a semblance of cheerfulness/confidence* ○ *bring the meeting to some semblance of order.*

semen /ˈsiːmen/ n [U] the whitish liquid containing SPERM produced by male animals.
  ▶ **seminal** /ˈseminl/ adj **1** (*often approv*) strongly influencing later developments: *a seminal idea/essay/speech/work* ○ *Her theories were seminal for educational reform.* **2** [usu attrib] of seed or semen: *the seminal fluid* ○ *a seminal duct.*

semester /sɪˈmestə(r)/ n (esp in US universities and colleges) either of the two divisions of the academic year: *the summer/winter semester.* Compare TERM 3, TRIMESTER.

semi /ˈsemi/ n (pl **semis** /ˈsemiz/) (*Brit infml*) a SEMI-DETACHED house.

semi- pref (used fairly widely with *adjs* and *ns*) half; partly: *semicircular* ○ *semi-detached* ○ *semifinal.*

semibreve /ˈsembriːv/ (*esp Brit*) (also *esp US* **whole note**) n (*music*) the longest written musical note in common use, equal to two minims (MINIM) in length. ⇨ picture at MUSIC.

semicircle /ˈsemisɜːkl/ n one half of a circle; a thing arranged in this shape: *a semicircle of chairs* ○ *sitting in a semicircle round the fire.* ⇨ picture at CIRCLE.
  ▶ **semicircular** /ˌsemiˈsɜːkjələ(r)/ adj having the shape of a semicircle: *a semicircular flower-bed.*

semicolon /ˌsemiˈkəʊlən; US ˈsemik-/ n the mark (;) used in writing and printing for separating parts of a complicated sentence or items in a detailed list. ⇨ App 3. Compare COLON¹.

semiconductor /ˌsemikənˈdʌktə(r)/ n (**a**) a substance that conducts electricity in certain conditions, but not as well as metals. (**b**) a device containing this, used esp in computing and electronics (ELECTRONIC).

semi-conscious /ˌsemiˈkɒnʃəs/ adj partly conscious: *An elderly woman was found semi-conscious on the floor of her kitchen.*

semi-detached /ˌsemi dɪˈtætʃt/ adj (of a house) joined to another house by one shared wall. ⇨ picture at HOUSE¹.

semifinal /ˌsemiˈfaɪnl/ n a match or round of a contest preceding the FINAL, eg in football or tennis.
  ▶ **semifinalist** /-ˈfaɪnəlɪst/ n a person or team taking part in a semifinal.

seminal ⇨ SEMEN.

seminar /ˈseminɑː(r)/ n **1** a small group of students at a university, etc meeting to discuss or study a particular topic with a teacher. **2** any meeting for discussion or training: *a one-day business management seminar.*

seminary /ˈseminəri; US -neri/ n a college for training priests or rabbis (RABBI).

semiotics /ˌsemiˈɒtɪks/ n [sing v] the study of signs and symbols and of their meaning and use, esp in writing. ▶ **semiotic** adj.

semiprecious /ˌsemiˈpreʃəs/ adj [usu attrib] (of a jewel) less valuable than the most precious types of jewel: *¸semiprecious ¹stones.*

semiquaver /ˈsemikweivə(r)/ (*esp Brit*) (also *esp US* **six¸teenth note**) n a musical note equal to half a QUAVER(2). ⇨ picture at MUSIC.

semi-skilled /ˌsemi ˈskɪld/ adj [usu attrib] (**a**) (of a worker) having some special training or qualifications, but less than a skilled worker: *a ¸semi-skilled ma¹chine operator.* (**b**) (of work) for such a worker: *semi-skilled jobs.*

Semitic /səˈmɪtɪk/ adj **1** of the group of races including the Jews and Arabs, and formerly the Phoenicians and Assyrians: *Semitic languages/peoples.* **2** Jewish.

semitone /ˈsemitəʊn/ (*US* **¹half-tone**) n half of a tone on the musical scale, eg the distance between C and C♯, or between E and F.

semi-vowel /ˈsemivaʊəl/ n a sound like a vowel that functions as a consonant, eg /w/, /j/.

semolina /ˌseməˈliːnə/ n [U] hard grains of wheat used for making PASTA, puddings (PUDDING), etc.

Semtex /ˈsemteks/ n [U] (*propr*) an explosive used esp to make bombs.

Sen abbr **1** Senator: *Sen John K Nordqvist.* **2** = SNR: *John F Davis Sen.* Compare JNR.

senate /ˈsenət/ n (often **the Senate**) **1** [CGp] the upper house of the law-making assembly in some countries, eg France, the USA and Australia: *a Senate committee/decision.* Compare CONGRESS 2, THE HOUSE OF REPRESENTATIVES. **2** [CGp, U] the governing council of certain universities. **3** [Gp] (in ancient Rome) the highest council of state.
  ▶ **senator** /ˈsenətə(r)/ n (often **Senator**, *abbr* **Sen**) a member of the senate: *the senior senator from New Hampshire.* **senatorial** /ˌsenəˈtɔːriəl/ adj [attrib]: *a senatorial decree.*

send /send/ v (pt, pp **sent** /sent/) **1(a)** ~ sth/sb (to sb/sth) to make sth/sb go or be taken somewhere without going or taking them oneself: [Vn] *send a letter/telegram/message* [Vnpr] *send goods/documents/information by courier* ○ *I've sent the children to bed.* ○ *His mother sent him to the bakery to get some bread.* [Vnp] *Send out the invitations to the party.* ○ *I'll send somebody round to collect it.* [Vnn, Vnpr] *We sent him a letter/We sent a letter to him.* [Vnn] *My parents send you their love/best wishes.* [Vn.that] *She* **sent word** *that she wouldn't be able to come.* (**b**) (*fml*) to send a message: [V.to inf] *She sent to say that she was safe and well.* **2** ~ sth (**out**) to transmit a signal, etc by radio waves: [Vn, Vnp] *The radio operator sent (out) an appeal for help.* **3** to make sth move sharply or quickly, often by force: [Vnpr] *Whenever he moved, the wound sent pains all along his arm.* [Vnp] *Satellites are being sent up all the time.* [Vn.in] *She bumped against the table and sent the plates crashing to the ground.* ○ *The blow* **sent** *him flying* (ie knocked him over). [Vnp] (*fig*) *The report sent share prices down a further 8p.* **4**(**a**) to make sb feel or behave in a particular way: [Vn-adj] *send sb mad/crazy/insane/berserk.* (**b**) ~ sb **to/into** sth to make sb enter a specified state: [Vnpr] *send sb to sleep* ○ *send sb into a rage/frenzy/fits of laughter* ○ *The news sent the Stock Exchange into a panic.* **IDM** **send sb** '**packing** (*infml*) to tell sb roughly or rudely to go away: *She tried to interfere, but I sent her packing.* **send sb to** '**Coventry** (*Brit*) to refuse to speak to sb, esp as a punishment by other members of a group: *People who smoke in the office complain of being sent to Coventry by the non-smoking majority.* **PHR V** ,**send a**'**way (to sb) (for sth)** = SEND OFF (FOR STH).

,**send sb** '**down** (*Brit*) **1** (*infml*) to order that sb be put in prison: *He was sent down for ten years for armed robbery.* **2** to order a student to leave a university for bad behaviour.

'**send for sth**; '**send for sb (to do sth)** to ask or order that sb be brought or delivered, or that sb should come: *send for a fresh supply of paper* ○ *send for a taxi/an ambulance/a doctor* ○ *send for sb to repair the TV.*

,**send sb** '**in** to order sb to go to a place in order to deal with a situation: *Soldiers were sent in to quell the riots.* ,**send sth** '**in** to send sth by post to a place where it will be dealt with: *Have you sent in your application for the job?*

,**send** '**off (for sth)** to write to sb to ask for sth to be sent to one by post: *I've sent off for those bulbs I saw advertised in the paper.* ,**send sb** '**off** (*Brit*) (of a REFEREE(1a)) to send a football player, etc off the playing field for breaking the rules of play. ,**send sth** '**off** to send sth by post: *Have you sent that letter off yet?*

,**send sth** '**on 1** to send sth to a destination in advance of one's own arrival time: *send on one's luggage.* **2** to post a letter again, directing it to sb's new address; to READDRESS sth.

,**send sth** '**out 1** to give sth out (GIVE¹) from itself; to EMIT sth: *The sun sends out light and warmth.* **2** to produce sth: *The trees send out new leaves in spring.* '**send sb to ...** to decide or order that sb should attend a particular place or institution: *They send their daughter to a boarding-school.* ○ *He was sent to hospital/to prison.*

,**send sb** '**up** (*US infml*) to send sb to prison. ,**send sb/sth** '**up** (*Brit infml*) to mock sb/sth, esp by copying them/it in a funny way: *comedians who send up members of the government.*

■ '**send-off** *n* an act of saying goodbye to sb: *She was given a good send-off at the airport.*

'**send-up** *n* an act of mocking sb/sth by copying them/it in a funny way: *Her book is a hilarious send-up of a conventional spy story.*

sender /'sendə(r)/ *n* a person who sends sth: *If undelivered, please return to sender* (eg on a letter).

senescent /sɪ'nesnt/ *adj* (*fml or medical*) becoming old: *senescent industries.* ▶ **senescence** /sɪ'nesns/ *n* [U].

senile /'si:naɪl/ *adj* having or showing the weaknesses and diseases of old age: *senile decay* ○ *He keeps forgetting where he lives — I think he's getting senile.*

▶ **senility** /sə'nɪləti/ *n* [U] the state of being senile.

■ **senile dementia** /ˌsi:naɪl dɪ'menʃə/ *n* [U] an illness of old people resulting in loss of memory, loss of control of the body's functions, etc.

senior /'si:niə(r)/ *adj* **1** ~ (**to sb**) high in rank or status compared with others: *a senior staff meeting* ○ *a senior lecturer* ○ *He is the senior partner in the firm.* ○ *She is senior to me, because she joined the company before me.* **2** (esp in sport) of or for people over the age of 18: *take part in senior competitions* ○ *He won his first senior cap as a 20-year-old.* **3** (*often* Senior, *abbr* Snr) (placed immediately after sb's name) being the parent of sb with the same name: *John Brown Senior.* **4** [attrib] (*Brit*) (of a school or section of a school) for children over the age of 11. Compare JUNIOR.

▶ **senior** *n* **1** a person who is older than oneself: *She is my senior by two years/two years my senior.* **2** (*Brit*) an older pupil or a member of a senior school: *The seniors are allowed into town during the lunch hour.* **3** (*US*) a student in her or his final year at a high school or college.

seniority /ˌsi:ni'ɒrəti; *US* -'ɔːr-/ *n* [U] **1** the state or fact of being senior in age, rank, etc: *Should promotion be based on merit or seniority?* **2** the extent to which sb is senior: *a doctor with five years' seniority over his colleague.*

■ ,**senior** '**citizen** *n* (*euph*) an old or retired person.

sensation /sen'seɪʃn/ *n* **1**(**a**) [C] a feeling in one's body resulting from sth that happens or is done to it: *a sensation of warmth/dizziness/falling* ○ *a tingling/burning sensation.* (**b**) [U] the ability to feel through the sense of touch: *lose all sensation in one's legs* ○ *Some sensation is coming back to my arm.* (**c**) [C *usu sing*] a general awareness or impression not caused by anything that can be seen or defined: *I had the strange sensation that I was being watched.* **2**(**a**) [C *usu sing*, U] a state of great surprise, excitement, interest, etc among a lot of people: *The news* **caused a** (*great*) **sensation.** (**b**) [sing] a person or thing that causes this state: *The band became a sensation overnight.*

▶ **sensational** /-ʃənl/ *adj* **1**(**a**) causing a sensation (2a): *a sensational crime/victory.* (**b**) (*derog*) deliberately trying to provoke interest by including material that is exciting or shocking: *a sensational newspaper/writer.* **2** (*infml*) extremely good; wonderful: *You look sensational in that dress.* ○ *The views from the top are sensational.* **sensationalism** /-ʃənəlɪzəm/ *n* [U] (*derog*) the deliberate use of shocking words, exciting stories, etc in order to provoke public interest or reaction: *the sensationalism of the popular press.* **sensationalist** /-ʃənəlɪst/ *adj*: *He rejected the story as sensationalist nonsense.* **sensationalize, -ise** /-ʃənəlaɪz/ *v* (*derog*) to treat sth in a way that is likely to cause public interest, excitement, etc: [Vn] *The event has been sensationalized by the media.* **sensationally** /-ʃənəli/ *adv*: *details of phone conversations sensationally revealed by the press* ○ (*infml*) *He is sensationally rich.*

sense /sens/ *n* **1** [C] any of the five powers of the body, ie sight, hearing, smell, taste and touch, by which a person or an animal perceives things: *the five senses* ○ *lose one's sense of smell* ○ *have a keen sense of hearing* ○ *sense-organs* (eg the nose, the eye, the ear, the tongue). ⇨ note at SENSIBLE. See also SIXTH SENSE. **2** [U, sing] (**a**) an appreciation or understanding of the value or worth of sth: *a sense of* the (ie the ability to know what is) *absurd/ ridiculous* ○ *not have much* **sense of humour** (ie not recognize and enjoy jokes, funny situations, etc) ○ *have no* **sense of direction** (ie be unable to find one's way easily). (**b**) consciousness or awareness of sth: *a sense of one's own importance/worth* ○ *have no sense of shame/guilt* ○ *feel a sense of security in her arms.* **3** [U] the ability to make reasonable judgements; practical wisdom: *have the sense to come in out of the rain* ○ *There's a lot of sense in what she says.* See also COMMON SENSE, HORSE SENSE. **4** [U] reason[1](4); good judgement: *What's the sense of doing that?* ○ *There's no sense in going alone* (ie It would be better not to). ○ ***Talk sense — what you're suggesting is impossible.*** **5** **senses** [pl] a normal state of mind; the ability to think clearly: *regain/come to one's senses* ○ *Threatening to leave him should* **bring him to his senses.** ○ *No one in their* (**right**) **senses** *would let a small child go out alone.* **6** [C] (**a**) a meaning of a word, phrase, etc: *a word with several senses* ○ *The sense of the word is not clear.* (**b**) a way in which a word, sentence, etc is to be understood: *in the strict/literal/figurative sense of the expression* ○ *I am a worker only in the sense that I work; I don't get paid for what I do.* ○ *What you say is true,* **in a sense.** **7** [sing] **the ~ of sth** *(fml)* the general feeling or opinion among a group of people: *The sense of the meeting was* (ie Most people present thought) *that he should resign.* **IDM** **beat, knock, drive, etc (some)** [1]**sense into sb** *(infml)* to change sb's behaviour, views, etc by severe or sometimes violent methods: *She's a wild uncontrollable girl, but that new school should knock some sense into her.* **come to one's** [1]**senses** to become conscious again after being unconscious: *When I came to my senses, I was lying in the gutter.* **make** [1]**sense 1** to have a meaning that is easily understood: *What you say makes no sense.* ○ *The words are jumbled up and don't make sense.* **2** to be sensible: *It doesn't make sense to buy such an expensive dress when it'll be out of fashion next year.* ○ *It would make sense to leave early.* **make** [1]**sense of sth** to understand sth that is difficult or has no clear meaning: *Can you make sense of this poem?* **see** [1]**sense** to start to be sensible: *It's time the government saw sense and abandoned this unworkable policy.* (**have**) **a sense of oc**[1]**casion** a feeling of the importance of an event, etc. **take leave of one's senses** ⇨ LEAVE[2].

▶ **sense** *v* **1** to become aware of sth that one cannot actually see, hear, etc: [Vn] *sense sb's sorrow/hostility* [V.that] *Although she didn't say anything, I sensed (that) she didn't like the idea.* [also V.wh]. **2** (of a machine, etc) to detect sth: [Vn] *an apparatus that senses the presence of toxic gases.*

senseless /'senslas/ *adj* **1** *(derog)* lacking any reason or purpose; foolish: *a senseless idea/action* ○ *senseless violence* ○ *It would be senseless to continue any further.* **2** [usu pred] unconscious: *fall senseless to the ground* ○ *beat/knock sb senseless.* ▶ **senselessly** *adv.*

sensibility /ˌsensə'bɪləti/ *n* **1** [UC usu *pl*] the ability to appreciate and respond in a delicate or SUBTLE(3) way to impressions and influences: *a man of fine sensibility and humour* ○ *artistic sensibilities.* **2** **sensibilities** [pl] the tendency to be easily offended or shocked: *wound/offend/outrage readers' sensibilities.* Compare SENSITIVITY 2.

sensible /'sensəbl/ *adj* **1** *(approv)* having or showing the ability to make sound judgements; reasonable: *a sensible person/idea/diet/suggestion* ○ *It was sensible of you to lock the door.* **2** [attrib] (of clothing, etc) practical rather than fashionable: *wear sensible shoes.* **3** [pred] **~ of sth** *(dated or fml)* aware of sth: *Are you sensible of the dangers of your position?*

▶ **sensibly** /-əbli/ *adv* in a sensible(1) way: *eat*

sensibly ○ *be sensibly dressed* ○ *They decided, quite sensibly, to postpone the broadcast for a few months.*

NOTE The noun **sense** can mean your ability to experience things in the world through different organs of the body: *the five senses of sight, smell, hearing, taste and touch.* It can also mean the ability to think in a practical way and make good judgements based on reason: *She talks a lot of good sense.* The adjective **sensitive** relates to the first meaning and to how easily you feel or experience something: *a soap for sensitive skin* ○ *He's a very sensitive child and gets upset easily.* **Sensible** relates to the second meaning and to making decisions based on reason: *She gave me some very sensible advice.* ○ *It wasn't very sensible to go climbing alone in such bad weather.*

sensitive /'sensətɪv/ *adj* **1 ~ (about/to sth)** easily offended or emotionally upset: *a frail and sensitive child* ○ *He's very sensitive about his baldness, so don't mention it.* ○ *A writer mustn't be too sensitive to criticism.* **2 ~ (to sth)** *(approv)* having or showing intelligent awareness or sympathetic understanding: *an actor's sensitive reading of a poem* ○ *be sensitive to the needs of others.* **3** needing to be treated with great care and caution so as not to cause trouble or offence: *sensitive military information* ○ *a* **sensitive area** *such as race relations.* ⇨ note at SENSIBLE. Compare INSENSITIVE. **4(a)** easily hurt or damaged: *the sensitive skin of a baby* ○ *A sensitive nerve in a tooth can cause great pain.* (**b**) **~ (to sth)** greatly or easily affected by sth: *be sensitive to penicillin* ○ *Photographic paper is highly sensitive to light.* **5 ~ (to sth)** (of instruments, etc) that can measure very small changes: *a sensitive balance/ barometer* ○ *(fig) The Stock Exchange is sensitive to likely political changes.*

▶ **sensitively** *adv.*
sensitivity /ˌsensə'tɪvəti/ *n* **1** [U] **~ (to sth)** the quality or degree of being sensitive: *the sensitivity of a writer* ○ *a case handled with great tact and sensitivity* ○ *sensitivity to pain/light/heat.* **2** **sensitivities** [pl] a tendency to be offended or emotionally upset: *take political/local sensitivities into account.* Compare SENSIBILITY 2.

sensitize, -ise /'sensətaɪz/ *v* **~ sth/sb (to sth)** (esp passive) to make sth/sb sensitive to sth: [Vnpr] *sensitize students to a poet's use of language* [Vn] *a photocopier using sensitized paper.*

sensor /'sensə(r)/ *n* a device that detects light, heat, pressure, etc: *security lights with an infrared sensor.*

sensory /'sensəri/ *adj* [usu attrib] of the physical senses or of sensation(1): *sensory organs/nerves* ○ *sensory deprivation.* ⇨ note at SENSUOUS.

sensual /'senʃuəl/ *adj* of, suggesting or giving physical, often sexual, pleasure: *sensual pleasure* ○ *the sensual curves of her body* ○ *He was darkly sensual and mysterious.* ⇨ note at SENSUOUS.

▶ **sensualist** *n* a person who enjoys physical pleasures, esp to excess.
sensuality /ˌsenʃu'æləti/ *n* [U] love or enjoyment of physical pleasure: *the sensuality of his poetry* ○ *Her appearance hinted at the languid sensuality that lay beneath the surface.*
sensually /-ʃuəli/ *adv.*

sensuous /'senʃuəs/ *adj* of, suggesting or giving pleasure to the senses: *a sensuous woman/gesture* ○ *his full sensuous lips* ○ *the sensuous appeal of her painting.* ⇨ note. ▶ **sensuously** *adv: sensuously swaying her hips.* **sensuousness** *n* [U]

NOTE Compare **sensory**, **sensual** and **sensuous**. **Sensory** is quite formal and refers to the process of receiving information through the senses: *sensory perceptions/organs.* **Sensual** and **sensuous** are very similar and refer to giving or causing physical, often sexual, pleasure: *a sensual person/caress* ○ *a* *sensuous mouth.* **Sensuous** also describes the physical pleasure produced by art, music, etc: *sensuous sounds/images/writing.*

sent *pt, pp* of SEND.

sentence /'sentəns; *US* -tns/ *n* **1** [C] (*grammar*) a set of words expressing a statement, a question or a command. Sentences usu contain a subject and a verb. In written English they begin with a capital letter and end with a full stop or an equivalent mark. **2** [C, U] (*law*) the punishment given by a lawcourt: *a jail/prison/custodial sentence* ○ *a death sentence* ○ *be* **under sentence of death** (ie condemned to die as a punishment) ○ *a life sentence* (ie the punishment of being sent to prison for life or a very long time) ○ *The judge* **passed/pronounced** *sentence (on the prisoner)* (ie said what the punishment would be). ○ *She has* **served** (ie completed) *her* **sentence** *and will now be released.*
▶ **sentence** *v* ~ sb (**to sth**) to state that sb is to have a certain punishment: [Vnpr] *sentence* ○ *a death sentence six months' imprisonment* [Vn.*to* inf] *The ringleaders were sentenced to be shot by a firing squad.* [Vn] *guidelines for the sentencing of juveniles* [Vnpr] (*fig*) *a crippling disease which sentenced him to a lifetime in a wheelchair.*

sententious /sen'tenʃəs/ *adj* (*fml derog*) expressing moral judgements in an attempt to sound impressive or wise: *a sententious speaker/remark.* ▶ **sententiously** *adv*: '*He should have thought of the consequences before he acted,*' *she concluded sententiously.*

sentient /'sentiənt; *Brit also* 'senʃnt/ *adj* [attrib] (*fml*) capable of perceiving or feeling things: *sentient beings.*

sentiment /'sentimənt/ *n* **1** [U] (*sometimes derog*) tender feelings of pity, romantic love, NOSTALGIA, etc which may be exaggerated or wrongly directed: *a love story full of cloying sentiment* ○ *There's no room for sentiment in business.* **2** (*fml*) (**a**) [U] general feeling or opinion: *an upsurge of anti-Western/ nationalist sentiment* ○ *Public sentiment is against any change to the law.* (**b**) [C] an attitude; an opinion: *a speech full of noble/lofty sentiments* ○ *This was a sentiment we all shared.* ○ *My sentiments exactly* (ie I agree)*!*

sentimental /ˌsenti'mentl/ *adj* **1** of or concerning the emotions, rather than reason: *have a sentimental attachment to one's birthplace* ○ *do sth for sentimental reasons* ○ *a watch with* **sentimental value** (ie one which is precious eg because it was given by sb one loves). **2** (*sometimes derog*) (**a**) (of things) expressing or causing tender emotions, eg pity, romantic love or NOSTALGIA, which may be exaggerated or wrongly directed: *sentimental music* ○ *a sloppy, sentimental love story.* (**b**) ~ (**about sb/ sth**) (of people) having such emotions: *She's very sentimental about animals.*
▶ **sentimentalist** /-təlɪst/ *n* (*sometimes derog*) a person who is sentimental(2b).
sentimentality /ˌsentimen'tæləti/ *n* [U] (*derog*) the quality of being too sentimental(2a): *the film is moving without degenerating into sentimentality.*
sentimentalize, -ise /-təlaɪz/ *v* (*derog*) to treat sb/ sth in a sentimental(2a) way: [V] *Be careful not to sentimentalize.* [Vn, Vpr] *He resists the temptation to sentimentalize (over) his ordeal.*
sentimentally /-təli/ *adv.*

sentinel /'sentɪnl/ *n* (*dated or fml*) a soldier whose job is to guard sth: (*fig*) *trees* **standing sentinel** *along the roadside.*

sentry /'sentri/ *n* a soldier placed outside a building, etc in order to watch or guard it: *People approaching the gate were challenged by the sentry.* ○ *be on* **sentry duty.**

■ '**sentry-box** *n* a small shelter for a sentry to stand in.

sepal /'sepl/ *n* (*botany*) any of the parts resembling leaves that lie under and support the petals of a flower.

separable /'sepərəbl/ *adj* ~ (**from sth**) that can be separated: *The question is not entirely separable from the financial one.* Compare INSEPARABLE. ▶ **separability** /ˌseprə'bɪləti/ *n* [U].

separate[1] /'seprət/ *adj* **1** ~ (**from sth/sb**) forming a unit by itself; existing apart; individual: *The children sleep in separate beds.* ○ *Violent prisoners are kept separate from the others.* ○ *They lead separate lives* (ie do not live or do things together). ○ *When the partnership ended, we* **went our separate ways.** **2** [usu attrib] different or distinct: *It happened on three separate occasions.* ○ *That is a separate issue and irrelevant to our discussion.*
▶ **separately** *adv* ~ (**from sb/sth**) as separate people or things; not together: *They are now living separately.* ○ *It is better to cook the stuffing separately from the turkey.*
separates *n* [pl] individual items of clothing, eg skirts, jackets, trousers, designed to be worn together in different combinations.
separatism /'sepərətɪzəm/ *n* [U] the policy of staying or becoming a separate group from other people, esp through political independence.
separatist /'sepərətɪst/ *n*: *right-wing separatists* ○ *a separatist organization/movement.*

separate[2] /'sepəreɪt/ *v* **1(a)** ~ (**sb/sth**) (**from sb/ sth**) to move apart or cause people or things to be or move apart; to divide or divide people or things: [Vn] *separate two dogs fighting* ○ *families separated by the war* [Vnpr] *separate the egg yolk from the white* ○ *This prisoner should be separated from the others.* ○ *separating fact from fantasy* [Vn, Vnpl] *Separate (out) the cotton fabrics from the rest of the wash.* [V, Vpr] *the engine separated (from its mounting) in flight.* (**b**) ~ (**out**) to stop being combined; to divide into individual elements: [V] *The yoghurt will separate when it is heated.* [Vp] *Oil and water always separate out.* **2** ~ (**from sb**) to leave another person's company: [V] *We talked for an hour before separating.* [also Vpr]. **3** ~ (**from sb**) to stop living together as a couple: [V] *After ten years of living together they decided to separate.* [Vpr] *She has separated from her husband.* **4** ~ sth (**from sth**) to lie or stand between two people, areas, countries, etc, keeping them apart: [Vn] *A deep gorge separates the two halves of the city.* ○ (*fig*) *Only 0.2 of a second separates the leaders.* [Vnpr] (*fig*) *Only 100 metres separated them from the border guards.* **5** to make sb/sth different in some way from sb/sth else: [Vnpr] *Her religious vocation separates her from the rest of us.* [Vn] *Politics is the only thing that separates us* (ie on which we disagree). ○ *The judges found it impossible to separate the two contestants* (ie They gave them equal scores). **IDM** **separate the** ‚**sheep from the** '**goats** to distinguish good people from bad people. **separate the** ‚**wheat from the** '**chaff** to distinguish valuable people or things from worthless ones: *sift through application forms to separate the wheat from the chaff.*
▶ **separated** *adj* ~ (**from sb**) no longer living together as a married couple, but not having legally ended the marriage: *I'm separated from my wife.* ○ *We're separated.*

separation /ˌsepə'reɪʃn/ *n* **1** ~ (**from sb/sth**) (**a**) [U] the action of separating people or things, or the state of being separate: *the separation of typhoid cases from other patients* ○ *the separation between church and state* ○ *Separation from his friends made him sad.* (**b**) [C] an instance or period of being separated: *after a separation of five years from his parents.* **2** [U, sing] an arrangement by which a married couple live apart but do not end the marriage: *decide on (a) separation.*

sepia /'si:piə/ *n* [U] **1** a brown substance used in inks and paints and, esp formerly, for printing photographs. **2** a rich reddish-brown colour.
▶ **sepia** *adj* [usu attrib] of a sepia colour: *an old sepia photograph.*

Sept *abbr* September: *12 Sept 1969.*

September /sep'tembə(r)/ *n* [U, C] (*abbr* **Sept**) the 9th month of the year, next after August.
For further guidance on how *September* is used, see the examples at *April.*

septet /sep'tet/ *n* a piece of music written for a group of seven instruments or singers.

septic /'septik/ *adj* infected with harmful bacteria: *A dirty cut may become/go septic.*
■ ¡**septic** ¡**tank** *n* a tank that holds waste from toilets until the action of bacteria makes it liquid enough to drain away.

septicaemia (*US* **-cemia**) /ˌseptɪ'si:miə/ *n* [U] (*medical*) infection of the blood; blood-poisoning (BLOOD[1]).

septuagenarian /ˌseptjuədʒə'neəriən; *US* -tʃuə-/ *n, adj* [attrib] (*fml*) a person between the ages of 70 and 79.

sepulchre (*US* **sepulcher**) /'seplkə(r)/ *n* (*arch*) a place for a dead body, esp one cut in rock or built of stone: *the Holy Sepulchre* (ie the one in which Jesus Christ was laid).
▶ **sepulchral** /sə'pʌlkrəl/ *adj* (*fml*) **1** [usu attrib] of a sepulchre, grave, etc or of burial: *a sepulchral statue.* **2** (*fml* or *joc*) looking or sounding sad and solemn: *speak in sepulchral tones.*

sequel /'si:kwəl/ *n* ~ (**to sth**) **1** a thing that happens after or as a result of an earlier event: *His speech had a most unfortunate sequel.* ○ *Famine is often the sequel to war.* **2** a novel, film, etc that continues the story of an earlier one, often using the same characters: *He is writing a sequel to his recent best seller.*

sequence /'si:kwəns/ *n* **1** [U,C] a set of events, numbers, actions, etc, in which each follows the one before continuously or in a particular order: *describe the sequence of events* (ie in the order in which they occurred) ○ *a sequence of dance movements* ○ *a sequence of playing-cards* (ie three or more next to each other in value, eg 10, 9, 8). **2** [C] a part of a film dealing with one scene or topic: *a thrilling sequence that includes a car chase.*
■ **the** ¡**sequence of** ¡**tenses** *n* [sing] (*grammar*) the rules according to which the tense of a subordinate clause (SUBORDINATE) depends on the tense of the main clause (MAIN[1]).

sequential /sɪ'kwenʃl/ *adj* following in order of time or place; forming a sequence: *sequential data processing.* ▶ **sequentially** /-ʃəli/ *adj*: *data stored/ accessed sequentially on a computer.*

sequester /sɪ'kwestə(r)/ *v* [Vn] (*law*) = SEQUESTRATE.
▶ **sequestered** *adj* [usu attrib] (*fml*) quiet and apart from other people: *a sequestered valley/spot/ site.*

sequestrate /'si:kwəstreɪt/ (also **sequester**) *v* [Vn] (*law*) to take possession of sb's property, funds, etc until a debt has been paid or other claims met. ▶ **sequestration** /ˌsi:kwə'streɪʃn/ *n* [U].

sequin /'si:kwɪn/ *n* a small circular shiny disc sewn onto clothing as an ornament: *a dress covered in gold sequins.*

sequoia /sɪ'kwɔɪə/ *n* a tree found in California that can live a long time and grow very tall.

seraph /'serəf/ *n* (*pl* **seraphim** /-fɪm/ or **seraphs**) (in the Bible) an ANGEL(1) of the highest order. Compare CHERUB.
▶ **seraphic** /sə'ræfɪk/ *adj* (*fml*) **1** like an ANGEL(2)

in beauty, goodness, etc: *a seraphic child/nature.* **2** feeling or showing great happiness: *a seraphic smile.*

sere = SEAR.

serenade /ˌserə'neɪd/ *n* **1** a song or tune sung or played at night, esp by a lover outside the window of the woman he loves. **2** a gentle piece of music in several parts, usu for a small group of instruments.
▶ **serenade** *v* [Vn] to sing or play a serenade to sb.

serendipity /ˌseren'dɪpəti/ *n* [U] (*fml*) the ability to make pleasant and unexpected discoveries entirely by chance.

serene /sə'ri:n/ *adj* calm and peaceful: *a serene sky* ○ *a serene look/smile* ○ *Throughout the crisis she remained serene and in control.* ▶ **serenely** *adv*: *He seemed serenely unaware that anything had gone wrong.* **serenity** /sə'renəti/ *n* [U]: *An atmosphere of serenity pervades the place.*

serf /sɜːf/ *n* **1** (formerly) a person forced to work on the land in a FEUDAL system. **2** a worker treated harshly or like a slave.
▶ **serfdom** /-dəm/ *n* [U] **1** the social and economic system under which land was cultivated by serfs: *abolish serfdom.* **2** the conditions of a serf's life: *released from his serfdom.*

serge /sɜːdʒ/ *n* [U] a type of strong woollen cloth used for making clothes: *a blue serge suit.*

sergeant /'sɑːdʒənt/ *n* (*abbrs* **Sergt**, **Sgt**) (also **sarge**) **1** (the title of) a NON-COMMISSIONED army officer with a rank above a CORPORAL[1]. ⇨ App 6. **2(a)** (*Brit*) (the title of) a police officer with a rank below that of an INSPECTOR(2). **(b)** (*US*) (the title of) a police officer with a rank below that of a captain or sometimes a LIEUTENANT.
■ ¡**sergeant-**¡**major** *n* **(a)** (*Brit*) (the title of) an army officer assisting the ADJUTANT of a regiment. **(b)** (*US*) (the title of) a NON-COMMISSIONED army officer of the highest rank. ⇨ App 6.

Sergt (also **Sgt**) *abbr* Sergeant: *Sergt (Colin) Hill* ○ *Sgt-Maj* (ie Sergeant-Major).

serial /'sɪəriəl/ *adj* **1** [usu attrib] of, in or forming a series. **2** [attrib] (of a story, etc) appearing in parts in a magazine, etc or on television or radio: *Our new drama serial begins at 7.30 this evening.*
▶ **serial** *n* a serial play, story, etc: *a detective/ drama serial.*
serialize, -ise /-riəlaɪz/ *v* to publish or broadcast sth as a serial: [Vn] *serialized on radio in twelve parts.* **serialization, -isation** /ˌsɪəriəlaɪ'zeɪʃn; *US* -lə'z-/ *n* [C, U].
serially /-iəli/ *adv.*
■ ¡**serial** ¡**killer** *n* a person who murders several people one after another.
¡**serial number** *n* a number that identifies one item in a series, eg on a cheque, a piece of equipment, etc.

series /'sɪəri:z/ *n* (*pl* unchanged) **1** a number of things, events, etc of a similar kind, esp placed or occurring one after another: *a series of lectures* ○ *a series of underground tunnels* ○ *a television/radio/ magazine series* ○ *a series of bad harvests* ○ *publish a new series of readers for students of English* ○ *the world series* (ie an annual series of baseball games played between the winning teams of the two major leagues (LEAGUE[1] 2) in the USA). **2** [C,U] an electrical circuit with the supply of current flowing directly through each component: *batteries connected in series* ○ *a series circuit/connection.* Compare PARALLEL.

serif /'serɪf/ *n* a short line at the top or bottom of some styles of printed letters: *printed in a serif typeface.* ⇨ picture. Compare SANSERIF.

serif   serif   sanserif

serious /'sɪəriəs/ *adj* **1** thinking in a careful solemn way; not silly: *a serious person/expression/manner* ○ *She looked very serious when she heard the news.* ○

Please be serious for a minute, this is very important. **2** [usu attrib] (of books, music, etc) needing or intended to be thought about carefully; not only for pleasure: *a serious play/discussion* ○ *a serious article about social problems.* **3** important because of possible danger or risk: *a serious illness/mistake/accident* ○ *That could cause serious injury.* ○ *The international situation is extremely serious.* **4** ~ **(about sb/sth)**; ~ **(about doing sth)** sincere; not meant as a joke: *a serious suggestion* ○ *Are you really serious about him* (ie Do you like or love him a lot?) ○ *Is she serious about wanting to be a pilot?*

▶ **seriously** *adv* **1** in a serious way: *speak seriously to her about it* ○ *be seriously ill/injured.* **2** (*infml*) (used at the beginning of a sentence when turning to a serious matter): *Seriously though, you could really hurt yourself doing that.* ⇨ note at HOPEFUL. **IDM** **take sb/sth seriously** to regard sb/sth as important and worth treating with respect: *She's so unreliable that you can't take anything she says seriously.* ○ *He takes (his) work very seriously.*

seriousness *n* [U] the state of being serious: *the seriousness of his expression* ○ *Do you realize the seriousness of the situation?* **IDM** **in all 'seriousness** (*infml*) very seriously; not as a joke: *You can't in all seriousness go out in a hat like that!*

sermon /ˈsɜːmən/ *n* **1(a)** a talk on a moral or religious subject, usu given by a priest during a religious service: *preach a sermon.* **(b)** such a talk in printed form: *a book of sermons.* **2** (*infml or joc*) a long talk about moral matters or about sb's faults, etc: *We had to listen to a long sermon from the manager about not wasting money.*

▶ **sermonize, -ise** /-aɪz/ *v* [V, Vpr] (*derog*) to give moral advice, esp when it is boring or not wanted.

serpent /ˈsɜːpənt/ *n* (*dated*) a snake, esp a large one.

▶ **serpentine** /ˈsɜːpəntaɪn; *US* -tiːn/ *adj* (*fml*) twisting and curving like a snake: *the serpentine course of the river.*

serrated

serrated edge

serrated /səˈreɪtɪd/ *adj* having teeth on the edge like a SAW²: *a knife with a serrated blade* ○ *serrated leaves.* ⇨ picture.

serried /ˈserid/ *adj* [usu attrib] (*dated or fml*) (of rows of people or things) arranged close together in order: *serried ranks/rows.*

serum /ˈsɪərəm/ *n* (*pl* **sera** /-rə/ or **serums**) **1(a)** [U] the thin liquid that remains from blood when the rest has clotted (CLOT 1). **(b)** [C, U] (*medical*) this liquid taken from certain animals and given to people to protect them against disease, poison, etc: *snakebite serum.* Compare VACCINE. **2** [U] any liquid like water in animal tissue, eg in a BLISTER(1).

servant /ˈsɜːvənt/ *n* **1** a person who works in sb else's household for wages, and often for food and lodging: *have/employ a large staff of servants.* **2** ~ **(of sb/sth)** a person who performs services for others, esp as an employee of a company or an organization: *a faithful servant of the company* ○ *a public servant* (ie a government employee). See also CIVIL SERVANT.

serve /sɜːv/ *v* **1** ~ **(sb)** **(as sth)** to work for sb, esp as a servant: [V-n] *serve as (a) gardener and chauffeur* [Vn] *He has served his master for many years.* [also Vn-n]. **2** to work or perform duties for a company, an organization, the armed forces, etc; to give service to sth/sb: [Vpr, Vnpr] *serve (a year) in the army* [V-n] *He served as a naval officer during the war.* [Vpr] *serve with the Royal Air Force* ○ *serve on* (ie be a member of) *a committee/board* ○ *serve under sb* (ie be under the command of a superior officer, leader, etc) [Vnadv] *Both as a civil servant and as a*

statesman he served his country well. ○ (*fig*) *This desk has served me well* (ie been very useful to me) *over the years.* [also V]. **3(a)** ~ **sb (with sth)**; ~ **sth (up) (to sb)** to give food to sb at a meal; to place food on the table at a meal: [Vpr] *a waiter serving at table* [V] *Who's going to serve?* [Vn] *Dinner is served* (ie is ready). [Vn-adj] *The wine should be served chilled.* [Vnpr, Vnn] *The hotel served lunch to us/served us with lunch/served us lunch.* [also Vn]. **(b)** ~ **sb (with sth)**; ~ **sth (to sb)** to help a customer or sell sth in a shop, etc: [V] *serve in a supermarket* [Vn] *Are you being served?* [Vnpr] *He served some sweets to the children.* **(c)** ~ **sb/sth (with sth)** (esp passive) to provide sb/sth with a useful or necessary service: [Vnpr] *The town is well served with public transport.* [also Vn]. **4** ~ **(for/as sth)** (*fml*) to satisfy a need or purpose; to be suitable for sth: [Vpr] *This room can serve for a study.* [V-n, V.*to* inf] *The photograph serves as a reminder/serves to remind us of the old days.* [V, Vn] *It's not exactly what I wanted but it will serve (my purpose).* **5** (of a portion of food) to be enough for sb/sth: [Vn] *This packet of soup serves two.* **6** to spend a period of time in a post, learning a trade, in prison, etc: [Vn] *serve a further term as governor* ○ *serve two years as an apprentice/a two-year apprenticeship* [Vnpr] *serve a life sentence for murder* ○ (*infml*) *He served time for fraud.* [Vn] *She's already served two aces this game.* [also Vnpr]. **7** ~ **sth (on sb)**; ~ **sb with sth** (*law*) to deliver sth formally to sb: [Vn] *serve notice* ○ *serve a summons/writ/warrant* [Vnpr] *serve a court order on sb/serve sb with a court order.* **8** ~ **(sth) (to sb)** (in tennis, etc) to start playing by hitting the ball to one's opponent: [V, Vpr] *It's your turn to serve (to me).* [Vn] *She's already served two aces this game.* [also Vnpr]. **IDM** **first come, first served** ⇨ FIRST². **if memory serves** ⇨ MEMORY. **serve sb 'right** (esp *with it*) (of sth unpleasant) to be what sb deserves: *'I got absolutely soaked.' 'It serves you right — I told you to take an umbrella.'* **serve one's/its 'turn** to be useful for a purpose or for a particular period: *I finally had to sell the car, but it had served its turn.* **serve sb's 'turn** to be good or useful enough for sb's purpose. **serve two 'masters** (usu in negative sentences) to follow two opposing parties, principles, etc at the same time. **PHRV** **serve sth 'out** (also **serve sth up**) to give portions of food to several people: *Shall I serve out the soup or would you like to help yourselves?* ○ *tomatoes served up on toast.* **2** to serve, work, etc until the end of a fixed period: *You'll have to serve out your notice before you leave the company.* **serve sth 'up 1** = SERVE STH OUT. **2** to give or offer sth: *She served up the usual excuses for being late.*

▶ **serve** *n* (in tennis, etc) an act or a manner of serving the ball: *a fast/powerful serve* ○ *Whose serve is it?* (ie Whose turn is it to serve?)

server *n* **1** (*computing*) a computer PROGRAM that controls or supplies information to several computers linked together; a device on which this is run: *a file/print server.* **2** a player who serves, eg in tennis. **3** (usu *pl*) an implement used for putting a portion of food onto sb's plate: *salad servers.*

serving *n* a portion of food for one person: *This recipe will be enough for four servings.*

service /ˈsɜːvɪs/ *n* **1** [U] ~ **(to sth)** work done or duties performed for a government, company, etc or in the armed forces: *ten years' service in the navy/police force* ○ *be declared unfit for* **active service** (ie fighting in a war, etc) ○ *conditions of service* ○ *a life of public service* ○ *be sentenced to 60 hours* **community service** (ie doing work for the community as a punishment) ○ *many years of faithful service to the company.* See also NATIONAL SERVICE. **2** [U] work done by a vehicle, machine, etc: *My car has given me excellent service.* ○ *You should get very good service from this computer.* **3** [C] **(a)** a department of people employed by the government or a public organization: *the ₁Civil 'Service* ○ *the ₁Diplo'matic Service* ○

the ₁National ¹Health Service ○ the ¹prison service ○ apply to (the) social services for help. See also SECRET SERVICE. (**b**) (usu pl) a branch of the armed forces: join the services (ie the navy, the army or the air force) ○ a service rifle/family. **4** [U] (dated) the state of being a servant; one's position as a servant: be in/go into service (ie be/become a domestic servant). **5** [C usu pl] ~ (**to sb/sth**) an amount of work done for another person or other people; a helpful act: You did me a great service by saying nothing. ○ They need the services of a good lawyer. ○ Her services to the state have been immense. **6** [C] (**a**) a system or an arrangement that meets public needs, esp for communication: a ¹bus/¹train service ○ a good ¹postal service ○ Essential services (ie the supply of water, electricity, etc) will be maintained. (**b**) a business that does work or supplies goods for customers, but does not make goods; such work or goods: banking and ¹insurance services ○ a new ¹carpet-cleaning service ○ a ¹service industry ○ the ¹service sector. **7** [U] the serving of customers in hotels, restaurants, etc; work done by domestic servants, hotel staff, etc: The food is good at this hotel, but the service is poor. ○ An extra 10% was added to the restaurant bill for service. ○ a quick-service restaurant. See also ROOM SERVICE, SELF-SERVICE. **8** [C] a ceremony of religious worship or the prayers, etc used at this: three services every Sunday ○ attend morning/evening ¹service ○ the ¹marriage/¹burial/com¹munion service. **9** [U,C] the maintenance and repair of a vehicle, machine, etc at regular intervals; an instance of this: take a car in for (a) service after 6000 miles (eg to have the oil changed, the tyres checked, etc) ○ a service for the central heating ○ We offer (an) excellent after-sales service. ○ a service department/engineer. **10** [C] a set of dishes, etc for serving food at table: a 30-piece ¹dinner service. **11** [U] (law) the formal delivery of sth: the service of a writ/summons. **12** [C] (**a**) (in tennis, etc) an act or a manner of serving the ball; a player's turn to serve: a fast service ○ Her service has improved. ○ Whose service is it? (**b**) (in tennis, etc) a part of a match in which sb serves: win/hold/lose/drop one's service ○ break sb's service (ie win a part of a match in which one's opponent serves) ○ a service game. **IDM at sb's ¹service** (fml) ready to help sb: If you need anything, I am at your service. (**be**) **of ¹service (to sb)** (fml) useful or helpful: Can I be of service to you in organizing the trip? **press sb/sth into service** ⇨ PRESS². **see ¹service** to serve in the armed forces: He saw service as an infantry officer in the last war. ○ He has seen service in many different parts of the world.

▶ **service** v **1** to maintain and repair a vehicle, machine, etc at regular intervals: [Vn] service a car/boiler/washing-machine ○ Has this heater been regularly serviced? **2** to supply a service(6a) or services to sth: [Vn] The area is well served by a number of local shops and other facilities. **3** to pay interest¹(5) on a loan: [Vn] The company hasn't enough cash to service its debts. **serviceable** adj (**a**) that can be used: The tyres are worn but still serviceable. (**b**) suitable for ordinary use or hard wear: serviceable clothes for children.

■ **¹service area** n an area near a MOTORWAY where petrol, food and drink, etc are sold.
¹service break n = BREAK² 6.
¹service charge n a sum added to a restaurant bill, eg 10% of the total, to pay for the service given by the staff: Does my bill include a service charge?
¹service flat n (Brit) a flat in which domestic service and sometimes meals, etc are provided and charged for in the rent.
¹service road n (Brit) a minor road, usu parallel to a main road, giving access to houses, shops, etc.
¹service station n = PETROL STATION.
serviceman /¹sɜːvɪsmən/ n (pl **-men** /-mən/; fem

servicewoman /-wʊmən/, pl **-women** /-wɪmɪn/) a member of the navy, army or air force.
serviette /ˌsɜːviˈet/ n (esp Brit) a piece of cloth or paper used at meals for protecting one's clothes and wiping one's lips and fingers; a NAPKIN: paper serviettes.
servile /¹sɜːvaɪl; US -vl/ adj (derog) too willing to obey or serve others; showing sb too much respect: servile flattery ○ I don't like his servile manner. ▶ **servility** /sɜːˈvɪləti/ n [U]: He displays a deference to his superiors which never becomes servility.
servitude /¹sɜːvɪtjuːd; US -tuːd/ n [U] (fml) the state of being forced to work for others and having no freedom: a life of poverty and servitude.
servo /¹sɜːvəʊ/ n (pl **-os**) (techn) a mechanism that controls a larger mechanism.
sesame /¹sesəmi/ n [U] a tropical plant grown for its seeds and their oil, which are used in cooking. See also OPEN SESAME.
session /¹seʃn/ n **1** a meeting or series of meetings of a parliament, lawcourt, etc for discussing or deciding sth: an emergency session of the State Legislature ○ the next session of parliament ○ The court is now **in session**. ○ Parliament is not **in session** during the summer. **2** a period of time spent doing a particular thing: a recording session ○ a training session ○ an all-night drinking session ○ After a couple of sessions at the gym, I feel a lot fitter. **3(a)** (esp Scot) a school or university year. (**b**) (US) a school term.

set¹ /set/ v (-tt-; pt pp **set**)
● **Placing in position 1** to put sth/sb in a particular place: [Vnpr] She set a tray down on the table. ○ They ate everything that was set before them. ○ The house is set (ie situated) in fifty acres of beautiful parkland. [Vnpr, Vnp] She set a tray (down) on the table. [Vnadv] Her eyes are set very close together. **2** ~ **sth to sth** (fml) to move or place sth so that it is near to or touching sth: [Vnpr] set pen to paper (ie begin to write). **3** (usu passive) to place the action of a play, novel, etc in a particular place or at a particular time: [Vnpr] The novel is set in pre-war London.
● **Causing to be in a particular state or to happen 4** to cause sb/sth to be in or reach the specified state: [Vnpr] The revolution set the country on the road to democracy. ○ The firm's accounts need to be set in order. ○ Her manner immediately set everyone at their ease. ○ She pulled the lever and set the machine in motion. [Vn-adj] The crowd watched as he set the bonfire alight. ○ The hijackers set the hostages free (ie released them). **5(a)** to make sb/sth begin to do sth: [Vn.ing] set a pendulum swinging ○ music to set your feet tapping ○ Her remarks set me thinking. (**b**) to make sb/oneself determined to do the specified task: I've set myself to finish the job by the end of the month.
● **Adjusting or arranging 6** to adjust sth so that it is ready for use or in position: [Vn] set the controls of a machine ○ set a trap ○ She set the camera on automatic. ○ I usually set my watch by (ie adjust it so that it shows the same time as) the clock in the town square. ○ She set the alarm for 7 o'clock (ie adjusted it so that it would ring then). **7** to arrange knives, forks, etc on a table for a meal: [Vnpr] Could you set the table for dinner? ○ The table is set for six guests. [also Vn]. **8** ~ **A in B** / ~ **B with A** (usu passive) to fix a precious stone firmly into a surface or an object: [Vnpr] She had the sapphire set in a gold ring. ○ Her bracelet was set with emeralds. **9** to arrange or fix sth; to decide on sth: [Vnpr] They haven't set a date for their wedding yet. ○ The government plans to set strict limits on public spending this year. [also Vn].
● **Creating 10** to establish sth so that others copy it

or try to achieve it: [Vn] *set a new fashion* ○ *set high safety standards* ○ *Imposing a lenient sentence for such a serious crime sets a dangerous precedent.* ○ *She set a new world record for the high jump.* ○ *I rely on you to set a good example.* **11** ~ sth (for oneself/sb) to give a task, problem, etc to be done, solved, achieved by oneself/sb: [Vn] *Who will be setting* (ie writing the questions in) *the French exam?* [Vnpr] *What books have been set* (ie are to be studied) *for A level English?* [Vnn, Vnpr] *She's set herself a difficult task/set a difficult task for herself.* [Vnn] *We must set ourselves precise sales targets for the coming year.*

● **Making or becoming firm or fixed 12** to become firm or hard from a soft or liquid state: [V] *Some kinds of concrete set more quickly than others.* ○ *Put the jelly in the fridge to set.* [V-adj] *The glue had set hard.* **13** (esp passive) to fix one's face or part of the body into a firm expression: [Vn] *Her jaw was set in a determined manner.* **14** to arrange hair while it is wet so that it will have a particular style when it dries: [Vn] *She had her hair washed and set.* **15**(**a**) to put a broken bone into a fixed position so that it will heal: [Vn] *The surgeon set her broken arm.* (**b**) [V] (of a broken bone) to heal in this way.

● **Presenting in the right form 16** (*techn*) to prepare a book, etc for printing: [Vn] *Books were previously set by hand but much of the work is now done by computer.* [also Vnpr]. **17** ~ sth (to sth) to provide music for words, a poem, etc so that it can be sung: [Vn, Vnpr] *Schubert set many of Goethe's poems (to music).* See also TYPESETTER.

● **Moving or flowing 18** (of the sun or moon) to go down below the horizon: [V] *In northern countries the sun sets much later in summer than in winter.* ○ *We sat and watched the sun setting.* Compare RISE[2] 13a, SUNSET.

IDM Idioms containing **set** are at the entries for the nouns or adjectives in the idioms, eg **set the pace** ⇨ PACE[1]; **set fair** ⇨ FAIR[2].

PHRV '**set about sb** (*dated infml*) to attack sb: *He set about the intruders with a stick.* '**set about sth / doing sth** (no passive) to begin a task; to start doing sth: *She set about the business of tidying her desk.* ○ *The new government must set about finding solutions to the country's economic problems.*

,**set sb a**'**gainst sb** (no passive) to make sb oppose a friend, relative, etc: *The civil war set brother against brother.* ○ *She accused her husband of setting their children against her.* **set sth (off) against sth 1** to judge sb/sth by comparing good or positive qualities with bad or negative ones: *The initial cost of a new car has to be set against the saving you'll make on repairs.* ○ *Set against the enormous benefits of the new technology, there is also a strong possibility that jobs will be lost.* **2** (*finance*) to declare certain business expenses as a way of reducing the amount of tax one must pay: *set capital costs (off) against tax.* ,**set sb/sth a**'**part (from sb/sth)** to make sb/sth different from or superior to others: *Her clear and elegant prose sets her apart from most other journalists.* ,**set sth a**'**part (for sth)** (usu passive) to keep sth for a special use or purpose: *One day a week was traditionally set apart for prayers and meditation.* ○ *Two rooms were set apart for use as libraries.*

,**set sth a**'**side 1** to place sth to one side: *Fry the onion for five minutes and then set it aside while you cook the fish.* **2** to save or keep money or time for a particular purpose: *She sets aside a bit of money every month.* ○ *I try to set aside a few minutes each day to do some exercises.* **3** to pay no attention to sth, esp temporarily, because other things are more important: *Let's set aside my personal feelings for a moment.* **4** (*law*) to state that a decision, sentence,

etc is not legally valid: *The verdict was set aside by the Appeal Court.*

,**set sth/sb** '**back (sth)** to delay the progress of sth/sb by the specified time: *The bad weather has set them back/set back their building programme several weeks.* ,**set sb** '**back sth** (*infml*) to cost sb the specified amount of money: *The repairs could set you back over £200.* ,**set sth** '**back (from sth)** (often passive) to place sth, esp a building, at a distance from sth: *The house is set well back from the road.*

,**set sb** '**down** (of a bus or train, or its driver) to stop and allow sb to get off: *Passengers may be set down and picked up only at the official stops.* ,**set sth** '**down 1** to write sth down on paper in order to record it: *Why don't you set your ideas down on paper?* **2** to give sth as a rule, principle, etc; to establish sth: *achieve the standards set down by the governing body.*

,**set** '**forth** (*fml*) to start a journey; to set out. ,**set sth** '**forth** (*fml*) to make sth known; to declare or present sth: *The Minister has set forth his views in a television broadcast.*

,**set** '**in** (of rain, bad weather, infection, etc) to begin and seem likely to continue: *I must get those bulbs planted before the cold weather sets in.* ○ *Those beams will need to be replaced; it looks as though woodworm has set in.* ,**set sth** '**in/into sth** (usu passive) to fix sth into a flat surface so that it does not project from it: *a plaque set into the wall.*

,**set** '**off** to begin a journey: *What time are you planning to set off tomorrow?* ○ *They've set off on a trip round the world.* ○ *We set off for London just after 10 o'clock.* ,**set sth** '**off 1** to make a bomb, etc explode: *A gang of boys were setting off fireworks in the street.* **2** to make an alarm start ringing: *If you open this door, it will set off the alarm.* **3** to cause a process or series of events to begin and continue: *Panic on the stock market set off a wave of selling.* **4** to make sth more noticeable or attractive by being placed near it: *That jumper sets off the blue of her eyes.* ,**set sb** '**off (doing sth)** to make sb start doing sth: *She's very sensitive — the slightest thing can set her off (crying).*

'**set on/upon sb** to attack sb suddenly: *I opened the gate, and was immediately set upon by a large dog.* '**set sb/sth on sb** to make a person or an animal attack sb suddenly: *The farmer threatened to set his dogs on us.*

,**set** '**out** to leave a place and begin a journey: *We set out at dawn.* ○ *They set out on the last stage of their journey.* ,**set sth** '**out 1** to arrange or display things: *We'll need to set out some chairs for the meeting.* ○ *Her work is always very well set out.* **2** to present ideas, facts, etc in an organized way, in speech or writing: *He set out his objections to the scheme.* ○ *She set out the reasons for her resignation in a long letter.* ○ *You haven't set out your ideas very clearly in this essay.* ,**set** '**out to do sth** to begin a job, task, etc with a particular aim or goal: *She set out to break the world land speed record.* ○ *They succeeded in what they set out to do.*

,**set** '**to** (*dated infml*) to begin doing sth in a busy or determined way: *The engineers set to on repair work to the bridge.* ○ *If we all set to we can finish the cleaning by lunchtime.*

,**set sb** '**up 1** to provide sb with the money, etc that is needed in order to do sth: *A bank loan helped to set him up in business.* ○ *Winning all that money in the lottery set her up for life.* **2** (*infml*) to make sb healthier, stronger, more lively, etc: *The break from work really set me up.* **3** (*infml*) to trick sb, esp putting them in danger or making them appear guilty of sth: *He denied the charges, saying the police had set him up.* ,**set sth** '**up 1** to place or build sth: *set up a monument/statue* ○ *The police set up roadblocks on routes leading out of the city.* **2** to make a piece of equipment, a machine, etc ready for use:

She set up her stereo in the living-room. **3** to make the necessary preparations so that sth can take place: *set up an experiment/a meeting.* **4** to establish or create sth: *set up (a) business* ○ *The company has set up several new branches in Scotland.* ○ *A government committee has been set up to look into the problems of drug abuse.* ○ *A fund will be set up for the dead men's families.* **5** to cause a process or a series of events to begin and continue: *The slump on Wall Street set up a chain reaction in stock markets around the world.* **6** to begin to make the specified loud noise: *set up a wailing sound.* ‚set **(oneself)** ¹**up (as sb)** to establish oneself in business (doing a particular job): *She took out a bank loan and set up on her own.* ○ *After leaving college, he set (himself) up as a freelance photographer.* ‚set **oneself** ¹**up as sb** to claim or pretend to be the specified type of person: *He sets himself up as a bit of an intellectual.*

■ ¹**set-aside** *n* [U] (*techn*) the system of paying farmers to withdraw land from agricultural production; land withdrawn in this way.

¹**set-back** *n* a difficulty or problem that delays sth or prevents it progressing: *Hopes of an early end to the strike received/suffered a severe set-back yesterday.* ○ *Defeat in the by-election is a major set-back for the ruling party.*

‚set ¹**book** (also ‚set ¹**text**) *n* (*Brit*) a book on which students must answer questions in an examination: *What are your set books for English A level?*

‚set-¹**to** *n* (*pl* **set-tos**) (*infml*) a fight or an argument: *They had a bit of a set-to.*

¹**set-up** *n* (usu *sing*) (*infml*) (**a**) the way in which sth is organized: *What's the set-up (like) in your company?* ○ *I've only been here for a couple of weeks and don't really know the set-up.* (**b**) an act of tricking sb, esp putting them in danger or making them appear guilty of sth: *She said it was a set-up and the drugs weren't hers.*

set² /set/ *n* **1** [C] (**a**) ~ **(of sth)** a group of similar things that belong together in some way: *a set of cutlery/golf clubs* ○ *a set of six dining chairs* ○ *a complete set of Dickens novels* ○ *a set of false teeth* ○ *a set of instructions* ○ *a new set of rules to learn* ○ *You can borrow my keys — I've got a spare set.* (**b**) a group of objects used together, eg for playing a game: *a chess set.* **2** [C] a piece of equipment for receiving radio or television signals: *Do not adjust your (TV) set.* **3** [C] (**a**) the scenery used for a play, film, etc: *a set designer* ○ *We need volunteers to help build and paint the set.* (**b**) a stage or place where a play or (part of) a film is performed: *The cast must all be on (the) set by 7 pm.* **4** [CGp] (*sometimes derog*) a group of people who spend a lot of time together socially or have similar interests, etc: *Oxford's literary set* ○ *the smart set* (ie rich, fashionable people). See also THE JET SET. **5** [sing] ~ **(of sth)** the way in which a particular part of one's body is held, esp showing determination: *She admired the firm set of his jaw.* **6** [C] (in a tennis match) a group of six or more games forming part of a match: *a five-set match* ○ *She won the first set easily.* **7** [C] (*mathematics*) a group of things having a shared quality. **8** [C] (in popular music) a series of songs or pieces of music performed by a musician or a group of musicians as part of a concert, etc: *We're playing the final set.* **9** [C] (*esp Brit*) a group of pupils with similar ability in a particular subject: *She's in the top biology set.* **10** (also **sett**) [C] a hole in the ground where a BADGER¹ lives. **11** [C] an act of setting (SET¹ 14) hair: *A shampoo and set costs £15.* **12** [C] a young plant, shoot, etc for planting: *onion sets.*

set³ /set/ *adj* **1** [usu attrib] fixed or arranged in advance: *Hotel meals are at set times.* ○ *There is a set procedure for making formal complaints.* ○ *Are there set hours of work in your company?* **2** fixed and not likely to change, as a result of habit: *She has very set*

ideas on bringing up children. ○ *As people get older they become more **set in their ways**.* **3** [attrib] (of a meal in a restaurant) offered at a fixed price, with a limited choice of dishes: *a set lunch/menu.* **4** [usu attrib] (of a person's expression) fixed; not natural: *a set smile* ○ *Her face took on a grim, set expression.* **5** [pred] ~ **(for sth / to do sth)** ready or prepared for sth/to do sth; likely to do sth: *We're all set to go.* ○ *Prices look set to rise again this month.* ○ *The Social Democrats look set for victory in the general election.* **6** [attrib] (of a book) that must be studied on a particular course. **IDM** **be (dead) set against sth / doing sth** strongly opposed to sth: *She's dead set against (the idea of) having children.* **be** ¹**set on sth / doing sth** to be determined to do sth: *She's set on a career in acting.* ○ *He was set on winning the championship.*

■ ‚set ¹**piece** *n* (**a**) an especially effective scene in a novel, film, play, etc arranged in a fixed or typical pattern or style: *The play contains a number of typical Stoppard set pieces.* (**b**) a carefully planned and practised military operation or football move.

set square /¹set skweə(r)/ *n* a flat piece of plastic or metal shaped like a TRIANGLE with one angle of 90°, used for drawing straight lines and angles.

sett /set/ *n* = SET² 10.

settee /se¹ti:/ *n* a long soft seat with a back and usu with arms, for two or more people.

setter /¹setə(r)/ *n* **1** a breed of dog with long hair that can be trained to find animals and birds in a hunt: *an Irish setter.* ⇨ picture at DOG¹. **2** (often in compounds) a person or thing that sets sth: *the setter of a trap/of crossword puzzles.* See also JET-SETTER, PACE-SETTER, TREND-SETTER.

setting /¹setɪŋ/ *n* **1(a)** a set of surroundings; the place at which sth happens: *The castle stands in a spectacular setting surrounded by hills.* ○ *The hotel provides the perfect setting for a holiday to remember.* (**b**) the place and time at which a play, novel, etc is set: *The setting of the play is Venice in the 1930s.* **2** a speed, height, temperature, etc at which a machine, etc can be set to operate: *The cooker has several temperature settings.* **3** a piece of metal in which a precious stone is fixed to form a piece of jewellery: *The ring has a ruby in a gold setting.* **4** a piece of music composed for a poem, etc: *Schubert's setting of a poem by Goethe.* **5** a complete set of equipment for eating (knife, fork, spoon, etc) provided for one person and arranged on a table: *place setting.*

settle¹ /¹setl/ *v* **1** ~ **sth (with sb)** to reach an agreement about sth; to end an argument or find a solution to a disagreement: [Vn] *settle a dispute/an argument/an issue* [Vnpr] *It's time you settled your differences with your father.* [V] *There is pressure on the unions to settle.* ○ *The parties in the lawsuit agreed to* **settle out of court** (ie come to an agreement without going to court). [also Vpr]. **2(a)** to make one's permanent home in a place: [Vpr] *settle in London/in Canada/in the country/near the coast* [Vadv] *She married and settled close to her parents' home.* (**b**) to make one's permanent home in a country or an area as a colonist (COLONY): [Vpr] *The Dutch settled in South Africa.* [Vn esp passive] (*fml*) *This area was settled by immigrants over a century ago.* **3** ~ **(on/over sth)** to fall from above and come to rest on sth; to stay for some time on sth: [V] *I don't think this snow will settle* (ie remain on the ground without melting). [Vpr] *The bird settled on a branch.* ○ *Dust had settled on everything.* ○ (*fig*) *An uneasy silence had settled over the waiting crowd.* **4** ~ **(back)** to make oneself comfortable in a new position: [Vpr, Vp] *settle (back) in one's armchair* [Vnpr] *He settled himself on the sofa to watch TV.* **5** (esp passive) to decide or arrange sth finally: [Vn] *That settles the matter.* ○ *Everything's settled. We're leaving on the nine o'clock train.* **6** to become or make sb/sth calm or relaxed: [V] *The baby wouldn't settle.* [Vn] *Have a drink to settle your stomach.* ○ *This pill will help to settle your nerves.* ○ *He seemed quite worried, but I managed to settle his mind.* **7 ~ (up) (with sb)** to pay what is owed, a bill, etc: [Vpr, Vp] *Have you settled (up) with her for the picture she sold you?* [Vp] *If you pay for both of us now, we can settle up later.* [V, Vn] *The insurance company took a long time to settle (her claim).* [Vn] *Please settle your bill before leaving the hotel.* **8** to sink slowly down; to make sth do this: [V] *The contents of the packet may have settled in transit.* [Vn] *Stir the coffee to settle the grounds.* **IDM** **settle a ˈscore (with sb); settle an old ˈscore** to hurt or punish sb who has harmed, cheated, etc one in the past. **settle/square an/one's acˈcount** ⇨ ACCOUNT[1]. **when the dust has settled** ⇨ DUST[1]. **PHRV** **ˌsettle ˈdown 1** to get into a comfortable position, either sitting or lying: *settle down for the night* ○ *She settled down in an armchair with the newspaper.* **2** to start having a quieter or more steady way of life; to get used to a new way of life, job, etc: *When are you going to marry and settle down?* ○ *She is settling down well in her new job.* **ˌsettle (sb) ˈdown** to become or make sb calm, less lively, excited, etc: *It took the class a while to settle down at the start of the lesson.* ○ *After all the recent excitement things have begun to settle down again.* ○ *The chairman tried to settle the audience down.* ○ *Settle down and be quiet!* **settle (down) to sth** to begin to give one's attention to sth: *Before you settle down to work, can I ask you a question?* **ˈsettle for sth** to accept sth that is seen as not quite satisfactory: *They had hoped to win the match easily but in the end had to settle for a draw.* ○ *We couldn't afford the house we really wanted, so we had to **settle for second-best**.* **ˌsettle ˈin / ˈinto sth** to move into a new home, job, etc and start to feel comfortable there: *We only moved house last week and we haven't settled in yet.* ○ *How are the children settling into their new school?* **ˈsettle on sth** to choose or make a decision about sth after thinking about it: *We've finally settled on Italy for our holidays.* ○ *Have they settled on a name for the baby yet?* **ˈsettle sth on sb** (*law*) to give money or property to sb formally, esp in a will: *He settled part of his estate on his son.*

settle² /ˈsetl/ *n* a wooden seat for two or more people, with a high back and arms, the seat often being the lid of a chest.

settled /ˈsetld/ *adj* **1** not changing or likely to change; steady: *long periods of settled weather* ○ *a settled family life.* **2** comfortable and at ease in a home, job, way of life, etc: *You'll feel more settled when you've been here a few weeks.*

settlement /ˈsetlmənt/ *n* **1(a)** [C] an official agreement that ends an argument or a dispute: *negotiate a peace/pay settlement* ○ *an **out-of-court settlement*** ○ *The strikers have **reached a settlement** with the employers.* **(b)** [U] the action of reaching such an agreement: *the settlement of a debt/dispute/claim.* **2** [C] (*law*) the terms, or a document stating the terms, on which money or property is given to sb; the money or property given in this way: *a divorce settlement.* **3(a)** [C] a village where a group of people have come to live and make their homes, usu where few or no people lived before: *Dutch and English settlements in North America* ○ *penal settlements in Australia.* **(b)** [U] the process of settling in such a place: *the gradual settlement of the American West.* **4** [U] the action of paying back money that was owed: *I enclose a cheque **in settlement of** your account.*

settler /ˈsetlə(r)/ *n* a person who goes to live permanently in a new developing country: *Welsh settlers in Argentina.*

seven /ˈsevn/ *n, pron, det* the number 7. **IDM** **at sixes and sevens** ⇨ SIX.
▶ **seven-** (in compounds) having seven of the thing specified: *a seven-day working week.*
seventh /ˈsevnθ/ *pron, det* 7th. — *n* each of seven equal parts of sth.
For further guidance on how *seven* and *seventh* are used, see the examples at *five* and *fifth*.

seventeen /ˌsevnˈtiːn/ *n, pron, det* the number 17.
▶ **seventeenth** /ˌsevnˈtiːnθ/ *n, pron, det.*
For further guidance on how *seventeen* and *seventeenth* are used, see the examples at *five* and *fifth*.

seventy /ˈsevnti/ **1** *n, pron, det* the number 70. **2** **the seventies** *n* [pl] the numbers, years or temperature from 70 to 79. **IDM** **in one's ˈseventies** between the ages of 70 and 80. ▶ **seventieth** /ˈsevntiəθ/ *n, pron, det.*
For further guidance on how *seventy* and *seventieth* are used, see the examples at *five* and *fifth*.

sever /ˈsevə(r)/ *v* (*fml*) **1 ~ sth (from sth)** to cut sth in two pieces or cut sth off sth: [Vn] *sever a rope* ○ *a severed limb/artery* [Vnpr] *His hand was severed from his arm.* **2** to end a relationship or connection; to break off (BREAK[1]) sth: [Vn] *sever all ties/links* ○ *sever relations with sb* ○ *She has severed her connection with the firm.*
▶ **severance** /ˈsevərəns/ *n* (*fml*) [U] the action or process of ending a relationship or connection: *the severance of diplomatic relations/of communications/ of family ties* ○ *a scheme of voluntary severance* (ie an agreement that sb will be paid a sum of money to leave their job). **ˈseverance pay** *n* [U] money paid to an employee whose contract is terminated by her or his employer.

several /ˈsevrəl/ *indef det, indef pron* more than three; some, but fewer than many **(a)** (*det*): *Several letters arrived this morning.* ○ *He's written several books about India.* ○ *Several more people than usual came to the lunchtime concert.* **(b)** (*pron*): *If you're looking for a photograph of Alice you'll find several in here.* ○ *Several of the paintings were destroyed in the fire.*
▶ **severally** /ˈsevrəli/ *adv* (*fml or law*) separately: *Partners are **jointly and severally liable** for the partnership's debts.*

severe /sɪˈvɪə(r)/ *adj* (**-r, -st**) **1 ~ (on/with sb/sth)** (of people or their behaviour) strict or harsh: *a severe look/punishment/measure* ○ *a severe critic* ○ *be severe with one's children* ○ *Was the judge too severe on her?* **2** very bad, intense or difficult: *a severe shortage* ○ *suffer severe damage/pain/injuries* ○ *severe frost/gales* ○ *a severe blow to her hopes* ○ *The bomb threat caused severe disruption to flights from Heathrow.* **3** demanding great skill, ability or patience: *a severe test of climbers' stamina* ○ *severe competition for university places.* **4** (of style, appearance, clothing, etc) without ornament; simple: *She wore a severe suit of plain grey with a white blouse.*
▶ **severely** *adv*: *punish sb severely* ○ *severely handicapped* ○ *His reputation was severely damaged.*
severity /sɪˈverəti/ *n* [U] the quality of being severe: *the severity (ie extreme cold) of the winter* ○ *The attacks continued with increasing severity.*

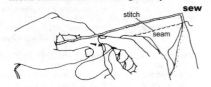
sew
stitch
seam

sew /səʊ/ *v* (*pt* **sewed**; *pp* **sewn** /səʊn/ or **sewed**) **(a)** to make stitches in cloth, etc with a needle and thread: [V] *sew by hand/by machine* [Vn, Vpr] *sew (round) the hem of a skirt.* ⇨ picture. **(b)** to make or attach sth with stitches: [Vn] *sew a dress/skirt* ∘ *a hand-sewn blouse* [Vnpr] *sew a button on(to) a shirt* [Vnp] *sew on a patch.* **PHRV** ,**sew sth** '**up 1** to join or mend sth by sewing: *sew up a seam.* **2** (esp passive) (*infml*) to bring sth, eg a business deal, to a favourable conclusion; to arrange sth in a satisfactory way: *sew up a deal* ∘ *By the end of the meeting everything was nicely sewn up.* ∘ *They have the computer magazine market all sewn up.*

▶ **sewing** *n* [U] **1** the activity of sewing: *enjoy sewing and knitting.* **2** the clothes, etc that are being sewn: *Where is my sewing?* ∘ *I've got a pile of sewing to do.* ∘ *a sewing table/basket.* '**sewing-machine** *n* a machine for sewing cloth.

sewage /'suːɪdʒ; *Brit also* 'sjuː-/ *n* [U] waste matter from human bodies, factories, towns, etc, usu flowing to treatment centres through special pipes: *chemically treated sewage* ∘ *sewage disposal.* Compare SEWERAGE.
■ '**sewage farm** *n* a place where sewage is treated, esp for use as MANURE.
'**sewage works** *n* [sing or pl *v*] a place where sewage is cleaned and made safe so that it can be allowed to go back into a river, etc.

sewer /'suːə(r); *Brit also* 'sjuː-/ *n* an underground pipe or passage that carries SEWAGE away to be treated or cleaned.

▶ **sewerage** /-ɪdʒ/ *n* [U] a system of sewers.

sewn *pp* of SEW.

sex /seks/ *n* **1(a)** [U] the state of being male or female; GENDER(2): *What sex is your dog?* ∘ *Anyone can apply, regardless of age, race or sex.* ∘ *sex discrimination* (ie treating sb differently because of their sex). **(b)** [C] either of the groups (*male* and *female*) into which living things are placed according to their functions in the process of producing young: *the opposite sex* ∘ *the conflict between the sexes.* See also THE FAIR SEX. **2** [U] **(a)** (also *fml* **sexual intercourse, intercourse**) ~ (**with sb**) the action of a man inserting his PENIS into a woman's VAGINA, usu leading to the release of SEMEN from the penis, as a result of which the woman may become pregnant: *have sex* (*with sb*) ∘ *They often had sex together.* ∘ *a sex manual* (ie giving information on sexual behaviour) ∘ *a sex shop* (ie selling pictures of sex, devices to make sex more enjoyable, etc). **(b)** sexual activity between two or more people in which they touch each other's body and sex organs: *gay sex.* **3** [U] physical attraction between two people and the activities that lead to and include sex(2): *sex education* ∘ *public attitudes to sex* ∘ *girls becoming interested in sex at an earlier age.*
▶ **sex** *v* to examine a creature in order to discover what sex(1a) it is: [Vn] *sexing young chicks.*
-sexed (forming compound *adjs*) having the specified amount of sexual desire: *over-sexed* ∘ *a highly-sexed youth.*
sexless *adj* **1** lacking sexual desire or activity: *a sexless relationship.* **2** neither male nor female: *a statue of strange sexless figures.*
sexy *adj* (**-ier, -iest**) (*infml*) **1** of or about sex(2): *a sexy book/film* ∘ *make sexy suggestions.* **2(a)** causing sexual desire: *You look very sexy in that outfit.* **(b)** feeling sexual desire: *I stopped feeling sexy after having the baby.* **sexily** *adv.* **sexiness** *n* [U].
■ '**sex abuse** *n* [U] illegal sexual activities, esp as practised on children by adults: *a child sex abuse case/enquiry.*
'**sex act** *n* an act of having sex: *take part in/perform sex acts.*
'**sex appeal** *n* [U] the quality of being attractive in a sexual way: *a man with lots of sex appeal.*
'**sex life** *n* a person's sexual activities: *a satisfying/flagging sex life.*
'**sex object** *n* a person, usu a woman, considered only in terms of her or his sexual attraction.

'**sex offender** *n* a person who has been found guilty of illegal sexual acts, esp with children.
'**sex-starved** *adj* (*infml*) not having enough opportunities for sex.
'**sex symbol** *n* a person generally considered to be ideal in terms of her or his appearance and sexual attraction: *a Hollywood sex symbol.*

sexism /'seksɪzəm/ *n* [U] unfair treatment of people, esp women, because of their sex, or the attitude that causes this: *blatant sexism in the selection of staff.*
▶ **sexist** /'seksɪst/ *adj* (*derog*) of or showing sexism: *sexist language* ∘ *a sexist person/attitude/joke.* — *n* (*derog*) a person who shows sexism or has a sexist attitude.

sexology /sek'sɒlədʒi/ *n* [U] the scientific study of human sexual behaviour. ▶ **sexologist** /sek'sɒlədʒɪst/ *n*.

sextant /'sekstənt/ *n* an instrument used esp formerly for measuring angles and distances, eg in order to determine the position of a ship.

sextet /seks'tet/ *n* **(a)** a group of six musicians performing together. **(b)** a piece of music for such a group.

sexton /'sekstən/ *n* a person whose job is to care for a church and its surroundings, ring the church bell, etc.

sexual /'sekʃuəl/ *adj* **1** involving physical attraction and sex(2): *sexual behaviour/relations/activity/desire* ∘ *Her interest in him is primarily sexual.* **2** of or concerned with the male and female parts or organs of a plant, an animal or a person: *sexual organs* (ie the PENIS, VAGINA, etc) ∘ *sexual reproduction in plants.* **3** of sex(1) or GENDER(2): *sexual differences/characteristics.*
▶ **sexuality** /ˌsekʃu'æləti/ *n* [U] the sexual nature or characteristics of sb: *explore one's sexuality.*
sexually /-əli/ *adv*: *sexually active* ∘ *a sexually transmitted disease* (eg AIDS).
■ ,**sexual 'intercourse** *n* [U] (*fml*) = SEX 2a.

Sgt (also **Sergt**) *abbr* sergeant.

sh /ʃ/ *interj* be quiet!; be silent!: *Sh! You'll wake the baby!*

shabby /'ʃæbi/ *adj* (**-ier, -iest**) **1(a)** (of things) in poor condition through much use or being badly cared for: *a shabby armchair/room* ∘ *shabby old clothes.* **(b)** (of people) untidy; badly dressed: *You look pretty shabby in those clothes.* **2** (of behaviour) mean and unfair; not honourable: *a shabby affair/excuse* ∘ *play a shabby trick on sb.* ▶ **shabbily** /'ʃæbɪli/ *adv*: *shabbily dressed* ∘ *I think you have been shabbily treated.* **shabbiness** *n* [U].

shack /ʃæk/ *n* a roughly built shed or hut.
▶ **shack** *v* **PHRV** ,**shack 'up (with sb / together)** (*sl*) (esp of a couple) to live together, esp when not married: *They've decided to shack up together in her flat.*

shackle
shackles
handcuffs

shackle /'ʃækl/ *n* **1** [C usu *pl*] either of a pair of metal rings linked by a chain, used for fastening a prisoner's wrists or ankles together. ⇨ picture. **2 shackles** [pl] **the ~s of sth** conditions, circumstances, etc that prevent one from acting or speaking freely: *the shackles of convention.*
▶ **shackle** *v* **1** [Vn] to put shackles on sb. **2** (esp passive) to prevent sb from acting or speaking

freely: [Vn] *be shackled by stupid and restricting laws.*

shade

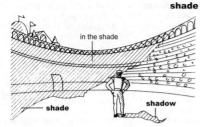

shade / ʃeɪd/ n **1** [U] ~ **(from sth)** a darker, usu cooler area behind sth, eg a building or tree, that blocks the sun's light and heat: *a temperature of 35°C* **in the shade** ○ *sit in the shade of a tree/wall* ○ *The trees give some welcome shade from the sun.* ⇨ picture. Compare SHADOW. **2** [C] (often in compounds) a thing that prevents light passing through or makes it less bright: *an* '*eye-shade* ○ *a new shade for the* '*lamp.* See also LAMPSHADE, SUNSHADE. **3** shades [pl] the ~s of sth (*rhet*) the darkness of sth: *the shades of evening/night.* **4** shades [pl] (*infml esp US*) = SUN-GLASSES. **5** [U] the darker part or parts of a picture: *There is not enough light and shade in your drawing.* **6** [C] a degree or depth of colour: *material in several shades of blue* ○ *choose a lighter shade.* **7(a)** [C] ~ **of sth** a slight difference in sth: *a word with many shades of meaning* ○ *people with all shades of opinion.* **(b)** [sing] a ~ **(better, worse, etc)** a small amount: *I think it's a shade warmer today.* ○ *She feels a shade better than yesterday.* **8** shades [pl] ~s **of sb/sth** (*infml*) reminders of sb/sth: '*Shades of Hitler!*' *I thought, as I listened to him haranguing the crowd.* ○ *shades of the 1950s.* **IDM** **put sb/sth in the** '**shade** to be very superior to sb/sth: *I can paint reasonably well, but her work puts mine in the shade.*

▶ **shade** v **1** ~ **sb/sth (from sth)** to prevent light from reaching sb/sth; to give shade(1) to sb/sth: [Vn] *shaded terraces* [Vnpr] *She shaded her eyes (from the sun) with her hand.* **2** [Vn] to provide a screen for a lamp, light, etc to reduce its brightness: [Vn] *There was a small shaded light by her bed.* **3** ~ **sth (in)** to make a part of a drawing, etc darker, eg with a mass of colour or with pencil lines, to give an effect of light and shade(5) or to emphasize a particular feature: [Vn] *the shaded areas on the map* [Vnp] *shade in a drawing.* **4** ~ **from sth into sth; ~ (off) into sth** (esp of colours) to change gradually into another colour: [Vpr, Vp] *scarlet shading (off) into pink* ○ (*fig*) *distrust of foreigners shading into racism.* **shading** n [U] the colour, pencil marks, etc that give an effect of darkness or emphasize a particular feature on a map, picture, etc.

shadow /'ʃædəʊ/ n **1(a)** [C] a dark area on a surface caused by an object standing between direct light and that surface: *The chair* **cast a shadow** *on the wall.* ○ *The shadows lengthened as the sun went down.* ○ (*fig*) *The bad news cast a shadow on/over our meeting* (ie made us sad). ⇨ picture at SHADE. **(b)** [U] (also shadows [pl]) darkness caused by an object blocking direct light: *Her face was in deep shadow.* ○ *a figure standing in the shadows.* **2** [C] a dark patch or area: *have shadows under the eyes* (eg because of illness or lack of sleep). **3** [C] **(a)** a person or animal that constantly follows sb: *The dog became his shadow and never left his side.* **(b)** a person, eg a DETECTIVE, who follows and watches sb closely and often secretly. **4** [sing] ~ **of sth** (usu in negative sentences) a very small amount of sth: *There is* **not a shadow of (a) doubt** *that he is guilty.* **5** [C] a thing that is not real or impossible to

obtain: *You can't spend your life chasing shadows.* **6** [sing] the ~ of sb/sth the strong influence of sb/sth: *the shadow of the approaching catastrophe* ○ *For years he lived* **in the shadow of** *his famous mother.* See also EYE-SHADOW, FIVE O'CLOCK SHADOW. **IDM** a shadow of one's/its former 'self not having the strength, influence, etc that one/it formerly had: *She used to be a great player, but now she's a mere shadow of her former self.*

▶ **shadow** v **1** to follow and watch sb closely and often secretly: *He was shadowed for a week by the secret police.* **2** to produce a shadow on sb/sth: [Vn] *Her face was shadowed by a wide-brimmed hat.* See also OVERSHADOW.

shadow adj [attrib] (*Brit politics*) (used to refer to leading members of the main political party in opposition to the government. A shadow minister studies the work of a particular government department, eg the Department of Education, and is likely to become a government minister if her or his party comes into power): *the Shadow Cabinet* ○ *the Shadow Foreign Secretary.*

shadowy adj **1** full of shadows: *the cool, shadowy interior of the church* ○ *a shadowy corner.* **2** [usu attrib] like a shadow; difficult to see or identify clearly: *a shadowy figure glimpsed in the twilight.* **3** [usu attrib] difficult to know much about; mysterious: *the shadowy world of the secret service.*

■ '**shadow-box** v [V] to box with an imaginary opponent. '**shadow-boxing** n [U].

shady /'ʃeɪdi/ adj (-ier, -iest) **1** giving shade from sunlight; situated in the shade: *a shady corner of the garden* ○ *We found a shady spot for our picnic.* **2** (*infml derog*) probably dishonest or illegal: *a shady deal* ○ *He's a rather shady character — I don't trust him.*

shaft /ʃɑːft; *US* ʃæft/ n **1(a)** the long narrow part of an ARROW or a SPEAR(1). **(b)** the long handle of a hammer or other tool, or eg of a golf club (GOLF). **2** [C] (often in compounds) a bar or rod joining parts of a machine or transmitting power in a machine. See also CRANKSHAFT. **3** [C] (often in compounds) a long narrow, usu VERTICAL, space, eg for a lift to move up and down in, for entry into a mine, or for allowing air into and out of a building: *a* '*lift shaft* ○ *a* '*mine shaft* ○ *a venti*'*lation shaft.* **4** [C] ~ **of sth** a long thin line of light: *a shaft of light/sunlight/ moonlight* ○ (*fig*) *a sudden shaft of inspiration.* **5** [C] either of the two poles between which a horse stands and to which it is fastened to pull a cart or carriage. **6** ~ **(of sth)** (*fml*) an amusing remark intended to hurt or provoke sb: *her brilliant shafts of wit.* **7** the shaft [sing] (*US infml*) harsh and unfair treatment, often involving deception: *give sb/ get the shaft.*

▶ **shaft** v [Vn] (*US infml*) to treat sb unfairly or harshly; to cheat sb.

shag¹ /ʃæg/ n [U] a strong type of tobacco cut into long thin pieces.

shag² /ʃæg/ v [V, Vn] (△ *Brit sl*) to have sex with sb.
▶ **shag** n.

shagged /ʃægd/ (also shagged 'out) adj [pred] (*Brit sl*) very tired.

shaggy /'ʃægi/ adj **(a)** (of hair, fur, etc) long, thick and untidy: *shaggy hair/eyebrows* ○ *a shaggy white beard.* **(b)** covered with long thick untidy hair, fur, etc: *a shaggy dog/coat.*

■ ,shaggy-'dog story n a very long joke, often with a silly and not very funny ending.

shah /ʃɑː/ n the title of the former ruler of Iran.

shake¹ /ʃeɪk/ v (*pt* shook /ʃʊk/; *pp* shaken /'ʃeɪkən/) **1(a)** to move or make sb/sth move with short quick movements from side to side or up and down: [V] *The whole building shakes when a train goes past.* [Vn] *Shake the bottle well before pouring.* ○ *He took her by the shoulders and shook her violently.*

[V.speech] = verb + direct speech   [V.*that*] = verb + *that* clause   [V.*wh*] = verb + *who, how,* etc clause

○ *Great sobs shook her whole body.* [Vnp] *The bumpy car ride shook us around a bit.* [V-adj] *A screw has shaken loose in the machine.* [Vn-adj] *He gently shook the children awake.* (**b**) to move sth in the specified direction by shaking: [Vnpr] *shake salt onto one's food* ○ *shake sand out of one's shoes* [Vnp] *shake the apples down from the tree.* (**c**) ~ (**with sth**) to make short quick movements that one cannot control, eg because one is cold or afraid; to TREMBLE(1a): [Vpr] *shaking with cold/laughter/fear/rage* ○ *He was clearly terrified and **shaking like a leaf.*** [Vn] *We laughed until our sides shook.* **2(a)** ~ **sb** (**up**) (not used in the continuous tenses) to disturb or upset sb greatly: [Vn] *be shaken by the news of sb's death* [Vn, Vnp] *They were badly shaken (up) in the accident.* (**b**) to make sth less certain; to reduce the strength of sth: [Vn] *shake sb's faith/confidence/ belief* ○ *Her theory has been shaken by this new evidence.* **3** ~ (**with sth**) (of the voice) to sound UNSTEADY(1), eg because one is upset or angry: [V, Vpr] *His voice shook (with emotion) as he announced the news.* **IDM** **shake one's ˈfist (at sb)** to show that one is angry with sb or threaten sb by shaking one's FIST. **shake sb's ˈhand; shake ˈhands (with sb); shake sb by the ˈhand** to take sb's hand and move it up and down as a greeting, or to express agreement, etc: *They shook hands on the deal.* **shake one's ˈhead** to turn one's head from side to side as a way of indicating 'no', or to express doubt, sorrow, disapproval, etc. **shake in one's ˈshoes** (*infml*) to be very frightened or nervous: *He was shaking in his shoes at the thought of facing his boss.* **shake a ˈleg** (*dated infml*) (esp imperative) to start to act; to hurry: *Come on, shake a leg, we're late already.* **PHRV** ˌ**shake ˈdown** to become familiar with a new situation and begin to function properly: *The new office staff are shaking down well.* ˌ**shake sb/sth ˈdown** (*US infml*) to search sb/sth thoroughly: *The police shook the club down, looking for narcotics.* See also SHAKEDOWN.

ˌ**shake sb ˈoff** to escape from sb; to get rid of sb: *shake off one's pursuers* ○ *She tried to shake him off but he continued to pester her.* ˌ**shake sth ˈoff** to get rid of sth: *The company has shaken off its rather old-fashioned image.* ○ *I can't seem to shake off this cold.* ˈ**shake on sth** to shake hands in order to confirm an arrangement, etc: *They shook on the deal.* ○ *Let's shake on it.* ˌ**shake sth ˈout** to open or spread sth by shaking: *shake out a newspaper/tablecloth/duster.* ˌ**shake sb ˈup** to surprise sb in order to make them think in a different way, become more active, etc: *We've got to shake up all these people with old-fashioned ideas.* ˌ**shake sth ˈup 1** to mix sth thoroughly by shaking: *Shake up the salad-dressing before you put it on.* **2** to make major changes in an organization, etc in order to make it more efficient, etc: *The company needs shaking up.*

▶ **shaker** *n* **1** (often in compounds) a container in which or from which sth is shaken: *a ˈcocktail shaker* ○ *a ˈsalt shaker.* **2 Shaker** a member of a US religious group. Shakers live a simple life and do not have sexual relations.

shaking *n* [sing] an act of shaking: *give sth a good shaking* (ie shake it well).

■ ˈ**shake-up** (also ˈ**shake-out**) *n* a major change to an organization, etc: *The only thing that will save the company is a radical shake-up of the way it is run.*

shake² /ʃeɪk/ *n* **1** [C usu *sing*] an act of shaking or being shaken: *a shake of the head* ○ *Give the jar a good shake.* **2 the shakes** [sing *v*] (*infml*) movements of the body that one cannot control, due eg to fear, illness or drinking too much alcohol: *get the shakes.* **3** [C] = MILK SHAKE. **IDM** **be no great shakes** ⇨ GREAT. **in two / a couple of ˈshakes**

(*infml*) in a moment; very soon: *Hang on! I'll be ready in two shakes!*

shakedown /ˈʃeɪkdaʊn/ *n* (*US infml*) a thorough search: *a shakedown of drug dealers.*

shaky /ˈʃeɪki/ *adj* **1** shaking or feeling weak because of fear, illness, etc: *a shaky voice* ○ *Her hands are shaky because she's nervous.* ○ *He looks a bit shaky on his feet.* **2** not firm and steady; not safe and reliable: *a shaky chair/table* ○ (*fig*) *a shaky marriage* ○ *The government is looking rather shaky at the moment.* ○ *You're **on shaky ground** with that argument.* ○ *The team recovered from a shaky start to score four goals in the second half.* ▶ **shakily** /-ɪli/ *adv.*

shale /ʃeɪl/ *n* [U] a type of soft rock that splits easily into thin flat pieces. ▶ **shaly** *adj.*

shall /ʃəl; *strong form* ʃæl/ *modal v* (*neg esp Brit* **shall not**; *contracted form* **shan't** /ʃɑːnt/; *pt* **should** /ʃʊd/; *neg* **should not**; *contracted form* **shouldn't** /ˈʃʊdnt/) **1** (indicating future predictions): *This time next week I shall be on holiday.* ○ *We shan't know the results until next week.* ○ *I said I should be glad to help.* **2** (*fml*) (indicating will or determination): *I shall write to you again at the end of the month.* ○ *He insisted that the papers should be destroyed.* ○ *She was determined that we should finish on time.* **3** (indicating offers or suggestions): *Shall I* (ie Would you like me to) *do the washing-up?* ○ *What shall we do this weekend?* ○ *Let's look at it again, shall we?* **4** (*fml*) (indicating orders or instructions): *Candidates shall remain in their seats until all the papers have been collected.* ○ *The lease stated that tenants should maintain the property in good condition.*

NOTE

1 PREDICTIONS

In British English, **shall** is sometimes used with *I* or *we* to predict a future event: *I shall be in touch with you again shortly.* The negative is **shall not** or **shan't**: *I shan't be free until 7 o'clock.* **Will** is also used with *I* and *we*, as well as with *you, he, she, it* and *they*. The negative is **won't**: *We won't stay long.*

You use **shall** for questions with *I* and *we*: *What shall I wear to the party?* **Will** is the usual future form in American English: *I will send the information tomorrow.* ○ *Will you be home for dinner?*

Shall and **will** are usually contracted to **'ll** in speaking: *She'll never finish in time.* ○ *It'll be our first family holiday for years.*

2 SUGGESTIONS

You use **Shall I…?** to make offers and **Shall we…?** to make suggestions, especially when you expect the other person to decide: *Shall I drive?* ○ *Shall we bring our swimming things?* This use is common especially in British English.

Shall or **can** are used to ask somebody else to make a suggestion: *Where shall/can we go for lunch?*

The question tag **shall I…?** (NOT 'will I?') is used to confirm that somebody agrees with your suggestion: *I'll make some sandwiches to take with us, shall I?*

shallot /ʃəˈlɒt/ *n* a vegetable like a small onion, with a very strong taste.

shallow /ˈʃæləʊ/ *adj* (**-er, -est**) **1** not deep; measuring a short distance between the top or the surface and the bottom: *shallow water* ○ *a shallow dish/bowl* ○ *the shallow end of the swimming-pool.* **2** (*derog*) (of a person) not thinking or capable of thinking seriously; (of ideas, remarks, etc) not showing serious thought: *He talks a lot, but I find him rather shallow and superficial.* ○ *a shallow expression of emotion.* **3** (of a person's breathing) taking in and sending out only a little air with each breath. Compare DEEP¹. ▶ **shallowly** *adv*: *breathing shallowly.*

[Vnn] = verb + noun + noun   [V-adj] = verb + adjective   For more help with verbs, see Study pages **B4–8**.

shallowness n [U].

shallows n [pl] a shallow place in a river or in the sea: *paddling in the shallows.*

sham /ʃæm/ v (-mm-) to pretend sth: [Vn] *sham illness/death/sleep* [V] *He's only shamming.*

▶ **sham** n (*usu derog*) **1** [C] (**a**) a person who pretends to be what he or she is not: *She claims to know all about computers but really she's a sham.* (**b**) (*usu sing*) a thing, feeling, etc that is not what sb pretends that it is: *His love was a sham — he only wanted her money.* ○ *Their marriage had become a complete sham.* **2** [U] pretended feeling, etc; deception: *They have intellectual pretentions but it is all sham.*

sham adj [attrib] (*usu derog*) pretended; not genuine: *a sham marriage* ○ *sham jewellery.*

shaman /ˈʃæmən, ˈʃɑːmən/ n (*pl* **shamans**) a priest in certain religions who is believed to be able to contact the gods or spirits and to cure people.

shamble /ˈʃæmbl/ v to walk or run in an awkward way, without raising one's feet properly: [V] *a shambling gait* [Vpr, Vp] *The old tramp shambled (off) down the road.* ⇨ note at SHUFFLE.

shambles /ˈʃæmblz/ n [sing v] (*infml*) a scene of complete disorder; a mess: *Your room is (in) a shambles. Tidy it up!* ○ *The government's economic policy is a complete shambles.*

shambolic /ʃæmˈbɒlɪk/ adj (*Brit infml joc*) not organized: *a shambolic figure* ○ *The department's accounting is shambolic.*

shame¹ /ʃeɪm/ n **1** [U] a feeling of distress and regret as a result of one's own wrongdoing, failure, foolish behaviour, etc or that of people one is associated with: *feel shame at having told a lie* ○ *hang one's head in shame* ○ **To my shame** (ie I feel shame that) *I never thanked him for his kindness.* **2** [U] the ability to feel shame: *How could you do such a thing? Have you no shame?* ○ *She is completely without shame.* **3** [U] loss of honour or respect as a result of wrongdoing, failure, etc: *bring shame on sb/oneself.* **4** a shame [sing] (*derog infml*) a thing that one feels is wrong or unfortunate or that one regrets: *It's **a crying shame** that we didn't buy the house when we had the money.* ○ *What a shame you didn't win.* ○ *Isn't it a shame that the rain spoiled our picnic?* IDM **put sb/sth to** ˈ**shame** to be greatly superior to sb/sth: *Your beautiful handwriting puts my untidy scrawl to shame.* ˈ**shame on you** you should feel shame about what you have done or said: *How could you treat her so badly? Shame on you!*

▶ **shameful** /-fl/ adj that should make sb feel shame: *shameful conduct/deceit.* **shamefully** /-fəli/ adv: *be shamefully treated.* **shamefulness** n [U].

shameless adj (*derog*) having or showing no feeling of shame: *shameless behaviour* ○ *act in a shameless way.* **shamelessly** adv. **shamelessness** n [U].

shaming adj making sb feel shame: *The experience was deeply shaming for us all.*

shame² /ʃeɪm/ v (**a**) to make sb feel shame¹(1): [Vn] *He was shamed by how much more work the others had done.* (**b**) to bring shame¹(3) upon sb: [Vn] *You've shamed your family.* PHRV ˈ**shame sb into doing sth** to persuade sb to do sth by making them feel shame: *shame sb into apologizing.*

shamefaced /ˌʃeɪmˈfeɪst/ adj showing feelings of shame: *a ˌshamefaced exˈpression/grin/aˈpology.* **shamefacedly** /-ˈfeɪstli/ adj.

shammy /ˈʃæmi/ (also **shammy leather**) n [U, C] (*infml*) = CHAMOIS-LEATHER.

shampoo /ʃæmˈpuː/ n **1** [C, U] (**a**) a liquid containing soap for washing the hair: *perfumed shampoos* ○ *Don't use too much shampoo.* (**b**) a similar substance for cleaning carpets, furniture covers, etc or for washing a car. **2** [C] an act of

washing the hair or of cleaning a carpet, etc: *give sb/sth a shampoo* ○ *a shampoo and set.*

▶ **shampoo** v (*pt, pp* **-pooed**; *pres p* **-pooing**) [Vn] to wash or clean hair, carpets, etc with shampoo.

shamrock /ˈʃæmrɒk/ n [C, U] a small plant with three leaves on each stem, the national symbol of Ireland: *wearing a/some shamrock on his lapel.*

shandy /ˈʃændi/ n (*esp Brit*) (**a**) [U] a drink made by mixing beer with LEMONADE or ginger ale (GINGER). (**b**) [C] a glass of this: *Two lemonade shandies, please.*

shanghai /ˌʃæŋˈhaɪ/ v (*pt, pp* **-haied** /-ˈhaɪd/; *pres p* **-haiing** /-ˈhaɪɪŋ/) ~ **sb** (**into doing sth**) (*infml*) to trick or force sb into doing sth: [Vnpr] *tourists shanghaied into buying expensive fakes* [also Vn].

shank /ʃæŋk/ n **1** the straight narrow part of an implement, etc: *the shank of an anchor/a key/a screw.* **2** (*usu pl*) (*often joc or derog*) a leg, esp the part between the knee and the ankle: *long thin shanks.* ⇨ picture at HORSE. IDM **on Shanks's** ˈ**pony/**ˈ**mare** (*dated infml joc*) on foot, not by car.

shan't short form of SHALL NOT.

shanty¹ /ˈʃænti/ n a roughly built hut or shed.

■ ˈ**shanty town** n an area inside or just outside a town, where poor people live in shanties.

shanty² (also ˈ**sea-shanty**, US **chanty**, **chantey**) /ˈʃænti/ n a song formerly sung by sailors while pulling ropes, etc.

shape¹ /ʃeɪp/ n **1** [C, U] the outer form or appearance of sth; the outline of an area, a figure, etc: *a round/square/oblong shape* ○ *an ashtray in the shape of a hand* ○ *people of **all shapes and sizes*** ○ *the odd shape of his nose* ○ *This room is rather an awkward shape.* ○ *a dress that hasn't got much shape* ○ *Many people would like to change their (body) shape.* ○ *The garden is round in shape.* **2** [C] a thing that is difficult to see properly; a form: *I could just see two dim shapes in the gloom.* ○ *A huge shape loomed up out of the fog.* **3** [U] (*infml*) condition; state: *She's **in good shape** (ie fit) after months of training.* ○ *What shape is the team in after its defeat?* ○ *The illness has left him in rather poor shape.* **4** [U] the nature, qualities or characteristics of sth: *the future shape of the health service* ○ *This decision affected the whole shape of politics in the 1930s.* IDM **get (oneself) into** ˈ**shape** to take exercise, etc in order to become fit: *I've been doing aerobics to get myself into shape.* **get/ knock/lick sth/sb into** ˈ**shape** to get sth/sb into an efficient or proper state; to arrange sth/sb properly: *We need a new manager to get the business into shape again.* **give shape to sth** to express sth clearly: *I'm having trouble giving shape to my ideas in this essay.* **in** ˈ**any shape (or form)** (*infml*) in whatever form sth appears or is presented: *I can't eat eggs in any shape or form.* **in** ˈ**shape** fit: *You'll never be in shape until you eat less and take more exercise.* **in the shape/form of sb/sth** (*infml*) appearing as sb/sth: *Help arrived in the shape of my next-door neighbour.* ○ *I received a nasty surprise in the shape of a letter from the taxman.* **out of** ˈ**shape 1** not having the usual shape: *This hat has been rather knocked out of shape.* **2** not fit: *I'm very out of shape — what form of exercise do you recommend?* **the** ˌ**shape of** ˌ**things to** ˈ**come** the way the future is likely to develop. **take** ˈ**shape** to take on a definite form; to become more organized: *A plan was beginning to take shape in my mind.* ○ *After months of work, the new book is gradually taking shape.*

▶ **shapeless** adj having no definite shape; not elegant in shape: *a shapeless mass/form/dress.* **shapelessly** adv. **shapelessness** n [U].

shape² /ʃeɪp/ v **1** ~ **sth (into sth)** to give a shape or form to sth: [Vnpr] *shape the clay into a ball* ○ *The lake is shaped like an 'S'.* [also Vn]. **2** to have a great influence on sb/sth; to determine the nature of sth: [Vn] *attitudes shaped by past experiences* ○ *These*

events helped to shape her future career. **3** ~ (**up**) to develop in a certain way: [V, Vp] *Our plans are shaping (up) well* (ie giving signs that they will be successful). [Vp] *How is the new team shaping up?* **4** (esp passive) to make a garment fit the shape of the body: [Vn] *The jacket is shaped* (ie becomes narrower) *at the waist.* **PHRV** ,shape 'up (*infml*) to improve one's behaviour, work harder, etc: *If you don't shape up you'll fail your exams.*
▶ **-shaped** (in compounds) having the specified shape: *an ,L-shaped 'room* ○ *have a ,pear-shaped 'figure* ○ *Rugby is played with an ,egg-shaped 'ball.*

shapely /'ʃeɪpli/ *adj* (**-ier, -iest**) (*approv*) (esp of a woman's body) having an attractive shape; well formed: *a shapely figure* ○ *shapely legs.*

shard /ʃɑːd/ (also **sherd** /ʃɜːd/) *n* a broken piece of clay, glass, metal, etc: *shards of pottery.*

share¹ /ʃeə(r)/ *n* **1** [C] ~ (**in/of sth**) a part or portion of a larger amount which is divided among several or many people, or to which several or many people contribute: *You can have my share of the cake.* ○ *We each pay an equal share of the bills.* ○ *Everyone who helped got a share in the profits.* **2** [U, sing] ~ (**in/of sth**) a person's part in sth done, received, etc by several people: *What share did he have in their success?* ○ *She must have her share of the blame* (ie accept that she was partly responsible). **3** [C] any of the equal parts into which the money of a business company is divided, giving the holder a right to a portion of the profits: *buy/hold 500 shares in an electronics company* ○ *shares valued at 60p each* ○ *share capital/dealing/prices* ○ *a share certificate.* **IDM** **get, etc a slice/share of the cake** ⇨ CAKE. **have, etc one's fair share of sth** ⇨ FAIR¹. **the lion's share** ⇨ LION. See also MARKET SHARE.
▶ **share** *v* **1(a)** ~ **sth** (**out**) (**among/between sb**) to give a share of sth to others: [Vnpr] *share the chocolates among the children* ○ *We shared the pizza between the four of us.* [Vnpr, Vnp] *The profits are shared (out) equally among the partners.* [also Vn]. (**b**) ~ (**sth**) (**with sb**) to have a share of sth with another or others: [Vn] *Let's share the last cake; you have half and I'll have half.* [Vnpr] *He offered to share the cost with me.* [also Vpr]. (**c**) ~ (**sth**) (**with sb**) to have or use sth with others; to have sth in common: [Vn] *share a bed/room/house* ○ *share sb's belief/faith/optimism* [V] *There's only one bedroom, so we'll have to share.* ○ *We both share the blame for the accident.* [Vnpr] *Can I share the book with you?* **2** ~ (**in**) **sth** to take part or become involved in an activity: [Vn, Vpr] *I also try to get the children to share (in) the housework.* **3** ~ **sth** (**with sb**) to tell sb about sth: [Vn, Vnpr] *She won't share her secret (with us).* [Vnpr] *I want to share my news with you.* **IDM** **share and share a'like** (*saying*) to share things equally: *Don't be so selfish — it's share and share alike in this house.*
■ '**share index** *n* a list that shows the current value of shares on the stock market (STOCK¹), based on the prices of a selected number of shares of major companies: *The Financial Times share index fell nine points to 1850.9.*
share-out *n* [sing] a distribution of sth: *a share-out of the profits.*

share² /ʃeə(r)/ *n* = PLOUGHSHARE.

sharecropper /'ʃeəkrɒpə(r)/ *n* (*esp US*) a farmer who gives part of her or his crop as rent to the owner of the land.

shareholder /'ʃeəhəʊldə(r)/ *n* an owner of shares in a business company.
▶ **shareholding** /-həʊldɪŋ/ *n* a portion of a business company owned in the form of shares: *own a majority shareholding.*

shariah /ʃəˈriːə/ *n* [U] the Muslim code of religious law.

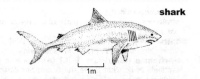
shark

shark /ʃɑːk/ *n* **1** a large sea fish with sharp teeth and a pointed FIN(1) on its back. There are several types of shark, some of which can attack people swimming. ⇨ picture. **2** (*infml derog*) a person who gets money from others dishonestly or lends money at very high interest rates: *a loan shark.*

sharp /ʃɑːp/ *adj* (**-er, -est**) **1** having a fine edge or point; that can cut or penetrate; not BLUNT(1): *a sharp knife/pin/needle* ○ *sharp teeth* ○ *The shears aren't sharp enough to cut the grass.* ○ (*fig*) *sharp features* (eg a pointed nose or chin). **2(a)** (of curves, bends, slopes, etc) changing direction suddenly: *a sharp bend in the road* ○ *a sharp turn to the left.* (**b**) [usu attrib] sudden and rapid: *a sharp drop in prices* ○ *a sharp rise in crime* ○ *a sharp intake of breath.* **3** clear; distinct: *a sharp outline* ○ *a sharp photographic image* (ie one with clear contrasts between areas of light and shade) ○ *in sharp focus* ○ *There is a sharp contrast between the lives of the poorest and the richest members of society.* **4** [usu attrib] (of sounds) high-pitched and loud: *sharp voices* ○ *There was a sharp knock on the door.* **5** (of food, etc) having an acid flavour or smell: *The lemon juice in this pudding makes it taste rather sharp.* **6** producing a strong physical sensation as if of cutting: *a sharp frost/wind* ○ *feel a sharp pain in the back.* **7** quickly aware of things; alert: *have sharp eyes/ears/reflexes* ○ *a sharp person/mind/intelligence* ○ *a sharp sense of humour* ○ *a sharp sense of smell* ○ *keep a sharp lookout* ○ *It was very sharp of you to notice that.* **8** ~ (**with sb**) (*derog*) intended or intending to criticize, injure, etc; harsh; severe: *sharp criticism/words/ remarks* ○ *She was rather sharp with me* (ie spoke harshly to me) *when I forgot my book.* ○ *have a sharp tongue* (ie often speak harshly or angrily). **9** often (*derog*) quick to take advantage of sb/sth, often dishonestly: *a sharp lawyer/accountant* ○ *She was too sharp for me* (ie was cleverer and so gained an advantage). **10** [usu attrib] (*infml*) (of clothes or sb's style of dressing) fashionable; SMART¹(2). **11** (*music*) (**a**) (of a sound, an instrument, etc) above the normal or correct pitch¹(2): *That note sounded sharp.* (**b**) (usu following *ns*) (of notes) raised half a tone¹(6): *in the key of C sharp minor.* ⇨ picture at MUSIC. Compare FLAT² 5. **IDM** **look 'sharp** to be quick; to hurry: *You'd better look sharp or you'll be late.* (**as**) ,**sharp as a 'needle**; (*US*) (**as**) ,**sharp as a 'tack** very intelligent and alert. **the 'sharp end (of sth)** (*infml*) the place or position of greatest difficulty or responsibility: *If anything goes wrong, I'm the one who's at the sharp end* (ie who has to suffer the consequences).
▶ **sharp** *n* (*symb* ♯) (*music*) a note raised by one SEMITONE, or the symbol used to indicate it: *a difficult piano piece full of sharps and flats.* Compare FLAT² 5, NATURAL 6.

sharp *adv* **1** (*infml*) (used after an expression indicating a time of day) exactly: *Please be here at seven (o'clock) sharp.* **2** (*infml*) suddenly: *stopped sharp* ○ *turn sharp left.* **3** (*music*) above the correct pitch²(1b): *sing sharp.*

sharpen /'ʃɑːpən/ *v* ~ (**sth**) (**up**) to become or make sth sharp: [Vn] *sharpen a pencil* ○ *This knife needs sharpening.* ○ *All this exercise has sharpened my appetite.* [Vnp] *This incident has sharpened up public awareness of the economic crisis.* [V] *Her eyes/senses sharpened* (ie became more alert). [Vnpr] *The pole had been sharpened to a point.* **sharpener**

/'ʃɑːpnə(r)/ *n* (usu in compounds) a device that sharpens things: *a* '*pencil-sharpener* ○ *a* '*knife-sharpener*.

sharpish *adj* rather sharp: *with a sharpish point at the end.* — *adv* (*infml*) quickly: *I want this room tidied up sharpish!*

sharply *adv* in a sharp way: *sharply pointed* ○ *prices dropping sharply* ○ *sharply contrasted styles* ○ *She spoke sharply to the child.* ○ *The road bends sharply.*

sharpness *n* [U]: *adjust the camera lens to obtain maximum sharpness.*

■ ¡**sharp-**'**eyed** *adj* able to see well; quick to notice things: *A* ¡*sharp-eyed po*'*lice officer spotted the stolen car.*

¡**sharp** '**practice** *n* [U] business dealings that are not entirely honest.

sharpshooter /'ʃɑːpʃuːtə(r)/ *n* a person who is skilled at shooting with a gun, etc.

shat *pt, pp* of SHIT *v*.

shatter /'ʃætə(r)/ *v* **1** to break or make sth break suddenly into small pieces: [V] *The vase hit the floor and shattered.* [Vn] *The explosion shattered all the windows.* ○ (*fig*) *an ear-shattering sound.* **2** (*infml*) to destroy sth completely: [V] *shatter sb's hopes* ○ *My illusions were shattered when I discovered that he'd lied to me for years.* **3** (*infml*) (esp passive) to upset or shock sb greatly: [Vn] *We were shattered by the news.* **4** (*infml*) (esp passive) to make sb extremely tired: [Vn] *We were absolutely shattered after the journey.*

▶ **shattering** /'ʃætərɪŋ/ *adj* **1** very disturbing; shocking: *a shattering experience* ○ *The news had a shattering effect on me.* **2** destroying sth completely: *The defeat was a shattering blow to her confidence.*
shatteringly *adv*.

■ '**shatter-proof** *adj* designed not to shatter: *shatter-proof glass for car windscreens.*

shave /ʃeɪv/ *v* **1** ~ **sth** (**off**) to cut hair off one's/sb's face, etc with a RAZOR: [V] *I cut myself shaving.* [Vn] *The nurse washed and shaved him.* ○ *Buddhist priests with shaved heads.* ○ *Do you shave your legs?* [Vnp] *He has shaved his beard off.* **2** ~ **sth** (**off/from sth**) to cut a very thin piece or pieces from the surface of wood, etc: [Vnpr] *shave a millimetre (of wood) off the bottom of the door* [also Vn]. ⇨ note at CLIP². **3** ~ **sth** (**off sth**) to reduce sth by a small amount: [Vnpr] *shave half a second off the world record* ○ *shave profit margins by 2%.*

▶ **shave** *n* an act of shaving: *I had a shave before I went out.* ○ *A sharp razor gives a close shave.* **IDM** a **close call/shave** ⇨ CLOSE¹.

shaven /'ʃeɪvn/ *adj* shaved: ¡*clean-*'*shaven* ○ *shaven heads.* ⇨ note at PROVE.

shaver (also **electric razor**) *n* an electrical tool for cutting hair off the face, etc.

shavings *n* [pl] very thin pieces of wood shaved off sth, esp with a plane²: *The floor of the carpenter's shop was covered with wood shavings.* ⇨ picture at PLANE².

■ '**shaving-brush** *n* a brush for spreading special thick soap over the face, etc before shaving.

'**shaving-cream**, '**shaving foam** *ns* cream or foam that one spreads over the face, etc before shaving.

shawl /ʃɔːl/ *n* a large piece of woollen material worn round the shoulders or head of a woman, or wrapped round a baby.

she /ʃi; *strong form* ʃiː/ *pers pron* (used as the subject of a *v*) **1** a female person or animal mentioned earlier or being observed now: '*What does your sister do?*' '*She's a dentist.*' ○ *Doesn't she* (ie the woman we are looking at) *look like her mother?* ○ *I stroked the cat and she rubbed against my leg.* **2** a thing regarded as female, eg a country or a ship, mentioned earlier or being observed now: *Nice car — how much did she cost?* Compare HER¹. ⇨ note at GENDER.

▶ **she** *n* [sing] a female: *What a lovely dog — is it a he or a she?*

she- (forming compound *ns*) female: *a* '*she-goat*/ *-wolf*.

sheaf /ʃiːf/ *n* (*pl* **sheaves** /ʃiːvz/) **1** a number of papers, etc lying one on top of the other and often tied together: *a sheaf of notes.* **2** a bunch of stalks of corn, wheat, etc tied together after being cut and left standing up so that they dry.

shear /ʃɪə(r)/ *v* (*pt* **sheared**; *pp* **shorn** /ʃɔːn/ or **sheared**) **1(a)** to cut the wool off a sheep: [Vn] *sheep shearing time.* (**b**) ~ **sth** (**off**) (esp passive) to cut off hair: [Vn, Vnp] *Her hair had been shorn (off).* ~ (**off**) to become twisted, or break off under pressure: [V, Vp] *The bolt sheared (off) and the wheel came off.* **PHRV** **be** '**shorn of sth** to have sth taken away; to be deprived (DEPRIVE) of sth: *The room looked bare, shorn of its rich furnishings.* ○ *a deposed king shorn of his former power.*

shears /ʃɪəz/ *n* [pl] a large cutting instrument shaped like SCISSORS, used for cutting hedges, etc and usu operated with both hands: *a pair of shears* ○ '*gardening shears.* ⇨ picture at SCISSORS.

sheath /ʃiːθ/ *n* (*pl* **sheaths** /ʃiːðz/) **1(a)** a cover fitting closely over the blade of a knife or other sharp weapon or tool: *He put the dagger back in its sheath.* ⇨ picture at KNIFE. (**b**) any similar protective covering: *the sheath round an electric cable.* **2** a rubber contraceptive (CONTRACEPTION) worn on the PENIS during sex; a CONDOM. **3** a woman's dress that fits the body closely: *a simple black silk sheath.*

■ '**sheath knife** *n* (*pl* **knives**) a knife with a fixed blade that fits in a sheath. ⇨ picture at KNIFE.

sheathe /ʃiːð/ *v* **1** (*fml*) to put sth into a SHEATH(1): [Vn] *He sheathed his sword.* **2** ~ **sth** (**in/with sth**) (esp passive) to put a protective covering on sth: [Vnpr] *electric wire sheathed with plastic* ○ *Her legs were sheathed in fine black nylons.* [Vn] *The tiger's claws are normally sheathed and are only extended when hunting.*

sheaves *pl* of SHEAF.

shebang /ʃɪ'bæŋ/ *n* **IDM** **the whole shebang** ⇨ WHOLE.

shebeen /ʃɪ'biːn/ *n* a place where alcoholic drinks are sold illegally.

shed¹ /ʃed/ *n* (often in compounds) a small simple building, usu made of wood or metal, used for storing things or sheltering animals, vehicles, etc: *a* '*tool-shed* ○ *a* '*wood-shed* ○ *a* '*coal-shed* ○ *a* '*cattle-shed* ○ *an* '*engine-shed* ○ *a* '*bicycle-shed.* ⇨ picture at HOUSE¹. Compare HUT. See also WATERSHED.

shed² /ʃed/ *v* (**-dd-**; *pt, pp* **shed**) **1** to lose sth by its falling off; to let sth fall or come off: [Vn] *Many trees shed their leaves in autumn.* ○ *This snake sheds its skin every year.* ○ *A lorry has shed its load on the motorway.* **2** (*fml*) to allow sth to pour out: [Vn] *shed tears* (ie cry) ○ *shed blood* (ie to injure or kill another person or other people). See also BLOODSHED. **3** to take or throw sth off; to remove or get rid of sb/sth: [Vn] *He shed his wet clothes and dried himself by the fire.* ○ *The duck's feathers shed water immediately.* ○ *Economic difficulties have forced many companies to shed staff.* ○ *This diet will help you to shed pounds* (ie weight) *in a matter of days.* ○ (*fig*) *You must learn to shed* (ie get rid of) *your inhibitions.* **4** ~ **sth** (**on/over sb/sth**) to spread or send sth out: [Vnpr] *The candles shed a soft glow over the room.* [also Vn]. **IDM** **cast/shed/throw light on sth** ⇨ LIGHT¹.

she'd /ʃiːd/ *short form* **1** she had. ⇨ note at HAVE. **2** she would. ⇨ WILL¹.

sheen /ʃiːn/ *n* [U] a smooth brightness; a shiny quality: *the sheen of silk* ○ *a shampoo to give your hair a beautiful sheen.*

sheep /ʃiːp/ *n* (*pl* unchanged) an animal with a thick coat kept on farms for its meat or its wool: *a flock of sheep* ○ *the bleating of sheep.* ⇨ picture. See also BLACK SHEEP, EWE, LAMB 1, RAM¹. **IDM** **count sheep** ⇨ COUNT¹. **like** '**sheep** too easily influenced

sheep

horn
fleece

ram
lamb
ewe

or led by others. **make** '**sheep's eyes at sb** (*infml*) to look at sb in a loving but foolish way. **one may/ might as well be hanged/hung for a sheep as a lamb** ⇨ HANG¹. **separate the sheep from the goats** ⇨ SEPARATE². **a wolf in sheep's clothing** ⇨ WOLF.

■ '**sheep-dip** *n* [U, C] a liquid which is used to kill insects, etc in a sheep's coat; the container in which sheep are put in order to treat them with this.

sheepdog /'ʃiːpdɒg/ *n* a dog trained to guard and control sheep; a type of dog bred originally for this purpose.

sheepfold /'ʃiːpfəʊld/ *n* an area in a field surrounded by a fence or wall where sheep are kept for safety.

sheepish /'ʃiːpɪʃ/ *adj* showing embarrassment because one has done sth wrong or foolish: *a sheepish grin* ○ *She came into the room looking rather sheepish.* ▶ **sheepishly** *adv*.

sheepskin /'ʃiːpskɪn/ *n* [U, C] the skin of a sheep with the wool still on it: *a sheepskin coat* ○ *sheepskin gloves.*

sheer¹ /ʃɪə(r)/ *adj* **1** [attrib] (often used for emphasis) complete; nothing more than: *sheer nonsense* ○ *a sheer waste of time* ○ *The sheer size of the building was enough to impress the visitors.* ○ *Her success was due to sheer hard work.* **2** [usu attrib] (of fabrics, etc) thin, light and almost transparent: *sheer nylon.* **3** very steep: *a sheer rock face/cliff* ○ *It's a sheer drop to the sea.*
▶ **sheer** *adv* straight up or down: *a cliff that rises sheer from the beach* ○ *The ground dropped away sheer at our feet.*

sheer² /ʃɪə(r)/ *v* **PHR V** ,**sheer a'way (from sth)** / ,**sheer 'off** to change direction suddenly, esp in order to avoid hitting sth: *The car sheered away, missing the lorry by inches.*

sheet¹ /ʃiːt/ *n* **1** a large rectangular (RECTANGLE) piece of thin cloth used on a bed. Sheets are often used in pairs, with one under the person sleeping and the other one over her or him: *put clean sheets on the bed.* **2(a)** a flat thin piece of any material, usu square or rectangular (RECTANGLE): *a sheet of glass/steel/plastic* ○ *sheet metal* (ie made into thin sheets). ⇨ note at PIECE¹. See also DUST-SHEET, FLY-SHEET. **(b)** a piece of paper for writing or printing on, etc, usu in a standard size: *a clean sheet of paper* (ie with no writing on it) ○ *a sheet of A4* ○ *Write each answer on a separate sheet.* ○ *Our free information sheet lists universities offering part-time courses.* See also BALANCE SHEET, BROADSHEET, CHARGE-SHEET, FACT-SHEET, NEWS-SHEET, SPREADSHEET, TIME SHEET. **3** a wide area of sth, covering the surface of sth else: *After the heavy frost the road was a sheet of ice.* **4** a wide mass of fire or water: *a sheet of flame* ○ *The rain came down in sheets* (ie very heavily). **IDM** **a clean sheet/slate** ⇨ CLEAN¹.
▶ **sheeting** *n* [U] **(a)** material, eg metal, plastic, etc, made into flat thin pieces: *a broken window covered with plastic sheeting* ○ *corrugated iron sheeting.* **(b)** material used for making sheets for beds.

■ ,**sheet 'lightning** *n* [U] lightning that appears as a broad area of light in the sky.

'**sheet music** *n* [U] music published on separate sheets that are not fastened together to form a book.

sheet² /ʃiːt/ *n* a rope or chain fastened to the lower corner of a sail to hold it and control the angle of the sail.

■ '**sheet anchor** *n* a person or thing that one depends on in a difficult situation: *The European Union can act as a sheet anchor for emerging democracies.*

sheikh (also **shaikh, sheik**) /ʃeɪk, ʃiːk/ *n* **1** an Arab leader; the head of an Arab village, tribe, etc. **2** a Muslim religious leader.
▶ **sheikhdom** /-dəm/ *n* an area of land ruled by a sheikh.

sheila /'ʃiːlə/ *n* (*Austral or NZ sl*) a girl or young woman.

shekel /'ʃekl/ *n* **1** [C] **(a)** the main unit of money in Israel. **(b)** an ancient silver coin used by the Jews. **2 shekels** [pl] (*infml joc*) money.

shelduck /'ʃeldʌk/ *n* (*pl* unchanged) a wild duck that lives on or near the coast.

shelf /ʃelf/ *n* (*pl* **shelves** /ʃelvz/) **1** a flat board, made eg of wood, metal or glass, fixed to a wall or forming part of a cupboard, etc for things to be placed on: *put up a shelf* ○ *the books on the top shelf* ○ *a shelf full of crockery* ○ *empty shelves in the supermarket.* **2** (*esp geology*) a thing resembling a shelf, esp a piece of rock projecting from a cliff or from the edge of a mass of land under the sea: *the continental shelf.* See also SHELVE². **IDM** **on the** '**shelf** (*infml*) **1** (of a person) treated as if no longer useful: *Retired people should not be made to feel left on the shelf.* **2** (*dated often sexist*) (esp of a woman who is not married) considered too old to be likely to get married: *Women used to think they were on the shelf at 30.*

■ '**shelf-life** *n* (*pl* **shelf-lives**) (usu *sing*) the length of time for which a stored item, esp food, remains in good condition: *packets of biscuits with a shelf-life of two or three weeks.*

shell /ʃel/ *n* **1(a)** [C, U] the hard outer covering of eggs, nuts, certain seeds and fruits, and also of certain animals: *Oysters, snails and tortoises all have shells.* ○ *collecting shells on the beach* ○ *walnut/ coconut/clam shells* ○ *broken pieces of shell.* ⇨ picture at NUT, SHELLFISH, SNAIL. See also EGGSHELL, SEA SHELL, TORTOISESHELL. **(b)** [C] an object resembling this: *pasta shells.* **2** [C] **(a)** the walls or outer structure of sth, eg a building or ship which is empty or destroyed inside: *Only the shell of the factory was left after the fire had been put out.* ○ (*fig*) *My life has been an empty shell since he died.* **(b)** any structure that forms a firm framework or outer covering: *the body shell of a car* ○ *The tunnel is lined with a concrete shell.* **3** [sing] the outward appearance of a person's character, mood, etc: *develop a shell of indifference.* **4** [C] **(a)** a metal case filled with explosive, to be fired from a large gun: *shell, mortar and sniper fire* ○ *The building was destroyed by an artillery shell.* Compare CARTRIDGE 1, SHOT¹ 4. **(b)** (*US*) = CARTRIDGE 1. **IDM** **come out of / go into, etc one's** '**shell** to become less/more shy or RESERVED; to start enjoying/avoiding the company of others: *She has really come out of her shell and is chatting to everyone.* ○ *Losing his job seems to have made him retire into his shell.*
▶ **shell** *v* **1** to remove the shell(1a) of sth: [Vn] *shell peas/peanuts/mussels* ○ *200g of shelled prawns.* **2** to fire shells (SHELL 4) at sb/sth: [Vn] *shell the enemy positions* [also V]. **PHR V** ,**shell 'out (sth) (for sth)** (*infml*) to pay money unwillingly: *The children expect me to shell out (the money) for their party.* **shelling** *n* [U] the firing of shells: *a night of heavy shelling.*

■ '**shell bean** *n* (*US*) a bean of which the seed is eaten and not the POD.

'**shell-shock** *n* [U] a nervous illness that can affect soldiers who have been in battle for a long time: *suffer from shell-shock.* '**shell-shocked** *adj* **1** suffering from shell-shock. **2** so shocked or confused that one is unable to think or act properly: *I felt totally shell-shocked when she told me he had died.*

'shell suit *n* a loose casual suit or single garment worn by men or women. Shell suits are made of a light, slightly shiny, material and are often brightly coloured. Compare TRACK SUIT.

she'll /ʃiːl/ *short form* she will. ⇨ WILL¹.

shellac /ʃəˈlæk, ˈʃelæk/ *n* [U] a substance similar to plastic in the form of thin sheets or flakes (FLAKE), used in making VARNISH(1a).

shellfire /ˈʃelfaɪə(r)/ *n* [U] attacks or explosions due to the firing of shells (SHELL 4): *The town came under regular/heavy shellfire.*

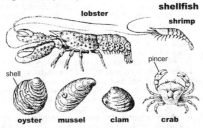

shellfish /ˈʃelfɪʃ/ *n* (*pl* unchanged) a type of water creature with a shell, esp one of the edible types: *Oysters, mussels, crabs and shrimps are all shellfish.* ⇨ picture.

shelter /ˈʃeltə(r)/ *n* **1** [U] ~ (**from sth**) the condition of being protected or kept safe, eg from rain, danger or attack: *Human beings need food, shelter and warmth.* ○ **take shelter** *from the rain* ○ *people desperately seeking shelter from the gunfire* ○ *She gave shelter to an escaped prisoner.* **2** [C] (often in compounds) (**a**) a structure built to give protection, esp from the weather or from attack: *They built a rough shelter from old pieces of wood and cardboard.* ○ *a 'bike shelter* (eg at a school, for pupils to leave their bicycles in) ○ *an 'air-raid/a 'fallout shelter.* See also BUS SHELTER. (**b**) a building provided, eg by a charity, for those in need, eg people without a home or badly treated animals: *a night shelter for the homeless* ○ *an animal shelter.*

▶ **shelter** *v* **1** (Vn, Vnpr) ~ **sb/sth** (**from sth/sb**) (**a**) to provide sb/sth with protection from the weather, danger, etc: [Vn] *The valley is sheltered by the mountains to the north.* ○ *shelter an escaped prisoner in one's home* [Vnpr] *trees that shelter a house from the wind* ○ *The wall sheltered the soldiers from the gunfire.* (**b**) to prevent sb/sth from having to face a difficult or unpleasant situation: [Vnpr] *He is trying to shelter his boss from criticism.* ○ *Is our country's industry sheltered from foreign competition?* [also Vn]. **2** ~ (**from sth**) to find a place that gives shelter; to take shelter: [Vpr] *shelter under the trees/behind a wall* ○ *shelter from the rain* ○ *political refugees sheltering in the US embassy* [also V]. **sheltered** *adj* **1** (of a place) not greatly exposed to bad weather: *find a sheltered spot for a picnic* ○ *a sheltered region.* **2** (*sometimes derog*) kept away from or not exposed to unpleasant circumstances, harmful influences, or the normal difficulties of life: *He had a sheltered life/childhood.* **3** (of houses or flats) designed for people, esp old people, to live fairly independently in, but with staff always available to help or look after them if necessary: *sheltered housing/accommodation for the elderly/disabled.*

shelve¹ /ʃelv/ *v* **1** to decide not to proceed with a plan, project, etc for a time, or to abandon it completely: [Vn] *Plans for a new theatre have had to be shelved because of lack of money.* **2** to put sth on a shelf or shelves, eg books in a library: [Vn] *The books had been shelved in the wrong order.*

▶ **shelving** *n* [U] shelves, or material for making them: *wooden shelving.*

shelve² /ʃelv/ *v* (of land) to slope downwards: [Vpr, Vp] *The beach shelves gently (down) to the sea.* See also SHELF 2.

shelves *pl* of SHELF.

shenanigans /ʃɪˈnænɪɡənz/ *n* [pl] (*infml*) **1** secret or dishonest activity: *political/financial/sexual shenanigans among the country's élite.* **2** playful tricks; MISCHIEF.

shepherd /ˈʃepəd/ *n* (*fem* **shepherdess** /ˌʃepəˈdes, ˈʃepədəs/) a person who looks after sheep.

▶ **shepherd** *v* to guide or direct people as if they were sheep: [Vnpr] *A guide shepherded us into the museum.* [Vnp] *The children were shepherded around by two teachers.*

■ **,shepherd's 'pie** (*Brit* also **,cottage 'pie**) *n* [U, C] a dish of minced (MINCE 1) meat baked with mashed (MASH *v*) potatoes on top.

sherbet /ˈʃɜːbət/ *n* [C, U] **1** (*Brit*) a sweet powder used to make FIZZY drinks or eaten on its own: *a bag of sherbet.* **2** (*US*) = SORBET.

sherd = SHARD.

sheriff /ˈʃerɪf/ *n* **1** (often **,High 'Sheriff**) (*Brit*) the chief officer appointed by the king or queen in counties and certain cities of England and Wales, with legal and ceremonial duties. **2** (*US*) an elected officer responsible for keeping law and order in a county.

sherry /ˈʃeri/ *n* (**a**) [U, C] a type of strong, yellow or brown wine, originally from southern Spain: *sweet/dry sherry* ○ *high-quality sherries* ○ *a sherry-glass* (ie a small narrow type of wine glass). (**b**) [C] a glass of this: *have a sherry before dinner.*

she's *short form* **1** /ʃiːz, ʃiz/ she is. ⇨ note at BE². **2** /ʃiːz/ she has. ⇨ note at HAVE.

Shetland /ˈʃetlənd/ *n* **1** (also **the Shetlands** [pl]) a group of islands off the north coast of Scotland. **2** (also **,Shetland 'wool**) [U] a soft fine wool from Shetland sheep: *a Shetland jumper.*

■ **,Shetland 'pony** *n* a small strong breed of pony with a rough coat.

shibboleth /ˈʃɪbəleθ/ *n* an old idea, principle or phrase that is no longer regarded by many as important or relevant: *elderly politicians still clinging to the outmoded shibboleths of party doctrine.*

shied *pt, pp* of SHY¹ *v*, SHY².

shield /ʃiːld/ *n* **1**(**a**) (esp formerly) a large piece of armour carried on the arm to protect the body when fighting. (**b**) a TROPHY(1) in the form of a shield: *win the school boxing shield.* (**c**) a drawing or model of a shield displaying a coat of arms (COAT). ⇨ picture at COAT OF ARMS. **2** ~ (**against sth**) a person or thing used to protect sb/sth, esp by forming a barrier: *The gunman used the hostages as a (human) shield.* ○ *This car polish is an effective shield against rust.* ○ (*fig*) *hide behind the shield of diplomatic immunity.* **3** a plate or screen that protects a machine or the person using it from damage or injury: *the shield round the handle of a chainsaw.*

▶ **shield** *v* **1**(**a**) ~ **sb/sth** (**against/from sth/sb**) to protect sb/sth by forming a barrier: [Vnpr] *shield sth from view* (ie prevent it being seen) ○ *shield one's eyes (from the sun) with one's hand* ○ *The police officer shielded the girl with his body.* ○ *The ozone layer shields the earth against/from harmful radiation.* [also Vn]. (**b**) to put a special plate, covering, etc over or around sth that could be dangerous: [Vn] *The gas flame should be properly shielded.* **2** ~ **sb** (**against/from sb/sth**) to protect sb from a harmful or unpleasant experience or influence: *You can't shield her from prosecution.* ○ *I tried to shield him against prying journalists.*

shift¹ /ʃɪft/ *v* **1** ~ (**sth**) (**from…**) (**to…**) (**a**) to change in emphasis, direction or FOCUS(1): [Vpr] *The*

---

action of the novel shifts from Paris to London. ○ *The balance of opinion has shifted away from state intervention in industry.* [V] *shifting alliances.* **(b)** to change the emphasis, direction or focus of sth: [Vnpr] *shift our resources/priorities to another project* ○ *Don't try to shift the responsibility from others.* **2** ~ (sth) (about/around) to move or move sth from one place or position to another: [V] *The cargo has shifted.* [Vp] *The tools slide around in the boot every time the car turns a corner.* [Vpr] *The wind shifted from east to north.* [Vn] *stage-hands shifting scenery* [Vnp] *The teacher shifted the desks around.* [Vnpr] *Help me shift the sofa away from the fire.* **3 (a)** to change or keep changing the position of one's body, eg because one is nervous or uncomfortable: [Vpr] *shift from one foot to the other* (ie while standing) [Vadv] *The audience shifted uneasily in their seats.* [also Vn]. **(b)** ~ **(oneself)** (*infml*) to move or leave a place: [V, Vn] *That's my seat you're sitting in, so shift (yourself)!* **(c)** (*Brit infml*) to move quickly: [V] *You'll have to shift if you want to get there by nine o'clock.* ○ *That car can really shift!* **4** ~ **out of sth / into sth**; ~ **up/down** (*US*) to change gear in a vehicle: [Vn] *shifting gear* [Vpr] *shift out of first into second* [Vp] *Shift up when you reach 30 mph.* **IDM** **shift one's 'ground** to change the basis of one's argument or change one's opinions during a discussion. **(the) ,shifting 'sands (of sth)** a situation that keeps changing, so that it is difficult to make sense of it or feel confident about it: *the shifting sands of world affairs.* **PHRV** **,shift for one'self** to manage without help from others: *When their parents died, the children had to shift for themselves.*

shift² /ʃɪft/ *n* **1** [C] ~ **(in sth)** a change of place, position, direction or tendency: *a gradual shift in the population away from the countryside to the towns* ○ *a shift in the direction of the wind* ○ *shifts in public opinion* ○ *a shift of emphasis/resources.* **2** [C] **(a)** a period of time worked by a group of workers who start work as another group finishes: *be on the 'day/'night shift at the factory* ○ *work an eight-hour shift* ○ *working in shifts* ○ *shift workers/work.* **(b)** [CGp] the workers in such a group: *The night shift has/have just come off duty.* Compare RELAY 2, RELIEF¹ 5. **3** a mechanism on a TYPEWRITER or computer KEYBOARD(1a) that allows capital letters or a different set of characters to be typed: *a 'shift-key.* **4** a woman's straight narrow dress.

shiftless /'ʃɪftləs/ *adj* (*derog*) lazy and lacking ambition.

shifty /'ʃɪfti/ *adj* (*infml derog*) seeming to be dishonest, eg because of the way one behaves; suspicious(2): *shifty eyes* ○ *He gave me a shifty look.* ○ *He looks rather a shifty character.* ▶ **shiftily** /-ɪli/ *adv*.

shilling /'ʃɪlɪŋ/ *n* **1** (until 1971) a British coin worth 12 old pennies; one 20th of a pound. **2** the basic unit of money in Kenya, Uganda and Tanzania.

shilly-shally /'ʃɪli ʃæli/ *v* (*pt, pp* **-shallied**) (*infml derog*) to be unable to make a decision; to hesitate: [V, Vp] *Stop shilly-shallying (about) and make your mind up.*

shim /ʃɪm/ *n* (*techn*) a thin strip of material used in machinery to make parts fit.

shimmer /'ʃɪmə(r)/ *v* to shine with a soft unsteady light: [V] *moonlight shimmering on the lake* ○ *the shimmering blue waters of the Mediterranean* ○ *The surface of the road shimmered in the heat.* ▶ **shimmer** *n* [U, sing] a shimmering light: *the shimmer of pearls/silk.*

shin /ʃɪn/ *n* the front part of the leg below the knee: *get kicked on the shin.* ⇨ picture at HUMAN. ▶ **shin** *v* (**-nn-**) **PHRV** **shin up/down (sth)** to climb up/down sth quickly, using the hands and legs to grip it: *shin up a tree/down the drainpipe.*

■ **'shin-bone** (also **tibia**) *n* the inner and usu larger of the two bones from the knee to the ankle.

'shin-guard (*Brit* also **'shin-pad**) *n* a pad worn to protect the shin when playing football, etc.

shindig /'ʃɪndɪg/ *n* (*infml*) **1** a lively and noisy party. **2** = SHINDY.

shindy /'ʃɪndi/ (also **shindig**) *n* (*dated infml*) (usu *sing*, only in the expression shown) a noisy disturbance or fight: *kick up a shindy.*

shine /ʃaɪn/ *v* (*pt, pp* **shone** /ʃɒn; *US* ʃəʊn/ or, in sense 3, **shined**) **1** to give out or reflect light; to be bright: [V] *I polished the glasses until they shone.* ○ *The sun was shining brightly.* [Vpr] *A streetlight was shining through the window.* ○ (*fig*) *His face shone with excitement.* [also Vp]. **2** to aim or point the light of a TORCH(1), etc in a specified direction: [Vpr] *The police shone a searchlight on the house.* [Vnadv] *Shine the torch over here.* **3** to polish sth: [Vn] *shine shoes/silver.* **4** ~ **(at/in sth)** to be excellent at sth: [V] *His speech at the conference gave him an opportunity to shine in front of the other delegates.* ○ *Her courage is a shining example to us all.* [Vpr] *He didn't shine at games.* **IDM** **a knight in shining armour** ⇨ KNIGHT. **make hay while the sun shines** ⇨ HAY. **rise and shine** ⇨ RISE². ▶ **shine** *n* [sing] the quality of reflecting light; brightness: *a shampoo that gives the hair a healthy shine* ○ *Give your shoes a good shine.* **IDM** **come rain, come shine**; **rain or shine** ⇨ RAIN¹. **take a 'shine to sb/sth** (*infml*) to begin to like sb/sth as soon as one sees or meets them/it: *I think that dog has taken a shine to me — it follows me everywhere.* **shiny** *adj* (**-ier, -iest**) (esp of a smooth surface) reflecting light; polished: *a shiny car* ○ *shiny black shoes* ○ *All the glasses are clean and shiny.*

shingle¹ /'ʃɪŋgl/ *n* [U] (*Brit*) a mass of small stones on a shore by the sea: *a shingle beach.* ▶ **shingly** /'ʃɪŋgli/ *adj*: *a shingly beach.*

shingle² /'ʃɪŋgl/ *n* (often *pl*) a small flat piece of wood used as a covering on roofs and walls. ⇨ picture at HOUSE¹. ▶ **shingled** *adj* covered with shingles.

shingles /'ʃɪŋglz/ *n* [sing *v*] a disease that affects the nerves and produces a band of painful spots on the skin. Compare HERPES.

ship¹ /ʃɪp/ *n* (often in compounds) a large boat carrying people or goods by sea: *a 'sailing-ship* ○ *a 'cargo ship* ○ *on board ship* ○ *go by ship* ○ *board a ship for India.* See also SPACESHIP, TROOP-SHIP, WARSHIP. **IDM** **jump ship** ⇨ JUMP¹.

ship² /ʃɪp/ *v* (**-pp-**) **1** to send or transport sth/sb, esp in a ship: [Vn] *Are the goods to be flown or shipped?* [Vnpr] *We ship goods to any part of the world.* [Vnp] *Fresh supplies are being shipped out by truck.* **2** (of a boat) to take in water over the side, eg in a storm: [Vn] *The canoe began to ship water.* **PHRV** **,ship sb/ sth 'off** (*infml*) to send sb/sth away to a place: *The children were shipped off to boarding-school at an early age.*

-ship *suff* (with *ns* forming *ns*) **1** the state of being sb; a person's status or office: *'friendship* ○ *'ownership* ○ *pro'fessorship.* **2** skill or ability as sth: *mu'sicianship* ○ *'scholarship.* See also -MANSHIP.

shipboard /'ʃɪpbɔːd/ *adj* [attrib] used or occurring on a ship: *shipboard life/routine.*

shipbuilder /'ʃɪpbɪldə(r)/ *n* a person or company that builds ships. ▶ **shipbuilding** *n* [U]: *the shipbuilding industry.*

shipload /'ʃɪpləʊd/ *n* as much cargo or as many passengers as a ship can carry: *set sail with a shipload of grain.*

shipmate /'ʃɪpmeɪt/ *n* a sailor on the same ship as another. See also MATE¹ 3.

shipment /'ʃɪpmənt/ *n* **1** [U] the process of transporting goods, esp by ship: *goods ready for shipment*

○ *arrange shipment by air.* **2** [C] a cargo or goods transported, esp by ship: *a shipment of grain for West Africa* ○ *food shipments.*

shipowner /ˈʃɪpəʊnə(r)/ *n* a person who owns a ship or ships.

shipper /ˈʃɪpə(r)/ *n* a person or company that arranges for goods to be shipped.

shipping /ˈʃɪpɪŋ/ *n* [U] **1** ships in general: *The canal is now open to shipping.* ○ *busy shipping lanes* ○ *the shipping forecast* (ie a report on the weather conditions at sea). **2** the transport of goods by ship: *the shipping of oil from the Middle East.*

shipshape /ˈʃɪpʃeɪp/ *adj* [usu pred] in good order; tidy: *It took us a long time to get the room shipshape after the party.*

shipwreck /ˈʃɪprek/ *n* [C, U] the loss or destruction of a ship at sea because of a storm, hitting rocks, etc: *salvage cargo from a shipwreck* ○ *suffer shipwreck.*
▶ **shipwreck** *v* (usu passive) to cause sb to suffer shipwreck: [Vn] *shipwrecked sailors* ○ *be shipwrecked on a desert island.*

shipyard /ˈʃɪpjɑːd/ *n* a place where ships are built or repaired: *shipyard workers.*

shire /ˈʃaɪə(r)/ *or, in compounds,* -ʃə(r)/ *n* (*Brit*) **1** [C] (*arch*) a county (now chiefly used in the names of certain counties, eg *Hampshire, Yorkshire*). **2 the shires** (also **the shire counties**) [pl] certain counties in central England which are mainly rural.
■ **ˈshire-horse** *n* a large powerful breed of horse used for pulling loads.

shirk /ʃɜːk/ *v* (*derog*) to avoid doing work, one's duty, etc because one is lazy, cowardly, not interested, etc: [V] *Stop shirking and get on with your work!* [Vn] *He never shirks responsibility.* [V.ing] *She always shirks making difficult decisions.* ▶ **shirker** *n*.

shirt /ʃɜːt/ *n* a piece of clothing made of cotton, etc and worn, esp by men, on the upper part of the body: *put on a clean shirt* ○ *wear a shirt and tie* ○ *a short-sleeved shirt.* See also NIGHTSHIRT, STUFFED SHIRT, SWEATSHIRT, T-SHIRT. ⇨ picture at JACKET.
IDM **keep one's ˈshirt on** (*infml*) (usu imperative) not to lose one's temper: *Keep your shirt on! It was only a joke.* **put one's ˈshirt on sb/sth** (*sl*) to bet all one's money on sb/sth: *He has put his shirt on the team winning the trophy.*
■ **ˈshirt-front** *n* the front part of a shirt, esp the stiff front part of a formal white shirt: *a starched shirt-front.*
ˈshirt-sleeve *n* a sleeve of a shirt. **IDM** **in (one's) ˈshirt-sleeves** not wearing a jacket over one's shirt: *It was a warm day and most of the spectators were in (their) shirt-sleeves.*
ˈshirt-tail *n* the part of a shirt that extends below the waist.

shirty /ˈʃɜːti/ *adj* ~ (**with sb/sth**) (*infml esp Brit*) angry; bad-tempered: *Don't get shirty with me!*

shit /ʃɪt/ *n* (*sl usu* ⚠) **1** [U] solid waste matter from the bowels; EXCREMENT: *a pile of dog shit on the pavement.* **2** [sing] an act of emptying solid waste matter from the bowels: *have/need a shit.* **3** [U] stupid remarks or writing; nonsense: *You do talk a load of shit!* See also BULLSHIT. **4** [C] (*derog*) an unpleasant person or one regarded with contempt: *He's an arrogant little shit.* **IDM** **in the ˈshit** in trouble: *I'll be in the shit if I don't get this work finished today.* **beat, kick, etc the ˈshit out of sb** to attack sb very violently so as to injure them. **not give a ˈshit (about sb/sth)** not to care at all: *He doesn't give a shit about anybody else.* **scare the shit out of sb** ⇨ SCARE.
▶ **shit** *v* (-tt-; *pt, pp* **shitted** or **shat** /ʃæt/) (*sl usu* ⚠) **1** [V] to empty solid waste from the bowels. [also Vn]. **2** [Vn] '~ **oneself** (**a**) to empty solid waste from the bowels accidentally. (**b**) to be very frightened.

shit *interj* (*sl usu* ⚠) (used to express anger, annoyance, disgust, etc): *Shit! I've missed the train!*
■ **ˌshit ˈscared** *adj* [pred] (*sl usu* ⚠) very frightened.

shitty /ˈʃɪti/ *adj* (*sl usu* ⚠) **1** very unpleasant; of very poor quality: *I'm not going to eat this shitty food.* **2** mean; very unfair: *What a shitty way to treat a friend!*

shiver /ˈʃɪvə(r)/ *v* ~ (**with sth**) to shake, esp because one feels cold or is frightened: [Vpr] *shivering with cold* ○ *She shivered in horror (at the thought).* [V] *The icy wind made him shiver.*
▶ **shiver** *n* **1** [C] an act of shaking because one is cold, frightened or excited: *The gruesome sight sent a shiver/sent shivers down my spine.* ○ *He gave a shiver of excitement.* **2 the shivers** [pl] a fit of shaking, because of fever or fear: *lying in bed with the shivers* ○ *Having to make a speech always gives me the shivers.*
shivery /ˈʃɪvəri/ *adj* shaking with cold, fear or illness: *feel cold and shivery.*

shoal¹ /ʃəʊl/ *n* (**a**) a large number of fish swimming together: *a shoal of herring* ○ *swimming in shoals.* (**b**) people or things in large numbers: *shoals of tourists/complaints/letters.*

shoal² /ʃəʊl/ *n* a shallow place in the sea, a bank of sand, etc, esp one that can be seen when the water level is low: *run aground on a shoal* ○ *steer away from the shoals.*

shock¹ /ʃɒk/ *n* **1** [C] a feeling caused by sth very unpleasant happening suddenly; the event, etc that causes this: *The news of his mother's death was a terrible shock to him.* ○ *The result of the election came as a shock to us all.* ○ *It gave me quite a shock to be told I was seriously ill.* See also CULTURE SHOCK. **2** [U] (*medical*) the state of extreme weakness caused by a physical injury that makes the volume or pressure of blood too low to circulate properly: *be in/go into shock through losing a lot of blood* ○ *suffer from shock after an accident* ○ *What is the correct medical treatment for shock?* See also SHELL-SHOCK. **3** [C] a violent shaking movement caused eg by an explosion: *earthquake shocks* ○ *The bumper is designed to absorb shock on impact.* **4** [C] = ELECTRIC SHOCK: *If you touch this live wire, you'll get/give yourself a shock.*
■ **ˈshock absorber** *n* a device fitted to a motor vehicle to reduce the effects of moving over rough ground. ⇨ picture at CAR.
ˈshock tactics *n* [pl] sudden, violent or offensive action taken for a purpose: *use shock tactics to get attention.*
ˈshock treatment (also **ˈshock therapy**) *n* [U] a way of treating mental illness by giving electric shocks (ELECTRIC) or a drug that has a similar effect.
ˈshock-troops *n* [pl] troops specially trained for violent attacks.
ˈshock wave *n* (esp *pl*) a movement of very high air pressure caused eg by an explosion: *shock waves transmitted by earthquakes.*

shock² /ʃɒk/ *v* **1** to cause an unpleasant feeling of surprise in sb: [Vn] *I was shocked at/by the news of her death.* [Vn.to inf] *It shocked me to hear of his illness.* **2** to offend or disgust sb: [V, Vn] *films intended to shock (the public)* [Vn.to inf] *He was shocked to hear his child swearing.* [Vn] *I'm not easily shocked, but that book really is obscene.*
▶ **shocker** *n* (*infml often joc*) a person or thing that is shocking, unacceptable or very bad: *I was a real shocker when I was young.* ○ *That film was an absolute shocker!*

shocking *adj* **1** very offensive, annoying or unacceptable: *shocking behaviour/words/insults* ○ *What she did was so shocking that I can hardly describe it.* **2** very unpleasant and sudden: *shocking news.* **3** (*infml*) very bad: *shocking weather* ○ *The food here is shocking.* **shockingly** *adv* **1** (*infml*) extremely: *a*

[V.speech] = verb + direct speech   [V.*that*] = verb + *that* clause   [V.*wh*] = verb + *who, how,* etc clause

shockingly expensive cigar. **2** very badly: *behave shockingly.* ˌ**shocking** ˈ**pink** *adj, n* a very bright pink colour: *wear a ˌshocking pink ˈdress.*

shock³ /ʃɒk/ *n* (usu **shock of hair**) a rough thick mass of hair on the head.

shockproof /ˈʃɒkpruːf/ *adj* (esp of a watch) designed to resist damage when knocked, dropped, etc.

shod¹ *pt, pp* of SHOE *v.*

shod² /ʃɒd/ *adj* (of a person) wearing shoes of a specified type or quality: *well shod for wet weather.*

shoddy /ˈʃɒdi/ *adj* (-**ier**, -**iest**) (*derog*) of poor quality; done or made badly: *shoddy goods/ workmanship.* ▶ **shoddily** *adv*: *shoddily made.* **shoddiness** *n* [U].

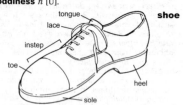

shoe

shoe /ʃuː/ *n* **1** an outer covering for a person's foot, usu made of leather or plastic: *a pair of shoes* ○ *walking shoes* ○ *put on/take off your (tennis) shoes* ○ *a shoe brush/shop* ○ *shoe polish.* ▷ picture. Compare BOOT¹ 1, SANDAL. See also SNOWSHOE. **2** = HORSESHOE. **IDM** **be in / put oneself in sb's shoes** to be in/ imagine oneself to be in sb else's position: *I wouldn't like to be in your shoes when they find out what you've done.* **fill sb's shoes** ▷ FILL¹. **if ˌI was/were in** ˈ**your shoes/place** (used to introduce a piece of advice): *If I were in your shoes he'd soon know what I thought of him.* **if the shoe fits** ▷ IF THE CAP FITS (CAP). **shake in one's shoes** ▷ SHAKE¹. **step into sb's shoes** ▷ STEP¹.
▶ **shoe** *v* (*pt, pp* **shod** /ʃɒd/) to fit a horse with a shoe or shoes: [Vn] *a blacksmith shoeing a pony.*

shoebox /ˈʃuːbɒks/ *n* **1** a box in which shoes are packed. **2** a very small room in which to live or work: *They put me in a shoebox of an office.*

shoehorn /ˈʃuːhɔːn/ *n* a device with a curved surface that is used for helping the heel to slide easily into a shoe.

shoelace /ˈʃuːleɪs/ (also **lace**) *n* a long piece of cord used to fasten a shoe: *a pair of shoelaces* ○ *tie/untie your shoelaces.* See also BOOTLACE.

shoemaker /ˈʃuːmeɪkə(r)/ *n* a person whose job is making or repairing shoes and boots. ▶ ˈ**shoemaking** *n* [U].

shoeshine /ˈʃuːʃaɪn/ *n* (*esp US*) an act of polishing sb's shoes, esp by sb whose job is to do this: *a shoeshine boy.*

shoestring /ˈʃuːstrɪŋ/ *n* (*esp US*) a SHOELACE. **IDM** **on a** ˈ**shoestring** (*infml*) using very little money: *travel round the world on a shoestring.*
▶ **shoestring** *adj* [attrib] (*infml*) spending very little money: *a shoestring budget.*

shone *pt, pp* of SHINE.

shoo /ʃuː/ *interj* (said to make animals or people, esp children, go away): *Shoo, all of you, I'm busy.*
▶ **shoo** *v* (*pt, pp* **shooed**) to make sb/sth go away by saying 'shoo' and often also waving one's hands or arms: [Vnp, Vnpr] *He shooed the children out (of the shop).*

shoo-in /ˈʃuː ɪn/ *n* (*US infml*) a candidate, team, etc that is thought certain to win.

shook *pt* of SHAKE¹.

shoot¹ /ʃuːt/ *v* (*pt, pp* **shot** /ʃɒt/) **1** ~ (**sth**) (**at sb/ sth**); ~ **sth** (**from sth**); ~ **sth** (**off**) to fire a gun or other weapon at sb/sth; to fire sth, eg a bullet or

missile from a gun, etc at sb/sth: [V] *Don't shoot — I surrender.* [Vn] *The guards were ordered to* **shoot on sight** *anyone trying to escape* (ie shoot them as soon as they saw them). [Vnpr] *He shot an arrow from his bow.* ○ *He shot his way out of the post office.* [Vpr] *troops shooting at the enemy* [Vnp] *shoot off several rounds of ammunition* [V.to inf] *The police only rarely* **shoot to kill** (ie try to kill the people they shoot at). **2** to kill or wound a person or an animal with a bullet, etc: [Vn] *She went out shooting rabbits.* ○ *He shot himself during a fit of depression.* [Vnpr] *One of the robbers was shot in the leg by police.* [Vn-adj] *Three people were shot dead during the robbery.* **3** to damage or remove sth by shooting: [Vnpr] *The gun/gunman shot a hole in the door.* [Vnp] *They shot the lock off.* **4** to be able to use a gun or similar weapon skilfully: [V, Vadv] *Can you shoot (well)?* [Vn] *Do you know how to shoot a pistol?* [Vadv] *learn to shoot straight.* **5** (of a gun or other weapon) to fire bullets, etc: [V, Vn] *This is just a toy gun — it doesn't shoot (real bullets).* [Vadv] *Get a rifle that shoots straight.* **6** to hunt esp birds and kill them with a gun, esp as a sport: [Vn] *shoot pheasants* [V] *go shooting.* **7**(**a**) to move or make sb/sth move suddenly or quickly in the specified direction: [Vpr] *The sports car shot past us.* ○ *A plane shot across the sky.* ○ *He shot out of the door after her.* [Vp] *She shot ahead on the last lap.* ○ *Flames were shooting up through the roof.* [Vnpr] *The driver was shot through the windscreen by the impact.* ▷ note at WHIZ. (**b**) (of pain) to move suddenly and quickly and be very sharp: [V] *have a shooting pain in the back* [Vpr] *The pain shot up her arm.* (**c**) ~ **sth at sb** (no passive) to direct sth at sb suddenly or quickly: [Vnpr] *journalists shooting questions at the candidates* [Vnpr, Vnn] *She shot an angry glance at him/shot him an angry glance.* **8** (*esp cinema*) to photograph or film sb/sth: [V] *Cameras ready? OK, shoot!* [Vn] *Where was the film shot?* ○ *shoot a car chase* [Vnpr] *The movie was shot in black and white.* [Vn.ing] *shoot a woman riding a horse.* **9** ~ (**at sth**) (in football, hockey, etc) to kick or hit the ball in an attempt to score a goal: [V, Vpr] *He should have shot (at goal) instead of passing.* **10** (*infml*) (in golf) to make a certain score in a complete round³(3b) or competition: [Vn] *She shot (a) 75 in the first round.* **11** (*esp US*) to play certain games: [Vn] *shoot pool.* **12** (*infml esp US*) (only imperative) to say what one wishes to say: [V] *You want to tell me something? OK, shoot!* **13** (*sl*) (no passive) to INJECT(1) a drug directly into one's blood: [Vn] *shoot heroin.* **14** (of a boat or a person in a boat) to move quickly through sth: [Vn] *shooting the rapids.* **IDM** **be/get** ˈ**shot of sth/sb** (*Brit infml*) to have sth no longer: *I'll be glad to get shot of this useless car.* **shoot one's** ˈ**bolt** (*infml*) to make one's final effort to achieve sth's aim. **shoot the** ˈ**breeze** (*US infml*) to have a casual conversation: *We sat around in the bar, shooting the breeze.* ˌ**shoot it** ˈ**out (with sb)** (*infml*) to fight against sb with guns, esp until one person or side is killed or captured by the other: *The gang decided to shoot it out with the police.* See also SHOOT-OUT. ˌ**shoot one's** ˈ**mouth off (about sth)** (*infml*) **1** to boast: *He's always shooting his mouth off about his success with women.* **2** to reveal sth that one should not reveal: *It's a secret, so don't go shooting your mouth off about it.* **shoot the** ˈ**works** (*US infml*) to gamble all one's money, resources, etc. **PHRV** ˌ**shoot sb/sth** ˈ**down 1** to make sb/sth fall to the ground by shooting them/it: *Several planes were shot down by enemy fire.* **2** to destroy or be very critical of sb's ideas, opinions, etc: *I suppose you'll shoot me down when I say this, but I think you're wrong and he's right.* ○ *His latest theory has been shot down in flames.* ˌ**shoot** ˈ**up 1** to grow very quickly: *Their kids have shot up since I last saw them.* **2** to rise suddenly by a large amount: *Ticket prices shot up last year.* ˌ**shoot sth** ˈ**up 1** to cause great damage to sth by shooting: *The gang-sters ran into the bar and started shooting it up.* **2** (*sl*) to INJECT(1) a drug directly into one's blood: *addicts shooting up heroin.*

▶ **shooting** *n* **1** [C, U] the shooting or killing of sb with a gun: *The number of shootings during rob-beries is increasing.* ○ *the shooting of unarmed civilians.* **2** [U] the sport of shooting guns at targets or to kill birds, animals, etc: *a shooting club* ○ *the shooting season* ○ *He enjoys riding, fishing and shoot-ing.* **'shooting-gallery** *n* a building or room where people shoot guns or rifles (RIFLE¹) for practice or to win prizes. **'shooting match** *n* IDM **the whole shooting match** ⇨ WHOLE. **,shooting 'star** (also **falling star**) *n* a small METEOR that burns as it enters the earth's atmosphere, appearing as a bright star travelling quickly across the sky. **'shooting-stick** *n* a stick with a sharp point at one end for sticking into the ground and a handle which opens to form a small seat at the other end.

■ **'shoot-out** *n* a battle fought with guns, esp until one person or side is killed or captured by the other: *The robbery led to a shoot-out between the robbers and the police.* See also PENALTY SHOOT-OUT.

shoot² /ʃuːt/ *n* **1** a new young growth(3) on a plant, bush or tree: *healthy green shoots* ○ *bamboo shoots.* **2** (*esp Brit*) an occasion when a group of people hunt and shoot esp birds for sport: *members of a grouse shoot.* **3** an occasion when a professional photo-grapher takes photographs for a particular purpose: *a shoot for a calendar.*

shooter *n* (esp in compound *n*s) a person or weapon that shoots. See also PEASHOOTER, SHARPSHOOTER, SIX-SHOOTER, TROUBLESHOOTER.

shop /ʃɒp/ *n* **1(a)** (*US* also **store**) a building or part of a building where goods or services are sold to the public: *a butcher's/chemist's shop* ○ *go to the shops* ○ *serve in a shop.* See also BOOKSHOP, CORNER SHOP. **(b)** (*US*) a small department of a large shop where spe-cial goods or services are sold to the public: *They have a little shop where they sell their handicrafts.* **2** (also **workshop**) (esp in compounds) a place where things are manufactured or repaired: *a ma'chine shop* ○ *a 'paint shop* (eg where cars are painted). IDM **all over the place/shop** ⇨ PLACE¹. **a bull in a china shop** ⇨ BULL¹. **,set up 'shop** to start a business: *She set up shop as a bookseller in the High Street.* **shut up shop** ⇨ SHUT. **talk shop** ⇨ TALK¹.

▶ **shop** *v* (**-pp-**) **1** ~ (**for sth**) (esp in the continuous tenses and with *go*) to go to a shop or shops to buy things: [V] *go shopping every day* ○ *She's gone shop-ping.* [Vpr] *I'm shopping for Christmas presents.* **2** (*Brit sl*) to tell the police about sb who has done sth illegal: [Vn] *The gang leader was shopped by a police informer.* PHRV **,shop a'round (for sth)** (*infml*) to search carefully for goods or services that are the best value or the most suitable: *shop around for the best deal on flights* ○ *Don't buy the first car you see — shop around a bit.* **shopper** *n* a person who is shopping: *crowds of Christmas shoppers.* **shopping** *n* [U] **1** the activity of shopping: *I'm going to do the/my shopping this afternoon.* ○ *a 'shopping bag/ basket.* See also WINDOW-SHOPPING. **2** goods bought in shops, esp food and household goods: *put the shopping in the car.* **'shopping centre** *n* a place where there are many shops close together, esp one that is specially planned and built. **'shopping mall** (also **mall**) *n* (*esp US*) a usu covered area that con-tains many shops and is closed to traffic.

■ **'shop assistant** (*Brit*) (*US* **sales clerk**) *n* a per-son who serves customers in a shop.

,shop-'floor *n* [sing] **1** the area in a factory where goods are made, in contrast with the offices, etc: *working **on the shop-floor*** ○ *a shop-floor worker.* **2** the workers in a factory, contrasted with the man-

agement: *How does the shop-floor feel about these changes?*

'shop-soiled (*Brit*) (*US* **'shopworn**) *adj* dirty or not in perfect condition as a result of being displayed or handled in a shop: *a sale of shop-soiled goods at half price.*

,shop-'steward *n* a trade union (TRADE¹) official elected by other members to represent them.

shopfront /'ʃɒpfrʌnt/ *n* the outside of a shop that faces the street.

shopkeeper /'ʃɒpkiːpə(r)/ (*US* also **'storekeeper**) *n* a person who owns or manages a shop, usu a small one.

shoplift /'ʃɒplɪft/ *v* to steal goods from a shop by deliberately leaving without paying for them: [V] *She started to shoplift as a fifteen-year-old.* ▶ **'shop-lifter** *n*: *Shoplifters will be prosecuted* (ie on a sign in a shop). **'shoplifting** *n* [U]: *be arrested for shop-lifting.*

shore¹ /ʃɔː(r)/ *n* **1** [C, U] the land along the edge of the sea or of any large area of water: *a house on the shore(s) of Lake Geneva* ○ *swim from the boat to the shore* ○ *go on shore* (eg of sailors from a ship). ⇨ picture at COAST¹. **2 shores** [pl] (*esp rhet*) a country, esp one with a coast: *visit foreign shores.* ⇨ note at COAST¹.

shore² /ʃɔː(r)/ *v* PHRV **,shore sth 'up 1** to support sth by placing a wooden beam or sth similar against or under it: *shore up the side of an old house to stop it falling down.* **2** to support sth that is weak or failing: *She used this evidence to shore up her argument.*

shoreline /'ʃɔːlaɪn/ *n* [usu *sing*] the edge of the sea or any large area of water: *The road follows the shoreline.*

shorn *pp* of SHEAR.

short¹ /ʃɔːt/ *adj* (**-er, -est**) **1(a)** measuring little or less than average from one end to the other: *a short line/dress/journey* ○ *short grass* ○ *It's only a short walk/distance from my house to the shops.* ○ *She's had her hair cut very short.* ○ *She walked with short, quick steps.* Compare LONG¹ 1. **(b)** of less than the average or required height: *a short person/ladder* ○ *too short to reach the top shelf.* Compare TALL. **2(a)** not lasting long; brief: *a short vacation/speech/film/ ceremony* ○ *write a short report* ○ *have a short mem-ory* (ie remember only things that have happened recently) ○ *The days get shorter* (ie hours of DAYLIGHT become fewer) *as winter approaches.* **(b)** [attrib] (of a period of time) seeming to have passed very quickly: *In two short years she became a star.* ○ *A few short months ago she had been a happy, fun-loving girl.* Compare LONG¹ 1. **3** [pred] ~ (**of sth**) not having a lot or enough of sth; lacking sth: *I must hurry, I'm a bit short of time.* ○ *I'm getting short of decent clothes.* ○ *She was short of ideas for her essay.* ○ (*infml*) *I'm a bit short* (ie of money) *this week.* **(b)** ~ **on sth** (*infml*) lacking or not having enough of a certain quality: *He's short on tact.* ○ *Her books are pretty short on originality.* **4** [pred] not adequate or plentiful; not easily available: *Water is short at this time of year.* **5** [pred] ~ (**of sth**) less than the stated or required number, amount or distance: *We've raised £2 000 but we're still £200 short of our target.* ○ *Her last throw was only 3 centimetres short of the world record.* ○ *This packet should contain 20 screws, but it's two short.* ○ *He was just short of his 80th birthday when he died.* ○ *The missile landed short of its target.* ○ *It took just short of two hours to do the work.* **6** [usu *pred*] ~ **for sth** being the shorter form of a name, word, etc; serving as an ABBREVIATION (ABBREVIATE) of sth: *'Ben' is usually short for 'Benja-min'.* **7(a)** [pred] ~ (**with sb**) (of a person) speaking or replying sharply and briefly to sb, eg because one is annoyed: *I'm sorry if I was a bit short with you when you phoned but I was rather busy at the time.*

S

(**b**) (of a remark) expressed sharply and briefly and suggesting that the speaker is annoyed: *He gave her a short, impatient answer.* **8** (of vowels or syllables) pronounced for a relatively brief time: *Compare the short vowel in 'pull' and the long vowel in 'pool'.* **9** [usu attrib] (of pastry) containing a lot of fat and crumbling (CRUMBLE 1) easily: *a flan with a short crust.* **IDM** **at short / at a moment's notice** ⇨ NOTICE. **be caught/taken 'short** (*infml*) **1** (*esp Brit*) to feel an urgent need to go to the toilet. **2** (*US*) to find oneself suddenly without enough of sth, esp money. **by a ¦short 'head** (*Brit*) (in horse-racing) by a distance of less than the length of a horse's head: *win/lose by a short head.* **cut a long story short** ⇨ LONG¹. **cut sth/sb 'short** to end sth suddenly and before the usual or natural time; to stop sb before they have finished: *a career tragically cut short by illness* ○ *I'm sorry to cut you short in mid-sentence.* **draw the short straw** ⇨ DRAW¹. **fall 'short of sth** to fail to reach a desired target or standard: *The money collected fell short of the amount required.* ○ *The trip fell short of our expectations.* **for 'short** being the shorter form of the specified name, word, etc: *Her name is 'Frances', or 'Fran' for short.* **full/short measure** ⇨ MEASURE². **give sb/sth / get short 'shrift** to dismiss sb/sth or be dismissed rapidly and without sympathy: *He went to complain to the boss, but got very short shrift.* **go 'short (of sth)** not to have enough of sth: *If you have a decent job, you'll never go short.* ○ *Many children go short of food.* **have / be on a short 'fuse** to have a tendency to get angry quickly and easily: *Be careful how you approach him, he's got a short fuse.* ○ *His temper was on a short fuse.* **in the long/short run** ⇨ RUN². **in the long/short term** ⇨ TERM. **in ¦short** in a few words; briefly: *Things couldn't be worse, financially: in short, we're broke.* **in ¦short 'order** quickly and without fuss: *They turned the business into a thriving concern in very short order.* **in ¦short sup'ply** not existing in large enough quantities to satisfy demand; SCARCE: *Fresh vegetables are in short supply at this time of year.* **little/nothing short of 'sth** little/nothing less than sth; almost or equal to sth: *Our escape was little short of miraculous.* ○ *This is nothing short of a disaster.* **make short 'work of sth/sb** to deal with or dispose of sth/sb quickly: *The team made short work of their opponents.* **out of / short of breath** ⇨ BREATH. **run 'short (of sth)** to have used most of one's supply of sth: *run short of petrol/time.* **sell sth/sb/oneself short** ⇨ SELL. **¦short and 'sweet** (*often ironic*) brief but pleasant: *Her visit was short and sweet — she barely came in the door.* **short of sth 1** without sth; unless sth happens: *Short of a miracle, we're certain to lose.* **2** apart from sth; without sth actually happening: *We did everything short of stealing to get the money.* **stop short** ⇨ STOP¹. **stop short of sth / doing sth** ⇨ STOP¹. **thick as two short planks** ⇨ THICK. ▶ **shortness** *n* [U]: *suffer from shortness of breath* (ie difficulty in breathing).
■ **¦short ¦back and 'sides** *n* [sing] a HAIRCUT in which the hair is cut very short at the sides and back of the head.
¦short-'change *v* (esp passive) **1** to give sb less than the correct amount of change²(4), esp deliberately: [Vn] *be short-changed in a shop.* **2** to give sb worse treatment than they deserve: [Vn] *The staff feel that they've been short-changed by the management.*
¦short 'circuit (also *infml* **short**) *n* a faulty connection in an electrical circuit, by which the current flows along the wrong route. **¦short-'circuit** (also *infml* **short**) *v* **1** to have or cause sth to have a short circuit: [V] *The lights short-circuited when I joined up the wires.* [also Vn]. **2** to avoid sth long and complicated by adopting a quicker simpler method:

[Vn] *short-circuit the normal procedures to get sth done quickly.*
¦short 'cut (also **'short cut**) (**a**) a route that makes a journey, walk, etc shorter: *I took a short cut across the field to get to school.* (**b**) a way of doing sth more quickly than when it is done in the usual way: *Becoming a doctor requires years of training — there are really no short cuts.*
¦short-'handed *adj* [usu pred] not having enough or as many as the usual number of staff, workers or helpers: *I'm sorry to keep you waiting — we're rather short-handed today.*
'short-haul *adj* [attrib] of or involving the transport of goods or passengers over relatively short distances: *short-haul flights/routes/aircraft.* Compare LONG-HAUL.
'short list *n* (usu *sing*) (*Brit*) a small number of candidates for a job, etc, selected from a larger number, and from which the successful candidate will be selected: *draw up a short list* ○ *There are three people on the short list.* **'short-list** *v* ~ **sb (for sth)** (esp passive) to put sb on a short list: [Vn, Vnpr] *I was short-listed (for the job) but I didn't get it.*
short-lived /ˌʃɔːt ˈlɪvd/; *US* ˈlaɪvd/ *adj* lasting for only a short time; brief: *a ˌshort-lived efˈfect/reˈlationship/sucˈcess* ○ *Her interest in tennis was very short-lived.*
¦short 'odds *n* [pl] (in betting) the strong possibility that sb/sth will win sth, so that if one bets on them one will win only a relatively small amount of money: *There will be short odds on his winning a fourth title.* Compare LONG ODDS.
¦short 'order *n* (*US*) an order in a restaurant for food that can be cooked quickly: *a ˌshort-order 'cook* (ie one whose job is to cook such orders).
¦short-'range *adj* [usu attrib] **1** (of missiles, etc) designed to travel over relatively short distances: *ˌshort-range ˌnuclear 'weapons.* Compare LONG-RANGE. **2** designed for or applying only to a limited period of time: *a ˌshort-range 'plan, 'project.*
'short-run *adj* [attrib] relating to or likely to last for only a short period: *ˌshort-run adˈvantages/'costs.*
¦short-'sighted *adj* **1** (also *esp US* **¦near-'sighted**) able to see clearly only things that are close: *wear glasses because one is short-sighted.* **2** having or showing lack of thought for what is likely to happen in the future: *a ˌshort-sighted 'person/'attitude/'policy.* See also NEAR-SIGHTED. Compare LONG-SIGHTED. **¦short-'sightedness** *n* [U]: *surgery to correct short-sightedness* ○ *political short-sightedness.*
¦short-'staffed *adj* [usu pred] not having enough staff or as many staff as usual; UNDERSTAFFED: *We're very short-staffed because a lot of people are off sick.*
¦short-'stay *adj* [attrib] in which one/sth stays only for a short period: *a ˌshort-stay 'hostel/'car park.*
¦short 'story *n* a piece of fiction that is shorter than a novel, esp one that deals with a single event or theme.
¦short 'temper *n* [sing] a tendency to become angry quickly and easily: *He has a very short temper.* ○ *Her short temper has made her many enemies.* **¦short-'tempered** *adj*: *Being tired often makes me short-tempered.*
¦short-'term *adj* [usu attrib] relating to or lasting for only a short period: *a ˌshort-term 'loan/a'greement/'goal/ap'pointment.* Compare LONG-TERM.
¦short-'termism *n* [U] consideration only of the near future.
¦short 'time *n* [U] employment for less than the usual working period, esp because there is not enough work to do: *workers on short time* ○ *ˌshort-time 'working.*
¦short 'wave *n* [C, U] (*abbr* **SW**) a radio wave with a FREQUENCY(2) greater than 3 MEGAHERTZ: *a ˌshort-wave 'radio/'broadcast.* Compare LONG-WAVE, MEDIUM-WAVE.

---

short² /ʃɔːt/ n (infml) **1** = SHORT CIRCUIT. **2** (Brit) (esp pl) a small strong alcoholic drink, esp of spirits spirit(9a). **3** a short film, esp one shown before the main film at a cinema. **IDM** **the long and short of it** ⇨ LONG². ▶ **short** v (infml) = SHORT-CIRCUIT: [V] The cable shorted. [also Vn].

shortage /ʃɔːtɪdʒ/ n [C,U] a lack of sth needed: food/fuel/housing shortages ○ a shortage of rice/ funds/equipment ○ The shop was forced to close owing to (a) shortage of staff. ○ There was no shortage of helpers.

shortbread /ʃɔːtbred/ (also **shortcake**) n [U,C] a crisp biscuit made with flour, sugar and a lot of butter.

shortcake /ʃɔːtkeɪk/ n [U] **(a)** (Brit) = SHORTBREAD. **(b)** a cake with a pastry base and cream and fruit on top: strawberry shortcake.

shortcoming /ʃɔːtkʌmɪŋ/ n (usu pl) a fault, eg in sb's character, a plan or a system; a DEFECT¹: She was fully aware of her own shortcomings. ○ despite the obvious shortcomings of the scheme.

shortcrust /ʃɔːtkrʌst/ (also ,shortcrust 'pastry) n [U] a type of pastry that crumbles (CRUMBLE 1) easily.

shorten /ʃɔːtn/ v to become or make sth shorter: [Vn] take two links out of the chain to shorten it ○ a shortened version of a talk [Vnpr] shorten one's journey by several miles [V] The days are beginning to shorten (ie There are fewer hours of DAYLIGHT). Compare LENGTHEN.

shortening /ʃɔːtnɪŋ/ n [U] fat used for making pastry.

shortfall /ʃɔːtfɔːl/ n ~ (in sth) an amount by which sth is less than required or expected: a shortfall in the annual budget ○ shortfalls in funding.

shorthand /ʃɔːthænd/ n [U] **1** (also esp US **stenography**) a method of writing what sb is saying as quickly as they are saying it, using special symbols and abbreviations (ABBREVIATE): take a shorthand and typing course ○ shorthand notes ○ take sth down in shorthand. Compare LONGHAND. **2** ~ (for sth) a shorter and simpler way of expressing or referring to sth: a shorthand description ○ Doctors use the term as shorthand for a variety of similar diseases.

shortly /ʃɔːtli/ adv **1(a)** a short time; not long: shortly afterwards ○ shortly before noon. **(b)** soon; in the near future: coming shortly to local cinemas ○ I'll be with you shortly. **2** sharply and briefly, usu indicating annoyance: 'Go away,' said Ruth shortly.

shorts /ʃɔːts/ n [pl] **1** short trousers that do not reach the knee, worn when playing sports or in hot weather or by children: a pair of tennis shorts ○ Women in shorts will not be allowed into the mosque. Compare TROUSERS. **2** (US) men's UNDERPANTS. Compare KNICKERS. See also BOXER SHORTS.

shot¹ /ʃɒt/ n **1** [C] ~ (at sb/sth) the firing of a single bullet from a gun, etc, or the sound this makes: take a shot at the enemy ○ fire a few shots ○ hear shots in the distance ○ Two of her shots hit the target. See also POT-SHOT. **2** [C] a person with the specified level of skill at shooting a gun, etc: a first-class/good/poor shot. **3** (also ,lead 'shot) [U] a large number of tiny balls of lead packed inside a CARTRIDGE(1) that is fired from a SHOTGUN. **4** [C] (pl unchanged) (formerly) a ball of stone or metal shot from a CANNON or large gun. Compare CARTRIDGE 1, SHELL 4. **5** ~ (at sb) a remark attacking or criticizing sb: His comment was meant as a shot at me. ○ fire the opening shots in a debate. See also PARTING SHOT. **6** [C] (sport) **(a)** (in eg tennis or golf) an act of hitting the ball: a backhand shot ○ Good shot! **(b)** (in eg football or hockey) an act of kicking or hitting the ball in an attempt to score a goal: have a shot at goal ○ The shot hit the post. **7** [C] **(a)** a photograph: a 'close-up shot ○ I got some good shots of people at the party. See also MUG SHOT. **(b)** a single continuous film

sequence: an action shot of a car chase. **8** [C] ~ (at sth / doing sth) an attempt to do, reach or achieve sth: have a shot at (solving) this problem ○ have a shot at the world record. **9** [C] the launching of a spacecraft or ROCKET(2b): the second space shot this year ○ a shot at Mars. **10** [C] (infml esp US) an injection (INJECT): Have you had your typhus shots yet? ○ The doctor gave him a shot of something to calm him down. **11** [C] (infml) a small amount of a strong alcoholic drink, esp of spirits (SPIRIT 9a): a shot of vodka. **12** (often **the shot**) [sing] a heavy ball used in shot-put (SHOT¹) competitions: put (ie throw) the shot. **IDM** a big noise/shot/name ⇨ BIG. call the shots/tune ⇨ CALL¹. a leap/shot in the dark ⇨ DARK². like a 'shot (infml) at once; without hesitating; immediately and eagerly: If I had the chance to go, I'd take it like a shot. a long shot ⇨ LONG¹. not by a long chalk/shot ⇨ LONG¹. a shot across the/sb's 'bows a statement or an action intended as a warning or threat to sb that one will take more serious action if they do not do what one wants. a shot in the 'arm a thing that encourages or gives fresh energy to sb/sth: The improved trade figures are a much-needed shot in the arm for the economy.
■ the 'shot-put n [sing] (also ,putting the 'shot) a sports contest in which competitors try to throw a shot(12) as far as possible.

shot² /ʃɒt/ adj **1** ~ (with sth) (of coloured cloth) woven so as to show different colours when looked at from different angles: shot silk ○ a black curtain shot with silver ○ (fig) brown hair shot with grey. **2** [usu pred] (infml) worn-out (WORN²); destroyed: Her patience was completely shot. ○ After the ordeal his nerves were shot to pieces. **IDM** be/get 'shot of sb/ sth (infml) to leave or make sb/sth leave: We'll soon be shot of this awful place. ○ By the end of the weekend I couldn't wait to get shot of them. shot through with sth containing much of a certain quality or feature; suffused (SUFFUSE) with sth: a statement shot through with feeling.

shot³ pt, pp of SHOOT¹.

shotgun /ʃɒtgʌn/ n a gun that fires cartridges (CARTRIDGE) containing shot¹(3), used esp in hunting: a shotgun blast ○ a double-barrelled shotgun. ⇨ picture at GUN.
■ ,shotgun 'wedding n (dated) a wedding between two people who are or feel forced to marry, eg because the woman is pregnant.

should /ʃəd; strong form ʃʊd/ modal v (neg **should not**; short form **shouldn't** /ʃʊdnt/) **1** (used to indicate what is right or wrong, appropriate or not appropriate, etc in the circumstances): You shouldn't drink and drive. ○ We should have checked the time before we left. ○ I shouldn't have trusted him so readily. ⇨ note. **2** (used for giving or asking for advice or recommending sth): Since you're so unhappy there, you should look for another job. ○ Should I phone him and apologize? ○ You really should go to India, it's a fantastic place. ○ I should (ie I think you should) wait a bit longer before making a decision. ○ (ironic) 'She doesn't think she'll get a job.' 'She should worry, with all her qualifications.' ⇨ note. **3** (Brit) (used for making polite requests): I should like to phone my lawyer. ○ We should be grateful for your help. **4** (used for saying that sth is likely or will probably happen): We should arrive before dark. ○ The roads should be less crowded today. ○ I should have finished the book by Friday. **5** (used for saying that sth expected has not happened): He should be happy, considering how successful he is. ○ It should be snowing now, according to the weather forecast. ○ The bus should have arrived ten minutes ago. **6** (Brit fml) (used esp after I or we to describe the consequence of an imagined event): If I was asked to work on Sundays I should resign. Compare WOULD 2. **7** (used after if and in *case* or in conditional sentences, to refer to a possible event or situation): *If you should change your mind, do let me know.* ○ *Should anyone phone* (ie If anyone phones)*, please tell them I'm busy.* ○ *In case you should need any help, here's my number.* **8** (used as the past tense of *shall* to report what sb has said): *He asked me what time he should come.* (ie He asked: 'What time shall I come?') *I said (that) I should be glad to help.* **9** (*Brit*) (used in a *that*-clause after verbs expressing a suggestion or an opinion): *I suggest that you should reconsider your position.* ○ *She recommended that I should take some time off.* ○ *He insisted that I should leave immediately.* **10** (used in a *that*-clause after many adjectives describing feelings): *I'm anxious that we should allow plenty of time.* ○ *I find it quite astonishing that he should be so rude to you.* **11** (used with *imagine, say, think*, etc for expressing opinions about which one is not completely certain): *I should imagine it will take about three hours.* ○ *I should say she's over forty.* ○ *'Is this enough food for everyone?' 'I should think so.'* ○ *'Will it matter?' 'I shouldn't think so.'* Compare WOULD 8. **12(a)** (used after a question word, esp *how*, for expressing annoyance at sb's question or request): *How should I know where you've left your bag?* **(b)** (used after a question word, esp *why*, for stating that there is no reason for sth or when refusing to do sth): *Why should I help him? He's never done anything for me.* **(c)** (used after a question word, esp *who* or *what*, for expressing surprise about an event or a situation): *I got on the bus and who should be sitting in front of me but my ex-wife!* **13** (used for telling sb that sth would amuse or surprise them if they saw or experienced it): *You should see him when he first gets up in the morning!* ○ *You should have seen her face when she found out!* **14** (used for expressing strong agreement): *'I know it's expensive but it will last for years.' 'I should hope so (too)!'* ○ *'Nobody will oppose it.' 'I should think not!'*

NOTE Should or ought to are used to say that something is the best thing or the right thing to do: *You should/ought to take the baby to the doctor's.* ○ *I should/ought to give up smoking.*

To talk about the past **should have** or **ought to have** are used: *You should have/ought to have been more careful.*

Had better is used to say what is the best thing to do in a situation that is happening now: *We'd better hurry or we'll miss the train.* ○ *It's very hot. You'd better not go out without a hat.*

Should not, ought not to or **must not** (or **shouldn't, oughtn't, mustn't,** especially in British English) are used to say that something is a bad idea or is the wrong thing to do: *The children oughtn't to watch so much television.* ○ *You mustn't miss this wonderful opportunity.*

To talk about the past **should not have** and **ought not to have** are used: *You shouldn't have said that!* ○ *I'm sorry, I ought not to have lost my temper.*

In American English **should** is used for suggestions and offers: *Should I make the coffee?* ○ *Should we meet you outside the theater?*

---

shoulder /ˈʃəʊldə(r)/ *n* **1** [C] **(a)** the part of the body between the top of each arm and the neck: *look back over one's shoulder* ○ **shrug one's shoulders** (ie as a gesture indicating that one does not know or is not interested) ○ *He slung the bag over his right shoulder.* ⇨ picture at HUMAN. ⇨ note at BODY. **(b)** a part of a garment covering this: *a jacket with padded shoulders.* **2 shoulders** [pl] **(a)** the part of the back between and including the shoulders: *a person with broad shoulders* ○ *carry a rucksack on one's shoulders* ○ *give a child a ride on one's shoulders.* **(b)** this part of the body regarded as bearing responsibilities, blame, etc: *shift the blame onto sb else's*

shoulders ○ *The burden of guilt has been lifted from my shoulders.* ○ *She has a lot (of responsibility) on her shoulders.* **3** [C,U] a piece of meat cut from the upper part of the front leg of an animal: *some/a shoulder of lamb* ○ *shoulder ham.* **4** [C] a part of a thing resembling a human shoulder in shape or position, eg on a bottle, a tool or a mountain. ⇨ picture at MOUNTAIN. See also HARD SHOULDER. **IDM** **be/stand head and shoulders above sb/sth** ⇨ HEAD[1]. **be looking over one's 'shoulder** to have the uncomfortable feeling that others are trying to catch, attack or harm one. **have a chip on one's shoulder** ⇨ CHIP[1]. **give sb/get the cold shoulder** ⇨ COLD[1]. **have a good head on one's shoulders** ⇨ HEAD[1]. **an old head on young shoulders** ⇨ OLD. **put one's shoulder to the 'wheel** to work hard at a task requiring a lot of effort: *Come on, everyone, (put your) shoulders to the wheel — we've got a lot to do.* **rub shoulders with sb** ⇨ RUB[1]. **(be / give sb) a shoulder to 'cry on** (to be) a person who gives sympathy and comfort to sb: *He was deeply unhappy and needed a shoulder to cry on.* **,shoulder to 'shoulder 1** working, fighting, etc together; united: *stand shoulder to shoulder with one's fellow-workers in the dispute.* **2** side by side: *sit shoulder to shoulder studying the map.* **straight from the shoulder** ⇨ STRAIGHT[2].

▶ **shoulder** *v* **1** to put sth onto one's shoulder or shoulders: [Vn] *She shouldered her backpack and set off along the road.* **2** to accept or take responsibility, blame, etc: [Vn] *shoulder the burdens of high office.* **3(a)** to push sb/sth out of the way with one's shoulder: [Vnadv] *He shouldered the police officer aside.* [also Vnpr]. **(b)** to force one's way in a particular direction with one's shoulder: [Vnpr] *He shouldered his way through the crowd.* [also Vnpl].

■ **'shoulder-bag** *n* a bag with a long strap that is hung over the shoulder.

'shoulder-blade *n* either of the two large flat bones at the top of the back; a SCAPULA. ⇨ picture at SKELETON.

,shoulder-'high *adj* at or to the height of the shoulders: *a shoulder-high wall* ○ *The victorious captain was carried shoulder-high by his team-mates.*

'shoulder-length *adj* (esp of hair) reaching down to the shoulders.

'shoulder-strap *n* **(a)** a narrow strip of material that goes over the shoulder to support a piece of clothing, eg a dress, a BRASSIÈRE or a NIGHTDRESS. **(b)** a strap attached to a bag so that it can be carried over one shoulder.

shout /ʃaʊt/ *n* **1** a loud call or cry: *shouts of joy/ alarm/excitement* ○ *Her warning shout came too late.* ○ *She was greeted with shouts of 'Long live the President!'* **2** (*infml esp Austral or NZ*) a person's turn to buy drinks: *What will you have? It's my shout.*

▶ **shout** *v* **1** ~ **sth (at/to sb)**; ~ **sth (out)** to say sth in a loud voice: [V] *There's no need to shout, I'm not deaf!* [Vnp] *The boys shouted out their names.* [V.speech] *'Go back!' she shouted.* [Vnpr] *Bill shouted a warning to me.* [Vn] *shout abuse/ encouragement* [V.that] *Ellen shouted that she couldn't hear properly.* [Vpr.that] *He shouted to me that the boat was sinking.* [Vpr.to inf] *I shouted at/to him to shut the gate.* **2** ~ **(out)** to call loudly or make a loud noise: [Vpr] *shout for joy* [Vnp] *She shouted out in pain.* [Vn-adj] *She shouted herself hoarse cheering on the team.* **PHRV** **'shout at sb** to speak to sb loudly and angrily: *Dad was always shouting at us.* **,shout sb 'down** to prevent sb from speaking or being heard by shouting: *The crowd kept shouting the speaker down.* **shouting** *n* [U] shouts: *The shouting stopped suddenly.* ○ *He waited till she was within shouting distance* (ie near enough to hear sth shouted). **IDM** **be all over bar the 'shouting** (*Brit*)

(of a performance, contest, etc) to be almost finished or decided, so that the final result is not in doubt.

NOTE Compare **shout, cry, yell** and **scream**. These verbs describe the different kinds of noise people make when they are angry, frightened or upset. People **cry out** as a sudden reaction to pain, fear or surprise: *She cried out in pain.* People **shout** when they are angry or want to get somebody's attention: *I was surprised to hear my parents shouting at each other.* ○ *'Close the doors please!' shouted the guard.*

Yell is to shout very loudly when you are frightened or excited, or in order to get somebody's attention: *We heard someone yelling for help.* ○ *'I can't hear you,' he yelled into the phone.* When people **scream** they make a very loud, high-pitched noise because they are in pain or are very frightened: *There was broken glass everywhere and people were screaming.* These verbs are also used instead of **say** to show ways of saying things, especially when writing direct speech: *'Get out!' she shouted/screamed/yelled.* ○ *'Who's there?' cried Alex.*

shove /ʃʌv/ v **1** to push sb roughly: [V] *The crowd was **pushing and shoving**.* [Vnpr] *He shoved her out of the way.* [Vnadv] *The policeman shoved me aside.* [also Vnp]. **2** (*infml*) to put sth casually or roughly in a place: [Vn, Vnp] *shove papers (away) in a drawer* [Vnpr] *Jack shoved his hands in his pockets.* ○ *'Where shall I put my case?' 'Shove it on the rack.'* **PHRV** ˌshove ˈoff (*infml*) (often *imperative*) to leave; to go away: *Just shove off and leave me alone!* ˌshove ˈup (*infml*) to move along, esp in order to make more room: *We can get one more in if you shove up.*
► **shove** n (usu *sing*) a rough push: *give sb/sth a good/hefty shove.* **IDM** **when push comes to shove** ⇨ PUSH[2].

shovel /ˈʃʌvl/ n **1** a tool like a SPADE[1] with curved edges, used for moving earth, snow, sand, etc: *workmen with picks and shovels.* ⇨ picture at SPADE. **2** a part of a large machine that moves earth, etc.
► **shovel** v (**-ll-**; *US* **-l-**) to lift or move sth with a shovel: [Vnp] *spend hours shovelling snow* [Vnp] *He shovelled up the broken glass into a bucket.* [Vnpr] *shovel earth into the hole* ○ (*fig derog*) *children shovelling food into their mouths.* ⇨ picture at SPADE.
shovelful /-fʊl/ n the amount that a shovel can hold: *two shovelfuls of earth.*

show[1] /ʃəʊ/ n **1** [C] any type of public entertainment, eg a theatre performance, a radio or television programme, or a CIRCUS: *a TV quiz show* ○ *a comedy show on radio* ○ *The most successful Broadway shows are often musicals.* See also CHAT SHOW. **2** [C, U] a public display or exhibition, eg of things in a competition or of new products: *a flower/horse/cattle show* ○ *the motor show* (ie where new models of cars are displayed) ○ *Many new computers are **on show** at the exhibition.* ⇨ note at EXHIBITION. **3** [C, U] (**a**) a thing done to give a particular impression, often a false one; an outward appearance: *put on a show of defiance/strength/friendship/sympathy* ○ *His public expressions of grief are nothing but show.* (**b**) a splendid or colourful display: *a fine show of blossom on the apple trees* ○ *all the glitter and show of the circus.* **4** [sing] (*infml*) anything that is happening; an organization, a business, an event, a project, etc: *She runs the whole show.* ○ *Let's **get this show on the road** (ie start work).* **5** [C usu *sing*] (*dated infml esp Brit*) a thing done or performed in a specified way: *put on/up a good show* (eg do well in a contest) ○ *It's a poor show* (ie very rude and disappointing) *if he can't even send you a card.* **IDM** **for ˈshow** intended to be seen but not used: *Those books are just for show — she never reads them.* **(jolly) good ˈshow!** (*dated Brit infml*) (used to ex-

press approval, congratulation or satisfaction). **a show of ˈhands** a group of people each raising a hand to vote for or against sth: *The issue was decided by a show of hands.* ○ *Who is in favour of the proposal? Can I have a show of hands, please?* **steal the show** ⇨ STEAL. **stop the show** ⇨ STOP[1].
► **showy** *adj* (**-ier, -iest**) (*often derog*) attracting attention by being bright, colourful or exaggerated: *a showy flower/finish.* **showily** /-ɪli/ *adv.* **showiness** n [U].
■ **ˈshow business** (also *infml* **showbiz**) n [U] the business of professional entertainment, esp in the theatre, in films or in television: *go/get into show business* ○ *show-business personalities.*
ˈshow-piece n a thing that is admired as an excellent example of its type.

show[2] /ʃəʊ/ v (*pt* **showed**; *pp* **shown** /ʃəʊn/ or, rarely, **showed**) **1** ~ **sth (to sb)** to make sth clear; to demonstrate sth: [V.*that*, Vn.*that*] *The figures clearly show (us) that her claims are false.* [Vn.*wh*] *I'll show him how to do it/what to do.* [Vnpr] *She showed the technique to her students.* [Vn] *Substantially increased funds show the high priority the government attaches to this scheme.* ○ *'I'm still your friend, you know.' 'Well, you've got a funny way of showing it!'* [Vnn] *They were shown the pointlessness of their actions.* [V.n *to* inf] *Her new book shows her to be a first-rate novelist.* **2(a)** to indicate sth to sb, esp by pointing: [Vn.*wh*] *Show me which picture you drew.* [Vnn] *I showed him the way out.* (**b**) to lead sb to the specified place or in the specified direction: [Vnpr] *We were shown into the waiting-room.* ○ *The stewardess showed us to our seats.* [Vnp] *Please show this lady out.* **3** ~ **sth (to sb)** to offer sth to sb for them to look at: [Vn] *You must show your ticket as you go in.* [Vnpr] *She has shown his letter to all her friends.* [Vnn] *They showed me their wedding photos.* **4** ~ **sth (at ...)** to make sth available for the public to see: [Vnpr] *The film is being shown at the local cinema.* [Vn] *She plans to show her paintings early next year.* **5(a)** to give evidence or proof of having a particular quality or characteristic: [Vn] *a soldier who showed great courage* ○ *The demand for steel is **showing signs of** slowing down.* [Vn-adj] *She showed herself unable to deal with money.* [V.n *to* inf] *He has shown himself to be ready to make compromises.* (**b**) to demonstrate a particular quality towards sb; to have a particular attitude towards sb: [Vn, Vnn] *The priest showed (me) great understanding.* [Vnpr] *They showed nothing but contempt for him.* **6** (*infml*) (no passive) to prove one's ability or worth to sb: [Vn] *They think I can't win, but I'll show them!* **7** to be or cause a feeling, etc to be noticeable: [Vpr] *Fear showed in his eyes.* [Vn] *She tried hard not to let disappointment show.* [Vn] *Her expression showed her disappointment.* ○ *Once again, the stubborn streak in her character showed itself.* ○ *Mr Cox began to **show signs of** impatience.* [Vnpr] *His annoyance showed itself in his face.* **8** to be or allow sth to be visible: [V] *Your petticoat is showing, Jane.* [Vp, Vpr] *His shirt was so thin that his vest showed through (it).* **9** to indicate a particular time, measurement, etc: [Vn] *The town hall clock showed midnight.* ○ *The end-of-year accounts show a loss.* **10** to be a picture of sb/sth; to illustrate sb/sth in a particular way; to represent sb/sth: [Vn-n] *The cartoon showed the Prime Minister as Superman.* [Vn-adj] *The photo shows her dressed in a black evening dress.* [Vn.*ing*] *In the portrait he is shown riding a horse.* **11** (*infml esp US*) to appear; to arrive: [V] *I waited for him all morning but he never showed.* See also SHOW UP. **12** (*US*) (*esp US*) to win third place or better in a horse-race (HORSE). **IDM** **fly/show/wave the flag** ⇨ FLAG[1]. **go ˈthrough/show one's ˈpaces** ⇨ PACE[1]. **go to ˈshow** to serve to prove or demonstrate: *It all/only goes to show what you can do when you really try.* **show (sb) a clean pair of**

'**heels** (*infml often joc*) to run from a place; to run away. **show sb the 'door** to ask sb to leave: *He insulted his host, and was promptly shown the door.* **show one's 'face** to appear amongst one's friends or in public: *She stayed at home, afraid to show her face.* **show one's 'hand/'cards** to reveal one's intentions or plans: *I suspect they're planning something but they haven't shown their cards yet.* **show sb / know / learn the ropes** ⇨ ROPE. **show one's 'teeth** to use one's power or authority to frighten or punish sb. **show 'willing** to show that one is ready to do sth, eg work hard or help, if required: *I don't think they need me, but I'll go anyway, just to show willing.* **(have) something, nothing, etc to 'show for sth** (to have) something, nothing, etc as a result of sth: *All those years of hard work, and nothing to show for it!* ○ *I've only got £100 to show for all the furniture I sold.* **PHRV ,show 'off** (*infml derog*) to try to impress others with one's abilities, wealth, intelligence, etc: *Do stop showing off — it's embarrassing.* See also SHOW-OFF. **,show sb/sth 'off** to try to make people notice sb/sth because one is proud of them/it: *a dress that shows off her figure* ○ *She was showing off her new husband at the party.* ○ *He likes to show off how well he speaks French.* **,show 'up** (*infml*) to arrive, often after a delay; to appear: *It was ten o'clock when he finally showed up.* ○ *We were hoping for a full team today but only five players showed up.* **,show (sth) 'up** to become or make sth become visible: *A fuel leak showed up on the infrared scanner.* ○ *Close inspection shows up the cracks in the stonework.* **,show sb 'up 1** (*Brit infml*) to make sb feel embarrassed by behaving badly in their company: *He showed me up by snoring during the concert.* **2** (*esp US*) to make sb feel embarrassed by doing sth better than them: *My daughter really showed me up when she beat me at tennis.*

▶ **showing** *n* **1** an act of showing a film: *two showings daily.* **2** (*usu sing*) evidence of the success, quality, etc of sb/sth: *the company's poor financial showing* ○ *On* (ie Judging by) *last week's showing, the team is unlikely to win today.*

■ '**show-off** *n* (*derog*) a person who tries to impress others: *Take no notice of him — you know what a show-off he is.*

showbiz /'ʃəʊbɪz/ *n* [U] (*infml*) = SHOW BUSINESS.

showcase /'ʃəʊkeɪs/ *n* **1** ~ (**for sb/sth**) a situation for showing sth favourably to a large number of people: *a trade fair designed as a showcase for British technology* ○ *The programme is a showcase for young talent.* **2** a case with a glass top or sides, for displaying articles in a shop, museum, etc. ▶ **showcase** *v* [Vn] *Several new bands were showcased there.*

showdown /'ʃəʊdaʊn/ *n* a final test, argument or fight to settle a dispute: *Management are seeking/ forcing/provoking a showdown with the unions.*

shower /'ʃaʊə(r)/ *n* **1(a)** a short period of rain or snow, etc: *be caught in a heavy shower* ○ *snow showers* ○ *scattered showers in the afternoon.* **(b)** a large number of things falling or arriving together: *a shower of sparks/stones* ○ (*fig*) *a shower of insults.* **2(a)** a device that produces a spray of water for washing; a small room containing this: *an electric shower* ○ *turn on the shower* ○ *shower gel* ○ *She's in the shower.* ○ *I'd like a room with a shower, please.* **(b)** a wash standing under such a device: *have a hot/cold/quick shower.* **3** (*US*) a party at which presents are given to a person, esp a woman about to get married or have a baby: *a bridal/baby shower.*

▶ **shower** *v* **1** to have a shower(2b): *He showered, changed and went out.* **2** ~ (**down**) **on sb/sth**; ~ **down** to fall in a shower(1b): [Vpr, Vp] *Ash from the volcano showered (down) on the nearby villages.* **3** ~ **sb with sth (a)** to cause a great number of things to fall on sb: [Vnpr] *The newly-weds were showered*

with confetti. ○ *The roof collapsed, showering us with dust and debris.* **(b)** to send or give sth to sb in large amounts: [Vnpr] *shower sb with gifts/shower gifts on sb.* ⇨ note at SPRAY².

showery /'ʃaʊəri/ *adj* (of the weather) with frequent showers of rain: *a showery day.*

showerproof /'ʃaʊəpruːf/ *adj* (of clothing) that can keep out light rain: *a showerproof jacket.*

showjumping /'ʃəʊdʒʌmpɪŋ/ *n* [U] the sport of riding a horse and jumping over barriers or fences: *a showjumping competition.*

showman /'ʃəʊmən/ *n* (*pl* **-men** /-mən/) **1** a person who enjoys attention and is skilled at making people notice her or him: *He's always been a great showman.* **2** a person who organizes public entertainments: *a travelling showman.*

▶ **showmanship** *n* [U] skill in attracting public attention, eg to sth one wishes to sell or to one's own abilities: *a brilliant piece of showmanship.*

shown *pp* of SHOW².

showroom /'ʃəʊruːm, -rʊm/ *n* a place where goods for sale are displayed: *You are welcome to browse in our showroom.* ○ *Ask at your nearest gas showroom.*

shrank *pt* of SHRINK.

shrapnel /'ʃræpnəl/ *n* [U] small pieces of metal which are scattered from an exploding bomb: *One child was injured by a piece of shrapnel.* ○ *shrapnel wounds.*

shred /ʃred/ *n* **1** (usu *pl*) a strip or piece torn, cut or scraped from sth larger: *His jacket was **torn/ripped to shreds** by the barbed wire.* ○ (*fig*) *My nerves are **in shreds** * (ie because of being very worried, tired, etc). **2** ~ **of sth** (usu *sing*, in negative sentences) a small amount of sth: *There is not a **shred of evidence** to support what he says.*

▶ **shred** *v* (**-dd-**) to tear, cut, etc sth into shreds: [Vn] *shredded cabbage* ○ *a machine for shredding waste paper.*

shredder *n* a device that shreds paper, eg so that no one can read what was printed on it.

shrew /ʃruː/ *n* **1** a small animal like a mouse, with a long nose. **2** (*dated*) a bad-tempered unpleasant woman.

▶ **shrewish** *adj* (esp of women) bad-tempered.

shrewd /ʃruːd/ *adj* (**-er**, **-est**) having or showing good and realistic judgement; ASTUTE: *a shrewd businesswoman/politician* ○ *make a shrewd guess/ investment.* ▶ **shrewdly** *adv*: *She eyed him shrewdly.* **shrewdness** *n* [U]: *He acted with characteristic shrewdness and insight.*

shriek /ʃriːk/ *v* **(a)** ~ (**with sth**); ~ (**out**) to give a sudden shout in a loud high voice: [Vpr] *shrieking with laughter/excitement* [V] *seagulls/sirens shrieking* [Vp] *shriek out in fright.* **(b)** ~ **sth** (**out**) to say sth in a loud high voice: [Vn, Vnpr] *shriek (out) a warning* [V.speech] *'I hate you,' he shrieked.* [also V.*that*].

▶ **shriek** *n* a loud high shout: *shrieks of delight/ laughter* ○ *The child let out/gave an ear-piercing shriek.*

shrift /ʃrɪft/ *n* **IDM** **give sb/sth / get short shrift** ⇨ SHORT¹.

shrill /ʃrɪl/ *adj* **1** (**-er**, **-est**) (of sounds, voices, etc) high-pitched and loud, esp in an unpleasant way: *a shrill cry/whistle* ○ *shrill laughter.* **2** (*sometimes derog*) (of a protest, demand, etc) loud and forceful: *shrill complaints/criticisms.* ▶ **shrilly** /'ʃrɪlli/ *adv*: *scream/screech shrilly* ○ *Her voice rose shrilly.* **shrillness** *n* [U].

shrimp /ʃrɪmp/ *n* **1** a small edible SHELLFISH found mainly in the sea. It becomes pink when boiled: *potted shrimps.* ⇨ picture at SHELLFISH. **2** (*joc* or *derog*) a very small person.

▶ **shrimping** *n* [U] the activity of catching shrimps: *a shrimping net.*

shrine /ʃraɪn/ *n* **1** ~ (**to sb/sth**); ~ (**for sb**) any place that is regarded as holy because of its associations with a special person or event: *a shrine to the Virgin Mary* ○ *make a pilgrimage to local shrines* ○ (*fig*) *Wimbledon is a shrine for all lovers of tennis.* **2** a container in which holy remains or objects are kept or where a holy person is buried.

shrink /ʃrɪŋk/ v (*pt* **shrank** /ʃræŋk/ or **shrunk** /ʃrʌŋk/; *pp* **shrunk**) **1(a)** (of clothes, material, etc) to become smaller, esp when washed in water that is too hot; to make clothes, material become smaller in this way: [V] *Will this shirt shrink in the wash?* [Vn] *The washing-machine shrank my sweater.* (**b**) to become smaller in size or amount: [V] *the shrinking countryside* [Vpr] *The workforce has shrunk from 20 000 to 6 000 in the past ten years.* **2** to move back or away from sth/sb, esp because of fear or disgust: [Vp] *shrink back in horror* [Vpr] *She shrank trembling against the wall.* **IDM** **a 'shrinking 'violet** (*joc*) a very shy person: *She's no shrinking violet — always ready to speak up for herself.* **PHRV** **'shrink from sth / doing sth** to be unwilling to do sth: *There's no point in shrinking from the truth.* ○ *He did not shrink from doing what was right.*
▶ **shrink** *n* (*sl joc*) a psychiatrist (PSYCHIATRY): *She sees her shrink once a week.*

shrinkage /ʃrɪŋkɪdʒ/ n [U] (**a**) the process of shrinking or the amount by which sth shrinks: *buy a bigger size to allow for shrinkage* ○ *There has been some shrinkage in our export trade.* (**b**) (in a shop, etc) the loss of profit because of goods being stolen: *Shrinkage costs the retail industry about £1.8 billion a year.*

shrunken /ʃrʌŋkən/ *adj* [usu attrib] having shrunk: *an old, shrunken apple* ○ *shrunken cheeks* ○ *the shrunken body of a starving child.*
■ **shrink-'wrapped** *adj* (of food, books, etc) wrapped tightly in a thin plastic covering: *shrink-wrapped 'cheese.*

shrivel /ʃrɪvl/ v (**-ll-**; *US* **-l-**) ~ (**up**) to shrink and WRINKLE(2) from heat or cold or because of being dry; to make sth shrink, etc in this way: [V, Vp] *The leaves had shrivelled (up) in the sun.* [Vn] *The heatwave is shrivelling potato stocks.* ▶ **shrivelled** (*US* **-eled**) *adj*: *an old man with a brown, shrivelled face.*

shroud /ʃraʊd/ n **1** (also **winding-sheet**) [C] a cloth in which a dead person is wrapped for burial. **2** [C] ~ **of sth** a thing that covers and hides sth: *shrouds of fog/smoke* ○ *cloaked in a shroud of mystery/ secrecy.* **3** **shrouds** [pl] the ropes supporting a ship's MAST(1).
▶ **shroud** *v* ~ **sth in sth** to cover or hide sth with sth: [Vnpr] *shrouded in darkness/mist* ○ *a crime shrouded in mystery.*

Shrove Tuesday /ˌʃrəʊv ˈtjuːzdeɪ, -di; *US* ˈtuːz-/ the day before the beginning of Lent. See also ASH WEDNESDAY, PANCAKE DAY.

shrub /ʃrʌb/ n a low plant or bush with several stems of wood: *evergreen shrubs* ○ *shrub roses* ○ *plant shrubs in the autumn.*
▶ **shrubbery** /ʃrʌbəri/ n [C,U] an area planted with shrubs: *plant a shrubbery* ○ *a clump of dense shrubbery.*

shrug /ʃrʌg/ v (**-gg-**) to raise one's shoulders slightly as a way of expressing doubt, lack of interest, etc: [V] *I asked her where Sam was, but she simply shrugged* (ie to show she did not know or care) *and said nothing.* [Vn] *He shrugged his shoulders and walked away.* **PHRV** **,shrug sth 'off** to dismiss sth as being unimportant: *The government is trying to shrug off blame for the economic crisis.* ○ *She shrugged off a minor knee injury in order to play in the final.*
▶ **shrug** *n* (usu *sing*) a movement of shrugging the shoulders: *give a resigned shrug (of the shoulders).*

shrunk ⇨ SHRINK.
shrunken ⇨ SHRINK.

shuck /ʃʌk/ n (*US*) an outer covering of a nut, etc.
▶ **shuck** *v* (*US*) to remove the shucks from sth: [Vn] *shuck peanuts/corn/peas.*
shucks *interj* (*US infml*) (used to express annoyance, regret, embarrassment, etc): *'It was great.' 'Shucks, I wish I'd been there!'*

shudder /ʃʌdə(r)/ v (**a**) ~ (**with sth**) to shake with fear, cold, etc: [Vpr] *shudder with apprehension/ disgust/fury* ○ *Just thinking about the accident makes me shudder.* [V.to inf] *I shudder to think how much this meal is going to cost.* (**b**) (of a vehicle, machine, building, etc) to make a strong shaking movement: [V] *The whole house shuddered as the bomb exploded.* [Vpr] *The bus shuddered to a halt/ stop.*
▶ **shudder** *n* a shuddering movement: *She gave a shudder (of relief/disgust).* ○ *The very thought of it sends shudders up my spine.*

shuffle /ʃʌfl/ v **1(a)** to walk by sliding along without lifting the feet completely off the ground: [V] *Walk properly — don't shuffle.* [Vpr] *The prisoners shuffled along the corridor.* [Vadv] *The queue shuffled forward slowly.* [Vp] *The old man shuffled off into the rain.* (**b**) to change one's position or move one's feet about while standing or sitting, because one is nervous, bored, etc: [V, Vn] *The audience began to shuffle (their feet) impatiently.* [Vpr] *The began to shuffle awkwardly from one foot to the other.* ⇨ note. **2(a)** to mix up a pack of cards before playing a card-game: [V] *Who is going to shuffle?* [Vn, Vnp] *She shuffled the cards (up).* (**b**) to move things or people around to different positions: [Vn, Vnp] *He shuffled the papers (around) on his desk, pretending to be busy.* [also Vnpr].
▶ **shuffle** *n* (usu *sing*) **1** a shuffling walk or movement: *hear a shuffle of feet.* **2** an act of mixing cards before a card-game: *give the pack/cards a good shuffle.* **3** = RESHUFFLE *n*.

NOTE Shuffle, shamble, stagger, stumble, waddle, hobble and limp all describe ways of walking slowly and with difficulty. **Shuffle** suggests moving with small steps and without lifting the feet off the ground completely: *The queue of prisoners shuffled towards the door.* **Shamble** suggests tired, careless steps: *an old man shambling along the road.*

People **stagger** when they cannot balance well, for example when carrying something heavy or when they are drunk: *They staggered into the airport with their heavy suitcases.* They **stumble** when they fall against things or cannot see where they are going: *She stumbled across the dark room and switched on the light.*

Waddle is often used humorously to describe moving from side to side like a duck while walking: *She waddled around the apartment, heavily pregnant.* People or animals **hobble** when they cannot walk easily because they are in pain, and they **limp** if one of their legs is injured or stiff: *I hobbled along the platform, step by painful step.* ○ *The bird was limping, dragging its injured wing along the ground.*

shun /ʃʌn/ v (**-nn-**) to avoid sth/sb: [Vn] *shun publicity/other people* ○ *She was shunned by her family.*

shunt /ʃʌnt/ v **1** (*infml*) (usu passive) to move sb/ sth to a different place, often a less important one: [Vnp] *She's been shunted off to a regional office.* ○ (*fig*) *After the speech any difficult questions were merely shunted aside* (ie not answered directly). [also Vpr]. **2(a)** to move a train, a carriage, etc slowly along a track or from one track to another: [Vnpr] *wagons shunted into a siding* [also Vn]. (**b**) [V,Vpr,Vnpr] (of a train) to be shunted.

shush /ʃʊʃ/ *interj* be silent!
▶ **shush** *v* to tell sb to be silent: [Vn] *He began to speak but was hastily shushed.*

[V. speech] = verb + direct speech   [V. *that*] = verb + *that* clause   [V. *wh*] = verb + *who, how,* etc clause

shut /ʃʌt/ v (-tt-; pt, pp **shut**) **1(a)** to move a door, lid, window, etc into a position where it closes an opening: [Vn] *Please shut the gate.* ○ *shut a drawer/ cold air vent* [Vnpr] *He shut the door on her/in her face* (ie wouldn't let her in). **(b)** (of a door, etc) to move or be able to be moved into such a position; to close: [V] *The window won't shut.* ○ *The supermarket doors shut automatically.* **2(a)** to close sth that is open; to close the lid, drawer, etc of sth: [Vn] *shut one's eyes/mouth* ○ *I can't shut my case — it's too full.* ○ *The cashier shut the till and locked it.* **(b)** (esp of the eyes or mouth) to close: [V] *His eyes shut and he fell asleep.* ○ *Her mouth opened and shut, but no sound came out.* **3** to fold together sth that opens out: [Vn] *shut a book/wallet.* **4** (*esp Brit*) (of a shop, bank, etc) to stop working or receiving customers: [V] *What time do the shops shut?* ○ *We shut after lunch on a Thursday.* ➪ note at CLOSE⁴. **IDM close/ shut the door on sth** ➪ DOOR. **keep one's mouth shut** ➪ MOUTH¹. **shut/slam the door in sb's face** ➪ DOOR. **shut one's ᵉars to sth/sb** to refuse to listen to sth/sb: *She decided to shut her ears to all the rumours.* **shut/close one's ᵉeyes to sth** ➪ EYE¹. **shut sb's ᵐmouth** (*infml*) to prevent sb from speaking, revealing secrets, etc. **shut your ᵐmouth/ᶠface!** (*sl*) be quiet!: *Shut your mouth, nobody asked you!* **shut up ˢshop** (*infml esp Brit*) to close one's business, stop trading, etc: *In the recession many small companies were forced to shut up shop.* **with one's eyes shut/closed** ➪ EYE¹. **PHRV ,shut sb/sth aᵂway** to put sb/sth in an enclosed place or away from others: *She shut the letters away where no one could find them.* ○ *I hate being shut away in the country.*

,**shut (sth) ᵈdown** (of a factory, etc) to stop working, esp permanently; to close a factory, etc: *A lot of local shops have shut down in the last few years.* ○ *They've shut down the chemical plant.*

,**shut sb/oneself ᶦin (sth)** to put sb/oneself in an enclosed place: *She shuts herself in her room for hours.* ○ *We're shut in* (ie surrounded) *by the hills here.* ○ *He tried to shut all thoughts of her out of his mind.* ○ *The government wants to shut the refugees out.*

,**shut sth ᶦin sth** to trap sth by closing sth on it: *I shut my finger in the car door.*

,**shut sth ᵒoff** to stop the supply or flow of sth, esp a gas or liquid: *Shut the water off before you mend the tap.* ,**shut sb/sth ᵒoff (from sth)** to prevent sb/sth from having contact with sth: *After the blizzard, we were completely shut off (from the outside world).*

,**shut sb/sth ᵒout (of sth)** to keep sb/sth out; to exclude sb/sth; to block sb/sth: *Those trees shut out the view.* ○ *He tried to shut all thoughts of her out of his mind.* ○ *The government wants to shut the refugees out.*

,**shut (sb) ᵘup** (*infml*) to stop or make sb stop talking: *Oh, shut up, you idiot!* ○ *Tell her to shut up.* ○ *She jabbed him with her elbow to shut him up.* ,**shut sth ᵘup** to close all the doors and windows of a house, etc: *We always shut up the house before going away.* ,**shut sb/sth ᵘup (in sth)** to confine sb; to put sth away: *The dog is kept shut up in its kennel all night.* ○ *She shuts her jewels up in a safe.* ▶ **shut** adj [pred]: *The door was shut.* ○ *She slammed the door shut.* ○ *Unfortunately the bank is shut now.*

■ ᶦ**shut-down** n the process of closing a factory, etc, either temporarily or permanently: *the nuclear reactor's automatic shut-down procedures* ○ *Since the shut-down, hundreds of miners have been out of work.*

shutter /ˈʃʌtə(r)/ n **1** a movable panel or screen that can be closed over a window to keep out light or thieves: *The shop doorway is fitted with rolling shutters.* **2** a device that opens to allow light to pass through the LENS of a camera: *hear the shutter click* ○ *adjust the shutter speed.*

▶ **shuttered** adj **(a)** with the shutters closed: *a shuttered room* ○ *The house was empty and shuttered.* **(b)** having shutters: *shuttered farmhouses/windows.*

shuttle /ˈʃʌtl/ n **1(a)** (in weaving) an instrument that pulls a thread across the width of the cloth, between the threads that pass along the length of it. **(b)** a device in a sewing-machine (SEW) that carries the lower thread to meet the upper thread to make a stitch. **2** an aircraft, a bus, etc that travels regularly between two places: *I'm flying to Boston on the shuttle.* ○ *There's a shuttle service between London and Edinburgh.* Compare SPACE SHUTTLE. **3** = SHUTTLECOCK.

▶ **shuttle** v [V, Vn] ~ **(sb) between A and B** to move sb or travel backwards and forwards between places: [Vpr, Vp] *reporters shuttling (back and forth) between conferences* [also Vnpr, Vnp].

shuttlecock /ˈʃʌtlkɒk/ n an object hit backwards and forwards in BADMINTON. Shuttlecocks are made of a round piece of rubber or CORK(1) with a ring of real or plastic feathers attached. ➪ picture.

shuttlecock

shy¹ /ʃaɪ/ adj (**shyer**, **shyest**) **1(a)** (of people) nervous and afraid or unwilling to speak in the presence of others: *a shy, retiring young man* ○ *He was too shy to speak to her.* ○ *The child isn't at all shy with adults.* **(b)** (of behaviour, etc) showing that one is nervous, afraid, etc in this way: *a shy look/smile.* **2** (of animals, birds, etc) unwilling to be seen by or be near people; easily frightened. **3** ~ **of sth / doing sth** afraid of doing sth or being involved in sth: *be shy of publicity* ○ *We are not shy of taking hard decisions.* **4** ~ **(on/of sth/sb)** (*US infml*) short of or lacking sth/sb: *We've plenty of wine, but we're shy on beer.* ○ *We are still two players shy (of a full team).* **IDM fight shy of sth** ➪ FIGHT¹. **once bitten, twice shy** ➪ ONCE.

▶ **shy** v (pt, pp **shied** /ʃaɪd/) ~ **(at sth)** (esp of a horse) to turn aside in fear or alarm: [Vpr] *The colt shied at a paper bag blowing in the wind.* [also V]. **PHRV ,shy aᵂway from sth / doing sth** to avoid doing or being involved in sth because of being shy or afraid, lacking confidence, etc: *I've always shied away from close friendships.*

-shy (forming compound adjs) avoiding or not liking the thing specified: ᶜ*camera-shy* (ie unwilling to be photographed) ○ *You've been ᵂwork-shy all your life.*

shyly adv: *smiling shyly.*

shyness n [U]: *try to overcome one's shyness.*

shy² /ʃaɪ/ v (pt, pp **shied** /ʃaɪd/) [Vn, Vnpr] (*dated infml*) to throw sth. See also COCONUT SHY.

shyster /ˈʃaɪstə(r)/ n (*infml esp US*) a dishonest person, esp a lawyer: *shyster politicians.*

SI /ˌes ˈaɪ/ abbr International System (of units of measurement) (French *Système International*): *SI units.* ➪ App 8.

Siamese /ˌsaɪəˈmiːz/ adj of Siam (now called Thailand), its people or its language.

▶ **Siamese** n **1(a)** [C] (pl unchanged) a native of Siam. **(b)** [U] the language of Siam. **2** [C] (pl unchanged) a Siamese cat.

■ ,**Siamese ᶜcat** (also **Siamese**) n a cat with short pale fur, a brown face and ears, and blue eyes. ,**Siamese ᵗtwins** n [pl] twins (TWIN 1) born with their bodies joined together in some way and sometimes sharing the same organs.

sibilant /ˈsɪbɪlənt/ adj like or produced with a sound like a long ᶜs': *the sibilant sound of whispering.*

▶ **sibilant** n a sibilant letter or sound made in speech, eg /s, z, ʃ, ʒ, tʃ, dʒ/.

sibling /ˈsɪblɪŋ/ n (*fml*) each of two or more people with the same parents; a brother or sister: *a situation common between siblings* ○ **sibling rivalry**.

sic /sɪk, siːk/ adv (*Latin*) (placed in brackets after a quoted word or phrase that seems to be wrongly spelled, not appropriate, etc, in order to show that it is quoted accurately): *The notice read: 'Skool (sic) starts at 9 am.'*

sick /sɪk/ *adj* (**-er, -est**) **1** physically or mentally ill: *a sick person/animal/plant ∘ She has been sick for weeks. ∘ He's off (work) sick.* **2** [usu pred] feeling that one wants to bring food from the stomach back out through one's mouth; wanting to VOMIT: *feeling sick ∘ You'll make yourself sick if you eat all those sweets. ∘ a sick feeling in the stomach ∘ Before going on stage I felt sick with fear.* ⇨ note. **3** [pred] ~ **of sb/sth/doing sth** (*infml*) bored with sb/sth; not liking sb/sth through having had too much of them/it: *I'm sick of waiting around like this. ∘ She has had the same job for years and is heartily sick of it. ∘ I'm sick of the sight of you!* **4** [pred] ~ **(at/about sth/doing sth)** miserable and disappointed or disgusted: *We were pretty sick about losing the match.* **5** (*infml*) (esp of humour) offensive because of appearing not to care about suffering, disease, death, etc: *a sick joke/mind ∘ She made a sick remark about dead babies.* **IDM** **be ˈsick** (*Brit*) to bring food back up from the stomach through the mouth; to VOMIT: *The cat's been sick on the carpet.* **eat oneself sick** ⇨ EAT. **fall ˈsick (with sth)**; (*fml*) **take ˈsick** to become ill: *He fell sick with malaria on a trip to Africa.* **go ˈsick** to report oneself as ill: *I couldn't face work on Monday so I went sick.* **make sb ˈsick** to disgust sb: *His hypocrisy makes me sick.* **(as) sick as a ˈparrot** (*Brit joc catchphrase*) disgusted or very disappointed. **sick at ˈheart** (*fml*) feeling great disappointment, fear or grief; unhappy: *She left her home reluctantly and sick at heart.* **sick to one's ˈstomach** (*US*) disgusted.

▶ **sick** *n* **1** [U] (*Brit infml*) food brought back up from the stomach through the mouth; VOMIT: *The basin was full of sick.* **2 the sick** [pl *v*] people who are ill: *All the sick and wounded were evacuated.*

sick *v* **PHRV** **ˌsick sth ˈup** (*Brit infml*) to bring food back up from the stomach through the mouth; to VOMIT sth: *The baby sicked up a little milk.*

-sick (forming compound *adjs*) feeling sick(2) as a result of travelling on a ship, plane, etc: *ˈseasick ∘ ˈairsick ∘ ˈtravel-sick ∘ ˈcarsick.* See also HOMESICK.

■ **ˌsick ˈheadache** *n* (*Brit*) a severe HEADACHE with vomiting (VOMIT).

ˈsick-leave *n* [U] permission to be absent from work, duty, etc because of illness; the period of such absence: *be granted sick-leave ∘ be on two weeks' sick-leave.*

ˈsick-pay *n* [U] pay given to an employee who is absent because of illness.

NOTE Be sick in British and American English means to bring food up from the stomach: *I think I'm going to be sick. ∘ She was continually sick during her pregnancy.* **Vomit** is used in medical contexts in both British and American English: *Symptoms of food poisoning may include diarrhoea and vomiting.* **Throw up** is the usual American expression and is also very common in British English: *The baby threw up all over the floor. ∘ The smell was so terrible we wanted to throw up.*

Being **ill** in British English and **sick** in American English means that you feel unwell or that you have a particular illness: *Dan felt so ill/sick he went straight back to bed. ∘ He was ill for some time before he died.* **Sick** is also used when talking about absence from work because of illness: *My secretary's off sick. ∘ He was on sick-leave following a heart attack.* It can also be used before a noun to mean **ill**: *She had a lot of experience nursing sick children.* **Ill** is not usually used before a noun. **Poorly** is also used in British English to mean ill, often by or about children: *Mama, are you poorly? ∘ Hospital staff described the man's condition as poorly but stable.*

sickbay /ˈsɪkbeɪ/ *n* a room or rooms, eg on a ship, for people who are ill.

sickbed /ˈsɪkbed/ *n* [sing] the bed of a person who is ill: *be on one's sickbed ∘ The President left his sickbed to attend the ceremony* (ie attended it although he was ill).

sicken /ˈsɪkən/ *v* **1** to make sb feel disgusted: [Vn] *Cruelty sickens me. ∘ I was sickened by the sight of the rotting corpses.* **2** ~ **(for sth)** (*Brit*) to begin to be ill; to become ill: [V] *He slowly sickened and died.* [Vpr] *She looks very pale. Is she sickening for something?*
▶ **sickening** *adj* **1** making one feel disgusted; very unpleasant: *a sickening sight/smell ∘ sickening cruelty ∘ The car hit the tree with a sickening crash.* **2** (*infml*) causing one trouble or annoyance: *It's sickening to think that we only missed the train by two minutes.* **sickeningly** *adv*.

sickle /ˈsɪkl/ *n* a tool with a curved blade on a short handle, used for cutting grass, corn, etc. ⇨ picture. Compare SCYTHE. See also HAMMER AND SICKLE.

sickle

■ **ˈsickle-cell** *n* a type of red blood cell in the shape of a sickle, found esp in a severe type of ANAEMIA.

sickly /ˈsɪkli/ *adj* **1** often ill: *a sickly child.* **2** not looking healthy; weak or faint: *sickly, dried-out plants ∘ a pale, sickly complexion ∘ He looked weak and sickly. ∘ She gave a sickly smile.* **3** unpleasant; making one feel sick(2): *a sickly smell/taste ∘ a sickly green colour ∘ (fig) a sickly, sentimental story.*

sickness /ˈsɪknəs/ *n* [U] **1** illness; bad health: *There's a lot of sickness in the village. ∘ They were absent because of sickness.* **2** [UC usu *sing*] a particular type of illness or disease: *sleeping sickness ∘ radiation sickness ∘ altitude sickness ∘ a sickness common in the tropics.* **3** [U] the feeling that one is likely to bring food back up from the stomach through the mouth: *The sickness passed after I lay down. ∘ The symptoms are fever and sickness.* See also MORNING SICKNESS.

■ **ˈsickness benefit** *n* [U] (*Brit*) money paid by the government to people who are absent from work because of illness: *be entitled to sickness benefit.* Compare SICK-PAY.

sickroom /ˈsɪkruːm, -rʊm/ *n* a room that is occupied by or kept ready for sb who is ill: *You should go to the sickroom if you're not feeling well.*

side¹ /saɪd/ *n* **1** [C esp *sing*] either of the two halves of a surface, an object or a place divided by an imaginary central line: *drive/walk along the left/right/shady/sunny side of the street ∘ go to the eastern side of the town ∘ satellite links to the other side of the world ∘ in the left side of the brain ∘ go over to the other/far side of the room ∘ Which side of the theatre would you like to sit?* **2** [C esp *sing*] either of two areas, etc divided by a line or boundary: *They stood on either side of the fence. ∘ He crossed the bridge to the other side of the river. ∘ the debit/credit side of an account.* **3** [C esp *sing*] **(a)** either the right or the left part of a person's body, esp from the base of the arm to the hip: *be wounded in the left side ∘ He was lying on his side.* **(b)** a place very near to this: *sit at/ by sb's side ∘ Fred stood on my left side. ∘ She refused to leave his side* (ie to leave him). **4** [C] **(a)** any of the surfaces of sth that is not the top or bottom, front or back: *a scratch on the side of the car ∘ A notice was stuck to the side of the filing cabinet. ∘ There is a garage built onto the side of the house. ∘ a side door/entrance/window ∘ The ship rolled **from side to side**.* **(b)** any of the surfaces of sth that is not the top or bottom: *A box has a top, a bottom and four sides.* **5** [C] the area near the edge or boundary of sth: *stand by the side of the car ∘ a table by the side of one's bed ∘ standing at the side of the road ∘ people* *sitting on both sides of the table* (ie on its two longer sides) ○ *the south side of the field/lake* ○ *We planted tulips along the side of the lawn.* See also FIRESIDE, SEASIDE. **6** [C] the upright or sloping surface round sth but not the top or bottom of it: *the side of the mountain* ○ *paintings on the sides* (ie walls) *of the cave* ○ *The side of the tin was dented.* See also HILLSIDE. **7** [C] either of the two surfaces of sth flat and thin, eg paper or cloth: *Write on one side of the paper only.* ○ *He told us not to write more than three sides.* ○ *Which is the right side of the material* (ie the one intended to be seen)*?* ○ *Both sides of the window were filthy.* ○ *side A/B of a record/tape.* **8** [C] (*esp mathematics*) any of the flat or nearly flat surfaces of a solid object: *the six sides of a cube.* **9** [C] (*mathematics*) any of the lines that form the boundaries of a flat shape: *the four sides of a square/rectangle/ parallelogram.* **10** [C] either of two people or groups involved in a dispute, contest, etc with each other: *the two sides in the strike* (ie employers and workers) ○ *There are faults on both sides.* **11** [C] (**a**) a position, an attitude or an opinion held by sb, eg in an argument: *She argued her side of the case well.* ○ *You must hear his side of things now.* ○ *Will you keep your side of the bargain?* (**b**) [C] an aspect of sth that is different from other aspects: *study all sides of a question* ○ *the gentle side of her character.* **12** [C] a sports team: *five-a-side football* ○ *the winning/losing side* ○ *pick sides* (ie choose who will play on each side) ○ *Austria has a strong side, and should win.* **13** [C] the branch of a family to which a particular person belongs, related either to that person's father or mother: *a cousin on my father's side* (ie a child of my father's brother or sister). **14** [C] either of the two halves of an animal that has been killed for meat: *a side of beef/bacon.* **15** [C] (*dated Brit infml*) a television channel: *Which side is the film on?* **IDM** **born on the wrong side of the blanket** ⇨ BORN. **come down on ˈone side of the fence or the ˈother** to make a choice between two alternatives: *The committee is considering the proposal and we're waiting to see which side of the fence it comes down on.* **err on the side of sth** ⇨ ERR. **from/on the wrong side of the tracks** ⇨ WRONG. **get on the right/wrong ˈside of sb** to please/annoy sb. **have got out of bed on the wrong side** ⇨ BED¹. **have sth on one's ˈside** to have sth as an advantage: *The climbers had exˈperience/ˈyouth/the ˈweather on their side.* **know which side one's bread is buttered** ⇨ KNOW. **laugh on the other side of one's face** ⇨ LAUGH. **let the ˈside down** (*esp Brit*) to fail to give one's friends, etc the help and support they expect, or to behave in a way that disappoints them: *You can always rely on Angela — she'd never let the side down.* **look on the bright side** ⇨ BRIGHT. **on/ from all ˈsides; on/from every ˈside** in/from all directions; everywhere: *be surrounded on all sides* ○ *Disaster threatens on every side.* **on the ˈbig, ˈsmall, ˈhigh, etc side** (*infml*) rather or too big, small, high, etc: *These shoes are a little on the large side.* **on the distaff side** ⇨ DISTAFF. **on the ˌright/ˌwrong side of ˈforty, ˈfifty, etc** (*infml often joc*) younger/ older than 40, 50, etc years of age. **on the safe side** ⇨ SAFE¹. **on the ˈside** (*infml*) **1** as an additional job or source of income: *a mechanic who buys and sells cars on the side.* **2** secretly: *He's married but he has a girlfriend on the side.* (**be**) **on the side of sb** (to be) a supporter of sb; holding the same views as sb: *Whose side are you on anyway?* (ie You should be supporting me.) ○ *I'm on George's side in this.* **on/to one ˈside 1** aside; out of one's way: *I put the broken glass to one side.* ○ *I left my bags on one side.* **2** to be dealt with later: *I put his complaint on one side until I had more time.* **the other side of the ˈcoin** the opposite or contrasting aspect of a matter: *Everyone assumes he's hard-working and conscientious but they don't know the other side of the coin.* **ˌside by**

ˈ**side 1** close together, facing in the same direction: *two children walking side by side.* **2** together: *The two communities exist happily side by side.* **3** supporting each other: *We stand side by side with you in this dispute.* **split one's sides** ⇨ SPLIT. **take sb on(to) one ˈside** to have a private talk with sb: *I took her on one side to explain my decision.* **take ˈsides (with sb)** to express support for sb in a dispute, etc: *You mustn't take sides in their argument.* ○ *She took sides with me against the bus driver.* **a thorn in sb's flesh/side** ⇨ THORN. **time is on sb's side** ⇨ TIME¹.

▶ **-sided** (forming compound *adjs*) having sides of the specified number or type: *a six-sided object* ○ *steep-sided hills* ○ *a glass-sided container.* See also ONE-SIDED.

■ ˈ**side-car** *n* a small vehicle attached to the side of a motor cycle (MOTOR) in which a passenger can ride.

ˈ**side dish** *n* an extra dish¹(2), eg a SALAD, usu served with a main course of a meal.

ˈ**side-effect** *n* (often *pl*) a secondary, usu unpleasant, effect of a drug, etc: *The drug has no adverse/ serious side-effects.*

ˈ**side-issue** *n* an issue that is less important than the main one: *Getting the money back is a side-issue. What really matters is the principle of the thing.*

ˌ**side-ˈon** *adv* (*Brit*) with the side of sth towards sth else: *The other car hit us side-on* (ie hit us from the side).

ˈ**side order** *n* (*esp US*) an item of food served to a person in addition to the main dish and on a separate plate: *a side order of French fries.*

ˈ**side-road** *n* a minor road leading off a main road.

ˈ**side-saddle** *adv* riding with both legs on the same side of the horse: *ride side-saddle.*

ˈ**side-splitting** *adj* (*infml*) extremely funny: *the clown's ˌside-splitting ˈantics.*

ˈ**side-street** *n* a minor street leading off a road in a town.

ˈ**side-swipe** *n* (*infml*) a critical remark about sb/ sth made while talking about sb/sth different: *When talking about the performance, she couldn't resist (taking) a side-swipe at the orchestra.*

ˈ**side-view** *n* a view of sth from the side: *The picture is/shows a side-view of the house.*

ˈ**side-whiskers** *n* [pl] patches of hair growing on the sides of a man's face down to, but not on, the chin.

side² /saɪd/ *v* **PHRV** ˈ**side with sb (against sb)** to support sb in an argument or dispute: *She always sides with her son against her husband.*

sideboard /ˈsaɪdbɔːd/ *n* **1** (*Brit*) (*US* **buffet**) [C] a piece of furniture, usu with drawers and cupboards, for storing plates, glasses, etc. **2 sideboards** (also **sideburns**) [pl] patches of hair growing on the side of a man's face in front of the ears. ⇨ picture at HAIR.

sideburns /ˈsaɪdbɜːnz/ *n* [pl] = SIDEBOARDS.

sidekick /ˈsaɪdkɪk/ *n* (*infml*) an assistant or close companion: *Leporello, Don Giovanni's comic sidekick.*

sidelight /ˈsaɪdlaɪt/ *n* **1** either of a pair of small lights at the front of a vehicle. ⇨ picture at CAR. **2** ~ **(on sb/sth)** a piece of information, usu given accidentally or in connection with another subject, that helps one to understand sb/sth: *The article about the theatre gave us a few sidelights on the character of its owner.*

sideline /ˈsaɪdlaɪn/ *n* **1** [C] an activity done in addition to one's main work, esp in order to earn extra money: *He's an engineer, but he repairs cars as a sideline.* **2 sidelines** [pl] the lines along the two long sides of a football pitch, tennis court, etc that mark the outer edges; the area just outside these: *The team's manager stood on the sidelines shouting instructions to the players.* **IDM** **on the ˈsidelines** observing sth but not directly involved in it: *The*

S

Prime Minister was content to watch from the side-lines as the issue was debated in parliament.

▶ **sideline** v [Vn] (*esp US*) to remove sb from a game, team, etc; to put sb out of action: [Vn] *Our best player has been sidelined by a knee injury.* ○ (*fig*) *The issue is in danger of being sidelined by more urgent business.*

sidelong /ˈsaɪdlɒŋ/ *adj* [attrib], *adv* (directed) to or from the side; sideways: *a sidelong glance* ○ *look sidelong at sb.* Compare SIDEWAYS.

sideshow /ˈsaɪdʃəʊ/ *n* **1** a small additional show or attraction at a CIRCUS, FAIR³(1), etc. **2** an activity of less importance than the main activity: *Offering cheap weekend fares was merely a sideshow to tempt more people to buy season tickets.*

sidestep /ˈsaɪdstep/ *n* a step to one side, esp to avoid sth/sb.

▶ **sidestep** v (-pp-) **1** to avoid sth, eg a blow, by stepping to one side: [Vn] *sidestep a tackle* (eg in football) [also V]. **2** to avoid answering a question, etc: [Vn] *He sidestepped the issue by saying it was not his responsibility.* [also V].

sidetrack /ˈsaɪdtræk/ v (*esp passive*) to lead sb into a discussion of sth that is not relevant to the main topic or issue: [Vn, Vnpr] *The lecturer was discussing the castle's history but got sidetracked by a question from the audience (into talking about religion).*

sidewalk /ˈsaɪdwɔːk/ *n* (*US*) = PAVEMENT 1.

sideways /ˈsaɪdweɪz/ *adv, adj* [attrib] **1** to, towards or from the side: *A crab moves sideways.* ○ *He looked sideways at me.* ○ *a sideways glance.* Compare SIDE-LONG. **2** with one side facing forwards: *The sofa will only go through the door sideways.* **IDM** **knock sb sideways** ⇨ KNOCK².

siding /ˈsaɪdɪŋ/ *n* **1** [C] a short track beside a main railway line, where trains can stand when they are not being used. **2** [U] (*US*) protective material used to cover the outside walls of buildings.

sidle /ˈsaɪdl/ v ~ **up/over (to sb/sth)**; ~ **along, past, away**, etc to move in the specified direction in a shy or nervous manner as if one does not want to be noticed: [Vpr] *He apologized and sidled out of the room.* [Vp] *She sidled over and whispered something in my ear.* ⇨ note at PROWL.

siege /siːdʒ/ *n* (**a**) a military operation in which an army tries to capture a town, etc by surrounding it and stopping the supply of food, etc to the people inside: *the siege of Troy* ○ *be in a state of siege* ○ *The city was **under siege** for eight months.* ○ *raise/lift* (ie end) *a siege* ○ *siege-guns.* (**b**) an operation by police, etc in which a building where people are living or hiding is surrounded for a long period of time in order to make them come out: *The siege was finally brought to an end when the terrorists surrendered.* **IDM** **lay ˈsiege to sth 1** to begin a siege of a town, building, etc. **2** to surround a building, esp in order to speak to or question the person or people living or working there: *Crowds of journalists laid siege to the star's flat.*

sienna /siˈenə/ *n* [U] a type of clay used for colouring paints, etc: *burnt sienna* (ie reddish-brown) ○ *raw sienna* (ie brownish-yellow).

sierra /siˈerə/ *n* (*esp in place-names*) a long range of steep JAGGED mountains, esp in Spain and America: *the Sierra Nevada.*

siesta /siˈestə/ *n* a rest or sleep taken in the early afternoon, esp in hot countries: *have/take a siesta.*

sieve

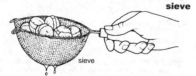

sieve

sieve /sɪv/ *n* an implement consisting of a wire or plastic net attached to a ring. Sieves are used for separating solids or large pieces of sth (which do not pass through) from liquids or very small pieces of sth (which do pass through). ⇨ picture. **IDM** **have a memory/mind like a ˈsieve** to have a very bad memory; to forget things easily.

▶ **sieve** v to put sth through a sieve: [Vnpr] *sieve the flour into a bowl* [also Vn].

sift /sɪft/ v **1(a)** to put a powder or other fine substance through a SIEVE: [Vn, Vnpr] *sift the flour/sugar (into a bowl).* (**b**) ~ **sth (out) from sth;** ~ **sth out** to separate sth from sth by putting it through a SIEVE: [Vnpr, Vnp] *sift (out) the lumps from the flour/the wheat from the chaff.* **2(a)** ~ **(through) sth** to examine sth very carefully, esp in order to separate the important or useful things from the rest: [Vn] *sift the evidence* [Vpr] *Investigators are sifting through the wreckage trying to find the cause of the crash.* (**b**) ~ **sth (out) from sth;** ~ **sth out** to separate sth from sth: [Vnp, Vnpr] *She looked quickly through the papers, sifting out (from the pile) anything that looked interesting.*

sigh /saɪ/ v **1** ~ **(with sth)** to take a long deep breath that can be heard, expressing sadness, relief, tiredness (TIRE¹), etc: [V] *She lay down on the bed sighing deeply.* [Vpr] *He sighed with relief on finding the key in his pocket.* **2** [V] (of the wind) to make a sound like sighing. **3** to express or say sth with a sigh: [V.speech] '*I'm afraid I can't help you,*' *she sighed.* **PHRV** **ˈsigh for sth/sb** (*fml*) to feel a deep sad desire for sth/sb that is lost, far away, etc: *sighing for his lost love.*

▶ **sigh** *n* an act or sound of sighing: *breathe/give/heave a sigh* ○ *with a deep sigh of relief/pleasure.*

sight¹ /saɪt/ *n* **1** [U] the ability to see; vision: *lose one's sight* (ie become blind) ○ *have good/poor sight and hearing* ○ *The disease has affected her sight.* **2** [U] ~ **of sth/sb** the action of seeing sth/sb: *After ten days at sea we had our first sight of land.* ○ *faint **at the sight of** blood.* **3** [U] the area or distance within which sb can see or sth can be seen: *She looked around for help but there was no one in sight.* ○ *He ate everything in sight.* ○ *The train came round the bend and into sight.* ○ *Put the parcel in the drawer out of sight.* ○ *They walked until they were out of sight of the house.* ○ *You must keep out of sight* (ie stay where you cannot be seen). ○ *The plane disappeared from sight.* ○ *She never let the child out of her sight.* ○ '*Get out of my sight*' (ie Go away)!' *he said angrily.* ○ (*fig*) *The end of the project is almost in/within sight.* **4(a)** [C] a thing that one sees or can see: *a museum recreating the sights and sounds of wartime Britain* ○ *The flowers are a lovely sight in spring.* ○ *Homeless people are now a familiar sight on our streets.* ○ *Victoria Station was a welcome sight to me after my long journey.* (**b**) **sights** [pl] the places of interest, esp in a town or city, that are often visited by tourists: *see the sights* ○ *If you come to Edinburgh I'll show you the sights.* **5 a sight** [sing] (*infml*) a person or thing that looks ridiculous, untidy, etc: *What a sight you look in those clothes!* **6** [C usu *pl*] a device that one looks through to aim a gun, etc or to observe sth through a TELESCOPE, etc: *the sights of a rifle* ○ *have sb/sth in one's sights.* **IDM** **at first glance/sight** ⇨ GLANCE. **at/on ˈsight** as soon as sb/sth is seen: *Soldiers were ordered to shoot on sight anybody trying to enter the building.* **catch sight of sb/sth** ⇨ CATCH¹. **hate, be sick of, etc the ˈsight of sb/sth** (*infml*) to hate, etc sb/sth very much: *I can't stand the sight of him!* ○ *My car breaks down so often that I'm beginning to hate the sight of it.* **heave in sight / into view** ⇨ HEAVE. **in the sight of sb / in sb's sight** (*fml*) in sb's opinion; in sb's view: *All men and women are equal in the sight of God.* **lose sight of sb/sth** ⇨ LOSE. **nowhere in sight** ⇨

S

NOWHERE. ‚out of ˈsight, ‚out of ˈmind (*saying*) we often forget people or things that are absent or can no longer be seen. **raise/lower one's ˈsights** to be more/less ambitious; to expect more/less: *If they can't afford a big house, they'll just have to lower their sights a little.* **set one's sights on sth / doing sth** to decide that one wants sth and try very hard to achieve it: *She's set her sights on winning the championship.* ○ *Tom's got his sights set on a career in acting.* **a (damn, etc) sight better, etc (than…); a (damn, etc) sight too good, etc** (*infml*) very much better, etc; far too good, etc: *This car's a (darned) sight better than my old one.* ○ *It's a (jolly) sight too expensive.* **a ‚sight for sore ˈeyes** (*infml*) a person or thing that one is relieved or pleased to see: *You're a sight for sore eyes — I thought you'd gone for good!* **sight unˈseen** without a chance to look at it before: *They bought the car sight unseen.*

▶ **sighted** *adj* able to see; not blind: *the blind and partially sighted.*

-sighted (in compound *adjs*) having the specified type of EYESIGHT: *short-/long-/far-sighted.*

■ **ˈsight-read** *v* [Vn] to play or sing music without looking at it or practising it before; to be able to do this. **ˈsight-reading** *n* [U].

sight² /saɪt/ *v* to manage to see sb/sth: [Vn] *After twelve days at sea, we sighted land.*

▶ **sighting** *n* an instance of sb/sth being seen: *several reported sightings of the escaped prisoner* ○ *the first sighting of a new star.*

sightless /ˈsaɪtləs/ *adj* unable to see; blind: *sightless eyes* ○ *a sightless species of bat.*

sightseeing /ˈsaɪtsiːɪŋ/ *n* [U] the activity of visiting places of interest as a tourist: *go sightseeing* ○ *a sightseeing tour of the city* ○ *We did a lot of sightseeing when we were in London.*

sign¹ /saɪn/ *n* **1** a mark, symbol, etc used to represent sth: *mathematical signs* (eg +, −, ×, ÷). **2** a board, notice, etc that directs sb towards sth, gives a warning, advertises a business, etc: *traffic signs* (eg for a speed limit or a bend in the road) ○ *a ˈshop-sign/ ˈpub-sign* ○ *Look out for a sign to the hospital.* ○ *The sign says it's 10 miles to Brighton.* **3** a gesture or movement made with the hand or head, used eg to give information or a command: *make the **sign of the cross*** (ie a movement in the shape of a cross made with the hand, eg in order to bless sb) ○ *She gave me a sign to sit down* (eg by pointing at a chair). **4** ~ **(of sth)** a thing that shows that sb/sth is present or exists, or that sth may happen: *signs of suffering on his face* ○ *some signs of improvement in her work* ○ *There wasn't a **sign of life** in the place* (ie There appeared to be no one present). ○ *The rain **shows no/little sign** of stopping.* ○ *All the signs are that things will get worse.* **5** (also ‚**sign of the ˈzodiac**) any of the 12 divisions of the ZODIAC, or the symbol representing it: *What sign were you born under?* See also STAR SIGN. **IDM** **a ‚sign of the ˈtimes** (*often derog*) a thing that shows the nature and quality of a particular period: *The rising level of crime is a sign of the times.*

■ **ˈsign language** *n* [U, C] a system of communication, eg for DEAF people, using gestures instead of words.

sign² /saɪn/ *v* **1** to write one's name on a document, etc, eg to show that one has written it, that it is genuine, or that one agrees with what it says: [Vn] *sign a letter/cheque/contract* ○ *sign one's autograph* [Vn-n] *sign oneself 'Azed'* ○ *an article signed 'Sirius'* [V, Vn] *Sign (your name) here, please.* **2** (no passive) to indicate eg a request or an order by making a gesture: [Vpr.*that*, Vpr.*wh*] *sign to sb that it is time to go/where to go* [Vn.*to* inf, Vpr.*to* inf] *The police officer signed (for) them to stop.* **3** ~ **(sb) (for/with/to sb/sth)** to be engaged or engage sb, eg as a sports player or musician, by signing a contract: [Vn] *Arsenal have just signed a new striker.* [Vpr] *He signed for Arsenal yesterday.* ○ *The band signed to/with Creature Records.* [also V, Vnpr]. **IDM** **sign on the dotted ˈline** (*infml*) to sign a document, etc that legally commits one, eg to buy sth: *Just sign on the dotted line and the car is yours.* **sign sb's / sign one's own ˈdeath-warrant** to do sth that will result in sb's/one's death, defeat, etc: *By informing on the gang, he was signing his own death-warrant.* **sign/take the pledge** ⇨ PLEDGE. **PHRV** ‚**sign sth aˈway** to lose one's rights, property, etc by signing a document, etc: *I'll never get married — it's like signing your life away.* **ˈsign for sth** to sign a form, etc to show that one has received sth: *The courier asked me to sign for the package.*

‚**sign (sb) ˈin/ˈout** to write one's/sb's name when one arrives at or departs from a place: *You must sign guests in when they enter the club.*

‚**sign ˈoff 1** (*Brit*) to end a letter: *She signed off with 'Yours ever, Janet'.* **2** to end a broadcast in some way, eg by playing a short piece of music: *This is your resident DJ signing off and wishing you all a pleasant weekend.*

‚**sign ˈon** (*Brit infml*) to register as an unemployed person.

‚**sign (sb) ˈon/ˈup (for sth)** to sign or make sb sign an agreement to do a job, become a soldier, etc: *sign on for five years in the army/for a secretarial course* ○ *The club has signed up a new goalkeeper this season.*

‚**sign sth ˈover (to sb)** to transfer the ownership of sth to sb by signing a document, etc: *She has signed the house over to her daughter.*

▶ **signing** *n* a person engaged, eg as a football player, by signing a contract: *the team's recent signings.*

signal¹ /ˈsɪɡnəl/ *n* **1** a sign, gesture or sound intended as a message, command, etc: *hand signals* (ie made by the driver of a car, etc to show which way he or she intends to turn) ○ *She flashed the torch as a signal.* ○ *He gave the signal for the race to begin.* ○ *He raised his arm as a signal for us to stop.* **2** any device or object placed to control traffic, give people a warning, etc: *traffic signals* (ie for cars, etc in the streets) ○ *The signal* (ie light) *was at/on red, so the train stopped.* **3(a)** any event or action that causes an activity to begin: *The President's arrival was the signal for an outburst of cheering.* **(b)** anything indicating that sth exists or is likely to happen: *Her speech yesterday was a signal that her views have changed.* **4** a sequence of electronic impulses or radio waves transmitted or received: *receive a signal from a satellite* ○ *an area with a poor/good TV signal.*

▶ **signal** *v* (**-ll-**; *US* **-l-**) ~ **(to sb/sth) (for sth)** to make a signal or signals; to communicate with sb in this way: [V] *He seems to be signalling.* [Vpr] *signal wildly with one's arms* [Vn, Vnpr] *signal a message (to sb)* [V.*that*, V.*wh*] *signal that one is going to turn/ which way one is going to turn* [Vpr] *signal to the troops for the attack to begin* [Vpr.*wh*] *signal to sb which way to go* [Vn.*to* inf, Vpr.*to* inf no passive] *signal (to) the waiter to bring the menu* [Vnpr] (*fig*) *signal one's discontent by refusing to vote* [Vn] (*fig*) *an event signalling a change in public opinion.* **signaller** (*US* **signaler**) /ˈsɪɡnələ(r)/ *n* a person who signals, esp a solider specially trained to do this.

■ **ˈsignal-box** *n* (*Brit*) a building beside a railway, from which railway signals are operated.

signal² /ˈsɪɡnəl/ *adj* [attrib] very good or bad; outstanding: *a signal victory/success/failure.* ▶ **signally** /-nəli/ *adv*: *You have signally failed to do what was expected of us.*

signalman /ˈsɪɡnəlmən/ *n* (*pl* **-men** /-mən/) **1** a person who operates signals on a railway. **2** a person trained to give and receive signals in the army or navy.

signatory /ˈsɪgnətri; US -tɔːri/ n ~ (**to sth**) a person, country, etc that has signed an agreement: *the signatories to a treaty* ∘ *the signatory powers*.

signature /ˈsɪgnətʃə(r)/ n **1(a)** [C] a person's name written by herself or himself: *a document with two signatures on it* ∘ *Her signature is almost illegible.* ∘ *He put his signature to the petition.* (**b**) [U] the action of signing sth: *a contract ready for signature.* **2** [C usu *sing*] a distinctive quality: *The film bears the unmistakable signature of its director.* See also KEY SIGNATURE.

■ ˈsignature tune (*Brit*) (also theme tune, US signature) n a brief tune used to introduce a particular broadcast or performer.

signet-ring /ˈsɪgnət rɪŋ/ n a ring for the finger with a design cut into it.

significance /sɪgˈnɪfɪkəns/ n [U] **1** the meaning or intention of sth: *I didn't understand the significance of his remark until later.* **2** importance: *a speech of great significance* ∘ *This information by itself is of little significance.* ∘ *Few people realized the significance of the discovery.* Compare INSIGNIFICANCE.

significant /sɪgˈnɪfɪkənt/ adj **1(a)** having a particular meaning: *Their change of plan is strange but I don't think it's significant.* (**b**) full of meaning: *a significant remark/look/smile.* **2** important; considerable: *make a significant saving* ∘ *a significant rise in profits.* Compare INSIGNIFICANT.

▶ **significantly** adv **1** in a way that has a special importance or meaning: *Significantly, he did not deny that there might be an election.* **2** to an important or considerable degree: *Profits have risen significantly.* ∘ *Nitrate levels are now significantly higher.*

signification /ˌsɪgnɪfɪˈkeɪʃn/ n (*fml* or *linguistics*) **1** [C] the meaning of a word, etc. **2** [U] the action of signifying (SIGNIFY 2) sth.

signify /ˈsɪgnɪfaɪ/ v (*pt, pp* -**fied**) (*fml*) **1** to be a sign of sth; to mean sth: [Vn] *Do the dark clouds signify rain?* ∘ *This signifies a change of attitude.* **2** to make sth known; to indicate sth: [Vn, V.*that*] *signify one's agreement/that one agrees* [Vnpr] *She signified her approval with a smile.* **3** (used esp in questions and negative sentences) to be of importance; to matter: [V] *It doesn't signify, so you needn't worry about it.*

signpost /ˈsaɪnpəʊst/ n a sign attached to a post, esp where roads meet, with arms pointing to places along the road and often showing the distances to them: *The signpost said 'Bristol 15 miles'.*

▶ **signpost** v **1** (esp passive) to provide a road, place, etc with signposts: [Vn] *The route is well signposted the whole way.* [Vnpr] *a big roundabout signposted to Newport and Abergavenny.* **2** to indicate a course, direction, etc: [Vn].*The language learning points are clearly signposted in terms that students can understand.* **signposting** n [U].

Sikh /siːk/ n a member of a religion (**Sikhism**) that developed from Hinduism in the 16th century and is based on a belief in only one God.

silage /ˈsaɪlɪdʒ/ n [U] grass or other green crops that are stored without first being dried and used to feed animals in winter.

silence /ˈsaɪləns/ n **1** [U] the condition of being quiet or silent; the absence of sound: *the silence of the night* ∘ *A scream broke/shattered the silence.* ∘ *In the library silence reigned* (ie it was totally silent). **2(a)** [U] the state of not speaking, answering sth spoken or silent, making comments, etc; the fact of not mentioning sth or revealing a secret: *All my questions (were) met with silence from him.* ∘ *They listened to him in silence.* ∘ *The teacher's stern look reduced him to silence.* ∘ *I can't understand her silence on this matter.* ∘ *I assume that your silence implies consent* (ie that by saying nothing you are

showing that you do not disagree). ∘ *After a year's silence* (ie a year during which she did not write), *I got a letter from her.* ∘ *They tried to buy his silence* (ie to pay him not to reveal a secret). (**b**) [C] a period during which sb is silent: *She became used to his long silences.* ∘ *a one-minute silence in honour of the dead* ∘ *There was a brief silence, followed by uproar.* ∘ (*joc*) *a deafening* (ie very noticeable) *silence.* **IDM** a **pregnant pause/silence** ⇨ PREGNANT. ˌsilence is ˈgolden (*saying*) it is often best not to say anything.

▶ **silence** v to make sb/sth become silent; to make sb/sth silent(er): [Vn] *Her critics refused to be silenced.* ∘ *His look of disapproval silenced her.* ∘ *silence the enemy's guns* (eg by destroying them) ∘ *Their doubts were not easily silenced.* **silencer** n (**a**) (*Brit*) (*US* **muffler**) a device that reduces the noise made by a vehicle's EXHAUST¹(2). ⇨ picture at CAR. (**b**) a device that reduces the noise made by a gun being fired.

silence *interj* be quiet: *'Silence!' he roared.*

silent /ˈsaɪlənt/ adj **1(a)** making little or no sound; not accompanied by any sound: *with silent footsteps* ∘ *the smooth, silent running of the engine* ∘ *The music stopped, and the room fell silent.* (**b**) not expressed aloud: *a silent prayer/protest* ∘ *I watched her in silent admiration.* **2(a)** not speaking; making no spoken or written comments: *The vast crowd fell silent.* ∘ *There were several questions I wanted to ask but I kept/remained silent.* ∘ *Everyone stood in shocked, silent groups.* ∘ *On certain important details the report is strangely silent.* (**b**) saying little: *He is the strong, silent type.* **3** (of films, esp before the 1930s) without a SOUNDTRACK(1): *a silent film/movie* ∘ *the silent screen.* **4** (of a letter) written but not pronounced: *The 'b' in 'doubt' and the 'w' in 'wrong' are silent.* ⇨ note at QUIET. **IDM** the ˌsilent maˈjority the people with moderate views who are unable or unwilling to express them publicly. ▶ **silently** adv: *standing silently beside him* ∘ *They drove on silently.*

■ ˌsilent ˈpartner n (*US*) = SLEEPING PARTNER.

silhouette /ˌsɪluˈet/ n (**a**) a dark outline of sb/sth seen against a light background: *the silhouettes of the trees against the evening sky.* (**b**) a picture showing sb/sth as a black shape against a light background: *paint sb in silhouette.*

▶ **silhouette** v ~ sb/sth (**against sth**) (usu passive) to make sth appear as a silhouette: [Vnpr] *stand silhouetted against the glow of the fire* [also Vn].

silica /ˈsɪlɪkə/ n [U] a compound of SILICON found in sand and in rocks such as QUARTZ.

silicate /ˈsɪlɪkeɪt/ n [C, U] any of the compounds of SILICA.

silicon /ˈsɪlɪkən/ n [U] (*symb* **Si**) a chemical element. Silicon is found in sand and in many rocks. It is used in making glass and in computers and electronic equipment. ⇨ App 7.

■ ˌsilicon ˈchip n a very small piece of silicon used to carry a complex electronic circuit.

silicone /ˈsɪlɪkəʊn/ n [U] any of a number of compounds of SILICON used to make paint, artificial rubber, VARNISH, etc: *a silicone breast implant.*

silk /sɪlk/ n **1** [U] (**a**) fine soft thread produced by silkworms (SILKWORM). (**b**) cloth or thread for sewing made from this: *dressed in silk* ∘ *a silk scarf/dress.* **2 silks** [pl] (*dated*) clothes made from silk; silk fabrics. **3** [C] (*Brit infml*) a lawyer (a Queen's or King's Counsel), who wears a silk GOWN(2) in court. **IDM** smooth as silk ⇨ SMOOTH¹.

■ ˌsilk-screen ˈprinting n [U] a method of printing that involves forcing ink through a design cut in a piece of fine material.

silken /ˈsɪlkən/ adj [usu attrib] **1** (*usu approv*) soft and smooth; shiny like silk: *a silken voice* ∘ *silken hair.* **2** (*esp rhet*) made of silk: *a silken gown.*

silkworm /ˈsɪlkwɜːm/ n a CATERPILLAR that spins silk around itself.

---

silky /ˈsɪlki/ *adj* (**-ier, -iest**) (*usu approv*) soft, fine, smooth, etc like silk: *silky hair/skin* ○ *a silky lining* ○ (*fig*) *a silky manner.* ▶ **silkiness** *n* [U].

sill /sɪl/ *n* a piece of wood, stone, etc forming the base of a window or a door: *She put a pot of geraniums on the sill.* See also WINDOW-SILL.

silly /ˈsɪli/ *adj* (**-ier, -iest**) (**a**) not showing thought or understanding; foolish: *a silly little boy* ○ *silly mistakes* ○ *Don't be silly!* ○ *What a silly thing to say!* (**b**) seeming ridiculous; CHILDISH: *play silly games.* **IDM** **play 'silly buggers** (*Brit sl*) to behave in a foolish or silly way: *Stop playing silly buggers and help me lift this.*
▶ **silliness** *n* [U].

silly (also ˌsilly ˈbilly) *n* (*infml*) (often used by or when speaking to children) a silly person: *Of course it won't hurt you, silly!*
■ **the 'silly season** *n* [sing] (*Brit*) the time, usu in the summer, when newspapers are full of unimportant stories because there is little news.

silo /ˈsaɪləʊ/ *n* (*pl* **-os**) **1(a)** a tall tower or underground place, usu on a farm, in which grass or other green crops are stored to be used as food for animals. (**b**) a tower or underground place for storing grain, cement, nuclear waste, etc. **2** an underground place where missiles are kept ready for firing.

silt /sɪlt/ *n* [U] sand, mud, etc carried by flowing water and left at the mouth of a river, in a harbour, etc.
▶ **silt** *v* **PHRV** ˌsilt (sth) 'up to become blocked or block sth with silt: *The harbour has silted up.* ○ *Sand has silted up the mouth of the river.*
silty *adj* covered with, full of or containing silt: *silty soils.*

silver /ˈsɪlvə(r)/ *n* **1** [U] (*symb* Ag) a chemical element. Silver is a shiny white precious metal used for ornaments, jewellery, coins, etc: *solid silver* ○ *a silver mine.* ▷ App 7. **2** [U] coins made of silver or of a metal looking like it: *£20 in notes and £5 in silver.* **3** [U] dishes, ornaments, etc made of silver: *Burglars stole all their silver.* **4** [C *usu sing*,U] = SILVER MEDAL: *Harris won (the) silver for Canada.* ○ *2 golds and 6 silvers.* **IDM** **born with a silver spoon in one's mouth** ▷ BORN. **cross sb's palm with silver** ▷ CROSS².
▶ **silver** *v* (*usu passive*) **1** to cover the surface or part of the surface of sth with silver or sth that looks like silver: [Vn] *a silvered crystal bowl.* **2** (*esp rhet*) to cause sth to become bright like silver: [Vn] *The edge of the spade was silvered from years of use.* ○ *The years have silvered her hair.*
silver *adj* made of or looking like silver: *a silver plate/dish/watch* ○ *a silver car/paint/thread* ○ *the silver moon.* **IDM** **every cloud has a silver lining** ▷ CLOUD¹.
silvery /ˈsɪlvəri/ *adj* **1** shiny or coloured like silver: *silvery fish* ○ *silvery grey hair.* **2** [attrib] (*approv*) (of sounds) high-pitched and clear: *the silvery notes of the little bells.*
■ ˌsilver 'birch *n* (*pl* unchanged or **birches**) a common tree with a pale grey bark.
ˌsilver 'jubilee *n* [C *usu sing*] the 25th anniversary of sth. Compare DIAMOND JUBILEE, GOLDEN JUBILEE.
ˌsilver 'medal (also **silver**) *n* [C *usu sing*] a medal awarded as second prize in a competition or race, esp in the Olympic Games: *win/take the silver medal.*
ˌsilver 'paper *n* [U] (*infml*) very thin sheets of tin or ALUMINIUM, used esp for wrapping cigarettes, chocolates, etc.
ˌsilver 'plate *n* [U] metal articles coated with silver.
ˌsilver-'plated *adj*: *silver-plated dishes/cutlery.*
the ˌsilver 'screen *n* [sing] (*rhet*) the cinema industry: *stars of the silver screen.*

ˌsilver-'tongued *adj* speaking in a way that charms or persuades people: *a ˌsilver-tongued 'lawyer.*
ˌsilver 'wedding *n* the 25th anniversary of a wedding: *My parents celebrate their silver wedding (anniversary) this year.* Compare DIAMOND WEDDING, GOLDEN WEDDING.

silverfish /ˈsɪlvəfɪʃ/ *n* (*pl* unchanged) a small insect without wings that is silver in colour and usu found in houses.

silversmith /ˈsɪlvəsmɪθ/ *n* a person who makes or sells silver articles.

silverware /ˈsɪlvəweə(r)/ *n* [U] articles made of silver or a metal that looks like silver, esp knives, forks, dishes, etc used at meals.

simian /ˈsɪmiən/ *adj* (*fml*) of or like a monkey or an APE: *simian arms.*

similar /ˈsɪmələ(r)/ *adj* ~ (**to sb/sth**); ~ (**in sth**) resembling sb/sth but not the same; like sb/sth: *We have similar tastes in music.* ○ *I reached a similar conclusion.* ○ *It is similar in taste to a banana.* ○ *The brothers look very similar.* Compare DISSIMILAR.
▶ **similarly** *adv* **1** in a similar way: *The two boys dress similarly.* **2** (used when indicating a connection between two facts, events, etc) also: *Similarly, the demand for copper has increased.*
similarity /ˌsɪməˈlærəti/ *n* ~ (**to sb/sth**); ~ (**between A and B**) **1** [U,sing] the state of being similar: *points of similarity between the two proposals* ○ *The species shows a great/close/striking/remarkable similarity to one found in parts of Africa.* **2** [C] ~ (**in/of sth**) (**to/with sth/sb**) a similar feature or aspect: *similarities in/of style/approach* ○ *It has/shows many similarities with/to the AIDS virus.*

simile /ˈsɪməli/ *n* [C,U] a comparison of one thing with another, eg 'as brave as a lion', 'a face like a mask': *use striking similes* ○ *Her style is rich in simile.* Compare METAPHOR.

simmer /ˈsɪmə(r)/ *v* **1** (esp in cooking) to stay or make sth stay almost at boiling point: [V] *Leave the soup to simmer.* [Vn] *Simmer the stew for at least an hour.* **2** ~ (**with sth**) to be filled with strong feelings which one has difficulty controlling: [Vpr] *simmer with rage/annoyance/excitement about sth* [also V]. **3** (of an argument, a dispute, etc) to develop for a time without any real anger or violence being shown: [V] *This row has been simmering for months.* **PHRV** ˌsimmer 'down (*infml*) to become calm after a period of anger, excitement, violence, etc: *Just simmer down and stop shouting.* ○ *Things have simmered down since the riots last week.*
▶ **simmer** *n* [sing] a period or condition of simmering (SIMMER 1): *bring to a gentle simmer.*

simper /ˈsɪmpə(r)/ *v* (**a**) to smile in a foolish insincere way: [V] *a simpering waiter.* (**b**) to say sth with such a smile: [V.speech] *'I never expected to win,' he simpered.*
▶ **simper** *n* [sing] a foolish insincere smile.
simperingly /ˈsɪmpərɪŋli/ *adv.*

simple /ˈsɪmpl/ *adj* (**-r, -st**) **1** easily done or understood; not causing difficulty: *a simple task/sum/problem/answer* ○ *written in simple English* ○ *The machine is quite simple to use.* **2** plain in form, design, etc; without much decoration or ornament: *simple food/furniture* ○ *The hotel is simple and informal.* ○ *enjoy a/the simple life* (ie a way of living without expensive goods, entertainments, etc) ○ *clothes that are simple but elegant.* **3** [usu attrib] (**a**) consisting of few parts or elements: *a simple design/tool/model* ○ *a simple sentence* (ie one with only a main clause) ○ *I'm afraid that the position is not as simple as that.* (**b**) not highly developed; basic in structure or function: *simple forms of life* ○ *a fairly simple system of classification.* **4** nothing more or other than: *give a simple unbiased account of events* ○ *It's a simple fact.* ○ *The reason is quite simple — I just like horses.* ○ *He didn't manage to sell it for the* *simple reason that* (ie because) *the price was too high.* **5(a)** natural(5), honest and frank: *behave in a simple, open way.* (**b**) not having a high position in society; ordinary: *I'm just a simple soldier.* **6(a)** easily deceived; foolishly ignorant: *He's not as simple as he looks.* (**b**) (*infml*) having abnormally low intelligence: *She doesn't understand you. She's a bit simple.* **7** (*grammar*) (used to describe the present or past TENSE² of an active verb that is formed without an auxiliary verb (AUXILIARY), as in *They grow coffee, She loved him, He came*): *the simple present/past tense.* **IDM** **pure and simple** ⇨ PURE.

▶ **simply** /ˈsɪmpli/ *adv* **1** in an easy way: *solved quite simply* ○ *Explain it as simply as you can.* **2** in a plain way: *be simply dressed* ○ *live simply.* **3** (used for emphasis) completely; absolutely: *His pronunciation is simply terrible.* ○ *I simply refuse to go!* **4** only; just; merely (MERE¹): *I bought the picture simply because I liked it.* ○ *Is success simply a matter of working hard?* **5** (used to introduce a summary of a situation): *Quite simply, we can't afford it.* ○ *It's simply that we like to deal with customers direct and not through an agent.*

■ ˌsimple ˈfracture *n* a fracture of a bone in which the bone does not penetrate the skin.

ˌsimple ˈinterest *n* [U] interest paid only on the sum of money invested, not on any interest added to it. Compare COMPOUND INTEREST.

ˌsimple-ˈminded *adj* (*often derog*) having or showing very little intelligence: *a simple-minded approach to the problem* ○ *He think I'm simple-minded enough to believe him.*

simpleton /ˈsɪmpltən/ *n* (*dated*) a person who is foolish, easily deceived or not very intelligent.

simplicity /sɪmˈplɪsəti/ *n* [U] (**a**) the quality of being easy, plain or natural(5): *the simplicity of the problem* ○ *the simplicity of her style* ○ *a character marked by frankness and simplicity* ○ *For simplicity's sake, we'll consider only the two largest categories.* (**b**) [C *usu pl*] anything that is easy, plain or natural: *the simplicities of country living.* **IDM** **be simˌplicity itˈself** to be very easy: *Cleaning the apparatus is simplicity itself — just wipe it over with a damp cloth.*

simplify /ˈsɪmplɪfaɪ/ *v* (*pt, pp* **-fied**) to make sth easy to do or understand; to make sth simple(1): [Vn] *a simplified text* (eg one for learners of the language) ○ *simplify the instructions so that children can understand them* ○ *That will simplify my task.*

▶ **simplification** /ˌsɪmplɪfɪˈkeɪʃn/ *n* (**a**) [U, sing] the action or process of simplifying sth: *a simplification of the rules.* (**b**) [C] a statement, situation, etc that is the result of simplifying sth: *That's a simplification — the reality is more complex.*

simplistic /sɪmˈplɪstɪk/ *adj* (*usu derog*) making difficult problems, issues, ideas, etc seem much simpler than they really are, eg in order to conceal sth: *a rather simplistic assessment of the situation.* ▶ **simplistically** /-klɪ/ *adv.*

simulacrum /ˌsɪmjuˈleɪkrəm/ *n* (*pl* **simulacra** /-krə/) (*fml*) a thing resembling or made to resemble sth.

simulate /ˈsɪmjuleɪt/ *v* **1** to pretend to have or feel an emotion: [Vn] *simulate anger/joy/interest.* **2** to create certain conditions by means of a model, etc, eg for study or training purposes: [Vn] *simulate a battle* ○ *The computer simulates conditions on the sea bed.* **3** to take the appearance of sth/sb: [Vn] *insects that simulate dead leaves* ○ *change colour to simulate the background.*

▶ **simulated** *adj* [usu attrib] artificial, but made to look, feel, etc like the real thing: *simulated fur/pearls.*

simulation /ˌsɪmjuˈleɪʃn/ *n* **1** [U] the action of simulating sth: *the simulation of genuine concern* ○ *the simulation of flight conditions.* **2** [C, U] the deliber-

ate making of certain conditions that could exist in reality, eg in order to study them or learn from them: *a computer simulation of a golf swing.*

simulator *n* any device designed to simulate certain conditions, eg flight, space travel, etc.

simultaneous /ˌsɪmlˈteɪniəs; *US* ˌsaɪm-/ *adj* ~ (**with sth**) happening or done at the same time as sth: *simultaneous demonstrations in London and New York* ○ *The conference delegates were provided with simultaneous translation of the speeches.* ▶ **simultaneously** *adv: The two drugs were developed simultaneously but quite independently.* ○ *All the eggs hatch simultaneously.* **simultaneity** /ˌsɪmltəˈneɪəti; *US* ˌsaɪmltəˈniːəti/ *n* [U].

sin¹ /sɪn/ *n* **1(a)** [U] the action of breaking a religious or moral law: *a life of sin.* (**b**) [C] an offence against such a law: *commit a sin* ○ *confess one's sins to a priest* ○ *the sin of gluttony.* See also DEADLY SIN, MORTAL SIN, ORIGINAL SIN. **2** [C] an action regarded as a serious fault or offence: *She treats being late for meals as an unforgivable sin.* ○ (*joc*) *It's a sin to stay indoors on such a fine day.* **IDM** **cover/hide a multitude of sins** ⇨ MULTITUDE. **be/do sth for one's sins** (*joc*) to be/do sth as a supposed punishment for sth: *I have to judge the local flower show for my sins!* **live in sin** ⇨ LIVE². **(as) miserable/ugly as ˈsin** (*infml*) very miserable/ugly.

▶ **sin** *v* (**-nn-**) ~ (**against sth**) to commit a sin or sins; to do wrong: [V] *He had sinned and repented.* [Vpr] (*fig*) *They sinned against the unwritten rules of the school.*

sinful /-fl/ *adj* (*rather fml*) wrong; wicked: *a sinful life* ○ (*infml*) *a sinful waste of good wine.* **sinfully** /-fəli/ *adv.* **sinfulness** *n* [U].

sinless *adj* (*fml*) never sinning; innocent. **sinlessness** *n* [U].

sin² *abbr* (*mathematics*) sine. Compare COS³.

since /sɪns/ *prep* (used with the present or past perfect tense) from a specified time in the past until a later past time, or until now: *She's been ill since Sunday.* ○ *I haven't eaten since breakfast.* ○ *She's been working in a bank since leaving school.* ○ *Since the party he had only spoken to her once.*

▶ **since** *conj* **1** (used with the present perfect, past perfect or simple present tense in the main clause) from a specified event in the past until a later past event, or until now: *Cath hasn't phoned since she went to Berlin.* ○ *It was the first time I'd had visitors since I'd moved into the flat.* ○ *How long is it since we last went to the cinema?* **2** because; as: *Since I haven't got her address I can't write to her.* **IDM** **ever since** ⇨ EVER.

since *adv* (used with the present or past perfect tense) from a specified time in the past until a later past time, or until now: *He left home two weeks ago and we haven't heard from him since.* ○ *She moved to London last May and has since got a job on a newspaper.* ○ *The original building has long since* (ie long before now) *been demolished.*

sincere /sɪnˈsɪə(r)/ *adj* (**-r, -st**) **1** (of feelings or behaviour) not pretended; genuine: *sincere affection/concern* ○ *Please accept my sincere thanks/apologies.* ○ *I think his offer of help was sincere.* **2** (of people) only saying things that one really means or believes: *a sincere well-wisher* ○ *Do you think she was being sincere when she said she liked my hat?* Compare INSINCERE.

▶ **sincerely** *adv:* thank sb *sincerely* ○ *yours sincerely/sincerely yours.* ⇨ note at YOUR.

sincerity /sɪnˈserəti/ *n* [U] the quality of being sincere; honesty: *the warmth and sincerity of his welcome.*

sine /saɪn/ *n* (*abbr* **sin**) (*mathematics*) (in a TRIANGLE with one angle of 90°) the RATIO between the length of the side opposite one of the angles of less than 90°

S

and the length of the longest side. Compare COSINE, TANGENT 2.

sinecure /'sɪnɪkjʊə(r), 'saɪn-/ n a position that requires no or little work, but gives the holder status or money.

sine die /ˌsaɪni 'daɪi:, ˌsɪneɪ 'di:eɪ/ adv (Latin fml esp law) without a date being fixed: *suspend a trial sine die.*

sine qua non /ˌsɪneɪ kwɑ: 'nəʊn/ n [sing] (Latin fml) an essential condition; a thing that is absolutely necessary: *Patience is a sine qua non for a good teacher.*

sinew /'sɪnju:/ n 1 [C, U] a tough cord of tissue joining a muscle to a bone. 2 sinews [pl] (a) physical strength; muscles. (b) (fml) the parts of a plan, a city, an organization, etc that give it strength: *A country's sinews are its roads and railways.*

▶ **sinewy** adj 1 having strong sinews or muscles; tough: *sinewy arms/legs.* 2 having or showing strength or vigour: *her sinewy prose style.*

sing /sɪŋ/ v (pt sang /sæŋ/; pp sung /sʌŋ/) 1 ~ (sth) (for/to sb) to make musical sounds with the voice in the form of a song, tune, etc: [V] *She always sings in the bath.* ○ *You're not singing in tune.* [Vn] *sing a song* ○ *Which part does he sing in the opera?* [Vp] *The birds were singing away happily outside.* [Vpr] *He sang to a piano accompaniment.* [Vnpr] *She was singing a lullaby to her child.* ○ *He sang the baby to sleep.* [Vn, Vnpr] *Will you sing me a song/sing a song for me?* [also V.speech]. 2 to make or move with a sound like a high-pitched whistle: [V, Vp] *The kettle was singing (away) on the cooker.* [Vpr] *The sound of the ocean singing in her ears.* ○ *A bullet sang past my ear.* IDM **sing a different 'song/'tune** to change one's opinion about or attitude towards sb/sth. **sing sb's/sth's 'praises** to praise sb/sth greatly: *The critics are certainly singing the praises of her new book.* PHRV ˌ**sing a'long (with sb/sth)**, ˌ**sing a'long (to sth)** to sing together with sb or while a musical instrument, record, etc is playing: *singing along to her favourite tune on the radio.* **'sing of sth** (dated or fml) to sing about and esp in praise of sth: *singing of man's struggle against oppression.* ˌ**sing 'up** (Brit) to sing more loudly: *Sing up, let's hear you.*

▶ **singer** n a person who sings, esp in public: *an opera singer* ○ *He's a ˌsinger-'songwriter.*

singing n [U] 1 the art of being a singer: *teach singing* ○ *a singing teacher* ○ *her singing career* ○ *He has a pleasant singing voice* (ie can sing pleasantly). 2 the action or sound of singing: *singing and dancing* ○ *their beautiful singing of the madrigal* ○ *I heard singing next door.*

■ **'sing-along** n = SINGSONG n 2: *a sing-along chorus.*

singe /sɪndʒ/ v (pres p singeing) (a) to burn sth slightly, usu by mistake: [Vn] *He leaned over the candle and singed his jacket.* (b) to be burnt in this way: [V] *the smell of singeing fur.*

▶ **singe** n a slight burn on cloth, etc.

single /'sɪŋgl/ adj 1 [attrib] (a) one only; not in a pair, group, etc: *a single red rose* ○ *do all the work in a single afternoon* ○ *the single European market* ○ *single-sex education* ○ *a single-storey house* ○ *There wasn't a single person I knew* (ie I knew no one at all) *at the party.* (b) considered on its own; separate: *the single most important event in the history of the world* ○ *She removed every single thing from the box.* 2 not married: *single men and women* ○ *remain single.* 3 [attrib] designed for, or used or done by, one person: *a single bed/sheet* ○ *reserve one single and one double room* (eg at a hotel). 4 [attrib] (Brit) (US one-way) (of a journey) only to a place, not there and back: *a single fare/ticket.* Compare RETURN² 2. IDM **Indian/single file** ⇨ FILE². **(in) ˌsingle 'figures** (in) figures less than ten: *Inflation is down to single figures* (ie under 10%).

▶ **single** n 1 [C] (infml) a single(4) ticket: *two singles to Leeds.* 2 [C] (dated) a record with only one short recording on each side: *a hit single.* Compare ALBUM 2, LP. 3 singles [pl] (esp US) people who are not married: *a club for singles* ○ *a singles bar/holiday.* 4 singles [sing v] a game played with one player rather than a pair of players on each side: *play (a) singles* ○ *the men's/women's singles in the golf tournament* ○ *a singles match.* 5 [C] (in cricket) a hit from which one run is scored.

single v PHRV ˌ**single sb/sth 'out (for sth)** to choose sb/sth from a group, eg for special attention: *Which would you single out as the best?* ○ *He was singled out for punishment.*

singleness n [U]: *show singleness of purpose* (ie concentrate on one goal, aim, etc).

singly /'sɪŋgli/ adv one by one; on one's own: *Do you teach your students singly or in groups?*

■ ˌ**single-'breasted** adj (of a coat or jacket) having only one set of buttons, so that the two front edges meet in the middle. Compare DOUBLE-BREASTED.

ˌ**single 'combat** n [U] fighting, usu with weapons, between two people: *meet in single combat.*

ˌ**single 'cream** n [U] (Brit) cream that does not contain a lot of milk fat. Compare DOUBLE CREAM.

ˌ**single-'decker** n a bus with only one level. Compare DOUBLE-DECKER.

ˌ**single-'handed** adj, adv done by one person with no help from others: *a ˌsingle-handed 'round-the-world race* ○ *do sth single-handed.* ˌ**single-'handedly** adv: *She won the game almost single-handedly.*

ˌ**single 'market** n an association of countries allowing free trade between its members, with a common currency and few restrictions on the movement of goods, money and people between countries.

ˌ**single-'minded** adj having or concentrating on one aim, purpose, etc: *I admire her single-minded determination to succeed.* **single-mindedly** adv: *work single-mindedly at sth.* **single-mindedness** n [U].

ˌ**single 'parent** n a parent who looks after a child or children without a partner: *a ˌsingle-parent 'family.*

singlet /'sɪŋglət/ n (Brit) (a) a man's garment without sleeves, worn under or instead of a shirt. (b) such a garment worn by runners, etc.

singsong /'sɪŋsɒŋ/ adj (of a way of speaking) with a repeated rising and falling rhythm: *He had a curious singsong voice.*

▶ **singsong** n 1 [sing] a singsong manner of speaking: *a distinct Welsh singsong.* 2 (also sing-along) [C] (infml) an informal occasion when a group of people sing songs together: *a singsong round the camp-fire.*

singular /'sɪŋgjələ(r)/ n (grammar) (abbreviated as sing in this dictionary) a form of a noun or verb which refers to one person or thing: *The verb must be in the singular.* ○ *The word 'clothes' has no singular.* Compare PLURAL.

▶ **singular** adj 1 (grammar) of or having the singular form: *a singular verb/noun/ending.* 2 (fml) (a) of an exceptionally high standard; remarkable: *a singular achievement.* (b) (dated) unusual; strange: *a singular style of dress.* **singularly** adv 1 very; in a remarkable way: *a singularly gifted pianist* ○ *The government has singularly failed to do anything about unemployment.* 2 (dated) unusually; in an odd way: *singularly attired.* **singularity** /ˌsɪŋgjuˈlærəti/ n [U] (fml) the strange or UNIQUE quality of sth: *the singularity of her voice.*

sinister /'sɪnɪstə(r)/ adj suggesting evil, or that sth bad may happen: *a pale, sinister figure lurking in the shadows* ○ *a sinister motive/conspiracy* ○ *There was something sinister about the man which made me feel uneasy.*

sink¹ /sɪŋk/ v (pt **sank** /sæŋk/; pp **sunk** /sʌŋk/) **1** to go down under the surface or towards the bottom of a liquid or soft substance: [V] *If you throw a stone into water, it sinks.* [V, Vpr] *The ship sank (to the bottom of the ocean).* [Vpr, Vp] *My feet sank (down) into the mud.* **2** to make a ship, etc go to the bottom of the sea: [Vn] *a battleship sunk by a torpedo.* **3** (*infml*) to prevent sb or sb's plans from succeeding; to ruin sth: [Vn] *The press want to sink his bid for the Presidency.* ○ *We'll be sunk if the car breaks down.* **4** to become lower; to fall slowly downwards: [V] *The foundations of the house are beginning to sink.* ○ *The sun was sinking in the west.* [Vpr] *The wounded animal sank to the ground, defeated.* [Vpr, Vp] *I sank (down) into an armchair.* **5** to decrease in value, number, amount, strength, etc: [V] *Share prices are sinking.* [Vpr] *The pound has sunk to its lowest recorded level against the dollar.* [V] *He is sinking fast* (ie will soon die). [Vpr, Vadv] (*fig*) *Stealing from your friends? How could you sink to this/sink so low?* **6** (of a person's voice) to become quieter: [Vpr] *Her voice sank to a whisper.* [also V]. **7(a)** to place sth in a hole made by digging: [Vn, Vnpr] *sink a post (into the ground).* **(b)** to make sth by digging: [Vn] *sink a well/shaft* [also Vnpr]. **8** to hit a ball so that it goes into a pocket or hole in SNOOKER(1), golf, etc: [Vnpr] *sink the red into the top pocket* [Vn] *He sank a 12-foot putt to win the match.* **9** (*infml*) to drink sth, esp a large amount of alcohol: [Vn] *They sank a whole bottle of gin between them.* **IDM** **be ˈsunk in sth** to be in a state of deep despair or deep thought: *She just sat there, sunk in gloom.* **one's heart sinks** ⇨ HEART. **sink one's ˈdifferences** to agree to forget what one disagrees about: *We must sink our differences in order to save the company.* **a/that ˈsinking feeling** (*infml*) an unpleasant feeling that one has when one realizes that sth bad has happened or is about to happen: *I had that horrible sinking feeling when I saw the ambulance outside the house.* **ˌsink or ˈswim** (to be in a situation where one will either fail totally or survive by one's own efforts): *With no more government aid the company was left to sink or swim.* **PHRV** **ˌsink ˈin /ˌsink ˈinto sth 1** (of liquids) to go down into another substance; to be absorbed in sth: *Rub the cream on your skin and let it sink in.* ○ *The rain sank into the dry ground.* **2** (of words, an event, etc) to be fully understood or realized: *He paused for a moment to let his words sink in.* ○ *It took a long time for the truth to sink in.* **ˈsink into sth** (no passive) to go gradually into a less active or happy state: *sink into sleep/a coma* ○ *She sank deeper into depression.* **ˌsink sth ˈinto sth 1** to make sth sharp go deeply into sth solid: *sink a knife into butter* ○ *The dog sank its teeth into my leg* (ie bit it). **2** to invest money in a business, etc: *They sank all their savings into the venture.*

sink² /sɪŋk/ n **(a)** a fixed open container, esp in a kitchen, with a water supply and a drain for waste water to flow away, used for washing dishes, cleaning vegetables, etc: *a sink unit* (ie a sink with drawers and cupboards underneath). **(b)** a similar, usu smaller, container for washing one's hands, etc, esp in a BATHROOM(1); a wash-basin (WASH²). **IDM** **everything but the kitchen sink** ⇨ KITCHEN.

sinker /ˈsɪŋkə(r)/ n a weight attached to a fishing line or net to keep it under water. **IDM** **hook, line and sinker** ⇨ HOOK¹.

sinner /ˈsɪnə(r)/ n (*rather fml*) a person who sins, esp habitually: *repentant sinners.*

Sino- (also **sino-**) /ˈsaɪnəʊ/ *comb form* Chinese; of China: *ˌSino-Japaˈnese.*

sinuous /ˈsɪnjuəs/ *adj* having many curves and twists; winding: *a sinuous snake* ○ *the sinuous movements of the dancer* ○ *the river's sinuous course.* ▸ **sinuously** *adv.*

sinus /ˈsaɪnəs/ n (*pl* **sinuses**) a hollow place in a bone, esp any of the spaces in the bones of the head that are connected to the inside of the nose.
▸ **sinusitis** /ˌsaɪnəˈsaɪtɪs/ n [U] the uncomfortable swelling of sinus tissues.

-sion ⇨ -ION.

sip /sɪp/ v (-pp-) ~ (**at**) sth to drink sth, taking a very small amount each time: [V] *He drank his tea, sipping noisily.* [Vn] *We sat in the sun, sipping lemonade.* [Vpr] *She sipped at her mineral water.*
▸ **sip** n a small amount of drink taken into the mouth: *He took a sip of brandy from the glass.*

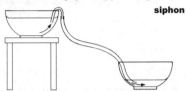

siphon

siphon /ˈsaɪfn/ n a pipe, tube, etc used for drawing liquid from one container to another, using the pressure of the atmosphere. ⇨ picture. See also SODA SIPHON.
▸ **siphon** v **PHRV** **ˌsiphon sth ˈinto / ˈout of sth**; **ˌsiphon sth ˈoff/ˈout** to transfer a liquid from one container to another using a siphon: *siphon petrol out of a car into a can* ○ *siphon off all the waste liquid.* **ˌsiphon sth ˈoff**; **ˌsiphon sth ˈfrom sth** (*infml often derog*) to transfer sth from one place to another, often unfairly or illegally: *She was siphoning off profits from the business into her own bank account.*

sir /sɜː(r)/ n **1(a)** (used as a formal or polite way of addressing a man): *Good morning, sir. Can I help you* (eg in a shop)? ○ *Are you ready to order, sir* (eg in a restaurant)? **(b)** (used esp in Britain as a form of address by children in school to a male teacher): *Please, sir, can I open the window?* Compare MISS¹ 2b. **2** **Sir** (used at the beginning of a formal letter to a company or an organization when one does not know the name of the person who will deal with the letter): *Dear Sir/Sirs.* **3** **Sir** /sə(r)/ (a title used before the first name of a KNIGHT(1) or BARONET): *Thank you, Sir ˈEdward.* ○ *Sir ˌJohn ˈJackson has arrived.* **IDM** **ˌno ˈsir!; no sirree!** /sɜːˈriː/ (*esp US infml*) certainly not: *Drink and drive! No sir!*

sire /ˈsaɪə(r)/ n **1** the male parent of an animal, esp a horse or pig: *the sire of many successful racehorses.* Compare DAM². **2** (*arch*) (used when addressing a King).
▸ **sire** v [Vn] to be the sire of an animal.

siren /ˈsaɪrən/ n **1** a device that makes a long loud sound or sounds as a signal or warning: *A police car raced past with its siren blaring.* ○ *The factory siren signalled the end of the night shift.* **2(a)** (in Greek myths) a sea creature, partly woman and partly bird in form, whose singing attracted sailors in ships towards the rocks. **(b)** a person, esp a woman, regarded as fascinating and dangerous.

sirloin /ˈsɜːlɔɪn/ n [U, C] beef cut from the best part of the back of a cow: *sirloin steak.*

sirocco /sɪˈrɒkəʊ/ n (*pl* -**os**) a hot, often wet, wind which blows from Africa into Southern Europe.

sisal /ˈsaɪsl/ n [U] a FIBRE(2,3) made from the leaves of a tropical plant and used for making rope, floor coverings, etc.

sissy (also **cissy**) /ˈsɪsi/ n (*infml derog*) a boy who lacks the qualities thought to be typical of boys, eg courage and a sense of adventure: *The other boys call me a sissy because I don't like games.*

sister /ˈsɪstə(r)/ n **1** a daughter of the same parents as oneself or the person mentioned: *my big/little* (ie older/younger) *sister* ○ *Have you any brothers and sisters?* ○ *She has been like a sister to me* (ie has behaved like a sister would). See also HALF-SISTER, STEPSISTER. **2** (used esp when addressing or referring to other members of a women's organization): *They supported their sisters in the dispute.* **3** (*US infml*) (used to address a woman): *Hey, sister, you dropped your bag.* **4** (*Brit*) a senior hospital nurse who is in charge of a WARD(1). See also CHARGE NURSE. **5 Sister** a member of certain female religious orders; a nun: *the Sisters of Charity.* **6** sth of the same type or made at the same time: *our sister company* ○ *After the disaster, tests were carried out on the tanker's sister ship.*

▶ **sisterhood** *n* **1** [U] the close relationship between women, esp in a women's organization. **2** [CGp] a society of women with shared interests or aims.

sisterly *adj* of or like a sister: *sisterly love* ○ *a sisterly kiss.*

■ **'sister-in-law** *n* (*pl* **sisters-in-law**) the sister of one's wife or husband; the wife of one's brother.

sit /sɪt/ *v* (**-tt-**; *pt, pp* **sat** /sæt/) **1(a)** to be in a position in which one's bottom is resting on a chair, the floor, etc and one's back is upright: [Vpr] *sitting on a stool/on the ground/in an armchair* ○ *sit at a table/desk* ○ *We sat at the back of the cinema.* [Vadv] *Sit still, Tommy!* **(b)** ~ **(sb)** **(down)**; ~ **oneself down** to move oneself or put sb else into this position: [Vp] *Please sit down.* [V] *Can you see anywhere to sit?* [Vpr, Vp] *She sat (down) on the bed and took her shoes off.* [Vnpr] *He lifted the child and sat her on the wall.* [Vnp] *Sit yourself down and tell us what happened.* **2** ~ **(for sb)** to be a model for an artist, a photographer, etc: [Vpr] *She sat for Augustus John.* [also V]. **3** (of eg dogs) to rest with the hind legs bent, the bottom on the ground and the front legs upright: [V] *She ordered the dog to sit.* [also Vpr]. **4(a)** (of birds) to rest on a branch, etc; to PERCH¹: [Vpr] *swallows sitting on the telephone wires* [also V]. **(b)** (of birds) to stay on the nest to keep the eggs warm: [V] *The hen sits for most of the day.* [also Vpr]. **5** (of a parliament, committee, lawcourt, etc) to be having a meeting; to be discussing business, dealing with a case, etc: [V] *The House of Commons was still sitting at 3 am.* **6** ~ (*for sth*) (*Brit*) to do an examination: [Vn, Vpr] *sit (for) an exam/a test.* **7** to be or remain in a particular position or state for a long time: *The book sat on my shelf for years before I read it.* [V-adj] *Those houses are just sitting empty.* **8** ~ **(on sb)** (of clothes) to fit the body in the specified way: [Vadv] *A jacket that sits well/loosely on sb.* **IDM** **be ˌsitting 'pretty** to be in a fortunate situation, esp when others are not: *I was the only person fully insured, so I'm sitting pretty.* **sit at sb's 'feet** to be sb's pupil or follower: *She sat at the feet of Freud himself.* **sit in 'judgement (on/over sb)** to judge sb's behaviour, esp when one has no right to do so: *How dare you sit in judgement on me?* **sit on the 'fence** to fail or refuse to decide between two proposals, courses of action, etc, eg because one is afraid or does not want to offend sb. **ˌsit 'tight 1** to remain where one is: *All the others left in a hurry, but I sat tight.* **2** to refuse to take action or change one's mind: *She threatened us with dismissal if we didn't agree, but we all sat tight.* **ˌsit 'up (and take notice)** (*infml*) suddenly to start paying attention to what is happening or being said: *I called her a hypocrite and that really made her sit up.* ○ *The news made us all sit up and take notice.* **PHRV** **ˌsit a'round/a'bout** (*often derog*) to sit doing nothing, esp while waiting for sb/sth or because one has nothing to do: *He just sits around listening to the radio all day.*

ˌsit 'back 1 to sit and rest comfortably in a chair: *I sat back and enjoyed a cup of tea.* **2** to take no action to help sb: *Everybody just sat back and did nothing.*

ˌsit 'by to take no action to stop sth bad happening: *How can the government just sit by and let this happen?*

'sit for sth (*Brit*) (no passive) to be the Member of Parliament for a specified place: *I sit for Bristol West.*

ˌsit 'in to occupy a building, room, etc as a protest. See also SIT-IN. **ˌsit 'in for sb** to do sb's job or perform sb's duties while they are away, ill, etc. Compare STAND IN. **ˌsit 'in on sth** to attend a meeting, etc without taking an active part, in order to learn, gain experience, etc: *A medical student sat in on the consultation.*

'sit on sth (no passive) to be a member of a committee, jury, etc: *How many people sit on the panel?* **2** (*infml usu derog*) to fail to deal with sth: *They have been sitting on my application for a month.* **'sit on sb** (*infml*) to stop sb's bad or awkward behaviour by taking firm action: *She can be very arrogant, and needs sitting on occasionally.*

ˌsit 'out to sit in the open air: *The garden's so lovely, I think I'll sit out.* **ˌsit sth 'out 1** to wait for sth unpleasant, boring, etc to finish: *sit out a storm.* **2** not to take part in a particular dance: *I think I'll sit this one out.*

'sit through sth to wait patiently until sth boring finishes: *I can't sit through a long flight without something to read.*

ˌsit 'up (for sb) not to go to bed until later than the usual time, esp because one is waiting for sb: *I'll get back late, so don't sit up (for me).* ○ *The nurse sat up with the patient all night.* ○ *We sat up late watching a show on TV.* **ˌsit (sb) 'up** to move oneself/sb into a sitting position: *The patient is well enough to sit up in bed now.* ○ *Sit up straight!*

▶ **sitter** *n* **1** a person whose portrait is being painted. **2** (*infml*) = BABYSITTER. **3** (*infml*) an easy catch or shot: *I missed an absolute sitter.*

sitting *n* **1** a period during which a lawcourt, parliament, etc conducts its normal business: *a long sitting.* **2** a period when a group of people eat a meal: *The dining-hall is small, so there are two sittings for lunch.* ○ *About 100 people can be served at one sitting* (ie at one time). **3** a period spent in one activity without interruption: *read a book at a single sitting.* **4** a period during which one is a model for an artist, photographer, etc: *The portrait was completed after six sittings.*

■ **'sit-down** *n* **1** a strike, demonstration, etc in which workers occupy a factory, public place, etc until their demands are considered or met: *stage a sit-down* ○ *a sit-down protest.* **2** [sing] (*Brit infml*) a short rest while sitting: *I just feel like a sit-down — let's find a café.* — *adj* [attrib] (of a meal) served to people sitting at tables. Compare BUFFET¹ 2.

'sit-in *n* a form of protest in which a group of people refuse to leave a factory, lecture hall, public place, etc: *They staged a sit-in at the city council offices.*

ˌsitting 'duck *n* a person or thing that is very easy to attack.

'sitting-room *n* (*esp Brit*) = LIVING-ROOM.

ˌsitting 'tenant *n* (*Brit*) a person renting and living in a flat, house, etc who has certain legal rights: *It's difficult to sell a house with a sitting tenant.*

'sit-up *n* an exercise to strengthen the stomach muscles, in which one lifts one's body from a lying position into a sitting position: *I do 50 sit-ups every morning.*

sitar /sɪ'tɑː(r), 'sɪtɑː(r)/ *n* an Indian musical instrument resembling a guitar, with a long neck and two sets of metal strings.

sitcom /'sɪtkɒm/ *n* (*infml*) = SITUATION COMEDY.

site /saɪt/ *n* **1** a place where a building, town, etc was, is or will be situated: *a town built on the site of* *a Roman fort* ○ *a site for a new school* ○ *deliver materials to a building site* ○ *The builders were on site early this morning.* **2** a place used for sth or where sth has happened: *the site of the battle* ○ *an archaeological site* ○ *a nuclear-testing site* ○ *Rescue workers rushed to the site of the plane crash.*

▶ **site** *v* to build sth in a particular place: [Vnpr] *a factory sited next to a railway line* [Vnadv] *Is it safe to site a power station here?*

situate /ˈsɪtʃueɪt/ *v* **1** (*fml*) (esp passive) to place or put a building or town in a particular position: [Vnpr] *The village is situated in a valley.* [Vnadv] *Where will the new headquarters be situated?* **2** (*fml*) to describe the circumstances surrounding an event, etc; to give the CONTEXT of sth: [Vnadv] *Let me try and situate the assassination historically.* [also Vnpr].

▶ **situated** *adj* [pred] (*fml*) (of a person) in circumstances of a specified kind: *Having six children and no income, I was badly situated.* ○ *How are you situated with regard to equipment* (ie Do you have all you need)?

situation /ˌsɪtʃuˈeɪʃn/ *n* **1** a set of circumstances or conditions, esp at a certain time; a position in which one finds oneself: *be in an embarrassing situation* ○ *get into/out of a difficult situation* ○ *the worsening diplomatic/financial situation* ○ *He briefly outlined the situation to us.* **2** the position of a town, building, etc in relation to its surroundings: *The house is in a beautiful situation overlooking the lake.* **3** (*fml*) a job: *find a new situation* ○ *Situations vacant/ Situations wanted* (ie the title of a section of a newspaper containing advertisements from people offering or looking for jobs). **IDM** **a chicken-and-egg situation** ⇨ CHICKEN. **save the day/situation** ⇨ SAVE[1].

■ ¦**situation ˈcomedy** (also *infml* **sitcom**) *n* a comedy programme on radio or television, based on a number of characters in an amusing situation.

six /sɪks/ *n, pron, det* the number 6. **IDM** **at ¦sixes and ˈsevens** (*infml*) in confusion; not well organized: *I haven't had time to arrange everything, so I'm all at sixes and sevens.*

▶ **sixth** /sɪksθ/ *pron, det* 6th. — *n* each of six equal parts of sth: *save a sixth of one's income.* ¦**sixth form** *n* [usu *sing*] (*Brit*) the two final years at school for pupils between 16 and 18 years old: *He's in the sixth form.* ○ *a sixth-form student/pupil* ○ *a ¦sixth-form college* (ie one for pupils of this age). ¦**sixth-former** *n* (*Brit*) a pupil in the sixth form. ¦**sixth ˈsense** *n* [sing] the ability to know sth without using the senses of sight, touch, smell, etc: *I had a kind of sixth sense that something terrible would happen.* For further guidance on how *six* and *sixth* are used see the examples at *five* and *fifth*.

¦**six-figure** *adj* [attrib] of more than 99 999 pounds, dollars, etc: *a six-figure salary.*

¦**six-pack** *n* a case of six bottles or cans, esp of beer.

¦**six-ˈshooter** (also ¦**six-gun**) *n* a REVOLVER that can hold six bullets.

sixfold /ˈsɪksfəʊld/ *adj, adv* ⇨ -FOLD.

sixpence /ˈsɪkspəns/ *n* (**a**) (in Britain) a small silver coin used before 1971, worth six old pennies. (**b**) this amount of money.

sixteen /ˌsɪksˈtiːn/ *n, pron, det* the number 16. ▶ **sixteenth** /ˌsɪksˈtiːnθ/ *n, pron, det.* ¦**six'teenth note** (*US*) *n* = SEMIQUAVER. For further guidance on how *sixteen* and *sixteenth* are used, see the examples at *five* and *fifth*.

sixty /ˈsɪksti/ *n, pron, det* **1** the number 60. **2** the sixties *n* [pl] numbers, years or temperature from 60 to 69. **IDM** **in one's ˈsixties** between the ages of 60 and 70. ▶ **sixtieth** /ˈsɪkstiəθ/ *n, pron, det.* For further guidance on how *sixty* and *sixtieth* are used, see the examples at *five* and *fifth*.

size[1] /saɪz/ *n* **1** [U, C] the dimensions, extent or

amount of sth/sb, esp in relation to sth/sb else: *It's about the size of a matchbox.* ○ *What's the size of your garden?* ○ *an area the size of Scotland* ○ *The house is just the right size for us.* ○ *Flowerpots come in all shapes and sizes.* ○ *Size isn't important; it's the quality that counts.* ○ (*Brit*) *They're both of a size* (ie about the same size). **2** [U, sing] the large extent, amount, etc of sth/sb: *The sheer size of the place is impressive.* ○ *It was a house of some size* (ie a fairly large one). ○ *I couldn't believe the size of his debts.* **3** [C] any of a number of standard measurements in which items, eg clothes or shoes, are made or sold: *It's the right/wrong size for me.* ○ *a size fifteen collar* ○ *an economy/a family/a large size packet of cereal* ○ *I take size nine shoes.* ○ *You need a smaller size.* ○ *Try this one for size* (ie to see if it is the right size). **IDM** **cut sb down to ˈsize** to show sb that they are not as important as they think. **that's about it / about the size of it** ⇨ ABOUT[1].

▶ **size** *v* [Vn] to mark the size(2) of sth. **PHR V** **size sb/sth ˈup** (*infml*) to form a judgement or an opinion of sb/sth: *We sized each other up at our first meeting.* ○ *He sized up the situation very quickly.*

sizeable (also **sizable**) /-əbl/ *adj* fairly large; considerable: *a sizeable town* ○ *Coming first in the race was, for him, a sizeable achievement.*

-sized (also **-size**) (forming compound *adjs*) having the specified size: *a medium-sized garden* ○ *a handy-sized dictionary* ○ *cut sth into equal-sized pieces.* See also PINT-SIZED.

size[2] /saɪz/ *n* [U] a sticky substance used to make material stiff or to prepare a wall for decoration.

▶ **size** *v* [Vn] to cover sth with size.

sizzle /ˈsɪzl/ *v* to make a hissing (HISS) sound, like that made by food frying in very hot fat: [V, Vp] *sausages sizzling (away) in the pan* ○ (*fig*) *a sizzling hot day.*

▶ **sizzle** *n* [sing] a sizzling sound.

sizzling *adj* very exciting: *sizzling guitar passages* ○ *The film contains several sizzling sex scenes.*

skate[1] /skeɪt/ *n* **1** (also ¦**ice-skate**) either of a pair of boots with steel blades fixed to the bottom for moving smoothly over ice. **2** = ROLLER-SKATE. **IDM** **get/put one's ˈskates on** (*infml*) to be quick; to hurry: *Get your skates on or you'll miss the bus.*

▶ **skate** *v* to move, dance, etc on skates: [V] *Can you skate?* [Vn] *skate a figure of eight* [Vpr] *skate round the rink* ○ *I hope it's cold enough to skate/go skating on the lake this winter.* **IDM** **be skating on thin ˈice** to be taking a risk: *We could ignore him and go direct to the chairman, but we'd be skating on very thin ice.* **PHR V** ¦**skate ˈover/ˈround sth** to avoid dealing with or talking about sth: *skate over a difficulty/a delicate issue* ○ *She skated round the likely cost of the plan.* ¦**skate through sth** to do sth quickly and easily: *I skated through the work and was finished by lunchtime.* **skater** *n* a person who skates: *a ¦figure/ˈspeed skater.* **skating** *n* [U] the sport of moving on skates: *a skating competition/ club.*

■ ¦**skating-rink** *n* **1** = ICE-RINK. **2** a smooth area used for roller-skating (ROLLER).

skate[2] /skeɪt/ *n* (*pl* unchanged or **skates**) a large flat sea-fish, often eaten as food.

skateboard /ˈskeɪtbɔːd/ *n* a short narrow board with small wheels fixed to it, which a person stands

sport or pleasure: *ride a skateboard.* ⇨ ᴋᴀᴛᴇ[1]. ▶ **skateboarder** *n.* **skateboard-**

..e /skɪˈdædl/ *v* [V] (*infml*) to go away or place quickly.

s.. skeɪn/ *n* a loosely wound length of wool, threa.., etc.

skeletal /ˈskelətl/ *adj* **1** of the ꜱᴋᴇʟᴇᴛᴏɴ(1) of a person or an animal: *skeletal deformities/diseases.* **2** very thin, eg because of hunger or disease: *skeletal figures dressed in rags.* **3** existing only in outline or as a framework: *a skeletal plan for new legislation.*

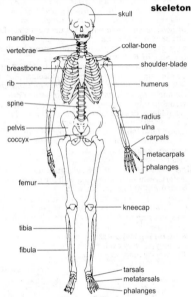

skeleton

- skull
- mandible
- vertebrae
- collar-bone
- breastbone
- shoulder-blade
- rib
- humerus
- spine
- radius
- pelvis
- ulna
- coccyx
- carpals
- metacarpals
- phalanges
- femur
- kneecap
- tibia
- fibula
- tarsals
- metatarsals
- phalanges

skeleton /ˈskelɪtn/ *n* **1** the framework of bones supporting the body of a person or an animal and protecting the organs in it: *The police have discovered a human skeleton.* ○ *The report described those who survived prison as 'walking skeletons'* (ie very thin because of hunger, illness, etc). ⇨ picture. **2** [usu *sing*] (**a**) any supporting structure or framework, eg of a building: *a skeleton of girders.* (**b**) an outline to which details are to be added: *the bare skeleton of a theory/an agreement.* **3** [attrib] having the smallest possible number of people, vehicles, etc needed to do sth: *a skeleton crew/staff* ○ *We only have a skeleton bus service on public holidays.* **ɪᴅᴍ** **a skeleton in the ˈcupboard** a secret, usu within a family, which would embarrass sb if it became known publicly.
■ **ˈskeleton key** *n* a key that will open several different locks.

skeptic = ꜱᴄᴇᴘᴛɪᴄ.

sketch /sketʃ/ *n* **1** a drawing made very quickly and not including much detail: *make a sketch of a face/scene* ○ *a pencil/charcoal sketch.* **2** a short account or description, giving only basic details: *give a quick sketch of how the changes will affect staff.* **3** a short funny play or piece of writing: *perform/do a sketch set in a doctor's waiting room* ○ *She writes satirical sketches for a magazine.*
▶ **sketch** *v* to draw sketches; to make a sketch of sb/sth: [V, Vn] *go into the park to sketch trees.* **ᴘʜʀ ᴠ** **ˌsketch sth ˈout** to give a general description or account of sth; to give an outline of sth: *sketch out proposals for a new road.* **ˌsketch sth ˈin** to give

more information or detail about sth: *You need to sketch in his character a bit more.*

sketchy *adj* (**-ier, -iest**) not complete; not having enough details: *a rather sketchy treatment of the subject* ○ *I have only a sketchy knowledge of Spanish history.* ○ *My recollections of the event are a bit sketchy.* **sketchily** *adv.* **ˈsketchiness** *n* [U].
■ **ˈsketch-book, ˈsketch-pad** *ns* a book of sheets of paper for sketching on.
ˈsketch-map *n* a map, usu drawn by hand, that shows only basic details.

skew /skjuː/ **1** to change sth from its usual position or direction; to ᴅɪꜱᴛᴏʀᴛ(2) sth: [Vn] *Party politics often skews decisions.* **2** to change direction suddenly: [Vp] *The ball skewed off at an angle.* [Vpr] *The car had skewed across the road into the ditch.*
▶ **skewed** *adj* ~ (**to/towards sth/sb**) **1** not normal or usual; distorted (ᴅɪꜱᴛᴏʀᴛ 3): *a skewed result/calculation/sense of humour/version of events* ○ *a guidebook skewed towards American visitors.* **2** not straight; ᴄʀᴏᴏᴋᴇᴅ(1): *Her spectacles were skewed.* See also ᴀꜱᴋᴇᴡ.
■ **skew-whiff** /ˌskjuːˈwɪf/ *adj* (*Brit infml*) not straight; ᴄʀᴏᴏᴋᴇᴅ(1): *He knocked my hat skew-whiff.* ○ (*fig*) *Some of his ideas are a bit skew-whiff.*

skewbald /ˈskjuːbɔːld/ *n, adj* (an animal, esp a horse) having patches of white and another colour, usu not black. Compare ᴘɪᴇʙᴀʟᴅ.

skewer /ˈskjuːə(r)/ *n* a long thin pointed piece of metal or wood that is pushed through meat to hold it together while cooking, or used to test whether sth is completely cooked.
▶ **skewer** *v* to push a skewer or sth similar through sth: [Vn] *skewer a fish* [Vnpr] *He skewered his foot on a nail.*

skiing

- binding
- boot
- ski
- pole

downhill skiing   **cross-country skiing**

ski /skiː/ *n* either of a pair of long narrow strips of wood, plastic, etc fixed to a person's boots so that he or she can move smoothly over snow: *a pair of skis* ○ *put on one's skis.*
▶ **ski** *adj* [attrib] relating to the sport of skiing: *ski equipment/slopes/resorts/instructions.*
ski *v* (*3rd pers sing pres t* **skis**; *pt, pp* **ski'd** or **skied**; *pres p* **skiing**) to move over snow on skis, esp as a sport: [V] *go skiing in Vermont* [Vpr] *I skied into a tree and broke my leg.* [Vp] *We skied down to the village.* **skier** /ˈskiːə(r)/ *n* a person who skis. **skiing** *n* [U] the activity or sport of moving on skis: *downhill/cross-country skiing* ○ *a skiing accident/holiday/instructor/lesson.* ⇨ picture.
■ **ˈski-bob** *n* a vehicle resembling a bicycle with skis instead of wheels, used for races on snow.
ˈski-jump *n* (**a**) a specially built steep slope that ends suddenly, with snow on it. People ski down it and then jump a long way through the air, landing on a lower slope. (**b**) a jump made from this. (**c**) a competition in which such jumps are made.
ˈski-lift *n* a device for pulling or carrying skiers up a slope.

skid /skɪd/ *v* (**-dd-**) (of a vehicle) to slide sideways suddenly on a surface covered with ice, oil, etc, or

as a result of turning too quickly: [V] *I/The car skidded and went straight into the wall.* [Vpr] *The car skidded off/across the road.* ○ *The car skidded to a halt and four men jumped out.* [also Vp].
▶ **skid** *n* an act of skidding: *steer into a skid* (ie in the direction in which the car has skidded). **IDM** **put the ˈskids under sb/sth** (*infml*) cause sb/sth to fail: *The government put the skids under the plan by stopping their research grant.*
■ **ˈskid-pan** *n* a surface specially prepared for drivers to practise skidding on.
skid row /ˌskɪd ˈrəʊ/ *n* [U] (*sl*) the poor area of a town where people who have no home or are often drunk gather: *He ended up on skid row.*

skies *pl* of SKY.

skiff /skɪf/ *n* a small light boat for rowing or sailing, usu for one person.

skiffle /ˈskɪfl/ *n* [U] (*esp Brit*) a type of music popular in the 1950s. It was a mixture of jazz and FOLK music and usu played by small groups: *a skiffle group.*

skilful (*US* **skillful**) /ˈskɪlfl/ *adj* ~ (**in sth / doing sth**) having or showing skill: *a skilful painter/driver/performer* ○ *a skilful performance* ○ *skilful in making decisions.* ▶ **skilfully** /-fəli/ *adv*: *a very skilfully handled press conference.*

skill /skɪl/ *n* **1** [U] ~ (**at/in sth / doing sth**) the ability to do sth well: *a job requiring great skill and attention to detail* ○ *his skill at mimicry/in marketing* ○ *a poet of considerable skill.* **2** [C] a specific skill or a particular type of skill: *the practical skills needed in carpentry* ○ *technical/communication/management skills* ○ *a skills shortage.*
▶ **skilled** *adj* **1** ~ (**in/at sth / doing sth**) (**a**) having skill; skilful: *a skilled negotiator* ○ *skilled at dealing with complaints.* (**b**) experienced; trained: *a highly-skilled craftsman* ○ *skilled staff.* **2** [attrib] (of work) needing skill: *Furniture-making is a skilled job.*

skillet /ˈskɪlɪt/ *n* (*US*) = FRYING-PAN.

skim /skɪm/ *v* (**-mm-**) **1** to remove cream, solid matter, etc from the surface of a liquid: [Vn] *skim milk* [Vnpr] *skim the cream from the milk* [also Vnp]. **2**(**a**) (no passive) to move quickly and lightly over a surface, not touching it or only occasionally touching it: [Vn, Vpr] *swallows skimming (over) the water* [Vn] *aircraft skimming the rooftops.* (**b**) to throw a flat stone low over water so that it bounces on the surface several times: [Vn, Vnpr] *skimming pebbles (over the lake).* **3** ~ (**through/over**) **sth** to read sth quickly, noting only the main points: [Vnpr] *His eyes skimmed the front page for her name.* [Vpr] *I try to skim through all the new scientific journals each month.* [also Vn].
■ ˌ**skimmed ˈmilk** (also ˌ**skim ˈmilk**) *n* [U] milk from which the cream has been skimmed.

skimp /skɪmp/ *v* ~ (**on sth**) to use or provide less of sth than is needed; to save money by spending less: [V] *Don't skimp by using margarine instead of butter.* [Vpr] *You should not skimp on insurance when booking your holiday.*
▶ **skimpy** *adj* (**-ier, -iest**) (*derog*) using or having less than the amount needed: *a rather skimpy meal* ○ *The dancers wore skimpy dresses.*

skin /skɪn/ *n* **1** [U, C usu *sing*] the outer covering of the body of a person or an animal: *have a dark/an olive/a fair skin* ○ *oily/dry skin* ○ *She has beautiful skin.* ○ *a skin disease.* **2** [C,U] (often in compounds) the skin of a dead animal with or without the fur: *skins laid out to dry* ○ *a* ˈ*rabbit-skin.* Compare FUR 1, HIDE². See also CALFSKIN, PIGSKIN, SHEEPSKIN, WINE-SKIN. **3**(**a**) [C,U] the outer covering of certain fruits or plants: *a banana skin* ○ *onion/potato skins.* Compare PEEL *n*, RIND, ZEST 3. (**b**) [C,U] the thin covering of a SAUSAGE: *Prick the skins before grilling.* (**c**) [C *sing*] any outer covering or case: *the metal skin of an aircraft.* **4** [C,U] the thin layer that forms on the

surface of certain liquids, eg boiled milk: *the skin on a milk pudding* ○ *a skin forming on paint in a pot.* **IDM** **be no skin off** ˈ**one's nose** (*infml*) not matter to one; not to affect or upset one: *It's no skin off* ˈ*my nose if you waste your money.* **by the** ˌ**skin of one's** ˈ**teeth** (*infml*) only just: *pass an exam by the skin of one's teeth* ○ *He escaped death by the skin of his teeth.* **get under sb's** ˈ**skin** (*infml*) **1** to annoy or irritate sb: *His endless complaints are getting under my skin.* **2** to interest or attract sb greatly: *The charm of the place soon gets under your skin.* **have got sb under one's** ˈ**skin** (*infml*) to be strongly attracted to sb. **jump out of one's skin** ⇨ JUMP¹. **save one's skin** ⇨ SAVE¹. (**nothing but / all**) **skin and** ˈ**bone** (*infml*) very thin: *He was all skin and bone after his illness.* (**have**) **a** ˌ**thin/thick** ˈ**skin** (to have) a character that makes one easily/not easily upset by criticism, insults, etc: *You need a thick skin to be a politician.*
▶ **skin** *v* (**-nn-**) (**a**) to take the skin off an animal: [Vn] *skin a rabbit.* (**b**) to injure oneself by accidentally scraping skin off eg one's knees: [Vn] *I skinned my elbow against the wall.* **IDM** **keep one's eyes peeled/skinned** ⇨ EYE¹. ˌ**skin sb a**ˈ**live** (used when threatening sb) to punish sb severely: *Your father'll skin you alive when he sees this!*
-skinned (forming compound *adjs*) having skin of the specified type: *dark-/light-skinned* ○ *pink-skinned.* See also THICK-SKINNED.

skinny *adj* (**-ier, -iest**) **1** (*infml usu derog*) very thin: *a skinny child* ○ *skinny legs.* **2** (of clothes) fitting closely: *a skinny black jumper.* ⇨ note at THIN.
■ ˌ**skin-**ˈ**deep** *adj* [usu pred] not deeply felt; not as important as it seems on the surface; SUPERFICIAL(3): *Any resentment he shows towards you is only skin-deep.* **IDM** **beauty is only skin-deep** ⇨ BEAUTY.
ˈ**skin-diving** *n* [U] the sport of swimming under water with a simple breathing apparatus but without a special diving-suit (DIVE¹). ˈ**skin-diver** *n*.
ˈ**skin-graft** *n* a SURGICAL operation in which skin taken from one part of sb's body is placed over another part to replace skin that has been burned or damaged.
ˌ**skin-**ˈ**tight** *adj* (of clothes) fitting very closely to the body: *a* ˌ*skin-tight* ˈ*dress* ○ *Her blouse was skin-tight.*

skinflint /ˈskɪnflɪnt/ *n* (*infml derog*) a person who does not like spending money, esp on other people.

skinful /ˈskɪnfʊl/ *n* (usu *sing*) (*Brit sl*) a large quantity of alcholic drink, enough to make a person drunk: *He'd had a skinful and got into a fight.*

skinhead /ˈskɪnhed/ *n* (*Brit*) a young person with very short hair, big boots, etc, esp one who is violent and aggressive.

skint /skɪnt/ *adj* [pred] (*Brit sl*) having no money: *I can't go on holiday this year — I'm absolutely skint.*

skipping-rope
(US jump rope)

skip
(US **jump**)

skip¹ /skɪp/ *v* (**-pp-**) **1** to move lightly and quickly, jumping off the ground a little with each step: [Vp, Vpr] *A child was skipping along (the road).* ○ *The lambs were skipping about (in the fields).* **2** (*Brit*) to jump over a rope which is held at both ends by oneself or by two other people and turned repeatedly over the head and under the feet: [V] *children skipping in the playground* ○ ˈ*skipping games.* ⇨

picture. **3** (*infml*) to go from one place, subject, etc
to another quickly: [Vp] *to skip over/across to Paris
for the weekend* [Vpr] *She kept skipping from one
topic of conversation to another.* **4** ~ **(out of ...)**; ~
off to leave a place secretly or in a hurry: [Vpr, Vn]
skip (out of) the country with the stolen money [Vp]
skip off without telling anyone. **5** (*infml*) to fail to
attend or have sth; to miss sth: *skip a lecture/an
appointment/a class* ○ *I often skip breakfast.* **6** to
omit part of a book when reading or studying:
[V, Vn] *I read the whole book without skipping (a
page).* [Vn] *Skip the first chapter/exercise and start
on page 25.* **IDM** **'skip it** (*infml*) (esp imperative) to
stop doing or saying sth: *If you're thinking of asking
me to lend you my car, (you can) skip it!*
▶ **skip** *n* a skipping movement: *How many skips can
you do without stopping?*
■ **'skipping-rope** (*Brit*) (*US* **'jump rope,** **'skip rope**)
n a length of rope, usu with handles at each end,
used esp by children or boxers for skipping. ⇨
picture.

skip² /skɪp/ *n* (*Brit*) a large, usu open, metal container used eg for carrying away old bricks,
rubbish, etc from a building site.

skipper /'skɪpə(r)/ *n* (**a**) the captain, esp of a small
ship or fishing boat. (**b**) (*infml*) the captain of a
sports team.
▶ **skipper** *v* to act as skipper of a boat, team, etc:
[Vn] *skipper a yacht* ○ *an all-woman crew, skippered
by Tracy Edwards.*

skirmish /'skɜːmɪʃ/ *n* **1** a fight between small
groups of soldiers, ships, etc, esp one that is not
planned: *a brief skirmish on the frontier.* **2** a fierce
argument, eg between political opponents: *a skirmish between the two party leaders.* Compare PITCHED
BATTLE.
▶ **skirmish** *v* [V] to take part in a skirmish. **skir-
misher** *n.* **skirmishing** *n* [U]: *Several people were
injured in the skirmishing between police and demonstrators.*

skirt /skɜːt/ *n* **1**(**a**) a piece of clothing for a woman
or girl that hangs from the waist: *a pleated/full/
long/short/straight skirt.* (**b**) the part of a dress,
coat, etc that hangs below the waist. **2** any of various types of guard or covering for the base of a
vehicle or machine: *the rubber skirt round the bottom of a hovercraft.* **IDM** **a bit of crumpet/fluff/
skirt/stuff** ⇨ BIT¹.
▶ **skirt** *v* to be on or move around the edge of sth:
[Vn] *The road skirts the town to the south.* [Vn, Vpr]
We skirted (round) the field and crossed the bridge.
PHR V **skirt 'round sth** to avoid referring to or
dealing with a topic, an issue, etc directly: *She
skirted round the problem of the high cost.*
■ **'skirting-board** (also **'skirting**) (*Brit*) (*US* **base-
board**) *n* [C, U] a narrow wooden board fixed along
the bottom of the walls inside a house.

skit /skɪt/ *n* ~ (**on sth**) a piece of humorous writing
or a short play that copies and mocks sb/sth: *a skit
on 'Macbeth'.*

skittish /'skɪtɪʃ/ *adj* (**a**) (of horses) easily excited;
difficult to control. (**b**) (of people) lively and playful:
skittish behaviour/movements. ▶ **skittishly** *adv.*
skittishness *n* [U].

skittle /'skɪtl/ *n* (*esp Brit*) **1** [C] a wooden or plastic
object shaped like a bottle, used in the game of
skittles. **2 skittles** [sing *v*] a game in which players
try to knock over as many skittles as possible by
rolling a ball at them. Compare TENPIN BOWLING.
IDM **beer and skittles** ⇨ BEER.

skive /skaɪv/ *v* ~ (**off**) (*Brit infml*) to avoid work, esp
by staying away or leaving early: [V] *'Where's Tom?'
'Skiving as usual!'* [Vp] *She always skives off early.*

skivvy /'skɪvi/ *n* (*Brit infml derog*) a usu female
servant, esp one who has to do boring jobs like
cleaning and washing: *I'm treated like a skivvy in
this house.*

▶ **skivvy** *v* (*pt, pp* **skivvied**) ~ (**for sb**) (*Brit infml*)
to work as or like a skivvy: [Vpr] *I refuse to skivvy
for you all the time!* [also V].

skua /'skjuːə/ *n* a large sea bird.

skulduggery (also **skullduggery**) /skʌl'dʌɡəri/ *n*
[U] (*often joc*) dishonest behaviour: *allegations of
political skulduggery.*

skulk /skʌlk/ *v* (*derog*) to hide or move around
secretly, esp when one is planning sth bad: [Vp, Vpr]
I don't want reporters skulking around (my house).
⇨ note at PROWL.

skull /skʌl/ *n* **1** the bone structure of the head
which protects and encloses the brain: *He fell off his
bike and fractured his skull.* ⇨ picture at SKELETON.
2 (*infml*) a person's head or brain: *How can I get it
into your thick skull that we can't afford a car?*
■ **skull and 'crossbones** *n* [sing] a picture of a
skull above two crossed bones, used formerly on the
flags of PIRATE(1) ships and now to warn of danger,
eg on bottles of poison.

skullcap /'skʌlkæp/ *n* a small round cap placed on
top of the head, worn esp by male Jews when praying and by Catholic bishops. ⇨ picture at HAT.

skunk

10 cm

skunk /skʌŋk/ *n* **1** (*US* **polecat**) [C] a small black
and white N American animal that can produce a
strong, unpleasant smell as a defence when attacked. ⇨ picture. **2** [C] (*infml derog*) a person
regarded with contempt. **IDM** **drunk as a skunk** ⇨
DRUNK.

sky /skaɪ/ *n* [U, sing] (usu **the sky** [sing], or **a sky** or
skies [pl] when following an *adj*) the space seen
when one looks upwards from the earth, where
clouds and the sun, moon and stars appear: *a clear
blue sky* ○ *a patch of blue sky* ○ *sunny/cloudy/grey
skies* ○ *birds flying across the sky* ○ *the night sky* ○
look up at the sky ○ *a starry sky/(the) starry skies* ○
The sky's gone very dark — I think it's going to rain.
○ *The sky has clouded over now.* **IDM** **the great sth
in the sky** ⇨ GREAT. **pie in the sky** ⇨ PIE. **praise,
etc sb/sth to the 'skies** to praise sb/sth very
highly: *It's not fair! Her work always gets praised to
the skies and mine is ignored.* **the sky's the 'limit**
(*infml saying*) there is no limit: *With talent like his,
the sky's the limit.*
■ **sky-'blue** *adj, n* [U] (of) the blue colour of the sky
with no clouds in it.
sky-'high *adj, adv* very high: *sky-high 'interest
rates* ○ *Property prices have gone sky-high.*
'sky-rocket *v* (of prices, etc) to rise to a very high
level: *Insurance costs have sky-rocketed.*

skydiving /'skaɪdaɪvɪŋ/ *n* [U] the sport of jumping
from an aircraft and falling for as long as one safely
can before opening one's parachute. **'skydiver** *n.*

skylark /'skaɪlɑːk/ *n* a small bird that sings pleasantly while it flies high up in the sky.

skylight /'skaɪlaɪt/ *n* a small window in a roof or
ceiling. ⇨ picture at HOUSE¹.

skyline /'skaɪlaɪn/ *n* the outline of buildings, trees,
hills, etc seen against the sky: *the New York skyline* ○
The dome of the cathedral dominates the skyline.

skyscraper /'skaɪskreɪpə(r)/ *n* a very tall modern
city building.

skywards /'skaɪwədz/ (also **skyward** /-wəd/) *adj,
adv* towards the sky; upwards: *pointing/looking skywards* ○ *flames shooting skywards.*

slab /slæb/ *n* a thick, flat, often rectangular or

The Commonwealth

The Queen with leaders of Commonwealth countries

English is spoken as a first language by over 300 million people and used as a means of communication by many more worldwide. One of the historical reasons for this is the spread of British rule during the British Empire. Now many of the countries which were once part of the Empire belong to a voluntary association, the **Commonwealth**. It is made up of fifty-one members, which are independent states, plus a number of dependencies (such as Bermuda, the Falkland Islands, Gibraltar, and, until 1997, Hong Kong) where Britain is responsible for defence, foreign affairs and internal security. All members recognize the British Queen as Head of the Commonwealth and in seventeen countries she is also Head of State. Members may have their own monarchies or be republics, like India.

The heads of government of the Commonwealth countries meet every two years to discuss matters of common interest. The aims of the Commonwealth are to combat discrimination, oppression and inequality and to promote world peace and cooperation on trade and development. There are strong cultural and sporting links among members. The Commonwealth Games are held every four years and are open to competitors from all member states.

The Commonwealth Games, 1990

United Kingdom constitution and government

The Constitution of the United Kingdom developed over time and is not written down in one place. It consists of various elements, including **statutes** (laws made by Parliament), important court cases and established practices.

The key principles of the constitution are the **rule of law** (everyone is subject to the laws of the land) and the **sovereignty of Parliament** (there are no restrictions on the laws that Parliament can pass).

The Queen's speech

The Monarch The process of transferring power from the monarch (the Queen or King) to the people began in the thirteenth century when King John was forced to restrict his power by signing the Magna Carta. Today, the monarch represents the people as **Head of State** but the real power lies in Parliament with the elected representatives of the people.

King John's seal

Parliament is made up of two chambers, the **House of Commons** and the **House of Lords**. Each autumn the monarch goes to **Westminster** for the **State Opening of Parliament** and reads out a speech which sets out the Government's plans for the year ahead.

The Houses of Parliament

Government front bench   Speaker   Opposition front bench

The House of Commons

back-benchers

The House of Commons has 650 **Members of Parliament (MPs)** who each represent a particular part of the country, a **constituency**. **General Elections** are held every five years, though the Prime Minister may **call** one earlier, and if an MP dies or retires a **by-election** is held in her or his constituency. MPs win their **seats** in parliament by a **majority vote** (or **first-past-the-post** system), that is, the **candidate** who wins the most votes becomes the MP for that constituency.

After a general election, the leader of the party which has the most seats in the House of Commons becomes **Prime Minister** and chooses ministers to be responsible for individual departments. These include the **Chancellor of the Exchequer**, who is responsible for the **Treasury** (finance ministry), the **Foreign Secretary**, responsible for the **Foreign and Commonwealth Office**, and the **Home Secretary**, responsible for domestic affairs. They, and a number of other im-portant ministers, form the **Cabinet**, which advises the Prime Minister. In the **House of Commons** they sit on the **front bench**, and other MPs from their party sit behind them (**back-benchers**). The main

The Prime Minister, John Major, and his wife

Opposition party sits in a similar arrange-ment facing them in the House, with their Leader and her or his **Shadow Cabinet** on the front benches. MPs from smaller parties also sit on the opposition benches. In the centre is the **Speaker**, who keeps order during debates.

The House of Lords has around 1200 members, made up of the two Archbishops and twenty-four bishops, **hereditary peers and peeresses**, who have inherited their title, and **life peers**, whose title is only for their lifetime and will not pass to their children.

United States constitution and government

The United States has a written constitution which sets out the principles of government. It was drawn up in 1787 and has so far been changed or **amended** twenty-six times. The first ten amendments, known together as the **Bill of Rights**, set down such basic rights as the freedom of speech, of religion and of the press.

To ensure that no individual or group has too much power, the constitution shares power between three groups, the **executive** (the President), the **legislative** (Congress) and the **judicial** (the courts), in such a way that each has a certain authority over the others (**a system of checks and balances**).

The President in front of the White House

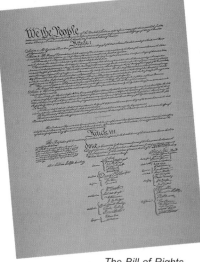

The Bill of Rights

When a candidate has been chosen by a party, he or she will **campaign** to win the election. The President is not elected directly by the people but by an **electoral college**. Voters in each state select a list of electors. The party in each state whose list receives the most votes wins the state and those electors then vote for their party's presidential candidate.

The President proposes new laws and changes in policy but Congress must agree before they are passed. The President is not a member of Congress and so cannot personally introduce bills there.

Bill Clinton campaigning for election

The President represents the country as **Head of State** but also has real political power. Elections for President are held every four years and no President may **hold office** for more than two **terms**. **Presidential candidates** are chosen by the political parties either through **Primaries** (direct elections) or at state **conventions** or **caucuses** (meetings of party representatives), depending on the state.

The House of Representatives

Congress consists of two houses, the **Senate** (to which each state elects two **senators** for a period of six years) and the **House of Representatives**, in which the number of **representatives** from each state depends on its population. Bills cannot become law until they have been passed by both houses, and if they are not passed by a two-thirds majority they can still be vetoed by the President. Bills must not conflict with the constitution.

The Federal government is responsible only for matters of national importance, such as foreign affairs, trade and defence.

The governments of the individual states are responsible for all other matters.

The Courts (⇨ **D7**) Federal judges are appointed by the President and confirmed by the Senate.

The highest court, the Supreme Court, has the power to judge whether a law passed by the government conforms to the constitution and whether the President has acted constitutionally. If it judges that the President's behaviour has been unconstitutional, he or she may be **impeached** (accused of a crime against the State).

The Capitol

The legal system in England and Wales

When the police believe that somebody has **committed a crime**, they arrest that person and the case is then **heard in court** and treated as a **criminal case**. The courts also deal with **civil cases**, where no crime has been committed, such as cases of divorce or disputes over property.

Magistrates Less serious criminal and civil cases are dealt with in the **Magistrates' Courts**, where there is no jury but a case is usually heard by two or three magistrates. Most **magistrates**, also known as **Justices of the Peace (JPs)**, work part-time and are not paid. They are given some training but do not need legal qualifications. A **clerk of the court** advises them on the law. When they have heard a case, the magistrates **reach a verdict** and where necessary decide what the punishment should be.

A Magistrates' Court

Magistrates also decide what should happen to somebody between the time they are arrested and the time when the case is heard in court. They may **grant bail** (allow the person to be free until the trial, if a sum of money is paid) or **remand** her or him **in custody** (keep the person in prison until the trial).

Judges More serious cases are heard by judges in the **crown courts** (for criminal cases) or the **county courts** (for civil cases). In civil cases, and in cases where the **defendant** has **pleaded guilty**, the judge sits alone, without a jury, and after hearing the case, makes a decision, or **judgement**.

If the person accused of a crime **pleads not guilty**, he or she is tried before a jury. When the evidence has been heard, the judge goes over the facts of the case (the **summing-up**) and explains the law to the

jury. If they **find the accused guilty**, the judge **passes sentence**, that is, decides what the punishment should be.

A solicitor's office

Solicitors are lawyers who do legal business for individuals and companies and also act as **advocates**, representing clients in court.

Barristers used to be the only lawyers allowed to appear as advocates in the higher courts. One advocate (the **Counsel for the Prosecution**) tries to prove in

A barrister

court that the accused committed the crime. The advocate representing the **defendant** (the **Counsel for the Defence**) tries to show that he or she is innocent. They **call witnesses** and question them about the facts of the case.

The jury in England and Wales is made up of twelve ordinary people aged between 18 and 65. When they have heard the evidence and the judge's summing-up, they **retire** to a special room to decide whether to **return a verdict of guilty** or **not guilty**. If they all agree, they have **reached a unanimous verdict**. If no more than two people disagree, the judge may ask for a **majority verdict**. If the accused is found guilty, he or she has the right to **appeal** and ask for the case to be heard by a higher court.

A judge

The legal system in the United States

The legal system in the United States is similar in many ways to the English system. One of the main differences is the existence of the United States **Constitution** which is interpreted by the highest court, the **Supreme Court** (⇨ **D4–5**). The nine **Supreme Court judges**, who are appointed by the President and approved by the Senate, can only be removed from office by **impeachment**.

Supreme Court judges

Judges Federal judges are also appointed for life by the President. They deal with **federal law**, which applies to the country as a whole, and with important cases involving citizens from different states. **State judges** hear cases involving the law of a particular state. They hold office for ten years and are usually elected, or confirmed in office by election.

The jury The number of people who make up a jury varies from state to state, but efforts are made to ensure that they represent a fair cross-section of society. Both the **defense** and the **prosecution** are allowed to reject a certain number of jury candidates. Except in minor cases, the defendant in a criminal case has the right to be tried by a jury, and many civil cases are also heard by a jury. In most states, the task of the jury is only to decide whether the defendant is innocent or guilty, while it is the judge who passes sentence.

The attorneys, who represent clients in court, have been trained at **law schools** and are licensed to practise only in certain states. If they wish to practise in a different state, they may have to take another exam. In a criminal case, the **prosecution attorney** is appointed by the **District Attorney** to prosecute the **defendant**. The **defense attorney** will be provided by the **Public Defender's Office** if the defendant cannot afford to engage her or his own lawyer. The prosecution may agree to charge the defendant with a less serious offence if he or she agrees to plead guilty. This is known as **plea bargaining**.

jury   prosecution attorney   defense attorney   judge

American courtroom

The vocabulary of English

In modern English, we can often express the same idea in different words. This is because English has over the centuries absorbed words from many different languages. For example, **fear**, **terror**, **alarm** and **fright** all have similar meanings but each came into English from a different language.

Anglo-Saxon English developed from Anglo-Saxon (also known as Old English), the language brought to Britain by Germanic tribes (the Angles, Saxons and Jutes) in the fifth century AD. These invaders gave England its name, 'the land of the Angles', and provided the language with many common basic terms.

Latin At the end of the sixth century, a group of monks came as missionaries from Rome to strengthen Christianity in Britain. The words which came into English from Latin at this time are mainly connected with religion and learning.

Old Norse In the ninth and tenth centuries, invaders came from Scandinavia and occupied a large part of eastern England. Many everyday words in modern English come from their language, Old Norse, which is related to Anglo-Saxon, and many place-names end in *-by,* from their word for village.

French When Britain was conquered by the Normans in 1066, French became the language of the ruling classes. Many words in modern English which describe government and the legal system, as well as terms connected with cooking, came from French at this time.

Latin and Greek Many words of Latin origin came into English through French, but the Renaissance of the fifteenth and sixteenth centuries brought a new interest in classical learning and an influx of words from Latin and Greek.

Worldwide Latin and Greek are still used as a source of new words, particularly in the field of science, but English speakers today take words from a wide variety of other languages for phenomena that have no existing English name.

ANGLO-SAXON

man	woman
breed	work
eat	house
shire	

LATIN

school	minister
pope	verse
candle	mass

OLD NORSE

sky	leg
call	take
dirt	
Whitby	

FRENCH

sovereign	court
govern	advise
braise	veal
mutton	

LATIN AND GREEK

physics	radius	history
architecture		
compute		
educate		

WORLDWIDE

telephone	futon
tea	video
tattoo	sauna

square piece of stone, wood or other solid substance: *a slab of marble/concrete* ○ *paved with stone slabs* ○ *massive slabs of rock* ○ *a fishmonger's slab* ○ *a slab of cheese/chocolate.* ⇨ note at PIECE¹.

slack¹ /slæk/ *adj* (**-er, -est**) **1** not tight or tense; loose: *a slack rope* ○ *his slack, half-open mouth* ○ *Let the reins go slack.* **2** (of business) not having many customers, sales, etc; not busy: *a slack period* ○ *times of slack demand* ○ *Trade is slack at the moment.* **3** (*derog*) (**a**) (of a person) not giving enough care and energy to a task: *be slack in one's work.* (**b**) not carefully or strictly done, planned, etc: *Discipline in the classroom is very slack.* ○ *The conference organization was rather slack.*
  ▶ **slack** *v* to be lazy; to avoid work: [V] *Stop slacking and get on with your work!* **PHR V** **slack 'off** to reduce activity, effort, speed, etc: *We're not so busy now, so we can slack off a bit.* ○ *The rain seems to be slacking off.* See also SLACKEN.
  slacker *n* (*infml*) a person who is lazy or avoids work.
  slackly *adv*: *a slackly open mouth.*
  slackness *n* [U].

slack² /slæk/ *n* [U] **1** the part of a rope, etc that hangs loosely: *too much slack in the tow-rope.* **2** a period or condition of not being active, used, etc: *There's plenty of slack in the economy.* **IDM** **take up the 'slack 1** (in industry) to improve the use of people and resources when they are not being fully or properly used. **2** to pull on a rope, etc so that it is no longer slack: *We took up the slack and then pulled as hard as we could.*

slack³ /slæk/ *n* [U] very small pieces of coal.

slacken /ˈslækən/ *v* **1** to become or make sth less tight: [Vn] *slacken the knot/rope/reins* ○ *He slackened his grip.* ○ *Her face/jaw/shoulders slackened.* **2** ~ (**sth**) (**off**) to become or make sth slower, less active, etc: [Vn] *We slackened our pace a little.* [Vp] *After months of being really busy at work, things are beginning to slacken off a bit.* [V] *The rain had slackened.* [Vnp, Vn] *Slacken (off) your speed as you approach the village.*

slacks /slæks/ *n* [pl] (*dated*) casual trousers for men or women: *a pair of slacks.*

slag /slæg/ *n* **1** the waste material that remains after metal has been removed from rock by heating it. **2** [C] (*Brit derog sl*) a woman whose appearance and sexual behaviour is thought not to be respectable.
  ▶ **slag** *v* (**-gg-**) **PHR V** **slag sb/sth 'off** (*Brit sl*) to say offensive and critical things about sb: *Now he's left, she's always slagging off her old boss.*
  ■ **'slag-heap** *n* a heap of slag(1) from a mine.

slain *pp* of SLAY.

slake /sleɪk/ *v* **1** to satisfy one's thirst: [Vn] *We slaked our thirst in a stream.* **2** (*techn*) (usu passive) to combine LIME¹(1) with water in a chemical process: *slaked lime.*

slalom /ˈslɑːləm/ *n* a SKI, water-ski (WATER¹) or CA-NOE race along a winding course marked by poles: *win the giant slalom* ○ *a slalom race/champion/course.*

slam /slæm/ *v* (**-mm-**) **1** to shut or make sth shut forcefully and loudly: [V, Vp, V-adj] *The door slammed (to/shut).* [Vn, Vn-adj] *She slammed the window (shut).* [Vnp] *He slammed the lid down.* **2** to put, push or throw sth into a specified place or position with great force: [Vnp] *slam the brakes on* ○ *He slammed down the phone/slammed the phone down.* [Vnpr] *She slammed the box on the table.* ○ *He was slammed against the wall by the explosion.* **3** (*infml*) to criticize sb/sth harshly: [Vn] *The plans were slammed by local conservation groups.* **IDM** **shut/slam the door in sb's face** ⇨ DOOR.
  ▶ **slam** *n* (usu *sing*) an act of slamming sth; the

noise of sth being slammed: *the slam of a car door.* See also GRAND SLAM.

slammer /ˈslæmə(r)/ *n* **the slammer** [sing] (*sl*) prison.

slander /ˈslɑːndə(r); *US* ˈslæn-/ *n* [C, U] a false spoken statement intended to damage sb's reputation; the legal offence of making such a statement: *a vicious slander* ○ *sue sb for slander.* Compare LIBEL.
  ▶ **slander** *v* to make such a false statement about sb: [Vn] *He was charged with slandering a government minister.*
  slanderous /-dərəs/ *adj*: *a slanderous attack/accusation.*

slang /slæŋ/ *n* [U] (abbreviated as *sl* in this dictionary) very informal words and expressions that are more common in spoken language and are not thought suitable for formal situations. Slang is sometimes restricted to one particular group of people, eg soldiers or children: *army/prison/teenage slang* ○ *a slang word/expression/term* ○ *'Grass' is criminal slang for 'informer'.* See also COLLOQUIAL, INFORMAL 3, RHYMING SLANG.
  ▶ **slang** *v* (*infml*) to attack sb using angry and offensive language: [Vn] *The two drivers were slanging each other in the middle of the road.*
  slangy *adj* containing a lot of slang: *a slangy style.*
  ■ **'slanging-match** *n* an argument in which each person uses angry and offensive language.

slant /slɑːnt; *US* slænt/ *v* **1** to lean or make sth lean in a particular direction; to be not straight or level: [V] *slanting eyes/rain* [Vpr] *handwriting that slants from left to right* [Vnpr] *Slant your skis a bit more to the left.* [also V]. **2** (*sometimes derog*) to present information from a particular point of view, esp in an unfair way: [Vnpr] *The report was slanted towards/in favour of the property developers.* [also Vn].
  ▶ **slant** *n* **1** a sloping position: *Her hat was set at a slant.* ○ *Cut the flower stems on the slant.* **2** ~ (**on sth/sb**) (*infml*) a particular point of view, from which sth/sb is seen or presented: *get a new slant on the political situation* ○ *They've decided to give the programme a more youthful slant.*

slap /slæp/ *v* (**-pp-**) **1** to hit sb/sth with the palm of the hand: [Vn, Vnpr] *She slapped his face/slapped him on the face.* [Vnpr] *He slapped me on the back and said 'Congratulations!'* Compare SMACK¹ *v*. **2** to put sth on a surface quickly and carelessly: [Vnpr] *slap the money on the counter* ○ *slap some paint onto a wall* [Vnp] *He slapped the book down on the desk.* **PHR V** **slap sb a'bout/a'round** to hit sb regularly or repeatedly: *He's been accused of slapping his wife around.* **slap sb/sth 'down** (*infml*) to stop sb talking, making suggestions, etc in a firm, usu unpleasant, way: *All his ideas were slapped down at the publicity meeting.* **slap sth on sb/sth** to issue an order demanding or forbidding sth: *slap a court order on sb* ○ *slap visa restrictions on tourists.* **slap sth 'on sth** (*infml*) to add an extra amount to the price of sth: *They've slapped 50p on the price of a packet of cigarettes.*
  ▶ **slap** *n* a blow with the palm of the hand: *She gave him a slap across the face.* ○ *He greeted me with a firm handshake and a slap on the back.* Compare SMACK¹ 1. **IDM** **slap and 'tickle** (*dated Brit infml joc*) lively kissing, etc between lovers: *a bit of slap and tickle on the sofa.* **a slap in the 'face** a rejection or an insult: *It was a real slap in the face when she refused to see me.* **a slap on the 'wrist** a warning or mild punishment: *I got a slap on the wrist for turning up late.*
  slap (also ˌslap-'bang) *adv* (*infml*) **1** directly; straight: *The car ran slap(-bang) into the wall.* **2** right; exactly: *She was standing slap(-bang) in the middle of the path, so I couldn't get past.*

slapdash /ˈslæpdæʃ/ *adj, adv* done or doing things

too quickly and carelessly: *slapdash work* ○ *a slap-dash worker* ○ *a slapdash approach/method.*

slap-happy /ˌslæp ˈhæpi/ *adj* (*infml*) cheerful, but too casual about serious things: *too slap-happy in his attitude to schoolwork.* Compare HAPPY-GO-LUCKY.

slapstick /ˈslæpstɪk/ *n* [U] a type of comedy based on simple, often rough, actions, eg hitting people, falling over, etc: *slapstick comedy.*

slap-up /ˈslæp ʌp/ *adj* [attrib] (*Brit infml*) (of a meal) large and very good: *a slap-up dinner at an expensive restaurant.*

slash /slæʃ/ *v* **1** to make a long cut in sth with a violent sweeping action, using a sharp object: [Vn] *The tyres on my car had been slashed.* ○ *She tried to kill herself by slashing her wrists.* [Vnpr] *His face had been slashed with a razor.* ○ *We had to **slash our way** through the undergrowth with sticks.* ⇨ note at CUT[1]. **2** to cut or reduce sth by a large amount: [Vn] *slash costs/prices/fares.* **PHR V** **'slash at sb/sth (with sth)** to make violent sweeping movements at sb/sth with a knife, etc: *slashing at the tall weeds with a stick* ○ *He slashed at his attacker with a knife.*

▶ **slash** *n* **1** [C] **(a)** a violent cutting movement with a knife, etc. **(b)** a long cut or wound made by this: *a razor slash* ○ (*fig*) *Her mouth was a slash of red lipstick.* **2** [C] = OBLIQUE *n.* ⇨ App 3. **3** a slash [sing] (*Brit sl*) an act of passing URINE: *have a quick slash.*

slat /slæt/ *n* (usu *pl*) a long thin narrow piece of wood, metal or plastic, esp one of a series in a piece of furniture, a fence, etc: *open/close the slats in a Venetian blind.*

▶ **slatted** *adj* having slats: *a bed with a slatted pine base.*

slate /sleɪt/ *n* **1(a)** [U] a dark grey rock that splits easily into thin flat layers: *a slate quarry.* **(b)** [C] a small thin piece of this, used for covering roofs: *slate tiles* ○ *a slate roof.* ⇨ picture at HOUSE[1]. **2** [C] a small sheet of slate in a wooden frame, used esp formerly in schools for children to write on. **3** [C] (*US*) a list of candidates in an election: *on the Democratic slate.* **IDM** **a clean sheet/slate** ⇨ CLEAN[1]. **wipe the slate clean** ⇨ WIPE.

▶ **slate** *v* **1** ~ sb/sth (for sth) (*Brit infml*) to criticize sb/sth severely, eg in a newspaper: [Vn] *slate a play/book/writer* ○ *The idea was slated by the committee.* [Vnpr] *They were slated for their poor performance.* **2** [Vn] to cover a roof with slates. **3** ~ sb (for sth) (*US infml*) (esp passive) to propose or choose sb for a job, position, etc: [Vnpr] *He was slated for promotion/the Presidency.* [Vn.to inf] *She was slated to appear in a new Spielberg movie.* **4** ~ sth (for ...) (esp passive) to plan that sth will happen at a specified time: [Vnpr, Vn.to inf] *a conference slated for next July/to take place in July.*

slaty *adj* of, like or containing slate(1): *slaty rock* ○ *a slaty blue colour.*

■ **ˌslate-ˈgrey** *adj* having the dark grey colour of slate(1): *slate-grey eyes.*

slattern /ˈslætən/ *n* (*dated derog*) a dirty untidy woman. ▶ **slatternly** *adj*: *a slatternly girl.*

slaughter /ˈslɔːtə(r)/ *n* [U] **1** the killing of animals, esp for food: *animals reared for slaughter.* **2** the cruel killing of many people at one time: *the widespread slaughter of innocent civilians.*

▶ **slaughter** *v* **1** to kill an animal, usu for food: [Vn] *slaughter pigs by humane methods.* **2** to kill people or animals violently and in large numbers: [Vn] *Men, women and children were slaughtered and whole villages destroyed.* **3** (*infml*) to defeat sb/sth completely in sport, a competition, etc: [Vn] *We were absolutely slaughtered by the home team.*

slaughterhouse /ˈslɔːtəhaʊs/ (also **abattoir**) *n* a place where animals are killed for food.

Slav /slɑːv/ *n* a member of any of the peoples of

Central and Eastern Europe who speak Slavonic languages.

▶ **Slavic** /ˈslɑːvɪk/ (also **Slavonic** /sləˈvɒnɪk/) *adj* of or relating to Slavs or their languages, which include Russian, Polish and Czech.

slave /sleɪv/ *n* **1** a person who is legally owned by sb and is forced to work for them: *treat sb like a slave* ○ *slave owners.* **2** ~ of/to sth a person who is completely dominated or influenced by sth: *a slave to duty/fashion/drink* ○ *the slave of ambition.*

▶ **slave** *v* ~ (away) (at sth) to work very hard: [Vpr, Vp] *slaving (away) at the housework for hours* [also V].

slaver *n* (esp formerly) a person or a ship involved in the business of buying and selling slaves.

slavery /ˈsleɪvəri/ *n* [U] **1** the state of being a slave: *sold into slavery.* **2** the practice of having slaves: *people working to abolish slavery.*

■ **ˈslave-driver** *n* (*derog*) a person who makes people work very hard: *My boss is a real slave-driver.*

ˌslave ˈlabour *n* [U] **(a)** work done by slaves; work that is hard and badly paid: *I left because the job was just slave labour.* **(b)** the people who do such work: *factories that employ only slave labour.*

ˈslave-trade *n* [sing] the buying and selling of people as slaves, esp in the 17th–19th centuries.

slaver /ˈslævə(r)/ *v* ~ (over sth) (of a person or an animal) to let liquid run out of one's mouth, esp because of excitement or hunger: [V] *slavering dogs* [Vpr] *slavering at the mouth over a plate of food.*

slavish /ˈsleɪvɪʃ/ *adj* (*derog*) following or copying sb/sth without original thought: *slavish devotion/loyalty/obedience* ○ *a slavish imitation of another writer's work.* ▶ **slavishly** *adv*: *slavishly following the rules.*

Slavonic = SLAVIC.

slay /sleɪ/ *v* (*pt* **slew** /sluː/; *pp* **slain** /sleɪn/) (*dated or fml or US*) to kill sb/sth in a violent way: [Vn] *soldiers slain in battle.*

sleaze /sliːz/ *n* **1** [U] SLEAZY material, conditions or behaviour: *the city's growing reputation for sleaze.* **2** [C usu *sing*] a person who behaves in a SLEAZY way.

sleazy /ˈsliːzi/ *adj* (**-ier, -iest**) (*infml*) (esp of a place) dirty and not respectable: *a sleazy club/hotel* ○ *a rather sleazy atmosphere.* ▶ **sleaziness** *n* [U].

sledge /sledʒ/ (also *esp US* **sled** /sled/) *n* a vehicle with long narrow strips of wood, metal, etc instead of wheels, for travelling over ice and snow. Larger types of sledge are pulled by horses or dogs and smaller ones are used for going down hills for sport or pleasure. ⇨ picture. Compare SLEIGH, TOBOGGAN.

sledge (esp US **sled**)

▶ **sledge** (also *esp US* **sled**; **-dd-**) [V, Vpr] (often **go sledging**) to ride on a sledge.

sledge-hammer /ˈsledʒ hæmə(r)/ *n* a large heavy hammer with a long handle.

sleek /sliːk/ *adj* (**-er, -est**) **1** smooth and shiny: *sleek hair/fur.* **2** (*sometimes derog*) (of a person) looking wealthy and comfortable in life: *sleek yuppies in their city suits.* **3** having an elegant smooth shape: *a sleek car/yacht* ○ *a sleek, modern design.* ▶ **sleekly** *adv*: *sleekly styled/groomed.* **sleekness** *n* [U].

sleep[1] /sliːp/ *n* **1** [U] the natural state of rest in which the eyes are closed and the mind and body are not active or conscious: *How many hours' sleep do you need every night?* ○ *I didn't get much sleep last night.* ○ *I can't **get to sleep** (ie succeed in sleeping)* ○ *Do you ever talk in your sleep?* ○ *The lecture was so boring that it nearly **sent**

me to sleep (ie made me fall asleep). ○ *Go to sleep now — it's late.* **2** [sing] a period of sleep: *have a good sleep* ○ *be in a deep sleep.* **IDM** **cry/sob oneself to 'sleep** to cry until one falls asleep. **,go to 'sleep** (*infml*) (eg of a limb) to lose the sense of feeling and become NUMB: *I've been sitting on the floor and my foot's gone to sleep.* **not get/have a wink of sleep** ⇨ WINK. **not lose sleep / lose no sleep over sth** ⇨ LOSE. **put sb to 'sleep** to make sb unconscious by using an anaesthetic (ANAESTHESIA): *be put to sleep for an operation.* **put sth to 'sleep** (*euph*) to kill an animal deliberately, eg because it is ill or badly injured: *When our dog was very old we had him put to sleep.*

▶ **sleepless** *adj* [usu attrib] without sleep: *have a sleepless night.* **sleeplessly** *adv.* **sleeplessness** *n* [U]: *suffer from sleeplessness.* See also INSOMNIA.

sleep² /sliːp/ *v* (*pt, pp* **slept** /slept/) **1** to be in a state of sleep; to be asleep: [V] *I couldn't sleep because of the noise.* ○ *sleeping accommodation* [Vadv] *sleep well/badly* [Vn, Vpr] *We slept (for) eight hours.* ○ *You slept right through (ie were not woken up by) the thunderstorm.* ○ *I slept (ie stayed the night) at a friend's house last night.* **2** (no passive) to have enough beds for the specified number of people: [Vn] *Our caravan can sleep six comfortably.* ○ *The hotel sleeps 300 guests.* **IDM** **let sleeping dogs 'lie** (*saying*) do not try to change a situation that could become a problem if sb interfered. **not sleep a wink** ⇨ WINK *n.* **sleep like a 'log** (*infml*) to sleep deeply, without interruption. **sleep 'rough** to sleep outdoors wherever one can: *He'd been sleeping rough for a week, in ditches and haystacks.* **sleep 'tight** (*infml*) (esp imperative) to sleep well: *Good night, sleep tight!* **PHRV** **,sleep a'round** (*infml*) to have sex with many partners. **,sleep 'in** (*esp US*) = LIE IN: *I get a chance to sleep in on Saturday.* **,sleep sth 'off** to recover from sth by sleeping: *sleep off a headache/a large meal* ○ *sleep it off* (ie after being drunk). **'sleep on sth** (*infml*) to delay deciding about sth until the next day, so that one has a chance to think about it: *Don't say now if you'll take the job — sleep on it first.* **,sleep 'out** to sleep outdoors. **,sleep together**; **,sleep with sb** (*euph*) to have a sexual relationship with sb, esp sb to whom one is not married: *He's going out with her, but I don't think he's sleeping with her/they're sleeping together.*

■ **'sleeping-bag** *n* a warm lined bag for sleeping in, eg when camping (CAMP¹ *v*).

'sleeping-car (also **'sleeping-carriage**) *n* a railway coach fitted with beds to sleep in.

,sleeping 'partner (also *esp US* **,silent 'partner**) *n* a partner who has invested money in a business company but who does not actually work in it.

'sleeping-pill *n* a PILL(1) containing a drug that helps sb to sleep.

,sleeping po'liceman *n* (*Brit infml*) a low ridge built across a road to make drivers slow down.

'sleeping sickness *n* [U] a serious tropical disease carried by the tsetse fly (TSETSE). It causes a feeling of wanting to go to sleep and can be fatal.

sleeper /'sliːpə(r)/ *n* **1(a)** (with an *adj*) a person who sleeps in the specified way: *a good/bad sleeper* ○ *a heavy/light sleeper* (ie one whom it is hard/easy to wake up). **(b)** a person who is asleep: *The net protects the sleeper from mosquitoes.* **2(a)** a night train with sleeping accommodation on it: *the London-to-Edinburgh sleeper.* **(b)** = SLEEPING-CAR. **(c)** a bed on such a train: *I've got a sleeper reserved on the overnight train.* **3** (*Brit*) (*US* **tie**) any of the heavy beams of concrete or wood on which the rails of a railway are fixed. **4** (*infml esp US*) a film, play, book, etc that achieves sudden unexpected success after attracting very little notice at first.

sleepwalk /'sliːpwɔːk/ *v* to walk around while

asleep: [V] *I found him sleepwalking in the kitchen.*
▶ **sleepwalker** *n.*

sleepy /'sliːpi/ *adj* (**-ier, -iest**) **1** needing or ready to go to sleep; tired: *feel/look sleepy* ○ *The heat and the wine made me sleepy.* **2** (of places) not very busy; without much activity: *a sleepy little village.* ▶ **sleepily** /-ɪli/ *adv*: *yawn sleepily.*

sleet /sliːt/ *n* [U] falling snow or HAIL¹(1) mixed with rain: *heavy rain, turning to sleet and snow.* ▶ **sleet** *v* (used with *it*, usu in the continuous tenses): [V] *It is sleeting* (ie Sleet is falling).

sleeve /sliːv/ *n* **1** a part of a garment that covers all or part of the arm: *He rolled up his sleeves and washed his hands.* ○ *a dress with short/long sleeves.* ⇨ picture at JACKET. See also SHIRT-SLEEVE. **2** (*US* also **jacket**) a paper or cardboard envelope for a record. Some records have a paper sleeve inside a cardboard sleeve: *a colourful sleeve design* ○ *sleeve notes* (ie notes about the music or the performers on a sleeve). **IDM** **an ace up one's sleeve** ⇨ ACE. **a card up one's sleeve** ⇨ CARD¹. **have a trick up one's sleeve** ⇨ TRICK. **laugh up one's sleeve** ⇨ LAUGH. **roll up one's sleeves** ⇨ ROLL². **(have/keep sth) up one's 'sleeve** (to have/keep sth) secret or in reserve for use when needed: *Luckily I had a speech up my sleeve for an occasion such as this.* **wear one's heart on one's sleeve** ⇨ WEAR¹.
▶ **-sleeved** (forming compound *adjs*) having sleeves of the specified type: *a ,long-/,short-/ ,loose-sleeved 'shirt.*

sleeveless *adj*: *a sleeveless sweater.*

sleigh /sleɪ/ *n* a SLEDGE¹, esp one pulled by a horse: *a sleigh ride.*

sleight /slaɪt/ *n* **IDM** **,sleight of 'hand 1** great skill in using the hands, esp in performing magic tricks. **2** a clever act of deception: *Last year's profits were more the result of financial sleight of hand than genuine growth.*

slender /'slendə(r)/ *adj* (**-er, -est**) **1(a)** (*approv*) (of people or their bodies) thin, esp in an attractive or graceful way: *a slender girl/figure/waist* ○ *slender fingers.* ⇨ note at THIN. **(b)** thin or narrow: *a wineglass with a slender stem.* **2** small in amount or size; not enough or barely enough: *slender resources/ hopes* ○ *people of slender means* (ie with little money) ○ *win by a slender margin/majority.* ▶ **slenderness** *n* [U].

slept *pt, pp* of SLEEP².

sleuth /sluːθ, sljuːθ/ *n* (*dated or joc*) a person who investigates crimes; a DETECTIVE: *an amateur sleuth.*

slew¹ *pt* of SLAY.

slew² (*US* also **slue**) /sluː/ *v* (esp of a vehicle) to turn or swing with force in a new direction: [Vp, Vpr] *The car slewed round/from side to side on the icy road.* [Vadv] *The van slewed sideways and hit the kerb.*

slew³ /sluː/ *n* [sing] ~ **of sth** (*infml esp US*) a large number or amount of sth: *a whole slew of problems.*

slice /slaɪs/ *n* **1** a thin wide flat piece cut off an item of food: *a slice of bread/meat/cake/cheese* ○ *a gin and tonic with a slice of lemon* ○ *Cut the cucumber into thin slices.* See also FISH-SLICE. ⇨ picture at BREAD. ⇨ note at PIECE¹. **2** (*infml*) a portion or share: *capture a large slice of the market* ○ *She must take a large slice of the credit for our success.* ○ *The team needed a fair slice of luck to win this game.* **3** (*sport*) (esp in golf) a poor stroke that makes the ball spin off in the wrong direction, ie to the right of a right-handed (RIGHT⁵) player. **IDM** **get, etc a slice/share of the cake** ⇨ CAKE. **a piece/slice of the action** ⇨ ACTION. **a ,slice of 'life** a film, play, book, etc that gives a very realistic view of ordinary life.
▶ **slice** *v* **1** ~ **sth (up)** to cut sth into slices: [Vnpr] *slice sth in half* [Vn, Vnpr] *slice (up) the meat/ cucumber/melon* [Vn] *a sliced loaf/a loaf of sliced bread.* **2** ~ **sth off (sth)** to cut sth from a larger piece: [Vnp, Vnpr] *slice a piece off (the joint)* [Vnpr]

[V] = verb used alone   [Vn] = verb + noun   [Vp] = verb + particle   [Vpr] = verb + prepositional phrase

(fig) He's sliced two seconds off the world record. [also Vnn]. **3** ~ **(through/into sth)** to cut smoothly or easily through sth: [Vpr] The axe sliced through the wood. ○ The falling slate sliced into his arm. [Vn] The bows of the ship sliced the water. **4** *(sport)* (esp in golf) to hit a ball with a slice(3): [Vn, Vnpr] She sliced her shot (into the rough).

slick /slɪk/ *adj* (**-er, -est**) **1(a)** *(sometimes derog)* done in a clever, smooth and efficient way, apparently without effort: *slick advertising/designs/presentation* ○ *slick movements/rhythms* ○ *The movie is full of slick* (ie clever, amusing) *dialogue*. **(b)** (of people) doing things in this way: *a slick performer/salesperson/negotiator* ○ *She's very slick, but I don't believe a word she says.* **2** smooth and SLIPPERY(1): *The roads were slick with wet mud.*

▶ **slick** (also **'oil slick**) *n* a thick patch of oil floating on the sea, esp from a damaged oil-tanker (OIL).
slick *v* ~ **sth (back/down)** to make hair flat using eg oil or cream: [Vnp] *boys with slicked-back hair and fancy clothes* [Vnpr] *His hair was slicked across his forehead.* [also Vn].
slicker *n* **1** *(infml esp US)* a slick(1a) person: *a city slicker* (ie slick by comparison with a person from the country). **2** *(US)* a long loose WATERPROOF coat.
slickly *adv.*
slickness *n* [U].

slide¹ /slaɪd/ *v* (*pt, pp* **slid** /slɪd/) **1** to move or move sth smoothly along an even, polished or SLIPPERY surface: [V, Vp] *I was sliding (about) helplessly on the ice.* [Vpr] *The ship slid into the water.* ○ *We slid down the grassy slope.* [Vp] *The drawers slide in and out easily.* [Vnpr] *I slid the rug in front of the fire.* ○ *She slid her hand along the rail.* [Vnadv] *Can the driver's seat be slid forward a little?* [V-adj] *The automatic doors slid open.* [also Vnp, Vn-adj]. **2** to move or move sth quickly, smoothly or quietly, eg so as not to be noticed: [Vp, Vpr] *slide into bed* ○ *She slid out while no one was looking.* [Vnpr] *He slid his arm around her waist.* ○ *He lifted the mat and slid the key under it.* [also Vnp]. **3** ~ **(into sth)** to change gradually to a lower or worse condition: [V] *House values may begin to slide.* ○ *He got depressed and began to **let things slide*** (ie to fail to do things or to organize them badly). [Vpr] *slide into bad habits/debt* ○ *The team is sliding down the league.* See also BACKSLIDE.
■ **'slide-rule** *n* an instrument like a ruler, for calculating numbers quickly. It is marked with logarithms (LOGARITHM), and has a central part that slides backwards and forwards.
sliding 'door *n* a door that slides across an opening rather than swinging away from it.
sliding 'scale *n* a scale¹(6) that makes one value or quantity dependent on another, eg so that they increase or decrease together: *Fees are calculated on a sliding scale according to income* (ie Richer people pay more).

slide² /slaɪd/ *n* **1** [sing] an act of sliding on ice or a smooth surface: *Let's go for a slide on the frozen pond.* **2** [C] a structure used esp by children for sliding down. **3** [C] a smooth stretch of ice or hard snow used esp by children for sliding on. **4** [C usu sing] a change to a lower or worse condition: *a slide in his fortunes/popularity* ○ *The dollar continued its slide on the foreign exchanges.* ○ *(infml) The economy is **on the slide**.* **5** [C] **(a)** a small piece of photographic film, usu held in a small frame and shown on a screen using a PROJECTOR; a transparency (TRANSPARENT): *a slide show/projector.* **6** [C] a glass plate on which sth is placed so that it can be looked at under a MICROSCOPE. ⇨ picture at MICROSCOPE. **7** [C] a sliding part of a machine or other device, eg the part of a TROMBONE shaped like a U. ⇨ picture at MUSICAL INSTRUMENT. See also LANDSLIDE.

slight¹ /slaɪt/ *adj* (**-er, -est**) **1(a)** not serious or

important; small: *a slight error/change/advantage/problem/headache* ○ *The bed was at a slight angle to the wall.* ○ *Her chances of success are slight.* ○ *do sth without the slightest difficulty* (ie with no difficulty at all) ○ *She takes offence at the slightest thing* (ie is very easily offended). **(b)** *(usu derog)* not worthy of serious attention; minor; unimportant: *Compared to his early work, this is a rather slight novel.* **2** not thick and strong; small; thin: *a slight figure/girl* ○ *The framework looks too slight to support such a heavy load.* **IDM not in the 'slightest** not at all: *You didn't embarrass me in the slightest.*

▶ **slightly** *adv* **1** to a small degree; a bit: *a slightly bigger house* ○ *The two chairs are slightly different.* ○ *The patient is slightly better today.* ○ *I know her slightly.* **2** in a slight(2) way: *She is small and slightly built.*
slightness *n* [U].

slight² /slaɪt/ *v* to treat sb rudely or without proper respect; to insult sb: [Vn] *She felt slighted because no one spoke to her.*

▶ **slight** *n* ~ **(on sb/sth)** an act or a remark that offends sb: *My comment was not meant as a slight (on you/your achievements).*

slim /slɪm/ *adj* (**-mmer, -mmest**) **1** *(approv)* not fat or thick; thin: *a slim person/figure/waist* ○ *Regular exercise is the best way to stay slim.* ○ *a slim volume of poetry* ○ *(fig) create a slimmer, more efficient car industry* (eg with fewer workers or factories). ⇨ note at THIN. **2** not as big as one would like or expect; small: *only a slim hope/chance/prospect of success* ○ *condemned on the slimmest of evidence.*

▶ **slim** *v* (**-mm-**) **1** to eat less or take exercise in order to lose weight and become slim: [V] *I'm trying to slim.* **2** ~ **sth (down) (to sth)** to reduce sth in numbers, size or scale: [Vn, Vnp, Vnpr] *slim (down) the factory's workforce (to/by around 200)* [Vnp] *a slimmed-down version of the earlier report.*
slimmer *n* a person who is slimming: *advice to slimmers.*
slimming *n* [U] the practice of trying to lose weight: *a slimming diet/magazine.*
slimness *n* [U].

slime /slaɪm/ *n* [U] any unpleasant liquid substance that is soft, SLIPPERY(1) or slightly thick: *There was a coating of slime on the unwashed sink.* ○ *the primeval slime from which all life developed* ○ *Snails and slugs leave a trail of slime.*

▶ **slimy** /'slaɪmi/ *adj* (**-ier, -iest**) **1** of, like or covered with slime: *The stones were slimy with weed.* **2** *(infml derog)* excessively polite in an insincere or dishonest way: *You slimy little creep!*

slimline /'slɪmlaɪn/ *adj* [attrib] small or thin in shape or design: *a slimline stereo system.*

sling /slɪŋ/ *n* **1** a band of material tied round the neck and used to support an injured arm: *have one's arm **in a sling**.* **2(a)** a band, belt, rope, etc in the form of a loop, in which an object may be raised, lowered or supported. **(b)** a similar device for carrying a baby. **3** (formerly) a loop of leather, etc, used for throwing stones.

▶ **sling** *v* (*pt, pp* **slung** /slʌŋ/) **1** *(infml)* to throw sth/sb carelessly or with force: [Vn, Vnpr] *slinging stones (at birds)* ○ *Sling it in the bin.* ○ *She slung her coat angrily into the car.* [Vnp, Vpr] *He was slung out (of the club) for fighting.* See also MUD-SLINGING. **2** to put sth somewhere so that it hangs loosely: [Vnpr] *sling a hammock between two tree-trunks* ○ *with her bag slung over her shoulder.* **IDM sling one's 'hook** *(Brit sl)* (used esp in the imperative) to go away.
slingshot /'slɪŋʃɒt/ *n* (*US*) = CATAPULT.

slink /slɪŋk/ *v* (*pt, pp* **slunk** /slʌŋk/) to move as if one feels guilty or ashamed, or does not want to be seen: [Vpr] *He was trying to slink into the house by the back door.* [Vp] *The dog slunk away with its tail between its legs.* ⇨ note at PROWL.

▶ **slinky** /'slɪŋki/ adj **1** (eg of movement or sound) smooth, graceful or SEDUCTIVE: *her slinky voice/ way of dancing.* **2** (of a woman's clothes) fitting closely to the curves of the body: *a slinky black dress.*

slip¹ /slɪp/ v (-pp-) **1(a)** ~ **(over)** **(on sth)** (esp of a person) to slide a short distance accidentally; to lose one's balance and fall or nearly fall in this way: [V] *The climber's foot slipped, and she fell.* [Vp, Vpr] *She slipped (over) on the ice and broke her leg.* **(b)** to slide accidentally out of the proper position or into a worse position: [V] *The truck turned sharply, causing its load to slip.* ○ *The razor/my hand slipped and I cut my chin.* [Vp, Vpr] *The straps keep slipping off (my shoulders).* **(c)** ~ **from / out of / through sth;** ~ **out/through** to fall, get away or escape from sth by being difficult to hold, or by not being held firmly: [Vpr] *The fish/vase slipped out of my hand.* ○ *He almost caught the ball, but it slipped through his fingers.* [Vn, V-adj] *The boat slipped (free from) its moorings.* [Vn] *The dog slipped its leash/collar.* [Vpr] (fig) *The champions could feel the trophy* **slipping from their grasp** (ie because they were losing). [Vp] (fig) *I didn't mean to say that — it just slipped out.* **(d)** to fail to grip or make proper contact with a surface: [V] *The wheels kept slipping on the wet road.* ○ *a slipping clutch* (ie of a car). **2** ~ **(into sth);** ~ **(from sth) to sth** to change to a lower, worse or different condition, esp when the change is slight, gradual or hardly noticed: [V] *Safety standards have slipped recently.* ○ *The director never lets the film's tension slip.* [Vp] *Share prices rose strongly in the morning, but slipped back in the afternoon.* [Vpr] *We've slipped behind schedule.* ○ *My bank balance has slipped into the red.* ○ *prevent the patient from slipping into unconsciousness* [Vn] *His popularity has slipped a lot.* **3** to fail to be noticed, thought of or remembered by sb: [Vn] *Your request completely* **slipped my attention.** ○ *It had slipped my mind/ memory that you were arriving today.* **4** (infml often joc) (only in the continuous tenses) to be less good, alert, strong, etc than usual: *That's three times in a row she's beaten me at tennis — I must be slipping.* **5** to go somewhere or move quietly, quickly or easily, eg in order not to be noticed, or without being noticed: [Vp] *The thief slipped out by the back door.* ○ *We slipped away to Paris for the weekend.* [Vpr] *She's just slipped out of the office for a moment.* ○ *The ship slipped out of the harbour at night.* [Vp] (fig) *This wine slips down very nicely* (ie is pleasant to drink). *The years slipped by.* **6** to put sth somewhere, esp quickly, quietly or secretly: [Vnpr] *slip an envelope into one's pocket* ○ *I tried to slip the note to him while the teacher wasn't looking.* ○ *I managed to slip a few jokes into my speech.* [Vnp] *She opened the door slightly and slipped a newspaper through.* [Vnn] *He slipped the waiter a tip.* **7** ~ **into / out of sth;** ~ **sth on/off** to put clothes on or take clothes off, esp quickly and easily: [Vpr] *slip into/out of a dress* [Vnp] *slip one's shoes on/off* [Vnpr] *slip a shawl over/round one's shoulders.* **IDM** **let sth 'slip 1** to miss or fail to take advantage of an opportunity, etc: *She let slip a chance to work abroad.* **2** to reveal sth accidentally or in a deliberately casual way while speaking: *I didn't let a word slip.* ○ *I let (it) slip that I was expecting a baby.* **roll/slip/trip off the tongue** ⇨ TONGUE. **slip through the 'net** to escape from sth that has been organized to catch or deal with one/it: *Police have attempted to interview everyone in the area but a few may have slipped through the net.* **PHRV** **slip a'way** (eg of an opportunity) to begin to disappear or be lost: *She could see her chances of victory slipping away.* **slip 'up (on sth)** (infml) to make a careless mistake: *The government slipped up badly in not releasing the documents sooner.* See also SLIP-UP.

■ **'slip-knot** n a knot that can slip easily along the

rope, etc on which it is tied, in order to make the loop tighter or looser.

'slip-on n, adj [attrib] (a shoe) made to be put on without fastening buttons or tying laces.

slipped 'disc n a disc(5) between the bones of the SPINE(1) that has moved out of place and causes pain.

'slip-road (also esp US **'access road**) n a road used for driving onto or off a MOTORWAY.

'slip-up n (infml) a careless mistake: *We cannot afford another slip-up like this one.*

slip² /slɪp/ n **1** (usu sing) an act of slipping (SLIP¹ 1): *One slip and you could fall off the cliff.* **2** a minor error caused eg by being careless or not paying attention: *He recited the whole poem without making a single slip.* ○ *There were a few slips in the translation.* ○ *One slip and you could lose the game.* See also FREUDIAN SLIP. **3** a small piece of paper, esp one for writing on or with printed information on: *a voting/ betting slip* ○ *write a phone number on a slip of paper* ○ *a salary slip* (ie giving details of money earned, tax paid, etc). See also PAYSLIP. **4** a loose garment without sleeves worn under a dress. **5** (in cricket) a fielder (FIELD²) placed to stop or catch balls which the batsman hits with a glancing (GLANCE) blow; a position occupied by such a fielder: *first/second/ third slip* ○ *Who is (at) first slip?* ○ *a slip fielder/catch* ○ *fielding* **in the slips.** **IDM** **give sb the 'slip** (infml) to escape or get away from sb who is following or chasing one: *I managed to give him the slip by hiding behind a wall.* **a 'slip of a boy, girl, etc** (dated) a small or thin, usu young, person: *She's only a slip of a thing, but she can run faster than all of us.* **a slip of the 'pen/'tongue** a minor error in writing/ speech: *A slip of the tongue made me say Robert instead of Richard.*

slippage /'slɪpɪdʒ/ n [U] (fml) **1** a usu slight or gradual fall in the amount, value, price or quality of sth: *some slippage of support for the government's policies.* **2** failure to keep a promise or meet a target set for achieving sth: *The railway authority builds a certain amount of slippage into its timetables.*

slipper /'slɪpə(r)/ n a loose light soft shoe worn in the house: *a pair of slippers.* See also CARPET-SLIPPERS.

▶ **slippered** adj wearing slippers.

slippery /'slɪpəri/ adj **1** (also infml **slippy**) (of a surface) difficult to hold, stand or move on without slipping because it is smooth, wet, polished, etc: *a slippery road/floor* ○ *Ice made the path slippery underfoot.* ○ *His hands were wet and slippery.* **2** (infml) (of a person) not to be trusted; not reliable: *Don't believe what he says — he's a slippery customer.* **3** (infml) (of a situation, topic, problem, etc) difficult to deal with; requiring careful thinking: *the rather slippery subject of race relations* ○ *You're on slippery ground if you start accusing him of dishonesty.* ○ *Freedom is a slippery concept* (eg because its meaning changes according to one's point of view). **IDM** **the/a slippery 'slope** a course of action that is difficult to stop once it has begun, and can lead to serious problems or disaster: *Television sponsorship is the slippery slope towards loss of editorial independence.*

slipshod /'slɪpʃɒd/ adj done or doing things without care; careless: *slipshod work/grammar/style* ○ *a slipshod worker/writer* ○ *You're too slipshod in your presentation.* ○ *The goal was a result of slipshod defence.*

slipstream /'slɪpstriːm/ n (usu sing) the stream of air behind an object, esp a vehicle, that is moving very fast: *riding* **in the slipstream** *of the cyclist in front.*

slipway /'slɪpweɪ/ n a sloping track leading down to water, on which ships are built or pulled up out of the water for repairs, or from which they are launched.

slit /slɪt/ *n* a long narrow cut, tear or opening: *eyes like slits* ○ *a long slit in her skirt* ○ *Make a slit in the piecrust.* Compare SLOT 1.
▶ **slit** *v* (**-tt-**; *pt*, *pp* **slit**) to make a slit in sth by cutting; to open sth by slitting: [Vn] *slit sb's throat* [Vnpr] *The jacket is slit up the back.* [Vn-adj] *slit an envelope open with a knife.*

slither /ˈslɪðə(r)/ *v* (**a**) to slide or slip with an unsteady movement, esp from side to side or in different directions: [Vpr] *slither down an icy slope* [Vp] *slithering around in the mud.* (**b**) to move along in a way similar to this, esp with one's body close to the ground: [Vp] *The snake slithered off (into the grass) as we approached.* [Vpr] *The soldiers slithered through the undergrowth/across the rocks.*
▶ **slithery** *adj* slithering or making sth/sb slither; SLIPPERY(1).

sliver /ˈslɪvə(r)/ *n* a small, thin or narrow piece of sth cut or broken off from a larger piece: *slivers of wood/glass/metal* ○ *Please cut me a small sliver of cheese.* ○ (*fig*) *A sliver of moonlight could be seen through the shutters.*

slob /slɒb/ *n* (*infml derog*) a person who is lazy or rude or who dresses carelessly: *Get out of bed, you fat slob!*

slobber /ˈslɒbə(r)/ *v* (*derog*) to let SALIVA fall from the mouth: [Vpr] *The baby had slobbered all over her bib.* [V] *his ugly, slobbering mouth.* **PHRV** **slobber over sb/sth** (*infml usu derog*) to show one's affection or desire for sb/sth too openly, esp so that it embarrasses other people: *I know he's fond of you but does he have to keep slobbering over you in public?*
▶ **slobber** *n* [U] (*infml*) SALIVA.

sloe /sləʊ/ *n* a small, very bitter wild PLUM(1a) with a dark purple skin: *sloe gin/liqueur.*

slog /slɒɡ/ *v* (**-gg-**) (*infml*) **1** (*esp sport*) to hit a ball very hard, but often without skill or accuracy: *slog the ball all round the ground* (ie in cricket) [also Vn, V]. **2** to work hard and steadily at sth, esp a long boring job: [Vp, Vpr] *a teacher slogging away at/slogging through a pile of marking.* **3** to walk or move steadily, with great effort or difficulty, in the specified direction, esp on foot: [Vpr] *slogging through the snow with heavy shopping bags* [also Vp, Vadv]. **IDM** **slog/sweat one's guts out** ⇨ GUT. **slog it 'out** to fight or struggle until a conclusion is reached: *two boxers slogging it out* ○ *The party leaders are slogging it out in a TV debate.*
▶ **slog** *n* (*infml*) **1** a hard stroke, esp in cricket. Compare SLUG³. **2** (*usu sing*) a period of hard work or effort, eg walking: *Marking the exam papers was quite a slog.* ○ *It's a long hard slog up the mountain.*

slogan /ˈsləʊɡən/ *n* a word or phrase that is easy to remember, used eg by a political party or in advertising to attract people's attention or to suggest an idea quickly: *political/advertising slogans* ○ *'Power to the people' is their campaign slogan.*

sloop /sluːp/ *n* a small ship with one MAST¹(1) and sails pointing forwards and backwards.

slop /slɒp/ *v* (**-pp-**) (**a**) (of liquids) to come out over the edge of a container, esp as a result of careless handling: [Vp] *As I put the bucket down, some water slopped out.* [Vpr] *The tea slopped into the saucer.* (**b**) to pour sth or cause it to come out of a container in this way: [Vnp] *She slopped the dirty water out onto the grass.* [Vnpr] *You've slopped food all down your shirt!* ○ *She slopped some beans onto my plate.* [also Vn]. **PHRV** **slop a'bout/a'round** (of liquids) to move around in a small space, esp a container: *Water was slopping around in the bottom of the boat.* **slop 'out** (esp in prison) to get rid of liquid waste, eg by pouring it down a toilet: *The prisoners have to slop out every morning.*

▶ **slop** *n* (usu *pl*) **1** food for pigs, usu the remains of food intended for people. **2** liquid or partly liquid waste, eg dirty waste water from sinks or baths: [attrib] *a 'slop-bucket.* **3** (*dated*) liquid food, eg milk or soup, esp for sick people.

slope /sləʊp/ *n* **1** [C] (**a**) a surface of which one end or side is higher than the other; a piece of rising or falling ground: *run up/down the slope* ○ *a grassy slope* ○ *a ski-slope.* See also NURSERY SLOPES. (**b**) (usu *pl*) an area of land that is part of a mountain or a range of mountains: *the lower slopes of Mount Everest* ○ *The storms will affect south-facing slopes of the Alps.* **2** [sing, U] the amount by which sth slopes: *Because of the slope of the roof, the snow cannot accumulate.* ○ *a 40° slope* ○ *a gentle/steep slope* ○ *measure the degree/angle of slope.* **IDM** **the/a slippery slope** ⇨ SLIPPERY.
▶ **slope** *v* to be at an angle so that one end or side is higher than the other: [V] *a sloping roof* ○ *The floor/ceiling slopes.* [Vpr, Vp] *The garden slopes gently (away/down) towards the river.* [Vadv] *Does your handwriting slope forwards or backwards?* **PHRV** **slope 'off** (*Brit infml*) to go away, esp without being noticed, eg in order to avoid doing work.

sloppy /ˈslɒpi/ *adj* **1** (*usu derog*) careless, UNTIDY or casual: *sloppy/work/typing/thinking* ○ *a sloppy worker/writer/dresser* ○ *Security procedures had become quite sloppy.* ○ *He changed out of his smart suit into a sloppy sweater and jeans.* **2** (*infml derog*) foolishly sentimental: *I hate sloppy romantic films.* **3** containing too much liquid: *sloppy porridge* ○ *The mixture is too sloppy.* ○ (*infml*) *She gave him a big sloppy kiss.* ▶ **sloppily** /-ɪli/ *adv*: *sloppily dressed* ○ *talking sloppily about love.* **sloppiness** *n* [U]: *There is no excuse for sloppiness in your work.*

slosh /slɒʃ/ *v* ~ (**sth**) **around/about** (*infml*) (**a**) (esp of a fairly large amount of liquid) to move around noisily inside a container: [Vpr] *water sloshing against the sides of the bath* [Vp] *I could hear the food sloshing around inside my stomach as I ran.* ○ (*fig*) *There's too much money sloshing around in professional tennis.* (**b**) to move liquid noisily or carelessly: [Vnpr] *slosh whitewash on the wall* [Vnadv] *He sloshes water all over the floor whenever he has a bath.* [also Vnp]. **PHRV** **slosh a'bout/a'round (in sth)** to move around noisily in sth liquid: *children sloshing about in puddles.* ⇨ note at SPRAY².
▶ **sloshed** *adj* [pred] (*sl esp Brit*) drunk.

slot /slɒt/ *n* **1** a narrow opening through which sth can be put: *put a coin in the slot* ○ *cut a slot in the box.* **2** a cut, a hole, an opening or a channel into which sth fits or along which sth slides: *a slot on a dashboard for a car radio* ○ *The curtain hooks run along a slot in the curtain rail.* **3** a position, a time or an opportunity for sth/sb, eg in a list, a programme of events or a series of broadcasts: *This record has occupied the Number One slot for the past 6 weeks.* ○ *fill the late-night current affairs slot on BBC 2.*
▶ **slot** *v* (**-tt-**) ~ (**sth/sb**) **in**; ~ (**sth/sb**) **into sth** to place sth/sb or be placed into a slot; to fit together by means of a slot: [Vpr] *The bolt slotted smoothly into place.* [Vnpr] *Slot the edge of the panel into the groove.* [Vnp] *Switch on the computer and slot in the disk.* ○ (*fig*) *Two minutes later he slotted in (ie scored) a second goal.* [Vp] *The tubes slot together like this.* [Vnp] *slot in an extra lesson* [Vnpr] *Can we slot her into a job in the sales department?* **IDM** **fall/slot into place** ⇨ PLACE¹. **slotted** *adj* (*esp techn*) (usu attrib) having a slot or slots in it: *a screw with a slotted head.*
■ **'slot-machine** *n* **1** a machine with a slot for coins, used eg for selling eg cigarettes or bars of chocolate. **2** (*esp US*) = FRUIT MACHINE.

sloth¹ /sləʊθ/ n [U] (fml) the sin or bad habit of being lazy.
▶ **slothful** /-fl/ adj (fml) lazy.

sloth² /sləʊθ/ n an animal of S America that lives in trees and moves very slowly.

slouch /slaʊtʃ/ v to stand, sit or move in a lazy way, often not quite upright: [V] Don't slouch! Stand/Sit up straight! [Vpr] She slouched past me with her hands in her pockets. [Vp] slouching about all day doing nothing.
▶ **slouch** n **IDM** **be no 'slouch (at sth/doing sth)** (infml) to be very good at sth or quick to do sth: She's no slouch on the guitar/at tennis.

slough¹ /slaʊ; US also sluː/ n (dated or rhet) **1** [C] a very soft wet area of land: The battlefield was a slough of mud and corpses. **2** [sing] ~ of sth a bad state of mind that is hard to change: be in a slough of despair/self-pity.

slough² /slʌf/ v ~ sth (off) to let skin, dead tissue, etc fall off; to cast sth off: [Vnp, Vn] a snake sloughing (off) its skin [Vnp] slough off dead skin cells by using a facial scrub. **PHRV** ,**slough sth 'off** to get rid of sth; to abandon sth: slough off one's responsibilities ○ a company trying to slough off its negative public image.

slovenly /'slʌvnli/ adj (derog) careless, untidy, dirty, etc in appearance, dress or habits: a slovenly waiter ○ a slovenly appearance/attitude. ▶ **slovenliness** n [U].

slow¹ /sləʊ/ adj (-er, -est) **1** not moving, acting or done quickly; taking a long time; not fast: a slow runner/vehicle/journey ○ walk at a slow pace ○ make a slow recovery from an illness ○ make slow progress ○ a tune played at a fairly slow tempo ○ Political evolution is a long slow process. **2** not quick to learn; finding things hard to understand: a slow child/learner ○ be slow at maths. **3** [pred] ~ to sth/to do sth; ~ (in/about) doing sth not doing things immediately; hesitating to act, speak, etc: (fml) be slow to anger ○ She was not slow to realize what was happening. ○ They were very slow (about) paying me. **4** not lively or active enough; SLUGGISH: The film's too slow (eg does not have enough exciting scenes). ○ Business is rather slow today (eg Not many goods are being sold). **5** [pred] (of watches and clocks) showing a time earlier than the correct time, often by a specified number of minutes: My watch is five minutes slow (eg It shows 1.45 when it is 1.50). Compare FAST¹ 3. **6** (of a route, method of transport, etc) not allowing or intended for great speed: the slow lane of the motorway ○ a slow train that stops at every station. Compare FAST¹ 1b. **7** (of photographic film) not very sensitive to light. Compare FAST¹ 4. **IDM** **quick/slow off the mark** ⇨ MARK¹. **quick/slow on the draw** ⇨ DRAW². **quick/slow on the uptake** ⇨ UPTAKE.
▶ **slowly** adv at a slow speed; not quickly: walk/speak/learn/react slowly ○ She slowly opened the door. ○ Slowly, things began to improve. ○ You ought to take it slowly until you feel fully fit again. **IDM** ,**slowly but 'surely** making slow but definite progress: Slowly but surely her condition improved.
slowness n [U].

■ ,**slow 'motion** n [U] (in a film, etc) the method of making action appear to happen more slowly than in real life: a scene filmed in slow motion ○ a ,slow motion 'replay.

slow² /sləʊ/ adv (-er, -est) (used esp in the comparative and superlative forms, or in compounds with participles) at a slow speed; slowly: Please walk a bit slower. ○ slow-moving traffic ○ He's a bit slow-minded (ie not very intelligent). **IDM** **go 'slow 1** (of workers) to work slowly, esp as a protest or to make their employer meet their demands. See also GO-SLOW. **2** to be less active than usual: You ought to go slow until you feel really well again. **go 'slow on sth** to show less enthusiasm for achieving sth: going slow on European integration.

slow³ /sləʊ/ v ~ (sth/sb) (down/up) to go or make sth/sb go at a slower speed: [Vp] Slow down/up a bit — I think it's the next road on the right. [V, Vpr] The train slowed (to a crawl) as it approached the station. [V, Vp] Output has slowed (up) a little. [Vnp] She slowed the car down and then stopped. [Vn, Vnp] All this luggage is slowing me down. ○ Lack of investment will slow (down) our economic growth. [also Vnpr]. **PHRV** ,**slow 'down/up** to work less hard: You must slow up a bit, or you'll make yourself ill.

slowcoach /'sləʊkəʊtʃ/ (US also 'slowpoke) n (infml) a person who moves, acts, works or thinks slowly: 'Come on, slowcoach, we're late already!'

slowpoke /'sləʊpəʊk/ n (US infml) = SLOWCOACH.

slow-worm /'sləʊwɜːm/ n a small European reptile with no legs, like a snake.

SLR /ˌes el 'ɑː(r)/ abbr (of a camera) single-lens reflex.

sludge /slʌdʒ/ n [U] **1** thick soft mud or a substance resembling this: some sludge in the bottom of the tank. **2** waste products from human bodies, factories, etc: chemical/toxic sludge.

slue (US) = SLEW².

slug¹ /slʌg/ n a small creature like a SNAIL without a shell that moves slowly and often eats garden plants. ⇨ picture at SNAIL.

slug² /slʌg/ n (infml esp US) **1** a bullet. **2** a small amount of any strong alcoholic drink: take a slug of whisky.

slug³ /slʌg/ v (-gg-) (US) [Vn] to hit sb hard, esp with the FIST. Compare SLOG. **IDM** **slug it out** to fight or compete fiercely until the contest is decided: The two teams slugged it out to the final whistle.

sluggish /'slʌgɪʃ/ adj moving slowly; not alert or lively: a sluggish stream/pulse ○ a sluggish economy ○ sluggish traffic/conversation ○ feel sluggish and lazy after eating too much. ▶ **sluggishly** adv. **sluggishness** n [U].

sluice /sluːs/ n (also 'sluice-gate, 'sluice-valve) n a sliding gate or other device for controlling the flow of water out of or into a canal, lake, etc: open the sluice-gates of a reservoir.
▶ **sluice** v **1** ~ sth (down/out) to wash sth with a stream of water: [Vnp] sluice out the stables [Vnpr, Vnp] We sluiced the muddy wheels (down) with a hose. [also Vn]. **2** (of water) to flow in the specified direction as if from a sluice: [Vpr] rain sluicing along the gutters.

slum /slʌm/ n **(a)** a street or district of old buildings in a poor dirty condition, often crowded with people: brought up in the slums of London ○ a slum area ○ slum children ○ slum clearance schemes. **(b)** (usu sing) a house or rooms in such a place: (fig) This place is a slum — can't you keep it tidy?
▶ **slum** v (-mm-) v (often derog or joc) (usu in the continuous tenses) to visit places that are at a lower social level than one's own, esp out of curiosity. **IDM** '**slum it** (infml) to choose or be forced to live in poor surroundings: While he was studying, Nick had to slum it in a tiny room.

slummy adj (derog) of or like a slum; dirty or untidy: a slummy district.

slumber /'slʌmbə(r)/ v (fml esp fig) to sleep: [V] slumbering peacefully ○ the slumbering threat of war.
▶ **slumber** n (often pl) (fml) a sleep: fall into a deep slumber ○ disturb sb's slumber(s).

slump /slʌmp/ v **1** to sit or fall heavily: [Vpr, Vp] Tired from her walk she slumped (down) onto the sofa. [also Vn]. **2** (of prices, trade, business activity) to fall suddenly or greatly: [V] Sales/Shares/Earnings have slumped. [Vpr] Profits slumped from £12 million to £1.4 million.
▶ **slump** n ~ (in sth) **1** a period when business is

bad, sales are few, etc: *a housing/an economic slump* ○ *a slump in the property market/in car sales.* Compare DEPRESSION 3, RECESSION 1. **2** a period when a person, a team, etc has little success, poor results, etc: *a slump in her career.*

slumped /slʌmpt/ *adj*: *They found her slumped over the steering-wheel.*

slung *pt, pp* of SLING *v.*

slunk *pt, pp* of SLINK.

slur /slɜ:(r)/ *v* (**-rr-**) **1** [Vn] to run sounds, words into each other so that they are not distinct: [Vn] *He was clearly drunk and kept slurring his words.* [also V.speech]. **2** [Vn] to play or sing musical notes so that each one runs smoothly into the next. **3** to harm sb's reputation by making unfair or false statements about them: [Vn] *slurring the company's public image.*
▶ **slur** *n* **1** ~ (**on sb/sth**) a statement, an accusation, etc that may damage the reputation of sb/sth, esp an unfair or false one: *cast a slur on sb* ○ *a legal error which resulted in a serious slur on his character.* **2** (*music*) the mark (⌢) or (⌣), used to show that two or more notes are to be played or sung smoothly and without a break. **3** a slurred sound.

slurp /slɜ:p/ *v* (*infml*) to make a loud noise with the lips as one eats or drinks sth; to make a noise like this: [Vn, Vnp] *He slurped (down) his soup greedily.* [also V, Vpr].
▶ **slurp** *n* (*usu sing*) (*infml*) a slurping sound.

slurry /ˈslʌri/ *n* [U] a thick liquid consisting of eg cement, clay, waste from farm animals, etc mixed with water.

slush /slʌʃ/ *n* [U] **1** soft, usu dirty, melting snow on the ground. **2** (*infml derog*) silly sentimental speech or writing: *a romantic novel full of slush.* ▶ **slushy** *adj*: *slushy pavements* ○ *slushy poetry* ○ *a slushy TV comedy.*
■ **slush fund** *n* (*derog*) a fund of money used for illegal purposes, esp by a political party: *create a slush fund to bribe influential officials.*

slut /slʌt/ *n* (*derog*) **(a)** a woman who has many casual sexual partners. **(b)** a woman who is untidy, careless, in dress or habits. ▶ **sluttish** *adj*: *a sluttish woman* ○ *sluttish behaviour.*

sly /slaɪ/ *adj* **1** (*often derog*) acting or done in a secret, often deceitful, way: *a sly political move* ○ (*joc*) *You sly old devil!* **2** (*usu attrib*) suggesting that one knows sth secret; knowing: *a sly grin/glance/look* ○ *a sly sense of humour.* **IDM** **on the ˈsly** secretly: *She must have been having lessons on the sly.*
▶ **slyly** *adv*: *She glanced slyly at him.* **slyness** *n* [U].

smack¹ /smæk/ *n* **1** a sharp blow given with the open hand; a SLAP: *give sb a smack in the face.* **2** (*infml*) a loud kiss: *a smack on the lips/cheek.* **3** a blow; a hit: *give the ball a hard smack* (eg with a bat in cricket). **4** (*usu sing*) a loud sharp sound: *We heard the smack as it hit the floor.*
▶ **smack** *v* **1** to strike sb with the open hand: [Vn] *I think it's wrong to smack children even when they misbehave.* **2 (a)** to put sth in the specified place noisily and with force: [Vnpr, Vnp] *He smacked the report (down) on my desk.* **(b)** to move so as to hit sb/sth with great force: [Vpr] *They accidentally smacked into each other and both fell over.* **IDM** **lick/smack one's lips** ⇨ LIP.
smack *adv* **1** in a sudden and violent way: *run smack into a brick wall* ○ *hit sb smack in the eye.* **2** (*US* **ˈsmack-dab**) directly; exactly: *It landed smack(-dab) in the middle of the carpet.*
smacker *n* (*infml*) **1** a loud kiss. **2** (*sl*) a British pound or US dollar: *one hundred smackers.*
smacking *n* [sing] an act of hitting sb with the open hand, esp as a punishment: *give sb a good smacking.*

smack² /smæk/ *v* **PHRV** **smack of sth** to have a suggestion or taste of sth, esp sth unpleasant: *beha-*

viour that smacks of guilt/dishonesty ○ *The official announcement smacks of a government cover-up.*

smack³ /smæk/ *n* [U] (*sl*) the drug HEROIN.

smack⁴ /smæk/ *n* a small boat for fishing: *a fishing smack.*

small /smɔ:l/ *adj* **1** not large in size, degree, number, value, etc: *a small house/town/room/car* ○ *a small claims court* (ie for minor legal claims) ○ *a small amount of money* ○ *This hat is too small for me.* ○ *Children learn better in small classes.* ○ *'I don't agree,' he said in a small* (ie quiet) *voice.* Compare BIG. ⇨ note. **2** young: *We have three small children.* ○ *We lived in the country when I was small.* **3** [usu attrib] **(a)** not as big as sth else of the same kind: *the small intestine.* **(b)** (of letters) not written or printed as capitals (CAPITAL¹ 3). **4** [usu attrib] not doing things on a large scale: *a small farmer/trader/shopkeeper/company* ○ *more help for small businesses.* **5** slight; unimportant: *make a few small changes to the report* ○ *There are only small differences between the two translations.* **6** [attrib] (used with uncountable nouns) little or no: *The government has small cause for optimism.* **IDM** **(be) grateful/thankful for small ˈmercies** (to be) relieved that a bad situation is not worse: *It may be cold but at least it's not raining — let's be thankful for small mercies.* **great and small** ⇨ GREAT. **in a big/small way** ⇨ WAY¹. **it's no/little/small wonder** ⇨ WONDER. **it's a ˌsmall ˈworld** (*saying*) one is likely to meet or hear about sb one knows wherever one goes. **look/feel ˈsmall** to look/feel inferior, stupid, weak, etc: *There's no need to make me look small in front of everybody!* **the still small voice** ⇨ STILL¹.
▶ **small** *adv* **1** into small pieces: *chop it up small.* **2** in a small size: *You can get it all in if you write very small.*
small *n* **1** **smalls** [pl] (*dated Brit infml*) small items of clothing, esp UNDERWEAR. **2** [sing] the narrow part of sth: *He felt a sharp pain in **the small of the/his back.***
smallish /ˈsmɔ:lɪʃ/ *adj* fairly small; quite small.
smallness *n* [U].
■ **ˈsmall ads** /ædz/ *n* [pl] (*Brit infml*) = CLASSIFIED ADVERTISEMENTS.
ˈsmall arms *n* [pl] weapons light enough to be carried in the hands: *small-arms fire.*
ˌsmall ˈbeer *n* [U] (*Brit infml*) a person or thing of no great importance or value: *It seems a lot of money but it's small beer to a large organization like that.*
ˌsmall ˈchange *n* [U] coins of low value: *I dropped some small change into the collecting tin.*
a ˌsmall ˈfortune *n* [sing] a lot of money: *The car cost me a small fortune.*
ˈsmall fry *n* [pl *v*] (*infml*) people thought to be unimportant.
the ˈsmall hours *n* [pl] the period of time soon after midnight: *working until/into the small hours.*
ˌsmall-ˈminded *adj* (*derog*) mean; not generous or forgiving. **ˌsmall-ˈmindedness** *n* [U].
the ˌsmall ˈprint *n* [U] the parts of a legal document, contract, etc which are often printed in small type and contain important details that are easy to miss: *Make sure you read all the small print before signing.*
ˌsmall-ˈscale *adj* **1** (of a map, drawing, etc) drawn to a small scale¹(5) so that few details are shown. **2** not great in size, extent, quantity, etc: *small-scale ˈfarming/ˈfarmers.* Compare LARGE-SCALE.
the ˌsmall ˈscreen *n* [sing] the television, contrasted with the cinema: *the film's first showing on the small screen.*
ˈsmall talk *n* [U] conversation about ordinary or unimportant matters, usu at a social event: *He has no small talk* (ie is not good at talking to people about ordinary or unimportant things).

'small-time adj [attrib] (infml derog) unimportant; PETTY(1a): a ¸small-time 'crook.

'small-town adj [attrib] typical of a small town; having limited knowledge and ideas about the outside world: ¸small-town 'attitudes.

NOTE Compare **small** and **little**. **Small** is the usual opposite of *big* or *large*. The comparative form is **smaller** and the superlative form is **smallest** and it can be modified by adverbs such as *rather* and *quite*: *Our house is smaller than yours but I think the garden is bigger.* ○ *It is a fairly small theatre with about 1 000 seats.* **Little** is often used to show feelings of affection, dislike or amusement, especially after other adjectives such as *pretty, ugly, nice, sweet*, etc: *She put her little arms round his neck and kissed him.* ○ *a beautiful little village in the mountains* ○ *It was the ugliest little dog you ever saw.* **Little** is used before names, as a diminutive: *Little Joanna had to spend Christmas in hospital.* ○ *Little Italy is an area of New York where many Italians live.* The comparative form **littler** and the superlative form **littlest** are not common.

smallholder /'smɔːlhəʊldə(r)/ n (Brit) a person who owns or rents a small piece of land for farming.

smallholding /'smɔːlhəʊldɪŋ/ n (Brit) a small piece of land used for farming.

smallpox /'smɔːlpɒks/ n [U] a serious, often fatal disease causing a high fever and leaving permanent marks on the skin: *a smallpox epidemic/vaccination.*

smarmy /'smɑːmi/ adj (Brit infml derog) (of people or their behaviour) trying to make oneself popular by praising sb or being very polite in an insincere way: *a smarmy salesman/smile.*

smart¹ /smɑːt/ adj (**-er, -est**) **1** (of people) clean, tidy and well dressed; wearing quite formal clothes: *You look very smart in your new suit.* **2** (of clothes, etc) clean, attractive and looking new: *a smart dress/suit* ○ *a smart car.* **3** (esp US) (of people or their actions, etc) having or showing intelligence; clever: *the smartest student in her class* ○ *a smart answer/idea* ○ *That's where the smart money is* (ie That is what clever people are investing in). **4** connected with fashionable rich people: *smart restaurants/hotels/shops* ○ *She mixes with the smart set.* **5** quick and sharp: *set off at a smart pace* ○ *a smart smack with the whip* ○ *a smart rebuke from the teacher.*
► **smarten** /'smɑːtn/ v **PHR V** ¸smarten (oneself/sb/sth) 'up (esp Brit) to make oneself/sb/sth more attractive: *You'll have to smarten (yourself) up a bit before you go out.* ○ *The hotel has been smartened up by the new owners.*
smartly adv: *smartly dressed* ○ *march smartly into the room* ○ *She knocked smartly on the door.*
smartness n [U].
■ **'smart alec** /-ælɪk/ (also **'smarty-pants**, **'smart-arse**) n (infml usu derog) a person who acts as if he or she is very clever or knows everything: *She's a real smart alec!*
'smart card n a small plastic card on which information is stored in electronic form: *The introduction of smart cards has revolutionized the banking system.*

smart² /smɑːt/ v **1** ~ (from sth) to cause or feel a sharp pain in a part of the body; to sting: [V] *The wound was beginning to smart a little.* [Vpr] *His eyes were smarting from the dust.* **2** ~ (from/over/under sth) to feel upset about a criticism, defeat, etc: [Vpr] *They're still smarting from their defeat in the final.* [also V].

smash /smæʃ/ v **1** ~ sth (up); ~ sth open to break sth or be broken violently and noisily into pieces: [Vpr] *the sound of a glass smashing (into/to pieces) on the floor* [Vn] *smash a window* [Vn,Vnp] *smash (up) all the furniture* [Vnpr] *smash the furniture to*

bits [Vn-adj] *The lock was rusty, so we had to smash the door open.* [V] *The windscreen had smashed.* **2(a)** to hit sth/sb very hard: [Vnpr] *smash sb in the face* ○ *He smashed the ball into the goal.* [Vn,Vnpr] *She fell and smashed her head (on the floor).* [also Vnp]. **(b)** [Vn, Vnpr] (in tennis, etc) to hit a ball downwards and very hard over the net. **3** ~ sth (up) to crash a vehicle: [Vn, Vnp] *She's smashed (up) her new car.* **4** (infml) to defeat or destroy or put an end to sth/sb: [Vn] *We are determined to smash terrorism.* ○ *Police have smashed the drug ring.* ○ *She's smashed the world record for this distance.* **5** to move with great force in the specified direction: [Vpr] *The car smashed into the wall.* ○ *The huge waves smashed against the rocks.* [Vnpr] *The elephant smashed its way through the trees.* **PHR V** ¸smash sth 'down to make sth fall down by hitting it hard and breaking it: *The fireman smashed the door down to reach the children.* ¸smash sth 'in to make a hole, etc in sth by hitting it with great force: *Vandals smashed the door in.* ○ (infml) *I'll smash your head in* (ie said as a threat to hit sb)*!* ¸smash sth 'up to destroy sth deliberately: *smash up telephone booths* ○ *Vandals broke into the pub and smashed the place up.*
► **smash** n **1** [sing] an act or a sound of smashing (SMASH 1): *the smash of breaking glass* ○ *The plate hit the floor with a smash.* **2** [C] a car crash: *We had an awful smash on the way to London.* **3** [C] (in tennis, etc) a way of hitting the ball downwards and very hard over the net: *develop a powerful smash.* **4** (also ¸smash 'hit) [C] (infml) a play, song, film, etc that is very successful and popular.
smashed adj [pred] (sl) drunk.
smasher n (infml esp Brit) an excellent, attractive, etc person or thing: *She's a real smasher!*
smashing adj (infml esp Brit) excellent: *We had a smashing holiday.*
■ ¸**smash-and-'grab** adj [attrib] (of a robbery (ROB), etc) in which the thief smashes a shop window to steal the goods on display: *a ¸smash-and-'grab raid.*

smattering /'smætərɪŋ/ n [sing] ~ (of sth) a slight knowledge, esp of a language: *have a smattering of French/chemistry.*

smear /smɪə(r)/ v **1(a)** ~ sth on/over sth/sb; ~ sth/sb with sth to spread an oily or sticky substance, eg paint, on sth/sb in a rough or careless way: [Vnpr] *smearing mud all over the wall* ○ *He had smeared grease on his overalls/smeared his overalls with grease.* ○ *Her face was smeared with blood.* **(b)** to make sth dirty or GREASY(1): [Vn] *Don't smear the glasses; I've just polished them.* **2** to damage sb's reputation, eg by saying bad things about them that are not true: [Vn] *The paper printed the story in an attempt to smear the President.* **3** to rub writing, a drawing, an outline, etc so that it is no longer clear: [Vn] *I accidentally smeared the ink before it was dry.*
► **smear** n **1** an oily or dirty mark made by smearing: *a smear of lipstick* ○ *smears of blood on the wall.* **2** an accusation that is not true but is intended to damage sb's reputation: *The story was a smear to discredit the prime minister.* ○ *a smear campaign.* **3** (also **'smear test**) a medical test in which a very small amount of tissue from a woman's CERVIX is removed and examined to check for CANCER cells: *a cervical smear* ○ *go for a regular smear.*

smell¹ /smel/ v (pt, pp **smelt** /smelt/ or **smelled**) **1(a)** (not used in the continuous tenses; often with *can* or *could*) to notice sth/sb by using the nose: [Vn] *Can you smell anything unusual?* ○ *The dog had smelt a rabbit.* [V.that] *I could smell (that) he had been smoking.* [Vn.ing no passive] *I could smell something burning.* ⇨ note at FEEL¹. **(b)** to put one's nose near sth and breathe in so as to discover or identify its smell: [Vn] *a dog smelling a lamppost* ○

Smell this and tell me what you think it is. **2** (not used in the continuous tenses) to be able to smell: [V] *Can birds smell?* **3(a)** (not used in the continuous tenses) to have an unpleasant smell: [V] *Your breath smells.* ○ *The fish has begun to smell.* **(b)** ~ (of sth) to have a smell of the specified type: [V-adj] *a bunch of sweet-smelling flowers* ○ *The dinner smells good.* [Vpr] *What does the perfume smell like?* ○ *The soup smells of garlic.* ○ *Her house smells of dogs.* **4** to be able to detect sth by instinct: [Vn] *He smelt danger.* [Vn, Vn.ing] (no passive): *I can smell trouble (coming).* **smell a** ¹**rat** (*infml*) to suspect that sth is wrong: *I smelt a rat when he started being so helpful!* **PHR V** ¸**smell sb/sth** ¹**out** to detect sb/sth by smelling: *The dogs are specially trained to smell out drugs.*

■ ¹**smelling-salts** *n* [pl] (esp formerly) a chemical with a very strong smell, kept in small bottles and used to revive people who have fainted (FAINT²).

smell² /smel/ *n* **1** [U] the ability to sense things with the nose: *Taste and smell are closely connected.* ○ *Dogs have an excellent sense of smell.* **2(a)** [C,U] a thing that is sensed by the nose; the quality that allows sth to be smelled: *a sweet/musty/delicious smell* ○ *a strong/faint smell of gas* ○ *There's a smell of cooking.* ○ *The smells from the kitchen filled the room.* ○ *The cream has no smell.* **(b)** [sing] an unpleasant smell: *There's a bit of a smell in here.* ○ *What a smell!* **3** [C usu *sing*] an act of smelling sth: *Have a smell of this egg and tell me if it's bad.*

▶ **smelly** *adj* (**-ier, -iest**) (*infml*) having a bad smell: *a smelly room/person* ○ *smelly feet/breath/fumes.*

smelt¹ /smelt/ *v* **1** to heat and melt ORE in order to obtain the metal it contains. **(b)** to obtain metal in this way: [Vn] *a copper-smelting works.*

▶ **smelter** *n* an apparatus for smelting metal.

smelt² *pt, pp* of SMELL¹.

smidgen /¹smɪdʒən/ *n* [sing] ~ (**of sth**) (*infml*) a small bit or amount: *'Do you want some sugar?' 'Just a smidgen.'*

smile /smaɪl/ *n* an expression of the face in which the corners of the mouth turn up, showing happiness, amusement, pleasure, etc: *with a warm/bright/friendly smile on his face* ○ *give sb a broad smile.* **IDM all** ¹**smiles** looking very happy, esp in contrast to one's earlier mood: *The worried look disappeared from her face and she was all smiles again.*

▶ **smile** *v* **1** ~ (**at sb/sth**) to give a smile or smiles: [V] *smile happily/with pleasure* ○ *He never smiles.* [Vpr] *I smiled at the child and she smiled back.* **2** to express sth by means of a smile: [Vn] *She smiled her approval.* [V.speech] *'Thank you,' smiled Paul.* **3** to give the specified type of smile: [Vn] *She smiled a bitter/satisfied smile.* **PHR V** ¹**smile on sb/sth** (*fml*) to look favourably on sb/sth: *Fortune smiled on us (ie We were lucky or successful).* **smilingly** *adv* with a smile or smiles.

smirk /smɜːk/ *n* a silly or unpleasant smile showing that one is pleased with oneself, knows sth that others do not know, etc: *Wipe that smirk off your face!*

▶ **smirk** *v* [V] to give a smirk.

NOTE Compare **smirk, sneer, frown, scowl** and **grimace**. These verbs describe expressions on people's faces when they are feeling various negative emotions. People **smirk** when they smile in a silly way to show that they are pleased with themselves, usually at the expense of somebody else. When people **sneer** they curl their top lip to express an attitude of superiority and contempt towards other people: *He's always sneering at my suggestions.* You **frown** by bringing your eyebrows together to show you are not pleased or cannnot understand something: *Mr Wilson frowned a great deal and always looked worried.* When people **scowl** they

twist their faces into an expression of anger, dissatisfaction, etc: *Behind his scowling face he was a kind old man.* When somebody **grimaces** they twist their whole face for a very short time as a reaction to pain or annoyance, or to cause laughter: *She grimaced when she realized there was no sugar in her coffee.*

smite /smaɪt/ *v* (*pt* **smote** /sməʊt/; *pp* **smitten** /¹smɪtn/) (*fml or joc*) **1** [Vn, Vnpr] to hit sb/sth hard; to strike sb/sth. **2** to have a great effect on sb: [Vn] *His conscience smote him.*

smith /smɪθ/ *n* = BLACKSMITH. See also GOLDSMITH, LOCKSMITH, SILVERSMITH.

smithereens /ˌsmɪðə¹riːnz/ *n* [pl] (used esp with *vs* meaning *break* or *destroy*) small pieces: *smash/blow sth (in)to smithereens.*

smithy /¹smɪði/ *n* a place where a BLACKSMITH works.

smitten¹ *pp* of SMITE.

smitten² /¹smɪtn/ *adj* [pred] **1** ~ (**with/by sb/sth**) (*esp joc*) having become suddenly very fond of sb, esp in a romantic way: *They've only met once but he's completely smitten with her.* **2** ~ **with/by sth** deeply affected by an emotion: *smitten with remorse for one's cruelty.*

smock /smɒk/ *n* **(a)** a loose comfortable garment like a shirt, worn esp by women: *a shapeless cotton smock.* **(b)** a long loose garment worn over other clothes to protect them from dirt, etc: *Smocks were formerly worn by farm-workers.* ○ *The artist's smock was covered in paint.* Compare OVERALL² 1.

smog /smɒɡ/ *n* [U] a mixture of smoke and FOG: *the smog of Victorian London.* ⇨ note at FOG.

smoke¹ /sməʊk/ *n* **1** [U] the white, grey or black gas produced by sth that is burning: *smoke from factory chimneys* ○ *The room was full of cigarette smoke.* ○ *a smoke alarm (ie a device that gives warning of a fire by detecting smoke).* **2** [C usu *sing*] (*infml*) an act or period of smoking tobacco: *They stopped work to have a smoke.* ○ *I haven't had a smoke all day.* **IDM go up in** ¹**smoke 1** to be completely burnt: *The whole row of houses went up in smoke.* **2** to result in failure; to leave nothing of value behind: *Hopes of an early end to the dispute have clearly gone up in smoke.* **(there is) no smoke without** ¹**fire** (*saying*) there is always some reason for a rumour: *He's denied having an affair with his secretary, but of course there's no smoke without fire.*

▶ **smokeless** *adj* [usu attrib] **1** burning with little or no smoke: *smokeless fuel.* **2** free from smoke: *a smokeless zone (ie an area where smoke, eg from factories, is not allowed).*

■ ¹**smoke-free** *adj* free from cigarette smoke: *smoke-free public transport (ie where smoking is not allowed).*

smoke² /sməʊk/ *v* **1(a)** to produce smoke or other visible gas: [V] *a smoking volcano* ○ *smoking factory chimneys.* **(b)** (of a fire indoors) to send smoke into the room instead of up the chimney: [V] *This fireplace smokes (badly).* **2(a)** to draw in smoke from burning tobacco or other substances through the mouth and let it out again: [Vn] *He smokes a pipe.* ○ *She smokes 20 (cigarettes) a day.* **(b)** to use cigarettes, etc in this way as a habit: [V] *Do you smoke?* ○ *She has never smoked.* **3** (esp passive) to preserve meat, fish, etc with smoke from wood fires to give it a special taste: [Vn] *smoked ham/salmon/mackerel.* **IDM put that in your pipe and smoke it** ⇨ PIPE¹. **PHR V** ¸**smoke sb/sth** ¹**out 1** to drive sb/sth out by means of smoke: *smoke out wasps from a nest.* **2** to force sb to leave a place where they are hiding or to make a secret publicly known: *He was determined to smoke out the leaders of the gang.*

▶ **smoker** *n* **1** a person who smokes tobacco regularly: *a heavy smoker (ie sb who smokes very often)* ○ *a smoker's cough.* **2** a carriage on a train where smoking is allowed: *Shall we sit in a smoker or a non-smoker?*

smoking *n* [U] the activity or habit of smoking cigarettes, etc: *'No Smoking'* (eg on a notice in a public place) ○ *Smoking isn't allowed in this cinema.* ○ *the smoking section of an aircraft.* '**smoking-jacket** *n* (esp formerly) a man's comfortable jacket, made eg of VELVET.

■ ˌsmoked ˈglass *n* [U] glass that has been specially made dark by smoke: *a smoked glass coffee table.*

smokescreen /ˈsməʊkskriːn/ *n* (**a**) a cloud of smoke used to hide military, naval, police, etc operations. (**b**) an action, explanation, etc designed to hide one's real intentions, activities, etc: *The export business was just a smokescreen for his activities as a spy.*

smokestack /ˈsməʊkstæk/ *n* (**a**) the tall chimney of a factory or ship. (**b**) (*US*) the metal chimney of a steam train (STEAM).

smoky /ˈsməʊki/ *adj* (**-ier, -iest**) **1(a)** producing a lot of smoke: *smoky chimneys/fires.* (**b**) full of or smelling of smoke: *the smoky atmosphere of a room/ an industrial town.* **2** like smoke in smell or taste: *smoky cheeses.* **3** like smoke in colour or appearance: *a pretty smoky glass* ○ *a smoky grey coat.*

smolder (*US*) = SMOULDER.

smooch /smuːtʃ/ *v* (*infml*) to kiss and hold sb closely, esp when dancing slowly: [V] *couples smooching on the dance floor.*

smooth¹ /smuːð/ *adj* (**-er, -est**) **1** having an even surface without points, lumps or rough patches: *a smooth skin/road/sheet of ice* ○ *a smooth sea* (ie calm, without waves) ○ *Marble is smooth to the touch* (ie feels smooth when touched). Compare ROUGH¹. **2** (of a liquid mixture) free from lumps; evenly mixed or beaten: *smooth custard* ○ *Mix the butter and sugar to a smooth paste.* **3** tasting pleasant; not harsh or bitter: *a smooth whisky/cigar.* **4** free from difficulties or problems: *as smooth a journey as possible* ○ *The new bill had a smooth passage through Parliament.* **5** moving evenly, without sudden starts or stops, etc: *a smooth ride in a car* ○ *a smooth crossing by sea* ○ *The aircraft made a smooth landing.* **6** flowing easily and evenly: *smooth verse* ○ *a smooth voice.* **7** (*often derog*) (esp of men) charming and polite, but often not sincere: *He's certainly a smooth operator/individual.* **IDM** (**as**) **smooth as ˈsilk** very smooth: *Her skin is still as smooth as silk.* **take the rough with the smooth** ⇨ ROUGH³.

▶ **smoothie** (*infml derog*) *n* a person, usu a man, who appears charming and polite but is often not sincere: *Don't trust him — he's a real smoothie!*

smoothly *adv* in a smooth manner: *The engine is running smoothly now.* ○ *'I don't want to bother you,' he said smoothly.* ○ *Things are not going very smoothly* (ie There have been a lot of problems, interruptions, etc).

smoothness *n* [U]: *the smoothness of her skin* ○ *the smoothness of the sea* ○ *The smoothness with which negotiations had proceeded surprised him.*

■ ˌsmooth-ˈtalking *adj* (*usu derog*) speaking in a flowing and charming way, usu to persuade sb to do sth: ˌsmooth-talking ˈsalesmen.

smooth² /smuːð/ *v* ~ sth (**away, back, down, out,** etc) to make sth smooth: [Vn, Vnpr] *smooth wood* (*with sandpaper*) ○ [Vn, Vnpr] *smooth (out) a sheet on a bed* ○ *A new leader could help to smooth (out) the party's difficulties.* **IDM** **smooth sb's/the ˈpath/ ˈway** to make progress easier: *talks aimed at smoothing the way to a treaty* ○ *Speaking the language fluently certainly smoothed our path.* **smooth sb's ruffled ˈfeathers** to make sb feel less angry or offended. **PHRV** ˌsmooth sth aˈway to make sth, esp problems or difficulties, disappear or become

less serious: *smooth away wrinkles/tension* ○ *Any differences between us were soon smoothed away.* ˌsmooth sth ˈover to make problems, etc seem less important or obvious: *An attempt was made to smooth over the disagreement between the two leaders.*

smorgasbord /ˈsmɔːɡəsbɔːd/ *n* [U] a variety of hot and cold SAVOURY(1) dishes from which one chooses and serves oneself: *Help yourself from the smorgasbord.*

smote *pt* of SMITE.

smother /ˈsmʌðə(r)/ *v* **1** ~ sb (**with sth**) to kill sb by covering their nose and mouth so that they cannot breathe; to SUFFOCATE sb: [Vnpr] *He smothered the baby with a pillow.* ○ (*fig*) *She felt smothered with kindness.* [also Vn]. **2** to EXTINGUISH(1) or reduce a fire by covering it with ashes, sand, etc: [Vn] *If you put too much coal on the fire at once you'll smother it.* [Vnpr] *She smothered the flames from the burning pan with a wet towel.* **3** to prevent sth from developing or being noticed; to suppress or STIFLE sth: [Vn] *smother a yawn/smile/giggle* ○ *I heard a smothered cry from the next room.* **4** ~ sth/sb with/in sth to cover sth/sb thickly, or with too much of sth: [Vnpr] *a pudding smothered in cream* ○ *smother a child with kisses.*

smoulder (*US* **smolder**) /ˈsməʊldə(r)/ *v* to burn slowly without a flame: [Vpr] *a cigarette smouldering in the ashtray* [Vpr] (*fig*) *Hate smouldered silently inside him.* ○ *She smouldered with jealousy.*

smudge /smʌdʒ/ *n* a dirty mark, often caused by rubbing sth with one's finger: *You've got a smudge of dust/paint on your cheek.*

▶ **smudge** *v* **1** to make a dirty mark or marks on sth: [Vn] *smudged lipstick* ○ *You've smudged my picture!* **2** (of ink, etc) to spread when rubbed, etc, making a dirty mark: [V] *Wet paint smudges easily.* ○ *Her mascara had smudged.* **smudgy** *adj*: *smudgy letters.*

smug /smʌɡ/ *adj* (*derog*) too pleased with or proud of oneself or one's achievements: *smile with smug satisfaction* ○ *Sue came in looking very smug.* ▶ **smugly** *adv*: *'We've already been there,' she said smugly.* **smugness** *n* [U].

smuggle /ˈsmʌɡl/ *v* ~ sth/sb (**into/out of/across/through sth**); ~ sth/sb **in/out/across/ through 1** to take, send or bring goods secretly and illegally into or out of a country, esp without paying customs duty: [Vn] *smuggle Swiss watches* [Vnpr] *smuggle drugs through customs* ○ *smuggle cattle across the border* [Vnp] *arrested for smuggling out currency.* **2** to send, take or bring sth/sb secretly to or from a place, esp when this is against the rules: [Vnpr] *smuggle people out of the country* ○ *smuggle a letter into prison* [also Vn, Vnp].

▶ **smuggler** /ˈsmʌɡlə(r)/ *n* a person who smuggles sth/sb: *drug smugglers* ○ *This cave was used by smugglers in the eighteenth century.*

smuggling /ˈsmʌɡlɪŋ/ *n* [U]: *a ˈdrug-smuggling operation* ○ *There's a lot of smuggling across this frontier.*

NOTE People **smuggle** goods from one country to another by taking them across a border secretly. These goods may be illegal, such as drugs, or they may be more expensive in the second country. Smugglers **run** guns, drugs and other banned dangerous items between countries, possibly as a regular activity: *Five people were arrested on drug-running charges.* Alcohol or recordings of music are **bootlegged** when they are produced secretly. When films, books, etc are copied and sold illegally they are **pirated**: *They pirated anything from videos to computer games.*

smut /smʌt/ *n* **1** [C] a small piece of dirt, ash, etc; a mark or spot made by this: *Some smuts from the chimney landed on his face and clothes.* **2** [U] (*infml*

S

derog) stories, pictures, etc that deal with sex in a rude or offensive way: *I object to newspapers full of smut.*

▶ **smutty** *adj* **1** (*infml derog*) (of talk, pictures, stories, etc) dealing with sex in an offensive way: *smutty books/jokes.* **2** marked with smuts (SMUT 1); dirty: *a child with a smutty face.*

snack /snæk/ *n* a small meal, usu eaten in a hurry, esp between main meals: *The children have a mid-morning snack of milk and biscuits.* ○ *I only have time for a snack at lunchtime.* ○ *a snack lunch* ○ *The pub serves bar snacks as well as a full lunchtime menu.*

▶ **snack** *v* [V, Vpr] ~ (**on sth**) (*infml*) to eat snacks between or instead of main meals.

■ **'snack bar** *n* a place where snacks may be bought: *We had coffee and sandwiches at the snack bar.*

snaffle /'snæfl/ *v* (*Brit infml*) to take sth for oneself, usu quickly before other people have an opportunity: [Vn] *They snaffled all the food before we got there.* ○ *A rival team snaffled one of their players.*

snag /snæg/ *n* **1** a small difficulty or obstacle, usu hidden, unknown or unexpected: *come across a snag* ○ *We hit* (ie were faced with) *several snags at the planning stage.* ○ *There must be a snag in it somewhere.* ○ *The snag is, I have no money.* **2** a rough or sharp object or part of sth. **3** a tear, hole or thread pulled out of place in material that has caught on sth rough or sharp: *I've got a snag in my tights.*

▶ **snag** *v* (**-gg-**) ~ (**sth**) (**on sth**) to catch or tear sth on sth rough or sharp; to become caught or torn in this way: [Vnpr] *He snagged his sweater on the wire fence.* [Vpr] *The net snagged on a rock on the seabed.* [also Vn, V].

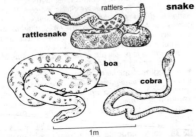

shell — snail
snail
slug

snail /sneɪl/ *n* a type of small soft animal, usu with a hard round shell on its back, which moves very slowly: *Snails have been eating our lettuces.* ⇨ picture. **IDM** **at a 'snail's pace** very slowly: *The traffic was moving at a snail's pace.*

snake

rattlers — snake
rattlesnake
boa
cobra
1m

snake /sneɪk/ *n* **1** any of various types of long reptile without legs, some of which are poisonous: *the scaly skin of the snake* ○ *a snake coiled up in the grass.* **2** a deceitful person. **IDM** **a ,snake in the 'grass** a deceitful person who pretends to be a friend.

▶ **snake** *v* ~ **a'cross, 'past, 'through, etc sth** to move in a twisting way like a snake; to follow a twisting, winding course in the specified direction: [Vpr, Vnpr] *The road snakes (its way) through the mountains.* [Vp] *The river snaked away into the distance.*

snaky *adj* like a snake: *snaky strands of hair.*

■ **'snake-bite** *n* [C, U] a wound or condition res-

ulting from being bitten by a poisonous snake: *be ill from a snake-bite* ○ *traditional remedies for snake-bite.*

'snake-charmer *n* an entertainer who can control snakes and make them seem to move to music.

,snakes and 'ladders *n* [sing *v*] (*Brit*) a game played on a board with counters (COUNTER² 1) which can move up pictures of ladders (to progress) or down pictures of snakes (to go back).

snakeskin /'sneɪkskɪn/ *n* [U] the skin of a snake, esp when made into leather for bags, etc: *shoes made of snakeskin* ○ *a snakeskin belt.*

snap¹ /snæp/ *v* (**-pp-**) **1** to break sth or be broken suddenly with a sharp noise: [V] *He stretched the rubber band till it snapped.* [Vp] *Suddenly the branch that he was standing on snapped off.* [Vn, Vnpr] *The great weight snapped the metal bar* (in two). [V] (*fig*) *After months of stress and worry, he finally snapped* (ie was unable to endure it any more). [also Vn, Vnp]. **2** to move or move sth into a certain position with a sudden sharp noise: [V-adj] *The box snapped open.* [Vnp] *She snapped down the lid of the box.* [Vn-adj] *She snapped her bag shut.* **3** ~ (**at sb/sth**) (of an animal) to make a sudden bite: [Vpr] *The terrier followed him down the path, snapping at his ankles.* [also V]. **4** ~ (**at sb**) to speak or say sth in a sharp, usu angry, voice: [V.speech] *'Come here at once,' she snapped.* [V, Vpr] *I'm sorry I snapped (at you) just now.* **5** (*infml*) to take a quick photograph of sb: [Vn, Vn.ing] *I snapped you (sunbathing) on the beach.* **IDM** **bite/snap sb's 'head off** ⇨ HEAD¹. **snap one's 'fingers** to make a sharp noise by moving the second or third finger quickly against the thumb, eg to attract sb's attention, mark the beat of music, etc: *He snapped his fingers to attract the waiter.* **,snap 'out of it/sth** (*infml*) (often imperative) to get quickly out of a bad or unhappy mood: *You've been miserable about losing her for months now — you really must snap out of it.* **,snap 'to it** (*infml*) (esp imperative) to start moving, working, etc quickly; to hurry up: *'I want those bricks moved; come on, snap to it!'* **PHRV** **,snap sth 'out** to say sth in a sharp or unpleasant way: *The sergeant snapped out an order.* **,snap sth 'up** to buy or seize sth quickly and eagerly: *The cheapest articles in the sale were quickly snapped up.*

snap² /snæp/ *n* **1** [C] an act or a sound of snapping (SNAP¹ 1,2,3): *The dog made a snap at the meat.* ○ *The oar broke with a snap.* **2** (also **snapshot**) [C] a photograph, usu one taken quickly: *She showed us her holiday snaps.* **3** [U] a card-game in which players call out 'snap' when two similar cards are laid down together: *play a game of snap.* **4** [sing] (*US infml*) a thing that is easy to do: *This job's a snap.* See also COLD SNAP, BRANDY-SNAP.

▶ **snap** *adj* [attrib] (*infml*) done, made, etc quickly and with little or no warning: *a snap election/decision* ○ *take a snap vote.*

snap *interj* (*infml*) **1** (said in the game of snap when one notices that two similar cards have been laid down). **2** (*Brit*) (said to draw attention to the fact that two things are similar): *Snap! You've got the same shoes as me.*

snappy *adj* (**-ier, -iest**) **1** (*infml*) lively; quick: *be snappy on one's feet* ○ *a snappy dancer.* **2** (*infml*) [usu attrib] fashionable; SMART¹(1,2): *a snappy outfit* ○ *She's a very snappy dresser.* **3** (also **snappish**) tending to talk to people in a sharp or bad-tempered way: *She's always snappy early in the morning.* **IDM** **,make it 'snappy; ,look 'snappy** (*infml*) (often imperative) to hurry up; to act quickly: *Look snappy! The bus is coming.* ○ *You'll have to make it snappy if you want to come too.* **snappily** *adv*: *'Go away,' she said snappily.* **snappiness** *n* [U].

■ **'snap-fastener** *n* (*US*) = PRESS-STUD.

[V.to inf] = verb + *to* infinitive   [Vn.inf (no *to*)] = verb + noun + infinitive without *to*   [V.*ing*] = verb + -*ing* form

snapdragon /ˈsnæpdrægən/ *n* a garden flower with flowers like small bags.

snapshot /ˈsnæpʃɒt/ *n* = SNAP² 2.

snare

snare /sneə(r)/ *n* **1** a trap for catching small animals and birds, esp one made with a loop of rope or wire: *The rabbit's foot was caught in a snare.* ⇨ picture. **2** *(fml)* a thing that is likely to trap or injure sb: *He fell victim to the sensual lures and snares of city life.*
▶ **snare** *v* to catch sth in a snare(1) or as if in a snare: [Vn] *snare a rabbit* ○ *(fig) snare a rich husband.*
■ **'snare drum** *n* a small drum with metal strings across one side to give it a sharp sound when played.

snarl¹ /snɑːl/ *v* **1** ~ **(at sb/sth)** (of dogs, etc) to show the teeth and GROWL(1) angrily: [Vpr] *The dog snarled at the milkman.* [also V]. **2** ~ **(sth) (at sb)** (of people) to speak in an angry bad-tempered voice: [Vn, Vnpr] *snarl abuse (at strangers)* [V.speech] *'Get out of here,' he snarled.*
▶ **snarl** *n* (usu *sing*) a sound or an act of snarling: *answer with an angry snarl* ○ *He bared his teeth in a snarl.*

snarl² /snɑːl/ *n* *(infml)* a confused state; a knot: *My knitting was in a terrible snarl.* ○ *His hair was full of snarls and impossible to comb.*
▶ **snarl** *v* **PHRV** **,snarl sth 'up** *(infml)* (usu passive) to make sth confused, mixed up, blocked, etc: *Her dress became snarled up in the pedals of her bike.* ○ *We got snarled up in the midday traffic.* **'snarl-up** *n* *(infml)* a confused or blocked state, esp of traffic: *a big snarl-up on the motorway.*

snatch /snætʃ/ *v* **1(a)** to take sth quickly or roughly: [V] *It's rude to snatch.* [Vnpr] *She snatched the letter from me/out of my hand.* [Vnp] *He snatched up the gun and fired.* [also Vn]. **(b)** ~ **sth away (from sth)** to take sth away from sth with a quick movement: [Vnp, Vnpr] *He snatched his hand away (from the flame).* **2** to steal sth/sb: [Vn] *Somebody snatched my wallet in the supermarket.* [Vnpr] *The baby had been snatched from its pram.* **3** to take or get sth quickly, esp when a chance to do so occurs: [Vn] *snatch an hour's sleep* ○ *snatch a meal between jobs* ○ *They managed to snatch victory in the last moments of the game.* **PHRV** **'snatch at sth 1** to try to take sth with the hands: *He snatched at the ball but did not catch it.* **2** to try eagerly to use sth: *snatch at every opportunity.*
▶ **snatch** *n* **1** (usu *pl*) **(a)** a short part, esp of sth heard or seen: *short snatches of song* ○ *overhear snatches of conversation.* **(b)** a short period of doing sth: *sleep in snatches* (ie not continuously). **2** a sudden attempt to seize sth quickly: *make a snatch at sth.*
snatcher *n* (often in compounds) a person who snatches sth and takes it away: *a baby snatcher* ○ *a handbag snatcher.*

snazzy /ˈsnæzi/ *adj* (**-ier, -iest**) *(infml)* (esp of clothes) fashionable and SMART¹(2): *a snazzy little hat* ○ *a very snazzy new car* ○ *She's a very snazzy dresser.* ▶ **snazzily** *adv*: *dress snazzily.*

sneak /sniːk/ *v* **1** ~ **(on sb) (to sb)** (Brit infml derog) (used esp by children) to tell an adult about the faults, wrongdoings, etc of another child: [Vpr] *She sneaked on her best friend to the teacher.* [also V]. **2** *(infml)* to take or do sth secretly, often without permission: [Vnpr] *sneak a chocolate from the box* [Vn] *sneak a look at the Christmas presents* [Vnn] *I* *managed to sneak him a note without the teacher seeing.* **3** to go quietly and secretly in the direction specified: [Vpr] *He sneaked out of the restaurant without paying.* [Vp] *The cat ate the food and sneaked off.* **PHRV** **,sneak 'up (on sb/sth)** to approach sb/sth quietly, staying out of sight until the last moment: *He enjoys sneaking up on his sister to frighten her.* ⇨ note at PROWL.
▶ **sneak** *n* *(infml)* a cowardly deceitful person, esp one who informs on others.
sneak *adj* [attrib] done or acting without warning; secret and unexpected: *a sneak attack.*
sneaker *n* (US) = PLIMSOLL: *He wore old jeans and a pair of sneakers.*
sneaking *adj* [attrib] (of a feeling) secret and RELUCTANT: *have a sneaking respect/sympathy for sb* ○ *I have a sneaking* (ie VAGUE(1a) but possibly right) *suspicion that he stole my wallet.*
sneaky *adj* *(infml derog)* done or acting in a secret or deceitful way: *sneaky behaviour* ○ *I think it's sneaky of the police to use unmarked cars.* **sneakily** *adv.*
■ **,sneak 'preview** *n* a special showing of a new film, exhibition, etc to certain people before it is shown to the public.
'sneak-thief *n* a person who steals things without using force, eg through open doors and windows.

sneer /snɪə(r)/ *v* ~ **(at sb/sth)** to curl the upper lip as a way of showing contempt for sb/sth; to laugh in a way that shows contempt: [Vpr] *He's always sneering at people less clever than he is.* [V.speech] *'What a ridiculous notion,' she sneered.* [also V]. ⇨ note at SMIRK.
▶ **sneer** *n* a look, smile, word, phrase, etc that shows contempt: *endure the jeers and sneers of one's enemies* ○ *He looked at me with a sneer of disdain.*
sneeringly /ˈsnɪərɪŋli/ *adv.*

sneeze /sniːz/ *n* a sudden noisy burst of air out through the nose and mouth, usu because the nose is irritated by dust, etc or because one has a cold: *coughs and sneezes* ○ *She let out a loud sneeze.*
▶ **sneeze** *v* to make a sneeze: [V] *Pollen in the air makes me sneeze.* ○ *Use a handkerchief when you sneeze.* **IDM** **not to be 'sneezed at/'sniffed at** *(infml)* worth considering or having; not to be rejected lightly: *A prize of £100 is not to be sneezed at.*

snicker /ˈsnɪkə(r)/ *v* to laugh in a suppressed, esp unpleasant, way; to SNIGGER: [V, Vpr] *She knew the children were snickering (at her) behind her back.* [also V.speech]. ⇨ note at GIGGLE. ▶ **snicker** *n.*

snide /snaɪd/ *adj (derog)* critical in an indirect unpleasant way: *snide remarks about the chairman's wife* ○ *He's always making snide comments about her appearance.*

sniff /snɪf/ *v* **1** to draw air in through the nose in a way that makes a sound, eg to stop the nose running or to express contempt: [V] *They all had colds and kept sniffing and sneezing.* **2(a)** ~ **(at) sth** to draw air in through the nose as one breathes, esp to discover or enjoy the smell of sth: [Vn] *sniff the sea air* [Vpr] *The dog was sniffing at the lamppost.* [also V]. **(b)** ~ **sth (up)** to draw sth up through the nose: [Vnp] *He sniffed the vapour up (through his nose).* [also Vn]. **(c)** *(infml)* to take a dangerous drug by breathing it in through the nose: [Vn] *sniff glue.* **3(a)** to say sth in a complaining way: [V.speech] *'Nobody understands me,' he sniffed.* **(b)** to say sth in a proud or disapproving way: [V.speech] *'I think you're all disgusting,' she sniffed.* **IDM** **not to be 'sneezed/'sniffed at** ⇨ SNEEZE. **PHRV** **'sniff at sth** to ignore or show contempt for sth: *I wouldn't sniff at the chance of a job, whatever it was.* **,sniff sb 'out** *(infml)* to discover sb; to find sb out: *sniff out the culprit* ○ *The police were determined to sniff out the ringleaders.*
▶ **sniff** *n* **1** an act or a sound of sniffing; a breath of

S

air, etc: *tearful sniffs* ○ *get a sniff of sea air* ○ *One sniff of this is enough to kill you.* ○ *'I'm going,' she said with a sniff.* **2** (usu *sing*) ~ **of sth** (*infml*) a small amount of sth: *They retreated at the first sniff of trouble.*

■ **'sniffer-dog** *n* (*infml*) a dog trained to find drugs or explosives by smell.

sniffle /'snɪfl/ *v* to SNIFF(1) slightly or repeatedly, esp because one is crying or has a cold: [V] *I wish you wouldn't keep sniffling.* [also V.speech].
▶ **sniffle** *n* an act or a sound of sniffling. **IDM get/ have the 'sniffles** (*infml*) to get/have a slight cold.

sniffy /'snɪfi/ *adj* (*infml*) showing contempt or disapproval: *Some people are rather sniffy about fast food.*

snifter /'snɪftə(r)/ *n* (*dated infml*) a small amount of an alcoholic drink: *have a quick snifter before the party.*

snigger /'snɪɡə(r)/ *n* a low unpleasant laugh, esp at sth rude or at another person's troubles, etc: *His bad jokes brought embarrassed sniggers from the audience.*
▶ **snigger** *v* ~ (**at sb/sth**) to laugh in a low unpleasant way: [Vpr] *What are you sniggering at?* ⇨ note at GIGGLE.

snip /snɪp/ *v* (**-pp-**) ~ (**at**) **sth** to cut sth sharply, esp with SCISSORS, in short quick strokes: [Vn, Vpr] *snip (at) a stray lock of hair* [Vnpr] *snip the corner off a carton of milk* [also Vnp].
▶ **snip** *n* **1** an act of snipping (SNIP): *with a few quick snips of the scissors* ○ *Snip, snip, snip went the shears.* **2** (*Brit infml*) a very cheap article; a BARGAIN¹(2): *It's a snip at only 50p!*

snipe¹ /snaɪp/ *n* (*pl* unchanged) a bird with a long straight bill that lives in wet regions. ⇨ picture.

snipe

snipe² /snaɪp/ *v* ~ (**at sb/sth**) **1** to shoot at sb from a hiding place, and usu from a distance: [V, Vpr] *terrorists sniping (at soldiers) from well-concealed positions.* **2** to make unpleasant critical remarks attacking sb/sth: [Vpr] *politicians sniping at each other to score party points* [also V].
▶ **sniper** *n* a person who shoots from a hiding place: *shot by snipers* ○ *sniper fire.*

snippet /'snɪpɪt/ *n* ~ (**of sth**) a small piece of information or news; a brief extract: *hear odd snippets of conversation.*

snivel /'snɪvl/ *v* (**-ll-**; *US* also **-l-**) (*derog*) (**a**) to cry and SNIFF(1) in a miserable way: [V] *Stop snivelling — I'm not going to hurt you!* (**b**) to complain, esp in a miserable, crying voice: [Vpr] *Don't keep snivelling about how poor we are.* [also V, V.speech].
▶ **snivelling** (*US* **sniveling**) *adj* [attrib] (*derog*) tending to cry and complain; miserable or weak: *a snivelling brat/letter.*

snob /snɒb/ *n* (*derog*) (**a**) a person who pays too much respect to social status and wealth, or who shows contempt for people of a lower social position: *Her husband's a terrible snob.* (**b**) a person who believes he or she has superior taste¹(5) or knowledge: *intellectual/cultural/musical snobs* ○ *Cars like this have a certain* **snob value/appeal.**
▶ **snobbery** /'snɒbəri/ *n* [U] (*derog*) attitudes and behaviour that are characteristic of a snob: *There is still a great deal of snobbery in our society.* ○ *intellectual snobbery.* See also INVERTED SNOBBERY.
snobbish (also *infml* **snobby**) *adj* (*derog*) of or like a snob: *He's quite snobbish about wine.* **snobbishness** *n* [U].

snog /snɒɡ/ *v* (**-gg-**) (*Brit infml*) to kiss and hold each other in a loving way: [V] *couples snogging in the back row of the cinema.*
▶ **snog** *n* [sing] (*Brit infml*) an act of snogging.

snook /snuːk/ *n* **IDM cock a snook at sb/sth** ⇨ COCK².

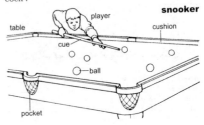

snooker

snooker /'snuːkə(r)/ *n* (**a**) [U] a game played with 15 red balls and 7 balls of other colours on a special table: *a snooker player/tournament/table.* ⇨ picture. Compare BILLIARDS, POOL² 3. (**b**) [C] a position in this game in which one player has made it very difficult for her or his opponent to play a shot within the rules.
▶ **snooker** *v* (esp passive) to leave an opponent in a snooker(b): [Vn] (*fig*) *be snookered by the taxman.*

snoop /snuːp/ *v* ~ (**around sth**); ~ (**around**) (*infml usu derog*) to look secretly round a place in order to find sth or obtain information, esp in ways that people do not consider proper or legal: [Vpr, Vp] *Someone was snooping around (outside) your house last night.* [Vpr] *journalists snooping into people's private affairs* [also V].
▶ **snooper** *n* (*usu derog*) a person who snoops: *They found a secluded spot out of sight of snoopers.*

snooty /'snuːti/ *adj* (*infml derog*) showing disapproval and contempt towards others, esp those of a lower social position: *a snooty letter refusing the invitation* ○ *He's too snooty to be seen drinking in the local pub.* ▶ **snootiness** *n* [U].

snooze /snuːz/ *v* (*infml*) to have a short or light sleep, esp during the day and usu not in bed: [V] *Dad was snoozing by the fire.*
▶ **snooze** *n* [sing] (*infml*) a short sleep: *I usually have a snooze after lunch.*

snore /snɔː(r)/ *v* to breathe roughly and noisily while sleeping: [V] *Does your husband snore?*
▶ **snore** *n* an act or sound of snoring: *His snores kept her awake.*

snorkel /'snɔːkl/ *n* a tube that allows a person to breathe air while swimming under water.
▶ **snorkel** *v* (**-ll-**; *US* **-l-**) to swim with a snorkel: [Vpr] *We snorkelled over the reef.* [also V]. **snorkelling** (*US* **-keling**) /'snɔːkəlɪŋ/ *n* [U] the activity or sport of swimming with a snorkel: *snorkelling equipment.*

snort /snɔːt/ *v* **1**(**a**) [V] (usu of animals, esp horses) to force air out loudly through the nose. (**b**) ~ (**at sth**) (of people) to make a similar sound as a way of showing eg annoyance, disgust or amusement: [Vpr] *snort with laughter/derision/rage at the suggestion* [V.speech] *'What a load of rubbish!' he snorted.* [also V]. **2** (*sl*) to take drugs through the nose: [Vn] *snort cocaine.*
▶ **snort** *n* **1** an act or sound of snorting: *give a snort of contempt/laughter* ○ *Her suggestion was greeted with snorts of derision.* **2** (*sl*) an act of taking drugs through the nose, or an amount taken in this way: *have a quick snort (of cocaine).*

snot /snɒt/ *n* [U] (*infml*) the soft or liquid substance inside the nose.
▶ **snotty** *adj* (*infml*) **1** (*often derog*) producing or covered with snot: *a child with a snotty nose* ○ *washing his snotty handkerchiefs.* **2** (also ,**snotty-'nosed**) (*derog*) showing a superior attitude towards others, esp those of a lower social position: *She's such a snotty little bitch.* ○ *a snotty voice/letter.*

snout /snaʊt/ n **1** the projecting nose and mouth of an animal, eg a pig: *Only the crocodile's snout was visible above the water.* ⇨ picture at BADGER¹, PIG. **2** the projecting front part of sth: *I found myself staring into the snout of a pistol.* **3** (*sl derog or joc*) a person's nose: *Get your snout out of* (ie Stop looking in) *my handbag!*

snow¹ /snəʊ/ n **1** [U] frozen water that falls to the ground from the sky in soft white flakes (FLAKE); a mass of this on the ground: *a heavy fall of snow* ○ *several inches of snow* ○ *Children were playing in the snow.* ○ *His hair was now as white as snow.* **2** **snows** [pl] falling or fallen snow: *the snows of Mount Everest* ○ *The snows came early that year.*

▶ **snowy** adj (**-ier, -iest**) **1(a)** covered with snow: *snowy streets/mountains* ○ *a snowy scene/landscape.* **(b)** with snow falling: *a snowy night/Christmas/ winter* ○ *The weather is often cold and snowy in January.* **2** as white as newly fallen snow: *snowy (white) tablecloths/petals/clouds.*

■ **snow-covered** (also *rhet* ˈsnow-clad) adj covered with snow: *snow-covered mountains/roofs.*
ˌsnow-ˈwhite adj (*esp rhet*) pure white: ˌsnow-white ˈhair/ˈhorses/ˈsheets.

snow² /snəʊ/ v **1** (used with *it*) to fall from the sky as snow: [V] *It snowed all day.* ○ *It was snowing when I woke up.* **2** [Vn] (*US infml*) to attempt to deceive or persuade sb by exaggerated or insincere talk. **PHR V** ˌsnow sb **ˈin**/**ˈup** (usu passive) to prevent sb from leaving a place because of heavy snow: *We were snowed in for three days by the blizzards.* ˌsnow sb ˈunder (with sth) (usu passive) to give sb so many things to do that they feel unable to deal with them all: *I'd love to accept your invitation but I'm completely snowed under.* ○ *We were absolutely snowed under with applications for the job.* ˌsnow sth ˈup (*Brit*) (usu passive) to block or cover sth, eg a road, with snow: *The driveway is still snowed up.*

snowball /ˈsnəʊbɔːl/ n **1** a mass of snow shaped into a firm ball: *children throwing snowballs at each other.* **2** (usu *sing*) a process or an activity that grows quickly in intensity, importance, etc: *The campaign for his release became an unstoppable snowball.* ○ *Such rumours can have a snowball effect.* **IDM** **not have a** ˌsnowball's chance in ˈhell**/a** ˌsnowball in ˈhell's chance (of doing sth) to have no chance at all.

▶ **snowball** v **1** to grow quickly in size, intensity or importance: [V] *Opposition to the scheme has snowballed.* **2** (only in the continuous tenses) to throw snowballs: [V] *children snowballing in the park.*

snowblower /ˈsnəʊbləʊə(r)/ n a machine for clearing snow from roads and paths by blowing it to one side.

snowbound /ˈsnəʊbaʊnd/ adj unable to travel, go out, etc because of heavy falls of snow: *a snowbound train* ○ *We were snowbound in the cottage for two weeks.*

snowcapped /ˈsnəʊkæpt/ adj (*rhet*) (of mountains and hills) covered in snow at the top.

snowdrift /ˈsnəʊdrɪft/ n a deep pile of snow blown together by the wind: *The train ran into a snowdrift.*

snowdrop /ˈsnəʊdrɒp/ n a small white flower appearing at the end of winter or in early spring. ⇨ picture at FLOWER.

snowfall /ˈsnəʊfɔːl/ n **(a)** [C] a fall of snow on one occasion: *A heavy snowfall overnight made travelling difficult.* **(b)** [U] the amount of snow that falls in a period of time in a particular place: *The average snowfall here is 10 centimetres a year.*

snowfield /ˈsnəʊfiːld/ n an area always covered with snow.

snowflake /ˈsnəʊfleɪk/ n any of the soft small groups of ice crystals that fall as snow: *snowflakes melting as they reach the ground.*

snowline /ˈsnəʊlaɪn/ n the level on mountains, etc above which snow never melts completely: *climb above the snowline.*

snowman /ˈsnəʊmæn/ n (*pl* **-men** /-men/) a figure of a man made with snow, esp by children for fun: *make/build a snowman.*

snowplough (*Brit*) (*US* **snowplow**) /ˈsnəʊplaʊ/ n a device or vehicle for clearing snow from roads or railways.

snowshoe /ˈsnəʊʃuː/ n a flat frame attached to the bottom of a shoe to allow a person to walk on deep snow without sinking in.

snowstorm /ˈsnəʊstɔːm/ n a heavy fall of snow, esp with a strong wind.

SNP /ˌes en ˈpiː/ abbr Scottish National Party (a Scottish political party which believes that Scotland should be independent of the rest of the United Kingdom).

Snr (also **Sen, Sr**) abbr Senior: *David Johnson Snr* (ie to distinguish him from his son with the same name).

snub¹ /snʌb/ v (**-bb-**) **(a)** to treat sb in a cold rude manner or deliberately ignore them: [Vn] *I tried to be friendly but she snubbed me completely.* **(b)** to refuse to accept or attend sth, esp as a mark of protest or contempt: *Leading players have consistently snubbed the tournament because of the poor prize money.*

▶ **snub** n ~ (**to sb**) words, behaviour, etc intended to snub sb: *His remarks in a radio interview are being interpreted as a deliberate snub to the prime minister.*

snub² /snʌb/ adj [attrib] (of a nose) short and turned up at the end.

snuck *pt*, *pp* of SNEAK 2,3.

snuff¹ /snʌf/ v [Vn, Vnp] ~ **sth** (**out**) to stop the flame of a candle burning. **IDM** ˈsnuff it (*Brit sl joc*) to die: *The hero snuffs it at the end of the movie.* **PHR V** ˌsnuff sth ˈout to destroy or end sth: *Her young life has been cruelly and senselessly snuffed out.*

snuff² /snʌf/ n [U] tobacco in the form of a powder that is taken into the nose by sniffing (SNIFF 2b): *take (a pinch of) snuff.*

snuffbox /ˈsnʌfbɒks/ n a small, usu decorated, box for holding SNUFF².

snuffle /ˈsnʌfl/ v **(a)** (esp of an animal) to make noises with the nose, as if smelling sth: [Vp] *The dog was snuffling around in the shed.* [also V, Vpr]. **(b)** to breathe noisily, esp because the nose is partly blocked or one is crying: *a child snuffling and coughing* [also V.speech].

▶ **snuffle** n **(a)** [C] an act or sound of snuffling: *the snuffles of a dog.* **(b)** [sing] (often **the snuffles** [pl]) (*infml*) a cold or an infection in the nose that causes sb to make such sounds: *have/get the snuffles.* Compare SNIFFLE.

snug /snʌg/ adj (**-gg-**) **1** (*approv*) warm and comfortable; sheltered from the cold: *a snug little house* ○ *I felt warm and snug in bed.* **2(a)** (*sometimes euph*) (esp of clothes) small or tight; fitting closely: *a snug-fitting coat* ○ *The jacket's a bit snug across the shoulders.* **(b)** fitting exactly: *The lid should be a snug fit.* **IDM** (**as**) **snug as a bug in a** ˈrug (*joc infml*) very snug(1).

▶ **snug** n (*Brit*) a small comfortable room, esp in a pub, with seats for only a few people.
snugly adv: *to be curled up snugly in bed* ○ *The village nestles snugly in a wooded valley.* ○ *The camera grip fits snugly into the hand.*

snuggle /ˈsnʌɡl/ v **(a)** ~ (**up to sb/sth**); ~ (**up/ down**) to lie or get close to sb/sth for warmth, comfort or affection: [Vp] *Emma snuggled up to/ against her mother.* ○ *Snuggle down and go to sleep.* [V-adj] *She snuggled closer.* [also Vpr, V]. **(b)** to place *sth* into a warm comfortable position: [Vnpr] *He snuggled his face into the pillow.*

so¹ /səʊ/ *adv* (used before *adjs* and *advs*) **1** (used to indicate the large extent or degree of sth): *Don't look so angry* (ie as angry as you appear now). ○ *After living there for so long, he must know the town very well.* **2** (used for emphasis) very; extremely: *The girls looked so pretty in their summer dresses.* ○ *I'm so glad to see you.* ○ *He sat there so quietly.* ○ *We have* ¹so *much to do.* ○ *Their attitude is so very English!* **3 not** ~ + *adj/adv* (+ **as ...**) not to the same extent (as ...): *It wasn't so bad as last time/as we expected.* ○ *The following day wasn't quite so warm.* ○ *I haven't enjoyed myself so much for a long time.* **4** ~ + *adj* + **a/an** + *n* (+ **as sb/sth**) (used in making comparisons): *He was not so quick a learner as his brother.* ○ *Is this so unusual a case* (ie more unusual than most)? **5** ~ + *adj/adv* + **(that)** ... to such an extent as to produce a particular result, cause a particular situation, etc: *He was so ill (that) we had to send for a doctor.* ○ *She spoke so quietly (that) I could hardly hear her.* ○ *I have so many books (that) I don't know what to do with them.* **6** ~ + *adj/adv* + **as to do sth** to such an extent that one does sth or sth becomes the case: *How could you be so stupid as to believe him?* ○ *(fml) Would you be so kind as to* lock the door when you leave? ○ *The weather wasn't so bad as to stop us travelling.* ○ *The sentence is so vague as to be meaningless.* **7** *(infml)* (used before *adjs* to indicate the size of sth) this: *The fish was about so big* (ie using one's hands to indicate the size). **IDM not so much** *sth* **as** ¹**sth** not one thing but rather sth else: *It's not so much a* ¹*hobby as a* ca¹*reer.* ○ *She's not so much poor as careless with money.* ¹**so many/much/long** (indicating a particular number, amount or period of time that can be different in each case or situation): *A recipe tells you that you need so many eggs, so much milk, that you have to cook the dish for so long, etc.* ○ *Write on the form that you stayed so many nights at so much per night.* ¹**so much** ¹**sth** a lot of sth, esp sth worthless: *His promises were just so much meaningless nonsense.* ¹**so much for** ¹**sb/** ¹**sth** there is nothing further to be said or done about sb/sth: *So much for our hopes of going abroad — we can forget it.* ○ *So much for our new secretary — she left after three days!* ¹**so much** ¹**so that ...** to such an extent that ...: *We are very busy — so much so that we won't be able to take time off this year.* **with not / without so much as** with not even sth: *Off he went, without so much as a 'goodbye'.*

so² /səʊ/ *adv* **1** (used for referring to sth previously mentioned without repeating it): *'Is he coming?' 'I believe/think so.'* ○ *I'm not sure if she'll succeed, but I certainly hope so.* ○ *'Will he resign?' 'It says so in the papers.'* ○ *I might be away next week. If so, I won't be able to see you.* **2** the case; true: *He thinks I dislike him but that simply isn't so.* ○ *'She's very unreliable.' 'Is that so?'* ○ *'Were you pleased when it happened?' 'Very much so.'* **3** (referring to sth already stated) this/that is what ...: *'Is it a good play?' 'So the critics say.'* ○ *George is going to help me, or so he says.* **4** also; and also: *He is divorced and so am I.* ○ *'We've been to Moscow.' 'So have I.'* **5** in this or that way; thus: *Stand with your arms out, so.* ○ *So it was that he finally returned home.* **6** (used to express agreement): *'You were at school with her.' 'So I was, I'd forgotten.'* ○ *'They won the championship five years ago.' 'So they did.'* ○ *'There's a funny smell coming from somewhere.' 'So there is.'* **7** (used esp by children for insisting that sth stated previously is not the case and that the opposite is true): *'You're not telling the truth, are you?' 'I am, so!'* **IDM and** ¹**so forth; and** ¹**so on (and** ¹**so forth)** (used for indicating things additional or similar to those already mentioned): *We discussed everything: when to go, what to see and so on (and so forth).* **or so** (used to

refer approximately to a number or amount): *There were* ¹*twenty or so* (ie about twenty) *people there.* ○ *We stayed for an* ¹*hour or so.* **so as to do sth** with the intention of doing sth: *He disconnected the phone so as not to be disturbed.* **so** ¹**be it** (used to indicate that one accepts sth and will not try to change it or cannot change it): *If he doesn't want to be involved, then so be it.* **so ... that** in such a way that; to such an extent that: *The programme has been so organized that none of the talks overlap.*

so³ /səʊ/ *conj* **1** (indicating the result of sth) and that is why; with the result that; therefore: *The shop was closed so I couldn't get any milk.* ○ *The manager was sick so I went in his place.* ○ *These glasses are very expensive so please be careful with them.* **2** *(infml)* (indicating purpose) with the intention that; in order that: *I gave you a map so you wouldn't get lost.* ○ *She whispered to me so no one else would hear.* **3** (used to introduce the next part of a story): *So now it's winter again and I'm still unemployed.* ○ *So after shouting and screaming for an hour she walked out in tears.* **4(a)** (used for introducing a statement after which one comments in a critical or contrasting way): *So I had a couple of drinks on the way home. What's wrong with that?* **(b)** = SO WHAT?: *'You've been drinking again.' 'So?'* **5** (used for introducing a topic of conversation): *So, what have you been doing today?* **6** (used for introducing a statement that concludes sth): *So, that's the end of tonight's show.* **7** (used for introducing a conclusion drawn from sth previously mentioned): *So there's nothing we can do about it.* **8** (used for introducing a statement expressing what is forced by the circumstances) in that case; therefore: *'The last bus has gone.' 'So, we'll have to walk.'* **9** (used before a question that follows from what was said previously): *'I've just been on a long trip.' 'So, how was it?'* **10** (used when stating that two events, situations, etc are similar) in the same way; also: *Just as large companies are having to cut back, so small businesses are being forced to close.* **IDM so that 1** with the aim that; in order that: *She worked hard so that everything would be ready in time.* **2** with the result that: *Nothing more was heard from him so that we began to wonder if he was dead.* **so** ¹**what?** *(infml)* (used for indicating that one thinks that what has been previously mentioned is not important and not worth caring about): *'He's fifteen years younger than me.' 'So* ¹*what?'* ○ *So* ¹*what if nobody else agrees with me?'*

so⁴ = SOH.

soak /səʊk/ *v* **1** ~ **(sth) (in sth)** to become thoroughly wet as a result of being placed in liquid or absorbing liquid; to make sth thoroughly wet in this way: [V] *Leave the dried beans to soak overnight.* [Vpr] *Those dirty dishes need to soak in soapy water for a while.* [Vn] *You'd better soak those jeans first or you'll never get them clean.* [Vnpr] *soak bread in milk.* **2** ~ **into/through sth;** ~ **in** (of a liquid) to enter or pass through sth; to penetrate sth: [Vpr] *The rain had soaked through his coat.* [Vp] *Clean up that wine on the carpet before it soaks in.* **3** *(infml)* to extract money from sb by charging or taxing them very heavily: [Vn] *soak the rich.* **PHRV** ¹**soak sth** ¹**off/**¹**out** to remove sth by soaking it in water: *soak out a stain from a shirt* ○ *soak a label off a jar.* ¹**soak sth** ¹**up 1** to take in or absorb a liquid: *Use a paper towel to soak up the cooking oil.* **2** to absorb sth into the senses or the mind: *soaking up the sunshine/the local atmosphere* ○ *He watched the film intently, soaking it all up.*

▶ **soak** *n* **1** (also **soaking**) an act of soaking (SOAK 1) sth: *Give the shirt a good soak/soaking.* **2** *(infml)* a person who drinks too much alcohol and is often drunk: *He's a dreadful old soak.*

soaked /səʊkt/ *adj* [pred] completely wet: *My*

clothes are completely soaked. ○ *blood-soaked bodies* ○ *We were caught in the rain and got* **soaked through/soaked to the skin.**

soaking /ˈsəʊkɪŋ/ (also ˌsoaking ˈwet) *adj* completely wet: *a soaking wet coat.*

so-and-so /ˈsəʊ ən səʊ/ *n* (*pl* **so-and-so's**) (*infml*) **(a)** an imaginary or unknown person; some person or other: *Let's suppose a Mr So-and-so registers at the hotel.* **(b)** (*derog*) a person that one is angry with or dislikes: *Some so-and-so has pinched my towel.* ○ *Our neighbour's a bad-tempered old so-and-so.*

soap /səʊp/ *n* **1** [U] a substance used with water for washing and cleaning, made of fat or oil combined with an ALKALI: *a bar of soap* ○ *soap bubbles* ○ *There's no soap in the bathroom.* ○ *Use plenty of soap and water.* **2** [C] (*infml*) = SOAP OPERA: *Do you watch any of the soaps on TV?*

▶ **soap** *v* to rub sth/sb/oneself with soap: [Vn] *soap a sponge* ○ *She soaped her skin and hair.* See also SOFT SOAP.

soapy *adj* (**-ier, -iest**) **1** full of soap: *warm soapy water.* **2** like soap in appearance, taste or smell.

■ ˈ**soap flakes** *n* [pl] very small thin pieces of soap, sold in a packet and used for washing clothes, etc.
ˈ**soap opera** *n* [C, U] (also *infml* **soap** [C]) a television or radio drama with continuing episodes (EPISODE 2) about the events and problems in the daily lives of the same group of characters: *a long-running radio soap opera.*
ˈ**soap powder** *n* [C,U] a powder made from soap and other substances, used for washing clothes.

soapbox /ˈsəʊpbɒks/ *n* a small temporary platform for standing on by sb making a speech in a public place: *soapbox oratory.*

soapstone /ˈsəʊpstəʊn/ *n* [U] a type of soft stone that feels like soap, used for making ornaments, etc.

soapsuds /ˈsəʊpsʌdz/ *n* [pl] = SUDS: *He was up to his elbows in soapsuds, washing his shirts.*

soar /sɔː(r)/ *v* **1** ~ **into sth** to rise quickly high into the air: [Vpr, Vp] *The rocket soared (up) into the air.* [also Vadv]. **2** to rise quickly to a high level or standard: [V] *soaring prices/profits/temperatures* ○ *Our spirits soared.* [Vpr] *Shares have soared to an all-time high.* **3** to fly very high in the air or to remain high in the air without using the wings or power: [Vpr] *seagulls soaring high above the cliffs* [also V, Vadv]. **4** to be very high or tall: [V] *a city of soaring skyscrapers* [Vpr] *cliffs soaring above the sea.*

sob /sɒb/ *v* (**-bb-**) **1** to cry noisily, drawing in breath frequently and making unhappy sounds: [V] *The child began to sob loudly.* [Vpr] *She sobbed into her pillow.* **2** to say sth while crying noisily: [V.speech] *'Help me,' he sobbed.* [Vnp] *She sobbed out her story.* ⇨ note at CRY¹. **IDM cry/sob oneself to sleep** ⇨ SLEEP¹. **sob one's ˈheart out** to cry very noisily and with great sorrow for a period: *She sobbed her heart out when he'd gone.*

▶ **sob** *n* an act or sound of sobbing: *give a sob* ○ *Her body shook with sobs.*

■ ˈ**sob story** *n* (*infml usu derog*) a story intended to make the listener or reader feel sympathy or sadness, esp one that fails to do this: *He told me a real sob story about how his wife had gone off with his best friend.*

sober /ˈsəʊbə(r)/ *adj* **1** not affected by alcohol; not drunk: *Were you completely sober when you said that?* ○ *I was as sober as a judge* (ie completely sober). ○ *He drinks a lot but always seems sober.* **2** serious and sensible; solemn: *a sober and hard-working young man* ○ *make a sober estimate of what is possible* ○ *a sober analysis of the facts.* **3** (of colour) not bright; plain: *a sober grey suit.*

▶ **sober** *v* to make sb serious, sensible and solemn: [Vn] *His gloomy news sobered us a little.* **PHRV** ˌ**sober (sb) ˈup** to become or make sb sober(1) after

drinking too much alcohol and getting drunk: *Put him to bed until he sobers up.* ○ *Some black coffee will help to sober you up.*

sobering *adj* making one feel serious and think carefully: *It's a sobering thought.* ○ *The news had a sobering effect.*

soberly *adv*: *decide sth soberly* ○ *soberly dressed.*

sobriety /səˈbraɪəti/ *n* [U] (*fml*) the state of being SOBER: *a man not noted for sobriety.*

Soc *abbr* Society: *Royal Geographical Soc.*

so-called /ˌsəʊ ˈkɔːld/ *adj* [usu attrib] (*often derog*) (used for suggesting that the word or words used for describing sb/sth are not appropriate): *Where are your ˌso-called ˈfriends now?* ○ *Our ˌso-called ˈvilla by the sea was a small bungalow two miles from the coast.*

soccer /ˈsɒkə(r)/ *n* [U] = ASSOCIATION FOOTBALL: *soccer players/teams* ○ *a soccer ball/match/stadium.*

sociable /ˈsəʊʃəbl/ *adj* fond of spending time with other people; friendly: *He has never really been the sociable type.* ○ *I'm not in a sociable mood.* **sociability** /ˌsəʊʃəˈbɪləti/ *n* [U] Compare ANTISOCIAL 2, UNSOCIABLE.

social /ˈsəʊʃl/ *adj* **1** [usu attrib] concerning the organization of and relations between people and communities: *social problems* ○ *social customs/change/reforms* ○ *groups threatening social order.* **2** [attrib] of or in society; of or concerning rank and position within society: *social class/background* ○ *one's social equals* (ie people of the same class as oneself in society) ○ *social advancement* (ie improvement of one's position in society). **3** [attrib] (of animals, etc) living in groups, not separately: *Most bees and wasps are social insects.* ○ *Man is a social animal.* **4** of or designed for activities in which people meet each other for pleasure: *have a busy social life* ○ *a social club* ○ *a social evening.* **5** SOCIABLE: (*infml*) *He's not a very social person.* See also UNSOCIAL.

▶ **social** (*US* also **sociable** /ˈsəʊʃəbl/) *n* an informal meeting or party organized by a group or club: *a church social.*

socially /-ʃəli/ *adv*: *I know him through work, but not socially.*

■ ˌ**social ˈclimber** *n* (*derog*) a person who wants to rise in social class and tries to be friendly with people of a higher social class in order to do so.
ˌ**social ˈconscience** *n* an awareness of and a desire to help in solving the social problems in the community: *have a strong social conscience.*
ˌ**social deˈmocracy** *n* [U] a form of SOCIALISM permitting greater individual freedom than socialism.
ˌ**social ˈdemocrat** *n* a supporter or member of a political party that believes in social democracy.
ˌ**social ˈdrinker** *n* a person who only drinks alcohol on social occasions.
ˌ**social ˈscience** *n* [U] (also ˌsocial ˈstudies [sing or pl *v*]) a group of subjects concerned with the study of people within society and including ECONOMICS, SOCIOLOGY, ANTHROPOLOGY, politics and geography.
ˌ**social seˈcurity** (*Brit*) (*US* **welfare**) *n* [U] government payments to people who are unemployed, ill, disabled (DISABLE), etc: *He's currently out of work and on social security.*
ˌ**social ˈservices** *n* [pl] organized government services providing help and advice to the community, esp concerning health, education, and HOUSING(1): *threatened cuts in the social services.*
ˈ**social work** *n* [U] work done to help people in the community with special needs, eg because of poverty or bad HOUSING(1): *She wants to do social work when she finishes college.* ˈ**social worker** *n* a person trained to do social work: *Social workers claimed the children were being ill-treated.*

socialism /ˈsəʊʃəlɪzəm/ *n* [U] **(a)** a political and economic theory that a country's land, transport, natural resources and chief industries should be owned and controlled by the whole community or by the State, and that wealth should be equally distributed: *the struggle to build socialism.* (**b**) a policy or practice based on this theory: *the struggle to build socialism.* Compare CAPITALISM, COMMUNISM, SOCIAL DEMOCRACY.

▶ **socialist** /'səʊʃəlɪst/ a supporter of socialism or a member of a socialist party. — *adj* in favour of, based on or connected with socialism: *a Socialist Party* ○ *socialist policies* ○ *socialist ideals/ideology/ beliefs.*

socialistic /ˌsəʊʃə'lɪstɪk/ *adj* having some of the features of socialism: *Some of her views are rather socialistic.*

socialite /'səʊʃəlaɪt/ *n* (*sometimes derog*) a person who is well-known in fashionable society and goes to a lot of fashionable parties, etc.

socialize, -ise /'səʊʃəlaɪz/ *v* **1** ~ (**with sb**) to mix socially with others in a friendly way: [V] *It's not a very friendly company — people don't socialize much outside work.* [Vpr] *an opportunity to socialize with new colleagues.* **2** ~ **sb** (**into sth / doing sth**) (*fml*) (usu passive) to make sb behave in a way that is acceptable in society: [Vn] *recent immigrants to the country who are not fully socialized* [also Vnpr]. **3** [Vn] (*fml*) (usu passive) to organize sth according to the principles of SOCIALISM.

▶ **socialization, -isation** /ˌsəʊʃəlaɪ'zeɪʃn; *US* -lə'z-/ *n* [U] (*fml*) the process of becoming socialized (SOCIALIZE 2).

society /sə'saɪəti/ *n* **1** [U] a system in which people live together in organized communities; people in general: *drugs, crime and other dangers to society* ○ *Society has a right to see law-breakers punished.* **2** [C, U] a community of people living in a particular country or region and having shared customs, laws, organizations, etc: *modern industrial societies* ○ *live in a multi-racial society* ○ *working-class society* ○ *the traditions of our society* ○ *the attitudes of Western society.* **3** [C] an organization of people formed for a particular purpose; a club; an association: *the school debating society* ○ *a co-operative society* ○ *a drama society.* See also BUILDING SOCIETY, FRIENDLY SOCIETY. **4** [U] the class of people who are fashionable, wealthy, influential or of high rank in a place; the upper class: **high society** (ie rich and important people) ○ *a society wedding.* **5** [U] (*fml*) the situation of being with other people; company(1): *avoid the society of other people.*

socio- *comb form* (**a**) of society (and…): *sociology* ○ *socio-cultural* ○ *socio-economic.* (**b**) of or relating to SOCIOLOGY (and…): *sociolinguistics.*

sociology /ˌsəʊsi'ɒlədʒi/ *n* [U] the scientific study of the nature and development of society and social behaviour. Compare ANTHROPOLOGY.

▶ **sociological** /ˌsəʊsiə'lɒdʒɪkl/ *adj*: *sociological theories/issues.* **sociologically** /-kli/ *adv.*
sociologist /-dʒɪst/ *n* an expert in sociology.

sock¹ /sɒk/ *n* a piece of clothing, usu made of wool, nylon or cotton, that is worn over the ankle and lower part of the leg, esp inside a shoe: *a pair of socks.* **IDM** **pull one's socks up** ⇨ PULL¹. **put a 'sock in it** (*dated Brit infml*) to be quiet; to stop talking or making a noise: *Can't you put a sock in it? I'm trying to work.*

sock² /sɒk/ *n* (*infml*) a strong blow, esp a hard punch: *give sb a sock on the jaw.*
▶ **sock** *v* (*infml*) to hit sb hard; to hit sb with a hard punch: [Vn, Vnpr] *He got terribly angry and socked me (in the face).* **IDM** **'sock it to sb** (*dated infml*) to attack sb or express oneself forcefully: *She really socked it to them in the meeting.*

socket /'sɒkɪt/ *n* **1** a natural or artificial hollow space into which sth fits or in which sth turns: *the eye socket* (ie the hollow space in a human or animal head for the eye). **2** (*US* also **outlet**) a device

socket (*US* also **outlet**)

socket (*US* also **outlet**)
plug
pin

into which an electric plug, a light BULB(2), etc fits in order to make a connection: *a socket at the back of a TV for the aerial.* ⇨ picture.

sod¹ /sɒd/ *n* (*Brit* △ *sl*) **1**(**a**) (used for expressing annoyance with or dislike of sb) a person: *You stupid sod!* ○ *The new boss is a mean sod!* (**b**) (used as a term of pity or sympathy) a person: *The poor old sod got the sack yesterday.* **2** a thing that is difficult or causes problems: *It was a sod of a job to mend it.*
▶ **sod** *v* (**-dd-**) (*Brit* △ *sl*) (only imperative) (used to express annoyance with sb/sth or to indicate that one does not care about sb/sth at all): [Vn] *Sod this car! It's always breaking down.* ○ *Sod it! I've left my wallet at the office.* ○ *Sod him! If he wants to behave like that, I don't care.* **IDM** **ˌsod 'all** (used when expressing anger) nothing at all; none at all: *He's done sod all (work) the whole day.* **PHRV** **ˌsod 'off** (usu imperative) to go away: *Sod off and leave me alone!*

sodding *adj* [attrib] (*Brit* △ *sl*) (used for emphasis when expressing annoyance): *What a sodding mess!* ○ *It's all your sodding fault!*

■ **Sod's ˈLaw** *n* [sing] (*Brit joc*) an imaginary rule of life according to which things tend to go wrong if they possibly can: *It's Sod's Law that it rains on the only day I can play tennis.*

sod² /sɒd/ *n* (*fml or rhet*) (**a**) [sing] a layer of earth with grass growing in it: *under the sod* (ie in one's grave). (**b**) [C] a piece of this that has been removed.

soda /'səʊdə/ *n* **1** [U] a chemical substance in common use, a compound of SODIUM: 'washing-soda (ie sodium carbonate (SODIUM) used for softening water, etc). See also CAUSTIC SODA, SODIUM BICARBONATE. **2** [U, C] = SODA WATER: *Add some soda to the whisky, please.* ○ *A whisky and soda, please.* **3** (also 'soda pop) [U, C] (*US*) a sweet FIZZY drink made with soda water, fruit flavour and sometimes ice-cream: *a glass of cherry soda* ○ *two lime sodas.*
■ **'soda-fountain** *n* (*esp US*) (**a**) (also **'soda siphon**) a device for supplying soda water. (**b**) a counter in a shop from which FIZZY drinks, ice-cream, etc are served.

'soda water *n* [U, C] water made FIZZY with carbon dioxide (CARBON) under pressure; this as a drink: *I won't have any wine — I'll just have (a) soda water.*

sodden /'sɒdn/ *adj* completely wet as a result of absorbing a lot of liquid: *My shoes are sodden from walking in the rain.* ○ (*fig*) *He staggered home sodden with drink* (ie very drunk).

sodium /'səʊdiəm/ *n* [U] a chemical element. Sodium is a silver-white metal that occurs naturally only in compounds. ⇨ App 7.
■ **ˌsodium biˈcarbonate** (also **biˌcarbonate of ˈsoda**, **ˈbaking soda**) (also *infml* **bicarb** /'baɪkɑːb/) *n* [U] a white compound in the form of crystals or powder that dissolves and is used in making FIZZY drinks, baking-powder (BAKE) and certain medicines.
ˌsodium ˈcarbonate (also **ˈwashing soda**) *n* [U] a white compound in the form of crystals or powder that dissolves and is used in making glass, soap and paper, and for softening water.
ˌsodium ˈchloride *n* [U] common table salt.

sodomy /'sɒdəmi/ *n* [U] ANAL sex(2b), esp between men.
▶ **sodomite** /'sɒdəmaɪt/ *n* (*dated fml*) a person practising sodomy.

sofa /ˈsəʊfə/ *n* a comfortable seat with raised arms and back, filled or covered with soft material and long enough for two or more people to sit on: *He was lying on the sofa watching TV.*
■ ˈsofa bed *n* a sofa that can be converted into a bed.

soft /sɒft; *US* sɔːft/ *adj* (**-er, -est**) **1** changing shape easily when pressed; not hard or firm to the touch: *soft ground/toffee/wax* ○ *margarine that is soft and easy to spread* ○ *She likes a soft pillow and a hard mattress.* Compare HARD¹ 1. **2** not hard as others are: *soft cheese* ○ *a soft pencil.* **3** (of surfaces) smooth and delicate to the touch: *as soft as velvet* ○ *soft skin* ○ *Our cat has very soft fur.* **4** [usu attrib] (of light, colours, etc) not bright or so bright as to be unpleasant: *a soft pink rather than a harsh red* ○ *lampshades that give a soft light* ○ *the soft glow of candlelight.* **5** (of outlines) not sharp or clear; not distinct: *the soft curves of the distant hills.* **6** with little force: *soft summer winds* ○ *a soft landing.* **7** (of sounds) quiet; gentle; not loud: *soft music in the background* ○ *in a soft voice* ○ *soft whispers.* **8** (*infml*) (of speech) not harsh or angry; gentle; mild: *His reply was soft and calm.* **9** ~ (**on sb/sth**); ~ (**with sb**) sympathetic and kind, esp to too great an extent; not strict or strict enough: *have soft parents* ○ *have a soft heart* ○ *She's too soft on the staff and they don't respect her.* ○ *Have the authorities gone soft on crime?* ○ *He's a bit too soft with his class to keep them under control.* Compare HARD¹ 5. **10** (*infml derog*) (**a**) lacking in determination, courage, etc; weak or sentimental: *Don't be so soft — there's nothing to be afraid of.* (**b**) foolish or silly: *He's gone soft in the head.* **11** ~ **on sb** (*infml*) feeling attraction for sb; very fond of or in love with sb: *I think he's quite soft on that new neighbour of his.* **12** (*infml derog*) not requiring hard work; without problems: *a soft job* (ie one that is easy or well paid) ○ *He has a very soft life really.* **13** (of drink) not alcoholic: *Would you like some wine or something soft?* ○ *I'd prefer a soft drink.* **14** (of water) free from mineral salts and therefore good for washing: *Don't use much soap powder — the water here is very soft.* Compare HARD¹ 13. **15** (of consonants) not sounding hard: *The letter 'c' is soft in 'city' and hard in 'cat'.* ○ *The letter 'g' is soft in 'gin' and hard in 'get'.* Compare HARD¹ 14. **IDM an easy/a soft touch** ⇨ TOUCH². **have a soft ˈspot for sb/sth** (*infml*) to be specially fond of sb/sth; to have particular affection for sb/sth: *He's a strange man, but I've always had a soft spot for him.*
▶ **softish** *adj* rather soft: *softish ice-cream.*

softly *adv* in a soft way: *softly shining lights* ○ *speak softly* ○ *She pressed his hand softly.* ○ *music playing softly in the background* ○ *treat children too softly* ○ *be softly spoken* (ie have a soft voice). ˌsoftly ˈsoftly *adj* [usu attrib] (of a plan for resolving sth) careful, SUBTLE(2), and without extreme action: *take a softly softly approach to street crime.* ▶ **softness** *n* [U]: *the softness of a baby's skin* ○ *criticize softness towards criminals.*

■ ˌsoft-ˈboiled *adj* (of eggs) boiled for a short time so that the YOLK is still soft. Compare HARD-BOILED.

ˌsoft ˈdrug *n* an illegal drug considered unlikely to cause addiction (ADDICT) or to be very harmful. Compare HARD DRUG.

ˌsoft ˈfruit *n* [C,U] small fruits without stones: *soft fruit like strawberries and currants.*

ˌsoft ˈfurnishings *n* [pl] curtains, cushions, furniture coverings, etc.

ˌsoft-ˈhearted *adj* kind, sympathetic and emotional: *He's always lending her money — he's too soft-hearted.* ○ *She's quite soft-hearted underneath that stern exterior.* Compare HARD-HEARTED. ˌsoft-ˈheartedness *n* [U].

ˌsoft ˈoption *n* (*often derog*) an alternative which is considered to be easier because it involves less effort, difficulty, etc: *He decided to take the soft*

option *and give in to their demands.* ○ *You might think this course is a soft option but I can assure you it isn't.*

ˌsoft ˈpalate *n* the back part of the roof of the mouth.

ˌsoft-ˈpedal *v* (**-ll-**; *US* **-l-**) ~ (**on**) sth (*infml*) to treat sth as not very serious or important; to give little or no emphasis to sth: [Vn, Vpr] *The government has been soft-pedalling (on) the question of teachers' pay.* [also V].

ˌsoft ˈporn *n* [U] films, pictures, books, etc that show or describe sexual activity but not in a very detailed or violent way. Compare HARD PORN.

ˌsoft ˈshoulder *n* (*US*) = VERGE 1a.

ˌsoft-ˈsoap *v* (*infml*) to say very pleasant things to sb in order to persuade them to do sth: [Vn] *Don't try to soft-soap me — I'm not changing my mind.* [also Vnpr].

ˌsoft-ˈspoken *adj* speaking or said with a gentle quiet voice: *a ˌsoft-spoken young ˈwoman.*

softball /ˈsɒftbɔːl; *US* ˈsɔːft-/ *n* (**a**) [U] a game similar to baseball but played on a smaller field with a larger soft ball. (**b**) [C] a ball used in this game.

soften /ˈsɒfn; *US* ˈsɔːfn/ *v* **1** to become or make sth softer or less hard: [V] *The butter will soften out of the fridge.* [Vn] *The lampshade will soften the light.* ○ *a lotion to soften the skin.* **2** to become or make sth less severe: [V] *His face softened and he almost smiled.* [Vn] *Age has softened his attitude.* **3** to reduce the force of sth: [Vn] *soften the impact of a collision* ○ *I tried to soften the blow by telling him that others had failed too.* **PHRV** ˌsoften sb ˈup (*infml*) to make sb unable or less able to resist an attack or being persuaded: *soften up the enemy with heavy bombing* ○ *Potential customers were softened up with free gifts before the sales presentation.*
▶ **softener** *n* [U,C] a chemical substance used for softening hard water; a device using this.

software /ˈsɒftweə(r); *US* ˈsɔːft-/ *n* [U] (*computing*) the data, programmes, etc not forming part of a computer but used when operating it. Compare HARDWARE.

softwood /ˈsɒftwʊd; *US* ˈsɔːft-/ *n* [C,U] wood from trees such as PINE¹ that is cheap to produce and can be cut easily. Compare HARDWOOD.

softy (also **softie**) /ˈsɒfti; *US* ˈsɔːfti/ *n* (*infml*) **1** (*derog*) a physically weak person: *Don't be such a softy — you can do it!* **2** a kind, sympathetic and sentimental person: *He's a real softie and sometimes people take advantage of him.* ○ *Despite her rather severe manner she's a softy at heart.*

soggy /ˈsɒgi/ *adj* (**-ier, -iest**) (*usu derog*) extremely wet and soft; heavy with water: *The ground was soggy after the heavy rain.* ○ *soggy bread/cornflakes.*
▶ **soggily** /-ɪli/ *adv.* **sogginess** *n* [U].

soh /səʊ/ (also **so, sol** /sɒl/) *n* (*music*) the fifth note of any major scale¹(6).

soil /sɔɪl/ *n* [C,U] **1** the upper layer of earth in which plants, trees, etc grow: *plant sth in soil* ○ *good/poor/rich soil* ○ *clay soils* ○ *soil erosion* ○ (*rhet*) *a man of the soil* (ie one who works on the land). ⇨ note at EARTH. **2** (*fml*) country; territory: *one's native soil* ○ *set foot on foreign soil.*
▶ **soil** *v* (*fml*) to make sth dirty: [Vn] *a basket for soiled sheets* (ie used ones that are waiting to be washed) ○ *They have never soiled their hands with manual work.* See also SHOP-SOILED.

soirée /ˈswɑːreɪ; *US* swɑːˈreɪ/ *n* (*fml*) a social gathering in the evening, esp for music or conversation.

sojourn /ˈsɒdʒən; *US* səʊˈdʒɜːrn/ *v* [V] (*fml*) to stay in a place away from one's home for a time.
▶ **sojourn** *n* (*fml*) a temporary stay in a place away from one's home: *a brief sojourn in the mountains.*

sol = SOH.

solace /ˈsɒləs/ *n* (**a**) [U] (*fml*) comfort or relief from

S

sorrow, anxiety, etc: *seek solace in alcohol* ○ *find solace in music.* (**b**) a thing that provides this: *His work was a real solace to him at this difficult time.*
▶ **solace** *v* [Vn] (*fml*) to give solace to sb; to comfort sb.

solar /ˈsəʊlə(r)/ *adj* [attrib] (**a**) of, concerning or related to the sun: *solar energy* ○ *solar time.* (**b**) using the sun's energy: *solar heating* ○ *solar-powered.*
■ ˌsolar ˈcell *n* a device that converts the energy of sunlight into electricity.
ˌsolar ˈplexus /ˈpleksəs/ *n* [sing] (**a**) a system of nerves at the back of the stomach. (**b**) (*infml*) an area of the stomach below the ribs (RIB 1): *a painful punch in the solar plexus.*
the ˈsolar system *n* [sing] the sun and all the planets which move around it.
ˌsolar ˈyear *n* the time it takes the earth to go round the sun once, approximately 365¼ days.

solarium /səˈleəriəm/ *n* (*pl* **solariums**) a room equipped with sun-lamps (SUN) or enclosed mainly by glass, where people go to expose themselves to real or artificial sunlight: *The new sports centre is fitted with saunas and solariums.*

sold *pt, pp* of SELL.

solder /ˈsəʊldə(r), ˈsɒldə(r); US ˈsɑːdər/ *n* [U] a soft mixture of metals used, when heated and melted, for joining metals, wires, etc together.
▶ **solder** *v* to join sth with solder: [Vn, Vnpr] *solder the wire* (*on/onto the plug*) [Vnadv] *solder the two pieces together.* ˈsoldering-iron *n* a tool used for soldering things.

soldier /ˈsəʊldʒə(r)/ *n* a member of an army, esp one who is not an officer: *soldiers in uniform* ○ *a soldier on duty/on leave.*
▶ **soldier** *v* PHRV **ˌsoldier ˈon** to continue doing or trying to achieve sth, despite difficulties: *He felt tired and ill but bravely soldiered on until the work was finished.* **soldiering** *n* [U] the life or activities of a soldier.
soldierly *adj* like or typical of a soldier: *a tall, soldierly man* ○ *soldierly qualities of bravery and discipline.*
soldiery /ˈsəʊldʒəri/ *n* [pl *v*] (*dated fml*) a body of soldiers, esp of a specified type: *well-disciplined soldiery.*
■ ˌsoldier of ˈfortune *n* a person who fights for any country or person who will pay her or him; a MERCENARY(2).

sole¹ /səʊl/ *n* **1** the bottom part of the foot, on which one walks and stands. ⇨ picture at FOOT¹. **2** the bottom part of a shoe or sock that covers the sole of the foot: *leather/rubber soles* ○ *These shoes need new soles and heels.* ⇨ picture at SHOE.
▶ **sole** *v* (usu passive) to put a new sole onto a shoe or boot: [Vn] *have a pair of shoes soled and heeled.*
-soled (forming compound *adjs*) with soles of the specified type: *rubber-soled boots.*

sole² /səʊl/ *n* (*pl* unchanged or **soles**) [C,U] an edible flat fish that lives in the sea: *grilled sole.*

sole³ /səʊl/ *adj* [attrib] **1** one and only; single: *the sole survivor of the crash* ○ *His sole concern was for the children.* ○ *Her sole reason for leaving was to get a job with more money.* **2** belonging to or restricted to one person or group; not shared: *have sole responsibility for sth* ○ *the sole owner* ○ *the sole agent.*
▶ **solely** /ˈsəʊlli/ *adv* alone; only; not involving sb/ sth else: *be solely responsible for the accident* ○ *Few people buy a car solely because of its fuel economy.* ○ *You shouldn't judge someone solely by their appearance.*

solecism /ˈsɒlɪsɪzəm/ *n* (*fml*) **1** a mistake in the use of language in speech or writing. **2** an offence against good manners or established acceptable behaviour: *commit a social solecism.*

solemn /ˈsɒləm/ *adj* **1** not happy or smiling; look-

ing very serious: *solemn faces* ○ *He looked very solemn as I told him the bad news.* **2** done, said, etc in a serious and sincere way: *a solemn promise/ undertaking/oath/vow.* **3** performed with dignity, esp for religious purposes; formal: *a solemn procession/ritual/ceremony.* ▶ **solemnly** *adv*: *speak/nod/watch/listen solemnly* ○ *Do you solemnly swear to tell the truth?*

solemnity /səˈlemnəti/ *n* (*fml*) **1** [U] the state or quality of being solemn: *writing of great beauty and solemnity* ○ *He was buried with great solemnity.* **2** [C usu *pl*] a solemn ceremony associated with a formal event or occasion: *observe the solemnities of the occasion.*

solemnize, -ise /ˈsɒləmnaɪz/ *v* (*fml*) to perform a religious ceremony, esp a wedding: [Vn] *solemnize a marriage in church.*

sol-fa /ˌsɒl ˈfɑː; US ˌsəʊl-/ *n* (in the teaching of singing) a method of representing musical notes by short words, ie *do, re, mi, fa, so, la, te.*

solicit /səˈlɪsɪt/ *v* **1** ~ (**sb**) (**for sth**); ~ (**sth**) (**from sb**) (*fml*) to ask sb eagerly or firmly for sth; to try to obtain sth: [Vpr, Vnpr] *solicit (sb) for money/solicit money (from sb)* [Vn] *solicit news/information/ opinions.* **2** (of a prostitute) to offer oneself to sb for sex, esp in a public place: [V] *be fined for soliciting* [Vn, Vpr] *prostitutes on the streets soliciting (for) clients.*

solicitor /səˈlɪsɪtə(r)/ *n* (*Brit*) a lawyer who prepares legal documents, eg for the sale of land or buildings, advises clients on legal matters, and sometimes speaks for them in the courts. Compare ADVOCATE *n* 2, BARRISTER.
■ Soˌlicitor-ˈGeneral *n* (*pl* Solicitors-General) one of the chief law officers in the British Government, next in rank below the Attorney-General (ATTORNEY).

solicitous /səˈlɪsɪtəs/ *adj* (*fml*) feeling or showing great concern for another person's welfare, interests, etc: *a solicitous host* ○ *be solicitous about sb's health.* ▶ **solicitously** *adv* (*fml*): '*Are you sure you're all right?*' *he asked solicitously.*

solicitude /səˈlɪsɪtjuːd; US -tuːd/ *n* [U] ~ (**for/about sb/sth**) (*fml*) anxious concern or care, esp about other people: *her solicitude for her children.*

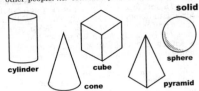

solid
cylinder   cube   sphere
cone   pyramid

solid /ˈsɒlɪd/ *adj* **1** not in the form of a liquid or gas; keeping its shape; firm: *solid fuels* (eg coal or wood) ○ *solid food* (ie not liquid or slightly liquid) ○ *solid objects* ○ *It was so cold that the village pond had frozen solid.* **2** without holes or spaces; not hollow: *a solid wall of rock* ○ *The club was packed solid* (ie very full or crowded). **3**(**a**) [attrib] of the same substance throughout; containing only one (specified) material: *a solid gold bracelet* ○ *solid silver cutlery.* (**b**) of one (specified) colour only: *apply strokes of solid blue to the painting.* **4** strong and firm in structure; that can support weight or resist pressure: *solid buildings/furniture* ○ *built on solid foundations* ○ *on solid ground.* **5** that can be depended on; reliable: *solid evidence/statistics* ○ *solid achievements* ○ *a good solid worker.* **6** in complete agreement; UNANIMOUS: *The government's policy has solid support from party members.* **7** [attrib or, informally, immediately after a *n*] without a break or pause; continuous: *The essay represents a solid* *week's work.* ○ *The phone never stopped ringing for two hours solid.* **8** (*geometry*) having three dimensions, ie length, width and thickness: *a solid figure* (eg a CUBE(1)) ○ *solid geometry* (ie the study of solid, not flat, figures). ⇨ picture. **IDM** **rock solid** ⇨ ROCK¹. **solid/steady as a rock** ⇨ ROCK¹.

solid *n* **1** a substance or an object that is solid, not a liquid or a gas: *Milk is a liquid; cheese is a solid.* ○ *The baby is not yet on solids* (ie eating solid foods). **2** (*geometry*) a figure of three dimensions, having length, width and thickness: *A cube is a solid.*

▸ **solidity** /sə'lɪdəti/ (*also* **solidness**) *n* [U] the quality or state of being solid: *the solidity of a building* ○ *lines and shadows which gave the picture a feeling of solidity* ○ *I was impressed by the solidity of the team's defence.*

solidly *adv* **1** in a firm and strong way: *a solidly-built house.* **2** continuously: *It rained solidly for three hours.* **3** agreeing with or supporting sb/sth completely: *We're all solidly behind you on this issue.*

solidarity /ˌsɒlɪ'dærəti/ *n* [U,C] unity, agreement and support resulting from shared interests, feelings, actions, sympathies, etc: *show solidarity in the face of opposition* ○ *class/international/social solidarity* ○ *solidarities of class.*

solidify /sə'lɪdɪfaɪ/ *v* (*pt, pp* **-fied**) ~ (**into sth**) **1** to become or make sth solid or hard: [V] *The paint had solidified in the tin.* [Vpr] *The mixture solidifes into toffee.* [Vn] *solidified rock.* **2** (of ideas, etc) to become more fixed and unlikely to change: [Vpr] *Vague objections to the system solidified into firm opposition.* [also V]. ▸ **solidification** /səˌlɪdɪfɪ'keɪʃn/ *n* [U]: *the solidification of volcanic rock.*

soliloquy /sə'lɪləkwi/ *n* [C,U] (an act of) speaking one's thoughts aloud, esp in a play when a character does this without another character being present on stage: *Hamlet's famous soliloquy* ○ *a playwright's use of soliloquy.*

▸ **soliloquize, -ise** /sə'lɪləkwaɪz/ *v* [V] (*fml*) to talk to oneself; to speak one's thoughts aloud, esp in a play.

solipsism /'sɒlɪpsɪzəm/ *n* [U] (*philosophy*) the theory that only the self exists or can be known. ▸ **solipsistic** /ˌsɒlɪp'sɪstɪk/ *adj*: *a solipsistic view of life.*

solitaire /ˌsɒlɪ'teə(r); *US* 'sɒlɪteər/ *n* **1** [U] a game for one person in which pieces are removed from their places on a special board after other pieces are moved over them. The aim is to finish with only one piece left on the board. **2** [U] (*US*) = PATIENCE 3. **3** [C] a single jewel; a piece of jewellery containing a single jewel: *a solitaire diamond/ring.*

solitary /'sɒlɪtri; *US* -teri/ *adj* **1(a)** [usu attrib] done or exisiting alone; without companions: *a solitary walk* ○ *lead a solitary life* ○ *one solitary tree on the horizon.* **(b)** fond of being alone; frequently spending time alone: *a solitary kind of person* ○ *Tigers are solitary animals.* **2** not often visited; in a lonely remote place: *a solitary island/valley.* ⇨ note at ALONE. **3** [usu attrib] (esp in negative sentences and questions) only one; single: *I can't think of a solitary occasion* (ie not even one) *when this happened.*

▸ **solitariness** *n* [U]: *the solitariness of the landscape* ○ *the enforced solitariness of some old people.*

solitary *n* **1** [U] (*infml*) = SOLITARY CONFINEMENT. **2** [C] (*fml*) a person who chooses to live completely alone; a HERMIT: *religious solitaries.*

■ **ˌsolitary conˈfinement** (also *infml* **solitary**) *n* [U] a punishment in which a prisoner is kept alone in a separate cell: *be put/kept/held in solitary confinement.*

solitude /'sɒlɪtjuːd; *US* -tuːd/ *n* [U] the state or situation of being alone without companions: *enjoy/seek solitude* ○ *a place of solitude.*

solo /'səʊləʊ/ *n* (*pl* **solos**) **1** a piece of music, dance, entertainment, etc performed by only one person: *a violin solo* ○ *sing/play/do a solo.* **2** a flight in which the pilot flies alone without an instructor (IN-STRUCT): *fly one's first solo.*

▸ **solo** *adj* [attrib], *adv* **1** (done) by one person alone; without being accompanied by anyone: *a solo attempt* ○ *his first solo flight* ○ *She wanted to fly solo across the Atlantic.* **2** (played or performed) by one instrument or performer; without being accompanied by another instrument or performer: *a fine solo performance on the flute* ○ *a piece for solo cello* ○ *sing solo.*

soloist *n* a person who performs a solo(1): *a violin soloist.*

solstice /'sɒlstɪs/ *n* either of the two times of the year at which the sun is furthest north or south of the EQUATOR: *the summer solstice* (ie about 21 June in the northern HEMISPHERE(2)) ○ *the winter solstice* (ie about 22 December in the northern hemisphere). Compare EQUINOX.

soluble /'sɒljəbl/ *adj* **1** ~ (**in sth**) that can be dissolved: *soluble aspirin* ○ *Glucose is soluble in water.* ○ *acid/alkali soluble soils.* **2** (*fml*) that can be solved or explained: *problems that are not readily soluble.*

▸ **solubility** /ˌsɒlju'bɪləti/ *n* [U].

solution /sə'luːʃn/ *n* **1** [C] ~ (**to sth**) a way of solving a problem, dealing with a difficult situation, etc: *try to find a better solution* ○ *There's no easy solution to this problem.* ○ *Refusing to talk about it is not the best solution.* **2** [C] ~ (**to sth**) an answer to a PUZZLE(2): *the solution to a crossword.* **3** [C,U] a liquid in which sth is dissolved; the state of being dissolved: *a solution of salt in water* ○ *salt in solution.* **4** [U] the process of dissolving a solid or a gas in liquid: *the solution of glucose in water.*

solve /sɒlv/ *v* **1** to find an answer to a problem, etc; to explain sth or make sth clear: [Vn] *solve a crossword puzzle/mathematical equation* ○ *solve a crime/mystery.* **2** to find a way of dealing with a difficult situation: [Vn] *solve the problem of enviromental pollution.*

▸ **solvable** *adj* that can be solved or explained: *problems that are not easily solvable.*

solver *n* (esp in compounds) a person who solves sth: *He's a good problem-solver.*

solvent /'sɒlvənt/ *adj* [usu pred] **1** having enough money to pay one's debts; not in debt: *a solvent company.* Compare INSOLVENT. **2** (*techn*) that can dissolve another substance: *solvent cleaners.*

▸ **solvent** *n* [U,C] a substance, esp a liquid, that can dissolve another substance: *industrial solvents for removing oil.*

solvency /-nsi/ *n* [U] the state of being solvent(1).

sombre (*US* **somber**) /'sɒmbə(r)/ *adj* **1** dark in colour; dull and gloomy (GLOOM): *sombre clothes* ○ *a sombre January day.* **2** sad and serious: *a sombre expression on his face* ○ *be in a sombre mood* ○ *a sombre occasion.* ▸ **sombrely** *adv*: *sombrely dressed.*

sombrero /sɒm'breərəʊ/ *n* (*pl* **-os**) a man's hat with a very wide BRIM(2), worn esp in Mexico.

some¹ /səm/ *indef det* (used in affirmative sentences, or in questions expecting a positive reply) **1** (used with uncountable *ns*) a certain amount of sth, but not a specified amount: *There's some ice in the fridge.* ○ *Some mail came for you this morning.* ○ *You left some money on the table.* ○ *Would you like some milk in your coffee?* ○ *There's some more wine in the kitchen, isn't there?* **2** (used with plural countable *ns*, usu referring to three or more) a certain number, but not a specified number: *Some children were playing in the park.* ○ *There were some papers on the desk.* ○ *Have some more vegetables.* ○ *If you put some pictures on the wall the room will look brighter.* ○ *Didn't you borrow some records of mine?* Compare ANY¹.

some² /sʌm/ *indef det* (usu stressed) **1** (used with countable and uncountable *ns*) **(a)** (used when referring to certain members of a group or certain types of a thing and not all of them): *Some people never seem to put on weight while others are always on a diet.* ○ *I like 'some modern music.* (**b**) a large number or amount of sth: *It's going to take some time to finish this.* ○ *She spoke at some length about the issue.* ○ *It was with some surprise that I heard the news.* ○ *We've known each other for some years now.* (**c**) a certain amount or number of sth but not a large one: *There is some hope that things will improve, I suppose.* ○ *She made some mistakes but her work was otherwise good.* ○ *I have some interest in the subject.* **2** (used with singular countable *ns*) a person, place, thing or time that is not known or not specified: *Some man at the door is asking to see you.* ○ *She won a competition in* **some** *newspaper or other.* ○ *I'll see you again some time, I'm sure.* **3** */also* səm/ (used with numbers) approximately: *He spent some twelve years of his life in Africa.* ○ *Some thirty people attended the funeral.* **4** (used before countable and uncountable *ns* at the beginning of a sentence for expressing negative opinions) no; no kind of: *Some kind of expert you are! You know even less than me.* ○ *'You might get the job.' 'Some chance! There will be lots of better candidates.'* **5** (used before countable and uncountable *ns* for expressing admiration or approval) (a) very good: *He's some player!* ○ *That's some achievement — you must be very proud.*

some³ /sʌm/ *indef pron* **1** a certain number or amount of people or things (**a**) (referring back to an item or items just mentioned): *Some disapprove of the idea.* ○ *You'll find some in the cupboard.* ○ *There's some (more) in the pot.* ○ *I already have some but it's not enough for six people.* (**b**) (referring forward to an item or items following): *We need some of the same colour paint.* ○ *There's some of it in the shed.* **2** a part of the whole number or amount being considered (**a**) (referring back to an item or items just mentioned): *All these students are good, but some work harder than others.* (**b**) (referring forward to an item or items following): *Some of the students had done their homework but most hadn't.* ○ *Some of the letter was illegible.* Compare ANY².

-some /-səm/ *suff* **1** (with *ns* and *vs* forming *adjs*) producing; likely to: *fearsome* ○ *quarrelsome* ○ *meddlesome.* **2** (with numbers forming *ns*) a group of the specified number: *threesome.*

somebody /'sʌmbədi/ *indef pron* (abbreviated as *sb* in this dictionary) = SOMEONE.

someday (also **some day**) /'sʌmdeɪ/ *indef adv* at some time in the future: *Someday we'll be together.* ○ *Some day he will be famous.* Compare SOME² 2.

somehow /'sʌmhaʊ/ (*US* also **someway**) *indef adv* **1** in some way; by some means: *We must stop him from seeing her somehow.* ○ *Somehow I must get a new job.* **2** for a reason that is not known or specified: *Somehow, I don't feel I can trust him.* ○ *I always knew she'd get the job, somehow.*

someone /'sʌmwʌn/ (also **somebody**) *indef pron* **1** some person: *There's someone at the door.* ○ *Someone from your office phoned.* ○ *If you saw someone drowning what would you do?* **2** an important person: *He thinks he's really somebody/someone.* ⇨ note at GENDER.

someplace /'sʌmpleɪs/ *indef adv* (*esp US*) = SOMEWHERE.

somersault /'sʌmәsɔːlt/ *n* a rolling movement in which sb turns their feet over their head on the ground or in the air: *turning somersaults* ○ *do a forward/backward somersault.*
▸ **somersault** *v* to perform a somersault or somersaults: [Vpr] *The car spun off the road and somersaulted over/into the hedge.* [also V].

something /'sʌmθɪŋ/ *indef pron* **1** (abbreviated as *sth* in this dictionary) a thing that is not known or specified: *There's something under the table.* ○ *I want*

something to eat. ○ *I wish there was something I could do to help.* ○ *There's something interesting on the front page.* ○ *If you don't like your job, why not do something about it?* ○ *There's something about his manner I don't like.* **2** a thing thought to be important or worth noting: *There's something* (ie some truth, some fact or opinion worth considering) *in what she says.* ○ *It's (really/quite) something* (ie a thing that one should feel happy about) *to have a job at all these days.* ○ *He's something in/He does something in* (ie He has a job connected with) *television.*
IDM or something (*infml*) or another thing similar to that mentioned: *She's writing a dictionary or something.* ○ *He hit a tree or something.* **something between, around, over, under, etc sth** a figure, measurement, etc of approximately the specified value: *She called at something after ten o'clock.* **something else** (*infml*) an exceptional person, thing, event, etc: *I've seen some fine players, but she's something else.* ¦**something like a 'sb/sth 1** partially similar to sb/sth: *We saw an animal something like a deer.* ○ *It tastes something like melon.* ○ *The tune goes something like this.* **2** approximately sb/sth: *It costs something like $35.* **something of a sth** to some degree the thing specified: *She found herself something of a celebrity.* ○ *I'm something of an expert on antiques.* **something or other** (*infml*) an unknown or forgotten thing: *He's a professor of something or other at Reading University.*

sometime (also **some time**) /'sʌmtaɪm/ *indef adv* at a time that is not specified: *I saw him sometime last summer.* ○ *Phone me some time next met.* Compare SOME² 2.
▸ **sometime** *adj* [attrib] (*fml*) formerly: *Thomas Atkins, sometime vicar of this parish.*

sometimes /'sʌmtaɪmz/ *indef adv* at some times but not all the time; occasionally: *He sometimes writes to me.* ○ *Sometimes I go by car.* ○ *Sometimes we went to the beach, but usually we just stayed by the hotel pool.*

someway /'sʌmweɪ/ *indef adv* (*US infml*) = SOMEHOW.

somewhat /'sʌmwɒt/ *indef adv* to some degree; rather: *I was somewhat surprised to see him.* ○ *He sounded somewhat confused.* ○ *The situation has changed somewhat since he last met.*

somewhere /'sʌmweə(r)/ (*US* also **someplace**) *indef adv* in, at or to some place: *I lost it somewhere between here and the station.* ○ *I've seen him somewhere before.* ○ *This year we're going somewhere else* (ie to a different place) *for our holidays.* **IDM or somewhere** or another similar place: *He went to school at Eton or somewhere.* **somewhere around, about, between, etc sth** a figure, amount, etc of approximately the specified value: *It was sold for somewhere in excess of £600.*
▸ **somewhere** *indef pron* some place: *I need to find somewhere to stay.* ○ *I know somewhere (where) we can go.*

somnambulism /sɒm'næmbjəlɪzəm/ *n* [U] (*fml*) the activity or habit of walking around while one is asleep. ▸ **somnambulist** /-lɪst/ *n*.

somnolent /'sɒmnələnt/ *adj* (*fml*) **1** almost asleep; SLEEPY(1): *feel rather somnolent after a large lunch.* **2** causing or suggesting sleep: *The noise of the stream had a pleasantly somnolent effect.*

son /sʌn/ *n* **1** [C] a male child of a parent: *I have a son and two daughters.* ○ *She has two grown-up sons.* ○ *Maxwell & Sons, Grocers.* (ie as the name of a business company). **2** [C *esp pl*] (*rhet*) a male member of a family, country, etc: *one of France's most famous sons.* **3** (a form of address used by an older man to a young man or boy): *'What's the matter with you, son?' asked the doctor.* ○ *'What is it you want to tell me, my son?' asked the priest.* ○ (*derog*) *Listen, son, don't start giving me orders.* **4 the Son** [sing] Jesus

Christ as the second person of the Trinity: *the Father, the Son and the Holy Spirit.* **IDM** **from father to son** ⇨ FATHER¹. **like father, like son** ⇨ FATHER¹.

■ **'son-in-law** *n* (*pl* **'sons-in-law**) the husband of one's daughter. Compare DAUGHTER-IN-LAW.

₁**son of a 'bitch** *n* (*pl* **sons of bitches**) (△ *sl*) a bad, cruel or very unpleasant person: *I'll kill that son of a bitch when I get my hands on him!*

sonar /ˈsəʊnɑː(r)/ *n* [U] a device or system for finding objects under water by means of reflected sound waves: *detected/located by sonar* ○ *Dolphins have a sense similar to our sonar.* Compare RADAR.

sonata /səˈnɑːtə/ *n* a piece of music composed for one instrument or two, one of which is usu the piano. Sonatas usu consist of three or four main divisions: *Beethoven's piano sonatas* ○ *a violin sonata.*

son et lumière /ˌsɒn eɪ ˈluːmjeə(r); US -luːmˈjeər/ *n* [U] (*French*) an entertainment held at night at a famous building or place, where its history is told and acted with special lighting and recorded sound: *a son et lumière show in the grounds of a ruined abbey.*

song /sɒŋ; US sɔːŋ/ *n* **1** [C] a piece of music with words that is sung: *a popular/pop/folk song* ○ *sing a song.* See also SWANSONG. **2** [U] music for the voice; singing: *burst into song* (ie suddenly begin singing). See also PLAINSONG. **3** [U] the musical call made by certain birds: *the song of the thrush.* **IDM** **for a 'song** (*infml*) at a very low price: *This table was going for a song at the market.* **sing a different song/tune** ⇨ SING. **(make) a song and 'dance (about sth)** (*infml derog*) (to make) a great fuss about sth, usu when it is unnecessary; to make sth widely known: *I know you're disappointed, but there's no need to make (such) a song and dance about it.*

▶ **songster** /-stə(r)/ *n* (*dated or rhet*) a person or bird that sings, esp pleasantly and often: *Robins, thrushes and blackbirds are the most commonly heard songsters in English gardens.*

songbird /ˈsɒŋbɜːd; US ˈsɔːŋ-/ *n* a bird noted for its musical call: *Blackbirds and thrushes are songbirds.*

songbook /ˈsɒŋbʊk; US ˈsɔːŋ-/ *n* a collection of songs with both words and music: *a children's songbook.*

songstress /ˈsɒŋstrəs; US ˈsɔːŋ-/ *n* (*dated or rhet*) a female singer.

songwriter /ˈsɒŋraɪtə(r); US ˈsɔːŋ-/ *n* a person who composes usu popular songs as a profession.

▶ **songwriting** *n* [U] the work of a songwriter.

sonic /ˈsɒnɪk/ *adj* relating to sound or the speed of sound: *sonic waves.*

■ ₁**sonic 'boom** *n* the explosive noise made when an aircraft passes the speed of sound. See also SUBSONIC, SUPERSONIC.

sonnet /ˈsɒnɪt/ *n* a poem with 14 lines, each of 10 syllables, and a fixed pattern of RHYME(1): *Shakespeare's sonnets.*

sonny /ˈsʌnɪ/ *n* (*infml sometimes derog*) (a form of address used by an older person to a young boy or young man): *Don't try to teach me my job, sonny.*

sonorous /ˈsɒnərəs; US səˈnɔːrəs/ *adj* (*fml*) **1** having a full deep sound: *a sonorous voice/tone.* **2** (of language, words, etc) sounding impressive and important: *a sonorous style of writing.* ▶ **sonority** /səˈnɒrəti; US -ˈnɔːr-/ *n* [U,C] (*fml*): *the sonority of the bass voices* ○ *rich orchestral sonorities.* **sonorously** *adv*: *speak sonorously.*

soon /suːn/ *adv* (**-er, -est**) **1** not long after the present time or the time mentioned; within a short time: *We'll soon be home.* ○ *We'll be home quite soon now.* ○ *We soon got there.* ○ *He'll be here very soon.* ○ *It will soon be five years since I started this job.* **2** (sometimes in the pattern **the sooner ... the sooner ...**) early; quickly: *'How soon can you be*

ready?' 'As soon as you like.'* ○ *Must you leave so soon?* ○ *She will be here sooner than you expect.* ○ *The sooner you begin the sooner you'll finish* (ie If you begin earlier you'll finish earlier). **IDM** **as 'soon as** (used as a *conj*) at the moment that; not later than the moment when: *He left as soon as he heard the news.* ○ *I'll tell him as soon as I see him.* **(just) as soon do sth (as do sth)** with equal willingness (as): *I'd (just) as soon stay at home as go for a walk.* *'Do you want to go out tonight?' 'I'd just as soon not.'* **least said soonest mended** ⇨ SAY. **no sooner said than 'done** (used esp in response to a question, request, etc) to indicate that sth has been done or will be done immediately). **no sooner ... than ...** immediately when or after: *He had no sooner/No sooner had he arrived than he had to leave again.* **soon after (sb/sth)** a short time after sb/sth: *He arrived ₁soon after 'three.* ○ *They left ₁soon after 'we did.* ○ *I rang for a taxi and it arrived soon 'after.* **the ₁sooner the 'better** as quickly as possible: *'When shall I tell him?' 'The sooner the better.'* **sooner do sth (than do sth)** rather do sth: *I'd sooner go for a walk than go shopping.* ○ *You don't have to come — you can stay at home if you'd sooner.* ○ *Go back there? I'd sooner emigrate!* ○ *Will you tell him, or would you sooner* (ie prefer it if) *I did?* ₁**sooner or 'later** one day; eventually, whether soon or later on: *You should tell her, because she'll find out sooner or later.* **sooner rather than later** in a short time instead of a longer time: *I hope we can sort it out sooner rather than later.*

soot /sʊt/ *n* [U] black powder in the smoke of wood, coal, etc: *sweep the soot out of the chimney* ○ *a fireplace blackened with soot.*

▶ **sooty 1** covered with soot; black with soot: *a sooty chimney.* **2** the colour of soot; black: *a sooty cat.*

soothe /suːð/ *v* **1** to make a person who is upset, anxious, etc quiet or calm; to calm or comfort sb: [Vn] *soothe a crying baby.* **2 ~ sth (away)** to make a pain less severe; to ease sth: [Vn] *soothe sb's backache by rubbing it* ○ *a cream that helps to soothe sunburn* [Vnp] *have a bath to soothe away aches and pains.* ▶ **soothing** *adj*: *soothing music* ○ *a soothing voice/lotion/massage.* **soothingly** *adv*: *'There's no need to worry,' he said soothingly.*

soothsayer /ˈsuːθseɪə(r)/ *n* (*arch*) a person who claims to be able to tell what will happen in the future.

sop /sɒp/ *n* (usu *sing*) **~ (to sb/sth)** (*often derog*) a thing offered to sb who is angry, not satisfied, etc in order to calm them or win their favour: *The change of policy is seen as a sop to the moderates in the party.*

▶ **sop** *v* (**-pp-**) **PHRV** ₁**sop sth 'up** to take up liquid, etc with sth that can absorb it: *Sop up the water with a paper towel.* ○ *He sopped up the gravy with a piece of bread.*

sopping *adj, adv* very wet: *Your clothes are sopping (wet)!*

sophisticated /səˈfɪstɪkeɪtɪd/ *adj* **1** having or showing a lot of experience of the world and social situations; knowing about fashion, culture, new ideas, etc: *a sophisticated young woman* ○ *wearing sophisticated clothes* ○ *have sophisticated tastes.* **2** able to understand difficult or complicated things: *Voters are much more sophisticated these days.* **3** complicated and refined; elaborate; SUBTLE(2): *a sophisticated computer system* ○ *a sophisticated analysis/discussion/argument.* See also UNSOPHISTICATED.

▶ **sophisticate** /səˈfɪstɪkeɪt/ *n* (*often ironic*) a sophisticated(1) person: *the sophisticates of the art world.* **sophistication** /səˌfɪstɪˈkeɪʃn/ *n* [U] the quality of being sophisticated: *the increasing power and sophistication of computers* ○ *She tried to cultivate an air of sophistication.*

S

S

sophistry /ˈsɒfɪstri/ n (fml) (**a**) [U] the use of clever but false arguments intended to deceive: *use sophistry to obscure the truth.* (**b**) [C] an instance or example of this: *the sophistries of clever politicians.*

sophomore /ˈsɒfəmɔː(r)/ n (US) a student in the second year of a course at a high school, college or university: *a sophomore class/year.*

soporific /ˌsɒpəˈrɪfɪk/ adj causing sleep: *a soporific drug.*

sopping ⇨ SOP.

soppy /ˈsɒpi/ adj (Brit infml derog) sentimental in a silly way: *a soppy film/love story* ○ *I'm soppy about animals.*

soprano /səˈprɑːnəʊ; US -ˈpræn-/ n (pl **-os** /-nəʊz/) [C] (*music*) (**a**) a singing voice of the highest range for a woman or boy. (**b**) a singer with such a voice: *The sopranos sang beautifully.* (**c**) a musical part written for a soprano voice: *sing soprano.*
▶ **soprano** adj [attrib] (of a musical instrument) with a range that is the highest of its type: *a soprano saxophone.*

sorbet /ˈsɔːbeɪ; US ˈsɔːrbət/ (*US* also **sherbet**) n [C,U] a frozen sweet food made from water, sugar and fruit juice: *a/some blackcurrant sorbet.*

sorcerer /ˈsɔːsərə(r)/ n (fem **sorceress** /ˈsɔːsərəs/) a person who is believed to practise magic, esp with the help of evil spirits: *a sorcerer in a children's fairy story.* Compare WIZARD 1.
▶ **sorcery** /ˈsɔːsəri/ n [U] the art, use or practice of magic, esp with evil spirits. Compare WITCHCRAFT.

sordid /ˈsɔːdɪd/ adj (derog) **1** (of conditions, places, etc) dirty and unpleasant: *a sordid slum* ○ *living in sordid poverty.* **2** (of people, behaviour, etc) not honest or moral; unpleasant: *a sordid affair* ○ *a person with a sordid past* ○ *I don't want to know all the sordid details.* ▶ **sordidly** adv. **sordidness** n [U].

sore /sɔː(r)/ adj **1**(**a**) (of a part of the body) hurting when touched or used; tender and painful: *have a sore finger/throat* ○ *My leg is still very sore.* (**b**) [usu pred] feeling pain: *She's still a bit sore after the operation.* See also SADDLE-SORE. **2** [usu pred] (*infml esp US*) upset and angry, esp because one has been treated unfairly: *She's sore about not being invited to the party.* **3** (fml or dated) serious; severe: *be in sore need of help.* **IDM** **a sight for sore eyes** ⇨ SIGHT[1]. **a ˌsore ˈpoint** a subject that makes sb feel upset or angry when it is mentioned: *Don't ask him about his job interview — it's rather a sore point with him at the moment.* **stand/stick out like a sore ˈthumb** to be very obvious, and often ugly in appearance: *The new office block sticks out like a sore thumb among the old buildings in the area.*
▶ **sore** n a painful place on the body where the skin or flesh is injured: *pressure sores caused by lying in bed all day.* See also CANKER SORE, COLD SORE.
sorely adv (fml) seriously; very greatly: *I was sorely tempted to complain, but I didn't.* ○ *Your financial help is sorely needed.* ○ *She was sorely missed at the reunion.*
soreness n [U]: *an ointment to reduce soreness and swelling.*

sorghum /ˈsɔːgəm/ n [U] a crop producing edible grains, grown in warm climates.

sorority /səˈrɒrəti; US -ˈrɔːr-/ n [CGp] (US) a women's social club in a college or university; its members. Compare FRATERNITY 2.

sorrel[1] /ˈsɒrəl; US ˈsɔːrəl/ n [U] a type of plant with a sour taste used to give flavour to food: *sorrel sauce/soup.*

sorrel[2] /ˈsɒrəl; US ˈsɔːrəl/ n **1** [U] a reddish-brown colour. **2** [C] a reddish-brown horse: *a sorrel mare/pony.*

sorrow /ˈsɒrəʊ/ n (**a**) [U] ~ (at/for/over sth) a feeling of sadness or distress caused esp by loss, disappointment or regret; grief: *express genuine/deep sorrow for having hurt sb* ○ *feel great sorrow at sb's death* ○ *have a lifetime of sorrow* ○ *He said his decision was made more in sorrow than in anger.* (**b**) [C] a particular cause of this feeling; a sad event: *the joys and sorrows of life* ○ *Her death was a great sorrow to everyone.* **IDM** **drown one's sorrows** ⇨ DROWN.
▶ **sorrow** v ~ (at/for/over sth) (fml) to feel, express or show sorrow: [Vpr] *sorrowing over his child's death* ○ *sorrowing at his misfortune* [V] *a sorrowing widow.*
sorrowful /-fl/ adj (rather fml) feeling, showing or causing sorrow: *a sorrowful occasion* ○ *a sorrowful face/look/voice.* **sorrowfully** /-fəli/ adv: *He shook his head sorrowfully.*

sorry /ˈsɒri; US ˈsɔːri/ adj (**-ier, -iest**) **1** [pred] ~ (**to do sth/that...**) feeling sadness or regret: *We were very sorry to hear of your father's death.* ○ *I'm sorry that you're leaving.* ○ *I'm sorry to tell you that your application has not been successful.* **2** [pred] ~ (**for/about sth**) full of shame and regret, esp about a past action: *Aren't you sorry for/about what you've done?* ○ *If you say you're sorry we'll forget what happened.* **3** (used to express mild regret, disagreement or refusal, and for making apologies and excuses): *I'm sorry, but I don't agree.* ○ *I'm sorry I'm late.* ○ *I'm sorry if I offended you.* ○ *'Can you lend me some money?' 'I'm sorry, I can't.'* **4** [attrib] (usu derog) in poor condition, esp causing pity: *a sorry sight* ○ *The house was in a sorry state.* **IDM** **be/feel sorry for sb** **1** to feel sympathy for sb: *I feel sorry for anyone who has to drive in this sort of weather.* **2** to feel pity for or mild disapproval of sb: *If he doesn't realize what he's done, then I'm sorry for him.* **better safe than sorry** ⇨ BETTER[2].
▶ **sorry** interj **1** (used for apologizing, making excuses, etc): *Sorry, did I knock your elbow?* ○ *Sorry I'm late.* **2** (esp Brit) (used when asking sb to repeat sth that one has not heard properly) what did you say?: *'My name's Jane Timms.' 'Sorry — Jane who?'*

sort[1] /sɔːt/ n **1** [C] a group or class of people or things that are alike in some way; a type: *He's the sort of person I really dislike.* ○ *What sort of paint are you using?* ○ *There's some sort of spice in it.* ○ *I won't tolerate this sort of behaviour/behaviour of this sort.* ○ *There are all sorts of (ie many types of) jobs you could do.* **2** [C usu sing] (infml) a type of character; a person: *a good/decent sort* ○ *He's not a bad sort really.* **IDM** **it takes all sorts (to make a world)** (saying) people vary very much in character and abilities (and this is a good thing). **nothing of the kind/sort** ⇨ KIND[2]. **of a ˈsort/of ˈsorts** (infml derog) of a poor or inferior type: *It was a holiday of sorts, but we weren't able to relax much.* **out of ˈsorts 1** feeling ill: *She's been rather out of sorts lately.* **2** in a bad temper; annoyed: *He's always out of sorts early in the morning.* **sort of** (infml) to some extent; in some way or other: *I sort of thought this might happen.* ○ *You sort of twist the ends together.* ○ *I feel sort of dizzy.* ○ *'Do you understand?' 'Sort of.'* ⇨ note at KIND[2]. **a sort of sth** (infml) an uncertain or unusual type of sth: *I had a sort of feeling he wouldn't come.*

sort[2] /sɔːt/ v ~ sth (out) (into sth); ~ sth (out) from sth to arrange things in groups; to separate things of one type, class, etc from things of other types, etc: [Vnp] *sort out the dirty washing* [Vnpr] *The computer sorts the words into alphabetical order.* ○ *The letters are sorted by postcode.* **IDM** **sort out the ˌmen from the ˈboys** to show or prove which people are truly brave, skilful, competent, etc: *a difficult mountain climb that will certainly sort out the men from the boys.* **PHRV** **ˌsort sth ˈout 1** to separate sth from a larger group: *Sort out the smaller plants and throw them away.* **2** (infml) to put sth in good order; to tidy sth: *sort out the kitchen cupboards.* ˌsort **sth/sb/oneself** ˈout to find a solution to a problem or to sb's/one's own problems, etc: *I'll leave you to sort this problem out.* ○ *If you come to me for advice I'll soon sort you out.* ○ *I need to sort my life/myself out a bit, before I start looking for a new job.* ˌsort **sb** ˈout (*infml*) to deal with sb, esp by punishing or attacking him: *Wait till I get my hands on him — I'll sort him out!* ˈsort **through sth** to go through a number of things, arranging them in groups: *sort through a pile of old photographs.*

sortie /ˈsɔːti/ *n* **1(a)** a brief trip away from one's home or base: *Apart from an occasional sortie into town to do some shopping, we stayed at home most of the time.* (**b**) an attempt to join, enter or do sth new: *His first sortie into politics was unsuccessful.* **2** a flight made by one aircraft during military operations: *a training/bombing sortie.* **3** an attack made by soldiers coming out from a position of defence: *carry out/make a sortie into enemy territory.*

SOS /ˌes əʊ ˈes/ *n* [sing] (**a**) a signal or message sent esp from a ship by radio, etc when one is in great danger and needs urgent help: *send an SOS to the coastguard* ○ *an SOS message.* (**b**) any urgent appeal for help, eg a radio broadcast to find relatives of a seriously ill person: *We heard the SOS about Bill's father on the car radio.* ○ (*joc*) *Our daughter sent us an SOS for some more money.* See also MAYDAY.

so-so /ˌsəʊ ˈsəʊ/ *adj* [pred], *adv* (*infml*) not very good; not very well; fairly good or well: *'How are you feeling today?' 'Only so-so.'* ○ *'What was the exam like?' 'So-so.'*

sot /sɒt/ *n* (*dated derog*) a person who gets drunk very often: *her drunken sot of a husband.*

sotto voce /ˌsɒtəʊ ˈvəʊtʃi/ *adj, adv* (*Italian fml or joc*) in a low voice, so as not to be heard by everyone: *a sotto voce remark* ○ *'You'll be sorry,' he added, sotto voce.*

sou /suː/ *n* [sing] (*infml*) (in negative sentences) a very small amount of money: *'Can you lend me 50p?' 'Sorry, I haven't a sou.'*

soufflé /ˈsuːfleɪ; *US* suːˈfleɪ/ *n* [C,U] a dish of eggs, milk and flour mixed with cheese, fruit, etc, beaten to make it light, and baked: *a/some lemon soufflé.*

sough /saʊ, sʌf/ *n* (*fml*) [sing] a whistling or rushing sound, like that made by the wind in trees: *the distant sough of the sea.*

sought *pt, pp* of SEEK.

soul /səʊl/ *n* **1** [C] (**a**) the spiritual part of a person, believed to exist after death: *Do you believe in the immortality of the soul?* **2** a person's moral or emotional nature or sense of identity: *Deep down in her soul she felt betrayed.* ○ *Music and dancing are their very soul.* **3** [C,U] strong and good human feeling; emotional, moral and intellectual energy, eg as revealed in works of art: *a man with no soul* ○ *a very polished performance, but lacking soul.* **4** [sing] the ~ **of sth** the perfect example of some virtue or quality: *He is the soul of honour/discretion.* **5** [C] a spirit of a dead person: *departed/immortal souls.* **6** [C] (**a**) (esp in negative sentences) a person: *There wasn't a soul to be seen* (ie No one was in sight). ○ *Don't tell a soul* (ie Do not tell anybody). (**b**) (with *adjs*, indicating affection, pity, etc) a person, child, etc: *He's a dear old soul.* ○ *She's lost all her money, poor soul.* **7** (also ˈsoul music) [U] a type of music made popular by African-Americans, expressing strong emotion: *the sound of soul* ○ *a soul singer.* **IDM** bare **one's heart/ soul** ⇨ BARE². body and soul ⇨ BODY. heart and soul ⇨ HEART. keep body and soul together ⇨ BODY. the life and soul of sth ⇨ LIFE. sell one's soul ⇨ SELL. upon my soul! (*dated*) (used as an exclamation of shock or surprise).

▶ **soulful** /-fl/ *adj* having, expressing or causing deep, usu sad, feeling: *a soulful look/voice/tune.*

soulfully /-fəli/ *adv: soulfully expressive eyes.* **soulfulness** *n* [U].

soulless /ˈsəʊlləs/ *adj* having or showing no concern for human feelings; without life, interest or comfort: *soulless work in the factory* ○ *soulless office buildings.*

■ ˈsoul-destroying *adj* (of work, etc) very boring, usu because a particular task is repeated many times: *a soul-destroying job.*

ˈsoul food *n* [U] (*US*) food traditionally associated with African-Americans in the southern USA.

ˈsoul mate *n* a person with whom one has a deep lasting friendship and understanding.

ˈsoul music *n* [U] = SOUL 7.

ˈsoul-searching *n* [U] deep examination of one's conscience and mind: *After a great deal of soul-searching he finally decided to leave home.*

sound¹ /saʊnd/ *n* **1(a)** [U] a sensation detected by the ear, caused by the VIBRATION of the air surrounding it: *Sound travels more slowly than light.* (**b**) [C] a thing that produces such a sensation; a thing that can be heard: *the sound of the wind/the sea/a car/ voices/breaking glass* ○ *the sound of music* ○ ˈvowel sounds (eg /uː, ʌ, ə/) ○ *I heard a strange sound outside.* ○ *He crept upstairs without a sound.* **2** [U] music, speech, etc recorded on a tape, as part of a film, etc or broadcast on radio or television: *a 'sound engineer* ○ *When was 'sound-recording invented?* ○ *Turn the sound down — the neighbours will complain.* **3** [U] the distance within which sth can be heard: *Their house is within (the) sound of the sea.* **IDM** by the ˈsound of it judging by what sb says and their attitude, tone of voice, etc: *They had a wonderful time by the sound of it.* like the look/ sound of sb/sth ⇨ LIKE¹. like, etc the sound of one's own ˈvoice (*derog*) to talk a lot or too much, usu without wanting to hear what others have to say: *She's much too fond of the sound of her own voice.*

▶ **soundless** *adj* without a sound; silent: *soundless footsteps.* **soundlessly** *adv*.

■ ˈsound barrier (also ˌsonic ˈbarrier) *n* [sing] the point at which an aircraft's speed is the same as that of sound waves, causing an explosive noise (a *sonic boom*): *break the sound barrier* (ie move faster than the speed of sound).

ˈsound bite *n* a short piece of recorded speech used esp in a news broadcast on television or radio: *a 30-second sound bite.*

ˈsound effect *n* (esp *pl*) a sound other than speech or music used in a film, play, etc to produce a realistic effect: *Taping your own sound effects is an interesting part of video movie making.*

ˈsound wave *n* a VIBRATION made in the air or some other medium by which sound is carried.

sound² /saʊnd/ *adj* (-**er**, -**est**) **1** in good condition; not hurt, diseased, injured or damaged: *sound teeth* ○ *a sound constitution* ○ *of sound mind* (ie not mentally ill) ○ *a house built on sound foundations* ○ *We arrived home safe and sound.* Compare UNSOUND 1. **2** based on reason, sense or judgement; reliable: *a sound argument/investment* ○ *sound advice* ○ *Her policies are environmentally sound.* Compare UN-SOUND 2. **3** [attrib] full and complete; thorough: *give sb a sound thrashing.* **4** careful and accurate; competent: *a very sound tennis player* ○ *a sound piece of writing.* **5** [usu attrib] (of sleep) not disturbed or interrupted: *I'm usually a sound sleeper.* ○ *a sound night's sleep.* **IDM** (as) sound as a ˈbell in perfect condition: *The doctor said I was as sound as a bell.*

▶ **sound** *adv* firmly; deeply: *be/fall sound asleep.*

soundly *adv* in a sound manner; thoroughly and fully: *a soundly based argument* ○ *be soundly beaten at chess* ○ *sleep soundly.*

soundness *n* [U]: *soundness of judgement* ○ *the soundness of the foundations.*

sound³ /saʊnd/ v **1** (not usu in the continuous tenses) **(a)** to give a specific impression when heard: [V-adj] *That music sounds beautiful.* ○ *His voice sounded hoarse.* ○ *His explanation sounds reasonable.* [V-n] *She sounds just the person we need for the job.* **(b)** ~ **(to sb) as if...** / **as though...** / **like...** to give the impression that...: *I hope I don't sound as if I'm criticizing you.* ○ *Your cough sounds as though it's getting worse.* ○ *It sounds to me like you need a holiday.* ⇨ note at FEEL¹. **2(a)** to produce a sound from sth; to make esp a musical instrument produce a sound: [Vn] *sound a trumpet/one's horn* ○ *The bell is sounded every hour.* **(b)** to give out a sound: [V] *The bell sounded for the end of the lesson.* **3** to give a signal by making a sound: [Vn] *sound the alarm* (eg by ringing a bell) ○ *sound the retreat* (eg by blowing a BUGLE). **4** (*techn*) (esp passive) to pronounce sth: [Vn] *The 'b' in 'dumb' is not sounded.* **IDM** **strike/ sound a note** ⇨ NOTE¹. **PHRV** **sound ˈoff (about/ against sth)** (*infml derog*) to talk or express one's opinions noisily about sth: *He's always sounding off about falling standards in education.*

▶ **-sounding** (forming compound *adjs*) having a specified sound or giving a mental impression of a specified kind: *loud-sounding pop music* ○ *a very grand-sounding name.*

■ **ˈsounding-board** *n* a means of making one's opinions, plans, etc known or of testing them before making them known: *The magazine became a sounding-board for its editor's political beliefs.* ○ *It's useful to have a colleague to act as a sounding-board before presenting ideas at meetings.*

sound⁴ /saʊnd/ v [V, Vn] to test or measure the depth of the sea, etc by using a line with a weight attached or an electronic instrument call an **echo- sounder**. **PHRV** **sound sb ˈout (about/on sth)** to try to discover sb's views, opinions, etc on sth, esp in a cautious or RESERVED way: *She has already sounded out her senior colleagues about her proposals for the department.*

▶ **soundings** *n* [pl] **1** careful questions asked in order to find out people's opinions on an issue: *take soundings (on sth)* ○ *What do your soundings show?* **2** measurements obtained by sounding (SOUND⁴ 1); the depth measured: *underwater soundings.*

sound⁵ /saʊnd/ *n* (often in place names) a narrow passage of water joining two larger areas of water; a STRAIT: ˌPlymouth ˈSound.

soundproof /ˈsaʊndpruːf/ *adj* made or constructed so that sound cannot pass through or in: *soundproof material* ○ *a soundproof studio.*

▶ **soundproof** *v* to make sth soundproof: [Vn] *I wish we could soundproof the boys' bedroom!*

soundtrack /ˈsaʊndtræk/ *n* **(a)** (the music, etc on) a track or band at the side of a cinema film which has the recorded sound on it. **(b)** the recorded music from a film, musical play, etc on a tape, disc, etc.

soup¹ /suːp/ *n* [U, C] liquid food made by cooking vegetables, meat, etc in water: *chicken/tomato/ vegetable soup* ○ *tinned/packet soups* ○ a ˈsoup-plate/ -spoon ○ *Will you have some soup before the meat course?* **IDM** **in the ˈsoup** (*Brit infml*) in trouble or difficulties: *If your Mum finds out what you've done, you'll really be in the soup!*

■ **ˈsoup-kitchen** *n* a place where soup and other food is supplied free to people with no money.

soup² /suːp/ *v* **PHRV** **soup sth ˈup** (*infml*) (esp passive) to increase the power of a car, etc by adjusting the engine: *a souped-up old mini* ○ (*fig*) *The 'new' film is just a souped-up version of the 1948 original.*

soupçon /ˈsuːpsɒn/ *n* [sing] ~ **(of sth)** (*sometimes joc*) a very small amount: *a soupçon of garlic in the salad* ○ *Do I detect a soupçon of malice in that remark?*

sour /ˈsaʊə(r)/ *adj* **1(a)** having a sharp taste, like

that of a LEMON or of fruit that is not ripe: *sour gooseberries* ○ *This apple is really sour!* **(b)** (esp of milk) tasting or smelling sharp and unpleasant from the action of bacteria; not fresh: *The milk's turned sour.* ○ *a sour smell.* **2** having or showing a bad temper or feelings of disappointment, hostility, dislike, etc: *a sour and disillusioned man* ○ *What a sour face she has!* ○ *The meeting ended on a sour note with several delegates walking out.* **IDM** **go/turn ˈsour** to stop being pleasant or favourable; to turn out badly: *Their relationship soon went sour.* ○ *His original enthusiasm has turned sour.* **sour ˈgrapes** (*saying*) (said when sb pretends that what they cannot have is of little or no value or importance): *He says he didn't want to marry her anyway, but that's just sour grapes.* See also SWEET-AND-SOUR.

▶ **sour** *v* to become or make sth sour: [Vn] *soured cream* ○ *The hot weather soured the milk.* [V] (*fig*) *His personality has soured.* [Vn] *The dispute soured relations between the allies.*

sourly *adv*.

sourness *n* [U]: *the sourness of the fruit* ○ *the sourness of her expression.*

■ **ˌsour ˈcream** *n* [U] cream that has been deliberately made sour by the addition of bacteria, and is used in cooking.

source /sɔːs/ *n* **1** a place from which sth comes or is obtained: *news from a reliable source* ○ *a limited source of income* ○ *renewable energy sources* ○ *Sex is a source of fascination for most of us.* **2** (esp *pl*) a person or document, etc providing information, esp for study: *He cited many sources for his book.* ○ *Government sources indicated yesterday that cuts may have to be made.* ○ *source material.* **3** the place where a river starts: *Where is the source of the Rhine?* **IDM** **at ˈsource** at the point of origin or beginning: *money taxed at source* (ie before it is given to an employee) ○ *Is the water polluted at source or further downstream?*

sourdough /ˈsaʊədəʊ/ *n* (*US*) [U] a type of dough with a sour taste used for making bread.

sourpuss /ˈsaʊəpʊs/ *n* (*infml*) a bad-tempered person: *She's an old sourpuss.*

souse /saʊs/ *v* **1** [Vn] to soak sb/sth in water; to throw water on or over sb/sth. **2** (esp passive) to put fish, etc into salty water, etc to preserve it: [Vn] *soused herrings.*

south /saʊθ/ [U, sing] (*abbr* S) *n* **1** (usu *the south*) the direction to one's right when one is facing the rising sun: *winds from the south* ○ *The town is to the south of* (ie further south than) *the capital.* ○ *Which way is south?* Compare EAST, NORTH, WEST. **2 the south, the South** the part of any country, etc that lies further south than other parts: *have a house in the South of France* ○ *He came to the south to look for a job.* See also THE DEEP SOUTH.

▶ **south** *adj* [attrib] **(a)** of, in or towards the south: *South Wales* ○ *the South Pacific* ○ *grow roses on a south wall* ○ *on the south coast.* **(b)** coming from the south: *a south wind* (ie blowing from the south).

south *adv* towards the south: *a south-facing garden* ○ *birds flying south for winter* ○ *The ship was sailing due south.* **IDM** **down ˈsouth** (*infml*) to or in the south: *go down south for a few days* ○ *They used to live in Ohio but they moved down south.*

southward /ˈsaʊθwəd/ *adj* going towards the south: *a southward course.*

southwards /ˈsaʊθwədz/ (also **southward**) *adv* towards the south: *driving southwards.* ⇨ note at FORWARD².

■ **ˌsouth-ˈeast** *n* [sing], *adj*, *adv* (*abbr* SE) (the direction or region) HALFWAY between south and east: *live in the south-east* ○ a ˌsouth-east ˈwind ○ *a house facing south-east.* **ˌsouth-ˈeasterly** *adj* **(a)** towards the south-east. **(b)** (of winds) blowing from the south-east. **ˌsouth-ˈeastern** /-ˈiːstən/ *adj* of, from or situated in the south-east: *the south-eastern states of the USA.* ˌsouth-ˈeastwards /-iːstwədz/ (also ˌsouth-ˈeastward) *adv* towards the south-east.

the ˌSouth ˈPole *n* [sing] the point of the Earth that is furthest south. ⇨ picture at GLOBE.

ˌsouth-ˈwest *n* [sing], *adj, adv* (*abbr* **SW**) (the direction or region) HALFWAY between south and west. ˌsouth-ˈwesterly *adj* (**a**) towards the south-west: *travel in a south-westerly direction.* (**b**) (of winds) blowing from the south-west. ˌsouth-ˈwestern /-ˈwestən/ *adj* of, from or situated in the south-west. ˌsouth-ˈwestwards /-ˈwestwədz/ (also ˌsouth-ˈwestward) *adv* towards the south-west.

southbound /ˈsaʊθbaʊnd/ *adj* travelling or leading towards the south: *a southbound train* ○ *the southbound lane of the motorway.*

southerly /ˈsʌðəli/ *adj, adv* **1** to, towards or in the south: *The plane flew off in a southerly direction.* **2** (of winds) blowing from the south: *southerly breezes.*

▶ **southerly** *n* (esp *pl*) a wind blowing from the south: *warm southerlies.*

southern /ˈsʌðən/ *adj* [usu attrib] of, from or situated in the south: *southern Europe* ○ *the Southern states of the USA* ○ *the southern hemisphere* (ie the southern half of the Earth). ⇨ picture at GLOBE.

▶ **southerner** *n* a person born or living in the southern part of a country: *a southerner now living up north.*

southernmost /-məʊst/ *adj* [usu attrib] furthest to the south: *the southernmost point of an island.*

southpaw /ˈsaʊθpɔː/ *n* (*infml*) a left-handed (LEFT²) person, esp in boxing.

souvenir /ˌsuːvəˈnɪə(r); *US* ˈsuːvənɪər/ *n* a thing taken, bought or received as a gift, and kept to remind one of a person, a place or an event: *a souvenir of my holiday* ○ *buy a souvenir programme of the concert* ○ *streets lined with souvenir and gift shops.*

sou'wester /ˌsaʊˈwestə(r)/ *n* a hat made to keep out the rain, with a long wide part at the back to protect the neck.

sovereign /ˈsɒvrɪn/ *n* **1** (*fml*) a person with the highest power in a country, esp a king or queen. **2** a former British gold coin, worth one pound.

▶ **sovereign** *adj* (*fml*) **1** (of power) without limit; highest: *have/exert sovereign power* ○ *a sovereign ruler.* **2** [attrib] (of a nation or state) fully independent and with complete freedom to govern itself: *become a sovereign state* ○ *be given sovereign rights.* **3** [attrib] (*fml*) very effective; excellent: *Education was seen as a sovereign remedy for all ills.*

sovereignty /ˈsɒvrənti/ *n* [U] (*fml*) **1** independent sovereign power: *economic/military/parliamentary sovereignty.* **2** the quality of being a country with this power: *respect an island's sovereignty.*

soviet /ˈsəʊviət, ˈsɒv-; *US* -viet/ *n* (*dated*) **1** [C] any of a number of elected local, district or national councils in the former USSR. **2** **the Soviets** [pl] (*esp US*) the people of the former USSR.

▶ **Soviet** *adj* [usu attrib] (*dated*) of or concerning the former USSR and its people: *Soviet Russia* ○ *the Soviet Union.*

sow¹ /səʊ/ *v* (*pt* **sowed**; *pp* **sown** /səʊn/ or **sowed**) **1** ~ **A** (**in/on B**) / ~ **B** (**with A**) to put or scatter seed in or on the ground; to plant land with seed: [Vn] *sow grass/lettuces* [Vnpr] *sow seeds in pots/rows* ○ *sow a field well with wheat* [V] *Water well after sowing.* **2** ~ **sth** (**in sth**) to spread or introduce feelings, ideas, etc: [Vnpr] *sow doubt in sb's mind* [Vn] *sow the seeds of* hatred/discontent. [IDM] **sow one's wild ˈoats** to go through a period of wild behaviour while young: *He sowed all his wild oats before he married.*

▶ **sower** *n* a person or thing that sows.

sow² /saʊ/ *n* a fully grown female pig. ⇨ picture at PIG. Compare BOAR, HOG 1.

soya bean /ˈsɔɪə biːn/ (also *esp US* **soy bean** /ˈsɔɪ biːn/) *n* a type of bean, originally from SE Asia, used as a substitute for animal PROTEIN in certain foods: *a soya bean casserole* ○ *soya flour/milk/oil.*

■ ˌsoya ˈsauce (also ˌsoy ˈsauce) *n* [U] a dark brown sauce made from soya beans. It has a salty taste and is used esp in Chinese and Japanese cooking: *stir-fried vegetables with soy sauce.*

sozzled /ˈsɒzld/ *adj* [pred] (*Brit infml*) very drunk: *He got absolutely sozzled at the Christmas party.*

spa /spɑː/ *n* a spring of mineral water (MINERAL) considered to be healthy to drink; a place where there is such a spring: *Cheltenham Spa* ○ *spa water.*

space¹ /speɪs/ *n* **1** [C] a gap or an area that is not filled between two or more objects or points: *a narrow/wide/small/large space* ○ *the spaces between words* ○ *There's a space here for your signature.* ○ *find a parking space* ○ *Are there any spaces left in the car park?* **2** [U] an area or a place that is not occupied and is available for use; room(3): *advertising space* ○ *office/housing space* ○ *luggage/storage space* ○ *There isn't much space left for your case.* ○ *Have you enough space to work in?* ⇨ note. **3** [C, U] a large area, esp of land not built on: *open spaces for children to play on* ○ *a country of wide open spaces* ○ *the freedom and space of the countryside.* **4** [U] the dimensions of height, depth and width in which all things exist and move: *He sat staring into space.* **5** (also ˌouter ˈspace) [U] the universe beyond the earth's atmosphere, in which all other planets and stars exist: *journey into/through space* ○ *the exploration of outer space* ○ *space flight.* **6** [C usu sing] an interval of time: (*with*)*in the space of two hours* (ie during a period not longer than two hours) ○ *a space of two weeks between appointments.* [IDM] **be cramped for room/space** ⇨ CRAMP². **watch this space** ⇨ WATCH¹.

■ ˌspace-age *adj* [attrib] (*dated*) very modern and advanced: *space-age technology/equipment.*

ˈspace-bar *n* a bar on a KEYBOARD(1), pressed to make spaces between words.

ˈspace heater *n* (*US*) an electric fire.

ˈspace probe *n* = PROBE 2.

ˈspace shuttle *n* a spacecraft designed for repeated use, eg between the earth and a space station.

ˈspace station *n* a large structure above the earth in space, used eg as a base for scientific research, as a launching pad for spacecraft, etc.

NOTE Space, **room**, **place** and **seat** all describe an area in a room, building, vehicle, etc which can be occupied by somebody or something. **Space** and **room** when they are uncountable are the most general words and describe an undefined area: *The wardrobe takes up too much room.* ○ *There's space next to the desk for a TV.* **Space** when it is countable means a specified area where you can put something: *There were no parking spaces left this morning.* **Place** and **seat** are both countable and are used to talk about specific places, usually for people to sit: *You'd better hurry and get a ticket or there won't be any places left.* ○ *I'd like two seats for tonight's performance.*

---

space² /speɪs/ *v* ~ **sth** (**out**) to arrange things with regular spaces between: [Vnpr] *space out the posts three metres apart* [Vnadv] *holes spaced 10 cm apart* ○ *plants evenly/equally/closely/widely spaced* ○ *The letter was well spaced* (ie typed, etc with a suitable amount of space between each line, etc). [also Vn].

▶ **spacing** *n* [U] the amount of space left between objects, words, etc in laying or setting sth out: *adjust the spacing to get the heading all on one line* ○ *Shall I use single or double spacing* (ie single or double spaces between the lines, eg when typing)?

■ ˌspaced ˈout *adj* [pred] (*infml*) not properly

S

conscious of things around one, esp because of drugs; feeling strange: *spaced out on acid.*

spacecraft /'speɪskrɑːft; *US* -kræft/ (*pl* unchanged) (also **spaceship**) *n* a vehicle for travelling in space: *spacecraft orbiting the earth.*

spaceman /'speɪsmæn/ *n* (*pl* **-men** /-men/; *fem* **spacewoman** /-wʊmən/, *pl* **-women** /-wɪmɪn/) a person who travels in outer space; an ASTRONAUT.

spaceship /'speɪsʃɪp/ *n* = SPACECRAFT.

spacesuit /'speɪssuːt; *Brit also* -sjuːt/ *n* a sealed suit covering the whole body and supplied with air, allowing sb to survive and move about in space.

spacial = SPATIAL.

spacious /'speɪʃəs/ *adj* having or providing a lot of space: *a very spacious kitchen ○ The accommodation was spacious and comfortable.* ▶ **spaciously** *adv*: *spaciously designed/laid out.* **spaciousness** *n* [U]: *White walls give a room a feeling of spaciousness.*

spade

shovel

spade

shovelling snow   digging the garden

spade[1] /speɪd/ *n* a tool for digging, with a long handle and a broad metal blade: *a garden spade ○ take a bucket and spade to the beach.* ⇨ picture. **IDM** **call a spade a spade** ⇨ CALL[1].
▶ **spadeful** /'speɪdfʊl/ *n* (*pl* **-fuls**) an amount of earth, etc carried on a spade: *three spadefuls of sand.*

spade[2] /speɪd/ *n* (**a**) **spades** [sing or pl *v*] one of the four suits (SUIT[1] 2) in a pack of cards. The cards in this suit have a black design shaped like pointed leaves with short stems: *the five of spades.* ⇨ picture at PLAYING-CARD. (**b**) [C] a card of this suit[1](2): *play a spade.* **IDM** **in spades** (*infml*) in large amounts or to a great extent: *She's certainly got ability — in spades.*

spadework /'speɪdwɜːk/ *n* [U] hard work done in preparation for sth: *I have to do all the spadework for the monthly committee meetings.* Compare GROUNDWORK.

spaghetti /spə'geti/ *n* [U] a type of Italian PASTA made in long thin sticks: *spaghetti Bolognese* (ie served with a sauce of meat, tomatoes, etc).

Spam /spæm/ *n* [U] (*propr*) a type of meat in tins, made from chopped cooked HAM(1) and usu eaten cold: *spam sandwiches.*

span[1] /spæn/ *n* **1** the length of time that sth lasts or continues: *a person's average life span ○ a short span of time ○ over a span of six years ○ a span of four generations ○ have a short concentration span* (ie be able to concentrate for only a short period of time). **2** the length of sth from one end to the other; the distance sth can reach: *He doesn't have a big enough span* (ie between the thumb and little finger) *to play both notes on the piano.* **3** a distance or part between the supports of an arch or a bridge: *The arch has a span of 60 metres.* ○ *The bridge crosses the river in a single span.* See also WING-SPAN.
▶ **span** (**-nn-**) *v* **1** to form a bridge or an arch over sth: [Vn] *a series of bridges spanning the river Thames ○ a busy road spanned by a footbridge.* **2** to extend over or across sth: [Vn] *research that spans a number of different subjects ○ a career spanning over*

30 years ○ Her life spanned almost the whole of the 19th century. **3** stretch one's hand across sth to touch sth at each end: [Vn] *Can you span an octave on the piano?*

span[2] /spæn/ *adj* **IDM** **spick and span** ⇨ SPICK.

span[3] /spæn/ (*arch*) *pt* of SPIN.

spangle /'spæŋgl/ *n* (*dated*) a tiny piece of shining metal or plastic used for decoration on a dress, etc, esp in large numbers: *leotards covered with silvery spangles.*
▶ **spangle** *v* ~ **sth** (**with sth**) (*passive*) to cover or decorate sth with or as if with spangles: [Vnpr] *a dress spangled with silver sequins* [also Vn].

spaniel /'spænjəl/ *n* a dog with large ears which hang down. There are several breeds of spaniel: *a cocker spaniel.* ⇨ picture at DOG[1].

Spanish /'spænɪʃ/ *adj* of Spain; of the people of Spain or their language: *Spanish dancing/food ○ My grandmother is Spanish.*
▶ **Spanish** *n* [U] the language of Spain: *Do you speak Spanish?*
■ **the Spanish Main** *n* [sing] the former name for the NE coast of S America and the Caribbean Sea near this coast.

spank /spæŋk/ *v* to hit sb, esp a child, with a open hand, esp on the bottom(3), as a punishment: [Vn] *We never spank our children.*
▶ **spank** *n* a blow with a flat hand, esp on the bottom(3).
spanking *n* a series of spanks; the act of hitting sb in this way: *That boy deserves a good spanking.* — *adj* [usu attrib] (*dated infml*) quick and lively: *We set off at a spanking pace.* — *adv* (*infml*) (used esp before *new* and *adjs* of colour) completely; absolutely: *a spanking new kitchen.*

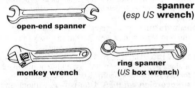
spanner
(*esp US* **wrench**)

open-end spanner

monkey wrench

ring spanner
(*US* **box wrench**)

spanner /'spænə(r)/ (*Brit*) (also *esp US* **wrench**) *n* a tool for gripping and turning a nut(2) on a screw, etc: *I'll need a spanner to change the back wheel.* ⇨ picture. **IDM** **(throw) a spanner in the works** (*Brit infml*) (to cause) a delay or problem in a plan, process, etc.

spar[1] /spɑː(r)/ *n* (**a**) a strong wooden or metal pole used to hold the sails, etc on a ship. (**b**) a structure that supports the wing of an aircraft.

spar[2] /spɑː(r)/ *v* (**-rr-**) ~ (**with sb**) **1** [V, Vpr] to make the movements of boxing but using only light blows, either in training or to test an opponent's defence. **2** to argue with sb, usu in a friendly way: [Vpr] *children sparring with each other* [also V].
■ **sparring partner** *n* **1** a person with whom a boxer fights when training. **2** (*infml*) a person with whom one enjoys frequent, usu friendly, arguments: *They've been sparring partners ever since they were at school together.*

spare[1] /speə(r)/ *adj* **1** extra to what is usu needed or used; kept for use when needed: *a spare bed/bedroom/room* (ie for guests) ○ *carry a spare wheel in the boot of the car ○ Take a spare jumper in case you get cold.* ○ *There's no spare room* (ie space) *in here for another desk.* ○ *Have you got a spare pen I could borrow? ○ Is that pen spare? ○ Sorry, I haven't got any spare cash on me. ○ There were no seats spare so we had to stand.* **2** (of time) for leisure; free: *Since starting my new job, I've had very little spare time. ○ What do you do in your spare time?* **3** (*esp fml*) (of people) thin: *a tall spare figure.* **4** simple and plain:

a few spare pieces of furniture ○ *a spare prose style.* **IDM go 'spare** (*Brit sl*) to become very annoyed or upset: *Your mum'll go spare if she finds out what you've done!*

▶ **spare** *n* a spare part for a machine, car, etc, esp an extra wheel for a car: *I've got a puncture and my spare is flat too!* ○ *I'll show you where the spares are kept.*

■ **¡spare 'part** *n* a part for a machine, car, etc used for replacing an old part that is damaged, broken, etc: *It's difficult to get spare parts for old washing-machines.*

¡spare 'rib *n* (usu *pl*) a RIB of PORK with most of the meat cut off: *barbecued spare-ribs.*

¡spare 'tyre (*US* **'tire**) *n* **1** an extra wheel for a car, etc. **2** (*infml joc*) a roll of fat around a person's waist.

spare² /speə(r)/ *v* **1** ~ **sb/sth (from sth)** to choose not to kill, hurt, harm, destroy, punish or criticize sb/sth: [Vn] *spare sb's life* (ie not kill them) ○ *They killed the men but spared the children.* ○ *Most of the area was demolished but the church was spared.* [Vnn, Vnpr] *He was spared (from) further humili-ation when the referee stopped the fight.* **2** to choose not to use, give or IMPOSE(1) sth: [Vnn] *Try to spare her as much distress as possible when you tell her.* ○ *You can spare yourself an unnecessary journey by phoning in advance.* ○ *Please spare me* (ie do not tell me) *the gruesome details.* [Vn] *No effort/trouble/expense was spared* (ie A lot of effort, etc was made) *to ensure our comfort.* **3(a)** ~ **sth (for sb/sth)** to have more than one needs of sth so that some of it is available for another person or purpose: [Vnpr] *Can you spare any money/old clothes for the homeless?* ○ *I can't spare the time for a holiday at the moment.* ○ *Spare a thought for* (ie Think about) *those less fortunate than you.* [Vn, Vnn] *Can you spare (me) a cigarette?* **(b)** (*infml*) to manage without sb, so that they are available for other jobs or activities: [Vn] *I can't spare him today — we need everybody here.* [also Vnpr]. **IDM no expense spared** ⇨ EXPENSE. **spare sb's 'blushes** (*Brit*) to save sb from an embarrassing situation: *A last-minute goal spared the champions' blushes.* **spare the rod and spoil the 'child** (*saying*) if you do not punish children, esp physically, when they do wrong, you will spoil their character. **to 'spare** that can be spared (SPARE 3); more than is needed; left over (LEAVE¹): *Do you have any milk to spare?* ○ *We caught the bus with only a few seconds to spare.* ○ *There is little time to spare* (ie We must act as quickly as possible).

▶ **sparing** /'speərɪŋ/ *adj* ~ **(with/of/in sth)** (*fml*) giving or using very little of sth; not wasting sth: *be sparing with the sugar* ○ *sparing of one's energy* ○ *He was not sparing in his advice to others.* ○ *They make sparing use of his talents.* **sparingly** *adv*: *Add garlic sparingly.*

spark /spɑːk/ *n* [C] **(a)** a tiny glowing piece of material thrown off from sth burning or produced when two pieces of a hard substance, eg stone or metal, are struck together: *Sparks from the fire were flying up the chimney.* ○ *The fireworks exploded in a shower of sparks.* ○ *Rubbing stones together produces sparks which can be used to start a fire.* ○ (*fig*) *Her criticism of council policy sent sparks flying* (ie caused a lot of argument). **(b)** a small flash of light produced by an electric current or impulse: *sparks from a faulty light switch* ○ *A spark ignites the mix-ture of air and petrol in a car engine.* **2(a)** [sing] ~ **of sth** a small amount of a particular quality: *with-out a spark of enthusiasm* ○ *a speech enlivened by the occasional spark of humour.* **(b)** [sing, U] energy or enthusiasm, esp a small amount which can cause sth greater to develop: *the creative spark which ig-nites the artist's imagination* ○ *All the spark seems to have gone out of her.* **IDM a bright spark** ⇨ BRIGHT.

▶ **spark** *v* **1** to produce a spark(1) or sparks: [V] *I tried to restart the engine, but it wouldn't spark.* ○ *The fire is sparking dangerously.* **2** [Vn] = SPARK STH OFF **PHRV ¡spark sth 'off** to be the immediate cause of sth, esp sth bad; to lead to sth: *an increase in consumer spending sparked off by tax cuts* ○ *His comment sparked off a quarrel between them.*

sparky /'spɑːki/ *adj* (*Brit infml*) full of energy or enthusiasm; lively: *a sparky sense of humour* ○ *I feel quite sparky this morning.*

■ **¡spark-plug** (*Brit* also **¡sparking-plug**) *n* a device for producing an electric spark which fires the pet-rol mixture in an engine: *I need a new set of spark-plugs.* ⇨ picture at CAR.

sparkle /'spɑːkl/ *v* ~ **(with sth) 1** to shine brightly with flashes of light: [V] *Her diamonds sparkled in the candlelight.* [Vpr] *pavements sparkling with frost* ○ *Her eyes sparkled with excitement.* **2** (*approv*) to be full of enthusiasm or humour: [V] *She always sparkles at parties.* [also Vpr].

▶ **sparkle** *n* [sing] **(a)** a flash of light: *the sparkle of sunlight on snow* ○ *There was a sudden sparkle as the fireworks were lit.* ○ (*fig*) *There was a sparkle of mischief in her eye.* **(b)** [U] a lively original quality: *a performance that lacked sparkle.*

sparkler /'spɑːklə(r)/ *n* a type of small FIREWORK, held in the hand, that produces showers of sparks (SPARK 1a) when lit.

sparkling /'spɑːklɪŋ/ *adj* **1** (also *infml* **sparkly**) shining with flashes of light: *the sparkling blue wa-ters of the Mediterranean.* **2** lively; brilliant; humorous: *sparkling conversation* ○ *a sparkling young woman* ○ *The champion was in sparkling form.* **3** (of drinks) producing tiny bubbles of gas: *sparkling wine.*

sparrow /'spærəʊ/ *n* a small brown and grey bird common in many parts of the world. There are several different types of sparrow.

sparrowhawk /'spærəʊhɔːk/ *n* a small HAWK¹(1) that eats smaller birds.

sparse /spɑːs/ *adj* (**-r, -st**) present only in small amounts; thin and scattered: *a sparse population* ○ *Vegetation becomes sparse higher up the mountain.* ○ *Television coverage of the event was rather sparse.* ▶ **sparsely** *adv*: *a sparsely furnished room* (ie one with little furniture) ○ *a sparsely populated region.* **sparseness** *n* [U].

spartan /'spɑːtn/ *adj* (*fml*) (of conditions) simple and harsh; without comforts or special pleasures: *the spartan life of a refugee camp* ○ *a spartan meal/diet.*

spasm /'spæzəm/ *n* **1** [C] a sudden, short but in-tense experience, feeling or period of activity: *a spasm of energy/excitement/fear/pain/coughing* ○ *Artistic inspiration comes in spasms.* **2** [C, U] a sud-den strong tightening of the muscles which one is unable to control: *muscular spasms* ○ *My back muscles were in/went into spasm.*

spasmodic /spæz'mɒdɪk/ *adj* **1** occurring or done for short periods at a time, at intervals which are not regular: *spasmodic efforts to clean the house* ○ *The attacks were spasmodic and ineffective.* **2** (*med-ical*) occurring in spasms: *spasmodic coughing.* ▶ **spasmodically** /-klɪ/ *adv*: *a spasmodically brilliant player.*

spastic /'spæstɪk/ *adj* (*medical*) suffering from ce-rebral palsy (CEREBRAL), and unable to control one's movements properly: *spastic children* ○ *spastic para-lysis.* ▶ **spastic** *n*: *a special school for spastics.*

spat¹ *pt, pp* of SPIT¹.

spat² /spæt/ *n* (*infml*) a small or unimportant quar-rel: *a spat between brother and sister.*

spat³ /spæt/ *n* (usu *pl*) a cloth or leather covering for the ankle formerly worn by men over the shoe and fastened at the side.

spate /speɪt/ *n* [sing] a large number of things or

S

events that occur suddenly and within a short period: *a spate of orders for our products* ○ *a recent spate of burglaries in the area.* **IDM in full spate** ⇨ FULL. **in (full)** ˈspate (of a river) flowing strongly at a much higher level than normal: *The Thames was in (full) spate.*

spatial (also **spacial**) /ˈspeɪʃl/ *adj* (*fml or techn*) relating to space as a physical dimension: *the spatial arrangement of atoms within the molecule* ○ *exercises to develop a child's spatial awareness* (ie the ability to judge the positions and distances of objects). ▶ **spatially** /-ʃəli/ *adv*.

spatter /ˈspætə(r)/ *v* (**a**) ~ **sth (on/over sb/sth)**; ~ **sb/sth (with sth)** to scatter drops of sth over sb/sth: [Vnpr] *spatter oil on one's clothes/spatter one's clothes with oil* ○ *As the bus passed it spattered us with mud.* ○ *the blood-spattered walls of the abattoir* [also Vn]. ⇨ note at SPRAY². (**b**) to fall noisily on a surface in large drops: [Vpr, Vp] *We heard the rain spattering (down) on the roof of the hut.* [Vn] *Mud spattered the pavements as the lorry roared past.*
▶ **spatter** (also **spattering**) *n* [sing] ~ (**of sth**) (**a**) a flat sound made by large drops of sth hitting a surface: *the spatter of rain on the windows.* (**b**) a small amount of sth: *a spatter of bullets* ○ *a spattering of applause.*

spatula /ˈspætʃələ/ *n* **1** a tool with a wide flat blade used for mixing and spreading things, esp in cooking and painting: *He scraped the mixture out of the bowl with a plastic/wooden spatula.* ⇨ picture at KITCHEN. **2** (*esp US*) = FISH-SLICE. **3** a thin wood or metal instrument used by a doctor for pressing the tongue down when examining the throat.

spawn /spɔːn/ *v* **1** (of fish, frogs (FROG 1), etc) to produce eggs: [V] *The salmon swim up-river to spawn.* [Vn] *Frogs spawn hundreds of eggs at a time.* **2** (*esp derog*) to produce sth, often in great numbers: [Vn] *departments which spawn committees and sub-committees* ○ *a new terrorist movement spawned by an alliance of extremist groups.*
▶ **spawn** *n* [U] (esp in compounds) the eggs of fish, frogs (FROG 1), etc. See also FROG-SPAWN.

spay /speɪ/ *v* to remove the ovaries (OVARY 1) of a female animal to prevent it breeding: [Vn] *Have you had your cat spayed?*

speak /spiːk/ *v* (*pt* **spoke** /spəʊk/; *pp* **spoken** /ˈspəʊkən/) ⇨ note. **1** to say words: [V] *He can't speak because of a throat infection.* ○ *The noise was so loud I could hardly hear myself speak.* [Vpr] *speak into a microphone* [Vadv] *Please speak more slowly.* **2(a)** ~ **of/about sth** to talk or say sth about sth; to mention sth: [Vpr] *She spoke about her plans for the future.* ○ *The witnesses spoke of a great ball of flame.* ○ *The area has been spoken of as a possible site for the new factory.* (**b**) ~ (**to sb**); (*esp US*) ~ (**with sb**) to have a conversation with sb; to address sb in words: [V] *I saw her in the street the other day but we didn't speak.* [Vpr] *Pay attention when I'm speaking to you!* ○ *I was speaking to/with him only yesterday.* ○ *The President refused to speak to/with the waiting journalists.* ○ *'Do you know him?' 'Not to speak to.'* (**c**) ~ (**to sb**); (*esp US*) ~ (**with sb**) to say sth to sb on the telephone: [Vpr] *May I speak to Susan* (ie at the beginning of a telephone conversation)? [V] *'Is that Susan?' 'Speaking* (ie Yes, this is Susan speaking).*' **3(a)** (not in the continuous tenses) to know and be able to use a language: [Vn] *He speaks several languages/a little Urdu/an unusual dialect.* ○ *Do you speak English?* (**b**) to say sth or express oneself in a particular language: [Vn] *What language are they speaking?* [Vn, Vpr] *I spoke (in) German at the meeting.* **4** ~ (**on/about sth**); ~ (**against sth**) to make a speech to an audience: [V] *speak in public* ○ *She spoke for forty minutes at the conference.* [Vpr] *I told him to speak on any subject he wanted.* ○ *speak in favour of/against the motion.* **5** to say or state sth:

[Vn] *speak the truth* ○ *He spoke only two words the whole evening.* **6** ~ (**to sb**) (usu in negative sentences) (*infml*) to be on friendly or polite terms with sb: [V, Vpr] *They're not speaking (to each other) after their argument.* **IDM actions speak louder than words** ⇨ ACTION. **be on** ˈspeaking terms (with **sb**) to be on friendly or polite terms; to be willing to talk to sb, esp after an argument: *She has not been on speaking terms with her parents for years.* **the facts speak for themselves** ⇨ FACT. **in a manner of speaking** ⇨ MANNER. **not to** ˈspeak of; **no sth/nothing to** ˈspeak of such a small amount of sth that it is not worth mentioning: *We haven't had any summer to speak of.* ○ *We've eaten no food to speak of today.* ○ *She has saved a little money, but nothing to* ˈspeak of. ˈroughly, ˈgenerally, ˈpersonally, etc speaking in a rough, general, etc way; from a general, personal, etc point of view: ˈ*Generally speaking, I don't like spicy food.* ○ ˈ*Personally speaking, I prefer the second candidate.* ○ *Napoleon was a giant among men, meta*ˈphorically speaking.* ○ *Environ*ˈmentally speaking, these products are quite harmful.* See also STRICTLY SPEAKING. ˌ**so to** ˈspeak (used with an unusual word, expression or image) one could say; as it were: *Teachers need to learn from their students, so to speak.* **speak for it**ˈself/ themˈselves to need no explaining; to have an obvious meaning: *Recent events speak for themselves.* **speak for one**ˈself to express one's opinion or wishes in one's own way: *I'm quite capable of speaking for myself, thank you!* **speak for your**ˈself (*joc or derog catchphrase*) you must not think that your opinions or wishes are shared by everyone: *'We all played very badly.' 'Speak for yourself, I think I played quite well!'* **speaking as sth** (used to indicate one's role, position or motive when expressing an opinion): *Speaking as a parent, I am very concerned about standards of education.* **speak one's** ˈmind to express one's views directly and honestly. **speak/talk of the devil** ⇨ DEVIL¹. **speak/talk the same language** ⇨ LANGUAGE. **speak** ˈvolumes about/for sth to be a strong illustration or strong evidence of sth: *These statistics speak volumes about the country's economic decline.* ○ *This letter speaks volumes for her honesty.* **speak** ˈwell/ˈill of sb (*fml*) to speak in a kind or positive/an unkind or negative way about sb: *Your teacher speaks well of you.* ○ *Don't speak ill of the dead.* **strictly speaking** ⇨ STRICTLY. **PHRV** ˈspeak for sb (no passive) to state the wishes or views of sb; to act as a representative for sb: *I can't speak for the others, but I'd love to come myself.* ○ *Our party speaks for the poor and unemployed.* ˈspeak of sth (*fml*) to indicate sth; to suggest sth: *Her behaviour speaks of suffering bravely borne.* ˌspeak ˈout (against sth) to say in a bold and clear manner what one thinks, esp in opposition to sth: *He was the only one to speak out against the closure of the hospital.* ○ *I will continue to speak out on matters of public concern.* ˈspeak to sb (about sth) (*infml*) to talk to sb in a severe way about sth that they should not have done: *This is the third time I've had to speak to you about being late.* ˌspeak ˈup to speak louder: *Please speak up — we can't hear you at the back.* ˌspeak ˈup (for sb/sth) to state clearly and freely what one thinks, esp on behalf of sb or in favour of sth: *It's time someone spoke up for the less privileged in our society.*
▶ **speaker** *n* **1(a)** a person who gives a talk or speech: *an interesting speaker* ○ *The party leader is a very good/poor (public) speaker.* (**b**) a person who is or was speaking: *I looked round to see who the speaker was.* ○ *The pronoun 'I' refers back to the speaker.* **2** a person who speaks a particular language: *French speakers/speakers of French* ○ *a fluent/native speaker of English.* **3** = LOUDSPEAKER: *Hi-fi systems generally have two speakers.* **4 the Speaker** the person who conducts business and

debates in a law-making assembly, eg the British House of Commons: *the Speaker of the House of Representatives.*

-speaking (forming compound *adjs*) speaking the specified language: *French-speaking Canada/ Canadians.*

■ **the ˌspeaking ˈclock** *n* [sing] (*Brit*) a telephone service that tells one what the current time is.

NOTE Speak and talk are used with similar meaning but **speak to** (**speak with** in American English) is often used in polite requests: *Can I talk to Susan?* ○ *I'd like to speak to the manager, please.* Talk suggests that two or more people are having a conversation: *We talked on the phone for nearly an hour.* Speak is used when one person is addressing a group: *A doctor spoke to the class about the dangers of smoking.* When it is transitive the object of **speak** is usually a language: *He speaks Italian.* ○ *What language do they speak in the Philippines?*

-speak /spiːk/ *suff* (forming uncountable *ns*) (*infml often derog*) the language or JARGON of a particular group, organization or subject: *computerspeak.*

speakeasy /ˈspiːkiːzi/ *n* (*US*) (formerly) a place where alcohol could be bought illegally, esp during PROHIBITION(3).

speakerphone /ˈspiːkəfəʊn/ *n* (*US*) a telephone that can be used without being held because it contains a MICROPHONE and a LOUDSPEAKER.

spear /spɪə(r)/ *n* **1** a weapon with a metal point on a long handle, used esp formerly for hunting and fighting: *brandish/throw/wield a spear.* **2** a long pointed leaf or stem, eg of grass, growing directly out of the ground.

▶ **spear** *v* to strike sb/sth with, or as if with, a spear; to kill sb/sth with a spear: [Vn] *They were standing in the river spearing fish.* ○ *She speared an olive with her fork.* [Vnpr] *He had been speared to death.*

spearhead /ˈspɪəhed/ *n* (usu *sing*) a person or group that begins or leads an attack or campaign: *The new party was the spearhead of popular discontent.*

▶ **spearhead** *v* to act as a spearhead for sth: [Vn] *spearhead a campaign for sexual equality.*

spearmint /ˈspɪəmɪnt/ *n* [U] a common variety of MINT¹(1) used to give flavour to food, etc, esp to sweets and TOOTHPASTE: *spearmint chewing-gum.* Compare PEPPERMINT.

spec¹ /spek/ *n* (*infml*) a detailed description of sth, required for a particular purpose: a SPECIFICATION (1,2).

spec² /spek/ *n* **IDM** **on ˈspec** (*Brit infml*) taking a chance; without being sure of obtaining what one wants: *I went to the concert on spec — I hadn't booked a seat.*

special /ˈspeʃl/ *adj* **1** [usu attrib] not common, usual or general; different from normal: *goods on* **special offer** (ie cheaper than usual) ○ *a school for children with* **special needs** (ie with learning difficulties, etc) ○ *He did it as a special favour.* **2** more important than others; particular: *What are your special interests?* ○ *She's a very special friend.* **3** [attrib] (**a**) designed or arranged for a particular purpose: *a special occasion* ○ *a special train* (eg for a holiday trip) ○ *You'll need a special tool to do that.* ○ *a special correspondent for The Times.* (**b**) used by or intended for a particular person; individual: *She has her own special way of doing things.* **4** [attrib] exceptional in amount, degree, quality, etc: *Take special care of it.* ○ *Why should we give you special treatment?* ○ *He takes no special trouble with his work.* Compare ESPECIAL.

▶ **special** *n* **1** a person or thing that is not of the usual or regular type, esp a police officer, a train or

an edition of a newspaper, etc: *an all night televisionspecial on the election* ○ *Specials were brought in to help the regular police force.* **2** (*US infml*) a reduced price in a shop or restaurant: *There's a special on coffee this week.* ○ *Coffee is* **on special** (ie being sold at a lower price than usual) *this week.*

specially /-ʃəli/ *adv* **1** for a particular purpose: *I came specially to see you.* ○ *I made this specially for your birthday.* **2** (also **especially**) exceptionally; particularly: *I enjoyed the evening, but the meal wasn't specially good.* ⇨ note at ESPECIAL.

■ **ˈSpecial Branch** *n* [Gp] (in Britain) the department of the police force that deals with national security: *be questioned by officers from Special Branch.*

ˌspecial ˈconstable *n* (*Brit*) a person trained to help the police force on particular occasions, esp during an emergency.

ˌspecial deˈlivery *n* [U] the delivery of a letter, parcel, etc by a special, usu faster, service instead of the normal post: *If you want the letter to arrive tomorrow send it (by) special delivery.*

ˌspecial efˈfects *n* [pl] special techniques in filming, or the scenes created by them. Special effects give an illusion of things that it would not normally be possible to film, eg ghosts, space travel, etc.

ˌspecial ˈlicence *n* (*Brit*) a licence allowing a couple to be married at a time or place not normally authorized.

ˌspecial ˈpleading *n* [U] (*law*) reasoning that unfairly favours one side of an argument.

specialism /ˈspeʃəlɪzm/ *n* a specialized area of study or work: *a degree with a specialism in Islamic art.*

specialist /ˈspeʃəlɪst/ *n* a person who is an expert in a particular branch of work or study, esp of medicine: *an ˈeye specialist* ○ *a specialist in computeraided design* ○ *get some specialist advice.* Compare GENERALIST.

speciality /ˌspeʃiˈæləti/ (also *esp US* **specialty** /ˈspeʃəlti/) *n* **1** a service or product for which a person, place, company, etc is well-known; a particularly good product or service: *Wood-carvings are a speciality of this village.* ○ *Home-made ice-cream is one of our specialities.* ○ *a shop selling speciality chocolates.* **2** an interest, an activity, a skill, etc to which sb gives particular attention or in which they specialize: *Her speciality is medieval literature.*

specialize, -ise /ˈspeʃəlaɪz/ *v* ~ (**in sth**) (**a**) to be or become an expert in a particular subject, branch of medicine, etc: [Vpr] *He specializes in oriental history.* [also V]. (**b**) to give particular attention to a subject, product, etc; to be well-known for sth: [Vpr] *a shop specializing in hand-made chocolates.*

▶ **specialization, -isation** /ˌspeʃəlaɪˈzeɪʃn; *US* -lə¹z-/ *n* [U].

specialized, -ised *adj* **1** designed or altered for a particular purpose: *specialized equipment.* **2** of or relating to a specialist: *specialized knowledge/ training.*

species /ˈspiːʃiːz/ *n* (*pl* unchanged) **1** a group of animals or plants within a GENUS(1). Members of a species are able to breed with each other but usu not with other species: *a rare species of beetle* ○ *the human species* ○ *Both species occur in this area.* Compare PHYLUM, CLASS 7, ORDER¹ 10, FAMILY 4. **2** (*infml*) a sort; a type: *an odd species of writer.*

specific /spəˈsɪfɪk/ *adj* **1** detailed and exact: *specific instructions* ○ *What are your specific aims?* **2** ~ (**to sth**) relating to one particular thing, etc; not general: *move from the general to the specific* ○ *beliefs that are specific to this part of Africa* ○ *The money is to be used for one specific purpose: the building of the new theatre.*

▶ **specifics** *n* [pl] particular aspects or details of

sth: *We all agreed on our basic aims, but when we got down to specifics it became more complicated.*

specifically /-kli/ *adv* in a specific manner; particularly: *You were specifically warned not to eat fish.* ○ *The houses are specifically designed for old people.*

specificity /ˌspesɪˈfɪsəti/ *n* [U] (*fml*) the quality of being specific: *The report's recommendations lack specificity.*

■ **spe**ˌ**cific** ˈ**gravity** *n* (*techn*) the mass of any substance in relation to an equal volume of water.

specification /ˌspesɪfɪˈkeɪʃn/ *n* **1** [C esp *pl*] the details describing the design and materials used to make sth: *specifications for (building) a garage* ○ *the technical specifications of a new car.* **2** a description of what is required: *look at the job specification* ○ *The offer did not meet our specifications.* **3** [U] the action of indicating exactly what is required: *the specification of blue as the colour of paint.*

specify /ˈspesɪfaɪ/ *v* (*pt, pp* -**fied**) (*esp fml*) to state sth clearly and definitely: [Vn] *The contract specifies red tiles, not slates, for the roof.* [V.that] *The regulations specify that calculators may not be used in the examination.* [also V.wh].

specimen /ˈspesɪmən/ *n* **1** a thing or part of a thing taken as an example of its group or class, esp for scientific research or for a collection: *There were some fine specimens of fossils in the museum.* ○ *a publisher's catalogue with specimen pages of a book.* **2** a sample, esp of URINE, to be tested for medical purposes: *supply specimens for laboratory analysis.* **3** (*infml*) a person of a specified type, esp one who is unusual in some way: *a fine physical specimen* ○ *The new librarian is an odd specimen, isn't he?*

specious /ˈspiːʃəs/ *adj* (*fml*) seeming right or true but actually wrong or false: *a specious argument.*

speck /spek/ *n* a very small spot; a tiny piece of dirt, etc: *specks of dust/soot* ○ *The ship was a mere speck on the horizon.*

speckle /ˈspekl/ *n* a small mark or spot, usu one of many, often occurring as natural markings on a background of a different colour: *brown speckles on a white egg.* Compare FRECKLE.

▶ **speckled** *adj* marked with speckles: *a speckled hen* ○ *speckled eggs.*

specs /speks/ *n* [pl] (*infml*) = GLASSES: *Has anyone seen my specs?*

spectacle /ˈspektəkl/ *n* **1(a)** a grand public display, procession, performance, etc: *The carnival parade was a magnificent spectacle.* **(b)** an impressive, remarkable or interesting sight: *The sunrise seen from high in the mountains was a tremendous spectacle.* **2** (*usu derog*) an object of attention, esp sb/sth unusual or ridiculous: *The poor fellow was a sad spectacle.* **IDM** **make a** ˈ**spectacle of oneself** to draw attention to oneself by behaving, dressing, etc in a ridiculous way in public: *make a spectacle of oneself by arguing with the waiter.*

spectacles /ˈspektəklz/ *n* [pl] (*dated or fml*) = GLASSES: *a pair of spectacles.*

▶ **spectacled** /-kəld/ *adj* wearing spectacles.

spectacular /spekˈtækjələ(r)/ *adj* **(a)** making a very fine display or show: *a spectacular display of fireworks.* **(b)** impressive or extraordinary: *a spectacular victory by the French athlete* ○ *a spectacular recovery from being three goals down.*

▶ **spectacular** *n* an impressive show or performance: *a Christmas TV spectacular.* **spectacularly** *adv*: *a spectacularly daring performance.*

spectator /spekˈteɪtə(r); US ˈspektərtər/ *n* a person who watches a show or game: *noisy spectators at a boxing match.*

■ **specˈtator sport** *n* a sport that attracts many spectators, eg football: *Many spectator sports are now televised.*

spectral /ˈspektrəl/ *adj* (*fml*) **1** of or like a

SPECTRE (1): *spectral figures.* **2** of a SPECTRUM(1,2): *spectral colours.*

spectre (*US* **specter**) /ˈspektə(r)/ *n* (*fml*) **1** a ghost: *haunted by spectres from the past.* **2** an unpleasant and frightening mental image of possible future trouble: *the spectre of unemployment/war.*

spectro- *comb form* of or concerned with a SPECTRUM(1,2): *spectrometer.*

spectrometer /spekˈtrɒmɪtə(r)/ *n* (*techn*) an instrument for measuring spectra (SPECTRUM 1): *a gamma-ray spectrometer.*

spectroscope /ˈspektrəskəʊp/ *n* (*techn*) an instrument for producing and examining spectra (SPECTRUM 1). ▶ **spectroscopic** /ˌspektrəˈskɒpɪk/ *adj*: *spectroscopic analysis.* **spectroscopy** *n* [U].

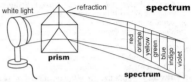

white light · refraction · **spectrum** · red · orange · yellow · green · blue · indigo · violet · prism · **spectrum**

spectrum /ˈspektrəm/ *n* (*pl* **spectra** /ˈspektrə/) **1** an image of a band of colours as seen in a RAINBOW, usu described as red, orange, yellow, green, blue, INDIGO and VIOLET(2): *A spectrum is formed by a ray of light passing through a prism.* ⊳ picture. **2** a series of bands of sound: *the sound spectrum.* **3** (usu *sing*) a complete or wide range of related qualities, ideas, etc: *cover a broad spectrum of interests* ○ *views from across the political spectrum.* ⊳ note at PLURAL.

speculate /ˈspekjuleɪt/ *v* **1** ~ (**about/on/upon sth**) to form opinions without having definite or complete knowledge or evidence; to guess: [Vpr] *speculate about/upon the future* ○ *speculate as to the cause of sth* ○ *I wouldn't like to speculate on the reasons for her resignation.* [V.that] *I can only speculate that he left willingly.* [also V, V.wh]. **2** ~ (**in sth**) to buy and sell goods or stocks and shares in the hope of making a profit through changes in their value, but with the risk of losing money: [Vpr] *speculate in oil shares* ○ *speculating on the stock market* [also V].

▶ **speculator** *n* a person who speculates (SPECULATE 2).

speculation /ˌspekjuˈleɪʃn/ *n* **1(a)** [U] ~ (**over/about/upon/on sth**) the action of speculating (SPECULATE 1): *There was much speculation over the cause of the crash/his resignation.* **(b)** [C] an opinion reached in this way; a guess: *Our speculations proved totally wrong.* **2** [U] ~ (**in sth**) the activity of speculating (SPECULATE 2): *speculation in oil* ○ *dishonest speculation in property development.*

speculative /ˈspekjələtɪv; *US also* ˈspekjəleɪtɪv/ *adj* **1** concerned with or formed as a result of SPECULATION(1): *speculative philosophy* ○ *His conclusions are purely speculative (ie based on reasoning, not facts).* **2** (of business activity) involving the risk of loss: *speculative investment.*

sped *pt, pp* of SPEED *v.*

speech /spiːtʃ/ *n* **1** [U] **(a)** the power or action of speaking: *We express our thoughts through speech.* ○ *His illness left him without the power of speech.* ○ *Speech impediments like stuttering or stammering can usually be cured.* ○ *freedom of speech* (ie the freedom to say openly in public what one thinks, esp on social and political matters). **(b)** a manner or way of speaking: *His speech was slurred: he'd clearly been drinking.* **2** [C] **(a)** ~ (**on/about sth**) a formal talk given to an audience: *make/deliver/give a speech on/about racism* ○ *a very boring after-dinner speech.* **(b)** a usu long group of lines to be spoken by an actor in a play: *He has some marvellous speeches in the next scene.* See also FIGURE OF SPEECH.

▶ **speechless** *adj* unable to speak, esp because of strong feeling: *speechless with rage/surprise* ○ *Anger left him speechless.* **speechlessly** *adv.* **speechlessness** *n* [U].

■ **'speech day** *n* a school celebration held once a year at which there are speeches and prizes are presented.

ˌ**speech 'therapy** *n* [U] special treatment to help people with speech and language problems to speak more clearly. ˌ**speech 'therapist** *n*.

speechify /ˈspiːtʃɪfaɪ/ *v* (*pt, pp* **-fied**) (*infml usu derog*) (esp in the continuous tenses) to make a speech or speeches in a POMPOUS way; to talk as if making a speech: [V] *town councillors speechifying at the opening of a new building.*

speed /spiːd/ *n* **1** [U] the quality of being quick or rapid: *act with speed and decisiveness* ○ *a quick burst of speed* ○ *Speed is his greatest asset as a tennis player.* ○ *The* **speed of events** *in Europe is forcing governments to take action.* ○ *Her leg healed with remarkable speed.* **2** [C, U] the rate at which sb/sth moves: *at a speed of 50 kilometres an hour* ○ *move at (a) very slow speed* ○ *travel* **at top speed** ○ *driving at* **high/low speeds**. **3** [C] (**a**) a measurement of how sensitive photographic film is to light: *What's the speed of the film you're using?* (**b**) the time taken by a camera SHUTTER(2) to open and close: *different shutter speeds* ○ *a photograph taken at a speed of* 1/250 of a second. **4** [U] (*sl*) a drug to produce a sense of excitement and energy. **5** [C] (esp in compounds) a gear: *a* ˌ**ten-speed 'bicycle**. **IDM** **at 'speed** at high speed; fast: *It's dangerous to go round corners at speed.* **full pelt/tilt/speed** ⇨ FULL. **full speed/ steam ahead** ⇨ FULL. **more haste, less speed** ⇨ HASTE. **pick up speed** ⇨ PICK¹. **a turn of speed** ⇨ TURN².

▶ **speed** *v* (*pt, pp* **sped** /sped/; in senses 2 and 3 **speeded**) **1** to move along or go quickly: [Vpr] *cars speeding past the school* [Vadv] *He sped downstairs and flung open the door.* [also Vp]. **2** to make sth move or happen quickly: [Vn] *The drugs will help speed her recovery.* [also Vnpr]. **3** (usu in the continuous tenses) to drive or go faster than the speeds allowed by law: [V] *The police caught him speeding.* **PHRV** ˌ**speed (sth) 'up** to increase or make sth increase speed: *The train soon speeded up.* ○ *They've speeded up production of the new car.*

speeding *n* [U] the traffic offence of driving at an illegal or dangerous speed: *be fined £250 for speeding.*

speedy *adj* (**-ier, -iest**) **1** moving quickly; fast: *They've got some very speedy players.* **2** coming, done, etc without delay: *wish sb a speedy recovery from illness.* **speedily** *adv*: *The situation must be resolved as speedily as possible.*

■ **'speed limit** *n* the highest speed at which it is legal to travel on a particular stretch of road: *keep to/within the speed limit* ○ *exceed the speed limit* ○ *The speed limit on this stretch of road is 40 mph.*

'speed trap *n* a system used by the police to catch people driving vehicles faster than the speed limit.

'speed-up *n* (usu *sing*) (*infml*) an increase in speed: *a speed-up in the rate of production.*

speedboat /ˈspiːdbəʊt/ *n* a motor boat (MOTOR) designed to go at high speeds.

speedometer /spiːˈdɒmɪtə(r)/ *n* an instrument showing the speed of a motor vehicle: *The speedometer is faulty.* ⇨ picture at CAR.

speedway /ˈspiːdweɪ/ *n* **1** [U] (*Brit*) the sport of racing motor cycles (MOTOR) on a special track: *Do you like speedway?* **2** [C] (*US*) a road on which fast driving is allowed.

speedwell /ˈspiːdwel/ *n* a small wild plant with bright blue flowers.

speleology /ˌspiːliˈɒlədʒi/ *n* [U] the scientific study

and exploring of caves. ▶ **speleologist** /ˌspiːliˈɒlədʒɪst/ *n*.

spell¹ /spel/ *v* (*pt, pp* **spelt** /spelt/ or **spelled** /speld/) **1(a)** to name or write the letters of a word in their correct order: [Vn] *How do you spell my name?* [Vnpr] *You can also spell Catharine with a 'K'.* [Vn-n] *You spell his name P-A-U-L.* (**b**) to put the letters of words together in the correct or accepted order: [V] *I've never been able to spell.* [Vn] *Why don't you learn to spell my name (correctly)?* **2** (of letters) to form words when put together in a particular order: [Vn] *C-A-T spells cat.* **3** to have sth as a result; to mean sth: [Vn] *The failure of their crops spelt disaster for the farmers.* **PHRV** ˌ**spell sth 'out 1** to make sth clear and easy to understand; to explain sth simply: *My instructions were simple enough — do I have to spell them out again?* **2** to say aloud or write the letters of a word in their correct order: *Could you spell that word out for me again?*

▶ **speller** *n* a person who spells in a particular way: *She's a good/poor speller.*

spelling *n* **1** [U] (**a**) the ability of a person to spell: *His spelling is terrible.* ○ *They were given a* ˌ**spelling test**. (**b**) the action or process of forming words correctly from individual letters: *a* ˌ**spelling mistake**. **2** [C] the way a word is spelt: *Which is the better spelling: Tokio or Tokyo?* ○ *English and American spelling(s).*

spell² /spel/ *n* **1(a)** [C] words which when spoken are thought to have magical power: *a book of spells* ○ *The wizard recited a spell.* (**b**) [C usu *sing*] a state or condition caused by sb speaking such words: *cast/ put a spell on sb* ○ *be under a spell*. **2** [*sing*] a fascinating or very attractive quality that a person or thing has; a strong influence: *under the spell of her beauty* ○ *the mysterious spell of music*.

spell³ /spel/ *n* **1** a period of time during which sth lasts: *a long spell of warm weather* ○ *rest for a short spell* ○ *She had a* **dizzy spell** *and was forced to sit down*. **2** ~ (**at/on sth**) a period of activity or duty, esp one which two or more people share: *take a spell at the wheel of the car* (eg when two people are sharing the driving) ○ *have a spell on the typewriter*.

spellbinding /ˈspelbaɪndɪŋ/ *adj* holding the attention completely: *a spellbinding performance/quality*.

▶ **spellbound** /-baʊnd/ *adj* [usu *pred*] with the attention held as if by a magical spell: *listen spellbound* ○ *He has the personality and presence to hold audiences spellbound*.

spelt *pt, pp* of SPELL¹.

spend /spend/ *v* (*pt, pp* **spent** /spent/) **1** ~ (**on sth**) to give or pay money for goods, services, etc: [V] *Advertisements aim to persuade people to spend.* [Vn] *She's spent all her money.* [Vnpr] *He spends too much (money) on clothes.* **2** ~ **sth** (**on sth/(in) doing sth**) (**a**) to use time, etc for a purpose: [Vnpr] *spend a lot of time and effort on a project/in explaining a plan* [Vn.ing] *spend one's entire life caring for other people.* (**b**) to use all of sth; to EXHAUST²(2) sth: [Vn] *Their energy was completely spent.* ○ *They went on firing until they had spent all their ammunition.* ○ *The storm quickly spent itself* (ie lost all its force and ended). [also Vnpr]. See also SPENT. **3** to pass time: [Vnpr] *spend a weekend in Paris* ○ *She spent her childhood on the east coast.* [Vnadv] *How do you spend your spare time?* **IDM** **spend the 'night with sb/together** (*euph*) to stay with sb for a night and have sex with them. **spend a 'penny** (*Brit infml euph*) to use the toilet: *I'm just going to spend a penny.*

▶ **spender** *n* a person who spends money in a particular way: *a big/an extravagant spender.*

spending *n* [U] money spent or available to be spent: *The government has reduced public/defence/ welfare spending.* ○ *spending cuts* ○ *Consumer spending rose this year by £70 million.* **'spending money**

n [U] money available for minor expenses, eg entertainments: *How much spending money did you take with you on holiday?*

spendthrift /'spendθrɪft/ *n* a person who spends money too freely or wastes money.

spent /spent/ *adj* (a) [usu attrib] used: *a spent match* ○ *a spent cartridge/bullet.* (b) (*fml*) very tired: *He returned home spent and cold.*

sperm /spɜːm/ *n* **1** [C] (*pl* unchanged or **sperms**) a male cell that can combine with a female egg to develop young: *He has a low sperm count* (ie has few sperm cells and so is not very FERTILE(2)). **2** [U] the liquid produced by a male animal containing sperm; SEMEN.
  ▶ **spermicide** /-ɪsaɪd/ *n* [U, C] a substance that kills sperm. **spermicidal** /ˌspɜːmɪ'saɪdl/ *adj* [attrib]: *spermicidal jelly.*
  ■ '**sperm bank** *n* a place where sperm is stored for future use in artificial insemination (ARTIFICIAL).
  '**sperm whale** *n* a type of large WHALE, hunted for the oily substance contained in its head.

spermatozoon /ˌspɜːmətə'zəʊɒn/ *n* (*pl* **spermatozoa** /-'zəʊə/) (*biology*) a SPERM(1).

spew /spjuː/ *v* **1** ~ (**sth**) (**up**) (*esp infml*) to VOMIT; to be sick: [Vp] *spewing up in the basin* [Vnp] *She spewed up the entire meal.* [V] *It makes me want to spew.* [also Vn]. **2** to rush out or make sth rush out in a stream: [Vpr] *Water spewed out of the hole.* [Vn] *The volcano is spewing molten lava.* [Vpr] *Industrial effluent continues to spew into our rivers.* [also Vp, Vnp].

sphagnum /'sfægnəm/ *n* (*pl* **sphagna** /'sfægnə/) a type of MOSS that grows in wet areas.

sphere /sfɪə(r)/ *n* **1(a)** (*geometry*) a solid figure that is entirely round, ie with every point on the surface at an equal distance from the centre. ⇨ picture at SOLID. (b) any object having approximately this shape, eg a ball. **2(a)** a range or extent of interest, activity, influence, etc: *states formerly within the Russian sphere of influence* ○ *be distinguished in many different spheres* (eg in the arts, literature and politics) ○ *Such matters are outside my sphere (of responsibility.* (b) a group in society; a social class: *She moves in a different sphere to me.*
  ▶ **spherical** /'sferɪkl/ *adj* shaped like a sphere: *a spherical object.*
  spheroid /'sfɪərɔɪd/ *n* a solid object that has approximately the shape of a sphere.
  -sphere *comb form* (forming *n*s) a region surrounding a planet, esp the Earth: *ionosphere* ○ *atmosphere.*
  ▶ **-spheric** (also **-spherical**) (forming *adj*s): *atmospheric.*

sphincter /'sfɪŋktə(r)/ *n* (*anatomy*) a ring of muscle that surrounds an opening in the body and can contract to close it: *the anal sphincter.*

sphinx /sfɪŋks/ *n* (esp **the Sphinx**) a stone figure or statue of a monster with a lion's body and a human or an animal's head. Such statues were common in ancient Egypt. In Greek myths the Sphinx spoke in riddles (RIDDLE[1] 1): *a sphinx-like* (ie mysterious) *smile.*

spic (also **spick**) /spɪk/ *n* (⚠ *sl offensive esp US*) a person from a country where Spanish is spoken, eg a Mexican or Puerto Rican.

spice /spaɪs/ *n* **1(a)** [C] any of various types of substance obtained from plants and used in cooking. Spices have a strong taste and smell: *Ginger, nutmeg, cinnamon, pepper and cloves are common spices.* (b) [U] such substances considered as a group: *mixed spice* ○ *a spice jar/rack.* **2** [U] extra interest or excitement: *a story that lacks spice* ○ *add a bit of spice to their lives.* Compare SALT 5.
  ▶ **spice** *v* ~ **sth** (**up**) (**with sth**) **1** to add flavour to sth with spice: [Vnp] *He spiced up the soup with some chilli powder.* [Vn] *spiced apples* [Vnadv] *Her curries are usually highly/heavily spiced.* [also Vnpr]. **2**

(usu passive) to add a different element, eg humour, to give interest or variety to sth: [Vnp] *something to spice up your love-life* [Vnpr] *a horror movie spiced with dark humour.*

spicy *adj* (-ier, -iest) **1** flavoured with spice; smelling or tasting of spice: *Do you like spicy food?* **2** exciting or interesting, esp because of being slightly shocking, sexually frank, etc: *spicy stories about the star's extramarital affairs.* **spiciness** *n* [U].

spick[1] /spɪk/ *adj* **IDM** ,**spick and 'span** [usu pred] neat, clean and tidy: *They always keep their kitchen spick and span.*

spick[2] = SPIC.

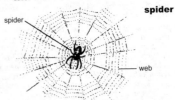

spider

spider

web

spider /'spaɪdə(r)/ *n* a small creature with eight thin legs. Many spiders spin webs (WEB 1) to trap insects as food. ⇨ picture.
  ▶ **spidery** /'spaɪdəri/ *adj* (esp of HANDWRITING) having long thin bent lines like a spider's legs: *written in her spidery scrawl.*

spied *pt, pp* of SPY *v.*

spiel /ʃpiːl, spiːl/ *n* (*infml usu derog*) a long or fast speech, usu intended to persuade sb or as an excuse: *The salesman gave us a long spiel about why we should buy his product.*

spigot /'spɪgət/ *n* a usu wooden plug used to close the hole of a barrel, etc or to control the flow of liquid from a tap .

spike /spaɪk/ *n* **1** [C] a hard thin pointed piece of metal, wood, etc; a sharp point: *sharp spikes on top of the railings in the park* ○ *hair lacquered into spikes.* **2(a)** [C] any of a set of metal points attached to the sole of a sports shoe to prevent one slipping while running. (b) **spikes** [pl] shoes fitted with these, used for running: *a pair of spikes.* **3** [C] a long pointed group of flowers on a single stem: *spikes of lavender.*
  ▶ **spike** *v* **1** to strike or injure sth/sb/oneself with a spike: [Vnpr] *spike oneself/one's leg on a nail* [also Vn]. **2** ~ **sth** (**with sth**) (*infml*) to add alcohol or a drug to a drink: [Vnpr] *Coke spiked with rum* [also Vn]. **IDM** **spike sb's 'guns** to spoil the plans of an opponent.
  spiked /'spaɪkt/ *adj* with a spike or spikes on: *a spiked helmet* ○ *spiked running shoes.*
  spiky *adj* (-ier, -iest) **1** having sharp points: *spiky plants/leaves* ○ *spiky hair.* **2** (*infml*) (of people) easily offended and difficult to please. **spikiness** *n* [U].

spill /spɪl/ *v* (*pt, pp* **spilt** /spɪlt/ or **spilled**) (of liquid) to run or fall over the edge of a container; to allow or cause liquid to do this: [V] *I knocked my mug and the coffee spilt.* [Vp] *He knocked the bucket over and all the water spilt out.* [Vpr] *Tears spilled down her cheeks.* [Vn] *The water jug was too full and I spilt some.* [Vnpr] *Who has spilt/spilled the coffee on the carpet?* [Vp, Vpr] (*fig*) *The fans spilled (out) from the stadium into the streets.* ⇨ picture at POUR. **IDM** **cry over spilt milk** ⇨ CRY[1]. **spill the 'beans** (*infml*) to reveal secret information, esp without intending to do so. **spill 'blood** (*fml*) to kill or injure people: *Much innocent blood is spilt in war.* **PHRV** ,**spill 'over** to fill one place and so move into another; to OVERFLOW(3): *The meeting spilt over from the hall into the corridor.* ○ (*fig*) *Unrest has spilt over into areas outside the city.* See also OVERSPILL.

▶ **spill** n **1** a fall from a horse, bicycle, etc: *have/ take a nasty spill.* **2** = SPILLAGE 2: *an* 'acid spill. **IDM** **thrills and spills** ⇨ THRILL n.

spillage /'spilidʒ/ n **1** [U] the action of spilling sth. **2** [C] (**a**) (also **spill**) an instance of sth being spilled: *prevent further oil/chemical spillages.* (**b**) an amount of sth that is spilt: *mop up the spillage.*

spin /spin/ v (**-nn-**; pt **spun** /spʌn/ or arch **span** /spæn/; pp **spun**) **1(a)** ~ sth (**round**) to make sth turn rapidly round and round a central point: [Vn] *spin the ball* (eg in cricket or tennis) ○ *They spun a coin to decide who should start.* (**b**) to move round and round rapidly: [Vp] *The revolving sign was spinning round and round in the wind.* ○ *The blow sent him spinning back against the wall.* [Vpr] *He watched the couples spinning around the dancehall.* [V] (fig) *My head is spinning* (ie I feel DIZZY). **2** ~ (**round/around**) to turn quickly: [Vp] *She spun round to face him.* [Vpr] *She spun on her heel and flounced out.* **3** ~ (**A into B**)/(**B from A**) to form thread from wool, cotton, silk, etc by making it into fine lengths and twisting it; to spin YARN(1) from wool, etc in this way: [Vnpr] *spin goat's hair into wool/spin wool from goat's hair.* [V] *She sat by the window, spinning.* [also Vn]. **4** (of a SPIDER, SILK-WORM, etc) to produce fine silk or material like silk from the body in order to make a WEB(1), COCOON(1), etc: [Vn] *spiders spinning their webs.* **5** [Vn] = SPIN-DRY. **IDM** **spin (sb) a** 'yarn, 'tale, etc to tell a usu long story, often in order to deceive sb: *The old sailor loves to spin yarns about his life at sea.* ○ *He spun us this unlikely story about being trapped for hours in a broken lift.* **PHRV** ,spin a'long (sth) to move along rapidly on wheels: *The car was spinning merrily along (the road).* ,spin sth 'out to make sth last as long as possible: *spin out the visit by talking* ○ *spin one's money out until next pay-day.*

▶ **spin** n **1** [U, C] a turning or spinning movement: *The bowler gave (a) spin to the ball.* ○ *spin bowling* ○ *He gambled his money on one spin of the wheel* (eg at a game of ROULETTE). **2** [C usu sing] a fast spinning movement of an aircraft as it descends rapidly: *go/ get into a spin* ○ *come/get out of a spin.* **3** [C] (infml) a short ride for pleasure, esp in a car: *Let's go for a spin in my new car.* **IDM** **in a flat spin** ⇨ FLAT¹.

spinner 1 a person who makes thread, etc by spinning: *spinners and weavers.* **2** = SPIN BOWLER. See also MONEY-SPINNER.

spinning n [U] the art or occupation of spinning wool, etc into thread. 'spinning-wheel n (esp formerly) a simple household machine for spinning thread by means of a large wheel operated with the foot.

■ 'spin bowler (also **spinner**) n (in cricket) a bowler who bowls the ball with a spinning movement.

,spin-'dry (pt, pp **-dried**) (also **spin**) v [Vn] to dry washed clothes by spinning them in a revolving drum¹(2) to remove excess water. ,spin-'drier n a machine for doing this. Compare TUMBLE-DRIER.

'spin-off n ~ (**from sth**) a benefit or product that is produced during or following the main activity: *commercial spin-offs from research work* ○ *The TV series was a spin-off from the movie.*

spina bifida /,spaɪnə 'bɪfɪdə/ n [U] (medical) a condition in which certain bones of the SPINE(1) are not properly developed at birth, often causing PARALYSIS in the limbs.

spinach /'spinitʃ; Brit also -idʒ/ n [U] a common garden plant with dark green leaves which are eaten as a vegetable, usu cooked but sometimes raw: *spinach soup.*

spinal /'spaɪnl/ adj [usu attrib] of or relating to the SPINE(1): *a spinal injury.*

■ ,spinal 'column n (usu sing) the SPINE(1).

,spinal 'cord n (usu sing) a mass of nerve fibres

enclosed in the SPINE(1), connecting all parts of the body with the brain.

spindle /'spindl/ n **1** a thin rod on which thread is twisted or wound during spinning. **2** a bar or pin which turns or on which sth, eg an AXLE, turns.

▶ **spindly** /'spindli/ adj (infml often derog) very long or tall and thin: *spindly legs* ○ *a few spindly plants.*

spine /spaɪn/ n **1** the row of bones along the back of humans and some animals; the BACKBONE(1): *He sustained an injury to his spine when he fell off his horse.* ⇨ picture at SKELETON. **2** any of the sharp parts like needles on certain plants and animals: *Hedgehogs and porcupines have spines, and so do some cactuses.* **3** the part of the cover of a book where the pages are joined together. The spine of a book is visible when it is in a row on a shelf. It usu shows the book's title.

▶ **spineless** adj **1** (derog) (of people) weak, cowardly or easily frightened. **2** (of animals) having no SPINE(1).

spiny adj full of or covered with spines (SPINE 2); prickly: *a spiny fish.*

■ 'spine-chilling adj frightening in an exciting way: *a spine-chilling horror story.*

spinet /spi'net; US 'spinət/ n (esp formerly) a type of musical instrument played like a piano.

spinnaker /'spinəkə(r)/ n a large extra sail on a racing YACHT used when sailing with the wind coming from behind. ⇨ picture at YACHT.

spinney /'spini/ n (Brit) a small wood.

spinster /'spinstə(r)/ n (sometimes derog) a woman who has not been married, esp an older woman: *an elderly spinster.* Compare BACHELOR 1.

▶ **spinsterhood** /-hʊd/ n [U] the state of being a spinster.

spinsterish adj (often derog) like or typical of a spinster: *her solitary, spinsterish life.*

spiral

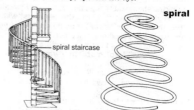

spiral staircase

spiral /'spaɪrəl/ adj **1** moving in a continuous curve that winds round a central point: *a spiral staircase* ○ *A snail's shell is spiral in form.* ⇨ picture.

▶ **spiral** n **1(a)** a line passing in a continuous curve around a central point. (**b**) an object that has a spiral shape: *spirals of dust whipped up by the wind.* **2** a continuous increase or DECREASE in sth, or in two or more things together: *the vicious spiral of rising wages and prices* ○ *the destructive spiral of violence in the inner cities* ○ *Sales suffered yet another downward spiral.*

spiral v (**-ll-**; US also **-l-**) **1** to move in a spiral course: [Vpr] *The falling leaf spiralled to the ground.* [Vadv] *The smoke spiralled upwards.* [also Vp]. to increase rapidly and continuously: [V] *Prices/ Interest rates are still spiralling.* ○ *Spiralling costs are forcing some businesses to cut staff.* [also Vadv]. **PHRV** ,spiral 'down to decrease continuously: *prices spiralling steadily down.*

spirally adv.

spire /'spaɪə(r)/ n a pointed structure, esp on a church tower: *a magnificent view of the spires of the city.* Compare STEEPLE. ⇨ picture at CHURCH.

spirit /'spirit/ n **1** [U, C] a person's mind or feelings as distinct from her or his body; a person's soul: *He*

S

is troubled in spirit/His spirit is troubled. ○ (infml) I might go for a run **if the spirit moves me** (ie if I feel like it). **2** [C] the soul thought of as separate from the body; a soul without a body; a ghost: the spirits of the dead ○ He is dead, but his spirit lives on. ○ It was believed that people could be possessed by evil spirits. See also THE HOLY SPIRIT. **3** [C] (dated) a magical creature, eg a fairy or an ELF. **4** [C] (always with an adj) a person of the specified type, emotion or temper: a brave/proud/generous/mean/free spirit ○ kindred spirits ○ one of the leading spirits of the reform movement. **5** [U] willingness to assert oneself; courage; liveliness: show a little **fighting spirit** ○ break sb's spirit (ie destroy sb's will, independence, etc) ○ Although they lost, the team played with tremendous spirit. **6** [U, sing] feelings of loyalty to a group, team, society, etc: They have (an) amazing **team spirit**. ○ There's not much **community spirit** round here. See also PUBLIC SPIRIT. **7** [sing] a state of mind or mood; an attitude: do sth in a spirit of fun/mischief ○ approach sth **in the wrong/right spirit** ○ 'OK, I'll try.' 'That's the spirit (ie the right attitude).' ○ The party was successful because everyone **entered into the spirit of the thing**. **8(a)** [sing] a characteristic quality or mood of sth: the spirit of the times ○ the pioneer spirit ○ the Christmas spirit. **(b)** [U] the real or intended meaning or purpose of sth: obey the spirit, not the letter (ie the narrow meaning of the words) of the law. **9(a)** [C usu pl] (esp Brit) a strong alcoholic drink: I don't drink whisky or brandy or any other spirits. **(b)** [U] alcohol for industrial, etc use: insects preserved in spirit. See also METHYLATED SPIRITS, SURGICAL SPIRIT, WHITE SPIRIT. **10** spirits [pl] a person's feelings or state of mind: in **high spirits** (ie cheerful) ○ in **low/poor spirits** (ie sad or depressed) ○ raise sb's spirits (ie make sb more cheerful) ○ A glass of brandy will help you to keep your spirits up. **IDM** in 'spirit in one's thoughts: I shall be with you **in spirit** (ie thinking about you though not with you physically). **raise sb's spirits** ⇨ RAISE. the **,spirit is 'willing (but the ,flesh is 'weak)** (saying) one's intentions and wishes are good but weakness, love of pleasure, etc prevent one from acting according to them.

▶ spirit v **PHRV** ,spirit sb/sth a'way/'off to take or carry sb/sth away in a quick, secret or mysterious manner, as if by magic: The band were spirited away at the end of the concert before their fans could get near them.

spirited /'spɪrɪtɪd/ adj [usu attrib] full of spirit(5); lively; forceful: a spirited attack/reply/conversation ○ a spirited horse. **spiritedly** adv.

-spirited (forming compound adjs) having the mood or state of mind specified: ,mean-'spirited ○ ,high-spirited 'children.

spiritless adj **1** depressed or unhappy: The old man seemed dejected and spiritless. **2** not having or showing liveliness or courage; without spirit(5).

■ **'spirit-level** (also **level**) n a glass tube partly filled with water or alcohol, with a bubble of air inside. Spirit-levels are used to test whether sth is level by the position of the bubble.

spiritual /'spɪrɪtʃuəl/ adj [usu attrib] **1** of the human spirit(1) or soul; not of physical things: concerned about sb's spiritual welfare ○ the modern world's lack of spiritual values. Compare MATERIAL². **2** of the Church or of religion: The Pope is the spiritual leader of many Christians. Compare TEMPORAL 1. **IDM** one's **,spiritual 'home** a place where one is, or thinks one could be, happiest; a country to which one feels more strongly attached than to one's own country.

▶ **spiritual** (also ,Negro 'spiritual) n a religious song of the type originally sung by black slaves in America.

spirituality /ˌspɪrɪtʃu'æləti/ n [U] the state or quality of being concerned with spiritual matters.

spiritually /-tʃuəli/ adv: a spiritually impoverished culture.

spiritualism /'spɪrɪtʃuəlɪzəm/ n [U] belief in the possibility of receiving messages from the spirits of the dead; practices based on this belief.

▶ **spiritualist** /-ɪst/ n a person who believes in or practises spiritualism.

spit¹ /spɪt/ v (-tt-; pt, pp spat /spæt/ or esp US spit) **1** ~ sth **(out)** to make liquid, food, etc come out of one's mouth, often with force: [Vn] He was spitting blood after being hit in the mouth. [Vnpr] The baby spat its food onto the table. [Vnp] He took one sip of the wine and spat it out. **2(a)** to pass SALIVA out from the mouth with force: [V] He's inclined to spit when he talks quickly. [Vpr] The boys were spitting out of the classroom window. **(b)** ~ **(at sb)** to do this as a sign of contempt or anger: [Vpr] She spat at him in his face. [also V]. **3(a)** ~ sth **(out)** to say sth violently or forcefully: [Vnpr, Vnp] She spat (out) curses at me. [also Vn, V.speech]. **(b)** to make a short sharp explosive noise to show anger: [V] He walked off spitting with fury. [Vpr] The cat spat at the dog. **4** (of a fire, hot fat, etc) to make a short sharp explosive noise; to throw sth out violently and noisily: [V] fried bacon spitting in the pan ○ Wet logs spit as they burn. **5** (Brit infml) (used with it, in the continuous tenses) to rain lightly: [V] It's not raining heavily any more, but it's still spitting a bit. **IDM** the **very/living/spitting image** ⇨ IMAGE. **spit it 'out** (infml) to say what you want to say quickly and briefly: 'What exactly are you trying to tell me? Come on, spit it out!'

▶ **spit** n **1** [U] liquid that forms in the mouth; SALIVA. **2** [C usu sing] an act of spitting. **IDM** be the **dead spit of sb** ⇨ DEAD. ,spit and 'polish thorough cleaning and polishing of equipment, esp by soldiers: give it some extra spit and polish.

spit² /spɪt/ n **1** a long thin metal rod pushed through meat, etc to hold and turn it while it is cooked over a fire: chicken roasting/turning on a spit. **2** a small narrow point of land that extends into the sea or a lake.

spite /spaɪt/ n [U] an unkind desire to hurt, annoy or offend sb; MALICE: I'm sure he only said it out of spite. **IDM** in 'spite of sth not being prevented by sth; regardless of sth; despite sth: They went out in spite of the rain. ○ In spite of all our efforts we failed. in **'spite of oneself** although one did not intend or expect to do so: He found himself smiling in spite of himself.

▶ **spite** v (only used in the infinitive with to) to upset, annoy or offend sb deliberately: [Vn] The neighbours play loud music every evening just to spite us. **IDM** cut off one's nose to spite one's face ⇨ NOSE¹.

spiteful /-fl/ adj showing or caused by spite; full of spite: a spiteful comment ○ He's just being spiteful. **spitefully** /-fəli/ adv. **spitefulness** n [U].

spitfire /'spɪtfaɪə(r)/ n a person with a fierce temper.

spittle /'spɪtl/ n [U] liquid that forms in the mouth; SALIVA.

spittoon /spɪ'tuːn/ n (esp formerly) a container for spitting into.

spiv /spɪv/ n (dated Brit sl derog) a man who makes money by dishonest business dealings and dresses so as to try and make others believe he is wealthy and successful.

splash /splæʃ/ v **1** ~ sth **(about)**; ~ sth **(on/onto/over sb/sth)**; ~ sb/sth **(with sth)** to make a liquid fly up through the air in drops; to make sb/sth wet by doing this: [Vn] Stop splashing me! [Vnpr] splash water on/over the floor ○ She splashed her face with cold water. ○ splash paint onto the canvas [Vnp] splash water around [Vp] The children love splash-

---

[Vnn] = verb + noun + noun   [V-adj] = verb + adjective   For more help with verbs, see Study pages **B4–8.**

ing about in the bath. ⇨ note at SPRAY². **2** (of a liquid) to fly about and fall in drops: [Vpr] *Water splashed onto the floor.* [Vp] *The rain splashed down all day.* [also V]. **3** to move through water making drops of it fly everywhere: [Vpr] *splash through puddles* [Vpr, Vnpr] *We splashed (our way) across the stream.* **4** ~ **sth (with sth)** (usu passive) to decorate sth with patches of colour, paint, etc: [Vnpr] *a bath towel splashed with blue and green* [also Vn]. **PHRV** **ˈsplash sth across sth** to display a news story, photograph, etc in a prominent position: *The story was splashed across the front page of the newspaper.* **ˌsplash aˈbout/aˈround** to spend money freely: *He thinks he can win friends by splashing money/ dollars about.* **ˌsplash ˈdown** (esp of a spacecraft) to land in water: *The astronauts splashed down in the Pacific.* See also SPLASHDOWN. **ˌsplash ˈout (on sth)** (*Brit infml*) to spend money freely on sth: *She splashed out on a new pair of shoes.*
▶ **splash** *n* **1** a sound or an act of splashing: *He fell into the pool with a splash.* **2** a mark, spot, etc made by splashing: *There are some splashes of mud on your skirt.* **3** a bright patch of colour: *The towel was dark blue with orange splashes.* **4** (*dated Brit infml*) a small quantity of a liquid added to a drink: *a splash of soda-water.* **IDM** **make, etc a ˈsplash** (*infml*) to do sth or happen in such a way as to attract attention, create excitement, etc: *She has made quite a splash in literary circles with her first book.* ○ *Their engagement created a terrific splash in the popular press.*

splashdown /ˈsplæʃdaʊn/ *n* a landing of a space-craft in the sea: *Splashdown is scheduled for 0500 hours.*

splat /splæt/ *n* (*infml*) a sharp sound as of sth wet striking a surface: *The tomato hit the wall with a splat.* ▶ **splat** *adv*: *The omelette fell splat onto the floor.*

splatter /ˈsplætə(r)/ *v* (**a**) (of large drops of liquid) to fall or hit sth noisily: [Vpr] *rain splattering on the roof* [also Vp]. (**b**) ~ **sb/sth (with sth)** to SPLASH(1) sb/sth with a liquid: [Vnpr] *overalls splattered with paint* ○ *A passing car splattered him with mud.* [also Vn, Vnpl]. ⇨ note at SPRAY².

splay /spleɪ/ *v* ~ **(sth) (out)** to make sth become wider at one end or more apart: [Vn] *splayed fingers* (ie spread outwards) [Vnp] *His legs were splayed out at an awkward angle.* [V, Vp] *The pipe splays (out) at one end.*
▶ **splay** *adj* [usu attrib] (esp of feet) broad, flat and turned outwards. **ˌsplay-ˈfooted** *adj* having splay feet.

spleen /spliːn/ *n* **1** [C] an organ of the body near the stomach, which regulates the quality of the blood: *an enlarged/a ruptured spleen.* ⇨ picture at DIGESTIVE. **2** [U] (*fml or dated*) bad temper: *a fit of spleen* ○ *vent one's spleen on sb.* See also SPLENETIC.

splendid /ˈsplendɪd/ *adj* **1** magnificent; very im-pressive: *a splendid sunset/house/achievement* ○ *The hotel stands in splendid isolation surrounded by moorland.* **2** (*infml*) very fine; excellent: *a splendid dinner/holiday* ○ *What a splendid idea!* ▶ **splendid** *interj* (*dated*) (used to express approval or pleasure). **splendidly** *adv*: *Keep going — you're doing splen-didly.*

splendour (*US* **splendor**) /ˈsplendə(r)/ *n* (**a**) [U] the state or quality of being splendid or grand: *the splendour of the stained glass windows* ○ *Can the city recapture its former splendour?* (**b**) **splendours** [pl] the splendid, magnificent, etc features or qualities of sth: *the spendours of Rome* (ie its fine buildings, etc).

splenetic /spləˈnetɪk/ *adj* (*fml*) habitually bad-tempered.

splice /splaɪs/ *v* [Vn] **1** to join two ends of rope by weaving the strands of one into the strands of the other. **2** to join two pieces of wood, tape, film, etc at the ends. **IDM** **get ˈspliced** (*Brit infml*) to get mar-ried: *Tim (and Mary) finally got spliced last week.*
▶ **splice** *n* a place in a film, tape, rope, etc where it has been joined.

splint /splɪnt/ *n* a piece of wood, metal, etc tied to an injured arm or leg to keep it in the right position while it heals: *have/put a leg in splints.*

splinter /ˈsplɪntə(r)/ *n* a small thin sharp piece of wood, metal, glass, etc broken off a larger piece: *remove a splinter from one's finger* ○ *splinters of ice.* ⇨ note at PIECE¹.
▶ **splinter** *v* **1** ~ **(sth) (into/to sth)** to break or make sth break into splinters: [V] *The mirror cracked but did not splinter.* [Vnpr] *The waves smashed the boat against the rocks, splintering it to pieces.* [also Vpr, Vn]. **2** ~ **(off)** to separate from a larger group: [Vp] *extremists who splintered off from the army of liberation.*
■ **ˈsplinter group** *n* a small group that has separ-ated from a larger one, esp in politics.

split /splɪt/ *v* (**-tt-**) (*pt, pp* **split**) **1** ~ **(sth) (up) (into sth)** (of a group of people) to separate or divide into two or more often opposing groups or parties; to cause a group to divide in this way: [Vpr, Vp] *The children split (up) into small groups.* [Vn, Vnpr] *This issue has split the party (from top to bottom).* [also V, Vnpl]. **2** to divide or make sth break into two or more parts, esp from end to end: [Vn] *The wood has split.* [Vn, Vnpr] *She split the log (in two) with an axe.* [Vnpr] *A skilled person can split slate into layers.* [also Vpr, Vnp]. **3** ~ **(sth) (open)** to break open or make sth break open: [V-adj] *The parcel had split open in the post.* [V] *His coat had split at the seams.* [Vn-adj] *He fell and split his head open on the pavement.* **4** to divide sth into several parts; to divide and share sth: [Vn] *split the cost of the meal* [Vnpr] *Would you like to split a bottle with me?* ○ *They split the money between them.* ○ *For the pur-poses of the survey we've split the town into four areas.* **5** (*sl esp US*) to leave a place: [V] *It's boring here — let's split.* **IDM** **split the ˈdifference** (when making a business deal, etc) to settle on an amount between two proposed amounts. **split ˈhairs** (*derog*) to make very small and unnecessary distinctions in an argument. **split an inˈfinitive** (in speaking or writing) to place an adverb between *to* and the infinitive, as in *to quickly read a book.* This is considered by some people to be bad style. **split one's ˈsides (laughing / with laughter)** to laugh wildly. **split the ˈticket** (*US politics*) to vote for candidates of more than one party. **PHRV** **ˌsplit (sth) aˈway/ˈoff (from sth)** to separate from or separate sth from a larger body or group: *The group have split away/off from the official union.* ○ *The storm has split the branch off from the main tree trunk.* **ˈsplit on sb (to sb)** (*Brit infml*) to tell sb in authority sth about a person that will get her or him into trouble: *Billy's friend split on him to the teacher.* **ˌsplit ˈup (with sb)** (*infml*) to end a friendship, relationship or marriage; to separate: *He used to play in a rock band before it split up.* ○ *John has just split up with his girlfriend.*
▶ **split** *n* **1** [C] ~ **(between A and B)**; ~ **(with sb/ sth)** a division or separation, esp resulting from a disagreement: *the split between the Prime Minister and the Cabinet* ○ *splits in/within the Conservative Party* ○ *a solo career following his split with the band.* **2** [C] a crack or tear¹ made by splitting: *mend a split in a skirt.* **3** [C] a sweet dish made from fruit, esp a banana cut in two along its length, with cream, ice-cream, etc on top: *a banana split.* **4** [C] an act or instance of being split. **5** **the splits** [pl] a position taken eg by a dancer or by a GYM-NAST in which the legs are stretched across the floor in opposite directions with the rest of the body upright: *do the splits.*

S

splitting *adj* [attrib] (esp of a HEADACHE) very painful: *I've got a splitting headache.*

■ **split 'ends** *n* [pl] hair on a person's head that is split at the ends.

split in'finitive *n* (*grammar*) an infinitive with an adverb placed between *to* and the verb, as in *to quickly read a book*, considered by some people to be bad style.

split-'level *adj* (of a room, a set of rooms, etc) having parts at different levels on the same floor¹(3): *a split-level bedroom.*

split 'peas *n* [pl] dried peas split into halves.

split perso'nality *n* a mental condition in which a person behaves sometimes with one set of emotions, actions, etc, and sometimes with another set. Compare SCHIZOPHRENIA.

split 'pin *n* a metal pin with the pointed end split so that it can be opened flat to hold the pin in position.

split 'second *n* a very short moment of time: *For a split second, I thought he was going to jump.* **'split-second** *adj* [attrib] very rapid or accurate: *The plan depends on split-second 'timing.*

splotch /splɒtʃ/ (*Brit* also **splodge** /splɒdʒ/) *n* a dirty mark or spot of ink, paint, etc; a patch of colour, light, etc: *splotches of red and gold.* ▶ **splotchy** (*Brit* also **splodgy**) *adj*: *a splotchy pattern.*

splurge /splɜːdʒ/ *n* (*infml*) (usu *sing*) **1** an act of spending money freely: *I had a splurge and bought two new suits.* **2** an expensive event or display intended to attract attention: *a splurge of celebrity guests.*

▶ **splurge** *v* ~ (**sth**) (**on sth**) to spend money freely: [Vnpr] *She won £500 and then splurged it all on new clothes.* [also V, Vn, Vpr].

splutter /'splʌtə(r)/ *v* **1** (also **sputter**) ~ **sth** (**out**) to speak or say sth in a quick confused way, eg from excitement or anger: [V.speech] '*But, but…you can't!*' *he spluttered.* [Vn, Vnp] *splutter (out) a few words of apology.* [Vn] to make a series of spitting (SPIT² 2) sounds: *She jumped into the water and came up coughing and spluttering.* [Vpr] *The engine spluttered into life* (ie started).

▶ **splutter** *n* a spluttering sound: *The candle gave a few faint splutters and then went out.*

spoil /spɔɪl/ *v* (*pt, pp* **spoilt** /spɔɪlt/ or **spoiled** /spɔɪld/) **1** to turn sth good into sth useless, worthless or unpleasant; to ruin sth: *camping trips spoilt by bad weather* ○ *spoilt ballot papers* (ie not valid because not properly marked) ○ *The new road has completely spoiled the character of the town.* ○ *The bad news has spoilt my day.* ○ *Don't spoil your appetite by eating between meals.* **2(a)** to harm the character of sb, esp a child, by lack of discipline or too much attention, praise, etc: [Vn] *a spoilt child* ○ *She spoils those children of hers.* **(b)** to pay great attention to the comfort and wishes of sb/oneself: [Vn] *Everybody enjoys being spoiled from time to time.* ○ *Have another chocolate — go on, spoil yourself.* **3** (of food, etc) to become bad or no longer fit to be used, eaten, etc: [V] *It will spoil if you don't put it in the fridge.* **IDM** **be 'spoiling for sth** to be very eager for a quarrel, an argument, etc: *I could see he was spoiling for a fight.* **be spoilt for 'choice** to have so many possibilities to choose from that it is difficult to make a decision. **spare the rod and spoil the child** ⇨ SPARE². **too many cooks spoil the broth** ⇨ COOK *n*.

▶ **spoil** *n* [U] (usu **the spoils** [pl]) **1** goods stolen from a place, eg by thieves or by an army in time of war: *The robbers divided up the spoils.* **2** profits, benefits, etc gained from sth: *the spoils of high office* ○ *share out the spoils of the estate.*

spoilage /'spɔɪlɪdʒ/ *n* [U] the decay of food, etc.

spoiler *n* **(a)** a device on an aircraft to slow its speed by interrupting the flow of air over it. **(b)** a

similar device on a vehicle to prevent it being lifted off the road when travelling very fast.

spoilsport /'spɔɪlspɔːt/ *n* a person who spoils the enjoyment of others, eg by not wanting to take part in an activity with them: *Don't be such a spoilsport!*

spoke¹ /spəʊk/ *n* any of the bars or wire rods that connect the centre of a wheel to its outer edge, eg on a bicycle. ⇨ picture at BICYCLE. **IDM** **put a 'spoke in sb's wheel** (*Brit*) to prevent sb from carrying out their plans.

spoke² *pt* of SPEAK.

spoken *pp* of SPEAK.

▶ **-spoken** (forming compound *adjs*) speaking in a specified way: *well-spoken* ○ *a soft-spoken man.*

■ **'spoken for** *adj* [pred] already claimed, owned or reserved: *I'm afraid you can't sit there — those seats are spoken for.*

the spoken 'word *n* [sing] language expressed in speech.

spokesman /'spəʊksmən/ *n* (*pl* **-men** /-mən/; *fem* **spokeswoman** /-wʊmən/, *pl* **-women** /-wɪmɪn/) ~ (**for sb/sth**) a person who speaks on behalf of a group, esp one who makes statements to journalists: *Labour's housing spokeswoman* ○ *a spokesman for the government denied the rumours.* ⇨ note at GENDER.

spokesperson /'spəʊkspɜːsn/ *n* (*pl* **-persons** or **-people**) ~ (**for sb/sth**) a person who speaks on behalf of a group: *They chose Robert Powell as their spokesperson.*

sponge /spʌndʒ/ *n* **1** [C] a type of simple sea creature with a light elastic body structure full of holes that can absorb water easily. **2(a)** [C] a part of a sponge or a piece of a similar artificial soft light substance with many holes in it that can absorb liquid and is used for washing or cleaning: *a bath sponge* (ie for washing one's body in the bath) ○ *clean the sink with a sponge.* **(b)** [U] this artificial soft light substance used for filling eg cushions: *a chair filled with sponge.* **3** [C, U] = SPONGE CAKE: *a chocolate sponge.* **IDM** **throw in the 'sponge/'towel** (*infml*) to admit that one is defeated and stop trying.

▶ **sponge** *v* **1(a)** ~ **sb/oneself/sth** (**down**) to wipe, wash or clean sb/oneself/sth with a sponge(2a): [Vn] *sponge a wound* [Vnp] *He sponged down the car with clean water.* **(b)** ~ **sth** (**off/out/up**) to remove sth using a sponge(2a): [Vn, Vnp] *sponge (out) a stain in the carpet* ○ *sponge (up) wine that has been spilt.* **2** ~ (**sth**) (**from/off sb**); ~ (**on sb**) (*infml derog*) to live at sb else's expense; to take money, food, etc from sb without giving or intending to give anything in return: [V, Vn] *She sponges (meals) all the time.* [Vpr] *James is always sponging off/on his friends.* **sponger** *n* a person who sponges (SPONGE *v* 2).

spongy *adj* soft, elastic and able to absorb water like a sponge: *spongy moss.* **sponginess** *n* [U].

■ **'sponge bag** *n* (*Brit*) a small WATERPROOF bag for holding one's soap, TOOTHPASTE, TOOTHBRUSH, etc, esp when one is travelling.

'sponge cake *n* [C, U] a soft light cake made with eggs, sugar and flour.

sponge 'pudding *n* [C, U] a PUDDING like a sponge cake.

sponsor /'spɒnsə(r)/ *n* **1** a person or firm that pays for a radio or television programme, or for a musical, artistic or sporting event, usu in return for advertising: *Royal Insurance, sponsors of the Royal Shakespeare Company.* **2** a person who pays money to charity after another person has completed a specified activity: *We need more sponsors for next week's charity walk.* **3** a person or company that pays for sb's training: *an athlete in need of a sponsor.* **4** a person who introduces a proposal, eg for a new law: *the sponsor of a new immigration bill.* **5** a person who agrees to be officially responsible for another: *act as sb's sponsor when they visit your country.*

▶ **sponsor** *v* to act as a sponsor for sb/sth: [Vn] *a firm sponsoring a new opera production* ○ *sponsor an athlete/a bill/a visitor* [Vn] *a sponsored walk* (ie one over a fixed distance in aid of charity before which those taking part get sponsors).

sponsorship *n* [U] (**a**) financial support from a sponsor: *get sponsorship for a concert/an expedition* ○ *a sponsorship deal.* (**b**) the action of sponsoring sb/sth or of being sponsored: *seek industrial sponsorship.*

spontaneity /ˌspɒntəˈneɪəti/ *n* [U] the quality of being SPONTANEOUS(1b): *the spontaneity of a performance.*

spontaneous /spɒnˈteɪniəs/ *adj* (**a**) done, happening, said, etc because of a sudden impulse from within, not planned or caused or suggested by sth/sb outside: *a spontaneous offer of help* ○ *spontaneous applause.* (**b**) natural, not deliberately used or developed: *a spontaneous manner/style of writing.* ▶ **spontaneously** *adv*: *react spontaneously.*
■ spon₁taneous com'bustion *n* [U] the burning of a mineral or vegetable substance caused by chemical changes, etc inside it, not by the application of fire from outside.

spoof /spuːf/ *n* (*infml*) **1** ~ (**of/on sth**) a humorous copy or PARODY of sth in which its main features are exaggerated and mocked: *a spoof horror movie.* **2** a trick played on sb as a joke.

▶ **spoof** *v* (*infml*) to copy sb/sth by exaggerating and mocking them/it: [V, Vn] *an actor spoofing (emotions).*

spook /spuːk/ *n* (*infml usu joc*) a ghost: *Are you afraid of spooks?*

▶ **spook** *v* (*infml esp US*) (**a**) to frighten sb/sth suddenly: [Vn] *Something in the bushes spooked her horse.* (**b**) ~ (**at sth**) to become suddenly frightened by sth: [Vpr] *spook at the sight of a gun* [also V].
spooky *adj* (**-ier, -iest**) (*infml*) strange in a way that causes fear; ghostly (GHOST): *a spooky old house.*

spool /spuːl/ *n* (*esp US*) = REEL¹.

▶ **spool** *v* to attach sth to or release sth from a spool: [Vnp] *spool thread in/out* [Vnpr] *spool tape onto a reel.*

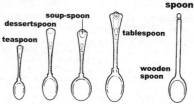

spoon

soup-spoon
dessertspoon
teaspoon
tablespoon
wooden spoon

spoon /spuːn/ *n* (often in compounds) (**a**) an implement consisting of a shallow bowl on a handle, used for stirring, serving and eating food: *a large wooden 'spoon* ○ *a 'soup-spoon* ○ *eat ice-cream with a spoon.* ⇨ picture. See also DESSERTSPOON, TABLESPOON, TEASPOON. (**b**) an amount that this can hold; a spoonful (SPOON): *two spoons of sugar, please.* **IDM born with a silver spoon in one's mouth** ⇨ BORN.

▶ **spoon** *v* to lift and move sth with a spoon: [Vnpr] *spoon sugar from the packet into a bowl* [Vnp] *greedily spooning up her soup.*
spoonful /-fʊl/ *n* (*pl* **-fuls**) the amount that a spoon can hold: *a heaped spoonful of sugar.*

spoonerism /ˈspuːnərɪzəm/ *n* an often humorous result of accidentally changing round the initial sounds of two or more words when speaking, eg *well-boiled icicle* for *well-oiled bicycle.*

spoonfeed /ˈspuːnfiːd/ *v* (*pt, pp* **-fed**) (**a**) [Vn] to feed a baby, etc using a spoon. (**b**) ~ **sth to sb; ~ sb**

(**with sth**) (*esp derog*) to give sb too much help or information, or to teach sb in a way that does not give them the opportunity to think for themselves: [Vn] *Some teachers spoonfeed their students.* [also Vnpr, Vnn].

spoor /spʊə(r)/ *n* [C] a track or smell left by a wild animal, enabling it to be followed.

sporadic /spəˈrædɪk/ *adj* happening or seen only occasionally or in a few places; occurring at intervals that are not regular: *sporadic showers* ○ *sporadic raids/gunfire/fighting.* ▶ **sporadically** /-kli/ *adv.*

spore /spɔː(r)/ *n* (*botany*) any of the tiny cells like seeds by which certain plants reproduce: *Ferns, mosses and fungi produce spores.*

sporran /ˈspɒrən/ *n* a flat bag, usu made of leather or fur, that is worn by men in front of the KILT as part of the Scottish national dress.

sport /spɔːt/ *n* **1**(**a**) [U] (*US* usu **sports** [pl]) physical activity done for exercise and pleasure, usu in a special area and according to fixed rules: *She plays a lot of sport.* ○ *He's very fond of sport.* (**b**) [C] a particular form of such activity: *team sports* ○ *Hockey, volleyball, football and tennis are all sports.* ○ *Which sports do you like best?* ○ *country sports* (eg hunting, fishing and shooting) ○ *sports coverage on TV* ○ *a 'sports field.* See also BLOOD SPORTS, FIELD SPORTS, SPECTATOR SPORT, WINTER SPORTS. **3** [U] (*fml*) amusement or fun: *say sth in sport* (ie not seriously meaning it; as a joke) ○ *make sport of* (ie joke about) *sb/sth.* **4** [C] (*infml*) (**a**) a person who reacts in a generous, cheerful and pleasant way, even in an awkward situation: *Please be a sport and lend me your bike.* (**b**) a person who reacts in the specified way in sport or similar activities when things do not go well for her or him: *a good/bad sport.* **5** [C] (*infml esp Austral*) (used as a friendly form of address, esp to a man): *How are you doing, sport!* **6** [C] (*biology*) a plant or an animal that is different in an unusual way from the normal type.

▶ **sport** *v* **1** to have or wear sth with pride for others to see: [Vn] *sport a moustache/a diamond ring/a flower in one's buttonhole.* **2** (usu in the continuous tenses) to play; to amuse oneself: [V, Vp] *seals sporting (about/around) in the water.*
■ 'sports car *n* a low fast car, often with a roof that can be folded back.
'sports day (*Brit*) (*US* 'field day) *n* a day on which the pupils of a school compete in sports events, with parents as spectators.
'sports jacket *n* a man's jacket for informal wear, not part of a suit. ⇨ picture at JACKET.

NOTE Sport is a general word for games and activities involving physical effort. Football, basketball, cricket, etc are types of **sport** or **games**: *There is tremendous enthusiasm in the States for the game of baseball.* **Games** such as chess and cards are played indoors and involve mental skills. You can play a **game of** tennis, squash, backgammon, etc. A tennis or football (soccer in American English) **match** is an important game played in front of an audience. A **football game** in American English refers to American football. A **race** is a running event to find out who is the fastest. People compete against each other in many different sports and skills to win **competitions** or **contests**: *He won a national singing contest.* ○ *The US has won the Cup for the 16th time out of 19 contests.* ○ *a photography competition.* A **tournament** or **championship** is a series of contests which has one winner or **champion**: *the Wimbledon tennis tournament* ○ *the European Football Championship.*

sporting /ˈspɔːtɪŋ/ *adj* **1** [attrib] connected with or interested in sport: *a sporting event/occasion* ○ *a sporting family* ○ *She was one of my sporting heroes.*

2 fair and generous in one's behaviour or treatment of others: *It's very sporting of you to change your plans because of me.* **IDM** a ˌsporting ˈchance a reasonable chance of success: *give sb a sporting chance* ○ *We've still got a sporting chance of winning.*
▶ **sportingly** *adv*: *He sportingly agreed to play the point again.*

sportscast /ˈspɔːtskɑːst/ *n* (*US*) a television or radio broadcast of sports news or a sports event.
ˈ**sportscaster** *n* (*US*) a person who introduces and presents a sportscast.

sportsman /ˈspɔːtsmən/ *n* (*pl* **-men** /-mən/; *fem* ˈ**sportswoman** /-wʊmən/, *pl* **-women** /-wɪmɪn/) **1** a person who takes part in or is fond of sport. **2** a person who is fair when playing sport, obeys the rules and does not get angry if he or she loses.
▶ ˈ**sportsmanlike** *adj* behaving in a fair or generous way, esp when playing a sport or game: *a sportsmanlike attitude/gesture.*
ˈ**sportsmanship** *n* [U] fair or generous behaviour, esp when playing a sport or game.

sportswear /ˈspɔːtsweə(r)/ *n* [U] clothes worn for playing sports or as casual clothing at other times.

sporty /ˈspɔːti/ *adj* (*infml*) **1** fond of or good at sport: *She's very sporty.* **2** (esp of clothes) attractive and noticeable: *a sporty shirt.* **3** (of cars) fast and elegant: *a sporty Mercedes.*

spot¹ /spɒt/ *n* **1(a)** a small, usu round, mark, different in colour or texture from the surface it is on: *a white skirt with red spots* ○ *Which has spots, the leopard or the tiger?* **(b)** a small mark on sth, esp one that should not be there: *spots of mud on her skirt.* **2** a small red mark on the skin caused eg by disease; a PIMPLE: *a teenage boy worried about his spots* ○ *She had chicken-pox and was covered in spots.* **3(a)** a particular place or area: *a nice picnic spot/spot for a picnic* ○ *stand **rooted to the spot** (ie unable to move)* ○ *This is the (very) spot where he was murdered.* See also BEAUTY SPOT, BLACK SPOT, HOT SPOT, TROUBLE-SPOT. **(b)** (*infml*) a place of entertainment: *a popular night spot.* **4** a feature or part of sth with the specified quality: *There are several weak spots in your argument.* ○ *That evening was the only **bright spot** (ie pleasant event) in an otherwise awful week.* **5** a small drop of a liquid: *Did you feel a few spots of rain?* **6** (usu *sing*) ~ **of** sth (*Brit infml*) a small amount of sth: *Are you ready for a spot of lunch?* ○ *I'm having **a spot of bother** (ie a bit of trouble) with my car.* **7** a place for an individual item of entertainment in a television, radio or theatre show: *a ten-minute guest spot on a radio programme* ○ *She has a regular cabaret spot at a local nightclub.* **8** a position in an order; a rank: *the number one spot in the pop charts.* **9** (*infml*) = SPOTLIGHT. **IDM** **change one's spots** ⇨ CHANGE¹. **have a soft spot for sb/ sth** ⇨ SOFT. **in a (tight) ˈspot** (*infml*) in a difficult position or situation: *I'm in a bit of a tight spot financially.* **knock spots off sb/sth** ⇨ KNOCK². **on the ˈspot 1** immediately; there and then (THERE¹): *He was hit by a falling tree and killed on the spot.* ○ *She was caught stealing and dismissed on the spot.* ○ *an on-the-spot parking fine.* **2** at the actual place where something is happening or has happened: *Let's go over to our reporter on the spot.* ○ *on-the-spot reporting* ○ *The police were on the spot within a few minutes of my telephone call.* **3** in a difficult position where one must respond or act in some way: *The interviewer's questions about her private life really **put her on the spot**.*

spot² /spɒt/ *v* (**-tt-**) **1** ~ **sb/sth (as sth)** (not in the continuous tenses) to see or find one person or thing from among many; to see, notice or recognize sb/sth when it is not easy to do so: [Vn] *He finally spotted just the shirt he wanted.* ○ *She spotted her friend in the crowd.* ○ *I can't spot the difference between them.* ○

Can you spot the flaw in their argument? [V.*wh*] *I soon spotted what the problem was.* [Vn.*in*] *He was spotted by police boarding a plane for Paris.* [Vn-n] *She has been spotted as a likely tennis star of the future.* **2** (*Brit infml*) (used with *it*) to rain slightly: [V] *It's beginning to spot.* [Vpr] *It's spotting with rain.* **3** ~ sth (**with** sth) (usu passive) to mark sth with a spot or spots: [Vnpr] *She wore an apron spotted with household stains.* [also Vn].
▶ **spotted** *adj* marked with a pattern of spots: *a spotted dog* ○ *a red spotted handkerchief.*

spotter *n* **1** (esp in compounds) a person who looks for a specified type of thing or person, as a HOBBY or a job: *a ˈtalent-spotter* (ie an agent who visits clubs, theatres, etc looking for new performers). See also TRAIN-SPOTTER. **2** a plane used for observing enemy positions, etc: *a police spotter plane.*

spotless *adj* **1** very clean and tidy: *He keeps his room spotless.* **2** (*fml*) without moral faults: *a spotless reputation.* **spotlessly** *adv*: *a spotlessly clean kitchen.*

spotty *adj* (*Brit infml*) **1** (*esp derog*) (of a person) having spots (SPOT¹ 2): *spotty youths* ○ *a spotty complexion/back.* **2** marked with spots (SPOT¹ 1): *a spotty pattern/dress.* **3** not even in quality: *a spotty performance.*

■ ˌspot ˈcheck *n* a check made suddenly and without warning on a person or thing chosen by chance: *The campaign against drinking and driving will include spot checks on motorists.*
ˌspot ˈon *adj* [pred] (*Brit infml*) exactly right; accurate: *His assessment of the situation was spot on.* ○ *Your budget figures were spot on this year.*

spotlight /ˈspɒtlaɪt/ *n* **1** (also **spot**) [C] a lamp used for sending a strong beam of light directly onto a particular place or person, eg on the stage of a theatre. **2 the spotlight** [sing] great public attention: *This week the spotlight is on the world of fashion.* ○ *a sportsman who likes to be **in the spotlight** (ie getting a lot of attention or publicity).*
▶ **spotlight** *v* (*pt, pp* **spotlit** /-lɪt/ or, esp in sense 2, **spotlighted**) **1** to direct a spotlight onto sb/sth: [Vn] *a spotlit stage.* **2** to draw or direct attention to sth; to show sth very clearly: *The report has spotlighted real deprivation in the inner cities.* Compare HIGHLIGHT *v*.

spouse /spaʊs, spaʊz/ *n* (*fml or law*) a husband or wife: *Fill in your spouse's name here.*

spout /spaʊt/ *n* [C] **1** a pipe or tube projecting from a container, eg on a TEAPOT, through which liquid can be poured: *The spout is chipped so it doesn't pour very well.* **2** a stream of liquid coming out with great force. **IDM** **up the ˈspout** (*Brit infml*) **1** in a difficult or HOPELESS(1) condition or position: *My holiday plans are completely up the spout.* ○ *If the press hears about this we're all up the spout.* **2** (*infml*) wrong; not accurate: *His estimate of the cost was totally up the spout.* **3** (*infml*) wasted; lost for no good reason: *The money I spent just went up the spout because I couldn't claim any of it back.*
▶ **spout** *v* **1(a)** ~ (**from** sth / **out**) (of a liquid) to come out of sth in a stream with great force: [Vpr] *blood spouting from a wound in his neck* [Vp] *The pipe had broken and oil was spouting out.* [also V]. **(b)** ~ sth (**from** sth / **out**) to send out a liquid in a stream with great force: [Vn] *volcanoes spouting ash and lava* [Vnp] *a broken pipe spouting out water* [also Vnpr]. **2** [V] (of a WHALE) to send a stream of water up through a hole in the head. **2** (*infml usu derog*) to speak at length or in a confident manner, as if making a speech: [Vnpr] *spouting his peculiar ideas to anyone who will listen* [Vn] *He can spout Shakespeare for hours.* [V] *When we got back the party chairman was still spouting.* [also Vnp, Vpr].

sprain /spreɪn/ *v* to injure a joint in the body, esp a

wrist or an ankle, by suddenly twisting it so that there is pain and usu swelling: [Vn] *sprain one's wrist* ○ *have a sprained ankle.*
▶ **sprain** *n* an injury caused in this way: *a bad sprain.*

sprang *pt* of SPRING³.

sprat /spræt/ *n* a small edible European sea-fish of the HERRING family.

sprawl /sprɔːl/ *v* (*often derog*) **1** to sit, lie or fall with the arms and legs spread out in a relaxed or awkward way: [Vpr] *He was sprawling in an arm-chair in front of the TV.* [V] *I tripped over the dog and fell sprawling.* **2** to spread in an untidy way in different directions over a large area: [V] *sprawling handwriting* [Vpr, Vp] *suburbs that sprawl (out) into the countryside.*
▶ **sprawl** *n* [UC usu *sing*] **1** a large area covered with buildings without any formal plan: *the city's suburban sprawl.* **2** a sprawling position or movement.
sprawled *adj* sitting or lying with one's arms and legs spread in a relaxed or awkward way: *They lay sprawled on the floor by the fire.* ○ *He knelt by the sprawled body of his dead child.*

spray¹ /spreɪ/ *n* **1(a)** a small branch of a tree or plant, with its leaves and flowers. (**b**) an artificial ornament of a similar shape: *a spray of diamonds.* **2** a bunch of cut flowers, etc arranged in an attractive way, eg as a decoration or BOUQUET(1): *She carried a spray of pink roses.*

spray² /spreɪ/ *n* **1** [U, C]   **spray**
liquid sent through the
air in tiny drops, eg by
the wind or through an
apparatus: ¹*sea spray* (ie
blown from waves) ○
*spray from a hosepipe/
waterfall* ○ *a fine spray
of liquid mud* ○ (*fig*) *a spray of bullets.* **2(a)** [U, C] (esp in compounds) a substance that is forced out of a special container, eg an AEROSOL, as fine drops: ¹*fly-spray* ○ *spray paint/perfume.* See also HAIRSPRAY. (**b**) [C] a device, eg an AEROSOL, used for applying a liquid in this form: *Where's the fresh-air spray?* ○ *I've lost my throat spray.* ○ *a spray can.* ⇨ picture.
▶ **spray** *v* **1** ~ *sth* (**on/onto/over sb/sth**); ~ *sb/sth* (**with sth**) (**a**) to apply a liquid to sth in the form of tiny drops from a container, eg an AEROSOL: [Vn, Vnpr] *spraying paint (onto a new car)* ○ *a farmer spraying his crops (with pesticide).* (**b**) to scatter sth, esp a liquid on sb/sth or over an area: [Vnpr] *A car drove through the puddle and sprayed me with water.* ○ *spray a target with bullets.* [also Vn]. **2** ~ (**out**) (**over, across, etc sb/sth**) (of a liquid) to be forced out in tiny drops: [Vpr, Vp] *Water sprayed (out) over the floor from the burst pipe.* [also V]. **sprayer** *n* (**a**) a person who sprays sth, usu as part of a job: *He's a paint sprayer in the local factory.* (**b**) an apparatus for spraying: *a crop sprayer.*
■ ¹**spray-gun** *n* a device used to spray paint, etc under pressure onto a surface.
¹**spray-on** *adj* [attrib] (*Brit*) that can be sprayed onto sth/sb from a container: *spray-on hair lacquer.*

NOTE Compare **spray**, **shower**, **spatter**, **splatter**, **splash** and **slosh**. These verbs all describe different ways of spreading liquids and other substances. They can all be used both transitively (you *splash* something) and intransitively (something *splashes*).
You **spray** fine drops of a liquid such as a perfume or a chemical by pressing a button or squeeezing a handle on a container: *Potatoes are sprayed after harvesting with a pesticide to stop mould.* **Shower** usually suggests a large amount of water, dust, etc falling in small drops on somebody or something by accident: *People in the street were showered with broken glass from the explosion.*

Spatter suggests large amounts of paint, mud, etc being thrown at something or somebody and making it or them dirty: *Passing traffic spattered us with melting snow.* Blood, paint, etc is **splattered** over a surface when it is thrown or spread in an uncontrolled way: *The wall behind them was splattered with their own blood.*
Splash means to make somebody or something wet with drops of a liquid, usually water: *Don't let the oil splash you.* **Slosh** suggests large amounts of water moving, or being thrown or poured in a careless way: *There was some water in the boat, sloshing about under our feet.*

spread /spred/ *v* (*pt, pp* **spread**) **1(a)** ~ **A on B** to put a substance onto a surface and form it into an even layer: [Vnpr] *spread butter on bread/glue on paper.* (**b**) ~ **B with A** to cover a surface with a substance in this way: [Vnpr] *spread bread with butter.* (**c**) to be capable of being put onto a surface in this way: [Vadv] *Butter spreads more easily when it's softer.* [also V]. **2** ~ *sth* (**out**) (**on/over sth**) to extend the surface area, width or length of sth, eg by opening it fully or unfolding (UNFOLD) it: [Vn] *The bird spread its wings.* [Vnpr] *spread a cloth on the table* [Vnp] *spread out one's arms* ○ *spread a map out on the floor.* **3** to become or make sth widely or more widely suffered, felt, known, available or used: [V] *The disease is spreading fast.* ○ *Use of computers spread rapidly during that period.* [Vpr] *Fear spread through the village.* ○ *The strike has already spread to other factories.* [Vn] *Flies spread disease.* [Vnpr] *He spread the news around the town.* **4** to become or cause sb/sth to be distributed over a large area: [Vadv, Vpr] *Settlers soon spread inland/across the country.* [Vnpr] *The company gradually spread its branches all over the continent.* [also Vnadv]. **5** to cover or make sth cover a larger or increasing area: [Vpr] *The desert spreads for hundreds of miles.* [Vpr] *The city has spread into what used to be countryside.* ○ *Water had leaked out and was spreading over the floor.* [Vn, Vnpr] *Take care not to spread that dirt (on the carpet).* [also Vn]. **6** ~ *sth* (**over sth**) to distribute sth over a period of time: [Vn, Vnpr] *spread the payments (over three months)* [Vnpr] *a course of studies spread over three years.* **IDM** **spread like** ¹**wildfire** (esp of rumours, reports or disease) to spread among a group of people very quickly: *The news spread like wildfire.* **spread one's** ¹**net** to extend one's power or influence. ¹**spread oneself** to occupy a lot of space, eg by lying with one's limbs extended: *Since there was no one else in the compartment I was able to spread myself.* **spread one's** ¹**wings** to extend one's activities and interests or start new ones: *We hope college life will help him to spread his wings a bit.* **PHRV** ¹**spread (sb/oneself)** ¹**out** to separate from others in a group so as to move over or occupy a wider area: *The search party spread out over the moor.* ○ *Don't all sit together, spread yourselves out.*
▶ **spread** *n* **1** (usu *sing*) ~ (**of sth**) (**a**) the extent, width or area covered by sth: *the spread of a bird's wings.* (**b**) an extent of space or time; a stretch of sth: *a huge spread of unspoilt countryside* ○ *a spread of 100 years.* (**c**) the range or variety of sth: *The survey reveals a wide spread of opinion.* **2** [U] the process or action of spreading (SPREAD 3,4,5) or being spread: *the spread of disease/crime/education* ○ *the spread of a city into the surrounding areas.* See also MIDDLE-AGED SPREAD. **3** [C] a newspaper or magazine article, advertisement, etc, esp one covering more than one printed column: *a double-page spread.* See also CENTRE SPREAD. **4** [C] (*infml*) a large and impressive meal: *We were treated to a magnificent spread.* **5** [U, C] a soft food that is put in a layer on bread, etc; a PASTE¹(3): *chocolate spread* ○ *cheese spreads.* **6** [C] (*US infml*) a large farm or RANCH:

[V] = verb used alone   [Vn] = verb + noun   [Vp] = verb + particle   [Vpr] = verb + prepositional phrase

They've got a huge spread in California. See also
BEDSPREAD.

spreader *n* **1** a thing used for spreading sth: *a
flexible spreader for glue.* **2** a person who makes sth
more widely known, available, etc: *a spreader of
gossip.*

■ ₁spread-¹eagle *v* (esp passive) put sb/oneself into a
position with the arms and legs spread out: [Vn] *The
blow spread-eagled him against the wall.* ○ *Sunbathers
lay spread-eagled on the grass.*

spreadsheet /¹spredʃiːt/ *n* (computing) a computer
PROGRAM(1) into which one enters sets of figures in
columns or rows which can be moved around and
used for calculating; a display or PRINTOUT produced
from such a PROGRAM(1): *enter the data into/onto a
spreadsheet.*

spree /spriː/ *n* (infml) a short period of lively and
enjoyable activity in which one does not feel any
restraint: *go on a spending/shopping spree* ○ *a
drunken spree.*

sprig /sprɪg/ *n* ~ (of sth) a small stem with leaves on
it taken from a plant or bush: *a sprig of holly/
parsley/heather* ○ *decorate a dish with a sprig of
mint.*

▶ **sprigged** *adj* (esp of fabrics) decorated with designs or patterns of sprigs.

sprightly /¹spraɪtli/ *adj* lively and full of energy: *a
sprightly 72-year-old* ○ *He's surprisingly sprightly for
an old man.* ▶ **sprightliness** *n* [U].

spring

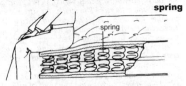

spring

spring¹ /sprɪŋ/ *n* **1** [C] a device of twisted, bent or
coiled (COIL) metal or wire that can be pushed,
pulled or pressed but which returns to its original
shape or position when released: *a watch spring* ○
the springs in an armchair ○ *a spring ¹mattress* (ie
one containing springs in a frame) ○ *Don't bounce on
the bed — you'll break the springs!* ➭ picture. **2** [C]
a place where water comes naturally to the surface
from under the ground: *a cool mountain spring* ○
visit some hot springs ○ *¹spring water.* **3** [U] an
elastic quality; the ability to return to the original
shape after pressure has been released: *The old bed
has lost most of its spring.* **4** [U, sing] a lively, cheerful
quality: *walk with a spring in one's step.* **5** [C] a
quick sudden jump upwards or forwards: *With an
easy spring the cat reached the branch.*

▶ **springy** *adj* (-ier, -iest) **1** returning to the original shape after being pushed, pulled, stretched,
etc; elastic: *a springy bed* ○ *The turf felt springy
under our feet.* **2** light and confident: *a youthful
springy step.*

■ ₁spring-¹loaded *adj* containing a spring¹(1) that
presses one part against another: *a ₁spring-loaded
¹hinge.*

₁spring ¹tide *n* a tide at which there is the greatest
rise or fall of water, occurring soon after the new
and full moon each month. Compare NEAP TIDE.

spring² /sprɪŋ/ *n* [U, C] the first season of the year,
coming between winter and summer, in which
plants begin to grow. Spring lasts from March to
May in the northern parts of the world: *spring
flowers/weather* ○ *In (the) spring leaves begin to grow
on the trees.* See also VERNAL. **IDM** **full of the joys
of spring** ➭ FULL.

■ ₁spring ¹chicken *n* **1** a young chicken for eating.
2 (joc) (usu after a negative) a young person: *She's
no spring chicken, is she?*

₁spring-¹clean *v* to clean a house, room, etc thor-

oughly: [V, Vn] *I'm going to spring-clean (the house)
this weekend.* **spring-clean** *n* [sing] (also US
₁spring-¹cleaning [U, sing]): *give the place a good
spring-clean(ing).*

₁spring ¹greens *n* [pl] (Brit) tender young CABBAGE
plants cooked and eaten as a vegetable.

₁spring ¹onion (US scallion) *n* a small young onion
with a thin white round part at the bottom and a
green stem and leaves, usu eaten raw.

₁spring ¹roll *n* a Chinese food consisting of a thin
pastry case filled with vegetables and sometimes
meat.

spring³ /sprɪŋ/ *v* (pt **sprang** /spræŋ/; pp **sprung**
/sprʌŋ/) **1** to jump quickly or suddenly, esp from
the ground in a single movement; to move suddenly
upwards or forwards: [Vpr] *spring out of bed/into
action/to one's feet* ○ *A cat sprang out of the bushes.*
[Vp] *He sprang up and rushed to the door.* ➭ note at
JUMP¹. **2** to move, open or close sharply and suddenly: [V-adj] *The box sprang open.* [Vp] *The branch
sprang back and hit me in the face.* **3** to operate or
cause sth to be operated by means of a mechanism:
[Vn] *spring a mine* (ie cause it to explode) ○ *spring a
trap* (ie cause it to close suddenly) [Vpr] *The engine
sprang into life.* **4** (infml) to help a prisoner, etc to
escape: [Vnpr] *spring a convict from jail* [also Vn].
IDM **come/spring to mind** ➭ MIND¹. **spring a
¹leak** (of a boat, ship, container, etc) to develop a
hole through which water or another liquid enters
or goes out. **PHRV** **¹spring from sth/...** **1** to have
sth as a source or origin; to originate from sth: *He
sprang from peasant stock.* ○ *Hatred often springs
from fear.* **2** (infml) to appear suddenly or unexpectedly from a place: *Where on earth did you spring
from?* **¹spring sth on sb** (infml) to present, introduce or propose sth suddenly to sb as a surprise or
without warning: *spring bad news/a surprise on sb* ○
I hate to spring this on you at such short notice.
₁spring ¹up to appear, develop, grow, etc quickly or
suddenly: *weeds springing up everywhere* ○ *New
houses are springing up all over the town.* ○ *Doubts
have begun to spring up in my mind.*

springboard /¹sprɪŋbɔːd/ *n* **1** a strong flexible
board from which a person can jump high before
diving (DIVE¹) or performing a gymnastic (GYM-
NASTICS) movement. **2** ~ (to/for sth) a starting point
that helps one to become involved in an activity:
*The college debating society was a natural spring-
board for her career in politics.*

springbok /¹sprɪŋbɒk/ *n* a small S African GAZELLE
that can jump high into the air.

springer /¹sprɪŋə(r)/ *n* a small dog of the SPANIEL
breed.

springtime /¹sprɪŋtaɪm/ *n* [U] the season of spring:
*The blossom on the trees looks lovely in (the) spring-
time.*

sprinkle /¹sprɪŋkl/ *v* ~ A (on/onto/over B); ~ B
(with A) to scatter or throw sth in small drops or
pieces; to scatter small drops or pieces of sth on sth:
[Vnpr] *sprinkle water on a dusty path/sprinkle a
dusty path with water* ○ *sprinkle pepper on one's
food/sprinkle one's food with pepper* [also Vn, Vnp].
➭ note at SCATTER.

▶ **sprinkle** *n* (usu sing) a small amount of sth
scattered over sth: *a sprinkle of salt* ○ (fig) *a sprinkle
of grey in her hair.*

sprinkler /¹sprɪŋklə(r)/ *n* **1** a device for sprinkling
water onto a lawn, etc. ➭ picture at HOUSE¹. **2** a
device inside a building which automatically
sprinkles water if there is a rise in temperature
caused by fire: *a ¹sprinkler system.*

sprinkling /¹sprɪŋklɪŋ/ *n* ~ (of sth/sb) (usu sing) a
small amount or number of sth: *a sprinkling of
rain/parmesan* ○ *Apart from a sprinkling of early
shoppers, the streets were empty.*

sprint /sprɪnt/ *v* to run a short distance very fast: [V] *He had to sprint to catch the bus.* [Vpr] *He sprinted past the other runners just before the finishing line.* [Vp] *She sprinted off/away into the distance.* [Vn] *She sprinted the length of the road.* ⇨ note at RUN[1].

▶ **sprint** *n* **1** a race in which the competitors run or move fast over a short distance: *a 100 metre sprint* ○ *a swimming/cycling sprint.* **2** (usu *sing*) an act of running or moving as quickly as possible: *Her sudden sprint in the middle of the race left the others behind.* ○ *He broke into a sprint and just reached the station on time.*

sprinter *n* a person who takes part in sprint races: *I'm a long-distance runner, not a sprinter.*

sprite /spraɪt/ *n* a fairy, an ELF or a GOBLIN.

spritzer /ˈsprɪtsə(r)/ *n* a drink consisting of wine mixed with soda water (SODA).

sprocket /ˈsprɒkɪt/ *n* any of several teeth (TOOTH 2) on a wheel that connect with the links of a chain or the holes in a film or in paper or tape. ⇨ picture at BICYCLE.

sprout /spraʊt/ *v* **1** ~ (**up**) (**from sth**) (**a**) (of plants or vegetables) to produce new leaves, shoots, etc: [V] *We can't use these potatoes — they've all started to sprout.* [Vpr] *new buds sprouting from the trees* [also Vp]. (**b**) to begin to grow or develop: [Vpr] *Hair sprouted from his chest.* [V, Vp] *Small businesses sprouted (up) all over the country.* **2** to develop, produce or start to grow sth: [Vn] *When do deer first sprout horns?* ○ *Tom has sprouted a beard since we saw him last.*

▶ **sprout** *n* **1** = BRUSSELS SPROUT. **2** a new shoot on a plant. See also BEAN SPROUTS.

spruce¹ /spruːs/ *adj* tidy and clean in appearance; SMART[1](1).

▶ **spruce** *v* **PHR V** ˌ**spruce (oneself/sb)** ˈ**up** to make oneself/sb tidy and clean and SMART[1](1): *He spruced (himself) up for the interview.* ○ *They were all spruced up for the party.*

spruce² /spruːs/ *n* (**a**) [C] a fir-tree (FIR) with many leaves like needles. (**b**) [U] its soft wood, used eg in making paper.

sprung¹ /sprʌŋ/ *pp* of SPRING[3].

sprung² /sprʌŋ/ *adj* fitted with springs (SPRING[1] 3): *a sprung floor/mattress/seat.*

spry /spraɪ/ *adj* (esp of older people) lively and active: *At 80, he's still remarkably spry.*

spud /spʌd/ *n* (*infml esp Brit*) a potato: *peeling spuds.*

spume /spjuːm/ *n* [U] (*fml*) FOAM(1), esp on waves.

spun *pp* of SPIN.

spunk /spʌŋk/ *n* [U] **1** (*dated infml*) courage; spirit. **2** (*Brit sl*) SEMEN.

▶ **spunky** *adj* (*dated infml*) having spunk(1); brave and determined.

spur /spɜː(r)/ *n* **1** either of a pair of sharp projecting points or, esp formerly, small wheels with sharp points, worn on the heels of a rider's boots and used for urging a horse to go faster: *a pair of spurs.* **2** (usu *sing*) ~ (**to sth**) a thing that acts as an encouragement to or reason for action or effort: *the spur of poverty* ○ *a spur to greater efficiency.* **3** an area of high ground extending from a mountain or hill. **4** a road or railway track that leads from the main road or line: *a* ˈ*spur road.* **IDM** **on the** ˌ**spur of the** ˈ**moment** as a result of a sudden impulse, without previous planning: *I bought the house on the spur of the moment.* ○ *a* ˌ*spur-of-the-moment* iˈ*dea.* **win one's** ˈ**spurs** ⇨ WIN.

▶ **spur** *v* (**-rr-**) ~ **sb/sth** (**to / on to sth**); ~ **sb/sth** (**on**) to encourage sb as a reason for sb to act or make an effort; to stimulate sb/sth: [Vnpr, Vnp] *Her magnificent goal spurred the whole team (on) to victory.* [Vnp] *He was spurred on by fierce ambition.* [Vn.to inf] *Failure spurred her to try harder.* [also Vn].

spurious /ˈspjʊəriəs/ *adj* **1** not genuine; false or FAKE: *spurious claims/documents/evidence.* **2** based on false reasoning: *a spurious argument.* ▶ **spuriously** *adv*.

spurn /spɜːn/ *v* to reject or refuse sb/sth in a way that shows contempt for them/it: [Vn] *a spurned lover* ○ *spurn sb's offer of help* ○ *She spurned his advances.*

spurt /spɜːt/ *v* **1**(**a**) ~ (**out**) (**from sth**) (of liquids, flames, etc) to burst out in a sudden stream: [Vpr] *There was water spurting from a broken pipe.* [Vp] *Blood spurted out from the wound.* [also Vadv]. (**b**) ~ **sth** (**out**) to produce liquids, flames, etc in a sudden stream: [Vn, Vnp] *The volcano spurted (out) molten lava.* **2** to increase one's speed suddenly and for a short time: [V, Vpr] *He spurted (past the others) as they approached the line.* [also Vp].

▶ **spurt** *n* **1** a sudden stream of liquid, flames, etc bursting out: *The water came out with a spurt.* **2** a sudden increase in speed, effort, activity, etc for a short time: *put on* (ie make) *a spurt* ○ *make a spurt for the finishing line* ○ *a sudden spurt of energy* ○ *working in spurts.*

sputter /ˈspʌtə(r)/ *v* **1** to make a series of quiet explosive sounds: [V] *a sputtering oil lamp* ○ *The engine sputtered feebly and then stopped.* **2** = SPLUTTER 1: [V.speech] *'What do you mean?' he sputtered.* [also V, Vn].

sputum /ˈspjuːtəm/ *n* [U] (*medical*) liquid coughed up from the throat or lungs, esp as a sign of certain diseases: *blood in the sputum.*

spy /spaɪ/ *n* **1** a person who tries to get secret information about another country, organization, etc, esp one employed by a government to do this: *suspected of being a spy* ○ *spy stories* ○ *a spy plane/ satellite* (ie one used for observing the activities of an enemy). **2** a person who secretly watches and reports on what others do, where they go, etc: *police spies* (ie people employed by the police to watch suspected criminals). Compare MOLE[2] 2.

▶ **spy** *v* (*pt, pp* **spied**) **1** to be a spy; to collect secret information about another country, organization, etc: [V, Vpr] *She was accused of spying (for the enemy).* **2** (*fml or joc*) (usu not in the continuous tenses) to observe or notice sb/sth: [Vn] *We spied three figures in the distance.* [Vn.ing] *I spied someone coming up the garden path.* **IDM** ˌ**spy out the** ˈ**land** to gather information in order to assess a situation before acting: *I got to the restaurant early to spy out the land before she arrived.* **PHR V** ˈ**spy on sb/sth** to watch sb/sth secretly: *spy on the enemy's movements* ○ *I'm sure my neighbours spy on me.*

Sq *abbr* (in street names) Square: *6 Hanover Sq.*

sq *abbr* (in measurements) square: *10 sq cm.*

squabble /ˈskwɒbl/ *v* ~ (**with sb**) (**about/over sth**) to quarrel noisily, esp about unimportant matters: [V, Vpr] *They spent the whole evening squabbling (over what to watch on TV).*

▶ **squabble** *n* a noisy quarrel, esp about sth unimportant.

squad /skwɒd/ *n* [CGp] (**a**) a small group of soldiers working or being trained together. (**b**) (in sport) a group of players or competitors forming a team: *the Olympic squad* ○ *select a squad of 20 players.* (**c**) a section of a police force that deals with a particular crime or type of crime: *an anti-terrorist squad* ○ *fraud/drugs squad.*

▶ **squaddie** *n* (*Brit sl*) a young soldier: *a bunch of squaddies.*

■ ˈ**squad car** *n* a police car.

squadron /ˈskwɒdrən/ *n* [CGp] **1** a group of military aircraft forming a unit in an air force (AIR[1]). **2** a unit of troops.

■ ˈ**squadron leader** *n* an officer commanding a squadron in an air force (AIR[1]). ⇨ App 6.

squalid /ˈskwɒlɪd/ *adj* (*derog*) **1** very dirty and

unpleasant, esp because of poverty or lack of care: *squalid housing* ○ *live in squalid conditions.* **2** having or showing low moral standards; SORDID: *a squalid tale of greed and corruption.* See also SQUALOR.

squall /skwɔːl/ *n* **1** a sudden violent wind, often with rain or snow. **2** a loud cry of pain or fear, esp from a baby.
▶ **squalling** *adj* crying noisily and frequently: *a squalling baby.*
squally *adj* having squalls (SQUALL 1): *squally showers.*

squalor /'skwɒlə(r)/ *n* [U] the state of being dirty and unpleasant; dirty and unpleasant conditions: *the squalor of the slums* ○ *live in squalor.* See also SQUALID.

squander /'skwɒndə(r)/ *v* ~ **sth** (**on sb/sth**) to waste sth foolishly or carelessly: [Vn] *squander a chance/an opportunity* ○ *squander one's youth* ○ *squander a two-goal lead* [Vnpr] *He squandered all his money on gambling.*

square¹ /skweə(r)/ *adj* **1** having four equal sides and four angles of 90°; having the shape of a square²(1): *a square room/table.* ⇨ picture at QUADRILATERAL. **2(a)** (used after a unit of measurement) measuring the specified amount on each of four sides: *a carpet six metres square.* **(b)** (used after a number to give a measurement of area): *a/one square metre* ○ *9 square metres of carpet* ○ *an area of 36 square metres.* ⇨ App 2. **3** having or forming a right angle (RIGHT¹), exactly or roughly; not curved: *square corners* ○ *a square jaw.* **4** broad or solid in shape: *a woman of square frame/build.* **5** [pred] ~ (**with sth**) level with or parallel to sth: *tables arranged square with the wall.* **6** [pred] **(a)** properly arranged or organized: *We should get everything square before we leave.* **(b)** (of accounts) settled; balanced: *get one's accounts square* ○ *Here's the £10 I owe you — that makes us square now.* **7** fair; honest: *a square deal* ○ *square dealings* (eg in business) ○ *I want you to be square with me.* **8** (*dated infml derog*) out of touch with new ideas, styles, etc; old-fashioned; conventional. **IDM** **be (all) 'square (with sb) 1** (in sport) to have equal scores: *all square at the ninth hole* (ie in a golf match). **2** with neither person in debt to the other: *If I give you £10, we can call it all square, can't we?* **a square 'meal** a large and satisfying meal: *He looks as though he hasn't had a square meal for months.* **a square 'peg (in a round 'hole)** (*Brit*) a person whose character or abilities make her or him not suitable for or comfortable in a job or position.
▶ **square** *adv* directly; not at an angle: *hit sb square on the jaw.* **IDM** **fair and square** ⇨ FAIR².
squarely *adv* **1** directly centred; not to one side: *look sb squarely in the eye* ○ *Her hat was set squarely on her head.* **2** in a fair and honest way: *act squarely.* **3** directly: *Economists have put the blame for the crisis squarely on the government.* **IDM** **fairly and squarely** ⇨ FAIRLY.
▪ ¡**square 'brackets** *n* [pl] the marks [ ]. ⇨ App 3.
'**square dance** *n* (*US*) a dance in which sets of four couples dance together, starting by facing inwards from four sides.
'**square knot** *n* (*US*) = REEF KNOT.
¡**square 'root** *n* a number greater than 0, which when multiplied by itself gives a particular specified number: *The square root of 16 is 4.* ○ *What is the square root of 81?*

square² /skweə(r)/ *n* **1** [C] **(a)** (*geometry*) a shape with four straight sides of equal length and four angles of 90°. ⇨ picture at QUADRILATERAL. Compare RECTANGLE. **(b)** a thing having this shape: *the squares on a chess board* ○ *break the chocolate into squares* ○ *wear a silk square round one's neck.* **2(a)** [C] an open area in a town, usu with four sides,

surrounded by buildings: *a market square* ○ *Trafalgar Square.* **(b) Square** [sing] (*abbr* **Sq**) (in addresses) the buildings and streets surrounding such an area: *He lives at 95 Russell Square/Sq.* **3** [C] the number obtained when a number is multiplied by itself: *The square of 7 is 49.* ○ *49 is a perfect square.* **4** [C] (*techn*) an instrument in the shape of a T or an L for drawing or measuring right angles (RIGHT¹): *use a T-square.* See also SET SQUARE. **5** (*dated infml*) a person who rejects or is out of contact with new ideas, styles, etc: *I'm basically a bit of a square.* **IDM** **back to square 'one** a return to the beginning of a project, task, etc because no progress has been made: *That idea hasn't worked, so it's/we're back to square one.*
▪ '**square-bashing** *n* [U] (*infml*) marching exercises done by soldiers on a parade-ground (PARADE).

square³ /skweə(r)/ *v* **1** ~ **sth** (**off**) to make sth have straight sides and right angles (RIGHT¹): [Vnp] *square off some wooden planks to make bookshelves* ○ *It's got rounded not squared corners.* **2** to make sth straight or level: [Vn] *square one's shoulders* (eg to show one is ready to act). **3** (usu passive) to mark sth into squares: [Vn] *squared paper.* **4** (usu passive) to multiply a number by itself: [Vn] *3 squared is 9.* ○ $y^2 = y \times y$ (ie y squared). **5** (*infml*) to give sb esp money in order to obtain their help in sth dishonest: [Vn] *The guards had to be squared before they would let us through.* [Vn.to inf] *He has been squared to say nothing to the police.* **6** (*infml*) to pay an account: [Vn] *We squared the bill and left.* **7** to make the scores, number of wins, etc of two competitors or teams level: [Vn] *Their victory has squared the series.* **IDM** **settle/square an/one's account** ⇨ ACCOUNT¹. **square the 'circle** to do sth that is impossible. **PHRV** ¡**square 'up (to sb/sth)** (*infml*) **1** to stand as if one is prepared to fight sb: (*fig*) *The government is squaring up for another battle with the unions.* ○ *They squared up (to each other) to fight.* **2** to face a difficult situation with courage and determination: *He must square up to the reality of being out of work.* ¡**square 'up (with sb)** to pay sb the money one owes, esp before leaving a restaurant: *Can I leave you to square up with the waiter?* ○ *You pay and we'll square up later.* '**square (sth) with sth** (*infml*) to be or make sth consistent with sth else: *Your theory doesn't square with the known facts.* ○ *The interests of farmers need to be squared with those of the consumer.* '**square sth with sb** (*infml*) to obtain approval for one's actions from sb: *I'm happy for you to proceed, but you'd better square it with the area manager first.*

squarish /'skweərɪʃ/ *adj* approximately square.

squash¹ /skwɒʃ/ *v* **1(a)** to press or crush sth so that it changes shape, becomes very soft, etc: [Vn] *squashed tomatoes* [Vn, Vn-adj] *He sat on his hat and squashed it (flat).* [Vnpr, Vnp] *He squashed his nose (up) against the shop window.* **(b)** to become crushed and soft and out of shape: [Vadv] *Peaches squash very easily.* **2** to force sth/sb/oneself into a small or restricted space: [Vpr] *Don't all try to squash into the kitchen at once.* [Vnpr] *They managed to squash forty people into the bus.* [Vnp] *She squashed her clothes down into the suitcase.* [Vnp] *There were ten of us in the flat, squashed together like sardines.* **3** to destroy a person's confidence and make them silent: [Vn] *I felt completely squashed by her sarcastic comments.* **4(a)** to stop sth; to crush sth: [Vn] *squash a revolt/rebellion.* **(b)** to reject an idea, a proposal, etc: [Vn] *My plan was firmly squashed by the committee.* **PHRV** ¡**squash (sb) 'up (against sb/sth)** to move or make sb move so close to sb/sth that they are uncomfortable: *We had to squash up to make room for two more people.* ○ *There were four of us squashed up against each other in the back of the car.*

---

squash

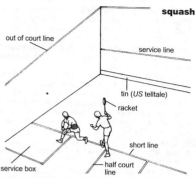

out of court line

service line

tin (*US* telltale)

racket

short line

service box

half court line

▶ **squash** *n* **1** [C usu *sing*] the state of being squashed (SQUASH 2): *It was a squash, but I managed to get everything into one suitcase.* ○ *The car seats six at a squash.* **2** [U, C] (*Brit*) a drink made from fruit juice and sugar to which one adds water: *a bottle/glass of orange/lemon squash* ○ *Two squashes, please.* **3** (also *fml* ˈsquash rackets) [U] a game played by two people with rackets and a small soft rubber ball, in a court enclosed by four walls: *a squash racket/ball/court/game* ○ *Do you play squash?* ⇨ picture.

squashy *adj* easily squashed (SQUASH 1a); soft: *a squashy chair* ○ *The pears have gone squashy* (ie too ripe).

squash² /skwɒʃ/ *n* (*pl* unchanged or **squashes**) [U, C] any of several large long or round vegetables with thick skins: *Pumpkins and marrows are varieties of squash.*

squat¹ /skwɒt/ *v* (**-tt-**) **1** ~ (**down**) (of people) to sit on one's heels with the knees bent up close to the body: [V, Vp] *The children squatted (down) by the fire.* ⇨ picture at KNEEL. **2** to occupy an empty building or settle on a piece of land without permission: [Vpr] *homeless people squatting in a derelict house* [also V].

▶ **squat** *n* **1** a squatting position; an exercise in which one moves into and out of this position: *do 40 press-ups and 20 squats every morning.* **2** a building occupied by people squatting (SQUAT¹ 2): *live in a squat.*

squatter *n* a person who occupies a building or land without permission: *claim squatters' rights* ○ *squatter camps* ○ *The squatters were evicted by the police.*

squat² /skwɒt/ *adj* short and thick: *a squat grey stone church* ○ *He was rather squat and heavy.*

squaw /skwɔː/ *n* a Native American woman or wife.

squawk /skwɔːk/ *v* **1** (esp of birds) to give a loud harsh cry, eg when frightened: [V] *The parrot squawked loudly.* **2** (*infml esp joc*) to complain loudly: [V.speech] *'He said what?' she squawked.* [also V].

▶ **squawk** *n* **1** a loud harsh cry: *give/let out a squawk.* **2** (*infml esp joc*) a loud complaint.

squeak /skwiːk/ *n* a short high-pitched cry or sound: *the squeak of a mouse* ○ *The door opened with a squeak.* ○ (*fig*) *They agreed without a squeak of protest.*

▶ **squeak** *v* **1** to make a squeak: [V] *a squeaking noise* ○ *These new shoes squeak.* **2** ~ **sth** (**out**) to say sth in a small high voice because one is nervous or excited: [Vpr] *The children jumped up and down, squeaking with excitement.* [V.speech] *'Let go of me!' he squeaked nervously.* [also V]. **3** to manage to win, pass, enter, etc with difficulty: [Vpr] *I managed with difficulty to squeak into the final round of the com-*

petition. [Vp] *He squeaked in with five minutes to spare.* [also Vadv].

squeaky *adj* making a squeaking sound: *a squeaky chair* ○ *speak in a squeaky voice.* ˌsqueaky ˈclean *adj* (*infml*) completely clean: (*fig*) *an all-American boy with a squeaky clean image.*

squeal /skwiːl/ *n* a long high-pitched cry or sound: *give a squeal of delight/anguish* ○ *the squeal of brakes/tyres.*

▶ **squeal** *v* **1** ~ (**with sth**) to make a squeal: [V] *The pigs were squealing.* [Vpr] *He squealed with pain.* **2** to speak in a high-pitched excited voice: [V.speech] *'I've caught a fish,' she squealed.* [also Vpr]. **3** ~ (**on sb**) (*sl*) to give secret information, esp to the police, about the criminal activities of a friend, colleague, etc: [V, Vpr] *How did they find him? Someone must have squealed (on him).*

squeamish /ˈskwiːmɪʃ/ *adj* **1** easily upset and likely to feel sick at eg the sight of blood: *be squeamish about killing spiders/seeing dead bodies.* **2** having strong moral views; too SCRUPULOUS: *Less squeamish nations will not hesitate to sell them arms.*

▶ **the squeamish** *n* [pl *v*] people who are squeamish: *an explicit and violent film, definitely not for the squeamish.*

squeamishly *adv.*

squeamishness *n* [U].

squeegee /ˈskwiːdʒiː/ *n* a tool with a rubber edge on a long handle, used for removing water, etc from smooth surfaces: *use a squeegee to clean the windows.*

squeeze /skwiːz/ *v* **1(a)** to hold and press on sth/sb from opposite sides, esp with the fingers: [Vn] *squeeze a tube of toothpaste* ○ *squeeze sb's hand* (eg as a sign of affection or sympathy) ○ *squeeze the trigger* (ie press it towards one) ○ *a doll that cries when you squeeze it* [Vn, Vnadv] *He hugged and squeezed her (tight).* **(b)** ~ **sth** (**out**) to twist sth firmly in order to remove water, etc from it: [Vnp] *Squeeze your swimming-costume out and hang it up to dry.* [also Vn]. **2(a)** ~ **sth** (**from / out of sth**); ~ **sth** (**out**) to get water or juice out of sth by pressing it or twisting it hard: [Vnpr] *squeeze the juice out of a lemon* [Vnp] *He took off his wet trousers and squeezed the water out.* ○ [Vnpr] (*fig*) *She felt as if every drop of emotion had been squeezed out of her.* **(b)** to force a substance out of a container by pressing on it with the fingers: [Vnpr] *squeeze paint from a tube* [Vnp] *squeeze out the glue.* **3** ~ (**sb/sth**) **into, through**, etc **sth**; ~ **through, in, past**, etc to force oneself/sb/sth into or through a narrow or restricted space: [Vpr] *squeeze into a very tight skirt* ○ *squeeze through a gap in the hedge/through a crowd* [Vpr, Vnpr] *squeeze (one's way) onto a crowded bus* [Vnpr] *She squeezed as many books onto the shelf as she could.* [Vp] *There were already six people in the lift, but he managed to squeeze in.* ○ *Can you squeeze past/by?* **4** to have a damaging effect on sth: [Vn] *High interest rates are squeezing industry hard.* ○ *The banks have had their profits squeezed this year.* **5** ~ **sth** (**out of sb**); ~ **sb** (**for sth**) to obtain sth by putting pressure on sb, threatening them, etc: [Vnpr] *squeeze more money out of taxpayers/taxpayers for more money* ○ *squeeze a promise out of sb* ○ *squeeze sb for information* [also Vn]. **PHRV** ˌsqueeze sb/sth ˈin to provide or find time for sth/sb, esp when one is very busy: *Dr Jackson's very busy this morning but she could probably squeeze you in between appointments.* ˌsqueeze sb/sth ˈout (of sth) to exclude sb/sth from sth: *an unsuccessful attempt to squeeze Egypt out of the trade negotiations* ○ *be squeezed out of the market/the medal winners* ○ *Colleagues on the committee had tried to squeeze her out.* ˌsqueeze (sb) ˈup (against sb/sth) to move close to sb/sth so that one is pressed tightly against them/it: *There'll be enough* *room if we all squeeze up a bit.* ○ *I had to sit squeezed up against the wall.*

▶ **squeeze** *n* **1** [C usu *sing*] an act of squeezing sth/sb: *give the tube another squeeze* ○ *She gave my hand a gentle squeeze.* **2** [C] a small amount of sth produced by squeezing: *a squeeze of lemon (juice).* **3** [sing] a state of being forced into a small or restricted space: *Seven people in the car was a bit of a squeeze.* ○ *It was a tight squeeze but we finally got all the clothes into the case.* **4** [C usu *sing*] difficulties caused by lack of money or resources: *a squeeze on manufacturing industries* ○ *a credit squeeze* (ie restrictions on borrowing money) ○ *She's just lost her job, so they're really feeling the squeeze.* **IDM** **put the 'squeeze on sb (to do sth)** (*infml*) to put pressure on sb to act in a particular way.

squeezer *n* (usu in compounds) a device for squeezing juice out of fruit: *a 'lemon-squeezer.*

squelch /skweltʃ/ *v* to make a wet sucking sound with the feet while walking: [V] *Her shoes squelched at every step.* [Vpr] *We squelched across the fields in the mud.* [also Vp].

▶ **squelch** *n* (usu *sing*) a squelching sound.
squelchy *adj*: *squelchy mud.*

squib /skwɪb/ *n* a small FIREWORK that jumps around as it burns before making a loud explosion. See also BANGER 3. **IDM** **a damp squib** ⇨ DAMP¹.

squid /skwɪd/ *n* (*pl* unchanged or **squids**) [C, U] a long sea creature with ten short arms round its mouth, sometimes eaten as food: *fried squid.* ⇨ picture at OCTOPUS.

squidgy /'skwɪdʒi/ *adj* (*infml esp Brit*) soft and wet: *squidgy raspberries* ○ *a nice squidgy cream cake.*

squiffy /'skwɪfi/ *adj* (*Brit infml*) slightly drunk.

squiggle /'skwɪgl/ *n* a line with twists and loops, sometimes intended to be a word or name: *Is this squiggle supposed to be a signature?* ○ *Three red squiggles on a white background — can you seriously call this art?* ▶ **squiggly** /'skwɪgli/ *adj*: *squiggly handwriting.*

squint /skwɪnt/ *v* **1** to look at sb/sth sideways or with eyes that are partly shut in order to see better or because of very bright light: [Vpr] *squint at/into the sun* ○ *squinting through the keyhole* ○ *Her eyes squinted against the brightness.* [Vnpr] *squinting her eyes against the smoke* [also V]. **2** [V] to have eyes that do not move together but each look in a different direction.

▶ **squint** *n* **1** a disorder of the eye muscles which causes each eye to look in a different direction: *He was born with a squint.* **2** (*Brit infml*) a short look: *Have/Take a squint at this.*

squire /'skwaɪə(r)/ *n* **1** (in titles **Squire**) (formerly) a man of high social status who owned land in a country area. **2** (*Brit infml or joc*) (used by a man as a friendly form of address to another man): *What can I get you, squire?* **3** (formerly) a young man who was an assistant to a KNIGHT(2) until becoming a knight himself.

squirearchy /'skwaɪərɑːki/ *n* [CGp] (esp formerly in England) people owning land, viewed esp as a class with political or social influence.

squirm /skwɜːm/ *v* **1** to move by twisting the body about: [Vp] *He was squirming around on the floor in agony.* [Vpr] *She managed to squirm out of his grasp and run for help.* **2** to feel great embarrassment or shame: [V] *It made him squirm to think how he'd messed up the interview.*

squirrel /'skwɪrəl; US 'skwɜːrəl/ *n* a small animal with a long thick tail and red or grey fur. Squirrels eat nuts and live in trees: *Red squirrels are now very rare in Britain.*

squirt /skwɜːt/ *v* (**a**) to force liquid, powder, etc out through a narrow opening in a thin stream or jet: [Vnpr] *squirt ketchup onto one's plate* ○ *Stop squirting water at me!* [also Vnp, Vn]. (**b**) (of liquid,

powder, etc) to be forced out in this way: [Vpr] *I dropped the hose and the water squirted all over me.* [Vp] *I squeezed the bottle and the sauce squirted out.* (**c**) ~ **sb/sth (with sth)** to cover sb/sth with liquid, powder, etc forced out in this way: [Vn] *Stop squirting me.* [Vnpr] *The little girl squirted us with (water from) her water-pistol.*

▶ **squirt** *n* **1(a)** a thin stream or jet of liquid, powder, etc: *a squirt of washing-up liquid.* (**b**) a small quantity of sth produced by squirting: *We only got a tiny squirt of tomato sauce with our chips.* **2** (*infml derog*) a person who is considered too confident and rather unpleasant: *He's such a little squirt.*

Sr *abbr* **1** = SNR. **2** (*religion*) Sister: *Sr Mary Frances.*

SS *abbr* **1** (written before two or more names) Saints. **2** /ˌes 'es/ (used before the name of a ship) steamship: *the ˌSS Tiˈtanic.*

St *abbr* **1** (written before a name) Saint: *St Peter.* See also S 1. **2** (used in an address) Street: *Fleet St.*

st *abbr* stone(7).

Sta *abbr* (esp on a map) Station: *Victoria Sta.*

stab /stæb/ *v* (**-bb-**) **1** to push a knife or pointed object into sb/sth: [Vn, Vnpr] *He had been stabbed (to death).* [Vnpr] *stab sb in the neck/chest/stomach* ○ *He stabbed the meat with his fork/stabbed his fork into the meat.* **2** ~ (**at**) **sb/sth (with sth)** to make forceful movements at sth with one's finger or a pointed object: [Vpr] *She stabbed angrily at the lift button.* [Vn] *He/His finger stabbed the air furiously.* [also Vnpr]. ⇨ note at NUDGE. **IDM** **stab sb in the 'back** (*infml*) to say or do sth to harm sb who trusts one; to betray sb.

▶ **stab** *n* **1** [C] an attempt to stab sb/sth or a wound inflicted by stabbing: *stab wounds* ○ *He received a stab in the chest.* **2** [C] a sudden sharp pain caused by or as if by stabbing: *a stab of pain in the chest* ○ *feel a stab of guilt/pity/fear/jealousy.* **3** [C usu *sing*] ~ (**at sth**) (*infml*) an attempt to do sth: *She found the test difficult but nevertheless made a good stab at it.* ○ *Anyone can have a stab at designing the new logo.* ○ *He made a wild stab at my name and got it completely wrong.* **IDM** **a ˌstab in the 'back** (*infml*) an act that harms sb, done by a person they thought was a friend: *Her refusal to support his campaign was a real stab in the back.*

stabbing *adj* [usu attrib] (esp of pain) very sharp and sudden: *have/feel a stabbing pain in the chest.* — *n* an incident in which a person is stabbed with a knife: *a dramatic increase in the number of stabbings in the city.*

stability /stə'bɪləti/ *n* [U] the quality or state of being STABLE¹(a): *preserve the stability of the dollar* ○ *economic/political stability.* Compare INSTABILITY.

stabilize, -ise /'steɪbəlaɪz/ *v* to become or make sth STABLE¹(a): [V] *His condition has now stabilized.* ○ *Let's wait until the situation stabilizes before we take a decision.* [Vn] *government measures to stabilize prices.*

▶ **stabilization, -isation** /ˌsteɪbəlaɪ'zeɪʃn; US -lə'z-/ *n* [U]: *the stabilization of currency exchange rates.*
stabilizer, -iser /'steɪbəlaɪzə(r)/ *n* a device that keeps sth STABLE¹(a), esp one that prevents an aircraft or a ship from rolling to one side, or one that helps to keep a child's bicycle upright: *He can now ride his bike without stabilizers.*

stable¹ /'steɪbl/ *adj* (**a**) firmly established; not likely to fail or change; steady: *a stable relationship/job/government* ○ *a house built on stable foundations* ○ *The patient's condition is stable.* ○ *Prices should remain stable for some months.* (**b**) (of a person) not easily upset or disturbed; balanced: *Mentally, she's not very stable.* (**c**) (of a substance) staying in the same chemical or atomic state: *an element forming stable compounds.* Compare UNSTABLE. See also STABILITY, STABILIZE. ▶ **stably** /'steɪbli/ *adv.*

stable² /'steɪbl/ *n* **1** a building in which horses are kept and fed: *lead a horse out of its stable* ○ *a stable door.* **2** (often *pl* with *sing* meaning and sometimes *sing v*) an organization that specializes in keeping horses for a particular purpose, and the horses owned by it: *a riding stables* ○ *He owns a racing stable(s).* **3** a club, a school, an organization, a company, etc providing the same background, values, standards, etc for people trained there: *actors from the same stable.* **IDM** **lock, etc the stable door after the horse has 'bolted** to try to prevent or avoid loss, damage, etc when it is already too late to do so.

▶ **stable** *v* to put or keep a horse in a stable: [Vn] *Where do you stable your pony?*
stabling *n* [U] accommodation for horses: *The house has stabling for 20 horses.*
■ **'stable-boy** (also **'stable-lad**) *n* a usu young person who works in a stable.

staccato /stəˈkɑːtəʊ/ *adj, adv* **(a)** (*music*) with each note played separately in order to produce short sharp sounds: *staccato notes* ○ *Play this phrase staccato.* **(b)** with short and sharp sounds: *a peculiar staccato voice* ○ *a staccato burst of high-pitched yelps.*

stack /stæk/ *n* **1** a pile or heap of sth, usu neatly arranged: *a wood stack* ○ *a stack of old newspapers* ○ *a display stack in a supermarket.* See also HAYSTACK. **2** (esp *pl*) ~ **of sth** (*infml*) a large number or quantity of sth: *stacks of money* ○ *a stack of washing-up* ○ *I've got stacks of work to do.* ○ *There's a whole stack of bills waiting to be paid.* **3** a tall chimney, esp on a factory. See also CHIMNEY-STACK, SMOKESTACK. **4** (*Brit*) a large high rock surrounded by sea. **5** (often *pl*) shelves in part of a library not open to the public, used to store books that are not often required by library users: *have a book brought up from the stacks.* **6** a number of aircraft flying in circles at different heights while waiting for permission to land at an airport. **IDM** **blow one's stack** ⇨ BLOW¹.

▶ **stack** *v* **1** ~ **sth (up)** to make sth into a stack or stacks; to pile sth up: [Vn] *stack chairs/boxes* [Vnpr] *stack logs into piles* [Vnpr, Vnp] *stack (up) the dishes on the draining-board.* **2** ~ **sth (with sth)** to put heaps or piles of things on or in a place: [Vn] *an evening job stacking shelves in a supermarket* [Vnpr] *The floor was stacked with books.* **3** ~ **sth (against sb)** to arrange sth so that one has an unfair advantage: [Vn] *I got bad cards the whole evening, which made me think that they had stacked the deck* (ie pack of cards). [also Vnpr]. **4** ~ **sth (up)** to fly or instruct aircraft to fly in a stack(6) while waiting to land: [Vn, Vnp] *The air traffic controllers stack (up) as many as fifty planes at a time.* [also V, Vp]. **IDM** **have the cards/odds stacked a'gainst one** to be unlikely to succeed in sth because conditions are not fair or favourable: *With financial problems like his, the odds are stacked heavily against him.* **PHR V** **,stack 'up (against sth)** (*US infml*) to compare with sth; to measure up (MEASURE¹) to sth: *How well does this washing-powder stack up against your usual brand?*

stadium /ˈsteɪdiəm/ *n* (*pl* **stadiums** or **-dia** /-diə/) a large sports field surrounded by seats for spectators: *a football stadium* ○ *build a new stadium for the Olympic Games.*

staff /stɑːf; *US* stæf/ *n* **1 (a)** [C usu *sing*, Gp] all the workers employed in a business, etc considered as a group: *the hotel staff* ○ *a staff of ten* ○ *We need more staff in the office.* ○ *We have 20 part-time members of staff.* ○ *The staff in this shop are very helpful.* ○ *staff shortages in the catering industry* ○ *They have had to take on/lay off a lot of staff.* **(b)** [pl *v*] the teachers in a school: *a head teacher and her staff* ○ *a new member of (the) staff* ○ *a staff room/meeting.* **2** [C usu *sing*, Gp] a group of senior army officers assisting a commanding officer: *the general staff* ○ *a 'staff*

officer. **3** (also **stave**) [C] (*music*) a set of five parallel lines on which music is written. ⇨ picture at CLEF. **4** [C] (*dated or fml*) a long stick used as a support when walking or climbing, as a weapon, or as a symbol of authority or sign of office: *The old man leant on a long wooden staff.* ○ *He entered holding his staff of office.* Compare STAVE¹ 1.

▶ **staff** *v* (usu passive) to provide an institution, etc with staff(1); to act as staff for sth: [Vn] *The school is staffed entirely by graduates.* ○ *There's nobody to staff the office today.* [Vnadv] *a well-staffed hotel* ○ *a fully-staffed department.* See also SHORT-STAFFED. **staffing** *n* [U]: *staffing arrangements/levels/problems.*
'staff nurse *n* (*Brit*) a hospital nurse ranking just below a sister(4).
'staff sergeant *n* **(a)** (*Brit*) a senior sergeant. **(b)** (*US*) a NON-COMMISSIONED officer ranking just above a sergeant.

stag /stæg/ *n* **1** an adult male DEER. ⇨ picture at DEER. Compare BUCK¹ 1, DOE, FAWN¹ 1, HART. **2** (*Brit*) a person who buys newly issued stocks and shares hoping to sell them quickly for a profit.
■ **'stag-night** (also **'stag-party**) *n* a party for men only, esp one for a man just before he gets married. Compare HEN-PARTY.

stage /steɪdʒ/ *n* **1** [C] a platform or an area, usu in a theatre, on which plays are performed to an audience: *He was on (the) stage for most of the play.* **2** **the stage** [sing] the acting profession; life and work in the theatre: *be on the stage* (ie be an actor) ○ *choose the stage as a career.* **3** [sing] a place where important events occur: *the political stage* ○ *a major figure on the international stage* ○ *Geneva has become the stage for many meetings of world leaders.* **4** [C] a point, period or step in the development, growth or progress of sth/sb: *At this stage it's impossible to know whether our plan will succeed.* ○ *At one stage he thought of giving up his job.* ○ *The baby has reached the 'talking stage.* ○ *The peace talks are now entering a critical/crucial stage.* ○ *The race is now in its final stage(s).* ○ *He taught me how to use the computer stage by stage.* **5** [C] **(a)** a part of a journey, race, etc: *She did the first stage of the trip by train.* **(b)** (*Brit*) a section of a bus route for which there is a fixed fare: *travel two stages for 50p.* **6** [C] a section of a spacecraft with a separate engine that falls off when its fuel is used up. See also LANDING-STAGE. **7** [C] (*dated infml*) = STAGECOACH. **IDM** **set the 'stage for sth** to prepare for sth; to make sth possible or easy: *The president's death set the stage for a military coup.*

▶ **stage** *v* **1** to present a play, etc on a stage: [Vn] *stage a new production of 'King Lear'.* **2** to arrange for and take part in an event: [Vn] *stage a protest rally/hunger strike* ○ *an event staged to mark the 500th anniversary of his death.* **3** to make sth happen: [Vn] *The dollar staged a recovery earlier today.* ○ *After five years in retirement, he staged a comeback in the boxing ring.* See also STAGING 1, STAGY.
■ **'stage direction** *n* a note in the text of a play telling actors where to move, how to perform, etc on stage.
,stage 'door *n* (usu *sing*) the entrance at the back of a theatre used by actors, theatre staff, etc: *fans waiting at the stage door for autographs.*
'stage fright *n* [U] nervous feelings felt by actors before or during a performance: *have/experience stage fright.*
'stage-hand *n* a person employed to help move scenery, etc in a theatre.
,stage 'left *adv* on the left side of a stage as viewed by an actor facing the audience.
,stage-'manage *v* to organize or arrange an event: [Vn.to inf] *The demonstration had been carefully stage-managed to coincide with the royal visit.* [also

[Vn]. **ˌstage-ˈmanager** n a person responsible for a theatre stage, equipment, scenery, etc during a play.

ˌstage ˈright adv on the right side of a stage as viewed by an actor facing the audience.

ˈstage-struck adj finding the theatre fascinating and wishing to become an actor: *His ten-year-old daughter is completely stage-struck.*

ˌstage ˈwhisper n words spoken quietly but distinctly by an actor, as if no one on stage can hear but intended to be heard by the audience.

stagecoach /ˈsteɪdʒkəʊtʃ/ (also **stage**) n (formerly) a public vehicle pulled by horses carrying passengers, and often mail, along a regular route.

stagecraft /ˈsteɪdʒkrɑːft; US -ˈkræft/ n [U] skill in presenting plays on a stage.

stagger /ˈstægə(r)/ v **1** to walk or move as if about to fall: [V] *I hit him hard and he staggered and fell.* [Vpr] *He staggered to his feet and continued the fight.* [Vadv] *I saw him staggering home drunk from the pub again last night.* [Vp,Vpr] *One man had managed to stagger out (of the wreckage).* [Vpr] (fig) *stagger under the weight/burden of one's responsibilities.* ⊏> note at SHUFFLE. **2** (usu passive) to astonish sb; to shock sb deeply: [Vn] *You will be staggered by the enormous variety of plants in her garden.* ○ *I was staggered to hear/when I heard of his death.* [Vn.that] *It staggers me that the government are doing nothing about it.* **3** to arrange events, hours of work, etc so that they do not start and finish at the same time: [Vn] *staggered office hours* ○ *stagger the annual holidays.*

▶ **staggering** /ˈstægərɪŋ/ adj astonishing; very difficult to believe: *a staggering achievement* ○ *earn a staggering £10 000 a week* ○ *I find their decision simply staggering.* **staggeringly** adv: *staggeringly beautiful.*

staging /ˈsteɪdʒɪŋ/ n [C,U] **1** a way or method of presenting a play on the stage: *an imaginative new staging of 'Macbeth'.* **2** a usu temporary platform or support for people working, eg on a building site.
■ **ˈstaging post** n a place at which people, aircraft, etc make a regular stop on a long journey.

stagnant /ˈstægnənt/ adj **1** (of water) not flowing or moving and so often smelling unpleasant: *stagnant pools* ○ *water lying stagnant in ponds and ditches.* **2** not developing or growing: *a period of stagnant growth* ○ *a stagnant economy* ○ *The market was stagnant last month.*

stagnate /stægˈneɪt; US ˈstægneɪt/ v **1** to stop developing or progressing: [V] *Profits have stagnated.* ○ *I feel I'm stagnating in this job.* ○ *His mind has stagnated since his retirement.* **2** to be or become STAGNANT(1): [V] *Water stagnating in dirty ponds.* ▶ **stagnation** /stægˈneɪʃn/ n [U]: *enter a period of economic/political stagnation.*

stagy /ˈsteɪdʒi/ adj (usu derog) (of behaviour) as if in a play; not natural: *stagy opulence* ○ *He gave a loud, stagy laugh.*

staid /steɪd/ adj (usu derog) serious and dull: *a staid institution/old gentleman* ○ *a museum which is trying to shed its rather staid image.*

stain /steɪn/ v **1(a)** ~ sth (with sth) (esp passive) to leave or make coloured patches or dirty marks on sth, esp ones that are difficult to remove: [V,Vadv] *Peach juice stains (very badly).* [Vn] *Unfortunately, the red wine stained the carpet.* [Vnpr] *fingers stained with nicotine* [Vn-adj] *The juice from the walnuts stained their fingers brown.* **(b)** to become or get stained: [Vadv] *Our beige carpet stains very easily.* [also V]. **2** to change the colour of eg wood or fabric by using a substance that penetrates the material: [Vn-adj] *He stained the wood dark brown.* [Vn] *We're going to stain the floor.* ○ *stain a specimen before looking at it through the microscope.* **3** to damage sb's reputation, etc: [Vn] *The incident with the actress certainly stained his political career.*

▶ **stain** n **1** [C] a dirty mark or patch of colour which is difficult to remove: *There's an ink stain on your shirt.* ○ *buy some stain remover* ○ *new stain-resistant fabrics.* **2** [U,C] a liquid used for staining wood, fabric, etc: *apply the stain thinly.* Compare DYE². **3** ~ (on sth) a thing that damages a person's reputation: *He left the court without a stain on his character.*
■ **ˌstained ˈglass** n [U] coloured glass, used esp to make windows in churches, etc: *ˌstained-glass ˈwindows.* ⊏> picture at CHURCH.

stainless steel /ˌsteɪnləs ˈstiːl/ n [U] a type of steel ALLOY¹ that does not normally RUST or CORRODE: *knives made of stainless steel* ○ *a stainless steel sink.*

stair /steə(r)/ n **(a) stairs** [pl] a set of steps from one floor of a building to another, usu inside it: *climb a long/short flight of stairs* ○ *at the foot/head of the stairs* (ie at the bottom/top of a set of stairs) ○ *I passed her on the stairs.* ○ *He came rushing down the stairs to greet her.* **(b)** [C] any one of these steps: *The child was sitting on the bottom stair.* ⊏> picture at STAIRCASE. **IDM above/below ˈstairs** (dated) in the owner's/the servants' part of the house: *Their affairs were being discussed below stairs* (ie by the servants).

▶ **stair** adj [attrib] on, belonging to or formed by a set of stairs: *a stair carpet/cupboard.*

NOTE Stairs or flights of stairs are found inside houses or other buildings: *As the lift was not working we started to climb the stairs.* A **staircase** is the part of the building including the stairs and the rail, and sometimes the walls and ceiling surrounding them: *We must redecorate the staircase.* ○ *a spiral staircase* ○ *a stone staircase.* **Steps** or flights of **steps** are usually made of stone or concrete and are found outside buildings. Individual **steps** make up a staircase or flight of steps: *I'll meet you on the steps of the museum.* ○ *There are 150 steps to the top of the tower.* ○ *I sat on the top step in the sunshine.*

staircase

banister

stair

landing

staircase /ˈsteəkeɪs/ (also **stairway**) n a set of stairs and its supporting structure, inside a building: *a wooden/stone staircase* ○ *a spiral staircase* (ie stairs winding round a central pillar). ⊏> picture. ⊏> note at STAIR.

stairway /ˈsteəweɪ/ n = STAIRCASE.

stairwell /ˈsteəwel/ n the part of a building containing the staircase.

stake /steɪk/ n **1** [C] a strong wood or metal stick, pointed at one end, that can be driven into the ground, eg to support a young tree, as a post for a fence, etc or to mark a particular spot. **2 the stake** [sing] (formerly) a wooden post to which a person was tied before being burnt to death as a punishment: *be burnt at the stake.* **3** [C usu pl] money, etc risked or gambled on the unknown result of a future event, eg a race or a card-game: *playing for high stakes* ○ *The stakes are high — if we don't win this contract, we go out of business.* **4** [C] money, etc invested by sb in an enterprise, giving them an interest or a share in it: *have/buy a stake in a company* ○ *He's taken a 10% stake in the business.* **5 stakes (a)** [pl] prize money, esp in horse-racing. **(b)**

(usu **Stakes**) [sing *v*] (esp in names) a horse-race (HORSE) in which all the owners of the horses in the race contribute to the prize money: *The Newmarket Stakes is always a popular race.* **IDM** at ¹**stake** to be won or lost; at risk: *This decision puts their lives at stake.* ○ *The future of this company is at stake.* **go to the** ¹**stake over sth** (*often joc*) to hold an opinion, a principle, etc at any cost: *I think I'm right on this issue but I wouldn't go to the stake over it.*
► **stake** *v* **1** to support sth with a stake(1): [Vn] *stake newly planted trees.* **2** ~ sth (**on sth**) to gamble or risk money, one's life, etc on sth: [Vnpr] *stake £25 on the favourite* (eg in horse-racing) ○ *I'd stake my life on it* (ie I am very confident about it). [also Vn]. **IDM** **stake (out) a/one's** ¹**claim (to sb/sth)** to declare a special interest in sb/sth; to claim a right to sb/sth: *In his speech the minister clearly staked a/his claim to the leadership of the party.* **PHRV** ¹**stake sth** ¹**out** (esp formerly) to mark an area with stakes in order to claim ownership of it. **2** to declare a special interest in or right to eg a place or an area of study: *He's staked out this corner of the sitting-room as his own.* **3** to watch a place continuously and secretly: *Detectives have been staking out the house for two days now.*
■ ¹**stake-out** *n* a continuous secret watch by the police.

stakeholder /ˈsteɪkhəʊldə(r)/ *n* a person, company, etc that has shares or an interest in a business or an industry: *The company is a 44% stakeholder in the Emerald oilfield.*

stalactite /ˈstæləktaɪt; US stəˈlæktaɪt/ *n* a long rock formation hanging down from the roof of a cave, formed over a long period by drops of water containing LIME¹. ⇨ picture.

stalagmite /ˈstæləgmaɪt; US stəˈlæg-/ *n* a rock formation on the floor of a cave, pointing upwards, formed over a long period from drops of water falling from the roof or from a STALACTITE. ⇨ picture at STALACTITE.

stale /steɪl/ *adj* **1** (esp of food) no longer fresh and often tasting or smelling unpleasant: *stale biscuits/bread/cake* ○ *the smell of stale cigarette smoke.* **2** no longer interesting or exciting because of having been heard, done, etc too often before; not new: *stale news/jokes/ideas* ○ *Their marriage has gone stale.* **3** no longer able to work, produce new ideas, perform, etc well because of having done sth for too long. ► **staleness** *n* [U].

stalemate /ˈsteɪlmeɪt/ *n* [UC usu *sing*] **1** a position of the pieces in a game of CHESS in which the player whose move it is cannot move without putting her or his king into CHECK²(4), with the result that neither player wins. **2** a stage of a dispute, contest, etc at which further action or progress by either side seems impossible: *end in stalemate* ○ *Negotiations have reached a (a) stalemate.*

stalk¹ /stɔːk/ *n* **1** the stem that supports a leaf, flower or fruit and joins it to another part of the plant: *pick roses with long stalks* ○ *eating a stalk of celery* ○ *remove the stalks from cherries.* ⇨ picture at FRUIT. **2** the main stem of a plant. ⇨ picture at FLOWER. **3** any thin structure supporting a part or an organ in certain animals: *The crab's eyes are at the end of short stalks.*

stalk² /stɔːk/ *v* **1** to move quietly and slowly towards an animal or a person in order to get near without being seen: [Vn] *hunters stalking deer* ○ *a rapist stalking his victim.* **2** to walk in a proud and angry way: [Vpr] *He stalked out of the room.* [Vp] *She*

stalked off/out without another word. **3** (*rhet*) (of eg an evil force) to move through a place in an unpleasant or threatening way: [Vn, Vpr] *Fear stalks (through) the town at night.* [Vn] *Ghosts are said to stalk the castle walls.*
► **stalker** *n* a person who stalks animals.
■ ¹**stalking horse** *n* a person or thing that is used to distract attention from sb's real plans or intentions: *He is seen as a stalking horse candidate and not as a serious challenger for the leadership.*

stall /stɔːl/ *n* **1** [C] (often in compounds) a table or small shop with an open front from which things are sold in a market, in a railway station, etc: *set up a stall* ○ *He runs a fruit stall.* **2** [C] (**a**) any small room, usu for one person: *stalls for changing in at the swimming-pool* ○ *a shower stall.* (**b**) a section of a stable or cattle shed for one animal. **3 stalls** [pl] (*Brit*) the seats in the part of a theatre that is nearest to the stage: *Our seats are in row 13 of the stalls.* **4** [C] any of several fixed seats, usu with the back and sides enclosed, in a church: *the* ¹*choir stalls.* **5** [C] a situation in which a vehicle's engine stops because it is not being supplied with enough power: *go into/get out of a stall.*
► **stall** *v* **1(a)** (of a vehicle or an engine) to stop suddenly because of not having enough power or speed: [V] *I/The car stalled at the traffic-lights.* (**b**) [V, Vn] (of a driver, pilot, etc) to cause a vehicle or an engine to do this. **2(a)** to avoid giving a definite answer or taking action, in order to get more time; to delay: [V] *Stop stalling and give me an answer!* [Vpr] *Don't let him go yet — see if you can stall for time.* (**b**) to avoid answering a person, etc in this way: [Vn] *stall one's creditors.* **3(a)** to prevent sth from happening or progressing: [Vn] *stall demands for a UN Security Council session.* (**b**) (of a situation) to stop making progress: [V] *Peace talks have stalled.*

stallholder /ˈstɔːlhəʊldə(r)/ *n* a person who runs a stall in a market, etc.

stallion /ˈstælɪən/ *n* a fully grown male horse, esp one used for breeding. Compare COLT 1, GELDING, MARE 1.

stalwart /ˈstɔːlwət/ *adj* [usu attrib] loyal and reliable, even when conditions are very difficult: *one of the team's most stalwart supporters.*
► **stalwart** *n* a loyal supporter of a political party, etc: *Labour Party stalwarts.*

stamen /ˈsteɪmən/ *n* (*botany*) any of the small thin male parts in the middle of a flower that produce POLLEN.

stamina /ˈstæmɪnə/ *n* [U] the ability to endure much physical or mental strain; great energy and strength: *a test of stamina* ○ *Marathon runners need plenty of stamina.* ○ *He doesn't have the stamina to be a teacher.*

stammer /ˈstæmə(r)/ *v* to speak with sudden pauses and a tendency to repeat the same sound or syllable rapidly, either because of having a speech problem or from fear, excitement, etc: [Vnp] *stammer out a request* [V.speech] *'I'm s-s-sorry,' she stammered.* [also V, Vn]. Compare STUTTER.
► **stammer** *n* (usu *sing*) a tendency to stammer: *He's always had a slight nervous stammer.*
stammerer /ˈstæmərə(r)/ *n* a person who stammers.

stamp¹ /stæmp/ *v* **1** to put one's foot down heavily on the ground: [Vn] *They walked up and down, stamping their feet to keep warm.* ○ *Rosie stamped her foot in annoyance.* [Vnp] *She stamped the soil down around the plant.* ○ *They stamped the fire out.* [V] *The audience was stamping and cheering.* [also Vnpr, Vn-adj]. **2** to walk with loud heavy steps: [Vp] *Don't stamp about like that, you'll wake everyone up.* [Vpr] *She stamped out of the room.* [also V]. ⇨ note. **3** ~ A (**on B**); ~ B (**with A**) to print the date, letters, a design, etc on paper, cloth or some other surface; to mark paper, etc with a design, an

official seal, etc: [Vn] *They didn't stamp my passport.*
○ *The librarian forgot to stamp my library books* (ie
with the date on which they should be returned).
[Vnpr] *crates of oranges stamped with the exporter's
trademark* [Vnn] *The file was stamped 'Top Secret'.*
4 (esp passive) to stick a stamp²(1) on a letter, etc:
[Vn] *The letter was addressed and sealed but had not
been stamped.* **5** (esp passive) to mark or affect sth
with a particular feeling or attitude: [Vnpr] *Reluctance was stamped all over their faces.* **6** ~ **sb as sth**
to indicate that sb has a particular quality; to mark
sb out (MARK²) as sth: [Vn-n] *This latest novel stamps
her as a genius.* **7** ~ **sth (out) (from sth)** to cut and
shape metal, etc into pieces by striking it with a
specially shaped tool: [Vnp] *a machine for stamping
out engine parts* [also Vn, Vnpr]. See also RUBBER-
STAMP. **v.** **PHR V** **'stamp on sth 1** to crush sth by
bringing one's foot down heavily on it: *She stamped
on the burning paper to put it out.* **2** to control or
suppress sth, esp by force: *The rebellion was soon
stamped on by the army.* **'stamp sth on sth** to cause
sth to have a lasting effect or influence: *stamp one's
personality/authority on a game* (ie as an outstanding player) ○ *The date is forever stamped on her
memory.* **¡stamp sth 'out** to remove, destroy or
suppress sth, esp by force or vigorous action: *stamp
out terrorism/a rebellion/vermin.*

■ **¡stamped addressed 'envelope** *n* (*abbr* SAE)
(*Brit*) an envelope on which one has written one's
own address and put a stamp: *For further details,
send a stamped addressed envelope to the following
address.* See also SELF-ADDRESSED.
'stamping-ground *n* (*infml*) a place where a particular person or animal may usually be found; a
favourite place or HAUNT: *I visited some of my old
stamping-grounds.*

NOTE Stamp, stomp, plod, trudge and tramp all
describe ways of walking with heavy steps. **Stamp**
refers to putting your feet down heavily when you
move, usually to show anger: *We could hear her
stamping around in the bathroom.* **Stomp** suggests
making a noise while walking in order to show
anger: *Peter slammed the door and stomped upstairs.*
Stomp can also suggest noisy walking or dancing:
*The entire crowd were stomping and singing to the
music.*
  Plod and **trudge** both mean to walk slowly for a
long time towards a particular destination. **Plod**
suggests a steady pace and **trudge** suggests a lot of
effort because of difficulty or bad weather: *We sat in
the hut waiting while a family of elephants plodded
past.* ○ *They trudged home through the deep snow.*
Tramp means to walk over a long distance, possibly
with no specific destination: *He tramped through the
rain looking for a place to sleep.*

stamp² /stæmp/ *n* **1(a)** (also *fml* **'postage stamp**) a
small piece of paper with an official design on it,
stuck on an envelope or a parcel to show that POST-
AGE has been paid: *a 26p stamp* ○ *a book of (postage)
stamps* ○ *I'd like three first-class stamps, please.* ○ *a
commemorative stamp* ○ *My hobby is collecting
stamps.* ○ *Would you like to see my* **'stamp album**? **(b)**
a similar piece of paper stuck on a document to
show that a particular amount of money has been
paid: *a TV licence stamp* ○ **'savings stamps.** **(c)** (also
'trading stamp) a similar piece of paper given to
customers when they buy things. When enough
stamps have been collected they can be exchanged
for various goods. **2** an instrument with which a
design, mark, etc is stamped on a surface: *a date
stamp.* See also RUBBER STAMP. **3** a design, words, etc
made by stamping sth onto a surface: *Have you got
many stamps in your passport?* ○ (*fig*) *The scheme has
the government's **stamp of approval**.* **4** an act or a
sound of stamping with the foot: *give a childish*

stamp of impatience. **5** (usu *sing*) (*fml*) a characteristic mark or quality: *Her work carries/bears the
unmistakable stamp of authority.* ○ *Their story has
the stamp of truth* (ie seems very likely to be true).
6 (usu *sing*) (*fml*) a kind or class: *men of a different
stamp.*
■ **'stamp-collecting** *n* [U] the activity of collecting
stamps (STAMP² 1a) as objects of interest or value.
'stamp-collector *n.*
'stamp-duty *n* a tax placed on certain types of legal
documents.
'stamp-pad *n* = INK-PAD.

stampede /stæm'piːd/ *n* **1** a sudden rush of frightened animals. **2** a sudden wild rush or mass
movement of people: *There was a stampede towards
the stage when the singer appeared.* ○ (*fig*) *the stampede to produce World Cup souvenirs.*
► **stampede** *v* **1(a)** (of animals or people) to run
wildly in a stampede: *The cattle stampeded
towards the river.* [also V]. **(b)** [Vn] to make animals
do this. **2** ~ **sb (into sth / doing sth)** to cause sb to
rush into doing sth that they have not considered
properly: [Vnpr] *Don't be stampeded into buying the
house.* [also Vn].

stance /stæns; *Brit also* staːns/ *n* (usu *sing*) **1** a
person's position or way of standing, esp in sports
such as cricket or golf when preparing to hit the
ball: *a good/natural stance.* **2** ~ **(on sth)** a moral or
intellectual attitude to sth, esp one that is expressed
publicly: *a cautious/positive/right-wing stance* ○
*take/adopt an uncompromising stance on immigra-
tion.* Compare POSTURE.

stanchion /'staːntʃən; *Brit also* 'staːn-/ *n* an upright
bar or post forming a support.

stand¹ /stænd/ *v* (*pt, pp* **stood** /stʊd/)
● **Being in an upright position** **1** to have or
keep an upright position: [V] *She was too weak to
stand.* ○ *After the bombing only a few houses were left
standing.* ○ *Don't just stand there — help your mother
with her bags!* ○ *I was standing only a few feet away.*
[Vadv] *Stand still while I take your photograph.*
[Vpr] *flamingos standing on one leg* [Vp] *We all stood
about in the corridor waiting.* **2** ~ **(up)** to get up
onto one's feet; to take an upright position: [V]
Everyone stood when the President entered. [Vp] *We
stood up in order to see better.* **3** to put sth/sb in an
upright position: [Vnpr] *Don't stand cans of petrol
near the fire.* ○ *I stood the little girl on a chair so that
she could see out of the window.* [Vnp] *Stand the
ladder up against the wall.* **4** (not in the continuous
tenses) to have a specified height: [Vn] *The tower
stands 60 metres high.*

● **Being in a place or condition** **5** to be in a
particular place; to be situated somewhere: [Vpr] *a
clock standing on the mantelpiece* [Vadv] *A tall poplar tree once stood here.* ○ *Further up the road stands
St John's Church.* **6** (of a vehicle, etc) to remain in
the same place: [Vpr] *the train standing at platform
3* ○ *The car stood at the traffic lights for a few
moments, then moved off.* **7** (of a liquid, mixture, etc)
to remain still and not flow or be disturbed: [V]
standing pools of rainwater ○ *Mix the batter and let it
stand for twenty minutes.* **8** to remain the same; to
remain valid: [V] *The agreement must stand* (ie cannot be altered or cancelled). ○ *My offer still stands.*
[Vpr] *His argument **stands or falls on** (ie is valid
or fails depending on the truth of) the assertion that
a language must be shared.* **9(a)** to be in the specified condition or situation: [V-adj] *The house has
stood empty for months.* ○ *The emergency services
stand ready to help if necessary.* ○ *She now stood
convicted of fraud.* ○ *'You're wrong about the date —
it was 1988.' 'I **stand corrected** (ie I accept that I
was mistaken).'* [Vadv] *I never know where I stand
with Tracey — one minute she's friendly, the next she
hardly speaks to me.* [V] *As things stand, there is*

little chance of a quick settlement of the dispute. (**b**) ~ **at sth** to be at the specified level, point of a scale, etc: [Vpr] *The church clock still stands at ten to four.* ◦ *Interest rates stand at an attractive 9%.* **10** to be in a situation where one is likely to do sth: [V.*to* inf] *stand to win/lose/gain* ◦ *You stand to make a lot of money from this deal.* **11** to have a particular attitude or opinion: [Vadv] *Where do you stand* (ie What is your opinion) *on these issues?* ◦ *stand firm against powerful pressure groups.*

● **Other meanings 12** (esp in negative sentences and in questions, with *can/could*; not in the continuous tenses or in the passive) to endure sth/sb; to bear sth/sb: [Vn] *He can't stand hot weather.* ◦ *I can't stand his mother!* ◦ *His heart won't stand the strain much longer.* [V.ing] *He can't stand being kept waiting.* [Vn.ing] *I can't stand people interrupting all the time.* **13** (no passive) to pay for sth for sb: [Vnadv] *stand drinks all round* [Vnn] *She was kind enough to stand us a meal.* **14** (*esp Brit*) (also *esp US* **run**) ~ (**for sth**) to be a candidate in an election: [Vpr] *stand for parliament* ◦ *stand for President* [V] *She stood unsuccessfully in the local elections.* See also STAND-ING.

IDM Idioms containing **stand** are at the entries for the nouns or adjectives in the idioms, eg **stand on ceremony** ⇨ CEREMONY; **make one's hair stand on end** ⇨ HAIR.

PHR V ⹁**stand a'side 1** to move to one side: *She stood aside to let us pass.* **2** to take no part in events; to do nothing: *Don't stand aside and let others do all the work.*

⹁**stand 'back (from sth) 1** to move back from a place: *The police ordered the crowd to stand back (from the building).* **2** to be situated away from sth: *The house stands back a little (from the road).*

⹁**stand 'by 1** to be present while sth bad is happening but not take any action to stop it: *How can you stand by and let him treat his dog like that?* **2** to be ready for action: *The troops are standing by.* See also STAND-BY. **'stand by sb** to support or help sb: *I'll stand by you whatever happens.* **'stand by sth** to be faithful to a promise, a decision, etc; to refuse to change sth: *She still stands by every word she said.*

⹁**stand 'down 1** to withdraw or resign from a position: *The President is standing down after five years in office.* **2** (*esp US*) (of a witness) to leave the stand²(6) in a lawcourt after giving evidence.

'stand for sth (no passive) **1** (not in the continuous tenses) to be an abbreviation (ABBREVIATE) of sth: *'The book's by T C Smith.' 'What does (the) 'T C' stand for?'* **2** (not in the continuous tenses) to represent sth: *I reject fascism and all it stands for.* **3** to be in favour of sth; to support sth: *a party that stands for racial tolerance.* **4** (*infml*) (in negative sentences) to tolerate sth: *I won't stand for any more of your rudeness!* ◦ *I'm not standing for it any longer.*

⹁**stand 'in (for sb)** to take sb's place; to DEPUTIZE for sb: *My assistant will stand in for me while I'm away.* See also STAND-IN.

⹁**stand 'out (from/against sth)** to be easily seen; to be noticeable: *She's the sort of person who stands out in a crowd.* ◦ *The bright lettering stands out well from/against the dark background.* ◦ *You must realize that he's not being honest with you — it stands out a mile* (ie very clearly)! ⹁**stand 'out (from sb/sth)** to be much better or more important than sb/sth: *In a long career, certain memories stand out from the rest.* ⹁**stand 'out for sth** (*infml*) to resist making an agreement and continue to press for better terms: *The nurses have been offered a 5% pay rise, but they're still standing out for 7%.*

⹁**stand 'over sb** to supervise or watch sb closely: *I don't like you standing over me while I am cooking.* ⹁**stand sb 'up** (*infml*) to fail to keep an appointment with sb, esp sb with whom one is having a romantic

or sexual relationship: *She was meant to be going out with Adam last night, but she stood him up.*

⹁**stand 'up for sb/oneself/sth** to speak or act in favour of sb/oneself/sth; to support sb/sth: *Always stand up for your friends.* ◦ *You must stand up for yourself/your rights.* ⹁**stand 'up (to sth)** to remain valid even when tested, examined closely, etc: *His argument simply doesn't stand up (to close scrutiny).* ◦ *I'm afraid this document will never stand up in a court of law.* ⹁**stand 'up to sb** to resist sb: *It was brave of her to stand up to those bullies.* ⹁**stand 'up to sth** (of materials, products, etc) to remain in good condition in spite of hard wear, etc: *This carpet is designed to stand up to a lot of wear and tear.*

■ **'stand-alone** *adj* that operates or is capable of operating independently: *stand-alone insurance policies* ◦ *a stand-alone computer.*

'stand-by *n* (*pl* **-bys**) a person or thing available as a substitute or in an emergency: *a stand-by electricity generator* ◦ *A plain dark suit is a reliable standby for most formal occasions.* **IDM** on **'stand-by** in a state of being ready to act, take part, etc: *Hendry was put on stand-by for Scotland's last match.* ◦ *The troops are on 24-hour stand-by* (ie ready to move within 24 hours of receiving the order). **'stand-by ticket** *n* a cheap ticket available when not all the tickets for a flight, a play, etc have been sold.

'stand-in *n* a person who takes the place of sb else, esp one who takes the part of an actor in dangerous scenes.

'stand-off *n* (*esp US*) a complete failure to reach agreement; a DEADLOCK: *a stand-off between management and unions.*

'stand-up *adj* [attrib] **1(a)** (of a COMEDIAN) giving a performance which consists of standing in front of an audience and telling a series of jokes: *a stand-up comic.* (**b**) (of comedy) performed in this way: *a stand-up comedy routine.* **2** (*esp Brit*) (of a fight, disagreement, etc) direct and violent: *I had a stand-up row with my boss today.* **3** (of a meal) eaten while standing: *a stand-up buffet.*

stand² /stænd/ *n* **1** [sing] an attitude towards sth; a position in an argument: *She has always **taken a firm/strong/tough stand** on nuclear disarmament.* **2** [C usu *sing*] a determined effort to resist attack, to argue one's case despite opposition, etc: *the rebels' last stand* ◦ *The troops **made a brave stand against** the enemy.* ◦ *The time has come to **make a stand** on the issue of environmental pollution.* **3** [C] (often in compounds) a small piece of furniture on which or in which sth may be placed: *an um'brella stand* ◦ *a 'cake stand* ◦ *a matching stand for your video recorder.* See also MUSIC STAND. **4** [C] (**a**) a table or similar structure from which goods are sold; a stall: *set up a market stand.* See also NEWS-STAND. (**b**) a table or an upright structure where things are displayed, advertised, etc: one of *the stands at a book fair.* **5** [C often *pl*] a large, usu sloping, structure at a sports ground containing rows of seats for spectators: *A cheer rose from the south stand.* ⇨ picture at FOOTBALL. See also GRAND-STAND. **6** [C usu *sing*] (*US*) the place where a witness in a lawcourt stands to give evidence: *Please **take the stand.*** **7** (*esp US*) a place where vehicles can wait for paying passengers: *a 'taxi stand* ◦ *a stand for six taxis.* See also ONE-NIGHT STAND.

standard /'stændəd/ *n* **1** (often *pl*) a level of quality: *a school which **sets high standards** of behaviour* ◦ *We provide a first-class standard of service.* ◦ *maintain/raise/improve safety standards.* **2** [C, U] a specified level of quality: *His work does not reach the **required standard.*** ◦ *I'm afraid your work is not **up to standard.*** ◦ *Local beaches fall short of/do not meet European standards of cleanliness.* **3** [pl] moral principles and behaviour: *a lowering of moral standards* ◦ *People's standards are not* *what they used to be.* See also DOUBLE STANDARDS. **4** a thing used as a test or measure: *industry standards ○ an international standard of weight ○ People were very poor then, by today's standards* (ie compared with people today). See also GOLD STANDARD. **5** a ceremonial flag, esp one associated with a particular person or group of people: *the royal standard.*

▶ **standard** *adj* **1** average, normal or usual: *pay the standard rate of tax ○ a standard-sized jar of coffee ○ It is standard procedure in museums to register objects as they are acquired. ○ Anti-lock brakes are standard/come as standard in all models.* **2** serving as, used as or conforming to a standard(4): *standard sizes of paper/units of weight.* **3** generally accepted as correct and widely used: *This is the standard textbook on the subject.* See also REVISED STANDARD VERSION. **4** (of spelling, pronunciation, grammar, etc) widely accepted as the usual form: *standard English.*

■ **'standard-bearer** *n* a prominent leader in a campaign, esp a political one: *a standard-bearer for women's rights.*

'standard lamp (*US* **'floor lamp**) *n* a tall lamp which has its base on the floor, used esp in a living-room (LIVING²).

ˌstandard of 'living *n* (*pl* ˌstandards of 'living) a level of comfort and wealth available to a person or group in a particular country, area, etc: *They have/ enjoy a high standard of living.*

ˌstandard 'time *n* [U] the time officially adopted for a country or part of it.

standardize, -ise /'stændədaɪz/ *v* to make sth conform to a fixed standard, shape, quality, type, etc: [Vn] *an attempt to standardize spelling ○ standardized electrical fittings.* ▶ **standardization, -isation** /ˌstændədaɪ'zeɪʃn/; *US* -dɪ'z-/ *n* [U]: *attempts to increase standardization in the computer industry.*

standing /'stændɪŋ/ *n* [U] **1** position or reputation; status: *a woman of some standing in the community ○ a scientist of good/high standing* (ie a respected one). **2** the length of time that sth has existed: *a debt/dispute/friendship of long standing.* See also LONG-STANDING.

▶ **standing** *adj* [attrib] **1(a)** remaining in force or use; permanent and established: *a standing army ○ a standing committee* (ie a permanent one that meets regularly). **(b)** continuing to be effective or valid: *We have a standing invitation to visit them when we're in the area. ○ a standing joke* (ie sth that regularly causes amusement). **2** (*esp sport*) done from a standing position: *a standing start/jump.*

■ **ˌstanding 'order** *n* **(a)** (also ˌbanker's 'order) a customer's instruction to a bank to pay a particular amount to sb else at regular intervals, eg for rent or MORTGAGE payments. Compare DIRECT DEBIT. **(b)** a rule or an order that remains valid and does not have to be repeated: *the standing orders of the House of Commons.*

ˌstanding o'vation *n* (usu *sing*) an enthusiastic expression of approval by people standing up from their seats to clap: *The soloist got a ten-minute standing ovation after her performance.*

'standing-room *n* [U] space for people to stand in, esp in a theatre, sports ground, etc: *There was standing-room only left in the concert hall.*

standoffish /ˌstænd'ɒfɪʃ/ *adj* cold and distant(3a) in manner or behaviour.

standpipe /'stændpaɪp/ *n* a VERTICAL pipe connected to a main water supply, used to provide water outside or at a distance from buildings.

standpoint /'stændpɔɪnt/ *n* (usu *sing*) a way of looking at things; a position from which things are seen and opinions are formed: *Try looking at it from the standpoint of the customer. ○ From a technical standpoint, this is a great advantage.*

standstill /'stændstɪl/ *n* [sing] a stop; a condition in which everything has stopped: *be at/come to/ bring sth to a standstill ○ Work is grinding to a standstill. ○ Traffic in the city is at a complete/virtual standstill.*

stank *pt* of STINK.

stanza /'stænzə/ *n* (*pl* stanzas) (*techn*) a group of lines forming a unit in some types of poem; a verse of poetry: *a ten-line stanza.*

staple¹ /'steɪpl/ *n* **1** a small thin piece of bent wire that is forced by a special instrument into sheets of paper to fasten them together. **2** a piece of metal in the shape of a U and with pointed ends. Staples are hammered into wood, etc to hold eg electrical wires in place.

▶ **staple** *v* to attach or secure sth with a staple or staples: [Vnp] *staple papers together* [Vnpr] *She stapled his photo onto the membership card.* **stapler** /'steɪplə(r)/ *n* a small instrument used for forcing staples into paper, etc.

staple² /'steɪpl/ *adj* [attrib] main or principal; standard: *the staple products/industries of a country ○ Rice is the staple diet in many Asian countries. ○ (fig) a staple part of comedy.*

▶ **staple** *n* (often *pl*) **1** a main product traded by a country or district: *Cotton is one of Egypt's staples.* **2** a main or principal element of sth, esp of a diet: *Bread, potatoes and other staples continue to rise in price. ○ Showbusiness history is a staple of Radio 2.*

star /stɑː(r)/ *n* **1** [C] **(a)** any one of the distant bodies appearing as a point of light in the sky at night: *The stars shone/twinkled brightly overhead. ○ Let's camp out under the stars. ○ There are no stars out* (ie no stars can be seen) *tonight.* See also POLESTAR, SHOOTING STAR, STARRY. **(b)** (*astronomy*) any large ball in outer space that is composed of gases and produces light, eg the sun. **2** [C] **(a)** an object, a decoration, often with 5 or 6 points, representing or thought to resemble a star by its shape: *Fix the star at the top of the Christmas tree. ○ Put a star* (ie an ASTERISK) *by his name.* **(b)** a mark of this shape used to indicate a category of excellence. The more stars sth is given, the better it is: *ˌfour-star 'petrol ○ a ˌfive-star ho'tel ○ This restaurant gets three stars in the guidebook.* **(c)** a metal BADGE in the shape of a star, worn to indicate rank: *a sheriff's star ○ a ˌtwo-star 'general.* **3** [C] a famous or brilliant singer, performer, sports player, etc: *a 'tennis star ○ a 'rock'/'pop star ○ the stars of stage and screen ○ several big Hollywood stars ○ a young actress with real star quality ○ give sb star treatment ○ He's got the star role in the new film.* See also ALL-STAR, FILM STAR. **4** [C often attrib] best one of a group: *She is my star pupil. ○ There is a prize of $25 for the magazine's star letter. ○ Billy's monkey was the star attraction at the pet show. ○ (infml) Thanks a lot — you're a star.* **5(a)** [C] (in ASTROLOGY) a planet, etc believed to influence a person's life, luck, personality, etc: *born under a lucky star* (ie successful and happy). See also ILL-STARRED. **(b) stars** [pl] a HOROSCOPE: *What do my stars say? ○ It's written in the stars.* **IDM** **reach for the stars** ⇨ REACH. **see 'stars** (*infml*) to have a feeling of seeing flashes of light, esp as a result of being hit on the head. **thank one's lucky stars** ⇨ THANK.

▶ **star** *v* (**-rr-**) **1** (usu *passive*) to mark sth with a star or an ASTERISK, esp in order to direct people's attention to it: [Vn] *The starred dishes on the menu are suitable for vegetarians.* **2(a)** ~ (**in sth**) to be a star(3) in a play, film, etc: [V] *She took many starring roles.* [Vpr] *She is to star in a movie about her life.* **(b)** ~ **sb** (**in sth**) to present sb as a star(3): [Vn] *a film starring Anthony Hopkins and Emma Thompson* [Vnpr] *The director wanted to star Michael Douglas in his new film.*

stardom /'stɑːdəm/ *n* [U] the status of being a

famous actor, performer, etc: *her rapid rise to star-dom* ○ *He is being groomed* (ie prepared and trained) *for stardom.*

starless *adj* with no stars to be seen: *a starless/sky/ night.*

■ **the ˌStars and ˈStripes** *n* [sing] the national flag of the USA.

ˈstar sign *n* (*infml*) any one of the 12 signs of the ZODIAC: *What's your star sign?* ○ *What star sign were you born under?*

ˈstar-studded *adj* containing a lot of famous performers: *He has assembled a star-studded cast for his new picture.*

ˌstar ˈturn *n* (*esp sing*) a main item in an entertainment or a performance: *The star turn in our show tonight will be a group of Chinese acrobats.*

starboard /ˈstɑːbəd/ *n* [U] the side of a ship or an aircraft that is on the right when one is facing forward: *alter course/come round to starboard* ○ *100 metres off the starboard bow.* Compare PORT².

starch /stɑːtʃ/ *n* (**a**) [U] a white CARBOHYDRATE food substance found in eg potatoes, flour and rice. (**b**) [U, C] food containing this: *cut down on starch.* (**c**) [U] this substance prepared in powder form or as a spray and used for making cotton clothes, etc stiff: *Spray starch on the shirt collars before ironing them.*
► **starch** *v* (*esp passive*) to make clothes, etc stiff using starch: [Vn] *starched white uniforms.*

starchy *adj* **1** containing a lot of starch: *starchy foods.* **2** (*infml derog*) very formal, stiff or conventional in manner: *a starchy middle-aged matron.*

stare /steə(r)/ *v* **1** ~ (**at sb/sth**) to look for a long time at sb/sth with the eyes wide open: [V] *It's rude to stare.* ○ *They all stared in/with amazement.* [Vpr] *She didn't like being stared at.* ○ *She was staring vacantly into the distance/into space.* ⇨ note at LOOK¹. **2** (of the eyes) to be wide open and fixed: [V] *He gazed at the scene with staring eyes.* [Vpr] *Her lifeless eyes stared at me.* **IDM** **be staring sb in the ˈface** to be obvious, easy or clear: *Defeat was staring them in the face* (ie seemed certain). ○ *The answer to the problem had been staring him in the face all the time.* **stark raving/staring mad** ⇨ STARK *adv.* **PHR V** **ˌstare sb ˈout** to stare at sb until they feel forced to lower their eyes or turn away: *The children were having a competition to see which one could stare the other out.*
► **stare** *n* a long fixed look: *give sb a cold/hard/ rude stare* ○ *We received a number of curious stares from passers-by.* ○ *Their news was greeted with a blank stare of disbelief.*

starfish /ˈstɑːfɪʃ/ *n* (*pl* unchanged) a flat sea creature in the shape of a star with five arms.

stark /stɑːk/ *adj* (**-er, -est**) **1(a)** severe and without comfort; bare¹(1b): *stark prison conditions* ○ *The landscape was grey and stark.* (**b**) [usu attrib] plain; basic: *the stark facts* ○ *Many are facing the stark reality of long-term unemployment.* **2** clearly obvious to the eye or the mind: *Her wealth is in stark contrast to the poverty all around her.* **3** [attrib] complete; absolute: *stark madness/terror.*
► **stark** *adv* **IDM** **ˌstark ˈnaked** completely naked. **ˌstark raving/staring ˈmad** completely mad.

starkly *adv*: *starkly different/evident* ○ *a style of architecture that contrasts starkly with that of a former age* ○ *The trees looked starkly black against the winter sky.*

starkness *n* [U]: *the starkness of the winter landscape/of their living conditions.*

starkers /ˈstɑːkəz/ *adj* [pred] (*Brit infml esp joc*) completely naked: *He was running down the road starkers.*

starlet /ˈstɑːlət/ *n* (*sometimes derog*) a young actor, esp a woman, who hopes to become a film star but is not yet very famous.

starlight /ˈstɑːlaɪt/ *n* [U] light from the stars: *walk home by starlight.*

starling /ˈstɑːlɪŋ/ *n* a small noisy bird with dark shiny feathers. ⇨ picture.

starling

starlit /ˈstɑːlɪt/ *adj* lighted by the stars: *a starlit night/scene.*

starry /ˈstɑːri/ *adj* (**-ier, -iest**) (**a**) lighted by stars: *a starry night/sky.* (**b**) shining like stars: *starry eyes.*
■ **ˌstarry-ˈeyed** *adj* (*infml often derog*) enthusiastic but not practical: *She's got some ˌstarry-eyed ˈnotion about reforming society.*

start¹ /stɑːt/ *n* **1(a)** [C] the beginning of a journey, an activity, a plan, a race, etc; the process or an act of starting: *make an early start (to one's journey)* ○ *She behaved badly from start to finish.* ○ *We won't finish the job today but we can make a start (on it).* ○ *I've written one page of my essay: it's not much but it's a start.* ○ *He knew from the start the idea was hopeless.* (**b**) **the start** [sing] the place where a race begins: *runners lined up at the start.* See also FALSE START. **2** [C usu *sing*] an opportunity for or help in starting: *give sb a fresh start* ○ *The money gave him just the start he needed.* **3** [C usu *sing*] an advantage gained or allowed in starting; the amount of this: *The smaller boys were given a start of 10 seconds in the race.* ○ *They didn't give me much of a start.* See also HEAD START. **4** [C usu *sing*] a sudden quick movement of surprise, fear, etc: *He sat up/woke up with a start.* ○ *You gave me quite a start* (ie surprised me). **IDM** **by/in fits and starts** ⇨ FIT⁴. **for a ˈstart** (used in an argument) as a first point: *I'm not buying it — I can't afford it for a start.* **get off to / have a flying start** ⇨ FLYING.

start² /stɑːt/ *v* ⇨ note at BEGIN. **1** ~ (**out**) to begin a journey; to leave: [V, Vp] *We plan to start (out) at 6 o'clock.* [Vpr] *I started after her* (ie followed her) *to tell her the news.* **2** to begin sth/to do sth; to begin to happen: [Vn] *I start work at 9 am.* ○ *I had to start* (ie begin using) *a new tin of paint.* ○ *He's just started a new job.* [V.to inf] *It started to rain.* [V.ing] *He started laughing.* ○ *I arrived after the play had started.* ○ *I've had enough criticism for one day — don't ˈyou start!* [Vnpr, Vpr] *They started (the concert) with a piece by Mozart.* **3** ~ (**on**) sth (**a**) to begin doing a job, an activity, a piece of work, etc: [Vn, Vnpr] *start (on) one's journey home* ○ *Have you started (on)* (ie begun to write or read) *your next book yet?* [Vnpr] *It's time to get started on/time we got started on* (ie began) *the washing up.* (**b**) ~ **sb on (doing) sth** to make sb begin doing sth: [Vnpr] *start babies on solid food.* **4(a)** (of a machine, etc) to begin operating: [V] *The car won't start.* (**b**) to make a machine, etc begin operating: [Vn] *I can't start the car.* **5** to bring sth into existence; to cause or enable sb/sth to begin or begin happening: [Vn] *start a fire* ○ *He decided to start a newspaper.* [Vnpr] *His uncle started him in business* (ie helped him, eg by giving money). [Vn.ing] *The news started me thinking.* ○ *The smoke started her coughing.* **6** ~ (**up**) (*fml*) (**a**) to make a sudden movement or change of position, eg because of fear, surprise or pain: [V] *She started at the sound of my voice.* [also Vp]. (**b**) to jump up suddenly: [V, Vp] *He started (up) from his seat.* **7** (*fml*) to move, rise or appear suddenly: [Vpr] *His eyes started out of his head* (ie suddenly opened wide, eg in surprise). **8** (*fml*) to drive an animal into the open from the place where it was hiding: [Vn] *start a hare.* **9** (*infml*) to complain or be critical: [V] *Don't you start — it's not my fault.* **IDM** **set/start/ keep the ball rolling** ⇨ BALL¹. **start a ˈfamily** to begin to have children: *They want to start a family but can't afford it at the moment.* **start (sth) from ˈscratch** to begin sth from the very beginning without advantage or preparation, esp when building or

S

developing sth: *He lost all his money and had to start again from scratch.* **start off on the right/wrong 'foot (with sb)** (*infml*) to begin sth, esp a relationship, in the right/wrong way: *He started off on the wrong foot by being rude to his new boss.* **'start something** (*infml*) to begin a fight, an argument, trouble, etc: *You shouldn't have been so rude to him — you've really started something now.* **to 'start with 1** in the first place; as the first point: *To start with we don't have enough money, and secondly we're too busy.* **2** at the beginning; to begin: *The club had only six members to start with.* ○ *I'll have melon to start with.* **PHRV** ,**start 'back 1** to begin to return: *Isn't it time we started back? It's getting dark.* **2** to jump or step back suddenly in fear, shock, surprise, etc: *He started back in alarm.*

'**start for...** to leave one place to go to another: *What time do you start for work?*

,**start 'off** to begin to move: *The horse started off at a steady trot.* ,**start off 'sth** to begin by doing sth: *The berries ,start off 'green but go red when they are ripe.* ,**start (sb) 'off (on sth)** to begin or make sb begin working on, doing, saying, etc sth: *It's impossible to stop him talking once he starts off.* ○ *What started her off on this crazy idea?*

,**start 'out (on sth)**; ,**start 'out (to do sth) 1** to begin a journey: *start out on a 20-mile walk* ○ *What time did you start out?* **2** (*infml*) to begin to do sth; to intend when starting: *start out in business* ○ *start out on a new career* ○ *start out to write/with the intention of writing a novel.*

,**start 'over** (*US*) to begin again: *She wasn't satisfied with our work and made us start (all) over.*

,**start (sth) 'up** to begin or begin working, running, happening, etc; to make sth do this: *start up a new company* ○ *The engine started up suddenly.* ○ *What started the argument up?* ○ *We couldn't start the car up.* ,**start (sb) 'up (in sth)** to cause sb to begin a career, working life, etc: *start up in business.* See also START-UP.

■ '**start-up** *n* [often *attrib*] an act of starting sth, esp of establishing a new business, etc: *the start-up costs of new ventures.*

starter /'stɑːtə(r)/ *n* **1** a person, horse, etc taking part in a race at the start: *Of the ten starters in the race only three finished.* Compare NON-STARTER. **2** a person who gives the signal for a race to start: *waiting for the starter's gun to fire.* **3** (usu with an *adj*) a person or thing that starts sth, esp in the way specified: *He was a late starter as a child* (ie He learned to talk, walk, etc later than most children). **4** a device for starting a machine, esp an engine: *a starter motor.* **5** (*esp Brit*) (*US* also **appetizer**) the first course of a meal, esp one with more than two courses: *What would you like as a starter?* **6** (often in compounds) a person or thing that starts: *a 'starter home* (ie one built specially for young people buying their first house) ○ *a 'starter kit/pack for home wine-making.* **IDM** **for 'starters** (*infml*) first of all; to start with: *What would you like (to eat) for starters?* ○ *We've got to decorate the house for starters — we can think about the garden after that.* **under ,starter's 'orders** (of horses, runners, etc ready to start a race) waiting for the order or signal to start.

starting-block /'stɑːtɪŋ blɒk/ *n* either of two blocks fixed to the ground against which a runner puts her or his feet at the start of a race.

starting-gate /'stɑːtɪŋ ɡeɪt/ *n* a barrier that is raised at the start of a race, allowing the horses, dogs, etc to start running.

starting-point /'stɑːtɪŋ pɔɪnt/ *n* a place or point from which sth begins: *We'll take this as the starting-point for our discussion.*

starting-price /'stɑːtɪŋ praɪs/ *n* the final ODDS(3) just before the start of a race.

startle /'stɑːtl/ *v* to give a sudden shock or surprise to a person or an animal; to make sb/sth move or jump suddenly from surprise: [Vn] *You startled me — I didn't hear you come in.* ○ *The sudden noise in the bushes startled her horse.* [Vn, Vn.to inf] *I was startled by the news of his death/startled to hear of his death.*

▶ **startled** /'stɑːtld/ *adj*: *a startled rabbit* ○ *a startled expression* ○ *She looked startled.*

startling /'stɑːtlɪŋ/ *adj* very surprising; astonishing; remarkable: *a startling result/achievement/revelation.* **startlingly** *adv*: *startlingly beautiful.*

starve /stɑːv/ *v* **1** to suffer severely or die from hunger; to make a person or an animal suffer or die in this way: [Vpr] *starve to death* [V] *pictures of starving children* ○ *wild animals starving in the drought* ○ (*infml*) [Vn] *She's starving herself to try to lose weight.* [also Vnpr]. **2** (*infml*) (used only in the continuous tenses) to feel very hungry: [V] *What's for dinner? I'm starving!* **PHRV** ,**starve sb into 'sth/'doing sth** to force sb to do sth by not allowing them to get food: *be ,starved into sur'render/sur'rendering.* ,**starve sb/sth of 'sth** (usu passive) to fail or refuse to give sb/sth what they need/it needs: *children ,starved of af'fection* ○ *Industry is being ,starved of technical exper'tise.* ,**starve sb 'out (of sth)** to force sb out of a place where they are hiding, etc by stopping supplies of food: *It took 8 days to starve them out (of the building).*

▶ **starvation** /stɑː'veɪʃn/ *n* [U] suffering or death caused by lack of food: *die of starvation* ○ *starvation wages* (ie too low to buy enough food) ○ *a starvation diet* (ie hardly enough food to keep one alive). ⇨ note at HUNGER.

stash /stæʃ/ *v* ~ *sth* (**away**) (*infml*) to store sth safely and secretly; to hide sth: [Vnpr, Vnp] *He has millions of dollars stashed (away) in Swiss bank accounts.* [also Vn].

▶ **stash** *n* (usu *sing*) (*infml*) a secret store: *The thieves never found my stash of money.*

stasis /'steɪsɪs/ *n* [U, C] (*pl* **stases** /-siːz/) (*fml*) a condition in which there is no change or development: *the dull stasis of provincial life.*

state¹ /steɪt/ *n* **1** [C] the condition in which a person or thing is, in appearance, mind, health, etc: *a confused state of mind* ○ *be in a state of shock* ○ *a poor state of health* ○ *in a state of undress* (ie naked) ○ *not in a fit state to drive* ○ *The house is in a very untidy state at the moment.* ○ *These buildings are in a bad state of repair* (ie need to be repaired). ○ *The government declared a state of emergency after the earthquake.* ○ *She was in a terrible state* (ie very upset, anxious, etc) *when we arrived.* **2** (also **State**) [C] a country considered as an organized political community controlled by one government; the territory occupied by this: *the State of Israel* ○ *member states of the European Union.* ⇨ note at COUNTRY 1. See also CITY-STATE, NATION-STATE, POLICE STATE, WELFARE STATE. **3** (also **State**) [C] an organized political community forming part of a country: *How many States are there in the United States of America?* ○ *the state of California.* Compare COUNTRY, PROVINCE 1. **4** (also **the State**) [U] the civil(2) government of a country: *matters/affairs of state* ○ *European heads of state* ○ *Church and State* ○ *free education provided by the state* ○ *state-owned/-sponsored/-controlled industries.* **5** [U] formal ceremony connected with high levels of government: *The Queen was in her robes of state.* ○ *The President was driven in state through the streets.* **6** **the 'States** [pl] (*infml*) the United States of America: *I've never been to the States.* **IDM** **in a good, etc state of repair** ⇨ REPAIR¹. **in/into a 'state** (*infml*) **1** in/into an excited or anxious state of mind: *She got herself into a state about her exams.* ○ *He was in a real state when I last saw him.* **2** dirty, untidy, etc:

What a state this place is in! **lie in state** ⊳ LIE². **a state of af'fairs** a set of circumstances; a situation: *What a shocking state of affairs!* **the state of 'play 1** the score, esp in cricket. **2** how opposite sides in a dispute stand in relation to one another: *What is the latest state of play in the disarmament talks?*

▶ **state** (also **State**) *adj* [attrib] **1** of, provided by or concerned with the state¹(4): ˌstate edu'cation ○ 'state schools (ie free schools run by public authorities) ○ ˌstate 'secrets ○ a ˌstate 'pension. **2** of, for or involving ceremony, used or done on ceremonial occasions: a ˌstate oc'casion ○ the ˌstate a'partments ○ a ˌstate 'visit (eg by a king or queen to another country) ○ the ˌstate opening of 'Parliament.

statehood *n* [U] the fact of being a state¹(2) and of having the rights and power of a state.

stateless *adj* (of a person) not recognized as a citizen of any country. **statelessness** *n* [U].

■ **the 'State Department** *n* the US government department of foreign affairs.

ˌ**state-of-the-'art** *adj* using the most modern or advanced techniques or methods: *a ˌstate-of-the-art com'puter program.*

ˌ**State's 'evidence** *n* [U] **IDM** ˌ**turn State's 'evidence** (*US*) = TURN KING'S/QUEEN'S EVIDENCE (EVIDENCE).

state² /steɪt/ *v* **1** to express sth in spoken or written words, esp carefully, fully and clearly: [Vn] *state one's views ○ an article in which she states the case for military action ○ There's no need to state the obvious* (ie obvious facts, etc). [V.*that*] *A police surgeon stated that the man had died from wounds to the chest and head.* [V.*wh*] *This report clearly states what the problems are.* **2** (usu passive) to arrange, fix, or announce sth in advance; to specify sth: [Vn] *at stated times/intervals ○ You must work the hours stated. ○ Follow the instructions (as) stated below.*

statecraft /'steɪtkrɑːft/ *n* [U] skill in managing state¹(4) affairs; statesmanship (STATESMAN).

stately /'steɪtli/ *adj* having dignity; impressive; grand: *a stately old woman ○ a stately bow.* ▶ **stateliness** *n* [U]: *a city famous for the stateliness and beauty of its buildings.*

■ ˌ**stately 'home** *n* (*Brit*) a large and grand house, usu of historical interest, esp one that the public may visit.

statement /'steɪtmənt/ *n* **1** [C] a thing that is stated: *The chairman is expected to make a public statement about the company's plans.* ○ (*fig*) *The artist regards his painting as a political statement.* **2** [C] a formal account of facts, views, problems, etc; a report: *an official statement ○ issue a statement to the press ○ The police asked the man to make a statement* (ie a written account of facts concerning a crime, used in court if legal action follows). **3** [U] (*fml*) the stating or expressing of sth in words: *When writing instructions, clarity of statement is the most important thing.* **4** [C] = BANK STATEMENT: *My bank sends me monthly statements.*

stateroom /'steɪtruːm, -rʊm/ *n* **1** [esp pl] a room used by important government members, members of a royal family, etc. **2** a private room on a ship.

Stateside /'steɪtsaɪd/ *adj, adv* (*US infml*) of, in or towards the USA: *a Stateside holiday ○ The play created a sensation Stateside.*

statesman /'steɪtsmən/ *n* (*pl* **-men** /-mən/; *fem* **stateswoman** /-wʊmən/, *pl* **-women** /-wɪmɪn/) a person who plays an important part in the management of State affairs, esp one who is skilled and experienced; a wise political leader: *an elder statesman of the party.*

▶ **statesmanlike** *adj* having or showing the qualities and abilities of a wise statesman: *a statesmanlike manner/role.*

statesmanship *n* [U] skill and wisdom in managing public affairs.

static /'stætɪk/ *adj* **1** not moving or changing: *a static society ○ be in a static relationship* (ie one that is dull and boring) ○ *a rather static performance of the play* (ie one in which there is little action, development of character, etc) ○ *House prices, which have been static for several months, are now rising again.* **2** (*physics*) (of force) acting by weight without producing movement: *static pressure.* Compare DYNAMIC 1.

▶ **static** *n* [U] **1** conditions in the atmosphere causing poor sound or picture quality on radio or television, marked by loud harsh noises: *There was too much static to hear their message clearly.* **2** (also ˌ**static elec'tricity**) electricity gathering on or in an object which cannot conduct a current: *My hair gets full of static in very dry weather.*

statics *n* [sing *v*] the branch of PHYSICS dealing with the forces that balance each other to keep objects in a state of rest.

station /'steɪʃn/ *n* **1(a)** a place where trains stop on a railway line; the buildings connected with this: *a railway/(US) railroad station ○ the station platform/ staff ○ I get off at the next station.* **(b)** a similar place where buses and coaches stop: *The bus leaves the bus/coach station at 9.42 am.* **2** (esp in compounds) a place, building, etc where a service is organized and provided, or specialized, esp scientific, work is done: *a po'lice/'fire station ○ a 'radar station ○ an agriˌcultural re'search station ○ a ˌnuclear 'power station.* **3** (esp in compounds) a company that broadcasts on radio or television; a building from which this is done: *satellite TV stations ○ a local radio station.* **4** (*dated or fml*) one's social position; rank or status: *people of all stations in life ○ He has ideas above his station.* **5** (*Austral*) a usu large sheep or cattle farm. **6** a small military or naval base or the people living in it: *He's returning to his army station.* **IDM** **panic stations** ⊳ PANIC. See also PETROL STATION, POLLING-STATION, SPACE STATION.

▶ **station** *v* (esp passive) to put sb, oneself, an army, etc at or in a certain place: [Vnpr] *Their regiment is stationed in Cyprus. ○ The police sergeant stationed himself by the back door.* [also Vnadv].

■ ˌ**station agent** *n* (*US*) = STATIONMASTER.

ˌ**Stations of the 'Cross** *n* [pl] a series of fourteen images or pictures telling the story of Christ's sufferings and death, at which prayers are said in certain churches.

'**station-wagon** *n* (*US*) = ESTATE CAR. ⊳ picture at HATCHBACK.

stationary /'steɪʃənri; *US* -neri/ *adj* **1** not moving or not intended to be moved: *remain stationary ○ hit a stationary vehicle ○ a stationary exercise bike.* **2** not changing in condition or quantity: *a stationary population.*

stationer /'steɪʃnə(r)/ *n* a person who runs a shop selling materials for writing, eg paper, pens and envelopes: *Is there a good stationer's (shop) near here?*

stationery /'steɪʃənri; *US* -neri/ *n* [U] materials for writing, eg paper, pens and envelopes: *order some more office stationery.*

stationmaster /'steɪʃnmɑːstə(r)/ (*US* also '**station agent**) a person in charge of a railway station.

statistics /stə'tɪstɪks/ *n* **(a)** [pl] a collection of information shown in numbers: *crime/unemployment statistics ○ use statistics to support an argument ○ Statistics show that out of 20 000 accidental deaths, 7 000 occurred in the home.* **(b)** [sing *v*] the science of collecting, classifying and analysing such information: *She's studying statistics at university.*

▶ **statistic** *n* an item of information expressed in numbers: *unearth a fascinating statistic.*

statistical /stə'tɪstɪkl/ *adj* of or shown by statistics: *statistical evidence.* **statistically** /-kli/ *adv*: *a statistically significant increase in health problems ○ To*

S

make these results statistically valid, we need to question more people.

statistician /ˌstætɪˈstɪʃn/ n a person who studies or works with statistics.

statuary /ˈstætʃuəri; US -ueri/ n [U] statues: a collection of marble statuary.

statue /ˈstætʃuː/ n a figure of a person, an animal, etc in stone, metal, etc, usu the same size as in real life or larger: erect a bronze statue of the Buddha ○ a Greek statue.

statuesque /ˌstætʃuˈesk/ adj (approv) (a) like a statue in size, dignity or lack of movement: remain in a statuesque position. (b) (esp of women) tall and graceful: her statuesque figure.

statuette /ˌstætʃuˈet/ n a small statue: A china statuette of a shepherdess stood on the table.

stature /ˈstætʃə(r)/ n [U] 1 the natural height of the body: be small in stature/short of stature. 2 importance and reputation gained by ability or achievement: a scientist of international stature ○ her growing political stature.

status /ˈsteɪtəs/ n [U] 1 the social, legal or professional position of sb/sth in relation to others: grant sb refugee status ○ be given equal status with other members of staff ○ Teachers don't have a very high status in this country. ○ There has been a decline in the country's economic status. See also MARITAL STATUS. 2 high rank or social position: seek status and security ○ He's very aware of his status.
■ **'status symbol** n a possession that is thought to show sb's high social rank, wealth, etc: He only bought the yacht as a status symbol — he doesn't use it very often.

status quo /ˌsteɪtəs ˈkwəʊ/ n the status quo [sing] the situation or state of affairs as it is now, or as it was before a recent change: upset/restore/preserve the status quo ○ conservatives who defend the status quo.

statute /ˈstætʃuːt/ n [C] 1 a law passed by an official ruling body and written down formally: a parliamentary/federal statue ○ It is laid down by statute. 2 any of the rules of an organization or institution: Under the statutes of the university, staff must retire at 65.
■ **'statute-book** n a collection of all the laws made by a government: It's not yet on the statute-book (ie not included in statute law).
'statute law n [U] all the statutes as a group. Compare CASE-LAW, COMMON LAW.

statutory /ˈstætʃətri; US -tɔːri/ adj [usu attrib] fixed, done or required by statute: statutory duties/guidelines/rights ○ statutory control of prices and incomes. ▶ **statutorily** adv.
■ **ˌstatutory 'rape** n [U] (US) the act of sex with a person under the age of full legal responsibility.

staunch /stɔːntʃ/ adj (-er, -est) firm and loyal in opinion and attitude: a staunch Christian/Conservative/Republican ○ a staunch supporter/defender of the EU ○ one of our staunchest allies. ▶ **staunchly** adv: staunchly committed/opposed to the changes.

stave¹ /steɪv/ n 1 a strong stick or pole: fence staves ○ riot police carrying staves. Compare STAFF 4. 2 any of the curved pieces of wood forming the side of a barrel, etc: a garden tub made of wooden staves. 3 (music) = STAFF 3.

stave² /steɪv/ v (pt, pp staved or stove /stəʊv/)
PHRV ˌstave sth **'in** to break or make a hole in sth: The side of the boat was stove in when it hit the rocks.
ˌstave sth **'off** (pt, pp staved) to keep sth bad away from one; to delay sth, esp temporarily: stave off disaster/danger/bankruptcy/hunger.

stay¹ /steɪ/ v 1(a) to remain or continue in the same place for a long or short time, permanently or temporarily, as specified by the context: [V] stay (at) home (ie not go out or to work) ○ I'm afraid I can't stay (ie I must leave now). [V-adj] stay late at the office [Vpr] stay in the house/in bed/in one's room ○ stay in teaching/journalism (ie not change one's job) ○ stay away from (ie not go to) school ○ Stay on this road for two miles then turn left. ○ They asked me to stay for/to dinner. [Vadv] Stay here until I come back. [V.to inf] We stayed to see what would happen. [Vn] I can only stay a few minutes. [Vp] I can't get my hat to stay on. ○ My trousers only stay up if I wear a belt. ▷ note at AND. (b) to continue in a certain state: [V-adj] stay awake ○ stay single (ie not marry) ○ He never stays sober for long. [Vp] The TV stays on all day at this place. [V-n] They stayed friends for years. ○ Everything has stayed the same. 2 to remain or live somewhere temporarily, esp as a visitor or a guest: [V] It's late — why don't you stay (ie for the night)? [Vpr] We stayed in a hotel. ○ I hope you will stay with us next time you visit Durham. ○ Jenny's staying in Dublin for a few days, but she now lives/is now living (ie has her home) in Belfast. [Vn] She **stayed the night** with me (ie slept at my house for the night). [also Vadv]. **IDM** **be here to 'stay/have come to 'stay** (infml) to be permanent and generally accepted: I hope that (the idea of) equality of opportunity for men and women has come to/is here to stay. **keep/stay/steer clear** ▷ CLEAR². **stay the 'course** to continue going to the end of sth difficult, eg a race, a task or a struggle: I don't think he's dedicated enough to stay the course. **stay one's 'hand** (arch or rhet) to hold oneself back from doing sth. **stay 'put** (infml) to remain where one/it is or is placed: We had thought of moving house but we've decided to stay put for a while. **PHRV** ˌstay be'hind (esp Brit) to remain at a place after others have left, esp to go home: They stayed behind after the party to help clear up. ○ The teacher told him to stay behind after class. ○ stay 'down (of food) to remain in the stomach, rather than be thrown up as VOMIT: She's so ill that nothing will stay down, not even water. ˌstay 'in to stay indoors: The doctor advised me to stay in for a few days. ˌstay 'on (at...) to remain at a place of study, employment, etc after others have left: He stayed on at university to do research. ˌstay 'out 1 to remain out of the house or in the open air, esp after dark: I don't like you staying out so late. 2 (of workers) to remain on strike: The miners stayed out for a whole year. ˌstay 'out of sth to remain at a point where one cannot be reached or affected by sb/sth: His father told him to stay out of trouble. ˌstay 'up to remain awake; not go to bed: The children were allowed to stay up for their favourite TV programme.
▶ **stay** n a period of staying; a visit: an overnight stay in Karachi ○ a two-week stay with my uncle. **IDM** **a ˌstay of exe'cution** (esp law) a delay in carrying out the order of a court: (fig) They were due to start demolishing the old theatre today but there's been a last-minute stay of execution.
stayer n a person or animal with the ability to keep going in a tiring race, competition, etc: He's proved himself a stayer over a long distance.
■ **'stay-at-home** n (infml usu derog) a person who rarely leaves her or his home to go anywhere or do anything new.
'staying power n [U] the ability to keep going; STAMINA: Long-distance runners need plenty of staying power.

stay² /steɪ/ n [C] a rope or wire supporting a ship's MAST(1), a pole, etc. See also MAINSTAY.

STD /ˌes tiː ˈdiː/ abbr (Brit) 1 sexually transmitted disease: an STD clinic. 2 subscriber trunk dialling (a system of making telephone calls without using an OPERATOR(2)): What's the STD code for Cambridge?

stead /sted/ n **IDM** in sb's/sth's 'stead (fml) in

sb's/sth's place; instead of sb/sth: *The old church was demolished and a modern office block built in its stead.* **stand sb in good ˈstead** to be useful or helpful to sb when needed: *Her languages will stand her in very good stead when she starts looking for a job.*

steadfast /ˈstedfɑːst; US -fæst/ *adj* ~ (**in sth / to sth**) (*fml approv*) firm and not changing; constant: *steadfast loyalty to one's country* ○ *remain steadfast in one's beliefs/to one's principles.* ▶ **steadfastly** *adv.* **steadfastness** *n* [U].

steady /ˈstedi/ *adj* (**-ier, -iest**) **1** firmly fixed, supported or balanced; not shaking or likely to fall over: *hold the camera steady* ○ *a steady gaze* ○ *He's not very steady on his legs after his illness.* ○ *Such fine work requires a good eye and a steady hand.* ○ *She was trembling with excitement but she kept her voice steady.* Compare UNSTEADY. **2** developing, etc gradually and in an even and regular way without being interrupted: *steady progress/improvement* ○ *a steady increase in the number of people unemployed* ○ *I've been getting a steady stream of letters on this subject.* **3** not changing; constant or regular: *move at a steady pace* ○ *steady breathing* ○ *a steady job/income* ○ *If you drive at a steady 50 miles an hour you will use less petrol.* ○ (*dated*) *a steady boyfriend/girlfriend* (ie with whom one has a serious relationship or one that has lasted for some time). **4** sensible and reliable: *a steady young man* ○ *a steady worker.* **IDM** **steady** (**ˈon**)! (*Brit infml*) (used as a warning) be careful; control yourself: *Steady on! You can't say things like that about someone you've never met.* ▶ **steadily** /ˈstedɪli/ *adv*: *work steadily* ○ *Prices are rising steadily.* ○ *The situation got steadily worse.* **steadiness** *n* [U].

steady *adv* **IDM** **go ˈsteady (with sb)** (*dated infml*) to have a sexual or romantic relationship with sb, in which one sees the other person regularly, esp over a period of time: *Are Tony and Jane going steady?* **solid/steady as a rock** ⇨ ROCK[1].

steady *v* (*pt, pp* **steadied**) to become or make sth/sb/oneself steady: [V] *Prices are steadying.* [Vn] *He thought he was going to fall and put a hand out to steady himself.* ○ *She had a drink to steady her nerves.* ○ *Her elder sister is a steadying influence on her.*

steak /steɪk/ *n* **1** [C,U] a thick flat piece of meat, esp (BEEF 1), for grilling (GRILL): *fillet/rump/sirloin steak* ○ *a steak-knife* (ie one with a special blade for eating steak with) ○ *Would you like your steak rare, medium or well-done?* **2** [U] BEEF(1) of less good quality, often cut into smaller pieces and used in pies, STEW, etc: *steak and kidney pie* ○ *braising steak.* **3** [C] a thick firm piece of fish: *cod/salmon steaks.*

■ **ˈsteak-house** *n* a restaurant that specializes in serving BEEF(1) steaks.

steal /stiːl/ *v* (*pt* **stole** /stəʊl/ *pp* **stolen** /ˈstəʊlən/) **1** ~ (**sth**) (**from sb/sth**) to take sth that belongs to another person without permission or legal right and usu secretly: [V] *It's wrong to steal.* [Vpr] *He stole from the rich to give to the poor.* [Vn] *Someone has stolen my watch.* ○ *I have had my watch stolen.* ○ *steal sb's ideas* ○ *They was arrested for receiving stolen goods.* [Vnpr] *He stole a towel from the hotel.* ⇨ note at ROB. **2** to obtain sth quickly or without being noticed: [Vn] *stolen kisses in shop doorways* ○ *steal a glance at oneself in the mirror.* **3** to move in the specified direction secretly and quietly, or without being noticed: [Vpr] *He stole into the room.* ○ *She stole up on me in the darkness.* ○ *The morning light was stealing through the shutters.* [also Vp]. ⇨ note at PROWL. **IDM** **steal a ˈmarch (on sb)** to gain an advantage over sb by doing sth secretly, or by acting before they do. **steal the ˈshow** to attract the most attention and praise, esp unexpectedly: *Despite fine acting by several well-known stars it was a young*

newcomer who stole the show. **steal sb's ˈthunder** to spoil sb's attempt to impress by acting before they do, making a better impression, etc.

▶ **steal** *n* [sing] (*infml esp US*) a thing that is for sale at an unexpectedly low price: *Ladies and gentlemen, it's a steal at only $50.*

stealth /stelθ/ *n* [U] the action of doing sth in a quiet or secret way: *Tracking wild animals requires great stealth.* ○ *The terrorists operate by stealth.*

▶ **stealth** *adj* [attrib] connected with a branch of technology that deals with making aircraft difficult to detect by RADAR, etc: *a stealth bomber.*

stealthy *adj* doing things, or done, with stealth: *stealthy movements.* **stealthily** /-ɪli/ *adv.*

steam /stiːm/ *n* [U] (**a**) the hot gas that water changes into when it boils: *steam coming out of a boiling kettle* ○ *The laundry was full of steam.* ⇨ note at WATER[1]. (**b**) the power obtained using this gas under pressure: *a steam brake/whistle* (ie worked by steam) ○ *the introduction of steam* (ie machines driven by steam) *in the 18th century.* **full speed/steam ahead** ⇨ FULL. **ˌget up /ˌpick up ˈsteam 1** (of a vehicle) to increase speed gradually. **2** (*infml*) to become gradually more powerful or involve more activity, etc: *The election campaign is beginning to get up steam.* **ˌlet off ˈsteam** (*infml*) to release energy or express strong emotions by behaving in a wild or noisy way: *The children were out in the playground letting off steam.* **ˌrun out of ˈsteam** (*infml*) to stop because one has no more energy or enthusiasm: *She was very keen on the plan at first but she seems to be running out of steam.* **under one's own ˈsteam** (*infml*) without help from others: *If I can't get a lift I'll have to get there under my own steam.*

▶ **steam** *v* **1** to send out steam: [V] *steaming hot coffee* [V, Vp] *The kettle was steaming (away) on the stove.* **2** to cook sth using steam: [Vn] *steamed pudding* ○ *Steam the fish for 10 minutes.* ⇨ note at COOK. **3**(**a**) to move in the specified direction using the power of steam: [Vpr] *a boat steaming up the Nile* ○ *The train steamed into/out of the station.* [also Vp]. (**b**) to move quickly in the specified direction: [Vpr] *Jeff steamed into the room and apologized for being late.* [also Vp]. **IDM** **be/get (all) steamed ˈup (about/over sth)** (*infml*) to become very angry or excited about sth: *Calm down — it's nothing to get steamed up about!* **PHRV** **ˌsteam sth ˈoff (sth)** to remove one piece of paper from another using steam to soften the glue sticking it together: *steam stamps off envelopes.* **ˌsteam sth ˈopen** to open an envelope, etc by using steam to soften the glue sticking it together: *She steamed the envelope open and read the letter.* **ˌsteam (sth) ˈup** to become or make sth covered with steam: *The car windows had steamed up.* **steamer** *n* **1** a boat or ship driven by steam. **2** a metal container with small holes in it, in which food is cooked using steam.

steamy *adj* **1** like steam or full of steam: *a steamy kitchen* ○ *a steamy jungle.* **2** (*infml*) showing or describing sexual activity; EROTIC: *steamy love scenes.*

■ **ˈsteam engine** *n* a train or engine driven by steam.

ˈsteam iron *n* an electric iron that can produce steam, making it easier to remove the creases (CREASE 1) from clothes.

ˈsteam shovel *n* (*esp US*) a machine for digging, originally worked by steam.

ˈsteam train *n* a train driven by steam: *a steam train enthusiast.*

steamboat /ˈstiːmbəʊt/ *n* a boat driven by steam, used esp formerly on rivers and along coasts.

steamroller /ˈstiːmrəʊlə(r)/ *n* a large slow vehicle with wide heavy wheels, used for making roads flat.

▶ **steamroller** *v* to crush or defeat sb/sth com-

pletely: [Vn] *steamrolling all opposition.* **PHRV**
¸**steamroller sb ¹into sth / doing sth** to force sb
into a situation or course of action.

steamship /'sti:mʃɪp/ *n* a ship driven by steam.

steed /sti:d/ *n* (*arch or rhet*) a horse: *my trusty steed.*

steel /sti:l/ *n* [U] **1(a)** a strong hard metal made of a
mixture of iron and CARBON(1), used for making
vehicles, tools, knives, machinery, etc: *It's made of
steel.* ○ *steel knives* ○ *a concrete and steel structure.* **(b)**
the industry that produces steel; the production of
steel: *the steel strike* ○ *deserted steel mills* ○ *the steel
areas of the north* ○ ¹*steel workers.* See also STAINLESS
STEEL. **2** (*arch or rhet*) weapons for fighting with:
the taste of cold steel. **IDM** **of ¹steel** of great
strength or courage: *a man of steel* ○ *nerves of steel.*
▶ **steel** *v* ~ **oneself (for/against sth)**; ~ **oneself (to
do sth)** to make oneself mentally or emotionally
stronger in order to be able to deal with sth unpleasant: [Vnpr] *She steeled herself for the task of telling
them the bad news.* [Vn.*to* inf] *He had to steel himself
to pick up the phone.* [also Vn].
steely *adj* like steel in colour, brightness or
strength: *his steely blue eyes* ○ *with steely determination.* **steeliness** *n* [U].
■ ¸**steel ¹band** *n* a band of musicians with instruments made from empty oil drums (DRUM¹ 2). Steel
bands originated in the West Indies.
¸**steel ¹wool** *n* [U] a mass of fine steel threads used
for making a surface smooth, for cleaning metal, etc.
Compare WIRE WOOL.

steelworks /'sti:lwɜ:ks/ *n* (*pl* unchanged) [sing or
pl *v*] a factory where steel is made.

steep¹ /sti:p/ *adj* (-er, -est) **1** (of a slope, stairs, etc)
rising or falling sharply, not gradually: *a steep path,
descent / hill / climb / gradient* ○ *I never cycle up that
hill — it's too steep.* **2** [usu attrib] (of a rise or fall in
an amount) sudden and very big: *a steep increase in
prices* ○ *The economy has gone into a steep decline.* **3**
(*infml*) (of a price or demand) too much; not reasonable; excessive: *£2 for a cup of coffee seems a bit steep
to me.*
▶ **steepen** /'sti:pən/ *v* to become or make sth
steep¹(1) or steeper: [V] *The path steepens as you
climb the hillside.* [also Vn].
steeply *adv.*
steepness *n* [U].

steep² /sti:p/ *v* **PHRV** ¹**steep sb / oneself / sth in sth**
(esp passive) to fill sth thoroughly with sth; to give
oneself / sb a thorough knowledge of sth: *a city
steeped in history* ○ *He steeped himself in the literature of ancient Greece and Rome.* ¹**steep sth in sth**
(esp passive) to put food in a liquid and leave it
there for some time, esp to soften it or give it
flavour: *plums steeped in brandy.*

steeple /'sti:pl/ *n* a tall tower with a SPIRE on top,
rising above the roof of a church. ⇨ picture at
CHURCH.

steeplechase /'sti:pltʃeɪs/ *n* **1** a long horse-race
(HORSE) in which the horses must jump over a series
of hedges and ditches. Compare FLAT-RACING. **2** a
long race in which people must jump over a series
of fences and ditches round a running track.
▶ **steeplechaser** *n* a person or horse competing in
steeplechases.

steeplejack /'sti:pldʒæk/ *n* a person who climbs
steeples, tall chimneys, etc to repair or paint them.

steer¹ /stɪə(r)/ *v* **1(a)** to direct or control the movement of a boat, car, etc: [V] *You steer and I'll push.*
[Vn, Vnpr] *steer a boat (into the harbour)* [Vpr] *steer
into the wind.* ⇨ note at TRAVEL. **(b)** (of a boat, car,
etc) to move in a particular direction as a result of
being steered by sb: [Vpr] *The boat steered round the
rocks.* [also Vadv]. **2** to guide sb's movements,
thoughts, etc: [Vnpr] *She steered me towards a table
in the corner.* ○ *He managed to steer the discussion
away from the subject of money.* ○ *The manual steers*

the user through the computer's main features. **3** to
follow a particular course: [Vadv] *steering north*
[Vn] *keep steering a northerly course* ○ (*fig*) *try to
steer a middle course between two extreme views.* **IDM**
keep/stay/steer clear ⇨ CLEAR².
▶ **steering** /'stɪərɪŋ/ *n* [U] the equipment or mechanism for steering a car, boat, etc: *power steering* ○
There is something wrong with the steering.
■ ¹**steering-column** *n* the part of a car or other
vehicle on which the steering-wheel is fitted.
¹**steering committee**, ¹**steering group** *ns* a committee that decides the order of certain business
activities and guides their general course.
¹**steering-wheel** (also **wheel**) *n* the wheel that the
driver turns in order to steer a vehicle. ⇨ picture at
CAR.

steer² /stɪə(r)/ *n* a young, usu castrated (CASTRATE),
male animal of the ox family, kept for its meat.
Compare BULL¹ 1, BULLOCK, OX 1.

steerage /'stɪərɪdʒ/ *n* [U] (formerly) the part of a
ship where accommodation was provided for passengers with the cheapest tickets: *travel steerage* ○
steerage passengers.

stellar /'stelə(r)/ *adj* [esp attrib] (*fml*) of a star or
stars: *stellar constellations.* Compare INTERSTELLAR.

stem¹ /stem/ *n* **1** the main long thin part of a plant
above the ground, or any of the smaller parts growing from this, from which the leaves or flowers
grow. ⇨ picture at FLOWER, FRUIT, FUNGUS. **2** a thin
part of sth, esp the narrow part of a WINEGLASS
between the base and the bowl, or the tube of a
tobacco pipe. **3** (*grammar*) the main part of a word
that remains the same when endings are added to it:
'Writ' is the stem of the forms *'writes'*, *'writing'* and
'written'. **IDM** **from ¸stem to ¹stern** from the front
to the back, esp of a ship: *The liner has been refitted
from stem to stern.*
▶ **stem** *v* (-mm-) **PHRV** ¹**stem from sth** to have sth
as its origin or cause: *discontent stemming from low
pay and poor working conditions* ○ *Her passion for
India stems from the time she spent there as a child.*
-¹**stemmed** (forming compound *adjs*) having a stem
or stems of the specified type: ¸*long-/*¸*short-/*
¸*thick-stemmed ¹glasses.*

stem² /stem/ *v* (-mm-) to stop sth which is flowing,
spreading or increasing: [Vn] *bandage a cut to stem
the bleeding* ○ *stem the flow of water from a burst pipe*
○ *an attempt to stem the tide of anti-government
feeling.*

stemware /'stemweə(r)/ *n* [U] (*US*) glasses and
glass bowls with a stem(2).

stench /stentʃ/ *n* (usu *sing*) a very unpleasant
smell: *the stench of rotting meat.*

stencil /'stensl/ *n* [C] **(a)** a thin sheet of metal,
cardboard, etc with a design or letters cut out of it,
used for putting this design, etc onto a surface when
ink or paint is applied to it. **(b)** a design, etc produced in this way: *decorate a wall with flower
stencils.*
▶ **stencil** *v* (-ll-; *US* also -l-) ~ **(A on B / B with A)** to
produce a design, etc by using a stencil; to mark a
surface with a stencil: [Vnpr] *stencil a pattern on
fabric* ○ *walls stencilled with flowers* [also V, Vn].

steno /'stenəʊ/ *n* (*pl* -os) (*infml esp US*) = STENO-
GRAPHER.

stenography /stə'nɒɡrəfi/ *n* [U] (*esp US*) = SHORT-
HAND.
▶ **stenographer** /-fə(r)/ *n* (*esp US*) a shorthand
typist (SHORTHAND).

stentorian /sten'tɔːrɪən/ *adj* (*fml*) (of a voice) loud
and powerful: *a stentorian roar.*

step¹ /step/ *v* (-pp-) to lift and put down one's foot,
or one foot after the other, in order to walk in the
direction or to the place specified: [Vpr] *step on sb's
foot* ○ *step in a puddle* ○ *step across a stream* ○ *step
into the house* ○ *step onto/off a train* [Vadv, Vp] *step*

forwards/back [Vadv] *step aside to let sb pass.* **IDM**
step into the ¹breach to take the place of sb who is
unexpectedly absent, in order to perform a particular task, do their job, etc: *Julie fell ill just before the
show so I was asked to step into the breach.* **step
into sb's ¹shoes** to take control of a task or job
from another person: *She stepped into her father's
shoes when he retired.* **¹step on it**; (US) **step on the
¹gas** (*infml*) to go faster, esp in a vehicle; to hurry:
You'll be late if you don't step on it. **step out of ¹line**
to behave badly or in a different way from what is
expected: *The teacher warned them that she would
punish anyone who stepped out of line.* **PHR V** ¸**step
a¹side/¹down** to leave an important job or position,
allowing another person to take one's place: *It's time
for me to step aside/down as chief executive and let a
younger person take over.*
¸**step ¹forward** to offer one's help, services, information, etc: *The organizing committee is
appealing for volunteers to step forward.*
¸**step ¹in** to become involved in a difficult situation,
an argument, etc, esp in order to help sb, stop sth
happening, etc: *If the police had not stepped in when
they did there would have been a serious incident.*
¸**step ¹out** (*esp US*) to leave a room, house, etc.
¸**step ¹up** to come forward: *She stepped up to collect
her prize.* ¸**step sth ¹up** to increase the amount,
speed or intensity of sth: *step up production* ○ *The
terrorists have stepped up their campaign of violence.*
■ **¹stepping-stone** *n* (**a**) a large stone or one of a
line of such stones that one can step on in order to
cross a stream, river, etc on foot. (**b**) a thing, event,
etc that allows sb to make progress or to begin to
achieve sth: *a first stepping-stone on the path to
success.*

step² /step/ *n* **1** [C] (**a**) an act of stepping once in
walking, running, dancing, etc: *He took a step towards the door.* ○ *Her boots sank further into the mud
with each step she took.* (**b**) the distance covered by a
step: *retrace one's steps* (ie go back) ○ *move a step
closer to the fire* ○ *It's only a few steps farther.* ○ *He
walked with us every step of the way.* (**c**) (also
¹**footstep**) a sound of sb walking: *We heard steps
outside.* (**d**) (*fml*) a particular way of walking: *She
felt pleased and her step was light.* **2** [C] one of a
series of actions taken in order to achieve sth: *the
first step on the road to recovery* ○ *This won't solve all
our problems, but it's a step in the right direction.* ○ *This has been a great step forward* (ie A lot
of progress has been made). ○ *What's the next step?*
(ie What must we do next?) ○ *The government is
taking steps* to ensure that the matter is properly
investigated. ○ *Our marketing methods put us a step/
several steps ahead of our main rivals.* **3** [C] a flat
surface, often one in a series, on which one's foot is
placed when going from one level to another: *a flight
of steps* ○ *Mind the step when you go down into the
cellar.* ○ *The child was sitting on the top/bottom step.*
See also DOORSTEP. ➪ picture at LADDER. ➪ note at
STAIR. **4** [C] any of a series of stages in a process; a
particular grade on a scale: *When do you get your
next step up* (ie When will you be promoted)? **5
steps** [pl] (*Brit*) a STEPLADDER: *a pair of steps* ○ *We
need the steps to get into the loft.* **6** [C often *pl*] a
series of movements of the feet, forming part of a
dance: *I don't know the steps for this dance.* **IDM**
break ¹step to change the way one is walking so
that one does not put the correct foot on the ground
at the same time as the people one is walking or
marching with. **change step** ➪ CHANGE¹. **fall into
¹step (with sb)** to change the way one is walking so
that one puts the correct foot on the ground at the
same time as the people one is walking or marching
with. **in / out of ¹step (with sb/sth) 1** putting/not
putting one's correct foot on the ground at the same
time as the people one is walking or marching with.

2 conforming/not conforming to what others are
doing or thinking: *He's out of step with modern ideas.*
mind/watch one's ¹step 1 to walk carefully. **2** to
behave or act carefully: *You'll be in trouble if you
don't watch your step.* ¸**step by ¹step** moving slowly
and gradually from one action or stage to the next:
I'll explain it to you step by step. ○ *a* ¸*step-by-step
in¹struction manual.*

step- /step-/ *pref* related as a result of one parent
marrying again. ➪ App 4.
■ **step-parent** /¹step peərənt/ *n* a STEPMOTHER or
STEPFATHER.

stepbrother /¹stepbrʌðə(r)/ *n* a son of one's STEP-
MOTHER or STEPFATHER by an earlier marriage.

stepchild /¹steptʃaɪld/ *n* (*pl* **-children** /-tʃɪldrən/) a
child of one's husband or wife by an earlier marriage.

stepdaughter /¹stepdɔːtə(r)/ *n* a daughter of one's
husband or wife by an earlier marriage.

stepfather /¹stepfɑːðə(r)/ *n* the man whom one's
mother has married after one's mother and father
have divorced (DIVORCE²) or one's father has died.

stepladder /¹steplædə(r)/ *n* a short folding ladder
that can stand on its own, with steps and usu a
small platform at the top. ➪ picture at LADDER.

stepmother /¹stepmʌðə(r)/ *n* the woman whom
one's father has married after one's father and
mother have divorced (DIVORCE²) or one's mother
has died.

steppe /step/ *n* (usu *pl*) a large area of land with
grass but few trees, esp in SE Europe and Siberia.
Compare PAMPAS, PRAIRIE, SAVANNAH, VELD.

stepsister /¹stepsɪstə(r)/ *n* a daughter of one's STEP-
MOTHER or STEPFATHER by an earlier marriage.

stepson /¹stepsʌn/ *n* a son of one's husband or wife
by an earlier marriage.

-ster *suff* (with *ns* and *adjs* forming *ns*) a person
connected with or having the quality of: *gangster* ○
trickster ○ *youngster.*

stereo /¹steriəʊ/ *n* (*pl* **-os**) (**a**) (also ¹**stereo system**)
[C] a CD player, CASSETTE player, radio, etc with two
separate speakers (SPEAK) so that different sounds
can be directed through each: *a car stereo.* Compare
MONO. See also PERSONAL STEREO. (**b**) [U] sound or a
recording using this system: *broadcast in stereo.* ►
stereo *adj* [attrib]: *a stereo recording/broadcast/
television.*

stereophonic /¸steriə¹fɒnɪk/ *adj* STEREO: *stereophonic sound.*

stereoscopic /¸steriə¹skɒpɪk/ *adj* seen as a three-
dimensional (THREE) picture; capable of seeing in
this way: *a stereoscopic image* ○ *stereoscopic vision.*

stereotype /¹steriətaɪp/ *n* [C] a fixed idea, image,
etc that many people have of a particular type of
person or thing, but which is often not true in
reality: *racial/sexual stereotypes* ○ *He doesn't conform to the usual stereotype of the city businessman
with a dark suit and briefcase.* ○ *the stereotype view of
women as housewives.* ► **stereotyped** *adj*: *a play
full of stereotyped characters.* **stereotypical**
/¸steriə¹tɪpɪkl/ *adj*: *a stereotypical portrayal of a gay
man.* **stereotyping** *n* [U]: *sexual stereotyping.*

sterile /¹steraɪl; US ¹sterəl/ *adj* **1** (of humans or
animals) not able to produce children or young:
Medical tests showed that he was sterile. Compare
FERTILE. **2** free from bacteria, etc: *sterile bandages* ○
An operating theatre should be completely sterile. **3**
(of discussion, communication, etc) not producing
any useful results: *a sterile debate.* **4** (of land) not
good enough to produce crops. **5** (*tech*) (of plants)
not producing fruit or seeds. **6** lacking individual
personality or imagination: *The room felt cold and
sterile.*
► **sterility** /stə¹rɪləti/ *n* [U]: *The disease can cause
sterility in men and women.* ○ *sterility of design.*

sterilize, -ise /'sterəlaız/ v **1** to make sth free from bacteria: [Vn] *sterilized milk* ○ *sterilized surgical instruments.* **2** to make a person or an animal unable to produce children or young, esp by removing or blocking the sex organs: [Vn] *After her fourth child she decided to be sterilized.* **sterilization, -isation** /ˌsterəlaı'zeıʃn; US -lə'z-/ n [U].

sterling /'stɜːlɪŋ/ n [U] British money: *the pound sterling* (ie the British £) ○ *payable in sterling or American dollars.* Compare POUND¹ 1a.
▶ **sterling** adj [usu attrib] of excellent quality; reliable; genuine: *her sterling work as an organizer.*
ˌsterling 'silver n [U] silver of a particular fixed standard of PURITY: *sterling silver jewellery.*

stern¹ /stɜːn/ adj (-er, -est) **(a)** serious and disapproving, not kind or cheerful; expecting to be obeyed: *a stern face/expression/voice* ○ *a stern warning/message* ○ *Her father looked rather stern.* **(b)** severe and strict: *The police are planning sterner measures to combat crime.* **IDM** **be made of sterner 'stuff** to have a stronger character and be more determined in dealing with problems than others: *Many would have given up, but Tim was made of sterner stuff.* ▶ **sternly** adv: *'Do as I say,' she said sternly.* **sternness** n [U].

stern² /stɜːn/ n [C] the back end of a ship or boat: *standing at/in the stern of the boat* ○ *walk towards the stern of a ship.* Compare BOW³. ⇨ picture at YACHT. **IDM** **from stem to stern** ⇨ STEM¹.

sternum /'stɜːnəm/ n (pl **sternums** or **sterna** /-nə/) (anatomy) = BREASTBONE.

steroid /'steroıd, 'stıəroıd/ n (chemistry) any of a number of chemical compounds produced naturally in the body, including certain hormones (HORMONE) and vitamins (VITAMIN). Steroids can be used to treat various diseases and are also sometimes used by sports players to improve their performance.

stertorous /'stɜːtərəs/ adj (fml) (of breathing or a person breathing) making a loud noise.

stethoscope /'steθəskəup/ n an instrument used by a doctor for listening to the beating of the heart, sounds of breathing, etc. It consists of a circular piece placed against the patient's chest, with two tubes leading to parts that fit in the doctor's ears.

stetson /'stetsn/ n a tall hat with a wide BRIM, worn esp by American cowboys (COWBOY). ⇨ picture at HAT.

stevedore /'stiːvədɔː(r)/ n a person whose job is to move goods on and off ships. See also DOCKER.

stew /stjuː; US stuː/ v to cook or allow sth to cook slowly in liquid in a closed dish, pan, etc: [V] *The meat needs to stew for several hours.* ○ *stewing steak/ beef* (ie beef suitable for stewing) [Vn] *stewed apple and custard.* **IDM** **let sb stew in their own 'juice** (infml) to leave sb to suffer from the unpleasant consequences of their own actions without helping them or trying to make them feel better: *Don't say anything to Jill yet — let her stew in her own juice for a bit.*
▶ **stew** n [U,C] a dish of meat, vegetables, etc cooked slowly in liquid in a closed dish: *a beef stew* ○ *have some more stew.* See also IRISH STEW. **IDM** **get (oneself)/be in a 'stew (about/over sth)** (dated infml) to become/be very worried, confused or upset about sth: *He's got himself in an awful stew over his exams.*

stewed adj [usu pred] **1** (of tea) tasting too strong and bitter because it has been left in the pot too long.

steward /stjuːəd; US 'stuːərd/ n **1** (fem **stewardess** /ˌstjuːə'des; US 'stuːərdəs/) a person who looks after the passengers on a ship, an aircraft or a train and who brings them meals, etc: *a ship's steward* ○ *an 'air stewardess.* **2** a person employed to manage another's property, esp a large house or land. **3** a person who helps to organize a large public event

eg a race or demonstration. **4** a person whose job is to arrange for the supply of food to a college, club, etc. See also SHOP STEWARD.
▶ **stewardship** n [U] (fml) the position and duties of a steward: *The estate prospered under his stewardship.*

Sth abbr South: *Sth Pole* (eg on a map).

stick¹ /stɪk/ n **1** [C] a short thin piece of usu dead wood: *collect dry sticks to start a fire* ○ *The boys attacked the police with sticks and stones.* **2** [C] (Brit) = WALKING-STICK: *My grandmother can't walk without a stick.* **3** [C] a long thin object used to hit and control the ball in certain sports, eg hockey and POLO. **4** [C] (often in compounds) a long thin piece of sth: *sticks of celery/chalk/charcoal/dynamite/ rhubarb.* See also CANDLESTICK, DRUMSTICK. **6** [C] a BATON(2) used by a CONDUCTOR(1). **5** [C usu pl] ~ **(of sth)** (infml) a piece of furniture: *These few sticks (of furniture) are all he has left.* **7** [C] (dated infml) a person of the specified type: *He's a funny old stick.* **8** **the 'sticks** [pl] (infml) country areas far from cities: *live (out) in the sticks.* See also CHOPSTICKS, COCKTAIL STICK, JOSS-STICK. **IDM** **be in a cleft stick** ⇨ CLEAVE¹. **the big stick** ⇨ BIG. **the carrot and the stick** ⇨ CARROT. **get the wrong end of the stick** ⇨ WRONG. **get/take stick (from sb) (for sth)** (infml) to be criticized or treated severely: *The government has taken a lot of stick from the press recently.* **give sb 'stick** (infml) to criticize or treat sb severely. **a rod/stick to beat sb with** ⇨ BEAT¹. **up sticks** ⇨ UP⁴.
■ **'stick insect** n a large insect with a body shaped like a stick of wood.

stick² /stɪk/ v (pt, pp **stuck** /stʌk/) **1(a)** ~ sth in/ into/through sth; ~ sth in/through to push a pointed object into, through, etc sth: [Vnpr] *Stick a fork into the meat to see if it's done.* ○ *Stick the pins through both pieces of material.* ○ *Don't stick your elbows into me.* [also Vnp]. **(b)** ~ in/into/through sth; ~ in/through (of sth pointed) to be pushed into or through sth and remain in position: [Vpr] *I found a nail sticking in the tyre.* [also Vp]. **2** to become or make sth fixed, joined or fastened with a sticky substance: [Vnpr] *stick a stamp on an envelope* [Vnp] *stick a broken cup (back) together* [V] *This glue's useless — it doesn't stick.* [Vpr] *The dough stuck to my fingers.* — also Vp, Vn]. **3** (infml) to put or fix sth in a position or place, esp quickly or carelessly: [Vnp] *stick up a notice on the notice-board* [Vnpr] *He stuck the pen behind his ear.* ○ *Stick the books on the table, will you?* **4** ~ **(in sth)** to be or become fixed in one place and unable to move: [V] *This drawer is sticking.* [Vpr] *The key has stuck in the lock.* ○ *The bus stuck in the mud.* **5** (infml) (in negative sentences and questions) to tolerate or accept sb/sth, esp an unpleasant person or situation: [Vn] *I don't know how you stuck that man for so long.* ○ *I can't stick this job any longer.* **6** (infml) to be or become established: [V] *They couldn't make the charges stick* (ie prove that they were true) ○ *He got the nickname 'Fatty' on his first day at school, and unfortunately the name has stuck* (ie has been used ever since). **IDM** **poke/stick one's nose into sth** ⇨ NOSE¹. **put/stick one's oar in** ⇨ OAR. **put/stick one's tongue out** ⇨ TONGUE. **stand/stick out like a sore thumb** ⇨ SORE. **stand/stick out a mile** ⇨ MILE. **stick/stop at 'nothing** to be willing to do anything to get what one wants, even if it is dishonest or wrong. **stick 'em 'up!** (infml) (said by an armed robber telling sb to raise their hands above their head). **stick in one's 'mind** (of a memory, an image, etc) to be remembered for a long time: *Memories of the accident stuck in my mind for ages.* **stick in one's 'throat** (infml) **1** to be difficult or impossible to accept: *It's the government's sanctimonious attitude that really sticks in my throat.* **2** (of words)

────────────────────────

[Vnn] = verb + noun + noun **[V-adj]** = verb + adjective For more help with verbs, see Study pages B4–8.

to be difficult or impossible to say: *I wanted to tell her, but the words stuck in my throat.* **stick one's 'neck out** (*infml*) to do or say sth bold which may be risky for oneself: *At this stage I don't want to stick my neck out by saying who will win.* **stick to one's 'guns** (*infml*) to refuse to change one's opinions, actions, etc in spite of criticism. **stick to one's 'last** to avoid doing things that one cannot do well.

PHR V ‚**stick a'round** (*infml*) to stay in or near a place, eg waiting for sth to happen or for sb to arrive: *Stick around, we may need you.*

'**stick at sth** to work in a steady and determined way at sth: *If we stick at it, we should finish the job today.*

'**stick by sb** (*infml*) to continue to support and be loyal to sb, esp through difficult times: *Her husband stuck by her in good times and bad.*

‚**stick sth 'down 1** to fasten the cover, etc of sth with glue, etc: *stick down (the flap of) an envelope.* **2** (*infml*) to write sth down: *Stick your names down on the list.*

‚**stick sth 'in/'into sth** to fix, fasten sth into a book, etc with glue, etc: *stick stamps into an album.*

‚**stick 'out** to be noticeable: *They wrote the notice in big red letters to make it stick out.* ‚**stick (sth) 'out** to be further out than sth else; to push sth further out than sth else: *His ears stick out.* ○ *She stuck her tongue out at me.* ○ *Don't stick your head out of the car window.* ‚**stick it/sth 'out** (*infml*) to continue with sth to the end, despite difficulties, etc: *He hates the job but he's determined to stick it out because he needs the money.* ‚**stick 'out for sth** (*infml*) to refuse to give up until one gets sth one wants: *They're sticking out for higher wages.*

'**stick to sth 1** to refuse to abandon or change sth: *'Would you like some wine now?' 'No, I'll stick to beer, thanks.'* ○ *Don't tell us what you think about it; just stick to the facts.* ○ *That's my story and I'm sticking to it.* **2** to continue doing sth, despite difficulties, etc: *stick to a job until it is finished.*

‚**stick to'gether** (*infml*) (of people) to remain friendly and loyal to one another: *If we keep calm and stick together, we'll be all right.*

‚**stick 'up** to extend upwards; to be upright: *The branch was sticking up out of the water.* ‚**stick sth 'up** (*infml*) to threaten the people in a place with a gun in order to rob it: *stick up a bank/post office.*

‚**stick 'up for sb/oneself/sth** to support or defend sb/oneself/sth: *stick up for yourself/your rights* ○ *Don't worry. If there's any trouble, I'll stick up for you.*

'**stick with sb/sth** (*infml*) to continue to support or keep one's connection with sb/sth: *I'm sticking with my original idea.* ○ *Stick with me and you'll be all right.*

■ '**stick-in-the-mud** *n* (*infml derog*) a person who resists change: *He's a real stick-in-the-mud.*

'**stick-on** *adj* [attrib] having glue, etc on the back; sticky: *stick-on labels.*

'**sticking-plaster** (also **plaster**) (*Brit*) (*US* **Band-aid**) *n* [C, U] (a small strip of) fabric, plastic, etc that can be stuck to the skin to protect a small wound or cut.

'**sticking-point** *n* a thing that prevents progress in a discussion, negotiation, etc: *a major sticking-point in the arms talks.*

'**stick-up** *n* (*infml*) a robbery (ROB) with a gun: *Don't move — this is a stick-up!*

sticker /'stɪkə(r)/ *n* **1** a sticky label with a picture or message on it, for sticking on a book, a file, a car window, etc: *a car sticker.* **2** (*infml approv*) a person who does not give up in spite of difficulties.

stickleback /'stɪklbæk/ *n* a small fish living in rivers, etc with sharp points on its back.

stickler /'stɪklə(r)/ *n* ~ **for sth** a person who thinks that a certain quality, type of behaviour, etc is very important and expects it of other people: *a stickler for accuracy/punctuality/discipline.*

stickpin /'stɪkpɪn/ *n* (*US*) = TIE-PIN.

sticky /'stɪki/ *adj* (**-ier, -iest**) **1** that sticks or tends to stick to anything which touches it: *sticky fingers covered in jam* ○ *sticky toffee.* **2** (*infml*) (**a**) (of weather) hot and damp: *a sticky August afternoon.* (**b**) (of a person) covered in sweat: *I'm all hot and sticky after my game of tennis.* **3** (*infml*) unpleasant; difficult: *a sticky situation* ○ *Their marriage is going through a sticky patch* (ie an unpleasant period of time). **4** [usu pred] (*Brit infml*) making or likely to make objections; not helpful: *The bank manager was a bit sticky about letting me have an overdraft.* **IDM come to a bad/sticky end** ⇨ END[1]. **a ‚sticky 'wicket** (*Brit*) a situation that is hard to deal with: *We're on a sticky wicket with these negotiations — they could easily fail.* ► **stickily** /-ɪli/ *adv.* **stickiness** *n* [U].

■ ‚**sticky 'tape** *n* [U] clear plastic tape which is sticky on one side, used for joining things together: *a parcel done up with string and sticky tape.* See also SELLOTAPE.

stiff[1] /stɪf/ *adj* (**-er, -est**) **1** not easily bent, folded, moved, changed in shape, etc: *stiff cardboard* ○ *a stiff drawer* (ie one that sticks) ○ *a stiff pair of shoes* ○ *have a stiff neck* (ie one that is painful and difficult to move) ○ *feel stiff* (ie have stiff muscles and joints) *after a long walk.* **2** thick and hard to stir; not liquid: *a stiff dough* ○ *Whisk the egg whites until stiff.* **3**(**a**) hard to do; difficult: *a stiff climb/exam.* (**b**) severe; tough: *face stiff opposition/competition* ○ *The judge imposed a stiff sentence.* **4** formal in manner, behaviour, etc; not friendly: *They received a rather stiff welcome.* **5** (*infml*) (of a price) high or too high: *pay a stiff membership fee.* **6** (of a wind, etc) blowing strongly: *a stiff breeze.* **7** (of an alcoholic drink) strong; containing a lot of alcohol: *That was a shock — I need a stiff drink!* **IDM stiff/straight as a ramrod** ⇨ RAMROD. (**keep**) **a stiff upper 'lip** (to show) an ability to appear calm when in pain, trouble, etc.

► **stiff** *adv* (*infml*) to an extreme degree; very much: *worried/scared/frozen stiff* ○ *The opera bored me stiff.*

stiffly *adv*: *stand/walk stiffly* ○ *'No, thank you,' he said stiffly.*

stiffness *n* [U].

■ ‚**stiff-'necked** *adj* (*fml derog*) proud and STUBBORN(1).

stiff[2] /stɪf/ *n* (*sl*) a dead body.

stiffen /'stɪfn/ *v* ~ (**sth**) (**up**) (**with sth**) to become or make sth stiff or stiffer: [V, Vp] *My back has stiffened (up) overnight.* [Vpr] *He stiffened with fear.* [Vnpr] *stiffen the collar of a shirt with starch* ○ (*fig*) [Vn] *The promise of a reward might stiffen their resolve* (ie make them braver). [also Vnp].

► **stiffener** /'stɪfnə(r)/ *n* a thing used to stiffen: *a collar/shoe stiffener.*

stiffening /'stɪfnɪŋ/ *n* [U] material used to stiffen a collar, a belt, etc.

stifle /'staɪfl/ *v* **1** to suppress or control sth: *stifle a yawn/laugh/cry/sob* [Vn] *The rebellion was quickly stifled.* ○ (*derog*) *stifle ideas/initiative/talent.* **2** to feel or make sb feel unable to breathe properly because of lack of fresh air: [V] *We were stifling in that hot room with all the windows closed.* [Vn] *Smoke filled the room and almost stifled the firemen.* **3** to make a fire stop burning: [Vn] *stifle the flames with a blanket.* ► **stifling** /'staɪflɪŋ/ *adj*: *a stifling room/smell/atmosphere* ○ *stifling heat* ○ *It's stifling in here — let's open a window.* **stiflingly** *adv*: *stiflingly hot.*

stigma /'stɪɡmə/ *n* [U, C usu *sing*] a bad reputation that sth has because many people disapprove of it, often unfairly: *There is still (a) social stigma attached to being unemployed.*

S

stigmata /ˈstɪgmətə, stɪgˈmɑːtə/ n [pl] marks resembling the wounds made by nails on the body of Christ. Some Christians believe that stigmata have appeared as holy marks on the bodies of certain saints.

stigmatize, -ise /ˈstɪgmətaɪz/ v ~ sb/sth (as sth) (fml) (usu passive) to describe or consider sb/sth as sth very bad, worthy of extreme disapproval, etc: [Vn-adj] ideas stigmatized as unnatural [also Vn-n, Vn].

stile /staɪl/ n a set of steps that help people to climb over a fence or wall, esp in the country. See also TURNSTILE.

stiletto /stɪˈletəʊ/ n (pl -os) **1** a small knife or tool with a narrow pointed blade. **2** (usu pl) (Brit infml) a woman's shoe with a very high narrow heel: wear stilettos/stiletto heels.

still¹ /stɪl/ adj (-er, -est) **1(a)** with little or no movement or sound; quiet and calm: still water ○ absolutely/completely/perfectly still ○ Please keep/stay/hold/sit/stand still while I take your photograph. **(b)** without wind: a still summer day. ⇨ note at QUIET. **2** [attrib] (of drinks) not containing bubbles of gas; not FIZZY: still cider/orange/mineral water. **IDM** the still small 'voice (of conscience) (rhet) a person's sense of right and wrong. still waters run 'deep (saying) a quiet or apparently calm person can have strong emotions, much knowledge or wisdom, etc.
▶ **still** n **1** [C] an ordinary photograph, contrasted with a motion picture, esp a single photograph from a cinema film: still photography ○ publicity stills from a new film. **2** the ~ of sth deep silence and calm: in the still of the night.
still v (fml) to become or make sth calm or at rest: [V] The wind/waves stilled. [Vn] She tried to still her doubts/fears.
stillness n [U] the quality of being still.
■ ˌstill 'life n **(a)** [U] the representation in painting or drawing of objects which are not living, eg fruit, flowers, etc: I prefer landscape to still life. **(b)** [C] (pl still lifes) a picture of this type.

still² /stɪl/ adv **1** up to and including the present time or the time mentioned: It's still raining. ○ Do you still live in London? ○ He still hopes/is still hoping to hear from her. ○ Will you still be here when I get back? ○ I still can't do it. ○ We could still change our minds. ○ She died ten years ago, but I think about her still. **2** (used for talking about an action or opinion that is not expected, because sth else makes it surprising): Although she felt ill, she still went to work. ○ He's treated you badly: still, he's your brother and you should help him. **3(a)** (used for making a comparative adj stronger): Tom is tall, but Mary is taller still. ○ The next day was warmer still. ○ It never stopped raining, and worse still, we got lost. **(b)** in addition; more: He came up with still more stories.

still³ /stɪl/ n an apparatus for making strong alcoholic drink: a whisky still. See also DISTIL 1b.

stillbirth /ˈstɪlbɜːθ/ n a birth at which the baby is born dead.

stillborn /ˈstɪlbɔːn/ adj **1** (of a baby) dead when born. **2** (of an idea or a plan) not developing further.

stilt /stɪlt/ n **1** either of a pair of poles with pieces on the side to support the feet. By standing on these pieces a person can walk raised above the ground. Stilts are used for fun, entertainment, etc: a pair of stilts ○ walk on stilts. **2** any of a set of posts or poles on which a building, etc is supported above the ground: a house built on stilts at the edge of a lake.

stilted /ˈstɪltɪd/ adj (derog) (esp of a manner of talking or writing) not natural or relaxed: a rather stilted conversation. ▶ **stiltedly** adv.

Stilton /ˈstɪltən/ n [U] a white English cheese with

blue lines of mould² running through it and a strong flavour.

stimulant /ˈstɪmjələnt/ n **1** a drug that makes one feel more alert or gives one more energy: Coffee and tea are mild stimulants. **2** ~ (to sth) an event, activity, etc that encourages greater or further activity: The tax cuts should act as a stimulant to further economic growth.

stimulate /ˈstɪmjuleɪt/ v **1** ~ sb/sth (to sth) to make sb/sth more active or alert; to encourage sb/sth: [Vnpr, Vn.to inf] This success stimulated him to even greater effort/to work even harder. [Vn] The exhibition has certainly stimulated interest in her work. **2** to make sth work or function: [Vn] Exercise stimulates circulation of the blood. [also Vn.to inf]. **3** to make sb interested and excited: [Vn] The lecture failed to stimulate me.
▶ **stimulating** adj **(a)** that makes sb more alert and active: the stimulating effect of a cold shower. **(b)** interesting or exciting: a stimulating discussion ○ I find his work very stimulating.
stimulation /ˌstɪmjuˈleɪʃn/ n [U]: intellectual/mental/sensory/sexual stimulation.

stimulus /ˈstɪmjələs/ n (pl stimuli /-laɪ/) ~ (to/for sth); ~ (to do sth) **1** a thing that encourages or excites sb/sth to activity, greater effort, etc: the stimulus of competition in business ○ Stress can provide us with a stimulus to achieve our goals. **2** a thing that produces a reaction in living things: produce a response to a stimulus ○ The nutrient in the soil acts as a stimulus to growth/to make the plants grow. ○ Does he respond to auditory stimuli (ie Does he react to the sounds around him)?

sting¹ /stɪŋ/ n **1** [C] a sharp, often poisonous, pointed part of certain insects and other creatures, used for wounding: the sting of a bee/wasp ○ The scorpion has a sting in its tail. ⇨ picture at SCORPION. **2** [C] a sharp pointed hair on the surface of the leaf of certain plants that causes pain when touched: Nettles have a nasty sting. **3** [C] a wound from the sting of an animal or a plant; the pain or mark caused by this: That bee gave me a nasty sting. ○ A jellyfish sting can be very painful. ○ Her face was covered in wasp stings. **4** [C, U] any sharp pain of body or mind: ointment to take the sting out of a burn ○ the sting of the wind in his face ○ the sting of remorse/jealousy. **IDM** a ˌsting in the 'tail an unpleasant feature of sth which only becomes clear at the end: The Chancellor's budget gave encouragement to industry, but there was a sting in the tail — the promise of future tax increases.

sting² /stɪŋ/ v (pt, pp stung /stʌŋ/) **1** to hurt or wound sb with or as if with a sting; to have the ability to do this: [V] a stinging blow/wind ○ Not all nettles sting. ○ I put some antiseptic on the cut and it really stung. [Vnpr] A bee stung me on the cheek. [Vn] The smoke is stinging my eyes. ○ He was stung (ie deeply upset) by their insults. **2** to feel sharp pain: [V] My eyes are stinging from the smoke. ○ His knee stung from the graze. **3** ~ sb (to/into sth/doing sth) to provoke sb by making them angry, upset or offended: [Vnpr] Their taunts stung him to action/into replying. [Vn] He launched a stinging attack on the government. **4** ~ sb (for sth) (infml) to charge sb too much money for sth: [Vnpr] Millions of home-owners may be stung for more tax. ○ How much did they sting you for? [also Vn].
■ ˈstinging-nettle n = NETTLE 1.

stingray /ˈstɪŋreɪ/ n a large wide flat fish that can cause severe wounds with its stinging tail.

stingy /ˈstɪndʒi/ adj (infml) spending, using or giving unwillingly; mean²(1): a stingy helping of food ○ Don't be so stingy with the cream! ○ He's very stingy about lending money. ▶ **stinginess** n [U].

stink /stɪŋk/ v (pt stank /stæŋk/ or stunk /stʌŋk/; pp stunk) (infml) **1** ~ (of sth) to have a very unpleasant and offensive smell: [V] *That fish in the fridge has gone bad — it stinks.* [Vpr] *Her breath stank of garlic.* **2** ~ **(of sth)** to seem very unpleasant, bad or dishonest: [V,Vpr] *The whole business stinks (of corruption)!* [V] *'What do you think of the idea?' 'Frankly, it stinks.'* **PHRV** ¦**stink sth 'out** to fill a place with a very unpleasant smell: *He stank the whole house out with his tobacco smoke.*

▶ **stink** *n* **1** [C] (*infml*) a very unpleasant smell: *What a stink!* **2** [sing] (*sl*) trouble; fuss: *The whole business caused quite a stink.* **IDM** **like 'stink** (*Brit sl*) intensely; very hard: *working like stink.*

stinker *n* (*infml*) **1** a thing that is very severe or difficult to do: *The maths exam was a real stinker.* **2** a very unpleasant person.

stinking *adj* [attrib] (*infml*) very bad or unpleasant: *I don't want your stinking money.* ○ *She's got a stinking cold.* — *adv* (*infml*) extremely; very: **stinking rich/drunk.**

■ **'stink bomb** *n* a small container that produces a very unpleasant smell when it is broken. Stink bombs are used for playing tricks on people.

stint /stɪnt/ *v* ~ **(on sth)**; ~ **oneself** (usu in negative sentences) to give only a small amount of sth, esp food: [Vpr] *You certainly didn't stint on the cream!* [Vn] *Have as much as you want — don't stint yourself.* [also V]. Compare UNSTINTING.

▶ **stint** *n* a person's fixed amount or period of work, etc: *I've done my stint in the kitchen for today.* ○ *Then I had a two-year stint as a security officer in Hong Kong.*

stipend /'staɪpend/ *n* a fixed sum of money paid regularly to sb, esp a priest or minister(3); a salary.

▶ **stipendiary** /staɪ'pendiəri; US -dieri/ *adj* receiving a stipend: *a stipendiary magistrate* (ie one who works for pay, not on a VOLUNTARY(2) basis).

stipple /'stɪpl/ *v* (esp passive) to paint or draw sth with small dots instead of lines: [Vn] *a stippled effect.*

stipulate /'stɪpjuleɪt/ *v* (*fml*) to state sth clearly and firmly as a requirement: [Vn] *agree to the terms stipulated in the contract* [V.*that*] *The job advertisement stipulated that all applicants should have at least 3 years' experience.* [also V.*wh*]. ▶ **stipulation** /ˌstɪpju'leɪʃn/ *n* [C,U]: *He agreed to take early retirement with the stipulation that he be allowed to keep his company car.*

stir /stɜː(r)/ *v* (-rr-) **1(a)** ~ **sth (with sth)** to move a spoon or sth similar round and round in a liquid, etc in order to mix it thoroughly: [Vn] *I've put sugar in your tea but I haven't stirred it.* ○ *Stir continuously until the mixture thickens.* [also Vnpr]. **(b)** ~ **sth into sth**; ~ **sth in** to add one substance to another in this way: [Vnpr] *Stir the dried fruit into the flour mixture.* [Vnp] *Stir in enough milk to form a soft dough.* **2** to move or make sth move slightly: [Vn] *A gentle breeze stirred the leaves.* [V] *Not a leaf was stirring* (ie There was no wind to move the leaves). ○ *No one stirs in this house before eight o'clock.* [Vn] *It's time to stir yourself and get to work.* **3** ~ **sb (to sth)** to excite sb or provoke strong feelings: [Vn] *a story that stirs the imagination* [Vnpr] *She was stirred to anger by the injustice of it all.* **4** (of a mood, feeling, etc) to begin to be felt: [Vpr] *A sense of longing began to stir in him.* [V] *There is a new optimism in the country — things are stirring.* **IDM** **stir the 'blood** to make sb excited or enthusiastic: *music that really stirs the blood.* **stir one's 'stumps** (*dated Brit infml*) to begin to move or move faster; to hurry. **PHRV** ¦**stir sb 'up** to provoke sb into action: *stir up peasants to revolt.* ¦**stir sth 'up 1** to cause trouble, etc, esp for other people: *stir up trouble/unrest/discontent.* **2** to stir sth thoroughly: *stir up the mud at the bottom of the pond.*

▶ **stir** *n* **1** [C] the action of stirring (STIR 1a) sth:

Give the rice a stir. **2** [sing] general excitement or shock: *Her resignation caused quite a stir.*

stirrer /'stɜːrə(r)/ *n* (*infml derog*) a person who likes causing trouble between other people.

stirring /'stɜːrɪŋ/ *adj* [usu attrib] very exciting: *a stirring TV drama.* — *n* ~ **(of sth)** a beginning of a feeling or an idea: *the first faint stirrings of revolution.*

■ **'stir-fry** *v* (*pt, pp* **-fried**) [Vn] to cook vegetables, meat, etc by frying them for a short time in very hot oil while stirring them. — *n* a dish made in this way.

stirrup /'stɪrəp/ *n* either of a pair of metal or leather loops that hang down from a horse's SADDLE to support a rider's feet: *put your feet in the stirrups.*

stitch /stɪtʃ/ *n* **1** [C] **(a)** a single act of passing a needle and thread into and out of material in sewing, or into and out of skin, etc to close a deep cut. ⇨ picture at SEW. **(b)** one complete turn of the wool round the needle in knitting. **2** [C] **(a)** a loop of thread, wool, etc made in this way: *make long/short/neat stitches* ○ *The cut in my hand needed five stitches.* **(b)** a piece of thread used to sew the edges of a wound together: *I'm having my stitches (taken) out today* (ie removed from a wound that has healed). **3** [C,U] (esp in compounds) a particular pattern of stitches or way of making stitches in sewing, knitting, etc: *an embroidery stitch.* **4** [C usu sing] a sudden sharp pain in the muscles at the side of the body, caused eg by running too hard: *Can we slow down and walk for a while? I've got a stitch.* **IDM** **drop a stitch** ⇨ DROP². **have not (got) a stitch 'on / not be wearing a 'stitch** (*infml*) to be naked. **in 'stitches** (*infml*) laughing a lot: *The play had us in stitches.* **a stitch in 'time (saves 'nine)** (*saying*) if one takes action or does a piece of work immediately, it may save a lot of extra work later.

▶ **stitch** *v* to mend, join or decorate sth with stitches; to sew sth: [Vn] *stitched pockets/sleeves* [Vnp] *Every sequin was stitched on by hand.* [Vnpr] *Can you stitch this button onto my shirt?* **PHRV** ¦**stitch sb 'up** (*Brit infml*) to betray or cheat sb: *He was stitched up by a former colleague.* ¦**stitch sth 'up 1** to join together or close sth by stitching: *stitch up a wound/a cut.* **2** (*Brit infml*) to complete sth, esp in a rough way: *stitch up a deal.*

stitching *n* [U] a row, group, etc of stitches: *The stitching has come undone.*

stoat /stəʊt/ *n* a small animal with brown fur that turns mainly white in winter. The white fur is called *ermine*. Stoats eat other animals, eg rabbits.

stock¹ /stɒk/ *n* **1** [C,U] a store of goods available for sale, distribution or use, eg in a shop: *The shop had a good stock of camping equipment.* ○ *Our new stock of winter coats will arrive soon.* ○ *Your order can be supplied from stock.* ○ *'Have you got copies of her book in stock?' 'No, I'm sorry, we're out of stock (of it) at the moment.'* **2** [C,U] ~ **(of sth)** a supply or amount of sth available for use, etc: *have a good stock of logs for the winter* ○ *Fuel/Food stocks are running low.* ○ *a country's housing stock* (ie all the houses available for living in) ○ *Stationery is kept in the stock cupboard.* **3** [U] farm animals: *buy some more breeding stock.* See also LIVESTOCK. **4** [C,U] money lent to a government at a fixed rate of interest: *government stock.* **5(a)** [U] the total value of the money, equipment, buildings, etc of a business company; capital²(1). **(b)** [C usu *pl*] a portion of this held by sb as an investment. Stocks differ from shares in that they are not issued in fixed amounts: *invest in stocks and shares.* **6** [U] a person's family or ancestors (of the type specified by the *adj*): *She comes from Welsh farming stock* (ie Her family were originally farmers in Wales). **7** [U] (*fml*) a person's reputation in the opinion of others: *His stock is high* (ie He is well thought of). **8** [C,U] a liquid made by cooking bones, meat, fish, vegetables, etc slowly in water, used in cooking, eg for soups: *gravy made with chicken stock.* **9** [C] the part of a gun that one holds against the shoulder when firing it: *a rifle stock.* **10** [C] a growing plant onto which a living stem from another plant is fixed to produce new growth. **11 stocks** [pl] a wooden structure with holes for the feet, and sometimes also for the hands, in which criminals were formerly locked as a punishment: *be put in the stocks.* Compare PILLORY *n.* **12** [U,C] a type of garden plant with brightly coloured sweet-smelling flowers. **IDM lock, stock and barrel** ⇨ LOCK¹. **on the 'stocks** being constructed or prepared: *Our new model is already on the stocks and will be available in the autumn.* **take 'stock (of sth)** to examine and make a list of all the goods in a shop, etc. See also STOCKTAKING. **take 'stock (of sb/ sth)** to consider and make a decision about a situation, sb's abilities, etc: *After a year in the job, she decided it was time to take stock (of her career).* See also LAUGHING-STOCK, ROLLING-STOCK.

▶ **stock** *adj* [attrib] **1** usually kept in stock and regularly available: *stock sizes ○ one of our stock items.* **2** commonly used; used too much, and therefore not interesting, effective, etc: *stock characters in soap opera ○ He replied to all questions with the stock answer: 'I have nothing to add.'*

■ **'stock-car** *n* **1** an ordinary car that has been strengthened for use in **stock-car racing**, a sport in which the cars are allowed to hit each other. **2** (*US*) a railway truck for carrying animals, esp cattle.

'stock-cube *n* a small cube of dried stock¹(8) used for making soup, etc: *beef stock-cubes.*

'stock exchange *n* a place where stocks and shares are publicly bought and sold; such business, or the people engaged in it: *the London Stock Exchange ○ companies listed/quoted/trading on the stock exchange ○ lose money on the stock exchange.*

,stock-in-'trade *n* [U] words, actions, behaviour, etc commonly used, displayed, etc by a particular person: *Flippant remarks are part of his stock-in-trade.*

'stock market *n* a stock exchange or the business conducted there: *dealings on the stock market ○ ,stock-market 'prices ○ a ,stock-market 'crash.*

stock² /stɒk/ *v* **1** to keep goods in stock; to keep a supply of sth: [Vn] *Do you stock batteries? ○ We stock all sizes.* **2** ~ **sth (with sth)** (esp passive) to provide or equip sth with goods or a supply of sth: [Vnadv] *a well-stocked shop/library/freezer* [Vnpr] *The museum shop is stocked with a wide range of souvenirs. ○ a garden stocked with rare plants* [also Vn]. **PHRV stock 'up (on/with sth) (for sth)** to collect and keep supplies of sth for a particular occasion or purpose: *stock up with food for Christmas ○ We'd better stock up on biscuits for when the children get back.*

▶ **stockist** /'stɒkɪst/ *n* a shop that sells goods of a particular type or made by a particular company: *available from all good stockists.*

stockade /stɒ'keɪd/ *n* a line or wall of strong upright, esp wooden, posts, built as a defence.

stockbroker /'stɒkbrəʊkə(r)/ (also **broker**) *n* a person or an organization that buys and sells stocks and shares for others. ▶ **stockbroking** *n* [U] the work of a stockbroker: *a stockbroking friend of mine ○ He's in stockbroking.*

stockholder /'stɒkhəʊldə(r)/ *n* (*esp US*) a person or an organization that owns stocks and shares.

stocking /'stɒkɪŋ/ *n* either of a pair of thin garments that fit closely over the legs and feet, worn esp by girls and women: *a pair of nylon/silk/woollen/cotton stockings.* Compare TIGHTS. See also BODY STOCKING. **IDM in one's ,stocking(ed) 'feet** wearing socks or stockings but not shoes.

■ **'stocking-filler** *n* (*Brit*) a present of small value, placed with others in a large sock or similar container and given at Christmas.

stockman /'stɒkmən/ *n* (*pl* **-men** /-mən/) (*Austral*) a man in charge of farm animals.

stockpile /'stɒkpaɪl/ *n* a large supply of goods, materials, etc collected and kept for future use, esp because they may become difficult to obtain, eg in a war: *a stockpile of nuclear weapons.* — *v* to collect and keep a stockpile of goods, materials, etc in this way: [Vn] *stockpiling raw materials.*

stock-still /,stɒk 'stɪl/ *adv* without movement: *remain/stay/stand stock-still.*

stocktaking /'stɒkteɪkɪŋ/ *n* **1** [U] the process of making a list of all the goods in a shop, etc: *The shop is closed for stocktaking.* **2** [U] a review of one's situation, position, resources, etc: *The committee called for a stocktaking of the current state of affairs.*

stocky /'stɒki/ *adj* (**-ier, -iest**) (usu of people) short, strong and solid in appearance: *a stocky little man.* ▶ **stockily** *adv: a stockily built man.*

stodge /stɒdʒ/ *n* [U] (*infml usu derog*) food that is heavy or solid and makes one feel very full, esp food with a lot of STARCH in it.

▶ **stodgy** /'stɒdʒi/ *adj* (*infml derog*) **1** (of food) heavy and solid: *stodgy puddings.* **2(a)** (of a book, etc) written in a boring way: *stodgy prose.* **(b)** (of a person) boring; not lively; dull.

stoic /'stəʊɪk/ *n* (*fml*) a person who can endure pain, discomfort or trouble without complaining or showing signs of feeling it.

▶ **stoical** /-kl/ (also **stoic**) *adj* of or like a stoic; enduring pain, etc without complaint: *remain stoical in the face of hardship ○ her stoic acceptance of death.* **stoically** /-kli/ *adv: suffer stoically.*

stoicism /'stəʊɪsɪzəm/ *n* [U] (*fml*) behaviour that is typical of a stoic: *She showed great stoicism during her husband's final illness.*

stoke /stəʊk/ *v* **1** ~ **sth (up) (with sth)** to add coal or some other fuel to a fire, etc: *The stoke the boiler/furnace (with coal)* [Vnp] *stoke up the fire.* **2** ~ **sth (up)** to encourage or increase an emotion, a tendency, etc: [Vn] *stoke fears of a property slump* [Vnp] *stoke up public anger.*

▶ **stoker** *n* a person who stokes a fire, etc, esp on a ship.

stole¹ *pt* of STEAL.

stole² /stəʊl/ *n* a women's garment consisting of a wide band of cloth or fur, worn around the shoulders.

stolen *pp* of STEAL.

stolid /'stɒlɪd/ *adj* (*usu derog*) (of a person) not easily excited; showing little or no emotion or interest: *a stolid character/manner ○ They sat in stolid silence.* ▶ **stolidly** *adv.* **stolidity** /stə'lɪdəti/ *n* [U].

stomach /'stʌmək/ *n* **1** [C] an organ of the body like a bag, into which food passes when swallowed and in which the first part of DIGESTION occurs: *have a stomach upset ○ have a sinking feeling in (the pit of) one's stomach* (eg because of fear, hunger or illness) ○ *It's unwise to swim on a full stomach* (ie when one has just eaten a meal). ○ *I don't like going to work on an empty stomach* (ie without having eaten anything). ⇨ picture at DIGESTIVE. **2** [C] (*infml*) the front part of the body between the chest and thighs; the ABDOMEN(1): *punch sb in the stomach.* **3** [U] **(a)** appetite for food: *I didn't have the stomach to eat anything at all.* **(b)** ~ **for sth** desire or eagerness for sth: *They had no stomach for a fight.* **IDM sb's eyes are bigger than their stomach** ⇨ EYE¹. **the pit of the/one's stomach** ⇨ PIT¹. **sick to one's stomach** ⇨ SICK. **turn one's 'stomach** to make one feel sick or disgusted: *The description of eye operations turned my stomach.*

▶ **stomach** *v* (esp in negative sentences or ques-

tions with *can, could*, etc) **1** to endure sth; to tolerate sth: [Vn] *I left before the end of the film — I couldn't stomach all the violence in it.* **2** to eat sth without feeling ill: [Vn] *I can't stomach seafood.*
■ **'stomach-ache** *n* [C, U] a continuing pain in the stomach or the bowels.
'stomach-pump *n* a pump with a flexible tube which can be inserted into the stomach through the mouth. It is used to remove esp poisonous substances from the stomach or to force liquid into it.

stomp /stɒmp/ *v* (*infml*) to move, walk, dance, etc in the specified direction with a heavy step: [Vp] *stomp about noisily* [Vpr] *She slammed the door and stomped out of the house.* ⇨ note at STAMP¹.

stone /stəʊn/ *n* **1** [U] (often used attributively or in compounds) a hard solid mineral substance that is not metallic; (a type of) rock: *a house built of (Cotswold) stone* ○ *stone walls/buildings/floors/statues* ○ *The ground is (as) hard as stone.* See also LIME-STONE, SANDSTONE, SOAPSTONE. **2** [C] a small piece of rock of any shape: *a pile of stones* ○ *Some children were throwing stones into the pond.* See also ROLLING STONE. **3** [C] (usu in compounds) a piece of stone shaped for a particular purpose: *These words are carved on the stone beside his grave.* See also GRAVE-STONE, MILLSTONE, PAVING-STONE, STEPPING-STONE, TOMBSTONE. **4** (also ₁**precious 'stone**) [C] a jewel: *a sapphire ring with six small stones.* **5** (also *esp US* **pit**) [C] (sometimes in compounds) a hard shell containing the nut or seed inside certain fruits: *cherry/plum/peach stones.* ⇨ picture at FRUIT. **6** [C] (esp in compounds) a small hard object that has formed in the BLADDER or KIDNEY and causes pain: *an operation to remove* ₁**kidney stones.** See also GALLSTONE. **7** [C] (*pl* unchanged) (*abbr* **st**) (*Brit*) a unit of weight; equal to 14 pounds: *He weighs over 10 stone.* ○ *two stone of potatoes.* ⇨ App 2. See also CORNERSTONE, DRYSTONE, FOUNDATION-STONE, HAILSTONE, LODESTONE. **IDM** **blood out of/from a stone** ⇨ BLOOD¹. **a heart of stone** ⇨ HEART. **kill two birds with one stone** ⇨ KILL. **leave no stone un¹turned** to try every possible course of action in order to achieve sth. **people in glass houses shouldn't throw stones** ⇨ PEOPLE. **a 'stone's throw** a very short distance: *We live a stone's throw from here/within a stone's throw of here.*
▶ **stone** *v* **1** to throw stones at sb, esp formerly as a punishment: [Vnpr] *be stoned to death* [also Vn]. **2** to remove the stones (STONE 5) from fruit: [Vn] *stoned date/olives.* **IDM** ₁**stone the 'crows** (*Brit sl*) (used as an exclamation of surprise, shock, disgust, etc): *Well, stone the crows, he's done it again!* **stoned** *adj* [usu pred] (*sl*) (**a**) very drunk. (**b**) under the influence of drugs, esp MARIJUANA.
'stoneless *adj* (*Brit*) without stones: *stoneless dates.*
■ the **'Stone Age** *n* [sing] the very early period of human history when tools and weapons were made of stone, not metal: *Stone Age settlements.*
₁**stone-'cold** *adj* completely cold: *The body was stone-cold.* ○ *This soup is stone-cold.* ₁**stone-cold 'sober** completely sober and not under the influence of alcoholic drinks.
₁**stone-'dead** *adj* completely dead.
₁**stone-'deaf** *adj* completely deaf. Compare TONE-DEAF.

stoneground /'stəʊngraʊnd/ *adj* (of flour) made by being crushed between heavy stones: *a stoneground wholemeal loaf.*

stonemason /'stəʊnmeɪsn/ *n* a person who cuts and prepares stone or builds with stone.

stonewall /ˌstəʊn'wɔːl/ *v* (*infml esp Brit*) to prevent the progress of a discussion, etc by refusing to answer questions or giving very long or VAGUE(1b) replies: [V, Vn] *a deliberate attempt to stonewall (the debate).*

stoneware /'stəʊnweə(r)/ *n* [U] pots, dishes, etc made from clay that contains a small amount of FLINT(1): *stoneware jars.*

stonewashed /'stəʊnwɒʃt; *US* -wɔːʃt/ *adj* (of a garment or fabric, esp DENIM) treated so as to produce a worn or faded appearance: *stonewashed jeans.*

stonework /'stəʊnwɜːk/ *n* [U] the stone parts of a building, etc esp those that are ornamental in design: *a church with beautiful stonework.*

stony /'stəʊni/ *adj* (**-ier, -iest**) **1** full of, covered in or having stones: *a stony beach* ○ *stony ground/soil.* **2** without feeling or sympathy: *a stony face/stare/look/gaze* ○ *maintain a stony silence* ○ ₁**stony-'hearted/-'faced.** **IDM** **flat/stony broke** ⇨ BROKE².
▶ **stonily** /-ɪli/ *adv* in a stony(2) manner: *She stared stonily out of the window.*

stood *pt, pp* of STAND¹.

stooge /stuːdʒ/ *n* **1** (*infml derog*) a person used by another to do routine or unpleasant work: *a government stooge.* **2** a person who performs in a comedy act and whose purpose is to appear foolish so that other performers can make jokes about her or him.

stool /stuːl/ *n* **1** (often in compounds) a seat without a back or arms: *a 'bar stool* ○ *a 'piano stool.* **2** = FOOTSTOOL. **3** (*fml or medical*) a piece of solid waste from the body. **IDM** **fall between two 'stools** (*Brit*) to fail to be or take either of two satisfactory alternatives: *You can't please both sides — if you try you may fall between two stools and please neither of them.*
■ **'stool-pigeon** *n* (*infml*) a person who helps the police to trap a criminal, eg by associating with criminals and getting secret information.

stoop /stuːp/ *v* **1** ~ (**down**) to bend forward and down: [V] *She stooped to look under the bed.* [Vp] *He stooped down to pick up the child.* **2** to have the head and shoulders habitually bent over: [V] *He's beginning to stoop with age* (ie as he gets older). **IDM** **stoop so 'low (as to do sth)** to lower one's moral standards so far as to do sth: *I never thought he'd stoop so low as to cheat on his best friend.* **PHRV** **'stoop to sth/doing sth** to lower one's moral standards to do sth: *He can behave badly at times but he'd never stoop to stealing.*
▶ **stoop** *n* (usu *sing*) a stooping position of the body: *walk with a slight stoop.*

stop¹ /stɒp/ *v* (**-pp-**) **1** to put an end to the movement, progress, etc of a person or thing: [Vn] *stop a taxi* ○ *Rain stopped play* (eg in cricket). ○ *Can you stop the printer once it's started?* ○ *Stop the car a minute, I want to look in that shop.* ○ *I had to stop somebody in the street to ask the way.* **2** to end or finish an activity: [Vn] *stop work* ○ *Stop it* (ie Do not do that)! [V.ing] *He never stops talking.* ○ *She's stopped smoking.* ○ *Will you stop making that awful noise!* ○ *Has it stopped raining yet?* **3** ~ **sb/sth (from) doing sth** to prevent sb from doing sth or sth from happening: [Vn] *I'm sure he'll go, there's nothing to stop him.* [V.n ing, Vn.ing, Vnpr] *You can't stop our going/us (from) going if we want to.* ○ *I only just managed to stop myself from shouting at him.* [Vn.ing, Vn] *We bandaged his wound but couldn't stop it bleeding/stop the bleeding.* **4(a)** to finish moving, happening or operating: [V] *What's the time? My watch has stopped.* ○ *Does this train stop at Oxford?* ○ *His heart has stopped.* ○ *The problem with her is that she doesn't know where/when to stop* (ie does not know when sth is no longer amusing, is offensive, etc and should not be continued). (**b**) to end an activity temporarily; to PAUSE: [V] *We stopped for a while to admire the scenery.* [V.to inf] *She never stopped to consider that others might object.* [Vadv] *She stopped dead* (ie stopped suddenly and completely) *when she saw me.* ⇨ note at AND. **5** ~ **sth (up) (with sth)** to fill or close a gap, hole, etc by blocking it with sth: [Vn] *stop a leak in a pipe/a gap in a hedge* ○ **stop one's ears** (ie cover them with one's hands to avoid hearing sth) [also Vnp, Vnpr]. **6** to refuse to give or allow sth normally given; to keep sth back: [Vn] *stop a cheque* (ie order a bank not to exchange it for cash) ○ *stop sb's wages.* **7** (*infml esp Brit*) to stay, esp for a short time: [V, Vpr] *Are you stopping (for supper)?* [Vpr] *We stopped at a campsite for a week.* **IDM** **the buck stops here** ⇨ BUCK³. **stick/stop at nothing** ⇨ STICK². **stop the 'rot** to stop or reverse a process where sth is becoming worse: *After a string of defeats they have stopped the rot with a convincing win.* **(stop (sb)) 'short** to stop or make sb stop doing sth suddenly or abruptly (ABRUPT): *He stopped short when he heard his name called.* ○ *I stopped him short before he could say any more.* **stop short of sth/doing sth** to be unwilling to go beyond a certain limit in one's actions: *He suspected his boss of acting dishonestly but stopped short of accusing him of anything.* **stop the 'show** to receive so much attention, APPLAUSE, etc from an audience that the performance, etc cannot continue. **PHRV** **,stop 'by**; **,stop 'round** to make a short visit to sb's house, etc: *Ask him to stop by for a drink.* **,stop 'in** (*Brit*) to stay indoors rather than go out: *I wasn't feeling well on Friday night so I stopped in.* **,stop 'off (at/in...)** to make a short break in a journey to do sth: *stop off at the pub on the way home.* **,stop 'out** (*Brit*) to stay out late at night: *stop out until three o'clock in the morning.* **,stop 'over (at/in...)** to break one's journey, esp when travelling by air for a short stay somewhere: *stop over in Rome for two days en route for the Middle East.* **,stop 'round** = STOP BY. **,stop 'up** to avoid going to bed until later than usual: *stop up (late) to watch a film on TV.*

■ **,stop-'go** *n* [U, esp attrib] (*Brit finance*) the policy of deliberately restricting and then encouraging economic activity, growth, etc: *a government's ,stop-go eco'nomic policy.*

'stop light *n* **1** a red traffic-light (TRAFFIC). **2** (*US*) = BRAKE LIGHT.

'stopping train *n* (*Brit*) a train that stops at many stations between main stations.

,stop 'press *n* [U] (*Brit*) late news added to a newspaper after printing has begun: *a 'stop-press announcement/report.*

stop² /stɒp/ *n* [C] **1** an act of stopping or state of being stopped: *make a short stop on a journey* ○ *Winchester will be the next stop.* ○ *The lift came to a stop on the second floor.* **2** a place where a bus, train, etc stops regularly, eg to allow passengers to get on or off: *Which stop do I get off at?* ○ *Is this a request stop?* See also BUS-STOP, PIT STOP. **3** a mark used in writing, esp a full stop (FULL). **4** (*music*) **(a)** a row of pipes in an organ² providing sounds of a particular quality. **(b)** a handle that the player pushes or pulls to control these. **5** (*phonetics*) a consonant sound produced by the sudden release of air that has been held back, eg /p, b, k, g, t, d/; as PLOSIVE. See also DOORSTOP. **IDM** **pull out all the stops** ⇨ PULL¹. **put an end/a stop to sth** ⇨ END¹.

stopcock /'stɒpkɒk/ (also **cock**) *n* a tap that controls the flow of liquid or gas through a pipe: *If a water-pipe bursts turn off the stopcock immediately.*

stopgap /'stɒpɡæp/ *n* a person or thing that acts as a temporary substitute for another: *stopgap measures in an emergency.*

stopover /'stɒpəʊvə(r)/ *n* a short stay somewhere between parts of a journey: *a two-day stopover in Delhi on the way to Hong Kong.*

stoppage /'stɒpɪdʒ/ *n* [C] **1** an interruption of an activity, esp of work in a factory, etc because of a strike¹(1): *a 24-hour stoppage at the local car plant.* **2**

stoppages [pl] (*Brit*) an amount of money taken by an employer from wages and salaries, for tax, National Insurance, etc. **3** a state of being blocked: *a stoppage in the pipe.*

stopper /'stɒpə(r)/ (*US* **plug**) *n* an object that fits into and closes an opening, esp the top of a bottle: *put the stopper back in the bottle.* ⇨ picture at BOTTLE.

▶ **stopper** *v* [Vn] to close sth with a stopper.

stopwatch /'stɒpwɒtʃ/ *n* a watch with a hand that can be stopped and started by pressing buttons, used to measure the time of a race, etc accurately.

storage /'stɔːrɪdʒ/ *n* [U] **1(a)** the storing of goods, etc: *extra storage space in the loft* ○ *put furniture into storage* ○ *a table that folds flat for storage.* **(b)** the space used or available for this: *food kept in cold storage* ○ *a storage compartment on a plane* ○ *a fuel/water storage tank* ○ *a storage jar.* **2** (*computing*) **(a)** the storing of information, etc on a computer: *data storage* ○ *computerized storage systems.* **(b)** the method or material used for this: *disk/tape storage.* **3** the cost of storing things: *pay storage.*

■ **'storage heater** *n* an electric heater that stores heat when electricity is cheaper, eg at night, and releases it later.

store /stɔː(r)/ *n* **1** [C] a quantity or supply of sth kept for use as needed: *have a good store of food in the house.* **2** [C usu *sing*] ~ **(of sth)** a large collection or amount: *a store of energy/knowledge* ○ *stores of pent-up anger and frustration.* **3** [C] **(a)** (*esp US*) (often in compounds) a shop: *a health food store.* See also DRUGSTORE. **(b)** a usu large shop selling many different types of goods: *a big department store* ○ *a DIY store.* See also CHAIN STORE. **4 stores** [pl] **(a)** goods, etc of a particular type, or for a special purpose: *medical/military stores.* **(b)** the supply of such goods or a place where they are kept: *available from stores.* **5** [C] (*computing*) a device in a computer for storing information. **IDM** **in store (for sb/ sth) 1** kept ready for future use: *He always keeps several cases of wine in store.* **2** coming in the future; about to happen: *I can see trouble in store.* ○ *There's a surprise in store for you.* **set (great/little/no/not much) 'store by sth** to consider sth to be of great, little, etc importance or value: *set great store by personal appearance/manners* ○ *He's never set much store by material possessions.*

▶ **store** *v* **1** ~ **sth (up/away)** to collect and keep sth for future use: [Vn, Vnp] *a squirrel storing (up) food for the winter* [Vnpr] *store information on computer* ○ *store in an airtight container.* **2** to put furniture, etc in a place where it can be kept safe: [Vn] *They've stored their furniture while they are abroad.* **3** ~ **sth (with sth)** (esp passive) to supply or fill sth with sth useful: [Vnpr] *a mind well stored with facts* [also Vn]. **4** to hold or contain sth: [Vn] *wooden casks for storing wine.*

storehouse /'stɔːhaʊs/ *n* (*pl* **-houses** /-haʊzɪz/) **(a)** a building where things are stored. **(b)** a person, place or thing that has or contains a lot of information: *This book is a storehouse of useful information.*

storekeeper /'stɔːkiːpə(r)/ *n* (*esp US*) = SHOP-KEEPER.

storeroom /'stɔːruːm, -rʊm/ *n* a room used for storing things, esp in a shop.

storey (*US* **story**) /'stɔːri/ *n* (*pl* **storeys**; *US* **stories**) a part of a building with rooms all at the same level; a floor¹(3): *a single-storey building* ○ *the upper/lower storey* ○ *an office block twenty storeys high* ○ *live on the third storey of a block of flats* ○ *a multi-storey car park.*

▶ **-storeyed** (*US* **-storied**) /-'stɔːrid/ (forming compound *adjs*) having the number of storeys specified: *a six-storeyed building.*

stork /stɔːk/ *n* a large, usu white, bird with a long beak, neck and legs. Storks feed in rivers, lakes etc and sometimes build their nests on the tops of high buildings.

storm /stɔːm/ n **1** [C] (often in compounds) very bad weather, with strong winds, rain and thunder, etc: *a thunderstorm/rainstorm/snowstorm/sandstorm* ○ *a dust-storm* ○ *a heavy/violent/raging storm* ○ *ride out/ weather* (ie come safely through or survive) *a storm* ○ *There's a storm brewing* (ie coming). **2** [C] ~ **(of sth)** a sudden violent display of strong feeling: *a storm of abuse/protest.* See also BRAINSTORM. **IDM** **any port in a storm** ⇨ PORT¹. **the calm before the storm** ⇨ CALM *n.* **the eye of the storm** ⇨ EYE¹. **a storm in a ¹teacup**; *(US)* **a tempest in a ¹teapot** a lot of anger or worry about sth unimportant. **take sth/sb by ¹storm 1** to capture sth by a violent and sudden attack: *take a city by storm.* **2** (of a play, an actor, a musician, etc) to have great and rapid success with people or in a place: *The play took the audience/Paris by storm.*
▶ **storm** *v* **1** ~ **(at sb)** to express violent anger; to shout angrily and loudly: [V.speech] *'Get out of here!' he stormed.* [also V, Vpr]. **2** to move or walk in a very angry or violent way in the direction specified: [Vpr] *storm out of the room* [Vp] *After the argument she stormed off.* **3** to attack or capture a place: [Vn] *the storming of the Bastille in 1789* [Vpr, Vnpr] *Troops stormed (their way) into the city.* [also Vnp, Vp].
stormy *adj* **(-ier, -iest)** **1** with strong winds, heavy rain, snow, etc: *stormy weather* ○ *a stormy night.* **2** full of strong feeling, violent arguments, etc: *a stormy discussion/debate/outburst* ○ *a stormy marriage/relationship.*
■ **¹storm cloud** *n* **(a)** a large black cloud coming before or with a storm: *storm clouds gathering on the horizon.* **(b)** (usu *pl*) a sign of sth dangerous or threatening: *Anxious employers can see the storm clouds of heavy tax increases ahead.*
¹storm-tossed *adj* damaged or blown about by storms: *a storm-tossed sea/ship.*
¹storm trooper *n* (esp formerly in Nazi Germany) a soldier specially trained for violent attacks.

story¹ /ˈstɔːri/ n **1** ~ **(about/of sb/sth)** **(a)** an account of past events, incidents, etc: *the story of Martin Luther King* ○ *stories of ancient Greece* ○ *You haven't heard the full/whole story.* ○ *The police didn't believe her story.* ○ *Many years later I returned to Africa — but that's another story.* See also LIFE STORY, HARD-LUCK STORY, SOB-STORY. **(b)** an account of invented or imagined events, etc: *a ¹love story* ○ *a short story by Chekhov* ○ *an adventure story for children* ○ *My father always used to tell us bedtime stories.* See also COCK-AND-BULL STORY, FAIRY STORY, GHOST STORY, TALL STORY. **2** (also **¹story-line**) the plot²(1) of a book, play, etc: *Her novels always have the same basic story(-line).* **3** (*journalism*) **(a)** a report of an item of news in a newspaper or magazine; an article²(2): *a front-page story* ○ *the cover story* (ie advertised on the cover of a magazine). See also LEAD STORY. **(b)** an event, a situation or material suitable for this: *be on the look-out for a good story.* **4** (*infml*) a false statement, description, etc; a lie: *Don't tell stories, Peter.* **IDM** **a likely story** ⇨ LIKELY. **the same old story** ⇨ SAME¹. **the story goes that … / so the story goes** people are saying (that …); so it is said: *She never saw him again — or so the story goes.* **tell its own tale/story** ⇨ TELL. **that's the ¹story of my ¹life** (*infml*) (said by sb when sth bad happens and they compare it to many similar experiences they have had in the past): *Another missed opportunity — that's the story of my life!* **to cut a long story short** ⇨ LONG¹.
■ **¹story-book** *n* a book of stories, usu for children: *Their love affair had a story-book ending* (ie It ended in a happy way, as most children's stories do).
story² *(US)* = STOREY.

storyteller /ˈstɔːritelə(r)/ *n* a person who tells stories.
▶ **¹storytelling** *n* [U] the art or practice of telling stories.

stoup /stuːp/ *n* a stone container for holy water in a church.

stout /staʊt/ *adj* **(-er, -est)** **1** [usu attrib] strong and thick: *stout walking shoes* ○ *a stout timber.* **2** (*esp euph*) (of a person) rather fat; built in a solid way: *She's growing rather stout.* ⇨ note at FAT¹. **3** [usu attrib] (*fml*) brave and determined: *a stout effort/ defence* ○ *a stout heart.*
▶ **stout** *n* [U, C] a strong dark beer.
stoutly *adv*: *stoutly built* ○ *He stoutly* (ie firmly) *refused to go.*
stoutness *n* [U].
■ **¹stout-¹hearted** *adj* (*fml*) brave and determined.

stove¹ /stəʊv/ *n* [C] an enclosed apparatus for cooking or heating rooms. Stoves operate by electricity or gas or by burning wood, coal or oil: *put a pan on the stove* ○ *a wood-burning stove.* Compare COOKER 1, FIRE¹ 3, HEATER.

stove² ⇨ STAVE².

stow /stəʊ/ *v* ~ **sth (away) (in sth)** to pack or store sth carefully and neatly, esp in its proper place: [Vnpr, Vnp] *stow clothes (away) in a trunk* [Vn, Vnpr] *stow cargo (in a ship's hold)* [Vnpr] *Passengers are requested to stow their hand-baggage in the lockers above the seats.* **PHRV** **stow away** to hide oneself as a STOWAWAY: *stow away on a ship bound for New York.*
▶ **stowage** /ˈstəʊɪdʒ/ *n* [U] space provided for stowing things in, esp on a boat or an aircraft or in a vehicle: *a vessel with excellent stowage (space).*

stowaway /ˈstəʊəweɪ/ *n* a person who hides in a ship or aircraft before its departure, in order to travel without paying or being seen.

straddle /ˈstrædl/ *v* **1** to sit or stand across sth with the legs wide apart and on each side of it: [Vn] *straddle a fence/ditch/horse.* **2** to extend across both sides of sth in space or time: [Vn] *The town straddles the border between the two counties.*

strafe /strɑːf; *US* streɪf/ *v* to attack sb/sth repeatedly with bullets or bombs from aircraft flying low over their target: [Vn] *strafe a beach.*

straggle /ˈstrægl/ *v* **1** to grow or spread in a way that is not regular or tidy: [V] *straggling hair/ hedges* [Vpr] *Small cottages straggle across the hillside.* **2** to move slowly alone or in small groups, usu behind and separated from the main group: [Vp, Vpr] *a few young children straggling along (behind their parents)* [V] *a straggling line of refugees.*
▶ **straggler** /ˈstræglə(r)/ *n* a person who straggles straggle(2): *The last stragglers are just finishing the race.*
straggly /ˈstrægli/ *adj* growing or hanging in a way that is not regular or tidy: *wet straggly hair.*

straight¹ /streɪt/ *adj* **1** without a bend or curve; extending or moving continuously in one direction only: *a straight line* ○ *straight hair* (ie without curls) ○ *straight-backed chairs* ○ *The road continues straight as an arrow for two miles.* ⇨ picture at HAIR. **2** [pred] properly positioned by being parallel to sth else; level or upright: *Is my tie straight?* ○ *His hat isn't on straight.* **3** [usu pred] arranged in proper order; tidy: *It took hours to get the house straight.* **4** honest; frank: *give a straight answer to a straight question* ○ *I don't think you're being straight with me.* ○ *It's time for some straight talking.* ○ *You can trust Peter — he's (as) straight as a die* (ie completely honest). **5** [attrib] involving only two clear alternatives; simple: *It was a straight choice between taking the job and staying out of work.* **6** [attrib] (in drama) serious; not concerned with comedy or musical theatre: *a straight play/actor.* **7**

[attrib] in continuous succession; CONSECUTIVE: *She's had ten straight wins and is in excellent form.* **8** (of an alcoholic drink) without water or anything else added; neat(5): *I like my vodka straight.* **9** (*infml*) (**a**) (of a person) conventional and conservative. (**b**) not HOMOSEXUAL: *straight men.* **IDM** **get sth right/straight** ⇨ RIGHT¹. **keep a straight 'face** to stop oneself from smiling or laughing when it is difficult to do so: *He has such a strange voice that it's difficult to keep a straight face when he's talking.* **put/set the record straight** ⇨ RECORD¹. **put/set sb straight (about/on sth)** to correct sb's mistake; to make sure that sb knows the correct facts, etc when they have the wrong idea or impression: *He seemed to think he could arrive for work whenever he liked, but I soon put him straight (about that).* **put sth 'straight** (*esp Brit*) to make sth tidy, properly arranged or in order: *Please put your desk straight before you leave the office.* **stiff/straight as a ramrod** ⇨ RAMROD. **the ˌstraight and 'narrow** (*infml*) the proper, honest and morally acceptable way of living: *He finds it difficult to stay on/keep to the straight and narrow for long.*

straight² /streɪt/ *adv* **1** not in a curve or at an angle; in a straight line: *sit up straight (ie without bending one's back)* ∘ *Keep straight on for two miles.* ∘ *Look straight ahead.* ∘ *The smoke rose straight up.* ∘ *He was too drunk to walk straight.* ∘ *I can't shoot straight (ie accurately at the target).* **2** by a direct route; without delaying or hesitating: *Come straight home/back.* ∘ *He went straight to Lagos, without stopping in Nairobi.* ∘ *She went straight from school to college.* ∘ *I'll come straight to the point — your work isn't good enough.* **3** honestly and directly; in a STRAIGHTFORWARD manner: *I told him straight that I didn't like him.* **4** continuously without a break: *work for 16 hours straight.* **IDM** **go 'straight** to live an honest life after being a criminal: *come out of prison and go straight.* **play 'straight (with sb)** to be honest and fair in the way in which one deals with sb: *I don't think you're playing straight with me.* **right/straight away/off** ⇨ RIGHT². **ˌstraight from the 'shoulder** (of criticism, etc) openly and honestly stated: *She gave it to me straight from the shoulder.* **ˌstraight 'out** directly and without hesitating: *I told him straight out that I thought he was lying.* ∘ *I didn't ask him to tell me — he just came straight out with it.* **ˌstraight 'up** (*Brit sl*) (used esp in asking and answering questions) honestly; really: *'I don't believe you got it for nothing.' 'Yes, I did — straight up!'* **think straight** ⇨ THINK¹.

straight³ /streɪt/ *n* **1** a straight part of a race track or course: *The two runners were level coming into the final straight.* See also THE HOME STRAIGHT. **2** (*infml*) a conventional person, esp a HETEROSEXUAL: *gays and straights.*

straightaway /ˌstreɪtə'weɪ/ *adv* immediately; straight away; at once: *Don't delay — do it straight away.*

straighten /'streɪtn/ *v* ~ (**sth**) (**up/out**) to become or make sth straight¹(1,2): [V,Vp] *The road finally straightens (out) after a series of bends.* [Vn] *straighten one's tie/skirt* [Vnp] *I damaged the front bumper of my car and had to get it straightened out.* **PHRV** **ˌstraighten sb 'out** (*infml*) to make sb understand clearly or correctly sth that they are confused or wrong about: *If you're unsure about office procedures, Jane will soon straighten you out.* **ˌstraighten sth 'out** to resolve or organize sth that is confused or in disorder: *I need time to straighten out my finances.* **ˌstraighten (oneself) 'up** to make one's body upright: *straighten (yourself) up and pay attention!* **ˌstraighten sth 'up** to make sth tidy: *You can't go out until you've straightened up your room.* ▶ **straightness** *n* [U].

■ **'straight man** *n* a member of a comedy team who makes remarks or creates situations for the main performer to make jokes about.

straightforward /ˌstreɪt'fɔːwəd/ *adj* **1** honest and frank, without trying to deceive sb or avoid sth: *be straightforward in one's business dealings* ∘ *a straightforward offer with no hidden disadvantages.* **2** easy to understand or do; not complicated; without difficulties: *a ˌstraightforward 'question/ap'proach* ∘ *written in ˌstraightforward 'language* ∘ *The rules are quite straightforward.* ▶ **straightforwardly** *adv.* **straightforwardness** *n* [U].

strain¹ /streɪn/ *v* **1** to injure part of the body/ oneself or make part of the body/oneself weak by too much effort: [Vn] *strain a muscle/one's heart* ∘ *strain one's eyes (eg by reading in a bad light)* ∘ *strain one's voice (ie by speaking or singing too long or too loudly)* ∘ *Those cases look very heavy — don't strain yourself.* **2** to make the greatest possible effort; to use all one's power, energy, etc in order to do sth: [Vn.to inf] *She spoke very quietly and I had to strain my ears to hear her.* [V.to inf] *People were straining to see what was going on.* [also V]. **3** to take or use sth to or beyond the limit of what is acceptable or possible: [Vn] *The dispute has severely strained relations between the two countries.* ∘ *Their constant complaints are straining my patience.* ∘ *The story certainly strains one's credulity (ie is very hard to believe).* **4** to pour food, etc through sth with a lot of small holes in it, eg a SIEVE or cloth, so as to separate solids from liquids: [Vn] *strain vegetables/ tea* [Vnpr, Vnp] *strain (off) the water from the boiled cabbage.* **IDM** **strain at the 'leash** (*infml*) to be eager to have the freedom to do what one wants: *youngsters straining at the leash to escape parental control.* **strain every 'nerve (to do sth)** to try as hard as one can: *The team will be straining every nerve to perform well.* **PHRV** **'strain at sth** to pull sth very hard or stretch sth very tightly: *rowers straining at the oars* ∘ *The dogs were straining at the lead, eager to be off.*

▶ **strained** *adj* **1** (of a situation) not relaxed or comfortable; tense or UNEASY: *There was a strained atmosphere throughout the meeting.* ∘ *Relations between the two families are rather strained.* **2** tired and worried or anxious: *She looked very strained when I last saw her — I think she's working too hard.* **3** not natural; produced by conscious effort rather than natural impulse: *a strained laugh.*

strainer *n* a device with a lot of small holes in it for straining (STRAIN 4) sth: *a 'tea strainer.*

strain² /streɪn/ *n* **1(a)** [C,U] a severe demand on mental or physical strength, resources, abilities, etc: *the **stresses and strains** of modern life* ∘ *There's a lot of strain at work because we're so busy.* ∘ *The transport system cannot cope with the strain of so many additional passengers.* ∘ *She has a lot of personal problems and is **under great strain.*** ∘ *Having to concentrate for so long was a real strain.* ∘ *I found it a strain making conversation with him.* (**b**) [U] a state in which one is worried, tense and very tired because of this: *suffering from nervous strain.* **2** [C,U] an injury to a part of the body caused by twisting a muscle or making too much effort: *a groin strain.* **3** [C,U] (**a**) the state of being stretched or pulled tightly: *The rope broke **under the strain.*** (**b**) a force causing this: *rope with a 100 kg **breaking strain.*** **4** [C usu *pl*] (*fml*) a part of a tune or piece of music being performed: *hear the strains of the church organ.*

strain³ /streɪn/ *n* **1** (usu *sing*) ~ (**of sth**) a tendency in a person's character: *There's a strain of madness in the family.* **2** a breed or type of animal, insect, plant, etc: *a new strain of wheat* ∘ *strains of mosquitoes that are resistant to insecticide.*

strait /streɪt/ *n* **1** [C often *pl* with *sing* meaning, esp in place names] a narrow passage of water connecting two seas or two large areas of water: *the Straits of Gibraltar* ○ *the Magellan Straits.* **2 straits** [pl] trouble; difficulty: *be* **in dire/desperate/ serious financial straits.**

straitened /ˈstreɪtnd/ *adj* [attrib] difficult because of poverty: *live* **in straitened circumstances/ times.**

strait-jacket /ˈstreɪtdʒækɪt/ *n* **1** a garment like a jacket with long arms which are tied to prevent the person wearing it from behaving violently. Strait-jackets are sometimes used for people who are mentally ill. **2** (*derog*) a thing that stops or restricts growth or development: *the strait-jacket of repressive taxation.*

strait-laced /ˌstreɪt ˈleɪst/ *adj* (*derog*) having or showing a very strict attitude to moral questions: *My parents are very strait-laced.* ○ *have strait-laced ideas about sex.*

strand¹ /strænd/ *n* (*arch or rhet*) the shore of a lake, sea or river.

▶ **strand** *v* (esp passive) **1** to cause esp a boat, a fish or a WHALE to be left on the shore and unable to return to the sea: [Vn] *The ship was stranded on a sandbank.* **2** to leave sb in a place where they are helpless, eg without money, friends or transport: [Vn] *I was stranded in a foreign country without a passport.*
stranded *adj*: *stranded tourists.*

strand² /strænd/ *n* **1(a)** each of the threads, wires, etc twisted together to form a rope or cable. **(b)** a single thread of string or material: *a strand of cotton hanging from the hem of a skirt.* **2** a single hair. **3** any of the various parts or aspects that together form the whole of sth: *drawing together the strands of the narrative.*

strange /streɪndʒ/ *adj* (**-r, -st**) **1** unusual; surprising; difficult to understand: *It's strange we haven't heard from him.* ○ *He wears the strangest clothes.* ○ *She has some very strange ideas.* ○ *I find their attitude strange.* ○ *It feels strange to be visiting the place again after all these years.* **2** ~ (**to sb**) not previously visited, seen or met; not familiar: *a strange country/town/neighbourhood* ○ *Never accept lifts from strange men.* ○ *At first the place was strange to me.* **3** having unpleasant feelings; not well: *It was terribly hot and I started to feel strange.* **4** not at ease or comfortable in a situation; feeling that one does not fit in (FIT²): *She felt very strange among these people she had never met before.* **IDM** ,**strange to** ˈ**say...** it is surprising or unusual that...: *Strange to say, I don't really enjoy television.*

▶ **strangely** *adv* in a strange(1) way: *She's been acting very strangely lately.* ○ *The house was strangely quiet.* ○ *It turned out we'd been at school together,* **strangely enough.**
strangeness *n* [U].

stranger /ˈstreɪndʒə(r)/ *n* **1** a person that one does not know or who is not familiar to one: *I'd met Anna before, but her friend was a* **complete/total stranger** *to me.* ○ *Our dog barks at strangers.* **2** a person who is in a place he or she does not know or know well, or with people he or she has not met before: *I'm a stranger in this town.* ○ *As a stranger, I just did what the others did.* **IDM** **be no/a** ˈ**stranger to sth** (*fml*) to be familiar/not familiar with sth as a result of having had experience of it: *He's no stranger to misfortune.*

strangle /ˈstræŋgl/ *v* **1** to kill sb by squeezing or gripping their throat tightly: [Vn] *He strangled her with her own scarf.* ○ (*infml*) *I could cheerfully strangle you for getting me into this mess!* ○ (*fig*) *This stiff collar is strangling me* (ie making it difficult for me to breathe). **2** to restrict or prevent the proper growth, operation or development of sth: [Vn] *The government's monetary policy is slowly strangling the economy.*

▶ **strangled** *adj* [attrib] (of the voice) restricted or partly suppressed: *a strangled cry/gasp.*
strangler *n* a person who kills sb by strangling them.

stranglehold /ˈstræŋglhəʊld/ *n* **1** a strong grip around sb's neck, with pressure on the throat, making breathing difficult: *get sb in a stranglehold.* **2** (usu *sing*) ~ (**on sth**) firm or complete control of sth, making it impossible for it to grow or develop properly: *The new tariffs have put a stranglehold on trade.*

strangulated /ˈstræŋgjuleɪtɪd/ *adj* **1** (*medical*) (of a part of the body) tightly squeezed so that blood cannot pass through it: [Vn] *a strangulated hernia.* **2** (of a voice) producing a restricted sound, eg because of fear or worry.

strangulation /ˌstræŋgjuˈleɪʃn/ *n* [U] the action of strangling (STRANGLE) sb/sth or the state of being strangled: *die of strangulation* ○ *the strangulation of individual freedom.*

strap /stræp/ *n* (esp in compounds) **1** [C] a strip of leather, cloth or other flexible material, often with a BUCKLE, used for fastening sth, keeping sth in place, carrying sth or holding onto sth: *an adjustable watch-strap* ○ *ankle straps on a shoe* ○ *bra straps* ○ *a rucksack with padded shoulder-straps* ○ *My camera strap has broken.* **2 the strap** [sing] (esp formerly) a punishment by beating with a narrow strip of leather; the strip of leather used for this.

▶ **strap** *v* **1** to hold, secure or fasten sth/sb with a strap or straps: [Vp, Vpr] *They strapped their equipment on(to their backs).* ○ *Make sure the passengers are strapped in(to their seats) before driving off.* [Vp] *The truck's load had been securely strapped down.* **2** ~ **sth (up)** to wrap strips of material around a wound, limb, etc: [Vn, Vnp] *His injured arm was tightly strapped (up).*
strapless /ˈstræpləs/ *adj* (esp of a dress or BRASSIERE) without straps.
strapped *adj* [pred] ~ (**for sth**) (*infml*) having little or not enough money: *I'm a bit strapped (for cash) at the moment — can I pay you later?*
strapping *adj* big, tall and strong: *They have four strapping children.*

strata *pl* of STRATUM.

stratagem /ˈstrætədʒəm/ *n* (*fml*) a trick, plan or scheme to deceive sb, esp an opponent: *adopt/devise a cunning stratagem.*

strategic /strəˈtiːdʒɪk/ (also **strategical** /-dʒɪkl/) *adj* [usu attrib] **1** forming part of a plan or an aim to achieve a specific purpose or to gain an advantage: *strategic planning/decisions* ○ *a strategic approach/argument* ○ *take up a strategic position* ○ *make a strategic move.* **2** (*military*) **(a)** (of an attack, a position, a plan, etc) that gives an advantage in a war: *a strategic alliance* ○ *strategic forces* ○ *strategic bombing* (eg of industrial areas and communication centres) ○ *an island of vital strategic importance.* **(b)** (of weapons, esp nuclear missiles) directed against an enemy's country rather than used in a battle: *strategic missiles.* Compare TACTICAL. ▶ **strategically** /-kli/ *adv*: *a strategically placed microphone* ○ *a strategically important target.*

strategy /ˈstrætədʒi/ *n* **1(a)** [C] a plan designed for a particular purpose: *devise economic strategies* ○ *work out a strategy to gain promotion* ○ *develop a new company/corporate strategy to beat the competition.* **(b)** [U] the process of planning sth or carrying out a plan in a skilful way: *By careful strategy she managed to get the office next to that of her boss.* Compare TACTIC. **2** [U,C] the art of planning and directing military activity in a battle or war; an instance of this: *military strategy* ○ *defence strategies.*

▶ **strategist** /-dʒɪst/ *n* a person skilled in planning things, esp military activity: *a military strategist* ○ *a* *brilliant strategist when it comes to business take-overs.*

stratify /'strætɪfaɪ/ v (pt, pp **-fied**) to arrange sth in layers or strata (STRATUM): *ancient pottery found in stratified layers of earth* ○ *a highly stratified society.*
▶ **stratification** /ˌstrætɪfɪ'keɪʃn/ n [U] the division of sth into layers or strata (STRATUM): *social stratification.*

stratosphere /'strætəsfɪə(r)/ n [sing] the layer of the earth's atmosphere between about 10 and 60 kilometres (KILOMETRE) above the surface of the earth. Compare IONOSPHERE.

stratum /'strɑːtəm; US 'streɪtəm/ n (pl **strata** /-tə/) **1** any of a series of layers, esp of rock, earth, etc: *a stratum of flint/gravel* ○ *geological/limestone strata.* **2** a level or class of a society: *people from all social strata.*

straw /strɔː/ n **1(a)** [U] the cut and dried stems of grain plants, eg wheat. Straw is used for making mats, hats, etc, for packing things to protect them, and as food for animals or for them to sleep on: *a straw hat* ○ *a stable filled with straw* ○ *a roof thatched* (ie covered) *with straw.* (**b**) [C] a single stem or piece of this. Compare HAY 1. **2** [C] thin tube of paper or plastic through which a drink is sucked into the mouth: *drinking lemonade through a straw.* **IDM** **clutch/grasp at 'straws** to try all possible means to escape from a difficult situation, even though there seems to be little hope of doing so: *I'm just clutching at straws, but is it possible that the doctors are wrong?* **draw the short straw** ⇨ DRAW¹. **the last/final 'straw** the final event, action, comment, etc that makes sth impossible to tolerate: *After all the problems I had with the job, not getting paid on time was the last/final straw.* **make bricks without straw** ⇨ BRICK. **not care a 'straw/two 'straws** ⇨ CARE². **a straw in the 'wind** a slight indication of how things may develop. **the straw that breaks/broke the camel's back** = THE LAST/FINAL STRAW.
■ **'straw-coloured** adj (US **-colored**) pale yellow: *straw-coloured hair.*
ˌ**straw 'poll** n a survey of public opinion that is not official: *A straw poll taken among local people showed that most did not want the new road to be built.*

strawberry /'strɔːbəri; US -beri/ n (**a**) [C] a soft juicy red fruit with tiny yellow seeds on the surface: *fresh strawberries and cream* ○ *strawberry jam.* (**b**) a plant on which this fruit grows. See also RUNNER 4.

stray /streɪ/ v **1** to move away from a group, the right path or place, etc with no particular destination or purpose: [Vpr] *stray into the path of an oncoming car* ○ *Young children should not be allowed to stray from their parents.* ○ *We strayed off the route because I didn't read the map correctly.* [V] *Some of the sheep have strayed.* **2** to leave the subject one is supposed to be thinking about or discussing: [Vpr] *My mind kept straying from the discussion (to other things).* ○ *We seem to have strayed from the point.*
▶ **stray** adj [attrib] **1** (of domestic animals) lost: *a home for stray dogs.* **2** separated from a group; not in the right place: *killed by a stray bullet* ○ *a few stray hairs.*
stray n **1** a domestic animal that has got lost or separated from its owner: *This dog must be a stray.* See also WAIF b. **2** a thing that is not in the right place or is separated from others of the same kind.

streak /striːk/ n ~ (**of sth**) **1** a long thin mark or line of a different substance or colour from its surroundings: *streaks of blood/oil/paint* ○ *streaks of grey in her hair* ○ *a streak* (ie flash) *of lightning.* **2** an element in a person's character, esp an unpleasant one: *a streak of jealousy/cruelty* ○ *have a jealous/mean/rebellious streak.* **3** a period of continuous

success or failure, eg in a sport: *a streak of good luck* ○ *hit* (ie have) *a winning/losing streak.*
▶ **streak** v **1** ~ **sth** (**with sth**) (esp passive) to mark sth with streaks (STREAK1): [Vn] *have one's hair streaked* [Vnpr] *white marble streaked with brown.* **2** (*infml*) to move very fast in the specified direction: [Vpr] *Tears streaked down his cheeks.* [Vp,Vpr] *She streaked away (from the rest) to win by several metres.* **3** [V] (*infml*) to run through a public place with no clothes on as a way of getting attention.
streaker n (*infml*) a person who streaks (STREAK v 3).
streaky adj marked with, having or full of streaks (STREAK 1): (*Brit*) *streaky bacon* (ie with layers of fat in it).

stream /striːm/ n **1** a small narrow river: *We waded across a shallow stream.* See also DOWNSTREAM, UPSTREAM, THE GULF STREAM. **2(a)** ~ (**of sth/sb**) a continuous flow of liquid or gas: *A stream of blood flowed from the wound.* ○ *He blew out a stream of cigar smoke.* See also BLOODSTREAM. (**b**) a constant movement of people or things: *a steady stream of traffic entering the city.* (**c**) a large number of things that happen one after the other: *a stream of complaints/telephone calls* ○ *be subject to a stream of abuse.* **3** the current or direction in which things are tending to move: *drift along with the stream* ○ *go against the stream of public opinion.* **4** (*esp Brit*) (in some schools) a group in which children of the same age and level of ability are placed: *the A/B/C stream.* **IDM** **on 'stream** happening or available; in operation: *More jobs will be coming on stream next year.* ○ *The project has been on stream for three years now.*
▶ **stream** v **1(a)** (of liquid) to move in a continuous flow; to pour out: [Vpr] *Sweat was streaming down his face.* [also Vp]. (**b**) (of people or things) to move in a continuous flow in a particular direction: [Vpr] *people streaming into the shop* ○ *traffic streaming out of the city* [also Vp]. **2** ~ (**with sth**) to produce a continuous flow of liquid: [V] *a streaming cold* (ie with much liquid coming from the nose) [Vpr] *a face streaming with blood/sweat/tears* [Vn] *a wound streaming blood.* **3** to float or wave at full length, esp in the wind: [Vp,Vpr] *Her hair streamed (out) in the wind.* ○ *Their scarves streamed (out) behind them.* **4** (*esp Brit*) (usu passive) to put children in streams (STREAM 4): [Vn] *Children are streamed according to ability.* **streamer** n **1** a long narrow flag. **2** a long narrow piece of coloured paper: *a room decorated for a party with balloons and streamers.* **streaming** n [U] the policy or action of placing children in streams (STREAM 4).
■ ˌ**stream of 'consciousness** n [U] (esp in literature) a continuous flow of ideas, thoughts and feelings as they are experienced by a person; a style of writing that expresses this without using the usual methods of description or conversation.

streamline /'striːmlaɪn/ v **1** to give sth a smooth even shape, so that it can move quickly and easily through air, water, etc: [Vn] *streamlined racing cars.* **2** to make a system, an organization, etc more efficient and effective, eg by using faster or simpler working methods: [Vn] *streamline a production process.*

street /striːt/ n (abbr **St**) a public road in a city, town or village with houses and buildings on one side or both sides: *cross the street* ○ *walk down/up the street* ○ *wander around the deserted streets* ○ *live in New York on 92nd street* ○ *people hanging around on street-corners* ○ *at street level* (ie on the ground floor) ○ *a 'street map/plan of York* ○ *street lights* ○ *street theatre* (ie plays, etc performed in the street): *My address is 122 Broad Street.* ○ *It's not safe to walk the streets at night.* ⇨ note at ROAD. See also BACKSTREET, HIGH STREET, SIDE-STREET. **IDM** **easy**

street ⇨ EASY¹. **the man in the street** ⇨ MAN¹.
(out) on the ˈstreets (*infml*) **1** without a home: *the problems of young people living on the streets* ○ *Unless I get a job soon, I'll be out on the streets.* **2** (*euph*) working as a prostitute. **ˈstreets ahead (of sb/sth)** (*infml*) much better, more advanced, etc than sb/sth: *a country that is streets ahead in terms of controlling environmental pollution* ○ *She is streets ahead of all the other players on the field.* **(right) up one's ˈstreet** (*infml*) within one's area of knowledge, interest, activity, etc: *This job seems right up your street.*

■ **ˈstreet credibility** (also *infml* **ˈstreet cred**) *n* [U] an image, a way of behaving, etc, that is acceptable to young people, esp those who have experienced or are concerned with the problems of real life: *You need to wear something with a bit more street cred.*
ˈstreet smart *adj* (*infml*) = STREETWISE.
ˈstreet value *n* (usu *sing*) a price for which sth illegal or illegally obtained can be sold: *Customs officers have seized drugs with a street value of over £1 million.*

streetcar /ˈstriːtkɑː(r)/ *n* (*US*) = TRAM.

streetwalker /ˈstriːtwɔːkə(r)/ *n* (*dated*) a prostitute who looks for customers on the streets.

streetwise /ˈstriːtwaɪz/ (also **street-smart** /ˈstriːt smɑːt/) *adj* (*infml*) having knowledge and experience of dealing with the difficulties of life in a big city.

strength /streŋθ/ *n* **1** [U] the quality of being strong; the amount of this that sb/sth has: *a person of great strength* ○ *possess great strength of character/mind/will* ○ *regain one's strength after an illness* ○ *the strength of the wind* ○ *add wine/spices/curry powder depending on the strength required* ○ *For a small woman she has surprising strength.* ⇨ note. **2** [U] the ability that sth has to resist force or hold heavy weights without breaking or being damaged: *the strength of a rope/box.* **3** [U] the extent to which a feeling or an opinion is strong: *the strength of public opinion/anger* ○ *a view that has gathered strength* (ie become stronger or more widely held) *in recent weeks* ○ *There is considerable strength of feeling on this issue.* **4** [C, U] the good qualities or abilities that a person or a thing has: *the strengths and weaknesses of an argument* ○ *The ability to keep calm is one of her many strengths.* ○ *His strength as a manager lies in his ability to communicate with people.* **6** [U] the number of people present or available; the full number of a group: *What is the strength of the workforce?* **IDM** **be at full/be below ˈstrength** to have the required/less than the required number of esp experienced or trained people: *The team will be back at full strength for the next match.* **bring sth/be up to (full) ˈstrength** to make sth reach/to be the required number: *We must bring the police force up to (full) strength.* **go from ˌstrength to ˈstrength** to progress with growing success: *Since her appointment the department has gone from strength to strength.* **in (full, great, etc) ˈstrength** in large numbers: *The police are out in strength on the streets.* **on the strength of sth** on the basis of sth; because of the influence of sth: *I got the job on the strength of your recommendation.* **a tower of strength** ⇨ TOWER.

▶ **strengthen** /ˈstreŋθn/ *v* to become or make sb/sth stronger: [V] *The wind has strengthened.* [Vn] *take up swimming to strengthen your muscles* ○ *repairs to strengthen the bridge* ○ *plans to strengthen the company's position in the market* ○ *This latest development has only strengthened my determination to leave.*

NOTE Compare **strength**, **power**, **force** and **vigour** (**vigor** in American English). **Strength** and **power** are used to talk about how strong somebody or something is. The **strength** of a person, or of some-

thing such as a bridge, is its ability to hold great weight: *I don't have the strength to carry you any further.* The **power** in part of a person's body, in a machine, or in something natural such as the wind, is the energy inside it that can be used to do something: *The power of the wind can be harnessed to produce electricity.*

Force and **vigour** relate to how much energy is used by somebody or something. The **force** of an explosion or a storm is how strong it is: *Our car was completely wrecked by the force of the collision.* A person's **vigour** is the energy with which he or she works: *She returned to work with renewed vigour after a long holiday.*

strenuous /ˈstrenjuəs/ *adj* **1** requiring great effort or energy: *a strenuous itinerary* ○ *strenuous work/ exercise/efforts* ○ *The next few weeks will be strenuous and demanding.* **2** making great efforts; ENERGETIC: *a strenuous defender of government policies.*
▶ **strenuously** *adv* with all one's energy: *strenuously oppose sth* ○ *She strenuously denies all the charges.*

streptococcus /ˌstreptəˈkɒkəs/ *n* (*pl* **-cocci** /-ˈkɒkaɪ/) (*medical*) any of a group of bacteria that cause serious infections and illnesses.

streptomycin /ˌstreptəʊˈmaɪsɪn/ *n* [U] (*medical*) an ANTIBIOTIC drug used for treating infections.

stress /stres/ *n* **1(a)** [U] pressure, tension or worry resulting from problems in one's life: *be under/ suffer from stress* ○ *In times of stress, she finds music a great relaxation.* ○ *Stress is believed to be a factor in several illnesses.* **(b)** [C usu *pl*] a thing that causes this: *emotional stresses* ○ *He finds the stresses of his job difficult to cope with.* **2** [U] ~ (**on sth**) special emphasis or importance given to sth: *She lays/puts great stress on punctuality.* ○ *I think the company places too much stress on cost and not enough on quality.* **3** [C, U] **(a)** an extra force used when pronouncing a particular word or syllable: *primary/secondary stress* ○ *In 'strategic' the stress is/ falls on the second syllable.* Compare INTONATION 1. **(b)** extra force used when making a particular sound in music: *Put a stress on the first note in each bar.* **4** [C, U] ~ (**on sth**) pressure put on sth that can damage it or make it lose its shape: *High winds put great stress on the structure.* ○ *a stress fracture of a bone* (ie one caused by such pressure).
▶ **stress** *v* **1** to give special emphasis or importance to sth; to emphasize sth: [Vn] *He stressed the importance of treating customers politely.* [V.*that*] *I must stress that what I say is confidential.* **2** to give extra force to a word or syllable when pronouncing it: [Vn] *You stress the first syllable in 'happiness'.*
stressed *adj* [pred] ~ (**out**) suffering from stress (1a); under great pressure so that one is tense, anxious or worried: *feel stressed* ○ *She has a heavy workload at the moment and is very stressed (out).*
stressful /-fl/ *adj* causing stress(1a): *She finds her new job very stressful.*
■ **ˈstress mark** *n* a mark used to indicate the stress(3a) on a syllable in a word: *In the word 'sympathetic'* /ˌsɪmpəˈθetɪk/ *the primary stress* (ˈ) *is on the third syllable, and the secondary stress* (ˌ) *is on the first syllable.*

stretch /stretʃ/ *v* **1(a)** to make sth longer, wider or looser, eg by pulling it: [Vn] *stretch a pair of gloves/ shoes.* **(b)** to become longer, wider, etc without breaking: [V] *The cardigan stretched when I washed it and now it's far too big for me.* ○ *The shoes will stretch after you've worn them a few times.* **2** to pull sth so that there are no loops or folds in it: [Vn-adj] *The mooring rope was stretched tight/taut.* [Vnpr] *The polythene was stretched over wire hoops.* [Vnp, Vnpr] *stretch a cable across (a gorge).* **3** to extend or push out a limb or part of the body and tighten the muscles, esp after waking or in order to

---

reach sth: [V] *He woke up, yawned and stretched.* [Vn] *stretch one's arms/legs* [Vpr] *She stretched across the table for the butter.* [Vp, Vnp] *He stretched out (his hand) to take the book.* [Vnp] *She stretched her arm towards the shelf but couldn't reach it.* **4(a)** ~ **sth (out) (to sth)** to make sth last longer than expected, esp by being careful how one uses it: [Vn, Vnpr] *stretch one's resources (to their limits)* [Vnp] *stretch out one's money* [Vnp] *I can probably stretch my stay to a full week.* **(b)** ~ **to sth** to last longer or be available for wider use than expected or intended: [Vadv] *I'd love a new coat if our money will stretch that far.* [Vpr] *Why don't you eat with us — I'm sure the food will stretch to five.* **5** to spread over an area or a period of time; to extend: [Vpr] *forests stretching for hundreds of miles* [Vp] *The road stretched out across the desert.* [Vp, Vpr] *The long summer vacation stretched ahead (of them).* **6** to make great demands on sb/sth; to use most or all of the capacity of sb/sth: [Vn] *The race really stretched him/his skill as a runner.* ○ *She has not really been stretched at school this term.* [Vnadv] *We can't take on any more work — we're fully stretched already.* [Vnpr] *The disaster stretched the city's emergency services to the limits.* **7** to use or adapt sth in a way that goes beyond a reasonable or acceptable limit: [Vn] *stretch the truth* (ie exaggerate or lie) ○ *stretch the meaning of a word.* **IDM** **bend/stretch the rules** ⇨ RULE. **stretch one's ¹legs** to go for a walk as exercise, esp after sitting for a time: *We stopped and got out of the car to stretch our legs.* **stretch a ¹point** to allow or do sth that is not usu acceptable, esp because of the particular circumstances: *She was hoping they would stretch a point and allow her to stay in the hostel an extra week.* **PHRV** **¡stretch (oneself) ¹out** to relax by lying at full length: *He stretched (himself) out on the sofa and fell asleep.*

▶ **stretch** *n* **1** [C] ~ **(of sth)** an area or extent of land or water: *a beautiful stretch of countryside* ○ *a long stretch of open road* ○ *a calm stretch of water.* **2** a period of time during which sth happens or is done continuously: *work in long stretches* ○ *a four-hour stretch on duty* ○ *She worked for six hours at a stretch.* **3** [C usu *sing*] an act of stretching one's limbs or body: *He got out of bed, had a good stretch and began to get dressed.* **4** [U] (often attrib) the capacity to stretch(1) or be stretched; an elastic quality: *This material has a lot of stretch in it.* ○ *stretch jeans/seat-covers/underwear.* **5** [C usu *sing*] (*sl*) a period of time spent in prison: *He did a stretch for armed robbery.* **6** [C usu *sing*] a straight part of a racing track: *be in the final/finishing stretch.* See also THE HOME STRETCH. **IDM** **at full stretch** ⇨ FULL. **not by any / by no stretch of the imagination** however hard one may try to believe or imagine sth: *By no stretch of the imagination could you call him ambitious.*

stretchy /ˈstretʃi/ *adj* (*infml*) that stretches (STRETCH 1) or can be stretched: *stretchy fabrics.*

■ **¹stretch marks** *n* [pl] marks left on a woman's body after she has been pregnant and the skin has been stretched.

stretcher /ˈstretʃə(r)/ *n* a framework of poles with a long piece of canvas attached between them, used for carrying a sick or injured person: *He's a stretcher case* (ie His injury is so bad that he needs a stretcher).

■ **¹stretcher-bearer** *n* a person who helps to carry a stretcher.

strew /struː/ *v* (*pt* **strewed**; *pp* **strewed** or **strewn** /struːn/) **1** ~ **A on/over B**; ~ **B with A** (esp passive) to scatter sth over a surface; to cover a surface with things: [Vnpr] *strew papers over the floor/strew the floor with papers* ○ *The battlefield was strewn with bodies.* [Vnadv] *In his room, dirty clothes were strewn everywhere.* **2** to lie scattered on or over a surface:

[Vn] *Papers strewed the floor.* ○ *a litter-strewn playground.* ⇨ note at SCATTER.

strewth /struːθ/ *interj* (*dated Brit sl*) (used to express surprise, annoyance, etc).

striated /straɪˈeɪtɪd; US ˈstraɪeɪtɪd/ *adj* (*fml or techn*) marked with lines or ridges: *flesh striated with veins and sinews.*

▶ **striation** /straɪˈeɪʃn/ *n* [C] (*fml*) a line or ridge.

stricken /ˈstrɪkən/ *adj* ~ **(by/with sth)** (esp in compounds) seriously affected by an unpleasant feeling or illness or placed in very difficult circumstances: *ˈgrief-/ˈpanic-/ˈpoverty-/ˈterror-stricken* ○ *be stricken with malaria/cancer/fever* ○ *Rescue teams raced to the stricken ship.*

strict /strɪkt/ *adj* (**-er**, **-est**) **1(a)** demanding that rules, esp those concerning behaviour, are obeyed or observed: *a strict teacher* ○ *a strict upbringing* ○ *She's very strict with her children.* **(b)** that must be obeyed or observed: *strict rules/instructions* ○ *give information in the strictest confidence.* **(c)** following rules or beliefs exactly: *a strict Catholic.* **2** clearly and exactly defined; PRECISE(2): *a strict understanding/interpretation* ○ *He's not a journalist in the strict sense (of the word).*

▶ **strictly** *adv* **1** in a strict manner: *be strictly brought up.* **2** completely; in all circumstances: *follow rules strictly* ○ *Smoking is strictly prohibited.* **3(a)** ~ **for sb/sth** only for sb/sth and no other: *an area reserved strictly for members* ○ *This machine is strictly for the use of staff.* **(b)** only of the specified nature and of no other: *an envelope marked 'strictly personal'.* **4** very; absolutely: *a book of strictly limited interest* ○ *do only work that is strictly necessary.* **IDM** **¹strictly speaking** if one uses words, applies rules, etc in their exact sense: *Strictly speaking, he's not qualified for the job.*

strictness *n* [U].

stricture /ˈstrɪktʃə(r)/ *n* **1** (usu *pl*) ~ **(on sb/sth)** (*fml*) a severe criticism; a remark expressing severe disapproval of sb/sth: *ignore strictures on one's clothing/attitudes.* **2** rules that restrict behaviour or action: *the strictures of religion* ○ *strictures against eating pork.*

stride /straɪd/ *v* (*pt* **strode**) **1** to walk with long steps in the specified direction: [Vpr] *stride along the road/across the fields* [Vp] *She turned and strode off.* **2** ~ **across/over sth** to cross sth with one long step: [Vpr] *stride over a ditch.*

▶ **stride** *n* **1** one long step; the distance covered by one long step: *He reached the door in three strides.* ○ *She's getting closer to the leader with every stride.* **2** a way of walking by taking long regular steps: *He walked in front of me and interrupted my stride.* **3** a thing that makes progress towards an aim: *Great strides have recently been made towards world peace.* ○ *This agreement is a significant stride in the pay talks.* **IDM** **get into one's ¹stride** to begin to do sth with confidence and at a good speed after being slow or hesitating: *She found the job difficult at first, but now she's really getting into her stride.* **take sth in one's ¹stride** to accept and deal with sth difficult or unpleasant without worrying or reacting too strongly: *Some people find retirement stressful, but he has taken it all in his stride.*

strident /ˈstraɪdnt/ *adj* **1** having a loud, harsh and sometimes unpleasant sound: *strident pop music* ○ *Her voice was strident and shrill.* **2** aggressive and harsh: *a strident opponent of government policy.* ▶ **stridency** /ˈstraɪdənsi/ *n* [U]. **stridently** *adv.*

strife /straɪf/ *n* [U] angry or violent disagreement; conflict: *industrial strife* ○ *a nation torn by political strife.*

strike¹ /straɪk/ *n* **1** an organized refusal to work by employees of a company, etc because of a disagreement over eg pay or conditions: *a miners' strike* ○ *a* strike by bus drivers ○ a general/an unofficial/a wildcat strike ○ call a strike ○ take strike action ○ an **all-out strike** (ie one in which all employees take part) ○ Air traffic controllers are **on strike**. ○ Engineering staff are threatening to **come/go out on strike**. See also HUNGER STRIKE. **2** a sudden attack, esp a military one: air/nuclear strikes. **3** (usu sing) a sudden discovery of sth valuable, esp gold or oil: a lucky strike. **4** (usu sing) an act of hitting or kicking sth/sb: It was a good strike but it went just wide of the goal.

■ ˈstrike pay n [U] money paid by a trade union to striking members during a strike officially recognized by the union.

ˈstrike-rate n (usu sing) the number of successes that sb has in relation to the number of attempts they make: a player with a high strike-rate.

strike² /straɪk/ v (pt, pp **struck** /strʌk/) **1(a)** to hit sb/sth hard or with force: [Vn] The ship struck a rock. ○ The tree was struck by lightning. [Vnpr] He struck his head on/against the ceiling. ○ The stone struck him on the forehead. ⇨ note at HIT¹. **(b)** to hit sb/sth with one's hand or a weapon: [Vn, Vnpr] She struck him (in the face). [Vnn] He struck the table a heavy blow with his fist. [Vn] Who struck the first blow (ie started the fight)? **(c)** ~ at sb/sth to aim a blow at sb/sth: [Vpr] He struck at me repeatedly with a stick. **(d)** to hit or kick a ball, etc: [Vnpr] He struck the ball into the net. [also Vn, Vnp]. **2(a)** to attack sb/sth, esp suddenly: [V] The lion crouched ready to strike. ○ Police fear that the killer may strike again. **(b)** ~ at sb/sth to cause damage to or have a serious effect on sb/sth: [Vpr] criticisms that **strike at the heart of** the party's policies ○ strike at the root of the problem. **3** (of disaster, disease, etc) to occur suddenly and have a harmful or damaging effect on sb/ sth: [V] Two days later tragedy struck. [Vn] The area was struck by an outbreak of cholera. **4** (not in the continuous tenses) (of a thought or an idea) to come into sb's mind suddenly: [Vn] An awful thought has just struck me. ○ I was struck by her resemblance to my aunt. [Vn.that] It strikes me that nobody is really in favour of the changes. [Vn.wh] It suddenly struck me how we could improve the situation. **5** ~ sb as sth to give sb a particular impression: [Vnadv] How does the idea strike you? [Vn-adj] The plan strikes me as ridiculous. [Vnn] She strikes me as a very efficient person. **6** (esp passive) to put sb suddenly into a specified state: [Vn-adj] be struck blind/dumb. **7** (of workers) to refuse to work as a protest: [V] Striking workers picketed the factory. [Vpr] The union has voted to strike for a pay increase of 10%. **8** to produce or make a match produce a flame when rubbed firmly against a rough surface: [Vn, Vnpr] strike a match (on a wall) [V] These matches are damp and won't strike. **9(a)** (of a clock) to indicate the time by sounding a bell, etc: [V, Vn] The clock has just struck (three). [Vn] The clock only strikes the hours. **(b)** (of time) to be indicated in this way: [V] Four o'clock had just struck on the church clock. **10** to produce a musical note, sound, etc by pressing a key or hitting sth: [Vn, Vnpr] strike a chord (on the piano). **11** to discover gold, minerals, oil, etc by digging or drilling (DRILL¹ v): [Vn] strike a rich vein of ore. **12** to make a coin, MEDAL, etc by stamping metal: [Vn] The Royal Mint will strike a commemorative gold coin. **IDM** be ˈstruck by/on/with sb/sth (infml) to be favourably impressed by sb/sth; to like sb/sth very much: I was really struck by the house and bought it immediately. ○ He's very much struck on his new girlfriend. **break/strike camp** ⇨ CAMP¹. **drive/strike a hard bargain** ⇨ HARD¹. **hit/strike home** ⇨ HOME³. **hit/strike the right/wrong note** ⇨ NOTE¹. **lightning never strikes twice** ⇨ LIGHTNING¹. **strike an ˈattitude / a ˈpose 1** to hold the body in a certain way or use gestures to create a particular impression: strike a pose for a photo-

graph. **2** to express oneself or behave in a way that is intended to communicate a particular attitude or feeling: He struck an attitude of defiance with a typically hard-hitting speech. **strike a ˈbalance (between A and B)** to find a sensible middle point between two demands, extremes, etc; to find a compromise: It was difficult to strike the right balance between justice and expediency. **strike a blow for/ against sth** to do sth on behalf of or in support of a belief, cause, principle, etc: By their action, they struck a blow for democracy. **strike/touch a chord** ⇨ CHORD. **strike fear, etc into sb / sb's heart** to cause sb to feel fear, etc: The news of the epidemic struck terror into the population. **strike ˈgold/ˈoil** to discover sth that is to one's advantage: She hasn't always been lucky with her boyfriends but she seems to have struck gold this time. **strike (it) ˈlucky** (infml) to have good luck in a particular matter: We certainly struck (it) lucky with the weather. **strike it ˈrich** (infml) to acquire a lot of money, esp suddenly or unexpectedly. **strike/sound a note** ⇨ NOTE¹. **strike while the iron is ˈhot** (saying) to make use of an opportunity immediately; to act while conditions are favourable. **within ˈstriking distance (of sth)** near enough to be reached or attacked easily: The hotel is within striking distance of the old town.

PHRV ˌstrike ˈback (at/against sb) to try to harm sb in return for an attack or injury one has received; to RETALIATE: He struck back at his critics with a passionate speech defending his policies.

ˌstrike sb ˈdown (esp passive) (of a disease, etc) to make sb unable to lead an active life; to make sb seriously ill or kill sb: be struck down by an assassin's bullet ○ He was struck down by cancer at the age of thirty.

ˌstrike sth ˈoff to remove sth with a sharp blow; to cut sth off: He struck off the rotten branches with an axe. ˌstrike sb/sth ˈoff (sth) to remove sb/sb's name from sth, esp from membership of a professional group: Strike her name off the list. ○ The doctor was struck off for incompetence.

ˈstrike on sth to get or find sth suddenly or unexpectedly: strike on a brilliant new idea ○ We struck on a wonderful little restaurant in one of the backstreets.

ˌstrike ˈout to start being independent; to start doing what one wants to do in life: strike out on one's own ○ She decided to strike out and start a new career.

ˌstrike ˈout (at sb/sth) **1** to aim a sudden violent blow or blows at sb/sth: He lost his temper and struck out wildly. **2** to attack sb/sth with words: In a recent article she strikes out at her critics. ˌstrike sth ˈout/ˈthrough to remove sth by drawing a line through it; to cross sth out (CROSS²): The editor struck out the whole paragraph. ˌstrike ˈout (for/ towards) sth to move in a vigorous and determined way (towards sth): strike out on foot for the distant hills ○ He struck out (ie started swimming) towards the shore.

ˌstrike ˈup (sth) (of a band, an ORCHESTRA, etc) to begin to play a piece of music: The band struck up (a waltz). ˌstrike ˈup sth (with sb) to begin a friendship, a relationship, etc, esp casually: He would often strike up conversations with complete strangers.

strikebound /ˈstraɪkbaʊnd/ adj unable to function because of a strike: The docks were strikebound for a week.

strikebreaker /ˈstraɪkbreɪkə(r)/ n a person who continues to work while other employees of the same organization are on strike¹(1), or who is employed in place of striking employees. See also BLACKLEG. ▶ **ˈstrike-breaking** n [U].

striker /ˈstraɪkə(r)/ n **1** a worker who is on strike¹(1). **2** (in football) a player whose main role is to attack and try to score goals. See also FORWARD⁴.

striking /ˈstraɪkɪŋ/ *adj* (**a**) attracting attention or interest because of being eg colourful, unusual or extreme: *a striking feature/example* ○ *striking colours/images* ○ *There is a **striking contrast** between her two novels.* (**b**) attracting attention because of being beautiful, HANDSOME, etc; attractive: *his striking good looks* ○ *a very striking young woman.* ▸ **strikingly** *adv*: *a strikingly handsome man* ○ *The two buildings are strikingly similar/different.*

string¹ /strɪŋ/ *n* **1**(**a**) [U] thin cord made of twisted threads, used for tying things together: *a ball/piece of string* ○ *tie up a parcel with string.* (**b**) [C] a length of this or similar material used eg to fasten or pull sth or to keep sth in place: *You move the puppet by pulling the strings.* ○ *The key is hanging on a string by the door.* See also DRAW-STRING, PURSE-STRINGS. **2** [C] (**a**) a tightly stretched piece of CATGUT, wire or nylon, eg on a VIOLIN, HARP or GUITAR, which produces a musical note when a bow is drawn across it or it is played with the fingers. ⇨ picture at MUSICAL INSTRUMENT. See also SECOND STRING. (**b**) (in tennis, etc) any of the long thin pieces of material woven together to form the part of a RACKET¹(1) used for hitting a ball, etc: *break a string.* **3 the strings** [pl] the stringed instruments (STRING²) in an ORCHESTRA: *The strings include violins, violas, cellos and double-basses.* ○ *The opening theme is taken up by the strings.* ⇨ picture at MUSICAL INSTRUMENT. **4** [C] (**a**) a set or series of things put together on a thread or cord: *a string of beads* ○ *a string of onions* ○ (*fig*) *The molecules join together to form long strings.* (**b**) a series of things or people coming closely one after the other: *a string of small lakes* ○ *a string of insults/lies/coincidences* ○ *a whole string of visitors.* **5** [C] (*computing*) a sequence of characters (CHARACTER 6). **IDM** **have two strings / a second, etc string to one's bow** ⇨ BOW¹. **one's mother's, wife's, etc apron-strings** ⇨ APRON. (**with**) **no ˈstrings attached / without ˈstrings** (*infml*) with no special conditions or restrictions: *an offer of £5 million in aid with no strings attached.* **pull strings** ⇨ PULL¹. **pull the strings** ⇨ PULL¹.
▸ **string** *adj* [attrib] **1** relating to or consisting of stringed instruments (STRING²): *a string quartet* ○ *a string band/orchestra.* **2** made with string¹(1) or sth like string: *a string bag/vest.*
stringy *adj* **1** long and thin, like string: *lank stringy hair.* **2** (esp of meat or beans) containing tough FIBRE(1) and so difficult or unpleasant to eat.
■ **ˌstring ˈbean** *n* = RUNNER BEAN.

string² /strɪŋ/ *v* (*pt, pp* **strung** /strʌŋ/) **1**(**a**) ~ sth (**up**) to hang or tie sth in place with a piece of string, rope, etc: [Vnpr] *Lanterns were strung in the trees around the pool.* [Vnp] *Flags had been strung up across the street.* (**b**) to hang or wind sth long and thin in a particular place: [Vnpr] *a long scarf strung around his neck/over the banister.* **2** ~ sth (**together**) to put a series of small objects, eg beads (BEAD 1), on a string: [Vnp] (*fig*) *carbon atoms strung together to form giant molecules* [Vnpr] (*fig*) *a line of cottages strung along the hillside* [also Vn]. **3** to put a string or strings on a bow¹(1), RACKET¹(1) or musical instrument, eg a VIOLIN: [Vnadv] *a loosely/tightly strung squash racket* [also Vn]. See also HIGHLY-STRUNG. **PHRV** **ˌstring sb aˈlong** to mislead sb deliberately, esp about one's own intentions or beliefs: *She has no intention of marrying him — she's just stringing him along.* **ˌstring aˈlong (with sb)** to stay with or accompany sb casually or as long as it is convenient: *She decided to string along with the others as she had nothing else to do.* **ˌstring (sth) ˈout 1** (esp passive) to spread things out at intervals in a line: *The Irish horse was in the lead, with the rest of the field strung out behind.* **2** to make sth last longer than expected or necessary: *stringing out the*

negotiations for a further six months. **ˌstring sth toˈgether** to combine words or phrases to form sentences: *I can just manage to string a few words of French together.* ○ *She managed to string together a few words of appreciation.* **ˌstring sb ˈup** (*infml*) to kill sb by hanging them, esp not legally: *If the crowd catch him, they'll string him up on the nearest tree.*
■ **ˌstringed ˈinstrument** *n* a musical instrument with strings that are played with the fingers or with a bow¹(2).

stringent /ˈstrɪndʒənt/ *adj* (*fml*) **1** (of a law, rule, etc) that must be obeyed; strict or severe: *stringent controls/standards/regulations.* **2** (of financial conditions) difficult because there is not enough money: *a stringent economic climate.* ▸ **stringency** /-nsi/ *n* [U, C]: *in these days of financial stringency* ○ *short-term economic stringencies.* **stringently** *adv*: *The regulations must be stringently applied/observed.*

stringer /ˈstrɪŋə(r)/ *n* a journalist who is not on the regular staff of a newspaper, but who often supplies stories for it.

strip¹ /strɪp/ *v* (**-pp-**) **1**(**a**) ~ sth (**from/off sth/sb**); ~ **sth/sb** (**of sth**); ~ **sth** (**away**) to remove a layer or layers of coverings, clothes, etc from sth/sb, esp so that it/they are completely bare: [Vn] *stripped wooden floors* [Vnpr] *strip paint off/from an old pine chest* ○ *The hillsides have been stripped of vegetation.* ○ *lead stripped from church roofs* [Vnp] *strip one's shirt off* [Vn, Vn-adj] *The bandits stripped him (naked) and beat him.* [Vnp] (*fig*) *strip away all pretence and speak openly.* (**b**) to remove all the things from a place and leave it empty: [Vn-adj] *Thieves stripped the house bare.* **2** ~ (**down**) (**to sth**); ~ (**off**) to take off all or most of one's clothes: [Vpr] *strip to the waist* (ie remove clothes from the upper part of one's body) [Vp] *strip down to* (ie remove all one's clothes except) *one's underwear* ○ *They stripped off and ran into the water.* [also V]. **3** ~ **sb of sth** to take away property or honours from sb: *He was stripped of all his possessions.* ○ *The general was stripped of his rank.* See also ASSET-STRIPPING. **PHRV** **ˌstrip sth ˈdown** to remove all the parts that can be detached from a machine, esp an engine, in order to examine, clean or repair it.
▸ **strip** *n* (usu *sing*) an act of removing one's clothes, esp in front of an audience: *do a strip.*
stripper *n* **1** [C] a performer who removes her or his clothes in front of an audience as a form of entertainment. **2** [C, U] (esp in compounds) a device or substance used for removing paint, etc: *ˈpaint-stripper.*
■ **ˈstrip club** (also *esp US* **ˈstrip joint**) *n* a club in which performers remove their clothes in front of an audience.

strip² /strɪp/ *n* **1** a long narrow piece of sth or area of land: *a strip of paper/land* ○ *Cut the meat into strips.* ○ *the Gaza Strip.* See also AIRSTRIP, LANDING-STRIP. **2** (*Brit*) (usu *sing*) clothes of a particular colour or colours worn by the members of a football team: *England are playing in the blue and white strip.* **3** (*US*) a street that has many shops, restaurants, etc: *He owns a liquor store out on the strip.* **IDM** **tear sb off a strip / tear a strip off sb** ⇨ TEAR².
■ **ˌstrip carˈtoon** (also **cartoon**) *n* (*Brit*) = COMIC STRIP.
ˈstrip light *n* a light that consists of a long glass tube, used esp in offices.
ˈstrip lighting *n* [U] a method of lighting using long glass tubes filled with glowing gas.

stripe /straɪp/ *n* **1** a long narrow band, usu of the same width throughout its length, on a surface that is different from it in colour or texture: *the tiger's stripes* ○ *a white tablecloth with red stripes* ○ *The plates have a blue stripe round the edge.* See also PINSTRIPE. **2** a mark, often in the shape of a V, that is worn on the uniform of eg a soldier or police officer to indicate rank: *How many stripes are there on a sergeant's sleeve?* ○ *She was awarded another stripe* (ie promoted to a higher rank).

▶ **striped** /straɪpt/ *adj* marked with or having stripes (STRIPE 1): *a striped shirt/suit/tie.* ⇨ picture at PATTERN.

stripy (also **stripey**) /'straɪpi/ *adj* (*infml*) = STRIPED: *a stripy blouse.*

stripling /'strɪplɪŋ/ *n* (*fml or joc*) a male person who is older than a boy but not yet a man; a youth: *He's a mere stripling.*

striptease /'strɪptiːz/ *n* [C,U] a form of entertainment, eg in a theatre, bar or club, in which a performer removes her or his clothes in a sexually exciting way in front of an audience.

strive /straɪv/ *v* (*pt* **strove** /strəʊv/ or **strived**; *pp* **striven** /'strɪvn/) (*fml*) **1** ~ (**for/after sth**) to try very hard or for a long time to obtain or achieve sth: [Vpr] *strive for success* [V.*to* inf] *strive to improve one's performance* [also V]. **2** ~ (**against sb/sth**) to fight hard against sb/sth: *strive against oppression.*

▶ **striving** *n* [U, sing]: *the/a relentless striving after perfection.*

strobe light /'strəʊb laɪt/ (also **strobe**) *n* a bright light that flashes rapidly on and off, eg in a DISCO(1).

strode *pt* of STRIDE.

stroke /strəʊk/ *n* **1** (*sport*) an act of striking a ball, eg with a bat or RACKET[1](1): *play a forehand stroke* ○ *What a beautiful stroke!* ○ *She won by two strokes* (ie in golf, took two fewer strokes than her opponent). **2** a single movement of the arm when hitting sth: *His punishment was six strokes of the cane.* **3** a mark made by moving a pen, brush, etc once across a surface: *paint with bold/thick (brush-)strokes* ○ *be removed from the register with a stroke of the pen.* **4** each of the sounds made by a bell or by a clock striking the hours: *At the first stroke, it will be exactly 9 o'clock.* ○ **on the stroke of** *three* (ie at 3.00 exactly). **5** (usu *sing*) an act of passing one's hand gently over a surface, usu several times: *give the cat/one's beard a stroke.* **6(a)** any of a series of repeated movements, esp in swimming or rowing: *long, powerful strokes* ○ *a fast/slow stroke* (ie in rowing). **(b)** (esp in compounds) a style of stroke in swimming: *The butterfly is the only stroke I can't do.* See also BACKSTROKE, BREAST-STROKE. **7** ~ (**of sth**) a single successful or effective action or event: *Your idea was a stroke of genius!* ○ *It was a stroke of luck that I found you here.* ○ *We'll have to get rid of him — he never does a stroke (of work).* ○ *It was a bold stroke to reveal the identity of the murderer on the first page.* See also MASTER-STROKE. **8** (*medical*) a sudden serious illness in the brain that can cause loss of the power to move or to speak clearly: *have/ suffer a stroke* ○ *The stroke left him partly paralysed.* Compare APOPLEXY. **IDM** **at a/one 'stroke** with a single immediate action: *They threatened to cancel the whole project at a stroke.* **put sb off their 'stroke** to cause sb to make a mistake or hesitate in what they are doing: *My speech went well until I was put off my stroke by an interruption.*

▶ **stroke** *v* **1** to pass the hand gently over a surface, usu several times: [Vn] *stroke a pet/one's beard/sb's hand.* **2** (*approv*) to strike a ball with a smooth controlled movement: [Vnpr] *She stroked the ball past her opponent.* [also Vnp].

stroll /strəʊl/ *v* to walk in a slow casual way: [Vpr, Vp] *strolling around (in) the park* [also V].

▶ **stroll** *n* a slow casual walk: *go for/have a stroll.*
stroller *n* **1** a person who is strolling: *Sunday-afternoon strollers in the park.* **2** (*US*) = PUSHCHAIR.

strong /strɒŋ/; *US* strɔːŋ/ *adj* (**-er** /-ŋgə(r)/; **-est** /-ŋgɪst/) **1(a)** (of people, animals or their bodies) physically powerful or healthy: *strong muscles/ arms/teeth* ○ *He's strong enough to lift a piano on his own.* ○ *He's as strong as an ox/a horse* (ie very

strong). **(b)** done with great physical power: *a strong push/blow/kick* ○ *She feels quite strong again now after her illness.* ○ *The old man's heart isn't strong enough to withstand a long journey.* ○ (*fig*) *have strong nerves* (ie be not easily frightened or worried). **(c)** (of a voice) loud and powerful: *an actor with a strong voice.* **2** not easily broken or damaged; well made; solid: *a strong stick/rope/structure* ○ *The chair wasn't strong enough to take his weight.* ○ *We need strong defences against the enemy.* **3** (of a physical or natural force) great; powerful; intense: *a strong wind/current* ○ *a strong magnet* ○ *Keep the plants away from strong sunlight.* **4** great in intensity or level: *a strong smell of gas* ○ *a strong feeling of nausea* ○ *She spoke with a strong Australian accent.* ○ *a strong influence* ○ *He is under strong pressure to resign.* ○ *a strong chance of winning* ○ *The school has a strong tradition of academic excellence.* Compare SLIGHT[1]. **5(a)** (of feelings, thoughts or opinions) felt, held or expressed with intensity: *a strong will/ belief/commitment/suspicion/interest* ○ *I had a strong impression that someone was following me.* ○ *There is strong support for/opposition to the government's policy.* ○ *have strong feelings* (ie opinions) *about sth.* **(b)** [attrib] (of a person) having such feelings or thoughts: *a strong believer/supporter/ opponent.* **6** great in number: *a strong police presence at the demonstration* ○ *A strong turnout is expected at the election.* **7** (used after numbers) (esp of a group) having the specified number of people in it: *a 5 000-strong army* ○ *The demonstrators were 100 000 strong.* **8** having a lot of power or influence: *a strong country/leader/army/union* ○ *have a strong personality* ○ *The company is in a strong position to increase its sales.* **9** (of a person) effective; skilful; able: *a strong player/team* ○ *a strong candidate for the job* (ie one who is likely to get it) ○ *a film with a strong cast* ○ *a student who is strong in physics but weak in English.* **10** based on proper reasoning or facts; convincing: *a strong argument/claim* ○ *strong evidence* ○ *You have a strong case for reinstatement.* **11** (of a relationship) close; firmly established; difficult to destroy: *a strong marriage* ○ *The party has strong links with the trade union movement.* **12** (*finance*) (of prices, currencies, etc) having a high or increasing value in relation to others: *strong share prices* ○ *a strong economy* ○ *The pound is getting stronger/weaker against the yen.* **13(a)** having a lot of flavour, esp of a distinctive kind: *strong mints/ radishes/cigarettes* ○ *This cheese tastes/smells rather strong.* **(b)** (esp of drinks) containing a lot of a substance; highly concentrated: *strong tea/coffee* ○ *a strong antiseptic solution.* **(c)** (of a drink) containing much alcohol: *Whisky is stronger than beer.* **14** having a powerful effect on the body: *a strong medicine/poison.* **15** (of a colour) bright or noticeable: *Strong colours suit you.* **16** forceful and extreme, almost to the point of being unacceptable: (*infml esp Brit*) *strong words/language* (ie swearing) ○ *It was a bit strong of him to call me a liar in front of the whole department.* **17** [usu attrib] **(a)** (*grammar*) (of a verb) forming the past tense by changing a vowel, eg *sing*, *sang*, not by adding *-d*, *-ed* or *-t*. **(b)** (*phonetics*) (of the pronunciation of some words) used when the word is stressed. For instance, the strong form of 'and' is /ænd/, rather than /ənd/, /ən/ or /n/, which are weak forms. Compare WEAK. **IDM** **be 'strong on sth 1** to be good at sth or doing sth: *I'm not very strong on dates* (ie I cannot easily remember the dates of important events). **2** to have a lot of ideas about sth; to concentrate on sth: *The report is strong on criticism, but short on practical suggestions.* ○ *The party is very strong on law and order.* **one's best/strongest card** ⇨ CARD[1]. **going 'strong** (*infml*) continuing an activity vigorously; continuing to be healthy: *The Kenyan runner is still going strong on the last lap.* ○ *She's 91 years old* and still going strong. ▶ **strongly** adv: a strongly-built boat ○ a light shining strongly ○ I **feel strongly that** (ie I firmly believe that) criminals should be punished. ○ He was strongly opposed to the idea. ○ a strongly-worded protest ○ The report is strongly critical of the government.

■ **'strong-arm** adj [attrib] involving threats, force or violence: use strong-arm methods/tactics against one's political opponents.

strong-'minded adj having a strong will or strong opinions; determined.

strongbox /'strɒŋbɒks/ n a strongly made, usu metal, box for keeping valuable things in.

stronghold /'strɒŋhəʊld/ n **1** a place where there is much support for a cause or a political party: a stronghold of republicanism/a republican stronghold. **2** a strongly built castle, fort, etc: guerrilla strongholds in the mountains.

strongman /'strɒŋmæn/ n (pl **-men** /-men/) a leader who rules by threats, force or violence: The country has been run by a succession of military strongmen.

strongroom /'strɒŋruːm, -rʊm/ n a room, eg in a bank, with thick walls and a strong solid door, where valuable items are kept.

strontium /'strɒntiəm; US -nʃiəm/ n [U] (symb **Sr**) a chemical element. Strontium is a soft silver-white metal. ⇨ App 7.

stroppy /'strɒpi/ adj (Brit sl) (of a person) bad-tempered; awkward to deal with: Don't **get stroppy** with me — it's not my fault!

strove pt of STRIVE.

struck pt, pp of STRIKE².

structuralism /'strʌktʃərəlɪzəm/ n [U] a method of analysing a subject, eg social sciences, PSYCHOLOGY (1), language or literature, which concentrates on the structure of a system and the relations between its elements, rather than on the individual elements themselves. ▶ **structuralist** /-rəlɪst/ n, adj [esp attrib]: a structuralist approach/analysis. Compare DECONSTRUCT.

structure /'strʌktʃə(r)/ n **1** [U] **(a)** the way in which sth is organized, built or put together: the structure of the human body ○ rules of sentence structure ○ the structure of a play ○ the molecular structure of DNA. **(b)** the state of being well planned or organized: Your essay lacks structure. **2** [C] a particular system, pattern, procedure or institution: a salary/career/management structure ○ the structures of a democratic society ○ economic/class structures ○ learn the basic structures of a language. **3** [C] a thing made of several parts put together in a particular way: The model is an odd-looking structure of balls and rods. ○ a single-storey structure ○ The Parthenon is a magnificent structure. ▶ **structure** v to give a structure to sth; to plan or organize sth: [Vn] look at the way society is structured ○ an intelligently structured essay [Vnpr] He structures his whole life around his weekly visits to his parents.

structural /'strʌktʃərəl/ adj [usu attrib] of or relating to a structure or structures: structural alterations to a building (eg removing internal walls to make rooms bigger) ○ a structural analysis. **structurally** /-rəli/ adv: The building is structurally sound.

strudel /'struːdl/ n [C, U] a cake made of fruit rolled up in thin pastry and baked: a slice of apple strudel.

struggle /'strʌɡl/ v **1** ~ (for sth); ~ (to do sth) to try very hard to do or achieve sth that is difficult: [Vpr] struggle for political recognition ○ The firm is struggling for survival. [V.to inf] We struggled to put up the tent in the howling gale. [V] The team has been struggling (ie not playing well) all season. **2** to make one's way with difficulty in the specified direction: [Vp] The chick finally broke through the shell

and struggled out. [Vpr] He struggled up the hill with his heavy shopping-bags. **3** ~ (against/with sth/sb) to try to overcome a problem or prevent sth undesirable from happening or continuing: [Vpr] struggle against corruption within the party ○ struggle with one's conscience [also V]. **4** ~ (with sb) (for sth) to compete or argue with sb, esp in order to obtain sth: [Vpr] rival leaders struggling for power ○ union leaders struggling with the management over levels of redundancy payments. **5(a)** ~ (against/with sb/sth) to move one's body vigorously, eg trying to get free: [V-adj] He finally managed to struggle free. [V, Vpr] He struggled (against his captors) but couldn't escape. [V.to inf] She struggled to get away from her attacker. [also V]. **(b)** ~ (with sb) to have a physical fight with sb: [Vpr] The shopkeeper struggled with the thief. [also V]. **PHR V** ,**struggle a'long/'on** to manage to continue in spite of great difficulties: We're struggling along on a tiny income.

▶ **struggle** n **1** a conflict or competition: the struggle for the championship ○ the struggle against tyranny ○ the 'class struggle ○ We will not surrender without a struggle. **2** a physical fight: There was a struggle, and the policeman was stabbed in the arm. **3** (usu sing) a difficult task requiring great effort: It was a real struggle to finish on time.

strum /strʌm/ v (**-mm-**) ~ (**on**) sth to play a GUITAR or similar instrument, esp in a simple way, moving one's hand up and down across the strings: [Vn, Vpr] strumming (on) my guitar [Vn] strum a tune [also V, Vp].

strumpet /'strʌmpɪt/ n (arch or joc derog) a female prostitute.

strung pt, pp of STRING².

■ **strung up** /,strʌŋ 'ʌp/ adj nervous, tense or excited: She gets very strung up before an exam.

strut¹ /strʌt/ n a rod or bar used to strengthen or support a structure: fix some wooden struts behind the fence to stop it blowing down.

strut² /strʌt/ v (**-tt-**) (often derog) to walk in an upright proud way: [Vp, Vpr] She strutted past us, ignoring our greeting. [V] strutting peacocks. **IDM** ,**strut one's 'stuff** (sl) to perform or dance, esp in a lively exciting way.

▶ **strut** n (usu sing) a proud upright way of walking.

strychnine /'strɪkniːn/ n [U] a poisonous substance used in very small amounts as a medicine.

stub /stʌb/ n **1** a short piece remaining after a pencil, cigarette, etc has been used: The crayon had been worn down to a stub. ○ (fig) The dog only has a stub of a tail (ie a very short one). **2** the small part of a cheque or ticket that remains, to be kept as a record, after the main part has been detached and given to sb.

▶ **stub** v (**-bb-**) ~ sth (against/on sth) to strike sth, esp one's toe, accidentally against sth hard, often causing pain: [Vn, Vnpr] I've stubbed my toe (on a rock). See also STUBBY. **PHR V** ,**stub sth 'out** to stop a cigarette, etc burning by pressing it against sth hard.

stubble /'stʌbl/ n [U] **1** the lower part of the stems of crops left in the ground after the top part has been cut and collected: a ban on burning stubble. **2** the short stiff hairs that grow on a man's face when he has not shaved recently: three days' stubble on his chin. See also DESIGNER STUBBLE.

▶ **stubbly** /'stʌbli/ adj like or showing stubble: a stubbly beard/chin.

stubborn /'stʌbən/ adj **1** (often derog) **(a)** determined not to change one's attitude or position; having a strong will: be too stubborn to apologize ○ She can be as stubborn as a mule (ie very stubborn). **(b)** not easily overcome: show stubborn resistance to change ○ a stubborn refusal to be involved. **2** difficult to move, change, remove or cure:

a stubborn cough that has lasted for weeks ○ *stubborn stains* ○ *You'll have to push hard — that door is a little stubborn.* ▶ **stubbornly** *adv*: *He stubbornly refused to pay.* **stubbornness** *n* [U].

stubby /'stʌbi/ *adj* (**-ier, -iest**) short and thick: *stubby fingers* ○ *a stubby tail.*

stucco /'stʌkəʊ/ *n* [U] PLASTER(1) or cement used for covering or decorating walls or ceilings. ▶ **stuccoed** *adj.*

stuck¹ *pt, pp* of STICK².

stuck² /stʌk/ *adj* [pred] **1** not able to move or be moved: *I can't open the door — it's stuck.* ○ *The boat is stuck in the mud.* ○ *We were stuck in a traffic jam for an hour.* ○ (*fig infml*) *I don't want to be stuck in a museum on a beautiful day like this!* **2** ~ (**on sth**) unable to find an answer or solution to sth: *I'm stuck on question 2.* **3** [pred] ~ **with sth/sb** (*infml*) having sth/sb one does not want: *I was stuck with an old car that I couldn't sell.* ○ *I'm stuck with my sister for the whole day.* ○ *Why am I always stuck with the ironing?* **4** ~ **on sb** (*dated infml*) very fond of sb; in love with sb: *He's really stuck on the new girl in his class.* **IDM** **get into / be stuck in a groove** ⇨ GROOVE. **get stuck 'in(to sth)** (*Brit infml*) to start doing sth enthusiastically: *We got stuck into the job immediately.*

stuck-up /ˌstʌk 'ʌp/ *adj* (*infml derog*) having a proud superior attitude towards others.

stud¹ /stʌd/ *n* **1(a)** a piece of jewellery attached to a small rod which is pushed through a hole in the ear, nose, etc: *diamond studs in her ears.* (**b**) a small object like a button with two heads, used esp formerly to fasten a collar or the front of a shirt. See also PRESS-STUD. **2(a)** a round raised piece of metal, usu one of many on the surface of sth, eg a belt or a shield, esp as an ornament: *a leather belt with metal studs.* (**b**) a nail or similar object on the sole of a shoe or boot, to allow it to grip the ground better: *screw-in studs for football boots.* ▶ **stud** *v* (**-dd-**) ~ **sth** (**with sth**) (usu passive) to decorate a surface with many studs, precious stones or similar objects: [Vn] *a studded leather belt* [Vnpr] *a crown studded with jewels* ○ (*rhet*) *a sea studded with small islands* ○ (*fig*) *He studded his speech with brilliant witticisms.* See also STAR-STUDDED.

stud² /stʌd/ *n* **1** [C, U] a place where animals, esp horses, are kept for breeding: *a stud-farm* ○ *a stud mare/dog* ○ *horses at stud* (ie available for breeding). **2** [C] (*sl*) a young man, who is thought to be very active sexually or who is regarded as a good sexual partner.

student /'stjuːdnt; US 'stuː-/ *n* **1(a)** a person, usu over the age of 16, who is studying at a university or college: *a 'history/'medical/B'A student* ○ *a student nurse/teacher* ○ *student grants/loans* (ie ones provided to students) ○ *the city's student population.* (**b**) (*esp US*) a boy or girl at school. **2** ~ **of sth** (*fml*) a person who observes or has a particular interest in sth: *a keen student of current affairs/human nature.* ▶ **studentship** *n* (*Brit*) an opportunity to do research or to study for a higher degree at a university, offered to a GRADUATE¹(1) usu with a GRANT or other small payment.

studied /'stʌdid/ *adj* carefully considered; deliberate: *reply with studied indifference* ○ *the studied elegance of his movements.*

studio /'stjuːdiəʊ; US 'stuː-/ *n* (*pl* **-os**) **1** a room from which radio or television programmes are regularly broadcast or in which they are recorded: *The Minister was interviewed at/in the BBC's Oxford studio.* ○ *a studio audience* (ie one in a studio, that can be seen or heard as a programme is broadcast). **2(a)** a place where cinema films are made or produced: *Was it filmed in a studio or on location?* Compare LOCATION 2. (**b**) (often *pl*) a cinema company: *She works for a major Hollywood studio.* ○ *a*

studio executive. **3** a room with equipment where musical or sound recordings are made. **4(a)** a room where an artist works: *a sculptor's/photographer's studio.* (**b**) a place where performers practise: *a dance studio.*
■ **'studio flat** (*Brit*) (also *esp US* **'studio apartment**) *n* a small flat, usu having a main room for living and sleeping in, with a small kitchen and a BATHROOM(1).

studious /'stjuːdiəs; US 'stuː-/ *adj* **1** spending a lot of time studying: *a studious child.* **2** [esp attrib] (*fml*) very careful; deliberate: *with studious politeness.* ▶ **studiously** *adv*: *He studiously ignored/ avoided us.*

study¹ /'stʌdi/ *n* **1(a)** [U] the activity of learning or gaining knowledge, esp from books: *devote all one's spare time to study* ○ *a room set aside for private study.* (**b**) **studies** [pl] such activity as pursued by a particular person, eg at a college or university: *return to one's studies after an illness.* (**c**) [U] the activity of gaining knowledge of a particular subject: *Entomology is the study of insects.* **2 studies** [pl] (used in the titles of certain academic subjects): *'business/'media/A'merican studies.* **3** [U] consideration; examination: *The proposals deserve careful study.* **4** [C] a detailed consideration or investigation of a subject: *make a study of the country's export trade* ○ *publish a study of Locke's philosophy* ○ *Scientific studies have shown that smoking causes cancer.* See also CASE-STUDY. **5** [C] a room, esp in sb's home, used for reading and writing. **6** [C] (**a**) a drawing or painting of a subject, esp one done for practice or before doing a larger picture: *a study of Chartres cathedral* ○ *a nude study.* (**b**) (*music*) a composition designed to give a player practice in technical skills. **7** [sing] ~ (**in sth**) a thing worth observing or learning from: *His face was a study in concentration.* ○ *Her efforts were a study in how not to hang wallpaper.* **IDM** **in a brown study** ⇨ BROWN.

study² /'stʌdi/ *v* (*pt, pp* **studied**) **1(a)** to give one's time and attention to learning about a subject, esp at a college or university: [Vpr] *study at Oxford University* [Vn, Vpr] *studying (for a degree in) medicine* [Vpr] *Like many American composers, he studied with/under Nadia Boulanger.* [V.to inf] *studying to be a doctor* [also V.wh]. (**b**) to engage in the activity of learning, esp by serious reading: [V] *He's in his bedroom, studying.* **2** to examine or consider sth very carefully: [Vn] *study the map/menu/timetable* ○ *Your proposal will be carefully studied before a decision is made.* [Vnpr] *Scientists are studying photographs of the planet for signs of life.*

stuff¹ /stʌf/ *n* **1** [U] (*infml*) (used instead of a more specific word when the name or type of sth is not known or when it does not matter) (**a**) a substance or material: *What's that brown stuff on your jacket?* ○ *The cushions are full of this rubbery stuff.* See also FOODSTUFF. (**b**) things, items, activities, etc: *Leave your stuff in the hall.* ○ *It's not the kind of stuff I usually read.* ○ *I like windsurfing, canoeing and stuff like that.* ○ *There's been some really good stuff on TV lately.* ○ *This is kids' stuff* (ie simple, suitable for children) *— let's try something more difficult.* **2** [U] (*fml*) the most important feature or quality of sth: *Real life is the stuff of all good novels.* ○ *We must find out what (kind of) stuff he is made of* (ie what sort of man he is, what his character is). See also HOT STUFF. **IDM** **be made of sterner stuff** ⇨ STERN¹. **a bit of crumpet/fluff/skirt/stuff** ⇨ BIT¹. **do one's 'stuff** (*infml*) to show what one is capable of; to perform: *It's your turn to sing now, so do your stuff.* **know one's stuff** ⇨ KNOW. **strut one's stuff** ⇨ STRUT². **stuff and 'nonsense** *interj* (*dated infml*) (used to dismiss sth that has been said as wrong or stupid): *Stuff and nonsense! You don't know what*

stuff

you're talking about. ,that's the 'stuff! (*infml approv*) that is good or what is needed.

stuff² /stʌf/ v **1(a)** ~ A (up) (with B) to fill sth tightly with sth: [Vn] *stuff envelopes* (ie fill a lot of envelopes with the same printed letter, etc) [Vn, Vnpr] *stuff a pillow (with feathers)* [Vnp] *My nose is stuffed up* (ie blocked, eg as the result of a cold). [Vn-adj] *The case was stuffed full of old clothes.* [Vnpr] (*fig*) *Don't stuff his head with silly ideas.* (**b**) ~ B into A / in to push sth tightly into sth: [Vnpr] *stuff feathers into a pillow* [Vnp] *She stuffed her clothes in and then tried to close the lid.* **2** to push sth quickly and carelessly in the specified place or direction: [Vnpr] *She stuffed the book in(to) her pocket.* [Vnp, Vnpr] *He stuffed the letter through the (door) and hurried away.* **3** ~ oneself/sb (with sth) (*infml*) to fill oneself/sb with food; to eat or make sb eat a lot or too much: [Vn, Vnpr] *She sat stuffing herself (with popcorn) all through the film.* **4** ~ sth (with sth) to put a thick PASTE¹ or small pieces of food into eg a chicken or other food before cooking it, to add more flavour: [Vn] *stuffed green peppers* (eg cooked with rice inside) [Vnpr] *turkey stuffed with sage and onion/chestnuts.* **5** (esp passive) to fill the empty dead body of an animal with enough material to restore it to its original shape, eg for exhibition in a museum: [Vn] *a stuffed tiger/owl.* **6** (*sl*) (used to express rejection of sth/sb) to do as one likes with sth/sb: [Vn] *You can stuff the job, I don't want it!* **IDM** get 'stuffed (*Brit derog sl*) (used to express contempt or rejection) to go away and stop annoying sb: *He wanted to borrow some money but I told him to get stuffed.* ,stuff one's 'face (*sl usu derog*) to eat a lot or too much: *He sat there, stuffing his face (with chocolates).*

▶ **stuffing** n [U] **1** (*US also* dressing) a mixture of food put inside a chicken, etc or meat or other food before it is cooked: *sage-and-onion stuffing.* **2** material used to fill cushions, soft furniture, toys, etc: *The stuffing is coming out of my pillow/mattress/doll.* **IDM** knock the stuffing out of sb ⇨ KNOCK².

■ ,stuffed 'shirt n (*infml derog*) a person whose behaviour or ideas are very formal or old-fashioned.

stuffy /'stʌfi/ adj (-ier, -iest) **1** not having much fresh air: *a stuffy room/atmosphere* ○ *Shall I open the window? It's a bit stuffy in here.* **2** (*infml derog*) formal, dull and rather old-fashioned: *a stuffy newspaper/club/tradition.* **3** (*infml*) (of the nose) blocked so that breathing is difficult. ▶ **stuffiness** n [U].

stultify /'stʌltɪfaɪ/ v (*pt, pp* -fied) (*fml*) to cause sb to feel bored or tired: [Vn] *the stultifying effect of work that never varies.*

stumble /'stʌmbl/ v **1** ~ (over sth) to fall or almost fall, esp as the result of accidentally hitting one's foot against sth: [V] *stumble and fall* [Vpr] *I stumbled over a tree root.* [also Vp, Vadv]. **2** ~ (over sth); ~ through sth to make a mistake or mistakes, eg when speaking or playing music: [Vpr] *She stumbled over the unfamiliar word but then continued.* ○ *The child stumbled through a piece by Chopin.* [V] *my first stumbling attempts at writing poetry.* **3** to move or walk in an unsteady way in the specified direction: [Vp] *stumbling around in the dark.* [Vpr] *A drunk stumbled past us.* ⇨ note at SHUFFLE. **PHR V** 'stumble across/on/upon sb/sth to find sth/sb unexpectedly or by chance: *Police investigating tax fraud stumbled across a drugs ring.* 'stumble into sth to become involved in a certain situation or place by accident: *I stumbled into acting, more by chance than anything else.*

▶ **stumble** n an act of stumbling.

■ 'stumbling-block n ~ (to sth) a problem or point that causes difficulty or prevents progress; an obstacle: *The failure to agree on manning levels is a major stumbling-block to settling the dispute.*

stump /stʌmp/ n **1** the bottom part of a tree left in the ground after the rest has fallen or been cut down. **2(a)** the end of sth or the part that is left after the main part has been cut or broken off, or has been worn down (WEAR¹): *the stump of a pencil/tooth.* (**b**) the remaining part of a limb that has been cut off. **3** (in cricket) any of the three upright wooden poles at which the ball is bowled: *the leg/middle/off stump.* ⇨ picture at CRICKET. **IDM** on the 'stump (*infml*) (esp of a politician before an election) going to different places and trying to raise support, esp by making speeches: *The Prime Minister is going out on the stump.* stir one's stumps ⇨ STIR.

▶ **stump** v **1** (*infml*) (esp passive) to be too difficult for sb: [Vn] *I'm stumped: I just don't know what to do.* ○ *Everybody was stumped by the problem.* **2** to walk in a stiff or noisy way: [Vp, Vpr] *He stumped out (of the room) in fury.* **3** [Vn] (*US*) to go around a region making political speeches, eg before an election. **4** [Vn] (of a wicket-keeper (WICKET) in cricket) to get a batsman out by touching the stumps with the ball while he is out of his CREASE(3). **PHR V** ,stump 'up (sth) (for sth) (*Brit infml*) to pay or provide a sum of money: *I'm always being asked to stump up (extra cash) for school outings.*

stumpy /'stʌmpi/ adj short and thick: *stumpy legs* ○ *a stumpy candle/tail.*

stun /stʌn/ v (-nn-) **1** to make a person or an animal unconscious by a blow, esp to the head: [Vn] *The fall stunned me for a moment.* **2** (esp passive) (**a**) to surprise or shock sb so much that they cannot think properly: [Vnpr] *be stunned into silence* [V] *I was stunned by the news of his death.* ○ *There was a stunned silence as she announced her resignation.* (**b**) to impress sb greatly: *stunned by her beauty/performance.*

▶ **stun** adj [attrib] (of a weapon) designed to stun people or animals: *a 'stun grenade.*

stunner n (*infml esp Brit*) a very attractive or impressive thing or person, esp a woman.

stunning adj (*infml*) (**a**) very attractive; beautiful: *You look stunning in that dress.* ○ *stunning scenery* ○ *a stunning achievement/performance/victory.* (**b**) very good or impressive. (**c**) surprising or shocking: *a stunning revelation.* **stunningly** adv: *stunningly attractive/beautiful.*

■ 'stun gun n a gun that stuns a person or an animal, eg by means of an electric shock, without causing any serious injury.

stung *pt, pp* of STING².

stunk *pp* of STINK.

stunt¹ /stʌnt/ n (**a**) (*sometimes derog*) an unusual act designed to attract attention: *a stunt to raise money for charity* ○ *It was just a publicity stunt.* ○ (*infml*) *Don't you ever pull a stunt like that again!* (**b**) a dangerous or difficult activity done as entertainment: *Her latest stunt is riding a motor cycle through a ring of flames.* ○ *a 'stunt pilot/rider/driver.*

■ 'stunt man n (*fem* 'stunt woman) a person who does dangerous stunts in place of an actor in a film, etc.

stunt² /stʌnt/ v to prevent sth/sb from growing or developing properly: [Vn] *stunted trees* ○ *the war stunted his artistic development.*

stupefy /'stju:pɪfaɪ; *US* 'stu:-/ v (*pt, pp* -fied) ~ sb (with sth) (esp passive) **1** to surprise or shock sb: [Vn] *her stupefying ignorance* ○ *I was stupefied by what I read.* **2** to make sb unable to think or feel properly; to make sb's senses less sharp: [Vnpr] *be stupefied with drink* [Vn] (*fig*) *the stupefying boredom of this repetitive work.*

▶ **stupefaction** /,stju:pɪ'fækʃn; *US* ,stu:-/ n [U] (*fml*) the state of being stupefied.

stupendous /stju:'pendəs; *US* stu:-/ adj (**a**) extremely great or large: *a stupendous mistake/*

explosion/appetite/amount. (**b**) extremely good or impressive: *a stupendous view from the balcony* ○ *The opera was quite stupendous!* ▶ **stupendously** *adv.*

stupid /'stjuːpɪd; *US* 'stuː-/ *adj* (**-er, -est**) **1** (*derog*) (**a**) slow to learn or understand things; not intelligent or clever: *The boy's not as stupid as you think.* ○ *Don't lie to me — I'm not stupid!* (**b**) showing lack of good judgement; foolish: *a stupid idea/mistake/accident* ○ *What a stupid thing to do!* ○ *You've locked us out, you stupid idiot!* **2** [attrib] (*infml*) (used to dismiss sth as unimportant or to show annoyance): *I don't want to hear your stupid secret anyway!* ○ *This stupid car won't start.*
▶ **stupidity** /stjuː'pɪdəti; *US* stuː-/ *n* **1** [U] the state of being stupid: *The accident was due to my own stupidity.* **2** [C usu *pl*] a stupid act or remark.
stupidly *adv*: *He grinned stupidly.* ○ *I stupidly left my car unlocked.*

stupor /'stjuːpə(r); *US* 'stuː-/ *n* [sing, U] the state of being nearly unconscious or not fully aware of what is happening, caused eg by shock, drugs or alcohol: *in a drunken stupor.*

sturdy /'stɜːdi/ *adj* (**-ier, -iest**) **1**(**a**) strong and firm: *a sturdy chair/suitcase/frame* ○ *sturdy footwear.* (**b**) (of people or their bodies) strong, fit and healthy: *a sturdy child* ○ *sturdy arms.* **2** determined; firm; sound: *sturdy resistance to the plan* ○ *sturdy common sense.* ▶ **sturdily** /-ɪli/ *adv*: *a sturdily built bicycle/ young man.* **sturdiness** *n* [U].

sturgeon /'stɜːdʒən/ *n* a large fish found in rivers. Sturgeons are eaten as food and also caught for their eggs (called *caviar*).

stutter /'stʌtə(r)/ *v* **1** = STAMMER. **2** (esp of a vehicle or an engine) to move or start with difficulty, making short sharp noises or movements: [Vpr] *The old plane stuttered along the runway.* [V] (*fig*) *a stuttering start to his career.*

sty¹ /staɪ/ *n* = PIGSTY.

sty² (also **stye**) /staɪ/ *n* (*pl* **sties** or **styes**) a sore red swelling on the edge of the EYELID(1).

Stygian /'stɪdʒiən/ *adj* [usu attrib] (*fml*) very dark: *Stygian darkness/gloom.*

style /staɪl/ *n* **1** [C, U] a distinctive manner of doing, performing or presenting sth: *her style of leadership/ management/teaching* ○ *a comedian with his own very personal style* ○ *sing the same song in a number of different styles* ○ *American-style hamburgers* ○ *I like his style* (ie the way he does things). See also LIFESTYLE. **2**(**a**) [C] a particular design or shape of sth, esp clothes: *the latest styles in dresses/shoes/ swimwear* ○ *wear one's hair in an unusual style* ○ *various styles of kitchen furniture.* See also HAIR-STYLE. (**b**) [U, sing] fashion in clothing, furniture, etc: *have a good sense of style* ○ *Her house is furnished in the latest style.* **3** [U] a fashionable or elegant quality: *She performs the songs with style and flair.* ○ *The piano gives the room a touch of style.* **4** [U] the way in which a work of art, a building, etc is characteristic of a particular historical period, place or person: *a building in Gothic/Romanesque/Tudor style* ○ *the architectural styles of ancient Greece.* **5** [C, U] (**a**) a manner of writing that is characteristic of a particular writer, historical period or type of literature: *make a study of Dickens's style* ○ *a poem in (the) classical style.* (**b**) the correct or conventional use of a language: *Is it correct/good English style to begin a sentence with 'but'?* ○ *follow* **house** '**style** (ie the conventions of spelling and punctuation (PUNC-TUATE) used by a particular publishing company). **6** [C] (*fml*) a title or form of address for a person: *The correct style when addressing an archbishop is 'Your Grace'.* IDM **cramp sb's style** ⇨ CRAMP². **in** (**great, grand, etc**) **style** in a grand or elegant way: *dine in style* ○ *We arrived in fine style in a hired limousine.* (**not/more**) **sb's** '**style** what sb likes: *Big cars are*

not my style. ○ *I don't like rock music; country-and-western is more my style.*
▶ **style** *v* **1** to design, shape or make sth in a particular, esp fashionable, style: [Vn] *have one's hair styled* [Vnadv] *an elegantly styled jacket.* **2** (*fml*) to give a title or form of address to sb/sth: [Vnadv] *the grandly styled 'Chancellor of the Duchy of Lancaster'* [Vn-n] *The country styles itself 'People's Democratic Republic'.* [also Vn]. PHRV '**style sth/ oneself on sth/sb** to copy the style, manner or appearance of sth/sb: *a Parisian café styled on a traditional English pub* ○ *a pop singer who styles himself on Elvis Presley.*
styling *n* [U] **1** the way in which sth is styled: *the car's elegant/modern styling.* **2** the activity of cutting and shaping hair: *styling brushes/mousse.*
stylish *adj* fashionable; having style(3): *stylish clothes/furniture* ○ *a stylish skier/dancer.* **stylishly** *adv.* **stylishness** *n* [U].
stylist /'staɪlɪst/ *n* **1** a person who cuts and shapes people's hair: *She had her hair done by a top stylist.* **2** a person, eg a writer, who has or tries to have a good or distinctive style.
▶ **stylistic** /staɪ'lɪstɪk/ *adj* [usu attrib] of or concerning literary or artistic style: *stylistic elements/ features/influences.* **stylistically** /-kli/ *adv.*
stylized, -ised /'staɪlaɪzd/ *adj* treated in a fixed, conventional or artificial style: *a stylized drawing of a bird* ○ *the highly stylized form of acting in Japanese theatre.* ▶ **stylization, -isation** /ˌstaɪlaɪ'zeɪʃn; *US* -lə'z-/ *n* [U].

stylus /'staɪləs/ *n* (*pl* **styluses**) a hard sharp needle that is fitted to a record-player (RECORD¹) and transmits sound on a record to equipment that reproduces it.

stymie /'staɪmi/ *v* (*pt, pp* **stymied**; *pres p* **stymieing** or **stymying**) (*infml*) (esp passive) to prevent sb from doing sth; to place difficulties or obstacles in sb's way: [Vn] *Their plans to open a new shop have been stymied by lack of funds.*

Styrofoam /'staɪrəfəʊm/ *n* [U] (*propr esp US*) = POLYSTYRENE: *Styrofoam coffee cups.*

suave /swɑːv/ *adj* (*sometimes derog*) (usu of a man) having a confident, smooth and elegant manner or appearance. ▶ **suavely** *adv.* **suavity** /-əti/ *n* [U].

sub /sʌb/ *n* (*infml*) **1** = SUBMARINE. **2** a substitute, esp in football or cricket. **3** money paid as a SUBSCRIP-TION(1a) to a club, etc. **4** a sub-editor.

sub- *pref* **1** (with *ns* and *adjs*) under; below: *subway* ○ *subsoil* ○ *submarine.* **2** (with *ns*) lower in rank; inferior: *sub-lieutenant* ○ *sub post office.* **3**(**a**) (esp with *adjs*) not quite; almost: *subnormal* ○ *substand-ard* ○ *subtropical.* (**b**) (esp with *ns*) less than; lower than: *subzero.* **4** (with *vs* and *ns*) (to form) a smaller or less important part of sth: *subdivide* ○ *subcommit-tee* ○ *subset* ○ *subspecies.* Compare UNDER-.

subaltern /'sʌbltən; *US* sə'bɔːltərn/ *n* (*Brit*) any officer in the army below the rank of captain.

sub-aqua /ˌsʌb 'ækwə/ *adj* [usu attrib] performed under water: *sub-aqua diving.*

subatomic /ˌsʌbə'tɒmɪk/ *adj* [usu attrib] (*techn*) of or concerning units of matter and energy that are smaller than atoms or occur in atoms: *subatomic 'particles/'physics.*

subcommittee /'sʌbkəmɪti/ *n* [CGp] ~ (**on sth**) a committee formed for a special purpose from among the members of a main committee: *the congressional subcommittee on Asian affairs.*

subconscious /ˌsʌb'kɒnʃəs/ *adj* of or concerning thoughts and feelings in the mind, which one is not fully aware of but which influence one's actions: *subconscious desires/urges/fears* ○ *the subconscious self.* Compare UNCONSCIOUS.
▶ **the/one's subconscious** *n* [sing] thoughts and feelings which one is not fully aware of, or the part

S

of the mind in which they occur: *memories buried deep in the subconscious.*

subconsciously *adv*: *I suppose that, subconsciously, I was reacting against my strict upbringing.*

subcontinent /ˌsʌb'kɒntɪnənt/ *n* a large land mass that forms part of a continent, esp the part of Asia that includes India: *the Indian subcontinent.*

subcontract /ˌsʌbkən'trækt; *US* -'kɒntrækt/ *v* ~ **sth (to sb)** (of a person or company responsible for doing a certain job of work) to give a contract to sb else to do part of the work: [Vnpr] *The company subcontracts its market research to a specialist consultancy.* [also Vn].

▶ **subcontract** /ˈsʌbkɒntrækt/ *n* a contract for sb to do work that has been subcontracted to them: *a plumber doing subcontract work.*

subcontractor /ˌsʌbkən'træktə(r); *US* -'kɒntræk-/ *n* a person or company that accepts and does subcontracted work.

subculture /ˈsʌbkʌltʃə(r)/ *n* the behaviour and practices associated with a particular group in society: *the teenage/hippy/gay subculture.*

subcutaneous /ˌsʌbkju'teɪniəs/ *adj* [usu attrib] under the skin: *a subcutaneous injection.*

subdivide /ˈsʌbdɪvaɪd, ˌsʌbdɪ'vaɪd/ *v* ~ **(sth) (into sth)** to divide sth or be divided into smaller divisions: [Vnpr] *Part of the building has been subdivided into offices.* [Vpr] *The religious group subdivided into a number of smaller sects.* [also V, Vn].

▶ **subdivision** *n* **1** /ˌsʌbdɪ'vɪʒn/ [U] the action or process of subdividing. **2** /'sʌbdɪvɪʒn/ [C] a thing produced by subdividing: *a subdivision of a postal area* ∘ *This section of the chapter has several subdivisions.*

subdue /səb'djuː; *US* -'duː/ *v* **1** to bring sb/sth under control by force; to defeat sb/sth: [Vn] *subdue the rebels* ∘ *(fig) government efforts to subdue inflation.* **2** to calm the feelings or emotions: *He was unable to subdue a mounting sense of excitement.*

▶ **subdued** /səb'djuːd; *US* -'duːd/ *adj* **1** not very loud, intense or noticeable: *a subdued conversation* ∘ *subdued lighting/colours* ∘ *a note of subdued excitement in her voice.* **2** not showing much excitement, interest or activity: *You're very subdued. What's wrong?* ∘ *The housing market is fairly subdued at the moment.*

sub-editor /ˌsʌb 'edɪtə(r)/ *n* a person whose job is to check and make changes to the text of a newspaper or magazine before it is printed.

subheading /'sʌbhedɪŋ/ *n* a word or phrase printed above any of the parts into which a piece of writing has been divided, eg in a newspaper.

subhuman /ˌsʌb'hjuːmən/ *adj* (*derog*) less than human; not worthy of a human being.

subject¹ /'sʌbdʒɪkt, -dʒekt/ *n* **1** [C] a thing or person that is being discussed or described; a topic or theme: *an unpleasant subject of conversation* ∘ *choose a subject for an essay* ∘ *a magazine article on the subject of divorce* ∘ *Space travel is a fascinating subject.* ∘ *Michael Jackson is the subject of a new biography.* ∘ *I have nothing more to say on that subject.* **2** [C] a branch of knowledge studied in a school, college, etc: *Physics and chemistry are my favourite subjects.* **3** a person or thing that is the main feature of a picture or photograph: *Focus the camera on the subject.* ∘ *Sailing-ships were a popular subject with 18th-century painters.* **4** [C] a person or thing being treated in a certain way or being used in experiments: *We need some male subjects for a psychology experiment.* **5** [sing] ~ **for/of sth** a thing or person that causes a specified response: *His real feelings became a subject for speculation.* ∘ *Care of the mentally handicapped has become a subject of fierce debate.* ∘ *His appearance was the subject for/of some critical comment.* **6** (*grammar*) **(a)** a word or phrase

in a sentence indicating who or what does the action stated by the verb, eg *the book* in *The book fell off the table.* Compare OBJECT¹ 4. **(b)** a word or phrase indicating the person(s) or thing(s) in a sentence about which sth is stated, eg *the house* in *The house is very old.* Compare PREDICATE¹. **(c)** a word or phrase in a PASSIVE sentence indicating who or what suffers or is affected by the action stated by the verb, eg *the tree* in *The tree was blown over during a storm.* **7** any member of a state¹(2) apart from its supreme ruler: *a British/French subject.* ⇨ note at CITIZEN. **IDM** **change the subject** ⇨ CHANGE¹.

■ **'subject-matter** *n* [U] the information or ideas contained in a book, speech, etc, esp as contrasted with the style in which they are presented: *the controversial subject-matter of his latest film.*

subject² /səb'dʒekt/ *v* **1** ~ **sb/sth to sth** to make sb/sth experience, suffer or be affected by sth: [Vnpr] *subject sb to criticism/ridicule/harassment/torture* ∘ *The city was subjected to repeated bombing raids.* ∘ *subject a substance to detailed analysis.* **2** ~ **sb/sth (to sth/sb)** to bring a country, etc or a person under one's control, esp by force: [Vn, Vnpr] *Ancient Rome subjected most of Europe (to its rule).* ▶ **subjection** /səb'dʒekʃn/ *n* [U]: *the city's frequent subjection to bombing raids* ∘ *The people were kept in subjection.*

subject³ /'sʌbdʒekt, -dʒɪkt/ *adj* **1** [pred] ~ **to sth** likely to have, suffer or be affected by sth: *Children are more subject to colds than adults.* ∘ *Flights are subject to delay after the heavy snowfall.* ∘ *The timetable is subject to alteration.* **2** [pred] ~ **to sth** depending on sth as a condition: *sold subject to contract* (ie provided that a contract is signed) ∘ *The plan is subject to the director's approval.* **3** [pred] ~ **to sth/sb** required to obey sth/sb; under the authority of sth/sb: *We are all subject to the law of the land.* **4** [attrib] under the control of sb else; not politically independent: *subject peoples.*

subjective /səb'dʒektɪv/ *adj* **1** (*sometimes derog*) based on personal taste or opinions: *a very subjective judgement of the play* ∘ *a highly subjective comment/description.* **2** (of ideas, feelings or experiences) existing in the mind and not provoked by things outside the mind: *a subjective impulse/sensation* ∘ *Our perception of things is often influenced by subjective factors, such as tiredness.* Compare OBJECTIVE.

▶ **subjectively** *adv*: *Much of what she says is true but I cannot identify with her ideas subjectively.*

subjectivism /səb'dʒektɪvɪzəm/ *n* [U] (*philosophy*) the theory that knowledge is subjective and that there is no external or absolute truth.

subjectivity /ˌsʌbdʒek'tɪvəti/ *n* [U]: *the subjectivity of the artist's vision.*

sub judice /ˌsʌb 'dʒuːdəsi, -seɪ/ *adj* (*Latin*) (esp pred) (of a legal case, esp in Britain) still being considered by a lawcourt, and therefore not to be discussed in public, eg in a newspaper.

subjugate /'sʌbdʒugeɪt/ *v* (*fml*) to overcome or defeat sb/sth; to gain control over sb/sth: [Vn] *a subjugated race* [Vnpr] *She was totally subjugated to the wishes of her husband.* ▶ **subjugation** /ˌsʌbdʒu'geɪʃn/ *n* [U].

subjunctive /səb'dʒʌŋktɪv/ *n* (*grammar*) **(a)** the subjunctive [U] the form of a verb that is often used to express eg wishes, uncertainty, possibility or condition. For example, in *I wish you were here, were* is in the subjunctive. **(b)** [C] a verb in this form. ▶ **subjunctive** *adj*: *the subjunctive mood.* Compare IMPERATIVE *n* 2, INDICATIVE 2, INFINITIVE.

sublet /ˌsʌb'let/ *v* (-tt-; *pt, pp* **sublet**) ~ **sth (to sb)** to rent to sb else all or part of a house or flat one is oneself renting from the owner: [Vnpr] *sublet a room to a friend* [also Vn].

sub-lieutenant /ˌsʌb lef'tenənt; *US* luː't-/ *n* a naval officer next in rank below a LIEUTENANT(2).

sublimate /ˈsʌblɪmeɪt/ v (*psychology*) to direct one's instincts, urges or energies, esp sexual ones, to other, usu more socially acceptable, activities: [Vn, Vnpr] *sublimating one's sex drive (in physical exercise).* ► **sublimation** /ˌsʌblɪˈmeɪʃn/ n [U].

sublime /səˈblaɪm/ adj **1** (*usu rhet*) of the best or most excellent kind; causing great admiration: *sublime beauty/scenery* ○ *her sublime devotion to the cause* ○ (*infml*) *The food was absolutely sublime.* **2** [attrib] (*often derog*) showing great confidence and lack of fear or concern for the consequences; extreme: *He shows sublime indifference to the sufferings of others.* **IDM** **from the sublime to the riˈdiculous** (of a sudden change) going from sth of great quality or importance to sth completely unimportant. ► **sublimely** adv: *be sublimely happy/indifferent* ○ *play the piano sublimely.* **sublimity** /səˈblɪməti/ n [U].

subliminal /ˌsʌblɪˈmɪnl/ adj perceived by or affecting the mind without one being aware of it: *the subliminal message of the text* (ie one not openly stated). ► **subliminally** adv.

sub-machine-gun /ˌsʌb məˈʃiːn ɡʌn/ n a light machine-gun (MACHINE) held in the hand for firing. ⇨ picture at GUN.

submarine /ˌsʌbməˈriːn, ˈsʌbməriːn/ n **1** an enclosed ship that can operate under water as well as on the surface: *a nuclear submarine* ○ *a submarine attack* ○ *be in/on/aboard a submarine.* **2** (also ˌsubmarine ˈsandwich) (*US*) a sandwich made from a long bread roll split along its length and filled with various types of food.

► **submarine** adj [attrib] (*fml or techn*) existing or placed under the surface of the sea: *submarine exploration* ○ *a submarine cable.*

submariner /sʌbˈmærɪnə(r); *US* ˈsʌbməriːnər/ n a member of a submarine's crew.

submerge /səbˈmɜːdʒ/ v **1(a)** to go under the surface of water, esp the sea: [V] *The submarine submerged to avoid enemy ships.* **(b)** to make sth go or be under the surface of water: [Vn] *a road submerged by flood water* ○ *The device is still able to operate even when totally submerged.* [also Vnpr]. **2** (usu passive) to hide or cover sth/sb completely: *be submerged by paperwork* (ie have so much that one cannot cope with it) ○ *The main argument was submerged in a mass of tedious detail.*

► **submerged** adj under the surface of water, esp the sea: *submerged forests* ○ *a partly-submerged wreck.*

submersible /səbˈmɜːsəbl/ adj (*techn*) that can be submerged in water: *a submersible pump/vessel.* — n a type of SUBMARINE(1) that operates under water for short periods: *explore the sea bed in a submersible.*

submersion /səbˈmɜːʃn; *US* -mɜːrʒn/ n [U].

submission /səbˈmɪʃn/ n **1(a)** [U] the action of presenting sth formally for consideration or for a decision to be made: *the submission of a claim/a petition/an appeal.* **(b)** [C] a document, statement, etc formally presented in this way: *The court has received a submission from the defence lawyers.* ○ *The examiner is under no obligation to mark late submissions* (ie pieces of work submitted late). **2** [U] the acceptance of defeat, or of another's power; the action or state of submitting to sb: *submission to authority* ○ *a gesture of submission* ○ *starve a city into submission* (ie force it to submit by not allowing it to receive supplies of food).

submissive /səbˈmɪsɪv/ adj ~ (**to sb**) willing to show obedience and yield to the authority of others: *a submissive gesture/daughter.* ► **submissively** adv. **submissiveness** n [U].

submit /səbˈmɪt/ v (**-tt-**) **1** ~ **sth (to sb/sth) (for sth)** to give sth to sb/sth so that it may be formally considered or so that a decision about it may be

made: [Vn] *submit an application/an estimate/a claim* [Vnpr] *submit plans to the council for approval* ○ *submit a painting for inclusion in an exhibition.* **2** (*esp law*) to suggest or argue: [V.*that*] *Counsel for the defence submitted that his client was clearly innocent.* ○ *The case, I submit, is not proven.* **3** ~ (**oneself**) (**to sb/sth**) to accept the authority, control or superior strength of sb/sth; to yield to sb/sth: [V] *I refuse to submit.* [Vpr] *submit to the enemy/one's opponent* ○ *submit to sb's authority/wishes* [Vnpr] *submit oneself to the decision of a court.*

subnormal /ˌsʌbˈnɔːml/ adj below the normal level of intelligence: *an educationally subnormal child.*

subordinate /səˈbɔːdɪnət/ adj **(a)** ~ (**to sb**) lower in rank or position: *be in a subordinate position to the head of the department.* **(b)** ~ (**to sth**) of less importance: *All other issues are subordinate to this one.*

► **subordinate** n a person who is subordinate to sb else: *delegate work to one's subordinates.*

subordinate /səˈbɔːdɪneɪt; *US* -dənət/ v ~ **sth (to sth)** to treat sth as of lesser importance than sth else: [Vnpr] *fears that safety considerations were being subordinated to commercial interests.* **subordination** /səˌbɔːdɪˈneɪʃn; *US* -dənˈeɪʃn/ n [U].

■ **suˌbordinate ˈclause** (also deˌpendent ˈclause) n (*grammar*) a clause, usu introduced by a CONJUNCTION(1), that provides further information about sth in the main sentence, eg *when it rang* in *She answered the phone when it rang.* Compare COORDINATE CLAUSE.

suborn /səˈbɔːn/ v (*fml*) to pay sb or use other methods to persuade them to do sth illegal, esp to tell lies in a lawcourt: [Vn] *suborn a witness.*

sub-plot /ˈsʌb plɒt/ n a plot of a play, novel, etc that is separate from but linked to the main plot.

subpoena /səˈpiːnə/ n (*law*) a written order[4] requiring a person to appear in a lawcourt: *serve a subpoena on a witness.*

► **subpoena** v to summon sb with a subpoena: [Vn] *subpoena a witness* [Vn-n, Vn.to inf] *The court subpoenaed her (to appear)* as a witness.

subscribe /səbˈskraɪb/ v **1** ~ (**to sth**) to arrange to receive a publication, esp a magazine, regularly by paying in advance: [V] *The magazine is trying to get more readers to subscribe.* [Vpr] *Which journals does the library subscribe to?* **2** ~ (**for**) **sth** (*finance*) to apply to buy shares (SHARE[3]): [Vpr] *How many shares can one subscribe for under this scheme?* [Vnadv] *The share issue was well subscribed.* [also Vn]. See also OVERSUBSCRIBED. **3** to apply to take part in sth: [Vnadv] *The half-day tour of Edinburgh is fully subscribed.* **4** ~ (**sth**) (**to sth**) to contribute a sum of money, esp regularly, to support a good cause(3), etc: [Vpr] *subscribe to a charity/party funds* [Vn, Vnpr] *How much did you subscribe (to the disaster fund)?* [also V]. **PHRV** **subˈscribe to sth** (*fml*) to agree with an opinion, a theory, etc: *Do you subscribe to her pessimistic view of the state of the economy?*

► **subscriber** n **1** a person who subscribes (SUBSCRIBE 1,2,4): *subscribers to New Scientist.* **2** (*Brit*) a person who rents a telephone line: *dial the code followed by the subscriber's personal number.* See also SUBSCRIPTION.

subscription /səbˈskrɪpʃn/ n **1** [C] ~ (**to sth**) **(a)** a sum of money paid for membership of a club, etc: *renew one's annual subscription.* **(b)** a sum of money given regularly to a CHARITY, etc: *a £20 subscription to Oxfam.* **2** [C] ~ (**to sth**) an arrangement by which one pays in advance for a fixed number of issues of a magazine: *take out a year's subscription to Country Life* ○ *a subscription form/fee.* **3** [U] the act of subscribing: *a monument paid for by public subscription.*

■ **sub'scription concert** *n* each of the concerts in a series for which tickets are sold in advance.

subsection /ˈsʌbsekʃn/ *n* a part of a section, esp in a legal document: *Please turn to subsection 563.*

subsequent /ˈsʌbsɪkwənt/ *adj* [attrib] later; following: *Subsequent events proved me wrong.* ○ *The first and all subsequent visits were kept secret.*

▶ **subsequently** *adv* afterwards: *They subsequently heard he had left the country.* ○ *Subsequently, the company went into liquidation.*

■ **subsequent to** *prep* (*fml*) following sth; after sth: *There have been further developments subsequent to our meeting.*

subservient /səbˈsɜːviənt/ *adj* ~ (**to sb/sth**) **1** (*often derog*) giving too much respect, obedience, etc: *a subservient manner, attitude.* **2** less important: *Everything else is subservient to the child's welfare.* ▶ **subservience** /-əns/ *n* [U].

subside /səbˈsaɪd/ *v* **1** to become less violent, active, intense, etc: [V] *The storm began to subside.* ○ *I took one aspirin and the pain gradually subsided.* ○ *He waited until the applause/laughter had subsided.* [Vpr] *The audience subsided into an expectant hush.* **2** (of water) to sink to a lower or to the normal level: [V] *The flood waters gradually subsided.* **3** [V] (of land) to sink to a lower level. **4** (of buildings, etc) to sink lower into the ground: [V] *Weak foundations caused the house to subside.* **5** (*infml joc*) to let oneself drop into a chair, etc: [Vpr] *subsiding into an armchair.*

▶ **subsidence** /səbˈsaɪdns, ˈsʌbsɪdns/ *n* [U,C] the process or an instance of an area of land subsiding: *a building damaged by subsidence* ○ *The railway line was closed because of (a) subsidence.*

subsidiary /səbˈsɪdiəri; *US* -dieri/ *adj* **1** ~ (**to sth**) connected to but of less importance, etc than sth else: *a subsidiary question/subject* ○ *All other issues are subsidiary to the need to provide food and medical supplies.* **2** (of a business company) controlled by another.

▶ **subsidiary** *n* a business company controlled by another company: *our Rome-based/Italian subsidiary* ○ *a subsidiary of General Motors.*

subsidize, -ise /ˈsʌbsɪdaɪz/ *v* to give a subsidy to sth/sb: [Vn] *subsidized industries.* ▶ **subsidization, -isation** /ˌsʌbsɪdaɪˈzeɪʃn; *US* -dəˈz-/ *n* [U]: *the subsidization of public transport.*

subsidy /ˈsʌbsədi/ *n* [C,U] money paid, esp by a government, eg to help support arts organizations or to reduce the costs of producing goods so that their prices can be kept low: *agricultural subsidies* ○ *increase/reduce the level of subsidy.*

subsist /səbˈsɪst/ *v* **1** ~ (**on sth**) (*fml*) to stay alive, esp with little food or money: [Vpr] *He subsisted mainly on vegetables and fruit.* [also V]. **2** (*fml*) to continue to exist: [V] *This pattern of industry still subsists in certain countries.*

▶ **subsistence** /-təns/ *n* [U] a means of staying alive: *be reduced to subsistence on bread and water* ○ *subsistence farming* (ie farming that produces only enough food for the farmer and her or his family to eat, leaving none to sell) ○ *a subsistence wage* (ie one that is only just enough to enable a worker to buy the basic necessities).

■ **sub'sistence level** *n* [U,C usu *sing*] a standard of living that only just provides the basic necessities: *exist at/above/below (the) subsistence level.*

subsoil /ˈsʌbsɔɪl/ *n* [U] a layer of soil lying immediately beneath the surface layer. Compare TOPSOIL.

subsonic /ˌsʌbˈsɒnɪk/ *adj* (flying at a speed) less than the speed of sound: *a subsonic speed/aircraft/flight.* Compare SUPERSONIC.

substance /ˈsʌbstəns/ *n* **1** [C] a particular type of matter: *a poisonous/chemical substance* ○ *a sticky substance* ○ *She tested positive to a banned substance* (ie drug). **2** [U] real physical matter that can be

touched, not just seen, heard or imagined: *They maintained that ghosts had no substance.* **3** [U] the quality of being based on facts: *malicious gossip, completely without substance* ○ *The commission's report gives substance to these allegations.* **4** [U] the most important or essential part of sth; the essential meaning: *the substance of the speech* ○ *I agree with the substance of what you say/with what you say in substance.* **5** [U] (*fml*) money; property: *a man/woman of substance* (ie a wealthy one).

substandard /ˌsʌbˈstændəd/ *adj* below the usual or required standard: *substandard goods.*

substantial /səbˈstænʃl/ *adj* **1** large in amount or value; considerable: *a substantial improvement/increase* ○ *obtain a substantial loan* ○ *win by a substantial majority* ○ *Her contribution to the discussion was substantial.* **2** [usu attrib] strongly built or made; large and solid: *a substantial house.* **3** [attrib] (*fml*) concerning the most important part of sth; essential: *We are in substantial agreement.*

▶ **substantially** /-ʃəli/ *adv* **1** to a considerable extent; greatly: *Their performance has substantially improved.* ○ *They contributed substantially to our success.* **2** for the most part; mainly: *Your assessment is substantially correct.*

substantiate /səbˈstænʃieɪt/ *v* (*rather fml*) to give facts to support a claim, statement, etc; to prove sth: [Vn] *Can you substantiate your accusations against him?* ▶ **substantiation** /səbˌstænʃiˈeɪʃn/ *n* [U].

substantive /səbˈstæntɪv, ˈsʌbstəntɪv/ *adj* (*fml*) genuine or actual; real: *make substantive changes.*

▶ **substantive** *n* (*dated grammar*) a noun.

substation /ˈsʌbsteɪʃn/ *n* a place which reduces the strength of electric power to make it suitable for domestic or business use.

substitute /ˈsʌbstɪtjuːt; *US* -tuːt/ *n* ~ (**for sb/sth**) a person or thing that replaces, acts for or serves as sb or sth else: *Everton substitute Mick Harris scored a minute from time.* ○ *This type of vinyl is no/a poor substitute for* (ie not as good as) *leather.* ○ *a substitute parent/player/teacher.*

▶ **substitute** *v* (**a**) ~ **sb/sth** (**for sb/sth**) to put or use sb/sth instead of sb/sth else: [Vnpr] *community health workers being substituted for district nurses* [Vn] *Johnson was substituted at half-time.* (**b**) ~ **for sb/sth** to act or serve as a substitute: [Vpr] *Can you substitute for me at the meeting?*

substitution /ˌsʌbstɪˈtjuːʃn; *US* -ˈtuːʃn/ *n* [U,C]: *the substitution of computer intelligence for other resources* ○ *Two substitutions were made during the match.*

substratum /ˈsʌbstrɑːtəm; *US* ˈsʌbstreɪtəm/ *n* (*pl* **substrata** /ˈsʌbstrɑːtə; *US* ˈsʌbstreɪtə/) a layer of sth, esp rock or soil, below another: *The plant grows well in almost any substratum.* ○ *substrata of society.*

substructure /ˈsʌbstrʌktʃə(r)/ *n* a structure that lies under or supports another structure; a base or foundation. Compare SUPERSTRUCTURE 1.

subsume /səbˈsjuːm; *US* -ˈsuːm/ *v* ~ **sth** (**in/into/under/within sth**) (*fml*) to include sth in a particular group: [Vnpr] *The three departments have now been subsumed under a single manager.* [also Vn].

subtend /səbˈtend/ *v* (*geometry*) (of a line or a CHORD(2)) to be opposite to an ARC(1) or angle: [Vn] *The chord AC subtends the arc ABC.* ○ *The side XZ subtends the angle XYZ.* ⇨ picture.

subterfuge /ˈsʌbtəfjuːdʒ/ *n* [U,C] a trick or deceitful way of achieving sth, esp one used to avoid a difficult situation: *gain sth by subterfuge* ○ *Her claim to be a journalist was simply a subterfuge to get into the theatre without paying.*

subterranean /ˌsʌbtəˈreɪniən/ *adj* under the

earth's surface; underground: *a subterranean passage/river/tunnel*.

subtitle /ˈsʌbtaɪtl/ *n* **1** a secondary or additional title of a book. **2** (usu *pl*) words that translate what is said in a film into a different language and appear on the screen at the bottom. Subtitles are also used, esp on television, to help deaf people.
▶ **subtitle** *v* (usu passive) to give a subtitle or subtitles to sth: [Vn-n] *The book is subtitled 'An Essay in Constructive Criticism'*. [also Vn]. Compare DUB.

subtle /ˈsʌtl/ *adj* (**-r, -st**) (*esp approv*) **1** difficult to detect or describe; fine[1](4): *a subtle charm/flavour/ style* ○ *subtle humour* ○ *a subtle distinction* ○ *subtle shades of pink*. **2** organized in a clever and complex way: *a subtle argument/design/strategy*. **3** able to perceive and describe fine[1](4) differences: *a subtle observer/critic/analyst* ○ *She has a very subtle mind*.
▶ **subtlety** /ˈsʌtlti/ *n* **1** [U] the quality of being subtle. **2** [C] a subtle distinction.
subtly /ˈsʌtli/ *adv*: *subtly different/coloured*.

subtotal /ˈsʌbtəʊtl/ *n* the total of a set of figures that are part of a larger group of figures.

subtract /səbˈtrækt/ *v* ~ **sth** (**from sth**) to take a number or quantity from another number or quantity: [Vn, Vnpr] *subtract 6 (from 9)* [Vnpr] *6 subtracted from 9 is 3* (ie 9–6=3). Compare ADD, DEDUCT. ▶ **subtraction** /səbˈtrækʃn/ *n* [U, C]: *a subtraction sum*.

subtropical /ˌsʌbˈtrɒpɪkl/ *adj* of or relating to regions near the tropical parts of the world: ˌsubtropical ˈplants ○ *a* ˌsubtropical ˈclimate.

suburb /ˈsʌbɜːb/ *n* a district away from the centre of a town or city, esp one where people live: *a suburb of London/a London suburb* ○ *a quiet residential suburb* ○ *live in the outer suburbs*.
▶ **suburban** /səˈbɜːbən/ *adj* **1** of or in a suburb: *a suburban street/shop/newspaper*. **2** (*derog*) limited in mental attitude or in style; dull or ordinary: *a rather suburban outlook on life*.
suburbanite /səˈbɜːbənaɪt/ *n* (*infml often derog*) a person who lives in the suburbs.
suburbia /səˈbɜːbiə/ *n* [U] (*often derog*) the suburbs, the people who live there and their way of life.

subvention /səbˈvenʃn/ *n* (*fml*) an amount of money given to support an industry, a theatre company, etc.

subversive /səbˈvɜːsɪv/ *adj* trying or likely to upset or destroy a political system, an accepted belief, etc from an inside position: *subversive activities/ propaganda* ○ *a subversive book/speaker/influence* ○ (*fml*) *ideas regarded as subversive of the existing social order*.
▶ **subversive** *n* a subversive person.
subversively *adv*.
subversiveness *n* [U].

subvert /səbˈvɜːt/ *v* **1** to destroy the authority of a political system, religion, etc: [Vn] *punish attempts to subvert public order*. **2** to make sb betray their moral values or loyalty: [Vn] *a diplomat subverted by a foreign power*. ▶ **subversion** /səbˈvɜːʃn; US -ˈvɜːrʒn/ *n* [U].

subway /ˈsʌbweɪ/ *n* **1** (*esp Brit*) a tunnel under a road or railway through which people can walk: *Use the subway to cross the road*. Compare UNDERPASS. **2** (*US*) an underground railway in a city: *travel by subway* ○ *a subway train/station*. Compare UNDERGROUND[2] 1 *n*, TUBE 4, METRO.

subzero /ˌsʌbˈzɪərəʊ/ *adj* (of temperatures) below zero.

succeed /səkˈsiːd/ *v* **1** ~ (**in sth / doing sth**) to do what one is trying to do; to achieve a desired aim; to be successful: [V] *Our plan succeeded*. [V, Vpr] *She's absolutely determined to succeed (in life)*. [Vpr] (*ironic*) *I tried to clean my watch, but only succeeded in breaking it*. Compare FAIL 1. **2** to come next after

sb/sth and take their/its place: [Vn, Vn-n] *Who succeeded Kennedy (as President)?* [Vn] *Exultation was quickly succeeded by despair*. **3** ~ (**to sth**) to gain the right to a title, property, etc when sb dies: [V, Vpr] *When the king died, his eldest son succeeded (to the throne)*. **IDM** **nothing succeeds like sucˈcess** (*saying*) success often leads to further successes.

success /səkˈses/ *n* **1** [U] the achievement of a desired aim, or of fame, wealth or social position: *He's hoping to* **make a success of** *the business*. ○ *The race ended in success for* (ie was won by) *the Irish horse*. ○ *I haven't had much success in finding a job*. **2** [C] a person or thing that succeeds: *He wasn't a success as a teacher*. ○ *Her rapid rise to the top has been one of the film industry's most remarkable success stories*. **IDM** **nothing succeeds like success** ⇨ SUCCEED. **a roaring success** ⇨ ROAR.
▶ **successful** /-fl/ *adj* having success: *a successful businesswoman/career/plan* ○ *My final attempt to fix it was successful*. **successfully** /-fəli/ *adv*.

succession /səkˈseʃn/ *n* **1** [C] a number of things or people following each other in time or order; a series: *a succession of wet days/defeats/poor leaders* ○ *three victories in (quick)succession*. **2** [U] the regular pattern of one thing or person following another in time or order: *the succession of the seasons*. **3** [U] the action, process or right of succeeding (SUCCEED 3) to a title, property, etc: *Who is first in line of succession to the throne?*

successive /səkˈsesɪv/ *adj* [attrib] coming one after the other without a break: *This was their fifth successive win*. ○ *Successive governments have failed to tackle the problem*. ▶ **successively** *adv*: *successively higher levels of radiation*.

successor /səkˈsesə(r)/ *n* ~ (**to sb/sth**) a person or thing that comes after and takes the place of sb/sth: *appoint a successor to the presidency* ○ *This car is the successor to our popular hatchback model*. Compare PREDECESSOR.

succinct /səkˈsɪŋkt/ *adj* (*approv*) expressed briefly and clearly: *His speech was short and succinct*. ▶ **succinctly** *adv*. **succinctness** *n* [U].

succour (*US* **succor**) /ˈsʌkə(r)/ *n* [U] (*fml*) help given to sb in need or in danger: *bring succour to the sick and wounded*.
▶ **succour** *v* [Vn] (*fml*) to give succour to sb.

succulent /ˈsʌkjələnt/ *adj* **1** (*approv*) (esp of fruit and meat) juicy and tasting good: *a succulent steak/ pear*. **2** (of plants) having leaves and stems that are thick and contain a lot of water.
▶ **succulence** /-əns/ *n* [U].
succulent *n* a succulent plant, eg a CACTUS.

succumb /səˈkʌm/ *v* ~ (**to sth**) (*fml*) to fail to resist an illness, an attack, etc; to yield to sth: [V] *The city succumbed after only a short siege*. [V, Vpr] *Several children have measles, and the others are bound to succumb (to it)*. [Vpr] *The driver later succumbed to* (ie died of) *his injuries*. [Vpr] (*joc*) *She succumbed to the temptation of a cream cake*.

such /sʌtʃ/ *det* **1(a)** (referring back to sth specified earlier) of this type: *He noticed her necklace. Such jewels must have cost thousands, he thought*. ○ *I've been invited on an Asian wedding. What happens on such occasions?* ○ *He said he hadn't got time or made some such excuse*. ○ *This isn't the only story of cruelty to children. Many such cases are reported every day*. **(b)** ~ **sth as/that...** (referring forward to sb/sth) of the type about to be specified: *Such a disaster as this had never happened to her before*. ○ *The knot was fastened in such a way that it was impossible to undo*. ○ *Such advice as* (ie the little advice that) *he was given proved almost worthless*. **2** ~ **sth** (**as/that...**) to the specified degree of importance, worth, etc: *He showed such concern that people took him to be a relative*. ○ *He's not such a fool as he looks*. ○ *It was such a boring speech (that) I fell asleep*. ○ *I'm afraid I* can't remember — it was such a long time ago. ○ Such is the influence of TV that it can make a person famous overnight. **3** (used for emphasis) so great; so very (much): She's got such talent. ○ We're having such a wonderful time. ○ I've had such a shock. ○ Why are you in such a hurry?

▶ **such** pron a person or thing of the type specified **(a)** (referring back): Cricket was boring. Such (ie That) was her opinion before meeting Ian! ○ She's a competent manager and has always been regarded as such by her colleagues. **(b)** ~ **as to do sth**; ~ **that...** (referring forward): The pain in her foot wasn't such as to stop her walking. ○ The damage was such that it would cost too much to repair. **IDM** **as such** as the word is usually understood; in the exact sense of the word: The new job is not a promotion as such but it has good prospects. **such as 1** like; for example: Wild flowers such as orchids and primroses are becoming rare. **2** everything that: Such as remains after tax will be yours when I die. **,such as it 'is** (used to apologize for the poor quality of sth): You're welcome to join us for supper, such as it is — we're only having soup and bread.
■ **'such-and-such** pron, det (a person or thing) of a particular type that does not need to be specified: Always say at the start of an application that you're applying for such-and-such (a job) because...

suchlike /'sʌtʃlaɪk/ pron, det (things) of the same type: You can buy string, glue, paper-clips and suchlike (items) at the local shop.

suck /sʌk/ v **1(a)** to draw liquid or air, etc into the mouth from sth by using the lip muscles: [Vnpr] suck the juice from an orange ○ suck milk through a straw. [Vnp, Vnpr] suck the poison out (of a wound) [Vn] a baby sucking its mother's breast [Vn-adj] suck an orange dry. **(b)** (of a pump, etc) to draw liquid or air out of sth: [Vnpr, Vnp] plants that suck (up) moisture from the soil [Vnp] The pump sucks air out through this valve. **2** ~ **(away) (at/on sth)** to perform the action of sucking sth: [Vpr, Vp] The baby sucked (away) at its bottle. [Vpr] The old man was sucking at his pipe. **3** to squeeze or roll sth with the tongue while holding it in the mouth: [Vn] suck a toffee ○ I used to suck my thumb as a child. **4** to pull sb/sth in the specified direction with great force: [Vnpr, Vnp] The canoe was sucked (down) into the whirlpool. [Vnp] Dangerous currents can suck swimmers under. **IDM** **milk/suck sb/sth dry** ⇨ DRY¹. **teach one's grandmother to suck eggs** ⇨ TEACH. **PHRV** **,suck sb 'in / 'into sth** (usu passive) to involve sb in an activity, an argument, etc, usu against their will: I don't want to get sucked into the debate about school reform. **,suck 'up (to sb)** (infml derog) to try to please sb by praising them excessively, helping them, etc: She's always sucking up to the teacher.
▶ **suck** n an act of sucking: have/take a suck (at sth).

sucker /'sʌkə(r)/ n **1** (infml) a person who is easily deceived: The world is full of suckers eager to waste their money. **2** ~ **for sb/sth** (infml) a person who cannot resist sb/sth or is very fond of sb/sth: I've always been a sucker for romantic movies. **3(a)** a special organ on the body of certain animals that enables them to stick to a surface: An octopus has suckers on its tentacles. **(b)** a usu rubber disc that sticks to a surface when pressed against it: toy arrows with suckers instead of sharp heads. **4** a shoot growing from the roots of a tree or bush, not from its branches. **5** (US infml) = LOLLIPOP.

suckle /'sʌkl/ v [Vn] to feed a baby or young animal with milk from the breast or from UDDER. ⇨ picture at COW.

sucrose /'suːkrəʊz, -rəʊs/ n [U] sugar obtained from sugar-cane (SUGAR) and sugar-beet (SUGAR).

suction /'sʌkʃn/ n [U] the removal of air from a

space, container, etc so that sth else can be drawn into it: Vacuum cleaners work by suction. ○ a suction pump/pad ○ Flies' feet stick to surfaces by suction.

sudden /'sʌdn/ adj happening, coming or done quickly and unexpectedly: a sudden decision/ change/increase ○ Their departure was very sudden. **IDM** **,all of a 'sudden** quickly and unexpectedly: All of a sudden, the front tyre burst. **,sudden 'death** a way of deciding the result of a game in which two or more competitors have equal scores by playing one more point or game. Whoever wins it wins the whole game: a ,sudden-death 'play-off. ▶ **suddenly** adv: The end came quite suddenly. ○ Suddenly, everyone started shouting and singing. **suddenness** n [U].

suds /sʌdz/ n [pl] **1** (also **soapsuds**) a mass of tiny bubbles (BUBBLE) on top of water to which soap has been added. **2** (US infml) beer.

sue /suː; Brit also sjuː/ v **1** ~ **(sb) (for sth)** to start a legal case in order to make a claim against sb: [Vn, Vnpr] If you don't complete the work, I will sue you (for damages) (ie for money to compensate for my loss). [also V, Vpr]. **2** ~ **for sth** (fml) to ask formally for sth, often in a lawcourt: [Vpr] sue for peace ○ She's suing for a divorce.

suede /sweɪd/ n [U] a type of leather with one side rubbed so that it has a soft, slightly rough surface: a suede coat ○ brown suede shoes.

suet /'suːɪt; Brit also 'sjuːɪt/ n [U] the hard fat from round the kidneys (KIDNEY) of cattle and sheep, used in cooking: a suet pudding (ie one made with flour and suet).

suffer /'sʌfə(r)/ v **1** ~ **(from/with/for sth)** to feel pain, discomfort, sorrow, etc: [Vpr] Do you suffer from (ie often have) headaches? ○ She's suffering from loss of memory. ○ He suffers terribly with (ie has pain in) his feet. ○ He made a rash decision and now he's suffering for it. [Vadv] She suffered terribly during her long illness. [also V]. **2** to experience sth unpleasant: [Vn] suffer pain/torture/defeat ○ suffer the consequences of one's actions ○ The company suffered huge losses in the recession. **3** to become worse in quality; to be badly affected: [V] Your studies will suffer if you play too much sport. ○ Her business suffered (eg made less profit) while she was ill. **IDM** **not/never suffer fools 'gladly** to refuse to be patient with people one thinks are foolish: She was an intellectual snob and not one to suffer fools gladly.
▶ **sufferer** /'sʌfərə(r)/ n a person who suffers, esp from an illness: arthritis sufferers.
suffering /'sʌfərɪŋ/ n **1** [U] pain of body or mind: There is too much suffering in the world. **2** **sufferings** [pl] feelings of pain, sorrow, etc: the physical and mental sufferings of the refugees.

sufferance /'sʌfərəns/ n [U] **IDM** **on 'sufferance** tolerated but not actually wanted: He's only here on sufferance.

suffice /sə'faɪs/ v ~ **(for sth/sb)** (fml) (not in the continuous tenses) to be enough for sb/sth; to be adequate: [V] One coat of paint should suffice. [Vpr] A week will suffice for what I need to do. [V.to inf] One example will suffice to illustrate what I mean. **IDM** **suffice (it) to say (that)...** (used to suggest that even though one could say more, what one does say should be enough to show what one means): I won't go into all the depressing details; suffice it to say that the whole affair was an utter disaster.

sufficient /sə'fɪʃnt/ adj ~ **(for sth/sb)**; ~ **(to do sth)** enough: sufficient money/time/fuel ○ Is £100 sufficient for your expenses? ○ Do we have sufficient (food) for ten people? ○ One aspirin should be sufficient to relieve the pain. Compare INSUFFICIENT.
▶ **sufficiency** /-nsi/ n [sing] ~ **(of sth)** (fml) an adequate quantity of sth: a sufficiency of nursing skills.
sufficiently adv: not sufficiently careful.

[Vnn] = verb + noun + noun   [V-adj] = verb + adjective   For more help with verbs, see Study pages **B4–8**.

suffix /'sʌfɪks/ n (abbreviated as *suff* in this dictionary) a letter or group of letters added at the end of a word to make another word, eg *-y* added to *rust* to make *rusty*, or *-en* in *oxen*. Compare PREFIX 1, AFFIX².

suffocate /'sʌfəkeɪt/ v **1** to die as a result of being unable to breathe; to kill sb by making them unable to breathe: [V] *Many passengers suffocated in the burning aircraft.* [Vn] *Two firemen were suffocated by the fumes.* ◦ (*fig*) *She felt suffocated* (ie restricted) *by all their rules and regulations.* **2** to have difficulty in breathing: [V] *I'm suffocating in here — can we open a window?*
  ▶ **suffocating** *adj* causing difficulty in breathing: *the suffocating heat of a tropical night* ◦ (*fig*) *a suffocating cloak of secrecy.*
  suffocation /ˌsʌfə'keɪʃn/ n [U]: *die of suffocation.*

suffragan /'sʌfrəgən/ *adj* [attrib] (of a bishop) appointed to help another bishop by managing part of his DIOCESE.
  ▶ **suffragan** *n* a suffragan bishop.

suffrage /'sʌfrɪdʒ/ n [U] the right to vote in political elections: *universal suffrage* (ie the right of all adults to vote) ◦ *The women's suffrage movement.*
  ▶ **suffragette** /ˌsʌfrə'dʒet/ n a member of a group of women who, in the early part of the 20th century, led a campaign in Britain for women's suffrage.

suffuse /sə'fjuːz/ v ~ sth (with sth) (esp passive) (esp of colour or light) to spread all over sth: [Vn] *A blush suffused his cheeks.* [Vnpr] *The evening sky was suffused with crimson.* ◦ (*fig*) *Her face was suffused with delight.*

sugar /'ʃʊgə(r)/ n **1(a)** [U] a sweet substance, often in the form of white or brown crystals, which is obtained from the juices of various plants. Sugar is used in cooking and for making drinks, etc sweet: *Don't eat too much sugar.* ◦ *Do you take sugar?* (ie Do you have it in your tea, etc?) ◦ *a sugar plantation/ refinery/bowl.* See also CASTOR SUGAR, ICING SUGAR. **(b)** [C] a lump or small amount of sugar: *How many sugars do you like in your coffee?* **2** [C] any of various sweet substances occurring naturally in plants, fruit, etc. **3** (*infml esp US*) (used as a form of address to sb one likes).
  ▶ **sugar** v to make sth sweet or cover sth with sugar: [Vn] *Is this tea sugared?* ◦ *sugared almonds.*
  IDM **sugar/sweeten the pill** ⇨ PILL.
  sugary /'ʃʊgəri/ *adj* **1** tasting of sugar; sweet: *sugary drinks/snacks.* **2** (*derog*) too sentimental; too pleasant, attractive, etc to be sincere: *a sugary love story.*
  ■ **'sugar-beet** n [U] a plant from whose large round roots sugar is made.
  'sugar-cane n [U] a tall tropical grass with thick stems from which sugar is made.
  ˌsugar-'coated *adj* **1** covered with sugar. **2** (*derog*) made to seem attractive: *a ˌsugar-coated 'promise.*
  'sugar-daddy n (*infml*) a rich man who is generous to a younger woman, usu in return for sex.
  'sugar-lump n a small CUBE of sugar, used to make tea, coffee, etc sweet.

suggest /sə'dʒest/ *US* səg'dʒ-/ v **1** ~ sb (for sth); ~ sth (to sb); ~ sb/sth (as sth) to put sth/sb forward as an idea or a candidate to be considered; to propose sth/sb: [Vn] *I suggest a tour of the museum.* [Vnpr] *Is there anyone you'd like to suggest for the job?* ◦ *There's something I want to suggest to you.* [V.that] *I suggest (that) we break for lunch now.* [V.wh] *Can you suggest how we might tackle the problem?* [V.ing] *He suggested taking the children to the zoo.* [Vn-n] *She suggested Paris as a good place for the conference.* [Vpr.that] *I suggested to the others that they might like to join us.* [also Vpr.wh]. **2** ~ sth (to sb) to put an idea, etc into sb's mind; to indicate(1b) sth: [Vn, Vnpr] *What do these symptoms suggest (to you)?* [V.that] *His cool response suggested that*

he didn't like the idea. [also Vpr.*that*]. **3** to state sth indirectly; to imply: [V.*that*, Vn] *'Are you suggesting that I'm a liar?'* *'I wouldn't suggest such a thing for a moment.'* **IDM** **sug'gest itself (to sb)** (*fml*) to come into sb's mind; to occur to sb: *Another possible explanation suggests itself (to me).*
  ▶ **suggestible** /-əbl/ *adj* easily influenced: *I did many stupid things when I was young and suggestible.* **suggestibility** /sə,dʒestə'bɪləti; *US* səg,dʒ-/ n [U].
  suggestive /-ɪv/ *adj* **1** ~ (of sth) putting particular ideas or associations into sb's mind: *music that is suggestive of warm summer days* ◦ *suggestive symbolism.* **2** making sb think of sex and sexual relationships: *He gave her a suggestive wink, and she blushed.* **suggestively** *adv.*

suggestion /sə'dʒestʃən; *US* səg'dʒ-/ n **1** [C] ~ (that...) an idea, plan, etc or person that is suggested or recommended: *What shall we do today — any suggestions?* ◦ *Several people made suggestions about/on how to raise funds.* ◦ *Janet was my first suggestion as chairperson.* ◦ *There's no suggestion that she should resign* (ie That would not even be a possibility). **2** [U] the action of suggesting sth: *On/ At your suggestion* (ie Because you suggested it) *I bought the more expensive model.* **3** [C usu *sing*] a slight amount or sign of sth; a hint(2): *speak English with the suggestion of a French accent.* **4** [U] the putting of an idea, etc into sb's mind through linking it to other ideas, pictures, etc: *Most advertisements work through suggestion.*

suicide /'suːɪsaɪd; *Brit also* 'sjuːɪ-/ n **1(a)** [U] the action of killing oneself intentionally: *He committed suicide.* **(b)** [C] an instance of this: *three suicides in one week.* **2** [C] a person who commits suicide. **3** [U] any action that may result in disaster for oneself: *Large-scale tax increases at this stage would be political suicide.*
  ▶ **suicidal** /ˌsuːɪ'saɪdl; *Brit also* ˌsjuːɪ-/ *adj* **1** of suicide; likely to lead to suicide: *suicidal tendencies* ◦ *be in a suicidal state.* **2** (of a person) likely to commit suicide; extremely depressed: *I was desperately unhappy, almost suicidal.* **3** likely to lead to disaster for oneself: *a suicidal policy.* **suicidally** /-dəli/ *adv*: *suicidally depressed.*

suit¹ /suːt; *Brit also* sjuːt/ n **1(a)** a set of outer garments of the same material, usu a jacket and trousers and sometimes a WAISTCOAT, or a jacket and skirt for a woman: *a 'business suit* ◦ *a ˌpin-stripe 'suit* ◦ *a ˌtwo-/ˌthree-piece 'suit* (ie of two/three garments) ◦ *a 'dress suit* (ie a man's formal evening suit). See also LOUNGE-SUIT, TROUSER SUIT, TRACK SUIT. **(b)** a set of clothing for a particular activity: *a 'diving suit* ◦ *a ˌsuit of 'armour.* See also BOILER SUIT, SPACESUIT, SWIMSUIT, WET SUIT. **2** any of the four sets forming a pack of cards: *The suits are spades, hearts, diamonds and clubs.* ⇨ picture at PLAYING-CARD. **3** (also **lawsuit**) a case in a lawsuit; legal proceedings: *file/bring a suit against sb* ◦ *a divorce suit.* **IDM** **follow suit** ⇨ FOLLOW. **in one's birthday suit** ⇨ BIRTHDAY.
  ▶ **-suited** (forming compound *adjs*) wearing a suit of the specified type: *sober-suited city businessmen.*
  suiting n [U] material for making suits: *men's suiting.*

suit² /suːt; *Brit also* sjuːt/ v **1** (esp of clothes, etc) to look attractive on sb: [Vn] *Does this skirt suit me?* ◦ *That colour doesn't suit your complexion.* [Vn.ing, Vn. to inf] *It doesn't suit you having/to have your hair cut short.* **2** (no passive; not in the continuous tenses) to be convenient for or acceptable to sb: [Vn] *The seven o'clock train will suit us very well.* ◦ *If you want to go by bus, that suits me fine.* ◦ *He can be very helpful, but only when it suits him.* [Vn. to inf] *Would it suit you to come at five?* **(b)** (usu in negative sentences) to be right or good for sb/sth: [Vn] *The*

S

[V] = verb used alone   [Vn] = verb + noun   [Vp] = verb + particle   [Vpr] = verb + prepositional phrase

suitable

climate here doesn't suit me. **IDM** **suit one's/sb's book** (*infml*) to be convenient or acceptable to one/ sb: *It suits my book if I never have to go there again.*

suit sb down to the 'ground (*Brit infml*) to be very convenient or appropriate for sb: *I've found a job that suits me down to the ground.* **suit one'self** (*infml*) (often imperative) to act entirely according to one's own wishes: *'I think I'll stay at home this evening.' 'Suit yourself.'* **PHRV** **suit sth to sth/sb** to make sth appropriate for sth/sb; to adapt sth to sth/ sb: *She suits her style to her readership.*

▶ **suited** *adj* [pred] ~ (**for/to sb/sth**) suitable or appropriate (for sb/sth): *He is not really suited for a teaching career.* ○ *He and his wife are ideally suited (to each other).*

suitable /ˈsuːtəbl; *Brit also* ˈsjuːt-/ *adj* ~ (**for/to sth/ sb**) right or appropriate for a purpose or an occasion: *a suitable candidate* ○ *clothes suitable for cold weather* ○ *a suitable place for a picnic* ○ *Would now be a suitable moment to discuss my report?* ▶ **suitability** /ˌsuːtəˈbɪləti; *Brit also* ˌsjuːt-/ *n* [U]. **suitably** /-əbli/ *adv*: *go to a party suitably dressed* ○ *He was suitably impressed when I told him I'd won.*

suitcase /ˈsuːtkeɪs; *Brit also* ˈsjuːt-/ *n* a case with flat sides and a handle, used for carrying clothes, etc when travelling. ⇨ picture at LUGGAGE.

suite /swiːt/ *n* **1(a)** a set of rooms in a hotel, etc: *The luxury suite consists of a bedroom, a bathroom and a sitting-room.* See also EN SUITE. **(b)** (*US*) an apartment; a flat. **2** a set of matching pieces of furniture: *a three-piece suite* (eg two chairs and a SOFA) ○ *a 'bathroom/'bedroom suite*. **3** a complete set of objects used together: *a suite of programs for a computer.* **4** (*music*) a piece of music consisting of three or more related parts, eg pieces selected from an opera: *a suite of classical dances.*

suitor /ˈsuːtə(r); *Brit also* ˈsjuː-/ *n* (*dated*) a man who wants to marry a particular woman: *She had rejected all her many suitors.*

sulfate (*US*) = SULPHATE.
sulfide (*US*) = SULPHIDE.
sulfur (*US*) = SULPHUR.

sulk /sʌlk/ *v* (*derog*) to be silent or bad-tempered because one is annoyed or upset: [V] *sulking teenagers* ○ *He sulked for days after being left out of the team.*

▶ **sulk** *n* (also **the sulks** [pl]) (*infml*) a period of sulking: *be in / go into a sulk* ○ *have (a fit of) the sulks.*

sulky *adj* having or showing a tendency to sulk: *a sulky person/look/mood.* **sulkily** /-ɪli/ *adv.* **sulkiness** *n* [U].

sullen /ˈsʌlən/ *adj* (*derog*) **1** silent, bad-tempered and gloomy (GLOOM): *a sullen person/look* ○ *All my attempts to amuse the children were met with sullen scowls.* **2** (*esp rhet*) dark and gloomy (GLOOM); DISMAL(1): *a sullen sky.* ▶ **sullenly** *adv.* **sullenness** *n* [U].

sully /ˈsʌli/ *v* (*pt, pp* **sullied**) (*fml or rhet*) to spoil or lower the value of sb's reputation, etc; to make sth dirty: *sully sb's name/honour* ○ *I refuse to sully my hands by accepting money from such an organization.*

sulphate (*US* **sulfate**) /ˈsʌlfeɪt/ *n* [C, U] a compound of sulphuric acid (SULPHUR) and a chemical element: *copper sulphate.*

sulphide (*US* **sulfide**) /ˈsʌlfaɪd/ *n* [C, U] a compound of SULPHUR and another chemical element.

sulphur (*US* **sulfur**) /ˈsʌlfə(r)/ *n* [U] (*symb* **S**) a chemical (ELEMENT 4). Sulphur is a pale yellow substance that burns with a bright flame and a strong smell, used in medicine and industry. ⇨ App 7.

▶ **sulphurous** (*US* **sulfurous**) /ˈsʌlfərəs/ *adj* of, like or containing sulphur: *a sulphurous smell* ○ *the volcano's sulphurous fumes.*

■ **sulphuric acid** (*US* **sulfu-**) /sʌlˌfjʊərɪk ˈæsɪd/ *n* [U] a very strong oily colourless acid.

sultan /ˈsʌltən/ *n* a ruler in certain Muslim countries: *the Sultan of Brunei.*

▶ **sultanate** /ˈsʌltəneɪt/ *n* **1** the position or period of rule of a sultan. **2** a territory ruled by a sultan: *the Sultanate of Oman.*

sultana /sʌlˈtɑːnə; *US* -tænə/ *n* a small RAISIN without seeds, used in cakes, etc.

sultry /ˈsʌltri/ *adj* **1** (of the weather, air, etc) very hot and HUMID: *a sultry summer afternoon.* **2** (of a woman, her appearance, etc) attractive in a way that suggests a passionate nature: *a sultry smile/ voice.* ▶ **sultriness** *n* [U].

sum /sʌm/ *n* **1** [C] ~ (**of sth**) an amount of money: *He was fined the sum of £200.* ○ *Huge sums have been invested in this project.* See also LUMP SUM. **2(a)** [C] usu *sing*) ~ (**of sth**) the total obtained by adding together numbers, amounts or items: *The sum of 5 and 3 is 8.* **(b)** (also **sum total**) [sing] **the** ~ **of sth** all of sth, esp when it is considered as not being enough: *I'm afraid that's the sum of my achievements today.* **3** [C often *pl*] a simple problem(2) that involves calculating numbers: *do a sum in one's head* ○ *be good at sums.*

▶ **sum** *v* (-**mm**-) **PHRV** **sum (sth) 'up 1** to give a brief summary of sth: *Before we end the meeting, perhaps I can sum up (what we have agreed).* **2** (of a judge) to give a summary of the evidence or arguments in a legal case. **sum sb/sth 'up** to form or express an opinion of sb/sth: *He summed up the situation immediately* (ie realized at once what was happening). ○ *I can best sum up her contribution to the project by saying that without her it would never have succeeded.* **summing-'up** *n* (*pl* **summings-up**) a speech in which a judge sums up the evidence or arguments in a legal case.

■ **sum 'total** *n* = SUM 2b.

summarize, -ise /ˈsʌməraɪz/ *v* to be or make a summary of sth: [Vn] *a talk summarizing the results of her recent research* [also V].

summary /ˈsʌməri/ *n* a brief statement of the main points of sth: *a news summary* ○ *a two-page summary of a government report.* **IDM** **in 'summary** as a brief statement of the main point(s): *In summary, this was a disappointing performance.*

▶ **summary** *adj* [usu attrib] **1** giving the main points only; brief: *a summary account of a long debate* ○ *summary financial statements.* **2** (*sometimes derog*) done or given immediately, without attention to details or formal procedure: *summary justice/ dismissal/execution.* **summarily** /ˈsʌmərəli; *US* səˈmerəli/ *adv*: *be summarily dismissed/executed.*

summation /sʌˈmeɪʃn/ *n* (usu *sing*) (*fml*) **1** a collection(2) of different parts forming a complete account or impression of sb/sth: *The exhibition was a summation of his life's work.* **2** a short account of the main points of sth; a summary: *begin a summation of the evidence presented.* **3** a total of numbers added together.

summer /ˈsʌmə(r)/ *n* [U,C] the warmest season of the year, coming between spring and autumn. Summer lasts from June to August in the northern parts of the world: *go on holiday in the summer* ○ *in the summer of 1989* ○ *this/next/last summer* ○ *a cool/hot/ wet summer* ○ *a lovely summer's day* ○ *summer sunshine* ○ *the summer holidays/vacation* ○ *have exams in the summer term.* See also INDIAN SUMMER. **IDM** **one swallow does not make a summer** ⇨ SWALLOW².

▶ **summery** /ˈsʌməri/ *adj* typical of or suitable for the summer: *summery weather* ○ *a summery dress.*

■ **summer camp** *n* (*esp US*) a place where children go during the summer for camping, sport and other activities.

'summer-house *n* a small hut in a garden, etc for sitting in in fine weather.

,**summer 'pudding** *n* [C, U] (*Brit*) a sweet dish made with berries covered with pieces of bread soaked in their juice.

'**summer school** *n* a course of lectures, etc held in the summer holidays, esp at a university or, in the USA, high school.

,**summer 'stock** *n* [U] (*US*) the production of special plays and other entertainments in summer in holiday resorts, etc; such plays, etc.

'**summer time** *n* (*Brit*) the period between March and October when in certain countries clocks are put forward one hour, giving long light evenings. Compare DAYLIGHT SAVING, SUMMERTIME.

summertime /'sʌmətaɪm/ *n* [U] the season of summer: *It's beautiful here in (the) summertime.*

summit /'sʌmɪt/ *n* **1** the highest point; the top, esp of a mountain: *climb to the summit* ○ (*fig*) *the summit of her career/ambition.* ➪ picture at MOUNTAIN. **2** a meeting between the heads of two or more governments, esp of the world's most powerful countries: *attend a summit in Washington* ○ *a summit talk/ meeting/conference* ○ *the summit powers.*

summon /'sʌmən/ *v* **1(a)** ~ sb (to sth) (*rather fml*) to send a message telling sb to come; to call people together: [Vnpr] *The shareholders were summoned to a general meeting.* [Vn, Vn.*to* inf] *We had to summon the doctor (to look at her).* [also Vnp]. **(b)** (*fml*) to order sb to appear in a lawcourt; to SUMMONS sb: [Vn.*to* inf] *I was summoned to appear before the magistrates.* [also Vn]. **2** (*fml*) to order a group of people to attend a meeting, etc; to CONVENE(1) sth: [Vn] *summon a conference* ○ *The Queen has summoned Parliament.* **3** ~ sth (**up**) to make a particular quality come as if from deep inside oneself, in an attempt to do sth: [Vn, Vnp] *I had to summon (up) all my courage to face him.* ○ *I can't summon (up) much enthusiasm for the project.* **PHR V** ,**summon sth 'up** to make a feeling, an idea, a memory, etc come into the mind; to EVOKE sth: *a smell which summons up memories of my childhood.*

summons /'sʌmənz/ *n* (*pl* **summonses** /-zɪz/) **1** an order to do sth, esp to come to do sth: *obey a summons.* **2** an order to appear in a lawcourt: *issue a summons* ○ *serve a summons on sb.*

➤ **summons** *v* ~ sb (**for sth**) to order sb to attend a lawcourt: [Vnpr] *He was summonsed for speeding.* [Vn.*to* inf] *She was summonsed to appear before the magistrate.* [also Vn].

sumo /'suːməʊ/ (also ,**sumo 'wrestling**) *n* [U] a Japanese style of wrestling (WRESTLE). To win, one fighter must force the other out of a marked circle or make him touch the ground with his body: *a ,sumo 'wrestler.*

sump /sʌmp/ *n* **1** the place under an engine that holds the engine oil. **2** a hole or hollow area into which waste³(2) liquid drains.

sumptuous /'sʌmptʃuəs/ *adj* looking expensive and splendid: *sumptuous food/meals* ○ *a sumptuous velvet dress.* ➤ **sumptuously** *adv*: *sumptuously dressed.* **sumptuousness** *n* [U].

Sun *abbr* Sunday: *Sun 1 June.*

sun /sʌn/ *n* **1** (also **the sun**) [sing] the star that shines in the sky during the day and gives the earth heat and light: *the sun's rays* ○ *The sun rises in the east and sets in the west.* ○ *A pale, wintry sun shone through the clouds.* **2** (usu **the sun**) [sing, U] the light and heat from the sun; SUNSHINE: *sit in the sun* ○ *have the sun in one's eyes* ○ *draw the curtains to shut out/let in the sun* ○ *feel the heat/warmth of the sun.* **3** [C] any star, esp one with planets moving round it. **IDM** **catch the sun** ➪ CATCH¹. **make hay while the sun shines** ➪ HAY. **a place in the sun** ➪ PLACE¹. **under the 'sun** anywhere in the world: *the best food under the sun* ○ *every country under the*

sun. **with the 'sun** when the sun rises or sets: *get up/go to bed with the sun.*

➤ **sun** *v* (-**nn**-) ~ **oneself** to sit or lie in the light of the sun: [Vn] *He sat in a deck-chair 'sunning himself.*

sunless *adj* without sun; receiving little or no light from the sun: *a sunless day/room.*

sunny *adj* (-**ier**, -**iest**) **1** bright with light from the sun: *a sunny day/room/garden.* **2** cheerful; happy: *a sunny smile/disposition.* ,**sunny-side 'up** *adv* (*infml*) (of an egg) fried on one side only.

■ '**sun-baked** *adj* **(a)** made hard by the heat of the sun: *sun-baked mud/fields.* **(b)** receiving a lot of light from the sun; very sunny: *sun-baked beaches.*

'**sun-blind** *n* (*Brit*) a curtain or piece of material fixed above a door or window and pulled down or across as a protection from the sun.

'**sun-drenched** *adj* (*approv*) receiving great heat and light from the sun: *sun-drenched Mediterranean beaches.*

'**sun-dress** *n* a dress without sleeves and cut low at the neck, worn in hot weather.

'**sun-glasses** *n* [pl] spectacles with dark glass in them to protect the eyes from bright sunlight: *a pair of sun-glasses.* See also DARK GLASSES.

'**sun-god** *n* the sun worshipped as a god.

'**sun-hat** *n* a hat made to protect the head and neck from sunlight.

'**sun-lamp** *n* a lamp producing ULTRAVIOLET light, with effects like those of sunlight. It is used for making the skin go brown.

'**sun lounge** (*Brit*) (*US* '**sun parlor**) *n* a room with large windows, situated so that it receives a lot of sunlight.

➤ '**sun lounger** *n* a chair with a seat long enough to support one's legs, used for sitting or lying in the sun.

■ '**sun-roof** (*Brit* also ,**sunshine 'roof**) *n* a part of the roof of a car that can be opened to let in air and sunlight.

'**sun-up** *n* [U] (*infml esp US*) = SUNRISE.

'**sun-worshipper** *n* (*infml*) a person who is very fond of lying in the sun: *The beach was crowded with sun-worshippers.*

sunbathe /'sʌnbeɪð/ *v* [V] to sit or lie in the sun, esp in order to make one's skin go brown.

sunbeam /'sʌnbiːm/ *n* a ray of sunlight.

sunbed /'sʌnbed/ *n* **1** a light, usu folding, chair with a seat long enough to support one's legs, used for sitting or lying in the sun. **2** a bed for lying on under a sun-lamp (SUN).

sunblock /'sʌnblɒk/ *n* [U, C] a substance for putting on the skin to protect it from the sun: *a sunblock cream.*

sunburn /'sʌnbɜːn/ *n* [U] the condition of having painful red skin because of spending too long in strong sunlight. Compare SUNTAN.

➤ **sunburned** /'sʌnbɜːnd/ (also **sunburnt** /'sʌnbɜːnt/) *adj* **(a)** suffering from sunburn: *sunburnt shoulders.* **(b)** (of a person or the skin) attractively brown from being in the sun.

sundae /'sʌndeɪ, -di/ *n* a dish of ice-cream with crushed fruit, fruit juice, nuts, etc: *a hot fudge sundae.*

Sunday /'sʌndeɪ, -di/ *n* (*abbr* **Sun**) **1** [C, U] the first day of the week (coming before Monday), a day of rest and worship for Christians: *Palm/Whit/ Remembrance Sunday* ○ *Would you like to come to Sunday lunch?* **2** [C usu *pl*] a newspaper published on a Sunday. **IDM** **for/in a month of Sundays** ➪ MONTH. **one's ,Sunday 'best** (*infml joc*) one's best clothes: *I put on my Sunday best for the occasion.*

■ '**Sunday school** *n* [C, U] a class held on Sundays at which children learn about the Christian religion.

For further guidance on how *Sunday* is used, see the examples at *Monday*.

sunder /ˈsʌndə(r)/ v [Vn, Vnpr] ~ sth/sb (from sth/ sb) (fml or rhet) to separate sth/sb, esp by force or for ever.

sundial

sundial /ˈsʌndaɪəl/ n a device using shadow to show the time. A pointed piece of metal, etc throws a shadow that moves round the numbers on a flat surface as the sun moves across the sky. ⇨ picture.

sundown /ˈsʌndaʊn/ n [U] (esp US) the time when the sun goes down and night begins.
▶ **sundowner** n (Brit infml) a usu alcoholic drink taken in the evening.

sundry /ˈsʌndri/ adj [attrib] various: sundry costs/ expenses ○ sundry items of food/clothing. **IDM** ˌall and ˈsundry (infml) everyone; all types of people: She invited all and sundry to her party.
▶ **sundries** n [pl] various, esp small, items not separately named: My expenses claim includes £15 for sundries.

sunflower /ˈsʌnflaʊə(r)/ n a garden plant with large yellow flowers that can grow very tall.

sung pp of SING.

sunk pp of SINK¹.

sunken /ˈsʌŋkən/ adj **1** [attrib] that has gone to the bottom of the sea: a sunken ship ○ sunken treasure. **2** (of cheeks, etc) hollow as a result of hunger, illness, etc: He was thin and emaciated, with sunken eyes. **3** [attrib] at a lower level than the area around: a sunken pond at the bottom of the garden.

sunlight /ˈsʌnlaɪt/ n [U] the light of the sun: bright/ direct/strong sunlight ○ a shaft/ray/pool of sunlight.

sunlit /ˈsʌnlɪt/ adj (usu attrib) lighted by the sun: a sunlit garden/scene/room.

sunrise /ˈsʌnraɪz/ n [UC usu sing] the time of the rising of the sun; dawn: get up at sunrise.
■ ˈsunrise industry n a new and expanding industry.

sunscreen /ˈsʌnskriːn/ n [U, C] a substance for putting on the skin to protect it from the sun: make sure you use an effective sunscreen.

sunset /ˈsʌnset/ n **1** [U] the time when the sun goes down and night begins: finish work at sunset. **2** [C] the appearance of the sky when the sun sets: watch a beautiful sunset.

sunshade /ˈsʌnʃeɪd/ n an umbrella for protecting sb from hot sun. Compare PARASOL.

sunshine /ˈsʌnʃaɪn/ n [U] **1** the light and heat of the sun: sit in the warm sunshine ○ brilliant spring sunshine. **2** (infml) happiness: She brought sunshine into our lives. **3** (Brit infml) (used for addressing sb, in a friendly or sometimes rude way): Hello, sunshine! ○ What do you think you're doing, sunshine? **IDM** a ray of sunshine ⇨ RAY¹.
■ ˌsunshine ˈroof n (Brit) = SUN-ROOF.

sunspot /ˈsʌnspɒt/ n any of the dark patches that sometimes appear on the sun's surface, causing electrical disturbances and interfering with radio signals.

sunstroke /ˈsʌnstrəʊk/ n [U] an illness caused by being exposed to the heat and light of the sun too much.

suntan /ˈsʌntæn/ n a brown colour of the skin caused by exposing it to the sun: get a good suntan ○ suntan oil/lotion/cream. Compare SUNBURN. ▶ **suntanned** adj: suntanned legs.

suntrap /ˈsʌntræp/ n a place that is sheltered from the wind: This garden is a real suntrap.

sup /sʌp/ v (-pp-) (Brit dialect) to drink or eat sth in small amounts: [Vn] They sat supping their beer.
▶ **sup** n [sing] (Brit dialect) an amount of liquid drunk: take a long sup of cold beer.

super¹ /ˈsuːpə(r)/; Brit also ˈsjuː-/ adj (infml) excellent; splendid: a super meal/book/dress/person.

super² /ˈsuːpə(r)/; Brit also ˈsjuː-/ n (Brit infml) a superintendent (SUPERINTEND), esp in the police force: the chief super.

super- pref **1(a)** (with ns and vs) above; over: super-structure ○ superimpose. **(b)** (with adjs and advs) superior to; more than: superhuman ○ supernaturally. **2** (esp with adjs) extremely; very: super-intelligent ○ super-rich. **3** (esp with ns) larger, more efficient, etc than the standard type: superglue ○ super-absorbent. Compare OVER-.

superabundant /ˌsuːpərəˈbʌndənt; Brit also ˌsjuː-/ (fml) much more than enough: a superabundant harvest. ▶ **superabundance** /-əns/ n [U, sing] ~ (of sth): a superabundance of energy.

superannuated /ˌsuːpərˈænjueɪtɪd; Brit also ˌsjuː-/ adj [usu attrib] (infml esp joc) (of people or things) too old; no longer fit or suitable for work or use: superannuated pop stars.
▶ **superannuation** /ˌsuːpərˌænjuˈeɪʃn; Brit also ˌsjuː-/ n [U] money paid towards a PENSION¹ that one gets when one retires; such a pension: a superannuation fund/scheme.

superb /suːˈpɜːb; Brit also sjuː-/ adj excellent; splendid: a superb player/meal/view ○ The weather was absolutely superb. ▶ **superbly** adv: superbly written ○ She played superbly.

supercharged /ˈsuːpətʃɑːdʒd; Brit also ˈsjuː-/ adj **(a)** (of an engine) given more power by being supplied with air or fuel at above normal pressure: an 8-cylinder supercharged car. **(b)** (infml) made stronger, more powerful or more effective: a super-charged version of the original plan.
▶ **supercharger** n a device that makes an engine supercharged.

supercilious /ˌsuːpəˈsɪliəs; Brit also ˌsjuː-/ adj (derog) thinking or showing that one thinks one is better than other people: a supercilious person/ smile/attitude. ▶ **superciliously** adv. **supercili-ousness** n [U].

supercomputer /ˈsuːpəkəmpjuːtə(r); Brit also ˈsjuː-/ n a powerful computer capable of dealing with complex tasks in a very short time.

superconductivity /ˌsuːpəˌkɒndʌkˈtɪvəti; Brit also ˌsjuː-/ n [U] (physics) the property of certain metals, at very low temperatures, to allow electricity to flow freely with no resistance(5).
▶ **superconductor** /ˈsuːpəkəndʌktə(r); Brit also ˈsjuː-/ n a metal that possesses superconductivity.

superego /ˌsuːpərˈiːgəʊ; Brit also ˌsjuː-/ n (pl -os) (usu sing) (psychology) the part of the mind that makes one aware of right and wrong and acts as a conscience to control one's behaviour. Compare EGO, ID.

superficial /ˌsuːpəˈfɪʃl; Brit also ˌsjuː-/ adj **1** of or on the surface only: a superficial wound ○ Superficial scratches can be easily removed. **2** appearing to be true or real until looked at more carefully: a superficial similarity. **3(a)** not thorough, deep or complete: a superficial book/description ○ have only a superficial knowledge of history ○ study botany at a very superficial level. **(b)** (derog) having no depth of understanding or feeling: a superficial mind/person. ▶ **superficiality** /ˌsuːpəˌfɪʃiˈæləti; Brit also ˌsjuː-/ n [U]: become bored by the superficiality of the conversation. **superficially** /-ʃəli/ adv: only superficially alike.

superfine /ˈsuːpəfaɪn; Brit also ˈsjuː-/ adj (esp

---

commerce) of extremely fine quality: *superfine linen/ cloth.*

superfluity /ˌsuːpəˈfluːəti; *Brit also* ˌsjuː-/ *n* [U, sing] ~ **(of sth)** too much of sth: *a superfluity of helpers.*

superfluous /suːˈpɜːfluəs; *Brit also* sjuː-/ *adj* more than is needed or wanted: *make a superfluous remark* (ie one that is unnecessary and rude) ○ *I won't bother you with all the superfluous details.* ○ *I soon realized that I was superfluous, and left.* ▶ **superfluously** *adv.*

superglue /ˈsuːpəgluː:; *Brit also* ˈsjuː-/ *n* [U] a very strong glue used in small quantities for household repairs, etc.

supergrass /ˈsuːpəɡrɑːs; *Brit also* ˈsjuː-/ *n* (*Brit infml*) a criminal who informs the police about the activities of a large number of other criminals. Compare GRASS[1] 4.

superhuman /ˌsuːpəˈhjuːmən; *Brit also* ˌsjuː-/ *adj* having more than normal human power, size, knowledge, etc: *show almost superhuman courage/ intelligence/strength.*

superimpose /ˌsuːpərɪmˈpəʊz; *Brit also* ˌsjuː-/ *v* ~ **sth (on sth)** to put sth on top of sth else, esp so that what is underneath can still be seen, heard, etc: [Vnpr] *a diagram of the new road layout superimposed on a map of the city* [also Vn].

superintend /ˌsuːpərɪnˈtend; *Brit also* ˌsjuː-/ *v* (*fml*) to manage and control workers, their work, etc; to supervise sb/sth: [Vn] *superintend the building work.*

▶ **superintendence** /-əns/ *n* [U]: *work done under the personal superintendence of the area manager.*

superintendent /-ənt/ *n* **1** a person who superintends: *a park superintendent.* **2(a)** (*Brit*) (the title of) a police officer next in rank above chief IN-SPECTOR: *Superintendent James Dobson.* **(b)** (*US*) (the title of) the head of a police department.

superior /suːˈpɪəriə(r); *Brit also* sjuː-/ *adj* **1** ~ **(to sb/sth)** better in quality than sth/sb else: *superior accommodation/intelligence* ○ *a superior product/ performance* ○ *She is clearly superior to the other candidates.* **2** ~ **(to sb)** higher in rank, importance or position: *a superior court* ○ *one's superior officer* ○ *be promoted to a superior position.* **3** (*derog*) showing that one thinks one is better than others: *a superior smile/look/manner* ○ *There's no need to be so superior.* Compare INFERIOR.

▶ **superior** *n* **1** (often *pl*) a person of higher rank, status or position: *one's social superiors* ○ *I need to discuss it with my superiors.* **2** (in titles) the head of a religious community: *the Father/Mother Superior.*

superiority /suːˌpɪəriˈɒrəti; *US* /-ˈɔːr-; *Brit also* ˌsjuː-/ *n* [U] ~ **(in sth)**; ~ **(to/over sth/sb)** the state of being superior: *feelings of superiority* ○ *superiority in numbers* ○ *military/technological superiority.*

■ **superiˈority complex** *n* a strong and unreasonable belief that one is better or more important than other people. Compare INFERIORITY COMPLEX.

superlative /suːˈpɜːlətɪv; *Brit also* sjuː-/ *adj* **1** of the highest degree or quality: *a superlative achievement/ performance.* **2** (*grammar*) of adjectives or adverbs that express the highest or a very high degree, eg *best, worst, slowest, most difficult.* Compare COMPARATIVE 3.

▶ **superlative** *n* a superlative form of an adjective or adverb: *It's hard to find enough superlatives to describe him!*

superlatively *adv*: *superlatively cooked/managed.*

superman /ˈsuːpəmæn; *Brit also* ˈsjuː-/ *n* (*pl* **-men** /-men/) a man with greater strength, ability, intelligence, etc than normal humans: *a kind of intellectual superman.*

supermarket /ˈsuːpəmɑːkɪt; *Brit also* ˈsjuː-/ *n* a large shop selling food, drink, household goods, etc. People choose what they want from the shelves and

pay for it as they leave: *queue/pay at a supermarket checkout.*

supernatural /ˌsuːpəˈnætʃrəl; *Brit also* ˌsjuː-/ *adj* that cannot be explained by the laws of science: *supernatural forces* ○ *a person believed to have supernatural powers.*

▶ **the supernatural** *n* [sing] supernatural forces, events, etc: *belief in the supernatural.*

supernaturally /-ˈnætʃrəli/ *adv.*

supernova /ˌsuːpəˈnəʊvə; *Brit also* ˌsjuː-/ *n* (*pl* **-novae** /-viː/ or **-novas**) (*astronomy*) a star that suddenly becomes very much brighter as a result of an explosion. Compare NOVA.

supernumerary /ˌsuːpəˈnjuːmərəri; *US* /ˌsuːpə-ˈnuːməreri; *Brit also* ˌsjuː-/ *adj* (*fml*) in excess of the normal number; extra: *supernumerary nursing staff.*

superpower /ˈsuːpəpaʊə(r); *Brit also* ˈsjuː-/ *n* any of the most powerful nations in the world.

supersede /ˌsuːpəˈsiːd; *Brit also* ˌsjuː-/ *v* to take the place of sth/sb that was present or used before: [Vn] *Steam locomotives have largely been superseded by diesel or electric trains.*

supersonic /ˌsuːpəˈsɒnɪk; *Brit also* ˌsjuː-/ *adj* faster than the speed of sound: *a supersonic aircraft* ○ *supersonic flight/speeds.* Compare SUBSONIC.

superstar /ˈsuːpəstɑː(r); *Brit also* ˈsjuː-/ *n* (*infml*) a very famous actor, singer, sports player, etc: *Hollywood superstars.*

superstition /ˌsuːpəˈstɪʃn; *Brit also* ˌsjuː-/ *n* (*often derog*) [U, C] the belief that certain events cannot be explained by reason or science, or that they bring good or bad luck; fear of what is unknown or mysterious: *behaviour based on fear and superstition* ○ *There's an old superstition that killing a spider brings you bad luck.*

▶ **superstitious** /-ˈstɪʃəs/ *adj* (*often derog*) **1** of, based on or caused by superstition: *superstitious beliefs/ideas/practices.* **2** believing in superstitions: *I never do anything important on Friday the 13th — I'm superstitious (about it).* **superstitiously** *adv.*

superstore /ˈsuːpəstɔː(r); *Brit also* ˈsjuː-/ *n* a very large shop which sells food or a wide variety of a particular type of goods: *a computer superstore.*

superstructure /ˈsuːpəstrʌktʃə(r); *Brit also* ˈsjuː-/ *n* **1** a structure built on top of sth else, eg the part of a building above the ground or the upper parts of a ship. Compare SUBSTRUCTURE. **2** the complex ideas, beliefs or systems in a society that have developed from more simple ones: *Human institutions and ideas are a superstructure built on economic reality.* Compare INFRASTRUCTURE.

supertanker /ˈsuːpətæŋkə(r); *Brit also* ˈsjuː-/ *n* a very large ship for carrying oil, etc.

supervene /ˌsuːpəˈviːn; *Brit also* ˌsjuː-/ *v* (*fml*) to occur as an interruption or a change to an existing situation: [V] *She was working well until illness supervened.*

supervise /ˈsuːpəvaɪz; *Brit also* ˈsjuː-/ *v* to watch sb/sth or check what sb has done to make sure that work, etc is done properly: [Vn] *supervise the building work* [V.n ing] *She supervised the removal men loading the lorry.* [also V].

▶ **supervision** /ˌsuːpəˈvɪʒn; *Brit also* ˌsjuː-/ *n* [U]: *Young children should not be left to play without supervision.* ○ *This drug should only be taken **under the supervision of** (ie as supervised by) a doctor.*

supervisor *n* a person who supervises sb/sth: *Essays should be handed in to your supervisor by the end of next week.* **supervisory** /ˌsuːpəˈvaɪzəri, ˈsuːpəvaɪzəri; *Brit also* sjuː-/ *adj* supervising: *supervisory duties/staff.*

supine /ˈsuːpaɪn; *Brit also* ˈsjuː-/ *adj* (*fml*) **1** lying flat on one's back with one's face upwards: *lie supine* ○ *You can do this exercise in a supine position.* Compare PRONE, PROSTRATE 1. **2** (*derog*) not acting when one

should because one is morally weak or lazy. ▸
supinely adv.

supper /'sʌpə(r)/ n [U, C] the last meal of the day, usu lighter and less formal than dinner: watch TV after supper ○ 'supper-time ○ What's for supper? ○ We'll have an early supper before we go out. ⇨ note at DINNER.

supplant /sə'plɑːnt; US -'plænt/ v (fml) to take the place of sb/sth; to replace sb/sth: [Vn] Computers will never completely supplant books. [Vn-n] The man he supplanted as party leader is now his most bitter opponent.

supple /'sʌpl/ adj that bends or moves easily; not stiff; flexible: supple leather ○ have a supple body ○ do exercises to keep you supple ○ Moisturizing cream keeps your skin soft and supple. ▸ **supply** (also **supplely**) /'sʌpli/ adv. **suppleness** n [U].

supplement /'sʌplɪmənt/ n **1** ~ (to sth) a thing added to sth else to improve or complete it: dietary/ vitamin supplements ○ The freelance design work provides a useful supplement to my ordinary income. **2(a)** an extra section, often in the form of a magazine, added to and sold with a newspaper: I read it in the Sunday colour supplement. **(b)** ~ (to sth) a book or section of a book that gives further information, treats a special subject, etc: the supplement to the Oxford English Dictionary. **3** an amount of money paid for an extra service, item, etc: There is a £10 supplement for a single room with its own bathroom.
▸ **supplement** /'sʌplɪment/ v ~ sth (with sth) to add to or complete sth with sth else: [Vn] work in the evenings to supplement one's student grant [Vnprp] a diet supplemented with vitamin tablets.

supplementary /ˌsʌplɪ'mentri/ adj ~ (to sth) additional; extra: a supplementary payment/pension.
■ **,supplementary 'benefit** n [U] (formerly in Britain) money paid regularly from government funds to people with low incomes. Compare INCOME SUPPORT.

supplicant /'sʌplɪkənt/ (also **suppliant** /'sʌpliənt/) n (fml) a person asking in a HUMBLE(1) way for sth: kneel as a supplicant at the altar (ie praying to God for sth).

supplication /ˌsʌplɪ'keɪʃn/ n [U, C] (fml) a very HUMBLE(1) request or prayer: kneel in supplication ○ He was deaf to my supplications.

supply /sə'plaɪ/ v (pt, pp **supplied**) **1** ~ sth (to sb); ~ sb (with sth) to give sb sth that is needed or useful; to provide sb with sth: [Vnprp] foreign governments supplying arms to the rebels ○ supply sb with information/food/fuel ○ His parents keep him well supplied with cash. **2** to provide enough of sth for a need; to fulfil sth: [Vn] foods supplying our daily vitamin requirements.
▸ **supply** n **1** [U] the action of supplying sth: a contract for the supply of various goods and services ○ a good source of supply ○ the supply of blood to the heart ○ You promised us fuel, but can you guarantee its supply? **2** [C often pl] a thing that is supplied; a stock or store of things provided or available: the gas-/water-supply ○ cut off the oxygen supply to the brain ○ arms/food/fuel supplies ○ adequate supplies of raw materials ○ Planes dropped food and medical supplies to the stranded villagers. **IDM** in short supply ⇨ SHORT¹.
supplier /sə'plaɪə(r)/ n a person or firm supplying goods, etc.
■ **sup,ply and de'mand** n [U] (economics) the amount of goods, etc available and the amount wanted by people. The relationship between these is often regarded as controlling economic activity and prices. See also THE MONEY SUPPLY.
sup'ply-side adj [attrib] (finance) of the policy of reducing taxes in order to stimulate economic growth: supply-side economics.

sup'ply teacher n a teacher employed to do the work of any other teacher who is absent through illness, etc.

support /sə'pɔːt/ v **1(a)** ~ sb/sth (in sth) to help sb/sth by one's approval or sympathy or by giving money: [Vn] support a cause/political party/reform ○ donate money to support a charity ○ The directors were trying to get rid of her, but her staff all supported her. ○ The American public stopped supporting the war in Vietnam. [Vnpr] Will you support me in my campaign for election? **(b)** to be a regular customer of or visitor to sth; to be a fan¹ of a team, etc: [Vn] Support your local theatre! ○ Which football team do you support? **2** to bear the weight of sth/sb/ oneself; to hold sth/sb/oneself in position: [Vn] a beam supporting a roof ○ The chair wasn't strong enough to support his weight. ○ He took hold of her arm to support her as she stumbled. ○ She was supporting herself on a pair of crutches. **3** to help to show that a theory, claim, etc is true; to confirm sth: [Vn] a theory that is not supported by the facts ○ What evidence do you have to support your accusation? **4** to provide sb/oneself with the money, etc needed to pay for food, accommodation, etc: [Vn] Mark has two children to support from his first marriage. ○ She doesn't earn enough to support herself. **5** to provide enough food and water to keep sb/sth alive: [Vn] It's amazing that such a barren landscape can support any form of life.
▸ **support** n **1** [U] ~ (for sth) help or encouragement given to sb/sth, esp in a difficult situation: a proposal that received little public support ○ He has the full support of his colleagues. ○ The company is providing financial support for this venture. ○ Can I rely on your support (ie Will you vote for me) in the election? ○ She has no visible means of support (ie no work, income, etc). ○ The theatre had to close owing to lack of support. See also MORAL SUPPORT. **2(a)** [C] a thing that bears the weight of sth or prevents it from falling: supports holding up a collapsing wall. **(b)** [U] the action of bearing the weight of sb/sth or of preventing them/it from falling: She held on to his arm for support. **3** [C] a person who gives help, sympathy, etc: When my father died, Jim was a great support. **IDM** in sup'port ready to give support: The police are patrolling the area, with the army in support. in support of sb/sth supporting sb/sth; in favour of sb/sth: speak in support of a ban on arms supplies.
supporter n a person who supports a political party, team, etc: a 'football supporter ○ a loyal supporter of the Prime Minister.
supporting adj [attrib] **1** (in the theatre and cinema) of secondary importance: a supporting actress/ cast/role. **2** helping to show that a theory, claim, etc is true: supporting evidence.
supportive /sə'pɔːtɪv/ adj (approv) giving help, encouragement or sympathy: She was very supportive during my father's illness.

suppose /sə'pəʊz/ v **1** to think, believe or assume that sth is true or probable: [V.that] What do you suppose he wanted? ○ What makes you suppose (that) I'm against it? ○ I don't suppose for a minute (that) he'll agree (ie I'm sure that he won't). ○ She'll be there today, I suppose. ○ I suppose you want to borrow money from me again (ie showing annoyance)? ○ We'll have to walk home, I suppose (ie showing reluctance). ○ I don't suppose you could help me (ie Please help me) with my homework. ○ It was generally supposed that she would be re-elected. [Vadv] 'Will he come?' 'Yes, I suppose so.' [Vn-adj, V.n to inf] (fml) Everyone supposes him (to be) poor, but he is really quite wealthy. [V.n to inf] (fml) It was widely supposed to have been lost during the war. **2** to pretend that sth is true; to take sth as a fact: [Vn] a theory which supposes the existence of other worlds *besides our own* [V.*that*] *Suppose (that) the news is true: what then?* ○ *Suppose you had a million pounds — how would you spend it?* [also V.n *to* inf]. **3** (used in the imperative, to make a suggestion) [V.*that*] *Suppose we don't tell anybody else about this.* **IDM** be **supposed to do/be sth 1** to be expected or required to do/be sth, eg because of a rule, law or custom: *Am I supposed to* (ie Should I) *clean all the rooms or just this one?* ○ *You're supposed to pay the bill by Friday.* ○ *They were supposed to be here an hour ago.* **2** (used in negative sentences) to be allowed to do/be sth: *You're not supposed to walk on the grass.* **3** (*infml*) to be generally thought or believed to do/be sth: *It's supposed to be a marvellous film.* ○ *She's supposed to have had hundreds of lovers.* ► **supposed** /sə'pəʊzd/ *adj* [attrib] (used to indicate that a statement or way of describing sb/sth is not true or correct): *His supposed confession was forged by the police.* ○ *The supposed beggar was really a police officer in disguise.* **supposedly** /sə'pəʊzɪdli/ *adv* according to what is supposed but not known for certain: *This picture is supposedly worth more than a million dollars.*

supposing (also **supposing that**) *conj* if we assume the fact or the possibility that; if: *Supposing (that) you are wrong, what will you do then?*

supposition /ˌsʌpə'zɪʃn/ *n* **1** [C] ~ (**that** ...) an idea that is thought to be true but has not been proved: *I am proceeding on the supposition that...* (ie assuming it to be true that...). **2** [U] the action of supposing that sth is true: *a newspaper article based entirely on supposition* (ie only on what the writer supposes to be true, not on fact).

suppository /sə'pɒzətri; *US* -tɔːri/ *n* a small piece of solid medicine placed in the RECTUM or VAGINA and left to dissolve.

suppress /sə'pres/ *v* **1** to put an end to sth, esp by force: [Vn] *suppress an uprising/a revolt* ○ *a drug that suppresses muscle spasms.* **2(a)** (*usu derog*) to prevent sth from being known or seen: [Vn] *try to suppress the truth about sth* ○ *suppress a newspaper* (ie prevent it from being published) ○ *The police have been accused of suppressing evidence relating to the trial.* **(b)** to prevent one's feelings from being expressed: [Vn] *suppress one's anger/amusement* ○ *He was unable to suppress a wry smile.* ► **suppressant** /sə'presnt/ *n* a thing that suppresses sth: *The chemical is believed to be an appetite suppressant.*

suppression /sə'preʃn/ *n* [U] the action of suppressing sth: *the suppression of a revolt/the truth* ○ *the suppression of one's anger.*

suppressor *n* **1** a thing or person that suppresses sb/sth: *the body's pain suppressors* ○ *the suppressor of the facts.* **2** a device fitted to an electrical apparatus to stop it causing poor quality sound or pictures on radio or television sets.

suppurate /'sʌpjʊəreɪt/ *v* (*fml*) (of a cut or wound) to have a thick yellow liquid (*pus*) forming inside it because of infection: [V] *a suppurating sore.* ► **suppuration** /ˌsʌpjʊ'reɪʃn/ *n* [U].

supra- /'suːprə/ *pref* above; beyond: *supranational* (ie going beyond national boundaries).

supreme /suː'priːm; *Brit also* sjuː-/ *adj* [usu attrib] **1** highest in rank or position: *the supreme ruler of a vast empire* ○ *the Supreme Commander of NATO* ○ *After a year without defeat, the team now reigns supreme as the finest in the country.* **2** most important; very great or greatest: *a supreme achievement* ○ *make the supreme sacrifice* (eg die for what one believes in) ○ *a supreme test of his commitment.* ► **supremacy** /suː'preməsi; *Brit also* sjuː-/ *n* [U] ~ (**over sb/sth**) the state of being supreme; a position of the highest power, authority or status: *achieve military supremacy over neighbouring countries* ○ *challenging Japan's supremacy in the field of*

electronics ○ *the dangerous notion of white supremacy* (ie that white races are better than others and should control them). **supremacist** /suː'preməsɪst; *Brit also* sjuː-/ *n*: *white supremacists.*

supremely /suː'priːmli; *Brit also* sjuː-/ *adv* in a supreme way; extremely: *supremely happy/confident.*

■ the ˌSupreme ˈBeing *n* [sing] (*fml*) God.

the Suˌpreme ˈCourt *n* [sing] the highest court in a state of the USA or in the whole of the USA.

supremo /suː'priːməʊ; *Brit also* sjuː-/ *n* (*pl* **-os**) a high-ranking manager or director: *an interview with fashion supremo Jean-Paul Gaultier.*

Supt *abbr* Superintendent (esp in the police force): *Supt (George) Hill.*

surcharge /'sɜːtʃɑːdʒ/ *n* ~ (**on sth**) an extra amount of money that one must pay in addition to the usual charge: *a 10% surcharge on imported goods.* ► **surcharge** *v* ~ **sb** (**on sth**) to demand a surcharge from sb: [Vnn] *They've surcharged us 10% on the price of the flight because of the rise in fuel prices.* [also Vn, Vnpr].

sure /ʃʊə(r); *Brit also* ʃɔː(r)/ *adj* (**-r, -st**) **1** [pred] ~ (**of/about sth**); ~ **that** ... ; ~ **what, etc** ... not doubting or seeming to doubt what one believes, knows, etc; confident that one is right: *I think he's coming, but I'm not quite sure.* ○ *I'm not sure when I saw her last.* ○ *Are you sure of your facts?* ○ *If you're not sure how to do it, ask me.* ○ *Can we be sure that she's telling the truth?* ○ *I think the answer's right but I'm not absolutely sure of it.* ○ *She felt sure that she had done the right thing.* Compare UNSURE 2. **2** [pred] ~ **of sth/doing sth** certain to receive, win, etc sth: *You're always sure of a warm welcome there.* ○ *England must win this game to be sure of qualifying for the World Cup.* **3** ~ **to do sth** definitely going to do sth; certain to do sth: *It's sure to rain.* ○ *You're sure to fail if you do it that way.* **4** true beyond doubt: *in the sure and certain knowledge that one is right* ○ *One thing is sure: I'm never lending money to Bob again.* ⇨ note at CERTAIN. **5** [usu attrib] able to be trusted or relied on: *a sure sign of economic recovery* ○ *There's only one sure way to do it.* ○ *She said goodbye to her son in the sure knowledge that he would be well looked after.* **6** [usu attrib] not hesitating or uncertain; steady and confident: *her sure touch at the keyboard.* **IDM** be **sure to do sth** don't fail to do sth: *Be sure to write and tell me all your news.* **for sure** (*infml*) without doubt: *I think he lives there but I couldn't say for sure.* ○ *It won't be easy, that's for sure.* ○ (*esp US*) '*Will you be there?*' '*For sure.*' **make ˈsure (of sth / that ...) 1** to discover whether sth is definitely so: *I think the door's locked, but I'd better go and make sure (it is).* **2** to do sth in order to be sure that sth else happens: *Our staff will do their best to make sure (that) you enjoy your visit.* ˈsure **of oneself** (*sometimes derog*) very confident of one's own abilities, ideas, etc: *He seems very sure of himself.* ˌsure ˈthing (*infml esp US*) yes; of course: '*Will you have one too?*' '*Sure thing!*' **to be ˈsure** (*fml*) I cannot deny (that); I admit: *He is clever, to be sure, but not very hard-working.*

► **sure** *adv* (*infml esp US*) certainly: *Do you want a game of tennis?*' '*Sure!*' ○ *It sure was cold!* **IDM** (**as**) **sure as eggs is ˈeggs**; (**as**) **sure as ˈfate**; (**as**) **sure as I'm standing ˈhere** (*infml*) very certainly: *He's dead, as sure as eggs is eggs.* (**as**) **sure as ˈhell** (*US infml*) very certainly: *I sure as hell wish I'd known that before.* ˌsure eˈnough (used to introduce a statement that confirms sth previously predicted, etc): *I said it would rain, and sure enough it did.*

sureness *n* [U] the quality of being sure: *a picture that shows the artist's sureness of touch* ○ *her sureness that she had done the right thing.*

■ **'sure-fire** adj [attrib] certain to be successful: *a ˌsure-fire recipe for sucˈcess* ○ *This is a sure-fire way to get publicity.*

ˌsure-**'footed** adj not likely to fall when walking or climbing. **sure-footedness** n [U].

surely /'ʃʊəli; *Brit also* 'ʃɔːli/ *adv* **1** (used to show that the speaker is certain or almost certain of what he or she is saying, or to express surprise at sth): *This is surely her best play.* ○ *He must surely have known you were unhappy.* ○ *Surely you're not going to eat that!* ○ *But they won't refuse, surely?* ○ *She has refused to help? Surely not!* ○ *'That's his wife.' 'His sister, surely?'* **2** (*esp fml*) without doubt; certainly: *This will surely cause problems.* ○ *If they don't receive food soon, they will surely die.* **3** (*infml esp US*) of course; yes: *'Can I borrow your car?' 'Surely.'* **IDM** **slowly but surely** ⇨ SLOWLY.

surety /'ʃʊərəti; *Brit also* 'ʃɔːr-/ *n* [C,U] **1** money given to support a promise that sb will pay their debts, perform a duty, etc; a guarantee: *offer £100 as (a) surety.* **2** a person who makes herself or himself responsible for the payment of debts, etc by sb else: *act as/stand surety for sb.* Compare SECURITY 3, BAIL¹.

crest   **surfing**   surfer   wave   trough   surfboard

surf /sɜːf/ *n* [U] the white part of waves as they fall on the shore or on rocks: *splashing about in the surf.* ▶ **surf** *v* [V] (also **go surfing**) to stand or lie on a SURFBOARD and ride towards the shore on a wave, as a sport. **surfer** *n.* See also WINDSURFER. **surfing** *n.* [U] the sport of riding on waves using a SURFBOARD. ⇨ picture.

surface /'sɜːfɪs/ *n* **1** [C] (**a**) the outside part of sth: *the earth's surface* ○ *the surface of a sphere.* (**b**) any of the sides of an object: *the polished surfaces of a diamond.* (**c**) the top or outside layer of sth: *the rough surface of the wall* ○ *an uneven road surface* ○ *clean/wipe all the kitchen surfaces* (ie the tops and sides of cupboards, etc) ○ *a work surface* (ie the top of a desk, table, etc) ○ *a surface wound* (ie not a deep one) ○ *surface transport* (ie road and rail travel) ○ *a surface worker* (ie sb who works above ground at a mine). **2** [C usu *sing*] the top of a body of liquid, eg the sea: *the smooth surface of the lake* ○ *bubbles rising to the surface (of a pool)* ○ *oil floating on the surface of the water* ○ *fish swimming just below the surface.* **3** [sing] the outward appearance of a person or thing, contrasted with feelings, qualities, etc which may not be seen at first: *She looks relaxed, but there are lots of tensions below the surface.* ○ *Look beyond the surface before you judge someone.* ○ *Doubts began to rise to the surface.* **IDM** **on the 'surface** when not observed, thought about, etc deeply or thoroughly: *On the surface, it seems like a good idea.* ○ *His charm is only on the surface.* **scratch the surface** ⇨ SCRATCH¹. ▶ **surface** *v* **1** ~ sth (with sth) to put a surface(1c) on sth: [Vnpr] *surfacing the area with concrete* [Vn] *The surfaced road ends at the farm.* **2** to come up to the surface of water: [V] *The ducks dived and surfaced again several metres away.* **3**(**a**) to appear again after a period of remaining hidden away from others, etc: [V] *Doubts/Fears/Problems began to surface.* ○ *I lost track of her for several years, but she* suddenly surfaced again in London. ○ *No further information has surfaced as yet.* (**b**) (*infml*) to wake from sleep or being unconscious: [V] *He finally surfaced at midday.*

■ **'surface area** *n* (usu *sing*) the size of the outside part of sth: *a leaf with a large surface area.*

'surface mail *n* [U] letters, etc carried by road, rail or sea, not by air.

ˌsurface **'tension** *n* [U] (*techn*) the property of liquids by which they form a layer at their surface and the tendency of this to make its area as small as possible.

ˌsurface-to-'air *adj* [attrib] (esp of missiles) fired from the ground or from ships and aimed at aircraft.

surfboard /'sɜːfbɔːd/ *n* a long narrow board used for surfing. ⇨ picture at SURFING.

surfeit /'sɜːfɪt/ *n* (usu *sing*) ~ (of sth) too much of sth, esp of food and drink: *Indigestion brought on by a surfeit of rich food.* ○ *a surfeit of programmes containing violence on television.* ▶ **surfeit** *v* ~ sb/oneself (with sth) (*fml*) (esp passive) to provide sb/oneself with too much of sth, esp food: [Vnpr] *be surfeited with pleasure* [also Vn].

surge /sɜːdʒ/ *v* **1** to move forward in or like waves: [V] *a surging river* ○ *surging crowds* [Vpr] *Floods surged along the valley.* [Vpr, Vadv] *Football fans surged (forward) into the stadium.* [also Vn]. **2** ~ (up) to increase suddenly and intensely: [V] *surging property prices* [Vpr, Vp] *Anger surged (up) inside him.* ▶ **surge** *n* ~ (of/in sth) **1** a forward or upward movement: *a tidal surge.* **2** a sudden rush or increase: *feel a surge of anger/pity/energy* ○ *a surge in the number of people out of work.*

surgeon /'sɜːdʒən/ *n* a doctor who performs medical operations: *a heart surgeon.* Compare PHYSICIAN. ■ ˌsurgeon **'general** *n* (*pl* surgeons general) (*US*) the head of a public health service or of a medical service in the armed forces.

surgery /'sɜːdʒəri/ *n* **1** [U] treatment of injuries or diseases that involves cutting or removing parts of the body: *need major/minor surgery* ○ *undergo abdominal/cosmetic surgery.* See also OPEN-HEART SURGERY, PLASTIC SURGERY. **2** (*Brit*) (**a**) [C] a place where a doctor, DENTIST, etc sees patients who come for advice or treatment: *a dental surgery.* (**b**) [C,U] the time during which a doctor, etc is available to see patients at the surgery: *morning/evening surgery* ○ *'surgery hours.* **3** [C] (*Brit*) a time when people can meet their Member of Parliament and ask her or him questions.

surgical /'sɜːdʒɪkl/ *adj* [attrib] of, by or for SURGERY(1): *surgical instruments/treatment/skills* ○ *a surgical ward* (ie for patients having operations). ▶ **surgically** /-kli/ *adv*: *The tumour was surgically removed.* ■ ˌsurgical **'spirit** *n* [U] (*Brit*) a clear liquid, consisting mainly of alcohol, used for cleaning wounds, etc.

surly /'sɜːli/ *adj* (-ier, -iest) bad-tempered and rude: *a surly child/face/manner.* ▶ **surliness** *n* [U].

surmise /sə'maɪz/ *v* (*fml*) to suppose sth without having evidence that makes it certain; to guess: [V.*that*] *We can only surmise (that) he must have had an accident.* [also V, Vn, V.speech]. ▶ **surmise** /'sɜːmaɪz/ *n* [U,C usu *sing*] (*fml*) a guess; guessing: *This is pure surmise on my part.*

surmount /sə'maʊnt/ *v* **1** to deal with a difficulty, etc; to overcome sth: [Vn] *She has had to surmount immense physical disabilities.* **2** to be or be placed on top of sth tall; to TOP² sth: [Vn] *The spire is surmounted by a weather-vane.* ▶ **surmountable** *adj* (of difficulties, etc) that can be overcome: *We still have some problems, but* *they're easily surmountable.* Compare INSURMOUNT-ABLE.

surname /ˈsɜːneɪm/ *n* a name shared by all the members of a family: *Smith is a common English surname.* Compare LAST NAME. ⇨ note at NAME[1].

surpass /səˈpɑːs; *US* -ˈpæs/ *v* ~ **sb/sth** (**in sth**) (*fml*) to do or be better than sb/sth: [Vn] *He set standards that are unlikely to be surpassed.* ◦ *The beauty of the scenery surpassed all my expectations.* [Vnpr] *She easily surpassed the other candidates in skill and motivation.*

▶ **surpassing** *adj* [attrib] (*dated or fml*) of high quality or degree; exceptional: *scenery of surpassing beauty.*

surplice /ˈsɜːplɪs/ *n* a loose, usu white, outer garment with wide sleeves worn by priests and singers in the CHOIR during religious services.

surplus /ˈsɜːpləs/ *n* [C, U] an amount that remains after one has used all one needs; an amount by which money received is greater than money spent: *food surpluses* ◦ *a trade surplus of £400 million* ◦ *Periods of great surplus were followed by periods of shortage.* ◦ *The balance of payments was in surplus last year* (ie The value of exports was greater than the value of imports). Compare DEFICIT.

▶ **surplus** *adj* ~ (**to sth**) more than is needed or used: *surplus labour/staff* (ie workers for whom there are no jobs) ◦ *surplus grain sold for export* ◦ *These items are surplus to requirements.*

surprise /səˈpraɪz/ *n* (**a**) [U] a feeling caused by sth happening suddenly or unexpectedly: *Their defeat caused little surprise* (ie was expected). ◦ *To my surprise, the plan succeeded.* ◦ *They lost, much to our surprise.* ◦ *Imagine our surprise on seeing her there.* ◦ *She looked up in surprise when I shouted.* ◦ *He expressed surprise that no one had offered to help.* (**b**) [C] an event or a thing that causes this feeling: *What a nice surprise!* ◦ *There were few surprises in the Chancellor's budget speech.* ◦ *Her letter came as a complete surprise (to me).* ◦ *He likes springing surprises on people.* ◦ *a surprise visit/attack/party.* **IDM** **sur,prise, sur'prise** (*infml often ironic*) (used when giving a surprise): *Surprise, surprise! I've bought you a present!* ◦ *One of the candidates was the manager's niece, and surprise, surprise,* (ie as one would expect) *she got the job.* **take sb/sth by sur'prise** to attack, capture, etc sb/sth unexpectedly or without warning: *The town was well defended so there was little chance of taking it by surprise.* **take sb by sur'prise** to happen unexpectedly, so as to shock sb slightly: *Her sudden resignation took us all by surprise.*

▶ **surprise** *v* **1** to make sb feel surprise: [Vn] *She's over 80? You surprise me!* ◦ *She was rather surprised by his rude behaviour.* ◦ *It wouldn't surprise me/I wouldn't be surprised if they got married soon.* [Vn.*to inf*] *Would it surprise you to know that I'm thinking of leaving?* **2** to attack, discover, etc sb suddenly and unexpectedly: [Vn] *surprise the opposition* (ie attack them when they are not prepared) [Vn.*ing*] *We came home early and surprised a burglar trying to break in.*

surprised *adj* ~ (**at/by sth/sb**) experiencing or showing a feeling of surprise: *wearing a surprised look on his face* ◦ *We were very surprised at the news.* ◦ *I'm surprised at you, behaving like that in front of the children.* ◦ *She was very surprised to see him there.* ◦ *I'm surprised (that) he didn't come.* ◦ *He was rather surprised by her reply.* ◦ *It's nothing to be surprised about.*

surprising *adj* causing surprise: *a surprising result* ◦ *It's (hardly) surprising (that) they lost.* ◦ *A surprising number of people came.* **surprisingly** *adv*: *Surprisingly, no one came.* ◦ *She looked surprisingly well.*

surreal /səˈriːəl/ *adj* very strange; not real, as in a dream, with ideas, images, etc appearing distorted or mixed together in an odd way: *His poems have a surreal quality.* ◦ *The play seems frighteningly surreal, yet it is based on truth.*

surrealism /səˈriːəlɪzəm/ *n* [U] a 20th-century movement in art and literature. Surrealism tries to express what is hidden in the mind by showing objects and events as seen in dreams, etc.

▶ **surrealist** /-lɪst/ *adj* [attrib] influenced by or showing surrealism: *a surrealist painter/painting.* — *n*: *Salvador Dali was a surrealist.*

surrealistic /sə,rɪəˈlɪstɪk/ *adj* **1** showing surrealism: *a surrealistic comedy.* **2** SURREAL: *a surrealistic dream.*

surrender /səˈrendə(r)/ *v* **1** ~ (**oneself**) (**to sb**) to stop resisting an enemy, etc; to yield: [V] *We shall never surrender.* [Vpr, Vnpr] *The hijackers finally surrendered (themselves) to the police.* [also Vn]. **2** ~ **sth/sb** (**to sb**) (*fml*) to give up possession of sth/sb when forced by others or by necessity; to hand sth/sb over (HAND[2]): [Vn] *surrender power/control* ◦ *He agreed to surrender all claims to the property.* [Vnpr] *They surrendered their guns to the police.* ◦ *Surrender an insurance policy in return for immediate payment.* **PHR V** **sur'render to sth** (*fml or rhet*) to allow a habit, an emotion, an influence, etc to control what one does: *He finally surrendered to his craving for drugs.*

▶ **surrender** *n* [U, C] ~ (**to sth/sb**) the action or an instance of surrendering: *sign a treaty of surrender* ◦ *insist on unconditional surrender* ◦ *She accused the government of a cowardly surrender to big-business interests.* ◦ *the surrender value of shares/an insurance policy.*

surreptitious /,sʌrəpˈtɪʃəs/ *adj* done or acting secretly or in a way that one does not want others to notice: *a surreptitious glance* ◦ *He started making surreptitious visits to the pub on his way home.* ▶ **surreptitiously** *adv*: *He glanced surreptitiously at his watch.*

surrogate /ˈsʌrəgət/ *n* ~ (**for sb/sth**) (*fml*) a person or thing that acts for or is used instead of another; a substitute: *She looked upon them as a surrogate family when her real parents were killed.* ◦ *a surrogate mother* (ie a woman who has a baby on behalf of another who is unable to have babies herself).

▶ **surrogacy** /ˈsʌrəgəsi/ *n* [U] the practice of acting or being used as a surrogate, esp as a surrogate mother.

surround /səˈraʊnd/ *v* (**a**) ~ **sb/sth** (**with sb/sth**) to move into position all round sb/sth, esp so as to prevent escape; to do this using sb/sth: [Vn] *Fire-fighters have surrounded the blaze.* [Vnpr] *They have surrounded the area with police.* ◦ (*fig*) *He likes to surround himself with* (ie live among) *beautiful things.* (**b**) ~ **sth/sb** (**with sth**) to be all round sth/sb: [Vn] *Tall trees surround the lake.* ◦ *The house is surrounded by beautiful countryside.* ◦ (*fig*) *Uncertainty still surrounds the appointment of a new director.* [Vnpr] *As a child I was surrounded with love and kindness.*

▶ **surround** *n* a usu ornamental border around an object: *a fireplace with a tiled surround.*

surrounding *adj* [attrib] that is around and nearby: *From the church tower you can get a splendid view of the village and the surrounding countryside.* **surroundings** *n* [pl] all the objects, conditions, etc that are around and may affect sb/sth; the environment: *live in pleasant surroundings* ◦ *In game parks one can watch wild animals in their natural surroundings.*

surtax /ˈsɜːtæks/ *n* [U] tax charged at a higher rate than the normal on income above a certain level.

surveillance /sɜːˈveɪləns/ *n* [U] careful watch kept on sb suspected of doing wrong: *The police are keeping the suspects under constant surveillance.* ◦ *a surveillance operation.*

survey /sə'veɪ/ v **1** to look carefully at all of sth/sb, esp from a distance: [Vn] *surveying the crowds from a balcony* ∘ *survey the countryside from the top of a hill* ∘ *Her blue eyes surveyed him coolly.* **2** to study and describe the general condition of sth: [Vn] *a speech in which she surveyed the whole state of the economy* ∘ *In this chapter, the author surveys recent developments in linguistics.* **3** to examine and record the area and features of a piece of land by measuring and calculating: [Vn] *survey a plot of land for building.* **4** (*Brit*) to examine a building, etc to make sure that its structure is in good condition: [Vn] *have a house surveyed before deciding to buy it.* **5** to investigate the behaviour, opinions, etc of a group of people, usu by questioning them: [Vn] *Of the 500 householders surveyed, 40% had dishwashers.*
▶ **survey** /'sɜːveɪ/ n **1** a general view, examination or description: *a comprehensive survey of modern music* ∘ *A quick survey of the street showed that no one was about.* **2** a map or plan made by surveying (SURVEY 3) an area: *an aerial survey* (ie made by taking photographs from an aircraft). **3** (*Brit*) an examination of the condition of a house, etc. **4** an investigation of the behaviour, opinions, etc of a group of people: *a public o'pinion survey* ∘ *Surveys show that 75% of people approve of the new law.* See also the ORDNANCE SURVEY.
surveyor /sə'veɪə(r)/ n **1** a person whose job is to survey(3,4) buildings, land, etc: *a chartered surveyor.* **2** (*Brit*) an official appointed to check the accuracy, quality, etc of sth: *surveyor of public works.* See also QUANTITY SURVEYOR.

survival /sə'vaɪvl/ n **1** [U] the state of continuing to live or exist, often in spite of difficulty or danger: *the miraculous survival of some people in the air crash* ∘ **the survival of the fittest** (ie the continuing existence of those animals and plants which are best adapted to their surroundings, etc) ∘ *fight for one's political survival* ∘ *sur'vival skills.* **2** [C] ~ (**from sth**) a person, thing or practice that has survived from an earlier time: *The ceremony is a survival from pre-Christian times.*

survive /sə'vaɪv/ v ~ (**from sth**); ~ (**on sth**) to continue to live or exist: [V] *the last surviving member of the family* ∘ *Of the six people in the plane when it crashed, only one survived.* [Vpr] *Many strange customs have survived from earlier times.* ∘ *I can't survive on £40 a week* (ie It is not enough for my basic needs). [V] (*fig*) *Life is hard at the moment, but we're surviving* (ie managing to overcome the difficulties). **2** to continue to live or exist in spite of nearly being killed or destroyed by sth: [Vn] *survive an earthquake/shipwreck* ∘ *Few buildings survived the bombing raids intact.* ∘ *The plants may not survive the frost.* **3** to remain alive after sb has died: [Vn] *The old lady has survived all her children.*
▶ **survivor** n a person who has survived: *send help to the survivors of the earthquake* ∘ *survivors from the original team* (ie members who remain in it while others have been replaced).

sus = SUSS.

susceptible /sə'septəbl/ adj **1** ~ **to sth** [pred] easily influenced or harmed by sth: *highly susceptible to flattery* ∘ *Children are more susceptible to some diseases than adults.* **2** easily influenced by feelings or emotions; sensitive: *a young man with a susceptible nature.* **3** [pred] ~ **of sth** (*fml*) allowing sth; capable of sth: *The facts are susceptible of various interpretations.*
▶ **susceptibility** /sə,septə'bɪləti/ n **1** [U] ~ (**to sth**) the state of being susceptible: *take advantage of her susceptibility* ∘ *susceptibility to disease.* **2** **susceptibilities** [pl] a person's feelings, considered as being easily hurt: *offend sb's susceptibilities.*

sushi /'suːʃi/ n [U] a Japanese dish consisting of small cakes of cold rice, esp with pieces of raw fish.

suspect /sə'spekt/ v **1** (not in continuous tenses) to have an idea of the existence, presence or truth of sth, without certain proof; to believe: [Vn] *He suspected an ambush.* [V.that] *I strongly suspect that they're trying to get rid of me.* ∘ *Most people don't, I suspect, realize this.* [also V.n to inf]. **2** to feel doubt about sth; to MISTRUST(2) sth: [Vn] *suspect sb's motives* ∘ *I suspect the truth of her statement.* **3** ~ **sb** (**of sth / doing sth**) to feel that sb is guilty of sth, without certain proof: [Vnpr] *He is suspected of drug dealing.* [Vn] *suspected criminals/terrorists* ∘ *Who do the police suspect?*
▶ **suspect** /'sʌspekt/ n a person suspected of a crime, etc: *The police are interrogating two suspects.* ∘ *He is a **prime suspect** in the murder case.*
suspect /'sʌspekt/ adj not to be relied on or trusted; possibly false: *His reasoning is suspect.* ∘ *The car has a suspect tyre* (eg one that is damaged and therefore dangerous).

suspend /sə'spend/ v **1** ~ **sth** (**from sth**) (*fml*) to hang sth up: [Vnpr] *A lamp was suspended from the ceiling above us.* [also Vn]. **2(a)** to prevent sth from being in effect for a time; to stop sth temporarily: [Vn] *suspend a rule* ∘ *Rail services are suspended indefinitely because of the strike.* ∘ *In the theatre we willingly **suspend disbelief** (ie temporarily believe that the characters, etc are real). ∘ *During the crisis, the constitution was suspended* (ie people did not have their normal civil rights). **(b)** to arrange that sth should happen at a later time; to delay sth: [Vn] *suspend introduction of the new scheme* ∘ *suspend judgement* (ie delay forming or expressing an opinion) ∘ *give a criminal a **suspended sentence*** (ie not order a prison sentence unless he or she commits a further offence). **4** ~ **sb** (**from sth**) (esp passive) to prevent sb officially from holding their usual position, carrying out their usual duties, etc for a time: [Vn] *The police officer was suspended while the complaint was investigated.* [Vnpr] *She was suspended from school for stealing.*
▶ **suspended** adj [pred] kept floating in air, liquid, etc: *particles suspended in water* ∘ *Smoke hung suspended in the still air.*
■ **su'spended ani'mation** n [U] the state of being alive but not conscious: (*fig*) *The whole project is in suspended animation while we wait for permission to proceed.*

suspender /sə'spendə(r)/ n **1** [C esp *pl*] (*Brit*) (*US* **garter**) a short elastic fastening for holding up a sock or STOCKING by its top. **2** **suspenders** [pl] (*US*) = BRACES.
■ **su'spender belt** n a woman's garment like a belt, worn round the waist, with fastenings for holding stockings (STOCKING) up.

suspense /sə'spens/ n [U] a feeling of tension, worry, etc about what may happen: *a story of mystery and suspense* ∘ *Don't **keep us in suspense** any longer — tell us what happened!*

suspension bridge

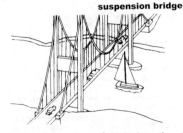

suspension /sə'spenʃn/ n **1** [U,C] the action of suspending sth or the condition of being suspended; an instance of this: *the suspension of a rule/law* ∘ *the suspension of a pupil from school* ∘ *They have*

S

appealed *against their suspensions.* **2** [U] the system of springs, etc by which a vehicle is supported on its wheels: *The poor suspension gives a rather bumpy ride.* ○ *a car with independent suspension* (ie for each wheel). ⇨ picture at CAR. **3** [C, U] a liquid with tiny pieces of solid matter floating in it; the state of such a liquid: *medicine in powder form held in suspension.* ■ **su'spension bridge** *n* a bridge suspended from steel cables supported by towers at each end. ⇨ picture.

suspicion /səˈspɪʃn/ *n* **1** [U, C] the feeling or thought, without certain proof, that sth is guilty of sth, that sth is wrong, or that sth is or is not the case: *regard sb with suspicion* ○ *He was arrested on suspicion of having stolen the money.* ○ *Her behaviour aroused no suspicion.* ○ *After a crime, suspicion naturally falls on the person who has a motive for it.* ○ *I have a sneaking suspicion that she is not telling me the truth.* ○ *It appears to be genuine, but I have my suspicions (about it).* ○ *My worst suspicions were confirmed when I read the letter.* **2** [sing] ~ (**of sth**) a slight taste or amount: *There was not the slightest suspicion of jealousy in her voice.* **IDM above su'spicion** too good, honest, etc to be suspected of wrongdoing: *Nobody who was near the scene of the crime is above suspicion.* **under su'spicion** suspected of wrongdoing.

suspicious /səˈspɪʃəs/ *adj* **1** ~ (**about/of sth/sb**) having or showing suspicion: *a suspicious look* ○ *I'm very suspicious about her motives.* ○ *He is suspicious of* (ie does not trust) *strangers.* **2** causing suspicion: *suspicious behaviour* ○ *a suspicious character* (ie sb who may be dishonest) ○ *You should inform the police if you see anything suspicious.* ▶ **suspiciously** *adv*: *acting suspiciously* ○ *Everything was suspiciously quiet.* ○ *This looks suspiciously like his handwriting.*

suss (also **sus**) /sʌs/ *v* (*Brit sl*) **1** ~ **sb/sth** (**out**) (**a**) to discover sb/sth: [Vn, Vnp] *I think I've got him/it sussed (out)* (ie I now understand him/it). (**b**) to investigate sth carefully: [Vp] *I want you to suss out the possibility of our doing a deal with them.* [also V.*wh*, V.*that*].

sustain /səˈsteɪn/ *v* **1(a)** to keep sb/sth alive or in existence: [Vn] *not enough oxygen to sustain life* ○ *Only the hope that the rescuers were getting nearer sustained the trapped miners* (ie kept them cheerful and enabled them to stay alive). ○ *enjoy a sustaining breakfast* (ie of food that gives strength). (**b**) to keep a sound, an effort, etc going; to maintain sth: [Vn] *sustain a note* (ie continue to play or sing it without interruption) ○ *make a sustained effort to finish off the work* ○ *The clapping was sustained for several minutes.* ○ *The author is to sustain his argument throughout the chapter.* **2** (*fml*) to experience or suffer sth: [Vn] *sustain a defeat/a loss* ○ *He sustained severe injuries to the head.* **3** (*law*) to decide that a claim, etc is valid: [Vn] *The court sustained his claim that the contract was illegal.* ○ *Objection sustained!* **4** (*fml*) to bear weight without breaking or falling: to support sth: [Vn] *The ice will not sustain your weight.*
▶ **sustainable** /-əbl/ *adj* that can be kept going or maintained: *sustainable economic growth* ○ *environmentally sustainable policies* (ie that do not harm the environment). **sustainability** /səˌsteɪnəˈbɪləti/ *n* [U].

sustenance /ˈsʌstənəns/ *n* [U] food and drink, or its power to keep sb alive and well: *weak from lack of sustenance* ○ *There's not much sustenance in a glass of lemonade.*

suture /ˈsuːtʃə(r)/ *n* (*medical*) a stitch or stitches made in sewing up a wound, esp following an operation.
▶ **suture** *v* [Vn] (*medical*) to sew up a wound.

svelte /svelt, sfelt/ *adj* (*approv*) (of a person) thin in a graceful attractive way: *a svelte figure.*

SW *abbr* **1** (*radio*) short wave. **2** South-West; South-Western: *SW Australia* ○ *London SW15 6QX* (ie as a POSTCODE).

swab /swɒb/ *n* (**a**) a piece of soft material used in medicine for cleaning wounds, etc or for taking samples, eg of MUCUS, for testing. (**b**) a sample taken in this way: *take a throat swab.*
▶ **swab** *v* (**-bb-**) **1** to clean or wipe sth with a swab: [Vnpr, Vn-adj] *swab the wound (clean) with cotton wool* [Vnpr] *swab the blood off sb's face* [also Vn]. **2** to clean sth with water using a cloth, etc: [Vn] *swab the decks.*

swaddle /ˈswɒdl/ *v* ~ **sb/oneself** (**in sth**) to wrap sb/oneself in warm clothes, etc: [Vnpr] *She sat by the fire, swaddled in a blanket.* [also Vn].
▶ **'swaddling-clothes** /ˈswɒdlɪŋ/ *n* [pl] (*dated*) strips of cloth used for swaddling a baby.

swag /swæg/ *n* **1** [C usu *pl*] (**a**) a carved ornament representing a hanging bunch of fruit and flowers. (**b**) a piece of material hanging in a similar way, esp as decoration. **2** [U] (*dated sl*) stolen goods.

swagger /ˈswægə(r)/ *v* (*often derog*) to walk or behave in a manner that is too proud or confident: [Vpr] *He swaggered into the room looking very pleased with himself.* [also V, Vp].
▶ **swagger** *n* [sing] (*sometimes derog*) a swaggering movement or way of behaving: *walk with a swagger.*
■ **'swagger stick** *n* (*Brit*) a short stick carried by a military officer.

swain /sweɪn/ *n* (*arch or joc*) a young male lover.

swallow¹ /ˈswɒləʊ/ *v* **1(a)** to cause or allow esp food or drink to go down the throat: [V] *Taking pills is easy — just put them in your mouth and swallow.* [Vn] *Chew your food properly before swallowing it.* (**b**) to use the muscles of the throat as if doing this, eg in fear: [V] *She swallowed hard, and turned to face her accuser.* **2** (*infml*) (**a**) to believe sth too easily: [Vn] *He flatters her outrageously, and she swallows it whole* (ie believes all of it). (**b**) to accept an insult, etc in a calm way or without protesting: [Vn] *He swallowed all the criticism without saying a thing.* **3** ~ **sb/sth** (**up**) to take sb/ sth into itself so that they/it can no longer be seen: [Vnp] *The jungle soon swallowed them up.* [Vn, Vnp] *The aircraft was swallowed (up) in the clouds.* [Vnp] (*fig*) *Many small firms are being swallowed up by large corporations* (ie taken over so that they disappear). (**b**) to use sth up completely: [Vnp] *The cost of the trial swallowed up all their savings.* [also Vn]. **4** to hide or suppress a feeling: [Vn] *She swallowed her anger and carried on.* ○ *I was forced to swallow my pride and ask for a loan.* **IDM swallow the 'bait** to accept sth that has been said, offered, etc to tempt one.
▶ **swallow** *n* (**a**) an act of swallowing. (**b**) an amount swallowed at one time: *take a swallow of beer.*

swallow² /ˈswɒləʊ/ *n* a small bird with long wings and a forked (FORK) tail that eats insects. Swallows visit northern countries in summer. **IDM one swallow does not make a 'summer** (*saying*) a single fortunate or satisfactory incident does not mean that what follows will be good.

swam *pt* of SWIM.

swami /ˈswɑːmi/ *n* a Hindu religious teacher.

swamp /swɒmp/ *n* [C, U] an area of land that is full of water; a MARSH.
▶ **swamp** *v* **1** to flood or fill sth with water: [Vn] *The sink overflowed and swamped the kitchen.* ○ *A huge wave swamped the boat.* **2** ~ **sb/sth** (**with sth**) (esp passive) to provide more of sth than can easily be dealt with: [Vnpr] *I've been swamped with work this year.* [Vn] *The embassy was swamped by a flood of visa applications.*
swampy *adj*: *swampy ground.*

swan

swan /swɒn/ *n* a large graceful, usu white, bird with a long thin neck that lives on rivers, lakes, etc. ⇨ picture.

▶ **swan** *v* (-nn-) **PHRV** ˌswan ˈoff/aˈbout/aˈround (*Brit infml derog*) to go around in a casual relaxed way which annoys other people: *She's swanning around the town in her new sports car.* ◦ *He's gone swanning of to Amsterdam for the weekend.*

swank /swæŋk/ *v* (*infml derog*) to behave in a way that shows one is proud of oneself; to boast: [V] *She's swanking just because she was told her essay was the best.*

▶ **swank** *n* (*infml derog*) **1** [U] behaviour or talk that is intended to impress people: *wear an expensive watch just for swank.* **2** [C] a person who swanks: *Don't be such a swank!*

swanky *adj* (-ier, -iest) (*infml derog*) fashionable and expensive: *They always stay in swanky hotels.* ◦ *Jill and her swanky friends.*

swansong /ˈswɒnsɒŋ/ *n* (usu *sing*) the last thing done or produced for the public by an artist, a composer, an actor, etc: *His performance as King Lear was to be his swansong before retiring.*

swap (also **swop**) /swɒp/ *v* (-pp-) ~ (**sth**) (**with sb**); ~ (**sb**) **sth for sth**; ~ **sth** (**over/round**) (*infml*) to exchange sth for sth else: [V, Vpr] *Does anybody want to swap (with me)?* [Vn] *I couldn't see the screen properly so we swapped seats.* ◦ *swap jokes/stories/information/ideas* [Vnpr] *I swapped my Peugeot for a Renault.* [Vnn] *I swapped him my John Coltrane cassette for his Miles Davis.* [also Vnp]. **IDM** **change/swap places** ⇨ PLACE¹.

▶ **swap** *n* (**a**) (usu *sing*) an act of swapping sth: *Shall we do a swap — your fishing-rod for my tennis racket?* (**b**) a thing swapped.

sward /swɔːd/ *n* [U] (*dated or rhet*) an area of grass.

swarm¹ /swɔːm/ *n* **1** a large number of insects or birds moving around together, eg bees following a queen bee: *a swarm of ants/locusts/starlings* ◦ *We watched the beekeeper putting the swarm back into the hive.* **2** (often *pl*) (*usu derog*) a large number of people; a crowd: *She's always surrounded by swarms of photographers.*

▶ **swarm** *v* **1** [V] (of bees) to move around in a swarm(1), esp following a queen bee. **2** to move in large numbers in the specified direction: [Vpr] *tourists swarming over all our ancient monuments* [Vp] *The crowd was swarming out through the gates.* **PHRV** ˈswarm with sb/sth to be full of people or things: *The capital is swarming with police.*

swarm² /swɔːm/ *v* **PHRV** swarm down/up sth to climb down/up sth by holding it with the hands and feet: *swarm down a rope/up a tree.*

swarthy /ˈswɔːði/ *adj* (of a person or the face) dark in colour: *a swarthy man/skin/complexion.*

swashbuckling /ˈswɒʃbʌklɪŋ/ *adj* [usu attrib] full of excitement and romantic adventure: *a swashbuckling tale of adventure on the high seas.*

swastika /ˈswɒstɪkə/ *n* a symbol in the form of a cross with its ends bent at right angles (RIGHT¹), formerly used as a Nazi EMBLEM. ⇨ picture at CROSS¹.

swat /swɒt/ *v* (-tt-) to hit sth/sb hard, esp with a flat object: [Vn] *swat a fly.*

▶ **swat** *n*: *take a swat at a wasp.*

swatter *n* an instrument, usu a flat piece of plastic or metal fixed to a handle, for swatting flies, etc.

swatch /swɒtʃ/ *n* a sample of fabric, wool, etc.

swathe¹ /sweɪð/ (also **swath** /swɒθ/) *n* a broad strip or area of plants or land: *a swathe of daffodils/forest.* **IDM** **cut a ˈswathe through sth 1** to destroy, kill, etc a considerable part of sth: *The new road cut a swathe through the countryside.* ◦ *Aids has already cut a swathe through New York's artistic community.* **2** to attract a lot of attention: *cut a swathe through society.*

swathe² /sweɪð/ *v* ~ **sb/sth** (**in sth**) to wrap sb/sth in several layers of fabric: [Vn] *Thick bandages swathed his head.* [Vnpr esp passive] *They were swathed in scarves and sweaters.* ◦ (*fig*) *The city lay swathed in fog.*

sway /sweɪ/ *v* **1** to move or swing slowly from side to side: [Vpr] *trees swaying in the wind* [V] *He swayed slightly, as if about to fall.* [Vn] *She swayed her hips seductively.* **2** to influence or change the opinions or actions of sb: [Vn] *a speech that swayed many voters* ◦ *He refused to be swayed by her argument.*

▶ **sway** *n* [U] **1** a movement from side to side: *walk with a sway of the hips.* **2** (*rhet*) rule or control: *The country was/fell under the sway of powerful invaders.* **IDM** **hold ˈsway** (**over sb/sth**) (*often rhet*) to have great power or influence over sb/sth; to be dominant: *areas of the country where the Labour Party holds sway.*

swear /sweə(r)/ *v* (*pt* **swore** /swɔː(r)/; *pp* **sworn** /swɔːn/) **1** ~ (**at sb/sth**) to use offensive words, esp when angry: [V] *She bumped her head in the doorway and swore loudly.* [Vpr] *The foreman is always swearing at the workers.* **2** (no passive) to say or promise sth very seriously or solemnly: [Vn] *I've never seen him before, I swear it.* [V.that] *She swore that she'd never seen him.* ◦ *I could have sworn (that)* (ie I was certain) *I heard a knock at the door.* [V.to inf] *I swore not to tell anybody about it.* **3** to make a solemn promise to do sth or a solemn statement about sth, esp in a lawcourt: [Vpr] *Witnesses have to swear on the Bible.* [Vn] *They have sworn (an oath of) allegiance to the crown.* [V.that] *Are you willing to swear in court that you saw him do it?* [V.to inf] *You have sworn to tell the truth.* See also SWORN².

IDM **swear ˈblind** (*infml*) to say that sth is definitely true: *She swore blind (that) she'd never received my letter.* **swear like a ˈtrooper** to use very rude or offensive language. **PHRV** ˈswear by sb/sth **1** to name sb/sth as a guarantee of what one is promising: *I swear by almighty God that I will tell the truth.* **2** (*infml*) to believe strongly that sth is useful, valuable, etc: *Most of my friends use word processors but I still swear by my old typewriter.* ˌswear sb ˈin (esp passive) to ask sb to swear an OATH(1) when they are appointed to a new position, responsibility, etc: *The President has to be sworn in publicly.* ◦ *Let the witness be sworn in.* ˈswear to sth (*infml*) to say definitely that sth is true: *I think I've met him before, but I wouldn't/couldn't swear to it* (ie I'm not completely sure).

■ ˈswear-word *n* an offensive word, often used to express one's anger, etc: *'Damn' and 'bloody' are common swear-words.*

sweat /swet/ *n* **1** [U] drops of a liquid similar to water that come through the skin when one is hot, ill, afraid, etc: *wipe the sweat from one's forehead* ◦ *After the race the sweat was running off them.* ◦ (*fig*) *They built it with the sweat of their brow* (ie by working very hard). Compare PERSPIRATION. **2 a** sweat [sing] the state of sweating or being covered with sweat: *I break out in a (cold) sweat when I think how near to death I was.* ◦ *work up a good sweat by running.* **3 a** sweat [sing] a state of great anxiety or distress: *She's in a real sweat about her* exams. **4** (*infml*) (**a**) [U] hard work or effort: *Making your own wine? It's not worth the sweat.* (**b**) **a sweat** [sing] a task, etc needing much effort: *Climbing all these stairs is a real sweat.* **IDM** **no** '**sweat** (*infml*) (used for saying that sth will not cause one difficulty) no problem: '*I'm sorry to give you so much extra work.*' '*No sweat!*'

▶ **sweat** *v* **1** to produce sweat: [V] *He was sweating heavily/profusely.* ∘ *The long climb made us sweat.* Compare PERSPIRE. **2** (*infml*) to be or remain in a state of anxiety: [V] *They all want to know my decision but I think I'll let them sweat a little* (ie by not telling them yet). **3** ~ (**over sth**) to work hard: [Vpr] *I really sweated over that essay.* **4** [Vn] (*Brit*) to heat meat, vegetables, etc slowly in a pan with fat or water, in order to extract the juices. **IDM** **slog/ sweat one's guts out** ⇨ GUT. **sweat** '**blood** (*infml*) to work very hard: *The staff have sweated blood to complete the work on time.* **PHRV** ,**sweat sth** '**off** to lose weight by exercising very hard: *I sweated off ten pounds in a week by playing squash every day.* ,**sweat sth** '**out** to cure a cold, fever, etc by sweating. ,**sweat it** '**out** to wait in a state of anxiety for sth to happen or end: *We just had to sit and sweat it out until the results were announced.*

sweaty *adj* (**-ier, -iest**) **1** covered or damp with sweat: *a sweaty T-shirt* ∘ *sweaty palms* ∘ *I'm all sweaty from running.* **2** causing sb to sweat: *a hot sweaty day.*

■ '**sweat-band** *n* a band of cloth worn round the head or wrist, for absorbing sweat.
,**sweated** '**labour** *n* [U] (*Brit derog*) work done for very low wages in bad conditions.
'**sweat gland** *n* an organ under the skin that produces sweat.

sweater /'swetə(r)/ *n* = JERSEY.

sweatshirt /'swet-ʃɜːt/ *n* a cotton JERSEY with long sleeves, often worn before and after sport.

sweatshop /'swet ʃɒp/ *n* (*derog*) a place where people work for low wages in bad conditions.

swede /swiːd/ (*US* also **rutabaga**) *n* [C, U] a large round yellow vegetable like a TURNIP. ⇨ picture at TURNIP.

sweep¹ /swiːp/ *v* (*pt, pp* **swept** /swept/) **1**(**a**) ~ **sth** (**from, off, into, etc sth**); ~ **sth** (**away, up, etc**) to remove dust, dirt, etc with a brush or by making a brushing movement with one's hand: [V] *Have you swept in here?* [Vnpr] *sweep the crumbs off the table/ into the dustpan* [Vnp] *sweep the dead leaves up.* (**b**) ~ **sth** (**out**) to clean sth by doing this: [Vn] *sweep the carpet/floor/yard* [Vnp] *sweep out the porch* [Vn-adj] *Has this room been swept clean?* **2** to move or push sth suddenly and with force: [Vnpr] *The current swept the logs down the river.* ∘ *We were almost swept off our feet by the waves.* ∘ (*fig*) *He was swept to power on a wave of popular support.* [Vnp] *She got swept along by the crowd.* ∘ *Many bridges were swept away by the floods.* ∘ (*fig*) *Many old laws and institutions were swept aside/away by the revolution.* **3** to move suddenly and with force over an area: [Vpr] *A huge wave swept over the deck.* ∘ *Rumours swept through the town.* [Vn] *Cold winds swept the plains.* ∘ (*fig*) *A wave of panic swept the country.* ∘ (*fig*) *The party swept the country* (ie won the election by a large majority). **4** to move in a smooth and impressive way: [Vp] *Without another word she swept out.* [Vpr] *The car swept up the drive to the front of the house.* **5** to extend in a long smooth curve: [Vpr] *The road sweeps round the lake.* [Vadv, Vp] *The beach sweeps (away) northwards as far as one can see.* **6** to pass over sth in order to examine it or search for sth: [Vn] *Searchlights swept the sky.* **7** to move over or along sth, touching it lightly: [Vn] *Her dress swept the ground as she walked.* **PHRV** ,**sweep sth** '**back** to brush hair back from the face: *Her auburn hair was swept back into an untidy bun.* **IDM** **sweep the**

'**board** to win all the prizes, money, games, etc: *Switzerland swept the board in the winter Olympics.*
,**sweep sb off their** '**feet** to fill sb with emotion, esp with love: *I was swept off my feet by her beauty and charm.* **sweep sth under the** '**carpet** to hide or conceal sth which might cause trouble or embarrassment: *The government are trying to sweep the affair under the carpet.*

▶ **sweeper** *n* **1** (in football) a defensive player whose position is behind the other defenders in order to try and stop anyone who passes them. **2**(**a**) a person whose job it is to sweep: *a road sweeper.* (**b**) a thing that sweeps: *a carpet sweeper.* See also MINESWEEPER.

sweepings *n* [pl] dust, rubbish, etc collected by sweeping the floor.

sweep² /swiːp/ *n* **1** [C usu *sing*] an act of sweeping sth: *Give the room a good sweep.* **2** [C] a smooth curving movement: *with a sweep of his arm/scythe.* **3** [C usu *sing*] a long, often curved, stretch of road, river, coast, etc: *the broad sweep of white cliffs round the bay.* **4** [U] the range or scope of sth: *His book covers the long sweep of the country's history.* **5** [C] a movement over an area, eg in order to search for sth or attack sb/sth: *The rescue helicopter made another sweep over the bay.* **6** [C] = CHIMNEY-SWEEP. **7** [C] = SWEEPSTAKE. **IDM** **make a clean sweep** ⇨ CLEAN¹.

sweeping /'swiːpɪŋ/ *adj* **1**(**a**) having a wide range or effect: *sweeping reforms/changes* ∘ *Councils will be given sweeping powers to impose fines.* (**b**) [usu attrib] complete; overwhelming (OVERWHELM): *a sweeping victory.* **2** (*derog*) (of statements, etc) not taking account of particular cases or exceptions; too general: *make a sweeping generalization.*

sweepstake /'swiːpsteɪk/ (also *infml* **sweep**) *n* (**a**) a type of gambling in which all the money bet on the result of a contest is paid to sb holding a winning ticket or a ticket corresponding to the winner. (**b**) a race, esp one for horses, on which money is bet in this way.

sweet¹ /swiːt/ *adj* (**-er, -est**) **1** tasting like sugar or honey; not sour, bitter or salty: *sweet apples/ biscuits/drinks* ∘ *sweet wine* ∘ *This cake is too sweet for me.* **2** smelling pleasant, esp like PERFUME: *The air was sweet with the scent of lilies.* ∘ (*fig*) *There's nothing like* ***the sweet smell of success.*** **3** pleasing to hear: *the sweet song of the blackbird* ∘ *The soprano's voice sounded clear and sweet.* **4** fresh and pure: *the sweet air of the countryside* ∘ *The spring water was sweet* (ie not salty, unpleasant, etc) *to the taste.* **5** giving satisfaction or pleasure: *a sweet feeling of freedom/success* ∘ ***Sweet dreams*** (ie said to sb going to sleep)! **6**(**a**) (*infml*) attractive and charming: *a sweet face/smile/gesture* ∘ *a sweet little dog/baby/cottage* ∘ *She looks sweet in that dress.* ⇨ note at NICE. (**b**) having or showing a pleasant nature; LOVABLE: *a sweet child/old lady* ∘ *a sweet temper/nature/disposition* ∘ *such a sweet-tempered/ sweet-natured girl* ∘ *It is sweet of you to have remembered us.* **IDM** **be** '**sweet on sb** (*dated infml*) to be fond of or in love with sb. **have a sweet** '**tooth** (*infml*) to like to eat sweet things. **in one's** ,**own sweet** '**time/'way** just as one pleases, or taking as long as one pleases, often in spite of the orders or wishes of others: *It's no use getting impatient with him — he'll do it in his own sweet time.* **keep sb** '**sweet** (*infml*) to be specially pleasant with sb in order to win favours: *I need to keep my boss sweet because I want to ask for some time off.* **short and sweet** ⇨ SHORT¹. **sweet** '**nothings** (*infml or joc*) words of affection exchanged by lovers: *She whispered sweet nothings in his ear.*

▶ **sweetish** *adj* rather sweet.

sweetly *adv* **1** in a sweet manner: *sweetly scented flowers* ∘ *sing/smile sweetly.* **2** smoothly and well:

The engine was running sweetly. ○ *All our plans are going sweetly.*

sweetness *n* [U] the quality of being sweet. **IDM** **(all) ,sweetness and 'light** (*ironic*) a display of mild and reasonable behaviour: *Yesterday he was rude and unpleasant to me but this morning he's all sweetness and light.*

■ **,sweet-and-'sour** *adj* [attrib] (of food) cooked in a sauce that contains sugar and either VINEGAR or LEMON: *Chinese ,sweet-and-sour 'pork.*

'sweet corn *n* [U] a type of MAIZE with sweet grains: *an ear of sweet corn.*

,sweet 'pea *n* a climbing garden plant with colourful sweet-smelling flowers.

,sweet po'tato *n* (*pl* **-os**) a tropical climbing plant with thick edible roots which are cooked as a vegetable. Compare YAM.

'sweet talk *n* [U] (*infml*) insincere praise used to persuade sb to do sth. **'sweet-talk** *v* ~ **sb (into sth / doing sth)** to use insincere praise to persuade sb to do sth: [Vnpr] *He tried to sweet-talk me into lending him my car.* [also Vn].

sweet² /swiːt/ *n* **1** [C often *pl*] (*Brit*) (*US* **candy** [U, C]) a small shaped piece of sweet substance, usu made with sugar and/or chocolate: *a packet of boiled sweets* ○ *You shouldn't eat sweets between meals.* ○ *a sweet shop.* **2** [C, U] (*Brit*) = DESSERT: *have some more sweet* ○ *What's for sweet?* **3** (used as a loving form of address): *Yes, my sweet.*

sweetbread /'swiːtbred/ *n* [C usu *pl*] the PANCREAS of a calf or lamb used as food.

sweeten /'swiːtn/ *v* **1** to become or make something sweet or sweeter: [V] *Fruit sweetens as it ripens.* [Vn] *tea sweetened with a little sugar.* **2** to make sth more pleasant or acceptable: [Vn] *The compliment failed to sweeten her disposition/mood.* ○ *Bonus shares will be thrown in to sweeten the deal.* **3** ~ **sb (up)** (*infml*) to make sb more likely to help, agree, etc, eg by offering gifts: [Vnp] *I'll sweeten her up a bit by inviting her to the party.* [also Vn]. **IDM** **sugar/sweeten the pill** ⇨ PILL.

▶ **sweetener** /'swiːtnə(r)/ *n* **1** [C, U] (a piece of) a substance used to sweeten food or drink, esp as a substitute for sugar. **2** [C] (*infml*) a thing given, especially dishonestly or illegally: *The firm offered her a large bonus as a sweetener.*

sweetheart /'swiːthaːt/ *n* **1** (used esp as a loving form of address, eg to a wife, husband, child, etc). **2** (*becoming dated*) a person that one loves: *They were childhood sweethearts.*

sweetie /'swiːti/ *n* (*infml*) **1** (*Brit*) (used esp by and when speaking to young children) a sweet²(1). **2** a kind person: *Thanks for helping, you're a sweetie.* **3** (used as a loving form of address): *Thank you, sweetie.*

swell /swel/ *v* (*pt* **swelled** /sweld/; *pp* **swollen** /'swəʊlən/ or **swelled**) **1(a)** ~ **(sth) (up) (with sth)** to become larger or rounder, eg because of pressure from inside; to make sth do this: [V] *Wood often swells when wet.* [Vpr, Vp] *His eyes swelled (up) with tears.* [Vp] *She twisted her ankle and it swelled up.* [also Vn, Vnpr, Vnp]. **(b)** ~ **(sth) (out)** to curve or make sth curve outwards: [V, Vp] *The sails swelled (out) in the wind.* [Vn, Vnp] *The wind swelled (out) the sails.* **2** ~ **(into/to sth)**; ~ **sth (to sth) (with sth)** to become or make sth greater in intensity, number, amount or volume: [Vpr] *The group of onlookers soon swelled (in)to a crowd.* ○ *The murmur swelled into a roar.* [Vn] *A number of extra costs have swelled the total.* ○ *I brought some friends along to* **swell the ranks** (ie join those already available to help, etc). ○ *Her actions helped* **swell the tide of** opposition. [also V, Vnpr]. **3** ~ **(sth) (with sth)** (of a person, the heart, etc) to feel full of intense emotion: [Vpr] *His breast/heart swelled with pride at his*

achievement. [also V, Vn, Vnpr]. See also GROUND SWELL.

▶ **swell** *n* **1** [sing] an act of swelling or the state of being swollen: *the swell of opposition to the proposals* ○ *the swell of her belly.* **2** [C] a slow moving of the sea with waves that do not break: *feel seasick in the heavy swell.* **3** [C] (*music*) a gradual increase in the volume of sound.

swell *adj* (*dated US infml*) excellent; very good, nice, etc: *That's a swell idea.* ○ *You look swell in that dress!*

swelling /'swelɪŋ/ *n* **1** [U] the condition of being swollen: *Wasp stings cause swelling and sharp pain.* **2** [C] an abnormally swollen place on the body: *He had a swelling on his knee.*

swelter /'sweltə(r)/ *v* (*infml*) to be so hot it is uncomfortable; to suffer from the heat: [V] *lie sweltering on a beach* ○ *The country is sweltering in a heatwave.* ▶ **sweltering** *adj*: *a sweltering (hot) day/ summer/climate.*

swept *pt, pp* of SWEEP¹.

swerve /swɜːv/ *v* to change direction suddenly: [V] *The car swerved sharply to avoid the child.* [Vpr] *The ball swerved to the left.* [also Vp].

▶ **swerve** *n* a swerving movement: *make a sudden swerve.*

swift¹ /swɪft/ *adj* (**-er, -est**) **1** ~ **(to do sth)** quick or rapid; PROMPT¹(1): *a swift response* ○ *He was swift to condemn the terrorist violence.* **2** that can move fast: *a swift runner/horse* ○ *a swift-flowing river.* ▶ **swiftly** *adv.* **swiftness** *n* [U].

swift² /swɪft/ *n* a small bird with long narrow wings that can fly with rapid curving movements.

swig /swɪɡ/ *v* (**-gg-**) ~ **sth (down)** (*infml*) to take a quick drink or drinks of sth, esp alcohol: [Vn, Vnpr] *swigging beer (from a bottle)* [Vnp] *swig down a glass of rum* [also Vpr].

▶ **swig** *n* an act of swigging: *take a long/deep swig of beer.*

swill /swɪl/ *v* **1(a)** ~ **sth (out/down)** (*Brit*) to pour large amounts of water, etc into, over or through sth to clean it: [Vnp] *swill down the front steps* ○ *He swilled his mouth out with antiseptic.* [also Vn]. **(b)** (of liquid) to flow or pour in the specified direction: [Vpr, Vp] *Water was swilling around in the bottom of the barrel.* **2** (*infml derog*) to drink sth in large quantities: [Vn] *swill beer/tea.*

▶ **swill** *n* [U] **1** scraps of waste food, usu mixed with water, for feeding to pigs. **2** (*US*) any liquid mess or waste.

swim /swɪm/ *v* (**-mm-**; *pt* **swam** /swæm/; *pp* **swum** /swʌm/) **1(a)** to move the body through water by using arms, legs, a tail, etc: [V] *I can't swim.* ○ *She swims like a fish* (ie very well). ○ *Let's go swimming.* [Vpr] *swim across the river* [Vadv] *swim underwater/upstream/ashore* [also Vp]. **(b)** to use particular movements to do this: [Vn] *swim breaststroke.* **(c)** to cover a distance by swimming: [Vn] *swim two lengths of the pool* ○ *swim the Channel.* **2** (usu in the continuous tenses) **(a)** ~ **(with sth)** to be flooded with liquid: [V, Vpr] *Her eyes were swimming (with tears).* [Vpr] *The bathroom floor was swimming with water.* **(b)** ~ **in sth** to be covered with liquid as if floating in it: [Vpr] *meat swimming in gravy.* **3(a)** to seem to be spinning round: [Vpr] *The room swam before his eyes/around him.* [also V]. **(b)** (of one's head) to feel as if everything is spinning round; to feel very confused: [V] *The whisky made his head swim.* **IDM** **sink or swim** ⇨ SINK¹.

▶ **swim** *n* an action or period of swimming: *go for/ have a swim.* **IDM** **in/out of the 'swim** (*infml*) aware of or involved/not aware of or involved in what is going on: *Although I'm retired, voluntary work keeps me in the swim (of things).*

swimmer *n* a person who swims, esp in the specified way: *a strong/good/fast swimmer.*

■ **'swimming-bath** n (esp pl) (Brit) a pool built indoors for swimming in.

'swimming-costume (also esp Brit **bathing-costume**, US also **bathing-suit**) n a garment worn for swimming.

'swimming-pool n an artificial pool for swimming in.

'swimming-trunks n [pl] a garment like short trousers or PANTS worn by men and boys for swimming: a pair of swimming-trunks.

swimmingly /'swɪmɪŋli/ adv (infml) pleasantly and smoothly: We're getting along swimmingly. ○ Everything went swimmingly (ie proceeded without difficulties).

swimsuit /'swɪmsuːt; Brit also -sjuːt/ n a garment worn for swimming, esp one worn by women and girls: a one-piece/two-piece swimsuit.

swimwear /'swɪmweə(r)/ n [U] clothing worn for swimming.

swindle /'swɪndl/ v (infml) ~ sb/sth (out of sth) to cheat sb/sth, esp in a business deal: [Vn] swindle an insurance company [Vnpr] Investors were swindled out of millions of pounds.

▶ **swindle** n (**a**) an act of swindling sb: an international swindle involving forged banknotes. (**b**) a person or thing that is presented wrongly in order to deceive people: The competition was a complete swindle.

swindler /'swɪndlə(r)/ n.

swine /swaɪn/ n **1** [C] (infml derog) (**a**) (used as a term of contempt or disgust): You rotten swine! (**b**) a very unpleasant or difficult thing: Those nails were real swines to get out. **2** [pl] (arch or fml) pigs: swine fever. **IDM pearls before swine** ⇨ PEARL.

swing¹ /swɪŋ/ v (pt, pp **swung** /swʌŋ/) **1** to move or make sth/sb move backwards and forwards or round and round while hanging or supported: [V, Vn] His arms swung/He swung his arms as he walked. [Vpr] The bucket was swinging from the end of a rope. [Vp] The gymnast swung round on the parallel bars. [also Vnpr]. **2** to move sb/oneself from one place to another by gripping sth and jumping, etc: [Vpr, Vp] The ape swung (along) from branch to branch. [Vnpr, Vnp] He swung himself (up) into the saddle. **3** to walk or run with an easy movement: [Vpr, Vp] The riders swung past us and away into the distance. **4** to move or make sth move in a curve: [Vpr] A car swung sharply round the corner. [Vp] The boom swung across. [Vn, Vnpr] She swung the axe (above her head). [Vnp] He swung the camera round in a broad arc. [V-adj, Vn-adj] The door (was) swung open/shut. **5** ~ (sth) (at sb/sth) to aim a blow at sb/sth: [Vpr] She swung at me with her fist. [Vn, Vnpr] They started swinging punches (at each other). [also V]. **6** ~ around/round to turn suddenly to face the opposite way: [Vp] She swung round (on him) angrily. ○ He swung round to confront his accusers. **7** ~ (sb) (from sth) to sth; ~ (sb) around/round (to sth) to change or make sb change suddenly from one opinion or mood, etc to another: [Vpr] Voters have/Voting has swung to the left. ○ He swings from wild optimism to total despair. [Vnp] Can you swing them round to my point of view? [also Vp, Vnpr]. **8** (of music) to have a strong rhythm: [V] a band/tune that really swings. **9** (infml) to succeed in obtaining or achieving sth, sometimes by slightly dishonest means: [Vnpr] I need to interview the play's director — can you swing it for me? [also Vn]. **IDM no room to swing a cat** ⇨ ROOM. **,swing into 'action** to act quickly: Immediately after the explosion the anti-terrorist squad swung into action.

swing² /swɪŋ/ n **1** [C] a swinging movement, action or rhythm: He took a wild swing at the ball. ○ the swing of a pendulum ○ walk with slight swing of the hips. **2** [C] a seat for swinging on, hung from above on ropes or chains: children playing/riding on

the swings. **3** [U] a type of jazz with a smooth rhythm, played esp by big dance bands in the 1930s. **4** [U, sing] strong rhythm in music: music with a swing (to it). **5** [C] an amount by which sth changes from one opinion, etc to another: Voting showed a 10% swing to Labour. ○ He is liable to abrupt swings of mood/mood swings (eg from happiness to despair). **IDM get into/the 'swing (of sth)** (infml) to adapt to a routine, etc: I've only been here for a week, so I haven't got into the swing of things yet. **go with a 'swing** (infml) **1** (of entertainment, etc) to be lively and enjoyable: The party certainly went with a swing. **2** (of music, poetry, etc) to have a strong rhythm. **in full swing** ⇨ FULL. **,swings and 'roundabouts** (infml esp Brit) a matter of balancing gains against losses: Higher earnings mean more tax, so it's all swings and roundabouts. ○ What you gain on the swings you may lose on the roundabouts.

▶ **swinging** adj (dated infml) lively and modern in style, attitudes, etc: the Swinging Sixties (ie 1960s).

■ **,swing-'door** n a door that opens in either direction and closes itself when released.

,swing-'wing n [usu attrib] a type of aircraft wing that can be moved forward for landing, etc and backward for rapid flight: a swing-wing bomber.

swingeing /'swɪndʒɪŋ/ adj [usu attrib] (esp Brit) **1** large in amount, number or range: swingeing fines/taxes/price increases ○ swingeing cuts in public services. **2** (of a blow) hard or forceful.

swipe /swaɪp/ v (infml) **1** ~ (**at**) sth/sb to hit or try to hit sth/sb with a quick swinging blow: [Vpr] He swiped at the ball and missed. [also Vn, Vnpr]. **2** (esp joc) to steal sth, esp by seizing it quickly: [Vn] Who's swiped my toothbrush?

▶ **swipe** n ~ (**at** sb/sth) (infml) **1** a quick swinging blow, or an attempt at this: have/take a swipe at the ball. **2** an attack on sb/sth in words: a vicious/satirical swipe at government policy.

swirl /swɜːl/ v (of air, water, etc) to move or flow with twists and turns and with varying speed; to make air, water, etc do this: [Vpr, Vp] dust swirling (around) in the streets [Vnpr] Smoke swirled up the chimney. [Vnpr, Vnp] She swirled the wine (round) in her glass.

▶ **swirl** n ~ (**of** sth) **1** a swirling movement: dancers spinning round in a swirl of bright colours. **2** a curled shape, esp as part of a pattern or design: strawberries topped with a swirl of cream.

swish¹ /swɪʃ/ v **1(a)** to swing sth through the air with a soft rushing sound: [Vn, Vnpr] The horse swished its tail from side to side. [also Vnp]. (**b**) to move with or make such a sound: [V] Her long gown swished as she walked. [Vpr] We swished through the long grass. [also Vp].

▶ **swish** n [sing] a swishing action or sound: The horse gave a swish of its tail. ○ the swish of curtains.

swish² /swɪʃ/ adj (infml esp Brit) fashionable or expensive: SMART¹(4): a swish hotel/restaurant.

Swiss /swɪs/ adj of Switzerland or its people.

▶ **Swiss** n (pl unchanged) a native of Switzerland.

■ **,Swiss 'roll** n a thin flat cake spread with jam, etc and rolled up.

,Swiss 'chard n [U] = CHARD.

switch /swɪtʃ/ n **1** a device for completing or breaking an electric circuit: a light switch ○ press the on/off switch. **2** (US) = POINT¹(18). **3** a change, esp a sudden one: a switch in policy/opinion ○ a switch from gas to electric ○ make a switch from publishing to teaching ○ Polls showed a switch to Labour. **4** a thin flexible shoot cut from a tree; a rod like this used for urging a horse, etc forward.

▶ **switch** v **1** ~ (sth) (over) (from sth) (to sth) to change or make sth change, esp suddenly: [Vpr] switch to modern methods [Vn] switch one's allegiance [Vpr, Vp] Many voters switched (back/over) to Labour. [Vnpr] switch the conversation to a different

---

[V.speech] = verb + direct speech   [V.that] = verb + that clause   [V.wh] = verb + who, how, etc clause

topic [Vnp] *Could you switch the TV over* (ie to a different channel)? [also V]. **2** ~ (sth) (with sb/sth); ~ (sth) over/round to exchange or make sb/sth exchange positions: [Vn] *Our glasses have been switched — this is mine.* [Vn, Vnpr] *Husband and wife should switch roles (with each other) occasionally.* [Vp] *You drive first and then we'll switch round/over.* [also V, Vpr, Vnpr]. **PHR V** ,**switch 'off** (*infml*) to become less interested, active, etc: *I switch off when he starts talking about cars.* ○ *After a busy day at work I just want to relax and switch off.* ,**switch (sth) 'off** to turn off electricity, etc or an appliance with a switch: *Switch off the gas/power at the mains.* ○ *Don't switch (the TV) off yet.* ,**switch (sth) 'on** to turn on electricity, etc or an appliance with a switch: *Switch on the light at the wall-socket.* ○ *Don't switch (the radio) on yet.*
 ■ '**switch-blade** *n* (*US*) = FLICK-KNIFE.
,**switched-'on** *adj* (*dated infml*) aware of what is going on or what is new or fashionable.

switchback /'swɪtʃbæk/ *n* **1** a railway or road that rises and falls sharply many times: *a switchback journey through the mountains with many ups and downs.* **2** (*esp Brit*) = ROLLER-COASTER.

switchboard /'swɪtʃbɔːd/ *n* a central panel in an office, etc with a set of switches for making telephone connections or operating electrical circuits; the staff controlling this: *the girl on the switchboard* ○ *switchboard operators* ○ *The switchboard has been busy all day.* ○ *Protesting viewers jammed the switchboard.*

swivel /'swɪvl/ *n* (*esp in compounds*) a link between two parts enabling one part to revolve without turning the other: *a swivel chair* (ie with a seat that can revolve on its base). **swivel** *v* (**-ll-**; *US* **-l-**) ~ (sth) (round) to turn or make sth turn on or as if on a swivel: [Vpr, Vp] *He swivelled (round) in his chair to face us.* [Vn, Vnp] *She swivelled the telescope (round).* [also V].

swollen¹ /'swəʊlən/ *pp* of SWELL.

swollen² /'swəʊlən/ *adj* grown bigger, wider, etc than usual; expanded: *He had twisted his ankle and it was badly swollen.* ○ *The river was swollen with the recent rains.*

swoon /swuːn/ *v* (**a**) ~ (over sb/sth) (*esp joc*) to be emotionally affected by sb/sth: [Vpr] *All the girls are swooning over the new history teacher.* [also V]. (**b**) (*dated*) to lose consciousness; to FAINT²: [Vpr] *He almost swoons at the sight of blood.* [also V]. ▶ **swoon** *n* [sing] (*dated*): *fall/go into a swoon.*

swoop /swuːp/ *v* (**a**) ~ (down) (on sb/sth) to come down suddenly with a rushing movement: [Vp] *The owl swooped down on the mouse.* [Vpr] *Planes swooped (low) over the ship.* [V, Vpr] (*fig*) *Detectives swooped (on the house) at dawn.*
 ▶ **swoop** *n* ~ (on sth/sb) (**a**) a swooping movement. (**b**) a sudden and unexpected attack: *Police made a dawn swoop.* **IDM** **at/in one fell swoop** ⇨ FELL⁴.

swop = SWAP.

sword /sɔːd/ *n* a weapon with a long thin metal blade and a protected handle: *draw/sheathe one's sword* (ie take it out of/put it into its SHEATH(1a)). ⇨ picture. **IDM** **cross swords** ⇨ CROSS². **put sb to the 'sword** (*dated or rhet*) to kill sb with a sword. **a sword of 'Damocles** /'dæməkliːz/ (*fml*) an unpleasant or terrible thing that may happen to sb at any time and causes a feeling of anxiety and danger: *The possibility of losing her job hung over her like a sword of Damocles all year.* **turn swords into 'ploughshares** (*rhet*) to stop fighting and return to peaceful activities.
 ■ '**sword dance** *n* a dance between and over swords placed on the ground, or one in which swords are waved or hit together.

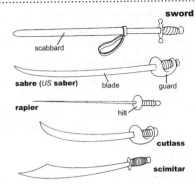

sword
scabbard
sabre (*US* **saber**) blade guard
rapier hilt
cutlass
scimitar

swordfish /'sɔːdfɪʃ/ *n* (*pl* unchanged) a large sea-fish with an extremely long thin pointed upper jaw.

swordplay /'sɔːdpleɪ/ *n* [U] fighting with swords.

swordsman /'sɔːdzmən/ *n* (*pl* **-men** /-mən/) a person who is skilled in the use of a sword: *a fine swordsman.*
 ▶ **swordsmanship** /-mənʃɪp/ *n* [U] skill in the use of a sword.

swore *pt* of SWEAR.

sworn¹ *pp* of SWEAR.

sworn² /swɔːn/ *adj* [attrib] **1** made with a solemn promise to tell the truth: *a sworn statement/affidavit.* **2** extreme and determined to remain so: *be sworn enemies.*

swot /swɒt/ *v* (**-tt-**) ~ (up) (on sth); ~ (for sth); ~ sth up (*Brit infml*) to study sth very hard, esp in preparation for an exam: [Vpr] *swotting for the exams* [Vnp, Vp] *I'm swotting up (on) my history.* [also V].
 ▶ **swot** *n* (*often derog*) a person who swots.

swum *pp* of SWIM.

swung *pt, pp* of SWING¹.

sybaritic /ˌsɪbə'rɪtɪk/ *adj* (*fml usu derog*) very fond of comfort and pleasure: *a sybaritic lifestyle.*

sycamore /'sɪkəmɔː(r)/ *n* **1** [C] (**a**) (*esp Brit*) a large tree of the MAPLE family. (**b**) (*esp US*) a plane-tree (PLANE³). **2** [U] the valuable hard wood of the sycamore.

sycophant /'sɪkəfænt/ *n* (*fml derog*) a person who tries to gain people's favour by insincere praise or always agreeing with them. ▶ **sycophancy** /'sɪkəfənsi/ *n* [U]. **sycophantic** /ˌsɪkə'fæntɪk/ *adj*: *a sycophantic smile/speech.*

syllable /'sɪləbl/ *n* any of the units into which a word may be divided, usu consisting of a vowel sound with a consonant before and/or after it: *'Arithmetic' is a word of four syllables/a four-syllable word.* ○ (*fig*) *I never received a syllable of thanks* (ie I received no thanks at all). **IDM** **in words of one syllable** ⇨ WORD.

syllabub /'sɪləbʌb/ *n* [C, U] a dish of cream mixed vigorously with sugar, wine, fruit juice, etc until stiff.

syllabus /'sɪləbəs/ *n* (*pl* **syllabuses** or **syllabi** /'sɪləbaɪ/) a list of subjects, topics, texts, etc included in a course of study: '*Hamlet' is on this year's English literature syllabus.* Compare CURRICULUM.

syllogism /'sɪlədʒɪzəm/ *n* (*techn*) a form of reasoning in which a conclusion is drawn from two statements, eg *All men must die; I am a man; therefore I must die.*
 ▶ **syllogistic** /ˌsɪlə'dʒɪstɪk/ *adj* a syllogistic argument.

sylphlike /'sɪlflaɪk/ *adj* (*approv or joc*) thin and graceful: *I wish I had your sylphlike figure.*

sylvan /'sɪlvən/ *adj* (*arch or rhet*) (**a**) of the woods: *sylvan glades.* (**b**) having woods; rural: *a sylvan setting.*

symbiosis /ˌsɪmbaɪˈəʊsɪs/ n [U] (*biology*) the relationship between two living creatures of different species that live close together and depend on each other in various ways: *the symbiosis between a plant and the insect that fertilizes it.* **symbiotic** /-ˈɒtɪk/ *adj*: (*fig*) *the symbiotic relationship between church and state.*

symbol /ˈsɪmbl/ n **1** ~ (of sth) an image, object, etc that suggests or refers to sth else: *The cross is the symbol of Christianity.* ○ *The lion is the symbol of courage.* ○ *The motor bike for me is a symbol of freedom.* See also SEX SYMBOL, STATUS SYMBOL. **2** ~ (for sth) (abbreviated as *symb* in this dictionary) a mark or sign with a particular meaning, eg the written notes in music or the letters standing for the chemical elements: *algebraic symbols* ○ *On maps, a cross is the symbol for a church.* ○ *Au is the chemical symbol for gold.*

▶ **symbolic** /sɪmˈbɒlɪk/ *adj* ~ (of sth) of, using or used as a symbol: *The cross is symbolic of Christianity.* ○ *The two leaders publicly shook hands in a symbolic gesture of friendship.* **symbolically** /-klɪ/ *adv.*

symbolism /ˈsɪmbəlɪzəm/ n [U] the use of symbols to represent things, esp in art and literature; the symbols used in this way: *poetry full of religious symbolism.* **symbolist** /ˈsɪmbəlɪst/ n [often attrib] an artist, a writer, etc who habitually uses symbols: *the symbolist poet Arthur Rimbaud.*

symbolize, -ise /ˈsɪmbəlaɪz/ v to be a symbol of sth: [Vn] *a picture of a red disc with rays coming from it, symbolizing the sun* ○ *More than any other figure he symbolizes his country's struggle for independence.*

symmetry /ˈsɪmətrɪ/ n [U] **1** the exact match in size and shape between the two halves of sth, as if one half were reflected in a mirror: *the perfect symmetry of the building.* **2** the attractive regular way in which parts are arranged: *the symmetry of her features.*

▶ **symmetrical** /sɪˈmetrɪkl/, **symmetric** *adjs* (of a design, etc) having two halves which are the same in size and shape; showing symmetry: *the symmetrical arrangement of the gardens* ○ *The plan of the ground floor is completely symmetrical.* Compare ASYMMETRIC. **symmetrically** /-klɪ/ *adv.*

sympathetic /ˌsɪmpəˈθetɪk/ *adj* **1** ~ (to/towards/with sb) feeling, showing or resulting from sympathy: *a sympathetic look/smile/remark* ○ *feel sympathetic towards sb who is suffering* ○ *He was enormously sympathetic when my father died.* **2** [pred] ~ (to sth/sb) showing favour or approval: *The management was sympathetic to the idea of a bonus suggested by the union.* **3** easy to like; pleasant: *I don't find her a very sympathetic person.* ▶ **sympathetically** /-klɪ/ *adv.*

sympathy /ˈsɪmpəθɪ/ n **1** [U] ~ (for/towards sb) the ability to share in the feelings of others; a feeling of pity and sorrow for sb: *feel great sympathy for sb* ○ *She showed no sympathy when I told her I was in trouble.* ○ *He deserves sympathy for the way he has been treated.* **2** sympathies [pl] shared emotions or opinions, or the expression of these: *You have my deepest sympathies on the death of your wife.* ○ *My sympathies are/lie with the workers in this dispute.* ○ *Some members of the party are thought to have fascist sympathies.* **3** [U] ~ (between sb and sb) friendship and understanding between people who have similar opinions or tastes: *A bond of sympathy developed between members of the group.* **IDM** **have no, some, etc ˈsympathy with sb/sth** to be unable/able to share sb's views, etc: *I have some sympathy with that point of view.* **in ˈsympathy (with sb/sth)** showing support or approval for a cause, etc: *The steel workers came out in sympathy with the miners* (ie went on strike to show support for them). ○ *I am broadly in sympathy with*

the aims of the party. **out of ˈsympathy with sb/sth** feeling unable to support or give approval to sb/sth: *She found herself out of sympathy with many of her younger colleagues.*

▶ **sympathize, -ise** /ˈsɪmpəθaɪz/ v ~ (with sb/sth) to feel or express sympathy or support: [V, Vpr] *I sympathize (with you) — I had a similar unhappy experience myself.* [Vpr] *We have long sympathized with the aims of the Green Party.*
sympathizer, -iser n a person who sympathizes, esp one who supports a cause or a political party: *Socialist sympathizers.*

symphony /ˈsɪmfənɪ/ n a long complex musical composition for a large ORCHESTRA, usu in three or four parts (*movements*): *Beethoven's ninth symphony* ○ *a symphony orchestra.*
▶ **symphonic** /sɪmˈfɒnɪk/ *adj* of or like a symphony: *Mozart's symphonic works.*

symposium /sɪmˈpəʊzɪəm/ n (*pl* symposia /-zɪə/) **1** a small conference or meeting to discuss a particular subject. **2** a collection of essays by several people on a particular subject, published as a book: *contribute to a symposium on environmental issues.*

symptom /ˈsɪmptəm/ n **1** a change in the body that indicates an illness: *the rash that is a symptom of measles.* **2** a sign of the existence of sth bad: *The demonstration is a symptom of discontent among the students.*
▶ **symptomatic** /ˌsɪmptəˈmætɪk/ *adj* ~ (of sth) being a symptom of sth: *Chest pains may be symptomatic of heart disease.* ○ *Is inflation symptomatic of economic decline?*

synagogue /ˈsɪnəgɒg/ n a building where Jews meet for religious worship and teaching.

synapse /ˈsaɪnæps, ˈsɪn-/ n (*anatomy*) a connection between two nerve cells. ▶ **synaptic** /saɪˈnæptɪk, sɪn-/ *adj.*

sync (also **synch**) /sɪŋk/ n [U] (*infml*) = SYNCHRONIZATION: *The film sound-track is out of sync with/not in sync with the picture.*

synchromesh /ˈsɪŋkrəʊmeʃ/ n [U] a device in a vehicle's GEARBOX that makes the parts turn at the same speed and thus allows gears to be changed smoothly.

synchronize, -ise /ˈsɪŋkrənaɪz/ v ~ (sth) (with sth) to operate, move, turn, etc at the same time, speed, etc; to make sth do this: [V] *The wheels must synchronize as they revolve.* [Vpr] *The sound in a movie must synchronize with the action.* [Vn] *Let's synchronize our watches* (ie set them to show exactly the same time). ○ *synchronized swimming* (ie by groups in formation, as a sport) [also Vnpr]. ▶ **synchronization, -isation** /ˌsɪŋkrənaɪˈzeɪʃn; US -nəˈz-/ (also *infml* sync) n [U].

synchronous /ˈsɪŋkrənəs/ *adj* (*fml*) occurring or existing at the same time: *synchronous events.*

syncopated /ˈsɪŋkəpeɪtɪd/ *adj* (*techn*) (of music) in which the strong beats have been made weak and the weak beats made strong: *syncopated rhythms.* ▶ **syncopation** /ˌsɪŋkəˈpeɪʃn/ n [U].

syndicalism /ˈsɪndɪkəlɪzəm/ n [U] the theory that factories, businesses, etc should be owned and managed by the workers employed in them.
▶ **syndicalist** /-kəlɪst/ n a supporter of syndicalism.

syndicate /ˈsɪndɪkət/ n a group of people or business companies combined to pursue a common interest.
▶ **syndicate** /ˈsɪndɪkeɪt/ v (usu passive) to publish an article, a CARTOON(1), etc in many different newspapers or magazines by making it available to a central organization that distributes it: [Vn] *His column is syndicated throughout the world.* **syndication** /ˌsɪndɪˈkeɪʃn/ n [U].

syndrome /ˈsɪndrəʊm/ n **1** (*medical*) a set of symptoms (SYMPTOM) which together indicate a particular disease or abnormal condition. **2** any set of opinions, events, actions, etc that are characteristic of a particular condition: *Unemployment, inflation and low wages are all part of the same economic syndrome.* See also DOWN'S SYNDROME.

synergy /'sɪnədʒi/ *n* [U, C] the combined effect of two or more things, processes, etc that exceeds the sum of their individual effects: *the synergy achieved by merging the two companies.*

synod /'sɪnɒd, -nəd/ *n* an official assembly of church members to discuss and decide on matters of religious teaching, church policy and administration, etc: *the General Synod of the Church of England.*

synonym /'sɪnənɪm/ *n* a word or phrase with the same or nearly the same meaning as another in the same language: *'Shut' and 'close' are synonyms.*

▶ **synonymous** /sɪ'nɒnɪməs/ *adj* ~ **(with sth)** having the same meaning: *The verbs 'shut' and 'close' are synonymous.* ○ *'Slay' is synonymous with 'kill' (though it is more forceful and rather dated).* ○ *(fig) Wealth is not necessarily synonymous with generosity* (ie Rich people are not always generous). Compare ANTONYM.

synopsis /sɪ'nɒpsɪs/ *n* (*pl* **synopses** /-siːz/) a summary of a book, play, etc: *The programme gives a brief synopsis of the plot.*

▶ **synoptic** /sɪ'nɒptɪk/ *adj* [attrib] of or forming a synopsis.

■ **the Synoptic 'Gospels** *n* [pl] (in the Bible) the gospels of Matthew, Mark and Luke, which describe events in a similar way, unlike that of John, which is very different.

syntax /'sɪntæks/ *n* [U] (*linguistics*) (the rules of grammar for) the arrangement of words into phrases and of phrases into sentences.

▶ **syntactic** /sɪn'tæktɪk/ *adj* of syntax: *syntactic differences between English and French.* **syntactically** /-kli/ *adv.* Compare GRAMMAR 1, MORPHOLOGY 2.

synthesis /'sɪnθəsɪs/ *n* (*pl* **syntheses** /-siːz/) **1(a)** [U] the combining of separate things, esp ideas, to form a complex whole: *develop a new theory by the synthesis of several earlier theories.* **(b)** [C] a thing that is produced in this way; a composition: *Her art is a synthesis of modern and traditional techniques.* **2(a)** the chemical production of a substance in plants and animals: *the body's synthesis of nucleic acids.* **(b)** [U] the artificial production of a substance that occurs naturally in plants and animals: *produce rubber from petroleum by synthesis.*

▶ **synthesize, -ise** /'sɪnθəsaɪz/ *v* **1** to combine parts into a whole: [Vn] *The two elements are synthesized by a chemical process.* **2** to make sth by SYNTHESIS(2): [Vn] *new chemicals synthesized by man* ○ *synthesized music/speech* (ie produced with electronic equipment).

synthesizer, -iser *n* an electronic machine for producing different sounds. Synthesizers are used as musical instruments, esp for copying the sounds of other instruments, and for reproducing speech sounds: *play the synthesizer* ○ *a voice/speech synthesizer.*

synthetic /sɪn'θetɪk/ *adj* **1** made by SYNTHESIS(2b); artificial: *synthetic chemicals/fabrics/fertilizers.* **2** (*infml derog*) not genuine or natural; false: *the salesman's synthetic friendliness.*

▶ **synthetic** *n* an artificial substance or fibre: *natural fibres and synthetics.*

synthetically /-kli/ *adv*: *a synthetically produced drug.*

syphilis /'sɪfɪlɪs/ *n* [U] an infectious disease passed from one person to another by sexual contact.

▶ **syphilitic** /ˌsɪfɪ'lɪtɪk/ *adj* of or suffering from syphilis.

syringe /sɪ'rɪndʒ/ *n* a device for sucking liquid in and forcing it out again in a thin stream. Syringes are used in medicine, gardening, cooking, etc: *a garden syringe.* See also HYPODERMIC *n* 1. ▷ picture at INJECTION.

▶ **syringe** *v* to clean sth or spray liquid onto sth with a syringe: [Vn] *syringe a wound/plant.*

syrup /'sɪrəp/ *n* [U] **1** water in which sugar is dissolved; (heavy) syrup ○ 'cough syrup (ie syrup with medicine in it, taken to ease coughing). **2** any thick sweet liquid, eg TREACLE: *golden syrup* ○ *maple syrup on pancakes.*

▶ **syrupy** *adj* **1** of or like syrup: *Heat the liquid until it is thick and syrupy.* **2** (*derog*) too sentimental: *a syrupy love-story.*

system /'sɪstəm/ *n* **1** [C] a group of things or parts working together as a whole: *a railway system* ○ *a stereo system* ○ *the country's telephone system* ○ *a system of ropes and pulleys.* See also CENTRAL NERVOUS SYSTEM, DIGESTIVE SYSTEM, PUBLIC-ADDRESS SYSTEM, SOLAR SYSTEM. **2** [C] a human or animal body as a whole, including its internal organs and processes: *The poison has passed into his system.* ○ *Too much alcohol is bad for your system.* See also IMMUNE SYSTEM. **3** [C] a set of ideas, theories, procedures, etc according to which sth is done: *a system of philosophy* ○ *the decimal system* ○ *the democratic system of government* ○ *the British legal system* ○ *a new system for processing application forms.* See also OPERATING SYSTEM. **4** **the system** [sing] (*infml usu derog*) the traditional methods, practices and rules existing in a society, an institution, a business, etc, esp regarded as unfair or too rigid, etc: *You can't beat the system* (ie You must accept it). **IDM** **get sth out of one's 'system** (*infml*) to get rid of a strong feeling or desire by expressing it openly or trying to fulfil it: *Why don't you tell me what's wrong? You'll feel better when you've got it out of your system.*

▶ **systematic** /ˌsɪstə'mætɪk/ *adj* **1** done or acting according to a system or plan: *a series of systematic experiments* ○ *He's very systematic in everything he does.* **2** (*derog*) carefully planned in advance to hurt or destroy sb/sth: *a systematic attempt to ruin sb's reputation* ○ *the systematic use of torture.* **systematically** /-kli/ *adv*: *Someone had systematically broken every window in the building.*

systematize, -ise /'sɪstəmətaɪz/ *v* to arrange sth according to a carefully organized system: [Vn] *make increased efforts to systematize health care.* **systematization, -isation** /ˌsɪstəmətaɪ'zeɪʃn; US -tə'z-/ *n*.

systemic /sɪ'stemɪk; *Brit also* sɪ'stiːmɪk/ *adj* **1** of or affecting the whole of the body. **2** (of substances used to treat plants) entering by the roots or shoots and spreading through all the tissues: *systemic fungicides/insecticides.* **systemically** /-kli/ *adv*.

■ **'systems analysis** *n* [U] analysis of all the steps in an operation in order to decide how to perform it most efficiently, esp using a computer. **'systems analyst** *n* an expert in systems analysis.

Tt

T (also **t**) /tiː/ n (pl **T's**, **t's** /tiːz/) the 20th letter of the English alphabet: *'Committee' is spelt with two t's.* **IDM dot one's/the i's and cross one's/the t's** ⇨ DOT. **to a 'T/'tee** (*infml*) in every detail; exactly: *The film captures the flavour of the period to a T.* ∘ *His new job suits him to a T.*

■ **'T-bone** n a bone shaped like the letter T, esp one in a piece of BEEFSTEAK: *a T-bone steak.*

'T-junction n (*Brit*) a place where one road joins another but does not cross it, thus forming the shape of a T.

'T-shirt (also **teeshirt**) n a casual shirt with short sleeves and no buttons, or just a few buttons at the top.

TA /ˌtiː 'eɪ/ abbr (in Britain) Territorial Army.

ta /tɑː/ interj (*Brit infml*) thank you.

tab /tæb/ n **1** a small projecting piece of cloth, metal, paper, etc, esp one by which sth can be held, hung, fastened or identified: *To open, pull tab* (eg on a can of beer). ∘ *Insert the cardboard tabs into the slots* (eg to make a box). ∘ *a 'name-tab* (eg sewn onto clothes). **2** = TABULATOR: *a tab key.* **3** (*US*) a bill[1](1) or price. **IDM keep tabs on sb/sth** (*infml*) to keep sb/sth under observation; to check sth regularly or constantly: *keep tabs on private phone calls made by members of staff.* **pick up the bill/tab** ⇨ PICK[1].

Tabasco /tə'bæskəʊ/ n [U] (*propr*) a hot-tasting red sauce made from spices and peppers.

tabby /'tæbi/ (also **tabby cat**) n a cat that has grey or brownish fur marked with dark lines or patches.

tabernacle /'tæbənækl/ n **1** [C] a place of worship used by certain Protestant or other Churches: *a Baptist/Mormon tabernacle.* **2** [C] (in the Roman Catholic Church) a container holding the sacred bread and wine of the Eucharist. **3 the tabernacle** [sing] (*Bible*) the small movable place of worship used by the Israelites while they were wandering in the desert.

table /'teɪbl/ n **1** a piece of furniture consisting of a flat top supported on one or more legs: *The box is on/under the table.* ∘ *sit at the table* ∘ *the ˌkitchen 'table* ∘ *a ˌbedside 'table* ∘ *a 'billiard-table* ∘ *reserve a table (for two) at a restaurant* ∘ *a 'table lamp* ∘ *lay/set the table* (ie prepare it for a meal with plates, knives, forks, etc). ⇨ picture at SNOOKER. See also COFFEE-TABLE, DINING-TABLE, DRESSING-TABLE, THE NEGOTIATING TABLE, OPERATING-TABLE, ROUND-TABLE, TRESTLE-TABLE. **2** people sitting at a table for a meal or other activity: *enough bridge players to make 4 tables* ∘ *His jokes amused the whole table.* **3(a)** a list of facts or figures arranged in an ordered way, esp in columns: *a table of contents* (ie a summary of what a book contains) ∘ *a table showing how prices and earnings have increased since 1945* ∘ *'logarithm tables.* **(b)** a list of sports teams or players showing their current positions in a competition: *If Chelsea wins, they go (to the) top of the league table.* **(c)** = MULTIPLICATION TABLE: *learn one's tables* ∘ *Do you know your six times table?* See also THE PERIODIC TABLE. **IDM at/around the 'breakfast, 'dinner, etc table**; **'table during a meal**: *lively conversation at/around the breakfast table* ∘ *Children must learn to behave at table.* **drink sb under the table** ⇨ DRINK[2]. **lay/put one's cards on the table** ⇨ CARD[1]. **on the 'table 1** (*Brit*) offered for consideration or discussion: *Management have put several new proposals on the table.* **2** (*esp US*) (of a

proposal, etc) left for discussion until some future date. **turn the 'tables (on sb)** to reverse a situation so as to put oneself in a position of superiority. **wait at table**; **wait on table**; **wait tables** ⇨ WAIT[2].

▶ **table** v **1** (*Brit*) to present sth formally for discussion, eg a motion or report in parliament: [Vn] *table a proposal/an offer/a bid* ∘ *table a question in parliament* ∘ *The Opposition have tabled several amendments to the bill.* **2** [Vn] (*US*) to leave sth, eg a proposal, etc, to be discussed at some future date.

■ **'table manners** n [pl] proper behaviour while eating at a table with others.

'table-mat n a mat placed under a hot plate or dish, etc to protect the surface of a table.

'table tennis n [U] = PING-PONG.

'table-top n the flat part that forms the surface of a table. — adj [attrib] suitable to be placed or used on a table: *a table-top sewing-machine.*

tableau /'tæbləʊ/ n (pl **tableaux** /-ləʊ, -ləʊz/) a dramatic, striking or attractive scene, esp one presented on stage without words or movement: *a tableau in which the dancers form themselves into the shape of a heart* ∘ *The sea presented an ever-changing series of tableaux from my bedroom window.*

tablecloth /'teɪblklɒθ/ n a cloth for covering a table, esp during meals.

table d'hôte /ˌtɑːbl 'dəʊt/ n [U] a restaurant meal consisting of a limited range of dishes served at a fixed price: *The table d'hôte menu offers good value.* Compare À LA CARTE.

tablespoon /'teɪblspuːn/ n **1** a large spoon used esp for serving food at table. ⇨ picture at SPOON. **2** (also **tablespoonful** /-fʊl/) the amount held by a tablespoon: *add 2 tablespoons/tablespoonfuls of water/flour.*

tablet /'tæblət/ n **1** a small measured amount of medicine in a hard solid form: *Take two of the tablets three times daily before meals.* **2** a flat block of stone with words cut or written on it, esp one fixed to a wall in memory of an important person or event: *a memorial tablet engraved with the name of the school's founder.*

tableware /'teɪblweə(r)/ n [U] (*fml*) plates, bowls, knives, forks and other items used for meals.

tabloid /'tæblɔɪd/ adj [attrib] (of a newspaper) having pages that are half the size of those of larger newspapers, and usu containing light or popular news stories: *the tabloid press* ∘ (*often derog*) *tabloid journalism.*

▶ **tabloid** n a tabloid newspaper: *The First Family gets a lot of coverage in the tabloids.* Compare BROADSHEET 1.

taboo /tə'buː/ n (pl **taboos**) ~ **(against/on sth) 1** a cultural or religious custom that forbids people to do, touch, use or talk about a certain thing: *the taboo against incest* ∘ *tribal taboos* ∘ *Death is one of the great taboos in our culture.* **2** a general agreement not to discuss or to do sth: *There's a taboo on smoking in this office.*

▶ **taboo** adj forbidden by a taboo: *Sex is no longer the taboo subject it used to be.* ∘ *Any mention of politics is taboo in his house.*

■ **ta'boo words** n [pl] words that are often considered offensive, shocking or rude, eg because they refer to sex, the body or race. Taboo words are marked ⚠ in this dictionary.

tabular /'tæbjələ(r)/ *adj* (*fml*) arranged or presented in a table(3a) or list: *statistics presented in tabular form.*

tabulate /'tæbjuleɪt/ *v* [Vn] to arrange facts or figures in the form of a table(3a) or list. ▶ **tabulation** /ˌtæbju'leɪʃn/ *n* [U, C].

tabulator (*fml*) (also **tab**) *n* a device on a KEYBOARD (1a) for advancing to a series of set positions in tabular work.

tacit /'tæsɪt/ *adj* [usu attrib] understood without being put into words; implied: *give tacit agreement/ approval/support* ∘ *The grim expression on his face was a tacit admission of failure.* ▶ **tacitly** *adv*.

taciturn /'tæsɪtɜ:n/ *adj* saying very little; not communicating a lot. ▶ **taciturnity** /ˌtæsɪ'tɜ:nəti/ *n* [U].

tack /tæk/ *n* **1** [U, sing] the general tendency or direction of sb's actions, words or thoughts: *be on the right/wrong tack* ∘ *It would be unwise to **change tack** now.* ∘ *I was unable to persuade her with offers of money, so I tried a different tack.* **2** [C] (*nautical*) (of boats with sails) a course at an angle to the front of the boat, sailed with the wind blowing towards one side: *on the port/starboard tack* (ie with the wind on the left/right side). **3** [C] a small nail with a broad head, esp one used for securing a carpet to the floor: *a box of tacks* ∘ *a 'carpet tack.* See also THUMB-TACK. **4** [C] a long loose stitch used in fastening pieces of cloth together loosely or temporarily. **IDM** **get down to brass tacks** ⇨ BRASS. **sharp as a tack** ⇨ SHARP.
▶ **tack** *v* **1** to fix sth in place with a tack(3) or tacks: [Vnp] *tack down the carpet* [Vnpr] *tack a poster to the wall.* **2** to sew or fasten sth with tacks (TACK 4): [Vnpr] *tack a ribbon onto a hat* [Vn, Vnp] *tack (up) the hem of a dress* [V] *tacking stitches/ threads.* **3** (*nautical*) to move from one tack(2) to another; to sail continually from one course to another in this way: [Vpr] *tack to port/starboard* ∘ *The yacht tacked towards the mainland.* [Vp] *tacking back and forth* [also V]. **PHR V** **tack sth 'on(to sth)** (*infml*) to add sth as an extra item: *a cover charge tacked onto the bill* ∘ *The last paragraph seems to have been tacked on as an afterthought* (eg It bears little relation to what has gone before).

tackle /'tækl/ *v* **1** to deal with or overcome sth awkward or difficult: [Vnadv] *tackle a problem head-on* (ie in a bold and vigorous way) ∘ *The government is determined to tackle inflation.* [Vn] *I think I'll tackle the decorating next weekend.* **2(a)** (eg in football or hockey) to try to take the ball from an opponent: [V] *no good at tackling* [Vn] *He was tackled just outside the penalty area.* **(b)** (in Rugby) to seize and stop an opponent who is holding the ball. **3** ~ **sb (about/on sth)** to speak to or approach sb about an awkward matter: [Vnpr] *When are you going to tackle your brother about that money he owes me?* [Vn] *He tackled me as I was about to leave the office.*
▶ **tackle** *n* **1** [C] an act of tackling sb in football, Rugby, etc: *The policeman brought the bank-robber to the ground with a flying tackle.* **2** [U] equipment for a sport or other activity: *'fishing-tackle.* **3** [U] (*techn*) a set of ropes and other equipment for lifting, pulling or restraining sth. See also BLOCK AND TACKLE.
tackler /'tæklə(r)/ *n* (*sport*) a player who tackles sb: *renowned as a hard tackler.*

tacky /'tæki/ *adj* **1** (*infml*) of poor quality or in poor taste, though perhaps bright and colourful: *tacky advertising/souvenirs/restaurants.* **2** (of paint, glue, etc) slightly sticky; not quite dry.

taco /'tɑ:kəʊ/ *n* (*pl* **-os**) a Mexican dish consisting of a folded, often crisp, PANCAKE(1) with eg meat or vegetables and often spices inside.

tact /tækt/ *n* [U] skill at not offending people or at creating a favourable impression by saying or doing the right thing: *She showed great tact in dealing with a tricky situation.* ∘ *Criticizing one's colleagues requires tact and diplomacy.*
▶ **tactful** /-fl/ *adj* having or showing tact: *It would have been more tactful to say nothing.* **tactfully** /-fəli/ *adv*: *She refused their invitation firmly but tactfully.*
tactless *adj* lacking tact: *His remarks about her appearance were extremely tactless.* **tactlessly** *adv*. **tactlessness** *n* [U].

tactic /'tæktɪk/ *n* **(a)** (often *pl*) a plan or method used to achieve sth, often against an opponent: *use strong-arm/surprise/delaying tactics* ∘ *The defence lawyers held a meeting to discuss tactics.* ∘ *Companies are always looking for the best tactic to attract customers.* ∘ *Some workers questioned the union's tactics in calling for an immediate strike.* **(b) tactics** [sing or pl *v*] the art of placing or moving fighting forces in a battle: *skilled in tactics.* Compare STRATEGY 1.
▶ **tactical** /-kl/ *adj* [usu attrib] **1** of or relating to tactics: *a tactical advantage/error.* **2** planning or planned skilfully in one's own interest, often with little regard for principle or immediate advantage: *a tactical retreat/decision/alliance* ∘ *tactical voting* (ie voting not for the candidate or party one prefers but for another that is more likely to defeat the candidate, etc one wishes to be defeated). **3** (esp of weapons) used against enemy forces at short range: *tactical missiles/bombing.* Compare STRATEGIC. **tactically** /-kli/ *adv*: *vote tactically* ∘ *The enemy were numerically weaker but tactically superior.*
tactician /tæk'tɪʃn/ *n* an expert in tactics: *He is a fine player and one of the best tacticians in the game.*

tactile /'tæktaɪl; US -tl/ *adj* (*fml*) of or using the sense of touch: *tactile organs/sensations/ communication* ∘ *The materials used by the artist have a strong tactile quality.*

tad /tæd/ *n* **a tad** [sing] (*infml esp US*) (used esp as an *adv*) a very small amount; a little: *just a tad more milk* ∘ *I was a tad disappointed she didn't come.*

tadpole /'tædpəʊl/ *n* the form of a FROG(1) or TOAD (1) at the stage when it lives under water and has gills (GILL¹ 1) and a tail.

taffeta /'tæfɪtə/ *n* [U] a shiny fabric like silk, used esp for making dresses.

taffy (*US*) = TOFFEE.

tag /tæg/ *n* **1** [C] (often in compounds) a label or device attached to sth/sb, eg to identify it/them: *put 'name-tags on all one's belongings* ∘ *a 'gift-tag* (eg tied to a Christmas present) ∘ *The police use electronic tags to monitor the whereabouts of young offenders on probation.* See also PRICE TAG. **2** [C] a name or phrase applied to sb/sth, that describes them/it in some way: *His stage successes have earned him the tag of 'the new Olivier'.* ∘ *If the new bridge is to avoid the 'white elephant' tag, more traffic must be encouraged to use it.* **3** [C] (*linguistics*) a word or phrase that is added to a sentence for emphasis, eg *I do* in *Yes, I do*: *a 'tag question* (ie a tag in the form of a question, eg *isn't it?, won't you?, aren't they?*). **4** (also **tig**) [U] a children's game in which one child chases the others and tries to touch one of them.
▶ **tag** *v* (**-gg-**) ~ **(with sth)** **(a)** to attach a tag(1) or similar mark to sth/sb: [Vn] *The birds were tagged so that their migration patterns could be studied.* [Vnpr] *I've tagged the relevant pages with yellow stickers.* **(b)** to give a tag(2) to sth/sb: [Vn-n] *The President wishes to avoid being tagged as a 'lame duck'.* [also Vnpr]. **PHR V** **ˌtag 'along (behind/with sb)** to accompany sb; to follow sb closely: *children tagging along behind their mother* ∘ *If you're going to the cinema, do you mind if I tag along (with you)?* **ˌtag sth 'on (to sth)** to add sth as an extra item; to

attach sth: *a postscript tagged on at the end of a letter.*

■ **'tag day** *n* (*US*) = FLAG-DAY.

tagliatelle /ˌtæljəˈteli/ *n* [U] a form of PASTA in thin flat strips.

tail /teɪl/ *n* **1** [C] the movable part at the end of the body of a bird, an animal or a fish: *a dog wagging its tail.* ⇨ picture at FISH¹, HORSE, SCORPION. See also CAT-O'-NINE-TAILS, PONY-TAIL. **2** [C] a thing like a tail in its shape or position: *the tail of a comet/a kite/an aircraft/a procession.* ⇨ picture at AIRCRAFT. **3** [C] (*infml*) a person following or watching sb, usu without being seen by them: *The police put a tail on him to check his movements.* **4** tails [pl] (also **tailcoat** [C]) a man's long coat, divided at the back into two pieces which become narrower towards the bottom. Tails are worn as part of formal dress, eg at weddings: *dressed in top hat, white tie and tails.* Compare DINNER-JACKET, MORNING COAT. **5** tails [sing *v*] the side of a coin without the head of a person on it, as a choice when the coin is tossed (TOSS 5). Compare HEADS. **IDM** **have, etc one's tail between one's 'legs** (*infml*) to be ashamed or depressed, eg after being defeated or spoken to severely. **have, etc one's tail up** to be confident and performing well: *The champion is unbeatable when his tail is up.* **heads or tails?** ⇨ HEAD¹. **make head or tail of sth** ⇨ HEAD¹. **nose to tail** ⇨ NOSE¹. **on sb's 'tail** following sb closely. **a sting in the tail** ⇨ STING¹. **the tail wagging the 'dog** a situation in which a minor part of sth is controlling or determining the course of the whole. **turn 'tail** to run away from a fight or a dangerous situation: *As soon as they saw us coming they turned tail and ran.* ▶ **tail** *v* to follow sb closely, esp to watch where they go and what they do: [Vnpr] *She tailed him to his hotel.* [also Vn]. **PHRV** **ˌtail 'back** (of traffic) to form a TAILBACK: *Traffic is tailing back five miles from the scene of the accident.* **ˌtail a'way/'off** to become smaller in amount, strength or intensity: *The number of tourists starts to tail off in October.* ○ *'I'd like to help, but...,' his voice tailed away.*

-tailed (forming compound *adjs*) having a tail of the specified type: *'long-tailed* ○ *'curly-tailed.*

tailless *adj*: *Manx cats are tailless.*

■ **ˌtail-'end** *n* (usu *sing*) ~ (of sth) the very last part of sth: *the tail-end of the procession/concert* ○ *I only heard the tail-end of their conversation.*

'tail-light (*US* **'tail-lamp**) *n* a red light at the back of a car, bicycle or train. ⇨ picture at CAR.

'tail wind *n* a wind blowing from behind a travelling vehicle, an aircraft, a runner, etc. Compare HEAD WIND.

tailback /ˈteɪlbæk/ *n* a long line of traffic that extends back from sth blocking the road.

tailboard /ˈteɪlbɔːd/ *n* = TAILGATE a.

tailcoat /ˈteɪlkəʊt/ *n* [C] = TAILS.

tailgate /ˈteɪlgeɪt/ *n* (**a**) (also **tailboard**) a movable board at the back of a lorry or cart. It can be lowered or removed when loading or taking things off the vehicle. (**b**) a door that opens upwards at the back of a HATCHBACK. ▶ **tailgate** [V, Vn] (*US infml*) to drive too closely behind another vehicle.

tailor /ˈteɪlə(r)/ *n* a person who makes men's clothes, esp one who makes suits, jackets, etc for individual customers: *go to the tailor('s) to be measured for a suit.* ▶ **tailor** *v* ~ sth to/for sb/sth to make or adapt sth for a particular purpose, person or type of person: [Vnpr, Vn.to inf] *homes tailored to the needs of/to suit the elderly* [Vnadv] *a specially tailored insurance policy.* **tailored** *adj* (of clothes) made in a particular style; well-made: *a (loosely/finely) tailored jacket.*

tailoring *n* [U] **1** the style of a garment or the way

it is made: *the elegant tailoring of the jacket.* **2** the activity or business of a tailor.

■ **ˌtailor-'made** *adj* **1** made by a tailor: *a ˌtailor-made 'suit.* **2** ~ (for sth/sb) made for a particular purpose, person, etc: *a car with a tailor-made engine* (ie specially designed for that car) ○ *Our units are tailor-made to fit/for the customer's kitchen.* ○ *(fig) He seems tailor-made* (ie perfectly suited) *for the job.*

tailpiece /ˈteɪlpiːs/ *n* a part added to the end of sth, eg a piece of writing, to make it longer or to complete it.

tailplane /ˈteɪlpleɪn/ *n* the HORIZONTAL part or surface of the tail of an aircraft.

tailspin /ˈteɪlspɪn/ *n* (usu *sing*) **1** a downward spinning movement of an aircraft, esp one out of control, in which the tail makes wider circles than the front. **2** a situation which is getting worse rapidly or is out of control: *The economy is in a tailspin.*

taint /teɪnt/ *n* (usu *sing*) ~ (of sth) a trace of some bad quality or decay or infection: *an administration anxious to be free from the taint of corruption.* ▶ **taint** *v* ~ sth (with sth) (esp passive) to affect sth with a taint: [Vn] *tainted meat/drinking-water* ○ *His reputation was tainted by the scandal.* [Vnpr] *Their relationship is tainted with jealousy.*

take¹ /teɪk/ *v* (*pt* **took** /tʊk/; *pp* **taken** /ˈteɪkən/) **1** ~ sth/sb (with one); ~ sth (to sb) (**a**) to carry sth/sb or accompany sb from one place to another: [Vn, Vnpr] *Don't forget to take your umbrella (with you) when you go.* [Vnpr] *It's your turn to take the dog for a walk.* ○ *She takes her children to school by car.* [Vnpr, Vnp] *Take this glass of water (up) to your father.* [Vnp] *The thief was taken away in a police van.* [Vn.ing] *I'm taking the children swimming later.* [Vnn] *She took him some flowers when she went to see him in hospital.* (**b**) to cause sb/sth to advance or make progress: [Vnpr] *Her energy and talent took her to the top of her profession.* ○ *The next chapter takes us* (ie the reader) *from 1919 to 1933.* ○ *The new loan takes the total debt to £100 000.* [Vnadv] *I'd like to take my argument a stage further.* **2** to get hold of sth/sb, esp with the hands or arms: [Vn] *I passed him the rope and he took it.* ○ *Free newspapers: please take one.* ○ *Would you mind taking* (ie holding) *the baby for a moment?* ○ *Take three eggs and beat them gently.* [Vn, Vnpr] *take sb's hand/take sb by the hand* [Vnpr] *She took a cigarette from the packet.* ○ *He took her in his arms and kissed her.* [Vnp] *He took a book down from the top shelf.* ○ *She opened the drawer and took out a pair of socks.* **3**(**a**) to remove sth from its proper place without permission or by mistake: [Vn] *Someone has taken my gloves.* ○ *Did the burglars take* (ie steal) *anything of value?* [Vnpr] *Someone's taken some money out of/from my bank account.* (**b**) ~ sth from sth / out of sth to remove or obtain sth from a particular place or source: [Vnpr] *The scientists are taking water samples from the river.* ○ *The loan repayments will be taken out of your bank account.* ○ *Today's lesson is taken from St Mark's Gospel.* ○ *Part of her article is taken straight* (ie copied) *from my book on the subject.* ○ *The machine takes its name from its inventor.* (**c**) ~ sth from sth (not in the continuous tenses) to reduce one number by the value of another; to SUBTRACT sth from sth: [Vnpr] *If you take 5 from 12, you're left with 7.* **4** ~ sth (from sb) (not usu in the continuous tenses) to gain possession of sth; to capture sth/sb; to win sth: [Vn, Vnpr] *The English army tried to take the town (from the French).* [Vn] *The invaders took many prisoners.* ○ *He took my bishop with his queen* (ie in a game of CHESS). ○ *Our bull took first prize at the agricultural show.* ○ *The company took 15 per cent of the market last year.* [Vn-n] *The enemy took him prisoner/He was taken prisoner by the enemy.* **5** (not usu in the continuous tenses) to accept or receive sth/sb: [Vn] *If they offer me the job, I'll take it.* ○ *Will*

T

you take £2 000 for the car (ie sell it for £2000)? ○ *The shop took* (ie sold goods worth a total of) *£50 000 last week.* ○ *She was accused of taking bribes.* ○ *Does the hotel take traveller's cheques/advance bookings?* ○ *Please transfer the call and I'll take it in my office.* ○ *Why should I* **take the blame** *for somebody else's mistakes?* ○ *If you* **take my advice,** *you'll have nothing more to do with him.* ○ *The workers would never agree to take a cut in wages.* [Vn-n] *I'd like you to take this bracelet as a gift.* [Vn.to inf] *Do you take this woman to be your wife?* **6** (not usu in the continuous tenses) to accept sb as eg a client, customer or patient: [Vn] *Dr Brown takes some private patients.* ○ *The school doesn't take girls* (ie only has boys as pupils). ○ *Ask the hotel manager if they take pets.* **7** (not in the continuous tenses) to have enough space for sth/sb; to be able to hold or contain a certain quantity: [Vn] *The tank takes 12 gallons.* ○ *This bus can take 60 passengers.* ○ *I don't think the shelf will take any more books.* **8** (not usu in the continuous tenses) to experience a physical force or weight: [Vn] *The shop-front took the full force of the explosion.* ○ *Will the ropes be able to take the strain* (ie without breaking)? [Vn, Vnpr] *Let your shoulders take the weight/Take the weight on your shoulders.* ○ *He took the blow* (ie The blow hit him) *on the chest.* **9** (not usu in the continuous tenses) to be able to endure or tolerate sth; to bear sth: [Vn] *She can't take criticism.* ○ *I don't think I can take much more of this heat.* ○ *I'm not taking any more of your insults!* ○ *Tell me the bad news — I can take it.* ○ *I find his political views a little hard to take.* **10** to react to sth/sb in the specified way: [Vnadv] *'How did he take the news of her death?' 'He took it surprisingly well* (ie He was not too upset by it).*'* ○ *These threats are not to be taken lightly.* **11** ~ **sth as sth** (not in the continuous tenses) to understand, interpret or consider sth in a particular way: [Vn-n] *She took what he said as a compliment.* [Vn.to inf] *What did you take his comments to mean?* [Vnadv] *How am I supposed to take that remark?* ○ *Taken overall, the project was a success.* **12** ~ **sb/sth for sb/sth** (not in the continuous tenses) to suppose, assume or consider sb/sth to be sb/sth, esp wrongly: [Vnpr] *Even the experts took the painting for a genuine Van Gogh.* ○ *Do you take me for a fool?* [Vn.to inf] *I took you to be an honest man.* **13** (not in the continuous tenses) to understand sth correctly: [Vn] *I don't think she took my meaning.* **14** to rent or find a place to live or stay: [Vn] *We're taking a cottage in Brittany for a month.* **15** to choose or buy sth: [Vn] *I'll take the grey jacket, please.* **16** (*fml*) to buy a newspaper or a magazine regularly: [Vn] *She takes The Guardian.* **17** to eat, drink, etc sth: [Vn] *The baby isn't old enough to take solid food.* ○ *Do you take sugar in your coffee?* ○ *The main evening meal is taken around 7 o'clock.* ○ *The doctor has given me some pills to take for my cough.* ○ *He takes drugs* (ie illegal drugs), *regularly.* ○ *Have you ever taken cocaine?* **18** (no passive; often with *it*) **(a)** to need or require the specified time to complete a task or process: [Vn] *The journey from the airport to the university takes about an hour and a half.* [Vnn] *It took her three hours to mend her bike.* [Vn.to inf] *That cut is taking a long time to heal.* ○ *It'll* **take time** (ie a long time) *(for her) to recover from the illness.* [Vadv, Vnadv] *I'll just have a shower before we go out; I won't take long/it won't take (me) long.* **(b)** to need or require the specified amount, quality, action or person to complete a certain task or process: [Vn.to inf] *It would take a lot of strength/a very strong man to lift that weight.* ○ *It only takes one careless driver to cause a serious accident.* ○ *It doesn't take much to make her angry.* [Vn] (*infml*) *She didn't take much persuading* (ie She was easily persuaded). [also Vnn]. **19** (not in the continuous tenses) to wear a particular size in shoes or clothes: [Vn] *What size*

shoes do you take? ○ *He takes a 42-inch chest.* **20** (not in the continuous tenses) to be able to function using sth; to require sth in order to function: [Vn] *My car takes unleaded petrol.* ○ *What type of batteries does this radio take?* **21** (*grammar*) (not in the continuous tenses) (eg of a verb) to have or require sth when used in a sentence or other structure: [Vn] *The verb 'eat' takes a direct object.* ○ *The verb 'rely' takes the preposition 'on'.* **22** to do an examination or a test, etc in order to obtain a qualification: [Vn] *She takes her finals next summer.* ○ *When are you taking your driving test?* **23** (*Brit fml*) to be awarded or obtain a degree: [Vn] *She took a first in English at Leeds University.* **24** to study an academic subject: [Vn] *She plans to take a course in applied linguistics.* ○ *The pupils have to choose what subjects they are going to take for GCSE.* **25** to find out and record sth; to write sth down: [Vn] *The policeman took my name and address.* ○ *Did you take notes at the lecture?* ○ *My secretary hates taking letters.* **26** to make sth by photography; to photograph sth/sb: [Vn] *take a photograph/picture/snapshot of sth/sb* ○ *have one's picture taken.* **27** to test or measure sth: [Vn] *take sb's pulse/temperature/blood pressure* ○ *The tailor took my measurements for a new suit.* **28** to use a certain method or procedure to find out people's opinions: [Vn] *Why don't we take a vote on it?* **29** to use sth as a means of transport; to go by sth: [Vn] *take the bus/plane/train* ○ *I was late so I took a taxi to work.* **30** to use a road or path as a route to go to a place: [Vn] *I usually take the M6 when I go to Scotland.* ○ *Take the second turning on the right after the station.* **31** go over or round sth: [Vnadv] *The horse took the first fence beautifully.* ○ *You took that corner much too fast.* [also Vn, Vnpr]. **32** (eg in football) to perform a certain type of kick or movement in order to bring the ball into play: [Vn] *take a penalty/free kick/corner/throw-in.* **33** (not usu in the continuous tenses) to hold or adopt an opinion or attitude: [Vn] *He takes the view that people should be responsible for their own actions.* ○ *Parents should take an interest in their children's hobbies.* ○ *I took an instant dislike to him.* ○ *The government is taking a tough line on drug abuse.* ○ *We need to take a different approach to the problem.* **34** to believe or predict that sth will happen: [V.n to inf] *I take Brazil to win the World Cup.* **35** to adopt a course of action in order to achieve sth: [Vn] *The government is taking action/measures/steps to combat drug abuse.* **36** (usu imperative) to consider sth/sb as an example: [Vn] *A lot of women manage to bring up families and go out to work at the same time — take Angela, for example.* **37** to sit down in a chair, etc: [Vn] *Come in, take a seat.* ○ *The orchestra are just taking their seats.* **38** ~ **sb (for sth)** to conduct or be in charge of a class, a lesson or a religious service: [Vn] *Mr Perkins will take the evening service.* [Vnpr] *The head teacher usually takes us for French.* **39** To become fully attached or absorbed; to become a full part of sth: [V] *The skin graft failed to take.* ○ *The dye won't take* (ie will not colour things) *in cold water.* **40** (*sl*) to have sex with sb: [Vn] *He took her on the sofa.* **41** to carry out or perform the action indicated by the noun: [Vn] *take* (ie have) *a break/a holiday/a nap* ○ *take* (ie have) *a bath/a shower/a wash* ○ *take a look/a walk/a deep breath* ○ *take a bite out of a sandwich* ○ *take a shot at goal.* **IDM** Most idioms containing **take** are at the entries for the nouns or adjectives in the idioms, eg **take the biscuit** ⇨ BISCUIT; **take sb's temperature** ⇨ TEMPERATURE. **have (got) what it 'takes** (*infml*) to have the qualities, etc needed to be successful. **take sth/sb as it 'comes / as they 'come** to accept or tolerate sth/sb without wishing it/them to be different or without thinking about it/them very much in advance: *She takes life as it comes.* ○ *I'm not thinking about winning the championship; I just take each*

[V.*to* inf] = verb + *to* infinitive   [Vn.inf (no *to*)] = verb + noun + infinitive without *to*   [V.*ing*] = verb + *-ing* form

game as it comes. **'take it (that...)** to assume or suppose: *I take it you won't be coming to Sophie's party.* ○ *Are we to take it (from your answer) that you refuse to cooperate?* **take it from 'me (that...)** (*infml*) you can believe me absolutely when I say what I am about to say: *Take it from me — he'll be a millionaire before he's 30.* **take it on/upon oneself to do sth** to decide to do sth without asking for permission: *You can't take it upon yourself to make important decisions like that.* ○ *He took it upon himself to record their work for future generations.* **take it or 'leave it** (esp imperative; used to indicate that one does not care if sb accepts or rejects one's offer): *I'm not giving you more than £20 for it — take it or leave it.* **take it / a lot 'out of sb** to make sb physically or mentally tired: *This job certainly takes it out of you.* **take some / a lot of 'doing** (*infml*) to require a lot of effort or time; to be very difficult to do: *Did you move all this furniture on your own? That must have taken some doing!* ○ *It'll take a lot of doing to read all these reports by Monday.* **you can't take sb 'anywhere** (*infml often joc*) the specified person cannot be trusted to behave well in public or in polite company: *His manners are appalling — you can't take him anywhere!* **PHRV** ,**take sb a'back** (esp passive) to shock or surprise sb: *I was somewhat taken aback by his rudeness.* ○ *She seemed taken aback at this suggestion/that I had recognized her.*

,**take 'after sb** (no passive) to resemble an older member of one's family, esp one's mother or father, in appearance or character: *Your daughter doesn't take after you at all.*

,**take a'gainst sb/sth** (*Brit*) to begin to feel a dislike of sb/sth: *Why have you suddenly taken against her?*

,**take sb/sth a'part** (*infml*) **1** (in sport) to defeat sb easily: *Sampras took Courier apart in the third set.* ○ *We were simply taken apart by the opposition.* **2** to criticize sb/sth severely: *Her second novel was taken apart by the critics.* ,**take sth a'part** to separate a machine, etc into the different parts of which it is made: *Let's take the radio apart and see what's wrong with it.*

,**take sth 'away 1** to make a feeling or sensation disappear: *The doctor has given me some tablets to take away the pain.* ○ *Nothing can take away the anguish of losing a child.* ○ *Anxiety has taken away his appetite.* **2** (*US* ,**take sth 'out**) to buy a cooked dish at a restaurant and carry it away to eat eg at home: *Two fish and chips to take away, please.* ,**take sth/sb a'way (from sth/sb)** to remove sth/sb from sth/sb: *These books must not be taken away from the library.* ○ *The child was taken away from its parents on the recommendation of social workers.* ,**take sth a'way (from sth)** to reduce one number by the value of another; to SUBTRACT sth from sth: *If you take 4 away from 10, that leaves 6.* ○ *10 take away 4 is 6.* ,**take (sth) a'way from sth** to make the effect or value of sth seem weaker, smaller or less impressive: *I don't wish to take (anything) away from his achievements, but he couldn't have done it without our help.*

,**take sth 'back 1** (of a shop) to agree to accept or receive back goods that were previously bought there, eg because they are faulty or of the wrong size: *We only take goods back if the customer can produce the receipt.* **2** to admit that sth one said was wrong or that one should not have said it: *I take back what I said (about you being selfish).* ,**take sb 'back (to...)** to cause sb's thoughts to return to a past time; to make sb remember sth: *The smell of the sea took him back to his childhood.* ○ *Hearing those old songs takes me back a bit.*

,**take sth 'down 1** to remove sth from a high level: *Will you help me take the curtains down?* ○ *The notice*

has now been taken down. **2** to remove a structure, esp by separating it into pieces: *take down a tent/ fence/Christmas tree* ○ *Workmen arrived to take down the scaffolding.* **3** to lower a garment worn below the waist without actually removing it: *take down one's trousers/underpants/skirt* ○ *The little boy's mother took down his shorts.* **4** to write sth down in order to make a record of it: *Reporters took down every word of his speech.* ○ *Anything you say may be taken down and used as evidence against you.*

,**take sb 'in 1** to allow sb to stay in one's home, sometimes for payment: *She takes in lodgers.* ○ *He was homeless, so we took him in.* **2** (often passive) to make sb believe sth that is not true; to deceive sb: *She took me in completely with her story.* ○ *Don't be taken in by his charming manner; he's completely ruthless.* ,**take sth 'in 1** to absorb sth into the body, eg by breathing or swallowing: *Fish take in oxygen through their gills.* **2** to make a garment narrower or tighter, eg by removing material or adding stitches: *This dress needs to be taken in at the waist.* **3** to include or cover sth: *The tour takes in six European capitals.* ○ *Her lecture took in all the recent developments in the subject.* **4** to go to see or visit sth, eg a film or museum, when one is in a place for a different purpose: *I generally take in a show when I'm in New York on business.* **5** to note sth with the eyes; to observe sth: *He took in every detail of her appearance.* ○ *She took in the scene at a glance.* **6** to understand or absorb sth that one hears or reads: *I hope you're taking in what I'm saying.* ○ *Halfway through the chapter I realized I hadn't taken anything in.*

,**take 'off 1** (of an aircraft) to leave the ground and begin to fly: *The plane took off an hour late.* ○ (*fig*) *Let your imagination take off* (ie be completely free). **2** to leave the ground when jumping: *The jumper's feet must be behind the line when she takes off.* **3** (*infml*) to start moving or running suddenly or in a hurry: *When he saw me coming he took off in the opposite direction.* **4** (*infml*) (of eg an idea or a product) to become successful or popular very quickly or suddenly; (of sales of a product) to increase very quickly: *The new dictionary has really taken off.* ○ *Sales of home fax machines have taken off in recent years.* ,**take (oneself) 'off (to...)** (*infml*) to leave a place: *You can't just take (yourself) off when you feel like it.* ○ *She's taken herself off to the country for a quiet weekend.* ,**take sb 'off 1** to copy sb's voice, actions or manner in an amusing way: *She takes off the director to perfection.* **2** (in entertainment or sport) to make sb leave the stage or the field of play: *The audience were clearly not amused. 'Take him off!' they yelled.* ○ *The injured player was taken off and replaced by a substitute.* Compare SEND SB OFF. ,**take sth 'off 1** to remove an item of clothing from one's/ sb's body: *take off one's coat/hat/shoes/skirt/glasses* ○ *The little boy's mother took off his shorts.* **2** to remove part of sb's/one's body, esp hair: *The hairdresser asked me how much he should take off.* ○ *I wish you'd take (ie shave) off that beard!* ○ *The explosion nearly took off his arm.* **3** to stop a series of performances of eg a play or a film: *The show was taken off because of poor audiences.* ,**take sb 'off (sth)** to rescue sb from eg a ship or an oil platform: *The crew were taken off (the wrecked vessel) by helicopter.* **take sb off sth** (often passive) to remove sb from a job or position: *The officer leading the inquiry has been taken off the case.* ,**take sth 'off (sb)** to remove a duty or responsibility from sb; to relieve sb of sth: *Employing a nurse will take the burden off his wife.* ○ *The defeat of her main rival has taken some of the pressure off (the champion).* ,**take sth 'off sb** to remove sth from sb's possession, usu against their will: *She was playing with a sharp knife, so I took it off her.* ,**take sth 'off (sth) 1** to remove or detach sth from a surface or an object:

[V.speech] = verb + direct speech   [V.*that*] = verb + *that* clause   [V.*wh*] = verb + *who, how*, etc clause

take the lid off a jar ○ *take off the doll's head* ○ *Would you mind taking your foot off my hand?* **2** to remove an item from a list or similar document: *The next time I saw the list, my name had been taken off (it).* ○ *The soup has been taken off the menu.* **3** to remove an amount of money in order to reduce a price, cost or payment: *Five per cent was added to VAT last year, and this year it's been taken off again.* **4** to have the specified period of time as a holiday or break from work: *take the day/morning/afternoon off* ○ *I'm taking next week off (work).* ˌtake sth ˈoff sth to cause a product to be no longer on sale: *Doctors recommended that the drug should be taken off the market.* ○ *The magazine has been taken off the shelves.*

ˌtake ˈon sth to begin to have a particular characteristic, quality or appearance; to assume sth: *The chameleon can take on the colours of its background.* ○ *Her face/eyes took on a hurt expression.* ○ *His voice took on a more serious tone.* ˌtake sb ˈon **1** to employ sb; to engage sb: *take on new staff* ○ *She was taken on as a graduate trainee.* **2** to accept sb as one's opponent in a game, contest or conflict: *take sb on at snooker/tennis/chess* ○ *Ajax will take on Juventus in this year's European Cup Final.* ○ *The rebels took on the entire Roman army.* ˌtake sth/sb ˈon to decide to do sth; to UNDERTAKE(1) sth; to accept sth/sb: *take on extra work* ○ *She took on greater responsibilities when she was promoted.* ○ *I can't take on any new clients at present.* **2** (of eg a bus, plane or ship) to allow sth/sb to enter; to take sth/sb on board: *The bus stopped to take on more passengers.* ○ *The ship took on more fuel at Freetown.*

ˌtake sb ˈout to accompany sb that one has invited eg to the theatre or a restaurant: *He wants to take her out but he's too shy to ask.* ○ *I took my wife out to dinner/for a meal on her birthday.* ˌtake sth/sb ˈout (*infml*) to destroy sth or kill sb; to put sth/sb out of action: *Enemy missiles took out two of our planes.* ˌtake sth ˈout **1** to remove or extract a part of the body: *She's gone into hospital to have her appendix taken out.* ○ *How many teeth did the dentist take out?* **2** to obtain an official document or a service: *take out an insurance policy/a mortgage/a patent.* **3** (*US*) = TAKE STH AWAY 2. ˌtake sth ˈout (against sb) to issue a document that requires sb to appear in court: *The police have taken out a summons against the driver of the car involved in the accident.* ˌtake sth ˈout (of sth) **1** to remove sth from inside sth: *Take your hands out of your pockets.* ○ *She put her bag on the seat and took out her camera.* **2** to obtain money by withdrawing it from a bank account: *How much do you need to take out (of your account)?* **3** to remove or transfer an amount of money from sth: *Monthly contributions to the pension scheme will be taken out of your salary.* **4** to make sth disappear from sth: *Cold water should take that stain out of your skirt.* ○ *The author had to take out all the references to real people.* ˌtake it/sth ˈout on sb to behave in an unpleasant way towards sb because one feels angry, disappointed, etc, esp when it is not their fault that one feels this way: *I know you've had a bad day — but there's no need to take it out on me!* ˌtake sb ˈout of themselves to make sb forget their worries and become less concerned with their own thoughts and situation: *A weekend with her family would help to take her out of herself.*

ˌtake (sth) ˈover to gain control of a country, a political party, etc: *The army is threatening to take over if civil unrest continues.* ○ *Has the party been taken over by extremists?* ○ (*fig*) *His character changes completely when jealousy takes over.* ˌtake sth ˈover to acquire or gain control of a business company, esp by obtaining the support of most of the people owning shares in it: *The firm has been taken over by an American conglomerate.* ˌtake (sth) ˈover (from sb) to take control or responsibility for sth, esp in place of sb else: *Peter will take over as*

managing director when Bill retires. ○ *George is taking over the running of our American operation.* ○ *Would you like me to take over (the driving) for a while?*

ˌtake sb ˈthrough sth to help sb learn, practise or become familiar with sth, eg by reading or commenting on each part in turn: *The director took us through the play scene by scene.* ○ *I still don't understand the contract. Can you take me through it again?*

ˈtake to ... to go away to a place, esp to escape from an enemy or from danger: *take to the forest/hills/caves* ○ *The crew took to the lifeboats when the ship was torpedoed.* ˈtake to sb/sth **1** to start liking sb/sth: *I didn't take to her husband at all.* ○ *He hasn't taken to his new school.* **2** to develop an ability for sth: *She took to tennis as if she'd been playing it all her life.* ˈtake to sth / doing sth to begin to do sth as a habit: *I've given up cigarettes and taken to smoking a pipe.* ○ *She's taken to drink* (ie has started to drink a lot of alcohol).

ˌtake ˈup to continue, esp starting after sb/sth else has finished: *This chapter takes up where the last one left off.* ˌtake ˈup sth to fill or occupy an amount of space or time: *This table takes up too much room.* ○ *Her time is fully taken up with writing.* ○ *I won't take up any more of your time.* ˌtake sth ˈup **1** to clear sth away or remove sth by lifting it: *The carpets/floorboards had to be taken up when the house was rewired.* **2** to make eg a garment or curtains shorter: *This skirt needs taking up.* Compare LET STH DOWN 2. **3** to learn or start to perform a certain activity, esp for pleasure: *take up gardening/golf/yoga* ○ *She has taken up* (ie begun to learn to play) *the oboe.* **4** to start or begin sth, esp a job: *She has taken up a job as a teacher.* ○ *She takes up her duties/responsibilities next week.* **5** to add one's voice to sth; to join in sth: *take up a chorus/refrain/song* ○ *The whole crowd took up the cry: 'Long live the King!'* ○ *Their protests were later taken up by other groups of workers.* **6** to continue sth that has been interrupted, not mentioned for some time, or not finished by sb else: *She took up the story where John had left off.* ○ *I'd like to take up the point you raised earlier.* **7** to move into a certain position or arrangement: *Our troops took up defensive positions on high ground overlooking the river.* **8** to accept sth that is offered or available: *take up a challenge* ○ *She took up his offer of a drink.* ○ *Their case was taken up by a famous lawyer.* ˌtake ˈup with sb (*infml*) to begin to be friendly with or spend a lot of time with sb, esp sb unpleasant or with a bad reputation: *She's taken up with an unemployed actor.* ˌtake sb ˈup on sth **1** to question or challenge sb about sth; to argue with sb about sth: *I must take you up on that point.* ○ *I'd like to take you up on what you said about unemployment.* **2** (*infml*) to accept a challenge, a bet, an offer, etc from sb: *'I bet I can run faster than you.' 'I'll take you up on that.'* ○ *Thanks for the invitation — we may take you up on it some time.* ˌtake sth ˈup with sb to speak or write to sb about sth that they may be able to deal with or help one with: *I'm thinking of taking the matter up with my MP.* be ˌtaken ˈup with sth/sb to have much of one's time and energies occupied by sth/sb: *She's very taken up with voluntary work at the moment.*

be ˈtaken with sb/sth to find sb/sth attractive or interesting: *We were all very taken with his fiancée.* ○ *I think he's rather taken with the idea.*

■ ˈtake-away (*US* ˈtake-out) *n* (**a**) a restaurant selling cooked food to be taken away and eaten elsewhere: *I'm too tired to cook — let's get something from the Chinese take-away.* ○ *a take-away restaurant/meal.* (**b**) a meal bought at such a restaurant: *I feel like an Indian take-away tonight.*

ˈtake-home pay *n* [U] the amount of one's wages or salary remaining after taxes and other contributions have been paid out of it.

¹**take-off** n **1** [C,U] the point at which an aircraft, etc leaves the ground and starts to fly: *a smooth take-off* ○ *The crash occurred only a minute after take-off.* ○ (*fig*) *Our company is poised for take-off* (ie great success). **2** [C,U] the moment when the feet leave the ground in jumping. **3** [C] ~ (**of sb**) (*infml*) the act of copying sb's voice or behaviour in a humorous way: *She does a brilliant take-off of the boss.*

¹**take-over** n **1** the act of taking control of a company by buying most of its shares: *the take-over of DanAir by British Airways* ○ *a* ¹*take-over bid.* **2** the act of taking over a country, a territory or an organization: *a military take-over* ○ *prevent the take-over of the Party by extremists.*

¹**take-up** n [sing, U] the degree to which sth is accepted by the people to whom it is offered or available: *The company reports a 70 per cent take-up of its share offer.*

NOTE Both **take** and **last** are used in talking about duration of time. **Take** is used to talk about the amount of time you need in order to go somewhere or to do something. **Take** must be used with an expression of time: *How long will the flight take?* ○ *It takes a long time to get home in the evenings.* ○ *It took (me) four hours to write this essay.*

   Last is used to talk about the amount of time an event continues for: *The movie lasted nearly three hours.* ○ *The strike did not last very long.* It does not always need an expression of time: *I hope this good weather lasts.* ○ *Do you think their marriage will last?* You also use **last** to say that you have enough of something for a period of time or for a particular purpose: *Do we have enough bread to last till tomorrow?* ○ *I knew the money I had borrowed wouldn't last long.*

take² /teɪk/ n **1** (*cinema*) a sequence of film photographed at one time without stopping the camera: *shoot the scene in a single take.* **2** (usu *sing*) an amount of money taken or received, eg in tax or in return for tickets sold: *The take was shared equally by the two contestants.* **IDM on the ¹take** (*sl*) regularly taking bribes (BRIBE): *They claim that a senior police officer is on the take (from known criminals).*

taker /ˈteɪkə(r)/ n **1** (usu *pl*) a person who accepts an offer or takes a bet: *There's still some cake left — any takers* (ie does anyone want some)? ○ *The bookies were offering odds of 3 to 1, but there were few takers.* **2** a person who takes sth: *drug/hostage/risk takers* ○ *It's better to be a giver than a taker.*

takings /ˈteɪkɪŋz/ n [pl] the amount of money that a shop, theatre, etc gets from selling goods, tickets, etc: *count the day's takings.*

talcum powder /ˈtælkəm paʊdə(r)/ (also **talc** /tælk/) n [U] a fine soft powder, usu with a pleasant smell, which is put on the skin to make it feel smooth and dry.

tale /teɪl/ n **1(a)** a story, often one that is simple to read or understand: *Chaucer's 'Canterbury Tales'* ○ *tales of adventure* ○ *The film is a hilarious tale of a family picnic that goes badly wrong.* See also FAIRY TALE. **(b).** a series of real events, told in the manner of a story: *He told me the tale of how he escaped from prison.* **2** a rumour, a piece of gossip or an excuse, often false or invented: *I've heard some odd tales about her.* **IDM live, etc to tell the tale** ⇨ TELL. **an old wives' tale** ⇨ OLD. **tell its own tale/story** ⇨ TELL. **tell tales** ⇨ TELL. **thereby hangs a tale** ⇨ HANG¹.

talent /ˈtælənt/ n **1** [C,U] ~ (**for sth**) a natural skill or ability at sth: *have immense artistic talent* ○ *She possesses a remarkable talent for music.* ○ *His work shows great talent.* **2** [U] a person or people with natural skill or ability: *There's always room for new/fresh talent in the music business.* ○ *a talent*

show/competition ○ *He's the most exciting new foot balling talent to emerge for years.* **3** [U] (*Brit sl*) sexually attractive people: *eyeing up the local talent.*
▶ **talented** adj having talent: *a highly/a hugely/an immensely talented musician.*
■ ¹**talent-scout** (also ¹**talent-spotter**) n a person whose job is to find talented new performers for the entertainment industry, sports teams, etc.

talisman /ˈtælɪzmən/ n (*pl* **talismans**) [C] an object that is thought to have magic powers and to bring good luck.

talk¹ /tɔːk/ v **1** ~ (**to/with sb**) (**about/of sth/sb**) to say things; to speak in order to give information or to express ideas, feelings, etc: [Vadv] *talk non-stop* [V] *We talked* (ie to each other) *for almost an hour.* ○ *I could hear them talking downstairs.* [Vpr] *He was talking to/with a friend.* ○ *What are they talking about?* ○ *She talked of applying for another job.* ○ *Are they talking in Spanish or Portuguese?* ○ *You can always talk to me if you've got a problem.* ⇨ note at SPEAK. **2** to have the power of speech: [V] *children learning to talk.* **3** to discuss sth: [Vn] *talk business/ politics/football.* **4** to express sth in words: [Vn] *She talks a lot of sense.* ○ *You're talking rubbish/ nonsense.* **5** to use a particular language when speaking: [Vn] *talk French.* **6** to bring oneself into a certain condition by talking: [Vn-adj] *talk oneself hoarse.* **7** to GOSSIP: [V] *We must stop meeting like this — people are beginning to talk!* [Vpr] *You'll have to be more discreet if you don't want to get yourself talked about.* **8** to give information to sb, esp unwillingly: [V] *The police questioned him for hours but he refused to talk.* **9** to copy the sounds of human speech: [V] *You can teach some parrots to talk.* **IDM know what one's talking about** ⇨ KNOW. **look who's ¹talking** (*infml*) you should not say such things about others since you are just as bad yourself. **money talks** ⇨ MONEY. **now you're ¹talking** (*infml*) I like what you are saying, suggesting, etc: *Take the day off? Now you're talking!* **speak/talk of the devil** ⇨ DEVIL¹. **speak/talk the same language** ⇨ LANGUAGE. ¹**talk about ...** (*infml*) (used for emphasizing sth): ¹*Talk about ex¹pensive! I've never known a place like it.* **talk the hind legs off a ¹donkey** (*infml*) to talk continuously, esp until other people become bored. **talking of sb/sth** while on the subject of sb/sth: *Talking of Jim, have you heard that he's getting married?* **talk ¹shop** (*usu derog*) to discuss one's work with people one works with, esp when in the company of other people: *I had lunch with Clive and Peter and they talked shop the whole time.* **talk through one's ¹hat** to talk nonsense. **talk ¹turkey** (*infml esp US*) to talk openly and directly. **talk one's way out of sth / doing sth** to avoid sth by clever talking: *I'd like to see him talk his way out of this one* (ie this trouble he has got into). ¹**you can/can't talk** (*infml*) = LOOK WHO'S TALKING (TALK¹). **you're a fine one to talk** (*infml*) = LOOK WHO'S TALKING (TALK¹). **PHR V** ¹**talk at sb** to speak to sb without listening to their replies: *You can't have a proper conversation with him — he just talks at you all the time.*
   ¹**talk ¹back (to sb)** to reply rudely to an order or a criticism from sb in authority: *She doesn't like her pupils to talk back to her.*
   ¹**talk sb ¹down** to stop sb speaking by talking loudly or forcefully. ¹**talk sb/sth ¹down** to help a pilot or an aircraft to land by giving radio instructions from the ground. ¹**talk ¹down to sb** to speak to sb as if they are less clever, important, etc than oneself: *I can't stand politicians who talk down to the public.*
   talk sb into / out of doing sth to persuade sb to do/not to do sth: *He talked his father into lending him the car.* ○ *I tried to talk her out of leaving.*
   ¹**talk sth ¹out** to discuss sth thoroughly and reach a

conclusion: *Sometimes it's better to talk out a problem than to keep it to yourself.*

,**talk sth** '**over (with sb)** to discuss sth thoroughly, esp to reach an agreement or a decision: *talk over your problems with sb* ○ *Her parents talked it over and decided to give her their permission.*

,**talk** '**round sth** to discuss sth without dealing with the most important point: *We wasted a whole hour talking round the problem instead of discussing ways of solving it.* ,**talk sb** '**round (to sth)** to persuade sb to accept or agree to sth: *We finally managed to talk them round (to our way of thinking).*

,**talk sb/sth** '**up** (*US*) to praise sb/sth, esp in an exaggerated way: *talk up the tourist attractions to encourage more visitors.*

▶ **talkative** /'tɔːkətɪv/ *adj* liking or tending to talk a lot: *a very talkative child* ○ *Are you feeling all right? You're not very talkative this evening.*

talker *n* **1** (esp with an *adj*) a person who talks in the specified way: *a brilliant/constant/reluctant talker* ○ *She's a great talker* (ie She talks a lot). **2** a person who talks a lot but does not act: *Don't rely on him to do anything — he's just a talker.*

■ '**talking-point** *n* a topic that is discussed or argued about: *The main talking-point at the conference was the new tax on imports.*

'**talking-to** *n* [sing] an angry talk in which sb is criticized for sth they have done wrong: *That child needs a good talking-to.*

talk² /tɔːk/ *n* **1** [C] a conversation or discussion: *I had a long talk with my boss about my career prospects.* ○ *We'll have to have a serious talk about this soon.* **2** [U] (**a**) talking, esp without action, results or the right information: *Don't worry — his threats are just talk.* ○ *Politicians are all talk — they never actually do anything.* ○ *There's too much talk and not enough work being done.* (**b**) rumour or gossip: *There's (some) talk of a general election.* **3** [C] a lecture or speech: *She gave a talk on her visit to China.* **4** talks [pl] formal discussions or negotiations: *arms talks* ○ *The latest round of pay talks has broken down.* ○ *Further talks aimed at producing peace will be held next month.* **5** [U] (esp in compounds) a way of speaking, esp for a particular purpose: '*baby-talk* ○ '*sales talk.* see also SMALL TALK, SWEET TALK. **IDM** **fighting talk/words** ⇨ FIGHT¹.

the talk of sth the main subject of conversation in a place: *Her resignation was the talk of the office.*

■ '**talk show** *n* (*esp US*) = CHAT SHOW.

NOTE A **talk** is an informal speech to a small audience on a particular subject: *Chris will give an illustrated talk on his expedition to Antarctica.* A **speech** is made to a lot of people on a formal occasion: *Martin Luther King's most famous speech* ○ *Several people made speeches at the wedding.* **Talks** are formal meetings between politicians at which they talk to each other about political problems, etc: *After ten hours of talks no agreement was reached.* ○ *The peace talks will be held in Geneva.* If you **have a talk** with somebody, you talk to them about a problem or about something that worries you: *I need to have a serious talk with you.*

Discussion refers to a serious talk about an interesting or important subject: *There has been a lot of discussion in schools on environmental issues.* ○ *After the film there will be a discussion.* **Conversation** is usually social and friendly, often for the exchange of ideas and information: *Television has killed the art of conversation.* ○ *We had an interesting conversation over lunch.*

A **chat** is an informal and often short conversation to exchange personal news: *I phoned Mary for a chat.* **Gossip** means talking about other people and their private lives in an unpleasant way: *You shouldn't listen to the gossip you hear in this village — most of it isn't true.*

talkie /'tɔːki/ *n* (often *pl*) (*dated esp US*) a cinema film with sound, not just pictures. See also WALKIE-TALKIE.

tall /tɔːl/ *adj* (-**er**, -**est**) **1** (of people or things) of more than average height; not short: *the tallest girl in the class* ○ *a tall tree/chimney/building* ○ *She's taller than me.* Compare SHORT¹ 1b. **2** of a specified height: *Tom is over six feet tall.* ⇨ note at HIGH¹. **IDM** **walk tall** ⇨ WALK¹. ▶ **tallness** *n* [U].

■ ,**tall** '**order** *n* [sing] (*infml*) a difficult task or an unreasonable request: *That's rather a tall order considering how little time we have.*

,**tall** '**story** *n* (*infml*) a story that is difficult to believe and unlikely to be true.

tallboy /'tɔːlbɔɪ/ (*Brit*) (*US* **highboy**) *n* a tall piece of furniture with drawers for clothes, etc.

tallow /'tæləʊ/ *n* [U] animal fat used for making candles, soap, etc.

tally /'tæli/ *n* a record of amounts, or a score in a game: *a match tally of 14 points* ○ *Keep a tally of how much you spend.*

▶ **tally** *v* (*pt, pp* **tallied**) ~ (**with sth**) (of statements, amounts, etc) to correspond; to be consistent with sth: [V] *These figures don't tally.* [Vpr] *Luckily for you, his story tallies with yours.*

Talmud /'tælmʊd; *US* 'tɑːl-/ *n* **the Talmud** [sing] a collection of ancient writings on Jewish law and tradition. ▶ **Talmudic** /ˌtæl'mʊdɪk/ *adj*.

talon /'tælən/ *n* (usu *pl*) a CLAW(1), esp of a bird of prey (BIRD): *an eagle's talons.*

tambourine /ˌtæmbə'riːn/ *n* (*music*) a round musical instrument like a shallow drum with metal discs around the edge. It is played by being shaken or hit with the hand.

tame /teɪm/ *adj* (-**r**, -**st**) **1** (of animals or birds) not wild or afraid of people: *The birds are so tame they will eat from your hand.* **2** [attrib] (*joc*) (of people) willing to be told what to do: *She gets her tame husband to help her with domestic chores.* **3** not exciting or interesting; dull: *a novel with rather a tame ending* ○ *I find the scenery around here a little tame.*

▶ **tame** *v* make (sth) tame or easy to control: [Vn] *taming wild animals* ○ *All attempts to tame the elements* (eg control the weather) *have failed.* **tamer** *n* (usu in compounds) a person who tames and trains wild animals: *a* '*lion-tamer.*

tamely *adv*: *accept criticism tamely.*

tameness *n* [U]: *I was surprised at the tameness of the animals.*

tamp /tæmp/ *v* **PHRV** ,**tamp sth** '**down** to press sth down firmly, esp so as to fit it into a small space: *tamp down the tobacco in a pipe.*

tamper /'tæmpə(r)/ *v* **PHRV** '**tamper with sth** to interfere with or alter sth without authority: [Vpr] *Someone has been tampering with the lock.* [Vpr] *The records of the meeting had been tampered with.*

tampon /'tæmpɒn/ *n* a specially shaped piece of soft material that a woman places inside her VAGINA to absorb blood during her period(4).

tan¹ /tæn/ *v* (-**nn**-) **1** (of a person or the skin) to become brown as a result of being exposed to the sun; to make sb brown in this way: [V] *My skin tans easily.* [Vn] *You look very tanned — have you been on holiday?* ○ *tanning cream* (ie to prevent the skin burning in the sun or to make it brown artificially). **2** [Vn] to make animal skin into leather by treating it with chemicals. **IDM** **tan sb's** '**hide** (*dated infml*) to beat sb hard and repeatedly as a punishment.

▶ **tan** *n* **1** [C] the brown colour of normally white skin after it has been exposed to the sun: *get a good tan* ○ *My tan's beginning to fade.* **2** [U, sing] a yellowish-brown colour: *Do you have these shoes in (a) tan?*

tan *adj* yellowish-brown: *tan leather gloves.*

tanner *n* a person who tans (TAN¹ 2) skins to make leather.

tannery /'tænəri/ *n* a place where skins are tanned (TAN¹ 2) to make leather.

tan² /tæn/ *abbr* (*mathematics*) tangent.

tandem /'tændəm/ *n* a bicycle with seats and pedals for two riders, one behind the other. **IDM** **in 'tandem (with sb/sth)** **1** one behind another: *drive/ride in tandem*. **2** together; at the same time and in corresponding ways: *The two systems are designed to work in tandem*. ○ *He and his wife run the business in tandem* (ie as partners).

tandoori /tæn'dʊəri/ *n* [U] (often attrib) a type of Indian food cooked over CHARCOAL(1) in a clay oven: *tandoori chicken* ○ *a tandoori restaurant*.

tang /tæŋ/ *n* (usu *sing*) a sharp taste, flavour or smell: *a sauce with a tang of lemon juice*. ▶ **tangy** /'tæŋi/ *adj*: *a tangy aroma/sauce/flavour*.

tangent /'tændʒənt/ *n* **1** (*geometry*) a straight line that touches the outside of a curve but does not cross it. ➪ picture at CIRCLE. **2** (*abbr* **tan**) (*mathematics*) the ratio of the lengths of the sides opposite and next to an angle in a right-angled (RIGHT¹) TRIANGLE(1). Compare COSINE, SINE. **IDM** **go/fly off at a 'tangent** to change suddenly from one subject or action, etc to another: *Stick to the point — don't keep going off at a tangent*. ▶ **tangential** *adj* having only a slight or indirect connection with sth: *a tangential argument*. **tangentially** *adv*.

tangerine /ˌtændʒə'riːn; *US* 'tændʒəriːn/ *n* **1** [C] a small sweet orange with a loose skin. **2** [U] a deep orange-yellow colour.

tangible /'tændʒəbl/ *adj* **1** [usu attrib] clear and definite; real: *tangible advantages/benefits/rewards* ○ *tangible proof* ○ *the company's tangible assets* (eg its buildings, machinery, etc). **2** (*fml*) that can be perceived by touch: *the tangible world*. ▶ **tangibly** /-əbli/ *adv*.

tangle /'tæŋgl/ *n* [C] **1** a confused mass of string, hair, etc that cannot easily be separated: *brush the tangles out of a dog's fur* ○ *a tangle of branches* ○ *The wool got in a dreadful tangle*. **2** a confused state; a state of disorder: *I got into a tangle trying to follow the instructions*. ○ *His financial affairs are in a complete tangle*. **3** (*infml*) an argument, a fight or a disagreement: *They got into a tangle about politics and started shouting at each other*. ▶ **tangle** *v* ~ (**sth**) (**up**) (usu passive) to twist sth or become twisted into a confused mass: [Vnp] *Don't let those ropes get tangled up*. [V] *I have the sort of hair that tangles easily*. [also Vn,Vp]. **PHRV** **'tangle with sb/sth** to become involved in an argument or a fight with sb/sth: [Vpr] *I shouldn't tangle with Peter — he's bigger than you*. **tangled** *adj*: *a tangled affair* ○ *tangled hair/wire/undergrowth*.

tango /'tæŋgəʊ/ *n* (*pl* **-os** /-gəʊz/) a South American dance for two people, with a strong distinctive rhythm; music for such a dance: *dance/do the tango*. ▶ **tango** *v* (*pt, pp* **-goed**; *pres p* **-going**) [V] to dance the tango.

tangy ➪ TANG.

tank

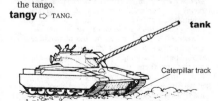

Caterpillar track

tank /tæŋk/ *n* **1(a)** a large container, usu for liquid or gas: *the 'petrol-tank of a car* ○ *keep tropical fish in a glass tank* ○ *a leak from the cold water tank in the roof*. ➪ picture at CAR. **(b)** (also **'tankful** /-fʊl/) the

contents of this: *We drove there and back on one tank of petrol*. **2** a military vehicle covered with a strong metal case and armed with guns. It can travel over very rough ground using wheels that move inside metal tracks. ➪ picture. ▶ **tank** *v* **PHRV** **be/get ,tanked 'up** (*sl*) to be/become drunk: *We got really tanked up on whisky and beer*.

tanker *n* (**a**) a ship, a lorry or an aircraft that carries oil, petrol, gas etc in large quantities: *an oil tanker*.

tankard /'tæŋkəd/ *n* a large, usu metal, container with a handle, esp one from which beer is drunk. ➪ picture at CUP¹.

tanner ➪ TAN¹.

tannery ➪ TAN¹.

tannic /'tænɪk/ *adj* of TANNIN.

tannin /'tænɪn/ *n* [U] any of various compounds found in the bark of certain trees and the fruit of many plants. It is used esp in preparing leather and in making wine.

Tannoy /'tænɔɪ/ *n* (*Brit propr*) a system with loudspeakers (LOUDSPEAKER) used for making announcements in a public place: *an announcement made over/on the Tannoy*.

tantalize, -ise /'tæntəlaɪz/ *v* to make a person or an animal desire sth which they cannot or may not be able to have or do: [Vn] *Give the dog the bone — don't tantalize him*. ○ *He was tantalized by the possibility of visiting the places he had read about*. ▶ **tantalizing, -ising** *adj*: *a tantalizing prospect/smell of food*. **tantalizingly, -isingly** *adv*: *tantalizingly just out of reach*.

tantamount /'tæntəmaʊnt/ *adj* [pred] ~ **to sth** equal in effect to sth: *The King's request was tantamount to a command*. ○ *Her statement is tantamount to a confession of guilt*.

tantrum /'tæntrəm/ *n* a sudden display of anger, esp by a child or sb behaving like one: *have/throw a tantrum* ○ *temper tantrums*.

tap¹ /tæp/ *n* **1** (also *esp US* **faucet**) a device for controlling the flow of liquid or gas out of a pipe or container: *hot and cold taps* (eg on a sink or bath) ○ *turn the tap on/off* ○ *Don't leave the taps running* (ie Turn them off). Compare VALVE 1. **2** an act of fitting a device to a telephone so that calls can be listened to secretly: *put a tap on sb's phone*. **IDM** **on 'tap 1** (of beer, etc) in a barrel with a tap; on DRAUGHT(4). **2** available whenever needed: *have a supply of reliable workers on tap*. ▶ **tap** *v* (**-pp-**) **1(a)** to draw liquid from a container: [Vn] *tap a cask of cider*. **(b)** ~ **sth** (**off**) (**from sth**) to draw liquid through the tap of a barrel: [Vnp] *tap off some beer* [also Vn,Vnpr]. **2** to cut the bark of a tree in order to collect the SAP¹: [Vn] *tap rubber-trees* [also Vnpr,Vnp]. **3** to extract or obtain a supply of sth from a source: [Vn] *vast mineral wealth waiting to be tapped* ○ *schemes to tap the skills of retired people*. **4** to fit a device to a telephone line so that calls can be listened to secretly: [Vn] *I think my phone is being tapped*. **PHRV** **'tap sb for sth** (*Brit infml*) to persuade sb to give one sth one needs: *tap sb for a loan*.

■ **'tap root** *n* the main root of a plant, growing straight downwards.

'tap water *n* [U] water supplied through pipes to taps in a building.

tap² /tæp/ *v* (**-pp-**) (**a**) to hit sb/sth gently with a quick light blow: [Vpr] *Who's that tapping at the window?* [Vp] *When I left he was still tapping away on his typewriter*. [Vnpr] *tap sb on the shoulder* [Vnp,Vnpr] *tap out a beat on a drum* [also V,Vn]. (**b**) to strike sth against sth else: [Vnpr] *tapping her fingers on the table* [Vn,Vnpr] *Everyone was tapping their feet (to the rhythm)*.

▶ **tap** *n* a quick light blow or the sound of one: *They heard a tap at the door.* ○ *He felt a tap on his shoulder.* ○ *She gave the lid a few gentle taps to loosen it.*

■ ¹**tap-dance** *n* a dance in which an elaborate rhythm is tapped with the feet, for which the dancer wears special shoes. — *v* [V]. ¹**tap-dancer** *n*. ¹**tap-dancing** *n* [U].

tape /teɪp/ *n* **1** [C, U] a narrow strip of material used for fastening sth or as a label: *a metre of linen tape* ○ *The seat covers are held in place by tapes.* ○ *a name-tape* (ie sewn into a garment and showing the owner's name). **2(a)** [U] a long thin strip of MAGNETIC(1) material, used for recording sounds, pictures or information: *recording tape* ○ *I've got all the Beethoven symphonies on tape.* See also MAGNETIC TAPE, VIDEOTAPE. **(b)** [C] a CASSETTE or REEL¹(a) with tape wound round it, on which music, conversations, etc are recorded: *The police seized various books and tapes.* ○ *Shall I put on a tape?* ○ *a blank tape* (ie one on which nothing has been recorded). **3** [U] a strip of paper or other flexible material with a sticky substance on one side, used for sticking things together: *adhesive tape* ○ *fix a notice to a wall with tape.* See also INSULATING TAPE, MASKING TAPE, SCOTCH TAPE. **4** [C] a narrow strip of material stretched across a track at the place where a race will finish: *He broke the tape* (ie finished the race) *half a second ahead of his rival.* **5** [C] = RED TAPE, TAPE-MEASURE, TICKER-TAPE.

▶ **tape** *v* **1(a)** to tie or fasten sth with tape(1): [Vn, Vnp] *tape (up) a bundle.* **(b)** to fasten or attach sth with tape(3): [Vnpr] *tape the flap of an envelope down* [Vnpr] *tape a message onto a door.* **2** to record sb/sth on tape(2) using a special machine: [Vn, Vnpr] *tape a concert (off/from the radio)* [Vn] *taped music/messages.* **IDM** **have (got) sb/sth ¹taped** *(infml esp Brit)* to understand sb/sth fully; to have become able to deal with sb/sth successfully: *It took me a while to learn the rules of the game but I think I've got them taped now.*

■ ¹**tape deck** *n* a machine for recording sounds on tape(2), usu as one component in a HI-FI system.

¹**tape-measure** (also **tape**, ¹**measuring tape**) *n* a strip of plastic, cloth or flexible metal marked for measuring the length of sth.

¹**tape-record** *v* to record sth on tape(2): [Vn] ¹*tape-recorded* ¹*interviews.* ¹**tape recorder** *n* a machine for recording sounds on tape(2) and playing back the recording. ¹**tape recording** *n* a recording made on a tape(2).

taper¹ /ˈteɪpə(r)/ *v* **1** ~ (sth) (off) (to sth) to become or make sth become gradually narrower: [Vpr, Vp] *a blade that tapers (off) to a fine point* [Vn] *The trouser legs are slightly tapered.* [also V, Vnp]. Compare FLARE². **2** ~ (sth) off to become or cause sth to become less: [Vp] *The number of applicants for the course has been tapering off recently.* [Vnp] *taper off production of an old model.*

taper² /ˈteɪpə(r)/ *n* **1** a length of thread covered in wax like a very thin candle: *put a taper to the fire to light it.* **2** (usu *sing*) the degree to which sth becomes gradually narrower or the part that does this: *jeans with a slight taper.*

tapestry /ˈtæpəstri/ *n* [C, U] a large piece of cloth into which threads of coloured wool are woven or sewn by hand to make pictures or designs: *medieval tapestries* ○ *a tapestry cushion cover* ○ *(fig) Meeting strange people like that is all part of life's rich tapestry.*

▶ **tapestried** *adj* hung or decorated with tapestries.

tapeworm /ˈteɪpwɜːm/ *n* a long flat creature that lives as a PARASITE(1) in the intestines (INTESTINE) of people or animals.

tapioca /ˌtæpiˈəʊkə/ *n* [U] hard white grains ob-

tained from the CASSAVA plant which are cooked and eaten as food.

tapir /ˈteɪpə(r)/ *n* a small animal similar to a pig with a long flexible nose, found in tropical America and Malaysia.

tar /tɑː(r)/ *n* [U] **1** a thick black sticky liquid that becomes hard when cold. Tar is obtained from coal and is used esp in making roads. **2** a similar substance formed by burning tobacco: *low-tar cigarettes.*

▶ **tar** *v* (-rr-) to cover sth with tar(1): [Vn] *a tarred road/roof.* See also TARMAC a. **IDM** **tar and ¹feather sb** to put tar(1) on sb and then cover them with feathers, as a punishment. **tarred with the same ¹brush (as sb)** having or considered to have the same faults as sb.

taramasalata /ˌtærəməsəˈlɑːtə/ *n* [U] *(Brit)* an edible, usu pink, PASTE¹(3) made from the eggs of certain fish.

tarantula /təˈræntʃələ/ *n* a large spider. Many types of tarantula are hairy and some are poisonous.

tardy /ˈtɑːdi/ *adj* *(fml)* **1** slow to act, move or happen: *be tardy in offering help* ○ *tardy progress* ○ *a tardy response.* **2** late: *a tardy arrival* ○ *(US) be tardy for/to school.* ▶ **tardily** /-ɪli/ *adv.* **tardiness** *n* [U].

target /ˈtɑːgɪt/ *n* **1(a)** an object that a person tries to hit in shooting practice or in certain sports, esp a round board with circles on it: *shoot off target* (ie fail to hit it). ⇨ picture at ARCHERY. **(b)** a place, a person or an object that people aim at when shooting or attacking: *bomb military targets* ○ *fire at a moving target.* **2** ~ (for sth) a person or thing against which criticism, dislike, contempt, etc is directed: *become a target for scorn/hate/derision.* **3** a result aimed at; a goal or an OBJECTIVE *n*: *meet one's export targets* ○ *Sales so far this year are on target* (ie likely to reach the desired level). ○ *a target date* (ie one set for completing a project, etc).

▶ **target** *v* (-t-) ~ sth (at/on sth/sb) (usu passive) to aim sth at sb/sth; to direct sth towards sb/sth: [Vnpr] *missiles targeted on Britain* ○ *a sales campaign targeted at the youth market* [Vn] *a new magazine that targets the elderly.*

tariff /ˈtærɪf/ *n* **1** a list of fixed charges, esp for rooms, meals, etc at a hotel. **2** a tax paid on imports: *raise tariff barriers against foreign goods.* Compare TAX 1.

Tarmac /ˈtɑːmæk/ *n* [U] **(a)** *(propr)* (also **tarmacadam**) a material for making road surfaces, consisting of broken stone mixed with TAR(1). **(b)** **tarmac** (*US* also **blacktop**) an area with a Tarmac surface, esp at an airport: *The plane taxied along the tarmac.* See also MACADAM.

▶ **tarmac** *v* (-ck-) *(Brit)* to cover a surface with Tarmac: [Vn] *I'm getting the front drive tarmacked.*

tarn /tɑːn/ *n* (often in names) a small lake among mountains.

tarnish /ˈtɑːnɪʃ/ *v* **1** (esp of metal) to lose its brightness by being exposed to air or damp; to make sth lose brightness in this way: [V] *mirrors that have tarnished with age* [Vn] *The brasswork needs polishing — it's badly tarnished.* **2** to damage sb's reputation: [Vn] *The new manager is determined to improve the club's somewhat tarnished image.*

▶ **tarnish** *n* [C, U] marks or loss of brightness on metal: *remove the tarnish from silver.*

tarot /ˈtærəʊ/ *n* [sing] a set of special cards with pictures on them, used for predicting people's futures: *tarot cards* ○ *interpret the tarot.*

tarpaulin /tɑːˈpɔːlɪn/ *n* [C, U] a large sheet of canvas made WATERPROOF, esp by being treated with TAR(1): *a truck covered by a tarpaulin.*

tarragon /ˈtærəgən/ *n* [U] a plant whose leaves are used for adding flavour to food and VINEGAR: *dried tarragon.*

tarry¹ /ˈtæri/ *v* (*pt, pp* **tarried**) [V, Vpr] *(arch or rhet)* to delay coming to or going from a place; to LINGER (1,2).

tarry² /ˈtɑːri/ adj of, like or covered with TAR(1).

tart¹ /tɑːt/ n a shallow pie containing fruit or other sweet filling, usu not covered with pastry: *a strawberry/jam tart*. Compare FLAN.

tart² /tɑːt/ adj **1** having an unpleasant sharp taste: *The stewed apple needs a bit more sugar — it's still a bit tart.* **2** [usu attrib] sharp in manner; unkind or sarcastic (SARCASM): *a tart reply/tone.* ▶ **tartly** adv: *'They had their opportunity,' Jill replied tartly.* **tartness** n [U].

tart³ /tɑːt/ n (sl) **1** a prostitute. **2** (Brit derog) a girl or woman whose behaviour or appearance is deliberately intended to attract sexual partners.
▶ **tart** v **PHRV** ˌtart oneself ˈup (infml esp Brit) (esp of a woman) to make oneself more attractive by dressing in fashionable clothes, putting on make-up (MAKE¹), jewellery, etc: *tarting herself up for the disco.* ˌtart sth ˈup (esp Brit) to decorate or improve the appearance of sth: *They've tarted up the restaurant but the food hasn't improved.*

tartan /ˈtɑːtn/ n (a) [C,U] a pattern on material of coloured lines crossing at right angles (RIGHT¹), esp one associated with a Scottish CLAN(1): *the traditional MacLeod tartan.* (b) [U] fabric woven with such a pattern: *a tartan skirt.*

tartar¹ /ˈtɑːtə(r)/ n [U] a hard substance that forms on the teeth. Compare PLAQUE².

tartar² /ˈtɑːtə(r)/ n a person who has a violent temper, esp sb in authority.

tartar sauce (also **tartare sauce**) /ˌtɑːtə(r) ˈsɔːs/ n [U] a cold sauce made of mayonnaise with chopped onions, capers (CAPER²), etc and eaten esp with fish.

task /tɑːsk; US tæsk/ n a piece of work that has to be done, esp a hard or unpleasant one: *a daunting/ formidable/thankless task.* ○ *Our first task is to establish a system.* ○ *I set myself the task of cleaning the gutters.* ○ *Becoming fluent in a foreign language is no easy task* (ie is difficult). ⇨ note at WORK¹. **IDM** take sb to ˈtask (about/for/over sth) to criticize sb severely for sth: *He was taken to task for not trying at school.* ○ *She took the government to task over its economic record.*
▶ **task** v ~ sb with sth/to do sth (fml) (usu passive) to give sth to sb as a task: [Vnpr] *tasked with guaranteeing security during the Pope's visit* [also Vn.to inf].
■ ˈtask force (a) a military force assembled and sent to a particular place. (b) a group of people assembled to deal with a particular problem.

taskmaster /ˈtɑːskmɑːstə(r); US -mæstər/ n a person who is strict in making others work hard: *Our teacher is **a hard taskmaster.***

tassel /ˈtæsl/ n a bunch of threads tied at one end and hanging from a cushion, hat, etc as decoration. ⇨ picture.
▶ **tasselled** (US **tasseled**) adj decorated with a tassel or tassels.

tassel
— tassel

taste¹ /teɪst/ n **1** [U] the sense by which a flavour is recognized: *Having a bad cold affects one's sense of taste.* **2** [C,U] the flavour of sth, causing a particular sensation when it comes into contact with the tongue: *Sugar has a sweet taste.* ○ *I don't like the taste of this cheese.* ○ *The soup had very little taste.* **3** [C usu sing] a small quantity of food or drink taken as a sample: *Just have a taste of this cheese!* **4** [sing] a brief experience of sth: *It was my **first taste** of life in a big city.* ○ *Although we didn't know it, this incident was **a taste of things to come.*** **5** [C,U] ~ (for sth) an interest in or preference for sth: *That trip gave me a taste for foreign travel.* ○ *have expensive tastes in clothes* ○

*Modern art is not **to everyone's taste.*** **6** [U] the ability to choose, recognize or enjoy what is considered appropriate or of good quality: *have excellent taste in art/music* ○ *a room furnished with taste* ○ *He's got more money than taste.* **IDM** an acquired taste ⇨ ACQUIRE. (be) in good, bad, poor, the best of, the worst of, etc ˈtaste showing taste¹(6) or lack of it; appropriate/not appropriate: *I thought his jokes were in very poor taste.* leave a bad/nasty ˈtaste in the mouth (of events, experiences, etc) to be followed by feelings of disgust, shame, etc. there's no accounting for taste ⇨ ACCOUNT². to ˈtaste (esp in cooking) in the quantity preferred: *Add salt to taste.*
▶ **tasteful** /-fl/ adj showing taste¹(6): *tasteful furniture.* **tastefully** /-fəli/ adv: *tastefully decorated.*
tasteless adj **1** having no flavour: *a tasteless soup.* **2** lacking in taste¹(6); not appropriate: *tasteless jokes.* **tastelessly** adv.
tasty adj (-ier, -iest) having a strong and pleasant flavour: *a tasty dish/meal/morsel.*
■ ˈtaste bud n (usu pl) any of the small cells on the tongue by which flavours in food and drink are recognized.

taste² /teɪst/ v **1** (not used in the continuous tenses; often with can) to be able to recognize flavours in food and drink: [Vn] *Can you taste the garlic in the stew?* [also V]. **2** ~ (of sth) to have a certain specified flavour: [V-adj] *taste sour/bitter/sweet* [Vpr] *It tastes strongly of mint.* **3** to test the flavour of sth by eating or drinking a small amount of it: [Vn] *Please taste the soup and tell me if it needs more salt.* ⇨ note at FEEL¹. **4** to eat or drink food or liquid: [Vn] *They hadn't tasted hot food for over a week.* ○ *That's the best wine I've ever tasted.* **5** to have a brief experience of sth: [Vn] *taste power/freedom/failure/ defeat.*
▶ **taster** n a person whose job is to judge the quality of wine, tea, etc by tasting it.
tasting n an event at which sth is tasted (TASTE² 3): *go to a wine tasting.*
-tasting (forming compound adjs) having the specified flavour or taste: *sweet-tasting* ○ *fresh-tasting.*

tat¹ /tæt/ n [U] (Brit infml) cheap goods of poor quality and little or no use: *a shop selling dreadful old tat.*

tat² /tæt/ n **IDM** tit for tat ⇨ TIT².

ta-ta /tæ ˈtɑː/ interj (Brit infml) goodbye.

tattered /ˈtætəd/ adj torn, old and in generally poor condition: *tattered documents/jeans/flags.*

tatters /ˈtætəz/ n [pl] torn pieces of cloth: *His clothes hung in tatters.* **IDM** in tatters destroyed; ruined: *The court case left his reputation/life/career in tatters.* ○ *Government policy is in tatters.*

tattle /ˈtætl/ n [U] (derog) talk about unimportant things; gossip. See also TITTLE-TATTLE.

tattoo¹ /təˈtuː; US tæˈtuː/ n (pl tattoos) **1** [C] a public display of military marching, music and exercises. **2** [sing] a military signal given by beating a drum: *beat the tattoo.* **3** [C] an act of tapping sth rapidly and continuously: *He beat a loud tattoo on the table with his fingers.*

tattoo² /təˈtuː; US tæˈtuː/ n (pl tattoos) a picture or pattern on a person's skin made by making small holes in it and filling them with coloured dye: *His arms were covered in tattoos.*
▶ **tattoo** v to mark sb's skin with a tattoo: [Vn] *get tattooed in a local shop* [Vnpr] *He had a ship tattooed on his arm.*

tatty /ˈtæti/ adj (-ier, -iest) (infml) in poor condition, esp as a result of being used for a long time or not being cared for; SHABBY(1): *tatty old clothes* ○ *a tatty office.*

taught pt, pp of TEACH.

taunt /tɔːnt/ v ~ sb (with sth) to try to make sb angry or upset by saying insulting things to them or by mocking them: [Vnpr] *The other children taunted him with remarks about his size.* [also Vn].

▶ **taunt** *n* (often *pl*) a taunting remark: *ignoring the taunts of the crowd.*

Taurus /'tɔːrəs/ *n* (**a**) [U] the second sign of the ZODIAC, the Bull. (**b**) [C] a person born under the influence of this sign. ▶ **Taurean** *n, adj.* ⇨ picture at ZODIAC. ⇨ note at ZODIAC.

taut /tɔːt/ *adj* **1** stretched tightly: *a taunt string* ○ *taut skin.* **2** (of muscles or nerves) tense: *a taut body.* **3** (of writing, a film, a performance, etc) with no irrelevant parts; tightly controlled: *a taut plot/ play.* ▶ **tautly** *adv.* **tautness** *n* [U].

tauten /'tɔːtn/ *v* [V, Vn] to become or make sth become TAUT.

tautology /tɔː'tɒlədʒi/ *n* [U, C] ~ (**on sth**) the saying of the same thing more than once in different ways without making one's meaning clearer or more forceful; an instance of this. ▶ **tautological** /ˌtɔːtə'lɒdʒɪkl/, **tautologous** /tɔː'tɒləgəs/ *adjs.*

tavern /'tævən/ *n* (*arch or rhet*) a pub; an INN.

tawdry /'tɔːdri/ *adj* **1** intended to be attractive but cheap and of poor quality: *tawdry jewellery/ furnishings.* **2** showing lack of moral principle and causing contempt: *a tawdry affair/scandal/tale.* ▶ **tawdriness** *n* [U].

tawny /'tɔːni/ *adj* brownish-yellow: *the lion's tawny mane.*

tax /tæks/ *n* [C, U] money that has to be paid to the government. People pay tax according to their income and businesses pay tax according to their profits. Tax is also often paid on goods and services: *a property/sales tax* ○ *tax increases/cuts* ○ *pay over £1 000 in taxes.* Compare DUTY 3, TARIFF 2. See also INCOME TAX, INDIRECT TAX, VALUE ADDED TAX. **IDM** a **tax on sth** a strain on sth: *a tax on one's health/ patience/strength.*

▶ **tax** *v* **1** to put a tax on sb/sth; to require sb to pay tax: [Vn] *tax luxury goods* ○ *tax rich and poor alike* [Vn] *My income is taxed at source* (ie Tax is taken from it before it is paid to me). **2** to pay tax on sth, esp a vehicle (so that one is allowed to use it on roads): [Vn] *The car is taxed until July.* **3** to make heavy demands on sb/sth; to strain sb/sth: [Vn] *All these questions are beginning to tax my patience.* **IDM** **tax one's/sb's 'brain(s)** to set oneself/sb a difficult mental task: *This crossword will really tax your brain.* **PHRV** **'tax sb with sth / doing sth** (*fml*) to accuse sb of sth, esp by showing them evidence of their wrongdoing; to CONFRONT(2) sb with sth: *She was taxed with negligence/ with having been negligent.* **taxable** *adj* on which tax is required to be paid: *taxable income/earnings.*

taxing *adj* tiring or demanding; requiring great physical or mental effort: *a taxing job.*

■ **'tax avoidance** *n* [U] the arrangement of one's financial affairs so that one only pays the minimum amount of tax required by law.

ˌ**tax-de'ductible** *adj* (of expenses) that may be deducted (DEDUCT) from income before the amount of tax to be paid is calculated.

'tax disc *n* (*Brit*) a small paper disc displayed on the WINDSCREEN of a vehicle to show that the tax permitting the vehicle to be used on roads has been paid.

'tax evasion *n* [U] illegal and deliberate failure to pay tax.

ˌ**tax-e'xempt** *adj* not subject to the payment of tax: *a ˌtax-exempt 'savings scheme.*

ˌ**tax-'free** *adj* on which no tax has to be paid: *a ˌtax-free 'bonus.*

'tax haven *n* a country where income tax, etc is low and where people go to live or businesses are registered because taxes are higher in their own countries.

'tax inspector *n* = INSPECTOR OF TAXES.

'tax relief *n* [U] a reduction in the amount of tax one is required to pay, eg because one is paying for a MORTGAGE.

'tax return *n* a statement of one's personal income, used by the government tax office for calculating the amount of tax one must pay.

'tax shelter *n* a means of organizing business affairs so as to reduce payment of tax to a minimum.

taxation /tæk'seɪʃn/ *n* [U] (**a**) the system of raising money by taxes: *the separate taxation of husbands and wives.* (**b**) money that has to be paid as taxes: *reduce/increase taxation.*

taxi /'tæksi/ (also **'taxi-cab, cab**) *n* a car with a driver that may be hired for journeys, esp one with a METER[1] that records the fare to be paid: *call/hail/ hire/take a taxi.*

▶ **taxi** *v* (of an aircraft) to move slowly along the ground before taking off or after landing: [Vpr] *The plane was taxiing along the runway.* [also Vp].

■ **'taxi rank** (also **'taxi stand**) *n* a place where taxis park while waiting to be hired.

taxidermy /'tæksɪdɜːmi/ *n* [U] the art of stuffing (STUFF[2] 5) dead animals, birds and fish so that they look like living ones, usu for display.

▶ **taxidermist** /-mɪst/ *n* a person who practises taxidermy.

taxman /'tæksmæn/ *n* (*pl* **-men** /-men/) **1** [C] a person whose job is to collect taxes. **2** **the taxman** [sing] (*infml*) the government department that is responsible for collecting taxes: *He had been cheating the taxman for years.*

taxonomy /tæk'sɒnəmi/ *n* (**a**) [U] the scientific process of classifying living things. (**b**) [C] a particular system of classifying things.

▶ **taxonomic** /ˌtæksə'nɒmɪk/ *adj.*

taxonomist /tæk'sɒnəmɪst/ *n* a person who practises taxonomy.

taxpayer /'tækspeɪə(r)/ *n* a person who pays taxes, esp income tax.

TB /ˌtiː'biː/ *abbr* tuberculosis: *be vaccinated against TB.*

T-bone ⇨ T.

tbsp (*pl* **tbsps**) *abbr* tablespoonful: *Add 3 tbsps sugar.*

tea /tiː/ *n* **1**(**a**) [U] the dried leaves of the tea bush: *a pound of tea.* (**b**) [U] a drink made by pouring boiling water onto the dried leaves of the tea bush. Milk and sugar may also be added: *a cup/mug/pot of tea* ○ *China/lemon/iced tea* ○ *Shall I make (the) tea?* (**c**) [C] a cup of this: *Two teas, please.* **2** [U] a drink made by pouring boiling water onto the leaves of other plants: *camomile/mint/herb tea.* **3** [U, C] (**a**) a light meal taken in the afternoon, usu with sandwiches, biscuits or cakes, and tea to drink: *We usually have tea at four o'clock.* See also CREAM TEA, HIGH TEA. (**b**) (in some areas or among some social classes of Britain) a cooked meal taken in the early evening: *have (your) tea as soon as you get home from school.* ⇨ note at DINNER. **IDM** **sb's cup of tea** ⇨ CUP[1]. **not for all the tea in 'China** not even for a great reward: *I wouldn't marry him for all the tea in China!*

■ **'tea bag** *n* a small thin paper bag containing tea leaves onto which boiling water is poured in order to make a drink of tea.

'tea break *n* (*Brit*) (in an office or a factory) a short period of time when people stop working and drink tea, coffee, etc.

'tea caddy (also **caddy**) *n* (*esp Brit*) a tin in which tea is kept for daily use.

'tea chest *n* (*Brit*) a light wooden box lined with metal, in which tea is transported. Tea chests are sometimes used for transporting personal possessions, eg when moving to another home.

'tea cloth *n* (*Brit*) = TEA TOWEL.

[V.*to* inf] = verb + *to* infinitive   [Vn.inf (no *to*)] = verb + noun + infinitive without *to*   [V.*ing*] = verb + *-ing* form

¹**tea cosy** n a cover placed over a TEAPOT to keep the tea inside it warm.

¹**tea-leaf** n (pl **-leaves**) any of the leaves left at the bottom of a TEAPOT after tea has been poured or in a cup after tea has been drunk: *throw away the tea-leaves* ○ *She said she could tell my fortune from the tea-leaves in my cup.*

¹**tea party** n a social occasion at which tea(1b) is served, esp in the late afternoon.

¹**tea-service** n = TEASET.

¹**tea-table** n a usu small table at which tea(3a) is served.

¹**tea towel** (Brit) (also ¹**tea cloth**, US ¹**dishtowel**) n a small towel for drying washed dishes, knives, forks, etc.

¹**tea trolley** (Brit) (US ¹**tea wagon**, ¹**teacart**) n a small table on wheels, used for serving tea. ⇨ picture at TROLLEY.

teacake /'tiːkeɪk/ n (Brit) a small flat cake, usu eaten hot with butter at tea(3a): *toasted teacakes.*

teacart /'tiːkɑːt/ n (US) = TEA TROLLEY.

teach /tiːtʃ/ v (pt, pp **taught** /tɔːt/) **1(a)** to show sb how to do sth so that they will be able to do it themselves: [Vn.to inf, Vn.wh] *He taught me (how) to drive.* **(b)** ~ sth (to sb/sth) to give sb information about a particular subject; to help sb learn sth: [Vn] *teach French/history/judo* [Vnn, Vnpr] *She teaches advanced students English/teaches English to advanced students.* **(c)** to do this for a living: [V] *She teaches at our local school.* [Vn] *He taught mathematics/woodwork for many years.* ⇨ note. **2** to encourage people to accept sth as a fact or principle: [Vn] *Christ taught forgiveness* (ie that we should forgive people who harm us, etc) [V.that] *He taught that the earth revolves around the sun.* [Vn.to inf] *My parents taught me never to tell lies.* [also Vn.that,Vnn]. **3** (infml) (no passive) to persuade sb not to do sth again by making them suffer so much that they are afraid to do it: [Vn, Vn.to inf] *So you lost all your money? That'll teach you (to gamble).* [Vnn] *It taught him a lesson he never forgot.* (used as a threat) [Vn.to inf] *I'll teach you to call* (ie punish you for calling) *me a liar!* **IDM** **teach one's grandmother to suck ¹eggs** (infml) to tell or show sb how to do sth that they can already do well, and probably better than oneself. **(you can't) teach an old dog new ¹tricks** (saying) (one cannot) successfully make old people change their ideas, methods of work, etc. **teach ¹school** (US) to be a teacher in a school.

▶ **teachable** adj **1** (of a subject) that can be taught. **2** (of a person) able to learn by being taught.

teacher n a person who teaches, esp in a school: *my English teacher.* Compare HEAD¹ 14.

teaching n **1** [U] the work of a teacher: *She wants to go into teaching as a career.* **2** [U, C often pl] that which is taught; a DOCTRINE: *the teaching(s) of the Church.*

NOTE Compare **teach, lecture, train, educate, coach** and **instruct**. **Teach** is used in most formal and informal situations and can refer to an academic subject or a practical skill for any age group: *John teaches history at a secondary school/to undergraduates.* ○ *My mother taught me how to swim.* **Lecture** is used instead of **teach** in universities: *He lectures in Psychology.* **Educate** refers to the development of knowledge and intellectual skills, especially children's. This usually happens through the formal **education** system of schools and universities: *Their son is being educated at a private school.* **Train** means to give somebody the instruction and practice they need in order to learn a job or skill: *The dogs are trained to guard the house from intruders.* ○ *The staff need more training in how to use*

computers. **Train** can also mean to practise a sport or physical skill so that you are very good at it: *Top athletes train for several hours a day.* **Coach** is also used to describe non-formal teaching, either of an academic subject or of a sport: *The children are being coached for the exam by their teacher.* ○ *He's the best player I've ever coached.* **Instruct** means to teach people a skill, or to show them how to do something practical: *She instructed the trainee nurses in giving injections.*

teacup /'tiːkʌp/ n a cup in which tea is served. **IDM** **a storm in a teacup** ⇨ STORM.

teak /tiːk/ n [U] the strong hard wood of a tall Asian tree, used esp for making furniture: *a teak table.*

teal /tiːl/ n (pl unchanged) a small wild duck.

team /tiːm/ n [CGp] **1** a group of players forming one side in certain games and sports, eg football and cricket: *Which team do you play for?* ○ *Leeds was/were the better team.* **2** a group of people working together: *a sales team* ○ *He's a good team person* (ie He works well with others). **3** two or more animals pulling a cart, carriage, etc together.

▶ **team** v **PHRV** ¹**team ¹up (with sb)** to work together with sb, esp for a common purpose: *team up with a Japanese manufacturer* ○ *The two companies have teamed up to develop a new racing car.* ¹**team sb/sth with sb/sth** (usu passive) to combine or match people or things: *a red jacket teamed with a black miniskirt.*

■ ¹**team-mate** n a member of the same team or group as oneself.

¹**team ¹spirit** n [U] (approv) willingness to act for the good of one's team rather than one's individual advantage.

teamster /'tiːmstə(r)/ n (US) a lorry driver.

teamwork /'tiːmwɜːk/ n [U] organized effort as a team: *The success of the project was largely the result of good teamwork.*

teapot /'tiːpɒt/ n **1** a container with a SPOUT(1), a handle and a lid, in which tea is made and from which it is poured into cups, etc. ⇨ picture at POT¹. **IDM** **a tempest in a teapot** = A STORM IN A TEACUP.

tear¹ /teə(r)/ v (pt **tore** /tɔː(r)/; pp **torn** /tɔːn/) **1(a)** to pull sth apart or into pieces with force: [Vn] *a torn handkerchief* [Vnpr] *tear a sheet of paper in two* ○ *He tore his shirt on a nail.* [Vn-adj] *tear a parcel open* [also Vnp]. ⇨ note at CUT¹. **(b)** ~ sth in sth to make a hole or split in sth by force: [Vnpr] *The explosion tore a hole in the wall.* **2(a)** to remove sth from sth else by pulling it sharply: [Vnpr] *tear a page out of a book/a notice from a wall* [Vnp] *He tore his clothes off* (ie took them off very quickly) *and dived into the lake.* **(b)** ~ oneself/sb/sth from sb/sth to pull oneself/sb/sth away from sb/sth by force: [Vnpr] *The child was torn from its mother's arms.* [Vn-adj] *She tore herself loose from his grasp.* **3** to become torn: [Vadv] *This material tears easily.* [V] *Don't pull the pages so hard or they will tear.* **4** to injure a muscle, TENDON, etc by stretching it too much: [Vn] *a torn ligament.* **5** (esp passive) to destroy the peace of sth: [Vn] *a country torn by war* [Vnp] *Ethnic conflict is tearing the region apart.* **6** to move in the specified direction very quickly or in an excited way: [Vp] *cars tearing past* [Vpr] *She tore out of the house shouting 'Fire!'* **IDM** **pick/pull/tear sb to pieces** ⇨ PIECE¹. **pick/pull/tear sth to pieces** ⇨ PIECE¹. **tear sth a¹part, to ¹shreds, to ¹bits, etc** to destroy or defeat sth completely; to criticize sb/sth harshly: *tear sb's hopes to shreds* ○ *The critics tore her new play to pieces.* ¹**tear at one's/sb's ¹heart** to affect one/sb emotionally very much: *an issue that tears at the heart of every American.* **tear one's ¹hair (out)** (infml) to show great anxiety, anger, etc: *My boss is tearing her hair out about the delay in the schedule.* ¹**tear the ¹heart out of sth** to destroy the most important part or aspect of sth: *riots that tore the heart out of Los Angeles.* **(be in) a tearing** 'hurry, 'rush, **etc** (to be) in a very great hurry: *There's no need to be in such a tearing hurry — we've got plenty of time.* **tear sb ˌlimb from 'limb** (*often joc*) to attack sb very violently. **tear sb 'off a strip; tear a 'strip off sb** (*infml*) to speak angrily to sb who has done sth wrong. ˌ**that's 'torn it** (*infml*) that has spoilt our plans. **wear and tear** ▷ WEAR². PHRV 'tear at sth (with sth) to attack sth violently, esp by cutting or tearing it: *He tore at the meat with his bare hands.* ˌtear oneself a'way **(from sb/sth)** to leave sb/sth unwillingly: *Tear yourself away from the television and come out for a walk.* **be torn between A and B** to have to make a painful choice between two things or people: *She was torn between love and duty.* ˌtear sth 'down to bring sth to the ground; to DEMOLISH(1a) sth: *They're tearing down these old houses to build a new office block.* ˌtear 'into sb/sth to attack sb/sth physically or with words. ˌtear sth 'up to destroy a document, etc by tearing it into pieces: *She tore up all the letters he had sent her.* ○ (*fig*) *He accused the government of tearing up* (ie not honouring) *the negotiated agreement.*

▶ **tear** *n* a hole or split caused by tearing: *The sheet has a tear in it.*

tear² /tɪə(r)/ *n* [C usu *pl*] a drop of salty water that comes from the eye when one cries, etc: *A tear rolled down his cheek.* ○ *Her eyes filled with tears.* ○ *shed/ weep bitter tears* ○ *a story that moved/reduced us to tears* (ie made us cry) ○ *He burst into tears* (ie began to cry). ○ *She was in tears* (ie crying) *over the death of her puppy.* ○ *Most classical music bores me to tears* (ie makes me very bored). IDM **crocodile tears** ▷ CROCODILE.

▶ **tearful** /-fl/ *adj* crying or ready to cry: *her tearful face* ○ *She became very tearful when she talked about the last time she saw him.* **tearfully** /-fəli/ *adv.*

■ 'tear-drop *n* a single tear.

'tear-gas *n* [U] gas that causes severe discomfort in the eyes, making them fill with tears. It is sometimes used by the police or the army to control crowds.

'tear-jerker *n* (*infml*) a story, film, etc designed to make people feel very sad in sympathy with the characters.

tearaway /'teərəweɪ/ *n* (*infml*) a person who behaves in a wild way or is not responsible or reliable: *Her son's a bit of a tearaway.*

tearoom /'tiːruːm, -rʊm/ (also 'teashop) *n* (*esp Brit*) a small restaurant or CAFÉ in which tea, coffee, cakes and sandwiches are served.

tease /tiːz/ *v* **1** to try to provoke sb in a playful or unkind way: [V] *Don't take what she said seriously — she was only teasing.* [Vnpr] *The other boys used to tease him because of/about his accent.* [Vn] *Stop teasing the cat* (eg by pulling its tail). **2** to try to attract sb sexually, esp while refusing to satisfy their desire: [V] *flirting and teasing* [also Vn]. **3** to pull sth gently apart into separate pieces: [Vnpr] *tease wool into strands* [also Vn]. **4** [Vn] (*US*) = BACKCOMB. PHRV ˌtease sth 'out to remove knots from hair, wool, etc by gently pulling or brushing it: (*fig*) *tease out the truth with persistent questions.*

▶ **tease** *n* (usu *sing*) a person who is fond of teasing (TEASE 1,2) others: *What a tease she is!*

teaser *n* (*infml*) (usu *sing*) a problem that is difficult to solve: *This one's a real teaser.* See also BRAIN-TEASER.

teasingly *adv* in order to tease(1,2) sb; in a way that teases: *She smiled at him teasingly.*

teasel (also **teazel, teazle**) /'tiːzl/ *n* a plant with large prickly flowers.

teaset /'tiːset/ (also **tea-service**) *n* a set of cups,

saucers (SAUCER 1), plates, a TEAPOT, a small JUG and a sugar bowl, used for serving tea(3a).

teaspoon /'tiːspuːn/ *n* (**a**) a small spoon for stirring or putting sugar into tea or other drinks. ▷ picture at SPOON. (**b**) an amount that this can hold: *Add two teaspoons of salt.*

▶ 'teaspoonful /-fʊl/ *n* (*abbr* **tsp**) an amount that a teaspoon can hold: *two teaspoonfuls of coffee.*

teat /tiːt/ *n* **1** an animal's NIPPLE(1a). ▷ picture at COW¹. **2** (*Brit*) (also *esp US* **nipple**) a rubber object with a small hole in it that is fitted to the end of a child's bottle and through which it can suck the milk, etc in the bottle.

teatime /'tiːtaɪm/ *n* [U] (*Brit*) the time at or during which tea(3) is taken.

tech /tek/ *n* (usu *sing*) (*infml*) a college or school offering courses in technical subjects: *do an engineering course at the local tech.* See also HIGH-TECH.

technical /'teknɪkl/ *adj* **1** [usu attrib] of or involving applied and industrial sciences: *a technical education* ○ *technical advances/achievements.* **2** [usu attrib] of a particular subject, art or craft, or its techniques: *the technical terms used in botany* ○ *the technical difficulties of colour printing* ○ *a musician with great technical skill but not much feeling.* **3** (of a book, etc) requiring specialized knowledge; using terms in a particular specialized way: *The article is rather technical in places.* **4** [attrib] that involves a strict interpretation of the law or of a set of rules: *The prosecution opened with a legal argument over a crucial technical point.*

▶ **technicality** /ˌteknɪ'kæləti/ *n* **1** a technical(2) term or point: *We got a lawyer to explain the legal technicalities to us.* **2** a detail of no real importance: *a mere technicality.*

technically /-kli/ *adv* **1** with reference to the technique displayed: *a technically accomplished violinist.* **2** according to the facts of a case, the exact meaning of words, etc; strictly: *Although technically (speaking) you may not have lied, you certainly haven't been entirely honest.*

■ 'technical college *n* (*Brit*) a college offering students courses in technical and other subjects after they have left school.

ˌtechnical 'hitch *n* a temporary failure or difficulty, esp one caused by a mechanical fault.

technician /tek'nɪʃn/ *n* **1** a person who is skilled in maintaining a particular type of equipment or machinery: *laboratory/aircraft technicians.* **2** an expert in the techniques of a particular science or craft.

Technicolor /'teknɪkʌlə(r)/ *n* [U] **1** (*propr*) a process of colour photography used for cinema films. **2** (usu **technicolour**) (*infml*) vivid or artificially brilliant colour: *The fashion show was a technicolour extravaganza.*

technique /tek'niːk/ *n* (**a**) [C] a method of doing or performing sth, esp in the arts or sciences: *applying modern techniques to a traditional craft.* (**b**) [U, sing] skill in this: *The singer displayed a flawless technique.*

techno- *comb form* of the applied sciences: *technology* ○ *technocrat.*

technocrat /'teknəkræt/ *n* an expert in science, ENGINEERING, etc, esp one who believes that a country's industry should be managed by technical experts. ▶ **technocratic** /ˌteknə'krætɪk/ *adj.*

technology /tek'nɒlədʒi/ *n* (**a**) [U] the scientific study and use of applied sciences, eg ENGINEERING. (**b**) [U, C] the application of this to practical tasks in industry: *recent advances in medical technology* ○ *new computer technologies.* See also HIGH TECHNOLOGY.

▶ **technological** /ˌteknə'lɒdʒɪkl/ *adj: a major technological breakthrough* ○ *technological changes/*

advances. **technologically** /-kli/ *adv: technologically advanced.*

technologist /tek'nɒlədʒɪst/ *n* an expert in technology.

teddy bear /'tedi beə(r)/ (also **teddy**) *n* a soft toy bear.

Teddy boy /'tedi bɔɪ/ (also **ted** /ted/) *n* (*Brit infml*) (in the 1950s) a young man who refused to accept conventional attitudes, styles of dress, etc. Teddy boys wore clothes similar to those of the Edwardian period (1901–10) and were fond of rock and roll (ROCK³) music.

tedious /'ti:diəs/ *adj* too long, slow or dull; boring: *The work is tedious.* ○ *We had to sit through several tedious speeches.* ▶ **tediously** *adv.* **tediousness** *n* [U].

tedium /'ti:diəm/ *n* [U] (*rather fml*) the state of being bored; boredom (BORE²): *She longed for something to relieve the tedium of everyday life.*

tee /ti:/ *n* (**a**) (in golf) a flat area from which a player hits the ball when beginning to play each hole. (**b**) a small piece of wood, plastic, etc that a golf player pushes into the ground and uses to support the ball when hitting it from this area. **IDM to a T/tee** ⇨ T.

▶ **tee** *v* (*pt, pp* **teed**) **PHRV** **tee 'off** to play a golf ball from a tee. ,**tee sb 'off** (*US sl*) to make sb angry or annoyed. ,**tee (sth) 'up** to prepare to play a golf ball by placing it on a tee.

teem¹ /ti:m/ *v* **PHRV** 'teem with sth (esp in the continuous tenses) to have sth in great numbers: *a river teeming with fish* ○ *City streets teeming with tourists.* ○ *His mind is teeming with bright ideas.*

▶ **teeming** *adj* present in great numbers: *the city's teeming millions* ○ *teeming insects.*

teem² /ti:m/ *v* ~ (**with sth**)/(**down**) (esp in the continuous tenses) (of water, rain, etc) to fall heavily; to pour: [V] *a teeming downpour* [Vpr] *It was teeming with rain.* [Vp] *The rain was teeming down.*

teenage /'ti:neɪdʒ/ (also *infml esp US* **teen** /ti:n/) *adj* [attrib] between 13 and 19 years old; of or for people of this age: *teenage fashions/problems* ○ *teen magazines/music* ○ *teenage children.*

▶ **teenaged** *adj* between 13 and 19 years old: *have a teenaged daughter.*

teenager /'ti:neɪdʒə(r)/ (also *infml esp US* **teen**) *n* a person between 13 and 19 years old: *music popular with teenagers.*

teens /ti:nz/ *n* [pl] the years of a person's age from 13 to 19: *be in one's (early/late) teens.*

teeny /'ti:ni/ (also **teeny-weeny** /,ti:ni 'wi:ni/, **teensy** /'ti:nzi/, **teensy-weensy** /,ti:nzi 'wi:nzi/) *adj* (**-ier, -iest**) (*infml*) tiny.

teeny-bopper /'ti:ni bɒpə(r)/ *n* (*dated infml*) a young teenager (TEENAGE), esp a girl, who eagerly follows current fashions in clothes, pop music, etc.

teeshirt /'ti:ʃɜːt/ *n* = T-SHIRT.

teeter /'ti:tə(r)/ *v* to stand or move in an unsteady way: [Vp] *She was teetering along/about/around in very high-heeled shoes.* [Vpr] *He teetered drunkenly on the edge of the pavement.* ○ (*fig*) *teetering on the brink/edge of disaster* [also V].

■ '**teeter-totter** *n* (*US*) = SEE-SAW 1.

teeth *pl* of TOOTH.

teethe /ti:ð/ *v* (usu in the continuous tenses) (of a baby) to have its first teeth starting to grow: [V] *Babies like to chew something when they're teething.*

■ '**teething troubles** (also '**teething problems**) *n* [pl] minor problems that can occur in the early stages of a new project or when a new product becomes available for the first time.

teetotal /,ti:'təʊtl/ *adj* (in favour of) never drinking alcoholic drinks: *He's (strictly) teetotal.*

▶ **teetotalism** *n* [U].

teetotaller (*US* also **teetotaler**) /-tlə(r)/ *n* a person who is teetotal.

TEFL /,ti: i: ef 'el, 'tefl/ *abbr* teaching of English as a foreign language. Compare TESL, TESOL.

Teflon /'teflɒn/ *n* [U] (*propr*) a substance used to form a surface on cooking implements, pans, etc that prevents food sticking to them.

tel *abbr* telephone (number): *tel 01865-56767.*

tel(e)- *comb form* **1** over a long distance; far: *telepathy* ○ *telescopic.* **2** of television: *telefilm* ○ *teletext.* **3** relating to TELECOMMUNICATIONS: *teleordering* ○ *telemarketing.*

telecommunications /,telikə,mju:nɪ'keɪʃnz/ (also *infml* **telecoms** /'telikɒmz/) *n* [pl] communications by radio, telephone, television, cable, TELEGRAPH or SATELLITE(1).

telecottage /'telikɒtɪdʒ/ *n* a room or small building in a rural area filled with computer equipment for the shared use of people living in the area.

telegram /'teligræm/ (also *Brit* **telemessage**) *n* a message sent by TELEGRAPH and then delivered in written or printed form: *send/receive a telegram (of congratulations/condolence).* Compare CABLE 2b.

telegraph /'teligrɑːf; *US* -græf/ *n* [U] a means of sending messages by the use of electric current along wires.

▶ **telegraph** *v* (**a**) [V, Vpr, Vn, Vnpr] to send a message by telegraph. (**b**) [Vn.to inf] to send instructions to sb by telegraph. Compare FAX.

telegraphic /,teli'græfik/ *adj* suitable for or sent by telegraph. **telegraphically** /-kli/ *adv.*

telegraphy /tə'legrəfi/ *n* [U] the process of communicating by telegraph: *wireless telegraphy.*

■ '**telegraph-pole** (also **-post**) *n* a pole supporting wires for telegraph or telephone messages.

telemessage /'telimesɪdʒ/ *n* (*Brit*) = TELEGRAM.

telemetry /tə'lemətri/ *n* [U] the process of automatically recording the readings of an instrument and transmitting them over a distance, usu by radio: *telemetry data/systems.*

teleology /,ti:li'ɒlədʒi/ *n* [U] the theory that events and developments are meant to fulfil a purpose and happen because of that. ▶ **teleological** /,ti:liə'lɒdʒɪkl/ *adj: a teleological view of history.*

telepathy /tə'lepəθi/ *n* [U] the communication of thoughts or feelings from one mind to another without the normal use of the senses: *She felt there was some telepathy between them.*

▶ **telepathic** /,teli'pæθik/ *adj* (**a**) of or using telepathy. (**b**) (of a person) able to communicate by telepathy: *How did you know what I was thinking? You must be telepathic.* **telepathically** /-kli/ *adv.*

telephone /'telifəʊn/ (also **phone**) *n* (**a**) [U] a system of sending sound, esp the human voice, to a distance by wire or radio: *make a telephone call* ○ *a telephone conversation* ○ *order goods over the telephone* ○ *You can always reach* (ie contact) *me by telephone.* (**b**) [C] an instrument used for this: *a mobile/portable phone* ○ *a car phone* ○ *answer the telephone* (ie pick up the RECEIVER(1) to receive a call) ○ *put the telephone down* (ie replace the RECEIVER(1)) ○ *The telephone hasn't stopped ringing all day* (ie There have been a lot of calls). **IDM on the** '**telephone 1** using the telephone: *She's on the telephone at the moment.* ○ *You're wanted* (ie Somebody wants to speak to you) *on the telephone.* **2** (*Brit*) connected to the telephone system: *They've just moved and they're not on the telephone yet.*

▶ **telephone** (also **phone**) *v* to use a telephone in order to speak to sb: [V] *Will you write or telephone?* [Vn, Vnpr] *telephone an order (to head office)* [V.to inf, Vn.to inf] *He telephoned (his wife) to say he'd be late.* [also Vnp].

telephonist /tə'lefənɪst/ *n* = OPERATOR 2.

telephony /tə'lefəni/ *n* [U] the process of sending sound by telephone.

■ '**telephone box** (also '**telephone booth**, '**telephone kiosk**) *n* = PHONE BOX.

'telephone directory (also **'phone directory**, **'telephone book**, **'phone book**) *n* a book listing the names, addresses and telephone numbers of people in a particular area who have a telephone.

'telephone exchange (also **exchange**) *n* a place where telephone lines are connected so that people can speak to each other.

'telephone number (also **'phone number**) *n* the number of a particular telephone, used in making a call to it. ⇨ note.

'telephone tapping (also **'phone tapping**) *n* [U] the practice of connecting a secret device to a telephone in order to listen to people's telephone conversations.

NOTE Telephone numbers in Britain consist of a *national code* for the city or town, usually of five figures starting with 01, followed by a number of between three and seven figures: *Oxford (01865) 56767.* The national code (also known as the *STD code*) is used when making a call outside the local area. Telephones in most large cities, eg London, have a four-figure national code followed by a seven-figure number: *0171-246 8022.*

All numbers are said separately. 0 is pronounced /əʊ/: *o one eight six five, five six seven six seven ○ o one seven one, two four six, eight o double two.* When giving a telephone number on the phone, the city or town rather than the code is often used: *Oxford five six seven six seven.*

Telephone numbers in the USA consist of a three-figure *area code* followed by a seven-figure number. The area code is only used when dialling from one region, city, etc to another (ie when *calling long distance/making a long distance call).* The first three numbers are separated from the last four by a hyphen: *(202) 234-5678.* Both the area code and the prefix are spoken as a series of three separate numbers.) 0 is pronounced /əʊ/, or said as *zero: two o two, two three four.* The last four figures may be said separately *(five six seven eight)* or as two sets of tens *(fifty-six seventy-eight).* If the last four numbers end in 00 or 000, they are usually treated as hundreds or thousands: *five o two, five six hundred (502-5600) ○ four nine nine, five thousand (499-5000).*

Note that fax numbers are treated similarly in Britain and in the USA. Business firms, etc often have a single telephone number from which callers may be connected to a three- or four-figure internal *extension (number): Oxford 56767 Ext 429 ○ (202) 234-5678 (x3201).*

telephoto lens /ˈtelifəʊtəʊ ˈlenz/ *n* a LENS that produces a large image of a distant object being photographed.

teleprinter /ˈteliprɪntə(r)/ (*US* **teletypewriter**) *n* a piece of equipment for automatically printing out messages that have been typed on a machine in another place and sent by telephone lines.

teleprompter /ˈteliprɒmptə(r)/ *n* a device used by speakers or performers on television. It is placed next to the camera and displays the words that are to be spoken. Compare AUTOCUE.

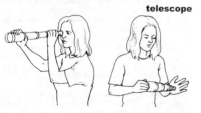

telescope

telescope /ˈteliskəʊp/ *n* an instrument shaped like a tube, with lenses (LENS 1) to make distant objects

appear larger and nearer: *look at the moon through a telescope.* ⇨ picture. See also RADIO TELESCOPE.

▶ **telescope** *v* **1** [V, Vn] to become or make sth shorter by sliding sections inside one another. ⇨ picture. **2** ~ **sth (into sth)** to reduce sth so that it occupies less space or time: [Vnpr] *Three episodes have been telescoped into a single programme.* [also Vn].

telescopic /ˌtelɪˈskɒpɪk/ *adj* **1** of or using a telescope; making things look larger as a telescope does: *a telescopic view of the moon ○ a telescopic sight* (eg on a rifle). **2** having sections which slide inside one another: *a telescopic aerial/umbrella.* **telescopically** /-kli/ *adv.*

teletext /ˈtelitekst/ *n* [U] a service providing news and other information on the television screens of paying customers.

telethon /ˈteləθɒn/ *n* a very long television programme, broadcast to raise money for charity.

teletypewriter /ˌteliˈtaɪpraɪtə(r)/ *n* (*US*) = TELEPRINTER.

television /ˈtelɪvɪʒn/ (also *Brit infml* **telly**) *n* (*abbr* **TV**) **1** (also **'television set**) [C] a piece of electrical equipment with a glass screen which shows broadcast programmes with moving pictures and sounds: *a colour/black-and-white television ○ turn the television set on/off.* See also CLOSED-CIRCUIT TELEVISION. **2** [U] the programmes broadcast on a television set: *spend the evening watching television ○ a television documentary.* **3** [U] the process of sending out programmes for people to watch on their television sets: *satellite/cable television ○ a television camera.* **4** [U] the business of producing and broadcasting television programmes: *a television announcer ○ She works in television.* **IDM** **on (the) 'television** broadcasting or being broadcast by television: *The Prime Minister, speaking on television, denied reports that... ○ Is there anything good on (the) television tonight?*

▶ **televise** /ˈtelɪvaɪz/ *v* to broadcast sth by television: [Vn] *televise the Olympic Games/a novel by Jane Austen ○ a televised debate/match.*

teleworking /ˈteliwɜːkɪŋ/ *n* [U] the practice of working at home while communicating with one's office and other places by computer.

telex /ˈteleks/ *n* **(a)** [U] a system of communication using telephone lines. A message is typed on a machine in one place, then sent by telephone to a machine in another place which immediately prints it out. **(b)** [C] a message sent or received by telex: *Several telexes arrived this morning.* **(c)** [C] (*infml*) a machine for sending and receiving messages by telex.

▶ **telex** *v* [Vn, Vnpr, Vn.*that*] ~ **sth (to sb)** to send a message or communicate with sb by telex.

tell /tel/ *v* (*pt, pp* **told** /təʊld/) **1** ~ **sth (to sb)** to make sth known, esp in spoken or written words: [Vn] *tell jokes/stories* [Vnpr] *He told the news to everybody in the office.* [Vnn] *Did she tell you her name?* [Vn.*that*] *They've told us (that) they're not coming.* [Vn.*wh*] *Tell me where you live. ○ I can't tell you* (ie I cannot find words to express) *how happy I am.* [Vnadv] *They've split up — or so I've been told/so I'm told* (ie That is what I have been told). [Vn] (used for emphasis): *It's not cheap, I can 'tell you. ○ It's impossible, I tell you!* **2** to give information to sb: [Vnn] *This book tells you all you need to know about buying a house.* [Vnn, Vn.*wh*] *This gauge tells you the amount of petrol you have left/how much petrol you have left.* [Vn.to inf] *The instructions tell you to replace the filter every 3 months.* [also Vn.*that*]. **3** to express sth in words: [Vn] *tell lies/the truth.* ⇨ note at SAY. **4** to reveal a secret: [V] *Promise you won't tell.* ○ (*infml*) *kiss and tell* (ie reveal one's love affairs). **5(a)** to decide or determine; to know definitely: [V] *It may rain or it may* not. *It's hard to tell.* [V.*that*] *You can tell (that) he's angry when he starts shouting a lot.* [V.*wh*] *How do you tell when to change gear?* ○ *The only way to tell if you like something is by trying it.* (**b**) ~ **A from B** (esp with *can/could/be able to*) to distinguish one thing or person from another: [Vn] *I can't tell the difference between margarine and butter* (ie cannot identify them by their tastes). [Vnpr] *Can you tell Tom from his twin brother?* [Vnadv] *It's difficult to tell them apart.* [V.*wh*] *These kittens look exactly alike — how can you tell which is which?* **6** ~ (**on sb**) to produce a noticeable effect: [V,Vpr] *The strain was beginning to tell (on the rescue team).* [Vpr] *Her lack of experience told against her* (ie was a disadvantage to her). **7** to order, direct or advise sb: [Vn.*to* inf] *Tell him to wait.* ○ *The doctor told me to eat more fresh fruit.* ○ *I kept telling myself to keep calm* (ie kept repeating it mentally). [Vnn] *Do what I tell you.* [Vnadv] *Children must* **do as they're told.** [Vn] *You* **won't be told** (ie won't obey orders or listen to advice)*, will you?* ⟹ note at ORDER². **IDM** **all** ˈ**told** with all people, items, etc counted and included: *There are 23 guests coming, all told.* **hear tell of sth** ⟹ HEAR. **I/I'll** ˌ**tell you** ˈ**what** (*infml*) (used to introduce a suggestion): *I'll tell you what — let's go to the cinema instead.* **I** ˈ**told you (so)** (*infml*) I warned you that this would happen: *He loves to say 'I told you so!' when things go wrong.* **know/tell sb a thing or two** ⟹ THING. ˌ**live, etc to** ˌ**tell the** ˈ**tale** to survive a difficult or dangerous experience so that one can tell others what really happened. **see/tell sth a mile off** ⟹ MILE. **tell me a**ˈ**nother!** (*infml*) I don't believe you. **tell its own tale/story** to explain itself, without any further explanation or comment being needed: *The empty whisky bottle rolling on the floor told its own tale.* **tell** ˈ**tales (about sb)** to make known another person's secrets, wrongdoings, faults, etc: *Someone's been telling tales about me, haven't they?* **tell the** ˈ**time**; (*US*) **tell** ˈ**time** to read the time from a clock, etc: *She's only five — she hasn't learnt to tell the time yet.* **tell sb where to get** ˈ**off / where they get** ˈ**off** (*infml*) to warn sb that their behaviour is unacceptable and will no longer be tolerated. **there's no knowing/saying/ telling** ⟹ KNOW. **to tell (you) the** ˈ**truth** (used when confessing or admitting sth): *To tell the truth, I fell asleep in the middle.* **you can never** ˈ**tell**; **you never can** ˈ**tell** you can never be sure, eg because appearances are often misleading. **you're telling** ˈ**me!** (*infml*) I completely agree with you. **PHR V** ˈ**tell of sth** to make sth known; to give an account of sth: *notices telling of the proposed job cuts.* ˌ**tell sb** ˈ**off (for sth / doing sth)** (*infml*) to speak angrily to sb for doing sth wrong: *You'll get told off if you're caught doing that.* ○ *I told the boys off for making so much noise.* ˈ**tell on sb** (*infml*) to reveal sb's activities, esp to a person in authority: *John caught his sister smoking and told on her.*

▶ **telling** *adj* having a noticeable or important effect: *a telling argument/example/remark.* **tellingly** *adv.*

■ ˌ**telling-**ˈ**off** *n* (usu *sing*) an instance of speaking to sb angrily because they have done sth wrong: *His teacher gave him a telling-off for being late three days running.*

ˈ**tell-tale** *n* (*infml derog*) a person, esp a child, who reports another's secrets, wrongdoings, etc: *Don't be such a tell-tale!* — *adj* [attrib] revealing or indicating sth: *tell-tale clues/marks/signs/sounds* ○ *the tell-tale smell of cigarette smoke* (ie revealing that sb has been smoking).

teller /ˈtelə(r)/ *n* **1** a person who receives and pays out money in a bank: *automatic teller machines.* **2** a person appointed to count votes, esp in a parliament. **3** (esp in compounds) a person who tells stories, etc: *a* ˈ*story-teller* ○ *a marvellous teller of* ˈ*jokes.* See also FORTUNE-TELLER.

telly /ˈteli/ *n* [U, C] (*Brit infml*) (a) television: *What's on telly tonight?*

temerity /təˈmerəti/ *n* [U] (*fml*) very bold or confident behaviour, esp when considered to be rude or lacking in respect: *He ran the company like a dictator and no one* **had the temerity to** *question his judgement.*

temp¹ /temp/ *n* (*infml*) a temporary employee, esp a secretary.

▶ **temp** *v* (*infml*) to do temporary work: [V] *He's been temping for over a year now and wants a permanent job.*

temp² *abbr* temperature: *temp 65°F.*

temper¹ /ˈtempə(r)/ *n* (**a**) [C] a state of the mind as regards being angry or calm: *be in a bad/good temper* (ie angry/cheerful) ○ *Tempers rose/cooled/flared.* ○ *After an hour of waiting, tempers began to fray.* (**b**) [C usu *sing*, U] the tendency to become angry easily: *learn to control one's temper* ○ *have a (short/quick/ nasty) temper* ○ *fly into a temper* ○ *a fit of temper* ○ *He's been in a (bad/foul/filthy) temper all morning.* **IDM** **keep/lose one's** ˈ**temper** to succeed/fail in controlling one's anger.

▶ -**tempered** /-ˈtempəd/ (forming compound *adjs*) having or showing the specified type of temper: ˌ*good-/*ˌ*bad-*ˈ*tempered* ○ *a* ˌ*hot-tempered* ˈ*man* ○ *a* ˌ*sweet-tempered* ˈ*child.*

temper² /ˈtempə(r)/ *v* **1** to bring metal to the required degree of hardness (HARD¹) by heating and then cooling; to harden other materials such as glass or clay: [Vn] *tempered steel.* **2** ~ **sth (with sth)** to make the effects of sth less severe by balancing it with sth else: [Vnpr] *temper justice with mercy* [also Vn].

tempera /ˈtempərə/ *n* [U] paint consisting of colouring matter mixed with egg and water: *painting in tempera.*

temperament /ˈtemprəmənt/ *n* [C, U] a person's nature as it affects the way he or she thinks, feels and behaves: *a man with an artistic/a nervous temperament* ○ *To be a champion, skill is not enough — you have to have the right temperament.* ○ *Actors often display a lot of temperament* (ie are emotional or easily excited).

▶ **temperamental** /ˌtemprəˈmentl/ *adj* **1** (*often derog*) liable to unreasonable changes of mood; not calm or consistent: *He's a very temperamental player* (ie plays well or badly according to his mood). ○ (*joc*) *My car is a bit temperamental* (ie is likely to break down, fail to start, etc). **2** caused by a person's temperament: *a temperamental aversion to hard work.* **temperamentally** /-təli/ *adv*: *be temperamentally unsuited to the job.*

temperance /ˈtempərəns/ *n* [U] **1** the practice of controlling and restraining one's behaviour, the amount one eats and drinks, etc. **2** drinking no, or almost no, alcoholic drinks: *a temperance society* (ie one promoting temperance). Compare INTEMPERANCE.

temperate /ˈtempərət/ *adj* **1** (*techn*) (of a climate or region) having a mild temperature without extremes of heat or cold: *temperate zones.* **2** (*fml*) behaving with TEMPERANCE(1); keeping one's behaviour, language, etc under control: *Please be more temperate in your language.* Compare INTEMPERATE. ▶ **temperately** *adv.*

temperature /ˈtemprətʃə(r); *US* also -tʃʊər/ *n* [C, U] the degree of heat or cold in a body, room, country, etc: *keep the house at an even temperature* ○ *keep the wine at* **room temperature** ○ *a rise/drop in temperature* ○ *Heat the oven to a temperature of 200°C.* ○ *a climate without extremes of temperature* ○ *some places have had temperatures in the 90s* (ie over 90° Fahrenheit). ⟹ note. **IDM** **get/have/run a** ˈ**temperature** to get/have an abnormally high temperature of the body: *He was very sick and had/was running a* *(high) temperature.* **raise the temperature** ⇨ RAISE. **take sb's ¹temperature** to measure the temperature of sb's body with a THERMOMETER: *The nurse took my temperature twice a day.*

NOTE Temperatures in Britain were traditionally measured using the **Fahrenheit** scale (°F). The **Celsius** or **Centigrade** (°C) system is now officially used, although many people still refer to degrees Fahrenheit. The Fahrenheit scale is still used in the USA for non-scientific purposes: *The temperature will fall to minus five tonight (-5°C). ○ It must be ninety-five this afternoon (95°F). ○ The normal temperature of the human body is 37°C. ○ She's ill in bed with a temperature of a hundred and two (102°F).*

tempest /ˈtempɪst/ *n (fml or rhet)* a violent storm.
IDM a tempest in a ¹teapot = A STORM IN A TEACUP.
▶ **tempestuous** /temˈpestʃuəs/ *adj* **(a)** *(fml or rhet)* affected by a violent storm: *a tempestuous sea/wind.* **(b)** violently excited; passionate: *a tempestuous love affair.*

template /ˈtempleɪt/ *n* a pattern, usu of thin board or metal, used as a guide for cutting metal, stone, wood, cloth, etc.

temple¹ /ˈtempl/ *n* a building used for the worship of a god or gods, esp in religions other than Christianity: *the temple of Zeus at Olympia ○ a Greek/Roman/Hindu/Buddhist/temple ○ (fig) Architecturally, the building is a temple to modernism.*

temple² /ˈtempl/ *n* the flat part at each side of the forehead. ⇨ picture at HEAD¹.

tempo /ˈtempəʊ/ *n (pl* **-os** or, in sense 1, **tempi** /ˈtempiː/) **1** the speed or rhythm of a piece of music: *in waltz tempo ○ Your tempo is too slow.* **2** the pace of any movement or activity: *the exhausting tempo of city life ○ At this point the narrative tempo of the novel changes.*

temporal /ˈtempərəl/ *adj* **1** *(fml)* of the affairs of the world, eg politics; of this life, not spiritual: *one's temporal desires/needs.* Compare SPIRITUAL. **2** *(fml)* of or relating to time: *a universe which has spatial and temporal dimensions.* **3** *(anatomy)* of the temple(s) of the head: *the left/right temporal lobe.*

temporary /ˈtemprəri; US -pəreri/ *adj* lasting or meant to last for a limited time only; not permanent: *temporary accommodation/employment ○ a temporary secretary ○ This arrangement is only temporary.* Compare PERMANENT. ▶ **temporarily** /ˈtemprərəli; US ˌtempəˈrerəli/ *adv*: *The theatre is temporarily closed for redecoration.* **temporariness** *n* [U].

temporize, -ise /ˈtempəraɪz/ *v (fml)* to delay making a decision, giving a definite answer or stating one's purpose, in order to gain time: [V] *The peace plan is merely a temporizing device.*

tempt /tempt/ *v* ~ **sb (into sth / doing sth)** **1** to persuade or try to persuade sb to do sth, esp sth wrong or unwise: [Vnpr] *They tried to tempt her (into staying) with offers of promotion.* [Vn.to inf] *Nothing would tempt me to join the army.* [also Vn]. **2** to make sb feel a desire for sth; to attract sb: [Vnpr] *The warm weather tempted us into going for a swim.* [Vn.to inf] *I am tempted to take the day off.* [also Vn]. **IDM tempt ¹fate/¹providence** to take a risk: *Having escaped injury in the car crash she felt it would be tempting fate to start driving again.*
▶ **tempter** *n* a person who tempts sb.
tempting *adj* attractive; inviting: *a tempting offer ○ That cake looks very tempting. ○ It's tempting to speculate about what might have happened.* **temptingly** *adv.*
temptress /ˈtemptrəs/ *n (usu joc)* a woman who tempts sb, esp sexually.

temptation /tempˈteɪʃn/ *n* **1** [U] the action of tempting sb or the state of being tempted: *the temptation of easy profits ○ yield/give way to temptation ○*

resist temptation ○ **put temptation in sb's way** (ie tempt them). **2** [C] a thing that tempts or attracts sb: *The open cake tin was too strong a temptation for him to resist.*

ten /ten/ *n, pron, det* the number 10. **IDM** **ˌten to ¹one** very probably: *Ten to one he'll be late.*
▶ **ten-** (in compounds) having ten of the thing specified: *a ten-gallon drum.*
tenth /tenθ/ *pron, det* 10th. — *n* each of ten equal parts of sth.
■ **ˌten ¹pence** (also **ˌten pence ¹piece, ten p, 10p**) /ˌten ¹piː/ *n (Brit)* a coin worth ten pence.
For further guidance on how *ten* and *tenth* are used, see the examples at *five* and *fifth.*

tenable /ˈtenəbl/ *adj* **1** that can be defended successfully against opposition or attack: *a tenable position ○ The view that the earth is flat is no longer tenable.* Compare UNTENABLE. **2** [pred] ~ **(for...)** (of an office or a position) that can be held for a certain time: *The lectureship is tenable for a period of three years.*

tenacious /təˈneɪʃəs/ *adj* **1** keeping a firm hold on an object, a principle, a course of action, etc; not letting go of sth readily: *a tenacious adversary/defence ○ She shows a tenacious loyalty to her friends.* **2** (of an idea, influence, etc) difficult to escape from; persistent (PERSIST): *a tenacious belief in a discredited myth.* ▶ **tenaciously** *adv*: *Though seriously ill, he still clings tenaciously to life.* **tenacity** /təˈnæsəti/ *n* [U]: *compete with skill and tenacity.*

tenant /ˈtenənt/ *n* a person who pays rent to a LANDLORD(1) for the use of a room, a building, land, etc: *evict tenants for non-payment of rent ○ (Brit) council tenants* (ie paying rent to the local council) *○ a tenant farmer* (ie one who does not own the land he cultivates). See also SITTING TENANT.
▶ **tenancy** /-ənsi/ **(a)** [U] the use of land or buildings as a tenant: *take over the tenancy of a farm.* **(b)** [C] a period of this: *hold a life tenancy of a house.*
tenant *v* (usu passive) to occupy sth as a tenant: [Vn] *houses tenanted by farm workers.*

tench /tentʃ/ *n (pl* unchanged) a European fish of the CARP¹ family that lives in rivers, lakes, etc.

tend¹ /tend/ *v* **1** to care for or look after sb/sth: [Vn] *nurses tending (the wounds of) the injured ○ shepherds tending their sheep.* **2** *(US)* to serve customers in a shop, bar, etc: [Vn] *tend the store ○ tend bar.*

tend² /tend/ *v* **1** to be likely to behave in a certain way or to have a certain characteristic or influence: [V.to inf] *I tend to go to bed earlier during the winter. ○ We tend to think of this as a modern problem, but it has existed for centuries. ○ Women tend to live longer than men. ○ Recent laws have tended to restrict the freedom of the press. ○ It tends to rain here a lot in the summer.* **2** ~ **to/towards sth** to take a certain direction: [Vpr] *He tends towards extreme views.* [also Vadv].
▶ **tendency** /ˈtendənsi/ *n* **1** ~ **(to/towards sth)/(to do sth)** a way a person or thing tends to be or behave: *a tendency to fat/towards fatness/to get fat ○ have/show homicidal tendencies.* **2** a direction in which sth moves or changes; a TREND: *Prices continue to show an upward tendency* (ie to increase).

tendentious /tenˈdenʃəs/ *adj (derog)* (of a speech, a piece of writing, etc) intended to promote a particular cause or point of view, and so likely to cause argument or disagreement: *tendentious party propaganda.* ▶ **tendentiously** *adv.* **tendentiousness** *n* [U].

tender¹ /ˈtendə(r)/ *adj* **(-er, -est)** **1** easily moved to pity or sympathy; kind: *have a tender heart.* **2** loving; gentle: *give sb tender looks ○ bid sb a tender farewell ○ She needs a lot of tender loving care. ○ (ironic) I was left to the tender mercies of the guards.* **3** (of food) easy to bite through; soft: *tender meat ○ Boil the beans until they are tender.* **4** easily

---

[Vnn] = verb + noun + noun   [V-adj] = verb + adjective   For more help with verbs, see Study pages **B4–8**.

damaged or hurt; delicate: *tender young plants* (eg ones that can be harmed by frost). **5** painful when touched; sensitive: *My leg is still very tender where it was bruised.* **6** [attrib] (of age) early; not yet mature: *leave home* **at the tender age of** *15* ○ *a child of tender years.*

▶ **tenderize, -ise** /'tendəraɪz/ *v* to make meat more tender, eg by beating it: [Vn] *tenderized steak.*
tenderly *adv.*
tenderness *n* [U].
■ ˌtender-ˈhearted *adj* having a kind and gentle nature; tender¹(1,2).

tender² /'tendə(r)/ *v* **1** ~ (**for sth**) to make an offer to carry out work, supply goods, etc at a stated price: [V] *competitive tendering* [Vpr] *Firms were invited to tender for the construction of the new motorway.* **2** ~ **sth** (**to sb**) (*fml*) to offer or present sth formally: [Vn, Vnpr] *He has tendered his resignation (to the Prime Minister).*
▶ **tender** (also *esp US* **bid**) *n* a formal offer to supply goods or carry out work at a stated price: **put work out to tender** (ie ask for such offers) ○ *put in/make/submit a tender for sth* ○ *accept the lowest tender.* See also LEGAL TENDER.

tender³ /'tendə(r)/ *n* **1** (esp in compounds) a person who looks after or tends sth: *tenders of gardens.* **2** a truck attached to a steam engine, carrying fuel and water.

tenderloin /'tendələɪn/ *n* [U] (*esp US*) the most tender middle part of a LOIN(1) of beef or pork.

tendon /'tendən/ *n* a strong band or cord of tissue that joins muscle to bone: *strain a tendon.*

tendril /'tendrəl/ *n* any of the short thin stems growing from a climbing plant by which it attaches itself to sth, eg a wall.

tenement /'tenəmənt/ (*US* also ˈtenement-house) *n* a large building with apartments or rooms rented cheaply, esp in a poor area of a city: *live in a crumbling tenement* ○ *a tenement block.*

tenet /'tenɪt/ *n* a principle or belief held by a person or group and forming part of a larger system of beliefs: *This is one of the basic tenets of the Christian faith.*

tenfold /'tenfəʊld/ *adj, adv* ⇨ -FOLD.

tenner /'tenə(r)/ *n* (*Brit infml*) a £10 note; £10: *I'll give you a tenner for your old bike.*

tennis

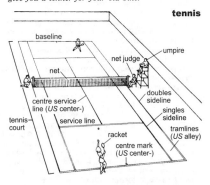

baseline
umpire
net judge
net
centre service line (*US* center-)
tennis court
service line
racket
doubles sideline
singles sideline
tramlines (*US* alley)
centre mark (*US* center-)

tennis /'tenɪs/ (also ˌlawn ˈtennis) *n* [U] a game in which two or four players hit a ball with rackets (RACKET¹ 1) backwards and forwards across a net on a specially marked playing area: *a tennis player/tournament.* ⇨ picture. See also SET² 6.
■ ˈtennis-ball *n* a ball used in playing tennis.
ˈtennis-court *n* a specially marked area on which tennis is played. ⇨ picture.
ˌtennis ˈelbow *n* [U] a painful swelling of the elbow caused by playing tennis, etc.

ˈtennis-racket *n* a RACKET¹(1) used in playing tennis.
ˈtennis shoe *n* a light canvas or leather shoe suitable for tennis or for general casual wear.

tenon /'tenən/ *n* a projecting end of a piece of wood shaped to fit into a MORTISE to make a joint.

tenor¹ /'tenə(r)/ *n* [sing] **the ~ of sth 1** the general routine, course or character of sth: *Nothing disturbed the even tenor of her life.* ○ *At this point the whole tenor of the meeting changed.* **2** the general meaning or sense of sth: *I know enough of the language to grasp the general tenor of what is being said.*

tenor² /'tenə(r)/ *n* (*music*) (**a**) the highest normal adult male singing voice. (**b**) a singer with such a voice. Compare ALTO, BARITONE. (**c**) a musical part written for a tenor voice: *sing tenor.*
▶ **tenor** *adj* [attrib] (of a musical instrument) with a range about that of a tenor voice: *a tenor saxophone.*

tenpin /'tenpɪn/ *n* any of the ten objects with the shape of a bottle that players try to knock down in a game of tenpin bowling.
▶ ˌtenpin ˈbowling *n* [U] (*US* also **tenpins** [pl]) a game in which players try to knock down tenpins by rolling a ball and hitting them, esp in a bowling-alley (BOWLING). See also BOWLING 1, SKITTLE 2.

tense¹ /tens/ *adj* **1**(**a**) (of a person) anxious, nervous or worried; not relaxed: *He's a very tense person.* ○ *look tense and under pressure.* (**b**) (of a situation, an event, a period, etc) causing an anxious, nervous or worried feeling: *a tense moment/atmosphere/meeting* ○ *The game is getting very tense.* **2** with muscles tight rather than relaxed: *faces tense with anxiety.* **3** stretched tightly: *a tense wire.*
▶ **tense** *v* ~ (**sth**) (**up**) to become or make sb/sth become tense¹(2): [V] *She tensed, hearing the noise again.* [Vn, Vnp] *He waited for the race to start, his muscles tensed (up).* [also Vp]. **IDM** **be/get tensed up** to be/become tense¹(1a): *Players get very tensed up before a match.*
tensely *adv.*
tenseness *n* [U].

tense² /tens/ *n* (*grammar*) any of the forms of a verb that may be used to indicate the time of the action or state expressed by the verb: *the present/past/future tense.*

tensile /'tensaɪl; *US* 'tensl/ *adj* **1** [attrib] relating to the extent to which sth can stretch without breaking: *the tensile strength of wire/rope.* **2** that can be stretched: *tensile cable.*

tension /'tenʃn/ *n* **1** [U] the state of being stretched tight or the extent to which sth is stretched tight: *Massage helps relieve the tension in one's muscles.* ○ *adjust the tension of a violin string/a tennis-racket.* **2** [U] mental, emotional or nervous strain; anxiety: *suffer from (nervous) tension* ○ *a headache caused by tension* ○ *She felt considerable tension before the exam.* See also PMT. **3** [U, C usu *pl*] ~ (**between A and B**) a situation in which people feel aggressive or UNFRIENDLY towards each other, and which may develop into conflict or violence: *racial/political/social tension(s)* ○ *The incident has further increased the tension between the two countries.* **4** [C, U] ~ (**between A and B**) a situation in which different forces, elements, influences, etc are in opposition to each other: *There is tension between the aims of the management and the wishes of the staff.*
▶ **tension** *v* (*techn*) to produce tension(1) in sth: [Vn] *tensioned nets* [Vn] *tensioning cables.*

tent /tent/ *n* a shelter made of canvas, etc supported by poles and ropes fixed to the ground, and used esp for camping: *put up/take down a tent.*
▶ **tented** *adj* consisting of a tent or tents; filled with tents: *tented accommodation* ○ *a tented camp/village.*

■ **'tent-peg** *n* = PEG¹ 2b. ⇨ picture at PEG.

tentacle /'tentəkl/ *n* **1** [C] a long thin flexible part extending from the body of certain creatures, used for feeling or holding things or for moving: *Snails and octopuses have tentacles.* ⇨ picture at OCTOPUS. **2 tentacles** [pl] (*often derog*) the influence of a large place, organization, system, etc which is regarded as being hard to escape: *the spreading tentacles of government bureaucracy.*

tentative /'tentətɪv/ *adj* done or said without certainty that it is right, definite or final; not confident: *make a tentative suggestion/arrangement* ○ *reach a tentative conclusion.* ▸ **tentatively** *adv*: *played rather too tentatively* ○ *step tentatively into the water.* **tentativeness** *n* [U].

tenterhooks /'tentəhʊks/ *n* [pl] **IDM** **(be) on 'tenterhooks** in a state of anxiety or excitement when waiting to find out what will happen: *We were kept on tenterhooks for hours while the judges were deciding the winners.*

tenth ⇨ TEN.

tenuous /'tenjuəs/ *adj* **1** so weak or slight that it hardly exists: *a rather tenuous argument* ○ *keep a tenuous hold on life* ○ *preserve tenuous links with one's former friends.* **2** extremely thin: *the tenuous threads of a spider's web.* ▸ **tenuously** *adv*.

tenure /'tenjə(r)/ *n* [U] **1** the act or a period of holding an important, esp political, position: *He knew that tenure of high political office was beyond him.* ○ *The tenure of the US Presidency is four years.* **2** the legal right to occupy property or land: *a fixed-period tenure* ○ *security of tenure* (ie the right to continue renting property). **3** the right to remain permanently in one's job, esp as a university teacher: *be granted tenure after six years' probation.*

tepee /'ti:pi:/ *n* a tent made of skins or bark on a frame of poles, used, esp formerly, by Native Americans. See also WIGWAM.

tepid /'tepɪd/ *adj* **1** slightly but not very warm: *The water was tepid.* **2** not enthusiastic: *His campaign received only tepid support.* Compare LUKEWARM.

tequila /tə'ki:lə/ *n* [U] a strong alcoholic drink made in Mexico from a tropical plant.

tercentenary /ˌtɜːsen'ti:nəri; *US* ˌtɜːsen'tenəri/ *n* the 300th anniversary of sth: *the tercentenary of the school's foundation* ○ *tercentenary celebrations.*

term /tɜːm/ *n* **1** a word or phrase used as the name of sth, esp one connected with a particular subject or used in a particular type of language: *'The nick' is a slang term for 'the police station'.* ○ *technical/legal/scientific terms* ○ *a term of affection/address.* **2** a period of time for which sth lasts; a fixed or limited time: *a long term of imprisonment* ○ *during the President's first term of office* ○ *the term of an agreement.* See also MID-TERM 1. **3** any of the three or four periods in the year during which classes are held in schools, universities, etc: *the autumn/spring/summer term* ○ *end-of-term examinations* ○ *during/in term(-time).* See also SEMESTER. **4** (*fml*) the end or completion of a particular period of time: *a pregnancy approaching its term* ○ *His life had reached its natural term.* **5** (*mathematics*) each of the quantities or expressions in a series, RATIO, etc. **IDM** **a contradiction in terms** ⇨ CONTRADICTION. **in the 'long/ 'short term** in the distant/near future; over a period lasting until the distant/near future: *We must aim for world peace in the long term.* ○ *policies effective only in the short term.* See also LONG-TERM, SHORT-TERM.

▸ **term** *v* (*fml*) to describe sb/sth by using a certain term(1): [Vn-adj] *term an offer unacceptable* [Vnn] *He has often been termed a genius.* See also TERMS.

termly *adj* happening or relating to each term(3): *termly fees.*

terminal /'tɜːmɪnl/ *adj* **1(a)** (of an illness or disease) leading to death, esp slowly; that cannot be cured: *terminal cancer.* **(b)** (of a person) suffering from such an illness or disease: *a terminal case/ patient.* **2** certain to lead to the end or destruction of sth: *an industry in terminal decline.*

▸ **terminal** *n* **1** a place or building where journeys by train or bus begin or end. See also TERMINUS. **2** a building at an airport or in a town where air passengers arrive and depart. **3** a point of connection in an electric circuit: *the positive/negative terminals* (eg of a battery). **4** an apparatus, usu consisting of a KEYBOARD(1a) and a screen, that connects the user with a computer system.

terminally /-nəli/ *adv*: *a hospice for the terminally ill.*

terminate /'tɜːmɪneɪt/ *v* **1** (*fml*) to come to or bring sth to an end: [V] *The meeting terminated in disorder.* [Vn] *terminate sb's contract* ○ *terminate a pregnancy* (eg by means of an ABORTION). **2** (of a train or bus) to end a journey somewhere and go no further: [Vpr] *This train will terminate at the next station.* [also Vadv].

termination /ˌtɜːmɪ'neɪʃn/ *n* **1** [U,C] the action or an instance of terminating (TERMINATE 1) sth or the state of being terminated: *the termination of an agreement.* **2** [C] (*medical*) an ABORTION.

terminology /ˌtɜːmɪ'nɒlədʒi/ *n* **1** [U,C] the technical terms used in a particular subject: *a word not used except in medical terminology* ○ *various scientific terminologies.* **2** [U] words used with particular specific meanings: *misunderstandings caused by differences of terminology.* ▸ **terminological** /ˌtɜːmɪnə'lɒdʒɪkl/ *adj*.

terminus /'tɜːmɪnəs/ *n* (*pl* **termini** /'tɜːmɪnaɪ/ or **terminuses** /-nəsɪz/) (*Brit*) the last station at the end of a railway line or the last stop on a bus route. See also TERMINAL *n* 1.

termite /'tɜːmaɪt/ *n* a small insect like an ANT, found chiefly in tropical areas, that does a lot of damage by eating wood.

terms /tɜːmz/ *n* [pl] **1** conditions offered, demanded or accepted in an agreement or arrangement: *peace terms* ○ *according to the terms of the contract* ○ *a failure to agree on the terms of a settlement.* **2** conditions relating to buying, selling or paying for sth: *get credit on easy terms* (eg allowing a buyer to pay over a long period) ○ *enquire about terms for renting a house.* **3** a way of expressing oneself/sth: *I wish to protest in the strongest possible terms.* ○ *He referred to your work in very flattering terms.* ○ *I explained in simple terms.* **IDM** **be on good, friendly, bad, etc 'terms (with sb)** to have a good, etc relationship: *I didn't know you and she were on such intimate terms* (ie were such close friends). ○ *I've always been on excellent terms with my staff.* **be on speaking terms** ⇨ SPEAK. **come to terms (with sb)** to reach an agreement. **come to 'terms with sth** to accept sth unpleasant over a period of time: *She's learnt to come to terms with her disability.* **in no uncertain terms** ⇨ UNCERTAIN. **in terms of 'sth; in 'sth terms 1** with regard to the particular aspect specified; as regards sth: *The job is great in terms of salary but there are disadvantages.* ○ *Let us consider the problem in political terms.* **2** from the basis of sth: *She judges everyone in terms of her own standards.* **on equal terms** ⇨ EQUAL. **on one's own / on sb's 'terms** with conditions that one/sb else decides: *I'm prepared to accept a reorganization of my department, but only on my own terms.*

■ **ˌterms of 'reference** *n* [pl] the range established for an inquiry, investigation, etc: *The committee decided that the matter lay outside/within its terms of reference.* See also TERM.

tern /tɜːn/ *n* a sea bird with long pointed wings and a forked (FORK) tail.

terrace /'terəs/ *n* **1** [C] (*esp Brit*) (often in street names) a continuous row of similar houses joined together in one block: *6 Olympic Terrace* ○ *a terrace-house* (ie one of those in such a row). ⇨ picture at HOUSE¹. **2 terraces** [pl] an area of wide shallow steps at a sports STADIUM where spectators stand and watch matches: *watch from the terraces*. **3** [C] a paved (PAVE) area beside a house or restaurant where people can sit, eat, etc: *a sun terrace*. See also PATIO. **4** [C] a raised level area of ground or a series of these into which the side of a hill is shaped so that it can be cultivated.

▶ **terraced** *adj* **1** formed into a terrace(4) or terraces: *a terraced hillside/garden*. **2** (*esp Brit*) forming part of or consisting of a terrace(1) or terraces: *a terraced house/street*.

terracing *n* [U] terraced ground or a terraced structure.

terracotta /ˌterəˈkɒtə/ *n* [U] **1** clay that has been baked but not glazed (GLAZE), used for making pots, etc: *a terracotta vase*. **2** the reddish-brown colour of terracotta.

terra firma /ˌterə ˈfɜːmə/ *n* [U] dry land; the ground, contrasted with water or air: *glad to be back on terra firma again* (eg after a trip by boat or aircraft).

terrain /təˈreɪn/ *n* [C, U] a stretch of land, with regard to its natural features: *hilly/marshy/rough terrain* ○ *difficult terrain for cycling*.

terrapin /ˈterəpɪn/ *n* a small TURTLE(2) found in rivers and lakes in N America.

terrestrial /təˈrestriəl/ *adj* **1** of or living on land: *the terrestrial parts of the world* ○ *terrestrial species*. **2** of the planet Earth. Compare CELESTIAL 2. **3** (of communications systems) operating on earth, not by SATELLITE(1): *terrestrial TV channels*. See also EXTRATERRESTRIAL.

terrible /ˈterəbl/ *adj* **1** very unpleasant or serious; causing one to feel very unhappy or upset: *a terrible war/accident/murder* ○ *hear some terrible news* ○ *terrible toothache* ○ *The heat was terrible*. **2** having a very unpleasant or uncomfortable feeling: *I feel terrible — I'm going to bed*. **3** of very low quality or standard; very bad: *What a terrible meal!* ○ *This essay is terrible.* ○ *I'm terrible at tennis.* **4** [attrib] very great: *make a terrible fuss about nothing* ○ *I'm in a terrible mess*.

▶ **terribly** /-əbli/ *adv* **1** very: *a terribly good book* ○ *I'm terribly sorry*. **2** very badly: *She suffered terribly when her son was killed*.

terrier /ˈteriə(r)/ *n* a small dog. There are several different types of terrier. See also BULL-TERRIER, FOX-TERRIER.

terrific /təˈrɪfɪk/ *adj* **1** [attrib] very great; extreme: *a terrific storm* ○ *driving at a terrific speed*. **2** (*infml*) excellent; wonderful: *He's doing a terrific job.* ○ *The view was terrific*.

▶ **terrifically** /-kli/ *adv* (*infml*) extremely: *terrifically clever/generous/rich*.

terrify /ˈterɪfaɪ/ *v* (*pt, pp* **-fied**) to make sb very frightened; to fill sb with TERROR(1a): [Vn] *The risks involved terrify me.* [Vnpr] *They terrified their victims into handing over large sums of money*.

▶ **terrified** *adj* ~ **(of sb/sth)**; ~ **(at sth)** very frightened; filled with TERROR(1a): *terrified of spiders/heights/the dark* ○ *He was terrified at the prospect of flying for the first time*.

terrifying *adj*: *a terrifying experience*. **terrifyingly** *adv*.

terrine /teˈriːn/ *n* [U, C] cooked food in the form of a firm PASTE¹(3); PÂTÉ.

territorial /ˌterəˈtɔːriəl/ *adj* of a country's or a ruler's territory: *territorial possessions* ○ *have territorial claims against another country* (ie claim part of its territory).

▶ **Territorial** *n* (in Britain) a member of the Territorial Army.

territoriality /ˌterəˌtɔːriˈæləti/ *n* [U].

territorially *adv*.

■ **the ‚Territorial ˈArmy** *n* [Gp] (in Britain) a military force of people who are not professional soldiers but who train as soldiers in their free time.

‚**territorial ˈwaters** *n* [pl] the sea near a country's coast and under its control: *fishing illegally in foreign territorial waters*.

territory /ˈterətri; *US* -tɔːri/ *n* **1** [C, U] land or an area of land under the control of a country or ruler: *Turkish territory* ○ *occupying enemy territory* ○ *conquer new territories*. **2** [U] land of a specified nature: *fertile territory*. **3 Territory** [C] a country or an area forming part of the USA, Australia or Canada but not ranking as a state or province: *North West Territory*. **4** [C, U] an area for which sb has responsibility with regard to a particular type of work or activity: *Our representatives cover a very large territory*. **5** [C, U] an area claimed as belonging to one person, group or animal and defended against others who try to enter it: *He seems to regard that end of the office as his territory.* ○ *Mating blackbirds will defend their territory against intruders.* **6** [U] an area of knowledge, activity or discussion: *Legal problems are Andrew's territory* (ie He handles them). ○ *Mail-order business is very much unknown territory for us.*

terror /ˈterə(r)/ *n* **1(a)** [U] extreme fear: *run away in terror* ○ *scream with terror* ○ *be in terror of one's life* (ie afraid of being killed) ○ *She lives in terror of* (ie is constantly afraid of) *losing her job.* ○ *strike terror into sb* (ie make them very frightened). See also REIGN OF TERROR. **(b)** [C] an instance of this: *have a terror of heights* ○ *The terrors of the night were past*. **2** [C] a person or thing that causes extreme fear: *street gangs that are the terror of the neighbourhood* ○ *Death holds no terrors for* (ie does not frighten) *me*. **3** [C] (*infml*) a person or an animal that causes one trouble or annoyance: *Their children are absolute terrors.*

▶ **terrorize, -ise** /ˈterəraɪz/ *v* to cause great fear by being aggressive or violent so that others do not defend themselves or oppose one: [Vn] *local gangs terrorizing the neighbourhood* [Vnpr] *villagers terrorized into leaving their homes*.

terrorism /ˈterərɪzəm/ *n* [U] the use of violence for political aims or to force a government to act, esp because of the fear it causes among the people: *appalling acts of terrorism*.

▶ **terrorist** /ˈterərɪst/ *n* a person who takes part in terrorism: *The terrorists are threatening to blow up the hijacked plane.* ○ *terrorist attacks*.

■ **ˈterror-stricken** *adj* filled with terror.

terry /ˈteri/ *n* [U] a cotton fabric with raised loops of thread, used for towels, etc.

terse /tɜːs/ *adj* using few words and perhaps not friendly or polite: *written in a terse style* ○ *a terse statement/person*. ▶ **tersely** *adv*. **terseness** *n* [U].

tertiary /ˈtɜːʃəri; *US* -ʃieri/ *adj* third in order, rank, importance, etc: *tertiary education* (ie at university or college level) ○ *tertiary* (ie very severe) *burns*. Compare PRIMARY, SECONDARY.

Terylene /ˈterəliːn/ *n* [U] (*propr*) a synthetic fabric used esp for making clothes.

TESL /ˈtesl/ *abbr* teaching of English as a second language. Compare TEFL, TESOL.

TESOL /ˈtiːsɒl, ˈtesɒl/ *abbr* (*esp US*) teaching of English to speakers of other languages: *a TESOL conference*. Compare TEFL, TESL.

tessellated /ˈtesəleɪtɪd/ *adj* (of a pavement) made from small flat pieces of stone of various colours arranged in a pattern.

test /test/ *n* **1** a short examination of knowledge or ability, consisting of questions that must be answered or activities that must be carried out: *give the pupils a test (paper) in arithmetic* ○ *an I'Q/ in'telligence test* ○ *a ˈdriving-test* (ie to obtain a driv-

[V.speech] = verb + direct speech   [V.that] = verb + *that* clause   [V.wh] = verb + *who, how*, etc clause

ing licence) ○ *take/pass/fail a test.* **2** a medical examination conducted in order to check or discover sb's condition: *an ¹eye test* ○ *a test for AIDS/ cancer* ○ *a ¹pregnancy test.* See also BLOOD TEST, BREATH TEST, MEANS TEST. **3** a trial or an experiment intended to show whether sth works or works well: *carry out tests on a new product.* See also ACID TEST, FIELD-TEST, ROAD TEST. **4** (*infml*) = TEST MATCH. **IDM** **put sb/sth to the ¹test** to find out whether sb/sth has the required qualities: *The government's policies have not yet been put to the test.* **stand the test of ¹time,** etc to prove to be reliable or of lasting value over a long period: *fine old buildings that have stood the test of centuries.*

▶ **test** *v* ~ (sb/sth) (for sth); ~ sb/sth (on sb/sth) to carry out a test(1,2,3) or tests on sb/sth: [V] *teachers discussing methods of testing* [Vn] *a **tried and tested** (ie reliable) remedy* ○ *testing nuclear weapons under the sea* ○ *have one's eyesight/hearing tested* ○ *The long climb tested our powers of endurance.* [Vpr] *test for pollution in the water/test the water for pollution* [Vnpr] *Many people are against new drugs being tested on animals.* See also MEANS-TESTED. **IDM** **test the ¹waters** to find out what the situation is before taking action or forming an opinion: *test the waters before launching a sales campaign.*

testable *adj* that can be tested: *testable theories.*
tester *n* a person who tests sth: *drug testers.*
testing *adj* difficult to deal with and requiring certain qualities or abilities: *testing assignments* ○ *a testing situation.*

■ **¹test case** *n* a legal case or other procedure whose result is expected to be used in settling similar cases in the future: *The outcome of these wage talks is seen as a test case for future pay negotiations.*
¹test drive *n* a drive taken to judge the performance or quality of a car one is thinking of buying. **¹test-drive** *v* (*pt* -drove; *pp* -driven) [Vn] to take a car for a test drive.
¹test match (also *infml* **test**) *n* a cricket or Rugby match between teams of certain countries, usu one of a series during a tour.
¹test pilot *n* a pilot whose job is to fly newly designed aircraft in order to test their performance.
¹test ¹run *n* = TRIAL RUN.
¹test-tube *n* a glass tube, closed at one end, used in chemical experiments. ⇨ picture. **¹test-tube baby** *n* a baby that is born through artificial insemination (ARTIFICIAL), or that develops elsewhere than in a mother's body. See also IN VITRO.

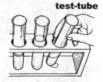

test-tube

testament /'testəmənt/ *n* (*fml*) **1** (usu *sing*) ~ (to sth) a thing that provides clear proof of sth: *The new model is a testament to the skill and dedication of the workforce.* **2** = WILL⁴ 5. See also NEW TESTAMENT, OLD TESTAMENT.

testes *pl* of TESTIS.

testicle /'testɪkl/ *n* either of the two male sex glands (GLAND) in which SPERM(1) are produced. ⇨ picture at REPRODUCTION. ▶ **testicular** *adj*: *testicular cancer.*

testify /'testɪfaɪ/ *v* (*pt, pp* -fied) **1** ~ (to sth); ~ (against / for / in favour of sb) to give evidence; to make a formal statement, esp as a witness in court: [V] *summoned to testify in court/before a grand jury* [Vpr] *The teacher testified to the boy's honesty.* ○ *Two witnesses testified against her and one in her favour.* [V.that] *He testified under oath that he had not been at the scene of the crime.* **2** ~ to sth (*fml*) to be evidence of sth; to demonstrate sth: [Vpr] *These events merely testify to the need for a change in the law.* [also V.that]. See also TESTIMONY.

testimonial /ˌtestɪ'məʊniəl/ *n* **1** a formal statement written by a former employer about sb's abilities or qualifications, for use eg when applying for a job. Compare REFERENCE 8. **2** a thing given to sb to show appreciation of their services or achievements: *a testimonial match* (ie to honour or raise money for a particular player).

testimony /'testɪməni; US -məʊni/ *n* **1** [U, C] a written or spoken statement of evidence, esp one given by a witness in court: *According to the witness's testimony, you were present when the crime was committed.* ○ *first-hand testimonies.* **2** [U, sing] ~ (to sth) a thing that is evidence of or demonstrates sth: *The pyramids are (a) testimony to the Ancient Egyptians' engineering skills.* See also TESTIFY.

testis /'testɪs/ *n* (*pl* **testes** /-tiːz/) (*anatomy*) a TESTICLE.

testosterone /te'stɒstərəʊn/ *n* [U] a HORMONE produced in the testicles (TESTICLE) that is capable of developing and maintaining male characteristics in the body.

testy /'testi/ *adj* easily annoyed or irritated; bad-tempered: *a testy person/reply.* ▶ **testily** /-ɪli/ *adv*: *reply testily.*

tetanus /'tetənəs/ *n* [U] a disease in which the muscles, esp of the jaw, become stiff. It is caused by bacteria entering the body through cuts or wounds. Compare LOCKJAW.

tetchy /'tetʃi/ *adj* bad-tempered; angry without good reason: *a tetchy person/mood/remark.* ▶ **tetchily** /-ɪli/ *adv.*

tête-à-tête /ˌteɪt ɑː 'teɪt/ *n* a private conversation between two people: *have regular tête-à-têtes with sb* ○ *a cosy tête-à-tête lunch.*

tether /'teðə(r)/ *n* a rope or chain by which an animal is tied to sth, allowing it to move around within a small area. **IDM** **at the end of one's tether** ⇨ END¹.
▶ **tether** *v* ~ sth (to sth) to tie an animal with a tether: [Vn, Vnpr] *He tethered his horse (to a tree).*

tetr(a)- *comb form* four: *tetrahedron* (ie a figure with four sides).

Teutonic /tjuː'tɒnɪk; US tuː-/ *adj* **1** of the Germanic peoples or their languages. **2** [usu attrib] showing qualities thought to be typical of German people: *Teutonic thoroughness.*

text /tekst/ *n* **1** [U] the main written or printed part of a book or page, contrasted with notes, illustrations, etc: *too much text and not enough pictures* ○ *The index refers the reader to pages in the text.* **2(a)** [C] the written form of a speech, a play, an article, etc: *the full text of the President's speech* ○ *As an actor, I keep going back to the text when I'm working on my performance.* **(b)** [U] any form of written material: *a computer that can process text.* **3** [C] **(a)** a book, play, etc studied for an examination: *'Hamlet' is a set text this year.* **(b)** a piece of writing about which questions are asked in an examination or a lesson; a passage(6): *Read the text carefully and then answer the questions.* **4** [C] a sentence or short passage from the Bible, etc used as the subject of a SERMON(1) or discussion: *I take as my text…*
▶ **textual** /'tekstʃuəl/ *adj* [usu attrib] of or in a text: *textual criticism* ○ *textual errors.*

textbook /'tekstbʊk/ *n* **1** a book giving instruction in a subject, used esp in schools, etc: *a grammar textbook.* **2** [attrib] conforming to what is considered the best or most acceptable way of doing sth: *a textbook example of how the game should be played.* Compare COPYBOOK.

textile /'tekstaɪl/ *n* any cloth or woven material: *factories producing a range of textiles* ○ *get a job in textiles* ○ *the textile industry.*

texture /'tekstʃə(r)/ *n* [C, U] **1** the way a surface, substance or fabric looks or feels to the touch, ie whether it is rough, smooth, hard, soft, etc: *the texture of wool/stone/leather* ○ *soil with a fine/coarse texture* ○ *the tone and texture of a painting*. **2** the way food or drink tastes or appears, ie whether it is rough, smooth, light, heavy, etc: *a sauce with a creamy texture* ○ *cakes with light textures*. **3** the way in which a piece of music or literature is constructed, with regard to the way in which its parts are combined: *a play with a dense texture* ○ *splendid instrumental textures*.

▶ **textural** /ˈtekstʊərəl/ *adj* of or relating to texture: *the textural characteristics of rock*.

textured *adj* (esp in compounds) having a distinct or specified texture: *textured* (ie not smooth) *wallpaper* ○ *The walls have a textured finish*. ○ *a ˌsmooth-textured ˈwine*.

-th *suff* **1** (with a few *vs* and *adjs* forming *ns*): *growth* ○ *width*. **2** (with simple numbers except *one, two* and *three* forming ORDINAL numbers): *sixth* ○ *fifteenth* ○ *hundredth*.

thalidomide /θəˈlɪdəmaɪd/ *n* [U] a sedative (SEDATE²) drug formerly given to pregnant women until it was found that some of them gave birth to babies with deformed (DEFORM) or missing limbs.

than /ðən; *rare strong form* ðæn/ *conj* (used after a comparative *adj* or *adv* to introduce a clause or phrase in which a comparison is expressed): *He's never more annoying than when he's trying to help*. ○ *She's a better player than (she was) last year*. ○ *He loves me more than you do*. ○ *You should know better than to behave like that*.

▶ **than** *prep* **1** (used before a *n* or *pron* to express a comparison): *He learns more quickly than the others*. ○ *I'm older than her*. ○ *Nobody understands the situation better than you*. ○ *There was more whisky in it than soda*. **2** (used after *more* or *less* for comparing amounts, numbers, distances, etc): *It cost me more than $100*. ○ *It never takes more than an hour*. ○ *He can't be more than fifteen*. ○ *It's less than a mile to the beach*. **3** (used after a clause beginning with *no sooner, hardly, barely* or *scarcely* for expressing that one thing happened almost immediately after another): *No sooner had I sat down than there was a loud knock at the door*. ○ *Hardly/Barely/Scarcely had we arrived than the problems started*. See also OTHER THAN, RATHER THAN.

thank /θæŋk/ *v* ~ **sb** (**for sth / doing sth**) to express gratitude to sb: [Vn] *There's no need to thank me — I was only doing my job*. [Vnpr] *We thanked them for all their help*. ○ (*ironic*) *He won't thank you* (ie He will be annoyed with you) *for leaving him to clear everything up*. **IDM** **have oneself/sb to thank (for sth)** (*ironic*) to be responsible/hold sb responsible for sth: *She has only herself to thank for what happened*. ○ *Who do we have to thank for this fiasco?* **I'll thank you for sth / to do sth** (used in making strong formal requests or commands, usu indicating annoyance): *I'll thank you to mind your own business*. ○ **ˌno, ˈthank you** (used for refusing an offer, a proposal, etc politely): *'Would you like some more coffee?' 'No, thank you.'* **thank ˈGod/ˈgoodness/ ˈheaven(s)** (used for expressing relief): *Thank God you're safe!* **thank one's ˈlucky stars** to feel very grateful because one has been very lucky: *You can thank your lucky stars (that) nothing worse happened*. **ˈthank you (for sth / doing sth)** (used for expressing gratitude or accepting an offer, etc): *Thank you (very much) for lending me your bike*.

▶ **thankful** /-fl/ *adj* (**a**) [attrib] ~ (**to do sth**); ~ (**that** ...) pleased and relieved about sth good that has happened: *You should be thankful to have escaped/that you have escaped with only minor injuries*. (**b**) ~ (**for sth**) grateful: *a thankful prayer* ○ *I am thankful for your enthusiasm and support*. **IDM** **grateful/thankful for small mercies** ⇨ SMALL.
thankfully /-fəli/ *adv* **1** in a thankful way: *I ac-*

cepted the invitation thankfully. **2** (qualifying a whole sentence) I/we are glad; fortunately (FORTUNATE): *Thankfully, it has stopped raining at last*. ○ *There was, thankfully, no real damage done*. ⇨ note at HOPEFUL.

thankless *adj* (of an action) unpleasant to do and not likely to earn one any thanks from others: *perform a thankless task*.

thanks *n* [pl] ~ (**to sb**) (**for sth**) expressions of gratitude: *give thanks to God* ○ *My heartfelt/warmest thanks to you all*. ○ **Many thanks** *for all your hospitality*. See also VOTE OF THANKS. **IDM** **no thanks to sb/sth** despite sb/sth; without any help or contribution from sb/sth: *It's no thanks to you (that) we arrived on time — your short cuts weren't short cuts at all!* **thanks to sb/sth** (sometimes ironic) because of sb/sth: *The fête was a great success, thanks to the fine weather and a lot of hard work*. ○ *We're £200 worse off, (and it's all) thanks to you!* — *interj* (*infml*) ~ (**for sth / doing sth**) thank you: *'Would you like some more cake?' 'No thanks.'* ○ *Thanks a lot for the loan/for lending me the money*. ○ *'Here's your change.' 'Thanks very much.'* **IDM** **thanks a ˈmillion** thank you very much.

■ **ˈthank-you** *n* an expression of thanks: *Have you said your thank-yous to Mrs Brown for the party?* ○ *She walked away without so much as a thank-you.* ○ *thank-you letters*.

thanksgiving /ˌθæŋksˈgɪvɪŋ/ *n* [U] **1** the expression of gratitude, esp to God. **2 Thanksgiving (Day)** a public holiday in the USA (on the fourth Thursday in November) and in Canada (on the second Monday in October), originally a day for giving thanks to God for the HARVEST(1).

that¹ /ðæt/ *det* (*pl* **those** /ðəʊz/) **1** (used for referring to a specific person or thing, esp when he, she or it is not near the speaker or as near to the speaker as another): *Look at that man standing there*. ○ *That box is bigger than this one*. ○ *How much are those apples at the back?* ○ *Where did that noise come from?* ○ *Who are those people over there?* Compare THIS. **2** (used for referring to sb/sth already mentioned or believed to be known or understood by the reader or person listening): *I was still living with my parents at that time/in those days*. ○ *That incident changed their lives*. ○ *Have you read that incredible story about her in the papers?* ○ *That friend of his was rather strange, wasn't he?* ○ *That dress of hers is too short*. **3** (used before a *n* after which further information is given to specify exactly who or what is being referred to): *Have you forgotten about that money I lent you last week?* ○ *Those students who failed the exam will have to take it again*. ○ *Who was that man you were talking to?*

that² /ðæt/ *pron* (*pl* **those** /ðəʊz/) **1** (used for referring to a specific person or thing, esp when he, she or it is not near the speaker or as near the speaker as another): *That's Peter at the bus-stop*. ○ *Who's that?* ○ *Hello. Is that Heather?* ○ *That's a nice dress*. ○ *Those look riper than these*. **2** (used for referring to sb/sth already mentioned, known or understood): *What can I do about that?* ○ *That was a really stupid thing to say*. ○ *Do you remember when we went to Norway? That was a good holiday*. ○ *That's exactly what I think*. ○ *Is that what he told you?* **3** (used esp in the plural for specifying particular people or things): *Those I like most are usually very expensive*. ○ *Those present were in favour of a change*. ○ **There are those who** *say* (ie Some people say) *she should never have been appointed*. **4** (used for specifying sth/sb of a particular type): *His reaction was that of a man losing his patience*. ○ *My best friends are those I've known the longest*. ○ *Salaries here are higher than those in my country*. **IDM** **and (all) ˈthat** (*infml*) and everything else connected with an activity, a situation, etc; and so on: *Did you*

bring the documents and (all) that? **that is (to say)**
1 which means: *He's a local government adminis-*
trator, that is to say a Civil Servant. **2** to be specific:
She's a housewife — when she's not teaching English,
that is. ₁**that's** ˈ**that** that is the end of the matter,
subject, etc and there is nothing further to do or
say: *I'm not going to let you use my car, and that's*
that.

that³ /ðæt/ *adv* so; to that extent or degree: *I can't*
walk that far (ie as far as that). ○ *They've spent* ˈ*that*
much (ie as much as is indicated). ○ *It's about* ˈ*that*
long (ie as long as is indicated). ○ *It isn't all that*
cold (ie not as cold as you are suggesting or not very
cold). ○ (*infml*) *I was that frightened I didn't know*
what to do.

that⁴ /ðət; *rare strong form* ðæt/ *conj* **1** (used for
introducing a clause that is the subject or object of a
v): *She said that the book was based on a true story.* ○
I thought that 9 May would be the date of the election.
○ *It's possible that he hasn't received the letter.* ○ *That*
she had no interest in him was obvious to us all. **2**
(*rhet*) (used for expressing wishes and regrets): *Oh*
that I could see him again! ○ *That I should see a child*
of mine arrested for selling drugs!

that⁵ /ðət; *rare strong form* ðæt/ *rel pron* **1** (used for
introducing a defining clause after a *n*) (**a**) (as the
subject of the *v* in the clause): *The letter that came*
this morning was from my father. ○ *The woman that*
spoke to me in the shop used to live near me in Exeter.
○ *Who was it that won the last World Cup?* (**b**) (as the
object of the *v* in the clause, but often omitted in this
position): *The watch (that) you gave me keeps perfect*
time. ○ *The person (that) I have to phone lives in*
Bombay. (**c**) (as the object of a *prep* in the clause,
but often omitted in this position): *The photographs*
(that) you're looking at were taken by my brother. ○
The man (that) I was talking to had just arrived from
Canada. ⇨ note at WHOM. **2** (used for introducing a
clause after a superlative, *the*, *only*, *all*, etc): *Shake-*
speare is the greatest English writer that ever lived. ○
The only part of the meal (that) I really liked was the
dessert. ○ *All that I have is yours.* **3** (used instead of
when after an expression of time): *the year that my*
father died ○ *the day that war broke out* ○ *It was only*
later/not until later that I started to feel better.

thatch /θætʃ/ *n* **1**(**a**) [U, C usu *sing*] a roof made of
dried straw, reeds (REED 1) or similar material:
Lights gleamed beneath the overhanging thatch. (**b**)
[U] straw, reeds (REED 1), etc used for making a roof:
a roof of thatch/a thatch roof. **2** [sing] (*infml*) thick
hair on the head.
▶ **thatch** *v* to cover a roof or building with thatch:
[Vn] *a thatched cottage* [Vnpr] *a hut thatched with*
palm leaves. **thatcher** *n* a person whose job is
thatching roofs. **thatching** *n* [U] **1** the skill of
putting thatch on roofs. **2** straw, etc used in making
a thatch.

thaw /θɔː/ *v* **1**(**a**) ~ (**sth**) (**out**) to become or make
sth liquid or soft after being frozen: [V] *All the snow*
has thawed. [V, Vp] *leave frozen food to thaw (out)*
before cooking [Vn, Vnpr] *thaw (out) frozen orange*
juice. (**b**) (used only with *it*) (of the weather) to
become warm enough to melt snow and ice: [V] *It's*
starting to thaw. Compare DEFROST, DE-ICE, MELT 1,
UNFREEZE 1. ⇨ note at WATER¹. **2** (of people, their
behaviour, etc) to become less formal and more
friendly in manner: [V] *Anglo-French relations have*
thawed considerably since the dispute over farming
quotas.
▶ **thaw** *n* (usu *sing*) **1** a period of warmer weather
that causes ice and snow to melt: *The sudden thaw*
caused widespread flooding. **2** a situation or period
in which people, countries, etc are less HOSTILE(1a)
and more friendly with each other: *a gradual thaw*
in relations with China.

the /ðə, ði; *strong form* ðiː/ *def art* ⇨ note at SCHOOL¹.
1 (used for referring to sb/sth that has already been
mentioned or can be understood): *A boy and a girl*
were sitting on a bench. The boy was smiling but the
girl looked angry. ○ *There was an accident here yes-*
terday. A car hit a tree and the driver was killed. **2**
(used for introducing a particular person or thing
when one is explaining which one is meant): *the*
house at the end of the street ○ *the birds of Borneo* ○
We still haven't solved the main problem. ○ *The people*
I met there were very friendly. ○ *Do you like the food*
in this country? ○ (*infml*) *The way she talks, you'd*
think she was an expert. **3** (used when the person or
thing referred to is the normal or obvious one): *The*
milkman was late this morning. ○ *Have you seen the*
paper? ○ *The children are in the garden.* ○ *Did you*
enjoy the play? ○ *Would you pass the salt, please?* **4**
(used esp with superlative *adjs*, *first*, *last*, *next*, etc):
the best day of your life ○ *the hottest day of the*
summer ○ *What was the last thing I said?* ○ *The scarf*
was exactly the right colour. **5** (used before an OR-
DINAL): *for the third time* ○ *the 4th of July* ○ *during the*
nineteenth century ○ *You're the third person to ask me*
that. **6** (used when there is only one of sth or one
group): *the sun/moon/sky/stars* ○ *the town centre* ○
the top of the mountain ○ *the Pacific Ocean* ○ *the*
Queen/President. **7** (used with an *adj* to make a *n*
that refers to all members of a group or nation or to
all things or people of a particular type): *The rich get*
richer and the poor get poorer. ○ *the elderly/the unem-*
ployed ○ *the French.* **8** (used before the plural of a
surname to refer to the whole family or to a married
couple): *Don't forget to invite the Jordans.* **9** (used
with a singular countable *n* to mean the whole
species): *The chimpanzee is an endangered species.*
10 (used for referring to objects or devices in general): *Who invented the toilet?* ○ *The computer has*
changed our way of life. ○ *I heard it on the radio.* **11**
(used to refer to a musical instrument or dance in a
general way): *learn how to play the cello* ○ *dance the*
polka. **12** enough of sth: *He hasn't got the intelli-*
gence (required). ○ *I wanted it but I didn't have the*
money. **13** (used in front of a unit of measure to
mean 'every'): *My car does forty miles to the gallon.* ○
I work freelance and am paid by the hour/word. **14**
(used to refer to a period of time in a general way):
I'm usually out during the day. ○ *in the 1990s.* **15**
(used to indicate that the person or thing referred to
is well-known or important): *Michael Crawford? Not*
ˈ*the Michael Crawford?* ○ *The family reunion was* ˈ*the*
social event of the year. **IDM** **the more, less,**
etc...the more, less, etc... (used to indicate that
the increase/decrease in one amount or degree of
sth affects the increase/decrease in amount or degree of sth else): *The more she thought about it, the*
more depressed she became. ○ *The more luxurious the*
hotel, the more expensive it usually is. ○ *The less said*
about the whole affair, the happier I'll be.

theatre (*US* **theater**) /ˈθɪətə(r); *US* ˈθiːətər/ *n* **1** [C]
(**a**) a building or outdoor area where plays and
similar entertainments are performed: *West End/*
Broadway theatres ○ *an open-air theatre.* (**b**) a cinema. **2** **the theatre** [sing] (**a**) theatres in general,
esp as a form of entertainment: *Do you often go to*
the theatre? (**b**) the work of writing, producing and
acting in plays: *She wants to go into the theatre.* **3**
[U] plays considered as a form of entertainment;
drama: *a study of Greek theatre* ○ *enjoy live theatre* ○
current ideas about what makes good theatre (ie
what is effective when performed). **4** [C] a room or
hall for lectures, etc with seats in rows rising one
behind another: *a lecture theatre.* **5** [C usu *sing*] ~
of sth (*rhet*) the place in which a war or other
conflict takes place: *a new theatre of civil war* ○ *the*
political theatre. **6** [C] = OPERATING THEATRE: *a*
theatre sister (ie a nurse who assists during operations).
■ ˈ**theatre-goer** *n* a person who goes regularly to
see plays performed.

theatrical /θɪˈætrɪkl/ *adj* **1** [usu attrib] of or for the theatre: *theatrical performances* ○ *a theatrical company/career.* **2** (of behaviour) exaggerated; not natural; done in order to create an effect: *theatrical gestures.*
▶ **theatricality** /θɪˌætrɪˈkæləti/ *n* [U] the exaggerated or artificial style or effect of sth: *I was fascinated by the sheer theatricality of the event.*
theatrically /-kli/ *adv*: *theatrically challenging* ○ *behave theatrically.*
theatricals *n* [pl] theatrical performances: *amateur theatricals.*

thee /ðiː/ *pron* (*arch or dialect*) (the object form of *thou*) you.

theft /θeft/ *n* [C, U] an act or the crime of stealing: *A number of thefts have been reported recently.* ○ *be guilty of theft.*

their /ðeə(r)/ *possess det* **1** of or belonging to them: *Their parties are always fun.* ○ *Which is their house?* ○ *Their fame rests entirely on one recording.* **2** (used instead of *her* or *his* to refer to a person whose sex is not known or not considered relevant): *If anyone telephones ask for their number so I can call them back.*
▶ **theirs** /ðeəz/ *possess pron* of or belonging to them: *Theirs are the children with very fair hair.* ○ *It's a favourite place of theirs.* ➪ note at GENDER.

theism /ˈθiːɪzəm/ *n* [U] belief in the existence of a God or gods. Compare MONOTHEISM, POLYTHEISM.

them /ðəm; *strong form* ðem/ *pers pron* **1** (used when referring to people or things as the object of a *v* or of a *prep*): *Tell them the news.* ○ *What are you doing with those matches? Give them to me.* ○ *Did you eat all of them?* **2** (used instead of *him* or *her* to refer to a person whose sex is not known or not considered relevant): *If anyone/a customer comes in before I get back, ask them to wait.* ➪ note at GENDER. **IDM** ˌ**them and** ˈ**us** rich or powerful people contrasted with ordinary people like the speaker(s): *attempt to eradicate the 'them and us' attitude in industrial relations.*

thematic /θɪˈmætɪk, θiː-/ *adj* of or related to a theme: *thematic maps/material.* ▶ **thematically** /-kli/ *adv*: *ideas that are thematically linked.*

theme /θiːm/ *n* [C] **1** the subject of a talk, a piece of writing or a person's thoughts; a topic: *The theme of our discussion was 'World Peace'.* **2** (*music*) a short tune that is repeated or developed in a piece of music: *variations on a theme.* **3** (*Brit*) = SIGNATURE TUNE: *the theme from 'Eastenders'.*
■ ˈ**theme park** *n* a large area for public amusement, containing entertainments which are connected with a single idea: *a Disneyland theme park.*
ˈ**theme song** (also ˈ**theme tune**) *n* (**a**) a tune that is often repeated in a musical play or film. (**b**) = SIGNATURE TUNE.

themselves /ðəmˈselvz/ *reflex, emph pron* (only taking the main stress in sentences when used for emphasis) **1** (*reflex*) (used when the people or animals performing an action are also affected by it): *They seemed to be enjoying themselves.* ○ *The children were arguing amongst themselves.* **2** (*emph*) (used for emphasizing *they* or *them*): *They themˈselves had had a similar experience.* ○ *Denise and Martin paid for it themˈselves.* ○ *The teachers were too surprised to comment.* **IDM** (**all**) **by them**ˈ**selves 1** alone: *They wanted to spend the evening by themselves.* **2** without help: *Alan and Jack built the shed (all) by themselves.*

then /ðen/ *adv* **1** (referring to a time in the past or future) (**a**) at that time: *We were living in Wales then.* ○ *I'll see you on Friday — we can discuss it then.* ○ *Jackie Kennedy, as she then was* (ie as her name was at that time), *was still only in her twenties.* [attrib] *the wife of the then Prime Minister.* (**b**) (used after a *prep*) that time: *From then on he refused to talk about it.* ○ *We'll have to manage without a television until then.* ○ *She'll have retired by then.* Compare NOW 1. **2** next; after that; afterwards: *I'll have soup first and then chicken.* ○ *We had a week in Rome and then went to Vienna.* ○ *Finish writing that report, then you can go home.* **3** (used in lists) and also: *We'll invite Imogen and Sandy, Rob and Kathy, and then there's Laura, Joanna, Catherine and Louise.* **4**(**a**) in that case; therefore: *If it's not on the table then it'll be in the drawer.* ○ *Offer to take him out for lunch, then* (ie as a result of this) *he'll be in a better mood.* ○ *You'll be looking for a new secretary then?* (**b**) (used for emphasis) considering what has been said or done: *So that's it then — you've nothing more to tell me?* **IDM** (**but**) **then a**ˈ**gain** (used to introduce a contrasting idea or piece of information): *I might go to the party, but then again I might not.* **then and there** = THERE AND THEN.

thence /ðens/ *adv* (*arch or fml*) from there: *They travelled by rail to the coast and thence by boat to America.*

thenceforward /ˌðensˈfɔːwəd/ (also **thenceforth** /ˌðensfɔːθ/) *adv* (*fml*) starting from that time: *He decided that thenceforward he would look at all incoming orders.*

theo- *comb form* of God or a god: *theology.*

theodolite /θɪˈɒdəlaɪt/ *n* an instrument used by surveyors (SURVEY) for measuring angles.

theology /θɪˈɒlədʒi/ *n* **1** [U] the study of the nature of God and of the foundations of religious belief: *a theology student.* **2** [C] a set of religious beliefs: *rival theologies.*
▶ **theologian** /ˌθiːəˈləudʒən/ *n* an expert in theology.
theological /ˌθiːəˈlɒdʒɪkl/ *adj*: *a theological college/ debate.* **theologically** /-kli/ *adv.*

theorem /ˈθɪərəm/ *n* a rule or general principle in MATHEMATICS, often expressed in symbols: *the binomial theorem* ○ *Pythagoras' theorem.*

theoretical /ˌθɪəˈretɪkl/ *adj* **1** concerned with the theory of a subject: *ideas presented within a theoretical framework* ○ *a theoretical physicist* ○ *This book is too theoretical; I need a practical guide.* Compare PRACTICAL 1. **2** probably or possibly true, but not confirmed or tested in practice: *The British player's greater experience gives him a theoretical advantage.* ○ *The monarch has the theoretical power to dismiss the government.* ▶ **theoretically** /-kli/ *adv*: *Theoretically we could still win, but it's not very likely.*

theory /ˈθɪəri/ *n* **1** [C, U] a set of properly argued ideas intended to explain facts or events: *Darwin's theory of evolution.* **2** [U] the principles on which a subject of study is based: *music/educational/ economic theory.* **3** [C] an opinion or idea, not necessarily based on reasoning: *different theories about how to bring up children* ○ *He has a theory that wearing hats makes men go bald.* ○ *'So if anyone tries to break in, the alarm will go off?' 'That's the theory.'* **4** [U] ideas, beliefs or claims about sth, which may not be found to be true: *It sounds fine in theory, but will it work (in practice)?* Compare PRACTICE 1.
▶ **theorist** /ˈθɪərɪst/ (also **theoretician** /ˌθɪərəˈtɪʃn/) *n* a person who forms, develops or studies theories about a particular subject: *political theorists.*
theorize, -ise /ˈθɪəraɪz/ *v* ~ (**about** sth) to form a theory or theories about sth: [Vpr] *We were theorizing about the ideal form of secondary education.* [Vn] (*fml*) *Morality has been extensively theorized by philosophers.* [also V, V.*that*]. **theorizing, -ising** *n* [U].

theosophy /θɪˈɒsəfi/ *n* [U] any of several religious

systems that aim at a direct knowledge of God by means of meditation (MEDITATE) or prayer.

therapeutic /ˌθerəˈpjuːtɪk/ *adj* (**a**) of or connected with healing: *the therapeutic properties of foods.* (**b**) having a good general effect on the body or the mind: *the therapeutic effects of sea air* ○ *I find listening to music quite therapeutic.*
▶ **therapeutically** /-klɪ/ *adv*.
therapeutics *n* [sing *v*] the branch of medicine concerned with curing disease.

therapy /ˈθerəpi/ *n* **1** [U, C] any treatment designed to improve a health problem or DISABILITY or to cure an illness: *She's having/undergoing therapy for breast cancer.* ○ *natural/alternative therapies* (eg ones that do not involve manufactured medicines or drugs). **2** [U] = PSYCHOTHERAPY. ⇨ note at PSYCHOLOGY. See also CHEMOTHERAPY, GROUP THERAPY, OCCUPATIONAL THERAPY, PHYSIOTHERAPY, RADIOTHERAPY, SPEECH THERAPY.
▶ **therapist** /ˈθerəpɪst/ *n* a specialist who treats people using a particular type of therapy.

there¹ /ðeə(r)/ *adv* **1(a)** in, at or to that place: *It's there, right in front of you!* ○ *We're nearly there* (ie We have nearly arrived). ○ *If John sits here, Mary can sit there.* ○ *We liked the hotel so much that we're going there again next year.* ○ *I can see something moving out there.* (**b**) (used after a *prep*) that place or thing: *Put the keys under there.* ○ *I'm not going in there!* ○ *He was born in Oxford, or somewhere near there.* (**c**) (used at the beginning of a sentence to indicate where sb/sth is. If the subject is not a *pron* it follows the *v*): *There it is: just to the right of the church.* ○ *There's the statue I was telling you about.* Compare HERE 1. **2** (used esp with *be* and *go* to express annoyance, excitement, anxiety, relief, etc. If the subject is not a *pron* it follows the *v*): '*There goes the last bus.* ○ *Look, Tom, there it goes!* ○ *There you are! I've been looking for you for over an hour.* ○ *There's/ There goes the school bell — I must run.* **3(a)** (used after *that* + *n* for emphasis): *That woman there is the boss's wife.* (**b**) (used to emphasize a call or greeting): *You there! Come back!* ○ *Hello there! Lovely to see you again!* **4** at or with reference to a particular point, eg in a story or an argument: *Don't stop there. What did you do next?* ○ *There I have to disagree with you, I'm afraid.* **IDM** **here and there** ⇨ HERE. **ˌthere and ˈback** to and from a place: *Can I get there and back in a day?* **ˌthere and ˈthen**; **ˌthen and ˈthere** at that time and place; immediately: *I took one look at the car and offered to buy it there and then.* **ˌthere's ˈsth for you** that is a particularly good example of sth: *She visited him every day he was in hospital. There's deˈvotion for you.* ○ (*ironic*) *He didn't even say thank you. There's ˈgratitude for you.* **ˌthere you ˈare** (used when giving sb a thing they want or have asked for): *There you are. I've brought your newspaper.* **2** (used to show how easy sth is when explaining or demonstrating sth): *You switch on, wait until the screen lights up, push in the disk and there you are!* ○ *There you are! I told you it was straightforward.* **ˌthere you ˈgo/go aˈgain** (used to criticize sb for behaving in a way that is typical of them): *There you go again — jumping to conclusions on the slightest evidence.*
▶ **there** *interj* (used to express eg triumph, annoyance or encouragement): *There (now)! What did I tell you?* (ie You can see that I was right). ○ *There! You've gone and woken the baby!* ○ *There! That didn't hurt too much, did it?* **IDM** **ˌso ˈthere!** (used to indicate that one is determined not to change one's attitude or opinion): *Well, you can't have it, so there!* **ˌthere, ˈthere!** (used to comfort a small child): *There, there! Never mind, you'll soon feel better.*

there² /ðə(r); *strong form* ðeə(r)/ *adv* (used in place of a subject with *be* and a few other verbs, esp when referring to sb/sth for the first time): *There's a man*

(*standing/waiting) at the bus-stop.* (Compare: *The man is (standing/waiting) at the bus-stop.*) ○ *There are two men at the bus-stop.* ○ *There's a man and a woman at the bus-stop.* ○ *There's been an accident.* ○ *There seems (to be) no doubt about it.* ○ *There appeared to be anybody willing to help.* ○ *I don't want there to be any misunderstanding.* ○ *There comes a time* (Compare: *The time comes*) *when dying seems preferable to staying alive.* ○ *There once lived a poor farmer who had four sons.* **IDM** **ˈthere's a good boy, girl, dog, etc** (used to praise or encourage small children or animals): *Finish your lunch, there's a good boy.*

thereabouts /ˌðeərəˈbaʊts/ (*US* also **thereabout** /ˌðeərəˈbaʊt/) *adv* (**a**) near that place: *The factory is in Leeds or somewhere thereabouts.* (**b**) near that number, quantity or time: *I'll be home at 8 o'clock or thereabouts.*

thereafter /ðeərˈɑːftə(r); *US* -ˈæf-/ *adv* (*fml*) after that: *You will be accompanied as far as the border; thereafter you must find your own way.* ○ *She retired in 1953 and died shortly thereafter.*

thereby /ˌðeəˈbaɪ/ *adv* (*fml*) by that means or action: *They paid cash, thereby avoiding any problems with tax.*

therefore /ˈðeəfɔː(r)/ *adv* for that reason: *He is out of the country and therefore unable to attend the meeting.*

therefrom /ˌðeəˈfrɒm/ *adv* (*fml or law*) from that; from it: *milk, and all food products derived therefrom.*

therein /ˌðeərˈɪn/ *adv* (**a**) (*fml or law*) in that place: *the house and all the possessions therein.* (**b**) (*fml*) in that fact, point, or issue: ***Therein** lies the crux of the matter.*

thereof /ˌðeərˈɒv/ *adv* (*fml or law*) of that; of it: *the original document, together with all copies thereof.*

thereon /ˌðeərˈɒn/ *adv* (*fml or law*) on that; on it: *The deeds to the land stipulate that no trees may be planted thereon.* ○ *the results of the survey and subsequent decisions based thereon.*

thereto /ˌðeəˈtuː/ *adv* (*fml or law*) to that; to it: *the agreement and the documents appended thereto.*

thereupon /ˌðeərəˈpɒn/ *adv* (*fml*) immediately after that; as an immediate result of that: *Thereupon he got up and walked out.*

therm /θɜːm/ *n* a unit of heat, used esp in measuring a gas supply.

thermal /ˈθɜːml/ *adj* [esp attrib] **1** of, relating to or containing heat: *thermal energy* ○ *thermal units* (ie for measuring heat) ○ *a thermal nuclear reactor.* **2** keeping sth/sb warm by preventing heat from escaping: *thermal insulation/underwear.*
▶ **thermal** *n* **1** [C] a rising current of warm air used eg by a glider (GLIDE) to gain height. **2** **thermals** [pl] thick UNDERWEAR worn for outdoor activities, eg climbing and sailing.

therm(o)- *comb form* of heat: *thermonuclear* ○ *thermometer.*

thermodynamics /ˌθɜːməʊdaɪˈnæmɪks/ *n* [sing *v*] the branch of science dealing with the relations between heat and other forms of energy. ▶ **thermodynamic** *adj*.

thermometer /θəˈmɒmɪtə(r)/ *n* an instrument for measuring temperature. ⇨ picture.

thermometer

thermonuclear /ˌθɜːməʊˈnjuːklɪə(r); *US* -ˈnuːklɪər/ *adj* of or using nuclear reactions that occur only at very high temperatures: *a thermonuclear device/explosion/reaction.*

Thermos /ˈθɜːməs/ (also **ˈThermos flask**, *US* **ˈTher-**

mos bottle/ *n* (*propr*) a small container used esp for keeping drinks hot or cold; a vacuum flask (VA-CUUM).

thermostat /'θɜːməstæt/ *n* a device for regulating temperature automatically, eg in an oven or in central heating (CENTRAL): *adjust/turn down the thermostat.* ► **thermostatic** /ˌθɜːmə'stætɪk/ *adj* **thermostatically** /-kli/ *adv*: *thermostatically controlled.*

thesaurus /θɪ'sɔːrəs/ *n* (*pl* **thesauruses** /-rəsɪz/ or **thesauri** /θɪ'sɔːraɪ/) a book containing words and phrases arranged according to their meanings.

these ⇨ THIS.

thesis /'θiːsɪs/ *n* (*pl* **theses** /'θiːsiːz/) **1** a statement or theory supported by arguments: *The author's central thesis is that freedom is incompatible with equality.* **2** a long written essay submitted by a candidate for a higher university degree: *a PhD/ Master's thesis.* Compare DISSERTATION.

Thespian (also **thespian**) /'θespiən/ *adj* (*joc or rhet*) of acting or the theatre: *The family has strong Thespian traditions.*
► **Thespian** (also **thespian**) *n* (*joc or rhet*) an actor.

they /ðeɪ/ *pers pron* (used as the subject of a *v*) **1** people, animals or things previously mentioned: *'Where are John and Liz?' 'They went for a walk.'* ○ *I've got two sisters. They're both doctors.* ○ *They* (eg The things you are carrying) *go on the bottom shelf.* **2** (used to refer to a person without specifying the sex, eg after *someone* or *nobody*): *If anyone arrives late they'll have to wait outside.* ⇨ note at GENDER. **3** people in general: *They say we're going to have a hot summer.* ○ *They've* (ie People in authority have) *sent us another form to fill in.* Compare THEM.

they'd /ðeɪd/ *short form* **1** they had. ⇨ note at HAVE. **2** they would. ⇨ WILL¹, WOULD.

they'll /ðeɪl/ *short form* they will. ⇨ WILL¹.

they're /ðeə(r)/; *US weak form* ðər/ *short form* they are. ⇨ note at BE².

they've /ðeɪv/ *short form* they have. ⇨ note at HAVE.

thick /θɪk/ *adj* (**-er**, **-est**) **1(a)** having a relatively great distance between opposite surfaces or sides; fat¹(3): *a thick slice of bread* ○ *a thick book* (ie with a lot of pages) ○ *a thick line drawn with a blunt pencil* ○ *a thick coat/pullover/carpet* ○ *thick fingers/lips.* **(b)** having a specified distance between opposite sides or surfaces: *The ice on the lake is over six inches thick.* **2** ~ (**with sth/sb**) having a large number of parts, objects or people close together: *a thick forest* ○ *His hair is thick and wavy.* ○ *in the thickest part of the crowd* ○ *The garden was thick with weeds.* ○ *The building was thick with reporters.* **3** (of a liquid or similar substance) relatively stiff or heavy; not flowing easily: *thick soup/paint/glue.* **4** (of a substance in the air or the atmosphere) present in large quantities: *thick fog/smoke/clouds.* **5(a)** (of an ACCENT(3)) very noticeable; strong; difficult to understand: *speak in a thick brogue.* **(b)** (of the voice) not clear or distinct, eg because one has a cold: *You sound a bit thick this morning!* **6** (*infml*) of low intelligence; stupid: *He's a bit thick.* **7** ~ (**with sb**) (*infml*) very close or friendly; sharing secrets: *John is very thick with Anne.* **IDM** **a bit thick** ⇨ BIT¹. **blood is thicker than water** ⇨ BLOOD¹. **give sb/get a thick 'ear** (*sl*) to punish sb/to be punished with a blow, esp on the ear. **have, etc a thick 'head** (*infml*) **1** to have pain or a dull feeling in one's head, eg as the result of a cold or drinking too much alcohol: *He woke up with a very thick head.* **2** to be stupid. **a thin/thick skin** ⇨ SKIN. **(as) thick as 'thieves** (*infml*) (of two or more people) very close or friendly; sharing secrets. **(as) thick as two short 'planks** (*sl*) very stupid. **thick/thin on the ground** ⇨ GROUND¹.
► **thick** *adv* thickly: *snow lying thick on the ground* ○ *Don't spread the butter too thick.* **IDM** **lay it on**

thick/with a 'trowel to make sth seem better, worse, etc than it really is; to exaggerate: *I laid it on thick to impress the interviewer.* **thick and 'fast** rapidly and in great numbers: *Offers of help are coming in thick and fast.* **thick on the 'ground** (*infml*) available in large numbers or amounts: *Promising young players are thick on the ground these days.*
thick *n* [U] **IDM** **in the 'thick of sth** in the busiest or most crowded part of sth; deeply involved in sth: *He's always in the thick of it/things.* ○ *We were in the thick of the fight.* **through ,thick and 'thin** in spite of all the difficulties: *He remained loyal to me through thick and thin.*

thicken /'θɪkən/ *v* to become or make sth thicker: [V] *I walked home through the thickening fog.* [Vn] *Use flour to thicken the gravy.* [Vnpr] *a stew thickened with lentils.* **IDM** **the plot thickens** ⇨ PLOT².

thickening /'θɪkənɪŋ/ *n* [U, sing] the process of becoming thicker: *She was aware of a thickening round her waist.*

thickly *adv*: *thickly sliced/buttered bread* ○ *a thickly wooded area* ○ *'I've got a terrible cold,' she said thickly.*

thickness *n* **1** [U,C] the quality or degree of being thick: *Snow fell to a thickness of several centimetres.* ○ *Sew in a lining to give the coat some extra thickness.* ○ *The wood is available in four different thicknesses.* **2** [C] a layer: *The town was buried under a great thickness of volcanic ash.* **3** [C] a part of sth that is thick or between two opposite surfaces: *steps cut into the thickness of the wall.*
■ **,thick-'headed** *adj* stupid.
,thick-'skinned *adj* not sensitive to criticism or insults.

thicket /'θɪkɪt/ *n* a mass of plants, bushes or small trees growing close together: *a thicket of overgrown rose-bushes* ○ (*fig*) *a thicket of microphones.*

thickset /ˌθɪk'set/ *adj* (of a person) having a broad heavy body.

thief /θiːf/ *n* (*pl* **thieves** /θiːvz/) a person who steals, esp secretly and without violence: *a 'car/'jewel thief.* Compare BURGLAR, ROBBER. See also THEFT. **IDM** **honour among thieves** ⇨ HONOUR¹. **thick as thieves** ⇨ THICK.
► **thieve** /θiːv/ *v* (*infml*) (usu in the continuous tenses) to be a thief; to steal things: [V] *You've been thieving again, haven't you?* ○ (*infml*) *Take your thieving hands off my radio!* **thieving** *n* [U]: *a life of thieving.*

thigh /θaɪ/ *n* **(a)** the part of the human leg between the knee and the hip: *the thigh-bone.* ⇨ picture at HUMAN. See also FEMUR. **(b)** the upper part of the legs or back legs of other animals: *chicken thighs.*

thimble /'θɪmbl/ *n* a small cap of metal or plastic worn on the end of the finger to protect it and push the needle when one is sewing.
■ **thimbleful** /-fʊl/ *n* (*pl* **-fuls**) a very small quantity, esp of liquid to drink.

thin /θɪn/ *adj* (**-nner**, **-nnest**) **1** having opposite surfaces or sides relatively close together; small in width or thickness: *a thin line/wire* ○ *a thin sheet of metal/slice of bread/layer of glue* ○ *thin fingers/lips* ○ *a thin cotton dress* ○ *The ice is too thin to stand on.* ○ *The walls are so thin you can hear what they're saying in the next room.* ○ *The rope was wearing thin in one place.* **2** (*sometimes derog*) not having much flesh on the body: *a tall, thin man* ○ *have thin legs* ○ *thin cattle* ○ *Her illness had left him looking pale and thin.* Compare FAT¹ 1. ⇨ note. **3** lacking strength or confidence; weak: *a thin voice/smile.* **4** (of a substance in the air or the atmosphere) not present in large quantities; not thick or DENSE(2): *a thin mist* ○ *thin clouds* ○ *We had difficulty breathing in the thin mountain air.* **5** containing a lot of liquid and relatively little solid substance: *thin gravy.* **6**

having a relatively small number of parts, objects or people scattered widely: *His hair's/He's getting rather thin on top* (ie He is starting to lose his hair). ○ *a region with a thin population* ○ *a thin audience.* **7** small in amount: *thin profits/support* ○ *Trading on the stock market has been thin.* **8** of poor quality or lacking some important ingredient: *a thin* (ie not convincing) *excuse* ○ *a thin* (ie easily discovered) *disguise* ○ *I found her latest novel pretty thin.* **IDM be skating on thin ice** ⇨ SKATE¹. **have a thin 'time (of it)** *(infml)* to have a lot of trouble or difficulty; to fail often: *The team's been having a thin time (of it) recently — not a single win in two months.* **thick/ thin on the ground** ⇨ GROUND¹. **the thin end of the 'wedge** *(esp Brit)* an event, an action or a demand that seems unimportant but is likely to lead to others that are much more important or serious: *Newspaper editors regard the government's intention to regulate the press as the thin end of the wedge.* **a thin/thick skin** ⇨ SKIN. **through thick and thin** ⇨ THICK. **vanish, etc into thin 'air** to disappear completely, often suddenly or in a mysterious way. **wear thin** ⇨ WEAR¹.

▶ **thin** *adv* thinly: *Don't spread it too thin.*

thin *v* (-nn-) ~ (sth) (out); ~ sth (down) to become or make sth less thick or fewer in number: [V] *The clouds thinned and the sun came out.* ○ *He/His hair is thinning on top.* [Vp] *The traffic was thinning out.* [Vnp] *thin out seedlings* (ie remove some to help others to grow better) [Vnp, Vnpr] *thin (down) paint with white spirit* [also Vn]. **PHRV** **thin 'down** (of a person) to become thinner; to lose weight: *He's thinned down a lot since he went on a diet.*

thinly *adv*: *thinly sliced ham* ○ *Sow the plants quite thinly.* ○ *She smiled thinly.* ○ *His novel is a thinly disguised autobiography.*

thinner /'θɪnə(r)/ *n* [U, C] (also **thinners** [pl]) any of various substances added to paint, VARNISH(1a), etc to make it less thick.

thinness /'θɪnnəs/ *n* [U].

■ **thin-'skinned** *adj* sensitive to criticism or insults.

NOTE Compare **thin**, **skinny**, **underweight**, **slim**, etc. When describing people with very little fat on their bodies, **thin** is the most usual word: *Steve is tall and thin and has brown hair and blue eyes.* It can also be used in a negative way, suggesting weakness or bad health: *Mother looked thin and tired after her long illness.*

It is often thought desirable to be **slim** or **slender**. **Slim** is often used to describe women who have controlled their weight by diet or exercise: *She has a beautifully slim figure.* **Lean** is usually used to describe a man who is thin and muscular: *At 58, he's lean and fit and still very attractive.*

Bony is often used to describe parts of the body such as the hands or face. **Skinny** and **scrawny** are negative and can suggest that a person or an animal is small or weak: *A few scrawny chickens were busy searching for scraps of food.* **Underweight** is used in medical contexts: *Women who smoke risk giving birth to underweight babies.* **Emaciated** describes a serious condition resulting from lack of food.

thine /ðaɪn/ *possess pron* *(arch)* the thing or things belonging to you.

▶ **thine** *possess det* *(arch)* (the form of *thy* before a vowel or an 'h') of or belonging to you; your.

thing /θɪŋ/ *n* **1** [C] any object whose name is not stated: *What's that thing on the table?* ○ *She's very fond of 'sweet things* (ie sweet foods). ○ *There wasn't a thing* (ie There was nothing) *to eat.* ○ *I haven't a thing to wear* (ie I have no suitable clothes). **2** **things** [pl] objects, clothing or tools belonging to sb or used for a particular purpose: *Don't forget your 'swimming things* (ie your costume and towel). ○

Have you packed your things for the journey? ○ *Put your things* (eg your coat and hat) *on and let's go.* ○ *my 'painting things* ○ *kitchen things* (eg pans, plates, spoons). **3** **things** [pl] (with an *adj* following) all that can be described in the specified way: *interested in (all) things Japanese/electrical.* **4(a)** [C] any fact, event, situation, action or activity: *A terrible thing has happened.* ○ *I like camping, climbing and that sort of thing.* ○ *a difficult thing to do* ○ *I've done a lot of things today.* ○ *There's another thing I want to ask you about.* ○ *I find the whole thing very boring.* ○ *The usual thing is to shake hands when you meet somebody for the first time.* ○ *The main thing to remember is to switch off the burglar alarm.* ○ *say/do the right/wrong thing* (ie what is most/least appropriate or polite) ○ *I didn't say a thing* (ie I said nothing). ○ *The strange thing is, she didn't tell me her name.* ○ *I know just the thing to cheer you up.* **(b)** **things** [pl] circumstances, conditions or matters that are not specified: *Things are going from bad to worse.* ○ *As things stand, we'll never finish on time.* ○ *Think things over before you decide.* ○ *All things considered, we're doing quite well.* **5** [C] (used of a person or an animal, expressing eg affection, pity or contempt): *You poor things, you look worn out!* ○ *My cat's very ill, poor (old) thing.* ○ *You stupid thing!* **IDM** **A is 'one thing, B is an'other** B is much more difficult, important or serious than A and cannot really be compared with it: *Teasing is one thing, threats of violence are quite another.* **,all/,other things being 'equal** provided that circumstances remain the same: *All things being equal, we should finish the job tomorrow.* **all things to all 'men/ 'people 1** changing one's attitudes or opinions in order to please everyone and offend no one: *He has no strong views of his own, but tries to be all things to all men/people.* **2** (of things) that can be interpreted or used differently by different people to their satisfaction. **amount to / come to / be the same thing** ⇨ SAME¹. **be the done thing** ⇨ DONE². **be onto a good 'thing** *(infml)* to have found a job, situation or style of life that is pleasant, easy or profitable. **chance would be a fine thing** ⇨ CHANCE¹. **a ,close/,near 'thing** a fine balance between eg success and failure, life and death, doing or not doing sth: *We managed to win, but it was a close thing.* **do one's own 'thing** *(infml)* to follow one's own interests; to do what one likes; to be independent: *He's always done his own thing.* **,first/,last 'thing** early in the morning/late in the evening: *I always take the dog for a walk last thing before going to bed.* **,first things 'first** the most important matters must be dealt with before others: *First things first, though — how about a cup of coffee?* **for 'one thing** (used to introduce a reason for sth): *'Why don't you buy a car?' 'Well, for one thing, I can't afford it.'* **have/ want it/things both ways** ⇨ BOTH¹. **have a 'thing about sb/sth** *(infml)* **1** to be greatly attracted by or interested in sb/sth, often to an unreasonable degree: *He's got a thing about French girls.* **2** to have a strong or unreasonable dislike of sb/sth: *I've got a thing about spiders.* **hear things** ⇨ HEAR. **it is, was, etc a 'good thing (that)...** it is, etc fortunate that...: *It's a good thing I brought my umbrella.* **know / tell sb a 'thing or two (about sth/sb)** *(infml)* to know/tell sb some useful information or gossip about sth/sb: *She's been married five times, so she should know a thing or two about men.* ○ *He seems perfectly respectable, but I could tell you a thing or two about him.* **make a 'thing of sth** *(infml)* to make a fuss about sth: *I don't want to make a (big) thing of it but you did say you would tidy up.* **not know, etc the first 'thing about sth/ sb** to know nothing at all about sth/sb: *I've lived next door to him for years but I don't know/couldn't tell you the first thing about him.* **(just) ,one of those 'things** an unfortunate event or experience

---

[V.*to* inf] = verb + *to* infinitive   [Vn.inf (no *to*)] = verb + noun + infinitive without *to*   [V.*ing*] = verb + -*ing* form

that one must accept as a normal part of life: *Well, never mind, it's just one of those things.* ˌone **(damned, etc) thing after a**ˈ**nother** a succession of unpleasant or undesirable events. **(not)** ˌquite **the (done)** ˈ**thing** (not) that which is considered socially acceptable: *It wasn't quite the done thing for women to drink in pubs in those days.* **the real thing/McCoy** ⇨ REAL. ˈ**see things** (*infml*) to experience an illusion; to see or think one sees sth/sb that is not really there: (*joc*) *Am I seeing things or is that Roy over there?* **sure thing** ⇨ SURE. **take it/ things easy** ⇨ EASY². **there's only** ˌone **thing** ˈ**for it** there is no other possible course of action: *There's only one thing for it: we'll have to borrow the money.* **the** ˌ**thing (about sth/sb)** ˈ**is** (used to draw attention to an important fact or matter): *The thing is, can we actually afford a new car?* ○ *The thing about her is that she's completely honest.* **a** ˌ**thing of the** ˈ**past** a thing that is old-fashioned or no longer exists: *The art of writing letters seems to be a thing of the past.* ˌ**things that go** ˌ**bump in the** ˈ**night** (*joc*) mysterious or frightening noises at night, sometimes thought to be caused by ghosts. **(what) with** ˌ**one thing and a**ˈ**nother** (*infml*) because of various duties, problems or distracting events: *What with one thing and another, I completely forgot your birthday.*

thingummy /ˈθɪŋəmi/ (also **thingumajig** /ˈθɪŋəmədʒɪɡ/, **thingumabob** /ˈθɪŋəməbɒb/, **thingy** /ˈθɪŋi/) *n* (*infml*) a person or thing whose name one does not know or has forgotten or does not wish to mention.

think¹ /θɪŋk/ *v* (*pt, pp* **thought** /θɔːt/) **1** ~ **(about sth)** to use the mind in an active way to form connected ideas: [V] *Are animals able to think?* ○ *I'm sorry, I didn't think* (ie said when one has offended sb accidentally). ○ *Let me think a moment* (ie Give me time before I answer). [Vpr] *Philosophers have thought about this problem for centuries.* See also THINK ABOUT STH/SB, THINK ABOUT (DOING) STH. **2** (not used in the continuous tenses) to have a particular idea, opinion or belief about sth/sb: [V.that, Vadv] *'Do you think (that) it's going to rain?' 'Yes, I think so.'* [V.that] *I think this is their house but I'm not sure.* ○ *I thought I heard a scream.* ○ *Am I right in thinking that you once lived here?* ○ *Don't think you'll get away with this!* ○ *Who do you think you are* (ie Why are you behaving in this proud, superior way)? ○ *I think he ought to resign.* ○ *He ought to resign, I think.* ○ *We'll need about 20 chairs, I should think.* [Vn-adj, V.that] *Do you think it likely/that it is likely?* [Vn.to inf] *a species long thought to be extinct* ○ *He's thought to be one of the richest men in Europe.* ○ *The galaxy is much larger than was previously thought.* [V.wh] *I don't care what anyone thinks, I'm going to marry her.* **3** to have or form an intention or a plan about sth: [V.that] *I think I'll go for a swim.* [Vpr] *I'm thinking in terms of about 200 guests.* [V.to inf] *I didn't think* (ie It did not occur to me) *to tell her.* **4** (used esp in the continuous tenses) to have ideas, words or images in one's mind: [Vn] *You're very quiet. What are you thinking?* [V.wh, Vpr.wh] *I was just thinking (to myself) what a long way it is.* [V.speech] *Here goes, she thought.* **5** (no passive) **(a)** to form an idea of sth; to imagine sth: [V.wh] *We couldn't think where you'd gone.* ○ *Think how nice it would be to see them again.* [V.that] *I can't think that he would be so stupid.* **(b)** to expect sth: [Vn] *Who'd have thought it* (eg of a surprising event)? [V.that] *I never thought (that) I'd see her again.* [V.to inf] (*fml*) *Who would have thought to find you here?* **6** (*infml*) (no passive) to direct one's thoughts in a certain manner, or to a certain subject: [V-adj] *Let's think positive.* ○ *You need to think big* (ie be ambitious). [Vn] *If you want to make money you've got to* ˈ**think money.** **IDM** **come to** ˈ**think of it** (used when one

suddenly recalls sth or when sth suddenly occurs to one): *Come to think of it, he did mention seeing you.* **I** ˈ**thought as much** that is what I expected or suspected: *'He said he'd forgotten.' 'I thought as much.'* **if/when you** ˈ**think about it** (used to draw attention to a fact that is not obvious or has not previously been noticed): *When you think about it, her behaviour was a little unusual.* **see/think fit** ⇨ FIT¹. **think a**ˈ**gain** to consider the situation again and perhaps change one's idea or intention: *Perhaps we need to think again about privatization.* ○ *If you think I'm going to lend you my car you can think again!* **think a**ˈ**loud** to express one's thoughts as they occur. **think** ˈ**better of it / of doing sth** to decide not to do sth after thinking further about it: *Rosie was about to protest but thought better of it.* **think (the)** ˈ**better of sb** to have a higher opinion of sb: *She has behaved appallingly — I must say I thought better of her.* **think nothing** ˈ**of it** (used as a polite response to an APOLOGY or expression of thanks). **think** ˈ**nothing of (doing) sth** to consider an activity to be normal and not particularly unusual or difficult: *She thinks nothing of walking thirty miles a day.* **think** ˈ**straight** to think in a clear or logical way: *I'm so tired I can hardly think straight.* **think** ˈ**twice about (doing) sth** to think carefully before deciding to do sth: *You should think twice about employing someone you've never met.* **think the world, highly, a lot, not much, poorly, little, etc of sb/sth** (not used in the continuous tenses) to have a very good, poor, etc opinion of sb/ sth: *He thinks the world of his daughter.* ○ *His work is highly thought of by the critics.* ○ *What do you think of my new dress?* **PHR V** ˈ**think about sth/sb 1** to direct one's thoughts to sth/sb; to occupy one's mind with sth/sb: *Do you ever think about your childhood?* ○ *I can't stop thinking about her.* **2** to consider sth/sb; to take sth/sb into account: *Don't you ever think about other people?* ○ *All he ever thinks about is money.* ˈ**think about (doing) sth** to consider or examine a request or a possible course of action to see if it is desirable or practical: *I'll think about it and let you know tomorrow.* ○ *She's thinking about changing her job.* ○ *She's thinking seriously about her future.*

ˌ**think a**ˈ**head (to sth)** to direct one's thoughts to a future event or situation and plan for it: *Thinking ahead to our next meeting…*

ˌ**think** ˈ**back (to sth)** to recall(1) sth in the past: *I keep thinking back to the day I arrived here.*

ˌ**think for one**ˈ**self** to form one's opinions and make decisions without depending on others.

ˈ**think of sth/sb 1** to have an image or idea of sth/ sb in one's mind: *When I made those remarks, I wasn't thinking of anyone in particular.* **2** to consider sth/sb; to take sth/sb into account: *There are so many things to think of when buying a house.* ○ *You can't expect me to think of everything!* **3** to form an idea and offer it as a suggestion: *Can anybody think of a way to raise money?* ○ *'What shall we do now?' 'I'll think of something.'* ○ *Have you thought of a name for the baby yet?* **4** (esp after *can*) to remember sth/sb: *I can think of at least three occasions when he arrived late.* ○ *I can't think of his name at the moment.* **5** to consider sth/sb from a certain point of view: *I think of this place as my home.* ○ *She is thought of as a possible future director.* ˈ**think of (doing) sth 1** to consider the possibility of doing sth, without reaching a decision or taking action: *They're thinking of moving to America.* ○ *I did think of resigning, but I decided against it.* **2** to imagine an actual or a possible situation: *Just think of the expense!* ○ *I couldn't think of letting you take the blame* (ie I would not allow that to happen). ○ *She would never think of marrying me.*

ˌ**think sth** ˈ**out** to consider or plan sth carefully:

Think out your answer before you start writing. ∘ *It's a very well thought out scheme.*

ˌthink sth ˈover to consider sth carefully, esp before reaching a decision: *Please think over what I've said.* ∘ *I'd like more time to think things over.*

ˌthink sth ˈthrough to consider a problem or a possible course of action fully.

ˌthink sth ˈup (*infml*) to produce an idea or a plan; to invent or DEVISE sth: *think up novel ways of raising money* ∘ *Can't you think up a better excuse than that?*

■ ˈthink-tank *n* a group of experts providing advice and ideas on political, social or economic matters.

think² /θɪŋk/ *n* [sing] (*infml*) an act of thinking: *I'll have a think and let you know tomorrow.* **IDM** **have (got) another think ˈcoming** to be forced to change or abandon one's opinions or plans: *If you think I'm going to pay all your bills you've got another think coming.*

thinkable /ˈθɪŋkəbl/ *adj* [pred] that can be imagined as sth that could possibly happen or be true: *Unemployment has reached a level that would not have been thinkable ten years ago.*

thinker /ˈθɪŋkə(r)/ *n* **1** a person who thinks seriously, and often writes about important things, eg philosophy or science: *Einstein was one of the greatest thinkers of the 20th century.* **2** a person who thinks deeply: *Helen's a charming woman but she's not much of a thinker.* See also FREETHINKER.

thinking /ˈθɪŋkɪŋ/ *adj* [attrib] able to consider serious matters; intelligent: *All thinking people must hate violence.*
▶ **thinking** *n* [U] (**a**) the process of considering sth mentally; reasoning: *do some hard/quick thinking* (ie think deeply). See also LATERAL THINKING. (**b**) ideas or opinions: *What's your current thinking on this question?* See also WISHFUL THINKING. **IDM** **to ˈmy way of thinking** ⇨ WAY¹.
■ ˈthinking-cap *n* **IDM** **put one's ˈthinking-cap on** (*infml*) to try to solve a problem by thinking about it.

third /θɜːd/ *pron, det* 3rd.
▶ **third** *n* **1** each of three equal parts of sth. **2** ~ (**in sth**) (*Brit*) a lower than average pass grade for a university degree: *She got a third in biology.*
For further guidance on how *third* is used, see the examples at *fifth*.
thirdly *adv* as the third item in a list, an argument, etc. ⇨ note at FIRST².
■ ˌthird-ˈclass *adj* (*derog*) of very low status: *I don't want to live in a ˌthird-class ˈcountry.*
the ˌthird deˈgree *n* [sing] long and severe questioning; the use of violence or threats to make sb confess or give information.
ˌthird ˈparty *n* (*fml*) another person in addition to the two main people involved: *He divulged details of our private conversation to a third party.* ˌthird-party inˈsurance *n* [U] insurance that gives the holder insurance cover against damage or injury caused by herself or himself to other people.
the ˌthird ˈperson *n* [sing] (*grammar*) a set of pronouns and verb forms relating to one or more things or people that are being spoken about: *'Has' is the third-person singular of the verb 'have'.* ∘ *The author refers to herself throughout in the third person* (ie using 'she', 'her', etc instead of 'I', 'me', etc).
ˌthird-ˈrate *adj* (*derog*) of very poor quality: *a ˌthird-rate ˈfilm/ˈactor.*
the ˌThird ˈWorld *n* [sing] the poor or developing countries of Africa, Asia and Latin America: *income-generating projects in the Third World* ∘ *ˌthird-world ˈcountries.*

thirst /θɜːst/ *n* **1**(**a**) [U, sing] the feeling caused by a desire or need to drink: *quench* (ie satisfy) *one's thirst with a long drink of water* ∘ *Working in the sun soon gave us a* (*powerful*) *thirst.* (**b**) [U] suffering

caused by this: *They lost their way in the desert and died of thirst.* **2** [sing] ~ (**for sth**) a strong desire for sth that one tries hard to satisfy: *a/the thirst for knowledge/fame/revenge.*
▶ **thirst** *v* [V] (*arch*) to feel a need to drink. **PHR V** ˈthirst for sth to be eager for sth: *thirsting for revenge.*
thirsty *adj* (**-ier, -iest**) **1** ~ (**for sth**) feeling thirst: *be/feel thirsty* ∘ *All this talking is making me thirsty.* ∘ (*fig*) *The team is thirsty for success.* **2** (*infml*) causing thirst: *Gardening is thirsty work.* **3** ~ (**for sth**) dry; in need of water: *thirsty crops* ∘ *The soil is thirsty for rain.* **thirstily** /-ɪli/ *adv*: *They drank thirstily.*

thirteen /ˌθɜːˈtiːn/ *n, pron, det* the number 13. ▶ **thirteenth** /ˌθɜːˈtiːnθ/ *n, pron, det.*
For further guidance on how *thirteen* and *thirteenth* are used, see the examples at *five* and *fifth*.

thirty /ˈθɜːti/ *n, pron, det* **1** the number 30. **2** the **thirties** *n* [pl] the numbers, years or temperature from 30 to 39. **IDM** **in one's thirties** between the ages of 30 and 40. ▶ **thirtieth** /ˈθɜːtiəθ/ *n, pron, det.*
For further guidance on how *thirty* and *thirtieth* are used, see the examples at *fifty*, *five* and *fifth*.

this /ðɪs/ *det, pron* (*pl* **these** /ðiːz/) **1** (used to refer to a person, a thing, a place or an event that is close to the speaker or writer, esp when compared with another): *Come here and look at this picture.* ∘ *These chairs are more comfortable than those.* ∘ *Is this the book you mean?* ∘ *Whose (shoes) are these?* ∘ *How long have you been living in this country?* ∘ *What's all this noise (about)?* **2** (used to refer to sth/sb previously mentioned): *We received an anonymous letter. This letter contained some startling allegations.* ∘ *What were these men doing?* ∘ *The boy was afraid and the dog had sensed this.* ∘ *What's this I hear about you getting married?* **3** (used to introduce sth/sb): *This is my husband.* ∘ *Listen to this: a boy in Mexico has won a million dollars.* ∘ *Do it like this* (ie in the way I am showing you). **4** (used with days or periods of time related to the present): *this* (ie the current) *week/month/year* ∘ *this morning* (ie today in the morning) ∘ *Do you want me to come this Tuesday* (ie Tuesday of this week) *or next Tuesday?* ∘ *Do it this minute* (ie now)! ∘ *He never comes to see me these days* (ie now, as compared with the past). ⇨ note at TIME¹. **5** (*infml*) (used before a *n* followed by a possessive, often indicating the attitude of the speaker to a thing or person): *When are we going to see this car of yours?* ∘ *These jeans of mine have been all around the world with me.* ∘ *This friend of hers is supposed to be very rich.* **6** (*infml*) (used to draw attention to a particular person or thing that one is describing): *There was this peculiar man sitting opposite me in the train.* ∘ *I've been getting these pains in my chest, Doctor.* **IDM** ˌthis and ˈthat; ˌthis, ˌthat and the ˈother various things or activities: *'What did you talk about?' 'Oh, this and that.'*
▶ **this** *adv* to this degree; so: *It's about this high* (ie as high as I am showing you with my hands). ∘ *I didn't think we'd get this far.* ∘ *Can you afford this much* (eg as much as you have given me)? Compare THAT¹,².

thistle /ˈθɪsl/ *n* a wild plant with prickly leaves and purple, white or yellow flowers. The thistle is the national symbol of Scotland. ⇨ picture at FLOWER.
thistledown /ˈθɪsldaʊn/ *n* [U] a very light soft substance that contains THISTLE seeds and is blown from thistle plants by the wind: *as light as thistledown.*

thither /ˈðɪðə(r)/ *adv* (*arch*) to or towards that place. **IDM** **hither and thither** ⇨ HITHER.
tho' ⇨ THOUGH.
thong /θɒŋ; *US* θɔːŋ/ *n* **1** a narrow strip of leather, used eg as a fastening or a whip. **2** (*US*) = FLIP-FLOP.
thorax /ˈθɔːræks/ *n* (*pl* **thoraxes** or **thoraces**

/ˈθɔːrəsiːz/ **1** (*anatomy*) the part of the body between the neck and the stomach; the chest. **2** (*biology*) the middle of the three main sections of an insect to which the legs and wings are attached. ⇨ picture at INSECT.

thorn /θɔːn/ *n* **1** [C] a sharp pointed growth(3) on the stem of certain plants, eg roses. **2** [C, U] a tree or bush with thorns: *a thorn hedge/scrub* ◦ *hedges of thorn*. See also BLACKTHORN, HAWTHORN. **IDM** **a thorn in sb's ˈflesh/ˈside** a person or thing that continually annoys sb or prevents them doing sth: *He's been a thorn in my side ever since he joined this department.*
▶ **thorny** *adj* (-ier, -iest) **1** having thorns (THORN 1): *a thorny bush/twig.* **2** causing difficulty or disagreement: *a thorny problem/subject/issue.*

thorough /ˈθʌrə; *US also* ˈθʌrəʊ/ *adj* **1(a)** done completely and with great attention to detail; not SUPERFICIAL(3a): *give the room a thorough cleaning* ◦ *have a thorough knowledge/understanding of the subject* ◦ *We aim to provide a thorough training in all aspects of the work.* **(b)** (of people) doing things in this way: *He's a slow worker but very thorough.* **2** [attrib] (*derog*) to the fullest degree; complete: *That woman is a thorough nuisance.*
▶ **thoroughly** *adv*: *The work had not been done very thoroughly.* ◦ *He's a thoroughly nasty person.*
thoroughness *n* [U] the quality of being thorough(1).

thoroughbred /ˈθʌrəbred/ *adj* (esp of a horse) bred from a single breed; of pure or PEDIGREE stock: *a thoroughbred racehorse.*
▶ **thoroughbred** *n* a thoroughbred animal, esp a horse. See also PURE-BRED.

thoroughfare /ˈθʌrəfeə(r)/ *n* a public road or street used by traffic, esp a major road in a city or town: *The Strand is one of London's busiest thoroughfares.*

thoroughgoing /ˌθʌrəˈɡəʊɪŋ/ *adj* [usu attrib] **(a)** thorough: *a ˌthoroughgoing ˈrevision of the text.* **(b)** to the greatest possible degree: *a ˌthoroughgoing ˈMarxist.*

those ⇨ THAT¹ˑ².

thou /ðaʊ/ *pers pron* (*arch*) (used as the second person singular subject of a *v*) you.

though (also **tho'**) /ðəʊ/ *conj* **1** despite the fact that; although: *She won first prize, though none of us had expected it.* ◦ *The food was delicious, though expensive.* ◦ *Though they lack official support they continue their struggle.* ◦ *Strange though it may seem* (ie Although it seems strange), *the tallest boy is the youngest.* **2** (used to introduce a clause at the end of a sentence) all the same; but: *I'll try to come, though I doubt I'll be there on time.* ◦ *He'll probably say no, though it's worth asking.* ⇨ note at ALTHOUGH.
▶ **though** *adv* in spite of this; however: *Our team lost. It was a good game, though.* ◦ *A peace agreement was drawn up. The delegates, though, refused to sign it.*

thought¹ *pt, pp* of THINK¹.

thought² /θɔːt/ *n* **1** [C often *pl*] **(a)** an idea or opinion produced by thinking: *I wrote down my thoughts as they came into my head.* ◦ *think sad thoughts* ◦ *I've had a terrible thought — what if she's had an accident?* ◦ *Let me have your thoughts on* (ie Tell what you think about) *the subject.* ◦ *He keeps his thoughts to himself* (ie does not tell others what he is thinking). **(b)** mental attention given to sth/sb: *Although she's far away she's still in our thoughts.* ◦ *Her thoughts turned to* (ie She started to think about) *what the children were doing.* **2(a)** [U] the power or process of thinking: *psychologists trying to explain the nature of thought* ◦ *be deep/lost in thought* (ie concentrating so much on one's thoughts that one is unaware of one's surroundings). **(b)** consideration; care; mental attention: *After a moment's thought, she gave her answer.* ◦ *He acted without proper thought.* ◦ *I've read your proposal and given it some serious thought.* ◦ *Not enough thought has gone into this essay.* ◦ **Spare a thought** *for those less fortunate than you.* **3** [U] ideas in eg philosophy, politics or science associated with a particular person, group or period of history: *modern/scientific/Greek thought.* **4** [U, C often *pl*] ~ **of** (doing) sth an intention: *You can give up all/any thought(s) of marrying Emma.* ◦ *The thought of resigning never crossed my mind* (ie never occurred to me). **IDM** **food for thought** ⇨ FOOD. **give pause for thought** ⇨ PAUSE. **a penny for your thoughts** ⇨ PENNY. **perish the thought** ⇨ PERISH. **ˌsecond ˈthoughts**; (*US*) **ˌsecond ˈthought** a change of opinion after considering sth again: *We had second thoughts about buying the house when we met the neighbours.* ◦ **On second thoughts** *I think I'd better go now.* **a school of thought** ⇨ SCHOOL¹. **ˈthat's a thought** that's an important point; that's a good idea: *'Why don't you try the other key?' 'That's a thought.'* **without a second ˈthought** (*Brit*) immediately; without stopping to consider sth further: *He did it without a second thought for the risks involved.*
▶ **thoughtful** /-fl/ *adj* **1** thinking deeply; absorbed in thought: *You're looking very thoughtful.* ◦ *His face took on a thoughtful expression.* **2** showing signs of careful thought: *a player who has a thoughtful approach to the game.* **3** showing consideration for the needs of others: *It was very thoughtful of you to send the flowers.* **thoughtfully** /-fəli/ *adv*: *She nodded thoughtfully.* **thoughtfulness** *n* [U]: *his thoughtfulness for others.*
thoughtless *adj* showing a lack of concern about the possible consequences of one's actions: *a thoughtless remark* ◦ *I haven't offered you a drink. How thoughtless of me!* **thoughtlessly** *adv*. **thoughtlessness** *n* [U].
■ **ˈthought-provoking** *adj* causing people to think seriously about certain matters: *a thought-provoking article.*

thousand /ˈθaʊznd/ *n, pron, det* (*pl* unchanged or **thousands**) **1** (after *a, one*, a number or an indication of quantity) the number 1 000: *ten thousand pounds.* ⇨ App 2. **2** (usu **thousands** [pl]) many; a lot: *We're giving away thousands of prizes.* ◦ *They've been here for thousands of years.* ◦ *I've got **a thousand and one** things to do.*
▶ **thousandth** /ˈθaʊznθ/ *n, pron, det* 1 000th: *a/one thousandth of a second* ◦ *the city's thousandth anniversary.*
For further guidance on how *thousand* and *thousandth* are used, see the examples at *hundred* and *hundredth*.

thousandfold /ˈθaʊzndfəʊld/ *adj, adv* ⇨ -FOLD.

thrash /θræʃ/ *v* **1** [Vn] to beat a person or an animal with a stick or whip, esp as a punishment. **2** ~ **(sth) (about/around)** to make violent movements, esp hitting sth with repeated blows: [Vp, Vnp] *a drowning man thrashing (his arms) about in the water* [also Vn, V]. **3** (*infml*) to defeat sb heavily in a contest: [Vn] *Chelsea were thrashed 6–1 by Leeds.* **4** [Vn] = THRESH **PHRV** **ˌthrash sth ˈout 1** to discuss sth thoroughly and honestly: *call a meeting to thrash out the problem.* **2** to produce sth by discussion of this kind: *After much argument we thrashed out a plan.*
▶ **thrash** *n* (*sl*) a party with music, dancing, etc: *have a thrash after the exams.*
thrashing *n* **1** an act of beating sb severely: *give sb/get a good thrashing.* **2** (*infml*) a severe defeat: *The Redskins celebrated their 8–1 thrashing of the Patriots.*

thread /θred/ *n* **1(a)** [U] cotton, wool, silk or nylon spun into thin strands and used for sewing: *a needle and thread* ◦ *a robe embroidered with gold thread.*

(b) [C] a single strand of a piece of fabric, etc: *the delicate threads of a spider's web* ○ *Her ring caught a thread in the cushion cover.* **2** [C] ~ **(of sth)** a very thin thing resembling a thread: *fine red threads in the marble* ○ *A thread of light emerged from the keyhole.* **3** [C often *pl*] an idea, a theme or a feature that is part of sth greater: *There is a melancholy thread running through all her poetry.* ○ *The author skilfully weaves/pulls the different threads of the plot together.* ○ **lose the thread** *of* (ie be no longer able to follow) *an argument* ○ **pick up the thread(s)** *of a conversation* (ie continue it after an interruption). **4** [C] the ridge around the length of a screw or similar object which allows it to be fastened in place by twisting. ⇨ picture at SCREW. **5 threads** [pl] (*US sl*) clothes. **IDM** **hang by a hair / a thread** ⇨ HANG[1]. **lose the thread** ⇨ LOSE. **pick up the pieces/ threads** ⇨ PICK[1].

▶ **thread** *v* **1(a)** to pass thread, string, etc through sth: [Vn, Vnpr] *thread a needle (with cotton)* [Vnpr] *thread cotton through (the eye of) a needle.* (b) (usu passive) to sew threads of a specified type into sth: [Vnpr] *a robe threaded with gold and silver.* **2** to put beads (BEAD 1a) on a thread: [Vn, Vnpr] *threading pearls (on a string) to make a necklace.* **3** to pass eg film, tape or string through sth and into the required position for use: [Vnpr] *thread film into/ through a projector* ○ *thread tinsel around the branches of the Christmas tree* [also Vnp, Vn]. **4** ~ **(sth) between/through sth** to move oneself or sth carefully or skilfully through a place, often changing direction to avoid sb/sth: [Vnpr] *threading his way through the crowded streets* ○ *She threaded her car slowly between the holes in the road.* [also Vpr]. **threaded** *adj* (*techn*) having a thread(4).

threadbare /ˈθredbeə(r)/ *adj* **1** (of eg cloth or clothing) old and worn thin: *a threadbare carpet/coat.* **2** not adequate or effective: *a threadbare argument/ plot.*

threat /θret/ *n* **1** [C] ~ **(to do sth)** an expression of one's intention to punish or harm sb, esp if they do not do as one wishes: *make/utter threats (against sb)* ○ *a ˈdeath threat* ○ *They did not carry out their threat to cut off the water-supply.* **2(a)** [U, C usu *sing*] the possibility of trouble, danger or ruin: *The factory is under threat/facing the threat of closure.* ○ *a country under the constant threat of flooding.* **(b)** [C usu *sing*] a person or thing likely to cause trouble, danger, etc: *a strong team but no threat to the current leaders* ○ *Terrorism is/poses a threat to the whole country.*

threaten /ˈθretn/ *v* **1(a)** ~ sb **(with sth)** to make a threat or threats against sb; to try to influence sb by threats: [Vnpr] *threaten an employee with dismissal* ○ *My attacker threatened me with a gun.* ○ *threaten sb's life* (ie to kill sb) [also V]. **(b)** to use sth as a threat: [Vn] *He threatened legal action.* ○ *The threatened strike has been called off.* [V.to inf, V.that] *The hijackers threatened to kill/that they would kill all the passengers if their demands were not met.* **2** to seem likely to occur or to do sth undesirable: [V] *When war threatens, people act irrationally.* [V.to inf] *a mistake that threatens to be costly* ○ *This dispute threatens to split the party.* [Vn] *The clouds threatened rain.* **3** to be a threat to sb/sth: [Vn] *This dispute is threatening party unity.* [Vnpr] *a species threatened with extinction.*

▶ **threatening** *adj* **1** expressing a threat of harm or violence: *threatening behaviour/gestures/letters.* **2** indicating that bad weather is likely: *a threatening sky* (ie full of dark clouds). **threateningly** *adv*: *glare threateningly.*

three /θriː/ *n, pron, det* the number 3. **IDM** **in twos and threes** ⇨ TWO.
For further guidance on how *three* is used, see the examples at *five*.

▶ **three-** (in compounds) having three of the thing specified: *a ˌthree-storey ˈbuilding* ○ *a ˌthree-legged ˈstool* ○ *a ˌthree-day ˈconference.*

■ ˌ**three-ˈD** (also **3-D**) *n* [U] the quality of having, or appearing to have, the dimensions of length, width and depth: *see everything in three-D* ○ *a ˌthree-D ˈimage* ○ *ˌthree-D ˈglasses* (ie enabling flat pictures to be viewed with the illusion of depth).

ˌ**three-diˈmensional** *adj* having, appearing to have or relating to the dimensions of length, width and depth: *ˌthree-dimensional ˈobjects/computer ˈgraphics/geˈometry* ○ *a three-dimensional effect* (ie the illusion of depth in a flat picture).

three-legged race /ˌθriː ˈleɡɪd reɪs/ *n* a race in which competitors run in pairs, the right leg of one runner being tied to the left leg of the other.

ˌ**three-line ˈwhip** *n* (*Brit*) a written notice to Members of Parliament from their party leader telling them that they must attend a debate and vote in a particular way.

ˈ**three-piece** *adj* [attrib] consisting of three separate parts or pieces: *a ˌthree-piece ˈsuit* (ie a set of clothes consisting of trousers, a jacket and a WAISTCOAT) ○ *a ˌthree-piece ˈsuite* (ie a set of three pieces of furniture, usu a SOFA and two armchairs (ARMCHAIR)).

ˌ**three-point ˈturn** *n* a method of turning a car, etc in a small space by driving forwards, then backwards, then forwards again in a series of curves.

ˈ**three-ply** *adj* (of wool, wood, etc) having three strands or thicknesses.

ˌ**three-ˈquarter** *adj* [attrib] three quarters of the size of a whole: *a ˌthree-quarter length ˈcoat* (ie reaching to just below the knee).

ˌ**three-ˈway** *adj* happening or operating in three ways or directions or between three people: *a three-way telephone conversation.*

threefold /ˈθriːfəʊld/ *adj, adv* ⇨ -FOLD.

threepence /ˈθriːpens* formerly* ˈθrepəns/ *n* [U] (*Brit*) (esp formerly) the sum of three pence.

threepenny bit /ˌθrepəni ˈbɪt/ (also ˌthreepenny ˈpiece /-ˈpiːs/) *n* (*Brit*) (formerly) a coin worth three pence.

threesome /ˈθriːsəm/ *n* a group of three people, eg playing music or playing a game together.

thresh /θreʃ/ *v* [V, Vn] to separate grains of corn, etc from the rest of the plant, using a machine or, esp formerly, by beating it with an implement held in the hand.

threshold /ˈθreʃhəʊld/ *n* **1** the floor or ground at the bottom of a DOORWAY, considered as the entrance of a house, building or room: *standing at/on the threshold* ○ *cross the threshold* (ie enter). **2** (usu *sing*) the point just before a new situation, period of life, etc begins: *be on the threshold of victory/ adulthood* ○ *We are at the threshold of a new era in medicine.* **3** a particular level or standard: *New TV channels have to pass a quality threshold before they are allowed to broadcast.* **4** a physical or mental limit below which a person does not react, eg to a sound, a feeling or an influence: *above/below the threshold of consciousness* ○ *have a high/low pain threshold* (ie be able to endure much/little pain).

threw *pt* of THROW[1].

thrice /θraɪs/ *adv* (*arch*) three times.

thrift /θrɪft/ *n* **1** [U] the habit of saving money and spending it carefully. **2** (also **thrift institution**) [C] (*US*) an institution that offers facilities for saving and borrowing money. **3** [U] a plant with bright pink flowers that grows by the sea.

▶ **thrifty** *adj* (**-ier, -iest**) showing thrift(1).

thrill /θrɪl/ *v* to excite or please sb very much: [Vn] *The film is thrilling audiences all over the world.* ○ *I was thrilled by your news.* **PHRV** ˈ**thrill to sth** to feel excited at sth: *Audiences will thrill to the hero's daring exploits.*

▶ **thrill** n (**a**) a feeling of being thrilled: *He gets his thrills from rock-climbing.* (**b**) an experience causing this: *It was a real thrill to meet the Queen.* ○ *the thrill of a live performance* ○ (*infml derog*) *cheap thrills* (ie entertainment that is exciting, but has little lasting value or quality). (**c**) a wave of physical feeling accompanying strong emotion: *feel a thrill of joy/fear/horror.* **IDM** (**the**) **thrills and 'spills** (*infml*) the excitement of dangerous sports or entertainments, as experienced by sb watching or taking part: *all the thrills and spills of the circus.*
thrilled *adj* [usu pred] ~ (**about/at/with sth**); ~ (**to do sth**) very pleased or excited: *The children were thrilled to bits/(US) pieces at their presents.* ○ *We were absolutely thrilled to hear your wonderful news.*
thriller n a novel, play or film with an exciting plot, esp one involving crime: *a thriller writer.*
thrilling *adj* causing excitement: *a thrilling experience/story/race.* **thrillingly** *adv.*

thrive /θraɪv/ v ~ (**on sth**) to live, continue, grow or develop well and vigorously: [V] *a thriving industry/community/garden* ○ *These animals rarely thrive in captivity.* [Vpr] *He thrives on* (ie is stimulated by) *criticism.*

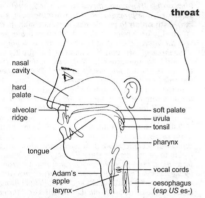

throat

nasal cavity
hard palate
alveolar ridge
tongue
Adam's apple
larynx
soft palate
uvula
tonsil
pharynx
vocal cords
oesophagus (*esp US* es-)

throat /θrəʊt/ n (**a**) the passage in the neck through which food and air are taken into the body: *A fish bone got stuck in her throat.* ○ *I've got a sore throat; I think I may be getting a cold.* ○ *The victim's throat had been cut/slit.* ⇨ picture. (**b**) the front part of the neck: *grab sb by the throat.* ⇨ picture at HEAD¹. **IDM cut one's own 'throat** to act in such a way as to harm oneself or one's interests. **force, thrust, ram, etc sth down sb's 'throat** (*infml derog*) to try to make sb accept or listen to one's views or beliefs against their will: *I don't like having her extremist ideas rammed down my throat.* **have, etc a frog in one's throat** ⇨ FROG. **have, etc a lump in one's/the throat** ⇨ LUMP¹. **jump down sb's throat** ⇨ JUMP¹. **stick in one's throat** ⇨ STICK².
▶ **-throated** (forming compound *adjs*) having a throat of the specified type or colour: *a deep-throated roar* ○ *a red-throated bird.*
throaty *adj* (**a**) produced deep in the throat: *a rich, throaty laugh.* (**b**) sounding harsh: *a throaty voice/cry/cough.* **throatily** /-ɪli/ *adv.*

throb /θrɒb/ v (**-bb-**) ~ (**with sth**) **1** (of a part of the body) to feel pain in a series of fast regular beats: [V] *His head throbbed* (ie He had a bad HEADACHE(1)). ○ *My feet were throbbing after the long walk.* [also Vpr]. **2** to beat or sound with a strong regular rhythm: [V] *a throbbing pain/drumbeat* ○ *The ship's engines throbbed quietly.* [Vpr] *a voice throbbing with emotion* ○ *The blood was throbbing in my veins.* ○ *Her heart was throbbing with excitement.*

▶ **throb** n a steady continuous beat: *the throb of distant drums* ○ *throbs of pain/desire.*

throes /θrəʊz/ n [pl] **IDM in the throes of sth / of doing sth** in the middle of an activity, a process or a situation, esp a very difficult or painful one: *be in the throes of childbirth/of moving house.*

thrombosis /θrɒmˈbəʊsɪs/ n (*pl* **thromboses** /-ˈbəʊsiːz/) [C,U] (*medical*) a serious condition caused by the formation of a CLOT(1) of blood in a blood-vessel (BLOOD¹) or in the heart. See also CORONARY THROMBOSIS.

throne /θrəʊn/ n **1** [C] a special chair or seat used by a king, queen or bishop during ceremonies. **2 the throne** [sing] the office or position of a king or queen: *Queen Elizabeth II succeeded to the throne in 1952.* ○ *the heir to the throne of Spain/the Spanish throne* ○ *come to/accede to/ascend the throne* (ie become king or queen) ○ *when Henry VIII was on the throne* (ie was king). Compare CROWN¹ 1c. **IDM the power behind the throne** ⇨ POWER.

throng /θrɒŋ; *US* θrɔːŋ/ n a crowded mass of people or animals: *a throng/throngs of busy shoppers* ○ *She pushed her way through the throng (of onlookers).*
▶ **throng** v (**a**) to move as a crowd in a certain direction: [Vpr] *The children thronged into the assembly hall.* [Vpr, V.to inf] *People are thronging to (see) his new play.* [also Vp, Vadv]. (**b**) ~ **sth (with sb/sth)** (of a crowd) to be in or fill a place: [Vn] *Crowds thronged the main square of the city.* [Vnpr] *The airport was thronged with weary travellers.*

throttle /ˈθrɒtl/ v **1** to seize sb by the throat and stop them breathing: [Vn] *He throttled the guard with his bare hands.* **2** to take away sth that is necessary for sth to function or survive: [Vn] *She accused the government of throttling the freedom of the press.* ○ *The city is being throttled by traffic congestion.* **PHRV ˌthrottle (sth) 'back/'down** to control the supply of fuel or power in order to reduce the speed of an engine or a vehicle.
▶ **throttle** n a device controlling the supply of fuel or power to an engine, eg the ACCELERATOR(1) in a car: *open up the throttle* (ie increase the speed) ○ *driving along at full throttle* (ie with the throttle completely open).

through¹ /θruː/ *prep* For the special uses of *through* in phrasal verbs, look at the verb entries. For example, the meaning of **get through sth** is given in the phrasal verb section of the entry for **get**. **1**(**a**) passing from one end or side of an opening, a channel or a passage to the other: *The train is going through a tunnel.* ○ *The burglar got in through the window.* ○ *The water flows into the tank through this pipe.* ○ *The sand ran through* (ie between) *my fingers.* (**b**) (used with verbs denoting senses) from one side of an object or a substance to the other: *You can see through glass.* ○ *He could just make out three people through the mist.* ○ *I could hear their conversation through the wall.* ○ *I can't feel anything through these gloves.* (**c**) passing from one side to the other of an object or a surface: *His knees have gone through* (ie made holes in) *his jeans.* ○ *The bullet went straight through him.* ○ *The blood soaked through his shirt and stained his jacket.* ○ *You need a sharp knife to cut through the knot.* (**d**) moving in sth or between things by which one is surrounded; among: *The path led through the trees to the river.* ○ *The doctor pushed through the crowd to get to the injured man.* ○ *She made her way through the traffic to the other side of the road.* ○ *I walked home through the fog.* (**e**) moving or travelling from one side or end of a place to another: *The Charles River flows through Boston.* ○ *Cars are not allowed to go through the city centre.* ○ *We had to wade through the river to the opposite bank.* ○ *The dog rushed straight through the flower-bed.* ○ *running through the narrow streets.* Compare ACROSS². **2** from the beginning to the end of an activity, a situation or a period of time: *He will not live through the night* (ie He will die before morning). ○ *The children are too young to sit through a long concert.* ○ *She nursed me through my long illness.* ○ *I'm halfway through (reading) his second novel.* **3** (also *infml* **thru**) (*US*) up to and including sth; until sth: *stay in London Tuesday through Friday.* **4(a)** (indicating the agent or means by which sth happens) by or because of sth: *You can only achieve success through hard work.* ○ *I heard of the job through a newspaper advertisement.* ○ *It was through you* (ie as a result of your help) *that Shirley and I were able to meet again.* **(b)** (indicating the cause or reason of sth happening): *We missed the plane through being held up on the M25.* ○ *The accident happened through no fault of mine.* **5** past a barrier which is established for a particular purpose: *How did you manage to get all those cigarettes through Customs?* ○ *He drove through a red light* (ie passed it when he should have stopped). **6** successfully past a particular stage or test: *get a Bill through Parliament* ○ *The teacher's job is to help the students through their exams.* ○ *All the top teams are safely through the first round.*

through² /θruː/ *adv part* For the special uses of **through** in phrasal verbs, look at the verb entries. For example, the meaning of **carry sth through** is given in the phrasal verb section of the entry for **carry**. **1** from one side or end of sth to the other: *Put the coffee in the filter and let the water run through.* ○ *The tyre's flat — the nail has gone right through.* ○ *We're coming to a farmyard — I suppose we can just walk through.* ○ *The onlookers stood aside to let the doctor through.* ○ *The flood was too deep to drive through.* **2** from the beginning to the end of sth: *Don't tell me how it ends — I haven't read it all the way through yet.* ○ *The baby slept right through* (ie did not wake up in the night). **3** past a barrier which is established for a particular purpose: *The light was red but the ambulance drove straight through.* **4** successfully past a particular stage or test: *Our team is through to* (ie has reached) *the semifinals.* **5(a)** travelling through a place without stopping: *'Did you stop in Oxford on the way?' 'No, we drove straight through.'* **(b)** (esp of trains) going direct to a destination without passengers needing to change to another train: *This train goes straight through to Edinburgh.* **6** connected by telephone: *Ask to be put through to me personally.* ○ *I tried to ring you but I couldn't get through* (eg because the line was engaged or faulty). ○ *You're through now* (ie You can begin to speak). **7** [pred] **~ (with sth/sb)** (*esp US*) (indicating that sb has finished with sth or that a relationship with sb is finished): *Are you through with that newspaper?* ○ *Keith and I are through* (ie have ended our relationship). **8** (after an *adj*) completely: *We got wet through.* **IDM** **,through and ¹through** completely; in every respect: *He's an Englishman through and through* (ie He has many typically English characteristics).

through³ /θruː/ *adj* [attrib] **1** (of a vehicle) going to a destination without stopping in a local area: *through traffic* ○ *There's a through train to Leeds.* **2** (of a route) allowing a continuous journey: *No through road* (ie The road is closed at one end).

throughout /θruːˈaʊt/ *adv* **1** in every part: *The house was painted white throughout.* ○ *Certain names in the book were underlined throughout.* **2** during the whole time of sth: *His voice faltered occasionally but he held the audience's attention throughout.*

▶ **throughout** *prep* **1** in or into every part of sth: *The news quickly spread throughout the country.* ○ *References to pain occur throughout the poem.* **2** during the whole time of sth: *Food was scarce*

throughout the war. ○ *Throughout his life he had always smoked heavily.*

throughput /ˈθruːpʊt/ *n* [U, sing] (*techn*) the quality of goods, number of people, etc going through a process, esp in a specified period of time: *a huge increase in the throughput of patients* ○ *a weekly throughput of 30 000 crates.*

throw¹ /θrəʊ/ *v* (*pt* **threw** /θruː/; *pp* **thrown** /θrəʊn/) **1** to send sth from one's hand through the air with some force by moving the arm: [Vadv] *How far can you throw?* [Vn, Vnpr] *Stop throwing stones (at the dog)!* [Vnp] *She threw the ball up and caught it again.* [Vnn] *Please throw me that towel.* ○ [Vnpr] *She threw it to me.* ○ (*fig*) *She threw* (ie gave) *me an angry look.* **2** to make sb/sth move suddenly and forcefully in the specified direction or manner: [Vnpr] *The boat was thrown onto the rocks.* ○ *She threw herself into his arms.* [Vnp] *The waves threw up a drenching spray.* [Vn-adj] *I threw open the windows to let the smoke out.* **3** to turn or move a part of the body quickly or violently in the specified direction: [Vnp] *He threw back his head and roared with laughter.* ○ *She threw up her hands in horror at the idea.* [Vnpr] *I ran up and threw my arms round him.* ○ (*fig*) *The party threw its weight behind* (ie supported) *the proposal.* **4 ~ sth around/over sb/ sth; ~ sth on/off** to put clothes, etc on or take them off quickly or carelessly: [Vnpr] *He threw a blanket over the injured man.* [Vnp] *He threw on his uniform.* ○ *She threw off her coat.* **5** to make sb fall quickly or violently to the ground: [Vn] *Two jockeys were thrown in the second race.* [Vn, Vnpr] *The wrestler succeeded in throwing his opponent (to the floor).* **6** [Vn] **(a)** to let a DICE(1a) fall after shaking it. **(b)** to obtain a number by doing this: *He threw three sixes in a row.* **7** (*techn*) to shape a clay pot, dish, etc on a potter's wheel (POTTER²): [Vn] *a hand-thrown vase.* **8** (*infml*) to disturb or confuse sb: [Vn] *The news of her death really threw me.* ○ *The speaker was completely thrown by the interruption.* **9** (esp passive) to cause sb/sth to be in a certain state: [Vnpr] *Hundreds were thrown out of work.* ○ *We were thrown into confusion by the news.* ○ *The problem was suddenly thrown into sharp focus.* **10** to direct sth at sb/sth: [Vnpr] *throw doubt on the verdict* ○ *throw the blame on sb* ○ *throw threats/insults/accusations at sb* [Vnp] *He threw the question back at me* (ie expected me to answer it myself). [also Vn]. **11(a)** to project or cast light, shade, etc: [Vn, Vnpr] *The trees threw long shadows (across the lawn).* **(b)** to project one's voice firmly and clearly in a particular direction: [Vnpr] *She threw her voice to the crowd of onlookers.* **12** to deliver a punch: [Vn] *In the struggle several punches were thrown.* **13** to move a switch, etc so as to operate it. **14** to have a sudden fit of bad temper, violent emotion, etc: [Vn] *She regularly throws tantrums.* **15** (*infml*) to give a party: [Vn] *throw a graduation party.* **IDM** Idioms containing **throw** are at the entries for the nouns or adjectives in the idioms, eg **throw the book at sb** ⇨ BOOK¹.
PHRV **,throw sth a¹bout/a¹round 1** to scatter sth: *Don't throw litter about like that.* **2** to spend money very freely.

throw oneself at sth/sb 1 to rush violently at sth/ sb. **2** (*infml derog*) (of a woman) to be too eager in trying to attract a man: *Everyone can see she's just throwing herself at him.*

,throw sth a¹way 1 (also **,throw sth ¹out**) to dispose of sth that is no longer wanted: *That rubbish — you can throw it away.* ○ *It's time we threw that old chair out.* **2** to fail to make use of sth; to waste sth: *throw away an opportunity/advantage* ○ *She threw away a career as a journalist.* **3** (of actors, etc) speak words in a deliberately casual way: *This speech is meant to be thrown away.*

,throw sb ¹back on sth (usu passive) to force sb to rely on sth because nothing else is available: *The*

television broke down so we were thrown back on our own resources (ie had to entertain ourselves). ￼
,**throw sth** ˈ**in 1** to include sth with what one is selling or offering, without increasing the price: *You can have the piano for £90, and I'll throw in the stool as well.* **2** to make a remark, etc casually.
,**throw oneself/sth** ˈ**into sth** to begin to do sth enthusiastically: *throwing themselves into their work* ○ *We threw all our energies into making the farm a success.*
,**throw sth/sb** ˈ**off** to manage to stop having sth or being troubled by sth/sb: *throw off a cold/a troublesome acquaintance/one's pursuers.*
ˈ**throw oneself on sb/sth** (*fml*) to rely entirely on sb/sth: *He was clearly guilty and could only throw himself on the mercy of the court.*
,**throw sb** ˈ**out 1** to force sb to leave a place: *The drunk was thrown out (of the pub).* **2** to distract or confuse sb; to make sb make a mistake: *Do keep quiet or you'll throw me out in my calculations.*
,**throw sth** ˈ**out 1** to say sth in an apparently casual way: *throw out a hint/a suggestion/an idea* ○ *She threw out a challenge to her opponents.* **2** to reject a proposal, an idea, etc. **3** = THROW STH AWAY 1.
,**throw sb** ˈ**over** to desert or abandon sb: *When he became rich he threw over all his old friends.*
,**throw sb to**ˈ**gether** to bring people into contact with each other, often casually: *Fate had thrown them together.* ○ *As the only English speakers, we were inevitably thrown together.* ,**throw sth to**ˈ**gether** to make or produce sth in a hurry: *I'll just throw together a quick supper.*
,**throw (sth)** ˈ**up** to VOMIT food. ▷ note at SICK.
throw sth up (*Brit*) **1** to resign from sth: *throw up one's job* ○ *You've thrown up a very promising career.* **2** to bring sth to people's notice: *Her research has thrown up some interesting facts.* **3** to build sth suddenly or in a hurry.

▶ **thrower** *n* a person who throws sth: *a javelin thrower* ○ *stone throwers.* See also FLAME THROWER.
■ ˈ**throw-away** *adj* [attrib] **(a)** intended to be thrown away as rubbish after being used only once or a few times: *throw-away cups/razors* ○ (*derog*) *the throw-away society* (ie that throws things away without using them again). **(b)** spoken in a deliberately casual way; not emphasized: *a throw-away remark.*
ˈ**throw-back** *n* [C usu *sing*] a person or thing that shows the characteristics of sb/sth in the past: *Such attitudes are a throw-back to Victorian times.*
ˈ**throw-in** *n* (in football) an act of throwing in the ball after it has gone outside the area of play.

throw² /θrəʊ/ *n* **1** an act of throwing sth: *a well-aimed throw* ○ *It's your throw* (eg your turn to throw the DICE(1a)). **2** a distance to which sth is or may be thrown: *a throw of 70 metres.* **IDM** **a stone's throw** ▷ STONE. **a** ˈ**throw** (*infml*) each; per item: *sell the posters at £5 a throw.*

thru (*infml*) = THROUGH¹ 3.

thrush¹ /θrʌʃ/ *n* a bird   **thrush**
with a brownish back
and brown spots on its
breast. ▷ picture.

thrush² /θrʌʃ/ *n* [U] **(a)**
an infectious disease
producing white patches
in the mouth and throat,
esp in children. **(b)** a similar disease affecting the
VAGINA.

thrust /θrʌst/ *v* (*pt, pp* **thrust**) **1** to push sth/sb/ oneself suddenly or violently: [Vnpr] *thrust a tip into the waiter's hand* [Vpr, Vnpr] *He thrust (his way) through the crowd.* [Vnp] (*fig*) *My objections were thrust aside* (ie dismissed). ○ *She tends to thrust herself forward too much* (ie to assert herself too much). ~ **at sb** (**with sth**)/ ~ **sth at sb** to make a forward stroke at sb with a weapon: [Vpr, Vnpr] *He*

thrust at me with a knife/thrust a knife at me. **PHR V** ˈ**thrust sth/sb on/upon sb** to force sb to accept sth/sb or to deal with sth/sb: *Some people have greatness thrust upon them* (ie become famous without wishing or trying to be). ○ *She is rather annoyed at having three extra guests suddenly thrust on her.*

▶ **thrust** *n* **1** [C] an act or movement of thrusting: *killed by a bayonet thrust.* **2(a)** a strong attack in war or in a contest: *a deep thrust into the opponent's territory.* **(b)** a critical remark aimed at sb. **3** [U] the forward force produced by a jet engine, a ROCKET(2b), etc. **4** [U] the main point or theme of sb's remarks: *What was the thrust of his argument?* **IDM** **the cut and thrust** ▷ CUT².
thruster *n* a small engine used to provide extra or correcting thrust(3), esp on a spacecraft.

thruway /ˈθruːweɪ/ *n* (*US*) = EXPRESSWAY.

thud /θʌd/ *n* a low dull sound like that of a blow on sth soft: *He fell off the ladder and hit the ground with a dull thud.*
▶ **thud** *v* (**-dd-**) to move, fall or hit sth with a thud: [Vpr] *the sound of branches thudding against the walls of the hut* [also Vp].

thug /θʌɡ/ *n* an aggressive person; a violent criminal.
▶ **thuggery** /ˈθʌɡəri/ *n* [U] aggressive or violent behaviour.
thuggish /ˈθʌɡɪʃ/ *adj.*

thumb /θʌm/ *n* **(a)** a short thick finger set apart from the other four. ▷ picture at HAND¹. **(b)** the part of a glove covering this. **IDM** **be all fingers and thumbs** ▷ FINGER¹. **a rule of thumb** ▷ RULE. **stand/stick out like a sore thumb** ▷ SORE. **thumbs** ˈ**up/**ˈ**down** (a phrase or gesture used to indicate success or approval/failure or rejection): *give sb/sth the thumbs up* ○ *I'm afraid it's thumbs down for your new proposal.* **twiddle one's thumbs** ▷ TWIDDLE. **under sb's** ˈ**thumb** completely under sb's influence or control: *She's got him under her thumb.*
▶ **thumb** *v* **IDM** **thumb a** ˈ**lift** to try to get a free ride in a motor vehicle by signalling with one's thumb. **thumb one's** ˈ**nose at sb/sth** to make a rude gesture at sb/sth by putting one's thumb against the end of one's nose. **PHR V** ˈ**thumb through sth** to turn over the pages of a book, etc: *thumbing through the dictionary.* See also WELL-THUMBED.
■ ˈ**thumb index** *n* a set of places for the fingers or thumbs cut in the edge of a book and often labelled with letters. A thumb index is used to identify the position of the various sections in the book, eg the words beginning with a certain letter in a dictionary.
ˈ**thumb-tack** *n* (*US*) = DRAWING-PIN.

thumbnail /ˈθʌmneɪl/ *n* the nail at the tip of the thumb.
▶ **thumbnail** *adj* [attrib] briefly written: *a thumbnail sketch/portrait/description.*

thumbscrew /ˈθʌmskruː/ *n* (esp formerly) an instrument used to TORTURE(1) sb by crushing the thumb.

thump /θʌmp/ *v* **1** to strike or knock sth heavily, esp with the FIST: [Vpr] *Someone thumped on the door.* [Vn] *The two boys started thumping each other.* [Vnp] (*fig*) *He thumped out a tune* (ie played it loudly) *on the piano.* [also Vn-adj, Vnpr]. **2** to beat strongly: [V, Vpr] *My heart was thumping (with excitement).* See also TUB-THUMPER.
▶ **thump** *n* **(a)** a heavy blow: *give sb a thump.* **(b)** a noise made by this: *The sack of cement hit the ground with a thump.*
thumping *adj* [attrib] (*infml*) big: *a thumping defeat* ○ *win by a thumping majority.* — *adv* (*infml*) extremely: *a thumping great lie.*

thunder /ˈθʌndə(r)/ *n* **(a)** [U] the loud noise that

---

follows a flash of lightning: *a crash/peal/roll of thunder* ○ *There's thunder in the air* (ie Thunder is likely). (**b**) [U, sing] any similar noise: *the thunder of the guns/jets/drums* ○ *a/the thunder of applause.* **IDM** **blood and thunder** ⇨ BLOOD¹. **steal sb's thunder** ⇨ STEAL.

▶ **thunder** *v* **1** (used with *it*) to make the noise of thunder: [V] *It thundered all night.* **2(a)** to make a loud deep noise: [V] *thundering hooves* [Vpr] *A voice thundered in my ear.* (**b**) to move in the specified direction making a loud deep noise: [Vp] *heavy trucks thundering along/by/past* [Vp] *The train thundered through the station.* **3** ~ **against sth/at sb** to shout, complain, etc very loudly and angrily against sth/sb: [Vpr] *reformers thundering against corruption* [V.speech] '*How dare you speak to me that way?' he thundered.* [also Vnp].
thunderous /-dərəs/ *adj* very loud: *thunderous applause.* **thunderously** *adv.*
thundery /-dəri/ *adj* (of weather) giving signs of thunder: *a thundery day.*

thunderbolt /ˈθʌndəbəʊlt/ *n* **1** a flash of lightning with a crash of thunder. **2** a very sudden or terrible event or statement: *Her sudden resignation came as a thunderbolt to the whole company.*

thunderclap /ˈθʌndəklæp/ *n* a crash of thunder.

thundercloud /ˈθʌndəklaʊd/ *n* a large dark cloud that can produce lightning and thunder.

thunderstorm /ˈθʌndəstɔːm/ *n* a storm with thunder and lightning and usu heavy rain.

thunderstruck /ˈθʌndəstrʌk/ *adj* [usu pred] amazed; extremely surprised and shocked.

Thur (also **Thurs**) *abbr* Thursday: *Thurs 26 June.*

Thursday /ˈθɜːzdeɪ, -di/ *n* [C, U] (*abbrs* **Thur**, **Thurs**) the fifth day of the week, next after Wednesday. For further guidance on how *Thursday* is used, see the examples at *Monday.*

thus /ðʌs/ *adv* (*fml*) **1** in this way; like this: *Hold the wheel in both hands, thus.* **2** as a result of this; therefore: *He is the eldest son and thus heir to the title.* **IDM** **thus far** = SO FAR (FAR¹).

thwart /θwɔːt/ *v* ~ **sb** (**in sth**) (esp passive) to prevent sb doing what they intend to; to oppose a plan, etc successfully: [Vn] *thwarted ambitions* [Vn, Vnpr] *He was thwarted (in his aims) by bad luck.*

thy /ðaɪ/ (also before a vowel **thine** /ðaɪn/) *possess det* (*arch*) your.

thyme /taɪm/ *n* [U] a plant with sweet-smelling leaves that are used in cooking.

thyroid /ˈθaɪrɔɪd/ (also **ˈthyroid gland**) *n* an organ at the front of the neck, producing a substance which controls the body's growth and development.

thyself /ðaɪˈself/ *reflex, emph pron* (*arch*) yourself.

ti /tiː/ *n* (*music*) the 7th note of any major scale¹(6).

tiara /tiˈɑːrə/ *n* **1** a small crown decorated with jewels, worn by a woman, eg a princess, on ceremonial occasions. **2** a crown worn by the Pope.

tibia /ˈtɪbiə/ *n* (*pl* **tibiae** /-biiː/) (*anatomy*) = SHINBONE. ⇨ picture at SKELETON.

tic /tɪk/ *n* a quick repeated movement of a muscle, esp in the face, that cannot be controlled: *have a nervous tic.*

tick¹ /tɪk/ *n* **1** a short, light, regularly repeated sound, esp that of a clock or watch. **2** (*Brit infml*) a moment: *Just wait a tick!* ○ *I'll only be a couple of ticks.* **3** (*US* **check**) a mark put beside a sum or an item in a list to show that it has been checked or done or is correct. Compare X² 4. ⇨ picture.

tick (*US* **check**)

tick (*US* check)

▶ **tick** *v* **1** ~ (**away**) (of a clock, etc) to make a series of ticks (TICK¹ 1): [V] *listen to the clock ticking/ the ticking of the clock* [Vp] *While we waited the taxi's meter kept ticking away.* **2** ~ **sth** (**off**) to put a tick¹(3) beside a sum, an item on a list, etc: [Vn] *tick the appropriate box* [Vn, Vnpr] *tick (off) the names of those present* [Vnp] *The jobs that are done have been ticked off.* **IDM** **what makes sb ˈtick** (*infml*) what makes sb behave in the way they do: *I've never really understood what makes her tick.* **PHRV** ,**tick aˈway/ˈby/ˈpast** (of time) to pass: *Meanwhile the minutes were ticking away.* ,**tick sth aˈway** (of a clock, etc) to mark the passage of time: *The station clock ticked away the minutes.* ,**tick sb ˈoff** (*Brit infml*) to speak to sb angrily because they have done sth wrong: *get ticked off for careless work.* ,**tick ˈover** (*esp Brit*) (esp in the continuous tenses) **1** (of an engine) to run slowly in NEUTRAL(2) without supplying power to a vehicle, etc: *keep the engine ticking over.* **2** (of activities) to continue in a routine way: *Just try and keep things ticking over while I'm away.*
■ ,**ticking-ˈoff** *n* (*pl* **tickings-off**) (*Brit infml*) an instance of speaking to sb angrily for doing sth wrong: *give sb a good ticking-off.*

,**tick-ˈtock** *n* (usu *sing*) the sound of a large clock ticking.

tick² /tɪk/ *n* **1** any of various small insects that suck blood. **2** (*Brit sl*) an unpleasant or worthless person.

tick³ /tɪk/ *n* [U] (*infml esp Brit*) credit: *buy goods on tick.*

ticker /ˈtɪkə(r)/ *n* (*sl*) a person's heart: *His ticker's not very strong.*
■ **ˈticker-tape** *n* [U] (*esp US*) (**a**) paper tape giving information from an automatic printing machine: *read the stock market prices off the ticker-tape.* (**b**) this or similar material thrown from windows to greet a famous person: *get a ticker-tape reception.*

ticket /ˈtɪkɪt/ *n* **1** [C] a written or printed piece of card or paper that gives the holder a certain right, eg to travel by plane, bus, etc or to a seat in a cinema: *buy a ticket to Manchester* ○ *a ticket office/ machine* ○ *I've booked two tickets for the theatre.* ○ *Admission by ticket only* (eg as a notice outside a hall). See also MEAL-TICKET, RETURN TICKET, SEASON TICKET. **2** [C] a label attached to sth, giving details of its price, size, etc. **3** [C usu *sing*] (*esp US*) a list of the candidates put forward by one party in an election: *run for office on the Republican ticket* ○ *a dream ticket* (ie an ideal pair of candidates standing together for political office). **4** [C] an official notice of an offence against traffic regulations: *get a parking/ speeding ticket.* **5** **the ticket** [sing] (*dated infml*) the correct or desirable thing: *All packed up and ready to go? That's the ticket.* **IDM** **just the job/ticket** ⇨ JOB. **split the ticket** ⇨ SPLIT.

▶ **ticket** *v* [Vn] (esp passive) to put a ticket(2) on an article for sale. **ticketing** *n* [U] the process of issuing tickets.

ticking /ˈtɪkɪŋ/ *n* [U] strong material for making MATTRESS and PILLOW covers.

tickle /ˈtɪkl/ *v* **1** to touch or stroke sb lightly, esp in a sensitive place, so as to cause a slightly uncomfortable sensation, often making them laugh: [Vnpr] *tickle sb in the ribs* ○ *She tickled my nose with a feather.* [V, Vn] *This blanket tickles (me).* **2** to produce a slightly uncomfortable sensation: [V] *My nose tickles.* **3** to amuse sb or provoke a certain feeling in them: [Vn] *The idea tickled her curiosity/vanity.* ○ *I was highly tickled by the thought.* **IDM** **be tickled ˈpink** (*infml*) to be extremely pleased or amused: *I'm tickled pink that my essay won the prize.* **take/tickle sb's fancy** ⇨ FANCY³.
▶ **tickle** *n* an act or sensation of tickling: *I've got a tickle in my throat — I think I may be getting a cold.* **IDM** **slap and tickle** ⇨ SLAP *n.*

ticklish /ˈtɪklɪʃ/ *adj* **1** (of a person) sensitive to being tickled: *I'm terribly ticklish.* **2** (*infml*) (of a problem) difficult to deal with: *a ticklish task for the local authorities.*

tick-tack-toe /ˌtɪk tæk ˈtəʊ/ *n* [U] (*US*) = NOUGHTS AND CROSSES.

tidal /ˈtaɪdl/ *adj* relating to or affected by tides: *a tidal river/estuary/barrage.*
■ ˌtidal ˈwave *n* **1** a great ocean wave, eg one caused by an EARTHQUAKE. **2** ~ (**of sth**) a great wave of popular enthusiasm, protest, etc: *carried along on a tidal wave of hysteria.*

tidbit (*US*) = TITBIT.

tiddler /ˈtɪdlə(r)/ *n* (*infml*) **1** a very small fish. **2** a very small thing or child.

tiddly /ˈtɪdli/ *adj* (*infml*) **1** (*esp Brit*) slightly drunk: *I feel a bit tiddly.* **2** (*Brit*) very small: *Two tiddly cheese biscuits? You can't call that a proper meal!*

tiddly-winks /ˈtɪdli wɪŋks/ *n* [U] a game in which players try to make small plastic discs jump into a cup by pressing them on the edge with a larger disc.

tide /taɪd/ *n* **1**(**a**) [C, U] a regular rise and fall in the level of the sea, caused by the attraction of the moon and sun: *at high/low tide* ○ *the ebb and flow of the tide.* See also NEAP TIDE, SPRING TIDE. (**b**) [C] the water moved by this: *driftwood washed up by the tide* ○ *The tide is (coming) in/(going) out.* ○ *Swimmers should beware of strong tides.* **2** [C usu *sing*] a direction in which opinion, events, luck, etc seem to move; a TREND: *a rising tide of discontent* ○ **stem the tide** *of opposition* ○ *The tide turned in our favour.* **3** [U] (*arch*) (in compounds) a time or season of the year: *ˈyule-tide* ○ *ˈChristmastide.* **IDM** **go, swim, etc with/against the tide** to agree with/oppose the attitudes, opinions, etc of most other people. **time and tide wait for no man** ⇨ TIME¹.
▶ **tide** *v* **PHRV** ˌtide sb ˈover (**sth**) to help sb during a difficult period by providing what they need: *Can you lend me some money to tide me over until I get my pay cheque?*

tidemark /ˈtaɪdmɑːk/ *n* **1** a mark made by the sea on a beach at the highest point of a tide. **2** (*Brit joc*) a line left round the inside of a bath, etc by dirty water.

tidings /ˈtaɪdɪŋz/ *n* [pl] (*arch or joc*) news: *Have you heard the good/glad tidings?*

tidy /ˈtaɪdi/ *adj* (**-ier**, **-iest**) **1**(**a**) arranged neatly and in order: *a tidy room/desk/garden* ○ *She keeps her house very tidy.* (**b**) having the habit of keeping things neat and in order: *a tidy boy* ○ *tidy habits* ○ *have a tidy mind* (ie be able to think in a clear and sensible way). Compare UNTIDY. **2** [attrib] (*infml*) (esp of a sum of money) fairly large; considerable: *She left a tidy fortune when she died.* ○ *It must have cost a tidy sum.*
▶ **tidily** *adv.*
tidiness *n* [U].

tidy *n* (esp in compounds) a holder for various small items: *a ˈdesk tidy* (ie for pens, paper-clips (PAPER), etc) ○ *a ˈsink tidy* (ie for bits of kitchen waste).

tidy *v* (*pt, pp* **tidied**) ~ (**sth/sb/oneself**) (**up**) to make sth/sb/oneself tidy: [Vp] *spend all morning tidying up* [V] *Who's been tidying in here?* [Vn, Vnp] *You'd better tidy this room (up) before the guests arrive.* [Vnp] *I must tidy myself up* (ie make myself look clean and neat). ○ (*fig*) *The new laws are intended to tidy up some of the outstanding issues in this area.* **PHRV** ˌtidy sth aˈway (*Brit*) to put sth in a certain place, esp where it cannot be seen, so that a room appears tidy: *Tidy away your toys when you've finished playing.* ˌtidy sth ˈout (*Brit*) to remove unnecessary items from sth and arrange the rest neatly: *tidy out one's drawers/a cupboard.*

tie¹ /taɪ/ *n* **1** (also **necktie**) a strip of material worn round the neck under the collar and tied with a knot in front: *wear a suit and tie.* See also BOW-TIE, OLD SCHOOL TIE. ⇨ picture at JACKET. **2** a piece of cord,

wire, etc used for fastening or tying sth: *ties for sealing plastic bags.* **3** (*techn*) (**a**) a rod or beam holding parts of a structure together. (**b**) (*US*) = SLEEPER 3. **4** (usu *pl*) a thing that unites people; a BOND(1): *the ties of friendship* ○ *family ties* ○ *The firm has ties with an American corporation.* **5** a thing that limits a person's freedom of action: *He doesn't want any ties; that's why he never married.* **6** a situation in a game or competition when two or more competitors or teams have the same score: *The match ended in a tie.* Compare DRAW² 2. **7** a sports match between two or more competing teams or players: *the first leg of the Cup tie between Aberdeen and Barcelona.* **8** (in written music) a curved line over two notes of the same pitch¹(2) that are to be played or sung as one. ⇨ picture at MUSIC.
■ ˈtie-break (also ˈtie-breaker) *n* a means of deciding the winner when competitors have equal scores: *The first set* (ie of a tennis match) *was won on the tie-break.*
ˈtie-pin (*US* also ˈstickpin, ˈtie-tack) *n* an ornamental pin for holding a tie¹(1) in place.

tie² /taɪ/ *v* (*pt, pp* **tied**; *pres p* **tying**) **1** to fasten sth/sb with rope, string, etc: [Vnpr] *tie a dog to a lamp-post* [Vn] *Shall I tie the parcel or use tape?* [Vnp] *The prisoner's hands were tied together.* **2** ~ **sth** (**on**) to fasten sth to or round sth/sb by means of its strings, etc: [Vnp] *tie on a label* [Vnpr] *Could you tie this apron round me?* [also Vn]. **3**(**a**) to arrange string, etc to form a knot or bow: [Vn] *tie a ribbon/scarf/tie/cravat* [Vn, Vnp] *tie (up) one's shoelaces* [Vnpr] *She tied her hair in(to) a bun.* (**b**) to make a knot or bow in this way: [Vnpr] *tie a knot in a piece of rope* [also Vn]. **4** to be fastened: [Vpr] *Does this sash tie in front or at the back?* [also Vadv]. **5** ~ **sth to sth** (esp *passive*) to connect or link sth to sth else: [Vnpr] *a party still tied to outdated policies* ○ *The fortunes of the company are tied to the success of the industry as a whole.* **6** ~ (**sb**) (**with sb**) (**for sth**) to make the same score as another competitor or team: [V, Vpr] *The two teams tied (with each other).* [Vnpr usu *passive*] *Britain are tied with Italy for second place.* **7** (*music*) to join notes with a tie¹(8): [Vn] *tied crotchets.* **IDM** **bind/tie sb hand and foot** ⇨ HAND¹. **have one's hands free/tied** ⇨ HAND¹. **tie sb/oneself into/(up) in ˈknots** to become or make sb very confused. ˌtie the ˈknot (*infml*) to get married.
PHRV ˌtie sb/oneself ˈdown (**to sth**) to restrict sb/oneself, eg to certain conditions or a fixed occupation or place: *refuse to be tied down by petty restrictions* ○ *Children do tie you down, don't they?* ˌtie ˈin (**with sth**) (of information or facts) to agree or be connected: *This evidence ties in with what we already know.* ˌtie (**sth**) ˈup to attach a boat to a fixed object or the land: *We tied (the boat) up alongside the quay.* ˌtie sb ˈup 1 to tie sb's legs together or tie them to sth with rope so that they cannot move or escape: *The thieves left the night-watchman tied up and gagged.* **2** (usu *passive*) to occupy sb so that they have no time for other things: *I'm tied up in a meeting until 3 pm.* ˌtie sth ˈup 1 to fasten sth with cord, rope, etc: *tie up a rubbish sack.* **2** to attach an animal to sth by means of a rope or chain: *It's cruel to leave a dog tied up all day.* **3** (often *passive*) to connect or link sth to sth else: *Her behaviour is tied up with her feelings of guilt.* **4** (often *passive*) to invest money, so that it is not easily available for use: *Most of his capital's tied up in property.* **5** to make conditions restricting the use or sale of property, etc. **6** to bring work, progress, etc to a stop: *The strike tied up production for a week.*
▶ **tied** *adj* [attrib] (of a house) rented to sb on condition that they work for the owners: *a ˌtied ˈcottage.* ˌtied ˈhouse *n* (*Brit*) a pub that is owned or controlled by a particular company and sells the beer which that company produces. Compare FREE HOUSE.

■ **'tie-dye** *v* [Vn] to produce coloured patterns on fabric by tying parts of it so that they receive less of the dye than other parts when the fabric is treated with dye.

'tie-in *n* ~ **(with sth)** **1** a joint promotion of related products, eg a book and a film: *a TV tie-in* ○ *a tie-in with the band's latest album.* **2** any connection or association.

'tie-on *adj* [attrib] (of a label, etc) that may be attached to sth by being tied.

'tie-up *n* **1** ~ **(with sb/sth)** an instance of two groups, companies, etc joining together: *a tie-up with Singapore Airlines.* **2** (*esp US*) a stopping of work, progress, etc: *a traffic tie-up.*

tier /tɪə(r)/ *n* a row or level of a structure, or an organization consisting of several rows or levels placed one above the other: *a wedding-cake with three tiers/a three-tier wedding-cake* ○ *the third tier of local government administration.* ➪ picture at LAYER.

▶ **tiered** *adj* arranged in tiers: *tiered seating* ○ *a tiered interest rate structure.*

-tiered (forming compound *adjs*) having the specified number of tiers: *a three-tiered cake* ○ *a two-tiered system.*

tiff /tɪf/ *n* a slight argument between friends or lovers: *She's had a tiff with her boyfriend.*

tig /tɪg/ *n* [U] (*Brit*) = TAG 4.

tiger /'taɪɡə(r)/ *n* a large fierce Asian animal of the cat family, having a yellowish coat with black bands: *She **fought like a tiger** to keep her children.* See also PAPER TIGER. ➪ picture at CAT.

▶ **tigerish** /'taɪɡərɪʃ/ *adj* like a tiger, esp (of a person) acting with fierce energy.

tight /taɪt/ *adj* (**-er, -est**) **1** fixed, fastened or drawn together firmly; hard to move or undo: *a tight knot* ○ *keep a tight hold on the rope* ○ *My belt's too tight — I need to let it out a bit.* ○ *The drawer is so tight I can't open it.* **2** fitting closely: *a tight joint* ○ *These shoes are too tight for me.* Compare LOOSE[1] 6b. See also AIRTIGHT, SKIN-TIGHT, WATERTIGHT. **3(a)** with things or people arranged closely: *a tight mass of fibres* ○ *a tight schedule* (ie leaving little time to spare) ○ *With six of us in the car it was a **tight squeeze**.* **(b)** (of a game, etc) with evenly matched competitors: *a tight race/match/contest.* **5** (of a situation) difficult or dangerous: *Having no money put me in a **tight corner/spot**.* **5** (of control, etc) strictly applied: *tight security/constraints/sanctions.* **6** fully stretched: *a tight rope/rein* ○ *The cord was stretched tight.* ○ *My chest feels rather tight* (eg because of ASTHMA). **7** (of a curve, turn, etc) changing direction sharply: *a tight bend in the road.* **8** [usu pred] (*infml*) drunk: *I got a bit tight at the party.* **9** (of money) not available to spend; SCARCE: *We can't go to Florida this year — money's too tight.* **10** (*infml derog*) not willing to spend or give much money; mean²(1): *She's very tight with her money.* **IDM** **keep a tight 'rein on sb/sth** to allow little freedom to sb/sth.

▶ **tight** *adv* tightly (not used before a past participle: *packed tight* but *tightly packed*): *Hold tight!* **IDM** **sit tight** ➪ SIT. **sleep tight** ➪ SLEEP².

tightly *adv* in a tight manner: *hold/hug/grip sb tightly* ○ *tightly sealed.*

tightness *n* [U].

■ **,tight-'fisted** *adj* not willing to spend or give much money; tight(10).

,tight-'knit *adj* (of a family, community, etc) having a strong sense of identity or close links between members.

,tight-'lipped *adj* keeping the lips pressed firmly together, esp to restrain one's emotion or to keep silent.

tighten /'taɪtn/ *v* ~ **(sth) (up) (a)** to become or make sth become tight or tighter: [Vn, Vnp] *tighten (up)*

the ropes/one's belt* [Vn] *This screw needs tightening.* ○ *She tightened her lips disapprovingly.* [V] *His grip on her arm tightened.* [also Vp, Vpr, Vnpr]. **(b)** to become or make sth stricter: [Vnp] *tighten up security* [V] *Controls have gradually tightened.* [also Vp, Vpr, Vn, Vnpr]. Compare LOOSEN, SLACKEN 1. **IDM** **tighten one's 'belt** to eat less food, spend less money, etc because there is little available: *The management warned of the need for further belt-tightening* (ie care with money, resources, etc). **PHRV** **,tighten 'up (on sth)** to become more careful or strict: *The police are tightening up on drunken driving.*

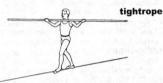

tightrope

tightrope /'taɪtrəʊp/ *n* a rope stretched tightly high above the ground, used esp by performers in a CIRCUS(1): *a tightrope walker.* ➪ picture. **IDM** **tread/walk a 'tightrope** to proceed in a situation which allows little freedom of action and in which an exact balance must be preserved: *The government is walking a difficult tightrope in wanting to reduce interest rates without pushing up inflation.*

tights /taɪts/ *n* [pl] **1** (*US* **pantihose, pantyhose**) a garment fitting closely over the hips, legs and feet, worn by girls and women: *a pair of cotton tights.* Compare STOCKING. **2** a similar garment covering the legs and body, worn by dancers, etc.

tigress /'taɪɡrəs/ *n* a female tiger.

tilde /'tɪldə/ *n* **1** a mark (˜) placed over the Spanish *n* when it is pronounced /nj/ (as in *cañon*), or the Portuguese *a* or *o* when the sound is produced through the nose (as in *São Paulo*). The tilde is also placed over certain vowels in the International Phonetic Alphabet to indicate that the vowel sound is produced through the nose, as in *penchant* /'pɒ̃ʃɒ̃/. **2** a mark (~) used in this dictionary in certain parts of an entry to replace the word in dark type at the head of the entry.

tile /taɪl/ *n* **1** a flat piece of baked clay or other material used in rows for covering roofs, walls, floors, etc: *cover the wall with cork tiles* ○ *insulate the ceiling with expanded polystyrene tiles* ○ *carpet tiles* (ie carpet sold in small squares for laying in rows). ➪ picture at HOUSE¹. **2** any of the small flat pieces used in certain board games. **IDM** **(out) on the 'tiles** (*sl*) enjoying oneself away from home, esp getting drunk or behaving wildly.

▶ **tile** *v* to cover a surface with tiles: [Vn] *a tiled bathroom.*

tiling *n* [U] an area covered with tiles: *drill two holes into the tiling.*

till¹ ➪ UNTIL.

till² /tɪl/ *n* a drawer in which money is kept behind the counter in a shop, bank, etc or in a cash register (CASH). **IDM** **have, etc one's fingers in the till** ➪ FINGER¹.

till³ /tɪl/ *v* [Vn] to prepare and use land for growing crops.

▶ **tillage** /'tɪlɪdʒ/ *n* [U] (*dated*) **1** the action or process of tilling land. **2** tilled land.

tiller /'tɪlə(r)/ *n* a bar used to turn the RUDDER(a) of a small boat. ➪ picture at YACHT. Compare HELM.

tilt /tɪlt/ *v* to move or make sth move into a sloping position: [V, Vpr, Vp] *This table tends to tilt (to one side/over).* [V, Vpr] (*fig*) *Popular opinion has tilted (in favour of the Socialists).* [Vpr] *She sat listening, with her head tilted slightly to one side.* [Vn] *Don't tilt your chair or you'll fall over!* [Vnp] *Tilt the barrel* *forward to empty it.* [also Vnpr]. **IDM tilt at 'windmills** to waste one's energy fighting imaginary enemies. **PHR V 'tilt at sb/sth** to attack sb/sth in speech or writing: *a satirical magazine tilting at public figures.*

▶ **tilt** *n* (usu *sing*) **1** a sloping position: *with a tilt of his head* ○ *the table is on/at a slight tilt.* **2** a meeting between opponents; an attack in speech, writing, etc: *have a tilt at sb.* **IDM full pelt/tilt/speed** ⇨ FULL.

tilth /tɪlθ/ *n* [U] soil that has been dug and prepared for planting: *flowers that require a fine tilth with plenty of moisture.*

timber /'tɪmbə(r)/ *n* **1** [U] **(a)** (*US* also **lumber**) wood prepared for use in building or carpentry (CARPENTER): *a 'timber-merchant* ○ *a 'timber-yard* (ie where timber is stored, bought and sold, etc) ○ *a timber-framed house.* **(b)** trees suitable for this; woods or forests: *cut down/fell timber.* **2** [C usu *pl*] a piece of wood, esp a beam, used in building a house or ship: *roof/floor timbers.*

▶ **timber** *interj* (used as a warning that a tree is about to fall after being cut).

timbered /'tɪmbəd/ *adj* (of buildings) built of wooden beams or with a framework of these.

timbre /'tæmbə(r)/ *n* a characteristic quality of sound produced by a particular voice or musical instrument.

time¹ /taɪm/ *n* **1** [U] **(a)** all the years of the past, present and future: *past/present/future time* ○ *The world exists in space and time.* **(b)** the passing of these taken as a whole: *As time passed they saw less and less of each other.* ○ *Time has not been kind to her looks* (ie She is no longer as beautiful as she was). ○ *(old) Father Time* (ie this process represented as an old man) ○ *Time heals all wounds.* **2** [U] time as measured by a conventional standard: *Greenwich Mean Time* ○ *Time in California is eight hours behind London.* **3** [U] a portion or measure of time: *That will take time* (ie cannot be done quickly). ○ *We've been here for some time* (ie for a fairly long time). ○ *I don't have (much) time for reading these days.* ○ *I'll be back in six months'/ten minutes' time.* ○ *We have no time to lose* (ie We must hurry). ○ *What a waste of time!* ○ *We must lose/waste no time in responding to the threat.* ○ *I spent most of my time (in) sightseeing.* ○ *Playing chess helped to pass the time.* ○ *I'm rather pressed for time* (ie in rather a hurry). **4 a time** [sing] a period of time, either long or short: *What a (long) time you've been!* ○ *We waited for a time and then went home.* ○ *I lived in Egypt for a time.* **5** [U] a point of time stated in hours and minutes of the day: *What time is it?/What is the time? (on you.)*? ⇨ App 2. **6** [U,C] a period of time measured in units, ie years, months, hours, etc: *The winner's time was 11.6 seconds.* ○ *He ran the mile in record time* (ie faster than any previous runner). ○ *Although she came second their times were only a tenth of a second apart.* ⇨ App 2. **7** [U] time spent in work or leisure: *get plenty of time off* (ie time not working) ○ *spare/free time* ○ *full-/part-time employment* ○ *paid time and a half/double time* (ie at one and a half times/twice the usual rate). See also SHORT TIME. **8** [U,C] a point or period of time used, available or suitable for sth: *'lunch-time* ○ *by the time we reached home○I agreed at the time but later I changed my mind.* ○ *This is not the time to bring up that subject.* ○ *Spring is my favourite time of year.* ○ *Shall we fix a time for the next meeting?* ○ *It's time we were going/time for us to go* (ie We should leave now). ○ *War and suffering had left the children old before their time.* ○ *Time's up* (ie The time allowed for sth is ended). **9** [C] **(a)** an occasion; an instance: *this/that/another/next/last time* ○ *the time before last* ○ *for the first/second/last time* ○ *I've told you countless times not to do that.* ○ *He failed his driving test five times.* ○ *She looks more*

lovely every time I see her. ○ *Sometimes she's fun to be with; at other times she can be very moody.* **(b)** the experience sb has of a particular occasion: *We had a great time at the fair.* ○ *What sort of time did you have?* **10** [C often *pl*] **(a)** a period of time associated with particular events, people, etc: *in 'Stuart times/ the time of the 'Stuarts* (ie when the Stuart kings ruled) ○ *in 'ancient/prehis'toric/'recent times* ○ *Mr Curtis was the manager in 'my time* (ie when I was working there). ○ *The Beatles were a bit before my 'time* (ie before the period I can remember or became interested in pop music). **(b)** a period of time associated with certain conditions, experiences, etc: *in time(s) of danger/hardship/prosperity* ○ *University was a good time for me.* ○ *Times are hard for the unemployed.* ○ *Times have changed* (ie things are different from how they used to be). **11** [U] (*music*) **(a)** a type of rhythm: *in 'waltz/'march time* ○ *beating time to the music.* **(b)** the rate at which a piece of music is to be played: *quick time.* See also DOWN TIME, EXTRA TIME, HALF-TIME, OPENING-TIME, PRIME TIME, SMALL-TIME, STANDARD TIME. **IDM (and) about 'time ('too)** (*infml*) and this is sth that should have happened some time ago: *I hear old Fred got promoted last week — and about time too, I'd say.* **ahead of 'time** earlier than expected. **ahead of one's 'time** having ideas that are too advanced for the period in which one lives. **all the 'time 1** during the whole of the time in question: *That letter I was searching for was in my pocket all the time* (ie while I was searching for it). **2** always: *You can't be a businessman all the time* (ie You have to develop other interests, etc). **at all 'times** always: *Our staff are available to help you at all times.* **at the best of times** ⇨ BEST³. **at 'one time** at some period in the past; formerly: *At one time I used to go skiing every winter.* **at the same time** ⇨ SAME¹. **at a 'time** in sequence; separately: *Don't try to do everything at once — take it a bit at a time.* ○ *Take the pills two at a time.* **at 'my, 'your, 'his, etc time of life** at my, your, his, etc age: *He shouldn't be playing squash at his time of life* (ie He is too old for it). **at 'times** sometimes: *I get very depressed at times.* **beat time** ⇨ BEAT¹. **behind the 'times** old-fashioned in one's ideas, methods, etc. **better luck next time** ⇨ BETTER¹. **bide one's time** ⇨ BIDE. **the big time** ⇨ BIG. **borrowed time** ⇨ BORROW. **buy time** ⇨ BUY. **do 'time** (*sl*) to serve a prison sentence: *He's done time for armed robbery.* **every 'time** whenever possible; whenever a choice can be made: *Some people enjoy mixing with the rich and famous, but not me — give me ordinary people every time.* **for old times' sake** ⇨ OLD. **for the time 'being** until some other arrangement is made: *You'll have your own office soon but for the time being you'll have to share one.* **from ₁time to 'time** now and then; occasionally. **gain time** ⇨ GAIN². **give sb a hard time** ⇨ HARD¹. **(in) 'half the time 1** (in) a much shorter time than expected: *If you'd given the job to me I could have done it in half the time.* **2** a considerable time; too long a time: *I'm not surprised he didn't finish the test: he spent half the time looking out of the window.* **have an easy time** ⇨ EASY¹. **have a hard, rough, tough, etc time (of it)** to experience a period of difficulty, unhappiness, etc; to be treated unfairly: *She had a hard time after her husband died.* **have a hard time doing sth** ⇨ HARD¹. **have/give sb a high old time** ⇨ HIGH¹. **have a lot of time for sb/ sth** (*infml*) to be enthusiastic about or interested in sb/sth. **have no time for sb/sth** to be unable or unwilling to spend time on sb/sth; to dislike sb/sth: *I've no time for lazy people/laziness.* **have a thin time** ⇨ THIN. **have the ₁time of one's 'life** (*infml*) to be exceptionally happy or excited: *The children had the time of their lives at the circus.* **have time on one's 'hands / time to 'kill** (*infml*) to have nothing to do. **have a whale of a time** ⇨ WHALE.

(it is) ˌhigh/aˌbout ˈtime the time is past when sth should have happened or been done: *It's high time you stopped fooling around and started looking for a job.* ○ *Isn't it about time we were going?* **in the course of time** ▷ COURSE¹. **in the fullness of time** ▷ FULLNESS. **in good time** early: *There wasn't much traffic so we got there in very good time.* **(all) in good ˈtime** after a reasonable or appropriate space of time, but not immediately: *'Can we have lunch now — I'm hungry.' 'All in good time.'* **in the nick of time** ▷ NICK¹. **in (less than) ˈno time** very quickly. **in one's own good ˈtime** at the time or rate that one decides oneself: *There's no point getting impatient with her; she'll finish the job in her own good time.* **in one's own sweet time/way** ▷ SWEET¹. **in one's own time** in one's free time; outside working hours. **in one's ˈtime** at a previous period or on a previous occasion in one's life: *I've seen some slow workers in my time but this group are the slowest by far.* **in ˈtime** sooner or later; eventually: *You'll learn how to do it in time.* **in time (for sth / to do sth)** not late: *Will I be in time for the train/to catch the train?* **in / out of ˈtime** *(music)* in/not in the correct time¹(11): *tapping one's fingers in time to/with the music.* **it's all, etc a matter of time** ▷ MATTER¹. **keep ˈtime 1** (of a clock or watch) to show the correct time: *My watch always keeps excellent time.* **2** to sing or dance in time¹(11). **keep up, move, etc with the ˈtimes** to change one's attitudes, behaviour, etc according to what is now usual. **kill time** ▷ KILL. **long time no see** ▷ LONG¹. **make good, etc ˈtime** to complete a journey quickly: *We made excellent time and reached our destination by midday.* **make up for lost time** ▷ LOST². **ˈmany's the time (that); ˈmany a time** many times; frequently: *Many's the time (that) I've visited Rome.* ○ *I've visited Rome many a time.* **mark time** ▷ MARK². **ˌnine times out of ˈten; ˌninety-nine times out of a ˈhundred** almost always. **(there is) no time like the ˈpresent** *(saying)* now is the best time to do sth. **once upon a time** ▷ ONCE. **on ˈtime** neither late nor early; happening at the correct time: *The train arrived (right/bang) on time.* **pass the time of day** ▷ PASS¹. **play for ˈtime** to try to gain time by delaying. **quite some time** ▷ QUITE. **a sign of the times** ▷ SIGN¹. **a stitch in time** ▷ STITCH. **take one's ˈtime (over sth / to do sth / doing sth) 1** to use as much time as one needs, without hurrying: *Take your time — there's no rush.* **2** *(ironic)* to be late or too slow: *You certainly took your time getting here!* **tell time; tell the time** ▷ TELL. **ˌtime after ˈtime; ˌtime and (time) aˈgain; ˌtimes without ˈnumber** on many occasions; repeatedly. **time and tide wait for ˈno man** *(saying)* no one can delay the passing of time, so one should not leave until later a favourable opportunity to do sth. **time hangs ˈheavy (on one's ˈhands)** time passes too slowly, esp because one has nothing to do. **time is on sb's ˈside** sb can afford to wait before doing or achieving sth: *Although she failed the exam she has time on her side: she'll still be young enough to take it again next year.* **the time is ˈripe for sth/sb to do sth** it is the right moment for (doing) sth. **the time of ˈday** the hour as shown by a clock. **time ˈwas (when) ...** there has been a time when...: *Time was you could get a good three-course meal for less than a pound.* **time (alone) will ˈtell, etc** it will become obvious with the passing of time: *Time will show which of us is right.* **watch the time** ▷ WATCH¹. **work, etc against ˈtime** to work, etc as fast as possible so as to finish by a specified time.

■ **ˌtime-and-ˈmotion** *adj* [attrib] concerned with measuring the efficiency of industrial and other operations: *a time-and-motion study.*
ˈtime bomb *n* a bomb that can be set to explode after a certain period of time: *(fig) Next year's trial*

of the former minister is a political time-bomb for the government.
ˈtime capsule *n* a container holding objects typical of the present time, buried for discovery in the future.
ˈtime-consuming *adj* taking or needing much time: *Some of the more time-consuming jobs can now be done by machines.*
ˈtime frame *n* a period of time used or available for sth: *We expect to complete the project within a fairly short time frame.*
ˈtime-honoured *(US* -honored*) adj* (esp of a custom, etc) respected because of long tradition.
ˈtime-lag *n* an interval of time between two connected events: *the time-lag between a flash of lightning and the thunder.*
ˈtime-lapse *adj* [attrib] *(techn)* (of photography) using individual pictures taken at long intervals to film a process. When these are shown at normal speed, the action seems much faster.
ˈtime-limit *n* a limit of time within or by which sth must be done: *set a time-limit for the completion of a job.*
ˌtime ˈout *n (US)* a short period of rest from activity, esp during a game.
ˈtime-scale *n* a period of time in which a sequence of events takes place; the successive stages of a process, an operation, etc: *What's the time-scale on this job?*
ˈtime-server *n (derog)* a person who regularly changes his opinions to those which are in fashion or held by people in power, esp for personal advantage. **ˈtime-serving** *adj, n* [U]: *time-serving bureaucrats.*
ˈtime-share *n* [U] an arrangement in which several people have joint ownership of a holiday home and

---

1 Expressing time

When referring to days, weeks, etc in the past, present and future the following expressions are used, speaking from a point of view in the present.

	past	present	future
morning afternoon evening	yesterday morning, etc	this morning, etc	tomorrow morning, etc
night	last night	tonight	tomorrow night
day	yesterday	today	tomorrow
week	last week	this week	next week
month	last month	this month	next month
year	last year	this year	next year

2 Prepositions of time

in (the)	
parts of the day (not night)	*in the morning(s), etc*
months	*in February*
seasons	*in (the) summer*
years	*in 1995*
decades	*in the 1920s*
centuries	*in the 20th century*

on (the)	
days of the week	*on Saturday(s)*
dates	*on (the) 20th (of) May*
specific days	*on Good Friday*
	on New Year's Day
	on my birthday
	on the following day

at (the)	
clock time	*at 5 o'clock*
	at 7.45 pm
night	*at night*
holiday periods	*at Christmas*
	at the weekend

---

agree to use it each at different times of the year: *time-share apartments.*

time sheet *n* a piece of paper, etc on which the number of hours a person works are recorded.

time signal *n* a sound or sounds indicating the exact time of day.

time signature *n* (*music*) a sign at the start of a piece of music, usu in the form of numbers, showing the number of beats in each bar. ⇨ picture at MUSIC.

time-span *n* a period of time.

time switch *n* a switch that can be set to operate automatically at a certain time: *The central heating is on a time-switch.*

time warp *n* (in science fiction) an imaginary situation in which people or things belonging to one point in time can be moved to another, so that eg the past or the future becomes the present.

time-worn *adj* worn or damaged by age: *a time-worn expression* (ie one that is used too often).

time zone *n* a region of the Earth where a common standard time is used: *After the long flight it took us a while to adjust to the new time zone.*

time² /taɪm/ *v* **1** to choose the time or moment for sth; to arrange the time of sth: [Vnadv] *You've timed your trip well — the weather's at its best.* ○ *His remark was well/badly timed* (ie made at the right/wrong moment). [Vnpr] *Kick-off is timed for 2.30.* [Vn.*to* inf esp passive]: *The train is timed to connect with the ferry.* ○ *The bomb was timed to explode during the rush hour.* **2** (*sport*) to make a stroke or strike the ball at a certain moment: [Vnadv] *He timed that shot beautifully.* [also Vn]. **3** to measure the time taken by a process or an activity, or by a person doing it: [Vn] *Please will you time my egg for me — I like it boiled for 4½ minutes.* [Vn,V.*wh*] *Time me while I do/Time how long it takes me to do two lengths of the pool.* [Vnpr] *The winner was timed at 4 minutes 3.56 seconds.*

▸ **timer** *n* (often in compounds) a person or device that times sth: *an oven timer.* See also EGG-TIMER, OLD-TIMER.

timing *n* **1** [U] (**a**) the choosing or controlling of the time when an action or event occurs: *a 'timing device* ○ *The timing of the announcement was rather unexpected.* (**b**) skill in this, as a way of achieving the desired result: *an actor with brilliant comic timing* (ie one who knows the funniest moment to deliver a line) ○ *He's not playing his shots well — his timing is faulty.* ○ *Split-second timing is essential for the plan to succeed.* **2** [C] a particular point or period of time when sth occurs: *Please check your flight timings carefully.*

timekeeper /'taɪmkiːpə(r)/ *n* a person or device that records time spent doing sth, esp at work.

timeless /'taɪmləs/ *adj* (*fml or rhet*) **1** not appearing to be affected by the passing of time: *her timeless beauty* ○ *His work has a timeless quality.* **2** existing throughout all time; permanent: *Certain truths are timeless.* ▸ **timelessly** *adv.* **timelessness** *n* [U].

timely /'taɪmli/ *adj* occurring at just the right time: *I was grateful for your timely intervention.* ○ *This has been a timely reminder of the importance of the alliance.* ▸ **timeliness** *n* [U].

timepiece /'taɪmpiːs/ *n* (*fml*) a clock or watch.

times /taɪmz/ *prep* multiplied by: *Five times two is/equals ten* (ie 5 × 2 = 10). ▸ **times** *n* [pl] (used in comparisons, to show how much more, better, easier, etc sth is than sth else): *This book is three times as long as/three times longer than/three times the length of that one.* ○ (*infml*) *This method is a hundred times better.*

timetable /'taɪmteɪbl/ (also *esp US* **schedule**) *n* a list showing the time at which certain events will take place: *a school timetable* (ie showing the time of each class) ○ *a train/bus/ferry timetable* ○ *the govern-ment's timetable for the reforms* ○ *I've got a very busy timetable this week* (ie a lot of appointments, etc).

▸ **timetable** *v* to plan sth according to a timetable: [Vnpr] *the classes timetabled for this evening* [also Vn]. **timetabling** *n* [U].

timid /'tɪmɪd/ *adj* easily frightened; shy: *as timid as a rabbit.* ▸ **timidity** /tɪ'mɪdəti/ *n* [U]. **timidly** *adv.*

timorous /'tɪmərəs/ *adj* (*fml*) nervous and easily frightened. ▸ **timorously** *adv.* **timorousness** *n* [U].

timpani /'tɪmpəni/ *n* [sing or pl *v*] a set of large drums in an ORCHESTRA. See also KETTLEDRUM.

▸ **timpanist** /'tɪmpənɪst/ *n* a person who plays the timpani.

tin /tɪn/ *n* **1** [U] (*symb* **Sn**) a chemical element. Tin is a soft white metal often combined with other metals or applied as a protective covering for iron and steel: *a tin box/roof/tray* ○ *a 'tin mine.* ⇨ App 7. **2** (also **tin can**, *esp US* **can**) [C] (**a**) a metal container in which food is sealed to preserve it: *open a tin of beans.* ⇨ picture at CAN. (**b**) the contents of this: *He ate a whole tin of stew.* (also *esp US* **can**) [C] (**a**) a metal container with a lid for holding liquids such as paint, glue, etc. (**b**) the contents of this. **4** [C] a metal container for keeping or cooking food in: *a 'biscuit tin* ○ *a 'roasting tin.*

▸ **tin** *v* (**-nn-**) (also *esp US* **can**) (esp passive) to seal food in a tin(2a) to preserve it: [Vn] *tinned sardines/peas/peaches.*

tinny *adj* (*derog*) **1** (of metal objects) not strong or solid: *a cheap tinny radio.* **2** having a thin metallic sound: *a tinny piano.*

■ **,tin 'can** *n* = TIN 2.

,tin 'foil *n* [U] very thin metal sheets used for wrapping and packing things: *a roll of tin foil.* Compare SILVER PAPER.

,tin 'hat *n* (*infml*) a soldier's steel HELMET.

'tin-opener (*Brit* also **'can-opener**) *n* a device or tool for opening tins of food.

'tin plate *n* [U] iron or steel sheets coated with tin.

'tin-tack *n* a short nail made of iron coated with tin.

,tin 'whistle (also **penny whistle**) *n* a simple musical instrument, played by blowing, with six holes for the different notes.

tincture /'tɪŋktʃə(r)/ *n* [C,U] ~ (**of** sth) (*techn*) a drug dissolved in alcohol for use as a medicine: *a/some tincture of iodine/quinine.*

tinder /'tɪndə(r)/ *n* [U] any dry substance that burns easily, eg wood.

■ **'tinder-box** *n* (formerly) a box containing tinder with a FLINT(2) and steel, used for lighting a fire: (*fig*) *There is much racial tension and the whole area is a tinder-box* (ie violence could easily break out).

tine /taɪn/ *n* (*techn*) any of the points or sharp parts of eg a fork, barbed wire (BARB) or a deer's ANTLER.

ting /tɪŋ/ *n* a sharp clear ringing sound: *the ting of a bicycle bell.* Compare TINKLE 1.

■ **ting-a-ling** /,tɪŋ ə 'lɪŋ/ *adv* making a series of tings: *The bell went ting-a-ling.*

tinge /tɪndʒ/ *v* ~ sth (**with** sth) (usu passive) **1** to add a small amount of colour to sth: [Vnpr] *hair tinged with grey* [also Vn]. **2** to add a small amount of a particular quality to sth: [Vnpr] *admiration tinged with envy* [also Vn].

▸ **tinge** *n* (esp *sing*) ~ (**of** sth) a slight colouring or trace: *blue with a tinge of green* ○ *There was a tinge of melancholy in her voice.*

tingle /'tɪŋgl/ *v* ~ (**with** sth) **1** (of a person or part of the body) to have a slight prickly or stinging feeling: [Vpr] *fingers tingling with cold* [V] *The slap she gave him made his cheek tingle.* ○ *a tingling sensation.* **2** to be affected or excited by an emotion: [Vpr] *tingling with excitement/indignation* [also V].

▸ **tingle** *n* (usu *sing*) a tingling feeling: *have a tingle in one's fingertips* ○ *feel a tingle of anticipation/curiosity.*

tinker /'tɪŋkə(r)/ n (**a**) a person belonging to a group with no fixed home that travels from place to place, often in caravans (CARAVAN 1): *a tinker woman.* (**b**) (esp formerly) a person travelling from place to place repairing pans, kettles (KETTLE), etc.
▶ **tinker** v ~ (**with sth**) to try to repair or improve sth in a casual way, often to no useful effect: [Vpr] *He likes tinkering with old radios.* [Vpr, Vp] *Who's been tinkering (around) with the wiring?* [Vpr] (*fig*) *Tinkering with the tax system won't solve the country's economic problems.* [also V].

tinkle /'tɪŋkl/ n (usu *sing*) **1** (also **tinkling** [sing, U]) a series of short, soft or light ringing sounds: *the tinkle of a small bell/of breaking glass/of ice being stirred in a drink.* **2** (*Brit infml*) a telephone call: *Give me a tinkle when you get home.*
▶ **tinkle** v to make a tinkle: [V] *the sound of tinkling glasses* ○ *tinkling laughter.*

tinny ⇨ TIN.

tin-pan alley /ˌtɪn pæn 'æli/ n [sing without a or the] (*dated infml sometimes derog*) people who compose, perform and publish popular music and the type of life they live: *He's been in tin-pan alley for twenty years.*

tinpot /'tɪnpɒt/ adj [attrib] (*derog*) inferior or worthless: *a tinpot little dictator.*

tinsel /'tɪnsl/ n [U] a bright shiny metallic substance used in strips or threads as a decoration: *decorate a Christmas tree with tinsel.*

tinseltown /'tɪnsltaʊn/ n (*infml*) Hollywood in California, the centre of the US film industry.

tint /tɪnt/ n **1** a shade or variety of a colour: *tints of green in the sky at dawn* ○ *white with a bluish tint.* **2(a)** a weak dye for colouring the hair. (**b**) the act or result of colouring the hair in this way: *She had a tint.*
▶ **tint** v (esp passive) to apply or give a tint to sth; to colour sth slightly: [Vn] *tinted glass/glasses* (ie made slightly darker) ○ *blue-tinted hair.*

tiny /'taɪni/ adj (**-ier, -iest**) very small: *a tiny baby/ cottage* ○ *Only a tiny minority hold such extreme views.*

-tion ⇨ -ION.

tip¹ /tɪp/ n **1(a)** the pointed or thin end of sth: *the tips of one's fingers/toes* ○ *the tip of one's nose* ○ *the tip of an animal's tail/a bird's wing* ○ *walk to the northern tip of the island.* See also FINGERTIP. (**b**) a small part or piece fitted to the end of sth: *the tip of an arrow/a billiard cue* ○ *a walking-stick with a rubber tip.* See also FELT-TIP PEN, FILTER TIP. **IDM on the tip of one's 'tongue** (of eg a word) almost or just about to be remembered: *His name's on the tip of my tongue, but I just can't think of it.* **the tip of the 'iceberg** the small noticeable part of a much larger situation or problem, that remains hidden: *Over 100 burglaries are reported every month, and that's just the tip of the iceberg* (ie many more occur but are not reported).
▶ **tip** v (**-pp-**) ~ **sth (with sth)** (usu passive) to fit a tip to sth; to cover or treat the tip of sth with sth: [Vnpr] *The table-legs were tipped with rubber.* ○ *a diamond-tipped drill* ○ *The tribes tip their spears with poison.* [also Vn].

tip² /tɪp/ v (**-pp-**) **1(a)** ~ **sth (up/over)** to make sth fall or turn over by putting too much weight or pressure on one side or end of it: [Vnp] *tip up a glass* ○ *She tipped over a chair in her rush to leave.* ○ *Careful! You'll tip the boat over* (ie turn it upside down). [Vnpr] (*fig*) *These tax increases could tip the economy into recession.* (**b**) ~ (**up/over**) to fall in this way: [Vp] *The glass tipped over and crashed to the floor.* [also V, Vpr]. **2(a)** to place sth at an angle to its normal position: [Vnp] *Tip the box up* (ie upside down) *and empty it.* ○ *He tipped his hat down over his forehead.* [also Vnadv, Vnpr, Vn]. (**b**) to move at an angle to the normal position: [Vadv] *The front seat*

tips forward/back. [also V, Vpr, Vp]. **3** (*Brit*) to make things in a container come out by holding or turning it at an angle: [Vn, V] *No rubbish to be tipped here/No tipping* (eg as a notice). [Vnpr] *He tipped the dirty water down the drain.* ○ *The train stopped abruptly, nearly tipping me out of my seat.* [also Vnp]. **4(a)** to touch or strike sth lightly, esp at the edge: [Vn] *The ball just tipped (the edge of) his racket.* (**b**) to make sth move in the specified direction by doing this: [Vnpr] *The goalkeeper tipped the ball over the bar.* [also Vnp]. **IDM tip the 'balance/ 'scale** to be the deciding factor for or against sth/ sb: *Her greater experience tipped the balance in her favour and she got the job.*
▶ **tip** n (*Brit*) **1** a place where rubbish may be left: *the municipal 'refuse tip* ○ *take a broken old refrigerator to the tip.* Compare DUMP n 1. **2** (*infml*) a dirty or untidy place: *Their house is an absolute tip.*
■ **'tipper lorry** (also **'tipper truck**) (*Brit*) (US **'dump truck**) n a lorry with a large container at the back which can be raised at one end to tip out the contents.

tip³ /tɪp/ n **1** a small sum of money given to sb, eg a waiter (WAIT²), as a personal reward for their services: *He left a tip under his plate.* **2(a)** a small but useful piece of practical advice: *a handy tip for removing grass stains from clothing* ○ *useful tips on how to prepare for the exam.* (**b**) a private or expert piece of advice about what is likely to happen eg in a horse-race (HORSE) or on the stock market (STOCK¹): *a hot* (ie very good) *tip for the Derby.*
▶ **tip** v (**-pp-**) **1** to give sb a tip³(1): [Vnn] *tip the taxi-driver 50p* [also Vn]. **2** ~ **sb/sth** (**as sth/to do sth**) to give a tip³(2b) about sth/sb; to predict sth: [Vn] *tip the winner* (ie name the winner of a race or contest before it takes place) [Vn-n, V.n to inf] *He has been widely tipped as the President's successor/to succeed the President.* **IDM tip sb the 'wink** (*Brit infml*) to give sb private information; to warn sb secretly: *I don't want him to know I'm here — please tip me the wink when he's gone.* **PHRV ,tip sb 'off** (*infml*) to give sb advance information about sth, eg a crime: *He tipped off the police about the robbery.*
■ **'tip-off** n advance information about sth, eg a crime: *Acting on a tip-off (from an informant), the police raided the gang's hide-out.*

tippet /'tɪpɪt/ n (**a**) a long piece of fur, etc worn by a woman round the neck and shoulders, with the ends hanging down in front. (**b**) a similar article of clothing worn by judges, clergy, etc.

tipple /'tɪpl/ n (usu *sing*) (*infml*) an alcoholic drink: *indulging in his favourite tipple.*
▶ **tipple** v (*infml*) [V, Vn] to drink alcohol, esp frequently in small amounts. **tippler** /'tɪplə(r)/ n.

tipster /'tɪpstə(r)/ n a person, eg a journalist, who gives advice about the horses, teams, etc likely to win a particular race or contest so that people can bet on them.

tipsy /'tɪpsi/ adj (*infml*) slightly drunk.

tiptoe /'tɪptəʊ/ n **IDM on 'tiptoe** on the tips of one's toes; with one's heels raised off the ground: *stand on tiptoe to see over the crowd* ○ *walk on tiptoe so as not to wake the baby.*
▶ **tiptoe** v to walk quietly and carefully on tiptoe: [Vpr, Vp] *She tiptoed (across) to the bed where Clare lay asleep.* [also V]. ⇨ note at PROWL.

tiptop /ˌtɪp'tɒp/ adj (*infml*) of the highest quality; excellent: *The course is in ˌtiptop conˈdition for the tournament.*

TIR /ˌti: aɪ 'ɑ:(r)/ abbr (esp on lorries in Europe) international road transport (French *Transport International Routier*).

tirade /taɪ'reɪd; US 'taɪreɪd/ n ~ (**against sb/sth**) a long angry speech of criticism or accusation: *He launched into a long tirade against the government.*

tire¹ /'taɪə(r)/ v (**a**) to lose energy; to become in need of sleep or rest: [V] *She's got so much energy — she never seems to tire.* ○ *Some of the British runners are beginning to tire.* (**b**) to make sb feel this way: [Vn] *The long walk tired me.* **PHRV** '**tire of (doing) sth** to lose interest in sth: *Children soon tire of new toys.* ○ (*derog*) *He never tires of telling me how much he earns.* ,**tire sb/oneself** '**out** to tire sb/oneself greatly or too much: *Don't run too fast; you'll tire yourself out.* ○ *I'm always tired out by the time I get home from work.*

▶ **tired** /ˈtaɪəd/ *adj* **1** [esp pred] feeling that one would like to sleep or rest: *feel/look tired* ○ *get/grow tired* ○ *I'm tired; I think I'll go to bed.* ○ *have tired eyes/feet.* **2** [pred] ~ **of sb/sth;** ~ **of doing sth** having lost interest in sb/sth; bored with sb/sth: *I'm sick and tired of (listening to) your criticisms.* ○ *You soon get tired of eating the same thing every day.* **3** (*derog*) boring, esp from being too familiar or well known: *The film had a rather tired plot.* ○ *see the same tired old faces at every party.* **tiredness** *n* [U].

tireless /ˈtaɪələs/ *adj* not tiring easily; showing a lot of energy: *a tireless campaigner* ○ *tireless work* ○ *He was tireless in his efforts on our behalf.* **tirelessly** *adv*: *work tirelessly for peace.*

tiresome /ˈtaɪəsəm/ *adj* causing trouble; annoying: *Selling your house can be a tiresome business.* ○ *The children were being rather tiresome.* **tiresomely** *adv*.

tiring /ˈtaɪərɪŋ/ *adj* making one feel tired, esp because of the effort involved: *a tiring journey/day* ○ *The work is very tiring.*

tire² (*US*) = TYRE. ➪ picture at BICYCLE, CAR.

'**tis** /tɪz/ *short form* (*arch*) it is.

tissue /ˈtɪʃuː; *Brit also* ˈtɪsjuː, ˈtɪʃjuː/ *n* **1** [U,C] any of the masses of cells of particular types of which animals or plants are made: *muscle/nerve/brain/scar tissue* ○ *the organs and tissues that make up the human body.* **2** [C] a piece of soft paper that absorbs liquids and is thrown away after use, esp one used as a HANDKERCHIEF: *a box of tissues.* **3** (also '**tissue-paper**) [U] very thin soft paper used for wrapping and packing things. **4** [C usu *sing*] ~ (**of sth**) a number of parts, facts or ideas connected closely together, often in a complex way: *His story is a tissue of lies.*

tit¹ /tɪt/ *n* a small bird, often with a dark top to the head. There are several types of tit. See also BLUE TIT.

tit² /tɪt/ *n* **IDM** ,**tit for** '**tat** a situation in which eg a blow, an injury or an insult is given in return for one received: *He hit me so I hit him back — it was tit for tat.* ○ *a series of tit-for-tat killings by rival gangs.*

tit³ /tɪt/ *n* (△ *sl*) (**a**) (esp *pl*) a woman's breast. (**b**) = NIPPLE(1).

Titan (also **titan**) /ˈtaɪtn/ *n* a person of great size, strength, intelligence or importance.

▶ **titanic** /taɪˈtænɪk/ *adj* very great or intense: *The two of them are locked in a titanic struggle for control of the company.*

titanium /tɪˈteɪniəm/ *n* [U] (*symb* Ti) a chemical element. Titanium is a grey metal used in making various strong light materials. ➪ App 7.

titbit /ˈtɪtbɪt/ (*US* **tidbit** /ˈtɪdbɪt/) *n* **1** a specially attractive bit of food: *She always keeps some titbits to give to her cat.* **2** ~ (**of sth**) a small but interesting piece of news or gossip: *titbits of information/scandal.*

tithe /taɪð/ *n* (formerly) one tenth of the annual produce of a farm, paid as a tax esp to support the church.

■ '**tithe barn** *n* a BARN(1) built to store tithes in.

titillate /ˈtɪtɪleɪt/ *v* (*often derog*) to stimulate or excite sb, esp sexually: [V] *titillating pictures of half-naked women* [Vn] *The book has no artistic merit — its sole aim is to titillate the reader.* ▶ **titillation** /ˌtɪtɪˈleɪʃn/ *n* [U].

title /ˈtaɪtl/ *n* **1** [C] the name of a book, poem, picture, etc: *The theme of the poem is stated in the title.* ○ *the title track from their latest CD* (ie the song with the same title as the disc) ○ *She has sung the title role in 'Carmen'* (ie the role of Carmen in that opera). **2** [C] a particular published work, eg a book or newspaper, considered as all the copies of that work: *The company publishes about 20 new titles each year.* **3** [C] (**a**) a word or phrase, often used together with a person's name, showing eg her or his social rank or official position: *The President's official title is 'Commander in Chief'.* ○ *He inherited the title of Duke from his father.* ○ *She has a title* (ie is of noble birth). (**b**) a word or short form, eg *Mr, Mrs* or *Doctor,* used before a person's name, and by which he or she prefers or has a right to be addressed: *State your name and title.* **4** [C] (*sport*) the official position of being the best player or team by having beaten all the others: *win the world heavyweight/the British 800-metres title* ○ *a '*title fight *(eg in boxing).* **5** [U,C] ~ (**to sth / to do sth**) (*law*) a right or claim, esp to the ownership of property: *disputing the country's title to govern the islands.*

▶ **title** *v* (usu passive) to give a title(1) to sth: [Vn-n] *a novel/film intriguingly titled 'The Man Who Died Twice'* [also Vnadv]. Compare ENTITLE 1.

titled *adj* having a title(3a); of noble birth: *a titled lady.*

■ '**title-deed** *n* a legal document proving sb's right to a property.

'**title-holder** *n* (*sport*) a person or team that has defeated all other competitors in a contest: *the current Olympic title-holder.*

'**title-page** *n* a page at the front of a book giving the title and the author's name.

titter /ˈtɪtə(r)/ *v* to give a short nervous laugh: [V] *There was an embarrassing pause on stage and the audience began to titter.* [also Vpr, V.speech]. ▶ **titter** *n*: *titters of mirth.* ➪ note at GIGGLE.

tittle-tattle /ˈtɪtl tætl/ *n* [U] silly or worthless talk; gossip: *The rumours were no more than idle tittle-tattle.*

titular /ˈtɪtjələ(r); *US* -tʃə-/ *adj* [attrib] (*fml*) having a certain title(3a), position or status but no real authority: *the titular Head of State.*

tizzy /ˈtɪzi/ (also **tizz** /tɪz/) *n* (usu *sing*) (*infml*) a state of nervous excitement or confusion: *be in/get in(to) a tizzy .*

T-junction ➪ T.

TNT /ˌti: en ˈti:/ *abbr* trinitrotoluene (a powerful explosive).

to¹ /*before consonants* tə; *before vowels* tu; *strong form* tuː/ *prep* For the special uses of **to** in phrasal verbs, look at the verb entries. For example, the meaning of **see to sth** is given in the phrasal verb section of the entry for **see¹**. **1(a)** in the direction of sth; towards sth: *walk to the office* ○ *fall to the ground* ○ *on the way to the station* ○ *point to sth* ○ *hold sth (up) to the light to examine it* ○ *turn to the left/right* ○ *travelling from town to town/place to place* ○ *go to Majorca for one's holidays* ○ *the next train to Baltimore* ○ *He was taken to hospital for treatment.* (**b**) ~ **the sth** (**of sth**) situated in a specified direction from sth: *the mountains to the north/east of here* ○ *Pisa lies to the west (of Florence).* ○ *cars parked at an angle to the pavement.* **2** towards a condition, state or quality; reaching a particular state: *inspire sb to action* ○ *bring/reduce/move sb to tears* (ie make sb cry) ○ *rise to power* ○ *a move to the left* (ie in politics) ○ *He tore the letter to pieces.* ○ *She sang her baby to sleep.* ○ *Wait until the traffic lights change from red to green.* **3** as far as sth; reaching sth: *The garden extends to the river bank.* ○ *Her dress reached down to her ankles.* ○ *soaked to the skin* ○ *cooked to perfection.* **4** (indicating the end of a range): *count (from 1) to 10* ○ *I like all kinds of music from opera to reggae.* ○ *The*

American runner went from first to last on the final lap. **5(a)** until and including a moment in time: *from Monday to Friday* ○ *from morning to night* ○ *I watched the programme from beginning to end.* ○ *The old King's servant was faithful to the end/last.* **(b)** before the start of sth: *How long is it to lunch?* ○ *only 8 more days to my birthday.* **6** (used in telling the time) before an exact hour on the clock: *ten (minutes) to two* ○ *It's (a) quarter to six.* Compare PAST² 1. **7** (used to introduce the indirect object of certain verbs or phrases): *He gave it to his sister.* ○ *(fml) To whom did she address the letter?* ○ *(infml) Who did she address the letter to?* ○ *make a contribution to the fund* ○ *I'll explain to you where everything goes.* ○ *He shouted to his friend to come back.* **8** of or belonging to sth/sb; for sth/sb: *the key to the door* ○ *secretary to the managing director* ○ *the Japanese ambassador to France* ○ *the words to a tune* ○ *the solution to a problem.* **9** directed towards or concerning sth/sb: *a threat to world peace* ○ *his claim to the throne* ○ *Her speech contained a reference to Abraham Lincoln.* **10** (indicating a relationship with sb): *She's married/engaged to an Italian.* ○ *She played Ophelia to Laurence Olivier's Hamlet.* **11** (used to introduce the second element of a comparison or ratio): *I prefer walking to climbing.* ○ *We won by six goals to three.* ○ *This wine is inferior/superior to the wine we bought last week.* ○ *Compared to me, he's rich.* ○ *odds of 100 to 1.* **12** making a certain value or quantity: *There are 100 pence to the pound* (ie £1 = 100p). ○ *There are 2.54 centimetres to the inch.* **13** (indicating a rate): *This car does 30 miles to the gallon.* ○ *get 9 francs to the pound.* Compare PER. **14** (indicating a possible range or an appropriate value): *20 to 30 years of age* ○ *3 to 4 centimetres long.* **15** in honour of sb/sth: *drink to sb/to sb's health* ○ *a monument to (the memory of) the soldiers who died in the war.* **16** close enough to be touching sb/sth: *dance cheek to cheek* ○ *Cars were bumper to bumper on the motorway.* **17** while sth else is happening or being done: *sing to the accompaniment of a guitar* ○ *She left the stage to prolonged applause.* **18** (used after *vs* of motion, eg *come, go, rush*) with the intention of giving sth: *come to our aid/assistance/rescue.* **19** (used after words describing feelings) towards sb/sth: *The villagers are hostile to strangers.* ○ *She's devoted to her family.* **20** (indicating sb's reaction to sth) causing sth: *To my surprise/delight/dismay the Labour Party won the election.* ○ *To my embarrassment, I forgot his birthday.* **21** (used esp after *vs* of perception, eg *seem, appear, feel, look, smell*) in the opinion of sb; from sb's point of view: *It feels like velvet to me.* ○ *It sounded like crying to me.* ○ *To the police, the burglary had the look of a professional job.* **22** satisfying sb/sth: *Her new hairstyle isn't really to my liking.*

to² /*before consonants* tə; *before vowels* tu; *strong form* tuː/ (often used immediately before the basic form of a *v* in the infinitive. The following are some of the main uses of *to* + the infinitive) **1** (used as the object of many *vs*, esp those labelled in this dictionary as V.*to* inf, V.n.*to* inf, Vn.*to* inf, Vpr.*to* inf): *He wants to go.* ○ *We had hoped to finish by four o'clock.* ○ *They like us to arrive on time.* ○ *She persuaded him to tell the truth.* ○ *He shouted to us to wait for him.* **2** (used as the subject or complement of a clause): *To be able to speak openly and freely again was wonderful.* ○ *His aim is to become the next president.* **3** (used after many *ns* and *adjs*, indicated in the entries for these as ~ **to do sth**): *the determination to succeed* ○ *the desire/wish to study medicine* ○ *the right to reply* ○ *be happy to see sb* ○ *be unwilling to continue* ○ *be ready to leave.* **4** (expressing purpose or intention): *They came (in order) to wish me luck.* ○ *She's working hard to earn money for their holiday.* ○ *Our products are made to last.* **5** (used to indicate that one action immediately follows or leads to another): *I reached*

the station (only) to discover that my train had already left. ○ *She looked through the window to see her husband asleep in his chair.* **6** (used after *how, what, where, who,* etc): *I don't know what to say.* ○ *Can you tell me where to find a bank?* **7** (used after *too* + *adj/adv* to explain the comment): *too hot to go out* ○ *driving too fast to be able to stop in time.* **8** (*fml*) (used after the present and past simple of *be* to indicate obligation): *You are not to talk during the exam.* ○ *She was to be here at 8.30 but she didn't arrive.* **9** (used alone to avoid repeating a *v* used earlier in the sentence): *I'd like to play chess but I don't know how to* (ie play). ○ *I told him to buy some milk but he forgot to* (ie buy some milk).

to³ /tuː/ *adv part* (usu of a door) in or into a closed position; shut: *Push the door to.* For the special uses of **to** in phrasal verbs, look at the verb entries. For example, the meaning of **set to** is given in the phrasal verb section of the entry for **set¹**. **IDM** ˌ**to and** ˈ**fro** backwards and forwards: *walking to and fro* ○ *journeys to and fro between London and Paris.*

toad /təʊd/ *n* **1** an animal like a frog that lives on land but breeds in water. ⟹ picture at FROG. **2** (used as an insult): *You repulsive little toad!*
■ ˌ**toad-in-the-**ˈ**hole** *n* [U] (*Brit*) a dish consisting of sausages (SAUSAGE) baked in BATTER².

toadstool /ˈtəʊdstuːl/ *n* a small FUNGUS(1) shaped like an UMBRELLA(1). Many types of toadstool are poisonous. ⟹ picture at FUNGUS. Compare MUSHROOM.

toady /ˈtəʊdi/ *n* (*derog*) a person who treats sb more important or of higher social status with excessive respect in the hope of personal gain or advantage.
▶ **toady** *v* (*pt, pp* **toadied**) ~ (**to sb**) (*derog*) to behave like a toady: [Vpr] *toadying to the boss* [also V].

toast¹ /təʊst/ *n* [U] bread sliced (SLICE *v* 1) and made brown and crisp by placing it close to direct heat, eg under a GRILL(1a): *make some toast for breakfast* ○ *a poached egg on toast* ○ *two slices/rounds of (buttered) toast.* **IDM** **have sb on** ˈ**toast** (*Brit infml*) to have sb completely in one's power. **warm as toast** ⟹ WARM¹.
▶ **toast** *v* **(a)** to make sth brown and crisp by heating it: [Vn] *a toasted (cheese) sandwich* ○ *toasted almonds.* **(b)** to warm oneself, one's feet, etc beside a fire: [Vn] *toast one's toes in front of the fire.* **toaster** *n* an electrical device for toasting slices of bread.
ˈ**toasting-fork** *n* a fork with a long handle used for toasting bread, etc in front of a fire.
toasty *adj* (*US*) warm and comfortable.
■ ˈ**toast rack** *n* (*Brit*) an object for holding slices of toast, ready for people to eat. ⟹ picture at RACK¹.

toast² /təʊst/ *v* to wish happiness or success to sb/sth by raising one's glass of wine, etc and drinking at the same time as other people: [Vn] *toast the bride and groom* ○ *We toasted the success of the new company.*
▶ **toast** *n* **1** an act of toasting sb/sth: *propose/drink a toast to sb* ○ *reply/respond to the toast.* **2** a person, etc toasted: *This performance will make him the toast of the whole club.* **IDM** **drink a toast to sb/sth** ⟹ DRINK².

toastmaster /ˈtəʊstmɑːstə(r); *US* -mæs-/ *n* a person who announces the toasts (TOAST² *n* 1) and introduces speakers at a formal meal.

tobacco /təˈbækəʊ/ *n* (*pl* **-os**) [C, U] the dried leaves of a plant that are used for making cigarettes, for smoking in a pipe or for chewing (CHEW): *tobacco smoke.*
▶ **tobacconist** /təˈbækənɪst/ *n* a shopkeeper who sells cigarettes, tobacco for pipes, etc.

toboggan /təˈbɒɡən/ *n* a vehicle for travelling on snow, esp down a slope. It consists of a flat seat attached to two narrow metal or wooden parts that slide easily on snow. Compare SLEDGE.

▶ **toboggan** v to use a toboggan: [V, Vpr] *go tobogganing (down the hill).*

toccata /tə'kɑːtə/ n (pl **toccatas**) (*music*) a composition, usu for ORGAN²(1) or HARPSICHORD, which includes difficult passages designed to demonstrate the player's skill.

tod /tɒd/ n **IDM** **on one's 'tod** (*Brit infml*) on one's own; alone: *I spent the whole evening sitting here on my tod.*

today /tə'deɪ/ n [U] **1** this day: *Today is her 100th birthday.* ○ *Have you seen today's paper?* ○ *We're leaving a week (from) today.* **2** the present period or time: *today's young people.*
▶ **today** adv **1** on this day. **2** at the present period; NOWADAYS: *Today such diseases are rare.*

toddle /'tɒdl/ v **1** (of a young child) to walk with short UNSTEADY(1) steps: *Has she started toddling yet?* [also Vp,Vpr]. **2** (*infml*) to walk or go: [Vp] *toddle round to see a friend* ○ *I think we should be toddling along/off (ie should leave) now.* [also Vpr].
▶ **toddler** /'tɒdlə(r)/ n a child who has only recently learnt to walk.

toddy /'tɒdi/ n [C, U] a drink made with strong alcohol, sugar, hot water and sometimes spices.

to-do /tə'duː/ n [sing] (*infml*) a fuss: *She made a great to-do about his forgetting her birthday.*

toe /təʊ/ n **1(a)** any of the five small parts at the front of the human foot: *I stubbed my toe on the chair-leg, and it's bleeding.* ⇨ picture at FOOT¹. **(b)** any of the similar parts of an animal's foot. **2** the part of a sock, shoe, etc that covers the toes. ⇨ picture at SHOE. **IDM** **dig one's heels/toes in** ⇨ DIG¹. **from head to foot/toe** ⇨ HEAD¹. **from top to toe** ⇨ TOP¹. **on one's 'toes** ready for action; alert; busy: *My boss regularly checks on what we're all doing, just to keep us on our toes.* **tread on sb's toes** ⇨ TREAD.
▶ **toe** v (*pt, pp* toed; *pres p* toeing) **IDM** **toe the (party) 'line** (*US* also **toe the 'mark**) to obey the orders and express the opinions of one's group or party; to conform.
■ **'toe-hold** n **1** a very small space on a cliff just big enough to put a foot on while climbing. **2** a point from which one can start to make progress in an activity: *Thanks to this contract, the firm has gained a toe-hold in the North American market.*

toecap /'təʊkæp/ n a strong metal or leather covering over the front part of a shoe or boot.

toenail /'təʊneɪl/ n the pale hard layer over the tip of each of one's toes. ⇨ picture at FOOT¹.

toff /tɒf/ n (*dated Brit infml*) a person who wears elegant clothes and appears to be rich or of a high social class.

toffee /'tɒfi/ US /'tɔːfi/ (*US* also **taffy** /'tæfi/) n **(a)** [U] a hard sticky brown sweet substance made by heating sugar, butter and water together: *a lump of toffee* ○ *treacle toffee.* **(b)** [C] a small piece of this: *a tin of toffees.* **IDM** **can't do sth for 'toffee** (*Brit infml*) is/are completely unable to do sth: *She can't sing for toffee!*
■ **'toffee-apple** (*Brit*) (*US* **candy apple**) n an apple covered with a thin layer of toffee and fixed on a stick.
'toffee-nosed adj (*Brit infml*) behaving as if one thinks one is better than other people, esp those in a lower social class; snobbish (SNOB).

tofu /'təʊfuː/ (also **bean curd**) n [U] a substance like soft white cheese made from SOYA BEAN milk and used in cooking.

tog¹ /tɒg/ v (**-gg-**) **PHRV** **tog oneself 'out/'up (in sth)** (*infml*) to put on clothes for a particular occasion or activity: *children togged out in their Sunday best* ○ *walkers getting togged up for a day on the hills.*
▶ **togs** n [pl] (*infml*) clothes: *sport/cricketing togs.*

tog² /tɒg/ n (*Brit*) a unit of measurement of the warmth of clothes and quilts (QUILT): *a 13.5 tog duvet.*

toga /'təʊgə/ n (pl **togas**) a loose outer garment worn by the citizens of ancient Rome.

together /tə'geðə(r)/ adv part For the special uses of **together** in phrasal verbs, look at the verb entries. For example, the meaning of **pull oneself together** is given in the phrasal verb section of the entry for **pull**¹. **1** with each other; with another person or other people; with different things: *They've gone for a walk together.* ○ *We grew up together in the same village.* ○ *Get all the ingredients together before you start cooking.* **2** so as to form one unit, group, mixture, etc: *glue/nail two boards together* ○ *Mix the sand and cement together, then add water.* ○ **Taken together**, these factors are highly significant. ○ *He's got more money than the rest of us put together.* **3** in or into agreement: *negotiations aimed at bringing the two sides in the dispute closer together* ○ *The party is absolutely together on this issue.* **4** at the same time: *All my troubles seem to come together.* ○ *They were all talking together and I couldn't understand a word.* **IDM** **get it to'gether** (*infml*) to get things/oneself organized or under control: *She would be a very good player if only she could get it together.* **together with 1** including: *Together with the Johnsons, there were 12 of us in the villa.* **2** in addition to; as well as: *I sent them my order, together with a cheque for £40.*
▶ **together** adj (*infml approv*) well organized and confident: *He's incredibly together for someone so young.*
togetherness n [U] a comfortable feeling created when people are happy: *create a feeling of togetherness.*

toggle¹ /'tɒgl/ n a fastening consisting of a short piece of wood, plastic, etc that is put through a loop, eg instead of a button on a coat.

toggle² /'tɒgl/ v [V, Vn] (*esp computing*) to press the same key or keys in order to start using a new style or FORMAT(3) and to stop using it.
■ **'toggle switch** n an electrical switch operated by a short lever which is moved up and down or backwards and forwards.

toil /tɔɪl/ v (*esp rhet*) **1** ~ (**away**) (**at/over sth**) to work very hard or for a long time: [V] *peasants toiling in the fields* [Vpr] *students toiling over their homework* [also Vp]. **2** to move slowly and with difficulty, esp in the specified direction: [Vpr] *The bus toiled up the steep hill.* [also Vp, Vadv].
▶ **toil** n [U] (*esp rhet*) work that is hard and makes one very tired: *after a hard day's toil.* ⇨ note at WORK¹.
toiler n.

toilet /'tɔɪlət/ n **1** [C] **(a)** a large bowl attached to a drain through which one sits on or stands over when one wants to get rid of waste matter from the body: *I need to go to (ie use) the toilet.* ○ *Somebody's forgotten to flush the toilet.* ○ *toilet facilities* ○ *the toilet seat.* **(b)** a room containing a toilet: *a hotel room with its own bathroom and toilet.* **(c)** a room or small building containing several toilets, each in a separate smaller room: *Where's the ladies' toilet, please?* **2** [U] (*dated*) the process of washing and dressing oneself, arranging one's hair, etc.
▶ **toiletries** /'tɔɪlətriz/ n [pl] products used in washing, cleaning one's teeth, etc, eg soap, SHAMPOO (1), TOOTHPASTE, etc.
■ **'toilet paper** (also **'toilet tissue**) n [U] paper for wiping oneself clean after using a toilet.
'toilet roll n (*Brit*) a roll of toilet paper. ⇨ picture at ROLL¹.
'toilet soap n [U, C] soap used for washing oneself.
'toilet-train v [Vn] (*esp passive*) to teach a small child how to use the toilet. **'toilet-training** n [U].

T

'toilet water n [U, C] PERFUME(1) with water added, for use on the skin.

> **NOTE** In British English the **toilet** in people's houses can also be called the **lavatory**, or informally the **loo**. In public places, especially on signs, the words **toilets**, **Gents** (for men's toilets) or **Ladies** (for women's toilets) are used: *Excuse me, where are the toilets please?* You might also see **WC** or **public conveniences** on some signs. In American English the most common word is the **bathroom**. In public places the **rest room**, the **ladies' room** or the **men's room** are used.

toils /tɔɪlz/ n [pl] ~ **(of sth)** *(fml)* traps; difficulties: *caught in the toils of war/the law.*

toing /'tuːɪŋ/ n ,**toing and 'froing** movement or travelling backwards and forwards: *There was a lot of toing and froing between the two embassies before the agreement was signed.*

token /'təʊkən/ n **1** a round piece of metal or plastic used to operate certain machines or as a form of payment: *a car-park token* ∘ *Tokens for the cigarette machine are available at the bar.* **2** a piece of paper, usu attached to a greetings card, which one can exchange for a particular range of goods, eg books, or for any goods in a particular shop: *a £20 'book/'record/'gift token.* Compare VOUCHER 1. **3** a sign or symbol of sth; evidence of sth: *Please accept this small gift **as a token of/in token of** my affection.* **IDM by the same token** ⇨ SAME[1].
> **token** adj [attrib] involving very little effort, commitment (COMMIT) or force and intended only as a symbol or GESTURE(2): *The advancing army encountered only token resistance.* ∘ *a token attempt/payment/strike* ∘ *put in a token appearance at the office party.*

tokenism n *(derog)* [U] the principle or practice of agreeing in a very small way to the demands of minority groups, etc simply in order to win favour with such groups or to satisfy legal requirements.

told pt, pp of TELL.

tolerable /'tɒlərəbl/ adj **1** that can be tolerated: *The climate here is hot but tolerable.* Compare INTOLERABLE. **2** fairly good; acceptable: *a tolerable price* ∘ *be in tolerable health.*
> **tolerably** /-əbli/ adv fairly; quite: *He plays the piano tolerably well.*

tolerate /'tɒləreɪt/ v **1** to allow for sth that one does not like or agree with to happen or continue: [Vn] *a government that refuses to tolerate opposition* ∘ *Bad language will not be tolerated.* [V.n ing] *I will not tolerate your behaving in this way.* **2** to endure sb/sth without complaining, etc; to put up (PUT) with sb/sth: [Vn] *tolerate heat/noise/pain* ∘ *How can you tolerate that awful woman?* **3** to be able to take a drug, etc or be given a treatment without harm: [Vn] *The body cannot tolerate such large amounts of radiation.*
> **tolerance** /'tɒlərəns/ n **1** [U] ~ **(of/for sb/sth)** the willingness or ability to tolerate sb/sth: *religious/racial tolerance* ∘ *He has a low tolerance for stupidity.* ∘ *Rats have developed a tolerance of/for certain poisons.* **2** [C,U] *(techn)* the amount by which the size, weight, etc of sth can vary without causing problems: *working to a tolerance of 0.0001 of an inch/to very fine tolerances.*
> **tolerant** /-rənt/ adj ~ **(of/towards sb/sth)** having or showing tolerance: *a tolerant man* ∘ *He was very tolerant of his daughter's passion for loud music.* **tolerantly** adv.
> **toleration** /,tɒlə'reɪʃn/ n [U] the action or practice of tolerating sth/sb: *religious toleration.*

toll¹ /təʊl/ n **1(a)** money paid for the use of eg a road or bridge. **(b)** *(US)* a charge for a telephone call calculated at a higher rate than a local call: *a 'toll call.* **2** the number of people or animals killed or injured in particular circumstances: *the death-toll in the earthquake/on the roads/after the massacre* ∘ *The final toll could rise to over 2 000.* **IDM take a heavy 'toll / take its 'toll (of sth)** to cause damage, injuries or deaths: *The war took a heavy toll of human life.* ∘ *Every year at Christmas drunk drivers take their toll.*
> ▪ **'toll-bridge** n a bridge at which a toll¹(1a) is charged.
> ,**toll-'free** adj *(US)* (of a telephone call) paid for by the person receiving the call: *Call this number toll-free for further information.*
> **'toll-road** n a road that one must pay a toll¹(1a) to travel on.

toll² /təʊl/ v ~ **(for sb/sth)** to ring a bell with slow regular strokes, esp to announce a death or at a funeral: [Vn] *The church sexton tolled the bell.* ∘ *(fig) This decision tolls the death knell for the shipbuilding industry.* **(b)** ~ **(for sb/sth)** (of a bell) to sound in this way: [Vn] *The church bell tolled the hour.* [also V].
> ▶ **toll** n [sing] the sound of a tolling bell.

tollbooth /'təʊlbuːθ; *Brit also* -buːð/ n a small building where tolls (TOLL¹ 1a) are collected.

Tom /tɒm/ n **IDM any/every ,Tom, ,Dick and 'Harry** *(usu derog)* people in general, rather than the people one knows: *We don't want any Tom, Dick and Harry using the club bar.*

tom /tɒm/ n = TOM-CAT.

tomahawk /'tɒməhɔːk/ n a light AXE(1) used as a tool or weapon by Native Americans. ⇨ picture at AXE.

tomato /tə'mɑːtəʊ; *US* tə'meɪtəʊ/ n (pl **-oes**) a juicy, usu red, fruit eaten raw, eg in a SALAD(1a), or cooked as a vegetable: *tomato juice/sauce/soup/ketchup* ∘ *tomato plants.* ⇨ picture at SALAD.

tomb /tuːm/ n a grave built of stone under or above the ground: *bury/lay sb in a tomb.*

tombola /tɒm'bəʊlə/ n [C, U] *(Brit)* a game in which people pick tickets out of a revolving drum¹(2) and certain tickets then win prizes.

tomboy /'tɒmbɔɪ/ n a girl who enjoys rough noisy activities. ▶ **tomboyish** adj.

tombstone /'tuːmstəʊn/ n a large flat stone covering or standing at the end of a grave, on which the name of a dead person is written: *a marble/granite tombstone.*

tom-cat /'tɒm kæt/ (also **tom**) n a male cat.

tome /təʊm/ n *(fml or joc)* a large heavy book, esp a serious one: *a hefty/weighty tome.*

tomfoolery /tɒm'fuːləri/ n [U, C usu pl] silly behaviour or activities: *get up to all kinds of tomfoolery.*

tommy-gun /'tɒmi gʌn/ n a light machine-gun (MACHINE).

tommy-rot /'tɒmi rɒt/ n [U] *(dated infml)* nonsense.

tomorrow /tə'mɒrəʊ/ n [U] **1** the day after today: *Today is Tuesday so tomorrow is Wednesday.* ∘ *Tomorrow is going to be fine and dry according to the weather forecast.* ∘ *tomorrow morning/afternoon/evening/night* ∘ *The announcement will appear in tomorrow's newspapers.* ⇨ note at MORNING. **2** the near future: *Who knows what changes tomorrow may bring?* ∘ *tomorrow's world.* **IDM the day after tomorrow** ⇨ DAY.
> ▶ **tomorrow** adv on the next day after today: *She's getting married tomorrow.* ∘ *See you this same time tomorrow, then.* **IDM jam tomorrow** ⇨ JAM¹.

tom-tom /'tɒm tɒm/ n **(a)** a long narrow African or Asian drum played with the hands. **(b)** a similar drum used eg in JAZZ bands.

ton /tʌn/ n **1** [C] a measure of weight, in Britain 2 240 lb (**long ton**) and in the USA 2 000 lb (**short ton**). ⇨ App 2. Compare TONNE. **2** [C] a measure of the capacity of a ship (1 ton = 100 CUBIC(1a) feet): *a 20 000-ton liner.* **3 tons** [pl] ~**s (of sth)** *(infml)* a lot:

They've got tons of money. ○ *I've still got tons (of work) to do.* **IDM** **do a/the** ˈ**ton** (*Brit sl*) to drive at a speed of 100 miles per hour or more: *He got caught doing a ton on the motorway.* **(come down on sb) like a ton of** ˈ**bricks** (*infml*) (to criticize or punish sb) very severely.

tonal /ˈtəʊnl/ *adj* **1** of (a) tone[1](1) or tones. **2** (*music*) relating to the character of a tune and the key[1](3a) in which it is played.

▶ **tonality** /təʊˈnæləti/ *n* [U, C] (*music*) the character of a tune resulting from the key in which it is played.

tone[1] /təʊn/ *n* **1** [C] a sound with reference to its quality, pitch[1](2) and strength: *the ringing tones of an orator's voice* ○ *a piano with an excellent tone.* **2** [C] a quality of voice expressing a particular emotion, attitude, etc: *speak in an angry/an impatient/ an aggrieved tone* ○ *a tone of command/reproach/ regret* ○ *People spoke in hushed tones.* ○ *Don't speak to me in that tone (of voice)* (eg in that unpleasant or critical way). **3** [sing] the general spirit or character of sth: *The overall tone of the book is gently nostalgic.* ○ *She* **set the tone for/of** *the meeting with a firm statement of company policy.* ○ *His jokes were quite funny but they did* **lower the tone** *(of the occasion) somewhat.* **4** [C] a shade of a colour: *a carpet in warm tones of brown and orange* ○ *Choose a colour that matches your skin tone.* **5** [U] (of the body) the state of being firm and strong: *good muscular tone.* **6** [C] (*music*) any one of the five larger intervals between one note and the next which, together with two semitones (SEMITONE), form an OCTAVE(a). **7** [C] a sound heard on a telephone line: *get the dialling/ringing/engaged tone* ○ *Please speak after the tone* (eg as an instruction on an ANSWERPHONE). **8** [C] (*linguistics*) the pitch[1](2) level of a syllable in speaking: *In 'Are you ill?' there is usually a rising tone on 'ill' , while in 'He's ill' there is usually a falling tone on 'ill'.*

▶ **-toned** (forming compound *adjs*) having the specified tone[1](1,2,4): *silver-toned trumpets.*

toneless *adj* lacking colour, spirit or expression; dull or flat in sound: *answer in a toneless voice.*
tonelessly *adv.*

■ **tone-**ˈ**deaf** *adj* unable to distinguish accurately between different musical notes.

ˈ**tone-poem** *n* (*music*) a piece of music for ORCHESTRA, intended eg to describe a place or express an idea in music.

tone[2] /təʊn/ *v* **PHRV** ˌ**tone sth** ˈ**down 1** to make sth less intense, extreme, etc: *You'd better tone down the more outspoken passages in your article.* **2** to make a colour less bright: *tone down the reds.* ˌ**tone** ˈ**in (with sth)** to match sth in colour: *The new curtains tone in beautifully with the carpet.* ˌ**tone sth** ˈ**up** to make one's body stronger, fitter, etc: *Regular exercise tones up the muscles.*

toner /ˈtəʊnə(r)/ **1** [C] a device for making the body firmer and stronger: *an electrical body toner.* **2** [U, C] a liquid or cream used for making the skin firm and smooth: *a good toner for oily skin.*

tongs

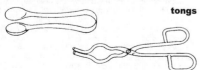

tongs /tɒŋz/ *n* [pl] **1** a device with two movable parts which are joined at one end, used for picking up and holding things: *(a pair of)* ˈ*sugar/*ˈ*coal/*ˈ*ice/* ˈ*salad tongs.* ⇨ picture. **2** a device that is heated and used for curling hair: *hair/curling tongs.* **IDM** **be/go at it / each other hammer and tongs** ⇨ HAMMER[1].

tongue /tʌŋ/ *n* **1** [C] the soft organ in the mouth, used in tasting, swallowing, etc and, by people, in speaking. ⇨ picture at THROAT, TOOTH. ⇨ note at BODY. **2** [U, C] the tongue of an animal, cooked and eaten as food: *sliced ox tongue.* **3** [C] (*fml or rhet*) a language: *He speaks English, but his native tongue is German.* ○ *speak in tongues* (ie in strange or unknown languages). See also MOTHER TONGUE. **4** [C usu *sing*] a manner of speaking: *She has a very sharp tongue.* **5** [C] anything that is shaped like a tongue: *a tongue of flame* ○ *a narrow tongue of land jutting out into the sea* ○ *the tongue of a shoe* (ie the piece of leather under the laces). ⇨ picture at SHOE. **IDM** **bite one's tongue** ⇨ BITE[1]. **find one's voice/ tongue** ⇨ FIND[1]. **get one's** ˈ**tongue round/ around sth** to manage to pronounce a difficult word or name correctly. **has the cat got your tongue?** ⇨ CAT. **have a loose tongue** ⇨ LOOSE[1]. **hold one's peace/tongue** ⇨ PEACE. **loosen sb's tongue** ⇨ LOOSEN. **mind/watch one's** ˈ**tongue** to be careful what one says in order not to upset or offend sb. **on the tip of one's tongue** ⇨ TIP[1]. **put/ stick one's** ˈ**tongue out** to show one's tongue outside one's lips, eg to a doctor or as a rude gesture: *Don't you dare stick your tongue out at me!* **roll/ slip/trip off the** ˈ**tongue** to sound natural, smooth and elegant, although not necessarily sincerely (SINCERE) meant: *compliments tripping easily off the tongue.* **a slip of the pen/tongue** ⇨ SLIP[2]. **tongues wag** (*infml*) people are eagerly passing on a rumour or piece of gossip to others: *Their affair has really set* ˈ*tongues wagging.* **with (one's) tongue in (one's)** ˈ**cheek** not intending to be serious: *write/ joke with tongue in cheek.*

▶ **-tongued** (forming compound *adjs*) having the specified manner of speaking: *sharp-tongued* ○ *eviltongued.*

■ ˌ**tongue-in-**ˈ**cheek** *adj* not intended seriously: *tongue-in-cheek remarks.*

ˈ**tongue-tied** *adj* not able to speak because one is shy or nervous.

ˈ**tongue-twister** *n* a word or phrase that is difficult to pronounce correctly or quickly, eg *She sells sea shells on the seashore.*

tonic /ˈtɒnɪk/ *n* **1** [C, U] **(a)** a medicine that increases one's strength or energy, taken esp after an illness or when one is tired. **(b)** a substance for giving health and strength, etc to a part of one's body: *a skin/hair tonic.* **2** [C usu *sing*] anything that makes people feel healthier or happier: *The good news was a tonic for us all.* **3** [C, U] = TONIC WATER: *a gin and tonic.* **4** [C] (*music*) the first note of a scale of 8 notes.

■ ˈ**tonic water** (also **tonic**) *n* [U, C] a FIZZY mineral water (MINERAL), often mixed with a strong alcoholic drink, esp GIN or VODKA: *a bottle of* ˈ*tonic water.*

tonight /təˈnaɪt/ *n* [U] **(a)** the present evening or night: *Here are tonight's football results.* **(b)** the evening or night of today: *Tonight will be cloudy.*

▶ **tonight** *adv* **(a)** on or during the present evening or night: *It's cold tonight.* **(b)** on or during the evening or night of today: *Are you doing anything tonight?*

tonnage /ˈtʌnɪdʒ/ *n* [U, C] **1** the size of a ship, expressed in tons (TON 2). **2** the total amount of weight of sth: *British Rail's annual freight tonnage* ○ *the total tonnage of bombs dropped in the war.*

tonne /tʌn/ *n* 1 000 kilograms; a metric ton (METRIC). ⇨ App 2. Compare TON 1: *a record grain harvest of 236m tonnes* ○ *a 17-tonne truck.*

tonsil /ˈtɒnsl/ *n* either of two small organs at the sides of the throat near the root of the tongue: *have one's tonsils out* (ie have them removed by a doctor). ⇨ picture at THROAT.

▶ **tonsillitis** /ˌtɒnsəˈlaɪtɪs/ *n* [U] an infection of the tonsils in which they become swollen and sore.

T

tonsure /ˈtɒnʃə(r)/ *n* a part of the head from which the hair has been shaved, esp of a person about to become a priest or monk.

too /tuː/ *adv* **1** (usu placed at the end of a clause) also: *They all wanted to go to the cinema, so I went too.* ○ *He speaks French, Italian, Spanish and Romanian too.* ⇨ note at ALSO. **2** (used before *adjs* and *advs*) to a higher degree or more than is allowed, desirable, good, etc: *drive too fast* ○ *These shoes are much too small for me.* ○ *We can't ski because there's too little snow.* ○ *This is too large a helping for me/ This helping is too large for me.* ○ *It's too long a journey to make in one day.* ○ *Accidents like this happen **all too** (ie much too) often.* **3** what is more; to make the situation worse: *She broke her leg last week — and on her birthday, too!* ○ *I've lost an earring — it was an expensive one* ˈtoo. **4** very; absolutely: *I'm not too sure if this is right.* ○ *You are really too kind.* ○ *She's **none too** (ie not very) clever.* ▪ **be too** ˈ**much for sb 1** to demand more skill or strength than sb has: *A cycling holiday would be too much for him at the moment.* **2** to be more than can be tolerated: *The noise finally became too much for me so I went in and complained.*

took *pt* of TAKE¹.

tool /tuːl/ *n* **1** a usu metal instrument held in the hand and used for making or repairing sth: *garden tools* ○ *a* ˈ*tool-kit* (ie a set of tools in a box or bag) ○ *power tools* (ie using electricity) ○ *The most useful tools to have are a screwdriver, a hammer and a saw.* **2** anything that helps one to do one's job: *research tools like questionnaires* ○ *The computer is now an indispensable/invaluable tool in many businesses.* ○ *the tools of one's* ˈ*trade* (ie the things one needs in order to do one's job). ⇨ note at MACHINE. **3** a person who is used or exploited by another: *The country's prime minister was a mere tool in the hands of the president.* **4** (△ *sl*) the PENIS. ▪ **down tools** ⇨ DOWN³.
▪ **tool** *v* **PHRV** ˌ**tool (sth/sb/oneself)** ˈ**up** (*Brit*) to equip a factory, etc with the necessary tools to produce sth: *the cost of tooling up for a new model.*

tooled *adj* decorated with a design made by pressing with a heated tool(1): *books bound in leather and tooled in gold.*

toot /tuːt/ *n* [C] a short high sound made by a horn or whistle.
▪ **toot** *v* to make a toot: [Vpr] *toot at a cyclist* [Vn] *The driver tooted his horn as he approached the bend.* [V] *She tooted as she drove away.*

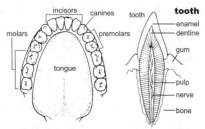
incisors   canines   tooth   **tooth**
molars   premolars   enamel / dentine / gum / pulp / nerve / bone
tongue

tooth /tuːθ/ *n* (*pl* **teeth** /tiːθ/) **1** [C] each of the hard white structures in the mouth which are used for biting and chewing (CHEW) food: *brush/clean one's teeth* ○ *He lost two front teeth in the fight.* ○ *She had to have a tooth out at the dentist's.* ○ *tooth decay* ○ *have false teeth* ○ *He spoke through **clenched teeth**.* ○ *She* **sank her teeth into** (ie bit into) *a thick slice of toast.* ⇨ picture. See also WISDOM TOOTH. **2** [C] a narrow pointed part of an object: *the teeth of a saw/ gear/cog* ○ *The comb had a lot of teeth missing.* **3 teeth** [pl] (*Brit infml*) effective force: *an organization with teeth.* **IDM armed to the teeth** ⇨ ARM².

bare one's/its teeth ⇨ BARE². **by the skin of one's teeth** ⇨ SKIN. **cast, fling, throw, etc sth in sb's** ˈ**teeth** (*rhet*) to criticize sb for sth they have done wrong. **cut a** ˈ**tooth** have a tooth growing out through the GUM¹. **cut one's** ˈ**teeth on sth** to gain experience from sth. **fight, etc tooth and** ˈ**nail** to fight or struggle for sth as hard as one can. **get/ take the bit between one's/the teeth** ⇨ BIT². **get one's** ˈ**teeth into sth** to work with energy and interest on sth demanding: *He wants a job he can get his teeth into.* **grit one's teeth** ⇨ GRIT *v*. **have a sweet tooth** ⇨ SWEET¹. **in the teeth of sth 1** in spite of sth: *The new policy was adopted in the teeth of fierce criticism.* **2** directly against the wind, etc: *in the teeth of a howling gale.* **a kick in the teeth** ⇨ KICK². **lie through one's teeth** ⇨ LIE¹. **long in the tooth** ⇨ LONG¹. **set sb's** ˈ**teeth on edge** (esp of a sharp sound or taste) to make sb feel physically uncomfortable. **show one's teeth** ⇨ SHOW².
▪ **toothed** /tuːθt; *Brit also* tuːðd; *US also* ˈtuːθəd/ *adj* [attrib] **1** having teeth: *a toothed whale.* **2** (in compounds) having teeth of the specified type: *a saw-toothed wheel.*

toothless *adj* **1** without teeth: *a toothless old man.* **2** without power or force: *The committee will be toothless unless the law is changed.*

toothy *adj* having or showing many, large or noticeable teeth: *a toothy grin.* See also TEETHE.

toothache /ˈtuːθeɪk/ *n* [U, C usu *sing*] a pain in a tooth or teeth. (*Brit*) *I've got toothache.* ○ *I've got a/ the toothache.*

toothbrush /ˈtuːθbrʌʃ/ *n* a brush for cleaning the teeth. ⇨ picture at BRUSH¹.

toothpaste /ˈtuːθpeɪst/ *n* [U] paste used on a brush for cleaning the teeth: *squeeze a tube of toothpaste.*

toothpick /ˈtuːθpɪk/ *n* a short pointed piece of wood or plastic used for removing bits of food from between the teeth.

toothsome /ˈtuːθsəm/ *adj* (*fml*) (esp of food) pleasant; DELICIOUS(1).

tootle /ˈtuːtl/ *v* (*infml*) **1** ~ (**on sth**) to make a series of short high sounds: [Vpr, Vp] *tootling (away) on his trumpet* [also V]. **2** to go in the specified direction in a casual way: [Vp] *She tootled off without saying a word.* [also Vpr].

top¹ /tɒp/ *n* **1** [C esp *sing*] (**a**) the highest part or point of sth: *get/climb to the top of Mount Everest* ○ *at the top of the stairs* ○ *My office is at the top of the building.* ○ *five lines from the top of the page.* See also TREETOP. (**b**) the upper surface of sth: *polish the top of the table/the* ˈ*table-top.* **2** [sing] ~ (**of sth**) the highest or most important rank or position: *rise to/ make it to/reach the top* (ie achieve fame, success, etc) ○ *He's at the top of his profession.* ○ *This decision came* **from the top** (ie was made by the most senior people).* ○ *Miami finished the season (at the) top of the football league.* ○ *We've got a lot of things to do, but packing is* **top of the list.** **3** [C] a thing forming or covering the upper part of sth: *the top of the milk* (ie the layer of cream floating on it) ○ *He took off his pyjama top.* **4** [C] a thing that covers or closes sth; a lid: *the top of a felt-tip pen* ○ *a bottle with a screw-top* ○ *Where's the top for this can of paint?* **5** [C] a garment covering the upper part of the body: *I need a top to go with these shorts.* **6** [U] = TOP GEAR: *You shouldn't be in top.* **7 tops** [pl] (*dated infml*) a person or thing of the best quality: *Among the sports superstars she's (the) tops.* **8** [sing] (in baseball) the first half of an inning (INNINGS). **9** [C usu *pl*] the leaves of a plant which is grown chiefly for its root: *We give the carrot tops to the rabbit.* **IDM at the top of the** ˈ**tree** in the highest position or rank in a profession, career, etc. **at the top of one's** ˈ**voice** as loudly as possible: *cheering/shouting/screaming at the top(s) of their voices.* **blow one's top** ⇨ BLOW¹. **bottom/top of the pile** ⇨ PILE¹. **come out**

on **top** to finish in first position; to be the winner: *In any argument he always tends to come out on top.* **from top to bottom** completely; thoroughly: *We searched the house from top to bottom.* **from top to toe** completely; all over: *dressed in green from top to toe.* **get on top of sb** to be too much for sb to manage, bear, etc: *All this extra work is getting on top of him.* **get on top of sth** to manage to do, finish or control sth: *How will I ever get on top of all this work?* **in the first/top flight** ⇨ FLIGHT¹. **off the top of one's head** (*infml*) (of sth said) without previous thought or preparation: *I can't remember the name off the top of my head.* ○ *He's talking off the top of his head* (ie What he says may not be correct). **on top 1** above; on the highest point or surface: *a cake with icing on top* ○ *Stand on top and look down* ○ *He's going bald on top* (ie of his head). **2** in a leading position; in control: *She was on top throughout the match.* **3** in addition: *He borrowed £50 and asked me to lend him my car on top.* **on top of sth/sb 1** over or above sth/sb; covering sth/sb: *Put this magazine on top of the others.* ○ *Many people were crushed when the building collapsed on top of them.* **2** in addition to sth: *He gets commission on top of his salary.* **3** very close to sth/sb: *There is no privacy when houses are built on top of each other like that.* **(be/feel) on top of the world** happy or proud, esp because of success or good luck. **over the top** (*abbr* OTT) (*infml esp Brit*) to an exaggerated or excessive degree: *The ending of the film is completely over the top.* ○ *an over-the-top performance.* **take sth from the top** (*infml*) to go back to the beginning of sth and repeat it: *OK, everybody, let's take it from the top.* **up top** (*Brit infml*) in the head: *He hasn't got very much up top* (ie He isn't very intelligent).
▶ **top** *adj* [usu attrib] highest in position, rank or degree: *a room on the top floor* ○ *one of the world's top scientists* ○ *top jobs/people* ○ *travelling at top speed.*

topless *adj* (**a**) (of a woman) having the breasts and upper part of the body bare: *a topless waitress.* (**b**) (of a woman's garment) exposing the breasts: *a topless dress.* — *adv* with the breasts bare: *sunbathe/go topless.*

topmost /'tɒpməʊst/ *adj* [attrib] highest: *the topmost branches of the tree.*

■ **top brass** *n* [Gp] (*infml*) senior officers or officials: *All the top brass attended the ceremony.*

top-class *adj* of the highest quality or standard: *a top-class performance.*

top dog *n* (usu *sing*) (*infml*) a person, group or country that is superior to others: *She's determined to show that she's still (the) top dog in this event.*

the top drawer *n* [sing] (*Brit*) the highest social position: *She's out of the top drawer.* ▶ **top-drawer** *adj*.

■ **top-dressing** *n* [C, U] MANURE or fertilizer (FERTILIZE) put onto the surface of a field and not dug or ploughed (PLOUGH *v*) into the soil.

top-flight *adj* of the highest quality; the best: *a top-flight hotel/'diplomat.*

top gear *n* [U] the highest gear in a motor vehicle: *change up into top gear.*

top hat (also *infml* **topper**) a man's tall black or grey hat, worn with formal dress. ⇨ picture at HAT.

top-heavy *adj* **1** too heavy at the top and therefore likely to fall over. **2** (of an organization) having too many senior staff: *The civil service has become top-heavy.*

top-notch *adj* (*infml*) excellent; of the highest quality: *a top-notch lawyer.*

top-of-the-range *adj* [usu attrib] the most expensive of a group of similar products: *a top-of-the-range camcorder.*

top-ranking *adj* [attrib] of the highest rank or importance; senior: *top-ranking police officers.*

top secret *adj* that must be kept absolutely secret,

esp from other governments: *a file of top secret information* ○ *a top-secret mission.*

the top ten *n* [pl] the ten most popular pop records each week: *She's a great singer, but her records never get into/make the top ten.*

top² /tɒp/ *v* (**-pp-**) **1**(**a**) to be higher than sth; to SURPASS sth: [Vn] *Exports have topped the £80 million mark.* (**b**) to be in first position: [Vn] *His latest book is currently topping the best-sellers list.* **2** (esp passive) to provide or be a top for sth: [Vnpr] *ice-cream topped with chocolate sauce* ○ *a roof topped with two strange-looking chimneys.* **3** to remove the top of a plant, fruit, etc while preparing it as food: [Vn] *top and tail* (ie remove the ends from) *gooseberries.* **4** (esp in golf) to hit a ball above the centre: [Vn] *I topped it badly and it only went a few yards.* **5** [Vn] (*sl*) to kill oneself/sb, esp by hanging (HANG¹ 6). **IDM** **head/top the bill** ⇨ BILL¹. **PHR V** **top sth off (with sth)** to finish or complete sth successfully: *The meal was topped off with a delicious chocolate mousse.* **top (sth) out** to complete a building by adding the highest stone, etc. **top (sth) up** to add an amount of sth to the amount already present: *top up with petrol/oil* ○ *top up a car battery* ○ *top up a mortgage* (ie borrow more) ○ (*infml*) *Let me top you up* (ie refill your glass).
▶ **topping** *n* [C, U] anything put on top of a cake, etc to add flavour: *a range of fruit-flavoured toppings* ○ *You pay £3 for the basic pizza and 75p for each extra topping.*
■ **top-up** *n* more of sth added to an amount to bring it back to the original level: *a top-up loan from the bank* ○ *Who's ready for a top-up* (ie another drink)?

top³ /tɒp/ *n* a toy that spins on a point when it is turned round rapidly by hand or by a string.

topaz /'təʊpæz/ *n* (**a**) [U] a transparent yellow mineral. (**b**) [C] a precious stone cut from this.

topcoat /'tɒpkəʊt/ *n* **1** the last of several coats of paint applied to a surface. Compare UNDERCOAT. **2** (*dated*) an OVERCOAT.

topi (also **topee**) /'təʊpi; *US also* təʊ'piː/ *n* a hard hat worn to give protection from the sun in very hot countries.

topiary /'təʊpiəri; *US* -ieri/ *n* [U] the art of cutting bushes into ornamental shapes such as birds and animals.

topic /'tɒpɪk/ *n* a subject of a discussion, a talk, a programme, an essay, etc: *a topic of conversation* ○ *Is drug abuse a suitable topic for a school debate?* ○ *We discussed a wide range of topics.*
▶ **topical** /-kl/ *adj* of interest at the present time: *a play full of topical allusions to well-known people* ○ *a topical theme.* **topicality** /ˌtɒpɪˈkæləti/ *n* [U, sing]: *Because of recent events, the film has taken on an unexpected topicality.* **topically** /-kli/ *adv*.

topknot /'tɒpnɒt/ *n* hair gathered into a small knot on the top of the head.

topography /tə'pɒɡrəfi/ *n* [U] the features of a place or district, esp the position of its rivers, mountains, roads, buildings, etc: *describe the local topography.* ▶ **topographical** /ˌtɒpəˈɡræfɪkl/ *adj*: *a topographical map.* **topographically** /-kli/ *adv*.

topper /'tɒpə(r)/ *n* (*infml*) = TOP HAT.

topping¹ ⇨ TOP².

topping² /'tɒpɪŋ/ *adj* (*dated Brit infml*) excellent.

topple /'tɒpl/ *v* **1**(**a**) ~ (**over**) to move from side to side and fall: [Vpr] *houses toppling into the sea* [Vp] *The pile of books toppled over onto the floor.* (**b**) to make (sth) fall in this way: [Vn] *The explosion toppled the old chimney.* **2** to cause sb to lose their position of power or authority: [Vn, Vnpr] *the crisis threatens to topple the government* (*from power*).

topside /'tɒpsaɪd/ *n* [U] (*Brit*) a joint of BEEF(1) cut from the upper part of the leg.

topsoil /'tɒpsɔɪl/ *n* [U] the layer of soil near the

surface: *The heavy rain had washed away the top-soil.* Compare SUBSOIL.

topsy-turvy /ˌtɒpsi ˈtɜːvi/ *adj, adv* (*infml*) in or into a state of great confusion: *Don't go into my bedroom — everything's all topsy turvy.* ○ *This sudden development turned all our plans topsy-turvy.*

tor /tɔː(r)/ *n* a small hill with rocks at the top, esp in parts of SW England.

torch /tɔːtʃ/ *n* **1** (*also esp US* **flashlight**) a small electric lamp that runs on a battery and is held in the hand: *shine a torch on sth/sb* ○ *He flashed his torch quickly round the garden.* **2** (*US*) = BLOWLAMP. **3** a piece of wood wrapped in esp oily cloth which is lit and held in the hand to give light. **IDM carry a torch for sb** ⇨ CARRY. **put sth to the ˈtorch** to set fire to sth deliberately.
▶ **torch** *v* to set fire to sth deliberately: [Vn] *buses torched by rioters.*

torchlight /ˈtɔːtʃlaɪt/ *n* [U] the light of a TORCH or torches: *put up the tent by torchlight* ○ *a torchlight procession* (ie one in which burning torches are carried).

tore *pt* of TEAR[1].

toreador /ˈtɒriədɔː(r); *US* ˈtɔːr-/ *n* (esp in Spain) a person who fights bulls (BULL[1]), esp while riding a horse.

torment /ˈtɔːment/ *n* (**a**) [UC usu *pl*] severe physical or mental suffering: *be in great torment* ○ *years of mental torment* ○ *suffer the torments of remorse/jealousy.* (**b**) [C usu *sing*] a thing or person that causes this: *His shyness made public speaking a constant torment to him.*
▶ **torment** /tɔːˈment/ *v* **1** to make sb suffer very much: [Vn] *be tormented by hunger/anxiety/mosquitoes.* **2** annoy sb for fun: [Vn, Vnpr] *They enjoy tormenting their teacher (with silly questions).*
tormentor /tɔːˈmentə(r)/ *n* a person who torments sb/sth: *The dog bared its teeth at its tormentors.*

torn *pp* of TEAR[1].

tornado /tɔːˈneɪdəʊ/ *n* (*pl* **-oes**) a violent storm with very strong circular winds over a small area: *The town was hit by a tornado.*

torpedo /tɔːˈpiːdəʊ/ *n* (*pl* **-oes**) a bomb, shaped like a tube, that is fired under the water from a ship or SUBMARINE(1) and aimed at other ships.
▶ **torpedo** *v* (*pt, pp* **torpedoed**; *pres p* **torpedoing**) **1** [Vn] to attack or sink a ship with a torpedo or torpedoes. **2** to destroy or ruin a policy, an event, an institution, etc: [Vn] *Continued fighting between local militias has torpedoed the peace talks.*

torpid /ˈtɔːpɪd/ *adj* (*fml*) not active; with very slow or no movement: *lie around in a torpid state.*

torpor /ˈtɔːpə(r)/ *n* [U] (*fml*) the state of being TORPID; lack of energy: *a state of torpor induced by the tropical heat* ○ *sink into a torpor of laziness.*

torque /tɔːk/ *n* [U] (*techn*) a twisting force causing machinery to ROTATE(1): *The more torque an engine has, the bigger the load it can pull in the same gear.*

torrent /ˈtɒrənt; *US* ˈtɔːr-/ *n* **1** a strong fast stream, esp of water: *raging mountain torrents* ○ *rain pouring down in torrents.* **2** a large amount of sth released suddenly and violently: *a torrent of abuse/bad language.*
▶ **torrential** /təˈrenʃl/ *adj* like a torrent: *torrential rain.*

torrid /ˈtɒrɪd; *US* ˈtɔːr-/ *adj* **1** (of a climate or country) very hot and dry: *a torrid summer.* **2** full of intense, esp sexual, emotion: *a torrid love affair.*

torsion /ˈtɔːʃn/ *n* [U] (*techn*) a twisting, esp of one end of sth while the other end is held fixed.

torso /ˈtɔːsəʊ/ *n* (*pl* **-os**) (**a**) the main part of the human body, not including the head, arms and legs. (**b**) a statue of this part of the body only.

tort /tɔːt/ *n* (*law*) a private or civil(4) wrong for which a person may have to pay compensation.

tortilla /tɔːˈtiːə/ *n* a round thin Mexican PANCAKE(1) made with eggs and corn flour, usu eaten hot with a filling of meat, etc.

tortoise /ˈtɔːtəs/ *n* a reptile with a hard shell, that moves very slowly. ⇨ picture.

tortoiseshell /ˈtɔːtəʃel, ˈtɔːtəʃel/ *n* **1** [U] the hard shell of a TURTLE(1), esp the type with yellow and brown markings, used for making combs, small ornaments, etc. **2** [C] a cat with black, white and brownish-orange markings. **3** [C] a type of BUTTER-FLY(1) with orange and brownish markings.

tortuous /ˈtɔːtʃuəs/ *adj* **1** full of twists and turns: *a tortuous mountain track* ○ *a tortuous route/journey.* **2** (*usu derog*) (of a policy, etc) not plain or direct; too complex: *a tortuous argument* ○ *tortuous logic.* ▶ **tortuously** *adv.*

torture /ˈtɔːtʃə(r)/ *n* **1**(**a**) [U] the action or practice of deliberately causing sb severe pain as a punishment or in order to force them to say or do sth: *the widespread use of torture* ○ *Some prisoners died under torture.* ○ *a torture chamber.* (**b**) [C] a method of doing this: *barbaric tortures.* **2** [U, C] great physical or mental suffering; an instance of this: (*joc*) *Having to sit through the junior school orchestra's concert was sheer torture!*
▶ **torture** *v* **1** to inflict great pain on sb: [Vn] *There is evidence that political prisoners are regularly tortured.* **2** to cause sb great physical or mental suffering: [Vn] *be tortured by fear/doubt.* **torturer** /ˈtɔːtʃərə(r)/ *n.*

Tory /ˈtɔːri/ *n, adj* (a member) of the British Conservative Party: *the Tory Party conference* ○ *Tory policies.* ▶ **Toryism** *n* [U].

tosh /tɒʃ/ *n* [U] (*Brit infml*) nonsense; rubbish: *He talks a load of tosh sometimes.*

toss /tɒs; *US* tɔːs/ *v* **1**(**a**) to throw sth lightly or carelessly or easily, esp in the specified direction: [Vnn, Vnpr] *toss the ducks some bread/toss some bread to the ducks.* (**b**) [Vn, Vnpr, Vnp] (esp of a BULL[1](1)) to throw sb up with the horns. **2** to move one's head sharply upwards, esp to show that one does not like or care about sth: [Vn] *She just tossed her head and walked off.* [also Vnp]. **3** to move or make sb/sth move from side to side or up and down: [V, Vp] *branches tossing (about) in the wind* [V] *I couldn't sleep, but kept tossing and turning in bed all night.* [Vn, Vnp] *The boat was tossed (up and down) by the waves.* [also Vpr, Vnpr]. **4** to shake or turn food to cover it with a liquid such as oil, etc: [Vn] *toss the salad* [Vnpr] *Now toss the pasta in melted butter.* **5** ~ (**up**); ~ (**sb**) **for sth** to throw a coin into the air in order to decide sth by chance, according to which side is facing upwards when it lands: [Vp] *Who's going to cook tonight? Let's toss up.* [Vnpr] *There's only one cake left — I'll toss you for it.* [also Vpr, Vn, Vnpr]. **PHRV** ˌtoss **(oneself) ˈoff** (△ *Brit sl*) to MASTURBATE. ˌtoss sth ˈoff to produce sth quickly and without much thought or effort: *I can toss off my article for the local newspaper in half an hour.* ˌtoss sth ˈoff/ˈback to drink sth rapidly. ˌtoss ˈup (*infml*) (to try) to decide between two alternatives: *I tossed up whether to tell her now or later.*
▶ **toss** *n* a tossing action or movement: *win/lose on the toss* (ie of a coin) ○ *take a toss* (ie be thrown from

a horse) ○ *with a scornful toss of the head.* **IDM**
argue the toss ⇨ ARGUE. **not give a 'toss (about
sb/sth)** (*sl*) not to care at all.

■ **'toss-up** *n* [sing] (*infml*) a situation in which
either of two alternatives is equally possible: *Both
players are equally good so it's an absolute toss-up
who will win.* ○ *Where shall we eat? It's a toss-up
between an Indian or a Chinese restaurant.*

tot¹ /tɒt/ *n* **1** a small child: *a TV programme for tiny
tots.* **2** a small glass of alcoholic drink, esp spirits:
a tot of whisky.

tot² /tɒt/ *v* **(-tt-)** **PHRV** ,**tot (sth) 'up** (*infml*) to add
up: *Tot up how much you've spent.* ○ *It's surprising
how the bills tot up.*

total /ˈtəʊtl/ *adj* [usu attrib] **1** complete; absolute:
total silence ○ *live in total ignorance (of sth)* ○ *That's
total nonsense!* ○ *a total eclipse of the sun/moon* (ie
one in which the sun/moon is completely covered
over) ○ *a total waste of time.* **2** being the full number
or amount: *the total number of casualties* ○ *The total
result was disappointing.* ○ *The firm made a total
profit of £200 000.*
▶ **total** *n* a total number or amount: *What does the
total come to?* ○ *We raised a **grand total** of £460 for
charity.* ○ *England scored a total of 436 runs.* See also
RUNNING TOTAL. **IDM** **in 'total** altogether: *That will
cost you £7.50 in total.*
total *v* **(-ll-;** *US* also **-l-)** **1** to amount to sth: [Vn] *He
has debts totalling more than £2 million.* **2** ~ **sth/sb
(up)** to count the total of sth/sb: [Vnp] *The scores
were totalled up and the winner announced.* [also
Vn]. **3** [Vn] (*US sl*) to destroy sth, esp a car, completely.

totality /təʊˈtæləti/ *n* (*fml*) the total number or
amount; the whole of sth.

totally /ˈtəʊtəli/ *adv* completely; utterly (UTTER¹):
totally blind ○ *I totally forgot about it.*

totalitarian /təʊˌtæləˈteəriən/ *adj* (*usu derog*) of a
system of government in which there is only one
political party, usu demanding that people submit
totally to the requirements of the State: *a totalitarian regime.* ▶ **totalitarianism** /-ɪzəm/ *n* [U].

tote¹ /təʊt/ *n* (*infml*) a method of betting on horses
in which the total amount of money bet on each race
is divided among those who bet on the winner:
betting on the tote.

tote² /təʊt/ *v* (*infml*) to carry sth: [Vn] *uniformed
men toting guns* ○ *gun-toting soldiers* [Vnp] *I've been
toting this bag round all day.* [also Vnpr].

totem /ˈtəʊtəm/ *n* **(a)** a natural object, esp an animal, regarded by Native Americans as the symbol
of a family or tribe; an image of this. **(b)** a person or
thing treated with very great or too much respect:
the outdated totems of the Victorian age.
■ **'totem-pole** *n* a tall wooden pole carved or
painted with a series of totems.

t'other /ˈtʌðə(r)/ *adj, pron* (*dialect or joc*) the other.

totter /ˈtɒtə(r)/ *v* **1** to rock or shake as if about to
fall: [V] *The building tottered briefly and then collapsed in a heap of rubble.* ○ (*fig*) *a tottering economy.*
2 to walk or move in an unsteady way, esp in the
direction specified: [Vpr] *The child tottered across
the room.* ○ *She tottered to her feet.* [also V, Vp].

toucan /ˈtuːkæn/ *n* a tropical American bird with
brightly coloured feathers and a very large beak.

touch¹ /tʌtʃ/ *v* **1** (of two or more things, surfaces,
etc) to be or come so close together that there is no
space between: [V] *The two wires were touching.* [Vn]
One of the branches was just touching the water. ○
*These seats are so high that my feet don't touch the
ground.* ○ *Don't let your coat touch the wall — the
paint's still wet.* **2** to put one's hand or fingers onto
sb/sth: [Vn] *Don't touch that dish — it's very hot!* ○
Can you touch your toes (ie reach them with your

hands)? [Vnpr] *He touched her gently on the cheek.* **3**
to move or interfere with sb/sth; to harm sb/sth:
[Vn] *I told you not to touch my things!* ○ *He says I
twisted his arm, but I never even touched him!* ○
*Fortunately the paintings were not touched by the
fire.* ○ *What he did was perfectly legal — the police
can't touch* (ie arrest) *him for it.* **4** (usu in negative
sentences) to eat or drink even a little of sth: [Vn]
You've hardly touched your meal. ○ *She never touches
alcohol.* **5** to make sb feel sympathetic or sad: [Vn] *a
sad story that touched us all deeply* ○ *I could see she
was touched by what he said.* **6** (*dated or fml*) to
affect or concern sth/sb: [Vn] *a region that has never
been touched by industry* ○ *matters touching/that
touch us all.* **7** (usu in negative sentences) to be as
good as sb/sth in skill, quality, etc: [Vn] *No one can
touch him* (ie He is the best) *as a designer/in design* ○
*There's nothing to touch mountain air for giving you
an appetite.* **8** to reach a certain level, etc: [Vn]
touch the depths of despair ○ *The speedometer was
touching 120 mph.* ○ *After touching 143, the share
price fell back to 108 by the close of trading.* **IDM** **be
touched with sth** to have a slight quantity of sth:
hair touched with grey ○ *an atmosphere touched with
nostalgia.* **hit/touch a nerve** ⇨ NERVE. **not touch
sb/sth with a 'bargepole** (*Brit infml*) to refuse to
have or be associated with sth/sb: *I can't think why
she wants to marry that awful man — I wouldn't
touch him with a bargepole.* **strike/touch a chord**
⇨ CHORD. **touch 'bottom** to reach the worst possible state or condition: *The property market seems
to have touched bottom.* ,**touch 'wood** (*Brit*); (*US*)
,**knock on 'wood** (*catchphrase*) (an expression
used, often while touching sth made of wood, in the
usu humorous hope of avoiding bad luck): *I've been
driving for 20 years and never had an accident —
touch wood!* **PHRV** ,**touch 'down 1** (of an aircraft)
to land. **2** (in Rugby) to score a TRY²(2) by putting the
ball on the ground behind the other team's goal line.
'touch sb for sth (*sl*) to get sb to give one money as
a loan or by begging: *He tried to touch me for a fiver.*
,**touch sth 'off** to make sth start: *His arrest touched
off a riot.* '**touch on/upon sth** to mention or deal
with a subject briefly: *The article hardly touches on
the central issue in the whole debate.* ,**touch sb 'up**
(*sl*) to touch sb sexually, usu in a way that is unexpected or welcome. ,**touch sth 'up** to improve
sth by making small changes: *touch up some
scratches with a bit of paint.*

touch² /tʌtʃ/ *n* **1** [C usu *sing*] an act of touching: *I
felt the touch of her hand on my arm.* ○ *That pile of
books looks as though it will collapse at the slightest
touch.* **2** [U] the ability to perceive things or their
qualities by touching them: *Blind people rely a lot on
(their sense of) touch.* See also MIDAS TOUCH. **3** [sing]
the way sth feels when touched: *be soft/cold/warm
to the touch* ○ *material with a smooth, silky touch.* **4**
[C] a small detail: *That was a nice touch.* ○ *She's
putting the finishing touches on her latest novel.*
5 [sing] **a** ~ (**of sth**) a slight quantity; a trace: *'Do
you take sugar?' 'Just a touch.'* ○ *There's a touch of
frost in the air.* ○ *I think the sauce needs a touch more
garlic.* ○ *I've got a touch of flu.* **6** [sing] a manner or
style of working, performing, etc: *play the piano
with a light/heavy/firm/delicate touch* ○ *service with
a personal touch* ○ *a computer graphics programme
that gives your work the professional touch.* **7** [sing]
a person's special skill: *I can't do the crossword
today — I must be losing my touch.* **8** [U] (in
football and Rugby) the area outside the lines at the
side of the pitch: *kick the ball into touch.* **IDM** **at a
'touch** if touched, however lightly: *The machine
stops and starts at a touch.* **the common touch** ⇨
COMMON¹. **in/out of 'touch (with sb)** in/not in
communication: *Let's keep in touch.* ○ *Do get in touch
soon* (eg by phone). ○ *Our head office can put you in
touch with a branch in your area.* ○ *I'll be in touch*

again towards the end of the week. ○ *We've been out of touch with Roger for years now.* **in / out of 'touch with sth** having/not having information about sth: *keep in touch with current events by reading the newspapers.* **an easy / a soft 'touch** (*sl*) a person who readily gives or does sth if asked. **lose touch** ⟹ LOSE. **a touch** (with an *adj* or *adv*) slightly: *It's a touch colder today.* ○ *She hit the ball a touch too hard.*
■ **,touch-and-'go** *adj* [usu pred] (*infml*) uncertain as to the result: *It was touch-and-go whether we would get to the airport in time.* ○ *She was so ill that it was touch-and-go whether she would live or not.*
,touch 'football *n* [U] (*US*) a form of football in which touching is used instead of tackling (TACKLE 2a).
'touch-line *n* a line marking the side of a football field.
'touch-type *v* [V] to type without looking at the keys.

touchdown /'tʌtʃdaʊn/ *n* **1** an aircraft's landing. **2** (in American football) a score made by taking the ball across the other team's goal line.

touché /tuːˈʃeɪ; *US* tuːˈʃeɪ/ *interj* (*French*) (used in an argument or a discussion to show that one accepts a good or clever point made by sb else).

touched /tʌtʃt/ *adj* [pred] **1** made to feel sympathy, pleasure or gratitude: *I was very touched by/touched to receive your kind letter.* **2** (*infml*) slightly mad.

touching /'tʌtʃɪŋ/ *adj* causing feelings of pity or sympathy: *a touching sight/story/scene* ○ *I find her loyalty rather touching.* ▶ **touchingly** *adv*.

touchstone /'tʌtʃstəʊn/ *n* a thing providing a standard or test of quality, etc: *a touchstone of artistic excellence* ○ *a touchstone by/against which later operas were judged.*

touchy /'tʌtʃi/ *adj* **(a)** easily offended or upset: *He's very touchy about his baldness.* **(b)** (of a subject, situation, etc) that may easily offend or upset people: *The programme dealt admirably with the touchy subject of incest.* ▶ **touchiness** *n* [U].

tough /tʌf/ *adj* (**-er, -est**) **1** not easily cut or broken; strong: *tough leather boots* ○ *tough material/plastic.* **2** not easily weakened by pain or difficulty; HARDY (1): *These animals need to be tough to survive the arctic winter.* ○ *He should recover — he's pretty tough.* **3** (*esp US*) rough; violent: *one of the toughest areas of the city* ○ *He often plays the **tough guy** in Hollywood movies.* **4** (*derog*) (of food, esp meat) hard to cut or chew; not tender. **5** ~ (**on/with sb/sth**) severe or harsh in attitude or treatment: *tough measures to deal with terrorism* ○ *take a tough line with offenders* ○ *be tough on crime/criminals* ○ *It's time to **get tough with** football hooligans.* **6** difficult: *a tough assignment/problem/journey* ○ *It's tough finding a job these days.* ○ *She's had rather a tough time lately.* ○ *Her successor will find her **a tough act to follow** (ie will find it difficult to do as well as her).* **7** ~ (**on sb**) (*infml*) unfortunate **(a)** (showing sympathy): *That's tough!* (ie Bad luck!) ○ *It's rather tough on him getting ill just before his holiday.* **(b)** (showing a lack of sympathy): *'I haven't got any money.' 'Tough!'* ○ *It's 'your tough luck if you lose her.* **IDM a hard/tough nut** ⟹ NUT. **(as) tough as old 'boots** (*infml*) very tough(1,2,4). **tough 'luck 1** (used to show sympathy). **2** (*ironic*) used to show that one does not really care about sb's bad luck): *If you don't like it that's just tough luck.*
▶ **tough** *n* (*dated infml*) a rough and violent person.
toughen /'tʌfn/ *v* ~ (**sth/sb**) (**up**) to become or make sth/sb tough or tougher: [Vn] *toughened glass* ○ *The government plans to toughen the immigration laws.* [Vnp] *His parents made him join the army to toughen him up.* [also V, Vp].
toughness *n* [U]: *physical/mental toughness.*
■ **,tough-'minded** *adj* realistic and determined in attitude; not sentimental.

toupee /'tuːpeɪ; *US* tuːˈpeɪ/ *n* a patch of false hair worn to cover a part of the head where hair has been lost; a small WIG.

tour /tʊə(r); *Brit also* tɔː(r)/ *n* **1** a journey for pleasure during which various places of interest are visited: *a round-the-world tour* ○ *a coach tour of northern France* ○ *a cycling/walking tour* ○ *tour operators.* See also PACKAGE TOUR. **2** a brief visit to or through a place: *a conducted/guided tour of St Paul's Cathedral* (ie made by a group led by a guide) ○ *go on a tour round the museum* ○ *The head teacher is making a **tour of inspection** of all the classrooms* (eg to see that they are all tidy). ⟹ note at JOURNEY. **3** an official series of visits for the purpose of playing matches, giving performances, etc: *a lecture tour* ○ *the Australian cricket team's forthcoming tour of England* ○ *The orchestra is currently **on tour** in Germany.*
▶ **tour** *v* ~ (**in sth**) to make a tour of or in a place: [Vn, Vpr] *They're touring (in) India.* [Vn] *The play will tour the provinces next month.* [also V].

tour de force /,tʊə də 'fɔːs/ *n* (*pl* **tours de force** /,tʊə də 'fɔːs/) (*French*) an extremely skilful performance or achievement: *a theatrical/musical tour de force.*

tourism /'tʊərɪzəm; *Brit also* 'tɔːr-/ *n* [U] the business of providing accommodation and services for people visiting a place: *Tourism is the country's major industry.*
▶ **tourist** /'tʊərɪst; *Brit also* 'tɔːr-/ *n* **1** a person who is travelling or visiting a place for pleasure: *London is full of foreign tourists in the summer.* ○ *a 'tourist attraction* ○ *a tourist infor'mation centre.* **2** (*sport*) a member of a team on tour(3): *the Australian tourists.* **touristy** *adj* (*infml derog*) full of tourists; designed to attract tourists: *The village has become terribly touristy.*
■ **'tourist class** *n* [U] (on aircraft and ships) second class.
'tourist trap *n* (*infml*) a place that attracts tourists but charges them too much money, etc.

tournament /'tʊənəmənt, 'tɔːn-, 'tɜːn-/ *n* a contest involving a number of competitors, esp one in which the loser at each stage leaves the competition until only the winner remains: *a tennis tournament* ○ *reach the final in a chess tournament.* ⟹ note at SPORT.

tourniquet /'tʊənɪkeɪ; *US* 'tɜːrnəkət/ *n* a piece of cloth, elastic, etc tied tightly round an arm or a leg to stop blood flowing from a wound.

tousle /'taʊzl/ *v* (usu passive) to make esp hair untidy: [Vn] *a girl with blue eyes and fair tousled hair.*

tout /taʊt/ *v* **1** ~ (**for sth**) to try to get people to buy one's goods or services, esp by approaching them directly: [Vpr] *touting for custom/business* [Vn] *touting one's wares* [also V]. **2** [V, Vn] (*Brit*) (*US* **scalp**) to sell tickets for sports events, concerts, etc at a price higher than the official one. **3** ~ **sb/sth** (**as sth**) to offer or propose sb/sth in the hope that people will believe or accept them/it: [Vn-n] *She is frequently touted as the next leader of the party.* [Vn] *They are always touting statistics about the safety of their product.*
▶ **tout** *n* (*Brit*) (*US* **scalper**) a person who touts tickets.

tow /təʊ/ *v* to pull sth along with a rope, chain, etc: [Vn] *tow a caravan* [Vnp] *If you park your car here the police might tow it away.* [also Vnpr]. ⟹ note at PULL[2].
▶ **tow** *n* (usu *sing*) an act of towing sth: *My car won't start — can you give me a tow?* **IDM in tow 1** (*infml*) with sb/sth following behind: *He had his whole family in tow.* **2** (of a damaged ship, etc) being towed: *The trawler took us in tow.* **on 'tow** (esp as a sign on the back of a damaged vehicle) being towed.

■ **'tow-bar** *n* a bar fitted to the back of a vehicle for towing a CARAVAN(1a), etc.

'tow-path *n* a path along the bank of a river or canal, formerly used by horses towing boats (called barges).

'tow-rope *n* a rope used for towing.

towards /təˈwɔːdz; *US* tɔːrdz/ (*also* **toward** /təˈwɔːd; *US* tɔːrd/) *prep* **1** in the direction of sb/sth: *walk towards the river* ○ *look out towards the sea* ○ *He came running towards me.* ○ *She had her back towards the door.* **2** moving closer to achieving sth: *a first step towards political unity* ○ *make progress towards (reaching) an agreement.* **3** in relation to sb/sth: *He has a rather patronizing attitude towards younger people.* ○ *The local people are always very friendly towards tourists.* **4** with the aim of obtaining or contributing to sth: *The money will go towards (the cost of) a new school.* ○ *£30 a month from your salary goes towards a pension fund.* **5** near a point in time: *It gets cooler towards evening.* ○ *He's getting towards retirement age.*

towel /ˈtaʊəl/ *n* a piece of cloth or paper for drying oneself or wiping things dry: *a 'hand-/'bath-towel* ○ *a paper 'towel* ○ *a heated towel-rail.* **IDM** **throw in the sponge/towel** ⇨ SPONGE. See also SANITARY TOWEL, TEA TOWEL.

▶ **towel** *v* (**-ll-**; *US* **-l-**) [Vn, Vnpr, Vnp] ~ **oneself/sb (down)** (**with sth**) to dry oneself/sb with a towel.

towelling (*US* **toweling**) *n* [U] thick soft cloth used esp for making towels: *a towelling bathrobe.*

tower /ˈtaʊə(r)/ *n* a tall narrow building or part of a building. Towers form part of many churchs and castles: *a clock/church tower* ○ *the Tower of London* ○ *the Eiffel Tower.* ⇨ picture at CHURCH. Compare SPIRE. See also CONTROL TOWER, COOLING TOWER, IVORY TOWER, WATCH-TOWER, WATER TOWER. **IDM** **a ˌtower of 'strength** a person who can be relied on to help, protect or comfort others.

▶ **tower** *v* **PHRV** **ˌtower aˈbove/ˈover sb/sth 1** to be much higher or taller than people or things close by: *The mountain towered above us.* ○ *At six feet, he towers over his mother.* **2** to be much greater than others in ability, quality, fame, etc: *She towers over the other sopranos of her generation.*

towering /ˈtaʊərɪŋ/ *adj* [attrib] **1** extremely high or tall: *the towering cliffs/peaks.* **2** (of anger, etc) very great: *be in a towering rage.* **3** (*approv*) very great: *a towering intellectual achievement.*

■ **'tower block** *n* (*Brit*) a very tall block of flats or offices.

town /taʊn/ *n* **1(a)** [C] a place with many houses, shops and other buildings that is larger than a village but smaller than a city: *drive through the centre of town* ○ *the historic town of Cambridge* ○ *Norwich is my **home town*** (ie where I was born or have lived for a long time). **(b)** [CGp] the people who live in a town: *The whole town turned out to welcome the team home.* **2** [sing, U] towns or cities, esp as contrasted with the country: *What are the advantages of living in the town?* ○ *town life.* **3** [U] (after a *prep* and without *the* or *a*) **(a)** the main part of a town where the shops, banks, etc are: *I'm going into town — do you want me to get you anything?* ○ *be in/out of town* (ie in/away from a particular town that is understood or has been referred to). **(b)** the main town or city of an area, eg London for people in the south of England: *go **up to town** to see a play.* See also BOOM TOWN, COUNTY TOWN, DORMITORY TOWN, GHOST TOWN, SHANTY TOWN, SMALL-TOWN. **IDM** **go to 'town (on sth)** (*infml*) to do sth with great energy or enthusiasm, esp by spending a lot of money: *When they give parties they really go to town.* ○ *The papers have really gone to town on the royal wedding* (ie written about it at great length). **a man about town** ⇨ MAN¹. **(out) on the 'town** (*dated or joc*) visiting places of entertainment such as theatres

and clubs in a town or city, esp at night. **paint the town red** ⇨ PAINT².

■ **ˌtown ˈcentre** *n* (*esp Brit*) the main part of a town, where the shops are. Compare DOWNTOWN.

ˌtown ˈcrier (*also* **crier**) *n* (esp formerly) a person employed to make official announcements in public places.

ˌtown ˈhall *n* a building containing local government offices and usu a hall for public meetings, concerts, etc.

'town house *n* **1** a house in town owned by sb who also has one in the country. **2** a modern house built as part of a planned group or row of houses.

ˌtown ˈplanning *n* [U] the control of the growth and development of a town, including its buildings, roads, etc, esp by a local authority.

townee /taʊˈniː/ (*also* **townie** /ˈtaʊni/) *n* (*derog*) a person who iives in a town or city, esp one who is ignorant of country life.

townscape /ˈtaʊnskeɪp/ *n* the view of a town, eg from a distance or in a picture: *an industrial townscape.*

townsfolk /ˈtaʊnsfəʊk/ (*also* **townspeople** /ˈtaʊnzpiːpl/) *n* [pl] the people of a town.

township /ˈtaʊnʃɪp/ *n* **1** a small town; the people living in a small town. **2** (in South Africa) a town or an area of a town intended for use by black people. **3** (in the USA or Canada) a division of a county as a unit of local government.

toxaemia (*also* **toxemia**) /tɒkˈsiːmiə/ *n* [U] (*medical*) = BLOOD-POISONING.

toxic /ˈtɒksɪk/ *adj* poisonous: *toxic drugs* ○ *illegal dumping of toxic waste.*

▶ **toxicity** /tɒkˈsɪsəti/ *n* [U] the quality or degree of being toxic: *substances with low/high toxicity.*

toxicology /ˌtɒksɪˈkɒlədʒi/ *n* the scientific study of poisons. **toxicologist** /-dʒɪst/ *n*.

toxin /ˈtɒksɪn/ *n* a poisonous substance, esp one formed by bacteria in plants and animals and causing a particular disease: *eliminate toxins from the body.*

toy /tɔɪ/ *n* **1** a thing to play with, esp for a child: *cuddly toys* ○ *a toy-shop.* **2** (*often derog*) a thing intended for fun rather than for serious use: *executive toys* ○ *His latest toy is a personal computer.*

▶ **toy** *adj* [attrib] **1** made as a copy of the specified thing and used for playing with: *a toy car/gun/soldier.* **2** (of a dog) of a small breed or variety, kept as a pet: *a toy poodle.*

toy *v* **PHRV** **'toy with sth 1** to consider sth casually or without serious intent: *I've been **toying with the idea** of moving abroad.* **2** to handle or move sth carelessly or without thinking: *toying with a pencil* ○ *She was just toying with her food, as if she wasn't really hungry.*

■ **'toy boy** *n* (*infml*) a woman's much younger male lover.

trace¹ /treɪs/ *n* **1** [C, U] a mark, an object or a sign showing what has existed or happened: *traces of prehistoric habitation* ○ *The police have been unable to find any trace of the gang.* ○ *We've lost **all trace of** him* (ie We no longer know where he is). ○ *The ship had vanished **without trace**.* **2** [C] a very small amount: *The post-mortem revealed traces of poison in her stomach.* ○ *He spoke without a trace of bitterness.*

■ **'trace element** *n* a substance occurring or needed only in extremely small amounts, esp in the soil, for the proper growth of plants.

trace² /treɪs/ *v* **1** ~ **sb/sth (to sth)** to find or discover sb/sth after looking carefully for them/it: [Vn] *attempts to trace a missing 5-year-old* ○ *I cannot trace the letter to which you refer.* **2(a)** ~ **sth (back) (to sth)** to find the origin or cause of sth: [Vnp] *He traces his descent back to the Pilgrim Fathers.* [Vnpr] *The cause of the fire was traced to a faulty fuse-box.* [also Vn]. **(b)** to describe a process or the develop-

ment of sth: [Vn] *Her book traces the town's history from Saxon times to the present day.* **3** to follow a series of marks, signs, etc to where they lead: [Vn] *archaeologists tracing the course of a Roman road* [Vnpr] *They traced the footprints to an old shed.* **4** ~ **sth (out)** to indicate sth in outline: [Vnp] *Those who came later followed the policies he had traced out.* [also Vn, Vnpr]. **5** [Vn] to copy a map, drawing, etc by drawing on transparent paper placed over it.
▶ **traceable** *adj* that can be traced: *a tradition that is traceable to the 15th century.*

tracer *n* **1** a bullet or shell(4) whose course is made visible by a line of smoke, etc left behind it: *tracer bullets.* **2** a RADIOACTIVE substance that can be detected as it passes through eg the human body, by the RADIATION(2) it produces. It is used for investigating a chemical or BIOLOGICAL process.

tracing *n* a copy of a map, drawing, etc made by drawing on transparent paper placed on top of it.
tracing-paper *n* [U] strong transparent paper for making copies of maps, drawings, etc.

trace³ /treɪs/ *n* (usu *pl*) either of the two long fastenings by which a horse is attached to and pulls a carriage, etc. ⇨ picture at HARNESS. **IDM** **kick over the traces** ⇨ KICK¹.

tracery /'treɪsəri/ *n* [U,C] (**a**) an ornamental pattern made of stone in a church window, etc. ⇨ picture at CHURCH. (**b**) a pattern resembling this: *the tracery of veins on a leaf.*

trachea /trə'kiːə; *US* 'treɪkiə/ *n* (*pl* **tracheas** or, in scientific use, **tracheae** /-kiːiː/) (*anatomy*) the passage leading down from the throat, through which one breathes; the WINDPIPE. ⇨ picture at RESPIRATORY.

tracheotomy /ˌtræki'ɒtəmi; *US* ˌtreɪki-/ *n* (*medical*) an operation to cut a hole in sb's TRACHEA, esp to help them to breathe.

track /træk/ *n* **1** (usu *pl*) a line or series of marks left by a moving vehicle, person, animal, etc: *'tyre tracks in the mud* ∘ *fresh 'bear tracks* ∘ *We followed his tracks through the snow.* **2** a course taken by sth/sb: *the track of a storm/comet/satellite* ∘ *The police are on the track of* (ie pursuing) *the escaped prisoner.* **3** a path or rough road: *a muddy track through the forest* ∘ *'sheep tracks on the hillside.* See also CART-TRACK. **4(a)** [C,U] two parallel rails for trains to travel along: *lay some new track* ∘ *The train left the track and crashed down a bank.* (**b**) [C] (*US*) a railway platform: *The train for Chicago is on track 9.* ⇨ note at PATH. **5** a prepared course or circuit for racing: *a 'cycling/'running/'greyhound/'motor-racing track.* See also DIRT-TRACK, RACETRACK. **6(a)** a section of a CD, record¹(3) or tape recording: *Here is a track from her new album.* (**b**) a channel of a recording tape: *a sixteen-track tape recorder.* (**c**) (*computing*) a section of a DISK(2) in which information is stored. **7** a continuous belt of metal plates round the wheels of a tank(2), bulldozer (BULLDOZE), etc, on which it moves. **8** a rail along which sth, eg a curtain, is moved. **IDM** **from/on the wrong side of the tracks** ⇨ WRONG. **hot on sb's/ sth's tracks/trail** ⇨ HOT. **in one's 'tracks** (*infml*) where one is; suddenly: *He fell dead in his tracks.* ∘ *Your question stopped him in his tracks* (ie surprised him and stopped him talking). **jump the rails/ track** ⇨ JUMP¹. **keep/lose track of sb/sth** to keep/fail to keep informed about sb/sth: *lose (all) track of time* (ie forget what time it is) ∘ *It's hard to keep track of* (ie keep in contact with) *all one's old school friends.* **make 'tracks (for...)** (*infml*) to leave for a place: *It's time we made tracks (for home).* **off the beaten track** ⇨ BEAT¹. **on the right/ wrong track** thinking or acting in the right/wrong way: *We haven't found a cure yet, but I'm sure we're on the right track.* See also ONE-TRACK MIND, SOUNDTRACK.

▶ **track** *v* **1** ~ **sb/sth (to sth)** to follow the course or movements of sb/sth: [Vn] *track a satellite/ missile using radar* [Vnpr] *The police tracked the terrorists to their hide-out.* **2** (*cinema*) (of a camera) to move along while filming: [V] *a tracking shot* [also Vpr, Vp]. **PHRV** ˌ**track sb/sth 'down** to find sb/sth by searching: *track down the kidnappers* ∘ *I finally tracked down the reference in a dictionary of quotations.* **tracker** *n* a person who tracks wild animals. **'tracker dog** *n* a dog used for finding criminals or explosives.
▪ **'track events** *n* [pl] sports events that are races run on a track(5), ie not jumping, etc. Compare FIELD EVENTS.
'tracking station *n* a place from which the movements of missiles, aircraft, etc are tracked by RADAR or radio.
'track record *n* the past achievements of a person or an organization: *He has an excellent track record* (ie has been very successful) *as a salesman.* ∘ *a company with a poor track record.*
'track suit (also **jogging suit**) *n* a warm loose pair of trousers and matching jacket worn for sports practice or as casual clothes. Compare SHELL SUIT.

tract¹ /trækt/ *n* **1** a large area of land: *huge tracts of forest/desert.* **2** (*anatomy*) a system of connected parts like tubes along which sth passes: *the di'gestive/re'spiratory/'urinary tract.*

tract² /trækt/ *n* a short essay, esp on a religious or political subject.

tractable /'træktəbl/ *adj* (*fml*) (**a**) (of people) easy to control or influence. (**b**) (of things) easy to deal with: *a less tractable problem/subject.* ▶ **tractability** /ˌtræktə'bɪləti/ *n* [U].

traction /'trækʃn/ *n* [U] **1** the action of pulling sth along a surface; the power used in this: *electric/ steam traction.* **2** (*medical*) treatment that involves continuous pulling on a limb, etc: *She's injured her back and is in traction for a month.* **3** the ability of a tyre or wheel to grip the ground without sliding: *Winter tyres give increased traction in mud or snow.* ▪ **'traction-engine** *n* a vehicle, powered by steam or DIESEL(2), formerly used for pulling heavy loads.

tractor /'træktə(r)/ *n* **1** a powerful motor vehicle used esp for pulling farm machinery. ⇨ picture at PLOUGH. **2** (also **truck tractor**) (*US*) the part of a tractor-trailer (TRACTOR) in which the driver sits. ▪ **'tractor-trailer** *n* (*US*) a large vehicle with two or more sections connected by flexible joints so that it can turn more easily. ⇨ picture at LORRY.

trad /træd/ (also **trad jazz**) *n* [U] (*infml*) traditional JAZZ, ie in the style of the 1920s, with free playing against a background of fixed rhythms and harmonies.

trade¹ /treɪd/ *n* **1(a)** [U] ~ **(with sb/sth)** the exchange of goods or services for money or other goods; buying and selling: *In the past twenty years, Japan's trade with Europe has greatly increased.* ∘ *Trade is always good* (ie Many goods are sold) *over the Christmas period.* ∘ *a trade agreement/deficit/ route.* See also FREE TRADE. (**b**) [C] ~ **(in sth)** a business of a particular kind: *be in the 'cotton/ 'furniture/'book trade* (ie make or sell cotton, furniture, etc) ∘ *The country earns most of its income from the tourist trade.* ∘ *do a brisk trade in* (ie sell a lot of) *cut-price jewellery.* See also RAG TRADE. **2(a)** [U,C] a way of making a living, esp a job that involves training and special skills: *be a butcher/ carpenter/tailor by trade* ∘ *The college offers courses in a variety of trades.* ⇨ note at JOB. (**b**) **the trade** [Gp] the people or companies engaged in a particular area of business: *offer discounts to the trade* ∘ *We sell cars to the trade* (ie to firms that sell cars to the general public). See also STOCK-IN-TRADE. **IDM** **do a roaring trade** ⇨ ROARING. **a jack of all trades** ⇨

JACK¹. **ply one's trade** ⇨ PLY². **the tricks of the trade** ⇨ TRICK.

■ **'trade gap** n (usu sing) the difference between the value of a country's imports and exports: *a widening/worsening trade gap.*

'trade mark n **1** a registered design or name used to identify a company's goods. **2** a distinctive characteristic: *a startling use of colour that is this artist's special trade mark.*

'trade name n **1** a name used to identify a particular type or BRAND(1) of a widely available product: *Aspirin in various forms is sold under a wide range of trade names.* **2** a name taken and used by a person or company for business purposes.

'trade price n the price charged by the company manufacturing a product to a company that will sell it to sb else.

,**trade 'secret** n **1** a device or technique used by a company in manufacturing its products, etc and kept secret from other companies or the general public. **2** (*infml*) a fact, etc that one is not willing to reveal.

,**trade 'union** (also ,**trades 'union, union,** *US* **'labor union**) n an organized association of employees engaged in a particular type of work, formed to protect their interests, improve conditions of work, etc. ,**trade-'unionism** (also ,**trades-'unionism**) n [U] the system of trade unions. ,**trade-'unionist** (also ,**trades-'unionist**) n a member of a trade union. **the** ,**Trades** ,**Union 'Congress** n [sing] (*Brit*) (*abbr* **TUC**) the association of representatives of British trade unions.

'trade wind n a strong wind continually blowing towards the EQUATOR and then to the west.

trade² /treɪd/ v **1(a)** ~ **(in sth) (with sb)** to buy and sell things; to engage in trade: [V] *a company which has ceased trading* (ie gone out of business) ○ *America's trading partners* (ie the countries with which it trades) [Vpr] *a firm which trades in arms/textiles/grain* ○ *an increase in the number of firms trading with Russia* ○ *The firm is trading* (ie doing business) *at a profit/loss.* **(b)** to buy and sell a particular item, product, etc: [Vn] *the volume of shares traded on the Stock Exchange* ○ *Tons of ivory are illegally traded every year.* **2** ~ **at sth** (*US*) to buy goods at a particular shop: [Vpr] *Which store do you trade at?* **3** ~ **(sb) sth (for sth)** to exchange sth for sth else: [Vnpr] *She traded her roller-skates for Bill's radio.* [Vnn] *I'll trade you my stamp collection for your model boat.* [Vn] (*fig*) *neighbours trading insults.* **PHRV** ,**trade sth 'in (for sth)** to give a used article as part of the payment for a new article: *He traded in his car for a new model.* ,**trade sth 'off (against sth)** to exchange sth for sth else which one wants very much when one cannot have or do both: *The company is prepared to trade off its up-market image against a stronger appeal to teenage buyers.* **'trade on sth** (*esp derog*) to make use of sth for one's own advantage: *He traded on the gullibility of the public.*

▶ **tradeable** (also **tradable**) /-əbl/ adj that can be exchanged for money or goods.

trader n a person who trades; a merchant. ⇨ note at DEALER.

trading n [U] business; the process of buying and selling: *brisk/thin trading on the Stock Exchange.*

■ **'trade-in** n a used article given as part of the payment for a new article: *an old car's trade-in value.*

'trade-off n ~ **(between sth and sth)** the balancing of various factors in order to achieve the best combination; a compromise: *a trade-off between efficiency in use and elegance of design.*

'trading estate n (*Brit*) an area designed to be occupied by a number of industrial and commercial firms. Compare INDUSTRIAL ESTATE.

'trading post n a small town in a remote area used as a centre for buying and selling goods.

'trading-stamp n a stamp that is given by certain shops, etc to their customers and may be exchanged later for goods or cash.

tradesman /'treɪdzmən/ n (*pl* **-men** /-mən/) **1** a person who comes to people's homes to deliver goods. **2** a shopkeeper.

tradespeople /'treɪdzpiːpl/ n [pl] people engaged in trade¹(2a).

tradition /trə'dɪʃn/ n **(a)** [U] the passing of beliefs or customs from one generation to the next: *By tradition, people play practical jokes on 1 April.* ○ *We decided to break with* (ie not observe) *tradition and not send any cards this Christmas.* **(b)** [C] a belief or custom passed on in this way; any established method, practice, etc: *literary traditions* ○ *It's a tradition to sing 'Auld Lang Syne' on New Year's Eve.* ○ *He sees himself as a Romantic poet in the tradition of Wordsworth and Coleridge.*

▶ **traditional** /-ʃənl/ adj according to or being tradition: *country people in their traditional costumes* (ie of a type worn for many centuries) ○ *It's traditional in America to eat turkey on Thanksgiving Day.* **traditionalism** /-ʃənəlɪzəm/ n [U] respect or support for tradition, esp as contrasted with modern or new practices. **traditionalist** /-ʃənəlɪst/ n a person who follows or supports tradition: *traditionalist attitudes.* **traditionally** /-ʃənəli/ adv: *In England, turkey is traditionally eaten on Christmas Day.*

traduce /trə'djuːs; *US* -'duːs/ v [Vn] (*fml*) to say damaging false things about sb/sth, esp to make people think badly about them/it. ▶ **traducer** n.

traffic /'træfɪk/ n [U] **1** vehicles moving along a road or street: *heavy/light traffic* ○ *local/motorway traffic* ○ *a traffic diversion* ○ *There's usually a lot of traffic at this time of day.* ○ *Traffic was brought to a standstill by the accident.* **2** the movement of ships or aircraft along a route: *cross-channel traffic* (ie ships crossing the English Channel) ○ *commercial air traffic.* **3** the number of people or the amount of goods moved from one place to another by road, rail, sea or air: *an increase in commuter/freight/goods/passenger traffic.* **4** ~ **(in sth)** illegal trading: *the traffic in drugs/arms/stolen goods.*

▶ **traffic** v (-ck-) ~ **(in sth)** to trade, esp illegally: [V] *drug trafficking* [Vpr] *illegal trafficking in works of art.* **trafficker** n: *a drugs trafficker.*

■ **'traffic circle** n (*US*) = ROUNDABOUT² (1).

'traffic cop n (*US infml*) a police officer who directs traffic, esp where roads meet or cross.

'traffic island (also **island, refuge, safety island,** *US* **safety zone**) n a raised area in the middle of a road dividing two streams of traffic, esp for use by people crossing the road on foot.

'traffic jam n a long line of vehicles that cannot move or that can only move very slowly, eg because there is so much traffic on the road.

'traffic-light (*US* **'stoplight**) n (usu *pl*) an automatic signal that controls road traffic, esp where roads meet or cross, by means of red, orange and green lights.

'traffic warden n (*Brit*) a person whose job is to check that people do not park in the wrong place or for longer than is allowed, and to report on those who do.

tragedy /'trædʒədi/ n **1** [C, U] a terrible event that causes great sadness: *Investigators are searching the wreckage of the plane to try to find the cause of the tragedy.* ○ *The whole affair ended in tragedy.* ○ *It's a tragedy* (ie extremely unfortunate) *for this country that such a great musician died so young.* **2(a)** [C] a serious play with a sad ending: *Shakespeare's tragedies and comedies.* **(b)** [U] the branch of drama that consists of such plays: *Greek tragedy.* Compare COMEDY 1.

T

[V] = verb used alone   [Vn] = verb + noun   [Vp] = verb + particle   [Vpr] = verb + prepositional phrase

▶ **tragedian** /trəˈdʒiːdiən/ *n* **1** a writer of tragedies. **2** an actor in tragedy.

tragedienne /trəˌdʒiːdiˈen/ *n* a woman acting in tragedy.

tragic /ˈtrædʒɪk/ *adj* **1** causing great sadness; very unfortunate: *a tragic accident/mistake/loss* ○ *Hers is a tragic story.* ○ *The effect of the pollution on the beaches is absolutely tragic.* ○ *It's tragic that she died so young.* **2** [attrib] of or in the style of TRAGEDY(2b): *one of our finest tragic actors.* ▶ **tragically** /-kli/ *adv*: *her tragically short life.*

tragicomedy /ˌtrædʒiˈkɒmədi/ *n* [C, U] **(a)** a play with elements of both comedy and TRAGEDY(2b); this branch of drama. **(b)** any event containing both these elements. ▶ **tragicomic** /-ˈkɒmɪk/ *adj*.

trail /treɪl/ *n* **1** a mark or sign in the form of a long line left by sth or sb passing by: *tourists who leave a trail of litter everywhere they go* ○ *The hurricane left a trail of destruction behind it.* See also VAPOUR TRAIL. **2** a path, esp through rough country: *a trail through the forest.* See also NATURE TRAIL. **3** a path, route or series of actions followed for a particular purpose: *a tourist trail* (ie of famous buildings) ○ *politicians on the campaign trail* (ie travelling around to attract support). **4** a track, sign or smell left behind that can be followed, esp in hunting: *The police are still on the trail of the escaped prisoner.* **IDM** **blaze a trail** ⇨ BLAZE³. **hot on sb's/sth's tracks/trail** ⇨ HOT.

▶ **trail** *v* **1** to drag sth or be dragged behind: [Vpr] *Her long skirt was trailing along/on the floor.* [Vn] *a bird trailing a broken wing* [Vnpr] *I trailed my hand in the water as the boat drifted along.* [also V, Vp, Vnpl]. ⇨ note at PULL¹. **2** to walk or move in a tired way, esp behind or later than others: [Vp] *The tired children trailed along behind their parents.* [Vpr] *We trailed around the shops for hours.* ○ *(fig)* [Vp, Vpr] *This country is still trailing far behind (others) in computer research.* **3** ~ (by/in sth) (usu in the continuous tenses) to be losing a game or other contest: [Vpr] *trailing by two goals to one at half-time* ○ *trailing in third place* [also V]. **4** (of plants) to grow over a surface, downwards or along the ground with long winding stems: [V] *trailing ivy* [Vpr] *roses trailing over the walls.* **5** ~ sb/sth (to sth) to follow the trail of sb/sth: [Vn] *trail a criminal/a wild animal* [also Vnpr]. See also TRACK *v* 1. **PHRV** **,trail aˈway/ˈoff** (of speech) to become gradually quieter and then stop, esp because one is shy, confused, etc: *Her voice trailed away to a whisper.*

■ **ˈtrail-blazer** *n* a person who does sth new or original; a PIONEER(1). **ˈtrail-blazing** *adj* [usu attrib] *(approv) trail-blazing work in scientific research.*

trailer /ˈtreɪlə(r)/ *n* **1(a)** a truck or other container with wheels pulled by another vehicle: *a car towing a trailer* ○ *carry camping equipment in a trailer.* **(b)** *(esp US)* = CARAVAN 1a. **2** a series of short extracts from a film or television programme, shown in advance to advertise it.

train¹ /treɪn/ *n* **1** a railway engine with several carriages or trucks linked to and pulled by it: *a ˈpassenger/ˈcommuter/ˈgoods/ˈfreight train* ○ *ˈexpress/ˈstopping trains* ○ *get on/off a train* ○ *catch/take/get the 7.15 train to London* ○ *You have to change trains at Didcot.* ○ *Don't miss the train.* ○ *I prefer to travel by train rather than driving.* ○ *The train pulled into/out of the station.* ○ *a ˈtrain driver.* See also STEAM TRAIN. **2** a number of people or animals, etc moving in a line: *a ˈcamel train* ○ *a ˈbaggage train* (ie people and animals transporting bags, equipment, etc). **3** (usu *sing*) ~ (of sth) a sequence of connected events, thoughts, etc: *His phone call interrupted my train of thought.* ○ *Loss of a loved one brings all sorts of other losses in its train* (ie as a result of it). **4** the part of a long dress

or ROBE(2) that trails behind the person wearing it. See also GRAVY TRAIN. **IDM** **put/set sth in ˈtrain** *(fml)* to prepare or start sth: *That telephone call set in train a whole series of events.*

■ **ˈtrain set** *n* a toy train that runs on a model track.

ˈtrain-spotter *n* a person who collects the numbers of railway engines he or she has seen, as a HOBBY. **ˈtrain-spotting** *n* [U].

train² /treɪn/ *v* **1(a)** ~ sb (as sth/in sth) to teach a person or an animal to perform a particular job or skill well, or to behave in a particular way, by regular instruction and practice: [Vn] *There is a shortage of trained nurses.* [Vn-n, Vnpr] *He was trained as an engineer/in engineering.* [Vn.to inf] *a dog trained to help blind people.* ⇨ note at TEACH. **(b)** ~ (as sth / in sth) to be taught in this way: [V-n] *He trained for a year as a secretary.* [V.to inf] *She trained to be a lawyer.* [also V]. **2** (esp passive) to make one's mind or senses quick to perceive things, esp by practice or instruction: [Vn] *The surveyor examined the wall with a trained eye.* [Vn.to inf] *You need to train your mind to think positively.* **3** ~ (sb/ sth) (for sth) to become physically fit by exercise and diet; to make a person or an animal do this: [Vpr] *The challenger has been training hard for the big fight.* [Vn] *My aunt trains horses.* **4** to make a plant grow in a required direction: [Vnpr] *train roses against/along/over/up a wall* [also Vn]. **PHRV** **ˈtrain sth on sb/sth** to point or aim a gun, camera, HOSE¹, etc at sb/sth: *He trained his binoculars on the distant figures.*

▶ **trainee** /ˌtreɪˈniː/ *n* a person being trained for a job, etc: *a ˌtrainee ˈsalesman.*

trainer *n* **1** a person who trains people or animals: *teacher-trainers* ○ *a guide-dog trainer.* **2** (also **ˈtraining shoe**) (usu *pl*) a soft shoe worn by sports players while exercising, or as casual wear: *a pair of trainers.*

training *n* [U] the process of preparing sb or being prepared for a sport or job: *be in training for a match/competition/race* ○ *One hour each week is set aside for staff training.* **ˈtraining college** *n* (*Brit*) a college that trains people for a trade or profession: *a teacher training college.*

trainman /ˈtreɪnmən/ *n* (*pl* **-men** /-mən/) (*US*) a member of the crew operating a railway train.

traipse /treɪps/ *v* (*infml*) to walk in a tired way: [Vpr] *We spent the whole afternoon traipsing round the shops.* [also Vp].

trait /treɪt; *Brit also* treɪ/ *n* an element in sb's personality; a distinguishing characteristic: *personality traits* ○ *Her fondness for hard work is a family trait.*

traitor /ˈtreɪtə(r)/ *n* ~ (to sb/sth) a person who betrays a friend, her or his country, a cause, etc: *he was seen as a traitor to the socialist cause.* **IDM** **,turn ˈtraitor** to become a traitor.

▶ **traitorous** /ˈtreɪtərəs/ *adj* (*fml*) of or like a traitor: *traitorous behaviour.*

trajectory /trəˈdʒektəri/ *n* the curved path of sth that has been fired, hit or thrown into the air, eg a missile: *a bullet's trajectory* ○ *(fig) the likely trajectory of the economy* (ie the way it will probably develop).

tram /træm/ (also **tramcar** /ˈtræmkɑː(r)/, *US* **streetcar, trolley**) *n* a vehicle that carries passengers, and is usu driven by electricity. Trams run on rails laid along the streets of a town.

tramlines /ˈtræmlaɪnz/ *n* [pl] **1** rails for a TRAM. **2** (*Brit infml*) (*US* **alley**) a pair of parallel lines on a tennis or BADMINTON court marking the extra area used when four people are playing. ⇨ picture at TENNIS.

trammel /ˈtræml/ *v* (**-ll-**; *US* **-l-**) (*fml or rhet*) [Vn] (esp passive) to take away sb's freedom of action; to restrict or limit sb. Compare UNTRAMMELLED.

▶ **trammels** *n* [pl] (*fml or rhet*) things that restrict or limit one's freedom to move, act, etc: *the trammels of tradition.*

tramp /træmp/ *v* **1** to walk with heavy or noisy steps: [Vp] *We could hear him tramping about upstairs.* [Vp] *They came tramping through the kitchen leaving dirty footmarks.* **2** to travel across an area on foot, esp for a long distance and often in a tired way: [Vpr] *tramping over the moors* [Vn, Vpr] *We tramped (for) miles and miles without finding anywhere to stay.* [Vn] *tramp the streets looking for work* [also Vp]. ⇨ note at STAMP¹.

▶ **tramp** *n* **1** [C] a person with no fixed home or occupation who wanders from place to place. **2** [C usu *sing*] a long walk: *go for a tramp.* **3** [sing] the ~ **of sb/sth** the sound of sb's heavy steps: *hear the tramp of marching feet.*

■ ¹**tramp steamer** *n* a ship that does not travel on a regular route but carries goods between many different ports.

trample /ˈtræmpl/ *v* **1** ~ **sth/sb (down)** to tread heavily on sth/sb so as to cause damage or destruction: [Vn, Vnp] *The campers had trampled the corn (down).* [Vnadv] *The flowers lay trampled underfoot.* [Vpr, Vp] *I don't want those people trampling (about) all over my garden.* [Vnpr] *The crowd panicked and ten people were trampled to death.* **2** ~ **on/upon sth/sb (a)** to crush or harm sth by treading on it: [Vpr] *Don't trample on the flowers.* **(b)** to fail to consider sb's feelings, rights, etc; to treat sb/sth with contempt: [Vpr] *I refuse to be trampled on any longer!*

trampoline /ˈtræmpəliːn/ *n* a sheet of strong material attached by springs to a frame, used for jumping high into the air and doing rolling or turning movements in the air.

▶ **trampoline** *v* to use a trampoline: [V] *enjoy trampolining.*

tramway /ˈtræmweɪ/ *n* the rails forming a route for a TRAM.

trance /trɑːns; *US* træns/ *n* **1** a state like sleep, caused eg by being hypnotized (HYPNOSIS): *go/fall into a trance* ∘ *put/send sb into a trance* ∘ *come out of a trance* ∘ *a trance-like state.* **2** a state in which one concentrates on one's thoughts and does not notice what is happening around one: *She's been in a trance all day — I think she's in love.*

tranche /trɑːnʃ/ *n* (*Brit finance*) a portion, esp of money or shares (SHARE¹ 3): *the first tranche of the company's new share issue.*

tranquil /ˈtræŋkwɪl/ *adj* quiet and peaceful: *a tranquil scene/pond/sea* ∘ *lead a tranquil life in the country.* ▶ **tranquillity** (*US* also **tranquility**) /træŋˈkwɪlət i/ *n* [U]: *an atmosphere of peace and tranquillity.* **tranquilly** *adv.*

tranquillize, -ise (*US* also **tranquilize**) /ˈtræŋkwəlaɪz/ *v* to make a person or an animal calmer or unconscious, esp by means of a drug: [Vn] *the tranquillizing effect of the music* ∘ *The game wardens tranquillized the rhinoceros with a drugged dart.*

▶ **tranquillizer, -iser** *n* a drug for making an anxious person feel calm, or for tranquillizing animals: *She's on* (ie is taking) *tranquillizers.*

trans- *pref* (with *adjs*) across; beyond: *transatlantic* ∘ *trans-Siberian.* **2** (with *vs*) into another place or state: *transplant* ∘ *transform.*

transact /trænˈzækt/ *v* ~ **sth (with sb)** (*fml*) to conduct or carry out business, esp involving two people or organizations: [Vn] *transact a deal/ negotiations* [Vnpr] *business transacted with a client.*

transaction /trænˈzækʃn/ *n* **1** [U] ~ (**of sth**) the conducting of business: *the transaction of official/ routine/government/public business.* **2** [C] a piece of business done: *cheque/credit/cash transactions* ∘ *legal/commercial/property transactions.*

transatlantic /ˌtrænzətˈlæntɪk/ *adj* [esp attrib] **1**

crossing the Atlantic: *a transatlantic flight/yacht/ telephone call.* **2** concerning countries on both sides of the Atlantic: *transatlantic cooperation.* **3** on or from the other side of the Atlantic: *transatlantic* (eg American) *visitors to Europe* ∘ *speak with a transatlantic drawl.*

transcend /trænˈsend/ *v* (*fml*) to be or go beyond the normal limits of sth: [Vn] *issues that transcend party politics* ∘ *Such matters transcend human knowledge* (ie We cannot know about them).

transcendent /trænˈsendənt/ *adj* (*fml approv*) extremely great; supreme: *a writer of transcendent genius.* ▶ **transcendence** /-dəns/ *n* [U].

transcendental /ˌtrænsenˈdentl/ *adj* [usu attrib] going beyond the limits of human knowledge, experience or reason, esp in a religious or spiritual way: *a transcendental experience.*

▶ **transcendentalism** /ˌtrænsenˈdentəlɪzəm/ *n* [U] a philosophy that stresses belief in transcendental things and the importance of spiritual rather than material existence. **transcendentalist** /-təlɪst/ *n.*

■ ˌ**transcenˌdental mediˈtation** *n* [U] (*abbr* **TM**) a method of freeing oneself from problems, anxiety, etc by thinking deeply in silence and repeating a special phrase to oneself over and over again.

transcontinental /ˌtrænzɪˌkɒntɪˈnentl; *US* ˌtræns-/ *adj* crossing a continent: *a transcontinental highway/railway.*

transcribe /trænˈskraɪb/ *v* **1** ~ **sth (into sth)** to represent sth in or convert sth into a written or printed form: [Vnpr] *transcribe a tune into musical notation* [Vn-n] *The word 'the' is transcribed (as) /ðə/ in phonetic symbols.* **2** ~ **sth (from sth)** to copy sth in writing: [Vnpr] *a novel transcribed from the author's original manuscript* [also Vn, V]. **3** ~ **sth (for sth)** to change the written form of a piece of music so that it can be played on a different instrument or sung by a different voice: [Vnpr] *a piano piece transcribed for the guitar* [also Vn].

▶ **transcript** /ˈtrænskrɪpt/ *n* **1** (also **transcription**) a written or printed copy of spoken words: *a transcript of the trial/speech.* **2** (*esp US*) a copy of an official record of a student's work, showing courses taken and grades achieved.

transcription /trænˈskrɪpʃn/ *n* **1** [U] the action or process of transcribing sth: *errors made in transcription.* **2** [C] **(a)** = TRANSCRIPT 1. **(b)** a written representation of sth: *the phonetic transcription of a word.* **(c)** a musical piece produced by transcribing (TRANSCRIBE 3) a piece of music: *a transcription for piano duet/of Beethoven's Fifth Symphony.*

transducer /trænzˈdjuːsə(r); *US* -ˈduːsər/ *n* (*techn*) a device for producing an electrical impulse from another form of energy, eg pressure.

transept /ˈtrænsept/ *n* (*architecture*) either of the two wide parts of a church shaped like a cross, which are built at right angles (RIGHT¹) to the main central part: *the north/south transept of the cathedral.* Compare NAVE. ⇨ picture at CHURCH.

transfer¹ /trænsˈfɜː(r)/ *v* (**-rr-**) **1** ~ **sth/sb (from...) (to...)** to move sth/sb from one place to another: [Vnpr] *The patient was transferred to another hospital.* ∘ *transfer money between bank accounts/into another bank account* ∘ *Our head office has been transferred from London to Cardiff.* [Vn] (*fig*) *transfer one's affections/allegiance* (ie become fond of/ loyal to sb else) [Vnpr] *Don't try to transfer the blame (on)to somebody else.* **2(a)** ~ **(sb/sth) (from...) (to...)** to change or move sb to another group, occupation or service: [Vpr, Vnpr] *He has (been) transferred from the warehouse to the accounts department.* [Vpr] *The patient wants to transfer to another doctor.* [also Vn, V]. **(b)** ~ **sb (from ...) (to ...)** (esp in football) to sell or give a player to another club: [Vnpr] *He was transferred from Arsenal to Manchester United.* [also Vn]. **3** ~ **(from ...)**

(to ...) to change to another place, route or means of transport during a journey: [Vpr] *We had to transfer from the south to the north terminal to catch a plane home* ∘ *The passengers had to transfer onto coaches because the railway line was blocked.* [also V]. **4** ~ **sth (to sb)** to hand over the possession of property or certain rights to sb else: [Vnpr] *He transferred ownership of the land to his nephew.* [also Vn]. **5** ~ **(sth) (from sth) (to sth)** to express or copy sth using a different medium; to be expressed or copied in this way: [Vnpr] *transfer computer data from disk to tape* [Vpr] *Her novels don't transfer easily to the cinema.* [also Vn, V].

▶ **transferable** /-ˈfɜːrəbl/ *adj* that can be transferred: *This ticket is not transferable* (ie It may only be used by the person to whom it is issued). **transferability** /ˌtrænsˌfɜːrəˈbɪləti/ *n* [U].

transference /ˈtrænsfərəns; *US* trænsˈfɜːrəns/ *n* [U] the action of transferring sth or the process of being transferred: *the transference of heat from the liquid to the container.*

transfer² /ˈtrænsfɜː(r)/ *n* **1** [U, C] **(a)** the action of transferring sth/sb or an instance of being transferred: *the transfer of currency from one country to another* ∘ *He has asked for a transfer to the company's Paris branch.* See also CREDIT TRANSFER. **(b)** an act or the process of transferring a sports player to another club: *the first goal he has scored since his transfer from/to Dallas* ∘ *a ˈtransfer fee/request* ∘ *be on the transfer list* (ie available to join another club). **2(a)** [U, C] an act of changing to a different place, vehicle or route during a journey: *The transfer from the airport to the hotel is included in the price.* **(b)** [C] (*US*) a ticket that allows a passenger to continue her or his journey on another bus or train. **3** [C] (*esp Brit*) a picture or design that is removed from a piece of paper and stuck onto a surface, esp by being pressed or heated.

transfigure /trænsˈfɪgə(r)/ *v* (*fml*) (usu passive) to change the appearance of sb/sth, esp so as to make them/it nobler or more beautiful: [Vn] *Her usually solemn face is transfigured when she smiles.* ▶ **transfiguration** /ˌtrænsˌfɪgəˈreɪʃn; *US* -gjəˈr-/ *n* [U, C].

transfix /trænsˈfɪks/ *v* (*fml*) (usu passive) to make sb unable to move, think or speak because of fear, surprise, etc: [Vnpr] *be transfixed with disbelief* [Vn] *We stood transfixed as the car toppled over the cliff.*

transform /trænsˈfɔːm/ *v* ~ **sth/sb (from sth) (into sth)** to change the appearance or character of sth/sb completely: [Vn] *A fresh coat of paint can transform a room.* ∘ *She used to be terribly shy, but a year abroad has completely transformed her* (ie so that she is no longer shy). [Vnpr] *The building of the canal has transformed the area from desert into fertile farmland.*

▶ **transformation** /ˌtrænsfəˈmeɪʃn/ *n* [C, U] ~ **(from sth) (to sth)** the action or an instance of transforming sth/sb; the state of being transformed: *the country's transformation from dictatorship to democracy* ∘ *His character seems to have undergone a complete transformation.*

transformer *n* an apparatus for increasing or reducing the voltage (VOLT) of an electric power supply, to allow a particular piece of electrical equipment to be used.

transfusion /trænsˈfjuːʒn/ (also **blood transfusion**) *n* [C, U] an act or the process of putting one person's blood into another person's body: *The injured man had lost a lot of blood and had to be given a transfusion.* ∘ (*fig*) *The project badly needs a transfusion of cash.*

transgenic /ˌtrænzˈdʒenɪk; *US* ˈtræns-/ *adj* (*biology*) (of an animal or a plant) having GENETIC material introduced from another type of animal or plant.

transgress /trænzˈgres; *US* træns-/ *v* **1** (*fml*) to go beyond the limit of what is morally or legally ac-

ceptable: [Vn] *transgress the bounds of decency.* **2** ~ **(against sth)** [V, Vpr] (*arch*) to offend against a moral or religious principle; to SIN¹ *v.*

▶ **transgression** /trænzˈgreʃn; *US* træns-/ *n* [C, U]. **transgressor** *n* (*fml*) a person who transgresses.

transient /ˈtrænziənt; *US* ˈtrænʃnt/ *adj* **1** lasting for only a short time; brief; temporary: *transient moods/problems.* Compare TRANSITORY. **2** staying or working in a place for a short time only, before moving on: *a city with a large transient population* (ie of students or temporary workers).

▶ **transience** /-əns/ *n* [U]: *the transience of human life.*

transient *n* a transient(2) person: *Most of the farm labourers are transients.*

transistor /trænˈzɪstə(r), -ˈsɪst-/ *n* **1** a small electronic device used in radios, televisions and similar appliances, for controlling an electrical signal as it passes along a circuit. **2** (also **tranˌsistor ˈradio**) a radio with transistors, esp a small one that can be carried.

transit /ˈtrænzɪt, -sɪt/ *n* **(a)** [U] the process of going or being taken or transported from one place to another: *goods delayed or lost in transit.* **(b)** [U, C usu sing] the act of going through a place on the way to somewhere else: *ships making the transit through the Panama Canal* ∘ *Transit passengers should wait in the transit lounge* (ie at an airport). ∘ *a transit visa* (ie one allowing a person to pass through a country but not to stay there).

■ **ˈtransit camp** *n* a camp providing temporary accommodation, esp for refugees (REFUGEE).

transition /trænˈzɪʃn, -ˈsɪʃn/ *n* [U, C] ~ **(from sth) (to sth)**; ~ **(between sth and sth)** the process or a period of changing from one state or condition to another: *the transition from childhood to adult life* ∘ *the transition between the old tax system and the new one* ∘ *Will the country be able to make a peaceful transition to democracy?* ∘ *go through a period of transition.* ▶ **transitional** /-ʃənl/ *adj: a transitional stage/period* ∘ *a transitional government* (ie one holding power temporarily during a period of change). **tranˌsitional reˈlief** *n* [U] (*Brit*) money available for reducing tax payments for a temporary period after the introduction of a new tax system, for people who would normally have to pay a much greater amount than under the old system.

transitive /ˈtrænsətɪv/ *adj* (*grammar*) (of a verb) that is used with a direct object either expressed or understood. Simple transitive verbs are labelled Vn in this dictionary. Compare INTRANSITIVE. ▶ **transitively** *adv.*

transitory /ˈtrænsətri; *US* -tɔːri/ *adj* lasting for only a short time; brief; temporary: *the transitory nature of his happiness* ∘ *Their success was only transitory.* Compare TRANSIENT 1.

translate /trænsˈleɪt/ *v* **1** ~ **(sth) (from sth) (into sth)** to change sth spoken or esp written from another language: [V] *He didn't understand Greek, so I offered to translate.* [Vnpr] *translate an article into Dutch* [Vn-n] *'Suisse' had been wrongly translated as 'Sweden'.* [Vnpr] (*fig*) *Can someone translate this legal jargon into plain English for me?* [also Vn]. Compare INTERPRET 3. **2** to be translated or be capable of being translated into another language: [Vadv] *Most poetry doesn't translate well.* [V-n] *The Welsh name translates as 'Land's End'.* **3** ~ **(sth) into sth** to express sth or to be expressed in a different, esp a more practical form: [Vnpr] *It's time to translate our ideas into action.* [Vpr] *The Party's favourable image doesn't always translate into votes.*

▶ **translation** /-ˈleɪʃn/ *n* **1** [U] the activity of translating: *errors in translation* ∘ *the translation of theories into practice.* **2** [C, U] a text or word that is translated: *make/do a translation of a document* ∘ *a rough/a literal/an exact translation* ∘ *The usual* translation of 'glasnost' is 'openness'. ○ *read Homer* **in translation** (ie in a different language from that in which he wrote).

translator *n* a person who translates writing or speech, esp as a job. Compare INTERPRETER.

transliterate /træns'lɪtəreɪt/ *v* ~ **sth** (**into/as sth**) to write words or letters in or as the letters of a different alphabet: [Vn, Vnpr] *transliterate Greek place-names (into the Roman alphabet)* [also Vn-n]. ▶ **transliteration** /ˌtrænsˌlɪtə'reɪʃn/ *n* [C, U].

translucent /træns'luːsnt/ *adj* allowing light to pass through but not transparent: *bathroom windows made of translucent glass* ○ *pale, translucent skin.* ▶ **translucence** /-sns/ (also **translucency** /-snsi/) *n* [U]: *the shimmering translucency of her fine silk gown.*

transmigration /ˌtrænzmaɪ'greɪʃn; *US* ˌtræns-/ *n* [U] the passing or a person's soul after death into another body.

transmission /træns'mɪʃn/ *n* **1** [U] the action or process of transmitting sth or of being transmitted: *the transmission of disease* ○ *the transmission of computer data along telephone lines* ○ *a break in transmission* (ie of a radio or television broadcast) *due to a technical fault.* **2** [C] a radio or television broadcast: *a live transmission from Washington.* **3** [U, C] the system of gears, etc by which power is passed from the engine to the wheels in a motor vehicle: *a car fitted with (an) automatic transmission.*

transmit /træns'mɪt/ *v* (-tt-) **1** ~ **sth** (**from…**) (**to…**) (**a**) to produce a signal by electronic means such as radio waves that can be heard by people elsewhere: [Vnpr] *signals transmitted from a satellite* [Vn] *transmit a Mayday call* [also V]. (**b**) to broadcast a radio or television programme: [Vn, Vnpr] *The World Cup final is being transmitted live (to over fifty countries).* **2** ~ **sth/itself** (**from…**) (**to…**) to pass sth from one person, place or thing to another: [Vnadv] *sexually transmitted diseases* [Vnpr] *They unwittingly transmit their own fears to their children.* [also Vn].
▶ **transmitter** *n* **1** a device or set of equipment for transmitting radio or other electronic signals. **2** a person or creature or thing that transmits sth: *The mosquito is a transmitter of disease.*

transmute /trænz'mjuːt/ *v* ~ **sth** (**into sth**) (*fml*) to change sth into a different substance, nature or form: [Vnpr] *It was once thought that ordinary metal could be transmuted into gold.* ○ *transmute personal feelings into poetry* [also Vn]. ▶ **transmutation** /ˌtrænzmjuː'teɪʃn/ *n* [C, U].

transnational /ˌtrænz'næʃnəl/ *adj* (*esp commerce*) operating in or between many different countries, without being based in any particular one: *transnational organizations/corporations.* Compare MULTI-NATIONAL.

transom /'trænsəm/ *n* **1** a bar of eg wood or stone across the top of a door or window. ⇨ picture at CHURCH. **2** (*esp US*) a window above the transom of a door or of a larger window.

transparent /træns'pærənt/ *adj* **1** allowing light to pass through so that objects behind can be seen clearly: *a box with a transparent lid* ○ *the pure, transparent waters of the lake.* Compare TRANSLU-CENT. **2** about which there can be no doubt or mistake; obvious: *a transparent lie* ○ *his straightforwardness and transparent honesty.* **3** (*approv*) easily understood; accessible; simple or clear: *a transparent style of writing.*
▶ **transparency** /-rənsi/ *n* **1** [U] the state or quality of being transparent: *a plastic with the transparency of glass.* **2** [C] a photograph printed on transparent plastic, so that it can be viewed when a light is shone through it; a slide²(5).

transparently *adv*: *be transparently honest/obvious.*

transpire /træn'spaɪə(r)/ *v* **1** (used with *it* and a *that*-clause; not usu in the continuous tenses) to become known; to prove to be so: [V.*that*] *This, it later transpired, was untrue.* ○ *It transpired that the gang had had a contact inside the bank.* **2** to happen: [V] *You're meeting him tomorrow? Let me know what transpires.*

transplant /træns'plɑːnt; *US* -'plænt/ *v* **1** ~ **sth** (**in/into sth**) to remove a growing plant with its roots still attached and plant it elsewhere: [Vnpr] *Transplant the seedlings into peaty soil.* [also Vn]. **2** ~ **sth** (**from sb/sth**) (**to/into sb/sth**) to take tissue or an organ from one person, animal or part of the body and put it into another: [Vnpr] *transplant a kidney into a 10-year-old boy* [Vn] *Patients often reject transplanted organs.* Compare IMPLANT 1. **3** ~ **sb/sth** (**from…**) (**to…**) to move sb/sth to a different place or environment: [Vnpr] *He hated being transplanted from his home in the country to the noise and bustle of the city.* [also Vn].
▶ **transplant** /'trænsplɑːnt; *US* -plænt/ *n* (**a**) [C] an instance of transplanting (TRANSPLANT 2) an organ, etc: *have a bone-marrow transplant* ○ *a heart transplant operation/patient.* Compare IMPLANT *n.* (**b**) [U] the transplanting of an organ, etc: *organs available for transplant.*
transplantation /ˌtrænsplɑːn'teɪʃn; *US* -plæn-/ *n* [U]: *the ethics of organ transplantation.*

transport¹ /'trænspɔːt/ *n* **1** (*US* also **transportation**) [U] (**a**) vehicles, roads, railways, etc for carrying people or goods from one place to another: *road/rail transport* ○ *I normally travel by/on public transport* (ie on trains or buses, not in a car). ○ *She works for London Transport as a bus driver.* (**b**) a vehicle or a method of travel: *His bicycle is his only means of transport.* ○ *My car is being repaired so I'm without transport at the moment.* (**c**) [U] the activity of carrying goods on vehicles: *regulations governing the transport of dangerous chemicals* ○ *transport costs/charges.* **2** [C] a ship, an aircraft or some other vehicle for carrying large loads, eg troops or supplies: *Military transports were used to evacuate the civilian populations.* ○ *a transport aircraft.* **3** **transports** [pl] ~ **of sth** (*rhet*) strong feelings: *in transports of joy/delight/grief.*
■ **'transport café** *n* (*Brit*) a CAFÉ beside a main road providing cheap food, esp for lorry drivers.

transport² /træn'spɔːt/ *v* **1**(**a**) to take sth/sb from one place to another in a vehicle: [Vnpr] *She was transported to hospital by helicopter.* [also Vn]. (**b**) to carry sth/sb somewhere by means of a natural process: [Vn, Vnpr] *The seeds are transported by/on the wind.* ○ *Blood transports oxygen around the body.* (**c**) to take sb/sth to a different state or context: [Vnpr] *European political institutions were transported to Africa.* ○ *The book transports you into another world.* [also Vn]. **2** (*esp formerly*) to send sb to a distant place against their will, eg as a punishment: [Vnpr] *British convicts were transported to Australia for life.* [also Vn].
▶ **transportable** /-əbl/ *adj* that can be transported.
transportation /ˌtrænspɔː'teɪʃn/ *n* [U] **1** (*esp US*) = TRANSPORT¹ 1. **2** the action of transporting eg criminals or the process of being transported: *sentenced to transportation.*
transported *adj* [pred] ~ (**with sth**) (*rhet*) affected by strong, usu pleasant, emotions: *transported with joy/delight* ○ *I was utterly transported by her performance.*
transporter /træn'spɔːtə(r)/ *n* a large vehicle used for carrying heavy objects, eg vehicles: *a car/tank/rocket transporter.*

transpose /træn'spəʊz/ *v* **1** to cause two or more things to change places: [Vn] *Two letters were acci-*

dentally transposed, and 'hand' got printed as 'hnad'. **2** ~ **sth (from ...) to ...**; ~ **sth into sth** to move or adapt sth to a different place or environment: [Vnpr] *The director transposes Shakespeare's play from 16th-century Venice to present-day England.* **3** ~ **sth (from sth) (into/to sth)** (*music*) to write or play an existing piece of music in a different key: [Vnpr] *transposing the song into D minor* [also V, Vnpl]. ▶ **transposition** /ˌtrænspə'zɪʃn/ *n* [C, U].

transsexual /trænz'sekʃuəl/ *n* (**a**) a person who emotionally feels herself or himself to be a member of the other sex. (**b**) a person who has had her or his external sexual organs removed or altered in order to resemble the other sex.

transubstantiation /ˌtrænsəbˌstænʃi'eɪʃn/ *n* [U] (*religion*) the belief that the bread and wine in the Eucharist are changed after they have been blessed into the body and blood of Christ, though their appearance does not change.

transverse /'trænzvɜːs/ *adj* [usu attrib] lying or acting across sth: *a transverse bar joining two posts.*

transvestite /trænz'vestaɪt/ *n* a person who dresses in the clothes of the opposite sex, esp for sexual pleasure. ▶ **transvestism** /trænz'vestɪzəm/ *n* [U] the practice of being a transvestite.

trap /træp/ *n* **1(a)** a plan for harming, capturing or detecting sb: *Don't go in there. It's a trap.* ○ *The thieves were caught in a police trap.* (**b**) a trick or clever action designed to make sb betray their ideas, reveal a secret, etc: *You fell right into my trap.* ○ *Is this question a trap?* (**c**) (usu *sing*) an unpleasant situation from which it is hard to escape: *Some women see marriage as a trap.* ○ *I fell into the trap of taking on new debts to pay off my old ones.* See also BOOBY TRAP, DEATH-TRAP, POVERTY TRAP, RADAR TRAP. **2** a device for catching animals: *lay/set/bait a trap* ○ *The mouse was caught in a trap.* See also MOUSE-TRAP. **3** a device or place where the specified thing collects: *a sediment trap.* See also TOURIST TRAP. **4** a light carriage with two wheels, pulled by a horse. **5** a cage from which a GREYHOUND is released at the start of a race: *The favourite has been drawn in trap 4.* **6** = TRAPDOOR. **7** (*sl*) mouth: *Shut your trap!*
▶ **trap** *v* (**-pp-**) **1** to keep sb in a place from which they want to move but cannot: [Vn] *Help! I'm trapped.* ○ *be trapped by the rising tide* [Vnadv] *The lift broke down and we were trapped inside.* [Vnpr] *They were trapped in the burning hotel.* ○ (*fig*) *He was trapped in an unhappy marriage.* **2** to catch sth somewhere, usu accidentally, so that it is stuck and cannot easily be moved: [Vnpr] *My jacket was trapped in the car door.* [Vn] *The pain was caused by a trapped nerve.* **3** to keep sth in a particular place and prevent it from escaping: [Vnpr] *The filter traps dust from the air.* ○ *a special fabric that traps body heat* [Vnpr] *harmful gases trapped in the earth's atmosphere.* **4** ~ **sb (into sth/doing sth)** to catch sb by a trick: [Vn, Vnpr] *The question was meant to trap him (into revealing his true identity).* **5** to catch an animal in a trap: [Vn] *It's cruel to trap birds.* [V] *The tribesmen obtain food by hunting and trapping.*
trapper *n* a person who traps animals, esp for their fur.

trapdoor /'træpdɔː(r)/ (also **trap**) *n* a door in a floor, ceiling or roof.

trapeze /trə'piːz; *US* træ-/ *n* a swing with a narrow seat suspended high above the ground. Trapezes are used esp by CIRCUS(1) performers: *a trapeze artist.*

trapezium /trə'piːziəm/ *n* (*pl* **trapeziums**) (*geometry*) **1** (*Brit*) (*US* **trapezoid**) a flat shape with four straight sides, one pair of opposite sides being parallel and the other pair not parallel. ⇨ picture at QUADRILATERAL. **2** (*US*) = TRAPEZOID 1.

trapezoid /'træpəzɔɪd/ *n* (*geometry*) **1** (*Brit*) (*US* **trapezium**) a flat shape with four straight sides, none of which are parallel. ⇨ picture at QUADRILATERAL. **2** (*US*) = TRAPEZIUM 1.

trappings /'træpɪŋz/ *n* [pl] the outward signs, objects and ceremonies associated with a particular situation, esp wealth or high status: *a big car, a country house, and all the other trappings of success* ○ *He had the trappings of high office but no real power.*

trash /træʃ/ *n* [U] **1** (*derog*) objects, ideas, writing, etc of poor quality: *He dismisses a lot of modern art as trash.* **2** (*US*) household or other waste, esp paper, cardboard or other dry material: *take out the trash.* Compare GARBAGE 1a. **3** (*US infml derog*) people that one does not respect: *white trash* (ie poor or deprived (DEPRIVE) white people).
▶ **trash** (*US infml*) to damage or destroy sth, esp in anger or as a protest: [Vn] *Vandals broke into the studio and trashed all the equipment.*
trashy *adj* of poor quality: *trashy novels/souvenirs.*
■ **'trash can** *n* (*US*) = DUSTBIN.

trauma /'trɔːmə; *US* 'traʊmə/ *n* (*pl* **traumas**) [U, C] **1(a)** (*psychology*) an emotional shock producing a lasting harmful effect. (**b**) [often *pl*] (*infml*) an unpleasant experience that causes one distress or anxiety: *going through the trauma(s) of divorce/of moving to a new house.* **2** (*medical*) an injury.
▶ **traumatic** /trɔː'mætɪk; *US* traʊ-/ *adj* **1** (of an experience) unpleasant; causing distress: *Our journey home was pretty traumatic.* ○ *a traumatic period in European history.* **2** (*techn*) of or causing trauma of the mind or the body.
traumatize, -ise /'trɔːmətaɪz; *US* 'traʊ-/ *v* (esp passive) to cause great shock or distress to sb: [Vn] *The team were utterly traumatized by their defeat.*

travail /'træveɪl, trə'veɪl/ *n* [U, C usu *pl*] (*arch or rhet*) an unpleasant experience or situation that involves a lot of effort or suffering: *the country's economic travails.*

travel /'trævl/ *v* (**-ll-**; *US* **-l-**) **1(a)** to make a journey or journeys: [V] *I love travelling.* ○ *We had been travelling for over a week.* [Vpr] *travel to work/across Africa* [Vadv] *travel abroad* [Vp] *We travelled down (to London) by car.* (**b**) to cover a distance in travelling; to make a journey, across, through, etc an area: [Vn] *He's travelled the whole world.* ○ *travel forty miles to work each day.* ⇨ note. **2** to move or go: [Vadv] *Light travels faster than sound.* ○ *News travels quickly these days.* [Vpr] *The billiard ball travelled across the table.* [Vp] (*fig*) *The author travels back (in time) to his youth.* **3** (of a product) to be still of good quality after a long journey: [Vadv] *Some wines do not travel well.* [also V]. **4** (*infml*) to move very fast: [Vn] *At top speed it can really travel.*
▶ **travel** *n* **1** [U] the activity or action of travelling: *'rail/'air/'space travel* ○ *foreign travel* ○ *Travel in the mountains can be slow and dangerous.* ○ *'travel books/writers* ○ *'travel arrangements/insurance.* **2** **travels** [pl] travelling or journeys, esp abroad: *She wrote an account of her travels in China.* ○ *I met many interesting people on my travels.* ⇨ note at JOURNEY. **3** [U] the extent, rate or type of movement of a mechanical part: *There's too much travel on the brake, it needs tightening.*
travel (also esp *US* **travelling**) *adj* [attrib] (of things) designed to be used when travelling: *a 'travel bag/rug/cot.*
travelled (*US* **traveled**) *adj* (usu in compounds) **1** (of a person) having travelled to a lot of places: *a well-/much-/widely-travelled journalist.* **2** (of a road, etc) used by people travelling: *This route was once much travelled.*
traveller (*US* **traveler**) /'trævələ(r)/ *n* **1** a person who is travelling or who often travels: *the famous traveller, writer and broadcaster* ○ *Travellers can expect further disruption on the railways today.* ○

special fares for frequent/business travellers. **2** (*esp Brit*) a person with no fixed home, esp one living in a community or camp that moves from place to place: *New Age Travellers.* **3** a travelling sales representative. See also COMMERCIAL TRAVELLER.

'traveller's cheque (*US* **'traveler's check**) *n* a cheque for a fixed amount, sold by a bank or travel agent, and easily exchanged for cash in foreign countries.

travelling (*US* **traveling**) *adj* [attrib] **1** making journeys or going from place to place: *a travelling circus/musician/exhibition* ○ *Roadworks inconvenience* **the travelling public.** **2** (*esp US*) = TRAVEL *adj.* — *n* [U]: *Travelling in the mountains can be dangerous at this time of year.* ○ *'travelling expenses* ○ *my 'travelling companions.* **,travelling 'salesman** *n* = COMMERCIAL TRAVELLER.

travelogue (*US* also **travelog**) /'trævəlɒg; *US* -lɔ:g/ *n* a film, broadcast or piece of writing about travel.

■ **'travel agent** *n* a person or firm whose job is making arrangements for people wishing to travel, eg obtaining tickets or reserving hotel rooms: *I arranged my trip through my local travel agent.* **'travel agency** *n* a firm or office of travel agents.

NOTE The person who **drives** a car, bus or train is the person in control of it. You also **ride** a bicycle, **ride** a horse, **sail** a boat or a ship (whether it has sails or an engine) and **fly** a plane. You **steer** a car, bicycle or ship when you turn it in a particular direction. When you travel as a passenger, you **ride in** a car, bus or train, **sail in** a ship, and **fly in** a plane. When you talk about methods of transport you can say **go by** car, **by** bicycle, **by** train, etc. You also **go by** boat/ship or **by** sea, and **go by** plane/**by** air: *I always go to work by bus.* ○ *You can get to Ireland by ship or by air.* When you walk you travel **on** foot.

traverse /trə'vɜ:s/ *v* to travel or extend across an area: [Vn] *skiers traversing the slopes* ○ *The road traverses a wild and mountainous region.*
▶ **traverse** /'trævɜ:s/ *n* **1(a)** (in mountain climbing) an act of walking across a steep cliff or rock, not climbing up or down it. **(b)** a place where this is possible or necessary. **2** (*techn*) a part of a structure that lies across another.

travesty /'trævəsti/ *n* ~ (**of sth**) (*often derog*) a false, absurd or distorted representation of sth; an inferior substitute for sth: *The trial was a travesty of justice.* ○ *His account of our meeting was a travesty (of what actually happened).*
▶ **travesty** *v* (*pt, pp* **-tied**) to make or be a travesty of sth: [Vn] *lesser novelists travestying the style of Dickens.*

trawl /trɔ:l/ *v* **1** ~ (**through**) **sth** (**for sth/sb**) to search through a large amount of material or a group of people, looking for a particular type of thing or person: [Vnpr, Vpr] *The police are trawling (through) their files for similar cases.* [Vpr] *dealers trawling for bargains at the local antiques market* [Vnpr, Vn] *Major companies trawl the universities (looking) for potential graduate trainees.* **2** ~ (**for sth**) to fish for sth using a large net with a wide opening or with a line to which many short lines and hooks are attached: [Vpr] *trawling for mackerel* [also V].
▶ **trawl** *n* **1** a search through a large amount of material or among a large group of people: *a trawl of/through new publications* ○ *a trawl for information.* **2** (also **'trawl-net**) a large net with a wide opening, dragged along the bottom of the sea by a boat. **3** (also **'trawl-line**) (*US*) a long line, used when fishing at sea, to which many short lines with hooks are attached.
trawler *n* a boat used in trawling (TRAWL 2).

tray /treɪ/ *n* **1(a)** a flat piece of wood, metal or

plastic with raised edges, used for carrying or holding things, esp food: *a 'tea-tray* ○ *Take her some breakfast on a tray.* ○ *Plant the seeds in a plastic tray filled with soil.* **(b)** a quantity of sth carried on a tray: *The waiter brought a tray of drinks.* **2** (*esp Brit*) (in compounds) a flat piece of metal or a shallow container, used for cooking food on in an oven: *a 'baking/'roasting tray.* See also IN-TRAY, OUT-TRAY.

treacherous /'tretʃərəs/ *adj* **1** behaving so as to betray sb/sth; intending or intended to betray sb: *a treacherous person* ○ *treacherous schemes/thoughts.* **2** dangerous, esp when seeming to be safe: *treacherous currents* ○ *The roads were icy, making driving conditions treacherous.*
▶ **treacherously** *adv.*
treachery /'tretʃəri/ *n* [C,U] behaviour that involves betraying sb/sth, esp secretly; an instance of this: *an act of treachery.*

treacle /'tri:kl/ (*Brit*) (*US* **molasses**) *n* [U] a thick sticky dark liquid produced from sugar. Compare SYRUP 2.
▶ **treacly** /'tri:kli/ *adj* **1** like treacle: *a treacly brown liquid.* **2** (*derog*) too sentimental: *treacly music.*

tread /tred/ *v* (*pt* **trod** /trɒd/; *pp* **trodden** /'trɒdn/ or **trod**) **1** ~ (**on, etc sth/sb**) to set one's foot down; to walk or step: [Vpr] *You're treading on my toe.* ○ *Mind you don't tread in that puddle.* [Vadv] (*fig*) *It is a sensitive issue so we must tread* (ie speak, proceed) *carefully.* [V] (*rhet*) *The expedition took us to places where no one had trod before.* **2** ~ **sth** (**in/down/out**) to press or crush sth with the feet: [Vn] *tread grapes* (ie to make wine) [Vnp] *Tread the earth down around the roots after planting.* [Vnpr] *Don't tread ash into the carpet!* **3** to make a path, etc by walking: [Vn] *a well-trodden path along the cliff edge.* IDM **be on/tread the boards** ⇨ BOARD¹. **,tread on sb's 'heels** follow sb closely. **,tread on sb's 'toes** (*infml*) to offend or annoy sb: *I don't want to tread on anybody's toes so I'll keep quiet.* **tread/walk a tightrope** ⇨ TIGHTROPE. **,tread 'water** to keep oneself upright in deep water by making treading movements with the legs. PHR V **'tread on sb**; (*US*) **'step on sb** (*infml*) to act without regard for sb or their feelings, while trying to gain an advantage for oneself: *You can't just go around treading on people.*
▶ **tread** *n* **1** [sing] a manner or sound of walking: *walk with a heavy tread.* **2** [C] the upper surface of a step or stair. **3** [C,U] the moulded pattern on the surface of a tyre that is in contact with the road: *Driving with worn treads can be dangerous.* **4** [C,U] the moulded pattern on the sole of a shoe.

treadle /'tredl/ *n* (esp formerly) a device worked by the foot to drive a machine: *a treadle sewing machine.*

treadmill /'tredmɪl/ *n* **1** tiring or boring routine work: *I'd like to escape from the office treadmill.* **2** (esp formerly) a large upright wheel turned by the weight of people or animals treading on steps round its inside edge, and used to drive machinery.

treason /'tri:zn/ (also **high treason**) *n* [U] the crime of betraying one's country, eg by helping its enemies during a war, or of trying to kill its ruler. ▶ **treasonable** /'tri:zənəbl/ *adj: a treasonable offence* (ie one that can be punished as treason).

treasure /'treʒə(r)/ *n* **1** [U] gold, silver, jewels, etc: *buried treasure.* **2** [C esp *pl*] a highly valued object: *'art treasures.* **3** [C] a person who is much loved or valued: *She's an absolute treasure — I couldn't do without her.*
▶ **treasure** *v* **1** to value sth highly: [Vn] *I treasure his friendship.* **2** to keep sth as precious or greatly loved: [Vn] *my most treasured possession* ○ *I shall always treasure the memory of our time together.*
treasurer /'treʒərə(r)/ *n* a person responsible for

the money, bills, etc of a club, a society or an organization.

■ ¹**treasure-house** n a place where valuable things are kept: *a treasure-house of antiques* ○ *The film archives are a cultural treasure-house.*

¹**treasure hunt** n (**a**) a game in which players try to find a hidden object. (**b**) a search for treasure.

¹**treasure trove** /trəʊv/ n **1** [U,C] treasure that is found hidden and whose owner is unknown. **2** [C] a place, book, etc containing many useful or beautiful things: *The shop is a treasure trove of curiosities, gifts and gadgets.*

treasury /ˈtreʒəri/ n **1 the Treasury** [Gp] (in Britain and certain other countries) the government department that controls public money. **2** [C] a place where treasure is stored.

treat /triːt/ v **1** ~ sb (**as/like sth**) to act or behave in a certain way towards sb/sth: [Vnadv] *I hate people who treat animals badly.* [Vnpr] *You should treat people with more consideration.* ○ *People sometimes treat new technology with suspicion.* [Vn-n] *He treats me as (if I were) a complete idiot.* **2** ~ **sth as sth** to consider sth in a certain way: [Vn-n] *I decided to treat his remark as a joke* (eg instead of being offended by it). **3** to deal with or discuss a subject, work of art, etc: [Vnpr] *The question is treated at greater length in the next chapter.* [also Vn, Vnadv]. **4** ~ sb/sth; ~ sb (**for sth**) to give medical care or attention to a person or a condition: [Vn] *a new drug for treating rheumatism* ○ *Last year the hospital treated 40 cases of malaria.* [Vnpr] *She was treated for sunstroke.* **5** ~ **sth** (**with sth**) to apply a process or a substance to sth to protect it, preserve it, etc: [Vnpr] *wood treated with creosote* ○ *treat crops with insecticide* [also Vn]. **6** ~ **sb/oneself** (**to sth**) to give sb/oneself sth enjoyable, eg special food or entertainment, at one's own expense: [Vnpr] *She treated each of the children to an ice-cream.* ○ *I decided to treat myself to a taxi* (eg instead of walking). ○ *We were treated to an impromptu dance display by local schoolchildren.* [also Vn]. **IDM treat sb like** ¹**dirt / a** ¹**dog** (*infml*) to treat sb with no respect at all: *They treat their workers like dirt.*

▶ **treat** n **1** a thing that gives great pleasure, esp sth unexpected or not always available: *Smoked salmon — what a treat!* ○ *I'm taking the children to the pantomime as a treat.* ○ *The concert is a real treat for lovers of light opera.* **2** an act of treating (TREAT 6) sb to sth: *This is my treat* (ie I will pay). **IDM trick or treat** ⇨ TRICK. **n. a treat** (*Brit infml*) extremely well or good: *The new knife sharpener works a treat.* ○ *He looked a treat in his uniform.*

treatable *adj*: *a treatable condition/infection.*

treatise /ˈtriːtɪs, -tɪz/ n ~ (**on sth**) a long written work dealing thoroughly with one subject.

treatment /ˈtriːtmənt/ n **1** [U] the process or manner of behaving towards or dealing with a person or thing: *undergoing medical treatment* ○ *the brutal treatment of political prisoners* ○ *Certain city areas have been singled out for special treatment.* **2** [C] a thing done to relieve or cure an illness or correct a problem, etc: *receive treatment for shock/minor injuries/lung cancer* ○ *an effective treatment for dry rot.* **3** [U,C] a manner of dealing with or discussing a subject, work of art, etc: *Shakespeare's treatment of madness in 'King Lear'.*

treaty /ˈtriːti/ n **1** [C] a formal agreement between two or more countries: *the Treaty of Rome* ○ *ratify a treaty* ○ *sign a* ¹*peace treaty with a neighbouring country.* **2** [U] (*techn*) a formal agreement between people, esp when buying and selling goods or property: *works of art sold by private treaty* (ie instead of by public AUCTION, etc).

treble¹ /ˈtrebl/ *det, adj* [usu attrib] three times as much or as many: *He earns treble my salary.* ○ *a treble whisky.*

▶ **treble** v to become or make sth three times as much or as many: [Vn] *He's trebled his earnings in two years.* [V] *The magazine's circulation has trebled since last year.* [Vpr] *Profits have trebled to £2.4 million.*

treble² /ˈtrebl/ n **1** [U] the high-pitched part of the sound given out by a radio, music system, etc: *turn up the treble on the stereo.* **2** [C] (**a**) a boy's high-pitched singing voice. (**b**) a boy with such a voice: *a choir of trebles.* (**c**) a part for such a voice: *He sings treble.*

▶ **treble** *adj* [attrib] high-pitched in tone: *a treble voice* ○ *a treble recorder* ○ *the treble clef* (ie the symbol in music showing that the notes following it are high in pitch¹(2)). Compare BASS¹.

tree /triː/ n a tall plant that can live a long time. Trees have a thick central wooden stem (the *trunk*) from which branches grow, usu bearing leaves: *an oak/ash/elm tree* ○ *a Christmas tree* ○ *cut down a tree* ○ *plant a tree* ○ *a clump of trees* ○ *shelter under the trees.* Compare BUSH 1a, SHRUB. See also FAMILY TREE, GUM-TREE. **IDM at the top of the tree** ⇨ TOP¹. **bark up the wrong tree** ⇨ BARK². **grow on trees** ⇨ GROW. **not see the wood for the trees** ⇨ WOOD.

▶ **treed** *adj* planted with trees: *a treed area.*

treeless *adj* without trees: *a treeless plain.*

■ ¹**tree house** n a structure built in the branches of a tree, usu for children to play in or on.

¹**tree line** n a level of land, eg on a mountain, above which trees will not grow: *There's still some snow above the tree line.*

treetop /ˈtriːtɒp/ n (esp pl) the branches at the very top of a tree: *birds nesting in the treetops.*

trefoil /ˈtrefɔɪl/ n **1** a plant whose leaves are each divided into three similar parts, eg CLOVER. **2** an ornament or design shaped like a trefoil leaf.

trek /trek/ n (**a**) a long hard journey, esp on foot: (*fig*) *It's quite a trek into town.* (**b**) a long hard walk lasting several days or weeks, esp in mountains. People go on a trek as a form of holiday: *a Himalayan trek.*

▶ **trek** v (-kk-) to make a trek: [V] **go trekking** in *Nepal* ○ *a trekking holiday* [also Vpr, Vp]. See also PONY-TREKKING.

trellis /ˈtrelɪs/ n [C,U] a light framework of crossing strips of wood, plastic, etc used esp to support climbing plants and often fastened to a wall. ⇨ picture at HOUSE¹.

tremble /ˈtrembl/ v **1**(**a**) ~ (**with sth**) to shake from fear, cold, weakness, etc: [V] *He opened the letter with trembling hands.* [Vpr] *Her voice trembled with rage.* ○ *We were trembling with excitement.* (**b**) to shake slightly: [V] *leaves trembling in the breeze.* **2** to be very anxious or afraid: [Vpr] *I tremble at the thought of a Labour government.* [V.to inf] *She trembled to think what might have happened to him.* [also V].

▶ **tremble** n (usu sing) a feeling, movement or sound of trembling: *a tremble of excitement/panic* ○ *There was a slight tremble in his voice.*

trembly /ˈtrembli/ *adj* (*infml*) trembling: *I felt all trembly.*

tremendous /trəˈmendəs/ *adj* **1** very great: *a tremendous explosion* ○ *I've got a tremendous amount of work to do.* ○ *They had the most tremendous row.* **2** (*infml*) very good; extraordinary: *a tremendous film/pianist/experience* ○ *He's a tremendous walker* (ie He walks a lot). ▶ **tremendously** *adv*: *work tremendously hard* ○ *I still miss him tremendously.*

tremolo /ˈtremələʊ/ n (pl **-os**) (*music*) a special effect made in playing a musical instrument or singing by repeating the same note or two notes rapidly. Compare VIBRATO.

tremor /ˈtremə(r)/ n **1** a slight shaking: *There was a tremor in her voice.* ○ ¹*earth tremors* (eg during an

EARTHQUAKE). **2** a wave of excited feeling: *tremors of fear/delight/excitement.*

tremulous /ˈtremjələs/ *adj* (*fml*) **1** shaking slightly because of being nervous, weak or excited: *in a tremulous voice* ◦ *with a tremulous hand.* **2** nervous, afraid or uncertain: *a tremulous look/smile/laugh.* ► **tremulously** *adv.*

trench /trentʃ/ *n* a ditch dug in the ground, eg as a drain or to give soldiers shelter from enemy fire: *irrigation trenches* ◦ *The workmen dug a trench for the new water-pipe.* ◦ *trench warfare.*
■ **ˈtrench coat** *v* a long loose coat, worn esp to keep off rain, with a belt and pockets in the style of a military coat.

trenchant /ˈtrentʃənt/ *adj* (of comments, arguments, etc) strongly and effectively expressed: *trenchant wit/criticism.* ► **trenchantly** *adv.*

trend /trend/ *n* a general tendency or direction: *economical/political/financial trends* ◦ *a growing trend towards smaller families* ◦ *follow the latest trends in fashion* ◦ *The underlying trend of inflation is still upwards.* ◦ *Our products set* (ie start) *the trend for others to follow.*
► **trendy** *adj* (**-ier, -iest**) (*infml*) fashionable: *trendy clothes/shops.* — *n* (*Brit infml usu derog*) a trendy person: *middle-class trendies.* **trendily** *adv.* **trendiness** *n* [U].
■ **ˈtrend-setter** *n* a person who leads the way in fashion, new ideas, etc. **ˈtrend-setting** *adj* [attrib]: *a trend-setting new sports car.*

trepidation /ˌtrepɪˈdeɪʃn/ *n* [U] great worry or fear about sth unpleasant that may happen: *We drove to the hospital full of fear and trepidation.* ◦ *I waited for my exam results with some trepidation.*

trespass /ˈtrespəs/ *v* **1** ~ (**on sth**) to enter sb's land or property without their permission or other authority: [V,Vpr] *He told me I was trespassing (on private land).* **2** [V,Vpr] ~ (**against sb**) (*arch or Bible*) to do wrong; to commit a sin. **PHRV** **ˈtrespass on sth** (*fml*) to make unfair use of sth; to take advantage of sth: *I mustn't trespass on your time/hospitality any longer.*
► **trespass** *n* **1** [C,U] (an act or instance of) trespassing: *an accidental trespass* ◦ *the law of trespass.* **2** [C] (*arch or Bible*) a sin or wrongdoing.
trespasser *n* a person who trespasses: *Trespassers will be prosecuted* (eg on a notice).

tress /tres/ *n* [C usu *pl*] (*rhet*) a long mass of hair, esp of a woman: *combing her dark tresses.*

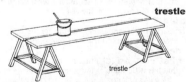

trestle

trestle /ˈtresl/ *n* a wooden or metal structure with two pairs of sloping legs. Trestles are used in pairs to support a flat surface, eg the top of a table. ⇨ picture.
■ **ˈtrestle-table** *n* a table supported on trestles.

tri- *pref* (with *ns* and *adjs*) three: *triangle* ◦ *tricolour* ◦ *trilingual.* Compare BI-, DI-.

triad /ˈtraɪæd/ *n* **1** a group or set of three related people or things. **2** (also **triad**) a Chinese secret organization involved in criminal activities.

triage /ˈtriːɑːʒ; *US* triˈɑːʒ/ *n* [U] (esp in a hospital) the process or a system of assessing how seriously ill or injured people are and treating the most serious cases first: *operate a triage system* ◦ *a triage nurse.*

trial /ˈtraɪəl/ *n* **1** [U,C] a formal examination of evid-

ence in a lawcourt, by a judge and often a JURY(1), to decide if sb accused of a crime is guilty or not: *face trial on drug trafficking charges* ◦ *be put on trial for fraud* ◦ *go on/stand trial for murder* ◦ *trial by jury* ◦ *imprisonment without trial* ◦ *The case comes up for trial* (ie will be heard in court) *next month.* ◦ *The defendant claimed that he had not had a fair trial.* **2** [C,U] an act or a process of testing the ability, quality, performance, etc of sb/sth, esp before a final decision is reached about them/it: *put a car through safety trials* ◦ *The new vaccine has undergone extensive trials.* ◦ *a trial of strength* (ie a contest to see who is stronger) ◦ *employ sb for a trial period/on a trial basis* ◦ *a trial separation* (ie of a couple whose marriage is in difficulties) ◦ *You can have the washing-machine **on trial** for a week.* **3** [C usu *pl*] a sports contest to find the best players for an important event: *trials for the Commonwealth Games.* **4** [C usu *pl*] an event at which animals compete or perform: *horse/sheepdog trials.* **5** [C] ~ (**to sb**) a difficult or annoying person, thing or experience: *the **trials and tribulations** of being an artist* ◦ *Sitting through her lecture was a real trial.* **IDM** **ˌtrial and ˈerror** the process of solving a problem after trying various methods and learning from one's failures: *learn by trial and error.*
■ **ˌtrial ˈrun** a test of the quality, popularity, performance, etc of sth: *The programme was given a trial run to gauge viewers' reactions.* Compare DRY RUN.

triangle

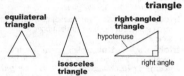

equilateral triangle

right-angled triangle

hypotenuse

isosceles triangle

right angle

triangle /ˈtraɪæŋgl/ *n* **1**(**a**) (*geometry*) a flat shape with three straight sides and three angles. ⇨ picture. (**b**) anything shaped like this: *a triangle of blue silk* ◦ *a triangle of grass beside the path* ◦ *cut the cake into triangles.* **2** (*music*) a musical instrument (MUSICAL) consisting of a metal rod bent in the shape of a triangle that the player strikes with another small metal rod. **3** a situation involving three people, ideas, opinions, etc: *a love triangle.* See also ETERNAL TRIANGLE.

triangular /traɪˈæŋgjələ(r)/ *adj* **1** shaped like a TRIANGLE(1): *a triangular garden/window.* **2** involving three people: *a triangular contest in an election* (ie one with three candidates).

triangulation /traɪˌæŋgjuˈleɪʃn/ *n* [U] (*techn*) a method of determining distance and position by measuring the distance between two fixed points and then measuring the angle from each of these to a third point.

triathlon /traɪˈæθlən, -lɒn/ *n* a sports event in which each competitor takes part in three different sports, eg running, swimming and cycling (CYCLE).

tribal /ˈtraɪbl/ *adj* [usu attrib] of a tribe or tribes: *tribal loyalties/languages/societies/wars.*
► **tribalism** /ˈtraɪbəlɪzəm/ *n* [U] **1** the behaviour, attitudes and loyalties that result from belonging to a tribe, esp in opposition to other tribes. **2** the state of being organized in a tribe or tribes.

tribe /traɪb/ *n* **1** a group of people of the same race and sharing the same language, religion, customs, etc, often led by a CHIEF(1): *a member of the Tembu tribe* ◦ *the twelve tribes of ancient Israel.* **2** (*usu derog*) a group or class of people: *Politicians! I hate the whole tribe of them!* **3** (often *pl*) (*infml joc or derog*) a large number of people: *tribes of drunken hooligans* ◦ *What a tribe* (ie large family) *they've got!* **4** (*biology*) a group of related animals or plants.

tribesman /ˈtraɪbzmən/ n (pl **-men** /-mən/; fem **tribeswoman** /-wʊmən/, pl **-women** /-wɪmɪn/) a member of a tribe(1).

tribulation /ˌtrɪbjuˈleɪʃn/ n [C,U] (rhet or joc) great trouble or suffering: a time of great tribulation ○ the tribulations of modern life.

tribunal /traɪˈbjuːnl/ n [CGp] a group of people with the authority to settle certain types of dispute: a rent tribunal (ie one hearing appeals against high rents) ○ a disciplinary tribunal ○ The tribunal dismissed all the complaints against him. See also INDUSTRIAL TRIBUNAL.

tributary /ˈtrɪbjətri; US -teri/ n a river or stream that flows into a larger one or into a lake: The Avon is a tributary of the Severn. ► **tributary** adj [attrib]: tributary streams/rivers.

tribute /ˈtrɪbjuːt/ n **1** [C,U] an act, a statement or a gift that is intended to show one's respect or admiration, esp for a dead person: floral tributes (ie gifts of flowers) ○ stand in silent tribute to those who died in the war ○ a musical entertainment entitled 'A Tribute to Noel Coward' ○ Her colleagues **paid tribute** to her outstanding loyalty and commitment to the firm. **2** [sing] a ~ (to sth/sb) an indication of how effective sth is: His recovery is a tribute to the doctors' skill. **3** [C,U] (esp formerly) money or valuable objects given by one country or ruler to another, esp in return for protection or for not being attacked.

trice /traɪs/ n **IDM** **in a trice** very quickly or suddenly: In a trice he was gone.

triceps /ˈtraɪseps/ n (pl unchanged) (anatomy) the large muscle at the back of the upper arm. Compare BICEPS.

trick /trɪk/ n **1(a)** a plan or an act intended to deceive sb: They had to think of a trick to get past the guards. ○ a 'trick question ○ Don't you ever **pull that trick** again! ○ (fig) It must be a **trick of the light** (ie that makes one see sth that is not there). See also CONFIDENCE TRICK, DIRTY TRICK. **(b)** an act intended to annoy sb or cause them minor discomfort so that one can laugh at them: **play a trick on sb** ○ The children's favourite trick is filling the sugar bowl with salt. ○ I could have sworn I gave it to her yesterday — my memory must be **playing tricks**. **2** a skilful act performed for entertainment: conjuring tricks ○ card tricks ○ She had trained her dog to do tricks (eg to stand on its back legs). **3** (C esp sing) the exact or best way of doing sth; a particular technique; a KNACK(1): **The trick is to** hold your breath while you aim. ○ I've never learnt the trick of folding shirts properly. **4** a characteristic habit; a MANNERISM(1): He has an annoying trick of saying 'You know?' after every sentence. ○ My car has developed the trick of stalling on steep hills. **5** the cards played in a single round of a card-game, the point scored by winning such a round: take/win a trick. See also HAT TRICK. **IDM** **sb's bag/box of 'tricks** (infml) a whole set of plans, actions, techniques or resources available to sb. **be up to one's (old) 'tricks** (infml) to be acting in a characteristic way that sb disapproves of: There's some money missing from my purse — you've been up to your tricks again, haven't you? **do the job/trick** ⇨ JOB. **every trick in the 'book** every method or technique that can be used to achieve what one wants: He'll try every trick in the book to stop you winning. **have a 'trick up one's sleeve** to have an idea, plan, etc that can be used if it becomes necessary. **not miss a trick** ⇨ MISS². **teach an old dog new tricks** ⇨ TEACH. **,trick or 'treat** (esp US) (said by children who visit houses at Hallowe'en and threaten to do silly or annoying things if they do not receive sweets or other small gifts). **the ,tricks of the 'trade** clever ways of doing things, known to and used by people experienced in a particular job: She's only been with

us a month so she's still learning the tricks of the trade. **the whole bag of tricks** ⇨ WHOLE.
► **trick** v **1** to deceive sb: [Vn] You've been tricked. **2 (a)** ~ **sb into sth/doing sth** to make sb do sth by means of a trick: [Vnpr] She tricked him into marriage/into marrying her. **(b)** ~ **sb out of sth** to make sb lose sth by means of a trick; to cheat sb of sth: [Vnpr] Her partner tried to trick her out of her share. **PHRV** **,trick sb/oneself/sth 'out (in/with sth)** to put decorations or ornaments on sth; to dress oneself/sb in bright or fine clothes: She was tricked out in fur jacket and boots.

trickery /-əri/ n [U] dishonest acts intended to deceive people; deception.

trickster /-stə(r)/ n a person who cheats people; a swindler (SWINDLE).

tricky adj (-ier, -iest) **(a)** requiring skill and good judgement; difficult or awkward: a tricky situation/problem/decision ○ Getting ashore here is tricky. **(b)** (of people or their actions) difficult to deal with or trust; deceitful; crafty (CRAFT): He's a tricky character to do business with.

trickle /ˈtrɪkl/ v **1** to flow or make sth flow slowly in a thin stream: [Vpr] tears trickling down her cheeks [Vnpr] trickle a little oil over the sliced tomato [also Vp]. **2** to go or move somewhere slowly or gradually; to make sth do this: [Vpr] People have begun trickling into the hall. ○ The ball trickled into the hole. [Vnpr] He trickled the ball into the hole. [Vp] News is starting to trickle out. **PHRV** **,trickle 'down** (esp of money) to spread from rich to poor people through the economic systems of a country.
► **trickle** n **1** a thin flow of liquid: The stream is reduced to a mere trickle in summer. **2** (usu sing) ~ (of sth) a small amount coming or going slowly: a trickle of information/visitors.
■ **'trickle charger** n a device that runs on electricity and is used to put a charge¹(7) into a battery.

tricksy /ˈtrɪksi/ adj (infml usu derog) done or presented in a way that is clever or complicated: a film full of tricksy camera-work that fails to disguise a weak story.

tricolour (US **tricolor**) /ˈtrɪkələ(r); US ˈtraɪkʌlər/ n **(a)** [C] a flag with three bands or blocks of different colours. **(b)** **the Tricolour** [sing] the French national flag, with wide upright bands of blue, white and red.

tricycle /ˈtraɪsɪkl/ (also infml **trike**) n a vehicle similar to a bicycle but with one wheel at the front and two at the back.

trident /ˈtraɪdnt/ n a long fork with three points, esp one that Neptune or Britannia is shown holding as a symbol of power over the sea.

tried pt, pp of TRY¹.

triennial /traɪˈeniəl/ adj lasting for or happening every three years: a triennial competition.

trier ⇨ TRY¹.

trifle /ˈtraɪfl/ n **1** [C] a thing, a matter or an activity that has little value or importance: He busies himself with trifles and avoids doing what's really important. ○ £1 000 is a mere trifle to her. **2** [C,U] a sweet dish made of cake and sometimes fresh fruit, usu soaked in wine or jelly, and covered with custard and cream. **IDM** **a trifle** slightly; a very small amount: She was a trifle envious of his success. ○ Lenny relaxed a trifle. ○ You acted a trifle (too) hastily.
► **trifle** v **PHRV** **'trifle with sb/sth** (esp in negative sentences) to treat lightly or in a casual way sb/sth that deserves serious attention or respect: He's **not a man to be trifled with**. **trifling** /ˈtraɪflɪŋ/ adj not important; TRIVIAL: a few trifling errors ○ the trifling sum of £2.

trigger /ˈtrɪgə(r)/ n **1** a small device that releases a spring when pressure is applied, esp so as to fire a gun: squeeze the trigger ○ have one's finger on the trigger (ie be ready to shoot). ⇨ picture at GUN. **2** ~ (for sth) an event or a thing that is the immediate cause of a particular reaction: *the trigger for change* ○ *chemical triggers in the brain* ○ *His resignation was the trigger that brought about the company's collapse.*

▶ **trigger** *v* ~ **(off)** to be the cause of a sudden, often violent reaction; to start sth: [Vn, Vnp] *The riots were triggered (off) by a series of police arrests.* [Vnp] *The smoke triggered off the alarm.*

■ **'trigger-happy** *adj* (*infml derog*) ready to react violently, esp by shooting, even when only slightly provoked.

trigonometry /ˌtrɪɡəˈnɒmətri/ *n* [U] the branch of MATHEMATICS that deals with the relationship between the sides and angles of triangles (TRIANGLE 1).

▶ **trigonometric** /ˌtrɪɡənəˈmetrɪk/, **-metrical** /-kl/ *adj*.

trike /traɪk/ *n* (*infml*) = TRICYCLE.

trilby /ˈtrɪlbi/ *n* a man's soft hat with a narrow BRIM(2) and the top part pushed in from front to back.

trill /trɪl/ *v* **1** to make a repeated sharp high sound: [V] *A phone trilled on the desk.* [Vp] *The canary was trilling away in its cage.* [also V.speech]. **2** to pronounce the letter 'r' with a trill while vibrating (VIBRATE 2) the tongue: [Vn] *trill one's r's.*

▶ **trill** *n* **1** a repeated sharp high sound made eg by the voice or a bird. **2** (*music*) two notes a tone¹(6) or a SEMITONE apart played or sung quickly several times one after the other.

trillion /ˈtrɪljən/ *n, pron, det* **1** (*US*) the number 1 000 000 000 000; one million million. **2** (*Brit*) the number 1 000 000 000 000 000 000; one million million million.

For further guidance on how *trillion* is used, see the examples at *hundred*.

trilogy /ˈtrɪlədʒi/ *n* a group of three related novels, operas, etc.

trim¹ /trɪm/ *v* (**-mm-**) **1(a)** to make sth neat or smooth by cutting away untidy parts: [Vn] *trim the top of a hedge* [Vn, Vnp] *trim one's beard (back).* **(b)** ~ **sth (off sth / off)** to reduce sth by cutting or removing what is unnecessary: [Vn, Vnpr] *The article's too long. Can you trim it (by a quarter)?* [Vnp, Vnpr] *Trim the excess fat off (the meat).* [Vnpr] *I trimmed an inch off the hem of this skirt.* [Vn] *Tax increases will undoubtedly trim public spending.* ⇨ note at CLIP². **2** ~ **sth (with sth)** to decorate sth, esp round its edges: [Vnpr] *trim a dress with lace* ○ *a hat trimmed with flowers* [also Vn]. **3** [Vn] to arrange sails to suit the wind.

▶ **trim** *n* **1** [U] good order or condition; the state of being ready or fit¹(1): *be/keep in good/proper/ excellent trim* ○ *She's got a month to get into trim for the race.* **2** [C usu *sing*] an act of cutting hair, esp by a small amount: *How much is it just for a trim?* **3** [U, sing] decorations for clothes, furniture, etc, esp along the edges and often of a different colour or material from the rest: *a yard of gold trim* ○ *The car is available with (a) black or red trim* (ie seat covers).

trimmer *n* an instrument that trims (TRIM¹ 1a): *an electric hedge trimmer.*

trimming *n* **1** trimmings [pl] **(a)** the special things that traditionally accompany sth: *roast turkey and all the trimmings* (ie vegetables, stuffing, etc) ○ *a church wedding with all the trimmings.* **(b)** pieces cut off when sth is trimmed: *pastry trimmings.* **2** [U, C esp *pl*] material, eg lace, used to decorate sth.

trim² /trɪm/ *adj* (*approx*) **1** slim, elegant or fit¹(1): *a trim waistline/figure* ○ *She keeps herself trim.* **2** neat and tidy; in good order: *a trim garden/moustache.*

trimaran /ˈtraɪməræn/ *n* a boat built like a CATAMARAN but with three parallel hulls (HULL¹) instead of two.

trimester /traɪˈmestə(r)/ *n* (*US*) **1** a period of three months. **2** each of three terms in an academic year.

trinity /ˈtrɪnəti/ *n* **1 the Trinity** [sing] (in the Christian religion) the union of Father, Son and Holy Spirit as one God. **2** [C] (*fml*) a group of three things or people.

trinket /ˈtrɪŋkɪt/ *n* a small ornament, piece of jewellery, etc of little value.

trio /ˈtriːəʊ/ *n* (*pl* **-os**) **1(a)** [CGp] a group of three people playing music or singing together. **(b)** [C] a piece of music for such a group: *a piano trio* (eg for piano, VIOLIN and CELLO). **2** [CGp] a set or group of three people or things: *A trio of number 9 buses came by.*

trip /trɪp/ *v* (**-pp-**) **1(a)** ~ **(over/up)**; ~ **(over/on sth)** to catch one's foot on sth and fall or nearly fall: [V, Vpr] *She tripped (over the cat) and fell.* [Vpr, Vp] *Be careful you don't trip (up) on the loose rug.* **(b)** ~ **sb (up)** to cause sb to do this: [Vn, Vnp] *He tried to trip me (up).* **2** to walk, run or dance with quick light steps: [Vp, Vpr] *She came tripping along (the garden path).* ○ (*fig*) [V] *a melody with a light tripping rhythm.* **3** to release a switch or catch²(3); to operate a mechanism by doing this: [Vn] *trip the shutter of a camera* ○ *If anyone tries to open this door it trips the alarm.* **4** [V, Vp] ~ **(out)** (*sl*) to be under the influence of a drug that makes one HALLUCINATE.

IDM **roll/slip/trip off the tongue** ⇨ TONGUE. **PHR V** **ˌtrip (sb) 'up** to make a mistake, reveal a secret, etc; to cause sb to do this: *I tripped up in the interview and said something rather silly.* ○ *The lawyer was trying to trip the witnesses up* (ie confuse them with questions).

▶ **trip** *n* **1** a journey, esp a short one for pleasure or for a particular purpose: *a day-trip to the seaside* ○ *during my last trip to London* ○ *a honeymoon trip to Venice* ○ *a ˈshopping/ˈbusiness/ˈstudy trip* ○ *a ˈboat/ ˈcoach/ˈhelicopter trip.* See also EGO-TRIP, FIELD TRIP, ROUND TRIP. ⇨ note at JOURNEY. **2** (*sl*) an experience caused by taking a drug that makes one HALLUCINATE: *an acid* (ie LSD) *trip* ○ *a good/bad trip.* **3** an act of tripping (TRIP 1) or being tripped; a fall or near fall.

tripper *n* a person making a short journey for pleasure: *The beach was packed with trippers.*

■ **'trip-wire** *n* a wire stretched close to the ground, which works a trap or warning device, etc when a person or an animal trips against it.

tripartite /traɪˈpɑːtaɪt/ *adj* [usu attrib] (*fml*) having three parts or involving three people, groups, etc: *a tripartite division* ○ *tripartite discussions.*

tripe /traɪp/ *n* [U] **1** the LINING(2) of a cow's stomach used as food: *boiled tripe and onions.* **2** (*sl*) **(a)** nonsense: *Don't talk tripe!* **(b)** writing, music, etc of low quality: *I don't read that tripe.*

triple /ˈtrɪpl/ *adj* [usu attrib] **1** having three parts or involving three people, groups, etc: *The plan has a triple purpose* (ie three purposes). ○ *a triple alliance* (ie between three countries) ○ *The cinema's showing a triple bill of* (ie a programme consisting of three) *horror movies.* **2** three times as much or as many: *travelling at triple the speed* ○ *a triple gold medallist* ○ *a triple murderer* (ie one who has killed three people).

▶ **triple** *v* to become or make sth three times as much or as many: [V] *Output has tripled in two years.* [also Vn].

triply /ˈtrɪpli/ *adv.*

■ **the 'triple jump** *n* [sing] an ATHLETIC(2) contest of jumping as far forward as possible with three jumps. The first jump lands on one foot, the second on the other and the third on both feet.

triplet /ˈtrɪplət/ *n* **1** (usu *pl*) any of three children or animals born to the same mother at one time: *His wife gave birth to triplets.* **2** (*music*) a group of three equal notes to be performed in the time usually taken to perform two of the same kind. **3** a set of three things.

triplicate /ˈtrɪplɪkət/ n **IDM** **in triplicate** consisting of three copies all looking the same, of which one is the original one: *submit an application in triplicate.*

tripod /ˈtraɪpɒd/ n a support with three legs for a camera, TELESCOPE, etc.

tripper ⇨ TRIP.

triptych /ˈtrɪptɪk/ n a picture or carved design on three panels fixed side by side, esp one placed over an ALTAR(1) in a church.

trite /traɪt/ adj (of a phrase, an opinion, etc) too often used and so dull; not new or original.

triumph /ˈtraɪʌmf/ n **1** [U] the state of feeling great satisfaction or joy as the result of success or victory: *shouts of triumph* ○ *The winning team returned home in triumph.* **2** [C] a great achievement or success: *one of the triumphs of modern science* ○ *She scored a resounding triumph over her old rival.*
▶ **triumph** v ~ **(over sb/sth)** to be successful; to gain a victory: [V] *Common sense triumphed in the end.* [Vpr] *triumph over one's difficulties* (ie overcome them).
triumphal /traɪˈʌmfl/ adj [usu attrib] of or for a triumph; celebrating a triumph: *a triumphal arch* (ie one built to honour a victory in war) ○ *a triumphal parade/procession.*
triumphant /traɪˈʌmfənt/ adj (**a**) very successful: *her triumphant return to the London stage.* (**b**) showing great satisfaction or joy about a victory: *a triumphant cheer/smile.* **triumphantly** adv.

triumvirate /traɪˈʌmvərət/ n a ruling group of three people: *The company is run jointly by a triumvirate of directors.*

trivet /ˈtrɪvɪt/ n a metal stand²(3), usu with three legs, for holding hot pans, etc, or formerly for cooking pots, etc placed over a fire.

trivia /ˈtrɪviə/ n [pl] (*usu derog*) unimportant things, details or pieces of information.

trivial /ˈtrɪviəl/ adj (*often derog*) of little importance; concerned with unimportant things: *a trivial matter/offence* ○ *a trivial TV game show* ○ *raise trivial objections to sth.*
▶ **triviality** /ˌtrɪviˈæləti/ n (*derog*) (**a**) [U] the state of being trivial. (**b**) [C] a trivial thing: *waste time on trivialities.*
trivialize, -ise /ˈtrɪviəlaɪz/ v (*derog*) to make a subject, problem, etc seem trivial: [Vn] *Serious events are too often trivialized by the media.* **trivialization, -isation** /ˌtrɪviəlaɪˈzeɪʃn; US -lə¹z-/ n [U].
trivially /-iəli/ adv.

trod pt of TREAD.

trodden pp of TREAD.

troglodyte /ˈtrɒɡlədaɪt/ n a person living in a cave, esp in PREHISTORIC times.

troika /ˈtrɔɪkə/ n a group of three people working together, esp as political leaders of a country.

Trojan /ˈtrəʊdʒən/ n, adj (an inhabitant) of Troy, an ancient city in Asia Minor: *the Trojan war* (ie between the Greeks and the Trojans, as described by Homer).
■ ¸**Trojan** ¹**horse** a person or thing used secretly to cause the ruin of an enemy, an opponent, a rival organization, etc.

troll¹ /trəʊl/ v ~ **(for sth)** to fish by pulling a line with BAIT(1) on through the water behind a boat: [Vpr] *trolling for pike* [also V].

troll² /trəʊl/ n (in Scandinavian myths) an imaginary being that looks like an ugly person and may be either very large and evil or very small, friendly and full of tricks.

trolley /ˈtrɒli/ n (pl **-eys**) **1** (*Brit*) a cart on wheels

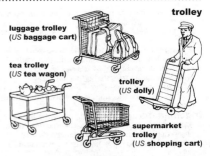

trolley

luggage trolley
(*US* **baggage cart**)

tea trolley
(*US* **tea wagon**)

trolley
(*US* **dolly**)

supermarket trolley
(*US* **shopping cart**)

that can be pushed or pulled along and is used for moving goods : *a* ¹*luggage trolley* ○ *a* ¹*supermarket trolley.* ⇨ picture. ⇨ picture at GOLF. **2** a small table on wheels for transporting or serving food, etc: *a* ¹*drinks trolley.* See also TEA TROLLEY. **3** (*US*) = TRAM. **IDM** **off one's** ¹**trolley** (*sl*) slightly mad; crazy.
■ ¹**trolley bus** n a bus driven by electricity from a cable above the street.

trollop /ˈtrɒləp/ n (*dated derog*) a woman who is untidy or whose sexual behaviour is considered too free.

trombone /trɒmˈbəʊn/ n a large brass musical instrument with a sliding tube used to raise or lower the note. ⇨ picture at MUSICAL INSTRUMENT.
▶ **trombonist** /trɒmˈbəʊnɪst/ n a person who plays a trombone.

troop /truːp/ n **1** troops [pl] soldiers: *an army of 50 000 troops* ○ *demand the withdrawal of foreign troops.* **2** [C] a large group of people or animals, esp when moving: *a troop of schoolchildren.* **3** [C] a unit of soldiers in armoured (ARMOUR) vehicles or of ARTILLERY(2) or of CAVALRY. **4** [C] a local group of Scouts (SCOUT 2).
▶ **troop** v (with a plural subject) to come or go together as a troop or in large numbers: [Vpr] *children trooping out of school* [also V, Vp]. **IDM** ¸**troop the** ¹**colour** (*Brit*) to perform a ceremony of carrying a regiment's flag along ranks of soldiers, esp on the birthday of the king or queen.
troop adj [attrib] of soldiers: *troop carriers/movements/reductions.*
trooper n **1** a soldier in an armoured (ARMOUR) unit or a CAVALRY unit. **2** (*US*) a member of a State police force. **IDM** **swear like a trooper** ⇨ SWEAR.
■ ¹**troop-ship** n a ship for transporting soldiers.

trope /trəʊp/ n (*fml*) a word or phrase used in a FIGURATIVE(1) way, eg a METAPHOR(a).

trophy /ˈtrəʊfi/ n **1** an object such as a silver cup or shield that is awarded as a prize, esp for winning a sports contest: *the Wimbledon* ¹*tennis trophy.* **2** an object taken or kept as proof of success in hunting, war, etc: *a set of antlers and other trophies.*

tropic /ˈtrɒpɪk/ n **1** [C usu *sing*] a line of LATITUDE(1) 23° 27' north (**the tropic of Cancer**) or south (**the tropic of Capricorn**) of the EQUATOR. ⇨ picture at GLOBE. **2 the tropics** [pl] the region between the two tropics, with a hot climate.
▶ **tropical** /-kl/ adj of, like or found in the tropics: *tropical forests/diseases/fish* ○ *a tropical climate.* **tropically** /-kli/ adv.

troposphere /ˈtrɒpəsfɪə(r); US ˈtrəʊp-/ n the **troposphere** [sing] a layer of the atmosphere that extends from about 6–10 kilometres upwards from the earth's surface.

Trot /trɒt/ n (*sl usu derog*) a Trotskyist.

trot /trɒt/ v (-tt-) **1(a)** [V, Vpr, Vp] (of a horse, etc or a rider) to move at a steady pace that is faster than a walk but slower than a CANTER. (**b**) to ride a horse, etc at such a pace: [Vnpr] *She trotted her pony round the field.* [also Vn,Vnpr]. **(a)** (of a person) to run without hurrying, taking short steps: [Vp] *The child was trotting along beside its parents.* [also Vpr,V]. **(b)** (*infml*) to walk or go, usu at a normal pace, in the specified direction: [Vp] *I'd better be trotting along now.* [also Vpr]. ⇨ note at RUN¹. **PHR V** ˌtrot **sth** ˈout (*infml derog*) to produce the same information, explanations, etc repeatedly for sb to hear or see: *They keep trotting out the same old excuses about the struggling economy.*

▶ **trot** *n* **1** [sing] a trotting pace: *go at a steady trot.* **2** [C] a period of trotting: *go for a trot.* **3** the **trots** [pl] (*sl*) DIARRHOEA: *get the trots.* **IDM** on the ˈtrot (*infml*) **1** one after the other: *lose eight games on the trot.* **2** continually busy: *I've been on the trot all day.* ○ *Her new job certainly keeps her on the trot.*

trotter *n* **1** a horse bred and trained for trotting. **2** (usu *pl*) a pig's foot, esp as food.

troth /trəʊθ; *US* trɔːθ/ *n* (*arch*) **IDM** **plight one's troth** ⇨ PLIGHT².

Trotskyism /ˈtrɒtskiɪzəm/ *n* [U] the political or economic ideas of Leon Trotsky, esp the belief that SOCIALISM should be established throughout the world by revolution.

▶ **Trotskyist** /ˈtrɒtskiɪst/ (also **Trotskyite** /-skiaɪt/) *n, adj* (a supporter) of Trotskyism.

troubadour /ˈtruːbədɔː(r)/ *n* a French travelling poet and singer in the 11th–13th centuries.

trouble /ˈtrʌbl/ *n* **1** [C,U] worry, pain, difficulty, danger, etc or a situation causing this: *We're **having trouble with** our new car.* ○ *My teeth are **giving** (ie causing) **me trouble**.* ○ *If we're late, there'll be **trouble*** (ie an unpleasant situation, perhaps involving punishment). ○ *He could **make trouble (for us)** if he wanted to.* ○ *family **trouble(s)*** (eg disagreements between parents and children) ○ *Our troubles are not over yet.* ○ *The idea soon **ran into trouble**.* ○ *The trouble* (ie problem) *(with you) is you're too selfish.* ○ *What's the trouble* (ie What's wrong)? **2(a)** [U] ~ **(to sb)** extra work or effort; BOTHER *n*(1): *I don't want to be any trouble (to you).* ○ *Were the children much trouble?* ○ *I can come back tomorrow — it's no trouble.* ○ *Repairing it is **more trouble than it's worth**.* ○ *I'm sorry to have **put you to so much trouble**.* **(b)** [sing] (*rather fml*) a thing that causes extra effort or difficulty: *It's a delicious dish but rather a trouble to prepare.* **3** [C,U] disputes, fighting, etc; UNREST: *the troubles in Northern Ireland* ○ *The firm's been hit by a lot of labour trouble* (eg strikes). **4** [U] **(a)** illness: *heart/liver trouble* ○ *a history of mental trouble.* **(b)** faulty operation, eg of a machine or vehicle: *My car's got clutch trouble.* **IDM** **ask for trouble/it** ⇨ ASK. **get into ˈtrouble** to cause trouble for oneself, eg by making a mistake: *Even an experienced climber can get into trouble.* ○ *He got into trouble with the police* (eg was arrested). **get sb into ˈtrouble 1** to cause trouble for sb: *Don't mention my name or you'll get me into trouble.* **2** (*infml euph*) to make a woman who is not married pregnant: *He got his girlfriend into trouble.* **give (sb) (some, no, any, etc) ˈtrouble** to cause trouble: *The video's been giving (us) a lot of trouble* (ie not working properly). **go to a lot of, considerable, etc trouble (to do sth)** to do sth even though it involves effort, difficulty, etc: *Thank you for going to so much trouble to find what I was looking for.* **in ˈtrouble 1** in a situation that involves danger, punishment, pain, worry, etc: *If we can't keep to the schedule, we'll be in (a lot of) trouble.* ○ *He's in trouble with the police over drugs.* **2** (*infml euph*) (of a woman who is not married) pregnant: **look for ˈtrouble** (*infml*) to behave in a way that is likely to provoke an argument, violence, etc: *drunken youths who roam the streets looking for trouble.* **take trouble over sth / with sth / to do sth /**

doing sth to use much care and effort in doing sth: *We took a lot of trouble to find the right person for the job.* **take the trouble to do sth** to do sth even though it involves effort or difficulty: *Decent journalists should take the trouble to check their facts.*

▶ **trouble** *v* **1** to cause worry, pain or disturbance to sb: [Vn] *be troubled by illness/doubt/bad news* ○ *My back's been troubling me.* ○ *a troubled look* ○ *What troubles me is that…* ○ *I'm sorry to trouble you, but could you tell me the time?* **2** ~ **(about sth)** (*rather fml*) (used esp in questions and negative sentences) to let oneself be worried or concerned about sth: [V,Vpr] *'Do you want me to post it for you?' 'No, don't trouble (about it), thank you.'* [V.*to* inf] *I rushed into the room without even troubling to knock.* **3** ~ **sb for sth / to do sth** (*fml*) (used with *may* or *might* in polite requests): [Vnpr] *May I trouble you for the salt?* [Vn.*to* inf] *Might I trouble you to give me a lift to the station?* **IDM** **pour oil on troubled water** ⇨ POUR.

ˈ**troublesome** /-səm/ *adj* giving trouble; causing annoyance, pain, etc: *a troublesome child/problem/cough.*

■ ˈ**trouble spot** *n* a place where trouble regularly occurs, esp a country where there is a war: *the world's major trouble spots.*

troublemaker /ˈtrʌblmeɪkə(r)/ *n* a person who often causes trouble, esp by involving others in trouble. ▶ **troublemaking** *n, adj* [U].

troubleshooter /ˈtrʌblʃuːtə(r)/ *n* a person who helps to settle disputes, eg in industrial relations, or who finds and corrects faults in machinery, etc: *industry troubleshooters.*

trough /trɒf; *US* trɔːf/ *n* **1** a long narrow open box for animals to feed or drink from. ⇨ picture at PIG. **2** a shallow channel that allows liquid to drain away. **3** (in METEOROLOGY) a long narrow region of low air pressure between two regions of higher pressure. Compare RIDGE 3. **4** a time of very low economic performance or little activity: *signs of recovery from the trough of recession* ○ *the **peaks and troughs** of any company's production schedule.* **5** a low area between two waves or ridges. ⇨ picture at SURFING.

trounce /traʊns/ *v* to defeat sb heavily: [Vn] *Wales were trounced 5–0 by Poland.*

troupe /truːp/ *n* [CGp] a group of actors and entertainers, esp those of a CIRCUS(1) or ballet: *a* ˈ*dance troupe.*

▶ **trouper** *n* **1** a member of a troupe: *an old stage trouper.* **2** (*infml approv*) a loyal reliable person: *Thanks for helping, you're a real trouper.*

trousers /ˈtraʊzəz/ (also *esp US* **pants**) *n* [pl] an outer garment that reaches from the waist to the ankles (or, as **short trousers**, to just above the knees) and is divided into two parts to cover the legs: *a pair of grey trousers* ○ *I was still in **short trousers*** (ie still only a boy) *at the time.* **IDM** **catch sb with their pants/trousers down** ⇨ CATCH¹. **wear the pants/trousers** ⇨ WEAR¹.

▶ **trouser** *adj* [attrib] of or for trousers: *trouser buttons/legs/pockets* ○ *a trouser press.* ˈ**trouser suit** *n* (*Brit*) (*US* **pantsuit**) a woman's suit of jacket and trousers.

trousseau /ˈtruːsəʊ/ *n* (*pl* **trousseaus** or **trousseaux** /-səʊz/) (*dated*) the clothes and other possessions collected by a BRIDE to begin married life with.

trout /traʊt/ *n* (*pl* unchanged) **1(a)** [C] a fish that lives in rivers, lakes, etc and is good to eat. There are several types of trout. **(b)** [U] the flesh of this fish as food: *a piece of smoked trout.* **2** (usu **old trout**) (*infml*) (often as a form of address) a bad-tempered or annoying old woman.

trove /trəʊv/ *n* ⇨ TREASURE TROVE.

trowel /ˈtraʊəl/ *n* **1** a small tool with a flat blade, used for spreading cement, PLASTER(1), etc. **2** a small garden tool with a curved blade for lifting plants, digging holes, etc. **IDM** **lay it on thick / with a trowel** ⇨ THICK *adv*.

truant /'truːənt/ *n* **1** a child who stays away from school without permission. **2** a person who avoids doing her or his work or duty. **IDM** **play 'truant** (*Brit*); (*US*) **play 'hooky** /'hʊki/ to stay away from school as a truant.
▶ **truancy** /-ənsi/ *n* [U] the practice of staying away from school without permission: *an increase in truancy rates.*

truce /truːs/ *n* an agreement between enemies or opponents to stop fighting for a certain time: *declare/negotiate/break a truce* ○ *a three-day truce.*

truck¹ /trʌk/ *n* **1** (*Brit*) an open railway vehicle for carrying goods. **2** (*esp US*) = LORRY. ⇨ picture at LORRY. **3** a vehicle which is open at the back, used for transporting goods, animals, soldiers, etc: *a farm/an army truck.* **4** a vehicle for carrying goods which is pushed or pulled by hand. See also FORK-LIFT TRUCK, PICK-UP 1.
▶ **trucker** *n* (*esp US*) a person whose job is driving a lorry.
trucking *n* [U] (*US*) the business of carrying goods by lorry.

truck² /trʌk/ *n* [U] (*US*) fresh vegetables, fruit, etc grown for the market. **IDM** **have/want no truck with sb/sth** to refuse to deal or associate with sb; to refuse to tolerate or consider sth: *I'll have no truck with extremists/extremism.*
■ **'truck farm** *n* (*US*) = MARKET GARDEN. **'truck farmer** *n*. **'truck farming** *n* [U].

truculent /'trʌkjələnt/ *adj* (*derog*) tending to quarrel or to be bad-tempered; aggressive: *truculent behaviour* ○ *He became very truculent and started arguing with me angrily.* ▶ **truculence** /-ləns/ *n* [U]. **truculently** *adv*.

trudge /trʌdʒ/ *v* to walk slowly or with difficulty because one is tired, on a long journey, etc: [Vpr, Vp] *trudging (along) through the deep snow* [Vn] *He trudged 20 miles.* [also V, Vadv]. ⇨ note at STAMP¹.
▶ **trudge** *n* (usu *sing*) a long difficult walk.

true /truː/ *adj* (**-r, -st**) **1** corresponding to known facts: *a true story* ○ *Is it true you're getting married?* ○ *British theatre is seriously underfunded — and the same is true of/for the film industry.* ○ *'We've always found somewhere to stay before.' 'True, but we may not always be so lucky.'* ○ *Unfortunately what you say is all/only too true.* ○ *Her story simply doesn't ring* (ie sound) *true.* ○ *You never said a truer word!* **2** [*esp attrib*] rightly called what one/it is called; real(2), genuine or sincere: *true love* ○ *The frog is not a true reptile.* ○ *He claimed to be the true heir.* ○ *She's a true professional.* **3** [*esp attrib*] exact; accurate: *a true copy of a document* ○ *The painting is a true likeness of her.* ○ *His aim was true.* ○ *Do newspapers give us a true analysis of what's going on in the world?* **4** ~ (**to sth**) loyal; faithful: *a true friend/ patriot* ○ *remain true to one's principles* ○ *be true to one's word* (ie do as one has promised). **5** [*esp pred*] fitted or placed in its proper, esp upright, position: *Is the wheel true?* ○ *Make sure the post is true before the concrete sets.* **IDM** **come 'true** (of a hope, wish, etc) to really happen; to become fact: *It's like a dream come* (ie that has come) *true.* **one's true 'colours** (*often derog*) one's real character; what one is actually like: *Once he achieved power he showed (himself in) his true colours.* **true to sth** being or acting as one would expect from sth: *True to form* (ie As usual), *he arrived late.* ○ *The movie is very true to life* (ie realistic). ○ *Plants grown from seed are not always true to type* (ie exactly like the plant that produced the seed).
▶ **true** *adv* **1** truly: *She spoke truer than she knew.*

2 accurately: *The arrow flew straight and true to its mark.*
true *n* **IDM** **,out of 'true** not in its proper or accurate position: *The door is out of true.*
■ **,true-'blue** *adj* completely faithful and loyal, esp to traditional principles: *a ,true-blue 'Tory sup-porter.*
,true-'life *adj* [attrib] that really happened: *a ,true-life ad'venture.*
,true 'north *n* [U] north according to the earth's AXIS(1), not magnetic north (MAGNETIC).

truffle /'trʌfl/ *n* **1** a type of edible FUNGUS(1) that grows underground and is enjoyed for its rich fla-vour. **2** a soft sweet made of a chocolate mixture.

trug /trʌg/ *n* a shallow basket used for carrying garden tools, plants, etc.

truism /'truːɪzəm/ *n* a statement that is obviously true, esp one that does not say anything important, eg *Nothing lasts for ever.*

truly /'truːli/ *adv* **1** in a sincere and genuine way: *truly grateful/sorry/upset.* **2** completely; really; to a great degree: *a truly generous act* ○ *Her last novel was truly awful.* **3** honestly and accurately: *Tell me truly what you think.* **IDM** **well and truly** ⇨ WELL¹. ⇨ note at YOUR.

trump /trʌmp/ (also **trump card**) *n* (in certain card-games) a card of a suit¹(2) that is chosen to have a particular game to have a higher value than the other three suits: *Hearts are trumps.* ○ *He took my ace with a low trump.* **IDM** **,come/turn up 'trumps** (*infml*) **1** to be especially helpful or generous: *No-body else in the family gave anything for the raffle, but my sister came up trumps.* **2** to do or happen better than expected: *The team turned up trumps on the day.*
▶ **trump** *v* **1** ~ **sth** (**with sth**) to take a card or trick(5) with a trump: [Vn, Vnpr] *She trumped my ace (with a six).* **2** to beat sth that sb says or does by saying or doing sth even better: [Vn] *They were trumped by another firm that made a higher offer.*
PHRV **,trump sth 'up** (usu passive) to invent a false excuse, accusation, etc in order to harm sb: *arrested on a trumped-up charge.*
■ **'trump card** *n* (**a**) = TRUMP *n*. (**b**) a very valuable or the most valuable resource that one has and may use, esp as a surprise, to gain an advantage: *Our rivals seem to hold all the trump cards.* ○ *Finally she played her trump card and threatened to resign.*

trumpery /'trʌmpəri/ *n, adj* [attrib] (*dated derog*) (objects that are) bright or attractive but of little value: *trumpery ornaments.*

trumpet /'trʌmpɪt/ *n* **1** a brass musical instrument played by blowing. It consists of a curved metal tube that becomes wider at the end, and has three valves (VALVE 3) for varying the notes: *play the trumpet* ○ *a trumpet blast/call.* ⇨ picture at MUSICAL INSTRU-MENT. **2** a thing shaped like a trumpet, esp the open flower of a DAFFODIL. ⇨ picture at FLOWER. **IDM** **blow one's own trumpet** ⇨ BLOW¹.
▶ **trumpet** *v* **1** (*often derog*) to state sth in public loudly and with force: [Vn] *He's always trumpeting his opinions.* **2** [V] (of an elephant) to make a loud noise like that of a trumpet. **trumpeter** *n* a person who plays a trumpet.

truncate /trʌŋ'keɪt; *US* 'trʌŋkeɪt/ *v* (esp passive) to make sth shorter by cutting off the top or end: [Vn] *a truncated pyramid* ○ *They published my article in truncated form.*

truncheon /'trʌntʃən/ (also **baton**) *n* a short thick stick carried as a weapon, esp by police officers.

trundle /'trʌndl/ *v* to roll or move heavily and slowly, esp in the specified direction; to make sth do this: [Vnpr] *A goods train trundled past.* [Vnpr] *She was trundling a wheelbarrow along the path.* [also Vpr, Vnp].

trunk /trʌŋk/ n **1** [C] the thick main stem of a tree, from which the branches grow. **2** [C usu *sing*] the main part of the human body apart from the head, arms and legs. ⇨ picture at HUMAN. See also TORSO. **3** [C] a large strong box with a lid for storing or transporting clothes or other things. ⇨ picture at LUGGAGE. **4** [C] the long nose of an elephant. **5** **trunks** [pl] SHORTS(1) worn by men or boys for swimming, boxing, etc. **6** [C] (*US*) the boot¹(2) of a car. ⇨ picture at CAR.

■ 'trunk call n (*dated esp Brit*) a telephone call to a distant place in the same country.

'trunk road n (*Brit*) an important main road.

truss /trʌs/ n **1** a framework, eg of beams, supporting a roof, bridge, etc. **2** a special belt with a pad worn by a person suffering from a HERNIA.

▶ **truss** v **1** ~ sth/sb (up) (with sth) to tie sth/sb securely: [Vn] *truss a chicken* (ie fasten its legs and wings securely before cooking it) [Vnpr, Vnp] *The thieves had trussed the guard (up) with rope.* **2** [Vn] (usu passive) to support a roof, bridge, etc with trusses (TRUSS 1).

trust¹ /trʌst/ n **1** [U] ~ (in sb/sth) the belief or willingness to believe that one can rely on the goodness, strength, ability, etc of sb/sth: *A good marriage is based on trust.* ○ *I have absolute trust in the (skill of the) doctors.* ○ *I put my trust in you.* ○ *You've betrayed my trust* (eg told a secret or not kept a promise). **2** [U] responsibility; care: *a position of great trust* ○ *The children were left in the trust of a girl of 15.* **3** [C] (*law*) (**a**) an arrangement by which a group of people or an organization holds money or property given to sb and uses it for that person's benefit: *In his will he created trusts for his children.* ○ *She inherits £50 000, to be held in trust for her until she is 21.* (**b**) an amount of money or property held and used in such a way: *10 per cent of the trust was to be used for the children's education.* (**c**) a group of people or an organization that holds and controls money or property given or lent to them by other people and uses it for the public good to encourage cultural activities or preserve old buildings: *The project is financed by a charitable trust.* ○ *a wildfowl trust.* See also THE NATIONAL TRUST, UNIT TRUST. **4** [C] an association of business firms formed to reduce competition, control prices, etc: *anti-trust laws.* **IDM** take sth on 'trust to accept or believe what sb says without evidence or investigation: *I can't prove it — you'll just have to take it on trust.*

▶ **trusting** adj showing trust; not suspicious: *have a trusting nature.*

■ 'trust fund n money that is held in trust(3a) for sb: *set up a trust fund.*

'trust territory n a territory governed by the United Nations Organization or by a country appointed by the United Nations Organization.

trust² /trʌst/ v **1** to have or place trust¹(1) in sb/sth; to treat sb/sth as reliable: [Vn] *They're not to be trusted.* ○ *I trust you implicitly.* ○ *You can't always trust what the papers say.* **2** to depend on sb to do sth, use sth, look after sth, etc properly or safely: [Vnpr] *I can't trust that boy out of my sight.* ○ *I'd trust him with my life.* [Vn.to inf] *Can I trust you to post this letter?* ○ (*ironic*) *Trust you* (ie It is typical of you) *to forget my birthday!* **3** (*fml*) to hope, esp with confidence: [V.that] *I trust (that) she's not seriously ill.* ○ *You've no objection, I trust.* **PHRV** 'trust in sb/sth to have confidence in sb/sth: *trust in providence* ○ *You must trust in your own judgement.* 'trust to sth/sb to risk leaving decisions about the progress of events to sth/sb: *trust to luck/fate/fortune* ○ *At such times you have to trust to instinct.*

trustee /trʌˈstiː/ n **1** a person who is responsible for managing a trust¹(3b): *I've been asked to act as (a) trustee for my godson.* **2** a member of a group of people managing the business affairs of an institu-

tion: *a trustee of the National Gallery.* **3** a country given responsibilities for governing a particular territory by the United Nations Organization.

▶ **trusteeship** /-ʃɪp/ n **1** [U,C] the position of a trustee. **2** [U] the responsibility for governing a particular territory given to a country by the United Nations Organization.

trustworthy /ˈtrʌstwɜːðɪ/ adj worthy of trust; reliable: *I've always found her honest and trustworthy.*

▶ **trustworthiness** n [U].

trusty /ˈtrʌstɪ/ adj (*arch or joc*) worthy of trust; reliable: *my trusty old bicycle.*

▶ **trusty** n a prisoner who is given special privileges or responsibilities because of good behaviour.

truth /truːθ/ n (*pl* truths /truːðz/) **1** [U] the quality or state of being true: *There's no truth/not a word of truth in what he says.* **2(a)** [U] that which is true: *the whole truth* ○ *the search for (the) truth* ○ *I want you to tell (me) the truth* (ie speak honestly, not lie). ○ *We found out the truth about him.* ○ *The (plain) truth is, I forgot about it.* (**b**) [C] a fact, belief, etc that is accepted as true: *believe in the eternal truths like freedom and justice.* See also HOME TRUTH. **IDM** in truth (*fml*) truly; really: *It was in truth a miracle.* the moment of truth ⇨ MOMENT. to tell the truth ⇨ TELL.

▶ **truthful** /-fl/ adj **1** (of a person) honest in what he or she says; never lying. **2** (of statements) true. **truthfully** /-fəlɪ/ adv. **truthfulness** n [U].

try¹ /traɪ/ v (*pt, pp* tried) **1** to make an attempt or effort: [V] *I don't know if I can come, but I'll try.* [V.to inf] *Try to be here on time.* ○ *I tried hard not to laugh.* ○ *You haven't even tried to lift it.* ○ *Don't try to swim across the river.* [Vn] *He's trying his best/hardest/utmost* (ie as much as he can). (In informal use, *try to* + infinitive is often replaced by *try and* + infinitive, esp in the imperative, and *don't/didn't try to* by *don't/didn't try and*: *Please try and come if you can. I'm leaving — don't try and stop me.*) ⇨ note at AND. **2** to use, do or test sth in order to see whether it is satisfactory, effective, enjoyable, etc: [Vn] *I've tried this new detergent, with excellent results.* ○ *'Would you like to try some raw fish?' 'Why not, I'll try anything once.'* [V.ing] *Have you ever tried wind-surfing?* ○ *Try phoning his home number.* [Vn] *Try that door* (ie Try opening it to see if it is locked or to find what is on the other side). [Vnpr] *Don't try any funny stuff with me!* ○ *Let's try the table in a different position.* ○ *Try these shoes for size.* ○ *I think we should try her for the job.* **3(a)** ~ sb (for sth) to hold a trial of sb: [Vnpr] *He was tried for murder.* [also Vn]. (**b**) (esp passive) to examine and decide a case¹(5a) in a lawcourt: [Vn] *The case was tried before a jury.* **4** to be hard to bear for sb/sth: [Vn] *Three hours of unnecessary delay had sorely tried my patience.* **IDM** do/try one's damnedest ⇨ DAMNEDEST. do/try one's utmost ⇨ UTMOST. try one's 'hand (at sth) to attempt sth, eg a skill or a sport, for the first time: *I'd like to try my hand at water-skiing.* try one's 'luck (at sth) to do sth that involves risk or luck, hoping to succeed: *I think I'll try my luck at roulette.* **PHRV** 'try for sth to make an attempt to get or win sth: *try for a scholarship/an Olympic medal/a job in the Civil Service.* ,try sth 'on 1 to put on clothing, etc to see if it fits and how it looks: *Try on the shoes before you buy them.* **2** (*Brit infml*) to behave badly or try to deceive sb, knowing that it is wrong but hoping that no one will object: *Don't try anything on with me, or you'll be sorry.* ,try 'out for sth (*US*) to compete for a position, to be a member of sth, etc: *She's trying out for the part of Cleopatra.* ,try sb/sth 'out (on sb) to test or use sb/sth in order to see how good, effective, etc they are/it is: *try out a new young quarter-back* ○ *The drug has not been tried out on humans yet.*

▶ **tried** adj [attrib] that has been proved to be

effective, reliable, etc: *a tried and tested* remedy ○ *a tried and true friend*.

trier *n* a person who tries hard and always does her or his best: *He's not very good but he's a real trier*.

trying *adj* difficult or annoying; hard to deal with: *She can be very trying at times.* ○ *I've had a trying day.*

■ **'try-on** *n* (*Brit infml*) an attempt to do sth that one does not expect to be allowed to do, while hoping no one will object.

'try-out *n* a test of the qualities or performance of a person or thing: *give sb/sth a try-out*.

try² /traɪ/ *n* **1** ~ (**at sth/doing sth**) an attempt: *I'll give it a try.* ○ *It's worth a try.* ○ *He had three tries at mending the lock and finally gave up.* **2** (in Rugby football) an act by a player of touching down the ball behind the opponents' goal-line (GOAL), which also entitles her or his side to a kick at goal: *score a try*. Compare CONVERT¹ 3.

tsar (also **tzar**, **czar**) /zɑː(r)/ *n* the title of the former EMPEROR of Russia.

▶ **tsarina** (also **tzarina**, **czarina**) /zɑːˈriːnə/ *n* the title of the former EMPRESS of Russia.

tsetse /ˈtsetsi/ (also **'tsetse fly**) *n* a tropical African fly that feeds on human and animal blood and can cause sleeping sickness (SLEEP²) by its bite.

T-shirt ⇨ T.

tsp (*pl* **tsps**) *abbr* teaspoonful: *Add 2 tsps sugar*.

T-square ⇨ SQUARE² 5.

tub /tʌb/ *n* **1(a)** (often in compounds) a wide, open, usu round, container used for washing clothes, holding liquids, growing plants, etc: *garden tubs*. ⇨ picture at BUCKET. **(b)** a similar small, usu plastic, container for food, etc: *a tub of ice-cream/cottage cheese/margarine*. **(c)** (also **tubful** /-fʊl/) an amount held by a tub: *a tub of hot water*. **2** = BATH-TUB. **3** (*infml esp joc*) a slow awkward boat: *a leaky old tub*.

■ **'tub-thumper** *n* (*infml derog*) a public speaker with a loud and violent or dramatic manner. **'tub-thumping** *n* [U], *adj*.

tuba /ˈtjuːbə; *US* ˈtuː-/ *n* a long brass musical instrument of low pitch¹(2). ⇨ picture at MUSICAL INSTRUMENT.

tubby /ˈtʌbi/ *adj* (*rather infml*) short and fat: *a tubby little man*. ⇨ note at FAT¹.

tube /tjuːb; *US* tuːb/ *n* **1** [C] a long hollow pipe or CYLINDER(1b) of metal, glass, rubber, etc for holding or transporting liquids, gases, etc: *a laboratory full of jars, tubes and other containers* ○ *Blood flowed along the tube into the bottle.* See also INNER TUBE, TEST-TUBE. **2** [C] ~ (**of sth**) a container with a cap(4), made of thin flexible metal or plastic and used for holding thick liquids, etc ready for use: *a tube of glue/ointment* ○ *squeeze toothpaste from/out of a tube*. **3** [C usu *pl*] a hollow organ in the body, shaped like a tube: *bronchial/Fallopian/Eustachian tubes*. **4 the tube** (also **the underground**) [U, sing] (*Brit infml*) the underground railway system in London: *travel to work by tube/on the tube* ○ *take a/the tube to Victoria* ○ *tube trains/tickets*. Compare SUBWAY 2. **5** [C] = CATHODE-RAY TUBE.

▶ **tubeless** *adj* [usu attrib] (of a tyre) having no inner tube (INNER).

tubing *n* [U] a length of tube(1); tubes: *two metres of copper/plastic tubing*.

tubular /ˈtjuːbjələ(r); *US* ˈtuː-/ *adj* **1** consisting of tubes; made of pieces shaped like tubes: *tubular scaffolding* ○ *tubular steel chairs*. **2** long, round and hollow like a tube: *tubular flowers*.

tuber /ˈtjuːbə(r); *US* ˈtuː-/ *n* a short thick round part of an underground stem or root which stores food and from which new plants will grow: *potato/dahlia tubers*.

▶ **tuberous** /ˈtjuːbərəs; *US* ˈtuː-/ *adj* **1** of or like a tuber. **2** having or producing tubers.

tuberculosis /tjuːˌbɜːkjuˈləʊsɪs; *US* tuː-/ *n* [U]

(*abbr* **TB**) a serious infectious disease in which swellings appear on body tissue, esp the lungs.

▶ **tubercular** /tjuːˈbɜːkjələ(r); *US* tuː-/ *adj* of, causing or affected with tuberculosis: *a tubercular infection/lung*.

TUC /ˌtiː juː ˈsiː/ *abbr* (in Britain) Trades Union Congress.

tuck¹ /tʌk/ *v* **1(a)** ~ **sth into sth**; ~ **sth in/up** to push, fold or turn the ends or edges of clothes, paper, etc so that they are hidden or held in place: [Vnpr] *Tuck your jeans into your boots.* [Vnp] *tuck one's shirt in* (eg into one's trousers) ○ *She tucked up her skirt and waded into the river.* ○ *The sheets were tucked in neatly* (ie around the bed). ○ *tuck the flap of an envelope in.* **(b)** to pull sth together into a small space: [Vnpr, Vnp] *The nurse tucked her hair (up) under her cap.* ○ *He sat with his legs tucked (up) under him.* **2** to put sth away where it is safe, comfortable or tidy: [Vnpr] *The hen tucked its head under its wing.* [Vnp] *He tucked the map away in a drawer.* **3** to put sth round sb/sth in order to make them comfortable, warm, etc: *tuck a blanket round sb's knees/legs*. **PHRV** **,tuck sth a'way** (*infml esp Brit*) to eat a lot of food. **,tuck sth/oneself a'way** (*infml*) to store or hide sth/oneself: *He's got a fortune tucked away in a Swiss bank account.* ○ *The farm was tucked away in the hills.* ○ *She likes to tuck herself away in her room for hours.* **,tuck sb 'in/'up** to make sb, esp a child, comfortable in bed by pulling the sheets and blankets (BLANKET 1) tightly round them: *The children are all safely tucked up (in bed).* **,tuck 'into sth/'in** (*infml esp Brit*) to eat sth with a healthy appetite: *He was tucking into a large plate of spaghetti.* ○ *Come on, tuck in, everybody!*

■ **'tuck-in** *n* (usu *sing*) (*Brit infml*) a large meal: *have a good tuck-in*.

tuck² /tʌk/ *n* **1** [C] a flat fold of material sewn into a garment, etc to make it fit better or for ornament: *The dress was slightly too big so I took a tuck in the waist.* **2** [U] (*dated Brit infml*) food, esp sweets, cakes, etc that children enjoy: *a school tuck shop*.

tucker /ˈtʌkə(r)/ *n* **IDM** **one's best bib and tucker** ⇨ BEST¹.

Tue (also **Tues**) *abbr* Tuesday: *Tues 9 March*.

Tuesday /ˈtjuːzdeɪ, -di; *US* ˈtuː-/ *n* [C, U] (*abbrs* **Tue**, **Tues**) the third day of the week, next after Monday. For further guidance on how *Tuesday* is used, see the examples at *Monday*.

tuft /tʌft/ *n* a bunch of hair, feathers, grass, etc growing or held together at the base.

▶ **tufted** *adj* having, or growing in, a tuft or tufts: *a tufted carpet*.

tug /tʌg/ *v* (**-gg-**) **(a)** ~ (**at**) **sth** to pull sth hard or violently: [Vpr] *tug at sb's elbow/sleeve* (eg to attract attention) ○ (*fig*) *It's a poignant story that really **tugs at the heartstrings*** (ie makes one feel sad). [Vn] *Don't tug my hair!* [Vn-adj] *He tugged the door open.* [V] *We tugged so hard that the rope broke.* **(b)** to pull sth/sb hard in a particular direction: [Vnpr] *The wind nearly tugged my umbrella out of my hand.* [also Vnp].

▶ **tug** *n* **1** a sudden hard pull: *I felt a tug at my sleeve.* ○ *She gave her sister's hair a sharp tug.* **2** (also **'tugboat**) a small powerful boat for pulling ships, esp into harbour or up rivers.

■ **,tug of 'love** *n* [sing] (*Brit infml*) a dispute over who is to have the main care of a child, esp one between parents who are no longer living together or married: *a tug-of-love drama.*

,tug of 'war *n* [sing, U] a contest in which two teams pull at opposite ends of a rope until one drags the other over a central line.

tuition /tjuˈɪʃn; *US* tuˈ-/ *n* [U] **(a)** (*rather fml*) teaching or instruction, esp of individuals or small groups: *have private tuition in French* ○ *tuition fees*.

(b) a sum of money charged for this, esp in colleges and universities.

tulip /'tjuːlɪp; US 'tuː-/ n a garden plant growing from a BULB(1) in spring, with a large, brightly coloured flower, shaped like a cup, on a tall stem. ⇨ picture at FLOWER.

tulle /tjuːl; US tuːl/ n [U] a soft fine silk or nylon material like net, used esp for veils (VEIL 1a) and dresses.

tumble /'tʌmbl/ v **1(a)** to fall or make sb/sth fall, esp in a sudden helpless way, often without serious injury: [Vpr] *tumble down the stairs/off a bicycle/out of a tree* [Vp] *Toddlers keep tumbling over.* [Vn, Vnp] *The children tumbled* (ie pushed) *each other (over) in the snow.* [also V, Vadv, Vnpr, Vnadv]. **(b)** to fall rapidly in value or amount: [V] *Share prices tumbled on the stock market.* **2** ~ **into / out of sth**; ~ **in/out** to move or rush in the specified direction in disorder or confusion: [Vpr] *I threw off my clothes and tumbled into bed.* ○ *The children tumbled into/out of the car.* [Vp] *My shopping bag broke and everything tumbled out.* **3** to roll quickly backwards or forwards over and over or up and down: [Vp] *The puppies were tumbling about on the floor.* [Vpr] *The water tumbled over the rocks.* [also V]. **PHRV** ,**tumble 'down** to fall into ruin; to collapse: *The old barn is practically tumbling down.* '**tumble to sth** (*infml*) to understand a situation, hidden meaning, etc: *I finally tumbled to the fact that she was seeing someone else.*

▶ **tumble** n **1** [C] a helpless or violent fall: *have/ take a nasty tumble.* **2** [sing] an untidy or confused state: *bedclothes in a tumble on the floor.* See also ROUGH-AND-TUMBLE.

■ ,**tumble-'drier** (also ,**tumbler-'drier**) n (*Brit*) a machine for drying washed clothes in a heated drum¹(2) that spins round and round.

tumbledown /'tʌmbldaʊn/ adj [attrib] falling or fallen into ruin: *a tumbledown old shack.*

tumbler /'tʌmblə(r)/ n **1(a)** a drinking glass with a flat bottom, straight sides and no handle or stem¹(2). ⇨ picture at GLASS. **(b)** (also **tumblerful** /-fʊl/) the amount held by a tumbler: *a tumbler of milk.* **2** an ACROBAT who turns somersaults (SOMERSAULT), esp on the ground. **3** the part of a lock that holds the BOLT¹(1) until lifted by a key.

■ **tumbler-drier** n (*Brit*) = TUMBLE-DRIER.

tumbleweed /'tʌmblwiːd/ n [U] a plant growing like a bush in desert areas of N America, parts of which break off in autumn and are rolled about by the wind.

tumbril /'tʌmbrəl/ n an open cart, esp of the kind used to carry condemned people to the GUILLOTINE(1) during the French Revolution: *tumbrils rolling through the streets.*

tumescent /tjuː'mesnt; US tuː-/ adj (*fml*) (esp of parts of the body) swelling or swollen, eg as a result of sexual excitement. ▶ **tumescence** /-sns/ n [U].

tummy /'tʌmi/ n (*infml*) stomach: *lying on one's tummy* ○ *have a tummy-ache* ○ *one's tummy-button* (ie NAVEL).

tumour (*US* **tumor**) /'tjuːmə(r); US 'tuː-/ n an abnormal mass of new tissue growing in or on part of the body: *benign/malignant tumours* ○ *die of a 'brain tumour.* See also GROWTH 4a.

tumult /'tjuːmʌlt; US 'tuː-/ n [U, sing] (*fml*) **1(a)** a lot of confused or excited noise, esp of a large mass of people: *struggle to be heard above the tumult.* **(b)** a state of confusion, excitement or public disturbance causing such a noise: *the tumult of war* ○ *The demonstration broke up in tumult.* **2** a troubled or confused state of mind: *Her mind was in a tumult.*

▶ **tumultuous** /tjuː'mʌltʃuəs; US tuː-/ adj **1** noisy because of the strong feelings involved: *tumultuous applause* ○ *receive a tumultuous welcome.* **2** in a state of disorder or confusion: *tumultuous crowds/events.*

tumulus /'tjuːmjələs; US 'tuː-/ n (*pl* **tumuli** /-laɪ/) a large pile of earth built over a burial place in ancient times. See also BARROW².

tun /tʌn/ n a large barrel for beer, wine, etc.

tuna /'tjuːnə; US 'tuːnə/ n (*pl* unchanged or **tunas**) **(a)** (also **tunny**) [C] a large sea-fish, eaten as food. **(b)** (also '**tuna-fish**) [U] its flesh as food.

tundra /'tʌndrə/ n [U, C] a large flat Arctic region of Europe, Asia and N America. No trees grow on it and the ground below the surface layer of soil is always frozen.

tune¹ /tjuːn; US tuːn/ n [C, U] a series of musical notes that give a piece of music its main character, making it pleasing, easy to remember, etc or otherwise: *whistle a catchy tune* ○ *hymn tunes* ○ *He gave us a tune on his guitar.* ○ *A lot of modern music has no tune (to it).* See also SIGNATURE TUNE, THEME TUNE. **IDM** **call the shots/tune** ⇨ CALL¹. **change one's tune** ⇨ CHANGE¹. **dance to sb's tune** ⇨ DANCE². **he who pays the piper calls the tune** ⇨ PAY². ,**in / ,out of 'tune (with sb/sth)** **1** at/not at the correct musical pitch¹(2): *The violin is not quite in tune with the piano.* ○ *The choir was (singing) distinctly out of tune in places.* **2** in/not in agreement or emotional harmony: *feel out of tune with one's surroundings/companions.* **sing a different song/ tune** ⇨ SING. **to the tune of sth** **1** using the tune of sth: *Sing it to the tune of Yankee Doodle.* **2** (*infml*) to the usu considerable sum or amount of sth: *offer sb sponsorship to the tune of £2 million a year.*

▶ **tuneful** /-fl/ adj having a pleasing tune; melodious (MELODY). **tunefully** /-fəli/ adv. **tunefulness** n [U].

tuneless adj (*usu derog*) without a tune; not melodious (MELODY). **tunelessly** adv. **tunelessness** n [U].

tune² /tjuːn; US tuːn/ v **1** to adjust a musical instrument to the correct pitch¹(2): [Vn] *tune a guitar.* **2** [Vn] to adjust an engine, etc so that it runs smoothly and efficiently. **3** ~ **sth (to sth)** to adapt or adjust sth so that it is suitable or correct for a particular purpose, situation, etc: [Vn, Vnpr] *His speech was finely tuned (to what the audience wanted to hear).* **PHRV** ,**tune 'in (to sth)** to adjust a radio, television, etc so that it receives a particular programme: *tune in to the BBC World Service* ○ *Tune in next week at the same time!* ,**tune (sth) 'up** to adjust musical instruments so that they can play together in harmony: *The orchestra were tuning up as we entered the hall.*

▶ **tuned** adj [pred] ~ **(in) (to sth)** having a radio, etc adjusted to a particular programme: *Stay tuned (to this wavelength) for the latest sports news.* ○ *You're not properly tuned in.* ,**tuned 'in** adj [pred] ~ **(to sth)** aware of or able to understand sth: *She seems to be tuned in to the needs of ordinary people.*

■ '**tuning-fork** n a small metal instrument with two arms that produces a particular note¹(5a) when struck, and is used in tuning musical instruments.

tuner /'tjuːnə(r); US 'tuː-/ n **1** (esp in compounds) a person who tunes musical instruments, esp pianos. **2** the part of a radio, television, etc that selects signals of a particular FREQUENCY(2).

tungsten /'tʌŋstən/ n [U] (*symb* **W**) a chemical element. Tungsten is a hard grey metal used esp in making steel. ⇨ App 7.

tunic /'tjuːnɪk; US 'tuː-/ n **1(a)** a loose outer garment, often without sleeves, that reaches to about the knees and is sometimes worn with a belt at the waist. **(b)** a similar garment with open sleeves that reaches to the hips and is worn over trousers or a skirt by women or girls. **2** a shaped jacket worn as part of a uniform by police officers, soldiers, etc.

tunnel /'tʌnl/ n **(a)** an underground passage, eg for a road or railway through a hill or under a river or the sea: *the Channel Tunnel* (ie between England and France) ○ *The train went into a tunnel.* **(b)** a similar underground passage made by an animal: *Moles dug tunnels under the lawn.* **IDM** **light at the end of the tunnel** ⇨ LIGHT[1].

▶ **tunnel** *v* (**-ll-**; *US* **-l-**) to dig a tunnel, esp in the specified direction: [V, Vp] *The prisoners had escaped by tunnelling (out).* [Vpr] *The engineers had to tunnel through solid rock.* [Vnpr, Vnp] *The rescuers tunnelled their way (in) to the trapped miners.* [Vn] *tunnel a hole/shaft/passage.*

■ ,**tunnel** '**vision** *n* **1** a condition in which one cannot see well things that are not straight ahead of one. **2** (*derog*) an inability to see or understand the wider aspects of a situation, an argument, etc.

tunny /'tʌni/ *n* = TUNA a.

tuppence /'tʌpəns/ *n* (*Brit infml*) = TWOPENCE. **IDM** **not care/give** '**tuppence for sb/sth** to consider sb/sth worthless or unimportant. ▶ **tuppenny** /'tʌpəni/ *adj* [attrib] (*Brit infml*) = TWOPENNY.

turban /'tɜːbən/ *n* (**a**) a head-dress for men, worn esp by Muslims and Sikhs. It is made by winding a length of cloth tightly round the head. (**b**) a woman's hat resembling this.

▶ **turbaned** /'tɜːbənd/ *adj* wearing a turban.

turbid /'tɜːbɪd/ *adj* (*fml*) (of liquids) thick and full of mud; not clear: *the turbid floodwaters of the river* ∘ (*fig*) *his turbid (ie confused) imagination.*

turbine /'tɜːbaɪn/ *n* a machine or motor driven by a wheel which is turned by a current of water, steam, air or gas.

turbocharger /'tɜːbəʊtʃɑːdʒə(r)/ (also **turbo**, *pl* **-os**) *n* an apparatus driven by a TURBINE that gets its power from an engine's EXHAUST[1](1) gases. It sends the mixture of petrol and air into the engine at high pressure, making it more powerful. ▶ **turbocharge** *v*: [Vn] *turbocharged engines.*

turbojet /ˌtɜːbəʊ'dʒet/ *n* (**a**) a TURBINE engine that produces forward movement by means of a jet of hot EXHAUST[1](1) gases. (**b**) an aircraft that gets its power from this type of engine.

turboprop /ˌtɜːbəʊ'prɒp/ *n* (**a**) a TURBINE used as a TURBOJET and also to drive a propeller (PROPEL). (**b**) an aircraft that gets its power from this.

turbot /'tɜːbət/ *n* (*pl* unchanged) [C, U] a large flat fish that lives in European seas and is highly valued as food: *grilled turbot.*

turbulent /'tɜːbjələnt/ *adj* **1**(**a**) in a state of disturbance, confusion or conflict: *turbulent crowds/ factions* ∘ *the city's turbulent history.* (**b**) not controlled or calm; likely to cause trouble: *her turbulent emotions.* **2** (of air or water) moving in a violently disturbed way: *turbulent waves* ∘ *turbulent weather conditions.*

▶ **turbulence** /-ləns/ *n* [U] **1** disturbance, confusion or conflict: *political turbulence* ∘ *The country is in a state of turbulence.* **2** violent or unsteady movement of air or water: *We experienced severe turbulence during the flight.*

turbulently *adv.*

turd /tɜːd/ *n* (*sl*) **1** a lump of solid waste matter passed from the body: *dog turds.* **2** (⚠) an unpleasant or worthless person.

tureen /tjuˈriːn, təˈriːn/ *n* a deep dish with a lid from which soup or vegetables are served at table.

turf /tɜːf/ *n* (*pl* **turfs** or **turves** /tɜːvz/) **1**(**a**) [U] short grass and the surface layer of soil it grows in, held together by the roots: *soft, springy turf* ∘ *lay turf* (eg to make a lawn) ∘ (*rhet*) *the hallowed turf of Wimbledon.* (**b**) [C] a piece of this cut from the ground. **2** **the turf** [sing] the sport of horse-racing, or the course on which a particular race is run: *champions of the turf.* **3** [U] (*infml esp US*) one's own familiar territory: *on my own turf.*

▶ **turf** *v* to cover ground with turf: [Vn] *a newly-turfed lawn.* **PHRV** ,**turf sb/sth** '**out (of sth)**, ,**turf sb** '**off (sth)** (*Brit infml*) to force sb/sth to leave a place; to throw sb/sth out or away: *He was turfed off*

the committee. ∘ *You'd have more room in your wardrobe if you turfed out all your old clothes.*

■ '**turf accountant** *n* (*Brit fml*) a BOOKMAKER.

turgid /'tɜːdʒɪd/ *adj* **1** (*derog*) (of language, style, etc) elaborate and difficult to understand; boring: *turgid prose.* **2** thick with mud, etc and swollen: *the turgid waters of the river.* ▶ **turgidity** /tɜːˈdʒɪdəti/ *n* [U].

turkey /'tɜːki/ *n* (*pl* **-eys**) **1**(**a**) [C] a large bird bred to be eaten, esp at Christmas and, in the USA, at Thanksgiving. (**b**) [U] its flesh as food: *a slice of roast turkey.* **2** (*US infml*) (**a**) a failure: *His latest movie is a real turkey.* (**b**) a silly or useless person: *That's not the way to do it, you turkey.* **IDM** **cold turkey** ⇨ COLD[1]. **talk turkey** ⇨ TALK[1].

Turkish /'tɜːkɪʃ/ *adj* of Turkey, its people or its language.

▶ **Turkish** *n* [U] the language of Turkey.

■ ,**Turkish** '**bath** *n* a type of bath in which one sits in a room of hot air or steam, followed by washing, MASSAGE, etc.

,**Turkish** '**coffee** *n* [U, C] very strong, usu very sweet, black coffee.

,**Turkish de**'**light** *n* [U] a sweet food consisting of lumps of a substance like jelly which has added flavour and colour and is covered with soft sugar.

turmeric /'tɜːmərɪk/ *n* [U] a powder used as a spice to give colour and flavour to food, esp CURRY[1]. It is made from the root of an E Indian plant.

turmoil /'tɜːmɔɪl/ *n* [U, sing] a state of great disturbance, confusion or uncertainty: *The country was in (a) turmoil during the strike.*

turn[1] /tɜːn/ *v*

● **Movement around a central point** **1** to move or make sth move round a central point or an AXIS(1); to ROTATE(1) (sth): [Vpr] *The earth turns on its axis once every 24 hours.* [V] *The hands of a clock turn very slowly.* ∘ *The wheels of the car began to turn.* ∘ *I can't get the screw to turn.* [Vn] *Can you turn it?* ∘ *She turned the handle but the door wouldn't open.* [Vnpr] *He turned the key in the lock.* ∘ *She turned the steering-wheel sharply to the left to avoid a cyclist.* **2** ~ (**sb/sth**) (**over**) to move or make sb/sth move so that a different side faces outwards or upwards: [Vp] *If you turn over you might find it easier to get to sleep.* ∘ *The car skidded, turned over and burst into flames.* [Vnp] *Grill the meat on one side, then turn it over and grill the other side.* [Vn] *He sat there idly turning the pages of a book.* [Vnpr] *She turned the chair on its side to repair it.* [Vnadv] *You've turned your sweater inside out.* [Vnp] *Turn the record over and put on* (ie start to play) *the other side.* **3**(**a**) to change position or direction or make sb/sth do this so as to face or start moving in the specified direction: [Vadv] *About/Left/Right turn!* (ie as military commands) [V] *We turned and headed for home.* [V.to inf] *She turned to look at me.* [Vpr] *He turned towards her.* ∘ (*fig*) *Her thoughts turned to* (ie She began to think about) *her dead husband.* [Vnpr] *He turned his back to the wall.* [Vp, Vnp] *She turned (her face) away in disgust.* (**b**) (of the tide) to start to come in or go out: [V] *The tide is turning — we'd better get back.* **4** to aim or point sth in the specified direction: [Vnpr] *Police turned water-cannon on the rioters* (ie to make them stop and go away). ∘ *They turned their dogs on us.* ∘ *She turned her eyes towards him.* ∘ (*fig*) *It's time to turn our attention to the question of money.*

● **Putting or sending something into a particular place or condition** **5** to make or let sb/ sth go into the specified place or state: [Vnpr] *turn a horse into a field* [Vnadv] *turn a boat adrift* [Vn-adj] *The police questioned him for three days before turning him loose again.* **6** to fold sth in the specified way: [Vnp] *She turned down the blankets and*

[V.*to* inf] = verb + *to* infinitive   [Vn.inf (no *to*)] = verb + noun + infinitive without *to*   [V.*ing*] = verb + *-ing* form

climbed into bed. ○ *He turned up the collar of his coat and hurried out into the rain.*

● **Changing direction 7** ~ (**round**) **sth** to go round sth: [Vn, Vpr] *The car turned (round) the corner and disappeared from sight.* **8** (of a river, road, etc) to curve in the specified direction: [V-n] *The river turns north at this point.* [Vpr] *The road turns to the left after the church.* **9** (no passive) to perform the specified movement by moving one's body in a circle: [Vn] *turn cartwheels/somersaults.*

● **Changing state or form 10**(**a**) to become or make sb/sth become: [V-adj, Vn-adj] *The milk turned sour in the heat/The heat turned the milk sour.* [V-adj] *He turned nasty when we refused to give him the money.* ○ *Leaves turn brown in autumn.* ○ *The weather has turned cold and windy.* [V-n] *She turned a deathly shade of white when she heard the news.* ○ *He's a lawyer turned politician* (ie He was formerly a lawyer but is now a politician). ➪ note at BECOME. (**b**) (not in the continuous tenses) to reach or pass the specified age or time: [Vn] *She turned forty last June.* ○ *It's turned midnight.* **11** ~ (**sb/sth**) (**from A**) **to/into B** to pass or change sb/sth from one condition or state to another one: [Vpr] *Caterpillars turn into butterflies.* ○ *Water turns into ice when it freezes.* ○ *His expression turned from bewilderment to horror.* [Vnpr] *The experience has turned him into a sad and bitter man.* ○ *The witch turned the prince into a frog.* ○ *The novel was turned into a successful Hollywood movie.* **12** (of the stomach) to have a sick feeling; to make the stomach have a sick feeling: [V, Vn] *The sight of the greasy stew made my stomach turn/turned my stomach.* **13** to become or make sth sour: [Vn] *The thundery weather has turned the milk.* [also V]. **14** to shape sth on a LATHE: [Vn] *turn a chair leg.*

IDM Most idioms containing **turn** are at the entries for the nouns or adjectives in the idioms, eg **not turn a hair** ➪ HAIR; **turn a deaf ear** ➪ DEAF. **as it/things turned** '**out** as was shown or proved by later events: *I didn't need my umbrella, as it turned out* (ie because it didn't rain). **be well, badly, etc turned** '**out** to be well, badly, etc dressed: *She's always so elegantly turned out.* **turn round and do sth** (*infml*) to say or do sth that one does not like or is upset by, esp in a way that surprises one: *How could she turn round and say that, after all I've done for her?*

PHRV ,**turn** (**sb**) **a**'**gainst sb** to stop being friendly towards sb or to make sb do this: *She turned against her old friend.* ○ *After the divorce he tried to turn the children against their mother.*

,**turn a**'**round** = TURN ROUND.

,**turn sb a**'**way** (**from sth**) to refuse to allow sb to enter a place; to refuse to give help or support to sb: *Hundreds of people were turned away from the stadium* (eg because it was full). ○ *They had nowhere to stay so I couldn't turn them away.*

,**turn** (**sb/sth**) '**back** to return the way one has come or to make sb/sth do this: *The weather became so bad that they had to turn back.* ○ *The project must go ahead: there can be no turning back.* ○ *Our car was turned back at the border.*

,**turn sb/sth** '**down** to reject or refuse to consider an offer, a proposal, etc or the person who makes it: *He tried to join the army but was turned down* (flat) *because of poor health.* ○ *He asked her to marry him but she turned him down/turned down his proposal.* ,**turn sth** '**down** to adjust a COOKER(1), radio, etc in order to reduce the heat, noise, etc: *Don't forget to turn down the gas after half an hour.* ○ *Please turn the volume down — it's much too loud.*

,**turn** '**in 1** to face or curve inwards: *Her feet turn in as she walks.* **2** (*infml*) to go to bed: *It's late — I think I'll turn in.* ,**turn sb** '**in** (*infml*) to take sb to the police to be arrested: *She threatened to turn him in.*

,**turn sth** '**in 1** to give back sth that one no longer needs; to return sth: *You must turn in your kit* (ie uniform, etc) *before you leave the army.* **2** to give a finished piece of esp written work to a teacher, etc: *She turned in a really first-rate essay on George Orwell.* **3** to stop doing sth; to abandon sth: *The job was damaging his health so he had to turn it in.* **4** to register or achieve a score, performance, etc: *The champion turned in a superb performance to retain his title.* ,**turn** '**in on oneself** to become too concerned with one's own problems and stop communicating with others: *She's really turned in on herself since Peter left her.*

,**turn sth** ,**inside** '**out / ,upside** '**down 1** to make a place very untidy when one is searching for sth: *The burglars had turned the house inside out.* **2** to change sth completely, causing confusion: *The new manager turned the old systems upside down.*

,**turn** '**off** (**sth**) to leave one road in order to travel on another: *Is this where we turn off/where the road turns off for Hull?* ○ *We turned off the motorway at Lancaster.* ,**turn** (**sb**) '**off** (*infml*) to lose or make sb lose interest, sometimes sexually; to make sb feel bored or disgusted: *I'm afraid I turned off when they started talking about pig-farming.* ○ *Men with beards turn me off.* ,**turn sth** '**off 1** to stop the flow of electricity, gas, water, etc by using a switch, tap, etc: *turn off the light/oven* ○ *They've turned off the water while they repair a burst pipe.* **2** to stop a radio, television, etc by pressing a button, moving a switch, etc: *Please turn the television off before you go to bed.*

'**turn on sb** to attack sb suddenly and unexpectedly: *His old dog suddenly turned on him and bit him in the leg.* ○ *Why are you all turning on me* (ie criticizing or blaming me)? '**turn on sth** to have sth as its main topic: *The discussion turned on the need for better public health care.* '**turn on sth / doing sth** (*Brit*) to depend on sth: *Much turns on the outcome of the current peace talks.* ,**turn sb** '**on** (*infml*) to excite or stimulate sb, esp sexually: *Jazz has never really turned me on.* ○ *She gets turned on by men in uniform.* ,**turn** (**sb**) '**on** (**to sth**) (*US*) to take or persuade sb to take an illegal drug, esp for the first time: *He turned her on to heroin.* ,**turn sth** '**on** to make a COOKER(1), a radio, etc start functioning by moving a switch, button, etc: *turn on the light/television/central heating* ○ *Turn on the gas and light the oven.* ○ *Could you turn on the bath* (ie make the water start flowing) *for me while you're upstairs?* ○ (*fig*) *He really knows how to turn on the charm* (ie become very charming).

,**turn** '**out 1** to be present at an event; to appear, assemble or attend: *A vast crowd turned out to watch the procession.* ○ *Not many men turned out for duty.* **2** (used with an *adv* or *adj*, or in questions after *how*) to happen in the specified way; to result: *If the day turns out wet we may have to change our plans.* ○ *Despite our worries, everything turned out well in the end.* ,**turn** (**sth**) '**out** to point or make sth point outwards: *Her toes turn out.* ○ *She turned her toes out.* ,**turn sth** '**out** to produce sth/sb: *The factory turns out 900 cars a week.* ○ *The school has turned out some first-rate pupils.* ,**turn sth** '**out 1** to switch a light or fire off: *Remember to turn out the lights before you go to bed.* **2** to empty sth or clean it thoroughly by removing the contents: *turn out the attic/one's drawers* ○ *The teacher ordered him to turn out his pockets.* ,**turn sb** '**out** (**of/from sth**) to force sb to leave a place: *My landlord is turning me out at the end of the month.* ○ *She got pregnant and was turned out of the house by her parents.* ,**turn** '**out to be sb/sth**; ,**turn** '**out that ...** to be discovered to be sb/sth; to prove(2) to be: *She turned out to be a friend of my sister/It turned out that she was a friend of my sister.* ○ *The job turned out to be harder than we thought.*

[V.speech] = verb + direct speech   [V.*that*] = verb + *that* clause   [V.*wh*] = verb + *who, how*, etc clause

,**turn** '**over** (of an engine) to start running: *It was so cold that the engine wasn't turning over at all.* ,**turn sth** '**over** 1 to cause an engine to start running. 2 to think about sth carefully; to consider sth thoroughly: *She kept turning over the events of the day in her mind.* 3 to do business worth the specified amount: *The company turns over £150 million a year.* 4 (of a shop) to sell out and replace its stock: *A supermarket turns over its stock very rapidly.* 5 (*sl*) to rob a place: *Burglars had turned the shop over.* ,**turn sb** '**over to sb** to deliver sb to the control or care of sb else, esp sb in authority: *Customs officials turned the man over to the police.* ,**turn sth** '**over to sb** to give the control or management of sth to sb: *He turned the business over to his daughter.*

,**turn** '**round/a'round** (of a ship or an aircraft) to prepare for a journey after completing the one before it: *These cruise ships can turn round in two days.* ,**turn (sb/sth)** '**round** to face or make sb/sth face in a different direction: *Turn round and let me look at your back.* ○ *Turn your chair round to the fire.* '**turn to sb/sth** to go to sb/sth for help, advice, etc: *She has nobody she can turn to.* ○ *The parish priest is someone to whom people can turn in difficult times.* ○ *After the failure of his marriage he turned to drink.* ,**turn** '**up 1** to be found, esp by chance, after being lost: *Don't worry about your missing wallet — I'm sure it'll turn up.* 2 to arrive; to make one's appearance: *We arranged to meet at the cinema at 7.30, but he never turned up.* 3 (of an opportunity) to happen, esp by chance; to present itself: *He's still hoping something (eg a job or a piece of good luck) will turn up.* ,**turn sth** '**up 1** to increase the volume(4) of a radio, television, etc: *I can't hear the radio very well — could you turn it up a bit?* 2 to make a garment shorter by folding and sewing it up at the bottom: *These trousers are too long — they'll need turning up/to be turned up.* 3 to discover sth by digging: *The farmer turned up some old coins while ploughing the field.* ○ *The soil had been turned up by the plough.*

■ '**turn-about** *n* a sudden and complete change of policy, opinion, etc: *The government's sudden turn-about on taxation surprised political commentators.*

'**turn-around** *n* = TURN-ROUND.

'**turn-off** *n* 1 a road that leads away from a larger or more important one: *This is the turn-off for the airport.* 2 (*usu sing*) (*infml*) a person or thing that makes one feel bored, disgusted or not sexually attracted: *Smelly feet are definitely a turn-off as far as I'm concerned.*

'**turn-on** *n* (*usu sing*) (*infml*) a person or thing that excites or stimulates sb, esp sexually: *She thinks hairy chests are a turn-on!*

'**turn-round** (also '**turn-around**) (*usu sing*) *n* 1 the process of unloading (UNLOAD 1) a ship or an aircraft at the end of one journey and loading it again for the next one. 2 a complete change in a situation or a trend, esp from bad to good: *We have witnessed a remarkable turn-round in the company's fortunes.*

'**turn signal** *n* (*US*) = INDICATOR 2b.

'**turn-up** *n* 1 [C *usu pl*] the end of a trouser leg folded upwards on the outside: *Turn-ups are becoming fashionable again.* 2 [sing] (*Brit infml*) an unusual or unexpected happening or event; a surprise: *The champion beaten in the first round? That's a turn-up for the book!*

turn² /tɜːn/ *n* 1 [C] an act of turning sth/sb round; a turning movement: *give the handle a few turns.* 2 [C] a change of direction; a point at which this occurs: *take a left/right turn.* See also THREE-POINT TURN, U-TURN. 3 [C] a bend or corner in a road: *a lane full of twists and turns* ○ *Slow down as you approach the turn.* Compare TURNING. 4 [C] a development or new tendency in sth: *an unfortunate turn of events* ○ *Matters have taken an unexpected turn.* ○

Business has taken a turn for the better/worse. 5 [C *usu sing*] a time when each member of a group must or may do sth: *Please wait (until it is/for) your turn to be served.* ○ *Whose turn is it to do the washing-up?* ○ *I'll take a turn at the steering-wheel.* 6 [C] (*becoming dated*) a short walk: *I think I'll take a turn round the garden.* 7 [C] a short performance by an actor, a singer, etc: *a comedy/song-and-dance/variety turn.* See also STAR TURN. 8 (*infml*) (**a**) [sing] a shock to sb's nerves: *You gave me quite a turn, bursting in like that!* (**b**) [C] (*dated or joc*) a feeling of illness: *She's had one of her turns.* **IDM** **at every** '**turn** everywhere or all the time: *She found her plans blocked at every turn.* **by** '**turns** having the specified qualities, etc one after the other repeatedly: *Her book is funny and frightening by turns.* **do sb a good/bad** '**turn** to do sth that helps/hinders sb. **done, etc to a** '**turn** (of meat, etc) cooked for exactly the right length of time. **in (his, its, etc)** '**turn** one after the other; in succession: *The girls called out their names in turn.* ○ *This led to greater production, which in (its) turn led to greater profits.* **not do a hand's turn** ⇨ HAND¹. **on the** '**turn** about to change or go a different way: *His luck is on the turn.* ○ *This milk is on the turn* (ie about to become sour). ,**one good** ,**turn deserves a'nother** (*saying*) one should help or be kind to others who have been kind to one in the past. ,**out of** '**turn 1** before or after one's turn²(5). 2 not at the correct or permitted time: *speak out of turn* (ie in an offensive or foolish way). **serve one's/its turn** ⇨ SERVE. **take** '**turns (at sth); take sth in** '**turns** to do sth one after the other: *You can't both use the bike at once — you'll have to take (it in) turns.* **(do sth)** ,**turn and** ,**turn a'bout** (to do sth) one after another or in succession. **the** ,**turn of the** '**year/century** the time when a new century starts: *turn-of-the-century buildings* (ie ones built at this time). **a** ,**turn of** '**mind** a way of thinking about things in the specified way: *have an academic/a practical/a scientific turn of mind.* **a** ,**turn of** '**phrase** a way of expressing or describing sth: *an apt/a succinct/a witty turn of phrase.* **a** ,**turn of the** '**screw** an extra amount of pressure, cruelty, etc added to a situation that is already difficult to bear or understand. **a** ,**turn of** '**speed** a sudden increase in one's speed or rate of progress; the ability to achieve this: *She put on an impressive turn of speed in the last lap.*

turncoat /'tɜːnkəʊt/ *n* (*derog*) a person who changes from one side, party, etc to another.

turning /'tɜːnɪŋ/ *n* a place where one road leads off from another: *take the wrong turning* ○ *Take the second turning on/to the left.*

■ '**turning-circle** *n* the smallest possible circle in which a vehicle can turn without reversing so as to be pointing in the opposite direction.

'**turning-point** *n* ~ (**in sth**) a time when an important change or development takes place: *Getting a new job proved to be a turning-point in her life.* ○ *The discovery of a vaccine was the turning-point in the fight against smallpox.*

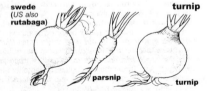

swede (US also rutabaga) turnip
parsnip turnip

turnip /'tɜːnɪp/ *n* [C,U] a plant with a round white (or white and purple) root used as a vegetable.

turnout /'tɜːnaʊt/ *n* (*usu sing*) 1 the number of people who attend a match, meeting, etc: *There was* a good/high/low turn-out at yesterday's meeting. **2** the way in which sb is dressed: *The teacher praised the children for their neat turn-out.* **3** (*esp Brit*) an act of emptying a drawer, a room, etc and throwing away things that are not needed: *These drawers are full of rubbish — it's time I had a good turn-out.*

turnover /'tɜːnəʊvə(r)/ *n* **1** [sing] the amount of money taken in a business within a certain period of time: *The firm has an annual turnover of £75 million.* ○ *make a profit of £2 000 on a turnover of £20 000.* **2** [sing] the rate at which employees leave a factory, company, etc and are replaced: *Why does the company have such a rapid turnover of staff?* **3** [sing] the rate at which goods are sold and replaced in a shop. **4** [C] a type of small pie made by folding a piece of pastry round a filling of fruit, jam, etc: *an apple turnover.*

turnpike /'tɜːnpaɪk/ *n* (*US*) a road for fast traffic which drivers must pay to drive on.

turnstile /'tɜːnstaɪl/ *n* a revolving gate that allows one person at a time to enter or leave eg a football ground or museum.

turntable /'tɜːnteɪbl/ *n* **1** the flat round revolving surface on which a record¹(3) is placed to be played. **2** a flat round revolving platform onto which a train engine or other vehicle runs to be turned round.

turpentine /'tɜːpəntaɪn/ (also *infml* **turps** /tɜːps/) *n* [U] a strong-smelling colourless liquid used esp for making paint thinner and for cleaning paint from brushes, etc.

turpitude /'tɜːpɪtjuːd; *US* -tuːd/ *n* [U] (*fml*) the state or quality of being wicked; DEPRAVITY.

turquoise /'tɜːkwɔɪz/ *n* **1** [C,U] a blue or greenish-blue precious stone: *a turquoise brooch.* **2** [U] a greenish-blue colour: *pale turquoise.* ▶ **turquoise** *adj*: *a turquoise dress.*

turret /'tʌrət/ *n* **1** a small tower on top of a larger tower or at the corner of a building or wall, eg of a castle. **2** a low flat, usu revolving, steel structure on a ship, an aircraft, a tank(2), etc where the guns are fixed and which protects people firing them: *a warship armed with twin turrets.*
▶ **turreted** *adj* having a turret(1) or turrets: *a turreted castle.*

turtle /'tɜːtl/ *n* **1** a large reptile that lives in the sea and has a large hard round shell. **2** (*US*) any reptile with a large shell, eg a TORTOISE or a TERRAPIN. ⇨ picture at TORTOISE. **IDM** **turn 'turtle** (*infml*) (of a boat) to turn over completely while sailing.
■ **'turtle-dove** *n* a wild DOVE¹(1) with a pleasant soft call. Turtle-doves are regarded as very loving birds.
'turtle-neck **1** a garment, esp a JERSEY(1), with a high part fitting closely round the neck. **2** (*US*) = POLO-NECK. ⇨ picture at NECK.

turves *pl* of TURF.

tusk /tʌsk/ *n* either of a pair of very long pointed teeth that project from the mouth of certain animals, eg the WALRUS and wild BOAR(1). See also IVORY.

tussle /'tʌsl/ *n* (*infml*) a struggle or fight, esp in order to get sth; a close contest: *We had a real tussle with the travel agent to get our money refunded.*
▶ **tussle** *v* ~ (**with sb**) to struggle or fight to get sth: [Vpr] *We had to tussle with the company to obtain more information.* [also V].

tussock /'tʌsək/ *n* a small area of grass that is thicker or higher than the grass growing round it.

tut /tʌt/ (also **tut-tut** /ˌtʌt 'tʌt/) *interj, n* (used as the written or spoken way of representing the sound expressing disapproval, annoyance, etc made by putting the tongue behind the teeth and sucking in air once or repeatedly): *give a tut(-tut) of disapproval.* ▶ **tut** (also **tut-tut**) *v* (**-tt-**) [V]: *She tut-tutted with impatience.*

tutelage /'tjuːtəlɪdʒ; *US* 'tuː-/ *n* [U] (*fml*) **1** protection of and authority over a person, country, etc:

parental tutelage. **2** teaching; instruction: *be under the tutelage of a master craftsman.*

tutor /'tjuːtə(r); *US* 'tuː-/ *n* **1** a private teacher, esp one who teaches a single pupil or a very small group: *a tutor in a private language school.* **2(a)** (*Brit*) a university teacher who supervises the studies of a student: *I have to see my tutor about my essay.* **(b)** (*US*) an assistant lecturer (LECTURE) in a college. **3** a book of instruction in a particular subject, esp music: *a violin tutor.*
▶ **tutor** *v* **(a)** ~ **sb** (**in sth**) to act as a tutor(1,2) to sb; to teach sb: [Vnpr] *tutor students for an examination* ○ *tutor sb in mathematics* [also Vn]. **(b)** to work as a tutor: [V] *Her work was divided between tutoring and research.*

tutorial /tjuː'tɔːrɪəl; *US* tuː-/ *adj* of a tutor(1,2) or her or his work: *tutorial classes* ○ *a tutorial college/group.* — *n* a period of instruction given, esp to one or two students, by a tutor(1,2) in a university: *have/give/miss a tutorial.*

tutti-frutti /ˌtuːti 'fruːti/ *n* (*pl* **-fruttis**) **(a)** [U] an ice-cream that contains various types of fruit and sometimes nuts. **(b)** [C] a portion of this.

tutu /'tuːtuː/ *n* a ballet dancer's short skirt made of many layers of stiff material that stick out from the waist.

tu-whit, tu-whoo /təˌwɪt tə'wuː/ *n* (used to represent the cry of an OWL).

tuxedo /tʌk'siːdəʊ/ *n* (*pl* **-os** or **-oes**) (also *infml* **tux** /tʌks/) (*US*) = DINNER-JACKET.

TV /ˌtiː 'viː/ *abbr* television: *What's on TV tonight?* ○ *We're getting a new colour TV.*

twaddle /'twɒdl/ *n* [U] speech or writing that is foolish, dull or of bad quality: *I've never heard such utter twaddle!* ○ *The novel is sentimental twaddle.*

twang /twæŋ/ *n* **1** a sound made when a tight string, esp on a musical instrument, is pulled and released: *the twang of a guitar.* **2** the quality of speech sounds produced through both the nose and the mouth: *speak with a twang* ○ *a slight Cockney twang.*
▶ **twang** *v* to make or cause sth to make a twang(1): [Vn] *Someone was twanging a guitar in the next room.* [also V].

twat /twɒt; *Brit also* twæt/ *n* (△ *sl*) **1** the outer female sex organs. **2** (*derog*) an unpleasant or stupid person.

tweak /twiːk/ *v* **1** to hold and twist sth sharply: [Vn] *She tweaked his ear playfully.* **2** [Vn] (*infml*) to adjust the controls of a machine, etc carefully.
▶ **tweak** *n* a sharp twist or pull: *He gave the boy's ear a painful tweak.*

twee /twiː/ *adj* (*Brit infml derog*) pretty, but too sweet and sentimental: *wallpaper with a twee design of shepherdesses and pink ribbon.*

tweed /twiːd/ *n* **1** [U] woollen cloth with a rough surface, often woven with mixed colours: *a tweed jacket.* **2** **tweeds** [pl] clothes made of tweed: *dressed in thick tweeds.*
▶ **tweedy** *adj* (*infml esp Brit*) **(a)** (of clothes) made, or appearing to be made, of tweed: *tweedy jackets.* **(b)** often dressed in tweeds: *The pub was full of tweedy farmers.*

tweet /twiːt/ *n* a short high-pitched sound made by a small bird: *'Tweet tweet,' went the canary.*

tweeter /'twiːtə(r)/ *n* a small LOUDSPEAKER for reproducing high notes. Compare WOOFER.

tweezers /'twiːzəz/ *n* [pl] a small implement with two thin arms for picking up very small things, pulling out hairs, etc: *a pair of tweezers.*

twelve /twelv/ *n, pron, det* the number 12: *the twelve disciples of Jesus.*
▶ **twelve-** (forming compound *adjs*) having twelve of the thing specified: *a twelve-storey building.*
twelfth /twelfθ/ *n, pron, det* 12th.

For further guidance on how *twelve* and *twelfth* are used, see the examples at *five* and *fifth*.

twelvemonth /'twelvmʌnθ/ *n* (*dated*) a year.

twenty /'twenti/ **1** *n*, *pron*, *det* the number 20. **2** **the twenties** *n* [pl] the numbers, years or degrees of temperature from 20 to 29. **IDM** **in one's twenties** between the ages of 20 and 30.
▶ **twentieth** /'twentiəθ/ *n*, *pron*, *det* 20th.

twenty- (forming compound *adjs*) having twenty of the thing specified: *a twenty-volume dictionary*.
For further guidance on how *twenty* and *twentieth* are used, see the examples at *five* and *fifth*.
■ **,twenty-'first** *n* [sing] (*infml*) a person's 21st birthday: *I got a CD player for my twenty-first*.
,twenty 'pence (also **,twenty pence 'piece**, **,twenty 'p, 20p**) *n* (*Brit*) a coin worth twenty new pence.
,twenty-,twenty 'vision *n* [U] normal ability to see: *The doctor said he had twenty-twenty vision.*

twerp /twɜːp/ *n* (*infml*) a stupid, irritating or worthless person.

twice /twaɪs/ *adv* **1** two times: *I've already seen the show twice.* ○ *The tablets should be taken twice a day.* ○ *a twice-weekly/-monthly/-yearly event.* **2** double in quantity, rate, etc: *She does twice as much work as her brother.* ○ *He's twice her age.* **IDM** **be 'twice the man/woman (that sb is)** to be much better, stronger, etc: *How dare you criticize him? He's twice the man (that) you are!* **lightning never strikes twice** ⇨ LIGHTNING[1]. **once bitten, twice shy** ⇨ ONCE. **once or twice** ⇨ ONCE. **think twice about sth** ⇨ THINK[1]. **twice 'over** not just once but twice: *After all the repair bills I reckon I've paid for it twice over* (ie paid twice the original cost).

twiddle /'twɪdl/ *v* ~ (**with**) **sth** to twist or turn sth, esp because one is nervous, bored, etc: [Vpr] *He twiddled with the radio knob until he found the right programme.* [Vn] *She sat twiddling the ring on her finger.* **IDM** **twiddle one's thumbs** to move one's thumbs round each other with one's fingers linked together, esp because one has nothing to do or is waiting for sth to happen: *We sat around for hours drinking coffee and twiddling our thumbs.*
▶ **twiddly** /'twɪdli/ *adj* (*infml*) awkward to handle, play, etc: *a tricky piano piece with lots of twiddly bits.*

twig[1] /twɪg/ *n* a small thin branch that grows out of a larger branch on a bush or tree: *use dry twigs to start a fire.*

twig[2] /twɪg/ *v* (**-gg-**) (*Brit infml*) to realize or understand sth: [V, Vn] *I gave him another clue, but he still didn't twig (the answer).* [V.*wh*] *I finally twigged what he meant.* [also V.*that*].

twilight /'twaɪlaɪt/ *n* [U] **1(a)** the faint light just after the sun has gone down: *I couldn't see their faces clearly in the twilight.* **(b)** the period of this: *a walk along the beach at twilight.* **2** **the ~ (of sth)** (*rhet*) the last stages of sth, when it becomes weaker or less important: *in the twilight of his career* ○ *his twilight years.* **3** a state in which things are not clearly known or understood: *live in a twilight world of truth and half-truth.*
▶ **twilit** /'twaɪlɪt/ *adj* lit in a faint way by twilight: *in the twilit gloom.*
■ **'twilight zone** *n* an uncertain area or condition between others that are more clearly defined: *Wrestling is in a twilight zone between sport and entertainment.*

twill /twɪl/ *n* [U] a strong cloth woven with DIAGONAL ridges across its surface: *cotton twill trousers.*

twin /twɪn/ *n* **1** [C] (often attrib) either of a pair of children or young animals born of the same mother at the same time: *She is expecting twins.* ○ *my twin brother/sister* ○ *twin lambs.* See also IDENTICAL TWINS, SIAMESE TWINS. **2** [C] (often attrib) either of a pair of similar, usu matching, things: *The plate was one of a pair, but I broke its twin.* ○ *There are twin*

holes on each side of the instrument. ○ *a ship with twin* (ie two similar) *propellers* ○ *the twin objectives of democracy and modernization.*
▶ **twin** *v* (**-nn-**) ~ **sth (with sth)** (esp *passive*) **(a)** [Vn, Vnpr] to join two people or things closely together. **(b)** (*Brit*) to establish a special link between two towns in different countries, eg by organizing social or sporting visits: [Vnpr] *Oxford is twinned with Bonn.* [also Vn].
■ **,twin 'bed** *n* either of a pair of single beds in a room for two people. **,twin-'bedded** *adj* (eg of a hotel room) having twin beds.
,twin 'bedroom *n* a room, eg in a hotel, having a pair of single beds.
,twin-'engined *adj* (of an aircraft) having two engines.
'twin set *n* (*Brit*) a woman's matching JERSEY(1) and CARDIGAN.
,twin 'town *n* either of a pair of towns, usu in different countries, that have established special links with each other: *Oxford and Bonn are twin towns.* ○ *Oxford's twin town in France is Grenoble.*

twine /twaɪn/ *n* [U] strong thread or string made by twisting two or more strands of thread together: *a ball of twine.*
▶ **twine** *v* ~ (**sth**) **round/around/through sth** to twist or wind round sth; to make sth do this: [Vpr] *vines twining round a tree* [Vnpr] *She twined her arms around my neck.*

twinge /twɪndʒ/ *n* **1** a short sudden feeling of pain: *get occasional twinges of rheumatism.* **2** a short sharp, usu unpleasant, thought or feeling: *a twinge of conscience/fear/guilt/regret/remorse.*

twinkle /'twɪŋkl/ *v* **1** to shine with a light that changes constantly from bright to faint: [V] *stars twinkling in the sky* ○ *The lights of the town twinkled in the distance.* **2** ~ (**with sth**) (**at sb**) (of sb or their eyes) to have a bright lively expression esp because one is amused: [Vpr] *Her eyes twinkled with mischief.* ○ *His mother twinkled at him over the rim of her teacup.* [also V].
▶ **twinkle** *n* [sing] **1** a twinkling light: *We could see the distant twinkle of the harbour lights.* **2** a bright amused expression of the eyes: *She said it with a twinkle in her eye(s).*
twinkling /'twɪŋklɪŋ/ *n* [sing] (*infml*) a very short time: *It was all over in a twinkling.* **IDM** **in the ,twinkling of an 'eye** very quickly: *It all happened in the twinkling of an eye.*

twirl /twɜːl/ *v* **1** to turn or make sth turn quickly and lightly round and round; to spin sth: [Vnpr] *He walked along briskly, twirling his cane in the air.* ○ *She sat twirling the stem of the glass in her fingers.* [also Vn]. **2** to move quickly round and round; to spin: [Vp, Vpr] *She twirled round (the room) happily.* [also V]. **3** to twist or curl sth, esp with the fingers: [Vn] *He kept twirling his moustache.* [also Vnpr].
▶ **twirl** *n* **1** a rapid circular movement: *She did a twirl in front of the mirror.* **2** a twirled mark or sign: *He signs his name with a fancy twirl at the end.*

twist[1] /twɪst/ *v* **1(a)** ~ **sth** (**round sth/round**) to wind sth round sth else: [Vnpr] *I twisted the bandage round her knee.* [Vn] *The telephone wire has got twisted* (ie wound around itself). [also Vnp]. **(b)** to move or grow by winding round sth: [Vpr] *The snake twisted round my arm.* [also Vp]. **2** ~ **sth (into sth)** to turn or wind threads, etc to make them into a rope, etc: [Vnpr] *We twisted the bed sheets into a rope and escaped by climbing down it.* [also Vn]. **3(a)** to change the natural shape of sth; to distort sth: [Vnpr] *He twisted his face into a grin.* [also Vn]. **(b)** to be distorted in this way: [V] *The metal frame tends to twist under pressure.* [also Vnpr]. **4(a)** to turn sth round; to revolve sth: [Vnpr] *Twist the knob to the right channel.* [Vnp] *I twisted my head round to reverse the car.* ○ *I can't twist the lid off.* [also Vn].

[V.*to* inf] = verb + *to* infinitive [Vn.inf (no *to*)] = verb + noun + infinitive without *to* [V.*ing*] = verb + *-ing* form

(**b**) to turn round; to revolve: [Vp] *I twisted round in my seat to speak to her.* ○ *The cap should twist off easily.* [also V, Vpr]. **5** (of roads, etc) to change direction often; to wind: [V] *Downstream the river twists and turns a lot.* [Vp, Vpr] *The path twisted down (the hillside).* **6** to injure a part of one's body, esp a joint, by turning it sharply: [Vn] *I've twisted my ankle.* **7** to give deliberately false meaning to words, etc: [Vn] *The papers twisted everything I said.* **IDM** **turn/twist the knife** ⇨ KNIFE. **twist sb's ¦arm** (*infml*) to persuade or force sb to do sth: *She'll let you borrow the car if you twist her arm.* **twist sb round one's little ¦finger** (*infml*) to persuade sb to do anything that one wants: *Jane has always been able to twist her parents round her little finger.*

▶ **twisted** *adj* **1** bent or crushed; not in the original shape: *a twisted smile* ○ *The car was now just a pile of twisted metal.* **2** (of a person's mind or behaviour) abnormal in an unpleasant way; perverted (PERVERT).

twister *n* (*infml*) **1** a person who lies or cheats. **2** (*US*) a violent storm caused by a revolving column of air; a WHIRLWIND. See also TONGUE-TWISTER.

twist² /twɪst/ *n* **1** [C] an act of twisting sth; a twisting movement: *He gave my arm a twist.* ○ *With a violent twist, he wrenched off the handle.* ○ *Give the rope a few more twists.* **2** [C] (**a**) a thing formed by twisting: *a rope full of twists* ○ *a twist of paper* (ie a small paper packet with the ends twisted to seal it). (**b**) a winding or twisting: *a twist of smoke* ○ *a shell with a spiral twist.* (**c**) a place where a path, etc turns: *a twist in the road* ○ *the **twists and turns** of the river.* **3** [C] a change or development: *the **twists and turns** in the economy* ○ *by a strange **twist of fate*** ○ *The story has an odd twist at the end.* **4** the twist [sing] a dance with a twisting movement of the body, popular in the 1960s: *do the twist.* **IDM** **get one's knickers in a twist** ⇨ KNICKERS. **round the bend/twist** ⇨ BEND².

▶ **twisty** *adj* full of twists (TWIST² 2): *a twisty road.*

twit¹ /twɪt/ *n* (*Brit infml often joc*) a stupid or annoying person: *He's an arrogant little twit!* ○ *Don't be a twit!*

twit² /twɪt/ *v* (**-tt-**) [Vn, Vnpr] ~ **sb** (**about/with sth**) (*dated*) to mock sb, esp in a friendly way.

twitch /twɪtʃ/ *n* **1** a sudden rapid, but usu not deliberate, movement of a muscle, etc: *I thought the mouse was dead, but then it gave a slight twitch.* **2** a sudden pull: *I felt a twitch at my sleeve.*

▶ **twitch** *v* **1** to move or make sth move with a twitch or twitches: [V] *The dog's nose twitched as it smelt the meat.* [Vpr] *Her face twitched with pain.* [also Vn]. **2** to give sth a small sharp pull: [Vpr] *He twitched nervously at his tie.* [Vn] *She twitched the corner of the rug to straighten it.* [Vnpr] *The wind twitched the paper out of my hand.*

twitchy *adj* (*infml*) worried or frightened; nervous: *People are beginning to get twitchy about all these rumours.* **twitchily** *adv.* **twitchiness** *n* [U].

twitter /ˈtwɪtə(r)/ *v* **1** [V] (of birds) to make a series of light short sounds. **2** ~ (**on**) (**about sth**) (*infml*) to talk rapidly in an excited or nervous way: [V] *Stop twittering!* [Vpr, Vp] *What is he twittering (on) about?* [V.speech] *'It's so marvellous to see you!' she twittered.*

▶ **twitter** *n* [sing] **1** the sound of birds twittering: *the twitter of sparrows.* **2** (*infml*) a state of nervous excitement: *a twitter of suspense and anticipation.*

two /tuː/ *n, pron, det* the number 2. Compare SECOND¹. **IDM** **a ¦day, ¦moment, ¦pound, etc or two** one or a few days, moments, pounds, etc: *May I borrow it for a day or two?* **in ¦two** in or into two pieces or halves: *The vase fell and broke in two.* ○ *She cut the cake in two and gave me half.* **in ¦twos and**

¦threes two or three at a time; in small numbers: *Applications for the job are coming in slowly in twos and threes.* **it takes two to do sth** (*saying*) one person cannot be entirely responsible for making a happy or an unhappy marriage, starting an argument, etc. **or two** (after a singular *n*) or more: *After a ¦minute or two we saw him.* ○ *I haven't seen him for a ¦year or two.* **put ¦two and ¦two to¦gether** to guess the truth from what one sees, hears, etc: (*joc*) *He's inclined to put two and two together and make five* (ie imagine that things are worse, more exciting, etc than they really are). **that makes ¦two of us** (*infml*) I am in the same position or hold the same opinion: *'I'm finding this party extremely dull.' 'That makes two of us!'*

For further guidance on how *two* is used, see the examples at *five*.

▶ **two-** (in compounds) having two of the thing specified: *a two-room flat.*

■ **¦two ¦bits** *n* [pl] (*US infml*) 25 cents. **¦two-bit** *adj* [attrib] (*US infml*) not very good, important, interesting, etc: *some two-bit dictator.*

¦two-di¦mensional *adj* having or appearing to have length and breadth but no depth: *a ¦two-dimensional ¦image* ○ (*fig*) *a ¦two-dimensional ¦character* (ie one that is not very interesting).

¦two-¦edged *adj* (**a**) (of a knife, sword, etc) having two sharp edges. (**b**) having two possible and opposite meanings or effects at the same time: *a ¦two-edged re¦mark* ○ *Publicity is a ¦two-edged ¦sword/ ¦weapon.*

¦two-¦faced *adj* deceitful or insincere.

¦two-¦handed *adj* (**a**) with or for both hands: *a two-handed stroke in tennis* ○ *a two-handed sword.* (**b**) done by or for two people: *a two-handed performance.*

¦two ¦pence (also **¦two pence ¦piece, ¦two ¦p, 2p**) *n* (*Brit*) a coin worth two pence.

¦two-¦piece *n, adj* (a set) consisting of two matching garments, eg a skirt and a jacket or trousers and a jacket: *a ¦two-piece ¦suit.*

¦two-ply *adj* (of wool or wood) having two strands or thicknesses.

¦two-¦seater *n* a vehicle or aircraft with seats for two people.

¦two-time *v* [V, Vn] (*infml*) to deceive sb, esp a lover, by not being faithful.

¦two-tone *adj* [attrib] having two colours or sounds: *two-tone shoes* ○ *a two-tone car horn.*

¦two-¦way *adj* [usu attrib] (**a**) (of a switch) allowing electric current to be turned on or off from either of two points. (**b**) (of a road or street) in which traffic travels in both directions. (**c**) (of traffic) in lanes travelling in both directions. (**d**) (of radio equipment, etc) for sending and receiving signals. (**e**) (of communication between people, etc) operating in both directions: *a ¦two-way ¦process.* **¦two-way ¦mirror** *n* a panel of glass that can be seen through on one side and is a mirror on the other.

twofold /ˈtuːfəʊld/ *adj, adv* **1** twice as much or as many: *a twofold increase* ○ *Her original investment had increased twofold.* **2** consisting of two parts: *a twofold task.*

twopence /ˈtʌpəns; *US* ˈtuːpens/ (also **tuppence**) *n* (*Brit*) **1** (esp formerly) the sum of two pence. **2** even the smallest amount: *I don't give twopence for/don't care twopence what they think.* ○ *It's not worth twopence.*

twopenny /ˈtʌpəni; *US also* ˈtuːpeni/ (also **tuppenny**) *adj* (*Brit*) (esp formerly) costing or worth two pence: *a ¦twopenny ¦stamp.*

■ **twopenny-halfpenny** /ˌtʌpni ˈheɪpni/ *adj* (*Brit infml*) not worthy of consideration or respect; worthless: *some twopenny-halfpenny little reporter.*

twosome /ˈtuːsəm/ *n* a group of two people, eg playing a game or taking part in a leisure activity together.

tycoon /taɪˈkuːn/ n (*infml*) a wealthy and powerful person in business or industry: ˈ*property*/ˈ*publishing tycoons.*

tying ⇨ TIE².

tyke /taɪk/ n (*infml*) a small child, esp one who behaves badly: *a greedy little tyke.*

type¹ /taɪp/ n **1** ~ **(of sth)** a class or group of people or things that have characteristics in common; a kind: *different racial types* ○ *a rare blood type* ○ *all types of job(s)/jobs of all types* ○ *Burgundy-type wines* ○ *Which type of coffee do you prefer?* ○ *A bungalow is/Bungalows are a type of house.* ○ *I love this/these type of games.* **2** ~ **(of sth)** a person, a thing, an event, etc considered as a representative example of a class or group: *not the type of party I enjoy* ○ *the old-fashioned type of gentleman* ○ *just the type of situation to avoid* ○ *I don't think she's the artistic type.* ○ *He's true to type* (ie behaves as sb of his class, group, etc may be expected to behave). **3** (*infml*) a person of a specified character: *a brainy type* ○ *He's not my type (of person)* (ie We have little in common).

▶ **type** v (*techn*) to classify sth/sb according to its type: [Vn] *patients typed by age and blood group.*

type² /taɪp/ n **1(a)** [C] a small block, esp of metal, with a raised letter or figure, etc on it, for use in printing. **(b)** [U] a set, supply, kind or size of these: *set sth in bold/italic type.*

▶ **type** v ~ **sth (out/up)** to write sth using a TYPE-WRITER or word processor (WORD): [V, Vp] *typing (away) with four fingers* [Vn, Vnp] *This letter will need to be typed (out) again.* **typing** (also ˈ**typewriting**) n [U] **1** the use of a TYPEWRITER or word processor (WORD); skill at doing this: *practise typing* ○ *typing paper* ○ *a typing pool* (ie a group of people who share a firm's typing work). **2** writing produced on a TYPEWRITER or word processor (WORD): *two pages of typing.*

typist /ˈtaɪpɪst/ n a person who types, esp one employed to do so: *a fast/slow typist* ○ *a shorthand typist.*

typecast /ˈtaɪpkɑːst; *US* -kæst/ v (*pt, pp* **typecast**) (esp passive) to give an actor the kind of role which he or she has often played successfully before or which seems to fit his or her personality: [Vn-n] *avoid being typecast as a gangster* [also Vn].

typeface /ˈtaɪpfeɪs/ (also **face**) n a set of types (TYPE²) in a particular design: *headings printed in a different typeface from the text.*

typescript /ˈtaɪpskrɪpt/ n [C, U] a text or document written in type²: *We receive several new typescripts every week.* ○ *The poems arrived in (fifty pages of) typescript.*

typesetter /ˈtaɪpsetə(r)/ n a person, company or machine that sets type² for printing.

typesetting /ˈtaɪpsetɪŋ/ n [U] the setting of type² for printing: *computer typesetting equipment.*

typewriter /ˈtaɪpraɪtə(r)/ n a machine for producing writing similar to print. The person using it presses keys which cause raised metal letters, etc to strike the paper, usu through a RIBBON(3) treated with ink: *an electric typewriter* ○ *a typewriter ribbon/keyboard.* Compare WORD PROCESSOR.

typewritten /ˈtaɪprɪtn/ adj written using a TYPEWRITER or word processor (WORD): *typewritten pages/letters/manuscripts.*

typhoid /ˈtaɪfɔɪd/ (also ˌ**typhoid** ˈ**fever**) n [U] a serious, sometimes fatal, disease that attacks the

bowels and produces fever. It is caused by infected food or drink: *a typhoid epidemic.*

typhoon /taɪˈfuːn/ n a violent tropical storm in the western Pacific. Compare HURRICANE, CYCLONE.

typhus /ˈtaɪfəs/ n [U] an infectious disease with fever, great weakness and purple spots on the body.

typical /ˈtɪpɪkl/ adj ~ **(of sb/sth) 1** having the distinctive qualities of a particular type of person or thing; representative: *a typical Scot/teacher/gentleman* ○ *a typical French meal* ○ *a typical cross-section of the population.* **2** characteristic of a particular person or thing: *It was typical of her to forget.* ○ *He responded with typical enthusiasm.* ○ *On a typical* (ie normal, average) *day we receive about fifty letters.* ○ *Such decoration was a typical feature of the baroque period.* ○ (*infml*) *The train's late again — typical!*

▶ **typically** /-kli/ adv **1** representing a particular type of person or thing: *typically American hospitality.* **2** characteristic of a particular person or thing: *Typically, she had forgotten her keys again.* ○ *They typically cost about £12.*

typify /ˈtɪpɪfaɪ/ v (*pt, pp* **-fied**) (usu not in the continuous tenses) to be a representative example or characteristic sign of sb/sth: [Vn] *Now a millionaire, he typifies the self-made man.* ○ *His whole attitude is typified by aggressive remarks like these.*

typist ⇨ TYPE².

typography /taɪˈpɒɡrəfi/ n [U] **1** the art or practice of printing. **2** the style or appearance of printed matter: *a high standard of typography.*

▶ **typographer** /taɪˈpɒɡrəfə(r)/ n a person skilled in typography.
typographical /ˌtaɪpəˈɡræfɪkl/, **typographic** /ˌtaɪpəˈɡræfɪk/ adjs. **typographically** /-kli/ adv.

tyrannical /tɪˈrænɪkl/ (also *fml* **tyrannous** /ˈtɪrənəs/) adj of or like a TYRANT; obtaining obedience by force or threats: *a tyrannical regime* ○ *be brought up by a cruel and tyrannical mother.*

tyrannize, -ise /ˈtɪrənaɪz/ v ~ **(over) sb/sth** to rule sb/sth as a TYRANT; to treat sb in an unfair or cruel way: [Vpr] *tyrannize over the weak* [Vn] *He tyrannizes his family.*

tyranny /ˈtɪrəni/ n **1(a)** [U] the unfair, severe or cruel use of power or authority: *victims of oppression and tyranny* ○ (*fig*) *These days, it seems, we must all submit to the tyranny of the motor car.* **(b)** [C esp *pl*] an instance of this: *the tyrannies of Nazi rule.* **2(a)** [U, C] the rule of a TYRANT. **(b)** [C] a country under this rule.

tyrant /ˈtaɪrənt/ n a severe or cruel ruler, esp one who has obtained complete power by force: (*fig*) *Her boss is a complete tyrant.*

tyre (*US* **tire**) /ˈtaɪə(r)/ n a covering fitted round the edge of a wheel to absorb shocks. Tyres are usu made of rubber filled with air or covering an inner tube filled with air: *a bicycle tyre* ○ *a spare tyre* ○ *a burst/flat/punctured tyre* ○ *check the tyre pressure* ○ *Your tyres are badly worn.* ⇨ picture at BICYCLE, CAR.

tyro /ˈtaɪrəʊ/ n (*pl* **-os**) a person who has little or no experience of sth or is beginning to learn sth: *a tyro movie producer.*

tzar = TSAR.

tzarina = TSARINA.

Uu

U¹ (also **u**) /juː/ *n* (*pl* **U's**, **u's** /juːz/) the 21st letter of the English alphabet: *'Ursula' begins with (a) U/'U'*. ■ **U-boat** *n* (esp in World War II) a German SUBMARINE(1).

'U-turn /'juː tɜːn/ *n* **1** a turn of 180° by a vehicle so that it can move forwards in the opposite direction: *do a U-turn* ○ *No U-turns* (ie as a sign on certain roads). **2** (*infml*) a complete change in policy, attitude, intention or action: *another spectacular U-turn by the government*.

U² /juː/ *adj* (*dated Brit infml or joc*) thought to be characteristic of the upper class: *very U behaviour*. Compare NON-U.

U³ /juː/ *abbr* (*Brit*) (of films) universal; suitable for anyone, including children: *a U certificate*.

UAE /ˌjuː eɪ 'iː/ *abbr* United Arab Emirates.

ubiquitous /juːˈbɪkwɪtəs/ *adj* [esp attrib] (*fml or joc*) seeming to be everywhere or in several places at the same time: *the French labourer's ubiquitous blue overalls*.
▶ **ubiquity** /juːˈbɪkwəti/ *n* [U] (*fml*) the quality of being ubiquitous.

U-boat ⇨ U¹.

UCAS /'juːkæs/ *abbr* (*Brit*) Universities and Colleges Admissions Service (an official body that processes applications to study at universities).

UDA /ˌjuː diː 'eɪ/ *abbr* Ulster Defence Association.

udder /'ʌdə(r)/ *n* an organ shaped like a bag that hangs between the back legs of a cow, a female goat, etc and produces milk. ⇨ picture at COW¹.

UDR /ˌjuː diː 'ɑː(r)/ *abbr* Ulster Defence Regiment.

UEFA /juːˈiːfə/ *abbr* Union of European Football Associations: *the UEFA Cup*.

UFO (also **ufo**) /ˌjuː ef 'əʊ, 'juːfəʊ/ *abbr* (*pl* **UFOs** or **ufos**) unidentified flying object: *UFO sightings*.
▶ **u'fology** /juːˈfɒlədʒi/ *n* [U] the study of UFOs.

ugh *interj* (the written form of a sound like /ɜː, ʊx/, etc made to indicate disgust or horror, and usu accompanied by an appropriate expression): *Ugh! How can you eat that stuff?*

ugly /'ʌɡli/ *adj* (**-ier**, **-iest**) **1** unpleasant, esp to look at: *an ugly face/child/building* ○ *an ugly wound/scar*. **2** HOSTILE(1a) or threatening; likely to provoke violence: *ugly threats/rumours/insinuations* ○ *The situation in the streets was turning/growing ugly*. ○ *The crowd was in an ugly mood*. ○ *Racial violence is beginning to* **rear/raise its ugly head** *again*. **IDM** **miserable/ugly as sin** ⇨ SIN¹. ▶ **ugliness** *n* [U]. ■ ˌ**ugly 'duckling** *n* a person who at first seems dull or unlikely to succeed but who later becomes successful, much admired, etc.

UHF /ˌjuː eɪtʃ 'ef/ *abbr* (*radio*) ultra-high frequency. Compare VHF.

UHT /ˌjuː eɪtʃ 'tiː/ *abbr* (of milk or food made from milk) ultra heat treated, ie processed in a way that will make it last for a long time: *UHT milk*.

UK /ˌjuː 'keɪ/ *abbr* United Kingdom, ie Great Britain and Northern Ireland: *a ˌUK 'citizen* ○ *the team from the UK*. ⇨ note at BRITISH.

ukulele /ˌjuːkə'leɪli/ *n* a musical instrument like a small GUITAR with four strings.

ulcer /'ʌlsə(r)/ *n* a sore area containing poisonous matter on the outside of the body or on the surface of an internal organ: *a gastric ulcer* ○ *I've got an ulcer on the inside of my mouth*. See also DUODENAL ULCER.
▶ **ulcerate** /'ʌlsəreɪt/ *v* to become or cause sth to become affected with an ulcer or ulcers: [Vn] *Some drugs can ulcerate the stomach lining*. [also V]. **ulceration** /ˌʌlsə'reɪʃn/ *n*: *severe ulceration of the legs*.

ulna /'ʌlnə/ *n* (*pl* **ulnae** /-niː/) (*anatomy*) the inner and thinner of the two bones in the part of the human arm between the hand and the elbow. ⇨ picture at SKELETON. Compare RADIUS 3a.

ulterior /ʌl'tɪəriə(r)/ *adj* [attrib] (*fml*) other than what is obvious or admitted; kept hidden: *Jim had an* **ulterior motive** *in buying me a drink — he wants to borrow my van*.

ultimate /'ʌltɪmət/ *adj* [attrib] **1** being or happening at the end of a process; last or final: *our ultimate aim/goal* ○ *Management must take ultimate responsibility for the late delivery*. ○ *Nuclear weapons are the ultimate deterrent*. **2** (*infml*) being the most extreme of its kind; best or worst; greatest: *the ultimate challenge* ○ *suffer the ultimate embarrassment of public ridicule*. **3** from which everything else originates; basic or fundamental: *the ultimate truths of philosophy and science*.
▶ **ultimate** *n* [sing] **the ~ (in sth)** (*infml*) the best, most advanced, etc of its kind: *the ultimate in modern kitchen design*.
ultimately *adv* **1** in the end; finally: *Ultimately, you'll have to make the decision yourself*. **2** at the most basic level: *All matter ultimately consists of atoms*.

ultimatum /ˌʌltɪ'meɪtəm/ *n* (*pl* **ultimatums**) a final demand or statement to sb that certain conditions must be met or that something must be done and that otherwise action will be taken against them: **deliver/issue an ultimatum to** *a foreign government*.

ultra- *pref* (used before a wide range of *adjs*) **1** extremely; excessively: *ultra-conservative* ○ *ultra-modern*. **2** beyond a specified limit or extent: *ultra-violet* ○ *ultra-high*. Compare INFRA-.

ultramarine /ˌʌltrəmə'riːn/ *adj*, *n* [U] (of a very bright blue colour).

ultrasonic /ˌʌltrə'sɒnɪk/ *adj* (of sounds) higher in pitch¹(2) than can be heard by a human being: *ultrasonic waves*.

ultrasound /'ʌltrəsaʊnd/ *n* [U] ULTRASONIC sound: *an ultrasound scan* (eg to examine a baby still inside its mother).

ultraviolet /ˌʌltrə'vaɪələt/ *adj* [usu attrib] (**a**) (*physics*) (of RADIATION(1b) or light) with a WAVELENGTH(1) that is just beyond the purple end of the range of colours that humans can see: *ultraviolet rays* (ie those that cause the skin to go darker). (**b**) of or using such RADIATION(1b) or light: *an ultraviolet lamp* ○ *ultraviolet treatment* (ie for skin diseases). Compare INFRARED.

ululate /'juːljuleɪt/ *v* (*fml*) to give a long cry; to HOWL(1) or WAIL. ▶ **ululation** /-leɪʃn/ *n* [U, C].

um /ʌm, əm/ *interj* (used to express the sound made when a speaker hesitates or is not sure what to say next): *Well, um, I'm not sure about that*. See also ER.

umber /'ʌmbə(r)/ *n* [U] a reddish-brown colour.

umbilical cord /ʌmˌbɪlɪkl 'kɔːd/ *n* the flexible tube of tissue connecting a baby to its mother before birth.

---

umbrage /ˈʌmbrɪdʒ/ n **IDM** take ˈumbrage (at sth) (fml or joc) to feel offended, insulted or upset by sth: He took umbrage at the way he was described in her book.

umbrella /ʌmˈbrelə/ n **1** a device with a folding frame of metal rods covered with material and a handle, held over the head to protect one from rain: a rolled/furled umbrella ○ put up an umbrella. Compare PARASOL, SUNSHADE. **2** (fig) any protecting force or influence: sheltering under the American nuclear umbrella ○ Police operated under the umbrella of the security forces. **3** [esp attrib] (fig) a thing that contains or includes various different elements or parts: an umbrella organization/group ○ 'Ball games' is an umbrella term for a variety of different sports.

umlaut /ˈʊmlaʊt/ n (in Germanic languages) a sign consisting of two dots placed over a vowel to indicate a change in its pronunciation, eg der Mann/die Männer (= the man/the men) in German.

umpire /ˈʌmpaɪə(r)/ n (in certain sports, eg hockey and baseball) a person in charge of a game who makes decisions during it and makes sure that the rules are obeyed. ⇨ picture at BASEBALL, CRICKET¹, TENNIS. Compare REFEREE 1a.
▸ **umpire** v to act as umpire in a game, etc: [V] We need someone to umpire. [also Vn].

umpteen /ˌʌmpˈtiːn/ pron, det (infml) a great many; a very large number of: I've told this story umpteen times. ○ We tried umpteen shops but we couldn't find what we wanted. ▸ **umpteenth** /ˌʌmpˈtiːnθ/ pron, det (infml) For the ˌumpteenth ˈtime, I tell you I don't know!

UN /ˌjuː ˈen/ abbr United Nations: the UN Secretary-General. See also UNO.

un- pref **1** (with adjs, advs and ns) not: unable ○ unconsciously ○ untruth. **2(a)** (with vs forming vs that describe the opposite or reverse of a process): unlock ○ undo ○ unfold. **(b)** (with ns forming vs that describe removing sth): unearth ○ unmask.

> **NOTE** The opposites of adjectives, nouns and verbs are often formed by adding a negative prefix. It is not possible to predict whether **un-**, **in-**, or **dis-** is used with a particular word and the correct form must be learned.
> **un-**: unexpected, unhappy, unlikely
> **in-**: inadequate, insincere, infinite
> **il-**: before the letter 'l': illogical
> **im-**: before the letters 'b', 'm' and 'p': imbalance, immature, impossible
> **ir-**: before the letter 'r': irresponsible
> **dis-**: dislike, distrust, disobedient, disqualify
> Words formed with **non-** describe the absence of a particular quality or action: a non-stick pan ○ He's a non-smoker. ○ The flight from Japan to London is non-stop.

'un /ən/ pron (infml) one: That's a good 'un (eg a good photograph, joke, etc)!

unabashed /ˌʌnəˈbæʃt/ adj not ashamed, embarrassed or discouraged in circumstances in which others might be: She appeared unabashed by all the media attention. ▸ **unabashedly** /-ˈʃɪdli/ adv.

unabated /ˌʌnəˈbeɪtɪd/ adj [usu pred] without any reduction in intensity or strength: The gales continued unabated.

unable /ʌnˈeɪbl/ adj [pred] ~ to do sth (rather fml) not having the ability, opportunity or authority to do sth: She is unable to walk. ○ I tried to contact him but was unable to. ○ I am unable to comment on this point.

unabridged /ˌʌnəˈbrɪdʒd/ adj (of a novel, play, speech, etc) published, performed, etc in full, without being made shorter in any way: an unabridged edition/version of 'War and Peace'.

unacceptable /ˌʌnəkˈseptəbl/ adj that cannot be

accepted, approved of or allowed: unacceptable terms/arguments ○ Torture is totally unacceptable in a civilized society. ▸ **unacceptably** /-bli/ adv: unacceptably low standards.

unaccompanied /ˌʌnəˈkʌmpənid/ adj **1** (fml) without a person going together with sb/sth: Children unaccompanied by an adult will not be admitted. ○ unaccompanied luggage/baggage (ie travelling separately from its owner). **2** (music) performed without anyone else playing or singing at the same time: sing unaccompanied.

unaccountable /ˌʌnəˈkaʊntəbl/ adj **1** that cannot be explained: an unaccountable increase in cases of the disease ○ For some unaccountable reason, the letter never arrived. **2** ~ (to sb/sth) (fml) not required to explain or justify one's actions; not ACCOUNTABLE: government departments that are unaccountable to the general public.
▸ **unaccountably** /-əbli/ adv in a way that cannot be explained; without any obvious reason: He was unaccountably absent from the meeting.

unaccounted /ˌʌnəˈkaʊntɪd/ adj [pred] ~ for **1** not present and not able to be found: One passenger is still unaccounted for. ○ Investigators found that thousands of pension contributions were unaccounted for. **2** not explained: His disappearance is unaccounted for.

unaccustomed /ˌʌnəˈkʌstəmd/ adj **1** ~ to sth / doing sth (of people) not in the habit of doing sth: I am unaccustomed to such hard work/to working so hard. **2** not characteristic, usual or normal: his unaccustomed silence ○ enjoy the unaccustomed luxury of expensive hotels.

unacknowledged /ˌʌnəkˈnɒlɪdʒd/ adj **1** not recognized or appreciated but deserving to be: an unacknowledged master of his craft ○ Her contribution to the research went largely unacknowledged. **2** not admitted or accepted as existing: unacknowledged feelings.

unacquainted /ˌʌnəˈkweɪntɪd/ adj ~ with sth not familiar with sth: visitors unacquainted with the local customs.

unadorned /ˌʌnəˈdɔːnd/ adj without decoration; plain: unadorned walls ○ Her language is simple and unadorned.

unadulterated /ˌʌnəˈdʌltəreɪtɪd/ adj **1** (esp of food) not mixed with other substances; pure. **2** [usu attrib] (infml) complete; absolute; SHEER¹(1): He's talking unadulterated nonsense.

unadventurous /ˌʌnədˈventʃərəs/ adj **(a)** not willing to take risks, try sth new, etc: an unadventurous cook. **(b)** not involving anything new or exciting: lead an unadventurous life.

unaffected /ˌʌnəˈfektɪd/ adj **1** ~ (by sth) not changed or affected by sth: People's rights are unaffected by the new laws. ○ The children seem unaffected emotionally by their parents' divorce. **2** natural in behaviour or style; not PRETENTIOUS: welcome sb with unaffected pleasure ○ He was his normal unaffected self.

unafraid /ˌʌnəˈfreɪd/ adj ~ (of sth); ~ (to do sth) not afraid; not lacking in courage: a businessman unafraid of taking risks ○ be unafraid to give an honest opinion.

unaided /ʌnˈeɪdɪd/ adj not assisted by sb/sth; without help: generations unaided by modern devices ○ He can now walk unaided.

unalloyed /ˌʌnəˈlɔɪd/ adj (fml) not mixed with sth else, eg with negative feelings; pure: The whole evening was an unalloyed pleasure.

unalterable /ʌnˈɔːltərəbl/ adj that cannot be changed: unalterable laws/decisions.

unaltered /ʌnˈɔːltəd/ adj that has not changed or been changed: a practice that remained unaltered for centuries.

unambiguous /ˌʌnæmˈbɪgjuəs/ adj clear in meaning; that cannot be interpreted in more than one way: *an unambiguous statement/answer.* ▶ **unambiguously** adv.

unambitious /ˌʌnæmˈbɪʃəs/ adj **1** without ambitions in life. **2** not involving anything new, exciting or demanding: *an unambitious itinerary/novel.*

un-American /ˌʌn əˈmerɪkən/ adj **1** against what are thought to be normal American customs or values: *State control is a very un-American notion.* **2** against the political interests of the USA: *the former House Committee on Un-American Activities.*

unanimous /juˈnænɪməs/ adj (a) ~ (in sth) with all in agreement on a decision or an opinion: *The environmental lobby is unanimous in its opposition to the proposed new bypass.* (b) (of a decision, an opinion, etc) agreed with by everybody in a group: *He was elected by a unanimous vote.* ○ *The decision was unanimous.*
▶ **unanimity** /ˌjuːnəˈnɪməti/ n [U] complete agreement about sth among a group: *There was a remarkable unanimity at the meeting.*
unanimously adv: *The motion was passed unanimously.*

unannounced /ˌʌnəˈnaʊnst/ adj without previous warning or arrangement, and therefore unexpected: *an unannounced extra item on the programme* ○ *He arrived unannounced.*

unanswerable /ʌnˈɑːnsərəbl; US ʌnˈæn-/ adj that cannot be answered or contradicted (CONTRADICT 1): *an unanswerable question* ○ *His case is unanswerable.*

unanswered /ʌnˈɑːnsəd/ adj that has not been answered or replied to: *unanswered letters* ○ *Several questions about the crime* **remain unanswered.**

unanticipated /ˌʌnænˈtɪsɪpeɪtɪd/ adj that is not expected or predicted: *unanticipated costs/setbacks.*

unappealing /ˌʌnəˈpiːlɪŋ/ adj not attractive or pleasant: *The prospect of studying for five years was distinctly unappealing.*

unappetizing, -ising /ʌnˈæpɪtaɪzɪŋ/ adj (of food) unpleasant, or appearing likely to be unpleasant, to eat.

unappreciated /ˌʌnəˈpriːʃieɪtɪd/ adj not appreciated or realized: *He felt that his efforts were unappreciated.*

unapproachable /ˌʌnəˈprəʊtʃəbl/ adj (of a person) difficult to talk to because not friendly, too formal, etc.

unarguable /ʌnˈɑːgjuəbl/ adj that cannot be disputed: *unarguable facts.* ▶ **unarguably** adv: *unarguably one of our greatest dancers.*

unarmed /ˌʌnˈɑːmd/ adj (a) without weapons: *unarmed civilians* ○ *He walked into the camp unarmed.* (b) not using weapons: *soldiers trained in* ˌun-armed ˈcombat.

unashamed /ˌʌnəˈʃeɪmd/ adj feeling or showing no guilt or embarrassment: *unashamed delight/fervour.*
▶ **unashamedly** /ˌʌnəˈʃeɪmɪdli/ adv: *unashamedly pursuing one's own interests.*

unasked /ˌʌnˈɑːskt; US ʌnˈæskt/ adj **1** without being asked: *The meeting ended but the all-important question still remained unasked.* **2** without having been invited: *She came to the party unasked.*
■ **unasked-for** adj without being asked for or requested: *unasked-for advice.*

unassailable /ˌʌnəˈseɪləbl/ adj (a) that cannot be defeated or defeated: *an unassailable fortress* ○ *Manchester United have (built up) an unassailable lead at the top of the premier division.* (b) that cannot be questioned or disputed: *Her position/argument is unassailable.*

unassisted /ˌʌnəˈsɪstɪd/ adj not helped by anyone or anything.

unassuming /ˌʌnəˈsjuːmɪŋ; US ˌʌnəˈsuː-/ adj not drawing attention to oneself or to one's abilities, achievements or status; modest: *a gentle and unassuming person/manner.*

unattached /ˌʌnəˈtætʃt/ adj **1** not connected with or belonging to a particular body, group, etc: *be unattached to any political organization.* **2** not married or having a regular BOYFRIEND or GIRLFRIEND.

unattainable /ˌʌnəˈteɪnəbl/ adj that cannot be achieved or reached: *unattainable targets/goals/ambitions.*

unattended /ˌʌnəˈtendɪd/ adj **1** with the owner not present: *unattended vehicles/baggage.* **2** ~ (to) without being supervised or attended to: *leave the shop counter/telephone unattended* ○ *old correspondence still unattended to* ○ *They daren't leave their children unattended for even a moment.*

unattractive /ˌʌnəˈtræktɪv/ adj not pleasant or desirable; not attractive: *an unattractive personality/place.* ▶ **unattractively** adv.

unauthorized, -ised /ʌnˈɔːθəraɪzd/ adj for which official permission has not been given: *unauthorized computer access* ○ *unauthorized entry* (ie into a building or part of one) ○ *an unauthorized biography* (ie one for which the subject has not given permission).

unavailable /ˌʌnəˈveɪləbl/ adj [usu pred] ~ (to sb/sth) not available: *files unavailable to researchers* ○ *The Minister was* **unavailable for comment.** ▶ **unavailability** n [U]: *problems caused by the unavailability of staff.*

unavailing /ˌʌnəˈveɪlɪŋ/ adj (fml) without success; not achieving the desired result; VAIN(3): *All our efforts were unavailing.*

unavoidable /ˌʌnəˈvɔɪdəbl/ adj that cannot be avoided: *unavoidable delays.* ▶ **unavoidably** /-əbli/ adv: *unavoidably absent/detained .*

unaware /ˌʌnəˈweə(r)/ adj [pred] ~ (of sth / that…) not conscious of or having knowledge of sth; ignorant of sth: *He was unaware of my presence/that I was there.* ○ *be socially/politically unaware.*
▶ **unawareness** n [U].

unawares /-ˈweəz/ adv when not expected; so as to surprise sb: *She came upon him unawares as he was searching her room.* ○ *His violent outburst* **caught/ took me** (completely) **unawares.**

unbalance /ˌʌnˈbæləns/ v to upset the balance of sb/sth; to disturb sb/sth: [Vn] *Over-production is unbalancing the economy.*
▶ **unbalanced** adj **1** [esp pred] (of a person) mad; mentally abnormal: *mentally unbalanced.* **2** [esp attrib] giving too much or too little emphasis to sth; not balanced: *an unbalanced diet* ○ *the unbalanced reporting of some newspapers.*

unban /ˌʌnˈbæn/ v to allow sth that was previously forbidden: [Vn] *Opposition parties have now been unbanned.*

unbearable /ʌnˈbeərəbl/ adj that cannot be tolerated or endured: *unbearable pain* ○ *I find his rudeness/the heat unbearable.* ▶ **unbearably** /-əbli/ adv: *unbearably hot/selfish.*

unbeatable /ʌnˈbiːtəbl/ adj (a) that cannot be defeated or beaten (BEAT¹ 5a): *The Brazilian team is regarded as unbeatable.* (b) the best of a particular type; that cannot be improved: *unbeatable prices/discounts/value.*

unbeaten /ʌnˈbiːtn/ adj not having been defeated or beaten (BEAT¹ 5a): *an unbeaten team* ○ *His time of 3 minutes 2 seconds remains unbeaten.*

unbecoming /ˌʌnbɪˈkʌmɪŋ/ adj (fml) **1** not suiting a particular person: *an unbecoming shade of green.* **2** ~ (to/of sb) not appropriate or acceptable and attracting criticism: *tactics unbecoming to an Olympic gold medallist.*

unbeknown /ˌʌnbɪˈnəʊn/ (also **unbeknownst** /ˌʌnbɪˈnəʊnst/) adj ~ **to sb** without the specified person knowing or being aware: *Unbeknown to his* *family, he had lost the job.* ○ *He was, unbeknownst to her, already married.*

unbelief /ˌʌnbɪˈliːf/ *n* [U] (*fml*) lack of belief or the state of not believing, esp in God, a religion, etc. Compare DISBELIEF.

▶ **unbelievable** /ˌʌnbɪˈliːvəbl/ *adj* **1** so great as to be difficult to believe: *unbelievable cruelty/skill/ luck/stupidity.* **2** difficult to believe and very annoying: *It's unbelievable that he should have been promoted and not you.* **3** that cannot be believed or is unlikely to be true: *an unbelievable story.* See also INCREDIBLE. **unbelievably** /-əbli/ *adv*: *unbelievably hot/cheap/stupid.*

unbeliever *n* a person who does not believe, esp in God, a religion, etc.

unbelieving *adj* feeling or showing that one does not believe sb/sth: *She stared at me with unbelieving eyes.* See also INCREDULOUS.

unbend /ˌʌnˈbend/ *v* (*pt, pp* **unbent** /ˌʌnˈbent/) **1** to become less strict or formal in behaviour or attitude: [V] *Eventually she unbent and gave her permission.* **2** to change or make sb/sth change from a bent position; to become or make sth/sth straight from a bent position: [V, Vn] *exercises that involve bending and unbending (the back).*

▶ **unbending** *adj* (*often derog*) refusing to change one's demands, opinions, decisions, etc; not yielding: *the unbending attitude of the authorities.*

unbiased /ʌnˈbaɪəst/ *adj* not favouring or emphasizing one side or aspect at the expense of another; IMPARTIAL: *unbiased advice/reporting* ○ *an unbiased referee.*

unbidden /ʌnˈbɪdn/ *adv* (*fml*) **1** without having been asked, invited or ordered: *walk in unbidden.* **2** without conscious effort: *memories/images coming unbidden to one's mind.*

unbleached /ʌnˈbliːtʃt/ *adj* not made whiter by the use of chemicals: *unbleached cotton/flour.*

unblemished /ʌnˈblemɪʃt/ *adj* not spoilt, damaged or marked in any way: *have an unblemished reputation for honesty* ○ *unblemished fruit.*

unblinking /ʌnˈblɪŋkɪŋ/ *adj* without blinking (BLINK 1): *an unblinking stare/gaze.*

unblock /ˌʌnˈblɒk/ *v* to clean sth, eg a pipe, by removing matter that is blocking it: [Vn] *unblock a drain.*

unborn /ˌʌnˈbɔːn/ *adj* [usu attrib] not yet born: *ˌunborn ˈchildren/ˈcalves* ○ *generations as yet unborn.*

unbounded /ʌnˈbaʊndɪd/ *adj* without or seeming to be without limits; BOUNDLESS: *unbounded confidence/enthusiasm.*

unbowed /ˌʌnˈbaʊd/ *adj* not defeated; not ready to stop fighting: *The losing team left the field **bloody but unbowed**.*

unbreakable /ʌnˈbreɪkəbl/ *adj* that cannot be broken: *unbreakable plastics/toys* ○ *the unbreakable spirit of the defenders.*

unbridgeable /ʌnˈbrɪdʒəbl/ *adj* (of divisions between people) that cannot be reduced or removed: *an unbridgeable gap/gulf between the two sides in the dispute.*

unbridled /ʌnˈbraɪdld/ *adj* [usu attrib] not controlled or kept within limits: *unbridled hatred/ enthusiasm/lust.* Compare BRIDLE *v* 2.

unbroken /ʌnˈbrəʊkən/ *adj* **1** not interrupted or disturbed: *ten hours of unbroken sleep* ○ *the unbroken silence of the woods.* **2** (of records in sport, etc) not beaten (BEAT[1] 5a). **3** (of a horse, etc) not made TAME(1); not easy to ride.

unbuckle /ˌʌnˈbʌkl/ *v* [Vn] to undo or make loose the BUCKLE of a belt, etc.

unburden /ˌʌnˈbɜːdn/ *v* ~ **oneself/sth (of sth) (to sb)** (*fml*) to talk to sb about one's problems, esp so as to reduce one's anxiety, deal with the situation

more sensibly, etc: [Vnpr] *She preferred to unburden herself to me rather than to her husband.* [also Vn].

unbutton /ˌʌnˈbʌtn/ *v* to undo the buttons of clothes: [Vn] *unbutton one's/sb's shirt.*

▶ **unbuttoned** *adj* informal; relaxed: *her unbuttoned style of management.*

uncalled-for /ʌnˈkɔːld fɔː(r)/ *adj* not fair, justified or necessary in the circumstances: *Your rude remarks were quite uncalled-for.*

uncanny /ʌnˈkæni/ *adj* (**a**) not natural; mysterious and slightly frightening: *The silence was uncanny.* ○ *I had an uncanny feeling that I was being watched.* (**b**) not easily explained; extraordinary: *She has an uncanny ability to be in the right place at the right time.* ○ *The resemblance between them is uncanny.* ▶ **uncannily** /-ɪli/ *adv.*

uncapped /ˌʌnˈkæpt/ *adj* (*Brit*) (in sport) not having played for a national team: *Three previously uncapped players have been selected.*

uncared-for /ʌnˈkeəd fɔː(r)/ *adj* not looked after (LOOK[1]); neglected (NEGLECT): *uncared-for children/ gardens.*

uncaring /ʌnˈkeərɪŋ/ *adj* (*derog*) not sympathetic about the problems or suffering of others: *uncaring employers* ○ *be selfish and uncaring.*

unceasing /ʌnˈsiːsɪŋ/ *adj* continuing all the time; INCESSANT: *unceasing efforts/conflict.* ▶ **unceasingly** *adv.*

uncensored /ʌnˈsensəd/ *adj* (of a film, book, account, etc) not having been censored (CENSOR *v*): *the uncensored version of the incident.*

unceremonious /ˌʌnˌserəˈməʊniəs/ *adj* sudden; roughly or rudely done: *his unceremonious departure/dismissal.* ▶ **unceremoniously** *adv* (*derog*) *He was unceremoniously sent home.*

uncertain /ʌnˈsɜːtn/ *adj* **1**(**a**) [usu pred] ~ (**about/ of sth**) feeling doubt about sth; not knowing sth definitely; not sure: *be/feel uncertain (about) what to do* ○ *uncertain about/of one's legal rights.* **2** not known definitely; that cannot be confidently predicted or described: *The outcome is still uncertain.* ○ *The industry faces an uncertain future.* **3** not to be depended on; unreliable: *As a player, her form at the moment is uncertain.* **4** likely to vary; tending to change frequently: *uncertain weather* ○ *a man of uncertain temper.* **5** not confident; HESITANT: *the baby's first uncertain steps.* **IDM in ˌno unˌcertain ˈterms** clearly and forcefully: *I told him what I thought of him in no uncertain terms!*

▶ **uncertainly** *adv* without confidence; hesitantly (HESITANT): *speak/smile uncertainly.*

uncertainty /ʌnˈsɜːtnti/ *n* (**a**) [U] the state of being uncertain: *There is some uncertainty about when the game is due to start.* (**b**) [C esp *pl*] a thing that is uncertain or causes one to be uncertain: *the uncertainties of life* ○ *political/economic uncertainty.*

unchallengeable /ʌnˈtʃælɪndʒəbl/ *adj* that cannot be challenged, questioned or disputed: *an unchallengeable fact/judgement/reason.*

unchallenged /ʌnˈtʃælɪndʒd/ *adj* **1** not doubted or questioned: *unchallenged decisions/authority* ○ *I can't let such a statement go unchallenged.* **2** not opposed: *the party's unchallenged domination of the country.* **3** not being stopped and asked to explain who one is, what one is doing, etc: *enter a restricted area unchallenged.*

unchangeable /ʌnˈtʃeɪndʒəbl/ *adj* that cannot be changed: *unchangeable patterns.*

unchanged /ʌnˈtʃeɪndʒd/ *adj* that has not changed or been changed: *an unchanged team* ○ *My opinion remains unchanged.*

unchanging /ʌnˈtʃeɪndʒɪŋ/ *adj* remaining the same; not changing: *unchanging customs/principles.*

uncharacteristic /ˌʌnˌkærəktəˈrɪstɪk/ *adj* ~ (**of sb**) not characteristic or typical of sb; unusual for

sb: *make an uncharacteristic mistake* ○ *Such behaviour is uncharacteristic of her.*
▶ **uncharacteristically** *adv* be uncharacteristically rude.

uncharitable /ˌʌnˈtʃærɪtəbl/ *adj* unkind, harsh and not sympathetic: *uncharitable remarks/thoughts* ○ *I don't want to be uncharitable, but she's not a terribly good cook.*

uncharted /ˌʌnˈtʃɑːtɪd/ *adj* **1** not marked on a map or chart: *an uncharted island.* **2** not previously explored; not familiar: *the uncharted depths of human emotions* ○ *The party is sailing in **uncharted waters*** (ie is in a situation it has never been in before).

unchecked /ˌʌnˈtʃekt/ *adj* (*derog*) not resisted or restrained: *rumours spreading unchecked* ○ *This abuse of human rights must not **go unchecked**.*

uncivil /ʌnˈsɪvl/ *adj* not polite; rude: *be uncivil to the neighbours.* See also INCIVILITY.

uncivilized, -ised /ʌnˈsɪvəlaɪzd/ *adj* (*derog*) **1** (of people or places) not having developed a modern way of life; BACKWARD(3): *an uncivilized society/country.* **2** (of behaviour, etc) not acceptable according to one's moral principles or standards: *uncivilized treatment of prisoners.*

unclaimed /ˌʌnˈkleɪmd/ *adj* not claimed as being owned by or owed to sb: *unclaimed property/prizes.*

uncle /ˈʌŋkl/ *n* **1(a)** a brother of one's father or mother, or the husband of one's aunt: *my uncle Jim.* ⇨ App 4. **(b)** a man whose brother or sister has a child: *Now you're an uncle.* **2** (*infml*) (used by children, esp before a first name to address or refer to an adult male friend of the family). **IDM bob's your uncle** ⇨ BOB⁴.
■ ˌUncle ˈSam *n* (*infml*) the United States of America.
ˌUncle ˈTom *n* (*US infml derog*) a black person who is eager to please or serve white people.

unclean /ˌʌnˈkliːn/ *adj* **(a)** dirty or not pure, and so likely to cause disease: *unclean premises.* **(b)** not good or pure in a moral or religious way: *unclean thoughts.*

unclear /ˌʌnˈklɪə(r)/ *adj* **1** not obvious: *His motives are unclear.* **2** not easy to see, hear or understand: *an unclear explanation* ○ *Her reply was unclear.* **3** not definite or firm: *Our plans are unclear at the moment.* **4** ~ **(about sth)** (of a person) not fully understanding sth; uncertain about sth: *I'm unclear (about) what you want me to do.*

uncluttered /ˌʌnˈklʌtəd/ *adj* (*approv*) not containing too many objects, details, or elements: *an uncluttered room/design/style.*

uncoil /ˌʌnˈkɔɪl/ *v* to become or make sth straight from a coiled (COIL) position: [V,Vn] *The snake slowly uncoiled (itself).* [Vn] *uncoil a cable.*

uncoloured (*US* **uncolored**) /ˌʌnˈkʌləd/ *adj* having no colour or no colour added: *plain, uncoloureu glass.*

uncomfortable /ʌnˈkʌmftəbl; *US* -fərt-/ *adj* **1** not physically comfortable: *uncomfortable chairs/shoes* ○ *lie in an uncomfortable position.* **2** feeling or causing one to feel anxious or embarrassed: *Your letter was an uncomfortable reminder of what I owe you.* ○ *He looked uncomfortable when the subject was mentioned.* **3** not pleasant to accept: *an uncomfortable truth/fact.*
▶ **uncomfortably** /-əblɪ/ *adv* **1** in a way that is not physically comfortable: *uncomfortably cramped.* **2(a)** in a way that causes one to feel anxious: *The exams are getting uncomfortably close.* **(b)** in a way that shows that one is anxious or embarrassed: *My question made him shift uncomfortably in his seat.*

uncommitted /ˌʌnkəˈmɪtɪd/ *adj* ~ **(to sth/sb)** not having given support to a particular person, side, idea, etc: *parties appealing to uncommitted voters* ○ *Some workers remain uncommitted to the project.*

uncommon /ʌnˈkɒmən/ *adj* **1** not happening or done often; unusual: *an uncommon sighting/occurrence* ○ *Instances of the disease are uncommon in this country.* **2** (*fml*) unusual in extent; great: *act with uncommon haste.*
▶ **uncommonly** *adv* (*fml*) to an unusual extent: *an uncommonly gifted child.*

uncommunicative /ˌʌnkəˈmjuːnɪkətɪv/ *adj* unwilling to talk very much or to give opinions.

uncompetitive /ˌʌnkəmˈpetətɪv/ *adj* (*commerce*) not cheaper or of better quality than others of the same type: *an uncompetitive industry/product.*

uncomplaining /ˌʌnkəmˈpleɪnɪŋ/ *adj* not complaining: *He puts up with everything in the same uncomplaining way.* ▶ **uncomplainingly** *adv*.

uncompleted /ˌʌnkəmˈpliːtɪd/ *adj* not having been completed: *an incompleted project/symphony.*

uncomplicated /ʌnˈkɒmplɪkeɪtɪd/ *adj* simple; STRAIGHTFORWARD(2): *an uncomplicated attitude/job.*

uncompromising /ʌnˈkɒmprəmaɪzɪŋ/ *adj* not willing or showing that one is willing to change one's attitude, position, etc: *She is known for her uncompromising opposition to a single European currency.* ▶ **uncompromisingly** *adv*.

unconcern /ˌʌnkənˈsɜːn/ *n* [U] lack of care or interest in matters where it might be expected: *She received the news with apparent unconcern.*

unconcerned /ˌʌnkənˈsɜːnd/ *adj* **1** ~ **(with sth/sb)** not feeling or showing that one cares about or is interested in sth: *be quite unconcerned with questions of morality.* **2** ~ **(about/at/by sth)** not worried or anxious about sth: *He drove on, apparently unconcerned about the noise the engine was making.* ▶ **unconcernedly** /ˌʌnkənˈsɜːnɪdlɪ/ *adv*.

unconditional /ˌʌnkənˈdɪʃənl/ *adj* not subject to any conditions or terms; absolute: *an ˌunconditional surˈrender/ˈoffer.* ▶ **unconditionally** /-ʃənəlɪ/ *adv*: *support sb unconditionally.*

unconditioned /ˌʌnkənˈdɪʃnd/ *adj* (of behaviour) not influenced by experience; done by instinct. Compare CONDITIONED REFLEX.

unconfirmed /ˌʌnkənˈfɜːmd/ *adj* (of information) not proved to be true; not confirmed: *ˌunconfirmed reˈports/ˈrumours.*

uncongenial /ˌʌnkənˈdʒiːnɪəl/ *adj* not pleasant or friendly; not causing one to feel relaxed: *uncongenial company* ○ *an uncongenial atmosphere.*

unconnected /ˌʌnkəˈnektɪd/ *adj* ~ **(with sth)** not related or connected in any way: *The two crimes are apparently unconnected.* ○ *The accident was unconnected with the building work being carried out on the site.*

unconscionable /ʌnˈkɒnʃənəbl/ *adj* [attrib] (*fml or joc*) excessive; greater or longer than is reasonable: *You take **an unconscionable time** getting dressed!*

unconscious /ʌnˈkɒnʃəs/ *adj* **1(a)** not conscious(1): *knock sb unconscious* ○ *She was unconscious for days after the accident.* **2** ~ **of sb/sth** not aware of sth; not realizing sth: *be unconscious of any change* ○ *She is unconscious of the effect she has on her colleagues.* **3** done or existing without one realizing; not intended: *act with unconscious arrogance* ○ *unconscious jealousy/humour.*
▶ **the unconscious** *n* [sing] (*psychology*) that part of one's mental activity of which one is not aware, but which can be detected and understood through the skilled analysis of dreams, behaviour, etc. Compare SUBCONSCIOUS.
unconsciously *adv* without being aware: *Perhaps, unconsciously, I have done something to offend her.*
unconsciousness *n* [U] the state of being unconscious(1): *lapse/fall into unconsciousness.*

unconsidered /ˌʌnkənˈsɪdəd/ *adj* **1** (of remarks, actions, etc) said or done without enough consideration or thought. **2** not considered serious because of little value or importance: *unconsidered trifles.*

unconstitutional /ˌʌnˌkɒnstɪˈtjuːʃənl; US -ˈtuːʃənl/ *adj* contrary to the rules of a political system or organization: *an unconstitutional law/election.*

uncontaminated /ˌʌnkənˈtæmɪneɪtɪd/ *adj* not harmed or spoilt by sth: *an uncontaminated water supply.*

uncontentious /ˌʌnkənˈtenʃəs/ *adj* not likely to cause argument or be considered offensive: *an uncontentious remark.*

uncontested /ˌʌnkənˈtestɪd/ *adj* without any opposition: *an uncontested election.*

uncontrollable /ˌʌnkənˈtrəʊləbl/ *adj* that cannot be controlled, prevented or restricted: *uncontrollable anger/panic/joy* ○ *an uncontrollable urge to sneeze.* ▶ **uncontrollably** *adv: shake uncontrollably.*

uncontrolled /ˌʌnkənˈtrəʊld/ *adj* **1** not subject to official control: *uncontrolled immigration.* **2** that cannot be controlled: *uncontrolled aggression.*

uncontroversial /ˌʌnˌkɒntrəˈvɜːʃl/ *adj* not causing or likely to cause disagreement: *an uncontroversial measure/policy/opinion.*

unconventional /ˌʌnkənˈvenʃənl/ *adj* not following what is considered normal practice or behaviour: *have unconventional views.* ▶ **unconventionally** *adv: dress unconventionally.*

unconvinced /ˌʌnkənˈvɪnst/ ~ **(of sth / that…)** not certain about sth, despite what one has been told: *She was very persuasive but I remain unconvinced.* ○ *The jury were unconvinced of his innocence/that he was innocent.*

unconvincing /ˌʌnkənˈvɪnsɪŋ/ *adj* failing to make sb believe sth or to impress sb: *unconvincing evidence* ○ *give an unconvincing performance.* ▶ **unconvincingly** *adv: lie unconvincingly.*

uncooked /ˌʌnˈkʊkt/ *adj* not cooked; raw: *The steak was uncooked in the middle.*

uncool /ˌʌnˈkuːl/ *adj (sl)* not considered acceptable by fashionable young people.

uncooperative /ˌʌnkəʊˈɒpərətɪv/ *adj* not willing to be helpful to others or do what they ask: *an uncooperative witness/patient.*

uncoordinated /ˌʌnkəʊˈɔːdɪneɪtɪd/ *adj* **1(a)** (of a person) not able to control one's movements: *He's too uncoordinated to play tennis well.* **(b)** (of movements or parts of the body) not controlled: *uncoordinated limbs.* **2** not well organized: *an uncoordinated campaign.*

uncork /ˌʌnˈkɔːk/ *v* [Vn] to remove the CORK(2) from a bottle.

uncountable /ʌnˈkaʊntəbl/ *adj* too many to be counted: *uncountable galaxies.*
■ **un₁countable ˈnoun** (also **ˈuncount noun**) *n* (*grammar*) a noun that cannot be made PLURAL(1) or preceded by *a* or *an*, eg *water, money, vegetation.* In this dictionary uncountable nouns are marked [U].

uncouple /ˌʌnˈkʌpl/ *v* ~ **sth (from sth)** to remove the connection between two vehicles, eg railway carriages: [Vn, Vnpr] *uncouple the front of a train (from the rest of it).*

uncouth /ʌnˈkuːθ/ *adj* lacking in good manners; not refined: *uncouth laughter* ○ *an uncouth young man.*

uncover /ʌnˈkʌvə(r)/ *v* **1** to remove a cover or covering from sth: [Vn] *leave the saucepan uncovered.* **2** to discover sth previously secret or unknown: [Vn] *uncover the truth* ○ *Agents have uncovered a plot to assassinate the President.*

uncritical /ˌʌnˈkrɪtɪkl/ *adj* ~ **(of sth/sb)** (*usu derog*) unwilling or unable to criticize sb/sth: *an uncritical attitude/view* ○ *uncritical supporters of the government.* ▶ **uncritically** /-ɪkli/ *adv.*

uncrossed /ˌʌnˈkrɒst; US -ˈkrɔːst/ *adj* (Brit) (of a cheque) not crossed (CROSS⁵ 2).

uncrowded /ʌnˈkraʊdɪd/ *adj* not filled with a large number of people: *uncrowded resorts/trains.*

uncrowned /ˌʌnˈkraʊnd/ *adj* (of a king or queen) not yet crowned (CROWN² 1). **IDM** the **₁uncrowned ˈking/ˈqueen (of sth)** the person considered to be the most talented or successful in a certain group or field.

unction /ˈʌŋkʃn/ *n* [U] the action of anointing (ANOINT) sb/sth with oil as a religious ceremony: *extreme unction* (ie this ceremony performed on sb who is about to die).

unctuous /ˈʌŋktjuəs/ *adj (fml)* praising sb or trying to please them in a way that is insincere and unpleasant: *speak in unctuous tones.* ▶ **unctuously** *adv.*

uncurl /ˌʌnˈkɜːl/ *v* ~ **(sth/oneself)** to become straight or make sth/oneself become straight from a curled position: [V, Vn] *The cat uncurled (itself) sensuously.* [Vn] *She uncurled her legs from under her.*

uncut /ˌʌnˈkʌt/ *adj* **1(a)** not cut into separate pieces: *uncut loaves of bread.* **(b)** (of plants) not cut and therefore still growing: *uncut hedges.* **2** (of a book, film, etc) not made shorter or censored (CENSOR *v*): *the original uncut version.* **3** (of a precious stone) not shaped by cutting: *uncut diamonds.*

undamaged /ʌnˈdæmɪdʒd/ *adj* not damaged or spoilt: *There was a slight collision but my car was undamaged.* ○ *He emerged from the court case with his reputation undamaged.*

undated /ˌʌnˈdeɪtɪd/ *adj* **1** without a date written or printed on it: *an undated letter/painting.* **2** of which the date is not known: *undated archaeological remains.*

undaunted /ʌnˈdɔːntɪd/ *adj* [usu pred] (*rhet*) not discouraged by difficulty, danger, or disappointment: *He remounted and rode on, undaunted by his fall.*

undecided /ˌʌndɪˈsaɪdɪd/ *adj* [pred] **1** not settled or resolved: *The (outcome of the) match is still undecided.* **2** ~ **(about sth/sb)** not having made a decision about sth: *I'm still undecided (about) who to vote for.*

undeclared /ˌʌndɪˈkleəd/ *adj* **(a)** (of goods on which duty(3) should be paid) not declared (DECLARE 3) or shown to CUSTOMS(b) officers. **(b)** (of income) not declared (DECLARE 3) to the tax authorities.

undefeated /ˌʌndɪˈfiːtɪd/ *adj* (esp in sport) not having lost or been defeated: *be undefeated in 13 matches* ○ *the undefeated world champion.*

undefended /ˌʌndɪˈfendɪd/ *adj* **1** not protected or guarded: *an undefended frontier.* **2** without any defence being made: *undefended cases* (ie in lawcourts).

undefined /ˌʌndɪˈfaɪnd/ *adj* not having a clear or definite form; VAGUE(1) in nature: *undefined powers* ○ *She found him, in some undefined way, rather strange.*

undemanding /ˌʌndɪˈmɑːndɪŋ/ *adj* **1** not requiring a lot of effort: *an undemanding job.* **2** (of a person) not tending to insist on attention or action from others: *an undemanding child/boss.*

undemocratic /ˌʌndeməˈkrætɪk/ *adj* contrary to or not acting according to the principles of DEMOCRACY(1a): *undemocratic decisions* ○ *an undemocratic regime.*

undemonstrative /ˌʌndɪˈmɒnstrətɪv/ *adj* not expressing one's feelings openly; RESERVED.

undeniable /ˌʌndɪˈnaɪəbl/ *adj* that cannot be disputed or denied; certainly true: *undeniable facts* ○ *His charm is undeniable, but I still don't trust him.* ▶ **undeniably** /-əbli/ *adv: undeniably impressive/beautiful.*

under /ˈʌndə(r)/ *prep* **1** in, to or through a position that is below or beneath sth: *The cat was under the table.* ○ *Have you looked under the bed?* ○ *Let's shelter* *under those trees.* ○ *He threw himself under a bus.* ○ *The water flows under the bridge.* ○ (*fig*) *What sign of the zodiac were you born under?* Compare OVER² 1. **2** below the surface of sth; covered by sth: *Most of the iceberg is under the water.* ○ *The Channel Tunnel goes under the sea.* ○ *She slipped under the bedclothes.* ○ *Are you wearing a vest under your shirt?* **3** in or to a position next to and lower than sth: *a ladder placed under a window.* **4(a)** younger than a specified age: *Nobody under eighteen is allowed to buy alcohol.* ○ *If you are 25 or under you can buy cheaper tickets.* See also UNDER AGE. ⇨ note at AGE¹. (**b**) less than a specified amount, distance or time: *an annual income of under £10 000* ○ *It's under a mile from here to the post office.* ○ *It took us under an hour.* Compare OVER² 2. **5(a)** working for or in the control of sb: *The restaurant is under new management.* ○ *She has a staff of 19 working under her.* (**b**) ruled or governed by sb: *Britain under the Tories* ○ *The country is now under martial law.* ○ *Under its new conductor, the orchestra has established an international reputation.* (**c**) according to an agreement, a law or a system: *Six suspects are being held under the Prevention of Terrorism Act.* ○ *Under the terms of the lease you had no right to sublet the property.* ○ *Is the radio still under guarantee?* **6** carrying sth: *She was struggling under the weight of three suitcases.* ○ *The wall collapsed under the strain.* **7(a)** being in a particular state or condition: *buildings under repair/construction* ○ *matters under consideration/discussion/investigation.* (**b**) being affected by sb/sth: *feeling under stress* ○ *He's very much under the influence of the older boys.* ○ *You'll be under (an) anaesthetic, so you won't feel a thing.* **8(a)** using a particular name: *open a bank account under a false name* ○ *She also writes under the pseudonym of Barbara Vine.* (**b**) found in a particular part of a book, list, etc: *If it's not under 'sport', try looking under 'games'.* **9** being planted with sth: *fields under wheat.*

▶ **under** *adv part* **1** under water: *If you take a deep breath you can stay under for more than a minute.* ○ *The ship went under* (ie sank) *on its first voyage.* **2** in or into an unconscious state: *She felt herself going under.*
under *adj* [attrib] lower; situated underneath: *the under layer* ○ *the under surface of a leaf.*

under- *pref* **1** (with *ns*) (**a**) below: *undergrowth* ○ *undercurrent.* (**b**) a person younger than a specified age: *under-fives.* (**c**) lower in position or rank: *under-secretary* ○ *undergraduate.* **2** (with *adjs, vs* and their related forms) not enough: *underripe* ○ *undercooked* ○ *underdeveloped.* Compare SUB-.

underachieve /ˌʌndərəˈtʃiːv/ *v* [V] (*euph*) to do less well than was expected, esp in school work.
▶**underachievement** *n* [U]. **underachiever** *n.*

underarm /ˈʌndərɑːm/ **1** *adj* [attrib] in, of or for the ARMPIT: *underarm hair/perspiration/deodorant.* **2** *adj, adv* (in sport) with the hand kept below the level of the shoulder: *an underarm service* ○ *bowl/serve/throw underarm.* Compare OVERARM.

underbelly /ˈʌndəbeli/ *n* [sing] **1** an area, a region, etc that is weak and exposed to attack: *The trade deficit remains the soft underbelly of the US economy.* **2** a hidden, unpleasant or criminal part of society: *murderers, rapists and the rest of humanity's dark underbelly.*

underbid /ˌʌndəˈbɪd/ *v* (**-dd-**; *pt, pp* **underbid**) [Vn] make a lower bid than sb else, eg when competing for a contract.

underbrush /ˈʌndəbrʌʃ/ *n* [U] (*US*) = UNDERGROWTH.

undercarriage /ˈʌndəkærɪdʒ/ (also **landing-gear**) *n* an aircraft's landing wheels and their supports:

raise/lower the undercarriage. ⇨ picture at AIRCRAFT.

undercharge /ˌʌndəˈtʃɑːdʒ/ *v* ~ (**sb**) (**for sth**) to charge sb too low a price for sth, usu by mistake: [Vn, Vnn, Vnpr] *He undercharged me (£1) (for the book).* [also V, Vpr]. Compare OVERCHARGE 1.

underclass /ˈʌndəklɑːs/ *n* a social class that is very poor or has very low status.

underclothes /ˈʌndəkləʊðz/ *n* [pl] (also *fml* **underclothing** /-kləʊðɪŋ/ [U]) = UNDERWEAR.

undercoat /ˈʌndəkəʊt/ *n* [U, C] a layer of paint under the final coat; the paint used for making this: *apply the undercoat first.* Compare TOPCOAT.

undercover /ˌʌndəˈkʌvə(r)/ *adj* [usu attrib] **1** doing things secretly or done secretly: ˌundercover ˈpayments. **2** involved in spying (SPY *v*) on people while appearing to work with or for them: ˌundercover ˈagents/acˈtivities/organiˈzations.

undercurrent /ˈʌndəkʌrənt/ *n* ~ (**of sth**) a feeling, influence or TREND, esp one that is against the main or most obvious one: *I detect an undercurrent of resentment towards the new proposals.*

undercut /ˌʌndəˈkʌt/ *v* (**-tt-**; *pt, pp* **undercut**) **1** to offer goods or services at a lower price than one's competitors: [Vnpr] *They're undercutting us by 5%.* [also Vn]. **2** to make sb/sth weaker or less firm: [Vn] *concessions made to try and undercut the opposition.*

underdeveloped /ˌʌndədɪˈveləpt/ *adj* (of a country, etc) not having achieved a high level of economic development. ▶ **underdevelopment** *n* [U].

underdog /ˈʌndədɒg; *US* -dɔːg/ *n* a person, team, etc thought to be in a weaker position, and therefore not likely to win a competition, fight, etc: *Before the match we were definitely the underdogs.*

underdone /ˌʌndəˈdʌn/ *adj* not thoroughly cooked: *nicely underdone vegetables* ○ *The beef was underdone and quite unpalatable.*

underestimate /ˌʌndərˈestɪmeɪt/ *v* **1** to guess that the amount of sth is lower than it really is: [Vn] *underestimate the cost/danger/difficulty of the expedition* ○ *We underestimated the time it would take to get there.* **2** to think that sb/sth is not as good or strong as they/it really is: *Never underestimate your opponent* (ie think that you will beat her or him easily). Compare UNDERRATE.
▶ **underestimate** /-mət/ *n* an estimate that is too low: *The number of deaths on the roads predicted for the year proved to be a serious underestimate.* Compare OVERESTIMATE.

underexpose /ˌʌndərɪkˈspəʊz/ *v* (esp passive) (in photography) to allow too little light to reach a film: [Vn] *an underexposed photograph.* Compare OVEREXPOSE 1.

underfed /ˌʌndəˈfed/ *adj* having had too little food to eat: *underfed animals/children.*

underfloor /ˌʌndəˈflɔː(r)/ *adj* [attrib] situated beneath the floor: ˌunderfloor ˈheating (eg using warm air).

underfoot /ˌʌndəˈfʊt/ *adj* [attrib], *adv* under one's feet; on the ground: *soft underfoot conditions* ○ *The snow underfoot was soft and deep.* ○ *It was muddy underfoot.* ○ *Many of her plants had been **trampled underfoot** by the children playing in the garden.*

undergarment /ˈʌndəgɑːmənt/ *n* (*dated or fml*) a piece of clothing worn under a shirt, dress, etc next to the skin.

undergo /ˌʌndəˈgəʊ/ *v* (*pt* **underwent** /-ˈwent/; *pp* **undergone** /-ˈgɒn; *US* -ˈgɔːn/) **1** to experience or endure sth unpleasant or painful: [Vn] *undergo great hardship/suffering/privation.* **2** to be put through a process, etc: [Vn] *undergo major surgery/reform/repair* ○ *The country underwent a great many changes after the war.*

undergraduate /ˌʌndəˈgrædʒuət/ n a university or college student who has not yet taken her or his first degree: *Cambridge undergraduates* ∘ *undergraduate courses/grants/students.* Compare GRADUATE¹, POST-GRADUATE.

underground¹ /ˌʌndəˈgraʊnd/ adv **1** under the surface of the ground. **2** in or into a secret place to hide from sb/sth: *He went underground to avoid capture.*

underground² /ˈʌndəgraʊnd/ adj [attrib] **1** under the surface of the ground: *underground passages/ caves* ∘ *an underground car park.* **2** operating secretly, esp against a ruling power: *the French underground resistance movement during World War II* ∘ *the underground press.*

▶ **underground** n **the underground 1** (also *Brit infml* **the tube**, *US* **the subway**) [sing] the underground railway: *travel by underground* ∘ *fares on the London Underground* ∘ *underground stations.* **2** [Gp] a secret, esp political, organization or its activities: *work for/join/contact the underground.*

undergrowth /ˈʌndəgrəʊθ/ (*US* **underbrush**) n [U] a mass of bushes, etc growing close together, esp under trees: *clear a path through the dense undergrowth.*

underhand /ˌʌndəˈhænd/ adj (*derog*) done or doing things in a secret and dishonest way: *employ ˌunderhand ˈtactics* ∘ *What you did was mean and underhand.*

underlay /ˈʌndəleɪ/ n [U, C] a layer of thick material placed under a carpet to protect it: *Some carpets have a foam rubber underlay attached to them.*

underlie /ˌʌndəˈlaɪ/ v (*pt* **underlay** /ˌʌndəˈleɪ/; *pp* **underlain** /-ˈleɪn/) (*fml*) (no passive) to form the basis of an action, a theory, etc: *the internal processes that underlie the way we perceive and think* ∘ *A similar theme underlies much of his work.*

▶ **underlying** adj [attrib] **1** existing in relation to a situation but not immediately obvious: *an underlying assumption/trend* ∘ *Unemployment may be an underlying cause of the rising crime rate.* **2** existing under sth: *the underlying rock formation.*

underline /ˌʌndəˈlaɪn/ (also **underscore**) v **1** [Vn] to draw a line under a word, etc. **2** to emphasize a fact, point, difference, etc: [Vn, V.*wh*] *The huge response to our appeal underlines how much the public really care.* [also Vn, V.*that*].

underling /ˈʌndəlɪŋ/ n (*derog*) a person with a lower rank or an inferior position.

underlying /ˌʌndəˈlaɪɪŋ/ ⇨ UNDERLIE.

undermanned /ˌʌndəˈmænd/ adj (of a ship, factory, etc) having too few people to function properly. Compare OVERMANNED, UNDERSTAFFED.

undermine /ˌʌndəˈmaɪn/ v **1** to make sth weaker at the base, eg by digging a tunnel: [Vn] *cliffs undermined by the sea.* **2** to make sth/sb gradually weaker or less effective: [Vn] *undermine sb's position/reputation/authority* ∘ *Repeated failure had not undermined his confidence.*

underneath /ˌʌndəˈniːθ/ prep beneath sth; below sth: *The coin rolled underneath the piano.* ∘ *She found a lot of dust underneath the sofa.* ∘ *Life-jackets are situated underneath the seats.*

▶ **underneath** adv beneath; below: *There's a pile of newspapers in the corner — have you looked underneath?* ∘ *This jacket's too big, even with a sweater underneath.* ∘ *A lot of noise was coming from the flat underneath.* ∘ (*fig*) *He seems bad-tempered but he's very soft-hearted underneath.*

underneath n [sing] the lower surface or part of sth: *the underneath of a car/shelf/sofa.*

undernourished /ˌʌndəˈnʌrɪʃt/ adj not provided with enough food of the right kind for good health and normal growth: *The children grow up severely undernourished.* Compare MALNOURISHED. ▶ **undernourishment** /-ˈnʌrɪʃmənt/ n [U].

underpants /ˈʌndəpænts/ (also *infml* **pants**) n [pl] a piece of clothing worn next to the skin, covering the lower part of the body and sometimes the top part of the legs. In British English underpants are worn by men and boys; in US English they are worn by either sex: *put on some/a pair of clean underpants.* Compare KNICKERS 1.

underpass /ˈʌndəpɑːs; *US* -pæs/ n **1** a road that goes under another road or a railway. Compare OVERPASS. **2** an underground passage by which people can walk under a road or railway. Compare SUBWAY 1.

underpay /ˌʌndəˈpeɪ/ v (*pt, pp* **underpaid** /-ˈpeɪd/) ~ **sb (for sth)** (esp passive) to pay an employee, etc too little money: [Vn] *Nurses complain of being overworked and underpaid.* [Vnpr] *He underpaid me for the work (by £10).* Compare OVERPAY.

underpin /ˌʌndəˈpɪn/ v (**-nn-**) **1** [Vn] to support a wall, etc from below with concrete, etc. **2** to form the basis for an argument, a claim, etc; to support or strengthen sth: [Vn] *His theories are underpinned by sound reasoning.* ∘ *The strength of the dollar is underpinned by the growth in world wealth.*

underplay /ˌʌndəˈpleɪ/ v **1** to make sth seem less important than it really is: [Vn] *The government is desperately trying to underplay the significance of the opinion polls.* **2** to give less force to sth than expected: [Vn] *The romantic element in the music was somewhat underplayed.* Compare OVERPLAY.

underprivileged /ˌʌndəˈprɪvəlɪdʒd/ adj having a lower standard of living or fewer rights than normal in a society: *special holidays for underprivileged children.* ▶ **the underprivileged** n [pl v]: *her work among the underprivileged.*

underrate /ˌʌndəˈreɪt/ v to have too low an opinion of sb/sth: [Vn] *underrate an opponent/achievement* ∘ *an underrated play/actor* ∘ *As a writer, he's seriously underrated.* Compare OVERRATE, UNDERESTIMATE 2.

underscore /ˌʌndəˈskɔː(r)/ v [Vn] = UNDERLINE.

undersea /ˈʌndəsiː/ adj [attrib] below the surface of the sea: *undersea exploration.*

under-secretary /ˌʌndəˈsekrətri; *US* -teri/ n **1** (also **Permanent Under-Secretary**) (in Britain) a senior civil servant (CIVIL) in charge of a government department. **2** (also **Parliamentary Under-Secretary**) (in Britain) a minister of relatively low status in certain government departments.

undersell /ˌʌndəˈsel/ v (*pt, pp* **undersold** /-ˈsəʊld/) to sell goods at a lower price than one's competitors: [Vn] *Our goods are never undersold* (ie Our prices are the lowest). ∘ *They're underselling us.*

undershirt /ˈʌndəʃɜːt/ n (*US*) = VEST¹ 1a.

underside /ˈʌndəsaɪd/ n [sing] the side or surface that is underneath; the bottom: *She found a label stuck to the underside of the table.*

undersigned /ˌʌndəˈsaɪnd/ **the undersigned** n (*pl* unchanged) (*fml*) the person who has signed at the bottom of a document: *We, the undersigned declare that...*

undersized /ˌʌndəˈsaɪzd/ adj of less than the usual size: *The cubs were weak and undersized.*

undersold *pt, pp* of UNDERSELL.

understaffed /ˌʌndəˈstɑːft; *US* -ˈstæft/ adj (of a school, a hospital, an office, etc) having too few people to function properly: *We are seriously understaffed.* Compare OVERSTAFFED, UNDERMANNED.

understand /ˌʌndəˈstænd/ v (*pt, pp* **understood** /-ˈstʊd/) (not used in the continuous tenses) **1(a)** to know the meaning of words, a language, a person's character, etc: [Vn] *understand the instructions/ rules/conditions* [V, Vn] *I'm not sure that I fully understand (you).* [Vn] *I can understand French perfectly.* [V.*wh*, Vn] *I don't understand (a word of) what he's saying.* **(b)** to perceive the meaning or importance of sth; to perceive the explanation for or

cause of sth: [Vn] *Do you understand the difficulty of my position?* [V.wh] *I don't understand why he came/ what the problem is.* [V.n ing] *I just can't understand him/his taking the money.* **2** to have a sympathetic awareness of sb/sth; to know how to deal with sb/ sth: [Vn] *understand children/machinery/modern music* ○ *We understand each other, even if we don't always agree.* [V.that, V.n ing] *I quite understand that you need a change/understand your needing a change.* [V.wh] *He understands how hard things have been for you.* [also V]. **3** (*usu fml*) (**a**) to be aware from information received that...; to gather(3): [V.that] *I understand (that) she is in Paris.* ○ *Am I to understand that you refuse?* [Vn] *The situation, as I understand it, is very serious.* [V.to inf] *I understood him to say that he would co-operate.* ○ *Senior ministers are understood to have opposed the plan.* (**b**) (usu passive) to assume that sth is the case; to take sth for granted (GRANT): [V.that] *Your expenses will be paid, that's understood.* **4** (esp passive) to supply or insert an omitted word or phrase mentally: [Vn] *In the sentence 'I can't drive', the object 'a car' is understood.* **IDM give sb to believe/understand** ⇨ GIVE¹. **make oneself under'stood** to make one's meaning clear: *He doesn't speak much English but he can make himself understood.*
▶ **understandable** /-əbl/ *adj* (**a**) that one might expect; natural or reasonable. (**b**) (of a meaning, an explanation, etc) that can be understood: *The instructions were not readily/easily understandable.* ○ *understandable delays/objections/motives.* **understandably** /-əbli/ *adv* for reasons that one can accept or feel sympathy for: *She was understandably annoyed.* ○ *Understandably, he's reluctant to talk about it.*

understanding /ˌʌndəˈstændɪŋ/ *n* **1** [U] the power of clear thought; intelligence: *mysteries beyond human understanding.* **2** [U,sing] ~ (**of sth**) knowledge of the meaning, importance or cause of sth: *I have only a limited understanding of French.* **3** [U,sing] the ability to tolerate sb/sth or show INSIGHT(1a); sympathetic awareness: *no real understanding between husband and wife* ○ *work for a better understanding between the nations of the world.* **4**(**a**) [U] ~ (**of sth**) (*usu fml*) the opinion sb has of the meaning of sth: *My understanding was that we were to meet here.* (**b**) [C usu *sing*] an informal agreement: *try to* **come to / reach an understanding** *with management about pay* ○ *We have an understanding that/There is an understanding between us that we will not sell to each other's customers.* **IDM on the understanding that...; on this understanding** on condition that...; on this condition: *I lent him the money on the understanding that he would pay me back the next day.*
▶ **understanding** *adj* able to tolerate or show sympathy towards others' feelings and views: *an understanding approach/smile/parent.*

understate /ˌʌndəˈsteɪt/ *v* **1** to state that sth is smaller or less important than it really is: [Vn] *The figures probably understate the real growth rate.* ○ *It would be wrong to understate the seriousness of the problem.* **2** to state or express sth in a very controlled way: [Vn] *understate one's views/feelings* ○ *She gave a beautifully understated performance as Ophelia.* Compare OVERSTATE.
▶ **understatement** /ˈʌndəsteɪtmənt/ *n* (**a**) [C] a statement that expresses an idea, etc in a very weak way: *To say that he was displeased is an understatement* (ie He was very angry). (**b**) [U] the action or practice of understating sth: *The Foreign Secretary expressed the government view with typical understatement.*

understudy /ˈʌndəstʌdi/ *n* ~ (**to sb**) a person who learns the part of another actor in a play, etc in order to be able to take her or his place if necessary:

(*fig*) *The Vice-President often acts as understudy to the President.*
▶ **understudy** *v* (*pt, pp* **-died**) to learn a part in a play, etc as an understudy; to act as an understudy to sb: [Vn] *understudy (the role of) Ophelia* ○ *She once understudied Marilyn Monroe.*

undertake /ˌʌndəˈteɪk/ *v* (*pt* **undertook** /-ˈtʊk/; *pp* **undertaken** /-ˈteɪkən/) (*fml*) **1** to make oneself responsible for sth; to engage in sth: [Vn] *undertake a mission/task/project* ○ *She undertook the organization of the whole scheme.* **2** to agree or promise to do sth: [V.to inf] *He undertook to finish the job by Friday.* [also V.that].
▶ **undertaking** /ˌʌndəˈteɪkɪŋ/ *n* **1** a task, etc that one has undertaken (UNDERTAKE 1); an enterprise: *a commercial/financial undertaking* ○ *Getting married is a serious undertaking.* **2** ~ (**that... / to do sth**) (*fml*) a promise or guarantee: *a written undertaking that the loan would be repaid* ○ *She gave a solemn undertaking to accept the court's ruling.*

undertaker /ˈʌndəteɪkə(r)/ (*US also* **mortician**) *n* a person whose business is to prepare dead people for burial, etc and arrange funerals.
▶ **undertaking** /ˈʌndəteɪkɪŋ/ *n* [U] the business of an undertaker.

undertone /ˈʌndətəʊn/ *n* **1** (often *pl*) a low or quiet tone: *speak in an undertone/in (low) undertones.* **2** ~ (**of sth**) a partly hidden feeling, quality, meaning, etc existing as well as the obvious one: *Her speech contained ominous undertones of what was to come.* Compare OVERTONE. **3** a thin or weak colour: *pink with an undertone of mauve.*

undertow /ˈʌndətəʊ/ *n* [sing] a current below the surface of the sea, moving in the opposite direction to the surface current. An example is the current caused by the backward flow of a wave after it breaks on a beach: *The pull of the undertow can drag swimmers out to sea.*

undervalue /ˌʌndəˈvæljuː/ *v* to put too low a value on sb/sth: [Vn] *undervalued share prices* ○ *Learning a foreign language is generally undervalued in this country.* ○ *I felt that my work was being undervalued.*

underwater /ˌʌndəˈwɔːtə(r)/ *adj* situated, used or done below the surface of the water: *underwater 'caves/'cameras/ex'plorers.* ▶ **underwater** *adv*: *The seal disappeared underwater.*

underwear /ˈʌndəweə(r)/ *n* [U] (also **underclothes** [pl], *fml* **underclothing** [U]) clothes worn under other clothes and next to the skin: *thermal underwear* ○ *She packed one change of underwear* (eg a BRA, PANTS(1b) and TIGHTS(1)).

underweight /ˌʌndəˈweɪt/ *adj* below the usual, legal or stated weight: *an underweight baby* ○ *You are only slightly underweight for* (ie in relation to) *your age.* ⇨ note at THIN. Compare OVERWEIGHT 1.

underwent /ˌʌndəˈwent/ *pt* of UNDERGO.

underworld /ˈʌndəwɜːld/ *n* [sing] **1** the part of society that lives by organized crime: *police contacts in the London underworld.* **2** the **underworld** (in myths) a place under the earth where the spirits of dead people live.

underwrite /ˌʌndəˈraɪt/ *v* (*pt* **underwrote** /-ˈrəʊt/; *pp* **underwritten** /-ˈrɪtn/) **1** [Vn] to accept responsibility for an insurance policy, thus guaranteeing payment in case loss or damage occurs. **2** (*finance*) to promise to buy, at an agreed price, the portion of a business company that is not bought by the public: [Vn] *The shares were underwritten by the Bank of England.* **3** to agree to pay for an enterprise: [Vn] *The government underwrote the initial costs of the scheme.*
▶ **'underwriter** *n* a person or an organization that underwrites insurance policies, esp for ships.

undeserved /ˌʌndɪˈzɜːvd/ *adj* unfair; not deserved: *an undeserved punishment* ○ *He has an undeserved reputation for meanness.* ▶ **undeservedly**

/-dɪˈzɜːvɪdli/ *adv*. **undeserving** /ˌʌndɪˈzɜːvɪŋ/ *adj* ~ **(of sth)**: *The film was undeserving of serious consideration* (ie It was very bad).

undesirable /ˌʌndɪˈzaɪərəbl/ *adj* **1** likely to cause trouble or difficulties; not wanted: *The drug has no undesirable side-effects.* ○ *Military intervention is highly undesirable.* **2** (of people, their habits, etc) not welcomed or accepted by others: *She's a most undesirable influence.*
▶ **undesirable** *n* (usu *pl*) an undesirable person: *drunks, vagrants and other undesirables* ○ (*joc*) *The club hires a bouncer to keep out undesirables.*
undesirably /-əbli/ *adv*.

undetected /ˌʌndɪˈtektɪd/ *adj* not discovered or detected: *The disease **went/remained undetected** for several years.* ▶ **undetectable** /-əbl/ *adj*: *This plane is virtually undetectable by radar.*

undeterred /ˌʌndɪˈtɜːd/ *adj* not discouraged or deterred (DETER): *undeterred by failure* ○ *It was raining heavily but he set out undeterred.*

undeveloped /ˌʌndɪˈveləpt/ *adj* **1** not fully grown or developed: *undeveloped fruit/muscles/organs.* **2** not yet used for agriculture, building, etc: *undeveloped land* ○ *undeveloped resources/sites.*

undid /ʌnˈdɪd/ *pt* of UNDO.

undies /ˈʌndiz/ *n* [pl] (*infml*) (esp women's) UNDERCLOTHES: *She appeared in her undies.*

undifferentiated /ˌʌndɪfəˈrenʃieɪtɪd/ *adj* having parts that are not distinct: *an undifferentiated hubbub of voices.*

undignified /ʌnˈdɪɡnɪfaɪd/ *adj* not showing proper dignity; looking foolish: *The meeting turned into an undignified brawl.*

undiluted /ˌʌndaɪˈluːtɪd/ *Brit also* -ˈljuːtɪd/ *adj* not made weaker by being mixed with another substance, feeling, etc: *undiluted wine* ○ *undiluted enthusiasm.*

undiminished /ˌʌndɪˈmɪnɪʃt/ *adj* not made smaller or less: *continue with undiminished vigour.*

undischarged /ˌʌndɪsˈtʃɑːdʒd/ *adj* (*finance*) (of a person who owes money) still legally required to pay back money that is owed: *an **undischarged bankrupt**.* Compare DISCHARGE[1] 3b.

undisciplined /ʌnˈdɪsəplɪnd/ *adj* lacking discipline: *undisciplined children/emotions.*

undisclosed /ˌʌndɪsˈkləʊzd/ *adj* not revealed or made known: *It was bought for an undisclosed sum.*

undiscovered /ˌʌndɪsˈkʌvəd/ *adj* not found or found out about: *a previously undiscovered artist.*

undisguised /ˌʌndɪsˈɡaɪzd/ *adj* not hidden; open and obvious: *undisguised joy/contempt.*

undisputed /ˌʌndɪˈspjuːtɪd/ *adj* **1** that cannot be doubted or questioned: *undisputed facts/rights.* **2** accepted as the best or without EQUAL: *the undisputed champion/market leader.*

undisturbed /ˌʌndɪˈstɜːbd/ *adj* not disturbed or interfered with: *The bones had lain undisturbed for centuries.*

undivided /ˌʌndɪˈvaɪdɪd/ *adj* **IDM** **give one's undivided at'tention (to sth/sb)**; **get/have sb's undivided at'tention** to concentrate fully on sth/sb; to be the one thing or person that sb attends to: *You have my (full and) undivided attention.* ○ *Tom seldom got his mother's undivided attention.*

undo /ʌnˈduː/ *v* (*pt* **undid** /ʌnˈdɪd/; *pp* **undone** /ʌnˈdʌn/) **1** to release knots, buttons, etc; to open a parcel, an envelope, etc: *My zip has **come undone**.* ○ *I can't undo my shoelaces.* ○ *undo some knitting* (ie take the strands apart). Compare DO UP, DO STH UP. **2** to cancel the effect of sth: [Vn] *He undid most of the good work of his predecessor.* ○ *It's not too late to try and undo the damage.*
▶ **undoing** /ʌnˈduːɪŋ/ *n* [sing] (*fml*) a person's ruin or failure, or the cause of this: *lead/contribute to sb's undoing* ○ *Drink was his undoing.*

undone *adj* [pred] **1** not tied or fastened; opened: *Your buttons are all undone.* **2** not done; not finished: *Most of the work was left undone.* **3** (*fml* or *dated*) ruined or defeated: *a great talent undone by drink and drugs.*

undoubted /ʌnˈdaʊtɪd/ *adj* [attrib] not doubted or questioned: *her undoubted ability/talent as an athlete.* ▶ **undoubtedly** *adv*: *The painting is undoubtedly genuine.*

undreamed-of /ʌnˈdriːmd ɒv/ (*also* **undreamt-of** /ʌnˈdremt ɒv/) *adj* not thought to be possible; not imagined: *undreamed-of wealth/success* ○ *We now travel round the world in a way previously undreamt-of.*

undress /ʌnˈdres/ *v* **1** to take off one's clothes: [V] *undress and get into bed.* **2** to remove the clothes of sb/sth: [Vn] *undress a child/doll.*
▶ **undress** *n* [U] (*fml*) having no clothes on: *wander round the bedroom **in a state of undress**.*
undressed *adj* [usu pred] with one's clothes off; naked: *Are you undressed yet?* ○ *It's time the children got undressed.*

undrinkable /ʌnˈdrɪŋkəbl/ *adj* not fit to be drunk, because not pure or of poor quality: *This wine is quite undrinkable.*

undue /ˌʌnˈdjuː; *US* -ˈduː/ *adj* [attrib] (*fml*) more than is right or proper; excessive: *with ˌundue ˈhaste* ○ *show undue concern over sb/sth* ○ *put undue pressure on sb.*

undulate /ˈʌndjuleɪt; *US* -dʒə-/ *v* to have the movement or appearance of a wave: [V] *undulating hills.*
▶ **undulation** /ˌʌndjuˈleɪʃn; *US* -dʒə-/ *n* [C,U] a smooth curving shape or movement: *The hills fell in gentle undulations to the sea.*

unduly /ˌʌnˈdjuːli; *US* -ˈduːli/ *adv* (*fml*) more than is right or proper; excessively: *I hope I'm not being unduly pessimistic.* ○ *Sampras should not worry unduly about his next opponent.*

undying /ʌnˈdaɪŋ/ *adj* [attrib] lasting for ever: *undying love/gratitude/loyalty.*

unearned /ˌʌnˈɜːnd/ *adj* **1** not gained by working: *ˌunearned ˈincome* (eg from interest on investments). **2** not deserved: *ˌunearned ˈpraise.*

unearth /ʌnˈɜːθ/ *v* ~ **sth (from sth)** **1** to find sth in the ground by digging: [Vn] *unearth buried treasure* ○ *The dog has unearthed some bones.* [also Vnpr]. **2** to find sth by chance or by searching; to discover sth and make it known: [Vnpr] *I unearthed my old diaries from the attic.* [Vn] *unearth new facts about Stalin's regime.*

unearthly /ʌnˈɜːθli/ *adj* **1** mysterious or frightening; SUPERNATURAL: *wild, unearthly music* ○ *The silence was unearthly.* **2** [attrib] (*infml*) unreasonable, esp because too early: *In my last job I had to get up at **an unearthly hour**.* Compare UNGODLY 2, UNHOLY 2.

uneasy /ʌnˈiːzi/ *adj* **1(a)** ~ **(about/at sth)** troubled or anxious: *have an uneasy conscience* (ie feel guilty) ○ *I'm uneasy in my mind about the risks involved.* **(b)** making one feel worried; disturbing: *I had an uneasy suspicion that all was not well.* ○ *His look made her feel uneasy.* **2** not safe or settled: *an uneasy truce/silence/relationship* ○ *pass an uneasy night.*
▶ **unease** /ʌnˈiːz/ (*also* **uneasiness** /ʌnˈiːzinəs/) *n* [U] anxiety or DISCONTENT(a): *I waited for her return with **growing unease**.* ○ *There is deep unease among union members.*
uneasily /ʌnˈiːzɪli/ *adv*: *He shifted uneasily in his chair.*

uneatable /ʌnˈiːtəbl/ *adj* (of food, etc) not fit to be eaten. Compare INEDIBLE.

uneaten /ʌnˈiːtn/ *adj* not eaten: *She had left her food uneaten.*

uneconomic /ˌʌnˌiːkəˈnɒmɪk, ˌʌnˌek-/ *adj* not

likely to make a profit; not economic(2): ¡uneconomic ¹factories/¹industries/¹processes.

uneconomical /ˌʌnˌiːkəˈnɒmɪkl, ˌʌnˌek-/ adj not using resources in the best way; not efficient: *uneconomical cars.* ▶ **uneconomically** -kli/ adv.

unedifying /ʌnˈedɪfaɪɪŋ/ adj making one feel disapproval; offensive: *the unedifying sight of her husband getting drunk.*

uneducated /ʌnˈedʒukeɪtɪd/ adj **1** suggesting a lack of the type of education, social background or good manners considered desirable: *uneducated speech/handwriting.* **2** having received little or no formal education at a school.

unemotional /ˌʌnɪˈməʊʃənl/ adj (*sometimes derog*) not having or showing strong feelings: *The English are sometimes accused of being unemotional.*

unemployable /ˌʌnɪmˈplɔɪəbl/ adj not likely to obtain a job because lacking in skills or qualifications.

unemployed /ˌʌnɪmˈplɔɪd/ adj without a paid job but available to work.
▶ **the unemployed** n [pl v] people who do not have a job: *the plight of the nation's unemployed.*

unemployment /ˌʌnɪmˈplɔɪmənt/ n [U] (**a**) the number of people without a paid job: *reduce unemployment* (eg by creating new jobs) ○ *the rising level of unemployment* ○ *the monthly unemployment figures.* (**b**) the state of being without a paid job: *throughout the period of your unemployment.*
■ **unem¹ployment benefit** (*US* also **unem¡ployment compen¹sation**) n [U] money paid by the State or (in the USA) a trade union to a worker who cannot find employment.

unending /ʌnˈendɪŋ/ adj **1** lasting for ever: *unending struggle to stay alive.* **2** (*infml*) frequently repeated: *I'm tired of your unending complaints.*

unenviable /ʌnˈenviəbl/ adj bad or unpleasant; not desirable: *I had the **unenviable task** of telling them about the staff cuts.*

unequal /ʌnˈiːkwəl/ adj **1** in which the different sides, groups, etc do not have the same advantages, rights, etc; not fair or balanced: *an unequal bargain/contest* ○ *unequal pay and conditions* (ie for men and women) ○ *The protesters finally gave up the unequal struggle and went home.* **2** ~ (**in sth**) different in size, amount, etc: *The twins are unequal in height.* **3** [pred] ~ **to sth** (*fml*) not strong, clever, etc enough to do sth: *I feel unequal to the task.* ▶ **unequally** /-kwəli/ adv.

unequalled /ʌnˈiːkwəld/ adj superior to all others: *His record as a show-jumper is unequalled.*

unequivocal /ˌʌnɪˈkwɪvəkl/ adj (*fml*) having only one possible meaning; clear: *an unequivocal statement* ○ *Her answer was an unequivocal 'no'.* ▶ **unequivocally** /-kəli/ adv: *state one's intentions unequivocally.*

unerring /ʌnˈɜːrɪŋ/ adj always right or accurate: *her unerring accuracy/good taste/instinct for a bargain.* ▶ **unerringly** adv.

UNESCO (also **Unesco**) /juːˈneskəʊ/ abbr United Nations Educational, Scientific and Cultural Organization.

unethical /ʌnˈeθɪkl/ adj not morally acceptable; not based on moral principles: *unethical decisions/practices.* ▶ **unethically** /-kli/ adv.

uneven /ʌnˈiːvn/ adj **1** not level, smooth or regular: *an uneven pavement/floor/surface* ○ *The ground was rough and uneven.* **2** not regular or consistent; varying: *have an uneven pulse* ○ *work of uneven quality* ○ *His body trembled and his voice was uneven.* **3** (of a contest, match, etc) with one side much better than the other. ▶ **unevenly** adv. **unevenness** n [U].

uneventful /ˌʌnɪˈventfl/ adj in which nothing very interesting, unusual or exciting happens: *an uneventful journey.*

unexceptionable /ˌʌnɪkˈsepʃənəbl/ adj (*fml*) that

cannot be criticized; entirely satisfactory: *The group's objectives were unexceptionable.*

unexceptional /ˌʌnɪkˈsepʃənl/ adv not outstanding or unusual; ordinary.

unexciting /ˌʌnɪkˈsaɪtɪŋ/ adj dull; not exciting.

unexpected /ˌʌnɪkˈspektɪd/ adj causing surprise because not expected: ¡unexpected ¹guests/¹changes/ re¹sults ○ *His reaction was quite unexpected.*
▶ **the unexpected** n [sing] an event, etc that is not expected: *We must be ready to cope with the unexpected.*
unexpectedly adv: *return unexpectedly* ○ *an unexpectedly high electricity bill.*
unexpectedness n [U].

unexplained /ˌʌnɪkˈspleɪnd/ adj without an adequate explanation; mysterious: *unexplained reasons/motives* ○ *The disappearance of the aircraft remains unexplained.*

unfailing /ʌnˈfeɪlɪŋ/ adj (*approv*) **1** never coming to an end; constant: *her unfailing patience/good humour/devotion.* **2** [usu attrib] that can be relied on; certain: *I know we can count on your unfailing cooperation and support.*
▶ **unfailingly** adv at all times: *unfailingly courteous.*

unfair /ˌʌnˈfeə(r)/ adj **1** ~ (**on/to sb**) not right or just; not fair: ¡unfair ¹treatment/compe¹tition ○ *an ¡unfair de¹cision/com¹parison/ad¹vantage* ○ *She sued her employer for unfair dismissal.* ○ *It's unfair on/to the candidates to raise their hopes too soon.* **2** not following normal rules or principles: ¡unfair ¹play (eg in a football match) ○ ¡unfair ¹trading. ▶ **unfairly** adv: *be unfairly treated.* **unfairness** n [U].

unfaithful /ʌnˈfeɪθfl/ adj ~ (**to sb/sth**) **1** having a sexual relationship with sb other than one's husband, wife or lover: *Her husband is unfaithful to her).* **2** (*dated*) not loyal: *an unfaithful servant.* ▶ **unfaithfulness** n [U].

unfamiliar /ˌʌnfəˈmɪliə(r)/ adj **1** ~ (**to sb**) not known at all or not well-known: *His face was unfamiliar to me.* ○ *working in new and unfamiliar surroundings.* **2** [pred] ~ **with sth** (*fml*) not having knowledge or experience of sth: *I'm unfamiliar with this type of computer.* ▶ **unfamiliarity** /ˌʌnfəˌmɪliˈærəti/ n [U].

unfashionable /ʌnˈfæʃnəbl/ adj not fashionable or popular at a particular time: *live in an unfashionable part of town.*

unfasten /ʌnˈfɑːsn/ n to undo sth that is fastened: [Vn] *unfasten one's belt/cotton/watch.*

unfathomable /ʌnˈfæðəməbl/ adj (*fml*) **1** too strange or difficult to be understood: *an unfathomable mystery.* **2** so deep that the bottom cannot be reached: *the ocean's unfathomable depths.*

unfavourable (*US* **unfavorable**) /ʌnˈfeɪvərəbl/ adj ~ (**to/for sb/sth**) not favourable; showing lack of approval or support; not suitable: *create an unfavourable impression* ○ *The play received unfavourable reviews* ○ *Conditions are unfavourable for sailing.* ▶ **unfavourably** (*US* **-vorably**) adv.

unfeeling /ʌnˈfiːlɪŋ/ adj lacking in care or sympathy for others; not sensitive: *He's an unfeeling brute.* ○ *She often appears cold and unfeeling.*

unfeigned /ʌnˈfeɪnd/ adj not pretended; genuine or sincere: *unfeigned delight.*

unfettered /ʌnˈfetəd/ adj not controlled or restricted; free: *unfettered market forces* ○ *be unfettered by rules and regulations.*

unfinished /ʌnˈfɪnɪʃt/ adj not complete; not finished: *have some unfinished business to attend to.*

unfit /ʌnˈfɪt/ adj **1** ~ (**for sth / to do sth**) (**a**) not of the required or an acceptable standard; not suitable: *food unfit for human consumption* ○ *houses unfit for people to live in.* (**b**) (also **unfitted** /ʌnˈfɪtɪd/) lacking the ability needed; not capable: *She is unfit*

U

for public office ○ *He is unfit to drive in his present state* (eg because he is drunk). **2** not perfectly healthy and fit: *Lack of exercise had made him very unfit.* ▶ **unfitness** *n* [U].

unflagging /ˌʌnˈflægɪn/ *adj* not decreasing in amount or intensity: *unflagging energy/zeal* ○ *listen with unflagging attention.* ▶ **unflaggingly** *adv.*

unflappable /ˌʌnˈflæpəbl/ *adj* (*infml esp Brit*) remaining calm in a crisis: *Even my normally unflappable secretary was showing signs of strain.* ▶ **unflappability** /ˌʌnˌflæpəˈbɪləti/ *n* [U].

unflattering /ʌnˈflætərɪŋ/ *adj* not helping a person's appearance, reputation, etc: *an unflattering hairstyle* ○ *unflattering remarks.*

unflinching /ʌnˈflɪntʃɪŋ/ *adj* not showing fear or reluctance (RELUCTANT) in the face of danger, difficulty, etc: *unflinching courage/determination.* ▶ **unflinchingly** *adv.*

unfocused (also **unfocussed**) /ʌnˈfəʊkəst/ *adj* **1** (of eyes or sight) not looking at anything particular: *her unfocused gaze.* **2** not clearly organized or defined: *The book suffers from an excess of unfocused detail.*

unfold /ʌnˈfəʊld/ *v* **1(a)** to spread flat sth that has been folded: [Vn] *unfold a map/tablecloth* ○ *The bird unfolded its wings.* **(b)** to be able to be pulled open from a folded position: [Vpr] *The seat unfolds into a bed.* [also V]. **2(a)** to be revealed or made known: [V] *as the story/plot unfolds.* **(b)** to reveal sth: [Vn, Vnpr] *She unfolded her plans (to us).*

unforeseen /ˌʌnfɔːˈsiːn/ *adj* not known in advance; unexpected: *ˌunforeseen ˈcircumstances/deˈvelopments/ˈdifficulties.*

unforgettable /ˌʌnfəˈgetəbl/ *adj* (*usu approv*) that will stay for ever in the memory: *an unforgettable experience/moment.*

unforgivable /ˌʌnfəˈgɪvəbl/ *adj* that cannot be forgiven or excused: *unforgivable behaviour* ○ *It was unforgivable of me to mislead you like that.* ▶ **unforgivably** *adv.*

unforgiving /ˌʌnfəˈgɪvɪŋ/ *adj* not willing to forgive people's faults, wrongdoings, etc: *His face was hard and unforgiving.*

unformed /ʌnˈfɔːmd/ *adj* not having developed fully: *have some rough unformed ideas.*

unfortunate /ʌnˈfɔːtʃənət/ *adj* **1** having or showing bad luck: *an unfortunate start to the trip* ○ *I was unfortunate enough to lose my keys.* **2** contrary to what one would have liked; that one regrets: *a most unfortunate choice of words* ○ *It is unfortunate that you missed the meeting.*
▶ **unfortunate** *n* (*esp pl*) (*dated or rhet*) an unfortunate person: *Unlike these unfortunates, I do have a job.*
unfortunately *adv* ~ (**for sb**): *I can't come, unfortunately.* ○ *Unfortunately for him, he was proved wrong.* ○ *The notice is most unfortunately phrased.*

unfounded /ʌnˈfaʊndɪd/ *adj* with no basis in fact: *unfounded rumours* ○ *Her worries were proved largely unfounded.*

unfreeze /ˌʌnˈfriːz/ *v* (*pt* **unfroze** /-ˈfrəʊz/; *pp* **unfrozen** /-ˈfrəʊzn/) **1** to THAW(1a) or allow sth that has been frozen to THAW(1a): [Vn] *unfreeze some chops* [also Vn]. Compare DEFROST, DE-ICE, MELT 1. **2** (*finance*) to remove official controls on the economy, etc: [Vn] *unfreeze assets/prices/trade restrictions.*

unfriendly /ʌnˈfrendli/ *adj* ~ (**to/towards sb**) not kind or sympathetic: *an unfriendly look/gesture/attitude* ○ *He was distinctly unfriendly towards me.*

unfulfilled /ˌʌnfʊlˈfɪld/ *adj* not satisfied; not fulfilled: *She feels unfulfilled in her present job.* ○ *an unfulfilled ambition.*

unfurl /ˌʌnˈfɜːl/ *v* **(a)** (of sth that has been rolled or folded) to spread open: [V] *The leaves were gradually*

unfurling. **(b)** to make sth do this: [Vn] *unfurl a banner/sail.*

unfurnished /ʌnˈfɜːnɪʃt/ *adj* without furniture: *We rented the flat unfurnished.*

ungainly /ʌnˈgeɪnli/ *adj* awkward; not graceful: *He walked in long ungainly strides.* ▶ **ungainliness** *n* [U].

ungodly /ʌnˈgɒdli/ *adj* **1** (*dated or fml*) not showing respect for God; wicked: *lead an ungodly life.* **2** [attrib] (*infml*) unreasonable; not convenient: *Why are you phoning at this **ungodly hour*** (ie so late at night)? Compare UNEARTHLY 2, UNHOLY 2.

ungovernable /ʌnˈgʌvənəbl/ *adj* (*fml*) **1** impossible or difficult to control; violent: *fly into an ungovernable rage/temper* ○ *a man of ungovernable passions.* **2** not easy to govern because of using violence and showing no respect for the law: *The region had become virtually ungovernable.*

ungracious /ʌnˈgreɪʃəs/ *adj* not polite or showing good manners: *an ungracious public remark about her rival* ○ *It was ungracious of me not to acknowledge your help.* ▶ **ungraciously** *adv.*

ungrammatical /ˌʌngrəˈmætɪkl/ *adj* contrary to the rules of grammar: *ungrammatical sentences/utterances.* ▶ **ungrammatically** /-kli/ *adv.*

ungrateful /ʌnˈgreɪtfl/ *adj* ~ (**to sb**) (**for sth**) not showing that one appreciates sb else's help, kindness, etc towards one; not grateful: *You ungrateful child.* ▶ **ungratefully** /-fəli/ *adv.*

unguarded /ʌnˈgɑːdɪd/ *adj* **1** not guarded: *The prisoner was left unguarded.* **2** (of remarks, etc) careless; not well considered: *unguarded gossip* ○ *catch sb in an unguarded moment* (ie When they are not expecting it).

unhappy /ʌnˈhæpi/ *adj* (**-ier, -iest**) **1(a)** sad or miserable; not happy: *look/sound unhappy* ○ *an unhappy occasion/atmosphere/face.* **(b)** ~ (**about/at/with sth**) anxious about or not satisfied with sth: *Investors were unhappy about the risk.* **2** unfortunate; that is or should be regretted: *an unhappy coincidence/chance* ○ *What has led to this unhappy state of affairs?* **3** [usu attrib] (*fml*) not suitable or appropriate: *an unhappy choice of words.*
▶ **unhappily** /-ɪli/ *adv* **1** in an unhappy way: *She sighed unhappily.* **2** contrary to what one would have liked: *Unhappily (for me), my appeal was rejected.*
unhappiness *n* [U].

unhealthy /ʌnˈhelθi/ *adj* **1** not having or showing good health: *an unhealthy complexion* ○ *unhealthy-looking plants* ○ (*fig*) *the unhealthy state of the economy.* **2** harmful to health: *an unhealthy climate/diet* ○ *living in damp unhealthy conditions.* **3** abnormal: *show an unhealthy interest in death.* ▶ **unhealthily** /-ɪli/ *adv*: *eat very unhealthily.* **unhealthiness** *n* [U].

unheard /ʌnˈhɜːd/ *adj* [usu pred] **(a)** with no one willing to pay attention and take action: *My protests went unheard.* **(b)** not heard: *a previously unheard piece of music.*
■ **unheard-of** /ʌnˈhɜːd ɒv/ *adj* not previously known or done; very unusual: *It was almost/virtually unheard-of for anyone to complain.*

unheeded /ʌnˈhiːdɪd/ *adj* heard or noticed but not responded to: *Their warnings went unheeded.*

unhelpful /ʌnˈhelpfl/ *adj* not helpful: *make an unhelpful suggestion.* ▶ **unhelpfully** *adv.*

unheralded /ʌnˈherəldɪd/ *adj* with no advance information or warning: *He arrived totally unheralded.*

unhesitating /ʌnˈhezɪteɪtɪŋ/ *adj* immediate; without delay or doubt: *an unhesitating response.* ▶ **unhesitatingly** *adv*: *He replied unhesitatingly.*

unhindered /ʌnˈhɪndəd/ *adj* with nothing stopping the progress of sb/sth: *have unhindered access to the files.*

unhinge /ʌnˈhɪndʒ/ v (esp passive) to make sb mentally ill: [Vn] *be unhinged by grief* ○ *The shock unhinged his mind.*

unholy /ʌnˈhəʊli/ adj [attrib] **1** wicked or dangerous; harmful to the interests of other people: *an* **unholy alliance** *between architects and planners.* **2** (*infml*) (used as an intensifier) very great; terrible: *leave things in an unholy mess* ○ *making an unholy row.*

unhook /ʌnˈhʊk/ v ~ sth (from sth) to remove sth from a hook; to undo the hooks of sth: [Vnpr] *unhook a picture from the wall* [Vn] *She unhooked her bra.*

unhoped-for /ʌnˈhəʊpt fɔː(r)/ adj not hoped for or expected: *an unhoped-for piece of good luck.*

unhurried /ʌnˈhʌrid/ adj calm and relaxed; not done, etc too quickly: *unhurried movements* ○ *a nice unhurried lunch.*

unhurt /ʌnˈhɜːt/ adj [usu pred] not hurt or harmed: *The driver escaped unhurt.*

unhygienic /ˌʌnhaɪˈdʒiːnɪk/ adj not clean, and therefore harmful to health: *unhygienic food preparation.*

uni- comb form having or consisting of one: *unilateral* ○ *unisex.*

UNICEF /ˈjuːnɪsef/ abbr United Nations Children's Fund (the branch of the United Nations concerned with the health and education of children throughout the world).

unicorn /ˈjuːnɪkɔːn/ n (in myths) an imaginary animal like a horse with one long horn on its forehead. ⇨ picture at COAT OF ARMS.

unidentifiable /ˌʌnaɪˈdentɪfaɪəbl/ adj that cannot be identified: *unidentifiable noises.*

unidentified /ˌʌnaɪˈdentɪfaɪd/ adj that has not been identified: *an unidentified species of insect* ○ *information from unidentified sources.*

■ ˌuniˌdentified ˌflying ˈobject (*abbr* UFO) n = FLYING SAUCER.

uniform¹ /ˈjuːnɪfɔːm/ n [C, U] the special set of clothes worn by all members of an organization or a group at work, or by children at school: *a military/police/nurse's uniform* ○ *soldiers/sailors in uniform* ○ *The hat is part of (the) school uniform.*

▶ **uniformed** adj wearing uniform: *uniformed security guards.*

uniform² /ˈjuːnɪfɔːm/ adj not varying; the same in all cases and at all times: *of uniform length/size/shape/colour* ○ *be kept at a uniform temperature.* ▶ **uniformity** /ˌjuːnɪˈfɔːməti/ n [U, sing]: *the drab uniformity of the modern world* ○ *Among teenagers the pressures for uniformity are strong.* ○ *There is a broad uniformity in working hours throughout the industry.* **uniformly** adv: *Reaction to the cuts was uniformly hostile.* ○ *The practice was not uniformly adopted until the late 19th century.*

unify /ˈjuːnɪfaɪ/ v (*pt, pp* **-fied**) to join or link people or things together to form one unit, or to make them similar to each other: [Vn] *an attempt to unify the nation* ○ *a unified transport system* ○ *Is religion a unifying force?* ▶ **unification** /ˌjuːnɪfɪˈkeɪʃn/ n [U]: *the unification of Germany.*

unilateral /ˌjuːnɪˈlætrəl/ adj done by or affecting one person, group or country without the agreement of another or the others: *take unilateral action* ○ *unilateral decisions/declarations* ○ *unilateral disarmament.* Compare BILATERAL, MULTILATERAL. ▶ **unilaterally** /-rəli/ adv: *a decision taken unilaterally.*

unimaginable /ˌʌnɪˈmædʒɪnəbl/ adj that cannot be imagined; very great: *poverty on an unimaginable scale* ○ *People behave in a way that would have been unimaginable twenty years ago.* ▶ **unimaginably** adv.

unimaginative /ˌʌnɪˈmædʒɪnətɪv/ adj not having

or showing imagination: *His work is sound but totally unimaginative.*

unimpaired /ˌʌnɪmˈpeəd/ adj not spoilt or damaged: *unimpaired vision.*

unimpeachable /ˌʌnɪmˈpiːtʃəbl/ adj (*fml approv*) that cannot be doubted or questioned: *evidence from an unimpeachable source* ○ *She has an unimpeachable moral character.* ▶ **unimpeachably** /-əbli/ adv.

unimpeded /ˌʌnɪmˈpiːdɪd/ adj with nothing blocking or stopping sth: *a seat with an unimpeded view of the stage.*

unimportant /ˌʌnɪmˈpɔːtnt/ adj not important: *He hates wasting time on unimportant details.* ○ *I'm a very unimportant member of the organization.*

unimpressed /ˌʌnɪmˈprest/ adj ~ (by/with sb/sth) not impressed: *We were distinctly unimpressed by/with the food in the hotel.*

unimpressive /ˌʌnɪmˈpresɪv/ adj not creating a good or strong impression: *In their first match the team's performance was unimpressive.*

uninformative /ˌʌnɪnˈfɔːmətɪv/ adj not providing enough information: *The notes were brief and uninformative.*

uninformed /ˌʌnɪnˈfɔːmd/ adj not having or showing sufficient knowledge or information about sth: *an uninformed view/opinion/judgement* ○ *Her colleagues had deliberately kept her uninformed.*

uninhabited /ˌʌnɪnˈhæbɪtɪd/ adj with no people living there: *an uninhabited island.*

uninhibited /ˌʌnɪnˈhɪbɪtɪd/ adj (of a person's behaviour, actions, etc) showing that one is not worried about the reactions of others; natural: *uninhibited laughter.* ▶ **uninhibitedly** adv.

uninitiated /ˌʌnɪˈnɪʃieɪtɪd/ adj without special knowledge.

▶ **the uninitiated** n [pl v] people without special knowledge or experience: *To the uninitiated, the system seems extremely complicated.*

uninspired /ˌʌnɪnˈspaɪəd/ adj not imaginative or inspiring; dull: *an uninspired speech/performance/painting.*

uninspiring /ˌʌnɪnˈspaɪərɪŋ/ adj not producing interest or excitement: *The book is fascinating, despite its uninspiring title.*

unintelligent /ˌʌnɪnˈtelɪdʒənt/ adj not intelligent; not clever: *a very unintelligent remark.*

unintelligible /ˌʌnɪnˈtelɪdʒəbl/ adj ~ (to sb) impossible to understand: *a pop song with totally unintelligible lyrics* ○ *What they were saying was unintelligible to me.* ▶ **unintelligibly** /-əbli/ adv.

unintentional /ˌʌnɪnˈtenʃənl/ adj not done, etc deliberately: *unintentional humour/rudeness.* ▶ **unintentionally** adv.

uninterested /ʌnˈɪntrəstɪd/ adj ~ (in sb/sth) having no interest or feelings about sb/sth because one does not find them/it interesting: *He is completely uninterested in anything to do with politics.* ⇨ note at INTEREST².

uninterrupted /ˌʌnˌɪntəˈrʌptɪd/ adj without a break; with nothing stopping or blocking sth: *have an uninterrupted view of the mountains* ○ *It's a place where I can work uninterrupted by the telephone.* *She spoke uninterrupted for two hours.*

uninviting /ˌʌnɪnˈvaɪtɪŋ/ adv not attractive: *The hotel room was bare and uninviting.*

union /ˈjuːnɪən/ n **1** [C] (**a**) = TRADE UNION: *union leaders/members/officials.* (**b**) an association or a club formed by uniting people or groups: *the Rugby Union* ○ *members of the Students' Union.* (**c**) a group of states or countries which join together: *the former Soviet Union.* **2** [U, sing] ~ (of A with B / between A and B) the action of uniting two or more things, groups, etc or the state of being united: *work towards monetary union* ○ *support the union between*

U

our two parties/the union of our party with yours. **3**
(*fml*) (**a**) [U] the state of being in agreement or
harmony: *live together in perfect union.* (**b**) [C] an
example of this, esp a marriage: *a happy union,
blessed with six children.*

▶ **unionize, -ise** /-aɪz/ *v* to organize people into a
trade union (TRADE¹): [Vn] *a unionized workforce.*
unionization, -isation /ˌjuːniənaɪˈzeɪʃn; US -nəˈz-/
n [U]: *a high level of unionization within the steel
industry.*

■ **the ˌUnion ˈJack** *n* [sing] the national flag of the
United Kingdom.

unionist /ˈjuːniənɪst/ *n* (**a**) a member of a trade
union (TRADE¹) or a supporter of trade unions. (**b**)
Unionist a person who supports political union, esp
between Britain and Northern Ireland. ▶ **unionism**
/ˈjuːniənɪzəm/ *n* [U].

unique /juˈniːk/ *adj* **1**(**a**) unlike anything else; being the only one of its type: *a unique design* ○
Everyone's fingerprints are unique. (**b**) better or
greater than any other; special: *a unique opportunity*
○ *be in a* **unique position** *to do sth* ○ *a unique
ability/achievement.* **2** [pred] ~ **to sb/sth** belonging
to or connected with only one person, group or
thing: *psychological processes unique to humans* ○
The wallaby is unique to Australia. **3** (*infml*) very
unusual: *a rather unique little restaurant.* ▶
uniquely *adv*: *a uniquely difficult situation* ○ *She is
uniquely suited to the job.* **uniqueness** *n* [U].

unisex /ˈjuːnɪseks/ *adj* designed for and used by
both sexes: *unisex fashions* ○ *a unisex hairdresser's
salon.*

unison /ˈjuːnɪsn, ˈjuːnɪzn/ *n* **IDM** **in unison (with
sb/sth)** saying, singing or doing the same thing at
the same time as sb else: *The last verse will be sung
in unison.* ○ *'Do you want to go to the beach?' 'Yes!'
they shouted in unison.*

unit /ˈjuːnɪt/ *n* **1** a single thing, person or group that
is complete in itself, although it can be part of sth
larger: *a family unit* ○ *a course book with twenty
units.* **2** a fixed amount or number used as a standard of measurement: *a unit of currency* ○ *The metre is
a unit of length.* ○ *a bill for fifty units of electricity.* **3**
a group of people who perform a special function in
a larger organization: *an inˌtensive ˈcare unit in a
hospital* ○ *a training/research unit.* **4** a small machine that performs a special function or that is part
of a larger machine: *a ˌwaste diˈsposal unit* ○ *the
central ˈprocessing unit in a computer.* **5** a piece of
furniture or equipment, that is designed to fit with
others and has a particular use: *matching kitchen
units* ○ *storage units.* **6**(**a**) the smallest whole number; the number 1: *The number 34 consists of three
tens and four units.* (**b**) any whole number from 0 to
9: *a column for the tens and a column for the units.*
▶ **unitary** /ˈjuːnətri; US -teri/ **1** single; of a unit(1):
the unitary family ○ *present a unitary image.* **2**
combining or combined in one group: *unitary policing* ○ *unitary development plans.*

■ **ˌunit ˈprice** *n* the price charged for each single
item of goods of the same type.

ˌunit ˈtrust (*Brit*) (US **mutual fund**) *n* a company
that invests money provided by its members in
various organizations and schemes. The fund of
money is divided into units that individuals can buy
or sell: *Investing in a unit trust reduces risks for
small investors.*

Unitarian /ˌjuːnɪˈteəriən/ *n, adj* (**a**) (a member) of the
Christian religious sect which rejects the doctrine
of the TRINITY(1) and believes that God is one person: *the Unitarian Church.* ▶ **Unitarianism** /-ɪzəm/
n [U].

unite /juˈnaɪt/ *v* **1** ~ (**sb/sth**) (**with sb/sth**) to become or make people or things become one; to come
or bring people or things together: [Vn] *the common
interests that unite our two countries* [V.to inf] *The*

two parties have united to form a coalition. [Vnpr]
*After three years in prison, he was again united with
his wife and family.* **2** ~ (**in sth / doing sth**) to act or
work together: [Vpr] *We should unite in fighting
poverty and disease.* [also V].

▶ **united** *adj* **1** joined together for a common purpose: *present a united front to the opposition* ○ *The
party is united behind its leaders.* **2** joined politically: *the campaign for a united Ireland* ○ *the United
States of America.* **3** joined together by love or
sympathy: *a very united family.* **unitedly** *adv*.

■ **the Uˌnited ˈKingdom** *n* [sing] (*abbr* (**the**) **UK**)
England, Scotland, Wales and Northern Ireland. ⊏>
note at BRITISH.

the Uˌnited ˈNations *n* [sing or pl *v*] (*abbr* (**the**)
UN) an organization of many countries formed to
encourage peace in the world and to deal with problems between nations.

the Uˌnited ˈStates (of Aˈmerica) *n* [sing or pl *v*]
(*abbrs* (**the**) **US, USA**) a large country in N America
consisting of 50 states and the District of Columbia.

unity /ˈjuːnəti/ *n* **1** [U] the state of being united or in
agreement: *live together in unity* ○ *political/national/
economic unity.* **2** [U] (in art, etc) the state of presenting a complete and pleasing whole: *The design
lacks unity.* **3** [C] a thing consisting of parts that
form a whole. **4** [U] (*mathematics*) the number 1.

Univ *abbr* University: *London Univ* ○ *Univ of Buffalo.*

universal /ˌjuːnɪˈvɜːsl/ *adj* connected with, affecting
or done by all people or things in the world or in a
particular group: *universal suffrage* (ie the right of
all the people in a country to vote) ○ *There is universal agreement on this issue.* ○ *Such beliefs are by no
means universal.*

▶ **universality** /ˌjuːnɪvɜːˈsæləti/ *n* [U].

universally /-səli/ *adv* by everyone or in every
case: *be universally accepted/admired/believed/
recognized* ○ *The rules do not apply universally.*

universe /ˈjuːnɪvɜːs/ *n* **1 the universe** [sing] everything that exists, including the earth, the stars, the
planets, space, etc. **2** [C] a system of stars, planets
etc: *Are there other universes outside our own?*

university /ˌjuːnɪˈvɜːsəti/ *n* the highest level of educational institution, in which students study for
degrees and academic research is done: *the university of East Anglia* ○ *a university student/lecturer/
professor* ○ *She's studying medicine at Edinburgh
University.* ○ *He's hoping to go to university next year.*
⊏> note at SCHOOL¹.

unjust /ˌʌnˈdʒʌst/ *adj* not just; not deserved: *an
unjust law/accusation/dismissal.* ▶ **unjustly** *adv*: *be
treated unjustly by the authorities* ○ *an unjustly neglected composer.*

unjustifiable /ˌʌnˈdʒʌstɪfaɪəbl/ *adj* that cannot be
justified or excused: *unjustifiable behaviour/
expenditure* ○ *take an unjustifiable risk.* ▶ **unjusti-
fiably** /-əbli/ *adv*.

unjustified /ˌʌnˈdʒʌstɪfaɪd/ *adj* not justified; not necessary: *She received a lot of unjustified criticism.*

unkempt /ˌʌnˈkempt/ *adj* (esp of a person's hair or
clothes) not kept tidy: *a long ˌunkempt ˈbeard* ○ *his
unkempt appearance* ○ *The garden looks rather unkempt.*

unkind /ˌʌnˈkaɪnd/ *adj* ~ (**to sb/sth**) not friendly or
thoughtful (THOUGHT²); cruel: *an unkind remark* ○
What an unkind thing to say! ○ *Don't be so unkind to
your brother.* ▶ **unkindly** *adv*: *He treated her very
unkindly.* ○ *My remarks were not meant unkindly.*
unkindness *n* [U].

unknowable /ˌʌnˈnəʊəbl/ *adj* that cannot be
known: *an unknowable secret* ○ *God is unknowable.*

unknowing /ˌʌnˈnəʊɪŋ/ *adj* [usu attrib] not being
aware; not knowing: *He was the unknowing cause of
all the misunderstanding.* ▶ **unknowingly** *adv*: *She
had unknowingly picked up the wrong suitcase.*

unknown /ˌʌnˈnəʊn/ adj ~ (**to sb**) **1** not known or identified: *The side-effects of the drug are as yet unknown (to scientists).* ∘ *The accident was due to unknown causes.* **2** not famous or well known: *The parts are all played by unknown actors.* **IDM** an ˌunknown ˈquantity a person or thing whose qualities are not yet known: *The new sales director is still a bit of an unknown quantity.* **unknown to sb** without the knowledge of sb: *Quite unknown to me, she'd gone ahead and told him.*
▶ **unknown** n (**a**) (usu **the unknown**) [sing] things or places that are not known about: *a journey into the unknown* ∘ *fear of the unknown.* (**b**) [C] a person who is not well known: *The leading role is played by a complete unknown.* (**c**) [C] an unknown factor: *There are still many unknowns about the US proposals.* (**d**) [C] (*mathematics*) a quantity that is not yet determined: *x and y are unknowns.*

unlace /ˌʌnˈleɪs/ v [Vn] to undo the laces of shoes, boots, etc.

unladen /ˌʌnˈleɪdn/ adj (of a vehicle) not loaded: *a lorry with an ˌunladen ˈweight of 3000 kilograms.*

unlawful /ˌʌnˈlɔːfl/ adj (fml) against the law; illegal: *be charged with unlawful possession of drugs.* ▶ **unlawfully** /-fəli/ adv.

unleaded /ˌʌnˈledɪd/ adj (of petrol) not containing lead: *a car converted to run on unleaded (fuel).* Compare LEAD-FREE.

unlearn /ˌʌnˈlɜːn/ v [Vn] to forget sth bad, wrong, etc deliberately: *You must start by unlearning all the bad habits your previous piano teacher taught you!*

unleash /ˌʌnˈliːʃ/ v ~ **sth** (**against/on/upon sb/sth**) to release sb/sth powerful or destructive: [Vn] *unleash the forces of nuclear power* ∘ *The government's proposals unleashed a storm of angry protest in the press.* [also Vnpr].

unleavened /ˌʌnˈlevnd/ adj (of bread) made without YEAST and so flat and heavy.

unless /ən'les/ conj if...not; on the condition that; except if or when: *You'll fail your exams unless you work harder.* ∘ *Unless something unexpected happens, I'll see you tomorrow.* ∘ *'Would you like some coffee?' 'Not unless you've already made some.'* ∘ *Come at 8 o'clock unless I phone.* ∘ *I sleep with the window open unless it's really cold.*

NOTE Unless cannot be used in conditional sentences which describe imaginary situations or imaginary events: *We would have had a lovely holiday if it hadn't rained.* (This is an imaginary situation because it DID rain so the holiday was NOT lovely.) ∘ *I'll be sorry if she doesn't come to the party.* (This is an imaginary event because you do not know if she will come.) **Unless** and **if...not** can often be used in the same way when you are describing a condition that will end or change a real situation: *You can't play football this evening if you don't do/unless you do your homework.* ∘ *We'll miss the train if we don't hurry/unless we hurry.*
Unless (not **if...not**) is often used to introduce an extra idea after the main statement: *She hasn't got any hobbies — unless you call watching TV a hobby.* ∘ *Have a cup of tea — unless you'd prefer a cold drink?*

unlike /ˌʌnˈlaɪk/ prep **1** different from sth; not like sth: *Her latest novel is quite unlike her earlier work.* ∘ *The scenery was unlike anything I'd seen before.* ∘ *Actually, their house is not unlike our own.* **2** not typical of sb/sth: *It's very unlike him to be so late.* **3** in contrast to sb/sth: *Unlike me, my husband likes to get up early.* ∘ *She was very well behaved, unlike most of the other children.*
▶ **unlike** adj [pred] different: *They are so unlike that nobody would think they're sisters.*

unlikely /ʌnˈlaɪkli/ adj (**-ier, -iest**) **1** not likely to happen; not expected; not probable: *It is unlikely to*

rain/that it will rain. ∘ *They're a most unlikely couple — they seem to like completely different things.* ∘ *His condition is unlikely to improve.* ∘ *In the unlikely event of a breakdown, life-jackets will be provided.* **2** [attrib] difficult to believe: *an unlikely story.* ▶ **unlikelihood** /ʌnˈlaɪklihʊd/, **unlikeliness** /-nəs/ ns [U].

unlimited /ʌnˈlɪmɪtɪd/ adj not limited; very great in number or quantity: *He seems to have unlimited wealth.* ∘ *Our car hire rates include unlimited mileage.*

unlined /ˌʌnˈlaɪnd/ adj **1** (of a garment, etc) without a layer of thin material inside: *an ˌunlined ˈskirt* ∘ ˌunlined ˈcurtains. **2** not marked with lines: ˌunlined ˈpaper ∘ *a smooth, unlined complexion.*

unlisted /ˌʌnˈlɪstɪd/ adj **1** not in a published list, esp of stock exchange (STOCK[1]) prices: *an unlisted company* ∘ *the unlisted securities market.* **2** (*US*) = EX-DIRECTORY.

unlit /ˌʌnˈlɪt/ adj **1** without lighting: *an ˌunlit ˈcorridor.* **2** not set burning: *an ˌunlit cigaˈrette.*

unload /ˌʌnˈləʊd/ v **1**(**a**) ~ (**sth**) (**from sth**) to remove things from a vehicle or ship, esp after they have been transported by it: [V] *We all helped to unload.* [Vnpr] *unload bricks from a lorry* [Vn] *unload a ship.* (**b**) (of vehicles, ships, etc) to have a load removed: [V] *Lorries may only park here when loading or unloading.* **2** to remove bullets from a gun or the film from a camera: [Vn] *an unloaded gun/camera.* **3** ~ **sth/sb** (**on/onto sb**) (*infml*) to pass sb/sth that is not wanted to sb else; to get rid of sb/sth: [Vnpr] *Do you mind if I unload the children onto you this afternoon?* ∘ *Don't unload your problems onto me.* [also Vn]. Compare OFFLOAD.

unlock /ˌʌnˈlɒk/ v **1** to undo the lock of sth using a key: *unlock the front door.* **2** to release sth by, or as if by, unlocking: *attempt to unlock the creative talents of young people* ∘ *exploration to unlock the secrets of the ocean bed.*
▶ **unlocked** adj not locked: *The police have warned motorists not to leave their cars unlocked.*

unlooked-for /ˌʌnˈlʊkt fɔː(r)/ adj (fml) not expected: *unlooked-for developments/happiness.*

unloose /ˌʌnˈluːs/ (also **unloosen** /ʌnˈluːsn/) v to make sth loose; to undo sth: [Vn] *He unloosed his belt.* ⇨ note at LOOSE[1].

unlovely /ˌʌnˈlʌvli/ adj not attractive: *an unlovely building.*

unlucky /ʌnˈlʌki/ adj not lucky; having or bringing bad luck: *Thirteen is often considered an unlucky number.* ∘ *We were very unlucky with the weather on holiday.* ∘ *They were unlucky not to win.*
▶ **unluckily** adv unfortunately: *Unluckily (for him), he did not get the job.*

unmade /ˌʌnˈmeɪd/ adj **1** (of a bed) not neatly arranged for sleeping in. **2** (Brit) (of a road) without a hard surface: *The footpath begins at the end of a narrow unmade road.*

unmanageable /ʌnˈmænɪdʒəbl/ adj that cannot be controlled easily: *dry, unmanageable hair* ∘ *The conflict may grow to unmanageable proportions.*

unmanly /ʌnˈmænli/ adj (of behaviour) not characteristic of or appropriate for men.

unmanned /ˌʌnˈmænd/ adj (of a machine, vehicle, etc) not having or needing sb to control or operate it; operated automatically or without a crew: *an ˌunmanned ˈspacecraft* ∘ *an ˌunmanned ˌlevel ˈcrossing.*

unmannerly /ʌnˈmænəli/ adj (fml) without good manners; not polite.

unmarried /ˌʌnˈmærid/ adj not married; single: *an ˌunmarried ˈmother* ∘ *He remained unmarried all his life.*

unmask /ˌʌnˈmɑːsk; US -ˈmæsk/ v to reveal the true

character of sb/sth; to expose sb/sth: [Vn] *unmask the culprit* ○ *unmask a plot/conspiracy.*

unmatched /ˌʌnˈmætʃt/ *adj* that cannot be matched; without an EQUAL: *an achievement that remains unmatched to this day.*

unmemorable /ʌnˈmemərəbl/ *adj* that cannot be remembered because it was not special; too difficult to remember: *an unmemorable speech.*

unmentionable /ʌnˈmenʃənəbl/ *adj* [usu attrib] too shocking or embarrassing to be mentioned or spoken about: *an unmentionable disease.*

unmet /ˌʌnˈmet/ *adj* (esp of a requirement) not satisfied: *children whose needs remain unmet* ○ *satisfy unmet demand.*

unmindful /ʌnˈmaɪndfl/ *adj* [pred] ~ **of sb/sth** (*fml*) not considering sb/sth; forgetting sb/sth: *be unmindful of the time.*

unmissable /ʌnˈmɪsəbl/ *adj* that one must not miss because it is so good: *an unmissable production.*

unmistakable /ˌʌnmɪˈsteɪkəbl/ *adj* obvious; impossible to mistake for sth else: *the unmistakable sound of her laughter* ○ *The family resemblance is unmistakable.* ▶ **unmistakably** /-əbli/ *adv*: *Her voice was unmistakably English.*

unmitigated /ʌnˈmɪtɪɡeɪtɪd/ *adj* [usu attrib] total; complete; absolute: *an unmitigated disaster* ○ *unmitigated delight.*

unmolested /ˌʌnməˈlestɪd/ *adj* [usu pred] not disturbed or attacked by sb; not prevented from doing sth: *The terrorists operated unmolested for weeks.* ○ *They allowed him to leave unmolested.*

unmoved /ˌʌnˈmuːvd/ *adj* [pred] **1** not affected by feelings of pity, sympathy, etc: *It's impossible to remain unmoved by the reports of the famine.* **2** in the same position: *Share prices remained unmoved.*

unnamed /ˌʌnˈneɪmd/ *adj* (esp of a person) whose name is not given or not known: *works by an unnamed artist* ○ *information from an unnamed source.*

unnatural /ʌnˈnætʃrəl/ *adj* **1** different from what is normal or expected; not natural: *unnatural behaviour* ○ *It is unnatural for the weather to be so warm in April.* **2** different from usual and generally accepted behaviour: *unnatural desires/vice.* **3** not genuine: *an unnatural laugh/voice.* ▶ **unnaturally** /-rəli/ *adv*: *Not unnaturally, she was greatly upset by her father's sudden death.* ○ *The house was unnaturally quiet.*

unnecessary /ʌnˈnesəsri; *US* -seri/ *adj* (**a**) not needed or desirable: *All that preparation was quite unnecessary.* ○ *My presence at the meeting was unnecessary.* (**b**) [usu attrib] more than is necessary; excessive: *go to unnecessary expense* ○ *take an unnecessary risk* ○ *suffer unnecessary pain.* (**c**) (of remarks, etc) not required in a situation and likely to be offensive: *an unnecessary reference to his previous marriage.* ▶ **unnecessarily** /ʌnˈnesəsərəli; *US* ˌʌnˌnesəˈserəli/ *adv*: *unnecessarily complicated instructions* ○ *You're worrying quite unnecessarily.*

unnerve /ʌnˈnɜːv/ *v* to make sb lose confidence or courage; to make sb feel nervous: [Vn] *His silence unnerved me.* ▶ **unnerving** *adj*: *an unnerving silence* ○ *She found the whole experience rather unnerving.* **unnervingly** *adv*: *The models were unnervingly lifelike.*

unnoticed /ˌʌnˈnəʊtɪst/ *adj* [usu pred] not observed or noticed: *She slipped out of the meeting unnoticed.* ○ *His kindness did not go unnoticed.*

unnumbered /ˌʌnˈnʌmbəd/ *adj* not marked with a number: *unnumbered theatre tickets/seats.*

UNO /ˈjuːnəʊ/ *abbr* United Nations Organization. See also UN.

unobtainable /ˌʌnəbˈteɪnəbl/ *adj* that cannot be obtained: *Unfortunately, it is unobtainable in most shops.* ○ (*Brit*) *I keep getting the unobtainable tone* (ie on the telephone).

unobtrusive /ˌʌnəbˈtruːsɪv/ *adj* (*usu approv*) not too obvious or easily noticeable: *an unobtrusive design* ○ *a shy, unobtrusive man* ○ *She tried to make herself unobtrusive so that she could overhear their conversation.* ▶ **unobtrusively** *adv*: *The buildings blend unobtrusively into the surrounding countryside.*

unoccupied /ˌʌnˈɒkjupaɪd/ *adj* **1** empty; not occupied: *find an unoccupied table* ○ *unoccupied hospital beds* ○ *The house had been left unoccupied for several years.* **2** (of a region or country) not under the control of foreign troops: *unoccupied territory.* **3** not busy: *My grandmother was never unoccupied for long.*

unofficial /ˌʌnəˈfɪʃl/ *adj* not accepted or approved by a person or people in authority; not official: *an ˌunofficial ˈstrike* ○ *an ˌunofficial ˈstatement.* ▶ **unofficially** /-ʃəli/ *adv*.

unopposed /ˌʌnəˈpəʊzd/ *adj* not opposed or stopped by sb/sth: *She was elected unopposed.* ○ *The bill was given an unopposed second reading in Parliament.*

unorthodox /ʌnˈɔːθədɒks/ *adj* different from what is usual, traditional or acceptable: *unorthodox beliefs/opinions/methods* ○ *He's a rather unorthodox teacher.* Compare HETERODOX.

unpack /ˌʌnˈpæk/ *v* ~ (**A from**) **B**; ~ (**A**) to take out things packed in a bag, case, etc: [V, Vn] *We unpacked (our suitcases) as soon as we arrived.* [Vn, Vnpr] *unpack one's books/clothes (from the case).*

unpaid /ˌʌnˈpeɪd/ *adj* **1** not yet paid: *an ˌunpaid ˈbill/ˈdebt.* **2**(**a**) (of people) not receiving payment for work done: *an ˌunpaid ˈbaby-sitter.* (**b**) done or taken without payment: *do ˌunpaid ˈwork for charity* ○ *take unpaid leave.*

unpalatable /ʌnˈpælətəbl/ *adj* (*fml*) **1** ~ (**to sb**) (of ideas, suggestions, etc) not easy to accept: *unpalatable advice/facts/truths* ○ *face an unpalatable choice.* **2** not pleasant to taste.

unparalleled /ʌnˈpærəleld/ *adj* so great, etc that it has no EQUAL: *unparalleled beauty/courage/strength/ success* ○ *an economic crisis unparalleled in modern times.*

unparliamentary /ˌʌnˌpɑːləˈmentri/ *adj* contrary to the accepted rules of behaviour in Parliament: *unparliamentary language.*

unpatriotic /ˌʌnˌpætriˈɒtɪk/ *adj* not supporting one's own country.

unpick /ˌʌnˈpɪk/ *v* to take out stitches from sth: [Vn] *unpick a hem/seam* ○ *I had to unpick all the stitching and start again.*

unplaced /ˌʌnˈpleɪst/ *adj* not one of the first three to finish in a race or contest: *The horse was unplaced in its first four races.*

unplayable /ˌʌnˈpleɪəbl/ *adj* **1** (in sport, of a ball, etc) too well hit by one's opponent to return; too difficult to play. **2** (of ground) not in a fit condition to be played on: *Heavy rain made the pitch virtually unplayable.* **3**(**a**) (of music) too difficult to be played. (**b**) (of an instrument) too old or damaged to be played.

unpleasant /ʌnˈpleznt/ *adj* not pleasant: *unpleasant smells/weather* ○ *an unpleasant surprise* ○ *I found his manner extremely unpleasant.* ▶ **unpleasantly** *adv*.

unpleasantness *n* [U, C] bad feeling or quarrelling between people; an instance of this: *I don't want any unpleasantness with the neighbours.*

unplug /ˌʌnˈplʌɡ/ *v* (-gg-) to take the plug of a piece of electrical equipment out of the SOCKET(2): [Vn] *Please unplug the TV before you go to bed.* ○ *If I'm very busy, I unplug the phone.* Compare PLUG STH IN.

unpopular /ʌnˈpɒpjələ(r)/ *adj* ~ (**with sb**) not popular; not liked or enjoyed by a person, a group or people in general: *an unpopular author/design/style/leader* ○ *a decision which proved unpopular with most of the residents.* ▶ **unpopularity** /ˌʌnˌpɒpjuˈlærəti/ *n* [U]: *the unpopularity of the present government.*

unprecedented /ʌnˈpresɪdentɪd/ *adj* never having happened, been done or been known before: *crime on an unprecedented scale* ○ *unprecedented levels of unemployment* ○ *a situation unprecedented in the history of the school.*

unpredictable /ˌʌnprɪˈdɪktəbl/ *adj* (**a**) that cannot be predicted: *unpredictable weather* ○ *an unpredictable result.* (**b**) (of a person) whose behaviour cannot be predicted: *unpredictable moods* ○ *You never know how she'll react: she's so unpredictable.*

unpremeditated /ˌʌnpriːˈmedɪtertɪd/ *adj* not planned in advance: *an unpremeditated attack/murder.*

unprepared /ˌʌnprɪˈpeəd/ *adj* not ready or prepared in advance: *You caught me unprepared.* ○ *I was completely unprepared for his reaction.*

unprepossessing /ˌʌnˌpriːpəˈzesɪŋ/ *adj* not making a good or strong impression; not attractive: *a man of unprepossessing appearance* ○ *an unprepossessing little office.*

unpretentious /ˌʌnprɪˈtenʃəs/ *adj* (*approv*) not trying to appear special, clever, important, etc: *written in a simple and unpretentious style* ○ *He's one of the most unpretentious people I've ever met.*

unprincipled /ʌnˈprɪnsəpld/ *adj* without moral principles; dishonest: *unprincipled behaviour* ○ *an unprincipled and selfish man.*

unprintable /ʌnˈprɪntəbl/ *adj* (of words or comments) too offensive or shocking to be printed: *shout unprintable insults at sb.*

unproblematic /ˌʌnˌprɒbləˈmætɪk/ *adj* not having or causing problems: *Relations between the two countries are unproblematic.*

unproductive /ˌʌnprəˈdʌktɪv/ *adj* not producing enough; not producing the desired result: *an unproductive discussion/meeting.* ▶ **unproductively** *adv.*

unprofessional /ˌʌnprəˈfeʃənl/ *adj* **1** (esp of behaviour) not reaching or opposed to the standards expected in a particular profession: *be dismissed for unprofessional conduct.* **2** (of a piece of work, etc) not done with the skill or care of a trained professional: *He made a very unprofessional job of the wallpapering.* ▶ **unprofessionally** /-ʃənəli/ *adv*: *act unprofessionally.*

unprofitable /ʌnˈprɒfɪtəbl/ *adj* **1** not making enough financial profit: *unprofitable industries.* **2** not bringing any benefit; wasted: *unprofitable study.* ▶ **unprofitably** *adv.*

unprompted /ʌnˈprɒmptɪd/ *adj* (of an answer or action) not said or done, etc as the result of a suggestion or request: *an unprompted offer of help.*

unpronounceable /ˌʌnprəˈnaʊnsəbl/ *adj* (of a word, esp a name) too difficult to pronounce.

unproven /ʌnˈpruːvn/ *adj* not proved or tested: *unproven theories.*

unprovoked /ˌʌnprəˈvəʊkt/ *adj* (esp of an attack) not caused by anything done or said: *unprovoked aggression/assaults.*

unpublished /ʌnˈpʌblɪʃt/ *adj* not published: *unpublished material/papers.*

unpunished /ʌnˈpʌnɪʃt/ *adj* [pred] not punished: *Such crimes must not go unpunished.*

unqualified /ˌʌnˈkwɒlɪfaɪd/ *adj* **1**(**a**) ~ (**as sth / for sth / to do sth**) without legal or official qualifications for doing sth: *ˌunˌqualified inˈstructors/ˈstaff.* (**b**) [pred] ~ (**to do sth**) (*infml*) not competent or knowing enough to do sth: *an unqualified opinion* ○ *I feel unqualified to speak on the subject.* **2** /ʌnˈkwɒlɪfaɪd/ [usu attrib] not limited or restricted;

total: *deserve unˌqualified ˈpraise* ○ *an unˌqualified sucˈcess* ○ *give sth one's unˌqualified apˈproval.*

unquenchable /ʌnˈkwentʃəbl/ *adj* that cannot be satisfied: *unquenchable desire/ambition/curiosity* ○ *have an unquenchable thirst.*

unquestionable /ʌnˈkwestʃənəbl/ *adj* that cannot be doubted or disputed; certain: *unquestionable honesty/integrity/authority.* ▶ **unquestionably** /-əbli/ *adv*: *This design is unquestionably the best.*

unquestioned /ʌnˈkwestʃənd/ *adj* not doubted or questioned: *unquestioned authority/beliefs/loyalty.*

unquestioning /ʌnˈkwestʃənɪŋ/ *adj* done without asking questions, expressing doubt, etc: *unquestioning obedience/acceptance.* ▶ **unquestioningly** *adv*: *obey orders unquestioningly.*

unquiet /ʌnˈkwaɪət/ *adj* [usu attrib] (*fml*) not calm or at ease: *all the signs of an ˌunquiet ˈmind.*

unquote /ˌʌnˈkwəʊt/ *n* **IDM** **quote (…unquote)** ⇨ QUOTE *n.*

unravel /ʌnˈrævl/ *v* (**-ll-**; *US* **-l-**) **1** to undo twisted, knitted or woven threads; (of such threads) to separate or come undone: [Vn] *try to unravel a great tangle of string* [V] *My knitting has started to unravel.* **2** to come apart; to collapse: [V] *Our plans began to unravel.* **3** to make sth clear; to explain sth: [Vn] *unravel the secrets of the animal kingdom* ○ *Detectives are still trying to unravel the mystery.*

unread /ʌnˈred/ *adj* (of a book, etc) that has not been read: *a pile of ˌunread ˈnewspapers* ○ *The manuscript was returned unread.*

unreadable /ʌnˈriːdəbl/ *adj* **1** (*derog*) (of a book, etc) too dull or too difficult to be worth reading. **2** = ILLEGIBLE.

unreal /ˌʌnˈrɪəl; *US* -ˈriːəl/ *adj* (of an experience) not seeming real; very strange, as if imagined: *The whole evening seemed strangely unreal.* ▶ **unreality** /ˌʌnriˈæləti/ *n* [U]: *An air of unreality hung over the whole ceremony.*

unrealistic /ˌʌnrɪəˈlɪstɪk; *US* -riːə-/ *adj* not realistic; not showing or accepting things as they really are: *unrealistic demands/expectations of sth* ○ *I thought the film was rather unrealistic.* ▶ **unrealistically** *adv.*

unreasonable /ʌnˈriːznəbl/ *adj* (of people or their behaviour) not fair to others; expecting too much; not reasonable: *take an unreasonable risk* ○ *She makes unreasonable demands on her children.* ○ *Am I being unreasonable in asking you to help me?* ▶ **unreasonably** /-əbli/ *adv.*

unreasoning /ʌnˈriːzənɪŋ/ *adj* (*fml*) (of a person or of attitudes, beliefs, etc) not using or guided by reason: *an unreasoning fear/hatred.*

unrelated /ˌʌnrɪˈleɪtɪd/ *adj* not related or connected: *two completely unrelated events* ○ *On holiday I like to do things that are totally unrelated to my work.*

unrelenting /ˌʌnrɪˈlentɪŋ/ *adv* (**a**) not becoming less strong or severe; continuous: *unrelenting criticism/pressure* ○ *Her success came through unrelenting hard work.* (**b**) (of a person) not willing to show pity; cruel: *a stern and unrelenting figure.* ▶ **unrelentingly** *adv*: *unrelentingly cruel.*

unreliable /ˌʌnrɪˈlaɪəbl/ *adj* not reliable; that cannot be trusted: *an unreliable memory* ○ *The trains are notoriously unreliable.* ▶ **unreliability** /ˌʌnrɪˌlaɪəˈbɪləti/ *n* [U].

unrelieved /ˌʌnrɪˈliːvd/ *adj* (*derog*) not changing; continuing: *an unrelieved diet of potatoes* ○ *She sank into a state of unrelieved gloom.*

unremarkable /ˌʌnrɪˈmɑːkəbl/ *adj* ordinary; not special: *an unremarkable childhood/life/building.*

unremarked /ˌʌnrɪˈmɑːkt/ *adj* (*fml*) [usu pred] not noticed: *His absence went unremarked.*

unremitting /ˌʌnrɪˈmɪtɪŋ/ *adj* never stopping: *He will be remembered for his unremitting efforts to*

U

protect wildlife. ▶ **unremittingly** *adv: The rain continued unremittingly.*

unrepeatable /ˌʌnrɪˈpiːtəbl/ *adj* **1** that cannot be repeated or done again: *unrepeatable bargains/offers.* **2** too offensive or shocking to be said again: *unrepeatable swear-words.*

unrepentant /ˌʌnrɪˈpentənt/ *adj* showing no regret for sth bad one has done: *an unrepentant murderer* ○ *He died unrepentant.*

unrepresentative /ˌʌnˌreprɪˈzentətɪv/ *adj* not typical or characteristic of a group: *an unrepresentative sample/minority.*

unrequited /ˌʌnrɪˈkwaɪtɪd/ *adj* (*fml*) (esp of love) not returned or rewarded: *unrequited passion.*

unreserved /ˌʌnrɪˈzɜːvd/ *adj* **1** (of seats, etc) not kept for the use of a particular person; not reserved: *unreserved theatre tickets.* **2** (*fml*) without hiding one's feelings or thoughts; complete: *offer unreserved approval/support/thanks.*
▶ **unreservedly** /ˌʌnrɪˈzɜːvɪdli/ *adv* completely; openly: *apologize/speak unreservedly.*

unresponsive /ˌʌnrɪˈspɒnsɪv/ *adj* ~ (**to sth**) not willing or able to react to sb/sth in a suitable or positive way: *a politician who is unresponsive to the mood of the country* ○ *an unresponsive child.*

unrest /ʌnˈrest/ *n* [U] a state of disturbance in which people are angry or dissatisfied and likely to protest or fight: *political/social unrest.*

unrestrained /ˌʌnrɪˈstreɪnd/ *adj* not controlled: *unrestrained anger/violence.*

unripe /ˌʌnˈraɪp/ *adj* not yet ripe: *unripe bananas.*

unrivalled (*US* **unrivaled**) /ʌnˈraɪvld/ *adj* having no EQUAL; better than everyone or everything else of the same type: *have an unrivalled knowledge of antiques* ○ *The hotel enjoys an unrivalled position overlooking the lake.*

unroll /ʌnˈrəʊl/ *v* **1** to open sth rolled up; (of sth rolled up) to open out: [Vn] *unroll a carpet/map/sleeping-bag* [also V]. **2** (of a series of events) to happen one after the other: [V] *watch events/history unroll.*

unruffled /ʌnˈrʌfld/ *adj* calm: *an unruffled sea* ○ *He remained unruffled by their accusations.*

unruly /ʌnˈruːli/ *adj* not easy to control or manage: *unruly behaviour* ○ *an unruly child/crowd* ○ *unruly hair.* ▶ **unruliness** *n* [U].

unsafe /ʌnˈseɪf/ *adj* not safe; dangerous: *Be careful — the ladder is unsafe.* ○ *The water is unsafe to swim in.*

unsaid /ʌnˈsed/ *adj* [pred] thought but not spoken: *Some things are better left unsaid.*

unsaleable /ʌnˈseɪləbl/ *adj* that cannot be sold because no one wants to buy it.

unsalted /ʌnˈsɔːltɪd, -ˈsɒlt-/ *adj* (esp of food) without added salt: *unsalted butter.*

unsatisfactory /ˌʌnˌsætɪsˈfæktəri/ *adj* not satisfactory; not good enough: *His work is highly unsatisfactory.*

unsaturated /ʌnˈsætʃəreɪtɪd/ *adj* (of fats) not having chemicals combined in a way that is harmful to health; not saturated (SATURATE). Compare POLYUNSATURATED.

unsavoury (*US* **unsavory**) /ʌnˈseɪvəri/ *adj* **1** (of people or their behaviour) offensive or unpleasant: *unsavoury habits* ○ *an unsavoury character/reputation.* **2** having an unpleasant taste or smell.

unscathed /ʌnˈskeɪðd/ *adj* [pred] not hurt: *The hostages emerged from their ordeal unscathed.*

unscientific /ˌʌnˌsaɪənˈtɪfɪk/ *adj* not scientific; not done in a careful logical way: *an unscientific approach to a problem.*

unscramble /ˌʌnˈskræmbl/ *v* to change a word or message in code into a form that can be understood: [Vn] *unscramble a computer password.*

unscrew /ˌʌnˈskruː/ *v* (**a**) to undo sth by turning it or by removing screws: [Vn] *unscrew the door-handle* ○ *There are four screws to unscrew.* (**b**) to undo or become undone by turning: [V] *The lid of this jar won't unscrew.* [Vn] *I can't unscrew the lid.*

unscripted /ʌnˈskrɪptɪd/ *adj* (of a speech, broadcast, etc) made without a prepared script: *a language course based on unscripted dialogues.*

unscrupulous /ʌnˈskruːpjələs/ *adj* without moral principles; not honest or fair: *unscrupulous business methods/practices* ○ *an unscrupulous property developer.* ▶ **unscrupulously** *adv.* **unscrupulousness** *n* [U].

unseat /ˌʌnˈsiːt/ *v* **1** to throw sb off a horse, bicycle, etc: [Vn] *The leading horse stumbled, unseating its rider.* **2** to remove (sb) from a position of power: [Vn] *a move to unseat the party leader.*

unseeded /ʌnˈsiːdɪd/ *adj* not selected as a seed(4) in a sports contest: *unseeded players.*

unseeing /ˌʌnˈsiːɪŋ/ *adj* (*rhet*) with the eyes open, but not noticing anything: *He stared, unseeing, into the distance.*

unseemly /ʌnˈsiːmli/ *adj* (*dated or fml*) (of behaviour, etc) not proper or suitable: *unseemly mirth/violence* ○ *There was an unseemly scramble for the best seats.* ▶ **unseemliness** *n* [U].

unseen /ˌʌnˈsiːn/ *adj* (**a**) without being seen; not visible: *I managed to slip out of the room unseen.* ○ *unseen effects/forces/powers.* (**b**) not previously seen: *unseen dangers/difficulties/obstacles* ○ *an unseen translation in an examination.* **IDM** **sight unseen** ⇨ SIGHT¹.

unselfconscious /ˌʌnselfˈkɒnʃəs/ *adj* not worried about or not aware of what other people think of one's behaviour. ▶ **unselfconsciously** *adv.*

unselfish /ʌnˈselfɪʃ/ *adj* willing to put the needs of others before one's own needs, wishes, etc: *her unselfish devotion to her children.* ▶ **unselfishly** *adv.*

unsentimental /ˌʌnˌsentɪˈmentl/ *adj* not having or expressing tender emotions; not sentimental.

unsettle /ˌʌnˈsetl/ *v* to disturb the normal calm state of sth/sb; to upset sth/sb: [Vn] *Moving house seems to have unsettled the children.*
▶ **unsettled** *adj* (**a**) not calm or relaxed; upset: *an unsettled stomach* ○ *I still feel rather unsettled in my job.* (**b**) that may change: *a period of unsettled weather* ○ *Our plans are still unsettled.* (**c**) (of an argument, etc) not resolved: *unsettled differences of opinion.* (**d**) (of a bill, etc) not yet paid: *unsettled debts.*

unshakeable /ʌnˈʃeɪkəbl/ *adj* (of a feeling or an attitude) that cannot be changed; absolutely firm: *unshakeable confidence/courage/loyalty* ○ *an unshakeable belief in the goodness of humanity.*

unshaven /ʌnˈʃeɪvn/ *adj* not recently shaved: *He looked pale and unshaven.*

unsightly /ʌnˈsaɪtli/ *adj* not pleasant to look at; ugly: *an unsightly scar* ○ *unsightly rubbish tips.*

unskilled /ʌnˈskɪld/ *adj* not having or needing special skill or training: *unskilled workers* ○ *unskilled labour.*

unsociable /ʌnˈsəʊʃəbl/ *adj* not enjoying the company of other people; not friendly. Compare ANTISOCIAL 2.

unsocial /ʌnˈsəʊʃl/ *adj* **1** outside the normal times of working: *work unsocial hours.* **2** = UNSOCIABLE.

unsolicited /ˌʌnsəˈlɪsɪtɪd/ *adj* not asked for: *unsolicited help/advice/support* ○ *unsolicited comments/criticisms* ○ *unsolicited mail* (eg for advertising purposes).

unsolved /ˌʌnˈsɒlvd/ *adj* not solved: *an unsolved mystery/problem.*

unsophisticated /ˌʌnsəˈfɪstɪkeɪtɪd/ *adj* **1** not having or showing much experience of the world and

---

[V.*to* inf] = verb + *to* infinitive   [Vn.inf (no *to*)] = verb + noun + infinitive without *to*   [V.*ing*] = verb + *-ing* form

social situations: *unsophisticated tastes/people*. **2** not complicated or refined; basic: *unsophisticated equipment/methods*.

unsound /ʌnˈsaʊnd/ *adj* **1** in poor condition; weak: *The roof is (structurally) unsound*. **2** containing mistakes; not reliable: ˌunsound ˈreasoning/ˈjudgement/ adˈvice ○ *The idea has been criticized as legally unsound*. **IDM** of ˌunsound ˈmind (*law*) not responsible for one's actions because of a mental illness or condition. ▶ **unsoundness** *n*: *the unsoundness of his argument* ○ *Her unsoundness of mind is evident*.

unsparing /ʌnˈspeərɪŋ/ *adj* ~ (**in sth**) **1** giving freely and generously: *be unsparing in one's efforts*. **2** severe; not caring about people's feelings: *Her descriptions of the poverty and suffering are unsparing and unforgettable*. ▶ **unsparingly** *adv*: *give unsparingly of one's time and money* ○ *He drove himself unsparingly*.

unspeakable /ʌnˈspiːkəbl/ *adj* (*usu derog*) that cannot be described in words, esp because it is so bad: *unspeakable cruelty/suffering*. ▶ **unspeakably** /-əbli/ *adv*.

unspecified /ʌnˈspesɪfaɪd/ *adj* not stated clearly or definitely: *The story takes place at an unspecified date*.

unspectacular /ˌʌnspekˈtækjələ(r)/ *adj* ordinary; not exciting or special: *a nice but unspectacular wedding*.

unstable /ʌnˈsteɪbl/ *adj* **1** likely to move or fall: *an unstable load* (eg on a truck) ○ *unstable walls/ chairs*. **2** likely to change suddenly: *be emotionally/ mentally unstable* ○ *unstable share prices* ○ *The political situation remains highly unstable*.

unstated /ʌnˈsteɪtɪd/ *adj* not stated or declared: *unstated assumptions/reasons*.

unsteady /ʌnˈstedi/ *adj* (**-ier, -iest**) **1** likely to fall, move or shake: *She is still unsteady on her feet after the illness*. ○ *an unsteady hand/voice* ○ *an unsteady ladder*. **2** not regular: *an unsteady pulse* ○ *His work is rather unsteady*. ▶ **unsteadily** /-ɪli/ *adv*: *walk/ move unsteadily*. **unsteadiness** *n* [U]: *I hoped he wouldn't hear the unsteadiness in my voice*.

unstinting /ʌnˈstɪntɪŋ/ *adj* ~ (**in sth**) given or giving freely and generously: *unstinting generosity/ support/praise* ○ *She was unstinting in her efforts to help*. ▶ **unstintingly** *adj*: *She worked unstintingly to help homeless people*.

unstoppable /ʌnˈstɒpəbl/ *adj* (*esp infml*) that cannot be stopped or prevented: *an unstoppable rise in prices* ○ *the unstoppable march of progress*.

unstructured /ʌnˈstrʌktʃəd/ *adj* without structure or organization: *an unstructured meeting/way of life*.

unstuck /ʌnˈstʌk/ *adj* **IDM** ˌcome unˈstuck **1** to become separated from sth to which it was stuck or fastened: *The flap of the envelope had come unstuck*. **2** (*infml*) to fail completely; to fail to achieve what is intended, with bad results: *Their plans came badly unstuck*. ○ *If you keep taking such risks, you'll come unstuck one day*.

unsubstantiated /ˌʌnsəbˈstænʃieɪtɪd/ *adj* (*fml*) stated but not proved to be true by evidence: *unsubstantiated allegations/claims*.

unsuccessful /ˌʌnsəkˈsesfl/ *adj* not successful: *His efforts to get a job were unsuccessful*. ○ *She made several unsuccessful attempts to see him*. ▶ **unsuccessfully** *adv*.

unsuitable /ʌnˈsuːtəbl; *Brit also* -ˈsjuː-/ *adj* ~ (**for sb/sth**) not right or appropriate for a particular person, purpose, occasion, etc: *reject unsuitable applicants* ○ *films that are unsuitable for children*. ▶ **unsuitability** *n* [U]. **unsuitably** *adv*.

unsuited /ʌnˈsuːtɪd; *Brit also* -ˈsjuː-/ *adj* **1** ~ (**to sth / do sth**) not having the required or appropriate qualities for sth: *measures that are unsuited to im-*

prove the economy ○ *He proved unsuited to a position of responsibility*. **2** ~ (**to sb/sth**) so different or opposed as to be unable to exist well together: *Their relationship was an unhappy one because they were totally unsuited (to each other)*.

unsullied /ʌnˈsʌlɪd/ *adj* not spoiled by anything; still pure or in the original state: *the unsullied emotions of childhood* ○ *have an unsullied reputation*.

unsung /ˌʌnˈsʌŋ/ *adj* [usu attrib] not praised or recognized but deserving to be: *the unsung heroes of the war*.

unsupported /ˌʌnsəˈpɔːtɪd/ *adj* **1** not physically supported: *sections of a structure left unsupported*. **2** not supported by evidence or facts: *an unsupported declaration*. **3** not assisted or supported by sb/sth else: *a naval attack unsupported by aircraft*.

unsure /ʌnˈʃʊə(r); *Brit also* -ˈʃɔː(r)/ *adj* [pred] **1** ~ (**of oneself**) having little confidence in oneself: *He's rather unsure of himself*. **2** ~ (**about/of sth**) not knowing sth certainly; uncertain: *I'm unsure of the facts*. ○ *We were unsure (about) who was to blame*.

unsurpassed /ˌʌnsəˈpɑːst/ *adj* better or greater than any other: *The quality of workmanship is unsurpassed*. ○ *crime figures unsurpassed in recent history*.

unsurprised /ˌʌnsəˈpraɪzd/ *adj* [pred] ~ (**at/by sth**); ~ (**to do sth**) not surprised: *She appeared totally unsurprised by the news*. ○ *We were unsurprised to find the house empty*.

unsurprising /ˌʌnsəˈpraɪzɪŋ/ *adj* not causing surprise: *It's unsurprising that people with dogs walk more than others*. ▶ **unsurprisingly** *adv*.

unsuspected /ˌʌnsəˈspektɪd/ *adj* **1** of which one was not previously aware; not predicted or known about: *Then an unsuspected problem arose*. ○ *show previously unsuspected talent*. **2** not suspected of doing sth wrong: *He left quietly, unseen and unsuspected*.

unsuspecting /ˌʌnsəˈspektɪŋ/ *adj* feeling no suspicion; not aware of the presence of danger: *He had crept up on his unsuspecting victim from behind*.

unsustainable /ˌʌnsəˈsteɪnəbl/ *adj* that cannot be maintained at the same rate, level, etc.

unsweetened /ˌʌnˈswiːtnd/ *adj* (of food or drink) without sugar or a similar substance having been added: *unsweetened orange juice*.

unswerving /ʌnˈswɜːvɪŋ/ *adj* ~ (**in sth**) steady or constant; not changing or becoming weaker: *unswerving loyalty/devotion/belief* ○ *He is unswerving in pursuit of his aims*.

unsympathetic /ˌʌnˌsɪmpəˈθetɪk/ *adj* **1** ~ (**to/ towards sb**) not feeling or showing sympathy: *a cold, unsympathetic man* ○ *She tends to be unsympathetic to those less fortunate than herself*. **2** ~ (**to/ towards sth**) not in agreement with sth; not supporting an idea, aim, etc: *He is unsympathetic towards any kind of liberal policy*. ▶ **unsympathetically** *adv*.

unsystematic /ˌʌnˌsɪstəˈmætɪk/ *adj* not organized into a clear and efficient system: ˌunsysteˌmatic ˈworking methods. ▶ **unsystematically** *adv*.

untainted /ʌnˈteɪntɪd/ *adj* ~ (**by sth**) not damaged or spoilt by sth unpleasant or undesirable: *a politician untainted by scandal*.

untalented /ʌnˈtæləntɪd/ *adj* without talent: *an untalented actor*.

untamed /ˌʌnˈteɪmd/ *adj* **1** (of land) still in its original state because people have not changed or cultivated it: *an untamed wilderness*. **2** (of animals) wild; not having been trained by humans: *untamed wildlife*. **3** (of a person) not controlled or influenced by others; behaving freely and naturally: *an untamed genius*.

untangle /ˌʌnˈtæŋgl/ *v* **1** to remove the knots, twisted parts, etc from sth; to free sth that has become twisted: [Vn] *untangle knitting wool* [Vnpr] *She untangled her skirt from the barbed wire.* **2** to make sth that is complicated or confusing clear or understood: [Vn] *untangle a mystery/sb's financial affairs.*

untapped /ˌʌnˈtæpt/ *adj* not yet used or exploited: *an untapped source of wealth/talent* ○ *draw on untapped reserves of strength.*

untenable /ʌnˈtenəbl/ *adj* (of a theory, position, etc) that cannot be defended against attack or criticism; that cannot be maintained: *untenable arguments/claims* ○ *The allegations against him have left his position as minister untenable.*

untested /ˌʌnˈtestɪd/ *adj* not tested; of unknown quality or value: *an untested assumption* ○ *untested medical treatment.*

unthinkable /ʌnˈθɪŋkəbl/ *adj* too unlikely or undesirable to be considered as a possibility: *Defeat was unthinkable.* ○ *To abandon such an old tradition is unthinkable.*

unthinking /ʌnˈθɪŋkɪŋ/ *adj* said, done, etc without proper consideration of the consequences; thoughtless (THOUGHT²): *unthinking remarks/criticisms.* ▶ **unthinkingly** *adv.*

untidy /ʌnˈtaɪdi/ *adj* (**-ier**, **-iest**) **1** not neat or properly arranged: *an untidy desk/kitchen/cupboard* ○ *untidy hair/writing.* **2** (of a person) not doing things in a neat or well organized way: *an untidy worker.* ▶ **untidily** /-ɪli/ *adv.* **untidiness** *n* [U].

untie /ʌnˈtaɪ/ *v* to undo sb/sth that is tied; to remove sth that ties sb/sth: [Vn] *untie a dog/parcel/prisoner* ○ *untie a rope/string/ribbon.*

until /ənˈtɪl/ (also **till**) (*till* more informal; *until* usu preferred in initial position) *conj* (**a**) as far as the time when: *Let's wait until the rain stops.* ○ *Don't start till I arrive.* ○ *Continue in this direction until you see a sign.* (**b**) before the time when sth happens and not after it: *Until she spoke I hadn't realized she was foreign.* ○ *I won't stop shouting until you let me go.* ○ *No names are being released until the relatives have been told.*
▶ **until** (also **till**) *prep* as far as the specified time or event: *wait until tomorrow* ○ *It may last till Friday.* ○ *Nothing happened until 5 o'clock.* ○ *The street is full of traffic from morning till night.* ○ *Until now I have always lived alone.* ○ *She continued working up until her death.* ○ *Don't open it till your birthday.* ○ *She was a bank clerk until the war, when she trained as a nurse.*

untimely /ʌnˈtaɪmli/ *adj* **1** happening too soon or sooner than normal: *her **untimely death** at 25.* **2** happening at a time that is not suitable: *an untimely arrival/remark.*

untiring /ʌnˈtaɪərɪŋ/ *adj* ~ (**in sth**) (*approv*) continuing at the same rate without loss of energy or enthusiasm: *untiring campaigners for peace* ○ *She is untiring in her efforts to help the homeless.*

untitled /ˌʌnˈtaɪtld/ *adj* having no TITLE(1): *an untitled work/poem.*

unto /ˈʌntu, -tə/ *prep* (*arch*) **1** to sth: '*Once more unto the breach, dear friends, once more.*' **2** until sth: *swear to be faithful unto death.*

untold /ˌʌnˈtəʊld/ *adj* **1** [attrib] too many or too much to be counted, measured, etc: *untold suffering/damage* ○ *a man of untold wealth.* **2** not told to anyone: *Theirs is an untold story.*

untouchable /ʌnˈtʌtʃəbl/ *adj* **1** that cannot be touched or affected in any way: *an untouchable world record* ○ *As long as he stays in South America he is untouchable by the British authorities.* **2** (in India) of a HINDU social class (or *caste*) regarded by other classes as the lowest.
▶ **untouchable** *n* a member of the untouchable(2) class.

untouched /ʌnˈtʌtʃt/ *adj* **1** ~ (**by sth**) not affected

or changed in any way: *an island untouched by progress* ○ *Big corporations were untouched by the recession.* **2** not damaged in any way: *Some buildings were left untouched by the hurricane.* **3** (of food) without any eaten: *He left his meal untouched.*

untoward /ˌʌntəˈwɔːd; US ʌnˈtɔːrd/ *adj* (*fml*) not expected and not convenient; unfortunate and awkward: *untoward occurrences* ○ *We all behaved as if nothing untoward had happened.*

untrained /ˌʌnˈtreɪnd/ *adj* not formally trained: *untrained staff* ○ *an untrained pet* ○ *To the untrained eye, the picture is simply a mass of coloured dots.*

untrammelled (*US* also **-meled**) /ʌnˈtræmld/ *adj* (*fml*) not restricted; not restrained: *a life untrammelled by legal restraints.*

untreated /ˌʌnˈtriːtɪd/ *adj* **1** not receiving medical treatment: *If untreated, the illness can become severe.* **2** (of substances) not made safe by chemical or other treatment: *untreated sewage.* **3** (of wood) not treated with substances to preserve it.

untried /ˌʌnˈtraɪd/ *adj* not yet tried or tested to discover quality or value: *She chose two untried actors for the leading roles.*

untrue /ʌnˈtruː/ *adj* **1** not true; contrary to fact: *The allegations were shown to be untrue.* **2** ~ (**to sb/sth**) (*fml*) not loyal or faithful: *She was untrue to him.*

untrustworthy /ʌnˈtrʌstwɜːði/ *adj* that cannot be trusted; not reliable.

untruth /ʌnˈtruːθ/ *n* **1** [C] (*pl* **-truths** /-ˈtruːðz/) (*fml euph*) a statement that is not true; a lie. **2** [U] lack of truth.
▶ **untruthful** /ʌnˈtruːθfl/ *adj* saying or consisting of sth that is not true: *an untruthful man* ○ *untruthful claims.* **untruthfully** /-fəli/ *adv.*

unturned /ˌʌnˈtɜːnd/ *adj* **IDM** **leave no stone unturned** ⇨ STONE.

untutored /ˌʌnˈtjuːtəd; US -ˈtuː-/ *adj* (*fml*) not having been formally taught about sth: *To my untutored ear, your voice sounds almost professional.*

untypical /ʌnˈtɪpɪkl/ *adj* ~ (**of sb/sth**) not typical: *an untypical example* ○ *He behaved in a way that was untypical of him.* ▶ **untypically** *adv.*

unusable /ˌʌnˈjuːzəbl/ *adj* that cannot be used because of being in such poor condition: *My typewriter is now very old and practically unusable.*

unused¹ /ˌʌnˈjuːzd/ *adj* never having been used: *an ˌunused ˈenvelope/stamp.*

unused² /ʌnˈjuːst/ *adj* [pred] ~ **to sth/doing sth** not having experienced sth much or at all and therefore not familiar with it: *We were unused to city life* ○ *to living in a city and found it strange at first.*

unusual /ʌnˈjuːʒuəl/ *adj* **1** rare or different from what is usual or normal: *This bird is an unusual winter visitor in these parts.* ○ *It's unusual for him to be so rude.* **2** (*esp approv*) remarkable or interesting because different from others: *a singer with a most unusual voice.*
▶ **unusually** /-ʒəli/ *adv* **1** to an extent that is different from what is usual or expected: *an unusually high/low rainfall for January.* **2** in a way that is not usual or typical: *Unusually for him, he wore a tie.* ○ *We had an unusually frank conversation.*

unutterable /ʌnˈʌtərəbl/ *adj* [attrib] (*fml*) too great, intense, etc to be expressed in an adequate way in words: *unutterable sadness* ○ *He's an unutterable bore.* ▶ **unutterably** /-əbli/ *adv*: *unutterably weary.*

unvarnished /ʌnˈvɑːnɪʃt/ *adj* **1** not varnished (VARNISH *v*). **2** [attrib] (of a statement, etc) basic or plain, with nothing added or exaggerated: *the plain unvarnished truth.*

unveil /ˌʌnˈveɪl/ *v* **1** to remove a covering from sth, esp as part of a public ceremony: [Vn] *unveil a statue/monument/plaque/portrait.* **2** to show or announce sth publicly for the first time: [Vn] *unveil*

[Vnn] = verb + noun + noun   [V-adj] = verb + adjective   For more help with verbs, see Study pages **B4–8**.

new models at the Motor Show ○ *She unveiled her plans for restructuring the company.* **3** to remove one's VEIL(1); to remove a veil from sth/sb: [V, Vn] *The bride unveiled (herself) at the end of the wedding ceremony.*

unvoiced /ˌʌnˈvɔɪst/ *adj* (of thoughts, etc) not expressed in words.

unwaged /ˌʌnˈweɪdʒd/ *adj* (*Brit euph*) having no paid employment. ▶ **the unwaged** *n* [pl *v*]: *half-price tickets for the unwaged.*

unwanted /ˌʌnˈwɒntɪd/ *adj* not wanted; considered undesirable or of no use; that one wishes to get rid of: *an unwanted pregnancy* ○ *feel unwanted* ○ *give unwanted clothes to charity.*

unwarranted /ʌnˈwɒrəntɪd; *US* -ˈwɔːr-/ *adj* not justified or necessary: *an unwarranted invasion of privacy.*

unwary /ʌnˈweəri/ *adj* not cautious or aware of possible danger, problems, etc: *The land is full of holes and other traps for the unwary walker.* ○ *Unwary buyers may be fooled by this offer.* ▶ **the unwary** *n* [pl *v*]: *Tax is a minefield for the unwary.*

unwashed /ˌʌnˈwɒʃt/ *adj* not washed: *a pile of unwashed dishes.*

unwavering /ʌnˈweɪvərɪŋ/ *adj* not changing or becoming weaker in any way: *unwavering determination/ambition.* ▶ **unwaveringly** *adv.*

unwelcome /ʌnˈwelkəm/ *adj* not wanted, desirable or pleasant; not welcome(1): *an unwelcome visitor* ○ *hear unwelcome news.*

unwelcoming /ʌnˈwelkəmɪŋ/ *adj* **1** (of a person) not friendly towards sb visiting or arriving: *The locals were distinctly unwelcoming.* **2** (of a place) not attractive and appearing uncomfortable to be in: *She went back to her cold unwelcoming house.*

unwell /ʌnˈwel/ *adj* [pred] ill: *She said she was feeling unwell and went home.*

unwholesome /ˌʌnˈhəʊlsəm/ *adj* **1** harmful to health: *an unwholesome climate* ○ *unwholesome food.* **2** not morally acceptable; not considered natural: *unwholesome reading for a child.* **3** appearing not healthy: *an unwholesome pallor.*

unwieldy /ʌnˈwiːldi/ *adj* **1** (of an object) awkward to move or control because of its shape, size or weight: *long, unwieldy poles.* **2** (of a system or group) too big or badly organized to function efficiently: *the unwieldy bureaucracy of centralized government.*

unwilling /ʌnˈwɪlɪŋ/ *adj* ~ (**to do sth**) not wanting to do sth; not willing; RELUCTANT: *They were forced to become unwilling partners in the scheme.* ○ *The public are usually unwilling to accept change.* ▶ **unwillingly** *adv*: *agree unwillingly to a request.* **unwillingness** *n* [U]: *His unwillingness to accept the truth annoyed me.*

unwind /ˌʌnˈwaɪnd/ *v* (*pt, pp* **unwound** /-ˈwaʊnd/) **1** ~ (**sth**) (**from sth**) to become undone after being wound in a ball, etc or round sth; to undo sth that is in this state: [V] *The rope began to unwind and the boat drifted away.* [Vn] *unwind a ball of wool/a reel of thread/a roll of bandage* [Vn, Vnpr] *He unwound the scarf (from his neck).* [also Vpr]. **2** to begin to relax after a period of work or tension: [V] *Music helps me to unwind after a hard day's work.* ○ *After a few drinks, he began to unwind and talk more openly.*

unwise /ˌʌnˈwaɪz/ *adj* not wise; foolish: *an unwise decision/move/step* ○ *It was unwise (of you) to reject his offer.* ▶ **unwisely** *adv.*

unwitting /ʌnˈwɪtɪŋ/ *adj* [attrib] (*fml*) doing sth without being aware of it or intending to do it: *unwitting accomplices in the crime* ○ *his unwitting participation in illegal activities.* ▶ **unwittingly** *adv*: *I think I may have unwittingly offended him.*

unwonted /ʌnˈwəʊntɪd/ *adj* (*fml*) not usual or expected: *He spoke with unwonted candour.*

unworkable /ʌnˈwɜːkəbl/ *adj* not practical or possible to carry out successfully; not FEASIBLE: *an unworkable plan/proposal/scheme.*

unworldly /ʌnˈwɜːldli/ *adj* not interested or involved in the practical or material aspects of life: *an unworldly man/outlook/idealism.*

unworried /ʌnˈwʌrid/ *adj* not worried; calm; relaxed: *appear unworried by criticism.*

unworthy /ʌnˈwɜːði/ *adj* **1** ~ (**of sth/sb**) not deserving sth/sb: *The idea is unworthy of serious consideration.* ○ *I am unworthy of such an honour.* **2** ~ (**of sb/sth**) not acceptable from sb/sth of good character: *conduct unworthy of a public figure.* **3** lacking worth or MERIT(1): *fighting for an unworthy cause.* ▶ **unworthiness** *n* [U].

unwound *pt, pp* of UNWIND.

unwrap /ʌnˈræp/ *v* to undo the covering that wraps sth: [Vn] *unwrap a parcel/present.*

unwritten /ˌʌnˈrɪtn/ *adj* not written down: *It's an unwritten law/rule* (ie one that is based on custom and practice and so generally understood and accepted, although it is not written down or official).

unyielding /ʌnˈjiːldɪŋ/ *adj* ~ (**in sth**) not changed or affected by pressure or influence, etc; firm: *The mattress was hard and unyielding.* ○ *She is unyielding in her opposition to the plan.*

unzip /ˌʌnˈzɪp/ *v* to undo the ZIP that fastens sth; to become undone in this way: [Vn] *unzip one's jeans/a dress* [V] *His jacket unzipped as he ran.*

up¹ /ʌp/ *adv part* For the special uses of **up** in phrasal verbs, look at the verb entries. For example, the meaning of **break up** is given in the phrasal verb section of the entry for **break¹**. **1** to or in an upright position: *I stood up to ask a question.* ○ *He jumped up from his chair.* ○ *It didn't take long to put the tent up.* Compare DOWN¹ 1. **2** to or in a higher place, position, condition, degree, etc: *Lift your head up.* ○ *Pull your socks up.* ○ *We got into the lift and went up.* ○ *Prices are still going up* (ie rising). ○ *Put the book up on the top shelf.* ○ *The sun was coming up* (ie rising) *as we left.* ○ *He lives up in the mountains.* ○ *Drive with the car windows up.* ○ *We were two goals up* (ie ahead of the other team) *at half-time.* Compare DOWN¹ 2. **3** facing upwards: *Lay the cards face up on the table.* ○ *Carry the box this side up.* **4** (of a computer, etc) working; in operation. **5** ~ (**to sb/sth**) to the place where sb/sth is and no further: *He came up (to me) and asked the time.* ○ *She went straight up to the door and knocked loudly.* ○ *A car drove up and he got in.* **6(a)** to an important place, esp a large city: *go up to San Francisco for the day.* **(b)** (*Brit*) to a university, esp Oxford or Cambridge: *She is going up to Oxford in October.* **(c)** to a place in the north of a country: *We're going up to Edinburgh soon.* ○ *They've moved up north.* Compare DOWN¹ 4. **7** into pieces: *She tore the paper up.* ○ *The road is up* (ie with the surface broken or removed while being repaired). **8(a)** completely: *We ate all the food up.* ○ *The stream has dried up.* **(b)** more loudly or clearly: *Turn the radio up.* ○ *Could you speak up, please?* **(c)** more strongly: *The wind is getting up.* **9** (of a period of time) finished; over: *Time's up. Stop writing and hand in your papers.* **10** onto a surface where it is displayed or visible: *hang a picture up* ○ *put/stick/pin up a notice.* **11** out of bed: *It's time to get up!* ○ *I stayed up late* (ie did not go to bed until late) *last night.* **12** (*infml*) happening; going on (esp of sth unusual or unpleasant): *I heard a lot of shouting — what's up?* ○ *I could tell something was up by the look on their faces.* **13** into a closed position: *lock up a door* ○ *Do your coat up, it's cold.* **14** (of hair) into a raised position on top of or at the back of the head: *put one's hair up* ○ *You look nice with your hair up.*

IDM **be up to sb 1** to be sb's duty or responsibility: *It's up to us to help those in need.* ○ *It's not up to you to tell me how to do my job.* **2** to be left to sb to decide: *Shall we go to the cinema or stay at home? It's up to you.* **be up with sb** be a source of discomfort, etc or a cause of illness, etc: *What's up with him? He looks furious.* **not be ¹up to much** to be of poor quality or standard; to be not very good: *His work isn't up to much.* **up against sth** (*infml*) facing problems, difficulties or opposition: *He came up against the local council.* ○ *She's really **up against it** (ie faced with big problems).* **up against sth/sb** in or into contact with sth/sb: *The ladder was leaning up against the wall.* ○ *The passengers were pressed up against each other in the crowded train.* ¸**up and a¹bout** out of bed and active again, esp after illness. ¸**up and ¹down 1** in one direction and then in the opposite direction: *She kept walking up and down outside the house.* **2** moving upwards and downwards: *jump up and down* ○ *The boat bobbed up and down on/in the water.* **3** sometimes good and sometimes bad: *Things have been rather up and down for me recently.* **up before sb/sth** appearing in front of sb in authority for a judgement to be made about sth one has done: *He was/came up before the local magistrate for speeding.* **up for sth 1** due for sth; having reached the point in time when sth is necessary: *My passport is up for renewal.* **2** on offer for sth: *The house is up for auction/sale.* **3** being considered for sth, esp as a candidate: *put oneself up for election* ○ *I'm up for promotion at work.* **up to sth 1** as or to a maximum number or amount: *count up to twenty slowly* ○ *I can take up to six people in my car.* **2** as far as a particular level, number, amount, point, etc: *The temperature went up to 35°.* ○ *House prices are now up to the level of two years ago.* **3** (also **up until sth**) not further or later than sth; until sth: *Read up to page 100.* ○ *Up to now he's been very quiet.* ○ *Up until the war she had never lived alone.* **4** as high or as good as sth: *My exam results were not up to the college's requirements.* ○ *His latest book isn't up to his usual standard.* **5** (also **up to doing sth**) physically or mentally capable of sth: *He's not up to the job.* ○ *I don't feel up to going to work today.* **6** (*infml*) occupied or busy with sth, esp sth bad: *What's he up to?* ○ *I'm sure he's **up to no good** (ie doing sth bad).* ○ *What tricks has she been up to?* **up (with) sb/sth** (used to express support for a person, a group or an institution): *Up (with) the working classes!*

up² /ʌp/ *prep* **1** to or in a higher position somewhere: *run up the stairs* ○ *further up the valley.* **2** along or further along a road, street, etc: *drive up the wrong street* ○ *go up the road to the shops.* **3** towards the source of a river: *a pleasure trip up the Thames.* **IDM** **up and down sth** in one direction and then in the opposite direction along sth: *walk up and down the platform* ○ *look up and down the corridor.* ¸**up ¹yours!** (⚠ *sl*) (said to sb as a way of expressing extreme anger, dislike or contempt, esp as a result of sth they have said or done).

up³ /ʌp/ *adj* **1** [pred] (*infml*) cheerful; happy or excited: *He's been really up since getting that job.* Compare DOWN¹ 1. **2** [attrib] directed or moving upwards: *an up stroke* ○ *the up escalator.*

up⁴ /ʌp/ *v* (**-pp-**) (*infml or joc*) (followed by *and* and another *v*) to get up or move suddenly: [V] *She upped and left without a word.* **2** (*infml*) to increase the price or value of sth: [Vn] ○ *He's upped his offer to £300.* **IDM** ¸**up ¹sticks** (*Brit*) to move with all one's possessions in order to live and work in another place: *They upped sticks and moved to France.*

up⁵ /ʌp/ *n* **1** [sing] the part of a ball's path in which it is still moving upwards after bouncing on the ground: *Try to hit the ball on the up.* **IDM** **be on the** ¸**up-and-¹up** (*infml*) **1** (*Brit*) to be improving, becoming more successful, etc all the time: *Business is on the up-and-up.* **2** (*US*) to be honest or sincere: *She seems to be on the up-and-up.* ¸**ups and ¹downs** good

and bad luck, experiences, events, etc: *We've certainly had our ups and downs.*

up- *pref* (with *ns*, *vs* and their related forms) higher: *upland* ○ *upgrade.*

up-and-coming /ˌʌp ən ¹kʌmɪŋ/ *adj* [usu attrib] (*infml*) making good progress and likely to succeed or become popular: *an ¸up-and-coming young ¹actor.*

upbeat /¹ʌpbiːt/ *adj* cheerful and enthusiastic: *be in an upbeat mood* ○ *The conference ended on a distinctly upbeat note.* Compare DOWNBEAT 1.

upbraid /ʌp¹breɪd/ *v* ~ **sb (for sth / doing sth)** (*fml*) [Vn, Vnpr] to criticize sb severely for doing sth wrong.

upbringing /¹ʌpbrɪŋɪŋ/ *n* (usu *sing*) the treatment and education one receives as a child, esp from parents: *have a strict religious upbringing.*

upcoming /¹ʌpkʌmɪŋ/ *adj* (*esp US*) due to happen or take place soon: *a review of upcoming events.*

up-country /ˌʌp¹kʌntri/ *adj, adv* in or towards the INTERIOR(2) of a country, esp a large one: ¸*up-country ¹districts* ○ *travel up-country.*

update /ˌʌp¹deɪt/ *v* **1** to make sth more modern or UP-TO-DATE, eg by adding new parts to it or replacing old parts: [Vn] *update production methods/computer systems* ○ *update a dictionary/file/law.* **2** ~ **sb (on sth)** to give sb the latest information about sth: [Vn, Vnpr] *I updated the committee (on our progress).* ► **update** /¹ʌpdeɪt/ *n*: *an update on the political situation* ○ *Maps need regular updates.*

up-end /ˌʌp¹end/ *v* to place sth upside down or so that one of its ends is at the top: [Vn] *I up-ended the crate and sat on it.* ○ (*fig*) *He was up-ended (ie knocked over) as he ran towards the goal.*

upfield /ˌʌp¹fiːld/ *adj, adv* (in sport) in or to a position at the opponents' end of the field: *kick the ball upfield.*

upfront /ˌʌp¹frʌnt/ *adj* **1** honest; open; frank: *be upfront about one's private life.* **2** [usu pred] (of a payment) in advance: *upfront charges.* See also UP FRONT (FRONT).

upgrade /ˌʌp¹greɪd/ *v* ~ **sb/sth (to sb/sth)** to raise sb/sth to a higher grade or rank: [Vn] *I'm hoping to get my job upgraded.* [Vnpr] *She was upgraded to (the post of) senior designer.* Compare DOWNGRADE. ► **upgrade** /¹ʌpgreɪd/ *n*: *a major upgrade of hotel facilities.*

upheaval /ʌp¹hiːvl/ *n* [C, U] a great or complete change involving disturbance, confusion, trouble, etc: *political/social upheavals* ○ *Moving to a new house causes such (an) upheaval.*

uphill /ˌʌp¹hɪl/ *adj* **1** sloping upwards: *an ¸uphill ¹road/¹climb* ○ *The last mile is all uphill.* **2** [attrib] needing great effort; very difficult: *an ¸uphill ¹task/¹struggle.* ► **uphill** *adv* up a slope: *walk uphill.*

uphold /ʌp¹həʊld/ *v* (*pt, pp* **upheld** /-¹held/) **1** to support or confirm a decision, belief, etc which has been questioned: [Vn] *uphold a verdict/sentence at the end of an appeal* ○ *uphold a policy/principle.* **2** to maintain a custom, etc: *uphold ancient traditions.* ► **upholder** *n*: *upholders of tradition.*

upholster /ʌp¹həʊlstə(r)/ *v* ~ **sth (in/with sth)** to provide furniture with padding (PAD²), springs and covering material: [Vn, Vnpr] *upholster a sofa (in leather).* ► **upholsterer** /-stərə(r)/ *n* a person whose trade is to upholster furniture.

upholstery /-stəri/ *n* [U] **1** upholstered seats, etc or the material used to make these. **2** the trade of an upholsterer.

upkeep /¹ʌpkiːp/ *n* [U] the cost or process of keeping sth in good condition and repair: *I can't afford the upkeep of a large house and garden.*

upland /¹ʌplənd/ *n* (often *pl*) the higher or INLAND(a) parts of a country: *the barren upland(s) of central Spain* ○ *an upland region.*

uplift /ˌʌpˈlɪft/ *v* to raise sb's spirits, so that they feel cheerful or have hope: [Vn] *an uplifting sermon* ○ *We were/felt uplifted by his inspiring words.*
▶ **uplift** /ˈʌplɪft/ *n* [U] the action of uplifting sb or the feeling of being uplifted: *an uplift in team morale.*
uplifted *adj* (of hands, arms, etc) raised; lifted up: *sing with arms uplifted.*

up-market /ˌʌp ˈmɑːkɪt/ *adj* (of products, services, etc) designed to appeal to or satisfy people in the higher social classes: *an upmarket 'restaurant/ 'shop/'car.* Compare DOWN-MARKET. ▶ **up-market** *adv*: *go/move up-market.*

upon /əˈpɒn/ *prep* (*fml*) = ON[1] 1,4b,9,10,13,18. **IDM** (almost) uˈpon one (of sth in the future) approaching; about to arrive or happen: *Christmas is almost upon us again.*

upper /ˈʌpə(r)/ *adj* [attrib] **1** higher in place or position; situated above another, esp similar, part: *the upper lip/arm/jaw* ○ *one of the upper rooms/ floors/windows.* **2** situated on higher ground or to the north or far INLAND: *Upper Egypt* ○ *the upper (reaches of the) Thames.* **3** higher in rank or wealth: *the upper levels of society* ○ *salaries/people in the upper income bracket.* Compare LOW[1] 6. **IDM** gain, get, etc the ˌupper ˈhand to get, etc the advantage or control over sb: *The progressive wing of the party has now clearly gained the upper hand.* **a stiff upper lip** ▷ STIFF[1].
▶ **upper** *n* **1** the part of a shoe or boot above the sole: *leather uppers.* **2** (*sl*) a drug that stimulates, giving energy and a cheerful feeling. Compare DOWNER 1. **IDM** on one's ˈuppers (*Brit infml*) having very little money; poor.
■ ˌupper ˈcase *n* [U] capital letters (CAPITAL[1] 3), esp in printing or typing: *an upper-case 'A'.* Compare LOWER CASE.
the ˌupper ˈclass *n* [CGp] the people who belong to the highest social class, esp because of being born into it: *belong to the upper class(es)* ○ *The upper class has/have always had influence.* ○ *an ˌupper-class 'accent/'background.*
the ˌupper ˈcrust *n* [Gp] (*infml or joc*) the highest social class; the upper class: *belong to the upper crust.*
ˈupper-cut *n* (in boxing) a punch delivered upwards with the arm bent.
the ˌUpper ˈHouse *n* [sing] the higher, usu smaller, branch of a national assembly, eg the House of Lords in Britain or the Senate of the US Congress.

uppermost /ˈʌpəməʊst/ *adj* highest in place, position or importance: *the uppermost branches of a tree* ○ *executives in the uppermost levels* ○ *These thoughts were uppermost in my mind.*
▶ **uppermost** *adv* on or to the highest or most important position: *Put the box down with this side uppermost.* ○ *She has always placed her career uppermost.*

uppity /ˈʌpəti/ *adj* (*infml derog*) behaving as if one is more important than other people; ARROGANT.

upraised /ˌʌpˈreɪzd/ *adj* (esp of a part of the body) raised in the air: *They saluted him with ˌupraised 'arms.*

upright /ˈʌpraɪt/ *adj* **1** with a straight back rather than bent; straight up; ERECT[1](1): *his upright bearing/posture/stance.* **2** strictly honest or honourable: *an upright citizen* ○ *be upright in one's business dealings.* **IDM** bolt upright ▷ BOLT[3].
▶ **upright** *adv* in or into an upright(1) position: *sit/ stand/hold oneself upright.*
upright *n* **1** a post or rod placed upright(1), esp as a support: *The ball bounced off the left upright of the goal.* **2** = UPRIGHT PIANO.

■ ˌupright piˈano (also **upright**) *n* a piano with the strings arranged vertically (VERTICAL). ▷ picture at PIANO[1].

uprising /ˈʌpraɪzɪŋ/ *n* an act by a group of people suddenly and violently starting to fight against those in power; a rebellion (REBEL): *an armed uprising.*

uproar /ˈʌprɔː(r)/ *n* [U,sing] **1** a lot of noise made by people shouting, esp because they are angry: *The meeting ended in (an) uproar.* **2** a large amount of public criticism and argument: *There was (an) uproar over the tax increases.*
▶ **uproarious** /ʌpˈrɔːriəs/ *adj* [esp attrib] (**a**) very noisy, esp with a lot of laughter: *an uproarious welcome/evening/debate.* (**b**) very funny. **uproariously** *adv*: *laugh uproariously* ○ *uproariously funny.*

uproot /ˌʌpˈruːt/ *v* **1** to pull a tree, plant, etc out of the ground together with its roots: [Vn] *trees uprooted by the floods.* **2** ~ **oneself** (from sth ...) to leave or make sb leave a place where one has settled or where they have settled: [Vnpr] *They decided to uproot themselves from their London home and move to the country.* [also Vn].

upset /ʌpˈset/ *v* (-tt-; *pt, pp* upset) **1** to make sb/ oneself unhappy or worried; to cause sb emotional distress: [Vn] *Don't upset yourself — no harm has been done.* ○ *The sight of animals suffering always upsets me.* ○ *It upsets me when you say things like that.* ○ *The accident was a most upsetting experience.* **2** to cause sb to feel ill in the stomach; to have a bad effect on the stomach: [Vn] *Cheese often upsets her/ her stomach.* **3** to cause sth to go wrong; to cause sth not to proceed in the normal or intended way: [Vn] *upset the balance of power* ○ *Bad weather has upset the train timetable.* **4** to turn or knock sth over, esp accidentally: [Vn] *upset one's cup/the milk/a plate of biscuits* ○ *A large wave upset the boat.* **IDM** upset the/sb's ˈapple-cart to spoil a plan or ruin an arrangement.
▶ **upset** /ˌʌpˈset/ *adj* **1** unhappy, worried or disappointed about sth: *I'm very upset about having to miss the party.* ○ *He was upset that she hadn't written.* **2** (of the stomach) disturbed and not working properly, esp because of sth drunk or eaten: *have an ˌupset 'stomach.*
upset /ˈʌpset/ *n* **1** [C,U] an act of upsetting sb/sth or the state of being upset: *That's the second upset I've had this week.* ○ *The affair caused her much emotional upset.* **2** [C] a stomach disorder: (*infml*) *in bed with a tummy upset.* **3** [C] (in sport) an unexpected result: *Their victory was quite an upset.*

upshot /ˈʌpʃɒt/ *n* [sing] the ~ (of sth) the final result or outcome: *The upshot of it all was that he resigned.*

upside-down (also **upside down**) /ˌʌpsaɪd ˈdaʊn/ *adj, adv* **1** with the upper part underneath instead of on top: *That picture is upside down.* ○ *Turn the plate upside down.* ○ *Why is he reading his newspaper upside-down?* **2** in or into total disorder or confusion: *I'm redecorating my room so everything's upside down at the moment.* ○ *Burglars had turned the house upside-down.*

upstage /ˌʌpˈsteɪdʒ/ *adj, adv* at or towards the back of a theatre stage: *an ˌupstage 'door* ○ *move upstage.*
▶ **upstage** *v* to take attention from sb towards oneself by doing sth more noticeable: [Vn] *She upstaged her more experienced team-mates with a dazzling display of skill.*

upstairs /ˌʌpˈsteəz/ *adv* up the stairs; to or on an upper floor: *walk/go upstairs* ○ *I thought I heard a noise upstairs.* ○ *I was upstairs when it happened.* Compare DOWNSTAIRS. **IDM** kick sb upstairs ▷ KICK[1].
▶ **upstairs** *adj* situated on an upper floor: *an ˌupstairs 'room/'window.*

U

[V.speech] = verb + direct speech   [V.*that*] = verb + *that* clause   [V.*wh*] = verb + *who, how,* etc clause

upstairs n [sing] (*infml*) the upper floor of a house, etc: *A bungalow does not have an upstairs.*

upstanding /ˌʌpˈstændɪŋ/ *adj* [attrib] (*fml or rhet*) **1** honest, respectable and of good reputation: *upstanding members of the city council.* **2** strong and healthy: *a fine upstanding young man.*

upstart /ˈʌpstɑːt/ *n* (*derog*) a person who has suddenly risen to wealth or a high position, esp one considered ARROGANT and annoying by others: *I'm not taking orders from that young upstart!* ○ *upstart bureaucrats.*

upstate /ˌʌpˈsteɪt/ *adv, adj* in or to the part of a State that is far from its main cities, esp the northern part: ˌupstate New ˈYork ○ *We go upstate every summer for our vacation.*

upstream /ˌʌpˈstriːm/ *adv, adj* in the direction from which a river, etc flows; against the current: *row/swim/walk upstream* ○ *Factories upstream (from us) are polluting the water.* Compare DOWNSTREAM.

upsurge /ˈʌpsɜːdʒ/ *n* (usu *sing*) (a) ~ (**in sth**) a sudden great increase in sth: *an upsurge in sales* ○ *the recent upsurge in violent crime.* (b) ~ (**of sth**) a sudden appearance of sth, esp a strong feeling: *an upsurge of anger/enthusiasm.*

upswing /ˈʌpswɪŋ/ *n* ~ (**in sth**) an upward movement or TREND; an increase in sth previously decreasing: *This event led to an upswing in the party's popularity.* Compare UPTURN.

uptake /ˈʌpteɪk/ *n* [sing] an act of taking in a substance; the amount of a substance taken in: *the body's oxygen uptake.* **IDM** ˌquick/ˌslow on the ˈuptake quick/slow to understand what is meant or what is happening: *You'll have to explain it to me carefully — I'm not very quick on the uptake.*

uptight /ˌʌpˈtaɪt/ *adj* ~ (**about sth**) (*infml*) **1** tense or nervous: *get uptight about exams/interviews.* **2** annoyed or HOSTILE(1b): *He gets very uptight at the mere mention of the subject.*

up-to-date /ˌʌp tə ˈdeɪt/ *adj* **1** modern or fashionable: ˌup-to-date ˈclothes/iˈdeas/ˈbooks/ˈmethods. **2** having or including the most recent information: *an* ˌup-to-date ˈdictionary/reˈport. See also UP TO DATE (DATE¹).

up-to-the-minute /ˌʌp tə ðə ˈmɪnɪt/ *adj* [attrib] **1** very modern or fashionable: ˌup-to-the-minute ˈtechˈnology. **2** having or including the most recent information possible: *an* ˌup-to-the-minute acˈcount of the ˈriots.

uptown /ˌʌpˈtaʊn/ *adj, adv* (*US*) in or to the outer districts of a town: ˌuptown New ˈYork ○ *go/drive/stay uptown.* Compare DOWNTOWN.

upturn /ˈʌptɜːn/ *n* ~ (**in sth**) an upward movement or TREND in business, luck, etc; an improvement: *an upturn in the sales figures* ○ *Her luck seems to have taken an upturn/to be* **on the upturn.** Compare UPSWING.
  ▶ **upturned** /ˌʌpˈtɜːnd/ *adj* turned upwards or UPSIDE DOWN(1): *a slightly* ˌupturned ˈnose ○ *sitting on an* ˌupturned ˈcrate.

upward /ˈʌpwəd/ *adj* [usu attrib] moving, leading or pointing to a higher place, point or level: *an upward glance/climb* ○ *the upward trend in prices.*
  ▶ **upward** (also **upwards** /-wədz/) *adv* towards a higher place, point or level: *The missile rose slowly upward into the sky.* ○ *Property prices are moving upwards.* ⇨ note at FORWARD².
  ˈ**upwards** *of prep* more than a specified approximate number: *Upwards of a hundred people came to the meeting.*
  ■ ˌ**upward moˈbility** *n* [U] movement into a higher social class or level of income. ˌ**upwardly ˈmobile** *adj* showing or wanting to show upward mobility: *upwardly mobile young executives.*

upwind /ˌʌpˈwɪnd/ *adj, adv* ~ (**of sb/sth**) in the direction from which the wind is blowing: *sail*

upwind ○ *If we're upwind of the animal it may smell our scent.*

uranium /juˈreɪniəm/ *n* [U] (*symb* **U**) a chemical element. Uranium is a heavy grey RADIOACTIVE metal used esp as a source of nuclear energy. ⇨ App 7.

Uranus /ˈjʊərənəs, jʊˈreɪnəs/ *n* the planet 7th in order from the sun.

urban /ˈɜːbən/ *adj* [usu attrib] of, relating to or living in a city or town: *urban areas* ○ *urban life* ○ *urban renewal (ie the repairing of old buildings, etc)* ○ *the urban population/poor.* Compare RURAL.
  ▶ **urbanize, -ise** /-aɪz/ *v* (esp passive) to make a rural area, a village, etc more like a town or city by building a lot of new houses, factories, etc: [Vn] *urbanized localities* ○ *Africa's most urbanized country.* **urbanization, -isation** /ˌɜːbənaɪˈzeɪʃn; *US* -nəˈz-/ *n* [U].

urbane /ɜːˈbeɪn/ *adj* (*fml*) having or showing refined manners; elegant and SOPHISTICATED 1: *an urbane man/manner.* ▶ **urbanely** *adv.* **urbanity** /ɜːˈbænəti/ *n* [U].

urchin /ˈɜːtʃɪn/ *n* **1** (also ˈ**street urchin**) (*derog*) a very poor and dirty child with no home, living in a town or city: *little urchins tugging at our clothes.* **2** = SEA URCHIN.

Urdu /ˈʊədu; *Brit also* ˈɜːduː/ *n* [U] a language related to HINDI but with many Persian words, used esp in Pakistan.

-ure *suff* **1** (with *vs* forming *ns*) the action or process of: *closure* ○ *failure* ○ *seizure.* **2** (with *vs* or *ns* forming *ns*) a group or thing having a specific function: *legislature* ○ *prefecture.*

urea /jʊəˈrɪə/ *n* [U] a colourless substance contained esp in URINE, which can be manufactured for use as a fertilizer (FERTILIZE).

urethra /jʊəˈriːθrə/ *n* (*pl* **urethras**) (*anatomy*) the tube by which URINE passes from the BLADDER(1) out of the body. ⇨ picture at REPRODUCTION.
  ▶ **urethral** *adj.*

urethritis /ˌjʊərəˈraɪtɪs/ *n* [U] an infection of the urethra.

urge /ɜːdʒ/ *v* **1** to try hard to persuade sb to do sth: [Vn.to inf] *He urged me to reconsider my decision.* [V.*that*] *She urged that there should be no violence during the demonstration.* [also Vn]. **2** ~ **sth** (**on/upon sb/sth**) to recommend or advise sth strongly: [Vn] *I urge caution.* [Vn.to inf] *Motoring organizations are urging drivers not to travel today unless it is absolutely necessary.* [Vnpr] *The government urged on/upon industry the importance of low pay settlements.* **3** to make an animal move more quickly, using force or encouragement: [Vnpr, Vnadv] *urge a horse up a slope/forward* [also Vnp]. **PHR V** ˌ**urge sb ˈon (to sth)** to encourage sb to do, start or continue sth: *supporters urging their team on* ○ *Urged on by his colleagues, he stood for election.*
  ▶ **urge** *n* a strong desire or impulse: *sexual urges* ○ *get/have/feel a sudden urge to travel.*

urgent /ˈɜːdʒənt/ *adj* **1** requiring immediate attention or action: *an urgent message/case/appeal for food aid* ○ *It is most urgent that I see you today.* ○ *My car is* **in urgent need of** *repair.* **2** showing that one believes sth needs immediate attention or action: *speak in an urgent whisper.* ▶ **urgency** /-dʒənsi/ *n* [U]: *a matter of the greatest urgency* ○ *There was a note of urgency in her voice.* **urgently** *adv*: *Medical supplies are urgently needed.* ○ *He said he wanted to see me urgently.*

urine /ˈjʊərɪn/ *n* [U] the waste liquid that collects in the BLADDER(1) and is then passed from the body.
  ▶ **urinal** /ˈjʊərɪnl; *Brit also* jʊəˈraɪnl/ *n* (a) a bowl or other FITTING²(1) attached to the wall in a public toilet for men, into which they urinate (URINE). (b) a room containing such bowls, etc.
  urinary /ˈjʊərɪnəri; *US* -neri/ *adj* [usu attrib] of urine or the parts of the body through which it passes: *a urinary infection* ○ *the urinary tract.*

urinate /'jʊərɪneɪt/ v [V] to pass urine out from the body.

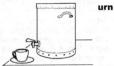

urn

urn /ɜːn/ n **1** a tall vase, usu with a stem and a base, esp one used for holding the ashes of a cremated (CREMATE) person. ⇨ picture. **2** (esp in compounds) a large metal container with a tap, in which tea, coffee, etc is made or from which it is served, eg in a CAFÉ or CANTEEN(1): *a tea urn.* ⇨ picture.

us /əs; *strong form* ʌs/ *pers pron* (used as the object of a v or a prep; also used by itself independently and after be) **1** me and another or others; me and you: *She gave us a picture as a wedding present.* ○ *We'll take the dog with us.* ○ *Hello, it's us back again!* Compare WE. **2** (*Brit sl*) me: *Give us the newspaper, will you?* **3** (*infml*) the company, organization, etc for which one works: *How long have you been with us now?*

US /ˌjuː 'es/ *abbr* United States (of America): *a US citizen.*

USA /ˌjuː es 'eɪ/ *abbr* United States of America: *a visa for the USA.* ⇨ note at AMERICAN.

USAF /ˌjuː es eɪ 'ef/ *abbr* United States Air Force.

usage /'juːsɪdʒ, 'juːzɪdʒ/ n **1** [U,C] the way in which words are used in a language: *current English usage* ○ *It's not a word in common usage.* **2** [U] the way in which sth is used; the extent to which sth is used: *statistics on drug usage* ○ *With normal usage, the equipment should last for many years.*

use¹ /juːz/ v (*pt, pp* used /juːzd/) **1** ~ sth (for sth / doing sth); ~ sth (as sth) to employ sth for a purpose; to do sth with: [Vn] *Do you know how to use a drill?* ○ *May I use your phone?* ○ *Use your common sense!* ○ *words that are only used in certain contexts* ○ *What kind of toothpaste do you use?* [Vnpr] *A hammer is used for driving in nails.* ○ *She uses her unmarried name for professional purposes.* [Vn-n] *use a saucer as an ashtray* [Vn.to inf] *We used the money to buy a new car.* ○ *They used force to persuade him.* **2** to exploit sb/sth to one's own advantage: [Vn] *He felt he'd been used.* [Vnpr, Vn.to inf] *She simply used us for her own ends/to get what she wanted.* [Vn-n] *He used the bad weather as an excuse for not coming.* **3** to do sth with some of a substance and so reduce the total amount of it: [Vnadv] *Use the milk sparingly, there's not much left.* [Vnpr] *We only used a gallon of petrol for the journey.* See also USED¹,², USED TO. **IDM** **I, etc could use sth** (*infml*) I, etc would very much like sth: *Phew! I could use a drink!* **use one's 'loaf** (*Brit infml*) to use one's intelligence: *Don't keep asking me what to do, use your loaf!* **PHRV** ,**use sth 'up** to use all of sth, so that no more is left: *use up all one's strength/energy* ○ *I've used up all the glue.* ○ *She used up the chicken bones to make soup.*

▶ **usable** /'juːzəbl/ *adj* [pred] that can be used; that is fit to be used: *The tyres are worn but still usable.*

use² /juːs/ n **1** [U, sing] ~ (of sth) the action of using sth or the state of being used: *the use of electricity for heating* ○ *an ingenious use of wind power* ○ *the use of force* ○ *keep sth for one's own use* ○ *funds for use in emergencies* ○ *a liquid for external use only* (ie that must not be swallowed) ○ *build cabins for use as holiday homes* ○ *This car park is for the use of customers only.* **2** [C,U] a purpose for which sth is used; a way in which sth can be used: *a tool with many uses* ○ *find a (new) use for sth* ○ *the use of language in a legal context.* **3** [U] ~ (of sth) **(a)** the

right or opportunity to use sth, eg sth belonging to sb else: *allow a tenant use of the garden* ○ *I have the use of the car this week.* **(b)** the power or ability to use one's mind or body: *have full use of one's mental faculties* ○ *lose the use of one's legs* (ie become unable to walk). **4** [U] value or advantage: *What's the use of worrying about it?* ○ *Its no use pretending you didn't know.* ○ *Do you want this old typewriter? It's of no use to me.* **5** [U] (*fml*) custom, practice or habit: *Long use has accustomed me to it.* **IDM** **come into / go out of 'use** to start/stop being used: *When did this word come into common use?* ○ *The city's trams will go out of use next year.* **have its/their/one's 'uses** to be useful but not ideal: *I don't like that cupboard but I suppose it has its uses.* **have no 'use for sb** to be unable to tolerate sb; to dislike sb: *I've no use for people who don't try.* **have no 'use for sth** to consider that one no longer needs sth: *I've no further use for my old cassette player, so you can have it.* **in 'use** being used: *We couldn't play tennis because the courts were all in use.* **make 'use of sth/sb** to use or benefit from sth/sb: *Make full use of every chance you have to speak English.* ○ *She has not made good use of her talents.* **put sth to good 'use** to gain benefit from sth one already has: *He'll be able to put his languages to good use in the new job.*

used¹ /juːzd/ *adj* [usu attrib] that has belonged to or been used by sb previously; second-hand (SECOND¹): *used clothes* ○ *a used-car dealer.*

used² /juːst/ *adj* ~ **to sth / doing sth** familiar with or accustomed to sth as a result of experience of it: *be quite used to hard work/working hard* ○ *The food here seemed strange at first but I soon became/got used to it.*

NOTE Compare **be used to**, **get used to** and **used to**.

To **be used to something / to doing something** means that you are familiar with something or with doing a particular thing, so that it is not a problem: *The people on this island are used to tourism.* ○ *I was not used to catching buses; I usually drove everywhere.*

To **get used to something / to doing something** means that you become familiar with something or with doing a particular thing, so that it is not a problem any longer: *The heat in India was very intense but I got used to it after a while.* ○ *I don't think I could ever get used to living in a big city after living in the country.*

Used to do/be something (only in the past tenses) describes a past habit or something existing only in the past: *I used to smoke but I gave up five years ago.* ○ *When I was a kid there used to be a school over there.*

used to /'juːst tə; *before vowels and finally* 'juːst tu/ *modal v* (*neg* **didn't use to** /-juːs/; *Brit also* *dated or formal* **used not to**, *short form* **usedn't to** /'juːsnt tə/, *before vowels and finally* /'juːsnt tu/) (expressing a frequent or continuous action or state in the past; in questions and negative sentences usu with did): *I used to live in London.* ○ *Life here is much easier than it used to be.* ○ *You used to smoke a pipe, didn't you?* ○ *I didn't use to like her.* ○ (*dated or fml*) *I usedn't to like her.*

NOTE We usually use the auxiliary verb **did** to make negatives and questions with the verb **used to**: *I didn't use to like classical music.* ○ *Did Jane use to have long hair?* ○ *There used to be a cinema here didn't there?* These forms are usually spoken and are sometimes spelt *did...used to* and *didn't used to*. Many people think these spellings are incorrect.

People also say or write **used not to**: *We used not to be friends.* The negative and question patterns *usedn't to*, and *used you to...?* are old-fashioned or very formal, and not very common.

useful /ˈjuːsfl/ *adj* **1** that can be used for a practical purpose; that helps one to do sth; helpful: *a useful gadget/book/hint* ○ *Videos are useful things to have in the classroom.* **2** of use or value to sb/sth: *do sth useful with one's life* ○ *Is there any way I can be useful while you're cooking?* ○ *Don't just sit watching television —* **make yourself useful!** **3** (*infml*) good; very satisfactory: *He's a very useful player.* ○ *That could be a useful score.*
▶ **usefully** /-fəli/ *adv*: *Is there anything I can usefully do here?* ○ *The money raised could more usefully be spent on new equipment.*
usefulness /-fəlnəs/ *n* [U] the state of being useful or possible to use: *She questioned the usefulness of his research.*

useless /ˈjuːsləs/ *adj* **1** not fulfilling the intended purpose: *All our efforts were useless.* ○ *It's useless arguing/to argue with them.* ○ *A car is useless without petrol.* ○ *The book's full of lovely pictures but it's useless as a guide.* **2** ~ (**doing sth/to do sth**) certain not to achieve the desired result: *I realized that it was useless to protest.* **3** (*infml*) having no ability or skill at sth: *I'm useless at sewing.* **4** having no purpose; giving no benefit to anyone: *a useless existence.* ▶ **uselessly** *adv*. **uselessness** *n* [U].

user /ˈjuːzə(r)/ *n* a person or thing that uses sth: *drug-users/road-users* ○ *users of public transport* ○ *the average user of database software.*
▶ **user-friendly** /ˌjuːzə ˈfrendli/ *adj* (esp of equipment, systems, etc) easy for people who are not experts to use or understand: *a user-friendly keyboard/hi-fi system* ○ *Dictionaries should be as user-friendly as possible.*

NOTE User-friendly means 'easy to use or understand' and usually describes computers and other machines. When **friendly** is combined with other words, especially nouns, it means 'sympathetic or kind to'. The most common combinations are **environmentally friendly** (ie not harmful to the environment) and **ozone-friendly** (ie not harmful to the layer of the gas ozone around the earth). People often make up new words using **friendly** with this meaning: *Germany has many bicycle-friendly towns.* ○ *My garden could be described as 'bird-friendly'.* ○ *How can schools make science more girl-friendly?*

usher /ˈʌʃə(r)/ *n* **1** a person who shows people where they should sit in a cinema, church, public hall, etc. **2** an official who allows people into and out of a lawcourt.
▶ **usher** *v* to lead sb to the place where they should go or sit, esp formally: [Vnpr] *The girl ushered me along the aisle to my seat.* [Vnp] *I was ushered in and then the interview started.* **PHR V** **usher sth ˈin** to mark the start of sth; to cause sth to begin: *The new government ushered in a period of prosperity.*
usherette /ˌʌʃəˈret/ *n* a girl or woman who leads people to their seats, esp in a cinema or theatre.

USN /ˌjuː es ˈen/ *abbr* United States Navy.

USS /ˌjuː es ˈes/ *abbr* United States Ship: *USS Oklahoma*. Compare HMS.

USSR /ˌjuː es es ˈɑː(r)/ *abbr* (the former) Union of Soviet Socialist Republics.

usual /ˈjuːʒuəl/ *adj* that happens or is done in many or most instances: *make all the usual excuses* ○ *She arrived later than usual.* ○ *As is usual with children, they soon got tired.* ○ *When the accident happened, the usual crowd gathered.* ○ *He wasn't his usual self.* **IDM** **as usual** in the same way as previously; as is usual: *You're late, as usual.* ○ *As usual, there weren't many people at the meeting.* ○ *Despite her problems, she carried on working as usual.* **business as usual** ⇨ BUSINESS.
▶ **usually** /ˈjuːʒuəli/ *adv* (abbreviated as *usu* in this dictionary) in the way that is usual or normal; most often: *What do you usually do on Sundays?* ○ *He's usually early.* ○ *We're more than usually busy today.*

usurer /ˈjuːʒərə(r)/ *n* (*dated usu derog*) a person who lends money at excessively high rates of interest(5).

usurp /juːˈzɜːp/ *v* (*fml*) to take sb's position of power or importance illegally or by force: [Vn] *usurp the throne* ○ (*fig*) *Streets intended for pedestrians are being usurped by motorists.* ▶ **usurpation** /ˌjuːzɜːˈpeɪʃn/ *n* [U]. **usurper** *n*.

usury /ˈjuːʒəri/ *n* [U] (*dated usu derog*) the practice of lending money at excessively high rates of interest(5).

utensil /juːˈtensl/ *n* a useful household tool or object: *cooking/kitchen utensils* (eg pots, pans, spoons).

uterus /ˈjuːtərəs/ *n* (*pl* **uteruses**) (*anatomy*) a WOMB. ⇨ picture at REPRODUCTION. ▶ **uterine** /ˈjuːtəraɪn/ *adj*: *uterine tumours*. See also INTRA-UTERINE DEVICE.

utilitarian /ˌjuːtɪlɪˈteəriən/ *adj* **1** designed to be useful and practical rather than attractive; functional (FUNCTION): *The furniture throughout is plain and utilitarian.* **2** based on or supporting the belief that actions are good if they are useful or benefit the greatest number of people.
▶ **utilitarianism** *n* [U] a philosophy based on utilitarian(2) principles.

utility /juːˈtɪləti/ *n* **1** [U] the quality of being useful: *a computer system of maximum utility* ○ *the utility value of a dishwasher.* **2** [C] a service provided for the public, eg an electricity, water or gas supply: *try to restore utilities after a storm* ○ *the administration of public utilities.*
▶ **utility** *adj* [attrib] that can fulfil several different functions efficiently: *a utility vehicle* ○ *a utility player* (ie one who can play equally well in several different positions, eg in football).
■ **uˈtility room** *n* a room, esp in a private house, containing large fixed domestic appliances: *a utility room with space for a washing-machine and tumble-drier.*

utilize, -ise /ˈjuːtəlaɪz/ *v* (*fml*) to use sth for a practical purpose; to make use of sth: [Vn] *utilize all available resources* [Vn-n] *utilize solar power as a source of energy.* ▶ **utilization, -isation** /ˌjuːtəlaɪˈzeɪʃn; *US* -ləˈz-/ *n* [U].

utmost /ˈʌtməʊst/ (also **uttermost** /ˈʌtəməʊst/) *adj* [attrib] greatest; most extreme: *of the utmost importance* ○ *with the utmost care* ○ *pushed to the utmost limits of endurance.*
▶ **the utmost** (also **the uttermost**) *n* [sing] the greatest, or most extreme extent or amount possible: *enjoy oneself to the utmost* ○ *My patience was tested to the uttermost.* **IDM** **do/try one's ˈutmost (to do sth)** to try as hard as one can: *I did my utmost to stop them.*

Utopia /juːˈtəʊpiə/ *n* [C, U] an imaginary place or state of things in which everything is perfect: *a vain quest for a political Utopia.*
▶ **Utopian** (also **utopian**) /-piən/ *adj* (*usu derog*) having or aiming for Utopia; idealistic (IDEALISM); not realistic: *Utopian ideals.*
utopianism *n* [U].

utter¹ /ˈʌtə(r)/ *adj* [attrib] (used as an intensifier) complete; total; absolute: *utter despair/nonsense/confusion* ○ *an utter waste of time* ○ *her utter delight/astonishment* ○ *You're an utter fool!* ▶ **utterly** *adv*: *Men and women are so utterly different.* ○ *We utterly failed to convince them.*

utter² /ˈʌtə(r)/ *v* (a) to make a sound or sounds with the mouth or voice: [Vn] *utter a sigh/a cry of pain.* (b) to say sth; to express sth in speech: [Vn] *utter threats* ○ *He never uttered a word (of protest).*
▶ **utterance** /ˈʌtərəns/ *n* (*fml*) **1** [U] the action of expressing ideas, etc in words: *give utterance to one's feelings/thoughts/views.* **2** [C] words spoken; a statement: *private/public utterances.*

uttermost = UTMOST.
U-turn ⇨ U¹.
uvula /ˈjuːvjələ/ *n* (*pl* **uvulas** or, in scientific use, **uvulae** /-liː/) (*anatomy*) a small piece of flesh that hangs from the back of the roof of the mouth above the throat. ⇨ picture at THROAT.

Vv

V¹ (also **v**) /viː/ n (pl **V's, v's** /viːz/) **1** the 22nd letter of the English alphabet: *Vivienne begins with (a) V/ 'V'.* **2** a thing shaped like a V: *planes flying in a V (formation).*
■ **'V-neck** n a style of NECKLINE in the shape of a V at the front. ⇨ picture at NECK. **'V-neck** (also **'V-necked**) adj having a V-neck: *a ₁V-neck 'sweater.*
'V-sign n a sign made with the first and second fingers spread to form a V. It can be used either to indicate victory (with palm outwards), or as a rude gesture (with palm inwards): *give/make a V-sign.*
V² abbr volt(s): *a 1.5 V battery.* Compare W² 1.
V³ (also **v**) symb the Roman NUMERAL for 5.
v abbr **1** verse: *St Luke ch 12 vv 4–10.* **2** (also **vs**) (esp in sporting or legal use) versus (ie against): *England v West Indies* ○ *the case of Regina vs Reed* (ie in a lawcourt). **3** (infml) very: *I was v pleased to get your letter.*
vac /væk/ n (Brit infml) **1** a university VACATION. **2** a vacuum cleaner (VACUUM).
vacancy /'veɪkənsi/ n **1** [C] an available room in a hotel, etc: *I'm sorry, we have no vacancies.* **2** [C] ~ **(for sb/sth)** an available job or position: *fill a vacancy* ○ *We have vacancies for secretaries with word-processing experience.* **3** [U] lack of ideas or intelligence; the state of being empty: *the vacancy of his stare/expression.*
vacant /'veɪkənt/ adj **1** not filled or occupied; empty: *a vacant position/hotel room/seat* ○ *Situations Vacant* (ie at the head of a newspaper column advertising jobs) ○ *Is the lavatory vacant?* ⇨ note at EMPTY¹. **2** showing no sign of thought or intelligence; blank: *a vacant stare/look* ○ *a vacant mind.* ▶ **vacantly** adv: *look/gaze vacantly into space.*
■ ₁**vacant pos'session** n [U] (used in house advertisements, etc) ownership of a house, etc after anyone previously living in it has moved out.
vacate /və'keɪt; US 'veɪkeɪt/ v (fml) to leave a place or position: [Vn] *vacate one's seat/hotel room* ○ *The squatters were ordered to vacate the premises.*
vacation /və'keɪʃn; US veɪ-/ n **1** [C] (also Brit infml **vac**) any of the intervals between terms in universities and lawcourts: *the Christmas/Easter vacation* ○ *the long vacation* (ie in the summer) ○ *vacation work.* Compare RECESS 1a. **2** [C,U] (esp US) = HOLIDAY 1a: *take a/some vacation* ○ *be on vacation.* ⇨ note at HOLIDAY.
▶ **vacation** v [V, Vpr] ~ **(at/in ...)** (US) to have a holiday at or in a place.
vaccinate /'væksɪneɪt/ v ~ **sb/sth (against sth)** to protect sb/sth against a disease by injecting (INJECT 1) VACCINE into the blood: [Vnpr] *have one's dog vaccinated against rabies* [also Vn]. Compare IMMUNIZE, INOCULATE. ▶ **vaccination** /₁væksɪ'neɪʃn/ n [C,U]: *have a polio vaccination* ○ *vaccination against smallpox.*
vaccine /'væksiːn; US væk'siːn/ n [U,C] a substance that is put into the blood and protects the body from a disease by causing a very mild form of it: *a polio/rabies vaccine.* Compare SERUM 1b.
vacillate /'væsəleɪt/ v ~ **(between sth and sth)** (fml usu derog) to keep changing one's mind; to have first one emotion or opinion and then another repeatedly: [V] *a weak and vacillating leader* [Vpr] *She vacillated between hope and fear.* Compare OSCILLATE 1. ▶ **vacillation** /₁væsə'leɪʃn/ n [C,U] (fml usu

derog): *her vacillation(s) over whether or not to resign.*
vacuity /və'kjuːəti/ n [U] (fml) lack of purpose, meaning or intelligence: *the total vacuity of government thinking.*
vacuous /'vækjuəs/ adj (fml) showing or suggesting lack of thought or intelligence: *a vacuous expression/smile* ○ *a charming but vacuous person.* ▶ **vacuously** adv. **vacuousness** n [U].
vacuum /'vækjuəm/ n (pl **vacuums**) **1(a)** a space that is completely empty of all matter or gas. **(b)** a space in a container from which the air has been completely or partly removed: *create a perfect vacuum.* **2** (usu sing) a situation in which sb/sth is no longer present and their/its place has not yet been filled: *There has been a vacuum in his life since his wife died.* ○ *The fall of the old regime left a **power vacuum** that the nationalists attempted to fill.* **IDM** **in a 'vacuum** isolated from other people, facts, events, etc: *Professional training cannot take place in a vacuum.*
▶ **vacuum** v ~ **sth (out)** (infml) to clean sth with a vacuum cleaner (VACUUM): [Vn] *vacuum the stairs/carpet* [also V].
■ **'vacuum cleaner** n an electrical appliance that sucks dust, dirt, etc into a bag attached to it.
'vacuum flask (also **flask**, US **'vacuum bottle**) n a container with a double wall that encloses a vacuum, used for keeping the contents hot or cold. Compare THERMOS.
'vacuum-packed adj (esp of foods) sealed in a pack from which most of the air has been removed.
'vacuum pump n a pump that creates a partial vacuum in a container.
vade-mecum /₁vɑːdi 'meɪkəm/ n a small useful reference book: *a fisherman's vade-mecum.*
vagabond /'vægəbɒnd/ n (dated usu derog) a person who wanders from place to place without a settled home or job, esp one considered lazy or dishonest.
vagary /'veɪgəri/ n (usu pl) a strange or sudden change that is difficult to predict: *the vagaries of the weather/the postal service.*
vagina /və'dʒaɪnə/ n (pl **vaginas**) (anatomy) the passage in a woman or female animal from the outer sex organs to the WOMB. ⇨ picture at REPRODUCTION. ▶ **vaginal** /və'dʒaɪnl/ adj: *a vaginal infection.*
vagrant /'veɪgrənt/ n (fml or law) a person without a settled home or regular work: *a shelter for vagrants.*
▶ **vagrancy** /'veɪgrənsi/ n [U] the condition or offence of being a vagrant: *be arrested on a vagrancy charge.*
vagrant adj: *vagrant children.*
vague /veɪg/ adj (**-r, -st**) **1(a)** not clearly expressed or perceived: *a vague promise/rumour* ○ *vague memories/hopes/feelings* ○ *I haven't the vaguest idea/ notion* (ie I don't know at all) *what you mean.* **(b)** not specific or exact: *The terms of the agreement were deliberately vague.* ○ *She can only give a vague description of her attacker.* **2(a)** (of a person) not sure about needs, intentions, etc: *be vague in/about one's plans* ○ *I'm still vague about what you want.* **(b)** (of a person's looks or behaviour) suggesting a lack of attention or clear thought: *give a vague smile/*

gesture. **3** not clearly identified; not distinct: *the vague outline of a ship in the fog.*

▶ **vaguely** *adv* **1** in a way one cannot specify: *Her face is vaguely familiar.* **2** roughly; approximately: *He pointed vaguely in my direction.* ○ *The map of Italy vaguely resembles a boot.* **3** in a way that shows a lack of attention or clear thought: *smile/gesture vaguely.*

vagueness *n* [U].

vain /veɪn/ *adj* (**-er, -est**) **1** having too high an opinion of one's looks, abilities, etc; too proud. **2** [usu attrib] producing no result; useless: *a vain attempt* ○ *in the vain hope of persuading him.* **3** [attrib] (*dated or rhet*) having no value; empty: *vain promises.* **IDM in** ˈ**vain** without success: *I tried in vain to sleep.* **2** useless: *All our efforts were in vain.* **take sb's name in vain** ⇨ NAME¹. See also VANITY.

▶ **vainly** *adv* **1** without success: *trying to find the keyhole in the dark.* **2** in a vain(1) manner; too proudly (PROUD).

vainglorious /ˌveɪnˈɡlɔːrɪəs/ *adj* (*dated or fml derog*) extremely proud and VAIN(1); boasting too much.

valance /ˈvæləns/ *n* a short curtain hung round the frame of a bed, above a window or under a shelf. Compare PELMET.

vale /veɪl/ *n* (*arch*, except in place names) a valley: *the Vale of the White Horse.*

valediction /ˌvælɪˈdɪkʃn/ *n* (*fml*) [C,U] (words used in) saying goodbye, esp on serious occasions.

▶ **valedictory** /-tərɪ/ *adj* [usu attrib] (*fml*) serving as or accompanying a valediction: *a valedictory message/gift.*

valency /ˈveɪlənsɪ/ (also *esp US* **valence**) *n* (*chemistry*) the power of an atom to combine with others, measured by the number of HYDROGEN atoms it can DISPLACE(1) or combine with: *Carbon has a valency of 4.*

valentine /ˈvæləntaɪn/ *n* (**a**) (also **valentine card**) a greetings card sent on St Valentine's Day (14 February) to a person one loves, often without giving one's name. (**b**) a person to whom one sends such a card: *Will you be my valentine?*

valet /ˈvæleɪ, ˈvælɪt/ *n* (**a**) a man's personal male servant who looks after his clothes, serves his meals, etc. (**b**) a hotel employee with similar duties.

▶ **valet** /ˈvælɪt/ *v* to clean the inside of a car: [Vn] *a car valeting service.*

valiant /ˈvælɪənt/ *adj* (*esp fml or rhet*) brave or determined: *valiant warriors/efforts* ○ *She made a valiant attempt to laugh.* ▶ **valiantly** *adv: Tom tried valiantly to rescue the drowning man.*

valid /ˈvælɪd/ *adj* **1** (of arguments, reasons, etc) well based or logical; sound²(2): *raise valid objections to a plan* ○ *The point you make is perfectly valid.* Compare INVALID¹. **2(a)** legally effective because made or done with the correct procedure: *a valid claim/contract* ○ *The marriage was held to be valid.* (**b**) that can be legally used or accepted: *a valid passport* ○ *a bus pass valid for one month* ○ *A cheque card is not a valid proof of identity.*

▶ **validity** /vəˈlɪdətɪ/ *n* [U] **1** the state of being logical: *question the validity of an argument/assumption.* **2** the state of being legally acceptable: *test the validity of a decision.*

validly *adv*.

validate /ˈvælɪdeɪt/ *v* **1** to show that sth is reasonable or logical: [Vn] *validate a theory/an argument.* See also INVALIDATE. **2** to make sth legally valid: [Vn] *validate a contract/marriage/passport.* ▶ **validation** /ˌvælɪˈdeɪʃn/ *n* [U,C].

valise /vəˈliːz; *US* vəˈliːs/ *n* (*dated*) a small bag for clothes, etc during a journey.

Valium /ˈvælɪəm/ *n* (*propr*) [U] a drug used to reduce stress and nervous tension.

valley /ˈvælɪ/ *n* an area of land between hills or

mountains, often with a river flowing through it; the land through which a river flows: *the Thames Valley.* ⇨ picture at MOUNTAIN.

valour (*US* **valor**) /ˈvælə(r)/ *n* [U] (*fml or rhet*) courage, esp in war: *display great valour* ○ *soldiers decorated* (ie given awards) *for valour.* **IDM discretion is the better part of valour** ⇨ DISCRETION.

valuable /ˈvæljuəbl/ *adj* **1** worth a lot of money: *a valuable collection of paintings.* **2** very useful or important: *valuable research work* ○ *valuable advice/help/information* ○ *We're wasting valuable time.* ⇨ note at INVALUABLE.

▶ **valuables** *n* [pl] valuable things, esp small personal possessions, jewellery, etc: *recover stolen valuables.*

valuation /ˌvæljuˈeɪʃn/ *n* **1(a)** [U,C] the action or an instance of estimating, esp professionally, how much money sth is worth: *property/land/stock valuation* ○ *Surveyors carried out a valuation of our house.* (**b**) [C] a financial value that is estimated in this way: *Experts put/set a high valuation on the painting.* **2** [U,C] the action or an instance of judging the quality or worth of sb/sth: *She puts a high valuation on Eliot's plays.*

value /ˈvæljuː/ *n* **1(a)** [C,U] the worth of sth in terms of money or other goods for which it can be exchanged: *a decline in the value of the dollar/pound* ○ *pay above/below the market value for sth* ○ *rising property values* ○ *gain/appreciate/go up in value* ○ *drop/fall/go down in value* ○ *order software to the value of £700.* (**b**) [U] the worth of sth compared with the price paid for it: *This tea is excellent value at 39p a packet.* ○ *Charter flights give/offer the best value for (your) money.* ○ *This great value-for-money offer is only available to society members.* **2** [U] the quality of being useful or important: *the value of regular exercise* ○ *be of great/little/some/no value to sb* ○ *have a high energy/nutritional value* ○ *The story has very little news value.* **3 values** [pl] moral or professional standards of behaviour; principles: *cultural/family/social values* ○ *preserve traditional values* ○ *Young people have a different set of values from their parents.* **4** [C] (*mathematics*) a number or quantity represented by a letter: *Find the value of x.* See also FACE VALUE, MARKET VALUE, STREET VALUE.

▶ **value** *v* **1** ~ **sth (at sth)** to estimate how much money sth is worth: [Vnpr] *He valued the house for me at $80 000.* [also Vn]. **2** ~ **sth/sb (as sth)** (not used in the continuous tenses) to have a high opinion of sth/sb: [Vn] *value sb's advice* ○ *value truth above all else* ○ *a valued contribution/possession* ○ *a valued client/customer* [Vn-n] *I value her as a friend.*

valuer *n* a person whose profession is to estimate how much property, land, etc is worth.

valueless *adj* without value or effect; worthless. ⇨ note at INVALUABLE.

■ ˌ**value** ˈ**added tax** *n* [U] (*abbr* **VAT**) a tax charged on the price of goods and services. It can be charged at each stage of the production process, but can be claimed back from the government by the companies involved. The final customer cannot claim it back.

ˈ**value judgement** *n* (*derog*) an estimate of moral, artistic, etc worth based on personal opinion rather than facts: *make value judgements.*

valve /vælv/ *n* **1** a mechanical device for controlling the flow of air, liquid or gas, allowing it to move in one direction only: *inlet/outlet valves* ○ *the valve of a bicycle tyre* ○ *a safety/exhaust valve.* ⇨ picture. ⇨ picture at BICYCLE. Compare TAP¹ 1. **2** a structure in the heart or in a vein, etc allowing the blood to flow in one direction only. **3** a device in certain brass musical instruments for changing the note. ⇨ picture at MUSICAL INSTRUMENT. See also BIVALVE.

vamp /væmp/ *n* (*dated infml often derog*) (esp in the

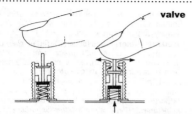

valve

1920s and 1930s) a woman who uses her sexual attractions to make men do what she wants.

vampire /'væmpaɪə(r)/ *n* **1** the body of a dead person that is believed by some to leave its grave at night and suck the blood of living people. **2** (also **'vampire bat**) a large tropical bat that sucks the blood of other animals.

van

van¹ /væn/ *n* **1** a covered vehicle, with no side windows, for transporting goods or people: *the 'baker's van* ○ *a 'furniture/re'moval van* ○ *a po'lice van* (ie for transporting police officers or prisoners) ○ *a 'van driver.* ⇨ picture. **2** (*Brit*) a closed railway carriage for bags, mail or goods, or for the use of the guard: *the 'luggage van* ○ *the 'guard's van.*

van² /væn/ *n* **the van** [sing] (*dated*) the leading part of an advancing army, fleet, etc: *positioned **in the van**.*

vanadium /və'neɪdiəm/ *n* [U] (*symb* V) a chemical element. Vanadium is a hard whitish metal used for strengthening some types of steel. ⇨ App 7.

V and A /ˌviː ən 'eɪ/ *abbr* (*Brit infml*) Victoria and Albert Museum (in London): *visit the V and A.*

vandal /'vændl/ *n* a person who deliberately destroys or damages works of art, public and private property, the beauties of nature, etc for no good reason.
▶ **vandalism** /-dəlɪzəm/ *n* [U] behaviour characteristic of vandals: (*fig*) *The withdrawal of arts subsidies is an act of cultural vandalism.*
vandalize, -ise /-dəlaɪz/ *v* (esp passive) to destroy or damage works of art, property, etc for no good reason: [Vn] *The public telephones had all been vandalized.*

vane /veɪn/ *n* **1** = WEATHER-VANE. **2** the sail of a WINDMILL or a similar device with a flat surface that is acted on or moved by wind or water.

vanguard /'vænɡɑːd/ *n* **the vanguard** [sing] **1** the leading part of an advancing army or fleet. **2** the leaders of a movement or of opinion, fashion, etc: *be in the vanguard of social change.* Compare REARGUARD.

vanilla /və'nɪlə/ *n* (**a**) [U] a substance used as a flavour in sweet foods. It is obtained from the tropical vanilla plant or produced artificially: *vanilla ice-cream/essence.* (**b**) [U] ice-cream made with vanilla: *Do you want chocolate, vanilla or strawberry?* (**c**) [C] a portion of this ice-cream: *one vanilla and one pistachio, please.*

vanish /'vænɪʃ/ *v* **1(a)** to disappear completely and suddenly: [V] *The thief vanished into the crowd.* ○ *My pen seems to have vanished without trace.* (**b**) [V] to stop existing; to fade away (FADE 2): [V] *He's one of a vanishing breed of political idealists.* ○ *Our prospects/hopes of success have vanished.*
■ **'vanishing-point** *n* [sing] (*techn*) the point in the distance at which parallel lines appear to meet.

vanity /'vænəti/ *n* **1** [U] excessive pride in one's appearance, achievements, etc: *She spoke without a trace of vanity.* ○ *Her remarks had injured his vanity.* **2** [U] (*fml*) the quality of being worthless or useless: *the vanity of human ambitions.* **3 vanities** [pl] things or acts that are worthless or show excessive pride: *the vanities of the world of fashion.* See also VAIN.

vanquish /'væŋkwɪʃ/ *v* [Vn] (*fml*) to defeat an opponent, etc; to overcome sb/sth.

vantage point /'vɑːntɪdʒ pɔɪnt/ *n* a position from which one views or considers sth: *From their vantage point on the cliff, they could watch the ships coming and going.* ○ *From the vantage point of the 20th century the war seems to have achieved little.*

vapid /'væpɪd/ *adj* (*fml*) dull or not interesting: *the vapid conversation bored her.* ▶ **vapidity** /væ'pɪdəti/ *n* [U].

vaporize, -ise /'veɪpəraɪz/ *v* [V, Vn] to turn into gas or make sth turn into gas. ▶ **vaporization, -isation** /ˌveɪpəraɪ'zeɪʃn; *US* -rə'z-/ *n* [U].

vapour (*US* **vapor**) /'veɪpə(r)/ *n* **1** [C, U] gas in the form of steam, smoke or other substances spread about or hanging in the air: *water vapour* ○ *petrol vapours.* **2 the vapours** [pl] (*arch* or *joc*) a sudden feeling that one is about to FAINT²: *have/get (an attack of) the vapours.*
▶ **vaporous** /'veɪpərəs/ *adj* (*fml*) full of or like vapour: *vaporous clouds of mist/smoke/steam.*
■ **'vapour trail** *n* a trail of clouds of water vapour left in the sky by an aircraft.

variable /'veəriəbl/ *adj* **1** varying; likely to change: *variable pressure/rainfall/weather/speed* ○ *Winds are mainly light and variable.* ○ *His mood/temper is variable.* ○ *The quality of the hotel food is distinctly variable.* **2** that can be varied: *a variable timer control* ○ *variable lighting.*
▶ **variable** *n* (often *pl*) a variable thing or quantity: *With so many variables, the exact cost is difficult to estimate.* ○ *Temperature was a variable in the experiment.* Compare CONSTANT *n.*
variability /ˌveəriə'bɪləti/ *n* [U] the quality of being variable; the tendency to vary.
variably /-əbli/ *adv.*

variance /'veəriəns/ *n* [U, C] the extent to which sth varies or differs from sth else: *the evolutionary variance within a species* ○ *a note with subtle variances of pitch.* **IDM** **at variance (with sb/sth)** (*fml*) disagreeing or having a difference of opinion with sb; in conflict with sth: *The two of them are at variance (with each other) over certain key policy issues.* ○ *Her theory is at variance with the known facts.*

variant /'veəriənt/ *n* a thing that differs from other things or from a standard: *The story has many variants.* ▶ **variant** *adj*: *variant forms of spelling.*

variation /ˌveəri'eɪʃn/ *n* **1** [C, U] ~ (in/of sth) the action or an instance of varying; (a) change: *Prices have not shown much variation this year.* ○ *Currency exchange rates are always subject to variation.* ○ *The dial records very slight variations in pressure.* **2** [C] ~ (on sth) (**a**) a thing that differs from others in the same general group: *This soup is a spicy variation of a traditional favourite.* ○ *Picasso painted several variations on this theme.* (**b**) (*music*) a REPETITION(1) of a simple MELODY in a different, and usu more complicated, form: *a set of variations on a theme by Mozart* ○ *piano/orchestral variations* ○ (*fig*) *His numerous complaints are all variations on a theme* (ie about the same thing).

varicose veins /ˌværɪkəʊs 'veɪnz/ *n* [pl] a condition in which the veins of the legs become swollen and painful.

varied /'veərid/ *adj* **1** of different types: *varied opinions/scenes/menus* ○ *Holiday jobs are many and varied.* **2** showing changes or variety: *lead a full* *and varied life* ○ *My experience is not sufficiently varied.*

variegated /ˈveərɪəgeɪtɪd/ **1** *adj* marked with differently coloured patches, spots, etc: *a plant with variegated leaves/flowers* ○ *This specimen is richly variegated in colour.* **2** of different types: *a variegated assortment of people/buildings/opinions.* ▶ **variegation** /ˌveərɪəˈgeɪʃn/ *n* [U].

variety /vəˈraɪətɪ/ *n* **1** [U] the quality of not being the same, or not being the same at all times: *offer/show/lack variety* ○ *a life full of change and variety* ○ *We all need variety in our diet.* **2** [sing] ~ (**of sth**) a number or range of different things: *a large/wide variety of patterns to choose from* ○ *He resigned for a variety of reasons.* **3** [C] ~ (**of sth**) a class of things that differ from others in the same general group; a member of such a class: *different varieties of English* ○ *grow rare varieties of orchid.* **4** (*US* also **vaudeville**) [U] a form of television or theatre entertainment consisting of a series of acts, eg singing, dancing, comedy, etc: *a vaˈriety show/theatre/artist.*
■ **vaˈriety store** *n* (*US*) a shop selling a wide range of small cheap items.

various /ˈveərɪəs/ *adj* **1** of several types, unlike one another: *tents in various (different) shapes and sizes* ○ *Her hobbies are **many and various**.* **2** [attrib] more than one; individual and separate: *for various reasons* ○ *at various times* ○ *write under various names.*
▶ **variously** *adv* (*fml*) differently according to the particular case, time, place, etc: *He was variously described as a hero, a genius and a fool.*

varnish /ˈvɑːnɪʃ/ *n* [U, C] **1(a)** a liquid that is applied to wood, metal, paintings, etc and forms a hard shiny transparent surface when dry. Varnish is available in many different colours: *give the shelves a coat of varnish.* **(b)** the hard shiny surface formed by this: *Someone's scratched the varnish on my desk.* Compare LACQUER 1. **2** (*Brit*) = NAIL VARNISH.
▶ **varnish** *v* to put varnish on sth: [Vn] *a highly varnished table-top* ○ *sand and varnish a chair* ○ *Some women varnish their toe-nails.*

varsity /ˈvɑːsətɪ/ *n* **1** (*dated Brit infml*) (not used in names) a university, esp Oxford or Cambridge: *a varsity match.* **2** (*US*) a team representing a university, college or school, esp in sports competitions: *a varsity football game.*

vary /ˈveərɪ/ *v* (*pt, pp* **varied**) **1** ~ (**in sth**) to be different in size, volume, strength, etc: [Vpr] *These fish vary in weight from 3 lb to 5 lb.* [V] *Opinions vary widely on this point.* **2** ~ (**with sth**); ~ (**from sth to sth**) to change, esp according to some factor: [Vpr] *Prices vary with the seasons.* ○ *Her mood varied from optimism to extreme depression.* [V] *Our routine never varies.* ○ *We all tried to hit it with varying degrees of success.* ➪ note at CHANGE¹. **3** to make sth different by introducing changes: [Vn] *vary a programme/route* ○ *Try varying the pace/speed at which you work.*

vascular /ˈvæskjələ(r)/ *adj* of or containing veins or tubes through which liquids flow in the bodies of animals or in plants: *vascular disease/tissue.*

vase /vɑːz; *US* veɪs, veɪz/ *n* a container without handles, usu made of glass, china, etc and used for holding cut flowers or as an ornament.

vasectomy /vəˈsektəmɪ/ *n* (*medical*) an operation to remove part of each of the tubes in a man's body that carry SPERM, after which he is unable to make a woman pregnant.

Vaseline /ˈvæsəliːn/ *n* [U] (*propr*) a thick yellowish substance used as an OINTMENT, etc.

vassal /ˈvæsl/ *n* **1** (in the Middle Ages) a man who promised to fight for and be loyal to a king or lord, in return for the right to hold land. **2** a person or nation that is dependent on another: *vassal states/kingdoms.*

vast /vɑːst; *US* væst/ *adj* [usu attrib] **1** very large in area, size, quantity or degree; huge: *a vast expanse of desert/water/snow* ○ *a vast crowd/throng/gathering* ○ *His business empire was vast.* **2** (*infml*) very great: *in the vast majority of cases* ○ *make a vast difference.*
▶ **vastly** *adv* (used for emphasis) very greatly: *children of vastly different ages* ○ *be vastly experienced.*
vastness *n* [U, C]: *lost in the vastness(es) of space.*

vat /væt/ *n* a large container for holding liquids, esp in industry: *distilling/fermenting vats.*

VAT /ˌviː eɪ ˈtiː, væt/ *abbr* value added tax: *Prices include 15% VAT.*

Vatican /ˈvætɪkən/ *n* the **Vatican** (**a**) [sing] the group of buildings in Rome where the Pope lives. (**b**) [Gp] the administrative centre of the Roman Catholic Church.

vaudeville /ˈvɔːdəvɪl/ *n* [U] (*US*) = VARIETY 4.

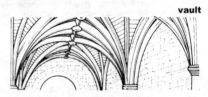
vault

vault¹ /vɔːlt/ *n* **1** a roof in the form of an arch or a series of arches. ➪ picture at CHURCH. **2(a)** an underground room used for storing things at a cool temperature: *ˈwine-vaults.* (**b**) a similar room beneath a church or in a CEMETERY, used for burials: *in the family vault.* (**c**) a similar room, esp in a bank and protected by locks, alarms, thick walls, etc, used for keeping valuable items safe. **3** a covering like the arch of a roof: (*rhet*) *the vault of heaven* (ie the sky).
▶ **vaulted** *adj* having a vault¹(1) or vaults; built in the form of a vault: *a vaulted roof/ceiling.*

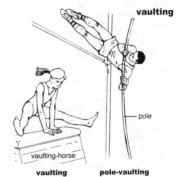
vaulting

pole

vaulting-horse

vaulting   pole-vaulting

vault² /vɔːlt/ *v* ~ (**over sth**) to jump in a single movement over or onto an object with a hand or hands resting on it or with the help of a pole: [Vn, Vpr] *vault (over) a fence* [Vpr] *The jockey vaulted lightly into the saddle.* [V] (*fig fml*) *vaulting* (ie very great, excessive) *ambition.* ➪ picture.
▶ **vault** *n* a jump made by vaulting. See also POLE-VAULT.
■ **ˈvaulting-horse** *n* a wooden apparatus for practice in vaulting. ➪ picture.

vaunted /ˈvɔːntɪd/ *adj* [usu attrib] (*fml derog*) praised too highly; boasted about: *The bank's **much-vaunted** security system failed completely.*

VC /ˌviː ˈsiː/ *abbr* **1** Vice-Chancellor. **2** Victoria Cross (a medal for special bravery awarded to members of the British and Commonwealth armed forces): *be awarded the VC* ○ *Col James Blunt VC*.

VCR /ˌviː siː ˈɑː(r)/ *abbr* video cassette recorder.

VD /ˌviː ˈdiː/ *abbr* venereal disease.

VDU /ˌviː diː ˈjuː/ *abbr* (*computing*) visual display unit: *a VDU operator/screen*. ⇨ picture at COMPUTER.

veal /viːl/ *n* [U] the flesh of a calf used as meat: *veal cutlets*.

vector /ˈvektə(r)/ *n* **1** (*mathematics*) a quantity that has both size and direction, eg VELOCITY. Compare SCALAR. **2** (*techn*) a course taken by an aircraft. **3** (*biology*) an insect, etc that carries a particular disease or infection. See also CARRIER 5.

veep /viːp/ *n* (*US infml*) a vice-president (VICE-).

veer /vɪə(r)/ *v* (**a**) to change direction or course, esp suddenly: [V] *The plane veered wildly*. [Vpr] *The car suddenly veered off the road*. [Vp] *The wind has veered round (to the north)*. (**b**) (of a conversation or of sb's behaviour or opinion) to change suddenly: [Vpr] *The discussion veered away from religion and round to politics*. ○ *Her mood veered between shame and anger*.

veg /vedʒ/ *n* [U, C] (*pl* unchanged) (*Brit infml*) a vegetable or vegetables: *He likes the traditional* **meat and two veg** *for his main meal*.

vegan /ˈviːgən/ *n* a person who neither eats nor uses any animal products, eg eggs, silk, leather: *a vegan diet*.

vegetable /ˈvedʒtəbl/ *n* **1** a plant or part of a plant eaten as food: *Potatoes, beans and onions are all vegetables*. ○ *green vegetables* (eg CABBAGE(1), LETTUCE, etc) ○ *a root vegetable* (eg a potato, CARROT(1), etc) ○ *a salad of raw vegetables* ○ *a vegetable garden/patch/plot* ○ *vegetable oils* (eg in MARGARINE) ○ *vegetable matter* (ie plants in general). Compare ANIMAL, FRUIT, MINERAL. **2(a)** a person who is physically alive but not capable of much mental activity or movement, eg because of injury or illness: *Severe brain damage turned him into a vegetable*. (**b**) a person who has a dull life: *Stuck at home like this, she felt like a vegetable*.

■ ˌvegetable ˈmarrow *n* (*Brit*) = MARROW[2].

vegetarian /ˌvedʒəˈteəriən/ *n* a person who, for moral, religious or health reasons, eats no meat: *a vegetarian meal/diet/restaurant*. Compare VEGAN.
▶ **vegetarianism** /-ɪzəm/ *n* [U] the practice of being a vegetarian.

vegetate /ˈvedʒəteɪt/ *v* to live a dull life with little activity or interest: [V] *vegetating at home without a job*.

vegetation /ˌvedʒəˈteɪʃn/ *n* [U] plants in general; plants found in a particular environment: *the luxuriant vegetation of tropical rain forests* ○ *There is little vegetation in the desert*.

vehement /ˈviːəmənt/ *adj* showing or caused by strong feeling; passionate: *a vehement protest/denial/attack* ○ *He has a vehement dislike of loud pop music*. ▶ **vehemence** /-məns/ *n* [U]. **vehemently** *adv*: *The charge was vehemently denied*.

vehicle /ˈviːəkl; *US also* ˈviːhɪkl/ *n* **1** (*esp fml*) a thing used for transporting goods or people, esp on land, such as a car, lorry or cart: *motor vehicles* (ie cars, buses, lorries, etc) ○ *vehicle licensing laws* (eg for motor vehicles) ○ *a space vehicle* (ie for carrying people into space). **2** ~ (**for sth**) a means by which thought, feeling, etc can be expressed: *Art may be used as a vehicle for propaganda*. ○ *The play is an ideal vehicle for her talents*.
▶ **vehicular** /vəˈhɪkjələ(r); *US* viː-/ *adj* (*fml*) intended for or consisting of vehicles: *vehicular access* ○ *The road is closed to vehicular traffic*.

veil /veɪl/ *n* **1** [C] (**a**) a covering of fine net or other usu transparent material worn, esp by women, to protect or hide the face, or as part of a hat, etc: *a bridal veil* ○ *She raised/lowered her veil*. (**b**) a piece of linen, etc worn by nuns over the head and shoulders. **2** [sing] a thing that hides or disguises sth: *a veil of mist over the hills* ○ *Their work is carried out behind a veil of secrecy*. **IDM** **draw a veil over sth** ⇨ DRAW[1]. **take the ˈveil** to become a nun.
▶ **veil** *v* to cover sb/sth with or as if with a veil: [Vn] *A thin mist veiled the lake*. ○ *She veiled her eyes with her hand*. Compare UNVEIL. **veiled** *adj* **1** partly hidden: *a thinly veiled threat/warning*. **2** wearing a veil(1): *a veiled Muslim woman*.

vein /veɪn/ *n* **1** [C] any of the tubes carrying blood from all parts of the body to the heart: *the jugular vein* ○ *Royal blood runs in his veins*. Compare ARTERY. **2** [C] any of the thin tubes forming the framework of a leaf or of an insect's wing. **3** [C] a narrow strip of a different colour in certain types of stone, eg marble, or in certain cheeses. **4** [C] a crack or channel in rock, filled with a certain mineral; a SEAM(2): *a vein of gold*. **5** [sing] ~ (**of sth**) a distinctive feature or quality: *have a vein of melancholy in one's character* ○ *A rich vein of humour runs through her work*. **6** [sing] a manner or style; a mood: *in lighter/more serious vein* ○ *The rest of her letter continues in the same/in similar vein*.
▶ **veined** /veɪnd/ *adj* marked with or having veins: *a veined hand/leaf* ○ *veined marble* ○ *blue-veined cheese* (eg Stilton).
veining /ˈveɪnɪŋ/ *n* [U] a pattern of lines or veins: *marble with greenish veining*.

velar /ˈviːlə(r)/ *n, adj* (*phonetics*) (a speech sound, eg /k/, or /g/) made by placing the back of the tongue against or near the back part of the mouth.

Velcro /ˈvelkrəʊ/ *n* [U] (*propr*) a material for fastening clothes, etc consisting of two nylon strips, one rough and one smooth, which stick to each other when pressed together.

veld (also **veldt**) /velt/ *n* [U] (in S Africa) flat open land with grass and no trees. Compare PAMPAS, PRAIRIE, SAVANNAH, STEPPE.

vellum /ˈveləm/ *n* [U] **1** material used formerly for writing on or for binding (BIND 3) books, originally made from calf, goat or lamb skin. **2** smooth paper of good quality for writing on.

velocity /vəˈlɒsəti/ *n* [U, C] (*esp techn*) the speed of sth, esp in a given direction: *gain/lose velocity* ○ *the velocity of light* ○ *a high-velocity rifle/bullet* ○ *Gazelles can move with an astonishing velocity*.

velour (also **velours**) /vəˈlʊə(r)/ *n* [U] a woven fabric like VELVET or FELT[1]: *a velour coat*.

velvet /ˈvelvɪt/ *n* [U] a woven fabric, esp of silk or nylon, that is thick and soft on one side: *a velvet jacket/curtain*.
▶ **velvety** *adj* (*approv*) soft like velvet: *a horse's velvety nose* ○ *her velvety brown eyes*.

velveteen /ˌvelvəˈtiːn/ *n* [U] a cotton fabric like velvet.

venal /ˈviːnl/ *adj* (*fml*) (**a**) ready to accept money for doing sth dishonest: *venal politicians and lawyers*. (**b**) (of conduct) characteristic of a venal person: *venal practices/sins*. ▶ **venality** /viːˈnæləti/ *n* [U].

vendetta /venˈdetə/ *n* **1** a dispute between families in which murders are committed in return for previous murders. **2** a series of harmful or offensive actions directed by one person against another: *conduct/pursue a personal vendetta against a hated rival*.

vending-machine /ˈvendɪŋ məʃiːn/ *n* a machine operated by coins for the sale of small items, eg cigarettes, drinks or sandwiches.

vendor /ˈvendə(r)/ *n* **1** (esp in compounds) a person who sells food or other small items from a stall in the open air: *ˈstreet vendors* ○ *ˈnews-vendors* (ie people selling newspapers). **2** (*law*) a person selling a house or other property. Compare PURCHASER.

veneer /vəˈnɪə(r)/ n **1** [C, U] a thin layer of wood or plastic glued to the surface of cheaper wood, for furniture, etc: *maple/walnut veneer.* **2** [sing] ~ (**of sth**) (*usu derog*) an appearance of concern or order, etc covering or disguising the true nature of sb/sth: *acquire a thin veneer of Western civilization.* Compare GLOSS¹ 2.

▶ **veneer** v [Vn, Vnpr] ~ **sth** (**with sth**) to put a veneer(1) on a surface.

venerable /ˈvenərəbl/ adj **1** [usu attrib] (*fml*) deserving great respect, esp because of age or character: *a venerable scholar* ∘ *the venerable ruins of the abbey.* **2** [attrib] (*religion*) (**a**) (in the Church of England) the title of an ARCHDEACON. (**b**) (in the Roman Catholic Church) the title of sb thought to be very holy but not yet made a saint. ▶ **venerability** /ˌvenərəˈbɪləti/ n [U].

venerate /ˈvenəreɪt/ v ~ **sb/sth** (**as sth**) (*fml*) to respect sb/sth greatly; to regard sb/sth as sacred: [Vn] *venerate the memory of one's dead ancestors* [Vn-n] *Such men were venerated as prophets.* ▶ **veneration** /ˌvenəˈreɪʃn/ n [U]: *The relics were objects of veneration.*

venereal /vəˈnɪəriəl/ adj relating to diseases spread by sexual contact: *a venereal infection.*
■ **ve,nereal di'sease** n [C, U] (*abbr* **VD**) a disease spread by sexual contact: *Gonorrhea and syphilis are venereal diseases.*

venetian blind /vəˌniːʃn ˈblaɪnd/ n a window screen with wooden, metal or plastic strips going across that can be adjusted to let in light and air as desired.

vengeance /ˈvendʒəns/ n [U] ~ (**on/upon sb**) the paying back of an injury that one has suffered; revenge(1a): *take/seek/wreak vengeance for the bombing* ∘ *He swore vengeance on his child's killer.* **IDM** **with a 'vengeance** (*infml*) to a greater degree than is expected or desired; in the fullest sense: *After a poor season last year, he's back in the team with a vengeance.* ∘ *Recession has hit the industry with a vengeance.*

vengeful /ˈvendʒfl/ adj (*fml*) showing a desire for revenge. ▶ **vengefully** /-fəli/ adv.

venial /ˈviːniəl/ adj [esp attrib] (*fml*) (of a sin or fault) not serious; that can be excused.

venison /ˈvenɪsn, ˈvenɪzn/ n [U] the flesh of a deer used as meat: *roast venison.*

venom /ˈvenəm/ n [U] **1** the poisonous liquid in the bite or sting of a snake, SCORPION, etc. **2** strong bitter feeling or language; hatred: *There was anger and venom in her voice.*
▶ **venomous** /ˈvenəməs/ adj **1** (of a snake, etc) producing venom. **2** full of hatred or spite: *a venomous look/remark.* **venomously** adv.

venous /ˈviːnəs/ adj (*techn*) of, full of or contained in the veins: *venous blood.*

vent¹ /vent/ n **1** an opening that allows air, gas, liquid, etc to pass out of or into a confined space: *air/heating vents.* **2** the opening in the body of a bird, fish, reptile or other small animal, through which waste matter is passed out. **IDM** **give (full) vent to sth** to express sth freely: *She gave vent to her feelings in a violent outburst.*
▶ **vent** v ~ **sth** (**on sb**) to express a strong feeling, esp anger, freely: [Vnpr] *He vented his rage/wrath/spleen on his long-suffering wife.* [also Vn].

vent² /vent/ n a long cut at the bottom of the back or side of a coat or jacket.

ventilate /ˈventɪleɪt; US -təleɪt/ v **1** to allow air to enter and move freely through a room, building, etc: [Vn] *ventilate the galleries of a coal-mine* ∘ *The kitchen is well-/poorly-ventilated.* **2** (*fml*) to discuss or examine an issue, a complaint, etc in public: [Vn] *These issues have been well ventilated in the press.* Compare HYPERVENTILATE.
▶ **ventilation** /ˌventɪˈleɪʃn; US -təˈleɪʃn/ n [U]: *the*

ventilation shaft of a coal-mine ∘ *The window may be opened to increase ventilation.* ∘ *The ventilation system isn't working.*
ventilator /ˈventɪleɪtə(r); US -təl-/ n a device or an opening for ventilating a room, etc.

ventricle /ˈventrɪkl/ n (*anatomy*) **1** each of the two lower parts of the heart, whose function is to pump blood around the body. Compare AURICLE 2. **2** a hollow part of various organs, esp the brain.

ventriloquism /venˈtrɪləkwɪzəm/ n [U] the art of producing voice sounds so that they seem to come from a person or place at a distance from the speaker.
▶ **ventriloquist** /-kwɪst/ n a person who is skilled in ventriloquism: *a ventriloquist's dummy.*

venture /ˈventʃə(r)/ n a project or an undertaking (UNDERTAKE), esp a commercial one involving a risk of failure: *embark on a new venture* ∘ *a joint venture between government and business* ∘ *The car-hire firm is their latest business venture.* ∘ *venture capital* (ie money invested in a new enterprise, esp a risky one). See also ENTERPRISE 1.

▶ **venture** v (*fml*) **1** to dare to go somewhere dangerous or unpleasant: [Vpr] *venture into the water/over the wall* ∘ *venture too near the edge of a cliff* [Vp] *I'm not venturing out in this rain.* [Vpr] (*fig*) *In her new book she ventures into the supernatural.* **2** to dare to say sth in a cautious way or without confidence: [Vn] *venture an opinion/objection/explanation* [V.to inf] *May I venture to suggest a change in the rules?* ∘ *I venture to disagree.* [V.speech] *'I wonder if I can help,' she ventured.* **3** ~ **sth** (**on sth**) to take the risk of losing or failing in sth: [Vnpr] *I ventured a small bet on the first race.* [also Vn]. **IDM** **nothing 'venture, nothing 'gain/'win** (*saying*) one cannot expect to achieve anything if one never takes risks. **PHRV** **'venture on/upon sth** to dare to attempt sth: *venture on a trip up the Amazon.*

venturesome /-səm/ adj (*fml*) ready to take risks; daring: *young children becoming more venturesome in their use of language.*

venue /ˈvenjuː/ n a place where people agree to meet, esp for a sports contest or music concert: *a last-minute change of venue* ∘ *London's newest pop venue.*

Venus /ˈviːnəs/ n the planet second in order from the sun, next to the Earth.

veracity /vəˈræsəti/ n [U] (*fml*) truth: *I don't doubt the veracity of your story.*

veranda (US also **porch**)

veranda (also **verandah**) /vəˈrændə/ (US also **porch**) n a platform with an open front and a roof which extends along the side or sides of a house, etc: *sitting on the veranda.* ⇨ picture. Compare PATIO.

verb /vɜːb/ n (*grammar*) (abbreviated as v in this dictionary) a word or phrase indicating an action, an event or a state, eg *bring, happen, exist*: *an irregular verb* ∘ *modal/phrasal verbs* ∘ *transitive/ intransitive verbs.*

verbal /ˈvɜːbl/ adj **1** of or in words: *verbal skills* (ie reading and writing) ∘ *non-verbal communication* (ie gestures, expressions of the face, etc). **2** spoken, not written: *a verbal explanation/agreement/warning/ reminder.* **3** (*grammar*) of verbs: *a noun performing a verbal function.*

▶ **verbally** /'vɜːbəli/ *adv* in spoken words, not in writing.

■ ˌ**verbal** ˈ**noun** (also **gerund**) *n* (*grammar*) a noun derived (DERIVE 2) from a verb, eg *swimming* in the sentence *Swimming is a good form of exercise.*

verbalize, -ise /'vɜːbəlaɪz/ *v* (*fml*) to express ideas or feelings in words: [Vn] *She tried to verbalize her doubts and fears.* [also V].

verbatim /vɜː'beɪtɪm/ *adj, adv* exactly as spoken or written; word for word: *a verbatim report* ○ *report a speech verbatim.*

verbiage /'vɜːbiɪdʒ/ *n* [U] (*fml derog*) the use of too many words, or of more difficult words than are needed, to express an idea, etc: *wade through the verbiage of an official report* (ie read it with difficulty).

verbose /vɜː'bəʊs/ *adj* (*fml derog*) using or containing more words than are needed : *a verbose speaker/speech/style.* ▶ **verbosity** /vɜː'bɒsəti/ *n* [U] (*fml*).

verdant /'vɜːdnt/ *adj* (*fml or rhet*) (of grass, plants, fields, etc) fresh and green: *verdant hills/meadows.*

verdict /'vɜːdɪkt/ *n* **1** a decision reached by a JURY on a question of fact in a law case: *return a verdict of guilty/not guilty* ○ *arrive at/reach a verdict* ○ *a majority verdict of 8 to 4.* See also OPEN VERDICT. **2** ~ (**on sth/sb**) a decision or an opinion given after testing, examining or experiencing sth: *The coroner recorded a verdict of accidental death.* ○ *The by-election result is seen as a verdict on the whole government.* ○ *What's your verdict on the play — did you enjoy it?*

verdigris /'vɜːdɪgriː; *US* 'vɜːrdəgrɪs/ *n* [U] a greenish-blue substance that forms on copper, brass and BRONZE(1) surfaces, as RUST forms on iron.

verge /vɜːdʒ/ *n* (**a**) (*Brit*) (*US* **soft shoulder**) the land beside a road: *Cars may not park on/along the grass verge.* (**b**) a strip of grass along the edge of a path, etc. **IDM on/to the verge of sth/doing sth** at or close to the point where sth new begins or takes place: *on the verge of war/success/bankruptcy* ○ *She looked on the verge of tears.*
▶ **verge** *v* **PHRV** ˈ**verge on sth** to be very close or similar to sth; to be approaching sth: *a situation verging on the ridiculous* ○ *I was treated with suspicion that verged on hostility.*

verger /'vɜːdʒə(r)/ *n* (*esp Brit*) a Church of England official who looks after a church and acts as an attendant.

verify /'verɪfaɪ/ *v* (*pt, pp* **-fied**) to make sure or show that sth is true, accurate or justified; to check or confirm sth: [Vn] *verify statements/allegations/facts* ○ *verify the figures/details of a report* ○ *Subsequent events tended to verify our initial fears.* [V.that, V.wh] *The computer will verify that/whether the data has been loaded correctly.* ▶ **verifiable** /'verɪfaɪəbl/ *adj*: *verifiable facts.* **verification** /ˌverɪfɪ'keɪʃn/ *n* [U]: *proposals for the verification of strategic arms reductions* (ie for checking that arms have been removed or destroyed).

verisimilitude /ˌverɪsɪ'mɪlɪtjuːd; *US* -tuːd/ *n* [U] (*fml*) the appearance of being true or real: *To add verisimilitude, the stage is covered with sand for the desert scene.*

veritable /'verɪtəbl/ *adj* [attrib] (*fml or joc*) correctly named or called; real; complete: *The book is a veritable goldmine for anyone interested in rare coins.*

verity /'verəti/ *n* **1** [C usu *pl*] (*fml*) an idea, a principle, etc generally thought to be true; a fundamental fact: *the eternal verities of life.* **2** [U] (*arch*) truth.

vermicelli /ˌvɜːmɪ'tʃeli/ *n* [U] PASTA made in long thin threads, like SPAGHETTI but much thinner. It is often added to soups.

vermilion /və'mɪliən/ *adj, n* [U] (of) a bright red colour.

vermin /'vɜːmɪn/ *n* [pl *v*] **1** certain wild animals and birds which are harmful to crops and farm animals and birds: *put down/exterminate vermin* ○ *Rats, foxes, moles and rabbits are usually treated as vermin.* Compare PEST 1. **2** insects sometimes found on the bodies of human beings and other animals: *fleas, lice and other vermin* ○ *a room alive/crawling with vermin.* **3** people who are very unpleasant or harmful to society.
▶ **verminous** /-əs/ *adj* covered with vermin(2): *verminous children.*

vermouth /'vɜːməθ; *US* vər'muːθ/ *n* [U] a strong white wine, often mixed with other drinks as a COCKTAIL.

vernacular /və'nækjələ(r)/ *n* (usu **the vernacular**) [C usu *sing*] **1** a language or form of a language spoken in a particular country or region or by a particular group, as compared with a formal or written language: *the black American vernacular* ○ *learn to speak the local vernacular.* **2** a style of architecture concerned with ordinary buildings as compared with large or grand ones. ▶ **vernacular** *adj*: *vernacular idioms/buildings.*

vernal /'vɜːnl/ *adj* [attrib] (*fml or rhet*) of, in or appropriate to the season of spring: *the vernal equinox.*

verruca /və'ruːkə/ *n* (*pl* **verrucas** or, in medical use, **verrucae** /-kiː/) a small hard infectious growth (4a) on the skin, usu on the bottom of the feet.

versatile /'vɜːsətaɪl; *US* -tl/ *adj* (*approv*) **1** turning easily or readily from one subject, skill or occupation to another: *a versatile cook/writer/athlete* ○ *a versatile mind.* **2** (of a tool, a machine, a substance, a food, etc) having many uses: *Few cooking ingredients are as versatile as eggs.* ▶ **versatility** /ˌvɜːsə'tɪləti/ *n* [U].

verse /vɜːs/ *n* **1** [U] writing arranged in lines, often with a regular rhythm or RHYME scheme; poetry: *Most of the play is written in verse, but some of it is in prose.* ○ *a verse translation of Homer's 'Iliad'.* Compare PROSE. **2** [C] a group of lines forming a unit in a poem or song: *a hymn of/with six verses.* **3 verses** [pl] (*dated*) poetry: *a book of humorous verses.* **4** [C] any one of the short numbered divisions of a chapter in the Bible. **IDM chapter and verse** ⇨ CHAPTER. See also BLANK VERSE, FREE VERSE, HEROIC VERSE.

versed /vɜːst/ *adj* ~ **in sth** [pred] knowing about or skilled in sth: *well versed in the art of cooking/in the ways of the world.*

versify /'vɜːsɪfaɪ/ *v* (*pt, pp* **-fied**) (*fml sometimes derog*) to write verse.
▶ **versification** /ˌvɜːsɪfɪ'keɪʃn/ *n* [U] (*fml*) the art of writing verse or the style in which verse is written. **versifier** *n* (*sometimes derog*): *amateur versifiers.*

version /'vɜːʃn, 'vɜːʒn; *US* 'vɜːrʒn/ *n* **1** an account of an event, etc from the point of view of one person: *There were contradictory versions of what actually happened.* **2(a)** a special form of sth made: *the standard/de luxe version of a car* ○ *the original/final version of a play.* (**b**) a specially adapted form of a book, piece of music, etc: *the radio/film version of 'Jane Eyre'* ○ *an orchestral version of a suite for strings.* See also the AUTHORIZED VERSION, THE REVISED STANDARD VERSION, THE REVISED VERSION.

verso /'vɜːsəʊ/ *n* (*pl* **-os**) the page on the left side of an open book: *on the verso page.* Compare RECTO.

versus /'vɜːsəs/ *prep* (*abbrs* **v, vs**) (*esp sport or law*) against sb/sth: *Kent versus Surrey* (eg in cricket) ○ *Rex versus Crippen* ○ *the advantage of better job opportunities versus the inconvenience of moving house and leaving one's friends.*

vertebra /'vɜːtɪbrə/ *n* (*pl* **vertebrae** /-riː/) each of the sections of the BACKBONE: *the cervical vertebrae.* ⇨ picture at SKELETON.

▶ **vertebral** /-rəl/ *adj: the vertebral column* (ie the BACKBONE).

vertebrate /ˈvɜːtɪbrət/ *n, adj* (a creature) having a BACKBONE: *Mammals, birds, reptiles, amphibians and fishes are vertebrates.*

vertex /ˈvɜːteks/ *n* (*pl* **vertices** /-tɪsiːz/ or **vertexes**) **1** (*mathematics*) (**a**) the point of a TRIANGLE(1), CONE(1), etc opposite the base. (**b**) a point where two lines meet to form an angle. **2** (*techn*) the highest point or top of sth.

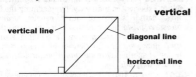

vertical
vertical line
diagonal line
horizontal line

vertical /ˈvɜːtɪkl/ *adj* (of a line, pole, etc) going straight up or down from a level surface or from top to bottom in a picture, etc; upright: *the vertical axis of a graph* ∘ *a vertical take-off aircraft* (ie one that rises straight up into the air without needing a RUNWAY) ∘ *The cliff was almost vertical.* ∘ *There was a vertical drop to the sea.* ⇨ picture.

▶ **vertical** *n* a vertical line, part or position: *The wall is several degrees off the vertical* (ie not vertical by that amount).

vertically /-kli/ *adv.*

vertigo /ˈvɜːtɪɡəʊ/ *n* [U] a feeling of losing one's balance, caused esp by looking down from a great height: *suffer from (an attack of) vertigo.*

▶ **vertiginous** /vɜːˈtɪdʒɪnəs/ *adj* (*fml*) of or causing vertigo: *a vertiginous drop/descent* ∘ (*fig*) *vertiginous heights of linguistic extravagance.*

verve /vɜːv/ *n* [U] enthusiasm, spirit or vigour, esp in art: *write/sing/act with verve* ∘ *The performance lacked verve.*

very¹ /ˈveri/ *adv* **1** (used as an intensifier before *adjs, advs* and *dets*) in a high degree; extremely: *very small/hot/useful* ∘ *very quickly/soon/far* ∘ *very much/few* ∘ *'Are you busy?' 'Not very.'* ∘ *'Do you like it?' 'Very much so.'* **2** (before a superlative *adj, pron* or *own*) in the fullest sense: *the very best quality* ∘ *the very first to arrive* ∘ *by six o'clock at the very latest* ∘ *your very own cheque-book.* **3** exactly: *sitting in the very same seat.*

■ ˌvery high ˈfrequency *n* [U] (*abbr* **VHF**) a radio FREQUENCY(2) of 30 to 300 MEGAHERTZ.

NOTE Very is used to modify adjectives and past participles used as adjectives: *I am very hungry.* ∘ *He is very interested in music.*

Very much is used to modify verbs: *She likes Beethoven very much.* ∘ *We enjoyed staying with you very much.*

Much or **very much** can modify past participles: *Grandma was much loved by everyone.*

---

very² /ˈveri/ *adj* [attrib] (usu after *the, this/that* or *her/his/its/our/their/your*) **1** itself, himself, etc and no other; actual; truly such: *This is the very book I want.* ∘ *At that very moment the phone rang.* ∘ *You're the very man I want to see.* ∘ *These pills are the very thing for your cold.* ∘ *Those were her very words.* **2** extreme: *at the very end/beginning.* **3** (used to emphasize a *n*): *He knows our very thoughts* (ie our thoughts themselves, even our most secret ones). ∘ *The very idea/thought* (ie The idea alone, quite apart from the reality) *of going abroad delighted him.* ∘ *The very idea!* (ie That is not a practical or proper suggestion.) ∘ (*Brit*) *Sardine tins can be the very devil* (ie very difficult) *to open.* **IDM** **before sb's very eyes** in sb's presence; in front of sb: *Before our*

very eyes he produced a puppy from the hat. **the very/living/spitting image** ⇨ IMAGE.

Very light /ˈveri laɪt/ *n* a coloured light fired at night from a gun, eg as a sign of distress from a ship.

vesicle /ˈvesɪkl/ *n* **1** (*anatomy or biology*) a small bag or hollow structure in the body of a plant or an animal. **2** (*medical*) a small swelling filled with liquid under the skin; a BLISTER(1).

vespers /ˈvespəz/ *n* [sing or pl *v*] (in the Christian Church) a church service or prayers in the evening. Compare EVENSONG, MATINS.

vessel /ˈvesl/ *n* **1** (*fml*) a ship or boat, esp a large one: *ocean-going vessels* ∘ *cargo vessels.* **2** (*fml*) any hollow container, esp one used for holding liquids, eg a barrel, bowl, bottle or cup. **3** a structure like a tube in the body of an animal or a plant, trans-porting or holding blood or other liquid: *blood-vessels.*

vest¹ /vest/ *n* **1**(**a**) (*Brit*) (*US* **undershirt**) a garment worn under a shirt, etc next to the skin: *cotton/string/thermal vests.* (**b**) a special garment covering the upper part of the body: *a bullet-proof vest* ∘ *a running vest.* **2** (*US*) = WAISTCOAT.

vest² /vest/ *v* ~ **sth** (**in sb/sth**); ~ **sb/sth** (**with sth**) (*fml*) (usu passive) to give sth as a firm or legal right to sb/sth: [Vnpr] *vest sb with authority* ∘ *Copyright is vested in the author.* ∘ *Parliament is vested with the power of making laws.* [also Vn].

■ ˌvested ˈinterest *n* a personal interest in a state of affairs, usu with an expectation of gaining sth: *You obviously have a vested interest in Tim's resigna-tion* (eg because you may get his job). ∘ *Powerful vested interests* (ie people with a vested interest) *are opposing the plan.*

vestibule /ˈvestɪbjuːl/ *n* **1** (*fml*) an entrance hall, eg where hats and coats may be left: *the vestibule of a church/theatre/hotel.* **2** (*US*) an enclosed space be-tween passenger coaches on a train.

vestige /ˈvestɪdʒ/ *n* **1** a small remaining part of what once existed; a trace: *the last vestiges of the old colonial regime* ∘ *Not a vestige of the abbey remains.* **2** (esp in negative sentences) a very small amount: *There's not a vestige of truth in the rumour.*

▶ **vestigial** /veˈstɪdʒiəl/ *adj* [usu attrib] (*fml or techn*) remaining as a vestige: *vestigial traces of an earlier culture* ∘ *It is possible to see the vestigial remains of rear limbs on some snakes.*

vestment /ˈvestmənt/ *n* (esp *pl*) a ceremonial gar-ment, esp one worn by a priest in church: *clerical/holy/sacred vestments.*

vestry /ˈvestri/ *n* a room or building attached to a church, where the priest can prepare for the service by dressing in ceremonial clothes, etc. ⇨ picture at CHURCH.

vet¹ /vet/ *n* = VETERINARY SURGEON.

vet² /vet/ *v* (**-tt-**) (*Brit*) to examine sb/sth carefully, eg to make sure that sb is suitable for a special job, that a product is of good quality, etc: [Vn] *All new staff are carefully vetted for security reasons.* ∘ *The holiday accommodation is thoroughly vetted by us before being included in our brochure.*

vet³ /vet/ *n* (*US infml*) = VETERAN 2.

vetch /vetʃ/ *n* [U, C] a plant of the pea family. There are several types of vetch, one of which is often used to feed cattle.

veteran /ˈvetərən/ *n* **1** a person with a lot of experi-ence, esp as a soldier: *war veterans* ∘ *a veteran politician/golfer.* **2** (also *infml* **vet**) (*US*) any former member of the armed forces: ˈVeterans Day (ie a holiday held on 11 November in memory of the end of World Wars I and II).

■ ˌveteran ˈcar *n* (*Brit*) a car made before 1916, esp before 1905: *a veteran Rolls Royce* ∘ *a veteran car rally.* Compare VINTAGE 2.

V

veterinary /ˈvetrənri; US ˈvetərəneri/ adj [attrib] of or for the diseases and injuries of farm and domestic animals: *veterinary medicine/studies.*

■ ˌveterinary ˈsurgeon n (fml) (also esp Brit vet, US veterinarian /ˌvetərɪˈneərɪən/) a person who is skilled in the treatment of animal diseases and injuries.

veto /ˈviːtəʊ/ n (pl -oes) ~ (on sth) **1** [C,U] the right to reject or forbid a decision or proposal of a law-making body, committee, etc: *use the presidential veto* ○ *exercise the power/right of veto.* **2** [C] a refusal to allow sth: *the government's veto on large-scale company mergers.*
▶ **veto** v (pres p **vetoing**) to use one's right to reject or forbid sth: [Vn] *The President vetoed the tax cuts.*

vex /veks/ v (esp passive) (dated or fml) to make sb angry or annoyed, esp with small or unimportant matters: [Vn.*that*] *It vexed her that she had forgotten Peter's birthday.* [also Vn].
▶ **vexation** /vekˈseɪʃn/ n (dated or fml) **(a)** [U] the state of being annoyed or worried: *His behaviour has caused me great vexation.* **(b)** [C esp pl] a thing that causes annoyance or worry: *life's little vexations.*
vexatious /vekˈseɪʃəs/ adj (dated or fml) annoying or worrying.
vexed adj **1** ~ (**at/with sb/sth**) worried or upset: *She looked distinctly vexed.* **2** (of a problem, etc) much discussed and difficult to deal with: *tackle the vexed issue/question of immigration.*
vexing adj: *vexing problems.*

VHF /ˌviː eɪtʃ ˈef/ abbr (radio) very high frequency: *programmes broadcast on VHF* ○ *a VHF radio.* Compare UHF.

via /ˈvaɪə, ˈviːə/ prep by way of sth; through sth: *go from London to Washington via New York* ○ *information sent via a computer network* ○ *He got into photography via a Fine Arts degree.*

viable /ˈvaɪəbl/ adj **1** that can be done; that will work; possible: *a viable plan/proposition/method* ○ *be commercially/politically/economically viable* ○ *There's no viable alternative.* **2** (biology) capable of developing and surviving independently: *viable organisms.* ▶ **viability** /ˌvaɪəˈbɪləti/ n [U]: *commercial/economic/financial viability.*

viaduct /ˈvaɪədʌkt/ n a long bridge, usu with many arches, carrying a road or railway across a river, valley, etc.

vial /ˈvaɪəl/ n = PHIAL.

vibes /vaɪbz/ n **1** [pl] (sl) = VIBRATIONS: *get good/bad vibes from sth.* **2** [sing or pl v] (infml) = VIBRAPHONE: *a jazzy vibes backing.*

vibrant /ˈvaɪbrənt/ adj **1** full of life and energy; exciting: *a vibrant atmosphere/performance* ○ *She looked in vibrant health.* **2** (esp of colours) bright and striking: *vibrant pinks and yellows* ○ *vibrant designs/patterns.* **3** (of sounds) strong or powerful: *vibrant tunes.* ▶ **vibrancy** /-brənsi/ n [U].

vibraphone /ˈvaɪbrəfəʊn/ n [C] (also infml **vibes** [sing or pl v]) an electric musical instrument like a XYLOPHONE, often used in JAZZ.

vibrate /vaɪˈbreɪt; US ˈvaɪbreɪt/ v **1** to move or make sth move very quickly and continuously from side to side; to shake: [V] *The whole house vibrates whenever a heavy truck passes.* [also Vn]. **2** to produce or make sth produce a sound with rapid slight variations of pitch[1](2): [V] *The strings of a piano vibrate when the keys are struck.* [also Vn].
▶ **vibrator** /-tə(r)/ n a device that vibrates, esp one used in MASSAGE or for sexual pleasure.

vibration /vaɪˈbreɪʃn/ n **1** [U,C] a continuous rapid shaking movement or sensation: *engine noise and vibration levels* ○ *vibrations caused by heavy lorries passing the window.* **2 vibrations** (also **vibes**) [pl] (sing **vibe**) (infml) a mood or atmosphere produced by a particular person, thing, place, etc: *pick up good/bad/negative vibrations.*

vibrato /vɪˈbrɑːtəʊ/ n [U,C] (pl **-os**) (music) a shaking effect in singing or on a musical instrument, consisting of rapid slight variations in pitch[1](2). Compare TREMOLO.

vicar /ˈvɪkə(r)/ n (in the Church of England) a priest in charge of a church and the area around it (called a *parish*). Compare CURATE, MINISTER[1] 3, PRIEST, RECTOR 1a.
▶ **vicarage** /ˈvɪkərɪdʒ/ n the house of a vicar.

vicarious /vɪˈkeərɪəs; US vaɪˈk-/ adj [esp attrib] **1** felt or experienced indirectly, by imagining the feelings, activities, etc of other people: *vicarious pleasure/satisfaction/pride* ○ *He got a vicarious thrill out of watching his son score the winning goal.* **2** (fml) done, felt or experienced by one person on behalf of another: *vicarious punishment/suffering.* ▶ **vicariously** adv.

vice[1] /vaɪs/ n **1(a)** [U] evil actions; wickedness: *sink into a life of vice.* **(b)** [C] a particular form of this: *Greed is a terrible vice.* Compare VIRTUE 1. **2** [C] (infml or joc) a fault or bad habit: *Chocolates are one of my little vices!* **3** [U] certain types of criminal behaviour, esp associated with sex, drugs or gambling: *He was arrested by the vice squad for drug-trafficking.*

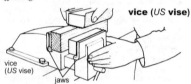

vice (US vise)

vice (US vise)

jaws

vice[2] (US **vise**) /vaɪs/ n a metal tool with a pair of jaws that hold a thing securely while work is done on it: (fig) *He held my arm in a vice-like* (ie very firm) *grip.*

vice- comb form **1** acting as an assistant to or in place of sb: *vice-president* ○ *vice-chancellor.* **2** next in importance to the rank specified: *vice admiral.* ➪ App 6.

viceregal /ˌvaɪsˈriːgl/ adj of a VICEROY.

viceroy /ˈvaɪsrɔɪ/ n a person governing a colony, province, etc as the representative of a king or queen.

vice versa /ˌvaɪs ˈvɜːsə, ˌvaɪsɪ-/ in the opposite way to what has just been said: *ˌWe help ˈthem and ˌvice ˈversa* (ie they help us).

vicinity /vəˈsɪnəti/ n **the vicinity** [sing] ~ (**of sth**) the area round a place: *crowds gathering in the vicinity of Trafalgar Square* ○ *There's no hospital in the immediate vicinity.*

vicious /ˈvɪʃəs/ adj **1** acting or done with evil intentions; cruel and violent: *vicious assault/attack/murder* ○ *He's not a vicious person.* **2** (of animals) fierce and dangerous: *a vicious dog.* **3** (infml) violent or severe: *a vicious wind/headache* ○ *a vicious spiral of rising prices.* **4** (fml) full of VICE[1](3). ▶ **viciously** adv: *fight/kick/swear viciously.* **viciousness** n [U].
■ ˌvicious ˈcircle n a continuing situation in which one problem or need leads to another and the new problem makes the first problem worse: *I need experience to get a job but without a job I can't get experience — it's a vicious circle.*

vicissitude /vɪˈsɪsɪtjuːd; US -tuːd/ n (usu pl) (fml) a change in a person's circumstances, or in the way sth develops: *try to deal with the vicissitudes of life/love.*

victim /ˈvɪktɪm/ n **1** a person, an animal or a thing that is injured, killed or destroyed as the result of crime, bad luck, an accident, etc: *murder/rape vic-*

tims ○ *earthquake/accident/famine victims* ○ *the innocent victim of an attack* ○ (*fig*) *He is the victim of his own success* (eg because working too hard has made him ill). **2** a person who is tricked: *the victim of a hoax/practical joke/conspiracy.* **3** a living creature killed and offered as a religious sacrifice: *a sacrificial victim.* **IDM** **fall 'victim (to sth)** to be hurt, killed, damaged or destroyed by sth: *Thousands fell victim to the epidemic.* ○ *Many plants have fallen victim to the sudden frost.*

victimize, -ise /'vɪktɪmaɪz/ *v* ~ **sb (for sth / doing sth)** to make sb suffer unfairly, esp because one does not like them or their opinions, etc: [Vn] *I was victimized at school because I didn't like games.* [Vnpr] *Union leaders claimed that some members had been victimized* (eg by being dismissed) *for taking part in the strike.* ▶ **victimization (-isation)** /ˌvɪktɪmaɪ'zeɪʃn; *US* -mə'z-/ *n* [U].

victor /'vɪktə(r)/ *n* (*fml*) the winner of a battle, contest, game, etc: *the victors and the vanquished* ○ *He finally emerged the victor after a close-fought contest.*

Victorian /vɪk'tɔːriən/ *adj* **1** of, living in or originating from the rule of Queen Victoria (1837–1901): *Victorian novels/poets/houses* ○ *the Victorian age/ era/period.* **2** having the qualities and attitudes thought to have been characteristic of people in Britain in the 19th century: *Victorian attitudes to sex* (ie ones stressing control of sexual desires or activity) ○ *Victorian values* (eg hard work, family loyalty, pride in one's country, etc).
▶ **Victorian** *n* a person living at the time when Queen Victoria ruled.

victory /'vɪktəri/ *n* (**a**) [U] success in a war, contest, game, etc: *celebrate/declare victory* ○ *lead the team to victory* ○ *victory parades/processions/celebrations.* (**b**) [C] an instance or occasion of this: *win a narrow/decisive/resounding victory in the election* ○ *gain/score a victory over the home team.* **IDM** **romp home / to victory** ⇨ ROMP.
▶ **victorious** /vɪk'tɔːriəs/ *adj* ~ (**in sth**); ~ (**over sb/sth**) having gained a victory: *a victorious battle/ campaign* ○ *the victorious players/team* ○ *be victorious in war.* **victoriously** *adv.*

victuals /'vɪtlz/ *n* [pl] (*dated*) food and drink.

video /'vɪdiəʊ/ *n* (*pl* -**os**) **1** [U] the process of recording, reproducing or broadcasting films on magnetic tape (MAGNETIC), using a special camera and a television: *use video in schools* (ie as a teaching aid) ○ *We recorded the whole wedding on video.* ○ *The film is coming out on video soon.* ○ *a video cassette.* **2** [C] (**a**) a recording or broadcast made by using video: *watching/making/showing videos* ○ *a pop video* ○ *a home video* (ie recorded by a person with no special skill, on ordinary equipment) ○ *The firm produced a short promotional video.* ○ *video shops/libraries.* (**b**) = VIDEO CASSETTE RECORDER: *programme the video to record a TV programme.* (**c**) (also ˌvideo ca'ssette) a film, etc recorded on a video tape: *take the videos back to the library.*
▶ **video** *v* (*pres p* **videoing**) (also **videotape**) to record moving pictures on videotape or videodisc: [Vn] *video a TV programme.*
■ 'video camera *n* a camera for taking video film. See also CAMCORDER.
'video game *n* a game played using a home computer, etc in which the player controls images on a television screen.
ˌvideo 'nasty *n* (*infml*) a video film showing offensive scenes of sex and violence.
ˌvideo ca'ssette recorder *n* (*abbr* VCR) (also video, ˌvideo ca'ssette player, 'video recorder) a device which, when linked to a television, can record and show programmes, etc on videotape or VIDEODISC.

videodisc /'vɪdiəʊdɪsk/ *n* [U,C] a plastic disc on

which films, etc can be recorded for showing on a television screen.

videotape /'vɪdiəʊteɪp/ *n* [U,C] a magnetic tape (MAGNETIC) used for recording television pictures and sound. ▶ **videotape** *v* [Vn] = VIDEO *v*.

vie /vaɪ/ *v* (*pt, pp* **vied** /vaɪd/; *pres p* **vying** /'vaɪɪŋ/) ~ **with sb (for sth / to do sth)**; ~ **for sth** (*fml*) to compete eagerly with sb for sth: [Vpr] *children vying for their mother's attention* ○ *The two new restaurants vied with each other to attract customers.*

view¹ /vjuː/ *n* **1** [U] the ability to see sth or to be seen from a particular place: *The lake came into view/We came in view of the lake as we turned the corner.* ○ *The sun disappeared from view behind a cloud.* ○ *A cloud hid the sun from view.* ○ *She was soon lost from view among the crowd.* ○ *The man in front was obstructing my view of the stage.* **2** [C] what can be seen from a particular place, esp fine natural scenery: *a room with a view of the sea* ○ *a book of postcards with 10 different views of London* ○ *There is a wonderful view from the top of the church tower.* ○ *You'll get a better view of the pianist if you stand up.* **3** (also **viewing**) [C] a special chance to see or inspect sth: *be invited to a private view of an art exhibition.* **4** [C *esp pl*] ~ (**about/on sth**) a personal opinion or attitude; a thought or comment on sth: *have/hold/express/air strong political views* ○ *oppose/support sb's views on education* ○ *What is your view on the subject?* ○ *In my view it was a waste of time.* ○ *He takes the view that all politicians are liars.* See also POINT OF VIEW. **5** [sing] a way of understanding or interpreting a subject, series of events, etc: *The scientific/legal/medical view is that...* ○ *a highly controversial view of modern art* ○ *take a realistic/favourable/pessimistic view of the problem* ○ *This book gives readers an inside view of political life.* **IDM** **a bird's-eye view** ⇨ BIRD. **have, etc sth in 'view** (*fml*) to have, etc sth as a clear idea, intention, plan, etc in one's mind: *At that time I had no particular plans in view.* **heave in sight / into view** ⇨ HEAVE. **in full view** ⇨ FULL. **in view of sth** taking sth into account; considering sth: *In view of the weather, the event will now be held indoors.* **on 'view** being shown to the public: *Our entire range is now on view at your local showroom.* **take a dim view of sth** ⇨ DIM. **take the long view** ⇨ LONG¹. **with a view to doing sth** (*fml*) with the intention or hope of doing sth: *He is decorating the house with a view to selling it.*

view² /vjuː/ *v* (*fml*) **1** to consider sth in the mind; to regard sth/sb as sth: [Vn] *How do you view your chances of success?* [Vnpr] *Viewed from the outside, the offer seems genuine.* [Vn-n] *He views it as a temporary job.* ○ *They view all tourists with suspicion.* ○ *The problem should not be viewed in isolation.* **2** to look at or watch sth carefully: [Vn] *view the match through binoculars* ○ *The film hasn't been viewed by the censor.* **3** to inspect a house, property, etc with the idea of buying it: [Vn] *open for viewing between 10.00 and 12.00.* **4** to watch television: [V] *the viewing public.*
▶ **viewer** /'vjuːə(r)/ *n* **1** a person who views sth: *viewers of the current political scene* ○ *paintings intended to shock the viewer.* **2** a person watching a television programme or a film: *regular viewers of the current series* ○ *suitable for adult/younger viewers.* **3** a device for viewing transparent photographs.

viewdata /'vjuːdeɪtə/ *n* [U] an information system in which computer data is sent along telephone lines and displayed on a television screen: *book a holiday through viewdata.*

viewfinder /'vjuːfaɪndə(r)/ *n* a device on a camera showing the area that will be photographed: *look through the viewfinder.* ⇨ picture at CAMERA.

viewpoint /'vjuːpɔɪnt/ *n* = POINT OF VIEW.

V

vigil /'vɪdʒɪl/ n a period of staying awake, esp at night, in order to keep watch or to pray: *keep a hospital bedside vigil* ○ *hold a candlelight vigil for peace.*

vigilant /'vɪdʒɪlənt/ adj (*fml*) looking out for possible danger, trouble, etc: *remain/stay vigilant against car theft.* ▶ **vigilance** /-əns/ n [U]: *police vigilance* ○ *She stressed the need for constant vigilance.* **vigilantly** adv.

vigilante /ˌvɪdʒɪ'lænti/ n (*sometimes derog*) a member of a group of people who try to prevent crime and disorder in a community, esp because the police are not dealing adequately with it.

vignette /vɪn'jet/ n **1** a short piece of writing or acting about a particular person, place or event: *a series of charming vignettes of Edwardian life.* **2(a)** a small picture or design, esp on the first page of a book. **(b)** a photograph or drawing, esp of a person's head and shoulders.

vigour (*US* **vigor**) /'vɪgə(r)/ n [U] **(a)** physical strength or energy: *work with renewed vigour and enthusiasm* ○ *feeling full of vigour.* **(b)** being forceful in thought, language, style, etc: *She responded to his angry accusations with equal vigour.* ⇨ note at STRENGTH.

▶ **vigorous** /'vɪgərəs/ adj **(a)** strong, active or full of energy: *avoid vigorous exercise* ○ *conduct a vigorous campaign* ○ *vigorous supporters of human rights.* **(b)** using forceful language, etc: *a vigorous debate* ○ *the poem's vigorous rhythms.* **vigorously** adv: *work/ play vigorously* ○ *shake sb's hand vigorously* ○ *argue vigorously in support of sth.*

Viking /'vaɪkɪŋ/ n a member of a race of Scandinavian people who attacked and sometimes settled in parts of N and W Europe, including Britain, in the 8th to the 11th centuries: *Viking invaders.*

vile /vaɪl/ adj (**-r, -st**) **1** extremely disgusting: *a vile smell/taste* ○ *use vile language.* **2** morally bad; wicked: *make vile accusations* ○ *Bribery is a vile practice.* **3** (*infml*) extremely bad: *vile weather* ○ *be in a vile temper/mood.* ▶ **vilely** /'vaɪlli/ adv. **vileness** n [U].

vilify /'vɪlɪfaɪ/ v (*pt, pp* **-fied**) (*fml*) to say unpleasant or insulting things about sb: [Vn] *She was vilified by the press for her unfashionable views.* ▶ **vilification** /ˌvɪlɪfɪ'keɪʃn/ n [U]: *face public vilification.*

vilia /'vɪlə/ n **1** (*Brit*) (usu as part of an address) a large house in a district outside the centre of a town or city: *live at 3 Albert Villas.* **2** a house where people stay on holiday, eg by the sea, in the countryside, etc: *rent a holiday villa in Spain.* **3** a country house with a large garden, esp in southern Europe. **4** (in Roman times) a country house or farm with an estate attached to it.

village /'vɪlɪdʒ/ n **1(a)** [C] a group of houses, shops, etc, usu with a church and situated in a country district: *the village school/church/pub.* **(b)** [CGp] the community of people who live there: *The whole village is involved in the fête.* Compare HAMLET, TOWN. **2** [C] (*US*) the smallest unit of local government.

▶ **villager** /'vɪlɪdʒə(r)/ n a person who lives in a village: *local villagers.*

villain /'vɪlən/ n **1(a)** a person who is guilty or capable of great wickedness: *He's no saint, but he's no villain either.* **(b)** (*Brit sl*) a criminal: *The police have caught the villains who broke into an old people's home.* **2** (in a story, play, etc) a character whose evil actions or motives (MOTIVE) are important to the plot: *a pantomime/tragic villain.* Compare HERO. **IDM** **the ˈvillain of the piece** (*esp joc*) a person or thing responsible for some trouble, damage, etc: *It is hard to identify the real villain of the piece in such a situation.*

▶ **villainous** /'vɪlənəs/ adj characteristic of a villain; extremely bad: *He plays the part of the villainous Captain Hook.* **villainy** n [U,C] (*fml*) wicked behaviour or a wicked act.

villein /'vɪleɪn/ n (in medieval Europe) a person who worked on land rented from a lord and who had to serve his lord.

vim /vɪm/ n [U] (*dated infml*) energy or vigour: *feel full of vim.*

vinaigrette /ˌvɪnɪ'gret/ n [U,C] a mixture of oil, VINEGAR, various types of HERB, etc, used for putting on SALAD.

vindicate /'vɪndɪkeɪt/ v (*fml*) **1** to clear sb/sth of blame or suspicion: [Vn] *The report fully vindicated the unions.* ○ *I consider that I've been completely vindicated.* **2** to show or prove the truth, justice, value, etc of sth that has been disputed: [Vn] *Subsequent events vindicated his suspicions.* ○ *Her demand for compensation was vindicated by the tribunal.* ▶ **vindication** /ˌvɪndɪ'keɪʃn/ n [U,C] (*fml*): *seek vindication of a claim* ○ *insist on a public vindication.*

vindictive /vɪn'dɪktɪv/ adj having or showing a desire for revenge; not forgiving: *a vindictive person/act/comment* ○ *She can be extremely vindictive.* ▶ **vindictively** adv: *'It serves them right,' he thought vindictively.* **vindictiveness** n [U].

vine /vaɪn/ n **1** a climbing plant whose fruit is the GRAPE: *'vine leaves* ○ *a row of vines.* **2** a thin stem of a plant that climbs or grows along the ground.

vinegar /'vɪnɪgə(r)/ n [U] a liquid with a very sharp taste used with certain foods: *onions pickled in vinegar* ○ *Do you want vinegar on your chips?*

▶ **vinegary** /'vɪnɪgəri/ adj **1** of or like vinegar in smell or taste: *This wine tastes rather vinegary.* **2** bad-tempered; unkind.

vineyard /'vɪnjəd/ n an area planted with vines (VINE 1) for making wine.

vingt-et-un /ˌvæ̃t eɪ 'ɜː/ n [U] (*French*) = PONTOON[1].

vino /'viːnəʊ/ n [U] (*infml joc*) wine.

vintage /'vɪntɪdʒ/ n **(a)** [C,U] wine produced in a particular season; the quality of this: *1959 was an excellent vintage.* ○ *What vintage (ie year) is this wine?* ○ *vintage claret/port* ○ *a vintage year for champagne.* **(b)** [C usu *sing*] the period or season of gathering grapes (GRAPE) for making wine: *The vintage was later than usual.*

▶ **vintage** adj [attrib] **1(a)** characteristic of a period in the past and of high quality: *vintage TV drama.* **(b)** (used before names) representing the best work of a particular person: *This movie is vintage Chaplin.* **2** (*Brit*) (of a vehicle) made between 1917 and 1930: *vintage cars.* Compare VETERAN CAR.

vintner /'vɪntnə(r)/ n (*dated*) a person whose business is selling wines.

vinyl /'vaɪnl/ n [U,C] tough flexible plastic used for making records, book covers, floor tiles, etc.

viola /vi'əʊlə/ n a musical instrument with strings played with a bow[1](2). A viola is similar to but larger than a VIOLIN. ⇨ picture at MUSICAL INSTRUMENT.

violate /'vaɪəleɪt/ v **1** to break or be contrary to a rule, principle, treaty, etc: [Vn] *violate international law/human rights.* **2** to disturb sth; to fail to respect sth: [Vn] *violate the peace* ○ *She felt that her privacy had been violated.* **3** to disturb or break into a sacred place: [Vn] *violate a tomb/shrine.* **4** (*fml or euph*) [Vn] to force a woman or girl to have sex; to RAPE[1] sb. ▶ **violation** /ˌvaɪə'leɪʃn/ n [U,C]: *be in open violation of the treaty* ○ *gross violations of human rights.* **violator** n.

violent /'vaɪələnt/ adj **1(a)** using, showing or caused by physical force that is intended to hurt or kill sb: *violent crime* ○ *a violent attack/assault/struggle* ○ *meet with/die a violent death* (eg be murdered) ○ *watch a violent film* (ie one in which many people are hurt or killed) ○ *Students were involved in violent clashes with the police.* ○ *He has a tendency to become/turn violent.* (**b**) using, showing or caused by very strong emotion: *fly into a violent rage* ○ *use violent language* ○ *take a violent dislike to sb.* **2** very bad or strong: *violent winds/storms/earthquakes* ○ *violent toothache* ○ *a violent contrast/change.*

▶ **violence** /-əns/ *n* [U] **1(a)** violent behaviour intended to hurt or harm sb: *crimes/acts/outbreaks/threats of violence* ○ *condemn the use of violence against demonstrators* ○ *TV violence/violence on TV* ○ *They are ready to **do violence** to anyone who stands in their way.* (**b**) very strong feeling that is not controlled: *views expressed with some violence.* **2** very strong physical force: *the violence of the storm/crash.*

violently *adv*: *kick/struggle/react violently* ○ *be violently ill/sick* ○ *He fell violently in love with her.*

violet /ˈvaɪələt/ *n* **1** [C] a small wild or garden plant, usu with sweet-smelling purple or white flowers. **2** [U] the colour of wild violets; bluish-purple. ⇨ picture at SPECTRUM. **IDM** **a shrinking violet** ⇨ SHRINK.

▶ **violet** *adj* having the bluish-purple colour of wild violets: *violet eyes.*

violin /ˌvaɪəˈlɪn/ *n* a musical instrument with strings. It is held under the chin and played with a bow[1](2). ⇨ picture at MUSICAL INSTRUMENT. ▶ **violinist** *n*: *a solo violinist.*

VIP /ˌviː aɪ ˈpiː/ *abbr* (*infml*) very important person: *give sb/get (the) VIP treatment* (ie special favours and privileges) ○ *the VIP lounge* (eg at an airport).

viper /ˈvaɪpə(r)/ *n* a poisonous snake found in Africa, Asia and Europe.

virago /vɪˈrɑːɡəʊ/ *n* (*pl* **os**) (*derog*) a fierce and forceful woman.

viral ⇨ VIRUS.

virgin /ˈvɜːdʒɪn/ *n* **1** [C] a person, esp a girl or woman, who has never had sex. **2 the (Blessed) Virgin** [sing] the Virgin Mary, mother of Jesus Christ: *believe in the virgin ˈbirth* (ie that Mary was a virgin before and after giving birth to Jesus).

▶ **virgin** *adj* [usu attrib] in an original or natural condition: *virgin snow* ○ *virgin olive oil* ○ *virgin forest/soil/land* (ie that has never been cultivated).

virginity /vəˈdʒɪnəti/ *n* [U] the state of being a virgin: *keep/lose one's virginity.*

virginal /ˈvɜːdʒɪnl/ *adj* of or suitable for a virgin: *dressed in virginal white.*

Virginia creeper /vəˌdʒɪniə ˈkriːpə(r)/ (*US* also **woodbine**) *n* [U] an ornamental climbing plant often grown on walls, with large leaves which turn red in the autumn.

Virgo /ˈvɜːɡəʊ/ *n* (**a**) [U] the 6th sign of the ZODIAC, the Virgin ⇨ picture at ZODIAC. (**b**) [C] (*pl* **-os**) a person born under the influence of this sign. ⇨ picture at ZODIAC. ⇨ note at ZODIAC.

virile /ˈvɪraɪl; *US* ˈvɪrəl/ *adj* (*usu approv*) **1** (of men) having a lot of sexual vigour or power: *virile young males.* **2** having or showing typically male strength or energy: *virile sports/games.*

▶ **virility** /vəˈrɪləti/ *n* [U] **1** sexual power in men: *feel a need to prove/assert one's virility* ○ *He drives fast cars as symbols of his virility.* **2** strength or energy: *political/economic virility.*

virology /vaɪˈrɒlədʒi/ *n* [U] the scientific study of viruses (VIRUS 1) and virus diseases. ▶ **virologist** /vaɪˈrɒlədʒɪst/ *n*.

virtual /ˈvɜːtʃuəl/ *adj* [attrib] almost or nearly the thing described, but not completely: *He's become a **virtual recluse** since his wife died.* ○ *We sat in virtual silence on the way home.* ○ *She married a virtual stranger.*

▶ **virtually** /-tʃuəli/ *adv* almost: *virtually certain/impossible/identical/invisible* ○ *These animals are virtually extinct.* ○ *Virtually all of it has been destroyed.* ○ *Virtually everyone I knew was there.*

■ ˌvirtual reˈality *n* [U] a system in which images that look like real objects are created by computer and appear to surround a person wearing special equipment: *virtual reality video games.*

virtue /ˈvɜːtʃuː/ *n* **1(a)** [U] behaviour that shows high moral standards; goodness: *lead a life of virtue* ○ *No one would describe him as a **paragon of virtue**.* (**b**) [C] a particular form of this; a good habit: *extol/praise the virtue of hard work* ○ (*saying*) *Patience is a virtue.* Compare VICE[1] 1. **2** [C, U] an attractive or useful quality; an advantage: *The plan has the great virtue of being flexible/of flexibility.* ○ *He was extolling the virtues of private education.* ○ *The director has made a virtue of the film's limited budget.* **IDM** **by virtue of sth** on account of or because of sth: *They are paid more by virtue of their seniority.* ○ *She got the job by virtue of being the only one to apply.* **make a ˌvirtue of neˈcessity** to do sth good willingly, even though one has to do it anyway: *Being short of money, I made a virtue of necessity and gave up smoking.* **of easy virtue** ⇨ EASY[1].

▶ **virtuous** /ˈvɜːtʃuəs/ *adj* **1** having or showing moral virtue: *virtuous behaviour* ○ *a virtuous person.* **2** (*derog* or *joc*) claiming to have or show better behaviour or higher moral principles than others: *He's feeling all virtuous because he's washed the car!* **virtuously** *adv*.

virtuoso /ˌvɜːtʃuˈəʊzəʊ, -ˈəʊsəʊ/ *n* (*pl* **virtuosos** or **virtuosi** /-ziː, -siː/) **1** a person who is exceptionally skilful at doing sth, esp playing a musical instrument or singing: *a cello virtuoso* ○ *a virtuoso pianist* ○ *jazz virtuosos.* **2** [attrib] showing unusually great skill: *a virtuoso display/performance.*

▶ **virtuosity** /ˌvɜːtʃuˈɒsəti/ *n* [U] the skill of a virtuoso: *orchestral/technical virtuosity* ○ *a display of breathtaking/dazzling virtuosity.*

virulent /ˈvɪrələnt, -rjəl-/ *adj* **1** [esp attrib] (of a disease or poison) extremely harmful: *a virulent form of flu.* **2** (*fml*) showing strong or bitter hostility: *virulent criticism* ○ *make a virulent attack on the media.* ▶ **virulence** /-ləns/ *n* [U]. **virulently** *adv*: *be virulently opposed to change.*

virus /ˈvaɪrəs/ *n* (*pl* **viruses**) **1(a)** a simple living thing, smaller than bacteria, which causes infectious disease: *the flu/rabies/AIDS virus* ○ *a virus infection.* Compare MICROBE. (**b**) (*infml*) a disease caused by one of these: *contract/transmit a virus* ○ *There's a virus going round the office* (ie making people ill). **2** (*computing*) a hidden code within a computer program intended to cause errors and destroy stored information.

▶ **viral** /ˈvaɪrəl/ *adj* of, like or caused by a virus: *a viral infection.*

visa /ˈviːzə/ *n* a stamp or mark put on a PASSPORT by officials of a foreign country to show that the holder may enter, pass through or leave their country: *entry/transit/exit visas* ○ *apply for an American visa* ○ *renew/extend a visa.*

visage /ˈvɪzɪdʒ/ *n* (*joc* or *rhet*) a person's face: *his beaming visage.*

vis-à-vis /ˌviːz ɑː ˈviː/ *prep* (*French*) **1** in relation to sth: *a difference of opinion about Britain's role vis-à-vis Europe.* **2** in comparison with sth: *The Channel Tunnel should not be given an unfair advantage vis-à-vis other forms of cross-Channel transport.*

viscera /ˈvɪsərə/ *n* (usu **the viscera**) [pl] (*anatomy*) the large internal organs of the body, eg the heart, the lungs, the bowels, etc.

▶ **visceral** /ˈvɪsərəl/ *adj* **1** (*fml*) (of feelings, etc) not rational; following one's instincts: *the sheer*

V

visceral excitement of a motor-bike ride. **2** (*anatomy*) of the viscera.

viscose /ˈvɪskəʊz, -əʊs/ *n* [U] an artificial material used in making clothes, etc: *This material is 50% viscose.*

viscount /ˈvaɪkaʊnt/ *n* **1** a British nobleman ranking higher than a BARON(1) but lower than an EARL. **2** the title of the eldest son of an EARL: *Viscount Linley.*
▶ **viscountcy** /-tsi/ *n* the title or rank of a viscount.
viscountess /ˈvaɪkaʊntəs/ *n* **1** a viscount's wife or widow. **2** a female viscount.

viscous /ˈvɪskəs/ *adj* (of a liquid) not flowing freely; thick and sticky: *viscous oil* ○ *a highly viscous fluid.*
▶ **viscosity** /vɪˈskɒsəti/ *n* [U]: *control the viscosity of blood* ○ *high viscosity oil.*

vise /vaɪs/ *n* (*US*) = VICE².

visible /ˈvɪzəbl/ *adj* ~ (**to sb/sth**) **1** that can be seen; in sight: *The hills were barely visible through the mist.* ○ *This star is not visible to the naked eye.* Compare INVISIBLE 1. **2** noticeable; clear; obvious: *visible improvements/differences/changes* ○ *The only visible damage was a broken headlight.*
▶ **visibility** /ˌvɪzəˈbɪləti/ *n* [U] **1** the fact or state of being visible: *companies trying to increase their visibility in the market* (ie to make people more aware of their products and services). **2** the extent to which the light or weather enables one to see things at a distance: *planes grounded because of poor/low/bad visibility* ○ *Visibility was down to 100 metres in the fog.*
visibly /-əbli/ *adv* in a noticeable way: *be visibly offended/ill/shocked* ○ *She was visibly shaken by the experience.*

vision /ˈvɪʒn/ *n* **1** [U] (**a**) the power of seeing; sight: *have good/perfect/poor/blurred/normal vision* ○ *within/outside one's field of vision* (ie that one can/cannot see from a certain point). (**b**) the ability to think about or plan the future with great imagination or wisdom: *a statesman of (great breadth of) vision* ○ *be rather lacking in vision.* **2** [C] (**a**) a dream or similar experience, esp of a religious kind: *Jesus came to Paul in a vision.* (**b**) (esp *pl*) a thing experienced powerfully in the imagination, esp concerning the future: *a political/economic vision* ○ *conjure up visions of married bliss* ○ *I had visions of us getting completely lost.* **3** [C] ~ **of sth** (*rhet*) a person or sight of unusual beauty: *She was a vision of loveliness.* **4** [U] the picture on a television or cinema screen: *We apologize for the loss of vision in certain areas.* See also TUNNEL VISION.

visionary /ˈvɪʒənri; *US* -ʒəneri/ *adj* **1** (*approv*) having or showing the ability to think about or plan the future with great imagination or wisdom: *visionary leaders/writers/* ○ *visionary insights/experiences.* **2** having or showing great imaginative or artistic power: *visionary poetry.*
▶ **visionary** *n* (*usu approv*) a person who has visionary ideas: *True visionaries are often misunderstood by their own generation.*

visit /ˈvɪzɪt/ *v* **1**(**a**) to go or come to see a person, place, etc either socially or on business or for some other purpose: [Vn] *visit friends/relatives* ○ *visit the dentist/doctor* ○ *Most tourists in London visit Trafalgar Square.* [V] 'visiting hours (ie when relations and friends can see patients at a hospital). (**b**) to go or come to see a person, a place, an institution, etc in order to make an official examination or check: [V] *The school inspector is visiting next week.* [Vn] *The restaurant is visited regularly by public health officers.* **2** to stay temporarily at a place or with a person: [V] *We don't live here, we're just visiting.* [Vn] *I'm going to visit my aunt for a few days.* **PHRV** 'visit sth on/upon sb/sth (*arch*) to inflict punishment, etc on sb/sth: *visit the sins of the fathers upon*

the children (ie make the children suffer for their parents' sins). **visit with sb** (*US infml*) to spend time with sb, esp for an informal talk: *Please stay and visit with me for a while.*
▶ **visit** *n* **1** ~ (**to sb/sth**) (**from sb/sth**) an act or period of visiting; a temporary stay: *his first visit to his wife's parents/to Paris* ○ *pay a visit to a friend/a doctor/a client* ○ *be/come/go on a visit to the seaside* ○ *a social/state visit* ○ *receive regular visits from one's landlord.* **2** (*US infml*) an informal talk: *We had a nice visit on the phone.* See also FLYING VISIT.
visiting *adj* [attrib] teaching for a fixed period at another university or college: *a visiting professor.*
'**visiting-card** (*Brit*) (*US* 'calling-card) *n* a small card with one's name, address, company, etc printed on it, which one leaves with clients, social contacts etc.

NOTE You **visit** somebody for a short time: *She visited her father in hospital every day.* You can also **visit** a place: *There are no fewer than 80 castles to visit in Wales.* You can use **come and stay** or **go and stay** when you visit somebody for a few days or longer: *Come and stay with us for the weekend.* ○ *My cousin Tom has invited me to go and stay with him in Canada.*

You **call on** somebody for an official purpose: *A representative of the company will call on you tomorrow.* You **call in on** a friend for a short time, often when you are on the way to somewhere else: *We could call in on Patrick on the way to your mother's.* You **drop by** at somebody's house, or **drop in on** somebody, if you make a short unplanned visit to friends or family: *Let's drop in on Nicky when we're in Bristol, shall we?* ○ *Drop by any time for a coffee.*

visitation /ˌvɪzɪˈteɪʃn/ *n* [C, U] (*fml*) **1** ~ (**of/from sb/sth**) an official visit, esp to inspect sb/sth: *a visitation of the sick* (ie made by a clergyman as part of his duties) ○ (*joc*) *visitations from the Tax Inspector.* **2** ~ (**of/from sb/sth**) an unexpected appearance of sth, eg a ghost: *a visitation of beings from outer space* ○ *strange dreams and visitations.* **3** ~ (**of sth**) a disaster considered as a punishment from God: *a visitation of plague.*

visitor /ˈvɪzɪtə(r)/ *n* ~ (**to sb/sth**) (**from sb/sth**) **1**(**a**) a person who visits a person or place: *I live alone and don't have/get many visitors.* ○ *We've got visitors (coming) this weekend.* ○ *She is a frequent visitor to the gallery.* (**b**) a person who stays temporarily at a place or with a person: *Rome welcomes millions of visitors each year.* **2** a bird that lives in an area temporarily or at a certain season: *summer/winter visitors to these shores.* See also HEALTH VISITOR.
■ '**visitors' book** *n* a book in which visitors write their names, addresses and sometimes comments, eg at a private house, a hotel or a place of public interest.

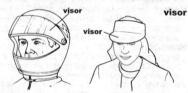

visor   visor

visor /ˈvaɪzə(r)/ *n* **1** a part of a HELMET, that can be pulled down to protect the eyes and face: *a motorcycle helmet with a visor.* ⇨ picture. **2** a piece of plastic, cloth, etc worn above the eyes to protect them from the sun. ⇨ picture. **3** a small movable screen in a car that protects the driver's eyes from the sun.

vista /ˈvɪstə/ *n* (*fml*) **1** a beautiful view, eg of natural scenery, a city, etc: *the broad vistas of parkland visible from the tower.* **2** a long series of scenes,

---

events, etc that one can look back on or forward to: *This discovery opens up new vistas of research for scientists.*

visual /'vɪʒʊəl/ *adj* of or concerned with seeing or sight: *visual images/effects* ○ *the visual arts* (ie painting, cinema, theatre, etc) ○ *a good visual memory* ○ *He takes photographs as a visual record of the places he has visited.* ○ *Her designs have a strong visual appeal.*
▶ **visual** *n* a picture, map, piece of film, etc, used to make an article or a talk easier to understand or more appealing: *His lecture was accompanied by some striking visuals.*

visualize, -ise /-aɪz/ *v* to form a mental picture of sb/sth; to see sb/sth in one's mind: [Vn] *I remember meeting him but I just can't visualize him.* [V.ing] *She can't visualize doing a job like that.* [V.n ing] *I can't visualize myself ever getting married.* [Vn-n] *I visualize their house as a sort of tumbledown mansion.* **visualization, -isation** /ˌvɪʒʊəlaɪ'zeɪʃn; *US* -lə'z-/ *n* [U, C]: *powers of visualization.*

visually /'vɪʒʊəli/ *adv* **1** in seeing: *visually handicapped/impaired* (ie blind or nearly blind). **2** in appearance: *a visually exciting display of primitive art.*
■ ˌvisual ˈaid *n* (esp *pl*) a picture, film, VIDEO(2a), etc used in teaching to help people to learn or understand sth.
ˌvisual diˈsplay unit *n* (*abbr* **VDU**) (*computing*) a device resembling a TELEVISION screen, which is connected to a computer and on which information stored in the computer can be displayed.

vital /'vaɪtl/ *adj* **1** ~ (**to/for sth**) essential to the existence, success, or operation of sth: *vital information* ○ *The timing was of vital importance.* ○ *The police **perform/play** a vital role in our society.* ○ *It is absolutely vital that this should be kept secret.* **2** [attrib] connected with or essential to life: *The heart performs a vital bodily function.* ○ *He received several bullet wounds but was not hit in any of the vital organs.* **3** (*approv*) energetic or lively; full of life: *She's a very vital person.*
▶ **vitally** /'vaɪtəli/ *adv* extremely: *Education is vitally important for the country's future.*
the vitals *n* [pl] (*dated or joc*) the important organs of the body, eg the heart and brain.
■ ˌvital staˈtistics *n* [pl] (*Brit infml*) the measurements of a woman's BUST¹(2), waist and hips.

vitality /vaɪ'tæləti/ *n* [U] liveliness and energy; vigour: *She is bursting with vitality and new ideas.* ○ *The music has a wonderful freshness and vitality.*

vitamin /'vɪtəmɪn; *US* 'vaɪt-/ *n* any of a number of organic substances which are present in certain foods and are essential to the health and growth of humans and animals: *Oranges are rich in vitamin C.* ○ *breakfast cereals enriched with vitamins* ○ *vitamin deficiency* ○ ˈvitamin pills.

vitiate /'vɪʃieɪt/ *v* (*fml*) to spoil the quality or reduce the force of sth: *inflationary wage increases that have vitiated much of the country's recent economic history.*

viticulture /'vɪtɪkʌltʃə(r), 'vaɪt-/ *n* [U] (*techn*) the science or practice of growing grapes (GRAPE), esp for use in making wine.

vitreous /'vɪtriəs/ *adj* (*techn*) hard, shiny and transparent like glass: *vitreous enamel/china/porcelain.*

vitrify /'vɪtrɪfaɪ/ *v* (*pt, pp* **-fied**) [V, Vn] to change or make sth change into glass or a substance similar to glass, esp by heat. ▶ **vitrification** /ˌvɪtrɪfɪ'keɪʃn/ *n* [U].

vitriol /'vɪtriɒl/ *n* [U] very cruel and bitter comments or criticism: *He poured out a stream of vitriol against foreign interference.*
▶ **vitriolic** /ˌvɪtri'ɒlɪk/ *adj* full of bitter hatred and anger: *a vitriolic letter* ○ *launch a vitriolic attack on sb.*

vitro ⇨ IN VITRO.

vituperation /vɪˌtjuːpə'reɪʃn; *US* vaɪˌtuː-/ *n* [U] (*fml*) cruel and angry criticism. ▶ **vituperative** /vɪ'tjuːpərətɪv; *US* vaɪ'tuːpəreɪtɪv/ *adj*: *His book was published to some extremely vituperative reviews.*

viva /'vaɪvə/ *n* (*Brit infml*) = VIVA VOCE: *I've finished my written exams but I still have to do a viva.*

vivacious /vɪ'veɪʃəs/ *adj* (*approv*) (esp of a woman) having or showing a lively attractive personality: *I remember his daughter as a charming, pretty and vivacious girl.* ○ *She gave a vivacious laugh.* ▶ **vivaciously** *adv*. **vivacity** /vɪ'væsəti/ *n* [U]: *dances performed with great vivacity.*

viva voce /ˌvaɪvə 'vəʊtʃi/ (also *Brit infml* **viva**) *n* a spoken examination, esp in British universities.

vivid /'vɪvɪd/ *adj* **1** (of light or colour) strong and bright; intense: *She looked at me with those vivid blue eyes of hers.* **2** creating ideas, images, etc easily: *a vivid imagination.* **3** producing strong clear pictures in the mind: *a vivid description/account* ○ *a vivid memory/recollection/dream.* ▶ **vividly** *adv*: *I vividly remember/recall the day I first met him.* **vividness** *n* [U]: *the frightening vividness of the dream.*

vivisection /ˌvɪvɪ'sekʃn/ *n* [U] the practice of performing operations, etc on live animals for the purposes of scientific research: *the anti-vivisection lobby.*

vixen /'vɪksn/ *n* **1** a female fox. **2** (*dated*) an unpleasant and bad-tempered woman.

viz /vɪz/ *abbr* that is to say; in other words (Latin *videlicet*): *I shall confine my remarks to a certain class of creative person, viz authors.*

V-neck ⇨ V¹.

vocabulary /və'kæbjələri; *US* -leri/ *n* **1** [C] the total number of words in a language: *When did the word 'bungalow' first enter the vocabulary?* **2** [C, U] all the words known to a person or used in a particular book, subject, etc: *a wide/limited/rich vocabulary* ○ *Tim has an average vocabulary for a 3-year-old.* ○ *one's active vocabulary* (ie the words one knows and uses) ○ *one's passive vocabulary* (ie the words one understands but does not use) ○ *enrich/increase/extend one's vocabulary.* **3** (*infml*) (also **vocab** /'vəʊkæb/) [U, C] a list of words with their meanings, esp one that accompanies a TEXTBOOK(1) in a foreign language. Compare GLOSSARY.

vocal /'vəʊkl/ *adj* **1** [usu attrib] of, for or produced by the voice: *the vocal organs* (ie the tongue, lips, etc) ○ *The cantata has a difficult vocal score.* ○ *Callas's vocal range was astonishing.* **2** expressing one's opinions or feelings freely and often loudly: *He is a very vocal critic of the government's transport policy.* ○ *The protesters are a small but vocal minority.*
▶ **vocal** *n* (often *pl*) the sung part of a piece of JAZZ or pop music: *backing vocals* ○ *In this recording Armstrong himself is on vocals.*
vocalist /'vəʊkəlɪst/ *n* a singer, esp in a JAZZ or pop group: *the lead/guest vocalist.* Compare INSTRUMENTALIST.
vocally /'vəʊkəli/ *adv* **1** in a way that uses the voice: *a charming if vocally limited performance.* **2** in an energetic, noisy and determined way: *protest vocally.*
■ ˌvocal ˈcords *n* [pl] the part of the LARYNX that produces the voice. ⇨ picture at THROAT.

vocalize, -ise /'vəʊkəlaɪz/ *v* (*fml*) to say or sing sounds or words; to use words to express sth: [Vn] *He finds it hard to vocalize his feelings.*
▶ **vocalization, -isation** *n* (*fml*) (**a**) [C] a word or sound produced by the voice: *the vocalizations of animals.* (**b**) [U] the process of producing a word or sound with the voice.

vocation /vəʊ'keɪʃn/ *n* **1** [C] ~ (**for/to sth**) a strong

V

feeling that one is specially fitted for a certain type of work or way of life: *have a religious vocation/a vocation to the priesthood* ∘ *Nursing is a vocation as well as a profession.* **2** [C usu *sing*] a person's job or profession: *She feels she's found her true vocation (in life).* ∘ *You've missed your vocation* (ie You are following the wrong career) — *you should have been an actor.*
▸ **vocational** /-ʃənl/ *adj* of or relating to the qualifications and preparation needed for a particular job: *do a vocational course* ∘ *vocational guidance/training* (eg for students about to leave school).

vocative /ˈvɒkətɪv/ *n* (*grammar*) a special form of a noun, a pronoun or an adjective used in some languages when addressing a person or thing.
▸ **vocative** *adj* of or in the vocative.

vociferous /vəˈsɪfərəs; *US* vəʊ-/ *adj* noisy and forceful in expressing one's feelings or opinions: *vociferous complaints/protests/demands* ∘ *a vociferous group of demonstrators.* ▸ **vociferously** *adv*: *be vociferously opposed to sth.*

vodka /ˈvɒdkə/ *n* [U, C] a strong colourless alcoholic drink made esp in Russia and Eastern Europe from grain, potatoes, etc: *a vodka and lime.*

vogue /vəʊg/ *n* [C usu *sing*] ~ (**for sth**) a current fashion: *a vogue for unusual pets/large families/health foods* ∘ *Black is **in vogue** again.* ∘ *Short hair has **come back into vogue.*** ∘ *His novels had a great vogue ten years ago.*

voice /vɔɪs/ *n* **1** [C, U] the sound or sounds produced through the mouth, esp by a person speaking or singing: *I can hear voices through the wall.* ∘ *Keep your voice down* (ie Don't speak loudly). ∘ *recognize sb's voice* ∘ *speak in a loud/rough/husky/gentle voice* ∘ *lower one's voice* (ie speak more quietly) ∘ *He has a good singing voice.* ∘ *When did his voice break* (ie become deep like a man's)? ∘ *Her voice shook/trembled with emotion.* ∘ *'There you are,' said a voice behind me.* ∘ *Don't take that **tone of voice** with me!* ∘ *He was **in good voice** (ie singing well) at the concert tonight.* **2** [sing] (**a**) ~ (**in sth**) the right to express one's opinion, etc in spoken or written words; influence: *The workers want a voice in the decision-making process.* (**b**) [sing] a particular attitude or opinion expressed: *listen to the voice of reason/experience/dissent* ∘ *a newspaper that represents the voice of the people.* **3** [sing] (*grammar*) a form or set of forms of a verb in which either the person or thing that does sth is the subject of the verb (*the active voice*) or the person or thing that is affected by the action of the verb is the subject (*the passive voice*). **4** [U] (*phonetics*) a sound produced by VIBRATION of the vocal cords (VOCAL), used in the pronunciation of vowels and certain consonants, ie /b, d, g, dʒ, v, ð, z, m, n, ŋ, w, r, l, j/. **IDM** **at the top of one's voice** ⇨ TOP[1]. **find one's voice/tongue** ⇨ FIND[1]. **give voice to sth** to express one's feelings, worries, etc: *Many of the workers at the meeting gave voice to their fears about job security and the future of the company.* **like, etc the sound of one's own voice** ⇨ SOUND[1]. **make one's 'voice heard** to express one's feelings, opinions, etc in such a way that they are noticed and taken into account: *This programme gives ordinary viewers a chance to make their voice(s) heard.* **raise one's voice** ⇨ RAISE. **the still small voice** ⇨ STILL[1]. **with ˌone 'voice** as a group; with everyone agreeing: *The various opposition parties speak with one voice on this issue.*
▸ **voice** *v* **1** to express one's feelings, etc in words: [Vn] *A spokesman voiced the workers' dissatisfaction.* ∘ *Some people are nervous about voicing their opinions in public.* **2** (*phonetics*) to produce a sound with voice(4): [Vn] *voiced consonants.*
-voiced (forming compound *adj*s) having a voice of the specified kind: *loud-voiced* ∘ *gruff-voiced.*

voiceless *adj* (*phonetics*) (of a sound) produced without voice(4). The consonants /p, t, k, tʃ, f, θ, s, ʃ, h/ are voiceless.
■ **'voice-box** *n* = LARYNX.
'voice-over *n* (in a film, television programme, etc) an explanation or account given by sb who is not seen: *She earns a lot of money doing voice-overs for TV commercials.*

void /vɔɪd/ *n* (usu *sing*) (*fml or rhet*) a large empty space: *Below him there was nothing but a black void.* ∘ *an aching void left by the loss of her child* ∘ *Who will fill the political void created by his death?*
▸ **void** *adj* (*fml*) **1** empty. **2** [pred] ~ **of sth** without sth; lacking sth: *Her face was void of all interest.* Compare DEVOID. **3** (of a contract, etc) not valid or legal: *The agreement was declared void.* **IDM** **null and void** ⇨ NULL.
void *v* [Vn] **1** (*fml*) to empty sth, esp the contents of one's bowels or BLADDER. **2** (*law*) to declare that sth is not valid.

voile /vɔɪl/ *n* [U] a very thin fine material made of cotton, wool or silk.

vol *abbr* (*pl* **vols**) volume: *Complete Works of Byron Vol 2.*

volatile /ˈvɒlətaɪl; *US* -tl/ *adj* **1** (*techn*) (of a liquid) changing rapidly into a gas. **2(a)** (*esp derog*) (of a person) changing quickly from one mood to another: *a highly volatile personality/disposition/nature.* (**b**) (of a situation) likely to change suddenly or sharply; not STABLE[1]: *volatile stock markets/exchange rates* ∘ *a volatile political situation.* ▸ **volatility** /ˌvɒləˈtɪləti/ *n* [U].

vol-au-vent /ˈvɒl ə vɒ̃; *US* ˌvɔːl əʊ ˈvɑːn/ *n* a small case of light pastry filled with meat, fish, etc in a rich sauce.

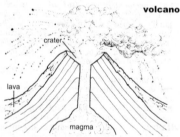

volcano

crater

lava

magma

volcano /vɒlˈkeɪnəʊ/ *n* (*pl* ~**es**) a mountain with a large opening on the top, and sometimes others on the side, through which melted rocks and gases escape with great force, or have done so in the past: *looking down into the crater of an extinct volcano* ∘ *An active volcano may erupt at any time.* ⇨ picture.
▸ **volcanic** /vɒlˈkænɪk/ *adj* [esp attrib] of, like or produced by a volcano: *volcanic eruptions/gases/rocks* ∘ *a volcanic island* ∘ *volcanic activity.*

vole /vəʊl/ *n* a small animal resembling a rat or mouse, which lives in fields or near rivers: *a 'water-vole.*

volition /vəˈlɪʃn; *US* vəʊ-/ *n* [U] (*fml*) the process of using one's will in choosing sth, making a decision, etc: *She left entirely of **her own volition.***

volley /ˈvɒli/ *n* **1** a number of bullets, stones, etc fired or thrown at the same time: *A volley of shots rang out.* ∘ *Police fired a volley over the heads of the crowd.* Compare SALVO. **2** a number of questions, comments, etc directed at sb together or in quick succession: *a volley of abuse/insults/protest* ∘ *She was subjected to a volley of questions by waiting journalists.* **3** (in tennis or football) a stroke or kick with which the ball is played before it touches the ground: *She hit a forehand volley into the net* (ie in tennis).

▶ **volley** *v* (in tennis or football) to hit or kick the ball before it touches the ground: [Vpr, Vnpr] *He volleyed (the ball) into the net.*

volleyball /ˈvɒlibɔːl/ *n* [U] a game in which opposing teams of players hit a ball backwards and forwards over a high net with their hands while trying not to let it touch the ground on their own side.

volt /vəʊlt/ *n* (*abbr* **v**) a unit for measuring the force of an electrical current: *a high security fence with 5 000 volts passing through it.*

▶ **voltage** /ˈvəʊltɪdʒ/ *n* [U, C] electrical force measured in volts: *high/low voltage* ◦ *the voltage of a battery.*

volte-face /ˌvɒlt ˈfɑːs/ *n* (*usu sing*) (*rather fml*) a complete change of attitude, opinion, policy, etc: *This represents a complete volte-face in government thinking.*

voluble /ˈvɒljʊbl/ *adj* (*fml sometimes derog*) (**a**) (of a person) talking a lot, usu very quickly. (**b**) (of speech) expressed in many words and usu fast: *voluble protests.* ▶ **volubly** /ˈvɒljʊbli/ *adv.*

volume /ˈvɒljuːm; *US* -jəm/ *n* **1** [C] (**a**) (*abbr* **vol**) a book, esp one of a matching set or a series: *an encyclopedia in 20 volumes* ◦ *Volume 2 of Shaw's Complete Works is missing.* (**b**) (*infml*) a single book: *a library of over 12 000 volumes* ◦ *a slim volume of poetry.* (**c**) several issues of a magazine, etc designed to be put together to form a book: *'New Scientist', volume 142, 1994.* **2** [U, C] the amount of space in a container or that a substance occupies: *jars of different volumes* ◦ *Allow the dough to rise until it has doubled in volume.* ⇨ picture. Compare AREA 1b. **3** [C] a large amount or quantity of sth: *the sheer volume of business/work* ◦ *an increasing volume of traffic* ◦ *handling record volumes of mail* ◦ (*infml*) *Volumes of black smoke poured from the chimney.* **4** [U] (**a**) the amount of sound produced by sth: *The TV was on at full volume.* ◦ *The music doubled in volume.* ◦ *the volume control knob.* (**b**) the switch on a radio, etc for controlling this: *turn the volume up/down.* **IDM speak volumes about/for sth** ⇨ SPEAK.

volume

volume = 27m³
27 cubic metres (*US* meters)

voluminous /vəˈluːmɪnəs/ *adj* (*fml* or *joc*) **1** (of clothes) using a lot of material; very full(6): *voluminous skirts/petticoats.* **2** (of writing) great in quantity: *keep up a voluminous correspondence with sb* ◦ *voluminous reports.* ▶ **voluminously** *adv.*

voluntary¹ /ˈvɒlntri; *US* -teri/ *adj* **1** acting, done or given willingly: *The prisoner made a voluntary statement.* ◦ *Attendance is purely voluntary.* ◦ *Charities rely on voluntary donations/contributions.* ◦ *The firm went into voluntary liquidation.* **2** working, done or maintained without payment: *do voluntary work in the local hospital* ◦ *fund-raising by voluntary groups* ◦ *The organization/service is run on a voluntary basis.* **3** (of movements of the body) controlled by the will: *voluntary muscles.* Compare INVOLUNTARY.

▶ **voluntarily** /ˈvɒlntrəli; *US* ˌvɒlənˈterəli/ *adv* **1** willingly; without being forced: *I didn't have to ask them to leave; they went voluntarily.* **2** without payment; free of charge: *The fund is voluntarily administered.*

voluntary² /ˈvɒlntri; *US* -teri/ *n* a piece of music played before, during or after a church service, usu on an organ²(1).

volunteer /ˌvɒlənˈtɪə(r)/ *n* **1** ~ (for sth / to do sth) a person who offers to do sth without being forced: *volunteers to run the Christmas show* ◦ *We need a volunteer for the post of treasurer.* ◦ *Few volunteers*

came forward. **2** a person who joins the armed forces of her or his own free will: *volunteer troops/forces.* Compare CONSCRIPT *n.* **3** a person who works for an organization but is not paid for what he or she does: *a volunteer helper/driver.*

▶ **volunteer** *v* **1** ~ (to do sth); ~ (sth) (for sth) to offer to do or give sth without being forced: [V.to inf] *Jill volunteered to organize a petition.* [Vpr] *Several staff members volunteered for early retirement.* [Vnpr] *She volunteered her services for the summer fair.* [also V]. **2** to suggest sth without being asked: [Vn] *volunteer advice/information* [V.speech] *'Tim's busy but I'll come,' he volunteered.* [also V.that]. **3** ~ (for sth) to join the army, etc of one's own free will: [Vpr] *volunteer for military service* [V.to inf] *volunteer to join the navy.* **4** to suggest sb for a job or an activity: [Vnpr] *My wife volunteered me for the washing-up.* [also Vn, Vn.to inf].

voluptuary /vəˈlʌptʃuəri; *US* -ueri/ *n* (*fml usu derog*) a person who enjoys physical pleasures.

voluptuous /vəˈlʌptʃuəs/ *adj* **1** (of a woman) having a full, round and sexually attractive figure: *the voluptuous curves of her body.* **2** giving or suggesting great pleasure to the senses: *voluptuous crimson velvet* ◦ *voluptuous harmonies.* ▶ **voluptuously** *adv.* **voluptuousness** *n* [U].

vomit /ˈvɒmɪt/ *v* ~ sth (up) to bring food from the stomach back out through the mouth; to be sick(2): [V] *We gave her salt and water to make her vomit.* [Vn] *vomit blood* [Vp] *He vomited up all he had eaten.* ◦ (*fig*) *factory chimneys vomiting forth black smoke.* ⇨ note at SICK.

▶ **vomit** *n* [U] food from the stomach brought back out through the mouth: *He had choked to death on his own vomit.*

voodoo /ˈvuːduː/ *n* [U] a religion practised esp in the West Indies involving WITCHCRAFT and magic.

voracious /vəˈreɪʃəs/ *adj* **1** wanting or eating great quantities of food: *a voracious eater* ◦ *have a voracious appetite.* **2** hungry for knowledge or information: *a voracious reader* ◦ *have a voracious interest in new ideas.* ▶ **voraciously** *adv*: *read/eat voraciously.* **voracity** /vəˈræsəti/ *n* [U].

vortex /ˈvɔːteks/ *n* (*pl* **vortexes** or **vortices** /-tɪsiːz/) a mass of water or air that spins round and round so fast that it pulls objects into its centre: *cosmic vortices* ◦ (*fig*) *be drawn into the vortex of high society.*

votary /ˈvəʊtəri/ *n* ~ (of sb/sth) (*fml*) a person who worships or is devoted to sb/sth.

vote /vəʊt/ *n* **1** [C] ~ (for/against sb/sth); ~ (on sth) a formal indication of one's choice between two or more people, courses of action, etc, made eg by marking a special piece of paper or by raising one's hand: *cast/record one's vote* ◦ *take/hold a vote on sth* ◦ *settle/decide/resolve the matter by a vote* ◦ *put sth to the vote* (ie decide a matter by voting) ◦ *The Labour candidate received/polled 8 000 votes.* ◦ *The measure was passed/defeated by 9 votes to 6.* ◦ *The vote went against him.* **2 the vote** [sing] (**a**) votes given by a particular group of people, eg at a political election: *attempts to win the teenage/immigrant/Scottish vote.* (**b**) the votes made in an election: *split the vote* (eg between rival opposition parties) ◦ *The Socialists got 35% of the vote.* **3 the vote** [sing] the right to vote, esp in political elections: *US nationals get the vote at 18.* **IDM cast a/one's vote** ⇨ CAST¹.

▶ **vote** *v* ~ (for/against sb/sth); ~ (on sth) to indicate formally one's choice of candidate in an election, one's preferred course of action, etc: [Vpr] *vote by ballot/proxy/post* ◦ *vote for/against the motion* ◦ *If we cannot agree, let's vote on it.* [Vn] *Vote Morris/Labour on polling day!* ◦ *I voted 'No' in the referendum.* [V] *Are you old enough to vote?* [Vadv] *How did you vote?* [V.to inf] *The workers voted to continue the strike.* **2** to elect sb to a position of authority by a majority of votes: [Vn-n] *I was voted* *chairman.* **3** to agree to give or provide sb/oneself with sth: [Vnn] *The directors have just voted themselves a large pay increase.* **4** (esp passive) to declare sth to be good, bad, etc: [Vn-n] *The show was voted a success.* [Vn-adj] *The judges voted my cake the best.* **5** (*infml*) (no passive) to suggest or propose: [V.*that*] *I vote (that) we stay here.* **IDM** ˌvote with one's ˈfeet to indicate one's opinion by going or not going somewhere: *The villagers voted with their feet by staying away from the meeting.* **PHRV** ˌvote sb/sth ˈdown to reject or defeat sb/sth by voting against them/it. ˌvote sb ˈin/ˈout/ˈon/ˈoff; ˌvote sb ˈinto/ˈout of/ˈonto/ˈoff sth to elect sb to, or reject sb from, a position of authority: *vote the Liberals in* ○ *She was voted out of office/off the board.* ˌvote sth ˈthrough to approve sth or bring a proposal, etc into force by voting for it: *Congress voted the bill through without a debate.*

voter *n* a person who votes or has the right to vote, esp in a political election: *canvass voters* ○ *policies designed to woo voters.* See also FLOATING VOTER.

voting *n* the action of formally indicating one's choice of candidate, preferred course of action, etc: *the first round of voting* ○ *a new system of voting* ○ *tactical voting* ○ *a* ˈvoting paper/slip ○ ˈvoting patterns.

■ ˌvote of ˈconfidence *n* (usu *sing*) a vote taken to show general support for a leader, government, etc: *pass a vote of confidence in sb.*

ˌvote of ˌno ˈconfidence *n* (usu *sing*) a vote taken to express lack of support for a leader, government, etc: *survive a vote of no confidence.*

ˌvote of ˈthanks *n* a speech asking an audience to show their appreciation of sb/sth, esp by clapping (CLAP[1]): *propose a vote of thanks.*

votive /ˈvəʊtɪv/ *adj* [usu attrib] presented, esp in church, to fulfil a promise made to God: *votive offerings/candles.*

vouch /vaʊtʃ/ *v* **PHRV** ˈvouch for sb/sth to take responsibility for or express confidence in a person; to guarantee that sb has a good character: *I can vouch for him/for his honesty.* ˈvouch for sth to confirm a claim, often by producing evidence to support it or using one's own experience to reach a decision: *Experts vouch for the painting's authenticity.*

voucher /ˈvaʊtʃə(r)/ *n* **1** (*Brit*) a small printed piece of paper which can be exchanged for certain goods or services, or which allows one a reduction in the price of sth: *This voucher entitles you to £5 off the cost of a meal for 2.* See also GIFT VOUCHER, LUNCHEON VOUCHER. **2** a piece of paper showing that money has been paid for goods, etc received; a RECEIPT(2).

vouchsafe /vaʊtʃˈseɪf/ *v* ~ sth (to sb) (*dated or fml*) to give sth to sb as a gift or privilege: [Vnpr] *He vouchsafed to me certain family secrets.* [also Vn-n, V.speech].

vow /vaʊ/ *n* a solemn promise, esp a religious one: *keep/break one's* ˈmarriage vows ○ *take a vow of silence/celibacy.*

▶ **vow** *v* to swear, promise or declare sth solemnly; to make a vow about sth: [Vn] *They vowed revenge.* [V.*that*] *He vowed that one day he would return.* [V.*to* inf] *She vowed never to speak to him again.* [also V.speech].

vowel /ˈvaʊəl/ *n* (*phonetics*) **(a)** a speech sound in which the mouth is open and the tongue is not

touching the top of the mouth, the teeth, etc, eg /ɑ:, e, ɔ:/: *vowel sounds* ○ *Each language has a different vowel system.* **(b)** a letter used to represent such a sound, eg (in English) a, e, i, o, u. Compare CONSONANT[1]. See also DIPHTHONG.

vox pop /ˌvɒks ˈpɒp/ *n* [U] (*infml*) public opinion, esp as expressed in short television or newspaper interviews with ordinary people on matters of current interest.

voyage /ˈvɔɪɪdʒ/ *n* a long journey, esp by sea or in space: *a transatlantic voyage* ○ *go on/make a voyage from Mombasa to Goa* ○ *the voyages of the Starship Enterprise* ○ (*fig*) *Archaeology takes us on a voyage into the past.* ⇨ note at JOURNEY.

▶ **voyage** *v* (*fml*) to go on a voyage; to travel: [Vpr] *voyaging across the Indian Ocean/through space.*

voyager /ˈvɔɪɪdʒə(r)/ *n* (*dated*) a person making a voyage, esp to unknown parts of the world by sea.

voyeur /vwaɪˈɜ:(r)/ *n* a person who gets pleasure from secretly watching the sexual activities of others. ▶ **voyeurism** /vwaɪˈɜ:rɪzəm/ *n* [U] **voyeuristic** /ˌvwaɪɜ:ˈrɪstɪk/ *adj*: *voyeuristic excitement.*

VP /ˌvi: ˈpi:/ *abbr* Vice-President.

vs *abbr* = v 2.

V-sign ⇨ V[1].

vulcanized, -ised /ˈvʌlkənaɪzd/ *adj* (esp of rubber) treated with SULPHUR, etc at great heat to make it stronger and more elastic.

vulgar /ˈvʌlɡə(r)/ *adj* **1** lacking in good taste, not refined: *a vulgar display of wealth* ○ *a loud and vulgar laugh.* **2** likely to offend many people; rude or OBSCENE: *a vulgar gesture/suggestion/joke.*

▶ **vulgarity** /vʌlˈɡærəti/ *n* [U] the quality of being vulgar: *the vulgarity of his jokes* ○ *That dress is the height of vulgarity.*

vulgarize, -ise /ˈvʌlɡəraɪz/ *v* [Vn] to spoil sth by making it too ordinary or well-known. **vulgarization, -isation** /ˌvʌlɡəraɪˈzeɪʃn; *US* -rəˈz-/ *n* [U].

vulgarly *adv* in a vulgar way; not in good taste: *a vulgarly furnished house.*

■ ˌvulgar ˈfraction *n* a fraction represented by numbers above and below a line, eg ¾ or ⅝. ⇨ App 2. Compare DECIMAL *n*.

vulnerable /ˈvʌlnərəbl/ *adj* ~ (to sth/sb) that can be hurt, harmed or attacked easily, esp because of being small or weak: *Young birds are very vulnerable to predators.* ○ *a vulnerable point in NATO's defences* ○ *be vulnerable to abuse/blackmail/criticism* ○ *a company vulnerable to takeover bids* ○ *His wife's death left him feeling vulnerable and depressed.* ○ *The election defeat puts the party leader in a vulnerable position.* ▶ **vulnerability** /ˌvʌlnərəˈbɪləti/ *n* [U] ~ (to sth): *factors affecting people's vulnerability to heart disease* ○ *The earthquake highlighted the vulnerability of elevated bridges and roads.* **vulnerably** /-əbli/ *adv.*

vulpine /ˈvʌlpaɪn/ *adj* (*fml*) of or like a fox: *a vulpine smile.*

vulture /ˈvʌltʃə(r)/ *n* **1** a large bird, usu with the head and neck almost bare of feathers, that eats the flesh of dead animals: *vultures circling/wheeling above us.* **2** a person who seeks benefit or profit from the troubles or sufferings of others: *press vultures eager to interview the grieving widow.*

vulva /ˈvʌlvə/ *n* (*pl* **vulvas**) (*anatomy*) the outer opening of the female sex organs.

vv *abbr* verses.

vying *pres p* of VIE.

Ww

W¹ (also **w**) /ˈdʌbljuː/ n (pl **W's**, **w's** /ˈdʌbljuːz/) the 23rd letter of the English alphabet: *William begins with (a) W/'W'*.

W² abbr **1** watt; watts: *a 60W light bulb.* Compare V² 2. **2** west; western: *WNY* (ie western New York state) ○ *London W5 5HY* (ie as a POSTCODE).

wacky /ˈwæki/ adj (**-ier**, **-iest**) (*infml esp US*) funny in a slightly mad way; crazy: *a wacky comedian.*

wad /wɒd/ n **1** a mass of soft material: *a wad of cotton wool soaked in antiseptic.* **2** a quantity of documents, paper money, etc folded or rolled together: *He pulled a wad of £10 notes out of his pocket.*

wadding /ˈwɒdɪŋ/ n [U] soft material used eg to wrap round things in order to protect them or sewn inside a coat to make it warmer.

waddle /ˈwɒdl/ v (*often derog*) to walk with short steps, swinging from side to side, like a duck: [Vpr] *A short plump man came waddling towards me.* [also V, Vp]. ⇨ note at SHUFFLE. ▶ **waddle** n [sing]: *walk with a waddle.*

wade /weɪd/ v **1** ~ (**across/through**) (**sth**) to walk with an effort, esp through water or mud: [Vp, Vpr] *There's no bridge — we'll have to wade across (the stream).* [Vpr] *They had to wade knee-deep through mud and debris to reach the trapped men.* [also V]. **2** (*US*) to play in water: [V] *children wading in the pool.* Compare PADDLE². **PHRV** ˌwade ˈin (*infml*) to enter a discussion, an argument, etc in a confident forceful way: *She waded in with a fierce attack on company policy.* ˌwade ˈinto sb/sth (*infml*) to attack sb/sth vigorously: *She waded into him as soon as he got home.* ˌwade ˈthrough sth to spend a lot of effort and time completing a boring or unpleasant task: *I spent the whole day wading through the paperwork on my desk.*
▶ **wader** n **1** (also ˈwading bird) [C] any of several birds with long legs that feed in shallow water. **2** **waders** [pl] high boots that reach up to the THIGH(1), worn eg when fishing: *a pair of waders.*

wadi /ˈwɒdi/ n (in the Middle East and N Africa) a valley or channel that is dry except when it rains.

wafer /ˈweɪfə(r)/ n **1(a)** a very thin crisp sweet biscuit eaten with ice-cream. **(b)** a biscuit made of very thin wafers and a sweet filling: *a packet of chocolate wafers.* **2** a small thin round piece of special crisp bread used in Holy Communion. **3** a very thin slice of sth: *thin wafers of silicon.*
■ ˌwafer-ˈthin adj very thin: *ˌwafer-thin ˈmints* ○ *Our profit margin is already wafer-thin.*

waffle¹ /ˈwɒfl/ n (*esp US*) a crisp cake made of cooked BATTER² with a pattern of squares on it, often eaten with SYRUP.
■ ˈwaffle-iron n a metal implement used for cooking waffles.

waffle² /ˈwɒfl/ v (*Brit infml derog*) to talk or write, esp at great length, without saying anything very important or sensible: [Vpr] *What is she waffling about now?* [Vp] *He waffled on for hours but no one was listening.* [also V]. ▶ **waffle** n [U] (*infml*): *The report looks impressive but it's mostly waffle.* ○ *He talked a lot/load of waffle.*

waft /wɒft; US wæft/ v to pass or make sth pass lightly and gently through the air: [Vpr] *The sound of their voices came wafting across the lake.* [Vp] *Delicious smells wafted up from the kitchen.* [Vnpr]

The scent of the flowers was wafted along by the breeze. [also Vnp].
▶ **waft** n a smell carried through the air: *wafts of perfume/cigar smoke.*

wag¹ /wæg/ v (**-gg-**) to move or make a part of one's body move quickly from side to side or up and down: [V] *The dog's tail wagged.* [Vn] *The dog wagged its tail excitedly.* [Vnpr] *wag one's finger at sb* (ie to show one's disapproval). Compare WAGGLE, WIGGLE. **IDM** **the tail wagging the dog** ⇨ TAIL. **tongues wag** ⇨ TONGUE.
▶ **wag** n a wagging movement.

wag² /wæg/ n (*dated*) a person who enjoys making jokes. ▶ **waggish** /ˈwægɪʃ/ adj (*dated*): *waggish humour.* **waggishly** adv.

wage¹ /weɪdʒ/ n (usu pl except in certain phrases and when used before another noun) a regular, usu weekly, payment made or received for work or services: *wages of £200 a week/a weekly wage of £200* ○ *Wages are paid on Fridays.* ○ *Tax and insurance are deducted from your wages.* ○ *a wage increase/rise of 3%* ○ *The staff have agreed to a voluntary **wage freeze*** (ie a situation in which wages are not increased for a time). ⇨ note at INCOME. See also LIVING WAGE, MINIMUM WAGE. Compare SALARY.
■ ˈwage-claim n a claim made by employees for a higher rate of pay. Compare PAY-CLAIM.
ˈwage-earner n a person who works for wages: *We have two wage-earners in the family.*
ˈwage-packet n = PAY-PACKET.

wage² /weɪdʒ/ v ~ sth (**against/on sth**) to begin and continue a war, campaign, etc: [Vn, Vnpr] *wage war (against/on a neighbouring country)* [Vnpr] *wage a campaign against sex discrimination.*

wager /ˈweɪdʒə(r)/ v (*dated or fml*) **(a)** ~ **on sth** to be so confident that sth is true or will happen that one would be willing to bet money on it: [V.that] *You won't find better goods anywhere else, I'll wager.* ○ *I'll/I'd wager that she knows more about it than she's saying.* [Vpr] *I wouldn't wager on him succeeding.* **(b)** ~ (**sth**) (**on sth**) to bet money on sth: [Vn, Vnpr] *wager £50 (on a horse)* [also Vpr, V].
▶ **wager** n (*dated or fml*) a bet: *lay/make a wager* ○ *win a wager.*

waggle /ˈwægl/ v (*infml*) to move or make sth move with short movements from side to side or up and down: [V] *His bottom waggles when he walks.* [Vn] *She can waggle her ears.* Compare WAG¹, WIGGLE.

wagon (*Brit* also **waggon**) /ˈwægən/ n **1** (*US* **freight car**) an open railway truck for carrying goods such as coal. **2** a vehicle with four wheels pulled by horses or oxen (OX) and used for carrying heavy loads. See also CART. **IDM** **on the ˈwagon** (*infml*) having given up drinking alcohol, either temporarily or permanently: *be/go on the wagon.* See also STATION-WAGON.

wagon-lit /ˌvægɒn ˈliː/ n (pl **wagons-lits** /ˌvægɒn ˈliː/) a sleeping-car (SLEEP²) on railways in Continental Europe.

wagonload /ˈwægənləʊd/ n an amount of goods carried in a WAGON.

wagtail /ˈwægteɪl/ n a small bird with a long tail that moves constantly up and down when the bird is standing or walking.

wah-wah /ˈwɑː wɑː/ n [U] (*music*) an effect achieved

[V] = verb used alone   [Vn] = verb + noun   [Vp] = verb + particle   [Vpr] = verb + prepositional phrase

on electric instruments, esp the GUITAR, which varies the quality of the sound: *a wah-wah pedal.*

waif /weɪf/ *n* (**a**) a small, very thin person, esp a child: *She's such a poor little waif — I don't think she eats enough.* (**b**) a person, esp a child, without a home, or an animal without an owner: *a kindly old lady who takes in waifs and strays.* ▸ **waiflike** *adj*: *a small waiflike figure.*

wail /weɪl/ *v* (**a**) ~ (**about/over sth**) to cry or complain about sth in a loud, usu high-pitched, voice: [V] *The sick child was wailing miserably.* [V.speech] *'I've lost my mummy!' she wailed.* [V.to inf] *The cat was wailing to be let out of the room.* [Vpr] (*fig*) *There's no use wailing about/over past mistakes.* [also Vn]. ⇨ note at CRY. (**b**) (of things) to make a similar sound: [V] *the wailing cry of a seagull* ∘ *Ambulances raced by with sirens wailing.* ∘ *You can hear the wind wailing in the chimney.*

▸ **wail** *n* (**a**) a cry in a loud high voice, esp one expressing pain or grief: *The child burst into loud wails.* (**b**) a sound similar to this: *the wail of sirens.* **wailing** *n* [U]: *The child's wailing kept us awake at night.*

wainscot /ˈweɪnskət/ *n* (*arch*) = SKIRTING-BOARD.

waist /weɪst/ *n* (**a**) the part of the body between the ribs (RIB 1) and the hips, usu narrower than the chest and the stomach: *She tied the rope round her waist.* ∘ *She has a 26-inch waist.* ∘ *The workmen were stripped to* (ie wearing nothing above) *the waist.* ∘ *He is paralysed from the waist down* (ie cannot move his legs). ∘ *waist measurements.* (**b**) the part of a garment that goes round this: *take a skirt in at the waist.*

▸ **waisted** *adj* (of a garment) narrower at the waist: *a waisted jacket.*

-waisted (forming compound *adjs*) having the type of waist specified: ˌnarrow-ˈwaisted ∘ *a* ˌhigh-waisted ˈdress (ie with its waist above the waist of the person wearing it).

■ ˌwaist-ˈdeep *adj, adv* up to the waist: *The water was waist-deep.* ∘ *wade waist-deep into the river.*

ˌwaist-ˈhigh *adj, adv* high enough to reach the waist: *The grass had grown waist-high.*

waistband /ˈweɪstbænd/ *n* the strip of cloth that forms the waist of a garment, esp at the top of trousers or a skirt: *an elasticated waistband.*

waistcoat /ˈweɪskəʊt/; *US* ˈweskət/ (*US also* **vest**) *n* a short garment with buttons down the front, but without sleeves, usu worn under a jacket or coat and often forming part of a man's suit.

waistline /ˈweɪstlaɪn/ the measurement of the body round the waist: *a narrow/slim waistline* ∘ *Regular exercise will help improve your waistline.*

wait¹ /weɪt/ *v* **1** ~ (**for sb/sth**) to stay where one is or delay acting, etc for a specified time or until sb/sth comes or until sth happens: [Vadv] *'Have you been waiting long?'* [Vn, Vpr] *'I've been waiting (for) twenty minutes.'* [V] *Tell him I can't see him now, he'll have to wait.* ∘ *The President agreed to speak to the waiting journalists.* [V.to inf] *The chairman is waiting to begin the meeting.* [Vpr] *Wait for me!* ∘ *Wait for a bus/at a bus-stop* ∘ *We are waiting for the rain to stop.* ∘ *You'll have to wait until the end of the month before I can pay you.* ∘ *This is just the opportunity I've been waiting for.* ∘ (*infml ironic*) *I was just waiting for* (ie expecting) *that to happen.* ⇨ note. **2** to wait and watch for sth: [Vn] *You will just have to wait your turn* (ie wait until your turn comes). Compare AWAIT. **3** to be left until a later time before being dealt with: [V, Vpr] *It can wait (until tomorrow); it's not urgent.* **4** (of a vehicle) to stop for a short time during a journey: [V] *No Waiting* (ie on a notice to indicate that vehicles must not stop at the side of the road even for a short time) *[fig] The train was waiting at the signal for 20 minutes.* **IDM** **I, they, etc can't wait for sth / to do sth** I am, they

are, etc very excited about sth that is going to happen or be done: *The children can't wait for Christmas.* ∘ *I can't wait to read his latest novel.* **keep sb ˈwaiting** to cause sb to wait or be delayed, eg because one arrives late: *I'm sorry to have kept you waiting.* **time and tide wait for no man** ⇨ TIME¹. ˌ**wait and ˈsee** to wait and find out what will happen before taking action: *We'll just have to wait and see — there's nothing we can do at the moment.* ∘ *a wait-and-see attitude.* ˈ**wait for it** (*infml*) (used to introduce a surprising piece of news or information): *When he leaves school he wants to be — wait for it — an astronaut!* **wait a minute/second** (used when one has just noticed sth or has had a sudden idea): *Wait a minute, this isn't the right key.* **what are we ˈwaiting for?** (*infml*) let us do what we have agreed or planned. **what are you ˈwaiting for?** (*infml ironic*) why don't you do sth that you have to or want to do, since there is nothing to stop you doing it: *Your dinner's on the table — what are you waiting for?* **(just) you ˈwait** (used to emphasize a threat, a warning or a promise): *I'll be famous one day, just you wait!* **PHRV** ˌ**wait aˈbout/aˈround** to stay in a place, without doing anything particular to do, eg because sb who is expected has not arrived: *The building was locked, so we had to wait around in the car park.* ˌ**wait beˈhind** to stay after other people have gone, esp to speak to sb privately: *Please wait behind after class today.* ˌ**wait ˈin** (*Brit*) to stay at home, esp because sb is expected to come: *I waited in all day but the plumber never came.* ˌ**wait ˈup** (*US*) (esp imperative) to wait for sb to join one: *Wait up — you're walking too fast for me.* ˌ**wait ˈup (for sb)** to delay going to bed until sb comes home: *I'll be back very late tonight, so don't wait up (for me).*

▸ **wait** *n* [sing] ~ (**for sth/sb**) an act or a time of waiting: *We had a long wait for the bus.* **IDM** **lie in wait** ⇨ LIE².

■ ˈ**waiting game** *n* [sing] a policy of delaying taking action so that one may act more effectively later: *The police are playing a waiting game outside the house where the armed man is hiding.*

ˈ**waiting-list** *n* ~ (**for sth / to do sth**) a number of people who are waiting for service, treatment, etc that is not yet available, and who will receive it when it becomes available: *put sb on a waiting-list* ∘ *a hospital waiting-list* (eg for operations) ∘ *There's a long waiting-list for tickets/to join the golf club.*

ˈ**waiting-room** *n* (**a**) a room in a station where people can sit while they are waiting for trains. (**b**) a room eg just outside a doctor's SURGERY(2a), where people wait to see the doctor.

NOTE Compare **wait for** and **expect**. *I'm expecting him to arrive soon* means that I'm sure he will arrive soon. *I'm waiting for him to arrive* means that I am staying here until he arrives at a particular time. **Waiting** describes what you are doing, usually for a short time, before something happens: *Let's wait here until it's time to go.* ∘ *I'm waiting to see the dentist.* **Expecting** suggests that something will definitely happen in the future: *She's expecting a baby.* ∘ *The fall in profits had been expected.*

wait² /weɪt/ *v* **IDM** **wait at ˈtable**; (*US*) **wait on ˈtable**; **wait ˈtables** (esp as a job) to serve food and drink to people, and do associated tasks such as clearing dirty dishes. **wait on sb hand and ˈfoot** to attend to all sb's needs: *He seemed to expect to be waited on hand and foot.* **PHRV** ˈ**wait on sb** to act as a servant for sb, esp by serving food and drink at a meal. See also LADY-IN-WAITING.

▸ **waiter** *n* (*fem* **waitress** /ˈweɪtrəs/) a person employed to serve customers at their tables in a restaurant, etc: *ask the waitress for the bill* ∘ *I tried to catch the waiter's attention.* See also DUMB WAITER.

waive /weɪv/ *v* (*fml*) to choose not to insist on sth in a particular case, even though one has a legal or official right to do so: [Vn] *waive a claim/right/rule* ○ *We have decided to waive the tuition fees in your case.*

▶ **waiver** /ˈweɪvə(r)/ *n* (*law*) a document that records the waiving of a legal right, etc: *sign a collision damage waiver* (ie an insurance policy for sb who hires a car, removing their financial responsibility for accidents involving other vehicles).

wake¹ /weɪk/ *v* (*pt* **woke** /wəʊk/; *pp* **woken** /ˈwəʊkən/) **1(a)** ~ (**up**) (**to sth**) to stop sleeping: [V, Vp] *What time do you usually wake (up) in the morning?* [Vadv] *I woke early this morning.* [Vp] *Wake up! It's eight o'clock.* [Vpr] *I woke to the sound of running water.* ○ *She had just woken from a deep sleep.* [V.*to* inf] *He woke to find himself alone in the house.* (**b**) ~ *sb* (**up**) to cause sb to stop sleeping: [Vn, Vnp] *Try not to wake the baby (up).* ○ *I was woken (up) by a noise downstairs.* Compare AWAKE¹, AWAKEN. **2** (*rhet* or *fml*) to cause sb to experience thoughts or feelings that had been forgotten or suppressed: *The incident woke memories of his past sufferings.* **PHRV** ˌwake ˈup to become lively or alert: *You'll have to wake up a bit if you're going to pass your exams.* ˌwake sb ˈup to cause sb to become lively or alert: *A cold shower will soon wake you up.* ○ *The audience needs waking up.* ˌwake ˈup to sth to become aware of sth; to realize sth: *It's time you woke up to the fact that you've got to earn your living.* ○ *He hasn't yet woken up to the seriousness of the situation.*

▶ **wakeful** /-fl/ *adj* (**a**) not sleeping or unable to sleep: *The children were still wakeful even though it was well past their bedtime.* (**b**) (of a period at night) spent with little or no sleep. **wakefully** /-fəli/ *adv.* **wakefulness** *n* [U].

waken /ˈweɪkən/ *v* **1** to wake or make sb wake from sleep: [V] *She wakened at dawn.* [Vn] *I was wakened by the sound of a car starting.* [also Vpr, Vnpr]. **2** to cause sb to experience thoughts or feelings that have been suppressed: [Vn] *waken a deep concern in people.*

waking *n* [U, often attrib] the state of not being asleep: *a dream-like state between sleeping and waking* ○ *She spends all her waking hours/moments/life caring for others.*

wake² /weɪk/ *n* **IDM** **in the wake of sth** coming after or following sth: *The fierce storm left a trail of destruction in its wake.* ○ *Outbreaks of disease occurred in the wake of the drought.*

wake³ /weɪk/ *n* (esp in Ireland) a social gathering, esp at night, for the purpose of watching over a dead person's body before it is buried.

walk¹ /wɔːk/ *v* **1(a)** (of a person) to move along at a slow or moderate pace by lifting up and putting down each foot in turn: [V] *The baby is learning to walk.* [V, Vp] *She was singing to herself as she walked (along).* [Vpr] *He walked into the room/past the church/towards me.* [Vn] *I've walked ten miles today.* [also Vadv]. Compare RUN¹, TROT 2. (**b**) to travel in this way rather than in a vehicle, etc: [V] *'How did you get here?' 'I walked.'* [Vadv] *I missed the bus and had to walk home.* [also Vpr, Vp]. (**c**) (often **go walking**) to travel in this way for exercise or pleasure: [V] *We are going walking (in the country) this weekend.* [Vpr] *I walked across Scotland last summer.* (**d**) [V] (of animals, esp horses) to move at the slowest pace, always having at least two feet on the ground. Compare GALLOP, TROT 1. **2** to go with sb as they walk; to take an animal for a walk: [Vnpr] *He walked her to her car.* [Vnadv] *I'll walk you home.* [Vn] *He's out walking the dog.* **3** to go through a place on foot: [Vn] *walk the moors* ○ *I've walked the length and breadth of the country.* **4** [V] (*rhet* or *dated*) (of a ghost) to appear. **IDM** **float/walk on air**

➪ AIR¹. **run before one can** ˈwalk to try to do difficult tasks before one has learnt the basic skills: *Don't try to run before you can walk.* **tread/walk a tightrope** ➪ TIGHTROPE. **walk before one can** ˈrun to learn the basic skills before trying to do more difficult tasks. **walk sb off their** ˈfeet (*infml*) to tire sb by making them walk too far or too fast. **walk the** ˈplank (formerly) to be forced, esp by pirates (PIRATE 1), to walk along a board placed over the side of a boat, so that one falls into the sea. **walk** ˈtall to feel proud and confident. **PHRV** ˌwalk aˈway from sth to avoid doing sth or refuse to do sth: *You can't just walk away from your responsibilities.* ˌwalk aˈway/ˈoff with sth (*infml*) **1** to steal sth: *Somebody walked off with my pen.* **2** to win a prize easily: *She walked away with the gold medal.* ˌwalk ˈinto sth (*infml*) **1** to become caught in an unpleasant situation, esp because one has not been careful enough to avoid it: *They set a trap for him and he walked right into it.* **2** to succeed in getting a job without having to make an effort: *She walked into a job at the bank as soon as she graduated.* ˌwalk ˈinto sth/sb to knock against sth/sb while walking: *She wasn't looking where she was going and walked straight into me.* ˌwalk ˈout (*infml*) (of workers) to stop working and go on strike suddenly. ˌwalk ˈout (of sth) to leave a meeting suddenly before the end, esp as a protest. ˌwalk ˈout on sb (*infml*) to abandon or leave sb: *He had a row with his wife and just walked out on her.* ˌwalk ˈover sb (*infml*) **1** to defeat sb thoroughly in a contest: *The visiting team was much too strong — they walked all over us.* **2** to treat sb without respect: *You mustn't let her walk (all) over you like that.* ˌwalk ˈup (to sb/sth) to walk towards sb/sth; to approach sb/sth: *A stranger walked up to me and shook my hand.* ○ *She walked up to the desk and asked to see the manager.*

■ ˈwalk-in *adj* [attrib] **1** (esp of a WARDROBE(1) or cupboard) large enough to walk into. **2** (*US*) (of an APARTMENT(1)) having its own entrance.

ˌwalk-ˈon *adj* [usu attrib] (of a part in a play) very small and without any words to say.

ˈwalk-out *n* **1** a sudden strike by workers. **2** a sudden angry departure from a meeting.

ˈwalk-over *n* **1** an easy victory in a game or contest: *The match was a walk-over for the visiting team.* **2** a victory achieved without actually competing, eg because one's opponent fails to arrive: *The British player had a walk-over in the first round.* Compare BYE¹ 2.

ˈwalk-up *n* (*US*) (**a**) a usu tall building, esp of flats, with stairs but no lift. (**b**) a flat, office, etc in such a building. — *adj* [attrib]: *a walk-up apartment.*

▶ **walker** *n* a person who walks, esp for exercise or enjoyment.

walk² /wɔːk/ *n* **1** [C] a journey on foot, esp for pleasure or exercise: *Let's go for a walk.* ○ *have a pleasant walk across the fields* ○ *She took the dog for a walk.* **2** [sing] the time it takes to walk somewhere or the distance to a place when walking: *The station is ten minutes' walk/a ten-minute walk from my house.* ○ *It's only a short walk to the beach.* **3** [sing] a person's manner or style of walking: *I recognized him at once by his walk.* **4** the act or speed of walking rather than running: *The horse slowed to a walk after its long gallop.* **5** [C] a path or route for walking: *There are some lovely walks in the surrounding countryside.* **IDM** **cock of the walk** ➪ COCK¹. **a walk of** ˈlife a person's occupation, profession or position in society: *She has friends from all walks of life.*

walkabout /ˈwɔːkəbaʊt/ *n* **1** an informal walk among a crowd by an important visitor, esp a royal person or the president of a country: *go on a* *walkabout.* **2** [C,U] (in Australia) a period of wandering in the bush(2) by an Aboriginal: *go walkabout.*

walkie-talkie /ˌwɔːki ˈtɔːki/ *n* (*infml*) a small radio that can be carried with one, used for transmitting or receiving messages.

walking /ˈwɔːkɪŋ/ *n* [U] the activity of going for walks, esp for exercise or enjoyment: *Walking is good exercise.* ○ *walking boots* ○ *a walking holiday in Scotland.*

▶ **walking** *adj* [attrib] (*infml*) (used with *ns* referring to things) being a human or living version of the specified thing: *She's a walking ˈdictionary/ encycloˈpaedia* (ie She knows a lot of words/facts).

■ ˈ**walking papers** *n* [pl] (*US infml*) the letter or notice dismissing sb from a job: *He was given his walking papers.*

ˈ**walking-stick** (also **stick**) *n* a stick carried or used as a support when walking.

Walkman /ˈwɔːkmən/ *n* (*pl* **-mans**) (*propr*) a small CASSETTE player with HEADPHONES that can be worn by sb walking about.

walkway /ˈwɔːkweɪ/ *n* a passage or path for walking along.

wall /wɔːl/ *n* **1(a)** a continuous upright solid structure made of stone, brick or concrete, used for enclosing, dividing or protecting sth, eg an area of land: *fields divided by stone walls* ○ *a garden wall* ○ *The old town had a wall all round it.* See also SEA WALL. **(b)** any of the upright sides of a building or room: *The castle walls were very thick.* ○ *Hang the picture on the wall opposite the window.* ⇨ picture at HOUSE¹. **2** a thing that forms a barrier or stops one making progress: *The mountain rose up in a steep wall of rock.* ○ *The tidal wave formed a terrifying wall of water.* ○ (*fig*) *The investigators were confronted by a wall of silence.* **3** the outer layer of a hollow structure, esp an organ or a cell of an animal or a plant: *the abdominal wall* ○ *the wall of an artery/a blood-vessel.* **IDM** **bang, etc one's head against a brick wall** ⇨ HEAD¹. **come/run up against a brick ˈwall** to reach a situation which prevents further progress: *There was a lot of bureaucracy involved and I kept coming up against a brick wall.* **a fly on the wall** ⇨ FLY². **have one's back to the wall** ⇨ BACK¹. **to the ˈwall** into a difficult situation from which there is little hope of escape: *Many firms have gone to the wall in this recession.* ○ *Charities have been squeezed dry and pushed to the wall.* **up the ˈwall** (*infml*) crazy or angry: *That noise is driving/sending me up the wall.* ○ *I'll go up the wall if it doesn't stop soon.* ˌ**walls have ˈears** (*saying*) people might be listening to what is being said, even though they are not in the room: *Be careful what you say — even the walls have ears!* **the writing on the wall** ⇨ WRITING.

▶ **wall** *v* (esp passive) to surround or enclose sth with a wall or walls: [Vn] *a walled city/garden.* **PHRV** ˌ**wall sth ˈin/ˈoff** to enclose or separate sth with a wall: *Part of the yard had been walled off.* ˌ**wall sth ˈup** to block an opening with a wall or bricks: *a walled-up door/fireplace/passage.* See also STONEWALL.

walling *n* [U] **1** the material from which a wall is built: *stone/concrete walling.* **2** the action or skill of building a wall or walls: *a firm that does paving and walling.*

■ ˌ**ˈwall-ˈmounted** *adj* fixed onto a wall: *ˌwall-mounted ˈlights.*

wall-painting *n* a picture painted directly on the surface of a wall; a FRESCO or MURAL.

ˌ**wall-to-ˈwall** *adj, adv* **1** (of a floor covering) that covers the whole floor of a room: *a ˌwall-to-wall ˈcarpet* ○ *a room carpeted wall-to-wall.* See also FITTED 1. **2** (*infml*) continuous; happening all the time: *wall-to-wall TV sports coverage.*

wallaby /ˈwɒləbi/ *n* an Australian animal like a small KANGAROO.

wallah /ˈwɒlə/ *n* (*infml*) (in India) a person connected with a specified occupation or task: *office wallahs.*

wallet /ˈwɒlɪt/ (*US also* **billfold**, **pocket-book**) *n* a small flat folding case made of leather or plastic which is carried in the pocket and used esp for holding paper money, credit cards (CREDIT¹), etc. Compare PURSE 1.

wallflower /ˈwɔːlflaʊə(r)/ *n* **1** a common garden plant that has sweet-smelling, usu orange or brownish-red, flowers in late spring. **2** (*infml*) a person who has no one to dance with or is too shy to dance at a party.

wallop /ˈwɒləp/ *v* (*infml*) **1** to hit sb/sth very hard: [Vn] *My father used to wallop me if I told lies.* [also Vnpr]. **2** (in a contest, match, etc) to defeat sb thoroughly: [Vn] *We walloped them 6–0.*

▶ **wallop** *n* (usu *sing*) (*infml*) a heavy powerful blow: *He fell on the floor with a terrific wallop.*

walloping *n* (usu *sing*) (*infml*) **(a)** an act of hitting sb hard or repeatedly: *She threatened the children with a walloping.* **(b)** a heavy defeat: *Our team got a real walloping yesterday.*

walloping *adj* [attrib] (*infml*) very big: *He had to pay a walloping (great) fine.*

wallow /ˈwɒləʊ/ *v* **1** ~ (**about/around**) (**in sth**) to lie and roll about in mud or water because it is enjoyable to do so: [Vpr, Vp] *a hippopotamus wallowing (about) in the mud.* [Vpr] *wallow in a hot bath.* **2** ~ (**in sth**) to take pleasure in a feeling or situation, esp in a SELFISH way: [Vpr] *wallow in grief/self-pity* ○ *He wallowed in his new-found fame.*

▶ **wallow** *n* [sing] an act of wallowing: *have a good wallow in the bath.*

wallpaper /ˈwɔːlpeɪpə(r)/ *n* [U] paper, usu with a coloured design on it, used for covering the walls of a room.

▶ **wallpaper** *v* to put wallpaper onto the walls of a room: [V, Vn] *spend the weekend wallpapering (the bedroom).*

Wall Street /ˈwɔːl striːt/ *n* the US financial centre and stock exchange (STOCK¹) in New York City: *Share prices fell on Wall Street today.* ○ *Wall Street responded quickly to the news.* Compare CITY 4.

wally /ˈwɒli/ *n* (*Brit infml*) a stupid or foolish person: *Don't be such a wally!*

walnut /ˈwɔːlnʌt/ *n* [C] **(a)** an edible nut with a rough surface and a hard, round, light brown shell in two halves. ⇨ picture at NUT. **(b)** (also **ˈwalnut tree**) [C] a tree on which this nut grows. **(c)** [U] the brown wood of the walnut tree, used in making furniture: *a walnut table.*

walrus /ˈwɔːlrəs/ *n* a large animal that lives in the sea in Arctic regions, similar to a SEAL¹ but with two long tusks (TUSK).

■ ˌ**walrus mouˈstache** *n* (*infml*) a long thick MOUSTACHE that hangs down on each side of the mouth.

waltz /wɔːls; *US* wɔːlts/ *n* **(a)** a slow graceful dance for couples. **(b)** music for this, with three beats (BEAT² 2) in each bar¹(4).

▶ **waltz** *v* **1** to dance a waltz: [V, Vpr] *dancers waltzing (round the room).* **2** (*infml*) to walk or proceed in the specified direction in a casual confident way: [Vp] *She waltzed up and announced that she was leaving.* [Vpr] *I don't like him waltzing into the house as if he owned it.* ○ *He waltzed through his exams.* **PHRV** ˌ**waltz ˈoff with sth** (*infml*) to leave with sth: *He's just waltzed off with my cigarette lighter!*

wan /wɒn/ *adj* **(a)** (of a person) pale and looking ill or tired: *She was looking pale and wan after her ordeal.* **(b)** (of a person's expression) indicating that one is ill, tired, nervous, unhappy, etc: *a wan smile* ○

(fig) the wan light of a winter's morning. ▶ **wanly** *adv: smile wanly.*

wand /wɒnd/ n **1** (also **magic wand**) a thin stick or rod held in the hand by a magician (MAGIC) or a fairy when performing magic or magic tricks: *The fairy godmother waved her (magic) wand.* **2** any small thin stick or rod. **IDM** **wave a magic wand** ⇨ WAVE¹.

wander /'wɒndə(r)/ v **1(a)** to walk around in an area or go from place to place, often without any special purpose: [Vpr] *wander through the countryside/around town* [Vp] *We wandered around for hours looking for the house.* [Vn] *The child was found wandering the streets alone.* [also V]. **(b)** to go slowly and casually in the specified direction: [Vp] *She wandered off towards the station.* ∘ *(fig) Her thoughts wandered back to her youth.* **2** ~ **(from/off sth)**; ~ **(away/off)** to move away from the place where one ought to be or from a group: [Vp] *Peter had wandered away from his mother.* ∘ *The child wandered off and got lost.* [Vpr] *They had wandered from the path and found themselves at the foot of a steep cliff.* ∘ *(fig) Don't wander from the subject — stick to the point.* **3** (of a road or river) to follow a winding path or course: [Vpr, Vp] *The road wanders (along) through the range of hills.* [also V]. **4** (of a person's mind) to stop concentrating on sth and become occupied with sth else: [V] *I could see that their attention was beginning to wander.* ∘ *I'm sorry, could you repeat that? My mind was wandering.*
▶ **wander** n [sing] (*infml*) an act of wandering (WANDER 1): *She went for a little wander round the park.*

wanderer /'wɒndərə(r)/ n a person who keeps travelling from place to place with no permanent home.

wanderings /'wɒndərɪŋz/ n [pl] journeys from place to place, often with no particular purpose: *He finally returned from his wanderings and settled down.*

wanderlust /'wɒndəlʌst/ n [U] a strong desire to travel.

wane /weɪn/ v **1** [V] (of the moon) to show a gradually decreasing area of brightness after being full. Compare WAX² 1. **2** to become gradually smaller, weaker, less powerful or less important: [V] *The power of the landowners waned during this period.* ∘ *Her enthusiasm for the whole idea was waning rapidly.* **IDM** **wax and wane** ⇨ WAX².
▶ **wane** n **IDM** **on the 'wane** gradually decreasing; waning (WANE 2): *By this time his political influence was on the wane.*

wangle /'wæŋgl/ v ~ **sth (out of sb)** (*infml*) to get sth that one wants by tricking or persuading sb or by means of a clever plan: [Vn] *I'd love to go to the match tomorrow — do you think you can wangle it?* ∘ *She managed to wangle an invitation to the reception.* [Vnpr] *I'll come if I can wangle some money out of my parents.* [also Vnn]. **IDM** **wangle one's way 'into / 'out of sth / doing sth** to get sth that one wants or avoid sth that one does not want by tricking or persuading sb or by means of a clever plan: *I don't know how he wangled his way into such a well-paid job.* ∘ *He managed to wangle his way out of paying.*

wank /wæŋk/ v [V] (△ *Brit sl*) to MASTURBATE.
▶ **wank** n (usu *sing*) (△ *Brit sl*) an act of masturbating (MASTURBATE).
wanker (△ *Brit sl*) **1** (*derog*) a stupid or useless person, esp a man. **2** a person who masturbates (MASTURBATE).

wanna /'wɒnə/ (*infml esp US*) **1** want to: *I wanna go home now.* **2** want a: *I wanna drink.*

wannabe /'wɒnəbi/ n (*sl derog esp US*) a person who wants to be like sb else and so behaves, dresses, etc in order to seem like them: *pop star wannabes.*

want¹ /wɒnt; *US also* wɔːnt/ v **1** to have a desire for sth; to wish for sth: [Vn] *They want a bigger house.* ∘

The staff want a pay increase. [V.to inf] *She wants to go to Italy.* [V.n to inf] *She wants me to go with her.* ∘ *I didn't want that to happen.* ∘ *I want it (to be) done as quickly as possible.* [V.n ing] *I don't want you arriving late.* [Vn-n] *The people want him as their leader.* ⇨ note. **2** to require or need sth: [Vn] *We'll want more furniture for the new office.* ∘ *Let me know how many copies you want.* [V.ing, V.to inf] *The plants want watering/want to be watered daily.* [V.ing] *I'm sure you don't want reminding of the need for discretion.* **3** (*infml*) (not after *I* or *we*) should or ought to: [V.to inf] *You want to be more careful.* ∘ *They want to make sure they're not cheated.* **4** ~ **sb (for sth)** (usu *passive*) to require sb to be present somewhere; need sb for a particular purpose: [Vn] *You are wanted immediately in the director's office.* [Vn, Vnpr] *He is wanted (for questioning) by the police* (eg in connection with a crime). **5** [Vn] to feel sexual desire for sb. **6** (*fml*) to lack sth: [Vn] *He doesn't want courage.* **IDM** **have/want it/things both ways** ⇨ BOTH¹. **not want to 'know (about sth)** to take no interest in sth because one does not care about it or because it is too much trouble: *I asked him for help but he didn't want to know (about my problems).* **want none of sth** ⇨ NONE. **waste not, want not** ⇨ WASTE¹. **PHRV** **'want for sth** (esp in questions or negative sentences) (*fml*) to suffer because of a lack of sth: *Those children want for nothing* (ie have everything they need). **,want 'in / 'out** (*infml*) to want to come in/go out: *The dog wants in — it's scratching at the door.* **,want 'in / 'into sth** (*infml esp US*) to wish to be involved in sth: *He wants in on the deal.* **,want 'out / 'out of sth** (*infml esp US*) to want to stop being involved in sth: *He told them that he wanted out (of the gang).*

NOTE **Would you like...?** is the most usual polite question form for offers and invitations: *Would you like a cup of coffee?* ∘ *Would you like to come to lunch?* **Do you want...?** is very direct and is not used in formal situations: *Do you want a piece of chocolate?* ∘ *We're going to the cinema tonight. Do you want to come with us?* **Would you care ...?** is a much more formal way of asking or inviting: *Would you care for another slice of cake?* ∘ *Would you care to come with me?*

want² /wɒnt; *US also* wɔːnt/ n **1** [C usu *pl*] a desire for sth; a need or requirement: *He is a man of few wants.* ∘ *This book meets a long-felt want* (ie has been needed for a long time). ∘ *The hotel staff saw to all our wants.* **2** [U, sing] ~ **of sth** lack of sth: *a want of food and medical supplies* ∘ *The plants died from want of water.* **3** [U] the state of being poor and lacking the essential things in life; poverty: *live in want* ∘ *Their health has suffered from years of want.* **IDM** **for want of sth** because of a lack of sth: *She decided to accept the offer for want of anything better.* ∘ *He couldn't get a job, though **not for want of** trying.* **in want of sth** needing sth: *The house is in want of repair.*

wanting /'wɒntɪŋ; *US also* 'wɔːn-/ adj [pred] ~ **(in sth)** (*fml*) lacking sth: *She's certainly not wanting in confidence.* **IDM** **be found wanting** ⇨ FIND¹.

wanton /'wɒntən/ adj **1** [esp *attrib*] (of an action) done deliberately for no good reason: *wanton cruelty/damage/waste* ∘ *the wanton destruction of a historic building.* **2** (*fml*) playful: *in a wanton mood.* **3** (*dated fml*) having or showing a strong interest in sex, esp with many partners. ▶ **wantonly** adv: *Many of our forests have been wantonly cut down.* **wantonness** n [U].

war /wɔː(r)/ n **1(a)** [U] a state of fighting between nations or groups within a nation using military force: *the horrors of war* ∘ *the outbreak* (ie beginning) *of war* ∘ *declare/wage war on sb* ∘ *The border incident led to war between the two countries.* ∘ *They*

W

have been **at war** (with each other) for the last four years. ○ The government wanted to avoid war at all costs. **(b)** [C] an instance or a period of such fighting: He had fought in two wars. ○ If a war breaks out, many other countries will be affected. Compare BATTLE. See also CIVIL WAR, COLD WAR, PHONEY WAR, POSTWAR. **2(a)** [C, U] a state of competition, conflict or hostility: the class war ○ a trade war ○ A state of war existed between the rival companies. See also PRICE WAR. **(b)** [sing] ~ (against/on sb/sth) great efforts made to deal with or end sth unpleasant and undesirable: Little progress has been made in the war against/on crime. **IDM** go to 'war (against/with sb/sth) to start fighting a war against sb/sth: go to war against/with one's enemies. **have been in the 'wars** (infml or joc) to have been hurt or injured: You look as if you've been in the wars — what have you been doing?

▶ **warring** adj [attrib] engaged in a war or conflict: warring tribes/factions.

■ 'war crime n a terrible act committed during a war, which is contrary to international law: be prosecuted for war crimes. 'war criminal n a person who commits or is found guilty of a war crime.

'war cry n a word or phrase shouted by people entering a battle in order to encourage each other and frighten the enemy. Compare BATTLE-CRY.

'war-dance n a dance performed by the members of a tribe, eg before battle or to celebrate a victory.

'war-game n **(a)** a practice battle used as a military training exercise. **(b)** a game in which models representing troops, ships, etc are moved about on maps.

,war of at'trition n [sing] a war or conflict in which each side tries to make the other stop fighting by maintaining the same position or attitude over a long period.

,war of 'nerves n [sing] an attempt to defeat one's opponents by putting mental pressure on them and gradually destroying their confidence and courage.

,war of 'words n [sing] a state or period of opposition between people in which each side criticizes or insults the other(s): As the election approaches the war of words between the main political parties becomes more intense.

'war-torn adj [attrib] (of a place) severely damaged by war or suffering greatly as a result of war: a war-torn city.

warble /'wɔːbl/ v **(a)** (esp of a bird) to sing with constantly changing notes: [V] larks warbling in the sky. **(b)** (of a person) to say or sing sth in a warbling manner: [Vn] warble a few songs [also V, V.speech].

▶ **warble** n (usu sing) the sound of sb/sth warbling: (fig) the warble of a telephone.

warbler /'wɔːblə(r)/ n a bird that warbles.

ward /wɔːd/ n **1** a separate part or room in a hospital for a particular group of patients: a children's/maternity/surgical ward ○ a public/private ward. **2** a division of a city, etc that elects and is represented by a COUNCILLOR in local government: There are three candidates standing for election in this ward. **3** a person, esp a child, who is being cared for by a GUARDIAN(2) or is under the protection of a lawcourt: She invested the money on behalf of her ward. ○ The child was made a **ward of court.**

▶ **ward** v **PHRV** ,ward sb/sth 'off to prevent sth dangerous or unpleasant from affecting or harming one: ward off blows/disease/danger/intruders.

wardship n [U] the state of being a ward(2).

-ward suff (with advs forming adjs) in the direction of: backward ○ eastward ○ homeward. ▶ **-wards** (also esp US **-ward**) (forming advs): onward(s) ○ forward(s).

warden /'wɔːdn/ n **1** a person responsible for supervising a place, making sure rules are obeyed, etc:

a countryside warden ○ the warden of a youth hostel. See also GAME-WARDEN, TRAFFIC WARDEN. **2** (Brit) the title of the heads of certain colleges and other institutions: the Warden of Merton College, Oxford. **3** (US) the GOVERNOR(2a) of a prison.

▶ **wardenship** n [U] the position of being a warden.

warder /'wɔːdə(r)/ n (fem **wardress** /'wɔːdrəs/) (Brit) a person who works as a guard in a prison.

wardrobe /'wɔːdrəʊb/ n **1** a place where clothes are stored, usu a large cupboard with shelves and a rail for hanging things on. **2** (usu sing) a person's collection of clothes: buy a new winter wardrobe. **3** a stock of costumes worn by actors in a theatre company.

■ 'wardrobe mistress n (masc 'wardrobe master) a person responsible for looking after the costumes in a theatre company.

wardroom /'wɔːdruːm, -rʊm/ n a place in a WARSHIP where the officers live and eat.

ware /weə(r)/ n **1** [U] (esp in compounds) **(a)** manufactured goods of the specified type: 'ironware ○ 'handmade ware ○ alu'minium ware. See also HARDWARE, SILVERWARE. **(b)** pottery (POTTER²) of the specified type or made for a particular purpose: porcelain ware. See also EARTHENWARE, OVENWARE. **2** **wares** [pl] articles offered for sale, esp in the street or in a market: advertise/display/sell/peddle one's wares.

warehouse /'weəhaʊs/ n **(a)** a building where large quantities of goods are stored before being sent abroad, to shops, etc. **(b)** a building where furniture is stored for its owners.

▶ **warehousing** n [U] the practice of storing things in a warehouse: warehousing costs/facilities.

warfare /'wɔːfeə(r)/ n [U] **(a)** the activity of fighting a war, esp of a particular type: guerrilla/modern/nuclear warfare. See also BIOLOGICAL WARFARE, CHEMICAL WARFARE, GERM WARFARE. **(b)** an aggressive or violent conflict or struggle: There is open warfare between the opponents of the new road scheme and those in favour of it.

warhead /'wɔːhed/ n the explosive head of a missile or bomb: equipped with a nuclear warhead.

warhorse /'wɔːhɔːs/ n **1** (formerly) a horse used in battle. **2** a soldier, politician, etc who has fought in many campaigns.

warily ⇨ WARY.

wariness ⇨ WARY.

warlike /'wɔːlaɪk/ adj **(a)** fond of or skilled in fighting wars: a warlike nation. **(b)** aggressive; showing a desire for conflict or war: warlike politicians ○ He entered the meeting in a warlike frame of mind.

warlord /'wɔːlɔːd/ n (sometimes derog) a person commanding groups of people fighting against other groups within a country: rival/local warlords.

warm¹ /wɔːm/ adj (-er, -est) **1(a)** of or at a fairly high temperature, between cool and hot: gusts of warm air ○ The weather is a bit warmer today. ○ Food for a baby should be warm, not hot. **(b)** (of a person or part of the body) having the normal body temperature and feeling comfortable: The patient must be kept warm. ○ have warm hands and feet ○ Come and get warm by the fire. **(c)** (of clothing) made of material that prevents the body from becoming cold: warm gloves ○ Put on your warmest clothes before you go out to play in the snow. Compare COLD¹, HOT. **2** showing enthusiasm; HEARTY(1): warm applause/congratulations/thanks ○ a warm recommendation ○ give sb a warm welcome/reception. **3** having or showing affection or kind friendly feelings: She is a warm and sympathetic person. ○ He has a warm heart. **4** (of colours, sounds, etc) creating a pleasant, comfortable and relaxed feeling: The room was furnished in warm reds and browns. ○ the warm and mellow tones of the cello. **5** [pred] (esp in a game) near to guessing the answer or finding sb/sth hid-

den: *Am I getting warmer?* ○ *You're not even warm.*
Shall I give you a clue? **IDM** **keep sb's ¹seat, etc**
warm (for them) (*infml*) to occupy a seat, post, etc
temporarily so that it is available for sb later. **make**
it/things ¹warm for sb (*infml*) to make things unpleasant or make trouble for sb: *His political*
opponents have been making things warm for him
lately. **(as) warm as ¹toast** (*infml*) very warm;
pleasantly warm: *We lit the fire and were soon as*
warm as toast.
> **warmly** *adv*: *warmly dressed* ○ *He thanked us all*
warmly. ○ *I can warmly recommend it.*
warmth /wɔːmθ/ *n* [U] **1(a)** the state of being
warm: *the warmth of the room.* **(b)** moderate heat:
enjoy the warmth of the sun ○ *The seeds need warmth*
to germinate. **2(a)** strength of feeling; enthusiasm:
He was touched by the warmth of their welcome. **(b)** a
friendly attitude towards other people: *She's efficient*
at her job but she lacks warmth.
■ **‚warm-¹blooded** *adj* (of animals) having a fairly
high blood temperature that does not change as the
temperature varies around them. Compare COLD-
BLOODED, HOT-BLOODED.
‚warm-¹hearted *adj* kind, friendly and sympathetic. Compare COLD-HEARTED.

warm² /wɔːm/ *v* ~ (**sth/sb**) (**up**) to become or make
sth/sb become warm or warmer: [V, Vp] *The milk is*
warming (up) on the stove. [Vn, Vnp] *I'll warm (up)*
some milk. [Vn] *warm oneself/one's hands by the fire.*
IDM **warm the ¹cockles (of sb's ¹heart)** to make
sb feel pleased or happy. **PHRV** **‚warm sth ¹over**
(*US*) = WARM STH UP. **¹warm to/towards sb** to begin
to like sb: *I warmed to her immediately.* ○ *He's not*
somebody one warms to easily. **¹warm to/towards**
sth to become more interested in or enthusiastic
about sth: *The speaker was now warming to her*
theme. ○ *I must say I'm beginning to warm towards*
the idea. **‚warm ¹up 1** to prepare for physical exercise or the performance of sth by practising gently
before it: *warm up before a race.* **2** (of a machine, an
engine, etc) to run for a short time in order to reach
the temperature at which it will operate efficiently:
Let the engine warm up before you drive off. **‚warm**
(**sb/sth**) **¹up** to become or make sb/sth become more
lively or enthusiastic: *The party soon warmed up.* ○
warm up an audience with a few jokes. **‚warm sth**
¹up; (*US*) **warm sth over** (*sometimes derog*) to heat
previously cooked food again for eating: *warm up*
yesterday's stew. See also GLOBAL WARMING, HOUSE-
WARMING.
> **warmer** *n* (esp in compounds) a thing or device
that warms sth, a part of the body, etc: *a towel*
warmer ○ *a hand warmer.*
■ **¹warming-pan** *n* a round metal pan with a lid and
a long handle, formerly filled with hot coal and used
for warming a bed.
¹warm-up *n* an act or a period of preparing for
physical exercise, a performance, etc by practising
gently: *warm-up exercises* ○ *She hurt her wrist dur-*
ing the warm-up.

warm³ /wɔːm/ *n* [sing] **1 the warm** a warm atmosphere or place: *Come out of the cold street into the*
warm. **2** an act of warming sth: *She gave his coat a*
warm by the fire.

warmonger /¹wɔːmʌŋgə(r)/ *n* (*derog*) a person who
tries to cause a war or who favours starting a war.
> **warmongering** *n* [U] actions, speeches, etc inten-
ded to cause war.

warn /wɔːn/ *v* **1** ~ **sb (of sth)**; ~ **sb about/against**
sb/sth; ~ **sb against doing sth** to inform sb in
advance of sth, esp possible danger or sth unpleasant that is likely to happen, so that they can try to
avoid it: [V.speech] *'Mind the step,' she warned.* [Vn]
I tried to warn him, but he wouldn't listen. ○ *If you*
warn me in advance, I'll have your order ready for
you. [Vnpr] *She was warned of the danger of driving*

the car in that state. ○ *He warned us against pick-*
pockets. ○ *The police have warned shopkeepers about*
the forged banknotes. [Vpr, Vnpr] *The police are*
warning (motorists) of possible delays. [Vn.*that*]
They warned her that if she did it again she would be
sent to prison. [Vn.*wh*] *I had been warned what to*
expect. **2** to advise sb to do or not to do sth: [Vn.*to*
inf] *They were warned not to climb the mountain in*
such bad weather. **PHRV** **‚warn sb ¹off (sth / doing**
sth) 1 to tell sb to leave or stay away from a place,
eg from private land: *The farmer warned us off (his*
land) when we tried to camp there. **2** to tell sb not to
do sth or to stop doing sth because it will have bad
consequences for them: *His doctor has warned him*
off (drinking) alcohol.
> **warning** *n* [C,U] a statement, an event, etc that
warns sb about sth: *She received/was given a written*
warning about her conduct. ○ *a gale warning to*
shipping ○ *Let that be a warning to you* (ie Let
that mistake, accident, etc teach you to be more
careful in future). ○ *warning lights/shots* ○ *The at-*
tack occurred without warning (ie unexpectedly). ○
The speaker sounded a note of warning (ie spoke of
possible risk or danger).

warp¹ /wɔːp/ *v* **1** to become or make sth become
bent or twisted from the usual or natural shape, esp
because of the effects of heat or damp: [V] *The wood*
began to warp. [Vn] *The hot sun had warped the*
cover of the book. **2** to make sb/sth abnormal in a
way that is unacceptable: [Vn] *a warped mind/sense*
of humour ○ *His judgement was warped by self-*
interest.

warp² /wɔːp/ *n* **1** the warp [sing] (in weaving) the
threads on a LOOM¹ over and under which other
threads (the *weft* or *woof*) are passed to make cloth.
▷ picture at WEAVE. **2** [C usu *sing*] a bend or twist:
The wood has developed a slight warp. ○ (*fig*) *a warp*
in sb's character. See also TIME WARP.

warpaint /¹wɔːpeɪnt/ *n* [U] **(a)** paint put on the body
before battle, esp formerly by Native Americans. **(b)**
(*infml joc*) make-up (MAKE¹): *She never goes out with-*
out putting her warpaint on!

warpath /¹wɔːpɑːθ; *US* -pæθ/ *n* **IDM** **(be/go) on the**
¹warpath (*infml*) angry and wanting to be aggressive towards sb: *Look out — the boss is on the*
warpath again!

warrant /¹wɒrənt; *US* ¹wɔːr-/ *n* **1** [C] ~ **(for sth)** **(a)**
a written order from a judge, etc, giving the police
authority to do sth: *issue a warrant for sb's arrest.*
See also DEATH-WARRANT, SEARCH WARRANT. **(b)** a
document that entitles the holder to receive goods,
money, services, etc: *a travel warrant* ○ *a warrant*
for dividends on shares. **2** ~ **for sth / doing sth** [U]
(*fml*) a reason that justifies an action: *There was no*
warrant for such behaviour. Compare UNWARRANTED.
> **warrant** *v* to justify sth; to make sth necessary or
appropriate in the circumstances: [Vn] *A minor in-*
cident like this scarcely warrants the media attention
it has received. ○ *Further investigation is clearly war-*
ranted. **IDM** **I('ll) warrant (you)** (*dated*) I am sure of
it and you can be sure of it too.
warranty /¹wɒrənti; *US* ¹wɔːr-/ *n* [C,U] a written or
printed guarantee, esp one given to the buyer of an
article, promising to repair or replace it if necessary
within a specified period: *buy a car without a war-*
ranty ○ *The machine is still under warranty.*
■ **¹warrant-officer** *n* an officer ranking between
commissioned officers (COMMISSION) and NON-
COMMISSIONED officers. ▷ App 6.

warren /¹wɒrən; *US* ¹wɔːrən/ *n* = RABBIT WARREN:
The old town is a warren of narrow streets and
alleys.

warrior /¹wɒriə(r); *US* ¹wɔːr-/ *n* **1** (*fml*) (esp formerly) a person who fights in battle; a soldier: *a*
warrior race (ie one that is fond of or skilled in

W

fighting). **2** a member of a tribe who fights for his tribe: *a Zulu warrior*.

warship /ˈwɔːʃɪp/ *n* a ship for use in war.

wart /wɔːt/ *n* a small hard dry growth(4a) on the skin. **IDM** ˌwarts and ˈall (*infml*) including faults and features that are not attractive: *You agreed to marry me, warts and all!* ○ *a warts-and-all biography*.

▶ **warty** *adj* covered in warts.

■ ˈwart-hog *n* an African wild pig with two large tusks (TUSK) and growths like warts on its face.

wartime /ˈwɔːtaɪm/ *n* [U] a period of time when there is a war: *wartime rationing* ○ *Special regulations were introduced in wartime*. Compare PEACE-TIME.

wary /ˈweəri/ *adj* (**-ier, -iest**) ~ (**of sb/sth**) cautious because aware of or fearing possible danger or problems: *wary investors* ○ *She is wary of strangers*. ○ *I kept a wary eye on the children*. ○ *You should be wary of trusting someone like that.* ▶ **warily** /-rəli/ *adv*: *They approached us warily*. **wariness** *n* [U].

was /wəz; *strong form* wɒz; *US also* wʌz/ ⇨ note at BE².

wash¹ /wɒʃ/ *n* **1** [C usu *sing*] an act of cleaning sth/ sb/oneself or of being cleaned with water and usu soap: *He looks as if he needs a good* (ie thorough) *wash*. ○ *have a **wash and brush up*** (ie wash oneself and make oneself tidy, brush one's hair, etc) ○ *a cold wash* (ie a wash in cold water) ○ *Please give the car a wash*. ○ *The colour has faded after only two washes*. **2 the wash** [*sing*] a quantity of clothes, sheets, etc washed together at one time: *take the wash out of the machine* ○ *All my shirts are **in the wash***. **3** [*sing*] disturbed water, eg behind a moving ship; the sound made by this: *the wash made by the steamer's propellers* ○ *hear the wash of the waves against the side of the boat*. **4** [C] a thin layer of colour painted on a surface. See also MOUTHWASH. **IDM** **come out in the ˈwash** (*infml*) of mistakes, problems, etc) to come right or be put right eventually, without any harm being done: *Don't worry, I'm sure it'll all come out in the wash*.

wash² /wɒʃ/ *v* **1(a)** to make sth/sb clean by using water and usu soap: [Vn] *These clothes will have to be washed*. ○ *Have these glasses been washed?* [Vn-adj] *The beach had been washed clean by the tide*. **(b)** to make oneself, esp one's face and hands, clean by using water and usu soap: [Vn] *Go and wash yourself*. [V] *I had to wash and dress in a hurry*. **(c)** (of clothes, fabrics, etc) to be able to be washed without losing colour, shrinking, etc: [Vadv] *This sweater washes well*. [V] *The dress won't wash — it's got to be dry-cleaned*. **2** (of water) to flow in the specified direction: [Vpr] *waves washing against the side of a boat* ○ *Water washed over the deck*. **3** (esp passive) (of water) to carry sb/sth in the specified direction: [Vnp] *debris washed along by the flood* ○ *The body was washed out to sea*. [Vnadv] *Pieces of the wreckage were washed ashore*. ○ *He was washed overboard in the storm*. [also Vnpr]. **4** to pour water through GRAVEL, etc in order to find gold: [Vn] *washing ore*. **5** (only in questions or negative sentences) ~ (**with sb**) (*infml*) to be accepted or believed by sb: [V, Vpr] *That excuse simply won't wash (with me)*. **IDM** **wash one's dirty linen in ˈpublic** (*derog*) to discuss or argue about one's personal affairs in public. **wash one's ˈhands of sb/sth** to refuse to be responsible for or involved with sb/sth: *I've washed my hands of the whole sordid business*. **PHRV** ˌwash **sb/sth** aˈway (of water) to remove or carry sb/sth away to another place: *footprints washed away by the rain* ○ *Their house was washed away in the flood*. ˌwash sth ˈdown (**with sth**) **1** to clean sth by using a stream or jet of water: *wash down the decks* ○ *wash down a car with a hose*. **2** to drink sth after, or at the

same time as, eating sth: *For lunch we had bread and cheese, washed down with beer*.

ˌwash (sth) ˈoff; ˌwash sth ˈoff sth to remove sth or be removed from a fabric or the surface of sth by washing: *Those grease stains won't wash off*. ○ *Wash that mud off (your boots) before you come in*.

ˌwash ˈout (of a dirty mark) to be removed from a fabric by washing: *These ink stains won't wash out*. ˌwash sth ˈout **1** to wash the inside of sth in order to remove dirt, etc: *wash out the empty bottles*. **2** (of rain) to make a game, an event, etc end early or prevent it from starting: *The match was completely washed out*. ○ *Torrential rain washed out most of the weekend's events*.

ˌwash ˈover sb (*infml*) to happen or relate to sb without affecting them: *All the criticism she's had seems to have washed right over her*.

ˌwash ˈup **1** (*Brit*) to wash the dishes, glasses, knives, forks, etc after a meal. See also WASHING-UP. **2** (*US*) to wash one's face and hands. ˌwash sth ˈup (*Brit*) **1** to wash things, eg dishes after a meal: *Have you washed up all the plates?* **2** (of water) to carry sth to the shore: *Cargo from the wrecked ship was washed up on the shore*.

▶ **washable** /-əbl/ *adj* that can be washed without being damaged: *washable clothes/fabrics/paint* ○ *machine washable* (ie that can be washed in a washing-machine (WASHING)).

■ ˈwash-basin (also basin, *US* ˈwash-bowl, sink) *n* a large bowl, usu fixed to a wall in a BATHROOM and fitted with taps for washing one's hands, etc in. Compare SINK².

ˈwash-cloth *n* (*US*) = FLANNEL 2.

ˌwashed ˈout *adj* **(a)** (of fabric or colour) faded by washing: *ˌwashed out ˌblue ˈoveralls*. **(b)** (of a person) pale and tired: *She looks washed out after her illness*.

ˌwashed ˈup *adj* (*infml*) **(a)** having failed or having no chance of succeeding: *Their marriage was washed up long before they separated*. **(b)** having failed because one is no longer good enough: *a washed up singer/actor/sportsman*.

ˈwash-out *n* (*infml*) a person, event, etc that is a complete failure: *The party/new manager was a total wash-out*.

washboard /ˈwɒʃbɔːd/ *n* a board with ridges on it used esp formerly for rubbing clothes on when washing them.

washday /ˈwɒʃdeɪ/ *n* [C usu *sing* without *a* or *the*] (*dated*) a day on which clothes are washed, esp when this is the same day every week: *Monday was always washday in our family*.

washer /ˈwɒʃə(r)/ *n* **1** a small flat ring made of rubber, metal or plastic placed between two surfaces, eg under a nut(2), to make a screw or joint tight. ⇨ picture at BOLT. **2** (*infml*) a washing-machine (WASHING): *a washer-drier* (ie a machine that both washes and dries clothes). See also DISH-WASHER.

washing /ˈwɒʃɪŋ/ *n* **1** [C, U] an act or the action of washing sth or of being washed: *The sweater had shrunk after repeated washing(s)*. ○ *Washing is a chore*. **2** [U] clothes being washed or waiting to be washed: *hang the washing on the line to dry* ○ *put a load of washing in the machine*.

■ ˈwashing-machine *n* an electric machine for washing clothes.

ˈwashing-powder *n* [U] soap or DETERGENT in the form of powder for washing clothes.

ˈwashing-soda *n* [U] = SODIUM CARBONATE.

ˌwashing-ˈup *n* [U] **(a)** the task of washing dishes, etc after a meal: *do the **washing-up***. **(b)** the dishes, etc needing to be washed after a meal: *The washing-up had been left in the sink*. **washing-ˈup liquid** *n* [U] liquid DETERGENT for washing dishes, etc.

washroom /'wɒʃruːm, -rʊm/ n (US euph) a toilet, esp in a public building. ⇨ note at TOILET.

washstand /'wɒʃstænd/ n (esp formerly, in houses without a supply of water to a BATHROOM or bedroom) a special table in a bedroom that holds a BASIN(2a) and JUG for washing oneself with.

wasn't /'wɒznt; US also 'wʌznt/ ⇨ BE¹.

WASP (also **Wasp**) /wɒsp/ abbr (esp US usu derog) White Anglo-Saxon Protestant: a typically Wasp attitude.

wasp /wɒsp/ n a black and yellow flying insect that can sting: a wasp sting.
▶ **waspish** adj sharply unpleasant or bad-tempered: a waspish voice/remark. **waspishly** adv. **waspishness** n [U].

wastage /'weɪstɪdʒ/ n [U] **1(a)** [U, sing] loss or destruction of sth, esp sth valuable that has not been used carefully: food wastage ○ a wastage of natural resources. **(b)** [U] an amount that is wasted: You must allow for five per cent wastage in transit. **2** [U] loss of employees because they retire or move to other jobs: reduce staff by natural wastage.

waste¹ /weɪst/ v **1** ~ sth (on sb/sth) to use more of sth than is necessary; to use sth carelessly: [V] waste time/food/electricity/energy [Vpr] Why waste money on clothes you don't need? **2** (esp passive) to do sth that does not produce the desired result: [Vn] We had a wasted journey — they weren't there. **3** ~ sth (on sb) (esp passive) to give or say sth that is not appreciated: [Vn, Vnpr] Your humour is wasted (on them), I'm afraid. [Vnpr] Good cooking is wasted on him; he doesn't care what he eats. **4** (usu passive) to fail to make full or good use of sb/sth: [Vn] It was a wasted opportunity. ○ She's wasted in her present job. **IDM** **waste one's 'breath** to talk or give advice without having any effect: They won't listen, so don't waste your breath. **,waste not, 'want not** (saying) if you never waste anything, esp food or money, you will always have it when you need it. **PHRV** **,waste a'way** (of a person) to become thin or weak, esp because of disease or worry.
▶ **waster** n **1** (often in compounds) a person or thing that wastes sth: a time-waster ○ Many household machines are great energy wasters. **2** a person who spends her or his time and money foolishly or carelessly, without thinking about the future. Compare WASTREL.

wasting adj [attrib] (of a disease) that makes a person become steadily weaker and thinner.

waste² /weɪst/ n **1** [U, sing] the action or an instance of using too much of sth unnecessarily, or of using things carelessly and without effect: a waste of time/money/energy/effort ○ The goods should be handled carefully to avoid waste. **2** [U] material, food, etc that is no longer needed and is (to be) thrown away: nuclear/toxic waste ○ A lot of household waste can be recycled. ○ The kitchen is fitted with a waste disposal unit. **3** [C usu pl] a large area of land where people cannot live or grow things: desert wastes ○ the icy wastes of the Antarctic. **IDM** **go to 'waste** to be wasted: I hate to see all that food going to waste.
▶ **wasteful** /-fl/ adj using more of sth than is necessary; causing waste: a wasteful use of energy/natural resources. **wastefully** /-fəli/ adv. **wastefulness** n [U].
■ **'waste-basket** (also **'waste-bin**) n (US) = WASTE-PAPER BASKET.
'waste pipe n a pipe for carrying away water which has been used or is not needed, eg dirty water from a bath.

waste³ /weɪst/ adj [usu attrib] **1** (of an area of land) not used, cultivated or built on, because it is not being suitable for such purposes: The stolen car was found on a piece of waste ground. **2** no longer useful and so to be thrown away: waste materials produced by the manufacturing process ○ waste water. **IDM** **lay sth 'waste** (rhet) to destroy sth completely: land laid waste by war.
■ **,waste 'paper** n [U] paper that is not wanted and is to be thrown away. **,waste-'paper basket** (Brit) (US **'waste-basket**, **'waste-bin**) n a basket or other container for waste paper, etc.
'waste product useless material produced by living things or during a manufacturing process.

wasteland /'weɪstlænd/ n [U, C] an empty area of land that is not or cannot be used, esp because it has been damaged in some way: an industrial wasteland ○ (fig) a cultural/spiritual wasteland.

wastrel /'weɪstrəl/ n (rather fml) a lazy person who wastes her or his time, money, etc.

watch¹ /wɒtʃ/ v **1** to look at sb/sth with attention; to observe sb/sth: [Vn] watch television/a football match [V, Vn] Watch (me) carefully. [V] 'Would you like to play?' 'No thanks — I'll just watch.' [V.to inf] He watched to see what would happen. [V.wh] They watched where they went. [Vn.ing] She watched the children playing. [Vn.inf (no to)] She watched the children cross the road. **2** ~ (over) sb/sth to guard or protect sb/sth; to look after sb/sth: [Vn, Vpr] Could you watch (over) my clothes while I have a swim? **3** (infml) to be careful about sb/sth; to give special attention to sth: [Vn] Watch yourself (ie Do not fall, do sth foolish, etc)! ○ You'd better watch your language (ie be careful what you say)! ○ I have to watch every penny (ie be very careful about what I spend). [V.wh] Watch what you say! **IDM** **mind/watch one's tongue** ⇨ TONGUE. **mind/watch one's step** ⇨ STEP². **watch the 'clock** (infml) to be careful not to work longer than the required time; to think more about when one's work will finish than about the work itself. **'watch it** (infml) (esp imperative) to be careful. **watch this 'space** (infml catchphrase) wait for further developments to be announced: I can't tell you any more about it yet, but watch this space. **watch the 'time** to stay aware of what time it is, eg to avoid being late for sth. **watch the 'world go by** to observe others while doing nothing oneself: We sat in a café watching the world go by. **PHRV** **'watch for sb/sth** to look and wait for sb to appear or for sth to happen: You'll have to watch for the right moment to make a move. **,watch 'out** (esp imperative) to take care: Watch out! There's a car coming. **,watch 'out for sb/sth 1** to keep looking so that one does not miss sb/sth: The staff were asked to watch out for forged bank-notes. **2** to be careful about sth: Watch out for the stairs — they're rather steep.
▶ **watcher** n (often in compounds) a person who watches sth, esp one who is interested in observing or studying a particular thing or activity regularly: seasoned soap opera watchers. See also BIRD-WATCHER, CLOCK-WATCHER.
■ **,watching 'brief** n [sing] the action of observing what a group, esp a political organization, is doing in order to protect people's interests: have/keep/maintain a watching brief on local government activity.

watch² /wɒtʃ/ n **1** [C] a small instrument for showing the time, worn on a strap on the wrist: wind/set a watch ○ My watch is fast/slow. Compare CLOCK¹ 1. See also STOPWATCH, WRIST-WATCH. **2** [sing] a person or group of people that watches sb/sth: The police put a watch on the suspect's house. **3** [C] a fixed period of work, usu four hours, on a ship, done by different members of the crew in turn: the middle watch (ie midnight to 4 am). **IDM** **keep a close eye/watch on sb/sth** ⇨ CLOSE¹. **keep 'watch (for sb/sth)** to stay watching, guarding, etc: We took it in turns to sleep while the others kept watch. **on 'watch** on duty, eg as a member of a ship's crew or as a guard. **(be) on (the) 'watch (for sb/sth)** (to be) watching carefully for sb/sth, esp for possible danger: *Tourists were warned to be on the watch for thieves.*

▶ **watchful** /-fl/ *adj* watching or observing closely; ALERT: *She kept a **watchful** eye on the children.* **watchfully** /-fəli/ *adv.* **watchfulness** *n* [U].

■ **'watch-strap** (*Brit*) (*US* **'watchband**) *n* a strap for fastening a watch to the wrist.

'watch-tower *n* a high tower from which guards, soldiers, etc keep watch.

watchdog /'wɒtʃdɒg; *US* -dɔːg/ *n* (**a**) a dog that is kept to guard property, esp a house. (**b**) a person or group that protects people's rights when they buy sth or use a service: *a consumer watchdog ○ the government's pollution watchdog, the National Rivers Authority.*

watchmaker /'wɒtʃmeɪkə(r)/ *n* a person who makes and repairs watches and clocks.

watchman /'wɒtʃmən/ *n* (*pl* **-men** /-mən/) a person employed to guard a building, eg a bank, an office building or a factory, esp at night: *a night watchman.*

watchword /'wɒtʃwɜːd/ *n* a word or phrase that expresses the beliefs or aims of a party or group: *Safety is our watchword.* Compare SLOGAN.

water¹ /'wɔːtə(r)/ *n* **1** [U] (**a**) a liquid without colour, smell or taste that falls as rain, is in lakes, rivers and seas, and is used for drinking, washing, etc: *a glass of water ○ 'drinking water ○ Fish live in (the) water.* See also FRESHWATER, SALT-WATER, SEA WATER. (**b**) this liquid as supplied to homes, factories, etc in pipes: *water rationing/shortages ○ There is hot and cold running water in all the bedrooms. ○ The water was turned off for several hours each day during the drought. ○ The pipe burst and water flowed everywhere.* See also TAP WATER. (**c**) a mass of this liquid, esp a lake, river or sea: *Don't go too near the edge or you'll fall in the water. ○ Several fields are under water (ie flooded) after the heavy rain.* (**d**) the surface of a lake, river, sea, etc: *float on the water ○ swim under (the) water.* See also BARLEY WATER, GRIPE-WATER, ICE-WATER, MINERAL WATER, SODA WATER, TONIC WATER. **2 waters** [pl] (**a**) the mass of water in a lake, river, etc: *the clear blue waters of the Mediterranean ○ flood waters.* (**b**) the sea near a particular country: *British (territorial) waters ○ in home/foreign waters.* **3** [U] the state or level of the tide: *(at) high/low water.* **IDM** **be in / get into hot water** ⇨ HOT. **blood is thicker than water** ⇨ BLOOD¹. **bread and water** ⇨ BREAD¹. **by water** using a boat, ship, etc for travel or transport. **a fish out of water** ⇨ FISH¹. **hell or high water** ⇨ HELL. **hold 'water** (*infml*) (of an argument, an excuse, a theory, etc) to seem real or true enough to be believed. **in deep water** ⇨ DEEP¹. **keep one's head above water** ⇨ HEAD¹. **like a duck to water** ⇨ DUCK¹. **like 'water** (*infml*) in great quantities: *spend money like water ○ The wine flowed like water at the party.* **a lot of / much water has flowed, etc under the 'bridge** many things have happened since an event, etc and the situation is different now. **make/pass 'water** (*fml*) to urinate (URINE). **muddy the waters** ⇨ MUDDY *v.* **pour/throw cold water on sth** ⇨ COLD¹. **pour oil on troubled water** ⇨ POUR. **still waters run deep** ⇨ STILL¹. **test the waters** ⇨ TEST *v.* **throw the baby out with the bath water** ⇨ BABY. **tread water** ⇨ TREAD. **(like) water off a 'duck's 'back** (of criticisms, etc) without any effect (on sb): *Their comments were (like) water off a duck's back.* **water under the 'bridge** an event, a mistake, etc that has already happened and cannot be changed, so there is no point in worrying about it: *The divorce was very painful but it's all water under the bridge now.*

▶ **waterless** *adj* (esp of an area of land) without water: *waterless deserts/regions.*

■ **'water-bed** *n* a MATTRESS for sleeping on, made of rubber or plastic and filled with water.

'water-bird *n* any bird that lives near and walks or swims in water, esp rivers, lakes, etc.

'water-biscuit *n* a thin crisp biscuit that is not sweet and is usu eaten with butter and cheese.

'water-borne *adj* **1** (of goods) carried by water. **2** (of diseases) spread by water: *Cholera is a water-borne disease.*

'water-bottle (*Brit*) (*US* **canteen**) *n* a plastic or metal container for carrying water to drink, used by walkers, soldiers, etc. See also HOT-WATER BOTTLE.

'water-buffalo *n* (*pl* unchanged or **-oes**) a common domestic Indian animal like a large cow.

'water-butt *n* a large barrel for collecting rain as it flows off a roof.

'water-cannon *n* (*pl* unchanged or **-cannons**) a machine that produces a powerful jet of water, used eg by the police to break up crowds.

'water-closet *n* (*dated*) (*abbr* WC) a toilet.

'water-colour (*US* **-color**) *n* (**a**) **'water-colours** [pl] colours mixed with water, not oil, used in painting. (**b**) [C] a picture painted with such paints. **'water-colourist** (*US* **-colorist**) *n* a person who paints with water-colours.

'water-cooled *adj* cooled by water circulating round it: *a water-cooled nuclear reactor.*

'water cooler *n* a device for cooling and storing water for drinking.

'water-hole (also **'watering-hole**) *n* a place, esp in a hot country, in which water collects and where animals go to drink.

'water-ice *n* [U, C] frozen water flavoured with fruit juice and sugar; a portion of this.

'water jump *n* a place where horses or runners have to jump over water in a race, eg a fence with water beside it.

'water-level *n* (**a**) the surface of water in a lake, pool or container, etc: *below the water-level.* (**b**) the height of this: *build a dam to raise the water-level.*

'water-lily *n* a plant that grows in water with large round floating leaves and white, yellow or pink flowers.

'water-line *n* the line along which the surface of the water touches a ship's side.

'water-main *n* a large underground pipe that supplies water to buildings, etc.

'water-meadow *n* a field near a river that is flooded regularly, esp in winter: *fertile water-meadows.*

'water-melon *n* [C, U] a large, dark green MELON with juicy red flesh and black seeds: *eating a slice of water-melon.*

'water-mill *n* a mill for grinding corn, etc that uses water, esp from a river, to make it work.

'water-pistol *n* a toy gun that shoots jets of water.

'water polo *n* [U] a game played by two teams of people swimming who try to throw a ball into a goal.

'water-power *n* [U] power obtained from flowing or falling water, used to drive machinery or produce electricity.

'water-rat (also **water-vole**) *n* an animal like a rat that swims in water and lives in a hole beside a river, lake, etc.

'water-rate *n* (*Brit*) a charge made for the use of water from a public water-supply.

'water-resistant *adj* that does not let water through easily: *water-resistant sun-cream.*

'water-ski *n* (*pl* **-skis**) (usu *pl*) either of a pair of long flat boards on which a person stands in order to SKI on water. — *v* (*pt, pp* **-skied**; *pres p* **-skiing**) to SKI on water while being pulled by a fast boat: [V] *go water-skiing.*

'water-softener *n* [C, U] a device or substance that removes certain minerals, esp chalk, from water.

'water-supply *n* (usu *sing*) (**a**) a system of providing and storing water. (**b**) the amount of water stored for a town, district, building, etc: *a clean/ contaminated water-supply.*

'water-table *n* the level at and below which water is found in the ground: *The water-table has gone down because of the lack of rain.*

'water-tower *n* a tall structure with a tank of water at the top from which water is supplied to buildings, etc at a steady pressure.

'water-vole *n* = WATER-RAT.

'water-wheel *n* a wheel turned by a flow of water, used esp formerly to work machinery.

'water-wings *n* [pl] plastic or rubber bags filled with air, worn on the shoulders by a person who is learning to swim.

> **NOTE** When water is **heated** to 100 degrees Celsius, it **boils** and becomes **steam**. When steam touches a cold surface, it **condenses** and becomes water again. When water is **cooled** below 0 degrees Celsius, it **freezes** and becomes **ice**. If the temperature increases, the ice **melts**. When **frozen** food or **icy** weather becomes warmer, we say it **thaws**. Frozen food **thaws** or **defrosts** when you take it out of the freezer.

water² /'wɔːtə(r)/ *v* **1** to pour water on plants, etc: [Vn] *water a flowerbed/lawn* ○ *The garden needs watering.* **2** to give water to an animal to drink: [Vn] *water the horses.* **3** (of the eyes) to become full of tears; (of the mouth) to produce SALIVA: [V] *The smoke made my eyes water.* ○ *The delicious smell from the kitchen made our mouths water.* **4** (usu passive) (esp of rivers) to flow through an area of land and provide it with water: [Vn] *a country watered by many rivers.* **5** to add water to a drink, esp to an alcoholic one to make it less strong: [Vn] *watered wine.* **PHRV** ,water sth 'down **1** to make a liquid weaker by adding water: *He'd been serving watered-down beer to his customers.* **2** to make a speech, piece of writing, etc less forceful or offensive by changing or leaving out certain details: *This is a watered-down version of the original proposal.*
■ ,watered 'silk *n* [U] a silk fabric that has a shiny surface with markings like waves on it.

watering-can /'wɔːtərɪŋ kæn/ *n* a metal or plastic container with a handle and a long SPOUT, used for pouring water on plants. See also ROSE² 3.

'watering-hole *n* = WATER-HOLE.

'watering place *n* (*dated esp Brit*) a place where people go to drink mineral waters or bathe for their health; a SPA.

watercourse /'wɔːtəkɔːs/ *n* an artificial channel of water.

watercress /'wɔːtəkres/ *n* [U] a plant that grows in streams and pools. Its leaves have a strong taste and are often used in salads (SALAD).

waterfall /'wɔːtəfɔːl/ *n* a stream or river that falls from a height, eg over rocks or a cliff.

waterfowl /'wɔːtəfaʊl/ *n* (*pl* unchanged) (usu *pl*) a bird that swims and lives near or on water, esp a duck or a GOOSE(1).

waterfront /'wɔːtəfrʌnt/ *n* a street, part of a town, etc that is next to water, eg a harbour or the sea: *cafés on the waterfront.*

waterlogged /'wɔːtəlɒgd; *US* -lɔːgd/ *adj* (**a**) (of land) so full of water that it cannot hold any more and becomes flooded: *The match had to be abandoned because the pitch was waterlogged.* (**b**) (of a boat, wood, etc) so full of water that it can no longer float.

Waterloo /ˌwɔːtə'luː/ *n* **IDM** meet one's Waterloo ⇨ MEET¹.

watermark /'wɔːtəmɑːk/ *n* **1** a symbol or design in some types of paper, which can be seen when the paper is held against the light. **2** a mark that shows

how much the water in a river, etc has risen or fallen: *the high watermark.*

waterproof /'wɔːtəpruːf/ *adj* that does not let water through: *a waterproof jacket* ○ *Is your watch waterproof?*
> **waterproof** *n* (often *pl*) a piece of clothing made from waterproof material: *You'll need waterproofs* (ie a waterproof jacket and trousers).
waterproof *v* [Vn] to make sth waterproof.

watershed /'wɔːtəʃed/ *n* (**a**) a line of high land where streams on one side flow into one river or sea, and streams on the other side flow into a different river or sea. (**b**) an event or a period of time that marks an important change: *a cultural/historical/political watershed* ○ *The General Strike was a watershed in British industrial relations.*

waterside /'wɔːtəsaɪd/ *n* [sing] the edge of a river, lake or sea: *stroll along the waterside* ○ *waterside plants.*

waterspout /'wɔːtəspaʊt/ *n* a column of water rising from the sea into the sky as a result of a WHIRLWIND.

watertight /'wɔːtətaɪt/ *adj* **1** made or closed so that water cannot get in or out: *a watertight compartment/joint/seal.* **2**(**a**) (of an excuse, etc) impossible to prove false. (**b**) (of an agreement) carefully prepared and written so that it contains no mistakes or weaknesses and is easy for everyone to understand.

waterway /'wɔːtəweɪ/ *n* a river, canal, etc along which ships can travel: *inland waterways* ○ *a navigable waterway.*

waterworks /'wɔːtəwɜːks/ *n* **1** [sing or pl *v*] a building with pumping machinery for supplying water to an area. **2** [pl] (*infml euph*) the organs of the body through which URINE is passed. **IDM** turn on the 'waterworks (*infml derog*) to start crying, esp in order to get sympathy or attention.

watery /'wɔːtəri/ *adj* **1**(**a**) of or like water: *a watery liquid/fluid* ○ (*fig rhet*) *go to a watery grave* (ie die by drowning). (**b**) (*usu derog*) containing too much water: *watery soup/gravy.* **2** weak; pale: *watery sunshine.* **3**(**a**) full of water: *Her eyes were red and watery.* (**b**) (*Brit*) suggesting that there will be rain: *a watery sky.*

watt /wɒt/ *n* (*abbr* W) a unit of electrical power: *a 60-watt light-bulb.*
> **wattage** /'wɒtɪdʒ/ *n* [U] an amount of electrical power expressed in watts: *low-wattage bulbs/lamps/ heaters.*

wattle¹ /'wɒtl/ *n* [U] sticks woven together as a material for making fences, walls, etc.
■ ,wattle and 'daub *n* [U] wattle covered with mud or clay and used, esp formerly, for making the walls of houses.

wattle² /'wɒtl/ *n* a loose piece of red skin that hangs down from the head or throat of a bird, eg a TURKEY(1a).

wave¹ /weɪv/ *v* **1** (of a fixed object) to move freely and loosely, eg in the wind: [V] *a field of waving corn* [Vpr] *a flag waving in the breeze* ○ *branches waving in the wind.* **2** ~ (at/to sb); ~ sth (at sb); ~ sth about to move one's hand or sth held in one's hand from side to side in the air in order to attract attention or as a greeting, signal, etc: [V] *He waved when he saw us.* [Vpr] *They waved at/to us from across the road.* [Vn, Vnp, Vnpr] *She waved her arms (about) (in the air).* [Vn, Vnpr] *The demonstrators were waving banners and placards (at passers-by).* [Vn, Vnn, Vnpr] *wave (sb) goodbye/wave goodbye to sb.* **3** to show that a person or vehicle should move in the specified direction, by waving one's hand: [Vnp] *She waved them away impatiently.* ○ *The policeman waved us on* (ie indicated that we should continue). **4** (of hair) to curl slightly: [Vadv] *His hair waves naturally.* [Vn] *She has had her hair*

[V.speech] = verb + direct speech   [V.*that*] = verb + *that* clause   [V.*wh*] = verb + *who, how*, etc clause

waved. **IDM** **fly/show/wave the flag** ⇨ FLAG¹. **wave a magic 'wand** to solve a problem as if by magic: *He expects someone to wave a magic wand and find him a job.* **PHRV** ˌwave sth a'side to dismiss an objection, etc as not important or relevant: *My reservations about the plan were waved aside.* ˌwave sth/sb 'down to signal to a vehicle or its driver to stop, by waving one's hand.

wave² /weɪv/ *n* **1** [C] **(a)** a moving ridge of water, esp on the sea, caused by the wind and tide: *boats bobbing in/on the waves* ○ *Huge waves crashed onto the beach.* ○ *He sat in the water and let the waves break over him.* ⇨ picture at SURF. **(b)** a group of people or things that is seen as moving like a wave: *waves of tourists* ○ *a new wave of invaders* ○ *The pain comes and goes in waves.* **2 the waves** [pl] *(fml)* the sea: *The ship sank beneath the waves.* **3** [C] a movement of the hand from side to side as a greeting, etc; an act of waving: *With a quick wave of his hand, he was gone.* **4** [C] a curving shape in part of a person's hair: *Her hair has natural waves.* See also PERMANENT WAVE. **5** [C] a sudden increase and spread of a condition, an emotion or an influence affecting a person or group: *a wave of anger/enthusiasm/hysteria* ○ *a 'crime wave.* See also HEATWAVE, SHOCK WAVE. **6** [C] **(a)** the movement or process by which heat, light, sound, magnetism (MAGNET), ELECTRICITY, ETC IS SPREAD OR CARRIED: *radio waves.* **(b)** a single curve in the course of this. See also MEDIUM WAVE, MICROWAVE. **IDM** **make 'waves** *(infml)* to cause trouble; to disturb a peaceful situation: *Some people seem to enjoy making waves.* **the crest of a/ the wave** ⇨ CREST.

▶ **wavelet** /'weɪvlət/ *n* a small wave of water: *gentle wavelets on a sandy shore.*

wavy *adj* having curves: *a wavy line* ○ *wavy hair.*

waveband /'weɪvbænd/ *n* = BAND² 6a.

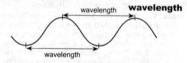

wavelength /'weɪvleŋθ/ *n* **1** the distance between two corresponding points in a sound, light or ELECTROMAGNETIC wave. **2** the length of the radio wave that a particular radio station uses for broadcasting its programmes. **IDM** **on a different/the same wavelength** having a different/the same way of thinking as sb else and therefore not able/able to understand them easily: *I'm afraid he and I are on totally different wavelengths.*

waver /'weɪvə(r)/ *v* **1** to be or become weak or unsteady: [V] *He felt his courage begin to waver.* ○ *Her steady gaze did not waver.* [Vpr] *He never wavered in his determination to succeed.* ○ *His voice wavered with emotion.* **2** ~ (**between sth and sth**) to hesitate, esp about making a decision or choice; dither: [V] *We haven't bought the house yet — we're still wavering.* [Vpr] *She's wavering between a career as a teacher and going into politics.* **3** (esp of light) to move in an unsteady way: [V] *wavering shadows.*

▶ **waverer** /'weɪvərə(r)/ *n: The strength of his argument convinced the last few waverers.*

wax¹ /wæks/ *n* [U] **1** (also **beeswax**) **(a)** a soft sticky yellow substance produced by bees and used by them for making HONEYCOMB cells. **(b)** this substance after special treatment, used for making candles, models, etc. **2** any of various solid fat or oily substances that melt easily, used for making candles, polish, etc: *a wax candle* ○ *wax polish.* See also PARAFFIN WAX, SEALING WAX. **3** a yellow substance like wax that is produced in the ears.

▶ **wax** *v* **(a)** to polish sth with wax: [Vn] *wax the floor/the furniture/the car.* **(b)** (esp passive) to

cover sth with wax: [Vn] *waxed paper/thread* ○ *a waxed jacket.* **(c)** to remove hair from a part of the body by using wax: [Vn] *wax one's legs.*

waxen /'wæksn/ *adj* *(fml)* smooth or pale like wax: *a waxen face.*

waxy *adj* having a surface or texture like wax: *waxy skin* ○ *waxy potatoes* ○ *leaves with a waxy coating.*

wax² /wæks/ *v* **1** [V] (of the moon) to appear gradually larger until its full form is visible. Compare WANE 1. **2** *(rhet)* to become as specified when speaking or writing about sth: [V-adj] *He waxed lyrical about/on the subject of new business methods.* **IDM** ˌwax and 'wane to increase and then decrease in strength or importance over a period of time: *Throughout history empires have waxed and waned.*

waxwork /'wækswɜːk/ *n* **(a)** [C] an object made of wax, esp the model of a person: *waxwork figures.* **(b)** **waxworks** [sing or pl *v*] a place where wax models of famous people are shown to the public.

way¹ /weɪ/ *n* **1** [C] (often in compounds) **(a)** a place for walking, travelling, etc along; a path, road, street, etc: *a way across the fields* ○ *a covered way between two buildings.* See also HIGHWAY, RAILWAY, SLIPWAY, WATERWAY. **(b)** **Way** the name of certain roads or streets: *No 26, Churchill Way.* **2** [C usu *sing*] **(a)** ~ (**from… to…**) a route, road, etc taken in order to reach a place: *the way into/out of a building* ○ *the best/quickest/right/shortest way from A to B* ○ *tell sb the way* ○ *Which way do you usually go to town?* ○ *He asked me the way to London.* ○ *I didn't go on the main road — I went the pretty way.* ○ *(fig) find a way out of one's difficulty* ○ *(fig) argue, bluff, talk, trick, etc one's way into/out of sth* (ie enter, escape, etc by arguing, etc) ○ *(fig) fight, force, shoulder, etc one's way across, into, etc sth* (ie cross, enter, etc sth by fighting, etc). **(b)** the route along which sb/sth is moving or would move if there was space: *find a way through the undergrowth* ○ *We had to pick our way along the muddy track.* ○ *There was a lorry blocking the way.* ○ *Get out of my way!* **3** [C usu *sing*] (in phrases after *which*, *this*, *that*, etc) (in) a specified direction: *'Which way did he go?' 'He went that way.'* ○ *Look this way, please.* ○ *If the tree falls that way, it will damage the house.* ○ *Look both ways* (ie to right and left) *before crossing the road.* ○ *They weren't looking our way* (ie towards us). ○ *Make sure that the sign's the right way up.* ○ *The arrow is pointing the wrong way.* ○ *(fig) Which way* (ie For which party) *will you vote?* **4** [C] **(a)** a method, style or manner of doing sth: *What is the best way to clean this?* ○ *She showed them the (right) way to do it.* ○ *I like the way you've done your hair.* ○ *There are several ways of doing it.* **(b)** (after *my*, *his*, *her*, etc) a course of action desired or chosen by sb: *My way doesn't work — let's try it your way.* ○ *We all have our favourite ways of doing certain things.* ○ *Try to find your 'own way to express the idea.* **(c)** a particular manner or style of behaviour: *speak in a kindly way* ○ *He has some rather odd ways.* ○ *She doesn't mean to be rude — it's just her 'way.* ○ *It is not her 'way to be selfish* (ie She is not selfish by nature). ○ *I don't like the way he looks at me.* ○ *It's disgraceful the way they spoil their children.* **5** [sing] (esp after *long*, *little*, etc) a distance or period of time between two points: *It's only a little way to the station.* ○ *We are a long way from the coast.* ○ *There's still a long way to go.* ○ *The roots go a long way down.* ○ *Your birthday is still a long way off/away.* **6** [sing] *(infml)* an area near a place; a particular part of a country: *It's been quite sunny down 'our way.* ○ *Please visit us next time you're over this way.* **7** [C] a particular aspect of sth; a respect¹(3): *Can I help you in any way?* ○ *She is in no way* (ie not at all) *to blame.* ○ *She helped us in every possible way.* **IDM** **across/over the 'way** (of a house, etc) on the other side of the street: *My sister* *lives over the way.* ₁**all the ᴵway 1** (also the ₁**whole ᴵway**) during the entire journey; during the whole period of a time: *She smoked non-stop all the way to London.* **2** completely: *We'll support you all the way.* ᴵ**be / be ᴵborn / be ᴵmade that/this way** (*infml*) (of a person) to behave or do things in a particular manner because it is part of one's character: *I can't change — I was born this way.* **be ₁set in one's ᴵways** to have habits, attitudes, etc that one is too old to change. **by a long way** ⇨ LONG¹. **by the ᴵway** (used to introduce a comment or question that is not directly related to the main subject of conversation): *Oh, by the way, there is a telephone message for you.* ◦ *What did you say your name was, by the way?* **by way of sth** by a route that includes the place mentioned: *They are travelling to the south of France by way of Paris.* **by way of / in the way of sth** as sth; for sth: *What are you thinking of doing by way of a holiday this year?* ◦ *By way of an introduction, I shall explain some of the historical background.* ◦ *The town doesn't offer much in the way of entertainment.* **change one's ways** ⇨ CHANGE¹. **clear the way** ⇨ CLEAR³. **come one's ᴵway** to occur or present itself to one: *An opportunity like that doesn't often come my way.* **cut both/two ᴵways** (of an action, argument, etc) to have two opposite effects or results. **divide, split, etc sth two, three, etc ᴵways** to share sth among two, three, etc people. **either way; one way or the other** whichever one of two possibilities, actions, etc happen or is chosen: *We could meet today or tomorrow — I don't mind either way.* **feel one's way** ⇨ FEEL¹. **find one's way** ⇨ FIND¹. **get into / out of the way of (doing) sth** to acquire/lose the habit of doing sth. **get/have one's own ᴵway** to get or do what one wants, often in spite of opposition: *She always gets her own way in the end.* **give ᴵway** to break or collapse: *The floorboards were rotten and finally gave way.* ◦ *Her legs seemed to give way under her and she fainted.* **give ᴵway (to sb/sth) 1** to yield (to sb/sth): *We must not give way to their demands.* **2** to allow sb/sth to be or go first: *Give way to traffic coming from the right.* **3** to let oneself be overcome by sth: *She gave way to despair.* **give way to sth** to be replaced by sth: *The storm gave way to bright sunshine.* **go far / a long way** ⇨ FAR¹. **go far / a long way towards sth / doing sth** ⇨ FAR¹. **go out of one's ᴵway (to do sth)** to take particular care and trouble to do sth: *When we first moved in, our neighbours went out of their way to help us.* **go one's own ᴵway** to act independently or as one chooses, esp against the advice of others: *Whatever you suggest, she will always go her own way.* **go sb's way 1** to travel in the same direction as sb: *I'm going your way, so I can give you a lift.* **2** (of events, etc) to be favourable to sb: *Things certainly seem to be going our way.* **go the way of all ᴵflesh** (*saying*) to live and die as other people do; to suffer the same changes, dangers, etc as other people. **the hard way** ⇨ HARD¹. **have come a long way** ⇨ LONG¹. **have/want it/ things both ways** ⇨ BOTH¹. **have it/things/ everything one's ᴵown way** to have what one wants, esp by opposing others: *All right, have it your own way — I'm tired of arguing.* **have a way with sb/sth** to have a particular talent for dealing with sb/sth: *have a way with difficult children/motor bikes.* **have one's way with sb** (*fml or joc*) to have sex with sb, possibly against their wishes. **in a bad ᴵway** ill or in serious trouble. **in a big/small way** on a large/small scale: *He's got himself into trouble in a big way.* ◦ *She collects antiques in a small way.* **in her, his, its, etc (own) ᴵway** by her, etc own standards, which may be unusual or different from those of the speaker: *In its (own) way the house is quite attractive.* **in the family way** ⇨ FAMILY. **in ₁more ways than ᴵone** (used to draw attention to the fact that the statement made has more than one meaning): *It's a very difficult situation, in more ways than one.* **in one's own sweet time/way** ⇨ SWEET¹. **in a ᴵway; in ᴵone way; in ᴵsome ways** to a certain extent but not entirely: *In some ways, I can understand why she wants to move.* **in the ordinary way** ⇨ ORDINARY. **in the/one's ᴵway** stopping sb/ one from doing sth or moving: *I'm afraid your car is in the way.* ◦ *I left them alone, as I felt I was in the way.* ◦ *Can you move, please, you're in my way.* **know one's way around** ⇨ KNOW. **laugh all the way to the bank** ⇨ LAUGH. **lead the way** ⇨ LEAD¹. **look the other ᴵway** to avoid seeing sb/sth, deliberately: *When the children started squabbling on the train, she just pretended to look the other way.* **lose one's way** ⇨ LOSE. **make one's ᴵway (to/towards sth)** to go; to make progress: *Passengers are requested to make their way to the exit doors.* ◦ *She's finding it hard to make her way in a business dominated by men.* **make ᴵway (for sb/sth)** to allow sb/sth to pass. **mend one's ways** ⇨ MEND. **not know where / which way to look** ⇨ KNOW. **(there are) no two ways a'bout it** (*saying*) there is only one correct or suitable way to act, speak or think with regard to sth: *It was the wrong decision — there are no two ways about it.* ₁**no ᴵway** (*infml*) under no circumstances: *Climb up that cliff? No way!* ◦ *There's no way we can afford a car at the moment.* ₁**one way and a'nother** taking into account all that has happened or all aspects of sth: *She's been very successful, one way and another.* ₁**one way or a'nother** by some means, method, etc; somehow: *We must finish the job this week one way or another.* **one way or the other** ⇨ EITHER WAY. **on one's/the ᴵway** in the process of going or coming: *I'd better be on my way* (ie I must leave) *soon.* ◦ *I'll buy some bread on the/ my way home.* **on the ᴵway** (*infml*) (of a baby) coming soon but not yet born: *She has two children and another one on the way.* **on the way ᴵout 1** in the process of leaving: *I bumped into him on the way out.* **2** going out of fashion or favour: *I thought hairstyles like that were on the way out.* **the ₁other way ᴵround 1** in the opposite position or direction: *Shouldn't that picture be the other way round?* **2** the opposite of what is expected or supposed: *Usually I'm early and you're late, but this time it's the other way round.* **out of harm's way** ⇨ HARM. ₁**out of the ᴵway 1** far from a town or city: *a tiny ₁out-of-the-way ᴵvillage in Cornwall.* **2** (in negative sentences) exceptional; strange; unusual: *He has done nothing out of the way yet.* **3** finished; dealt with: *I've done all the ironing, so that's out of the way.* **a/the parting of the ways** ⇨ PARTING. **pave the way** ⇨ PAVE. **pay one's/its way** ⇨ PAY². **pick one's way** ⇨ PICK¹. **point the way** ⇨ POINT². **rub sb up the wrong way** ⇨ RUB¹. **see, etc the error of one's ways** ⇨ ERROR. **see one's ᴵway ('clear) to doing sth** to find that it is possible or convenient to do sth: *I can't see my way clear to finishing the work this month.* ◦ *Could you see your way to lending me £50 for a couple of days?* **see which way the ᴵwind is blowing** to see what is likely to happen before doing sth: *I'd like to see which way the wind is blowing before applying for another job.* **smooth sb's/the path/way** ⇨ SMOOTH². **(not) stand in sb's ᴵway** (not) to prevent sb from doing sth: *If you want to study music, we won't stand in your way.* **take the easy way out** ⇨ EASY¹. **talk one's way out of sth / doing sth** ⇨ TALK¹. **that's the way the cookie ᴵcrumbles** (*infml esp US*) that is the situation and we cannot change it, so we must accept it. **to ᴵmy way of ᴵthinking** in my opinion. **under ᴵway** having started and making progress: *The project is now well under way.* **a/sb's way of ᴵlife** the normal pattern of social or working life of a person or group: *She adapted easily to the French way of life.* **the ₁way of the ᴵworld** the way that most people behave; the way that things happen:

Life is unfair, but that's the way of the world. ¡**ways and 'means** the methods and resources for doing sth, esp providing money. **where there's a will, there's a way** ⇨ WILL¹. ¡**work one's 'way through college, round the world, etc** to have a job or series of jobs while studying, travelling, etc: *She had to work her way through law school.* ¡**work one's way 'through sth** to read or do sth from beginning to end: *We are still working our way through all the application forms.* ¡**work one's way 'up** to be promoted regularly to a higher position in a company: *He worked his way up from junior clerk to sales director.*

way² /weɪ/ *adv* (*infml*) (used with a *prep* or an *adv* and usu not in negative sentences) very far; to a considerable extent: *She finished the race way ahead of the other runners.* ○ *The shot was way off target.* ○ *The price is way above what we can afford.* ○ *The initial estimate was way out* (ie completely wrong). ○ (*esp US*) *This skirt is way* (ie much) *too long.* **IDM** **'way back** a long time ago: *I first met him way back in the 'fifties.*

■ ¡**way-'out** *adj* (*dated infml*) unusual and strange; not conventional: *¡way-out 'clothes/'fashions/i'deas.*

wayfarer /'weɪfeərə(r)/ *n* (*dated*) a traveller, esp on foot.

waylay /weɪ'leɪ/ *v* (*pt, pp* **waylaid** /-'leɪd/) to wait for and stop sb who is passing, esp in order to ask them for sth or to attack them: *I got waylaid on my way to work by some tourists who'd got lost.*

waymark /'weɪmɑːk/ *n* (*Brit*) a natural or artificial object used to indicate a route for people walking, riding bicycles, etc. ▶ **waymarked** /-mɑːkt/ *adj*: *waymarked paths.*

-ways *suff* (with *ns* forming *adjs* and *advs*) in the specified direction: *lengthways* ○ *sideways.*

wayside /'weɪsaɪd/ *n* (usu *sing*) (land at) the side of a road or path: *wayside cottages* ○ *growing by the wayside.* **IDM** **fall by the 'wayside** to fail to continue or make progress in sth.

wayward /'weɪwəd/ *adj* not easily controlled; rather wild: *a wayward child.* ▶ **waywardness** *n* [U].

WC /ˌdʌbljuː 'siː/ *abbr* **1** water-closet. ⇨ note at TOILET. **2** West Central: *London WC2B 4PH* (ie as a POSTCODE).

we /wi; *strong form* wiː/ (used as the subject of a *v*) **1** I and another person or other people; I and you: *We've moved to Plymouth.* ○ *We'd* (ie the company would) *like to offer you a job.* ○ *Why don't we go and see it together?* **2** people in general: *We all know someone who has been burgled.* **3** (*fml*) (used instead of *I* by a king, queen or POPE as by a writer in a formal context). Compare THE ROYAL 'WE'.

weak /wiːk/ *adj* (**-er, -est**) **1(a)** having little strength or energy; not physically strong: *She is still weak after her illness.* ○ *He was too weak to walk far.* ○ *Her legs felt weak.* **(b)** likely to break: *That bridge is too weak to carry heavy traffic.* **2** (of a person's character) easy to influence; not firm: *He's too weak to be a good leader.* ○ *In a weak moment* (ie When I was easily persuaded), *I said he could borrow the car.* **3** not financially strong, sound or successful: *a weak currency/economy/market.* **4** not functioning properly: *a weak heart* ○ *a weak stomach* (ie one that is easily upset by food) ○ *My eyesight is rather weak.* **5** of a low standard; lacking in skill, etc: *a weak team* ○ *She was rather weak at maths at school.* **6** not convincing or forceful: *weak arguments/evidence* ○ *a story with a weak ending.* **7** not easily seen or heard: *a weak light/signal/sound.* **8** done without enthusiasm or energy: *a weak smile* ○ *He made a weak attempt to look cheerful.* **9** (of liquids) containing a high proportion of water: *weak tea.* **10(a)** (*grammar*) (of verbs) forming the past tense, etc by adding *-d, -ed* or *-t* (eg *walk, walked* or *waste, wasted*)

and not by changing a vowel (eg *run, ran* or *come, came*). **(b)** (*phonetics*) (of the pronunciation of certain words) used when the word is not stressed. For instance, the weak form of 'and' is /ən/ or /n/ as in *bread and butter* /ˌbred n 'bʌtə(r)/. Compare STRONG. **IDM** ¡**weak at the 'knees** (*infml*) hardly able to stand because of emotion, fear, illness, etc: *The shock made me go all weak at the knees.* ¡**weak in the 'head** (*infml*) stupid: *You must be weak in the head if you believe that.*

▶ **the 'weak** *n* [pl *v*] people who are poor, sick or without power.

weaken /'wiːkən/ *v* **1** to become or make sb/sth weak or weaker: [Vn] *weakened by disease/hunger/injury* ○ *The fall in productivity has weakened the economy.* [V] *His influence on the party is steadily weakening.* **2** to become or make sth less determined or certain about sth: [Vn] *weaken sb's confidence/resolve* [V] *They have not yet agreed to our requests but they are clearly weakening.*

weakling /'wiːklɪŋ/ *n* (*derog*) a weak person or animal: *Don't be such a weakling!*

weakly *adv* in a weak manner: *smile weakly.*

weakness *n* **1** [U, C] the state of being weak: *weakness of character* ○ *the weakness of the dollar/pound* ○ *New evidence revealed the weakness of the prosecution's case.* **2** [C] a fault or lack of strength, eg in a person's character; a weak part of sth: *It's important to know your own strengths and weaknesses.* ○ *structural weaknesses* ○ *Can you spot the weakness in her argument?* **3** [C usu *sing*] ~ (**for sth/sb**) a special or foolish enjoyment of sth/sb: *have a weakness for chocolate.*

weal /wiːl/ *n* a raised mark on the skin made by hitting with a stick, whip, etc.

wealth /welθ/ *n* **1** [U] **(a)** a large amount of money, property, etc: *a man of great wealth* ○ *Nobody knew how she had acquired her wealth.* **(b)** the state of being rich: *Wealth had not brought them happiness.* ○ *The country's wealth is based on trade.* **2** [sing] ~ **of sth** a large amount or number of sth: *a wealth of opportunity* ○ *a book with a wealth of illustrations.*

▶ **wealthy** *adj* (**-ier, -iest**) having wealth; rich.

wean /wiːn/ *v* [Vn, Vnpr] ~ **sb/sth** (**off sth**) (**on to sth**) to gradually stop feeding a baby or young animal with its mother's milk and start feeding it with solid food. **PHRV** ¡**'wean sb (away) from sth/doing sth** to make sb stop doing sth, esp gradually: *wean sb (away) from drugs/drinking/gambling.* ¡**'wean sb on sth** (esp passive) to make sb experience sth regularly, esp from an early age: *young tennis stars weaned on competitive matchplay.*

weapon /'wepən/ *n* **1** a thing designed or used for causing physical harm, eg a bomb, gun, knife, sword, etc: *a deadly weapon* ○ *nuclear weapons* ○ *They were carrying weapons.* **2** an action or a procedure used to defend oneself or get what one wants in a conflict or contest: *Their ultimate weapon is the threat of an all-out strike.* ○ *Humour was his only weapon against their hostility.*

▶ **weaponry** /-ri/ *n* [U] weapons: *a range of sophisticated weaponry.*

wear¹ /weə(r)/ *v* (*pt* **wore** /wɔː(r)/; *pp* **worn** /wɔːn/) **1** to have sth on one's body, esp clothing, as an ornament, etc: [Vn] *wear a beard/coat/hat/ring/watch* ○ *Bowler hats are not often worn nowadays.* ○ *She was wearing sun-glasses.* ○ *She never wears green* (ie green clothes). [Vnpr] *He wore a gold chain round his neck.* [Vn-adj] *She wears her hair long* (ie has long hair). ⇨ note. **2** to have a certain look on one's face: [Vn] *He/His face wore a puzzled frown.* ○ (*fig*) *The house wore a neglected look.* **3** to become or make sth less strong, new, useful, etc through continuous use or rubbing: [V-adj] *The sheets have worn thin.* [V] *The carpets are starting to wear.* [Vnpr] *I have worn my socks into holes.* [Vn-adj] *The stones*

had been worn smooth by the constant flow of water. [also Vn]. **4** to make a hole, path, etc in sth by constant rubbing, use, etc: [Vnpr] *I've worn holes in my socks.* ○ *The children have worn a path across the field where they walk each day to school.* ○ *The water had worn a channel in the rock.* **5** to endure or be capable of enduring continued use: [V, Vadv] *You should choose a fabric that will wear (well)* (ie last a long time). [Vadv] *Fashion shoes often wear very badly* (ie do not last long). ○ *(fig) Despite her age she had worn well* (ie still looked quite young). **6** (*Brit infml*) (esp in questions and negative sentences) to accept or tolerate sth, esp sth that one does not approve of: *He wanted to sail the boat alone but his parents wouldn't wear it.* **IDM** **wear one's 'heart on one's 'sleeve** to allow one's emotions, esp one's love for sb, to be seen. **wear the 'pants/'trousers** (*often derog*) (esp of a woman) to be the dominant person in a relationship, esp a marriage: *It's quite clear who wears the trousers in that house!* **wear 'thin** to begin to fail: *My patience is beginning to wear very thin.* ○ *Don't you think that joke's wearing a bit thin* (ie because we've heard it so many times)? **PHRV** **,wear (sth) a'way** to become or make sth become thin, no longer visible, etc by constant use: *The inscription on the coin had worn away.* ○ *The steps had been worn away by the feet of thousands of visitors.*
,wear (sth) 'down to become or make sth become gradually smaller, thinner, etc: *The tread on the tyres has (been) worn down to a dangerous level.* **,wear sb/sth 'down** to make sb/sth weaker by constant attack, nervous strain, etc: *She was worn down by overwork.* ○ *This relentless pressure is beginning to wear down his opponent's resistance.* **,wear (sth) 'off** to disappear or remove sth gradually: *The pain is slowly wearing off.* ○ *Children love new toys, but the novelty soon wears off.* ○ *The dishwasher has worn the glaze off the china.* **,wear 'on** (of time) to pass, esp at a pace that seems slow: *As the evening wore on, she became more and more nervous.* **,wear (sth) 'out** to become or make sth become thin or weak and useless, through so much use: *Her patience had/was at last worn out.* ○ *I wore out two pairs of boots on the walking tour.* **,wear oneself/ sb 'out** to make sb very tired: *They were worn out after a long day spent working in the fields.* ○ *Just listening to his silly chatter wears me out.*
▶ **wearable** /ˈweərəbl/ *adj* suitable to be worn: *a wardrobe of clothes that are no longer wearable.*
wearer /ˈweərə(r)/ *n* a person who is wearing sth: *These shoes will damage the wearer's feet.*
wearing /ˈweərɪŋ/ *adj* that makes one feel tired: *I've had a wearing day.* ○ *My elderly mother finds shopping very wearing.*

NOTE You **wear** clothes, including gloves, scarves, belts and glasses, and also perfume on your skin: *Do you have to wear a suit for work?* ○ *I've been wearing glasses for ten years.* You can also say you **have** something **on**: *She had on some very unusual earrings.* ○ *He ran outside without any shoes on.* You **carry** objects with you when you go somewhere, especially in your hands or arms: *He wasn't wearing his raincoat, he was carrying it over his arm.* ○ *She always carries an umbrella in her briefcase.*

wear² /weə(r)/ *n* [U] **1** the wearing of clothes; the state of being worn as clothing: *casual clothes for everyday wear* ○ *Cotton is suitable for wear in summer.* **2** (esp in compounds) things worn as clothes for a particular purpose or of a particular type: *'children's/'ladies'/'men's wear* ○ *formal/informal wear* ○ *'sportswear.* See also FOOTWEAR, UNDERWEAR. **3(a)** the amount or type of use sth has over a period of time: *This carpet will stand very heavy wear.* **(b)** the damage or loss of quality caused when sth is

used a lot or for a long time: *My shoes are showing (signs of) wear.* **4** the capacity sth has for continuing to be used: *There is still a lot of wear left in that old coat.* **IDM** **,wear and 'tear** damage, loss of quality, etc caused by ordinary use: *The insurance policy does not cover damage caused by normal wear and tear.* **the worse for wear** ⇨ WORSE.

weary /ˈwɪəri/ *adj* (**-ier, -iest**) **1(a)** very tired, esp as a result of effort or stress: *weary in body and mind* ○ *They felt weary after all their hard work.* **(b)** ~ **of sth/doing sth** no longer interested in or enthusiastic about sth; tired of sth: *The people are growing weary of the war.* ○ *I am weary of (listening to) her endless complaints.* **2(a)** causing one to feel tired or bored: *a weary journey/wait* ○ *the last weary mile of their climb.* **(b)** showing that one is tired: *a weary sigh/smile.*
▶ **wearily** /ˈwɪərəli/ *adv.*
weariness *n* [U].
wearisome /ˈwɪərɪsəm/ *adj* causing one to feel tired or bored: *wearisome complaints/tasks.*
weary *v* **1** ~ **sb (with sth)** to make sb feel tired, annoyed or lacking in patience: [Vn] *She was wearied by the constant noise.* [also Vnpr]. **2** ~ **of sb/sth; ~ of doing sth** (*fml*) to lose one's interest in or enthusiasm for sth: *She began to weary of her companions.*

weasel /ˈwiːzl/ *n* a small fierce animal with reddish-brown fur, a long thin body and short legs. Weasels kill and eat other small animals. Compare ERMINE, FERRET, STOAT.
▶ **weasel** *v* (-ll-; *US* -l-) **PHRV** **,weasel 'out (of sth)** (*infml derog esp US*) to avoid doing sth that one ought to do or has promised to do.
■ **'weasel words** *n* [U] (*infml esp US*) statements that are deliberately not clear or frank, used when one wishes to avoid committing oneself to a definite statement.

weather¹ /ˈweðə(r)/ *n* [U] the condition of the atmosphere at a certain place and time, with reference to temperature and the presence of rain, sunshine, wind, etc: *cold/sunny/warm/wet/windy weather* ○ *a weather-chart/-map* ○ *We had marvellous weather on our trip.* ○ *The weather is very changeable.* ○ *The success of the crop depends on the weather.* ○ *if the weather breaks/holds* (ie if the present good weather changes/continues) ○ *We shall play the match tomorrow, weather permitting* (ie if the weather is fine). Compare CLIMATE 1. **IDM** **in 'all weathers** in all kinds of weather, both good and bad: *She's out in all weathers, tending her garden.* **keep a 'weather eye (open) on sth** to be alert and ready in case of trouble. **make heavy weather of sth** ⇨ HEAVY. **under the 'weather** (*infml*) feeling slightly ill or depressed: *be/feel/look under the weather* ○ *She's been a little under the weather recently.*
■ **'weather-beaten** *adj* (esp of sb's skin) brown, rough and lined or damaged because one has spent a lot of time outside in the sun and wind: *the weather-beaten face of an old sailor.*
'weather forecast *n* a description of what the weather will probably be like for the next day or few days, esp one broadcast on radio or television.
'weather station *n* a building used for observing and recording weather conditions.
'weather-vane *n* a metal object that is put in a high place, esp on top of a building, and turns round easily in the wind in order to show which direction it is blowing from.

weather² /ˈweðə(r)/ *v* **1** to change or make sth change shape or colour because of the action of the sun, rain, wind, etc: [Vpr] *Teak weathers to a greyish colour.* [Vn] *rocks weathered by wind and water* [also V]. **2** to come safely through a difficult period, etc; to survive sth: [Vn] *weather a crisis.*

W

weatherboard /ˈweðəbɔːd/ (*US* **clapboard**) *n* each of a series of boards fixed so that they OVERLAP(1) on the side of a building to protect it from wind and rain. ▶ ˈweatherboarded *adj*: *weatherboarded huts*. ˈweatherboarding *n* [U].

weathercock /ˈweðəkɒk/ *n* a weather-vane (WEATHER¹) in the shape of a COCK¹(1). ⇨ picture at CHURCH.

weatherman /ˈweðəmæn/ *n* (*pl* **-men** /-men/) (*infml*) a person who describes and forecasts the weather, esp on television or radio.

weatherproof /ˈweðəpruːf/ *adj* that can keep out rain, snow, wind, etc: *weatherproof clothing*.

weave /wiːv/ *v* (*pt* **wove** /wəʊv/ or, in sense 4, **weaved**; *pp* **woven** /ˈwəʊvn/ or, in sense 4, **weaved**) **1(a)** (~ **A** (**from B**); ~ **B** (**into A**) to make fabric, etc by passing threads or strips across, over and under other ones, by hand or on a machine called a *loom*: [Vn] *a tightly woven piece of cloth* [Vnpr] *cloth woven from silk and wool* ∘ *weave a basket from strips of willow* ∘ *weave woollen yarn into cloth* [Vnp] *weave threads together*. ⇨ picture. (**b**) to work at a LOOM¹, making cloth: [V] *The women earn their living by weaving*. **2** ~ **A** (**out of / from B**); ~ **B** (**into A**) to twist flowers, bits of wood, etc together to make sth: [Vn, Vnpr] *weave a garland (out of primroses)* [Vnpr] *weave primroses into a garland* [also Vnp]. **3** ~ **sth** (**into sth**) to put facts, events, etc together into a story or a connected whole: [Vn] *weave a plot/a magic spell* ∘ *The lives of four different couples are woven into the narrative*. **4** to move along by twisting and turning to avoid things that are in one's way: [Vpr, Vnpr] *weave (one's way) through a crowd* [Vp] *weave in and out through the traffic* [Vpr] *The road weaves through a range of hills*. [also Vnp]. **IDM** **get cracking/weaving** ⇨ CRACK¹.
▶ **weave** *n* the way in which material is woven; a style of weaving: *the delicate, airy weave of her fabrics*.
weaver *n* a person whose job is weaving cloth.

web /web/ *n* **1** a net of fine threads made by a SPIDER or some other spinning creature to catch insects in: *a spider's web*. ⇨ picture at SPIDER. See also COBWEB. **2** ~ (**of sth**) a complex series or structure with many connecting parts: *create a web of companies across Europe* ∘ *a web of lies/intrigue*. **3** a piece of skin joining together the toes of certain birds and animals that swim, eg ducks and frogs (FROG).
▶ **webbed** *adj* (of the foot of a bird or an animal) having the toes joined by webs (WEB 3).

webbing /ˈwebɪŋ/ *n* [U] strong bands of woven material used for supporting the springs in seats, for making tidy the edges of carpets, and for making belts, etc.

we'd /wiːd, wid/ *short form* **1** we had. ⇨ note at HAVE. **2** we would. ⇨ WILL¹, WOULD¹.

Wed (also **Weds**) *abbr* Wednesday: *Wed 4 May*.

wed /wed/ *v* (*pt, pp* **wedded** or **wed**) (*dated or journalism*) (not in the continuous tenses) to marry: [V, Vn] *Rock star to wed (top model)* (eg introducing a newspaper story).
▶ **wedded** *adj* [pred] **1** ~ **to sth** unable to give sth up; devoted to sth: *He is wedded to his work/to the idea of European union*. **2** ~ **to sth** united or combined with sth: *beauty wedded to simplicity*. **3** (*dated or fml*) (**a**) legally married: *one's (lawful) wedded wife/husband*. (**b**) of or in marriage: *wedded bliss*.

wedding /ˈwedɪŋ/ *n* a marriage ceremony and the party which usually follows it: *a wedding dress/reception/invitation/present* ∘ *There will be a wedding in the village church on Saturday*. ∘ *We have been invited to their daughter's wedding*. ∘ *Today is our wedding anniversary*. See also SHOTGUN WEDDING, WHITE WEDDING.
■ ˈwedding breakfast *n* (*Brit*) a special meal after a marriage ceremony for the couple who have just got married and their families and friends.
ˈwedding cake *n* [C, U] a rich iced (ICE²) cake, often with several levels, that is cut up and eaten at a wedding party. Pieces are also sometimes sent to absent friends.
ˈwedding ring *n* a ring that is given during a marriage ceremony and worn afterwards to show that the person wearing it is married: *Wedding rings are usually worn on the third finger of the left hand*.

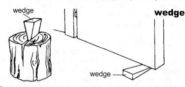

wedge /wedʒ/ *n* **1(a)** a piece of wood or metal that has one thick end and one narrow sharp end, used eg to split wood or rock or to keep things apart: *put a wedge under the door to keep it open*. ⇨ picture. (**b**) a thing shaped like or used as a wedge: *a wedge of cake/cheese* (ie a piece cut from a large round cake/cheese). ⇨ note at PIECE¹. **2** a golf club³(2) with a head like a wedge, used for hitting the ball high into the air. **IDM** **drive a wedge between sb and sb** ⇨ DRIVE¹. **the thin end of the wedge** ⇨ THIN.
▶ **wedge** *v* **1** to fix sth firmly or force sth apart using a wedge: [Vn-adj] *wedge a door open* [Vn] *The window doesn't stay closed unless you wedge it*. **2** to pack or squeeze sth/sb/oneself tightly into a space: [Vnpr] *wedge packing material into the spaces round the vase* ∘ *I was so tightly wedged between two other passengers that I couldn't get off the bus*. [also Vnp].

wedlock /ˈwedlɒk/ *n* [U] (*fml or law*) the state of being married: *born in/out of wedlock* (ie of parents who are/are not married).

Wednesday /ˈwenzdeɪ, -di/ *n* [C, U] (*abbrs* **Wed**, **Weds**) the fourth day of the week, next after Tuesday.
For further guidance on how *Wednesday* is used, see the examples at *Monday*.

wee¹ /wiː/ *adj* **1** (*esp Scot*) small in size: *the poor wee fellow*. **2** (*infml*) very small in amount or extent; tiny: *I'll have a wee drop of cream in my coffee*. ∘ *We'll be a wee bit late, I'm afraid*.

wee² /wiː/ (also **wee-wee** /ˈwiː wiː/) *n* (*infml*) (used esp by or when talking to young children) (**a**) [sing] an act of urinating (URINE): *have/do a wee(-wee)*. (**b**) [U] URINE.
▶ **wee** (also **wee-wee**) *v* (*pt* (**wee-**)**weed**) [V] (*infml*) (used esp by or when talking to young children) to URINATE.

weed /wiːd/ *n* **1(a)** [C] a wild plant growing where it is not wanted, esp among crops or garden plants: *The garden is overgrown with weeds*. ∘ *She spent the afternoon pulling up weeds in the flowerbeds*. (**b**) [U] any of several plants without flowers that grow in water and form a green floating mass: *The pond is full of weed*. **2** [C] (*infml derog*) (**a**) a person with a thin weak body. (**b**) a person who has a weak character: *Don't be such a weed!* **3** (*infml*) (**a**) **the weed** [sing] (*dated or joc*) tobacco or cigarettes: *I wish I could give up the weed* (ie stop smoking). (**b**) [U] MARIJUANA.
▶ **weed** *v* to take out weeds from the ground: [Vn, V] *I've been busy weeding (in) the garden*. **PHR V** ˌweed sth/sb **'out** to remove or get rid of people, animals or things that are not wanted or less good from a group: *weed out the weakest plants* ∘ *weed out corrupt party officials*.

weedy adj (**a**) full of or covered with weeds (WEED 1a). (**b**) (infml derog) having a thin weak body: a weedy little man.
■ '**weed-killer** n [C,U] a substance that destroys weeds: spray the lawn with weed-killer.

week /wiːk/ n **1(a)** a period of seven days, thought of as either from Sunday to Saturday or from Monday to Sunday: last/next/this week ○ early next week ○ at the end of last week ○ What day of the week is it? ○ He comes to see us once a week. (**b**) any period of seven days: a six weeks' course ○ a week ago today (ie seven days) ○ three weeks ago yesterday (ie 22 days ago) ○ They are going on a trip for two weeks. ○ I'll be away for no more than a week. See also HOLY WEEK. **2(a)** the six days apart from Sunday: During the week, the road is very busy but there is very little traffic on Sundays. (**b**) the five days other than Saturday and Sunday: They live in town during the week and go to the country for the weekend. ○ I never have time to go to the cinema in the week. (**c**) the period in a week when one works: a 35-hour week ○ The government is introducing a shorter working week. ○ How many lessons are there in the school week? **IDM** the other day/morning/evening/week ⇨ OTHER. today, tomorrow, Monday, etc '**week** seven days after today, tomorrow, Monday, etc: I'll see you on Thursday week. ,**week after** '**week** (infml) continuously for many weeks: Week after week the drought continued. ,**week by** '**week** as the weeks pass: Week by week he grew a little stronger. **week** ,**in, week** '**out** every week without exception: Every Sunday, week in, week out, she writes to her parents. **a** ,**week last** '**Monday,** '**yesterday, etc** (esp Brit) seven days before last Monday, yesterday, etc: It was a week yesterday (that) we heard the news. **a** ,**week next/on/this** '**Monday;** a ,**week to**'**morrow, etc** seven days after next Monday, tomorrow, etc: It's my birthday a week on Monday.
▶ **weekly** adj, adv (happening, done, published, etc) once a week or every week: weekly payments ○ a weekly shopping trip ○ Wages are paid weekly. ○ The machine must be checked weekly. — n a newspaper or magazine that is published once a week.

weekday /'wiːkdeɪ/ n any day except Sunday (and usu Saturday): Trains run more frequently on weekdays than on Saturday or Sunday. ○ Weekdays are always busy here. ○ weekday opening times.

weekend /ˌwiːk'end/ (US '**weekend**) n (**a**) Saturday and Sunday: The office is closed at/(US) on the weekend. ○ He has to work (at) weekends. See also DIRTY WEEKEND. (**b**) Saturday and Sunday or a slightly longer period as a holiday or rest: a weekend in the country ○ spend the weekend at home ○ a weekend cottage/visit. See also LONG WEEKEND.
▶ **weekender** n a person who spends the weekend away from home; a weekend visitor: Many of the cottages in the village are now owned by weekenders.

weeklong /'wiːklɒŋ/ adj lasting for a week: a week-long course/visit.

weeny /'wiːni/ adj (infml) tiny: Weren't you just a weeny bit scared? See also TEENY.

weep /wiːp/ v (pt, pp **wept** /wept/) **1** ~ (**for/over sb/ sth**) (rather fml) to cry: [V] The music made me weep. [Vpr] weep for joy ○ a mother weeping over the death of her child [Vn] weep bitter tears of disappointment [V.to inf] She wept to see him in such a state [V.speech] 'Don't go,' he wept. ⇨ note at CRY[1]. **2** (esp in the continuous tenses) (esp of a wound) to give out liquid: [V] His legs were covered with weeping sores (ie ones which had not healed).
▶ **weep** n [sing] an act of weeping: After the children left home I had a little weep.

weeping adj [attrib] (of certain trees) having branches that hang downwards: a weeping birch/ willow.

weepy adj (infml) (**a**) sad and tending to cry easily:

She is still feeling weepy. (**b**) (of a film, story, etc) tending to make one cry; sentimental: a weepy ending. — n (infml) a sad or sentimental film, play, etc.

weevil /'wiːvl/ n a type of small BEETLE with a hard shell that feeds on grain, nuts and other seeds, and destroys crops.

weft /weft/ n the **weft** [sing] (in weaving) the threads woven across, over and under the threads lying on the LOOM[1]. ⇨ picture at WEAVE. See also WARP[2].

weigh /weɪ/ v **1** to measure how heavy sth is by means of scales (SCALE[3] 1), a balance, etc: [Vn] He weighed himself on the bathroom scales. ○ The load must be weighed before it is put in the washing-machine. ○ He weighed the stone in his hand (ie estimated how heavy it was by holding it). **2** to show a certain weight when put on scales (SCALE[3] 1), etc: [Vadv] How much do you weigh? (ie How heavy are you?) [V-n] She weighs 60 kilos. ○ (infml) These cases weigh a ton (ie are very heavy) — what have you got in them? **3(a)** ~ sth (**with/against sth**) to consider carefully the relative value or importance of sth: [Vn] weighing the pros and cons [Vnpr] weigh one plan against another ○ weigh the advantages of the investment against the risks involved. (**b**) ~ sth (**up**) to consider sth carefully: [Vn] weigh the consequences of an action/the evidence [Vnp] weigh up one's chances of success. **4** to lift an anchor out of the water and into a boat before sailing: [Vn] We **weighed anchor. 5** ~ (**with sb**) (**against sb/sth**) to be considered important when sb/sth is being judged; to have influence on sb: [Vpr] His criminal record weighed heavily against him (with the jury). ○ Her past achievements weighed in her favour as a candidate. **IDM** weigh one's '**words** to choose carefully words that express exactly what one means: I must weigh my words to avoid any misunderstanding. **PHRV** ,**weigh sb** '**down** to make sb feel anxious or depressed: weighed down by worry and overwork ○ The responsibilities of the job are weighing her down. ,**weigh sb/sth** '**down** to make sb/sth bend by being heavy: The porter was weighed down by all the luggage. ○ The branches were weighed down with ripe apples.
,**weigh** '**in (at sth)** (of a boxer, JOCKEY, etc) to be weighed before a contest, race, etc: He weighed in at several pounds below the limit. ,**weigh** '**in (with sth)** (infml) to join in a discussion, an argument, etc by saying sth important or convincing; to contribute forcefully: At that point, the chairman weighed in with a strong defence of company policy.
'**weigh on sb/sth** to make sb anxious; to worry sb: The responsibilities weigh (heavily) on him. ○ It was obvious that something was weighing on her mind. ,**weigh sth** '**out** to measure a quantity of sth by weight: weigh out a kilo of tomatoes ○ Weigh out all the ingredients before you start making the cake. ,**weigh sb** '**up** to form an opinion of sb by observing or talking to them, etc: For most of the interview he sat in silence, weighing me up.
■ '**weigh-in** n (pl -**ins**) (usu sing) a check on the weight of a boxer, JOCKEY, etc, made just before a fight, race, etc.
'**weighing-machine** n a machine for weighing people or things that are too heavy to be weighed on a simple balance.
'**weighing-scale** n (usu pl) a balance used for weighing.

weighbridge /'weɪbrɪdʒ/ n a machine for weighing vehicles and their loads, usu with a platform set into the road, onto which the vehicles can be driven.

weight[1] /weɪt/ n **1** [U] a measure of how heavy sb/ sth is, expressed according to a particular system of measurement, eg in kilograms or pounds: Bananas are usually sold by weight. ○ It's nearly 10 kilos in *weight.* ○ *She is of average weight for her height.* ○ *You must eat less if you want to lose/take off weight* (ie become less heavy). ○ *He's put on/gained weight* (ie become heavier) *since he gave up smoking.* See also OVERWEIGHT, UNDERWEIGHT. ⇨ App 2. **2** [U] the quality of being heavy: *Lead is often used because of its weight.* ○ *The weight of the overcoat made it uncomfortable to wear.* **3** [C, U] a unit(s) or system of units by which weight is measured and expressed: *tables of weights and measures.* ⇨ App 2. **4** [C] **(a)** a piece of metal known to weigh a particular amount, used with scales (SCALE³ 2) for weighing things: *a 2 lb weight.* **(b)** a heavy object, esp one used to keep sth in position: *a clock worked by weights* ○ *put small weights in the hem of a curtain* ○ *The doctor said he must not lift heavy weights.* See also PAPERWEIGHT. **5** [sing] ~ **(of sth)** **(a)** a heavy load to be supported: *The pillars have to support the weight of the roof.* ○ *The weight of the water from the burst pipe caused the ceiling to collapse.* **(b)** a great responsibility or worry: *The news was certainly a weight off my mind.* ○ *The full weight of decision-making falls on her.* **6** [U] importance, strength or influence: *arguments of great weight* ○ *Recent events give added weight to their campaign.* ○ *The jury were convinced by the weight of the evidence against her.* ○ *Your opinion carries weight with the chairman.* **IDM** **pull one's weight** ⇨ PULL¹. **throw one's 'weight about/around** (*infml*) to use one's authority too aggressively in order to achieve what one wants. **weight of 'numbers** the combined power, strength, influence, etc of a group which is larger than another: *They won the argument by sheer weight of numbers.* **worth one's/its weight in gold** ⇨ WORTH.

▶ **weightless** *adj* having no weight, or with no weight relative to the surroundings because of the absence of GRAVITY(1). **weightlessness** *n* [U]: *become accustomed to weightlessness in a spacecraft.*

weighty *adj* (**-ier, -iest**) (*rather fml*) **1** showing or requiring serious thought; important or influential: *weighty arguments/decisions/matters.* **2** having great weight; difficult to bear: *a weighty tome/burden.* **weightily** /-ɪli/ *adv.* **weightiness** *n* [U].

weight² /weɪt/ *v* **1** ~ **sth (down) (with sth)** **(a)** to attach a weight¹(4b) to sth in order to keep it in the right position: [Vn] *weighted doors* [Vn, Vnp] *The net is weighted (down) to keep it below the surface of the water.* **(b)** ~ **sth (with sth)** to make sth heavier with a weight¹(4b): [Vnpr] *The stick had been weighted with lead.* **2** (esp passive) to plan or arrange sth in a way that favours a particular person or group: [Vnpr] *a law weighted against/towards/in favour of those owning land.*

▶ **weighting** *n* [U] (*Brit*) extra pay or allowances given in special cases, eg to people working in cities because it costs more to live there: *a London weighting allowance.*

weightlifting /'weɪtlɪftɪŋ/ *n* [U] the activity of lifting heavy objects as a sport or as exercise. ▶ **'weightlifter** *n*.

weir /wɪə(r)/ *n* **1** a wall or barrier built across a river in order to control the flow of water or change its direction. **2** a fence made of branches put across a stream in order to make a pool where fish may be caught.

weird /wɪəd/ *adj* (**-er, -est**) **1** strange and sometimes frightening because not natural or normal: *Weird shrieks were heard in the darkness.* **2** (*infml derog*) odd; not usual or conventional: *weird clothes/hairstyles* ○ *I found some of her poems a bit weird.* ○ *a garden full of weird and wonderful* (ie unusual and interesting) *plants.* ▶ **weirdly** *adv.* **weirdness** *n* [U].

weirdo /'wɪədəʊ/ *n* (*pl* **-os** /-əʊz/) (*infml usu derog*)

a person who behaves, dresses, etc in a way that is odd or not conventional; an ECCENTRIC person.

welcome /'welkəm/ *adj* **1** received with or giving pleasure: *a welcome change/rest/sight/visitor* ○ *Your offer of a loan is extremely welcome just now.* ○ *I had the feeling that we were not welcome at the meeting.* ○ *We've been made most welcome in the village* (ie accepted in a friendly way). **2** [pred] ~ **to sth/to do sth (a)** freely allowed or invited to take sth or to do sth: *She's welcome to stay here whenever she likes.* ○ *I don't want these books any more — you're welcome to them.* **(b)** (*ironic*) free to have sth or to do sth because the speaker does not want to have it or to do it: *If anyone thinks they can do this job any better, they are welcome to it/welcome to try!* ○ *As far as I'm concerned, if it's my desk she wants, she's welcome to it!* **IDM** **you're 'welcome** (used as a polite reply to thanks): *'Thanks for the lift.' 'You're welcome.'*

▶ **welcome** *interj* (a greeting used by a person who is already in a place to one who is arriving): *Welcome back/home!* ○ *Welcome on board!* ○ *Welcome to England!*

welcome *n* a greeting or RECEPTION, esp a kind or glad one: *an enthusiastic/a hearty/a warm welcome* ○ *The victorious team were given a tumultuous welcome when they arrived home.* ○ *She was touched by the warmth of their welcome.* **IDM** **outstay/overstay one's 'welcome** to stay too long as a guest, when one's host would prefer one to leave.

welcome *v* **1** ~ **sb (to sth)** to greet sb arriving in a place: [V] *a welcoming smile* [Vn] *They were there at the door to welcome us.* [Vnpr] *She welcomed the delegates to the conference.* [Vnpr, Vnp] *It is a pleasure to welcome you (back) on the show.* **2(a)** to be glad to have sth; to receive sth with pleasure or satisfaction: [Vn] *The changes were welcomed by everybody.* ○ *I'd welcome any comments you may care to make on my report.* **(b)** to receive or react to sth in the specified manner: [Vn] *welcome the news with amazement/indifference/enthusiasm* [Vnadv] *welcome a suggestion coldly/enthusiastically.*

weld /weld/ *v* **1(a)** ~ **A and B (together); ~ A (on)to B** to join pieces of metal together by hammering or pressing them, usu when the metal is softened by heat, or by using an OXYACETYLENE flame or an electric ARC(3): [Vn] *weld a broken axle* [Vnp] *weld parts together* ○ *The car has had a new wing welded on.* [also Vnpr]. **(b)** [Vn] to make sth by joining pieces of metal in this way. **2** ~ **sb/sth into sth; ~ sth together** to unite people or things into an effective whole: [Vnpr] *weld a bunch of untrained recruits into an efficient fighting force* [Vnp] *The crisis helped to weld the team together.* Compare FORGE² 2b.

▶ **weld** *n* a joint made by welding.

welder *n* a person whose job is making welded joints, eg in a car factory.

welfare /'welfeə(r)/ *n* [U] **1** the good health, happiness, comfort, etc of a person or group: *the welfare of the nation* ○ *Parents are responsible for the welfare of their children.* ○ *We are concerned about his welfare.* **2** practical care for the health, safety, etc of a particular group: *student/animal welfare* ○ *a child welfare clinic* ○ *the government's Social Welfare Department.* **3** (*US*) = SOCIAL SECURITY: *welfare payments.*

■ **,welfare 'state** (often **the ,Welfare 'State**) **(a)** *n* [C usu sing] a system of caring for the citizens of a country through a range of services, family allowances, free medical care and homes for old people provided by the State: *the possibility of cuts in the Welfare State.* **(b)** [C] a country that has such a system: *Britain's responsibilities as a welfare state.*

'welfare work *n* [U] **(a)** organized efforts to care for the health, safety and interests of a group of people, eg employees in a factory or disabled

W

(DISABLE) people. (**b**) (*US*) the work of people employed in the government's social services (SO-CIAL) department. **'welfare worker** *n*.

well¹ /wel/ *adv* (**better** /'betə(r)/; **best** /best/) **1** (usu placed after the *v*, and after the direct object if the *v* is transitive) in a good, right or satisfactory way: *The children behaved well.* ○ *She speaks English very well.* ○ *The conference was very well organized.* ○ *Does the job pay well?* ○ *Well done/played/run!* (ie expressing admiration for sb's achievement) ○ *I hope everything is **going well** (ie is satisfactory) **with** you.* ○ *Things didn't **go well for** the company at first, but everything is fine now.* ○ *The plan didn't work out very well.* ○ *Investing in industry is money well spent.* ○ *Do these colours **go well** (ie look nice) **together**?* Compare ILL² 1. **2(a)** with praise or approval: *She* **spoke well of** *the nurses and the way she had been looked after.* (**b**) in a kind way: *They treated me very well.* Compare ILL² 2. **3** thoroughly and completely: *Shake the mixture well.* ○ *The surface must be well prepared before you start to paint.* ○ *His shoes were always well polished.* ○ *I don't know him very well.* ○ *I'm well* (ie fully) *able to manage on my own.* **4** (after *can*, *could*, *may*, *might*) with good reason; probably; easily: *You may well be right.* ○ *I might well consider it later.* ○ *I **can't very well** leave now.* ○ *I couldn't very well refuse to help them, could I?* ○ *'They've split up, you know.' 'I **can well believe it**.'* ○ *It may well be that the train is delayed.* **5** to a great extent or degree: *I don't know exactly how old he is, but he's well over/past forty.* ○ *She was driving at well over the speed limit.* ○ *lean well forward/back in one's chair* ○ *It was well worth waiting for.* ○ *Temperatures are well up in the thirties.* **6** (*sl*) very: *The film was* 'well *good*. **IDM** **as well (as sb/sth)** in addition to sb/sth/doing sth: *Are they coming as well?* ○ *He grows flowers as well as vegetables.* ○ *She is a talented musician as well as being a photographer.* ⇨ note at ALSO. **be** ,well **'out of sth** (*infml*) to be fortunate that one is not involved in sth. **be** ,well '**up in sth** to know a lot about sth: *He's well up in all the latest developments in the industry.* **bloody well** ⇨ BLOODY². **do oneself 'well** to provide oneself with comforts, nice things, etc. **do 'well 1** to be successful: *Jack is doing very well at school.* ○ *The business did well last year.* **2** (only in the continuous tenses) to be making a good recovery from an illness, etc: *Mother and baby are doing well* (ie after a birth). **do 'well by sb** to treat sb generously. **do 'well for oneself** to become successful or wealthy. **do 'well out of sb/sth** to make a profit out of or obtain money from sb/sth. **do 'well to do sth** (esp as a warning) to be sensible or wise to do sth: *You would do well to concentrate more on his work.* ○ *You did well to sell when the price was high.* **fucking well** ⇨ FUCK. **jolly well** ⇨ JOLLY. **leave/let well a'lone**; (*US*) **let well enough alone** not to interfere with sth that is satisfactory or adequate: *Any changes in the rule would be very difficult to implement so it's better to leave well alone.* **may/might (just) as well do sth** to do sth because it seems best in the circumstances, though often reluctantly (RELUCTANT): *Since nobody else wants the job, we might as well let him have it.* **mean well** ⇨ MEAN¹. **one may/might as well be hanged/hung for a sheep as a lamb** ⇨ HANG¹. **pretty much/nearly/well** ⇨ PRETTY. ,very 'well (used to indicate that one agrees or will do what has been ordered, suggested, etc): *Very well, doctor, I'll try to take more exercise.* ○ *Oh, very well, if you insist.* ,well and '**truly** (*infml*) completely: *By that time we were well and truly lost.* '**well away 1** having made good progress: *By the end of the month, we'll be well away.* **2** (*infml*) drunk or fast asleep. ,well 'in (**with sb**) (*infml*) regarded by sb as a close friend; accepted: *She seems to be well in with the right people.* ,well '**off** in a good position, esp financially: *His family is*

not very well off. ○ *Some people don't know when they're well off* (ie do not appreciate their fortunate position). ○ *As usual, it's the less well-off who will suffer most.* ,well '**off for sth** having plenty of sth: *We're well off for storage space in the new flat.*

■ Many compound *adjs* are formed from *well* with a past participle. They are usu hyphenated when attributive but not hyphenated when predicative. Those which are usu hyphenated in both positions are shown below in examples. The comparative and superlative forms of these *adjs* are usu formed with *better* and *best*.

,well-ad'**justed** *adj* (of a person) having a balanced attitude and approach to life: *work experience that helps young people mature into well-adjusted adults.*

,well-ad'**vised** *adj* sensible; wise: *a* ,well-advised '*move* ○ *You would be well advised to* (ie You ought to) *reconsider your decision.*

,well-ap'**pointed** *adj* having all the necessary equipment, furniture, etc: *a* ,well-appointed/ho'tel/ a'partment/'office.

,well-'**balanced** *adj* (**a**) (of a person) sensible and emotionally in control: *healthy,* ,well-balanced young '*people* ○ *You need to be very well balanced to cope with the stress of a job like that.* (**b**) (of a meal or a diet) containing a sensible variety of what the body requires for good health.

,well-be'**haved** *adj* behaving in a way that other people approve of: *a* ,well-behaved '*child*/'*dog*.

'**well-being** *n* [U] a state of being healthy, happy, etc: *economic/psychological well-being* ○ *have a sense of well-being.*

,well-'**born** *adj* from a noble family.

,well-'**bred** *adj* having or showing good manners: *She was too well-bred to show her disappointment.* Compare ILL-BRED.

,well-'**built** *adj* (**a**) (usu *approv*) (of a person) big and solid with strong muscles. (**b**) (a building) strongly made or constructed.

,well-con'**nected** *adj* friendly with or related to rich, influential or socially superior people.

,well-'**cut** *adj* (of clothes) made well and therefore probably expensive: *a* ,well-cut '*suit*.

,well-de'**fined** *adj* clearly indicated; easy to see or understand: *a* ,well-defined '*pattern*.

,well-dis'**posed** *adj* ~ (**towards sb/sth**) (**a**) sympathetic or friendly to sb: *She seemed well disposed towards us.* (**b**) approving a plan, etc; ready to help: *The committee are well disposed towards the idea.* Compare ILL-DISPOSED.

,well-'**done** *adj* (of food, esp meat) cooked thoroughly or for a long time: *He prefers his steak well done.* Compare RARE², UNDERDONE.

,well-'**dressed** *adj* wearing fashionable or expensive clothes: *This is what today's well-dressed man is wearing.*

,well-'**earned** *adj* much deserved: *a* ,well-earned '*rest* ○ ,well-earned '*praise*.

,well-e'**stablished** *adj* that has existed and operated successfully for a long time: *a* ,well-established '*firm* ○ ,well-established pro'*cedures*.

,well-'**fed** *adj* having good meals regularly: *The cat looked sleek and well fed.*

,well-'**founded** *adj* based on good evidence: ,well-founded su'*spicions*.

,well-'**groomed** *adj* (of a person) looking clean, tidy and carefully dressed.

,well-'**heeled** *adj* (*infml*) rich: *a restaurant with many* ,well-heeled '*customers*.

,well-in'**formed** *adj* having or showing knowledge or information about many subjects or about one particular subject: ,well-informed o'*pinion*/'*quarters*/ '*sources*.

,well-in'**tentioned** *adj* intended or intending to be helpful, useful, etc: *She reacted angrily to my* ,well-intentioned re'*marks*. ○ *He's well-intentioned but not very good at getting things done.*

W

well-'kept adj carefully looked after; in good condition: rows of houses with ,well-kept 'gardens ○ (fig) a ,well-kept 'secret.

well-'known adj known to many people; familiar or famous: ,well-known 'actors/'facts/'landmarks/ quo'tations ○ Her books are not very well known.

well-'meaning adj acting or done, etc with good intentions, but often not having the desired effect: She began to resent the constant enquiries from well-meaning friends and relatives.

well-'meant adj done, said, etc with good intentions but not having the desired effect.

well-'oiled adj (a) (sl) drunk: He was already well-oiled before he arrived. (b) operating smoothly: the well-oiled political machine.

well-pre'served adj (a) (of an old person) not showing many signs of old age; looking young. (b) (of old things) in good condition: a well-preserved Renaissance painting.

well-'read adj having read many books, and therefore having gained a lot of knowledge.

well-'rounded adj (a) (of a person's body) pleasantly round in shape. (b) (of a person) having a fully developed personality or varied abilities: educating children to be well-rounded individuals. (c) [usu attrib] wide and varied: a ,well-rounded edu'cation.

well-'run adj managed efficiently: a ,well-run ho'tel/'company.

well-'spoken adj speaking correctly or in an elegant way.

well-'thought-of adj (of a person) respected, admired and liked: He is well thought of in government circles.

well-thought-'out adj carefully planned.

well-'thumbed adj (of a book, etc) with pages that are dirty at the edges because of being read many times.

well-'timed adj done, said, etc at the right time or at an appropriate time: Your remarks were certainly well timed. ○ a ,well-timed inter'vention. Compare ILL-TIMED.

well-to-'do adj wealthy.

well-'tried adj often used and therefore known to be reliable: a ,well-tried 'method/'remedy.

well-'trodden adj (of a road or path) much used.

well-'turned adj (fml) expressed in an elegant way: a ,well-turned 'compliment/'phrase.

well-'versed adj [pred] ~ (in sth) knowing a lot about sth; experienced: well-versed in the art of flattery.

'well-wisher n a person who hopes that another will be happy, successful, healthy, etc: They received many letters of sympathy from well-wishers.

well-'worn adj (a) (of a phrase, etc) used so often that it has little meaning and sounds dull. (b) (of clothes, objects, etc) used a lot and therefore rather old or untidy: a ,well-worn 'jacket/'briefcase.

well² /wel/ adj (**better** /'betə(r)/; **best** /best/) **1** [usu pred] in good health: I don't feel very well. ○ Is she well enough to travel? ○ Get well soon! (eg on a card) ○ I'm better now, thank you. ○ He's not a well man. ⇨ note at HEALTHY. **2** [pred] in a satisfactory state or position: It seems that all is not well at home. **3** [pred] sensible or desirable: It would be well to start early. **IDM** ,all very 'well (for sb)... (infml ironic) (used to indicate that one is not happy or in agreement with what sb has said or done): It's all very well (for 'you) to say you want a new car, but I'm the one who will have to pay for it. ,all well and 'good (infml) good but not completely satisfactory: An extra day's leave is all well and good, but what about the bonus we were promised? (just) as 'well (to do sth) sensible or appropriate: It would be (just) as well to phone and say we may be late.

well³ /wel/ interj **1** (used to express surprise or anger): Well, who would have thought it? ○ Well, well — I would never have guessed it! ○ Well, what

a thing to say! **2** (used to express relief): Well, thank goodness that's over! ○ Well, here we are at last! **3** (also **oh well**) (used to show that one accepts that sth cannot be changed): Oh well, there's nothing we can do about it. ○ Well, it can't be helped. **4** (also **very well**) (used to express agreement or understanding): Very well, then, I'll accept your offer. **5** (used when agreeing rather unwillingly that sth may be true): Well, you may be right. **6** (used when continuing a conversation after a pause, or to change the subject): Well, as I was saying,... ○ Well, the next day... ○ Well, let's move on to the next item. **7** (used to express uncertainty): 'Do you want to come?' 'Well, I'm not sure.' **8** (used with questions to indicate that one is waiting for sb to say sth): Well, are you going to tell us or not? **9** (used to mark the end of a conversation, etc): Well, I'd better be going now. **10** (used to give the speaker time to think of what he or she wants to say): I think it happened, well, towards the end of last summer. **11** (used when one wants to correct or change sth that one has just said): There were thousands of people there — well, several hundred anyway. **IDM** well I 'never ('did)! (infml) (used to express surprise or annoyance).

well⁴ /wel/ n **1**(a) a deep hole in the ground, usu lined with brick or stone, for obtaining water from under the ground: dig/drill/sink a well ○ The villagers get their water from a well. (b) an oil well. **2** an enclosed deep and narrow space, eg one extending from the top to the bottom of a building and containing a staircase or lift(1). **3** (Brit) a space in a lawcourt in front of the judge where lawyers sit, separated from the rest of the court by rails. See also INK-WELL.

▶ **well** v ~ (**out/up**) to flow or rise to the surface and SPILL over: [Vpr, Vp] Anger was welling up inside him.

we'll /wi:l, wil/ short form **1** we shall. ⇨ SHALL. **2** we will. ⇨ WILL¹.

wellington /'welɪŋtən/ (also ,**wellington 'boot**, infml **welly**) n (esp Brit) a rubber boot, usu reaching almost to the knee and worn to protect the foot from water, mud, etc: a pair of wellingtons/wellington boots. ⇨ picture at BOOT¹.

wellnigh /,wel'naɪ/ adv (fml or rhet) almost: It was ,wellnigh im'possible to see anything in the fog.

welly /'weli/ n (Brit infml) = WELLINGTON: a pair of green wellies.

Welsh /welʃ/ adj of Wales, its people or its language: the Welsh coastline ○ Welsh poetry.

▶ **Welsh** n **1** [U] the Celtic language of Wales. **2** the Welsh [pl] the people of Wales.

■ ,**Welsh 'dresser** n (Brit) a piece of wooden furniture with cupboards and drawers in the lower part and shelves in the upper part. ⇨ picture at DRESSER.

,**Welsh 'rarebit** (also **rarebit**) n a dish of melted cheese on TOAST¹(1).

welsh /welʃ/ v ~ (**on sth**) (derog) to fail to do sth that one has promised to do: [Vpr] He welshed on the deal. [also V].

Welshman /'welʃmən/ (pl **-men** /-mən/) n a man who lives in or comes from Wales.

welt /welt/ n a mark left on the skin by a heavy blow, esp with a whip.

welter /'weltə(r)/ n [sing] ~ **of sth/sb** a confused mixture of things or people: a welter of information/ legislation/criticism.

welterweight /'weltəweɪt/ n a boxer weighing between 61 and 67 kilograms, next above LIGHTWEIGHT (2): a welterweight champion/contest.

wench /wentʃ/ n (arch or joc) a young woman.

wend /wend/ v (arch or rhet) to go; to leave: It's time we were **wending our way** (ie We must go).

Wendy house /'wendi haʊs/ n (pl **houses**

W

/haʊzɪz/) a small toy house like a tent for children to play in.

went *pt* of GO[1].

wept *pt, pp* of WEEP.

were /wə(r); *strong form* wɜ:(r)/. ⇨ note at BE[2].

we're /wɪə(r)/ *short form* we are. ⇨ note at BE[2].

weren't /wɜ:nt/ *short form* were not. ⇨ note at BE[2].

werewolf /'weəwʊlf/ *n* (*pl* -**wolves** /-wʊlvz/) (in stories) a person who changes, or is capable of changing, into a WOLF, esp at the time of the full moon.

Wesleyan /'wezliən/ *n, adj* (a member) of the Methodist Church founded by John Wesley.

west /west/ *n* [U, sing] (*abbr* **W**) **1** (usu **the west**) the direction in which the sun sets; one of the four main points of the COMPASS[1](1): *The rain is coming from the west.* ∘ *Bristol is in the west of England.* ∘ *She lives to the west of* (ie further west than) *Paris.* Compare EAST, NORTH, SOUTH. **2 the West** Europe, N America and Canada contrasted with Eastern countries. **3 the West** (*US*) the western side of the USA: *She's lived in the West* (eg California) *for ten years now.* See also MIDWEST, THE WILD WEST.
▸ **west** *adj* [attrib] **1** in or towards the west: *West Africa* ∘ *She lives on the west coast.* **2** (of winds) from the west: *a west wind.* See also WESTERLY.
west *adv* towards the west: *three miles west of here* ∘ *The garden faces west.*

westward /'westwəd/ *adj* towards the west: *in a westward direction.*

westwards /'westwədz/ (also **westward**) *adv: travel westward(s).* ⇨ note at FORWARD[2].
■ **the West Country** *n* [sing] (*Brit*) the south-west (SOUTH) region of Britain, esp Cornwall, Devon and Somerset: *a West-Country village.*

the West End *n* [sing] (*Brit*) the area of London that includes most theatres, fashionable and expensive shops, etc: *a West-End cinema.* Compare THE EAST END.

the West Indies *n* [pl] the islands of Central America, including Cuba and the Bahamas. **West Indian** *adj, n.*

westbound /'westbaʊnd/ *adj* travelling or leading towards the west: *westbound traffic* ∘ *the westbound carriageway of the motorway.*

westerly /'westəli/ *adj* **1** [attrib] in or towards the west: *in a westerly direction.* **2** [usu attrib] (of winds) from the west: *westerly gales.*
▸ **westerly** *n* a wind blowing from the west: *light westerlies.*

western /'westən/ (also **Western**) *adj* [attrib] of, from or living in the west part of the world or of a specified region: *western customs/philosophies* ∘ *Western Australia.* See also COUNTRY-AND-WESTERN.
▸ **western** *n* a film or book about the life of cowboys (COWBOY 1) in the western part of the USA, esp in the second half of the 19th century.

westerner *n* (**a**) a native or inhabitant of the West, ie Europe, N America and Canada: *a country in Asia visited by few westerners.* (**b**) a native or an inhabitant of the western part of a country, esp the USA.

westernize, -ise /-aɪz/ *v* to make an Eastern country, person, etc more like one in the West, esp in ways of living and thinking, institutions, etc: [Vn] *The island became fully westernized after the war.*

westernization, -isation /,westənaɪ'zeɪʃn; *US* -nə'z-/ *n* [U].

westernmost /-məʊst/ *adj* situated furthest west: *the westernmost tip of the island.*

wet /wet/ *adj* (-**tter**, -**ttest**) **1** covered or soaked with liquid, esp water: *wet clothes/grass/roads* ∘ *Her cheeks were wet with tears.* ∘ *Did you get wet* (eg in the rain)? ∘ *dripping/soaking/wringing* (ie thoroughly) *wet.* Compare DRY[1] 1. **2** (of weather, etc) raining: *a wet day* ∘ *a wet climate* ∘ *It was the wettest*

October for many years. Compare DRY[1] 2. **3**(**a**) (of ink, paint, cement, etc) recently applied and not yet dry or set: *Be careful — the plaster is still wet.* (**b**) (of sth covered with paint, etc) not yet dry or set: *Don't touch the door — it's wet.* **4** (*Brit infml derog*) (**a**) (of a person) without energy, strength or courage. (**b**) (of Conservative politicians) favouring moderate rather than extreme policies. **IDM** (**still**) **wet behind the ears** (*infml derog*) not mature or experienced, eg in a job. **wet through** thoroughly soaked: *We got wet through.* ∘ *My shirt is wet through.*
▸ **wet** *n* **1 the wet** [sing] wet weather; rain: *Come in out of the wet.* **2** [U] liquid, esp water: *There's some wet on the carpet.* **3** [C] (*Brit derog*) (**a**) a dull or weak person. (**b**) a Conservative politician who favours moderate rather than extreme policies: *Tory wets.*

wet *v* (*pt, pp* **wet** or **wetted**) to make sth wet: [Vn] *Wet the clay a bit more before you start to mould it.* **IDM** **wet the/one's bed** (not passive; past tense usu *wet*) to pass URINE from the body when in bed and asleep. **wet one's whistle** (*dated infml*) to have a drink, esp an alcoholic one. **wetting** *n* [sing] an instance of becoming or being made wet: *get a thorough wetting in the heavy rain.*

wetly *adv: The leaves glistened wetly in the rain.*

wetness *n* [U].
■ **wet blanket** *n* (*infml derog*) a person who spoils other people's fun by disapproving of it or refusing to join in.

wet dream *n* a sexually exciting dream that results in an ORGASM.

wet fish *n* [U] (*Brit*) fresh raw fish for sale in a shop, etc.

wet-nurse *n* (esp formerly) a woman employed to feed another woman's baby with milk from her own breast.

wet suit *n* a rubber garment worn to keep warm by people swimming under water or sailing.

wetback /'wetbæk/ *n* (*US infml*) a Mexican person who enters the USA illegally.

wetlands /'wetləndz/ *n* [pl] damp areas of land: *preserve natural wetlands.* ▸ **wetland** *adj* [attrib]: *wetland birds/plants.*

we've /wi:v, wiv/ *short form* we have. ⇨ note at HAVE.

whack /wæk/ *v* [Vn, Vnpr] (*infml*) to hit or beat sb/ sth hard.
▸ **whack** *n* **1** a heavy blow, or a sharp sound made by this: *He gave the ball a terrific whack.* **2** (usu sing) ~ (**at sth**) (*infml*) an attempt: *I failed my test first time, but I'm having another whack at it.* **3** (usu sing) (*infml*) a share: *We already pay a fair whack in taxation.* ∘ *Some people are not doing their whack.*

whacked *adj* [usu pred] (*infml*) (of a person) very tired; exhausted: *I'm absolutely whacked!*

whacking *n* (*infml*) a beating. — *adj* [attrib] (*infml*) big: *a whacking lie.* — *adv* (*infml*) very: *a whacking great bruise.*

whale /weɪl/ *n* a very large animal that lives in the sea and looks like a huge fish. There are several different types of whale, some of which are hunted: *a sperm whale* ∘ *killer whales.* **IDM** **have a whale of a time** (*infml*) to enjoy oneself very much; to have a very good time: *The children had a whale of a time at the fair.*
▸ **whaler** *n* (**a**) a ship used for hunting whales. (**b**) a person who hunts whales.

whaling *n* [U] the activity of hunting and killing whales, esp for their oil.

whalebone /'weɪlbəʊn/ *n* [U] a thin hard flexible substance found in the upper jaw of certain types of whale. Whalebone was used formerly to make the cloth of certain garments stiffer: *whalebone corsets.*

W

[V] = verb used alone   [Vn] = verb + noun   [Vp] = verb + particle   [Vpr] = verb + prepositional phrase

wham /wæm/ *interj, n* (*infml*) a sudden heavy blow, or the sound made by this: *The door flew open and — wham! — hit me in the face.*
▶ **wham** *v* (**-mm-**) (*infml*) to hit sth/sb violently; to move sth quickly, noisily or forcefully: [Vnpr] *He whammed the ball into the back of the net.* [also Vn, Vnpl].

whammy /ˈwæmi/ *n* (*infml esp US*) an action, event, etc that has a powerful or unpleasant effect on or creates special problems for sb/sth: *Labour's policy of high interest rates and higher taxes will hit every family in the land — it's a **double whammy**.*

wharf /wɔːf/ *n* (*pl* **wharfs** or **wharves** /wɔːvz/) a structure made of wood or stone beside the sea, a river, etc where ships may wait to have goods brought on or off.

what[1] /wɒt/ *interrog det* (used for asking sb to specify one or more things, places, people, etc): *What time/date is it?* ○ *What books have you got on the subject?* ○ *What number did you ring?* ○ *What kind of music do you like?* ⇨ note at WHICH.
▶ **what** *interrog pron* (used for asking sb to specify one or more things, etc): *What did you say?* ○ *What (ie What job) does he do?* ○ *What are you reading/sewing/thinking?* ○ *What's the time/date?* ○ *What does it mean?* ○ *What do you want to do now?* **IDM** **and 'what not** (*infml*) and other things of the same type: *It's full of old toys, books and what not.* **get / give sb what 'for** (*Brit infml*) to be punished/punish sb severely: *I'll give her what for if she does that again.* **what for?** for what purpose or reason?: *What is this tool for?* ○ (*infml*) *What did you do that for?* (ie Why did you do that?) ○ *'I need to go to the doctor.' 'What for?'* **what if?** what would happen if?: *What if the train is late?* ○ *What if she forgets to bring it?* **what 'of it?**; so **'what?** (*infml*) (used when admitting that sth is true, but to question whether it is important or whether sb is going to do anything about it): *Yes, I wrote it. What of it?* **what's 'what** (*infml*) what things are useful, important, etc: *She certainly knows what's what.* **what with sth** (used to list various causes): *What with the cold weather and my bad leg, I haven't been out for weeks.*
■ **'what-d'you-call-him/-her/-it/-them** (also **'what's-his/-her/-its/-their-name**) *n* (used instead of a name that one cannot remember): *She's just gone out with old what-d'you-call-him.*

what[2] /wɒt/ *det* the thing or things or people that: *I spent what little time I had with my family.* ○ *What family and friends I still have live abroad.*
▶ **what** *pron* the thing or things that: *What you say may well be true.* ○ *No one knows what will happen next.*

what[3] /wɒt/ *det, adv* (used in exclamations): *What (awful) weather we're having!* ○ *What a lovely view!* ○ *What big feet you've got!*
▶ **what** *interj* **1** (*infml*) (used when one has not heard what sb has said): *What? Can you say that again?* **2** (*infml*) (used to show that one has heard sb who is trying to get one's attention): *'Hey, Bill!' 'What?' 'Where's the corkscrew?'* **3** (used with emphasis to show disbelief or surprise): *'I've won a trip to New York.' 'What?'* ○ *'It will cost £500.' 'What?'*

whatever /wɒtˈevə(r)/ *det, pron* **1** any or every (thing): *We will be grateful for whatever amount you can afford.* ○ *You can eat whatever you like.* **2** regardless of what: *Whatever we do, some people will criticize it.* ○ *Keep calm, whatever happens.* **IDM** **or what'ever** (*infml*) or anything of a similar type: *There's a useful cupboard under the stairs for brushes, boots or whatever.*
▶ **whatever** *interrog pron* (expressing surprise or confusion) what: *Whatever do you mean?* ○ *Whatever*

can it be? ○ *Whatever happened to old Sam?* ○ *Now you've lost your jacket. **Whatever next?***
whatever (also **whatsoever**) *adv* (used after *no* + a noun, *nothing, none*, etc for emphasis): *There can be no doubt whatever about it.* ○ *'Are there any signs of improvement?' 'None whatsoever.'*

whatnot /ˈwɒtnɒt/ *n* [U without *a* or *the*] (*infml*) (used to refer to sth without naming or describing it): *a drawer full of bits of paper, pencils and whatnot. They never miss family occasions — you know, weddings and funerals and whatnot.*

wheat /wiːt/ *n* [U] (**a**) the grain from which flour for bread, etc is made: *wheat flour.* (**b**) the plant that produces this: *a field of wheat* ○ *grow/plant wheat.* ⇨ picture at CEREAL. **IDM** **separate the wheat from the chaff** ⇨ SEPARATE[2].
■ **'wheat germ** *n* [U] the centre of the wheat grain, which is especially healthy to eat.

wheedle /ˈwiːdl/ *v* (*derog*) (**a**) ~ **sth (out of sb)** to obtain sth by repeated requests or insincere praise: [V] *a wheedling tone of voice* [Vnpr] *She wheedled the money out of her father.* ○ *He managed to wheedle his way into the party.* ○ *He wheedled his way into the building.* [V.speech] *'Oh go on, please,' he wheedled.* [also Vn]. (**b**) ~ **sb (into doing sth)** to persuade sb to do sth by repeated requests or insincere praise: [Vnpr] *The children wheedled me into letting them go to the film.* [also Vn].

wheel /wiːl/ *n* **1** [C] (**a**) a circular object that turns around a rod at its centre, as on cars, bicycles, etc or as part of a machine, etc. ⇨ picture at BICYCLE. (**b**) (esp in compounds) a thing like a wheel, eg a machine of which a wheel is an essential part: *a potter's 'wheel.* See also CATHERINE WHEEL, FERRIS WHEEL, MILL-WHEEL, WATER-WHEEL. **2** [C *usu sing*] = STEERING-WHEEL: *Here's a picture of me **at the wheel** of my new car.* ○ *This is the first time I've sat behind the wheel since the accident.* ○ *Do you want to **take the wheel** (ie drive) for a bit?* **3 wheels** [pl] (*infml*) a motor vehicle, esp a car: *I can't come — I don't have any wheels.* **IDM** **oil the wheels** ⇨ OIL. *v.* **put one's shoulder to the wheel** ⇨ SHOULDER. **put a spoke in sb's wheel** ⇨ SPOKE[1]. **reinvent the wheel** ⇨ REINVENT. **,wheels within 'wheels** a situation in which complicated or secret influences, reasons, etc affect what happens and how people behave: *There are wheels within wheels in this organization — you never really know what's going on.*
▶ **wheel** *v* **1**(**a**) to push or pull a vehicle with wheels: [Vn, Vnpr] *wheel the barrow (across the garden)* [also Vnp]. (**b**) to carry sb/sth in a vehicle with wheels: [Vnpr] *I was wheeled to the operating theatre on a sort of trolley.* [also Vn, Vnp]. **2**(**a**) to move in a curve or circle: [V, Vp] *Birds wheeled (about) in the sky above us.* [also Vpr]. (**b**) ~ **(round/around)** to turn round quickly so as to face another way: [Vp] *He wheeled round to face them.* [also V]. **IDM** **,wheel and 'deal** (*infml*) (esp in the continuous tenses) to negotiate or make business deals in a clever, sometimes dishonest, way: *There will be a lot of wheeling and deal before an agreement is reached.* **PHRV** **,wheel sth 'out** (*infml derog*) to produce an explanation, an excuse, a piece of evidence, etc that has often been heard or seen before: *wheel out the same tired old arguments.*
-wheeled (forming compound *adjs*) having the specified number of wheels: *a ,sixteen-wheeled 'lorry.*
-wheeler (forming compound *ns*) a vehicle with the specified number of wheels: *a ,three-'wheeler.*
wheelie *n* (*sl*) an act of riding a bicycle or motor cycle (MOTOR) balancing on the back wheel, with the front wheel off the ground: *do a wheelie.*
■ **'wheel-house** *n* a small enclosed cabin on a ship where the pilot, etc stands at the wheel to steer.

wheelbarrow /'wiːl-
bærəʊ/ (also **barrow**)
n an open container
for moving small loads
in, with a wheel at one
end, and two legs and
two handles at the other.
⇨ picture.

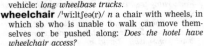

wheelbarrow

wheelbase /'wiːlbeɪs/
n (usu *sing*) the distance
between the front and
back AXLE of a motor
vehicle: *long wheelbase trucks.*

wheelchair /'wiːltʃeə(r)/ *n* a chair with wheels, in
which sb who is unable to walk can move themselves or be pushed along: *Does the hotel have
wheelchair access?*

wheeler-dealer /ˌwiːlə 'diːlə(r)/ *n* (*infml*) a person
who is skilled at making business deals, sometimes
dishonestly.

wheelwright /'wiːlraɪt/ *n* a person who makes and
repairs esp wooden wheels for carts, etc.

wheeze /wiːz/ *v* (**a**) to breathe noisily and with
difficulty, eg because of a sore throat: [V] *He was
coughing and wheezing all night.* (**b**) to say, sing, etc
sth while breathing noisily or with difficulty:
[V.speech] *'I've got a sore throat,' he wheezed.*
▸ **wheeze** *n* **1** a sound of wheezing: *He has a slight
wheeze in his chest.* **2** (*Brit infml*) a good idea, esp a
joke or trick: *a clever wheeze.*
wheezy *adj* making a wheezing sound: *a wheezy
chest/laugh/voice* ○ *My cold's getting better but I'm
still a bit wheezy.* **wheezily** /-ɪli/ *adv.* **wheeziness**
n [U].

whelk /welk/ *n* a small edible sea creature that lives
in a shell.

whelp /welp/ *n* a young animal of the dog family; a
PUPPY or CUB.
▸ **whelp** *v* [Vn] (*fml*) (of a female dog, WOLF, etc) to
give birth to young.

when /wen/ *interrog adv* at what time; on what
occasion: *When can you come?* ○ *When did he die?* ○ *I
don't know when he died.* ○ *When were you living in
Spain?*
▸ **when** *rel adv* **1** (used after *time, day, month*, etc)
at or on which: *Sunday is the day I can relax.* ○ *There
are times when I wonder why I do this job.* ○ *It was
the sort of morning when everything goes wrong.* **2** at
which time; on which occasion: *The last time I went
to Scotland was in May, when the weather was beautiful.*
when *pron* what/which time: *Until when can you
stay?* ○ *I saw her last Friday, since when I've phoned
her twice.*
when *conj* **1** at or during the time that: *It was
raining when we arrived.* ○ *When he saw me, he
waved.* ○ *When I'm in London, I usually go to the
theatre.* **2** since; considering that: *How can they
expect to learn anything when they never listen.* **3**
although; despite the fact that: *She claimed to be 18,
when I know she's only 16.*

whence /wens/ *adv* (*arch or fml*) from where: *They
returned whence they came.*

whenever /wen'evə(r)/ *conj* **1** at any time, regardless of when: *I can meet you whenever you like.* **2**
every time that; as often as: *Whenever she comes, she
brings a friend.* ○ *The roof leaks whenever it rains.* ○
We try to help whenever possible. **IDM or when'ever**
(*infml*) or at any time: *It's not urgent — we can do it
next week or whenever.*
▸ **whenever** *interrog adv* (expressing surprise)
when: *Whenever did you find time to do all that
cooking?*

where /weə(r)/ *interrog adv* in or to what place or
position: *Where do you live?* ○ *Where does she come
from?* ○ *I wonder where she comes from.* ○ *Where* (ie

At what point) *did I go wrong in my calculations?* ○
Where are you going for your holidays? ○ *Where is all
this leading?* (ie What is the conclusion of what you
are saying?)
▸ **where** *rel adv* **1** (used after words or phrases
that refer to a place) at, in or to which (place): *the
place where you last saw it* ○ *one of the few countries
where people drive on the left.* **2** at which place: *We
then moved to Paris, where we lived for six years.*
where *conj* (in) the place in which: *Put it where we
can all see it.* ○ *Where food is hard to find, few birds
remain throughout the year.* ○ (*fig*) *That's where
you're wrong.*

whereabouts /ˌweərə'baʊts/ *interrog adv* in or
near what place; where: *Whereabouts did you find it?*
▸ **whereabouts** /'weərəbaʊts/n [sing or pl *v*] the
place where sb/sth is: *His whereabouts is/are unknown.*

whereas /ˌweər'æz/ *conj* **1** (*fml*) in contrast or
comparison with the fact that; while: *He earns
£10 000 a year whereas she gets at least £30 000.* ○ *We
thought she was rather arrogant, whereas in fact she
was just very shy.* **2** (*esp law*) (at the beginning of
sentences in official documents) taking into consideration the fact that.

whereby /weə'baɪ/ *rel adv* (*fml*) by which: *a new
system whereby all staff have to carry identification
cards.*

wherefore /'weəfɔː(r)/ *n* **IDM the whys and
wherefores** ⇨ WHY.

wherein /weər'ɪn/ *rel adv* (*fml*) in which; in what;
in what respect: *a situation wherein it is hard to
decide what is right and wrong.*

whereupon /ˌweərə'pɒn/ *conj* after which; and
then: *She laughed at him, whereupon he walked out.*

wherever /weər'evə(r)/ *conj* **1** in any place; regardless of where: *Sit wherever you like.* ○ *I'll find him,
wherever he is.* ○ *He comes from Boula, wherever that
may be* (ie and I don't know where that is). **2(a)** in
all places that; everywhere: *Wherever she goes, there
are crowds of people waiting to see her.* (**b**) in all
instances that; in every case when; whenever: *It is
important that, wherever possible, children grow
up knowing both their parents.* **IDM or wher'ever**
(*infml*) or any other place: *foreign tourists from
Spain, France or wherever.*
▸ **wherever** *interrog adv* (expressing surprise)
where: *Wherever did you get that hat?*

wherewithal /'weəwɪðɔːl/ *n* the **wherewithal** [sing]
(*rhet or joc*) the money, etc needed for sth: *My
parents found the wherewithal to send me to a cheap
fee-paying school.*

whet /wet/ *v* (**-tt-**) to excite or stimulate sb's desire,
interest, etc: [Vn] *Magazines often publish short extracts from new novels to **whet your appetite** (ie
make you want more).*

whether /'weðə(r)/ *conj* **1** (used before a clause or
an infinitive that expresses or suggests a choice
between two alternatives) (**a**) (used as the object of
vs like *know, consider, doubt, question, wonder*, etc):
I don't know whether I'll be able to come. ○ *We'll be
told tomorrow whether we're needed or not.* ○ *We were
wondering whether to go today or tomorrow.* (Note
that when there are two alternative clauses separated by *or, whether* is repeated.) *I asked him whether
he had done it all himself or whether someone had
helped him.* Compare IF 4. (**b**) (after *adjs* and *preps*):
*She was undecided whether she should accept his
offer.* ○ *It was not clear whether the riots were political or religious.* ○ *He hesitated about whether to drive
or take the train.* ○ *It all depends on whether it rains
or not.* (**c**) (used as the subject or complement of a
sentence): *It's doubtful whether there'll be any seats
left.* ○ *The question is whether to go to Munich or
Vienna.* **2** (used to indicate that the statement being
made applies whichever of the alternatives given

happens or is true): *You are entitled to a free gift whether you apply by post or by phone.* **IDM** **whether or not** (used to introduce two possibilities which cannot both be true): *Whether or not it rains/ Whether it rains or not, we're playing football on Saturday.* ○ *Let me know whether or not you're interested.* ○ *She'll go to their wedding, whether you like it or not.* ⇨ note at IF.

whetstone /ˈwetstəʊn/ *n* a shaped stone used for sharpening cutting tools.

whew (also **phew**) /fjuː/ *interj* (used as the written form of any of various sounds made by breathing out strongly or whistling to express surprise, relief, alarm or EXHAUSTION): *Whew! That was a lucky escape!*

whey /weɪ/ *n* [U] the thin liquid that remains after sour milk has formed curds (CURD).

which /wɪtʃ/ *interrog det* (used to ask sb to specify one or more people or things from a limited number): *Which way is quicker — going by bus or by train?* ○ *Which Mr Smith do you mean — the one who teaches history or the one who teaches music?* ○ *Which languages did you study at school?* ○ *Ask him which platform the Boston train leaves from.* Compare WHAT¹. ⇨ note.

▶ **which** *interrog pron* (used to ask sb to specify one or more people or things from a limited number): *Which is your favourite subject?* ○ *Which of the boys is tallest?* ○ *Here are the chairs. Tell me which are worth buying.* ○ *The twins are so much alike that I can't tell / I don't know which is which* (ie I cannot distinguish one from the other).

which *rel pron* (used to refer to sth previously mentioned): *Tyson threw a punch after the bell which ended the first round.* ○ *Houses which overlook the lake cost more.* ○ *She banged into something solid which she immediately grabbed hold of.* ○ *Read the passage to which I referred in my talk.* ○ *His best film, which won several awards, was about the life of Gandhi.* ○ *His new car, for which he paid £15 000, has already had to be repaired.* ○ *'I don't know what I'm going to do with you,' Maggie said, which only made us laugh even more.*

which *rel det* (*rather fml*) (used to refer back to the preceding *n* or statement): *The postman comes at 6.30 in the morning, at which time I am usually still asleep.* ○ *He may of course agree immediately, in which case all this effort will be a waste of time.*

NOTE Which and what are both used to ask questions about people and things. **Which** is used before a noun when there is a limited number of possible answers: *Which car is yours — the Ford or the Volvo?* ○ *Which teacher do you have for history?* **What** is often used when there is a wide choice of possible answers: *What sort of food do you like?* ○ *What are your favourite television programmes?* When referring to people, we often use **which** in a more formal style, even if there is a wide choice of possible answers: *Which/What writers do you admire most?* Only **which** can be followed by **of**: *Which of his plays have you seen?*

whichever /wɪtʃˈevə(r)/ *det, pron* **1** (used when one is defining the feature or quality of sth that is important in making a decision, in order for sth to happen, etc): *Take whichever hat suits you best.* ○ *We'll eat at whichever restaurant is cheaper.* ○ *You will receive a cash payment on your 65th birthday or after ten years, whichever is later.* ○ *Whichever of you comes first will receive a prize.* ○ *The form read 'Are you single/married/divorced/separated? (Strike out whichever does not apply.)'* **2** regardless of which: *Whichever you buy, there is a six-month guarantee.* ○ *It takes three hours, whichever route you take.* ○ *The situation is an awkward one, whichever way you look at it.*

whiff /wɪf/ *n* (usu *sing*) ~ (**of sth**) (**a**) a smell, esp one that is only smelt for a short period of time: *a strong whiff of cigar smoke* ○ *He caught a whiff of perfume as he leaned towards her.* (**b**) a trace or HINT(2): *a whiff of danger/scandal* ○ *There was a whiff of something he didn't like about the whole business.*

while¹ /waɪl/ (also *esp Brit* **whilst** /waɪlst/) *conj* **1**(**a**) during the time that; when: *He fell asleep while (he was) watching television.* ○ *While I was in Madrid there was a carnival.* ○ *She wrote her first novel while still at school.* (**b**) at the same time as: *While Mary was writing the letter, the children were playing outside.* ○ *I like listening to the radio while driving to work.* ○ *The first team lost 6–0, while the juniors were also beaten.* **2** (used to show a contrast): *I drink black coffee while David prefers it with cream.* ○ *English is understood all over the world while Turkish is spoken by only a few people outside Turkey itself.* **3** (*fml*) although; in spite of the fact that: *While I admit that there are problems, I don't agree that they cannot be solved.*

while² /waɪl/ *n* [sing] a period of time: *She worked in a bank for a while before studying law.* ○ *For a long while we had no news of him.* ○ *I'll be back in a little while.* ○ *It took quite a while* (ie a long time) *to find a hotel.* ○ *We waited for three hours, all the while hoping that someone would come and fetch us.* **IDM** **once in a while** ⇨ ONCE. **worth sb's while** ⇨ WORTH.

▶ **while** *v* **PHR V** **while sth aˈway** to pass a period of time in a relaxed way: *We whiled away the time at the airport reading magazines.* ○ *It's easy to while a few hours away in a museum.*

whim /wɪm/ *n* a sudden desire or idea, esp an unusual or unreasonable one: *I know it's an odd thing to ask. Just call it an old man's whim.* ○ *It's just something I bought on a whim.* ○ *Staff are moved from one department to another at the whim of the boss.* ○ *She seems ready to cater to/indulge* (ie satisfy) *his every whim.* ○ *follow the whims of fashion.*

whimper /ˈwɪmpə(r)/ *v* (**a**) (of a person or an animal) to make a series of low weak sad cries, esp with fear or pain: [V] *A child in a bed nearby began to whimper.* ○ *She was making little whimpering noises of concern.* (**b**) to say sth in this way: [V.speech] *'Please don't leave me alone,' he whimpered.* ⇨ note at CRY¹.

▶ **whimper** *n* a low weak sad cry; a whimpering sound: (*fig*) *The conference ended less with a bang than with a whimper* (ie in a way that was weak and not impressive).

whimsy /ˈwɪmzi/ *n* [U] odd or playful behaviour or humour: *The dabs of colour in his paintings sometimes verge on decorative whimsy.*

▶ **whimsical** /ˈwɪmzɪkl/ *adj* unusual and rather playful; CAPRICIOUS but charming: *a whimsical sense of humour* ○ *Much of his work has a whimsical quality.* **whimsically** /-kli/ *adv*.

whine /waɪn/ *n* (usu *sing*) (**a**) a long high-pitched, usu unpleasant or annoying, sound such as that made by a SIREN, etc: *the steady whine of a mechanical saw.* (**b**) a long high-pitched complaining cry, esp one made by a dog or a child. (**c**) a complaining tone of voice: *speak in a high, nasal whine.*

▶ **whine** *v* **1** to make a whine: [V] *a whining voice* ○ *In the background, a drill whined.* [V] *The dog sat outside the door whining (to be let in).* **2** (*derog*) to complain, esp about unimportant things: [V] *Do stop whining!* [Vpr] *What is that child whining about now?* [V.speech] *'I want to go home,' he whined.*

whinge /wɪndʒ/ *v* (*pres p* **whingeing** or **whinging**) (*Brit infml derog*) to complain, esp constantly and about sth unimportant, in a way that irritates others: [V] *The President should stop whingeing and start leading.* [Vp, Vpr] *She whinged (on) about how miserable she was.*

whinny /ˈwɪni/ *n* a gentle NEIGH.

▶ **whinny** *v* (*pt, pp* **whinnied**) to make a whinny: [V, Vpr] *The horse whinnied (with pleasure).*

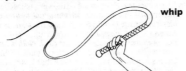

whip

whip¹ /wɪp/ *n* **1** [C] a length of cord or strip of leather fastened to a handle, used esp for urging on an animal or for striking a person or an animal as a punishment: *The jockey was fined for excessive use of the whip.* ○ *He cracked his whip and the horse leapt forward.* ⇨ picture. See also HORSEWHIP. **2** [C] (**a**) (in Britain and the USA) an official of a political party who has the authority to maintain discipline among its members, esp to make them attend and vote in important government debates: *the chief whip.* (**b**) (*Brit*) a written instruction from this official: *a ˌthree-line ˈwhip* (ie one with three lines drawn under it to show that it is very urgent). **3** [C, U] a dish consisting of cream, eggs, etc that have been stirred into a soft light mass with fruit, chocolate, etc: *caramel/strawberry whip.* **IDM** **a fair crack of the whip** ⇨ FAIR¹. **have, etc the ˈwhip hand (over sb)** to be in a position where one has power or control over sb: *The management had the whip hand and it was useless to resist.*

▶ **whippy** *adj* (of a stick, etc) that bends easily; flexible.

whip² /wɪp/ *v* (**-pp-**) **1** to beat a person or an animal with a whip, esp as a punishment: [Vn] *Prisoners were whipped to get confessions out of them.* **2** ~ **sth (up) (into sth)** to stir cream, eggs etc rapidly with a fork or some other instrument in order to make a stiff light mass: [Vn] *coffee with **whipped cream*** [Vnp, Vnpr] *Whip the ingredients (up) into a smooth paste.* **3** to move rapidly or suddenly in the direction specified: [Vpr] *Icy winds whipped across the open plain.* [Vp] *She whipped round just as he was about to attack her from behind.* ○ *The branch whipped back and hit me in the face.* **4** to move sth quickly to, from, etc a particular place: [Vnp] *The intruder whipped out a knife.* [Vnpr] *The wind whipped several slates off the roof.* ○ *She suddenly whipped the mask from her face.* **5** (*dated Brit infml*) to steal sth: [Vn] *Who's whipped my umbrella?* **PHRV** ˌ**whip sb/sth ˈon** to urge a person or an animal to go faster, work harder, etc: *He whipped his armies on relentlessly.* ˌ**whip sth/sb ˈup 1** to make people become excited, enthusiastic, etc: *They're trying to whip up support for their candidate.* ○ *The crowd was whipped up into a frenzy by the speaker.* **2** (*infml*) to prepare a meal, etc very quickly: *I can easily whip you up a snack of some kind.*

▶ **whipping** *n* [C, U] a beating, esp with a whip, as a punishment. ˈ**whipping-boy** *n* a person who is regularly made to take the blame and punishment for the faults of others. Compare SCAPEGOAT. ˈ**whipping cream** *n* [U] cream that is suitable for whipping (WHIP² 2).

■ ˈ**whip-round** *n* (*Brit infml*) a collection of contributions of money from a group of people: *We had a whip-round (to buy a Christmas present) for the office cleaners.*

whiplash /ˈwɪplæʃ/ *n* a blow with a whip.

■ ˈ**whiplash injury** *n* an injury to the neck caused by a sudden quick movement of the head: *She suffered a whiplash injury in a car crash.*

whipper-snapper /ˈwɪpə snæpə(r)/ *n* (*dated infml*

derog) a young and unimportant person who behaves in a way that others think is too bold and confident.

whippet /ˈwɪpɪt/ *n* a small thin dog similar to a GREYHOUND, often used for racing.

whir ⇨ WHIRR.

whirl /wɜːl/ *v* **1** to move or make sb/sth move quickly round and round: [V] *the whirling blades of the fan* [Vpr] *seagulls whirling over the ship* [Vnp] *The wind whirled up the fallen leaves.* [Vnpr] *He whirled his partner round the dance floor.* **2** to move or make sb/sth move rapidly in the specified direction: [Vpr] *The houses whirled past us as the train gathered speed.* [Vp] *He whirled round, startled.* [Vnp] *We were whirled away/off in a waiting taxi.* [also Vnpr]. **3** (of the brain, senses, etc) to seem to go round and round, so that one feels confused or excited: [V] *I couldn't sleep: my mind was still whirling from all I had seen and heard.*

▶ **whirl** *n* [sing] **1** a whirling movement: *the whirl of the propeller blades* ○ (*fig*) *The performers danced round in a whirl of colour.* **2** a rapid succession of activities: *an endless whirl of parties* ○ *be thrust into the **social whirl**.* **3** a state of confusion: *My mind is in a complete whirl.* **IDM** **give sth a ˈwhirl** (*infml*) to try sth as an experiment, to see if it is suitable, enjoyable, etc: *The job doesn't sound very exciting but I'll give it a whirl.*

whirligig /ˈwɜːlɪɡɪɡ/ *n* **1** a toy that spins round and round, esp a top³. **2** = ROUNDABOUT² 2.

whirlpool /ˈwɜːlpuːl/ *n* (**a**) a place in a river or the sea where there are strong currents moving in circles: *be sucked into the whirlpool* ○ (*fig*) *Her mind was a whirlpool of questions.* (**b**) a special heated pool like this for relaxing in: *The hotel has a sauna, whirlpool and steam bath.*

whirlwind /ˈwɜːlwɪnd/ *n* a column of air that turns round and round very rapidly: *She went through the house like a whirlwind, cleaning each room in turn.* ○ (*fig*) *He's a whirlwind of energy and enthusiasm.* **IDM** **reap the whirlwind** ⇨ REAP.

▶ **whirlwind** *adj* [attrib] very rapid: *a whirlwind romance* ○ *a whirlwind tour of Europe.*

whirr (also **whir**) /wɜː(r)/ *n* (usu *sing*) a continuous low sound such as that made by the regular movement of part of a machine or the wings of a bird: *the whirr of a fan/motor/propeller.*

▶ **whirr** (also **whir**) *v* to make a whirr: [V] *whirring helicopters* ○ *The coffee machine made a series of whirring and clicking sounds.*

whisk /wɪsk/ *n* **1** a device for stirring eggs, cream, etc very fast: *an electric whisk.* ⇨ picture. **2** a quick light brushing movement: *a whisk of a horse's tail.*

whisk
(also **egg beater**)

▶ **whisk** *v* **1(a)** to take sb/sth away or in the specified direction quickly and suddenly: [Vnp] *The waiter whisked away the plates before we had finished.* [Vnpr] *She was whisked to the top floor in the executive lift.* (**b**) to go away or in the specified direction quickly and suddenly: [Vp] *He whisked off before I could speak to him.* [also Vpr]. **2** to beat eggs, etc into a stiff light mass: [Vnp] *Whisk all the ingredients together.* [Vn] *Whisk the egg whites until stiff.* **3** to move sth quickly through the air with a light sweeping movement: [Vn] *The horse whisked its tail angrily.*

whisker /ˈwɪskə(r)/ *n* **1** [C] any of the long stiff hairs that grow near the mouth of a cat, rat, etc. **2** **whiskers** [pl] (*dated or joc*) the long hair growing on

W

a man's face: *wearing a wig and false whiskers.* Compare BEARD¹ a. **IDM** **be the cat's whiskers/ pyjamas** ⇨ CAT. **be, come, etc within a whisker of sth / doing sth** (*Brit*) to be or come extremely near to sth/doing sth: *The two firms are now within a whisker of agreeing on a deal.* **by a 'whisker** by a very small amount or margin: *She won the race by a whisker.*

▶ **whiskered** /'wɪskəd/ (also **whiskery** /'wɪskəri/) *adj* having whiskers.

whisky (*Brit*) (*US or Irish* **whiskey**) /'wɪski/ *n* (**a**) [U] a strong alcoholic drink made from malted (MALT) grain, esp BARLEY(a) or RYE: *a bottle of whisky.* (**b**) [C] a type of this: *This is a very good whisky.* (**c**) [C] a glass of this: *Two large whiskies, please.*

whisper /'wɪspə(r)/ *v* **1** to speak or say sth quietly, using only one's breath, so that only the people closest to one can hear: [V] *Don't you know it's rude to whisper?* [V.speech] *'Can you meet me tonight?' he whispered.* [Vnpr] *He leaned over and whispered something in her ear.* [V.that, Vpr.that] *She whispered (to me) that she was afraid.* [also Vpr, Vn, Vpr.to inf]. **2** (of leaves, the wind, etc) to make soft sounds: [Vpr] *A gentle breeze was whispering in/through the trees.* [also V].

▶ **whisper** *n* **1** a whispering sound or low voice: *He spoke in whispers.* ○ *Her voice dropped to a whisper.* See also STAGE WHISPER. **2** a rumour: *I've heard whispers that the firm is likely to go bankrupt.*

■ **'whispering campaign** *n* unpleasant rumours about sb intended to damage their reputation and deliberately passed from person to person.

whist /wɪst/ *n* [U] a card-game for two pairs of players.

■ **'whist drive** *n* a series of games of whist played by several sets of partners at different tables, with certain players moving after each round to the next table.

whistle /'wɪsl/ *n* **1(a)** a clear high-pitched sound made by forcing breath through a small hole between partly closed lips: *Bob gave a long low whistle.* ○ *The crowd drowned his speech with whistles and jeers.* (**b**) a similar sound made by a machine: *the shrill/piercing whistle of a steam engine.* (**c**) a high-pitched singing sound made by a bird. See also WOLF-WHISTLE. **2(a)** an instrument used to produce a clear high-pitched sound, esp as a signal: *The referee blew (a short blast on) his whistle.* (**b**) the sound of this: *The whistle went for the end of the match.* **IDM** **blow the whistle on sb/sth** ⇨ BLOW¹. **clean as a whistle** ⇨ CLEAN¹.

▶ **whistle** *v* **1(a)** to make the sound of a whistle: [V] *She whistled in amazement.* ○ *A train whistled in the distance.* (**b**) to produce a tune in this way: [Vn] *He whistled the national anthem as he walked along.* (**c**) to make a signal to sb/sth or show one's attitude in this way: [Vpr] *She whistled for her dog.* [Vpr.to inf] *He whistled to his friend to come out of his hiding-place.* [Vn] *The crowd booed and whistled its disapproval.* **2** to move rapidly making a noise like a whistle: [Vpr] *A bullet whistled past his head.* ○ *The wind whistled through a crack in the door.* [also Vp]. **IDM** **whistle in the 'dark** to pretend not to be afraid. **PHRV** **'whistle for sth** (*infml*) to wish for or expect sth without any chance of getting it: *If he wants his money now he'll have to whistle for it — I'm broke!*

■ **'whistle-stop** *n* **1** (*US*) a small railway station where trains stop only when signalled to do so. **2** [attrib] (of a trip, etc) consisting of a series of brief stops at a lot of places: *be/go on a **whistle-stop tour** of the country.*

Whit /wɪt/ *n* [U often attrib] = WHITSUN: *the Whit weekend.*

■ **‚Whit 'Sunday** *n* the 7th Sunday after Easter; Pentecost.

whit /wɪt/ *n* [sing] (usu in negative sentences) the smallest amount: *It won't make a/one whit of difference to the final outcome.*

white¹ /waɪt/ *adj* (**-r, -st**) **1** of the very palest colour, like fresh snow or milk: *strong white teeth* ○ *white blossom* ○ *white bread* ○ *She painted the walls white.* ○ *Her hair has turned white* (eg with age). ○ *new improved washing powders that wash clothes 'whiter than white'* ○ *a white-coated doctor.* Compare BLACK¹. See also SNOW-WHITE. **2** of a race that has pale skin: *Her attacker was a white youth in his twenties.* ○ *the end of white rule in South Africa.* **3** ~ (**with sth**) (of a person) pale as a result of emotion or illness: *He was white with fury.* ○ *She went as white as a sheet when she heard the news.* **4** (of tea or coffee) with milk or cream added. **5** (of wine) pale yellow in colour: *a bottle of dry white wine* ○ *'A glass of wine, please.' 'Red or white?'* **IDM** **black and white** ⇨ BLACK². **(in) black and white** ⇨ BLACK². **bleed sb white** ⇨ BLEED. **in black and white** ⇨ BLACK².

▶ **whiten** /'waɪtn/ *v* to become or make sth white or whiter: [V] *He clenched his fists until his knuckles whitened.* [Vn] *whiten one's tennis shoes* ○ *a whitening agent used in paper-making.*

whiteness *n* [U]: *the pure whiteness of her skin* ○ *the clinical whiteness of the room.*

whitish *adj* very pale and almost white; fairly white: *a whitish blue* ○ *a whitish fungal growth on the wood.*

■ **‚white 'ant** *n* a TERMITE.

‚white-'collar *adj* [usu attrib] (**a**) working in an office rather than eg operating machines in a factory: *professional and white-collar workers.* Compare BLUE-COLLAR. (**b**) of or relating to people working in offices: *white-collar jobs/unions.*

‚white 'corpuscle (also **'white cell**) *n* any of the cells in the blood that fight infection. Compare RED CORPUSCLE.

‚white 'elephant *n* [C usu *sing*] a possession or thing that is useless and often expensive to maintain: *The new office block has become an expensive white elephant.*

‚white 'flag *n* a symbol of surrender: *show/wave the white flag.*

‚white 'heat *n* [U] the high temperature at which metal looks white.

‚white 'hope *n* [sing] (*infml*) a person who is expected to bring success to a team, group, etc: *He was once the **great white hope** of the Party.*

‚white 'horses *n* [pl] waves in the sea with white tops on them.

‚white-'hot *adj* (**a**) extremely hot: *ladles pouring out white-hot metal.* (**b**) very intense: *white-hot conviction/passion.*

the 'White House *n* (**a**) [sing] the official residence of the President of the USA in Washington, DC. (**b**) [Gp] the US President and her or his advisers: *The White House has denied the report.* ○ *White House aides.*

‚white 'knight *n* a person or an organization that rescues a company from being bought by another company at too low a price.

‚white 'lie *n* a harmless or small lie, esp one told in order to avoid hurting sb.

‚white 'light *n* [U] ordinary light that is colourless. ⇨ picture at SPECTRUM.

‚white 'meat *n* [U] (**a**) meat from a bird, eg chicken, or VEAL or PORK. (**b**) meat from the breast of a cooked chicken or other bird. Compare RED MEAT.

'white-out *n* a heavy SNOWSTORM in which it is impossible to see anything. Compare BLACKOUT.

‚White 'Paper *n* (*Brit*) a report published by the

government about its policy on a matter that is to be considered by Parliament. Compare GREEN PAPER.

ˌwhite ˈpepper n [U] pepper made by grinding dried pepper seeds from which the dark outer covering has been removed. Compare BLACK PEPPER.

ˌwhite ˈsauce n [U] a sauce made from butter, flour and milk: *Add cheese to the white sauce.*

ˌwhite ˈspirit n [U] (*esp Brit*) a light type of petrol used eg as a cleaning substance: *remove paint from the brushes with white spirit.*

ˌwhite ˈstick n a long thin white rod carried by blind people to help them walk around without knocking things and to indicate to others that they are blind.

ˌwhite-ˈtie n a man's white bow-tie (BOW¹): *dressed in white tie and tails.* ˌwhite-ˈtie adj (of social occasions) at which full formal evening dress (EVENING) is worn: *Is it a white-tie affair?*

ˌwhite ˈwater n [U] a fast shallow stretch of water; rapids (RAPID): *white-water rafting.*

ˌwhite ˈwedding n a traditional wedding, esp in a church, at which the BRIDE wears a white dress.

ˌwhite ˈwine n [U, C] wine that is pale yellow in colour, made from green grapes (GRAPE): *a bottle of dry/sweet white wine.*

white² /waɪt/ n **1** [U] a white colour or PIGMENT. **2(a)** [U] white clothes or material: *dressed all in white.* (**b**) whites [pl] white clothes, esp as worn for sports: *tennis whites ∘ Don't wash whites with brightly coloured clothes.* **3** [C, U] the transparent substance that surrounds the YOLK of an egg and becomes white when beaten (BEAT¹ 3) or cooked: *whisked egg whites ∘ Use the whites of two eggs.* ⇨ picture at EGG. **4** [C] a member of a race with a pale skin; a Caucasian. **5** [C *esp pl*] the white part of the eye: *He could see the whites of her eyes glinting in the dim light.* **IDM** **black and white** ⇨ BLACK².

whitebait /ˈwaɪtbeɪt/ n [U] very small young fish that are fried and eaten whole.

Whitehall /ˈwaɪthɔːl/ n (**a**) [U] a street in London where a lot of Government offices are situated: *Rumours are circulating in Whitehall.* (**b**) [Gp] the British Government: *Whitehall is/are refusing to confirm the reports. ∘ Whitehall officials.*

whitewash /ˈwaɪtwɒʃ/ n **1** [U] chalk or LIME¹ in powder form that is mixed with water and used for painting houses. **2** [U, C] the process or an instance of deliberately hiding sb's errors, faults, etc: *The Opposition dismissed the report as a whitewash.* **3** [C] (*sport infml*) a thorough defeat: *They completed the whitewash with a 9–0 win in the last game.*
▶ **whitewash** v **1** to put whitewash(1) on a wall, etc: [Vn] *pretty, whitewashed villages.* **2** to try to make sb or sb's reputation appear to be honest, without blame, etc by deliberately hiding errors, faults, etc.

whither /ˈwɪðə(r)/ adv (*arch or rhet*) to what place or state: *Whither (ie What is the likely future of) the shipping industry?*

whiting /ˈwaɪtɪŋ/ n (*pl* unchanged) a small sea-fish with white flesh.

Whitsun /ˈwɪtsn/ (also **Whit** /wɪt/) n the seventh Sunday after Easter and the days close to it.

whittle /ˈwɪtl/ v ~ **A** (**from B**); ~ **B** (**into A**) to make sth from a piece of wood by repeatedly cutting small slices from it: [Vnpr] *whittling a tent-peg from a stick/a stick into a tent-peg* [also Vn]. **PHRV** ˌwhittle sth aˈway to remove or decrease sth gradually: *Inflation has steadily whittled away their savings.* ˌwhittle sth ˈdown to reduce the size or number of sth gradually: *The number of employees is being slowly whittled down in order to reduce costs.*

whizz¹ (also **whiz**) /wɪz/ v (**a**) to move fast through the air with a whistling sound: [Vpr] *A bullet whizzed past my ear.* [also Vp]. (**b**) (*infml*) to move or go very fast: [Vpr] *The little trains were whizzing*

round and round the track. [Vp] *whizz over to France for the week end.*

NOTE Compare **zoom, whizz, shoot, dart** and **nip**. They are all followed by a preposition or an adverb. **Whizz** and **zoom** both describe fast noisy movement, usually of a vehicle. **Zoom** suggests the low noise of an engine: *At about 3 o'clock in the morning we heard a low-flying aircraft zooming over the house.* **Whizz** sometimes suggests a high whistling sound: *Fireworks whizzed up into the sky.*

Shoot and **dart** mean the sudden fast movement of a person, an animal or a thing: *A car shot out of a side road and nearly hit me. ∘ The waiter darted out of sight into the kitchen.* **Nip** is used mostly in spoken British English and means to go somewhere quickly for a particular purpose: *She's just nipped out to do some shopping. ∘ A bike is ideal for nipping through traffic.*

whizz² (also **whiz**) /wɪz/ n (*infml*) a person who is extremely good at sth: *a computer whizz ∘ She's a whizz at maths.*
■ ˈwhizz-kid (also ˈwhiz-kid) n (*infml esp US*) a person who becomes successful at sth very quickly: *a technology whizz-kid ∘ a whizz-kid guitarist.*

who /huː/ interrog pron **1** (used as the subject of a v to ask about the name, identity or function of one or more people): *Who is the woman in the black hat? ∘ I wonder who phoned this morning. ∘ Who are those men in white coats? ∘ Do you know who broke the window?* **2** (*infml*) (used as the object of a v or *prep*): *Who did you see at church? ∘ Who are you phoning? ∘ Who shall I give it to? ∘ Who's the money for?* Compare WHOM. **IDM** **who am ˈI, who are ˈyou, etc, to do sth?** what right, authority, etc have I, have you, etc to do sth: *Who are you to tell me I can't park here?* **(know, learn, etc) who's ˈwho** to be informed about people's names, jobs, status, etc: *You'll soon find out who's who in the office.*
▶ **who** rel pron **1(a)** (in clauses which define the preceding n): *the man/men who wanted to meet you ∘ The people who called yesterday want to buy the house.* (**b**) (in clauses which do not define the preceding n but give further information about it): *My wife, who is out at the moment, will phone you when she gets back. ∘ Mrs Smith, who has a lot of teaching experience, will be joining us in the spring.* **2** (used as the object of a v or *prep*) (**a**) (in clauses which define the preceding n, where it can be omitted): *The couple (who) we met on the ferry have sent us a card. ∘ The boy (who) I was speaking to is the son of my employer.* (**b**) (in clauses which do not define the preceding n, where it cannot be omitted): *Mary, who we were talking about earlier, has just walked in.* ⇨ note at WHOM.

WHO /ˌdʌbljuː eɪtʃ ˈəʊ/ abbr World Health Organization (an international organization that aims to fight and control disease).

whoa /wəʊ/ interj (used as a command to a horse, etc to make it stop or stand still).

who'd /huːd/ short form **1** who had. ⇨ HAVE³. **2** who would. ⇨ WILL¹, WOULD.

whodunnit (also **whodunit**) /ˌhuːˈdʌnɪt/ n (*infml*) a story or play about a murder in which the person who does it is only revealed at the end: *her latest whodunnit.*

whoever /huːˈevə(r)/ (also *arch* **whosoever**) pron **1** the person who: *Whoever says that is a liar. ∘ Send it to whoever is in charge of sales.* **2** regardless of who: *Whoever it is wants to speak to me, tell them I'm busy. ∘ Tell whoever you like — I don't care.*
▶ **whoever** interrog pron (expressing surprise) who: *Whoever heard of such a thing!*

whole /həʊl/ adj **1** [attrib] full; complete: *three whole days ∘ We drank a whole bottle each. ∘ The* *whole town was destroyed by the earthquake.* ○ *The whole country* (ie All the people in it) *mourned the death of the president.* ○ *I've sold the whole lot* (ie everything). ○ *Let's forget the whole affair/matter/thing.* ○ *Tell me the whole truth.* ⇨ note at HALF¹. **2** not broken or damaged: *cook sth whole* (ie without cutting it into pieces) ○ *swallow sth whole* (ie without chewing (CHEW) it). **IDM** **go the whole 'hog** (*infml*) to do sth thoroughly or completely: *We painted the kitchen, and then decided to go the whole hog and redecorate the other rooms as well.* **the whole bag of 'tricks / ca'boodle / she'bang / 'shooting match** (*infml*) the entire collection of facts or things; everything: *I just threw the whole caboodle in the back of the car.* ○ *They bought the house, the land, the stables — the whole shooting match.* **a 'whole lot** (*infml*) very much; a lot: *I'm feeling a whole lot better.* **a 'whole lot (of sth)** (*infml*) a large number or amount: *There were a whole lot of people I didn't know.* ○ *I lost a whole lot of money.* **with all one's heart / one's whole heart** ⇨ HEART.

▶ **whole** *n* **1** [C] a thing that is complete in itself: *Four quarters make a whole.* ○ *As members of society we are all parts of a greater whole.* ⇨ note at HALF¹. **2** [sing] ~ **of sth** (*esp Brit*) all that there is of sth: *She spent the whole of the year in hospital.* **IDM** **as a 'whole 1** as one thing or piece and not as separate parts: *Is the collection going to be divided up or sold as a whole?* **2** in general: *The population as a whole is/are in favour of the reform.* **on the whole** considering everything: *On the whole, I'm in favour of the idea.*

wholeness *n* [U].

wholly /'həʊlli/ *adv* completely; entirely: *not a wholly successful book* ○ *I'm not wholly convinced by your argument.*

■ **,whole 'milk** *n* [U] milk that has not had any fat removed.

'whole note *n* (*US*) = SEMIBREVE.

,whole 'number *n* (*mathematics*) a number that consists of one or more units, with no fractions.

wholefood /'həʊlfuːd/ *n* [U] (also **wholefoods** [pl]) food that has not been processed or refined and is free from artificial substances: *a whole food restaurant.*

wholegrain /'həʊlgreɪn/ *adj* made with or containing whole grains, eg of wheat: *wholegrain mustard.*

wholehearted /,həʊl'hɑːtɪd/ *adj* (*approv*) without doubts; full and complete: *give ,wholehearted sup'port.* ▶ **wholeheartedly** *adv*: *be wholeheartedly in favour of the scheme.*

wholemeal /'həʊlmiːl/ *n* [U] flour that is made from whole grains of wheat, etc including the HUSK: *wholemeal bread.*

wholesale /'həʊlseɪl/ *n* [U esp attrib] the selling of goods, esp in large quantities, to shopkeepers for them to sell to the public: *the wholesale market* ○ *wholesale prices.* Compare RETAIL.

▶ **wholesale** *adv* in large quantities and at a price that allows the person buying sth to sell it again at a profit: *We buy our supplies wholesale.*

wholesale *adj* [attrib] (*esp of sth bad*) happening or done on a large scale: *the wholesale slaughter of innocent people.*

wholesale *v* to sell goods to people who will sell them to others: [Vn] *a drug wholesaling company.* **wholesaler** *n*.

wholesome /'həʊlsəm/ *adj* **1(a)** good for one's health: *plain but wholesome meals.* **(b)** suggesting a healthy condition: *have a wholesome appearance.* **2** morally good or worthy: *a wholesome influence.* Compare UNWHOLESOME. ▶ **wholesomeness** *n* [U].

wholewheat /'həʊlwiːt/ *n* [U] whole grains of wheat, including the HUSK: *wholewheat flour/bread.*

who'll /huːl/ *short form* who will. ⇨ WILL¹.

wholly ⇨ WHOLE.

whom /huːm/ *interrog pron* (*fml*) (used as the object of a *v* or *prep*) which person or people: *Whom did they invite?* ○ *To whom should I write?*

▶ **whom** *rel pron* (*fml*) **1** (used as the object of a *v* or *prep* introducing a clause that defines the person mentioned): *The author whom you criticized in your review has written a letter in reply.* ○ *The person to whom this letter was addressed died three years ago.* **2** (used esp in formal written English as the object of a *v* or *prep* in a clause that refers to but does not define the person mentioned): *My mother, whom I'm sure you remember, died recently.* ○ *She was betrayed by her daughter, in whom she placed so much trust.*

NOTE **Whom** is not used very often in spoken English. **Who** is usually used as the object pronoun, especially in questions: *Who did you invite to the party?*

Whom is necessary after prepositions: *To whom should I address the letter?*, This pattern is very formal and is used especially in writing. In spoken English we say: *Who should I address the letter to?*, putting the preposition at the end of the sentence.

In defining relative clauses the object pronoun **whom** is usually changed to **who** or **that**, or left out completely: *The family (whom/who/that) we stayed with were very kind.* In non-defining relative clauses **whom** or **who** (but not **that**) is used and the pronoun cannot be left out: *Our doctor, whom/who we all liked very much, retired last week.* This pattern is not used very much in spoken English.

whomsoever /,huːmsəʊ'evə(r)/ *rel pron* (*fml*) (used as the object of a *v* or *prep*) which person or people: *He's free to marry whomsoever he chooses.*

whoop /wuːp, huːp/ *n* **1** a loud cry, esp one expressing joy or excitement: *They opened the parcel with whoops of delight.* **2** a harsh sound made by sb with whooping cough (WHOOP).

▶ **whoop** *v* to give a loud cry of joy or excitement: [V] *singing and whooping with glee.* **IDM** **,whoop it 'up** /wuːp; *US* wʊp/ (*infml*) to take part in noisy celebrations: *After their victory they were whooping it up all night long.*

■ **'whooping cough** /'huːpɪŋ kɒf; *US* -kɔːf/ *n* [U] an infectious disease, esp of children, with a series of coughs followed by a HARSH(1) gasp for breath.

whoopee /wʊ'piː/ *interj* (expressing joy).

▶ **whoopee** *n* **IDM** **make 'whoopee** (*dated infml*) to celebrate noisily.

whoops /wʊps/ *interj* (*infml*) **(a)** (used when one has almost had an accident, broken sth, etc): *Whoops! I nearly dropped the tray.* **(b)** (used to express regret or embarrassment when one has accidentally said something rude, revealed a secret, etc).

whoosh /wʊʃ, wuːʃ/ *n*, *interj* (*infml*) a sudden movement accompanied by a rushing sound: *a whoosh of flame* ○ *The car sped past us with a whoosh.* ○ *I lit the firework and — whoosh! — it shot up into the air.*

▶ **whoosh** *v* [V, Vpr, Vp] (*infml*) to make a whoosh or move with a whoosh.

whopper /'wɒpə(r)/ *n* (*infml*) **1** a very big thing of its type: *The fisherman had caught a whopper.* **2** a big lie: *If she said that, she was telling a real whopper.*

whopping /'wɒpɪŋ/ (*infml*) *adj* very big: *a whopping lie* ○ *a whopping $74 million loss.*

▶ **whopping** *adv* (*infml*) very: *a whopping great hole in the ground.*

whore /hɔː(r)/ *n* (*dated or derog*) **(a)** a prostitute. **(b)** a woman who is not sexually faithful to one man or who has sex with a lot of men.

■ **'whore-house** *n* (*dated or derog*) a house where prostitutes work; a BROTHEL.

who're /'huːə(r)/ *short form* who are. ⇨ BE¹.

whorl /wɜːl/ *n* **1** a curved line or mass of sth forming a rough circle: *send up whorls of dust.* **2** a complete circle formed by the ridges of a FINGER-PRINT. **3** a ring of leaves, flowers, etc round the stem of a plant.

who's /huːz/ *short form* **1** who is. ⇨ BE¹. **2** who has. ⇨ HAVE².

whose /huːz/ *interrog pron, interrog det* of whom: *Whose (house) is that?* ○ *I wonder whose (book) this is.*
▶ **whose** *rel det* (**a**) of whom: *the boy whose father is a singer* ○ *the people whose house was broken into last week.* (**b**) of which: *the house whose front door has a glass panel* (ie instead of *the house with a front door with a glass panel*).

whosoever /ˌhuːsəʊˈevə(r)/ *pron* (*arch*) = WHOEVER.

who've /huːv/ *short form* who have. ⇨ HAVE².

why /waɪ/ *interrog adv* **1** for what reason or purpose: *Why were you late?* ○ *Why did you buy those shoes?* ○ *Tell me why you did it.* ○ *Do you know why the door is locked?* ○ *'I want you to tidy the kitchen.' 'Why me?'* **2** (used before a *v* to suggest that sth is unacceptable or unnecessary): *Why get upset just because you got a bad mark?* ○ *Why bother to write? We'll see him tomorrow.* **IDM** **why ˈever** (used to express surprise) why: *Why ever didn't you tell us before?* ˌwhy ˈnot (used to make or agree to a suggestion): *Why not write to her?* ○ *'Let's go to the cinema.' 'Why not?'*
▶ **why** *rel adv* (used esp after *reason*) for which: *the reason why he left her* ○ *That is (the reason) why I came early.*
why *interj* (*dated or US*) (expressing surprise, impatience, etc): *Why, Jane, it's you!* ○ *Why, it's easy — a child could do it!*
why *n* **IDM** **the ˌwhys and (the) ˈwherefores** the reasons: *I don't need to hear all the whys and the wherefores, just tell me what happened.*

WI *abbr* **1** (esp in addresses) West Indies. **2** /ˌdʌbljuːˈaɪ/ (*Brit*) Women's Institute (an organization of women in country areas who meet regularly to take part in cultural activities, learn traditional skills, etc).

wick /wɪk/ *n* (**a**) a length of string in the centre of a candle, the top end of which is lit and burns as the wax melts. ⇨ picture at CANDLE. (**b**) (in lamps, etc) a length of woven material through which oil is drawn up to be burnt: *trim the wick of a lamp.* **IDM** **get on sb's ˈwick** (*Brit infml*) to annoy sb continually.

wicked /ˈwɪkɪd/ *adj* (**-er, -est**) **1** (of people or their actions) morally bad; evil: *a wicked man/deed* ○ *That was a wicked thing to do.* ○ (*joc*) *They do a wicked creamy chocolate dessert* (ie one that is nice to eat but very bad for one's figure). **2** intended to harm or capable of harming sb: *a wicked blow* ○ *a wicked-looking knife.* **3** tending to annoy or shock people in a playful way; MISCHIEVOUS: *a wicked sense of humour* ○ *take a wicked delight in sth.* **4** (*sl*) very good: *Their new CD is really wicked.*
▶ **the wicked** *n* [pl] **IDM** **(there's) no peace, rest, etc for the ˈwicked** (*saying usu joc*) people who do wrong have and must expect a life full of fear, worry, etc.
wickedly *adv*: *smile wickedly* ○ *wickedly funny* ○ *The knife gleamed wickedly in the moonlight.*
wickedness *n* [U].

wicker /ˈwɪkə(r)/ *n* [U] thin flexible sticks of wood woven together, esp to make baskets or furniture: *a wicker chair.*

wickerwork /ˈwɪkəwɜːk/ *n* [U] thin flexible sticks of wood woven together; baskets, furniture, etc made of these: *wickerwork chairs.*

wicket /ˈwɪkɪt/ *n* (**a**) (in cricket) either of the two sets of three upright sticks (called *stumps*) with pieces of wood (called *bails*) lying across the top.

The ball is bowled at the wicket and it is defended by the batsman: *take a wicket* (ie dismiss a batsman) ○ *Surrey are four wickets down/have lost four wickets* (ie Four of their batsmen have been dismissed). ⇨ picture at CRICKET. (**b**) the stretch of ground between the two wickets: *Don't walk on the wicket.* **IDM** **keep ˈwicket** to act as a wicket-keeper (WICKET). **a sticky wicket** ⇨ STICKY.
■ **ˈwicket-keeper** *n* (in cricket) a player who stands behind the wicket in order to stop balls that the batsman misses, or to catch balls that the batsman hits, etc. ⇨ picture at CRICKET.

wicket-gate /ˈwɪkɪt geɪt/ *n* a small gate, esp at the side of a large one.

wide /waɪd/ *adj* (**-r, -st**) **1**(**a**) measuring a lot from side to side; not narrow: *a wide river* ○ *The gap in the fence was just wide enough for the sheep to get through.* ○ (*fig*) *He won by a wide margin.* ○ *There are wide differences between the two parties.* Compare BROAD¹ 1. (**b**) having the specified width: *a two-inch-wide ribbon* ○ *The room is twelve feet long and ten feet wide.* **2** including a great variety of people or things: *the whole wide world* ○ *a wide selection/vocabulary/audience* ○ *wide influence/support* ○ *a manager with wide experience of industry* ○ *The affair raises wider issues of national interest.* ○ *Health in its widest sense refers to both physical and mental well-being.* **3** fully open: *She stared at him with eyes wide.* ○ *Someone had left the door wide open.* **4** ~ (**of sth**) far from the point aimed at: *Her shot was wide (of the target).* **IDM** **be/fall wide of the ˈmark** to fail to be accurate; to be far from the point aimed at: *His guesses were all very wide of the mark.* **give sb/sth a wide ˈberth** to remain at a distance from sb/sth: *These small creatures can be very fierce so it is advisable to give them a wide berth.*
▶ **wide** *adv* to a great extent; fully: *with legs wide apart* ○ *Open your mouth wide.* **IDM** **cast one's net wide** ⇨ CAST¹. **far and near/wide** ⇨ FAR¹. **wide ˈopen** (of a contest) with no competitor who is certain to win. **wide ˈopen (to sth)** exposed to attack, etc: *be wide open to criticism.* ˌwide aˈwake *adj* [usu pred] (**a**) fully awake. (**b**) ~ (**to sth**) fully conscious or aware of things: *He felt wide awake to his surroundings.*
wide *n* (in cricket) a ball that is judged to be bowled where the batsman cannot reach it.
-wide (forming *adjs* and *advs*) extending to the whole of sth: *a nationwide search* ○ *travelled world-wide.*
widely *adv* **1** to a large extent or degree: *We differ widely in our political views.* **2** over a large area or range; among a large number of people: *widely scattered* ○ *It is widely known that…* ○ *His books are widely read in Europe.*
■ ˌwide-angle ˈlens *n* a camera LENS that can give a wider field of vision than a standard lens.
ˈwide boy *n* (*dated Brit infml derog*) a man who is regularly involved in dishonest business deals.
ˌwide-ˈeyed *adj* with eyes fully open because of fear, great surprise, etc: *The children watched in wide-eyed amazement.*
ˌwide-ˈranging *adj* covering a large area or many subjects: *be given ˌwide-ranging ˈpowers* ○ *a ˌwide-ranging ˈspeech.*

NOTE Compare **wide** and **broad**. **Wide** is the most general word but **broad** is used to describe parts of the body: *a broad nose* ○ *broad shoulders.* Otherwise **broad** is used in more formal or literary language, to describe features of the countryside, etc: *a broad river* ○ *a broad stretch of meadowland.*

widen /ˈwaɪdn/ *v* to become or make sth wider: [Vpr, Vp] *Here the stream widens (out) into a river.* [Vn] *The road is being widened.* ○ *He wants to widen* *his knowledge of the subject.* [V] *There is a widening gap between rich and poor.*

widespread /ˈwaɪdspred/ *adj* found or distributed over a large area or number of people: *widespread damage/confusion.*

widgeon /ˈwɪdʒən/ *n* (*pl* unchanged or **widgeons**) a type of wild duck.

widow /ˈwɪdəʊ/ *n* a woman whose husband has died and who has not married again: *a ¹war widow ○ She has been a widow for ten years.*
▶ **widow** *v* (usu passive) to make sb a widow or WIDOWER: [Vn] *She was widowed at an early age.* **widowed** *adj* [attrib]: *his widowed father.*
▶ **ˈwidowhood** *n* [U] the state or period of being a widow.

widower /ˈwɪdəʊə(r)/ *n* a man whose wife has died and who has not married again.

width /wɪdθ, wɪtθ/ *n* **1(a)** [U, C] the measurement from one side of sth to the other side of it: *10 metres in width ○ measure the width of the floor ○ The carpet is available in various widths.* ⇨ picture at DIMENSION. **(b)** [C] a piece of material of a particular width: *You'll need two widths of fabric for each curtain.* **2** [C] the distance between the sides of a swimming-pool (SWIM): *She can swim two widths now.* Compare BREADTH. **3** [U] the state of extending over a large range of subjects, attitudes, etc: *width of experience/opinion.*

widthways /ˈwɪdθweɪz, ˈwɪtθ-/ *adv* along the width and not the length: *The fabric was folded widthways.*

wield /wiːld/ *v* **1** to hold sth and use it as a weapon, tool, etc: [Vn] *wield an axe/a sword/a tennis racket.* **2** to have and be able to use power, etc: [Vn] *wield authority/control/power.*

wiener /ˈwiːnə(r)/ *n* (*US*) = FRANKFURTER.

wife /waɪf/ *n* (*pl* **wives** /waɪvz/) a married woman, esp when considered in relation to her husband: *the doctor's wife ○ She's his second wife.* **IDM** **husband and wife** ⇨ HUSBAND. **an old wives' tale** ⇨ OLD. **the world and his wife** ⇨ WORLD.
▶ **wifely** *adj* (*dated or joc*) of, like or expected of a wife: *wifely duties/virtues.*

wig /wɪɡ/ *n* a covering for the head made of real or artificial hair. Wigs are worn eg to hide the fact that one is BALD, by actors as part of their costume, or in a lawcourt by judges, etc: *She disguised herself with a blonde wig and dark glasses.* Compare TOUPEE. See also BIGWIG.

wigging /ˈwɪɡɪŋ/ *n* (usu *sing*) (*dated Brit infml*) an instance of speaking angrily to sb for having done sth wrong; a REBUKE.

wiggle /ˈwɪɡl/ *v* (*infml*) to move or make sth move from side to side with rapid short movements: [Vn] *The baby was wiggling its toes.* [V] *Their bottoms wiggled as they danced.* Compare WAG¹, WAGGLE.
▶ **wiggle** *n* (*infml*) a wiggling movement.
wiggly /ˈwɪɡli/ *adj* (*infml*) **(a)** not straight; wavy (WAVE²): *a wiggly line.* **(b)** moving with a wiggle: *a wiggly worm.*

wigwam /ˈwɪɡwæm; *US* -wɑːm/ *n* a hut or tent made by fastening mats or animal skins over a framework of poles, esp as used formerly by Native Americans. See also TEPEE.

wild /waɪld/ *adj* (**-er, -est**) **1** [usu attrib] **(a)** (of animals, birds, etc) living free in natural conditions; not TAME or kept in a house or on a farm: *a wild boar/cat/duck ○ filming wild animals.* **(b)** (of plants or fruit) growing in natural conditions; not cultivated: *wild flowers ○ wild roses/strawberries.* **2** [usu attrib] (of a person, tribe, etc) considered to be at a primitive stage of human development. **3** (of scenery, an area of land, etc) not cultivated or settled by people: *a wild mountain region.* **4** affected by storms or strong winds: *a wild night/sea.* **5** out of control; without discipline: *He led a wild life in his youth. ○*

He's made friends with rather a wild crowd. **6** full of strong feeling; very angry, excited, passionate, etc: *wild laughter/applause ○ The crowd went wild with delight. ○ It makes me wild* (ie very angry) *to see such cruelty. ○ She had a wild look on her face.* **7** [pred] ~ **about sth/sb** (*infml*) extremely enthusiastic about sth/sb: *The children are wild about their new puppy.* **8** not carefully aimed or planned, and perhaps rather foolish: *a wild aim/guess/shot ○ a wild idea/scheme.* **9** (*infml*) very good, enjoyable or exciting: *a really wild movie/holiday.* **IDM** **beyond one's wildest ˈdreams** far more, better, etc than one could ever have imagined or hoped for. **run ˈwild** (of an animal, a plant, a person, etc) to develop freely without any control: *Those boys have been allowed to run wild.* **sow one's wild oats** ⇨ SOW¹.
▶ **wild** *n* **(a) the wild** [sing] a natural state or environment: *animals living in the wild.* **(b) the wilds** [pl] (*sometimes derog*) remote areas, usu not cultivated, where few people live: *the wilds of Scotland ○ live out in the wilds* (ie far from towns, etc).
wildly *adv* **(a)** in a wild manner: *rush wildly from room to room ○ talk wildly* (ie in an exaggerated or a very emotional way). **(b)** extremely: *a wildly exaggerated account ○ wildly funny.*
wildness *n* [U].

■ **ˈwild card** *n* **1** (in card-games) a card that can be given the value of another card by the person holding it. **2** (*sport*) an opportunity to enter a competition without having to take part in qualifying matches, be ranked at a particular level, etc: *He was given a wild card to take part in the tournament. ○ a wild card entry.*
ˌwild-ˈgoose chase *n* a foolish and HOPELESS(1) search for sth/sb that does not exist or can only be found elsewhere: *The hoaxer had sent the police on a wild-goose chase.*
the ˌWild ˈWest *n* [sing] the western States of the USA during the period when they were being settled by Europeans and there was little respect for the law: *films about the Wild West.*

wildcat /ˈwaɪldkæt/ *adj* [attrib] (of strikes) begun suddenly by workers, without official support.

wildebeest /ˈwɪldəbiːst/ *n* (*pl* unchanged or **wildebeests**) = GNU.

wilderness /ˈwɪldənəs/ *n* (usu *sing*) **1** an area that is not cultivated or settled; a desert: *the Arctic wilderness.* **2** ~ (**of sth**) an area where grass and other plants grow without any control: *The garden had been neglected for years and was now a wilderness of weeds. ○ (fig) a wilderness of old abandoned cars.* **IDM** **in the ˈwilderness** no longer in an important or influential position, esp in politics: *After a few years in the wilderness he was reappointed to the Cabinet.*

wildfire /ˈwaɪldfaɪə(r)/ *n* **IDM** **spread like wildfire** ⇨ SPREAD *v.*

wildfowl /ˈwaɪldfaʊl/ *n* (*pl* unchanged) any of the types of birds that are shot or hunted as game¹(6), esp ducks and geese (GOOSE).

wildlife /ˈwaɪldlaɪf/ *n* [U] wild animals and birds: *the conservation of wildlife ○ a wildlife sanctuary.*

wiles /waɪlz/ *n* [pl] tricks intended to deceive or attract sb: *She used all her feminine wiles to get her way.*

wilful (*US also* **willful**) /ˈwɪlfl/ *adj* (*derog*) **1** [usu attrib] (of sth bad) done intentionally; deliberate: *wilful damage/misconduct/murder/neglect.* **2** (of a person) determined to do as one wishes: *a wilful child.* ▶ **wilfully** /-fəli/ *adv*: *wilfully ignore instructions.* **wilfulness** *n* [U].

will¹ /wɪl/ *modal v* (*short form* **'ll** /l/; *neg* **will not**, *short form* **won't** /wəʊnt/; *pt* **would** /wəd, *strong form* wʊd/, *short form* **'d** /d/; *neg* **would not**, *short form* **wouldn't** /ˈwʊdnt/). **1(a)** (used for talking about or predicting the future): *Next year will be our* *tenth wedding anniversary.* ○ *He'll start school this year, won't he?* ○ *You'll be in time if you hurry.* ○ *How long will you be staying in Paris?* ○ *Fred said he'd be leaving soon.* ○ *By next year all the money will have been spent.* ⇨ note at SHALL. **(b)** (used for talking about what is probable or expected in the present): *That'll be the doctor now!* ○ *They'll be home by this time.* ○ *You'll have had dinner already, I suppose.* **2(a)** (used when making requests): *Will you send this letter for me, please?* ○ *You'll water the plants while I'm away, won't you?* ○ *I asked him if he wouldn't mind calling later.* **(b)** (used when giving an order): *You'll do it this minute!* ○ *Will you be quiet!* **3** (to be willing or ready to do sth): *I'll check this letter for you, if you want.* ○ *We won't lend you any more money.* ○ *He wouldn't ride on my motor bike — he was too frightened.* ○ *We said we would keep them.* ○ *I will admit that it wasn't a very sensible thing to do.* **4(a)** (used for stating general truths or facts): *If it's made of wood it will float.* ○ *Engines won't run without lubricants.* **(b)** (indicating a particular fact): *This jar will hold a kilo.* ○ *The door won't open!* **5** (used for describing habits in the present or past): *She'll listen to music, alone in her room, for hours.* ○ *He would spend hours in the bathroom or on the telephone.* **6** (used to suggest the speaker's annoyance about sth): *He 'will comb his hair at the table, even though he knows I don't like it.* ○ *He 'would keep telling those dreadful stories.*

will² /wɪl/ *v* (only used in the simple present tense; 3rd pers sing **will**) (*dated or fml*) to wish: [V] *Call it what you will, it's still a problem.* ○ *You're free to travel where you will in the country.* **IDM** **if you 'will** (*fml*) if you prefer to express it in these terms: *He became her senior adviser — her deputy, if you will.*

will³ /wɪl/ *v* **1** to try to make sth happen or to make sb/oneself do sth by using one's mental powers: [Vn] *As a child he thought that his grandmother's death had happened because he had willed it.* [V.n *to* inf, Vnp] *The crowd were cheering her, willing her to win/willing him on.* [V.n *to* inf] *Closing his eyes, he willed himself to relax.* [Vnpr] *Gripping the steering wheel tightly she tried to will the van up the hill.* **2** (*fml*) to intend sth; to desire sth: [Vn] *This happened because God willed it.* [also V.*that*]. **3** ~ **sth** (**to sb**) (*fml*) to leave property, etc to sb after one has died by means of a will⁴(5): [Vnpr] *He willed most of his money to charity.* [Vnn] *Father willed me the house and my sister his stocks and shares.*

will⁴ /wɪl/ *n* **1** [U, sing] mental power by which one can direct one's thoughts and actions or influence those of others. See also FREE WILL. **2(a)** [U, sing] (also **will-power** [U]) mental control that one can use over one's own impulses: *have a strong/weak will* ○ *He has no will of his own.* ○ *She shows great strength of will.* **(b)** [U, C] strong desire; determination: *Despite her terrible injuries, she hasn't lost the will to live.* ○ *There was a clash of wills among committee members.* **3** [U] the specified feeling that a person has towards others: *bear sb no ill will.* See also GOODWILL. **4** [U] that which is desired by sb: *try to do God's will* ○ *It is the will of Allah.* **5** [C] a legal document in which sb states to whom they want their property and money to be given after their death: *one's last will and testament* ○ *Have you made a/your will?* **IDM** **against one's 'will** not according to one's wishes; unwillingly: *I was forced to sign the agreement against my will.* **at 'will** where, when, etc one wishes: *come and go at will* ○ *The animals are allowed to wander at will in the park.* **where there's a ͵will there's a 'way** (*saying*) a person with sufficient determination will always find a way of doing sth. **with the best will in the world** ⇨ BEST¹. **with a 'will** willingly and enthusiastically: *They set to work with a will.*

▶ **-willed** (forming compound *adjs*) with a will of a specified type: *strong-willed* ○ *weak-willed.*
■ **'will-power** *n* [U] = WILL 2a.

willies /'wɪliz/ *n* **the willies** [pl] (*infml*) a nervous feeling: *Being alone in that gloomy house gave me the willies.*

willing /'wɪlɪŋ/ *adj* **1(a)** ready or eager to help: *willing assistants.* **(b)** [pred] ~ (**to do sth**) having no objection to doing sth or to sth being done: *Are you willing to accept responsibility?* **2** [attrib] done, given, etc readily or enthusiastically: *willing cooperation/help/support.* **IDM** **God willing** ⇨ GOD. **show willing** ⇨ SHOW². **the spirit is willing** ⇨ SPIRIT. ▶ **willingly** *adv*: *He willingly agreed to give her a lift.* '*Will you help me?*' '*Willingly.*' **willingness** *n* [U, sing]: *Job knowledge can be less important than (a) willingness to learn.*

will-o'-the-wisp /͵wɪl ə ðə 'wɪsp/ *n* **1** a bluish moving light that is sometimes seen at night on soft wet ground, caused by the burning of natural gases. **2** a person or thing that is impossible to catch or reach: *You shouldn't hope to find perfect happiness — it's just a will-o'-the-wisp.*

willow /'wɪləʊ/ *n* **(a)** [C] a tree or bush with thin flexible branches and long narrow leaves, often growing near water. There are several different types of willow. **(b)** [U] its wood, used esp for making cricket bats.
▶ **willowy** *adj* (*approv*) (of a person) tall, thin and graceful: *a willowy young actress.*
■ **'willow-pattern** *n* [U] a traditional blue and white Chinese design that includes a picture of a willow tree and a river, used esp on plates, etc: *a willow-pattern dinner service.*

willy /'wɪli/ *n* (*Brit infml*) (used esp by or when speaking to young children) a PENIS.

willy-nilly /͵wɪli 'nɪli/ *adv* whether one wants it or not: *He was forced willy-nilly to sit through a lot of boring speeches.*

wilt¹ /wɪlt/ *v* **1(a)** (of a plant or flower) to bend downwards, grow pale and die: [V] *The leaves are beginning to wilt.* **(b)** (usu passive) to cause a plant or flower to do this: [Vn] *plants wilted by the heat.* **2** to become less strong or less keen; to grow weak, tired, etc: [V] *The spectators were wilting visibly in the hot sun.* ○ *Helen's indignation wilted.*

wilt² /wɪlt/ (*arch*) 2nd pers sing pres *t* of WILL¹,².

wily /'waɪli/ *adj* (**-ier, -iest**) clever at getting what one wants; CUNNING: *as wily as a fox* ○ *a wily and potentially dangerous politician.*

wimp /wɪmp/ *n* (*infml derog*) a weak and nervous person, esp a man: *Don't be such a wimp, of course you won't fall off!*
▶ **wimpish** *adj* (*infml derog*) of or like a wimp: *wimpish behaviour.*

wimple /'wɪmpl/ *n* a head covering made of cloth folded round the head and neck, worn by women in the Middle Ages and now by certain nuns.

win /wɪn/ *v* (**-nn-**; *pt, pp* **won** /wʌn/) **1** to be successful in a battle, contest, race, etc; to do best: [V] *Which team won?* ○ *The Miami Dolphins are sure to win/are the favourites to win.* [Vpr] *France won by six goals to two.* [Vn] *win a bet/wager* ○ *win a war/ championship/tournament/election* ○ *win an argument.* **2** ~ **sth** (**from sb**) to obtain or achieve sth as the result of a bet, competition, race, etc: [Vn] *She won first prize/a holiday (in the lottery).* [Vnn] *You've won yourself a trip to America.* [Vnpr] *The Conservatives won the seat (ie in Parliament) from Labour at the last election.* **3(a)** to obtain or achieve sth one wants, esp as a result of hard work or determination: [Vn] *win the right to vote* ○ *They are trying to win support/approval for their proposal.* ○ *The President has failed to win an overall majority.*

W

[V.speech] = verb + direct speech　　　[V.*that*] = verb + *that* clause　　　[V.*wh*] = verb + *who, how,* etc clause

(b) ~ **sth for sb/sth** to cause sb to obtain or achieve sth: [Vnn] *Her performance won her much critical acclaim.* [also Vnpr]. **IDM carry/win the day** ⇨ DAY. **nothing venture, nothing gain/win** ⇨ VENTURE *v*. **win (sth) ,hands 'down** (*infml*) to win easily, by a large margin: *The local team won (the match) hands down.* **,win or 'lose** whether one succeeds or fails: *Win or lose, it should be a very good match.* **win one's 'spurs** (*fml*) to achieve distinction or fame. **you, one, etc ,can't 'win** (*infml*) there is no way of achieving success or of pleasing people: *If I don't send her flowers she says 'You never send me flowers', and if I do she says 'What are you feeling guilty about?' I just can't win!* **PHR V ,win sth/sb 'back** to regain sth/sb one has lost: *The party must try to win back the support it has lost.* ○ *He hoped to win her love back.* **,win sb 'over/ 'round (to sth)** to gain sb's support or favour, esp by persuading them to like one: *She's against the idea, but I'm sure I can win her over.* **,win 'out/'through** (*infml*) to come successfully through a difficult period; to achieve success eventually: *It's not going to be easy but I'm sure we'll win through in the end.*

▶ **win** *n* a victory in a game, contest, etc: *It's their first defeat after ten successive wins.* Compare LOSS.
winner *n* **1** a person, horse, etc that wins: *the five lucky winners of our competition* ○ *a Nobel prize winner* ○ *The winner was presented with a trophy.* ○ *It's difficult to pick a winner from so many excellent runners.* Compare LOSER. **2** (*infml*) a thing, an idea, etc that is successful: *Their latest model is certain to be a winner.*
winning *adj* **1** [attrib] that wins or has won: *the winning horse/number/ticket.* **2** [usu attrib] attractive; causing people to like one: *a winning smile* ○ *winning ways.* **'winning-post** *n* (*esp Brit*) a post that marks the end of a race: *Your horse was first past the winning-post.*
winnings /'wɪnɪŋz/ *n* [pl] money that is won, esp by betting or gambling: *collect one's winnings* ○ *This prize has taken his winnings this year to over $350 000.*

wince /wɪns/ *v* ~ **(at sth)** to show pain, distress or embarrassment by a slight movement of the muscles in the face: [V, Vpr] *She winced (with pain) as she stood on his injured foot.* [Vpr] *I still wince at the memory of the stupid things I did.* ▶ **wince** *n* (usu sing).

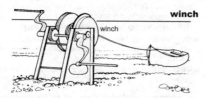

winch

winch /wɪntʃ/ *n* a machine for lifting or pulling heavy objects by means of a rope or chain wound round a drum¹(2).
▶ **winch** *v* to move sb/sth by using a winch: [Vnpr] *winch a glider off the ground* (ie pull it along by means of a winch until it rises into the air) [Vnp] *The helicopter winched the survivors up* (eg out of the sea) *to safety.*

wind¹ /wɪnd/ *n* **1** [C, U] (also **the wind**) (used with *a* or in the plural when referring to the type of wind or its direction; used with *much, little*, etc when referring to its strength, etc) air moving as a result of natural forces: *trees blown down by strong/high/ gale-force winds* ○ *a light wind* ○ *a cold/biting north wind* (ie one blowing from the north) ○ *The curtains were flapping backwards and forwards in the wind.* ○ *The wind was howling round the chimneys.* ○ *A gust of wind blew my hat off.* ○ *The wind has dropped* (ie is less strong) *now.* ○ *a shift in wind direction* ○ *The day was very still, without a breath of wind.* See

also CROSSWIND, DOWNWIND, TAIL WIND. **2** [U] breath, esp as needed for continuous exercise or for blowing into a musical instrument: *be short of wind* ○ *After running hard I had to stop and regain my wind* (ie wait until I could breathe more easily). See also SECOND WIND. **3** [U] (*Brit*) (*US* **gas**) air that has been swallowed with food or drink, or gas that forms in the stomach or intestines (INTESTINE) and causes discomfort: *get a baby's wind up* (ie cause it to BELCH by gently hitting its back). **4** [U] words that are not sincere; boasting talk: *He's just full of wind, the pompous old fool!* **5(a)** [U] a group of wind instruments (WIND¹): *music for wind and strings.* **(b) the wind** [Gp] the players of the wind instruments (WIND¹) in an ORCHESTRA: *the wind section.* **IDM break 'wind** (*euph*) to release air from the intestines (INTESTINE) through the ANUS. **get 'wind of sth** to hear a rumour that sth is happening; to hear about sth secret: *Our competitors must not be allowed to get wind of our plans.* **get/have the 'wind up (about sth)** (*infml*) to become/be frightened. **in the 'wind** about to happen: *They sensed that there was something in the wind.* **it's an ill wind** ⇨ ILL¹. **like the 'wind** very fast: *She ran like the wind.* **put the 'wind up sb** (*infml*) to make sb frightened; to alarm sb. **sail close/near to the wind** ⇨ SAIL². **see which way the wind is blowing** ⇨ WAY¹. **a straw in the wind** ⇨ STRAW. **take the 'wind out of sb's sails** to cause sb to lose their confidence or pride, eg by doing or saying sth that they do not expect: *The government's concession on pensions has taken much of the wind out of the Opposition's sails.* **throw, etc caution to the 'winds** ⇨ CAUTION. **a wind / the winds of 'change** (used esp by journalists) an influence that causes change; a tendency to change: *It would be foolish to defy the winds of change.*

▶ **windless** *adj* without wind: *a windless day.*
windy *adj* (**-ier, -iest**) **1(a)** with much wind: *wet and windy conditions* ○ *It was a windy day.* **(b)** exposed to strong winds: *a windy hillside.* **2** (*infml derog*) (of language) using a lot of long words in order to impress people, without necessarily being very clear: *windy phrases.*

■ **'wind-blown** *adj* **(a)** carried by the wind: *,wind-blown 'snow.* **(b)** made untidy by the wind: *,wind-blown 'hair.*
'wind-break *n* a row of trees or a hedge or fence that provides protection from the wind.
'wind chill *n* [U] the combined effect of low temperature and wind on the body or a surface: *take into account the wind chill factor.*
'wind farm *n* an area of land on which there are a lot of windmills (WINDMILL 1b).
'wind instrument *n* a musical instrument in which sound is produced by the player blowing a current of air through or across a MOUTHPIECE: *Flutes and clarinets are wind instruments.* Compare WOODWIND.
'wind-sock *n* a canvas tube, open at both ends, that hangs at the top of a pole, eg on an AIRFIELD, to show the direction of the wind.

wind² /wɪnd/ *v* **1** to make sb too tired to be able to breathe properly for a short time: [Vn] *We were winded by the steep climb.* ○ *The punch in the stomach momentarily winded him.* **2** [Vn] to help a baby to release wind¹(3) from its stomach by gently hitting its back. See also LONG-WINDED.

wind³ /waɪnd/ *v* (*pt, pp* **wound** /waʊnd/) **1** to follow a curving or twisting course: [V] *winding alleys and backstreets* [Vpr, Vnpr] *The river winds (its way) along a narrow valley.* [Vadv] *The path winds steeply upwards.* [also Vp]. **2** to twist or COIL string, wool, etc round and round itself so that it forms a ball, or to twist it onto a REEL¹, etc: [Vnpr, Vnp] *wind wool (up) into a ball* [also Vn]. **3(a)** ~ **sth round sb/sth;** ~ **sb/sth in sth** to fold sth round sb/sth closely; to

---

[Vnn] = verb + noun + noun   [V-adj] = verb + adjective   For more help with verbs, see Study pages **B4–8**.

wrap sb/sth in sth: [Vnpr] *wind a bandage round one's finger.* (**b**) ~ **itself round sb/sth** to become twisted round sb/sth: *The shirt flew off the washing line and wound itself round the apple tree.* **4**(**a**) to turn a handle round and round: [Vn] *You operate the trapdoor by winding this handle.* (**b**) to cause sth to move in the specified direction by turning a handle, pressing a button, etc: [Vnp] *wind a video back/ forward/on* ○ *wind a car window down/up* ○ *wind in a fishing line* [also Vnpr]. **5** ~ **sth** (**up**) to cause a mechanism to operate, eg by turning a key to tighten the spring: [Vn] *wind one's watch* [Vnp] *He wound up the clockwork toys.* See also WIND-UP.

PHR V ,wind 'down 1 (of a person) to relax, esp after a period of stress or excitement: *This year has been frantically busy for us — I need a month's rest to wind down.* **2** (of a clock or watch) to go slowly and then stop. ,wind sth 'down to bring sth to an end gradually over a period of time: *The government has decided to wind down its nuclear programme.* ,wind 'up (*infml*) (of a person) to arrive finally in a place; to end up (END²): *We eventually wound up (staying) in a little hotel by the sea.* ○ *I always said he would wind up in prison.* ,wind (sth) 'up to finish a speech, etc: *The speaker had just begun winding up when the door was flung open.* ○ *If we all agree, let's wind up the discussion.* ,wind sb/sth 'up to cause sb/sth to reach a high level of excitement or stress: *He gets so wound up when he's arguing.* ○ (*Brit infml*) *Are you deliberately winding me up* (ie annoying me)? See also WIND-UP. ,wind sth 'up to stop running a business, company, etc and close it completely: *wind up one's affairs.*

▶ **wind** *n* a single turn made in winding (WIND³ 5) sth: *Give the handle another couple of winds.*

■ **'winding-sheet** *n* = SHROUD.

'wind-up *adj* [attrib] (of a mechanical device) that is operated by turning a key or LEVER(2): *wind-up toys/windows* ○ *an old-fashioned wind-up gramophone.* — *n* (*infml*) a deliberate attempt to annoy or provoke sb: *Is this some kind of a wind-up?*

windbag /'wɪndbæg/ *n* (*infml derog*) a person who talks a lot but says nothing important.

windcheater /'wɪndtʃiːtə(r)/ (*esp Brit*) (*US* also **windbreaker** /'wɪndbreɪkə(r)/) *n* a jacket designed to protect the person wearing it from the wind.

windfall /'wɪndfɔːl/ *n* **1** an unexpected gift of money, piece of good luck, etc: *The publicity the case has attracted may bring a windfall for the book's author.* ○ *windfall profits.* **2** a fruit, esp an apple, that has been blown off a tree by the wind.

windlass /'wɪndləs/ *n* a machine for pulling or lifting things, consisting of a rope or chain that winds round a HORIZONTAL drum¹(2); a WINCH. ⇨ picture at WINCH.

windmill /'wɪndmɪl/ *n* (**a**) a mill worked by the action of wind on long projecting arms (*sails*) that turn on a central SHAFT(2). ⇨ picture. (**b**) a similar tall thin structure used to change the power of the wind into electricity. **IDM** **tilt at windmills** ⇨ TILT.

windmill
sail

window /'wɪndəʊ/ *n* **1**(**a**) an opening in the wall or roof of a building, car, etc that has glass in it so that light can pass through and people can see in and out. Some windows can be opened to let fresh air enter: *She was standing at the window, staring out.* ○ *He opened the bedroom window.* ○ *He prefers to travel in a seat near the window.* See also BAY WINDOW, DORMER, FRENCH WINDOW, PICTURE WINDOW, SASH WINDOW. (**b**) a piece of glass in the frame of a window: *stained-glass*

windows in a church ○ *a plate-glass window* ○ *The ball smashed a window.* (**c**) the space behind the window of a shop where goods are displayed for sale: *I saw the vase in the window of an antique shop.* ○ *a window display.* **2** a small part of a container, an envelope, etc that one can see through: *fold the letter so the address can be seen through the window of the envelope.* **3** (*computing*) an area of a computer screen within a frame in which information of a particular type can be displayed. **4** a time when conditions for doing sth are favourable: *Disagreement in the Labour Party has given the government a* **window of opportunity** *to press ahead with new legislation.* **IDM** **fly/go out of the 'window** (*infml*) to be no longer in existence; to disappear: *With the failure of the peace talks all hopes of a swift end to the war have flown out of the window.* **a window on the 'world** a means of observing and learning about people, esp those of other countries.

▶ **windowless** *adj* without windows: *working in a small, windowless office.*

■ **'window-box** *n* a long narrow box fixed outside a window, in which plants are grown.

'window-dressing *n* [U] (**a**) the art or skill of arranging goods in an attractive way in shop windows. (**b**) (*derog*) the presenting of facts, etc in a way that looks attractive but may be misleading: *The company's support of scientific research is just window-dressing.*

'window-pane *n* a piece of glass for or in a window: *rain beating down against the window-pane.* ⇨ picture at HOUSE¹.

'window shade *n* (*US*) = BLIND³.

'window-shopping *n* [U] the activity of looking at goods displayed in shop windows, usu without intending to buy anything: *go window-shopping.*

'window-sill (also **'window-ledge**) *n* a narrow shelf below a window, either inside or outside: *Place the bulbs on a sunny window-sill.* ⇨ picture at HOUSE¹.

windpipe /'wɪndpaɪp/ *n* the passage from the throat through which air reaches the lungs. ⇨ picture at RESPIRE.

windscreen /'wɪndskriːn/ (*Brit*) (*US* **windshield**) *n* a glass window across the front of a motor vehicle: *a heated/tinted windscreen* ○ *Her windscreen shattered.* ⇨ picture at CAR.

■ **'windscreen wiper** (*Brit*) (also **wiper**, *US* **'windshield wiper**) *n* a blade with a rubber edge that wipes a windscreen clear of rain, snow, etc. It is operated by power from the vehicle's battery. ⇨ picture at CAR.

windshield /'wɪndʃiːld/ *n* (**a**) (*US*) = WINDSCREEN. (**b**) a glass or plastic screen that provides protection from the wind, eg at the front of a motor cycle (MOTOR).

windsurfer /'wɪndsɜːfə(r)/ *n* (**a**) (*US propr* **Windsurfer**) a long board, similar to a SURFBOARD, with a sail. (**b**) a person who moves across water on this.
▶ **'windsurf** *v* to move across water on a windsurfer: [V] *Most visitors came to sail or windsurf.* **windsurfing** *n* [U]. ⇨ picture.

windsurfing

windswept /'wɪndswept/ *adj* (**a**) (of a place) exposed to strong winds: *a windswept hillside.* (**b**) (of a person's appearance) untidy after being blown about by the wind: *windswept hair.*

windward /'wɪndwəd/ *adj, adv* on or to the side from which the wind is blowing: *the windward side of the boat.* Compare LEE, LEEWARD.
▶ **windward** *n* [U] the side or direction from which the wind is blowing: *sail to windward.*

windy ⇨ WIND¹.

wine /waɪn/ n **1** [U, C] an alcoholic drink made from the juice of grapes (GRAPE) that has been left to FERMENT¹: *open a bottle of wine* ○ *dry/sweet wine* ○ *a glass of red/white/rosé/sparkling wine* ○ *vintage wines.* **2** [U, C] an alcoholic drink made from plants or fruits other than grapes (GRAPE): *apple/cowslip/rice wine.* **3** (also **wine red**) [U] a dark red colour: *a wine velvet evening dress.*
▶ **wine** **IDM** **,wine and 'dine (sb)** to entertain sb or be entertained with food and drink: *We were wined and dined very well.* ○ *The town offers many opportunities for wining and dining.*
■ **'wine bar** n (*Brit*) a bar¹(1) or small restaurant where wine is the main drink available. ⇨ note at INN.
'wine cellar n **(a)** an underground room where wine is stored. **(b)** (also **cellar**) wine stored in this: *He has an excellent wine cellar.*
,wine 'cooler n (*US*) a drink made with wine, fruit juice and FIZZY water.
'wine list n a list of wines available in a restaurant, etc: *an extensive wine list* ○ *Waiter, could we have the wine list, please?*
,wine 'vinegar n [U] VINEGAR that is made from wine.

wineglass /'waɪnɡlɑːs/ n a glass for drinking wine from. ⇨ picture at GLASS.

winery /'waɪnəri/ n (*esp US*) a place where wine is made.

wing /wɪŋ/ n **1** [C] **(a)** either of the pair of limbs covered in feathers that a bird uses to fly. **(b)** either of a pair of similar parts that an insect or a bat² uses to fly: *The moth opened its wings.* ⇨ picture at BUTTERFLY. **2** [C] a part that projects from the side of an aircraft and supports it in the air. ⇨ picture at AIRCRAFT. **3** [C] a part of a building that projects from the main part: *the east/west wing of a house* ○ *build a new wing of a hospital.* **4** (*Brit*) (*US* **fender**) [C] a projecting part of the body of a car, etc above a wheel: *a dent in the wing* ○ *The nearside wing was damaged in the collision.* ○ *a wing mirror.* ⇨ picture at CAR. **5** [C usu *sing*] a part of an organization, esp a political party, that holds particular views or has a particular function: *the radical wing of the Labour Party.* See also THE LEFT WING, THE RIGHT WING. **6** [C] (*sport*) **(a)** either side of the playing area in football, hockey, etc: *playing on the wing* ○ *kick the ball out to the wing.* **(b)** (also **winger**) (in football, hockey, etc) either of the attacking players whose place is towards the side of the playing area: *the team's new left wing.* **7** the wings [pl] (in a theatre) the area to the right and left of the stage that is hidden from the audience by curtains, scenery, etc: *She stood watching the performance from the wings.* **IDM clip sb's wings** ⇨ CLIP². **(wait, etc) in the 'wings** ready to do sth, esp to do sb's job when they leave: *The chairman's successor is already waiting in the wings.* **on the 'wing** (*esp rhet*) (of a bird, bat², etc) while it is flying: *photograph butterflies on the wing.* **spread one's wings** ⇨ SPREAD v. **take 'wing** (*rhet*) to fly up or away: (*fig*) *His imagination took wing.* **under sb's/one's 'wing** being helped by sb/one and shown by them/one what to do, where things are, etc, esp when one is in a new place or situation: *She immediately took the new secretary under her wing.* ○ *He spent several years under the wing of a top Australian tennis coach.*
▶ **wing** v **1** to travel on wings; to fly: [Vpr, Vnpr] *planes winging their way across the sky.* **2** [Vn] to wound a person in the arm or a bird in the wing.
winged /wɪŋd/ adj (often forming compound adjs) having wings, esp of the specified number or type: *winged insects* ○ *delta-winged aircraft.*
winger /'wɪŋə(r)/ n (*sport*) = WING 6b: *Chris Waddle,*

the England winger. See also LEFT-WINGER, RIGHT-WINGER.

wingless adj (esp of insects) without wings.
■ **'wing commander** n an officer in the Royal Air Force. ⇨ App 6.
'wing-nut n a nut(2) with two projecting parts so that it can easily be turned by the thumb and a finger. ⇨ picture at BOLT.
'wing-span n the distance between the end of one wing and the end of the other when the wings are fully stretched: *a bird with a two-foot wing-span* ○ *the wing-span of a glider.*

wingding /'wɪŋdɪŋ/ n (*US infml*) a wild party.

wink /wɪŋk/ v **1** ~ **(at sb)** to close one eye very briefly and open it again, esp as a private signal to sb: *Jack winked conspiratorially* [Vpr] *He winked at me to show that he was playing a joke on the others.* **2** (*rhet*) (of a light, star, etc) to flash quickly on and off: [V] *We could see the lighthouse winking in the distance.* **IDM as easy as winking** ⇨ EASY¹. **PHRV 'wink at sth** to pretend that one has not noticed sth, eg bad behaviour.
▶ **wink** n an act of winking, esp as a signal: *He gave me a meaningful/knowing wink.* See also FORTY WINKS. **IDM a nod is as good as a wink** ⇨ NOD n. **not get/have a 'wink of sleep; not sleep a 'wink** not to sleep at all: *The neighbours were having a party and we didn't get a wink of sleep.* **tip sb the wink** ⇨ TIP³ v.

winkle /'wɪŋkl/ (*Brit*) (also **periwinkle**) n a small edible SHELLFISH.
▶ **winkle** v **PHRV ,winkle sb/sth 'out (of sth)** (*infml*) to get sb/sth out of a place slowly and with difficulty: *I'm sure he'd like to come for a walk with us if we can winkle him out of his study.* **,winkle sth 'out (of sb)** (*infml*) to obtain information, etc from sb with difficulty: *She's very clever at winkling secrets out of people.*

winner ⇨ WIN.

winning ⇨ WIN.

winnow /'wɪnəʊ/ v ~ **sth (from sth)** [Vn, Vnpr] to blow a current of air through grain in order to remove the CHAFF¹. **PHRV winnow sb/sth down/out** to reduce the number in a set of people or things gradually until only the best ones are left.

wino /'waɪnəʊ/ n (pl **-os**) (*infml*) a person who is unable to stop drinking alcohol, esp cheap wine.

winsome /'wɪnsəm/ adj (*fml*) (of people or their manner) attractive and pleasant: *a winsome smile.* ▶ **winsomely** adv.

winter /'wɪntə(r)/ n [U, C] the last and coldest season of the year. Winter lasts from December to February in the northern parts of the world: *a mild/hard winter* ○ *Many trees lose their leaves in winter.* ○ *They worked on the building all through the winter.* ○ *The team are touring India this winter.* ○ *winter weather* ○ *a winter coat.* **IDM in the dead of winter** ⇨ DEAD n.
▶ **winter** v (*fml*) to spend the winter: [Vpr] *It became fashionable to winter in Italy.* [V] *The swans' wintering grounds.*
wintry /'wɪntri/ adj **(a)** of or like winter; cold and dark: *a wintry landscape* ○ *wintry light/weather.* **(b)** not friendly: *a wintry smile.*
■ **,winter 'sports** n [pl] sports that people do on snow or ice: *skiing, skating and other winter sports.*

wintertime /'wɪntətaɪm/ n [U] the period or season of winter: *The days are shorter in (the) wintertime.*

wipe /waɪp/ v **1(a)** ~ **sth (on sth)** to remove dirt, liquid, etc from sth by rubbing its surface with a cloth, a piece of paper, etc: [Vn, Vn-adj] *She wiped the table (clean)* [Vnpr] *She wiped her hands on a tea towel.* ○ *Please wipe your feet* (ie remove the dirt from your shoes) *on the mat.* ○ *Don't wipe your nose on your sleeve!* [Vn] *wipe one's eyes* (ie to remove tears) ○ *Who's going to wipe the dishes* (ie dry them after they have been washed)? [Vnp] *wipe down* (ie all over) *the kitchen door.* (**b**) to rub a cloth, etc over a surface: [Vnpr] *wipe a damp sponge across one's face.* **2**(**a**) ~ sth from/off sth; ~ sth away/off/up to clear or remove sth by wiping: [Vnpr] *Alison wiped the tears from her eyes.* ○ *wipe the writing off the blackboard* [Vnp] *wipe off one's make-up* ○ *wipe up the spilt milk* ○ *All the fingerprints have been wiped off.* [Vnpr] *(fig infml) Wipe that stupid grin off your face* (ie Stop grinning (GRIN))! (**b**) ~ sth (off/from sth) to remove sth that was recorded on a tape, etc: [Vn, Vnpr] *He found he had wiped the recording (off the tape) by mistake.* [Vnpr] *(fig) The stock market ended 30 points down, wiping $12 billion off share values.* **IDM** **wipe the ˈfloor with sb** *(infml)* to defeat sb thoroughly in an argument or a contest. **wipe sb/sth off the ˌface of the ˈearth / off the ˈmap** to destroy sb/sth completely. **wipe the slate ˈclean** to forget past faults or offences; to make a fresh start. **PHRV** ˌwipe sth ˈout 1** to destroy sth completely: *the campaign to wipe out malaria* ○ *Whole villages were wiped out in the bombing raids.* **2** to cancel sth: *This year's losses have wiped out last year's profits.* **3** to clean the inside of a bowl, etc by rubbing it with a cloth: *Can you wipe out the wine-glasses for me?*

▶ **wipe** *n* **1** an act of wiping sth: *give the table mats a quick wipe.* **2** a thin piece of cloth or soft paper soaked in a liquid that cleans away dirt and bacteria: *Remember to take nappies and baby wipes.*

wiper *n* = WINDSCREEN WIPER.

wire /ˈwaɪə(r)/ *n* **1**(**a**) [U,C] metal in the form of thin flexible thread; a piece of this: *a coil of copper wire* ○ *cut off a length of wire* ○ *Leave the cookies to cool on a wire rack.* ○ *wire coat-hangers.* See also BARBED WIRE, HIGH WIRE, TRIP-WIRE. (**b**) [C,U] a piece of wire used to carry electric current or signals: ˈfuse wire* ○ ˈtelephone wires. (**c**) [U,sing] a barrier, framework, fence, etc made from wire: *The hamster had got through the wire at the front of its cage.* **2** [C] *(infml esp US)* a TELEGRAM: *send sb a wire.* **IDM** **get one's ˈwires crossed** *(infml)* to be mistaken or confused about what sb is saying or has said: *We seem to have got our wires crossed. I thought you were coming yesterday.* **a live wire** ⇨ LIVE[1]. **pull strings; pull wires** ⇨ PULL[1].

▶ **wire** *v* **1** ~ A (on) to B; ~ A and B together to fasten or join one thing to another with wire: [Vnp] *The two pieces of wood were wired together.* [also Vnpr]. **2** *(esp passive)* (**a**) to connect sth to a supply of electricity by means of wires: [Vn] *The house is not wired yet.* [Vnp] *As soon as the equipment is wired up, you can use it.* [also Vnpr]. (**b**) to connect sth/sb to a piece of equipment: [Vnp] *Researchers were wired up with microphones before asking people their views.* [Vpr] *I was wired for sound before being interviewed on TV.* **3**(**a**) *(infml esp US)* to send sb a message by TELEGRAM: [Vn] *I'll wire my parents.* [Vpr.to inf] *He wired to his brother to send some money.* [Vn.that, V.that] *She wired (us) that she would be delayed.* [also Vn.to inf, Vpr.that]. (**b**) ~ sth to sb *(infml esp US)* to send sth to sb by means of a TELEGRAM: [Vnpr, Vnn] *wire money to sb/wire sb money* (ie instruct a bank by TELEGRAM to give money to sb). **wiring** /ˈwaɪərɪŋ/ *n* [U] the system of wires used for supplying electricity to a building, machine, etc: *The wiring is faulty and needs to be replaced.*

wiry /ˈwaɪəri/ *adj* (**-ier, -iest**) (**a**) (of a person) thin but strong. (**b**) stiff and flexible, like wire: *wiry hair.*
■ ˈwire-cutter* *n* *(esp pl)* a tool for cutting wire: *a pair of wire-cutters.*

ˌwire ˈnetting *n* [U] wire woven into a network, used eg for fences.

ˈwire-tapping *n* [U] the activity of listening to other people's telephone conversations by making a secret connection to the telephone line.

ˌwire ˈwool *n* [U] *(Brit)* a mass of very fine pieces of wire, used for cleaning and polishing things. Compare STEEL WOOL.

wireless /ˈwaɪələs/ *n* *(dated)* (**a**) [C] a radio receiving set; a radio(3a): *I heard it on the wireless.* (**b**) [U] the sending and receiving of radio signals: *broadcast by wireless.*

wisdom /ˈwɪzdəm/ *n* [U] **1** the ability to make good and serious judgements because of one's experience and knowledge; the quality of being wise: *moral wisdom* ○ *I question the wisdom of giving a child so much money.* **2** *(fml)* wise thoughts, observations, etc: *listen to sb's* **pearls of wisdom** ○ *the conventional/received wisdom* (ie the generally accepted view) ○ *a woman of great* **wit and wisdom**.
■ ˈwisdom tooth *n* any of the four large teeth at the back of the mouth which usu appear when one is about 20 years old.

wise[1] /waɪz/ *adj* (**-r, -st**) having or showing good judgement based on knowledge and experience: *a wise old man* ○ *a wise choice/decision/precaution/friend* ○ *I'm sure you're wise to wait a few days.* ○ *I'm* **older and wiser** *after 10 years in the business.* Compare UNWISE. **IDM** **be ˌwise after the eˈvent** *(often derog)* to be able to explain sth after it has happened but without having predicted it: *We now know what we should have done — it's easy to be wise after the event.* **be/get ˈwise to sth/sb** *(infml esp US)* to be/become aware of sth or of sb's qualities or behaviour: *He thought he could fool me but I got wise to him.* **none the ˈwiser; not any the ˈwiser** knowing no more than before: *Even after listening to his explanation I'm none the wiser.* **put sb ˈwise (to sth)** *(infml esp US)* to inform sb about sth.
▶ **wise** *v* **PHRV** ˌwise ˈup (to sth) *(infml esp US)* to become aware or informed of sth: *It's about time he wised up to the fact that times have changed.*
wisely *adv.*
■ ˈwise guy *n* *(infml derog)* a person who speaks or behaves as if he or she knows more than other people: *OK, wise guy, what do we do now?*

wise[2] /waɪz/ *n* **IDM** **in no wise** *(arch or rhet)* not at all: *Drug use among young people is in no wise decreasing.*

-wise *suff* (with *ns* forming *adjs* and *advs*) **1** in the manner or direction of: *likewise* ○ *clockwise* ○ *anticlockwise* ○ *lengthwise.* **2** *(infml)* with reference to; as far as sth is concerned: *businesswise* ○ *weatherwise.*

wisecrack /ˈwaɪzkræk/ *n* *(infml)* a clever remark or joke.
▶ **wisecrack** *v* [V] to make wisecracks.

wish /wɪʃ/ *v* **1**(**a**) (with *that* often omitted and the *that*-clause usu in the past tense) to want sth that cannot now happen or that probably will not happen: [V.that] *I wish you hadn't told me all this.* ○ *She wished she had* (ie was sorry she had not) *stayed at home.* ○ *I wish I knew what was going to happen.* ○ *I wish he weren't/wasn't so bad every night.* ○ *I wish I were rich.* [Vn-adj] *He's dead and it's no use wishing him alive again.* (**b**) ~ (for sth) to say or feel that one wants sth, esp sth that can only be achieved by good luck or magic: [Vpr] *It's no use wishing for things you can't have.* ○ *What more could one wish for?* (ie Everything is perfect.) [V] *Shut your eyes and wish.* (**c**) *(fml)* to demand or want sth: [Vn] *I'll do it if that's what you wish.* [V.to inf] *I don't wish* (ie mean) *to be rude, but that's not what you said yesterday.* ○ *She wishes to be alone.* [V.n.to inf] *Do you wish me to leave now?* ⇨ note at HOPE. **2** to say that one hopes sb will have sth, eg as a greeting: [Vnn] *We wish you a Merry Christmas!* ○ *They wished us a pleasant journey.* ○ *His colleagues wished him happiness on his retirement.* ○ *Wish me luck!* **IDM** **(just) as you ˈwish** I am prepared to agree with you or to do what you want: *We can meet at my house or yours,*

W

just as you wish. **PHRV** ˌwish sth aˈway to try to get rid of something by wishing that it did not exist: *These problems can't be wished away, you know.* ˈwish sb/sth on sb (*infml*) (in negative sentences) to want to pass an unpleasant task, visitor, etc on to sb else: *It's not a job I'd wish on anybody.*

▶ wish *n* **1** [C] (**a**) ~ (**to do sth**); ~ (**for sth**) a desire or longing, or an expression of this: *She expressed a wish to be alone.* ○ *He had no wish to intrude on their privacy.* ○ *If you had three wishes what would you choose?* ○ *Her wish came true* (ie She got what she wished for). ○ *You have deliberately acted against my wishes.* (**b**) a thing that is wished for: *You will get your wish.* **2** wishes [pl] ~es (**for sth**) hopes for sb's happiness or welfare, or the expression of these: *with best wishes* (eg at the end of a letter) ○ *We all send our best wishes* (*for your recovery*). **IDM** your wish is my comˈmand (*joc*) I am ready to do whatever you ask. See also DEATH-WISH.

wishful /-fl/ *adj* (*fml*) having or expressing a wish: *It is nothing but a wishful fantasy.* ˌwishful ˈthinking *n* [U] belief based on wishes and not on facts: *There is no evidence to suggest that this forecast is anything but wishful thinking.*

wishbone /ˈwɪʃbəʊn/ *n* a bone shaped like a V between the neck and the breast of a chicken, duck, etc. When the bird is being eaten, the wishbone is sometimes pulled apart by two people, and the one who gets the larger part makes a wish.

wishy-washy /ˈwɪʃi wɒʃi; *US* -wɔːʃi/ *adj* (*derog*) weak in colour, character, quality, etc: *a wishy-washy blue* ○ *a wishy-washy liberal* (ie one whose ideas are not clearly defined).

wisp /wɪsp/ *n* ~ (**of sth**) **1** a small thin bunch, piece or amount of sth: *a wisp of hair/hay/straw/grass* ○ *a wisp of smoke.* **2** a small thin person: *a wisp of a girl.*

▶ wispy *adj* like a wisp or in wisps; not thick or full: *wispy hair/clouds.*

wisteria (also wistaria) /wɪˈstɪəriə/ *n* [U] a climbing plant with long hanging bunches of pale purple or white flowers.

wistful /ˈwɪstfl/ *adj* full of or expressing sad or VAGUE(1) longing, esp for sth that is past or that one cannot have: *wistful eyes* ○ *a wistful mood.* ▶ wistfully /-fəli/ *adv*: *sighing wistfully* ○ *'If only I had known you then,' he said wistfully.* wistfulness *n* [U].

wit /wɪt/ *n* **1**(**a**) [U] the ability to combine words, ideas, etc to produce a clever type of humour: *have a biting/dry/lively/quick wit* ○ *a book full of the wit and wisdom of her 30 years in politics.* (**b**) [C] a person who has or is famous for this: *a well-known wit and raconteur.* **2** [U] (also wits [pl]) quick understanding; intelligence: *a battle of wits* ○ *be frightened/scared/terrified out of one's wits* (ie very frightened) ○ *a chance to pit your wits against* (ie compete with) *our current quiz champion* ○ *It should not be beyond the wit of man to resolve this dispute.* See also HALFWIT. **IDM** at one's wits' ˈend not knowing what to do or say because one is very worried: *I'm at my wits' end worrying about how to pay the bills.* have/keep one's ˈwits about one to be/remain alert and ready to act: *You need to keep your wits about you when you're driving in London.* live by one's wits ⇨ LIVE². to ˈwit (*dated fml*) that is to say: *He seems to have rejected or ignored the committee's main point, to wit, the need for a larger market for coal.*

▶ witless *adj* foolish or stupid: *a witless remark* ○ *be bored/scared witless.*

-witted (forming compound *adjs*) having a particular type of intelligence: ˌdim-ˈwitted ○ ˈsharp-witted. See also QUICK-WITTED.

witty *adj* (-ier, -iest) full of clever humour: *a witty*

speaker/remark. witticism /ˈwɪtɪsɪzəm/ *n* a witty remark. wittily /-ɪli/ *adv*.

witch /wɪtʃ/ *n* (**a**) (esp formerly) a woman thought to have evil magic powers. Witches are often described in fairy stories as wearing a pointed hat and flying on a BROOMSTICK. (**b**) (*derog*) an ugly old woman.

■ the ˈwitching hour *n* [sing] the time when witches are active or sth magical happens, esp midnight.

ˈwitch-doctor *n* (esp formerly in Africa) a doctor with supposed magic powers. Compare MEDICINE MAN.

ˈwitch-hunt *n* (*usu derog*) a campaign directed against people who hold views that are considered unacceptable or a threat to society, etc: *a political witch-hunt.*

witchcraft /ˈwɪtʃkrɑːft; *US* -kræft/ *n* [U] the use of magic powers; esp evil ones.

witch-hazel /ˈwɪtʃ heɪzl/ *n* [U] a liquid obtained from the bark of a N American tree, used for treating minor injuries.

with /wɪð, wɪθ/ *prep* For the special uses of with in phrasal verbs, look at the verb entries. For example, the meaning of bear with sb/sth is given in the phrasal verb section of the entry for bear². **1**(**a**) in the company or presence of sb/sth: *She lives with her parents.* ○ *I went on holiday with a friend.* ○ *Are you coming with us?* ○ *I've got a client with me at the moment.* ○ *Could you put these plates away with the others.* ○ *If you mix blue with yellow you get green.* ○ *Does this tie go with this shirt?* ○ *The money is on the table with the shopping-list.* (**b**) in the care, charge or possession of sb: *I left a message for you with your secretary.* ○ *The keys are with reception.* **2** having or carrying sth: *a girl with* (ie who has) *red hair* ○ *a person with a knowledge of German* ○ *a jacket with a hood* ○ *a house with a swimming-pool* ○ *a man with a suitcase* ○ *They're both in bed with flu.* ○ *He looked at her with a hurt expression.* **3**(**a**) (indicating the tool or instrument used): *feed the baby with a spoon* ○ *sew with cotton thread* ○ *prop the door open with a chair* ○ *You can only see it with a microscope.* ○ *He hit it with a hammer.* ○ *It was easy to translate with a dictionary.* (**b**) (indicating the material or item used): *fill the bowl with water* ○ *sprinkle the dish with salt* ○ *The truck was loaded with timber.* ○ *The floor was covered with broken glass.* ○ *The bag was stuffed with dirty clothes.* **4**(**a**) agreeing with or supporting sb/ sth: *Are you with us on this issue?* (**b**) in opposition to sth; against sth: *fight/argue/quarrel with sb* ○ *in competition with our rivals* ○ *play tennis with sb* ○ *at war with a neighbouring country* ○ *I had an argument with my boss.* **5** because of sth; on account of sth: *blush with embarrassment* ○ *tremble with fear* ○ *shaking with laughter* ○ *Her fingers were numb with cold.* **6** (indicating the manner, circumstances or condition in which sth is done or takes place): *I'll do it with pleasure.* ○ *She performed a somersault with ease.* ○ *He acted with discretion.* ○ *She sleeps with the window open.* ○ *He welcomed her with open arms.* ○ *Don't stand with your hands in your pockets.* ○ *With your permission, sir, I'd like to speak.* **7** in the same direction as sth: *sail with the wind* ○ *swim with the tide* ○ *The shadow moves with the sun.* **8** because of and at the same time as sth: *The shadows lengthened with the approach of sunset.* ○ *Skill comes with practice.* ○ *Good wine will improve with age.* **9** in regard to, towards or concerning sb/sth: *careful with the glasses* ○ *angry with the children* ○ *pleased with the result* ○ *inconsistent with an earlier statement* ○ *a problem with accommodation* ○ *They fell in love with each other.* ○ *What can he want with me?* ○ *What can you do with a chess set?* **10** in the case of sb/sth; as regards sb/sth: *With these students it's pronunciation that's the problem.* ○ *It's a very busy time with* *us at the moment.* **11** and also sth; including sth: *The meal with wine came to £15 each.* ○ *With preparation and marking a day's work works 12 hours a day.* ○ *The week cost us over $500 but that was with skiing lessons.* **12** being an employee or a client of an organization: *I hear he's with ICI now.* ○ *She acted with a touring company for three years.* **13** (indicating separation from sth/sb): *I could never part with this ring.* ○ *Can we dispense with the formalities?* **14** considering one fact in relation to another: *With only two days to go we can't afford to relax.* ○ *She won't be able to help us, with all her family commitments.* ○ *It's much easier compared with last time.* **15** in spite of sth; despite sth: *With all her faults I still love her.* **16** (used in exclamations): *Off to bed with you!* ○ *Down with the Tories!* **IDM** be **'with me/you** (*infml*) to be able to follow what sb is saying: *Are you with me?* ○ *I'm afraid I'm not quite with you.* **'with it** (*infml*) **1** knowing about current fashions and ideas; fashionable: *Come on — get with it!* ○ *a new with-it magazine for teenagers.* **2** understanding what is happening around one; alert: *I'm not very with it today.* **with 'that** immediately after that; then: *He muttered a few words of apology and with that he left.*

withdraw /wɪθˈdrɔː, wɪðˈd-/ *v* (*pt* **withdrew** /-ˈdruː/; *pp* **withdrawn** /-ˈdrɔːn/) **1** ~ **sb/sth (from sth)** **(a)** to move or take sb/sth back or away: [Vn, Vnpr] *The general refused to withdraw his troops from the town.* [Vnpr] *The old coins have been withdrawn from circulation.* [Vn] *The workers have threatened to withdraw their labour* (ie go on strike). **(b)** to remove money from a bank account, etc: [Vn] *I'd like to withdraw £500 please.* **2** (*fml*) to take back a promise, an offer, a statement, etc: [Vn] *withdraw a job application ○ Unless the contract is signed immediately, the offer will be withdrawn.* **3** ~ **(from sth)** to go back or away from a place, an event, etc or from other people: [V] *Heavy bombardment forced the army to withdraw.* [Vpr] *She's beginning to withdraw into herself* (ie stop communicating with other people). ○ *He was forced to withdraw from the race because of injury.*
▶ **withdrawal** /-ˈdrɔːəl/ *n* **1(a)** [U] the action of withdrawing sth/sb or of being withdrawn: *the withdrawal of labour/supplies/support/troops ○ the withdrawal of a product from the market ○ She is showing signs of withdrawal* (ie of not wanting to communicate with other people) *and depression.* **(b)** [C] an instance of this: *You can make withdrawals of up to £250 a day from your account.* **2** [U] the process of stopping taking a drug which one's body has become used to, often accompanied by unpleasant reactions: *get **withdrawal symptoms** after giving up smoking.*
withdrawn *adj* (of a person) not wanting to communicate with others: *He's become increasingly withdrawn since his wife's death.*

wither /ˈwɪðə(r)/ *v* **1** (esp of plants) to dry up and die; to make a plant, etc do this: [V] *The flowers will wither if you don't put them in water soon.* [Vn] *The hot sun had withered the leaves.* **2** ~ **(away)** to become weaker, often before disappearing completely: [Vp] *Their hopes gradually withered away.* [also V].
▶ **withered** *adj* [usu attrib] **1** (of plants) dried and dead: *withered leaves.* **2** (of people or parts of the body) thin and weak because of disease, old age, etc: *withered limbs.*
withering /ˈwɪðərɪŋ/ *adj* (of a look, remark, etc) intended to make sb feel silly or ashamed: *withering sarcasm/scorn ○ She gave him a withering look.*
witheringly *adv*.

withers /ˈwɪðəz/ *n* [pl] the highest part of the back of a horse, between the shoulders. ⇨ picture at HORSE.

withhold /wɪðˈhəʊld, wɪθˈh-/ *v* (*pt, pp* **withheld** /-ˈheld/) ~ **sth (from sb/sth)** to refuse to give sth; to keep sth back: [Vn] *withhold one's consent/permission* [Vn, Vnpr] *He was charged with deliberately withholding information from the police.*

within /wɪˈðɪn/ *prep* **1(a)** after not more than the specified period of time: *I should be back within an hour.* ○ *If you don't hear anything within seven days, phone again.* **(b)** ~ **(of sth)** not further than the specified distance from sth: *a house within a mile of the station ○ The town has three fast-food restaurants within a hundred metres (of each other).* ○ *Is it within walking distance?* **2** inside the range or limits of sth: *We are now **within sight of** (ie able to see) the island.* ○ *There is a bell within the patient's reach.* ○ *He finds it hard to live within his income/means* (ie without spending more than he earns). ○ *I'd prefer you to keep this information within the family* (ie known only by members of the family). ○ *We are now within range of enemy fire.* **3** (*fml*) inside sth/sb: *The noise seems to be coming from within the building.* ○ *Despite her grief, she found a hidden strength within herself.*
▶ **within** *adv* (*fml*) inside: *Cleaner required. Apply within.*

without /wɪˈðaʊt/ *prep* **1** not having, experiencing or showing sth: *two days without food ○ a whole night without sleep ○ a skirt without pockets ○ You can't leave the country without a passport.* ○ *The letter had been posted without a stamp.* ○ *I've come out without any money.* ○ *She spoke without much enthusiasm.* ○ *They were received without ceremony* (ie in an informal manner). **2** in the absence of sb/sth; not accompanied by sb/sth: *He said he couldn't live without her.* ○ *Don't go without me.* **3** not using or taking sth: *Can you see without your glasses? ○ Don't go out without your coat.* **4** (used with the *-ing* form to mean 'not'): *She entered the room without knocking.* ○ *He left without saying goodbye.* ○ *Try and do it without making any mistakes.* ○ *The party was organized without her knowing anything about it.*
▶ **without** *adv part* not having or showing sth: *Do you want a room with a bath or one without?* ○ *If there's no sugar we'll have to do/manage without.*

withstand /wɪðˈstænd, wɪθˈs-/ *v* (*pt, pp* **withstood** /-ˈstʊd/) (*rather fml*) to endure sth without giving in, collapsing, wearing out, etc; to resist sth: [Vn] *withstand attacks/pressure/high winds ○ building materials made to withstand extremes of temperature.*

witless ⇨ WIT.

witness /ˈwɪtnəs/ *n* **1** [C] **(a)** (also **'eye-witness**) a person who sees an event take place and is therefore able to describe it to others: *Were there any witnesses (at the scene) of the accident?* **(b)** a person who gives evidence in a lawcourt after swearing to tell the truth: *a defence/prosecution witness ○ appear as (a) witness for the defence/prosecution ○ The witness was cross-examined by the defending counsel.* **(c)** a person who is present at an event, esp the signing of a document, in order to confirm that it took place: *We need someone to act as (a) witness when we sign the contract.* **2** (*fml*) **(a)** [U] what is said about an event, etc, esp in a lawcourt; evidence: *give witness on behalf of an accused person.* **(b)** [C usu sing] a thing serving as evidence: *This village is a witness to the ravages of war.* **IDM** be **'witness to sth** **1** to see an event take place: *I was witness to a terrible accident.* **2** to be able to confirm that an event took place: *We're both witness to the fact that she lied.* **bear witness** ⇨ BEAR². See also JEHOVAH'S WITNESS.
▶ **witness** *v* **1** to be present at sth and see it: [Vn] *witness an accident/a murder/a quarrel ○ We were witnessing one of the most important scientific developments of the century.* ○ (*fml*) *Weather forecasters are not always right: witness* (ie look at the example of) *their recent mistakes.* **2** to be the place, period,

institution, etc in which certain events take place: [Vn] *Europe witnessed massive political change in the late 1980s.* ○ *The retail trade is witnessing a sharp fall in sales.* **3** to be a witness to the signing of a document, esp by also signing the document oneself: [Vn] *witness the signing of a contract* ○ *witness a signature/treaty/will.* **4** ~ **to sth** (*law or fml*) to give evidence about sth in a lawcourt, etc: [Vpr] *witness to the truth of a statement.*

■ **ˈwitness-box** (*Brit*) (*US* **ˈwitness-stand**) *n* the place in a lawcourt where a witness stands to give evidence.

witter /ˈwɪtə(r)/ *v* ~ **(on) (about sth)** (*infml usu derog*) to speak in a long and sometimes boring way about sth unimportant: [Vpr, Vp] *What are you wittering (on) about?* [also V].

witticism ⇨ WIT.

wittingly /ˈwɪtɪŋli/ *adv* aware of what one is doing; intentionally: *It is clear that, wittingly or unwittingly, he had offended her.*

witty ⇨ WIT.

wives *pl* of WIFE.

wizard /ˈwɪzəd/ *n* **1** (esp in fairy stories) a man who has magical powers. **2** a person with extraordinary skills and abilities: *a financial/computer wizard.*

▶ **wizardry** /-dri/ *n* [U] **1** the practice of magic. **2** extraordinary skill or power: *financial/technical wizardry.*

wizened /ˈwɪznd/ *adj* reduced in size because of age, with many small folds in the skin: *a wizened old woman* ○ *a face wizened with age* ○ *wizened apples.*

woad /wəʊd/ *n* [U] a blue dye with which the ancient Britons used to paint their bodies.

wobble /ˈwɒbl/ *v* ~ **(sth) (about/around)** to move or make sth move from side to side in an unsteady way: [V] *This table wobbles.* ○ *He was very fat and his stomach wobbled as he ran.* [Vp, Vpr] *A child came wobbling along (the pavement) on a bicycle.* [V] (*fig*) *Her voice sometimes wobbles on high notes.* [Vn, Vnp] *Please don't wobble the desk (about) when I'm trying to write.* [also Vnpr].

▶ **wobble** *n* (usu *sing*) a wobbling movement.

wobbly /ˈwɒbli/ *adj* (*infml*) tending to move in an unsteady way from side to side: *a wobbly tooth/chin* ○ *a wobbly line* (ie not drawn straight) ○ *wobbly jelly* ○ *He is still a bit wobbly (on his legs) after his illness.* — *n* IDM **throw a ˈwobbly** (*Brit infml*) to have a fit of nervous anger: *My parents threw a wobbly when I told them.*

wodge /wɒdʒ/ *n* ~ **(of sth)** (*Brit infml*) a large piece or amount: *a thick wodge of ten-pound notes.*

woe /wəʊ/ *n* (*dated or fml or joc*) **1** [U] great sorrow or distress: *a tale of woe.* **2 woes** [pl] things that cause sorrow or distress; troubles: *financial/economic woes.* IDM **woe beˈtide sb**; **ˈwoe to sb** (*fml or joc*) there will be trouble for sb: *Woe betide anyone who arrives late!* ○ *Woe to the person who dares to criticize her!* **ˌwoe is ˈme!** *interj* (*arch or joc*) how unhappy I am!

woebegone /ˈwəʊbɪɡɒn; *US* -ɡɔːn/ *adj* (*fml*) looking unhappy: *a woebegone child/expression/face.*

woeful /ˈwəʊfl/ *adj* (*fml*) **1** full of sorrow; very sad: *a woeful cry/look/sight.* **2** (*usu attrib*) very bad; deserving disapproval: *display woeful ignorance.* ▶ **woefully** *adv* /-fəli/ *The preparations were woefully inadequate.*

wog /wɒɡ/ *n* (⚠ *Brit sl offensive*) a person who does not have a white skin.

wok /wɒk/ *n* a large pan shaped like a bowl, used for cooking esp Chinese food. ⇨ picture at PAN[1].

woke *pt* of WAKE[1].

woken *pp* of WAKE[1].

wold /wəʊld/ *n* (esp *pl*, in the names of places) (in Britain) a piece of high open land that is not cultivated: *the Lincolnshire wolds.*

jackal   wolf   wolf

wolf /wʊlf/ *n* (*pl* **wolves** /wʊlvz/) a wild animal that looks like a dog and that lives and hunts in groups: *a pack of wolves* ○ *a she-wolf with her cubs.* IDM **cry wolf** ⇨ CRY[1]. **keep the ˈwolf from the door** to have enough money to avoid hunger and need: *I earn enough to keep the wolf from the door.* **a lone wolf** ⇨ LONE. **throw sb to the ˈwolves** to leave sb to be roughly treated or criticized without trying to help or defend them. **a wolf in sheep's ˈclothing** a person who appears friendly or harmless but is really an enemy.

▶ **wolf** *v* ~ **sth (down)** to eat sth in a very quick and hungry way: *He wolfed down his breakfast and rushed out.*

wolfish *adj* of or like a wolf: *a wolfish grin.*

■ **ˈwolf-whistle** *n* a rising and falling whistle sound made by a man to show that he finds a woman, esp one passing in the street, attractive. — *v* [V, Vpr] ~ **(at sb)** to make a wolf-whistle.

wolfhound /ˈwʊlfhaʊnd/ *n* a very large dog originally used for hunting wolves: *an Irish wolfhound.*

woman /ˈwʊmən/ *n* (*pl* **women** /ˈwɪmɪn/) **1** [C] an adult human female being: *men, women and children* ○ *a single/married/divorced woman* ○ *I'd prefer a woman doctor to examine me.* ○ *a ˈwoman friend* ○ *my ˈwomen friends.* **2** [C] a wife, female lover or GIRLFRIEND: *He's got a new woman, I think.* **3** [sing without *a* or *the*] female human beings in general; the female sex: *the age-old differences between man and woman.* **4** [C] a female worker or woman under the authority of sb else: *In the old days we had a woman who used to come in and do the cleaning.* **5** (used as a form of address, esp in a lively, angry or IMPATIENT(1b) way): *Don't just stand there, woman — do something!* IDM **be twice the man/woman** ⇨ TWICE. **the inner man/woman** ⇨ INNER. **make an honest woman of sb** ⇨ HONEST. **a man/woman of parts** ⇨ PART[1]. **a man/woman of his/her word** ⇨ WORD. **a man/woman of the world** ⇨ WORLD.

▶ **-woman** (forming compound *ns*) **1(a)** (with *ns*) a woman who lives in the place specified: *a countrywoman.* **(b)** (with *adjs* and *ns*) a female native of the country specified: *an Irishwoman.* **2** (with *ns*) a woman concerned with sth: *a ˈhorsewoman* ○ *a ˈsportswoman.* Compare -MAN.

womanish *adj* (*derog*) (of a man) like a woman; suitable for women but not for men: *He has a rather womanish manner.*

womanize, -ise /-aɪz/ *v* [V] (*usu derog*) (of a man) to have sexual affairs with many women. **womanizer, -iser** *n*: *He's a terrible womanizer.*

womanly *adj* (*approv*) like a woman; FEMININE: *a womanly figure* ○ *womanly qualities/virtues.* **womanliness** *n* [U].

■ **ˌWomen's Libeˈration** (also *infml* **ˌWomen's ˈLib** /lɪb/) *n* [U] the freedom of women to have the same social and economic rights as men; the movement that aims to achieve this. **ˌWomen's ˈLibber** *n* (*dated infml*) a person who supports or promotes Women's Liberation.

the ˈwomen's movement *n* [sing] the social and political movement promoting the idea that men and women should have equal rights in society, and aiming to achieve this by legal means and by changing people's attitudes.

womanhood /ˈwʊmənhʊd/ [U] **1** the state of being a woman: *grow to/reach womanhood.* **2** women in general: *German womanhood.*

[V.*to* inf] = verb + *to* infinitive   [Vn.inf (no *to*)] = verb + noun + infinitive without *to*   [V.*ing*] = verb + *-ing* form

womankind /'wʊmənkaɪnd/ n [U] (fml) women in general: *the sufferings of womankind.*

womb /wuːm/ n (anatomy) (in women and certain other female animals) the organ in which the baby or young is carried while it develops before birth. ⇨ picture at FEMALE.

wombat /'wɒmbæt/ n an Australian wild animal like a small bear, the female of which carries its young in a pocket of skin on its body.

womenfolk /'wɪmɪnfəʊk/ n [pl] (fml or joc) women, esp the women of a family or community considered together: *The dead soldiers were mourned by their womenfolk.* Compare MENFOLK.

won pt, pp of WIN.

wonder /'wʌndə(r)/ n **(a)** [U] a feeling of surprise and delight, caused by sth beautiful, unusual or unexpected: *They were filled with wonder at the sight.* ○ *We gazed at the painting in silent wonder.* **(b)** [C] a thing or an event that causes this feeling: *the wonders of modern technology* ○ *the seven wonders of the ancient world* ○ *a wonder drug* (ie one that has extremely good effects). **IDM** **a chinless wonder** ⇨ CHINLESS. **do/work miracles/wonders** ⇨ MIRACLE. **it's no/little/small 'wonder (that)...** it is not/not very surprising: *No wonder you were late!* ○ *Small wonder (that) he was so tired!* **it's a 'wonder (that)...** it's surprising or strange that ...: *It's a wonder (that) no one was hurt.* **a nine days' wonder** ⇨ DAY. **wonders will never 'cease** (saying usu ironic) (expressing surprise and pleasure at sth, often sth unimportant): *'I've washed the car for you.' 'Wonders will never cease!'*

▶ **wonder** v **1(a)** ~ (about sth) to feel CURIOUS(1) about sth; to ask oneself questions: [V.wh] *I wonder who he is.* ○ *I wonder why she left in such a hurry.* ○ *I was beginning to wonder what had happened to you.* [Vpr] *I was just wondering about that myself.* [V.speech] *'What will happen now?' she wondered.* **(b)** (used as a polite way of introducing a request or question) [V.wh] *I wonder if/whether you could help me.* ○ *I was wondering if you were free this evening.* **2** ~ (at sth) (fml) to feel great surprise and admiration: [V] *He could do nothing but stand and wonder.* [Vpr] *Her grace and beauty can only be wondered at.* [V.that] *I don't wonder (that) you got angry — I would have done too.* **IDM** **I shouldn't 'wonder** (infml) I should not be surprised (to discover): *He charges it all to his expense account, I shouldn't wonder.*

wonderful /-fl/ adj **(a)** good, pleasant or enjoyable: *a wonderful day/person/opportunity* ○ *My holiday was absolutely wonderful.* ○ *It's wonderful to see you again.* ○ *It's wonderful that they managed to escape.* **(b)** causing wonder; remarkable: *It's wonderful what they can do these days.* **wonderfully** /-fəli/ adv **(a)** extremely; extremely well: *wonderfully happy/healthy/relaxed* ○ *Everything worked out wonderfully.* **(b)** unusually; surprisingly (SURPRISE): *She is wonderfully active for her age.*

wonderingly /'wʌndrɪŋli/ adv: *She looked at him wonderingly.*

wonderment n [U] pleasant surprise; wonder(1a): *They gazed at the food in wonderment.*

wondrous /'wʌndrəs/ adj (arch or fml) wonderful: *a wondrous sight.* **wondrously** adv.

wonderland /'wʌndəlænd/ n (usu sing) a land or place full of wonderful things.

wonky /'wɒŋki/ adj (Brit infml) unsteady or weak: *a wonky chair.*

wont /wəʊnt; US wɔːnt/ adj [pred] ~ (to do sth) (dated or rhet) in the habit of doing sth; used to doing sth: *He was wont to fall asleep during meals.* ▶ **wont** n [sing] (fml or rhet) a custom; a habit: *She got up early, as was her wont.*

won't short form will not. ⇨ WILL¹.

woo /wuː/ v (pt, pp **wooed**) **1** to try to obtain the

support of sb: [Vn] *woo voters/investors/clients* [also Vnp, Vnpr, Vn.to inf]. **2** (dated) [Vn] to try to gain the love of a woman in order to marry her.

wood /wʊd/ n **1(a)** [U] the hard material that the trunk and branches of a tree are made of. **(b)** this substance, cut and used as building material, fuel, etc: *Most furniture is made of wood.* ○ *He chopped some wood for the fire.* ○ *wood-carving* ○ *a wood floor.* See also FIREWOOD. **(c)** [C] a particular type of this: *Pine is a soft wood.* See also HARDWOOD, SOFTWOOD. **2** [C often pl] an area of land, smaller than a forest, covered with growing trees: *go for a walk in the wood(s).* **3** [C] (sport) a bowl²(1). **4** [C] a golf club with a head made of wood. Compare IRON¹ 4, DEAD WOOD. **IDM** **from the 'wood** (of alcoholic drinks) from a wooden barrel: *beer from the wood.* **neck of the woods** ⇨ NECK. **not see the ,wood for the 'trees** to fail to see or understand the main point, subject, etc because one is paying too much attention to details: *If you add too many notes to the text, the reader won't be able to see the wood for the trees.* **,out of the 'wood(s)** (infml) (usu with a negative) free from trouble or difficulties: *She's regained consciousness, but she's not out of the woods* (ie sure to recover) *yet.* **touch wood** ⇨ TOUCH¹.

▶ **wooded** adj (of land) covered with growing trees: *a wooded valley.*

wooden /'wʊdn/ adj **1** [esp attrib] made of wood: *wooden furniture/fences/toys.* **2** (of sb's behaviour) stiff and awkward; not natural: *The acting was rather wooden, I thought.* **woodenly** adv stiffly and awkwardly: *The lines were delivered woodenly.*

woodenness n [U]. **the ,wooden 'spoon** n [sing] (Brit infml) an imaginary prize that is thought of as being won by the person, team, etc coming last in a race, competition, etc.

woody adj **(a)** covered with growing trees: *a woody hillside.* **(b)** of or like growing wood: *a plant with woody stems.*

■ **'wood pulp** n [U] wood broken or crushed into small pieces and used for making paper.

woodblock /'wʊdblɒk/ n each of the small pieces of wood used in making a floor, often arranged in a pattern: *a woodblock floor.*

woodchuck /'wʊdtʃʌk/ n (US) a small N American animal of the SQUIRREL family.

woodcock /'wʊdkɒk/ n (pl unchanged) [C] a brown bird hunted for food or sport. It has a long straight beak, short legs and a short tail.

woodcut /'wʊdkʌt/ n a print made from a design, drawing, etc cut in a block of wood.

woodcutter /'wʊdkʌtə(r)/ n (dated) a person whose job is cutting down trees.

woodland /'wʊdlənd/ n [U] land covered with trees; woods: *ancient/mixed/local woodland* ○ *woodland scenery.*

woodlouse /'wʊdlaʊs/ n (pl **-lice**) /-laɪs/ a small creature like an insect that lives in decaying wood, damp soil, etc.

woodman /'wʊdmən/ (also **'woodsman** /-zmən/) n (pl **-men** /-mən/) a man who works in a wood or forest, looking after and sometimes cutting down trees.

woodpecker /'wʊdpekə(r)/ n a bird that climbs trees and taps them rapidly with its beak to find insects. ⇨ picture.

woodpecker
— beak

woodpigeon /'wʊdpɪdʒɪn/ n a large wild pigeon.

woodshed /'wʊdʃed/ n a shed where wood is stored, esp for fuel.

woodwind /'wʊdwɪnd/ n [Gp] the set of musical

instruments in an ORCHESTRA which are mostly made of metal or wood and are played by blowing; the players of these: *The flute, the clarinet and the oboe are woodwind instruments.* ○ *the woodwind section.* ⇨ picture at MUSICAL INSTRUMENT.

woodwork /'wʊdwɜːk/ *n* [U] **1** things made of wood, esp the wooden parts of a building, eg doors, stairs, etc: *The woodwork is painted white* ○ (*joc*) *He hit the woodwork* (ie the wooden frame of the goal) *twice before scoring.* **2** (also **'woodworking**) the activity or skill of making things from wood.

woodworm /'wʊdwɜːm/ *n* (**a**) [C] a worm that eats wood, making many small holes in it. (**b**) [U] the holes caused by this: *The beams are riddled with woodworm.*

woof[1] /wʊf/ *interj, n* (*infml*) the barking sound made by a dog.

woof[2] /wuːf; *US also* wʊf/ *n* = WEFT.

woofer /'wuːfə(r)/ *n* a LOUDSPEAKER designed to reproduce low notes accurately. Compare TWEETER.

wool /wʊl/ *n* (**a**) [U] the fine soft hair that forms the coats of sheep, goats and certain other animals: *These goats are specially bred for their wool.* (**b**) [U] thread, cloth, clothing, etc made from this: *a ball of knitting wool* ○ *a wool coat/blanket.* **IDM** **pull the wool over sb's eyes** ⇨ PULL[1]. See also COTTON WOOL, DYED-IN-THE-WOOL, STEEL WOOL, WIRE WOOL.

▶ **woollen** (*US* **woolen**) /'wʊlən/ *adj* [usu attrib] made entirely or partly of wool: *woollen material/blankets/gloves.* **woollens** (*US* **woolens**) *n* [pl] clothes made of wool, esp knitted ones: *a special wash programme for woollens.*

woolly (*US* **wooly**) /'wʊli/ *adj* **1**(**a**) covered with wool or hair like wool: *woolly sheep* ○ *the dog's woolly coat.* (**b**) like or made of wool; woollen: *a woolly hat.* **2** (also **woolly-'headed**, **woolly-'minded**) *adj* (*Brit*) (of people or their minds, arguments, ideas, etc) not thinking clearly; not clearly expressed or thought out. — *n* (*infml*) a woollen garment, esp a JERSEY(1): *wearing winter woollies.* **woolliness** *n* [U].

■ **'wool-gathering** *n* [U] lack of attention to sth because one is thinking of other things.

woozy /'wuːzi/ *adj* (*infml*) feeling unsteady, confused or sick, esp as a result of drinking too much alcohol.

wop /wɒp/ *n* (⚠ *sl offensive*) a person from southern Europe, esp an Italian.

word /wɜːd/ *n* **1**(**a**) [C] a sound or group of sounds that expresses a meaning and forms an independent unit of a language: *What's the Spanish word for table?* ○ *Tell me what happened in your own words.* ○ *He couldn't put his feelings into words* (ie express them). ○ *I have no words/can't find words to express* (ie I have no adequate way of indicating) *my gratitude.* (**b**) [C] this represented as letters or symbols, usu with a space on either side: *That word is not spelled correctly.* ○ *The words in the dictionary are arranged in alphabetical order.* See also FOURLETTER WORD, HOUSEHOLD WORD. **2**(**a**) [C] anything said; a remark or statement: *a word/a few words of advice/sympathy/warning* ○ *a man/woman of few words* (ie one who does not talk very much) ○ *Can I have a quick word with you?* ○ *I don't believe a word of his story.* ○ *She left without a word.* (**b**) **words** [pl] things that are said, contrasted with things that are done: *We want fewer words and more deeds.* See also WAR OF WORDS. **3** [sing] a promise or guarantee: *I never doubted/questioned her word.* ○ *I give you my word that this won't happen again.* ○ *We only have his word for it that the cheque is in the post.* ○ *As I expected, they kept/broke their word.* ○ *I trust her not to go back on her word.* **4** [sing] (*dated or fml*) (**a**) (without *a* or *the*) a piece of news; a message: *Please send (me)/leave word of your safe arrival/ that you have arrived safely.* (**b**) **the word** the

rumour: *The word is that he's left the country.* **5** (usu **the word**) [sing] a spoken command or signal: *Stay hidden until I give the word.* ○ *He likes to think that his word is law* (ie his commands will be obeyed). **6 the Word** (also the **word of 'God**) [sing] the Bible and its teachings: *preach the Word.* **IDM** **actions speak louder than words** ⇨ ACTION. **be as good as one's word** to do what one has promised to do: *You'll find that she's as good as her word.* **be lost for words** ⇨ LOST[2]. **be not the 'word for sth/sb** (*infml*) to be an inadequate description of sth/sb: *Lazy isn't the word for it! He never does any work at all.* **breathe a word** ⇨ BREATHE. **by word of 'mouth** in spoken, not written, words: *The news spread by word of mouth.* **a dirty word** ⇨ DIRTY[1]. **eat one's words** ⇨ EAT. **fighting talk/words** ⇨ FIGHT[1]. **(right) from the word 'go** (*infml*) right from the start: *She knew (right) from the word go that it was going to be difficult.* **(not) get a word in 'edgeways** (not) to be able to interrupt sb who talks a great deal. **hang on sb's words / on sb's every word** ⇨ HANG[1]. **not have a good word to 'say for sb/sth** (*infml*) not to say anything at all favourable about sb/sth: *He doesn't have/seldom has a good word to say for his brothers.* **have, etc the last word** ⇨ LAST[1]. **have a word in sb's 'ear** to speak to sb privately. **have 'words (with sb) (about sth)** to quarrel or argue with sb about sth: *I could hear them having words in the next room.* **in 'other words** expressed in a different way; that is to say: *It was a perfectly ordinary day; in other words, I went to work and came home again.* **(not) in so many 'words** (not) in exactly the same words as are claimed or reported to have been used: *'Did she say she hated you?' 'Not in so many words but it was obvious that she did.'* **in a 'word** briefly: *In a word, I think he's a fool.* **in words of one 'syllable** using very simple language. **the last word** ⇨ LAST[1]. **a man/woman of his/her 'word** a person who does what he or she has promised to do. **mum's the word!** ⇨ MUM[2]. **(upon) my 'word!** (*dated or fml*) (an exclamation expressing surprise): *My word, you're back early!* **not know the meaning of the word** ⇨ KNOW. **not mince words** ⇨ MINCE. **not a 'word (to sb) (about sth)** don't say anything: *Not a word (to Mary) (about what I've told you)!* **the operative word** ⇨ OPERATIVE. **a play on words** ⇨ PLAY[2]. **the printed word** ⇨ PRINT[2]. **put in/say a (good) 'word for sb** say sth in sb's favour in order to help them. **put 'words into sb's mouth** to suggest that sb has said sth when they have not: *She accused the journalist of putting words into her mouth.* **say/be one's last/final 'word (on sth)** to give/be one's final opinion or decision: *That's unlikely to be her last word on the subject.* **say the word** ⇨ SAY. **take sb at their 'word** to assume that sb means exactly what they say or promise. **take sb's 'word for it (that …)** to accept that what sb says is true or correct: *I can't prove I'm not lying — you'll just have to take my word for it.* **take the 'words (right) out of sb's mouth** to say what sb else was about to say. **too funny, outrageous, sad, shocking, etc for 'words** so funny, etc that it cannot be expressed in words; extremely funny, etc: *The whole situation was too stupid for words.* **weigh one's words** ⇨ WEIGH. **word for 'word** in exactly the same or (when translated) exactly equivalent words: *His story matches yours almost word for word.* ○ *a word-for-word ac'count/trans'lation.* **sb's word is as good as their 'bond** sb's promise can be relied upon completely. **one's word of 'honour** a solemn promise: *I give you my word of honour I didn't do it.*

▶ **word** *v* (esp passive) to express sth in particular words: [Vnadv] *a carefully worded reminder* ○ *Be careful how you word your reply.* [also Vnpr]. **wording** *n* [U,C usu *sing*] the words used to express sth;

the way in which sth is expressed: *a complicated form of wording.*

wordless *adj* (*fml*) not expressed in words: *wordless grief/sympathy.* **wordlessly** *adv.*

wordy *adj* (*derog*) using or expressed in too many words: *an eloquent, if rather wordy, speech.* **wordily** /-ɪli/ *adv.* **wordiness** *n* [U].

■ ˌword-ˈperfect (*US* ˌletter-ˈperfect) *adj* able to say or repeat sth from memory without making any mistakes.

ˈ**word processor** *n* a computer that records typed words, diagrams, etc and displays them on a screen, where they can be corrected or changed and then automatically printed. Compare TYPEWRITER. ˈ**word processing** *n* [U] work on a word processor: *word-processing skills.*

wordplay /ˈwɜːdpleɪ/ *n* [U] the clever or amusing use of words, esp involving a word that has two meanings or different words that sound the same.

wore *pt* of WEAR¹.

work¹ /wɜːk/ *n* **1** [U] the use of physical strength or mental power in order to do or make sth: *His success was due to sheer hard work.* ○ *The work of building the bridge took six months.* ○ *Years of research work have failed to produce a cure for the disease.* ○ *The study of butterflies has been her life's work.* ○ *He never does a stroke of* (ie any) *work.* ○ *She put/set them to work painting the fence.* ○ *The work of calculating tax deductions is done by computer.* See also DONKEY-WORK. ⇨ note. **2** [U] (**a**) tasks that need to be done: *There is plenty of work to be done in the garden.* ○ *I have some work for you to do.* See also FIELDWORK, HOMEWORK 1. (**b**) materials needed or used for this: *She took her work* (eg books and papers) *with her into the garden.* ○ *She often brings work* (eg files and documents) *home with her from the office.* ○ *His work was spread all over the floor.* See also PAPERWORK. **3** [U] (**a**) a thing or things produced as a result of work: *an exhibition of the work of young sculptors* ○ *Is this all your own work?* (ie Did you do it without help from others?) ○ *The craftsmen sell their work to visitors.* ○ *She produced an excellent piece of work in the final examination.* (**b**) the result of an action; what is done by sb: *The damage to the painting is the work of vandals.* **4** [U] (**a**) what a person does as an occupation, esp in order to earn money; employment: *It is difficult to find work in the present economic climate.* ○ *When did you start work here?* ○ *She had been out of work* (ie without a job) *for a year.* ○ *She's now back in work* (ie She has a job) *again.* ○ *Police work is mainly routine.* ○ *The accountant described his work to the sales staff.* ○ *full-time/part-time/unpaid/ voluntary work* ○ *work experience* ○ *work clothes.* See also PIECE-WORK, SOCIAL WORK. (**b**) (without *the*) a place where one does this: *She goes to/leaves for work at 8 o'clock.* ○ *What time do you arrive at/get to work in the morning?* ○ *I have to leave work early today.* ○ *Her friends from work came to see her in hospital.* **5** [C often *pl*] a book, piece of music, painting, etc: *the collected/complete works of Tolstoy* ○ *He recognized the sketch as an early work by Degas.* Compare WORK OF ART, OPUS. **6** [U] (*physics*) the use of force to produce movement. See also JOULE. **7** (in compounds) (**a**) (forming words for things made of the specified material or the activity of making them): ˈ*wickerwork* ○ ˈ*woodwork* ○ ˈ*metalwork.* (**b**) (forming words for things made or work done with the specified tool): ˈ*needlework* ○ ˈ*brushwork.* (**c**) (forming words for decoration of a specified type): ˈ*latticework* ○ ˈ*paintwork.* (**d**) (forming words for structures of the specified type): ˈ*framework* ○ ˈ*network* ○ ˈ*bodywork.* **8 the works** [pl] the moving parts of a machine, etc; the mechanism: *the works of a clock.* **9 works** [pl] (esp in compounds) operations involving building or repair: ˈ*roadworks* ○ ˌ*public*

ˈ**works.** **10 works** [sing or pl *v*] (esp in compounds) a place where industrial or manufacturing processes are carried out: *an engi*ˈ*neering works* ○ *a* ˈ*brick-works* ○ *There has been an accident at the works.* ⇨ note at FACTORY. **11 the works** [pl] (*infml*) everything: *She was wearing a tiara, a diamond necklace and a gold bracelet — the works!* **IDM** **all in a day's work** ⇨ DAY. **at** ˈ**work** having an effect; operating: *She suspected that secret influences were at work.* **at** ˈ**work (on sth)** busy doing sth: *He is still at work on the painting.* ○ *Danger — men at work!* (ie on a road sign). **dirty work** ⇨ DIRTY¹. **get (down) to / set to** ˈ**work (on sth / to do sth)** to begin; to make a start. **give sb/sth the** ˈ**works** (*infml*) **1** to give or tell sb everything. **2** to give sb/sth the full or best possible treatment: *They gave the car the works and it looks like new.* **3** to treat sb harshly or violently. **go/set about one's** ˈ**work** to do/start to do one's work: *She went cheerfully about her work.* ˌ**good** ˈ**works** kind acts to help others. **have one's** ˈ**work cut out (doing sth)** (*infml*) to have difficulty doing sth, esp in the available time: *You'll have your work cut out getting there by nine o'clock.* **make hard work of sth** ⇨ HARD¹. **make light work of sth** ⇨ LIGHT³. **make short work of sth/sb** ⇨ SHORT¹. **many hands make light work** ⇨ HAND¹. **a nasty piece of work** ⇨ NASTY. **nice work if you can get it** ⇨ NICE. **shoot the works** ⇨ SHOOT¹. **a spanner in the works** ⇨ SPANNER. **too much like hard work** ⇨ HARD¹. **the work of a** ˈ**moment,** ˈ**second, etc** a thing that takes a very short time to do: *It was the work of a few minutes to hide the damage.*

■ ˈ**work-basket** (*Brit*) (*US* ˈ**work-bag**) *n* a container for sewing materials, eg thread and needles.

ˌ**work of** ˈ**art** *n* (*pl* **works of art**) a picture, poem, building, statue, etc: *a display of works of art* ○ (*fig*) *The decoration on the cake was a work of art.*

ˈ**work-shy** *adj* (*derog*) having a reputation for not working hard; lazy.

ˈ**work surface** *n* = WORKTOP.

ˈ**work table** *n* a table on which work is done, esp one with drawers for eg sewing materials.

NOTE Work, labour and toil are uncountable nouns meaning work as physical or mental activity. **Work** is the most general: *Looking after children all day is hard work.* **Labour** suggests a lot of physical effort: *I was trained as a builder so I'm used to manual labour.* **Toil** is a formal or literary word and means hard work over a long period of time: *A lifetime of hard toil on the farm made him look old and tired.*

Job and **task** are countable nouns meaning a piece of work that a person does. **Job** is general and may be difficult or easy, pleasant or unpleasant: *I have a few jobs to do in the house this morning.* ○ *I've been given the enjoyable job of presenting the prizes.* **Job** can also mean an occupation: *She's had the same job for five years.* A **task** is usually a small job which you may not enjoy, and may not want to do: *The teacher gave the children some holiday tasks.* **Task** can also mean something important that must be done in order to achieve something bigger in the future: *The police face a very difficult task dealing with the increase in violent crime.*

Piece of work is used when referring to work involving writing, art or mental skills: *I have three pieces of written work to do by the end of term.* It can also mean the finished piece of writing, drawing, etc: *Make sure each child puts a piece of their work on the wall.*

work² /wɜːk/ *v* **1** ~ **(away) (at/on sth);** ~ **(under sb)** to do sth that involves physical or mental activity, esp in one's job: [Vp, Vpr] *I've been working (away) at my essay all day.* [Vn, Vpr] *Staff work (for) 35 hours per week.* [Vpr] *I worked under her* (ie with her as my manager) *for two years.* ○ *He is working on*

a new novel. ○ *This craftsman works in leather* (ie makes leather goods). **2 ~ (for sb/sth)** to have a job: [V] *Most people have to work in order to live.* ○ *She isn't working now* (eg because she has not got a job or has retired). [Vpr] *She works for an engineering company.* **3** to make oneself/sb work: [Vnadv] *She works herself too hard.* [also Vnpr]. **4 ~ against/for sth** to make efforts to defeat sth or to achieve sth: [Vpr] *a statesman who works for peace* [V.*to* inf] *The committee is working to get the prisoners freed.* **5(a)** (of a machine, device, etc) to function; to operate: [V] *a lift/bell/switch that doesn't work* [Vadv] *The gears work smoothly.* [Vpr] *It works by electricity.* **(b)** to make a machine, device, etc operate: [Vn] *Do you know how to work the lathe?* ○ *The machine is worked by wind power.* **6 ~ (on sb/sth)** to have the desired result or effect on sb/sth: [V, Vpr] *Did the cleaning stuff work (on that stain)?* (ie Did it remove it?) [V] *My plan worked, and I got them to agree.* [Vpr] *His charm doesn't work on me* (ie does not affect or impress me). **7** to manage or operate sth so as to gain benefit from it: [Vn] *work a mine/an oil well* ○ *work the land* (ie cultivate it) ○ *He works the North Wales area* (eg selling a company's goods). **8** to cause or produce sth as a result of effort: [Vn] *work mischief/havoc/magic* ○ *work a cure/change/ miracle.* **9 ~ sth (into sth)** to make or shape sth by eg hammering, pressing or stretching it: [Vn] *work gold/iron* ○ *work clay* (ie mix water into it) ○ *work dough* (ie when making bread) [Vnpr] *work the mixture into a paste.* See also WROUGHT. **10 ~ sth (on sth)** to sew a design onto a piece of cloth; to EMBROIDER sth: [Vn, Vnpr] *work (a floral pattern on) a cushion cover.* **11** (of a person's features) to move violently: to TWITCH: [V] *He stared at me in horror, his face working.* **12** to move or pass into or through sth, usu gradually: [Vp, Vnp] *Rain has worked (its way) in through the roof.* [Vpr] *The back of your shirt has worked out of your trousers.* [also Vnpr]. **13** to become or make sth free, loose, etc through pressure, rapid movement, etc: [V-adj, Vn-adj] *I was tied up, but managed to work (myself) free.* ○ *The screw had worked (itself) loose.* [Vnpr] *Work the nail out of the wood.* **IDM** Most idioms containing **work** are at the entries for the nouns or adjectives in the idioms, eg **work to rule** ⇨ RULE; **work like a charm** ⇨ CHARM¹. **ˈwork it** (*infml*) to arrange matters in a particular way: *Can you work it so that we get free tickets?* **PHRV** ˌwork aˈround/ ˈround to sth/sb to approach a topic, subject, etc gradually: *It was some time before he worked around to what he really wanted to say.*
ˌwork sth ˈin to try to include sth: *Can't you work in a few more jokes?*
ˌwork sth ˈoff **1** to earn money in order to be able to pay a debt: *work off a large bank loan.* **2** to make sth less in amount or intensity: *work off one's anger on sb* ○ *work off excess weight by regular exercise.*
ˌwork ˈout **1** to develop in a specified way; to turn out (TURN¹): *Things have worked out quite well for us.* **2** to train the body by vigorous physical exercise: *I work out regularly to keep fit.* **3** to be capable of being solved: *The sum/problem doesn't work out.*
ˌwork sb ˈout to understand sb's character: *I've never been able to work her out.* ˌwork sth ˈout **1** to calculate sth: *I've worked out your share of the cost at £10.50.* **2** to find the answer to sth; to solve sth: *work out a problem/puzzle/coded message* ○ *Can you work out what these squiggles mean?* **3** to plan or DEVISE sth: *I've worked out a new marketing strategy.* ○ *a well worked-out scheme.* **4** (usu passive) to remove all the coal, minerals, etc from a mine over a period of time: *a worked-out silver mine.* ˌwork ˈout at sth to be equal to sth; to have sth as a total: *What does our share of the bill work out at?*
ˌwork sb ˈover (*sl*) to beat sb thoroughly, eg to

make them give one information: *He'd been worked over by the gang because he couldn't pay.*
ˌwork ˈround to sth/sb ⇨ WORK AROUND/ROUND TO STH/SB.
ˈwork to sth to follow a plan, TIMETABLE, etc: *work to a budget* ○ *We're working to a very tight deadline* (ie We have little time in which to do the work).
ˈwork towards sth to try to reach or achieve a goal: *We're working towards common objectives.*
ˌwork sth ˈup to develop or improve sth gradually: *work up support for the party* ○ *I can't work up any enthusiasm for his idea.* ˌwork sb/oneself ˈup (into sth) to make sb/oneself gradually reach a state of great excitement, anger, anxiety, etc: *Don't work yourself up/get worked up over such a trivial matter.* ˌwork sth ˈup into sth to bring sth to a more complete or more satisfactory state: *I'm working my notes up into a dissertation.* ˌwork ˈup to sth to develop to a point of great intensity, etc: *The music worked up to a rousing finale.* ○ *I wonder what all this is working up to?*
■ ˌwork-to-ˈrule *n* a form of protest by workers, in which they strictly observe rules made by their employers and the terms of their contracts, and refuse to work for any extra time.

workable /ˈwɜːkəbl/ *adj* **1** that can be done, used, etc successfully; practical: *This plan simply isn't workable.* **2** (of a mine, etc) that is profitable to work²(7). **3** that can be spread, shaped, etc: *The glue remains workable for 15 minutes.*

workaday /ˈwɜːkədeɪ/ *adj* [usu attrib] not unusual or especially interesting; ordinary: *simple workaday food.*

workaholic /ˌwɜːkəˈhɒlɪk/ *n* (*infml usu derog*) a person who has a strong desire to work hard and finds it difficult to stop working.

workbench /ˈwɜːkbentʃ/ *n* a table used for doing practical jobs, esp working with wood or metal.

workbook /ˈwɜːkbʊk/ *n* a book for students that gives information on a subject together with exercises to help them to practise what they have learned.

workday /ˈwɜːkdeɪ/ (also **working day**) *n* a day on which one usu does one's job: *Saturday is a workday for him.*

worker /ˈwɜːkə(r)/ *n* **1(a)** (often in compounds) a person who works, esp one who does a particular type of work: *car/factory/office/rescue workers.* See also BLUE-COLLAR, GUEST WORKER, WHITE-COLLAR. **(b)** a person who works in the specified way: *a good/ hard/quick/slow worker.* **(c)** (*infml*) a person who works hard: *That girl is certainly a worker!* **2** an employee, esp one who does MANUAL work: *Workers are in dispute with management about the pay freeze.* ○ *worker participation in decision-making.* **3** a female bee which works in a colony of bees but does not reproduce: *a worker bee.* Compare DRONE¹.

workforce /ˈwɜːkfɔːs/ *n* [CGp] the total number of workers who are employed in a company or factory, or who are available for work: *Ten per cent of the workforce will be made redundant.*

workhorse /ˈwɜːkhɔːs/ *n* a person or machine that is relied upon to do hard work.

workhouse /ˈwɜːkhaʊs/ *n* (*pl* **-houses** /-ˈhaʊzɪz/) (*Brit*) (formerly) a public institution where very poor people were sent to live and given work to do.

working /ˈwɜːkɪŋ/ *adj* [attrib] **1(a)** having a job; employed: *The meeting must be held at a time convenient for working mothers.* ○ *the working population of the country* (ie the people in it that work). **(b)** having a job that involves physical labour: *a working men's club* ○ *My father was just a simple working man.* **2** of, for or suitable for work: *My working hours are (from) 9 to 5.* ○ *She was still dressed in her working clothes.* ○ *The union has negotiated a 35-hour working week.* ○ *She had spent* *all her working life in the factory.* ○ *Working conditions in the industry have improved greatly.* ○ *a working breakfast/lunch* (ie one during which business is discussed). **3** functioning or able to function: *a working model of a steam engine* ○ *The government has a working majority* (ie one that is sufficient to allow it to govern). **4** that is good enough as a basis for work, argument, etc and may be improved later: *a working hypothesis/theory* ○ *That's only the book's working title — we'll probably call it something else eventually.* ○ *She has a working knowledge of French.* **IDM** **in running/working order** ⇨ ORDER¹.

▶ **working** *n* **1** [C] a mine, etc that is being or has been worked (WORK² 7): *We went exploring in some disused tin workings.* **2 workings** [pl] *~s* **(of sth)** the processes involved in the way a machine, an organization, a part of the body, etc operates: *the workings of the human mind* ○ *It is impossible to understand the workings of such a huge organization.*

■ **,working 'capital** *n* [U] capital that is needed and used in running a business, and not invested in its buildings, equipment, etc.

the ,working 'class *n* [sing] (also **the ,working 'classes** [pl]) the social class whose members generally do paid MANUAL or industrial work: *represent the interests of the working class* ○ *working-class attitudes/families/origins* ○ *She comes from a working-class background.* Compare MIDDLE CLASS.

,working 'day *n* **(a)** = WORKDAY. **(b)** the part of the day during which work is done: *The union is campaigning for a shorter working day.*

'working party *n* a group of people appointed, eg by a government department, to investigate sth and report or advise on it: *set up a working party to look into the matter.*

workload /'wɜːkləʊd/ *n* an amount of work to be done by sb: *have a heavy workload* ○ *reduce/increase sb's workload.*

workman /'wɜːkmən/ *n* (*pl* **-men** /-mən/) **(a)** a man who is employed to do physical or MANUAL work: *workmen cleaning the drains.* **(b)** a person who works in the specified way: *a good/bad workman* ○ *skilled/unskilled workmen.*

▶ **'workmanlike** *adj* of or like a good workman; practical and skilful: *She did a very workmanlike job on it.* ○ *The team gave a typically workmanlike performance.*

'workmanship *n* [U] **(a)** a person's skill in working: *They admired her workmanship.* **(b)** the quality of this as seen in sth that has been made: *Our new washing-machine keeps breaking down — it's entirely due to shoddy workmanship.*

'workmate /'wɜːkmeɪt/ (*Brit*) *n* a person with whom one works, often doing the same job, in an office, a factory, etc.

workout /'wɜːkaʊt/ *n* a period of vigorous physical exercise or training: *I like to have a workout in the gym every day.*

workplace /'wɜːkpleɪs/ *n* [C] (often **the workplace** [sing]) the place where people work, eg an office or a factory: *introduce new technology into the workplace.*

workroom /'wɜːkruːm, -rʊm/ *n* a room in which work is done: *The jeweller has a workroom at the back of his shop.*

worksheet /'wɜːkʃiːt/ *n* a paper on which work that has been done or is in progress is recorded.

workshop /'wɜːkʃɒp/ *n* **(a)** a room or building in which machines, etc are made or repaired. **(b)** a period of discussion and practical work on a particular subject, in which a group of people share their knowledge and experience: *a 'poetry/'theatre workshop.*

workstation /'wɜːksteɪʃn/ a place in an office, etc where a person works, esp with a computer.

worktop /'wɜːktɒp/ (also **work surface**) *n* a flat surface in a kitchen, on top of a cupboard, etc, used eg for preparing food on.

world /wɜːld/ *n* **1 the world** [sing] the earth with all its countries and peoples: *a journey round the world* ○ *travel (all over) the world* ○ *the rivers and oceans of the world* ○ *The whole world would be affected by a nuclear war.* ○ *Which is the largest city in the world?* ○ *English is a world language* (ie is used everywhere in the world). **2 the world** [sing] everything that exists; the universe: *the creation of the world.* **3** [sing] a particular part of the earth or the part known at a particular time: *the western world* ○ *the English-speaking world* (ie those parts where English is spoken as the first language) ○ *the Roman world* (ie the part of the earth that the Romans knew). See also THE NEW WORLD, THE OLD WORLD, THE THIRD WORLD. **4** [C] a planet like the earth: *There may be other worlds out there.* **5** [sing] the state of human existence: *this world and the next* (ie life on earth and existence after death) ○ *the world to come* (ie life after death) ○ *come into the world* (ie be born) ○ *It's a sad world where there is such terrible suffering.* **6 the world** [sing] **(a)** the way different people behave or live; human affairs: *He showed no interest in the world around him.* ○ *She's gone off to see the world for a year before she starts university.* ○ *He's too young to understand the ways of the world.* **(b)** possessions and physical pleasures: *the temptations of the world* ○ *She decided to renounce the world and enter a convent.* **7 the world** [sing] **(a)** everybody: *The whole world seemed to be at the party.* ○ *She felt that the (whole) world was against her.* ○ *There's no need to tell the whole world about it!* **(b)** people with conventional attitudes: *I don't care what the world thinks.* **8** [C] (often in compounds) people or things belonging to a particular group, area of activity or interest, etc: *the animal/insect world* ○ *the world of art/politics/sport* ○ *the racing/scientific/theatre world* ○ *The medical world is divided on this issue.* **IDM** **be ,all the 'world to sb** to be loved by and very important to sb. **be not long for this world** ⇨ LONG³. **be 'worlds apart** to be completely different in attitudes, opinions, etc: *Politically, they're 'worlds apart.* **the best of both worlds / all possible worlds** ⇨ BEST³. **brave new world** ⇨ BRAVE. **come/go 'down/'up in the world** to become less/more important in society or successful in one's career: *They've come up in the world since I lrst met them.* **dead to the world** ⇨ DEAD. **the end of the world** ⇨ END¹. **for all the world as if... / like sb/sth** (usu expressing surprise) exactly as if...: *She behaved for all the world as if nothing unusual had happened.* ○ *He looked for all the world like a naughty schoolboy caught stealing apples.* **(not) for (all) the 'world** (not) for any reason at all: *I wouldn't sell that picture for all the world.* **how, etc on earth / in the 'world** ⇨ EARTH. **(be/live) in a world of one's 'own** (to live) without sharing one's thoughts, ideas or feelings with others. **it's a small world** ⇨ SMALL. **a man/woman of the 'world** ɘ person with a lot of experience of life, esp one who is not easily surprised or shocked. **the next world** ⇨ NEXT¹. **on top of the world** ⇨ TOP¹. **,out of this 'world** (*infml*) absolutely wonderful, magnificent, beautiful, etc: *The meal was out of this world.* **set the 'world on fire** (*infml*) to be very successful and gain the admiration of other people. **watch the world go by** ⇨ WATCH¹. **the way of the world** ⇨ WAY¹. **what is the world 'coming to?** (used as an expression of disapproval, surprise or shock, esp at changes in people's attitudes or behaviour): *When I listen to the news these days, I sometimes wonder what the world is coming to.* **a window on the world** ⇨ WINDOW. **with the best will in the world** ⇨ BEST¹. **(all) the ,world and his 'wife** (*Brit infml*) everybody; a large number of people: *The world and his wife were in*

W

Brighton that day! **the ˌworld is one's ˈoyster** one is in a position to take the opportunities that life has to offer: *With talent like that, the world is his oyster.* **a/the ˈworld of difference, good, etc** (*infml*) a lot of difference, good, etc: *There's a world of difference between a packet of frozen peas and peas picked freshly from the garden.* ○ *That trip* **did** *him* **the world of good.** **the (whole) world ˈover** everywhere: *People are basically the same the world over.* **the worst of all worlds** ⇨ WORST.

▶ **worldly** *adj* **1** [attrib] of or concerned with the physical world rather than a spiritual life: *one's worldly goods* (ie one's possessions) ○ *worldly power/ success.* **2** having or showing a wide experience of life, and so not easily shocked: *After ten years in London, she's much more worldly than she was.* **worldliness** *n* [U]. **ˌworldly-ˈwise** *adj* [U] having great experience of life and so not easily deceived.

■ **ˈworld-beater** *n* a person or thing that is better than all others: *She has enough talent as a player to be a world-beater.*

ˌworld-ˈclass *adj* as good as the best in the world: *a ˌworld-class ˈwriter/ˈathlete* ○ *ˌworld-class hoˈtels/ wines.*

ˌworld-ˈfamous *adj* known throughout the world: *a ˌworld-famous ˈpop star* ○ *His books are world-famous.*

ˌworld ˈpower *n* a country that has great influence in international politics.

ˌworld ˈwar *n* a war that involves many countries: *the First/Second World War.*

ˈworld-weary *adj* bored with life or tired of living.

worldwide /ˈwɜːldwaɪd/ *adj* found in or affecting the whole world: *worldwide economic trends* ○ *a ˌworldwide ˈmarket.*

▶ **ˌworldˈwide** *adv* everywhere in the world: *Our product is sold worldwide.*

earthworm **worm**

worm /wɜːm/ *n* **1(a)** [C] a long thin creature with no bones or limbs, which lives in soil: *birds looking for worms.* ⇨ picture. See also EARTHWORM. **(b) worms** [pl] long thin creatures that live inside the bodies of people or animals and can cause illness: *The dog has worms.* **(c)** [C] (esp in compounds) an insect at the stage of development when it looks like a short worm: *The apples are full of worms.* See also SILKWORM, WOODWORM. **2** [C usu *sing*] (*infml derog*) (often as a form of address) a person who is not respected because he or she is considered morally weak, dishonest, etc. **IDM a can of worms** ⇨ CAN¹. **the ˌworm will ˈturn** a person who is normally quiet and does not complain will protest when the situation becomes too hard to bear.

▶ **worm** *v* **1** to give an animal medicine that causes worms to be passed out of the body in the FAECES: [Vn] *All horses should be regularly wormed.* **2** to twist and turn one's body in order to move in a specified direction: [Vnpr] *They had to* **worm their way** *through the narrow tunnel.* [also Vnp]. **PHRV** **ˌworm one's way / oneself ˈinto sth** (*usu derog*) to obtain the confidence or affection of sb, esp in order to gain some advantage for oneself: *She used flattery to worm her way/herself into his confidence.* **ˌworm sth ˈout (of sb)** to obtain information, etc from sb over a period of time by constantly and cleverly questioning them: *We eventually wormed the truth out of her.*

wormy *adj* containing many worms: *a wormy apple.*

■ **ˈworm-cast** *n* a small winding tube of earth that is pushed up to the surface of the ground by a worm as it moves through soil.

wormeaten /ˈwɜːmiːtn/ *adj* full of holes made by worms (WORM 1c) or woodworms (WOODWORM).

wormwood /ˈwɜːmwʊd/ *n* [U] a plant with a bitter flavour, used in making certain alcoholic drinks and medicines.

worn¹ *pp* of WEAR¹.

worn² /wɔːn/ *adj* **1** damaged by use or wear: *These shoes are looking rather worn.* **2** (of a person) looking very tired: *She came back pale and worn.* ■ **ˌworn-ˈout** *adj* **1** used or worn so often that it can no longer be used: *a ˌworn-out ˈcoat* ○ (*fig*) *ˌworn-out iˈdeas.* **2** [usu pred] (of a person) very tired: *You look worn-out after your long journey.*

worrisome /ˈwʌrɪsəm/ *adj* (*dated*) causing worry.

worry /ˈwʌri/ *v* (*pt, pp* **worried**) **1** ~ (**about/over sb/ sth**) to be anxious and troubled about sb/sth: [V] *'Don't worry,' she said,* putting an arm round his shoulder. ○ *Don't worry if you can't finish it.* [Vpr] *Your parents are worrying about you: please write to them.* ○ *Stop worrying about the money — we'll manage somehow.* ○ *He's always worrying over nothing at all.* [also V.*that*]. **2** ~ **sb/oneself (about sb/sth)** to make sb/oneself anxious or troubled about sb/sth: [Vn] *What worries me is how I'm going to tell the children.* ○ *Many people are worried by the possibility of a nuclear accident.* [Vn-adj] *She worried herself sick/She was worried sick about her missing son.* [Vn.*that*] *It worries me that they haven't answered my letters.* **3** ~ **sb (with sth)** to annoy or disturb sb; to BOTHER sb: [Vn] *Don't worry her now — she's busy.* ○ *The noise doesn't seem to worry them.* [Vnpr] *Don't worry him with a lot of silly questions.* **4** (esp of a dog) to seize sth with the teeth and shake or pull it repeatedly: *The farmer said my dog had been worrying his sheep.* **IDM** **ˌnot to ˈworry** (*infml*) it does not matter; it is not important: *We've missed the train, but not to worry — there's another one in ten minutes.*

▶ **worried** *adj* ~ (**about sb/sth**); ~ (**that…**) feeling or showing worry about sb/sth; anxious: *be worried about one's weight/job/husband* ○ *a worried look* ○ *You look/sound worried.* ○ *I was worried that you wouldn't find me.* ○ *Worried relatives waited at the airport.* ○ *'Shall we meet on Thursday or Friday?' 'I'm not worried* (ie I don't mind) *— either day would be OK.'* ○ *You* **had me worried** *for a minute — I thought you said 50% not 15%.* **worriedly** *adv*.

worrier *n* a person who worries a lot.

worry *n* **1** [U] the state of being worried; anxiety: *His parents were frantic with worry.* ○ *Worry and illness had made him prematurely old.* **2** [C] a thing that causes one to worry; a cause of anxiety: *He has a lot of financial worries at the moment.* ○ *I don't want to listen to all his problems — I've got enough worries of my own.* **3** [C usu *sing*] a responsibility: *You don't have to do anything about transport — that's my worry.*

worrying *adj* **1** causing worry: *His attitude is extremely worrying.* **2** full of worry: *It was a very worrying time for them.* **worryingly** *adv*: *worrying/ high levels of radiation.*

worse /wɜːs/ *adj* (comparative of BAD¹) **1** ~ (**than sth / doing sth**) bad to a greater degree or on a greater scale; less good or desirable: *The weather got worse during the day.* ○ *The interview was far/ much worse than he had expected.* ○ *prevent an* **even worse** *tragedy* ○ *The economic crisis is getting worse and worse.* ○ *Don't tell her that — you'll only* **make things/matters worse.** Compare WORST. **2** [pred] in or into worse health: *If he gets any worse, we must phone for the doctor.* Compare BETTER¹. **IDM** **sb's bark is worse than their bite** ⇨ BARK². **come off ˈworse/ˈworst** to lose a fight, contest, etc or suffer more compared with others. **go from ˌbad to ˈworse** (of a bad condition, situation, etc) to become even worse: *We were hoping for an improvement but things have gone from bad to worse.* ˌworse ˈluck! (*Brit infml*) (used to indicate that one is disappointed about sth): *I shall have to miss the party, worse luck!*

▶ **worse** *adv* **1** less well: *I'm not a very good player, but Graham plays worse than I do.* Compare WORST *adv*. **2** more intensely than before: *It's raining worse than ever.* **IDM** ˌworse ˈoff to be poorer, unhappier, etc than before: *The increase in taxes means that we'll be £30 a month worse off.* ○ *I've only broken my arm; other patients are far worse off than me.*

worse *n* [U] more problems or bad news: *I'm afraid there is worse to come.* **IDM** be none the ˈworse (for sth) to be not harmed by sth: *The children were none the worse for their adventure.* be the worse for ˈdrink to be drunk. can/could do ˈworse than do sth to be sensible to do sth: *If you want a safe investment, you could do a lot worse than put your money in a building society.* a change for the better/worse ⇨ CHANGE². for better or worse ⇨ BETTER³. so much the better/worse ⇨ BETTER³. the ˌworse for ˈwear (*infml*) **1** in poor condition because of being used a lot: *My old dictionary is looking a bit the worse for wear.* **2** drunk: *Bill came home from the office party considerably the worse for wear.*

worsen /ˈwɜːsn/ *v* to become or make sth worse: [V] *a steadily worsening economic situation* ○ *The patient's condition worsened during the night.* [Vn] *The drought has worsened their chances of survival.*

worship /ˈwɜːʃɪp/ *n* **1** [U] (**a**) the practice of showing respect for God or a god, eg by praying or singing with others at a service(8): *perform an act of worship* ○ *bow one's head in worship* ○ *devil worship.* (**b**) a ceremony for this: *Morning worship begins at 11 o'clock.* **2** [U] admiration or love felt for sb/sth. See also HERO-WORSHIP. **3** his, your, etc Worship [C] (*esp Brit*) (a formal and polite way of addressing or referring to a MAGISTRATE or a MAYOR): *His Worship, the Mayor of Chester* ○ *No, your Worship.*

▶ **worship** *v* (**-pp-**; *US* **-p-**) **1** [Vn] to show respect and honour to God or a god. **2** to attend a church service: [V] *the church where they had worshipped for years.* **3** to feel great love and admiration for sb/sth, esp to such an extent that one cannot see their/its faults: [Vn] *You can see she worships him.* ○ *worship sb from afar* (ie not tell them one's feelings). **worshipper** (*US* **worshiper**) *n* a person who worships sb/sth: *regular worshippers at St Andrew's Church* ○ *rows of sun-worshippers lying on the beach.* **worshipful** /-fl/ *adj* **1** (*fml*) showing or feeling respect and admiration for sb. **2 Worshipful** (*esp Brit*) (a title used to address or refer to particular people or groups): *the Worshipful Company of Goldsmiths.*

worst /wɜːst/ *adj* (superlative of BAD¹) worse than any other person or thing of a similar kind; most bad: *one of the worst cases of child abuse he'd ever seen* ○ *It was the worst storm for years.* ○ *This is the worst essay I've ever read.* ○ *What you've told me confirms my worst fears* (ie proves they were right). Compare WORSE. **IDM** be one's ˌown worst ˈenemy to be the cause of one's own problems: *Her indecisiveness makes her her own worst enemy.* come off worse/worst ⇨ WORSE.

▶ **worst** *adv* worse than anyone or anything else of a similar kind: *The worst hit* (ie most badly affected) *area of the country was the south-west.* ○ *Manufacturing industry was worst affected by the fuel shortage.* ○ *He is one of the worst dressed men I know.* ○ *Worst of all, I lost the watch my father had given me.* Compare WORSE *adv*.

worst *n* **the worst** [sing] the part, situation, possibility, etc that is worse than any other: *The worst of*

the storm was over. ○ *When they did not hear from her, they feared the worst.* ○ *I was prepared for the worst when I saw the wrecked car.* ○ *She was always optimistic, even when things were at their worst.* ○ *The worst of it is that I can't even be sure if they received my letter.* **IDM** at (the) ˈworst if the worst happens: *At worst this may mean the end of her playing career.* ○ *At the very worst, he'll have to pay a fine.* bring out the best/worst in sb ⇨ BEST³. do one's ˈworst to be as awkward or unpleasant as possible: *Let them do their worst — we'll fight them every inch of the way!* get the ˈworst of it to be defeated: *The dog had been in a fight and had obviously got the worst of it.* if the ˌworst comes to the ˈworst if circumstances become too difficult or dangerous: *If the worst comes to the worst, we'll just have to sell the house.* the worst of ˈall (possible) worlds all the disadvantages of every situation: *The country has ended up with the worst of all worlds: inflation, unemployment and food shortages.*

worst *v* [Vn] (*dated or fml*) (usu passive) to defeat sb in a fight or contest.

worsted /ˈwʊstɪd/ *n* [U] a fine wool cloth used for making trousers, skirts, etc: *a grey worsted suit.*

worth /wɜːθ/ *adj* [pred] (usu used like a *prep*) **1** be ~ sth having a particular value: *Our house is worth about £60 000.* ○ *I paid only $3 000 for this painting, but it's worth a lot more.* **2** (of a person) having money and possessions of a particular value: *He's worth about £10 million.* **3** ~ sth / doing sth likely to bring enjoyment, benefit, profit, etc: *It's not worth the effort/the trouble.* ○ *The scheme is worth a try.* ○ *This book is well worth reading.* ○ *He felt that his life was no longer worth living.* ○ *Don't bother washing your car every week — it's not worth it.* ○ *It's an idea that's worth considering.* See also WORTHWHILE. **IDM** a bird in the hand is worth two in the bush ⇨ BIRD. for ˌall one/it is ˈworth with all one's energy and effort: *It's a marvellous part, and she plays it for all it's worth.* ○ *They're promoting their new course for all they're worth.* for ˌwhat it's ˈworth (used when offering one's opinion about sth): *So that's what I think, for what it's worth.* the game is not worth the candle ⇨ GAME¹. more than one's job's worth ⇨ JOB. not worth a ˈdamn, ˈstraw, a red ˈcent, a tinker's ˈcuss, etc (*infml*) worthless: *Their promises are not worth a damn.* not worth the paper it's ˈwritten on (of a contract, an agreement, etc) having no value because one of the people who signed it has no intention of honouring it. ˌworth every ˈpenny completely justifying the cost: *The trip cost a lot but it was worth every penny.* ˌworth one's ˈsalt good at one's job: *Any teacher worth her salt knows that.* ˌworth one's/its ˌweight in ˈgold very useful or valuable: *A good mechanic is worth his weight in gold.* ˌworth sb's ˈwhile profitable or interesting to sb: *It would be (well) worth your while to come to the meeting.* ○ *They promised to make it worth her while* (ie pay her well) *to take part.*

▶ **worth** *n* [U] **1** ~ of sth (following a *n* indicating amount) (**a**) the amount of sth that a specified sum of money will buy: *The thieves stole £5 000 worth of jewellery.* (**b**) the amount of sth that will last for a specified length of time: *two weeks' worth of groceries.* **2**(**a**) financial value: *items of great/little worth.* (**b**) use and practical or moral value: *a man of great worth.* **worthless** *adj* **1** having no value or use: *worthless old chairs* ○ *worthless promises.* ⇨ note at INVALUABLE. **2** (of a person) having no good qualities: *a worthless character.* **worthlessness** *n* [U]: *a sense of his own worthlessness.*

worthwhile /ˌwɜːθˈwaɪl/ *adj* important, interesting or rewarding enough to justify the time, money or effort that is spent: *It's worthwhile taking the trouble to explain a job fully to new employees.* ○ *Nursing is a* *very ₁worthwhile ca¹reer.* ○ *The journey was long, but seeing him again made it all worthwhile.*

worthy /'wɜːði/ *adj* (**-ier, -iest**) **1** [pred] ~ **of sth / to do sth** deserving sth or to do sth: *a statement worthy of contempt* ○ *Her achievements are worthy of the highest praise.* ○ *She said she was not worthy to accept the honour they had offered her.* **2** [usu attrib] (**a**) deserving respect or consideration: *a worthy cause* ○ *a worthy winner* ○ *a worthy but rather boring play about racism.* (**b**) (*usu joc*) (esp of a person) deserving respect: *the worthy citizens of the town.* **3** [pred] ~ **of sb/sth** (*usu approv*) (**a**) good enough to be suitable for sth: *It was difficult to find words worthy of the occasion.* (**b**) typical of sb/sth: *It was a performance worthy of a master.*
▸ **worthily** /-ɪli/ *adv.*
worthiness *n* [U].

worthy *n* (*esp joc*) an important person: *All the local worthies have been invited to the ceremony.*

-worthy (forming compound *adjs*) deserving of or suitable for the thing specified: *noteworthy* ○ *trustworthy* ○ *roadworthy* ○ *newsworthy.*

would /*strong form* wʊd; *weak forms* wəd, əd/ *modal v* (*short form* **'d** /d/; *neg* **would not**; *short form* **wouldn't** /'wʊdnt/) **1** (used instead of **will** after verbs in the past tense, when reporting what sb has said): *He said he would be here at 8 o'clock.* (ie He said, 'I will be there at 8 o'clock'). ○ *She asked me if I'd give her a lift home.* ○ *They told me that they probably wouldn't come.* See also WILL¹. **2**(**a**) (used for describing the consequence of an imagined event): *She'd look better with shorter hair.* ○ *If you went to see him, he would be delighted.* ○ *Hurry up! It would be a pity to miss the beginning of the play.* ○ *She'd be a fool to accept it* (ie if she accepted). (**b**) (used for describing an action or event that would have happened if sth else had happened first): *If I had seen the advertisement in time I would have applied for the job.* ○ *They would never have met if she hadn't gone to Emma's party.* **3** (used after *so that/in order that* to express purpose or result): *She burned the letters so that her husband would never read them.* **4** (used after *wish* to express what one wants to happen): *I wish you'd be quiet for a minute* ○ *He wishes (that) she would leave him.* **5** (used to indicate that sb/sth was not willing or refused to do sth): *She wouldn't go to the dentist, even though she was in considerable pain.* ○ *My car wouldn't start this morning.* **6**(**a**) (used in polite requests): *Would you mind paying me in cash, please?* ○ *Would you open the door for me, please?* (**b**) (used in polite offers or invitations): *Would you like a sandwich?* ○ *Would you have dinner with me on Friday?* **7** (used with *like, love, hate, prefer, be glad/happy,* etc to express preferences): *I'd love a coffee.* ○ *I'd hate you to think I was criticizing you.* ○ *I'd be only too glad to help.* ○ *Where would you like to sit?* **8** (used with *imagine, say, think,* etc for expressing opinions about which one is not certain): *I would imagine the journey will take about an hour.* ○ *I'd say he was about fifty.* **9** (used when describing habits or repeated actions in the past): *When my parents were away, my grandmother would look after me.* ○ *He'd always be the first to offer to help.* **10** (used when commenting on characteristic behaviour): *'She said it was your fault.' 'Well, she ¹would say that, wouldn't she? She's never liked me.'* ○ *It ¹would rain* (ie How typical it is of the weather that it should rain) *on our wedding day!*
■ **would-be** *adj* [attrib] hoping to become the type of person specified: *a would-be artist/model/author.*

wound¹ /wuːnd/ *n* **1** an injury to part of the body, esp one caused by a weapon with cutting or tearing of the flesh: *a knife/stab wound* ○ *a gaping wound in his chest* ○ *He died after receiving two bullet wounds in the head.* ○ *His wounds healed slowly.* **2** ~ (**to sth**) an injury to a person's feelings, reputation, etc: *deep*

psychological wounds ○ *The defeat was a wound to his pride.* **IDM** **lick one's wounds** ⇨ LICK. **rub salt into the wound / sb's wounds** ⇨ RUB¹.
▸ **wound** *v* (esp passive) **1** to cause a wound: [Vn] *Ten people were killed and thirty seriously wounded.* [Vnpr] *The guard was wounded in the leg.* **2** to hurt sb's feelings, reputation, etc: [Vn] *He was/felt deeply wounded by their disloyalty.* **the wounded** *n* [pl *v*] wounded people: *Many of the wounded died on their way to hospital.* **wounding** *adj* hurting a person's feelings: *he found her remarks deeply wounding.*

> **NOTE** Wound and **injure** are both used in talking about damage to the body. They are often used in the passive. A person can be **wounded** by a knife, gun or other weapon. It is a deliberate action, connected with fighting or war: *He was wounded in the civil war.* ○ *Soldiers shot and wounded a man crossing the border.* **Wounded** is also sometimes an adjective: *His wounded leg collapsed under him.*
> In an accident, for example involving a car or a machine, a person might be **injured**: *Five people were seriously injured in last night's train crash.* Somebody might also **injure** a part of the body while playing sport: *She injured her shoulder playing tennis.* **Injured** is also sometimes an adjective: *an injured knee.* **Hurt** may be as serious as **injure**, or it may be used to talk about a minor pain: *They were badly hurt in a car accident.* ○ *I hurt my back lifting that box.*
> Somebody might have a **wound** or an **injury** on a part of the body which has been damaged: *a head wound* ○ *gunshot wounds* ○ *The wound healed rapidly and the stitches were removed after 10 days.* ○ *It was a serious injury and may affect her career.* ○ *Helmets protect the players from brain injuries.*

wound² *pt, pp* of WIND³.

wove *pt* of WEAVE.

woven *pp* of WEAVE.

wow¹ /waʊ/ (also **wowee** /ˌwaʊ'iː/) *interj* (*infml*) (expressing great surprise or admiration): *Wow! You look terrific!*
▸ **wow** *n* [sing] (*sl*) a very great success: *She's a wow with all the boys.*
wow *v* ~ **sb** (**with sth**) (*infml esp US*) to impress sb greatly: [Vnpr] *He wowed Broadway with a brilliant performance.* [also Vn].

wow² /waʊ/ *n* [U] variation in the pitch¹(2) of sounds reproduced from a record or tape, resulting from changes in the speed of the motor. Compare FLUTTER *n* 4.

WPC /ˌdʌbljuː piː 'siː/ *abbr* (in Britain) woman police constable: *WPC (Linda) Green.* Compare PC 2.

wpm /ˌdʌbljuː piː 'em/ *abbr* words per minute: *50 wpm* (ie when typing).

WRAC /ræk, ˌdʌbljuː aːr eɪ 'siː/ *abbr* (in Britain) Women's Royal Army Corps.

wrack ⇨ RACK².

WRAF /ræf, ˌdʌbljuː aːr eɪ 'ef/ *abbr* (in Britain) Women's Royal Air Force.

wraith /reɪθ/ *n* the ghost or image of a person seen shortly before or after her or his death: *a wraith-like figure* (ie a very thin pale person).

wrangle /'ræŋgl/ *n* ~ (**with sb**) (**about/over sth**) a usu long and complicated argument: *They were involved in a long legal wrangle with the company over payment.*
▸ **wrangle** *v* ~ (**with sb**) (**about/over sth**) to argue angrily and usu for a long time about sth: [Vpr] *They're still wrangling over the financial details.* [also V]. **wrangling** *n* [U, C]: *hours of procedural wrangling* ○ *a week of political/diplomatic wranglings.*

wrap /ræp/ *v* (**-pp-**) **1** ~ **sth** (**up**) (**in sth**) to cover or enclose sth completely in eg paper or plastic: [Vnpr, Vnp] *The Christmas presents were wrapped*

[V.*to* inf] = verb + *to* infinitive   [Vn.inf (no *to*)] = verb + noun + infinitive without *to*   [V.*ing*] = verb + *-ing* form

(up) in shiny green paper. [Vn] *individually wrapped chocolates* [Vnpr] (*fig*) *hills wrapped in mist*. See also GIFT-WRAP, SHRINK-WRAPPED. **2(a)** ~ **sth round/around sb/sth** to wind a piece of material round sb/sth as a covering or for protection: [Vnpr] *wrap a scarf round one's neck/a bandage round one's ankle*. **(b)** ~ **sb/sth in sth** to cover sb/ sth with a piece of material: [Vnpr] *wrap a baby in a blanket*. **IDM** be ,**wrapped** ¦**up in sb/sth** to be so involved with sb/sth that one does not notice other people or things: *They are completely wrapped up in their children.* ○ *She was so wrapped up in her work that she didn't realize how late it was.* **PHRV** ,**wrap (it)** ¦**up** (*usu imperative*) (*sl*) to stop talking or making a noise. ,**wrap (sb/oneself)** ¦**up** to put warm clothes on sb/oneself: *Wrap up warm(ly)! It's very cold outside.* ,**wrap sth** ¦**up** (*infml*) to complete sth, eg a discussion or an agreement, in a satisfactory way: *I had already wrapped up a couple of deals by lunch-time.* ○ *That just about wraps it up for today, gentlemen.* ,**wrap sth** ¦**up (in sth)** to present an idea or a piece of information in a way that is difficult for people to understand: *Why does he have to wrap up even a simple statement in such complicated language?*
▶ **wrap** *n* **1** [C] a loose scarf or SHAWL. **2** [U] paper or plastic used for wrapping food, etc in: *plastic food wrap.* **IDM** under ¦**wraps** (*infml*) secret or hidden: *The documents will stay/be kept under wraps for ten more years.*
wrapper *n* a piece of paper, etc that is wrapped round sth when it is bought, eg to protect it or to keep it clean: *chocolate/sweet wrappers.*
wrapping *n* [U, C] material used for covering or packing sth: *Put plenty of wrapping round the glass ornaments when you pack them.* ○ *They tore the wrappings off the presents.* ¦**wrapping paper** *n* [U] usu coloured paper for wrapping parcels or presents.

wrath /rɒθ; *US* ræθ/ *n* [U] (*dated or fml*) great anger: *the wrath of God* ○ *incur sb's wrath* ○ *vent one's wrath on sb.* ▶ **wrathful** /-fl/ *adj.* **wrathfully** *adv.*

wreak /riːk/ *v* ~ **sth (on sb)** (*rather fml*) to do great harm or damage to sb/sth; to cause violence, destruction, etc: [Vnpr] *wreak one's fury/revenge on sb* ○ *His heavy drinking **wreaked havoc on** his family.* [also Vn].

wreath /riːθ/ *n* (*pl* **wreaths** /riːðz/) **1(a)** an arrangement of flowers and leaves twisted or woven into a circle or similar shape. Wreaths are used for decoration or placed on graves, etc as a mark of respect: *a funeral wreath* ○ *We laid wreaths at the war memorial.* ○ *Every Christmas a holly wreath was hung on the front door.* **(b)** a circle of flowers or leaves worn as a mark of honour round a person's head: *a laurel wreath.* **2** a ring of smoke, cloud, etc: *wreaths of mist.*

wreathe /riːð/ *v* **1** ~ **sth (in/with sth)** (*usu passive*) to cover or surround sth: [Vnpr] *stems wreathed with clusters of purple flowers* ○ *The hills were wreathed in mist.* ○ (*fig*) *Her face was **wreathed in** smiles* (ie She was smiling a lot). [also Vn]. **2** (of smoke, mist, etc) to move slowly in rings: [Vadv] *smoke wreathing upwards* [also Vpr, Vp].

wreck /rek/ *n* **1(a)** a ship that has sunk or has been badly damaged: *Two wrecks block the entrance to the harbour.* See also SHIPWRECK. **(b)** a vehicle, an aircraft, etc that has been badly damaged, esp in an accident: *The car was reduced to a smouldering wreck.* **2** (*usu sing*) (*infml*) a person whose health, esp mental health, has been seriously damaged: *Worry about the business has turned her into a nervous/gibbering wreck.*
▶ **wreck** *v* **1** (esp passive) to damage a ship so much that it sinks or can no longer sail: [Vn] *The ship was wrecked off the coast of France.* Compare SHIPWRECK *v.* **2** to damage or destroy sth: [Vn] *The*

road was littered with wrecked cars. ○ *Vandals completely wrecked the train.* **3** to spoil sth completely: *The weather wrecked all our plans.* ○ *He's wrecked his chances of ever getting promotion.* **wrecker** *n* **1** a person who causes damage or destruction. **2** (*US*) a vehicle used for removing cars, lorries, etc that have been damaged, etc.
wreckage /'rekɪdʒ/ *n* [U] the remains of sth that has been wrecked: *Wreckage of the aircraft was scattered over a wide area.* ○ *A few survivors were pulled from the wreckage.* ○ (*fig*) *He is trying to salvage something from the wreckage of his political career.*

wren /ren/ *n* a very small brown bird that often has its tail upright.

wrench /rentʃ/ *v* **1** ~ **sth off (sth)**; ~ **sb/sth away** to twist or pull sb/sth violently away from sth: [Vnpr] *wrench a door off its hinges* [Vnp] *I wrenched my arm away.* [Vn-adj] *wrench the door open* ○ *He managed to wrench himself free.* **2** to injure a joint, eg one's ankle or shoulder, by twisting it: [Vn] *She must have wrenched her knee when she fell.*
▶ **wrench** *n* **1** [C *usu sing*] a sudden and violent twist or pull: *She stumbled and gave her ankle a painful wrench.* **2** [sing] an act of leaving sb/sth that causes one pain or distress: *Leaving home was a terrible wrench for me.* **3** [C] a type of SPANNER that can be adjusted to grip and turn nuts (NUT 2) of different sizes. See also MONKEY WRENCH.

wrest /rest/ *v* **PHRV** ¦**wrest sth from sb/sth** (*rather fml*) **(a)** to take sth away from sb, esp after a violent struggle: *He wrested the gun from my grasp.* **(b)** to obtain sth from sb/sth after trying hard for a long time: *wrest a confession from sb* ○ *Foreign investors are trying to wrest control of the firm from the family.*

wrestle /'resl/ *v* ~ **(with sb)** to fight sb, esp as a sport, by holding them and trying to throw or force them to the ground: [V] *Can you wrestle?* [Vpr] *Armed guards wrestled with the intruders.* ○ *He wrestled his opponent to the floor/ground.* **PHRV** ¦**wrestle with sth** to struggle to deal with sth difficult: *wrestle with a problem/one's conscience* ○ *The pilot was wrestling with the controls.*
▶ **wrestle** *n* (*usu sing*) **1** a fight involving wrestling. **2** ~ **(with sth)** a hard struggle: *a wrestle with one's conscience.*

wrestling
wrestler

wrestler /'reslə(r)/ *n* a person who takes part in wrestling as a sport.
wrestling /'reslɪŋ/ *n* [U] the sport in which people wrestle: *watch (the) wrestling on television.*

wretch /retʃ/ *n* **1** a very unfortunate or unhappy person: *a poor half-starved wretch.* **2** (*often joc*) an evil or wicked person: *He's a despicable wretch.* ○ *You wretch! You've eaten my cake!*

wretched /'retʃɪd/ *adj* **1** very unhappy; miserable: *I felt wretched about not being able to help her.* ○ *His migraine made him feel wretched* (ie ill and miserable) *all morning.* ○ *people living in wretched poverty.* **2** of very poor quality; very bad: *wretched weather.* **3** [attrib] (*infml*) (used to express annoyance): *The wretched car won't start again!* ○ *I'm sick of the whole wretched business.* ▶ **wretchedly** *adv.* **wretchedness** *n* [U]: *a life of utter wretchedness.*

wriggle /'rɪgl/ *v* **(a)** to twist and turn with quick short movements: [V, Vp] *Stop wriggling (about) and sit still!* [Vn] *The baby was wriggling its toes.* **(b)** to move in the specified direction with wriggling movements: [V-adj, Vn-adj] *The thieves left her tied up but she wriggled (her arms/herself) free.* [Vpr]

The fish wriggled out of my fingers. [Vpr, Vnpr] *They managed to wriggle (their way) through the thick hedge.* [also Vp, Vnp]. **PHRV** ‚wriggle ˈout of sth / doing sth** (*infml*) to avoid having to do sth one does not want to do, eg by making excuses: *It's your turn to make the beds — don't try to wriggle out of it.* ○ *The Minister managed to wriggle out of answering the question.*

▶ **wriggle** *n* (usu *sing*) a wriggling movement.

wring /rɪŋ/ *v* (*pt, pp* **wrung** /rʌŋ/) **1(a)** ~ sth (out) to twist and squeeze sth in order to remove liquid from it: [Vn, Vnpr] *He wrung the clothes (out) before putting them on the line to dry.* (**b**) ~ sth out (of sth) to remove liquid from sth in this way: [Vnpr] *Wring the water out of your swimming costume.* [also Vnp]. **2** [Vn] to twist a bird's neck in order to kill it. **IDM** ‚wring one's ˈhands** to squeeze and twist one's hands together as a sign of anxiety, sadness or despair: *It's no use just wringing our hands — we must do something to help.* ‚wring sb's ˈneck** (*infml*) (used as an expression of anger or as a threat) to act violently towards sb: *If I find the person who scratched my car, I'll wring his neck!* **PHRV** ~ sth out of / from sb** to obtain sth from sb with effort or difficulty, esp by putting mental or emotional pressure on them: [Vnpr] *wring a confession from sb* ○ *They managed to wring a promise out of her.*

▶ **wringer** /ˈrɪŋə(r)/ *n* a device with a pair of rolling bars between which washed clothes are passed so that water is squeezed out. Compare MANGLE².

■ ‚wringing ˈwet** *adj* (esp of clothes) very wet; soaking.

wrinkle /ˈrɪŋkl/ *n* **1** (usu *pl*) a small fold or line in the skin, esp one of those on the face that are caused by age: *She's beginning to get wrinkles around her eyes.* **2** a small fold, usu one of many, in a piece of material, eg paper or cloth: *She ran her hand over her skirt to try to remove the wrinkles.* Compare CREASE 1. **3** (*infml*) a useful suggestion or HINT(3).

▶ **wrinkle** *v* **1** to tighten the skin of the face, esp the nose and forehead, into lines or folds: [Vn] *She wrinkled her nose in distaste.* **2** to form wrinkles: [V] *The paper has wrinkled where it got wet.* **wrinkled** /ˈrɪŋkld/ *adj* having or showing wrinkles: *his old wrinkled face* ○ *wrinkled peaches.* **wrinkling** *n* [U] the process of forming wrinkles: *Overexposure to the sun can cause premature wrinkling.*

wrinkly /ˈrɪŋkli/ *adj* having wrinkles: *an old apple with a wrinkly skin.*

wrist /rɪst/ *n* the part of the body between the hand and the arm; the joint on which the hand moves. ▷ picture at HAND. **IDM** a slap on the wrist** ▷ SLAP *n*. ■ ˈwrist-watch** *n* a watch designed to be fastened around the wrist.

writ /rɪt/ *n* ~ (for sth) a formal document, issued to sb by a lawcourt or a person in authority, stating a legal obligation: *serve* (ie officially deliver) *a writ for libel on sb/serve sb with a writ for libel* ○ *The patient's solicitors issued a writ against the doctor, alleging negligence.* See also HOLY WRIT.

▶ **writ** (*arch*) *pp* of WRITE. **IDM** ‚writ ˈlarge** (*fml or rhet*) **1** clear and obvious: *Disappointment was writ large on their faces.* **2** in an exaggerated form: *Their political philosophy is just selfishness writ large.*

write /raɪt/ *v* (*pt* **wrote** /rəʊt/; *pp* **written** /ˈrɪtn/) **1** to make letters or other symbols on a surface, usu paper, esp with a pen or pencil: [V] *The children are learning to read and write.* [Vpr] *I haven't got anything to write with.* ○ *Please write on both sides of the paper.* ○ *You may write in ink or pencil.* [Vn, Vpr]

write (in) capitals / Chinese characters / shorthand [Vn] *write one's name* [Vnpr] *The teacher wrote the answers on the blackboard.* [Vn-n] *The 'b' had been wrongly written as a 'd'.* **2(a)** to compose sth in written form: [Vn] *write a book / film script / symphony / speech* ○ *He writes poetry in his spare time.* ○ *Who wrote 'Pride and Prejudice'?* [Vnpr] *He writes a weekly column for the local newspaper.* [Vnn] *Can you write me a summary of what happened, please.* (**b**) ~ (about / of sth) to state, mention or discuss sth in a book or an article: [Vpr] *A lot has been written about this.* ○ *Ancient historians wrote of a lost continent beneath the ocean.* [V] *No decision has yet been made at the time of writing.* [V.*that*] *In his latest book, he writes that the theory has since been disproved.* [also V.speech]. (**c**) ~ (about / on sth) to work as an author or a journalist: [V] *When did you start writing?* [Vpr] *She writes (on / about politics) for a weekly magazine.* **3** ~ (sth) (to sb) to write and send a letter to sb: [V, Vpr] *I'll write (to you) soon.* [V.*to* inf, V.*ing*] *They wrote to thank us / wrote thanking us for the present.* [Vnn, Vnpr] *She wrote him a long letter / wrote a long letter to him.* [Vn] (*esp US*) *Write me while you're away.* [Vn.*that*] (*esp US*) *He wrote me that he would be arriving on Wednesday.* [also V.*that*]. **4** to put information on a sheet of paper or in the appropriate places on a form: [Vn] *He wrote eight pages on question 1 and didn't have time for questions 2 and 3.* ○ *A doctor may write up to 30 prescriptions a day.* [Vnn] *I haven't any cash. I'll have to write you a cheque.* **5** (of a pen, pencil, etc) to be capable of being used for writing: [V] *This pen won't write.* [also Vadv]. **6** ~ (sth) to / onto sth (*computing*) to record data in the memory of a computer or other storage device: [Vpr, Vnpr] *write (a file) directly to / onto the hard disk.* **IDM** be written all over sb's ˈface** (usu of a quality or an emotion) to be very obvious from the expression on sb's face: *Guilt was written all over his face.* have sth / sb written all ˈover it** (*infml*) to be obviously the specified thing or to have obviously been written or done by the specified person: *a performance with star quality written all over it.* nothing (much) to write ˈhome about** (*infml*) not outstanding or exceptional; ordinary: *The play was nothing (much) to write home about.* not worth the paper it's written on** ▷ WORTH. **PHRV** ‚write aˈway (to sb/sth) (for sth)** ▷ WRITE OFF/AWAY (TO SB/STH) (FOR STH).

‚write ˈback (to sb)** to write and send a letter in reply to sb: *I wrote back (to him) immediately to thank him for the invitation.*

‚write sth ˈdown 1** to put sth down in writing on paper; to make a written note or record of sth: *Write down the address before you forget it.* **2** (*commerce*) to reduce the value of assets (ASSET 2), stock, etc: *All stocks over six months old were written down to 50%.* ○ *the written-down value of the stock.* See also WRITE-DOWN.

‚write ˈin (to sb/sth) (for sth)** to write a letter to an organization or a company, eg to order sth or express an opinion: *Thousands of people have written in to us for a free sample.* ○ *She wrote in to complain.* ‚write sb/sth ˈin** (*US politics*) to add an extra name to a list of candidates on a ballot paper (BALLOT 1a); to vote for sb in this way. ‚write sth ˈinto sth** to include sth as part of an agreement, etc: *A penalty clause was written into the contract.*

‚write ˈoff/aˈway (to sb/sth) (for sth)** to write to an organization or a company to order sth or to ask for information about sth: *I've written off (to the manufacturer) for further details.* ‚write sth ˈoff 1** (*esp commerce*) to recognize that sth is a loss or failure; to cancel a debt: *write off a debt / loss* ○ *write off £5 000 for depreciation of machinery.* **2** to damage sth, esp a vehicle, so badly that it is not worth repairing: *The driver escaped with minor injuries but the car was completely written off.* See also WRITE-

OFF. ¦write sb/sth ¦**off** to regard sb/sth as a failure: *He lost this match, but don't write him off (as a future champion).* ¦write sb/sth ¦**off as sth** to regard sb/sth as unimportant or not worth paying attention to: *It's easy to write him off as just an eccentric old bore.* ¦**write sth ¦out 1** to put information in the appropriate order on a form, etc: *write out a cheque/ prescription/job application.* **2** to copy sth: *Write out each word ten times to help you remember it.* ¦**write sb ¦out (of sth)** to remove a character from a continuing drama series on television or radio: *She was written out (of the series) after 20 years in the role.* ¦**write sth ¦up 1** to make a full written record of sth: *write up one's lecture notes/the minutes of a meeting ○ write up one's diary (ie until the current date).* **2** to write a review of a performance or an account of an event, usu for a newspaper: *I'm writing up the play for the local paper.* See also WRITE-UP.

▶ **written** *adj* expressed in writing rather than in speech: *a written request/agreement/confession ○ written evidence/permission ○ Students have to take both an oral and a written examination.* **the ¦written ¦word** *n* [sing] language expressed in writing: *the power of the written word.*

■ ¦**write-down** *n* (*commerce*) a reduction in the value of assets (ASSET 2), etc: *a £100 000 write-down in the value of the property.*

¦**write-off** *n* **1** a thing, esp a vehicle, that is so badly damaged that it is not worth repairing: *After the accident, the car was a complete write-off.* **2** (*commerce*) an act of cancelling a debt because there is no chance that it will be paid.

¦**write-up** *n* a written or published account of an event, a review of a play, etc: *His performance got/ was given an enthusiastic write-up in the local press.*

writer /ˈraɪtə(r)/ *n* **1** a person whose job or regular occupation is writing eg books, stories or articles: *a writer of poetry ○ a travel/science/cookery writer ○ French/17th-century writers.* See also SCRIPTWRITER. **2** (with an *adj*) a person who forms letters in a particular way when writing: *a neat/messy writer.* **3** a person who has written a particular thing: *the writer of this letter/article/computer program.*

■ ¦**writer's ¦cramp** *n* [U] a pain or stiff feeling in the hand caused by writing for a long time.

writhe /raɪð/ *v* to move or twist the body continually, esp because of great pain: [V, Vp] *She was writhing (about) on the floor in agony.* [V] *the writhing bodies of the dancers ○ The snake writhed and hissed.*

writing /ˈraɪtɪŋ/ *n* **1** [U] (**a**) the activity or occupation of writing eg books, stories or articles: *I do a bit of writing in my spare time. ○ She doesn't earn much from her writing.* (**b**) books, stories, articles, etc: *an excellent piece of writing ○ travel/religious/critical writing ○ women's writing (ie by women).* (**c**) the literary style of such material: *He is admired for the elegance of his writing.* **2 writings** [pl] written works, eg books or essays: *the writings of Dickens/ Freud.* **3** [U] the general activity or skill of writing: *a ¦writing-desk ○ ¦writing-paper ○ writing materials* (eg pens, paper, ink). **4** [U] written or printed words: *There is some writing on the side of the paper. ○ The writing on the stone was very faint.* **5** [U] the way in which a person forms letters when writing; HANDWRITING(b): *I can never read your writing. ○ He's got awful writing.* **IDM** **in ¦writing** in written form, esp in a document or contract: *You must get his agreement in writing. ○ If you have any complaints, please put them in writing.* **the ¦writing (is) on the ¦wall** (there are) clear signs that warn of failure, disaster or defeat: *Many see these pit closures as the writing on the wall for the whole mining industry.*

written *pp* of WRITE.

wrong /rɒŋ; *US* rɔːŋ/ *adj* **1** not true or correct: *He did the sum but got the wrong answer/got the answer wrong. ○ Her estimate of the cost was completely wrong.* **2** [pred] ~ (**about sth/sb**); ~ (**to do sth**) (of a person) not right about sb/sth; mistaken: *Events have proved that she was wrong/have proved her wrong. ○ You were wrong about him; he's an American after all. ○ We were wrong to assume that she'd agree. ○ You think you've beaten me, but **that's where you're wrong**. ○ Thousands of satisfied customers can't be wrong.* **3** [usu attrib] not required, suitable or the most desirable: *You're folding it the wrong way. ○ We discovered that we were on the wrong train. ○ The police arrested the wrong woman. ○ We came the wrong way/took a wrong turning. ○ I'm afraid you've got the wrong number (ie on the telephone). ○ You're holding the camera the wrong way up/round. ○ He's the wrong person for the job. ○ I realized that I had said the wrong thing when I saw her reaction.* **4** [pred] ~ (**with sb/sth**) (**a**) not operating or functioning correctly: *What's wrong with the engine? It's making an awful noise. ○ There's something wrong with my left eye — I can't see properly. ○ The doctor said there was nothing wrong with me.* (**b**) causing problems or difficulties; not as it should be; abnormal: *Is anything wrong? You look worried. ○ There's nothing wrong with our tax system; why change it? ○ What's wrong with telling the truth? (ie How can it be criticized?)* **5** [esp pred] ~ (**of/for sb**) (**to do sth**) not morally right; not just or honest: *It is (morally) wrong to steal. ○ You were wrong/It was wrong of you to take her bike without permission. ○ It is quite wrong for politicians to accept gifts from business people. ○ He told me he had done nothing wrong.* Compare RIGHT[1]. **IDM** **back the wrong horse** ⇨ BACK[4]. **bark up the wrong tree** ⇨ BARK[2]. **born on the wrong side of the blanket** ⇨ BORN. **catch sb on the wrong foot** ⇨ CATCH[1]. **from/on the ¦wrong side of the ¦tracks** (*US*) living in an area or a part of a town which is regarded as socially inferior. **get on the right/ wrong side of sb** ⇨ SIDE[1]. **get (hold of) the ¦wrong end of the ¦stick** (*infml*) to be completely mistaken in understanding what has been said: *You've got the wrong end of the stick — he doesn't owe me money, I owe him!* **have got out of bed on the wrong side** ⇨ BED[1]. **hit/strike the right/ wrong note** ⇨ NOTE[1]. **not be far off/out/wrong** ⇨ FAR[1]. **on the right/wrong side of forty, etc** ⇨ SIDE[1]. **on the right/wrong track** ⇨ TRACK. **put a foot wrong** ⇨ FOOT. **rub sb up the wrong way** ⇨ RUB[1]. **start off on the right/wrong foot** ⇨ START[2].

▶ **wrong** *adv* (used after *vs*) in a wrong manner; so as to produce the wrong result: *You guessed wrong. ○ You've spelt my name wrong. ○ He played the tune all wrong.* Compare WRONGLY. **IDM** **get sb ¦wrong** (*infml*) to fail to understand sb: *Please don't get me wrong, I'm not criticizing you.* **go ¦wrong 1** to make a mistake: *If you read the instructions, you'll see where you went wrong. ○ You can't go wrong with a book token (ie It is always an acceptable gift).* **2** (of a machine) to stop working properly: *The car radio has gone wrong again.* **3** to experience trouble: *Their marriage started to go wrong when he got a job abroad. ○ The experiment went disastrously wrong (ie had unexpected and very unpleasant results).* **put a foot wrong** ⇨ FOOT[1].

wrong *n* **1** [U] actions that are wrong: *He doesn't know the difference between right and wrong. ○ She could do no wrong in the opinion of her devoted followers.* **2** [C] (*fml*) an action that is morally wrong or not just: *They have done us a great wrong. ○ She complained of the wrongs she had suffered. ○ He is determined to **right the wrongs** done to his family.* **IDM** **in the ¦wrong** responsible for eg a mistake, an offence or a quarrel: *He admitted that he was in the wrong.* **the rights and wrongs of sth** ⇨ RIGHT[3].

wrong v (fml) (esp passive) to treat sb in a wrong or unfair way: [Vn] a wronged wife ○ He felt deeply wronged by the allegations.

wrongful /-fl/ adj [attrib] (esp law) not fair, just or legal: He sued his employer for wrongful dismissal/ the police for wrongful arrest. **wrongfully** /-fəli/ adv: be wrongfully convicted/imprisoned.

wrongly adv (used esp before a past participle or a v) in a wrong, mistaken or unfair way: wrongly spelt/labelled/translated ○ a wrongly addressed parcel ○ wrongly accused/convicted ○ I was wrongly informed that I had failed the examination. ○ He imagines, (quite) wrongly, that she loves him. ○ Rightly or wrongly, she refused to accept the offer (ie I do not know whether she was right or wrong to do so).

wrongness n [U].

■ **wrong-ˈfoot** v (Brit) (esp passive) to put sb in a difficult or embarrassing situation by doing sth they do not expect: [Vn] Her cleverly disguised lob completely wrong-footed her opponent. ○ I was wrong-footed by the interviewer's next question.

ˌwrong-ˈheaded adj having or showing bad judgement: ˌwrong-headed iˈdeas.

wrongdoer /ˈrɒnduːə(r)/ n (fml) a person who does sth dishonest or illegal.
▶ **wrongdoing** /ˈrɒnduːɪn/ n [U, C] illegal or dishonest behaviour: The company denies any wrongdoing. ○ be sorry for one's wrongdoings.

wrote pt of WRITE.

wrought /rɔːt/ v (fml or rhet) (used in the past tense only) caused sth to happen: [Vn] changes wrought in our society ○ The storm wrought havoc throughout southern Britain.
▶ **wrought** adj [attrib] **1** made or manufactured and decorated: elaborately wrought carvings. **2** (of metal) beaten or shaped by hammering.
■ **ˌwrought ˈiron** n [U] a tough form of iron used for decorative work: a ˌwrought-iron ˈbedstead/ˈgate/ ˈrailing. Compare CAST IRON.

wrung pt, pp of WRING.

wry /raɪ/ adj **1** indicating amused intelligent awareness of a situation; slightly mocking or cynical (CYNIC): She watched their fumbling efforts with wry amusement. ○ a wry grin/smile ○ The film is a wry and witty commentary on the 60s. **2** [usu attrib] (of a person's face, features, etc) twisted into an expression of disappointment, disgust or annoyance: pull a wry face. ▶ **wryly** adv: grin/smile wryly. **wryness** n [U].

wt abbr weight.

WYSIWYG (also **wysiwyg**) /ˈwɪziwɪg/ abbr (computing) what you see is what you get (indicating that what appears on a computer screen is in exactly the same form as what appears on a PRINTOUT of the same material).

W

X¹ (also **x**) /eks/ n (pl **X's, x's** /ˈeksɪz/) the 24th letter of the English alphabet: *'Xylophone' begins with (an) X/'X'.*

■ ¹**X-chromosome** n (*biology*) a CHROMOSOME that occurs as one of an IDENTICAL(2) pair in female cells to produce a female during REPRODUCTION(2), or combined with a single Y-chromosome (Y¹) in male cells to produce a male. Compare Y-CHROMOSOME.

¹**X-rated** adj (esp of films) thought to be not suitable for children under a certain age: *X-rated video movies.*

X² (also **x**) symb **1** the Roman NUMERAL for 10. **2** (indicating a kiss, esp at the end of a letter, etc): *Love from Kathy XXX.* **3** (indicating a vote for sb in an election): *Write X beside the candidate of your choice.* **4** (*Brit*) (indicating an error in written work). Compare TICK¹ 3. **5**(**a**) (*mathematics*) an unknown quantity: *4x = x + x + x + x.* (**b**) a person, a number, an influence, etc that is not known or not specified: *Mr and Mrs X.* **6** (indicating a position, eg on a map): *X marks the spot.*

xenophobia /ˌzenəˈfəʊbiə/ n [U] an intense dislike or fear of strangers or people from other countries: *Excessive patriotism can lead to xenophobia.* ► **xenophobic** /-ˈfəʊbɪk/ adj.

Xerox /ˈzɪərɒks/ n (*propr*) (**a**) a process for producing photographic copies of letters, documents, etc: *a Xerox machine.* (**b**) a photographic copy made using this process: *make/take a couple of Xeroxes of the contract.* Compare PHOTOCOPY.

► **xerox** v to produce copies of documents, etc by Xerox or a similar process: [Vn] *Could you xerox this letter please, Louise?*

-xion ⇨ -ION.

XL /ˌeks ˈel/ abbr (esp on clothing) extra large.

Xmas /ˈkrɪsməs, ˈeksməs/ n [C, U] (*infml*) (used as a short form, esp in writing) Christmas: *A merry Xmas to all our readers!*

X-ray /ˈeks reɪ/ n **1** (usu pl) a type of RADIATION(1b) that can penetrate solid objects and makes it possible to see into or through them. X-rays are commonly used by doctors to examine bones and organs inside the body: *an X-ray machine* (ie one that produces X-rays) ○ *X-ray therapy* (ie medical treatment using X-rays) ○ *An X-ray telescope examines and measures the X-rays emitted by stars.* **2**(**a**) a photograph made by X-rays, esp one showing bones or organs in the human body: *a chest X-ray ○ take an X-ray of sb's hand ○ The doctor studied the X-rays.* (**b**) (*infml*) a medical examination using X-rays: *go for an X-ray.*

► **X-ray** v to examine, photograph or treat a person or an animal, using X-rays: [Vn] *have one's lungs X-rayed.*

xylophone /ˈzaɪləfəʊn/ n a musical instrument consisting of parallel wooden or metal bars mounted on a frame. Each bar is a different length and produces a different note¹(5) when hit with small wooden hammers. Compare GLOCKENSPIEL. ⇨ picture at MUSICAL INSTRUMENT.

Yy

Y¹ (also **y**) /waɪ/ *n* (*pl* **Y's, y's** /waɪz/) the 25th letter of the English alphabet: '*Yak' begins with (a) Y/'Y*.
■ **'Y-chromosome** *n* (*biology*) a CHROMOSOME that occurs by itself and only in male cells, and produces a male after combining with an X-chromosome (X¹) during REPRODUCTION. Compare X-CHROMOSOME.
'Y-fronts *n* [pl] (*Brit propr*) men's UNDERPANTS, with seams (SEAM 1a) and an opening in the front sewn in the shape of a Y upside-down: *a pair of Y-fronts*.

Y² *abbr* **1** yen¹. **2** /waɪ/ (*US infml*) = YMCA, YWCA.

Y³ /waɪ/ *symb* (**a**) (also **y**) (*mathematics*) an unknown quantity: $x = y + 2$. (**b**) a second person, number or influence that is not known or not specified: *Mr X met Miss Y*.

-y¹ *suff* **1** (also **-ey**) (with *ns* forming *adjs*) full of; having the quality of: *dusty* ○ *icy* ○ *clayey*. **2** (with *vs* forming *adjs*) tending to: *runny* ○ *sticky*.

-y² *suff* **1** (with *vs* forming *ns*) the action or process of: *inquiry* ○ *expiry*. **2** (also **-ie**) (with *ns* indicating small size or, as a form of a name, indicating affection): *piggy* ○ *doggie* ○ *daddy* ○ *Susie*.

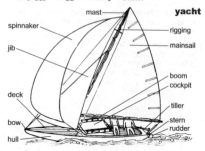

yacht

spinnaker
jib
deck
bow
hull
mast
rigging
mainsail
boom
cockpit
tiller
stern
rudder

yacht /jɒt/ *n* a light boat with sails and usu also an engine, used for pleasure trips or for racing: *a yacht club/crew/race*. ➪ picture. Compare DINGHY.
▶ **yachting** *n* [U] the activity of sailing in yachts for pleasure or as a sport: *a yachting holiday* ○ *go yachting*.

yachtsman /jɒtsmən/ *n* (*pl* **-men** /-mən/; *fem* **'yachtswoman** /-wʊmən/, *pl* **-women** /-wɪmɪn/) a person who sails a YACHT for pleasure or as a sport: *a round-the-world yachtsman*.

yahoo /ˌjɑːˈhuː/ *n* (*pl* **-oos**) a rude and violent person: *a yahoo 'attitude*.

yak /jæk/ *n* a type of OX(2) with long horns and long hair, found mainly in central Asia.

Yale /jeɪl/ (also **'Yale lock**) *n* (*Brit propr*) a type of lock with revolving internal parts, commonly used for doors: *have a Yale (lock) fitted* ○ *a Yale key*.

yam /jæm/ *n* **1** the edible root of a tropical climbing plant. **2** (*US*) a type of sweet potato.

yammer /ˈjæmə(r)/ *v* ~ (**on**) (**about sb/sth**) (*infml derog*) to talk noisily and continuously; to speak or complain in an irritating manner: [Vp] *They kept yammering on about how expensive everything was*. [also V, Vpr].

yang /jæŋ/ *n* [U] (in Chinese philosophy) the active bright male principle of the universe. Compare YIN.

Yank /jæŋk/ *n* (*Brit infml sometimes derog*) = YANKEE. ➪ note at AMERICAN.

yank /jæŋk/ *v* (*infml*) to pull sth with a sudden sharp movement: [Vn, Vpr] *She yanked (on) the rope and it broke*. [Vnpr, Vnp] *yank the bedclothes off (the bed)*.
▶ **yank** *n* (usu *sing*) a sudden sharp pull: *He gave the rope a yank*.

Yankee /ˈjæŋki/ (also **Yank**) *n* **1** (*Brit infml sometimes derog*) an inhabitant of the USA; an American: *Yankee hospitality*. **2** (*US*) (**a**) an inhabitant of any of the northern American States, esp those of New England. (**b**) a FEDERAL(3) soldier in the American Civil War.

yap /jæp/ *v* (**-pp-**) **1** ~ (**at sb/sth**) (esp of small dogs) to make short sharp barks (BARK² 1a): [Vpr] *yapping at the milkman* [also V]. **2** (*sl*) to talk noisily and foolishly, esp in an annoying way: [V] *Stop yapping!* [also Vpr, Vp].

yard¹ /jɑːd/ *n* **1**(**a**) an area outside a building, usu with a concrete or stone floor and often with a wall partly or completely surrounding it: *The prison yard* ○ *Children were playing ball in the yard at the back of the house*. See also BACKYARD 1a. (**b**) (*US*) = BACK-YARD 1b. **2** (usu in compounds) an area of land used for a special purpose or business: *a 'railway yard* ○ *a 'builder's yard*. See also BOATYARD, CHURCHYARD, FARMYARD, SCOTLAND YARD, SHIPYARD.

yard² /jɑːd/ *n* **1** (*abbr* **yd**) a unit of length, equal to 3 feet (36 inches) or 0.9144 of a metre: *I'll take two yards of this material, please*. ○ *We live only a few yards from the bus station*. ➪ App 2. **2** a long piece of wood fastened to a MAST(1) for supporting and spreading a sail.
▶ **yardage** /ˈjɑːdɪdʒ/ *n* [C, U] size measured in yards or square yards: *a considerable yardage of canvas* ○ *He knows the yardage of the whole golf-course*.
■ **'yard-arm** *n* either end of a yard²(2) supporting a sail.

yardstick /ˈjɑːdstɪk/ *n* ~ (**of sth**) a standard used for assessing the quality of people or things: *Durability is one yardstick of quality*. ○ *We need a yardstick to measure our performance by*.

yarn /jɑːn/ *n* **1** [U] thread, esp wool, that has been spun for knitting, weaving, etc. **2** [C] (*infml*) a story, esp one that is exaggerated or invented: *His excuse was that he caught the wrong train, but I think he was **spinning a yarn** (ie not telling the truth)*.

yarrow /ˈjærəʊ/ *n* [C, U] a plant with many small white or pinkish flowers that have a strong smell.

yashmak /ˈjæʃmæk/ *n* a piece of material covering most of the face, worn in public by Muslim women in certain countries.

yaw /jɔː/ *v* [V] (of a ship or an aircraft) to keep turning off a straight course. Compare PITCH² 5, ROLL² 7a. ▶ **yaw** *n* [C, U]: *the angle of yaw*.

yawl /jɔːl/ *n* a boat that has two masts (MAST 1), the second of which is short and near the back of the boat, and sails.

yawn /jɔːn/ *v* **1** to take a deep breath with the mouth wide open, usu when one is tired or bored: [V] *He stretched himself and yawned*. **2** (of large holes) to be wide open: [V] *A crevasse yawned at their feet*. ○ (*fig*) *a yawning gap/gulf between rich and poor*.
▶ **yawn** *n* **1** an act of yawning (YAWN 1). **2** (usu *sing*) (*infml derog*) a boring event, idea, etc: *The meeting was one big yawn from start to finish*.

yaws /jɔːz/ n [sing or pl v] a tropical skin disease causing large red swellings.

Y-chromosome ⇨ Y¹.

yd abbr (pl **yds**) a yard (a measurement): *12 yds of silk.* Compare FT, IN⁴.

ye¹ /jiː, weak form ji/ pers pron (arch) (pl of **thou**) you.

ye² /jiː, or pronounced as **the**/ det (used in the names of pubs, shops, etc as if it were the old-fashioned spelling) the: *Ye Olde Bull and Bush* (eg on a pub sign).

yea /jeɪ/ adv, n (arch) yes. Compare NAY 2.

yeah /jeə/ adv (infml) yes. **IDM** ˌoh ˈyeah? (used to show that one does not believe what has been said): *'I'm going to be rich one day.' 'Oh yeah?'*

year /jɪə(r); Brit also jɜː(r)/ n **1** [C] the time taken by the earth to travel once round the sun, about 365¼ days. **2** (also **calendar year**) the period from 1 January to 31 December, ie 365 days, or 366 in a leap year (LEAP), divided into 12 months: *in the year 1865* ○ *I shall be 18 this year.* ○ *a good year for strawberries* (ie a year in which there are many of them and they are cheap). See also LEAP YEAR, NEW YEAR. **3** [C] any continuous period of 365 days: *It's just a year (today) since I arrived here.* ○ *I arrived three years ago (today).* ○ *They're getting married in a year's time.* ○ *a ˌfive-year ˈforecast.* See also LIGHT-YEAR. **4** [C] a period of one year associated with a particular activity or organization: *the ˌacademic/ˌschool ˈyear* ○ *ˌfirst year ˈstudents* ○ *the ˌtax year.* See also FINANCIAL YEAR. **5** [C usu pl] age; time of life: *be twenty years old/of age* ○ *a seventy-year-old man* ○ *She looks young for (a woman of) her years* (ie looks younger than she is). ○ *He died in his sixtieth year* (ie at the age of 59). **6 years** [pl] (infml) a long time: *I've worked for this firm for years (and years).* ○ *It's years since we last met.* **IDM** ˌall (the) year ˈround throughout the year: *He swims in the sea all year round.* **donkey's years** ⇨ DONKEY. **man, woman, car, etc of the ˈyear** a person or thing chosen as outstanding in a particular activity during a particular year: *TV personality of the year.* **not/never in a hundred, etc ˈyears** absolutely not/never: *I'd never have thought of that in a million years.* **put ˈyears on sb** to make sb feel or look older: *The illness put years on him.* **take ˈyears off sb** to make sb feel or look younger: *Giving up smoking has taken years off her.* **the turn of the year/century** ⇨ TURN². **ˌyear after ˈyear** continuously for many years: *Year after year they went to Blackpool in August.* **ˌyear by ˈyear** as the years pass; each year: *Year by year their affection for each other grew stronger.* **the year ˈdot** (Brit); (US) **the ˌyear ˈone** (infml) a very long time ago: *I've been going there every summer since the year dot.* **year ˈin, year ˈout** every year without exception. **ˌyear of ˈgrace**; **ˌyear of our ˈLord** (fml) any specified year after the birth of Christ: *in the year of our Lord 1217* (ie 1217 AD).

▶ **yearly** adj, adv (occurring) every year or once a year: *a yearly conference/a conference held yearly.*

■ **ˌyear-ˈlong** adj [attrib] continuing for or throughout a year: *a ˌyear-long ˈlecture tour.*

ˌyear-on-ˈyear adj [attrib] (esp of figures, prices, etc) in the period of 12 months until a particular date: *a small year-on-year increase in house prices.*

ˌyear-ˈround adj throughout each year: *an island with ˌyear-round ˈsunshine* ○ *a ˌyear-round ˈsport.*

yearbook /ˈjɪəbʊk/ n **1** a book published once a year, giving details of events, etc of the previous year, esp those that concern a particular area of activity: *The British Music Yearbook.* **2** (US) a book containing photographs of the senior class in a school or university and details of school activities.

yearling /ˈjɪəlɪŋ/ n an animal, esp a horse, between one and two years old: *a race for yearlings.*

yearn /jɜːn/ v ~ (**for sb/sth**) to desire sth strongly and with great emotion: [V] *a yearning desire* [Vpr]

He yearned for his home and family. [V.to inf] *She yearned to return to her native country.*

▶ **yearning** n [C, U] ~ (**for sth/sb**); ~ (**to do sth**) a strong and emotional desire. **yearningly** adv.

yeast /jiːst/ n [C, U] a type of FUNGUS(1) used in making beer and wine, or to make bread rise²(16).

▶ **yeasty** adj tasting or smelling strongly of yeast; having a lot of bubbles on the surface, like yeast when it is developing.

yell /jel/ v **1** ~ (**out**) (**in/with sth**) to give a loud sharp cry or cries of pain, excitement, anger, etc: [Vp] *yell out in anguish/terror/pain* [Vpr] *yell with fear/agony/laughter* [V] *Stop yelling, can't you!* **2** ~ **at sb** (**about/for sth**); ~ (**out**) **sth** (**at sb/sth**) to speak or say sth in a yelling voice: [Vpr] *She's always yelling at him for being drunk.* [Vpr.to inf] *She yelled at the child to get down off the wall.* [Vn, Vnpr, Vnp] *The crowd yelled (out) encouragement (at the players).* [V.speech] *'Stay where you are!' she yelled.* ⇨ note at SHOUT.

▶ **yell** n **1** a loud cry of pain, excitement, etc: *a yell of terror* ○ *let out an ear-splitting yell.* **2** (US) an organized shout or CHEER used at a college to encourage a team, etc.

yellow /ˈjeləʊ/ adj **1(a)** of the colour of eg a ripe LEMON(1), an egg YOLK or gold. ⇨ picture at SPECTRUM. **(b)** (often offensive) having the light brown skin of certain eastern Asian peoples. **2** (infml derog) cowardly.

▶ **yellow** n **(a)** [C, U] the colour yellow: *a pattern of yellows and greens.* **(b)** [U] yellow clothes or material: *wearing yellow.*

yellow v to become or make sth yellow: [V] *yellowing autumn leaves* [V, Vn] *The manuscript had/was yellowed with age.*

yellowish, yellowy adjs rather yellow.

yellowness n [U].

■ **ˌyellow ˈcard** n (in football, etc) a card shown by the REFEREE(1a) to a player as a warning about bad behaviour on the field of play. Compare RED CARD.

ˌyellow ˈfever n [U] an infectious tropical disease that causes the skin to turn yellow.

ˌyellow ˈflag n **1** = FLAG⁴. **2** a flag coloured yellow, displayed by a ship on which sb has or may have an infectious disease.

ˌyellow ˈline n (in Britain) a yellow line painted at the side of a road to show that the parking of vehicles is restricted: *You can't park on a double yellow line.*

ˌYellow ˈPages n [pl] (propr) a telephone DIRECTORY, or a section of one, listing companies and organizations according to the goods or services they offer: *look in the Yellow Pages.*

the ˌyellow ˈpress n [sing] (Brit infml derog) newspapers that deliberately include material that is exciting or shocking in order to attract readers.

yellowhammer /ˈjeləʊhæmə(r)/ n a small bird, the male of which has a yellow head, neck and breast.

yelp /jelp/ n a short sharp cry of pain, anger, excitement, etc: *The dog let out a yelp as I trod on its paw.*

▶ **yelp** v [V] to give a yelp.

yen¹ /jen/ n (pl unchanged) the unit of money in Japan.

yen² /jen/ n (usu sing) ~ (**for sth / to do sth**) (infml) a strong desire: *I've always had a yen to visit Australia.*

yeoman /ˈjəʊmən/ n (pl **-men** /-mən/) (Brit) (formerly) a farmer who owned and worked his own land: *wealthy yeoman farmers.*

▶ **yeomanry** /-ri/ n [Gp] (Brit) **1** (formerly) farmers who owned their own land. **2** (formerly) a group of yeomen who chose to become soldiers and provided their own horses.

■ **ˌYeoman of the ˈGuard** n a member of the British king's or queen's BODYGUARD.

yes /jes/ interj **1(a)** (used for answering and saying that sth is true or correct): *'Is this painting by Picasso?' 'Yes, it is.'* ○ *'Don't you want to come with us?' 'Yes, of course I do.'* (**b**) (used to indicate that one agrees with what has been said): *'English is a difficult language.' 'Yes, but not as difficult as Chinese.'* ○ *'Isn't she sweet?' 'Yes.'* (**c**) (used for agreeing to a request): *'Can I borrow this book?' 'Yes, of course.'* **2** (used for accepting an invitation or offer): *'Coffee?' 'Yes, please.'* **3** (used for acknowledging one's presence or replying when one is called): *'Williams.' 'Yes, sir.'* ○ *'Waiter!' 'Yes, madam.'* **4** (used for asking what sb wants): *'Yes?' 'I'd like two tickets to Brighton, please.'* Compare NO *interj.* **IDM** ˌyes and ˈno partly true or correct and partly not: *'Are you enjoying your new job?' 'Well, yes and no. It's interesting but very hard work.'*

▶ **yes** *n* (*pl* **yeses** or **yesses** /ˈjesɪz/) an answer that shows one agrees, accepts sth, etc: *Can't you give me a straight (ie direct) yes or no?*

■ **yes-man** /ˈjes mæn/ *n* (*pl* **-men** /-men/) a weak person who always agrees with people in authority in order to gain their approval.

yesterday /ˈjestədeɪ, -dɪ/ *adv* on the day just past; on the day before today: *He only arrived yesterday.* ○ *I can remember it as if it were yesterday.* ○ *Where were you yesterday morning/afternoon/evening?* ⇨ note at MORNING.

▶ **yesterday** *n* [U, C often *pl*] **1** the day before today: *Yesterday was Sunday.* ○ *Where's yesterday's (news)paper?* **2** the recent past: *dressed in yesterday's fashions.* **IDM** be born yesterday ⇨ BORN. the day before yesterday ⇨ DAY.

yesteryear /ˈjestəjɪə(r)/ *n* [U] (*arch* or *rhet*) the recent past: *recalling pop stars of yesteryear.*

yet /jet/ *adv* **1(a)** (used in questions and negative sentences and after *vs* expressing uncertainty, usu at the end of the sentence. In British English *yet* is usu used with the present or past perfect tense, in American English with the simple past tense.) by this or that time; until now/then: *I haven't received a letter from him yet.* ○ *(US) I didn't receive a letter from him yet.* ○ *'Are you ready?' 'No, not yet.'* ○ *She was not yet sure if she could trust him.* ○ *I doubt if he's read it yet.* (**b**) now; as soon as this: *Don't go yet.* ○ *We don't need to start yet.* ⇨ note at ALREADY. (**c**) from now into the future for the specified length of time: *He'll be busy for ages yet.* ○ *They won't arrive for at least two hours yet.* **2** at this point in time, as before; still² (1): *We **have yet** to decide what action to take.* **3** (used with a *modal v*) at some time in the future: *We may win yet.* ○ (*rather fml*) *She may yet surprise us all.* **4** (used after superlatives) made, produced, written, etc until and including now/then: *the most comprehensive study yet of his music* ○ *the highest building yet constructed.* **5** (used before comparatives) even¹(2); still²(3b): *a recent and yet more improbable theory* ○ *advancing yet further* ○ *yet another example of his negligence.* **IDM** as ˈyet until now/then: *an as yet unpublished report* ○ *As yet little is known of the causes of the disease.* yet aˈgain once more: *Yet again we can see the results of hasty decision-making.*

▶ **yet** *conj* but at the same time; nevertheless: *slow yet thorough* ○ *She trained hard all year yet still failed to reach her best form.*

yeti /ˈjeti/ (also **Abominable Snowman**) *n* a large hairy creature like a man or a bear, reported to live in the highest part of the Himalayas.

yew /juː/ *n* (**a**) (also ˈ**yew-tree**) [C] a small tree which has dark green leaves all through the year, and small red berries. Yews are often planted near churches. (**b**) [U] the wood of this tree.

Y-fronts ⇨ Y¹.

YHA /ˌwaɪ eɪtʃ ˈeɪ/ *abbr* Youth Hostels Association.

yid /jɪd/ *n* (△ *sl offensive*) a Jew.

Yiddish /ˈjɪdɪʃ/ *adj, n* [U] (of) the international Jewish

language, a form of old German with words taken from Hebrew and several modern languages, used by Jews in or from eastern or central Europe: *speak (in) Yiddish* ○ *Yiddish songs.* Compare HEBREW 2.

yield /jiːld/ *v* **1** to produce or provide sth as a natural product, as a result or as profit: [Vn] *trees that no longer yield fruit* ○ *investment accounts yielding high interest* ○ *research that yields new insights into animal behaviour.* **2** ~ (**to sb/sth**) to allow oneself to be overcome by pressure; to stop opposing or resisting sb/sth: [V] *The town was forced to yield after a long siege.* [Vpr] *The government has not yielded to public opinion.* ○ *She yielded to temptation and had another chocolate.* **3** ~ sb/sth (**up**) (**to sb**) (*fml*) (**a**) to give control of sth to sb, esp unwillingly; to deliver or surrender sb/sth to sb: [Vnpr, Vnp] *The terrorists have yielded two of their hostages (up) to the police.* [also Vn]. (**b**) to reveal sth: [Vnp] *The universe is slowly yielding up its secrets to scientists.* [also Vn, Vnpr]. **4** to bend or break under pressure: [V] *Despite all our attempts to break it open, the lock would not yield.* ○ *The dam eventually yielded and collapsed under the weight of water.* **5** ~ (**to sb/sth**) (*esp US*) (of traffic) to allow other traffic to go first; to give way (WAY¹): [Vpr] *Drivers joining the freeway must yield to traffic in the outside lane.* [also V]. **6** ~ to sth to be replaced by sth: *Increasingly, farm land is yielding to property development.*

▶ **yield** *n* [U, C] the total amount that is produced: *a good/high/poor yield of wheat* ○ *What is the yield per acre?* ○ *the annual milk yield.*

yielding *adj* **1** likely to accept or submit to the wishes of others: *She lay soft and yielding in his arms.* **2** (of a substance) that can bend or move when pressed; soft rather than stiff.

yin /jɪn/ *n* [U] (in Chinese philosophy) the PASSIVE(1) dark female principle of the universe. Compare YANG.

yippee /jɪˈpiː; *US* ˈjɪpi/ *interj* (*infml*) (expressing pleasure or excitement).

YMCA /ˌwaɪ em siː ˈeɪ/ (also *US infml* **Y**) *abbr* Young Men's Christian Association: *stay at the YMCA (hostel).*

yob /jɒb/ (also **yobbo** /ˈjɒbəʊ/, *pl* **-os**) *n* (*dated Brit sl*) a rude, noisy or aggressive young person; a LOUT.

yodel /ˈjəʊdl/ *v* (**-ll-**; *US* **-l-**) [V, Vn] to sing a song or make a musical call in the traditional Swiss manner, with frequent changes from the normal voice to a very high voice and back again.

▶ **yodel** *n* a yodelling song or call.

yoga /ˈjəʊɡə/ *n* [U] **1** a Hindu philosophy that teaches control over the mind, senses and body in order to produce spiritual experience and the union of the individual soul with the spirit of the universe. **2** a system of exercises for the body and for controlling one's breathing, used in yoga or by people wanting to become fitter: *yoga classes.*

▶ **yogi** /ˈjəʊɡi/ *n* (*pl* **yogis**) a teacher of or an expert in yoga(1).

yoghurt (also **yogurt**, **yoghourt**) /ˈjɒɡət; *US* ˈjəʊɡərt/ *n* [U, C] a thick slightly sour liquid food, made from milk with bacteria added and often with fruit: *a breakfast of muesli and yoghurt* ○ *a carton of strawberry yoghurt.*

yoke /jəʊk/ *n* **1** [sing] ~ (**of sth/sb**) (*fml*) harsh treatment and lack of freedom that is difficult to bear: *throw off the yoke of slavery* ○ *under the yoke of a cruel master.* **2** [C] (**a**) a shaped piece of wood fixed across the necks of two animals, esp cattle, and attached to the cart, PLOUGH(1), etc they are pulling. ⇨ picture. (**b**) (*pl* unchanged) two animals working together with a yoke: *five yoke of oxen.* **3** [C] a piece

yoke

of wood shaped to fit across a person's shoulders forcarrying two equal loads, one on each side. **4** [C] the part of a garment fitting round the shoulders or hips and from which the heavier part of the garment hangs.
▶ **yoke** v **1** ~ **sth (to sth)**; ~ **sth and sth (together)** to put a yoke on an animal: [Vnpr] *yoke oxen to a plough* [Vnp] *yoke bullocks together* [also Vn]. **2** ~ **A and B (together) (in sth)** (*fml*) (usu passive) to link people, ideas, etc: [Vnpr, Vnp] *companies yoked (together) in a trilateral deal* [also Vn].

yokel /ˈjəʊkl/ n (*joc or derog*) a country person without much education; a BUMPKIN.

yolk /jəʊk/ n [C,U] the round yellow part in the middle of an egg: *Beat up the yolks of three eggs.* ⇨ picture at EGG¹.

Yom Kippur /ˌjɒm ˈkɪpə(r), kɪˈpʊə(r); US ˌjəʊm/ an annual Jewish holiday with fasting (FAST³) and prayers.

yomp /jɒmp/ v (*Brit sl esp military*) to march with heavy equipment over difficult country: [Vpr] *yomping across moorland* [also V, Vp].

yon /jɒn/ det (*arch or dialect*) that: *yon island/lass.* ▶ **yon** adv **IDM** **hither and yon** ⇨ HITHER.

yonder /ˈjɒndə(r)/ det, adj (*arch or dialect*) that is or that can be seen over there: *Do you see yonder clump of trees (ie that clump of trees over there)?* ▶ **yonder** adv: *Whose is that farm (over) yonder?*

yore /jɔː(r)/ n **IDM** **of yore** (*arch or rhet*) long ago: *in days of yore.*

Yorkshire pudding /ˌjɔːkʃə ˈpʊdɪŋ/ n [U,C] BATTER² that has been baked in an oven, often eaten with BEEF(1).

you /ju; US jə; *strong form* juː/ *pers pron* **1** the person or people being addressed (**a**) (used as the subject or object of a v or after a *prep*; also used after *be*): *You said you knew the way.* ○ *I thought she told you.* ○ *This is just between you and me* (ie not to be told to anyone else). ○ *I don't think that hairstyle is you* (ie It doesn't suit your appearance or personality). (**b**) (used with *ns* and *adjs* to address sb directly): *You girls, stop talking!* ○ *You silly fool, you've lost us the game.* **2** people in general; everyone or anyone; *You learn a language better if you visit the country where it's spoken.* ○ *Driving on the left is strange at first but you get used to it.* **IDM** **you and your ʹyours** you and your family and close friends: *Best wishes to you and yours.*
■ **you-all** /ˈjuː ɔːl/ *pers pron* (*esp southern US*) you (when more than one person): *Have you-all brought swimsuits?*

you'd /juːd/ *short form* **1** you had. ⇨ note at HAVE. **2** you would. ⇨ WILL¹, WOULD.

you'll /juːl/ *short form* you will. ⇨ WILL¹.

young /jʌŋ/ adj (**-nger** /-ŋgə(r)/; **-ngest** /-ŋgɪst/) **1** not far advanced in life, growth, development, etc; recently born or begun: *a young woman/animal/tree/nation* ○ *Are you younger or older than me?* Compare OLD 2. **2** (of a person's appearance, attitudes or behaviour) like a young person: *a young forty-year-old* ○ *He's sixty but he's very young in his outlook.* **3** not as mature or experienced as one would expect: *My daughter's thirteen but she's young for her age.* **4** of, for or characteristic of youth or young people: *young love/ambition/fashion* ○ *Those clothes she's wearing are much too young for her.* **5** (of a group) representing the young members of an organization: *the Young Conservatives* ○ *Young Farmers' clubs.* **6(a) the younger** (*fml*) (used before or after a person's name, to distinguish that person from an older person with the same name): *the younger Pitt* ○ *Pitt the younger.* Compare ELDER¹ 2. (**b**) (*infml becoming dated*) (used before a person's name, eg to distinguish a son from his father): *Young Jones is just like his father.* **7** (used to show one's superiority (SUPERIOR) over or contempt for

the person one is addressing): *Now listen to me, young man/lady/woman!* **8** (*rhet*) near the beginning: *The night is still young.* **IDM** **an angry young man** ⇨ ANGRY. **not as/so young as one used to be/as one (once) was** old or growing old and losing energy: *I can't play squash twice a week — I'm not as young as I was, you know!* **not getting any ʹyounger** becoming older: *The long walk to the shops tires me out — I'm not getting any younger, you know.* **an old head on young shoulders** ⇨ OLD. **young and ʹold (aʹlike)** everyone, regardless of age: *This is a book for young and old (alike).* ʹ**young at ʹheart** still feeling and behaving as one did when one was young.
▶ **young** n [pl] **1** young animals: *The female bird feeds its young until they leave the nest.* **2 the young** young people considered as a group: *a film that appeals specially to the young.*

youngish /ˈjʌŋɪʃ/ adj fairly young; quite young: *a youngish President.*

youngster /-stə(r)/ n a child; a young person: *She's still only a youngster.*

your /jɔː(r); US also jʊər; *weak form* jə(r)/ *possess det* **1** of or belonging to the person or people being addressed: *Excuse me, is this your seat?* ○ *Do you like your new job?* ○ *Your hair's going grey.* ○ *The post office is on your right.* **2** of or belonging to people in general: *Dentists advise you to have your teeth checked every six months.* ○ *In Japan you are taught great respect for your elders.* **3** (*often derog*) (used to indicate that sb/sth is well-known or often talked about): *I don't think much of your English weather.* ○ (*ironic*) *You and your bright ideas!* **4** (also **Your**) (used when addressing royal people, important officials, etc): *Your Majesty* ○ *Your Excellency.*
▶ **yours** /jɔːz; US jʊərz/ *possess pron* **1** of or belonging to you: *Is that book yours?* ○ *Is she a friend of yours?* ○ (*fml*) *Thank you for yours* (ie your letter) *of 25 May.* **2** (usu **Yours**, *abbr* **yrs**) (used in ending a letter): *Yours faithfully/sincerely/truly.* **IDM** **you and yours** ⇨ YOU.

NOTE Yours faithfully, Yours sincerely and, especially in American English, **Yours truly** are the most usual ways of ending formal letters, for example when writing to a bank, hotel, shop, etc. When you do not know the name of the person you are writing to, the correct style is to begin **Dear Sir** or **Dear Madam** or **Dear Sir or Madam** and to end with **Yours faithfully**. Sometimes you know the name, but you do not know the person, or you need to address somebody quite formally, for example a person you have only met once or twice. In this case begin **Dear Mr/Mrs/Miss/Ms Smith** and end **Yours sincerely**. In American English **Sincerely**, **Sincerely yours** and **Yours truly** are more often used.
If you know the person or are on equal terms with her or him, for example when writing to a colleague, you can use the first name and add **With best wishes**. **Yours**, **Best wishes**, **Love** or **Love from** are used for personal letters. **Love** and **Love from** are the most informal and used when writing to close friends or family.

Dear Madam, ...	Dear Mrs Brown, ...
Yours faithfully,	**Yours sincerely/truly,**
Jane Jones	Jane Jones
Dear Margaret, ...	Dear Maggie, ...
With best wishes,	Best wishes,
Yours sincerely/truly,	**Yours,**
Jane (Jones)	Jane
Dear Mum and Dad, ...	
Lots of love,	
Jane	

For further help with letter-writing, ⇨ App 3.

Y

you're /jʊə(r), jɔː(r); *US weak form* jər/ *short form* you are. ⇨ note at BE².

yourself /jɔːˈself; *weak form* jəˈself; *US* jʊərˈself/ (*pl* **-selves** /-ˈselvz/) *reflex, emph pron* (only taking the main stress when used for emphasis) **1** (*reflex*) (used when the person or people addressed both cause and are affected by an action): *Have you ¹hurt yourself?* ○ *En¹joy yourselves!* **2** (*emph*) (used to emphasize the person or people addressed): *You yourself are one of the chief offenders.* ○ *You can try it out for your¹selves.* ○ *Do it your¹self — I haven't got time.* **3** you: *We sell a lot of these to people like yourself.* ○ *'And yourself,' he replied, 'How are you?'* **IDM** **(all) by your¹self/your¹selves 1** alone: *How long were you by yourself in the house?* **2** without help: *Are you sure you did this exercise by yourself?*

youth /juːθ/ *n* (*pl* **youths** /juːðz/) **1** [U] the time when a person is young, esp the time before a child becomes an adult: *I (often went there in my youth.* ○ *He painted scenes from his youth* (ie ones that he remembered from the time when he was young). ○ *He is no longer in the first flush of youth.* Compare AGE¹ 2. **2** [U] (*fml*) the state or quality of being young: *Her youth gives her an advantage over the other runners.* ○ *She is full of youth and vitality.* Compare AGE¹ 2. **3** [C] (*often derog*) a young person, esp a young man: *The fight was started by some youths who had been drinking.* **4** (also **the youth**) [pl *v*] young people considered as a group: *the country's youth* ○ *the youth of today* ○ *youth training schemes.*
▶ **youthful** /-fl/ *adj* having qualities typical of young people; young or seeming young: *a youthful managing director* ○ *a youthful appearance* ○ *She's a very youthful sixty-five.* **youthfully** /-fəli/ *adv.* **youthfulness** *n* [U].
■ **'youth club** *n* a club for young people, offering a variety of social activities.
'youth hostel *n* a building in which cheap and simple food and accommodation are provided for esp young people on walking, riding, etc holidays.
'youth hostelling *n* [U] the practice of walking or riding from one youth hostel to another as a holiday activity: *go youth hostelling.*

you've /juːv; *weak form* juv/ *short form* you have. ⇨ note at HAVE

yowl /jaʊl/ *n* a long loud cry, esp of pain or distress.
▶ **yowl** *v* to make a yowl: [V] *I was kept awake by cats yowling all night.*

yo-yo /ˈjəʊ jəʊ/ *n* (*pl* **-os**) a toy consisting of two thick discs of wood or plastic attached to a length of string that is wound between them. The yo-yo can be made to move up or down the string when this is released and then pulled with a finger: *Share prices are going up and down like a yo-yo.*

yr *abbr* **1** (*pl* **yrs**) year: *valid for 3 yrs* ○ *children aged 4–11 yrs.* **2** your.

yrs *abbr* yours: *Yrs sincerely* (ie before a signature on a letter).

YTS /ˌwaɪ tiː ˈes/ *abbr* Youth Training Scheme.

yuan /juˈɑːn/ *n* (*pl* unchanged) the main unit of money in China.

yucca /ˈjʌkə/ *n* a tall plant with white flowers like bells, and stiff pointed leaves.

yuck (also **yuk**) /jʌk/ *interj* (*sl*) (used for expressing disgust, dislike, etc).
▶ **yucky** *adj* (*sl*) unpleasant; disgusting: *yucky school dinners.*

yule /juːl/ (also **yule-tide** /ˈjuːl taɪd/) *n* (*arch or rhet*) the festival of Christmas.
■ **'yule-log** *n* **1** a large log of wood traditionally burnt on Christmas Eve. **2** a chocolate cake made to look like a log of wood, eaten at Christmas.

yummy /ˈjʌmi/ *adj* (*infml*) (used esp in spoken English) nice to eat; DELICIOUS(1): *Mum's made us a yummy chocolate cake.*

yum-yum /ˌjʌm ˈjʌm/ *interj* (*infml*) (used for expressing pleasure while eating or when thinking about food).

yuppie (also **yuppy**) /ˈjʌpi/ *n* (*infml often derog*) a young professional person, esp one who earns a lot of money in a city job and is ambitious.

YWCA /ˌwaɪ dʌbljuː siː ˈeɪ/ (also *US infml* **Y**) *abbr* Young Women's Christian Association: *stay at the YWCA (hostel).*

Y

Zz

Z (also **z**) /zed; *US* zi:/ *n* (*pl* **Z's**, **z's** /zedz; *US* zi:z/) the 26th and last letter of the English alphabet: *Zebra begins with (a) Z/'Z'.* **IDM** **from A to Z** ⇨ A¹.

zany /'zeɪnɪ/ *adj* (**-ier**, **-iest**) (*infml*) unusual or ridiculous in an amusing way; ECCENTRIC(1): *a zany haircut/lifestyle/personality.*

zap /zæp/ *v* (**-pp-**) (*infml*) **1** ~ **sb** (**with sth**) to kill sb or make sb unconscious: [Vnpr] *He looked like a man zapped with 1000 volts.* [also Vn]. **2** to destroy or overcome sth: [Vn] *The radar got zapped.* ○ *It's vital to zap stress fast.* **3** [Vn] to switch off a television or make sth disappear from the screen of a computer. **4** to move or move sth suddenly or quickly in the specified direction: [Vpr] *Have you seen him zapping around town on his new motor bike?* [Vnpr, Vnp] *She zapped the ball (back) over the net.* [also Vp].

zeal /zi:l/ *n* [U] ~ (**for/in sth**); ~ (**to do sth**) (*fml*) great energy or enthusiasm: *show zeal for/in the cause* ○ *revolutionary/religious/missionary zeal.*
▶ **zealous** /'zeləs/ *adj* full of zeal; eager: *a zealous preacher/philanthropist* ○ *zealous determination.* **zealously** *adv*.

zealot /'zelət/ *n* (*often derog*) a person who is extremely enthusiastic about sth, esp religion or politics.
▶ **zealotry** /-rɪ/ *n* [U] (*fml often derog*) the attitude or behaviour of a zealot: *religious zealotry.*

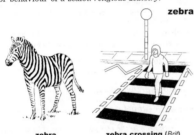

zebra

zebra   zebra crossing (*Brit*)

zebra /'zebrə, 'zi:brə/ *n* (*pl* unchanged or **zebras**) an African wild animal similar to a horse but with black or dark brown and white lines on its body: *zebra stripes.*
■ **¡zebra 'crossing** *n* (*Brit*) an area of road with broad white lines painted on it, at which vehicles must stop if people wish to walk across. ⇨ picture. Compare PEDESTRIAN CROSSING, PELICAN CROSSING.

Zeitgeist /'zaɪtgaɪst/ *n* (*German*) the characteristic mood or quality of a particular period of history as shown by the ideas, beliefs, etc of the time.

Zen /zen/ *n* [U] a Japanese form of Buddhism that emphasizes the importance of controlling or concentrating the mind more than learning from religious books: *Zen Buddhism.*

zenith /'zenɪθ/ *n* **1** the point in the sky directly above an observer. Compare NADIR 2. **2** the highest point of achievement: *reach the zenith of one's career/power/influence* ○ *At its zenith the Roman empire covered almost the whole of Europe.*

zephyr /'zefə(r)/ *n* (*dated or fml*) a soft gentle wind.

Zeppelin /'zepəlɪn/ *n* a type of large AIRSHIP used by the Germans in the First World War.

zero /'zɪərəʊ; *US also* 'zi:rəʊ/ *n, pron, det* **1** the number 0; NOUGHT(1): *Five, four, three, two, one, zero... We have lift-off!* **2(a)** a point between PLUS(2) (+) and MINUS(2) (–) numbers on a scale, esp on a THERMOMETER: *The thermometer fell to zero last night.* (**b**) a temperature, pressure, etc that is equivalent to zero on a scale: *It was ten degrees below zero last night* (ie -10°C, ten degrees below the temperature at which water freezes). ⇨ note at NOUGHT. **3(a)** the lowest point; nothing: *Prospects of success in the talks were put at zero.* (**b**) not any; none: *zero inflation/growth/profit* ○ *My interest in politics is zero* (ie I am not interested in it).
▶ **zero** *v* **PHR V** **¡zero 'in on sb/sth 1** to aim guns, etc at a particular target. **2** to fix one's attention on sb/sth; to concentrate on sb/sth: *zero in on the key issues for discussion.*
■ **'zero-hour** *n* [U] the time when an event, an attack, etc is planned to start: *Zero-hour is 3.30 am.* **¡zero-'rated** *adj* (of goods, services, etc) on which no value added tax (VALUE) is charged.

zest /zest/ *n* [U, sing] **1** the quality of being interesting, exciting, enjoyable, etc: *The element of risk gave (an) added zest to the whole experience.* **2** ~ (**for sth**) great enjoyment or excitement; enthusiasm: *have a zest for life* ○ *He entered into our plans with terrific zest.* **3** the outer skin of oranges, lemons (LEMON), etc, when used to give flavour in cooking. Compare PEEL *n*, RIND, SKIN 3. ▶ **zestful** /-fl/ *adj*.

zigzag /'zɪgzæg/ *n* a line or course that turns sharply left and then right repeatedly.
▶ **zigzag** *adj* [attrib]: *a zigzag road/path/pattern.*
zigzag *v* (**-gg-**) to go in a zigzag line: [Vpr] *The narrow path zigzags up the cliff.* [also V, Vp]. ⇨ picture at PATTERN.

zillion /'zɪljən/ *n* (*infml esp US*) a very large number: *She's a zillion times brainier than I am.*

zinc /zɪŋk/ *n* [U] (*symb* Zn) a chemical element. Zinc is a bluish-white metal used in the production of other metals and for covering iron, wire, etc to protect it against RUST(1). ⇨ App 7.

zing /zɪŋ/ *n* [U] (*infml*) liveliness, energy or interest: *The juice adds zing to drinks and desserts.*

Zionism /'zaɪənɪzəm/ *n* [U] a political movement concerned originally with establishing an independent Jewish state and now with developing the state of Israel. ▶ **Zionist** /'zaɪənɪst/ *n, adj*.

zip (*esp US* zipper)

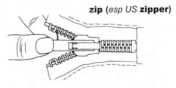

zip /zɪp/ *n* **1** (also *esp Brit* **'zip-fastener**, *esp US* **zipper**) [C] a device used for fastening clothes, bags, etc. A zip consists of two rows of metal or plastic teeth (TOOTH 2) that can be pulled together to close sth or pulled apart to open it: *The zip on my jacket is stuck.* ○ *Your zip's undone.* **2** [sing] a short sharp sound, eg of a bullet going through the air. **3** [U] (*infml*) energy; vigour.
▶ **zip** *v* (**-pp-**) **1** to fasten or undo clothes, bags, etc

with a zip(1): [Vn-adj] *She zipped the tent flap shut.*
[also Vn, Vnpr]. **2** to move with energy or speed in
the specified direction: [Vpr] *I'm just zipping into
town to buy some food.* [Vp] *After a slow beginning,
the play fairly zips along in the second act.* ⇨ note at
WHIZZ. **PHR V** **zip (sb/sth)** **'up** to fasten sth or be
fastened with a zip: *Will you zip me/my dress up,
please?* ○ *The jacket zips up to the collar for extra
warmth.*
▸ **zipped** *adj* fastening with a zip(1): *zipped pockets.*

Zip code /ˈzɪp kəʊd/ *n* (*US*) = POSTCODE.

zipper /ˈzɪpə(r)/ *n* (*esp US*) = ZIP 1.

zither /ˈzɪðə(r)/ *n* a musical instrument with many
strings stretched over a flat wooden box and played
with the fingers and a PLECTRUM.

signs of the zodiac

Aries	Taurus	Gemini
21 March–20 April	21 April–20 May	21 May–20 June

Cancer	Leo	Virgo
21 June–20 July	21 July–19/22 August	20/23 August–22 September

Libra	Scorpio	Sagittarius
23 September–22 October	23 October–21 November	22 November–20 December

Capricorn	Aquarius	Pisces
21 December–20 January	21 January–19 February	20 February–20 March

zodiac /ˈzəʊdiæk/ *n* (**a**) **the zodiac** [sing] an imaginary area of the sky containing the positions of
the sun, the moon and the main planets, divided
into 12 equal parts (**the signs of the zodiac**), named
after 12 groups of stars. ⇨ picture. (**b**) [C] a usu
circular DIAGRAM of these signs used in ASTROLOGY
to predict the future. See also HOROSCOPE. Compare
STAR SIGN. ▸ **zodiacal** /zəʊˈdaɪəkl/ *adj*.

NOTE The **signs of the zodiac** (also called **star
signs**) are used in **astrology** and **horoscopes**.
They are often called 'The Stars' in newspapers and
magazines. Your date of birth determines which
sign you are and this is supposed to have an influence on your personality. The signs of the zodiac are
studied by astrologers to predict the future: *'What
star sign are you?' 'I'm a Gemini.'* ○ *He's a typical
Pisces/a typical Piscean.* ○ *She was born under the
sign of Leo.* There is not always an adjective form
for the name of the sign.

zombie /ˈzɒmbi/ *n* **1** (*infml*) a dull slow person who

seems to act without thinking or not to be aware of
what is happening around her or him. **2** (in certain
African and Caribbean religions) a dead body that
has been made alive again by WITCHCRAFT.

zone /zəʊn/ *n* **1** an area or a region with a particular characteristic or use: *the erogenous zones of the
body* ○ *smokeless zones* (ie city areas in which only
fuels that produce little or no smoke may be used) ○
a war/demilitarized zone ○ *a no-fly zone* (ie one over
which aircraft are not allowed to fly). **2** an area that
is different from its surroundings in eg colour, texture or appearance: *When the needle enters the red
zone it indicates danger.* **3** any of the five parts into
which the earth's surface is divided by imaginary
lines parallel to the EQUATOR. These are **the torrid
zone, the North** and **South temperate zones,** and
the North and **South frigid zones. 4** any of several
areas within which there is a particular scale of
charges for eg making a telephone call, sending a
letter or travelling by bus or train: *postal charges to
countries in zone B* ○ *This ticket is valid for travel
between any stations in the central zone.*
▸ **zonal** /ˈzəʊnl/ *adj* relating to or arranged in
zones.
zone *v* **1** [Vn] to divide or mark a place into zones.
2 to specify that an area should be used for a
particular purpose: [Vnpr] *The land was zoned for
industrial use.* **zoning** *n* [U].

zonked /zɒŋkt/ *adj* [pred] ~ (**out**) (*sl*) **1** extremely
tired; exhausted (EXHAUST² 1): *I feel utterly zonked.* **2**
drunk or badly affected by a drug.

zoo /zuː/ *n* (*pl* **zoos**) (also *fml* **zoological gardens**
[pl]) a place, eg a park, where living wild animals
are kept for the public to see them and where they
can be studied and bred: *The children enjoy going to
the zoo.*
■ **'zoo-keeper** *n* a person employed in a zoo to care
for the animals.

zoo- *comb form* of or relating to animals or animal
life: *zoology.*

zoology /zəʊˈɒlədʒi; *Brit also* zuˈɒl-/ *n* [U] the scientific study of animals and their behaviour. Compare
BIOLOGY, BOTANY.
▸ **zoological** /ˌzəʊəˈlɒdʒɪkl; *Brit also* ˌzuːə-/ *adj* of
or relating to zoology. ˌ**zoological 'gardens** *n* [pl]
(*fml*) = zoo.
zoologist /zəʊˈɒlədʒɪst; *Brit also* zuˈɒl-/ *n* a person
who studies animals and their behaviour.

zoom /zuːm/ *v* **1** (of aircraft, cars, etc) to move very
quickly, esp making a continuous deep noise: [Vpr]
zooming along the motorway [Vadv] *The jet zoomed
low overhead.* [also Vp]. ⇨ note at WHIZZ. **2** (*infml*)
(of prices, costs, etc) to rise quickly and suddenly:
[V, Vp] *Overnight trading caused share prices to
zoom (up).* **PHR V** ˌ**zoom 'in (on sb/sth)**; ˌ**zoom
'out** (of cameras) to make the size of the object being
photographed appear bigger/smaller by using a
zoom lens (ZOOM).
▸ **zoom** *n* [sing] the sound of a vehicle zooming
past.
■ **'zoom lens** *n* a camera LENS(1) that can be adjusted to make the object being photographed
appear gradually bigger or smaller, so that it seems
to be closer or more distant.

zucchini /zuˈkiːni/ *n* (*pl* unchanged or **zucchinis**)
(*esp US*) = COURGETTE. ⇨ picture at MARROW².

Zulu /ˈzuːluː/ *n* a member of a Bantu people of southern Africa.
▸ **Zulu** *adj* of the Zulu people or their language.

Z

Appendix 1
Irregular verbs

This appendix lists all the verbs with irregular forms that are included in the dictionary, except for those formed with a hyphenated prefix (eg *pre-set*, *re-lay*) and the modal verbs (eg *can*, *must*). Irregular forms that are only used in certain senses are marked with an asterisk (eg *abode*). Full information on usage, pronunciation, etc is given at the entry.

Infinitive	Past tense	Past participle
abide	abided, *abode	abided, *abode
arise	arose	arisen
awake	awoke	awoken
be	was/were	been
bear	bore	borne
beat	beat	beaten
become	became	become
befall	befell	befallen
beget	begot, (*arch*) begat	begotten
begin	began	begun
behold	beheld	beheld
bend	bent	bent
beseech	besought, beseeched	besought, beseeched
beset	beset	beset
bet	bet, betted	bet, betted
bid	bid, *bade	bidden, *bid
bind	bound	bound
bite	bit	bitten
bleed	bled	bled
bless	blessed	blessed
blow	blew	blown
break	broke	broken
breed	bred	bred
bring	brought	brought
broadcast	broadcast	broadcast
browbeat	browbeat	browbeaten
build	built	built
burn	burnt, burned	burnt, burned
burst	burst	burst
bust	bust, busted	bust, busted
buy	bought	bought
cast	cast	cast
catch	caught	caught
chide	chided, chid	chided, chidden
choose	chose	chosen
cleave¹	cleaved, clove, cleft	cleaved, cloven, cleft
cleave²	cleaved, clave	cleaved
cling	clung	clung
come	came	come
cost	cost, *costed	cost, *costed
creep	crept	crept
cut	cut	cut
deal	dealt	dealt
dig	dug	dug
dive	dived; (*US*) dove	dived
do¹,²	did	done
draw	drew	drawn
dream	dreamt, dreamed	dreamt, dreamed

Infinitive	Past tense	Past participle
drink	drank	drunk
drive	drove	driven
dwell	dwelt; (*US*) dwelled	dwelt
eat	ate	eaten
fall	fell	fallen
feed	fed	fed
feel	felt	felt
fight	fought	fought
find	found	found
flee	fled	fled
fling	flung	flung
floodlight	floodlighted, floodlit	floodlighted, floodlit
fly	flew	flown
forbear	forbore	forborne
forbid	forbade	forbidden
forecast	forecast, forecasted	forecast, forecasted
foresee	foresaw	foreseen
foretell	foretold	foretold
forget	forgot	forgotten
forgive	forgave	forgiven
forgo	forwent	forgone
forsake	forsook	forsaken
forswear	forswore	forsworn
freeze	froze	frozen
gainsay	gainsaid	gainsaid
get	got	got; (*US*) gotten
give	gave	given
go	went	gone
grind	ground	ground
grow	grew	grown
hamstring	hamstrung	hamstrung
hang	hung, *hanged	hung, *hanged
have	had	had
hear	heard	heard
heave	heaved, *hove	heaved, *hove
hew	hewed	hewed, hewn
hide	hid	hidden
hit	hit	hit
hold	held	held
hurt	hurt	hurt
inlay	inlaid	inlaid
input	input, inputted	input, inputted
inset	inset	inset
interweave	interwove	interwoven
keep	kept	kept
kneel	knelt; (*esp US*) kneeled	knelt; (*esp US*) kneeled
knit	knitted, *knit	knitted, *knit
know	knew	known

Infinitive	Past tense	Past participle	Infinitive	Past tense	Past participle
lay	laid	laid	**prove**	proved	proved; (*US*) proven
lead	led	led			
lean	leant, leaned	leant, leaned	**put**	put	put
leap	leapt, leaped	leapt, leaped	**quit**	quit; (*Brit* also) quitted	quit; (*Brit* also) quitted
learn	learnt, learned	learnt, learned	**read** /riːd/	read /red/	read /red/
leave	left	left	**rebuild**	rebuilt	rebuilt
lend	lent	lent	**recast**	recast	recast
let	let	let	**redo**	redid	redone
lie[2]	lay	lain	**rehear**	reheard	reheard
light	lit, lighted	lit, lighted	**remake**	remade	remade
lose	lost	lost	**rend**	rent	rent
make	made	made	**repay**	repaid	repaid
mean	meant	meant	**rerun**	reran	rerun
meet	met	met	**resell**	resold	resold
miscast	miscast	miscast	**reset**	reset	reset
mishear	misheard	misheard	**resit**	resat	resat
mishit	mishit	mishit	**retake**	retook	retaken
mislay	mislaid	mislaid	**retell**	retold	retold
misread /ˌmɪsˈriːd/	misread /ˌmɪsˈred/	misread /ˌmɪsˈred/	**rewind**	rewound	rewound
misspell	misspelled, misspelt	misspelled, misspelt	**rewrite**	rewrote	rewritten
			rid	rid	rid
			ride	rode	ridden
misspend	misspent	misspent	**ring**	rang	rung
mistake	mistook	mistaken	**rise**	rose	risen
misunderstand	misunderstood	misunderstood	**run**	ran	run
			saw	sawed	sawn; (*US*) sawed
mow	mowed	mown, mowed			
offset	offset	offset	**say**	said	said
outbid	outbid	outbid	**see**	saw	seen
outdo	outdid	outdone	**seek**	sought	sought
outfight	outfought	outfought	**sell**	sold	sold
outgrow	outgrew	outgrown	**send**	sent	sent
output	output	output	**set**	set	set
outrun	outran	outrun	**sew**	sewed	sewn, sewed
outsell	outsold	outsold	**shake**	shook	shaken
outshine	outshone	outshone	**shear**	sheared	shorn, sheared
overcome	overcame	overcome	**shed**	shed	shed
overdo	overdid	overdone	**shine**	shone, *shined	shone, *shined
overdraw	overdrew	overdrawn			
overeat	overate	overeaten	**shit**	shitted, shat	shitted, shat
overfly	overflew	overflown	**shoe**	shod	shod
overhang	overhung	overhung	**shoot**	shot	shot
overhear	overheard	overheard	**show**	showed	shown, showed
overlay	overlaid	overlaid	**shrink**	shrank, shrunk	shrunk
overpay	overpaid	overpaid			
override	overrode	overridden	**shut**	shut	shut
overrun	overran	overrun	**sing**	sang	sung
oversee	oversaw	overseen	**sink**	sank	sunk
overshoot	overshot	overshot	**sit**	sat	sat
oversleep	overslept	overslept	**slay**	slew	slain
overspend	overspent	overspent	**sleep**	slept	slept
overtake	overtook	overtaken	**slide**	slid	slid
overthrow	overthrew	overthrown	**sling**	slung	slung
overwrite	overwrote	overwritten	**slink**	slunk	slunk
partake	partook	partaken	**slit**	slit	slit
pay	paid	paid	**smell**	smelt, smelled	smelt, smelled
plead	pleaded; (*US*) pled	pleaded; (*US*) pled			
			smite	smote	smitten
proofread /ˈpruːfriːd/	proofread /ˈpruːfred/	proofread /ˈpruːfred/	**sow**	sowed	sown, sowed
			speak	spoke	spoken

Infinitive	Past tense	Past participle
speed	sped, *speeded	sped, *speeded
spell	spelt, spelled	spelt, spelled
spend	spent	spent
spill	spilt, spilled	spilt, spilled
spin	spun, (*arch*) span	spun
spit	spat; (*esp US*) spit	spat; (*esp US*) spit
split	split	split
spoil	spoilt, spoiled	spoilt, spoiled
spotlight	spotlit, *spotlighted	spotlit, *spotlighted
spread	spread	spread
spring	sprang	sprung
stand	stood	stood
stave	staved, *stove	staved, *stove
steal	stole	stolen
stick	stuck	stuck
sting	stung	stung
stink	stank, stunk	stunk
strew	strewed	strewed, strewn
stride	strode	—
strike	struck	struck
string	strung	strung
strive	strove, strived	striven
sublet	sublet	sublet
swear	swore	sworn
sweep	swept	swept
swell	swelled	swollen, swelled
swim	swam	swum
swing	swung	swung
take	took	taken
teach	taught	taught
tear	tore	torn
tell	told	told

Infinitive	Past tense	Past participle
think	thought	thought
throw	threw	thrown
thrust	thrust	thrust
tread	trod	trodden, trod
typecast	typecast	typecast
unbend	unbent	unbent
underbid	underbid	underbid
undercut	undercut	undercut
undergo	underwent	undergone
underlie	underlay	underlain
underpay	underpaid	underpaid
undersell	undersold	undersold
understand	understood	understood
undertake	undertook	undertaken
underwrite	underwrote	underwritten
undo	undid	undone
unfreeze	unfroze	unfrozen
unwind	unwound	unwound
uphold	upheld	upheld
upset	upset	upset
wake	woke	woken
waylay	waylaid	waylaid
wear	wore	worn
weave	wove, *weaved	woven, *weaved
wed	wedded, wed	wedded, wed
weep	wept	wept
wet	wet, wetted	wet, wetted
win	won	won
wind[3] /waɪnd/	wound /waʊnd/	wound /waʊnd/
withdraw	withdrew	withdrawn
withhold	withheld	withheld
withstand	withstood	withstood
wring	wrung	wrung
write	wrote	written

Appendix 2
Numbers

Using numbers

Compound numbers

- You can find the numbers from one to twenty, and also *thirty, forty, fifty,* etc, in the main part of the dictionary. These are used to make compound numbers up to one hundred. In compound numbers, we put a hyphen between the words:

  thirty-five   sixty-seven

- Numbers over 10 are often written in figures but in some contexts, especially in order to avoid ambiguity, words are more appropriate. When writing a cheque we generally use words for the pounds or dollars and figures for the pence or cents:

  twenty-two pounds (and) 45 pence
  seventy-nine dollars (and) 30 cents

- Ordinal numbers such as *fifth, ninth* and *thirtieth* are also given in the dictionary. Compound ordinal numbers up to one hundred are formed by adding the ordinals *first, second, third,* etc to *twenty, thirty, sixty,* etc:

  twenty-first   eighty-seventh

- When ordinal numbers are written in figures, the last two letters of the written ordinal must be added:

  21st   22nd   23rd   24th   25th   etc

  Dates, however, can be written as:

  19 May 1995
  19th May 1995

Numbers over 100

- For numbers over 100, we say *six hundred and forty-two, seven hundred and ninety,* etc, using *and* to link the hundreds and the tens. When said aloud, *and* is pronounced /n/. The main stress falls on the final word of the number:

  ˌthree ˌhundred and ˌtwenty-ˈnine
  ˌfive ˌhundred and ˈsixty

  In American English *and* is often left out:

  ˌeight ˌhundred ˌninety-ˈtwo

  In a more mathematical context, we might say the individual figures instead:

  three two nine   five six zero

- Numbers between 100 and 199 can be written or spoken as *one hundred and four* or *a hundred and four.* We say *one hundred and four,* etc when we want to be precise. In informal contexts, or when we are giving only an approximate number or amount, we say *a hundred and four.* Compare:

  The total cost was one hundred and sixty-three pounds and five pence.

  The bill came to about a hundred and sixty pounds.

Numbers over 1000

- We can say and write numbers over 1000 in two ways. For 1200, for example, we can say *one thousand two hundred* or, more informally, *twelve hundred.*

- For numbers between 1000 and 1099, we can use *a* instead of *one* before *thousand*:

  one thousand and sixty
  a thousand and sixty

  However, if there are any hundreds in the number we would normally say:

  one thousand two hundred and sixty

- Larger numbers are usually said as:

  ˌtwenty-ˌeight ˈthousand, ˌone ˌhundred and ˌforty-ˈfour

  A comma is used after the thousands when a number is written in words. When the number is written in figures, a comma or, sometimes in British English, a space is used:

  28,144   28 144

  Numbers over a million are written in a similar way:

  2,600,830   2 600 830

  ˌtwo ˈmillion, ˌsix ˌhundred ˈthousand, ˌeight ˌhundred and ˈthirty

- Long numbers which do not stand for a quantity, such as bank account and telephone numbers, are usually grouped into twos, threes, fours or fives:

  My credit card number is:
  0432 9999 4567 9876.

  Dial 01865 56767 for more information.

  Each number is said individually.

Zero

- English has several names for the figure 0. *Zero* is the most precise word and is also most common in American English. *Nought*, *nothing* and *o* /əʊ/ are used in informal English (▷ note at NOUGHT). In both British and American English, *o* is used to represent 0 when saying bank account or telephone numbers.

Fractions

- Common fractions, written as ½, ¼, ⅓, are generally said as *a half*, *a quarter* or *a third*. *One* may be used instead of *a* for emphasis. For other fractions which are more commonly used in a technical or mathematical context, we say *one twelfth*, *one sixteenth*, etc. Fractions such as ⅔, ¾ and ⁷⁄₁₀ are said as *two thirds*, *three quarters* and *seven tenths*.

- When a fraction is used before a noun phrase, the word *of* is inserted:

  *a fifth **of** the annual turnover*

  *a quarter **of** all women*

  When *half* is used in this way, *a* is omitted, and *of* may also be left out:

  Half (of) the members voted against increasing subscriptions.

- If a fraction is used with an uncountable or a singular noun, the verb is generally singular:

  *A quarter of the money **has** already been spent.*

  *Two thirds of the area **is** flooded.*

  If the noun is singular but represents a group of people, the verb may be singular or plural:

  *A third of the population **is/are** in favour of the change.*

  If the noun is countable, the verb is plural:

  *Three quarters of all graduates **find** jobs within six months.*

- When a fraction follows a whole number we link them with *and*: 2¼ is said as *two and a quarter*; 3⁵⁄₁₆ is said as *three and five sixteenths*.

- More complex fractions, such as ⁷⁄₂₅₆, ³¹⁄₁₄₄ and ¹⁹⁄₅₆, are said as *seven over two five six*, *thirty-one over one four four* and *nineteen over fifty-six*.

Percentages

- Percentages are written in words as *twenty-five per cent* and in figures as *25%*.

- When they are used with a noun phrase as the subject of a sentence, the verb is singular or plural according to the pattern described for fractions:

  *90% of the land **is** cultivated.*

  *Eighty per cent of the workforce **is/are** against the strike.*

  *65% of children **play** computer games.*

Decimals

- In English, a *point* (.) is used instead of a comma when writing decimals. We also say *point* when speaking the number. The stress falls on the last figure:

  ˌtwenty-ˌsix point ˈtwo

  If there is more than one figure after the decimal point, we say each separately:

  26.23   ˌtwenty-ˌsix point ˌtwo ˈthree

  3.142   ˌthree point ˌone ˌfour ˈtwo

  In numbers less than one, for example 0.15, we say *zero point one five, point one five* or, sometimes in British English, *nought point one five*.

Numbers in time

Telling the time

- The twelve-hour system is used for most purposes. Morning, afternoon or evening is not specified when this is obvious:

  'What time is it, please?'
  'It's six o'clock.'

- There is often more than one way of saying the time:

  eleven thirty
  half past eleven
  half eleven (infml)

  The time is expressed in different ways in British and American English:

  It's (a) quarter to eight. (Brit)
  It's seven forty-five. (Brit)
  It's (a) quarter to/of eight. (US)

  It's (a) quarter past one. (Brit)
  It's one fifteen. (Brit)
  It's (a) quarter after one. (US)

  It's ten (minutes) past six. (Brit)
  It's six ten. (Brit)
  It's ten after six. (US)

It's five (minutes) to four. (Brit)
It's three fifty-five. (Brit)
It's five to/of four. (US)

The word *minutes* can be omitted after 5, 10, 20 and 25, but it is almost always used after other numbers:

It's eighteen minutes past/after nine.

- In a formal context, or when the time of day is not obvious, morning or evening is specified. We often use *am* meaning *in the morning* and *pm* meaning *in the afternoon* or *in the evening*:

Students should assemble at the main gate at 5pm.

He came round at three o'clock in the morning!

Note that we do not say:

~~three o'clock am~~

- The twenty-four hour clock is used in Britain for timetables and in some official letters and notices. In the USA it is used only for military purposes and on ships.

Times are spoken as:

0300   *(o) three hundred hours*
1345   *thirteen forty-five*
2305   *twenty-three o five*

There are two ways of saying midnight:

0000   *o o double o*
2400   *twenty-four hundred hours*

Duration

- The length of time something takes is expressed in hours, minutes and, where appropriate, seconds:

Cover the pan and simmer gently for one and a half hours.

He took just two minutes to knock out his opponent.

When *half* is used alone without another number, it does not have *a* before it or *of* after it:

The journey takes half an hour.

- Abbreviations are often used in written English:

Allow 4–5 hrs for the paint to dry.
The fastest time was 12 mins 26 secs.

Numbers in measurement

Both metric and non-metric systems of measurement are used in Britain. The choice depends on the situation and on the age of the speaker. The metric system is always used in a scientific context. In the USA, the metric system is much less widely used. Conversion tables between metric and non-metric systems are given at the end of this Appendix.

Length and height

- We talk about something being a particular measurement long, wide, high or thick:

The garden is 50 feet long.
He had a three-inch scar on his cheek.
The road rises to 2 288 m above sea level.
The ice was several centimetres thick.

- When we are describing people, we talk about how tall they are:

She's 1.63 metres tall.

When we use feet and inches we can say:

*He's only five **feet** four (inches).*
*He's only five **foot** four.*

Distance and speed

- Distance by road in Britain and the USA is measured in miles rather than kilometres:

It is 42 miles to Liverpool.
The signpost said: 'Liverpool 42'.

- When describing speed, we talk about miles per hour (mph), kilometres per hour (kph), kilometres per second, etc. In informal English, *per* is often replaced by *a* or *an*:

She was driving at 75 miles an hour.
a speed limit of 50 kph
a hundred-mile-an-hour police chase
Light travels at 299 792 kilometres per second.

- In Britain, distance in sport is usually measured in metres:

the women's 800 metres freestyle

In the USA, yards and miles are often used:

a six-mile run

Distance in horse-racing is measured in furlongs or miles:

The Derby is run over a distance of twelve furlongs or one and a half miles.

Dimension

- We often state the size of something in terms of its length and width, and sometimes also its height and depth. We say *by* but write '×' between each of the measurements:

  a room sixteen feet by twelve (16ft × 12ft)

  a table five foot by three foot by two foot six high (5ft × 3ft × 2ft 6in)

  The box measures 800 by 400 by 400 (millimetres) (800 × 400 × 400mm).

Area

- Land used for farming or as part of an estate is measured in acres or hectares:

  a house with 10 acres of grounds
  a 2 000 hectare farm

- Regions or areas of a country are usually measured in square miles or square kilometres:

  Dartmoor covers an area of more than 350 square miles.

  Population density is only 24 people per square kilometre (24/km²).

- Smaller areas are measured in square yards, feet or metres:

  5 000 square feet of office space
  15 square metres of carpet (eg 5m × 3m)

  As in the above examples, *square* is used immediately after a number when giving a measurement of area.

  When *square* follows both a number and a unit of measurement, the number indicates the length of each of the sides of something. Compare the previous example with:

  a carpet 15 metres square (15m × 15m)

Weight

- We usually buy food that is not packaged, for example at a delicatessen counter, in pounds and ounces. However, when food is in a packet, the weight is usually measured in kilograms or grams:

  Could I have a quarter (of a pound) of smoked ham, please, and half a pound of Cheddar?

  net weight 175g (on a packet of biscuits)

  Sometimes, both metric and non-metric weights are shown on packets.

- In Britain, a person's weight is measured in stones and pounds; in America, pounds only are used:

  She weighs 8st 10lb. (Brit)
  He's lost over three stone in a year. (Brit)
  My brother weighs 183 pounds. (US)

  Babies are weighed in pounds and ounces:
  The baby weighed 6lb 4oz at birth.

- In Britain, heavy items are now usually weighed in kilograms (informally kilos) or sometimes pounds. In the USA, pounds are used. Larger quantities are weighed in tons or tonnes:

  a car packed with 140 pounds of explosive
  a 40kg sack of gravel
  Our baggage allowance is only 20 kilos.
  The price of copper fell by £11 a tonne.

Capacity

- In Britain, we buy milk and beer in pints or half pints:

  a one-pint carton of milk
  Two pints of lager, please.

  In the USA, beer is sold in 12-ounce cans or bottles. Milk and juice are sold in pints, quarts or gallons. Note that American fluid ounces and pints are slightly smaller than British ones.

- Wine is sold in centilitres or litres. Other bottled drinks may also be sold in litres.

- In Britain, many other liquids are sold by the litre:

  half a litre of cooking oil
  5 litres of paint

  In the USA, fluid ounces or gallons are used:
  2 gallons of paint

- Petrol and diesel used to be sold in gallons in Britain but they are now sold in litres. In the USA, gallons are used.

- Small amounts of liquid are usually measured in millilitres in a scientific context, or as fluid ounces in cookery:

  100ml sulphuric acid
  Add 8fl oz milk and beat thoroughly.

Metric measures

(with approximate non-metric equivalents)

	Metric		Non-metric
Length	10 millimetres (mm)	= 1 centimetre (cm)	= 0.394 inch
	100 centimetres	= 1 metre (m)	= 39.4 inches/1.094 yards
	1000 metres	= 1 kilometre (km)	= 0.6214 mile
Area	100 square metres (m²)	= 1 are (a)	= 0.025 acre
	100 ares	= 1 hectare (ha)	= 2.471 acres
	100 hectares	= 1 square kilometre (km²)	= 0.386 square mile
Weight	1000 milligrams (mg)	= 1 gram (g)	= 15.43 grains
	1000 grams	= 1 kilogram (kg)	= 2.205 pounds
	1000 kilograms	= 1 tonne	= 19.688 hundredweight
Capacity	10 millilitres (ml)	= 1 centilitre	= 0.018 pint (0.021 US pint)
	100 centilitres (cl)	= 1 litre (l)	= 1.76 pints (2.1 US pints)
	10 litres	= 1 decalitre (dal)	= 2.2 gallons (2.63 US gallons)

Non-metric measures

(with approximate metric equivalents)

	Non-metric		Metric
Length		1 inch (in)	= 25.4 millimetres
	12 inches	= 1 foot (ft)	= 30.48 centimetres
	3 feet	= 1 yard (yd)	= 0.914 metre
	220 yards	= 1 furlong	= 201.17 metres
	8 furlongs	= 1 mile	= 1.609 kilometres
	1760 yards	= 1 mile	= 1.609 kilometres
Area		1 square (sq) inch	= 6.452 sq centimetres (cm²)
	144 sq inches	= 1 sq foot	= 929.03 sq centimetres
	9 sq feet	= 1 sq yard	= 0.836 sq metre
	4840 sq yards	= 1 acre	= 0.405 hectare
	640 acres	= 1 sq mile	= 259 hectares/ 2.59 sq kilometres
Weight	437 grains	= 1 ounce (oz)	= 28.35 grams
	16 ounces	= 1 pound (lb)	= 0.454 kilogram
	14 pounds	= 1 stone (st)	= 6.356 kilograms
	8 stone	= 1 hundredweight (cwt)	= 50.8 kilograms
	20 hundredweight	= 1 ton	= 1016.04 kilograms
British capacity	20 fluid ounces (fl oz)	= 1 pint (pt)	= 0.568 litre
	2 pints	= 1 quart (qt)	= 1.136 litres
	8 pints	= 1 gallon (gal)	= 4.546 litres
American capacity	16 US fluid ounces	= 1 US pint	= 0.473 litre
	2 US pints	= 1 US quart	= 0.946 litre
	8 US pints	= 1 US gallon	= 3.785 litres

Appendix 3
Punctuation and writing

This Appendix shows you how to use punctuation in written English. It also helps you to write down a conversation and shows you how to set out formal and informal letters.

Full stop (.)

A **full stop** or (*US*) **period** is used

- at the end of a sentence that is not a question or an exclamation:

  I knocked at the door. There was no reply. I knocked again.

- sometimes, though not in this dictionary, in abbreviations:

  Jan.   e.g.   a.m.

Comma (,)

Commas indicate a slight pause and are used to divide a sentence into several parts so that it is easier to follow its meaning. They are used

- to separate words in a list, though they are often omitted before *and*:

  a bouquet of red, pink and white roses
  tea, coffee, milk or hot chocolate

- to separate phrases or clauses:

  If you keep calm, take your time, concentrate and think ahead, then you're likely to pass your driving test.

  Worn out after all the excitement of the party, the children soon fell asleep.

- before and after a clause or phrase that gives additional, but not essential, information about the noun it follows:

  Mount Everest, the world's highest mountain, was first climbed in 1953.

  The Pennine Hills, which are very popular with walkers, are situated between Lancashire and Yorkshire.

  (No commas are used before and after a clause that **defines** the noun it follows:

  The hills that separate Lancashire from Yorkshire are called the Pennines.)

- to separate main clauses, especially long ones, linked by a conjunction such as *and, as, but, for, or*:

  We had been looking forward to our camping holiday all year, but unfortunately it rained every day.

- to separate an introductory word or phrase, or an adverb or adverbial phrase that applies to the whole sentence, from the rest of the sentence:

  Oh, so that's where it was!

  As it happens, however, I never saw her again.

  By the way, did you hear what happened to Sue's car?

- to separate a tag question from the rest of the sentence:

  It's quite expensive, isn't it?
  You live in Bristol, right?

- before or after 'he said', etc when writing down conversation:

  'Come back soon,' she said.

- before a short quotation:

  It was Disraeli who said, 'Little things affect little minds'.

Colon (:)

A **colon** is used

- to introduce a list of items:

  These are our options: we go by train and leave before the end of the show, or we take the car and see it all.

- in formal writing, before a clause or phrase that gives more information about the main clause:

  The garden had been neglected for a long time: it was overgrown and full of weeds.

  (A semicolon or a full stop, but not a comma, may be used instead of a colon here.)

- to introduce a quotation, which may be indented:

  As Kenneth Morgan writes:

    The truth was, perhaps, that Britain in the years from 1914 to 1983 had not changed all that fundamentally.

  Others, however, have challenged this view ...

Semicolon (;)

A **semicolon** is used

- instead of a comma to separate parts of a sentence that already contain commas:

  She was determined to succeed whatever the cost; she would achieve her aim, whoever might suffer on the way.

- in formal writing, to separate two main clauses, especially those not joined by a conjunction:

  The sun was already low in the sky; it would soon be dark.

Question mark (?)

A **question mark** is used

- at the end of a direct question:

  Where's the car?
  You're leaving already?

  (A question mark is not used at the end of an indirect question: *He asked if I was leaving.*)

- especially with a date, to express doubt:

  John Marston (?1575–1634)

Exclamation mark (!)

An **exclamation mark** or (*US*) **exclamation point** is used at the end of a sentence expressing surprise, joy, anger, shock or some other strong emotion:

  That's marvellous!
  'Never!' she cried.

In informal written English, more than one exclamation mark, or an exclamation mark and a question mark, may be used:

  'Your wife's just given birth to triplets.'
  'Triplets!?'

Apostrophe (')

An **apostrophe** is used

- with s to indicate that a thing or person belongs to somebody:

  my friend's brother
  the waitress's apron
  King James's crown/King James' crown
  the students' books
  the women's coats

- in short forms, to indicate that letters or figures have been omitted:

  I'm (I am)
  they'd (they had/they would)
  the summer of '89 (1989)

- sometimes, though not in this dictionary, with s to form the plural of a letter, a figure or an abbreviation:

  roll your r's
  during the 1990's
  MP's in favour of the motion

Hyphen (-)

A **hyphen** is used

- to form a compound from two or more other words:
  hard-hearted
  fork-lift truck
  mother-to-be

  to form a compound from a prefix and a proper name:
  pre-Raphaelite
  pro-European

  when writing compound numbers between 21 and 99 in words:
  seventy-three
  thirty-one

- sometimes, in British English, to separate a prefix ending in a vowel from a word beginning with the same vowel:
  co-operate
  pre-eminent

- after the first section of a word that is divided between one line and the next:
  decide what to do in order to avoid mistakes of this kind in the future

Dash (–)

A **dash** is used

- in informal English, instead of a colon or semicolon, to indicate that what follows is a summary or conclusion of what has gone before:

  Men were shouting, women were screaming, children were crying – it was chaos.

  You've admitted that you lied to me – how can I trust you again?

- singly or in pairs to separate a comment or an afterthought from the rest of the sentence:

  He knew nothing at all about it – or so he said.

Dots (...)

Three dots (also called an **ellipsis**) are used to indicate that words have been omitted, especially from a quotation or at the end of a conversation:

... challenging the view that Britain ... had not changed all that fundamentally.

Slash (/)

A **slash** or **oblique** is used

- to separate alternative words or phrases:

  have a pudding and/or cheese

  single/married/widowed/divorced (delete as applicable)

- to indicate the end of a line of poetry where the lines are not set separately:

  Wordsworth's famous lines, 'I wandered lonely as a cloud/That floats on high o'er vales and hills ...'

Quotation marks (' ' " ")

Single **quotation marks** or **inverted commas** are generally used in British English:

  'Help! I'm drowning!'

In American English, double quotation marks are used:

  "Help! I'm drowning!"

Quotation marks are used

- to enclose words and punctuation in direct speech:

  'Why on earth did you do that?' he asked. 'I'll fetch it,' she replied.

- to draw attention to a word that is unusual for the context, for example a slang expression, or to a word that is being used for special effect, such as irony:

  He told me in no uncertain terms to 'get lost'.

  Thousands were imprisoned in the name of 'national security'.

- to enclose the titles of articles, books, poems, plays, etc:

  Keats's 'Ode to Autumn'
  I was watching 'Match of the Day'.

- around short quotations or sayings:

  Do you know the origin of the saying: 'A little learning is a dangerous thing'?

Brackets ( )

Brackets (also called **parentheses**) are used

- to separate extra information or a comment from the rest of a sentence:

  Mount Robson (12972 feet) is the highest mountain in the Canadian Rockies.

  He thinks that modern music (ie anything written after 1900) is rubbish.

- to enclose cross-references:

  This moral ambiguity is a feature of Shakespeare's later works (see Chapter Eight).

- around numbers or letters in text:

  Our objectives are (1) to increase output, (2) to improve quality and (3) to maximize profits.

Square brackets ([ ])

Square brackets are used

- to enclose editorial comments:

  a notice reading 'Everything to be put away in it's [sic] proper place after use'

  constant references in her diary to 'Mr G[ladstone]'s visits'

- around words inserted to make a quotation grammatically correct:

  Britain in [these] years was without ...

Italics

In handwritten or typed text, and in the examples that follow, *italics* are indicated by underlining. Italics are used

- to show emphasis:

  I'm not going to do it – you are.
  ... proposals which we cannot accept under any circumstances

- to indicate the titles of books, plays, etc:

  Joyce's Ulysses
  a letter in The Times
  the title role in Puccini's Tosca

- for foreign words or phrases:

  the English oak (Quercus robur)

  I had to renew my permesso di soggiorno (residence permit).

Quoting conversation

When you write down a conversation, you normally begin a new paragraph for each new speaker. Quotation marks enclose the words spoken:

> *'You're sure of this?' I asked.*
> *He nodded grimly.*
> *'I'm certain.'*

Verbs used to indicate direct speech, for example *he said, she complained*, are separated by commas from the words spoken, unless a question mark or an exclamation mark is used:

> *'That's all I know,' said Nick.*
> *Nick said, 'That's all I know.'*
> *'Why?' asked Nick.*

When *he said* or *said Nick* **follows** the words spoken, the comma is placed inside the quotation marks, as in the first example above. If, however, the writer puts the words *said Nick* **within** the actual words Nick speaks, the comma is outside the quotation marks:

> *'That', said Nick, 'is all I know.'*

'But you said you loved me! "I'll never leave you, Sue, as long as I live." That's what you said, isn't it?'
Dave shrugged awkwardly.
'I don't remember exactly what I said,' he began, 'but ...'
'You liar!' Sue screamed, slapping his face. 'Lies, excuses, evasions – that's all I get from you. Well I've had enough. You understand?'
'Look, I said I was sorry.'
Fixing him with a withering glare, Sue muttered, 'You *will* be sorry, Dave. I promise you that.'

Writing letters

In a letter to a friend, you write your address, or a short form of it, at the top right of the letter, and then the date. You do not need to put the name and address of the person you are writing to.

In a formal letter, you put your own address in the top right-hand corner, and then the date. You put the name and address of the person you are writing to below and to the left of this. For help in choosing an appropriate beginning and ending for different types of letter, ⇨ note at YOUR.

Compare the layout and style of the following letters:

26 Windmill Road
Bromley
Kent BR2 6DP

15 January 1995

The Information Officer
Welsh Tourist Board
Brunel House
2 Fitzalan
Cardiff CF2 1UY

Dear Sir

I hope to have a holiday in North Wales this summer with my family.

Could you please send me a list of camp-sites in the area, and information about the facilities they offer.

My son and daughter would like to go pony-trekking; could you therefore also send me a list of riding centres that cater for children aged between 11 and 14?

Thank you very much.

Yours faithfully

Rachel Watts
Rachel Watts

26 Windmill Road
Bromley
Kent BR2 6DP

22 March

Dear Barbara

How are you and Tom? It seems ages since we saw you. I hope your new job is going well. David and I are both fine, and Lizzie is getting on well at her new school.

I'm writing now because I'm coming to Oxford next Tuesday for a meeting, and I wondered if we could meet for a pizza or something afterwards. Alternatively, I could just call round at your house for a little while on my way home. The meeting should be over by 5.30 at the latest.

Let me know what suits you. It would be lovely to see you if you have time.

Love from

Rachel

Appendix 4
Family relationships

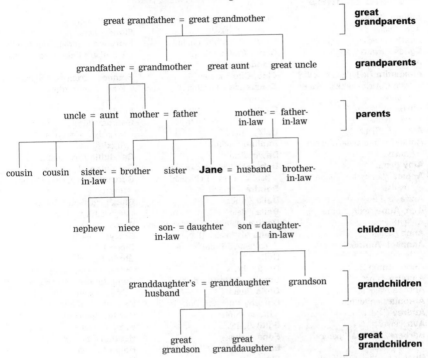

Jane's family

If Jane's husband dies or they get divorced, and Jane gets married to somebody else, her new husband will be the stepfather of her children. The children will be his stepdaughter and stepson.

If her new husband already has children from a previous marriage, those children will be Jane's children's stepbrothers and stepsisters.

If Jane and her second husband have children together, they will be her older children's half-brothers and half-sisters.

Appendix 5
Common first names

Short forms and pet names follow the name from which they are formed.

Female names

Abigail /'æbɪgeɪl/
Ada /'eɪdə/
Agatha /'ægəθə/; Aggie /'ægi/
Agnes /'ægnɪs/; Aggie /'ægi/
Aileen ⇨ Eileen
Alexandra /ˌælɪg'zɑːndrə; US -'zæn-/; Alex /'ælɪks/; Sandy /'sændi/
Alexis /ə'leksɪs/
Alice /'ælɪs/
Alison /'ælɪsn/
Amanda /ə'mændə/; Mandy /'mændi/
Amy /'eɪmi/
Angela /'ændʒələ/; Angie /'ændʒi/
Anita /ə'niːtə/
Ann, Anne /æn/; Annie /'æni/
Anna /'ænə/
Annabel, Annabelle /'ænəbel/
Anne, Annie ⇨ Ann
Annette /ə'net/
Anthea /'ænθɪə/
Antonia /æn'təʊnɪə/
Audrey /'ɔːdri/
Ava /'eɪvə/
Barbara, Barbra /'bɑːbrə/; Babs /bæbz/
Beatrice /'bɪətrɪs; US 'biːət-/
Becky ⇨ Rebecca
Belinda /bə'lɪndə/
Bernadette /ˌbɜːnə'det/
Beryl /'berəl/
Bess, Bessie, Beth, Betsy, Bett, Betty ⇨ Elizabeth
Brenda /'brendə/
Bridget, Bridgit, Brigid /'brɪdʒɪt/; Bid /bɪd/
Candice /'kændɪs/
Carla /'kɑːlə/
Carol, Carole /'kærəl/
Caroline /'kærəlaɪn/; Carolyn /'kærəlɪn/; Carrie /'kæri/
Catherine, Cathy ⇨ Katherine
Cecilia /sə'siːlɪə/
Cecily /'sesəli/; Cicely /'sɪsəli/
Celia /'siːlɪə/
Charlene /'ʃɑːliːn/
Charlotte /'ʃɑːlət/
Cheryl /'tʃerəl/
Chloe /'kləʊi/
Christina /krɪ'stiːnə/; Tina /'tiːnə/

Christine /'krɪstiːn/; Chris /krɪs/; Chrissie /'krɪsi/
Cindy ⇨ Cynthia, Lucinda
Clare, Claire /kleə(r)/
Claudia /'klɔːdɪə/
Cleo, Clio /'kliːəʊ/
Constance /'kɒnstəns/; Connie /'kɒni/
Cynthia /'sɪnθɪə/; Cindy /'sɪndi/
Daisy /'deɪzi/
Daphne /'dæfni/
Dawn /dɔːn/
Deborah /'debərə/; Debbie, Debby /'debi/; Deb /deb/
Deirdre /'dɪədri/
Delia /'diːlɪə/
Della /'delə/
Denise /də'niːz/
Diana /daɪ'ænə/; Diane /daɪ'æn/; Di /daɪ/
Dolly /'dɒli/
Dora /'dɔːrə/
Doreen, Dorene /'dɔːriːn/
Doris /'dɒrɪs/
Dorothy /'dɒrəθi/; Dot /dɒt/; Dottie /'dɒti/
Edith /'iːdɪθ/
Edna /'ednə/
Eileen /'aɪliːn/; Aileen /'eɪliːn/
Elaine /ɪ'leɪn/
Eleanor /'elənə(r)/; Eleanora /ˌelɪə'nɔːrə/; Ellie /'eli/
Eliza /ɪ'laɪzə/; Liza /'laɪzə/; Lisa /'liːsə/
Elizabeth, Elisabeth /ɪ'lɪzəbəθ/; Liz /lɪz/; Lizzie, Lizzy /'lɪzi/; Libby /'lɪbi/; Beth /beθ/; Betsy /'betsi/; Bett /bet/; Betty /'beti/; Bess /bes/; Bessie /'besi/
Ella /'elə/
Ellen /'elən/
Ellie ⇨ Eleanor
Elsie /'elsi/
Elspeth /'elspəθ/ (Scot)
Emily /'eməli/
Emma /'emə/
Erica /'erɪkə/
Ethel /'eθl/
Eunice /'juːnɪs/
Eve /iːv/; Eva /'iːvə/
Evelyn /'iːvlɪn, 'ev-/
Fay /feɪ/
Felicity /fə'lɪsəti/

Fiona /fi'əʊnə/
Flora /'flɔːrə/
Florence /'flɒrəns; US 'flɔːr-/; Flo /fləʊ/; Florrie /'flɒri; US 'flɔːri/
Frances /'frɑːnsɪs; US 'fræn-/; Fran /fræn/; Frankie /'fræŋki/
Freda /'friːdə/
Georgia /'dʒɔːdʒə/; Georgie /'dʒɔːdʒi/; Georgina /dʒɔː'dʒiːnə/
Geraldine /'dʒerəldiːn/
Germaine /dʒɜː'meɪn/
Gertrude /'gɜːtruːd/; Gertie /'gɜːti/
Gillian /'dʒɪlɪən/; Jill, Gill /dʒɪl/; Jilly /'dʒɪli/
Ginny ⇨ Virginia
Gladys /'glædɪs/
Glenda /'glendə/
Gloria /'glɔːrɪə/
Grace /greɪs/; Gracie /'greɪsi/
Gwendoline /'gwendəlɪn/; Gwen /gwen/
Hannah /'hænə/
Harriet /'hærɪət/
Hazel /'heɪzl/
Heather /'heðə(r)/
Helen /'helən/
Henrietta /ˌhenri'etə/
Hilary /'hɪləri/
Hilda /'hɪldə/
Ida /'aɪdə/
Imogen /'ɪmədʒən/
Ingrid /'ɪŋgrɪd/
Irene /aɪ'riːni, 'aɪriːn/
Iris /'aɪrɪs/
Isabel, (esp Scot) Isobel /'ɪzəbel/
Isabella /ˌɪzə'belə/
Ivy /'aɪvi/
Jacqueline /'dʒækəlɪn/; Jackie /'dʒæki/
Jan ⇨ Janet, Janice
Jane /dʒeɪn/; Janey /'dʒeɪni/
Janet /'dʒænɪt/; Janette /dʒə'net/; Jan /dʒæn/
Janice, Janis /'dʒænɪs; Jan /dʒæn/
Jean /dʒiːn/; Jeanie /'dʒiːni/
Jennifer /'dʒenɪfə(r)/; Jenny, Jennie /'dʒeni/
Jessica /'dʒesɪkə/; Jess /dʒes/; Jessie /'dʒesi/

Jill, Jilly ⇨ Gillian
Jo ⇨ Joanna, Josephine
Joan /dʒəʊn/
Joanna /dʒəʊˈænə/; Joanne
/dʒəʊˈæn/; Jo /dʒəʊ/
Jocelyn /ˈdʒɒslɪn/
Josephine /ˈdʒəʊzəfiːn/; Jo
/dʒəʊ/; Josie /ˈdʒəʊsi/
Jodie /ˈdʒəʊdi/
Joyce /dʒɔɪs/
Judith /ˈdʒuːdɪθ/; Judy
/ˈdʒuːdi/
Julia /ˈdʒuːliə/; Julie /ˈdʒuːli/
Juliet /ˈdʒuːliet/
June /dʒuːn/
Karen, Karin /ˈkærən/
Katherine, Catherine, (esp
US) -arine, Kathryn
/ˈkæθrɪn/; Kathy, Cathy
/ˈkæθi/; Kate /keɪt/; Katie,
Katy /ˈkeɪti/; Kay /keɪ/; Kitty
/ˈkɪti/
Kim /kɪm/
Kirsten /ˈkɜːstɪn/
Kitty ⇨ Katherine
Laura /ˈlɔːrə/
Lauretta, Loretta /ləˈretə/
Lesley /ˈlezli/
Libby ⇨ Elizabeth
Lilian, Lillian /ˈlɪliən/
Lily /ˈlɪli/
Linda /ˈlɪndə/
Lisa, Liza ⇨ Eliza
Livia /ˈlɪviə/
Liz, Lizzie, Lizzy ⇨ Elizabeth
Lois /ˈləʊɪs/
Lorna /ˈlɔːnə/
Louise /luˈiːz/; Louisa
/luˈiːzə/
Lucia /ˈluːsiə, also ˈluːʃə/
Lucinda /luːˈsɪndə/; Cindy
/ˈsɪndi/
Lucy /ˈluːsi/
Lydia /ˈlɪdiə/
Lyn(n) /lɪn/
Mabel /ˈmeɪbl/
Madeleine /ˈmædəlɪn/
Madge, Maggie ⇨ Margaret
Maisie /ˈmeɪzi/
Mandy ⇨ Amanda
Marcia /ˈmɑːsiə, also ˈmɑːʃə/;
Marcie /ˈmɑːsi/
Margaret /ˈmɑːɡrət/; Madge
/mædʒ/; Maggie /ˈmæɡi/;
(esp Scot) Meg /meg/; Peg
/peg/; Peggie, Peggy /ˈpeɡi/
Margery, Marjorie
/ˈmɑːdʒəri/; Margie /ˈmɑːdʒi/
Marlene /ˈmɑːliːn/
Maria /məˈriːə, also məˈraɪə/
Marian, Marion /ˈmæriən/

Marie /məˈriː, also ˈmɑːri/
Marilyn /ˈmærəlɪn/
Marion ⇨ Marian
Martha /ˈmɑːθə/
Martina /mɑːˈtiːnə/
Mary /ˈmeəri/
Maud /mɔːd/
Maureen /ˈmɔːriːn/
Mavis /ˈmeɪvɪs/
Meg ⇨ Margaret
Melanie /ˈmeləni/
Melinda /məˈlɪndə/
Michelle /mɪˈʃel/
Mildred /ˈmɪldrəd/
Millicent /ˈmɪlɪsnt/; Millie,
Milly /ˈmɪli/
Miranda /məˈrændə/
Miriam /ˈmɪriəm/
Moira /ˈmɔɪrə/
Molly /ˈmɒli/
Monica /ˈmɒnɪkə/
Muriel /ˈmjʊəriəl/
Nadia /ˈnɑːdiə/
Nancy /ˈnænsi/; Nan /næn/
Naomi /ˈneɪəmi/
Natalie /ˈnætəli/
Natasha /nəˈtæʃə/
Nell /nel/; Nellie, Nelly /ˈneli/
Nicola /ˈnɪkələ/; Nicky /ˈnɪki/
Nora /ˈnɔːrə/
Norma /ˈnɔːmə/
Olive /ˈɒlɪv/
Olivia /əˈlɪviə/
Pamela /ˈpæmələ/; Pam
/pæm/
Pat ⇨ Patricia
Patience /ˈpeɪʃns/
Patricia /pəˈtrɪʃə/; Pat /pæt/;
Patti, Pattie, Patty /ˈpæti/;
Tricia /ˈtrɪʃə/
Paula /ˈpɔːlə/
Pauline /ˈpɔːliːn/
Peg, Peggie, Peggy ⇨
Margaret
Penelope /pəˈneləpi/; Penny
/ˈpeni/
Philippa /ˈfɪlɪpə/
Phoebe /ˈfiːbi/
Phyllis /ˈfɪlɪs/
Polly /ˈpɒli/; Poll /pɒl/
Priscilla /prɪˈsɪlə/; Cilla /ˈsɪlə/
Prudence /ˈpruːdns/; Pru,
Prue /pruː/
Rachel /ˈreɪtʃl/
Rebecca /rɪˈbekə/; Becky
/ˈbeki/
Rhoda /ˈrəʊdə/
Rita /ˈriːtə/
Roberta /rəˈbɜːtə/
Robin /ˈrɒbɪn/
Rosalie /ˈrəʊzəli, also ˈrɒzəli/

Rosalind /ˈrɒzəlɪnd/; Rosalyn
/ˈrɒzəlɪn/
Rose /rəʊz/; Rosie /ˈrəʊzi/
Rosemary /ˈrəʊzməri/; Rosie
/ˈrəʊzi/
Ruth /ruːθ/
Sadie ⇨ Sarah
Sally /ˈsæli/; Sal /sæl/
Samantha /səˈmænθə/; Sam
/sæm/
Sandra /ˈsɑːndrə; US ˈsæn-/;
Sandy /ˈsændi/
Sandy ⇨ Alexandra, Sandra
Sarah, Sara /ˈseərə/; Sadie
/ˈseɪdi/
Sharon /ˈʃærən/
Sheila, Shelagh /ˈʃiːlə/
Shirley /ˈʃɜːli/
Sibyl ⇨ Sybil
Silvia, Sylvia /ˈsɪlviə/; Sylvie
/ˈsɪlvi/
Sonia /ˈsɒniə, also ˈsəʊniə/
Sophia /səˈfaɪə/
Sophie, Sophy /ˈsəʊfi/
Stella /ˈstelə/
Stephanie /ˈstefəni/
Susan /ˈsuːzn/; Sue /suː/;
Susie, Suzy /ˈsuːzi/
Susanna, Susannah
/suːˈzænə/; Suzanne
/suːˈzæn/; Susie, Suzy
/ˈsuːzi/
Sybil, Sibyl /ˈsɪbəl/
Sylvia, Sylvie ⇨ Silvia
Teresa, Theresa /təˈriːzə/;
Tess /tes/; Tessa /ˈtesə/; (US)
Terri /ˈteri/
Thelma /ˈθelmə/
Tina ⇨ Christina
Toni /ˈtəʊni/ (esp US)
Tracy, Tracey /ˈtreɪsi/
Tricia ⇨ Patricia
Trudie, Trudy /ˈtruːdi/
Ursula /ˈɜːsjʊlə/
Valerie /ˈvæləri/; Val /væl/
Vanessa /vəˈnesə/
Vera /ˈvɪərə/
Veronica /vəˈrɒnɪkə/
Victoria /vɪkˈtɔːriə/; Vicki,
Vickie, Vicky, Vikki /ˈvɪki/
Viola /ˈvaɪələ/
Violet /ˈvaɪələt/
Virginia /vəˈdʒɪniə/; Ginny
/ˈdʒɪni/
Vivien, Vivienne /ˈvɪviən/;
Viv /vɪv/
Wendy /ˈwendi/
Winifred /ˈwɪnɪfrɪd/; Winnie
/ˈwɪni/
Yvonne /ɪˈvɒn/
Zoe /ˈzəʊi/

Male names

Abraham /'eɪbrəhæm/; Abe /eɪb/
Adam /'ædəm/
Adrian /'eɪdriən/
Alan, Allan, Allen /'ælən/; Al /æl/
Albert /'ælbət/; Al /æl/; Bert /bɜːt/
Alexander /ˌælɪg'zɑːndə(r); US -'zæn-/; Alec /'ælɪk/; Alex /'ælɪks/; Sandy /'sændi/
Alfred /'ælfrɪd/; Alf /ælf/; Alfie /'ælfi/
Andrew /'ændruː/; Andy /'ændi/
Alistair, Alisdair, Alas- /'ælɪstə(r)/ (Scot)
Allan, Allen ⇨ Alan
Alvin /'ælvɪn/
Angus /'æŋgəs/ (Scot)
Anthony, Antony /'æntəni/; Tony /'təʊni/
Archibald /'ɑːtʃɪbɔːld/; Archie, Archy /'ɑːtʃi/
Arnold /'ɑːnəld/
Arthur /'ɑːθə(r)/
Auberon /'ɔːbərɒn/
Aubrey /'ɔːbri/
Barnaby /'bɑːnəbi/
Barry /'bæri/
Bartholomew /bɑː'θɒləmjuː/
Basil /'bæzl/
Benjamin /'bendʒəmɪn/; Ben /ben/
Bernard /'bɜːnəd/; Bernie /'bɜːni/
Bert ⇨ Albert, Gilbert, Herbert, Hubert
Bill, Billy ⇨ William
Bob, Bobby ⇨ Robert
Boris /'bɒrɪs/
Bradford /'brædfəd/; Brad /bræd/ (esp US)
Brendan /'brendən/ (Irish)
Brian, Bryan /'braɪən/
Bruce /bruːs/
Bud /bʌd/ (US)
Carl /kɑːl/
Cecil /'sesl; US 'siːsl/
Cedric /'sedrɪk/
Charles /tʃɑːlz/; Charlie /'tʃɑːli/; Chas /tʃæz/; Chuck /tʃʌk/ (US)
Christopher /'krɪstəfə(r)/; Chris /krɪs/; Kit /kɪt/
Chuck ⇨ Charles
Clarence /'klærəns/
Clark /klɑːk/ (esp US)
Claude, Claud /klɔːd/
Clement /'klemənt/
Clifford /'klɪfəd/; Cliff /klɪf/
Clint /klɪnt/ (esp US)

Clive /klaɪv/
Clyde /klaɪd/ (esp US)
Colin /'kɒlɪn/
Craig /kreɪg/
Curt /kɜːt/
Cyril /'sɪrəl/
Dale /deɪl/ (esp US)
Daniel /'dæniəl/; Dan /dæn/; Danny /'dæni/
Darrell /'dærəl/
Darren /'dærən/ (esp US)
David /'deɪvɪd/; Dave /deɪv/
Dean /diːn/
Dennis, Denis /'denɪs/
Derek /'derɪk/
Dermot /'dɜːmət/ (Irish)
Desmond /'dezmənd/; Des /dez/
Dick, Dickie, Dicky ⇨ Richard
Dirk /dɜːk/
Dominic /'dɒmɪnɪk/
Donald /'dɒnəld/; Don /dɒn/
Douglas /'dʌgləs/; Doug /dʌg/
Duane /duː'eɪn/; Dwane /dweɪn/ (esp US)
Dudley /'dʌdli/; Dud /dʌd/
Duncan /'dʌŋkən/
Dustin /'dʌstɪn/
Dwight /dwaɪt/ (esp US)
Eamonn, Eamon /'eɪmən/ (Irish)
Ed, Eddie, Eddy ⇨ Edward
Edgar /'edgə(r)/
Edmund, Edmond /'edmənd/
Edward /'edwəd/; Ed /ed/; Eddie, Eddy /'edi/; Ted /ted/; Teddy /'tedi/; Ned /ned/; Neddy /'nedi/
Edwin /'edwɪn/
Elmer /'elmə(r)/ (US)
Elroy /'elrɔɪ/ (US)
Emlyn /'emlɪn/ (Welsh)
Enoch /'iːnɒk/
Eric /'erɪk/
Ernest /'ɜːnɪst/
Errol /'erəl/
Eugene /'juːdʒiːn/; Gene /dʒiːn/ (US)
Felix /'fiːlɪks/
Ferdinand /'fɜːdɪnænd/
Fergus /'fɜːgəs/ (Scot or Irish)
Floyd /flɔɪd/
Francis /'frɑːnsɪs; US 'fræn-/; Frank /fræŋk/
Frank /fræŋk/; Frankie /'fræŋki/
Frederick /'fredrɪk/; Fred /fred/; Freddie, Freddy /'fredi/
Gabriel /'geɪbriəl/
Gareth /'gæreθ/ (esp Welsh)

Gary /'gæri/
Gavin /'gævɪn/
Gene ⇨ Eugene
Geoffrey, Jeffrey /'dʒefri/; Geoff, Jeff /dʒef/
George /dʒɔːdʒ/
Geraint /'geraɪnt/ (Welsh)
Gerald /'dʒerəld/; Gerry, Jerry /'dʒeri/
Gerard /'dʒerɑːd/
Gilbert /'gɪlbət/; Bert /bɜːt/
Giles /dʒaɪlz/
Glen /glen/
Godfrey /'gɒdfri/
Gordon /'gɔːdn/
Graham, Grahame, Graeme /'greɪəm/
Gregory /'gregəri/; Greg /greg/
Guy /gaɪ/
Hal, Hank ⇨ Henry
Harold /'hærəld/
Henry /'henri/; Harry /'hæri/; Hal /hæl/; Hank /hæŋk/ (US)
Herbert /'hɜːbət/; Bert /bɜːt/; Herb /hɜːb/
Horace /'hɒrɪs; US 'hɔːrəs/
Howard /'haʊəd/
Hubert /'hjuːbət/; Bert /bɜːt/
Hugh /hjuː/
Hugo /'hjuːgəʊ/
Humphrey /'hʌmfri/
Ian /'iːən/
Isaac /'aɪzək/
Ivan /'aɪvən/
Ivor /'aɪvə(r)/
Jack ⇨ John
Jacob /'dʒeɪkəb/; Jake /dʒeɪk/
Jake ⇨ Jacob, John
James /dʒeɪmz/; Jim /dʒɪm/; Jimmy /'dʒɪmi/; Jamie /'dʒeɪmi/ (Scot)
Jason /'dʒeɪsn/
Jasper /'dʒæspə(r)/
Jed /dʒed/ (esp US)
Jeff, Jeffrey ⇨ Geoffrey
Jeremy /'dʒerəmi/; Jerry /'dʒeri/
Jerome /dʒə'rəʊm/
Jerry ⇨ Gerald, Jeremy
Jesse /'dʒesi/ (esp US)
Jim, Jimmy ⇨ James
Jock ⇨ John
Joe ⇨ Joseph
John /dʒɒn/; Johnny /'dʒɒni/; Jack /dʒæk/; Jake /dʒeɪk/; Jock /dʒɒk/ (Scot)
Jonathan /'dʒɒnəθən/; Jon /dʒɒn/
Joseph /'dʒəʊzɪf/; Joe /dʒəʊ/
Julian /'dʒuːliən/
Justin /'dʒʌstɪn/

Keith /kiːθ/
Kenneth /ˈkenɪθ/; **Ken** /ken/;
  Kenny /ˈkeni/
Kevin /ˈkevɪn/; **Kev** /kev/
Kirk /kɜːk/
Kit ⇨ Christopher
Lance /lɑːns; US læns/
Laurence, Lawrence
  /ˈlɒrəns; US ˈlɔːr-/; Larry
  /ˈlæri/; Laurie /ˈlɒri US
  ˈlɔːri/
Len, Lenny ⇨ Leonard
Leo /ˈliːəʊ/
Leonard /ˈlenəd/; Len /len/;
  Lenny /ˈleni/
Leslie /ˈlezli/; Les /lez/
Lester /ˈlestə(r)/
Lewis /ˈluːɪs/; Lew /luː/
Liam /ˈliːəm/ (Irish)
Lionel /ˈlaɪənl/
Louis /ˈluːi; US ˈluːɪs/; Lou
  /luː/ (esp US)
Luke /luːk/
Malcolm /ˈmælkəm/
Mark /mɑːk/
Martin /ˈmɑːtɪn; US ˈmɑːrtn/;
  Marty /ˈmɑːti/
Matthew /ˈmæθjuː/; Matt
  /mæt/
Maurice, Morris /ˈmɒrɪs; US
  ˈmɔːrəs/
Max /mæks/
Mervyn /ˈmɜːvɪn/
Michael /ˈmaɪkl/; Mike
  /maɪk/; Mick /mɪk/; Micky,
  Mickey /ˈmɪki/
Miles, Myles /maɪlz/
Mitchell /ˈmɪtʃl/; Mitch /mɪtʃ/
Morris ⇨ Maurice
Mort /mɔːt/ (US)
Murray /ˈmʌri/ (esp Scot)
Myles ⇨ Miles
Nathan /ˈneɪθən/; Nat /næt/
Nathaniel /nəˈθæniəl/; Nat
  /næt/
Neal ⇨ Neil
Ned, Neddy ⇨ Edward
Neil, Neal /niːl/

Nicholas, Nicolas /ˈnɪkələs;
  US ˈnɪkləs/; Nick /nɪk/;
  Nicky /ˈnɪki/
Nigel /ˈnaɪdʒl/
Noel /ˈnəʊəl/
Norman /ˈnɔːmən/; Norm
  /nɔːm/
Oliver /ˈɒlɪvə(r)/; Ollie /ˈɒli/
Oscar /ˈɒskə(r)/
Oswald /ˈɒzwəld/; Oz /ɒz/;
  Ozzie /ˈɒzi/
Owen /ˈəʊɪn/ (Welsh)
Oz, Ozzie ⇨ Oswald
Patrick /ˈpætrɪk/ (esp Irish);
  Pat /pæt/; Paddy /ˈpædi/
Paul /pɔːl/
Percy /ˈpɜːsi/
Peter /ˈpiːtə(r)/; Pete /piːt/
Philip /ˈfɪlɪp/; Phil /fɪl/
Quentin /ˈkwentɪn; US -tn/;
  Quintin /ˈkwɪntɪn; US -tn/
Ralph /rælf, Brit also reɪf/
Randolph, Randolf
  /ˈrændɒlf/; Randy /ˈrændi/
  (esp US)
Raphael /ˈræfeɪəl/
Raymond /ˈreɪmənd/; Ray
  /reɪ/
Reginald /ˈredʒməld/; Reg
  /redʒ/; Reggie /ˈredʒi/
Rex /reks/
Richard /ˈrɪtʃəd/; Dick /dɪk/;
  Dickie, Dicky /ˈdɪki/; Rick
  /rɪk/; Ricky /ˈrɪki/; Richie,
  Ritchie /ˈrɪtʃi/
Robert /ˈrɒbət/; Rob /rɒb/;
  Robbie /ˈrɒbi/; Bob /bɒb/;
  Bobby /ˈbɒbi/
Robin /ˈrɒbɪn/
Roderick /ˈrɒdrɪk/; Rod /rɒd/
Rodge ⇨ Roger
Rodney /ˈrɒdni/; Rod /rɒd/
Roger /ˈrɒdʒə(r)/; Rodge
  /rɒdʒ/
Ronald /ˈrɒnəld/; Ron /rɒn/;
  Ronnie /ˈrɒni/
Rory /ˈrɔːri/ (Scot or Irish)
Roy /rɔɪ/

Rudolph, Rudolf /ˈruːdɒlf/
Rufus /ˈruːfəs/
Rupert /ˈruːpət/
Russell /ˈrʌsl/; Russ /rʌs/
Samuel /ˈsæmjuəl/; Sam
  /sæm/; Sammy /ˈsæmi/
Sandy ⇨ Alexander
Scott /skɒt/
Seamas, Seamus /ˈʃeɪməs/
  (Irish)
Sean /ʃɔːn/ (Irish or Scot)
Sebastian /səˈbæstiən/; Seb
  /seb/
Sidney, Sydney /ˈsɪdni/; Sid
  /sɪd/
Simon /ˈsaɪmən/
Stanley /ˈstænli/; Stan /stæn/
Stephen, Steven /ˈstiːvn/;
  Steve /stiːv/
Stewart, Stuart /ˈstjuːət; US
  ˈstuːərt/
Ted, Teddy ⇨ Edward
Terence /ˈterəns/; Terry
  /ˈteri/; Tel /tel/
Theodore /ˈθiːədɔː(r)/; Theo
  /ˈθiːəʊ/
Thomas /ˈtɒməs/; Tom /tɒm/;
  Tommy /ˈtɒmi/
Timothy /ˈtɪməθi/; Tim /tɪm/;
  Timmy /ˈtɪmi/
Toby /ˈtəʊbi/
Tom, Tommy ⇨ Thomas
Tony ⇨ Anthony
Trevor /ˈtrevə(r)/
Troy /trɔɪ/
Victor /ˈvɪktə(r)/; Vic /vɪk/
Vincent /ˈvɪnsnt/; Vince
  /vɪns/
Vivian /ˈvɪviən/; Viv /vɪv/
Walter /ˈwɔːltə(r)/, also
  ˈwɒltə(r)/; Wally /ˈwɒli/
Warren /ˈwɒrən; US ˈwɔːr-/
Wayne /weɪn/
Wilbur /ˈwɪlbə(r)/ (esp US)
Wilfrid, Wilfred /ˈwɪlfrɪd/
William /ˈwɪljəm/; Bill /bɪl/;
  Billy /ˈbɪli/; Will /wɪl/; Willy
  /ˈwɪli/

Appendix 6

Ranks in the armed forces

Royal Navy (RN)	United States Navy (USN)	
Admiral of the Fleet	Fleet Admiral (*wartime only*)	
Admiral (Adm)	Admiral (ADM)	
Vice Admiral (V Adm)	Vice Admiral (VADM)	
Rear Admiral (Rear Adm)	Rear Admiral (RADM)	
Commodore (Cdre)	Commodore (COMO)	
Captain (Capt)	Captain (CAPT)	**Commissioned officers**
Commander (Cdr)	Commander (CDR)	
Lieutenant Commander (Lt Cdr)	Lieutenant Commander (LCDR)	
Lieutenant (Lt)	Lieutenant (LT)	
Sub-lieutenant (Sub-Lt)	Lieutenant Junior Grade (LTJG)	
Acting Sub-Lieutenant (Act Sub-Lt)	Ensign (ENS)	
	Chief Warrant Officer (CWO)	**Warrant officer**
Midshipman	Midshipman	**Officer trainee**
Fleet Chief Petty Officer (FCPO)	Master Chief Petty Officer (MCPO)	
	Senior Chief Petty Officer (SCPO)	
Chief Petty Officer (CPO)	Chief Petty Officer (CPO)	
	Petty Officer 1st Class (PO1)	
	Petty Officer 2nd Class (PO2)	**Ratings (*Brit*)**
Petty Officer (PO)	Petty Officer 3rd Class (PO3)	**Non-commissioned officers (*US*)**
Leading Seaman (LS)	Seaman (SN)	
Able Seaman (AS)		
Ordinary Seaman (OD)		
Junior Seaman (JS)	Seaman Apprentice (SA)	
	Seaman Recruit (SR)	

British Army	United States Army	
Field Marshal (FM)	General of the Army (GEN)	
General (Gen)	General (GEN)	
Lieutenant General (Lt Gen)	Lieutenant General (LTG)	
Major General (Maj Gen)	Major General (MG)	
Brigadier (Brig)	Brigadier General (BG)	
Colonel (Col)	Colonel (COL)	**Commissioned officers**
Lieutenant Colonel (Lt Col)	Lieutenant Colonel (LTC)	
Major (Maj)	Major (MAJ)	
Captain (Capt)	Captain (CPT)	
Lieutenant (Lt)	First Lieutenant (1LT)	
Second Lieutenant (2nd Lt)	Second Lieutenant (2LT)	
Warrant Officer 1st Class (WO1)	Chief Warrant Officer (CWO)	**Warrant officers**
Warrant Officer 2nd Class (WO2)	Warrant Officer (WO)	
	Command Sergeant Major (CSM)	
	Sergeant Major (SGM)	
	First Sergeant (1SG)	
	Master Sergeant (MSG)	
	Sergeant First Class (SFC)	**Other ranks (*Brit*)**
Staff Sergeant (S/Sgt) / Colour Sergeant (C/Sgt)	Staff Sergeant (SSG)	**Non-commissioned officers (*US*)**
Sergeant (Sgt)	Sergeant (SGT)	
Corporal (Cpl)	Corporal (CPL)	
Lance-Corporal (LCpl)	Private First Class (PFC)	
Private (Pte)	Private (PVT)	

Royal Air Force (RAF)	United States Air Force (USAF)	
Marshal of the Royal Air Force	General of the Air Force	
Air Chief Marshal (ACM)	General (GEN)	
Air Marshal (AM)	Lieutenant General (LTG)	
Air Vice Marshal (AVM)	Major General (MG)	
Air Commodore (Air Cdre)	Brigadier General (BG)	**Commissioned**
Group Captain (Gp Capt)	Colonel (COL)	**officers**
Wing Commander (Wg Cdr)	Lieutenant Colonel (LTC)	
Squadron Leader (Sqn Ldr)	Major (MAJ)	
Flight Lieutenant (Flt Lt)	Captain (CAPT)	
Flying Officer (Fg Off)	First Lieutenant (1LT)	
Pilot Officer (Pt Off)	Second Lieutenant (2LT)	
Warrant Officer (WO)		**Warrant officer**
Flight Sergeant (FS)	Chief Master Sergeant (CMSGT)	
	Senior Master Sergeant (SMSGT)	
	Master Sergeant (MSGT)	
Chief Technician (Chf Tech)	Technical Sergeant (TSGT)	**Airmen** (*Brit*)
Sergeant (Sgt)	Staff Sergeant (SSGT)	
	Sergeant (SGT)	**Non-**
Corporal (Cpl)		**commissioned**
Junior Technician (Jnr Tech)		**officers** (*US*)
Senior Aircraftman (SAC)		
Leading Aircraftman (LAC)	Airman First Class (AFC)	
Aircraftman (AC)	Airman Basic (AB)	

Royal Marines (RM)	United States Marine Corps (USMC)	
General (Gen)	General (GEN)	
Lieutenant General (Lt Gen)	Lieutenant General (LTG)	
Major General (Maj Gen)	Major General (MG)	
Brigadier (Brig)	Brigadier General (BG)	
Colonel (Col)	Colonel (COL)	**Commissioned**
Lieutenant Colonel (Lt Col)	Lieutenant Colonel (LTC)	**officers**
Major (Maj)	Major (MAJ)	
Captain (Capt)	Captain (CPT)	
Lieutenant (Lt)	First Lieutenant (1LT)	
Acting Lieutenant (Act Lt)		
Second Lieutenant (2nd Lt)	Second Lieutenant (2LT)	
Warrant Officer 1st Class (WO1)	Warrant Officer 1st Class (WO1)	
	Warrant Officer 2nd Class (WO2)	**Warrant officers**
	Warrant Officer 3rd Class (WO3)	
Warrant Officer 2nd Class (WO2)	Warrant Officer 4th Class (WO4)	
Colour Sergeant (C/Sgt)	Sergeant Major (SGM)	
	Master Gunnery Sergeant (MGSGT)	
Sergeant (Sgt)	First Sergeant (1SGT)	**Other ranks**
	Master Sergeant (MSGT)	(*Brit*)
	Gunnery Sergeant (GSGT)	
	Staff Sergeant (SSGT)	**Non-**
	Sergeant (SGT)	**commissioned**
Corporal (Cpl)	Corporal (CPL)	**officers** (*US*)
	Lance-Corporal (LCPL)	
Lance-Corporal (LCpl)	Private First Class (PFC)	
Marine (Mne)	Private (PVT)	
Junior Marine (J Mne)		

Appendix 7
Chemical elements

Element	Symbol	Atomic number
actinium	Ac	89
aluminium	Al	13
americium	Am	95
antimony	Sb	51
argon	Ar	18
arsenic	As	33
astatine	At	85
barium	Ba	56
berkelium	Bk	97
beryllium	Be	4
bismuth	Bi	83
boron	B	5
bromine	Br	35
cadmium	Cd	48
caesium	Cs	55
calcium	Ca	20
californium	Cf	98
carbon	C	6
cerium	Ce	58
chlorine	Cl	17
chromium	Cr	24
cobalt	Co	27
copper	Cu	29
curium	Cm	96
dysprosium	Dy	66
einsteinium	Es	99
erbium	Er	68
europium	Eu	63
fermium	Fm	100
fluorine	F	9
francium	Fr	87
gadolinium	Gd	64
gallium	Ga	31
germanium	Ge	32
gold	Au	79
hafnium	Hf	72
hahnium	Ha	105
helium	He	2
holmium	Ho	67
hydrogen	H	1
indium	In	49
iodine	I	53
iridium	Ir	77
iron	Fe	26
krypton	Kr	36
lanthanum	La	57
lawrencium	Lr	103
lead	Pb	82
lithium	Li	3
lutetium	Lu	71
magnesium	Mg	12
manganese	Mn	25
mendelevium	Md	101

Element	Symbol	Atomic number
mercury	Hg	80
molybdenum	Mo	42
neodymium	Nd	60
neon	Ne	10
neptunium	Np	93
nickel	Ni	28
niobium	Nb	41
nitrogen	N	7
nobelium	No	102
osmium	Os	76
oxygen	O	8
palladium	Pd	46
phosphorus	P	15
platinum	Pt	78
plutonium	Pu	94
polonium	Po	84
potassium	K	19
praseodymium	Pr	59
promethium	Pm	61
protactinium	Pa	91
radium	Ra	88
radon	Rn	86
rhenium	Re	75
rhodium	Rh	45
rubidium	Rb	37
ruthenium	Ru	44
rutherfordium	Rf	104
samarium	Sm	62
scandium	Sc	21
selenium	Se	34
silicon	Si	14
silver	Ag	47
sodium	Na	11
strontium	Sr	38
sulphur	S	16
tantalum	Ta	73
technetium	Tc	43
tellurium	Te	52
terbium	Tb	65
thallium	Tl	81
thorium	Th	90
thulium	Tm	69
tin	Sn	50
titanium	Ti	22
tungsten	W	74
uranium	U	92
vanadium	V	23
xenon	Xe	54
ytterbium	Yb	70
yttrium	Y	39
zinc	Zn	30
zirconium	Zr	40

Appendix 8
SI units

The International System of Units (Système International d'Unités – SI) is an internationally agreed system of measurement that uses seven base units, with two supplementary units.

All other SI units are derived from the seven base units. In addition, multiples and sub-multiples (fractions) of units are expressed by the use of approved affixes.

Units

	Physical quantity	Name	Symbol
Base units	length	metre	m
	mass	kilogram	kg
	time	second	s
	electric current	ampere	A
	thermodynamic temperature	kelvin	K
	luminous intensity	candela	cd
	amount of substance	mole	mol
Supplementary units	plane angle	radian	rad
	solid angle	steradian	sr

Affixes

Multiple	Affix	Symbol
10	deca-	da
10^2	hecto-	h
10^3	kilo-	k
10^6	mega-	M
10^9	giga-	G
10^{12}	tera-	T
10^{15}	peta-	P
10^{18}	exa-	E

Sub-multiple	Affix	Symbol
10^{-1}	deci-	d
10^{-2}	centi-	c
10^{-3}	milli-	m
10^{-6}	micro-	μ
10^{-9}	nano-	n
10^{-12}	pico-	p
10^{-15}	femto-	f
10^{-18}	atto-	a

Appendix 9

Notes on usage

Throughout the dictionary you will find many notes on usage in English, indicated by the symbol **NOTE**. These notes are of various kinds. They may for example clarify points of grammar, or explain differences between British and American usage, or show the differences between groups of words with similar meanings. The list below gives the **entries** at which these notes can be found, and the words or language points covered at each.

a a; an
about about; on
above above; over
act achievement; act; deed; exploit; feat
affect affect; effect
afraid afraid; frightened; scared
age a man/woman/boy/girl of ... ; ... years old; a ... year-old; ... years of age; under/over ... ; the ... age group; in one's teens, twenties, etc; at/before/by the age of ...
agree agree; be agreed on
all all; both; half
allow allow; let; permit
allowance allowance; permission; permit
almost almost; hardly; nearly; scarcely
alone alone; by oneself; lonely; lonesome; on one's own; solitary
already already; yet
also also; as well; not ... either; too
although albeit; although; however; though
American American; Central/Latin/North/ South America; USA; Yank
among among; between
and come and ... ; go and ... ; try and ...
argument altercation; argument; fight; quarrel; row
arrange arrange; organize; plan
as as; as if; like
ask ask; beg; beseech; entreat; implore; request
awake awake; awaken; wake up; waken
bang bang; bash; bump; knock
be table of verb forms
bear bear; born; borne; have
beautiful attractive; beautiful; good-looking; handsome; pretty
become become; get; go; turn
been be; been; go; gone
before after; before; behind; in front of
begin begin; start
bi -
big big; great; great big; large; large number/amount/quantity
body table of bodily/facial expressions
border border; boundary; frontier
brand brand; make
break break; interlude; intermission; interval; pause; recess; rest
British Brit; British; Britisher; Briton
can able to; can; could; manage to; may
care care about; care for; take care of
cargo cargo; freight; goods
carry bear; carry; cart; hump; lug

cause bring about; cause; make
cent cent; dime; nickel; quarter
certain certain; sure
change alter; change; modify; vary
choose choose; opt for; pick; select
citizen citizen; national; subject
clip clip; prune; shave; trim
close close; closed; lock; shut
coast bank; beach; coast; seaside; shore
comprise composed of; comprise; consist of; constitute
continual continual; continuous
cook bake; barbecue; boil; broil; cook; deep-fry; fry; grill; roast; sauté; steam
country country; state; nation; land
cry cry; sob; wail; weep; whimper
cut chop; cut; hack; saw; slash; tear
dare
date ways of expressing dates in speech and writing
dealer dealer; merchant; trader
different different from/than/to
dimension broad; dimension; deep; depth; length; long; wide; width
dinner dinner; lunch; packed lunch; supper; tea
disability disabled; disability; handicap; (physically/mentally) handicapped; impaired hearing/speech/sight; partially ...
do table of verb forms
drip drip; leak; ooze; run; seep
due due to; owing to
each each (one of); every (one of)
earth earth; floor; ground; land; soil
ecology ecological; ecologically; ecology; environment; environmental; environmentally
eg eg; ie
elder elder; old; older
empty empty; full; occupied; vacant
especial especially; specially
exhibition demonstration; display; exhibition; fair; show
factory factory; mill; plant; works
fairly fairly; pretty; quite; rather
farther farther; further
fat chubby; fat; flabby; large; obese; overweight; plump; podgy; tubby
feel feel; hear; listen; look; see; smell; sound; taste
female female; feminine; male; man; masculine; neuter; woman

first first; firstly; second; secondly; third; thirdly

fish fish; fishes

floor ground/first/second floor

fog fog; haze; mist; smog

forward backward(s); eastward(s); forward(s); northward(s); southward(s); westward(s)

gender chairman; -ess; man; he/she; humanity; human race; man; mankind; people

giggle giggle; snicker; snigger; titter

half half; quarter; whole

happen happen; occur; take place

have² have; have got

have³ table of verb forms

healthy fit; healthy; well

high high; tall

hit beat; hit; strike

holiday holiday; leave; vacation

hope hope; wish

hopeful frankly; generally; hopefully; obviously; personally; sadly; seriously; thankfully; to begin with

hunger famine; hunger; starvation

-ic -ic; -ical

if if; whether

illness ailment; condition; disease; illness

income fee; income; pay; pay-day; salary; wages

inn bar; inn; pub; wine bar

interested disinterested; interested; not interested; uninterested

invaluable in-; inflammable; innumerable; invaluable; -less; non-flammable; numberless; priceless; worthless

-ize -ise; -ize

job employment; job; occupation; profession; trade

journey excursion; journey; travel; travels; trip; tour; voyage

jump bounce; jump; leap; spring

kind kind of; sort of

lady gentleman; lady; ladies and gentlemen

late the last; the latest; the latter

less fewer; less

let hire; let; rent

lie lay; lie

long a long time; long

look gawp; gaze; look; peer; stare

loose let loose; loose; loosen; unloosen

machine apparatus; device; gadget; implement; instrument; machine; tool

may be allowed to; can; may; mustn't

might could; may; might

mistake blunder; defect; error; fault; mistake

modal can; could; dare; may; might; must; need; ought to; shall; should; used to; will; would

morning in/on + afternoon/evening/ morning; tomorrow/yesterday/ this morning

much a lot of; (a) little; (a) few; lots; much

must have to; must; need to

name Christian name; family name; first/given name; forename; full/middle/last name; surname

need

neither either (of); neither; neither ... nor; none/any (of)

new contemporary; modern; new

next nearest; next

nice charming; delightful; enjoyable; friendly; good; kind; lovely; nice; pleasant; pretty; sweet

night at/by night; in/during the night

nought 0; nil; nought; zero

nudge jab; nudge; poke; prod; stab

occasion chance; occasion; opportunity

occurrence event; incident; occurrence

old aged; ancient; antique; elderly; old

one one; ones

order command; direct; instruct; order; tell

partner

path footpath; lane; path; track

penny p; pence; penny; piece

people people; person

piece bar; block; chunk; crumb; cube; flake; fragment; scrap; sheet; slab; slice; splinter; wedge

plural plural forms of words ending in -a/-on/-um/-us

present actual; current; present

presently

price charge; cost; price

prove prove; shave

prowl creep; lurk; prowl; sidle; skulk; slink; sneak; steal; tiptoe

psychology analysis; psychiatrist; psychiatry; psychologist; psychology; psychotherapist; psychotherapy; therapist; therapy

pull drag; draw; haul; pull; tow; trail

quiet calm; quiet; silent; still

quite quite; very

raise raise; rise

rare rare; scarce

re- pronunciation of verbs beginning with *re-*

reason cause; ground(s); justification; motive; reason

recent lately; not long ago; recently

recycle recyclable; recycle; recycled

relation relation; relations; relationship

rest balance; leftovers; relic; remainder; remains; remnants; residue; the rest

road alley; avenue; expressway; freeway; highway; lane; motorway; road; street

rob burgle; rob; steal

round around; round

run gallop; jog; race; run; sprint; trot

say say; tell

scatter scatter; sprinkle; strew

school hospital/church/prison/school with or without the definite article

Scottish Scotch; Scots; Scottish

scurry scamper; scurry; scuttle

sell flog; peddle; push; sell

sensible sense; sensible; sensitive

sensuous sensory; sensual; sensuous

shall shall; shan't; will; won't

should ought to; should

shout cry; scream; shout; yell

shuffle hobble; limp; shamble; shuffle; stagger; stumble; waddle

sick be sick; ill; poorly; sick; throw up; vomit

small little; small

smirk frown; grimace; scowl; smirk; sneer

smuggle bootleg; pirate; run; smuggle

space place; seat; space; room

speak speak; talk

sport championship; competition; contest; game; match; race; sport; tournament

spray shower; slosh; spatter; splash; splatter; spray

stair stair; staircase; steps

stamp plod; stamp; tramp; trudge

strength force; power; strength; vigour

take last; take

talk chat; conversation; discussion; gossip; speech; talk; talks

teach coach; educate; instruct; lecture; teach; train

telephone telephone numbers in UK and USA

temperature Celsius; Centigrade; Fahrenheit

thin bony; emaciated; lean; scrawny; skinny; slender; slim; thin; underweight

time in/on/at in expressions of time; last night, this morning, etc

toilet bathroom; Gents; Ladies; lavatory; loo; men's/ladies' room; public convenience; rest room; toilet; WC

travel drive; fly; go; ride; sail; steer

un- dis-; il-; in-; ir-; non-; un-

unless if ... not; unless

used² be/get used to; used to

used to

user environmentally, ozone, etc friendly; user-friendly

very much; very; very much

visit call on; call in on; come and stay; drop by; drop in on; go and stay; visit

wait expect; wait; wait for

want care for; want; would you like ... ?

water boil; condense; cool; defrost; freeze; frozen; ice; icy; melt; steam; thaw

wear carry; have on; wear

which what; when

whizz dart; nip; shoot; whizz; zoom

whom who; whom; that

wide broad; wide

work job; labour; piece of work; task; toil; work

wound hurt; injure; injury; wound; wounded

your Dear Sir/Madam; yours faithfully/sincerely/truly

zodiac astrology; horoscopes; signs of the zodiac; star signs; zodiac

Appendix 10
Defining vocabulary

In order to make the dictionary definitions easy to understand, we have written them using only the words in the following list. The words in the list were carefully chosen according to their frequency in the language and their value to students as a 'core vocabulary' of English. Inflected forms of the words listed (eg plural forms of nouns or *-ing* forms of verbs) are also used, but not words with suffixes added (eg *technical* is used but not *technically*).

Occasionally it has been necessary to use in a definition a word not in this list. When such a word occurs it is shown in SMALL CAPITAL LETTERS. If you do not know the meaning of this word, look it up at its alphabetical place in the dictionary.

Many of the words in the list have more than one meaning. We normally use them in definitions in their main or most common meaning, but when this is not the case we show this by indicating the sense number of the word in the dictionary. For example, the definition of **winch** (*noun*) is:

> a machine for lifting or pulling heavy objects by means of a rope or chain wound round a drum¹(2).

Here the word 'drum' is being used with a special meaning, shown in the dictionary as sense **2** in the first entry for **drum**.

Exceptions

The only exceptions to the list (ie words which are not in the list but which are not marked in a special way when they occur in definitions) are these:

(a) Proper names (beginning with a capital letter) of people, places, religions, institutions, etc, such as **Jesus**, **America**, **Islam**.

(b) Adjectives expressing shades of colour, eg **yellowish**, **reddish-brown**.

(c) Root words used in defining derivatives and compounds formed from them when these appear at the entry for the root words, eg 'bleary' used in the definitions for **blearily** and **bleary-eyed** at the entry for **bleary**.

a	achieve	advantage	alcohol	angle *n*
abandon	achievement	adventure	alcoholic *adj*	angrily
ability	acid	adverb	alert	angry
able	acknowledge	advertise	alike *adj*	animal
abnormal	acquire	advertisement	alive	ankle
abnormally	across *adv, prep*	advertising *n*	all *adv, det,*	anniversary
about *adv, prep*	act *n, v*	advice	pron	announce
above *adv, prep*	action	advise	allow	announcement
abroad	active	adviser	allowance	annoy
absence	actively	affair	almost	annoyance
absent *adj*	activity	affect	alone	annoying *adj*
absolute *adj*	actor	affection	along *adv, prep*	annual *adj*
absolutely	actual	afraid	aloud	another *det,*
absorb	actually	after *adv, prep*	alphabet	pron
abstract *adj*	adapt	afternoon	already	answer *n, v*
absurd	add	afterwards	also	anxiety
academic *adj*	addition	again	alter	anxious
accept	in addition to	against	alternative *n*	any *det, pron*
acceptable	additional	age *n*	although	anyone
acceptance	address *n, v*	agent	always	anything
access *n*	adequate	aggressive	ambition	anywhere
accessible	adjective	aggressively	ambitious	apart
accident	adjust	ago	among	apparatus
accidentally	adjustment	agree	amount *n, v*	apparently
accommodation	administration	agreement	amuse	appeal *n, v*
accompany	administrative	agricultural	amusement	appear
according to	admiration	agriculture	amusing *adj*	appearance
account *n*	admire	ahead	an	appetite
accumulate	admission	aid	analyse	apple
accuracy	admit	aim *n, v*	analysis	appliance
accurate	adopt	air *n*	ancestor	application
accurately	adult *n*	aircraft	ancient	apply
accusation	advance *v*	airport	and	appoint
accuse	in advance	alarm *n, v*	anger *n*	appointment

appreciate
appreciation
approach *n, v*
appropriate *adj*
approval
approve
approximately
arch *n*
architecture
area
argue
argument
arm *n*
armed *adj*
armour
arms *n*
army
around *adv,*
   prep
arrange
arrangement
arrest *v*
arrival
arrive
art
article
artificial
artificially
artist
artistic
as *adv, conj,*
   prep
   as well as
ash
ashamed
aside
ask
asleep
aspect
assemble
assembly
assert
assess
assist
assistant
associate *v*
association
assume
astonish
astonishing
at
   at last
   at least
   at once
atmosphere
atmospheric
atom
atomic
attach
attack *n, v*
attempt *n, v*
attend
attention

attitude
attract
attraction
attractive
audience
author
authority
automatic
automatically
autumn
available
average *adj, n*
avoid
awake *adj*
award *n, v*
aware
awareness
away
awkward

baby
back *adj, adv, n*
background
backwards
bacon
bacteria
bad-tempered
bad
badly
bag *n*
bake
balance *n, v*
ball *n*
ballet
band *n*
bank *n*
bar *n*
bare *adj*
bark *n*
barrel
barrier
base *n, v*
baseball
basic
basis
basket
bat *n*
bath *n*
batsman
battery
battle *n*
be
beach *n*
beak
beam *n*
bean
bear *n, v*
beat *n, v*
beautiful
beauty
because
because of
become

bed *n*
bedroom
bee
beer
before *adv, conj,*
   prep
beg
begin
beginning *n*
behalf
behave
behaviour
behind *adv,*
   prep
being *n*
belief
believe
believer
bell
belong
below *adv, prep*
belt *n*
bend *n, v*
beneath *adv,*
   prep
benefit *n, v*
berry
beside
best *adj, adv*
bet *n, v*
betray
better *adj, adv*
between
beyond *adj, adv*
bible
bicycle
bid *n*
big
bill *n*
bird
birth
birthday
biscuit
bishop
bit
bite *n, v*
bitter
black *adj, n*
blade
blame *n, v*
blank *adj*
bleed
bless
blind *adj*
block *n, v*
blood *n*
blow *n, v*
blue *adj, n*
board *n*
boast *v*
boat *n*
body
boil *v*

bold
bomb *n*
bone *n*
book *n*
boot *n*
border *n*
bored *adj*
boring *adj*
born
borrow
both *adj, adv,*
   pron
bottle *n*
bottom *n*
bounce *v*
boundary
bow /baʊ/ *n*
bowels
bowl *n, v*
box *n, v*
boxer
boxing *n*
boy
brain *n*
branch *n*
brass *n*
brave *adj*
bread
breadth
break *n, v*
breakfast *n*
breast *n*
breath
breathe
breathing *n*
breed *n, v*
brick *n*
bridge
brief *adj*
briefly
bright
brightly
brightness
brilliant
bring
broad *adj*
broadcast *n, v*
brother
brown *adj*
brush *n, v*
bubble *n*
bucket *n*
build *v*
building *n*
bullet
bunch *n*
burial
burn *n, v*
burst *v*
bury
bus
bush
business

busy
but
butter *n*
button *n*
buy *v*
buyer
by *adv, prep*

cable *n*
cage *n*
cake *n*
calculate
calculation
calf
call *n, v*
calm *n, v*
camera
camp *n*
campaign *n*
can *n, v*
canal
cancel
candidate
candle
cannot
canvas *n*
cap *n*
capable
capacity
capital *n*
captain *n*
capture *v*
car
card-game
card *n*
cardboard
care *n*
care *for*
career *n*
careful
carefully
careless
carelessly
cargo
carpet *n*
carriage
carry
   carry out
cart *n*
carve
case *n*
   in case
   in case of
cash *n*
cast *n, v*
castle
casual *adj*
casually
cat
catch *n, v*
category
cathedral
cattle

cause *n, v*
cave *n*
ceiling
celebrate
celebration
cell
cement *n*
cent
central
centre *n, v*
century
ceremonial
ceremony
certain
certainly
certainty
certificate
chain *n*
chair *n*
chalk *n*
challenge *n, v*
chance *n*
change *n, v*
channel *n*
character
characteristic
 adj, n
charge *n, v*
 in charge (of)
charity
charm *n*
charming *adj*
chart *n*
chase *v*
cheap
cheaply
cheat *v*
check *n, v*
cheek *n*
cheer *v*
cheerful
cheese
chemical *adj, n*
chemistry
cheque
chest
chicken *n*
chief *adj*
child, children
childhood
chimney
chin
chocolate
choice *n*
choose
chop *v*
church
cigarette
cinema
circle *n*
circuit
circular
circulate

circulation
circumstance
citizen
city
civil *adj*
claim *n, v*
class *n*
classical
classify
clause
clay
clean *adj, v*
clear *adj, v*
clearly
clergyman
clever
client
cliff
climate
climb *v*
clock
close *adj, adv, v*
closely
cloth
clothes *n*
clothing *n*
cloud *n*
club *n*
coach *n*
coal
coast *n*
coat *n*
code *n*
coffee
coin *n*
cold *adj, n*
collapse *n, v*
collar *n*
collect *v*
collection
college
colony
colour *n, v*
coloured *adj*
colourful
colouring *n*
colourless
column
comb *n, v*
combination
combine *v*
come
comedy
comfort *n, v*
comfortable
comfortably
comic *adj*
command *n, v*
comment *n, v*
commerce
commercial
commission *n*
commit

committee
common *adj*
 in common
commonly
communicate
communication
community
companion
company
compare
comparison
compensate
compensation
compete
competition
competitive
competitor
complain
complaint
complete *adj, v*
completely
complex *adj*
complicated *adj*
component
compose
composition
compound *n*
compromise *n*
compulsory
computer
conceal
concentrate *v*
conception
concern *n, v*
concert
conclusion
concrete *n*
condemn
condense
condition
conduct *n, v*
conference
confess
confidence
confident
confidently
confine
confirm
conflict *n*
conform
confuse
confusion
congress
connect
connection
conscience
conscious
consciousness
consequence
consider
considerable
consideration
consist

consistent
consonant
constant
constantly
constitute
construct
contact *n*
contain
container
contempt
contents
contest *n*
continent *n*
continually
continue
continuous
continuously
contract *n, v*
contrary *adj, n*
contrast *n, v*
contribute
contribution
control *n, v*
convenient
convention
conventional
conversation
convert *v*
convince
convincing *adj*
cook *n, v*
cooking *n*
cool *adj, v*
copper
copy *n, v*
cord
corn
corner *n*
corporation
correct *adj, v*
correctly
correspond
cosmetic
cost *n, v*
costume
cotton
cough *v*
could
council
count *n, v*
counter *n*
country
countryside
county
couple *n*
courage
course *n*
court *n*
cover *n, v*
covering *n*
cow *n*
coward
cowardly

crack *n, v*
crash *n, v*
crawl *v*
crazy
cream *n*
create
creative
creature
credit *n*
creep *v*
crew *n*
cricket
crime
criminal *adj, n*
crisis
crisp *adj*
critical
criticism
criticize
crop *n*
cross *n, v*
crowd *n, v*
crown *n*
cruel
cruelty
crush *v*
cry *n, v*
crystal
cultivate
cultural
culture
cup *n*
cupboard
cure *n, v*
curiosity
curl *n, v*
currency
current *adj, n*
currently
curse *n, v*
curtain *n*
curve *n, v*
cushion *n*
custom
customer
cut *n, v*
cycle *n*

daily *adj, adv*
damage *n, v*
damp *n*
dance *n, v*
dancer
danger
dangerous
dare *v*
dark *adj, n*
darkness
data
date *n*
daughter
dawn *n*
day

dead
deal *n*
deal with
dealing *n*
death
debate *n*
debt
decay *n, v*
deceitful
deceive
deception
decide
decimal *adj*
decision
declaration
declare
decorate
decoration
decrease *v*
deed
deep *adj, adv*
deeply
deer
defeat *n, v*
defence
defend
defensive
define
definite
definitely
degree
delay *n, v*
deliberate *adj*
deliberately
delicate
delight *n, v*
delightful
deliver
delivery
demand *n, v*
demonstrate
deny
depart
department
departure
depend
dependent *adj*
deposit *v*
depress
depressed *adj*
depressing *adj*
depression
depth
descend
describe
description
desert *n, v*
deserve
design *n, v*
desirable
desire *n, v*
desk
despair *n*

despite
destination
destiny
destroy
destruction
destructive
detach
detail *n, v*
detect
determination
determine
determined *adj*
develop
development
device
devil *n*
devote
diagram
diamond
dictionary
die
diet *n*
differ
difference
different
differently
difficult
difficulty
dig *v*
dignity
dimension
dinner
dip *v*
direct *adj, v*
direction
directly
director
dirt
dirty *adj*
disadvantage
disagree
disagreement
disappear
disappoint
disappointed *adj*
disappointment
disapproval
disapprove
disaster
disc
discharge *v*
discipline
discomfort
discourage
discover
discovery
discuss
discussion
disease
disguise *v*
disgust *n, v*
disgusting *adj*

dish *n*
dishonest
dishonestly
dislike *n*
dismiss
disorder
display *n, v*
dispose
dispute *n, v*
dissolve
distance *n*
distant
distil
distinct
distinction
distinctive
distinctly
distinguished
    adj
distort
distract
distress
distribute
distribution
district
disturb
disturbance
disturbing *adj*
ditch *n*
divide *v*
division
do *v*
doctor *n*
document *n*
dog *n*
dollar
domestic *adj*
dominant
dominate
door
dot *n*
double *adj*
doubt *n, v*
doubtful
down *adv, prep*
downward
downwards
drag *v*
drain *n, v*
drama
dramatic
draw *v*
drawer
drawing *n*
dream *n*
dress *n, v*
drink *n, v*
drive *n, v*
driver
drop *n, v*
drug *n*
drum *n*
drunk *adj*

dry *adj, v*
duck *n*
due *adj*
dull *adj*
during
dust *n*
duty
dye *n*

each
eager
eagerly
eagerness
ear
early *adj, adv*
earn
earth *n*
ease *n, v*
easily
east
eastern
easy
eat
eccentric
economic
economy
edge *n*
edible
educate
education
educational
effect *n*
effective
effectively
efficiency
efficient
efficiently
effort
egg *n*
eight *det, n,*
    pron
either *adv, det,*
    pron
elaborate *adj*
elastic *adj*
elbow *n*
elect
election
electric
electrical
electricity
electronic
elegant
element
elephant
eleven *det, n,*
    pron
else
elsewhere
embarrass
embarrassment
emergency
emotion

emotional
emotionally
emphasis
emphasize
empire
employ
employee
employer
employment
empty *adj, v*
enable
enclose
enclosure
encourage
encouragement
end *n, v*
ending *n*
endless
endure
enemy
energy
engage
engine
engineer
enjoy
enjoyable
enjoyment
enough *adv, det,*
    pron
enter
enterprise
entertain
entertainer
entertaining *adj*
entertainment
enthusiasm
enthusiastic
enthusiastically
entirely
entitle
entrance *n*
entry
envelope
environment
envy
equal *adj*
equally
equip
equipment
equivalent *adj*
error
escape *n, v*
especially
essay *n*
essential
establish
estate
estimate *n, v*
even *adj, adv*
evening
evenly
event
eventually

ever
every
everybody
everyone
everything
everywhere
evidence *n*
evil *adj, n*
exact *adj*
exactly
exaggerate
examination
examine
example
excellence
excellent
except *prep*
exception
exceptional
exceptionally
excess
excessive
excessively
exchange *n, v*
excite
excited *adj*
excitement
exciting *adj*
exclude
exclusive *adj*
exclusively
excuse *n, v*
execute
exercise
exercise
exhibition
exist
existence
expand
expect
expenditure
expense
expensive
experience *n, v*
experiment *n*
expert *adj, n*
explain
explanation
explode
exploit *v*
explore
explosion
explosive *adj, n*
export *n*
expose
exposure
express *v*
expression
extend
extent
external
extinct
extra *adj*

extract *n, v*
extraordinary
extreme *adj, n*
extreme
extremely
eye *n*

fabric
face *n, v*
fact
factor
factory
fade
fail *v*
failure
faint *adj*
fair *adj*
fairly
fairy
faith
faithful
fall *n, v*
false
falsely
fame
familiar
family
famous
fan *n*
far *adj, adv*
fare *n*
farm *n*
farmer
farming *n*
fascinating *adj*
fashion *n*
fashionable
fast *adj, adv*
fasten
fastening *n*
fat *adj, n*
fate
father *n*
fault *n*
favour *n, v*
favourable
favourably
favourite *adj*
fear *n, v*
feather *n*
feature *n*
feed *v*
feel *v*
feeling *n*
fellow
female *adj, n*
fence *n*
festival
fever
few *adj, det, pron*
fiction
field *n*

fierce
fiercely
fifth
fight *n, v*
figure *n*
file *n*
fill *v*
filling *n*
film *n, v*
final *adj*
finally
financial
financially
find *v*
find out
fine *adj*
finely
fingernail
finger *n*
finish *n, v*
fire *n, v*
fireplace
firm *adj, n*
firmly
first *adj, adv*
fish *n, v*
fit *adj, n, v*
fitting *adj*
five *det, n, pron*
fix *v*
flag *n*
flame *n*
flash *n, v*
flat *adj, n*
flavour *n, v*
fleet *n*
flesh *n*
flexible
flight *n*
float *v*
flood *n, v*
floor *n*
flour *n*
flow *n, v*
flower *n*
fluid *n*
fly *n, v*
fold *n, v*
follow
follower
fond
food
fool *n*
foolish
foolishly
foot *n*
football
for *prep*
forbid
force *n, v*
forceful
forcefully
forecast *v*

forehead
foreign
forest
forget
forgive
fork *n*
form *n, v*
formal
formally
formation
former
formerly
fort
fortunate
fortune
forward *adj, adv*
forwards
found
foundation
four *det, n, pron*
fourth
fox *n*
fraction
frame *n*
framework
frank *adj*
free *adj, adv, v*
freedom
freely
freeze *v*
frequent *adj*
frequently
fresh
friend
friendly
friendship
frighten
frightening *adj*
from
front *adj, n*
frost *n*
fruit *n*
fry *v*
fuel *n*
fulfil
full-time
full *adj*
fully
fun *n*
function *n, v*
fund *n*
fundamental
funeral
funny
fur
furniture
further *adj, adv*
furthest *adj, adv*
fuss *n*
future *adj, n*

gain *n, v*
gallery

gamble *v*
game *n*
gang *n*
gap
garden *n*
garment
gas *n*
gate *n*
gather *v*
gathering *n*
gear *n*
general *adj, n*
generally
generation
generous
generously
gentle
gently
genuine
gesture *n*
get
ghost *n*
gift
girl
give *v*
glad
glass *n*
glove
glow *v*
glue *n*
go *v*
goal
goat
god
gold *adj, n*
golden
golf
good *adj*
goods
goodbye
goodness
gossip *n*
govern
government
graceful
grade *n*
gradual
gradually
grain
grammar
grand
grandfather
grandmother
grass *n*
grateful
gratitude
grave *n*
great *adj*
greatly
greedy
green *adj*
greet
greeting *n*

grey *adj*
grief
grind *v*
grip *n, v*
ground *n*
group *n*
grow
growth
guarantee *n, v*
guard *n, v*
guess *n, v*
guest
guidance
guide *n, v*
guilt
guilty
gun *n*

habit
habitually
hair
hairy
half *det, n*
hall
hammer *n, v*
hand *n, v*
handle *n, v*
hang *v*
happen
happily
happiness
happy
harbour *n*
hard *adj, adv*
harden
hardly
hardship
harm *n, v*
harmful
harmless
harmony
harsh
harshly
hat
hate *v*
hatred
have
he
head-dress
head *n*
heal
health
healthy
heap *n*
hear
hearing *n*
heart
heat *n, v*
heating *n*
heaven
heavily
heavy *adj*
hedge *n*

heel *n*
height
hell
help *n, v*
helpful
helpless
hen
her *det, pron*
here
herself
hesitate
hide *v*
high-pitched
high-ranking
high *adj, adv*
highly
hill
him
himself
hip
hire *v*
his
historical
history
hit *n, v*
hockey
hold *n, v*
holder
hole *n*
holiday *n*
hollow *adj*
holy
home *adv, n*
honest
honestly
honesty
honey
honour *n, v*
honourable
hook *n*
hope *n, v*
hopeful
horizon
horn
horror
horse-racing
horse *n*
hospital
host *n*
hostility
hot-tasting
hot
hotel
hour
house *n*
household
how
however *conj, adv*
huge
human *adj, n*
humorous
humour

hundred
hunger *n*
hungry
hunt *n, v*
hurry *n, v*
hurt *v*
husband *n*
hut

I
ice-cream
ice *n*
idea
ideal *adj, n*
identify
identity
if
ignorant
ignore
ill *adj, adv*
illegal
illegally
illness
illusion
illustrate
illustration
image
imaginary
imagination
imaginative
imagine
immediate
immediately
impact *n*
implement *n*
imply
import *n*
importance
important
impossible
impress
impression
impressive
improve
improvement
impulse
in *adv, prep*
inability
inadequate
inch
incident
include
income
increase *n, v*
increasingly
independence
independent *adj*
independently
indicate
indication
indirect
indirectly
individual *adj, n*

indoors
industrial
industry
inevitable
infect
infection
infectious
inferior
inflict
influence *n, v*
influential
inform
informal
information
ingredient
inhabitant
inherit
injure
injury
ink *n*
inner
innocent *adj*
inquiry
insect
insert *v*
inside *adj, n, prep*
insincere
insist
inspect
inspection
instance
instead
instinct
institution
instruct
instruction
instrument
insult *n, v*
insulting *adj*
insurance
intellectual *adj*
intelligence
intelligent
intend
intense
intensely
intensity
intention
intentionally
interest *n, v*
interested *adj*
interesting *adj*
interfere
internal
international *adj*
interpret
interrupt
interruption
interval
into
introduce

introduction
invent
invention
invest
investigate
investigation
investment
invitation
invite
involve
inward
inwards
iron *n*
irrelevant
irritate
irritating *adj*
island
isolate
issue *n, v*
it
item
its
itself

jacket *n*
jam *n*
jaw *n*
jealous
jelly
jet *n*
jewel
jewellery
job
join *v*
joint *adj, n*
joke *n, v*
journalist
journey *n*
joy
judge *n, v*
judgement
juice
juicy
jump *n, v*
just *adj, adv*
justice
justify

keen *adj*
keep *v*
key *n*
kick *n, v*
kill *v*
killing *n*
kilogram
kind *adj, n*
kindness
king
kiss *n, v*
kitchen
knee *n*
kneel
knife *n*

knit *v*
knock *n, v*
knot *n*
know
knowledge

label *n*
labour *n*
lace *n*
lack *n, v*
ladder *n*
lake
lamb
lamp
land *n, v*
landing *n*
language
large
last *adj, adv, v*
late *adj, adv*
laugh *n, v*
laughter
launch *v*
lavatory
law-making
law
lawcourt
lawn
lawyer
lay *v*
layer *n*
lazy
lead /li:d/ *n, v*
lead /led/ *n*
leader
leaf *n*
lean *v*
learn
learning *n*
least *adv, det, pron*
leather
leave *v*
  leave out
lecture *n*
left *adj*
leg *n*
legal
legally
lend
length
less *adv, det, pron*
lesson
let *v*
letter
level *adj, n*
library
licence *n*
lid
lie *n, v*
life
lift *n, v*

light *adj, n, v*
lightly
lightning
like *adj, prep, v*
likely *adj*
limb
limit *n, v*
line *n, v*
link *n, v*
lion
lip
liquid *adj, n*
list *n*
listen
literary
literature
litre
little *adj, det, pron*
live *adj*
live *v*
liveliness
lively
living *adj*
load *n, v*
loan *n*
local *adj*
lock *n, v*
lodging *n*
log *n*
logic
logical
lonely
long *adj, adv*
look *n, v*
  look after
loop *n*
loose *adj*
loose-fitting
loosely
lord *n*
lorry
lose
loss
lot
  a lot
  lots
loud *adj, adv*
loudly
love *n, v*
lover
low *adj, adv*
lower *v*
loyal
loyalty
luck
lucky
lump *n*
lunch *n*
lung

machine
machinery

mad
madness
magazine
magic *adj, n*
magical
magistrate
magnificent
mail *n*
main *adj*
mainly
maintain
major *adj*
majority
make *v*
making *n*
male *adj, n*
man *n*
manage
management
manager
manner
manufacture *n, v*
many
map *n*
marble
march *n, v*
margin
mark *n, v*
market *n*
marking *n*
marriage
marry
mass *n*
mat *n*
match *n, v*
material *n*
matter *n, v*
mature *adj*
maximum *adj*
may *v*
me
meal
mean *adj, v*
meaning *n*
means *n*
measure *n, v*
measurement
meat
mechanical
mechanism
medical *adj*
medicine
medieval
medium *adj, n*
meet *v*
meeting *n*
melt
member
membership
memory
mend *v*
mental

mentally
mention *v*
mess *n*
message
messenger
metal
metallic
method
metre
metric
middle *adj, n*
midnight
might *v*
mild *adj*
mile
military
milk *n*
mill *n*
million
mind *n, v*
mine *n, pron*
mineral
minister *n*
minor *adj*
minute *n*
mirror *n*
miserable
miss *v*
missile
mist *n*
mistake *n, v*
mix *v*
mixture
mock *v*
model *n*
moderate *adj*
modern
modest
moment
money
monk
monkey *n*
month
mood
moon *n*
moral *adj*
morally
more *adv, det, pron*
morning
most *adv, det, pron*
mostly
mother *n*
motion *n*
motor *n*
motorist
mould *n, v*
mountain
mouse
mouth *n*
movable
move *n, v*

movement
much *adv, det, pron*
mud
multiply
murder *n, v*
muscle *n*
museum
music
musical *adj*
musician
must *v*
mutual
my
myself
mysterious
mystery
myth

nail *n*
naked
name *n, v*
narrow *adj*
nation
national *adj*
native *adj, n*
natural *adj*
naturally
nature
naval
navy *n*
near *adj*
near *adj, adv, prep*
nearly
neat
neatly
necessarily
necessary
necessity
neck *n*
need *n, v*
needle *n*
negative *adj*
negotiation
neither *adv, det, pron*
nerve *n*
nervous
nervousness
nest *n*
net *n*
network *n*
never
nevertheless
new
newly
news
newspaper
next *adj, adv*
next to
nice
night

nine *det, n, pron*
no *det, interj*
noble *adj*
nobleman
noise
noisily
noisy
none
nonsense
no one
nor
normal
normally
north
northern
nose *n*
not
note *n, v*
nothing
notice *n, v*
noticeable
noun
novel *n*
now
nowhere
nuclear
number *n, v*
nun
nurse *n*
nut
nylon

obedience
obey
object *n, v*
objection
obligation
observation
observe
observer
obstacle
obtain
obvious
obviously
occasion *n*
occasionally
occupation
occupy
occur
ocean
odd
of
off *adv, prep*
offence
offend
offender
offensive *adj*
offer *n, v*
offering *n*
office
officer
official *adj, n*
officially

often
oil *n*
oily
old
old-fashioned
omit
on *adv, prep*
once *adv, conj*
one *det, n, pron*
oneself
onion
only *adj, adv*
onto
open *adj, v*
opening *n*
openly
opera
operate
operation
opinion
opponent
opportunity
oppose
opposite *adj, n,*
   prep
opposition
or
orange *adj, n*
order *n, v*
  in order
   to/that
ordinary
ore
organ
organization
organize
origin
original *adj*
originally
originate
ornament *n*
ornamental
other *det, pron*
otherwise
ought
our
ours
ourselves
out
  out of
outcome
outdoor
outer
outline *n*
outside *adj, n,*
   prep
outstanding
outward
outwards
oven
over *adv, prep*
overcome
owe

own *det, pron, v*
owner
ownership
oxygen

pace *n*
pack *n, v*
packet
pad *n*
page *n*
pain *n*
painful
paint *n, v*
painter
painting *n*
pair *n*
pale *adj*
palm *n*
pan *n*
panel
paper *n*
paragraph
parallel *adj*
parcel *n*
parent
park *n, v*
parliament
part *n*
partial
partially
participate
particular *adj*
particularly
partly
partner *n*
party *n*
pass *n, v*
passage
passenger
passing *n*
passion
passionate
past *adj, n, prep*
pastry
patch *n*
path
patience
patient *adj, n*
patiently
pattern *n*
pause *n*
pay *n, v*
payment
peace
peaceful
pen *n*
penalty
pence
pencil *n*
penetrate
penny
people *n*
pepper *n*

per
perfect *adj*
perfectly
perform
performance
performer
perhaps
period
permanent
permanently
permission
permit *v*
person
personal
personality
personally
persuade
pet *n*
petrol
philosophy
photograph *n, v*
photographer
photographic
photography
phrase *n*
physical
physically
piano
pick *v*
picture *n*
pie
piece *n*
pig *n*
pile *n, v*
pillar
pilot *n*
pin *n, v*
pink *adj*
pipe *n*
pitch *n*
pity *n*
place *n, v*
plain *adj, n*
plan *n, v*
plane *n*
planet
planning *n*
plant *n, v*
plastic *adj, n*
plate *n*
platform
play *n, v*
player
playful
pleasant
pleasantly
please
pleased *adj*
pleasing *adj*
pleasure
plenty *n*
plot *n*
plug *n*

pocket *n*
poem
poet
poetry
point *n, v*
pointed *adj*
poison *n, v*
poisonous
pole *n*
police *n*
policy
polish *n, v*
polite
politely
politics
political
politically
politician
pool *n*
poor
pop *n*
popular
popularity
population
port
portion *n*
portrait
portray
position *n*
positive *adj*
positively
possess
possession
possibility
possible
possibly
post *n, v*
pot *n*
potato
pound *n*
pour
poverty
powder *n*
power *n*
powerful
practical *adj*
practice
practise
praise *n, v*
pray
prayer
precious
predict
prefer
preference
pregnant
prejudice *n*
preliminary
preparation
prepare
presence
present *adj, n, v*
preserve *v*

president
press *n, v*
pressure *n*
pretend
pretty *adj*
prevent
previous
previously
price *n*
prickly
pride
priest
primary *adj*
primitive *adj*
prince
princess
principal *adj*
principle
print *n, v*
printing *n*
prison
prisoner
private *adj*
privately
privilege
prize *n*
probable *adj*
probably
problem
procedure
proceed
proceedings
process *n, v*
procession
produce *n, v*
product
production
profession
professional *adj*
profit *n*
profitable
programme *n*
progress *n*
project *n, v*
prolong
prominent
promise *n, v*
promising *adj*
promote
promotion
pronoun
pronounce
pronunciation
proof *n*
proper
properly
property
proportion
proposal
propose
prostitute *n*
protect
protection

protective
protest *n, v*
proud *adj*
prove
provide
province
provoke
pub
public *adj, n*
publication
publicity
publicly
publish
pull *n, v*
pump *n, v*
punch *n*
punish
punishment
pupil
pure
purple *adj*
purpose
pursue
push *n, v*
put
put out (=
extinguish)

qualification
qualified *adj*
qualify
quality
quantity
quarrel *n, v*
quarter *n*
queen *n*
question *n, v*
quick *adj*
quickly
quiet *adj*
quietly
quite
quote *v*

rabbit *n*
race *n, v*
racing *n*
radio *n*
rail *n*
railway
rain *n, v*
raise *v*
range *n*
rank *n, v*
rapid
rapidly
rare
rarely
rat *n*
rate *n*
rather
raw
ray

reach *n, v*
react
reaction
read *v*
reader
readily
reading *n*
ready
real
realistic
reality
realize
really
reason *n*
reasonable
reasoning *n*
receive
recent
recently
recognize
recommend
record *n, v*
recording *n*
recover
recovery
red *adj, n*
reduce
reduction
refer
reference
refined *adj*
reflect
reform *n, v*
refusal
refuse *v*
regain
regard *n, v*
regardless
regiment *n*
region
register *n, v*
regret *n, v*
regular *adj*
regularly
regulate
regulation
reject *v*
rejection
relate to
related *adj*
relation
  in relation to
relationship
relative *adj*
relatively
relax
relaxed *adj*
release *n, v*
relevant
reliable
relief
relieve
religion

religious
reluctance
rely on
remain *v*
remains *n*
remark *n*
remarkable
remember
remind
remote
removal
remove *v*
renew
rent *n, v*
repair
repeat *v*
repeatedly
replace
replacement
reply *n, v*
report *n, v*
represent
representation
representative
  adj, n
reproduce
reptile
republic
reputation
request *n, v*
require
requirement
rescue *v*
research *n*
resemble
reserve *n, v*
residence
resign
resist
resistance
resolve *v*
resort *n*
resource
respect *n, v*
respectable
respond
response
responsibility
responsible
rest *n, v*
restaurant
restore
restrain
restraint
restrict
restriction
result *n, v*
retire
return *n, v*
reveal
revenge *n*
reverse *v*
review *n*

revive
revolution
revolve
reward *n*
rhythm
rice
rich
rid *v*
  get rid of
ride *n, v*
rider
ridge *n*
ridiculous
right *adj, adv, n*
rigid
ring *n, v*
ripe
rise *n, v*
risk *n, v*
risky
ritual *n*
rival *adj, n*
river
road
rob *n*
rock *n*
rod
role
roll *n, v*
romantic *adj*
roof *n*
room *n*
root *n*
rope *n*
rose
rot *v*
rough *adj*
roughly
round *adj, adv,
  n, prep*
route *n*
routine *n*
row /rəʊ/ *n, v*
royal *adj*
rub *v*
rubber
rubbish *n*
rude
rudely
ruin *n, v*
rule *n, v*
ruler
rumour *n*
run *n, v*
runner
rural
rush *n, v*

sacred
sacrifice *n*
sad
sadness
safe *adj*

safely	sensible	show *n, v*	smoothly	spiritual *adj*
safety	sensitive	shower *n*	snake *n*	spite *n*
sail *n, v*	sentence *n*	shrink *v*	snow *n*	in spite of
sailor	sentimental	shut *v*	so *adv, conj*	splendid
saint	separate *adj, v*	shy *adj*	so as (not) to	split *n, v*
sake	separately	sick *adj*	soak *v*	spoil *v*
salary	separation	side *n*	soap *n*	spoon *n*
sale	sequence	sideways	social *adj*	sport *n*
salt *n*	series	sight *n*	socially	sporting *adj*
salty	serious	sign *n, v*	society	spot *n*
same	seriously	signal *n, v*	sock *n*	spray *n, v*
sample *n*	servant	signature	soft	spread *n, v*
sand *n*	serve *v*	silence *n*	soften	spring *n*
sandwich *n*	service *n*	silent	soil *n*	square *adj, n*
satisfaction	set *n, v*	silk	soldier *n*	square
satisfactory	setting *n*	silly *adj*	sole *n*	stable *n*
satisfy	settle *v*	silver *n*	solemn	staff *n*
sauce	seven *det, n,*	similar	solemnly	stage *n*
save *v*	pron	similarly	solid *adj*	stair
say *v*	seventh	simple	solution	staircase
scale *n*	several	simply	solve	stake *n*
scatter	severe	sin *n*	some *det, pron*	stall *n*
scene	severely	since	somebody	stamp *n, v*
scenery	sew	sincere	somehow	stand *n, v*
scheme *n*	sex *n*	sing *v*	something	standard *adj, n*
school *n*	sexual	singer	sometimes	star *n*
science	sexually	singing *n*	somewhere	stare *v*
scientific	shade *n*	single *adj*	son	start *n, v*
scientist	shadow *n*	sink *n, v*	song	state *n, v*
scope	shake *v*	sister	soon	statement
score *n, v*	shallow	sit *v*	sore *adj*	station *n*
scrap *n*	shame *n*	site *n*	sorrow	statue
scrape *v*	shape *n, v*	situate	sorry	status
scratch *v*	share *n, v*	situation	sort *n*	stay *n, v*
screen *n*	sharp *adj*	six *det, n, pron*	soul	steadily
screw *n, v*	sharply	sixth	sound *adj, n, v*	steady *adj*
sea bird	shave *v*	size *n*	soup	steal *v*
sea-fish	she	sketch *n*	sour *adj*	steam *n*
sea	shed *n*	skilful	source	steel *n*
seal *n, v*	sheep	skilfully	south *adj, n*	steep *adj*
search *n, v*	sheet	skill	southern	steeply
season *n*	shelf	skilled	space *n*	steer *v*
seat *n*	shell *n*	skin *n*	spacecraft	stem *n*
second *adv, det,*	shelter *n, v*	skirt *n*	speak	step *n, v*
n, pron	shield *n*	sky *n*	speaker	stick *n, v*
secondary	shine *v*	slave *n*	special	sticky
secret *adj, n*	shiny	sleep *n, v*	specialist	stiff *adj*
secretly	ship *n*	sleeve	specialize	still *adj, adv*
section *n*	shirt	slender	specially	stimulate
secure *adj, v*	shock *n, v*	slice *n*	species	sting *n*
securely	shocking *adj*	slide *n, v*	specific	stir *v*
security	shoe *n*	slight *adj*	specify	stitch *n*
see *v*	shoot *n, v*	slightly	spectacle	stock *n*
seed *n*	shop *n, v*	slip *v*	spectator	stomach *n*
seek	shopkeeper	slope *n, v*	speech	stone *n*
seem	shopping *n*	slow *adj, v*	speed *n*	stop *n, v*
seize	shore *n*	slowly	spell *n, v*	storage
select *v*	short *adj*	small	spelling *n*	store *n, v*
selection	shorten	smart	spend	storm *n, v*
sell *v*	shot	smell *n, v*	spending *n*	story
send	should	smile *n, v*	spice *n*	straight *adj, adv*
senior *adj*	shoulder *n*	smoke *n, v*	spin *v*	strain *n*
sense *n*	shout *n, v*	smooth	spirit *n*	strand *n*

strange	supreme	tell	threat	traditionally
strangely	sure *adj*	temper *n*	threaten	traffic
stranger *n*	surely	temperature	three *det, n,*	trail *n*
strap *n*	surface *n*	temple	*pron*	train *n, v*
straw	surprise *n, v*	temporarily	throat	training *n*
stream *n*	surprised *adj*	temporary	through *adv,*	transfer *n, v*
street	surprising *adj*	tempt	*prep*	translate
strength	surround *v*	ten *det, n, pron*	throughout *adv,*	transmit
strengthen	surroundings	tend	*prep*	transparent
stress *n, v*	survey *n*	tendency	throw *n, v*	transport *n, v*
stretch *n, v*	survive	tender *adj*	thumb *n*	trap *n, v*
strict	suspect *v*	tennis	thunder *n*	travel *n, v*
strictly	suspend	tense *adj*	thus	traveller
strike *n, v*	suspicion	tense *n*	ticket *n*	tray
striking *adj*	suspicious	tension	tide *n*	treat *n, v*
string *n*	swallow *v*	tent	tidy *adj, v*	treatment
strip *n*	swear	tenth	tie *n, v*	tree
stroke *n*	sweat *n*	term *n*	tight *adj*	trial
strong-smelling	sweep *v*	terms *n*	tighten	tribe
strong	sweet-smelling	in terms of	tightly	trick *n, v*
strongly	sweet *adj, n*	terrible	time *n*	trim *v*
structure *n*	swell *v*	territory	tin *n*	trip *n*
struggle *n, v*	swelling *n*	test *n, v*	tiny	troop *n*
student	swim *v*	text	tip *n*	tropical
study *n, v*	swing *n, v*	texture	tire *v*	trouble *n, v*
stuff *v*	switch *n*	than *conj, prep*	tired *adj*	trousers
stupid	switch off/on	thanks *n*	tissue	truck
style *n*	sword	thank you	title *n*	true *adj*
subject *n*	syllable	that *conj, det,*	to *adv, prep*	truly
submit	symbol	*pron*	tobacco	trunk
substance	sympathetic	the	today	trust *n, v*
substitute *n*	sympathy	theatre	toe *n*	truth
succeed	system	theatrical	together	try *v*
success		their	toilet	tube
successful	table *n*	theirs	tolerate	tune *n*
successfully	tail *n*	them	tomorrow	tunnel *n*
succession	take *v*	theme	ton	turn *n, v*
successive	take off (of	themselves	tone *n*	turn off/on
such *det, pron*	planes, etc)	then	tongue *n*	twelve *det, n,*
suck *v*	talent	theory	tonight	*pron*
sudden	talented	there *adv*	too	twice
suddenly	talk *n, v*	therefore	tool *n*	twist *n, v*
suffer	tall	these *det, pron*	tooth	two *det, n, pron*
suffering *n*	tank	they	top *adj, n*	type *n, v*
sufficient	tap *n, v*	thick *adj*	topic	typical
sugar *n*	tape *n*	thickly	total *adj, n*	typically
suggest	target *n*	thickness	totally	tyre
suggestion	task	thief	touch *n, v*	
suit *n, v*	taste *n, v*	thin *adj*	tough *adj*	ugly
suitable	tax *n, v*	thing	tour *n*	unable
sum *n*	taxi *n*	think *v*	tourist	unacceptable
summary	tea	third *det, pron*	towards	unaware
summer	teach	thirst *n*	towel *n*	uncertain
summon	teacher	thirsty	tower *n*	uncertainty
sun *n*	teaching *n*	this *det, pron*	town	uncle
sunlight	team *n*	thorough	toy *n*	uncomfortable
superior *adj*	tear /tɪə(r)/	thoroughly	trace *n, v*	unconscious
supervise	tear /teə(r)/ *v*	those *det, pron*	track *n*	under *adv, prep*
supply *n, v*	technical	though *conj*	trade *n, v*	underground
support *n, v*	technique	thought *n*	trader	*adj, adv*
supporter	technology	thousand *det, n,*	trading *n*	underneath *adv,*
suppose	telephone *n*	*pron*	tradition	*prep*
suppress	television	thread *n*	traditional	understand

understanding *n*
undesirable
undo
unemployed
unexpected
unexpectedly
unfair
unfairly
unfortunate *adj*
unhappiness
unhappy
uniform *n*
unimportant
union
unit
unite
united *adj*
unity
universe
university
unkind
unknown *adj*
unless
unlikely
unnecessary
unpleasant
unreasonable
unsteady
untidy
until *conj, prep*
unusual
unusually
unwilling
unwillingly
unwise
up *adv, prep*
upon
upper
upright *adj, adv*
upset *adj, v*
upstairs
upward
upwards
urge *n, v*
urgent
us
use *n, v*

useful
useless
user
usual *adj*
usually

vacuum *n*
valid
valley
valuable
value *n, v*
van
variation
variety
various
vary
vegetable
vehicle
vein
verb
verse
version
very
victory
view *n, v*
vigorous
vigorously
vigour
village
violence
violent
violently
virgin
visible
visit *n, v*
visitor
visual *adj*
vivid
voice *n*
volume
vote *n, v*
vowel
voyage *n*

wage *n*
waist
wait *v*

wake *v*
walk *n, v*
wall *n*
wander *v*
want *v*
war *n*
warm *adj, v*
warmth
warn
warning *n*
wash *n, v*
waste *n, v*
watch *n, v*
water *n, v*
wave *n, v*
wax *n*
way
we
weak
weakness
wealth
wealthy
weapon
wear *n, v*
weather *n*
weave *v*
wedding *n*
week
weigh
weight *n*
welcome *adj,*
  n, v
welfare
well *adj, adv*
  as well as
well-known
west *adj, adv, n*
western *adj*
wet *adj*
what *det, pron*
whatever *adv,*
  det, pron
wheat
wheel *n*
when *adv, conj*
whenever *conj*
where *adv, conj*

wherever *conj*
whether
which *det, pron*
whichever *det,*
  pron
while *conj, n*
whip *n, v*
whistle *n, v*
white *adj, n*
who
whoever
whole *adj, n*
whom
whose *det*
why *adv*
wicked
wickedness
wicket
wide *adj*
widely
widespread
widow *n*
width
wife
wild *adj*
wildly
will *n, v*
willing *adj*
willingly
willingness
win *v*
wind /wɪnd/ *n*
wind /waɪnd/
window
wine *n*
wing *n*
winner
winter *n*
wipe *v*
wire *n*
wisdom
wise
wish *n, v*
with
withdraw
within *prep*
without *prep*

witness *n, v*
woman
wonder *n*
wonderful
wood
wooden
wool
woollen
word *n*
work *n, v*
worker
world
worm *n*
worry *n, v*
worse
worship *n, v*
worst *adj, adv*
worth *adj, n*
worthless
worthy *adj*
would
wound *n, v*
wrap *v*
wrist
write
writer
writing *n*
wrong *adj, n*
wrongdoing
wrongly

yard
year
yellow *adj*
yes
yesterday
yet *adv*
yield *n, v*
you
young *adj, n*
your
yours
yourself
youth

zero *det, n,*
  pron

Phonetic symbols
used in the dictionary

Consonants

p	pen	/pen/	s	so	/səʊ/
b	bad	/bæd/	z	zoo	/zu:/
t	tea	/ti:/	ʃ	shoe	/ʃu:/
d	did	/dɪd/	ʒ	vision	/'vɪʒn/
k	cat	/kæt/	h	hat	/hæt/
g	got	/gɒt/	m	man	/mæn/
tʃ	chain	/tʃeɪn/	n	no	/nəʊ/
dʒ	jam	/dʒæm/	ŋ	sing	/sɪŋ/
f	fall	/fɔ:l/	l	leg	/leg/
v	van	/væn/	r	red	/red/
θ	thin	/θɪn/	j	yes	/jes/
ð	this	/ðɪs/	w	wet	/wet/

Vowels and diphthongs

i:	see	/si:/	ʌ	cup	/kʌp/
i	happy	/'hæpi/	ɜ:	bird	/bɜ:d/
ɪ	sit	/sɪt/	ə	about	/ə'baʊt/
e	ten	/ten/	eɪ	say	/seɪ/
æ	cat	/kæt/	əʊ	go	/gəʊ/
ɑ:	father	/'fɑ:ðə(r)/	aɪ	five	/faɪv/
ɒ	got	/gɒt/	aʊ	now	/naʊ/
ɔ:	saw	/sɔ:/	ɔɪ	boy	/bɔɪ/
ʊ	put	/pʊt/	ɪə	near	/nɪə(r)/
u	actual	/'æktʃuəl/	eə	hair	/heə(r)/
u:	too	/tu:/	ʊə	pure	/pjʊə(r)/

(r) indicates that British pronunciation will have /r/ only if a
vowel sound follows directly; otherwise it is omitted. In American
pronunciation, every 'r' of the ordinary spelling is retained.

Sounds from other languages

/x/ represents a fricative sound as in /lɒx/
for Scottish **loch**, Irish **lough**.

The mark /˜/ over a vowel indicates a
nasal quality. Nasalized vowels may be
retained in certain words taken from
French, as in **penchant** /'pɒ̃ʃɒ̃/, **vingt-et-un**
/ˌvæt eɪ 'ɜ̃:/. The symbol /a/ is used for a
short open vowel, different from English
/æ/ or /ɑ:/, which some speakers retain in
French words such as **éclat** /eɪ'kla/.

Weak vowels /i/ and /u/

The sounds written /i:/ and /ɪ/ must
always be different, as in **heat** /hi:t/ compared with **hit** /hɪt/. But /i/ represents a
vowel that can be sounded in either way, or
as a sound which is a compromise between
them. In a word such as **happy** /'hæpi/,
younger speakers use a quality more like
/i:/ but short in duration. When /i/ is followed by /ə/ the sequence can also be
pronounced /jə/. So the word **dubious**,
shown in the dictionary as /'dju:biəs/ may
be pronounced as three syllables
/'dju:bɪəs/, or as two syllables /'dju:bɪəs,
'dju:bjəs/.

In the same way, the two vowels represented by /u:/ and /ʊ/ must be distinct but
/u/ represents a vowel that varies between
them. If /u/ is followed directly by a consonant sound, it can also be pronounced in
a third way, as /ə/. So **situation**, shown as

/ˌsɪtʃu'eɪʃn/, can be pronounced
/ˌsɪtʃu:'eɪʃn/ or /ˌsɪtʃʊ'eɪʃn/, and **stimulate**, shown as /'stɪmjuleɪt/, can be any of
/'stɪmju:leɪt, 'stɪmjʊleɪt, 'stɪmjəleɪt/.

The sequence /uə/ can additionally be
pronounced /wə/. So **actual**, shown as
/'æktʃuəl/ may be three syllables
/'æktʃu:əl/ or two syllables /'æktʃʊəl,
'æktʃwəl/.

Variant pronunciations

Many English words have two or more
common pronunciations. The dictionary
shows such alternatives separated by a
comma: **salt** /sɔ:lt, sɒlt/. The learner
should normally use the first pronunciation shown, but will almost certainly hear
the others as well. Only the most common
variants are shown, and the fact that a certain pronunciation is not included does not
necessarily mean that it is wrong.

Weak forms and strong forms

Certain very common words, eg **at, and,
for, can**, have two pronunciations. We give
the usual (weak) pronunciation first. The
second pronunciation (strong) must be
used if the word is stressed, and also generally when the word is at the end of a
sentence. For example:

● *I'm waiting for* /fə(r)/ *a bus.*
● *What are you waiting for* /fɔ:(r)/?